American Statistics Index 1984

ELEVENTH ANNUAL SUPPLEMENT

Covering Publications Issued January 1–December 31, 1984

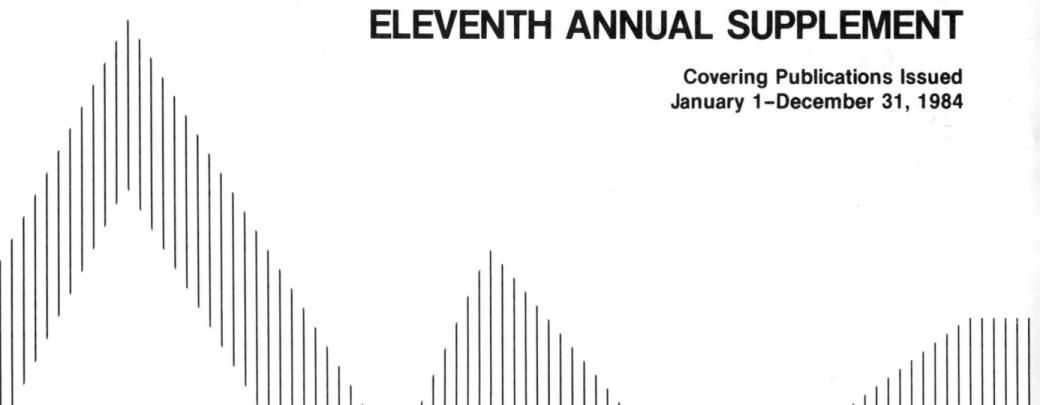

A comprehensive guide to the statistical publications of the U.S. Government

Index

 Congressional Information Service

Editorial Advisory Board

Hon. Richard Bolling, Former Representative from Missouri

Edward DiRoma New York Public Library

William Kingsley, American Council of Life Insurance

John W. Lehman Washington, D.C.

Robert R. Nathan Robert R. Nathan Associates

Conrad Taeuber Washington, D.C.

Special Consultant

Ruth Fine Washington, D.C.

Staff

Editorial Director Susan I. Jover

Director of Statistical Services Darlene J. Montgomery

Managing Editor Daniel Coyle Marie Fredell

Asst. Managing Editor, Abstracts David W. Tallerico

Review Editor, Index Vera L. McKee

Abstracting and Indexing Staff Michael Benigni Jane Bobba Lorraine V. Forte Jane A. Lean Virginia Pfeifle David B. Rice Shelley W. Walker Betsy H. Witte

Manager, Administrative Services Lee Mayer

Personnel Director Susie G. Schwarz

Assistant Personnel Director Anne F. Starbird

Personnel Assistant Karen W. Lucas

Director, Manufacturing William C. Smith

Plant Operations Manager William Idol

Micropublishing Production Staff Susan Anderson Tobi Barnhill Lukman Bazarah Rita Berry Patty Bettencourt Margarett Boyle Soon Chea Desmond Davis Frank Day Brezeetha Dhanireddy Donna Edwards Sharon Foster Kathleen Frazzetta Sharon Garey Christine Gass Jean Ann Gibson Kimberly Goba Christopher Gorczyca Rhonda Harris Norma Herbert Claire Keister Jeffrey Kessler Joyce Lowery Betty Lyles Kathleen Lyons Diana Machen Brian McCary Jane Miers Luke Murdock Tai Nguyen Edgar O'Bannon Jennifer Offenbacher Vatsaladevi Panneerselvam

Accuracy Editor Marilynne Imhoof

Editorial Assistant Patrice Morgan

Acquisitions Editors Mary E. Schiller, *Chief* Kevin G. Kendrick Phyllis R. Klun Susannah Livingston Loretta Saltzman

Documents Control Claire Goldman, *Chief* Don Crisostomo Ruth Sowash

Patricia Poppen Juanita Prather Margaret Reid Winnie Robertson Jean Shields Leonilza Silva Michelle Slaviero Victor Smith Poonam Srivastava Doris K. Stevens Mark Steo Nancy Taylor Betty Trinquero Terri Van Houten Rosario Vargas Lucy Villagra Mary Kay Williams Kim Wilson Bruce Woodhams Shaun Woolcock Jeffrey Zahn

Assistant Director of Research Mark Vonderhaar

Research Staff Marilynn Bynum George Codrea Jay Fletcher Sandra Friedman Cindy Friel Lois Gearhart Debra Green Mary Haygood Sarah Heron Angela Hitti Betty Leonard Eric Massant Vandana Mathur David Molenda Mary Phillips William Reilly Nina Schuster Jeffrey Showell Kate Talev

Director of Market Research Alexander D. McRae

Documents on Demand Sharon L. Schmedicke

Production Coordinator Dorothy W. Rogers

Production Services Supervisor Esther R. Aikens

Production Services Staff Helene E. Gaffney Elizabeth Naccarato Debra Turnell

National Sales Manager John P. Bell

Sales Representatives Thomas Ball John Cox Donald Crowley Paul Davidson Charles De Grasse Jane Edwards E. Donald Fitch Paul A. Hennrikus James Tucker

Marketing Services Coordinator Laima Rivers

Marketing Services Assistants Ellie Kasten Bethann Prather

Director, Communications Richard K. Johnson

Advertising, Publicity, and Promotion Staff Barbara Busby Jack Carey Shanon Huestis Marcia Taylor Leslie Wilson

Secretary to the President Karen L. Grossnickle

Secretary to VP Planning, Research and Development Helene Grant

Secretary to Sr. VP, Finance, Manufacturing & EDP Susan Savage

Staff Assistants Bonnie Balzer Caryl Dikkers Marian Fowler Charles Luther Delwin Martin Teresa McVeigh John Nazarian

---

GOV Z7554 .U5A46 11th Ed. Index Vol.

Congressional Information Service, Inc.

President Paul P. Massa

Vice President and Editorial Director Susan I. Jover

Vice President, Marketing James F. Connolly

Vice President, Planning, Research and Development Michael P. Stern

Vice President, Research Donald G. Tacheron

Sr. Vice President, Finance, Manufacturing & EDP Peter M. Bjornerud

Vice President, EDP & Technology Ralph James

Manager, Applications Programming William DeRoche

Software Engineers Mojtaba Anvari Andrew Ross

Systems Programmer Robert Better

Programmer/Analyst Yvonne Malcom

Computer Operators Susanna Ferro Mel Turner

Controller Max Venegas

Accounting Staff Stuart Abramowitz Barry Blacka Gina Bramante Susan Fasano Karen Hendren Sheila Moore Rita Skolnik Emmy Wong

---

ISSN 0091 - 1658
Key Title: American Statistics Index

The Library of Congress Cataloged the First Issue of This Title as Follows:

American Statistics Index, 1973- Washington. Congressional Information Service. annual.

"A comprehensive guide and index to the statistical publications of the U.S. Government."

1. United States-Statistics-Bibliography.
2. United States-Statistics-Abstracts. I. Congressional Information Service.

Z7554.U5A46	016.3173	73-82599
ISSN 0091 - 1658		MARC-S

International Standard Book Number For the Set: 0-88692-043-4 For Index Volume: 0-88692-044-2 For Abstract Volume: 0-88692-045-0

Published by Congressional Information Service, Inc. 4520 East-West Highway Bethesda, MD 20814 U.S.A.

A privately organized reference service.

Printed and Bound in the United States of America.

Copyright © 1985 by Congressional Information Service, Inc. All rights reserved.

CONTENTS

The American Statistics Index 1984 Annual Supplement is published in two volumes, the contents of which are summarized below.

Index

Detailed Table of Contents: Index Volume v

User Guide vii

Introduction to the American Statistics Index vii
Coverage of ASI Annual and Monthly Editions vii
Statistical Publications Covered by ASI viii
Organization of ASI Abstracts and Indexes ix
How ASI Abstracts Statistical Publications xi
How ASI Indexes Statistical Publications xii
Acquiring the Documents xx
Additional CIS Services xx
Sample Abstracts xxiii
Sample Search xxvi
Where To Write for Statistical Publications xxviii
Document Availability Symbols xxxii
Acronyms and Selected Abbreviations xxxiii
Issuing Agencies and ASI Accession Numbers xxxiv

Index by Subjects and Names 1

Index by Categories 871

Index by Titles 967

Index by Agency Report Numbers 1035

Guide to Selected Standard Classifications 1059

Abstracts

Detailed Table of Contents: Abstracts Volume

Issuing Agencies and ASI Accession Numbers v

User Guide xvii

Abstracts of Statistical Publications 1

Detailed Table of Contents: Index Volume

Index by Subjects and Names 1
(This index contains references to subjects, to corporate authors, and to individual authors of articles and publications.)

Index by Categories 871
(This index contains references to publications tables, and groups of tables that contain breakdowns of statistical data by State, by industry, by age, or by some other standard category.)

Geographic Breakdowns

By Census Division	871
By City	873
By County	877
By Foreign Country	880
By Outlying Area	887
By Region	890
By SMSA or MSA	898
By State	900
By Urban-Rural and Metro-Nonmetro	914

Economic Breakdowns

By Commodity	917
By Federal Agency	921
By Income	924
By Individual Company or Institution	926
By Industry	935
By Occupation	939

Demographic Breakdowns

By Age	942
By Disease	948
By Educational Attainment	949
By Marital Status	952
By Race	954
By Sex	959

Index by Titles 967
(This index contains an alphabetical listing of all publication titles abstracted.)

Index by Agency Report Numbers 1035
(This index contains a listing of all publications abstracted for which there are agency report numbers available, arranged by issuing agency.)

Guide to Selected Standard Classifications 1059
(This guide outlines the major standard classification systems used by various Federal agencies to arrange and present social and economic statistical data.)

Census Regions and Divisions	1059
Outlying Areas of the U.S.	1059
Standard Federal Administrative Regions	1059
Farm Production Regions	1059
Federal Reserve Districts	1060
Federal Home Loan Bank Districts	1060
Bureau of Labor Statistics Regions (and Regional Offices)	1060
Metropolitan Statistical Areas	1061
Consolidated Metropolitan Statistical Areas	1062
Cities with Population over 100,000	1063
Consumer Price Index Cities	1063
Standard Industrial Classification	1064
Standard Occupational Classification	1075
Standard International Trade Classification, Revision 2	1078

USER GUIDE

INTRODUCTION TO THE AMERICAN STATISTICS INDEX

The U.S. Government is the world's most important and prolific publisher of statistics. Federal agencies produce a continual flow of facts and figures on virtually every aspect of life in America and on most matters of worldwide concern.

Until the initiation of the American Statistics Index (ASI) and related services in 1972, use of Government statistics was hampered by the absence of adequate tools to identify relevant publications and pinpoint the data within them, as well as by the difficulty of locating and acquiring the publications themselves.

Major statistical agencies, such as the Census Bureau, index their own publications and disseminate them widely; other agencies issue publications lists and partial indexes; many agencies do neither. Nowhere in the Government is this wealth of data indexed, or even listed, completely. Many of these publications are not available through the Government Printing Office nor listed in its *Monthly Catalog;* and many are unavailable at depository libraries.

ASI aims to be a master guide and index to all the statistical publications of the U.S. Government. It was created to meet the need expressed in 1971 by the President's Commission on Federal Statistics, for "a central catalog of data available in government agencies . . . a single source in which one could locate all data currently collected by the Federal Government on a particular subject."

Specifically, the purpose of ASI is to perform the following functions, promptly and comprehensively:

- **Identify** the statistical data published by all branches and agencies of the Federal Government.
- **Catalog** the publications in which these data appear, providing full bibliographic information about each publication.
- **Announce** new publications as they appear.
- **Describe** the contents of these publications fully.
- **Index** this information in full subject detail.
- **Micropublish** virtually all the publications covered by ASI, thereby providing, on a continuing basis, reliable access to the statistics themselves.

To assure comprehensiveness, ASI staff members monitor all published document listings and regularly visit or contact over 500 Federal offices. In 1984, ASI collected, abstracted, and micropublished approximately 6,500 titles, including over 700 periodicals. To assure prompt coverage during the year, full abstracts and indexing for all publications, including statistical articles within individual issues of periodicals, are published in an ASI Monthly Supplement issued 5 to 6 weeks after the month in which publications are obtained. The source documents themselves are issued on ASI microfiche about one week later.

This ASI 1984 Annual, the Eleventh Annual Supplement, cumulates and enhances ASI Monthly Supplement coverage of Federal statistical publications issued during 1984. It is meant to be used in coordination with other ASI publications and services that provide comprehensive coverage of Federal statistical publications issued since the 1960s.

The following User's Guide discusses how the ASI system is organized; what kinds of statistical publications and statistics are issued by the Federal Government and accessible through ASI; how these publications are cataloged for retrieval through ASI; how their contents are abstracted and indexed in ASI; and where one can obtain the publications in hardcopy or on ASI microfiche.

COVERAGE OF ASI ANNUAL AND MONTHLY EDITIONS

ASI full coverage of U.S. Government statistical publications dates from the 1960s. This coverage is achieved through a base ASI Retrospective Edition, covering publications issued from 1960-73; Annual Supplement editions, each covering publications issued during a single year of coverage, 1974-84; and Monthly Supplement editions, issued throughout each year.

Each ASI edition is issued in 2 sections: an Abstracts Section that contains full descriptions of the content and format of each publication, organized by ASI accession number; and an Index Section that contains comprehensive subject and name, category, title, and report number indexes, with references keyed to abstract accession numbers.

The separate ASI editions are more fully described below.

ASI 1984 Eleventh Annual Supplement

The ASI 1984 Annual, the Eleventh Annual Supplement (covering publications issued Jan. 1-Dec. 31, 1984), cumulates coverage of all publications originally abstracted and indexed in the ASI 1984 Monthly Supplements. It replaces and fully supersedes those Monthly Supplements.

In addition, the 1984 Annual contains full abstracts and indexing for all periodicals actively being published in 1984. In this respect, it is also designed to serve as the base reference source for all periodicals currently publishing in 1985, and to be used in conjunction with the ASI 1985 Monthly Supplements for locating data contained in current periodicals. Abstracts of periodicals and other recurring publications in the 1984 Annual reflect the format and content of the latest issue received during the year, and include notations of any significant changes occurring during the year.

ASI 1985 Monthly Supplements

ASI 1985 Monthly Supplements provide current abstracts and indexing for all new publications issued during each month of 1985. These include wholly new publications, new items in series, and updates or new editions of annuals, semiannuals, or other publications covered in previous ASI editions.

Monthly Supplements may also include abstracts for some publications that were issued prior to 1985, but that only recently came to our attention. Such publications are covered, provided they are still current enough to be of general interest.

All statistical periodicals covered by ASI, whether quarterly, monthly, weekly, or daily, are reviewed by the ASI staff on a continuing basis, and the issues received are listed in each Monthly Supplement in the "Periodicals Received and Reviewed" section. However, Monthly Supplements do not re-abstract or re-index periodicals that have remained substantially unchanged since this 1984 Annual.

Only those periodicals that show significant changes in content or format since the basic description in this 1984 Annual are re-abstracted and indexed in the detail necessary to describe the change.

Periodical articles that contain statistical data are abstracted and indexed individually each month.

Monthly Supplements are issued 5 to 6 weeks after the end of the month covered, generally by the 10th-12th of each month.

ASI Retrospective Coverage

The base edition of ASI is the *1974 Annual and Retrospective Edition,* referred to hereafter as the Retrospective Edition. This edition provides comprehensive abstracting and indexing coverage of Federal Government statistical publications in print as of Jan. 1, 1974, as well as significant publications issued since the early 1960s.

In the case of repetitive or continuing publications, such as annuals or periodicals, which present continuing series of statistics over long periods of time, the Retrospective Edition does not describe each issuance published since 1960. Rather, it describes in full the format and contents of the most recent edition as of Jan. 1, 1974, and, where possible, characterizes major changes in format that have occurred in recent years.

The Retrospective Edition is supplemented by the following ASI Annual editions, which cover publications issued between 1974 and 1983:

The *ASI First Annual Supplement (Covering Publications Issued Jan. 1-Dec. 31, 1974)* was published in May 1975. It cumulates coverage of 1974 publications originally provided by ASI 1974 Monthly Supplements.

The *ASI Second Annual Supplement (Covering Publications Issued Jan. 1-Dec. 31, 1975)* was published in May 1976. It cumulates coverage of all 1975 publications originally provided by ASI 1975 Monthly Supplements.

The *ASI Third Annual Supplement (Covering Publications Issued Jan. 1-Dec. 31, 1976)* was published in May 1977. It cumulates coverage of all 1976 publications originally provided by ASI 1976 Monthly Supplements.

The *ASI 1977 Fourth Annual Supplement (Covering Publications Issued Jan. 1-Dec. 31, 1977)* was published in May 1978. It cumulates coverage of all 1977 publications originally provided by ASI 1977 Monthly Supplements.

The *ASI 1978 Fifth Annual Supplement (Covering Publications Issued Jan. 1-Dec. 31, 1978),* was published in May 1979. It cumulates coverage of all 1978 publications originally provided by ASI 1978 Monthly Supplements.

The *ASI 1979 Sixth Annual Supplement (Covering Publications Issued Jan. 1-Dec. 31, 1979)* was published in May 1980. It cumulates coverage of all 1979 publications originally provided by ASI 1979 Monthly Supplements.

The *ASI 1980 Seventh Annual Supplement (Covering Publications Issued Jan. 1-Dec. 31, 1980)* was published in May 1981. It cumulates coverage of all 1980 publications originally provided by ASI 1980 Monthly Supplements.

The *ASI 1981 Eighth Annual Supplement (Covering Publications Issued Jan. 1-Dec. 31, 1981)* was published in May 1982. It cumulates coverage of all 1981 publications originally provided by ASI 1981 Monthly Supplements.

The *ASI 1982 Ninth Annual Supplement (Covering Publications Issued Jan. 1-Dec. 31, 1982)* was published in early June 1983. It cumulates coverage of all 1982 publications originally provided by ASI 1982 Monthly Supplements.

The *ASI 1983 Tenth Annual Supplement (Covering Publications Issued Jan. 1-Dec. 31, 1983)* was published in early June 1984. It cumulates coverage of all 1983 publications originally provided by ASI 1983 Monthly Supplements.

STATISTICAL PUBLICATIONS COVERED BY ASI

Publications included in ASI cover a wide range of subjects, reflecting the many concerns of hundreds of central and regional Federal agencies. These issuing agencies are listed in the detailed table of contents in the Abstracts volume and in the list of "Issuing Agencies and ASI Accession Numbers" in the Index volume. ASI abstracts and indexes all Federal agency publications that contain social, economic, demographic, or natural resources data, and a selection of publications with scientific and technical data.

ASI includes all Federal publications that contain primary data of research value or secondary data collected on a special subject, and also special studies and analyses or other statistics-related materials. All types of publications are covered, whether published as periodicals, as special one-time reports, as items within a large continuing report series, or as annual or biennial reports.

For purposes of inclusion in ASI, the term "publication" is defined as all printed or duplicated materials that may be distributed by an agency to members of the public, whether on a broad or a limited basis. In a few cases, ASI has obtained single copies of materials that are not generally available for distribution, and has micropublished them for distribution. Press releases and other ephemera are included only if they contain basic data not readily available in another form.

The sections below describe selected examples of the approximately 6,500 titles covered every year by ASI.

Basic Social and Economic Statistical Data

Since its early organization, and as required by the U.S. Constitution, the Federal Government has been designated responsible for gathering basic national social and economic data. Today, six large Federal statistical agencies, each in a specialized field, have as their major function the regular collection, analysis, and publication of such data. Data published by these agencies are broadly characterized below:

- **Bureau of the Census** — Decennial 1980 Census of Population and Housing, economic and agricultural censuses, Census of Government, Current Housing Reports, Current Industrial Reports, monthly foreign trade data, and reports from the monthly Current Population Survey; also methodological studies, indexes, and guides.
- **Bureau of Labor Statistics** — Monthly reports on the Consumer Price Index and unemployment rate; other periodic, serial, and annual reports on prices, wages and hours, benefits, collective bargaining, work stoppages, and productivity.
- **Crop Reporting Board, Department of Agriculture** — Monthly to annual reports on every important U.S. crop, with data on production, yield, prices,

prospective plantings, and indicated production for the season.

- **Energy Information Administration —** Weekly to annual reports on U.S. production, consumption, stocks, trade, and prices of all major energy resources; finances and operations of oil companies, electric utilities, and other energy industries; and projections of energy supply and demand.
- **National Center for Health Statistics —** Monthly and annual collections of vital statistics; periodic surveys of the health condition of the population and of health care, personnel, and facilities.
- **National Center for Education Statistics —** Annual and other collections of data on elementary, secondary, and higher education schools, staff, students, finances, curricula, and graduates.

Many additional departments and agencies regularly compile primary data, both from required reports in their areas of responsibility and from special surveys; for example: Bureau of Mines' *Mineral Industry Surveys,* Justice Department's *Uniform Crime Reports* and victimization surveys, Treasury Department income tax statistics, Federal Reserve data on finances and banking, Department of Transportation data on highways and air traffic, National Science Foundation's *Surveys of Scientific Resources,* and Central Intelligence Agency studies of the economies of Communist countries.

Program Related Statistics

Almost all executive departments and administrative or regulatory agencies publish statistics on their own funding and programs.

These data cover agency financial statements, personnel, processing efficiency, workloads, accidents, persons served, and payments made. Some of these data have interest well beyond the functioning of the agency; for example, social security recipients and payments, food stamp recipients, aliens admitted, speed of handling court cases, nuclear power plant shutdowns and accidents, Federal civilian workforce, and military troop strengths.

ASI provides full coverage of these types of program statistics, but, where possible, selects agency-wide reports for inclusion, and excludes subagency reports that only repeat data in the reports of the larger unit.

For example, the basic financial publication for the entire Government, the *Budget of the U.S.,* is fully covered by ASI in both its brief and detailed versions; but ASI does not also cover budget requests or justifications from individual agencies. ASI generally covers the annual report of each separate agency, but not those of subagencies unless they include unique data. Also, ASI covers data on grants, contracts, and procurements, as reported by a large agency as a whole (such as DOD *Prime Contract Awards*), but usually excludes reports by individual divisions.

Special Studies

Many agencies produce a steady stream of monographs, analyses, and studies on subjects within their areas of activity; these are covered by ASI whenever they include statistical data of probable research value. Some agencies also undertake large special studies from time to time; examples of those covered by ASI are the 1972-73 Consumer Expenditure Survey and its annual updates beginning in 1980-81, which provide the basis for major Consumer Price Index revisions.

In some cases, special commissions are created specifically for the purpose of studying a problem of current concern. Studies of this nature have been covered by ASI beginning with those from the early 1960s. For instance, this 1984 Annual covers reports from the President's Private Sector Survey on Cost Control (Grace Commission) presenting proposals to reduce Federal budget deficits and agency operating costs.

Some original studies are included which, although not primarily quantitative in nature, present statistics unavailable anywhere else; a number of reports by the Commission on Civil Rights fall into this category. Other publications in ASI are primarily non-statistical, but may contain significant statistical sections. Congressional committee hearings and prints are prime examples.

Non-Tabular Statistics-Related Materials

Publications selected for inclusion in ASI generally contain statistical data in tabular form. However, maps, charts, listings, and narrative materials have also been covered if they provide aid in locating statistical data or in understanding statistical programs. Thus, we cover narrative discussions of statistical methodology, classification guides, directories, and bibliographies that include references to a significant body of statistical materials.

In general, we have attempted to cover all such material issued by the major statistical agencies, but we have applied somewhat more rigid standards for inclusion of material from other agencies.

Exclusions and Selective Coverage

The following kinds of material are either excluded from ASI or covered only on a selective basis:

- **Scientific and technical data —** Highly technical studies, scientific and experimental observations, engineering data, clinical medical studies, and animal laboratory studies are generally excluded from ASI. These data are disseminated through such information services as NTIS, NASA, ERIC, and the National Library of Medicine; ASI makes no attempt to duplicate this coverage.

  We do provide selective coverage of technical data with broad social or economic implications or particular current interest, as well as the less technical publications of technically oriented agencies. For instance, we do cover epidemiological studies; a large number of reports on energy resources, use, and conservation; EPA publications presenting monitoring data and pollution abatement measures and technologies; NOAA weather observations and forecasting techniques; and selected NASA publications.

- **Contract studies —** ASI coverage of contract studies by private organizations is typically limited to those that have been issued by a Federal agency as its own publication, either directly through the agency, through GPO, or through NTIS. In special cases, additional contract studies are covered that we would normally exclude but that have been recommended by an agency as being of particular importance.
- **Classified and confidential data —** These data are not included.
- **Congressional publications —** Congressional publications that contain substantial statistical information are included in ASI. However, ASI does not include any appropriations hearings, which contain primarily Federal program data, and which are abstracted and indexed in detail in the comprehensive *CIS/Index to Publications of the U.S. Congress.*

When ASI covers a congressional publication also covered by the CIS/Index, it is completely re-abstracted and indexed to highlight the statistical data.

ORGANIZATION OF ASI ABSTRACTS AND INDEXES

ASI provides access to statistical data through companion volumes of indexes and abstracts. In making a subject search, you should consult this 1984 Annual for descriptions of publications issued during 1984, and for basic descriptions of periodicals that continue publication in 1985. The 1985 Monthly Supplements will cover new publications issued during 1985, including new editions of annual reports, and will change and update information regarding 1985 issues of periodicals. To search for material issued prior to 1984, you should consult the ASI Retrospective Edition and the subsequent Annual Supplements.

ASI Indexes

Ordinarily, research in ASI will begin with the Index volume. The ASI indexes are designed to lead you to the information you seek from a variety of starting points. The four basic ASI indexes are designed to answer the following types of questions:

- **Subject and Name Index** — "What publications provide statistical data on cost of living and related matters?" and "What publications were issued by the Office of Management and Budget?"
- **Category Index** — "What publications provide cost of living data broken down by city, or some other geographic category?"
- **Title Index** — "What statistical data are included in a periodical entitled *Monthly Labor Review*?"
- **Agency Report Number Index** — "Where in ASI will I find reports in the BLS Bulletin 3015 series?"

Each ASI index reference will lead you to an abstract. Descriptive abstracts are provided for every publication; they are designed to tell you enough about the information content of the publication to enable you to decide whether or not it is likely to contain the specific data for which you are looking.

This system depends upon a basic key — the ASI accession number — which identifies publications (or specific parts of publications) in both the index and the abstract volumes.

ASI Accession Numbers

Each ASI abstract carries a unique accession number, which identifies not only the individual publication, but also the issuing agency and the publication type (see Sample Abstracts on p. xxiii-xxv for an illustration of how accession numbers appear on abstracts). The accession number has four basic components, the form and functions of which are described below.

- **Issuing Agency** — In the accession number for any one publication's abstract, the first two to four digits (up to the digit before the hyphen) are keyed to an overall coding scheme and represent the agency that issued the publication. (Coding for large agencies may be broken down by sub-agency or subject matter area.)
- **Publication type** — The last digit before the hyphen is keyed to the document's publication type, as follows:
  - 2 = Current periodicals, daily through semi-annual
  - 4 = annuals and biennials
  - 6 = publications in series
  - 8 = special and irregular publications
  - 1, 3, 5, 7, 9 = special series and special groups of publications (such as census reports or crop reports) that do not fall into one of the four basic types or which are most clearly represented if kept together under a special heading.
- **Sequential ASI serial number** — The digits after the hyphen form a unique serial number, sequentially assigned, basically in order of ASI acquisition, so that every publication has its own unique number that can be easily found in the Abstracts volumes of ASI.
- **Analytic number** — In many cases, ASI describes publications by using a main abstract in coordination with subordinate abstracts called "analytics," which are printed after the main abstract and are identified and sequenced by decimal numbers (.1, .2, or .3, etc.) following the main abstract accession number.

Analytics are frequently used to describe and individually index distinct parts of a large publication. They are also used to abstract and separately index the individual publications comprising a series, or the statistical articles appearing in individual issues of periodicals.

To use the ASI indexes and abstracts effectively, you do not need to know the ASI agency-coding or publication-

Sample: ASI Accession Numbers

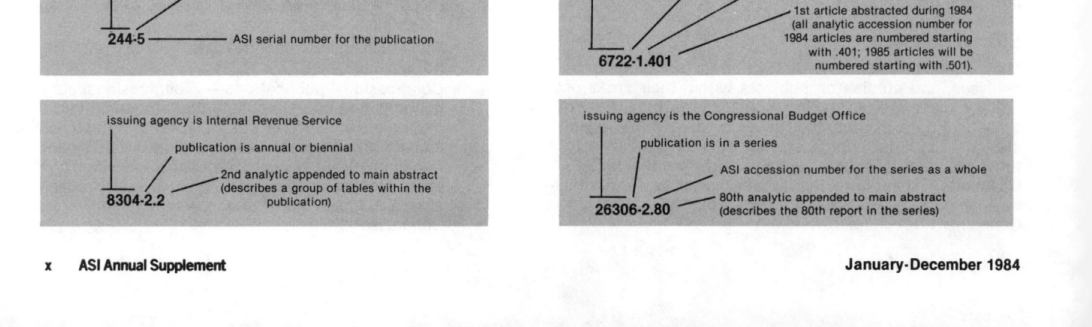

type coding schemes, which are incorporated into accession numbers, but familiarity with codes can speed interpretation of entries in the indexes.

Arrangement of Abstracts by Accession Number

All abstracts are arranged by accession number in ascending order. This system automatically catalogs all publications, first by issuing agency, then by publication type, and then by individual publication serial number. All index references are made to these accession numbers. For ease in referring from index to abstract, every page of abstracts in the Abstracts volume carries a locator number in the upper right or left corner.

Continuity of Accession Numbers

Generally, once ASI has assigned an accession number to a publication, all successive issues or updates of that publication will receive the same accession number. If the number is changed, cross-references between the old and new numbers are included in the abstracts. The accession number will change if, for example, the periodicity of the publication changes from quarterly to annual, or if the issuing agency of the publication changes.

HOW ASI ABSTRACTS STATISTICAL PUBLICATIONS

All ASI abstracts are original and are based upon examination of the entire document. Abstracts differ substantially in degree of detail, depending on the type of publications and the kind of data being described. However, all abstracts are written to fulfill certain objectives.

These objectives are to describe a publication fully enough to allow you to determine if it is likely to contain the specific statistical data you seek; to provide the bibliographic data you need to identify and locate the publication if you wish to borrow or acquire it; and to tell you where in the publication you can find the data, often with specific page ranges.

Guidelines for Describing Statistical Contents

In describing the basic subject matter or statistical data of a publication, ASI does not attempt to summarize observations or conclusions. Rather, we attempt to state consistently what a publication is about; what specific data are presented, from what source, and at what level of detail; and what relationship the publication has to other statistical series. In describing a publication, ASI abstractors observe the following guidelines:

- State the subject matter and purpose of the publication as a whole.
- Identify sources of data presented, whether primary (based on original collection) or whether selected or reprinted from other published sources.
- Describe, if data are primary, the sample type and size, the survey methodology, or the information reporting requirement by which the data were gathered.
- Specify time span and geographic coverage of the data (special methods, discussed below, are used to describe time coverage and currency of data in periodicals).
- State periodicity of data collection and publication.
- Indicate breakdowns of the data and the level of detail they provide.
- Outline physical contents of the publication, such as number of charts and tables, and presence of narrative discussion, appendices, bibliographies, and index. Include page ranges to indicate the quantity and location of each type of material.
- List individual titles of all tables in publications that present continuing time series data or data from basic censuses (handling of table listings is further discussed below).
- Review continuity and length of time series data, providing references to ASI abstracts of earlier publications in the series (with the exception of semiannual or annual reports bearing the same accession number) and any breaks in publishing continuity since ASI coverage began.
- Provide references to known related publications that present similar or identical source data in different analytical or publication formats.

In all cases, the aim is to specify as precisely as possible the actual data to be found in a publication. Particular pains are taken to distinguish among publications providing different data on similar subject matter.

Listing of Table Titles

For every publication, ASI attempts to identify, mention, and index the subjects and categories for which significant amounts of statistical data are presented. Often, the best way to describe in detail the data in a statistical publication is to list the titles of the tables it contains.

In general, ASI lists individual titles of tables that carry forward a continuing time series of data in biennial, annual or periodical publications. We also list table titles for publications presenting data from basic surveys and censuses. We usually list the titles exactly as they appear in the original publication. Where necessary for clarity or additional detail, these titles are augmented by material in brackets. Pagination for each table, or group of tables, is given.

Abstracts of special or irregular publications generally do not list tables, but describe the tables in varying degrees of detail, depending upon their number and complexity. If listing table titles is the clearest and briefest way to indicate the exact data present, it is done for any type of publication.

Special Aspects of Abstracts Describing Periodicals

This 1984 Annual contains full descriptions of all statistical periodicals that published any issues during 1984. Since most statistical periodicals retain constant format, features, and tables, it would be redundant to provide full abstracts for each issue. Therefore, abstracts of periodicals indicate the features common to all issues and list tables that appear in each issue or at regular intervals. Periodicals that were discontinued during 1984 are so annotated in this 1984 Annual; all others may be presumed to be continuing publication in 1985.

Statistical articles in periodicals are individually abstracted and indexed each month, and special tables that appear only in certain issues are listed. All such articles and special tables appearing in periodical issues during 1984 are included in this 1984 Annual.

In listing tables for periodicals, we do not give the time coverage of the data as a specific month or year, but describe it in a way that will apply to all issues. The abstracts do not include page ranges, which may change from issue to issue.

All abstracts of periodicals in this annual include a notation of issues received, reviewed, and microfilmed during 1984. The cover dates of the issues are labeled (P) if they approximate the publication date; or (D) if they represent the period covered by the data presented. The body of the abstract usually indicates the time lag between the data date and the publication date.

Periodical abstracts in the 1984 Annual serve as the base abstracts for continuing periodicals, to be used in conjunction with the 1985 Monthly Supplements. Issues of those periodicals received during 1985 will be listed in the Monthly Supplements "Periodicals Received and Reviewed" section as they are received, but will not be re-abstracted or re-indexed unless their contents change significantly.

Provision of Bibliographic Data

ASI abstracts for each publication provide, at a minimum, primary bibliographic information, such as title, date, collation, agency report number (if any), and periodicity. In addition, we include, whenever possible, the Superintendent of Documents classification number, the Library of Congress card number, the Government Printing Office (GPO) *Monthly Catalog* entry number, the GPO stock number, and the depository Item Number.

However, many Government publications covered in ASI have not been assigned all, or in some cases any, identification or classification numbers. Many of the publications we cover are not cataloged either in the GPO *Monthly Catalog* or in the issuing agency's own catalog or publication list, if one exists.

Each document abstract provides as much specific information on hardcopy availability as we are able to obtain at time of publication, and includes information on ASI microfiche availability and price. (For more information about the availability of documents or microfiche, see below "Acquiring the Documents.")

Usually, all bibliographic information for a publication is given at the head of the main abstract, following the title (see Sample Abstracts on p. xxiii-xxv for detailed labeling of bibliographic information provided). When analytic abstracts are being used to describe separate documents in a series, however (see sample abstract for publications in series), only bibliographic data common to the entire series are included in the main abstract, and information individual to each document is shown in its respective analytic abstract.

Frequently, a publication that is going to be cataloged by the GPO *Monthly Catalog* will not have been cataloged by the time ASI monthly abstracts are published. If such *Monthly Catalog* entries appear prior to the ASI Annual, information from them is included in the published Annual. Occasionally, items have not yet been covered in the *Monthly Catalog*, but are documents within continuing series for which established classification data exist; in such cases, we will publish classification data, based on precedent, in the absence of *Monthly Catalog* verification. In addition, ASI publishes bibliographic data revisions and additions in a special section at the end of each quarterly Monthly Supplement index volume. These revisions and additions are then cumulated annually and issued as separate pamphlets to supplement the bibliographic data in each past ASI Annual.

References to Publication Dates

When a date is included in the title of a publication, ASI prints it as part of the title; this date usually represents the period covered by the data or, sometimes, the year the report was prepared. When a date is given anywhere within a publication to indicate date of transmittal, final preparation, or printing, ASI lists this date in the bibliographic data. The user should remember, however, that schedules are often delayed and the publication may not actually have become available until later.

Some publications contain no date at all, and, for these, ASI lists in the bibliographic data the closest approximation it can determine of the year of actual release.

Uses of Main Abstracts and Analytic Abstracts

To handle the broad variety of materials it includes, ASI developed a flexible approach to document accessioning and abstracting. As described earlier in the section on the ASI accession number, we use a structured abstract system that provides for main abstracts and subordinate abstracts (analytics).

ASI uses analytics for the following purposes:

- To single out part of a publication for more detailed abstracting, or to divide the publication into parts, generally into groups of tables, which are then listed. Analytics may also be used for sections or chapters of a publication, each of which is then further described.
- To abstract individual publications in a series. The title and bibliographic data unique to the publication are given in the analytic; data common to the series as a whole are given in the main abstract.
- To abstract articles in periodicals. Article abstracts are identified by 3-digit analytics, beginning with .401 for the first article abstracted in 1984. Thus, article abstracts always follow table listings, which begin with .1.

ASI provides for each individual publication the descriptive information outlined in the above sections. For periodicals, annuals, or one-time publications, the basic information is usually given in the main abstract (see the Sample Abstracts on p. xxiii and xxiv).

For publications in series, information common to the series as a whole is given in the main abstract, and that peculiar to each individual publication in the series is given in its respective analytic (see Sample Abstract on p. xxv). This system allows complete descriptions of individual, related publications without extensive repetition of common characteristics.

The use of analytics also allows ASI to index to specific parts or even single tables in publications. Any index terms may be assigned to an analytic to indicate data specific only to that analytic, and the ASI accession number, with a decimal, will lead the user to it.

For example, the accession number 6224-2.2, under the index term "Counterfeiting and forgery," shows that the second analytic, not the publication as a whole, contains data on that topic. The main abstract, however, will contain the basic information on the subject, data type and source, and overall contents of the publication.

When index terms apply to the entire publication or to many of the analytics used, these terms are assigned to the main abstract only and are not repeated for the individual analytics to which they apply.

HOW ASI INDEXES STATISTICAL PUBLICATIONS

ASI indexes are designed to serve a wide range of needs and search approaches for locating statistical materials. To accomplish this, the following four separate indexes have been provided:

- **Index by Subjects and Names,** which contains references to specific subject areas, places, and personal and corporate authors.
- **Index by Categories** (and accompanying Guide to Selected Standard Classifications), which contains references to tabular data breakdowns by twenty-one common geographic, demographic, and economic categories (e.g., by State, by sex, or by specific industry).
- **Index by Titles**
- **Index by Agency Report Numbers**

This section reviews basic ASI objectives and policies in building these four indexes; provides instructions and suggestions for using each of them; and gives specific hints on which indexes to use for answers to a number of different types of questions.

INDEX BY SUBJECTS AND NAMES

The Index by Subjects and Names provides access to:

- **Subjects** of publications and of specific data within publications.
- **Place names,** including names of cities, counties, States, and foreign countries to which data relate.
- **Government agency names,** including the Federal national or regional agencies, commissions, or congressional committees that issue publications or that are the subjects of data contained in publications.
- **Major Government programs or proposals** to which data relate (e.g., Work Incentive Program, Medicare).
- **Special classes of publications or data** (e.g., publications under the terms "Opinion and attitude surveys," "Statistical programs and activities," "Projections," "Directories," and "Bibliographies").
- **Individual personal names, companies, and institutions,** both as authors and as subjects of publications.
- **Major surveys** through which significant bodies of data have been collected (e.g., Current Population Survey).

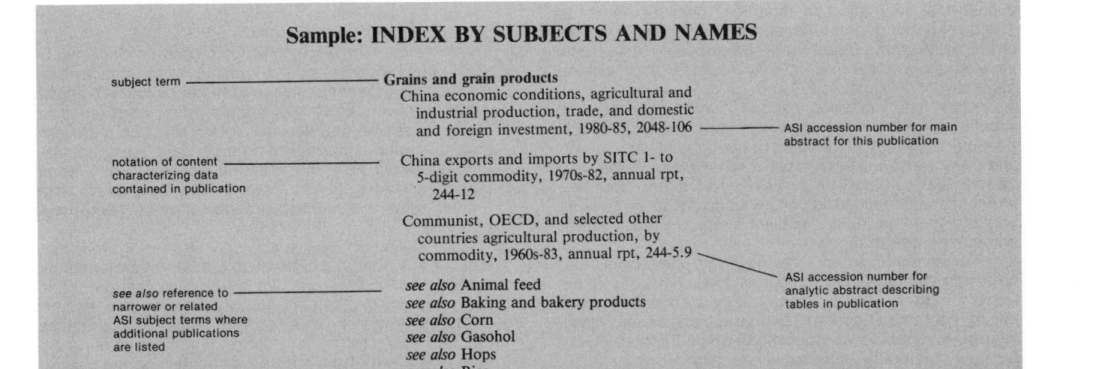

Sample: INDEX BY SUBJECTS AND NAMES

As illustrated in the above sample, this index consists of the following four basic structural elements:

- Subject and author terms (subject terms are based upon a controlled vocabulary).
- *See* and *see also* cross references directing the user to the appropriate index term or to terms under which additional related data may be found.
- Notations of content, which summarize the relevant data content and time coverage of each publication indexed to a particular term. Under an author's name the title is used as a notation of content.
- ASI accession numbers, which refer the user to the full ASI abstract for that publication.

ASI Subject Terms

Subject terms and cross references in the Index of Subjects and Names are based on a controlled vocabulary developed by ASI to meet the particular needs of ASI data coverage. This vocabulary is constantly reviewed and enlarged to respond to the ever expanding range of subjects receiving attention in Government publications.

Publications abstracted in ASI cover an extremely wide variety of subjects, and the data presented range from the very general to the very specific. In selecting subject index terms for the ASI controlled vocabulary, we have strived to maintain a middle level of specificity, which allows for adequate flexibility in indexing to specific subjects, but avoids too great a fragmentation and scattering of subject references. For example, in dealing with data on commodities, the ASI controlled vocabulary generally contains terms for commodity groups, such as the terms "Grains and grain products," "Animal feed," and "Baking and bakery products," found in the preceding sample. However, in the case of selected specific commodities, which are frequently dealt with in publications covered by ASI, we have established separate index terms (e.g., "Wheat," "Corn," "Rice," and "Soybeans" in the preceding sample).

ASI policy is to index to subject terms that reflect the principal subject matters and data contents of each publication abstracted. In addition, unusual items or items of special interest that occur in the body of a report or article, or in individual tables or groups of tables, will be indexed whether or not they relate to the primary focus of the publication at hand.

When indexing a publication to which a hierarchy of vocabulary terms might apply, we select the most specific applicable term or terms in the controlled vocabulary, and do not also index to broader or narrower terms that do not reflect so well its particular focus. But when the focus of the document is equally upon the more general and the more particular subject term, we place index entries under both terms.

For example, when indexing large compendia that present major data on commodities, we index both to the terms for commodity groups and also to those terms for specific commodities that have been established in the controlled vocabulary. Publications primarily focusing on a single commodity, such as wheat, corn, or rice, will be indexed only to the specific commodity terms and not to the more general term "Grains and grain products." Publications that focus on the general subject of grains, but contain a considerable amount of data on one or more of these specific commodities, will be indexed both to the specific commodity terms and to "Grains and grain products." Finally, publications that include some data on the specific commodities, but have a main focus that is on grains will be indexed only to "Grains and grain products."

Cross References

The *see also* references provided by ASI, such as those shown in the preceding sample, are designed to guide you to additional material to be found under the related or narrower terms cited, and to remind you of the need to check the Index by Categories where additional data may be available.

ASI also provides *see* references to aid in locating the specific form of phraseology of subject terms used by ASI. ("Great Plains," for example, is not a term used by ASI, but relevant entries will be found under the term "North Central States.")

Notations of Content

Each index entry under a subject or category term contains an ASI accession number and a "notation of content," a brief description of a report's subject matter or data content. These notations assist you in selecting relevant entries under any particular term and restricting the number of abstracts to which you need refer.

Notations of content are individually written for each publication indexed by ASI. They include, at a minimum, the main subject or subjects of the publication as they relate to the specific index term, and the data date. Additional information that may be noted, as relevant, includes geographic area of coverage, major data breakdowns, and periodicity of publication. Under an author term, the publication title is typically used as the notation of content. Elsewhere, the publication title is rarely used for this purpose.

In selecting the first words for notations of content, we have attempted to choose key words that will automatically group index entries according to their prime subject content. The key words perform some of the functions of a "second-level" index term (e.g., the word "China" used in the preceding sample to group entries relating to China). Although the informal type of grouping thus achieved can be helpful to you, these groups will not always bring together all related material. A complete search should include examination of all notations of content under a given term.

In general, only one notation of content for any one publication appears under a specific index term. This entry must reflect the full scope of the publication being indexed as it relates to that subject term. As a result, in many cases, the notation of content must be quite general, subsuming coverage of a great deal of specific data. In those cases, however, when the material relating to an index term is too diverse to be covered by a single notation of content, a second notation may be used under that term.

As stated above, usually only one notation of content for any one publication will appear under a specific index term. However, the wording of the notation of content for a single publication may be different for each of the index terms under which it appears. In such cases, the differences reflect an effort to relate the wording and initial key-word of the notation of content to the specific index term under which it appears.

For example, the publication in the above index sample with the notation of content, "Communist, OECD, and selected other countries agricultural production, by commodity, 1960s-83, annual rpt," contains data on a wide variety of additional economic subjects relating to communist and other countries. Under the index term "Communist countries," to reflect this broad scope, the notation of content reads "Economic conditions in Communist, OECD, and selected other countries, 1960s-83, annual rpt."

In all cases, it must be remembered that notations of content are brief and highly condensed guides, and cannot be used as substitutes for the abstracts. The full abstracts will further describe the extent and limitations of the data indicated in the index entry, and will often note the existence of related data that could not be indicated in the brief space occupied by the index entry.

Other Indexing Conventions

* **Alphabetization** — Following Library of Congress practice, ASI alphabetizes on a word-by-word basis. For example, "New Jersey" and "New York" precede "Newark," and "Fire departments" precedes

- "Firearms." It is important to know if there is a word break in a term, since a compound word like "Airlines" will follow all terms beginning with the word "Air" (i.e., "Air pollution"). Hyphenated words are alphabetized as if they were two separate words.
- **Proper Names —** These have been entered in natural word order. Thus, you will find "Department of Labor" rather than "Labor Department," and "Bureau of Labor Statistics" rather than "Labor Statistics Bureau." However, names of individuals always have last name first, such as "Little, Arthur D., Inc."
- **References to the United States —** Because of the nature and scope of most U.S. Government statistical publications, "U.S." is an implied prefix for many of the subjects in the ASI Subject Index. Thus, you will find "Army" rather than "U.S. Army," and "Foreign relations" rather than "U.S. Government-foreign relations." In agency titles, the prefix "U.S." has been dropped whenever possible, except where necessary to conform to *U.S. Government Manual* usage (e.g., U.S. Postal Service). In notations of content, "U.S." is always implied unless "foreign," "world," or "by country" is specified.

Making a Subject Index Search

If you are seeking a specific piece of information in ASI, you will often find it quickly by referring to the obvious subject term or terms, locating the relevant group of notations of content, and selecting the one or ones most pertinent to your search. You should then consult the abstract for a full description of the publication and its availability.

If such a search does not yield the information required, or if you desire a more complete survey of possible data on the subject, additional steps should be taken. As previously noted, your first step should be to consult the more specific and related *see also* terms listed under the relevant subject terms in order to obtain additional leads.

Your next step should be to consult more general terms that encompass the subject matter sought. Despite our efforts to index to the most specific available term, some statistical publications are so wide-ranging or so detailed in their subject coverage that it is impractical to include references to all the specific topics they mention. It is wise, therefore, when checking the specific subject term in which you are interested, also to check the more general terms related to it.

Searching the subject terms, however, is only part of making a successful subject search in ASI. For instance, a publication that contains data on agriculture may break down this data by hundreds of different commodities, one of which is likely to be grains. The existence of these breakdowns by category adds a new dimension to statistical data retrieval. To help the researcher locate this kind of information quickly, ASI has provided an Index by Categories, which is discussed in detail below.

A limited amount of overlapping (or "double posting") occurs between the Index by Subjects and Names and the Index by Categories. Detailed data subject matter shown in tabular breakdowns (e.g., occupational breakdowns) are always indexed in the Index by Categories. In selected cases, where tabular breakdowns or cross-tabulations provide an extensive or particularly significant body of data on a given subject, references to these data have been included in both the Index of Subjects and Names (e.g., indexed to the subject terms "Clerical workers," "Nurses and nursing," "Blue-collar workers," etc.) and the Index by Categories (e.g., "By Occupation"). The existence of this limited overlap should not mislead the user with respect to the large amount of additional data available through the Index by Categories.

INDEX BY CATEGORIES

As mentioned above, to provide a ready access to the multiplicity of detailed statistical data in tabular breakdowns and cross-classifications, ASI has created a special type of index: the Index by Categories. This index includes references to all publications that contain comparative tabular data broken down in any or several of the following twenty-one standard categories:

- **Geographic Categories —** By census division; By city; By county; By foreign country; By outlying area (territories of the U.S.); By Region; By SMSA or MSA; By State; and By urban-rural and metro-nonmetro.
- **Economic Categories —** By commodity; By Federal agency; By income; By individual company or institution; By industry; and By occupation.
- **Demographic Categories —** By age; By disease; By educational attainment; By marital status; By race; and By sex.

For easier use, index entries within each of the categories are grouped according to subject matter, under one of the following nineteen subheadings:

Agriculture and Food
Banking, Finance, and Insurance
Communications and Transportation
Education
Energy Resources and Demand
Geography and Climate
Government and Defense
Health and Vital Statistics
Housing and Construction
Industry and Commerce
Labor and Employment
Law Enforcement
Natural Resources, Environment, and Pollution
Population
Prices and Cost of Living
Public Welfare and Social Security
Recreation and Leisure
Science and Technology
Veterans Affairs

In those instances where a reference might logically fit under two or more of the subheadings, we have tried to select the most obvious one and to place it there. A brief listing of the kinds of material referenced under each subheading is given at beginning of the Index by Categories.

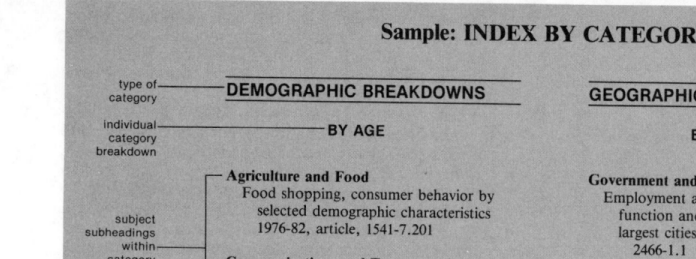

As illustrated in the above sample, this index consists of the following four basic structural elements:

- Category terms, for the twenty-one categories listed above.
- Subject subheadings, to group entries within each category by subject matter. These are listed above.
- Notations of content, which are used just as in the Index by Subjects and Names to characterize further the data indexed to the category.
- ASI accession numbers, which refer the user to the full ASI abstract for that publication.

In the Index by Categories, data in the specified categories can be identified with greater detail and specificity than in the Index by Subjects and Names. This index also provides the best and most complete source for locating comparative data on a wide variety of subjects.

Breakdowns in individual tables, to which references are made in the Index by Categories, may vary considerably in the detail provided. Breakdowns "By sex" are, by definition, complete. Breakdowns "By State" are usually, but not always, for all 50 States. However, detail in breakdowns of such categories as "By city," "By SMSA," "By Federal agency," "By industry," "By commodity," and "By occupation," varies widely. In the abstracts of publications containing such breakdowns, we have, when possible, tried to include an indication of the degree of detail provided (i.e., "by detailed industries," "by major cause of death," "for 20 large cities," etc.).

In searching the Index by Categories for very detailed data, such as those on a small city, minor industry, or other specific entity, you are likely to find several entries referring to publications that could possibly contain the information you want. You will usually find it necessary to go back to the abstract to ascertain which publication has or is most likely to have that information. In some cases, where a high degree of specificity is desired, an examination of the Index by Categories and the abstracts will help to narrow the field of possibilities, but it may still be necessary actually to examine the text of two or three publications to be certain the exact information needed is there.

Examples and further instructions for making various types of Category Index searches follow.

Making a Search by Geographic Categories

Much data on Chicago can be located under the term "Chicago, Ill." in the Index by Subjects and Names. These entries represent instances where Chicago is the principal subject of a publication or where a significant body of information relating to Chicago can be found. There are considerable additional data, however, to be found in individual tables that have a breakdown by city, including Chicago. These data are located in the Index by Categories under the term "By city."

Similarly, you can find data on individual States, counties, SMSAs, MSAs, or foreign countries in the Index by Categories. The number of places included in reports indexed to these categories may vary considerably. Breakdowns by State or county are usually complete, unless the notation of content indicates that data are limited to a specific part of the country, or to "large counties" or "selected counties." In the case of cities or foreign countries, there may be wider variation; when practical, the notation of content indicates the degree of detail provided (e.g., "447 largest cities" or "major States and cities" in the sample above). The abstract often provides further precision, sometimes even listing the cities covered.

Data on the regions of the U.S. can be found under the category "By region." Since, however, the different Federal agencies use a variety of regional delineations, such data may not be comparable from one report to another. To assist the user, ASI has provided lists of six major regional structures in the Guide to Selected Standard Classifications, further described below.

Making a Search by Economic Categories

The Index by Categories term "By Industry" will lead to reports and to individual tables which present a wealth of detailed data on both major and minor industries. These data can often be found only through the Index by Categories, since the Subject Index would become unwieldy if ASI attempted to index each column of every table.

In the same way as for cities, explained above, the notation of content will generally indicate the level of industry detail provided in each publication, and the abstract will specify further. In some cases, the degree of detail in the breakdowns may be based upon a standard classification system, such as the Standard Industrial Classification (SIC) which classifies all types of industries, businesses, and services for purposes of developing comparable statistical data. Whenever such a standard classification is used, this fact is noted in the abstract and frequently in the notation of content as well. Several of the most frequently used classifications, including the SIC, are listed in ASI's Guide to Standard Statistical Classifications, further described below.

The use of the SIC listing to find data on a specific industry is illustrated in the sample below. For example, if you want data on the typesetting industry, an industry for which there is no separate entry in the Subject Index, you can refer to the SIC listing to determine at what SIC level the typesetting service industry is specified. Since it is specified at the 4-digit level, you can then examine the entries under "By Industry" in the Category Index, and check the abstracts of likely references, to find reports and specific tables that present data broken down to the SIC 4-digit level.

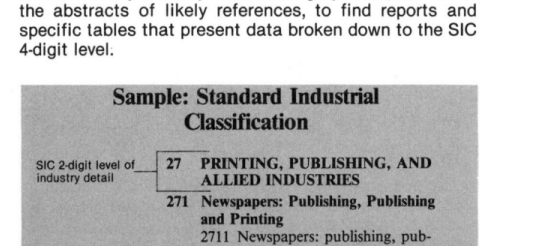

Very detailed data on commodities can be found in the same way, using the category term "By Commodity." The industry and commodity categories only partially overlap, since many firms produce a wide range of commodities but are classified only in the industry of their major activity. ASI policy is to follow the classification—industry-based or commodity-based—used by the publication. To make a complete search for such economic data, you will probably want to examine both categories.

Data shown for individual entities of all kinds, including companies or their brand name products, universities, hospitals, foundations, and government projects may be found under "By Individual Company or Institution." Category indexing is also provided for data "By Federal Agency," "By Occupation," and "By Income," including both salary levels and total family income.

Making a Search by Demographic Categories

When you want data about specific groups of the population, the Category Index is a versatile tool to augment the Subject Index. For example, the following subjects can be thoroughly searched using this two-pronged approach:

- **Women —** Data may be found under the subject terms "Women," "Women's employment," or "Maternity." Quantities of additional data may be found under the category term "By Sex."

- **Age groups —** Look under subject terms "Children," "Youth," or "Aged and aging." Look also under the category term "By Age."

- **Blacks —** Look under such subject terms as "Black Americans," "Black students," or "Racial discrimination." More data can be found under the category term "By Race."

- **The poor —** The subject term "Poverty" will lead to reports dealing specifically with the poor. Additional data can be extracted from reports with breakdowns "By Income," found in the Category Index.

- **Divorced persons —** The subject term "Marriage and divorce" will lead to reports specifically on this subject. The category term "By Marital Status" will lead to additional data.

In a similar way you can find data on demographic groups under the categories "By Occupation," "By Industry," "By Educational Attainment," or "By Disease."

Making a Search for Comparative Data

A major advantage of the Index by Categories is the ease with which it enables you to locate comparative data on a subject. This index is the logical starting point for such search questions as: "Which cities have the highest unemployment rate?" "Which States have the lowest taxes?" "Which are the largest industries in the U.S.; in specified States?" "Do people with more education really earn more money?" (These last two questions each combine two category terms: "By Industry" and "By State;" and "By Income" and "By Educational Attainment.") Data pertinent to these questions will also be found under the subject terms "Employment and unemployment, general;" "State and local taxes," etc. However, the most efficient search for such comparative data will begin with the Index by Categories.

ASI's Guide to Selected Standard Classifications

As stated above, Federal statistical data breakdowns are frequently presented in terms of several standard classification systems, and ASI abstracts generally make note of their use. To provide an easily accessible reference for the user, we have printed a number of major classification systems or lists in the "Guide to Selected Standard Classifications." The Guide, which appears at the end of the Index Section, includes the following listings:

- Census regions and divisions; outlying areas of the U.S.; Standard Federal Administrative Regions; farm production regions; Federal Reserve Districts; Federal Home Loan Bank Districts; Bureau of Labor Statistics Regions.
- Metropolitan Statistical Areas (MSAs); Consolidated Metropolitan Statistical Areas; cities with population over 100,000 (based on the 1980 Census of Population); and Consumer Price Index cities.
- Standard Industrial Classification (SIC), providing 1- to 4-digit codes for industry divisions through individual industries.
- Standard Occupational Classification, providing 1-to 4-digit codes for major and minor occupational groups.

* Standard International Trade Classification, a system of 3-digit codes for commodities in world trade, developed by the United Nations, used for foreign trade data, and consistent with the 7-digit codes used for U.S. import-export data.

Even when data breakdowns do not correspond with one of these standard classification systems, these listings can still serve as useful guides to what may be included in breakdowns at varying levels of detail (i.e., "by major

industry group" will approximate the 2-digit SIC level, and "by detailed industries" will approximate the 4-digit level).

Government publications that describe these and other standard classification systems, survey methods, glossaries, and directories are abstracted and microfilmed by ASI, and can usually also be obtained in hardcopy by the user. Such publications are generally indexed to "Methodology" or "Classifications" as well as to their respective subjects.

INDEX BY TITLES

This index lists titles of all publications covered by ASI in the 1984 Annual. It also lists titles of periodical articles, conference papers, and reports within larger publications when these are separately abstracted.

This index lists all main titles and also analytic titles of individual monographs within a series, except when series reports are essentially identical, e.g., a series of State reports or country reports. In these cases, the name of each State or country can be found in the Index by Subjects and Names; the reports will also be listed, usually in alphabetical order, in the Abstracts volume under the ASI accession number for the series. Series reports on individual commodities or industries are listed in the Index by Titles under the name of the commodity, followed by the name of the series, e.g., "Footwear, Current Industrial Report."

Titles are listed alphabetically in natural word order, as they appear in the abstract. ASI routinely omits initial articles (a, an, the) in titles, both in the abstracts and in this index. Titles that begin with Arabic numbers (e.g., "1984 Gas Mileage Guide") appear at the end of the index.

To assist users in locating a publication, we provide in certain cases alternate word orders for titles, including

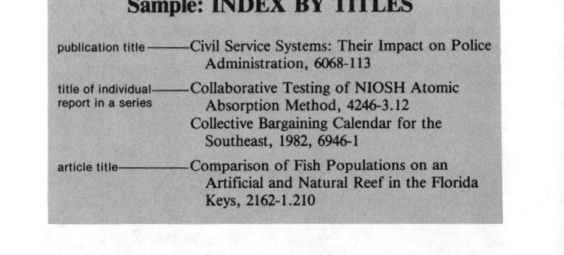

all of those beginning with Arabic numerals. For example, census reports are generally listed under the overall title of the census and under the title of the individual report as well.

Each title is followed by the ASI accession number, which directs the user to the abstract of the publication.

Anyone knowing the title of the publication desired can locate it most quickly in this index. Users should keep in mind that notations of content in the Index by Subjects and Names and in the Index by Categories bear no necessary relationship to a publication's title and should not be confused with it.

INDEX BY AGENCY REPORT NUMBERS

This index lists the report numbers assigned to publications by the issuing agency. It can be useful both for identifying one specific document and for locating an entire series of numbered publications.

We have grouped numbers in this index under the names of each issuing executive department, independent agency or commission, or congressional body, but

generally have not attempted to group them by bureau, office, or committee within a department or independent agency. (Frequently, the alphabetical prefixes of the numbers themselves serve to identify agencies.)

Exceptions to this general rule are Census Bureau publication numbers, which are preceded with the word "Census" so that they group together and are not intermixed with other Commerce Department reports. Also, the "DHHS" prefix in the Department of Health and Human Services report numbers has been omitted so that numbers will group more meaningfully.

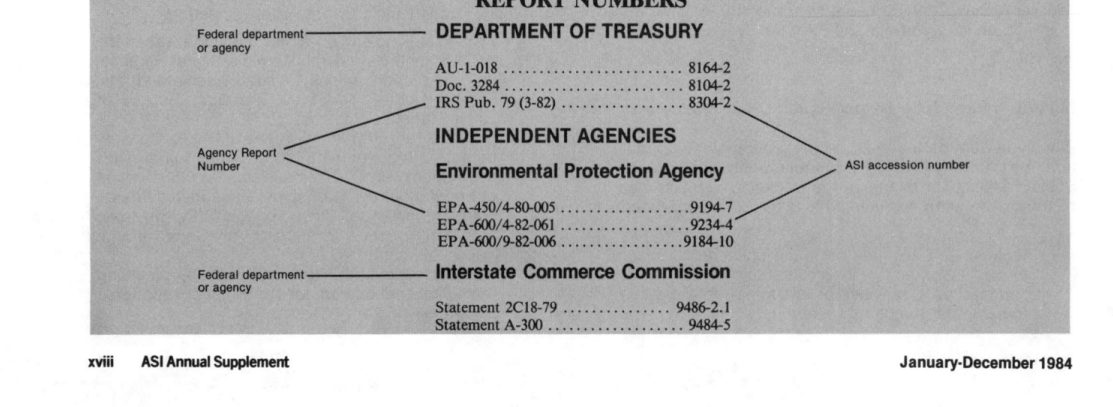

Suggestions for Making Information Searches

The "best" information search technique to use with ASI abstracts and indexes depends upon the type of information needed and upon the amount and type of information with which the search begins. Listed below are some examples of the types of information you can obtain through ASI, together with suggested routes for searching.

IN ORDER TO ...	YOU SHOULD ...		
Pinpoint specific statistical data on any subject treated in Federal Government publications.	Use the subject index.		ASI Monthly Supplements; the issues received each month will be listed.
		Locate continuing monthly or quarterly reports on a particular subject.	Look in the subject index. The notations of content include the periodicity of the reports.
Locate broad analyses of comprehensive studies.	Use the subject index; concentrate on the more general subject terms.	Determine the availability of comparable historical data.	Look in the Abstracts Section of each ASI edition, under the same accession number. The abstract will state whether the report is part of a continuing time series; e.g., "Twentieth annual report." Also, look in the abstract for references to earlier publications, changes in ASI accession numbers, or breaks in continuity.
Determine whether data are available for specific parts of the U.S., such as States, cities, or counties; for specific industries or commodities; or for specific groups of people, such as races, men and women, or age, income, or occupational groups.	Use both the subject and category indexes.		
Find comparative data for States, cities, foreign countries, Government agencies, commodities, industries, or groups of people.	Use the category index.	Locate the report of a specific Board or Commission.	Look in the subject index under the name of the issuing agency.
		Locate an agency publication list.	Look in the subject index under "Government publications lists."
Find out what Federal Reserve district Florida is in.	Look in the Guide to Selected Standard Classifications.		
Determine whether a large report, with a breakdown by trial industry, will include data on the dog food industry.	Look at the Standard Industrial Classification Codes listed in the Guide to Selected Standard Classifications to determine that the industry you are looking for has a 4-digit code. Look in the indexes for notations of content specifying detailed industry breakdowns. Look at the table listing in the abstract for tables specifying 4-digit detail.	Review the entire statistical output of any particular Federal Government agency or office.	Look in the detailed table of contents for the ASI accession number and page of the agency that interests you. Look in the Abstracts Section for all publications under this accession number.
		Find out how many Federal Government agencies publish data on the same subject.	Look in the subject index, at the ASI accession numbers following the notations of content. The first two to four digits (minus the digit before the hyphen) indicate the issuing agency of the publication.
Find data on Minneapolis.	Look in the subject index under "Minneapolis, Minn." Look also in the category index under "By city."	Locate a specific statistical article in a periodical.	Look in the title index or in the subject index under the author's name.
Be confident that you have found the latest data available.	Look at the dates in the notations of content that interest you in the ASI 1984 Annual. Check ASI 1985 Monthly Supplements under the same index terms to see if there are similar notations with later dates. ASI is current to 6-10 weeks after publication of the reports covered. If the notations of content indicate a periodical, locate the latest issue in the "Periodicals Received and Reviewed" section.	Determine the content of a specific publication when you know the title or agency report number.	Use the title index or the agency report number index to locate the pertinent abstract.
		Locate all the reports in a specific series.	Look in the title index of each edition of ASI under the title of the series. If it is a numbered series, use the agency report number index.
		Find a report you remember hearing about in the 1970s.	Start out by checking the ASI Retrospective Edition indexes, followed by successive Annual Supplements.
Find the latest issue of a periodical carrying forward a statistical time series.	Look in ASI 1984 Annual for description of the periodical. Look for the title in the "Periodicals Received and Reviewed" section of the latest	Locate reports describing specific statistical methods; locate reports containing projected data.	Look in the subject index under "Methodology;" look in the subject index under "Projections."

ACQUIRING THE DOCUMENTS

Once you have identified a publication that appears to contain the data you seek, you may wish to borrow or acquire the publication itself, either in its original hardcopy form or in microform.

Acquiring Documents From a Library

Although there are no complete collections in existence, Government documents can be found in many libraries, particularly those that have been designated as U.S. Government depository libraries. There are usually at least two depositories in each congressional district, approximately 1,300 throughout the country.

The publication abstracts that contain a bullet (•) and an Item Number indicate publications that have been made available to depository libraries by the Government Printing Office. However, fewer than 50 depositories receive *all* the publications that are theoretically available to them, and even these libraries receive only about three-quarters of all the publications covered by ASI.

Libraries that subscribe to the ASI Microfiche Library will have complete collections of the materials abstracted and indexed in ASI.

Requesting or Purchasing Publications From the Government

Whether or not they are sent to depositories, many Government publications can be purchased while the supply lasts, either from the Government Printing Office, or, in certain cases, from the National Technical Information Service, or the issuing agency.

If a publication listed in ASI is available for sale, the price and source, when known, are listed in the abstract. It should be noted that the prices of Government publications are subject to frequent change. The price listed is that printed on the publication or in the GPO *Monthly Catalog,* or is based on firm information about a later price from another source.

When the publication abstract contains a single dagger (†), inquiries should be addressed directly to the issuing agency in order to determine whether copies are available for distribution. Principal agency addresses are listed in the section labeled "Where to Write for Statistical Publications" (see p. xxviii).

Some publications intended for internal or official use only have been printed in small editions, and copies generally are not available for distribution. In some cases, the agency will honor a written request for a copy of one of these publications, but this will be decided by the agency on a case-by-case basis. Abstracts of publications in this category carry a double dagger (‡).

In some cases, we have been informed by the agency that there are absolutely no copies available for distribution outside the agency. Abstracts of publications in this category carry a diamond symbol (◆). In most of these cases, the agencies have cooperated with our attempt to make the data available to the public by permitting ASI to microfilm the publications for inclusion in the ASI Microfiche Library. The agency itself will not honor requests for publications that carry this symbol.

The ASI Microfiche Program

Because of the enormous difficulty of acquiring, cataloging, and maintaining a collection of all the publications covered by ASI, no complete hardcopy collection of these publications now exists in any library. For this reason, CIS has undertaken to make these publications available in American Standard microfiche on a continuing basis.

Our microfiche sheets measure 105 × 149 mm (approximately 4" × 6"), and contain up to 98 document pages. Each has an eye-readable "title header" that conclusively identifies the accession number, series title (if any), dates of periodical issues, and document title of each publication filmed. Documents are separated from each other, and they are plainly sequenced for file integrity and quick retrieval according to ASI accession number.

Researchers may view microfiche with the aid of a simple reader, such as those found in most libraries and offices. Individual pages from a microfiche can be reproduced in full size with the aid of a reader-printer; these machines are becoming increasingly available in libraries and offices.

With a few specific exclusions, all publications abstracted and indexed in ASI are available on ASI microfiche. The microfiche availability and unit count for a given publication are indicated by the notation "ASI/MF" in the publication's abstract. We have systematically excluded only publications that reprint other items in the ASI Microfiche Library, large or colored maps that are unsuitable for reproduction in standard microfiche, and large appendix volumes that are non-statistical, such as public hearing testimony, or highly technical.

Automatically updated collections of current publications, on silver-halide, archival-quality microfiche, are available on a subscription basis. Retrospective collections, shipped in their entirety and ready for use, may also be purchased. Collections may be ordered to contain the entire range of ASI publications, may be limited to "non-depository" publications (i.e., those not included in Government documents classes sent to depository libraries), or may be limited to publications of a single Government agency. For details, please write: CIS Library Services Manager.

ASI Documents on Demand

Since June 1, 1975, individual publications covered in ASI have been available on diazo microfiche or paper copy for purchase through our ASI DOCUMENTS ON DEMAND service. The price of any document is based on the "unit count" data indicated for the document, e.g. ASI/MF/3. (Note that a unit count of 3 is the minimum order for any document, regardless of size; each additional 100 pages or less equals 1 additional unit.) Please ask your librarian for additional ordering information; or contact CIS Customer Service Representative, P.O. Box 30056, Bethesda, MD 20814.

ADDITIONAL CIS SERVICES

Index to International Statistics and Statistical Reference Index

Beginning in January 1983, Congressional Information Service initiated publication of the Index to International Statistics (IIS), a comprehensive monthly index and abstracting service, covering the statistical publications of international intergovernmental organizations, including UN, OECD, EC, OAS, and approximately 30 other important organizations.

Since 1980, Congressional Information Service has published the Statistical Reference Index (SRI), a monthly abstract and index publication with annual cumulations, covering statistical reports from a broad range of U.S. sources other than the Federal Government. These sources include trade, professional, and other nonprofit associations; business organizations; commercial publishers; independent research centers; State government agencies; and university research centers. SRI has selected from these sources a cross-section of documents presenting basic national and State data on business, industry, finance, economic and social conditions, the environment, and the population.

SRI and IIS complement ASI's coverage of statistical materials by providing access to data not collected by the Federal Government and to alternative sources and analyses of data. Because the abstracting and indexing styles of the two publications are quite similar, researchers can use ASI, SRI, and IIS without significantly changing their search methods.

Most of the documents covered in SRI and IIS are included in their respective Microfiche Libraries, available on a subscription basis. For more information about SRI, IIS, and their microfiche programs, contact the CIS Marketing Department.

CIS On-Line Services

Through cooperative arrangements with on-line computer services, the CIS data base is made available to the public. This service makes possible direct on-line computer searching of the abstracts and indexing contained in all American Statistics Indexes and all CIS/Indexes, from our first publication to the present.

CIS/Indexes to Publications of the U.S. Congress

Since 1970, Congressional Information Service has published the CIS/Index, a monthly abstract and index publication with annual cumulations, which covers all publications of the U.S. Congress. Selected congressional publications containing statistical data are covered in ASI as well as CIS. Those covered by ASI are re-abstracted and re-indexed to focus on their statistical contents.

However, ASI does not repeat CIS/Index coverage of the wide range of congressional publications that contain no substantial statistical data. Nor does ASI abstract or index the publications of the Senate and House Appropriations Committees. Since CIS/Indexes provide detailed access to the extensive program statistics and background information contained in publications of these committees, we believe that reabstracting them for ASI would be a duplication of effort and service.

The CIS/Microfiche Library and CIS Documents on Demand services provide full-text availability of CIS/ Index publications in a manner paralleling ASI microfiche services.

Other Services

Beginning in January 1984, Congressional Information Service initiated publication of the CIS Federal Register Index, a comprehensive index covering all rules, proposed rules, notices, and Presidential documents contained in the daily *Federal Register.*

Congressional Information Service has also published an index to U.S. Congressional Committee Prints, covering the earliest publications through 1969; and, in 1981, began publishing an index to U.S. Congressional Committee Hearings, covering 1833-1969. Companion microfiche services provide full-text availability of documents covered by each index.

Additional CIS publications and microform collections are fully described in the CIS catalog, available upon request.

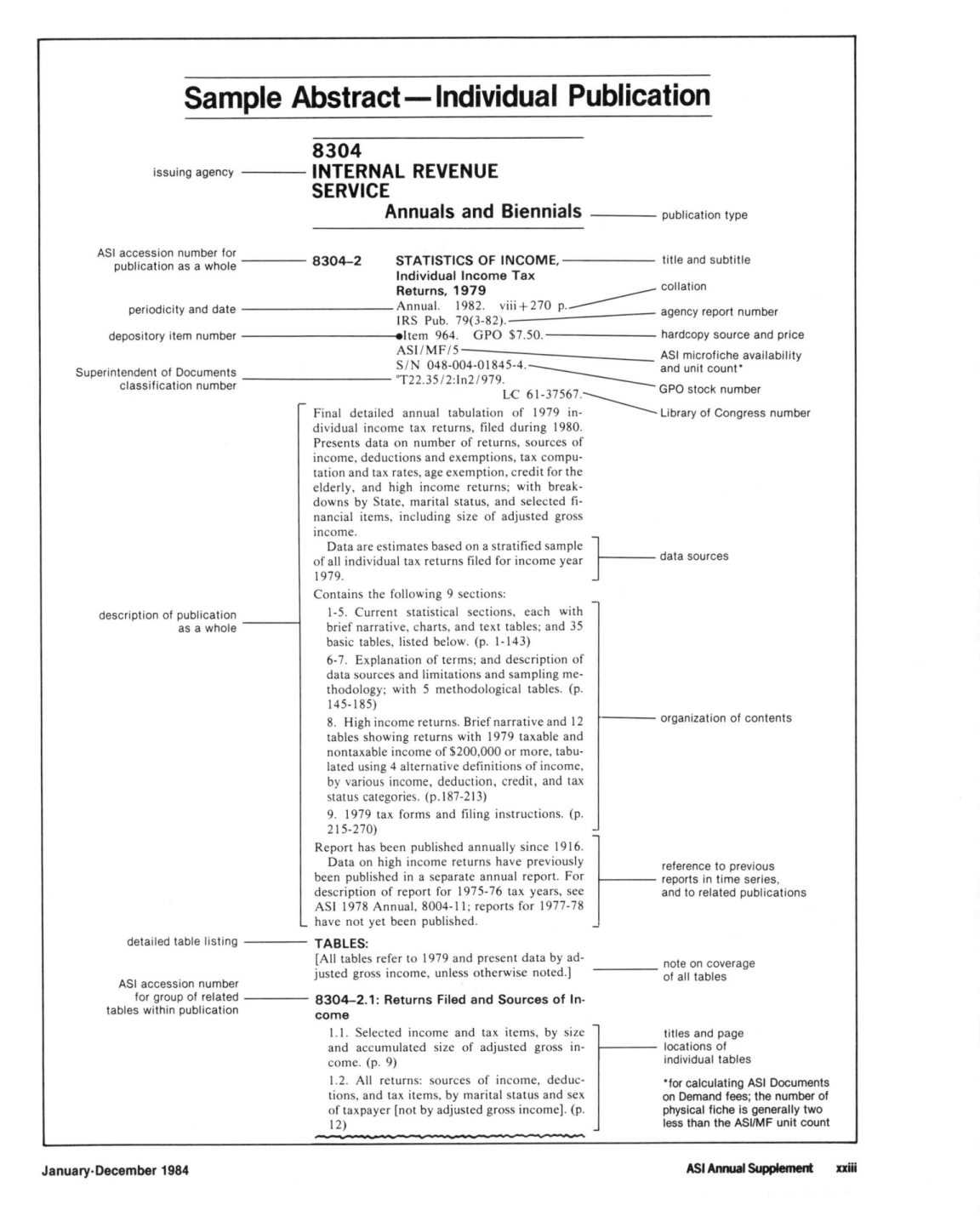

Sample Abstract — Individual Publication

Sample Abstract—Periodical Publication

6722 BUREAU OF LABOR STATISTICS: GENERAL

Current Periodicals

ASI accession number for periodical as a whole — **6722-1** — **MONTHLY LABOR REVIEW** — title of periodical

Monthly. Approx. 105 p. — approximate pagination of each issue

● Item 770.

GPO or BLS Regional Offices: $23.00 per yr.; single copy $3.00. ASI/MF/4 — ASI microfiche availability and unit count* per issue

S/N 029-001-80003-7.

°L2.6:(v.nos.&nos.) — Superintendent of Documents classification number

MC 81-9003. LC 15-02645. — Library of Congress number

GPO Monthly Catalog entry number

description of periodical as a whole:

a. Monthly journal on labor conditions; with current statistics on employment, earnings, prices, productivity, and labor-management relations.

Contains feature articles, individually described below; current labor statistics, with 37 tables, listed below; and the following regular features: *a.* Labor month in review.

b. Special labor force reports summaries, described below. Reports are also issued separately (see 6746-1).

TABLES:

[Most tables show monthly data for the past 13 months, up to either 30 or 60 days prior to the cover date of the issue.] — note on coverage of all tables

ASI accession number for group of related tables within publication — **6722-1.1: Employment and Unemployment: Household Data**

titles of individual tables:

1. Employment status of the noninstitutional population 16 years and over, selected years 1950-80.

2. Employment status, by sex, age, and race, seasonally adjusted [annual and monthly averages].

ARTICLES:

individual issue date, volume, and number — **SEPTEMBER 1982 Vol. 105, No. 9**

ASI accession number for abstract of article within individual issue — **6722-1.262: Labor Force Patterns of Students, Graduates, and Dropouts, 1981** — title, author, and page range of article within individual issue

By Anne McDougall Young (p. 39-42). Annual article on employment, unemployment, and school enrollment status of all youth and 1981 high school graduates and dropouts, 1980-81 with trends from 1960. Data are from the Current Population Survey.

Includes 4 tables showing labor force, employment, and labor force participation and unemployment rates of all youth, graduates, and dropouts, by school or college enrollment (as applicable), educational attainment, age, sex, and race or Hispanic origin.

Updates an article for 1980 (see ASI 1981 Annual, 6722-1.156).

*for calculating ASI Documents on Demand fees; the number of physical fiche is generally two less than the ASI/MF unit count

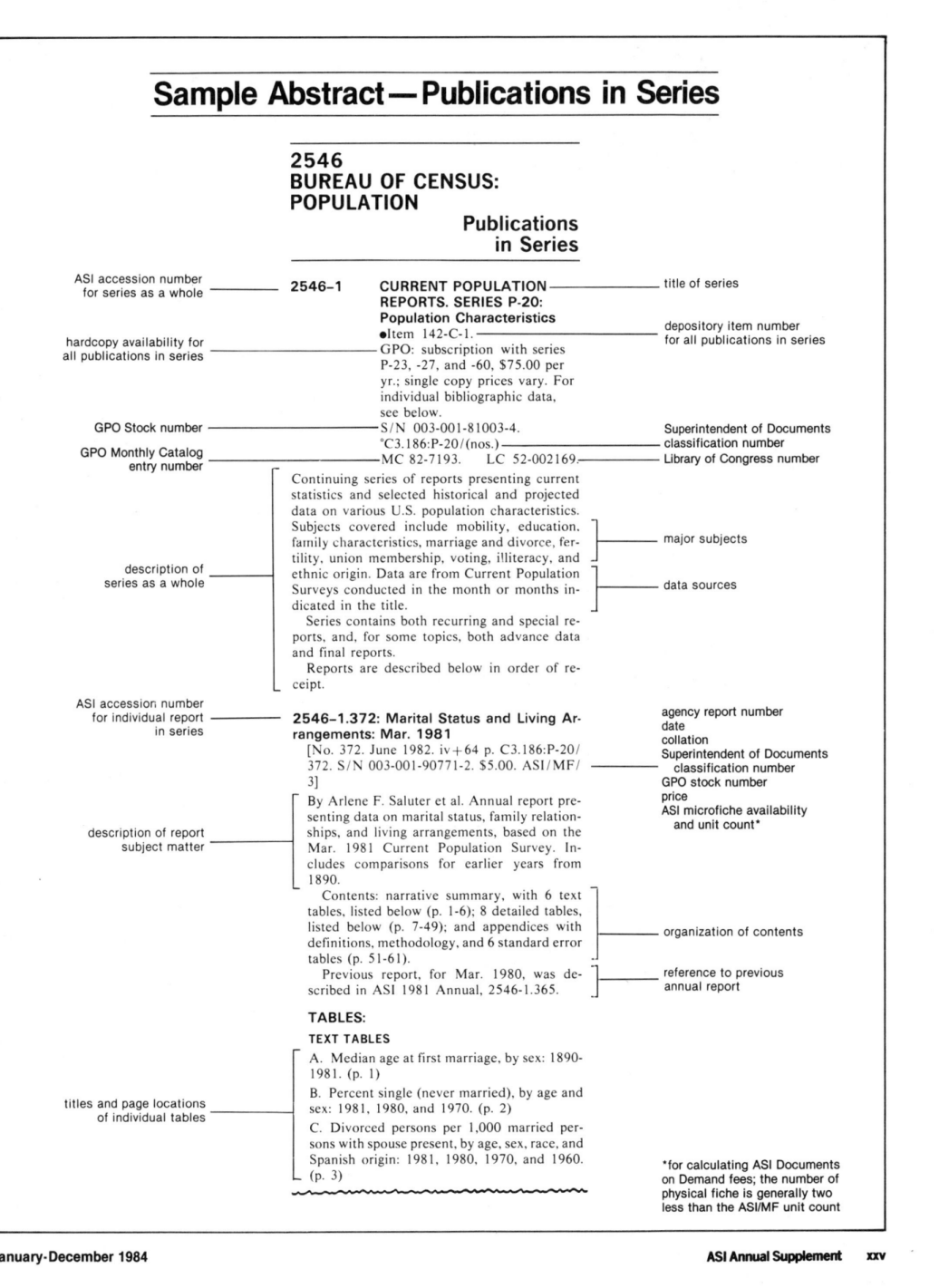

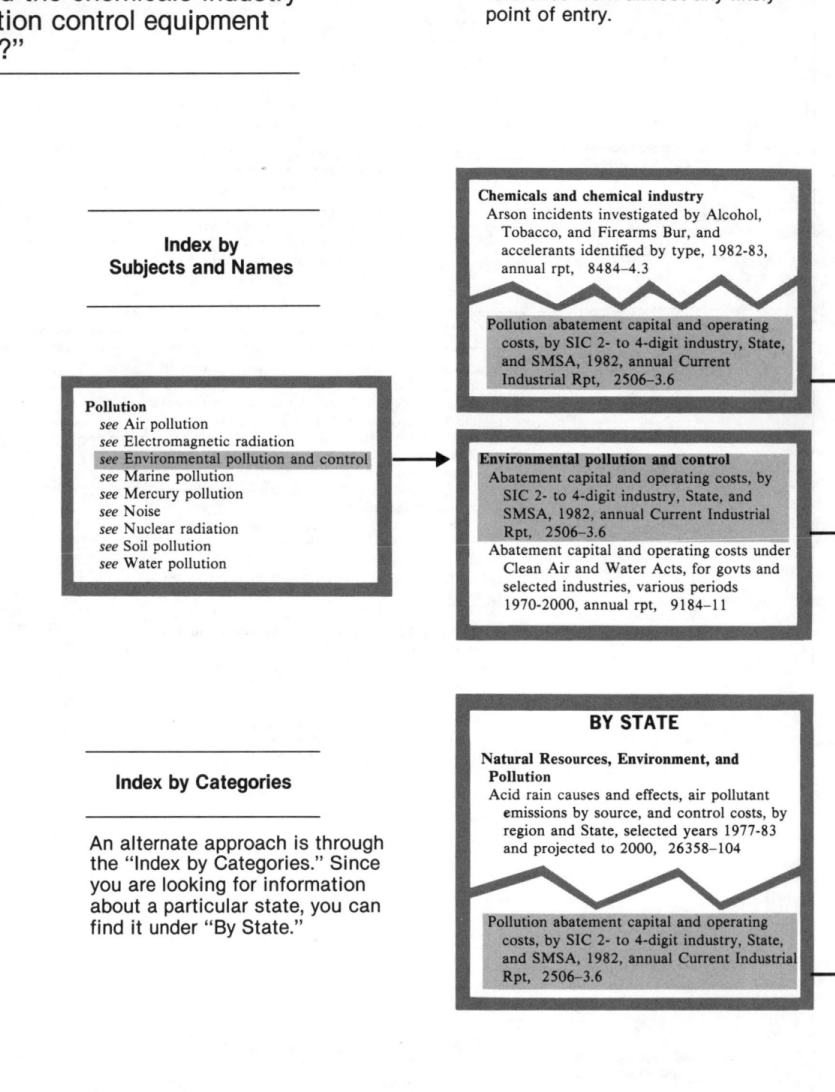

Step 2

Go from the index to the data description in the appropriate Abstracts volume

The ASI accession number in the index will lead to a publication entry that fully describes the document and pinpoints the tables containing the statistics you need.

Step 3

Retrieve the publication

The ASI abstract contains the bibliographic information you need to locate the publication in a library's hardcopy collection or to obtain it from the issuing source, if copies are available.

Alternatively, if you have access to an ASI Microfiche Library collecton, the ASI accession number will lead you directly to the correct microfiche. Or, individual publications abstracted in any ASI Monthly or Annual Supplement are available for purchase on microfiche directly from Congressional Information Service through our CIS & ASI Documents on Demand Service.

Order kits supplied to all ASI subscribers provide the necessary information about costs and how to place microfiche orders. (Details are also available by writing CIS, Customer Service Rep., P.O. Box 30056, Bethesda, MD 20814.

**2506
BUREAU OF CENSUS: MANUFACTURING
Publications in series**

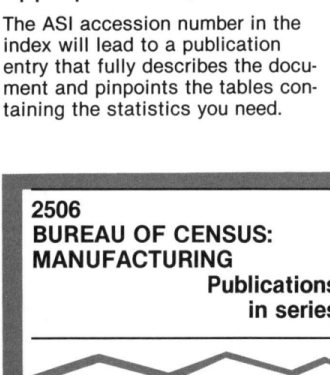

2506–3.6: Pollution Abatement Costs and Expenditures, 1982

[Annual. Feb. 1984. 74+App 12 p. MA200(82)-1. C3.158:MA200(82)-1. LC 77-646295. MC 84-11935. $4.00. ASI/MF/3]

Annual report for 1981 on pollution abatement control capital expenditures and operating costs, for U.S. by SIC 4-digit industry, for States by 2-digit industry, and for SMSAs. Data are from a survey of approximately 20,000 establishments selected as a subsample from the 57,000 1980 Annual Survey of Manufactures (ASM) establishments.

Contents: introduction, with 5 charts and 3 tables (p. 1-11); 14 tables, listed below (p. 12-74); and appendices, with facsimile survey form and SMSA definitions (12 p.).

TABLES:

[All data are for 1982 unless otherwise noted.

Tables 2-5 show data for establishments with 20 or more employees and are repeated for U.S. by SIC 2- to 4-digit industry (table A), for States by SIC 2-digit industry (table B), and for SMSAs (table C).

Forms of abatement are water, air, and solid waste.]

CAPITAL EXPENDITURES AND OPERATING COSTS

1A-1B. Pollution abatement capital expenditures and operating costs, by form of abatement, major [SIC 2-digit] industry group, and State, 1978-82. (p. 12-17)

2A-2C. Pollution abatement capital expenditures [by air and water pollution abatement technique (end-of-line and production process change), by type of air pollutant, and for solid waste]. (p. 18-29)

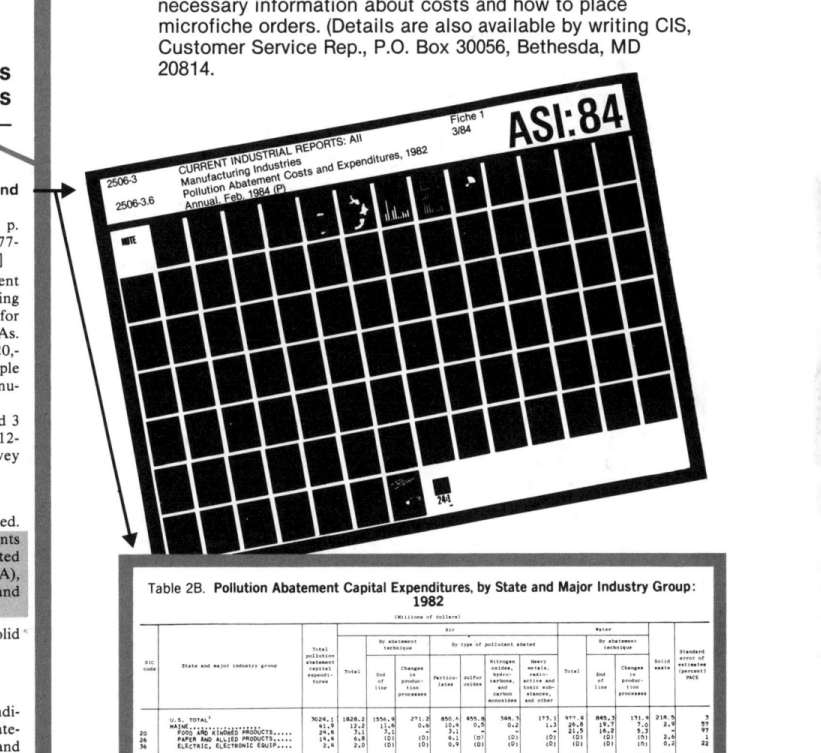

Where to Write for Statistical Publications

Publications abstracted in ASI are frequently available to the public from the Government Printing Office, the National Technical Information Service, or the issuing agency. In addition, a complete collection of abstracted publications is available in the ASI Microfiche Library.

Information about the source and availability of specific publications is given in each ASI abstract. (For illustrations, see the Sample Abstracts; for background information, see the section headed "Acquiring the Documents" on p. xx.)

The mailing addresses of GPO, NTIS, and principal issuing agency sources of publications are listed below.

When ordering publications from the issuing agency, requests should be directed to the specific subagency, Information Division, c/o the parent agency. Where the subagency has a separate mailing address, it is given.

There has been no attempt to list regional or field offices for every agency and subagency. Listings and addresses of these offices can be found in most agency catalogs, and in local telephone directories for the cities in which they are located.

Addresses have been provided for the sources of publications, periodicals, and/or specials and irregulars, which may be available only, or more conveniently, from offices in other locations than the central information office for an agency. Identification of other unusual sources will appear with the abstract of a publication.

GOVERNMENT PRINTING OFFICE (GPO)
Superintendent of Documents
Washington, DC 20402

NATIONAL TECHNICAL INFORMATION SERVICE (NTIS)
5285 Port Royal Rd
Springfield, VA 22161

EXECUTIVE OFFICE OF THE PRESIDENT
Publications Unit, Rm G236
New Executive Office Bldg
Washington, DC 20503

CENTRAL INTELLIGENCE AGENCY
Photoduplication Service
Library of Congress
Washington, DC 20540

COUNCIL OF ECONOMIC ADVISERS
New Executive Office Bldg
Washington, DC 20506

COUNCIL ON ENVIRONMENTAL QUALITY
722 Jackson Pl., N.W.
Washington, DC 20006

OFFICE OF MANAGEMENT & BUDGET
Publications Unit, Rm G236
New Executive Office Bldg
Washington, DC 20503

OFFICE OF SCIENCE AND TECHNOLOGY POLICY
New Executive Office Building
Washington, DC 20506

OFFICE OF THE U.S. TRADE REPRESENTATIVE
600 17th St., N.W.
Washington, DC 20506

DEPARTMENT OF AGRICULTURE
(Subagency Name)
Information Division
Washington, DC 20250

AGRICULTURAL MARKETING SERVICE
Information Staff
Rm 3068-S
Washington, DC 20250
Cotton Division
4841 Summer Ave.
Memphis, TN 38122

CROP REPORTING BOARD
5829 S. Building
Washington, DC 20250

FOREST SERVICE—Forest (and Range) Experiment Stations
Intermountain (INT)
324 25th St.
Ogden, UT 84401
North Central (NC)
1992 Folwell Ave.
St. Paul, MN 55108
Northeastern (NE)
370 Reed Rd
Broomall, PA 19008
Pacific Northwest (PNW)
P.O. Box 3890
Portland, OR 97208
Pacific Southwest (PSW)
1960 Addison St.
P.O. Box 245
Berkeley, CA 94701

Rocky Mountain (RM)
240 West Prospect St.
Fort Collins, CO 80526

Southeastern (SE)
200 Weaver Blvd.
Asheville, NC 28804

Southern (SO)
T-10210 Postal Services Bldg
701 Loyola Ave.
New Orleans, LA 70113

SOIL CONSERVATION SERVICE
(Western U.S.)
West Technical Service Center, Rm 511
511 N.W. Broadway
Portland, OR 97209

DEPARTMENT OF COMMERCE
(Subagency Name)
Office of Public Affairs
Washington, DC 20230

BUREAU OF ECONOMIC ANALYSIS
Information Services Division
1401 K St., N.W.
Washington, DC 20235

BUREAU OF THE CENSUS
Customer Services
Data User Services Division
Washington, DC 20233

NATIONAL BUREAU OF STANDARDS
Office of Information Activities
Rm 640, Administration Bldg
Washington, DC 20234

NATIONAL OCEANIC AND ATMOSPHERIC ADMINISTRATION
Office of Public Affairs
WSC-5
Rockville, MD 20852

Environmental Satellite, Data, and Information Service
Library and Information Services Division
Rockville, MD 20852

Environmental Research Laboratories
Public Information Office
Boulder, CO 80302

National Climatic Data Center
ESDIS
Federal Building
Asheville, NC 28801

National Marine Fisheries Service
Public Affairs, Page Two Bldg
3300 Whitehaven St., N.W.
Washington, DC 20235

National Ocean Service
Public Information Office
WSC-1
Rockville, MD 20852

National Weather Service
Rm 400, Gramax Bldg
8060 13th St.
Silver Spring, MD 20910

PATENT AND TRADEMARK OFFICE
Office of Information Service
Rm 1D01, CP3
Crystal Plaza, VA 20231

DEPARTMENT OF COMMERCE DISTRICT OFFICES
Suite 1050, 505 Marquette Ave., N.W.
Albuquerque, NM 87102

701 C St.
Anchorage, AK 99513

Suite 600, 1365 Peachtree St., N.E.
Atlanta, GA 30309

Rm 415, U.S. Customhouse
Baltimore, MD 21202

Suite 200, 908 S. 20th St.
Birmingham, AL 35205

441 Stuart St.
Boston, MA 02116

1312 Federal Bldg
Buffalo, NY 14202

3000 New Federal Office Bldg
Charleston, WV 25301

2120 Capitol Ave.
Cheyenne, WY 82001

55 E. Monroe St.
Chicago, IL 60603

550 Main St.
Cincinnati, OH 45202

Rm 600, 666 Euclid Ave.
Cleveland, OH 44114

Suite 172, 1835 Assembly St.
Columbia, SC 29201

Rm 7A5, 1100 Commerce St.
Dallas, TX 75242

Rm 177, New Customhouse
Denver, CO 80202

Rm 817, 210 Walnut St.
Des Moines, IA 50309

Rm 445, 231 W. Lafayette
Detroit, MI 48226

Rm 203, Federal Bldg
Greensboro, NC 27402

Rm 610-B, 450 Main St.
Hartford, CT 06103

Rm 4106, 300 Ala Moana Blvd
Honolulu, HI 96850

Rm 2625, 515 Rusk Ave.
Houston, TX 77002

Rm 357, 46 E. Ohio St.
Indianapolis, IN 46204

200 Pascagoula
Jackson, MS 39201

Rm 1840, 601 E. 12th St.
Kansas City, MO 64106

Suite 635, 320 W. Capitol Ave.
Little Rock, AR 72201

Rm 800, 11777 San Vincente Blvd
Los Angeles, CA 90049

Rm 636B, U.S. Post Office and Courthouse Bldg
Louisville, KY 40202

Rm 821, 25 W. Flagler St.
Miami, FL 33130

517 E. Wisconsin Ave.
Milwaukee, WI 53202

218 Federal Bldg
Minneapolis, MN 55401

Suite 1427, 1 Commerce Plaza
Nashville, TN 27239

2 Canal St.
New Orleans, LA 70130

Rm 3718, Federal Office Bldg
New York, NY 10007

4024 Lincoln Blvd
Oklahoma City, OK 73105

300 S. 19th St.
Omaha, NE 68102

9448 Federal Bldg
Philadelphia, PA 19106

Suite 2950, 201 N. Central Ave.
Phoenix, AZ 85073

2002 Federal Bldg
Pittsburgh, PA 15222

Rm 618, 1220 S.W. 3rd Ave.
Portland, OR 97204

Rm 120, 777 W. 2nd St.
Reno, NV 89503

8010 Federal Bldg
Richmond, VA 23240

120 S. Central Ave.
St. Louis, MO 63105

350 S. Main St.
Salt Lake City, UT 84101

450 Golden Gate Ave.
San Francisco, CA 94102

Rm 659, Federal Bldg
San Juan, PR 00918

125-29 Bull St.
Savannah, GA 31412

Rm 706, 1700 Westlake Ave., N.
Seattle, WA 98109

240 W. State St.
Trenton, NJ 08608

DEPARTMENT OF DEFENSE

Office of the Assistant Secretary of Defense (Public Affairs)
The Pentagon
Washington, DC 20301

Directorate for Information Operations and Reports (DIOR)
Suite 1204, 1215 Jefferson Davis Hwy.
Arlington, VA 22202-4302

DEFENSE LOGISTICS AGENCY
Defense Fuel Supply Center
Public Affairs
Bldg 8, Cameron Station
Alexandria, VA 22314

U.S. AIR FORCE PUBLICATIONS
Office of the Secretary of the Air Force
Office of Information
Public Information Division
Headquarters, USAF
Washington, DC 20330

U.S. ARMY PUBLICATIONS
Public Information Office
Office of the Chief of Information
Headquarters, Department of the Army
Washington, DC 20310

U.S. ARMY CORPS OF ENGINEERS
Public Affairs Office
Forrestal Bldg
Washington, DC 20314

U.S. ARMY CORPS OF ENGINEERS REGIONAL OFFICES

Alaska District
P.O. Box 7002
Anchorage, AK 99510

Detroit District
P.O. Box 1027
Detroit, MI 48231

Louisville District
P.O. Box 59
Louisville, KY 40201

Lower Mississippi Valley Division
P.O. Box 60
Vicksburg, MS 39180

Missouri River Division
Downtown Station, P.O. Box 103
Omaha, NE 68101

Mobile District
P.O. Box 2288
Mobile, AL 36628

Nashville District
P.O. Box 1070
Nashville, TN 37202

New England Division
424 Trapelo Rd
Waltham, MA 02154

New Orleans District
P.O. Box 60267
New Orleans, LA 70160

North Atlantic Division
90 Church St.
New York, NY 10007

North Central Division
536 S. Clark St.
Chicago, IL 60605

Ohio River Division
P.O. Box 1159
Cincinnati, OH 45201

South Atlantic Division
510 Title Bldg
30 Pryor St., S.W.
Atlanta, GA 30303

South Pacific Division
630 Sansome St.
San Francisco, CA 94111

Southwest Division
1114 Commerce St.
Dallas, TX 75242

U.S. NAVY PUBLICATIONS
Public Information Division
Office of Information
Department of the Navy
Washington, DC 20350

DEPARTMENT OF EDUCATION
(Specified Office)
400 Maryland Ave., S.W.
Washington, DC 20202

NATIONAL ASSESSMENT OF EDUCATIONAL PROGRESS (NAEP)
P.O. Box 2923
Princeton, NJ 08541

NATIONAL CENTER FOR EDUCATION STATISTICS (NCES)
Brown Bldg, Rm 418
Washington, DC 20202

NATIONAL INSTITUTE OF EDUCATION
1200 19th St., N.W.
Washington, DC 20506

DEPARTMENT OF ENERGY
(Subagency Name)
Washington, DC 20585

ENERGY INFORMATION ADMINISTRATION
National Energy Information Center
EI-20, Mail Station 1F048
1000 Independence Ave., S.W.
Washington, DC 20585

FEDERAL ENERGY REGULATORY COMMISSION
Public Information Office, Rm 1000
825 North Capitol St., N.E.
Washington, DC 20426

OAK RIDGE NATIONAL LABORATORY
Technical Information Center
P.O. Box 62
Oak Ridge, TN 37831

DEPARTMENT OF HEALTH AND HUMAN SERVICES
Office of Public Affairs
Rm 647-D, HHH Bldg
200 Independence Ave., S.W.
Washington, DC 20201

CENTERS FOR DISEASE CONTROL
1600 Clifton Rd, N.E.
Atlanta, GA 30333

FOOD AND DRUG ADMINISTRATION
HFE 88
5600 Fishers La.
Rockville, MD 20857

HEALTH CARE FINANCING ADMINISTRATION
648 East High Rise Bldg
6401 Security Blvd
Baltimore, MD 21235

HEALTH RESOURCES AND SERVICES ADMINISTRATION
(Subagency Name)
1443 Parklawn Bldg
5600 Fishers La.
Rockville, MD 20857

NATIONAL CENTER FOR HEALTH STATISTICS
Rm 1-57, Federal Center Bldg #2
3700 East-West Hwy
Hyattsville, MD 20782

NATIONAL CHILD SUPPORT ENFORCEMENT CENTER
Rm 820, 6110 Executive Blvd.
Rockville, MD 20852

NATIONAL CLEARINGHOUSE FOR ALCOHOL INFORMATION
P.O. Box 2345
Rockville, MD 20852

NATIONAL CLEARINGHOUSE FOR DRUG ABUSE INFORMATION
10A-53 Parklawn Bldg
5600 Fishers La.
Rockville, MD 20857

NATIONAL INSTITUTES OF HEALTH
Office of Information
Rm 307, Bldg 1
9000 Rockville Pike
Bethesda, MD 20205

NATIONAL INSTITUTE OF MENTAL HEALTH
Public Inquiries
Rm 11A-21, 5600 Fishers La.
Rockville, MD 20857

NATIONAL INSTITUTE FOR OCCUPATIONAL SAFETY AND HEALTH
Publications, DTS
4676 Columbia Parkway
Cincinnati, OH 45226

OFFICE OF HUMAN DEVELOPMENT SERVICES
Rm 3290, HHH Bldg
200 Independence Ave., S.W.
Washington, DC 20201

OFFICE ON SMOKING AND HEALTH
Rm 158, 5600 Fishers La.
Rockville, MD 20857

PUBLIC HEALTH SERVICE
Office of Public Affairs
Rm 740-G, HHH Bldg
200 Independence Ave., S.W.
Washington, DC 20201

SOCIAL SECURITY ADMINISTRATION
Printing and Records Management Branch
1121 Operations Bldg
6401 Security Blvd
Baltimore, MD 21235

DEPARTMENT OF HOUSING AND URBAN DEVELOPMENT
Publication Service Center
Rm B-258
Washington, DC 20410

OFFICE OF POLICY DEVELOPMENT AND RESEARCH
HUD USER
P.O. Box 280
Germantown, MD 20767

DEPARTMENT OF THE INTERIOR
(Subagency Name)
Office of Information
Washington, DC 20240

BUREAU OF MINES
Publication Distribution Section
4800 Forbes Ave.
Pittsburgh, PA 15213

U.S. GEOLOGICAL SURVEY
Distribution Branch
Text Products Section
604 South Pickett St.
Alexandria, VA 22304

DEPARTMENT OF JUSTICE
Office of Public Information
10th and Constitution Ave., N.W.
Washington, DC 20530

BUREAU OF PRISONS
320 1st St., N.W.
Washington, DC 20534

DRUG ENFORCEMENT ADMINISTRATION
1405 I St., N.W.
Washington, DC 20537

FEDERAL BUREAU OF INVESTIGATION
9th and Pennsylvania Ave., N.W.
Washington, DC 20535

FOREIGN CLAIMS SETTLEMENT COMMISSION OF THE U.S.
Vanguard Building
1111 20th St., N.W.
Washington, DC 20579

IMMIGRATION AND NATURALIZATION SERVICE
425 I St., N.W.
Washington, DC 20536

NATIONAL CRIMINAL JUSTICE REFERENCE SERVICE (NCJRS)
Box 6000
Rockville, MD 20850

OFFICE OF JUSTICE ASSISTANCE, RESEARCH AND STATISTICS
633 Indiana Ave., N.W.
Washington, DC 20531

DEPARTMENT OF LABOR

Office of Information, Publications, and Reports
200 Constitution Ave., N.W.
Washington, DC 20210

BUREAU OF LABOR STATISTICS
Information Office
GAO Bldg
441 G St., N.W.
Washington, DC 20212

BUREAU OF LABOR STATISTICS REGIONAL OFFICES

Region I
Rm 1603, JFK Federal Bldg
Government Center
Boston, MA 02203

Region II
1515 Broadway, Suite 3400
New York, NY 10036

Region III
3535 Market St.
P.O. Box 13309
Philadelphia, PA 19101

Region IV
1371 Peachtree St., N.E.
Atlanta, GA 30309

Region V
Federal Office Bldg
230 S. Dearborn St.
Chicago, IL 60604

Region VI
555 Griffin Square Bldg
Dallas, TX 75202

Regions VII and VIII
911 Walnut St.
Kansas City, MO 64106

Regions IX and X
450 Golden Gate Ave.
Box 36017
San Francisco, CA 94102

EMPLOYMENT AND TRAINING ADMINISTRATION
Rm 10426, 601 D St., N.W.
Washington, DC 20213

MINE SAFETY AND HEALTH ADMINISTRATION
Office of Information
Ballston Tower #3, Rm 902
4015 Wilson Blvd
Arlington, VA 22203

DEPARTMENT OF STATE

(Subagency Name)
Bureau of Public Affairs
Washington, DC 20520

DEPARTMENT OF TRANSPORTATION

OFFICE OF THE SECRETARY OF TRANSPORTATION
Office of Public & Consumer Affairs (S-81)
400 7th St., S.W.
Washington, DC 20590

FEDERAL AVIATION ADMINISTRATION
Public Inquiry Center (APA-420)
800 Independence Ave., S.W.
Washington, DC 20590

FEDERAL HIGHWAY ADMINISTRATION
Office of Public Affairs (HPA-1)
400 7th St., S.W.
Washington, DC 20590

FEDERAL RAILROAD ADMINISTRATION
Office of Public Affairs (ROA-30)
400 7th St., S.W.
Washington, DC 20590

MARITIME ADMINISTRATION
Office of Public Affairs (MAR-240)
400 7th St., S.W.
Washington, DC 20590

NATIONAL HIGHWAY TRAFFIC SAFETY ADMINISTRATION
400 7th St., S.W.
Washington, DC 20590

SAINT LAWRENCE SEAWAY DEVELOPMENT CORPORATION
Rm 814
800 Independence Ave., S.W.
Washington, DC 20591

URBAN MASS TRANSPORTATION ADMINISTRATION
Office of Public Affairs (UPA-1)
400 7th St., S.W.
Washington, DC 20590

U.S. COAST GUARD
Public Affairs Division (G-BPA)
2100 2nd St., S.W.
Washington, DC 20593

DEPARTMENT OF THE TREASURY

Public Affairs Office
15th and Pennsylvania Ave., N.W.
Washington, DC 20220

BUREAU OF ALCOHOL, TOBACCO AND FIREARMS
Office of Public Affairs
1200 Pennsylvania Ave., N.W.
Washington, DC 20226

BUREAU OF ENGRAVING AND PRINTING
Public Affairs Section, Rm 602-11A
14th and C Sts., S.W.
Washington, DC 20228

BUREAU OF GOVERNMENT FINANCIAL OPERATIONS
Pennsylvania Ave. and Madison Pl., N.W.
Washington, DC 20226

BUREAU OF THE MINT
Assistant to the Director for Public Affairs
501 13th St., N.W.
Washington, DC 20220

COMPTROLLER OF THE CURRENCY
Communications Division
490 L'Enfant Plaza East, S.W.
Washington, DC 20219

INTERNAL REVENUE SERVICE
Office of Public Affairs
1111 Constitution Ave., N.W.
Washington, DC 20224

OFFICE OF REVENUE SHARING
Office of Public Affairs
2401 E St., N.W.
Washington, DC 20226

U.S. CUSTOMS SERVICE
Office of Public Affairs
1301 Constitution Ave., N.W.
Washington, DC 20229

U.S. SECRET SERVICE
Office of Public Affairs
1800 G St., N.W.
Washington, DC 20223

INDEPENDENT AGENCIES

ACTION
Office of Public Affairs
Washington, DC 20525

AMERICAN BATTLE MONUMENTS COMMISSION
5127 Pulaski Bldg
Washington, DC 20314

APPALACHIAN REGIONAL COMMISSION
Archivist
1666 Connecticut Ave., N.W.
Washington, DC 20235

CIVIL AERONAUTICS BOARD
Publications Services Section, B-22
Washington, DC 20428

CONSUMER PRODUCT SAFETY COMMISSION
Bureau of Information and Education
Product Safety Information Division
5401 Westbard Ave.
Bethesda, MD 20207

ENVIRONMENTAL PROTECTION AGENCY
(Subagency Name)
401 M St., S.W.
Washington, DC 20460

Public Information Center
820 Quincy St., N.W.
Washington, DC 20011

ENVIRONMENTAL PROTECTION AGENCY REGIONAL OFFICES

Region I
Rm 2203, JFK Federal Bldg
Boston, MA 02203

Region II
Rm 1009, 26 Federal Plaza
New York, NY 10007

Region III
Curtis Bldg
6th and Walnut Sts.
Philadelphia, PA 19106

Region IV
345 Courtland St., N.E.
Atlanta, GA 30308

Region V
230 South Dearborn St.
Chicago, IL 60604

Region VI
First International Bldg
1201 Elm St.
Dallas, TX 75270

Region VII
324 E. 11th St.
Kansas City, MO 64106

Region VIII
1860 Lincoln St.
Denver, CO 80295

Region IX
215 Fremont St.
San Francisco, CA 94105

Region X
1200 6th Ave.
Seattle, WA 98101

EQUAL EMPLOYMENT OPPORTUNITY COMMISSION
2401 E St., N.W.
Washington, DC 20507

EXPORT-IMPORT BANK OF THE UNITED STATES
Public Affairs Office
811 Vermont Ave., N.W.
Washington, DC 20571

FARM CREDIT ADMINISTRATION
Information Division
1501 Farm Credit Dr.
McLean, VA 22102

FEDERAL COMMUNICATIONS COMMISSION
Public Information Office
1919 M St., N.W.
Washington, DC 20554

FEDERAL DEPOSIT INSURANCE CORPORATION
Information Office
550 17th St., N.W.
Washington, DC 20429

FEDERAL ELECTION COMMISSION
1325 K St., N.W.
Washington, DC 20463

FEDERAL EMERGENCY MANAGEMENT AGENCY
Office of Public Affairs
500 C St., S.W.
Washington, DC 20472

FEDERAL HOME LOAN BANK BOARD
Office of Communications
1700 G St., N.W.
Washington, DC 20552

FEDERAL HOME LOAN BANKS
Federal Home Loan Bank of Atlanta
Peachtree Center Station
P.O. Box 56527
Atlanta, GA 30343

Federal Home Loan Bank of Boston
P.O. Box 2196
Boston, MA 02106

Federal Home Loan Bank of Chicago
111 E. Wacker Dr.
Chicago, IL 60601

Federal Home Loan Bank of Cincinnati
2500 DuBois Tower
P.O. Box 598
Cincinnati, OH 45201

Federal Home Loan Bank of Dallas
500 E. John Carpenter Freeway
P.O. Box 619026
Dallas/Ft. Worth, TX 75261

Federal Home Loan Bank of Des Moines
907 Walnut St.
Des Moines, IA 50309

Federal Home Loan Bank of Indianapolis
1350 Merchants Plaza, South Tower
115 W. Washington St.
P.O. Box 60
Indianapolis, IN 46206

Federal Home Loan Bank of New York
One World Trade Center
New York, NY 10048

Federal Home Loan Bank of Pittsburgh
11 Stanwix St.
Gateway Center
Pittsburgh, PA 15222

Federal Home Loan Bank of San Francisco
600 California St.
P.O. Box 7948
San Francisco, CA 94120

Federal Home Loan Bank of Seattle
600 Stewart St.
Seattle, WA 98101

Federal Home Loan Bank of Topeka
3 Townsite Plaza
P.O. Box 176
120 East 6th St.
Topeka, KS 66601

FEDERAL HOME LOAN MORTGAGE CORPORATION
1770 G St., N.W.
Washington, DC 20552

FEDERAL MARITIME COMMISSION
Public Information Office
1100 L St., N.W.
Washington, DC 20573

FEDERAL MEDIATION AND CONCILIATION SERVICE
2100 K St., N.W.
Washington, DC 20427

FEDERAL RESERVE SYSTEM
Board of Governors
Publications Section
Division of Administrative Services
Washington, DC 20551

Federal Reserve Bank of Atlanta
Research Department
P.O. Box 1731
Atlanta, GA 30301

Federal Reserve Bank of Boston
Bank & Public Information Center
600 Atlantic Ave.
Boston, MA 02106

Federal Reserve Bank of Chicago
Publications Division
P.O. Box 834
Chicago, IL 60690

Federal Reserve Bank of Cleveland
Research Department
P.O. Box 6387
Cleveland, OH 44101

Federal Reserve Bank of Dallas
Research Department
Station K
Dallas, TX 75222

Federal Reserve Bank of Kansas City
Research Department
925 Grand Ave.
Kansas City, MO 64198

Federal Reserve Bank of Minneapolis
Office of Public Information
Minneapolis, MN 55480

Federal Reserve Bank of New York
Public Information Department
33 Liberty St.
New York, NY 10045

Federal Reserve Bank of Philadelphia
Public Services Department
Independence Mall
100 N. 6th St.
Philadelphia, PA 19106

Federal Reserve Bank of Richmond
Bank and Public Relations Department
P.O. Box 27622
Richmond, VA 23261

Federal Reserve Bank of St. Louis
Research Department
Box 442
St. Louis, MO 63166

Federal Reserve Bank of San Francisco
Research Information Center
P.O. Box 7702
San Francisco, CA 94120

FEDERAL TRADE COMMISSION
Public Reference Room
Rm 130
Washington, DC 20580

GENERAL SERVICES ADMINISTRATION
Director of Information
Washington, DC 20405

National Archives and Records Service
Publications Sales Branch
Washington, DC 20408

INTERSTATE COMMERCE COMMISSION
Public Information Office
Washington, DC 20423

MERIT SYSTEMS PROTECTION BOARD
1120 Vermont Ave., N.W.
Washington, DC 20419

NATIONAL AERONAUTICS AND SPACE ADMINISTRATION
Headquarters, Information Center
Washington, DC 20546

NATIONAL CREDIT UNION ADMINISTRATION
Office of Public Information
1776 G St., N.W.
Washington, DC 20456

NATIONAL FOUNDATION ON THE ARTS AND HUMANITIES
1100 Pennsylvania, Ave., N.W.
Washington, DC 20506

NATIONAL LABOR RELATIONS BOARD
1717 Pennsylvania Ave., N.W.
Washington, DC 20570

NATIONAL MEDIATION BOARD
1230 16th St., N.W.
Washington, DC 20036

NATIONAL SCIENCE FOUNDATION
Public Information Branch, Rm 531
1800 G St., N.W.
Washington, DC 20550

NATIONAL TRANSPORTATION SAFETY BOARD
Publications Unit
800 Independence Ave., S.W.
Washington, DC 20594

NUCLEAR REGULATORY COMMISSION
Attn: Sales Manager
Washington, DC 20555

OFFICE OF PERSONNEL MANAGEMENT
Office of Public Affairs
1900 E St., N.W.
Washington, DC 20415

PANAMA CANAL COMMISSION
425 13th St., N.W.
Washington, DC 20004

PENSION BENEFIT GUARANTY CORPORATION
2020 K St., N.W.
Washington, DC 20006

RAILROAD RETIREMENT BOARD
Division of Information Service
844 Rush St.
Chicago, IL 60611

SECURITIES AND EXCHANGE COMMISSION
Office of Public Information
450 5th St., N.W.
Washington, DC 20549

SELECTIVE SERVICE SYSTEM
600 E St., N.W.
Washington, DC 20435

SMALL BUSINESS ADMINISTRATION
Office of Public Affairs
1441 L. St., N.W.
Washington, DC 20416

SMITHSONIAN INSTITUTION
Office of Public Affairs
Washington, DC 20560

TENNESSEE VALLEY AUTHORITY
Suite 300, 412 First St., S.E.
Washington, DC 20444

Public Affairs Office
400 Commerce Ave.
Knoxville, TN 37902

Division of Energy Use and Distributor Relations
721 Power Building
Chattanooga, TN 37401

Division of Land and Forest Resources
Norris, TN 37828

Technical Library
Office of Agricultural and Chemical Development
Muscle Shoals, AL 35660

U.S. ARMS CONTROL AND DISARMAMENT AGENCY
Office of Public Affairs
320 21st St., N.W.
Washington, DC 20451

U.S. INFORMATION AGENCY
Office of Public Liaison
400 C St., S.W.
Washington, DC 20547

U.S. INTERNATIONAL DEVELOPMENT COOPERATION AGENCY
Office of Public Affairs
Washington, DC 20523

Agency for International Development
Director, Office of Public Affairs
Washington, DC 20523

AID Document and Information Handling Facility
Suite 100, 7222 47th St.
Chevy Chase, MD 20815

Overseas Private Investment Corporation
1129 20th St., N.W.
Washington, DC 20527

U.S. INTERNATIONAL TRADE COMMISSION
Office of the Secretary
Washington, DC 20436

U.S. POSTAL SERVICE
475 L'Enfant Plaza West, S.W.
Washington, DC 20260

VETERANS ADMINISTRATION
810 Vermont Ave., N.W.
Washington, DC 20420

SPECIAL BOARDS, COMMITTEES, AND COMMISSIONS

ADVISORY COMMISSION ON INTERGOVERNMENTAL RELATIONS
Suite 2000, Vanguard Bldg
111 20th St., N.W.
Washington, DC 20575

ADVISORY COMMITTEE ON FEDERAL PAY
Rm 205, 1730 K St., N.W.
Washington, DC 20006

ARCHITECTURAL AND TRANSPORTATION BARRIERS COMPLIANCE BOARD
Rm 1010 Switzer Bldg
330 C St., N.W.
Washington, DC 20202

BOARD FOR INTERNATIONAL BROADCASTING
Suite 400, 1201 Connecticut Ave., N.W.
Washington, DC 20036

BOARD OF FOREIGN SCHOLARSHIPS
Operations Staff
U.S. Information Agency
Washington, DC 20547

COMMISSION ON CIVIL RIGHTS
Publications Warehouse
621 N. Payne St.
Alexandria, VA 22314

COMMODITY FUTURES TRADING COMMISSION
Office of Public Information
2033 K St., N.W.
Washington, DC 20581

Suite 4600, 233 S. Wacker Dr.
Chicago, IL 60606

Rm 400, 4901 Main St.
Kansas City, MO 64112

510 Grain Exchange Building
Minneapolis, MN 55415

Suite 4747, One World Trade Center
New York, NY 10048

FEDERAL FINANCIAL INSTITUTIONS EXAMINATION COUNCIL
Comptroller of the Currency Bldg, 8th Fl.
490 L'Enfant Plaza East, S.W.
Washington, DC 20219

FEDERAL LABOR RELATIONS AUTHORITY
500 C St., S.W.
Washington, DC 20424

HARRY S. TRUMAN SCHOLARSHIP FOUNDATION
712 Jackson Place, N.W.
Washington, DC 20006

INTER-AMERICAN FOUNDATION
1515 Wilson Blvd, 5th Fl.
Rosslyn, VA 22209

INTERNATIONAL JOINT COMMISSION, U.S. AND CANADA
United States Section
2001 S St., N.W.
Washington, DC 20440

JAPAN-U.S. FRIENDSHIP COMMISSION
1875 Connecticut Ave., N.W.
Washington, DC 20009

MARINE MAMMAL COMMISSION
1625 I St., N.W.
Washington, DC 20006

MIGRATORY BIRD CONSERVATION COMMISSION
Department of the Interior Bldg
Washington, DC 20240

NATIONAL ADVISORY COUNCIL ON ADULT EDUCATION
Rm 323, 425 13th St., N.W.
Washington, DC 20004

NATIONAL ADVISORY COUNCIL ON CHILD NUTRITION
Rm 509, 3101 Park Center Dr.
Alexandria, VA 22302

NATIONAL ADVISORY COUNCIL ON CONTINUING EDUCATION
425 13th St., N.W., Rm 529
Washington, DC 20004

NATIONAL ADVISORY COUNCIL ON INDIAN EDUCATION
425 13th St., N.W.
Washington, DC 20004

NATIONAL ADVISORY COUNCIL ON INTERNATIONAL MONETARY AND FINANCIAL POLICIES
Rm 5455
Department of the Treasury
Washington, DC 20220

NATIONAL CAPITAL PLANNING COMMISSION
1325 G St., N.W.
Washington, DC 20576

NATIONAL COMMISSION FOR EMPLOYMENT POLICY
1522 K St., N.W., Rm 300
Washington, DC 20005

NATIONAL COMMISSION ON LIBRARIES AND INFORMATION SCIENCE
GSA Regional Office Bldg 3
Suite 3122
7th and D Sts., S.W.
Washington, DC 20024

NATIONAL NARCOTICS INTELLIGENCE CONSUMERS COMMITTEE
Drug Enforcement Administration
1405 I St., N.W.
Washington, DC 20537

PRESIDENT'S COMMITTEE ON EMPLOYMENT OF THE HANDICAPPED
Vanguard Bldg.
1111 20th St., N.W.
Washington, DC 20036

U.S. ADVISORY COMMISSION ON PUBLIC DIPLOMACY
Rm 1008, 1750 Pennsylvania Ave., N.W.
Washington, DC 20547

JUDICIAL BRANCH

ADMINISTRATIVE OFFICE OF U.S. COURTS
Washington, DC 20544

FEDERAL JUDICIAL CENTER
1520 H St., N.W.
Washington, DC 20005

SPECIAL COURTS
U.S. Court of International Trade
1 Federal Plaza
New York, NY 10007

U.S. Court of Claims
717 Madison Pl., N.W.
Washington, DC 20005

U.S. Tax Court
400 2nd St., N.W.
Washington, DC 20217

UNITED STATES CONGRESS
(House Committee Name)
U.S. House of Representatives
Washington, DC 20515
(Senate Committee Name)
U.S. Senate
Washington, DC 20510
(Joint Committee Name)
U.S. Congress
Washington, DC 20510

CONGRESSIONAL BUDGET OFFICE
Office of Intergovernmental Relations
2nd and D Sts., S.W.
Washington, DC 20515

LIBRARY OF CONGRESS
Publications Officer
Washington, DC 20540

OFFICE OF TECHNOLOGY AND ASSESSMENT
Office of Public Affairs
Washington, DC 20510

U.S. GENERAL ACCOUNTING OFFICE
Document Handling and Information
Services Facility
P.O. Box 6015
Gaithersburg, MD 20877

QUASI-OFFICIAL AGENCIES

AMERICAN NATIONAL RED CROSS
Office of Public Affairs and
Financial Development
17th and D Sts., N.W.
Washington, DC 20006

NATIONAL RAILROAD PASSENGER CORPORATION (AMTRAK)
Vice President, Public Affairs
400 North Capitol St., N.W.
Washington, DC 20001

U.S. RAILWAY ASSOCIATION
Public Affairs Office
955 L'Enfant Plaza North, S.W.
Washington, DC 20595

U.S. SYNTHETIC FUELS CORPORATION
1200 New Hampshire Ave., N.W.
Washington, DC 20856

Document Availability Symbols

The following abbreviations and symbols are used to indicate the availability of documents abstracted by ASI. The symbols are provided in the bibliographic data section given at the head of each abstract.

GPO For sale by Government Printing Office, Washington, D.C., 20402.

The GPO stock number (S/N) is also given. The price is given if it has been announced at the time ASI goes to press; GPO prices change frequently, however.

NTIS For sale by National Technical Information Service, 5285 Port Royal Rd., Springfield, Va., 22161.

Order number and price are also given if available.

† or ‡ Inquire of the issuing agency.

† Copies are available at the time the document is issued, usually free of charge, but supplies may be limited.

‡ Limited or restricted distribution has been specified by the agency. In some cases a request for a copy will be honored.

Addresses of major issuing agency offices are given in the Abstracts Volume, p. xxxvii; Index Volume, p. xxviii. If documents are available from another office, the name and address will be given in the bibliographic data section of the abstract.

◆ No distribution. Issuing agency has specified it should not be contacted.

ASI/MF Available on ASI microfiche. Microfiche collections are available in many libraries. The number following this notation indicates the unit count for ordering individual documents on microfiche through ASI "Documents on Demand." For information, see p. xx.

● **Item** Depository item number, assigned to classes of documents issued to depository libraries.

ACRONYMS AND SELECTED ABBREVIATIONS

The following acronyms and abbreviations may be used without further identification:

Abbreviation	Full Name
ADAMHA	Alcohol, Drug Abuse and Mental Health Administration
Admin	Administration
AEC	Atomic Energy Commission
AFDC	Aid to Families with Dependent Children
AID	Agency for International Development
Amtrak	National Railroad Passenger Corporation
Assn	Association
BEA	Bureau of Economic Analysis
Bibl	Bibliography
BLS	Bureau of Labor Statistics
Bull	Bulletin
Bur	Bureau
CAB	Civil Aeronautics Board
CBO	Congressional Budget Office
CCC	Commodity Credit Corporation
CDC	Centers for Disease Control
CETA	Comprehensive Employment and Training Act
CIA	Central Intelligence Agency
Conf	Conference
CPI	Consumer Price Index
CRS	Congressional Research Service
CY	Calendar year
DEA	Drug Enforcement Association
Dept	Department
Dev	Development
Div	Division
DOD	Department of Defense
DOE	Department of Energy
DOT	Department of Transportation
EC	European Community
EDA	Economic Development Administration
EIA	Energy Information Administration
EPA	Environmental Protection Agency
ERS	Economic Research Service
ESEA	Elementary and Secondary Education Act
Eximbank	Export-Import Bank
FAA	Federal Aviation Administration
FAO	Food and Agriculture Organization (UN)
FAS	Foreign Agricultural Service
FBI	Federal Bureau of Investigation
FCC	Federal Communications Commission
FDA	Food and Drug Administration
FDIC	Federal Deposit Insurance Corporation
Fed	Federal
FERC	Federal Energy Regulatory Commission
FHA	Federal Housing Administration
FHLB	Federal Home Loan Bank
FHLBB	Federal Home Loan Bank Board
FmHA	Farmers Home Administration
FPC	Federal Power Commission
FSLIC	Federal Savings and Loan Insurance Corporation
FTC	Federal Trade Commission
FY	Fiscal year
GAO	General Accounting Office
GATT	General Agreement on Tariffs and Trade
GDP	Gross Domestic Product
GNP	Gross National Product
Govtl	Governmental
GPO	Government Printing Office
GSA	General Services Administration
HCFA	Health Care Financing Administration
HHS	Department of Health and Human Services
HMO	Health Maintenance Organization
HRSA	Health Resources and Services Administration
HUD	Department of Housing and Urban Development
Hwy	Highway
ICC	Interstate Commerce Commission
IMF	International Monetary Fund
Info	Information
Inst	Institute
Instn	Institution
Intl	International
IRA	Individual retirement arrangement
IRS	Internal Revenue Service
ITA	International Trade Administration
MarAd	Maritime Administration
Mgmt	Management
MSA	Metropolitan Statistical Area (formerly SMSA)
NASA	National Aeronautics and Space Administration
Natl	National
NATO	North Atlantic Treaty Organization
NCES	National Center for Education Statistics
NCHS	National Center for Health Statistics
NIE	National Institute of Education
NIH	National Institutes of Health
NIMH	National Institute of Mental Health
NLRB	National Labor Relations Board
NOAA	National Oceanic and Atmospheric Administration
NRC	Nuclear Regulatory Commission
NSF	National Science Foundation
NTIS	National Technical Information Services
OAS	Organization of American States
OASDHI	Old-Age, Survivors, Disability, and Health Insurance Program
OCS	Outer continental shelf
OECD	Organization for Economic Cooperation and Development
OHDS	Office of Human Development Services
OMB	Office of Management and Budget
OPEC	Organization of Petroleum Exporting Countries
OSHA	Occupational Safety and Health Administration
PHS	Public Health Service
PPI	Producer Price Index
PRC	People's Republic of China
Pub	Publication
R&D	Research and Development
REA	Rural Electrification Administration
Res	Research
ROTC	Reserve Officers Training Corps
Rpt	Report
S&L	Savings and Loan Association
SALT	Strategic Arms Limitation Talks
SBA	Small Business Administration
SEC	Securities and Exchange Commission
SIC	Standard Industrial Classification
SITC	Standard International trade Classification
SMSA	Standard Metropolitan Statistical Area (see MSA)
SRS	Statistical Reporting Service
SSA	Social Security Administration
SSI	Supplemental Security Income
TSUSA	Tariff Schedules of the U.S., Annotated
TTPI	Trust Territory of the Pacific Islands
TVA	Tennessee Valley Authority
USDA	Department of Agriculture
USGS	U.S. Geological Survey
USIA	U.S. Information Agency
USITC	U.S. International Trade Commission
USPS	U.S. Postal Service
VA	Veterans Administration
VISTA	Volunteers in Service to America

Issuing Agencies and ASI Accession Numbers

Listed below are issuing agencies for all publications abstracted in this Annual. Agencies are arranged to reflect current departmental organizations.

EXECUTIVE OFFICE OF THE PRESIDENT

- 20 General
- 100 Office of Management and Budget
- 200 Council of Economic Advisers
- 240 Central Intelligence Agency
- 440 Office of the U.S. Trade Representative
- 480 Council on Environmental Quality

DEPARTMENT OF AGRICULTURE

- 1000 General
- 1120 Agricultural Cooperative Service
- 1180 Farmers Home Administration
- 1200 Forest Service
- 1240 Rural Electrification Administration
- 1260 Soil Conservation Service
- 1270 Office of Transportation
- 1290 Federal Grain Inspection Service
- Agricultural Marketing Service
  - 1300 General
  - 1309-
  - 1319 Commodity Reports
- 1350 Human Nutrition Information Service
- 1360 Food and Nutrition Service
- 1370 Food Safety and Inspection Service
- 1380 Packers and Stockyards Administration
- 1390 Animal and Plant Health Inspection Service
- Economic Research Service
  - 1500 General
  - 1520 International
  - 1540 National Economics
  - 1560 National Economics, Commodities
  - 1580 Natural Resources
  - 1590 Economic Development
- Statistical Reporting Service
  - 1610-
  - 1651 Crop Reporting Board
- 1700 Agricultural Research Service
- 1740 Cooperative State Research Service
- Agricultural Stabilization and Conservation Service
  - 1800 General
  - 1820 Commodity Credit Corp.
- 1920 Foreign Agricultural Service

DEPARTMENT OF COMMERCE

- 2000 General
- 2010 Bureau of Industrial Economics
- 2040 International Trade Administration
- 2060 Economic Development Administration
- 2100 Minority Business Development Agency
- National Oceanic and Atmospheric Administration
  - 2140 General
  - 2150 National Environmental Satellite, Data, and Information Service
  - 2160 National Marine Fisheries Service
  - 2170 National Ocean Service
  - 2180 National Weather Service
- 2210 National Bureau of Standards
- 2220 National Technical Information Service
- 2240 Patent and Trademark Office
- Bureau of Census
  - 2300 Bibliographies and Guides
  - 2320 General
  - 2330-
  - 2331 1982 Census of Agriculture
  - 2340 Agriculture
  - 2371-
  - 2373 1982 Census of Construction Industries
  - 2380 Construction
  - 2390-
  - 2391 1982 Census of Service Industries
  - 2395-
  - 2401 1982 Census of Retail Trade
  - 2403-
  - 2405 1982 Census of Wholesale Trade
  - 2410 Distribution and Service
  - 2420 Foreign Trade
  - 2453-
  - 2460 1982 Census of Governments
  - 2462-
  - 2466 Governments
  - 2473-
  - 2475 1980 Census of Housing
  - 2480 Housing
  - 2491 1982 Census of Manufactures
  - 2500 Manufacturing
  - 2511 1982 Census of Mineral Industries
  - 2531-
  - 2535 1980 Census of Population
  - 2540 Population
  - 2551 1980 Census of Population and Housing
  - 2573 1982 Census of Transportation
  - 2593 1982 Economic Censuses of Outlying Areas
  - 2620 Methodology
- 2700 Bureau of Economic Analysis
- 2800 National Telecommunications and Information Administration
- 2900 U.S. Travel and Tourism Administration

DEPARTMENT OF ENERGY

- 3000 General
- 3020 Office of the Secretary of Energy
- 3080 Federal Energy Regulatory Commission
- 3100 Economic Regulatory Administration
- 3160 Energy Information Administration
- 3210 Alaska Power Administration
- 3220 Bonneville Power Administration
- 3230 Southeastern Power Administration

3240 Southwestern Power Administration
3250 Western Area Power Administration
3300 Conservation and Renewable Energy
3350 Nuclear Energy
3360 Civilian Radioactive Waste Management
3400 International Affairs and Energy Emergencies

DEPARTMENT OF DEFENSE

3500 General
3540 Office of the Secretary of Defense
3560 Joint Chiefs of Staff
3600 Department of Air Force
3700 Department of Army
3750 Army Corps of Engineers
3800 Department of Navy
3900 Defense Agencies

DEPARTMENT OF HEALTH AND HUMAN SERVICES

4000 General

Public Health Service

4040 General
4060 Food and Drug Administration Health Resources and Services Administration
4100 General
4110 Bureau of Health Professions
National Center for Health Statistics
4120 Bibliographies and Guides
4140 General
4160 Methodology
4180 National Center for Health Services Research
Centers for Disease Control
4200 General
4240 National Institute for Occupational Safety and Health
National Institutes of Health
4430 General
4460 National Library of Medicine
4470 NIH Research Institutes

Alcohol, Drug Abuse and Mental Health Administration
4480 National Institute on Alcohol Abuse and Alcoholism
4490 National Institute on Drug Abuse
4500 National Institute of Mental Health

4600 Office of Human Development Services
4650 Health Care Financing Administration
Social Security Administration
4700 General
4740 Office of Research, Statistics, and International Policy

---

DEPARTMENT OF EDUCATION

4800 General
National Center for Education Statistics
4820 General
4830 Elementary and Secondary Schools
4840 Higher Education
4850 Libraries
4860 Adult and Vocational Education
4890 National Assessment of Educational Progress
4910 National Institute of Education
4940 Office of Special Education and Rehabilitative Services

DEPARTMENT OF HOUSING AND URBAN DEVELOPMENT

5000 General
5120 Community Planning and Development
5140 Housing (FHA)
5180 Policy Development and Research

DEPARTMENT OF INTERIOR

5300 General
5500 Fish and Wildlife Service

5540 National Park Service
Bureau of Mines
5600 General
5610 Mineral Industry Surveys
5660 Geological Survey
5700 Bureau of Indian Affairs
5720 Bureau of Land Management
5730 Minerals Management Service
5820 Bureau of Reclamation

DEPARTMENT OF JUSTICE

6000 General
6060 Office of Justice Assistance, Research and Statistics
6220 Federal Bureau of Investigation
6240 Bureau of Prisons
6260 Immigration and Naturalization Service

DEPARTMENT OF LABOR

6300 General
6360 Bureau of International Labor Affairs
6400 Employment and Training Administration
6460 Labor-Management Services Administration
6500 Employment Standards Administration
6560 Women's Bureau
6600 Occupational Safety and Health Administration
6660 Mine Safety and Health Administration
Bureau of Labor Statistics
6700 Bibliographies and Guides
6720 General
6740 Employment Analysis and Trends
6760 Prices and Living Conditions
6780 Wages and Industrial Relations
6820 Productivity and Technology
6840 Occupational Safety and Health
6860 Foreign Labor Conditions
6880 Methodology
6910 Regional Office 1, Boston
6920 Regional Office 2, New York

6940	Regional Office 4, Atlanta
6960	Regional Office 6, Dallas
6970	Regional Office 7 and 8, Kansas City

DEPARTMENT OF STATE

7000	General
7140	Bureau of Intelligence and Research
7180	Bureau of Consular Affairs

DEPARTMENT OF TRANSPORTATION

7300	General
7400	Coast Guard
7500	Federal Aviation Administration
7550	Federal Highway Administration
7600	Federal Railroad Administration
7700	Maritime Administration
7740	Saint Lawrence Seaway Development Corp.
7760	National Highway Traffic Safety Administration
7880	Urban Mass Transportation Administration

DEPARTMENT OF TREASURY

8000	General
8060	Office of Revenue Sharing
8100	Bureau of Government Financial Operations
8140	U.S. Customs Service
8160	Bureau of Engraving and Printing
8200	Bureau of the Mint
8240	Bureau of the Public Debt
8300	Internal Revenue Service
8400	Office of the Comptroller of Currency
8440	U.S. Savings Bonds Division
8460	U.S. Secret Service
8480	Bureau of Alcohol, Tobacco and Firearms

INDEPENDENT AGENCIES

9020	ACTION
9080	Appalachian Regional Commission
9140	Civil Aeronautics Board
9160	Consumer Product Safety Commission
	Environmental Protection Agency
9180	General
9190	Air
9200	Water
9230	Pesticides, Radiation, and Hazardous Materials
9240	Equal Employment Opportunity Commission
9250	Export-Import Bank
9260	Farm Credit Administration
9270	Federal Election Commission
9280	Federal Communications Commission
9290	Federal Deposit Insurance Corp.
9300	Federal Home Loan Banks
9310	Federal Home Loan Bank Board
9320	Federal Financing Bank
9330	Federal Maritime Commission
9360	Federal Reserve Board of Governors
	Federal Reserve Banks
9371	Federal Reserve Bank of Atlanta
9373	Federal Reserve Bank of Boston
9375	Federal Reserve Bank of Chicago
9377	Federal Reserve Bank of Cleveland
9379	Federal Reserve Bank of Dallas
9381	Federal Reserve Bank of Kansas City
9383	Federal Reserve Bank of Minneapolis
9385	Federal Reserve Bank of New York
9387	Federal Reserve Bank of Philadelphia
9389	Federal Reserve Bank of Richmond
9391	Federal Reserve Bank of St. Louis
9393	Federal Reserve Bank of San Francisco
9400	Federal Trade Commission
9410	Federal Home Loan Mortgage Corp.
9430	Federal Emergency Management Agency
9450	General Services Administration

9480	Interstate Commerce Commission
9490	Merit Systems Protection Board
9500	National Aeronautics and Space Administration
9530	National Credit Union Administration
9560	National Foundation on the Arts and the Humanities
9580	National Labor Relations Board
9610	National Transportation Safety Board
9620	National Science Foundation
9630	Nuclear Regulatory Commission
9660	Panama Canal Commission
9700	Railroad Retirement Board
9730	Securities and Exchange Commission
9740	Selective Service System
9760	Small Business Administration
9770	Smithsonian Institution
9800	Tennessee Valley Authority
9820	U.S. Arms Control and Disarmament Agency
9840	Office of Personnel Management
9850	U.S. Information Agency
9860	U.S. Postal Service
9880	U.S. International Trade Commission
	U.S. International Development Cooperation Agency
9900	General
9910	Agency for International Development
9920	Veterans Administration

SPECIAL BOARDS, COMMITTEES, AND COMMISSIONS

10040	Advisory Commission on Intergovernmental Relations
10100	Advisory Committee on Federal Pay
10170	Advisory Council on Social Security
10310	Board for International Broadcasting
11040	Commission on Civil Rights
11120	Commission on Fair Market Value Policy for Federal Coal Leasing
11710	Committee for Purchase from the Blind and Other Severely Handicapped

11920 Commodity Futures Trading Commission
13000 Federal Financial Institutions Examination Council
13360 Federal Labor Relations Authority
14310 Harry S. Truman Scholarship Foundation
14350 Interagency Task Force on Acid Precipitation
14420 Inter-American Foundation
14640 International Joint Commission, U.S. and Canada
14690 Japan-U.S. Friendship Commission
14730 Marine Mammal Commission
14820 Motor Carrier Ratemaking Study Commission
14870 National Advisory Council on Indian Education
15040 National Advisory Committee on Oceans and Atmosphere
15210 National Advisory Council on Continuing Education
15340 National Advisory Council on International Monetary and Financial Policies
15630 National Commission on Libraries and Information Science
15890 National Narcotics Intelligence Consumers Committee
16590 President's Committee on Employment of the Handicapped
16900 President's Private Sector Survey on Cost Control
17590 U.S. Advisory Commission on Public Diplomacy
17610 U.S. Architectural and Transportation Barriers Compliance Board
17890 White House Conference on Productivity

UNITED STATES COURTS

18200 Administrative Office of the U.S. Courts
18220 Special Courts
18400 Federal Judicial Center

UNITED STATES CONGRESS

House Committees
21140 House Aging Committee, Select
21160 House Agriculture Committee
21200 House Armed Services Committee
21240 House Banking, Finance and Urban Affairs Committee
21260 House Budget Committee
21340 House Education and Labor Committee
21360 House Energy and Commerce Committee
21380 House Foreign Affairs Committee
21400 House Government Operations Committee
21420 House Administration Committee
21440 House Interior and Insular Affairs Committee
21520 House Judiciary Committee
21560 House Merchant Marine and Fisheries Committee
21620 House Post Office and Civil Service Committee
21700 House Science and Technology Committee
21720 House Small Business Committee
21780 House Ways and Means Committee
21940 House Special Publications
21960 House Temporary Committees

Joint Committees
23840 Joint Economic Committee
23860 Joint Taxation Committee

Senate Committees
25140 Senate Aging Committee, Special
25160 Senate Agriculture, Nutrition, and Forestry Committee
25200 Senate Armed Services Committee
25240 Senate Banking, Housing, and Urban Affairs Committee
25260 Senate Commerce, Science and Transportation Committee
25310 Senate Energy and Natural Resources Committee
25320 Senate Environment and Public Works Committee
25360 Senate Finance Committee
25380 Senate Foreign Relations Committee
25400 Senate Governmental Affairs Committee
25520 Senate Judiciary Committee
25680 Senate Rules and Administration Committee
25720 Senate Small Business Committee, Select
25920 Senate Documents
25940 Senate Special Publications

General Accounting Office
26100 General
26111 Accounting and Financial Management
26113 Resources, Community and Economic Development
26115 Assistant Comptroller General
26117 Chief Economist
26119 General Government
26121 Human Resources
26123 National Security and International Affairs
26125 Information Management and Technology
26131 Program Evaluation and Methodology
26200 Government Printing Office
26300 Congressional Budget Office
26350 Office of Technology Assessment
26400 Library of Congress

QUASI-OFFICIAL AGENCIES

29250 American National Red Cross
29600 U.S. Railway Association
29650 U.S. Synthetic Fuels Corp.

Index by Subjects and Names

Index by Subjects and Names

This index contains references to subjects, to corporate authors, and to individual authors of articles and publications where the author's name appears on the title page.

References to individual items within a tabular breakdown (e.g., data about a particular State in a table that is broken down State

by State) have been included only on a selective basis. For complete references to information of this kind please use the Index by Categories, which begins on page 871.

For a discussion of how to make best use of both indexes, please see pages xiii-xviii.

Abandoned buildings

Arson incidents by occupancy of structure, average property value, and arrest rates, by type of property, 1983, annual rpt, 6224–2.1

Census of Housing, 1980: inventory, occupancy, and unit characteristics, changes from 1973 by region and inside-outside SMSAs and central cities, series, 2473–3

Housing occupancy and unit and household characteristics, by region and metro-nonmetro residence, 1983, biennial survey, 2485–1

Neighborhood and housing quality indicators and attitudes, and occupant characteristics, by urban- rural location and region, 1981, annual survey, 2485–7

Neighborhood and housing quality indicators and attitudes, by occupant and unit characteristics, region, and metro-nonmetro location, 1981, annual survey, 2485–2

Abbott, Julian

"Knowledge of Social Security: Survivor Families with Young Children", 4742–1.401

Abbott, P. O.

"Hydrology of Area 61, Northern Great Plains and Rocky Mountain Coal Provinces, Colorado and New Mexico", 5666–19.5

Abilene, Tex.

Census of Housing, 1980: occupancy and unit characteristics, by race, Hispanic origin, and city, SMSA rpt, 2473–1.58

Census of Population and Housing, 1980: detailed population and housing characteristics, by county, city, and census tract, SMSA rpt, 2551–2.58

Housing vacancy rates for single and multifamily units and mobile homes, by city and ZIP code, 1984, annual metro area rpt, 9304–19.21

see also under By SMSA or MSA in the "Index by Categories"

Abnormalities

see Birth defects

Abortion

Abortions, by patient sociodemographic

characteristics, pregnancy history, and procedure, 1980, US Vital Statistics final rpt, 4146–5.72

Death rates by sex, race, and age for 40 causes, projected for 10-year period, 1982 rpt, 4208–21

Deaths and death rates by detailed cause and demographic characteristics, 1979 and selected trends, US Vital Statistics annual rpt, 4144–2.1

Deaths and death rates related to pregnancy, 1981, US Vital Statistics advance rpt, 4146–5.78

Deaths and death rates related to pregnancy, 1982, US Vital Statistics advance rpt, 4146–5.81

Deaths by principal or contributing cause, with type of injury reported in accidental, poisoning, and violent deaths, by age, sex, and race, 1978, 4146–5.76

Health condition and health care resources, use, and expenditures, 1970s-82 with trends and projections 1900-2000, annual compilation, 4144–11

Hospital discharges and length of stay, by patient age and sex, facility size and ownership, procedure performed, and region, 1983, 4146–8.101

Hospital discharges and length of stay, by patient characteristics, facility size, procedure performed, diagnosis, and region, 1982, annual rpt, 4147–13.78

Legal abortions, and deaths from abortion and childbirth, by medical and sociodemographic characteristics, 1972-83, hearings, 21368–47

Legal abortions and rates, by State of occurrence, 1980, annual rpt, 4204–1.3

Medicaid funded abortions by justification, and expenditures, by State, FY78-83, annual rpt, 4654–9

Pregnancy health counseling effect on smoking, diet, delivery costs, and birth weight, by sociodemographic characteristics and pregnancy history, 1983 article, 4102–1.401

Statistical Abstract of US, social, political, and economic data, 1950s-83 and trends, annual rpt, 2324–1.1

Teenage girls births and sexual experience by race, abortions, and birth control use, by age, 1970s-80 with birth trends from 1920, hearings, 21968–29

Abrams, Richard K.

"Monetary Control: A Comparison of the

U.S. and Canadian Experiences, 1975-79", 9381–10.38

Abrasive materials

County Business Patterns: establishments, employees, and payrolls, by SIC 4-digit industry and county, 1981, annual State rpt series, 2326–8

County Business Patterns: establishments, employees, and payrolls, by SIC 4-digit industry and county, 1982, annual State rpt series, 2326–6

Employment, earnings, and hours, by SIC 4-digit nonfarm industry, monthly 1974-Feb 1984, annual update, 6744–4

Exports and imports of US, detailed SIC-based commodities by world area, 1983, annual rpts, 2424–6

Exports and imports of US, totals and as percent of domestic production, by SIC 2- to 5-digit commodity, 1981, annual rpt, 2424–3

Exports of US, detailed commodities by country of destination, monthly rpt, 2422–3

Exports of US, detailed Schedule B commodities by country of destination, 1983, annual rpt, 2424–9

Exports of US, detailed Schedule E commodities by mode of transport and world area and country of destination, 1983, annual rpts, 2424–5

Great Lakes trade, by SITC 3-digit commodity, port, vessel type, world area, and country, 1982, annual rpt, 7744–3

Imports of US, detailed Schedule A commodities by country and world area of origin, and mode of transport, 1983, annual rpts, 2424–2

Imports of US, detailed Schedule A commodities by country, monthly rpt, 2422–2

Imports of US, detailed TSUSA commodities by country of origin, 1983, annual rpt, 2424–4

Input-output structure of US economy, detailed interindustry transactions for 537 industries, and components of final demand, 1977 benchmark data, 2708–17

Manufacturing census, 1982: financial and operating data, by SIC 2- to 4-digit industry, State, SMSA, and county, preliminary census div rpt series, 2491–3

Abrasive materials

Manufacturing census, 1982: financial and operating data, for SIC 4-digit industries by product, preliminary rpt, 2491–1.243

Mineral industries census, 1982: financial and operating data, by SIC 2- to 4-digit industry, preliminary summary rpt, 2511–2.1

Minerals Yearbook, 1982, Vol 1: commodity reviews of production, reserves, supply, use, and trade, annual rpt, 5604–33

Minerals Yearbook, 1982, Vol 2 preprints: State reviews of production and sales by commodity, and business activity, annual rpt series, 5604–16

Minerals Yearbook, 1982, Vol 2: State reviews of production, sales, and firms, by commodity, and business activity, annual rpt, 5604–34

Minerals Yearbook, 1982, Vol 3: foreign country reviews of production, trade, and policies, by commodity, annual rpt, 5604–35

Minerals Yearbook, 1982, Vol 3 preprints: foreign country reviews of production, trade, and policies, by commodity, annual rpt series, 5604–17

Minerals Yearbook, 1983, Vol 1 preprints: commodity review of production, reserves, supply, use, and trade, annual rpt, 5604–15.3, 5604–15.53

Minerals Yearbook, 1983, Vol 3 preprints: foreign country reviews of production, trade, and policies, by commodity, annual rpt series, 5604–23

Occupational injuries and incidence, nonmetallic mineral mining and related operations, detailed analysis, 1982, annual rpt, 6664–1

Occupational injury and illness rates, by SIC 2- to 4-digit industry, 1982, annual rpt, 6844–1

Producer prices and indexes, by stage of processing and detailed commodity, monthly rpt, 6762–6

Producer prices and indexes, by stage of processing and detailed commodity, monthly 1983, annual supplement, 6764–2

Production, prices, trade, use, employment, tariffs, and stockpiling, by mineral commodity, with foreign comparisons, 1979-83, annual rpt, 5604–18

Waterborne commerce of US (domestic and foreign), freight by commodity, traffic, and passengers, by port and waterway, 1982, annual rpt, 3754–3

see also under By Commodity in the "Index by Categories"

Absenteeism

Allergy and Infectious Diseases Natl Inst activities, grants by instn, State, and country, and disease incidence and costs, FY60s-84, annual rpt, 4474–30

Coal mines and related operations, injury, employment, worktime, and productivity data, 1982, annual rpt, 6664–4

Disability (short-term) earnings lost, insurance benefits, sick leave, and work days lost by sex, by type of worker, 1948-81, article, 4742–1.417

Disability days, by age, region, metro-nonmetro location, and selected SMSA, 1980-81, 4147—10.146

DOE and contractor facility accidents, deaths, illnesses, radiation exposure, and property damage, by facility, 1982, annual rpt, 3004–24

Fed Govt civilian employee occupational injuries, deaths, and illnesses, by agency, 1982, annual rpt, 6604–1

Fed Govt programs and mgmt cost control proposals, 3-year savings by function and agency, and financial and operating data, 1960s-81, 16908–1.3, 16908–1.16, 16908–1.27

Hispanic Americans health services use, illness rates, and disability days, by socioeconomic characteristics, and compared to blacks and whites, 1978-80, 4147–10.147

Labor force not at work on day of survey, employed part-time, or unemployed, by reason, sex, race, Hispanic origin, region, and State, 1983, annual rpt, 6744–7

Labor force, special characteristics, Labor Statistics Handbook, 1947-82, annual rpt, 6724–1.2

Metal mines and related operations, injury, employment, and worktime data, 1982, annual rpt, 6664–3

Minerals (nonmetallic) mining and related operations injury, employment, and worktime data, 1982, annual rpt, 6664–1

Mines (sand and gravel) and related operations, injury, employment, and worktime data, 1982, annual rpt, 6664–2

Mines (stone) and related operations, injury, employment, and worktime data, 1982, annual rpt, 6664–5

Occupational health and safety State govt program staffing requirements, and occupational injury data, for selected States, selected years 1973-81, hearings, 21348–88

Occupational injuries, illnesses, and workdays lost, by SIC 2-digit industry, 1982-83, annual press release, 6844–3

Occupational injury and illness rates, by SIC 2- to 4-digit industry, 1982, annual rpt, 6844–1

Traffic accidents, circumstances, injuries, deaths, and characteristics of persons and vehicles involved, 1982, annual rpt, 7764–13

Veterans and nonveterans health condition, and veteran use of VA and non-VA hospitals by disease, by age, race, income, and metro-nonmetro location, various periods 1971-81, 9926–1.18

Workers compensation coverage by State, benefits, degree of disability, and employer costs, 1939-80, article, 4742–1.414

Abt Associates Inc.

"Citation Release", 6068–187

"Unreported Taxable Income from Selected Illegal Activities", 8008–112

Abu Dhabi

see United Arab Emirates

Accidents and accident prevention

Army active duty personnel health status and use of Army medical services in US and abroad, by treatment facility, monthly rpt, 3702–4.2

Children's accident prevention, parents safety precautions in 9 Massachusetts areas, 1980-82 survey, article, 4102-1.402

Index by Subjects and Names

Court caseloads for Federal district, appeals, and bankruptcy courts, by type of suit and offense, circuit, and district, quarterly rpt, 18202–1

Death rates by sex, race, and age for 40 causes, projected for 10-year period, 1982 rpt, 4208–21

Deaths and death rates, by cause and age, provisional 1982-83, US Vital Statistics annual rpt, 4144–7

Deaths and death rates, by cause, provisional data, monthly rpt, 4142–1

Deaths and death rates, by detailed geographic area, cause, and demographic characteristics, 1979, US Vital Statistics annual rpt, 4144–3

Deaths and death rates, by selected cause and demographic characteristics, 1981, US Vital Statistics advance rpt, 4146–5.78

Deaths and death rates, by selected cause and demographic characteristics, 1982, US Vital Statistics advance rpt, 4146–5.81

Deaths and death rates from accidents, by place, detailed cause, and demographic characteristics, 1979, US Vital Statistics annual rpt, 4144–2.1, 4144–2.5

Deaths and death rates from homicide, by location, circumstances, and victim characteristics, and years of life lost from homicide and other leading causes of death, 1970-78, 4205–38

Deaths by principal or contributing cause, with type of injury reported in accidental, poisoning, and violent deaths, by age, sex, and race, 1978, 4146–5.76

Deaths due to cold weather and related causes, by age, race, State, and city, selected periods 1962-83, 21148–30

Deaths from accidents by selected cause, 1981 with trends from 1960s and reduction goals for 1990, article, 4102–1.409

Disability Insurance beneficiaries sociodemographic and medical characteristics, 1977-79, annual rpt, 4744–20

Health condition and health care resources, use, and expenditures, 1970s-82 with trends and projections 1900-2000, annual compilation, 4144–11

Hospital discharges and length of stay, by patient characteristics, facility size, procedure performed, diagnosis, and region, 1982, annual rpt, 4147–13.78

Indian births, morbidity, and deaths and rates, and health services facilities and use, 1954-83, annual compilation, 4104–7

Infant deaths by detailed cause, geographic location, age, race, and sex, 1979, US Vital Statistics annual rpt, 4144–2.2

Injury rates, total and by place of accident, by age, region, metro-nonmetro location, and selected SMSA, 1980-81, 4147–10.146

Mobile and manufactured home safety standards, program inspections, enforcement actions, and accidents and casualties by victim characteristics, 1982-83, biennial rpt, 5004–4

Natl park system visitor deaths, by park and type of accident, 1973-83, annual rpt, 5544–6

Navy and Marine Corps disease incidence, medical care, and deaths, by diagnosis, 1978–79, annual rpt, 3804–1

Index by Subjects and Names

Navy personnel alcohol and drug abuse, and related deaths, courts-martial, discharges, and treatment program funding and staff, FY83, annual table, 3804–12

Nuclear power plant electrical systems, errors in operation and maintenance by circumstance, plant type, and system, 1977-81, 9638–51

Older persons by demographic, socioeconomic, and health characteristics, selected years 1900-81 and projected to 2050, Current Population Rpt, 2546–2.125

Pipeline safety regulations enforcement of DOT and States by pipeline type and State, and accidents and commodity losses, selected years 1973-FY84, GAO rpt, 26113–130

Pipelines for natural gas and hazardous liquids, accidents and casualties, and DOT and State govts safety standards enforcement, funding, and training activities, 1982, annual rpt, 7304–5

Statistical Abstract of US, social, political, and economic data, 1950s-83 and trends, annual rpt, 2324–1.1

Storms and unusual weather phenomena characteristics, casualties, and property damage, by State and outlying area, monthly listing, 2152–3

Subway accidents, deaths, injuries, and property damage, by type of accident and victim and cause, for 11 systems, 1983, annual rpt, 7884–5

Transit system financial and operating data, by mode, function, fleet size, and individual system, FY82, annual rpt, 7884–4

Transportation accident deaths, by mode, 1982-83, annual summary rpt, 9614–6

Transportation accident investigations and recommendations by Natl Transportation Safety Board, 1983, annual rpt, 9614–1

Transportation finances, operations, vehicles, equipment, accidents, and energy use, by mode of transport, 1955-84, annual rpt, 7304–2

see also Agricultural accidents and safety *see also* Aviation accidents and safety *see also* Electromagnetic radiation *see also* Fires and fire prevention *see also* Marine accidents and safety *see also* Mine accidents and safety *see also* Nuclear radiation *see also* Occupational health and safety *see also* Poisoning and drug reaction *see also* Product safety *see also* Railroad accidents and safety *see also* Traffic accidents and safety *see also* Traffic engineering *see also* Workers compensation *see also* under By Disease in the "Index by Categories"

Accounting and auditing

Air Force fiscal mgmt system operations and techniques, info for comptroller personnel, quarterly rpt, 3602–1

Census of Population, 1980: detailed socioeconomic and demographic characteristics, by age, sex, race, Hispanic origin, occupation, and industry, State rpt series, 2531–4

Census of Population, 1980: labor force, by sex, detailed occupation, and region, with comparison to 1970 census, supplementary rpt, 2535–1.12

Census of Service Industries, 1982: employment, establishments, receipts, and payroll, by SIC 2- to 4-digit kind of business, SMSA, county, and city, State rpt series, 2391–1

Census of Service Industries, 1982: employment, establishments, receipts, and payroll, by SIC 4-digit kind of business and State, preliminary rpt, 2390–2.19

Community Dev Block Grants and Urban Dev Action Grants, audits of grantees and findings, FY83, annual rpt, 5124–5

County Business Patterns: establishments, employees, and payrolls, by SIC 4-digit industry and county, 1981, annual State rpt series, 2326–8

County Business Patterns: establishments, employees, and payrolls, by SIC 4-digit industry and county, 1982, annual State rpt series, 2326–6

DOD procurement revolving fund accounting mgmt, costs and cost carryovers by cause and activity site, FY82-83, GAO rpt, 26111–22

Election campaign funding and activities of Fed Election Commission, and political action committees funding, 1983, annual rpt, 9274–1

Employment, earnings, and hours, by SIC 4-digit nonfarm industry, monthly 1974-Feb 1984, annual update, 6744–4

Fed Govt agencies internal audits and resolution of questioned costs, by selected agency, FY81-83, GAO rpt, 26111–24

Fed Govt agencies without inspectors general, internal audit activities, funding, and staff, by agency, FY83, GAO rpt, 26111–23

Fed Govt consolidated financial statements based on business accounting methods, FY82-83, annual rpt, 8104–5

Fed Govt programs and mgmt cost control proposals, 3-year savings by function and agency, and financial and operating data, 1960s-81, 16908–1

Franchises of firms engaged in distribution of goods and services by kind of business, establishments by State, and sales, 1982-84, annual rpt, 2014–5

GAO activities and operations, and resulting Fed Govt cost savings, FY83, annual rpt, 26104–1

GAO publications issued, 2nd half 1983, semiannual listing, 26102–1

GAO publications on automatic data processing, food, health, and land use, annual listing series, 26104–11

Hospital cost measurement for reimbursement, alternative methods including classification of disease severity, 1984 articles, 4652–1.425, 4652–1.426, 4652–1.427, 4652–1.428

Income tax return audits by IRS, FY83, annual rpt, 8304–3.3

Income tax returns and filers, by income level, filing and tax payment status, and amount of tax owed or refund, selected years 1978-82, article, 8302–2.408

Income tax returns of corporations, detailed income and tax items by industry, 1981, annual rpt, 8304–4

Income tax returns of partnerships, detailed data by industry, 1981 estimates, annual article, 8302–2.404

ACTION

Income tax returns of partnerships, receipts by source, deductions by type, and establishments, by selected industry, 1982, annual article, 8302–2.416

Income tax returns of sole proprietorships, detailed data by industry div and selected industry group, 1981, annual rpt, 8304–7

Income tax returns of sole proprietorships, receipts, deductions by type, payroll, and net income, by major industry, 1982, annual article, 8302–2.413

Input-output structure of US economy, detailed interindustry transactions for 537 industries, and components of final demand, 1977 benchmark data, 2708–17

Mental health agencies electronic accounting and budgeting systems description, design, and use, 1983 rpt, 4506–2.6

NYC metro area small business owners and accountants, assessment of economy, professional activities, and community problems, by county and industry div, 1983 survey, hearings, 21728–52.3

Occupational manpower needs and supply by detailed occupation, and educational and training program enrollees and grads by detailed field, 1982 and 1995, biennial rpt, 6744–3

Occupational Outlook Handbook, **1984-85** biennial rpt, 6744–1

Oil price and allocation regulations enforcement by DOE, and overcharge allegations, settlements, and refunds to States, by company, as of June 1983, hearing, 21368–50

Revenue sharing entitlements by State, and noncompliance audit cases by type, FY83 and cumulative through FY82, annual rpt, 8064–1.1

Savings and loan assn auditing firms concentration ratios, by FHLB district, 1976-80, article, 9312–1.403

Unemployment insurance overpayments detection and recovery from random audit program in selected States, 1975-82 and projected to FY86, GAO rpt, 26121–77

Wages of white-collar workers, by occupation, work level, and industry div, Mar 1984, annual rpt, 6784–2

see also Depreciation

see also Federal Inspectors General reports

see also under By Industry in the "Index by Categories"

Achievement tests

see Educational tests

Acid rain

see Air pollution

see Water pollution

Acquisitions, business

see Business acquisitions and mergers

Acrylics

see Plastics and plastics industry

ACTION

Activities, volunteer characteristics, and budget, by program, FY82, annual rpt, 9024–2

Budget of US Appendix, detailed budgets and personnel summaries, by agency, FY85, annual rpt, 104–3

Budget of US, appropriations, outlays, balances, and budget receipts, by govtl branch and agency, FY83, annual rpt, 8104–2

Cost control proposals for Fed Govt programs and mgmt, 3-year savings by function and agency, and financial and operating data, 1960s-81, 16908–1.5

ACTION

Older persons sociodemographic characteristics, and Fed Govt program participation and funding, 1983 with trends and projections 1900-2060, annual rpt, 25144–3.1

see also Retired Senior Volunteer Program *see also* VISTA

Adamczyk, Christine

"Comparative Analysis of Five PL 480 Title I Impact Evaluation Studies", 9918–13

Adams, Donald B.

"Definition and Measurement of Exchange Market Intervention", 9366–1.126

Adams, J. K.

"Method for Ranking Biological Habitats in Oil Spill Response Planning and Impact Assessment", 5508–87

Adams, Larry T.

"Labor Organization Mergers 1979-84: Adapting to Change", 6722–1.456

Adelberg, Sheldon

"Workload and Decision Trends: Statistical Highlights, FY80-82", 6006–2.32

Aden

see Yemen, South

Adhesives

see Chemicals and chemical industry

Administration

see Administration of justice *see* Administrative law and procedure *see* Executives *see* Health facilities administration *see* Industrial management *see* Public administration *see* School administration and staff

Administration for Children, Youth, and Families

see Office of Human Development Services

Administration for Handicapped Individuals *see* Office of Human Development Services

Administration for Public Services *see* Office of Human Development Services

Administration of justice

- Employment in criminal justice by job category and level of govt, and arrests for serious crimes in 5 States by disposition, Dec 1983 rpt, 6062–2.401
- Fed Govt programs and mgmt cost control proposals, CBO and GAO estimates of savings by function and agency, FY85-89, 26308–45
- Fed Govt programs and mgmt cost control proposals, 3-year savings by function and agency, and financial and operating data, 1960s-81, 16908–1.9
- Foreign human rights conditions in 162 countries, economic and military aid of US, and economic aid of intl organizations, 1981-83, annual rpt, 21384–3
- Govt census, 1982: city govt revenues by source, expenditures by function, debt, and assets, by State and city, 2457–4
- Govt census, 1982: county govt revenues by source, expenditures by function, debt, and assets, by State and county, 2457–3
- Govt census, 1982: employment, payrolls, and average earnings, by function, level of govt, State, county, population size, and inside-outside SMSAs, 2455–2
- Govt census, 1982: local govt employment by function, payroll, and average earnings, for individual counties, cities, and school and special districts, 2455–1

Govt census, 1982: State govt payments to local govts, by program, source of funds, level of govt, and State, with trends from 1902, 2460–3

- Govt finances, by level of govt, State, and for large cities and counties, 1981-83, annual rpt series, 2466–2
- Govt revenues by source and expenditures by function, natl income and product account, *Survey of Current Business*, monthly rpt, monthly and annual tables, 2702–1.24
- Judicial Conf semiannual proceedings and findings, 1984 annual rpt, 18204–5
- Justice Dept activities, by subagency, FY82, annual rpt, 6004–1
- Public opinion on taxes, tax policy, and intergovtl relations, 1972-84 surveys, annual rpt, 10044–2
- Wiretapping authorizations by offense, costs, persons involved, arrests, trials, and convictions, 1983, annual rpt, 18204–7

see also Administrative law and procedure *see also* Arrest *see also* Civil procedure *see also* Correctional institutions *see also* Courts *see also* Crime and criminals *see also* Criminal procedure *see also* Due process of law *see also* Evidence *see also* Extradition *see also* Federal aid to law enforcement *see also* Judges *see also* Judicial reform *see also* Juries *see also* Law enforcement *see also* Lawyers *see also* Legal aid *see also* Military law *see also* Parole and probation *see also* Pretrial detention and release *see also* Sentences, criminal procedure *see also* Trials *see also* Witnesses *see also* under names of specific types of courts (listed under Courts)

Administration on Aging

see Office of Human Development Services

Administrative agencies

see under Executive Office of the President *see* under Federal boards, committees, and commissions *see* under Federal executive departments *see* under Federal independent agencies

Administrative Conference of the U.S.

- Budget of US Appendix, detailed budgets and personnel summaries, by agency, FY85, annual rpt, 104–3
- Budget of US, appropriations, outlays, balances, and budget receipts, by govtl branch and agency, FY83, annual rpt, 8104–2

Administrative law and procedure

- AFDC programs and provisions of States under Social Security Act, FY82, annual rpt, 4704–9
- AFDC recipients and payments, applications by disposition, payment discontinuances by reason, and hearings by outcome, by State, quarterly rpt, 4742–6
- AFDC State admin agencies performance measures, caseloads, payments, and costs, by State, FY81, annual rpt, 4704–10

Index by Subjects and Names

- Airport security operations to prevent hijacking, screening results, enforcement actions, and hijacking attempts, 1st half 1984, semiannual rpt, 7502–5
- Alaska and Alaska Native corporation claims for Fed Govt land, status and Land Mgmt Bur conveyance problems, various dates 1978-FY84, GAO rpt, 26113–125
- Claims settlements arising out of Federal agency operations, FY83, annual rpt, 26104–1
- Coal lands of Fed Govt leasing activity, acreage, and reserves, by State, coal region, and tract, FY83, annual rpt, 5724–10
- Drivers license revocation and other drunk driving deterrence measures in selected States, and total and alcohol-related traffic deaths, 1980-82, 9618–10
- Fed Govt administrative law judges by agency and grade, various dates 1947-82, and New Jersey administrative law cases, FY80-84, hearings, 25528–96
- Fed Govt advisory committees, and members, staff, meetings, and costs, by agency, FY83, annual rpt, 9454–18
- Fed Govt programs and mgmt cost control proposals, 3-year savings by function and agency, and financial and operating data, 1960s-81, 16908–1
- Fed Govt programs under Ways and Means Committee jurisdiction, program operations and financing data for assessing budgetary requirements, by State, FY70s-83, 21788–117
- Food stamp recipient households size and composition, income, and income deductions allowed, Aug 1981, annual rpt, 1364–8
- Freedom of Info Act, requests to HHS received and denied, costs, and fees collected, 1983, annual rpt, 4004–21
- Justice Dept activities, by subagency, FY82, annual rpt, 6004–1
- Legal fees awarded private parties in cases against Federal, State, and local govts, by case, selected years 1977-83, 6008–19
- Natural gas and hazardous liquid pipelines accidents and casualties, and DOT and State govt safety activities, 1982, annual rpt, 7304–5
- Older persons discrimination in Fed Govt aid programs, Age Discrimination Act enforcement by 28 agencies, FY83, annual rpt, 4004–27
- Public lands mgmt adjudication, appeals, and hearings, FY83, annual rpt, 5724–1.3
- State govt revenues by source, expenditures by function, debt, and holdings by type, FY83, annual rpt, 2466–2.5
- Trade adjustment assistance eligibility and certification of workers and companies, by industry and labor union, 1975-83, annual rpt, 444–1.2
- Unemployment insurance State govt program admin, quality appraisal results, FY84, annual rpt, 6404–16
- US Attorneys civil and criminal case processing in district, appellate, and State courts, by district, FY83, annual rpt, 6004–2

see also Antitrust law *see also* Civil procedure *see also* Consumer protection

Index by Subjects and Names

Advertising

see also Environmental Impact Statements
see also Environmental pollution and control
see also Federal Inspectors General reports
see also Fuel allocation
see also Government and business
see also Labor law
see also Licenses and permits
see also Maritime law
see also Occupational health and safety
see also Price regulation
see also Public administration
see also Tax laws and courts
see also Tax protests and appeals
see also under names of individual regulatory commissions (listed under Federal independent agencies)

Administrative Office of the U.S. Courts

Budget of US Appendix, detailed budgets and personnel summaries, by agency, FY85, annual rpt, 104–3

Budget of US, appropriations, outlays, balances, and budget receipts, by govtl branch and agency, FY83, annual rpt, 8104–2

Caseloads (civil and criminal) and activity summary, for Federal district, appeals, and bankruptcy courts, 1975-June 1984, annual chartbook, 18204–9

Caseloads (civil and criminal) for Federal district, appeals, and special courts, year ended June 1983 and selected data from 1940, annual rpt, 18204–8

Caseloads (criminal), dispositions, convictions, and sentences of Federal defendants, by offense and district, as of June 1983 with trends from 1945, annual rpt, 18204–1

Caseloads, actions, procedure duration, judges, and jurors, by Federal district and appeals court, 1979-84, annual rpt, 18204–3

Caseloads for Federal district, appeals, and bankruptcy courts, by type of suit and offense, circuit, and district, quarterly rpt, 18202–1

Classification codes for US criminal titles and sections, with corresponding detailed offenses and severity levels, 1984, annual rpt, 18204–14

Judicial Conf semiannual proceedings and findings, 1984 annual rpt, 18204–5

Juror (grand and petit) usage and costs, trials, and trial days, by Federal district court, years ended June 1980-84, annual rpt, 18204–4

Wiretapping authorizations by offense, costs, persons involved, arrests, trials, and convictions, 1983, annual rpt, 18204–7

Administrators

see Executives

Admire, Jacqelyn B.

"Hypertension Control: Meeting the 1990 Objectives for the Nation", 4102–1.432

Adolescents

see Youth

Adoption

Budget of US, effects of Reagan Admin policy changes, by detailed program, FY85, annual rpt, 104–21

Fed Govt public welfare programs and tax expenditures benefitting children and youth, participation and funding for 71 programs, FY81-83, 21968–30

Foster care children permanent placement, Fed Govt incentive program funding and operations in 7 States, FY80-82, GAO rpt, 26121–81

Govt census, 1982: State govt payments to local govts, by program, source of funds, level of govt, and State, with trends from 1902, 2460–3

Immigrant and nonimmigrant visas issued and refused, and status adjustments, by class and nationality, FY77, annual rpt, 7184–1

Immigrant orphans adopted abroad and to be adopted, admissions to US by world region and country of birth, FY76-81, annual rpt, 6264–2

State govt social services spending by type and funding source, and admin of Fed Govt block grants, for 13 States, selected years FY80-84, GAO rpt, 26121–76

Adult day care

Census of Service Industries, 1982: employment, establishments, receipts, and payroll, by SIC 2- to 4-digit kind of business, SMSA, county, and city, State rpt series, 2391–1

Home mgmt and personal care assistance, noninstitutionalized adults needing services by living arrangement, sex, and age, annual average 1979-80, article, 4144–11.1

Older persons by demographic, socioeconomic, and health characteristics, selected years 1900-81 and projected to 2050, Current Population Rpt, 2546–2.125

Older persons receiving selected services from family and agencies, living arrangements, and need for home mgmt help, selected years 1977-82, article, 1702–1.409

Underground economy, household expenditures and participation by type of goods or service and sociodemographic characteristics, with methodology and bibl, 1981 survey, 8308–27

Adult education

Basic and secondary education programs, students, staff, and facilities, annual summary rpt, suspended, 4864–4

Computer specialists sociodemographic, educational, and employment characteristics, and Fed Govt support by agency, 1978, biennial Current Population Rpt, 2546–2.124

Condition of Education, detailed data on enrollment, staff, achievement, finances, curricula, and education effects on employment, 1982-83, annual rpt, 4824–1.4

Education Dept programs and activities, FY83, annual rpt, 4804–6

Education Dept programs funding, operations, and effectiveness, FY83, annual rpt, 4804–5

Enrollment and other data for adult and vocational education programs, by student sociodemographic characteristics, selected years 1975-81, annual rpt, 4824–2.21

Enrollment in academic, vocational, and continuing education, by student characteristics, Oct 1982, 4848–16

Fed Govt educational grants, State allocations by program, type of recipient agency, and State, FY83, annual rpt, 4804–8

Govt census, 1982: State govt payments to local govts, by program, source of funds, level of govt, and State, with trends from 1902, 2460–3

Indian Education Act, Fed Govt grants and fellowships awarded by State, FY83, and natl advisory council funding, FY73-84, annual rpt, 14874–1

Jail capacities, conditions, expenditures, and services, and socioeconomic and other characteristics of inmates, various dates 1976-82, 10048–59

Natl Advisory Council on Continuing Education activities, 1984 annual narrative rpt, 15214–1

Older persons sociodemographic characteristics, and Fed Govt program participation and funding, 1983 with trends and projections 1900-2060, annual rpt, 25144–3.1

Teaching degrees conferred by specialty and State, required credit hours, and instn officials attitudes, by instn type, 1970s-83, hearings, 21348–89

see also Vocational education and training

Advertising

Agricultural commodities generic advertising, activities and funding by source, selected years 1972-82, 1548–242

Air passenger and shipper complaints to CAB, by US and foreign air carrier and type of complaint, monthly rpt, 9142–20

Airline financial data, by carrier, carrier group, and for total certificated system, quarterly rpt, 9142–12

Airline operating and other costs, itemized for domestic and intl trunk and local service carriers, 1st half 1983, semiannual rpt, 9142–47

Bank financial and operating statements, functional cost analysis for Fed Reserve member banks with average and high earnings, by deposit size, 1982, annual rpt, 9364–6

Business statistics, detailed data for major industries and economic indicators, *Survey of Current Business,* monthly rpt, 2702–1.4

Census of Population, 1980: detailed socioeconomic and demographic characteristics, by age, sex, race, Hispanic origin, occupation, and industry, State rpt series, 2531–4

Census of Population, 1980: labor force, by sex, detailed occupation, and region, with comparison to 1970 census, supplementary rpt, 2535–1.12

Census of Service Industries, 1982: employment, establishments, receipts, and payroll, by SIC 2- to 4-digit kind of business, SMSA, county, and city, State rpt series, 2391–1

Census of Service Industries, 1982: employment, establishments, receipts, and payroll, by SIC 4-digit kind of business and State, preliminary rpt, 2390–2.5

Cigarette sales, market shares, advertising expenditures and methods, and tar and nicotine content, by cigarette type, selected years 1963-81, annual rpt, 9404–4

County Business Patterns: establishments, employees, and payrolls, by SIC 4-digit industry and county, 1981, annual State rpt series, 2326–8

County Business Patterns: establishments, employees, and payrolls, by SIC 4-digit industry and county, 1982, annual State rpt series, 2326–6

Advertising

Crime prevention media campaign, effects on public attitudes and activities, as of Nov 1981, 6068–183

Election campaign expenditures for network and local TV ads, and public opinion on TV influence, selected years 1972-83, hearings, 21428–7

Electric utilities privately owned, advertising and sales expenses, by company, 1982, annual rpt, 3164–23.2

Employment, earnings, and hours, by selected SIC 1- to 4-digit industry, State, and for 278 major labor areas, 1939-83, annual rpt, 6744–5

Employment, earnings, and hours, by SIC 4-digit nonfarm industry, monthly 1974-Feb 1984, annual update, 6744–4

Finances and operations, by SIC 2- to 4-digit industry, 1970s-83 and projected to 1988, annual rpt, 2014–4

Food consumer research and marketing devs, and consumption and price trends, quarterly rpt with articles, 1541–7

Food industry advertising expenditures by media type, and advertising to sales ratio by selected food item, 1970-79 with some trends from 1955, 1548–234

FTC budget authority and expenditures for regulatory analysis, by prospective regulation and contractor, 1983, hearings, 21528–56

Help-wanted advertising in New England States, Fed Reserve 1st District, monthly rpt, 9373–2.2

Help-wanted advertising index and ratio to unemployment, *Business Conditions Digest,* cyclical indicators, monthly rpt, 2702–3.3

Help-wanted advertising index and ratio to unemployment, *Business Conditions Digest,* historical supplement and methodology, 1947-82, 2708–31

Housing (multifamily rental) energy use and costs, conservation effect on rental marketing, and effect of utility bill payment methods on conservation efforts, 1970s-80s, 3308–73

Income tax returns of corporations, detailed income and tax items by industry, 1981, annual rpt, 8304–4

Income tax returns of sole proprietorships, detailed data by industry div and selected industry group, 1981, annual rpt, 8304–7

Income tax returns of sole proprietorships, receipts, deductions by type, payroll, and net income, by major industry, 1982, annual article, 8302–2.413

Input-output structure of US economy, detailed interindustry transactions for 537 industries, and components of final demand, 1977 benchmark data, 2708–17

Manufacturing census, 1982: financial and operating data, for SIC 4-digit industries by product, preliminary rpt, 2491–1.440

Military procurement competitive, noncompetitive, and formally advertised awards, and awards by statutory authority and pricing provision, FY74-1st half FY84, semiannual rpt, 3542–1.2

Military procurement competitive, noncompetitive, and formally advertised awards, by size, FY83, annual rpt, 3544–19

Milk order advertising and promotion programs finances, fees, and producer participation, by region, 1983, article, 1317–4.406

Multinatl corporation income reallocation through regulation of intercorporate transactions, by tax item, treaty status, asset size, industry, and tax haven country, 1982, 8008–110

Natural gas interstate pipeline company detailed financial and operating data, by firm, 1983, annual rpt, 3164–38

Postal Service operations, revenues by source, and employee characteristics, 1970s-83, and electronic mail promotion costs, FY82-87, hearings, 21628–55

Producer prices and indexes, by stage of processing and detailed commodity, monthly rpt, 6762–6

Producer prices and indexes, by stage of processing and detailed commodity, monthly 1983, annual supplement, 6764–2

Smoking and tobacco marketing legislation introduced and enacted in State legislatures, by State, 1982, annual rpt, 4204–13

see also Labeling

see also Sales promotion

see also under By Industry in the "Index by Categories"

Advisory Commission on Intergovernmental Relations

Budget of US Appendix, detailed budgets and personnel summaries, by agency, FY85, annual rpt, 104–3

Budget of US, appropriations, outlays, balances, and budget receipts, by govtl branch and agency, FY83, annual rpt, 8104–2

Federal, State, and local govt finances, policy, and intergovtl relations, series, 10046–8

Govt finances, by level of govt and State, selected years 1929-83, annual rpt, 10044–1

Intergovernmental Perspective, quarterly rpt, 10042–1

Jail capacities, conditions, expenditures, and services, and socioeconomic and other characteristics of inmates, various dates 1976-82, 10048–59

Local govt finances and population characteristics for cities and suburbs, by region and selected SMSA, selected years 1957-FY83, 10048–61

Programs and finances, 1983, annual rpt, 10044–3

Public works capital needs and intergovtl financing, by type of project and selected city, various periods 1950-83, 10048–60

R&D Fed Govt funding for all performers, by field and supporting agency, selected years FY60-84, annual rpt, 9627–20

Regulatory growth of Fed Govt effect on local compliance costs and funding, local officials assessment, and comparisons to State govt regulations, 1970s-82 with trends from 1900, 10048–58

Taxes, tax policy, and intergovtl relations, public opinion survey results, 1972-84, annual rpt, 10044–2

Advisory Committee on Federal Pay

Budget of US Appendix, detailed budgets and personnel summaries, by agency, FY85, annual rpt, 104–3

Budget of US, appropriations, outlays, balances, and budget receipts, by govtl branch and agency, FY83, annual rpt, 8104–2

Index by Subjects and Names

Fed Govt pay comparability with private industry, and recommended and actual pay increase, various dates 1971-84, annual rpt, 10104–1

Advisory Council on Historic Preservation

Budget of US Appendix, detailed budgets and personnel summaries, by agency, FY85, annual rpt, 104–3

Budget of US, appropriations, outlays, balances, and budget receipts, by govtl branch and agency, FY83, annual rpt, 8104–2

Advisory Council on Social Security

Medicare recommendations of Council, and trust fund and program operations, 1982 quadrennial rpt, 10178–1

AEC

see Atomic Energy Commission

Aeronautical engineering

see Aviation sciences

Aeronautical navigation

FAA activities and R&D for improvement of air traffic control and airway facilities and equipment under Natl Airspace System Plan, 1982-2000, annual rpt, 7504–12

FAA air traffic control and airway facilities and services, operations, and finances, FY83, annual rpt, 7504–37

FAA air traffic control facilities traffic levels, by airport and State, FY83, annual rpt, 7504–27

FAA air traffic control instrument flight rule aircraft handled, by user type, control center, and region, FY69-83 and forecast to FY95, annual rpt, 7504–15

FAA certifications for pilots and nonpilots, by type, age, sex, region, and State, 1983, annual rpt, 7504–2

Foreign and US astronautic and aeronautic events, comprehensive chronology, 1976, annual rpt, 9504–2

General aviation aircraft, hours flown, and equipment, by type, use, and model of aircraft, region, and State, 1982, annual rpt, 7504–29

see also Radar

Aerospace Corp.

"Underground Storage of Large Volumes of Crude Oil: The U.S. Strategic Petroleum Reserve Program", 3008–91

Aerospace industry

Business statistics, detailed data for major industries and economic indicators, *Survey of Current Business,* monthly rpt, 2702–1.20

Census of Population, 1980: detailed socioeconomic and demographic characteristics, by age, sex, race, Hispanic origin, occupation, and industry, State rpt series, 2531–4

Collective bargaining agreements expiring during year, covered workers by SIC 2-digit industry, firm, and union, with summary of key provisions, 1984, annual rpt, 6784–9

Communist, OECD, and selected other countries freight and carrier inventories, by mode of transport, 1960s-83, annual rpt, 244–5.10

County Business Patterns: establishments, employees, and payrolls, by SIC 4-digit industry and county, 1981, annual State rpt series, 2326–8

Index by Subjects and Names

County Business Patterns: establishments, employees, and payrolls, by SIC 4-digit industry and county, 1982, annual State rpt series, 2326–6

Employment, earnings, and hours, by selected SIC 1- to 4-digit industry, State, and for 278 major labor areas, 1939-83, annual rpt, 6744–5

Employment, earnings, and hours, by SIC 4-digit nonfarm industry, monthly 1974-Feb 1984, annual update, 6744–4

Finances and operations, by SIC 2- to 4-digit industry, 1970s-83 and projected to 1988, annual rpt, 2014–4

Financial statements for manufacturing, mining, and trade corporations, by selected SIC 2- to 3-digit industry, quarterly rpt, 2502–1

Foreign and US astronautic and aeronautic events, comprehensive chronology, 1976, annual rpt, 9504–2

Great Lakes trade, by SITC 3-digit commodity, port, vessel type, world area, and country, 1982, annual rpt, 7744–3

Income tax returns of corporations, detailed income and tax items by industry, 1981, annual rpt, 8304–4

Input-output structure of US economy, detailed interindustry transactions for 85 industries, and components of final demand, 1977, article, 2702–1.421

Input-output structure of US economy, detailed interindustry transactions for 537 industries, and components of final demand, 1977 benchmark data, 2708–17

Manufacturing census, 1982: financial and operating data, by SIC 2- to 4-digit industry, State, SMSA, and county, preliminary census div rpt series, 2491–3

Minority group and women employment, by occupational group and SIC 2- to 3-digit industry, 1981, annual rpt, 9244–1.1

Occupational injury and illness rates, by SIC 2- to 4-digit industry, 1982, annual rpt, 6844–1

R&D expenditures of US firms foreign affiliates, by selected industry, 1974-82, 9626–2.131

R&D industry expenditures, total and for 6 leading industries, projected 1984-85 with trends from 1975, 9626–2.145

R&D industry funding and employment of scientists and engineers, by industry group, firm size, and funding source, 1956-82, annual rpt, 9627–21

Sales, and new and backlog orders for military and nonmilitary customers, quarterly Current Industrial Rpt, 2506–12.22

Shipments, trade, consumption, and firms, by type of aircraft and aircraft engine, monthly Current Industrial Rpt, 2506–12.24

see also Aircraft

see also Missiles and rockets

see also under By Industry in the "Index by Categories"

Aetna Life Insurance Co.

Fed Govt civilian health benefit plans enrollment and premiums, for individual private and employee organization plans, FY81-82, annual rpt, 9844–1.2

AFDC

see Aid to Families with Dependent Children

Afghanistan

Agricultural and food production indexes, and production of selected commodities, by world region and country, 1974-83, annual rpt, 1524–5

AID economic assistance to developing countries, obligations and disbursements by country, quarterly rpt, 9912–4

AID educational program activities and project impacts in 12 developing countries, 1950s-82, 9916–11.8

AID irrigation and rural dev projects in Helmand Valley of Afghanistan, funding and effectiveness, 1949-79, 9916–3.18

AID loan repayment status and terms by program and country, and status of predecessor agency loans, quarterly rpt, 9912–3

Economic, social, and political summary data, by country, 1984, annual factbook, 244–11

Exports of US, detailed Schedule B commodities by country of destination, 1983, annual rpt, 2424–9

Exports of US, detailed Schedule E commodities by mode of transport and world area and country of destination, 1983, annual rpts, 2424–5

Imports of US, detailed Schedule A commodities by country and world area of origin, and mode of transport, 1983, annual rpts, 2424–2

Imports of US, detailed TSUSA commodities by country of origin, 1983, annual rpt, 2424–4

Loans and grants for economic and military assistance from US and intl agencies, by program and country, FY46-83, annual rpt, 9914–5

Military spending, arms trade, and armed forces size, with total govt spending and population, by country, 1972-82, annual rpt, 9824–1

Minerals Yearbook, 1982, Vol 3: foreign country reviews of production, trade, and policies, by commodity, annual rpt, 5604–35

Minerals Yearbook, 1982, Vol 3 preprints: foreign country review of production, trade, and policies, by commodity, annual rpt, 5604–17.88

Population size and growth rates, and latest available benchmark demographic data, by country, 1950-83, biennial rpt, 2324–4

Refugee resettlement program activities and funding, arrivals and population by country of origin and State, and employment and other characteristics, FY83, annual rpt, 4704–8

see also under By Foreign Country in the "Index by Categories"

Africa

Agricultural and food production indexes, and production of selected commodities, by world region and country, 1974-83, annual rpt, 1524–5

Agricultural exports and imports of US, by detailed commodity and country, FY83 and CY83, semiannual rpts, 1522–4

Agricultural exports of US to South Africa, Nigeria, and total sub-Saharan Africa, 1981-83, and forecast 1984, article, 1522–1.401

Africa

Agricultural situation in sub-Saharan Africa, by country, 1982-83 and outlook for 1984, annual rpt, 1524–4.10

Agricultural supply/demand, consumption per capita, and trade, by world area and country group, 1960s-82, 1528–181

Agricultural supply/demand, trade, and production, and socioeconomic data, by country, 1950s-77, 1528–179

Agricultural trade of US, by commodity and country, bimonthly rpt with articles, 1522–1

AID activities and funding by project and function, FY85, and developing countries summary socioeconomic data, 1970s-83, by country, annual rpt, 9914–3

AID community dev assistance to local govts in developing countries, program activities and funding, 1960s-80s, 9918–11

AID contracts and grants for technical and support services, by instn, country, and State, FY83, annual listing, 9914–7

AID economic assistance to developing countries, obligations and disbursements by country, quarterly rpt, 9912–4

AID Housing Guaranty Program financial statements, and projects by country, FY83, annual rpt, 9914–4

AID loan repayment status and terms by program and country, and status of predecessor agency loans, quarterly rpt, 9912–3

AID loans authorized, signed, and canceled, by country and world area, monthly rpt, 9912–2

China economic conditions, agricultural and industrial production, trade, and domestic and foreign investment, 1980-85, 2048–106

Defense and total govt expenditures, military imports, GNP, and intl reserves of countries receiving US economic aid, by country, 1976-81, annual rpt, 9914–1

Economic conditions and foreign marketing prospects in 46 Sub-Saharan countries, 1983 world region rpt, 2046–5.1

Energy production by type, and oil prices, trade, and consumption, by country group and selected country, monthly rpt, 242–5

Export sales and shipments of US grains, oilseed products, hides, skins, and cotton, by country, weekly rpt, 1922–3

Exports and imports of OECD, total and for 4 major countries, and US trade by country, by commodity, 1972-82, annual world region rpt, 244–13.4

Exports and imports of US (airborne), by world area and US customs district and city, monthly rpt, 2422–8

Exports and imports of US (waterborne), by type of service, commodity, country, route, and US port, 1982, annual rpt, 7704–2

Exports and imports of US (waterborne), by type of service, customs district, port, and world area, monthly rpt, 2422–7

Exports and imports of US, by commodity group, world area, selected country, US coastal area and port, and mode of transport, with seasonal adjustments, monthly rpt, 2422–9

Exports and imports of US, detailed SIC-based commodities by world area, 1983, annual rpts, 2424–6

Africa

Exports of US, detailed Schedule E commodities by mode of transport and world area and country of destination, 1983, annual rpts, 2424–5

Food production and needs, and related economic trends and outlook, for 67 developing countries, 1980-86, annual rpt, 1524–6

Food supply policies of 21 developing countries, with farm sector data, tariff income, and prices and imports of 5 grains, 1960s-81, 1528–168

Great Lakes trade, by SITC 3-digit commodity, port, vessel type, world area, and country, 1982, annual rpt, 7744–3

Immigrant and nonimmigrant visas of US issued and refused, and status adjustments, by class and nationality, FY77, annual rpt, 7184–1

Immigration, and alien residents, workers, visitors, deportations, and naturalizations, by country of birth, FY81, annual rpt, 6264–2

Imports of US, detailed Schedule A commodities by country and world area of origin, and mode of transport, 1983, annual rpts, 2424–2

Investment (foreign direct) of US, by world area and country, 1977-83, article, 2702–1.442

Investment (intl direct) worldwide, and US investment flows by major industry, by world region and country, 1982 and trends from 1950, annual rpt, 2044–25

Loans and grants for economic and military assistance from US and intl agencies, by program and country, FY46-83, annual rpt, 9914–5

Loans of large US banks to foreigners at all US and foreign offices, by country group and country, quarterly rpt, 13002–1

Military, social, and economic summary data, by world area and country, 1960s-80s, hearing, 25388–47.1

Military spending, arms trade, and armed forces size, with total govt spending and population, by country, 1972-82, annual rpt, 9824–1

Minerals production, reserves, and industry role in domestic economy and world supply, 1981, world region rpt, 5606–1.11

Minerals Yearbook, 1982, Vol 3: foreign country reviews of production, trade, and policies, by commodity, annual rpt, 5604–35

Minerals Yearbook, 1982, Vol 3 preprints: foreign country review of production, trade, and policies, by commodity, annual rpt, 5604–17.83, 5604–17.84

Multilateral dev banks economic dev projects, environmental and cultural impacts in developing countries, 1970s-83, hearings, 21248–80

Oil and gas undiscovered recoverable resources, cumulative production, and identified reserves, as of 1982, preliminary oil basin rpt, 5666–17.13

Population size and growth rates, and latest available benchmark demographic data, by country, 1950-83, biennial rpt, 2324–4

R&D Fed Govt funding for foreign performers, by world region and country, FY82-84, annual rpt, 9627–20.2

Refugee arrivals in US, by world area of origin and processing and nationality, monthly rpt, 7002–4, 7002–5

Refugee arrivals in US by world area of origin and State of settlement, and Fed Govt intl and domestic assistance costs, FY85, annual rpt, 7004–16

Refugee migration, settlement status, and assistance, by world area and country of origin and asylum, as of May 1984, annual rpt, 7004–15

Students in US and Soviet bloc training programs, by program type and Latin American country or world region of student origin, selected years 1972-82, GAO rpt, 26123–77

Terrorist (intl) incidents, casualties, and attacks on US targets, by attack type and world area, with chronology of events, 1983, annual rpt, 7004–13

Tide height and time daily at worldwide coastal points, 1985 predictions, annual rpt, 2174–2.3

Travel to and from US on US and foreign flag air carriers, by country, world area, and US port, monthly rpt, 7302–2

Travel to US and receipts by world area and selected country, 1960-83, and US Travel and Tourism Admin activities, 1983, annual rpt, 2904–6

USIA info center and reading room operations, by world region, country, and city, FY83, annual rpt, 9854–4

Weather conditions and effect on agriculture, by US region, State, and city, and world area, weekly rpt, 2152–2

Weather conditions and impact assessment, by world area and country, monthly rpt, 2152–9

Women sociodemographic, economic, and fertility characteristics, with comparisons to men, by country, 1960s-85, world region rpt, 2326–15.2

see also African Development Bank

see also African Development Fund

see also Algeria

see also Angola

see also Benin

see also Botswana

see also Burundi

see also Cameroon

see also Cape Verde

see also Central African Republic

see also Chad

see also Comoros

see also Congo

see also Djibouti

see also Egypt

see also Equatorial Guinea

see also Ethiopia

see also Gabon

see also Gambia

see also Ghana

see also Guinea

see also Guinea-Bissau

see also Ivory Coast

see also Kenya

see also Lesotho

see also Liberia

see also Libya

see also Madagascar

see also Malawi

see also Mali

see also Mauritania

Index by Subjects and Names

see also Mauritius

see also Morocco

see also Mozambique

see also Namibia

see also Niger

see also Nigeria

see also Rwanda

see also Sao Tome and Principe

see also Senegal

see also Seychelles Islands

see also Sierra Leone

see also Somalia

see also South Africa

see also Sudan

see also Swaziland

see also Tanzania

see also Togo

see also Tunisia

see also Uganda

see also Upper Volta

see also Zaire

see also Zambia

see also Zimbabwe

see also under By Foreign Country in the "Index by Categories"

African Development Bank

AID loan repayment status and terms by program and country, and status of predecessor agency loans, quarterly rpt, 9912–3

Environmental and cultural impacts of multilateral dev banks economic dev projects in developing countries, 1970s-83, hearings, 21248–80

Human rights conditions in 162 countries, economic and military aid of US, and economic aid of intl organizations, 1981-83, annual rpt, 21384–3

Loans and grants for economic and military assistance from US and intl agencies, by program and country, FY46-83, annual rpt, 9914–5

African Development Fund

Loan activity by purpose and country, and funds by source, FY83, annual rpt, 15344–1.9

Afro-Americans

see Black Americans

Aftalion, Florin

"Political Economy of French Monetary Policy", 9373–3.26

Agarwal, Vinod B.

"Mortgage Rate Buydowns: Further Evidence", 9412–2.408

Age

see Aged and aging

see Children

see Population characteristics

see Youth

see under By Age in the "Index by Categories"

Age Discrimination Act

Older persons discrimination in Fed Govt aid programs, Age Discrimination Act enforcement by 28 agencies, FY83, annual rpt, 4004–27

Aged and aging

Arizona nursing home patients aged 55 and older in urban and rural areas, impairment levels for specified functions, 1980, article, 4102–1.413

Bus industry collective ratemaking and regulatory reform impacts on operations, finances, and services to older persons and rural areas by State, 1970s-83, 14828–2

Index by Subjects and Names

Aged and aging

Census of Housing, 1980: inventory, occupancy, and unit characteristics, changes from 1973 by region and inside-outside SMSAs and central cities, series, 2473–3

Census of Housing, 1980: occupancy and unit characteristics of SMSAs and central cities, by race, Hispanic origin, and city, State and SMSA rpt series, 2473–1

Census of Population and Housing, 1980: detailed population and housing characteristics, by county, city, and census tract, State and SMSA rpt series, 2551–2

Census of Population, 1980: detailed socioeconomic characteristics, by county, city, and inside-outside SMSAs and central cities, State rpt series, 2531–3

City govt revenue sharing program allocations and use by function, and response to program cuts, by city size and region, 1982 survey, hearings, 25408–86.2

Criminal case disposition, effect of victim injury and other factors, and law enforcement official and victim attitudes, 1983 survey, 6068–185

Death rates by age and sex, and persons aged 65 and 80 and older share of population and deaths, selected years 1900-80, article, 4102–1.447

Death rates for persons 65 and over, by major cause, sex, and age, selected years 1940-80, 4147–3.25

Deaths due to cold weather and related causes, by age, race, State, and city, selected periods 1962-83, 21148–30

Discrimination against older persons in employment, Fed Govt Age Discrimination in Employment Act compliance activities, annual rpt, discontinued, 9244–8

Discrimination against older persons in Fed Govt aid programs, Age Discrimination Act enforcement by 28 agencies, FY83, annual rpt, 4004–27

Economic and demographic trends for IRS regions, districts, and service centers, 1972-82 and projected to 1990, annual rpt, 8304–8

Employment (part-time) of older persons in community services and program funding, by State and outlying area, FY84, press release, 6408–60

Fed Govt pension and health spending for older persons, by program and as percents of budget and GNP, 1965-85 with projections to 2040, 25148–28

Florida and California elderly migration by selected State of origin or destination, and Florida elderly, by sociodemographic and housing characteristics, 1970 and 1980, 4478–150

Food aid programs of Fed Govt and others, funding, participant characteristics, and nutrition and poverty data, 1970s-83, 028–20

Food aid programs of USDA, participants and costs by program and region, monthly rpt, 1362–14

Food aid programs of USDA, participants, monthly press release, 1362–13

Food stamp recipient households size and composition, income, and income deductions allowed, Aug 1981, annual rpt, 1364–8

Foreign aged population characteristics, with related health care data and vital statistics, by world area and selected country, 1950-80 and projected to 2020, 2546–10.12

Genetically abnormal human cell cultures available to researchers, and cultures shipped, 1984 annual listing, 4474–23

Govt census, 1982: State govt payments to local govts, by program, source of funds, level of govt, and State, with trends from 1902, 2460–3

Health care expenditures, costs, and insurance of older persons, effects of proposed Medicare cost share increase, selected years 1965-81, 25148–27

Health Care Financing Review, Medicare and Medicaid program activity, health care expenditures, and research, quarterly rpt with articles, 4652–1

Health care total and out-of-pocket expenditures of aged, by sociodemographic characteristics, poverty and health status, and degree of functional limitation, 1980, 4146–11.4

Health condition and health care resources, use, and expenditures, 1970s-82 with trends and projections 1900-2000, annual compilation, 4144–11

Health long-term care and financing alternatives for older persons, including nursing home insurance and use of home equity, 1984 conf papers, 4658–7

Health Services Research Natl Center grants and contracts, by program area, FY83, annual listing, 4184–2

HHS aid to each State and local govt or private instn, amount obligated, funding agency, and program, FY83, annual listing, 4004–3

Home equity mortgaged under 4 hypothetical instruments, effects on current income of elderly Baltimore, Md, residents, 1976, article, 9312–7.402

Home heating costs of low-income households, natural gas price decontrol effects, aid programs, and gas supply/demand data, by income level and State, 1970s-95, hearing, 25148–26

Hospital discharges and length of stay of aged and nonaged persons, by region, facility size, and diagnosis, 1981, 4146–8.98

Household living arrangements, family relationships, and marital status, by demographic characteristics, Mar 1983, annual Current Population Rpt, 2546–1.388

Households and housing detailed characteristics, and unit and neighborhood quality, by inside-outside central cities, 1979-82 surveys, SMSA rpt series, 2485–6

Households and housing unit characteristics, by region and metro-nonmetro residence, 1983, biennial survey, 2485–1

Housing and households characteristics, and low-income housing construction and availability, 1970s-83, hearing, 21968–28.1

Housing and neighborhood quality indicators and attitudes, and occupant characteristics, by urban-rural location and region, 1981, annual survey, 2485–7

Housing conditions of rural aged, selected householder and housing characteristics with comparisons to urban and nonaged population, 1979, 1598–193

Housing projects for older and handicapped persons, construction and rehabilitation loans of HUD, FY84, annual listing, 5004–6

Income and income sources of older persons, by OASDI beneficiary and poverty status, labor force participation, and demographic characteristics, 1982, biennial rpt, 4744–26

Income of older persons and percent in poverty, by household composition and sex, with comparisons to nonaged, selected years 1950-82, article, 4742–1.413

Income tax and social security tax burden of households and effect of indexing by income level, 1982, and Fed Govt revenues by source, FY60-89, press release, 8008–109

Income tax returns of elderly, by income statement and tax item and income level, 1981 with trends from 1977, article, 8302–2.412

Income tax returns of individuals, by filing and deduction characteristics and income level, 1983, annual article, 8302–2.414

Income tax returns of individuals, detailed data, 1982, annual rpt, 8304–2

Income tax returns with aged exemption, 1980, hearing, 21788–132

Injuries, deaths, and medical costs from selected consumer products use, by victim age, 1981-83, annual rpt, 9164–2

Job Training Partnership Act dislocated workers program performance standards guide for States, with data on previous programs, by State and client characteristics, FY81-82, 6408–59.2

Kentucky employment growth in 9-county rural area, labor force and establishment characteristics, 1979-80, 1598–194

Nutrition services for elderly, program operations and assessment, and participant sociodemographic, health, and diet characteristics, 1976 and 1982, 4608–16

NYC families caring for aged relatives, preference for social service and financial programs to provide assistance, 1980, article, 4652–1.403

OASDI and pension policy, impacts of increased life expectancy, with alternative sociodemographic projections to 2100, hearing, 25368–130

Older persons receiving selected services from family and agencies, living arrangements, and need for home mgmt help, selected years 1977-82, article, 1702–1.409

Population demographic and economic characteristics, 1982 with projections of population size to 2050, annual Current Population Rpt, 2546–2.119

Population demographic characteristics, and health condition and services use, for older persons entitled to both Medicare and Medicaid, 1980, article, 4652–1.433

Population of aged, by demographic, socioeconomic, and health characteristics, selected years 1900-81 and projected to 2050, Current Population Rpt, 2546–2.125

Aged and aging

Population size and change for metro and nonmetro areas and central cities by census div, and growth of areas with large black and aged populations, 1970-82, 2328–47

- Population sociodemographic characteristics of aged, and Fed Govt program participation and funding by agency, 1983 with trends and projections 1900-2080, annual rpt, 25144–3
- Poverty-level persons and families, by income source, hours of work, earnings, taxes, and family characteristics, various periods 1959-84, 21788–131
- Poverty population size, effect of counting public noncash transfers as income by recipient characteristics, 1979-83, 2626–2.52
- Poverty rate by family composition, and effect of noncash transfers, taxes, unemployment benefits, and business cycles, selected years 1959-82, hearings, 21788–141
- Poverty status and living arrangements of persons over 65, and poverty status of aged households receiving social security, 1981, annual rpt, 4744–3.1
- Poverty status of families and persons, by detailed socioeconomic characteristics, 1982, annual Current Population Rpt, 2546–6.40
- Poverty status of families and persons by selected characteristics, public welfare funding, and effect of counting transfer payments as income, selected years 1950-83, 25928–4
- Public housing under private mgmt, assessment by housing officials and managers, and tenants, with operating costs, crime, and rent delinquency by project type and location, 1982, 5188–103
- Recreation at outdoor Fed Govt facilities, Golden Age and Golden Access Passports issued, by agency, 1983, annual rpt, 5544–14
- Rural and nonrural aged persons population characteristics, and needs and costs of social services by type, 1970s-82 with trends from 1900, 21148–28
- Smoke alarm sound levels by brand, and response time by circumstances and for older and mentally retarded persons, 1983 rpt, 2218–70
- *Statistical Abstract of US,* social, political, and economic data, 1950s-83 and trends, annual rpt, 2324–1.1
- Tax expenditures, Fed Govt revenues foregone through income tax deductions and exclusions by type, and effect of Deficit Reduction Act, FY84-89, annual rpt, 21784–10
- Transit systems research publications, 2nd half FY83, semiannual listing, 7882–1
- Transportation needs and sociodemographic characteristics of older persons, selected years 1900-2030, 7308–183
- Veterans aged 55 and over, socioeconomic characteristics, economic resources, health care and status, and actual and expected use of VA benefits, 1983 survey, 9928–29
- Women's labor force and OASDHI participation by age, and pension coverage by sex, selected years 1939-82, hearing, 25368–131.1

see also Adult day care
see also Civil service pensions
see also Individual retirement arrangements
see also Medicare
see also Military pensions
see also Nursing homes
see also Old Age Assistance
see also Old-Age, Survivors, Disability, and Health Insurance
see also Pensions
see also Retirement
see also Social security
see also Social Security
see also Supplemental Security Income
see also Veterans benefits and pensions
see also under By Age in the "Index by Categories"

Agency for International Development

- Activities and funding of AID by project and function, FY85, and developing countries summary socioeconomic data, 1970-83, by country, annual rpt, 9914–3
- Cargo shipments and costs of Fed Govt by agency or program and route, and employment and economic impacts of US vessel preference, 1980, GAO rpt, 26117–30
- Central America economic assistance from AID by type of aid, for 7 countries, FY80-83, GAO rpt, 26123–55
- Community dev by local govts in developing countries, AID assistance program activities and funding, 1960s-80s, 9918–11
- Contracts and grants of AID for technical and support services, by instn, country, and State, FY83, annual listing, 9914–7
- Contracts and grants of AID to universities for technical assistance to foreign countries and other services, FY83, annual listing, 9914–6
- Cost control proposals for Fed Govt programs and mgmt, 3-year savings by function and agency, and financial and operating data, 1960s-81, 16908–1.10
- Currency (foreign) accounts owned by US under AID admin and by foreign govts with joint AID control, status by program and country, quarterly rpt, 9912–1
- Currency (foreign) holdings of US, detailed transactions and balances by program and country, 1st half FY84, semiannual rpt, 8102–7
- Defense and total govt expenditures, military imports, GNP, and intl reserves of countries receiving US economic aid, by country, 1976-81, annual rpt, 9914–1
- Dev assistance activities of AID, evaluation rpt series, 9916–11
- Dev assistance activities of AID, socioeconomic impacts, evaluation rpt series, 9916–1
- Dev assistance activities of AID, special study series, 9916–3
- Disaster preparedness and summary sociodemographic, political, and economic data, country rpt series, 9916–2
- Disasters, persons affected, deaths, damage, and aid by US and others, by country, FY83 and trends from FY64, annual rpt, 9914–12
- Economic and military assistance role in US foreign policy, with aid proposals by world region, FY85 with trends from FY74, 7008–38

Index by Subjects and Names

- Economic assistance to developing countries, obligations and disbursements by country, quarterly rpt, 9912–4
- Environmental monitoring staff and funding of AID and multilateral dev banks, FY83, hearings, 21248–80
- Foreign Service positions and union membership by agency, grievances, and pay rates, FY8l-83 with ambassador appointments from 1961, GAO rpt, 26123–64
- Free zones in developing countries, industry financial and operating data by country, with case studies for 5 countries, 1970s-82, 9918–10
- Housing finance and low-income housing projects in Asian developing countries, and activities of 2 countries, 1970s-82, annual conf proceedings, 9914–11
- Housing Guaranty Program financial statements, and projects by country, FY83, annual rpt, 9914–4
- Human rights conditions in 162 countries, economic and military aid of US, and economic aid of intl organizations, 1981-83, annual rpt, 21384–3
- Intl exchange and training programs of Fed Govt, participants by world region, and funding, by agency, FY83, annual rpt, 9854–8
- Latin America students in US and Soviet bloc training programs, by program type and student country, and summary by world region, selected years 1972-82, GAO rpt, 26123–77
- Liabilities (contigent) and claims paid by Fed Govt on federally insured and guaranteed contracts with foreign obligors, by country and program, periodic rpt, 8002–12
- Loan activity, terms, and purpose, by country, FY83, annual rpt, 15344–1.10
- Loan repayment status and terms by program and country, AID and predecessor agencies, quarterly rpt, 9912–3
- Loans and grants for economic and military assistance from US and intl agencies, by program and country, FY46-83, annual rpt, 9914–5
- Loans authorized, signed, and canceled, by country and world area, monthly rpt, 9912–2
- Philippines dev and military assistance funding from US, FY78-84 and proposed FY85-89, GAO rpt, 26123–54
- PL 480 Title I funding and socioeconomic impacts, with case studies for 5 countries, 1950s-81, 9918–13
- Private sector dev and socioeconomic conditions, effects of AID and other foreign assistance and govt policy, with case studies for 6 countries, 1960s-80, 9918–12
- R&D Fed Govt funding for all performers, by field and supporting agency, selected years FY60-84, annual rpt, 9627–20
- Voluntary agencies overseas foreign aid programs funding and expenditures, by agency, 1982/83, annual rpt, 9914–9
- Women sociodemographic, economic, and fertility characteristics, with comparisons to men, by country, 1960s-85, world region rpt series, 2326–15

Index by Subjects and Names

Aging Cell Culture Repository

Genetically abnormal human cell cultures available to researchers, and cultures shipped, 1984 annual listing, 4474–23

Agnello, Richard J.

"Economic Potential for Utilizing Minced Fish in Cooked Sausage Products", 2162–1.401

Agrarian reform

see Land reform

Agricultural accidents and safety

Deaths and death rates from accidents, by place, detailed cause, and demographic characteristics, 1979, US Vital Statistics annual rpt, 4144–2.5

Grain handling facility explosions, injuries, deaths, and cause, by company, FY83, annual rpt, 1294–1

Injuries and deaths from use of selected consumer products, by victim age and medical treatment status, 1982, annual rpt, 9164–6

Injuries, illnesses, and workdays lost, by SIC 2-digit industry, 1982-83, annual press release, 6844–3

Injuries of farm workers, by relationship to farm owner and injury severity, 1982, article, 1702–1.408

Injury and illness rates and causes, by SIC 2- to 4-digit industry, 1982, annual rpt, 6844–1

Pesticide use for crops and livestock, acreage treated, application methods, and use of safety equipment and professional services, 1982 survey, 1588–76

Washington State deaths by sex, cause, and detailed occupation, summary data from occupational mortality study, 1950-79, 4248–47

Agricultural chemicals

see Fertilizers

see Pesticides

Agricultural commodities

Advertising (generic) for agricultural commodities, activities and funding by source, selected years 1972-83, 1548–242

Agricultural Statistics, 1983, annual rpt, 1004–1

Census of Agriculture, 1982: farms, farmland, production and costs, and operator characteristics, preliminary State and county rpt series, 2330–1

Cold storage food stocks of 77 commodities, by region, 1983, annual rpt, 1631–11

Crop Reporting Board commodity publications, 1984 releases, annual listing, 1614–1

Developing countries agricultural supply/demand and market for US exports, with socioeconomic indicators, country rpt series, 1526–6

EC food supply/demand and market and support prices, with exchange rates, fertilizer price index, GDP, and population, by country, 1960-83, 1528–173

Foreign agricultural and food production indexes, and production of selected commodities, by world region and country, 1974-83, annual rpt, 1524–5

Input-output structure of US economy, detailed interindustry transactions for 85 industries, and components of final demand, 1977, article, 2702–1.421

Input-output structure of US economy, detailed interindustry transactions for 537 industries, and components of final demand, 1977 benchmark data, 2708–17

Production and farm finances, expenses by type, and domestic economic impact, selected years 1972-82 and preliminary 1983-84, annual rpt, 1544–19

Production itemized costs, receipts, and net returns, for 13 crops, 4 livestock types, and milk, by region, 1981-83, annual rpt, 1544–20

Research (agricultural) expenditures and scientist years, by topic, commodity, and performing organization, FY82, annual rpt, 1744–2

Small farms with sales under $2,500, acreage, finances, operations, and operator characteristics, by region and for 6 States, 1978, 1548–241

Statistical Abstract of US, social, political, and economic data, 1950s-83 and trends, annual rpt, 2324–1.3

Transportation census, 1982: trucks, by detailed characteristics, miles traveled, and type of product carried, State rpt series, 2573–1

Waterborne commerce of US (domestic and foreign), freight by commodity, traffic, and passengers, by port and waterway, 1982, annual rpt, 3754–3

see also Agricultural exports and imports

see also Agricultural marketing

see also Agricultural prices

see also Agricultural stocks

see also Animal feed

see also Animals

see also Citrus fruits

see also Cocoa and chocolate

see also Coffee

see also Corn

see also Cotton

see also Dairy industry and products

see also Fibers

see also Flowers and nursery products

see also Food and food industry

see also Food prices

see also Food supply

see also Fruit and fruit products

see also Grains and grain products

see also Gum and wood chemicals

see also Hides and skins

see also Honey and beekeeping

see also Hops

see also Livestock and livestock industry

see also Lumber industry and products

see also Meat and meat products

see also Nuts

see also Oils, oilseeds, and fats

see also Poultry industry and products

see also Rice

see also Seeds

see also Soybeans

see also Spices and herbs

see also Sugar industry and products

see also Tea

see also Tobacco industry and products

see also Vegetables and vegetable products

see also Wheat

see also Wool and wool trade

see also under By Commodity in the "Index by Categories"

Agricultural cooperatives

Agricultural Cooperative Service

Activities and programs of USDA, by subagency, FY83, annual rpt, 1004–3

Agricultural cooperative finances and operations, aggregate for top 100 assns by principal product and revenue source, FY82, annual rpt, 1124–3

Agricultural cooperatives activities, operations, finances, and current issues, monthly rpt articles, 1122–1

Agricultural cooperatives commercial farmer membership and use, by type and sales size of farm and region, 1980, 1128–32

Agricultural cooperatives, membership, activities, and finances, by commodity and selected State, 1900-80 with trends from 1863, 1128–30

Agricultural cooperatives, membership, and activities, by type of service, commodity, and State, FY51-1982, annual survey rpt, 1124–1

Dairy cooperatives itemized costs for manufacturing cheese, butter, and dry milk, plants, and plant capacity, 1981/82, 1128–25

Dairy cooperatives sales volume and market shares by commodity, and finances, by region, 1980 with trends from 1957, 1128–29

Eastern Europe grain production, consumption, and trade, and US farm cooperatives grain and oilseed export potential, for 4 countries, selected years 1960-90, 1128–27

Farm supply sales programs of agricultural cooperatives, services offered, inventory mgmt and marketing methods, sales force and compensation system, for 4 products, 1982, 1128–24

Grain cooperatives marketing, storage, and shipments by mode of transport, by grain type and region, FY80, 1128–28

Grain cooperatives storage and handling facilities, sales, exports, and financial condition, selected years 1974-82, 1128–31

Livestock producers membership in agricultural cooperatives, and patronage for marketing and supplies purchase, by region and farm sales size, 1980, 1128–26

Agricultural cooperatives

Agricultural production, marketing, trade, supply, food consumption, and food and nutrition programs, 1960s-83, annual chartbook, 1504–3

Agricultural Statistics, 1983, annual rpt, 1004–1.2

Argentina grain production, exports by firm, storage by facility type and port, and shipments to ports by mode of transport, by grain type, selected years 1954-81, 1528–185

Census of Agriculture, 1982: farms, farmland, production and costs, and operator characteristics, preliminary State and county rpt series, 2330–1

Census of Agriculture, 1982: farms, farmland, production, finances, and operator characteristics, by county, final State rpt series, 2331–1

Dairy cooperatives and percent share of producers and deliveries, by region, 1982 with trends from 1965, article, 1317–4.403

Agricultural cooperatives

Dairy cooperatives itemized costs for manufacturing cheese, butter, and dry milk, plants, and plant capacity, 1981/82, 1128–25

Dairy cooperatives sales volume and market shares by commodity, and finances, by region, 1980 with trends from 1957, 1128–29

Eastern Europe grain production, consumption, and trade, and US farm cooperatives grain and oilseed export potential, for 4 countries, selected years 1960-90, 1128–27

Election campaign finances and Fed Election Commission monitoring activities, 1984 Federal elections, biennial rpt series, 9276–2

Election campaign finances, election procedures, and Fed Election Commission monitoring activities, press release series, 9276–1

Election campaign funding and activities of Fed Election Commission, and political action committees funding, 1983, annual rpt, 9274–1

Farm finances, expenses by type, loans by purpose and source, and credit detail by Fed Reserve District, quarterly rpt, 9365–3.10

Farm sector investments in cooperatives, and cooperatives net worth, selected years 1940-84, annual rpt, 1544–16.2

Farm supply sales programs of agricultural cooperatives, services offered, inventory mgmt and marketing methods, sales force and compensation system, for 4 products, 1982, 1128–24

Finances and operations of cooperatives, aggregate for top 100 assns by principal product and revenue source, FY82, annual rpt, 1124–3

Finances, operations, activities, and current issues, for cooperatives, monthly rpt articles, 1122–1

Finances, operations, and membership, by commodity and selected State, 1900-80 with trends from 1863, 1128–30

Fishery cooperatives in US, Guam, and Puerto Rico, 1983, annual rpt, 2164–1.10

Grain cooperatives marketing, storage, and shipments by mode of transport, by grain type and region, FY80, 1128–28

Grain cooperatives storage and handling facilities, sales, exports, and financial condition, selected years 1974-82, 1128–31

Liberia socioeconomic impacts of AID rural dev assistance program, 1976-77, 9916–1.53

Livestock producers membership in agricultural cooperatives, and patronage for marketing and supplies purchase, by region and farm sales size, 1980, 1128–26

Membership, activities, and number of assns, by type of service, commodity, and State, FY51- 1982, annual survey rpt, 1124–1

Membership and use of cooperatives by commercial farmers, by type and sales size of farm and region, 1980, 1128–32

Oil and gas production, supply, and reserves of agricultural cooperatives, 1979 and 1982, article, 1561–16.403

Tobacco stocks held by grower cooperatives, by type, quarterly rpt, 1319–3

Agricultural credit

Agricultural cooperative finances and operations, aggregate for top 100 assns by principal product and revenue source, FY82, annual rpt, 1124–3

Agricultural production, marketing, trade, supply, food consumption, and food and nutrition programs, 1960s-83, annual chartbook, 1504–3

Agricultural Statistics, 1983, annual rpt, 1004–1

Agriculture Fact Book of US, compilation of data for 1983 with trends from 1940, annual rpt, 1004–14

Budget of US, effects of Reagan Admin policy changes, by detailed program, FY85, annual rpt, 104–21

Budget of US, loans and loan guarantees, and Admin proposed limits on credit assistance, by program, FY83-89, annual rpt, 26306–3.65

Budget of US, receipts by source and outlays by agency and program, monthly rpt, 8102–3

CCC finances and program operations, FY83, annual rpt, 1824–1

CCC loan activities by commodity, and agency operating results, monthly press release, 1802–7

Census of Agriculture, 1982: farms, farmland, production and costs, and operator characteristics, preliminary State and county rpt series, 2330–1

Cotton loan rates, and micronaire differentials of CCC, monthly rpt, annual tables, 1309–12.2

County Business Patterns: establishments, employees, and payrolls, by SIC 4-digit industry and county, 1982, annual State rpt series, 2326–6

Credit assistance costs, policies to improve measurement, with loan and loan guarantee data by program, and Federal and private credit instns operations, 1970-84, 26306–6.72

Farm finance and credit conditions, forecast 1984, conf summary, annual rpt, 9264–9

Farm finances, assets, expenses, cash flow, receipts, and loans, selected years 1971-85, annual rpt, 1544–13

Farm finances, assets, liabilities, income, receipts by commodity and State, and expenses, 1980-83 and trends from 1910, annual rpt, 1544–16

Farm finances, expenses by type, loans by purpose and source, and credit detail by Fed Reserve District, quarterly rpt, 9365–3.10

Farm finances, production, expenses by type, and domestic economic impact, selected years 1972-82 and preliminary 1983-84, annual rpt, 1544–19

Farm loans outstanding, by type of lender and State, 1960-83, biennial rpt, 1544–2

Farm non-real estate debt outstanding, by type of lender and district, as of Jan 1983, annual rpt, 9264–4

Farm production expenditures, detailed items by farm sales size and region, 1983, annual rpt, 1614–3

Farm production itemized costs, receipts, and net returns, for 13 crops, 4 livestock types, and milk, by region, 1981-83, annual rpt, 1544–20

Index by Subjects and Names

Farm production, prices, marketing, and trade, by commodity, forecast and current situation, monthly rpt, 1502–4

Farm real estate and other debt, by type of lender, 1980 benchmark data with revised estimates for 1970-82, 1548–230

Farm real estate credit-financed transfers, by type of lender and region, selected years 1945-84, annual rpt, 1541–8.5

Farm sector financial review, debt outlook, and rural banks condition, 1950s-83, article, 9362–1.401

Fed Govt aid to State and local govts, expenditures, and direct payments, by program, agency, and State, FY83, annual rpt, 2464–2

Fed Govt grants-in-aid for 13 program areas, FY82-84, annual article, 10042–1.402

Fed Govt loans, grants, and tax benefits to business, by program and economic sector, projected FY84-88 with effective tax rates for FY80-82, 26306–6.70

Fed Govt policy issues effect on agricultural and food prices, income, and trade, and crop support levels by program, Nov 1984, semiannual rpt, 1542–6

FmHA borrowers, by loan type, race, Hispanic origin, and State, annual rpt, suspended, 1184–11

FmHA farm ownership loan applicants socioeconomic characteristics, and average loan amounts, annual rpt, suspended, 1184–7

FmHA loan applications, by loan type, borrower race and Hispanic origin, State, and outlying area, annual rpt, discontinued, 1184–1

FmHA loans and borrower supervision activities in farm and housing programs, by type and State, monthly rpt, 1182–1

FmHA loans and grants by program and State, and summary of services, FY83 with trends from FY63, annual rpt, 1184–17

FmHA loans, by type, race, Hispanic origin, and State, quarterly rpt, 1182–5

FmHA operating loan applicants socioeconomic characteristics, and average loan amounts, annual rpt, suspended, 1184–9

FmHA operating loans, by State and use of funds, annual rpt, suspended, 1184–4

FmHA soil and water loan applicants socioeconomic characteristics, and average loan amounts, annual rpt, suspended, 1184–8

Grain loan support programs of USDA, activity and status by type of grain and State, monthly rpt, 1802–3

Honey loan activity of CCC, by State, weekly rpt, monthly tables, 1311–2

Korea (South) agricultural services projects of AID and Korea govt, economic impacts, 1950s-83, 9916–1.52

Mortgage debt interest, by State, 1979-82, annual rpt, 1544–18

Mortgage debt outstanding, by type of lender and district, as of Jan 1983, annual rpt, 9264–3

Mortgage loan activity, by type of lender, loan, and mortgaged property, monthly rpt, 5142–18

Mortgage transactions and holdings, by lender group and type of property and loan, quarterly rpt, 5142–30

Index by Subjects and Names

Agricultural exports and imports

North Central States agricultural credit conditions, earnings, and expenditures, Fed Reserve 9th District, quarterly rpt, 9383–11

North Central States farm credit conditions and economic devs, Fed Reserve 7th District, biweekly rpt, 9375–10

Portugal agricultural subsidies, profits, marketing margins, and consumer prices, by commodity or product, and effects of prospective EC membership, 1981, 1528–171

Southeastern States farm credit conditions and real estate values, Fed Reserve 5th District, quarterly rpt, 9389–17

Southwestern States farm credit conditions and real estate values, Fed Reserve 11th District, quarterly rpt, 9379–11

Storage facility and equipment loans to farmers under CCC grain program, by State, FY68-84, annual table, 1804–14

Storage facility and equipment loans to farmers under CCC grain program, by State, monthly table, 1802–9

Western States farm real estate values, and nonreal estate farm loan trends, monthly rpt, quarterly data, 9381–2

see also Agricultural quotas and price supports

see also Farm Credit System

Agricultural education

Agricultural research and extension program needs, and foreign and US supply/demand indicators by commodity and world area, 1950s-2020, 1008–47

Degrees conferred in higher education, by race, Hispanic origin, sex, level, and field, selected years 1949/50-1979/80, annual rpt, 4824–2.16

Foreign and US agricultural supply/demand, trade, and production, and socioeconomic data, by country, 1950s-77, 1528–179

Research funding for agriculture from Fed Govt and States, by region, State, and outlying area, FY78-82, GAO rpt, 26113–111

Science and engineering grad enrollment, fields of study, financial support, and other student and instn characteristics, 1975-82, annual survey, 9627–7

Science and engineering grads of 1980-81, employment characteristics or grad enrollment, by degree level, field, sex, and race, 1982, 9627–25

Teaching degrees conferred by specialty and State, required credit hours, and instn officials attitudes, by instn type, 1970s-83, hearings, 21348–89

Veterans education assistance program participation and costs under GI Bill and other programs, WW II through Sept 1983, annual rpt, 9924–22

Vocational education, detailed data on enrollment, achievement, curricula, and effects on employment, selected years 1980-82, annual rpt, 4824–1.3

see also Agricultural extension work

see also Agricultural sciences

Agricultural exports and imports

Agricultural policies of US effect on trade, with US and foreign trade by commodity and grain stocks by world area, various periods 1979-83, 1528–183

Agricultural production, marketing, trade, supply, food consumption, and food and nutrition programs, 1960s-83, annual chartbook, 1504–3

Agricultural situation and farm-related topics, monthly rpt, 1502–6

Agricultural Stabilization and Conservation Service programs, annual commodity fact sheet series, 1806–4

Agricultural Statistics, 1983, annual rpt, 1004–1

Business statistics, detailed data for major industries and economic indicators, *Survey of Current Business,* monthly rpt, 2702–1.11

Canada agricultural trade with US, effects of nontariff trade barriers, selected years 1955-81, 1528–175

CCC commodity exports in exchange for strategic material imports by world region and country, and strategic material stockpiles, various periods 1950-83, hearings, 21208–20

China economic conditions, agricultural and industrial production, trade, and domestic and foreign investment, 1980-85, 2048–106

China exports and imports, by commodity, world area, and country, quarterly rpt, 242–6

China exports and imports by SITC 1- to 5-digit commodity, 1970s-82, annual rpt, 244–12

Coastal environmental characteristics, fish, wildlife, and use, and population socioeconomic data, for individual areas, series, 5506–4

Communist country trade with US, by detailed commodity and country, quarterly rpt with articles, 9882–2

Developing countries agricultural supply/demand and market for US exports, with socioeconomic indicators, country rpt series, 1526–6

Developing countries disaster preparedness and summary sociodemographic, political, and economic data, country rpt series, 9916–2

Developing countries food production and needs, and related economic trends and outlook, for 67 countries, 1980-86, annual rpt, 1524–6

Developing countries food supply policies, with farm sector data, tariff income, and prices and imports of 5 grains, for 21 countries, 1960s-81, 1528–168

Developing countries govt policy, and AID and other foreign assistance, effects on private sector dev and socioeconomic conditions, with case studies for 6 countries, 1960s-80, 9918–12

Eastern Europe agricultural production and trade by commodity, food consumption, and farm inputs, for 6 countries, 1960-80 with projections to 1991, 1528–178

EC agricultural self-sufficiency and trade by selected product, with comparisons to other countries, selected years 1959/60-1983/84, hearing, 25368–135

EC trade with US by country, and total agricultural and nonagricultural trade, selected years 1958-83, annual rpt, 7144–7

Export sales and shipments of US grains, oilseed products, hides, skins, and cotton, by country, weekly rpt, 1922–3

Exports and imports between US and outlying areas, by detailed commodity and mode of transport, monthly rpt, 2422–4

Exports and imports, intl position of US and 4 OECD countries, and factors affecting US competition, quarterly pamphlet, 2042–25

Exports and imports of agricultural commodities, outlook and current situation, quarterly rpt, 1542–4

Exports and imports of US, and trade balance, by major commodity group, selected country, and world area, with seasonal adjustments, monthly rpt, 2422–6

Exports and imports of US, by agricultural commodity and country, bimonthly rpt with articles, 1522–1

Exports and imports of US, by commodity group, world area, selected country, US coastal area and port, and mode of transport, with seasonal adjustments, monthly rpt, 2422–9

Exports and imports of US by country, and trade shifts by commodity, USITC quarterly monitoring rpt, 9882–9

Exports and imports of US, by detailed agricultural commodity and country, FY83 and CY83, semiannual rpts, 1522–4

Exports and imports of US, by detailed agricultural commodity for 8 major commodity groups, monthly rpt, 1922–8

Exports and imports of US, by principal end-use category, 1965-83, annual rpt, 204–1.9

Exports and imports of US, detailed SIC-based commodities by world area, 1983, annual rpts, 2424–6

Exports and imports of US, totals and as percent of domestic production, by SIC 2- to 5-digit commodity, 1981, annual rpt, 2424–3

Exports and personal expenditures of US and world for selected agricultural commodities, by country, and export share of US farm income, various periods 1926-82, 1528–172

Exports, imports, and economic indicators by country and country group, and US trade policy actions, 1960s-83, annual rpt, 444–1.3

Exports, imports, tariffs, and industry operating data for agricultural products, 1979-83, TSUSA commodity rpt series, 9885–1

Exports of agricultural products and nonelectrical machinery, *Business Conditions Digest,* historical supplement and methodology, 1947-82, 2708–31

Exports of agricultural products and nonelectrical machinery, *Business Conditions Digest,* monthly rpt, 2702–3.9

Exports of manufactured and agricultural commodities, manufacturing production, and export-related employment, 1960s-82, State rpt series, 2046–3

Exports of US agricultural products and dollar exchange rate, percent changes for 12 countries, 1981-83, article, 9391–1.421

Exports of US, detailed commodities by country of destination, monthly rpt, 2422–3

Exports of US, detailed Schedule B commodities by country of destination, 1983, annual rpt, 2424–9

Agricultural exports and imports

Exports of US, detailed Schedule E commodities by mode of transport and world area and country of destination, 1983, annual rpts, 2424–5

Farm finance and credit conditions, forecast 1984, conf papers, annual rpt, 1004–16

Farm finance and credit conditions, forecast 1984, conf summary, annual rpt, 9264–9

Farm production, prices, marketing, and trade, by commodity, forecast and current situation, monthly rpt, 1502–4

Fed Govt policy issues effect on agricultural and food prices, income, and trade, and crop support levels by program, Nov 1984, semiannual rpt, 1542–6

Fed Govt programs and mgmt cost control proposals, 3-year savings by function and agency, and financial and operating data, 1960s-81, 16908–1.2

Food supply, trade, and use, by commodity, 1963-83, annual rpt, 1544–4.4

Foreign agricultural production, prices, and trade, by country, 1983 and outlook for 1984/85, annual world region rpt series, 1524–4

Foreign Agriculture, production, consumption, and policies, and US export dev and promotion, monthly rpt, 1922–2

Foreign and US agricultural production, prices, trade, and consumption, quarterly rpt with articles, 1522–3

Foreign and US agricultural production, trade, and climatic devs, weekly press release, 1922–4

Foreign and US agricultural supply/demand and production data, for selected US and world crops, and for US livestock and dairy products, periodic rpt, 1522–5

Foreign and US agricultural supply/demand, consumption per capita, and trade, by world area and country group, 1960s-82, 1528–181

Foreign and US agricultural supply/demand indicators by commodity and world area, and related research and extension program needs, 1950s-2020, 1008–47

Foreign and US agricultural supply/demand, trade, and production, and socioeconomic data, by country, 1950s-77, 1528–179

Foreign and US feed and livestock trade by product and world region, and ocean freight rates between selected countries of origin and destination, selected years 1960-82, 1528–177

Foreign and US fresh and processed fruit, vegetable, and nut production and trade, FAS monthly rpt with articles, 1925–34

Foreign exchange rate appreciation of dollar, effects on exports, stocks, and prices of wheat, corn, and soybeans, 1980-82 and for hypothetical 20-year period, 1528–174

Great Lakes trade, by SITC 3-digit commodity, port, vessel type, world area, and country, 1982, annual rpt, 7744–3

Import quotas and imports for selected commodities, by country of origin, monthly rpt, 8146–1

Imports detained by FDA, by product, shipper or manufacturer, country, and detention reasons, monthly listing, 4062–2

Imports injury to price-supported US agricultural industries, investigations with background financial and operating data for selected products, series, 9886–10

Imports of US, detailed Schedule A commodities by country and world area of origin, and mode of transport, 1983, annual rpts, 2424–2

Imports of US, detailed Schedule A commodities by country, monthly rpt, 2422–2

Imports of US, detailed TSUSA commodities by country of origin, 1983, annual rpt, 2424–4

Input-output structure of US economy, detailed interindustry transactions for 537 industries, and components of final demand, 1977 benchmark data, 2708–17

Intl transactions summary, including impact of oil imports and agricultural exports, 4th qtr 1982-4th qtr 1983, article, 9362–1.403

Meat and poultry inspection activities and personnel of Federal, State, and foreign govts, FY83, annual rpt, 1374–1

North Central States farm credit conditions and economic devs, Fed Reserve 7th District, biweekly rpt, 9375–10

OECD trade, total and for 4 major countries, and US trade by country, by commodity, 1972-82, annual world region rpt series, 244–13

Panama Canal commerce, by commodity, flag of vessel, and trade routes, FY82, annual rpt, 9664–3.2

Pests (plant) and pathogens found entering US, by country of origin, State, and method of interception, FY82, annual rpt, 1394–16

Port impact on local employment through transport of 5 commodities, by industry for 3 eastern ports, and demand for US coal by country, 1981, 7308–182

Price indexes for food and manufactured exports and imports, quarterly press release, 6762–13

Processed foods production and stocks by State, shipments, exports, materials used, and consumption, by product, periodic Current Industrial Rpt series, 2506–4

Research (agricultural) expenditures and scientist years, by topic, commodity, and performing organization, FY82, annual rpt, 1744–2

South America and Argentina agricultural exports, and coffee exports of Colombia and Brazil to US and world, market share analysis, 1960-79, 1528–169

Southeastern States agricultural conditions, Fed Reserve 8th District, quarterly rpt, 9391–13

Tariff Schedules of US, Annotated, classifications and rates of duty for detailed imported commodities, 1985 edition, 9886–13

TTPI socioeconomic, health, and govtl data, by TTPI govt, FY83 and selected trends, detailed annual rpt, 7004–6

Waterborne commerce of US (domestic and foreign), freight by commodity, traffic, and passengers, by port and waterway, 1982, annual rpt, 3754–3

see also Public Law 480

see also under names of specific commodities or commodity groups (listed under Agricultural commodities)

Index by Subjects and Names

Agricultural extension work

Agricultural research and extension program needs, and foreign and US supply/demand indicators by commodity and world area, 1950s-2020, 1008–47

Budget of US, effects of Reagan Admin policy changes, by detailed program, FY85, annual rpt, 104–21

Fed Govt aid to State and local govts, expenditures, and direct payments, by program, agency, and State, FY83, annual rpt, 2464–2

Korea (South) agricultural services projects of AID and Korea govt, economic impacts, 1950s-83, 9916–1.52

TVA agricultural dev program activities, and fertilizer shipments by fertilizer type, selected years 1935-81, 9808–68

Agricultural finance

Agricultural economics technical research, quarterly journal, 1502–3

Agricultural production, marketing, trade, supply, food consumption, and food and nutrition programs, 1960s-83, annual chartbook, 1504–3

Agricultural Statistics, 1983, annual rpt, 1004–1

Agriculture Fact Book of US, compilation of data for 1983 with trends from 1940, annual rpt, 1004–14

Business statistics, detailed data for major industries and economic indicators, *Survey of Current Business,* monthly rpt, 2702–1.11

Census of Agriculture, 1982: farms, farmland, production and costs, and operator characteristics, preliminary State and county rpt series, 2330–1

Census of Agriculture, 1982: farms, farmland, production, finances, and operator characteristics, by county, final State rpt series, 2331–1

Economic Indicators of the Farm Sector, assets, liabilities, income, and expenses, by State, 1979-82, annual rpt, 1544–18

Economic Indicators of the Farm Sector, assets, liabilities, income, and expenses, 1980-83 and trends from 1910, annual rpt, 1544–16

Economic Indicators of the Farm Sector, finances, production, expenses by type, and domestic economic impact, selected years 1972-82 and preliminary 1983-84, annual rpt, 1544–19

Economic Indicators of the Farm Sector, itemized production costs, receipts, and net returns, for 13 crops, 4 livestock types, and milk, by region, 1981-83, annual rpt, 1544–20

Farm business legal organization, finances, operations, tax rates, and State laws restricting farm corporations, 1960s-82, 1548–233

Farm debt, loans outstanding, and interest rates, by type of lender and State, 1960-83 with trends from 1940, biennial rpt, 1544–2

Farm debt to asset ratio, by southeastern State, 1979-83, article, 9371–1.424

Farm finance and credit conditions, forecast 1984, conf papers, annual rpt, 1004–16

Farm finance and credit conditions, forecast 1984, conf summary, annual rpt, 9264–9

Farm finances, assets, expenses, cash flow, receipts, and loans, selected years 1971-85, annual rpt, 1544–13

Index by Subjects and Names

Agricultural labor

Farm finances, expenses by type, loans by purpose and source, and credit detail by Fed Reserve District, quarterly rpt, 9365–3.10

Farm sector balance sheet, 1929-84, annual rpt, 204–1.8

Farm sector financial review, debt outlook, and rural banks condition, 1950s-83, article, 9362–1.401

Farmers prices received for major products and paid for farm inputs and living items, by commodity and State, monthly rpt, 1629–1

Farmers prices received for major products and paid for farm inputs, by commodity and State, 1983, annual rpt, 1629–5

Flow-of-funds accounts, assets and liabilities by type and economic sector, year-end outstandings, 1960-83, annual rpt, 9364–3

Flow-of-funds accounts savings, investments, and credit statements, quarterly rpt, 9365–3.3

Income tax returns of corporations, detailed income and tax items by industry, 1981, annual rpt, 8304–4

Income tax returns of corporations, summary data by industry div, 1981 estimates, annual article, 8302–2.403

Income tax returns of corporations with foreign tax credit, income and deductions by type, asset size, and selected industry group, 1980, article, 8302–2.415

Income tax returns of foreign subsidiaries of US corporations, income and tax data, by industry and asset size, 1980, article, 8302–2.410

Income tax returns of individuals, detailed data, 1982, annual rpt, 8304–2

Income tax returns of partnerships, detailed data by industry, 1981 estimates, annual article, 8302–2.404

Income tax returns of partnerships, receipts by source, deductions by type, and establishments, by selected industry, 1982, annual article, 8302–2.416

Income tax returns of sole proprietorships, detailed data by industry div and selected industry group, 1981, annual rpt, 8304–7

Income tax returns of sole proprietorships, receipts, deductions by type, payroll, and net income, by major industry, 1982, annual article, 8302–2.413

Income tax returns with investment credits, for individuals by income, and for sole proprietorships by industry, 1981, article, 8302–2.409

Land privately held, acreage and owners by owner characteristics, land use, and region, and purchase and improvement funding, 1978 survey, series, 1506–5

North Central States agricultural credit conditions, earnings, and expenditures, Fed Reserve 9th District, quarterly rpt, 9383–11

North Central States farm credit conditions and economic devs, Fed Reserve 7th District, biweekly rpt, 9375–10

North Central States farm investments, effective rates of Federal/State income and State/local property taxes, by category of structure and equipment and State, 1981-82, 1548–237

Southeastern States farm credit conditions and real estate values, Fed Reserve 5th District, quarterly rpt, 9389–17

Tax rates of Fed Govt and States, effect on farm investments under alternative depreciation methods and inflation rates, 1950-84, 1548–231

see also Agricultural cooperatives

see also Agricultural credit

see also Agricultural insurance

see also Agricultural production costs

see also Agricultural quotas and price supports

see also Agricultural subsidies

see also Farm Credit System

see also Farm income

see also Property value

Agricultural income

see Farm income

Agricultural industries

see Agricultural cooperatives

see Agricultural finance

see Agricultural labor

see Agricultural marketing

see Agricultural production

see Agricultural services

see Agricultural wages

see Agriculture

see Dairy industry and products

see Farms and farmland

see Flowers and nursery products

see Food and food industry

see Fruit and fruit products

see Grains and grain products

see Honey and beekeeping

see Livestock and livestock industry

see Meat and meat products

see Poultry industry and products

see Sugar industry and products

see Tobacco industry and products

see Vegetables and vegetable products

see Veterinary medicine

Agricultural innovations

AID dev assistance activities, socioeconomic impacts, evaluation rpt series, 9916–1

Budget of US, effects of Reagan Admin policy changes, by detailed program, FY85, annual rpt, 104–21

Expenditures and scientist years for agricultural research, by topic, commodity, and performing organization, FY82, annual rpt, 1744–2

Genetic resource (plant and animal) conservation, commercial uses, causes of depletion, and geographic sources, 1984 rpt, 5548–13

R&D Fed Govt funding, by function, agency, and program, selected years FY80-84 and proposed FY85, 26308–46

see also Biomass energy

Agricultural insurance

Farm production expenditures, detailed items by farm sales size and region, 1983, annual rpt, 1614–3

Farm production itemized costs, receipts, and net returns, for 13 crops, 4 livestock types, and milk, by region, 1981-83, annual rpt, 1544–20

Fed Crop Insurance Corp finances, and insurance participation and operations in 2 States by crop, 1980-84, GAO rpt, 26113–132

Fed Crop Insurance Corp program activities and costs, and FCIC and private insurance company gains and losses, 1980-84 with some trends from 1948, GAO rpt, 26113–119

Fed Crop Insurance Corp program operations and finances, for FCIC policies and private policies reinsured by FCIC, 1970s-84 with trends from 1948, hearing, 21168–28

Fed Govt programs and mgmt cost control proposals, 3-year savings by function and agency, and financial and operating data, 1960s-81, 16908–1.15

Agricultural labor

Agricultural production, marketing, trade, supply, food consumption, and food and nutrition programs, 1960s-83, annual chartbook, 1504–3

Agricultural products trade, tariffs, and industry operating data, 1979-83, TSUSA commodity rpt series, 9885–1

Agricultural Statistics, 1983, annual rpt, 1004–1.2

Census of Agriculture, 1982: farms, farmland, production and costs, and operator characteristics, preliminary State and county rpt series, 2330–1

Census of Agriculture, 1982: farms, farmland, production, finances, and operator characteristics, by county, final State rpt series, 2331–1

Census of Housing, 1980: structural, financial, and householder characteristics, by region and State, 2475–4

Census of Population and Housing, 1980: detailed population and housing characteristics, by county, city, and census tract, State and SMSA rpt series, 2551–2

Census of Population, 1980: detailed socioeconomic and demographic characteristics, by age, sex, race, Hispanic origin, occupation, and industry, State rpt series, 2531–4

Census of Population, 1980: detailed socioeconomic characteristics, by county, city, and inside-outside SMSAs and central cities, State rpt series, 2531–3

Census of Population, 1980: labor force, by sex, detailed occupation, and region, with comparison to 1970 census, supplementary rpt, 2535–1.12

Communist, OECD, and selected other countries economic statistics, 1960s-83, annual rpt, 244–5.2

County and City Data Book, detailed socioeconomic and demographic data for States, counties, and cities, selected years 1976-82, 2328–1

County Business Patterns: establishments, employees, and payrolls, by SIC 4-digit industry and county, 1982, annual State rpt series, 2326–6

Developing countries food supply policies, with farm sector data, tariff income, and prices and imports of 5 grains, for 21 countries, 1960s-81, 1528–168

Eastern Europe agricultural production and trade by commodity, food consumption, and farm inputs, for 6 countries, 1960-80 with projections to 1991, 1528–178

Economic indicators and components, current data and annual trends, monthly rpt, 23842–1.2

Employment and earnings, detailed data, monthly rpt, 6742–2.3, 6742–2.4, 6742–2.8

Employment and economic conditions, alternative BLS projections to 1995 with selected trends for 1959-82, 6728–29

Agricultural labor

Employment, by sector, major industry group, and sex, selected years 1850-1982, article, 6722–1.425

Employment, earnings, and hours, monthly press release, 6742–5

Employment situation, earnings, hours, and other BLS economic indicators, transcripts of BLS Commissioner's monthly testimony, periodic rpt, 23846–4

Employment, unemployment, and labor force, by demographic and employment characteristics, State, and for 30 metro areas and 11 large cities, 1983, annual rpt, 6744–7

Farm finances, assets, liabilities, income, receipts by commodity and State, and expenses, 1980-83 and trends from 1910, annual rpt, 1544–16

Farm finances, expenses by type, loans by purpose and source, and credit detail by Fed Reserve District, quarterly rpt, 9365–3.10

Farm finances, production, expenses by type, and domestic economic impact, selected years 1972-82 and preliminary 1983-84, annual rpt, 1544–19

Farm hired workers, sociodemographic characteristics, and farm/nonfarm income and workdays, by whether worked in Mar 1981, article, 6722–1.440

Farm labor and productivity, 1929-83, annual rpt, 204–1.8

Farm labor, farms, and labor costs, by labor and farm type and State, with immigrant labor law effect on farm work force, 1978, 1598–192

Farm labor, wages, hours, and perquisites, by State, quarterly rpt, 1631–1

Farm population employment by industry div, and unemployment, by region, 1983, annual rpt, 2544–1

Farm production expenses, by type and State, 1979-82, annual rpt, 1544–18

Farm production inputs, outputs, and productivity, by region, 1939-82, annual rpt, 1544–17

Farm production itemized costs, receipts, and net returns, for 13 crops, 4 livestock types, and milk, by region, 1981-83, annual rpt, 1544–20

Foreign and US agricultural supply/demand, trade, and production, and socioeconomic data, by country, 1950s-77, 1528–179

Foreign population size and growth rates, and latest available benchmark demographic data, by country, 1950-83, biennial rpt, 2324–4

Foreign women sociodemographic, economic, and fertility characteristics, with comparisons to men, by country, 1960s-85, world region rpt series, 2326–15

Handbook of Labor Statistics, employment, earnings, hours, and labor force characteristics, 1982 and trends, detailed annual rpt, 6724–1

Health insurance coverage of farmers, farm population, and managers, by insurance type and selected sociodemographic characteristics, 1976, 1598–191

Immigration, and alien residents, workers, visitors, deportations, and naturalizations, by country of birth, FY81, annual rpt, 6264–2

Index by Subjects and Names

Labor legislation enacted by 48 States, DC, and Guam, 1983, annual summary article, 6722–1.406

Mexico and US range and wildlife characteristics, problems, and research strategies and needs, 1981 conf papers, 1208–197

Minority group and women's employment, by occupational group, SIC 2- to 3-digit industry, State, and SMSA, 1981, annual rpt, 9244–1

Montana and North Dakota coal production, impact of mining on agricultural land availability and on farm income and production costs, by mining tract, 1982 rpt, 1588–79

Occupational manpower needs and supply by detailed occupation, and educational and training program enrollees and grads by detailed field, 1982 and 1995, biennial rpt, 6744–3

Occupational Outlook Handbook, 1984-85 biennial rpt, 6744–1

Productivity growth adjusted for wage and price controls of early 1970s, and regression results, by industry, 1948-81, article, 9381–1.407

Rural area situation and dev, periodic rpt articles, 1502–7

Small farms with sales under $2,500, acreage, finances, operations, and operator characteristics, by region and for 6 States, 1978, 1548–241

Washington State deaths by sex, cause, and detailed occupation, summary data from occupational mortality study, 1950-79, 4248–47

Watermelon grower-to-retailer handling costs and time, by handling phase and method, 1982, 1308–18

Women's employment and earnings, by labor force and socioeconomic characteristics, and compared to men, 1978-81 and trends from 1940s, 6568–29

Workers compensation law provisions of States and Fed Govt, by jurisdiction, as of July 1984, semiannual rpt, 6502–1

see also Agricultural accidents and safety
see also Agricultural productivity
see also Agricultural wages
see also Farm income
see also Migrant workers
see also Seasonal and summer employment
see also under By Occupation in the "Index by Categories"

Agricultural land
see Farms and farmland

Agricultural machinery and equipment

Agricultural Statistics, 1983, annual rpt, 1004–1.2

Air pollutant emission factors, by detailed source, 3rd edition, 1983-84 supplements, 9198–13

Capital (fixed), govt and private nonresidential structures and equipment, residential capital, and consumer-owned durable goods by item, 1980-83, annual article, 2702–1.433

Census of Agriculture, 1982: farms, farmland, production and costs, and operator characteristics, preliminary State and county rpt series, 2330–1

Census of Agriculture, 1982: farms, farmland, production, finances, and operator characteristics, by county, final State rpt series, 2331–1

China economic conditions, agricultural and industrial production, trade, and domestic and foreign investment, 1980-85, 2048–106

Communist, OECD, and selected other countries consumer and producer goods production, 1960s-83, annual rpt, 244–5.8

Cooperatives, membership, activities, and finances, by commodity and selected State, 1900-80 with trends from 1863, 1128–30

County Business Patterns: establishments, employees, and payrolls, by SIC 4-digit industry and county, 1981, annual State rpt series, 2326–8

County Business Patterns: establishments, employees, and payrolls, by SIC 4-digit industry and county, 1982, annual State rpt series, 2326–6

Cuba economic conditions, agricultural and industrial production and distribution, trade, and intl economic relations, 1970-82 and trends from 1957, 248–40

Eastern Europe agricultural production and trade by commodity, food consumption, and farm inputs, for 6 countries, 1960-80 with projections to 1991, 1528–178

Employment, earnings, and hours, by selected SIC 1- to 4-digit industry, State, and for 278 major labor areas, 1939-83, annual rpt, 6744–5

Employment, earnings, and hours, by SIC 4-digit nonfarm industry, monthly 1974-Feb 1984, annual update, 6744–4

Exports and imports of US, by agricultural commodity and country, bimonthly rpt with articles, 1522–1

Exports and imports of US, detailed SIC-based commodities by world area, 1983, annual rpts, 2424–6

Exports and imports of US, totals and as percent of domestic production, by SIC 2- to 5-digit commodity, 1981, annual rpt, 2424–3

Exports, imports, tariffs, and industry operating data for agricultural machinery, 1979-83, TSUSA commodity rpt, 9885–6.68

Exports, imports, tariffs, and industry operating data for miscellaneous machines and equipment, 1979-83, TSUSA commodity rpt, 9885–6.84

Exports of US, detailed commodities by country of destination, monthly rpt, 2422–3

Exports of US, detailed Schedule B commodities by country of destination, 1983, annual rpt, 2424–9

Exports of US, detailed Schedule E commodities by mode of transport and world area and country of destination, 1983, annual rpts, 2424–5

Farm finances, assets, expenses, cash flow, receipts, and loans, selected years 1971-85, annual rpt, 1544–13

Farm finances, assets, liabilities, income, receipts by commodity and State, and expenses, 1980-83 and trends from 1910, annual rpt, 1544–16

Farm finances, expenses by type, loans by purpose and source, and credit detail by Fed Reserve District, quarterly rpt, 9365–3.10

Index by Subjects and Names

Agricultural marketing

Farm finances, production, expenses by type, and domestic economic impact, selected years 1972-82 and preliminary 1983-84, annual rpt, 1544–19

Farm investments, effect of Fed Govt and State tax rates under alternative depreciation methods and inflation rates, 1950-84, 1548–231

Farm investments, effective rates of Federal/State income and State/local property taxes, by category of structure and equipment, for 7 North Central States, 1981-82, 1548–237

Farm production expenditures, detailed items by farm sales size and region, 1983, annual rpt, 1614–3

Farm production inputs, outputs, and productivity, by region, 1939-82, annual rpt, 1544–17

Farm production inputs supply, use, and prices, periodic situation rpt with articles, 1561–16

Farm production, prices, marketing, and trade, by commodity, forecast and current situation, monthly rpt, 1502–4

Farmers prices received for major products and paid for farm inputs and living items, by commodity and State, monthly rpt, 1629–1

Farmers prices received for major products and paid for farm inputs, by commodity and State, 1983, annual rpt, 1629–5

Foreign and US agricultural supply/demand, trade, and production, and socioeconomic data, by country, 1950s-77, 1528–179

Foreign market and trade for farm machinery and equipment, and user industry operations and demand, country market research rpts, 2045–13

Grain storage facility and equipment loans to farmers under CCC program, by State, FY68-84, annual table, 1804–14

Grain storage facility and equipment loans to farmers under CCC program, by State, monthly table, 1802–9

Great Lakes trade, by SITC 3-digit commodity, port, vessel type, world area, and country, 1982, annual rpt, 7744–3

Hog production, producer characteristics, facilities, and marketing, by type and size of enterprise and region, 1975 and 1980, 1568–248

Imports of tillage tools from Brazil, injury to US industry from foreign subsidized products, investigation with background financial and operating data, 1984 rpt, 9886–15.55

Imports of US, detailed Schedule A commodities by country and world area of origin, and mode of transport, 1983, annual rpts, 2424–2

Imports of US, detailed Schedule A commodities by country, monthly rpt, 2422–2

Imports of US, detailed TSUSA commodities by country of origin, 1983, annual rpt, 2424–4

Income tax returns of corporations, detailed income and tax items by industry, 1981, annual rpt, 8304–4

Income tax returns of sole proprietorships, detailed data by industry div and selected industry group, 1981, annual rpt, 8304–7

Income tax returns of sole proprietorships, receipts, deductions by type, payroll, and net income, by major industry, 1982, annual article, 8302–2.413

Industry finances and operations, by SIC 2- to 4-digit industry, 1970s-83 and projected to 1988, annual rpt, 2014–4

Input-output structure of US economy, detailed interindustry transactions for 85 industries, and components of final demand, 1977, article, 2702–1.421

Input-output structure of US economy, detailed interindustry transactions for 537 industries, and components of final demand, 1977 benchmark data, 2708–17

Korea (South) agricultural services projects of AID and Korea govt, economic impacts, 1950s-83, 9916–1.52

Manufacturing census, 1982: financial and operating data, by SIC 2- to 4-digit industry, State, SMSA, and county, preliminary census div rpt series, 2491–3

Manufacturing productivity, hours, and employment indexes, 1958-81, annual rpt, 6824–1.3

Minority group and women employment, by occupational group and SIC 2- to 3-digit industry, 1981, annual rpt, 9244–1.1

North Central States economic indicators, Fed Reserve 7th District monthly rpt, 9375–9

North Central States farm credit conditions and economic devs, Fed Reserve 7th District, biweekly rpt, 9375–10

Occupational injury and illness rates, by SIC 2- to 4-digit industry, 1982, annual rpt, 6844–1

Occupational Outlook Handbook, 1984-85 biennial rpt, 6744–1

OECD trade, total and for 4 major countries, and US trade by country, by commodity, 1972-82, annual world region rpt series, 244–13

Producer prices and indexes, by stage of processing and detailed commodity, monthly rpt, 6762–6

Producer prices and indexes, by stage of processing and detailed commodity, monthly 1983, annual supplement, 6764–2

R&D industry funding and employment of scientists and engineers, by industry group, firm size, and funding source, 1956-82, annual rpt, 9627–21

Shipments, trade, and consumption of farm machinery and lawn and garden equipment, by product, 1982-83, annual Current Industrial Rpt, 2506–12.1

Small farms with sales under $2,500, acreage, finances, operations, and operator characteristics, by region and for 6 States, 1978, 1548–241

Tractor production, shipments, trade, consumption, and firms, by tractor type, monthly Current Industrial Rpt, 2506–12.9

Transportation census, 1982: trucks, by detailed characteristics, miles traveled, and type of product carried, State rpt series, 2573–1

Turkey land improvement and farm machinery manufacturing, effectiveness of AID-Turkish govt joint assistance project, 1968-74, 9916–1.50

Watermelon grower-to-retailer handling costs and time, by handling phase and method, 1982, 1308–18

Wholesale trade census, 1982: employment, establishments, sales by commodity, and payroll, by SIC 4-digit kind of business and State, preliminary rpt series, 2403–1

Agricultural marketing

Advertising (generic) for agricultural commodities, activities and funding by source, selected years 1972-83, 1548–242

Agricultural production, marketing, trade, supply, food consumption, and food and nutrition programs, 1960s-83, annual chartbook, 1504–3

Agricultural Statistics, 1983, annual rpt, 1004–1

Agriculture Fact Book of US, compilation of data for 1983 with trends from 1940, annual rpt, 1004–14

Budget of US, effects of Reagan Admin policy changes, by detailed program, FY85, annual rpt, 104–21

Census of Population, 1980: labor force, by sex, detailed occupation, and region, with comparison to 1970 census, supplementary rpt, 2535–1.12

China economic conditions, agricultural and industrial production, trade, and domestic and foreign investment, 1980-85, 2048–106

Farm finance and credit conditions, forecast 1984, conf papers, annual rpt, 1004–16

Farm finances, production, expenses by type, and domestic economic impact, selected years 1972-82 and preliminary 1983-84, annual rpt, 1544–19

Farm production expenditures, detailed items by farm sales size and region, 1983, annual rpt, 1614–3

Farm production itemized costs, receipts, and net returns, for 13 crops, 4 livestock types, and milk, by region, 1981-83, annual rpt, 1544–20

Farm production, prices, marketing, and trade, by commodity, forecast and current situation, monthly rpt, 1502–4

Farm-retail food prices, marketing cost components, and industry finances and productivity, selected years 1967-83, annual rpt, 1544–9

Fed Govt programs and mgmt cost control proposals, 3-year savings by function and agency, and financial and operating data, 1960s-81, 16908–1.2

Food consumer research and marketing devs, and consumption and price trends, quarterly rpt with articles, 1541–7

Income from farm marketings, monthly by commodity, and by State, 1980-83, annual rpt, 1544–16

Income tax returns of corporations, detailed income and tax items by industry, 1981, annual rpt, 8304–4

Income tax returns of sole proprietorships, receipts, deductions by type, payroll, and net income, by major industry, 1982, annual article, 8302–2.413

Receipts (cash) from marketing of detailed commodities and commodity groups, by State and region, 1979-82, annual rpt, 1544–18

Research (agricultural) expenditures and scientist years, by topic, commodity, and performing organization, FY82, annual rpt, 1744–2

Small farms with sales under $2,500, acreage, finances, operations, and operator characteristics, by region and for 6 States, 1978, 1548–241

Trucking deregulation effects on marketing food and agricultural commodities, 1976-82, 1548–238

Agricultural marketing

Underground economy, household expenditures and participation by type of goods or service and sociodemographic characteristics, with methodology and bibl, 1981 survey, 8308–27

- Wholesale trade census, 1982: employment, establishments, finances, and operations, by SIC 2- to 4-digit kind of business, SMSA, county, and city, State rpt series, 2405–1
- Wholesale trade sales and inventories, by SIC 2- to 3-digit kind of business, monthly rpt, 2413–7
- Wholesale trade sales, inventories, purchases, and gross margins, by SIC 2- to 3-digit kind of business and type of ownership, 1983, annual rpt, 2413–13
- *see also* Agricultural cooperatives
- *see also* Agricultural exports and imports
- *see also* Agricultural prices
- *see also* Agricultural quotas and price supports
- *see also* Agricultural stocks
- *see also* Agricultural surpluses
- *see also* Consumer surveys
- *see also* Food inspection
- *see also* Food prices
- *see also* Market research
- *see also* under names of specific commodities or commodity groups (listed under Agricultural commodities)

Agricultural Marketing Service

- Activities and programs of USDA, by subagency, FY83, annual rpt, 1004–3
- Apple production, marketing, and prices in 4 Appalachian States, 1983/84 crop year, annual rpt, 1311–13
- Bean (dried) prices by State, and foreign and US production, use, stocks, and trade, weekly rpt, 1311–17
- Cost control proposals for Fed Govt programs and mgmt, 3-year savings by function and agency, and financial and operating data, 1960s-81, 16908–1.2, 16908–1.31
- Cotton (long staple) production, prices, exports, stocks, and mill consumption, monthly rpt, 1309–12
- Cotton acreage planted, by State and county, and fiber quality, by variety, 1980-84, annual rpt, 1309–6
- Cotton fiber and processing test results, by staple, region, State, and production area, seasonal biweekly rpt, 1309–3
- Cotton fiber and processing test results, by State, 1983, annual rpt, 1309–4
- Cotton fiber grade, staple, and mike, for upland and American Pima cotton by State, monthly rpt, 1309–11
- Cotton linters production, prices, stocks, use, and trade, monthly rpt, 1309–10
- Cotton prices at selected spot markets, futures prices at NYC exchange, and CCC loan rates, 1983/84 with some trends from 1920, annual rpt, 1309–2
- Cotton prices in 8 spot markets, futures prices at NYC exchange, farm prices, and CCC loan stocks, monthly rpt, 1309–1
- Cotton quality specifications, by State, 1983/84, annual rpt, 1309–7
- Cotton quality, supply, disappearance, and carryover, 1983-84, annual rpt, 1309–8
- Cottonseed quality factors, by State, 1983 crop, annual rpt, 1309–5

Index by Subjects and Names

- Dairy marketing and price data for selected cities, States, and regions, 1983, annual rpt, 1317–1
- Food purchases for domestic aid programs, by commodity, firm, and shipping point or destination, weekly rpt, 1302–3
- Fraud and abuse in USDA programs, audits and investigations, 2nd half FY84, semiannual rpt, 1002–4
- Fruit and vegetable shipments, and arrivals in 23 US and 5 Canada cities, by mode of transport and State or country of origin, 1983, annual rpt series, 1311–4
- Fruit and vegetable shipments by mode of transport, arrivals, and imports, by commodity and State and country of origin, weekly rpt, 1311–3
- Fruit and vegetable truck freight rates to 6 major markets, weekly by commodity and region, with monthly truck-mile costs, 1983, annual rpt, 1311–15
- Fruit and vegetable wholesale prices in NYC, Chicago, and selected shipping points, by crop, 1983, annual rpt, 1311–8
- Grain production, prices, trade, and export inspections by US port and country of destination, by grain type, weekly rpt, 1313–2
- Grain stocks by region and market city, and grain inspected for export, by type, weekly rpt, 1313–4
- Hay prices in 10 market areas, for baled alfalfa and prairie hay, weekly rpt, 1313–5
- Honey and sugar production, prices, trade, stocks, and marketing, and honey loan activity and processing awards of CCC, weekly rpt, 1311–2
- Hops production, stocks, use, and US trade by country, monthly rpt, 1313–7
- Livestock, meat, and wool, market news summary statistics by animal type and market, weekly rpt, 1315–1
- Milk order market major provisions, summary by Federal marketing area, as of July 1984, annual rpt, 1317–11
- Milk order market prices and detailed operations, by State and market area, monthly 1982-83, annual rpt, 1317–3
- Milk order market prices and detailed operations, monthly rpt with articles, 1317–4
- Molasses (feed) production, wholesale prices by market area, and US imports by customs district and country, weekly rpt, 1311–16
- Peach production, marketing, and prices in 4 Southeastern States and Appalachia, 1983, annual rpt, 1311–12
- Peanut production, prices, stocks, exports, use, inspection, and quality, by region and State, selected crop years 1974-83, annual rpt, 1311–5
- Peanut production, prices, trade by country, and stocks, weekly rpt, 1311–1
- Poultry and egg marketing and price data for selected regions, States, and SMSAs, monthly 1983, annual rpt, 1317–2
- Rice market activities, prices, inspections, sales, trade, supply, and use, for US and selected foreign markets, weekly rpt, 1313–8
- Tobacco leaf stocks, and products manufactured and sold, by type, quarterly rpt, 1319–3

- Tobacco prices, marketing, grades, and types for 3 classes, 1983 crop and 1983/84 season, annual rpt series, 1319–5
- Tobacco production, prices, stocks, taxes by State, and trade and foreign production by country, 1983, annual rpt, 1319–1
- Watermelon grower-to-retailer handling costs and time, by handling phase and method, 1982, 1308–18
- Wheat (durum) acreage, production, prices, stocks, use, and US and Canada exports by country, quarterly rpt, 1313–6
- Wool market foreign and domestic prices and trade, weekly and biweekly rpt, 1315–2
- *see also* Packers and Stockyards Administration

Agricultural pests

see Pests and pest control

Agricultural policies

- Advertising (generic) for agricultural commodities, activities and funding by source, selected years 1972-83, 1548–242
- Agricultural economics technical research, quarterly journal, 1502–3
- Agricultural policies of US effect on trade, with US and foreign trade by commodity and grain stocks by world area, various periods 1979-83, 1528–183
- *Agricultural Statistics, 1983,* annual rpt, 1004–1
- Developing countries food supply policies, with farm sector data, tariff income, and prices and imports of 5 grains, for 21 countries, 1960s-81, 1528–168
- Economic Research Service activities, funding, and staff in DC and other locations, by detailed branch and section, FY83, annual rpt, 1504–7
- Economic Research Service activities, funding, and staff in DC and other locations, by detailed branch and section, FY84, annual rpt, 1504–6
- Farm finance and credit conditions, forecast 1984, conf papers, annual rpt, 1004–16
- Farm policies and objectives, farm income, and net family income and net worth per farm, by farm sales class, 1982, article, 9381–1.411
- Fed Govt policy issues effect on agricultural and food prices, income, and trade, and crop support levels by program, Nov 1984, semiannual rpt, 1542–6
- Fed Govt programs and mgmt cost control proposals, 3-year savings by function and agency, and financial and operating data, 1960s-81, 16908–1.2
- *Foreign Agriculture,* production, consumption, and policies, and US export dev and promotion, monthly rpt, 1922–2
- Research (agricultural) expenditures and scientist years, by topic, commodity, and performing organization, FY82, annual rpt, 1744–2
- Soil conservation program policies of Fed Govt, attitudes of farmers and ranchers in 6 central US counties, 1982/83 survey, hearing, 25168–61
- *see also* Agricultural credit
- *see also* Agricultural exports and imports
- *see also* Agricultural finance
- *see also* Agricultural marketing
- *see also* Agricultural prices
- *see also* Agricultural quotas and price supports

Index by Subjects and Names

Agricultural production

see also Agricultural subsidies
see also Food prices
see also Land reform

Agricultural prices

- Agricultural economics technical research, quarterly journal, 1502–3
- Agricultural production, marketing, trade, supply, food consumption, and food and nutrition programs, 1960s-83, annual chartbook, 1504–3
- Agricultural situation and farm-related topics, monthly rpt, 1502–6
- *Agricultural Statistics, 1983,* annual rpt, 1004–1
- Business statistics, detailed data for major industries and economic indicators, *Survey of Current Business,* monthly rpt, 2702–1.2
- CCC commodities for sale, and prices, monthly press release, 1802–4
- Communist, OECD, and selected other countries economic statistics, 1960s-83, annual rpt, 244–5.2
- Crop and livestock supply/demand, farm and market prices, and commodity program operations, for selected commodities, 1983 and outlook for 1984, annual article, 9381–1.402
- Crop prices and production values, for detailed crops by State, 1981-83, annual rpt, 1621–2
- Crop Reporting Board commodity publications, 1984 releases, annual listing, 1614–1
- Economic and population time series data frequently used in statistical demand analyses, 1941-1982, annual rpt, 1544–21
- Economic indicators and components, current data and annual trends, monthly rpt, 23842–1.4
- Farm finance and credit conditions, forecast 1984, conf papers, annual rpt, 1004–16
- Farm production, prices, marketing, and trade, by commodity, forecast and current situation, monthly rpt, 1502–4
- Farm-retail food prices, marketing cost components, and industry finances and productivity, selected years 1967-83, annual rpt, 1544–9
- Farmers prices received for major products and paid for farm inputs and living items, by commodity and State, monthly rpt, 1629–1
- Farmers prices received for major products and paid for farm inputs, by commodity and State, 1983, annual rpt, 1629–5
- Fed Govt policy issues effect on agricultural and food prices, income, and trade, and crop support levels by program, Nov 1984, semiannual rpt, 1542–6
- Foreign agricultural production, prices, and trade, by country, 1983 and outlook for 1984/85, annual world region rpt series, 1524–4
- Foreign and US agricultural production, prices, trade, and consumption, quarterly rpt with articles, 1522–3
- Foreign and US agricultural supply/demand and production data, for selected US and world crops, and for US livestock and dairy products, periodic rpt, 1522–5
- Foreign and US indexes of consumer, producer, and major commodity prices, nonfarm wages, and currency value, US and 4 countries, bimonthly rpt, 2042–11

Foreign and US prices and US import prices, for selected commodities, bimonthly rpt with articles, 1522–1.1

- Foreign exchange rate appreciation of dollar, effects on exports, stocks, and prices of wheat, corn, and soybeans, 1980-82 and for hypothetical 20-year period, 1528–174
- Index of farm prices, and exports, 1972-82, 1528–172
- Indexes of prices received and paid by farmers, 1946-83, annual rpt, 204–1.8
- North Central States economic indicators, Fed Reserve 7th District monthly rpt, 9375–9
- North Central States farm credit conditions and economic devs, Fed Reserve 7th District, biweekly rpt, 9375–10
- OECD economic indicators, for US and 6 countries, biweekly rpt, 242–4
- Producer Price Index, by major commodity group and subgroup, and processing stage, monthly press release, 6762–5
- Producer prices and indexes, by stage of processing and detailed commodity, monthly rpt, 6762–6
- Producer prices and indexes, by stage of processing and detailed commodity, monthly 1983, annual supplement, 6764–2
- Southeastern States agricultural conditions, Fed Reserve 8th District, quarterly rpt, 9391–13
- Southeastern States financial and economic devs, Fed Reserve 6th District, monthly rpt with articles, 9371–1
- Western States economic indicators, Fed Reserve 12th District, quarterly rpt, 9393–1.3

see also Agricultural quotas and price supports

see also Food prices

see also under names of specific commodities or commodity groups (listed under Agricultural commodities)

Agricultural production

- Acid rain causes and effects, air pollutant emissions by source, and control costs, by region and State, selected years 1977-83 and projected to 2000, 26358–104
- Acreage planted and harvested, by crop and State, 1982-83 and planned as of June 1984, annual rpt, 1621–23
- Aerial survey R&D publications, and sources of natural resource and environmental data gathered by air- and spacecraft, quarterly listing, 9502–7
- Agricultural economics technical research, quarterly journal, 1502–3
- Agricultural production, marketing, trade, supply, food consumption, and food and nutrition programs, 1960s-83, annual chartbook, 1504–3
- Agricultural situation and farm-related topics, monthly rpt, 1502–6
- Agricultural Stabilization and Conservation Service programs, annual commodity fact sheet series, 1806–4
- *Agricultural Statistics, 1983,* annual rpt, 1004–1
- *Agriculture Fact Book of US,* compilation of data for 1983 with trends from 1940, annual rpt, 1004–14
- Biotechnology commercial uses, R&D funding and output, controls, and industry

financial and operating data, for US and 5 countries, 1970s-83 and estimated 1984-85, 26358–98

- Business statistics, detailed data for major industries and economic indicators, *Survey of Current Business,* monthly rpt, 2702–1.11
- Census of Agriculture, 1982: farms, farmland, production and costs, and operator characteristics, preliminary State and county rpt series, 2330–1
- Census of Agriculture, 1982: farms, farmland, production, finances, and operator characteristics, by county, final State rpt series, 2331–1
- Coastal environmental characteristics, fish, wildlife, and use, and population socioeconomic data, for individual areas, series, 5506–4
- Crop production value and average prices received by farmers, for detailed crops by State, 1981-83, annual rpt, 1621–2
- Crop Reporting Board commodity publications, 1984 releases, annual listing, 1614–1
- Exports and imports of US, totals and as percent of domestic production, by SIC 2- to 5-digit commodity, 1981, annual rpt, 2424–3
- Farm finance and credit conditions, forecast 1984, conf papers, annual rpt, 1004–16
- Farm finance and credit conditions, forecast 1984, conf summary, annual rpt, 9264–9
- Farm output and productivity indexes, 1929-83, annual rpt, 204–1.8
- Farm production inputs, outputs, and productivity, by region, 1939-82, annual rpt, 1544–17
- Farm production, prices, marketing, and trade, by commodity, forecast and current situation, monthly rpt, 1502–4
- Farms, production, acreage, and related data, by selected crop and State, monthly rpt, 1621–1
- Foreign and US agricultural production, prices, trade, and consumption, quarterly rpt with articles, 1522–3
- Foreign and US agricultural production, trade, and climatic devs, weekly press release, 1922–4
- Input-output structure of US economy, detailed interindustry transactions for 537 industries, and components of final demand, 1977 benchmark data, 2708–17
- Mexico and US range and wildlife characteristics, problems, and research strategies and needs, 1981 conf papers, 1208–197
- Montana and North Dakota coal production, impact of mining on agricultural land availability and on farm income and production costs, by mining tract, 1982 rpt, 1588–79
- Natl income and product, comprehensive accounts and components, *Survey of Current Business,* monthly rpt, 2702–1.21, 2702–1.22
- Reclamation programs of Fed Govt in western US, finances and operations by project and State, 1981-82, annual rpts, 5824–1
- Research (agricultural) expenditures and scientist years, by topic, commodity, and performing organization, FY82, annual rpt, 1744–2

Agricultural production

Small farms with sales under $2,500, acreage, finances, operations, and operator characteristics, by region and for 6 States, 1978, 1548–241

Southeastern States agricultural conditions, Fed Reserve 8th District, quarterly rpt, 9391–13

Statistical Abstract of US, social, political, and economic data, 1950s-83 and trends, annual rpt, 2324–1.3

TTPI socioeconomic, health, and govtl data, by TTPI govt, FY83 and selected trends, detailed annual rpt, 7004–6

Weather conditions and effect on agriculture, by US region, State, and city, and world area, weekly rpt, 2152–2

Weather events socioeconomic impacts and costs, heating and cooling degree days, and housing energy bills, by census div and State, monthly rpt, 2152–12

Weather phenomena and storm characteristics, casualties, and property damage, by State, monthly listing, 2152–3

see also Agricultural production costs

see also Agricultural productivity

see also Agricultural stocks

see also Aquaculture

see also Fertilizers

see also Food supply

see also Foreign agriculture

see also under names of specific commodities or commodity groups (listed under Agricultural commodities)

Agricultural production costs

Agricultural production, marketing, trade, supply, food consumption, and food and nutrition programs, 1960s-83, annual chartbook, 1504–3

Agricultural situation and farm-related topics, monthly rpt, 1502–6

Agricultural Statistics, 1983, annual rpt, 1004–1

Agriculture Fact Book of US, compilation of data for 1983 with trends from 1940, annual rpt, 1004–14

Census of Agriculture, 1982: farms, farmland, production and costs, and operator characteristics, preliminary State and county rpt series, 2330–1

Census of Agriculture, 1982: farms, farmland, production, finances, and operator characteristics, by county, final State rpt series, 2331–1

Farm finance and credit conditions, forecast 1984, conf papers, annual rpt, 1004–16

Farm finances, assets, expenses, cash flow, receipts, and loans, selected years 1971-85, annual rpt, 1544–13

Farm finances, assets, liabilities, income, receipts by commodity and State, and expenses, 1980-83 and trends from 1910, annual rpt, 1544–16

Farm finances, expenses by type, loans by purpose and source, and credit detail by Fed Reserve District, quarterly rpt, 9365–3.10

Farm finances, production, expenses by type, and domestic economic impact, selected years 1972-82 and preliminary 1983-84, annual rpt, 1544–19

Farm production expenditures, detailed items by farm sales size and region, 1983, annual rpt, 1614–3

Farm production expenses, by type and State, 1979-82 and trends from 1950, annual rpt, 1544–18

Farm production inputs supply, use, and prices, periodic situation rpt with articles, 1561–16

Farm production itemized costs, receipts, and net returns, for 13 crops, 4 livestock types, and milk, by region, 1981-83, annual rpt, 1544–20

Farm production, prices, marketing, and trade, by commodity, forecast and current situation, monthly rpt, 1502–4

Farm-retail food prices, marketing cost components, and industry finances and productivity, selected years 1967-83, annual rpt, 1544–9

Farmers prices received for major products and paid for farm inputs and living items, by commodity and State, monthly rpt, 1629–1

Farmers prices received for major products and paid for farm inputs, by commodity and State, 1983, annual rpt, 1629–5

Foreign and US agricultural supply/demand, trade, and production, and socioeconomic data, by country, 1950s-77, 1528–179

Income tax returns of corporations, detailed income and tax items by industry, 1981, annual rpt, 8304–4

Montana and North Dakota coal production, impact of mining on agricultural land availability and on farm income and production costs, by mining tract, 1982 rpt, 1588–79

Natural gas price changes effect on farm income and fertilizer use, 1980 and projected to 1990, 1548–240

Natural gas price decontrol alternatives effect on farm production by crop, prices, and fertilizer use and costs, 1982-90, model results, 1548–239

North Central States agricultural credit conditions, earnings, and expenditures, Fed Reserve 9th District, quarterly rpt, 9383–11

Pesticide use for crops and livestock, acreage treated, application methods, and use of safety equipment and professional services, 1982 survey, 1588–76

Small farms with sales under $2,500, acreage, finances, operations, and operator characteristics, by region and for 6 States, 1978, 1548–241

Southeastern States agricultural conditions, Fed Reserve 8th District, quarterly rpt, 9391–13

Southeastern States farm credit conditions and real estate values, Fed Reserve 5th District, quarterly rpt, 9389–17

Southeastern States soil conservation and water pollution reduction participants, costs, and acreage, by conservation method and State, selected years 1973-82, 1588–84

see also Agricultural marketing

see also Agricultural production

see also under names of specific commodities or commodity groups (listed under Agricultural commodities)

Agricultural productivity

Agricultural Statistics, 1983, annual rpt, 1004–1.2

Agriculture Fact Book of US, compilation of data for 1983 with trends from 1940, annual rpt, 1004–14

Index by Subjects and Names

China economic conditions, agricultural and industrial production, trade, and domestic and foreign investment, 1980-85, 2048–106

Farm output and productivity indexes, 1929-83, annual rpt, 204–1.8

Farm production inputs, land mgmt, and environmental effects, for 4 crops, 1940s-80 and projected to 2010, 9188–94

Farm production inputs, outputs, and productivity, by region, 1939-82, annual rpt, 1544–17

Farms, production, acreage, and related data, by selected crop and State, monthly rpt, 1621–1

Foreign agricultural production, prices, and trade, by country, 1983 and outlook for 1984/85, annual world region rpt series, 1524–4

Foreign and US agricultural supply/demand and production data, for selected US and world crops, and for US livestock and dairy products, periodic rpt, 1522–5

Foreign and US production, acreage, and yield for selected crops, forecasts by selected world region and country, FAS monthly rpt, 1925–28

Productivity of labor and capital, growth by SIC 1- to 2-digit industry, and measurement methods and bibl, various periods 1948-78 with trends from 1800, 2218–69

Research (agricultural) expenditures and scientist years, by topic, commodity, and performing organization, FY82, annual rpt, 1744–2

Research and extension program needs, and foreign and US agricultural supply/demand indicators by commodity and world area, 1950s-2020, 1008–47

see also Agricultural production costs

see also Fertilizers

see also under names of specific commodities or commodity groups (listed under Agricultural commodities)

Agricultural quotas and price supports

Acreage reduction payment-in-kind program costs, requirements, producer and diversion payments, and loan interest forgiven, by crop, as of 1983, hearing, 21788–138

Agricultural Stabilization and Conservation Service payment-in-kind acreage reduction program, ineligible participants and acreage, and estimated incorrect payments, by State and selected county, 1983, 1008–46

Agricultural Stabilization and Conservation Service producer payments under 26 programs, monthly rpt, 1802–10

Agricultural Stabilization and Conservation Service programs, annual commodity fact sheet series, 1806–4

Agricultural Statistics, 1983, annual rpt, 1004–1

Argentina grain and oilseed production, effect of agricultural price regulation, 1947-80, 1528–170

Budget of US, CBO analysis of revenue and spending alternatives and projections of economic indicators, FY85-89, annual rpt, 26304–3.3

Budget of US, effects of Reagan Admin policy changes, by detailed program, FY85, annual rpt, 104–21

Index by Subjects and Names

Agricultural sciences

Budget of US, receipts, outlays, and budget authority, by function and agency, FY84-89 revised estimates, midsession review of FY85 budget, annual rpt, 104–7

CCC finances and program operations, FY83, annual rpt, 1824–1

CCC loan activities by commodity, and agency operating results, monthly press release, 1802–7

Cost control proposals for Fed Govt programs and mgmt, CBO and GAO estimates of savings by function and agency, FY85-89, 26308–45

Cost control proposals for Fed Govt programs and mgmt, 3-year savings by function and agency, and financial and operating data, 1960s-81, 16908–1.2

Cotton (upland) acreage base, and base acreage planted and in conservation use, by region and State, 1982 and 1984, article, 1561–1.403

Cotton import quotas and imports under quota, by type and staple length, 1981/82-1982/83, FAS annual rpt, 1925–4.3

Cotton land diversion and deficiency payment program participation, acreage, and effect on yields, income, and expenses, 1982-85, article, 1561–1.404

Crop and livestock supply/demand, farm and market prices, and commodity program operations, for selected commodities, 1983 and outlook for 1984, annual article, 9381–1.402

Crop support levels by program, and Fed Govt policy issues effect on agricultural and food prices, income, and trade, Nov 1984, semiannual rpt, 1542–6

Dairy marketing and price data for selected cities, States, and regions, 1983, annual rpt, 1317–1

Dairy production by State, stocks, prices, and CCC price support activities, by product type, monthly rpt, 1627–3

Dairy products price support purchases, sales, donations, and inventories of CCC, monthly rpt, 1802–2

Developing countries food supply policies, with farm sector data, tariff income, and prices and imports of 5 grains, for 21 countries, 1960s-81, 1528–168

EC food supply/demand and market and support prices, with exchange rates, fertilizer price index, GDP, and population, by country, 1960-83, 1528–173

Farm finances, assets, expenses, cash flow, receipts, and loans, selected years 1971-85, annual rpt, 1544–13

Farm price support programs for 5 crops, and effects of alternative Fed Govt policies, FY56-83 with projections to FY88, 26306–6.71

Farm production by crop, prices, and fertilizer use and costs, effect of natural gas price decontrol alternatives, 1982-90, model results, 1548–239

Farm production, prices, marketing, and trade, by commodity, forecast and current situation, monthly rpt, 1502–4

Fed Govt aid to State and local govts, expenditures, and direct payments, by program, agency, and State, FY83, annual rpt, 2464–2

Fed Govt grants-in-aid for 13 program areas, FY82-84, annual article, 10042–1.402

Fed Govt loans, grants, and tax benefits to business, by program and economic sector, projected FY84-88 with effective tax rates for FY80-82, 26306–6.70

Feed grain production, acreage, stocks, use, trade, prices, and price supports, periodic situation rpt with articles, 1561–4

Grain and soybean import prices at Rotterdam, and EC import levies and supports, by type of grain, weekly press release, 1922–4

Grain loan support programs of USDA, activity and status by type of grain and State, monthly rpt, 1802–3

Grains and feed trade and export and support prices, US and major producer countries, FAS monthly rpt, 1925–2.4

Honey and sugar production, prices, trade, stocks, and marketing, and honey loan activity and processing awards of CCC, weekly rpt, 1311–2

Imports injury to price-supported US agricultural industries, investigations with background financial and operating data for selected products, series, 9886–10

Income of farm operators from Fed Govt programs, payments by State, 1979-82, annual rpt, 1544–18

Milk and dairy production, prices, consumption, and trade, quarterly situation rpt with articles, 1561–2

Milk order market major provisions, summary by Federal marketing area, as of July 1984, annual rpt, 1317–11

Milk order market prices and detailed operations, by State and market area, monthly 1982-83, annual rpt, 1317–3

Milk order market prices and detailed operations, monthly rpt with articles, 1317–4

Milk price support alternatives, effects on production, use, prices, and farm receipts, projected 1983/84-1988/89 and actual 1982/83, 1568–246

Milk price supports effect on production, use, prices, and farm receipts, by region and State, 1940s-83 and alternative projections to 1988/89, 1568–245

Peanut production, prices, trade by country, and stocks, weekly rpt, 1311–1

Portugal agricultural subsidies, profits, marketing margins, and consumer prices, by commodity or product, and effects of prospective EC membership, 1981, 1528–171

Prune (dried) production, trade, consumption, and stocks of US and 2 countries, EC subsidies, and US exports by country, 1982/83-1984/85, article, 1925–34.435

Rice price support loan activity of CCC, 1970-83, semiannual rpt, 1561–8.5

Tobacco production, trade, consumption, marketing, taxes, and price supports, quarterly situation rpt with articles, 1561–10

Tobacco quotas, support levels, and loan receipts, by type of tobacco, 1977-83, annual rpt, 1319–1

Tobacco support program of CCC, itemized costs, adequacy of assessed producer payments, and crop loans and accrued

interest, for flue-cured and burley tobacco, various periods 1981-84, GAO rpt, 26113–117

USDA agricultural surplus direct purchase program finances, and purchases and food received by schools by commodity, various periods 1936-83, 1548–243

Wheat and rye price supports and loan rates, periodic situation rpt with articles, 1561–12

Agricultural Research Service

Activities and programs of USDA, by subagency, FY83, annual rpt, 1004–3

Consumer goods prices and supplies, family finance, and home economics, quarterly rpt with articles, 1702–1

Dairy Herd Improvement Program activities and research, periodic rpt, 1702–2

Funding for agricultural research from Fed Govt and States, by region, State, and outlying area, FY78-82, GAO rpt, 26113–111

Sedimentation control, surveillance, and research activity of Fed Govt, by project, agency, region, and State, 1982, annual rpt, 5664–9

see also Cooperative State Research Service

Agricultural sciences

Agricultural economics technical research, quarterly journal, 1502–3

Budget of US, effects of Reagan Admin policy changes, by detailed program, FY85, annual rpt, 104–21

Carbon dioxide atmospheric levels, climatic effects and impacts of fossil and synthetic fuels use, deforestation, and land use patterns, research rpt series, 3406–3

Census of Population, 1980: detailed socioeconomic and demographic characteristics, by age, sex, race, Hispanic origin, occupation, and industry, State rpt series, 2531–4

Dairy Herd Improvement Program activities and research, periodic rpt, 1702–2

DOE R&D projects and funding at natl labs, universities, and other instns, FY83, annual summary rpt, 3004–18.1

Expenditures and scientist years for agricultural research, by topic, commodity, and performing organization, FY82, annual rpt, 1744–2

Fishery resources mgmt and R&D, Fed Govt grants by project and resulting publications, 1983, annual listing, 2164–3

Meteorological services and research of Fed Govt, programs and funding by agency, FY84-85, annual rpt, 2144–2

Occupational Outlook Handbook, 1984-85 biennial rpt, 6744–1

R&D-employed scientists and engineers salaries by degree, type of establishment, age, experience, and field, 1984, annual rpt, 3004–1

R&D expenditures by higher education instns and federally funded centers, by field, source of funds, instn, and State, FY82, annual rpt, 9627–13

R&D expenditures by source, and scientists education and employment, detailed data by field, selected years 1953-84, annual rpt, 9624–18

R&D expenditures of higher education instns, and science and engineering employment and grad students, by field, 1972-83, biennial rpt, 9627–24

Agricultural sciences

R&D Fed Govt facilities and services available for private sector use, by field of science, 1984 biennial listing, 2224–4

R&D Fed Govt funding, by function, agency, and program, selected years FY80-84 and proposed FY85, 26308–46

R&D Fed Govt funding for all performers, by field and supporting agency, selected years FY60-84, annual rpt, 9627–20

Research and extension program needs, and foreign and US agricultural supply/demand indicators by commodity and world area, 1950s-2020, 1008–47

Research funding for agriculture from Fed Govt and States, by region, State, and outlying area, FY78-82, GAO rpt, 26113–111

Research grants awarded competitively by USDA for agricultural science, food and nutrition, and energy dev, FY83, annual listing, 1744–1

Satellite Landsat system proposed transfer to private sector, uses and product sales by user type, and university programs and personnel by instn, 1973-85, 26358–100

Science and engineering doctoral degree recipients, by field, sex, race, age, citizenship, postgrad employment and study status, State, and instn, 1960-82, 9626–6.16

Science and engineering grads of 1980-81, employment characteristics or grad enrollment, by degree level, field, sex, and race, 1982, 9627–25

Scientists and engineers employed at universities and colleges, by field, sex, State, and instn, Jan 1983 and selected trends from 1967, annual survey, 9627–11

Scientists and engineers employed in energy-related fields, supply/demand and effects of R&D funding, by energy type, employer type, field, and age, 1962-91, annual rpt, 3004–19

Scientists, engineers, and technicians employed in private industry, by occupation and industry group, 1980-81, biennial rpt, 9627–23

Scientists, engineers, and technicians needed in defense and nondefense industries, and supply/demand, by field, 1981-87, 9628–71

Soviet Union-US science and technology exchange projects, man-hours, and funding, by Fed Govt agency and activity type, FY81-82, 7008–41

TVA activities, financial and operating data by program and facility, and power sales by customer, FY83, annual rpt, 9804–1

see also Agricultural education

see also Agricultural innovations

see also Biomass energy

Agricultural services

Census of Agriculture, 1982: farms, farmland, production and costs, and operator characteristics, preliminary State and county rpt series, 2330–1

Census of Agriculture, 1982: farms, farmland, production, finances, and operator characteristics, by county, final State rpt series, 2331–1

Census of Population, 1980: detailed socioeconomic and demographic characteristics, by age, sex, race, Hispanic origin, occupation, and industry, State rpt series, 2531–4

Cooperatives, membership, activities, and finances, by commodity and selected State, 1900-80 with trends from 1863, 1128–30

Cooperatives, membership, and activities, by type of service, commodity, and State, FY51-1982, annual survey rpt, 1124–1

Cotton ginning charges and related data, by State, 1983/84, annual rpt, 1564–3

County Business Patterns: establishments, employees, and payrolls, by SIC 4-digit industry and county, 1981, annual State rpt series, 2326–8

County Business Patterns: establishments, employees, and payrolls, by SIC 4-digit industry and county, 1982, annual State rpt series, 2326–6

Earnings by major industry group, and personal income per capita and by source, by region and State, 1929-82, 2708–40

Employment, wages, and hours of agricultural service workers, by selected State, quarterly rpt, 1631–1

Farm finances, assets, liabilities, income, receipts by commodity and State, and expenses, 1980-83 and trends from 1910, annual rpt, 1544–16

Farm finances, expenses by type, loans by purpose and source, and credit detail by Fed Reserve District, quarterly rpt, 9365–3.10

Farm finances, production, expenses by type, and domestic economic impact, selected years 1972-82 and preliminary 1983-84, annual rpt, 1544–19

Farm production expenditures, detailed items by farm sales size and region, 1983, annual rpt, 1614–3

Farm production itemized costs, receipts, and net returns, for 13 crops, 4 livestock types, and milk, by region, 1981-83, annual rpt, 1544–20

Foreign direct investment in US, major investors and investments by SIC 4-digit industry, transaction type and value, and location, 1983, annual rpt, 2044–20

Income tax returns of partnerships, detailed data by industry, 1981 estimates, annual article, 8302–2.404

Income tax returns of sole proprietorships, detailed data by industry div and selected industry group, 1981, annual rpt, 8304–7

Income tax returns of sole proprietorships, receipts, deductions by type, payroll, and net income, by major industry, 1982, annual article, 8302–2.413

Occupational injury and illness rates, by SIC 2- to 4-digit industry, 1982, annual rpt, 6844–1

Pesticide use for crops and livestock, acreage treated, application methods, and use of safety equipment and professional services, 1982 survey, 1588–76

see also Agricultural innovations

see also Veterinary medicine

Agricultural Stabilization and Conservation Service

Acreage reduction and diversion programs for wheat, feed grains, and cotton, base acreage enrolled, by State, irregular rpt, suspended, 1802–12

Acreage reduction payment-in-kind program, ineligible participants and acreage, and incorrect payments, by State and selected county, 1983, 1008–46

Index by Subjects and Names

Activities and programs of USDA, by subagency, FY83, annual rpt, 1004–3

Agricultural Statistics, 1983, annual rpt, 1004–1.2

Appalachia land stabilization and conservation program activities and funding, for 13 States, annual rpt, discontinued, 1804–3

CCC commodities for sale, and prices, monthly press release, 1802–4

CCC loan activities by commodity, and agency operating results, monthly press release, 1802–7

Computer systems for ASCS field offices, costs and savings by component, FY84-92, GAO rpt, 26125–27

Conservation practices in rural areas, Agricultural Conservation Program participation and payments, by State, FY83, annual rpt, 1804–7

Dairy products price support purchases, sales, donations, and inventories of CCC, monthly rpt, 1802–2

Emergency Conservation Program participation and payments for farmland restoration from natural disaster, by practice and State, FY83, annual rpt, 1804–22

Fertilizer production and trade, and consumption by region and State, 1983, annual rpt, 1804–6

Forestry Incentives Program, Fed Govt cost-sharing funds for private timberland improvement, by region and State, monthly rpt, 1802–11

Fraud and abuse in USDA programs, audits and investigations, 2nd half FY84, semiannual rpt, 1002–4

Grain loan support programs of USDA, activity and status by type of grain and State, monthly rpt, 1802–3

Pesticide production, trade, and sales, by type, 1980-82, annual rpt, 1804–5

Producer payments under 26 programs, monthly rpt, 1802–10

Programs of ASCS, annual commodity fact sheet series, 1806–4

Storage facility and equipment loans to farmers under CCC grain program, by State, FY68-84, annual table, 1804–14

Storage facility and equipment loans to farmers under CCC grain program, by State, monthly table, 1802–9

Water Bank Program agreements, acreage, and Fed Govt payments, by State, FY72-83, annual rpt, 1804–21

Water Bank Program agreements, acreage, and Fed Govt payments, by State, monthly rpt, 1802–5

see also Commodity Credit Corp.

Agricultural stocks

Acreage reduction payment-in-kind program costs, requirements, producer and diversion payments, and loan interest forgiven, by crop, as of 1983, hearing, 21788–138

Agricultural Stabilization and Conservation Service programs, annual commodity fact sheet series, 1806–4

Agricultural Statistics, 1983, annual rpt, 1004–1

Argentina grain production, exports by firm, storage by facility type and port, and shipments to ports by mode of transport, by grain type, selected years 1954-81, 1528–185

Index by Subjects and Names

Agricultural subsidies

Bean (dried) prices by State, and foreign and US production, use, stocks, and trade, weekly rpt, 1311–17

Catfish raised on farms, production, inventory, sales, prices, and imports, monthly release, 1631–14

Cattle and calves for beef and milk, inventory and value by State, 1982-84, semiannual press release, 1623–1

Cattle and calves on feed, inventory and marketings by State, monthly release, 1623–2

Census of Agriculture, 1982: farms, farmland, production and costs, and operator characteristics, preliminary State and county rpt series, 2330–1

Census of Agriculture, 1982: farms, farmland, production, finances, and operator characteristics, by county, final State rpt series, 2331–1

Coffee production, trade and quotas, and consumption, by country, with US and intl prices, FAS periodic circular, 1925–5

Cold storage food stocks by commodity and census div, and warehouse cold storage space in use, by State, monthly rpt, 1631–5

Cold storage food stocks of 77 commodities, by region, 1983, annual rpt, 1631–11

Cotton (long staple) production, prices, exports, stocks, and mill consumption, monthly rpt, 1309–12

Cotton linters production, prices, stocks, use, and trade, monthly rpt, 1309–10

Cotton production and trade, foreign and US, FAS monthly and annual rpt series, 1925–4

Cotton quality, supply, disappearance, and carryover, 1983-84, annual rpt, 1309–8

Crop Reporting Board commodity publications, 1984 releases, annual listing, 1614–1

Dairy products, commercial and Fed Govt storage holdings of butter, cheese, and nonfat dry milk, monthly rpt, 1317–4.2

Dairy products foreign and US production, consumption, and trade, FAS annual circular series, 1925–10

Dairy products holdings, total and Fed Govt, and USDA purchases, by region, monthly 1983, annual rpt, 1317–1.1

Developing countries food production and needs, and related economic trends and outlook, for 67 countries, 1980-86, annual rpt, 1524–6

Farm finance and credit conditions, forecast 1984, conf summary, annual rpt, 9264–9

Farm finances, assets, liabilities, income, receipts by commodity and State, and expenses, 1980-83 and trends from 1910, annual rpt, 1544–16

Farm finances, expenses by type, loans by purpose and source, and credit detail by Fed Reserve District, quarterly rpt, 9365–3.10

Farm finances, production, expenses by type, and domestic economic impact, selected years 1972-82 and preliminary 1983-84, annual rpt, 1544–19

Farm production, prices, marketing, and trade, by commodity, forecast and current situation, monthly rpt, 1502–4

Fats, oils, and related products foreign and US production and trade, FAS monthly and annual circular series, 1925–1

Feed grain and feedstuff production, prices, trade, and stocks, by feed type, weekly rpt, 1313–2

Feed grain production, acreage, stocks, use, trade, prices, and price supports, periodic situation rpt with articles, 1561–4

Fertilizer stocks, by season, 1983-84, annual rpt, 1804–6.1

Foreign and US agricultural supply/demand and production data, for selected US and world crops, and for US livestock and dairy products, periodic rpt, 1522–5

Foreign exchange rate appreciation of dollar, effects on exports, stocks, and prices of wheat, corn, and soybeans, 1980-82 and for hypothetical 20-year period, 1528–174

Fruit and nut production, prices, trade, stocks, and use, by selected crop, periodic situation rpt with articles, 1561–6

Grain and wheat stocks, by world region, average 1979-83, 1528–183

Grain cooperatives storage and handling facilities, sales, exports, and financial condition, selected years 1974-82, 1128–31

Grain futures contracts, stocks in deliverable position by type and grade, weekly tables, 11922–4

Grain, oilseed, and hay stocks on and off farms, and capacity of off-farm grain storage facilities, by State, 1978-83, 1641–17

Grain production, trade, stocks, and prices, foreign and US, FAS monthly and annual rpt series, 1925–2

Grain stocks by region and market city, and grain inspected for export, by type, weekly rpt, 1313–4

Grain stocks on and off farms and total in all positions, by crop, periodic rpt, 1621–4

Grain stocks, supply deviation, and effect on use, trade, and prices, for US and selected countries, various periods 1960-83, 1528–184

Hog production, producer characteristics, facilities, and marketing, by type and size of enterprise and region, 1975 and 1980, 1568–248

Honey and sugar production, prices, trade, stocks, and marketing, and honey loan activity and processing awards of CCC, weekly rpt, 1311–2

Hops production, stocks, use, and US trade by country, monthly rpt, 1313–7

Hops stocks held by growers, dealers, and brewers, Sept 1984, semiannual release, 1621–8

Imports injury to price-supported US agricultural industries, investigations with background financial and operating data for selected products, series, 9886–10

Livestock, meat, poultry, and egg production, prices, trade, stocks, and consumption, periodic situation rpt, 1561–7

Milk and dairy production, prices, consumption, and trade, quarterly situation rpt with articles, 1561–2

Milk pasteurized by ultra-high temperature, sales, production, stocks, costs, market shares, and prices, 1980, 1568–247

Mushroom imports injury to US industry, and stocks, production, sales, trade, and consumption, quarterly rpt, 9882–5

Peanut production, prices, stocks, exports, use, inspection, and quality, by region and State, selected crop years 1974-83, annual rpt, 1311–5

Peanut production, prices, trade by country, and stocks, weekly rpt, 1311–1

Peanut stocks, millings, and processing, Feb-July 1984, semiannual rpt, 1621–6

Potato and sweet potato production, stocks, and prices, 1982-83, annual rpt, 1621–11

Potato and sweet potato production, stocks, prices, acreage, and yield, 1978-82 and preliminary 1983, 1641–14

Potato production, stocks, processing, yields, and harvest losses, by State, periodic rpt, 1621–10

Rice market activities, prices, inspections, sales, trade, supply, and use, for US and selected foreign markets, weekly rpt, 1313–8

Rice production, prices, trade, stocks, and use, 1978-July 1984 and 1984/85 outlook, semiannual situation rpt, 1561–8

Rice stocks on and off farms and total, periodic rpt, 1621–7

Soybean stocks on and off farms, by State, various dates 1983-84, annual rpt, 1621–5

Sugar and sweeteners production, consumption, prices, supply, and trade, quarterly rpt with articles, 1561–14

Tobacco leaf stocks, and products manufactured and sold, by type, quarterly rpt, 1319–3

Tobacco production, prices, stocks, taxes by State, and trade and foreign production by country, 1983, annual rpt, 1319–1

Vegetable production, prices, stocks, and consumption, for selected fresh and processed crops, periodic situation rpt with articles, 1561–11

Walnut production, stocks, use, and exports of US and 4 countries, and EC export subsidy, selected years 1977-1984/85, article, 1925–34.429

Wheat (durum) acreage, production, prices, stocks, use, and US and Canada exports by country, quarterly rpt, 1313–6

Wheat and rye foreign and US production, prices, trade, stocks, and use, periodic situation rpt with articles, 1561–12

see also Agricultural surpluses

Agricultural subsidies

Advertising (generic) for agricultural commodities, activities and funding by source, selected years 1972-83, 1548–242

Agricultural Stabilization and Conservation Service producer payments under 26 programs, monthly rpt, 1802–10

Agricultural Statistics, 1983, annual rpt, 1004–1

Budget of US Appendix, detailed budgets and personnel summaries, by agency, FY85, annual rpt, 104–3

Budget of US, CBO analysis and review of FY85 budget by function, annual rpt, 26304–2

Budget of US, compact budgets by function, agency, and account, FY85 with projections to FY89, annual rpt, 104–2

Budget of US, effects of Reagan Admin policy changes, by detailed program, FY85, annual rpt, 104–21

Budget of US, loans and loan guarantees, and Admin proposed limits on credit assistance, by program, FY83-89, annual rpt, 26306–3.65

Agricultural subsidies

Budget of US, receipts by source and outlays by function, FY40-89 estimates revised for consistency with FY85 budget definitions, annual rpt, 104–12

Budget of US, receipts, outlays, and budget authority, by function and agency, FY84-89 revised estimates, midsession review of FY85 budget, annual rpt, 104–7

Budget of US, receipts, outlays, and budget authority, by function and agency, 1st revision of FY85 budget, annual rpt, 104–17

Census of Govts, 1982: State govt payments to local govts, by program, source of funds, level of govt, and State, with trends from 1902, 2460–3

Conservation practices in rural areas, Agricultural Conservation Program participation and payments, by State, FY83, annual rpt, 1804–7

Cost control proposals for Fed Govt programs and mgmt, CBO and GAO estimates of savings by function and agency, FY85-89, 26308–45

Cost control proposals for Fed Govt programs and mgmt, 3-year savings by function and agency, and financial and operating data, 1960s-81, 16908–1.2

EC export subsidies by commodity, FAS quarterly rpt, 1925–32.1

EC walnut export subsidy, 1982/83-1984/85, article, 1925–34.429

Farm finances, assets, liabilities, income, receipts by commodity and State, and expenses, 1980-83 and trends from 1910, annual rpt, 1544–16

Farm finances, production, expenses by type, and domestic economic impact, selected years 1972-82 and preliminary 1983-84, annual rpt, 1544–19

Farm income, payments by State and program, 1979-82 and trends from 1950, annual rpt, 1544–18

Fed Crop Insurance Corp program activities and costs, and FCIC and private insurance company gains and losses, 1980-84 with some trends from 1948, GAO rpt, 26113–119

Fed Crop Insurance Corp program operations and finances, for FCIC policies and private policies reinsured by FCIC, 1970s-84 with trends from 1948, hearing, 21168–28

Fed Govt aid to State and local govts, expenditures, and direct payments, by program, agency, and State, FY83, annual rpt, 2464–2

Fed Govt financial and nonfinancial domestic aid, 1984 annual comprehensive catalog, 104–5

Fed Govt grants-in-aid for 13 program areas, FY82-84, annual article, 10042–1.402

Fed Govt loans, grants, and tax benefits to business, by program and economic sector, projected FY84-88 with effective tax rates for FY80-82, 26306–6.70

Fraud and abuse in USDA programs, audits and investigations, 2nd half FY84, semiannual rpt, 1002–4

Fruit (deciduous) grower prices and processor net cost and subsidies in 4 countries and EC, 1982/83-1983/84, article, 1925–34.414

Govt revenues by source and expenditures by function, natl income and product account, *Survey of Current Business,* monthly rpt, monthly and annual tables, 2702–1.24

Korea (South) agricultural services projects of AID and Korea govt, economic impacts, 1950s-83, 9916–1.52

Land privately held, acreage and owners by owner characteristics, land use, and region, and purchase and improvement funding, 1978 survey, series, 1506–5

Loan programs of Fed Govt, direct and guaranteed loans outstanding by agency and program, *Treasury Bulletin,* quarterly rpt, 8002–4.10

Portugal agricultural subsidies, profits, marketing margins, and consumer prices, by commodity or product, and effects of prospective EC membership, 1981, 1528–171

Prune (dried) production, trade, consumption, and stocks of US and 2 countries, EC subsidies, and US exports by country, 1982/83-1984/85, article, 1925–34.435

Rice market activities, prices, inspections, sales, trade, supply, and use, for US and selected foreign markets, weekly rpt, 1313–8

Southeastern States soil conservation and water pollution reduction participants, costs, and acreage, by conservation method and State, selected years 1973-82, 1588–84

Tax expenditures, Fed Govt revenues foregone through income tax deductions and exclusions by type, and effect of Deficit Reduction Act, FY84-89, annual rpt, 21784–10

TTPI socioeconomic, health, and govtl data, by TTPI govt, FY83 and selected trends, detailed annual rpt, 7004–6

see also Agricultural quotas and price supports

Agricultural surpluses

Acreage reduction payment-in-kind program costs, requirements, producer and diversion payments, and loan interest forgiven, by crop, as of 1983, hearing, 21788–138

Agricultural Stabilization and Conservation Service programs, annual commodity fact sheet series, 1806–4

CCC commodities for sale, and prices, monthly press release, 1802–4

CCC finances and program operations, FY83, annual rpt, 1824–1

CCC loan activities by commodity, and agency operating results, monthly press release, 1802–7

Cotton prices in 8 spot markets, futures prices at NYC exchange, farm prices, and CCC loan stocks, monthly rpt, 1309–1

Dairy inventories of CCC, storage and spoilage costs of surplus butter, cheese, and nonfat dry milk, 1982-83, GAO rpt, 26113–120

Dairy products price support purchases, sales, donations, and inventories of CCC, monthly rpt, 1802–2

Farm finances, assets, liabilities, income, receipts by commodity and State, and expenses, 1980-83 and trends from 1910, annual rpt, 1544–16

Index by Subjects and Names

Grain loan support programs of USDA, activity and status by type of grain and State, monthly rpt, 1802–3

Grain stocks on and off farms and total in all positions, by crop, periodic rpt, 1621–4

Milk price support alternatives, effects on production, use, prices, and farm receipts, projected 1983/84-1988/89 and actual 1982/83, 1568–246

Milk price supports effect on production, use, prices, and farm receipts, by region and State, 1940s-83 and alternative projections to 1988/89, 1568–245

Rice stocks on and off farms and total, periodic rpt, 1621–7

see also Agricultural quotas and price supports

see also Agricultural stocks

see also Food assistance

see also Public Law 480

Agricultural Trade Development and Assistance Act

see Public Law 480

Agricultural transportation

see Agricultural marketing

Agricultural wages

Agricultural Statistics, 1983, annual rpt, 1004–1.2

Census of Agriculture, 1982: farms, farmland, production and costs, and operator characteristics, preliminary State and county rpt series, 2330–1

Census of Agriculture, 1982: farms, farmland, production, finances, and operator characteristics, by county, final State rpt series, 2331–1

Earnings by major industry group, and personal income per capita and by source, by region and State, 1929-82, 2708–40

Farm finances, assets, liabilities, income, receipts by commodity and State, and expenses, 1980-83 and trends from 1910, annual rpt, 1544–16

Farm hired workers, sociodemographic characteristics, and farm/nonfarm income and workdays, by whether worked in Mar 1981, article, 6722–1.440

Farm labor, farms, and labor costs, by labor and farm type and State, with immigrant labor law effect on farm work force, 1978, 1598–192

Farm labor, wages, hours, and perquisites, by State, quarterly rpt, 1631–1

Farm production expenditures, detailed items by farm sales size and region, 1983, annual rpt, 1614–3

Occupational Outlook Handbook, 1984-85 biennial rpt, 6744–1

Rural area situation and dev, periodic rpt articles, 1502–7

Texas farm household income, by income source and substate region, 1979, article, 9379–1.406

Wages (minimum) for farm and nonfarm workers under Fair Labor Standards Act, 1938-84, annual rpt, 4744–3.1

Agriculture

Agricultural Statistics, 1983, annual rpt, 1004–1

Agriculture Fact Book of US, compilation of data for 1983 with trends from 1940, annual rpt, 1004–14

Farm finance and credit conditions, forecast 1984, conf papers, annual rpt, 1004–16

Index by Subjects and Names

Farm finance and credit conditions, forecast 1984, conf summary, annual rpt, 9264–9

GAO publications on food, agriculture, and nutrition, 1981-83, annual listing, 26104–11.2

Handbook of Labor Statistics, employment, earnings, hours, and labor force characteristics, 1982 and trends, detailed annual rpt, 6724–1

Natl income and product, comprehensive accounts and components, *Survey of Current Business,* monthly rpt, monthly and annual tables, 2702–1.27

Pollution abatement capital and operating costs under Clean Air and Water Acts, for govts and selected industries, various periods 1970-2000, annual rpt, 9184–11

Small and minority-owned businesses finances and operations, Federal contracts by agency, and worker characteristics, by industry, race, sex, and State, 1950s-83, annual rpt, 9764–6

Statistical Abstract of US, social, political, and economic data, 1950s-83 and trends, annual rpt, 2324–1.3

Transportation census, 1982: trucks, by detailed characteristics, miles traveled, and type of product carried, State rpt series, 2573–1

see also Agricultural accidents and safety
see also Agricultural commodities
see also Agricultural credit
see also Agricultural education
see also Agricultural exports and imports
see also Agricultural extension work
see also Agricultural finance
see also Agricultural innovations
see also Agricultural insurance
see also Agricultural labor
see also Agricultural machinery and equipment
see also Agricultural marketing
see also Agricultural policies
see also Agricultural prices
see also Agricultural production
see also Agricultural production costs
see also Agricultural productivity
see also Agricultural quotas and price supports
see also Agricultural sciences
see also Agricultural services
see also Agricultural stocks
see also Agricultural subsidies
see also Agricultural surpluses
see also Agricultural wages
see also Botany
see also Census of Agriculture
see also Drought
see also Farm income
see also Farms and farmland
see also Fertilizers
see also Food and food industry
see also Foreign agriculture
see also Forests and forestry
see also Horticulture
see also Irrigation
see also Pesticides
see also Pests and pest control
see also Rural areas
see also Soils and soil conservation
see also Wildlife and wildlife conservation

Agriculture Department

see Department of Agriculture

Aguadilla, P.R.

see also under By SMSA or MSA in the "Index by Categories"

Aguirre, Rafael

"Current Status of the Natural Resources in the Northwest of Mexico", 1208–197

AID

see Agency for International Development

Aid to Blind

Beneficiary families and children, and total and average payments, by public assistance program and State, since 1940, monthly rpt, 4742–1.5

Benefits and beneficiary characteristics of OASDHI, Medicaid, SSI, and other social insurance and public welfare programs, selected years 1937-82, annual rpt, 4744–3.13

Benefits, beneficiaries below poverty level, and State expenditures for SSI and 3 earlier programs, selected years 1972-83, article, 4742–1.402

Outlying areas programs and provisions under Social Security Act, FY82, annual rpt, 4704–9

Outlying areas public assistance adult recipients and payments, by program, quarterly rpt, 4742–6.1

see also Supplemental Security Income

Aid to Families with Dependent Children

Alabama rural black population, education, employment, health services, and economic status, for 16 counties, selected years 1970-81, 11048–180

Beneficiaries and payments, applications by disposition, payment discontinuances by reason, and hearings by outcome, by State, quarterly rpt, 4742–6

Beneficiaries of AFDC including unemployed-parent segment and emergency assistance, monthly rpt, 4742–2

Beneficiaries of noncash public and employer-based transfer programs, by income source and socioeconomic characteristics, 1982, final Current Population Rpt, 2546–6.37

Beneficiary families and children, and total and average payments, by public assistance program and State, since 1940, monthly rpt, 4742–1.5

Benefit overpayments, payment error rates, and sanctions imposed, for food stamp, AFDC, and SSI programs, by State, various dates 1980-82, GAO rpt, 26113–136

Benefits and beneficiary characteristics of OASDHI, Medicaid, SSI, and other social insurance and public welfare programs, selected years 1937-82, annual rpt, 4744–3.11, 4744–3.13

Benefits per child for AFDC and foster home care, for selected States, 1974 and 1982, hearing, 21968–28

Budget of US, CBO analysis of revenue and spending alternatives and projections of economic indicators, FY85-89, annual rpt, 26304–3.3

Budget of US, effects of Reagan Admin policy changes, by detailed program, FY85, annual rpt, 104–21

Child Support Enforcement Program cost savings to AFDC, Federal and State govts, and public assistance programs, by State and selected city or county, FY76-85, 4748–37

Child Support Enforcement Program costs, cases, and collections, by State, FY82, semiannual rpt, 4002–5

Child Support Enforcement Program costs, cases, and collections, by State, FY83, annual rpt, 4004–29

Child Support Enforcement Program financial and operating data, FY79-83, annual rpt, 4004–16

Cost control proposals for Fed Govt programs and mgmt, 3-year savings by function and agency, and financial and operating data, 1960s-81, 16908–1.6, 16908–1.23

Costs and productivity of AFDC and food stamp programs in 8 States, 1973-82, GAO rpt, 26111–18

Deficit Reduction Act provisions related to AFDC, 1984 narrative article, 4742–1.423

Eligibility for AFDC under Omnibus Budget Reconciliation Act, effect on caseloads and recipient benefits and living costs, 1981-83, GAO rpt, 26131–11

Fed Govt programs under Ways and Means Committee jurisdiction, program operations and financing data for assessing budgetary requirements, by State, FY70s-83, 21788–117

Fed Govt public welfare programs and tax expenditures benefitting children and youth, participation and funding for 71 programs, FY81-83, 21968–30

Finances, programs, staff, and litigation of SSA, FY83, annual rpt, 4704–6

Food stamp recipient households size and composition, income, and income deductions allowed, Aug 1981, annual rpt, 1364–8

Fraud in Fed Govt benefit programs and other unreported taxable income from illegal activities, with methodology and bibl, 1970s-82, 8008–112

Fresno, Calif, economic, population, labor, and housing indicators, various periods 1974-85, hearing, 21248–84

Funding and participant characteristics for Fed Govt and other food aid programs, and nutrition and poverty data, 1970s-83, 028–20

Govt census, 1982: State govt payments to local govts, by program, source of funds, level of govt, and State, with trends from 1902, 2460–3

Income (household) and cash and noncash transfer program participation, by sociodemographic characteristics, quarterly rpt, 2542–2

Income (personal) by source including transfer payments, and social insurance contributions by type, by region, 1982, 2708–40

Income from transfer payments, natl income and product account, *Survey of Current Business,* monthly rpt, monthly and annual tables, 2702–1.23

Medicare and Medicaid eligibility, participation, covered services and use, and reimbursements and payments, various periods 1966-82, annual rpt, 4654–1

Michigan health funding, Blue Cross-Blue Shield and welfare participation, and unemployment, poverty, and food assistance by county, 1979-83, hearing, 21348–86

Aid to Families with Dependent Children

Poverty-level persons and families, by income source, hours of work, earnings, taxes, and family characteristics, various periods 1959-84, 21788-131

Public opinion on taxes, tax policy, and intergovtl relations, 1972-84 surveys, annual rpt, 10044-2

Refugee arrivals in US by world area of origin and State of settlement, and Fed Govt intl and domestic assistance costs, FY85, annual rpt, 7004-16

Research and statistical projects and techniques, and evaluation of public welfare programs, 1983 conf papers, 4704-11

State govt AFDC admin agencies performance measures, caseloads, payments, and costs, by State, FY81, annual rpt, 4704-10

State programs and provisions under Social Security Act, by State, FY82, annual rpt, 4704-9

Traffic accidents and casualties detailed direct and indirect costs, by characteristics of persons and vehicles involved, 1979-80, 7768-80

Wisconsin public welfare programs caseloads, selected vital statistics, and households in poverty, 1970s-83, hearings, 21788-141

Workfare program for AFDC recipients, participation and requirements in 16 States, Feb 1983, GAO rpt, 26131-9 *see also* Work Incentive Program

Aid to Permanently and Totally Disabled

Beneficiary families and children, and total and average payments, by public assistance program and State, since 1940, monthly rpt, 4742-1.5

Benefits and beneficiary characteristics of OASDHI, Medicaid, SSI, and other social insurance and public welfare programs, selected years 1937-82, annual rpt, 4744-3.13

Benefits, beneficiaries below poverty level, and State expenditures for SSI and 3 earlier programs, selected years 1972-83, article, 4742-1.402

Outlying areas programs and provisions under Social Security Act, FY82, annual rpt, 4704-9

Outlying areas public assistance adult recipients and payments, by program, quarterly rpt, 4742-6.1

see also Supplemental Security Income

Air bases

see Military bases, posts, and reservations

Air cargo

Accident circumstances, severity, and causes, for domestic and foreign air carriers in US operations, periodic rpt, 9612-1

Aircraft handled by instrument flight rule, by user type, FAA traffic control center, and region, FY69-83 and forecast to FY95, annual rpt, 7504-15

Aircraft registered with FAA, by type and characteristics of aircraft, carrier, make, State, and county, 1983, annual rpt, 7504-3

Aviation activity, detailed data on aircraft, air traffic, air carriers, personnel, airports, and FAA operations, 1974-83, annual rpt, 7504-1

China economic conditions, agricultural and industrial production, trade, and domestic and foreign investment, 1980-85, 2048-106

Communist, OECD, and selected other countries freight and carrier inventories, by mode of transport, 1960s-83, annual rpt, 244-5.10

Consumer complaints to CAB, by type of complaint and US and foreign air carrier, monthly rpt, 9142-20

Cuba economic conditions, agricultural and industrial production and distribution, trade, and intl economic relations, 1970-82 and trends from 1957, 248-40

DOD shipments of military and personal property, loss claims, passenger traffic, and costs, by mode of transport, quarterly rpt, 3702-1

Exports and imports between US and outlying areas, by detailed commodity and mode of transport, monthly rpt, 2422-4

Exports and imports of US (airborne), by world area and US customs district and city, monthly rpt, 2422-8

Exports and imports of US, by commodity group, world area, selected country, US coastal area and port, and mode of transport, with seasonal adjustments, monthly rpt, 2422-9

Exports of US, detailed Schedule E commodities by mode of transport and world area and country of destination, 1983, annual rpts, 2424-5

Finances, operations, vehicles, equipment, accidents, and energy use, by mode of transport, 1955-84, annual rpt, 7304-2

Financial and operating data for each certificated charter, and cargo carrier, quarterly rpt, 9142-30

Financial data for airlines, by carrier, carrier group, and for total certificated system, quarterly rpt, 9142-12

Freight yields and revenue ton-miles for major and all cargo domestic air carrier groups, quarterly rpt, 9142-35

Fruit and vegetable shipments, and arrivals in 23 US and 5 Canada cities, by mode of transport and State or country of origin, 1983, annual rpt series, 1311-4

Fruit and vegetable shipments by mode of transport, arrivals, and imports, by commodity and State and country of origin, weekly rpt, 1311-3

Hazardous material transport accidents, casualties, and property damage, by mode of transport, with DOT control activities, 1983, annual rpt, 7304-4

Imports of US, detailed Schedule A commodities by country and world area of origin, and mode of transport, 1983, annual rpts, 2424-2

Intercity freight ton-miles and energy consumption rates, by mode of transport, 1970-82, annual rpt, 3164-73

Intl services transactions by type, and sales, assets, and employment of US multinatl service firms by industry and world region, 1977-82, 2706-5.30

Tax (excise) collections of IRS, by source, quarterly press release, 8302-1

Traffic (passenger and cargo) and departures by aircraft type, by airline and US and foreign airport, aircraft type, and airline, 1982, annual rpt, 7504-35

Index by Subjects and Names

Traffic, aircraft, pilots, airport activity, and fuel use, forecast FY84-95 with FY79-83 trends, annual rpt, 7504-6

Traffic and financial data for airline industry, by carrier, FY83 with trends from FY73, annual rpt, 9144-1

Traffic, capacity, and performance, by carrier and type of operation, monthly rpt, 9142-13

Traffic, capacity, and performance for medium regional airlines, by carrier and certification status, quarterly rpt, 9142-44

Western States economic indicators, Fed Reserve 12th District, quarterly rpt, 9393-1.1

Air conditioning

Air pollutant and radiation indoor levels by emissions source, and household exposure and health effects by pollutant type, various periods 1966-83, hearings, 21708-102

Apartment market absorption rates and characteristics for nonsubsidized privately financed furnished and unfurnished units completed in 1982, annual Current Housing Rpt, 2484-2

Buildings heating and air conditioning fuel by type, for new private nonresidential and public buildings, by region, 1979-83, monthly rpt, annual tables, 2382-4.4

Census of Housing, 1980: inventory, occupancy, and unit characteristics, changes from 1973 by region and inside-outside SMSAs and central cities, series, 2473-3

Census of Housing, 1980: occupancy and unit characteristics of SMSAs and central cities, by race, Hispanic origin, and city, State and SMSA rpt series, 2473-1

Census of Population and Housing, 1980: detailed population and housing characteristics, by county, city, and census tract, State and SMSA rpt series, 2551-2

Construction industries census, 1982: financial and operating data, by SIC 4-digit industry and State, final rpt series, 2373-1

Construction industries census, 1982: financial and operating data, by SIC 4-digit industry and State, preliminary rpt, 2371-1.10

Cooling and heating degree days by State, and housing energy bills and departures from normal, by census div, monthly rpt, 2152-11, 2152-12

County Business Patterns: establishments, employees, and payrolls, by SIC 4-digit industry and county, 1981, annual State rpt series, 2326-8

County Business Patterns: establishments, employees, and payrolls, by SIC 4-digit industry and county, 1982, annual State rpt series, 2326-6

Employment, earnings, and hours, by selected SIC 1- to 4-digit industry, State, and for 278 major labor areas, 1939-83, annual rpt, 6744-5

Employment, earnings, and hours, by SIC 4-digit nonfarm industry, monthly 1974-Feb 1984, annual update, 6744-4

Energy aid of Fed Govt for low-income households, allocations and average benefits in 13 States, and public interest group assessment, FY81-83, GAO rpt, 26121-75

Index by Subjects and Names

Air Force

Energy aid of Fed Govt for low-income households, by income, aid type, and State, FY83, annual rpt, 4744–3.13

Energy conservation programs of utilities under natl conservation act, cost effectiveness and participating household characteristics, 1980s, 3308–69

Energy supply/demand and prices, by fuel type and consuming sector with foreign comparisons, 1949-83, annual rpt, 3164–74

Energy supply/demand and prices, by fuel type, sector, and end use, detailed trends and projections 1973-95, annual rpt, 3164–75

Energy use, by economic sector, end use, and energy source, 1983 and 2000, 2006–2.5

Energy use, costs, expenditures, and conservation, and household and housing characteristics, EIA survey series, 3166–7

Energy use in housing, and savings under alternative conservation strategies, by State, with model methodology and energy prices, selected years 1970-81, 21368–48

Energy use in nonresidential buildings, expenditures, and conservation, by building characteristics, EIA survey series, 3166–8

Equipment shipments, trade, and consumption, by product, 1983, annual Current Industrial Rpt, 2506–12.7

Exports and imports of US, detailed SIC-based commodities by world area, 1983, annual rpts, 2424–6

Exports, imports, tariffs, and industry operating data for fans, pumps, compressors, and cooling equipment, 1979-83, TSUSA commodity rpt, 9885–6.83

Exports of air conditioning and refrigeration equipment by world area, and imports, by product, biennial rpt, suspended, 2014–2

Exports of US, detailed commodities by country of destination, monthly rpt, 2422–3

Exports of US, detailed Schedule B commodities by country of destination, 1983, annual rpt, 2424–9

Exports of US, detailed Schedule E commodities by mode of transport and world area and country of destination, 1983, annual rpts, 2424–5

Florida and California elderly migration by selected State of origin or destination, and Florida elderly, by sociodemographic and housing characteristics, 1970 and 1980, 4478–150

Home mortgages (graduated payment) FHA-insured, financial, property, and mortgagor characteristics, for US and selected localities, quarterly rpt, 5142–42

Home mortgages (graduated payment) FHA-insured, financial, property, and mortgagor characteristics, for US and selected States, quarterly rpt, 5142–41

Home mortgages (graduated payment) FHA-insured, financial, property, and mortgagor characteristics, US summary, quarterly rpt, 5142–40

Home mortgages FHA-insured, financial, property, and mortgagor characteristics, for US and selected localities, quarterly rpt, 5142–2

Home mortgages FHA-insured, financial, property, and mortgagor characteristics, for US, selected States, and Puerto Rico, quarterly rpt, 5142–3

Home mortgages FHA-insured, financial, property, and mortgagor characteristics, quarterly rpt, 5142–1

Home mortgages FHA-insured, financial, property, and mortgagor characteristics, 1983, annual rpt, 5144–17

Home mortgages FHA-insured for low-cost homes, financial, construction, property, and mortgagor characteristics, quarterly rpt, 5142–4

Housing alteration and repair expenditures by characteristics of property and region, 1983, annual rpt, 2384–4

Housing alteration and repair expenditures, by type and property size, various periods 1963-83, article, 2012–1.406

Housing and households detailed characteristics, and unit and neighborhood quality, by inside-outside central cities, 1979-82 surveys, SMSA rpt series, 2485–6

Housing and neighborhood quality indicators and attitudes, and occupant characteristics, by urban-rural location and region, 1981, annual survey, 2485–7

Housing census, 1980: structural, financial, and householder characteristics, by region and State, 2475–4

Housing heating and air conditioning equipment shipments by type of fuel used, monthly rpt, 2012–1.6

Housing, new single and multifamily unit physical and financial characteristics, by region and metro-nonmetro location, 1979-83, annual rpt, 2384–1

Housing occupancy and unit and household characteristics, by region and metro-nonmetro residence, 1983, biennial survey, 2485–1

Housing units air conditioning status, for new 1-family and multifamily units, selected years 1966-83, annual rpt, 3164–73

Imports of US, detailed Schedule A commodities by country and world area of origin, and mode of transport, 1983, annual rpts, 2424–2

Imports of US, detailed Schedule A commodities by country, monthly rpt, 2422–2

Imports of US, detailed TSUSA commodities by country of origin, 1983, annual rpt, 2424–4

Income tax returns of sole proprietorships, detailed data by industry div and selected industry group, 1981, annual rpt, 8304–7

Injuries, deaths, and medical costs from consumer products use, and Consumer Product Safety Commission activities and recalls, by product type and brand, FY83, annual rpt, 9164–2

Natural gas utility marketing and servicing of household appliances and conservation equipment in US and Canada, by firm and product, 1978, hearing, 21368–54

Occupational Outlook Handbook, 1984-85 biennial rpt, 6744–1

OECD trade, total and for 4 major countries, and US trade by country, by commodity, 1972-82, annual world region rpt series, 244–13

Pacific Northwest electricity consumption and prices by end-use sector, and economic and demographic data, 1960s-83 and projected to 2005, annual rpt, 3224–2

Producer prices and indexes, by stage of processing and detailed commodity, monthly rpt, 6762–6

Producer prices and indexes, by stage of processing and detailed commodity, monthly 1983, annual supplement, 6764–2

Service industry census, 1982: employment, establishments, receipts, and payroll, by SIC 2- to 4-digit kind of business, SMSA, county, and city, State rpt series, 2391–1

Solar collector and photovoltaic module production, sales, and use, with listing of manufacturers, 1983, annual rpt, 3164–62

see also Cold storage and refrigeration

Air Force

Agent Orange exposed Air Force personnel diseases and disorders, by disease type, age, and officer status, 1984 rpt, 3604–3

Aides to officers, enlisted personnel authorized and assigned to perform personal services by race and sex, and program costs, by service branch, 1982-83, GAO rpt, 26123–53

Aircraft (C-5 and C-17 cargo) dimensions and operating characteristics, 1983, GAO rpt, 26123–81

Aircraft for DOD noncombat use, costs, Navy and Air Force requirements, and Navy losses, by aircraft type, selected years FY73-86, hearing, 21408–76

Base support costs by function, and personnel and acreage by installation, by service branch, FY85, annual rpt, 3504–11

Cost control proposals for Fed Govt programs and mgmt, 3-year savings by function and agency, and financial and operating data, 1960s-81, 16908–1.20

Manpower active duty strength, recruits, and reenlistment, by race, Hispanic origin, sex, and service branch, quarterly press release, 3542–7

Manpower of DOD, and organization, budget, weapons, and property, by service branch, State, and country, 1984 annual summary rpt, 3504–13

Manpower of DOD, by State, service branch, and major installation, as of Sept 1983, annual rpt, 3544–7

Manpower requirements and cost estimates, DOD budget detailed analysis, FY85, annual rpt, 3504–1

Manpower statistics on active duty, civilian, and reserve personnel, by service branch, monthly rpt, 3542–14

Manpower statistics on active duty, civilian, and retired personnel and dependents, FY83 and historical, annual rpt, 3544–1

Manpower strengths, and military pension earnings and program costs, under alternative policies, selected years FY71-2020, 26306–6.76

Manpower strengths in US and abroad, by service branch, world area, and country, quarterly news release, 3542–9

Manpower strengths of active duty, reserve, and civilian personnel, by service branch, selected years FY68-89, annual rpt, 3544–2

Air Force

- Manpower strengths, summary by service branch, monthly press release, 3542–2
- Medical facilities of DOD in US and abroad, beds, admissions, outpatient visits, and live births by service branch, quarterly rpt, 3542–15
- Medical personnel, trainees, and accessions by source, by occupation, specialty, and service branch, FY83, annual rpt, 3544–24
- Military weapons and troop strength of US and NATO compared to USSR and Warsaw Pact, as of Jan 1984, annual rpt, 3564–1
- NATO military commitment of US, Europe force strengths by service branch and costs by component, FY82 with trends from FY75, GAO rpt, 26123–71
- Radiation from 1940s-70s nuclear weapons tests, levels in air and water, and personnel exposure by military unit and job category, series, 3906–1
- Reserve forces manpower and equipment strengths, readiness, and funding, by reserve component, FY83, annual rpt, 3544–27
- Reserve forces manpower strengths and characteristics, by component, quarterly rpt, 3542–4
- Strategic military capability, force strengths, weapons, training, supplies, and requirements, by service branch, FY80-84 and projected to 1990, 3508–19
- Training and education programs of DOD, funding, staff, students, and facilities, by service branch and reserve component, FY85, annual rpt, 3504–5
- Women military personnel on active duty, by demographic and service characteristics and service branch, with comparisons to men, FY83, annual chartbook, 3544–26
- *see also* Department of Air Force

Air Force Academy
see Service academies

Air Force contracts and procurement
see Defense contracts and procurement

Air freight
see Air cargo

Air National Guard
see National guard

Air navigation
see Aeronautical navigation

Air piracy

- Hijacking attempts and airport security operations, screening results, and enforcement actions, 1st half 1984, semiannual rpt, 7502–5
- Hijacking attempts on US and foreign aircraft, summary data 1970-80, annual rpt, 7304–1
- Hijackings, on-board explosions, other crimes against civil aviation, and circumstances, US and worldwide, 1931-83, annual rpt, 7504–31
- Terrorist (intl) incidents, casualties, and attacks on US targets, by attack type and world area, with chronology of events, 1983, annual rpt, 7004–13

Air pollution

- Abatement capital and operating costs, by SIC 2- to 4-digit industry, State, and SMSA, 1982, annual Current Industrial Rpt, 2506–3.6
- Abatement capital and operating costs under Clean Air and Water Acts, for govts and selected industries, various periods 1970-2000, annual rpt, 9184–11
- Abatement capital expenditures, by pollution type and selected industry, 1973-84, annual article, 2702–1.423
- Abatement equipment shipments by industry, exports, and new and backlog orders, by product, 1983, annual Current Industrial Rpt, 2506–12.5
- Abatement expenditures and effect on economic indicators and industry operations, by major industry, projected under 3 pollution regulation alternatives 1983-95, 9188–84
- Abatement expenditures by govt, business, and consumers, 1972-82, annual article, 2702–1.407
- Abatement programs, emissions standards dev, monitoring, and enforcement, 1982, annual rpt, 9194–4
- Abatement R&D industry funding, by pollution type and funding source, 1973-82, annual rpt, 9627–21
- Abatement under Clean Air Act, emissions by source, standards, and effects on auto industry and health, 1970s-83, hearings, 25328–25
- Acid Precipitation Natl Assessment Program activities, and funding by Federal agency, 1983, annual rpt, 14354–1
- Acid rain and air pollution environmental effects, and methods for neutralizing acidified water bodies, summary research rpt series, 5506–5
- Acid rain causes and effects, air pollutant emissions by source, and control costs, by region and State, selected years 1977-83 and projected to 2000, 26358–104
- Acid rain causes and effects, air pollutant emissions by source in US and selected countries, and control costs, 1970s-83 and projected to 2000, 21368–52
- Acid rain causes and effects, air pollutant emissions by source in US and selected countries, control costs, and Fed Govt research funding, 1960s-82, 3408–27
- Alcohol fuel (ethanol) production in Tennessee Valley, feedstocks, facilities, tax incentives, and related farming data, by State, 1970s-83 and projected to 1992, 9808–69
- Canada-US border air pollution in Detroit-Windsor and Port Huron-Sarnia areas, annual rpt, discontinued, 14644–5
- Carbon dioxide atmospheric concentration increase effects on hydrologic conditions, projected for 26-35 years, 9188–95
- Carbon dioxide atmospheric levels, climatic effects and impacts of fossil and synthetic fuels use, deforestation, and land use patterns, research rpt series, 3406–3
- Carbon dioxide emissions, climatic effects, and control costs, projected under alternative emissions controls and energy use restrictions to 2100 with trends 1970s-80, reprint, 9188–88
- Carbon dioxide emissions from fossil fuel combustion, and growth rates, by country and country group, 1950-80, 3006–7.6
- Carbon dioxide emissions from fossil fuel combustion by fuel type, worldwide estimates based on total and non-oxidized fossil fuel production, 1950-81, 3008–94
- Carbon monoxide atmospheric concentrations and levels within buildings and along commuting and residential driving routes, for 4 cities, Jan-Mar 1981, 9198–110

Index by Subjects and Names

- Coal dev plans on Fed Govt lease lands in 12 regions under Fed Coal Mgmt Program, environmental and socioeconomic impacts to 2000, final statement series, 5726–4
- Coal transport environmental impacts by type and mode of transport, methodology for assessing alternative systems, 1983 rpt, 3408–28
- Coastal environmental characteristics, fish, wildlife, and use, and population socioeconomic data, for individual areas, series, 5506–4
- DOE-contractor nuclear facilities radioactive and nonradioactive releases, by type and site, 1982, annual rpt, 3004–23
- DOE R&D projects and funding at natl labs, universities, and other instns, FY83, annual summary rpt, 3004–18.1
- Electric power plant (coal-fired) sulfur dioxide emissions in eastern US, effect of alternative geographic area limits on power and coal industries, 1983 rpt, 3408–32
- Electric power plant coal and oil receipts and average cost by sulfur content and State, quarterly rpt, 3162–39
- Electric power plant coal deliveries, sulfur content, and quantity meeting sulfur content regulations, 1983, annual rpt, 3164–42
- Emission factors, by detailed source, 3rd edition, 1983-84 supplements, 9198–13
- Emissions levels for 5 pollutants, by detailed source, State, and Air Quality Control Region, 1981, annual rpt, 9194–7
- Emissions levels for 5 pollutants, by source, 1970-82 with trends from 1940, annual rpt, 9194–13
- Environmental quality and protection programs, costs, and Fed Govt enforcement, 1983, detailed annual rpt, 484–1
- Environmental quality, pollutant discharge by type, and EPA protection activities, 1970s-83, biennial summary rpt, 9184–16
- Environmental quality, pollutant discharge by type and source, and EPA protection activities and funding, 1970s-83, biennial regional rpt series, 9184–15
- EPA budget and full-time staff positions by type of activity, and grants to States, by program, FY75-84 and proposed FY85, 26308–47
- EPA Office of R&D environmental research plans, and outlays by program, FY84-88, annual rpt, 9184–10
- EPA pollution control research and grant assistance program activities, monthly rpt, 9182–8
- EPA publications in NTIS collection, quarterly listing, 9182–5
- Fluorocarbon, methane, and nitrous oxide atmospheric concentrations, 1960-2030, 9188–95
- Foreign market and trade for pollution control instruments and equipment, and user industry operations and demand, country market research rpts, 2045–17
- Govt census, 1982: State govt payments to local govts, by program, source of funds, level of govt, and State, with trends from 1902, 2460–3
- Great Lakes radioactivity discharges by source, and concentrations in environment, various periods 1963-82, annual rpt, 14644–1.2

Index by Subjects and Names

Air travel

Hazardous organic chemicals concentrations in air, by urban-rural location, city, and for areas with many potential sources, for 132 chemicals, 1970-80, 9198–109

Health condition and health care resources, use, and expenditures, 1970s-82 with trends and projections 1900-2000, annual compilation, 4144–11

Indoor air pollutant and radiation levels by emissions source, and household exposure and health effects by pollutant type, various periods 1966-83, hearings, 21708–102

Meteorological services and research of Fed Govt, programs and funding by agency, FY84-85, annual rpt, 2144–2

Nitrate and sulfate emissions, monitoring results by surveillance station, 1979 with trends by urban-rural area from 1971, 9198–107

NYC and New Jersey atmospheric levels of 28 volatile organic compounds, by site and urban-rural location, 1979-June 1981, 9198–108

Oil enhanced recovery technologies use and environmental impacts, by oil field, county, and State, 1970s-80 and projected to 2000, 3408–29

Pollution levels for 6 pollutants, and measurements exceeding natl standards, by site, 1983, annual rpt, 9194–5

Pollution levels for 6 pollutants, by source, region, and for large SMSAs, 1975-82, annual rpt, 9194–1

Solar and biomass energy use effects on air pollutant emissions, by region, projected to 2000, 3408–30

Southwestern US atmospheric concentrations of sulfur dioxide by city or site, and copper smelter emissions by plant, selected years 1974-82, hearing, 21448–31

Steel plant modernization capital investment under Clean Air Act compliance extension program, by firm, 1981-83, GAO rpt, 26113–138

Sulfur dioxide emissions reduction proposal effects on polluting industries and coal production, by region and State, projected to 2010, 9188–97

Transportation and related energy use, and air quality, for urban areas and Chicago area, late 1970s-82 and projected under lower auto emission standards to 1995, 3408–31

Turbidity of atmosphere, monitoring results by station and season, with description of model predicting urbanization effects, 1960s-76, 9198–106

Uranium mining operations, finances, and costs of alternative methods to meet emissions standards, for industry and selected mines, selected years 1948-90, 9188–96

see also Electromagnetic radiation
see also Motor vehicle exhaust
see also Nuclear radiation
see also Trace metals

Air raid shelters
see Fallout shelters

Air safety
see Aviation accidents and safety

Air traffic control

Budget of US, effects of Reagan Admin policy changes, by detailed program, FY85, annual rpt, 104–21

Collisions of aircraft, and near collisions by circumstances and State, by type of aircraft, various periods 1980-84, 7508–61

Employment at DOT, by subagency, State, and selected personnel characteristics, FY83, annual rpt, 7304–18

FAA activities and finances, and employees by region, FY82-83, annual rpt, 7504–10

FAA activities and R&D for improvement of air traffic control and airway facilities and equipment under Natl Airspace System Plan, 1982-2000, annual rpt, 7504–12

FAA air traffic control and airway facilities and services, operations, and finances, FY83, annual rpt, 7504–37

FAA air traffic control facilities traffic levels, by airport and State, FY83, annual rpt, 7504–27

FAA air traffic control facility operations and services, by service type, aviation category, and facility, 1974-83, annual rpt, 7504–1.2

FAA air traffic control instrument flight rule aircraft handled, by user type, control center, and region, FY69-83 and forecast to FY95, annual rpt, 7504–15

FAA aviation medicine research and studies, technical rpt series, 7506–10

FAA certifications for pilots and nonpilots, by type, age, sex, region, and State, 1983, annual rpt, 7504–2

Fed Govt programs and mgmt cost control proposals, 3-year savings by function and agency, and financial and operating data, 1960s-81, 16908–1.11

General aviation aircraft, hours flown, and equipment, by type, use, and model of aircraft, region, and State, 1982, annual rpt, 7504–29

Merit Systems Protection Board personnel action appeals from air traffic controllers, FY82, annual rpt, 9494–2.3

Occupational manpower needs and supply by detailed occupation, and educational and training program enrollees and grads by detailed field, 1982 and 1995, biennial rpt, 6744–3

Occupational Outlook Handbook, 1984-85 biennial rpt, 6744–1

Traffic, aircraft operations by type and passenger enplanements, by airport, region, and State, projected FY82-95 and trends from FY76, annual rpt, 7504–7

Traffic, aircraft, pilots, airport activity, and fuel use, forecast FY84-95 with FY79-83 trends, annual rpt, 7504–6

User fees to recover costs of 7 federally subsidized public service programs, by type of fee, user, and service, FY84-88, 26306–6.68

see also Aviation accidents and safety

Air transportation
see Airlines
see Airports and airways
see Military aviation

Air travel

China economic conditions, agricultural and industrial production, trade, and domestic and foreign investment, 1980-85, 2048–106

Communist and selected OECD countries passenger-kilometers flown on scheduled service, 1960s-83, annual rpt, 244–5.10

Consumer complaints to CAB, by type of complaint and US and foreign air carrier, monthly rpt, 9142–20

Cuba economic conditions, agricultural and industrial production and distribution, trade, and intl economic relations, 1970-82 and trends from 1957, 248–40

Deregulation of airlines in 1978, effect on industry operations and finances, air traffic patterns, and CAB programs, various periods FY76-84, 9148–56

Fed Govt programs and mgmt cost control proposals, 3-year savings by function and agency, and financial and operating data, 1960s-81, 16908–1

Finances, operations, vehicles, equipment, accidents, and energy use, by mode of transport, 1955-84, annual rpt, 7304–2

Foreign travel to US, by characteristics of visit and traveller, country, and State of destination, quarterly rpt, 2902–1

Passenger and cargo traffic, and departures by aircraft type, by airline and US and foreign airport, 1982, annual rpt, 7504–35

Passenger, cargo, and mail traffic, and airline operations, by type of service, air carrier, State, and country, 1974-83, annual rpt, 7504–1.4, 7504–1.6

Passenger traffic, aircraft, pilots, airport activity, and fuel use, forecast FY84-95 with FY79-83 trends, annual rpt, 7504–6

Passenger traffic, and aircraft operations by type, by airport, region, and State, projected FY82-95 and trends from FY76, annual rpt, 7504–7

Passenger traffic and airline service changes by city since 1978 deregulation, with market shares, fares, and load factors, quarterly rpt, 9142–42

Passenger traffic and capacity for US and intl operations of major trunk carriers, and seasonal adjustment factors, monthly rpt, 9142–19

Passenger traffic and financial data for airline industry, by carrier, FY83 with trends from FY73, annual rpt, 9144–1

Passenger traffic, capacity, and performance, by carrier and type of operation, monthly rpt, 9142–13

Passenger traffic, capacity, and performance for medium regional airlines, by carrier and certification status, quarterly rpt, 9142–44

Passenger traffic since 1978 deregulation, by major carrier, quarterly rpt, 9142–49

Passenger travel to and from US on US and foreign flag air carriers, by country, world area, and US port, monthly rpt, 7302–2

Passengers denied confirmed space on commercial flights, by carrier, monthly rpt, 9142–23

Southeastern States financial and economic devs, Fed Reserve 6th District, monthly rpt with articles, 9371–1

Statistical Abstract of US, social, political, and economic data, 1950s-83 and trends, annual rpt, 2324–1.3

Tax (excise) collections of IRS, by source, quarterly press release, 8302–1

Tax collections, refunds, and taxes due IRS, by State and region, and IRS court activity and operating expenses, FY83, annual rpt, 8304–3.3

Air travel

Ticket sales by type of distributor, and travel agency financial and operating data, 1970s-82, hearing, 25268–81

Western Area Power Admin agency-owned jet aircraft use, costs, and employee time savings, Oct 1981-May 1982 and Oct 1983-Feb 1984, 3006–5.8

Aircraft

- Air pollutant emission factors, by detailed source, 3rd edition, 1983-84 supplements, 9198–13
- Air pollution levels for 5 pollutants, by detailed source, State, and Air Quality Control Region, 1981, annual rpt, 9194–7
- Air traffic control and airway facilities and equipment, FAA improvement activities and R&D under Natl Airspace System Plan, 1982-2000, annual rpt, 7504–12
- Air traffic control and airway facilities and services, operations, and finances, FY83, annual rpt, 7504–37
- Airline deregulation in 1978, traffic and service changes by city, with market shares, fares, and load factors, quarterly rpt, 9142–42
- Airline operating and other costs, itemized for domestic and intl trunk and local service carriers, 1st half 1983, semiannual rpt, 9142–47
- Airline passenger and cargo traffic, and departures by aircraft type, by airline and US and foreign airport, 1982, annual rpt, 7504–35
- Airline traffic and financial data, by carrier, FY83 with trends from FY73, annual rpt, 9144–1
- Aviation activity, detailed data on aircraft, air traffic, air carriers, personnel, airports, and FAA operations, 1974-83, annual rpt, 7504–1
- Aviation traffic, aircraft, pilots, airport activity, and fuel use, forecast FY84-95 with FY79-83 trends, annual rpt, 7504–6
- Census of Population, 1980: detailed socioeconomic and demographic characteristics, by age, sex, race, Hispanic origin, occupation, and industry, State rpt series, 2531–4
- China economic conditions, agricultural and industrial production, trade, and domestic and foreign investment, 1980-85, 2048–106
- Communist, OECD, and selected other countries freight and carrier inventories, by mode of transport, 1960s-83, annual rpt, 244–5.10
- Costs of operating privately owned small planes by component, and Fed Govt mileage reimbursement rates, 1983, annual rpt, 9454–13.2
- County Business Patterns: establishments, employees, and payrolls, by SIC 4-digit industry and county, 1982, annual State rpt series, 2326–6
- Exports and imports of US, detailed SIC-based commodities by world area, 1983, annual rpts, 2424–6
- Exports and imports of US, totals and as percent of domestic production, by SIC 2- to 5-digit commodity, 1981, annual rpt, 2424–3
- Exports of US, detailed commodities by country of destination, monthly rpt, 2422–3

Index by Subjects and Names

- Exports of US, detailed Schedule B commodities by country of destination, 1983, annual rpt, 2424–9
- Exports of US, detailed Schedule E commodities by mode of transport and world area and country of destination, 1983, annual rpts, 2424–5
- FAA aviation medicine research and studies, technical rpt series, 7506–10
- FAA-registered aircraft, by type and characteristics of aircraft, carrier, make, State, and county, 1983, annual rpt, 7504–3
- Flight and engine hours, and shutdown rates, by aircraft and engine model for each air carrier, monthly rpt, 7502–13
- Foreign and US astronautic and aeronautic events, comprehensive chronology, 1976, annual rpt, 9504–2
- Foreign economic, social, and political summary data, by country, 1984, annual factbook, 244–11
- General aviation aircraft, hours flown, and equipment, by type, use, and model of aircraft, region, and State, 1982, annual rpt, 7504–29
- Great Lakes trade, by SITC 3-digit commodity, port, vessel type, world area, and country, 1982, annual rpt, 7744–3
- Imports of US, detailed Schedule A commodities by country and world area of origin, and mode of transport, 1983, annual rpts, 2424–2
- Imports of US, detailed Schedule A commodities by country, monthly rpt, 2422–2
- Imports of US, detailed TSUSA commodities by country of origin, 1983, annual rpt, 2424–4
- Input-output structure of US economy, detailed interindustry transactions for 85 industries, and components of final demand, 1977, article, 2702–1.421
- Input-output structure of US economy, detailed interindustry transactions for 537 industries, and components of final demand, 1977 benchmark data, 2708–17
- Instrument flight rule aircraft handled, by user type, FAA traffic control center, and region, FY69-83 and forecast to FY95, annual rpt, 7504–15
- Manufacturing census, 1982: financial and operating data, by SIC 2- to 4-digit industry, State, SMSA, and county, preliminary census div rpt series, 2491–3
- Manufacturing census, 1982: financial and operating data, for SIC 4-digit industries by product, preliminary rpt, 2491–1.398, 2491–1.399, 2491–1.400
- Marijuana cultivation control activity of State law enforcement agencies, and aid from Fed Govt and Natl Guard, 1983 survey, GAO rpt, 26119–64
- OECD trade, total and for 4 major countries, and US trade by country, by commodity, 1972-82, annual world region rpt series, 244–13
- Producer prices and indexes, by stage of processing and detailed commodity, monthly rpt, 6762–6
- Producer prices and indexes, by stage of processing and detailed commodity, monthly 1983, annual supplement, 6764–2

- Propeller shipments and exports, 1983, annual Current Industrial Rpt, 2506–12.23
- Shipments, trade, consumption, and firms, by type of aircraft and aircraft engine, monthly Current Industrial Rpt, 2506–12.24
- Soviet Union propaganda campaign against NATO nuclear missile deployment, and USSR and NATO nuclear arms and aircraft in place, 1977-83, narrative rpt, 9828–25
- Transportation finances, operations, vehicles, equipment, accidents, and energy use, by mode of transport, 1955-84, annual rpt, 7304–2
- Waterborne commerce of US (domestic and foreign), freight by commodity, traffic, and passengers, by port and waterway, 1982, annual rpt, 3754–3
- *see also* Aerospace industry
- *see also* Aviation accidents and safety
- *see also* Aviation fuels
- *see also* Helicopters
- *see also* Military aircraft
- *see also* under By Commodity in the "Index by Categories"

Aircraft accidents

see Aviation accidents and safety

Aircraft carriers

see Naval vessels

Airlines

- Air traffic control and airway facilities and equipment, FAA improvement activities and R&D under Natl Airspace System Plan, 1982-2000, annual rpt, 7504–12
- Aircraft registered with FAA, by type and characteristics of aircraft, carrier, make, State, and county, 1983, annual rpt, 7504–3
- Aviation activity, detailed data on aircraft, air traffic, air carriers, personnel, airports, and FAA operations, 1974-83, annual rpt, 7504–1
- Aviation activity forecasts, methodology, data sources, and coverage, Feb 1983 conf papers, annual rpt, 7504–28
- Aviation traffic, aircraft, pilots, airport activity, and fuel use, forecast FY84-95 with FY79-83 trends, annual rpt, 7504–6
- Budget of US, effects of Reagan Admin policy changes, by detailed program, FY85, annual rpt, 104–21
- Business statistics, detailed data for major industries and economic indicators, *Survey of Current Business,* monthly rpt, 2702–1.8
- Cash flows for all certificated carriers, quarterly rpt, 9142–34
- Collective bargaining agreements expiring during year, covered workers by SIC 2-digit industry, firm, and union, with summary of key provisions, 1984, annual rpt, 6784–9
- Commuter air carriers and air taxi accidents by seating capacity and cause, and deaths, 1975-82, GAO rpt, 26113–116
- Commuter airlines, air taxi, and general aviation fatal accidents, alcohol involvement, circumstances, and pilot characteristics, 1975-81, 9618–11
- Consumer complaints to CAB, by type of complaint and US and foreign air carrier, monthly rpt, 9142–20

Index by Subjects and Names

County Business Patterns: establishments, employees, and payrolls, by SIC 4-digit industry and county, 1981, annual State rpt series, 2326–8

County Business Patterns: establishments, employees, and payrolls, by SIC 4-digit industry and county, 1982, annual State rpt series, 2326–6

Deregulation of airlines in 1978, effect on industry operations and finances, air traffic patterns, and CAB programs, various periods FY76-84, 9148–56

Deregulation of airlines in 1978, resulting traffic and service changes by city, with market shares, fares, and load factors, quarterly rpt, 9142–42

Developing countries disaster preparedness and summary sociodemographic, political, and economic data, country rpt series, 9916–2

DOD shipments of military and personal property, loss claims, passenger traffic, and costs, by mode of transport, quarterly rpt, 3702–1

Employment, earnings, and hours, by selected SIC 1- to 4-digit industry, State, and for 278 major labor areas, 1939-83, annual rpt, 6744–5

Employment, earnings, and hours, by SIC 4-digit nonfarm industry, monthly 1974-Feb 1984, annual update, 6744–4

Energy supply/demand and prices, by fuel type, sector, and end use, detailed trends and projections 1973-95, annual rpt, 3164–75

Energy use and costs for domestic and intl operations, by US air carrier group, monthly rpt, 9142–21

Energy use, prices, and conservation and efficiency measures, by fuel type, end-use sector, selected industry, and region, 1960-83, annual rpt, 3164–73

Finances, operations, vehicles, equipment, accidents, and energy use, by mode of transport, 1955-84, annual rpt, 7304–2

Financial and operating data for each certificated charter, and cargo carrier, quarterly rpt, 9142–30

Financial data for airlines, by carrier, carrier group, and for total certificated system, quarterly rpt, 9142–12

Financing of airports by source, bond issues by region, and airport operations, by airport and operator type, FY75-83 and projected to FY93, 26306–6.75

Flight and engine hours, and shutdown rates, by aircraft and engine model for each air carrier, monthly rpt, 7502–13

Hijackings, on-board explosions, other crimes against civil aviation, and circumstances, US and worldwide, 1931-83, annual rpt, 7504–31

Income and profitability, by major carrier, 1972-83, annual rpt, 9144–37

Income tax returns of corporations, detailed income and tax items by industry, 1981, annual rpt, 8304–4

Income tax returns of sole proprietorships, detailed data by industry div and selected industry group, 1981, annual rpt, 8304–7

Income tax returns of sole proprietorships, receipts, deductions by type, payroll, and net income, by major industry, 1982, annual article, 8302–2.413

Income taxes paid, net income, and effective tax rates, by major carrier, 1968-83, annual rpt, 9144–34

Input-output structure of US economy, detailed interindustry transactions for 537 industries, and components of final demand, 1977 benchmark data, 2708–17

Intl operations of US combination carriers, traffic and financial data in Atlantic, Pacific, and Latin America regions, quarterly rpt, 9142–41

Minority group and women employment, by occupational group and SIC 2- to 3-digit industry, 1981, annual rpt, 9244–1.1

Occupational manpower needs and supply by detailed occupation, and educational and training program enrollees and grads by detailed field, 1982 and 1995, biennial rpt, 6744–3

Occupational Outlook Handbook, 1984-85 biennial rpt, 6744–1

Operating and other costs itemized for domestic and intl trunk and local service carriers, 1st half 1983, semiannual rpt, 9142–47

Operating unit costs for each system major and short-haul natl carrier, quarterly rpt, 9142–37

Passenger miles and trips, by transport mode, selected years 1929-81, 26358–97

Passenger traffic and capacity for US and intl operations of major trunk carriers, and seasonal adjustment factors, monthly rpt, 9142–19

Passenger traffic, capacity, yields, and load factors, changes for each system major and short-haul natl carrier, periodic rpt, 9142–45

Passengers denied confirmed space on commercial flights, by carrier, monthly rpt, 9142–23

Productivity, hours, and employment indexes for selected SIC 3- and 4-digit industries, 1954-82, annual rpt, 6824–1.4

Profit margins for major operators of large aircraft, by carrier group and carrier, quarterly rpt, 9142–43

Revenue ton-miles and freight yields for major and all cargo domestic air carrier groups, quarterly rpt, 9142–35

Scientists, engineers, and technicians employment in transportation, utilities, and retail and wholesale trade, by field of science and industry, 1982, 9628–72

Stock (common) average price for major carriers, and compared to New York Stock Exchange indexes, quarterly Dec 1977-June 1984, semiannual rpt, 9142–36

Subsidies of Fed Govt paid since 1979 to air carriers serving small communities, by carrier, monthly rpt, 9142–48

Traffic (passenger and cargo) and departures by aircraft type, by airline and US and foreign airport, 1982, annual rpt, 7504–35

Traffic and financial data for airline industry, by carrier, FY83 with trends from FY73, annual rpt, 9144–1

Traffic, capacity, and performance, by carrier and type of operation, monthly rpt, 9142–13

Traffic, capacity, and performance for medium regional airlines, by carrier and certification status, quarterly rpt, 9142–44

Airports and airways

Traffic levels, accidents, and deaths for airlines and general aviation, 1970-80, annual rpt, 7304–1

Traffic levels at FAA air traffic control facilities, by airport and State, FY83, annual rpt, 7504–27

see also Aerospace industry

see also Air travel

see also Airports and airways

see also Aviation accidents and safety

see also Pilots

see also under By Individual Company or Institution in the "Index by Categories"

see also under By Industry in the "Index by Categories"

Airports and airways

Airline deregulation in 1978, effect on industry operations and finances, air traffic patterns, and CAB programs, various periods FY76-84, 9148–56

Airport size and safety, and accidents at or near airports by circumstance, for total and selected airports, various periods 1964-81, 9618–12

Aviation activity, detailed data on aircraft, air traffic, air carriers, personnel, airports, and FAA operations, 1974-83, annual rpt, 7504–1

Aviation activity forecasts, methodology, data sources, and coverage, Feb 1983 conf papers, annual rpt, 7504–28

Bond tax-exempt issues for private activity, by purpose, face value, major industry, and State, 1983, article, 8302–2.417

Budget of US, effects of Reagan Admin policy changes, by detailed program, FY85, annual rpt, 104–21

Capital needs and intergovtl financing for public works, by type of project and selected city, various periods 1950-83, 10048–60

China economic conditions, agricultural and industrial production, trade, and domestic and foreign investment, 1980-85, 2048–106

Coastal environmental characteristics, fish, wildlife, and use, and population socioeconomic data, for individual areas, series, 5506–4

Construction put in place, permits authorized by region, State, and MSA, and Federal contract awards, by construction type, bimonthly rpt with articles, 2012–1

Developing countries disaster preparedness and summary sociodemographic, political, and economic data, country rpt series, 9916–2

DOT grant awards for transportation planning and safety programs, by region, State, and for 35 largest SMSAs, FY83, annual rpt, 7304–7

Exports and imports of US (airborne), by world area and US customs district and city, monthly rpt, 2422–8

FAA activities and finances, and employees by region, FY82-83, annual rpt, 7504–10

FAA activities and R&D for improvement of air traffic control and airway facilities and equipment under Natl Airspace System Plan, 1982-2000, annual rpt, 7504–12

FAA air traffic control and airway facilities and services, operations, and finances, FY83, annual rpt, 7504–37

Airports and airways

- FAA aviation medicine research and studies, technical rpt series, 7506–10
- Fed Govt aid to State and local govts, expenditures, and direct payments, by program, agency, and State, FY83, annual rpt, 2464–2
- Fed Govt Airport and Airway Trust Fund receipts, expenditures, assets, and liabilities, monthly rpt, 8102–9.5
- Fed Govt airport improvement program grants and activities, by State and airport, FY83, annual rpt, 7504–38
- Fed Govt grants for airport planning and dev projects, by sponsor, airport, and location, periodic press release series, 7506–8
- Fed Govt-owned real property inventory and costs, worldwide summary by location, agency, and use, 1983, annual rpt, 9454–5
- Fed Govt programs and mgmt cost control proposals, 3-year savings by function and agency, and financial and operating data, 1960s-81, 16908–1.11
- Fed Govt surplus personal property donations to State and local agencies and nonprofit instns, by region and State, FY83, annual rpt, 9454–22
- Financing of airports by source, bond issues by region, and airport operations, by airport and operator type, FY75-83 and projected to FY93, 26306–6.75
- Foreign economic, social, and political summary data, by country, 1984, annual factbook, 244–11
- Govt census, 1982: city govt revenues by source, expenditures by function, debt, and assets, by State and city, 2457–4
- Govt census, 1982: county govt revenues by source, expenditures by function, debt, and assets, by State and county, 2457–3
- Govt census, 1982: employment, payrolls, and average earnings, by function, level of govt, State, county, population size, and inside-outside SMSAs, 2455–2
- Govt census, 1982: State govt payments to local govts, by program, source of funds, level of govt, and State, with trends from 1902, 2460–3
- Govt employment and payroll, by function, level of govt, and jurisdiction, 1983, annual rpt series, 2466–1
- Govt finances, by level of govt, State, and for large cities and counties, 1981-83, annual rpt series, 2466–2
- Govt transportation revenues by source and expenditures, by level of govt and mode of transport, and Fed Govt aid by type, FY77-82, 7308–185
- Hijackings, on-board explosions, other crimes against civil aviation, and circumstances, US and worldwide, 1931-83, annual rpt, 7504–31
- Immigration, and alien residents, workers, visitors, deportations, and naturalizations, by country of birth, FY81, annual rpt, 6264–2
- Passenger travel to and from US on US and foreign flag air carriers, by country, world area, and US port, monthly rpt, 7302–2
- Security operations of airports to prevent hijackings, screening results, enforcement actions, and hijacking attempts, 1st half 1984, semiannual rpt, 7502–5

Traffic (passenger and cargo) and departures by aircraft type, by airline and US and foreign airport, 1982, annual rpt, 7504–35

- Traffic, aircraft operations by type and passenger enplanements, by airport, region, and State, projected FY82-95 and trends from FY76, annual rpt, 7504–7
- Traffic, aircraft, pilots, airport activity, and fuel use, forecast FY84-95 with FY79-83 trends, annual rpt, 7504–6
- Traffic and service changes by city since 1978 airline deregulation, with market shares, fares, and load factors, quarterly rpt, 9142–42
- Traffic levels at FAA air traffic control facilities, by airport and State, FY83, annual rpt, 7504–27
- Transit system (automated guideway) characteristics and itemized costs, for 16 systems in operation or under construction, 1982, annual rpt, 7884–6
- User fees to recover costs of 7 federally subsidized public service programs, by type of fee, user, and service, FY84-88, 26306–6.68
- Weather stations of Natl Weather Service, locations and regular observations made, 1984 annual listing, 2184–5
- *see also* Air traffic control
- *see also* Aviation accidents and safety

Ajman

see United Arab Emirates

Akhtar, M. A.

"Effects of Exchange Rate Uncertainty on German and U.S. Trade", 9385–1.405

Akielaszek, John

"Regional Survey of the Chemistry of Headwater Lakes and Streams in New England: Vulnerability to Acidification", 5506–5.15

Akron, Ohio

- Census of Housing, 1980: occupancy and unit characteristics, by race, Hispanic origin, and city, SMSA rpt, 2473–1.59
- Census of Population and Housing, 1980: detailed population and housing characteristics, by county, city, and census tract, SMSA rpt, 2551–2.59
- Housing vacancy rates for single and multifamily units and mobile homes, by city and ZIP code, 1984, annual metro area rpt, 9304–27.9
- *see also* under By City and By SMSA or MSA in the "Index by Categories"

Alabama

- Agricultural acreage by crop type, impact of TVA agricultural dev program in Alabama, 1936 and 1941, 9808–68
- Agriculture census, 1982: farms, farmland, production and costs, and operator characteristics, preliminary State summary and county rpts, 2330–1.1
- Agriculture census, 1982: farms, farmland, production, finances, and operator characteristics, by county, final State rpt, 2331–1.1
- Alcohol fuel (ethanol) production in Tennessee Valley, feedstocks, facilities, tax incentives, and related farming data, by State, 1970s-83 and projected to 1992, 9808–69
- Bank deposits in commercial and mutual savings banks and in US branches of foreign banks, by account type, instn, State, SMSA, and county, June 1983, annual rpt, 9295–3.9

Index by Subjects and Names

- Biomass Fuels Program of TVA, technologies and processes dev, costs, and resource requirements, 1970s-90s, series, 9806–9
- Black rural population of Alabama, education, employment, health services, and economic status, for 16 counties, selected years 1970-81, 11048–180
- Census of Housing, 1980: occupancy and unit characteristics of SMSAs and central cities, by race, Hispanic origin, and city, State rpt, 2473–1.2
- Census of Population and Housing, 1980: detailed population and housing characteristics, by county, city, and census tract, State rpt, 2551–2.2
- Census of Population, 1980: detailed socioeconomic and demographic characteristics, by age, sex, race, Hispanic origin, and industry, State rpt, 2531–4.2
- Coal (bituminous) mining production and related workers, wages by occupation, and benefits, by size of mine and union status, in 6 States and aggregate for Rocky Mountain States, July 1982 survey, 6787–6.198
- Coal dev plans on Fed Govt lease lands, environmental and socioeconomic impacts to 2000, final statement, 5726–4.8
- Collective bargaining calendar for Southeast US, 1984, annual rpt, 6946–1.68
- County Business Patterns: establishments, employees, and payrolls, by SIC 4-digit industry and county, 1982, annual State rpt, 2326–6.2
- Employment (nonagricultural) by industry div and SMSA, earnings, and hours, for 8 southeastern States, monthly press release, 6942–7
- Employment and unemployment in Alabama by SMSA and industry div, and planned capital investment and new jobs by selected firm, 1982-83, article, 9371–1.408
- Employment, earnings, and hours, by selected SIC 1- to 4-digit industry, State, and for 278 major labor areas, 1939-83, annual rpt, 6744–5.1, 6744–5.3
- Employment, prices, earnings, and union membership in 8 southeastern States, Oct 1982-83, annual rpt, 6944–2
- Environmental quality, pollutant discharge by type and source, and EPA protection activities and funding, 1970s-83, biennial regional rpt, 9184–15.4
- Exports of manufactured and agricultural commodities, manufacturing production, and export-related employment, 1960s-82, State rpt, 2046–3.1
- Financial and economic devs, Fed Reserve Bank of Atlanta monthly rpt with articles, 9371–1
- Fish and shellfish landings, prices, and cannery production, for Gulf States and North Carolina, by area, weekly rpt, 2162–6.3
- HHS aid to each State and local govt or private instn, amount obligated, funding agency, and program, FY83, annual listing, 4004–3.4
- Income (personal) per capita and by source, and earnings by industry div, by State, MSA, and county, 1977-82, annual regional rpt, 2704–2.6

Index by Subjects and Names

Alaska

Manufacturing census, 1982: financial and operating data, by SIC 2- to 4-digit industry, State, SMSA, and county, preliminary census div rpt, 2491–3.6

Mineral Industry Surveys, State review of production, 1983, advance annual rpt, 5614–6.1

Minerals Yearbook, 1982, Vol 2 preprints: State review of production and sales by commodity, and business activity, annual rpt, 5604–16.2

Minerals Yearbook, 1982, Vol 2: State reviews of production, sales, and firms, by commodity, and business activity, annual rpt, 5604–34

Population size, Apr 1980 and July 1982, and per capita income, 1979 and 1981, by county and city, State Current Population Rpt, 2546–11.1

Retail trade census, 1982: employment, establishments, sales, and payroll, by SIC 2- to 4-digit kind of business, SMSA, county, and city, State rpt, 2397–1.1

Savings and loan assns, FHLB 4th District insured members financial condition and operations, by SMSA, monthly rpt, 9302–1

Textile mill employment and average hours and earnings, for 8 Southeastern States, monthly press release, 6942–1

Water supply and quality, and effect of coal mining operations, for selected river basins in Eastern and Interior coal provinces, 1983 rpt, 5666–15.23

Water supply and quality in streams and lakes, and groundwater levels in wells, by drainage basin, 1982, annual State rpt, 5666–20.1

Water supply and quality in streams and lakes, and groundwater levels in wells, by drainage basin, 1983, annual State rpt, 5666–10.1

Water supply and quality in 8 southeastern States, with background socioeconomic data, 1960s-2020 with trends from 1930, 9208–119

Wood residue production and use in TVA region, by tree species group and residue type, for 44 counties, 1979, technical paper, 9806–2.36

see also Anniston, Ala.

see also Birmingham, Ala.

see also Florence, Ala.

see also Gadsden, Ala.

see also Huntsville, Ala.

see also Mobile, Ala.

see also Montgomery, Ala.

see also Tuscaloosa, Ala.

see also under By State in the "Index by Categories"

Alamogordo, N.Mex.

Wages of office and plant workers, by occupation, 1984 labor market area survey rpt, 6785–3.5

Alaska

Agriculture census, 1982: farms, farmland, production and costs, and operator characteristics, preliminary State summary and county rpts, 2330–1.2

Agriculture census, 1982: farms, farmland, production, finances, and operator characteristics, by county, final State rpt, 2331–1.2

Airline departures and seats scheduled weekly from Alaska, by city, Apr 1978 and 1984, article, 9142–42.405

Arctic Natl Wildlife Refuge resources, resident and visitor activities, and environmental impacts of energy exploration, 1983, annual update rpt, 5504–26

Army Corps of Engineers activities and projects, FY83 and trends from 1800s, annual rpt, 3754–1

Bank deposits in commercial and mutual savings banks and in US branches of foreign banks, by account type, instn, State, SMSA, and county, June 1983, annual rpt, 9295–3.19

Census of Housing, 1980: occupancy and unit characteristics of SMSAs and central cities, by race, Hispanic origin, and city, State rpt, 2473–1.3

Census of Population and Housing, 1980: detailed population and housing characteristics, by county, city, and census tract, State rpt, 2551–2.3

County Business Patterns: establishments, employees, and payrolls, by SIC 4-digit industry and county, 1982, annual State rpt, 2326–6.3

Electric power plant capacity and generation by fuel type, and marketing, for Alaska by utility, type of ownership, and location, 1983, annual rpt, 3214–2

Employment, earnings, and hours, by selected SIC 1- to 4-digit industry, State, and for 278 major labor areas, 1939-83, annual rpt, 6744–5.1, 6744–5.3

Energy supply/demand and prices, by fuel type and consuming sector with foreign comparisons, 1949-83, annual rpt, 3164–74

Energy supply/demand and prices, by fuel type, sector, and end use, with foreign comparisons, 1960-83 and projected to 1995, annual summary rpt, 3164–76

Environmental quality, pollutant discharge by type and source, and EPA protection activities and funding, 1970s-83, biennial regional rpt, 9184–15.10

Exports of manufactured and agricultural commodities, manufacturing production, and export-related employment, 1960s-82, State rpt, 2046–3.2

Fish and shellfish canned and frozen production, imports, landings, and prices, for Alaska and Northwest States, weekly rpt, 2162–6.5

HHS aid to each State and local govt or private instn, amount obligated, funding agency, and program, FY83, annual listing, 4004–3.10

Ice conditions of Bering Sea and Alaska north coast, monthly rpt, 2182–5

Income (personal) per capita and by source, and earnings by industry div, by State, MSA, and county, 1977-82, annual regional rpt, 2704–2.9

Land claims of Alaska and Alaska Native corporations for Fed Govt lands, status and Land Mgmt Bur conveyance problems, various dates 1978-FY84, GAO rpt, 26113–125

Land Mgmt Bur public lands admin and program activities in western States, FY82-84, annual rpt, 5724–13

Lumber production, prices, trade, and employment in Northwest US and British Columbia, quarterly rpt, 1202–3

Manufacturing census, 1982: financial and operating data, by SIC 2- to 4-digit industry, State, SMSA, and county, preliminary census div rpt, 2491–3.9

Mineral Industry Surveys, State review of production, 1983, advance annual rpt, 5614–6.2

Minerals resources of Alaska, production, claims on wildlife refuges, oil and gas leases, and exploratory wells, with maps and bibl, 1983, annual rpt, 5664–11

Minerals Yearbook, 1982, Vol 2 preprints: State review of production and sales by commodity, and business activity, annual rpt, 5604–16.3

Minerals Yearbook, 1982, Vol 2: State reviews of production, sales, and firms, by commodity, and business activity, annual rpt, 5604–34

Oil (Alaskan) potential exports to Japan, costs and benefits, with background data on oil prices, Pacific Basin supply/demand, and tankers, various periods 1918-99, hearings, 25388–45

Oil and gas companies production and exploration detailed expenditures, revenues, operating ratios, and sales volume, 1982, annual Current Industrial Rpt, 2506–8.11

Population size and components of change, by MSA and county, 1980-82, annual State Current Population Rpt, 2546–4.2

Population size, Apr 1980 and July 1982, and per capita income, 1979 and 1981, by county and city, State Current Population Rpt, 2546–11.2

Railroad freight revenues and tonnage in Alaska, by commodity, summary data, FY75-81, annual rpt, 7304–1

Retail trade census, 1982: employment, establishments, sales, and payroll, by SIC 2- to 4-digit kind of business, SMSA, and retail district, State rpt, 2401–1.2

Retail trade census, 1982: employment, establishments, sales, and payroll, by SIC 2- to 4-digit kind of business, SMSA, county, and city, State rpt, 2397–1.2

Savings and loan assns, FHLB 12th District members financial operations and housing industry indicators by State, monthly rpt, 9302–21

Service industry census, 1982: employment, establishments, receipts, and payroll, by SIC 2- to 4-digit kind of business, SMSA, county, and city, State rpt, 2391–1.2

Shipping industry impact on local economy, and port dev financing through user fees, by State, other area, industry, and port, 1970s-2020, hearings, 21568–34

Timber acreage and resources in Alaska, by species, ownership class, and inventory unit, 1967-74, series, 1206–9

Wages for 3 occupational groups, relative average levels in 78 labor market areas, 1983, annual press release, 6785–13

Wages of office and plant workers, by occupation, 1984 labor market area survey rpt, 6785–3.7

Water supply, and snow survey results, monthly State rpt, 1266–2.1

Waterborne commerce of US (domestic and foreign), freight by commodity, traffic, and passengers, by port and waterway, 1982, annual rpt, 3754–3.4

Alaska

Weather broadcasts for US ships, by major ocean area, as of Jan 1984, biennial rpt, 2184–3

Wholesale trade census, 1982: employment, establishments, finances, and operations, by SIC 2- to 4-digit kind of business, SMSA, county, and city, State rpt, 2405–1.2

see also Alaska Natives

see also Anchorage, Alaska

see also Gulf of Alaska

see also Pribilof Islands, Alaska

see also Trans-Alaska Pipeline System

see also under By State in the "Index by Categories"

Alaska Natives

Arctic Natl Wildlife Refuge resources, resident and visitor activities, and environmental impacts of energy exploration, 1983, annual update rpt, 5504–26

Budget of US, effects of Reagan Admin policy changes, by detailed program, FY85, annual rpt, 104–21

Census of Housing, 1980: occupancy and unit characteristics of SMSAs and central cities, by race, Hispanic origin, and city, State and SMSA rpt series, 2473–1

Census of Population and Housing, 1980: detailed population and housing characteristics, by county, city, and census tract, State and SMSA rpt series, 2551–2

Census of Population, 1980: detailed socioeconomic and demographic characteristics, by age, sex, race, Hispanic origin, occupation, and industry, State rpt series, 2531–4

Census of Population, 1980: detailed socioeconomic characteristics, by county, city, and inside-outside SMSAs and central cities, State rpt series, 2531–3

Census of Population, 1980: Indian and Alaska Native population and housing occupancy, by reservation, Alaska Native village, and other Indian area, supplementary rpt, 2535–1.16

Census of Population, 1980: migration since 1975, by State and selected demographic characteristics, supplementary rpt, 2535–1.13

County and City Data Book, detailed socioeconomic and demographic data for States, counties, and cities, selected years 1976-82, 2328–1

Employment and training programs for Indians and Alaska Natives, funding allocation under Job Training Partnership Act, by individual tribe and group, FY84, press release, 6408–57

Health clinic visits and ambulatory high use patients of Alaska Native Medical Center, by age and sex, and patient deaths, 1972-78, article, 4102–1.440

Health condition of Indians, births, morbidity, and deaths and rates, and health services facilities and use, 1954-83, annual compilation, 4104–7

Health programs for Indians and Alaska Natives, activities and funding for scholarships, care services, and facilities construction, by city, FY82, annual rpt, 4104–11

Housing and community dev program operations for Indians and Alaska Natives, FY82 with Community Dev Block Grant funding by tribe and State for FY81, annual rpt, 5004–5

Land claims of Alaska and Alaska Native corporations for Fed Govt lands, Land Mgmt Bur conveyance problems and status, various dates 1978-FY84, GAO rpt, 26113–125

Revenue sharing payments to States, local govts, Indian tribes, and Alaska Native villages, and entitlement computation data, FY84, series, 8066–1

Statistical Abstract of US, social, political, and economic data, 1950s-83 and trends, annual rpt, 2324–1.1

Alaska Power Administration

Activities, project operations, and financial statements, annual rpt, suspended, 3214–1

Budget appropriations proposed for Fed Govt energy programs, by office or dept and function, FY84-85, annual rpt, 3004–14

Budget of US, effects of Reagan Admin policy changes, by detailed program, FY85, annual rpt, 104–21

Cost control proposals for Fed Govt programs and mgmt, 3-year savings by function and agency, and financial and operating data, 1960s-81, 16908–1

Electric power plant capacity and generation by fuel type, and marketing, for Alaska by utility, type of ownership, and location, 1983, annual rpt, 3214–2

Electric power wholesale purchases and costs for individual REA borrowers, by supplier and State, 1940-83, annual rpt, 1244–5

Electric utilities privately owned, detailed financial and operating data by company, with summary data for other distributors by type, 1982, annual rpt, 3164–23

Albania

Background Notes, summary social, political, and economic data, 1984 rpt, 7006–2.40

Cuba economic conditions, agricultural and industrial production and distribution, trade, and intl economic relations, 1970-82 and trends from 1957, 248–40

Economic, social, and political summary data, by country, 1984, annual factbook, 244–11

Export licensing and monitoring activities under Export Admin Act, for selected commodities, and for Communist and other countries, FY83, annual rpt, 2044–22

Exports and imports of US with Communist countries, by detailed commodity and country, quarterly rpt with articles, 9882–2

Exports of US, detailed Schedule E commodities by mode of transport and world area and country of destination, 1983, annual rpts, 2424–5

Imports of US, detailed Schedule A commodities by country and world area of origin, and mode of transport, 1983, annual rpts, 2424–2

Imports of US, detailed TSUSA commodities by country of origin, 1983, annual rpt, 2424–4

Loans and grants for economic and military assistance from US and intl agencies, by program and country, FY46-83, annual rpt, 9914–5

Index by Subjects and Names

Military spending, arms trade, and armed forces size, with total govt spending and population, by country, 1972-82, annual rpt, 9824–1

Minerals Yearbook, 1982, Vol 3: foreign country reviews of production, trade, and policies, by commodity, annual rpt, 5604–35

Minerals Yearbook, 1983, Vol 3 preprints: foreign country review of production, trade, and policies, by commodity, annual rpt, 5604–23.2

Population size and growth rates, and latest available benchmark demographic data, by country, 1950-83, biennial rpt, 2324–4

Scientific document exchanges of Albania and PRC with USSR, 1948-61, 2326–9.7

see also under By Foreign Country in the "Index by Categories"

Albany, Ga.

Census of Housing, 1980: occupancy and unit characteristics, by race, Hispanic origin, and city, SMSA rpt, 2473–1.60

Census of Population and Housing, 1980: detailed population and housing characteristics, by county, city, and census tract, SMSA rpt, 2551–2.60

see also under By SMSA or MSA in the "Index by Categories"

Albany, N.Y.

Census of Housing, 1980: occupancy and unit characteristics, by race, Hispanic origin, and city, SMSA rpt, 2473–1.61

Census of Population and Housing, 1980: detailed population and housing characteristics, by county, city, and census tract, SMSA rpt, 2551–2.61

Housing and households detailed characteristics, and unit and neighborhood quality, by inside-outside central cities, 1980 survey, SMSA rpt, 2485–6.2

Public works capital needs and financing, by project type, level of govt, and selected jurisdiction, 1970s-83 and projected to 2000, hearing, 23848–181

Wages of office and plant workers, by occupation, 1984 SMSA survey rpt, 6785–11.9

see also under By City and By SMSA or MSA in the "Index by Categories"

Albany, Oreg.

Radioactivity levels at former AEC and Manhattan Project research and storage sites, 1978-82, 3406–1.39

Radioactivity levels at former AEC and Manhattan Project research and storage sites, 1979-82, 3406–1.37

Albrecht, Clare

"Average Wages for 1982 for Indexing Under the Social Security Act and the Automatic Determinations for 1984", 4706–2.119

Albuquerque, N.Mex.

Census of Housing, 1980: occupancy and unit characteristics, by race, Hispanic origin, and city, SMSA rpt, 2473–1.62

Census of Population and Housing, 1980: detailed population and housing characteristics, by county, city, and census tract, SMSA rpt, 2551–2.62

Homeless population and characteristics, and temporary shelter operations, use, and user characteristics, for selected cities, various periods 1979-84, hearing, 21248–85

Index by Subjects and Names

Alcohol use

Housing vacancy rates for single and multifamily units and mobile homes, by city and ZIP code, 1983, annual metro area rpt, 9304–19.8

Housing vacancy rates for single and multifamily units and mobile homes, by city and ZIP code, 1984, annual metro area rpt, 9304–19.18

Wages of office and plant workers, by occupation, 1984 labor market area survey rpt, 6785–3.9

see also under By City and By SMSA or MSA in the "Index by Categories"

Alcohol, Drug Abuse and Mental Health Administration

Contract awards, grants, and staff of ADAMHA, by Inst, program, and State, FY83, annual factbook, 4044–1

Cost control proposals for Fed Govt programs and mgmt, 3-year savings by function and agency, and financial and operating data, 1960s-81, 16908–1.7

Data projects and systems of HHS, by subagency, FY83-84, annual inventory, 4044–3

R&D Fed Govt funding for all performers, by field and supporting agency, selected years FY60-84, annual rpt, 9627–20

Research grants, awards, and fellowships of ADAMHA, by recipient, FY82, annual listing, 4044–13

see also National Institute of Mental Health

see also National Institute on Alcohol Abuse and Alcoholism

see also National Institute on Drug Abuse

Alcohol fuels

Auto methanol fuel, regulatory barriers to market dev, with supply/demand and auto fleet use and fuel economy, mid-1970s-82 and projected to 2000, GAO rpt, 26113–112

Auto use of alcohol fuels, effects on oil refinery finances and operations, projected to 2000 with trends 1964-80, 3308–75

Consumption, by fuel type, economic sector, and end use, 1983 and 2000, 2006–2.5

Corporate income tax returns, detailed income and tax items by industry, 1981, annual rpt, 8304–4

Cuba economic conditions, agricultural and industrial production and distribution, trade, and intl economic relations, 1970-82 and trends from 1957, 248–40

Exports, imports, tariffs, and industry operating data for monohydric alcohols, foreign and US, 1978-82, TSUSA commodity rpt supplement, 9885–4.37

Production costs, related employment, and Fed Govt subsidies and impact on farm income, for alcohol fuels, selected years 1978-90, GAO rpt, 26113–140

Production of gasohol and ethanol, plant capacity, tax exemptions and sales by State, and prices, 1983, annual rpt, 3304–9

Tennessee Valley ethanol production, feedstocks, facilities, tax incentives, and related farming data, by State, 1970s-83 and projected to 1992, 9808–69

see also Biomass energy

see also Gasohol

Alcohol use

Adolescent abuse, characteristics of victims and abuse, local agencies contacted, drug and alcohol involvement, and reciprocal violence, 1980-81 survey, 4608–18

Aircraft accidents in general aviation by State, circumstances, and pilots involved by age and blood alcohol level, 1981, annual rpt, 9614–3.1

Aircraft fatal accidents of commuter airlines, air taxis, and general aviation, alcohol involvement, circumstances, and pilot characteristics, 1975-81, 9618–11

Airline pilots terminated for medical reasons and reinstated by carrier, and aircraft accidents by age of flight crew, selected years 1960-81, hearing, 21148–34

Alcohol, Drug Abuse and Mental Health Admin staff, contract awards, and grants, by Inst, program, and State, FY83, annual factbook, 4044–1

Arrests and arrest rates, by offense, offender characteristics, population size, and State, 1970s-83, annual rpt, 6224–2.2

Births by outcome, and mother's sociodemographic, life style, and maternity characteristics, 1980, article, 4102–1.418, 4102–1.422

Blood lead levels by sociodemographic and behavioral characteristics, and potential workplace exposure, 1976-80, 4147–11.201

Budget of US, effects of Reagan Admin policy changes, by detailed program, FY85, annual rpt, 104–21

Children and youth benefitting from Fed Govt public welfare programs and tax expenditures, participation and funding for 71 programs, FY81-83, 21968–30

Consumption of food and nutrient intake by individuals, by food group, source, and socioeconomic characteristics, 1977-78 natl survey, final rpt series, 1356–4

Crime and criminal justice data, including justice expenditures and employment by level of govt, 1970s-82 with some trends from 1875, 6068–174

Death rates by sex, race, and age for 40 causes, projected for 10-year period, 1982 rpt, 4208–21

Deaths and death rates by detailed cause and demographic characteristics, 1979 and selected trends, US Vital Statistics annual rpt, 4144–2.1

Education Dept programs funding, operations, and effectiveness, FY83, annual rpt, 4804–5

Employee theft and misconduct in retail, hospital, and manufacturing establishments, by type and frequency of violation, 1978-80, 6068–178

Fed Govt plan to reduce drug abuse and trafficking, funding by agency and background data on drug use by substance, selected years FY81-85, biennial rpt, 024–1

Govt census, 1982: State govt payments to local govts, by program, source of funds, level of govt, and State, with trends from 1902, 2460–3

Health condition and health care resources, use, and expenditures, 1970s-82 with trends and projections 1900-2000, annual compilation, 4144–11

Health habits associated with 10 major death causes, prevalence of 8 risk factors in selected States, 1981-83 surveys, article, 4202–7.405

Health habits of adults, including physical activity, smoking, alcohol use, hypertension, and seat belt use, by age and sex, 1982, annual rpt, 4204–1.3

Heart attack and cancer incidence and deaths in men aged 35-59, effects of lowering blood cholesterol levels, with background data on other risk factors, 1973-83, 4478–145

HHS aid to each State and local govt or private instn, amount obligated, funding agency, and program, FY83, annual listing, 4004–3

High school classes of 1980 and 1982: educational and sociodemographic characteristics and expectations, natl longitudinal study, series, 4826–2

High school seniors use and assessment of drugs by type, alcohol, and cigarettes, by sex and region, 1975-83 surveys, annual rpt, 4494–4

High school seniors use of drugs, alcohol, and cigarettes, 1975-82, article, 4102–1.410

Homeless population and characteristics, and temporary shelter operations, use, and user characteristics, by region and selected city, 1983, 5188–108

Homeless population and characteristics, and temporary shelter operations, use, and user characteristics, for selected cities, various periods 1979-84, hearing, 21248–85

Hospital discharges and length of stay, by patient characteristics, facility size, procedure performed, diagnosis, and region, 1982, annual rpt, 4147–13.78

Hypertension prevalence among heavy alcohol users, by blood pressure and drinks consumed per day, 1984 article, 4102–1.434

Indian births, morbidity, and deaths and rates, and health services facilities and use, 1954-83, annual compilation, 4104–7

Israel and France urban youths use of selected drugs, alcohol, and cigarettes, by age and sex, 1977 and 1979, article, 4102–1.430

Jail capacities, conditions, expenditures, and services, and socioeconomic and other characteristics of inmates, various dates 1976-82, 10048–59

Mental health facilities, services, staff, and patient characteristics, 1970s-82 with trends from 1954, annual rpt, 4504–9

Mental hospitals of States and counties, patients and admissions by diagnosis, age, and State, FY81, annual rpt, 4504–2

Navy personnel alcohol and drug abuse, and related deaths, courts-martial, discharges, and treatment program funding and staff, FY83, annual table, 3804–12

Older persons by demographic, socioeconomic, and health characteristics, selected years 1900-81 and projected to 2050, Current Population Rpt, 2546–2.125

Pretrial citation release use, cost savings for law enforcement agencies, and failures to appear in court, by offense and selected jurisdiction, 1970s-82, 6068–187

Research grants, awards, and fellowships of ADAMHA, by recipient, FY82, annual listing, 4044–13

Research on alcoholism, treatment programs, and patient characteristics, quarterly journal, 4482–1

Research review of alcohol use, and health, economic, and social impacts, 1970s-81, 4488–4

Alcohol use

South Carolina manufacturing plants with selected employee health care services, by SIC 2-digit industry, 1982, article, 4102–1.408

State and local govt productivity measurement, with background data and output indexes for 7 govt services, various periods 1955-82, 6728–27

State govt alcohol, drug abuse, and mental health treatment funding, and admin of Fed Govt block grants, for 13 States, FY80-84, GAO rpt, 26121–87

Statistical Abstract of US, social, political, and economic data, 1950s-83 and trends, annual rpt, 2324–1.1

Treatment of alcohol- and drug abuse-related and other mental health disorders, outpatient visits in Baltimore, Md, and visit probability rates, 1981-82, article, 4102–1.449

see also Driving while intoxicated

Alcoholic beverages

see Alcohol use

see Beer and breweries

see Driving while intoxicated

see Liquor industry

see Wine and winemaking

Alcoholism

see Alcohol use

Alexandria, La.

Census of Housing, 1980: occupancy and unit characteristics, by race, Hispanic origin, and city, SMSA rpt, 2473–1.63

Census of Population and Housing, 1980: detailed population and housing characteristics, by county, city, and census tract, SMSA rpt, 2551–2.63

Housing vacancy rates for single and multifamily units and mobile homes, by city and ZIP code, 1984, annual metro area rpt, 9304–19.10

see also under By SMSA or MSA in the "Index by Categories"

Alexandria, Va.

see also under By City in the "Index by Categories"

Alfalfa

see Animal feed

see Seeds

Algal blooms

see Eutrophication

Algeria

Agricultural and food production indexes, and production of selected commodities, by world region and country, 1974-83, annual rpt, 1524–5

Agricultural situation in Middle East and North Africa, by country and commodity, 1983 and outlook for 1984, annual rpt, 1524–4.3

Cuba economic conditions, agricultural and industrial production and distribution, trade, and intl economic relations, 1970-82 and trends from 1957, 248–40

Economic, social, and political summary data, by country, 1984, annual factbook, 244–11

Exports of US, detailed Schedule B commodities by country of destination, 1983, annual rpt, 2424–9

Exports of US, detailed Schedule E commodities by mode of transport and world area and country of destination, 1983, annual rpts, 2424–5

Imports of US, detailed Schedule A commodities by country and world area of origin, and mode of transport, 1983, annual rpts, 2424–2

Imports of US, detailed TSUSA commodities by country of origin, 1983, annual rpt, 2424–4

Loans and grants for economic and military assistance from US and intl agencies, by program and country, FY46-83, annual rpt, 9914–5

Military aid of US, arms sales, and training programs costs and budget requests by program, world region, and country, FY83-85, annual rpt, 7144–13

Military spending, arms trade, and armed forces size, with total govt spending and population, by country, 1972-82, annual rpt, 9824–1

Minerals Yearbook, 1982, Vol 3: foreign country reviews of production, trade, and policies, by commodity, annual rpt, 5604–35

Minerals Yearbook, 1983, Vol 3 preprints: foreign country review of production, trade, and policies, by commodity, annual rpt, 5604–23.3

Natural gas and liquefied natural gas trade of US with 4 countries, by US pipeline company, 1982-83, annual article, 3162–4.406

Natural gas and liquefied natural gas transported, by State and country of origin and destination, 1982, article, 3162–4.409

Oil and gas undiscovered recoverable resources, cumulative production, and identified reserves, as of 1982, preliminary oil basin rpt, 5666–17.13

Oil production, and exports and prices to US, by major exporting country, detailed data, monthly rpt, 3162–24

Oil reserves, production, and resource lifespan under alternative production rates, for 3 countries, 1909-1982 with projections to 2100, 3166–9.8

Population size and growth rates, and latest available benchmark demographic data, by country, 1950-83, biennial rpt, 2324–4

see also under By Foreign Country in the "Index by Categories"

Alien workers

Farm labor, farms, and labor costs, by labor and farm type and State, with immigrant labor law effect on farm work force, 1978, 1598–192

Income (taxable) not reported on individual and corporate returns, and associated Federal revenue losses, by detailed legal and illegal source, 1973-81, 8308–26

TTPI socioeconomic, employment, health, and govtl data, by TTPI govt, FY83 and selected trends, detailed annual rpt, 7004–6.2

Visas issued and refused to immigrants and nonimmigrants, and status adjustments, by class and nationality, FY77, annual rpt, 7184–1

Workers admitted to US, FY76-81, annual rpt, 6264–2

see also Mexicans in the U.S.

Aliens

Drug Enforcement Admin cases against major drug traffickers by case characteristics, and agents assessment of activities, in 3 cities, 1979-82, GAO rpt, 26119–57

Index by Subjects and Names

Fed Govt programs and mgmt cost control proposals, 3-year savings by function and agency, and financial and operating data, 1960s-81, 16908–1.9

Haiti men at 2 US immigration processing centers, incidence of breast enlargement, Dec 1981-May 1982, article, 4102–1.451

Immigration, and alien residents, workers, visitors, deportations, and naturalizations, by country of birth, FY81, annual rpt, 6264–2

Resettlements and arrivals of refugees and aliens in US, by State, outlying area, country of birth and citizenship, age, sex, and sponsoring agency, monthly rpt, 4702–3

Statistical Abstract of US, social, political, and economic data, 1950s-83 and trends, annual rpt, 2324–1.1

Travel to and from US on US and foreign flag air carriers, by country, world area, and US port, monthly rpt, 7302–2

Visas issued and refused to immigrants and nonimmigrants, and status adjustments, by class and nationality, FY77, annual rpt, 7184–1

see also Alien workers

see also Citizenship

see also Foreign students

see also Immigration

see also Mexicans in the U.S.

see also Refugees

Alimony

see Child support and alimony

Allardice, David R.

"Small Issue Industrial Revenue Bond Financing in the Seventh Federal Reserve District", 9375–13.2

Allegheny County, Pa.

Radioactivity levels at former AEC and Manhattan Project research and storage sites, 1981, 3406–1.38

Allen, Edward W.

"World Cotton Trends and Competition", 1561–1.402

Allen, George

"Crop Quality Differences and Estimates of Corn for Feed Use", 1561–4.405

Allentown, Pa.

Census of Housing, 1980: occupancy and unit characteristics, by race, Hispanic origin, and city, SMSA rpt, 2473–1.64

Census of Population and Housing, 1980: detailed population and housing characteristics, by county, city, and census tract, SMSA rpt, 2551–2.64

Housing and households detailed characteristics, and unit and neighborhood quality, by inside-outside central cities, 1980 survey, SMSA rpt, 2485–6.7

see also under By City and By SMSA or MSA in the "Index by Categories"

Allergies

Natl Inst of Allergy and Infectious Diseases activities, grants by instn, State, and country, and disease incidence and costs, FY60s-84, annual rpt, 4474–30

see also under By Disease in the "Index by Categories"

Allied health personnel

DOD medical personnel, trainees, and accessions by source, by occupation, specialty, and service branch, FY83, annual rpt, 3544–24

Index by Subjects and Names

Health care services of selected medical practitioners, use by patient characteristics, 1980 survey with trends from 1963, 4146–12.4

Hospital employment, vacancies, and vacancy rates, by occupation and by hospital specialty, region, census div, and State, 1980, annual rpt, 4114–12

Manpower supply and education of health professionals, by occupation, demographic and professional characteristics, and location, 1950s-83 and projected to 2000, biennial rpt, 4114–8

Mental health clinical training funding by NIMH, by program and field, FY80-83, GAO rpt, 26121–86

Military reserve forces medical personnel and wartime requirements by occupation, and medical equipment costs, by reserve component, as of 1983, annual rpt, 3544–27.2

Minority group and women employment and training in health professions, by field, selected years 1962/63-1983/84, 4118–18

Navy and Marine Corps disease incidence, medical care, and deaths, by detailed diagnosis, and medical personnel and workloads, 1978-79, annual rpt, 3804–1

Occupational manpower needs and supply by detailed occupation, and educational and training program enrollees and grads by detailed field, 1982 and 1995, biennial rpt, 6744–3

Occupational Outlook Handbook, 1984-85 biennial rpt, 6744–1

Southeastern States health care resource availability, and employment by occupation, by facility type, by State and SMSA in Fed Reserve 6th District, 1970s-81, article, 9371–1.425

VA Medicine and Surgery Dept trainees, by detailed program and city, FY83, annual rpt, 9924–21

Wages of hospital workers by sex and occupation, and benefits, for 22 MSAs, Oct 1981 survey, 6787–6.201

see also Clinical laboratory technicians *see also* Dietitians and nutritionists *see also* Midwives

Allman, Dale N.

"1978-83 Increase in U.S. Business Failures", 9381–1.414

Alpena, Mich.

Wages of office and plant workers, by occupation, 1984 labor market area survey rpt, 6785–3.7

Alternative Solutions, Inc.

"U.S. Foundations Responsiveness to Puerto Rican Needs and Concerns: Foundation Giving to Puerto Rican Organizations 1979-81", 21788–137.1

Altman Foundation

Philanthropic grants of Altman Foundation in New York by recipient, and Foundation income and expenses, selected years 1913-82, hearings, 21788–137

Alton, Ill.

see also under By SMSA or MSA in the "Index by Categories"

Altoona, Pa.

Census of Population and Housing, 1980: detailed population and housing characteristics, by county, city, and census tract, SMSA rpt, 2551–2.65

see also under By SMSA or MSA in the "Index by Categories"

Aluminum and aluminum industry

Air pollutant emission factors, by detailed source, 3rd edition, 1983-84 supplements, 9198–13

Business statistics, detailed data for major industries and economic indicators, *Survey of Current Business,* monthly rpt, 2702–1.14

Castings (nonferrous) shipments and unfilled orders, by metal type, monthly Current Industrial Rpt, 2506–10.5

Census of Population, 1980: detailed socioeconomic and demographic characteristics, by age, sex, race, Hispanic origin, occupation, and industry, State rpt series, 2531–4

China economic conditions, agricultural and industrial production, trade, and domestic and foreign investment, 1980-85, 2048–106

Communist, OECD, and selected other countries minerals and metals production, by commodity, 1960s-83, annual rpt, 244–5.6

County Business Patterns: establishments, employees, and payrolls, by SIC 4-digit industry and county, 1981, annual State rpt series, 2326–8

County Business Patterns: establishments, employees, and payrolls, by SIC 4-digit industry and county, 1982, annual State rpt series, 2326–6

Electric power industrial demand model estimates, economic indicators, and supporting data for 5 industries, 1960s-80 with projections to 2000, 3008–87

Electric power sales of Columbia River system, by customer, FY83, annual rpt, 3224–1

Electric power sales, revenues, and prices of Bonneville Power Admin, by class of customer and individual purchaser, 1983, semiannual rpt, 3222–1

Employment, earnings, and hours, by SIC 4-digit nonfarm industry, monthly 1974-Feb 1984, annual update, 6744–4

Exports and imports of US, detailed SIC-based commodities by world area, 1983, annual rpts, 2424–6

Exports and imports of US, totals and as percent of domestic production, by SIC 2- to 5-digit commodity, 1981, annual rpt, 2424–3

Exports of US, detailed commodities by country of destination, monthly rpt, 2422–3

Exports of US, detailed Schedule B commodities by country of destination, 1983, annual rpt, 2424–9

Exports of US, detailed Schedule E commodities by mode of transport and world area and country of destination, 1983, annual rpts, 2424–5

Finances and operations, by SIC 2- to 4-digit industry, 1970s-83 and projected to 1988, annual rpt, 2014–4

Foreign minerals production, reserves, and industry role in domestic economy and world supply, country and world region rpt series, 5606–1

Foundry products imports effect on US industry, investigation with background financial and operating data, 1984 rpt, 9886–4.77

Futures trading in selected commodities, foreign currencies, Treasury securities, and stock indexes, NYC, Chicago, and other markets activity, monthly rpt, 11922–5

Great Lakes trade, by SITC 3-digit commodity, port, vessel type, world area, and country, 1982, annual rpt, 7744–3

Imports of US, detailed Schedule A commodities by country and world area of origin, and mode of transport, 1983, annual rpts, 2424–2

Imports of US, detailed Schedule A commodities by country, monthly rpt, 2422–2

Imports of US, detailed TSUSA commodities by country of origin, 1983, annual rpt, 2424–4

Input-output structure of US economy, detailed interindustry transactions for 537 industries, and components of final demand, 1977 benchmark data, 2708–17

Manufacturing census, 1982: financial and operating data, by SIC 2- to 4-digit industry, State, SMSA, and county, preliminary census div rpt series, 2491–3

Manufacturing census, 1982: financial and operating data, for SIC 4-digit industries by product, preliminary rpt series, 2491–1

Mineral industries census, 1982: financial and operating data, by SIC 2- to 4-digit industry, preliminary summary rpt, 2511–2.1

Mineral industries census, 1982: financial and operating data, including materials consumed, by SIC 4-digit industry and State, preliminary rpt, 2511–1.3

Mineral Industry Surveys, commodity review of production, trade, stocks, and consumption, monthly rpt, 5612–1.1

Mineral Industry Surveys, commodity review of production, trade, stocks, and consumption, quarterly rpt, 5612–2.2

Minerals Yearbook, 1982, Vol 1: commodity reviews of production, reserves, supply, use, and trade, annual rpt, 5604–33

Minerals Yearbook, 1982, Vol 2 preprints: State reviews of production and sales by commodity, and business activity, annual rpt series, 5604–16

Minerals Yearbook, 1982, Vol 2: State reviews of production, sales, and firms, by commodity, and business activity, annual rpt, 5604–34

Minerals Yearbook, 1982, Vol 3: foreign country reviews of production, trade, and policies, by commodity, annual rpt, 5604–35

Minerals Yearbook, 1982, Vol 3 preprints: foreign country reviews of production, trade, and policies, by commodity, annual rpt series, 5604–17

Minerals Yearbook, 1983, Vol 1 preprints: commodity review of production, reserves, supply, use, and trade, annual rpt, 5604–15.4, 5604–15.8

Minerals Yearbook, 1983, Vol 3 preprints: foreign country reviews of production, trade, and policies, by commodity, annual rpt series, 5604–23

Occupational injuries and incidence rates at metal mines and related operations, detailed analysis, 1982, annual rpt, 6664–3

Aluminum and aluminum industry

Occupational injury and illness rates, by SIC 2- to 4-digit industry, 1982, annual rpt, 6844–1

OECD trade, total and for 4 major countries, and US trade by country, by commodity, 1972-82, annual world region rpt series, 244–13

Pacific Northwest aluminum industry electricity use, operations, and energy and labor efficiency by plant, projected 1984-2003, annual rpt, 3224–2.4

Producer prices and indexes, by stage of processing and detailed commodity, monthly rpt, 6762–6

Producer prices and indexes, by stage of processing and detailed commodity, monthly 1983, annual supplement, 6764–2

Production (primary aluminum) plant ownership, capacity, and type and source of raw material and energy used, by plant, State, and country, June 1984, semiannual listing, 5602–5

Production, prices, trade, use, employment, tariffs, and stockpiling, by mineral commodity, with foreign comparisons, 1979-83, annual rpt, 5604–18

Productivity, hours, and employment indexes for selected SIC 3- and 4-digit industries, 1954-82, annual rpt, 6824–1.3

Shipments (defense and total), trade, consumption, and inventories of aluminum ingots and mill products, monthly Current Industrial Rpt, 2506–10.9

Stockpiling of strategic and critical materials, Fed Govt activities and inventories by commodity, Oct 1983-Mar 1984, semiannual rpt, 9432–1

Stockpiling of strategic materials, inventories, costs, and goals, by commodity, as of June 1984, semiannual rpt, 9452–7

Strategic minerals supply/demand, trade, and foreign and US industry devs by firm and country, by commodity, bimonthly rpt, 5602–4

Wages and benefits in nonferrous metal manufacturing, by occupation, size of establishment, union status, and metro-nonmetro location, 1981 survey, 6787–6.196

Waterborne commerce of US (domestic and foreign), freight by commodity, traffic, and passengers, by port and waterway, 1982, annual rpt, 3754–3

see also under By Commodity in the "Index by Categories"

see also under By Industry in the "Index by Categories"

Aluminum Co. of America

Tennessee Valley dams and reservoirs owned by ALCOA, elevations, storage, flows, and hydroelectric generating capacity use, 1981, annual rpt, 9804–7

Alvarez, Donato

"Productivity Trends in Manufacturing in the U.S. and 11 Other Countries", 6722–1.405

Amarillo, Tex.

Census of Housing, 1980: occupancy and unit characteristics, by race, Hispanic origin, and city, SMSA rpt, 2473–1.66

Census of Population and Housing, 1980: detailed population and housing characteristics, by county, city, and census tract, SMSA rpt, 2551–2.66

see also under By City and By SMSA or MSA in the "Index by Categories"

Ambulances

see Emergency medical service

Ambulatory aids

see Prosthetics and orthotics

American Association of Retired Persons Pharmacy Service

"Your Money Saving Guide, Generic Prescription Drugs You Can Trust", 25528–98

American Battle Monuments Commission

Budget of US Appendix, detailed budgets and personnel summaries, by agency, FY85, annual rpt, 104–3

Budget of US, appropriations, outlays, balances, and budget receipts, by govtl branch and agency, FY83, annual rpt, 8104–2

American Dental Association

Election campaign funding by political action committees and voting on FTC rules, for individual congressmen, 1978-82, hearings, 21428–7.2, 25688–6.2

American Forces Information Service

"Defense '84: Almanac", 3504–13

American Gas Association

"Actual and Forecasted Conservation in the Residential Gas Space Heating Market Through 1990", 21368–54

"Impact on Low Income and Elderly Consumers of Take-or-Pay and Indefinite Price Escalator Clauses in Gas Contracts", 25148–26

"1978 Survey of A.G.A. Gas Utility Merchandising Companies", 21368–54

American Indians

see Indians

American Medical Association

Election campaign funding by political action committees and voting on FTC rules, for individual congressmen, 1978-82, hearings, 21428–7.2, 25688–6.2

American Motors Corp.

Energy economy test results, 1985 model year, annual rpt, 3304–11

Energy use of autos and light trucks, economy standards and manufacturer compliance, and gas prices and taxes, with selected foreign comparisons, FY80-83 and projected to 2000, hearing, 21368–49

Safety of domestic and foreign autos and light trucks, crash test results of selected new models for model year to date, press release series, 7766–7

Sales, prices, and registrations of autos and auto products in US, and trade of 8 countries with US, by make and model, 1964-83, annual rpt, 9884–7

American National Red Cross

Blood program collection, production, and distribution activities, technical services, research, and processing fees, 1982/83, annual rpt, 29254–3

Program highlights and financial statements, 1982/83, annual rpt, 29254–1

American Psychological Association

Membership by State, 1970 and 1980, annual rpt, 4504–9.4

Index by Subjects and Names

American Revolution

see War

American Samoa

Bank deposits in commercial and mutual savings banks and in US branches of foreign banks, by account type, instn, State, SMSA, and county, June 1983, annual rpt, 9295–3.18

Employment, minimum wage rates, average earnings, and benefits, by industry and individual establishment, Nov 1983, biennial rpt, 6504–6

Environmental quality, pollutant discharge by type and source, and EPA protection activities and funding, 1970s-83, biennial regional rpt, 9184–15.9

Exports and imports between US and outlying areas, by detailed commodity and mode of transport, monthly rpt, 2422–4

Govt financial data, audits of Interior Dept Inspector General, FY83, annual rpt, 5304–15.4

HHS aid to each State and local govt or private instn, amount obligated, funding agency, and program, FY83, annual listing, 4004–3.9

Hwy Statistics, detailed data on traffic, govt finances, fuel use, vehicles, driver licenses, and hwy characteristics, 1983, annual rpt, 7554–1.6

Medical referrals (off-island) of TTPI and American Samoa, costs, and potential savings, by govt, FY83 with comparisons from FY78, GAO rpt, 26123–72

Minerals Yearbook, 1982, Vol 2: State reviews of production, sales, and firms, by commodity, and business activity, annual rpt, 5604–34

Population size and components of change, by outlying area, 1970-82, Current Population Rpt, 2546–3.127

Population size and components of change, by outlying area, 1980-83, Current Population Rpt, 2546–3.134

Population size and growth rates, and latest available benchmark demographic data, by country, 1950-83, biennial rpt, 2324–4

Port dev costs and financing through user fees, and shipping industry impact on local economy, by State, other area, industry, commodity, and port, 1970s-82, hearings, 21568–34.1

Water supply and quality in streams and lakes, and groundwater levels in wells, by drainage basin, 1983, annual State rpt, 5666–10.10

see also under By Outlying Area in the "Index by Categories"

American Schools and Hospitals Abroad

AID activities and funding by project and function, FY85, and developing countries summary socioeconomic data, 1970s-83, by country, annual rpt, 9914–3

American Society for Metals

"Quality Assessment of National Defense Stockpile Cobalt Inventory", 25208–27

American Stock Exchange

Trading volume on New York and American Stock Exchanges, monthly rpt, 9362–1.1

Trading volume, securities listed by type, and exchange finances, by stock exchange, selected years 1935-82, annual rpt, 9734–2.1, 9734–2.3

Index by Subjects and Names

Transactions volume and proceeds and new issue registrations, for US registered exchanges, SEC monthly rpt, 9732–1

American Telephone and Telegraph Co.

Costs, operating data, and billings for AT&T local and long distance lines, by State, 1980-82 with trends from 1970, 23848–176

Divestiture of AT&T, effect on telecommunications equipment industry, with background financial and operating data, 1984 rpt, 9886–4.75

Fiber optics displacement of copper in telecommunications, with Bell System use and copper and fiber optics industry data, 1978-88, 2048–104

Financial and operating data by company type, with fixed cost recovery from interstate revenue by Bell company and State, 1981-82 with trends from 1945, 26306–6.79

Financial, operating, and employment data of telephone and telegraph firms, detailed statistics, 1982, annual rpt, 9284–6

Labor-mgmt cooperative program for policy dev at AT&T, 1984 narrative article, 6722–1.419

Wages and employment in telephone and telegraph industry by occupation and sex, 1981, annual survey, 6787–6.199

Ames Laboratory

see also Department of Energy National Laboratories

Amey, Dorothy M.

"Veterans Administration Health Care: Planning for Future Years", 26306–6.78

Amick, David R.

"Evaluation of the Bonneville County DUI Accident Prevention Program (Project Safety)", 7762–9.404

Ammunition

Bombing (explosive and incendiary) and arson incidents by target, State, and circumstances, and explosives theft and recovery, 1982-83, annual rpt, 8484–4

Census of Population, 1980: detailed socioeconomic and demographic characteristics, by age, sex, race, Hispanic origin, occupation, and industry, State rpt series, 2531–4

County Business Patterns: establishments, employees, and payrolls, by SIC 4-digit industry and county, 1981, annual State rpt series, 2326–8

County Business Patterns: establishments, employees, and payrolls, by SIC 4-digit industry and county, 1982, annual State rpt series, 2326–6

DOD budget, itemized account of legislative history, FY84, annual rpt, 3504–7

DOD budget justification for procurement programs, by equipment type, service branch, and defense agency, FY83-86, annual rpt, 3504–14

DOD budget justification, programs, and policies, FY85, annual rpt, 3544–2

DOD expenditures for goods and services, by function, 1972-84, article, 2702–1.440

DOD outlays and obligations, by function and service branch, quarterly rpt, 3542–3

DOD procurement, prime contract awards by category, contract and contractor type, and service branch, FY74-1st half FY84, semiannual rpt, 3542–1

DOD procurement, prime contract awards by detailed procurement category, FY80-83, annual rpt, 3544–18

DOD procurement, prime contract awards for 25 commodity categories and R&D, by State and census div, FY81-83, annual rpt, 3544–11

DOD shipments of military and personal property, loss claims, passenger traffic, and costs, by mode of transport, quarterly rpt, 3702–1

DOD strategic capability, force strengths, weapons, training, supplies, and requirements, by service branch, FY80-84 and projected to 1990, 3508–19

Employment, earnings, and hours, by SIC 4-digit nonfarm industry, monthly 1974-Feb 1984, annual update, 6744–4

Exports and imports of US, detailed SIC-based commodities by world area, 1983, annual rpts, 2424–6

Exports and imports of US, totals and as percent of domestic production, by SIC 2- to 5-digit commodity, 1981, annual rpt, 2424–3

Exports of US, detailed commodities by country of destination, monthly rpt, 2422–3

Exports of US, detailed Schedule B commodities by country of destination, 1983, annual rpt, 2424–9

Exports of US, detailed Schedule E commodities by mode of transport and world area and country of destination, 1983, annual rpts, 2424–5

Fed Govt programs and mgmt cost control proposals, 3-year savings by function and agency, and financial and operating data, 1960s-81, 16908–1

Foreign market and trade for sporting goods and recreational equipment and vehicles, country market research rpts, 2045–14

Imports of US, detailed Schedule A commodities by country and world area of origin, and mode of transport, 1983, annual rpts, 2424–2

Imports of US, detailed Schedule A commodities by country, monthly rpt, 2422–2

Imports of US, detailed TSUSA commodities by country of origin, 1983, annual rpt, 2424–4

Income tax returns of corporations, detailed income and tax items by industry, 1981, annual rpt, 8304–4

Input-output structure of US economy, detailed interindustry transactions for 85 industries, and components of final demand, 1977, article, 2702–1.421

Input-output structure of US economy, detailed interindustry transactions for 537 industries, and components of final demand, 1977 benchmark data, 2708–17

Manufacturing census, 1982: financial and operating data, by SIC 2- to 4-digit industry, State, SMSA, and county, preliminary census div rpt series, 2491–3

Manufacturing census, 1982: financial and operating data, for SIC 4-digit industries by product, preliminary rpt, 2491–1.301

Occupational injury and illness rates, by SIC 2- to 4-digit industry, 1982, annual rpt, 6844–1

Producer prices and indexes, by stage of processing and detailed commodity, monthly rpt, 6762–6

Anchorage, Alaska

Producer prices and indexes, by stage of processing and detailed commodity, monthly 1983, annual supplement, 6764–2

Sealift Military Command operations for naval fleet support, and transport of DOD and AID cargo by route, quarterly rpt, 3802–2

Tax (excise) collections of IRS, by source, quarterly press release, 8302–1

Tax (excise) on hunting and fishing equipment, revenue of Fed Govt fish and wildlife restoration program by type of equipment, FY84, annual rpt, 5504–13

Waterborne commerce of US (domestic and foreign), freight by commodity, traffic, and passengers, by port and waterway, 1982, annual rpt, 3754–3

Amols, George

"Agricultural Finance Statistics, 1960-83", 1544–2

Amstutz, Daniel G.

"Outlook for U.S. Agricultural Trade", 1004–16.1

Amstutz, David E.

"Reexamination of Occurrence Rates for Accidental Oil Spills on the U.S. Outer Continental Shelf", 5738–1

Amtrak

see National Railroad Passenger Corp.

Anaheim, Calif.

Census of Housing, 1980: occupancy and unit characteristics, by race, Hispanic origin, and city, SMSA rpt, 2473–1.67

Census of Population and Housing, 1980: detailed population and housing characteristics, by county, city, and census tract, SMSA rpt, 2551–2.67

CPI by component for US city average, and by region, population size, and for 28 SMSAs, monthly press release, 6762–1

CPI by detailed component, for US city average, 28 SMSAs, and 4 regions by population size, monthly rpt, 6762–2

Housing and households detailed characteristics, and unit and neighborhood quality, by inside-outside central cities, 1981 survey, SMSA rpt, 2485–6.19

Housing unit starts and completions authorized by building permits in 20 MSAs, quarterly rpt, 2382–9

Housing vacancy rates for single and multifamily units and mobile homes, by city and ZIP code, 1983, annual metro area rpt, 9304–20.7

Wages of office and plant workers, by occupation, 1983 SMSA survey rpt, 6785–12.2

see also under By City and By SMSA or MSA in the "Index by Categories"

Anchorage, Alaska

Census of Housing, 1980: occupancy and unit characteristics, by race, Hispanic origin, and city, SMSA rpt, 2473–1.68

Census of Population and Housing, 1980: detailed population and housing characteristics, by county, city, and census tract, SMSA rpt, 2551–2.68

CPI by component for US city average, and by region, population size, and for 28 SMSAs, monthly press release, 6762–1

CPI by detailed component, for US city average, 28 SMSAs, and 4 regions by population size, monthly rpt, 6762–2

Anchorage, Alaska

see also under By City and By SMSA or MSA in the "Index by Categories"

Anderson, Ind.

Census of Housing, 1980: occupancy and unit characteristics, by race, Hispanic origin, and city, SMSA rpt, 2473–1.69

Census of Population and Housing, 1980: detailed population and housing characteristics, by county, city, and census tract, SMSA rpt, 2551–2.69

see also under By SMSA or MSA in the "Index by Categories"

Anderson, S.C.

Census of Housing, 1980: occupancy and unit characteristics, by race, Hispanic origin, and city, SMSA rpt, 2473–1.70

Census of Population and Housing, 1980: detailed population and housing characteristics, by county, city, and census tract, SMSA rpt, 2551–2.70

see also under By SMSA or MSA in the "Index by Categories"

Anderson, Theodore C.

"Costs and Indexes for Domestic Oil and Gas Field Equipment and Production Operations, 1983", 3164–45

"Indexes and Estimates of Domestic Well Drilling Costs, 1983 and 1984", 3164–67

Andorra

Background Notes, summary social, political, and economic data, 1984 rpt, 7006–2.41

Economic, social, and political summary data, by country, 1984, annual factbook, 244–11

Exports of US, detailed Schedule B commodities by country of destination, 1983, annual rpt, 2424–9

Imports of US, detailed TSUSA commodities by country of origin, 1983, annual rpt, 2424–4

Population size and growth rates, and latest available benchmark demographic data, by country, 1950-83, biennial rpt, 2324–4

see also under By Foreign Country in the "Index by Categories"

Andreassen, Arthur J.

"Economic Outlook for the 1990's: Three Scenarios for Economic Growth", 6728–29

Andrews, Michael D.

"Recent Trends in the U.S. Foreign Exchange Market", 9385–1.411

Andrilenas, Paul A.

"Current World Fertilizer Situation and Outlook, 1982/83-1992/93", 1004–16.1

Anemia

see Blood diseases and disorders

see Nutrition and malnutrition

Angelo, Luigi

"Processing and Refining Capacity of the Domestic Sugar Industry", 1561–14.401

"Sugarbeet and Sugarcane Grower Receipts, Production Costs, and Net Returns, 1981-83 Crops", 1561–14.403

"Sugarbeet and Sugarcane Production and Processing Costs: 1982 Crop", 1561–14.402

Angola

Agricultural and food production indexes, and production of selected commodities, by world region and country, 1974-83, annual rpt, 1524–5

Agricultural situation in sub-Saharan Africa, by country, 1982-83 and outlook for 1984, annual rpt, 1524–4.10

Cuba economic conditions, agricultural and industrial production and distribution, trade, and intl economic relations, 1970-82 and trends from 1957, 248–40

Economic conditions and foreign marketing prospects in 46 Sub-Saharan countries, 1983 world region rpt, 2046–5.1

Economic, social, and political summary data, by country, 1984, annual factbook, 244–11

Exports of US, detailed Schedule B commodities by country of destination, 1983, annual rpt, 2424–9

Exports of US, detailed Schedule E commodities by mode of transport and world area and country of destination, 1983, annual rpts, 2424–5

Imports of US, detailed Schedule A commodities by country and world area of origin, and mode of transport, 1983, annual rpts, 2424–2

Imports of US, detailed TSUSA commodities by country of origin, 1983, annual rpt, 2424–4

Loans and grants for economic and military assistance from US and intl agencies, by program and country, FY46-83, annual rpt, 9914–5

Military spending, arms trade, and armed forces size, with total govt spending and population, by country, 1972-82, annual rpt, 9824–1

Minerals Yearbook, 1982, Vol 3: foreign country reviews of production, trade, and policies, by commodity, annual rpt, 5604–35

Population size and growth rates, and latest available benchmark demographic data, by country, 1950-83, biennial rpt, 2324–4

see also under By Foreign Country in the "Index by Categories"

Animal and Plant Health Inspection Service

Activities and programs of USDA, by subagency, FY83, annual rpt, 1004–3

Animal protection, licensing, and inspection activities of USDA, and animals used in research, by State, FY83, annual rpt, 1394–10

Cattle brucellosis eradication, and testing of goats and swine, cooperative Federal-State program activities, by State, FY83, annual rpt, 1394–6

Cattle tuberculosis eradication and surveillance, cooperative Federal-State program activities, by State, FY83, annual rpt, 1394–13

Foreign and US animal disease outbreaks, quarterly rpt, 1392–3

Fraud and abuse in USDA programs, audits and investigations, 2nd half FY84, semiannual rpt, 1002–4

Hogs and pigs fed garbage, monthly rpt, discontinued, 1392–5

Plant pests and pathogens found entering US, by country of origin, State, and method of interception, FY82, annual rpt, 1394–16

Poultry Natl Improvement Plan, hatchery participation and flocks included, by disease program, region, and State, 1981-83, annual rpt, 1394–15

Animal diseases and zoonoses

Avian influenza effect on poultry and egg production and prices, and eradication program costs of Fed Govt, 1982-84, article, 1561–7.402

Index by Subjects and Names

Brucellosis eradication in cattle, and testing of goats and swine, cooperative Federal-State program activities, by State, FY83, annual rpt, 1394–6

Cases and incidence of infectious notifiable diseases and other public health concerns, by census div and State, 1982, annual rpt, 4204–1

Fishery resources mgmt and R&D, Fed Govt grants by project and resulting publications, 1983, annual listing, 2164–3

Foreign and US animal disease outbreaks, quarterly rpt, 1392–3

Livestock grazing on Natl Forest System lands, and losses from predators, poisonous plants, and other causes, by region and State, FY83, annual rpt, 1204–5

Plague (bubonic and pneumonia-inducing) deaths, and cases by onset date, patient characteristics, and source, 1983 and trends from 1950, article, 4202–7.408

Poultry Natl Improvement Plan, hatchery participation and flocks included, by disease program, region, and State, 1981-83, annual rpt, 1394–15

Poultry slaughtered under Fed Govt inspection, pounds certified, and condemnations by cause, by State, monthly rpt, 1625–3

Research (agricultural) expenditures and scientist years, by topic, commodity, and performing organization, FY82, annual rpt, 1744–2

Research funding for agriculture from Fed Govt and States, by region, State, and outlying area, FY78-82, GAO rpt, 26113–111

Tuberculosis eradication and surveillance in cattle, cooperative Federal-State program activities, by State, FY83, annual rpt, 1394–13

see also Food and waterborne diseases

see also Rabies

see also Veterinary medicine

Animal feed

Acreage planted and harvested, by crop and State, 1982-83 and planned as of June 1984, annual rpt, 1621–23

Acreage planting intended for 19 crops, by State, as of Feb 1984, annual rpt, 1621–22

Acreage, yield, and production of field crops, by State, 1978-82 and preliminary 1983, 1641–7

Agricultural Stabilization and Conservation Service feed grains program, 1960-84, annual fact sheet, 1806–4.10

Agricultural Stabilization and Conservation Service producer payments under 26 programs, monthly rpt, 1802–10

Agricultural Statistics, 1983, annual rpt, 1004–1

Agriculture census, 1982: farms, farmland, production and costs, and operator characteristics, preliminary State and county rpt series, 2330–1

Agriculture census, 1982: farms, farmland, production, finances, and operator characteristics, by county, final State rpt series, 2331–1

Agriculture Fact Book of US, compilation of data for 1983 with trends from 1940, annual rpt, 1004–14

Index by Subjects and Names

Animal feed

Air pollutant emission factors, by detailed source, 3rd edition, 1983-84 supplements, 9198–13

Argentina grain and oilseed production, effect of agricultural price regulation, 1947-80, 1528–170

Biotechnology commercial uses, R&D funding and output, controls, and industry financial and operating data, for US and 5 countries, 1970s-83 and estimated 1984-85, 26358–98

Cattle and calves on feed, inventory and marketings by State, monthly release, 1623–2

Cattle and hog feeding in Corn Belt and cattle feeding in Great Plains, selected costs at current rates, periodic situation rpt, 1561–7

China economic conditions, agricultural and industrial production, trade, and domestic and foreign investment, 1980-85, 2048–106

China exports and imports by SITC 1- to 5-digit commodity, 1970s-82, annual rpt, 244–12

Choline chloride from Canada and UK at less than fair value, imports injury to US industry, investigation with background financial and operating data, 1983 rpt, 9886–14.90

Choline chloride from Canada at less than fair value, imports injury to US industry, investigation with background financial and operating data, 1984 rpt, 9886–14.123

Cooperatives farm supply sales programs, services offered, inventory mgmt and marketing methods, and sales force and compensation system, for 4 products, 1982, 1128–24

Cooperatives, membership, activities, and finances, by commodity and selected State, 1900-80 with trends from 1863, 1128–30

County Business Patterns: establishments, employees, and payrolls, by SIC 4-digit industry and county, 1981, annual State rpt series, 2326–8

County Business Patterns: establishments, employees, and payrolls, by SIC 4-digit industry and county, 1982, annual State rpt series, 2326–6

Cows for milk, grains and other concentrates fed, monthly rpt, 1627–1

Dairy production by State, stocks, prices, and CCC price support activities, by product type, monthly rpt, 1627–3

Eastern Europe grain production, consumption, and trade, and US farm cooperatives grain and oilseed export potential, for 4 countries, selected years 1960-90, 1128–27

EC food supply/demand and market and support prices, with exchange rates, fertilizer price index, GDP, and population, by country, 1960-83, 1528–173

Employment, earnings, and hours, by SIC 4-digit nonfarm industry, monthly 1974-Feb 1984, annual update, 6744–4

Export sales and shipments of US grains, oilseed products, hides, skins, and cotton, by country, weekly rpt, 1922–3

Exports (total and to EC) and production of US corn gluten products and citrus pulp, 1960-83, hearing, 25368–135

Exports and imports of US, by agricultural commodity and country, bimonthly rpt with articles, 1522–1

Exports and imports of US, by detailed agricultural commodity and country, FY83 and CY83, semiannual rpts, 1522–4

Exports and imports of US, by detailed agricultural commodity for 8 major commodity groups, monthly rpt, 1922–8

Exports and imports of US, detailed SIC-based commodities by world area, 1983, annual rpts, 2424–6

Exports and imports of US, totals and as percent of domestic production, by SIC 2- to 5-digit commodity, 1981, annual rpt, 2424–3

Exports and personal expenditures of US and world for selected agricultural commodities, by country, and export share of US farm income, various periods 1926-82, 1528–172

Exports, imports, tariffs, and industry operating data for animal feed and ingredients, foreign and US, 1979-83, TSUSA commodity rpt, 9885–1.64

Exports of manufactured and agricultural commodities, manufacturing production, and export-related employment, 1960s-82, State rpt series, 2046–3

Exports of US, detailed commodities by country of destination, monthly rpt, 2422–3

Exports of US, detailed Schedule B commodities by country of destination, 1983, annual rpt, 2424–9

Exports of US, detailed Schedule E commodities by mode of transport and world area and country of destination, 1983, annual rpts, 2424–5

Farm finances, assets, liabilities, income, receipts by commodity and State, and expenses, 1980-83 and trends from 1910, annual rpt, 1544–16

Farm finances, expenses by type, loans by purpose and source, and credit detail by Fed Reserve District, quarterly rpt, 9365–3.10

Farm marketing cash receipts and production expenses, by State, 1979-82, annual rpt, 1544–18

Farm production expenditures, detailed items by farm sales size and region, 1983, annual rpt, 1614–3

Farm production inputs, land mgmt, and environmental effects, for 4 crops, 1940s-80 and projected to 2010, 9188–94

Farm production inputs, outputs, and productivity, by region, 1939-82, annual rpt, 1544–17

Farm production itemized costs, receipts, and net returns, for 13 crops, 4 livestock types, and milk, by region, 1981-83, annual rpt, 1544–20

FDA investigation and regulatory activities, quarterly rpt, 4062–3

Fish and fish products production by region and State, and trade, by species and product, 1982-83, annual rpt series, 2166–6

Foreign and US agricultural production, trade, and climatic devs, with US and Rotterdam dam prices and EC supports, weekly press release, 1922–4

Foreign and US agricultural supply/demand and production data, for selected US and world crops, and for US livestock and dairy products, periodic rpt, 1522–5

Foreign and US feed and livestock trade by product and world region, and ocean freight rates between selected countries of origin and destination, selected years 1960-82, 1528–177

Foreign and US grain production, trade, stocks, consumption, and prices, FAS monthly and annual rpt series, 1925–2

Futures trading in selected commodities, foreign currencies, and stock indexes, Chicago and other markets activity, monthly rpt, 11922–1

Futures trading in selected commodities, foreign currencies, Treasury securities, and stock indexes, NYC, Chicago, and other markets activity, monthly rpt, 11922–5

Great Lakes trade, by SITC 3-digit commodity, port, vessel type, world area, and country, 1982, annual rpt, 7744–3

Hay prices in 10 market areas, for baled alfalfa and prairie hay, weekly rpt, 1313–5

Hog production, producer characteristics, facilities, and marketing, by type and size of enterprise and region, 1975 and 1980, 1568–248

Hogs and pigs fed garbage, monthly rpt, discontinued, 1392–5

Imports of dairy products subject to quota and annual quotas, by commodity and country of origin, FAS monthly circular, 1925–31

Imports of US, detailed Schedule A commodities by country and world area of origin, and mode of transport, 1983, annual rpts, 2424–2

Imports of US, detailed Schedule A commodities by country, monthly rpt, 2422–2

Imports of US, detailed TSUSA commodities by country of origin, 1983, annual rpt, 2424–4

Input-output structure of US economy, detailed interindustry transactions for 537 industries, and components of final demand, 1977 benchmark data, 2708–17

Livestock-feed price ratios for corn-fed hogs and beef steers, monthly 1970-83, annual rpt, 1564–6.3

Manufacturing census, 1982: financial and operating data, by SIC 2- to 4-digit industry, State, SMSA, and county, preliminary census div rpt series, 2491–3

Manufacturing census, 1982: financial and operating data, for SIC 4-digit industries by product, preliminary rpt, 2491–1.18, 2491–1.19

Milk (nonfat dry) and whey powder for animal feed, wholesale prices in selected areas, 1983, annual rpt, 1317–1.4

Molasses (feed) production, wholesale prices by market area, and US imports by customs district and country, weekly rpt, 1311–16

OECD trade, total and for 4 major countries, and US trade by country, by commodity, 1972-82, annual world region rpt series, 244–13

Oils and fats production, consumption by end use, and stocks, by type, monthly Current Industrial Rpt, 2506–4.4

January-December 1984

ASI Annual Supplement 41

Animal feed

PL 480 commodity allocations for long-term credit sales, by country, quarterly press release, 1922–7

Portugal agricultural subsidies, profits, marketing margins, and consumer prices, by commodity or product, and effects of prospective EC membership, 1981, 1528–171

Prices received by farmers and production value for detailed crops by State, 1981-83, annual rpt, 1621–2

Prices received by farmers for major products, and paid for farm inputs and living items, by commodity and State, monthly rpt, 1629–1

Prices received by farmers for major products, and paid for farm inputs, by commodity and State, 1983, annual rpt, 1629–5

Producer prices and indexes, by stage of processing and detailed commodity, monthly rpt, 6762–6

Producer prices and indexes, by stage of processing and detailed commodity, monthly 1983, annual supplement, 6764–2

Production, acreage, stocks, use, trade, prices, and price supports, periodic situation rpt with articles, 1561–4

Production and farm finances, expenses by type, and domestic economic impact, selected years 1972-82 and preliminary 1983-84, annual rpt, 1544–19

Production, farms, acreage, and related data, by selected crop and State, monthly rpt, 1621–1

Production, prices, trade, and marketing, by commodity, current situation and forecast, monthly rpt, 1502–4

Production, prices, trade, and stocks, for feedstuffs and feed grains by type, weekly rpt, 1313–2

Productivity, hours, and employment indexes for selected SIC 3- and 4-digit industries, 1954-82, annual rpt, 6824–1.3

Rice market activities, prices, inspections, sales, trade, supply, and use, for US and selected foreign markets, weekly rpt, 1313–8

Seed exports of US, by type of seed, world region, and country, FAS quarterly rpt, 1925–13

Stocks of grains, oilseeds, and hay on and off farms, by State, 1978-83, 1641–17

Supply/demand, prices, and commodity program operations, for selected crops and livestock, 1983 and outlook for 1984, annual article, 9381–1.402

Waterborne commerce of US (domestic and foreign), freight by commodity, traffic, and passengers, by port and waterway, 1982, annual rpt, 3754–3

Wheat and rye foreign and US production, prices, trade, stocks, and use, periodic situation rpt with articles, 1561–12

Wildlife refuge revenues from economic and recreational uses, and refuge managers attitudes toward expanded use, FY81-83, GAO rpt, 26113–128

see also Pasture and rangeland

see also under By Commodity in the "Index by Categories"

Animal Health Institute

"Animal Drug Lag", 25528–98

Animal oils

see Oils, oilseeds, and fats

Animals

China economic conditions, agricultural and industrial production, trade, and domestic and foreign investment, 1980-85, 2048–106

China exports and imports by SITC 1- to 5-digit commodity, 1970s-82, annual rpt, 244–12

Exports and imports of US, by detailed agricultural commodity and country, FY83 and CY83, semiannual rpts, 1522–4

Exports and imports of US, detailed SIC-based commodities by world area, 1983, annual rpts, 2424–6

Exports and imports of US, totals and as percent of domestic production, by SIC 2- to 5-digit commodity, 1981, annual rpt, 2424–3

Exports of US, detailed commodities by country of destination, monthly rpt, 2422–3

Exports of US, detailed Schedule B commodities by country of destination, 1983, annual rpt, 2424–9

Exports of US, detailed Schedule E commodities by mode of transport and world area and country of destination, 1983, annual rpts, 2424–5

Imports of US, detailed Schedule A commodities by country and world area of origin, and mode of transport, 1983, annual rpts, 2424–2

Imports of US, detailed Schedule A commodities by country, monthly rpt, 2422–2

Imports of US, detailed TSUSA commodities by country of origin, 1983, annual rpt, 2424–4

Licensing, inspection, and protection of animals by USDA, and animals used in research, by State, FY83, annual rpt, 1394–10

NIH Research Resources Div activities, accomplishments, and funding, by program, FY83, annual rpt, 4434–12

Pet shop franchise business opportunities, 1984 annual listing, 2044–27

Transportation census, 1982: trucks, by detailed characteristics, miles traveled, and type of product carried, State rpt series, 2573–1

see also Animal diseases and zoonoses

see also Animal feed

see also Birds and bird conservation

see also Endangered species

see also Fish and fishing industry

see also Fishing, sport

see also Livestock and livestock industry

see also Marine mammals

see also Pasture and rangeland

see also Poultry industry and products

see also Rabies

see also Veterinary medicine

see also Wildlife and wildlife conservation

see also Wildlife refuges

see also Zoological parks

see also under By Commodity in the "Index by Categories"

Index by Subjects and Names

Ann Arbor, Mich.

Census of Housing, 1980: occupancy and unit characteristics, by race, Hispanic origin, and city, SMSA rpt, 2473–1.71

Census of Population and Housing, 1980: detailed population and housing characteristics, by county, city, and census tract, SMSA rpt, 2551–2.71

Home mortgage creative financing, effect on home sales price, model results for Ann Arbor, Mich, 1981, article, 9412–2.407

Wages of office and plant workers, by occupation, 1984 labor market area survey rpt, 6785–3.10

see also under By City and By SMSA or MSA in the "Index by Categories"

Annest, Joseph L.

"Blood Lead Levels for Persons Ages 6 Months-74 Years, U.S., 1976-80", 4147–11.201

Anniston, Ala.

Census of Housing, 1980: occupancy and unit characteristics, by race, Hispanic origin, and city, SMSA rpt, 2473–1.72

Census of Population and Housing, 1980: detailed population and housing characteristics, by county, city, and census tract, SMSA rpt, 2551–2.72

see also under By SMSA or MSA in the "Index by Categories"

Annual Housing Survey

Data coverage and availability for transportation industry statistics from Census Bur, 1983 pamphlet, 2326–7.61

Data coverage and availability of Census Bur publications, 1984 annual listing, 2304–2

Housing and financial characteristics, and unit and neighborhood quality, for 15 SMSAs, 1978, annual survey special supplement, 2485–8

Housing and households detailed characteristics, and unit and neighborhood quality, by inside-outside central cities, 1979-82 surveys, SMSA rpt series, 2485–6

Housing and neighborhood quality indicators and attitudes, and occupant characteristics, by urban-rural location and region, 1981, annual survey, 2485–7

Housing and neighborhood quality indicators and attitudes, by occupant and unit characteristics, region, and metro-nonmetro location, 1981, annual survey, 2485–2

Housing occupancy and unit and household characteristics, by region and metro-nonmetro residence, 1983, biennial survey, 2485–1

Annual Survey of Manufactures

Data coverage and availability of Census Bur publications, 1984 annual listing, 2304–2

Financial and operating data, 1980-81 survey reprints, hardbound vol, 2504–1

Antarctic

Climatological data mgmt for Antarctic, 1983 workshop proceedings, 2156–18.15

Marine Mammal Protection Act admin and populations, strandings, and catch permits by type and applicant, by species and location, Apr 1983-Mar 1984, annual rpt, 2164–11

Weather broadcasts for US ships, by major ocean area, as of Jan 1984, biennial rpt, 2184–3

Index by Subjects and Names

Anthropology

R&D expenditures of higher education instns, and science and engineering employment and grad students, by field, 1972-83, biennial rpt, 9627–24

R&D Fed Govt funding for all performers, by field and supporting agency, selected years FY60-84, annual rpt, 9627–20

Science and engineering doctoral degree recipients, by field, sex, race, age, citizenship, postgrad employment and study status, State, and instn, 1960-82, 9626–6.16

Science and engineering grad enrollment, fields of study, financial support, and other student and instn characteristics, 1975-82, annual survey, 9627–7

Science and engineering grads of 1980-81, employment characteristics or grad enrollment, by degree level, field, sex, and race, 1982, 9627–25

Anthropometry

see Body measurements

Antigua and Barbuda

- AID economic assistance to developing countries, obligations and disbursements by country, quarterly rpt, 9912–4
- AID loan repayment status and terms by program and country, and status of predecessor agency loans, quarterly rpt, 9912–3
- Economic, social, and political summary data, by country, 1984, annual factbook, 244–11
- Population size and growth rates, and latest available benchmark demographic data, by country, 1950-83, biennial rpt, 2324–4
- *see also* under By Foreign Country in the "Index by Categories"

Antimony

see Metals and metal industries

Antiques

- Exports, imports, tariffs, and industry operating data for art and antiques, 1979-83, TSUSA commodity rpt, 9885–7.58
- Exports of US, detailed commodities by country of destination, monthly rpt, 2422–3
- Exports of US, detailed Schedule B commodities by country of destination, 1983, annual rpt, 2424–9
- Imports of US, detailed Schedule A commodities by country, monthly rpt, 2422–2
- Imports of US, detailed TSUSA commodities by country of origin, 1983, annual rpt, 2424–4

Antitrust law

- American Telephone and Telegraph Co divestiture effect on telecommunications equipment industry, with background financial and operating data, 1984 rpt, 9886–4.75
- Biotechnology commercial uses, R&D funding and output, controls, and industry financial and operating data, for US and 5 countries, 1970s-83 and estimated 1984-85, 26358–98
- Bus industry collective ratemaking and regulatory reform impacts on operations, finances, and services to older persons and rural areas by State, 1970s-83, 14828–2

Court cases disposition and convictions in Federal district courts, as of June 1970-83, annual rpt, 18204–1

- DOT programs fraud and abuse, audits and investigations, 1st half FY84, semiannual rpt, 7302–4
- FTC investigative activity, litigation, and admin, FY82, annual rpt, 9404–1
- Justice Dept Antitrust Div and other subagency activities, FY82, annual rpt, 6004–1
- Retail prices set by manufacturers under fair-trade law by brand and product, with manufacturers, market concentration, and sales, by industry, selected years 1952-82, 9406–1.38
- *see also* Competition
- *see also* Economic concentration and diversification

Apartment houses

- Alteration and repair expenditures for housing, by type and property size, various periods 1963-83, article, 2012–1.406
- Alteration and repair expenditures for residential property, quarterly rpt, 2382–7
- Alteration and repair expenditures for residential property, 1979-83, annual rpt, 2384–4.1
- Appalachian States, FHLB 5th District housing vacancy rates for single and multifamily units and mobile homes, by ZIP code, annual metro area rpt series, 9304–27
- Arson incidents by occupancy of structure, average property value, and arrest rates, by type of property, 1983, annual rpt, 6224–2.1
- Bond tax-exempt issues by purpose, and Fed Govt mortgage bond revenue losses and borrower characteristics, selected years 1971-85, hearings, 21788–135
- Census of Govts, 1982: properties, govt-assessed value, sales, and tax rates, by property type, State, SMSA, county, and city, 2453–1
- Census of Housing, 1980: inventory, occupancy, and unit characteristics, changes from 1973 by region and inside-outside SMSAs and central cities, series, 2473–3
- Census of Housing, 1980: occupancy and unit characteristics of SMSAs and central cities, by race, Hispanic origin, and city, State and SMSA rpt series, 2473–1
- Census of Housing, 1980: structural, financial, and householder characteristics, by region and State, 2475–4
- Construction industries census, 1982: financial and operating data, by SIC 4-digit industry and State, final rpt series, 2373–1
- Construction industries census, 1982: financial and operating data, by SIC 4-digit industry and State, preliminary rpt series, 2371–1
- Construction put in place, value of new public and private structures, by type, monthly rpt, 2382–4
- Energy use and costs in multifamily rental housing, conservation effect on rental marketing, and effect of utility bill payment methods on conservation efforts, 1970s-80s, 3308–73

Apartment houses

- Energy use, costs, expenditures, and conservation, and household and housing chacteristics, survey series, 3166–7
- Fires (housing electrical) in 10 cities, by type of wiring and equipment involved and circumstances, 1980-81, 2218–71
- Florida and California elderly migration by selected State of origin or destination, and Florida elderly, by sociodemographic and housing characteristics, 1970 and 1980, 4478–150
- Housing and financial characteristics, and unit and neighborhood quality, for 15 SMSAs, 1978, annual survey special supplement, 2485–8
- Housing and households detailed characteristics, and unit and neighborhood quality, by inside-outside central cities, 1979-82 surveys, SMSA rpt series, 2485–6
- Housing and neighborhood quality indicators and attitudes, and occupant characteristics, by urban-rural location and region, 1981, annual survey, 2485–7
- Housing occupancy and unit and household characteristics, by region and metro-nonmetro residence, 1983, biennial survey, 2485–1
- HUD rental rehabilitation grants for low- and moderate-income housing, by community, 1984 press release, 5006–3.33
- HUD rental rehabilitation program allocations, by State, county, and city, FY85, press release, 5006–3.39
- HUD rental rehabilitation projects, owner minority status, funding, assisted units, and location for 141 projects, 1984 press release, 5006–3.38
- Market absorption rates and characteristics for nonsubsidized privately financed furnished and unfurnished units completed in 1982, annual Current Housing Rpt, 2484–2
- Market absorption rates and characteristics for nonsubsidized privately financed units completed in 1983, preliminary annual rpt, 2484–3
- Market absorption rates for apartments and condominiums, and completions by rent class and sales price, quarterly rpt, 2482–2
- Mortgage insurance funds of HUD, financial and property activity, and insurance written, monthly rpt, 5002–9
- Mortgage insurance of HUD in force, and property acquisitions and sales, quarterly rpt, 5002–3
- Mortgage loan activity, by type of lender, loan, and mortgaged property, monthly rpt, 5142–18
- New Communities program of HUD, activities, costs, land sales, and community and population characteristics, for 13 communities, 1970s-83, 5188–107
- New housing unit starts, by units per structure and metro-nonmetro location, and mobile home placements and sales price, by region, monthly rpt, 2382–1
- New housing units authorized, by public and private ownership, by region, div, State, selected MSA, and 4,700 permit-issuing places, monthly rpt, 2382–5
- New housing units authorized, by public and private ownership, State, and permit-issuing place, 1983, annual rpt, 2384–2

ASI Annual Supplement 43

Apartment houses

- New housing units completed and under construction, by units per structure, region, and inside-outside SMSAs, monthly rpt, 2382–2
- New multifamily housing physical characteristics, by region, 1979-83, annual rpt, 2384–1.3
- North Central States, FHLB 7th District housing vacancy rates for single and multifamily units and mobile homes, by ZIP code, annual metro area rpt series, 9304–18
- Pacific Northwest electricity consumption and prices by end-use sector, and economic and demographic data, 1960s-83 and projected to 2005, annual rpt, 3224–2
- Smoke alarm sound levels by brand, and response time by circumstances and for older and mentally retarded persons, 1983 rpt, 2218–70
- South Central States, FHLB 9th District housing vacancy rates for single and multifamily units and mobile homes by ZIP code, annual metro area rpt series, 9304–19
- Southeastern States financial and economic devs, Fed Reserve 6th District, monthly rpt with articles, 9371–1
- Vacancy and occupancy rates, and vacant housing characteristics, by region and metro-nonmetro location, selected years 1960-83, annual rpt, 2484–1
- Vacant housing characteristics and costs, and occupancy and vacancy rates, by region and metro-nonmetro location, quarterly rpt, 2482–1
- West Central States, FHLB 10th District housing vacancy rates for single and multifamily units and mobile homes, by ZIP code, annual metro area rpt series, 9304–22
- Western States, FHLB 11th District housing, employment, and economic indicators, by SMSA, quarterly rpt, 9302–18
- Western States, FHLB 11th District housing vacancy rates for single and multifamily units and mobile homes, by ZIP code, annual metro area rpt series, 9304–20
- Western States, FHLB 11th District member S&Ls financial operations and housing industry indicators by State, monthly rpt, 9302–17
- Western States, FHLB 12th District housing vacancy rates for single and multifamily units and mobile homes, by ZIP code, annual metro area rpt series, 9304–21
- Western States housing outlook and economic and demographic trends, FHLB 11th District, urban area rpt series, 9306–2
- *see also* Condominiums and cooperatives
- *see also* Rooming and boarding houses

Appalachia

- Agricultural Stabilization and Conservation Service producer payments under 26 programs, monthly rpt, 1802–10
- Apple production, marketing, and prices in 4 Appalachian States, 1983/84 crop year, annual rpt, 1311–13
- Budget of US, hwy dev funding, effects of Reagan Admin policy changes, FY85, annual rpt, 104–21
- Fed Govt aid to State and local govts, expenditures, and direct payments, by program, agency, and State, FY83, annual rpt, 2464–2
- HHS aid to each State and local govt or private instn, amount obligated, funding agency, and program, FY83, annual listing, 4004–3
- Housing vacancy rates for single and multifamily units and mobile homes in FHLB 5th District, by ZIP code, annual metro area rpt series, 9304–27
- Hwy system and access roads funding and completion status, by State, quarterly tables, 9082–1
- Land stabilization and conservation program activities and funding, for 13 States, annual rpt, discontinued, 1804–3
- Peach production, marketing, and prices in 4 Southeastern States and Appalachia, 1983, annual rpt, 1311–12
- Population by age and urban-rural location, and employment and net employment change by industry, selected years 1960-90, article, 9088–33
- Regional dev spending for each Appalachian State, by program area and source of funds, FY82, annual rpt, 9084–1
- Savings and loan assns, FHLB 5th District members financial condition and operations by SMSA, monthly rpt, 9302–8
- Water supply and quality, and effect of coal mining operations, for selected river basins in Eastern and Interior coal provinces, series, 5666–15
- Wood fuel removal program itemized costs to Forest Service in 3 central Appalachia natl forests, 1981, 1208–191
- *see also* under names of individual States

Appalachian Regional Commission

- Appalachia population by age and urban-rural location, and employment and net employment change by industry, selected years 1960-90, article, 9088–33
- Budget of US, appropriations, outlays, balances, and budget receipts, by govtl branch and agency, FY83, annual rpt, 8104–2
- Funding for Appalachian regional dev, by program area and source of funds, FY82, annual rpt, 9084–1
- Hwy system and access roads funding and completion status, by State, quarterly tables, 9082–1
- R&D Fed Govt funding for all performers, by field and supporting agency, selected years FY60-84, annual rpt, 9627–20

Apparel

see Clothing and clothing industry

Apples

see Fruit and fruit products

Appleton, Wis.

- Census of Housing, 1980: occupancy and unit characteristics, by race, Hispanic origin, and city, SMSA rpt, 2473–1.73
- Census of Population and Housing, 1980: detailed population and housing characteristics, by county, city, and census tract, SMSA rpt, 2551–2.73
- *see also* under By SMSA or MSA in the "Index by Categories"

Index by Subjects and Names

Appliances

see Household appliances and equipment

Apportionment

see Congressional apportionment

Apprenticeship

- Minorities and women in labor-mgmt, employer, and referral union apprentice programs, annual rpt, discontinued, 9244–7
- Occupational manpower needs and supply by detailed occupation, and educational and training program enrollees and grads by detailed field, 1982 and 1995, biennial rpt, 6744–3
- *Occupational Outlook Handbook,* 1984-85 biennial rpt, 6744–1
- Veterans education assistance program participation and costs under GI Bill and other programs, WW II through Sept 1983, annual rpt, 9924–22

Appropriations

see Budget of the U.S.

see Defense budgets and appropriations

Aptitude tests

see Educational tests

Aquaculture

- Agriculture census, 1982: farms, farmland, production, finances, and operator characteristics, by county, final State rpt series, 2331–1
- Catfish raised on farms, production, inventory, sales, prices, and imports, monthly release, 1631–14
- China economic conditions, agricultural and industrial production, trade, and domestic and foreign investment, 1980-85, 2048–106
- Colorado River Storage Project finances, water resource dev, power production, and other activities in western States, FY83, annual rpt, 5824–3
- Fish and eggs for stocking distributed from natl hatcheries, by species, hatchery, and jurisdiction, FY83, annual rpt, 5504–10
- Fish and shellfish of economic importance, biological, fishery, and mgmt data, literature review series, 2166–16
- Fish hatchery production, deliveries, and operating costs, and fishery assistance, by region, hatchery, and Fed Govt assistance station, FY82, annual rpt, 5504–9
- Japan fish landings, prices, trade by country, cold storage, and market devs, periodic press release, 2162–7
- Natl Forest System wildlife habitat and fishery improvements, use, and game population and harvest by species and forest, by region, FY83, annual rpt, 1204–31
- R&D and mgmt of fishery resources, Fed Govt grants by project and resulting publications, 1983, annual listing, 2164–3
- R&D Fed Govt facilities and services available for private sector use, by field of science, 1984 biennial listing, 2224–4
- Research grants awarded competitively by USDA for agricultural science, food and nutrition, and energy dev, FY83, annual listing, 1744–1

Arab Republic of Egypt

see Egypt

Arabian Peninsula

see Oman

see Qatar

Index by Subjects and Names

see Saudi Arabia
see United Arab Emirates
see Yemen, North
see Yemen, South

Arbitration

see Civil procedure
see Labor-management relations, general
see Labor-management relations in government
see Labor-management relations, local and regional

Archeology

Science and engineering doctoral degree recipients, by field, race, age, citizenship, postgrad employment and study status, State, and instn, 1960-82, 9626–6.16

Architect of the Capitol

- Budget of US Appendix, detailed budgets and personnel summaries, by agency, FY85, annual rpt, 104–3
- Budget of US, appropriations, outlays, balances, and budget receipts, by govtl branch and agency, FY83, annual rpt, 8104–2
- Budget of US, compact budgets by function, agency, and account, FY85 with projections to FY89, annual rpt, 104–2
- Expenditures for Capitol buildings and grounds, salaries, supplies, and services, 1st half FY84, semiannual rpt, 25922–2

Architectural Barriers Act

Building access for handicapped persons to Fed Govt or federally funded facilities, compliance activities and complaints by agency, FY83, annual rpt, 17614–1

Architecture

- Census of Population, 1980: detailed socioeconomic and demographic characteristics, by age, sex, race, Hispanic origin, occupation, and industry, State rpt series, 2531–4
- Census of Population, 1980: labor force, by sex, detailed occupation, and region, with comparison to 1970 census, supplementary rpt, 2535–1.12
- Census of Service Industries, 1982: employment, establishments, receipts, and payroll, by SIC 2- to 4-digit kind of business, SMSA, county, and city, State rpt series, 2391–1
- Census of Service Industries, 1982: employment, establishments, receipts, and payroll, by SIC 4-digit kind of business and State, preliminary rpt, 2390–2.18
- County Business Patterns: establishments, employees, and payrolls, by SIC 4-digit industry and county, 1981, annual State rpt series, 2326–8
- County Business Patterns: establishments, employees, and payrolls, by SIC 4-digit industry and county, 1982, annual State rpt series, 2326–6
- Degrees conferred in higher education, by race, Hispanic origin, sex, level, and field, selected years 1949/50-1979/80, annual rpt, 4824–2.16
- Employment, earnings, and hours, by selected SIC 1- to 4-digit industry, State, and for 278 major labor areas, 1939-83, annual rpt, 6744–5
- Employment, earnings, and hours, by SIC 4-digit nonfarm industry, monthly 1974-Feb 1984, annual update, 6744–4

Handicapped persons access to Fed Govt or federally funded buildings, compliance activities and complaints by agency, FY83, annual rpt, 17614–1

- Housing (earth-sheltered) design, energy efficiency, natural and nuclear hazard reduction, and costs, by selected SMSA, 1983 rpt, 3308–71
- Income tax returns of partnerships, detailed data by industry, 1981 estimates, annual article, 8302–2.404
- Income tax returns of sole proprietorships, detailed data by industry div and selected industry group, 1981, annual rpt, 8304–7
- Industry finances and operations, by SIC 2- to 4-digit industry, 1970s-83 and projected to 1988, annual rpt, 2014–4
- Input-output structure of US economy, detailed interindustry transactions for 537 industries, and components of final demand, 1977 benchmark data, 2708–17
- Natl Endowment for Arts activities and grants, FY83, annual rpt, 9564–3
- *Occupational Outlook Handbook,* 1984-85 biennial rpt, 6744–1

Arctic

Marine Mammal Protection Act admin and populations, strandings, and catch permits by type and applicant, by species and location, Apr 1983-Mar 1984, annual rpt, 2164–11

Area studies

Degrees conferred in higher education, by race, Hispanic origin, sex, level, and field, selected years 1949/50-1979/80, annual rpt, 4824–2.16

Area wage surveys

- Wages by occupation, and benefits for office and plant workers, annual labor market survey rpt series, 6785–3
- Wages by occupation, and benefits for office and plant workers in 70 SMSAs, 1983, annual rpt, 6785–1
- Wages by occupation, and benefits for office and plant workers, 1983, annual SMSA survey rpt series, 6785–12
- Wages by occupation, and benefits for office and plant workers, 1984, annual SMSA survey rpt series, 6785–11
- Wages by occupation, for office and plant workers in metro areas, by sex and region, July 1983, annual summary rpt, 6785–9
- Wages by occupation, for office and plant workers in selected labor market areas, 1983 surveys, annual summary rpt, 6785–6
- Wages by occupation, for office and plant workers in selected SMSAs, 1983 and 1984 surveys, annual rpt, 6785–5
- Wages for 3 occupational groups, relative average levels in 78 labor market areas, 1983, annual press release, 6785–13
- Wages for 4 occupational groups, relative average levels in 70 SMSAs, 1983, annual press release, 6785–8
- *see also* Industry wage surveys

Arecibo, P.R.

see also under By SMSA or MSA in the "Index by Categories"

Argentina

- Agricultural and food production indexes, and production of selected commodities, by world region and country, 1974-83, annual rpt, 1524–5

Argentina

- Agricultural exports of Argentina and total South America, and coffee exports of Colombia and Brazil to US and world, market share analysis, 1960-79, 1528–169
- Agricultural situation in Latin America, by country, 1981-83 and outlook for 1984, annual rpt, 1524–4.9
- Agricultural supply/demand, trade, and production, and socioeconomic data, by country, 1950s-77, 1528–179
- AID loan repayment status and terms by program and country, and status of predecessor agency loans, quarterly rpt, 9912–3
- *Background Notes,* summary social, political, and economic data, 1984 rpt, 7006–2.32
- Debt financing, income of 7 US bank holding companies, actual and in event of interest nonpayment, 1st qtr 1984, press release, 9368–77
- Economic conditions in Communist, OECD, and selected other countries, 1960s-83, annual rpt, 244–5
- Economic, social, and political summary data, by country, 1984, annual factbook, 244–11
- Economic trends in income, production, prices, employment, finances, and trade, 1984 semiannual rpt, 2046–4.18
- Exports and imports of US, by commodity and country, 1972-82, annual world region rpt, 244–13.2
- Exports of US, detailed Schedule B commodities by country of destination, 1983, annual rpt, 2424–9
- Exports of US, detailed Schedule E commodities by mode of transport and world area and country of destination, 1983, annual rpts, 2424–5
- Grain and oilseed production in Argentina, effect of agricultural price regulation, 1947-80, 1528–170
- Grain production, exports by firm, storage by facility type and port, and shipments to ports by mode of transport, by grain type, for Argentina, selected years 1954-81, 1528–185
- Imports of US, detailed Schedule A commodities by country and world area of origin, and mode of transport, 1983, annual rpts, 2424–2
- Imports of US, detailed TSUSA commodities by country of origin, 1983, annual rpt, 2424–4
- Loans and grants for economic and military assistance from US and intl agencies, by program and country, FY46-83, annual rpt, 9914–5
- Medical and health care equipment market and trade, and user industry operations and demand, 1984 country market research rpt, 2045–2.47
- Military aid of US, arms sales, and training programs costs and budget requests by program, world region, and country, FY83-85, annual rpt, 7144–13
- Military spending, arms trade, and armed forces size, with total govt spending and population, by country, 1972-82, annual rpt, 9824–1
- *Minerals Yearbook, 1982,* Vol 3: foreign country reviews of production, trade, and policies, by commodity, annual rpt, 5604–35

Argentina

Minerals Yearbook, 1982, Vol 3 preprints: foreign country review of production, trade, and policies, by commodity, annual rpt, 5604–17.5

Nuclear power generation in US and 18 non-Communist countries, monthly rpt, 3162–24.10

Nuclear power plant construction and operation status, and capacity, by plant, region, State, and selected country, 1983 and projected to 2020, annual rpt, 3164–57

Oil field equipment from 5 countries, injury to US industry from foreign subsidized imports and less than fair value sales, investigation with background financial and operating data, 1984 rpt, 9886–19.11

Population size and growth rates, and latest available benchmark demographic data, by country, 1950-83, biennial rpt, 2324–4

Raisin and dried prune stocks, production, and exports for 4 countries, 1982-83 and forecast 1984, article, 1925–34.416

Steel (carbon) wire rod from Spain and Argentina at less than fair value, imports injury to US industry, investigation with background financial and operating data, 1984 rpt, 9886–14.126

Steel from 5 countries, injury to US industry from foreign subsidized products and sales at less than fair value, investigation with background financial and operating data, 1984 rpt, 9886–19.8

Steel wire rod from 4 countries, imports injury to US industry from sales covered by foreign govt grants, investigation with background financial and operating data, 1980-83, 9886–15.47

Telecommunication equipment market and trade, and user industry operations and demand, 1984 country market research rpt, 2045–12.31

Wheat exports, total and for major producers by world area and country of destination, 1973/74-1983/84, FAS rpt, 1925–2.7

see also under By Foreign Country in the "Index by Categories"

Argon

see Gases

Argonne National Laboratory

- "Effects of Relaxing Automobile Emission Standards: A Generic Analysis and an Urban Case Study", 3408–31
- "Environmental Implications of Solar and Biomass Energy Growth", 3408–30
- "Inland Transport Modes for Coal and Coal-Derived Energy: An Evaluation Method for Comparing Environmental Impacts", 3408–28
- "Regional, New-Source Bubble Policy for Sulfur Dioxide Emissions in the Eastern U.S.", 3408–32

see also Department of Energy National Laboratories

Arizona

- Agriculture census, 1982: farms, farmland, production and costs, and operator characteristics, preliminary State summary and county rpts, 2330–1.4
- Agriculture census, 1982: farms, farmland, production, finances, and operator characteristics, by county, final State rpt, 2331–1.3

Bank deposits in commercial and mutual savings banks and in US branches of foreign banks, by account type, instn, State, SMSA, and county, June 1983, annual rpt, 9295–3.17

Census of Population and Housing, 1980: detailed population and housing characteristics, by county, city, and census tract, State rpt, 2551–2.4

Census of Population, 1980: detailed socioeconomic and demographic characteristics, by age, sex, race, Hispanic origin, and industry, State rpt, 2531–4.4

Copper mine expansion in Cananea, Mexico, effects on US air pollution and copper industry, with US and foreign industry data, 1960s-95, hearing, 21448–31

Copper smelting sulfur dioxide emissions of 8 plants in 2 States, under alternative emission standards, 1981-82, hearings, 25328–25

County Business Patterns: establishments, employees, and payrolls, by SIC 4-digit industry and county, 1982, annual State rpt, 2326–6.4

Employment, earnings, and hours, by selected SIC 1- to 4-digit industry, State, and for 278 major labor areas, 1939-83, annual rpt, 6744–5.1, 6744–5.3

Environmental quality, pollutant discharge by type and source, and EPA protection activities and funding, 1970s-83, biennial regional rpt, 9184–15.9

Exports of manufactured and agricultural commodities, manufacturing production, and export-related employment, 1960s-82, State rpt, 2046–3.3

Fish products imported through California and Arizona ports of entry, by country, weekly rpt, 2162–6.4

Forest biomass in Rocky Mountain States, conversion from volume to dry weight, for softwood and hardwood species, 1977, 1208–200

Fruit (citrus) production and use, by crop and State, 1977/78-1981/82, 1641–4

Health Care Cost-Containment System of Arizona, persons eligible and per capita costs for 4 providers, 1982, article, 4652–1.414

HHS aid to each State and local govt or private instn, amount obligated, funding agency, and program, FY83, annual listing, 4004–3.9

Hospitals and nursing homes in Arizona, finances and operations for specified facilities, and itemized expenses for selected cases, 1978-83, hearing, 21148–29

Income (personal) per capita and by source, and earnings by industry div, by State, MSA, and county, 1977-82, annual regional rpt, 2704–2.7

Manufacturing census, 1982: financial and operating data, by SIC 2- to 4-digit industry, State, SMSA, and county, preliminary census div rpt, 2491–3.8

Mineral Industry Surveys, State review of production, 1983, advance annual rpt, 5614–6.3

Minerals Yearbook, 1982, Vol 2 preprints: State review of production and sales by commodity, and business activity, annual rpt, 5604–16.4

Index by Subjects and Names

Minerals Yearbook, 1982, Vol 2: State reviews of production, sales, and firms, by commodity, and business activity, annual rpt, 5604–34

Population size, Apr 1980 and July 1982, and per capita income, 1979 and 1981, by county and city, State Current Population Rpt, 2546–11.3

Retail trade census, 1982: employment, establishments, sales, and payroll, by SIC 2- to 4-digit kind of business, SMSA, and retail district, State rpt, 2401–1.3

Savings and loan assns, FHLB 11th District members financial condition and operations by State, quarterly rpt, 9302–19

Savings and loan assns, FHLB 11th District members financial operations and housing industry indicators by State, monthly rpt, 9302–17

Service industry census, 1982: employment, establishments, receipts, and payroll, by SIC 2- to 4-digit kind of business, SMSA, county, and city, State rpt, 2391–1.3

Timber resources and removals in 9 Rocky Mountain States, and forest and rangeland area, by ownership, forest and tree characteristics, and State, 1977, 1208–201

Transportation census, 1982: trucks, by detailed characteristics, miles traveled, and type of product carried, State rpt, 2573–1.3

Water supply and quality in streams and lakes, and groundwater levels in wells, by drainage basin, 1982, annual State rpt, 5666–20.3

Water supply, and snow survey results, monthly State rpt, 1266–2.2

Wholesale trade census, 1982: employment, establishments, finances, and operations, by SIC 2- to 4-digit kind of business, SMSA, county, and city, State rpt, 2405–1.3

see also Phoenix, Ariz.

see also Tucson, Ariz.

see also under By State in the "Index by Categories"

Arkansas

- Agriculture census, 1982: farms, farmland, production and costs, and operator characteristics, preliminary State summary and county rpts, 2330–1.5
- Agriculture census, 1982: farms, farmland, production, finances, and operator characteristics, by county, final State rpt, 2331–1.4
- Bank deposits in commercial and mutual savings banks and in US branches of foreign banks, by account type, instn, State, SMSA, and county, June 1983, annual rpt, 9295–3.9
- Census of Housing, 1980: occupancy and unit characteristics of SMSAs and central cities, by race, Hispanic origin, and city, State rpt, 2473–1.5
- Census of Population and Housing, 1980: detailed population and housing characteristics, by county, city, and census tract, State rpt, 2551–2.5
- Census of Population, 1980: detailed socioeconomic and demographic characteristics, by age, sex, race, Hispanic origin, and industry, State rpt, 2531–4.5

Index by Subjects and Names

Employment by major nonagricultural industry, and average hours and earnings of manufacturing production workers, for 5 southwestern States, monthly rpt, 6962–2

Employment, earnings, and hours, by selected SIC 1- to 4-digit industry, State, and for 278 major labor areas, 1939-83, annual rpt, 6744–5.1, 6744–5.3

Employment, industrial relations, prices, and economic conditions in 5 Southwestern States, regional rpts series, 6966–1

Environmental quality, pollutant discharge by type and source, and EPA protection activities and funding, 1970s-83, biennial regional rpt, 9184–15.6

Exports of manufactured and agricultural commodities, manufacturing production, and export-related employment, 1960s-82, State rpt, 2046–3.4

HHS aid to each State and local govt or private instn, amount obligated, funding agency, and program, FY83, annual listing, 4004–3.6

Income (personal) per capita and by source, and earnings by industry div, by State, MSA, and county, 1977-82, annual regional rpt, 2704–2.6

Manufacturing census, 1982: financial and operating data, by SIC 2- to 4-digit industry, State, SMSA, and county, preliminary census div rpt, 2491–3.7

Mineral Industry Surveys, State review of production, 1983, advance annual rpt, 5614–6.4

Minerals Yearbook, 1982, Vol 2 preprints: State review of production and sales by commodity, and business activity, annual rpt, 5604–16.5

Minerals Yearbook, 1982, Vol 2: State reviews of production, sales, and firms, by commodity, and business activity, annual rpt, 5604–34

Population size and components of change, by MSA and county, 1980-82, annual State Current Population Rpt, 2546–4.4

Population size, Apr 1980 and July 1982, and per capita income, 1979 and 1981, by county and city, State Current Population Rpt, 2546–11.4

Retail trade census, 1982: employment, establishments, sales, and payroll, by SIC 2- to 4-digit kind of business, SMSA, county, and city, State rpt, 2397–1.4

Rice market activities, prices, inspections, sales, trade, supply, and use, for US and selected foreign markets, weekly rpt, 1313–8

Rice stocks on and off farms and total, periodic rpt, 1621–7

Savings and loan assns, FHLB 9th District insured members financial condition and operations by SMSA, monthly rpt, 9302–13

Service industry census, 1982: employment, establishments, receipts, and payroll, by SIC 2- to 4-digit kind of business, SMSA, county, and city, State rpt, 2391–1.4

Transportation census, 1982: trucks, by detailed characteristics, miles traveled, and type of product carried, State rpt, 2573–1.4

Water supply and quality in streams and lakes, and groundwater levels in wells, by drainage basin, 1982, annual State rpt, 5666–20.4

Wholesale trade census, 1982: employment, establishments, finances, and operations, by SIC 2- to 4-digit kind of business, SMSA, county, and city, State rpt, 2405–1.4

see also Craighead County, Ark.
see also Fayetteville, Ark.
see also Fort Smith, Ark.
see also Little Rock, Ark.
see also North Little Rock, Ark.
see also Pine Bluff, Ark.
see also Springdale, Ark.
see also Texarkana, Ark.
see also under By State in the "Index by Categories"

Arkansas River

Bridges over navigable waters, with type of bridge and use, owner, dimensions, and location, 1984 regional listing, 7406–5.2

Freight (waterborne domestic and foreign) by commodity, traffic, and passengers, by port and waterway, 1982, annual rpt, 3754–3.2

Water supply and quality in streams and lakes, and groundwater levels in wells, by drainage basin, 1980, annual State rpt series, 5666–12

Water supply and quality in streams and lakes, and groundwater levels in wells, by drainage basin, 1981, annual State rpt series, 5666–16

Water supply and quality in streams and lakes, and groundwater levels in wells, by drainage basin, 1982, annual State rpt series, 5666–20

Water supply and quality in streams and lakes, and groundwater levels in wells, by drainage basin, 1983, annual State rpt series, 5666–10

Arlington, Tex.

see also under By City and By SMSA or MSA in the "Index by Categories"

Armed services

Foreign military spending, arms trade, and armed forces size, with total govt spending and population, by country, 1972-82, annual rpt, 9824–1

see also Air Force
see also Armed services reserves
see also Army
see also Coast Guard
see also Department of Defense
see also Joint Chiefs of Staff
see also Marine Corps
see also Military personnel
see also Navy
see also Voluntary military service

Armed services reserves

Budget of DOD, expenditures for each service branch and total defense agencies, by function and State, FY85, annual rpt, 3544–23

Budget of DOD, itemized account of legislative history, FY84, annual rpt, 3504–7

Construction and renovation of military bases, DOD budget authorization requests, by DOD component, State, country, and project, FY85, annual rpt, 3544–15

Cost control proposals for Fed Govt programs and mgmt, 3-year savings by function and agency, and financial and operating data, 1960s-81, 16908–1.20

Arms control and disarmament

Cost of DOD base support by function, and personnel and acreage by installation, by service branch, FY85, annual rpt, 3504–11

Manpower active duty strength, recruits, and reenlistment, by race, Hispanic origin, sex, and service branch, quarterly press release, 3542–7

Manpower and equipment strengths, readiness, and funding, by reserve component, FY83, annual rpt, 3544–27

Manpower of DOD, and organization, budget, weapons, and property, by service branch, State, and country, 1984 annual summary rpt, 3504–13

Manpower statistics on active duty, civilian, and reserve personnel, by service branch, monthly rpt, 3542–14

Manpower strengths and characteristics, by reserve component, quarterly rpt, 3542–4

Manpower strengths and mobilization alert system efficiency, for selected Army Reserve and Natl Guard units, 1982-83 survey, GAO rpt, 26123–57

Manpower strengths of active duty, reserve, and civilian personnel, by service branch, selected years FY68-89, annual rpt, 3544–2

Military weapons and troop strength of US and NATO compared to USSR and Warsaw Pact, as of Jan 1984, annual rpt, 3564–1

Navy personnel, detailed statistics, quarterly rpt, 3802–4

Nuclear attack civil defense plans of Fed Emergency Mgmt Agency, funding and operations by component, FY81-84 and projected FY85-89, GAO rpt, 26123–61

Strategic military capability, force strengths, weapons, training, supplies, and requirements, by service branch, FY80-84 and projected to 1990, 3508–19

Training and education programs of DOD, funding, staff, students, and facilities, by service branch and reserve component, FY85, annual rpt, 3504–5

see also Coast Guard Reserve
see also National guard

Arms and munitions

see Arms control and disarmament
see Arms sales
see Bombs
see Defense contracts and procurement
see Defense expenditures
see Explosives
see Firearms
see Military assistance
see Military weapons
see Missiles and rockets
see Nuclear weapons

Arms control and disarmament

DOD budget, FY85 weapons system requests consistency with US policy and specified treaties, with funding FY83-87, annual rpt, 21384–4

Foreign military, social, and economic summary data by world area and country, and US-USSR relations, 1960s-80s, hearing, 25388–47

Soviet Union propaganda campaign against NATO nuclear missile deployment, and USSR and NATO nuclear arms and aircraft in place, 1977-83, narrative rpt, 9828–25

Arms control and disarmament

Treaties and other bilateral and multilateral agreements of US in force, by country, Jan 1984, annual listing, 7004–1

Treaties on arms control status, and Arms Control and Disarmament Agency activities, 1983, annual rpt, 9824–2

see also Arms sales

see also Defense expenditures

see also Strategic Arms Limitation Treaties

see also Strategic Arms Reduction Talks

Arms Control and Disarmament Agency

see U.S. Arms Control and Disarmament Agency

Arms Export Control Act

Foreign military training of US, students, costs, and revenue losses from reduced tuition by country, by service branch, FY79-83, GAO rpt, 26123–56

Arms sales

- Budget of DOD, justification, programs, and policies, FY85, annual rpt, 3544–2
- Budget of US Appendix, detailed budgets and personnel summaries, by agency, FY85, annual rpt, 104–3
- Budget of US, effects of Reagan Admin policy changes, by detailed program, FY85, annual rpt, 104–21
- Budget of US, Reagan Admin funding requests for foreign economic and military aid by program and country, FY82-85, annual rpt, 7004–14
- China exports and imports by SITC 1- to 5-digit commodity, 1970s-82, annual rpt, 244–12
- Cost control proposals for Fed Govt programs and mgmt, 3-year savings by function and agency, and financial and operating data, 1960s-81, 16908–1.17, 16908–1.31
- Debt to US of foreign govts and private obligors, by country and program, periodic rpt, 8002–6
- Developing countries arms transfers from US, USSR, and Europe, by weapon type and world region, 1974-82, 25948–3
- Developing countries receiving US economic aid, total govt and defense expenditures, military imports, GNP, and intl reserves by country, 1976-81, annual rpt, 9914–1
- Exports and imports of US, detailed SIC-based commodities by world area, 1983, annual rpts, 2424–6
- Foreign military aid of US and sales of arms, equipment, and training, by item and country, FY50-83, annual rpt, 3904–3
- Foreign military aid of US, arms sales, and training programs costs and budget requests by program, world region, and country, FY83-85, annual rpt, 7144–13
- Foreign military, social, and economic summary data by world area and country, 1960s-80s, hearing, 25388–47.1
- Foreign military spending, arms trade, and armed forces size, with total govt spending and population, by country, 1972-82, annual rpt, 9824–1
- Liabilities (contigent) and claims paid by Fed Govt on federally insured and guaranteed contracts with foreign obligors, by country and program, periodic rpt, 8002–12
- Philippines dev and military assistance funding from US, FY78-84 and proposed FY85-89, GAO rpt, 26123–54

Soviet Union and Warsaw Pact military weapons systems, assistance and presence worldwide, and force strengths, with selected US and NATO comparisons, as of 1984, 3508–14

Statistical Abstract of US, social, political, and economic data, 1950s-83 and trends, annual rpt, 2324–1.2

Treaties on arms control status, and Arms Control and Disarmament Agency activities, 1983, annual rpt, 9824–2

see also Military assistance

Army

- Aides to officers, enlisted personnel authorized and assigned to perform personal services by race and sex, and program costs, by service branch, 1982-83, GAO rpt, 26123–53
- Cost control proposals for Fed Govt programs and mgmt, 3-year savings by function and agency, and financial and operating data, 1960s-81, 16908–1.18, 16908–1.31
- Health status of Army personnel, and use of Army medical services in US and abroad by personnel, retirees, and dependents, monthly rpt, 3702–4
- Manpower active duty strength, recruits, and reenlistment, by race, Hispanic origin, sex, and service branch, quarterly press release, 3542–7
- Manpower assigned to critical occupation specialties by skill type, and working outside specialty at 5 installations, as of Mar 1982, GAO rpt, 26123–59
- Manpower of DOD, and organization, budget, weapons, and property, by service branch, State, and country, 1984 annual summary rpt, 3504–13
- Manpower of DOD, by State, service branch, and major installation, as of Sept 1983, annual rpt, 3544–7
- Manpower requirements and cost estimates, DOD budget detailed analysis, FY85, annual rpt, 3504–1
- Manpower statistics on active duty, civilian, and reserve personnel, by service branch, monthly rpt, 3542–14
- Manpower statistics on active duty, civilian, and retired personnel and dependents, FY83 and historical, annual rpt, 3544–1
- Manpower strengths, and military pension earnings and program costs, under alternative policies, selected years FY71-2020, 26306–6.76
- Manpower strengths in US and abroad, by service branch, world area, and country, quarterly news release, 3542–9
- Manpower strengths of active duty, reserve, and civilian personnel, by service branch, selected years FY68-89, annual rpt, 3544–2
- Manpower strengths, summary by service branch, monthly press release, 3542–2
- Medical facilities of DOD in US and abroad, beds, admissions, outpatient visits, and live births by service branch, quarterly rpt, 3542–15
- Medical personnel, trainees, and accessions by source, by occupation, specialty, and service branch, FY83, annual rpt, 3544–24
- Military weapons and troop strength of US and NATO compared to USSR and Warsaw Pact, as of Jan 1984, annual rpt, 3564–1

Index by Subjects and Names

- NATO military commitment of US, Europe force strengths by service branch and costs by component, FY82 with trends from FY75, GAO rpt, 26123–71
- Radiation from 1940s-70s nuclear weapons tests, levels in air and water, and personnel exposure by military unit and job category, series, 3906–1
- Reserve forces manpower and equipment strengths, readiness, and funding, by reserve component, FY83, annual rpt, 3544–27
- Reserve forces manpower strengths and characteristics, by component, quarterly rpt, 3542–4
- Reserve forces manpower strengths and mobilization alert system efficiency, for selected Army Reserve and Natl Guard units, 1982-83 survey, GAO rpt, 26123–57
- Strategic military capability, force strengths, weapons, training, supplies, and requirements, by service branch, FY80-84 and projected to 1990, 3508–19
- Training and education programs of DOD, funding, staff, students, and facilities, by service branch and reserve component, FY85, annual rpt, 3504–5
- Women military personnel on active duty, by demographic and service characteristics and service branch, with comparisons to men, FY83, annual chartbook, 3544–26

see also Army Corps of Engineers

see also Department of Army

see also National guard

Army bases

see Military bases, posts, and reservations

Army contracts and procurement

see Defense contracts and procurement

Army Corps of Engineers

- Activities and projects, FY83 and trends from 1800s, annual rpt, 3754–1
- Cost control proposals for Fed Govt programs and mgmt, 3-year savings by function and agency, and financial and operating data, 1960s-81, 16908–1.18, 16908–1.22, 16908–1.31
- Fish and shellfish landings, life cycles, and environmental needs, for selected species by region, with glossary and bibl, series, 5506–8
- Great Lakes and connecting channels water levels, recorded and expected, biweekly rpt, 3752–2
- Great Lakes water levels, surface and drainage area, depth, and volume, and connecting and outlet channel flows, various periods 1900-83, 3758–6
- Great Lakes water levels, trends and projections, monthly rpt, 3752–1
- Hydroelectric power generating capacity and plant characteristics, for Western States, FY83, annual rpt, 3254–1
- Port dredging hourly labor costs by component and occupation, and Army Corps of Engineers contract awards by region and company, 1970s-83, hearings, 21728–53
- Procurement, DOD prime contract awards by individual contractor, service branch, State and city, and country, FY83, annual listing, 3544–22
- Procurement, DOD prime contract awards in labor surplus areas, by service branch, State, and area, 1st half FY84, semiannual rpt, 3542–19

Index by Subjects and Names

Art

Recreation activities at Corps water resources dev projects, by district and project, 1982, annual rpt, 3754–5

Recreation construction for water resources dev projects of Army Corps of Engineers and Reclamation Bur, unfunded costs by project, FY82, GAO rpt, 26113–115

Recreation fees and collection costs, visitors, and capacity of outdoor Fed Govt, State, and private facilities, by managing agency and State, 1983, annual rpt, 5544–14

Sedimentation control, surveillance, and research activity of Fed Govt, by project, agency, region, and State, 1982, annual rpt, 5664–9

Southeastern Power Admin sales by customer, plants, and capacity, and financial statements of Southeastern Fed Power Program, FY83, annual rpt, 3234–1

Tennessee Valley river control and reservoir elevations, storage, flows, and hydroelectric generating capacity use, 1981, annual rpt, 9804–7

Waterborne commerce of US (domestic and foreign), freight by commodity, traffic, and passengers, by port and waterway, 1982, annual rpt, 3754–3

Wetlands environmental characteristics and mgmt, and Army Corps of Engineers projects for discharging dredged material on wetlands, 1950s-80, 26358–102

Arnett, Ross H., III

"Private Health Insurance: New Measures of a Complex and Changing Industry", 4652–1.430

Arnold, Gail D.

"Housing of the Rural Elderly", 1598–193

Arnow, Ted

"Water-Level and Water-Quality Changes in Great Salt Lake, Utah, 1847-1983", 5668–70

Arrest

Aircraft hijackings, on-board explosions, other crimes against civil aviation, and circumstances, US and worldwide, 1931-83, annual rpt, 7504–31

Airport security operations to prevent hijacking, screening results, enforcement actions, and hijacking attempts, 1st half 1984, semiannual rpt, 7502–5

Alcohol-related and total traffic deaths, and drunk driver license revocations and other deterrence measures in selected States, 1980-82, 9618–10

Alcohol, tobacco, firearms, and explosives arrests and seizures, by State, FY82, last issue of annual rpt, 8484–1.6

Aliens apprehended, deported, and required to depart, FY1892-1981, annual rpt, 6264–2

Arrests and arrest rates by offense, offender characteristics, and State, and juvenile arrests by disposition, by population size, 1970s-83, annual rpt, 6224–2.2

Crime and criminal justice data, including justice expenditures and employment by level of govt, 1970s-82 with some trends from 1875, 6068–174

Criminal case processing from arrest to sentencing, series, 6066–22

DC criminal cases involving drug users, and user and nonuser rates of detention, pretrial rearrest, and failure to appear in court, 1979-81, 6066–20.7

Disposition of arrests for serious crimes in 5 States, and criminal justice employment nationwide by job category and level of govt, Dec 1983 rpt, 6062–2.401

Drug (illegal) supply, use, casualties, treatment program and emergency room admissions in major cities, arrests, and seizures, by drug type, 1982, annual rpt, 15894–1

Drug abuse residential treatment program effectiveness indicators, with data on pre- and post-program characteristics of grads and dropouts, 1970-74 study, 4496–5.18

Drug and narcotics foreign production, acreage, eradication, and seizures, by substance, with labs destroyed and US aid, by country, 1981-85, annual rpt, 7004–17

Drug Enforcement Admin cases against major drug traffickers by case characteristics, and agents assessment of activities, in 3 cities, 1979-82, GAO rpt, 26119–57

Drug enforcement regional task force program investigation activities, funding, and personnel, with nationwide drug abuse data, 1983 annual rpt, 6004–17

Economic indicators relation to measures of social pathology including crime and death rates, various periods 1950-80, 23848–76

Homeless population and characteristics, and temporary shelter operations, use, and user characteristics, for selected cities, various periods 1979-84, hearing, 21248–85

Juvenile arrests for Crime Index offenses, and police assessments, staff, and programs for control of criminal activity by youth gangs in 27 cities, 1980-81, 6068–175

Marijuana cultivation control activity of State law enforcement agencies, and aid from Fed Govt and Natl Guard, 1983 survey, GAO rpt, 26119–64

Micronesia Federated States, arrests by type, and traffic and other accidents and deaths, Jan-Aug 1983, annual rpt, 7004–6.2

New York State mental patients released, felony arrest rate by arrest record, 1975, 6066–20.5

Panama Canal police charges and arrests, FY81-82, annual rpt, 9664–3.3

Peru cocaine addicts and arrested traffickers and users socioeconomic characteristics, and cocaine confiscated, 1974-78, intl conf papers, 7008–40

Police dept costs and operations, patrol car use, investigations, arrests, and recruit training, by city population size, 1982, 6066–21.1

Police dept performance, analyses of police activities effects on neighborhoods and citizens, 1977, compilation of papers, 6068–181

Robbery rates and circumstances, medical costs and property losses of victims, and offender and victim characteristics, 1960s-81, 6068–180

Statistical Abstract of US, social, political, and economic data, 1950s-83 and trends, annual rpt, 2324–1.1

Wiretapping authorizations by offense, costs, persons involved, arrests, trials, and convictions, 1983, annual rpt, 18204–7

Witness Security Program costs, participants by arrest record, and prosecutions by offense, offender type, and disposition, various periods FY70-83, GAO rpt, 26119–70

see also Trials

Arsenic

see Metals and metal industries

Arson

Bombing (explosive and incendiary) and arson incidents by target, State, and circumstances, and explosives theft and recovery, 1982-83, annual rpt, 8484–4

Bombing (explosive and incendiary) incidents, damage, injuries, and deaths, by target, State, and circumstances, 1983, annual rpt, 6224–5

Convictions, prison sentences, and average sentence lengths, by offense, offender class, and selected State, various periods 1971-84, 6066–19.10

Crime Index by population size and region, and offenses known to police by large city, Jan-June 1984, semiannual rpt, 6222–1

Crimes, arrests by offender characteristics, and rates, by offense, and law enforcement employees, by population size and jurisdiction, 1970s-83, annual rpt, 6224–2

Forest fire damage and causes, by State and region, 1981, annual rpt, 1204–4

Forest fires on Forest Service land and acres burned, by cause, forest, and State, 1983, annual rpt, 1204–6

Homicides, by circumstance and type of weapon, 1983, annual rpt, 6224–2.1

Income (taxable) not reported, by illegal source, with characteristics of persons involved, methodology, and bibl, 1970s-82, 8008–112

Investigation and prosecution of arsonists, by incident characteristics and outcome, motive, and type of evidence, for 4 jurisdictions, 1981, 6068–184

Prison terms actually served by selected State, and Illinois pretrial detention time credited to sentence, by offense, various periods 1977-83, 6066–19.7

Statistical Abstract of US, social, political, and economic data, 1950s-83 and trends, annual rpt, 2324–1.1

Terrorist (intl) incidents, casualties, and attacks on US targets, by attack type and world area, with chronology of events, 1983, annual rpt, 7004–13

Art

Census of Population, 1980: detailed socioeconomic and demographic characteristics, by age, sex, race, Hispanic origin, occupation, and industry, State rpt series, 2531–4

Census of Population, 1980: labor force, by sex, detailed occupation, and region, with comparison to 1970 census, supplementary rpt, 2535–1.12

Exports, imports, tariffs, and industry operating data for art and antiques, 1979-83, TSUSA commodity rpt, 9885–7.58

Exports of US, detailed commodities by country of destination, monthly rpt, 2422–3

Exports of US, detailed Schedule B commodities by country of destination, 1983, annual rpt, 2424–9

Art

Exports of US, detailed Schedule E commodities by mode of transport and world area and country of destination, 1983, annual rpts, 2424–5

Franchise business opportunities, by firm and kind of business, 1984 annual listing, 2044–27

Graphic presentation of socioeconomic data, use, dev, and standards, 1978 conf papers, 2626–2.51

Great Lakes trade, by SITC 3-digit commodity, port, vessel type, world area, and country, 1982, annual rpt, 7744–3

Imports of ivory carvings and jewelry, 1982, annual rpt, 5504–19

Imports of US, detailed Schedule A commodities by country and world area of origin, and mode of transport, 1983, annual rpts, 2424–2

Imports of US, detailed Schedule A commodities by country, monthly rpt, 2422–2

Imports of US, detailed TSUSA commodities by country of origin, 1983, annual rpt, 2424–4

Manufacturing census, 1982: financial and operating data, by SIC 2- to 4-digit industry, State, SMSA, and county, preliminary census div rpt series, 2491–3

Manufacturing census, 1982: financial and operating data, for SIC 4-digit industries by product, preliminary rpt, 2491–1.432

Occupational manpower needs and supply by detailed occupation, and educational and training program enrollees and grads by detailed field, 1982 and 1995, biennial rpt, 6744–3

Occupational Outlook Handbook, 1984-85 biennial rpt, 6744–1

Paints, inks, and related art items trade, tariffs, and industry operating data, 1979-83, TSUSA commodity rpt supplement, 9885–4.46

Service industry census, 1982: employment, establishments, receipts, and payroll, by SIC 2- to 4-digit kind of business, SMSA, county, and city, State rpt series, 2391–1

Tax return art appraisals accepted and rejected on estate, gift, and income tax cases, and valuation by taxpayers, IRS, and US courts, 1978-82, hearings, 21408–74

Arteriosclerosis

see Cardiovascular diseases

see Cerebrovascular diseases

see Circulatory diseases

Arthritis

see Musculoskeletal diseases

Artificial fibers

see Synthetic fibers and fabrics

Artificial organs

see Medical transplants

Artificial satellites

see Communications satellites

see Meteorological satellites

see Satellites

Artificial sweeteners

see Syrups and sweeteners

Arts and the humanities

Census of Population, 1980: detailed characteristics, by age, sex, race, Hispanic origin, occupation, and industry, State rpt series, 2531–4

Degrees conferred in higher education, by race, Hispanic origin, sex, level, and field, selected years 1949/50-1979/80, annual rpt, 4824–2.16

Index by Subjects and Names

Educational progress, natl assessment summary data for 7 learning areas, by characteristics of participants, selected years 1971-82, annual rpt, 4824–2.6

Educational services in underground economy, household expenditures and participation by type of instruction, 1981 survey, 8308–27

Funding of arts and humanities, by source and State, FY82-83 with trends from FY66, 21408–69

High school classes of 1980 and 1982: educational and sociodemographic characteristics and expectations, natl longitudinal study, series, 4826–2

Japan-US Friendship Commission educational and cultural exchange activities, grants, and trust fund status, FY83, annual rpt, 14694–1

Puerto Rico organizations in US and Puerto Rico, philanthropic grants received, by foundation, purpose, and recipient, 1979-81, hearings, 21788–137.1

Teaching degrees conferred by specialty and State, required credit hours, and instn officials attitudes, by instn type, 1970s-83, hearings, 21348–89

see also Antiques

see also Architecture

see also Art

see also Dance

see also Federal aid to arts and humanities

see also Foreign languages

see also Language and literature

see also Motion pictures

see also Museums

see also Music

see also Performing arts

see also Photography

see also Social sciences

see also Theater

Asbestos

see Nonmetallic minerals and mines

Asbury Park, N.J.

Census of Housing, 1980: occupancy and unit characteristics, by race, Hispanic origin, and city, SMSA rpt, 2473–1.223

Census of Population and Housing, 1980: detailed population and housing characteristics, by county, city, and census tract, SMSA rpt, 2551–2.223

Asheville, N.C.

Census of Housing, 1980: occupancy and unit characteristics, by race, Hispanic origin, and city, SMSA rpt, 2473–1.75

Census of Population and Housing, 1980: detailed population and housing characteristics, by county, city, and census tract, SMSA rpt, 2551–2.75

see also under By SMSA or MSA in the "Index by Categories"

Ashland, Ky.

Census of Housing, 1980: occupancy and unit characteristics, by race, Hispanic origin, and city, SMSA rpt, 2473–1.185

Census of Population and Housing, 1980: detailed population and housing characteristics, by county, city, and census tract, SMSA rpt, 2551–2.185

Housing vacancy rates for single and multifamily units and mobile homes, by city and ZIP code, 1984, annual metro area rpt, 9304–27.10

see also under By SMSA or MSA in the "Index by Categories"

Asia

Agricultural and food production indexes, and production of selected commodities, by world region and country, 1974-83, annual rpt, 1524–5

Agricultural exports and imports of US, by detailed commodity and country, FY83 and CY83, semiannual rpts, 1522–4

Agricultural situation in 4 East Asian countries, by commodity, 1983 and outlook for 1984, annual rpt, 1524–4.2

Agricultural situation in 5 South Asia countries, by commodity, 1970s-1983/84 and outlook for 1984/85, annual rpt, 1524–4.11

Agricultural supply/demand, consumption per capita, and trade, by world area and country group, 1960s-82, 1528–181

Agricultural supply/demand, trade, and production, and socioeconomic data, by country, 1950s-77, 1528–179

Agricultural trade of US, by commodity and country, bimonthly rpt with articles, 1522–1

AID activities and funding by project and function, FY85, and developing countries summary socioeconomic data, 1970s-83, by country, annual rpt, 9914–3

AID community dev assistance to local govts in developing countries, program activities and funding, 1960s-80s, 9918–11

AID contracts and grants for technical and support services, by instn, country, and State, FY83, annual listing, 9914–7

AID economic assistance to developing countries, obligations and disbursements by country, quarterly rpt, 9912–4

AID Housing Guaranty Program financial statements, and projects by country, FY83, annual rpt, 9914–4

AID loan repayment status and terms by program and country, and status of predecessor agency loans, quarterly rpt, 9912–3

AID loans authorized, signed, and canceled, by country and world area, monthly rpt, 9912–2

Carbon dioxide emissions from fossil fuel combustion, and growth rates, by country and country group, 1950-80, 3006–7.6

China economic conditions, agricultural and industrial production, trade, and domestic and foreign investment, 1980-85, 2048–106

Coal reserves, production, demand indicators, and trade, by country, selected years 1973-82 and alternative trade projections to 1995, annual rpt, 3164–77

Cuba economic conditions, agricultural and industrial production and distribution, trade, and intl economic relations, 1970-82 and trends from 1957, 248–40

Defense and total govt expenditures, military imports, GNP, and intl reserves of countries receiving US economic aid, by country, 1976-81, annual rpt, 9914–1

Export sales and shipments of US grains, oilseed products, hides, skins, and cotton, by country, weekly rpt, 1922–3

Exports and imports of OECD, total and for 4 major countries, and US trade by country, by commodity, 1972-82, annual world region rpt, 244–13.5

Index by Subjects and Names

Asian Americans

Exports and imports of US (airborne), by world area and US customs district and city, monthly rpt, 2422–8

Exports and imports of US (waterborne), by type of service, commodity, country, route, and US port, 1982, annual rpt, 7704–2

Exports and imports of US (waterborne), by type of service, customs district, port, and world area, monthly rpt, 2422–7

Exports and imports of US, by commodity group, world area, selected country, US coastal area and port, and mode of transport, with seasonal adjustments, monthly rpt, 2422–9

Exports and imports of US, detailed SIC-based commodities by world area, 1983, annual rpts, 2424–6

Exports of US, detailed Schedule E commodities by mode of transport and world area and country of destination, 1983, annual rpts, 2424–5

Food production and needs, and related economic trends and outlook, for 67 developing countries, 1980-86, annual rpt, 1524–6

Food supply policies of 21 developing countries, with farm sector data, tariff income, and prices and imports of 5 grains, 1960s-81, 1528–168

Great Lakes trade, by SITC 3-digit commodity, port, vessel type, world area, and country, 1982, annual rpt, 7744–3

Housing finance and low-income housing projects in Asian developing countries, and activities of 2 countries, 1970s-82, annual conf proceedings, 9914–11

Immigrant and nonimmigrant visas of US issued and refused, and status adjustments, by class and nationality, FY77, annual rpt, 7184–1

Immigration, and alien residents, workers, visitors, deportations, and naturalizations, by country of birth, FY81, annual rpt, 6264–2

Imports of US, detailed Schedule A commodities by country and world area of origin, and mode of transport, 1983, annual rpts, 2424–2

Investment (foreign direct) of US, by world area and country, 1977-83, article, 2702–1.442

Investment (intl direct) worldwide, and US investment flows by major industry, by world region and country, 1982 and trends from 1950, annual rpt, 2044–25

Loans and grants for economic and military assistance from US and intl agencies, by program and country, FY46-83, annual rpt, 9914–5

Loans of large US banks to foreigners at all US and foreign offices, by country group and country, quarterly rpt, 13002–1

Military aid of US, and sales of arms, equipment, and training, by item and country, FY50-83, annual rpt, 3904–3

Military aid of US, arms sales, and training programs costs and budget requests by program, world region, and country, FY83-85, annual rpt, 7144–13

Military, social, and economic summary data, by world area and country, 1960s-80s, hearing, 25388–47.1

Military spending, arms trade, and armed forces size, with total govt spending and population, by country, 1972-82, annual rpt, 9824–1

Minerals Yearbook, 1982, Vol 3: foreign country reviews of production, trade, and policies, by commodity, annual rpt, 5604–35

Minerals Yearbook, 1982, Vol 3 preprints: foreign country review of production, trade, and policies, by commodity, annual rpt, 5604–17.87

Multilateral dev banks economic dev projects, environmental and cultural impacts in developing countries, 1970s-83, hearings, 21248–80

Nuclear power plant spent fuel and demand for uranium and enrichment services, for US and non-Communist country groups, 1983 and projected to 2020, annual rpt, 3164–72

Population size and growth rates, and latest available benchmark demographic data, by country, 1950-83, biennial rpt, 2324–4

R&D Fed Govt funding for foreign performers, by world region and country, FY82-84, annual rpt, 9627–20.2

Refugee arrivals in US, by world area of origin and processing and nationality, monthly rpt, 7002–4, 7002–5

Refugee arrivals in US by world area of origin and State of settlement, and Fed Govt intl and domestic assistance costs, FY85, annual rpt, 7004–16

Refugee Indochinese population, arrivals, and departures, by country of origin and resettlement, camp, and ethnicity, monthly rpt, 7002–4

Refugee migration, settlement status, and assistance, by world area and country of origin and asylum, as of May 1984, annual rpt, 7004–15

Rice area, yield, production, stocks, trade, and use, for 3 Asia regions, 1960s-83 and 1983/84 forecast, FAS annual rpt, 1925–2.6

Students in US and Soviet bloc training programs, by program type and Latin American country or world region of student origin, selected years 1972-82, GAO rpt, 26123–77

Terrorist (intl) incidents, casualties, and attacks on US targets, by attack type and world area, with chronology of events, 1983, annual rpt, 7004–13

Travel to and from US, by world area and selected country, projected 1984-85, annual rpt, 2904–9

Travel to and from US on US and foreign flag air carriers, by country, world area, and US port, monthly rpt, 7302–2

Travel to US and receipts by world area and selected country, 1960-83, and US Travel and Tourism Admin activities, 1983, annual rpt, 2904–6

USIA info center and reading room operations, by world region, country, and city, FY83, annual rpt, 9854–4

Weather conditions and effect on agriculture, by US region, State, and city, and world area, weekly rpt, 2152–2

Weather conditions and impact assessment, by world area and country, monthly rpt, 2152–9

see also Afghanistan
see also Asian Development Bank
see also Bahrain
see also Bangladesh
see also Bhutan
see also Brunei
see also Burma
see also China, Peoples Republic
see also Hong Kong
see also India
see also Indonesia
see also Iran
see also Iraq
see also Israel
see also Japan
see also Jordan
see also Kampuchea
see also Korea, North
see also Korea, South
see also Kuwait
see also Laos
see also Lebanon
see also Macao
see also Malaysia
see also Maldives
see also Middle East
see also Mongolia
see also Nepal
see also Oman
see also Pakistan
see also Papua New Guinea
see also Philippines
see also Qatar
see also Saudi Arabia
see also Singapore
see also Southeast Asia
see also Sri Lanka
see also Syria
see also Taiwan
see also Thailand
see also Turkey
see also United Arab Emirates
see also Vietnam
see also Yemen, North
see also Yemen, South
see also under By Foreign Country in the "Index by Categories"

Asian Americans

Agriculture census, 1982: farms, farmland, production, finances, and operator characteristics, by county, final State rpt series, 2331–1

Births among Asian and Pacific Islands Americans by ethnic origin and sociodemographic and birth characteristics, with comparisons to blacks and whites, 1978-80, 4146–5.75

Cancer cases, incidence, deaths, and death rates, by body site, age, race, Hispanic origin, and sex, for 10 geographic areas, 1973-81, 4478–130

Census of Housing, 1980: occupancy and unit characteristics of SMSAs and central cities, by race, Hispanic origin, and city, State and SMSA rpt series, 2473–1

Census of Population and Housing, 1980: detailed population and housing characteristics, by county, city, and census tract, State and SMSA rpt series, 2551–2

Census of Population, 1980: Asian and Pacific Islander population, by detailed race and State, supplementary rpt, 2535–1.15

Census of Population, 1980: detailed socioeconomic and demographic characteristics, by age, sex, race, Hispanic origin, occupation, and industry, State rpt series, 2531–4

Asian Americans

Census of Population, 1980: detailed socioeconomic characteristics, by county, city, and inside-outside SMSAs and central cities, State rpt series, 2531–3

Census of Population, 1980: migration since 1975, by State and selected demographic characteristics, supplementary rpt, 2535–1.13

County and City Data Book, detailed socioeconomic and demographic data for States, counties, and cities, selected years 1976-82, 2328–1

Scientists and engineers employment by sector and activity, and share female, black, and Asian descent, by field, 1982, 9626–2.142

Statistical Abstract of US, social, political, and economic data, 1950s-83 and trends, annual rpt, 2324–1.1

Vocational training bilingual projects, participants, characteristics, and costs, by program, FY82, annual rpt, 4804–26

see also Pacific Islands Americans

Asian Development Bank

- Environmental and cultural impacts of multilateral dev banks economic dev projects in developing countries, 1970s-83, hearings, 21248–80
- Human rights conditions in 162 countries, economic and military aid of US, and economic aid of intl organizations, 1981-83, annual rpt, 21384–3
- Loan activity by purpose and country, and funds by source, FY83, annual rpt, 15344–1.8
- Loans and grants for economic and military assistance from US and intl agencies, by program and country, FY46-83, annual rpt, 9914–5

Asin, Ruth H.

"Person Trip Characteristics", 7556–6.11

Asparagus

see Vegetables and vegetable products

Asphalt and tar

see Petroleum and petroleum industry

Assassination

- Terrorist (intl) incidents, casualties, and attacks on US targets, by attack type and world area, with chronology of events, 1983, annual rpt, 7004–13

Assault

- Convictions, prison sentences, and average sentence lengths, by offense, offender class, and selected State, various periods 1971-84, 6066–19.10
- Court cases, dispositions, convictions, and sentences of Federal criminal defendants, by offense and district, as of June 1983 with trends from 1945, annual rpt, 18204–1
- Court criminal case disposition, effect of victim injury and other factors, and law enforcement official and victim attitudes, 1983 survey, 6068–185
- Crime and criminal justice data, including justice expenditures and employment by level of govt, 1970s-82 with some trends from 1875, 6068–174
- Crime Index by population size and region, and offenses known to police by large city, Jan-June 1984, semiannual rpt, 6222–1
- Crimes, arrests by offender characteristics, and rates, by offense, and law enforcement employees, by population size and jurisdiction, 1970s-83, annual rpt, 6224–2

Criminal case processing from arrest to sentencing, cases and processing time by disposition, dismissal reason, and offense, for 14 cities, 1979, 6066–22.1

- Economic indicators relation to measures of social pathology including crime and death rates, various periods 1950-80, 23848–76
- Law enforcement officer assaults, murders, and other deaths by circumstances, level of govt, agency, victim and offender characteristics, and location, 1983, annual rpt, 6224–3
- Minnesota crime sentencing guidelines by type and severity of offense, 1982, 10048–59
- Pretrial citation release use, cost savings for law enforcement agencies, and failures to appear in court, by offense and selected jurisdiction, 1970s-82, 6068–187
- Prison terms actually served by selected State, and Illinois pretrial detention time credited to sentence, by offense, various periods 1977-83, 6066–19.7
- Prisoners in State prisons median sentence, and admissions and releases by prisoner and sentencing characteristics, by offense and State, 1981 and trends from 1926, 6066–19.9
- School crime against students, teachers, and others, by offense, circumstances, and offender sex and race, 1974-76, 6066–20.2
- School crime, assaults and robberies of secondary students and teachers, 1972-83, 4918–13
- School crime, assaults and robberies of teachers and minority and all students, and vandalism incidents, 1976/77, 4808–12
- Terrorist (intl) incidents, casualties, and attacks on US targets, by attack type and world area, with chronology of events, 1983, annual rpt, 7004–13
- Victimization of households, by offense type, race of household head, and family income and urban-rural residence, 1975-83, periodic rpt, 6062–2.404
- Victimization rates and reports to police, by offense, 1973-83, 6062–2.405
- Victimization rates by type of offense, and victim and offense characteristics, Natl Crime Survey series, 6066–3
- Victims of crime, medical expenses and property loss, and median loss by victim characteristics, by offense type, 1975-81, 6066–19.6

see also Domestic violence

Assets and liabilities

see Business assets and liabilities, general

see Business assets and liabilities, specific industries

see Business inventories

see Personal debt

see Wealth

Assistance Payments Administration

see Social Security Administration

Association of South East Asian Nations

Background Notes, summary social, political, and economic data, 1983 rpt, 7006–2.9

Associations

Agricultural commodities generic advertising, activities and funding by source, selected years 1972-82, 1548–242

Index by Subjects and Names

- Census of Population, 1980: detailed socioeconomic and demographic characteristics, by age, sex, race, Hispanic origin, occupation, and industry, State rpt series, 2531–4
- Census of Population, 1980: detailed socioeconomic characteristics, by county, city, and inside-outside SMSAs and central cities, State rpt series, 2531–3
- Construction and building materials industries trade assns, professional societies, and labor unions, 1984 listing, article, 2012–1.405
- County Business Patterns: establishments, employees, and payrolls, by SIC 4-digit industry and county, 1982, annual State rpt series, 2326–6
- Credit union financial statements by region, State, and type of membership, for Federal and federally insured State unions, 1983, annual rpt, 9534–1
- Earnings by major industry group, and personal income per capita and by source, by region and State, 1929-82, 2708–40
- Employment by detailed occupation, for 29 SIC 2-digit nonmanufacturing industries, 1981 BLS survey, 6748–60
- Employment, earnings, and hours, by selected SIC 1- to 4-digit industry, State, and for 278 major labor areas, 1939-83, annual rpt, 6744–5
- Employment, earnings, and hours, by SIC 4-digit nonfarm industry, monthly 1974-Feb 1984, annual update, 6744–4
- Higher education instns, by type, location, and other characteristics, 1983/84 annual listing, 4844–3
- Income tax returns of corporations, detailed income and tax items by industry, 1981, annual rpt, 8304–4
- Input-output structure of US economy, detailed interindustry transactions for 537 industries, and components of final demand, 1977 benchmark data, 2708–17
- Minority group and women employment, by occupational group and SIC 2- to 3-digit industry, 1981, annual rpt, 9244–1.1
- Political action committee and other campaign funding, and Fed Election Commission monitoring activities, press release series, 9276–1
- Political action committee and other campaign funding, and Fed Election Commission monitoring activities, 1984 Federal elections, biennial series, 9276–2
- Political action committee campaign funding, by candidate and PAC, by State, 1960-82, hearings, 25688–6
- Political action committee campaign funding to individual congressmen, and public opinion on reform proposals and assn influence, 1970s-83, hearings, 21428–7
- Political action committee funding to reelect and defeat House and Senate members by candidate, and FEC activities and funding, 1983, annual rpt, 9274–1

see also Credit unions

see also Labor unions

see also Nonprofit organizations and foundations

see also Savings and loan associations

see also Tax exempt organizations

Index by Subjects and Names

Astronautics

see Astronauts
see Communications satellites
see Meteorological satellites
see Satellites
see Space medicine
see Space programs
see Space sciences

Astronauts

Foreign and US astronautic and aeronautic events, comprehensive chronology, 1976, annual rpt, 9504–2

Soviet Union and US astronauts, missions and flight times, 1961-83, annual rpt, 9504–6.1

Astronomy

Foreign and US astronautic and aeronautic events, comprehensive chronology, 1976, annual rpt, 9504–2

NASA project launch schedules and technical descriptions, press release series, 9506–2

NOAA scientific and technical publications, monthly listing, 2142–1

NSF grant and award recipients, by State, FY83, annual listing, 9624–11

NSF research programs, activities, and funding, FY82-83, annual rpt, 9624–6

R&D expenditures by higher education instns and federally funded centers, by field, source of funds, instn, and State, FY82, annual rpt, 9627–13

R&D expenditures by source, and scientists education and employment, detailed data by field, selected years 1953-84, annual rpt, 9624–18

R&D expenditures of higher education instns, and science and engineering employment and grad students, by field, 1972-83, biennial rpt, 9627–24

R&D Fed Govt facilities and services available for private sector use, by field of science, 1984 biennial listing, 2224–4

R&D Fed Govt funding, by function, agency, and program, selected years FY80-84 and proposed FY85, 26308–46

R&D Fed Govt funding for all performers, by field and supporting agency, selected years FY60-84, annual rpt, 9627–20

Science and engineering doctoral degree recipients, by field, sex, race, age, citizenship, postgrad employment and study status, State, and instn, 1960-82, 9626–6.16

Science and engineering grad enrollment, fields of study, financial support, and other student and instn characteristics, 1975-82, annual survey, 9627–7

Science and engineering grads of 1980-81, employment characteristics or grad enrollment, by degree level, field, sex, and race, 1982, 9627–25

Scientists and engineers employed at universities and colleges, by field, sex, State, and instn, Jan 1983 and selected trends from 1967, annual survey, 9627–11

Star position tables for land surveying use, 1984 annual rpt, 5724–7

Athayde, Dennis N.

"Final Report of the Nationwide Urban Runoff Program", 9208–122

Athens County, Ohio

Housing vacancy rates for single and multifamily units and mobile homes, by city and ZIP code, 1984, annual metro area rpt, 9304–27.8

Athens, Ga.

Census of Housing, 1980: occupancy and unit characteristics, by race, Hispanic origin, and city, SMSA rpt, 2473–1.76

Census of Population and Housing, 1980: detailed population and housing characteristics, by county, city, and census tract, SMSA rpt, 2551–2.76

see also under By SMSA or MSA in the "Index by Categories"

Athletics

see Physical education and training
see Sporting goods
see Sports and athletics

Atlanta, Ga.

Auto dealer repair workers, wages, and benefits, by occupation, size of establishment, and for 24 labor market areas, Nov 1982 survey, 6787–6.202

Cancer cases, incidence, deaths, and death rates, by body site, age, race, Hispanic origin, and sex, for 10 geographic areas, 1973-81, 4478–130

Census of Housing, 1980: occupancy and unit characteristics, by race, Hispanic origin, and city, SMSA rpt, 2473–1.77

Census of Population and Housing, 1980: detailed population and housing characteristics, by county, city, and census tract, SMSA rpt, 2551–2.77

CPI by component for US city average, and by region, population size, and for 28 SMSAs, monthly press release, 6762–1

CPI by detailed component, for US city average, 28 SMSAs, and 4 regions by population size, monthly rpt, 6762–2

Fruit and vegetable shipments, and arrivals in 23 US and 5 Canada cities, by mode of transport and State or country of origin, 1983, annual rpt, 1311–4.1

Hospital worker wages by sex and occupation, and benefits, for 22 MSAs, Oct 1981 survey, 6787–6.201

Housing and financial characteristics, and unit and neighborhood quality, for 15 SMSAs, 1978, annual survey special supplement, 2485–8

Housing and households detailed characteristics, and unit and neighborhood quality, by inside-outside central cities, 1982 survey, SMSA rpt, 2485–6.32

Housing water conservation programs and savings of water and energy, for selected cities and suburbs, 1980-83, 5188–109

Repair technicians and apprentices wages and benefits, for 5 types of electrical repair shops in 19 SMSAs, Nov 1981 survey, 6787–6.197

Wages by occupation, and benefits for office and plant workers, 1984 SMSA survey rpt, 6785–11.5

Atlantic City, N.J.

Census of Housing, 1980: occupancy and unit characteristics, by race, Hispanic origin, and city, SMSA rpt, 2473–1.78

Census of Population and Housing, 1980: detailed population and housing characteristics, by county, city, and census tract, SMSA rpt, 2551–2.78

Atlantic Ocean

Wages of office and plant workers, by occupation, 1984 labor market area survey rpt, 6785–3.9

see also under By SMSA or MSA in the "Index by Categories"

Atlantic Ocean

Coastal environmental and socioeconomic conditions, and potential impacts of oil and gas OCS leases, final statement series, 5736–1

Coastal environmental and wildlife characteristics, use, and mgmt, for individual ecosystems, series, 5506–9

Dumping of low-level radioactive wastes at 4 largest and all disposal sites, 1983 hearings, 21568–36

Dumping of waste materials, EPA permit program and intl London Dumping Convention activities, 1981-83, annual rpt, 9204–8

Exports and imports of US (waterborne), by type of service, commodity, country, route, and US port, 1982, annual rpt, 7704–2

Fish and eggs for stocking distributed from natl hatcheries, by species, hatchery, and jurisdiction, FY83, annual rpt, 5504–10

Fish and shellfish landings, life cycles, and environmental needs, for selected species by region, with glossary and bibl, series, 5506–8

Fish and shellfish landings, prices, trade, consumption, and industry operating data, for US with foreign comparisons, 1982-83, annual rpt, 2164–1

Fish catch quotas for US 200 mile zone, allocations by species and country, 1984 coastal area rpt, 7006–5.3

Fish landings, employment, gear used, and seafood production, for detailed species by State, 1977, annual rpt, 2164–2

Fishermen (ocean sport), fishing activities, and catch by species, by fisherman characteristics and State, for Atlantic and Gulf of Mexico coasts, 1979-80, 2166–17.2

Fishing (ocean sport) effort and catch, and Natl Marine Fisheries Service tagging and research activity, by species and location, 1983, annual rpt, 2164–7

Fishing (ocean sport and commercial) landings and allowable and potential catch of US and Canada, for 34 species in North Atlantic, 1983, annual rpt, 2164–14

Hurricanes and tropical storms in North Atlantic and Caribbean area, paths, surveillance, deaths, property damage, and landfall probabilities by city, 1983, annual rpt, 2184–7

Marine Mammal Protection Act admin and populations, strandings, and catch permits by type and applicant, by species and location, Apr 1983-Mar 1984, annual rpt, 2164–11

Mineral industries census, 1982: financial and operating data, by State and for 4 offshore regions, preliminary summary rpt, 2511–2.2

Oil and gas OCS reserves of Fed Govt, leasing and exploration activities, production, revenues, and costs, by ocean region, FY83, annual rpt, 5734–4

Oil and gas undiscovered recoverable resources, cumulative production, and identified reserves, as of 1982, preliminary oil basin rpt, 5666–17.15

Index by Subjects and Names

Atlantic Ocean

Oil, gas, and minerals dev, under Fed Govt OCS leases, with production, revenues, reserves, and oil spills, by State and ocean region, 1950s-82, annual rpt, 5734–3

Oil spill risk analyses for OCS proposed lease sale areas, series, 5736–2

Temperature of sea surface by ocean and for US coastal areas, and Bering Sea ice conditions, monthly rpt, 2182–5

Tidal current tables, daily time and velocity by station for US Atlantic coast, 1985, annual rpt, 2174–1.1

Tide height and time daily at worldwide coastal points, 1985 predictions, annual rpt, 2174–2.2, 2174–2.3

Vertebrates (marine) abundance and seasonal distribution off southeastern US coast, with oil and gas dev effects and lease status, early 1980s, 5508–85

Weather and tropical cyclones, quarterly journal with articles, 2152–8

Weather broadcasts for US ships, by major ocean area, as of Jan 1984, biennial rpt, 2184–3

see also Caribbean area

see also New York Bight

Atlantic Richfield Co.

Gasoline retail sales percent change in California for ARCO, other majors, and independents, and Trans-Alaska Pipeline owner companies financial data by company, 1981-83, hearing, 21728–51

Atmospheric sciences

Carbon dioxide atmospheric levels, climatic effects and impacts of fossil and synthetic fuels use, deforestation, and land use patterns, research rpt series, 3406–3

Census of Population, 1980: detailed socioeconomic and demographic characteristics, by age, sex, race, Hispanic origin, occupation, and industry, State rpt series, 2531–4

DOE R&D projects and funding at natl labs, universities, and other instns, FY83, annual summary rpt, 3004–18.1

DOE R&D projects and funding at natl labs, universities, and other instns, FY84, annual summary rpt, 3004–18.4

Forest research project descriptions and bibl, 1982, annual rpt, 1204–14

NOAA scientific and technical publications, monthly listing, 2142–1

NSF grant and award recipients, by State, FY83, annual listing, 9624–11

NSF research programs, activities, and funding, FY82-83, annual rpt, 9624–6

R&D-employed scientists and engineers salaries by degree, type of establishment, age, experience, and field, 1984, annual rpt, 3004–1

R&D expenditures by higher education instns and federally funded centers, by field, source of funds, instn, and State, FY82, annual rpt, 9627–13

R&D expenditures by source, and scientists education and employment, detailed data by field, selected years 1953-84, annual rpt, 9624–18

R&D expenditures of higher education instns, and science and engineering employment and grad students, by field, 1972-83, biennial rpt, 9627–24

R&D Fed Govt facilities and services available for private sector use, by field of science, 1984 biennial listing, 2224–4

R&D Fed Govt funding, by function, agency, and program, selected years FY80-84 and proposed FY85, 26308–46

R&D Fed Govt funding for all performers, by field and supporting agency, selected years FY60-84, annual rpt, 9627–20

Science and engineering doctoral degree recipients, by field, sex, race, age, citizenship, postgrad employment and study status, State, and instn, 1960-82, 9626–6.16

Science and engineering grad enrollment, fields of study, financial support, and other student and instn characteristics, 1975-82, annual survey, 9627–7

Scientists and engineers employed at universities and colleges, by field, sex, State, and instn, Jan 1983 and selected trends from 1967, annual survey, 9627–11

see also Meteorology

see also Stratosphere

Atomic bombs

see Fallout shelters

see Nuclear explosives and explosions

see Nuclear weapons

Atomic energy

see Nuclear power

see Power-generating plants and equipment

Atomic Energy Commission

Radiation from 1940s-70s nuclear weapons tests, levels in air and water, and personnel exposure by military unit and job category, series, 3906–1

Radioactive contamination of former AEC and Manhattan Project research and storage sites, test results series, 3406–1

Uranium resources research publications, 1976-83, listing, 3358–27

see also under names of agencies (listed under Department of Energy)

Atomic explosives

see Nuclear explosives and explosions

Atomic power plants

see Nuclear power

see Power-generating plants and equipment

Atomic weapons

see Nuclear weapons

Attitudes

see Opinion and attitude surveys

Attleboro, Mass.

see also under By SMSA or MSA in the "Index by Categories"

Attorneys-at-law

see Lawyers

Atwell, John K.

"Protecting American Agriculture: The VS Role", 1004–16.1

Auburn, Maine

Census of Housing, 1980: occupancy and unit characteristics, by race, Hispanic origin, and city, SMSA rpt, 2473–1.218

Census of Population and Housing, 1980: detailed population and housing characteristics, by county, city, and census tract, SMSA rpt, 2551–2.218

see also under By SMSA or MSA in the "Index by Categories"

Audiology

see Ear diseases and infections

see Hearing and hearing disorders

see Speech pathology and audiology

Audiovisual education

Libraries of colleges and universities, expenditures, holdings by type, use, staff by sex, and Federal grants received, 1979-82, biennial rpt, 4854–1

Medicine Natl Library activities, collections, and grants, FY81-83, annual rpt, 4464–1

see also Educational broadcasting

Auditing

see Accounting and auditing

Audits and Surveys

"Home Taping in America: 1983, Extent and Impact", 25528–100.1

Augusta, Ga.

Census of Housing, 1980: occupancy and unit characteristics, by race, Hispanic origin, and city, SMSA rpt, 2473–1.79

Census of Population and Housing, 1980: detailed population and housing characteristics, by county, city, and census tract, SMSA rpt, 2551–2.79

see also under By SMSA or MSA in the "Index by Categories"

Aurora, Colo.

see also under By City in the "Index by Categories"

Aurora, Ill.

see also under By SMSA or MSA in the "Index by Categories"

Austin, Tex.

Census of Housing, 1980: occupancy and unit characteristics, by race, Hispanic origin, and city, SMSA rpt, 2473–1.80

Census of Population and Housing, 1980: detailed population and housing characteristics, by county, city, and census tract, SMSA rpt, 2551–2.80

Housing vacancy rates for single and multifamily units and mobile homes, by city and ZIP code, 1983, annual metro area rpt, 9304–19.9

Housing vacancy rates for single and multifamily units and mobile homes, by city and ZIP code, 1984, annual metro area rpt, 9304–19.24

Wages of office and plant workers, by occupation, 1984 labor market area survey rpt, 6785–3.10

see also under By City and By SMSA or MSA in the "Index by Categories"

Australia

Agricultural and food production indexes, and production of selected commodities, by world region and country, 1974-83, annual rpt, 1524–5

Agricultural exports and imports of US, by detailed commodity and country, FY83 and CY83, semiannual rpts, 1522–4

Agricultural situation in North America and Oceania, by country and commodity, 1983 and outlook for 1984, annual rpt, 1524–4.1

Agricultural supply/demand, trade, and production, and socioeconomic data, by country, 1950s-77, 1528–179

Computers and computer equipment market and trade, and user industry operations and demand, 1983 country market research rpt, 2045–1.46

Economic conditions in Communist and OECD countries, 1982, annual rpt, 7144–11

Economic conditions in Communist, OECD, and selected other countries, 1960s-83, annual rpt, 244–5

Index by Subjects and Names — Automation

Economic indicators of 12 Pacific Basin countries or areas and US, quarterly rpt, 9393–9

Economic, social, and political summary data, by country, 1984, annual factbook, 244–11

Economic trends in income, production, prices, employment, finances, and trade, 1983 semiannual rpt, 2046–4.1

Economic trends in income, production, prices, employment, finances, and trade, 1984 annual rpt, 2046–4.77

Employment, labor force, and participation and unemployment rates by sex, in US and 9 OECD countries, various periods 1970-3rd qtr 1983, annual article, 6722–1.404

Energy prices and taxes by energy source and end-use sector, for US and 9 OECD countries, quarterly 1979-83, annual rpt, 3164–71

Exports and imports of OECD countries, by country, 1983, annual rpt, 7144–10

Exports and imports of US (waterborne), by type of service, customs district, port, and world area, monthly rpt, 2422–7

Exports and imports of US, by commodity group, world area, selected country, US coastal area and port, and mode of transport, with seasonal adjustments, monthly rpt, 2422–9

Exports and imports of US, detailed SIC-based commodities by world area, 1983, annual rpts, 2424–6

Exports of US, detailed Schedule B commodities by country of destination, 1983, annual rpt, 2424–9

Exports of US, detailed Schedule E commodities by mode of transport and world area and country of destination, 1983, annual rpts, 2424–5

Farm machinery and equipment market and trade, and user industry operations and demand, 1983 country market research rpt, 2045–13.3

Fruit (deciduous) grower prices and processor net cost and subsidies in 4 countries and EC, 1982/83-1983/84, article, 1925–34.414

Imports of US, detailed Schedule A commodities by country and world area of origin, and mode of transport, 1983, annual rpts, 2424–2

Imports of US, detailed TSUSA commodities by country of origin, 1983, annual rpt, 2424–4

Industrial process control equipment market and trade, and user industry operations and demand, 1984 country market research rpt, 2045–6.37

Intl transactions of US with 10 countries, 1981-83, *Survey of Current Business*, monthly rpt, annual table, 2702–1.31

Lab instruments market and trade, and user industry operations and demand, 1983 country market research rpt, 2045–10.18

Loans and grants for economic and military assistance from US and intl agencies, by program and country, FY46-83, annual rpt, 9914–5

Military aid of US, arms sales, and training programs costs and budget requests by program, world region, and country, FY83-85, annual rpt, 7144–13

Military pension lifetime earnings in US and 7 countries, as of 1983, 26306–6.76

Military spending, arms trade, and armed forces size, with total govt spending and population, by country, 1972-82, annual rpt, 9824–1

Minerals Yearbook, 1982, Vol 3: foreign country reviews of production, trade, and policies, by commodity, annual rpt, 5604–35

Minerals Yearbook, 1982, Vol 3 preprints: foreign country review of production, trade, and policies, by commodity, annual rpt, 5604–17.6

Population size and growth rates, and latest available benchmark demographic data, by country, 1950-83, biennial rpt, 2324–4

R&D Fed Govt funding for foreign performers, by world region and country, FY82-84, annual rpt, 9627–20.2

Raisin and dried prune stocks, production, and exports for 4 countries, 1982-83 and forecast 1984, article, 1925–34.416

Space launchings attaining Earth orbit or beyond, by country, 1957-83, annual rpt, 9504–9.1

Space satellites and other objects launched since 1957, quarterly listing, 9502–2

Sporting goods and recreational equipment and vehicles market and trade, 1983 country market research rpt, 2045–14.9

Steel from 5 countries, injury to US industry from foreign subsidized products and sales at less than fair value, investigation with background financial and operating data, 1984 rpt, 9886–19.8

Telecommunication equipment market and trade, and user industry operations and demand, 1983 country market research rpt, 2045–12.33

Weather conditions and effect on agriculture, by US region, State, and city, and world area, weekly rpt, 2152–2

Weather conditions and impact assessment, by world area and country, monthly rpt, 2152–9

Wheat exports, total and for major producers by world area and country of destination, 1973/74-1983/84, FAS rpt, 1925–2.7

Youth unemployment rates in Australia and US, by sex and age, Mar 1983 and trends from 1960s, article, 6722–1.462

see also under By Foreign Country in the "Index by Categories"

Austria

Agricultural and food production indexes, and production of selected commodities, by world region and country, 1974-83, annual rpt, 1524–5

Agricultural situation in Western Europe, by country and commodity, 1983 and outlook for 1984, annual rpt, 1524–4.6

Agricultural supply/demand, trade, and production, and socioeconomic data, by country, 1950s-77, 1528–179

AID loan repayment status and terms by program and country, and status of predecessor agency loans, quarterly rpt, 9912–3

Economic, social, and political summary data, by country, 1984, annual factbook, 244–11

Economic trends in income, production, prices, employment, finances, and trade, 1984 annual rpt, 2046–4.55

Exports and imports of OECD countries, by country, 1983, annual rpt, 7144–10

Exports and imports of US with Western Europe, and US market share and export opportunities for selected commodities, by country, 1982-84, 2048–105

Exports of US, detailed Schedule B commodities by country of destination, 1983, annual rpt, 2424–9

Exports of US, detailed Schedule E commodities by mode of transport and world area and country of destination, 1983, annual rpts, 2424–5

Imports of US, detailed Schedule A commodities by country and world area of origin, and mode of transport, 1983, annual rpts, 2424–2

Imports of US, detailed TSUSA commodities by country of origin, 1983, annual rpt, 2424–4

Loans and grants for economic and military assistance from US and intl agencies, by program and country, FY46-83, annual rpt, 9914–5

Military aid of US, arms sales, and training programs costs and budget requests by program, world region, and country, FY83-85, annual rpt, 7144–13

Military spending, arms trade, and armed forces size, with total govt spending and population, by country, 1972-82, annual rpt, 9824–1

Minerals Yearbook, 1982, Vol 3: foreign country reviews of production, trade, and policies, by commodity, annual rpt, 5604–35

Minerals Yearbook, 1982, Vol 3 preprints: foreign country review of production, trade, and policies, by commodity, annual rpt, 5604–17.7

Nuclear power plant construction and operation status, and capacity, by plant, region, State, and selected country, 1983 and projected to 2020, annual rpt, 3164–57

Population size and growth rates, and latest available benchmark demographic data, by country, 1950-83, biennial rpt, 2324–4

see also under By Foreign Country in the "Index by Categories"

Automation

Air traffic control and airway facilities and equipment, FAA improvement activities and R&D under Natl Airspace System Plan, 1982-2000, annual rpt, 7504–12

Air traffic control and airway facilities and services, operations, and finances, FY83, annual rpt, 7504–37

Employment and productivity and effects of technological change in 4 industries, 1960-90, 6828–23

Metalworking machinery industry computerized automation, by plant characteristics, for 6 industry groups and small plants, 1982 surveys, 23848–179

Natl Weather Service, effects of proposed reorganization and technological improvement on staff and expenditures, FY82 and projected to 2000, 2188–16

Robotics imports effects on US industry, investigation with background financial and operating data, 1977-83, 9886–4.65

Robots for industrial use, R&D, training, and employment impacts, US with comparisons to foreign countries, 1980s with projections to 1992, 26358–105

Automation

Robots installed for manufacturing, and jobs displaced and created by occupation, by type of robot use, 1980s-2000, hearings, 21728–54

Robots installed in US and selected foreign countries, by type, 1981, annual rpt, 9624–10.1

Southeastern States industrial robots by major industry, and State share of manufacturing employment, by State, 1984 survey, article, 9371–1.423

see also Computer use
see also Computers
see also Electronic funds transfer
see also Information storage and retrieval systems

Automobile exhaust
see Motor vehicle exhaust

Automobile industry
see Motor vehicle industry

Automobile insurance

Costs (direct and indirect) of traffic accidents and casualties, by characteristics of persons and vehicles involved, 1979-80, 7768–80

Costs of operating and owning autos and vans by component and vehicle size, for 12 years of operation, 1984 model year, annual rpt, 7304–2, 7304–2.3, 7554–21

Costs of operating autos and motorcycles by component and vehicle size or make, and Fed Govt mileage reimbursement rates, 1983, annual rpt, 9454–13

Farm production expenditures, detailed items by farm sales size and region, 1983, annual rpt, 1614–3

Automobile parking
see Parking facilities

Automobile repair

Census of Population, 1980: labor force, by sex, detailed occupation, and region, with comparison to 1970 census, supplementary rpt, 2535–1.12

Census of Service Industries, 1982: employment, establishments, receipts, and payroll, by SIC 2- to 4-digit kind of business, SMSA, county, and city, State rpt series, 2391–1

Census of Service Industries, 1982: employment, establishments, receipts, and payroll, by SIC 4-digit kind of business and State, preliminary rpt, 2390–2.9

Collective bargaining agreements expiring during year, covered workers by SIC 2-digit industry, firm, and union, with summary of key provisions, 1984, annual rpt, 6784–9

Costs (direct and indirect) of traffic accidents and casualties, by characteristics of persons and vehicles involved, 1979-80, 7768–80

Costs of operating and owning autos and vans by component and vehicle size, for 12 years of operation, 1984 model year, annual rpt, 7304–2, 7304–2.3, 7554–21

Costs of operating autos and motorcycles by component and vehicle size or make, and Fed Govt mileage reimbursement rates, 1983, annual rpt, 9454–13

Costs of warranty and nonwarranty repair by type, and auto dealer and independent repair shops, 1983 hearings, 25328–25

County Business Patterns: establishments, employees, and payrolls, by SIC 4-digit industry and county, 1981, annual State rpt series, 2326–8

County Business Patterns: establishments, employees, and payrolls, by SIC 4-digit industry and county, 1982, annual State rpt series, 2326–6

Earnings by major industry group, and personal income per capita and by source, by region and State, 1929-82, 2708–40

Employment, earnings, and hours, by selected SIC 1- to 4-digit industry, State, and for 278 major labor areas, 1939-83, annual rpt, 6744–5

Employment, earnings, and hours, by SIC 4-digit nonfarm industry, monthly 1974-Feb 1984, annual update, 6744–4

Employment, wages, and benefits of auto dealer repair workers, by occupation, size of establishment, and for 24 labor market areas, Nov 1982 survey, 6787–6.202

Farmers prices received for major products and paid for farm inputs, by commodity and State, 1983, annual rpt, 1629–5

Fed Govt motor vehicle fleet costs and operating data, by agency, FY83, annual rpt, 9454–9

Finances and operations, by SIC 2- to 4-digit industry, 1970s-83 and projected to 1988, annual rpt, 2014–4

Franchise business opportunities, by firm and kind of business, 1984 annual listing, 2044–27

Franchises of firms engaged in distribution of goods and services by kind of business, establishments by State, and sales, 1982-84, annual rpt, 2014–5

Income tax returns of corporations, detailed income and tax items by industry, 1981, annual rpt, 8304–4

Income tax returns of corporations with foreign tax credit, income and deductions by type, asset size, and selected industry group, 1980, article, 8302–2.415

Income tax returns of partnerships, detailed data by industry, 1981 estimates, annual article, 8302–2.404

Income tax returns of partnerships, receipts by source, deductions by type, and establishments, by selected industry, 1982, annual article, 8302–2.416

Income tax returns of sole proprietorships, detailed data by industry div and selected industry group, 1981, annual rpt, 8304–7

Income tax returns of sole proprietorships, receipts, deductions by type, payroll, and net income, by major industry, 1982, annual article, 8302–2.413

Income tax returns with investment credits, for individuals by income, and for sole proprietorships by industry, 1981, article, 8302–2.409

Input-output structure of US economy, detailed interindustry transactions for 85 industries, and components of final demand, 1977, article, 2702–1.421

Input-output structure of US economy, detailed interindustry transactions for 537 industries, and components of final demand, 1977 benchmark data, 2708–17

Occupational injury and illness rates, by SIC 2- to 4-digit industry, 1982, annual rpt, 6844–1

Occupational manpower needs and supply by detailed occupation, and educational and training program enrollees and grads by detailed field, 1982 and 1995, biennial rpt, 6744–3

Occupational Outlook Handbook, 1984-85 biennial rpt, 6744–1

Receipts for selected services, by SIC 2- to 4-digit kind of business, 1983, annual rpt, 2413–8

Retail trade census, 1982: employment, establishments, sales, and payroll, for tire, battery, and auto accessory dealers by State, preliminary rpt, 2395–1.11

Underground economy, household expenditures and participation by type of goods or service and sociodemographic characteristics, with methodology and bibl, 1981 survey, 8308–27

Virgin Islands economic censuses, 1982: employment, establishments, payroll, and receipts, by SIC 1- to 4-digit industry, island, and city, 2593–1

see also under By Industry in the "Index by Categories"

Automobile safety devices
see Motor vehicle safety devices

Automobiles

Agriculture census, 1982: farms, farmland, production, finances, and operator characteristics, by county, final State rpt series, 2331–1

Bankruptcy (personal), filers by debt type and other characteristics, selected years 1978-81, hearing, 25528–97.1

Bombing (explosive and incendiary) incidents, damage, injuries, and deaths, by target, State, and circumstances, 1983, annual rpt, 6224–5

Census of Housing, 1980: inventory, occupancy, and unit characteristics, changes from 1973 by region and inside-outside SMSAs and central cities, series, 2473–3

Census of Housing, 1980: occupancy and unit characteristics of SMSAs and central cities, by race, Hispanic origin, and city, State and SMSA rpt series, 2473–1

Census of Population and Housing, 1980: detailed population and housing characteristics, by county, city, and census tract, State and SMSA rpt series, 2551–2

Census of Population, 1980: detailed socioeconomic and demographic characteristics, by age, sex, race, Hispanic origin, occupation, and industry, State rpt series, 2531–4

Census of Population, 1980: detailed socioeconomic characteristics, by county, city, and inside-outside SMSAs and central cities, State rpt series, 2531–3

Census of Transportation, 1982: trucks, by detailed characteristics, miles traveled, and type of product carried, State rpt series, 2573–1

Communist, OECD, and selected other countries consumer and producer goods production, 1960s-83, annual rpt, 244–5.8

Commuting to work, householder principal mode of transport, distance, and travel time, by race, Hispanic origin, tenure, urban-rural location, and region, 1981, annual survey, 2485–7

Consumer expenditures for autos, and index of consumer sentiment, *Business Conditions Digest,* historical supplement and methodology of business indicators, 1947-82, 2708–31

Index by Subjects and Names

Automobiles

Consumer expenditures for autos, and index of consumer sentiment, *Business Conditions Digest,* monthly rpt, 2702–3.3

Costs of operating and owning autos and vans by component and vehicle size, for 12 years of operation, 1984 model year, biennial rpt, 7554–21

Costs of operating of autos by component and vehicle size, and Fed Govt mileage reimbursement rates, 1983, annual rpt, 9454–13.1

County Business Patterns: establishments, employees, and payrolls, by SIC 4-digit industry and county, 1982, annual State rpt series, 2326–6

Cuba economic conditions, agricultural and industrial production and distribution, trade, and intl economic relations, 1970-82 and trends from 1957, 248–40

Diesel car sales by make, 1970s-83, hearings, 25328–25

DOE in-house energy use, conservation investments, and savings, by type of use and fuel and field office, FY83, annual rpt, 3024–3

Drivers licensed by age and sex, and licensing policies, by State, 1982, annual rpt, 7554–16

Electric-powered vehicles, Fed Govt dev program implementation, FY83, annual rpt, 3304–2

Energy economy and miles traveled per car, annual data, monthly rpt, 3162–24.1

Energy economy and registrations, by type of vehicle, 1960-83, annual rpt, 3164–74.3

Energy economy measures for autos and light trucks of US, Japan, and Europe make, selected years 1960-83, annual rpt, 3164–73

Energy economy performance of autos and light trucks by make, and standards, 1978-85 model years, annual rpt, 7764–9

Energy economy test results for autos complying with California emission standards, 1984 model year, annual rpt, 3304–13

Energy economy test results, 1985 model year, annual rpt, 3304–11

Energy supply/demand and prices, by fuel type, sector, and end use, detailed trends and projections 1973-95, annual rpt, 3164–75

Energy use, by type of air pollutant source and fuel, and State, 1981, annual rpt, 9194–14

Energy use in transportation sector by mode, fuel supplies, and demographic and economic determinants of vehicle use, 1970s-83, annual rpt, 3304–5

Energy use of autos and light trucks, economy standards and manufacturer compliance, and gas prices and taxes, with selected foreign comparisons, FY80-83 and projected to 2000, hearing, 21368–49

Experimental vehicle designs and auto safety, 1982, conf proceedings, annual rpt, 7764–3

Exports and imports of autos and trucks by country, retail prices of selected US and Japan models, and industry operating data, monthly rpt, 9882–8

Exports and imports of US, detailed SIC-based commodities by world area, 1983, annual rpts, 2424–6

Exports and imports of US, totals and as percent of domestic production, by SIC 2- to 5-digit commodity, 1981, annual rpt, 2424–3

Exports, imports, tariffs, and industry operating data for motor vehicles and bodies and chassis, foreign and US, 1979-83, TSUSA commodity rpt, 9885–6.63

Exports of US, detailed Schedule B commodities by country of destination, 1983, annual rpt, 2424–9

Exports of US, detailed Schedule E commodities by mode of transport and world area and country of destination, 1983, annual rpts, 2424–5

Farm finances, assets, liabilities, income, receipts by commodity and State, and expenses, 1980-83 and trends from 1910, annual rpt, 1544–16

Farm finances, expenses by type, loans by purpose and source, and credit detail by Fed Reserve District, quarterly rpt, 9365–3.10

Farm finances, production, expenses by type, and domestic economic impact, selected years 1972-82 and preliminary 1983-84, annual rpt, 1544–19

Farm production expenditures, detailed items by farm sales size and region, 1983, annual rpt, 1614–3

Fed Govt motor vehicle fleet and mileage, GSA mgmt activities and finances, FY78-83, annual rpt, 9454–23

Fed Govt motor vehicle fleet costs and operating data, by agency, FY83, annual rpt, 9454–9

Fed Govt programs and mgmt cost control proposals, 3-year savings by function and agency, and financial and operating data, 1960s-81, 16908–1

Florida and California elderly migration by selected State of origin or destination, and Florida elderly, by sociodemographic and housing characteristics, 1970 and 1980, 4478–150

Forecasts for selected business activities and natl economic indicators, compilation of representative opinions, 1984, annual rpt, 9389–3

Franchises of firms engaged in distribution of goods and services by kind of business, establishments by State, and sales, 1982-84, annual rpt, 2014–5

Great Lakes trade, by SITC 3-digit commodity, port, vessel type, world area, and country, 1982, annual rpt, 7744–3

Housing census, 1980: structural, financial, and householder characteristics, by region and State, 2475–4

Housing units with cars and trucks available, by inside-outside central cities, 1979-82 surveys, SMSA rpt series, 2485–6

Hwy Statistics, detailed data on traffic, govt finances, fuel use, vehicles, driver licenses, and hwy characteristics, by State, 1983, annual rpt, 7554–1

Hwy Statistics, summary data on traffic, govt finances, fuel use, vehicles, and driver licenses, by State, 1982, annual rpt, 7554–24

Hwy traffic volume on rural roads and city streets, by region, monthly rpt, 7552–8

Hwy use taxes by tax type, and truck size and weight limits, economic effects on trucking industry, 1982-83 and projected 1984-87, hearings, 25328–24

Imports of autos and parts, *Business Conditions Digest,* historical supplement and methodology, 1947-82, 2708–31

Imports of autos and parts, *Business Conditions Digest,* monthly rpt, 2702–3.9

Imports of US, detailed Schedule A commodities by country and world area of origin, and mode of transport, 1983, annual rpts, 2424–2

Imports of US, detailed Schedule A commodities by country, monthly rpt, 2422–2

Imports of US, detailed TSUSA commodities by country of origin, 1983, annual rpt, 2424–4

Input-output structure of US economy, detailed interindustry transactions for 537 industries, and components of final demand, 1977 benchmark data, 2708–17

Intl trade position of US and 4 OECD countries, and factors affecting US competition, quarterly pamphlet, 2042–25

Loans for autos and other financial services of nonbank firms and bank holding companies, with financial and operating data by firm, 1981-82 with trends from 1962, technical paper, 9375–11.3

Loans for autos, auto sales related to usury limits in 2 States, and loans made and outstanding by lender type, various periods 1977-82, article, 9375–1.409

Loans for autos, monthly rpt, 23842–1.5

Loans from banks and finance companies, rates, terms, and related data, monthly rpt series, 9365–2

Manufacturing census, 1982: financial and operating data, for SIC 4-digit industries by product, preliminary rpt, 2491–1.393

Methanol fuel for autos, regulatory barriers to market dev, with supply/demand and auto fleet use and fuel economy, mid-1970s-82 and projected to 2000, GAO rpt, 26113–112

Michigan bankruptcy filings, by filer type, moving history, income, creditor action, debt and asset type, credit status, exemptions claimed, and county, 1979-81, hearings, 21528–57.3

Natl income and product, comprehensive accounts and components, *Survey of Current Business,* monthly rpt, 2702–1.21, 2702–1.22

North Central States economic indicators, Fed Reserve 7th District monthly rpt, 9375–9

OECD trade, total and for 4 major countries, and US trade by country, by commodity, 1972-82, annual world region rpt series, 244–13

Older persons population characteristics, and needs and costs of social services by type, by metro-nonmetro status, 1970s-82 with trends from 1900, 21148–28

Passenger miles and trips, by transport mode, selected years 1929-81, 26358–97

Personal consumption expenditures, natl income and product account, *Survey of Current Business,* monthly rpt, monthly and annual tables, 2702–1.23

Automobiles

Personal stocks of durable goods, by type, in current and constant dollars, 1980-83, annual article, 2702-1.433

Police dept costs and operations, patrol car use, investigations, arrests, and recruit training, by city population size, 1982, 6066-21.1

Producer prices and indexes, by stage of processing and detailed commodity, monthly rpt, 6762-6

Producer prices and indexes, by stage of processing and detailed commodity, monthly 1983, annual supplement, 6764-2

R&D projects on engines and power trains, DOE contracts and funding by recipient, FY83, annual rpt, 3304-17

Recalls of motor vehicles and equipment with safety-related defects, by make, quarterly listing, 7762-2

Rental of autos and trucks, industry receipts, 1983, annual rpt, 2413-8

Retail dealers business income tax returns, partnerships detailed data, 1981 estimates, annual article, 8302-2.404

Retail trade sales, inventories, purchases, gross margin, and accounts receivable, by SIC 2- to 4-digit kind of business and type of ownership, 1983, annual rpt, 2413-5

Retail trade sales of consumer goods including autos, and manufacturers orders and shipments, 1950-84, annual chartbook, 9364-2.3

Sales of domestic and imported cars, monthly rpt, quarterly data, 23842-1.1

Sales, prices, and registrations of autos and auto products in US, and trade of 8 countries with US, by make and model, 1964-83, annual rpt, 9884-7

Senate salaries, expenses, and contingent fund disbursements, by payee, detailed listings, 1st half FY84, semiannual rpt, 25922-1

Statistical Abstract of US, social, political, and economic data, 1950s-83 and trends, annual rpt, 2324-1.3

Tax (excise) collections of IRS, by source, quarterly press release, 8302-1

Tax provisions (State) for motor fuel, vehicle registration fees, and disposition of receipts, by State, as of Jan 1984, biennial rpt, 7554-37

Tax revenues, by level of govt, type of tax, State, and selected large counties, quarterly rpt, 2462-3

Theft of autos and other crime convictions, prison sentences, and average sentence lengths, by offender class and selected State, various periods 1971-84, 6066-19.10

Theft of autos and other Crime Index offenses by population size and region, and offenses known to police by large city, Jan-June 1984, semiannual rpt, 6222-1

Theft of autos and other offenses, actual prison terms served by selected State, various periods 1977-83, 6066-19.7

Theft of autos and other offenses, arrests by offender characteristics, and rates, by population size and jurisdiction, 1970s-83, annual rpt, 6224-2

Theft of autos and other offenses, victim medical expenses and property loss, and median loss by victim characteristics, 1975-81, 6066-19.6

Theft of autos and other offenses, victimization of households, by offense type, race of household head, and family income and urban-rural residence, 1975-83, periodic rpt, 6062-2.404

Theft of autos and other offenses, victimization rates and reports to police, 1973-83, 6062-2.405

Theft of autos and other offenses, victimization rates and victim characteristics, Natl Crime Survey series, 6066-3

Theft of autos, Federal court cases disposition, convictions, and sentences, by district, year ended June 1983 and trends from 1961, annual rpt, 18204-1

Transportation finances, operations, vehicles, equipment, accidents, and energy use, by mode of transport, 1955-84, annual rpt, 7304-2

Travel patterns, personal and household characteristics, auto use, and public transport availability, 1977 survey, series, 7556-6

Wholesale trade census, 1982: employment, establishments, sales by commodity, and payroll, by SIC 4-digit kind of business and State, preliminary rpt, 2403-1.1

Women's travel patterns, by employment and sociodemographic characteristics and type of child care used, 1980 survey, 7888-62

see also Automobile insurance
see also Automobile repair
see also Gasoline
see also Gasoline service stations
see also Motor vehicle exhaust
see also Motor vehicle industry
see also Motor vehicle registrations
see also Motor vehicle safety devices
see also Traffic accidents and safety

Autopsies

Performance of autopsies, by cause of death, age, race, and sex, 1979, US Vital Statistics annual rpt, 4144-2.1

Avery, David

"Alabama: Prospects Brighten for 1984", 9371-1.408

"Robot Corps in Southeastern Industry", 9371-1.423

Avery, Robert B.

"Survey of Consumer Finances, 1983", 9362-1.406

"Survey of Consumer Finances, 1983: A Second Report", 9362-1.411

Aviation

see Aeronautical navigation
see Aerospace industry
see Air traffic control
see Aircraft
see Airlines
see Airports and airways
see Astronauts
see Aviation accidents and safety
see Aviation fuels
see Aviation medicine
see Aviation sciences
see Civil aviation
see General aviation
see Military aviation
see Space medicine
see Space sciences

Index by Subjects and Names

Aviation accidents and safety

Accident circumstances and severity, by type of flying and aircraft, 1981, annual rpt, 9614-3

Accidents and deaths in transportation, by mode of transport, 1972-82, annual rpt, 7304-2

Air traffic control and airway facilities and services, operations, and finances, FY83, annual rpt, 7504-37

Airline and general aviation accidents and deaths, 1983, preliminary annual rpt, 9614-9

Airline and general aviation accidents, deaths, and rates, by type of service, 1974-83, annual rpt, 7504-1.9

Airline and general aviation accidents, deaths, rates, and Natl Transportation Safety Board investigations, 1974-83, annual rpt, 9614-1

Airline and general aviation traffic levels, accidents, and deaths, 1970-80, annual rpt, 7304-1

Airline pilots terminated for medical reasons and reinstated by carrier, and aircraft accidents by age of flight crew, selected years 1960-81, hearing, 21148-34

Airport security operations to prevent hijacking, screening results, enforcement actions, and hijacking attempts, 1st half 1984, semiannual rpt, 7502-5

Airport size and safety, and accidents at or near airports by circumstance, for total and selected airports, various periods 1964-81, 9618-12

Alcohol-related fatal accidents of comuter airlines, air taxis, and general aviation, by pilot characteristics and circumstances, 1975-81, 9618-11

Bombing (explosive and incendiary) and arson incidents by target, State, and circumstances, and explosives theft and recovery, 1982-83, annual rpt, 8484-4

Collisions of aircraft, and near collisions by circumstances and State, by type of aircraft, various periods 1980-84, 7508-61

Commuter air carriers and air taxi accidents by seating capacity and cause, and deaths, 1975-82, GAO rpt, 26113-116

Death rates by sex, race, and age for 40 causes, projected for 10-year period, 1982 rpt, 4208-21

Deaths and death rates by detailed cause and demographic characteristics, 1979 and selected trends, US Vital Statistics annual rpt, 4144-2.1

Deaths in transportation accidents, by mode, 1982-83, annual summary rpt, 9614-6

Employment at DOT, by subagency, State, and selected personnel characteristics, FY83, annual rpt, 7304-18

FAA aviation medicine research and studies, technical rpt series, 7506-10

General aviation and air carrier accident circumstances, severity, and causes, for US operations of domestic and foreign aircraft, periodic rpt, 9612-1

General aviation violations of FAA flight operations and maintenance standards, and FAA enforcement actions, annual rpt, discontinued, 7504-25

Hazardous material transport accidents, casualties, and property damage, by mode of transport, with DOT control activities, 1983, annual rpt, 7304-4

Index by Subjects and Names

Hijackings, on-board explosions, other crimes against civil aviation, and circumstances, US and worldwide, 1931-83, annual rpt, 7504–31

Injury and illness rates and causes, by SIC 2- to 4-digit industry, 1982, annual rpt, 6844–1

Law enforcement officer assaults, murders, and other deaths by circumstances, level of govt, agency, victim and offender characteristics, and location, 1983, annual rpt, 6224–3

Meteorological services and research of Fed Govt, programs and funding by agency, FY84-85, annual rpt, 2144–2

Occupational deaths, by industry div and cause, 1981-82, article, 6722–1.422

Safety programs, and accidents, injuries, deaths, hazards, and property damage, by mode of transport, 1983, annual rpt, 7304–19

see also Air traffic control

Aviation fuels

Airline operating and other costs, itemized for domestic and intl trunk and local service carriers, 1st half 1983, semiannual rpt, 9142–47

Aviation traffic, aircraft, pilots, airport activity, and fuel use, forecast FY84-95 with FY79-83 trends, annual rpt, 7504–6

Business statistics, detailed data for major industries and economic indicators, *Survey of Current Business,* monthly rpt, 2702–1.15

Consumption and costs for domestic and intl airline operations, by US carrier group, monthly rpt, 9142–21

Consumption, by fuel type, economic sector, census div, and State, 1960-82, State Energy Data System annual rpt, 3164–39

Consumption of energy, by type of air pollutant source and fuel, and State, 1981, annual rpt, 9194–14

Costs of operating privately owned small planes by component, and Fed Govt mileage reimbursement rates, 1983, annual rpt, 9454–13.2

Defense Fuel Supply Center procurement, prices, stocks, and other activities, FY83, annual rpt, 3904–6

Defense Fuel Supply Center procurement, prices, stocks, transport, and other activities and finances, FY83, annual rpt, 3904–8

Exports of US, detailed commodities by country of destination, monthly rpt, 2422–3

Foreign and US oil production, trade, and stocks, by product and country, 1982, annual rpt, 3164–50.3

Imports of US, detailed Schedule A commodities by country, monthly rpt, 2422–2

Natl Energy Policy Plan, energy supply, demand, and prices, by fuel and consuming sector, projected 1985-2010, biennial rpt, 3004–13

Price and volume of 13 oil products sold by gas plant operators and refiners, by end-use sector, PAD district, and State, monthly rpt, 3162–11

Prices and expenditures for fuels, by consuming sector, State, and fuel type, 1970-81, annual rpt, 3164–64

Producer prices and indexes, by stage of processing and detailed commodity, monthly rpt, 6762–6

Producer prices and indexes, by stage of processing and detailed commodity, monthly 1983, annual supplement, 6764–2

Production, reserves, and prices, by fuel type, and selected indicators of energy use, by State, 1982-83 with selected comparisons from 1971, annual rpt, 3164–60

Properties of aviation fuels, lab analysis, 1983, last issue of annual rpt, 3006–2.2

Refinery financial and operating impacts from auto use of alcohol fuels, projected to 2000 with trends 1964-80, 3308–75

Supply/demand and price forecasts, by fuel type, quarterly rpt, 3162–34

Supply/demand and prices, by energy resource and major producing and consuming country and sector, detailed data, monthly rpt, 3162–24

Supply/demand and prices, by fuel type and consuming sector with foreign comparisons, 1949-83, annual rpt, 3164–74

Supply/demand and prices, by fuel type, sector, and end use, detailed trends and projections 1973-95, annual rpt, 3164–75

Supply/demand and prices, by fuel type, sector, and end use, with foreign comparisons, 1960-83 and projected to 1995, annual summary rpt, 3164–76

Supply/demand of oil and refined products, refinery capacity and use, and OPEC, non-OPEC, and spot market prices, weekly rpt, 3162–32

Supply/demand, trade, stocks, and refining of oil and natural gas liquids, by detailed product, State, and PAD district, with fuel oil sulfur content, monthly rpt with articles, 3162–6

Supply/demand, trade, stocks, and refining of oil and natural gas liquids, by detailed product, State, and PAD district, and refineries in US and territories, 1983 annual rpt, 3164–2

Tax (excise) collections of IRS, by source, quarterly press release, 8302–1

Tax collections, refunds, and taxes due IRS, by State and region, and IRS court activity and operating expenses, FY83, annual rpt, 8304–3.3

Tax provisions (State) for motor fuel, vehicle registration fees, and disposition of receipts, by State, as of Jan 1984, biennial rpt, 7554–37

Transportation energy use by mode, fuel supplies, and demographic and economic determinants of vehicle use, 1970s-83, annual rpt, 3304–5

Transportation finances, operations, vehicles, equipment, accidents, and energy use and transport, by mode of transport, 1955-84, annual rpt, 7304–2

Waterborne commerce of US (domestic and foreign), freight by commodity, traffic, and passengers, by port and waterway, 1982, annual rpt, 3754–3

Aviation industry

see Aerospace industry

see Aircraft

see Airlines

Ayres, Robert U.

see Aviation accidents and safety

Aviation medicine

FAA aviation medicine research and studies, technical rpt series, 7506–10

see also Space medicine

Aviation sciences

Aerial survey R&D publications, and sources of natural resource and environmental data gathered by air- and spacecraft, quarterly listing, 9502–7

Engineers sociodemographic, educational, and employment characteristics, and Federal support by agency, 1978, Current Population Rpt, 2546–2.121

Foreign and US astronautic and aeronautic events, comprehensive chronology, 1976, annual rpt, 9504–2

NASA R&D funding to colleges and universities, by State, field of science, and instn, FY83, annual listing, 9504–7

R&D expenditures by higher education instns and federally funded centers, by field, source of funds, instn, and State, FY82, annual rpt, 9627–13

R&D expenditures by source, and scientists education and employment, detailed data by field, selected years 1953-84, annual rpt, 9624–18

R&D expenditures of higher education instns, and science and engineering employment and grad students, by field, 1972-83, biennial rpt, 9627–24

R&D Fed Govt facilities and services available for private sector use, by field of science, 1984 biennial listing, 2224–4

Science and engineering doctoral degree recipients, by field, sex, race, age, citizenship, postgrad employment and study status, State, and instn, 1960-82, 9626–6.16

Science and engineering grad enrollment, fields of study, financial support, and other student and instn characteristics, 1975-82, annual survey, 9627–7

Scientists and engineers employed at universities and colleges, by field, sex, State, and instn, Jan 1983 and selected trends from 1967, annual survey, 9627–11

Scientists, engineers, and technicians needed in defense and nondefense industries, and supply/demand, by field, 1981-87, 9628–71

see also Space sciences

Awards, medals, and prizes

Fed Govt Senior Executive Service employee admin, and program status and effectiveness, by agency and by executive and job characteristics, July 1979-Sept 1983, GAO rpt, 26119–51

Mint Bur activities and finances, production of medals and US and foreign coins, and gold and silver stocks and transactions, by office, FY83, annual rpt, 8204–1

see also Military awards, decorations, and medals

Ayres, Robert U.

"Final Report on Future Energy Consumption by the Industrial Chemicals Industry (SIC 28)", 3308–66.5

Bachrach, Christine A.

Bachrach, Christine A.
"Use of Contraception in the U.S., 1982", 4146–8.103

Baer, Herbert
"High Speed Rail in the Midwest", 9375–1.406

Bagshaw, Michael L.
"Forecasting the Money Supply in Time Series Models", 9377–9.8
"Forecasting Using Contemporaneous Correlations", 9377–9.11
"Velocity: A Multivariate Time-Series Approach", 9377–9.13

Bahamas
Economic, social, and political summary data, by country, 1984, annual factbook, 244–11
Exports of US, detailed Schedule B commodities by country of destination, 1983, annual rpt, 2424–9
Exports of US, detailed Schedule E commodities by mode of transport and world area and country of destination, 1983, annual rpts, 2424–5
Imports of US, detailed Schedule A commodities by country and world area of origin, and mode of transport, 1983, annual rpts, 2424–2
Imports of US, detailed TSUSA commodities by country of origin, 1983, annual rpt, 2424–4
Loans and grants for economic and military assistance from US and intl agencies, by program and country, FY46-83, annual rpt, 9914–5
Military aid of US, arms sales, and training programs costs and budget requests by program, world region, and country, FY83-85, annual rpt, 7144–13
Minerals Yearbook, 1982, Vol 3: foreign country reviews of production, trade, and policies, by commodity, annual rpt, 5604–35
Minerals Yearbook, 1983, Vol 3 preprints: foreign country review of production, trade, and policies, by commodity, annual rpt, 5604–23.85
Oil exports to US by OPEC and non-OPEC countries, monthly rpt, 3162–24.3
Population size and growth rates, and latest available benchmark demographic data, by country, 1950-83, biennial rpt, 2324–4
Tax evasion through nonresidents bank claims and deposits, direct investments, income payments, and other transactions in 5 Caribbean countries, 1978-82, 8008–106
see also under By Foreign Country in the "Index by Categories"

Bahr, Leonard M., Jr.
"Ecological Characterization of the Mississippi Deltaic Plain Region: A Narrative with Management Recommendations", 5506–4.2
"Ecology of Intertidal Oyster Reefs of the South Atlantic Coast: A Community Profile", 5506–9.2

Bahrain
Agricultural situation in Middle East and North Africa, by country and commodity, 1983 and outlook for 1984, annual rpt, 1524–4.3
AID economic assistance to developing countries, obligations and disbursements by country, quarterly rpt, 9912–4

Computers and computer equipment market and trade, and user industry operations and demand, 1984 country market research rpt, 2045–1.47
Economic, social, and political summary data, by country, 1984, annual factbook, 244–11
Economic trends in income, production, prices, employment, finances, and trade, 1984 semiannual rpt, 2046–4.42
Exports of US, detailed Schedule B commodities by country of destination, 1983, annual rpt, 2424–9
Exports of US, detailed Schedule E commodities by mode of transport and world area and country of destination, 1983, annual rpts, 2424–5
Imports of US, detailed Schedule A commodities by country and world area of origin, and mode of transport, 1983, annual rpts, 2424–2
Imports of US, detailed TSUSA commodities by country of origin, 1983, annual rpt, 2424–4
Loans and grants for economic and military assistance from US and intl agencies, by program and country, FY46-83, annual rpt, 9914–5
Military aid of US, arms sales, and training programs costs and budget requests by program, world region, and country, FY83-85, annual rpt, 7144–13
Military spending, arms trade, and armed forces size, with total govt spending and population, by country, 1972-82, annual rpt, 9824–1
Minerals Yearbook, 1982, Vol 3: foreign country reviews of production, trade, and policies, by commodity, annual rpt, 5604–35
Minerals Yearbook, 1982, Vol 3 preprints: foreign country review of production, trade, and policies, by commodity, annual rpt, 5604–17.88
Population size and growth rates, and latest available benchmark demographic data, by country, 1950-83, biennial rpt, 2324–4
Telecommunication equipment market and trade, and user industry operations and demand, 1982 country market research rpt, 2045–12.32
see also under By Foreign Country in the "Index by Categories"

Bail
see Pretrial detention and release

Bailey, W. J.
"Fuel Performance Annual Report for 1982", 9634–8

Baker, Allen
"Poultry and Egg Outlook", 1004–16.1

Baker, Jay
"Public Response to Hurricane Probability Forecasts", 2186–4.11

Baker, Joe G.
"Occupational Employment in Nuclear-Related Activities, 1983", 3004–11

Bakersfield, Calif.
Census of Housing, 1980: occupancy and unit characteristics, by race, Hispanic origin, and city, SMSA rpt, 2473–1.81
Census of Population and Housing, 1980: detailed population and housing characteristics, by county, city, and census tract, SMSA rpt, 2551–2.81

Index by Subjects and Names

Housing vacancy rates for single and multifamily units and mobile homes, by city and ZIP code, 1983, annual metro area rpt, 9304–20.4
Housing vacancy rates for single and multifamily units and mobile homes, by city and ZIP code, 1984, annual metro area rpt, 9304–20.16
Wages by occupation, and benefits for office and plant workers, 1984 labor market area survey rpt, 6785–3.7
see also under By City and By SMSA or MSA in the "Index by Categories"

Baking and bakery products
Air pollutant emission factors, by detailed source, 3rd edition, 1983-84 supplements, 9198–13
Bread (white pan) price indexes and farm-retail price spreads, periodic situation rpt with articles, 1561–12
Census of Population, 1980: detailed socioeconomic and demographic characteristics, by age, sex, race, Hispanic origin, occupation, and industry, State rpt series, 2531–4
Census of Population, 1980: detailed socioeconomic characteristics, by county, city, and inside-outside SMSAs and central cities, State rpt series, 2531–3
Consumption of food and nutrient intake by individuals, by food group, source, and socioeconomic characteristics, 1977-78 natl survey, final rpt series, 1356–4
Consumption, supply, trade, prices, expenditures, and indexes, by food commodity, 1963-83, annual rpt, 1544–4
County Business Patterns: establishments, employees, and payrolls, by SIC 4-digit industry and county, 1981, annual State rpt series, 2326–8
County Business Patterns: establishments, employees, and payrolls, by SIC 4-digit industry and county, 1982, annual State rpt series, 2326–6
CPI by detailed component, for US city average, 28 SMSAs, and 4 regions by population size, monthly rpt, 6762–2
EC food supply/demand and market and support prices, with exchange rates, fertilizer price index, GDP, and population, by country, 1960-83, 1528–173
Employment, earnings, and hours, by selected SIC 1- to 4-digit industry, State, and for 278 major labor areas, 1939-83, annual rpt, 6744–5
Employment, earnings, and hours, by SIC 4-digit nonfarm industry, monthly 1974-Feb 1984, annual update, 6744–4
Exports and imports of US, detailed SIC-based commodities by world area, 1983, annual rpts, 2424–6
Exports of US, detailed commodities by country of destination, monthly rpt, 2422–3
Exports of US, detailed Schedule B commodities by country of destination, 1983, annual rpt, 2424–9
Exports of US, detailed Schedule E commodities by mode of transport and world area and country of destination, 1983, annual rpts, 2424–5
Finances and operations, by SIC 2- to 4-digit industry, 1970s-83 and projected to 1988, annual rpt, 2014–4

Index by Subjects and Names

Bangladesh

Imports of US, detailed Schedule A commodities by country and world area of origin, and mode of transport, 1983, annual rpts, 2424–2

Imports of US, detailed Schedule A commodities by country, monthly rpt, 2422–2

Income tax returns of corporations, detailed income and tax items by industry, 1981, annual rpt, 8304–4

Income tax returns of sole proprietorships, detailed data by industry div and selected industry group, 1981, annual rpt, 8304–7

Income tax returns of sole proprietorships, receipts, deductions by type, payroll, and net income, by major industry, 1982, annual article, 8302–2.413

Input-output structure of US economy, detailed interindustry transactions for 537 industries, and components of final demand, 1977 benchmark data, 2708–17

Manufacturing census, 1982: financial and operating data, by SIC 2- to 4-digit industry, State, SMSA, and county, preliminary census div rpt series, 2491–3

Manufacturing census, 1982: financial and operating data, for SIC 4-digit industries by product, preliminary rpt, 2491–1.20, 2491–1.21

Minority group and women employment, by occupational group and SIC 2- to 3-digit industry, 1981, annual rpt, 9244–1.1

Occupational injury and illness rates, by SIC 2- to 4-digit industry, 1982, annual rpt, 6844–1

Pesticide (ethylene dibromide) residue in grain and grain foods, and effect of processing and cooking, by selected product, 1984 hearing, 25168–62

Portugal agricultural subsidies, profits, marketing margins, and consumer prices, by commodity or product, and effects of prospective EC membership, 1981, 1528–171

Prices (farm-retail) for foods, marketing cost components, and industry finances and productivity, selected years 1967-83, annual rpt, 1544–9

Producer prices and indexes, by stage of processing and detailed commodity, monthly rpt, 6762–6

Producer prices and indexes, by stage of processing and detailed commodity, monthly 1983, annual supplement, 6764–2

Productivity, hours, and employment indexes for selected SIC 3- and 4-digit industries, 1954-82, annual rpt, 6824–1.3

Retail trade sales and inventories, by kind of business, region, census div, and selected State, SMSA, and city, and seasonal adjustments, monthly rpt, 2413–3

Underground economy, household expenditures and participation by type of goods or service and sociodemographic characteristics, with methodology and bibl, 1981 survey, 8308–27

see also under By Commodity in the "Index by Categories"

Balance of payments

see International transactions

Balance of trade

see Foreign trade

see International transactions

Balance sheets

see Business assets and liabilities, general

see Business assets and liabilities, specific industries

see Business income and expenses, general

see Business income and expenses, specific industries

Balazik, Ronald F.

"Costs and Effects of Environmental Protection Controls Regulating U.S. Phosphate Rock Mining", 5608–143

Baldwin, Carliss Y.

"Return to Nursing Home Investment: Issues for Public Policy", 4652–1.417

Ballantyne, Harry C.

"Actuarial Status of the OASI and DI Trust Funds", 4742–1.410

"Long-Range Projections of Social Security Trust Fund Operations in Dollars", 4706–2.120

"Present Policies and Methods Regarding the Long-Term Adjustment of Benefits", 4742–1.420

Ballistic missiles

see Missiles and rockets

Baltimore and Ohio Railroad

Finances and operations of 7 commuter rail systems, and public agency cost reimbursement, 1980, 7888–61

Baltimore, Md.

Census of Housing, 1980: occupancy and unit characteristics, by race, Hispanic origin, and city, SMSA rpt, 2473–1.82

Census of Population and Housing, 1980: detailed population and housing characteristics, by county, city, and census tract, SMSA rpt, 2551–2.82

CPI by component for US city average, and by region, population size, and for 28 SMSAs, monthly press release, 6762–1

CPI by detailed component, for US city average, 28 SMSAs, and 4 regions by population size, monthly rpt, 6762–2

Fruit and vegetable shipments, and arrivals in 23 US and 5 Canada cities, by mode of transport and State or country of origin, 1983, annual rpt, 1311–4.1

Home equity mortgaged under 4 hypothetical instruments, effects on current income of elderly Baltimore, Md, residents, 1976, article, 9312–7.402

Homeless population and characteristics, and temporary shelter operations, use, and user characteristics, for selected cities, various periods 1979-84, hearing, 21248–85

Hospital worker wages by sex and occupation, and benefits, for 22 MSAs, Oct 1981 survey, 6787–6.201

Housing unit starts and completions authorized by building permits in 20 MSAs, quarterly rpt, 2382–9

Population size of top 25 cities, 1980 and 1982, press release, 2328–46

Port impact on local employment through transport of 5 commodities, by industry for 3 eastern ports, and demand for US coal by country, 1981, 7308–182

Wages by occupation, and benefits for office and plant workers, 1984 SMSA survey rpt, 6785–11.8

Waterborne commerce of US (domestic and foreign), freight by commodity, traffic, and passengers, by port and waterway, 1982, annual rpt, 3754–3.1

see also under By City and By SMSA or MSA in the "Index by Categories"

Bangladesh

Agricultural and food production indexes, and production of selected commodities, by world region and country, 1974-83, annual rpt, 1524–5

Agricultural situation in 5 South Asia countries, by commodity, 1970s-1983/84 and outlook for 1984/85, annual rpt, 1524–4.11

Agricultural supply/demand, trade, and production, and socioeconomic data, by country, 1950s-77, 1528–179

AID activities and funding by project and function, FY85, and developing countries summary socioeconomic data, 1970s-83, by country, annual rpt, 9914–3

AID economic assistance to developing countries, obligations and disbursements by country, quarterly rpt, 9912–4

AID loan repayment status and terms by program and country, and status of predecessor agency loans, quarterly rpt, 9912–3

Background Notes, summary social, political, and economic data, 1984 rpt, 7006–2.42

Economic conditions, investment and export opportunities, and trade practices, 1984 country market research rpt, 2046–6.9

Economic, social, and political summary data, by country, 1984, annual factbook, 244–11

Exports of US, detailed Schedule B commodities by country of destination, 1983, annual rpt, 2424–9

Exports of US, detailed Schedule E commodities by mode of transport and world area and country of destination, 1983, annual rpts, 2424–5

Food supply policies of 21 developing countries, with farm sector data, tariff income, and prices and imports of 5 grains, 1960s-81, 1528–168

Imports of US, detailed Schedule A commodities by country and world area of origin, and mode of transport, 1983, annual rpts, 2424–2

Imports of US, detailed TSUSA commodities by country of origin, 1983, annual rpt, 2424–4

Loans and grants for economic and military assistance from US and intl agencies, by program and country, FY46-83, annual rpt, 9914–5

Military aid of US, arms sales, and training programs costs and budget requests by program, world region, and country, FY83-85, annual rpt, 7144–13

Military spending, arms trade, and armed forces size, with total govt spending and population, by country, 1972-82, annual rpt, 9824–1

Minerals Yearbook, 1982, Vol 3: foreign country reviews of production, trade, and policies, by commodity, annual rpt, 5604–35

Minerals Yearbook, 1982, Vol 3 preprints: foreign country review of production, trade, and policies, by commodity, annual rpt, 5604–17.87

PL 480 Title I funding and socioeconomic impacts in developing countries, with case studies for 5 countries, 1950s-81, 9918–13

Bangladesh

Population size and growth rates, and latest available benchmark demographic data, by country, 1950-83, biennial rpt, 2324–4

- Rice area, yield, and production by crop, 1979/80-1983/84, FAS annual rpt, 1925–2.6
- *see also* under By Foreign Country in the "Index by Categories"

Bangor, Maine

- Census of Housing, 1980: occupancy and unit characteristics, by race, Hispanic origin, and city, SMSA rpt, 2473–1.83
- Census of Population and Housing, 1980: detailed population and housing characteristics, by county, city, and census tract, SMSA rpt, 2551–2.83
- *see also* under By SMSA or MSA in the "Index by Categories"

Bank deposit insurance

see Federal Deposit Insurance Corp.

see Federal Savings and Loan Insurance Corp.

Bank deposits

- Bank financial and operating statements, functional cost analysis for Fed Reserve member banks with average and high earnings, by deposit size, 1982, annual rpt, 9364–6
- Bank merger proposals receiving adverse Justice Dept appraisals, bank deposits, market shares and ratios, and merger disposition, June 1982-Dec 1983, article, 9375–1.404
- Bank mergers, concentration levels, and market deposits merged, by number of bank organizations in SMSA and county, simulated 1982, technical paper, 9366–1.136
- Banking and financial data, 1982, annual rpt, 9364–5
- Business statistics, detailed data for major industries and economic indicators, *Survey of Current Business,* monthly rpt, 2702–1.6
- Commercial and mutual savings bank deposits for US banks and US branches of foreign banks, by account type, instn, State, SMSA, and county, June 1983, annual rpt, 9295–3
- Commercial bank debits, deposits, and deposit turnover, by type of account, monthly rpt, 9365–2.5
- Commercial bank savings and time deposits, compounded annual rates of change, 1964-83, annual rpt, 9391–9.1
- Commercial insured banks profitability, finances, loans and terms, intl earnings, and operating ratios, 1980-83, annual article, 9362–1.409
- Concentration indicators for bank deposits, by State and for US and 7 OECD countries, various dates 1982-84, article, 9373–1.405
- *County and City Data Book,* detailed socioeconomic and demographic data for States, counties, and cities, selected years 1976-82, 2328–1
- Debits and turnover of demand and savings deposits, monthly rpt, 9362–1.1
- Economic indicators and components, current data and annual trends, monthly rpt, 23842–1.5
- Farm financial assets by type, 1940-84, annual rpt, 1544–16.2

FDIC bank examination activities and supervisory actions, 1983, annual rpt, 9294–1

- Fed Govt programs and mgmt cost control proposals, 3-year savings by function and agency, and financial and operating data, 1960s-81, 16908–1.26
- Fed Reserve Bank of Minneapolis financial statements, 1981-82, annual rpt, 9383–2
- Financial and business statistics, historic trends, 1984 annual chartbook, 9364–2.1, 9364–2.13
- Financial and business statistics, quarterly chartbook, 9362–2.1, 9362–2.7
- Financial and monetary conditions, selected US summary data, weekly rpt, 9391–4
- Financial, banking, and mortgage market activity, weekly release series, 9365–1
- Flow-of-funds accounts, assets and liabilities by type and economic sector, year-end outstandings, 1960-83, annual rpt, 9364–3
- Flow-of-funds accounts savings, investments, and credit statements, quarterly rpt, 9365–3.3
- Income tax proposals to encourage savings, and personal assets and liabilities by type, 1981, article, 8302–2.407
- Interest rate ceilings on bank deposits, effect of deregulation on home mortgage interest rates, various periods Apr 1975-Mar 1984, article, 9391–1.412
- Interest rates (explicit and implicit) on commercial bank deposits, by account type, 1976-82, article, 9387–1.403
- Interest rates on bank deposits, deregulation effect on deposits and bank financial performance, 1978-83, hearing, 21248–83
- Interest rates on time and savings deposits, maximum payable at federally insured instns, Dec 1983, annual rpt, 9364–1.2
- Intl transactions, *Survey of Current Business,* monthly rpt, quarterly tables, 2702–1.31
- Minority business Fed Govt funding, procurement, and subsidies, and deposits in minority-owned banks, by agency, FY69-83, annual rpt, 2104–5
- Monetary and Fed Govt budget trends, Fed Reserve Bank of St Louis monthly rpt, 9391–2
- Money market mutual funds and deposit accounts, and super negotiable orders of withdrawal accounts, interest rates, monthly Dec 1982-Sept 1983, article, 1702–1.401
- Money market mutual funds and deposit accounts balances, and correlation results for interest rates and flows by type of fund, various periods Dec 1982-June 1984, article, 9371–1.431
- New England States financial instn assets and liabilities, Fed Reserve 1st District, monthly rpt, 9373–2.5
- OASDHI beneficiaries with direct deposit of benefit checks, by age, sex, race, benefit amount, and State, as of Dec 1983, article, 4742–1.412
- OASDHI direct deposits, by type of bank account and beneficiary characteristics, 1982, annual rpt, 4744–3.6
- Pennsylvania bank, S&L, and savings bank deposit and commercial and industrial loan market shares, and loan activity, 1980-83, article, 9387–1.404

Index by Subjects and Names

- Small business loan and credit activities and assessment, effect of bank deregulation by business characteristics, 1980 and 1982 surveys, hearings, 21728–52.1
- Southeastern States banks by asset size, finances, and loans and deposits by type, Fed Reserve 5th District, various dates 1979-83, annual article, 9389–1.408
- Southeastern States economic indicators, by State, Fed Reserve 5th District, quarterly rpt, 9389–16
- Southeastern States, Fed Reserve 8th District banking and financial conditions, quarterly rpt, 9391–14
- Southeastern States financial and economic devs, Fed Reserve 6th District, monthly rpt with articles, 9371–1
- Tax evasion through nonresidents bank claims and deposits, direct investments, income payments, and other transactions in 5 Caribbean countries, 1978-82, 8008–106
- Trust assets of banks and trust companies, by type of asset and fund and State, 1983, annual rpt, 13004–1
- Western States depository instns financial activity by State, and large commercial banks by city, Fed Reserve 10th District, monthly rpt, 9381–11
- Western States economic indicators, Fed Reserve 12th District, quarterly rpt, 9393–1.5
- Western States, Fed Reserve 10th District depository instns deposits, loans, investments, and borrowings, monthly rpt, 9381–2
- *see also* Certificates of deposit
- *see also* Checking accounts
- *see also* Negotiable orders of withdrawal accounts
- *see also* Savings

Bank holding companies

- Argentina debt financing, effect on income of 7 US bank holding companies, actual and in event of interest nonpayment, 1st qtr 1984, press release, 9368–77
- Assets, offices, and deposits of bank holding companies, by State, 1982, annual rpt, 9364–5.11
- Fed Home Loan Bank System members, with assets of S&Ls, by instn, city, and State, 1983, annual listing, 9314–5
- Fed Reserve Bank of Dallas financial statements, 1982-83, annual rpt, 9379–2
- Financial ratios of involvement in nonbank subsidiaries and subsidiary performance, by bank holding company size, various periods 1978-82, article, 9377–1.406
- Financial services of nonbank firms and bank holding companies, with financial and operating data by firm, 1981-82 with trends from 1962, technical paper, 9375–11.3
- Florida multibank holding companies profits related to market position, concentration, and deposit growth, 1973-77, article, 9371–1.401
- Income tax returns of corporations, detailed income and tax items by industry, 1981, annual rpt, 8304–4
- Interstate bank offices by type, and electronic funds transfer networks, for Fed Reserve 7th District by State of origin and coverage, 1981-83, article, 9375–1.403

Index by Subjects and Names

Interstate bank service offices, including S&Ls, bank branches, and nonbank subsidiaries offering financial services, by instn and State, 1981-83, 9371–13

Interstate limited-service bank applications as of May 1984, and New England acquisitions and mergers effect on assets, by firm, Dec 1974-Sept 1983, article, 9373–1.409

Mergers of banks approved and denied by FDIC, and resources, deposits, and offices of merged banks, 1982, annual rpt, 9294–1.1

Bank reserves

see Banks and banking

Bankruptcy

Bank closures and brokered deposits of individual banks, Feb 1982-Oct 1983, and total business failures, 1950-Sept 1983, hearing, 21248–83

Banks (natl) domestic and intl operations, charters, mergers, and liquidations, by State and instn, and Comptroller of Currency activities, quarterly rpt, 8402–3

Banks requiring FDIC disbursement, depositors, deposits, and disbursements, by location and disbursement reason, 1983 with deposit losses from 1921, annual rpt, 9294–1.2

Business bankruptcy filings with SEC participation, by firm, FY83, annual rpt, 9734–2.7

Business Conditions Digest, cyclical indicators, by economic process, monthly rpt, 2702–3.3

Business Conditions Digest, historical supplement on economic, business, and financial conditions and cyclical fluctuations, with methodology, 1947-82, 2708–31

Business failures by industry div, 1978 and 1983, article, 9381–1.414

Business formation and failures, 1929-83, annual rpt, 204–1.7

Business statistics, detailed data for major industries and economic indicators, *Survey of Current Business,* monthly rpt, 2702–1.1

California business failures, plant closings, layoffs, and relocations, by plant, industry, county, and city, 1980-83, hearing, 21348–84.1

Court bankruptcy caseloads in Federal district courts and new judges needed, by circuit and district, various dates 1982-83, hearing, 25528–97

Court bankruptcy cases and admin in districts with and without case trustees, and staff and potential costs of nationwide trustee program, various periods 1979-83, annual rpt, 6004–15

Court caseloads for Federal district, appeals, and bankruptcy courts, by type of suit and offense, circuit, and district, quarterly rpt, 18202–1

Court civil and criminal casloads and activity summary, for Federal district, appeals, and bankruptcy courts, 1975-June 1984, annual chartbook, 18204–9

Credit Union Natl Admin insurance fund financial activity, and insured instns financial and operating data, FY83, annual rpt with semiannual update for 1st qtr FY84, 9534–7

Farm finances, assets, expenses, cash flow, receipts, and loans, selected years 1971-85, annual rpt, 1544–13

Farm operators leaving business and liquidating assets in Fed Reserve 5th District, by reason, quarterly rpt, 9389–17

Farmers operators leaving business in Fed Reserve 11th District, by reason and sales class, quarterly rpt, semiannual tables, 9379–11

FmHA loans and borrower supervision activities in farm and housing programs, by type and State, monthly rpt, 1182–1

IRS prosecutions, litigations, and interpretive law decisions, FY83 with comparisons to FY82, annual rpt, 8304–3.2

Personal bankruptcy, filers by debt type and other characteristics, and impacts in Connecticut and Michigan, various dates 1946-82, hearings, 21528–57

Personal bankruptcy, filers by debt type and other characteristics, selected years 1978-81, hearing, 25528–97.1

Social pathology measures including crime and death rates, relation to selected economic indicators, various periods 1950-80, 23848–76

Statistical Abstract of US, social, political, and economic data, 1950s-83 and trends, annual rpt, 2324–1.3

Bankruptcy Reform Act

Court bankruptcy cases and admin in districts with and without case trustees, and staff and potential costs of nationwide trustee program, various periods 1979-83, annual rpt, 6004–15

Banks and banking

Assets and liabilities of Fed Reserve member and nonmember banks, 1982-83, annual rpt, 9364–1.2

Assets, liabilities, loans, investments, and deposits for commercial banks, total and in and outside NYC, monthly rpt, 9362–1.1

Bombing (explosive and incendiary) and arson incidents by target, State, and circumstances, and explosives theft and recovery, 1982-83, annual rpt, 8484–4

Bombing (explosive and incendiary) incidents, damage, injuries, and deaths, by target, State, and circumstances, 1983, annual rpt, 6224–5

Business Conditions Digest, historical supplement on economic, business, and financial conditions and cyclical fluctuations, with methodology, 1947-82, 2708–31

Business statistics, detailed data for major industries and economic indicators, *Survey of Current Business,* monthly rpt, 2702–1.6

Census of Population, 1980: detailed socioeconomic and demographic characteristics, by age, sex, race, Hispanic origin, occupation, and industry, State rpt series, 2531–4

Census of Population, 1980: detailed socioeconomic characteristics, by county, city, and inside-outside SMSAs and central cities, State rpt series, 2531–3

Connecticut personal bankruptcy filings, by debt type, whether claiming Federal homestead exemption, and other characteristics, 1980, hearing, 21528–57.1

Banks and banking

Construction industries census, 1982: financial and operating data, by SIC 4-digit industry and State, final rpt series, 2373–1

Construction industries census, 1982: financial and operating data, by SIC 4-digit industry and State, preliminary rpt series, 2371–1

County Business Patterns: establishments, employees, and payrolls, by SIC 4-digit industry and county, 1981, annual State rpt series, 2326–8

County Business Patterns: establishments, employees, and payrolls, by SIC 4-digit industry and county, 1982, annual State rpt series, 2326–6

Debits, deposits and turnover, consumer credit, certificates of deposits, and loan interest rates, monthly rpt series, 9365–2

Deregulation of banks and other financial instns, implications for effective bank size, 1958-83, literature review, 9366–1.135

Developing countries free zones, industry financial and operating data by country, with case studies for 5 countries, 1970s-82, 9918–10

Earnings by major industry group, and personal income per capita and by source, by region and State, 1929-82, 2708–40

Employment by detailed occupation, for 29 SIC 2-digit nonmanufacturing industries, 1981 BLS survey, 6748–60

Employment, earnings, and hours, by selected SIC 1- to 4-digit industry, State, and for 278 major labor areas, 1939-83, annual rpt, 6744–5

Employment, earnings, and hours, by SIC 4-digit nonfarm industry, monthly 1974-Feb 1984, annual update, 6744–4

Farm finances, expenses by type, loans by purpose and source, and credit detail by Fed Reserve District, quarterly rpt, 9365–3.10

FDIC bank examination activities and supervisory actions, 1983, annual rpt, 9294–1

Fed Govt benefit payment by check and direct deposit, costs to agencies and banks, FY81, technical paper, 9366–1.139

Fed Govt credit assistance costs, policies to improve measurement, with loan and loan guarantee data by program, and Federal and private credit instns operations, 1970-84, 26306–6.72

Finances and operations, by SIC 2- to 4-digit industry, 1970s-83 and projected to 1988, annual rpt, 2014–4

Financial and business statistics, historic trends, 1984 annual chartbook, 9364–2

Financial and business statistics, quarterly chartbook, 9362–2

Financial and economic devs, Fed Reserve Bank of Boston bimonthly rpt articles, 9373–1

Financial and economic devs, Fed Reserve Bank of Chicago bimonthly rpt articles, 9375–1

Financial and economic devs, Fed Reserve Bank of New York quarterly rpt with articles, 9385–1

Financial and economic devs, Fed Reserve Bank of Philadelphia bimonthly rpt articles, 9387–1

Banks and banking

Financial and economic trends, compounded annual rates of change, 1964-83, annual rpt, 9391–9.1

Financial and monetary conditions, selected US summary data, weekly rpt, 9391–4

Financial and operating data, 1982, annual rpt, 9364–5

Financial, banking, and mortgage market activity, weekly release series, 9365–1

Financial instn deregulation, interstate banking, and bank performance and risks, 1984 conf papers, 9375–7

Financial performance of banks and bank deposits, effect of deposit interest rate deregulation, 1978-83, hearing, 21248–83

Financial ratios and stock dividends of Student Loan Marketing Assn compared to banks and 4 Fed Govt-sponsored credit assns, 1980-82, GAO rpt, 26121–71

FmHA loans and borrower supervision activities in farm and housing programs, by type and State, monthly rpt, 1182–1

Foreign branches of US banks, assets and liabilities by world region and country, quarterly rpt, 9365–3.7

Foreign branches of US banks, balance sheets, monthly rpt, 9362–1.3

Foreign direct investment of US, by selected major industry group and world area, 1980-82, annual article, 2702–1.430

Foreign loans, debts, exchange rates, and intl reserves, for US and selected countries, various periods 1949-84, conf papers, 9373–3.28

Foreign loans of US banks to non-OPEC developing countries, with terms and capital exposure, various periods 1977-83 and projected to 1990, article, 9362–1.407

Income tax returns of corporations, detailed income and tax items by industry, 1981, annual rpt, 8304–4

Income tax returns of corporations with foreign tax credit, income and deductions by type, asset size, and selected industry group, 1980, article, 8302–2.415

Income tax returns of foreign subsidiaries of US corporations, income and tax data, by industry and asset size, 1980, article, 8302–2.410

Income tax returns of partnerships, detailed data by industry, 1981 estimates, annual article, 8302–2.404

Income tax returns of partnerships, receipts by source, deductions by type, and establishments, by selected industry, 1982, annual article, 8302–2.416

Income tax returns of sole proprietorships, detailed data by industry div and selected industry group, 1981, annual rpt, 8304–7

Income tax returns of sole proprietorships, receipts, deductions by type, payroll, and net income, by major industry, 1982, annual article, 8302–2.413

Income taxes, effective rates, and selected financial data, for financial instns by type and individual firm, with comparisons to other industries, selected years 1960-82, hearing, 25368–129

Industrial banks, S&Ls, and savings banks authorized and offering negotiable orders of withdrawal accounts, and instns and deposits, by State, as of Dec 1983, press release, 9368–75

Input-output structure of US economy, detailed interindustry transactions for 537 industries, and components of final demand, 1977 benchmark data, 2708–17

Interstate bank service offices, including S&Ls, bank branches, and nonbank subsidiaries offering financial services, by instn and State, 1981-83, 9371–13

Intl banking facilities by State and ownership, and aggregate assets and liabilities, various dates 1981-83, article, 9391–1.409

Intl banking facilities of US and foreign banks in New York and other States, assets and liabilities, monthly rpt, 9365–2.22

Intl transactions of US, and economic and monetary trends for US and 10 major trading partners, quarterly rpt, 9391–7

Intl transactions, *Survey of Current Business,* monthly rpt, quarterly tables, 2702–1.31

Investments and loans of commercial banks, monthly rpt, 23842–1.5

Investments and loans of commercial banks, 1939-83, annual rpt, 204–1.5

Merger antitrust analysis geographic market definition for banking, literature review, 1984 technical paper, 9366–1.138

Mergers, concentration levels, and market deposits merged, by number of bank organizations in SMSA and county, simulated 1982, technical paper, 9366–1.136

Minority group and women employment, by occupational group and SIC 2- to 3-digit industry, 1981, annual rpt, 9244–1.1

Natl banks domestic and intl operations, charters, and mergers, quarterly rpt, 8402–3

Natl banks income, expenses, and dividends, *Treasury Bulletin,* quarterly rpt, 8002–4.19

New England States thrift and commercial banking instns financial statements, by type of instn and State, 1972 and 1982, annual rpt, 9304–3

Occupational injury and illness rates, by SIC 2- to 4-digit industry, 1982, annual rpt, 6844–1

Occupational manpower needs and supply by detailed occupation, and educational and training program enrollees and grads by detailed field, 1982 and 1995, biennial rpt, 6744–3

Occupational Outlook Handbook, 1984-85 biennial rpt, 6744–1

Productivity, hours, and employment indexes for selected SIC 3- and 4-digit industries, 1954-82, annual rpt, 6824–1.4

Profitability of insured commercial banks, finances, loans and terms, intl earnings, and operating ratios, 1980-83, annual article, 9362–1.409

Profitability of medium-sized commercial banks, financial ratios and asset and liability composition by profitability and region, 1972-81, research paper, 9371–10.20

Robberies, by type of premises, population size, and region, 1983, annual rpt, 6224–2.1

Robberies of banks, court cases by case processing, sentencing, and offender characteristics, and compared to other Fed Govt felony cases, 1979-80, periodic rpt, 6062–2.407

Index by Subjects and Names

Robberies of banks, Federal court cases disposition, convictions, and sentences, by district, year ended June 1983 and trends from 1961, annual rpt, 18204–1

Robberies of banks since 1935, and success rates, average amount stolen, and customers and employees killed, 1974-80, 6068–180

Small business loan and credit activities and assessment, effect of bank deregulation by business characteristics, 1980 and 1982 surveys, hearings, 21728–52.1

Southeastern States banks by asset size, finances, and loans and deposits by type, Fed Reserve 5th District, various dates 1979-83, annual article, 9389–1.408

Southeastern States, Fed Reserve 8th District banking and financial conditions, quarterly rpt, 9391–14

Statistical Abstract of US, social, political, and economic data, 1950s-83 and trends, annual rpt, 2324–1.3

Stock prices and balance sheet data for banks related to interest rate risk exposure, Jan 1976-Nov 1981, technical paper, 9387–8.82

Trust assets of banks and trust companies, by type of asset and fund and State, 1983, annual rpt, 13004–1

Western States economic indicators, Fed Reserve 12th District, quarterly rpt, 9393–1.5

see also Agricultural credit

see also Bank deposits

see also Bank holding companies

see also Checking accounts

see also Consumer credit

see also Credit

see also Credit cards

see also Credit unions

see also Electronic funds transfer

see also Eurocurrency

see also Export-Import Bank

see also Farm Credit System

see also Federal Financing Bank

see also Federal Home Loan Banks

see also Federal Reserve System

see also Federal Savings and Loan Insurance Corp.

see also Flow-of-funds accounts

see also Foreign exchange

see also Interest rates

see also Loans

see also Money supply

see also Mortgages

see also Negotiable orders of withdrawal accounts

see also Savings

see also Savings and loan associations

see also Savings banks

see also under By Industry in the "Index by Categories"

Banks for Cooperatives

see Farm Credit System

Banks, Vera J.

"Farm Population Trends by Farm Characteristics, 1975-80", 1598–144

Barbados

Agricultural and food production indexes, and production of selected commodities, by world region and country, 1974-83, annual rpt, 1524–5

Agricultural situation in Latin America, by country, 1981-83 and outlook for 1984, annual rpt, 1524–4.9

Index by Subjects and Names

AID economic assistance to developing countries, obligations and disbursements by country, quarterly rpt, 9912–4

Background Notes, summary social, political, and economic data, 1984 rpt, 7006–2.43

Economic conditions, income, production, prices, employment, and trade, 1984 annual country rpt, 2046–4.100

Economic, social, and political summary data, by country, 1984, annual factbook, 244–11

Exports of US, detailed Schedule B commodities by country of destination, 1983, annual rpt, 2424–9

Exports of US, detailed Schedule E commodities by mode of transport and world area and country of destination, 1983, annual rpts, 2424–5

Imports of US, detailed Schedule A commodities by country and world area of origin, and mode of transport, 1983, annual rpts, 2424–2

Imports of US, detailed TSUSA commodities by country of origin, 1983, annual rpt, 2424–4

Loans and grants for economic and military assistance from US and intl agencies, by program and country, FY46-83, annual rpt, 9914–5

Military spending, arms trade, and armed forces size, with total govt spending and population, by country, 1972-82, annual rpt, 9824–1

Minerals Yearbook, 1982, Vol 3: foreign country reviews of production, trade, and policies, by commodity, annual rpt, 5604–35

Minerals Yearbook, 1983, Vol 3 preprints: foreign country review of production, trade, and policies, by commodity, annual rpt, 5604–23.85

Population size and growth rates, and latest available benchmark demographic data, by country, 1950-83, biennial rpt, 2324–4

Rum imports (duty-free) of US under Caribbean Basin Initiative, by country, Jan-June 1983-84, annual rpt, 9884–15

see also under By Foreign Country in the "Index by Categories"

Barbato, Philip J.

"Federal State and Local Transportation Financial Statistics, FY77-82", 7308–185

Barber and beauty shops

- Census of Population, 1980: detailed socioeconomic and demographic characteristics, by age, sex, race, Hispanic origin, occupation, and industry, State rpt series, 2531–4
- Census of Population, 1980: labor force, by sex, detailed occupation, and region, with comparison to 1970 census, supplementary rpt, 2535–1.12
- Census of Service Industries, 1982: employment, establishments, receipts, and payroll, by SIC 2- to 4-digit kind of business, SMSA, county, and city, State rpt series, 2391–1
- County Business Patterns: establishments, employees, and payrolls, by SIC 4-digit industry and county, 1981, annual State rpt series, 2326–8
- County Business Patterns: establishments, employees, and payrolls, by SIC 4-digit industry and county, 1982, annual State rpt series, 2326–6

Employment, earnings, and hours, by SIC 4-digit nonfarm industry, monthly 1974-Feb 1984, annual update, 6744–4

Franchise business opportunities, by firm and kind of business, 1984 annual listing, 2044–27

Income tax returns of sole proprietorships, detailed data by industry div and selected industry group, 1981, annual rpt, 8304–7

Income tax returns of sole proprietorships, receipts, deductions by type, payroll, and net income, by major industry, 1982, annual article, 8302–2.413

Input-output structure of US economy, detailed interindustry transactions for 537 industries, and components of final demand, 1977 benchmark data, 2708–17

Occupational manpower needs and supply by detailed occupation, and educational and training program enrollees and grads by detailed field, 1982 and 1995, biennial rpt, 6744–3

Occupational Outlook Handbook, 1984-85 biennial rpt, 6744–1

Receipts for selected services, by SIC 2- to 4-digit kind of business, 1983, annual rpt, 2413–8

Senate salaries, expenses, and contingent fund disbursements, by payee, detailed listings, 1st half FY84, semiannual rpt, 25922–1

Underground economy, household expenditures and participation by type of goods or service and sociodemographic characteristics, with methodology and bibl, 1981 survey, 8308–27

Virgin Islands economic censuses, 1982: employment, establishments, payroll, and receipts, by SIC 1- to 4-digit industry, island, and city, 2593–1

see also under By Industry in the "Index by Categories"

Barges

- Argentina grain production, exports by firm, storage by facility type and port, and shipments to ports by mode of transport, by grain type, selected years 1954-81, 1528–185
- Coal-fired electric power plants, capacity, coal demand, and coal supply by mode of transport and region of origin, by State, for units planned 1983-92, annual rpt, 3088–18
- Coal transport environmental impacts by type and mode of transport, methodology for assessing alternative systems, 1983 rpt, 3408–28
- Construction financing guarantees of MarAd, by vessel type and firm, FY83, annual rpt, 7704–14.1
- Defense Fuel Supply Center procurement, prices, stocks, transport, and other activities and finances, FY83, annual rpt, 3904–8
- Finances, operations, vehicles, equipment, accidents, and energy use, by mode of transport, 1955-84, annual rpt, 7304–2
- Freight (waterborne domestic and foreign) by commodity, traffic, and passengers, by port and waterway, 1982, annual rpt, 3754–3
- Grain barge shipments from interior river points, by type, weekly rpt, 1313–2
- Grain rail and barge loadings, ship and container car availability, ocean freight rates, and export inspections, prices, and sales, weekly rpt, 1272–2

Baton Rouge, La.

Intermodal containers and equipment owned by US shipping and leasing companies, inventory by type and size, 1983, annual rpt, 7704–10

NYC ocean dumping of municipal wastes, and sewage production and disposal barge capacity and operating costs, 1970s-82 and projected to 2000, hearings, 21568–36

Oil and refined products stocks, and interdistrict shipments by mode of transport, monthly rpt, 3162–6.2

Oil and refined products stocks, and interdistrict shipments by mode of transport, 1983, annual rpt, 3164–2

Ports, port facilities by type, and inland waterways by size, by location, 1982-83, annual rpt, 7704–16

St Lawrence Seaway ships, cargo and passenger volumes, and toll revenues, 1981-82 and trends from 1959, annual rpt, 7744–2

Barite

see Nonmetallic minerals and mines

Barium

see Metals and metal industries

Barker, David

"Investment Tax Credit on Corporation Returns, 1980", 8302–2.405

Barley

see Animal feed

see Grains and grain products

Barnes, Allan M.

"Plague in the U.S., 1983", 4202–7.408

Barr, John S., III

"Issues Facing Cotton Producers", 1004–16.1

Barr, Pamela S.

"Gross State Product in New England", 9373–2.403

Barrientos, Celso S.

"El Nino-Southern Oscillation Episode of 1982-83", 2152–8.402

Barry, Robert D.

"Processing and Refining Capacity of the Domestic Sugar Industry", 1561–14.401

"U.S. Outlook for Sweeteners and Tropical Products", 1004–16.1

Barth, James R.

"Efficiency of the Treasury Bill Futures Market: Some Alternative Test Results", 9316–1.105

Barton, Weldon V.

"Family Farm: Government and Private Responsibilities", 1004–16.1

Basic Educational Opportunity Grants

see Student aid

Basketball

Injuries and deaths from use of selected consumer products and related activity, by victim age and sex, 1982, annual rpt, 9164–7

Bassett, Patricia M.

"Timber Resource Statistics for Eastern Washington", 1206–28.3

Baton Rouge, La.

- Census of Housing, 1980: occupancy and unit characteristics, by race, Hispanic origin, and city, SMSA rpt, 2473–1.84
- Census of Population and Housing, 1980: detailed population and housing characteristics, by county, city, and census tract, SMSA rpt, 2551–2.84
- Wages of office and plant workers, by occupation, 1984 labor market area survey rpt, 6785–3.6

Baton Rouge, La.

see also under By City and By SMSA or MSA in the "Index by Categories"

Battelle Memorial Institute
- "Health Effects of Occupational Exposure to Hazardous Chemicals: A Comparative Assessment with Notes on Ionizing Radiation", 9638–50
- "Report on 1984 National Survey of Compensation Paid Scientists and Engineers Engaged in Research and Development Activities", 3004–1
- *see also* Department of Energy National Laboratories

Batten, Dallas S.
- "Currency Substitution: A Test of Its Importance", 9391–1.418
- "How Robust Are the Policy Conclusions of the St. Louis Equation?: Some Further Evidence", 9391–1.417
- "Recent Decline in Agricultural Exports: Is the Exchange Rate the Culprit?", 9391–1.421
- "What Can Central Banks Do About the Value of the Dollar?", 9391–1.413

Batteries
see Electrical machinery and equipment

Battle Creek, Mich.
- Census of Housing, 1980: occupancy and unit characteristics, by race, Hispanic origin, and city, SMSA rpt, 2473–1.85
- Census of Population and Housing, 1980: detailed population and housing characteristics, by county, city, and census tract, SMSA rpt, 2551–2.85
- Wages by occupation, and benefits for office and plant workers, 1984 labor market area survey rpt, 6785–3.6
- *see also* under By SMSA or MSA in the "Index by Categories"

Battleships
see Naval vessels

Baum, Carlene
- "Drug Utilization in the U.S., 1982", 4064–12

Baum, Kenneth
- "Size Characteristics and Spending Patterns for Corn Belt Grain Farms in 1982, from the Farm Production Expenditure Survey", 1544–19.404

Baumes, Harry S., Jr.
- "Estimating Retail and Farm Marketing Relationships for U.S. Processed and Fresh Apples", 1561–6.401

Baumgartner, David C.
- "Fire Effects Appraisal System for Wisconsin", 1208–198

Bauxite
see Aluminum and aluminum industry

Bay City, Mich.
- Census of Housing, 1980: occupancy and unit characteristics, by race, Hispanic origin, and city, SMSA rpt, 2473–1.86
- Census of Population and Housing, 1980: detailed population and housing characteristics, by county, city, and census tract, SMSA rpt, 2551–2.86
- *see also* under By SMSA or MSA in the "Index by Categories"

Bayer, Amanda S.
- "Monetary Perspective on Underground Economic Activity in the U.S.", 9362–1.402

BEA
see Bureau of Economic Analysis

Beaches
see Lakes and lakeshores
see Seashores

Beans
see Vegetables and vegetable products

Bearings
see Machines and machinery industry

Beauchamp, David A.
- "Species Profiles: Life Histories and Environmental Requirements of Coastal Fishes and Invertebrates (Pacific Northwest), Chinook Salmon", 5506–8.22

Beaumont, Tex.
- Census of Housing, 1980: occupancy and unit characteristics, by race, Hispanic origin, and city, SMSA rpt, 2473–1.87
- Census of Population and Housing, 1980: detailed population and housing characteristics, by county, city, and census tract, SMSA rpt, 2551–2.87
- Housing vacancy rates for single and multifamily units and mobile homes, by city and ZIP code, 1984, annual metro area rpt, 9304–19.15
- Ships in Natl Defense Reserve Fleet at Beaumont harbor, Jan 1984, semiannual inventory, 7702–2
- Wages of office and plant workers, by occupation, 1984 labor market area survey rpt, 6785–3.6
- *see also* under By City and By SMSA or MSA in the "Index by Categories"

Beautification of the landscape
see Open space land programs
see Urban beautification

Beauty aids
see Cosmetics

Beauty parlors
see Barber and beauty shops

Beaver County, Pa.
see also under By SMSA or MSA in the "Index by Categories"

Beck, Herbert
- "Mortgage Industry in the Federal Republic of Germany", 9312–1.405

Beck, James L.
- "Burnout: Age at Release from Prison and Recidivism", 6006–2.31
- "Reliability in Guideline Application: Initial Hearings, 1982", 6006–2.33

Becker, Eugene H.
- "Employment and Unemployment Improvements Widespread in 1983", 6722–1.409
- "Self-Employed Workers: An Update to 1983", 6722–1.443

Becker, Stephanie
- "Local Finance: A Bootstraps Operation", 10042–1.403

Beecher, Gary R.
- "Generating Nutrient Data", 1004–16.1

Beer and breweries
- Business statistics, detailed data for major industries and economic indicators, *Survey of Current Business,* monthly rpt, 2702–1.11
- China economic conditions, agricultural and industrial production, trade, and domestic and foreign investment, 1980-85, 2048–106
- Consumption of food and nutrient intake by individuals, by food group, source, and socioeconomic characteristics, 1977-78 natl survey, final rpt series, 1356–4

Index by Subjects and Names

- Consumption, supply, trade, prices, expenditures, and indexes, by food commodity, 1963-83, annual rpt, 1544–4
- County Business Patterns: establishments, employees, and payrolls, by SIC 4-digit industry and county, 1981, annual State rpt series, 2326–8
- County Business Patterns: establishments, employees, and payrolls, by SIC 4-digit industry and county, 1982, annual State rpt series, 2326–6
- Cuba economic conditions, agricultural and industrial production and distribution, trade, and intl economic relations, 1970-82 and trends from 1957, 248–40
- EC food supply/demand and market and support prices, with exchange rates, fertilizer price index, GDP, and population, by country, 1960-83, 1528–173
- Employment, earnings, and hours, by selected SIC 1- to 4-digit industry, State, and for 278 major labor areas, 1939-83, annual rpt, 6744–5
- Employment, earnings, and hours, by SIC 4-digit nonfarm industry, monthly 1974-Feb 1984, annual update, 6744–4
- Exports and imports of US, by agricultural commodity and country, bimonthly rpt with articles, 1522–1
- Exports and imports of US, by detailed agricultural commodity and country, FY83 and CY83, semiannual rpts, 1522–4
- Exports and imports of US, detailed SIC-based commodities by world area, 1983, annual rpts, 2424–6
- Exports and imports of US, totals and as percent of domestic production, by SIC 2- to 5-digit commodity, 1981, annual rpt, 2424–3
- Exports of US, detailed commodities by country of destination, monthly rpt, 2422–3
- Exports of US, detailed Schedule B commodities by country of destination, 1983, annual rpt, 2424–9
- Exports of US, detailed Schedule E commodities by mode of transport and world area and country of destination, 1983, annual rpts, 2424–5
- Hops production, stocks, use, and US trade by country, monthly rpt, 1313–7
- Hops stocks held by growers, dealers, and brewers, Sept 1984, semiannual release, 1621–8
- Imports of US, detailed Schedule A commodities by country and world area of origin, and mode of transport, 1983, annual rpts, 2424–2
- Imports of US, detailed Schedule A commodities by country, monthly rpt, 2422–2
- Imports of US, detailed TSUSA commodities by country of origin, 1983, annual rpt, 2424–4
- Income tax returns of corporations, detailed income and tax items by industry, 1981, annual rpt, 8304–4
- Input-output structure of US economy, detailed interindustry transactions for 537 industries, and components of final demand, 1977 benchmark data, 2708–17
- Israel and France urban youths use of selected drugs, alcohol, and cigarettes, by age and sex, 1977 and 1979, article, 4102–1.430

Index by Subjects and Names

Belize

Manufacturing census, 1982: financial and operating data, by SIC 2- to 4-digit industry, State, SMSA, and county, preliminary census div rpt series, 2491–3

Producer prices and indexes, by stage of processing and detailed commodity, monthly rpt, 6762–6

Producer prices and indexes, by stage of processing and detailed commodity, monthly 1983, annual supplement, 6764–2

Production, removals, and stocks of beer and cereal beverages, by State, FY81-82, last issue of annual rpt, 8484–1.3

Production, stocks, materials used, and tax-free and taxable removals by State, for beer, monthly rpt, 8486–1.1

Productivity, hours, and employment indexes for selected SIC 3- and 4-digit industries, 1954-82, annual rpt, 6824–1.3

Retail trade census, 1982: employment, establishments, sales, and payroll, for liquor stores, by State, preliminary rpt, 2395–1.27

Rice prices paid by brewers, 1980/81-1983/84, semiannual rpt, 1561–8.3

Tax (excise) collections of IRS, by source, quarterly press release, 8302–1

Taxation and revenue systems, by type of tax and system, level of govt, and State, selected years 1958-83, annual rpt, 10044–1.3

Wholesale trade census, 1982: employment, establishments, sales by commodity, and payroll, by SIC 4-digit kind of business and State, preliminary rpt, 2403–1.37

Bees and beeswax

see Honey and beekeeping

Behavioral sciences

see Anthropology

see Psychology

see Social sciences

see Sociology

Belden, Sanford A.

"Future Family Farm Needs", 1004–16.1

Belgium

Agricultural and food production indexes, and production of selected commodities, by world region and country, 1974-83, annual rpt, 1524–5

Agricultural situation in Western Europe, by country and commodity, 1983 and outlook for 1984, annual rpt, 1524–4.6

Agricultural supply/demand, trade, and production, and socioeconomic data, by country, 1950s-77, 1528–179

AID loan repayment status and terms by program and country, and status of predecessor agency loans, quarterly rpt, 9912–3

Auto and auto products sales, prices, and registrations in US, and trade of 8 countries with US, by make and model, 1964-83, annual rpt, 9884–7

Auto safety and experimental vehicle designs, 1982, conf proceedings, annual rpt, 7764–3

Economic and monetary trends, compounded annual rates of change for US and 10 major trading partners, quarterly rpt, 9391–7

Economic conditions in Communist, OECD, and selected other countries, 1960s-83, annual rpt, 244–5

Economic, social, and political summary data, by country, 1984, annual factbook, 244–11

Economic trends in income, production, prices, employment, finances, and trade, 1984 semiannual rpt, 2046–4.56

Exports and imports of NATO countries with Council for Mutual Economic Assistance Europe members, by country, 1980-83, annual rpt, 7144–5

Exports and imports of NATO countries with PRC, by country, 1980-83, annual rpt, 7144–14

Exports and imports of OECD countries, by country, 1983, annual rpt, 7144–10

Exports and imports of US with Western Europe, and US market share and export opportunities for selected commodities, by country, 1982-84, 2048–105

Exports of US, detailed Schedule B commodities by country of destination, 1983, annual rpt, 2424–9

Exports of US, detailed Schedule E commodities by mode of transport and world area and country of destination, 1983, annual rpts, 2424–5

Fish and shellfish wholesale prices and market activity in 8 West Europe countries, weekly rpt, 2162–8

Food processing and packaging equipment market and trade, and user industry operations and demand, 1982 market research rpt, 2045–11.24

Food supply/demand and market and support prices, with exchange rates, fertilizer price index, GDP, and population, by EC country, 1960-83, 1528–173

Imports of US, detailed Schedule A commodities by country and world area of origin, and mode of transport, 1983, annual rpts, 2424–2

Imports of US, detailed TSUSA commodities by country of origin, 1983, annual rpt, 2424–4

Intl transactions of US with 10 countries, 1981-83, *Survey of Current Business,* monthly rpt, annual table, 2702–1.31

Lab instruments market and trade, and user industry operations and demand, 1983 country market research rpt, 2045–10.15

Loans and grants for economic and military assistance from US and intl agencies, by program and country, FY46-83, annual rpt, 9914–5

Manufacturing labor productivity and cost indexes for US and 11 OECD countries, 1960-82, annual article, 6722–1.405

Manufacturing productivity and unit labor cost indexes for US and 11 countries, 1950-82 and preliminary 1983, annual rpt, 6864–1

Military aid of US, arms sales, and training programs costs and budget requests by program, world region, and country, FY83-85, annual rpt, 7144–13

Military spending, arms trade, and armed forces size, with total govt spending and population, by country, 1972-82, annual rpt, 9824–1

Minerals Yearbook, 1982, Vol 3: foreign country reviews of production, trade, and policies, by commodity, annual rpt, 5604–35

Minerals Yearbook, 1983, Vol 3 preprints: foreign country review of production, trade, and policies, by commodity, annual rpt, 5604–23.8

Nuclear power generation in US and 18 non-Communist countries, monthly rpt, 3162–24.10

Nuclear power plant construction and operation status, and capacity, by plant, region, State, and selected country, 1983 and projected to 2020, annual rpt, 3164–57

Population size and growth rates, and latest available benchmark demographic data, by country, 1950-83, biennial rpt, 2324–4

Steel imports of US from EC and other countries, and US industry operating data, for 15 products limited under arrangement with EC, monthly rpt, 9882–10

see also under By Foreign Country in the "Index by Categories"

Belize

Agricultural situation in Latin America, by country, 1981-83 and outlook for 1984, annual rpt, 1524–4.9

AID activities and funding by project and function, FY85, and developing countries summary socioeconomic data, 1970s-83, by country, annual rpt, 9914–3

AID economic assistance to developing countries, obligations and disbursements by country, quarterly rpt, 9912–4

AID economic assistance to 7 Central American countries, by type of aid, FY80-83, GAO rpt, 26123–55

AID loan repayment status and terms by program and country, and status of predecessor agency loans, quarterly rpt, 9912–3

Economic, social, and political summary data, by country, 1984, annual factbook, 244–11

Exports of US, detailed Schedule B commodities by country of destination, 1983, annual rpt, 2424–9

Exports of US, detailed Schedule E commodities by mode of transport and world area and country of destination, 1983, annual rpts, 2424–5

Imports of US, detailed Schedule A commodities by country and world area of origin, and mode of transport, 1983, annual rpts, 2424–2

Imports of US, detailed TSUSA commodities by country of origin, 1983, annual rpt, 2424–4

Loans and grants for economic and military assistance from US and intl agencies, by program and country, FY46-83, annual rpt, 9914–5

Military aid of US, arms sales, and training programs costs and budget requests by program, world region, and country, FY83-85, annual rpt, 7144–13

Minerals Yearbook, 1982, Vol 3: foreign country reviews of production, trade, and policies, by commodity, annual rpt, 5604–35

Minerals Yearbook, 1982, Vol 3 preprints: foreign country review of production, trade, and policies, by commodity, annual rpt, 5604–17.86

Natural resources and hazards to resource dev, with data on mineral, energy, and water resources, by Central American country, 1981 with trends from 1977, 5668–71

Belize

Oil and gas undiscovered recoverable resources, cumulative production, and identified reserves, as of 1981, final world oil basin rpt, 5666–18.4

Population size and growth rates, and latest available benchmark demographic data, by country, 1950-83, biennial rpt, 2324–4

Refugees from Central America by country of origin and asylum, and aid from US and Mexico, FY82-1984, GAO rpt, 26123–70

see also under By Foreign Country in the "Index by Categories"

Bell, Donald

"How Social Security Payments Affect Private Pensions", 6722–1.431

"Surviving Spouse's Benefits in Private Pension Plans", 6722–1.426

Bell, Ralph

"Over-the-Counter Drugs: Factors in Adult Use of Sedatives, Tranquilizers, and Stimulants", 4102–1.435

Bell, William G.

"Transportation for Older Americans: Issues and Options for the Decade of the 1980's", 7308–183

Belleville, Ill.

see also under By SMSA or MSA in the "Index by Categories"

Belli, R. David

"Foreign Direct Investment in the U.S. in 1983", 2702–1.439

"U.S. Business Enterprises Acquired or Established by Foreign Direct Investors in 1983", 2702–1.418

Bellingham, Wash.

Census of Housing, 1980: occupancy and unit characteristics, by race, Hispanic origin, and city, SMSA rpt, 2473–1.88

Census of Population and Housing, 1980: detailed population and housing characteristics, by county, city, and census tract, SMSA rpt, 2551–2.88

Housing vacancy rates for single and multifamily units and mobile homes, by city and ZIP code, 1983, annual metro area rpt, 9304–21.5

see also under By SMSA or MSA in the "Index by Categories"

Beloit, Wis.

Census of Housing, 1980: occupancy and unit characteristics, by race, Hispanic origin, and city, SMSA rpt, 2473–1.193

Census of Population and Housing, 1980: detailed population and housing characteristics, by county, city, and census tract, SMSA rpt, 2551–2.193

Belongia, Michael T.

"Are Options on Treasury Bond Futures Priced Efficiently?", 9391–1.404

"Money Growth Variability and GNP", 9391–1.411

"Recent Decline in Agricultural Exports: Is the Exchange Rate the Culprit?", 9391–1.421

Beltran del Rio, Abel

"Problems and Prospects of the Mexican Economy in 1983-88", 21248–82

Bend, Oreg.

Housing vacancy rates for single and multifamily units and mobile homes, by city and ZIP code, 1984, annual metro area rpt, 9304–21.10

Benin

Agricultural and food production indexes, and production of selected commodities, by world region and country, 1974-83, annual rpt, 1524–5

Agricultural situation in sub-Saharan Africa, by country, 1982-83 and outlook for 1984, annual rpt, 1524–4.10

AID economic assistance to developing countries, obligations and disbursements by country, quarterly rpt, 9912–4

AID loan repayment status and terms by program and country, and status of predecessor agency loans, quarterly rpt, 9912–3

Economic conditions and foreign marketing prospects in 46 Sub-Saharan countries, 1983 world region rpt, 2046–5.1

Economic, social, and political summary data, by country, 1984, annual factbook, 244–11

Economic trends in income, production, prices, employment, finances, and trade, 1984 annual rpt, 2046–4.19

Exports of US, detailed Schedule B commodities by country of destination, 1983, annual rpt, 2424–9

Exports of US, detailed Schedule E commodities by mode of transport and world area and country of destination, 1983, annual rpts, 2424–5

Imports of US, detailed Schedule A commodities by country and world area of origin, and mode of transport, 1983, annual rpts, 2424–2

Imports of US, detailed TSUSA commodities by country of origin, 1983, annual rpt, 2424–4

Loans and grants for economic and military assistance from US and intl agencies, by program and country, FY46-83, annual rpt, 9914–5

Military aid of US, arms sales, and training programs costs and budget requests by program, world region, and country, FY83-85, annual rpt, 7144–13

Military spending, arms trade, and armed forces size, with total govt spending and population, by country, 1972-82, annual rpt, 9824–1

Minerals Yearbook, 1982, Vol 3: foreign country reviews of production, trade, and policies, by commodity, annual rpt, 5604–35

Minerals Yearbook, 1982, Vol 3 preprints: foreign country review of production, trade, and policies, by commodity, annual rpt, 5604–17.84

Population size and growth rates, and latest available benchmark demographic data, by country, 1950-83, biennial rpt, 2324–4

see also under By Foreign Country in the "Index by Categories"

Benker, Karen M.

"Significant Features of Fiscal Federalism, 1982-83 Edition", 10044–1

Benkovitz, C.

"Radioactive Materials Released from Nuclear Power Plants, Annual Report, 1981", 9634–1

Bennett, Barbara A.

"Bank Regulation and Deposit Insurance: Controlling the FDIC's Losses", 9393–8.407

Index by Subjects and Names

Bennett, James D.

"U.S. Production, Imports & Import/Production Ratios for Cotton, Wool & Man-Made Fiber Textiles & Apparel", 2044–14

Bennett, Veronica

"Consumer Demand for Product Deregulation", 9371–1.417

Benninga, Simon

"General Equilibrium Properties of the Term Structure of Interest Rates", 9387–8.91

Benton Harbor, Mich.

Census of Housing, 1980: occupancy and unit characteristics, by race, Hispanic origin, and city, SMSA rpt, 2473–1.89

Census of Population and Housing, 1980: detailed population and housing characteristics, by county, city, and census tract, SMSA rpt, 2551–2.89

see also under By SMSA or MSA in the "Index by Categories"

Bergen County, N.J.

see also under By SMSA or MSA in the "Index by Categories"

Bering Sea

Fish catch quotas for US 200 mile zone, allocations by species and country, 1984 coastal area rpt, 7006–5.2

Ice conditions of Bering Sea and Alaska north coast, monthly rpt, 2182–5

Oil spill risk analyses for OCS proposed lease sale areas, series, 5736–2

Berk, Marc L.

"Persons with Limitations of Activity: Health Insurance, Expenditures and Use of Services", 4186–3.19

Berkeley, Calif.

see also under By City in the "Index by Categories"

Berkeley Planning Associates

"Cost Study of the Small Business Development Center Delivery System and the Small Business Administration's (SBA's) Management Assistance Delivery System", 25728–36

Berkhouse, L. H.

"Operation CROSSROADS, 1946", 3906–1.42

"Operation SANDSTONE, 1948", 3906–1.41

Bermuda

Economic, social, and political summary data, by country, 1984, annual factbook, 244–11

Exports of US, detailed Schedule B commodities by country of destination, 1983, annual rpt, 2424–9

Exports of US, detailed Schedule E commodities by mode of transport and world area and country of destination, 1983, annual rpts, 2424–5

Imports of US, detailed Schedule A commodities by country and world area of origin, and mode of transport, 1983, annual rpts, 2424–2

Imports of US, detailed TSUSA commodities by country of origin, 1983, annual rpt, 2424–4

Loans and grants for economic and military assistance from US and intl agencies, by program and country, FY46-83, annual rpt, 9914–5

Population size and growth rates, and latest available benchmark demographic data, by country, 1950-83, biennial rpt, 2324–4

Index by Subjects and Names

Bibliographies

Tax evasion through nonresidents bank claims and deposits, direct investments, income payments, and other transactions in 5 Caribbean countries, 1978-82, 8008–106

see also under By Foreign Country in the "Index by Categories"

Bernstein, Edward M.

"Reflections on Bretton Woods", 9373–3.28

Berries

see Fruit and fruit products

Berry, Linda

"Loan Impacts in Home Energy Audit Programs: A Minnesota Example", 3308–72

Bertram, Kenneth M.

"Inland Transport Modes for Coal and Coal-Derived Energy: An Evaluation Method for Comparing Environmental Impacts", 3408–28

Beryllium

see Metals and metal industries

Bethlehem, Pa.

- Census of Housing, 1980: occupancy and unit characteristics, by race, Hispanic origin, and city, SMSA rpt, 2473–1.64
- Census of Population and Housing, 1980: detailed population and housing characteristics, by county, city, and census tract, SMSA rpt, 2551–2.64
- Housing and households detailed characteristics, and unit and neighborhood quality, by inside-outside central cities, 1980 survey, SMSA rpt, 2485–6.7
- *see also* under By SMSA or MSA in the "Index by Categories"

Betting

see Gambling

Beverages

- Census of Population, 1980: detailed socioeconomic and demographic characteristics, by age, sex, race, Hispanic origin, occupation, and industry, State rpt series, 2531–4
- China economic conditions, agricultural and industrial production, trade, and domestic and foreign investment, 1980-85, 2048–106
- China exports and imports by SITC 1- to 5-digit commodity, 1970s-82, annual rpt, 244–12
- Consumption of beverages, by age and sex, 1977/78, article, 1541–7.403
- Consumption of food and nutrient intake by individuals, by food group, source, and socioeconomic characteristics, 1977-78 natl survey, final rpt series, 1356–4
- Consumption, supply, trade, prices, expenditures, and indexes, by food commodity, 1963-83, annual rpt, 1544–4
- County Business Patterns: establishments, employees, and payrolls, by SIC 4-digit industry and county, 1981, annual State rpt series, 2326–8
- County Business Patterns: establishments, employees, and payrolls, by SIC 4-digit industry and county, 1982, annual State rpt series, 2326–6
- Employment, earnings, and hours, by selected SIC 1- to 4-digit industry, State, and for 278 major labor areas, 1939-83, annual rpt, 6744–5
- Employment, earnings, and hours, by SIC 4-digit nonfarm industry, monthly 1974-Feb 1984, annual update, 6744–4

Exports and imports of US, and trade balance, by major commodity group, selected country, and world area, with seasonal adjustments, monthly rpt, 2422–6

Exports and imports of US, by agricultural commodity and country, bimonthly rpt with articles, 1522–1

Exports and imports of US, by detailed agricultural commodity and country, FY83 and CY83, semiannual rpts, 1522–4

Exports and imports of US, detailed SIC-based commodities by world area, 1983, annual rpts, 2424–6

Exports of US, detailed commodities by country of destination, monthly rpt, 2422–3

Exports of US, detailed Schedule B commodities by country of destination, 1983, annual rpt, 2424–9

Exports of US, detailed Schedule E commodities by mode of transport and world area and country of destination, 1983, annual rpts, 2424–5

Great Lakes trade, by SITC 3-digit commodity, port, vessel type, world area, and country, 1982, annual rpt, 7744–3

Imports of US, detailed Schedule A commodities by country and world area of origin, and mode of transport, 1983, annual rpts, 2424–2

Imports of US, detailed Schedule A commodities by country, monthly rpt, 2422–2

Imports of US, detailed TSUSA commodities by country of origin, 1983, annual rpt, 2424–4

Income tax returns of corporations, detailed income and tax items by industry, 1981, annual rpt, 8304–4

Industry finances and operations, by SIC 2- to 4-digit industry, 1970s-83 and projected to 1988, annual rpt, 2014–4

Manufacturing census, 1982: financial and operating data, by SIC 2- to 4-digit industry, State, SMSA, and county, preliminary census div rpt series, 2491–3

Manufacturing census, 1982: financial and operating data, for SIC 4-digit industries by product, preliminary rpt series, 2491–1

Minority group and women employment, by occupational group and SIC 2- to 3-digit industry, 1981, annual rpt, 9244–1.1

Occupational injury and illness rates, by SIC 2- to 4-digit industry, 1982, annual rpt, 6844–1

OECD trade, total and for 4 major countries, and US trade by country, by commodity, 1972-82, annual world region rpt series, 244–13

Producer prices and indexes, by stage of processing and detailed commodity, monthly rpt, 6762–6

Producer prices and indexes, by stage of processing and detailed commodity, monthly 1983, annual supplement, 6764–2

Transportation census, 1982: trucks, by detailed characteristics, miles traveled, and type of product carried, State rpt series, 2573–1

Virgin Islands economic censuses, 1982: employment, establishments, payroll, and receipts, by SIC 1- to 4-digit industry, island, and city, 2593–1

see also Beer and breweries

see also Coffee

see also Liquor industry

see also Soft drink industry

see also Tea

see also Wine and winemaking

see also under By Commodity in the "Index by Categories"

Bhutan

- Economic, social, and political summary data, by country, 1984, annual factbook, 244–11
- Imports of US, detailed TSUSA commodities by country of origin, 1983, annual rpt, 2424–4
- Loans and grants for economic and military assistance from US and intl agencies, by program and country, FY46-83, annual rpt, 9914–5
- Population size and growth rates, and latest available benchmark demographic data, by country, 1950-83, biennial rpt, 2324–4
- *see also* under By Foreign Country in the "Index by Categories"

Bianchi, Suzanne M.

"Occupational Reclassification and Changes in Distribution by Gender", 6722–1.417

"Wives Who Earn More than Their Husbands", 2326–11.9

Bibliographies

- Acid rain causes and effects, air pollutant emissions by source in US and selected countries, control costs, and Fed Govt research funding, 1960s-82, 3408–27
- Aerial survey R&D publications, and sources of natural resource and environmental data gathered by air- and spacecraft, quarterly listing, 9502–7
- Air pollution and acid rain environmental effects, and methods of neutralizing acidified water bodies, summary research rpt series, 5506–5
- Alaska Arctic Natl Wildlife Refuge resources, resident and visitor activities, and environmental impacts of energy exploration, 1983, annual update rpt, 5504–26
- Alcohol use, and health, economic, and social impacts, review of research, 1970s-81, 4488–4
- Alcoholism research, treatment programs, and patient characteristics, quarterly journal, 4482–1
- Biomass Fuels Program of TVA, technologies and processes dev, costs, and resource requirements, 1970s-90s, series, 9806–9
- Birds (marine) on southeastern US coast, distribution, abundance, and oil spill effects, by species and State, 1820s-1982, 5508–72
- Birds protected under Migratory Bird Treaty Act, population characteristics and potential impact of Fed Govt coal leasing, for 25 species, 1900s-82, 5508–88
- Budget deficits effect on interest rates, regression results and bibl, various periods 1965-83, 8008–111
- Cancer Natl Inst epidemiology and biometry activities, staff, budget, and contract awards by project and recipient instn, FY83, annual rpt, 4474–29
- Coastal environmental and wildlife characteristics, use, and mgmt, for individual ecosystems, series, 5506–9

Bibliographies

Crime and criminal justice data, including justice expenditures and employment by level of govt, 1970s-82 with some trends from 1875, 6068–174

Education statistics summary compilation, 1980/81-1982/83 with selected trends from 1869, biennial rpt, 4804–27

Employment and unemployment current statistics and articles, Monthly Labor Review, 6722–1

Energy R&D and technology publications, quarterly listing, 9502–4

Energy research publications, monthly listing, 3002–2

Environmental pollution-related disease research activities and publications, Sept 1982-Aug 1983, annual rpt, 9184–9

Estuary environmental characteristics, fish, wildlife, uses, and mgmt, for individual estuaries, series, 5506–7

Fed Govt policy issues effect on agricultural and food prices, income, and trade, and crop support levels by program, Nov 1984, semiannual rpt, 1542–6

Fish and shellfish landings, life cycles, and environmental needs, for selected species by region, with glossary and bibl, series, 5506–8

Fish and shellfish of economic importance, biological, fishery, and mgmt data, literature review series, 2166–16

Fishery resources mgmt and R&D, Fed Govt grants by project and resulting publications, 1983, annual listing, 2164–3

Food aid programs of Fed Govt and others, funding, participant characteristics, and nutrition and poverty data, 1970s-83, 028–20

Foreign countries *Background Notes,* summary social, political, and economic data, series, 7006–2

Forest research project descriptions and bibl, 1982, annual rpt, 1204–14

Franchise business opportunities by firm and kind of business, and sources of aid and info, 1984 annual listing, 2044–27

Genetic resource (plant and animal) conservation, commercial uses, causes of depletion, and geographic sources, 1984 rpt, 5548–13

Genetically abnormal human cell cultures available to researchers, and cultures shipped, 1984 annual listing, 4474–23

Geological Survey and other publications, 1983, annual listing, 5664–4

Glaciology intl research summaries, methodology, and bibls, series, 2156–18

Head Start Project programs and effect on child dev, literature review with bibl, selected years 1970-83, 4608–17

Head Start Project programs effect on child dev, by characteristics of program, child, and family, literature review, selected years 1965-81, 4608–20

Health condition of Vietnam veterans, methodology for 3 CDC studies on effects of military service and Agent Orange exposure, Nov 1983 rpt, 4208–22

Health status measurement methodology, confs, and publications, quarterly listing, suspended, 4122–1

Hispanic Americans socioeconomic and demographic characteristics, and compared to non-Hispanics, selected years 1970-83, chartbook, 2328–48

Homeless population and characteristics, and temporary shelter operations, use, and user characteristics, by region and selected city, 1983, 5188–108

Housing finance technical analysis, quarterly rpt articles, 9312–7

Immunization research publications, 1984 annual listing, 4204–16

Income (legal) not reported on Federal income tax returns by source, and legal and illegal underground income, with bibl, 1974-81, article, 2702–1.419

Income (taxable) not reported, by illegal source, with characteristics of persons involved, methodology, and bibl, 1970s-82, 8008–112

Marijuana use, abstracts of research articles and rpts, 1974-82, 4496–1.31

Marine mammals protection, Fed Govt and intl regulatory and research activities, with bibl, 1983, annual rpt, 14734–1

Medicine Natl Library activities, collections, and grants, FY81-83, annual rpt, 4464–1

Mentally retarded and developmentally disabled treatment and services, university-affiliated facility funding, activities, and clients, 1980-FY83, 4608–19

Metals resource recovery through leaching technologies, characteristics of methods and operations, regulation, and research, series, 5606–6

Military weapons systems cost estimates, DOD methodology for rpts to Congress, with bibl, 1970s-83, GAO rpt, 26123–62

Minerals resources of Alaska, production, claims on wildlife refuges, oil and gas leases, and exploratory wells, with maps and bibl, 1983, annual rpt, 5664–11

Motor vehicles powered by electricity, Fed Govt dev program implementation, with bibl, FY83, annual rpt, 3304–2

NSF Science Resources Studies Div activities, project descriptions, and 1973-83 publications, 1983 annual listing, 9624–21

Occupational health risks from hazardous substances and radiation, by industry, occupation, age, and sex, with bibl and glossary, 1920s-82, 9638–50

Ocean dumping and pollution investigations and activities of NOAA, research and monitoring studies funded, and bibl, FY83, annual rpt, 2144–9

Ports, port facilities by type, and inland waterways by size, by location, 1982-83, annual rpt, 7704–16

Productivity of labor and capital, growth by SIC 1- to 2-digit industry, and measurement methods and bibl, various periods 1948-78 with trends from 1800, 2218–69

Radioactive materials transport surveillance program activities, results, and Fed Govt funding, by State, 1984 summary rpt, 9636–1.23

Radionuclide concentrations in cattle and wildlife near Nevada nuclear test site, 1957-81, last issue of annual rpt, 9234–5

Seat belt use, effects of driving circumstances and driver characteristics and attitudes, 1981 survey, 7768–82

Sedimentation control, surveillance, and research activity of Fed Govt, by project, agency, region, and State, 1982, annual rpt, 5664–9

Index by Subjects and Names

Shift work, effects of rotating schedules on productivity and health, 1983 bibl, 7506–10.29

Smoking and health research, article abstracts and indexes, 1983, annual rpt, 4044–8

Smoking and health research publications, bimonthly listing, 4042–1

Smoking related to chronic obstructive lung disease and deaths, by sociodemographic and smoking characteristics, literature review, 1984 annual Surgeon General rpt, 4044–6

Solar photovoltaic system R&D sponsored by DOE, project descriptions and publications, FY83, annual listing, 3304–20

Statistical Abstract of US, guide to sources, 1984 annual rpt, 2324–1

Telecommunications and Info Natl Admin research and engineering rpts, FY83, annual listing, 2804–3

Transit systems research publications, 2nd half FY83, semiannual listing, 7882–1

Underground economy, household expenditures and participation by type of goods or service and sociodemographic characteristics, with methodology and bibl, 1981 survey, 8308–27

Water supply and quality, and effect of coal mining operations, for selected river basins in Eastern and Interior coal provinces, series, 5666–15

Water supply and quality, and effect of coal mining operations, for selected river basins in Western coal provinces, series, 5666–19

Wetlands environmental characteristics, acreage, uses, and mgmt, by wetland type and region, 1950s-80, 26358–102

see also Computer data file guides

see also Government publications lists

Bicycles

Accident deaths in transportation, by mode, 1982-83, annual summary rpt, 9614–6

Accidents (fatal), circumstances, and characteristics of persons and vehicles involved, detailed data, 1982, annual rpt, 7764–10

Accidents, circumstances, injuries, deaths, and characteristics of persons and vehicles involved, 1982, annual rpt, 7764–13

Accidents, deaths, circumstances, and characteristics of persons and vehicles involved, series, 7766–13

Census of Housing, 1980: structural, financial, and householder characteristics, by region and State, 2475–4

Census of Population, 1980: detailed socioeconomic and demographic characteristics, by age, sex, race, Hispanic origin, occupation, and industry, State rpt series, 2531–4

Census of Population, 1980: detailed socioeconomic characteristics, by county, city, and inside-outside SMSAs and central cities, State rpt series, 2531–3

China economic conditions, agricultural and industrial production, trade, and domestic and foreign investment, 1980-85, 2048–106

Commuting to work, householder principal mode of transport, distance, and travel time, by race, Hispanic origin, tenure, urban-rural location, and region, 1981, annual survey, 2485–7

Index by Subjects and Names

Biological sciences

County Business Patterns: establishments, employees, and payrolls, by SIC 4-digit industry and county, 1981, annual State rpt series, 2326–8

County Business Patterns: establishments, employees, and payrolls, by SIC 4-digit industry and county, 1982, annual State rpt series, 2326–6

Exports and imports of US, detailed SIC-based commodities by world area, 1983, annual rpts, 2424–6

Exports and imports of US, totals and as percent of domestic production, by SIC 2- to 5-digit commodity, 1981, annual rpt, 2424–3

Exports of US, detailed commodities by country of destination, monthly rpt, 2422–3

Exports of US, detailed Schedule B commodities by country of destination, 1983, annual rpt, 2424–9

Exports of US, detailed Schedule E commodities by mode of transport and world area and country of destination, 1983, annual rpts, 2424–5

Foreign market and trade for sporting goods and recreational equipment and vehicles, country market research rpts, 2045–14

Imports of US, detailed Schedule A commodities by country and world area of origin, and mode of transport, 1983, annual rpts, 2424–2

Imports of US, detailed Schedule A commodities by country, monthly rpt, 2422–2

Imports of US, detailed TSUSA commodities by country of origin, 1983, annual rpt, 2424–4

Industry finances and operations, by SIC 2- to 4-digit industry, 1970s-83 and projected to 1988, annual rpt, 2014–4

Injuries and deaths from use of selected consumer products and related activity, by victim age and sex, 1982, annual rpt, 9164–7

Injuries and deaths from use of selected consumer products, by victim age and medical treatment status, 1982, annual rpt, 9164–6

Input-output structure of US economy, detailed interindustry transactions for 537 industries, and components of final demand, 1977 benchmark data, 2708–17

Manufacturing census, 1982: financial and operating data, for SIC 4-digit industries by product, preliminary rpt, 2491–1.407

Thefts, and total value of property stolen and recovered, by property type, 1983, annual rpt, 6224–2.1

Tires and tubes for bicycles from Taiwan at less than fair value, imports injury to US industry, investigation with background financial and operating data, 1984 rpt, 9886–14.106

Traffic accidents and deaths by characteristics of persons and vehicles involved and State, and Natl Hwy Traffic Safety Admin activities, 1961-81, annual rpt, 7764–1

Traffic accidents and occupant and non-occupant deaths, 1972-82, annual rpt, 7304–2

Virgin Islands economic censuses, 1982: employment, establishments, payroll, and receipts, by SIC 1- to 4-digit industry, island, and city, 2593–1

see also Mopeds

Bielsa, Lourdes M.

"Species Profiles: Life Histories and Environmental Requirements of Coastal Fishes and Invertebrates (South Florida), Pink Shrimp", 5506–8.26

Bigelow, Bruce E.

"Development of Corporate Incentive Programs for Motivating Safety Belt Use: A Review", 7762–9.409

Bilingual education

see Compensatory education

Billings, Mont.

- Census of Housing, 1980: occupancy and unit characteristics, by race, Hispanic origin, and city, SMSA rpt, 2473–1.90
- Census of Population and Housing, 1980: detailed population and housing characteristics, by county, city, and census tract, SMSA rpt, 2551–2.90
- Wages of office and plant workers, by occupation, 1984 SMSA survey rpt, 6785–11.8
- *see also* under By SMSA or MSA in the "Index by Categories"

Bills, Nelson L.

"Assessing Erosion on U.S. Cropland, Land Management and Physical Features", 1588–83

Biloxi, Miss.

- Census of Housing, 1980: occupancy and unit characteristics, by race, Hispanic origin, and city, SMSA rpt, 2473–1.91
- Census of Population and Housing, 1980: detailed population and housing characteristics, by county, city, and census tract, SMSA rpt, 2551–2.91
- Wages of office and plant workers, by occupation, 1984 labor market area survey rpt, 6785–3.9
- *see also* under By SMSA or MSA in the "Index by Categories"

Binghamton, N.Y.

- Census of Housing, 1980: occupancy and unit characteristics, by race, Hispanic origin, and city, SMSA rpt, 2473–1.92
- Census of Population and Housing, 1980: detailed population and housing characteristics, by county, city, and census tract, SMSA rpt, 2551–2.92
- Wages by occupation, and benefits for office and plant workers, 1984 labor market area survey rpt, 6785–3.10
- *see also* under By SMSA or MSA in the "Index by Categories"

Biological sciences

- Biotechnology commercial uses, R&D funding and output, controls, and industry financial and operating data, for US and 5 countries, 1970s-83 and estimated 1984-85, 26358–98
- Biotechnology firms, patents, and trade by country, and effect of industry growth on US drug and chemical trade, selected years 1979-2000, 9886–4.78
- Carbon dioxide atmospheric levels, climatic effects and impacts of fossil and synthetic fuels use, deforestation, and land use patterns, research rpt series, 3406–3
- Census of Population, 1980: detailed socioeconomic and demographic characteristics, by age, sex, race, Hispanic origin, occupation, and industry, State rpt series, 2531–4

Degrees conferred in higher education, by race, Hispanic origin, sex, level, and field, selected years 1949/50-1979/80, annual rpt, 4824–2.16

- DOE R&D projects and funding at natl labs, universities, and other instns, FY83, annual summary rpt, 3004–18.1
- DOE R&D projects and funding at natl labs, universities, and other instns, FY84, annual summary rpt, 3004–18.2
- Fish and shellfish of economic importance, biological, fishery, and mgmt data, literature review series, 2166–16
- Health and population research funded by 4 private organizations, project listing by topic, with funding data, 1981, annual rpt, 4474–16
- High school classes of 1980 and 1982: educational and sociodemographic characteristics and expectations, natl longitudinal study, series, 4826–2
- Marine Mammal Protection Act admin and populations, strandings, and catch permits by type and applicant, by species and location, Apr 1983-Mar 1984, annual rpt, 2164–11
- NASA R&D funding to colleges and universities, by State, field of science, and instn, FY83, annual listing, 9504–7
- NIH grants and awards for R&D, training, construction, and medical libraries, by location and recipient, FY83, annual listings, 4434–7
- NSF grant and award recipients, by State, FY83, annual listing, 9624–11
- NSF research programs, activities, and funding, FY82-83, annual rpt, 9624–6
- Nuclear industry nongovt employment by industry segment, occupation, and census div, and DOE and NRC nuclear employment, 1968-83, biennial rpt, 3004–11
- *Occupational Outlook Handbook,* 1984-85 biennial rpt, 6744–1
- Oceanographic data, stations and cruises recording data for World Data Center A by country, ship, and type of data, 1983, annual rpt, 2144–15
- Plant science R&D at higher education instns, funding by source, grad students, and staff, 1983, 9626–2.143
- Public health labs of States, pay scales and job requirements by occupation and State, FY81-83, annual rpt, 4204–7
- R&D and science-related Fed Govt funding and total and federally funded expenditures of universities and colleges, by instn and field of science, FY82, 9626–2.136
- R&D and science-related Fed Govt funding to higher education and nonprofit instns, by field, instn, agency, and State, FY82, annual rpt, 9627–17
- R&D-employed scientists and engineers salaries by degree, type of establishment, age, experience, and field, 1984, annual rpt, 3004–1
- R&D expenditures by higher education instns and federally funded centers, by field, source of funds, instn, and State, FY82, annual rpt, 9627–13
- R&D expenditures by source, and scientists education and employment, detailed data by field, selected years 1953-84, annual rpt, 9624–18

Biological sciences

R&D expenditures of higher education instns, and science and engineering employment and grad students, by field, 1972-83, biennial rpt, 9627–24

- R&D Fed Govt facilities and services available for private sector use, by field of science, 1984 biennial listing, 2224–4
- R&D Fed Govt funding, by function, agency, and program, selected years FY80-84 and proposed FY85, 26308–46
- R&D Fed Govt funding for all performers, by field and supporting agency, selected years FY60-84, annual rpt, 9627–20
- R&D funding by industry, program, and Federal agency, and high-technology trade performance, selected years 1960-FY84, 26306–6.77
- Science and engineering doctoral degree recipients, by field, sex, race, age, citizenship, postgrad employment and study status, State, and instn, 1960-82, 9626–6.16
- Science and engineering grad enrollment, fields of study, financial support, and other student and instn characteristics, 1975-82, annual survey, 9627–7
- Science and engineering grad program enrollment, by field, degree level, source of financial support, race, and Hispanic origin, 1975-81, 9626–2.134
- Science and engineering grad program enrollment by field, sources of financial support, and foreign students, 1975-82, 9626–2.141
- Science and engineering grads of 1980-81, employment and median salaries by level and field of degree, 1982, 9626–2.137
- Science and engineering grads of 1980-81, employment characteristics or grad enrollment, by degree level, field, sex, and race, 1982, 9627–25
- Scientists and engineers employed at universities and colleges, by field, sex, and instn, 1973-82, 9626–2.140
- Scientists and engineers employed at universities and colleges, by field, sex, State, and instn, Jan 1983 and selected trends from 1967, annual survey, 9627–11
- Scientists and engineers employed in energy-related fields, supply/demand and effects of R&D funding, by energy type, employer type, field, and age, 1962-91, annual rpt, 3004–19
- Scientists and engineers employment by sector and activity, and share female, black, and Asian descent, by field, 1982, 9626–2.142
- Scientists and engineers supply, employment, and education, by sex, race, Hispanic origin, and field, selected years 1965-83, biennial rpt, 9624–20
- Scientists, engineers, and technicians employed in private industry, by occupation and industry group, 1980-81, biennial rpt, 9627–23
- Scientists, engineers, and technicians needed in defense and nondefense industries, and supply/demand, by field, 1981-87, 9628–71
- Soviet Union-US science and technology exchange projects, man-hours, and funding, by Fed Govt agency and activity type, FY81-82, 7008–41

see also Botany
see also Genetics
see also Physiology
see also Zoology

Biological warfare agents

see Chemical and biological warfare agents

Biologics

see Pharmaceutical industry
see Vaccination and vaccines

Biomass energy

- Air pollutant emission effects of solar and biomass energy use, by region, and projected to 2000, 3408–30
- Budget of US, effects of Reagan Admin policy changes, by detailed program, FY85, annual rpt, 104–21
- Consumption by fuel type, and estimated supply from renewable resources, 1977 and projected 2000, hearing, 21448–30
- Consumption, by fuel type, economic sector, census div, and State, 1960-82, State Energy Data System annual rpt, 3164–39
- Consumption of energy, by type of air pollutant source and fuel, and State, 1981, annual rpt, 9194–14
- Cuba economic conditions, agricultural and industrial production and distribution, trade, and intl economic relations, 1970-82 and trends from 1957, 248–40
- DOE R&D projects and funding at natl labs, universities, and other instns, FY84, annual summary rpt, 3004–18.2
- Methane gas from straw- and manure-fed methane generator, research project technical characteristics, annual rpt, discontinued, 3304–14
- Natl Energy Policy Plan, energy supply, demand, and prices, by fuel and consuming sector, projected 1985-2010, biennial rpt, 3004–13
- Northeast and North Central regions biomass timber, green weight by biomass component and State, 1981, 1208–207
- Prices and expenditures for fuels, by consuming sector, State, and fuel type, 1970-81, annual rpt, 3164–64
- Research grants awarded competitively by USDA for agricultural science, food and nutrition, and energy dev, FY83, annual listing, 1744–1
- Research publications on energy of DOE and other sources, monthly listing, 3002–2
- Rocky Mountain States forest biomass, conversion from volume to dry weight, for softwood and hardwood species, 1977, 1208–200
- Southeast region biomass timber, trees, volume, and green weight by species, site and diameter class, and stand age, 1982, 1208–199
- Supply/demand and prices, by energy source and end-use sector and for 7 electric utilities, 1981-2000 with trends from 1960s, 3008–93
- Tennessee Valley ethanol production, feedstocks, facilities, tax incentives, and related farming data, by State, 1970s-83 and projected to 1992, 9808–69
- Timber harvest residue recovery for energy, cost-effectiveness of 3 logging systems, 1983 technical paper, 9806–2.37
- TVA Biomass Fuels Program, technologies and processes dev, costs, and resource requirements, 1970s-90s, series, 9806–9

Index by Subjects and Names

see also Alcohol fuels
see also Gasohol
see also Wood fuel

Biomedical engineering

- Biotechnology commercial uses, R&D funding and output, controls, and industry financial and operating data, for US and 5 countries, 1970s-83 and estimated 1984-85, 26358–98
- Biotechnology firms, patents, and trade by country, and effect of industry growth on US drug and chemical trade, selected years 1979-2000, 9886–4.78
- Census of Population, 1980: detailed socioeconomic and demographic characteristics, by age, sex, race, Hispanic origin, occupation, and industry, State rpt series, 2531–4
- DOD medical personnel, trainees, and accessions by source, by occupation, specialty, and service branch, FY83, annual rpt, 3544–24
- General Medical Sciences Natl Inst research programs and funding, FY83, annual rpt, 4474–12
- Genetically abnormal human cell cultures available to researchers, and cultures shipped, 1984 annual listing, 4474–23
- NIH Research Resources Div activities, accomplishments, and funding, by program, FY83, annual rpt, 4434–12
- R&D funding by industry, program, and Federal agency, and high-technology trade performance, selected years 1960-FY84, 26306–6.77
- Science and engineering doctoral degree recipients, by field, sex, race, age, citizenship, postgrad employment and study status, State, and instn, 1960-82, 9626–6.16
- Science and engineering grad enrollment, fields of study, financial support, and other student and instn characteristics, 1975-82, annual survey, 9627–7

Birch, Thomas W.

"Forest-Land Owners of New York", 1206–7.10

Birds and bird conservation

- Alaska Arctic Natl Wildlife Refuge resources, resident and visitor activities, and environmental impacts of energy exploration, 1983, annual update rpt, 5504–26
- California marine resources and environmental effects of proposed oil and gas dev, for 2 sanctuaries off central and northern coasts, 1980s and projected to 2006, hearing, 21448–30.1
- Coastal environmental and wildlife characteristics, use, and mgmt, for individual ecosystems, series, 5506–9
- Coastal environmental characteristics, fish, wildlife, and use, and population socioeconomic data, for individual areas, series, 5506–4
- Duck hunting stamp sales, with philatelic data and reproductions, 1983/84, annual fact sheet, 5504–25
- Environmental quality and protection programs, costs, and Fed Govt enforcement, 1983, detailed annual rpt, 484–1
- Estuary environmental characteristics, fish, wildlife, uses, and mgmt, for individual estuaries, series, 5506–7

Index by Subjects and Names

Births

Fish and Wildlife Service conservation and research project descriptions and results, by program, FY83, annual rpt, 5504–20

Forest, range, and associated waters use and mgmt assessment, and environmental impacts of Forest Service program options, 1977-2030 and trends from 1920, 1208–24

France Brittany coast oil spill cleanup and research costs, marine and tourism industry losses, and recreation losses of tourists and residents, 1971-79, 2178–13

Genetic resource (plant and animal) conservation, commercial uses, causes of depletion, and geographic sources, 1984 rpt, 5548–13

Great Lakes organochlorine residues in herring gull eggs, by monitoring site, selected years 1971-81, annual rpt, 14644–1.1

Imports of US, detailed TSUSA commodities by country of origin, 1983, annual rpt, 2424–4

Marine vertebrates off southeastern US coast, abundance and seasonal distribution, with oil and gas dev effects and lease status, early 1980s, 5508–85

Mexico and US range and wildlife characteristics, problems, and research strategies and needs, 1981 conf papers, 1208–197

Migratory Bird Treaty Act protected birds, population characteristics and potential impact of Fed Govt coal leasing, for 25 species, 1900s-82, 5508–88

Mourning dove population, by region and hunting and nonhunting State, 1984, annual rpt, 5504–15

Natl Forest System wildlife habitat and fishery improvements, use, and game population and harvest by species and forest, by region, FY83, annual rpt, 1204–31

Oil spill risk analyses for OCS proposed lease sale areas, series, 5736–2

Research of State fish and wildlife agencies, federally funded wildlife and bird projects and costs, by species and State, 1984, annual rpt, 5504–24

Southeastern US coast marine bird distribution, abundance, and oil spill effects, by species and State, 1820s-1982, 5508–72

Texas Padre and Mustang Islands, shorebird distribution, abundance, and oil spill effects, by species, 1979-81, 5508–86

Water Bank Program agreements, acreage, and Fed Govt payments, by State, FY72-83, annual rpt, 1804–21

Water Bank Program agreements, acreage, and Fed Govt payments, by State, monthly rpt, 1802–5

Wisconsin forest fires damage to timber, crops, game, waterfowl, and recreation sites, economic effects by county, 1980-82, 1208–198

Woodcock population and hunter harvest, by region and State, 1984 and trends from 1966, annual rpt, 5504–11

see also Hunting and trapping

see also Zoological parks

Birmingham, Ala.

Auto dealer repair workers, wages, and benefits, by occupation, size of establishment, and for 24 labor market areas, Nov 1982 survey, 6787–6.202

Census of Housing, 1980: occupancy and unit characteristics, by race, Hispanic origin, and city, SMSA rpt, 2473–1.93

Census of Population and Housing, 1980: detailed population and housing characteristics, by county, city, and census tract, SMSA rpt, 2551–2.93

Homeless population and characteristics, and temporary shelter operations, use, and user characteristics, for selected cities, various periods 1979-84, hearing, 21248–85

Housing and households detailed characteristics, and unit and neighborhood quality, by inside-outside central cities, 1980 survey, SMSA rpt, 2485–6.8

see also under By City and By SMSA or MSA in the "Index by Categories"

Birnbaum, Howard

"Managing Programs for the Elderly: Design of a Social Information System", 4652–1.402

Birth control

see Abortion

see Family planning

Birth defects

Agent Orange exposed Air Force personnel diseases and disorders, by disease type, age, and officer status, 1984 rpt, 3604–3

Birth defects, by region, 1977-81, annual rpt, 4204–1.3

Births by outcome, and mother's sociodemographic, life style, and maternity characteristics, 1980, article, 4102–1.422, 4102–1.423

Deaths and death rates, by cause and age, provisional 1982-83, US Vital Statistics annual rpt, 4144–7

Deaths and death rates by detailed cause and demographic characteristics, 1979 and selected trends, US Vital Statistics annual rpt, 4144–2.1

Deaths and death rates, by detailed geographic area, cause, and demographic characteristics, 1979, US Vital Statistics annual rpt, 4144–3

Deaths and death rates, by selected cause and demographic characteristics, 1981, US Vital Statistics advance rpt, 4146–5.78

Deaths and death rates, by selected cause and demographic characteristics, 1982, US Vital Statistics advance rpt, 4146–5.81

Deaths by principal or contributing cause, with type of injury reported in accidental, poisoning, and violent deaths, by age, sex, and race, 1978, 4146–5.76

Dental Research Natl Inst research and training funds awarded, by recipient instn, FY83, annual listing, 4474–19

Disability Insurance beneficiaries sociodemographic and medical characteristics, 1977-79, annual rpt, 4744–20

Head Start Project enrollment of handicapped children, by handicap, State, and for Indian and migrant programs, 1982, annual rpt, 4604–1

Hospital discharges and length of stay, by patient characteristics, facility size, procedure performed, diagnosis, and region, 1982, annual rpt, 4147–13.78

Infant deaths by detailed cause, geographic location, age, race, and sex, 1979, US Vital Statistics annual rpt, 4144–2.2

see also under By Disease in the "Index by Categories"

Birthplace

Aircraft hijackers, and date and place of birth and race or ethnic group, 1961-83, annual rpt, 7504–31.3

Births and birth rates, by detailed demographic characteristics and geographic area, 1979 and trends, US Vital Statistics annual rpt, 4144–1

Census of Agriculture, 1982: farms, farmland, production, finances, and operator characteristics, by island, final outlying area rpt, 2331–1.54

Census of Population and Housing, 1980: detailed population and housing characteristics, by county, city, and census tract, State and SMSA rpt series, 2551–2

Census of Population, 1980: detailed socioeconomic and demographic characteristics, by age, sex, race, Hispanic origin, occupation, and industry, State rpt series, 2531–4

Census of Population, 1980: detailed socioeconomic characteristics, by county, city, and inside-outside SMSAs and central cities, State rpt series, 2531–3

Deaths in US by State and by outlying area or country of birth, 1979, US Vital Statistics annual rpt, 4144–2.1

Foreign women sociodemographic, economic, and fertility characteristics, with comparisons to men, by country, 1960s-85, world region rpt series, 2326–15

Hispanic Americans socioeconomic and demographic characteristics, and compared to non-Hispanics, selected years 1970-83, chartbook, 2328–48

Immigration, and alien residents, workers, visitors, deportations, and naturalizations, by country of birth, FY81, annual rpt, 6264–2

Older persons by demographic, socioeconomic, and health characteristics, selected years 1900-81 and projected to 2050, Current Population Rpt, 2546–2.125

Refugee and alien arrivals and resettlements in US, by State, outlying area, country of birth and citizenship, age, sex, and sponsoring agency, monthly rpt, 4702–3

Refugee arrivals in US by world area of origin and State of settlement, and Fed Govt intl and domestic assistance costs, FY85, annual rpt, 7004–16

Refugee migration, settlement status, and assistance, by world area and country of origin and asylum, as of May 1984, annual rpt, 7004–15

Births

Asian and Pacific Islands Americans births by ethnic origin and sociodemographic and birth characteristics, with comparisons to blacks and whites, 1978-80, 4146–5.75

Births and birth and fertility rates, by State, provisional 1982-83, US Vital Statistics annual rpt, 4144–7

Births and birth rates, by demographic and birth characteristics, 1981 with trends from 1940, US Vital Statistics advance rpt, 4146–5.73

Births and birth rates, by detailed demographic characteristics and geographic area, 1979 and trends, US Vital Statistics annual rpt, 4144–1

Births

Births and birth rates, by parent and birth characteristics and infant condition at birth, 1982 and trends from 1940, US Vital Statistics annual advance rpt, 4146–5.79

Births, and birth rates for unmarried and all women, by race of child, age and Hispanic origin of mother, and State, 1980, 4147–21.42

Births, fertility rates, expected births, and childless women, by socioeconomic characteristics, June 1982, annual Current Population Rpt, 2546–1.386

Births, fertility rates, expected births, and childless women, by socioeconomic characteristics, June 1983, advance annual Current Population Rpt, 2546–1.385

Births, fertility rates, expected births, and childless women, by socioeconomic characteristics, June 1983, annual Current Population Rpt, 2546–1.393

Birthspacing by period of woman's birth and marriage, period of child's birth, and sociodemographic characteristics, June 1980, Current Population Rpt, 2546–1.387

Certificates of birth, death, marriage, and divorce, records availability and vital statistics records offices, by State, 1984 annual listing, 4124–7

Cesarean and total births in hospitals affiliated and not affiliated with medical schools, by characteristics of mother, birth, and hospital, 1977, 4186–6.4

County and City Data Book, detailed socioeconomic and demographic data for States, counties, and cities, selected years 1976-82, 2328–1

Developing countries govt policy, and AID and other foreign assistance, effects on private sector dev and socioeconomic conditions, with case studies for 6 countries, 1960s-80, 9918–12

Food aid special supplemental program for women, infants, and children, effectiveness and participant characteristics, 1973-82, GAO rpt, 26131–10

Foreign population size and growth rates, and latest available benchmark demographic data, by country, 1950-83, biennial rpt, 2324–4

Foreign women sociodemographic, economic, and fertility characteristics, with comparisons to men, by country, 1960s-85, world region rpt series, 2326–15

Health characteristics of infants, by mother's sociodemographic, lifestyle, and maternity characteristics, 1980, article, 4102–1

Health condition and health care resources, use, and expenditures, 1970s-82 with trends and projections 1900-2000, annual compilation, 4144–11

Hispanic Americans births and birth and fertility rates, by detailed Hispanic origin, characteristics of mother, birth, and prenatal care, and for 22 States, 1981, 4146–5.80

Indian births, morbidity, and deaths and rates, and health services facilities and use, 1954-83, annual compilation, 4104–7

Indian Health Service hospital admissions, discharges, births, total and occupied beds, length of stay, and outpatient visits, by area and facility, quarterly rpt, 4102–3

Low birth weight births by maternal risk including smoking, blood pressure, and blood value factors, by mothers age, race, and Hispanic origin, 1981, annual rpt, 4205–24

Low birth weight incidence and Apgar scores of infants, by infant and mother characteristics, birthplace, and attendant, 1978, article, 4102–1.414

Midwife-attended and out-of-hospital births, by mother's sociodemographic and prenatal care characteristics and infant race and birthweight, 1978-79 with trends from 1935, 4147–21.40

Military medical facilities of DOD in US and abroad, admissions, beds, outpatient visits, and live births, by service branch, quarterly rpt, 3542–15

Navy and Marine Corps disease incidence, medical care, and deaths, by detailed diagnosis, and medical personnel and workloads, 1978-79, annual rpt, 3804–1

Navy medical facilities, live births, by facility, quarterly rpt, 3802–1

Outlying area population size and components of change, by area, 1970-82, Current Population Rpt, 2546–3.127

Population demographic and economic characteristics, 1982 with projections of population size to 2050, annual Current Population Rpt, 2546–2.119

Population size and components of change, by MSA and county, 1980-82, annual State Current Population Rpt series, 2546–4

Population size and components of change, by outlying area, 1980-83, Current Population Rpt, 2546–3.134

Population size and components of change, by region and State, 1970-83, Current Population Rpt, 2546–3.133

Population size and components of change, by region and State, 1970s-83 with projections to 2050, annual Current Population Rpt, 2546–2.119

Population size and components of change, by region, census div, and State, July 1981-83, annual Current Population Rpt, 2546–3.128

Population size and components of change, projected under 3 fertility assumptions, 1982-2080 with trends from 1900, SSA actuarial rpt, 4706–1.92

Population size by single years of age, and components of change, by sex and race, projected 1983-2080, final Current Population Rpt, 2546–3.132

Poverty-level persons and families, by income source, hours of work, earnings, taxes, and family characteristics, various periods 1959-84, 21788–131

Pregnancy health counseling effect on smoking, diet, delivery costs, and birth weight, by sociodemographic characteristics and pregnancy history, 1983 article, 4102–1.401

Puerto Rico educational enrollment, finance, completions, curricula, and personnel by instn, and health and vital statistics, selected years 1970-83, hearings, 21348–93

Soviet Union industrial and agricultural production by selected commodity, and demographic trends and projections by Republic, 1950s-2000, hearings, 23848–180

Index by Subjects and Names

Statistical Abstract of US, social, political, and economic data, 1950s-83 and trends, annual rpt, 2324–1.1

Teenage girls births and rates, and distribution of births with low birth weight and Apgar scores, by mother and infant characteristics, 1970-81, 4147–21.41

Teenage girls births and sexual experience by race, abortions, and birth control use, by age, 1970s-80 with birth trends from 1920, hearings, 21968–29

TTPI budget, vital statistics, and health services data, often by TTPI govt, FY83 and selected trends, annual rpt, 7004–6.1

Vital statistics, births, marriages, divorces, and deaths, provisional data, monthly rpt, 4142–1

see also Abortion

see also Birth defects

see also Birthplace

see also Fertility

see also Fetal deaths

see also Illegitimacy

see also Infant mortality

see also Maternity

see also Obstetrics and gynecology

Bishop, Christine E.

"Return to Nursing Home Investment: Issues for Public Policy", 4652–1.417

Bisignano, Joseph

"Monetary Policy Regimes and International Term Structures of Interest Rates", 9393–8.401

Bismarck, N.Dak.

Census of Housing, 1980: occupancy and unit characteristics, by race, Hispanic origin, and city, SMSA rpt, 2473–1.94

Census of Population and Housing, 1980: detailed population and housing characteristics, by county, city, and census tract, SMSA rpt, 2551–2.94

see also under By SMSA or MSA in the "Index by Categories"

Bismuth

see Metals and metal industries

Bixby, Ann K.

"Benefits and Beneficiaries Under Public Employee Retirement Programs, 1980", 4742–1.403

"Public Social Welfare Expenditures, FY81-82", 4746–16.1

"Social Welfare Expenditures, 1981 and 1982", 4742–1.425

Black Americans

Agriculture census, 1982: farms, farmland, production, finances, and operator characteristics, by county, final State rpt series, 2331–1

Alabama rural black population, education, employment, health services, and economic status, for 16 counties, selected years 1970-81, 11048–180

Bankruptcy (personal), filers by debt type, employment and financial status, race, and Hispanic origin, 1982 survey, hearings, 21528–57.2

Cancer cases, incidence, deaths, and death rates, by body site, age, race, Hispanic origin, and sex, for 10 geographic areas, 1973-81, 4478–130

Census of Housing, 1980: inventory, occupancy, and unit characteristics, changes from 1973 by region and inside-outside SMSAs and central cities, series, 2473–3

Index by Subjects and Names

Black students

Census of Housing, 1980: occupancy and unit characteristics of SMSAs and central cities, by race, Hispanic origin, and city, State and SMSA rpt series, 2473–1

Census of Population and Housing, 1980: detailed population and housing characteristics, by county, city, and census tract, State and SMSA rpt series, 2551–2

Census of Population, 1980: detailed socioeconomic and demographic characteristics, by age, sex, race, Hispanic origin, occupation, and industry, State rpt series, 2531–4

Census of Population, 1980: detailed socioeconomic characteristics, by county, city, and inside-outside SMSAs and central cities, State rpt series, 2531–3

Census of Population, 1980: migration since 1975, by county and selected demographic characteristics, supplementary rpt, 2535–1.14

Census of Population, 1980: migration since 1975, by State and selected demographic characteristics, supplementary rpt, 2535–1.13

Central cities and suburbs population and employment, effect of region, neighborhood, population, and labor characteristics, 1970-80, technical paper, 9387–8.89

County and City Data Book, detailed socioeconomic and demographic data for States, counties, and cities, selected years 1976-82, 2328–1

Employment, unemployment, and labor force, by demographic and employment characteristics, State, and for 30 metro areas and 11 large cities, 1983, annual rpt, 6744–7

Employment, unemployment, and labor force participation by race, detailed Hispanic origin, and sex, quarterly rpt, 6742–18

Handbook of Labor Statistics, employment, earnings, hours, and labor force characteristics, 1982 and trends, detailed annual rpt, 6724–1

Health care services for elderly, knowledge, use, and factors affecting service quality, by race and Hispanic origin, 1984 article, 4652–1.406

Income and socioeconomic characteristics of persons, families, and households, detailed cross-tabulations, Current Population Rpt series, 2546–6

Marriages, divorces, and rates, by detailed demographic and geographic characteristics, 1979 and trends, US Vital Statistics annual rpt, 4144–4

Medical residents by specialty and race, and minority medical faculty by race and Hispanic origin, selected years 1980-83, 4102–1.412

Occupational employment and percent black, women, and part-time workers, by detailed occupation, 1982, biennial rpt, 6744–3

Population demographic, social, and economic characteristics, Current Population Rpt series, 2546–1

Population size and change for metro and nonmetro areas and central cities by census div, and growth of areas with large black and aged populations, 1970-82, 2328–47

Poverty population size, effect of counting public noncash transfers as income by recipient characteristics, 1979-83, 2626–2.52

Poverty status of young adults related to motivation, psychological factors, and family characteristics, by race and sex, 1970s-82, longitudinal studies, 4008–65

Scientists and engineers employment by sector and activity, and share female, black, and Asian descent, by field, 1982, 9626–2.142

Statistical Abstract of US, social, political, and economic data, 1950s-83 and trends, annual rpt, 2324–1.1

Vocational training bilingual projects, participants, characteristics, and costs, by program, FY82, annual rpt, 4804–26

see also Black colleges

see also Black students

see also Minority businesses

see also Racial discrimination

see also under By Race in the "Index by Categories"

Black colleges

Desegregation in higher education, Louisiana funding for black instn integration, and Virginia students needed to meet desegregation goals by race, by instn, selected years 1978-85, hearings, 21348–91

Directory of black colleges and universities, annual listing, discontinued, 4004–28

Enrollment, degrees conferred, revenues, and expenditures at predominantly black instns, 1981, annual rpt, 4824–2.13

Howard University salaries, academic standing, medical research, and library operations, and finances of Howard Inn, selected years 1976-83, GAO rpt, 26121–74

Natl Endowment for Humanities activities and grants, FY83, annual rpt, 9564–2

R&D and science-related Fed Govt funding to higher education and nonprofit instns, by field, instn, agency, and State, FY82, annual rpt, 9627–17

R&D expenditures by higher education instns and federally funded centers, by field, source of funds, instn, and State, FY82, annual rpt, 9627–13

Science and engineering grad enrollment, fields of study, financial support, and other student and instn characteristics, 1975-82, annual survey, 9627–7

Scientists and engineers employed at universities and colleges, by field, sex, State, and instn, Jan 1983 and selected trends from 1967, annual survey, 9627–11

Black lung

Benefit claims and benefits, and trust fund receipts by source and disbursements, 1982, annual rpt, 6504–3

Benefits, and beneficiaries with representative payees by age and relation to payee, by Fed Govt cash program, as of 1983, GAO rpt, 26121–85

Benefits, beneficiary characteristics, and trust funds of OASDHI, Medicaid, SSI, and other social insurance and public welfare programs, selected years 1950-82, annual rpt, 4744–3.9, 4744–3.10

Benefits by type under Federal black lung and State workers compensation programs, 1970-80, article, 4742–1.414

Benefits to miners, widows, and dependents reported monthly, and by State reported quarterly, monthly rpt, 4742–1.6, 4742–1.13

Benefits under each State and Federal workers compensation program by payment source, and State and black lung benefits by type, 1979-81, article, 4742–1.409

Benefits under State workers compensation programs and Fed Govt black lung program, 1980-82, article, 4742–1.424

Budget of US, effects of Reagan Admin policy changes, by detailed program, FY85, annual rpt, 104–21

Children and youth benefitting from Fed Govt public welfare programs and tax expenditures, participation and funding for 71 programs, FY81-83, 21968–30

Cost control proposals for Fed Govt programs and mgmt, 3-year savings by function and agency, and financial and operating data, 1960s-81, 16908–1.6

Exams for black lung, incidence among coal miners, and NIOSH research activities, annual rpt, suspended, 4244–1

Excise tax collections of IRS for black lung benefits, quarterly press release, 8302–1

Fed Govt black lung disability trust fund receipts, expenditures, assets, and liabilities, monthly rpt, 8102–9.10

HHS aid to each State and local govt or private instn, amount obligated, funding agency, and program, FY83, annual listing, 4004–3

SSA programs, finances, staff, and litigation, FY83, annual rpt, 4704–6

Tax collections, refunds, and taxes due IRS, by State and region, and IRS court activity and operating expenses, FY83, annual rpt, 8304–3.3

Taxes on coal for surface and underground mines, by type of tax and State, 1984 rpt, 11128–1

Black, Stuart C.

"Animal Investigation Program for the Nevada Test Site: 1957-81", 9234–5

Black students

Alabama rural black population, education, employment, health services, and economic status, for 16 counties, selected years 1970-81, 11048–180

Crime in public schools, assaults and robberies of teachers and minority and other students, and vandalism incidents, 1976/77, 4808–12

Digest of Education Statistics, detailed data on students, staff, finances, and facilities, 1982 and selected trends, annual rpt, 4824–2

Enrollment of persons aged 3-34, by grade level and student characteristics, Oct 1982, advance annual Current Population Rpt, 2546–1.391

Science and engineering grad enrollment, fields of study, financial support, and other student and instn characteristics, 1975-82, annual survey, 9627–7

Virginia higher education new enrollment, and students needed to meet desegregation goals, by race and instn, selected years 1978-85, hearings, 21348–91

see also under By Race in the "Index by Categories"

Blacksin, Jack

Blacksin, Jack
"Statistics of Income for Individuals: A Historical Perspective", 8308–28.1

Blaich, Oswald P.
"Argentina's Grain Marketing System", 1528–185

Blais, Lynn E.
"Do We Want Large Social Security Surpluses?", 9373–1.414

Blanchard, Bonnie M.
"Yellowstone Grizzly Bear Investigations, Report of the Interagency Study Team, 1982", 5544–4

Blanchfield, Lisa A.
"Environmental Surveillance for the INEL Radioactive Waste Management Complex and Other Areas, Annual Report, 1983", 3354–10

Blaylock, James R.
"Household Characteristics and the Demand for Vegetables and Potatoes", 1561–11.401
"Household Characteristics, Frequency of Use, and the Demand for Dairy Products", 1561–2.404
"Household Expenditures for Fruits, Vegetables, and Potatoes", 1548–236
"Scaling Household Nutrient Data", 1502–3.401

Blazer, Evelyn
"Livestock and Meat Statistics, 1983", 1564–6

Bleakly, Kenneth
"State Community Development Block Grant Program: The First Year's Experience", 5188–106

Blind
American Printing House for Blind, Fed Govt funding by agency and State, FY83, annual rpt, 2464–2
Disability Insurance beneficiaries sociodemographic and medical characteristics, 1977-79, annual rpt, 4744–20
Fed Govt minority group and handicapped employment, by race, Hispanic origin, disability, sex, and employment characteristics, as of Sept 1982, biennial rpt, 9844–27
Handicapped children early education research and service project activities and characteristics, and grants to States for program dev, 1983-84, annual listing, 4804–30
Head Start Project enrollment of handicapped children, by handicap, State, and for Indian and migrant programs, 1982, annual rpt, 4604–1
Income tax returns of individuals, detailed data, 1982, annual rpt, 8304–2
Mail (free) for blind and handicapped, USPS revenue forgone by class of mail, FY83, annual rpt, 9864–5.3
Mail (free) for blind and handicapped, volume and costs, FY83, annual rpt, 9864–2
Mail (free) for blind and handicapped, volume and weight, quarterly rpt, 9862–1
Mail (free) for blind, handicapped, and servicemen, USPS operating costs itemized by class of mail, FY83, annual rpt, 9864–4
Recreation at outdoor Fed Govt facilities, Golden Age and Golden Access Passports issued, by agency, 1983, annual rpt, 5544–14

Special education programs for handicapped children, enrollment, staff, and funding, by handicap, age, and State, 1981/82-1982/83, annual rpt, 4944–4
Tax expenditures, Fed Govt revenues foregone through income tax deductions and exclusions by type, and effect of Deficit Reduction Act, FY84-89, annual rpt, 21784–10
Vending stand concessions operated by blind on Federal and non-Federal property, and income, FY82-83, annual rpt, 4944–2
Veterans aged 55 and over, socioeconomic characteristics, economic resources, health care and status, and actual and expected use of VA benefits, 1983 survey, 9928–29
Vocational rehabilitation State agency expenditures, caseloads, rehabilitations, and staff, under Section 110 of the Rehabilitation Act, by State, FY82, annual rpt, 4944–9
Vocationally rehabilitated persons under State agency programs, by sociodemographic characteristics and disabling condition, FY79-81, annual rpt, 4944–6
Workshops for blind and handicapped, Fed Govt procurement of goods and services and participating workshops, FY78-82, annual rpt, 11714–1
see also Aid to Blind
see also Supplemental Security Income

Blood
Acquired immune deficiency syndrome (AIDS) cases, and research funding and activities, monthly rpt, 4042–2
Exports of US, detailed commodities by country of destination, monthly rpt, 2422–3
Exports of US, detailed Schedule B commodities by country of destination, 1983, annual rpt, 2424–9
Heart attack and cancer incidence and deaths in men aged 35-59, effects of lowering blood cholesterol levels, with background data on other risk factors, 1973-83, 4478–145
Lead levels in blood by sociodemographic and behavioral characteristics, and potential workplace exposure, 1976-80, 4147–11.201
Nutrition status of infants and children, blood and height-weight indicators, and low birth weight risk factors, by age, race, and Hispanic origin, 1981, annual rpt, 4205–24
Price indexes and prices for producers of blood and plasma products, monthly 1983, annual supplement, 6762–6, 6764–2
Red Cross blood program collection, production, distribution activities, technical services, research, and processing fees, 1982/83, annual rpt, 29254–3
Red Cross program operations and financial statements, 1982/83, annual rpt, 29254–1
see also Blood diseases and disorders
see also Blood pressure

Blood diseases and disorders
Deaths and death rates, by cause and age, provisional 1982-83, US Vital Statistics annual rpt, 4144–7

Index by Subjects and Names

Deaths and death rates by detailed cause and demographic characteristics, 1979 and selected trends, US Vital Statistics annual rpt, 4144–2.1
Deaths and death rates, by detailed geographic area, cause, and demographic characteristics, 1979, US Vital Statistics annual rpt, 4144–3
Deaths and death rates, by selected cause and demographic characteristics, 1981, US Vital Statistics advance rpt, 4146–5.78
Deaths and death rates, by selected cause and demographic characteristics, 1982, US Vital Statistics advance rpt, 4146–5.81
Disability Insurance beneficiaries sociodemographic and medical characteristics, 1977-79, annual rpt, 4744–20
Hospital discharges and length of stay, by patient characteristics, facility size, procedure performed, diagnosis, and region, 1982, annual rpt, 4147–13.78
Infant deaths by detailed cause, geographic location, age, race, and sex, 1979, US Vital Statistics annual rpt, 4144–2.2
Natl Heart, Lung, and Blood Inst activities and funding, with morbidity and mortality data, various periods 1940-88, annual rpt, 4474–22
Natl Heart, Lung, and Blood Inst, Advisory Council recommended programs and budget, FY85-89, annual rpt, 4474–11
Natl Heart, Lung, and Blood Inst organization, disease and mortality data, and funds and recipients, FY83 with trends from 1900, annual fact book, 4474–15
State govt maternal and child health funding, and admin of Fed Govt block grants, by program for 13 States, 1981-83, GAO rpt, 26121–70
see also Blood pressure
see also under By Disease in the "Index by Categories"

Blood pressure
Alcohol abuse and hypertension prevalence, by blood pressure and drinks consumed per day, 1984 article, 4102–1.434
Births of low birth weight by maternal risk including smoking, blood pressure, and blood value factors, by mothers age, race, and Hispanic origin, 1981, annual rpt, 4205–24
Child blood pressure and heart rate effects of reading aloud, results of study of Baltimore, Md, 5th graders, 1984 article, 4102–1.415
Costs of hypertension screening and treatment at 9 worksites, 1978-80, 4478–148
Deaths and death rates, by detailed geographic area, cause, and demographic characteristics, 1979, US Vital Statistics annual rpt, 4144–3
Health condition and health care resources, use, and expenditures, 1970s-82 with trends and projections 1900-2000, annual compilation, 4144–11
Health habits associated with 10 major death causes, prevalence of 8 risk factors in selected States, 1981-83 surveys, article, 4202–7.405
Health habits of adults, including physical activity, smoking, alcohol use, hypertension, and seat belt use, by age and sex, 1982, annual rpt, 4204–1.3

Index by Subjects and Names

Blue collar workers

Heart attack and cancer incidence and deaths in men aged 35-59, effects of lowering blood cholesterol levels, with background data on other risk factors, 1973-83, 4478–145

Hypertension prevalence and control, and change in death rates from all causes and cardiovascular disease, selected years 1971-82, article, 4102–1.432

Internist office visits and drugs provided, by characteristics of visit, patient, and physician, and location, 1980-81, 4147–13.80

Natl Heart, Lung, and Blood Inst activities and funding, with morbidity and mortality data, various periods 1940-88, annual rpt, 4474–22

Obstetrician-gynecologist office visits and drugs used, by visit reason, diagnosis, treatment, and patient and physician characteristics, 1980-81, 4147–13.76

Physicians (not office-based) visits by reason, diagnosis, treatment, patient and physician characteristics, and physician primary activity, 1980, 4147–13.77

State govt preventive health services funding by program, Fed Govt block grants, and opinions on State program admin, for 13 States, FY81-84, GAO rpt, 26121–88

Surgeon office visits and drugs provided, by characteristics of visit, patient, and physician, and location, 1980-81, 4147–13.79

Bloom, Abby L.

"Prospects for Primary Health Care in Africa: Another Look at the Sine Saloum Rural Health Project in Senegal", 9916–3.20

Bloomington, Ill.

Census of Housing, 1980: occupancy and unit characteristics, by race, Hispanic origin, and city, SMSA rpt, 2473–1.96

Census of Population and Housing, 1980: detailed population and housing characteristics, by county, city, and census tract, SMSA rpt, 2551–2.96

Housing vacancy rates for single and multifamily units and mobile homes, by county, city, and ZIP code, 1983, annual metro area rpt, 9304–18.2

see also under By SMSA or MSA in the "Index by Categories"

Bloomington, Ind.

Census of Housing, 1980: occupancy and unit characteristics, by race, Hispanic origin, and city, SMSA rpt, 2473–1.95

Census of Population and Housing, 1980: detailed population and housing characteristics, by county, city, and census tract, SMSA rpt, 2551–2.95

Wages by occupation, and benefits for office and plant workers, 1983 labor market area survey rpt, 6785–3.2

see also under By SMSA or MSA in the "Index by Categories"

Blount, Joseph H.

"Pelvic Inflammatory Disease: Incidence and Trends in Private Practice", 4202–7.404

Blue collar workers

Census of Housing, 1980: structural, financial, and householder characteristics, by region and State, 2475–4

Census of Population and Housing, 1980: detailed population and housing characteristics, by county, city, and census tract, State and SMSA rpt series, 2551–2

Census of Population, 1980: detailed socioeconomic and demographic characteristics, by age, sex, race, Hispanic origin, occupation, and industry, State rpt series, 2531–4

Census of Population, 1980: detailed socioeconomic characteristics, by county, city, and inside-outside SMSAs and central cities, State rpt series, 2531–3

Census of Population, 1980: labor force, by sex, detailed occupation, and region, with comparison to 1970 census, supplementary rpt, 2535–1.12

Disability (work-related), incidence among men aged 22-64 related to sociodemographic and employment characteristics and to self-evaluated mental stress, 1972-74, 4746–5.43

DOD-owned manufacturing and R&D facilities, operating data by selected SIC 2- to 3-digit industry, State, and SMSA, 1982, annual Current Industrial Rpt, 2506–3.4

Earnings of manufacturing production workers, by State, with adjustments for industrial mix variations, selected years 1973-82, article, 9373–1.407

Employee benefits in private industry, coverage by benefit type and provisions and occupational group, 1983, annual rpt, 6784–19

Employment and economic conditions, alternative BLS projections to 1995 with selected trends for 1959-82, 6728–29

Employment by detailed occupation, for 29 SIC 2-digit nonmanufacturing industries, 1981 BLS survey, 6748–60

Employment, earnings, and hours, by SIC 4-digit nonfarm industry, monthly 1974-Feb 1984, annual update, 6744–4

Employment, earnings, and hours, monthly press release, 6742–5

Employment situation, earnings, hours, and other BLS economic indicators, transcripts of BLS Commissioner's monthly testimony, periodic rpt, 23846–4

Employment, unemployment, and labor force, by demographic and employment characteristics, State, and for 30 metro areas and 11 large cities, 1983, annual rpt, 6744–7

Fed Govt civilian employment by occupation, total and for 25 agencies, as of Oct 1983, annual article, 9842–1.405

Fed Govt minority group and handicapped employment, by race, Hispanic origin, disability, sex, and employment characteristics, as of Sept 1982, biennial rpt, 9844–27

Fed Govt pay comparability with private industry, and recommended and actual pay increase, various dates 1971-84, annual rpt, 10104–1

Fed Govt programs and mgmt cost control proposals, 3-year savings by function and agency, and financial and operating data, 1960s-81, 16908–1.27

Foreign women sociodemographic, economic, and fertility characteristics, with comparisons to men, by country, 1960s-85, world region rpt series, 2326–15

Handbook of Labor Statistics, employment, earnings, hours, and labor force characteristics, 1982 and trends, detailed annual rpt, 6724–1

Imports injury to US industries from foreign subsidized products, investigations with background financial and operating data for selected industries and products, series, 9886–15

Imports injury to US industries from import sales at less than fair value, investigations with background financial and operating data, series, 9886–14

Imports injury to US industries from removal of duties on foreign subsidized products, investigations with background financial and operating data, series, 9886–18

Income of households, families, and persons, by detailed socioeconomic characteristics and region, 1982, annual Current Population Rpt, 2546–6.39

Manufacturing census, 1982: financial and operating data, by SIC 2- to 4-digit industry, State, SMSA, and county, preliminary census div rpt series, 2491–3

Manufacturing census, 1982: financial and operating data, for SIC 4-digit industries by product, preliminary rpt series, 2491–1

Minority group and women's employment, by occupational group, SIC 2- to 3-digit industry, State, and SMSA, 1981, annual rpt, 9244–1

Natl income and product, comprehensive accounts and components, *Survey of Current Business,* monthly rpt, monthly and annual tables, 2702–1.27

Occupational manpower needs and supply by detailed occupation, and educational and training program enrollees and grads by detailed field, 1982 and 1995, biennial rpt, 6744–3

Occupational Outlook Handbook, 1984-85 biennial rpt, 6744–1

Pension plans with postretirement benefit increases, participants and average increase by occupational group and plan characteristics, 1978-81, article, 6722–1.453

Poverty status of families and persons, by detailed socioeconomic characteristics, 1982, annual Current Population Rpt, 2546–6.40

Seat belt use by blue and white collar workers, results of Virginia projects to increase use, 1983, article, 7762–9.409

Southeastern States manufacturing production workers average hours and earnings, for 8 States, monthly press release, 6942–7

Southwestern States manufacturing production workers average hours and earnings, for 5 States, monthly rpt, 6962–2

Washington State deaths by sex, cause, and detailed occupation, summary data from occupational mortality study, 1950-79, 4248–47

Women's employment and earnings, by labor force and socioeconomic characteristics, and compared to men, 1978-81 and trends from 1940s, 6568–29

see also Area wage surveys

see also Industry wage surveys

see also under By Occupation in the "Index by Categories"

see also under names of specific industries or industry groups

Blue Cross-Blue Shield

Blue Cross-Blue Shield

Births (cesarean and total) in hospitals affiliated and not affiliated with medical schools, by characteristics of mother, birth, and hospital, 1977, 4186–6.4

Employee benefits in private industry, coverage by benefit type and provisions and occupational group, 1983, annual rpt, 6784–19

Fed Govt civilian health benefit plans enrollment and premiums, for individual private and employee organization plans, FY81-82, annual rpt, 9844–1.2

FTC budget authority and expenditures for regulatory analysis, by prospective regulation and contractor, 1983, hearings, 21528–56

Hospital and physician reimbursement by patient disease type and severity category, and patients in 2 or more categories by coverage type, FY80-83, article, 4652–1.426

Medicare program operations and admin efficiency, Blue Shield participants, and end-stage renal disease program activity, FY81, annual rpt, 4654–5

Michigan health funding, Blue Cross-Blue Shield and welfare participation, and unemployment, poverty, and food assistance by county, 1979-83, hearing, 21348–86

Older persons health status, health services use and expenditures by type, Medicare enrollment and reimbursement, and private insurance coverage, 1977-84, article, 4652–1.420

Premiums of private health insurance plans, and benefits by type of administering insurer and insurer at risk, 1983 and trends from 1965, article, 4652–1.430

Blyth, James E.

"Primary Forest Products Industry and Timber Use, Missouri, 1980", 1206–10.6

"Pulpwood Production in the North-Central Region, By County, 1982", 1204–19

Board for International Broadcasting

Budget of US Appendix, detailed budgets and personnel summaries, by agency, FY85, annual rpt, 104–3

Budget of US, appropriations, outlays, balances, and budget receipts, by govtl branch and agency, FY83, annual rpt, 8104–2

Radio Free Europe and Radio Liberty broadcast and financial data, with comparisons to other intl broadcasters, FY83, annual rpt, 10314–1

Board of Parole

see U.S. Parole Commission

Boarding houses

see Rooming and boarding houses

Boats and boating

Army Corps of Engineers water resources dev projects, recreation activities by district and project, 1982, annual rpt, 3754–5

Census of Population, 1980: detailed socioeconomic and demographic characteristics, by age, sex, race, Hispanic origin, occupation, and industry, State rpt series, 2531–4

Coastal environmental characteristics, fish, wildlife, and use, and population socioeconomic data, for individual areas, series, 5506–4

County Business Patterns: establishments, employees, and payrolls, by SIC 4-digit industry and county, 1981, annual State rpt series, 2326–8

County Business Patterns: establishments, employees, and payrolls, by SIC 4-digit industry and county, 1982, annual State rpt series, 2326–6

Employment, earnings, and hours, by selected SIC 1- to 4-digit industry, State, and for 278 major labor areas, 1939-83, annual rpt, 6744–5

Employment, earnings, and hours, by SIC 4-digit nonfarm industry, monthly 1974-Feb 1984, annual update, 6744–4

Energy use in transportation sector by mode, fuel supplies, and demographic and economic determinants of vehicle use, 1970s-83, annual rpt, 3304–5

Exports and imports of US, detailed SIC-based commodities by world area, 1983, annual rpts, 2424–6

Exports and imports of US, totals and as percent of domestic production, by SIC 2- to 5-digit commodity, 1981, annual rpt, 2424–3

Exports of US, detailed commodities by country of destination, monthly rpt, 2422–3

Exports of US, detailed Schedule B commodities by country of destination, 1983, annual rpt, 2424–9

Exports of US, detailed Schedule E commodities by mode of transport and world area and country of destination, 1983, annual rpts, 2424–5

Finances, operations, vehicles, equipment, accidents, and energy use, by mode of transport, 1955-84, annual rpt, 7304–2

Fishermen (ocean sport), fishing activities, and catch by species, by fisherman characteristics, State, and coastal region, series, 2166–17

Fishery and fish processing employment, firms, and vessels, 1950s-83, annual rpt, 2164–1.10

Fishing (ocean sport) effort and catch, and Natl Marine Fisheries Service tagging and research activity, by species and location, 1983, annual rpt, 2164–7

Fishing diesel and sail-assisted boats in Hawaiian waters, fuel use, earnings, and operating costs, with fuel and fish price indexes, various periods 1967-81, article, 2162–1.401

Foreign market and trade for sporting goods and recreational equipment and vehicles, country market research rpts, 2045–14

Govt census, 1982: State govt payments to local govts, by program, source of funds, level of govt, and State, with trends from 1902, 2460–3

Great Lakes trade, by SITC 3-digit commodity, port, vessel type, world area, and country, 1982, annual rpt, 7744–3

Idaho and Montana recreation sites of Forest Service, itemized operating and maintenance costs by type of site, 1980, 1208–202

Imports of US, detailed Schedule A commodities by country and world area of origin, and mode of transport, 1983, annual rpts, 2424–2

Imports of US, detailed Schedule A commodities by country, monthly rpt, 2422–2

Imports of US, detailed TSUSA commodities by country of origin, 1983, annual rpt, 2424–4

Income tax returns of corporations, detailed income and tax items by industry, 1981, annual rpt, 8304–4

Income tax returns of sole proprietorships, detailed data by industry div and selected industry group, 1981, annual rpt, 8304–7

Income tax returns of sole proprietorships, receipts, deductions by type, payroll, and net income, by major industry, 1982, annual article, 8302–2.413

Input-output structure of US economy, detailed interindustry transactions for 537 industries, and components of final demand, 1977 benchmark data, 2708–17

Manufacturing census, 1982: financial and operating data, by SIC 2- to 4-digit industry, State, SMSA, and county, preliminary census div rpt series, 2491–3

Manufacturing census, 1982: financial and operating data, for SIC 4-digit industries by product, preliminary rpt, 2491–1.405

Michigan bankruptcy filings, by filer type, moving history, income, creditor action, debt and asset type, credit status, exemptions claimed, and county, 1979-81, hearings, 21528–57.3

Minority group and women employment, by occupational group and SIC 2- to 3-digit industry, 1981, annual rpt, 9244–1.1

Natl forests recreation sites, area, and capacity, by type of activity, as of Nov 1983, annual rpt, 1204–28

Natl forests recreational use, visitor-days by State and activity, FY79-83, annual rpt, 1204–1.1

Natl forests recreational use, visitor-days by type of activity, forest, and State, FY83 with trends from 1924, annual rpt series, 1204–17

Papua New Guinea tuna landings by species, and fishery operating data and govt revenues generated, 1979-81, article, 2162–1.402

Producer prices and indexes, by stage of processing and detailed commodity, monthly rpt, 6762–6

Producer prices and indexes, by stage of processing and detailed commodity, monthly 1983, annual supplement, 6764–2

Recreation (outdoor) participation, by type of activity, projected 1985-2030, 1208–195

Registrations, use, and accident deaths, injuries, and property damage, by detailed cause, State, and outlying area, 1983, annual rpt, 7404–1

Retail trade census, 1982: employment, establishments, sales, and payroll, for boat dealers, by State, preliminary rpt, 2395–1.13

Tuna fleet, capacity, and processor investment in vessels by investment type, with tuna catch, prices, and imports, selected years 1932-80, 9406–1.39

User fees to recover costs of 7 federally subsidized public service programs, by type of fee, user, and service, FY84-88, 26306–6.68

Waterborne commerce of US (domestic and foreign), freight by commodity, traffic, and passengers, by port and waterway, 1982, annual rpt, 3754–3

see also Barges
see also Ferries
see also Inland water transportation
see also Marine accidents and safety
see also Ships and shipping

Boca Raton, Fla.

Census of Housing, 1980: occupancy and unit characteristics, by race, Hispanic origin, and city, SMSA rpt, 2473–1.369

Census of Population and Housing, 1980: detailed population and housing characteristics, by county, city, and census tract, SMSA rpt, 2551–2.369

Wages by occupation, and benefits for office and plant workers, 1984 labor market area survey rpt, 6785–3.3

see also under By SMSA or MSA in the "Index by Categories"

Body measurements

Birth weight, by detailed demographic characteristics and geographic area, 1979, US Vital Statistics annual rpt, 4144–1

Birth weight, effects of special supplemental food program for women, infants, and children, 1973-82, GAO rpt, 26131–10

Births and birth rates, by demographic and birth characteristics, 1981 with trends from 1940, US Vital Statistics advance rpt, 4146–5.73

Births and birth rates, by parent and birth characteristics and infant condition at birth, 1982 and trends from 1940, US Vital Statistics annual advance rpt, 4146–5.79

Child obesity and low height-for-age, for public food program participants aged 1-4, by race and Hispanic origin, 1982, article, 4202–7.403

Fetal deaths and rates, by gestation period, birth weight and order, race, age of mother, and geographic area, 1979, US Vital Statistics annual rpt, 4144–2.3

Health and Nutrition Examination Natl Survey, health and dental condition and body measurements by age, sex, and race, Vital and Health Statistics series, 4147–11

High school classes of 1980 and 1982: educational and sociodemographic characteristics and expectations, natl longitudinal study, series, 4826–2

Nutrition status of infants and children, blood and height-weight indicators, and low birth weight risk factors, by age, race, and Hispanic origin, 1981, annual rpt, 4205–24

Nutrition surveillance, blood values and other nutrition indicators by age, race, and Hispanic origin, 1982, annual rpt, 4204–1.3

Women's body measurements, methodology and summary results, 1983 technical rpt, 7506–10.28

see also Obesity

Boehm, Thomas P.

"Affordability of Alternative Mortgage Instruments: A Household Analysis", 9312–7.401

Boerger, Frank

"Port Requirements for the San Francisco Bay Area", 21568–34

Boertlein, Celia G.

"Geographical Mobility: Mar. 1981 to Mar. 1982", 2546–1.384

Bogorad, Lawrence

"Problems and Potentials of Genetic Engineering", 1004–16.1

Bogs

see Wetlands

Boise City, Idaho

see also under By City and By SMSA or MSA in the "Index by Categories"

Boise, Idaho

Census of Housing, 1980: occupancy and unit characteristics, by race, Hispanic origin, and city, SMSA rpt, 2473–1.97

Census of Population and Housing, 1980: detailed population and housing characteristics, by county, city, and census tract, SMSA rpt, 2551–2.97

Traffic accidents and costs avoided under Boise, Idaho, accident reduction program, and alcohol-related arrests, various periods 1975-81, article, 7762–9.406

Boland, Barbara

"Prosecution of Felony Arrests, 1979", 6066–22.1

Bolivia

Agricultural and food production indexes, and production of selected commodities, by world region and country, 1974-83, annual rpt, 1524–5

Agricultural exports of US to Latin America, by commodity, country group, and selected country, FY81-84 and forecast FY85, article, 1522–1.407

Agricultural situation in Latin America, by country, 1981-83 and outlook for 1984, annual rpt, 1524–4.9

Agricultural supply/demand, trade, and production, and socioeconomic data, by country, 1950s-77, 1528–179

AID activities and funding by project and function, FY85, and developing countries summary socioeconomic data, 1970s-83, by country, annual rpt, 9914–3

AID economic assistance to developing countries, obligations and disbursements by country, quarterly rpt, 9912–4

AID loan repayment status and terms by program and country, and status of predecessor agency loans, quarterly rpt, 9912–3

Background Notes, summary social, political, and economic data, 1983 rpt, 7006–2.1

Cocaine use, user characteristics, medical and botanical research, and South American production and legal policy and enforcement, 1979 intl conf papers, 7008–40

Disaster preparedness and summary sociodemographic, political, and economic data, 1970s-83, 9916–2.56

Economic, social, and political summary data, by country, 1984, annual factbook, 244–11

Economic trends in income, production, prices, employment, finances, and trade, 1984 annual rpt, 2046–4.9

Economic trends in income, production, prices, employment, finances, and trade, 1984 semiannual rpt, 2046–4.78

Exports and imports of US, by commodity and country, 1972-82, annual world region rpt, 244–13.2

Exports of US, detailed Schedule B commodities by country of destination, 1983, annual rpt, 2424–9

Exports of US, detailed Schedule E commodities by mode of transport and world area and country of destination, 1983, annual rpts, 2424–5

Imports of US, detailed Schedule A commodities by country and world area of origin, and mode of transport, 1983, annual rpts, 2424–2

Imports of US, detailed TSUSA commodities by country of origin, 1983, annual rpt, 2424–4

Loans and grants for economic and military assistance from US and intl agencies, by program and country, FY46-83, annual rpt, 9914–5

Military aid of US, arms sales, and training programs costs and budget requests by program, world region, and country, FY83-85, annual rpt, 7144–13

Military spending, arms trade, and armed forces size, with total govt spending and population, by country, 1972-82, annual rpt, 9824–1

Minerals Yearbook, 1982, Vol 3: foreign country reviews of production, trade, and policies, by commodity, annual rpt, 5604–35

Population size and growth rates, and latest available benchmark demographic data, by country, 1950-83, biennial rpt, 2324–4

see also under By Foreign Country in the "Index by Categories"

Bolle, Mary J.

"Measuring State OSHA Effectiveness Using Occupational Injury Rates: Problems and Prospects", 21348–88

Bolling, H. Christine

"Honduras: An Export Market Profile", 1526–6.3

Bolte, Irma M.

"Continuing Education for Maternal Child Health Nurses: A Means To Improve the Health Care of Mothers and Children", 4102–1.405

Bolts

see Hardware

Bolyard, Joan E.

"International Travel and Passenger Fares, 1983", 2702–1.417

Bomb shelters

see Fallout shelters

Bombs

Aircraft hijackings, on-board explosions, other crimes against civil aviation, and circumstances, US and worldwide, 1931-83, annual rpt, 7504–31

Airport security operations to prevent hijacking, screening results, enforcement actions, and hijacking attempts, 1st half 1984, semiannual rpt, 7502–5

Assaults, murders, and other deaths of law enforcement officers, by circumstances, level of govt, agency, victim and offender characteristics, and location, 1983, annual rpt, 6224–3

Bombing (explosive and incendiary) and arson incidents by target, State, and circumstances, and explosives theft and recovery, 1982-83, annual rpt, 8484–4

Bombing (explosive and incendiary) incidents, damage, injuries, and deaths, by target, State, and circumstances, 1983, annual rpt, 6224–5

Homicide and suicide rates for youth, by sex, race, and circumstances, selected

Bombs

years 1970-79, and stress and violent behavior reduction goals for 1990, 4102–1.437

Homicides, by circumstance and type of weapon, 1983, annual rpt, 6224–2.1

Terrorist (intl) incidents, casualties, and attacks on US targets, by attack type and world area, with chronology of events, 1983, annual rpt, 7004–13

see also Military weapons

see also Nuclear explosives and explosions

Bondar, Joseph

"Effects of OASDI Benefit Increase, Dec. 1983", 4742–1.407

"Social Security Beneficiaries Enrolled in the Direct Deposit Program, Dec. 1983", 4742–1.412

Bonds

see Government securities

see Municipal bonds

see Securities

see Surety bonds

see Tax exempt securities

Bonner and Moore Management Science "Impacts of Alcohol Fuels on the U.S. Refining Industry", 3308–75

Bonneville Power Administration

Budget appropriations proposed for Fed Govt energy programs, by office or dept and function, FY84-85, annual rpt, 3004–14

Budget of US, CBO analysis of revenue and spending alternatives and projections of economic indicators, FY85-89, annual rpt, 26304–3.3

Budget of US, effects of Reagan Admin policy changes, by detailed program, FY85, annual rpt, 104–21

Cost control proposals for Fed Govt programs and mgmt, 3-year savings by function and agency, and financial and operating data, 1960s-81, 16908–1

Electric power consumption and prices in Pacific Northwest by end-use sector, and economic and demographic data, 1960s-83 and projected to 2005, annual rpt, 3224–2

Electric power wholesale purchases and costs for individual REA borrowers, by supplier and State, 1940-83, annual rpt, 1244–5

Electric utilities privately owned, detailed financial and operating data by company, with summary data for other distributors by type, 1982, annual rpt, 3164–23

Energy conservation program activities and funding of Bonneville Power Admin, FY82 and estimated FY83-87, 3228–2

Operations, and Columbia River power system sales and financial statements, FY83, annual rpt, 3224–1

Sales, revenues, and prices, by class of customer and individual purchaser, 1983, semiannual rpt, 3222–1

Washington Public Power Supply System nuclear reactors construction financing, with regional economic impacts and power supply/demand, 1980s-2035, hearing, 21448–29

Books and bookselling

Census of Population, 1980: detailed socioeconomic and demographic characteristics, by age, sex, race, Hispanic origin, occupation, and industry, State rpt series, 2531–4

County Business Patterns: establishments, employees, and payrolls, by SIC 4-digit industry and county, 1981, annual State rpt series, 2326–8

County Business Patterns: establishments, employees, and payrolls, by SIC 4-digit industry and county, 1982, annual State rpt series, 2326–6

Employment, earnings, and hours, by selected SIC 1- to 4-digit industry, State, and for 278 major labor areas, 1939-83, annual rpt, 6744–5

Employment, earnings, and hours, by SIC 4-digit nonfarm industry, monthly 1974-Feb 1984, annual update, 6744–4

Exports and imports of US, detailed SIC-based commodities by world area, 1983, annual rpts, 2424–6

Exports and imports of US, totals and as percent of domestic production, by SIC 2- to 5-digit commodity, 1981, annual rpt, 2424–3

Exports, imports, tariffs, and industry operating data for books, magazines, newspapers, and other printed matter, foreign and US, 1978-82, TSUSA commodity rpt, 9885–2.28

Exports of US, detailed commodities by country of destination, monthly rpt, 2422–3

Exports of US, detailed Schedule B commodities by country of destination, 1983, annual rpt, 2424–9

Finances and operations, by SIC 2- to 4-digit industry, 1970s-83 and projected to 1988, annual rpt, 2014–4

GPO bookstores and other sources of Census Bur data, 1984 annual listing, 2304–2

GPO document sales program mgmt and finances, and bookstore operations by location, FY78-82, GAO rpt, 26111–17

Imports of US, detailed Schedule A commodities by country, monthly rpt, 2422–2

Imports of US, detailed TSUSA commodities by country of origin, 1983, annual rpt, 2424–4

Income tax returns of sole proprietorships, detailed data by industry div and selected industry group, 1981, annual rpt, 8304–7

Income tax returns of sole proprietorships, receipts, deductions by type, payroll, and net income, by major industry, 1982, annual article, 8302–2.413

Input-output structure of US economy, detailed interindustry transactions for 537 industries, and components of final demand, 1977 benchmark data, 2708–17

Occupational Outlook Handbook, 1984-85 biennial rpt, 6744–1

OECD trade, total and for 4 major countries, and US trade by country, by commodity, 1972-82, annual world region rpt series, 244–13

Personal stocks of durable goods, by type, in current and constant dollars, 1980-83, annual article, 2702–1.433

Retail trade census, 1982: employment, establishments, sales, and payroll, for direct selling establishments, by State, preliminary rpt, 2395–1.35

see also Libraries

see also Printing and publishing industry

Index by Subjects and Names

Booz, Allen and Hamilton, Inc.

"National Weather Service: A Strategy and Organization Concept for the Future", 2188–16

Booze, C. F., Jr.

"1980 and 1981 Accident Experience of Civil Airmen with Selected Visual Pathology", 7506–10.30

Boron

see Gases

Borowski, Allan

"Comparison of Youth Unemployment in Australia and the U.S.", 6722–1.462

Borowski, Marla

"Agricultural Policy: Objectives for a New Environment", 9381–1.411

Boston and Maine Railroad

Finances and operations of 7 commuter rail systems, and public agency cost reimbursement, 1980, 7888–61

Boston, Mass.

Auto dealer repair workers, wages, and benefits, by occupation, size of establishment, and for 24 labor market areas, Nov 1982 survey, 6787–6.202

Census of Housing, 1980: occupancy and unit characteristics, by race, Hispanic origin, and city, SMSA rpt, 2473–1.98

Census of Population and Housing, 1980: detailed population and housing characteristics, by county, city, and census tract, SMSA rpt, 2551–2.98

CPI by component for US city average, and by region, population size, and for 28 SMSAs, monthly press release, 6762–1

CPI by detailed component, for US city average, 28 SMSAs, and 4 regions by population size, monthly rpt, 6762–2

Fish and shellfish landings and prices at Boston and other New England ports, and total New England cold storage holdings, weekly rpt, 2162–6.2

Fruit and vegetable shipments, and arrivals in 23 US and 5 Canada cities, by mode of transport and State or country of origin, 1983, annual rpt, 1311–4.1

Govt budget of Boston and impact of reduced local revenue and Fed Govt aid, and other devs, FY80-86, article, 9373–1.406

Hospital worker wages by sex and occupation, and benefits, for 22 MSAs, Oct 1981 survey, 6787–6.201

Housing and households detailed characteristics, and unit and neighborhood quality, by inside-outside central cities, 1981 survey, SMSA rpt, 2485–6.30

Population size of top 25 cities, 1980 and 1982, press release, 2328–46

Repair technicians and apprentices wages and benefits, for 5 types of electrical repair shops in 19 SMSAs, Nov 1981 survey, 6787–6.197

Urban revitalization project in Boston, Mass, effect on business conditions by business type, size, and location, 1978 and 1980 surveys, hearings, 21788–140.2

Visual impairment survey methodology and results by age, in 3 SMSAs, Aug 1981-Dec 1982, 4478–147

Wages by occupation, and benefits for office and plant workers, 1984 SMSA survey rpt, 6785–11.10

see also under By City and By SMSA or MSA in the "Index by Categories"

Index by Subjects and Names

Botany

Carbon dioxide atmospheric levels, climatic effects and impacts of fossil and synthetic fuels use, deforestation, and land use patterns, research rpt series, 3406–3

Cocaine use, user characteristics, medical and botanical research, and South American production and legal policy and enforcement, 1979 intl conf papers, 7008–40

DOE R&D projects and funding at natl labs, universities, and other instns, FY83, annual summary rpt, 3004–18.1

High school class of 1982: science and math coursework and assessment, by sociodemographic and school characteristics and educational goal, 4826–2.14

R&D in botany and other plant sciences at higher education instns, funding by source, grad students, and staff, 1983, 9626–2.143

Research grants awarded competitively by USDA for agricultural science, food and nutrition, and energy dev, FY83, annual listing, 1744–1

Science and engineering doctoral degree recipients, by field, sex, race, age, citizenship, postgrad employment and study status, State, and instn, 1960-82, 9626–6.16

Science and engineering grad enrollment, fields of study, financial support, and other student and instn characteristics, 1975-82, annual survey, 9627–7

see also Flowers and nursery products

see also Forests and forestry

see also Fruit and fruit products

see also Horticulture

see also Plants and vegetation

see also Vegetables and vegetable products

Botswana

Agricultural situation in sub-Saharan Africa, by country, 1982-83 and outlook for 1984, annual rpt, 1524–4.10

AID activities and funding by project and function, FY85, and developing countries summary socioeconomic data, 1970s-83, by country, annual rpt, 9914–3

AID economic assistance to developing countries, obligations and disbursements by country, quarterly rpt, 9912–4

AID loan repayment status and terms by program and country, and status of predecessor agency loans, quarterly rpt, 9912–3

Economic conditions and foreign marketing prospects in 46 Sub-Saharan countries, 1983 world region rpt, 2046–5.1

Economic, social, and political summary data, by country, 1984, annual factbook, 244–11

Exports of US, detailed Schedule B commodities by country of destination, 1983, annual rpt, 2424–9

Exports of US, detailed Schedule E commodities by mode of transport and world area and country of destination, 1983, annual rpts, 2424–5

Food supply policies of 21 developing countries, with farm sector data, tariff income, and prices and imports of 5 grains, 1960s-81, 1528–168

Imports of US, detailed Schedule A commodities by country and world area of origin, and mode of transport, 1983, annual rpts, 2424–2

Imports of US, detailed TSUSA commodities by country of origin, 1983, annual rpt, 2424–4

Loans and grants for economic and military assistance from US and intl agencies, by program and country, FY46-83, annual rpt, 9914–5

Military aid of US, arms sales, and training programs costs and budget requests by program, world region, and country, FY83-85, annual rpt, 7144–13

Military spending, arms trade, and armed forces size, with total govt spending and population, by country, 1972-82, annual rpt, 9824–1

Minerals Yearbook, 1982, Vol 3: foreign country reviews of production, trade, and policies, by commodity, annual rpt, 5604–35

Minerals Yearbook, 1983, Vol 3 preprints: foreign country review of production, trade, and policies, by commodity, annual rpt, 5604–23.10

Population size and growth rates, and latest available benchmark demographic data, by country, 1950-83, biennial rpt, 2324–4

see also under By Foreign Country in the "Index by Categories"

Bottles

see Packaging and containers

Botulism

see Food and waterborne diseases

Boughton, James M.

"Alternatives to Intervention: Domestic Instruments and External Objectives", 9373–3.26

Boulder, Colo.

Auto dealer repair workers, wages, and benefits, by occupation, size of establishment, and for 24 labor market areas, Nov 1982 survey, 6787–6.202

Census of Housing, 1980: occupancy and unit characteristics, by race, Hispanic origin, and city, SMSA rpt, 2473–1.138

Census of Population and Housing, 1980: detailed population and housing characteristics, by county, city, and census tract, SMSA rpt, 2551–2.138

CPI by component for US city average, and by region, population size, and for 28 SMSAs, monthly press release, 6762–1

CPI by detailed component, for US city average, 28 SMSAs, and 4 regions by population size, monthly rpt, 6762–2

Employment, earnings, and CPI changes in Denver-Boulder, Colo, SMSA, 1983, annual rpt, 6974–2

Hospital worker wages by sex and occupation, and benefits, for 22 MSAs, Oct 1981 survey, 6787–6.201

Housing unit starts and completions authorized by building permits in 20 MSAs, quarterly rpt, 2382–9

Housing vacancy rates for single and multifamily units and mobile homes, by county, city, and ZIP code, 1983, annual SMSA rpt, 9304–22.1

Repair technicians and apprentices wages and benefits, for 5 types of electrical repair shops in 19 SMSAs, Nov 1981 survey, 6787–6.197

Wages by occupation, and benefits for office and plant workers, 1983 SMSA survey rpt, 6785–12.5

Brandt, Edward N., Jr.

see also under By SMSA or MSA in the "Index by Categories"

Bowe, Frank

"Disabled Women in America", 16598–4

Bowers, H. L.

"Trends in Nuclear Power Plant Capital Investment Cost Estimates, 1976-82", 9638–52

Bowers, Norman

"Employment and Unemployment Improvements Widespread in 1983", 6722–1.409

Bowman, Phillip J.

"Longitudinal Study of Black Youth: Issues, Scope and Findings. Part II, Final Report of the Project: Motivation and Economic Mobility of the Poor", 4008–65.2

Boycotts

Export Admin Act antiboycott provisions, violations and fines by company, and boycotts by firm type and country, FY83, annual rpt, 2044–22

Boyle, E. H., Jr.

"Chromium Availability, Market Economy Countries. A Minerals Availability Program Appraisal", 5606–4.12

Boynton, Robert D.

"Impacts of Nationwide Adoption of the California Solids Standards for Fluid Milk Product", 1561–2.405

Bozzelli, Joseph W.

"Volatile Organic Compounds in the Ambient Atmosphere of the New Jersey, New York Area", 9198–108

Bradbury, Katharine L.

"Making Ends Meet: Boston's Budget in the 1980s", 9373–1.406

"Urban Decline and Distress: An Update", 9373–1.413

Bradenton, Fla.

Census of Housing, 1980: occupancy and unit characteristics, by race, Hispanic origin, and city, SMSA rpt, 2473–1.99

Census of Population and Housing, 1980: detailed population and housing characteristics, by county, city, and census tract, SMSA rpt, 2551–2.99

see also under By SMSA or MSA in the "Index by Categories"

Bradstock, M. Kirsten

"Behavioral Risk Factor Surveillance, 1981-83", 4202–7.405

Brain diseases

see Cerebrovascular diseases

see Neurological disorders

Brand, Donald A.

"X-Ray Screening Protocol for Extremity Injuries", 4186–2.6

Brand, Horst

"Productivity in Making Air Conditioners, Refrigeration Equipment, and Furnaces", 6722–1.471

Brand names

see Labeling

see Trademarks

see under By Individual Company or Institution in the "Index by Categories"

Brandt, Edward N., Jr.

"Nutrition Monitoring and Research in the Department of Health and Human Services", 4102–1.454

"1981 National Urban Pesticide Applicator Survey", 1561–16.408

Brannon, M. Elizabeth

Brannon, M. Elizabeth

"Breast Feeding—the Community Norm. Report of a Workshop", 4102–1.455

Brass

see Metals and metal industries

Brazil

- Agricultural and food production indexes, and production of selected commodities, by world region and country, 1974-83, annual rpt, 1524–5
- Agricultural exports of US to Latin America, by commodity, country group, and selected country, FY81-84 and forecast FY85, article, 1522–1.407
- Agricultural situation in Latin America, by country, 1981-83 and outlook for 1984, annual rpt, 1524–4.9
- Agricultural supply/demand and market for US exports, with socioeconomic indicators, selected years 1969-82 and projected to 1990, country rpt, 1526–6.4
- Agricultural supply/demand, trade, and production, and socioeconomic data, by country, 1950s-77, 1528–179
- Agricultural tillage tools from Brazil, imports injury to US industry from foreign subsidized products, investigation with background financial and operating data, 1984 rpt, 9886–15.55
- AID economic assistance to developing countries, obligations and disbursements by country, quarterly rpt, 9912–4
- AID educational program activities and project impacts in 12 developing countries, 1950s-82, 9916–11.8
- AID loan repayment status and terms by program and country, and status of predecessor agency loans, quarterly rpt, 9912–3
- Cast iron pipe fittings from Brazil, imports injury to US industry from foreign subsidized products, investigation with background financial and operating data, 1984 rpt, 9886–15.53
- Castor oil hydrogenated products from Brazil, imports injury to US industry from removal of duties, investigation with background financial and operating data, 1984 rpt, 9886–18.13
- Cocoa bean production, Bahia State main and temporao crop, 1958/59-1983/84, FAS semiannual circular, 1925–9.2
- Coffee exports of Colombia and Brazil to US and world, market share analysis, 1983 rpt, 1528–169
- Economic and monetary trends, compounded annual rates of change for US and 13 trading partners, quarterly rpt annual supplement, 9391–7
- Economic conditions in Communist, OECD, and selected other countries, 1960s-83, annual rpt, 244–5
- Economic, social, and political summary data, by country, 1984, annual factbook, 244–11
- Economic trends in income, production, prices, employment, finances, and trade, 1983 semiannual rpt, 2046–4.2
- Economic trends in income, production, prices, employment, finances, and trade, 1984 semiannual rpt, 2046–4.57
- Eximbank loan guarantees and insurance currently provided and needed by Mexico and Brazil, and value of worldwide and US trade, 1981-84, hearings, 25248–97

Exports and imports of US, by commodity and country, 1972-82, annual world region rpt, 244–13.2

- Exports of US, detailed Schedule B commodities by country of destination, 1983, annual rpt, 2424–9
- Exports of US, detailed Schedule E commodities by mode of transport and world area and country of destination, 1983, annual rpts, 2424–5
- Food processing and packaging equipment market and trade, and user industry operations and demand, 1984 market research rpt, 2045–11.20
- Food supply policies of 21 developing countries, with farm sector data, tariff income, and prices and imports of 5 grains, 1960s-81, 1528–168
- Imports of US, detailed Schedule A commodities by country and world area of origin, and mode of transport, 1983, annual rpts, 2424–2
- Imports of US, detailed TSUSA commodities by country of origin, 1983, annual rpt, 2424–4
- Industrial process control equipment market and trade, and user industry operations and demand, 1984 country market research rpt, 2045–6.34
- Iron bars from Brazil, imports injury to US industry from sales covered by foreign govt grants, investigation with background financial and operating data, 1980-83, 9886–15.45
- Loans and grants for economic and military assistance from US and intl agencies, by program and country, FY46-83, annual rpt, 9914–5
- Medical and health care equipment market and trade, and user industry operations and demand, 1984 country market research rpt, 2045–2.53
- Military aid of US, arms sales, and training programs costs and budget requests by program, world region, and country, FY83-85, annual rpt, 7144–13
- Military spending, arms trade, and armed forces size, with total govt spending and population, by country, 1972-82, annual rpt, 9824–1
- *Minerals Minerals Yearbook, 1982,* Vol 3 preprints: foreign country review of production, trade, and policies, by commodity, annual rpt, 5604–17.11
- *Minerals Yearbook, 1982,* Vol 3: foreign country reviews of production, trade, and policies, by commodity, annual rpt, 5604–35
- Nuclear power generation in US and 18 non-Communist countries, monthly rpt, 3162–24.10
- Nuclear power plant construction and operation status, and capacity, by plant, region, State, and selected country, 1983 and projected to 2020, annual rpt, 3164–57
- Oil field equipment from 5 countries, injury to US industry from foreign subsidized imports and less than fair value sales, investigation with background financial and operating data, 1984 rpt, 9886–19.11
- Oranges and frozen juice concentrate production, consumption, and exports of Brazil Sao Paulo State, 1981/84, annual article, 1925–34.401

Index by Subjects and Names

- Oranges and frozen juice concentrate production, consumption, and exports of Brazil, 1981-83 and forecast 1983/84, article, 1925–34.420
- Population size and growth rates, and latest available benchmark demographic data, by country, 1950-83, biennial rpt, 2324–4
- Scissors and shears from Brazil, imports injury to US industry from removal of duties, investigation with background financial and operating data, 1983 rpt, 9886–18.12
- Steel imports of US from EC and other countries, and US industry operating data, for 15 products limited under arrangement with EC, monthly rpt, 9882–10
- Steel pipes and tubes from Brazil and Spain, injury to US industry from foreign subsidized and less than fair value imports, investigation with background financial and operating data, 1984 rpt, 9886–19.12
- Steel pipes from Brazil at less than fair value, imports injury to US industry, investigation with background financial and operating data, 1984 rpt, 9886–14.103
- Steel products from Brazil at less than fair value, imports injury to US industry, investigation with background financial and operating data, 1984 rpt, 9886–14.99
- Steel products from Brazil, imports injury to US industry from foreign subsidized products, investigation with selected financial and operating data, 1984 rpt, 9886–15.49
- Steel sheet from Brazil at less than fair value, imports injury to US industry, investigation with background financial and operating data, 1984 rpt, 9886–14.113, 9886–14.120
- Steel sheet from Brazil, injury to US industry from govt-subsidized and less than fair value imports, investigation with background financial and operating data, 1980-83, 9886–19.7
- Telecommunication equipment market and trade, and user industry operations and demand, 1982 country market research rpt, 2045–12.34
- Yarn (cotton) from Brazil, imports injury to US industry from removal of duties on foreign subsidized products, investigation with selected financial and operating data, 1984 rpt, 9886–18.14
- *see also* under By Foreign Country in the "Index by Categories"

Brazoria County, Tex.

see also under By SMSA or MSA in the "Index by Categories"

Bread

see Baking and bakery products

Bregger, John E.

"Current Population Survey: A Historical Perspective and BLS' Role", 6722–1.435

Bremerton, Wash.

- Census of Housing, 1980: occupancy and unit characteristics, by race, Hispanic origin, and city, SMSA rpt, 2473–1.100
- Census of Population and Housing, 1980: detailed population and housing characteristics, by county, city, and census tract, SMSA rpt, 2551–2.100
- Wages by occupation, and benefits for office and plant workers, 1984 labor market area survey rpt, 6785–3.4

Index by Subjects and Names

see also under By SMSA or MSA in the "Index by Categories"

Brenner, M. Harvey

"Estimating the Effects of Economic Change on National Health and Social Well-Being", 23848–76

Bretzfelder, Robert

"Regional Nonfarm Wages and Salaries Thus Far in the Recovery", 2702–1.412

"Regional Shifts in Personal Income by Industrial Component, 1959-83", 2702–1.443

Brewer, Elijah

"Discriminant Analysis of S&L Accounting Profits: 1976-81", 9316–2.47

Bribery

see Corruption and bribery

Bridgeport, Conn.

- Census of Housing, 1980: occupancy and unit characteristics, by race, Hispanic origin, and city, SMSA rpt, 2473–1.101
- Census of Population and Housing, 1980: detailed population and housing characteristics, by county, city, and census tract, SMSA rpt, 2551–2.101
- *see also* under By City and By SMSA or MSA in the "Index by Categories"

Bridges

- Army Corps of Engineers activities and projects, FY83 and trends from 1800s, annual rpt, 3754–1
- Capital needs and financing for public works, by project type, level of govt, and selected jurisdiction, 1970s-83 and projected to 2000, hearing, 23848–181
- Capital needs and intergovtl financing for public works, by type of project and selected city, various periods 1950-83, 10048–60
- Construction industries census, 1982: financial and operating data, by SIC 4-digit industry and State, preliminary rpt series, 2371–1
- Eastern US local govt hwy expenditures, per capita aid, and bridges by condition, by selected county and city, various periods 1965-80, article, 9377–1.405
- Hwy and bridge Fed Hwy Admin allocations, by project and State, FY85, 7556–3.2
- *Hwy Statistics,* detailed data on traffic, govt finances, fuel use, vehicles, driver licenses, and hwy characteristics, by State, 1983, annual rpt, 7554–1
- Ownership, type, use, dimensions, and location of bridges over navigable waters, 1984 regional listing series, 7406–5
- Repair projects for hwys and bridges funded by Fed Govt, and costs, for 7 States, FY81-82, GAO rpt, 26113–121
- Replacement and rehabilitation program of Fed Govt, funding by bridge and bridge status by State, 1983, annual rpt, 7554–27
- Steel (structural) imports, effect on US industry, investigation with background financial and operating data, 1984 rpt, 9886–4.79

Bridgeton, N.J.

- Census of Housing, 1980: occupancy and unit characteristics, by race, Hispanic origin, and city, SMSA rpt, 2473–1.362
- Census of Population and Housing, 1980: detailed population and housing characteristics, by county, city, and census tract, SMSA rpt, 2551–2.362

see also under By SMSA or MSA in the "Index by Categories"

Bristol, Conn.

- Census of Housing, 1980: occupancy and unit characteristics, by race, Hispanic origin, and city, SMSA rpt, 2473–1.102
- Census of Population and Housing, 1980: detailed population and housing characteristics, by county, city, and census tract, SMSA rpt, 2551–2.102
- *see also* under By SMSA or MSA in the "Index by Categories"

Bristol, Tenn.

- Census of Housing, 1980: occupancy and unit characteristics, by race, Hispanic origin, and city, SMSA rpt, 2473–1.195
- Census of Population and Housing, 1980: detailed population and housing characteristics, by county, city, and census tract, SMSA rpt, 2551–2.195
- *see also* under By SMSA or MSA in the "Index by Categories"

Bristol, Va.

see also under By SMSA or MSA in the "Index by Categories"

British Columbia, Canada

- Lumber production, prices, trade, and employment in Northwest US and British Columbia, quarterly rpt, 1202–3
- Tidal current tables, daily time and velocity by station for North America and Asia coasts, 1985, annual rpt, 2174–1.2

Britt, Douglas L.

"Liming of Acidified Waters: A Review of Methods and Effects on Aquatic Ecosystems", 5506–5.13

Broadcasting

see Educational broadcasting

see Political broadcasting

see Public broadcasting

see Radio

see Television

Brockton, Mass.

- Census of Housing, 1980: occupancy and unit characteristics, by race, Hispanic origin, and city, SMSA rpt, 2473–1.103
- Census of Population and Housing, 1980: detailed population and housing characteristics, by county, city, and census tract, SMSA rpt, 2551–2.103
- *see also* under By SMSA or MSA in the "Index by Categories"

Brody, Jacob A.

"Facts, Projections, and Gaps Concerning Data on Aging", 4102–1.447

Brodzinski, Richard

"Volatile Organic Chemicals in the Atmosphere: An Assessment of Available Data", 9198–109

Brogan, Mary

"Child Support Enforcement Statistics, FY83", 4004–29

Brokers

see Futures trading

see Real estate business

see Stockbrokers

Bromine

see Nonmetallic minerals and mines

Brookhaven National Laboratory

- "Assessment of Environmental Problems Associated with Increased Enhanced Oil Recovery in the U.S.: 1980-2000", 3408–29
- *see also* Department of Energy National Laboratories

Brumbaugh, Dan

Brooks, Barbara G.

"Occupational Radiation Exposure at Commercial Nuclear Power Reactors, 1982", 9634–3

Brooks, Nora L.

"Minifarms: Farm Business or Rural Residence?", 1548–241

Broomcorn

see Fibers

Brooms

see Household appliances and equipment

Brorsen, B. Wade

"Commodity Price Relationships in the Southern Plains", 1561–4.401

Broward County, Fla.

Foreign property ownership by individual Netherlands Antilles firms in Broward County, various periods 1978-83, hearings, 21408–71

Brown and Caldwell

"Residential Water Conservation Projects", 5188–109

Brown, Stephen P.

"Effects of Oil Prices and Exchange Rates on World Oil Consumption", 9379–1.405

Browne, Lynn E.

- "High Technology and Regional Economic Development", 9373–2.402
- "How Different Are Regional Wages? A Second Look", 9373–1.407
- "New England Economy and the Development of High Technology Industries", 9373–2.404

Brownsville, Tex.

- Census of Housing, 1980: occupancy and unit characteristics, by race, Hispanic origin, and city, SMSA rpt, 2473–1.104
- Census of Population and Housing, 1980: detailed population and housing characteristics, by county, city, and census tract, SMSA rpt, 2551–2.104
- Employment and economic impacts on Texas border of Mexican peso devaluation, for 6 counties and 2 SMSAs, 1970s-May 1983, hearing, 21788–133
- Employment in Mexico border US-owned plants, and peso devaluation, related to employment in 4 Texas SMSAs, 1978-83, article, 9379–1.402
- Wages of office and plant workers, by occupation, 1984 labor market area survey rpt, 6785–3.10
- *see also* under By SMSA or MSA in the "Index by Categories"

Broyles, Susan G.

- "College Costs: Basic Student Charges, 2-Year and 4-Year Institutions, 1983-84", 4844–10
- "Fall Enrollment in Colleges and Universities, 1982", 4844–2
- "Institutions of Higher Education: Index by State and Congressional District, 1983-84", 4844–11
- "1983-84 Education Directory, Colleges and Universities", 4844–3

Brubaker, Sterling

"Resource and Environmental Impacts of Trends in U.S. Agriculture", 9188–94

Brucellosis

see Animal diseases and zoonoses

Brumbaugh, Dan

"Federal Deposit Insurance as a Call Option: Implications for Depository Institution and Insurer Behavior", 9316–1.107

Brunei

Brunei

Economic, social, and political summary data, by country, 1984, annual factbook, 244–11

- Exports of US, detailed Schedule B commodities by country of destination, 1983, annual rpt, 2424–9
- Exports of US, detailed Schedule E commodities by mode of transport and world area and country of destination, 1983, annual rpts, 2424–5
- Imports of US, detailed Schedule A commodities by country and world area of origin, and mode of transport, 1983, annual rpts, 2424–2
- Imports of US, detailed TSUSA commodities by country of origin, 1983, annual rpt, 2424–4
- Loans and grants for economic and military assistance from US and intl agencies, by program and country, FY46-83, annual rpt, 9914–5
- Military aid of US, arms sales, and training programs costs and budget requests by program, world region, and country, FY83-85, annual rpt, 7144–13
- *Minerals Yearbook, 1982,* Vol 3: foreign country reviews of production, trade, and policies, by commodity, annual rpt, 5604–35
- *Minerals Yearbook, 1982,* Vol 3 preprints: foreign country review of production, trade, and policies, by commodity, annual rpt, 5604–17.87
- Oil reserves, production, and resource lifespan under alternative production rates, for 4 Asian countries, late 1800s-1982 and projected to 2030, 3166–9.9
- Population size and growth rates, and latest available benchmark demographic data, by country, 1950-83, biennial rpt, 2324–4
- *see also* under By Foreign Country in the "Index by Categories"

Bruno, G. A.

"U.S. Uranium Mining Industry: Background Information on Economics and Emissions", 9188–96

Bruno, Rosalind R.

"Educational Attainment in the U.S.: Mar. 1981 and 1980", 2546–1.390

Brunswick, Ga.

Wages of office and plant workers, by occupation, 1984 labor market area survey rpt, 6785–3.7

Bryan, Michael F.

"Outlook for Inflation", 9377–1.404 "Voluntary Export Restraints: The Cost of Building Walls", 9377–1.407

Bryan, Tex.

- Census of Housing, 1980: occupancy and unit characteristics, by race, Hispanic origin, and city, SMSA rpt, 2473–1.105
- Census of Population and Housing, 1980: detailed population and housing characteristics, by county, city, and census tract, SMSA rpt, 2551–2.105
- Housing vacancy rates for single and multifamily units and mobile homes, by city and ZIP code, 1984, annual metro area rpt, 9304–19.17

Bsevi, Giorgio

"Monetary Authorities' Reaction Functions and the European Monetary System", 9373–3.26

Index by Subjects and Names

Bucy, Michele

"Experimental Squid Jigging Off the Washington Coast", 2162–1.401

Budget of the U.S.

- Budget estimates and debt, cyclically adjusted assuming mid-level unemployment and GNP, and methodology, quarterly 1955-83, 2706–5.31
- Budget of US Appendix, detailed budgets and personnel summaries, by agency, FY85, annual rpt, 104–3
- Budget of US, appropriations, outlays, balances, and budget receipts, by govtl branch and agency, FY83, annual rpt, 8104–2
- Budget of US, authority balances in FY85 budget, by agency, FY83-85, annual rpt, 104–8
- Budget of US, brief overview, FY85, annual rpt, 104–6
- Budget of US, CBO analysis and review of FY85 budget by function, annual rpt, 26304–2
- Budget of US, CBO analysis of revenue and spending alternatives and projections of economic indicators, FY85-89, annual rpt, 26304–3
- Budget of US, CBO analysis of revenue and spending estimation errors in congressional concurrent resolutions, FY80-82, 26308–48
- Budget of US, compact budgets by function, agency, and account, FY85 with projections to FY89, annual rpt, 104–2
- Budget of US, effects of Reagan Admin policy changes, by detailed program, FY85, annual rpt, 104–21
- Budget of US, object class analysis of obligations, by branch of Fed Govt and selected depts and agencies, FY85 estimates, annual rpt, 104–9
- Budget of US, receipts and expenditures projected for FY85, annual article, 2702–1.406
- Budget of US, receipts by source and outlays by function, FY40-89 estimates revised for consistency with FY85 budget definitions, annual rpt, 104–12
- Budget of US, receipts, expenditures, and deficit estimates under Apr 1984 revisions to FY84-85 budgets, annual article, 2702–1.411
- Budget of US, receipts, expenditures, and deficit estimates under Aug 1984 revisions to FY84-85 budgets, annual article, 2702–1.429
- Budget of US, receipts, outlays, and budget authority, by function and agency, FY84-89 revised estimates, midsession review of FY85 budget, annual rpt, 104–7
- Budget of US, receipts, outlays, and budget authority, by function and agency, 1st revision of FY85 budget, annual rpt, 104–17
- Budget of US, special analyses of economic and social impact, FY85, annual rpt, 104–1
- Business statistics, detailed data for major industries and economic indicators, *Survey of Current Business,* monthly rpt, 2702–1.6
- Construction grants, loans, and loan guarantees of Fed Govt, by program and type of structure, FY80-83 and estimated FY84-85, annual article, 2012–1.404

Deficit, actual and assuming efficient tax system, FY75-83 and projected FY84-95, article, 9387–1.402

- Deficit and proposed reductions, projected FY84-88, hearings, 25408–86
- Deficit and surplus, *Business Conditions Digest,* historical supplement and methodology, 1947-82, 2708–31
- Deficit impacts on economy, projected FY84-88 with trends and foreign comparisons from 1946, conf papers, 9373–3.27
- Deficit-interest rate relationship, and deficit cyclical and structural components, various periods 1955-83 and projected FY84-89, article, 9391–1.415
- Deficit relationship to economic factors, FY83, article, 2702–1.408
- Deficits and fiscal policy of Fed Govt, with expenditures by level of govt, selected years 1929-83, article, 10042–1.401
- Deficits effect of unemployment and inflation increases and income tax indexing, 1980-83, article, 2702–1.427
- Deficits effect on economic indicators and trade balance of US and 4 countries, model results, various periods 1974-85, technical paper, 9366–7.102
- Deficits effect on inflation, and Fed Govt debt outstanding by holder, Reagan Admin mid-1983 outlook for FY83-84 with supporting data from 1949, article, 9371–1.402
- Deficits effect on interest rates and economic indicators, with govt borrowing and saving, for US and 6 OECD countries, 1975-83, technical paper, 9366–7.89
- Deficits effect on interest rates, regression results and bibl, various periods 1965-83, 8008–111
- Deficits, Fed Govt finances, and economic indicators, selected years 1962-83 and projected under cost control proposals to 2000, 16908–1.1
- Deficits, revenues, and debt of Fed Govt, and GNP and unemployment, cyclically adjusted estimates assuming middle-range unemployment, 1955-3rd qtr 1983, article, 2702–1.403
- Deficits, revenues, and expenditures, and effects of 1981-82 tax legislation, FY81 and FY86, article, 9383–6.401
- *Economic Report of the President* for 1984, economic effects of budget proposals, and trends and projections 1950s-89, annual hearings, 23844–4
- *Economic Report of the President* for 1984, Joint Economic Committee critique and policy recommendations, annual rpt, 23844–2
- Fed Govt agency budget requests and program costs and characteristics, CBO working paper series, 26306–3
- Fed Govt programs under Ways and Means Committee jurisdiction, program operations and financing data for assessing budgetary requirements, by State, FY70s-83, 21788–117
- Financial and business statistics, historic trends, 1984 annual chartbook, 9364–2.8
- Foreign military and economic aid of US, Reagan Admin budget requests by program and country, FY82-85, annual rpt, 7004–14

Index by Subjects and Names

Govt finances, quarterly chartbook, 9362–2.4

Natl income and product, comprehensive accounts and components, *Survey of Current Business,* monthly rpt, 2702–1.21

OASDI trust fund financial status, and Fed Govt budget balance adjusted for OASDI, various periods 1946-83, article, 9373–1.414

Older persons Fed Govt pension and health spending, by program and as percents of budget and GNP, 1965-85 with projections to 2040, 25148–28

Older persons sociodemographic characteristics, and Fed Govt program participation and funding by agency, 1983 with trends and projections 1900-2080, annual rpt, 25144–3

Postal Service pension and health benefits subsidized by Fed Govt trust funds, and subsidy reduction plans deficit impact, FY79-84 and projected to FY89, 26306–6.82

Receipts and outlays, FY29-85, and financing and debt, FY74-85, Council of Economic Advisers annual rpt, 204–1.6

Receipts and outlays, 1982, annual rpt, 9364–5.5

Receipts by source and outlays by agency and program, monthly rpt, 8102–3

Receipts by source and outlays by agency, *Treasury Bulletin,* quarterly rpt, 8002–4.1

Receipts by source and outlays by function, cumulative for fiscal year, annual trends, and quarterly data, monthly rpt, 23842–1.6

Statistical Abstract of US, social, political, and economic data, 1950s-83 and trends, annual rpt, 2324–1.2

Statistical programs of Fed Govt, funding by subject and agency, FY74-85, annual rpt, 104–10

see also Defense budgets and appropriations

see also Executive impoundment of appropriated funds

see also Fiscal policy

see also Nonappropriated funds

see also Public debt

Budgets

see Budget of the U.S.

see Cost of living

see Defense budgets and appropriations

see Foreign budgets

Buffalo, N.Y.

Census of Housing, 1980: occupancy and unit characteristics, by race, Hispanic origin, and city, SMSA rpt, 2473–1.106

Census of Population and Housing, 1980: detailed population and housing characteristics, by county, city, and census tract, SMSA rpt, 2551–2.106

CPI by component for US city average, and by region, population size, and for 28 SMSAs, monthly press release, 6762–1

CPI by detailed component, for US city average, 28 SMSAs, and 4 regions by population size, monthly rpt, 6762–2

Fruit and vegetable shipments, and arrivals in 23 US and 5 Canada cities, by mode of transport and State or country of origin, 1983, annual rpt, 1311–4.1

Hospital worker wages by sex and occupation, and benefits, for 22 MSAs, Oct 1981 survey, 6787–6.201

Repair technicians and apprentices wages and benefits, for 5 types of electrical repair shops in 19 SMSAs, Nov 1981 survey, 6787–6.197

Wages of office and plant workers, by occupation, 1983 SMSA survey rpt, 6785–12.2

Waterborne commerce of US (domestic and foreign), freight by commodity, traffic, and passengers, by port and waterway, 1982, annual rpt, 3754–3.3

see also under By City and By SMSA or MSA in the "Index by Categories"

Building abandonment

see Abandoned buildings

Building and loan associations

see Savings and loan associations

Building laws

see Building permits

see Zoning and zoning laws

Building materials

Acid Precipitation Natl Assessment Program activities, and funding by Federal agency, 1983, annual rpt, 14354–1

Agricultural cooperatives, membership, activities, and finances, by commodity and selected State, 1900-80 with trends from 1863, 1128–30

Air pollutant and radiation indoor levels by emissions source, and household exposure and health effects by pollutant type, various periods 1966-83, hearings, 21708–102

Air pollutant emission factors, by detailed source, 3rd edition, 1983-84 supplements, 9198–13

Air pollutant emissions in US and selected countries, control costs, and acid rain causes and effects, 1970s-83 and projected to 2000, 21368–52

Asphalt and tar roofing and siding shipments, by product and region, 1983, annual Current Industrial Rpt, 2506–8.6

Census of Construction Industries, 1982: financial and operating data, by SIC 4-digit industry and State, final rpt series, 2373–1

Census of Construction Industries, 1982: financial and operating data, by SIC 4-digit industry and State, preliminary rpt series, 2371–1

Census of Population, 1980: detailed socioeconomic and demographic characteristics, by age, sex, race, Hispanic origin, occupation, and industry, State rpt series, 2531–4

China economic conditions, agricultural and industrial production, trade, and domestic and foreign investment, 1980-85, 2048–106

Clay construction products production and shipments by region, trade, and consumption, by product, monthly Current Industrial Rpt, 2506–9.2

County Business Patterns: establishments, employees, and payrolls, by SIC 4-digit industry and county, 1981, annual State rpt series, 2326–8

County Business Patterns: establishments, employees, and payrolls, by SIC 4-digit industry and county, 1982, annual State rpt series, 2326–6

DOD procurement, prime contract awards by category, contract and contractor type, and service branch, FY74-1st half FY84, semiannual rpt, 3542–1

Building materials

Employment, earnings, and hours, by selected SIC 1- to 4-digit industry, State, and for 278 major labor areas, 1939-83, annual rpt, 6744–5

Employment, earnings, and hours, by SIC 4-digit nonfarm industry, monthly 1974-Feb 1984, annual update, 6744–4

Energy use and cost for building materials manufacture, by energy source and industry, 1970s-82, article, 2012–1.401

Energy use, prices, and conservation and efficiency measures, by fuel type, end-use sector, selected industry, and region, 1960-83, annual rpt, 3164–73

Exports and imports of US, detailed SIC-based commodities by world area, 1983, annual rpts, 2424–6

Exports and imports of US, totals and as percent of domestic production, by SIC 2- to 5-digit commodity, 1981, annual rpt, 2424–3

Exports, imports, tariffs, and industry operating data for bedroom furnishings and nontextile floor coverings, 1979-83, TSUSA commodity rpt supplement, 9885–7.61

Exports, imports, tariffs, and industry operating data for wood, paper, and printed matter, TSUSA commodity rpt series, 9885–2

Exports of US, detailed commodities by country of destination, monthly rpt, 2422–3

Exports of US, detailed Schedule B commodities by country of destination, 1983, annual rpt, 2424–9

Exports of US, detailed Schedule E commodities by mode of transport and world area and country of destination, 1983, annual rpts, 2424–5

Farm production expenditures, detailed items by farm sales size and region, 1983, annual rpt, 1614–3

Farmers prices received for major products and paid for farm inputs and living items, by commodity and State, monthly rpt, 1629–1

Farmers prices received for major products and paid for farm inputs, by commodity and State, 1983, annual rpt, 1629–5

Franchise business opportunities, by firm and kind of business, 1984 annual listing, 2044–27

Glass (flat) production, shipments, inventories, and trade, quarterly Current Industrial Rpt, 2506–9.6

Great Lakes trade, by SITC 3-digit commodity, port, vessel type, world area, and country, 1982, annual rpt, 7744–3

Home mortgages (graduated payment) FHA-insured, financial, property, and mortgagor characteristics, for US and selected localities, quarterly rpt, 5142–42

Home mortgages (graduated payment) FHA-insured, financial, property, and mortgagor characteristics, for US and selected States, quarterly rpt, 5142–41

Home mortgages (graduated payment) FHA-insured, financial, property, and mortgagor characteristics, US summary, quarterly rpt, 5142–40

Home mortgages FHA-insured, financial, property, and mortgagor characteristics, for US and selected localities, quarterly rpt, 5142–2

Building materials

Home mortgages FHA-insured, financial, property, and mortgagor characteristics, for US, selected States, and Puerto Rico, quarterly rpt, 5142–3

Home mortgages FHA-insured, financial, property, and mortgagor characteristics, quarterly rpt, 5142–1

Home mortgages FHA-insured, financial, property, and mortgagor characteristics, 1983, annual rpt, 5144–17

Home mortgages FHA-insured for low-cost homes, financial, construction, property, and mortgagor characteristics, quarterly rpt, 5142–4

Housing alteration and repair expenditures by characteristics of property and region, 1983, annual rpt, 2384–4

Housing, new single and multifamily unit physical and financial characteristics, by region and metro-nonmetro location, 1979-83, annual rpt, 2384–1

Hwy construction expenditures and contracts awarded for Federal-aid system, by type of material used and State, various periods 1944-83, annual rpts, 7554–29

Hwy construction material prices and indexes for Federal-aid system, by type of material and urban-rural location, quarterly rpt, 7552–7

Hwy construction materials prices on Federal-aid hwy system, 3rd qtr 1984, 7556–3.3

Hwy receipts by source, and expenditures by function, by level of govt and State, 1983, annual rpt, 7554–1.4

Imports of US, detailed Schedule A commodities by country, monthly rpt, 2422–2

Imports of US, detailed TSUSA commodities by country of origin, 1983, annual rpt, 2424–4

Income tax returns of corporations, detailed income and tax items by industry, 1981, annual rpt, 8304–4

Income tax returns of partnerships, detailed data by industry, 1981 estimates, annual article, 8302–2.404

Income tax returns of sole proprietorships, detailed data by industry div and selected industry group, 1981, annual rpt, 8304–7

Income tax returns of sole proprietorships, receipts, deductions by type, payroll, and net income, by major industry, 1982, annual article, 8302–2.413

Industry finances and operations, by SIC 2- to 4-digit industry, 1970s-83 and projected to 1988, annual rpt, 2014–4

Injuries and deaths from use of selected consumer products and related activity, by victim age and sex, 1982, annual rpt, 9164–7

Injuries, deaths, and medical costs from consumer products use, and Consumer Product Safety Commission activities and recalls, by product type and brand, FY83, annual rpt, 9164–2

Input-output structure of US economy, detailed interindustry transactions for 537 industries, and components of final demand, 1977 benchmark data, 2708–17

Manufacturing census, 1982: financial and operating data, by SIC 2- to 4-digit industry, State, SMSA, and county, preliminary census div rpt series, 2491–3

Manufacturing census, 1982: financial and operating data, for SIC 4-digit industries by product, preliminary rpt series, 2491–1

Minerals Yearbook, 1982, Vol 2: State reviews of production, sales, and firms, by commodity, and business activity, annual rpt, 5604–34

Minority group and women employment, by occupational group and SIC 2- to 3-digit industry, 1981, annual rpt, 9244–1.1

Nuclear power industry status and outlook, with reactor construction, utility financial and operating data, and foreign comparisons, 1970s-83 with projections to 2010, 26358–99

Occupational injury and illness rates, by SIC 2- to 4-digit industry, 1982, annual rpt, 6844–1

Ocean dumping of waste materials, EPA permit program and intl London Dumping Convention activities, 1981-83, annual rpt, 9204–8

Producer prices and indexes, by stage of processing and detailed commodity, monthly rpt, 6762–6

Producer prices and indexes, by stage of processing and detailed commodity, monthly 1983, annual supplement, 6764–2

Production, shipments, PPI, and stocks of building materials, by type, bimonthly rpt, 2012–1.5, 2012–1.6

Retail trade census, 1982: employment, establishments, sales, and payroll, for hardware stores by State, preliminary rpt, 2395–1.3

Retail trade sales and inventories, by kind of business, region, census div, and selected State, SMSA, and city, and seasonal adjustments, monthly rpt, 2413–3

Retail trade sales, inventories, purchases, gross margin, and accounts receivable, by SIC 2- to 4-digit kind of business and type of ownership, 1983, annual rpt, 2413–5

Scientists, engineers, and technicians employment in transportation, utilities, and retail and wholesale trade, by field of science and industry, 1982, 9628–72

Trade assns, professional societies, and labor unions of construction and building materials industries, 1984 listing, article, 2012–1.405

Transportation census, 1982: trucks, by detailed characteristics, miles traveled, and type of product carried, State rpt series, 2573–1

Virgin Islands economic censuses, 1982: employment, establishments, payroll, and receipts, by SIC 1- to 4-digit industry, island, and city, 2593–1

Waterborne commerce of US (domestic and foreign), freight by commodity, traffic, and passengers, by port and waterway, 1982, annual rpt, 3754–3

see also Cement and concrete

see also Clay industry and products

see also Insulation

see also Lumber industry and products

see also Paints and varnishes

see also Quarries and stone products

Index by Subjects and Names

Building permits

Business Conditions Digest, current data on economic, business, and financial conditions and cyclical fluctuations, monthly rpt, 2702–3

Business Conditions Digest, historical supplement on economic, business, and financial conditions and cyclical fluctuations, with methodology, 1947-82, 2708–31

Business statistics, detailed data for major industries and economic indicators, *Survey of Current Business,* monthly rpt, 2702–1.3

California (southern) housing demand by county, prices and sales, and costs after homeowner tax deductions, 1970s-80, hearing, 21148–31

California housing market, and Los Angeles average home price and mortgage rate, 1969-82 with economic indicators projected to 1989, 9306–1.1

Construction put in place, permits authorized by region, State, and MSA, and Federal contract awards, by construction type, bimonthly rpt with articles, 2012–1

Housing unit starts and completions authorized by building permits in 20 MSAs, quarterly rpt, 2382–9

New England States economic indicators, Fed Reserve 1st District, monthly rpt, 9373–2.3

New housing units authorized, by public and private ownership, by region, div, State, selected MSA, and 4,700 permit-issuing places, monthly rpt, 2382–5

New housing units authorized, by public and private ownership, State, and permit-issuing place, 1983, annual rpt, 2384–2

Nuclear power plant generation, capacity, and capacity utilization, monthly rpt, 3162–24.8

Southeastern States and 5 SMSAs economic indicators, Fed Reserve 8th District, quarterly rpt, 9391–15

Southeastern States economic indicators, by State, Fed Reserve 5th District, quarterly rpt, 9389–16

Southeastern States financial and economic devs, Fed Reserve 6th District, monthly rpt with articles, 9371–1

Western States, FHLB 11th District housing, employment, and economic indicators, by SMSA, quarterly rpt, 9302–18

Western States, FHLB 11th District member S&Ls financial operations and housing industry indicators by State, monthly rpt, 9302–17

Western States housing outlook and economic and demographic trends, FHLB 11th District, urban area rpt series, 9306–2

Western States housing permits issued, Fed Reserve 12th District, quarterly rpt, 9393–1.4

see also Zoning and zoning laws

Buildings

see Apartment houses

see Architecture

see Building materials

see Building permits

Index by Subjects and Names

see Commercial buildings
see Condominiums and cooperatives
see Construction industry
see Elevators
see Housing condition and occupancy
see Housing construction
see Housing maintenance and repair
see Industrial plants and equipment
see Prefabricated buildings
see Public buildings

Buiter, Willem H.
"Theory of Optimum Deficits and Debt", 9373–3.27

Bukoski, William
"Preventing Substance Abuse: The State of the Art", 4102–1.410

Bulgaria
Agricultural and food production indexes, and production of selected commodities, by world region and country, 1974-83, annual rpt, 1524–5

Agricultural production and trade by commodity, food consumption, and farm inputs, for 6 countries, 1960-80 with projections to 1991, 1528–178

Agricultural situation in Eastern Europe, by country, 1983 and outlook for 1984, annual report, 1524–4.7

Cuba economic conditions, agricultural and industrial production and distribution, trade, and intl economic relations, 1970-82 and trends from 1957, 248–40

Economic conditions in Communist, OECD, and selected other countries, 1960s-83, annual rpt, 244–5

Economic, social, and political summary data, by country, 1984, annual factbook, 244–11

Economic trends in income, production, prices, employment, finances, and trade, 1984 annual rpt, 2046–4.79

Export licensing and monitoring activities under Export Admin Act, for selected commodities, and for Communist and other countries, FY83, annual rpt, 2044–22

Exports and imports of NATO countries with Council for Mutual Economic Assistance Europe members, by country, 1980-83, annual rpt, 7144–5

Exports and imports of US with Communist countries, by detailed commodity and country, quarterly rpt with articles, 9882–2

Exports of US, detailed Schedule B commodities by country of destination, 1983, annual rpt, 2424–9

Exports of US, detailed Schedule E commodities by mode of transport and world area and country of destination, 1983, annual rpts, 2424–5

Imports of US, detailed Schedule A commodities by country and world area of origin, and mode of transport, 1983, annual rpts, 2424–2

Imports of US, detailed TSUSA commodities by country of origin, 1983, annual rpt, 2424–4

Military spending, arms trade, and armed forces size, with total govt spending and population, by country, 1972-82, annual rpt, 9824–1

Minerals Yearbook, 1982, Vol 3: foreign country reviews of production, trade, and policies, by commodity, annual rpt, 5604–35

Minerals Yearbook, 1982, Vol 3 preprints: foreign country review of production, trade, and policies, by commodity, annual rpt, 5604–17.12

Minerals Yearbook, 1983, Vol 3 preprints: foreign country review of production, trade, and policies, by commodity, annual rpt, 5604–23.12

Population size and growth rates, and latest available benchmark demographic data, by country, 1950-83, biennial rpt, 2324–4

Science and technology dev and transfer between USSR and other members of Council for Mutual Economic Assistance, 1940s-81, 2326–9.7

see also under By Foreign Country in the "Index by Categories"

Bureau of Alcohol, Tobacco and Firearms
Alcohol and tobacco production, removals, stocks, and materials used, by State, monthly rpts, 8486–1

Alcoholic beverages and tobacco production, stocks, and Fed Govt tax and enforcement activities, by State, FY81-82, last issue of annual rpt, 8484–1

Assaults, murders, and other deaths of law enforcement officers, by circumstances, level of govt, agency, victim and offender characteristics, and location, 1983, annual rpt, 6224–3

Bombing (explosive and incendiary) and arson incidents by target, State, and circumstances, and explosives theft and recovery, 1982-83, annual rpt, 8484–4

Cost control proposals for Fed Govt programs and mgmt, 3-year savings by function and agency, and financial and operating data, 1960s-81, 16908–1.12

Law enforcement activities of Alcohol, Tobacco, and Firearms Bur in 20 cities and nationwide, funding, and jobs to be transferred to Customs and Secret Service, 1979-82, hearings, 21528–55

Bureau of Budget
see Office of Management and Budget

Bureau of Census
Activities, publications, and user services of Census Bur, monthly rpt, 2302–3

Annual Survey of Manufactures, 1980-81: operating and financial data, rpt reprints, hardbound vol, 2504–1

Apartment and condominium completions by rent class and sales price, and market absorption rates, quarterly rpt, 2482–2

Apartment market absorption rates and characteristics for nonsubsidized privately financed furnished and unfurnished units completed in 1982, annual Current Housing Rpt, 2484–2

Apartment market absorption rates and characteristics for nonsubsidized privately financed units completed in 1983, preliminary annual Current Housing Rpt, 2484–3

Budgets and permanent staff positions appropriated for Commerce Dept agencies, FY84-85, annual rpt, 2004–6

Bunker fuels, oil, and coal laden in US on vessels engaged in foreign trade, by port, monthly rpt, 2422–5

Census of Agriculture, 1982: data coverage and availability for agriculture census and related statistics, 1984 guide, 2308–55

Census of Agriculture, 1982: farms, farmland, production and costs, and operator characteristics, preliminary State and county rpt series, 2330–1

Bureau of Census

Census of Agriculture, 1982: farms, farmland, production, finances, and operator characteristics, by county, final State rpt series, 2331–1

Census of Construction Industries, 1982: financial and operating data, by SIC 4-digit industry and State, final rpt series, 2373–1

Census of Construction Industries, 1982: financial and operating data, by SIC 4-digit industry and State, preliminary rpt series, 2371–1

Census of Govts, 1982: city govt revenues by source, expenditures by function, debt, and assets, by State and city, 2457–4

Census of Govts, 1982: county govt revenues by source, expenditures by function, debt, and assets, by State and county, 2457–3

Census of Govts, 1982: employment, payrolls, and average earnings, by function, level of govt, State, county, population size, and inside-outside SMSAs, 2455–2

Census of Govts, 1982: local govt employment by function, payroll, and average earnings, for individual counties, cities, and school and special districts, 2455–1

Census of Govts, 1982: properties, govt-assessed value, sales, and tax rates, by property type, State, SMSA, county, and city, 2453–1

Census of Govts, 1982: school districts revenues, expenditures, debt, and assets, by district and State, 2457–1

Census of Govts, 1982: State govt payments to local govts, by program, source of funds, level of govt, and State, with trends from 1902, 2460–3

Census of Housing, 1980: inventory, occupancy, and unit characteristics, changes from 1973 by region and inside-outside SMSAs and central cities, series, 2473–3

Census of Housing, 1980: occupancy and unit characteristics of SMSAs and central cities, by race, Hispanic origin, and city, State and SMSA rpt series, 2473–1

Census of Housing, 1980: structural, financial, and householder characteristics, by region and State, 2475–4

Census of Manufactures, 1982: financial and operating data, by SIC 2- to 4-digit industry, State, SMSA, and county, preliminary census div rpt series, 2491–3

Census of Manufactures, 1982: financial and operating data, for SIC 4-digit industries by product, preliminary rpt series, 2491–1

Census of Manufactures, 1982: textile mill machinery in place, by machine type and textile industry, special preliminary rpts, 2491–2

Census of Mineral Industries, 1982: financial and operating data, by SIC 2- to 4-digit industry and State, preliminary summary rpts, 2511–2

Census of Mineral Industries, 1982: financial and operating data, including materials consumed, by SIC 4-digit industry and State, preliminary rpt series, 2511–1

Census of Population and Housing, 1980: detailed population and housing characteristics, by county, city, and census tract, State and SMSA rpt series, 2551–2

Bureau of Census

Index by Subjects and Names

Census of Population, 1980: detailed socioeconomic and demographic characteristics, by age, sex, race, Hispanic origin, occupation, and industry, State rpt series, 2531–4

Census of Population, 1980: detailed socioeconomic characteristics, by county, city, and inside-outside SMSAs and central cities, State rpt series, 2531–3

Census of Population, 1980: population characteristics, selected and advance data, supplementary rpt series, 2535–1

Census of Population, 1980: selected socioeconomic data, with trends and projections 1960-2050, young readers pamphlet series, 2326–1

Census of Retail Trade, 1982: employment, establishments, sales, and payroll, by SIC 2- to 4-digit kind of business, SMSA, and retail district, State rpt series, 2401–1

Census of Retail Trade, 1982: employment, establishments, sales, and payroll, by SIC 2- to 4-digit kind of business, SMSA, county, and city, State rpt series, 2397–1

Census of Retail Trade, 1982: employment, establishments, sales, and payroll, by SIC 4-digit kind of business and State, preliminary rpt series, 2395–1

Census of Service Industries, 1982: employment, establishments, receipts, and payroll, by SIC 2- to 4-digit kind of business, SMSA, county, and city, State rpt series, 2391–1

Census of Service Industries, 1982: employment, establishments, receipts, and payroll, by SIC 4-digit kind of business and State, preliminary rpt series, 2390–2

Census of Transportation, 1982: trucks, by detailed characteristics, miles traveled, and type of product carried, State rpt series, 2573–1

Census of Wholesale Trade, 1982: employment, establishments, finances, and operations, by SIC 2- to 4-digit kind of business, SMSA, county, and city, State rpt series, 2405–1

Census of Wholesale Trade, 1982: employment, establishments, sales by commodity, and payroll, by SIC 4-digit kind of business and State, preliminary rpt series, 2403–1

Chemical, oil, rubber, and plastic production, shipments, stocks, and materials used, by detailed product, periodic Current Industrial Rpt series, 2506–8

Clay and glass production, shipments, trade, and stocks, by product, periodic Current Industrial Rpt series, 2506–9

Clothing and shoe industry production, shipments, trade, and consumption, by product, periodic Current Industrial Rpts series, 2506–6

Communist countries economies, special studies series, 2326–9

Computer data files, listing with irregular updates, 2302–5

Construction put in place, value of new public and private structures, by type, monthly rpt, 2382–4

Corporations financial statements for manufacturing, mining, and trade, by selected SIC 2- to 3-digit industry, quarterly rpt, 2502–1

Cost control proposals for Fed Govt programs and mgmt, 3-year savings by function and agency, and financial and operating data, 1960s-81, 16908–1.3

Cotton ginnings and production for 18 States, by county, 1983 crop, annual rpt, 2344–1

Cotton ginnings, by State and county, seasonal monthly rpt, 2342–2

Cotton ginnings, by State, seasonal semimonthly rpt, 2342–1

County and City Data Book, detailed socioeconomic and demographic data for States, counties, and cities, selected years 1976-82, 2328–1

County Business Patterns: establishments, employees, and payrolls, by SIC 4-digit industry and county, 1981, annual State rpt series, 2326–8

County Business Patterns: establishments, employees, and payrolls, by SIC 4-digit industry and county, 1982, annual State rpt series, 2326–6

Current Population Reports, demographic, social, and economic characteristics, series, 2546–1

Current Population Reports, demographic subjects, special study series, 2546–2

Current Population Reports, income and socioeconomic characteristics of persons, families, and households, detailed cross-tabulations, series, 2546–6

Current Population Reports, population estimates and projections, by region and State, series, 2546–3

Current Population Reports, population estimates for civilian, resident, and total population, monthly rpt, 2542–1

Current Population Reports, population size and components of change, by MSA and county, annual State rpt series, 2546–4

Current Population Reports, population size, Apr 1980 and July 1982, and per capita income, 1979 and 1981, by county and city, State rpt series, 2546–11

Data collection and use, IRS and other Fed Govt admin record research methods, 1984 annual conf papers, 8304–17

Data collection and use, IRS and other Fed Govt admin record research methods, 1984 compilation of papers, 8308–28

Data collection programs, missions, and appropriations of Fed Govt statistical agencies, and effect of budget cuts, FY80-84, GAO rpt, 26125–28

Data coverage policy for 1982 agriculture and economic censuses, and Federal agency data use, 1984 GAO narrative rpt, 26125–26

Economic censuses for 1982 and related statistics, data coverage and availability, 1984 guide, 2308–5

Economic Censuses of Virgin Islands, 1982: employment, establishments, payroll, and receipts, by SIC 1- to 4-digit industry, island, and city, 2593–1

Economic time series of Fed Govt, content, design, and methodology, research rpt and conf proceedings series, 2626–7

Export and import statistics country classifications, Census Bur codes and designations, revisions to 1981 base edition, 2428–3

Exports and imports between US and outlying areas, by detailed commodity and mode of transport, monthly rpt, 2422–4

Exports and imports of US (airborne), by world area and US customs district and city, monthly rpt, 2422–8

Exports and imports of US (waterborne), by type of service, customs district, port, and world area, monthly rpt, 2422–7

Exports and imports of US, and trade balance, by major commodity group, selected country, and world area, with seasonal adjustments, monthly rpt, 2422–6

Exports and imports of US, by commodity group, world area, selected country, US coastal area and port, and mode of transport, with seasonal adjustments, monthly rpt, 2422–9

Exports and imports of US, detailed SIC-based commodities by world area, 1983, annual rpts, 2424–6

Exports and imports of US, totals and as percent of domestic production, by SIC 2- to 5-digit commodity, 1981, annual rpt, 2424 3

Exports of US, detailed commodities by country of destination, monthly rpt, 2422–3

Exports of US, detailed Schedule B commodities by country of destination, 1983, annual rpt, 2424–9

Exports of US, detailed Schedule E commodities by mode of transport and world area and country of destination, 1983, annual rpts, 2424–5

Farm population, by employment and socioeconomic characteristics, 1983, annual rpt, 2544–1

Fed Govt aid to State and local areas, by type of payment, State, county, and city, FY83, annual rpt, 2464–3

Fed Govt aid to State and local govts, expenditures, and direct payments, by program, agency, and State, FY83, annual rpt, 2464–2

Fed Govt expenditures in States and local areas, Census Bur data collection, limitation, contributing agency costs, and opinions of congressional users, 1984 GAO rpt, 26111–20

Food products (processed) production and stocks by State, shipments, exports, materials used, and consumption, periodic Current Industrial Rpt series, 2506–4

Foreign countries population demographic data, methodology, and analyses, research rpt series, 2546–10

Foreign-owned US multiestablishment firms, employment, and payroll, by country, State, industry group, and foreign ownership share, 1981-82, annual rpt, 2324–6

Foreign population size and growth rates, and latest available benchmark demographic data, by country, 1950-83, biennial rpt, 2324–4

Foreign women sociodemographic, economic, and fertility characteristics, with comparisons to men, by country, 1960s-85, world region rpt series, 2326–15

Govt employment and payroll, by function, level of govt, and jurisdiction, 1983, annual rpt series, 2466–1

Govt finances, by level of govt, State, and for large cities and counties, 1981-83, annual rpt series, 2466–2

Index by Subjects and Names

Bureau of Economic Analysis

Hispanic Americans socioeconomic and demographic characteristics, and compared to non-Hispanics, selected years 1970-83, chartbook, 2328–48

Housing alteration and repair expenditures by characteristics of property and region, 1983, annual rpt, 2384–4

Housing alteration and repair expenditures, quarterly rpt, 2382–7

Housing and financial characteristics, and unit and neighborhood quality, for 15 SMSAs, 1978, annual survey special supplement, 2485–8

Housing and households detailed characteristics, and unit and neighborhood quality, by inside-outside central cities, 1979-82 surveys, SMSA rpt series, 2485–6

Housing and households selected characteristics, subject rpt series, 2486–1

Housing and neighborhood quality indicators and attitudes, and occupant characteristics, by urban-rural location and region, 1981, annual survey, 2485–7

Housing and neighborhood quality indicators and attitudes, by occupant and unit characteristics, region, and metro-nonmetro location, 1981, annual survey, 2485–2

Housing, new single and multifamily unit physical and financial characteristics, by region and metro-nonmetro location, 1979-83, annual rpt, 2384–1

Housing, new single-family units sold and for sale by price, stage of construction, months on market, and region, and seasonal adjustments, monthly rpt, 2382–3

Housing occupancy and unit and household characteristics, by region and metro-nonmetro residence, 1983, biennial survey, 2485–1

Housing prices and price index for new single-family units sold, by region, quarterly rpt, 2382–8

Housing starts, by units per structure and metro-nonmetro location, and mobile home placements and sales price, by region, monthly rpt, 2382–1

Housing unit starts and completions authorized by building permits in 20 MSAs, quarterly rpt, 2382–9

Housing units authorized, by public and private ownership, by region, div, State, selected MSA, and 4,700 permit-issuing places, monthly rpt, 2382–5

Housing units authorized, by public and private ownership, State, and permit-issuing place, 1983, annual rpt, 2384–2

Housing units completed and under construction, by region and units per structure, monthly rpt, 2382–2

Housing vacancy and occupancy rates, and vacant unit characteristics, by metro-nonmetro location and region, selected years 1960-83, annual rpt, 2484–1

Housing vacant unit characteristics and costs, and occupancy and vacancy rates, by region and metro-nonmetro location, quarterly rpt, 2482–1

Imports of US, detailed Schedule A commodities by country and world area of origin, and mode of transport, 1983, annual rpts, 2424–2

Imports of US, detailed Schedule A commodities by country, monthly rpt, 2422–2

Imports of US, detailed TSUSA commodities by country of origin, 1983, annual rpt, 2424–4

Income (household) and cash and noncash transfer program participation, by sociodemographic characteristics, quarterly rpt, 2542–2

Industry coding systems for statistical programs of 6 Federal agencies, comparability, workload, and updating cycles, 1984 rpt, 106–4.5

Lumber, furniture, and paper products production and shipments by region and State, inventories, trade, and consumption, periodic Current Industrial Rpt series, 2506–7

Machinery and equipment production, shipments, trade, stocks, consumption, orders, and firms, by product, periodic Current Industrial Rpt series, 2506–12

Manufacturing production, shipments, inventories, orders, and pollution control expenses, periodic Current Industrial Rpt series, 2506–3

Mental health statistics, natl reporting program historical overview, 1840-1983, narrative rpt, 4508–5

Metals (intermediate product) shipments, trade, and inventories, by product, periodic Current Industrial Rpt series, 2506–11

Metals (primary product) production, shipments, trade, inventories, and unfilled orders, by product, periodic Current Industrial Rpt series, 2506–10

Pocket Data Book, general data, biennial rpt, suspended, 2324–2

Population demographic and socioeconomic trends, special analyses series, 2326–11

Population size and change for metro and nonmetro areas and central cities by census div, and growth of areas with large black and aged populations, 1970-82, 2328–47

Population size of top 25 cities, 1980 and 1982, press release, 2328–46

Programs, funding, and employment of Commerce Dept agencies, FY83, annual rpt, 2004–1

Publications and data files of Census Bur, monthly listing, 2302–6

Publications, data coverage, and suggested uses of Census Bur products, series, 2326–7

Publications of Census Bur, data coverage and availability, 1984 annual listing, 2304–2

Publications of Commerce Dept, biweekly listing, 2002–1

Retail trade sales and inventories, by kind of business, region, census div, and selected State, SMSA, and city, and seasonal adjustments, monthly rpt, 2413–3

Retail trade sales, by kind of business, advance monthly rpt, 2413–2

Retail trade sales, inventories, purchases, gross margin, and accounts receivable, by SIC 2- to 4-digit kind of business and type of ownership, 1983, annual rpt, 2413–5

Service industries receipts, by SIC 2- to 4-digit kind of business, 1983, annual rpt, 2413–8

Ships and tonnage entering and clearing US Customs, by district and port of entry, 1983, annual rpt, 2424–7

State and local govt retirement systems, cash and security holdings and finances, quarterly rpt, 2462–2

Statistical Abstract of US, social, political, and economic data, 1950s-83 and trends, annual rpt, 2324–1

Tax revenues, by level of govt, type of tax, State, and selected large counties, quarterly rpt, 2462–3

Technical papers on survey methodology, programs, and measurement techniques, series, 2626–2

Textile imports, by product and country of origin, monthly rpt, 2422–1

Textile mill production, stocks, materials used, orders, and trade by country, by product and major State, periodic Current Industrial Rpt series, 2506–5

Voting age population, by congressional district, biennial rpt, discontinued, 2544–2

Wholesale trade sales and inventories, by SIC 2- to 3-digit kind of business, monthly rpt, 2413–7

Wholesale trade sales, inventories, purchases, and gross margins, by SIC 2- to 3-digit kind of business and type of ownership, 1983, annual rpt, 2413–13

Bureau of Consular Affairs

Cost control proposals for Fed Govt programs and mgmt, 3-year savings by function and agency, and financial and operating data, 1960s-81, 16908–1.10

Passport applications and estimated travel to Europe, monthly rpt, 7182–2

Passports issued, by holder characteristics, travel purpose, and country of destination, quarterly rpt, 7182–1

Visas issued and refused to immigrants and nonimmigrants, and status adjustments, by class and nationality, FY77, annual rpt, 7184–1

Bureau of Domestic Commerce

see International Trade Administration

Bureau of East-West Trade

see International Trade Administration

Bureau of Economic Analysis

Budgets and permanent staff positions appropriated for Commerce Dept agencies, FY84-85, annual rpt, 2004–6

Business Conditions Digest, current data on economic, business, and financial conditions and cyclical fluctuations, monthly rpt, 2702–3

Business Conditions Digest, historical supplement on economic, business, and financial conditions and cyclical fluctuations, with methodology, 1947-82, 2708–31

Data collection programs, missions, and appropriations of Fed Govt statistical agencies, and effect of budget cuts, FY80-84, GAO rpt, 26125–28

Economic research of BEA, preliminary rpts and specialized topics, staff paper series, 2706–5

Income (personal) per capita and by source, and earnings by industry div, by State, MSA, and county, 1977-82, annual regional rpts, 2704–2

Income (personal) per capita and by source, earnings by major industry group, and social insurance contributions, by region and State, 1929-82, 2708–40

Bureau of Economic Analysis

Industry coding systems for statistical programs of 6 Federal agencies, comparability, workload, and updating cycles, 1984 rpt, 106–4.5

Programs, funding, and employment of Commerce Dept agencies, FY83, annual rpt, 2004–1

Publications of Commerce Dept, biweekly listing, 2002–1

Survey of Current Business, detailed data for major industries and economic indicators, monthly rpt, 2702–1

Bureau of Engraving and Printing

Cost control proposals for Fed Govt programs and mgmt, 3-year savings by function and agency, and financial and operating data, 1960s-81, 16908–1.12

Currency and other products delivered by Bur of Engraving and Printing, annual rpt, discontinued, 8164–1

Bureau of Government Financial Operations

Budget of US, appropriations, outlays, balances, and budget receipts, by govtl branch and agency, FY83, annual rpt, 8104–2

Budget of US, receipts by source and outlays by agency and program, monthly rpt, 8102–3

Cost control proposals for Fed Govt programs and mgmt, 3-year savings by function and agency, and financial and operating data, 1960s-81, 16908–1.12

Fed Govt aid to State and local govt public service programs, annual rpt, discontinued, 8104–1

Fed Govt consolidated financial statements based on business accounting methods, FY82-83, annual rpt, 8104–5

Fed Govt trust fund receipts, expenditures, assets, and liabilities, for 9 funds, periodic rpt series, 8102–9

Foreign currency hodlings of US, detailed transactions and balances by country and program, 1st half FY84, semiannual rpt, 8102–7

Foreign currency purchases by US with dollars, by country, Oct 1983-Mar 1984, semiannual rpt, 8102–5

Foreign exchange rates offered by US disbursing offices, by country, quarterly rpt, 8102–6

Liabilities and other financial commitments, by Federal agency, as of Sept 1983, annual rpt, 8104–3

Receipts, outlays, and debt account transactions of Fed Govt, daily statement, 8102–4

Surety companies authorized to post bonds with Fed Govt, location and bonding limits, as of July 1984, annual listing, 8104–4

Bureau of Health Manpower

see Bureau of Health Professions

Bureau of Health Professions

County and SMSA health manpower and facilities data, users guide to computerized area resource file, 1983, annual rpt, 4114–11

Grants and contract awards for training and research programs, annual listing, suspended, 4114–1

Health professionals supply and education, by occupation, demographic and professional characteristics, and location, 1950s-83 and projected to 2000, biennial rpt, 4114–8

Hospital employment, vacancies, and vacancy rates, by occupation and by hospital specialty, region, census div, and State, 1980, annual rpt, 4114–12

Minority group and women employment and training in health professions, by field, selected years 1962/63-1983/84, 4118–18

Physician supply and ratio to population by State and county population size, and counties with shortages and needs, 1960-79 and projected 1982-94, 4118–52

Bureau of Health Services Research

see National Center for Health Services Research

Bureau of Indian Affairs

Assaults, murders, and other deaths of law enforcement officers, by circumstances, level of govt, agency, victim and offender characteristics, and location, 1983, annual rpt, 6224–3

Cherokee Indians Eastern Band of North Carolina, financial and operating data for Bur of Indian Affairs assistance programs, FY83, annual rpt, 5704–4

Cost control proposals for Fed Govt programs and mgmt, 3-year savings by function and agency, and financial and operating data, 1960s-81, 16908–1.9

Handicapped children public education program enrollment, staff, and funding, by handicap, age, and State, 1981/82-1982/83, annual rpt, 4944–4

Bureau of Industrial Economics

Air conditioning and refrigeration equipment exports by world area, and imports, by product, biennial rpt, suspended, 2014–2

Construction put in place, permits authorized by region, State, and MSA, and Federal contract awards, by construction type, bimonthly rpt with articles, 2012–1

Electric current characteristics, by country and selected city, 1984 rpt, 2018–8

Franchises of firms engaged in distribution of goods and services by kind of business, establishments by State, and sales, 1982-84, annual rpt, 2014–5

Industry finances and operations, by SIC 2- to 4-digit industry, 1970s-83 and projected to 1988, annual rpt, 2014–4

Input-output structure of US economy, detailed interindustry transactions for 537 industries, and components of final demand, 1977 benchmark data, 2708–17

Programs, funding, and employment of Commerce Dept agencies, FY83, annual rpt, 2004–1

Bureau of Intelligence and Research

Communist and and OECD countries economic conditions, 1982, annual rpt, 7144–11

EC trade with US by country, and total agricultural and nonagricultural trade, selected years 1958-83, annual rpt, 7144–7

Military aid of US, arms sales, and training programs costs and budget requests by program, world region, and country, FY83-85, annual rpt, 7144–13

NATO countries trade with Council for Mutual Economic Assistance Europe members, by country, 1980-83, annual rpt, 7144–5

Index by Subjects and Names

NATO countries trade with PRC, by country, 1983, annual rpt, 7144–14

OECD countries GNP and GNP growth, by country, 1973-83, annual rpt, 7144–8

OECD non-NATO countries trade with Europe Council for Mutual Economic Assistance members, annual rpt, discontinued, 7144–6

OECD non-NATO countries trade with PRC, annual rpt, discontinued, 7144–15

OECD trade, by country, 1983, annual rpt, 7144–10

Bureau of International Commerce

see International Trade Administration

Bureau of International Labor Affairs

Research contracts of Bur of Intl Labor Affairs, by project and contractor, FY73-84, annual listing, 6364–1

Bureau of Justice Statistics

see Office of Justice Assistance, Research and Statistics

Bureau of Labor Statistics

Collective bargaining agreements expiring during year, covered workers by SIC 2-digit industry, firm, and union, with summary of key provisions, 1984, annual rpt, 6784–9

Collective bargaining wage and benefit rate changes in labor-mgmt agreements, quarterly press release, 6782–2

Cost control proposals for Fed Govt programs and mgmt, 3-year savings by function and agency, and financial and operating data, 1960s-81, 16908–1.3

CPI by component for US city average, and by region, population size, and for 28 SMSAs, monthly press release, 6762–1

CPI by detailed component, for US city average, 28 SMSAs, and 4 regions by population size, monthly rpt, 6762–2

CPI components relative importance, for selected SMSAs, and US city average by region and population size, 1983, annual rpt, 6884–1

CPI planned 1987 revisions to urban areas sampled and index publication schedule, 1984 press release, 6888–29

Dallas-Fort Worth, Tex, SMSA employment, earnings, hours, and CPI changes, 1983 with trends from 1968, annual rpt, 6964–2

Data collection, analysis, and presentation methods, by program, 1984 handbook, 6888–1

Data collection programs, missions, and appropriations of Fed Govt statistical agencies, and effect of budget cuts, FY80-84, GAO rpt, 26125–28

Denver-Boulder, Colo, SMSA employment, earnings, and CPI changes, 1983, annual rpt, 6974–2

Department store inventory price indexes, July 1984, semiannual rpt, 6762–7

Earnings, hourly and weekly averages and Hourly Earnings Index, by industry div, monthly press release, 6742–3

Earnings of families by number of earners, and earnings and employment status of individual family members, quarterly rpt, 6742–19

Econometric methodology for measuring prices, labor costs, productivity, and wages, technical paper series, 6886–6

Economic indicators and labor force characteristics, selected years 1880-1995, chartbook, 6728–30

Index by Subjects and Names

Bureau of Labor Statistics

Educational attainment of labor force, by demographic and employment characteristics, 1984, press release, 6748–79

Employee benefits in private industry, coverage by benefit type and provisions and occupational group, 1983, annual rpt, 6784–19

Employment (nonagricultural) by industry div and SMSA, earnings, and hours, for 8 southeastern States, monthly press release, 6942–7

Employment and earnings, detailed data, monthly rpt, 6742–2

Employment and economic conditions, alternative BLS projections to 1995 with data for selected years 1959-82, 6728–29

Employment and price changes during recession and recovery, by selected employee characteristics, 1979-Jan 1984, 6728–28

Employment and wages of workers covered by State unemployment insurance laws and Fed Govt unemployment compensation, by SIC 4-digit industry and State, 1982, annual rpt, 6744–16

Employment by detailed occupation, for 29 SIC 2-digit nonmanufacturing industries, 1981 BLS survey, 6748–60

Employment by major nonagricultural industry, and average hours and earnings of manufacturing production workers, for 5 southwestern States, monthly rpt, 6962–2

Employment Cost Index and percent change by occupational group, industry div, region, and metro-nonmetro area, quarterly press release, 6782–5

Employment, earnings, and hours, by selected SIC 1- to 4-digit industry, State, and for 278 major labor areas, 1939-83, annual rpt, 6744–5

Employment, earnings, and hours, by SIC 4-digit nonfarm industry, monthly 1974-Feb 1984, annual update, 6744–4

Employment, earnings, and hours, monthly press release, 6742–5

Employment status of family members, by occupation, family composition, age of children, and other characteristics, 1983 and trends from 1940, 6746–1.253

Employment, unemployment, and labor force, by demographic and employment characteristics, State, and for 30 metro areas and 11 large cities, 1983, annual rpt, 6744–7

Employment, unemployment, and labor force, detailed data by sociodemographic and employment characteristics, and industry, 1940s-83, 6748–72

Export and import price indexes for food and manufactured products, quarterly press release, 6762–13

Handbook of Labor Statistics, employment, earnings, hours, and labor force characteristics, 1982 and trends, detailed annual rpt, 6724–1

Houston, Tex, SMSA employment, earnings, hours, and CPI changes, 1983 with trends from 1968, annual rpt, 6964–1

Industry coding systems for statistical programs of 6 Federal agencies, comparability, workload, and updating cycles, 1984 rpt, 106–4.5

Job tenure and occupational mobility of workers, by sociodemographic characteristics and industry div, as of Jan 1983, press release, 6748–76

Kansas City, Mo-Kans, SMSA employment, earnings, and CPI changes, with comparisons to total US, 1983, annual rpt, 6974–1

Labor force status monthly changes, by selected worker characteristics, 1981-82, biennial rpt, 6744–17

Living costs abroad, State Dept indexes, housing allowances, and hardship differential rates by country and major city, quarterly rpt, 6862–1

Manufacturing productivity and unit labor cost indexes for US and 11 countries, 1950-82 and preliminary 1983, annual rpt, 6864–1

Middle Atlantic States employment and price conditions, series, 6926–1

Minority group labor force participation, employment, and unemployment, by race, detailed Hispanic origin, and sex, quarterly rpt, 6742–18

Monthly Labor Review, current statistics and articles, 6722–1

New England States employment and price conditions, series, 6916–7

NYC metro area employment and prices, 1983, annual rpt, 6924–2

NYC metro area employment by industry div, monthly rpt, discontinued coverage, 6922–4

Occupational injuries and illnesses, data available from NTIS, by State, 1981, annual rpt, 6704–2

Occupational injuries, detailed accident circumstances and safety data, by body part injured, type of equipment used, or industry, series, 6846–1

Occupational injuries, illnesses, and workdays lost, by SIC 2-digit industry, 1982-83, annual press release, 6844–3

Occupational injury and illness rates, by SIC 2- to 4-digit industry, 1982, annual rpt, 6844–1

Occupational manpower needs and supply by detailed occupation, and educational and training program enrollees and grads by detailed field, 1982 and 1995, biennial rpt, 6744–3

Occupational Outlook Handbook, 1984-85 biennial rpt, 6744–1

Occupational trends and outlook, quarterly rpt, 6742–1

Producer Price Index, by major commodity group and subgroup, and processing stage, monthly press release, 6762–5

Producer prices and indexes, by stage of processing and detailed commodity, monthly rpt, 6762–6

Producer prices and indexes, by stage of processing and detailed commodity, monthly 1983, annual supplement, 6764–2

Productivity and costs of labor for private, nonfarm business, and manufacturing sectors, preliminary data, quarterly rpt, 6822–1

Productivity and costs of labor for private, nonfarm business, and manufacturing sectors, revised data, quarterly rpt, 6822–2

Productivity, hours, and employment indexes for selected SIC 3- and 4-digit industries, 1954-82, annual rpt, 6824–1

Productivity of labor and capital in manufacturing, all nonfarm business, and all private business, indexes and percent change, 1948-83, annual rpt, 6824–2

Retail prices for energy and food, and housing fuel consumption, by region, and for 28 SMSAs and US city average, monthly press release, 6762–8

Southeastern States employment conditions, series, 6946–1

Southeastern States employment, prices, earnings, and union membership in 8 States, Oct 1982-83, annual rpt, 6944–2

Southeastern States high technology employment and share of total employment, by State, 1982 and percent change 1975-82, press release, 6948–6

Southeastern States textile mill employment and average hours and earnings, for 8 States, monthly press release, 6942–1

Southeastern States textile mill employment, monthly 1951-83, annual summary rpt, 6944–1

Southwestern States employment, industrial relations, prices, and economic conditions, regional rpts series, 6966–1

Special Labor Force Reports, series, 6746–1

St Louis, Mo, SMSA employment, earnings, and CPI changes, 1983, annual rpt, 6974–3

State and local govt employee wage and benefit changes under collective bargaining, and workers affected, 1979-84, semiannual press release, 6782–6

State and local govt employment and payrolls, monthly rpt, 6742–4

State and local govt productivity measurement, with background data and output indexes for 7 govt services, various periods 1955-82, 6728–27

Statistical and analytical programs and publications, annual listing, suspended, 6704–1

Technological change, impact on productivity and employment in 4 industries, 1960-90, 6828–23

Unemployment and part-time employment, by race, Hispanic origin, sex, family composition, income, and poverty status, 1980-82, annual report, 6744–15

Unemployment, by duration, work experience during year, sex, race, and Hispanic origin, 1982-83, 6748–77

Unemployment levels and rates, by State and for 240 large SMSAs, monthly press release with Current Population Survey annual benchmark averages, 6742–12

Wage and benefit changes from collective bargaining or employer decisions, by industry group, monthly rpt, 6782–1

Wages by occupation, and benefits for office and plant workers, annual labor market survey rpt series, 6785–3

Wages by occupation, and benefits for office and plant workers in 70 SMSAs, 1983, annual rpt, 6785–1

Wages by occupation, and benefits for office and plant workers, 1983, annual SMSA survey rpt series, 6785–12

Wages by occupation, and benefits for office and plant workers, 1984, annual SMSA survey rpt series, 6785–11

Bureau of Labor Statistics

Wages by occupation, for office and plant workers in metro areas, by sex and region, July 1983, annual summary rpt, 6785–9

Wages by occupation, for office and plant workers in selected labor market areas, 1983 surveys, annual summary rpt, 6785–6

Wages by occupation, for office and plant workers in selected SMSAs, 1983 and 1984 surveys, annual rpt, 6785–5

Wages for 3 occupational groups, relative average levels in 78 labor market areas, 1983, annual press release, 6785–13

Wages for 4 occupational groups, relative average levels in 70 SMSAs, 1983, annual press release, 6785–8

Wages, hours, benefits, and employment, by occupation and selected geographic areas, industry surveys series, 6787–6

Wages of white-collar workers, by occupation, work level, and industry div, Mar 1984, annual rpt, 6784–2

Wages of workers covered by unemployment insurance, by industry div, State, and MSA, 1981-83, annual press releases, 6784–17

Women's labor force participation, by age, race, and family status, quarterly rpt, 6742–17

Women's labor force participation by marital status, and children by parent labor force status, by family composition, race, and Hispanic origin, Mar 1984 and trends from 1970, 6748–78

Youth labor force participation, by age group, Apr and July 1984 and change from 1983, annual press release, 6744–13

Youth summer employment, by sex, race, and class of worker, 1979-84, annual press release, 6744–14

Bureau of Land Management

Alaska and Alaska Native corporation claims for Fed Govt land, status and Land Mgmt Bur conveyance problems, various dates 1978-FY84, GAO rpt, 26113–125

Coal dev on Fed Govt lease land in Western US, surface and mineral rights by State, and environmental protection adequacy, various periods 1978-85, 26358–103

Coal dev plans on Fed Govt lease lands in 12 regions under Fed Coal Mgmt Program, environmental and socioeconomic impacts to 2000, final statement series, 5726–4

Coal Fed Govt leases, acreage, production, and prices, by State, and legal and mgmt issues, 1970s-83 with production projections to 2000, 11128–1

Coal lands of Fed Govt leasing activity, acreage, and reserves, by State, coal region, and tract, FY83, annual rpt, 5724–10

Cost control proposals for Fed Govt programs and mgmt, 3-year savings by function and agency, and financial and operating data, 1960s-81, 16908–1.9

Horse and burro wild herd areas in western States, population, adoption, and protection and mgmt costs, as of 1984, biennial rpt, 5724–8

Public land acreage and use, and mgmt activities and finances, annual State rpt series, 5724–11

Public lands, Fed Govt payments to local govts in lieu of property taxes by State, FY84, annual press release, 5724–9

Index by Subjects and Names

Public lands mgmt activities in western States, FY82-84, annual rpt, 5724–13

Public lands mgmt, grants, sales, and use, by State, FY83 and historical, annual rpt, 5724–1

Public lands sales of Land Mgmt Bur, prices of Nevada and California acreage, and effect on Forest Service land acquisition program, 1983, GAO rpt, 26113–122

Recreation fees and collection costs, visitors, and capacity of outdoor Fed Govt, State, and private facilities, by managing agency and State, 1983, annual rpt, 5544–14

Rocky Mountain forest and rangeland area, and timber resources and removals, by ownership, forest and tree characteristics, and State, 1977, 1208–201

Star position tables for land surveying use, 1984 annual rpt, 5724–7

Western US Fed Govt lands by agency and mining restriction status, and energy resources on potential wilderness areas and other lands, 1970s-81 and projected to 1990, 3308–68

Bureau of Mines

Aluminum primary production plant ownership, capacity, and type and source of raw material and energy used, by plant, State, and country, June 1984, semiannual listing, 5602–5

Cost control proposals for Fed Govt programs and mgmt, 3-year savings by function and agency, and financial and operating data, 1960s-81, 16908–1.9

Foreign minerals production, reserves, and industry role in domestic economy and world supply, country and world region rpt series, 5606–1

Helium (US-produced) market demand and Bur of Mines production, sales, and helium program financial statement, FY83, annual rpt, 5604–32

Japan specialty steel and ferroalloy raw material supply/demand, with industry market and manufacturing data, selected years 1970-81, 5608–144

Metals resource recovery through leaching technologies, characteristics of methods and operations, regulation, and research, series, 5606–6

Mineral Industry Surveys, commodity reviews of production, trade, and consumption, advance annual rpt series, 5614–5

Mineral Industry Surveys, commodity reviews of production, trade, stocks, and consumption, monthly rpt series, 5612–1

Mineral Industry Surveys, commodity reviews of production, trade, stocks, and consumption, quarterly rpt series, 5612–2

Mineral Industry Surveys, explosives and blasting agents consumption by type, industry, and State, 1983, annual rpt, 5614–22

Mineral Industry Surveys, phosphate rock production, sales, exports, and use, 1984 crop year, annual rpt, 5614–20

Mineral Industry Surveys, State reviews of production, 1983, advance annual rpt series, 5614–6

Minerals production, prices, trade, use, employment, tariffs, and stockpiling, by commodity, with foreign comparisons, 1979-83, annual rpt, 5604–18

Minerals Yearbook, 1982, Vol 1: commodity reviews of production, reserves, supply, use, and trade, annual rpt, 5604–33

Minerals Yearbook, 1982, Vol 2 preprints: State reviews of production and sales by commodity, and business activity, annual rpt series, 5604–16

Minerals Yearbook, 1982, Vol 2: State reviews of production, sales, and firms, by commodity, and business activity, annual rpt, 5604–34

Minerals Yearbook, 1982, Vol 3: foreign country reviews of production, trade, and policies, by commodity, annual rpt, 5604–35

Minerals Yearbook, 1982, Vol 3 preprints: foreign country reviews of production, trade, and policies, by commodity, annual rpt series, 5604–17

Minerals Yearbook, 1983, Vol 1 preprints: commodity reviews of production, reserves, supply, use, and trade, annual rpt series, 5604–15

Minerals Yearbook, 1983, Vol 3 preprints: foreign country reviews of production, trade, and policies, by commodity, annual rpt series, 5604–23

Natural gas composition and occurrence of helium, analyses of samples from individual wells and pipelines in 26 States and 2 countries, 1983, annual survey, 5604–2

Nonfuel minerals company mergers by SIC 1- to 4-digit industry of acquired and acquiring firm, assets, and earnings measures, various periods 1960-79, 5608–145

Nonfuel minerals foreign and US supply under alternative market conditions, reserves, and background industry data, series, 5606–4

Phosphate rock industry environmental protection costs, by control type and selected State, with background operating data, 1977-81 with cost projections to 1990, 5608–143

Publications and other material of Mines Bur, 1982, annual listing, 5604–40

Publications and patents of Mines Bur, monthly listing, 5602–2

Strategic minerals supply/demand, trade, and foreign and US industry devs by firm and country, by commodity, bimonthly rpt, 5602–4

Bureau of Motor Carrier Safety

see Federal Highway Administration

Bureau of Narcotics and Dangerous Drugs

see Drug Enforcement Administration

Bureau of Prisons

Activities of Justice Dept, by subagency, FY82, annual rpt, 6004–1

Assaults, murders, and other deaths of law enforcement officers, by circumstances, level of govt, agency, victim and offender characteristics, and location, 1983, annual rpt, 6224–3

Cost control proposals for Fed Govt programs and mgmt, 3-year savings by function and agency, and financial and operating data, 1960s-81, 16908–1.9

Fed Prison Industries operations and finances, FY83, annual rpt, 6244–3

Health services employment at Federal correctional instns, by occupation, instn, and region, monthly rpt, 6242–2

Index by Subjects and Names

Burundi

Prisoners in Federal correctional instns, by prison, security level, contract facility type, sex, and region, monthly and weekly rpts, 6242–1

Bureau of Reclamation

Colorado River Storage Project finances, water resource dev, power production, and other activities in western States, FY83, annual rpt, 5824–3

Cost control proposals for Fed Govt programs and mgmt, 3-year savings by function and agency, and financial and operating data, 1960s-81, 16908–1.9, 16908–1.31

Dams, reservoirs, and hydroelectric plants, listing of major foreign and US structures with location and characteristics, as of June 1983, 5828–13

Hydroelectric power generating capacity and plant characteristics, for Western States, FY83, annual rpt, 3254–1

Reclamation programs of Fed Govt in western US, finances and operations by project and State, 1981-82, annual rpts, 5824–1

Recreation construction for water resources dev projects of Army Corps of Engineers and Reclamation Bur, unfunded costs by project, FY82, GAO rpt, 26113–115

Recreation fees and collection costs, visitors, and capacity of outdoor Fed Govt, State, and private facilities, by managing agency and State, 1983, annual rpt, 5544–14

Sedimentation control, surveillance, and research activity of Fed Govt, by project, agency, region, and State, 1982, annual rpt, 5664–9

Water storage and carriage facilities of Reclamation Bur, by type, as of Sept 1983, annual listing, 5824–7

Bureau of Resources and Trade Assistance *see* International Trade Administration

Bureau of Security and Consular Affairs *see* Bureau of Consular Affairs

Bureau of Sport Fisheries and Wildlife *see* Fish and Wildlife Service

Bureau of Standards *see* National Bureau of Standards

Bureau of the Mint

Activities and finances of Mint Bur, production of medals and US and foreign coins, and gold and silver stocks and transactions, by office, FY83, annual rpt, 8204–1

Coin production of Bur, for US by denomination and mint, and for foreign countries, monthly table, 8202–1

Cost control proposals for Fed Govt programs and mgmt, 3-year savings by function and agency, and financial and operating data, 1960s-81, 16908–1.12

Bureau of the Public Debt

Cost control proposals for Fed Govt programs and mgmt, 3-year savings by function and agency, and financial and operating data, 1960s-81, 16908–1.12

Public debt issued, redeemed, and outstanding, by individual issue and source, monthly rpt, 8242–2

Savings bonds issued, redeemed, and outstanding, by series, monthly rpt, 8242–1

Bureaucracy *see* Federal employees *see* Government efficiency *see* International employees *see* Public administration *see* State and local employees

Burfisher, Mary E. "Cameroon: An Export Market Profile", 1526–6.6

Burglary *see* Robbery and theft

Burial and burial laws *see* Cemeteries and funerals *see* Military cemeteries and funerals

Burke, Jim "Antitrust Laws, Justice Department Guidelines, and the Limits of Concentration in Local Banking Markets", 9366–1.136

Burke, Vee "Cash and Non-Cash Benefits for Persons with Limited Income", 25928–4

Burkhead, Dan "Estimates of Poverty Including the Value of Noncash Benefits: 1979-82", 2626–2.50

"Estimates of Poverty Including the Value of Noncash Benefits: 1983", 2626–2.52

Burlington, N.C.

Census of Housing, 1980: occupancy and unit characteristics, by race, Hispanic origin, and city, SMSA rpt, 2473–1.107

Census of Population and Housing, 1980: detailed population and housing characteristics, by county, city, and census tract, SMSA rpt, 2551–2.107

see also under By SMSA or MSA in the "Index by Categories"

Burlington, Vt.

Census of Housing, 1980: occupancy and unit characteristics, by race, Hispanic origin, and city, SMSA rpt, 2473–1.108

Census of Population and Housing, 1980: detailed population and housing characteristics, by county, city, and census tract, SMSA rpt, 2551–2.108

see also under By SMSA or MSA in the "Index by Categories"

Burma

Agricultural and food production indexes, and production of selected commodities, by world region and country, 1974-83, annual rpt, 1524–5

Agricultural situation in Southeast Asia, by country and commodity, 1983 and outlook for 1984, annual rpt, 1524–4.5

Agricultural supply/demand, trade, and production, and socioeconomic data, by country, 1950s-77, 1528–179

AID activities and funding by project and function, FY85, and developing countries summary socioeconomic data, 1970s-83, by country, annual rpt, 9914–3

AID economic assistance to developing countries, obligations and disbursements by country, quarterly rpt, 9912–4

AID loan repayment status and terms by program and country, and status of predecessor agency loans, quarterly rpt, 9912–3

Background Notes, summary social, political, and economic data, 1984 rpt, 7006–2.44

Economic, social, and political summary data, by country, 1984, annual factbook, 244–11

Exports of US, detailed Schedule B commodities by country of destination, 1983, annual rpt, 2424–9

Exports of US, detailed Schedule E commodities by mode of transport and world area and country of destination, 1983, annual rpts, 2424–5

Imports of US, detailed Schedule A commodities by country and world area of origin, and mode of transport, 1983, annual rpts, 2424–2

Imports of US, detailed TSUSA commodities by country of origin, 1983, annual rpt, 2424–4

Loans and grants for economic and military assistance from US and intl agencies, by program and country, FY46-83, annual rpt, 9914–5

Military aid of US, arms sales, and training programs costs and budget requests by program, world region, and country, FY83-85, annual rpt, 7144–13

Military spending, arms trade, and armed forces size, with total govt spending and population, by country, 1972-82, annual rpt, 9824–1

Minerals Yearbook, 1982, Vol 3: foreign country reviews of production, trade, and policies, by commodity, annual rpt, 5604–35

Minerals Yearbook, 1983, Vol 3 preprints: foreign country review of production, trade, and policies, by commodity, annual rpt, 5604–23.13

Population size and growth rates, and latest available benchmark demographic data, by country, 1950-83, biennial rpt, 2324–4

see also under By Foreign Country in the "Index by Categories"

Burnham, Drusilla "Induced Terminations of Pregnancy: Reporting States, 1980", 4146–5.72

Burris, B. E. "Assessment of Potential Environmental Problems Concerning Water Availability", 9208–125

Burundi

Agricultural and food production indexes, and production of selected commodities, by world region and country, 1974-83, annual rpt, 1524–5

Agricultural situation in sub-Saharan Africa, by country, 1982-83 and outlook for 1984, annual rpt, 1524–4.10

AID activities and funding by project and function, FY85, and developing countries summary socioeconomic data, 1970s-83, by country, annual rpt, 9914–3

AID economic assistance to developing countries, obligations and disbursements by country, quarterly rpt, 9912–4

Economic conditions and foreign marketing prospects in 46 Sub-Saharan countries, 1983 world region rpt, 2046–5.1

Economic, social, and political summary data, by country, 1984, annual factbook, 244–11

Economic trends in income, production, prices, employment, finances, and trade, 1983 annual rpt, 2046–4.3

Exports of US, detailed Schedule B commodities by country of destination, 1983, annual rpt, 2424–9

Exports of US, detailed Schedule E commodities by mode of transport and world area and country of destination, 1983, annual rpts, 2424–5

Burundi

Imports of US, detailed Schedule A commodities by country and world area of origin, and mode of transport, 1983, annual rpts, 2424–2

Imports of US, detailed TSUSA commodities by country of origin, 1983, annual rpt, 2424–4

Loans and grants for economic and military assistance from US and intl agencies, by program and country, FY46-83, annual rpt, 9914–5

Military aid of US, arms sales, and training programs costs and budget requests by program, world region, and country, FY83-85, annual rpt, 7144–13

Military spending, arms trade, and armed forces size, with total govt spending and population, by country, 1972-82, annual rpt, 9824–1

Minerals Yearbook, 1982, Vol 3: foreign country reviews of production, trade, and policies, by commodity, annual rpt, 5604–35

Minerals Yearbook, 1982, Vol 3 preprints: foreign country review of production, trade, and policies, by commodity, annual rpt, 5604–17.83

Population size and growth rates, and latest available benchmark demographic data, by country, 1950-83, biennial rpt, 2324–4

see also under By Foreign Country in the "Index by Categories"

Buses

Accidents (fatal), circumstances, and characteristics of persons and vehicles involved, detailed data, 1982, annual rpt, 7764–10

Accidents (fatal), circumstances, and characteristics of persons and vehicles involved, 1983, annual rpt, 7764–14

Accidents, circumstances, injuries, deaths, and characteristics of persons and vehicles involved, 1982, annual rpt, 7764–13

Census of Housing, 1980: structural, financial, and householder characteristics, by region and State, 2475–4

Census of Population and Housing, 1980: detailed population and housing characteristics, by county, city, and census tract, State and SMSA rpt series, 2551–2

Census of Population, 1980: detailed socioeconomic and demographic characteristics, by age, sex, race, Hispanic origin, occupation, and industry, State rpt series, 2531–4

Census of Population, 1980: detailed socioeconomic characteristics, by county, city, and inside-outside SMSAs and central cities, State rpt series, 2531–3

Collective ratemaking and regulatory reform impacts on bus industry operations, finances, and services to older persons and rural areas by State, 1970s-83, 14828–2

Communist, OECD, and selected other countries consumer and producer goods production, 1960s-83, annual rpt, 244–5.8

County Business Patterns: establishments, employees, and payrolls, by SIC 4-digit industry and county, 1981, annual State rpt series, 2326–8

County Business Patterns: establishments, employees, and payrolls, by SIC 4-digit industry and county, 1982, annual State rpt series, 2326–6

Cuba economic conditions, agricultural and industrial production and distribution, trade, and intl economic relations, 1970-82 and trends from 1957, 248–40

DOD shipments of military and personal property, loss claims, passenger traffic, and costs, by mode of transport, quarterly rpt, 3702–1

Employment and finances of ICC-regulated carriers by mode of transport, and ICC activities, FY80-83 and trends, annual rpt, 9484–1

Employment, earnings, and hours, by SIC 4-digit nonfarm industry, monthly 1974-Feb 1984, annual update, 6744–4

Energy economy and registrations, by type of vehicle, 1960-83, annual rpt, 3164–74.3

Energy use in transportation sector by mode, fuel supplies, and demographic and economic determinants of vehicle use, 1970s-83, annual rpt, 3304–5

Exports, imports, tariffs, and industry operating data for motor vehicles and bodies and chassis, foreign and US, 1979-83, TSUSA commodity rpt, 9885–6.63

Exports of US, detailed commodities by country of destination, monthly rpt, 2422–3

Fed Govt motor vehicle fleet costs and operating data, by agency, FY83, annual rpt, 9454–9

Finances and operations of transit systems, by mode of transport, function, fleet size, and system, FY82, annual rpt, 7884–4

Finances, operations, equipment, passengers, employment, and payroll for Class I interstate motor carriers, by district, 1982, annual rpt, 9486–5.3

Finances, operations, vehicles, equipment, accidents, and energy use, by mode of transport, 1955-84, annual rpt, 7304–2

Great Lakes trade, by SITC 3-digit commodity, port, vessel type, world area, and country, 1982, annual rpt, 7744–3

Hwy-railroad grade-crossing accidents, detailed data by State and railroad, 1982, annual rpt, 7604–2

Hwy Statistics, detailed data on traffic, govt finances, fuel use, vehicles, driver licenses, and hwy characteristics, by State, 1983, annual rpt, 7554–1

Imports of US, detailed Schedule A commodities by country, monthly rpt, 2422–2

Income tax returns of sole proprietorships, detailed data by industry div and selected industry group, 1981, annual rpt, 8304–7

Japan auto, truck, and bus production, by make, 1982, hearings, 21788–134

Manufacturing census, 1982: financial and operating data, for SIC 4-digit industries by product, preliminary rpt, 2491–1.393

Occupational Outlook Handbook, 1984-85 biennial rpt, 6744–1

Passenger miles and trips, by transport mode, selected years 1929-81, 26358–97

Producer prices and indexes, by stage of processing and detailed commodity, monthly rpt, 6762–6

Producer prices and indexes, by stage of processing and detailed commodity, monthly 1983, annual supplement, 6764–2

Index by Subjects and Names

Productivity, hours, and employment indexes for Class I buses, 1954-82, annual rpt, 6824–1.4

Registrations of motor vehicles, by State and type of vehicle, 1982-83, annual summary rpt, 7554–24

Research publications on public transit, 2nd half FY83, semiannual listing, 7882–1

Ridership and selected revenue data, for individual large Class I motor carriers, quarterly rpt, 9482–13

Ridership for transit services, by service type, 1983 rpt, 7306–9.6

Safety inspections of motor carriers by Fed Hwy Admin, audits of driver qualification and vehicle operation records, and violations cited, 1982, annual rpt, 7554–38

Safety inspections of motor carriers on interstate hwys, violations cited, and vehicles and drivers ordered out of service, 1982, annual rpt, 7554–35

Safety inspections of motor carriers on interstate hwys, violations cited, and vehicles and drivers ordered out of service, May 1983, semiannual rpt, 7552–15

Safety programs, and accidents, injuries, deaths, hazards, and property damage, by mode of transport, 1983, annual rpt, 7304–19

Sales, prices, and registrations of autos and auto products in US, and trade of 8 countries with US, by make and model, 1964-83, annual rpt, 9884–7

State and local govt productivity measurement, with background data and output indexes for 7 govt services, various periods 1955-82, 6728–27

Tax provisions (State) for motor fuel, vehicle registration fees, and disposition of receipts, by State, as of Jan 1984, biennial rpt, 7554–37

Trolley and motor bus capital and operating costs, electrified railroad mileage by country, and subway system mileage by US city, selected years 1960-80, 3006–7.7

see also Motor vehicle exhaust

see also School busing

Bushnell, Pearsall, and Trozzo, Inc. "Economic Effects of Levying a User Charge on Foreign and Domestic Commerce To Finance Harbor Maintenance", 21568–34

Business

see Business acquisitions and mergers

see Business assets and liabilities, general

see Business cycles

see Business education

see Business energy use

see Business firms and establishments, number

see Business income and expenses, general

see Business inventories

see Business orders

see terms listed under Industry

Business acquisitions and mergers

Bank holding company interstate service applications, and New England acquisitions and mergers effect on assets, by firm, Dec 1974-Sept 1983, article, 9373–1.409

Bank merger antitrust analysis geographic market definition, literature review, 1984 technical paper, 9366–1.138

Index by Subjects and Names

Bank merger proposals receiving adverse Justice Dept appraisals, bank deposits, market shares and ratios, and merger disposition, June 1982-Dec 1983, article, 9375–1.404

Bank mergers and consolidations approved by Fed Reserve Board of Governors during 1983, annual rpt, 9364–1.2

Bank mergers approved and denied by FDIC, and resources, deposits, and offices of merged banks, 1982, annual rpt, 9294–1.1

Bank mergers, concentration levels, and market deposits merged, by number of bank organizations in SMSA and county, simulated 1982, technical paper, 9366–1.136

Banks (natl) domestic and intl operations, charters, mergers, and liquidations, by State and instn, and Comptroller of Currency activities, quarterly rpt, 8402–3

Banks in Midwest States, FHLB of Des Moines members merger activity, 1982-83, annual rpt, 9304–7

Business formation and failures, 1929-83, annual rpt, 204–1.7

Credit Union Natl Admin insurance fund financial activity, and insured instns financial and operating data, FY83, annual rpt with semiannual update for 1st qtr FY84, 9534–7

Financial services acquisitions, risk and earnings correlations and regression analysis, various periods 1970-82, article, 9371–1.416

Foreign direct investment in US by country, and finances, operations, and land ownership, by industry group for businesses acquired and established, 1982-83, annual article, 2702–1.418

Foreign direct investment in US, major investors and investments by SIC 4-digit industry, transaction type and value, and location, 1983, annual rpt, 2044–20

Franchises of firms engaged in distribution of goods and services by kind of business, establishments by State, and sales, 1982-84, annual rpt, 2014–5

Hospital Corp of America capital costs reimbursement from Medicare and Medicaid following acquisition of Hospital Affiliates Intl, 1981-82, GAO rpt, 26121–65

Labor union mergers, and affiliation and membership at time of merger, Jan 1979-Apr 1984, article, 6722–1.456

Minerals (nonfuel) company mergers by SIC 1- to 4-digit industry of acquired and acquiring firm, assets, and earnings measures, various periods 1960-79, 5608–145

Oil and coal industry acquisitions and joint ventures of foreign-affiliated US firms, Jan 1982-June 1983, annual rpt, 3024–2

Oil refineries in operation, and refineries bought and sold by company, by capacity, various dates 1980-85, article, 3162–6.401

Savings and loan assn acquisitions in Southeastern States related to market concentration and acquired S&L market share, 1974-81, article, 9312–1.401

Savings and loan assn mergers, characteristics of acquired and acquiring instns, for 3 merger types, 1980-83 with summary trends from 1970, article, 9312–1.402

Savings and loan assns merged through FSLIC aid, financial and merger data including volume of brokered deposits, 1982-Oct 1983, hearing, 21248–83

Securities brokerage services and finances of brokerage firms and New England banks and thrifts, and brokerage acquisitions by firm, selected years 1977-84, article, 9373–1.417

Business assets and liabilities, general

Business Conditions Digest, current data on economic, business, and financial conditions and cyclical fluctuations, monthly rpt, 2702–3

Corporations assets and liabilities, 1940-83, annual rpt, 204–1.7

Corporations financial statements for manufacturing, mining, and trade, by selected SIC 2- to 3-digit industry, quarterly rpt, 2502–1

Corporations historic financial and business statistics, 1984 annual chartbook, 9364–2.10

Economic indicators and components, current data and annual trends, monthly rpt, 23842–1.5

Employee stock ownership plans in developing countries, and firms finances and operations, with case studies of US and 3 countries, 1970s-82, 9916–3.19

Financial and business statistics, quarterly chartbook, 9362–2.5

Flow-of-funds accounts, assets and liabilities by type and economic sector, year-end outstandings, 1960-83, annual rpt, 9364–3

Flow-of-funds accounts savings, investments, and credit statements, quarterly rpt, 9365–3.3

Foreign corporation US affiliates, assets and employment by region and State, 1977 and 1981, annual rpt, 2044–25

Foreign firms US affiliates financial and operating data, by country of parent firm and industry div, 1980-81, article, 2702–1.402

Import and tariff provisions effect on US industries and products, investigations with background financial and operating data, series, 9886–4

Imports injury to US industries from removal of duties on foreign subsidized products, investigations with background financial and operating data, series, 9886–18

Income tax returns filed by type of filer, selected income items, summary data, quarterly rpt, 8302–2.1

Income tax returns of corporations, detailed income and tax items by industry, 1981, annual rpt, 8304–4

Income tax returns of corporations, summary data by industry div, 1981 estimates, annual article, 8302–2.403

Income tax returns of corporations with foreign tax credit, income and deductions by type, asset size, and selected industry group, 1980, article, 8302–2.415

Income tax returns of foreign subsidiaries of US corporations, income and tax data, by industry and asset size, 1980, article, 8302–2.410

Income tax returns of individuals, detailed data, 1982, annual rpt, 8304–2

Business assets and liabilities, specific industries

Interest rate volatility, effect on corporate debt maturity structure, Oct 1976-Oct 1982, technical paper, 9381–10.29

Intl investment position of US, net position and components, selected years 1897-1982, annual rpt, 2044–25

Manufacturing census, 1982: financial and operating data, for SIC 4-digit industries by product, preliminary rpt series, 2491–1

Manufacturing operating and financial data, 1980-81 Annual Survey of Manufactures rpt reprints, hardbound vol, 2504–1

Multinatl corporation income reallocation through regulation of intercorporate transactions, by tax item, treaty status, asset size, industry, and tax haven country, 1982, 8008–110

Partnership finances, tax deductions, and employment, by industry div and size, 1979, article, 8302–2.411

Pension fund terminations and value of reversion to sponsor, for 12 largest private terminations, 1980-83, article, 9385–1.406

Services intl transactions, and operations of US multinatl service firms and foreign affiliates, by industry and world region, 1977-82, 2706–5.30

Small and minority-owned businesses finances and operations, Federal contracts by agency, and worker characteristics, by industry, race, sex, and State, 1950s-83, annual rpt, 9764–6

Small business capital formation under securities law exemptions, effects on stocks offered, issuers, and purchasers, series, 9736–2

Statistical Abstract of US, social, political, and economic data, 1950s-83 and trends, annual rpt, 2324–1.3

see also Agricultural finance

see also Bankruptcy

see also Business assets and liabilities, specific industries

see also Business income and expenses, general

see also Business inventories

see also Capital investments, general

see also Depreciation

see also Foreign investments

see also Industrial plants and equipment

see also Investments

see also Mortgages

see also Operating ratios

Business assets and liabilities, specific industries

Agricultural cooperative finances and operations, aggregate for top 100 assns by principal product and revenue source, FY82, annual rpt, 1124–3

Agricultural cooperatives activities, operations, finances, and current issues, monthly rpt articles, 1122–1

Agricultural cooperatives for grain, storage and handling facilities, sales, exports, and financial condition, selected years 1974-82, 1128–31

AID Housing Guaranty Program financial statements, and projects by country, FY83, annual rpt, 9914–4

Airline cash flows for all certificated carriers, quarterly rpt, 9142–34

Airline financial and operating data for certificated, charter, and cargo carriers, quarterly rpt, 9142–30

Business assets and liabilities, specific industries

Airline financial data, by carrier, carrier group, and for total certificated system, quarterly rpt, 9142–12

Airline traffic and financial data, by carrier, FY83 with trends from FY73, annual rpt, 9144–1

Army morale, welfare, and recreation programs, revenue and expenses worldwide by activity and major command, FY82-83, annual rpt, 3704–12

Auto industry finances and operations by manufacturer, foreign competition, and consumer auto expenditures and attitudes toward car buying, selected years 1968-85, annual rpt, 2004–8

Bank balance sheet statements by Fed Reserve District, for major banks in NYC, and for US branches and agencies of foreign banks, weekly release, 9365–1.3

Bank deposit interest rate deregulation, effect on bank deposits and bank financial performance, 1978-83, hearing, 21248–83

Bank financial and operating statements, functional cost analysis for Fed Reserve member banks with average and high earnings, by deposit size, 1982, annual rpt, 9364–6

Bank financial statistics, historic trends, 1984 annual chartbook, 9364–2.13

Bank holding company interstate service applications, and New England acquisitions and mergers effect on assets, by firm, Dec 1974-Sept 1983, article, 9373–1.409

Bank holding company ratios of financial involvement in nonbank subsidiaries and subsidiary performance, by holding company size, various periods 1978-82, article, 9377–1.406

Bank profitability, finances, loans and terms, intl earnings, and operating ratios for insured commercial instns, 1980-83, annual article, 9362–1.409

Banking and financial data, 1982, annual rpt, 9364–5

Banking intl facilities by State and ownership, and aggregate assets and liabilities, various dates 1981-83, article, 9391–1.409

Banking intl facilities of foreign and US banks in New York State and total US, assets and liabilities, monthly rpt, 9365–2.22

Banks (insured commercial) and offices, and summary assets and liabilities, 1982-83, annual rpt, 9364–1.2

Banks (insured commercial and with foreign offices) assets and liabilities, by type of bank, monthly rpt, quarterly tables, 9362–1.4

Banks (natl) domestic and intl operations, charters, mergers, and liquidations, by State and instn, and Comptroller of Currency activities, quarterly rpt, 8402–3

Banks (US) foreign branches assets and liabilities, by world region and country, quarterly rpt, 9365–3.7

Banks and thrift instns in New England, financial statements by type of instn and State, 1972 and 1982, annual rpt, 9304–3

Banks foreign branches, balance sheets, monthly rpt, 9362–1.3

Banks in Fed Reserve 1st District, assets and liabilities, monthly rpt, 9373–2.5

Banks, S&Ls, and insurance companies financial and business statistics, quarterly chartbook, 9362–2.7

Bonneville Power Admin operations, and Columbia River power system sales and financial statements, FY83, annual rpt, 3224–1

Bus industry collective ratemaking and regulatory reform impacts on operations, finances, and services to older persons and rural areas by State, 1970s-83, 14828–2

Chrysler Corp Loan Guarantee Act implementation, with related financial and operating data, FY83, last issue of annual rpt, 8004–14

Colorado River Storage Project finances, water resource dev, power production, and other activities in western States, FY83, annual rpt, 5824–3

Conrail operations and US Railway Assn finances and activities, FY81-83, annual rpt, 29604–1

Construction industries census, 1982: financial and operating data, by SIC 4-digit industry and State, final rpt series, 2373–1

Construction industries census, 1982: financial and operating data, by SIC 4-digit industry and State, preliminary rpt series, 2371–1

Credit union assets, and distribution of assets and liabilities by type, 1976 and 1983, article, 9381–1.410

Credit union assets, member savings, and accounts, by asset and account size and for top 100 unions, 1981, hearing, 25368–129

Credit union financial statements by region, State, and type of membership, for Federal and federally insured State unions, 1983, annual rpt, 9534–1

Credit union membership, shares and loans, and asset size, for Federal and federally insured State unions by State, 1984 annual listing, 9534–6

Credit Union Natl Admin Central Liquidity Facility, financial performance, quarterly rpt, 9532–4

Credit Union Natl Admin insurance fund financial activity, and insured instns financial and operating data, FY83, annual rpt with semiannual update for 1st qtr FY84, 9534–7

Defense Fuel Supply Center procurement, prices, stocks, and other activities, FY83, annual rpt, 3904–6

Defense Fuel Supply Center procurement, prices, stocks, transport, and other activities and finances, FY83, annual rpt, 3904–8

Disabled American Veterans financial statements, 1982, GAO rpt, 26111–16

Electric and gas utility diversification activity by type, and finances and bond ratings by selected firm, various periods 1970-83, hearing, 21368–53

Electric utilities privately owned, detailed financial and operating data by company, with summary data for other distributors by type, 1982, annual rpt, 3164–23

Energy producers finances and operations, by energy type for US firms domestic and foreign operations, 1974-82, annual rpt, 3164–44

Index by Subjects and Names

Eximbank financial condition, and loan, credit, and insurance authorizations, by country, FY83, annual rpt, 9254–1

Farm Credit System banks financial statements, Dec 1979-83, annual rpt, 9264–5

Farm Credit System mortgage and other loans, and financial statements, 1982 and selected trends from 1961, annual rpt, 9264–2

FDIC balance sheet, 1982, and payoff and assumption cases and insurance fund net losses, 1965-83, article, 9393–8.407

FDIC officials and operations, 1983, annual rpt, 9294–1.2

Fed Financial Instns Examination Council financial statements, 1982-83, with summary data on financial instns by type, year ended June 1983, annual rpt, 13004–2

Fed Home Loan Bank of Atlanta financial statements, 1982-83, annual rpt, 9304–1

Fed Home Loan Bank of Boston financial statements, 1983, annual rpt, 9304–2

Fed Home Loan Bank of Chicago financial statements, 1982-83, annual rpt, 9304–4

Fed Home Loan Bank of Cincinnati financial statements, 1982-83, annual rpt, 9304–6

Fed Home Loan Bank of Dallas financial statements, 1982-83, annual rpt, 9304–11

Fed Home Loan Bank of Des Moines financial statements, 1982-83, annual rpt, 9304–7

Fed Home Loan Bank of Indianapolis financial statements, 1982-83, annual rpt, 9304–10

Fed Home Loan Bank of New York financial statements, 1982-83, annual rpt, 9304–12

Fed Home Loan Bank of Pittsburgh financial statements, 1982-83, annual rpt, 9304–13

Fed Home Loan Bank of San Francisco financial statements, 1982-83, annual rpt, 9304–14

Fed Home Loan Bank of Seattle financial statements, 1982-83, annual rpt, 9304–15

Fed Home Loan Bank of Topeka financial statements, 1982-83, annual rpt, 9304–16

Fed Home Loan Banks and S&Ls, financial condition and mortgage loan activity, monthly rpt with articles, 9312–1

Fed Home Loan Mortgage Corp activities and financial statements, 1983, annual rpt, 9414–1

Fed Reserve Bank of Atlanta financial statements, 1982-83, annual rpt, 9371–4

Fed Reserve Bank of Chicago financial statements, 1983, annual rpt, 9375–5

Fed Reserve Bank of Cleveland financial statements, 1982-83, annual rpt, 9377–5

Fed Reserve Bank of Dallas financial statements, 1982-83, annual rpt, 9379–2

Fed Reserve Bank of Kansas City financial statements, 1982-83, annual rpt, 9381–3

Fed Reserve Bank of Minneapolis financial statements, 1981-82, annual rpt, 9383–2

Fed Reserve Bank of New York financial statements, 1982-83, annual rpt, 9385–2

Fed Reserve Bank of Philadelphia financial statements, 1982-83, annual rpt, 9387–3

Fed Reserve Bank of Richmond financial statements, 1983, annual rpt, 9389–2

Index by Subjects and Names

Fed Reserve Bank of San Francisco financial statements, 1982-83, annual rpt, 9393–2

Fed Reserve Board and Reserve banks financial statements and employees, and review of monetary policy and economic devs, 1983, annual rpt, 9364–1

Fed Reserve payments services provided depository instns, financial statements, and costs and revenues by service and district bank, 1983, annual press release, 9364–9

Finance companies assets and liabilities and business credit, 1982, annual rpt, 9364–5.7

Finance companies holdings of bank loans and commercial paper, monthly rpt, 9365–2.7

Financial instn holdings, for banks in and outside NYC, and for thrift instns, monthly rpt, 9362–1.1

Govt Natl Mortgage Assn financial statements, and mortgage-backed securities program, FY82-83, annual rpt, 5144–6

GPO activities, finances, and production, FY83, annual rpt, 26204–1

Hospitals and nursing homes in Arizona, finances and operations for specified facilities, and itemized expenses for selected cases, 1978-83, hearing, 21148–29

Insurance industry (property and casualty) financial and operating data, investments, and tax liability, various periods 1951-82, hearing, 25368–128

Investment companies classification, assets, and location, Sept 1982, annual directory, 9734–1

Minerals (nonfuel) company mergers by SIC 1- to 4-digit industry of acquired and acquiring firm, assets, and earnings measures, various periods 1960-79, 5608–145

Mines Bur helium production and sales, and helium program financial statement, FY83, annual rpt, 5604–32

Motor and rail carriers regulated by ICC, employment and finances by mode of transport, and ICC activities, FY80-83 and trends, annual rpt, 9484–1

Motor carriers (Class I interstate) finances, operations, equipment, employment, and payroll, by district, 1982, annual rpt, 9486–5.3

Natural gas interstate pipeline company detailed financial and operating data, by firm, 1983, annual rpt, 3164–38

Natural gas supply, contract prices, pipeline operations and finances, and residential use, various periods 1966-1983/84, 3168–89

Nuclear power accident liability insurance under Price-Anderson Act, effects on industry finances and operations, with insurance coverage, claims, and costs, various periods 1957-82, 9638–49

Oil and gas companies production and exploration detailed expenditures, revenues, operating ratios, and sales volume, 1982, annual Current Industrial Rpt, 2506–8.11

Oil companies energy production and imports by type, and financial data, 1975-81, annual rpt, 3164–74

Business assets and liabilities, specific industries

Oil industry foreign-affiliated US firms, selected financial data, 1981-82, annual rpt, 3024–2

Overseas Private Investment Corp programs and finances, with list of insured projects and companies, FY83, annual rpt, 9904–2

Panama Canal Commission financial condition, FY81-82, annual rpt, 9664–3.1

Pension plan investment in Fed Govt mortgage-backed securities, yields by issuer, and fund assets by fund type, 1970s-82, conf papers, 5008–32

Philanthropic foundations assets and grants for 50 largest foundations, and for selected foundations by recipient, selected years 1975-82, hearings, 21788–137

Philanthropic foundations detailed financial and operating data, and stock holdings by instn, 1979 with selected trends from 1920, GAO rpt, 26119–53

Postal Service finances, organization, and services since 1775, and current operations, FY81-82, annual rpt, 9864–6

Postal Service operations, employment, productivity, and financial statements, FY79-83, annual rpt, 9864–1

Postal Service operations, finances, and employee productivity, performance, and compensation, FY83 with projections to FY85, annual rpt, 9864–5

Prison Industries (Federal) operations and finances, FY83, annual rpt, 6244–3

Public utility holding company finances, securities issued, and subsidiaries by type, by firm, FY83, annual rpt, 9734–2.6

Radio Free Europe and Radio Liberty broadcast and financial data, with comparisons to other intl broadcasters, FY83, annual rpt, 10314–1

Railroad finances and operations, detailed data by firm, class of service, and district, 1983, annual rpt, 9486–6.1

Red Cross program operations and financial statements, 1982/83, annual rpt, 29254–1

Rural Electrification Admin loans to power supply and distribution firms, and borrower operating and financial data, by firm and State, 1983, annual rpt, 1244–1

Savings and loan assn balance sheet items by State and SMSA, and finances of FHLBs, 1983, annual rpt, 9314–3

Savings and loan assns (FSLIC-insured), financial ratios of profitable and unprofitable S&Ls, selected years 1965-82, technical paper, 9316–2.47

Savings and loan assns and FSLIC-insured savings banks and S&Ls, assets, liabilities, and deposit and loan activity, monthly rpt, 9312–4

Savings and loan assns assets and liabilities, by FHLB district and State, selected years 1955-82, annual rpt, 9314–1

Savings and loan assns, FHLB System members assets by instn, city, and State, 1983, annual listing, 9314–5

Savings and loan assns, FHLB 4th District insured members financial condition and operations, by SMSA, monthly rpt, 9302–1

Savings and loan assns, FHLB 6th District insured members financial condition and operations by State, monthly rpt, 9302–11

Savings and loan assns, FHLB 6th District insured members financial condition and operations by State, quarterly rpt, 9302–23

Savings and loan assns, FHLB 8th District members financial operations by State and SMSA, monthly rpt, 9302–9

Savings and loan assns, FHLB 8th District members, locations, assets, and savings, 1984, annual listing, 9304–9

Savings and loan assns, FHLB 9th District insured members financial condition and operations by SMSA, monthly rpt, 9302–13

Savings and loan assns, FHLB 10th District insured members finances and operations by SMSA, monthly rpt, 9302–22

Savings and loan assns, FHLB 10th District members, locations, assets, and savings, 1984, annual listing, 9304–17

Savings and loan assns, FHLB 11th District members financial condition and operations by State, quarterly rpt, 9302–19

Savings and loan assns, FHLB 11th District members financial operations and housing industry indicators by State, monthly rpt, 9302–17

Savings and loan assns, FHLB 12th District members financial operations and housing industry indicators by State, monthly rpt, 9302–21

Savings instn assets and liabilities, by type of instn, 1980-82, annual rpt, 9364–5.4

Savings instn financial statistics, historic trends, 1984 annual chartbook, 9364–2.14

Savings instns, FHLB 1st District members, locations, and financial condition, 1984, annual listing, 9304–26

Savings instns, FHLB 2nd District members financial operations, by State, monthly rpt, 9302–14

Securities industry finances, for stockbrokers, investment firms, and individual stock exchanges, 1978-82, annual rpt, 9734–2.1, 9734–2.2

Shipping firms combined condensed financial statements, Dec 1981-82, annual rpt, 7704–14.5

Small Business Admin loan and contract activity by program, and balance sheets, FY83, annual rpt, 9764–1.1

Small Business Investment Companies finances, funding, licensing, and loan activity, 2nd half FY84, semiannual rpt, 9762–3

Smithsonian Instn finances, activities, and visitors, FY83, annual rpt, 9774–3

Southeastern Power Admin sales by customer, plants, and capacity, and financial statements of Southeastern Fed Power Program, FY83, annual rpt, 3234–1

Southwestern Fed Power System financial statements, electric power sales by customer, and project capacity, production, and costs, FY83, annual rpt, 3244–1

St Lawrence Seaway Dev Corp finances and activities, and seaway toll charges and cargo tonnage by type of cargo, 1983, annual rpt, 7744–1

Subway accidents, deaths, injuries, and property damage, by type of accident and victim and cause, for 11 systems, 1983, annual rpt, 7884–5

Business assets and liabilities, specific industries

Synthetic Fuels Corp financial statements, activities, and executive staff and salaries, FY83, annual rpt, 29654–1

Telegraph carriers financial and operating data, for 7 firms, quarterly rpt, 9282–1

Telephone and telegraph firms detailed financial, operating, and employment statistics, 1982, annual rpt, 9284–6

Telephone companies borrowing under rural telephone loan program, financial and operating data, 1983, annual rpt, 1244–2

Telephone operating and financial data by company type, with fixed cost recovery from interstate revenue by Bell company and State, 1981-82 with trends from 1945, 26306–6.79

Transit system deficits, effect of cost and service increases and ridership and fare decreases, and govt aid and system operating ratios, 1970-80, 7308–184

Transit system financial and operating data, by mode, function, fleet size, and individual system, FY82, annual rpt, 7884–4

Transportation finances, operations, vehicles, equipment, accidents, and energy use, by mode of transport, 1955-84, annual rpt, 7304–2

Trust assets of banks and trust companies, by type of asset and fund and State, 1983, annual rpt, 13004–1

TVA activities, financial and operating data by program and facility, and power sales by customer, FY83, annual rpt, 9804–1

TVA power program finances and operations, by plant and distributor, FY83, annual rpt, 9804–23

Washington Public Power Supply System nuclear reactors construction financing, with regional economic impacts and power supply/demand, 1980s-2035, hearing, 21448–29

Western Area Power Admin operations by plant, financial statements, and electric power sales by customer, FY83, annual rpt, 3254–1

see also Agricultural finance

see also Business income and expenses, specific industries

see also Business inventories

see also Capital investments, specific industries

see also Depreciation

see also Educational finance

see also under By Industry in the "Index by Categories"

Business cycles

Budget deficit-interest rate relationship, and deficit cyclical and structural components, various periods 1955-83 and projected FY84-89, article, 9391–1.415

Budget of US, deficit effect on inflation, and debt outstanding by holder, Reagan Admin mid-1983 outlook for FY83-84 with supporting data from 1949, article, 9371–1.402

Business Conditions Digest, current data on economic, business, and financial conditions and cyclical fluctuations, monthly rpt, 2702–3

Business Conditions Digest, historical supplement on economic, business, and financial conditions and cyclical fluctuations, with methodology, 1947-82, 2708–31

Current account balances of US, Japan, and West Germany, effects of business cycles, modeling results, 1970s-82 and projected 1983-86, technical paper, 9366–7.92

Economic conditions of US, with some foreign comparisons, 1960s-82 and alternative projections to 1992, hearing, 21248–79

Economic growth, with data on labor force, inflation, and productivity, 1953-83 with inflation and unemployment projections to 1988, article, 9373–1.402

Economic Report of the President for 1984, economic trends from 1929 and Reagan Admin proposals, annual rpt, 204–1

Economic trends and projections, 1970s-83, and Budget of US under current fiscal policy and alternatives, FY85-89, annual rpt, 26304–3.1

Employment and price changes during recession and recovery, by selected employee characteristics, 1979-Jan 1984, 6728–28

Employment change over business cycles, by worker characteristics and industry div, quarterly 1982-2nd qtr 1984 with trends from 1948, annual article, 6722–1.448

Employment situation, earnings, hours, and other BLS economic indicators, transcripts of BLS Commissioner's monthly testimony, periodic rpt, 23846–4

GNP components growth related to changes in negotiable orders of withdrawal accounts and other M1 components, various periods 1948-84, article, 9385–1.413

GNP related to M1 and nonfinancial sector debt, and velocity of targets during business expansion, various periods 1958-83, article, 9391–1.416

New England States economic recovery indicators, employment indexes, monthly rpt with articles, 9373–2

North Central States manufacturing and total employment, percent change for Fed Reserve 7th District States, various periods 1969-84, article, 9375–1.408

NYC metro area small business owners and accountants, assessment of economy, professional activities, and community problems, by county and industry div, 1983 survey, hearings, 21728–52.3

Poverty population by labor force status, and effect of public welfare changes and recession, by family status, FY82, 21788–139

Poverty rate by family composition, and effect of noncash transfers, taxes, unemployment benefits, and business cycles, selected years 1959-82, hearings, 21788–141

Recession and recovery effect on labor cost and price indexes, changes by index component, various periods 1949-82, article, 6722–1.464

Recession and recovery effect on labor cost and productivity indexes, changes by index component, various periods 1948-82, article, 6722–1.470

Recession, M1 and interest rates performance as leading indicators, various periods 1949-83, article, 9385–1.410

State and local govt grants from Fed Govt, expenditures by function, and business cycle effects on spending, various periods 1948-83, article, 9385–1.401

Index by Subjects and Names

Unemployment during business cycles, and by worker age, sex, occupation, industry div, reason, and duration, various periods 1969-82, article, 6722–1.444

Unemployment of men and women, by contributing factor, and change in industry share of labor force and unemployment, 1973-75 and 1981-82, article, 6722–1.432

Unemployment rate and components of change, growth rates for 6 recovery periods 2nd qtr 1954-2nd qtr 1984, and projected unemployment rate for 4th qtr 1985, article, 9373–1.415

Western States economic conditions, Fed Reserve 8th District with comparisons to total US, for periods of expansion and recession, 1970-1st qtr 1983, article, 9391–1.402

see also Economic indicators

Business districts

see Central business districts

Business diversification

see Economic concentration and diversification

Business education

Census of Population, 1980: detailed socioeconomic and demographic characteristics, by age, sex, race, Hispanic origin, occupation, and industry, State rpt series, 2531–4

County Business Patterns: establishments, employees, and payrolls, by SIC 4-digit industry and county, 1981, annual State rpt series, 2326–8

Degrees conferred in higher education, by race, Hispanic origin, sex, level, and field, selected years 1949/50-1979/80, annual rpt, 4824–2.16

Franchises of firms engaged in distribution of goods and services by kind of business, establishments by State, and sales, 1982-84, annual rpt, 2014–5

High school classes of 1980 and 1982: educational and sociodemographic characteristics and expectations, natl longitudinal study, series, 4826–2

Service industry census, 1982: employment, establishments, receipts, and payroll, by SIC 2- to 4-digit kind of business, SMSA, county, and city, State rpt series, 2391–1

Teaching degrees conferred by specialty and State, required credit hours, and instn officials attitudes, by instn type, 1970s-83, hearings, 21348–89

Vocational education, detailed data on enrollment, achievement, curricula, and effects on employment, selected years 1980-82, annual rpt, 4824–1.3

Vocational rehabilitation State agency expenditures, caseloads, rehabilitations, and staff, under Section 110 of the Rehabilitation Act, by State, FY82, annual rpt, 4944–9

Business efficiency

see Industrial management

see Labor productivity

see Operating ratios

see Productivity

Business energy use

Agricultural production, marketing, trade, supply, food consumption, and food and nutrition programs, 1960s-83, annual chartbook, 1504–3

Index by Subjects and Names

Business energy use

Agriculture census, 1982: farms, farmland, production and costs, and operator characteristics, preliminary State and county rpt series, 2330–1

Agriculture census, 1982: farms, farmland, production, finances, and operator characteristics, by county, final State rpt series, 2331–1

Air pollutant emission factors, by detailed source, 3rd edition, 1983-84 supplements, 9198–13

Air pollution levels for 5 pollutants, by detailed source, State, and Air Quality Control Region, 1981, annual rpt, 9194–7

Air pollution levels for 5 pollutants, by source, 1970- 82 with trends from 1940, annual rpt, 9194–13

Airline fuel use and costs for domestic and intl operations, by US carrier group, monthly rpt, 9142–21

Alaska electric power capacity and generation by fuel type, and marketing, by utility, type of ownership, and location, 1983, annual rpt, 3214–2

Aluminum primary production plant ownership, capacity, and type and source of raw material and energy used, by plant, State, and country, June 1984, semiannual listing, 5602–5

Bonneville Power Admin energy conservation program activities and funding data, FY82 and estimated FY83-87, 3228–2

Bonneville Power Admin sales, revenues, and prices, by class of customer and individual purchaser, 1983, semiannual rpt, 3222–1

Buildings (commercial) energy use under alternative heating, cooling, and air conditioning systems and control strategies, for 6 cities, 1983 rpt, 2218–68

Buildings heating and air conditioning fuel by type, for new private nonresidential and public buildings, by region, 1979-83, monthly rpt, annual tables, 2382–4.4

Buuilding materials manufacture, energy use and cost by source and industry, 1970s-82, article, 2012–1.401

Coal, coke, and breeze supply/demand, prices, trade, and stocks, by end-use sector and State, quarterly rpt with articles, 3162–37

Coal production and stocks by district, and shipments by district of origin, State of destination, consuming sector, and mode of transport, quarterly rpt, 3162–8

Coal receipts, consumption, stocks, and average price at electric utilities, by State, weekly rpt, monthly data, 3162–1.2

Coal supply/demand, projected 1983-95 with summary trends from 1865, annual rpt, 3164–68

Columbia River system electric power sales, by customer, FY83, annual rpt, 3224–1

Construction industries census, 1982: financial and operating data, by SIC 4-digit industry and State, final rpt series, 2373–1

Construction industries census, 1982: financial and operating data, by SIC 4-digit industry and State, preliminary rpt series, 2371–1

DOE in-house energy use, conservation investments, and savings, by type of use and fuel and field office, FY83, annual rpt, 3024–3

Electric and gas utility ratemaking and regulatory policy standards, and consumers and sales covered, by type of consumer and utility, 1983, annual rpt, 3104–7

Electric power plant (coal-fired) capacity, coal demand, and coal supply by mode of transport and region of origin, by State, for units planned 1983-92, 3088–18

Electric power plant (steam) fuel deliveries, costs, and quality, by fuel type, State, and utility, 1983, annual rpt, 3164–42

Electric power plant capacity, production, retail sales, and fuel stocks, use, and costs, by State, 1979-83, annual rpt, 3164–11

Electric power plant capital and operating detailed costs, capacity, and fuel use, by plant, plant type, utility, and State, 1982, annual rpt, 3164–9

Electric power plants and industrial facilities prohibited from oil and gas primary use, and exemption petitions, by facility, with summary fuel use, 1983, annual rpt, 3104–8

Electric power rate schedules, by user type, utility, and city, Jan 1984, annual rpt, 3164–40

Electric power sales of TVA, by customer, FY83, annual rpt, 9804–1

Electric power use indexes, by SIC 2- and 3-digit industry, monthly rpt, 9365–2.10

Electric utilities privately owned, sales revenues by company and consuming sector, with summary data for other distributors by type, 1982, annual rpt, 3164–23

Electric utility fuel cost, quality, use, receipts, and stocks, and power plant production, by energy source, State and utility, quarterly rpt, 3162–39

Electric utility production, fuel consumption, stocks, and costs by fuel type, and sales, by State, monthly rpt, 3162–35

Energy prices and expenditures for fuels and electricity, by consuming sector, State, and fuel type, 1970-81, annual rpt, 3164–64

Energy production, reserves, and prices, by energy type, and selected indicators of energy use, by State, 1982-83 with selected comparisons from 1971, annual rpt, 3164–60

Energy supply/demand and price forecasts, by fuel type, quarterly rpt, 3162–34

Energy supply/demand and prices, by energy resource and major producing and consuming country and sector, detailed data, monthly rpt, 3162–24

Energy supply/demand and prices, by energy source and end-use sector and for 7 electric utilities, 1981-2000 with trends from 1960s, 3008–93

Energy supply/demand and prices, by fuel type and consuming sector with foreign comparisons, 1949-83, annual rpt, 3164–74

Energy supply/demand and prices, by fuel type, sector, and end use, detailed trends and projections 1973-95, annual rpt, 3164–75

Energy supply/demand and prices, by fuel type, sector, and end use, with foreign comparisons, 1960-83 and projected to 1995, annual summary rpt, 3164–76

Energy supply/demand, prices, end use, and related technical and socioeconomic data, including impacts of US policy and intl devs, series, 3006–7

Energy use, by economic sector, end use, and energy source, 1983 and 2000, 2006–2.5

Energy use, by economic sector, State, census div, and detailed energy resource, 1960-82, State Energy Data System annual rpt, 3164–39

Energy use, by type of air pollutant source and fuel, and State, 1981, annual rpt, 9194–14

Energy use in nonresidential buildings, expenditures, and conservation, by building characteristics, EIA survey series, 3166–8

Energy use in transportation and other sectors, by fuel, selected years 1970-83, annual rpt, 3304–5

Energy use, per capita and by economic sector, State, and major energy resource, 1960-82, State Energy Data System annual supplement, 3164–55

Energy use, prices, and conservation and efficiency measures, by fuel type, end-use sector, selected industry, and region, 1960-83, annual rpt, 3164–73

Environmental quality and protection programs, costs, and Fed Govt enforcement, 1983, detailed annual rpt, 484–1

Farm energy use in Tennessee Valley, by type of fuel and State, 1970s-83, 9808–69

Farm finances, assets, liabilities, income, receipts by commodity and State, and expenses, 1980-83 and trends from 1910, annual rpt, 1544–16

Farm finances, expenses by type, loans by purpose and source, and credit detail by Fed Reserve District, quarterly rpt, 9365–3.10

Farm finances, production, expenses by type, and domestic economic impact, selected years 1972-82 and preliminary 1983-84, annual rpt, 1544–19

Farm production expenditures, detailed items by farm sales size and region, 1983, annual rpt, 1614–3

Farm production inputs supply, use, and prices, periodic situation rpt with articles, 1561–16

Farm production itemized costs, receipts, and net returns, for 13 crops, 4 livestock types, and milk, by region, 1981-83, annual rpt, 1544–20

Fertilizer production and trade, and consumption by region and State, 1983, annual rpt, 1804–6

Fishing diesel and sail-assisted boats in Hawaiian waters, fuel use, earnings, and operating costs, with fuel and fish price indexes, various periods 1967-81, article, 2162–1.401

Fuel oil (distillate and residual) and kerosene deliveries, by end use, PAD district, and State, selected years 1978-83, annual rpt, 3164–2

Hog production, producer characteristics, facilities, and marketing, by type and size of enterprise and region, 1975 and 1980, 1568–248

Business energy use

Industrial electric power cogeneration in 5 industries, and fuel use and utility supply/demand effects, by region, 1983-93, 3008–92

Industrial electric power demand model estimates, economic indicators, and supporting data for 5 industries, 1960s-80 with projections to 2000, 3008–87

Industrial energy demand, forecasting model description, detailed technology specifications, and energy use, for 27 SIC 2- to 4-digit industries, 1970s-80 and projected to 2000, 3308–66

Input-output structure of US economy, detailed interindustry transactions for 537 industries, and components of final demand, 1977 benchmark data, 2708–17

Manufacturing energy efficiency progress, and energy use by type, by SIC 2-digit industry, 1982, annual rpt, 3304–8

Manufacturing operating and financial data, 1980-81 Annual Survey of Manufactures rpt reprints, hardbound vol, 2504–1

Mineral industries census, 1982: financial and operating data, including materials consumed, by SIC 4-digit industry and State, preliminary rpt series, 2511–1

Motor fuel consumption by consuming sector, hwy-nonhwy use, and State, 1983, annual rpt, 7554–1.1

Natl Energy Policy Plan, energy supply, demand, and prices, by fuel and consuming sector, projected 1985-2010, biennial rpt, 3004–13

Natural and supplemental gas production, prices, trade, use, reserves, and pipeline company finances, by firm and State, monthly rpt with articles, 3162–4

Natural gas consumer prices, by consumer sector, census div, and State, 1983, preliminary annual rpt, 3164–4

Natural gas interstate pipeline company detailed financial and operating data, by firm, 1983, annual rpt, 3164–38

Natural gas price decontrol alternatives effect on supply/demand, prices, and home heating costs of low-income households, 1970s-95, hearing, 25148–26

Natural gas prices, reserves, consumption, and production, projected under alternative price controls 1983-95 with market data for various periods 1970-Mar 1984, 3008–96

New England States electricity and gasoline sales, Fed Reserve 1st District, monthly rpt, 9373–2.6

OECD energy prices and taxes by energy source and end-use sector, for US and 9 countries, quarterly 1979-83, annual rpt, 3164–71

Pacific Northwest electricity consumption and prices by end-use sector, and economic and demographic data, 1960s-83 and projected to 2005, annual rpt, 3224–2

Solar collector and photovoltaic module production, sales, and use, with listing of manufacturers, 1983, annual rpt, 3164–62

State govt energy conservation programs, Fed Govt financial and technical aid, and reported energy savings, by State, 1983, annual rpt, 3304–1

Steel industry finances and operations under proposed import quota, projected 1985-89 with selected foreign comparisons and trends from 1950, 26306–6.80

TVA electric power purchases of municipal and cooperative distributors, and prices and consumption by distributor and consumer sector, monthly rpt, 9802–1

TVA power program finances and operations, by plant and distributor, FY83, annual rpt, 9804–23

Uranium enrichment facilities operations, finances, uranium stocks, and energy use and capital investment by facility, FY83, annual rpt, 3354–7

Wood fuel consumption, by end-use sector, SIC 2-digit industry, region, State, and selected industrial and power plant, 1980-83, biennial rpt, 3164–78

see also Transportation energy use

Business failures

see Bankruptcy

Business firms and establishments, number

Agricultural cooperatives, membership, activities, and finances, by commodity and selected State, 1900-80 with trends from 1863, 1128–30

Agricultural cooperatives, membership, and activities, by type of service, commodity, and State, FY51-1982, annual survey rpt, 1124–1

Airlines (commuter and intrastate) operating in 1978 by region and State, and listing by city, by operation status in 1984, article, 9142–42.404

Alcoholic beverages and tobacco production, stocks, and Fed Govt tax and enforcement activities, by State, FY81-82, last issue of annual rpt, 8484–1

American Samoa minimum wage rates, employment, earnings, and benefits, by establishment and industry, Nov 1983, biennial rpt, 6504–6

Auto industry operations, trade, and registrations, foreign and US, selected years 1928-82, domestic content requirement hearings, 21788–134

Bank deposits in commercial and mutual savings banks and in US branches of foreign banks, by account type, instn, State, SMSA, and county, June 1983, annual rpt, 9295–3

Bank interstate offices by type, and electronic funds transfer networks, for Fed Reserve 7th District by State of origin and coverage, 1981-83, article, 9375–1.403

Bank interstate service offices, including S&Ls, bank branches, and nonbank subsidiaries offering financial services, by instn and State, 1981-83, 9371–13

Bankers' banks, shareholder, client, and total independent banks Statewide, by State, early 1984, article, 9371–1.415

Banking and financial data, 1982, annual rpt, 9364–5

Banking intl facilities by State and ownership, and aggregate assets and liabilities, various dates 1981-83, article, 9391–1.409

Banks (insured commercial) and offices, and summary assets and liabilities, 1982-83, annual rpt, 9364–1.2

Banks and thrift instns in New England, financial statements by type of instn and State, 1972 and 1982, annual rpt, 9304–3

Banks in Fed Reserve 5th District, by asset size, finances, and loans and deposits by type, various dates 1979-83, annual article, 9389–1.408

Index by Subjects and Names

Banks in Midwest States, FHLB of Des Moines members by type and State, 1982-83, annual rpt, 9304–7

Biotechnology firms, patents, and trade by country, and effect of industry growth on US drug and chemical trade, selected years 1979-2000, 9886–4.78

Bus industry collective ratemaking and regulatory reform impacts on operations, finances, and services to older persons and rural areas by State, 1970s-83, 14828–2

Business Conditions Digest, historical supplement on economic, business, and financial conditions and cyclical fluctuations, with methodology, 1947-82, 2708–31

Business statistics, detailed data for major industries and economic indicators, *Survey of Current Business,* monthly rpt, 2702–1.1

California business failures, plant closings, layoffs, and relocations, by plant, industry, county, and city, 1980-83, hearing, 21348–84.1

Chemicals (synthetic organic) production and sales by product, and listing of manufacturers, 1983, annual rpt, 9884–3

Coastal environmental characteristics, fish, wildlife, and use, and population socioeconomic data, for individual areas, series, 5506–4

Construction industries census, 1982: financial and operating data, by SIC 4-digit industry and State, final rpt series, 2373–1

Construction industries census, 1982: financial and operating data, by SIC 4-digit industry and State, preliminary rpt series, 2371–1

Cotton storage capacity, and total and chain operated warehouses, by region and State, selected years 1970-84, article, 1561–1.406

County and City Data Book, detailed socioeconomic and demographic data for States, counties, and cities, selected years 1976-82, 2328–1

County Business Patterns: establishments, employees, and payrolls, by SIC 4-digit industry and county, 1981, annual State rpt series, 2326–8

County Business Patterns: establishments, employees, and payrolls, by SIC 4-digit industry and county, 1982, annual State rpt series, 2326–6

Credit Union Natl Admin insurance fund financial activity, and insured instns financial and operating data, FY83, annual rpt with semiannual update for 1st qtr FY84, 9534–7

Dairy cooperatives and percent share of producers and deliveries, by region, 1982 with trends from 1965, article, 1317–4.403

Dairy cooperatives sales volume and market shares by commodity, and finances, by region, 1980 with trends from 1957, 1128–29

Dairy products production by type, and plants, by State, 1983, annual rpt, 1627–5

Department stores, by SMSA, monthly rpt, 2413–3

Index by Subjects and Names

Business firms and establishments, number

Developing countries free zones, industry financial and operating data by country, with case studies for 5 countries, 1970s-82, 9918–10

Fish and fish products production by region and State, and trade, by species and product, 1982-83, annual rpt series, 2166–6

Fishery and fish processing employment, firms, and vessels, 1950s-83, annual rpt, 2164–1.10

Forest industry establishments, employment, and payroll in Northeast, by SIC 2- to 4-digit industry, State rpt series, 1206–16

Franchises of firms engaged in distribution of goods and services by kind of business, establishments by State, and sales, 1982-84, annual rpt, 2014–5

Georgia job expansion in southern rural 10-county area, employment and establishments by worker and industry characteristics, 1976-81, article, 1502–7.401

Health maintenance organizations enrollment (total, Medicare, and Medicaid), finances, Fed Govt qualification status, and PHS loan activity, by HMO, FY83, annual rpt, 4044–2

Income tax returns filed by type, for US, IRS regions, and service center cities, 1972-82 and projected 1983-90, annual rpt, 8304–9.1

Income tax returns of foreign subsidiaries of US corporations, income and tax data, by industry and asset size, 1980, article, 8302–2.410

Income tax returns of partnerships, receipts by source, deductions by type, and establishments, by selected industry, 1982, annual article, 8302–2.416

Income tax returns of sole proprietorships, detailed data by industry div and selected industry group, 1981, annual rpt, 8304–7

Industry finances and operations, by SIC 2- to 4-digit industry, 1970s-83 and projected to 1988, annual rpt, 2014–4

Kentucky employment growth in 9-county rural area, labor force and establishment characteristics, 1979-80, 1598–194

Livestock packers purchases and feeding, and livestock markets, dealers, and sales, by region and State, 1981-82, annual rpt, 1384–1

Machinery and equipment production, shipments, trade, stocks, consumption, orders, and firms, by product, periodic Current Industrial Rpt series, 2506–12

Manufacturer-set retail prices under fair-trade law by brand and product, with manufacturers, market concentration, and sales, by industry, selected years 1952-82, 9406–1.38

Manufacturing census, 1982: financial and operating data, by SIC 2- to 4-digit industry, State, SMSA, and county, preliminary census div rpt series, 2491–3

Manufacturing census, 1982: financial and operating data, for SIC 4-digit industries by product, preliminary rpt series, 2491–1

Meat marketing and distribution establishments, sales, and per capita consumption, 1950s-82 with trends from 1929, 1548–232

Metals (intermediate product) shipments, trade, and inventories, by product, periodic Current Industrial Rpt series, 2506–11

Milk price supports effect on production, use, prices, and farm receipts, by region and State, 1940s-83 and alternative projections to 1988/89, 1568–245

Mineral industries census, 1982: financial and operating data, by SIC 2- to 4-digit industry and State, preliminary summary rpts, 2511–2

Mineral industries census, 1982: financial and operating data, including materials consumed, by SIC 4-digit industry and State, preliminary rpt series, 2511–1

Minerals Yearbook, 1982, Vol 2: State reviews of production, sales, and firms, by commodity, and business activity, annual rpt, 5604–34

Motor carriers (Class II) of property financial and operating data, by region, 1982, annual rpt, 9484–10

Northern Mariana Islands economic, govtl, and population data, FY83 with trends and projections, annual rpt, 7004–6.2

Oil refinery locations and capacities in US and territories, by company, Jan 1983, annual rpt, 3164–2

Partnership finances, tax deductions, and employment, by industry div and size, 1979, article, 8302–2.411

Pest control firms in urban areas, pesticide use by type, employment, and sales, by type of service, 1981 survey, article, 1561–16.408

Philanthropic foundations detailed financial and operating data, and stock holdings by instn, 1979 with selected trends from 1920, GAO rpt, 26119–53

Potato chip plants, 1982-83, annual rpt, 1621–11

Public utility holding company finances, securities issued, and subsidiaries by type, by firm, FY83, annual rpt, 9734–2.6

Retail trade census, 1982: employment, establishments, sales, and payroll, by SIC 2- to 4-digit kind of business, SMSA, and retail district, State rpt series, 2401–1

Retail trade census, 1982: employment, establishments, sales, and payroll, by SIC 2- to 4-digit kind of business, SMSA, county, and city, State rpt series, 2397–1

Retail trade census, 1982: employment, establishments, sales, and payroll, by SIC 4-digit kind of business and State, preliminary rpt series, 2395–1

Savings and loan assns and FSLIC-insured savings banks and S&Ls, assets, liabilities, and deposit and loan activity, monthly rpt, 9312–4

Savings and loan assns, by FHLB district and State, selected years 1955-82, annual rpt, 9314–1

Savings and loan assns, FHLB 6th District insured members financial condition and operations by State, quarterly rpt, 9302–23

Savings instns FSLIC-insured, offices, and savings deposits, by State, SMSA, and county, 1983, annual rpt, 9314–4

Securities brokers and investment firms, finances, and SEC registration, 1978-FY83, annual rpt, 9734 2.1, 9734–2.2

Service industry census, 1982: employment, establishments, receipts, and payroll, by SIC 2- to 4-digit kind of business, SMSA, county, and city, State rpt series, 2391–1

Service industry census, 1982: employment, establishments, receipts, and payroll, by SIC 4-digit kind of business and State, preliminary rpt series, 2390–2

Small and minority-owned businesses finances and operations, Federal contracts by agency, and worker characteristics, by industry, race, sex, and State, 1950s-83, annual rpt, 9764–6

Small business economic conditions, with comparisons to larger businesses, selected years 1979-83, annual rpt, 9764–1.1

Solar collector and photovoltaic module production, sales, and use, with listing of manufacturers, 1983, annual rpt, 3164–62

Statistical Abstract of US, social, political, and economic data, 1950s-83 and trends, annual rpt, 2324–1.3

Sulfuric acid production, establishments, and shipments, by census div and State, and trade, 1983, annual Current Industrial Rpt, 2506–8.13

Technology-intensive industry employment and establishments by industry and selected location, and venture capital investments by source, 1970s-82, 26358–107

Telephone operating and financial data by company type, with fixed cost recovery from interstate revenue by Bell company and State, 1981-82 with trends from 1945, 26306–6.79

Transit system financial and operating data, by mode, function, fleet size, and individual system, FY82, annual rpt, 7884–4

Transportation finances, operations, vehicles, equipment, accidents, and energy use, by mode of transport, 1955-84, annual rpt, 7304–2

Travel agency financial and operating data, and airline ticket sales by type of distributor, 1970s-82, hearing, 25268–81

TV and radio industry minority and women employment by occupation, and business owners, by race and State, with revenues and stations, 1971-81, hearing, 21368–45

TV and radio stations on the air, by class of operation, monthly press release, 9282–4

Uranium exploration, land acquisition expenditures, and employment, various periods 1966-83 and planned 1984-85, annual rpt, 3164–65

Uranium prices, deliveries, trade, stocks, secondary marketing, investment, and employment, selected years 1967-83 and for commitments to 2001, annual rpt, 3164–66

Uranium reserves and mining and milling industries operations and finances, with selected foreign comparisons, various periods 1964-83 and projected to 2000, 3008–95

Virgin Islands economic censuses, 1982: employment, establishments, payroll, and receipts, by SIC 1- to 4-digit industry, island, and city, 2593–1

Wholesale trade census, 1982: employment, establishments, finances, and operations, by SIC 2- to 4-digit kind of business, SMSA, county, and city, State rpt series, 2405–1

Business firms and establishments, number

Wholesale trade census, 1982: employment, establishments, sales by commodity, and payroll, by SIC 4-digit kind of business and State, preliminary rpt series, 2403–1

see also Bank holding companies
see also Farms and farmland
see also Foreign corporations
see also Franchises
see also Government corporations
see also Holding companies
see also Industrial plants and equipment
see also Minority businesses
see also Multinational corporations
see also Public utilities
see also Small Business Investment Companies

see also under By Individual Company or Institution in the "Index by Categories"
see also under By Industry in the "Index by Categories"

Business income and expenses, general

- Air pollutant emissions in US and selected countries, control costs, and acid rain causes and effects, 1970s-83 and projected to 2000, 21368–52
- Air pollutant sulfur dioxide emissions reduction proposal, effects on polluting industries and coal production by region and State, projected to 2010, 9188–97
- Business and financial statistics, quarterly chartbook, 9362–2.2
- *Business Conditions Digest,* current data on economic, business, and financial conditions and cyclical fluctuations, monthly rpt, 2702–3
- *Business Conditions Digest,* historical supplement on economic, business, and financial conditions and cyclical fluctuations, with methodology, 1947-82, 2708–31
- Business statistics, detailed data for major industries and economic indicators, *Survey of Current Business,* monthly rpt, 2702–1
- Coastal environmental characteristics, fish, wildlife, and use, and population socioeconomic data, for individual areas, series, 5506–4
- Corporate taxes and effective rates on US, foreign, and worldwide income, by major industry group, and share of Fed Govt receipts, 1980-82, 23868–14
- Corporations financial statements for manufacturing, mining, and trade, by selected SIC 2- to 3-digit industry, quarterly rpt, 2502–1
- Corporations financial statistics, monthly rpt, 9362–1.1
- Corporations historic financial and business statistics, 1984 annual chartbook, 9364–2.10
- Corporations profits and capital consumption allowances under alternative depreciation formulas, 1980-83, article, 2702–1.434
- Corporations profits by industry, 1929-83, and sources and uses of funds, 1946-83, annual rpt, 204–1.7
- *County and City Data Book,* detailed socioeconomic and demographic data for States, counties, and cities, selected years 1976-82, 2328–1
- Economic indicators and components, current data and annual trends, monthly rpt, 23842–1.1, 23842–1.3, 23842–1.5

Index by Subjects and Names

- Economic trends and projections, 1970s-83, and Budget of US under current fiscal policy and alternatives, FY85-89, annual rpt, 26304–3.1
- Economic trends, natl compounded annual rates of change, monthly rpt, 9391–3.2
- Election campaign finances and Fed Election Commission monitoring activities, 1984 Federal elections, biennial rpt series, 9276–2
- Employee stock ownership plans in developing countries, and firms finances and operations, with case studies of US and 3 countries, 1970s-82, 9916–3.19
- Enterprise zone and urban revitalization projects of State and local govts, effect on business and employment in selected areas, various dates 1972-83, hearing, 21788–140
- Environmental quality and protection programs, costs, and Fed Govt enforcement, 1983, detailed annual rpt, 484–1
- Financial services acquisitions, risk and earnings correlations and regression analysis, various periods 1970-82, article, 9371–1.416
- Forecasts for selected business activities and natl economic indicators, compilation of representative opinions, 1984, annual rpt, 9389–3
- Foreign direct investment in US by country, and finances, operations, and land ownership, by industry group for businesses acquired and established, 1982-83, annual article, 2702–1.418
- Foreign direct investment in US, by major industry group, world area, and selected country, 1980-83, annual article, 2702–1.439
- Foreign direct investment worldwide, and US investment flows by major industry, by world region and country, 1982 and trends from 1950, annual rpt, 2044–25
- Foreign firms US affiliates financial and operating data, by country of parent firm and industry div, 1980-81, article, 2702–1.402
- France Brittany coast oil spill cleanup and research costs, marine and tourism industry losses, and recreation losses of tourists and residents, 1971-79, 2178–13
- Franchises of firms engaged in distribution of goods and services by kind of business, establishments by State, and sales, 1982-84, annual rpt, 2014–5
- Fresno, Calif, economic, population, labor, and housing indicators, various periods 1974-85, hearing, 21248–84
- Georgia small businesses, effect of mgmt counseling on sales, employment, profits, and taxes paid, 1980-81, hearing, 25728–36
- Import and tariff provisions effect on US industries and products, investigations with background financial and operating data, series, 9886–4
- Imports from Communist countries, injury to US industries, investigations with background financial and operating data, selected industries and products, series, 9886–12
- Imports injury to US industries from foreign subsidized products and sales in US at less than fair value, investigations with background financial and operating data, series, 9886–19

- Imports injury to US industries from foreign subsidized products, investigations with background financial and operating data for selected industries and products, series, 9886–15
- Imports injury to US industries from import sales at less than fair value, investigations with background financial and operating data, series, 9886–14
- Imports injury to US industries from increased import sales, investigations with background financial and operating data, series, 9886–5
- Imports injury to US industries from removal of duties on foreign subsidized products, investigations with background financial and operating data, series, 9886–18
- Income (taxable) not reported on individual and corporate returns, and associated Federal revenue losses, by detailed legal and illegal source, 1973-81, 8308–26
- Income tax payments of corporations to Fed Govt, Budget of US estimates revised for consistency with FY85 budget definitions, FY40-89, annual rpt, 104–12
- Income tax returns filed by type of filer, selected income items, summary data, quarterly rpt, 8302–2.1
- Income tax returns of corporations, detailed income and tax items by industry, 1981, annual rpt, 8304–4
- Income tax returns of corporations, summary data by industry div, 1981 estimates, annual article, 8302–2.403
- Income tax returns of corporations with foreign tax credit, income and deductions by type, asset size, and selected industry group, 1980, article, 8302–2.415
- Income tax returns of elderly, by income statement and tax item and income level, 1981 with trends from 1977, article, 8302–2.412
- Income tax returns of foreign subsidiaries of US corporations, income and tax data, by industry and asset size, 1980, article, 8302–2.410
- Income tax returns of individuals, by filing and deduction characteristics and income level, 1983, annual article, 8302–2.414
- Income tax returns of individuals by tax return item, State, and occupation, and income by source and tax owed, by income level, selected years 1916-80, conf papers, 8308–28.1
- Income tax returns of individuals, detailed data, 1982, annual rpt, 8304–2
- Income tax returns of partnerships, receipts by source, deductions by type, and establishments, by selected industry, 1982, annual article, 8302–2.416
- Income tax returns of sole proprietorships, detailed data by industry div and selected industry group, 1981, annual rpt, 8304–7
- Income tax returns of sole proprietorships, receipts, deductions by type, payroll, and net income, by major industry, 1982, annual article, 8302–2.413
- Industry finances and operations, by SIC 2- to 4-digit industry, 1970s-83 and projected to 1988, annual rpt, 2014–4
- Industry R&D expenditures by funding source, and projected impact on output, employment, and hours of labor, by selected industry, various periods 1953-90, hearings, 25368–133

Index by Subjects and Names

Mail postage ratemaking and classification cases, processing, and participant costs and attitudes, 1970s-84, GAO rpt, 26119–63

Manufacturer-set retail prices under fair-trade law by brand and product, with manufacturers, market concentration, and sales, by industry, selected years 1952-82, 9406–1.38

Manufacturers capacity utilization rates and production indexes, sales, inventories, shipments, and orders, 1947-83, annual rpt, 204–1.3

Manufacturers under Fed Govt contract and owned by DOD, operating data by agency, selected SIC 2- to 4-digit industry, State, and SMSA, 1982, annual Current Industrial Rpt, 2506–3.4

Manufacturing and trade inventories, sales, and inventory/sales ratios, quarterly article, 2702–1.34

Manufacturing census, 1982: financial and operating data, for SIC 4-digit industries by product, preliminary rpt series, 2491–1

Manufacturing operating and financial data, 1980-81 Annual Survey of Manufactures rpt reprints, hardbound vol, 2504–1

Minority business mgmt and financial assistance from federally funded organizations, by region, State, and business characteristics, FY83, annual rpt, 2104–6

Multinatl and multistate corporations income under alternative State income tax treatment methods, by major industry, 1977, article, 9373–1.412

Multinatl corporation income reallocation through regulation of intercorporate transactions, by tax item, treaty status, asset size, industry, and tax haven country, 1982, 8008–110

Natl income and product, comprehensive accounts and components, *Survey of Current Business,* monthly rpt, 2702–1.21

Natl income and product, comprehensive accounts and components, *Survey of Current Business,* monthly rpt, monthly and annual tables, 2702–1.27

Partnership finances, tax deductions, and employment, by industry div and size, 1979, article, 8302–2.411

Pollution abatement capital and operating costs, by SIC 2- to 4-digit industry, State, and SMSA, 1982, annual Current Industrial Rpt, 2506–3.6

Pollution abatement capital and operating costs under Clean Air and Water Acts, for govts and selected industries, various periods 1970-2000, annual rpt, 9184–11

Pollution abatement expenditures, and effect on economic indicators and industry operations, by major industry, projected under 3 pollution regulation alternatives 1983-95, 9188–84

Pollution abatement expenditures of govt, business, and consumers, 1972-82, annual article, 2702–1.407

Port dev costs and financing through user fees, and shipping industry impact on local economy, by State, other area, industry, commodity, and port, 1970s-2020, hearings, 21568–34

Business income and expenses, general

Productivity and costs of labor for private, nonfarm business, and manufacturing sectors, preliminary data, quarterly rpt, 6822–1

Productivity and costs of labor for private, nonfarm business, and manufacturing sectors, revised data, quarterly rpt, 6822–2

R&D expenditures of US firms foreign affiliates, by selected industry, 1974-82, 9626–2.131

R&D funding by industry, program, and Federal agency, and high-technology trade performance, selected years 1960-FY84, 26306–6.77

R&D industry expenditures by funding source, and scientists and engineers employed, by SIC 2- and 3-digit industry, 1982 with trends from 1962, annual rpt, 9626–2.139

R&D industry expenditures, total and for 6 leading industries, projected 1984-85 with trends from 1975, 9626–2.145

R&D industry funding and employment of scientists and engineers, by industry group, firm size, and funding source, 1956-82, annual rpt, 9627–21

Retail trade census, 1982: employment, establishments, sales, and payroll, by SIC 2- to 4-digit kind of business, SMSA, and retail district, State rpt series, 2401–1

Retail trade census, 1982: employment, establishments, sales, and payroll, by SIC 2- to 4-digit kind of business, SMSA, county, and city, State rpt series, 2397–1

Retail trade census, 1982: employment, establishments, sales, and payroll, by SIC 4-digit kind of business and State, preliminary rpt series, 2395–1

Retail trade sales and inventories, by kind of business, region, census div, and selected State, SMSA, and city, and seasonal adjustments, monthly rpt, 2413–3

Retail trade sales, by kind of business, advance monthly rpt, 2413–2

Retail trade sales, inventories, purchases, gross margin, and accounts receivable, by SIC 2- to 4-digit kind of business and type of ownership, 1983, annual rpt, 2413–5

Retail trade sales of consumer goods including autos, and manufacturers orders and shipments, 1950-84, annual chartbook, 9364–2.3

Science Indicators, R&D expenditures, innovations, research, and higher education, with foreign comparisons, 1960s- 83, annual rpt, 9624–10

Security services expenditures, by level of govt and for private business by major industry, 1981, 6066–20.8

Service industries receipts, by SIC 2- to 4-digit kind of business, 1983, annual rpt, 2413–8

Service industry census, 1982: employment, establishments, receipts, and payroll, by SIC 2- to 4-digit kind of business, SMSA, county, and city, State rpt series, 2391–1

Service industry census, 1982: employment, establishments, receipts, and payroll, by SIC 4-digit kind of business and State, preliminary rpt series, 2390–2

Services intl transactions, and operations of US multinatl service firms and foreign affiliates, by industry and world region, 1977-82, 2706–5.30

Small and minority-owned businesses finances and operations, Federal contracts by agency, and worker characteristics, by industry, race, sex, and State, 1950s-83, annual rpt, 9764–6

Small business capital formation under securities law exemptions, effects on stocks offered, issuers, and purchasers, series, 9736–2

Small business employment and receipts size standards for Fed Govt contract awards by industry, and DOD contract awards data, 1970s-83, hearings, 21728–53

Small business loans and credit, operational expectations, and NYC metro area owners economic and professional attitudes, by industry div, 1980-83 surveys, hearings, 21728–52

Southeastern States and 5 SMSAs economic indicators, Fed Reserve 8th District, quarterly rpt, 9391–15

Southeastern States, financial and operating characteristics of 22 high performance firms and 10 largest banks, 1982-83, article, 9371–1.414

Statistical Abstract of US, social, political, and economic data, 1950s-83 and trends, annual rpt, 2324–1.3

Stock offerings gross proceeds for corporate common and preferred shares, by major industry div, SEC monthly rpt, 9732–1

Tax evasion through tax haven countries, with income, investments, and taxes withheld by country, various periods 1975- 83, hearings, 21408–71

Trade policy of Fed Govt, with data on US industry foreign trade and revenues, and Japan semiconductor industry subsidies, 1970s-83, hearings, 21368–46

Underground legal and illegal income, and legal income not reported on Federal income tax returns by source, with bibl, 1974-81, article, 2702–1.419

Virgin Islands economic censuses, 1982: employment, establishments, payroll, and receipts, by SIC 1- to 4-digit industry, island, and city, 2593–1

Weather events socioeconomic impacts and costs, heating and cooling degree days, and housing energy bills, by census div and State, monthly rpt, 2152–12

Wholesale trade census, 1982: employment, establishments, finances, and operations, by SIC 2- to 4-digit kind of business, SMSA, county, and city, State rpt series, 2405–1

Wholesale trade census, 1982: employment, establishments, sales by commodity, and payroll, by SIC 4-digit kind of business and State, preliminary rpt series, 2403–1

Wholesale trade sales and inventories, by SIC 2- to 3-digit kind of business, monthly rpt, 2413–7

Wholesale trade sales, inventories, purchases, and gross margins, by SIC 2- to 3-digit kind of business and type of ownership, 1983, annual rpt, 2413–13

see also Agricultural finance

see also Agricultural marketing

see also Agricultural production costs

see also Business assets and liabilities, general

see also Business income and expenses, specific industries

Business income and expenses, general

see also Capital investments, general
see also Depreciation
see also Economic indicators
see also Energy production costs
see also Farm income
see also Labor cost indexes
see also Operating ratios
see also Payroll
see also Production costs

Business income and expenses, specific industries

- Aerospace industry sales, and new and backlog orders, for military and nonmilitary customers, quarterly Current Industrial Rpt, 2506–12.22
- Agricultural cooperative finances and operations, aggregate for top 100 assns by principal product and revenue source, FY82, annual rpt, 1124–3
- Agricultural cooperatives activities, operations, finances, and current issues, monthly rpt articles, 1122–1
- Agricultural cooperatives for grain, storage and handling facilities, sales, exports, and financial condition, selected years 1974-82, 1128–31
- Agricultural cooperatives, membership, activities, and finances, by commodity and selected State, 1900-80 with trends from 1863, 1128–30
- Agricultural cooperatives, membership, and activities, by type of service, commodity, and State, FY51-1982, annual survey rpt, 1124–1
- AID Housing Guaranty Program financial statements, and projects by country, FY83, annual rpt, 9914–4
- Air cargo yields and revenue ton-miles, for major and all cargo domestic carrier groups, quarterly rpt, 9142–35
- Airline cash flows for all certificated carriers, quarterly rpt, 9142–34
- Airline deregulation in 1978, effect on industry operations and finances, air traffic patterns, and CAB programs, various periods FY76-84, 9148–56
- Airline financial and operating data for certificated, charter, and cargo carriers, quarterly rpt, 9142–30
- Airline financial data, by carrier, carrier group, and for total certificated system, quarterly rpt, 9142–12
- Airline income and profitability, by major carrier, 1972-83, annual rpt, 9144–37
- Airline income taxes paid, net income, and effective tax rates, by major carrier, 1968-83, annual rpt, 9144–34
- Airline intl operations, traffic and financial data for US combination carriers in Atlantic, Pacific, and Latin America regions, quarterly rpt, 9142–41
- Airline operating and other costs, itemized for domestic and intl trunk and local service carriers, 1st half 1983, semiannual rpt, 9142–47
- Airline operating unit costs for each system major and short-haul natl carrier, quarterly rpt, 9142–37
- Airline operations and passenger, cargo, and mail traffic, by type of service, air carrier, State, and country, 1974-83, annual rpt, 7504–1.6
- Airline profit margins, for major operators of large aircraft by carrier group and carrier, quarterly rpt, 9142–43

Index by Subjects and Names

- Airline traffic and financial data, by carrier, FY83 with trends from FY73, annual rpt, 9144–1
- Airport financing by source, bond issues by region, and airport operations, by airport and operator type, FY75-83 and projected to FY93, 26306–6.75
- Alcohol fuel (ethanol) production in Tennessee Valley, feedstocks, facilities, tax incentives, and related farming data, by State, 1970s-83 and projected to 1992, 9808–69
- Altman Foundation philanthropic grants in New York by recipient, and Foundation income and expenses, selected years 1913-82, hearings, 21788–137
- Aluminum industry electricity use, operations, and energy and labor efficiency by plant, for Pacific Northwest, projected 1984-2003, annual rpt, 3224–2.4
- Amtrak finances and operations, and Northeast Corridor rail improvement project goals, funding, and progress, FY83, annual rpt, 7604–9
- Army morale, welfare, and recreation programs, revenue and expenses worldwide by activity and major command, FY82-83, annual rpt, 3704–12
- Auto and auto products sales, prices, and registrations in US, and trade of 8 countries with US, by make and model, 1964-83, annual rpt, 9884–7
- Auto industry finances and operations by manufacturer, foreign competition, and consumer auto expenditures and attitudes toward car buying, selected years 1968-85, annual rpt, 2004–8
- Auto industry finances, employment, production, and cost increases to comply with Fed Govt pollution and safety standards, 1970s-83, annual rpt, 3304–5.4
- Auto industry operations, and trade by country, monthly rpt, 9882–8
- Auto industry operations, trade, and registrations, foreign and US, selected years 1928-82, domestic content requirement hearings, 21788–134
- Bank deposit interest rate deregulation, effect on bank deposits and bank financial performance, 1978-83, hearing, 21248–83
- Bank financial and operating statements, functional cost analysis for Fed Reserve member banks with average and high earnings, by deposit size, 1982, annual rpt, 9364–6
- Bank financial statistics, historic trends, 1984 annual chartbook, 9364–2.13
- Bank holding company income, actual and in event of Argentina nonpayment of debt interest, for 7 US multinatls, 1st qtr 1984, 9368–77
- Bank holding company ratios of financial involvement in nonbank subsidiaries and subsidiary performance, by holding company size, various periods 1978-82, article, 9377–1.406
- Bank income and expenses, Fed Reserve 5th District member banks, by State, 1983, annual rpt, 9389–10
- Bank income, expenses, and dividends, for Fed Reserve members, 1982, annual rpt, 9364–5.11

- Bank profitability, finances, loans and terms, intl earnings, and operating ratios for insured commercial instns, 1980-83, annual article, 9362–1.409
- Banking and financial data, 1982, annual rpt, 9364–5
- Banks (natl) domestic and intl operations, charters, mergers, and liquidations, by State and instn, and Comptroller of Currency activities, quarterly rpt, 8402–3
- Banks (natl) income, expenses, and dividends, *Treasury Bulletin,* quarterly rpt, 8002–4.19
- Banks and thrift instns in New England, financial statements by type of instn and State, 1972 and 1982, annual rpt, 9304–3
- Banks in Fed Reserve 5th District, by asset size, finances, and loans and deposits by type, various dates 1979-83, annual article, 9389–1.408
- Biotechnology commercial uses, R&D funding and output, controls, and industry financial and operating data, for US and 5 countries, 1970s-83 and estimated 1984-85, 26358–98
- Bonneville Power Admin operations, and Columbia River power system sales and financial statements, FY83, annual rpt, 3224–1
- Bonneville Power Admin sales, revenues, and prices, by class of customer and individual purchaser, 1983, semiannual rpt, 3222–1
- Bus industry collective ratemaking and regulatory reform impacts on operations, finances, and services to older persons and rural areas by State, 1970s-83, 14828–2
- Campground facilities privately owned, and financial and operating data, by region, 1982, annual rpt, 5544–14.5
- CCC loan activities by commodity, and agency operating results, monthly press release, 1802–7
- Chemicals (synthetic organic) production and sales by product, and listing of manufacturers, 1983, annual rpt, 9884–3
- Chrysler Corp Loan Guarantee Act implementation, with related financial and operating data, FY83, last issue of annual rpt, 8004–14
- Cigarette sales, market shares, advertising expenditures and methods, and tar and nicotine content, by cigarette type, selected years 1963-81, annual rpt, 9404–4
- Colorado River Storage Project finances, water resource dev, power production, and other activities in western States, FY83, annual rpt, 5824–3
- Communications satellite intl systems charges, operations, investment shares by country, and competition impacts, 1964-83 with projections to 2003, hearings, 25388–46
- Connecticut home health agencies total costs related to level of medical service and administrative spending, 1981, article, 4652–1.411
- Conrail operations and US Railway Assn finances and activities, FY81-83, annual rpt, 29604–1
- Construction industries census, 1982: financial and operating data, by SIC 4-digit industry and State, final rpt series, 2373–1

Index by Subjects and Names

Construction industries census, 1982: financial and operating data, by SIC 4-digit industry and State, preliminary rpt series, 2371–1

Copper mine expansion in Cananea, Mexico, effects on US air pollution and copper industry, with US and foreign industry data, 1960s-95, hearing, 21448–31

Credit card fraud losses, transactions by electronic funds transfer and other means, and potential for EFT crime, 1975-82, 6066–19.3

Credit union financial statements by region, State, and type of membership, for Federal and federally insured State unions, 1983, annual rpt, 9534–1

Credit Union Natl Admin Central Liquidity Facility, financial performance, quarterly rpt, 9532–4

Credit Union Natl Admin insurance fund financial activity, and insured instns financial and operating data, FY83, annual rpt with semiannual update for 1st qtr FY84, 9534–7

Disabled American Veterans financial statements, 1982, GAO rpt, 26111–16

Electric and gas utility diversification activity by type, and finances and bond ratings by selected firm, various periods 1970-83, hearing, 21368–53

Electric power plant capacity and generation by fuel type, and marketing, for Alaska by utility, type of ownership, and location, 1983, annual rpt, 3214–2

Electric power plant capital and operating detailed costs, capacity, and fuel use, by plant, plant type, utility, and State, 1982, annual rpt, 3164–9

Electric power purchases of municipal and cooperative distributors, and prices and consumption by distributor and consumer sector, for TVA, monthly rpt, 9802–1

Electric utilities privately owned, capital investment, finances, equity performance, and operating characteristics, 1950-82 with supply estimates to 2010, 3168–87

Electric utilities privately owned, detailed financial and operating data by company, with summary data for other distributors by type, 1982, annual rpt, 3164–23

Electric utility production, fuel consumption, stocks, and costs by fuel type, and sales, by State, monthly rpt, 3162–35

Energy conservation programs of utilities, financing, costs, participation, and energy savings, various periods 1981-84, hearing, 21368–54

Energy producers finances and operations, by energy type for US firms domestic and foreign operations, 1974-82, annual rpt, 3164–44

Energy production, dev, and distribution firms revenues and income, quarterly rpt, 3162–38

Eximbank financial condition, and loan, credit, and insurance authorizations, by country, FY83, annual rpt, 9254–1

Farm Credit System banks financial statements, Dec 1979-83, annual rpt, 9264–5

Farm Credit System mortgage and other loans, and financial statements, 1982 and selected trends from 1961, annual rpt, 9264–2

Business income and expenses, specific industries

FDIC officials and operations, 1983, annual rpt, 9294–1.2

Fed Crop Insurance Corp finances, and insurance participation and operations in 2 States by crop, 1980-84, GAO rpt, 26113–132

Fed Crop Insurance Corp program activities and costs, and FCIC and private insurance company gains and losses, 1980-84 with some trends from 1948, GAO rpt, 26113–119

Fed Crop Insurance Corp program operations and finances, for FCIC policies and private policies reinsured by FCIC, 1970s-84 with trends from 1948, hearing, 21168–28

Fed Financial Instns Examination Council financial statements, 1982-83, with summary data on financial instns by type, year ended June 1983, annual rpt, 13004–2

Fed Home Loan Bank of Atlanta financial statements, 1982-83, annual rpt, 9304–1

Fed Home Loan Bank of Boston financial statements, 1983, annual rpt, 9304–2

Fed Home Loan Bank of Chicago financial statements, 1982-83, annual rpt, 9304–4

Fed Home Loan Bank of Cincinnati financial statements, 1982-83, annual rpt, 9304–6

Fed Home Loan Bank of Dallas financial statements, 1982-83, annual rpt, 9304–11

Fed Home Loan Bank of Des Moines financial statements, 1982-83, annual rpt, 9304–7

Fed Home Loan Bank of Indianapolis financial statements, 1982-83, annual rpt, 9304–10

Fed Home Loan Bank of New York financial statements, 1982-83, annual rpt, 9304–12

Fed Home Loan Bank of Pittsburgh financial statements, 1982-83, annual rpt, 9304–13

Fed Home Loan Bank of San Francisco financial statements, 1982-83, annual rpt, 9304–14

Fed Home Loan Bank of Seattle financial statements, 1982-83, annual rpt, 9304–15

Fed Home Loan Bank of Topeka financial statements, 1982-83, annual rpt, 9304–16

Fed Home Loan Banks and S&Ls, financial condition and mortgage loan activity, monthly rpt with articles, 9312–1

Fed Home Loan Mortgage Corp activities and financial statements, 1983, annual rpt, 9414–1

Fed Reserve Bank of Atlanta financial statements, 1982-83, annual rpt, 9371–4

Fed Reserve Bank of Chicago financial statements, 1983, annual rpt, 9375–5

Fed Reserve Bank of Cleveland financial statements, 1982-83, annual rpt, 9377–5

Fed Reserve Bank of Dallas financial statements, 1982-83, annual rpt, 9379–2

Fed Reserve Bank of Kansas City financial statements, 1982-83, annual rpt, 9381–3

Fed Reserve Bank of Minneapolis financial statements, 1981-82, annual rpt, 9383–2

Fed Reserve Bank of New York financial statements, 1982-83, annual rpt, 9385–2

Fed Reserve Bank of Philadelphia financial statements, 1982-83, annual rpt, 9387–3

Fed Reserve Bank of Richmond financial statements, 1983, annual rpt, 9389–2

Fed Reserve Bank of San Francisco financial statements, 1982-83, annual rpt, 9393–2

Fed Reserve Board and Reserve banks financial statements and employees, and review of monetary policy and economic devs, 1983, annual rpt, 9364–1

Fed Reserve payments services provided depository instns, financial statements, and costs and revenues by service and district bank, 1983, annual press release, 9364–9

Financial instns income taxes, effective rates, and selected financial data, by instn type and firm, with comparisons to other industries, selected years 1960-82, hearing, 25368–129

Fishing diesel and sail-assisted boats in Hawaiian waters, fuel use, earnings, and operating costs, with fuel and fish price indexes, various periods 1967-81, article, 2162–1.401

Food prices (farm-retail), marketing cost components, and industry finances and productivity, selected years 1967-83, annual rpt, 1544–9

Govt Natl Mortgage Assn financial statements, and mortgage-backed securities program, FY82-83, annual rpt, 5144–6

GPO activities, finances, and production, FY83, annual rpt, 26204–1

GPO document sales program mgmt and finances, and bookstore operations by location, FY78-82, GAO rpt, 26111–17

Health maintenance organizations and prepaid health plans enrollment, use, and Fed Govt aid, FY83, annual rpt, 4104–8

Health maintenance organizations enrollment (total, Medicare, and Medicaid), finances, Fed Govt qualification status, and PHS loan activity, by HMO, FY83, annual rpt, 4044–2

Hospital Corp of America capital costs reimbursement from Medicare and Medicaid following acquisition of Hospital Affiliates Intl, 1981-82, GAO rpt, 26121–65

Hospitals and nursing homes in Arizona, finances and operations for specified facilities, and itemized expenses for selected cases, 1978-83, hearing, 21148–29

Howard University salaries, academic standing, medical research, and library operations, and finances of Howard Inn, selected years 1976-83, GAO rpt, 26121–74

Insurance company workers compensation income, expenses, and benefits paid by degree of disability, 1939-80, article, 4742–1.414

Insurance industry (property and casualty) financial and operating data, investments, and tax liability, various periods 1951-82, hearing, 25368–128

Kennedy Performing Arts Center income and expenses by type, and Fed Govt share of expenses, FY79-83, GAO rpt, 26119–60

Libraries of colleges and universities, expenditures, holdings by type, use, staff by sex, and Federal grants received, 1979-82, biennial rpt, 4854–1

Mineral industries census, 1982: financial and operating data, by SIC 2- to 4-digit industry and State, preliminary summary rpts, 2511–2

Business income and expenses, specific industries

Mineral industries census, 1982: financial and operating data, including materials consumed, by SIC 4-digit industry and State, preliminary rpt series, 2511–1

Minerals (strategic) supply/demand, trade, and foreign and US industry devs by firm and country, by commodity, bimonthly rpt, 5602–4

Minerals Yearbook, 1982, Vol 1: commodity reviews of industry economic conditions, supply/demand, and trade, annual rpt, 5604–33.3

Mines Bur helium production and sales, and helium program financial statement, FY83, annual rpt, 5604–32

Motor and rail carriers regulated by ICC, employment and finances by mode of transport, and ICC activities, FY80-83 and trends, annual rpt, 9484–1

Motor carrier passengers and selected revenue data, for individual large Class I motor carriers, quarterly rpt, 9482–13

Motor carriers (Class I) of household goods operating revenues, net income, and revenue tons, by firm, quarterly rpt, 9482–14

Motor carriers (Class I) of property financial and operating data, by region and firm, quarterly rpt, 9482–5

Motor carriers (Class I interstate) finances, operations, equipment, employment, and payroll, by district, 1982, annual rpt, 9486–5.3

Motor carriers (Class II) of property financial and operating data, by region, 1982, annual rpt, 9484–10

Motorcycle imports, sales, and inventories of foreign make, and prices and employment for domestic makes, quarterly rpt, 9882–12

Natural and supplemental gas production, prices, trade, use, reserves, and pipeline company finances, by firm and State, monthly rpt with articles, 3162–4

Natural gas interstate pipeline company detailed financial and operating data, by firm, 1983, annual rpt, 3164–38

Natural gas interstate pipeline sales, total and under minimum fee contract provision, by service type, contract date, and region, 1981, 3168–91

Natural gas supply, contract prices, pipeline operations and finances, and residential use, various periods 1966-1983/84, 3168–89

Nuclear power accident liability insurance under Price-Anderson Act, effects on industry finances and operations, with insurance coverage, claims, and costs, various periods 1957-82, 9638–49

Nuclear power industry status and outlook, with reactor construction, utility financial and operating data, and foreign comparisons, 1970s-83 with projections to 2010, 26358–99

Nuclear power plant construction costs and status, capacity, and revenue requirements, by plant and utility, various dates Dec 1983-Mar 1984, article, 9385–1.412

Nuclear power plant licensing 24-month delay, effect on utility financial performance and electric power prices, for plant completed May 1979, 9638–53

Nuclear power plant safety standards and research, design, licensing, construction, operation, and finances, with data by reactor, bimonthly rpt, 3352–4

Oil (Alaskan) potential exports to Japan, costs and benefits, with background data on oil prices, Pacific Basin supply/demand, and tankers, various periods 1918-99, hearings, 25388–45

Oil and gas companies production and exploration detailed expenditures, revenues, operating ratios, and sales volume, 1982, annual Current Industrial Rpt, 2506–8.11

Oil and gas finances by firm, and effect of income and excise tax provisions on firms, Fed Govt revenues, and investor tax returns, 1980 and projected to 1992, hearing, 21788–132

Oil and gas 5-year OCS leasing plan and proposed sale off California coast, acreage, costs, and benefits, various periods 1953-2006, hearing, 21448–30

Oil companies energy production and imports by type, and financial data, 1975-81, annual rpt, 3164–74

Oil industry foreign-affiliated US firms, selected financial data, 1981-82, annual rpt, 3024–2

Oil pipeline in Alaska, owner companies financial data, and retail gasoline competitive position in 2 States, by company, 1980-83, hearing, 21728–51

Oil price and allocation regulations enforcement by DOE, and overcharge allegations, settlements, and refunds to States, by company, as of June 1983, hearing, 21368–50

Oil refineries financial and operating impacts from auto use of alcohol fuels, projected to 2000 with trends 1964-80, 3308–75

Overseas Private Investment Corp programs and finances, with list of insured projects and companies, FY83, annual rpt, 9904–2

Panama Canal Commission financial condition, FY81-82, annual rpt, 9664–3.1

Pest control firms in urban areas, pesticide use by type, employment, and sales, by type of service, 1981 survey, article, 1561–16.408

Pharmaceutical industry R&D costs and finances, selected years 1962-83, hearing, 25528–98

Philanthropic foundations detailed financial and operating data, and stock holdings by instn, 1979 with selected trends from 1920, GAO rpt, 26119–53

Phosphate rock industry environmental protection costs, by control type and selected State, with background operating data, 1977-81 with cost projections to 1990, 5608–143

Postal Service electronic mail system message volume and profitability under proposed rate and service increases, FY82 and projected to FY87, 21408–70

Postal Service finances, organization, and services since 1775, and current operations, FY81-82, annual rpt, 9864–6

Postal Service operating costs, itemized by class of mail, FY83, annual rpt, 9864–4

Postal Service operations, employment, productivity, and financial statements, FY79-83, annual rpt, 9864–1

Index by Subjects and Names

Postal Service operations, finances, and employee productivity, performance, and compensation, FY83 with projections to FY85, annual rpt, 9864–5

Postal Service operations, revenues by source, and employee characteristics, 1970s-83, and electronic mail promotion costs, FY82-87, hearings, 21628–55

Postal Service revenue and mail volume by class, and special service transactions, quarterly rpt, 9862–1

Postal Service revenue, operating costs, and volume, FY83, annual rpt, 9864–2

Prison Industries (Federal) operations and finances, FY83, annual rpt, 6244–3

Public utility holding company finances, securities issued, and subsidiaries by type, by firm, FY83, annual rpt, 9734–2.6

Radio Free Europe and Radio Liberty broadcast and financial data, with comparisons to other intl broadcasters, FY83, annual rpt, 10314–1

Rail high-speed system planned from Chicago, capital and operating costs and profitability by speed class, frequency, and route, 1984 article, 9375–1.406

Railroad commuter systems financial and operating data for 7 systems, and public agency cost reimbursement, 1980, 7888–61

Railroad finances and operations, detailed data by firm, class of service, and district, 1983, annual rpt, 9486–6.1

Railroad finances, operations, and freight rates and shares, by commodity and railroad, 1970s-82, hearings, 25268–80

Railroad freight volume and revenues, by commodity and region of origin and destination, 1982, annual rpt, 7604–6

Railroad revenue, income, freight, and rate of return, by Class I freight railroad and district, quarterly rpt, 9482–2

Real estate broker industry structure and practices, sales commissions, and broker and consumer attitudes, selected years 1975-81, 9408–48

Real estate developers land and dev costs of HUD New Communities program, cumulative 1970-75, 5188–107

Recording industry operations and sales lost from home taping, home taping costs, and material taped by source, 1969-83, hearings with chartbook, 25528–100

Red Cross program operations and financial statements, 1982/83, annual rpt, 29254–1

Rural Electrification Admin loans to power supply and distribution firms, and borrower operating and financial data, by firm and State, 1983, annual rpt, 1244–1

Savings and loan assns (FSLIC-insured), financial ratios of profitable and unprofitable S&Ls, selected years 1965-82, technical paper, 9316–2.47

Savings and loan assns, FHLB 4th District members financial results related to market competition, regression results, 1973-82, article, 9302–2.402

Savings and loan assns, FHLB 6th District insured members financial condition and operations by State, monthly rpt, 9302–11

Savings and loan assns, FHLB 6th District insured members financial condition and operations by State, quarterly rpt, 9302–23

Index by Subjects and Names

Savings instns FSLIC-insured, income, expenses, and financial ratios, 2nd half 1983, semiannual rpt, 9312–6

Securities brokerage services and finances of brokerage firms and New England banks and thrifts, and brokerage acquisitions by firm, selected years 1977-84, article, 9373–1.417

Securities industry finances, for stockbrokers, investment firms, and individual stock exchanges, 1978-82, annual rpt, 9734–2.1

Semiconductor industry subsidies of Japan govt by program, with financial and operating data by firm, R&D, and comparisons to US industry, 1970s-83, hearings, 21368–46.1

Shipping firms combined condensed financial statements, Dec 1981-82, annual rpt, 7704–14.5

Ships in US merchant fleet, shipping costs, construction, employment, military availability, and Fed Govt subsidies, 1970s-1984 and projected to 2000, 26306–6.83

Small Business Admin loan and contract activity by program, and balance sheets, FY83, annual rpt, 9764–1.1

Small Business Investment Companies finances, funding, licensing, and loan activity, 2nd half FY84, semiannual rpt, 9762–3

Smithsonian Instn finances, activities, and visitors, FY83, annual rpt, 9774–3

Southeastern Power Admin sales by customer, plants, and capacity, and financial statements of Southeastern Fed Power Program, FY83, annual rpt, 3234–1

Southwestern Fed Power System financial statements, electric power sales by customer, and project capacity, production, and costs, FY83, annual rpt, 3244–1

St Lawrence Seaway Dev Corp finances and activities, and seaway toll charges and cargo tonnage by type of cargo, 1983, annual rpt, 7744–1

Steel industry finances and operations under proposed import quota, projected 1985-89 with selected foreign comparisons and trends from 1950, 26306–6.80

Steel industry financial and operating data, steel imports by source, and employment situation at Fairless Hills, Pa, plant, 1970s-90, hearing, 25528–94

Student Loan Marketing Assn activities, and financial ratios and stock dividends compared to banks and 4 Fed Govt-sponsored credit assns, 1980-82, GAO rpt, 26121–71

Synthetic Fuels Corp financial statements, activities, and executive staff and salaries, FY83, annual rpt, 29654–1

Telegraph carriers financial and operating data, for 7 firms, quarterly rpt, 9282–1

Telephone and telegraph firms detailed financial, operating, and employment statistics, 1982, annual rpt, 9284–6

Telephone companies borrowing under rural telephone loan program, and financial and operating data, 1983, annual rpt, 1244–2

Telephone operating and financial data by company type, with fixed cost recovery from interstate revenue by Bell company and State, 1981-82 with trends from 1945, 26306–6.79

Telephone operating data, costs, and billings for American Telephone and Telegraph Co local and long distance lines, by State, 1980-82 with trends from 1970, 23848–176

Transit system (automated guideway) characteristics and itemized costs, for 16 systems in operation or under construction, 1982, annual rpt, 7884–6

Transit system deficits, effect of cost and service increases and ridership and fare decreases, and govt aid and system operating ratios, 1970-80, 7308–184

Transit system financial and operating data, by mode, function, fleet size, and individual system, FY82, annual rpt, 7884–4

Transit system operations, tax burden related to ridership, fares, and govt funding, for selected States and cities, 1950s-82, reprint, 7888–59

Transit systems, expenditures by level of govt, and revenues by source, with distribution of commuter trips by mode of transport, 1980-82, article, 10042–1.404

Transportation finances, operations, vehicles, equipment, accidents, and energy use, by mode of transport, 1955-84, annual rpt, 7304–2

Travel agency financial and operating data, and airline ticket sales by type of distributor, 1970s-82, hearing, 25268–81

Trucking industry economic effects of tax and size and weight rules, and hwy use taxes and Trust Fund revenues by tax type, FY82-84 and projected to 1990, GAO rpt, 26117–31

TV and radio industry minority and women employment by occupation, and business owners, by race and State, with revenues and stations, 1971-81, hearing, 21368–45

TVA activities, financial and operating data by program and facility, and power sales by customer, FY83, annual rpt, 9804–1

TVA power program finances and operations, by plant and distributor, FY83, annual rpt, 9804–23

Uranium enrichment facilities operations, finances, uranium stocks, and energy use and capital investment by facility, FY83, annual rpt, 3354–7

Uranium exploration, land acquisition expenditures, and employment, various periods 1966-83 and planned 1984-85, annual rpt, 3164–65

Uranium mining operations, finances, and costs of alternative methods to meet emissions standards, for industry and selected mines, selected years 1948-90, 9188–96

Vending stand concessions operated by blind on Federal and non-Federal property, and income, FY82-83, annual rpt, 4944–2

Vietnam Veterans Memorial Fund receipts by source, and disbursements by item and payee, Apr 1979-Mar 1984, GAO rpt, 26111–21

Washington Public Power Supply System nuclear reactors construction financing, with regional economic impacts and power supply/demand, 1980s-2035, hearing, 21448–29

Watermelon grower-to-retailer handling costs and time, by handling phase and method, 1982, 1308–18

Business inventories

Western Area Power Admin operations by plant, financial statements, and electric power sales by customer, FY83, annual rpt, 3254–1

see also Agricultural finance

see also Agricultural marketing

see also Agricultural production costs

see also Business assets and liabilities, specific industries

see also Capital investments, specific industries

see also Depreciation

see also Educational finance

see also Energy production costs

see also Farm income

see also Operating ratios

see also Payroll

see also Production costs

see also under By Industry in the "Index by Categories"

Business inventories

Alcohol and tobacco production, removals, stocks, and materials used, by State, monthly rpts, 8486–1

Alcoholic beverages and tobacco production, stocks, and Fed Govt tax and enforcement activities, by State, FY81-82, last issue of annual rpt, 8484–1

Auto industry operations, and trade by country, monthly rpt, 9882–8

Auto production and inventories, and sales of domestic and imported new autos and trucks, 1983-84, annual article, 2702–1.438

Business and financial statistics, historic trends, 1984 annual chartbook, 9364–2.3

Business and financial statistics, quarterly chartbook, 9362–2.2

Business Conditions Digest, cyclical indicators, by economic process, monthly rpt, 2702–3.3

Business Conditions Digest, historical supplement on economic, business, and financial conditions and cyclical fluctuations, with methodology, 1947-82, 2708–31

Business statistics, detailed data for major industries and economic indicators, *Survey of Current Business,* monthly rpt, 2702–1

Chemical, oil, rubber, and plastic production, shipments, stocks, and materials used, by detailed product, periodic Current Industrial Rpt series, 2506–8

Clay and glass production, shipments, trade, and stocks, by product, periodic Current Industrial Rpt series, 2506–9

Construction industries census, 1982: financial and operating data, by SIC 4-digit industry and State, final rpt series, 2373–1

Cotton (long staple) production, prices, exports, stocks, and mill consumption, monthly rpt, 1309–12

Cotton linters production, prices, stocks, use, and trade, monthly rpt, 1309–10

Dairy production by State, stocks, prices, and CCC price support activities, by product type, monthly rpt, 1627–3

Department store inventory price indexes, July 1984, semiannual rpt, 6762–7

Economic indicators and components, and Fed Reserve 4th District business and financial conditions, monthly chartbook, 9377–10

Business inventories

Economic indicators and components, current data and annual trends, monthly rpt, 23842–1.3

Finished goods inventory in durable and nondurable manufacturing, related to stocks, orders, and employment stability objectives, Jan 1961-May 1981, technical paper, 9387–8.79

Finished goods inventory in durable and nondurable manufacturing, related to unfilled orders and employment stability objectives, 1st qtr 1963-2nd qtr 1981, technical paper, 9387–8.80

Food products (processed) production and stocks by State, shipments, exports, materials used, and consumption, periodic Current Industrial Rpt series, 2506–4

Forecasts for selected business activities and natl economic indicators, compilation of representative opinions, 1984, annual rpt, 9389–3

GPO document sales program mgmt and finances, and bookstore operations by location, FY78-82, GAO rpt, 26111–17

Hops stocks held by growers, dealers, and brewers, Sept 1984, semiannual release, 1621–8

Import and tariff provisions effect on US industries and products, investigations with background financial and operating data, series, 9886–4

Imports from Communist countries, injury to US industries, investigations with background financial and operating data, selected industries and products, series, 9886–12

Imports injury to US industries from foreign subsidized products and sales in US at less than fair value, investigations with background financial and operating data, series, 9886–19

Imports injury to US industries from foreign subsidized products, investigations with background financial and operating data for selected industries and products, series, 9886–15

Imports injury to US industries from import sales at less than fair value, investigations with background financial and operating data, series, 9886–14

Imports injury to US industries from increased import sales, investigations with background financial and operating data, series, 9886–5

Imports injury to US industries from removal of duties on foreign subsidized products, investigations with background financial and operating data, series, 9886–18

Income tax returns filed by type of filer, selected income items, summary data, quarterly rpt, 8302–2.1

Income tax returns of corporations, detailed income and tax items by industry, 1981, annual rpt, 8304–4

Income tax returns of partnerships, receipts by source, deductions by type, and establishments, by selected industry, 1982, annual article, 8302–2.416

Income tax returns of sole proprietorships, receipts, deductions by type, payroll, and net income, by major industry, 1982, annual article, 8302–2.413

Industry finances and operations, by SIC 2- to 4-digit industry, 1970s-83 and projected to 1988, annual rpt, 2014–4

Input-output structure of US economy, detailed interindustry transactions for 85 industries, and components of final demand, 1977, article, 2702–1.421

Input-output structure of US economy, detailed interindustry transactions for 537 industries, and components of final demand, 1977 benchmark data, 2708–17

Inventories and final business sales, 1946-83, annual rpt, 204–1.1

Lumber, furniture, and paper products production and shipments by region and State, inventories, trade, and consumption, periodic Current Industrial Rpt series, 2506–7

Machinery and equipment production, shipments, trade, stocks, consumption, orders, and firms, by product, periodic Current Industrial Rpt series, 2506–12

Manufacturers capacity utilization rates and production indexes, sales, inventories, shipments, and orders, 1947-83, annual rpt, 204–1.3

Manufacturers shipments, inventories, and orders, by industry, monthly Current Industrial Rpt, 2506–3.1

Manufacturing and trade inventories, sales, and inventory/sales ratios, quarterly article, 2702–1.34

Manufacturing census, 1982: financial and operating data, for SIC 4-digit industries by product, preliminary rpt series, 2491–1

Manufacturing operating and financial data, 1980-81 Annual Survey of Manufactures rpt reprints, hardbound vol, 2504–1

Metals (intermediate product) shipments, trade, and inventories, by product, periodic Current Industrial Rpt series, 2506–11

Metals (primary product) production, shipments, trade, inventories, and unfilled orders, by product, periodic Current Industrial Rpt series, 2506–10

Mineral Industry Surveys, commodity reviews of production, trade, stocks, and consumption, monthly rpt series, 5612–1

Mineral Industry Surveys, commodity reviews of production, trade, stocks, and consumption, quarterly rpt series, 5612–2

Minerals (strategic) supply/demand, trade, and foreign and US industry devs by firm and country, by commodity, bimonthly rpt, 5602–4

Mobile homes placed, average sales price, and dealer inventories, by region, monthly rpt, 2382–1

Motorcycle imports, sales, and inventories of foreign make, and prices and employment for domestic makes, quarterly rpt, 9882–12

Natl income and product, comprehensive accounts and components, *Survey of Current Business,* monthly rpt, 2702–1.21

Natl income and product, comprehensive accounts and components, *Survey of Current Business,* monthly rpt, monthly and annual tables, 2702–1.26

North Central States auto dealer inventories and other economic indicators, Fed Reserve 7th District monthly rpt, 9375–9

Nuclear power and weapons policy, fuel supply/demand, waste disposal and siting, environmental effects of radiation, and public attitudes, 1970s-82 with projections to 2000, 3008–88

Index by Subjects and Names

Production, shipments, PPI, and stocks of building materials, by type, bimonthly rpt, 2012–1.6

Retail trade sales and inventories, by kind of business, region, census div, and selected State, SMSA, and city, and seasonal adjustments, monthly rpt, 2413–3

Retail trade sales, inventories, purchases, gross margin, and accounts receivable, by SIC 2- to 4-digit kind of business and type of ownership, 1983, annual rpt, 2413–5

Seasonal adjustment methodology for economic time series, dev and design of Census Bur and other systems, with illustrative data, 1981 conf papers, 2626–7.5

Small business owners expectations of operations, expansion opportunity, and loan availability during coming quarter, July 1983 survey, hearings, 21728–52.2

Steel (stainless and alloy tool) production, employment, prices, and US importer inventories and unfilled orders, quarterly rpt, 9882–3

Textile mill production, stocks, materials used, orders, and trade by country, by product and major State, periodic Current Industrial Rpt series, 2506–5

Wholesale trade census, 1982: employment, establishments, finances, and operations, by SIC 2- to 4-digit kind of business, SMSA, county, and city, State rpt series, 2405–1

Wholesale trade sales and inventories, by SIC 2- to 3-digit kind of business, monthly rpt, 2413–7

Wholesale trade sales, inventories, purchases, and gross margins, by SIC 2- to 3-digit kind of business and type of ownership, 1983, annual rpt, 2413–13

see also Business orders

see also Coal stocks

see also Energy stocks and inventories

see also Petroleum stocks

Business machines

see Computers

see Office furniture and equipment

Business orders

Business and financial statistics, historic trends, 1984 annual chartbook, 9364–2.3

Business Conditions Digest, cyclical indicators, by economic process, monthly rpt, 2702–3.3

Business Conditions Digest, historical supplement on economic, business, and financial conditions and cyclical fluctuations, with methodology, 1947-82, 2708–31

Business statistics, detailed data for major industries and economic indicators, *Survey of Current Business,* monthly rpt, 2702–1

Economic indicators and components, current data and annual trends, monthly rpt, 23842–1.3

Finished goods inventory in durable and nondurable manufacturing, related to stocks, orders, and employment stability objectives, Jan 1961-May 1981, technical paper, 9387–8.79

Finished goods inventory in durable and nondurable manufacturing, related to unfilled orders and employment stability objectives, 1st qtr 1963-2nd qtr 1981, technical paper, 9387–8.80

Index by Subjects and Names

Machine tool orders by selected industry, trade, and shipments and Japan share of US market by type of tool, various dates 1972-84, hearing, 25388–48

Machinery and equipment production, shipments, trade, stocks, consumption, orders, and firms, by product, periodic Current Industrial Rpt series, 2506–12

Manufacturers capacity utilization rates and production indexes, sales, inventories, shipments, and orders, 1947-83, annual rpt, 204–1.3

Manufacturers shipments, inventories, and orders, by industry, monthly Current Industrial Rpt, 2506–3.1

Metals (primary product) production, shipments, trade, inventories, and unfilled orders, by product, periodic Current Industrial Rpt series, 2506–10

Minerals (strategic) supply/demand, trade, and foreign and US industry devs by firm and country, by commodity, bimonthly rpt, 5602–4

North Central States economic indicators, Fed Reserve 7th District monthly rpt, 9375–9

Ships in US merchant fleet, shipping costs, construction, employment, military availability, and Fed Govt subsidies, 1970s-1984 and projected to 2000, 26306–6.83

Steel (stainless and alloy tool) production, employment, prices, and US importer inventories and unfilled orders, quarterly rpt, 9882–3

Textile mill production, stocks, materials used, orders, and trade by country, by product and major State, periodic Current Industrial Rpt series, 2506–5

Busing

see School busing

Butter

see Dairy industry and products

Butters, Gerald R.

"Consumers' Experience with Real Estate Brokers: Report on the Consumer Survey of the FTC's Residential Real Estate Brokerage Investigation", 9408–48

Butz, Earl L.

"Historical Perspective", 1004–16.1

Buxton, Boyd M.

"Profitability of Milk Production in Selected States", 1561–2.403

Buxton, Freeman K.

"USDA's Revised Truck Fleet Cost", 1311–15

Buzzanell, Peter J.

"World Outlook for Sugar and Tropical Products", 1004–16.1

CAB

see Civil Aeronautics Board

Cable television

Copyright royalty fees collected for secondary cable TV transmissions and jukeboxes, FY82, annual rpt, 26404–2

Financial and operating data of cable TV industry, by region and State, annual rpt, discontinued, 9284–15

Minority group and women employment by occupation, and business owners, by race and State, with TV and radio revenues and stations, 1971-81, hearing, 21368–45

Cadmium

see Metals and metal industries

Cafferata, Gail L.

"Private Health Insurance Coverage of the Medicare Population", 4186–3.18

Caguas, P.R.

see also under By SMSA or MSA in the "Index by Categories"

Calcium

see Metals and metal industries

California

Agricultural cooperatives, membership, activities, and finances, by commodity and selected State, 1900-80 with trends from 1863, 1128–30

Agriculture census, 1982: farms, farmland, production and costs, and operator characteristics, preliminary State summary and county rpts, 2330–1.6

Agriculture census, 1982: farms, farmland, production, finances, and operator characteristics, by county, final State rpt, 2331–1.5

Auto fuel economy test results for models complying with California emission standards, 1984 model year, annual rpt, 3304–13

Bank deposits in commercial and mutual savings banks and in US branches of foreign banks, by account type, instn, State, SMSA, and county, June 1983, annual rpt, 9295–3.18

Bean (dried) prices by State, and foreign and US production, use, stocks, and trade, weekly rpt, 1311–17

Business failures, plant closings, layoffs, and relocations, for California by plant, industry, county, and city, 1980-83, hearing, 21348–84.1

Celery acreage planted and growing, by major producing State and area, monthly rpt, 1621–14

Census of Population and Housing, 1980: detailed population and housing characteristics, by county, city, and census tract, State rpt, 2551–2.6

Census of Population, 1980: detailed socioeconomic and demographic characteristics, by age, sex, race, Hispanic origin, and industry, State rpt, 2531–4.6

Coastal environmental and wildlife characteristics, use, and mgmt, for individual ecosystems, series, 5506–9

County Business Patterns: establishments, employees, and payrolls, by SIC 4-digit industry and county, 1982, annual State rpt, 2326–6.6

Drivers licenses renewed by mail and in person at California Motor Vehicles Dept, by driver age and accident and conviction rates, 1980-83, article, 7762–9.401

Employment, earnings, and hours, by selected SIC 1- to 4-digit industry, State, and for 278 major labor areas, 1939-83, annual rpt, 6744–5.1, 6744–5.3

Environmental quality, pollutant discharge by type and source, and EPA protection activities and funding, 1970s-83, biennial regional rpt, 9184–15.9

Exports of manufactured and agricultural commodities, manufacturing production, and export-related employment, 1960s-82, State rpt, 2046–3.5

Farm real estate market values in California, by use and crop, 1976-84, annual rpt, 1541–8.1

Fish market and cannery receipts, canned tuna and export fish prices, and imports by country of origin, for California, weekly rpt, 2162–6.4

Fishermen (ocean sport), fishing activities, and catch by species, by fisherman characteristics and State, for Pacific coast, 1979-80, 2166–17.1, 2166–17.3

Fishing catch and mean weight of marlin, for 2 southern California angling clubs, July-Nov of selected years 1945-80, article, 2162–1.401

Forests (natl) timber sales contract operations in Northwest US by forest and firm, and lumber supply/demand, FY76-1983 with trends from 1913, hearings, 25318–57

Fruit (citrus) production and use, by crop and State, 1977/78-1981/82, 1641–4

Gasoline retail sales percent change in California for ARCO, other majors, and independents, and Trans-Alaska Pipeline owner companies financial data by company, 1981-83, hearing, 21728–51

Hay prices in 10 market areas, for baled alfalfa and prairie hay, weekly rpt, 1313–5

Hazardous waste generation and disposal taxes in 3 States, and effects on waste mgmt, 1981-83, with assessment of 3 Fed Govt tax proposals, GAO rpt, 26113–124

HHS aid to each State and local govt or private instn, amount obligated, funding agency, and program, FY83, annual listing, 4004–3.9

Home mortgage creative financing, effect on home sales price, model results for California, 1975-82, article, 9412–2.402

Home mortgage prepayments, effect of rising interest rates, 1975-82, for California mortgages issued 1947-76, 9306–1.6

Housing demand by county, prices and sales, and costs after homeowner tax deductions, for southern California, 1970s-80, hearing, 21148–31

Housing market in California, and Los Angeles average home price and mortgage rate, 1969-82 with economic indicators projected to 1989, 9306–1.1

Income (personal) per capita and by source, and earnings by industry div, by State, MSA, and county, 1977-82, annual regional rpt, 2704–2.9

Land Mgmt Bur public lands sales, prices of Nevada and California acreage, and effect on Forest Service land acquisition program, 1983, GAO rpt, 26113–122

Lumber production, prices, trade, and employment in Northwest US and British Columbia, quarterly rpt, 1202–3

Manufacturing census, 1982: financial and operating data, by SIC 2- to 4-digit industry, State, SMSA, and county, preliminary census div rpt, 2491–3.9

Medicare and Medicaid payment limits effects on physician charges in California, by specialty, 1950s-84, 25368–127

Mineral Industry Surveys, State review of production, 1983, advance annual rpt, 5614–6.5

Minerals Yearbook, 1982, Vol 2 preprints: State review of production and sales by commodity, and business activity, annual rpt, 5604–16.6

California

Minerals Yearbook, 1982, Vol 2: State reviews of production, sales, and firms, by commodity, and business activity, annual rpt, 5604–34

- Motorcycle accidents, and licensing test results and costs, for 3 California licensing programs, 1976-78, article, 7762–9.402
- Oil and gas extraction production workers, wages, hours, and benefits, by occupation, region, and for 5 States, June 1982 survey, 6787–6.203
- Oil and gas field itemized equipment and operating costs and cost indexes, for 10 producing areas, 1981-83, annual rpt, 3164–45
- Oil and gas 5-year OCS leasing plan and proposed sale off California coast, acreage, costs, and benefits, various periods 1953-2006, hearing, 21448–30
- Older persons migrating to and from Florida and California by selected State of origin or destination, and Florida elderly, by sociodemographic and housing characteristics, 1970-80, 4478–150
- Peppers (dried chili and paprika) production and value, 1971-83, FAS annual rpt, 1925–15.1
- Plant closing provisions of Fed Govt and State law, corporate policies, collective bargaining agreements, and job loss in California and total US, 1982, article, 9377–1.401
- Population size and components of change, by MSA and county, 1980-82, annual State Current Population Rpt, 2546–4.5
- Population size, Apr 1980 and July 1982, and per capita income, 1979 and 1981, by county and city, State Current Population Rpt, 2546–11.5
- Rice market activities, prices, inspections, sales, trade, supply, and use, for US and selected foreign markets, weekly rpt, 1313–8
- Rice stocks on and off farms and total, periodic rpt, 1621–7
- Savings and loan assns, FHLB 11th District members financial condition and operations by State, quarterly rpt, 9302–19
- Savings and loan assns, FHLB 11th District members financial operations and housing industry indicators by State, monthly rpt, 9302–17
- Shipping industry impact on local economy, and port dev financing through user fees, by State, other area, industry, and port, 1970s-2020, hearings, 21568–34
- Tuna imports of US by country of origin, cannery receipts and production, and effect of reduced production on California economy, selected years 1977-82, article, 2162–1.403
- Water supply and quality in streams and lakes, and groundwater levels in wells, by drainage basin, 1982, annual State rpt, 5666–20.5
- Water supply and use in 3 areas with supply problems and total US, and methods to increase supply, selected years 1974-80 and projected to 2010, 9208–125
- Wholesale trade census, 1982: employment, establishments, finances, and operations, by SIC 2- to 4-digit kind of business, SMSA, county, and city, State rpt, 2405–1.5

see also Anaheim, Calif. *see also* Bakersfield, Calif. *see also* Chico, Calif. *see also* Fairfield, Calif. *see also* Fresno, Calif. *see also* Fresno County, Calif. *see also* Garden Grove, Calif. *see also* Lompoc, Calif. *see also* Long Beach, Calif. *see also* Los Angeles, Calif. *see also* Marin County, Calif. *see also* Modesto, Calif. *see also* Monterey, Calif. *see also* Napa, Calif. *see also* Oakland, Calif. *see also* Ontario, Calif. *see also* Oxnard, Calif. *see also* Petaluma, Calif. *see also* Porterville, Calif. *see also* Redding, Calif. *see also* Riverside, Calif. *see also* Sacramento, Calif. *see also* Salinas, Calif. *see also* San Bernardino, Calif. *see also* San Diego, Calif. *see also* San Diego County, Calif. *see also* San Francisco, Calif. *see also* San Jose, Calif. *see also* San Mateo County, Calif. *see also* Santa Ana, Calif. *see also* Santa Barbara, Calif. *see also* Santa Cruz, Calif. *see also* Santa Maria, Calif. *see also* Santa Rosa, Calif. *see also* Seaside, Calif. *see also* Simi Valley, Calif. *see also* Stockton, Calif. *see also* Torrance, Calif. *see also* Tulare, Calif. *see also* Vallejo, Calif. *see also* Ventura, Calif. *see also* Visalia, Calif. *see also* Yuba City, Calif. *see also* under By State in the "Index by Categories"

Cambodia

see Kampuchea

Cambridge Systematics, Inc.

"Impacts of Downtown Revitalization Projects on Small Business", 21788–140.2

Camden, N.J.

Air pollution levels for 28 volatile organic compounds in NYC and New Jersey, by site and urban-rural location, 1979-June 1981, 9198–108

Cameroon

- Agricultural and food production indexes, and production of selected commodities, by world region and country, 1974-83, annual rpt, 1524–5
- Agricultural situation in sub-Saharan Africa, by country, 1982-83 and outlook for 1984, annual rpt, 1524–4.10
- Agricultural supply/demand and market for US exports, with socioeconomic indicators, 1960s-83 and projected to 1990, country rpt, 1526–6.6
- Agricultural supply/demand, trade, and production, and socioeconomic data, by country, 1950s-77, 1528–179
- AID activities and funding by project and function, FY85, and developing countries summary socioeconomic data, 1970s-83, by country, annual rpt, 9914–3

Index by Subjects and Names

- AID and other foreign assistance, and govt policy, effects on private sector dev and socioeconomic conditions, with case studies for 6 countries, 1960s-80, 9918–12
- AID economic assistance to developing countries, obligations and disbursements by country, quarterly rpt, 9912–4
- AID loan repayment status and terms by program and country, and status of predecessor agency loans, quarterly rpt, 9912–3
- Economic conditions and foreign marketing prospects in 46 Sub-Saharan countries, 1983 world region rpt, 2046–5.1
- Economic conditions, investment and export opportunities, and trade practices, 1984 country market research rpt, 2046–6.4
- Economic, social, and political summary data, by country, 1984, annual factbook, 244–11
- Economic trends in income, production, prices, employment, finances, and trade, 1984 annual rpt, 2046–4.43
- Exports of US, detailed Schedule B commodities by country of destination, 1983, annual rpt, 2424–9
- Exports of US, detailed Schedule E commodities by mode of transport and world area and country of destination, 1983, annual rpts, 2424–5
- Imports of US, detailed Schedule A commodities by country and world area of origin, and mode of transport, 1983, annual rpts, 2424–2
- Imports of US, detailed TSUSA commodities by country of origin, 1983, annual rpt, 2424–4
- Loans and grants for economic and military assistance from US and intl agencies, by program and country, FY46-83, annual rpt, 9914–5
- Military aid of US, arms sales, and training programs costs and budget requests by program, world region, and country, FY83-85, annual rpt, 7144–13
- Military spending, arms trade, and armed forces size, with total govt spending and population, by country, 1972-82, annual rpt, 9824–1
- *Minerals Yearbook, 1982,* Vol 3: foreign country reviews of production, trade, and policies, by commodity, annual rpt, 5604–35
- *Minerals Yearbook, 1982,* Vol 3 preprints: foreign country review of production, trade, and policies, by commodity, annual rpt, 5604–17.82
- Population size and growth rates, and latest available benchmark demographic data, by country, 1950-83, biennial rpt, 2324–4
- *see also* under By Foreign Country in the "Index by Categories"

Campaign funds

- Fed Election Commission campaign funding and activities, and political action committees funding, 1983, annual rpt, 9274–1
- Fed Election Commission monitoring activities, and campaign finances, 1984 Federal elections, biennial rpt series, 9276–2
- Fed Election Commission monitoring activities, campaign finances, and election procedures, press release series, 9276–1

Index by Subjects and Names

Canada

Income tax returns of individuals, detailed data, 1982, annual rpt, 8304–2

Labor unions (maritime and other) congressional campaign expenditures, by party, 1981-82, hearings, 25388–45

Political action committee campaign funding by candidate and PAC, proposed candidate spending limits, voting rates by party, and political opinions, by State, 1960-82, hearings, 25688–6

Political action committee campaign funding, by House and Senate candidate, 1978-82 Federal elections, biennial rpt, 9274–4

Political action committee campaign funding to individual congressmen, and public opinion on reform proposals and assn influence, 1970s-83, hearings, 21428–7

Statistical Abstract of US, social, political, and economic data, 1950s-83 and trends, annual rpt, 2324–1.2

Tax expenditures, Fed Govt revenues foregone through income tax deductions and exclusions by type, and effect of Deficit Reduction Act, FY84-89, annual rpt, 21784–10

Camping

- Army Corps of Engineers water resources dev projects, recreation activities by district and project, 1982, annual rpt, 3754–5
- Coastal environmental characteristics, fish, wildlife, and use, and population socioeconomic data, for individual areas, series, 5506–4
- County Business Patterns: establishments, employees, and payrolls, by SIC 4-digit industry and county, 1982, annual State rpt series, 2326–6
- Fed Govt programs and mgmt cost control proposals, 3-year savings by function and agency, and financial and operating data, 1960s-81, 16908–1.31
- Fire (forest) damage and causes, by State and region, 1981, annual rpt, 1204–4
- Fires on Forest Service land and acres burned, by cause, forest, and State, 1983, annual rpt, 1204–6
- France Brittany coast oil spill cleanup and research costs, marine and tourism industry losses, and recreation losses of tourists and residents, 1971-79, 2178–13
- Franchise business opportunities, by firm and kind of business, 1984 annual listing, 2044–27
- Franchises of firms engaged in distribution of goods and services by kind of business, establishments by State, and sales, 1982-84, annual rpt, 2014–5
- Idaho and Montana recreation sites of Forest Service, itemized operating and maintenance costs by type of site, 1980, 1208–202
- Income tax returns of sole proprietorships, detailed data by industry div and selected industry group, 1981, annual rpt, 8304–7
- Income tax returns of sole proprietorships, receipts, deductions by type, payroll, and net income, by major industry, 1982, annual article, 8302–2.413
- Natl forests recreation sites, area, and capacity, by type of activity, as of Nov 1983, annual rpt, 1204–28
- Natl forests recreational use, visitor-days by State and activity, FY79-83, annual rpt, 1204–1.1

Natl forests recreational use, visitor-days by type of activity, forest, and State, FY83 with trends from 1924, annual rpt series, 1204–17

Natl park area visits and overnight stays, visitors, and vehicles, by State and park, 1983, annual rpt, 5544–12

Receipts and collection costs, visitors, and capacity of outdoor Fed Govt, State, and private facilities, by managing agency and State, 1983, annual rpt, 5544–14

Receipts for selected services, by SIC 2- to 4-digit kind of business, 1983, annual rpt, 2413–8

Recreation (outdoor) participation, by type of activity, projected 1985-2030, 1208–195

Service industry census, 1982: employment, establishments, receipts, and payroll, by SIC 2- to 4-digit kind of business, SMSA, county, and city, State rpt series, 2391–1

Virgin Islands economic censuses, 1982: employment, establishments, payroll, and receipts, by SIC 1- to 4-digit industry, island, and city, 2593–1

Campos, Victor

"Profiles of the Problems of Coca in Bolivia", 7008–40

Canada

- Abortions performed in 12 States and NYC, by State of residence and for non-US residents by selected area, 1980, US Vital Statistics final rpt, 4146–5.72
- Acid rain causes and effects, air pollutant emissions by source in US and selected countries, and control costs, 1970s-83 and projected to 2000, 21368–52
- Acid rain causes and effects, air pollutant emissions by source in US and selected countries, control costs, and Fed Govt research funding, 1960s-82, 3408–27
- Agricultural and food production indexes, and production of selected commodities, by world region and country, 1974-83, annual rpt, 1524–5
- Agricultural products trade with US, effects of nontariff trade barriers, selected years 1955-81, 1528–175
- Agricultural situation in North America and Oceania, by country and commodity, 1983 and outlook for 1984, annual rpt, 1524–4.1
- Agricultural supply/demand, trade, and production, and socioeconomic data, by country, 1950s-77, 1528–179
- Auto and auto products sales, prices, and registrations in US, and trade of 8 countries with US, by make and model, 1964-83, annual rpt, 9884–7
- Auto industry operations, trade, and registrations, foreign and US, selected years 1928-82, domestic content requirement hearings, 21788–134
- China exports and imports, by commodity, world area, and country, quarterly rpt, 242–6
- China trade and trade balances with world and major trading partners, by selected commodity, quarterly rpt, 242–6.1
- Choline chloride from Canada and UK at less than fair value, imports injury to US industry, investigation with background financial and operating data, 1983 rpt, 9886–14.90

Choline chloride from Canada at less than fair value, imports injury to US industry, investigation with background financial and operating data, 1984 rpt, 9886–14.123

Coal exports of US to Canada by mode of transport, and overseas, by district of origin, quarterly rpt, 3162–8

Coal reserves, production, demand indicators, and trade, by country, selected years 1973-82 and alternative trade projections to 1995, annual rpt, 3164–77

Codfish (dried salted) from Canada at less than fair value, imports injury to US industry, investigation with background financial and operating data, 1984 rpt, 9886–14.115

Computers and computer equipment market and trade, and user industry operations and demand, 1984 country market research rpt, 2045–1.51

Copper production, production costs, prices, wages, and productivity, for US and 3 countries, 1970s-83 and projected to 1989, 21368–55

Deaths in US by State and by outlying area or country of birth, 1979, US Vital Statistics annual rpt, 4144–2.1

Dollar holdings rate of return related to domestic real money stock for 5 OECD countries, regression results, various periods 1966-84, article, 9391–1.418

Drivers license requirements and admin, by State and Canada Province, 1984, biennial rpt, 7554–18

Economic and monetary trends, compounded annual rates of change for US and 10 major trading partners, quarterly rpt, 9391–7

Economic conditions, consumer and stock prices and production indexes, 6 OECD countries and US, *Business Conditions Digest,* monthly rpt, 2702–3.10, 2708–31

Economic conditions in Communist and OECD countries, 1982, annual rpt, 7144–11

Economic conditions in Communist, OECD, and selected other countries, 1960s-83, annual rpt, 244–5

Economic conditions, investment and export opportunities, and trade practices, 1983 country market research rpt, 2046–6.1

Economic indicators and oil use and imports for US and 6 OECD countries, and oil production by country, biweekly rpt, 242–4

Economic indicators and trade balance of US and 4 countries, effect of US budget deficits, model results, various periods 1974-85, technical paper, 9366–7.102

Economic indicators for 7 OECD countries and US, quarterly rpt, 2042–10

Economic indicators of 12 Pacific Basin countries or areas and US, quarterly rpt, 9393–9

Economic, social, and political summary data, by country, 1984, annual factbook, 244–11

Egg filler flats from Canada at less than fair value, imports injury to US industry, investigation with background financial and operating data, 1984 rpt, 9886–14.119

Canada

Electric power transactions of US with Canada and Mexico, by utility and US region, 1983, annual rpt, 3104–10

Employment, labor force, and participation and unemployment rates by sex, in US and 9 OECD countries, various periods 1970-3rd qtr 1983, annual article, 6722–1.404

Energy prices and taxes by energy source and end-use sector, for US and 9 OECD countries, quarterly 1979-83, annual rpt, 3164–71

Energy production by type, and oil prices, trade, and consumption, by country group and selected country, monthly rpt, 242–5

Export credit program activities of Eximbank and 6 OECD countries, 1982, annual rpt, 9254–3

Exports and imports, agreement devs, US trade relations, and USITC investigations, 1983, annual rpt, 9884–5

Exports and imports of NATO countries with Council for Mutual Economic Assistance Europe members, by country, 1980-83, annual rpt, 7144–5

Exports and imports of NATO countries with PRC, by country, 1980-83, annual rpt, 7144–14

Exports and imports of OECD countries, by country, 1983, annual rpt, 7144–10

Exports and imports of US (waterborne), by type of service, customs district, port, and world area, monthly rpt, 2422–7

Exports and imports of US, by commodity group, world area, selected country, US coastal area and port, and mode of transport, with seasonal adjustments, monthly rpt, 2422–9

Exports and imports of US, detailed SIC-based commodities by world area, 1983, annual rpts, 2424–6

Exports of US by selected commodity, and foreign and US economic and employment indicators and balance of payments, by world area and country, 1970s-83, annual rpt, 2044–26

Exports of US, detailed Schedule B commodities by country of destination, 1983, annual rpt, 2424–9

Exports of US, detailed Schedule E commodities by mode of transport and world area and country of destination, 1983, annual rpts, 2424–5

Farmland (US) owned by foreigners, acreage, value, and use, by State and county, and for 5 leading investor countries, 1983, annual rpt, 1584–3

Finance (intl) and financial policy, external factors affecting US economy, econometric model methodology and results for US and 4 countries, various periods 1964-75, 9368–78

Fishing (ocean sport and commercial) landings and allowable and potential catch of US and Canada, for 34 species in North Atlantic, 1983, annual rpt, 2164–14

Foreign exchange bank and nonbank activity, and currency futures turnover in US and 3 foreign markets, Mar 1980 and Apr 1983, article, 9385–1.411

Fruit and vegetable shipments, and arrivals in 23 US and 5 Canada cities, by mode of transport and State or country of origin, 1983, annual rpt series, 1311–4

Grain handling and rail transport system of Canada, financial and operating data and effects of limited capacity on grain and oilseed exports, selected years 1950-82, 1528–176

Great Lakes fisheries landings, US and Canadian summary, 1977, annual rpt, 2164–2.8

Health care resources, use, and per capita public expenditures, and selected population characteristics, for US and 6 countries, selected years 1975-81, 21148–33

Hogs and pork from Canada, effect on US industry, investigation with background financial and operating data, 1984 rpt, 9886–4.80

Hospital use by children by Canada Province and US region, and death rates, by diagnosis and sex, selected years 1977-79, 4147–5.1

Immigration, and alien residents, workers, visitors, deportations, and naturalizations, by country of birth, FY81, annual rpt, 6264–2

Imports of US, detailed Schedule A commodities by country and world area of origin, and mode of transport, 1983, annual rpts, 2424–2

Imports of US, detailed TSUSA commodities by country of origin, 1983, annual rpt, 2424–4

Industrial production indexes of 7 OECD countries and US, biweekly rpt, periodic article, 2042–24

Interest rate term structure in West Germany and Canada related to short-term US rates, 1973-82, article, 9393–8.401

Interest rates and budget balances of US and 6 OECD countries, 1973-83, annual rpt, 26304–3.1

Investment (foreign direct) in US, by major industry group, world area, and selected country, 1980-83, annual article, 2702–1.439

Investment (foreign direct) in US, major investors and investments by SIC 4-digit industry, transaction type and value, and location, 1983, annual rpt, 2044–20

Investment (foreign direct) of US, by selected major industry group and world area, 1982-83, annual article, 2702–1.430

Investment (foreign direct) of US, by world area and country, 1977-83, article, 2702–1.442

Investment (intl) position of US, net change by component, investment type, and world region, and for 2 countries, 1982-83, annual article, 2702–1.424

Loans and grants for economic and military assistance from US and intl agencies, by program and country, FY46-83, annual rpt, 9914–5

Lumber exports from Northwest US ports by selected country, and US imports from Canada, quarterly rpt, 1202–3

Manufacturing labor productivity and cost indexes for US and 11 OECD countries, 1960-82, annual article, 6722–1.405

Manufacturing productivity and unit labor cost indexes for US and 11 countries, 1950-82 and preliminary 1983, annual rpt, 6864–1

Index by Subjects and Names

Military aid of US, arms sales, and training programs costs and budget requests by program, world region, and country, FY83-85, annual rpt, 7144–13

Military pension lifetime earnings in US and 7 countries, as of 1983, 26306–6.76

Military spending, arms trade, and armed forces size, with total govt spending and population, by country, 1972-82, annual rpt, 9824–1

Minerals Yearbook, 1982, Vol 3: foreign country reviews of production, trade, and policies, by commodity, annual rpt, 5604–35

Minerals Yearbook, 1982, Vol 3 preprints: foreign country review of production, trade, and policies, by commodity, annual rpt, 5604–17.14

Molds (industrial) from Canada, effect on competing US industry, investigation with background financial and operating data, 1979-83, 9886–4.72

Money supply control based on interest rate targeting, for US and Canada, 1975-79, technical paper, 9381–10.38

Natural gas and liquefied natural gas trade of US with 4 countries, by US pipeline company, 1982-83, annual article, 3162–4.406

Natural gas and liquefied natural gas transported, by State and country of origin and destination, 1982, article, 3162–4.409

Natural gas composition and occurrence of helium, analyses of samples from individual wells and pipelines in 26 States and 2 countries, 1983, annual survey, 5604–2

Natural gas exports of US to Canada, Mexico, and Japan, 1980-83, annual rpt, 3024–2

Natural gas imports and contracted supply from Canada and Mexico, by US pipeline firm, 1982-83, annual rpt, 3164–33.6

Natural gas imports from Canada, by importing company and Canada supplier, actual 1981 and projected maximum under contract, hearings, 23848–177

Natural gas utility marketing and servicing of household appliances and conservation equipment in US and Canada, by firm and product, 1978, hearing, 21368–54

Nuclear power generation in US and 18 non-Communist countries, monthly rpt, 3162–24.10

Nuclear power plant construction and operation status, and capacity, by plant, region, State, and selected country, 1983 and projected to 2020, annual rpt, 3164–57

Nuclear power plant spent fuel and demand for uranium and enrichment services, for US and non-Communist country groups, 1983 and projected to 2020, annual rpt, 3164–72

Oil production, consumption, stocks, and exports and prices to US, by major exporting and consuming country, detailed data, monthly rpt, 3162–24

Population size and growth rates, and latest available benchmark demographic data, by country, 1950-83, biennial rpt, 2324–4

Potatoes from Canada at less than fair value, imports injury to US industry, investigation with background financial and operating data, 1983 rpt, 9886–14.89

Index by Subjects and Names

R&D Fed Govt funding for foreign performers, by world region and country, FY82-84, annual rpt, 9627–20.2

Rabies cases in animals and humans, for US and Mexico by State and for Canada by Province, 1980-82, annual rpt, 4205–28

Raspberries from Canada at less than fair value, imports injury to US industry, investigation with background financial and operating data, 1984 rpt, 9886–14.112

Real estate broker govt certification requirements, licenses, and exam results, by State and Canada Province, 1977-78, 9408–48

Space satellites and other objects launched since 1957, quarterly listing, 9502–2

St Lawrence Seaway ships, cargo and passenger volumes, and toll revenues, 1981-82 and trends from 1959, annual rpt, 7744–2

Steel imports of US from EC and other countries, and US industry operating data, for 15 products limited under arrangement with EC, monthly rpt, 9882–10

Travel to and from US and travel receipts and payments by world area, and travel to US by country, 1977-83, annual rpt, 2904–10

Travel to and from US, by world area and selected country, projected 1984-85, annual rpt, 2904–9

Travel to and from US on US and foreign flag air carriers, by country, world area, and US port, monthly rpt, 7302–2

Water supply in US and Canada, streamflow, well and reservoir levels, and dissolved solids and temperature in 6 US rivers, by station, monthly rpt, 5662–3

Waterborne commerce of US (domestic and foreign), freight by commodity, traffic, and passengers, by port and waterway, 1982, annual rpt, 3754–3.3

Weather broadcasts for US ships, by major ocean area, as of Jan 1984, biennial rpt, 2184–3

Wheat (durum) acreage, production, prices, stocks, use, and US and Canada exports by country, quarterly rpt, 1313–6

Wheat exports, total and for major producers by world area and country of destination, 1973/74-1983/84, FAS rpt, 1925–2.7

see also British Columbia, Canada
see also Montreal, Canada
see also Ontario, Canada
see also Ottawa, Canada
see also Toronto, Canada
see also Vancouver, Canada
see also Winnipeg, Canada
see also under By Foreign Country in the "Index by Categories"

Canal Zone

see Panama Canal
see Panama Canal Commission

Canals

Army Corps of Engineers activities and projects, FY83 and trends from 1800s, annual rpt, 3754–1

Bridges over navigable waters, with type of bridge and use, owner, dimensions, and location, 1984 regional listing series, 7406–5

Coastal environmental characteristics, fish, wildlife, and use, and population socioeconomic data, for individual areas, series, 5506–4

County Business Patterns: establishments, employees, and payrolls, by SIC 4-digit industry and county, 1982, annual State rpt series, 2326–6

Fed Govt reclamation projects in western US, electric power capacities and transmission miles, and water storage and carriage facilities, by State, FY81, annual rpt, 5824–1.1

Freight (waterborne domestic and foreign) by commodity, traffic, and passengers, by port and waterway, 1982, annual rpt, 3754–3

Reclamation Bur water storage and carriage facilities, by type, as of Sept 1983, annual listing, 5824–7

St Lawrence Seaway ships, cargo and passenger volumes, and toll revenues, 1981-82 and trends from 1959, annual rpt, 7744–2

Western Area Power Admin small-scale potential hydroelectric generation, site inventory, characteristics, and costs, by State and county, 1984 rpt, 3258–1

see also Panama Canal
see also Suez Canal

Cancer

see Carcinogens
see Neoplasms

Candy and confectionery products

Census of Population, 1980: detailed socioeconomic and demographic characteristics, by age, sex, race, Hispanic origin, occupation, and industry, State rpt series, 2531–4

Consumption of food and nutrient intake by individuals, by food group, source, and socioeconomic characteristics, 1977-78 natl survey, final rpt series, 1356–4

Consumption, supply, trade, prices, expenditures, and indexes, by food commodity, 1963-83, annual rpt, 1544–4

County Business Patterns: establishments, employees, and payrolls, by SIC 4-digit industry and county, 1981, annual State rpt series, 2326–8

County Business Patterns: establishments, employees, and payrolls, by SIC 4-digit industry and county, 1982, annual State rpt series, 2326–6

Employment, earnings, and hours, by SIC 4-digit nonfarm industry, monthly 1974-Feb 1984, annual update, 6744–4

Exports and imports of US, by agricultural commodity and country, bimonthly rpt with articles, 1522–1

Exports and imports of US, by detailed agricultural commodity and country, FY83 and CY83, semiannual rpts, 1522–4

Exports and imports of US, detailed SIC-based commodities by world area, 1983, annual rpts, 2424–6

Exports, imports, tariffs, and industry operating data for cocoa, chocolate, and confectionery products, 1979-83, TSUSA commodity rpt, 9885–1.67

Exports of US, detailed commodities by country of destination, monthly rpt, 2422–3

Exports of US, detailed Schedule B commodities by country of destination, 1983, annual rpt, 2424–9

Exports of US, detailed Schedule E commodities by mode of transport and world area and country of destination, 1983, annual rpts, 2424–5

Great Lakes trade, by SITC 3-digit commodity, port, vessel type, world area, and country, 1982, annual rpt, 7744–3

Imports of products containing sugar, injury to price-supported US sugar industries, investigation with background financial and operating data, 1983 rpt, 9886–10.7

Imports of US, detailed Schedule A commodities by country and world area of origin, and mode of transport, 1983, annual rpts, 2424–2

Imports of US, detailed Schedule A commodities by country, monthly rpt, 2422–2

Income tax returns of sole proprietorships, detailed data by industry div and selected industry group, 1981, annual rpt, 8304–7

Income tax returns of sole proprietorships, receipts, deductions by type, payroll, and net income, by major industry, 1982, annual article, 8302–2.413

Input-output structure of US economy, detailed interindustry transactions for 537 industries, and components of final demand, 1977 benchmark data, 2708–17

Manufacturers sales, shipments, trade, and consumption of selected ingredients, 1983, annual Current Industrial Rpt, 2506–4.5

Manufacturing census, 1982: financial and operating data, by SIC 2- to 4-digit industry, State, SMSA, and county, preliminary census div rpt series, 2491–3

Manufacturing census, 1982: financial and operating data, for SIC 4-digit industries by product, preliminary rpt, 2491–1.25, 2491–1.26

Occupational injury and illness rates, by SIC 2- to 4-digit industry, 1982, annual rpt, 6844–1

Producer prices and indexes, by stage of processing and detailed commodity, monthly rpt, 6762–6

Producer prices and indexes, by stage of processing and detailed commodity, monthly 1983, annual supplement, 6764–2

Productivity, hours, and employment indexes for selected SIC 3- and 4-digit industries, 1954-82, annual rpt, 6824–1.3

Underground economy, household expenditures and participation by type of goods or service and sociodemographic characteristics, with methodology and bibl, 1981 survey, 8308–27

see also Cocoa and chocolate
see also under By Commodity in the "Index by Categories"

Cans

see Packaging and containers

Canton, Ohio

Census of Housing, 1980: occupancy and unit characteristics, by race, Hispanic origin, and city, SMSA rpt, 2473–1.110

Census of Population and Housing, 1980: detailed population and housing characteristics, by county, city, and census tract, SMSA rpt, 2551–2.110

see also under By SMSA or MSA in the "Index by Categories"

Cantwell, Mimi

"Capital Punishment, 1982. National Prisoner Statistics", 6065–1

Canzoneri, Matthew B.

Canzoneri, Matthew B.
"Effects of Exchange Rate Variability on Output and Employment", 9366–7.97
"Monetary Policy Games and the Role of Private Information", 9366–7.103

Capacity utilization, industrial
see Industrial capacity and utilization

Cape Coral, Fla.
Census of Housing, 1980: occupancy and unit characteristics, by race, Hispanic origin, and city, SMSA rpt, 2473–1.161
Census of Population and Housing, 1980: detailed population and housing characteristics, by county, city, and census tract, SMSA rpt, 2551–2.161

Cape Verde
AID activities and funding by project and function, FY85, and developing countries summary socioeconomic data, 1970s-83, by country, annual rpt, 9914–3
AID economic assistance to developing countries, obligations and disbursements by country, quarterly rpt, 9912–4
AID loan repayment status and terms by program and country, and status of predecessor agency loans, quarterly rpt, 9912–3

Background Notes, summary social, political, and economic data, 1984 rpt, 7006–2.45

Disaster preparedness and summary sociodemographic, political, and economic data, 1970s-81., 9916–2.57

Economic conditions and foreign marketing prospects in 46 Sub-Saharan countries, 1983 world region rpt, 2046–5.1

Economic conditions, income, production, prices, employment, and trade, 1984 annual country rpt, 2046–4.123

Economic, social, and political summary data, by country, 1984, annual factbook, 244–11

Imports of US, detailed TSUSA commodities by country of origin, 1983, annual rpt, 2424–4

Loans and grants for economic and military assistance from US and intl agencies, by program and country, FY46-83, annual rpt, 9914–5

Military aid of US, arms sales, and training programs costs and budget requests by program, world region, and country, FY83-85, annual rpt, 7144–13

Military spending, arms trade, and armed forces size, with total govt spending and population, by country, 1972-82, annual rpt, 9824–1

Minerals Yearbook, 1982, Vol 3: foreign country reviews of production, trade, and policies, by commodity, annual rpt, 5604–35

Minerals Yearbook, 1982, Vol 3 preprints: foreign country review of production, trade, and policies, by commodity, annual rpt, 5604–17.84

Population size and growth rates, and latest available benchmark demographic data, by country, 1950-83, biennial rpt, 2324–4

see also under By Foreign Country in the "Index by Categories"

Capital District Regional Planning Commission
"Survey of Community Water Systems", 23848–181

Capital investments, general
Alabama employment and unemployment by SMSA and industry div, and planned capital investment and new jobs by selected firm, 1982-83, article, 9371–1.408

Business and financial statistics, historic trends, 1984 annual chartbook, 9364–2.2

Business and financial statistics, quarterly chartbook, 9362–2.2

Business Conditions Digest, current data on economic, business, and financial conditions and cyclical fluctuations, monthly rpt, 2702–3

Business Conditions Digest, historical supplement on economic, business, and financial conditions and cyclical fluctuations, with methodology, 1947-82, 2708–31

Capital (fixed), govt and private nonresidential structures and equipment, residential capital, and consumer-owned durable goods by item, 1980-83, annual article, 2702–1.433

Capital earned return and union and nonunion labor income, effect of union wage differential, 1971, technical paper, 9387–8.83

Computers and computer equipment foreign market and trade, and user industry operations and demand, country market research rpts, 2045–1

Corporations historic financial and business statistics, 1984 annual chartbook, 9364–2.10

Corporations profits and capital consumption allowances under alternative depreciation formulas, 1980-83, article, 2702–1.434

Cost of capital (net) for 35 types of structures and equipment, under 1980-82 tax laws, article, 9387–1.405

Economic and financial trends, natl compounded annual rates of change, 1964-83, annual rpt, 9391–9.2

Economic indicators and components, current data and annual trends, monthly rpt, 23842–1.5

Enterprise zone and urban revitalization projects of State and local govts, effect on business and employment in selected areas, various dates 1972-83, hearing, 21788–140

Expenditures for new plants and equipment, monthly rpt, 9362–1.1

Expenditures for new plants and equipment, 1947-84, annual rpt, 204–1.3

Expenditures for plant and equipment, actual and expected, by major industry group, quarterly article, 2702–1.33

Expenditures for plant and equipment, actual and expected, by major industry group, 1981-84, annual article, 2702–1.404

Expenditures for plant and equipment, by major industry group, 1982, annual rpt, 9364–5.6

Exports and imports of US, relative contributions of labor by type and capital to trade balance, selected years 1958-80, technical paper, 9381–10.30

Flow-of-funds accounts savings, investments, and credit statements, quarterly rpt, 9365–3.3

Index by Subjects and Names

Forecasts for selected business activities and natl economic indicators, compilation of representative opinions, 1984, annual rpt, 9389–3

Foreign economic indicators for 7 OECD countries and US, quarterly rpt, 2042–10

Foreign economic trends and implications for US, annual and semiannual country rpt series, 2046–4

Foreign firms US affiliates financial and operating data, by country of parent firm and industry div, 1980-81, article, 2702–1.402

Foreign food processing and packaging equipment market and trade, and user industry operations and demand, country market research rpts, 2045–11

Foreign trade zones operations and economic effects, with data on merchandise shipments, value added, employment, hours, and customs revenue, 1978-83, 9886–4.70

Franchise business opportunities by firm and kind of business, and sources of aid and info, 1984 annual listing, 2044–27

Franchise owner investment and initial outlay required, 1982, annual rpt, 2014–5.1

Gross private domestic fixed investment, 1929-83, annual rpt, 204–1.1

Import and tariff provisions effect on US industries and products, investigations with background financial and operating data, series, 9886–4

Imports from Communist countries, injury to US industries, investigations with background financial and operating data, selected industries and products, series, 9886–12

Imports injury to US industries from foreign subsidized products and sales in US at less than fair value, investigations with background financial and operating data, series, 9886–19

Imports injury to US industries from import sales at less than fair value, investigations with background financial and operating data, series, 9886–14

Imports injury to US industries from increased import sales, investigations with background financial and operating data, series, 9886–5

Imports injury to US industries from removal of duties on foreign subsidized products, investigations with background financial and operating data, series, 9886–18

Income tax credit for corporate investments, with data on returns, income, taxes, and investment value, by industry div and selected major group, 1974-80, article, 8302–2.405

Income tax proposals to encourage savings, and personal assets and liabilities by type, 1981, article, 8302–2.407

Income tax returns filed by type of filer, selected income items, summary data, quarterly rpt, 8302–2.1

Income tax returns with investment credits, for individuals by income, and for sole proprietorships by industry, 1981, article, 8302–2.409

Income taxes on corporate and personal capital related to capital formation and intl flows, 1984 technical paper, 8006–3.51

Index by Subjects and Names

Capital investments, specific industries

Industry finances and operations, by SIC 2- to 4-digit industry, 1970s-83 and projected to 1988, annual rpt, 2014–4

Input-output structure of US economy, detailed interindustry transactions for 537 industries, and components of final demand, 1977 benchmark data, 2708–17

Jamaica PL 480 Title I assistance effects on economic dev, with data on govt finance, economic indicators, demography, and dev programs, 1970s-81, 9916–1.51

Manufacturing census, 1982: financial and operating data, by SIC 2- to 4-digit industry, State, SMSA, and county, preliminary census div rpt series, 2491–3

Manufacturing census, 1982: financial and operating data, for SIC 4-digit industries by product, preliminary rpt series, 2491–1

Manufacturing operating and financial data, 1980-81 Annual Survey of Manufactures rpt reprints, hardbound vol, 2504–1

Natl income and product, comprehensive accounts and components, *Survey of Current Business,* monthly rpt, monthly and annual tables, 2702–1.26

Overseas Business Reports: economic conditions, investment and export opportunities, and trade practices, annual country market research rpt series, 2046–6

Overseas Business Reports: economic conditions, investment and export opportunities, and trade practices, world region rpt series, 2046–5

Pollution abatement capital and operating costs, by SIC 2- to 4-digit industry, State, and SMSA, 1982, annual Current Industrial Rpt, 2506–3.6

Pollution abatement capital and operating costs under Clean Air and Water Acts, for govts and selected industries, various periods 1970-2000, annual rpt, 9184–11

Pollution abatement capital expenditures, by pollution type and selected industry, 1973-84, annual article, 2702–1.423

Pollution abatement expenditures, and effect on economic indicators and industry operations, by major industry, projected under 3 pollution regulation alternatives 1983-95, 9188–84

Pollution abatement expenditures of govt, business, and consumers, 1972-82, annual article, 2702–1.407

Pollution control costs for aic rain abatement, by State and under alternative emissions control methods and standards, 1970s-83 and projected to 2000, 21368–52

Pollution control costs for carbon dioxide emissions, alternative forecasts to 2100 with trends 1970s-80, reprint, 9188–88

Pollution control costs for sulfur dioxide emissions, projected under alternative emissions control standards to 2010, 9188–97

Pollution control costs for sulfur dioxide emissions, 1960s-82, 3408–27

Pollution control instruments and equipment foreign market and trade, and user industry operations and demand, country market research rpts, 2045–17

Productivity of labor and capital, growth by SIC 1- to 2-digit industry, and measurement methods and bibl, various periods 1948-78 with trends from 1800, 2218–69

Productivity of labor and capital in manufacturing, all nonfarm business, and all private business, indexes and percent change, 1948-83, annual rpt, 6824–2

Productivity of labor, economic growth, and industrial policy dev, selected years 1947-82 with some projections to 1986, 26306–6.69

Productivity related to changes in capital and hours of labor inputs, 1984 technical paper, 9381–10.35

R&D expenditures by higher education instns and federally funded centers, by field, source of funds, instn, and State, FY82, annual rpt, 9627–13

Science Indicators, R&D expenditures, innovations, research, and higher education, with foreign comparisons, 1960s- 83, annual rpt, 9624–10

Small and minority-owned businesses finances and operations, Federal contracts by agency, and worker characteristics, by industry, race, sex, and State, 1950s-83, annual rpt, 9764–6

Small business capital formation under securities law exemptions, effects on stocks offered, issuers, and purchasers, series, 9736–2

Small business owners expectations of operations, expansion opportunity, and loan availability during coming quarter, July 1983 survey, hearings, 21728–52.2

see also Capital investments, specific industries

see also Depreciation

see also Foreign investments

see also Industrial plants and equipment

Capital investments, specific industries

Agricultural cooperative cash flow, asset disposals, working capital, and other finances, for 100 largest cooperatives by commodity group, 1982-83, article, 1122–1.412

Agricultural cooperative finances and operations, aggregate for top 100 assns by principal product and revenue source, FY82, annual rpt, 1124–3

Agricultural cooperatives, membership, and activities, by type of service, commodity, and State, FY51-1982, annual survey rpt, 1124–1

Airline cash flows for all certificated carriers, quarterly rpt, 9142–34

Airline financial data, by carrier, carrier group, and for total certificated system, quarterly rpt, 9142–12

Alcohol fuel (ethanol) production in Tennessee Valley, feedstocks, facilities, tax incentives, and related farming data, by State, 1970s-83 and projected to 1992, 9808–69

Auto industry finances and operations by manufacturer, foreign competition, and consumer auto expenditures and attitudes toward car buying, selected years 1968-85, annual rpt, 2004–8

Auto industry finances, employment, production, and cost increases to comply with Fed Govt pollution and safety standards, 1970s-83, annual rpt, 3304–5.4

Biotechnology commercial uses, R&D funding and output, controls, and industry financial and operating data, for US and 5 countries, 1970s-83 and estimated 1984-85, 26358–98

Bonneville Power Admin operations, and Columbia River power system sales and financial statements, FY83, annual rpt, 3224–1

Bus industry collective ratemaking and regulatory reform impacts on operations, finances, and services to older persons and rural areas by State, 1970s-83, 14828–2

Colorado River Storage Project finances, water resource dev, power production, and other activities in western States, FY83, annual rpt, 5824–3

Conrail operations and US Railway Assn finances and activities, FY81-83, annual rpt, 29604–1

Construction industries census, 1982: financial and operating data, by SIC 4-digit industry and State, final rpt series, 2373–1

Construction industries census, 1982: financial and operating data, by SIC 4-digit industry and State, preliminary rpt series, 2371–1

Copper production, production costs, prices, wages, and productivity, for US and 3 countries, 1970s-83 and projected to 1989, 21368–55

Electric power plant (nuclear and coal-fired) construction itemized cost estimates, and investment per kilowatt for 20 cities, 1980s-95, 9638–52

Electric power plant capital and operating detailed costs, capacity, and fuel use, by plant, plant type, utility, and State, 1982, annual rpt, 3164–9

Electric power systems equipment foreign market and trade, and user industry operations and demand, country market research rpts, 2045–15

Electric utilities privately owned, capital investment, finances, equity performance, and operating characteristics, 1950-82 with supply estimates to 2010, 3168–87

Electric utilities privately owned, detailed financial and operating data by company, with summary data for other distributors by type, 1982, annual rpt, 3164–23

Electronic component equipment foreign market and trade, and user industry operations and demand, country market research rpts, 2045–4

Electronic component manufacturing equipment foreign market and trade, and user industry operations and demand, country market research rpts, 2045–5

Energy producers finances and operations, by energy type for US firms domestic and foreign operations, 1974-82, annual rpt, 3164–44

Farm finances, assets, expenses, cash flow, receipts, and loans, selected years 1971-85, annual rpt, 1544–13

Farm finances, assets, liabilities, income, receipts by commodity and State, and expenses, 1980-83 and trends from 1910, annual rpt, 1544–16

Farm finances, expenses by type, loans by purpose and source, and credit detail by Fed Reserve District, quarterly rpt, 9365–3.10

Farm finances, production, expenses by type, and domestic economic impact, selected years 1972-82 and preliminary 1983-84, annual rpt, 1544–19

Capital investments, specific industries

Farm investments, effect of Fed Govt and State tax rates under alternative depreciation methods and inflation rates, 1950-84, 1548-231

Farm investments, effective rates of Federal/State income and State/local property taxes, by category of structure and equipment, for 7 North Central States, 1981-82, 1548-237

Farm machinery and equipment foreign market and trade, and user industry operations and demand, country market research rpts, 2045-13

Farm production expenditures, detailed items by farm sales size and region, 1983, annual rpt, 1614-3

Farm production expenses, by type and State, 1979-82, annual rpt, 1544-18

Farm production itemized costs, receipts, and net returns, for 13 crops, 4 livestock types, and milk, by region, 1981-83, annual rpt, 1544-20

Farm real estate value, sales, financing, taxes, and proposed use after purchase, by State, 1970s-84, annual rpt, 1541-8

Graphic industries equipment foreign market and trade, and user industry operations and demand, country market research rpts, 2045-3

Lab instruments foreign market and trade, and user industry operations and demand, country market research rpts, 2045-10

Machine tools and equipment foreign market and trade, and user industry operations and demand, country market research rpts, 2045-9

Medical and health care equipment foreign market and trade, and user industry operations and demand, country market research rpts, 2045-2

Mineral industries census, 1982: financial and operating data, by SIC 2- to 4-digit industry and State, preliminary summary rpts, 2511-2

Mineral industries census, 1982: financial and operating data, including materials consumed, by SIC 4-digit industry and State, preliminary rpt series, 2511-1

Minerals (strategic) supply/demand, trade, and foreign and US industry devs by firm and country, by commodity, bimonthly rpt, 5602-4

Mines Bur helium production and sales, and helium program financial statement, FY83, annual rpt, 5604-32

Motor and rail carriers regulated by ICC, employment and finances by mode of transport, and ICC activities, FY80-83 and trends, annual rpt, 9484-1

Motor carriers (Class I interstate) finances, operations, equipment, employment, and payroll, by district, 1982, annual rpt, 9486-5.3

Natural gas interstate pipeline company detailed financial and operating data, by firm, 1983, annual rpt, 3164-38

Natural gas pipeline and compressor station construction costs, 1979-82, annual rpt, 3084-3

Nuclear power industry status and outlook, with reactor construction, utility financial and operating data, and foreign comparisons, 1970s-83 with projections to 2010, 26358-99

Nuclear power plant capacity, generation, shutdowns, operation status and costs, and fuel, quarterly rpt, 3352-3

Nuclear power plant construction costs and status, and capacity, by plant and State, as of Mar 1984, annual rpt, 3164-69

Nuclear power plant construction costs and status, capacity, and revenue requirements, by plant and utility, various dates Dec 1983-Mar 1984, article, 9385-1.412

Nuclear power plant licensing 24-month delay, effect on utility financial performance and electric power prices, for plant completed May 1979, 9638-53

Oil and gas companies production and exploration detailed expenditures, revenues, operating ratios, and sales volume, 1982, annual Current Industrial Rpt, 2506-8.11

Oil and gas field itemized equipment and operating costs and cost indexes, for 10 producing areas, 1981-83, annual rpt, 3164-45

Oil pipeline in Alaska, owner companies financial data, and retail gasoline competitive position in 2 States, by company, 1980-83, hearing, 21728-51

Oil refineries financial and operating impacts from auto use of alcohol fuels, projected to 2000 with trends 1964-80, 3308-75

Panama Canal Commission financial condition, FY81-82, annual rpt, 9664-3.1

Rail high-speed system planned from Chicago, capital and operating costs and profitability by speed class, frequency, and route, 1984 article, 9375-1.406

Rural Electrification Admin loans to power supply and distribution firms, and borrower operating and financial data, by firm and State, 1983, annual rpt, 1244-1

Semiconductor industry subsidies of Japan govt by program, with financial and operating data by firm, R&D, and comparisons to US industry, 1970s-83, hearings, 21368-46.1

Southeastern Power Admin sales by customer, plants, and capacity, and financial statements of Southeastern Fed Power Program, FY83, annual rpt, 3234-1

Southwestern Fed Power System financial statements, electric power sales by customer, and project capacity, production, and costs, FY83, annual rpt, 3244-1

St Lawrence Seaway Dev Corp finances and activities, and seaway toll charges and cargo tonnage by type of cargo, 1983, annual rpt, 7744-1

Steel industry capital expenditures, by selected country, 1977-81, *Minerals Yearbook,* annual rpt, 5604-35.1

Steel industry domestic investment of foreign countries, 1978-81, *Minerals Yearbook,* annual rpt, 5604-35.1

Steel industry financial and operating data, steel imports by source, and employment situation at Fairless Hills, Pa, plant, 1970s-90, hearing, 25528-94

Steel plant modernization capital investment under Clean Air Act compliance extension program, by firm, 1981-83, GAO rpt, 26113-138

Index by Subjects and Names

Synthetic Fuels Corp financial statements, activities, and executive staff and salaries, FY83, annual rpt, 29654-1

Telecommunication equipment foreign market and trade, and user industry operations and demand, country market research rpts, 2045-12

Telegraph carriers financial and operating data, for 7 firms, quarterly rpt, 9282-1

Telephone and telegraph firms detailed financial, operating, and employment statistics, 1982, annual rpt, 9284-6

Telephone companies borrowing under rural telephone loan program, and financial and operating data, 1983, annual rpt, 1244-2

Transit system (automated guideway) characteristics and itemized costs, for 16 systems in operation or under construction, 1982, annual rpt, 7884-6

Transit system financial and operating data, by mode, function, fleet size, and individual system, FY82, annual rpt, 7884-4

Transportation finances, operations, vehicles, equipment, accidents, and energy use, by mode of transport, 1955-84, annual rpt, 7304-2

TVA activities, financial and operating data by program and facility, and power sales by customer, FY83, annual rpt, 9804-1

Uranium enrichment facilities operations, finances, uranium stocks, and energy use and capital investment by facility, FY83, annual rpt, 3354-7

Uranium exploration, land acquisition expenditures, and employment, various periods 1966-83 and planned 1984-85, annual rpt, 3164-65

Uranium mining operations, finances, and costs of alternative methods to meet emissions standards, for industry and selected mines, selected years 1948-90, 9188-96

Uranium prices, deliveries, trade, stocks, secondary marketing, investment, and employment, selected years 1967-83 and for commitments to 2001, annual rpt, 3164-66

Uranium reserves and mining and milling industries operations and finances, with selected foreign comparisons, various periods 1964-83 and projected to 2000, 3008-95

Vietnam Veterans Memorial Fund receipts by source, and disbursements by item and payee, Apr 1979-Mar 1984, GAO rpt, 26111-21

Washington Public Power Supply System nuclear reactors construction financing, with regional economic impacts and power supply/demand, 1980s-2035, hearing, 21448-29

Western Area Power Admin operations by plant, financial statements, and electric power sales by customer, FY83, annual rpt, 3254-1

see also Depreciation

see also Foreign investments

see also Industrial plants and equipment

Capital punishment

Crime and criminal justice data, including justice expenditures and employment by level of govt, 1970s-82 with some trends from 1875, 6068-174

Index by Subjects and Names

Executions since 1930, and prisoners under death sentence by prison control, sex, and region, by State, 1972-82, periodic rpt, 6062–2.406

Executions since 1930, and prisoners under death sentence, by prisoner characteristics, region, and State, 1982, annual rpt, 6065–1

Caprio, Gerard, Jr.

"Deficit-Savings Ratios as Indicators of Interest-Rate Pressure: A Collection of Notes", 9366–7.89

"Domestic Saving, Current Accounts, and International Capital Mobility", 9366–7.100

Caranza, Cesare

"Methods of Monetary Control in Italy, 1974-83", 9373–3.26

Carbon black

see Nonmetallic minerals and mines

Carbon monoxide

see Air pollution

Carcinogens

- Air pollution levels for 132 hazardous organic chemicals, by urban-rural location, city, and for areas with many potential sources, 1970-80, 9198–109
- Cigarette tar, nicotine, and carbon monoxide content in 207 varieties, 1982, periodic rpt, 9402–2
- Natl Cancer Inst contracts and grants, by contractor, instn, State, and city, FY83, annual listing, 4474–28
- Natl Cancer Inst epidemiology and biometry activities, budget, and contract awards by project and recipient instn, FY83, annual rpt, 4474–29
- Occupational health risks from hazardous substances and radiation, by industry, occupation, age, and sex, with bibl and glossary, 1920s-82, 9638–50
- Smoking and health research, article abstracts and indexes, 1983, annual rpt, 4044–8
- *see also* Nuclear radiation
- *see also* Radioactive materials

Cardiovascular diseases

- Agent Orange exposed Air Force personnel diseases and disorders, by disease type, age, and officer status, 1984 rpt, 3604–3
- Air pollutant and radiation indoor levels by emissions source, and household exposure and health effects by pollutant type, various periods 1966-83, hearings, 21708–102
- Airline pilots terminated for medical reasons and reinstated by carrier, and aircraft accidents by age of flight crew, selected years 1960-81, hearing, 21148–34
- Cholesterol blood levels, effects of lowering levels on heart attack and cancer incidence and deaths in men aged 35-59, with background data on other risk factors, 1973-83, 4478–145
- Death rates for persons 65 and over, by major cause, sex, and age, selected years 1940-80, 4147–3.25
- Death rates from cardiovascular disease and other causes, and hypertension prevalence and control, selected years 1971-82, article, 4102–1.432
- Deaths and death rates, by cause and age, provisional 1982-83, US Vital Statistics annual rpt, 4144–7

Deaths and death rates by detailed cause and demographic characteristics, 1979 and selected trends, US Vital Statistics annual rpt, 4144–2.1

Deaths and death rates, by detailed geographic area, cause, and demographic characteristics, 1979, US Vital Statistics annual rpt, 4144–3

Deaths and death rates, by selected cause and demographic characteristics, 1981, US Vital Statistics advance rpt, 4146–5.78

Deaths and death rates, by selected cause and demographic characteristics, 1982, US Vital Statistics advance rpt, 4146–5.81

Economic indicators relation to measures of social pathology including crime and death rates, various periods 1950-80, 23848–76

Education of consumers about cardiovascular disease and nutrition, effectiveness of Natl Heart, Lung, and Blood Inst and Giant Food, Inc, program in DC metro area, 1978-79, 4478–144

Environmental pollution-related disease research activities and publications, Sept 1982-Aug 1983, annual rpt, 9184–9

Health condition and health care resources, use, and expenditures, 1970s-82 with trends and projections 1900-2000, annual compilation, 4144–11

Hospital discharges and length of stay, by patient characteristics, facility size, procedure performed, diagnosis, and region, 1982, annual rpt, 4147–13.78

Natl Heart, Lung, and Blood Inst activities and funding, with morbidity and mortality data, various periods 1940-88, annual rpt, 4474–22

Natl Heart, Lung, and Blood Inst, Advisory Council recommended programs and budget, FY85-89, annual rpt, 4474–11

Natl Heart, Lung, and Blood Inst organization, disease and mortality data, and funds and recipients, FY83 with trends from 1900, annual fact book, 4474–15

Occupational deaths, by industry div and cause, 1981-82, article, 6722–1.422

Older persons by demographic, socioeconomic, and health characteristics, selected years 1900-81 and projected to 2050, Current Population Rpt, 2546–2.125

Smoking and health research, article abstracts and indexes, 1983, annual rpt, 4044–8

Smoking and health research publications, bimonthly listing, 4042–1

Soviet Union industrial and agricultural production by selected commodity, and demographic trends and projections by Republic, 1950s-2000, hearings, 23848–180

see also Blood pressure

see also under By Disease in the "Index by Categories"

Cargo

see Air cargo

see Freight

Carhart, Steven C.

"Macroeconomic and Energy Supply Integration", 3308–66.8

Caribbean area

- Agricultural and food production indexes, and production of selected commodities, by world region and country, 1974-83, annual rpt, 1524–5
- Agricultural exports and imports of US, by detailed commodity and country, FY83 and CY83, semiannual rpts, 1522–4
- Agricultural imports from US, by commodity and country, 1980-83, article, 1925–34.413
- Agricultural situation in Latin America, by country, 1981-83 and outlook for 1984, annual rpt, 1524–4.9
- Agricultural trade of US, by commodity and country, bimonthly rpt with articles, 1522–1
- AID activities and funding by project and function, FY85, and developing countries summary socioeconomic data, 1970s-83, by country, annual rpt, 9914–3
- AID economic assistance to developing countries, obligations and disbursements by country, quarterly rpt, 9912–4
- AID loan repayment status and terms by program and country, and status of predecessor agency loans, quarterly rpt, 9912–3
- AID loans authorized, signed, and canceled, by country and world area, monthly rpt, 9912–2
- *Background Notes,* summary social, political, and economic data, 1983 rpt, 7006–2.7, 7006–2.12
- Economic, social, and political summary data, by country, 1984, annual factbook, 244–11
- Elections in Latin America, votes and share of population voting by country and election type, selected years 1962-83, 7008–42
- Exports and imports of US (waterborne), by type of service, commodity, country, route, and US port, 1982, annual rpt, 7704–2
- Exports and imports of US (waterborne), by type of service, customs district, port, and world area, monthly rpt, 2422–7
- Exports of US, detailed Schedule B commodities by country of destination, 1983, annual rpt, 2424–9
- Exports of US, detailed Schedule E commodities by mode of transport and world area and country of destination, 1983, annual rpts, 2424–5
- Farmland (US) owned by Netherlands Antilles investors, acreage, value, and use, by State and county, 1983, annual rpt, 1584–3
- Fish landings and potential yield, consumption, and incidence of ciguatera, by Caribbean island, 1984 article, 2162–1.403
- Fish landings of US recreational fishermen, by ocean subregion and species, 1979-80, annual rpt, 2164–1.2
- Fish larvae abundance and distribution in Caribbean area, by fish species or group, summer 1972 and winter 1973, 2168–80
- Fishing (ocean sport) effort and catch, and Natl Marine Fisheries Service tagging and research activity, by species and location, 1983, annual rpt, 2164–7
- Food production and needs, and related economic trends and outlook, for 67 developing countries, 1980-86, annual rpt, 1524–6

Caribbean area

Food supply policies of 21 developing countries, with farm sector data, tariff income, and prices and imports of 5 grains, 1960s-81, 1528–168

Forests (tropical) status by country and world region, conservation methods, and mgmt role of US, foreign, and intl groups, 1977-80s and projected to 2000, 26358–101.1

Great Lakes trade, by SITC 3-digit commodity, port, vessel type, world area, and country, 1982, annual rpt, 7744–3

Human rights conditions in 162 countries, economic and military aid of US, and economic aid of intl organizations, 1981-83, annual rpt, 21384–3

Hurricanes and tropical storms in North Atlantic and Caribbean area, paths, surveillance, deaths, property damage, and landfall probabilities by city, 1983, annual rpt, 2184–7

Immigrant and nonimmigrant visas of US issued and refused, and status adjustments, by class and nationality, FY77, annual rpt, 7184–1

Immigration, and alien residents, workers, visitors, deportations, and naturalizations, by country of birth, FY81, annual rpt, 6264–2

Imports of US, detailed Schedule A commodities by country and world area of origin, and mode of transport, 1983, annual rpts, 2424–2

Imports of US, detailed TSUSA commodities by country of origin, 1983, annual rpt, 2424–4

Inter-American Foundation activities, grants, and fellowships, by country, FY83, annual rpt, 14424–1

Inter-American Foundation activities, 1984 narrative semiannual rpt, 14422–2

Investment (foreign direct) in US, by major industry group, world area, and selected country, 1980-83, annual article, 2702–1.439

Investment (foreign direct) of US, by world area and country, 1977-83, article, 2702–1.442

Investment (intl direct) worldwide, and US investment flows by major industry, by world region and country, 1982 and trends from 1950, annual rpt, 2044–25

Loans of large US banks to foreigners at all US and foreign offices, by country group and country, quarterly rpt, 13002–1

Military aid of US, arms sales, and training programs costs and budget requests by program, world region, and country, FY83-85, annual rpt, 7144–13

Military spending, arms trade, and armed forces size, with total govt spending and population, by country, 1972-82, annual rpt, 9824–1

Minerals Yearbook, 1982, Vol 3: foreign country reviews of production, trade, and policies, by commodity, annual rpt, 5604–35

Money orders of USPS sent to Latin America, volume and amount by area, 1983 hearings, 21628–55

Oil exports to US by OPEC and non-OPEC countries, monthly rpt, 3162–24.3

Population size and growth rates, and latest available benchmark demographic data, by country, 1950-83, biennial rpt, 2324–4

Refugee arrivals in US, by world area of origin and processing and nationality, monthly rpt, 7002–4, 7002–5

Refugee arrivals in US by world area of origin and State of settlement, and Fed Govt intl and domestic assistance costs, FY85, annual rpt, 7004–16

Refugee migration, settlement status, and assistance, by world area and country of origin and asylum, as of May 1984, annual rpt, 7004–15

Rum imports (duty-free) of US under Caribbean Basin Initiative, by country, Jan-June 1983-84, annual rpt, 9884–15

Students in US and Soviet bloc training programs, by program type and Latin American country or world region of student origin, selected years 1972-82, GAO rpt, 26123–77

Tax evasion through nonresidents bank claims and deposits, direct investments, income payments, and other transactions in 5 Caribbean countries, 1978-82, 8008–106

Tax evasion through tax haven countries, with income, investments, and taxes withheld by country, various periods 1975- 83, hearings, 21408–71

Travel to and from US and travel receipts and payments by world area, and travel to US by country, 1977-83, annual rpt, 2904–10

Weather conditions and impact assessment, by world area and country, monthly rpt, 2152–9

Weather stations of Natl Weather Service, locations and regular observations made, 1984 annual listing, 2184–5

Weather stations of Upper Air Observational Network, by US and foreign location, 1984 annual listing, 2184–6

Women sociodemographic, economic, and fertility characteristics, with comparisons to men, by country, 1960s-85, world region rpt, 2326–15.1

see also Antigua and Barbuda

see also Bahamas

see also Barbados

see also Bermuda

see also Caribbean Common Market

see also Cuba

see also Dominica

see also Dominican Republic

see also Grenada

see also Haiti

see also Jamaica

see also Puerto Rico

see also St. Christopher and Nevis

see also St. Lucia

see also St. Vincent and The Grenadines

see also Trinidad and Tobago

see also Virgin Islands

see also under By Foreign Country in the "Index by Categories"

Caribbean Common Market

Agricultural exports and imports of US, by detailed commodity and country, FY83 and CY83, semiannual rpts, 1522–4

Carlin, Thomas A.

"Who Gets Rural Jobs?", 1004–16.1

Carlino, Gerald A.

"Declining City Productivity and the Growth of Rural Regions: A Test of Alternative Explanations", 9387–8.90

Index by Subjects and Names

"Inflationary Expectations and the Consumer", 9387–8.92

Carlisle, Pa.

see also under By SMSA or MSA in the "Index by Categories"

Carlozzi, Nicholas

"International Capital Mobility and the Coordination of Monetary Rules", 9387–8.85

"Structure, Parameterization and Solution of a Multicountry Simulation Model", 9387–8.84

Carman, Clifford M.

"Dairy Outlook", 1004–16.1

"Participation in the Milk Diversion Program", 1561–2.402

Carnes, Richard B.

"Meatpacking and Prepared Meats Industry: Above-Average Productivity Gains", 6722–1.428

Carney, Samuel M.

"Distribution of Waterfowl Species Harvested in States and Counties During 1971-80 Hunting Seasons", 5508–18

Carpets

see Textile industry and fabrics

Carpools

see Commuting

Carson, Carol S.

"Underground Economy: An Introduction", 2702–1.419, 2702–1.428

Cartels

EC trade promotion policies and financing by industry, and effect on competing US industries, 1970s-82, 9886–4.73

see also Organization of Petroleum Exporting Countries

Carter, Charlie

"Alabama: Prospects Brighten for 1984", 9371–1.408

"Economic Influence of Retirees on Selected Southeastern Communities", 9371–1.420

"Surge in Bankruptcies: Is the New Law Responsible?", 21528–57

Carter, Patricia W.

"U.S. Civil Airmen Statistics, 1983", 7504–2

Cartography

Census of Population, 1980: detailed socioeconomic and demographic characteristics, by age, sex, race, Hispanic origin, occupation, and industry, State rpt series, 2531–4

Fed Govt programs and mgmt cost control proposals, 3-year savings by function and agency, and financial and operating data, 1960s-81, 16908–1.3

Geological Survey programs and funding, FY78-83, annual rpt, 5664–8

Glaciology intl research summaries, methodology, and bibls, series, 2156–18

Population socioeconomic data graphic presentation use, dev, and standards, 1978 conf papers, 2626–2.51

Satellite Landsat system proposed transfer to private sector, uses and product sales by user type, and university programs and personnel by instn, 1973-85, 26358–100

Satellite systems (foreign and US) for civil observation, data product revenue, and proposed transfer of Fed Govt system to private sector, selected years 1978-FY84, 2148–47

Index by Subjects and Names

see also Maps

Case, Robert A.

"North Atlantic Tropical Cyclones, 1983", 2152–8.401

Casper, Wyo.

Census of Housing, 1980: occupancy and unit characteristics, by race, Hispanic origin, and city, SMSA rpt, 2473–1.111

Census of Population and Housing, 1980: detailed population and housing characteristics, by county, city, and census tract, SMSA rpt, 2551–2.111

see also under By SMSA or MSA in the "Index by Categories"

Cassidy, Henry J.

"Estimates of Losses from Short Puts", 9316–1.102

"Review of the Federal Home Loan Bank Board's Adjustable-Rate Mortgage Regulations and the Current ARM Proposal", 9316–1.104

Casstevens, Thomas W.

"On-Farm Water Management in Aegean Turkey, 1968-74", 9916–1.50

Castellanos-Vera, Aradit

"Observations on the Distribution, Abundance, and Productivity of the Osprey in the Ojo de Liebre-Guerrero Negro Lagoon, B.C.S., Mexico", 1208–197

Castillo, Julian

"The Hispanic Population: An Overview", 16598–5

Castor beans

see Vegetables and vegetable products

Castor oil

see Oils, oilseeds, and fats

Catalogs

see Bibliographies

see Directories

see Government publications lists

Caterinicchio, Russell P.

"Relative Intensity Measures: Pricing of Inpatient Nursing Services Under Diagnosis-Related Group Prospective Hospital Payment", 4652–1.424

Cathcart, James B.

"Phosphate-Rock Resources of the U.S.", 5668–74

Cattle

see Dairy industry and products

see Livestock and livestock industry

CATV

see Cable television

Cavaiola, Lawrence J.

"Analysis of Administration Strategic Arms Reduction and Modernization Proposals", 26306–6.73

Cedar Falls, Iowa

Census of Housing, 1980: occupancy and unit characteristics, by race, Hispanic origin, and city, SMSA rpt, 2473–1.367

Census of Population and Housing, 1980: detailed population and housing characteristics, by county, city, and census tract, SMSA rpt, 2551–2.367

see also under By SMSA or MSA in the "Index by Categories"

Cedar Rapids, Iowa

Census of Housing, 1980: occupancy and unit characteristics, by race, Hispanic origin, and city, SMSA rpt, 2473–1.112

Census of Population and Housing, 1980: detailed population and housing characteristics, by county, city, and census tract, SMSA rpt, 2551–2.112

see also under By City and By SMSA or MSA in the "Index by Categories"

Celery

see Vegetables and vegetable products

Cement and concrete

Air pollutant emission factors, by detailed source, 3rd edition, 1983-84 supplements, 9198–13

Air pollution abatement equipment shipments by industry, exports, and new and backlog orders, by product, 1983, annual Current Industrial Rpt, 2506–12.5

Business statistics, detailed data for major industries and economic indicators, *Survey of Current Business,* monthly rpt, 2702–1.18

Census of Population, 1980: detailed socioeconomic and demographic characteristics, by age, sex, race, Hispanic origin, occupation, and industry, State rpt series, 2531–4

China economic conditions, agricultural and industrial production, trade, and domestic and foreign investment, 1980-85, 2048–106

Communist, OECD, and selected other countries consumer and producer goods production, 1960s-83, annual rpt, 244–5.8

County Business Patterns: establishments, employees, and payrolls, by SIC 4-digit industry and county, 1981, annual State rpt series, 2326–8

County Business Patterns: establishments, employees, and payrolls, by SIC 4-digit industry and county, 1982, annual State rpt series, 2326–6

Cuba economic conditions, agricultural and industrial production and distribution, trade, and intl economic relations, 1970-82 and trends from 1957, 248–40

Employment, earnings, and hours, by selected SIC 1- to 4-digit industry, State, and for 278 major labor areas, 1939-83, annual rpt, 6744–5

Employment, earnings, and hours, by SIC 4-digit nonfarm industry, monthly 1974-Feb 1984, annual update, 6744–4

Energy use and cost for building materials manufacture, by energy source and industry, 1970s-82, article, 2012–1.401

Exports and imports of US, detailed SIC-based commodities by world area, 1983, annual rpts, 2424–6

Exports and imports of US, totals and as percent of domestic production, by SIC 2- to 5-digit commodity, 1981, annual rpt, 2424–3

Exports, imports, tariffs, and industry operating data for hydraulic cement, 1979-83, TSUSA commodity rpt supplement, 9885–5.17

Exports of US, detailed commodities by country of destination, monthly rpt, 2422–3

Exports of US, detailed Schedule B commodities by country of destination, 1983, annual rpt, 2424–9

Exports of US, detailed Schedule E commodities by mode of transport and world area and country of destination, 1983, annual rpts, 2424–5

Foreign minerals production, reserves, and industry role in domestic economy and world supply, country and world region rpt series, 5606–1

Great Lakes trade, by SITC 3-digit commodity, port, vessel type, world area, and country, 1982, annual rpt, 7744–3

Hwy construction expenditures and contracts awarded for Federal-aid system, by type of material used and State, various periods 1944-83, annual rpt, 7554–29.6

Hwy construction material prices and indexes for Federal-aid system, by type of material and urban-rural location, quarterly rpt, 7552–7

Hwy construction materials prices on Federal-aid hwy system, 3rd qtr 1984, 7556–3.3

Hwy construction materials used per $1 million of total expenditures on Federal-aid system, by State, 1980-82, annual rpt, 7554–29.2

Imports of US, detailed Schedule A commodities by country and world area of origin, and mode of transport, 1983, annual rpts, 2424–2

Imports of US, detailed Schedule A commodities by country, monthly rpt, 2422–2

Imports of US, detailed TSUSA commodities by country of origin, 1983, annual rpt, 2424–4

Income tax returns of corporations, detailed income and tax items by industry, 1981, annual rpt, 8304–4

Income tax returns of sole proprietorships, detailed data by industry div and selected industry group, 1981, annual rpt, 8304–7

Input-output structure of US economy, detailed interindustry transactions for 537 industries, and components of final demand, 1977 benchmark data, 2708–17

Manufacturing census, 1982: financial and operating data, by SIC 2- to 4-digit industry, State, SMSA, and county, preliminary census div rpt series, 2491–3

Manufacturing census, 1982: financial and operating data, for SIC 4-digit industries by product, preliminary rpt series, 2491–1

Mineral Industry Surveys, commodity review of production, trade, and consumption, 1983, advance annual rpt, 5614–5.5

Mineral Industry Surveys, commodity review of production, trade, stocks, and consumption, monthly rpt, 5612–1.2

Minerals Yearbook, 1982, Vol 1: commodity reviews of production, reserves, supply, use, and trade, annual rpt, 5604–33

Minerals Yearbook, 1982, Vol 2 preprints: State reviews of production and sales by commodity, and business activity, annual rpt series, 5604–16

Minerals Yearbook, 1982, Vol 2: State reviews of production, sales, and firms, by commodity, and business activity, annual rpt, 5604–34

Minerals Yearbook, 1982, Vol 3 preprints: foreign country reviews of production, trade, and policies, by commodity, annual rpt series, 5604–17

Minerals Yearbook, 1983, Vol 1 preprints: commodity review of production, reserves, supply, use, and trade, annual rpt, 5604–15.15

Cement and concrete

Minerals Yearbook, 1983, Vol 3 preprints: foreign country reviews of production, trade, and policies, by commodity, annual rpt series, 5604–23

Occupational injuries and incidence rates at stone mines and related operations, detailed analysis, 1982, annual rpt, 6664–5

Occupational injury and illness rates, by SIC 2- to 4-digit industry, 1982, annual rpt, 6844–1

Producer prices and indexes, by stage of processing and detailed commodity, monthly rpt, 6762–6

Producer prices and indexes, by stage of processing and detailed commodity, monthly 1983, annual supplement, 6764–2

Production, prices, trade, use, employment, tariffs, and stockpiling, by mineral commodity, with foreign comparisons, 1979-83, annual rpt, 5604–18

Production, shipments, PPI, and stocks of building materials, by type, bimonthly rpt, 2012–1.5, 2012–1.6

Productivity, hours, and employment indexes for selected SIC 3- and 4-digit industries, 1954-82, annual rpt, 6824–1.3

Transportation census, 1982: trucks, by detailed characteristics, miles traveled, and type of product carried, State rpt series, 2573–1

Waterborne commerce of US (domestic and foreign), freight by commodity, traffic, and passengers, by port and waterway, 1982, annual rpt, 3754–3

see also under By Commodity in the "Index by Categories"

see also under By Industry in the "Index by Categories"

Cemeteries and funerals

Census of Population, 1980: detailed socioeconomic and demographic characteristics, by age, sex, race, Hispanic origin, occupation, and industry, State rpt series, 2531–4

Census of Population, 1980: labor force, by sex, detailed occupation, and region, with comparison to 1970 census, supplementary rpt, 2535–1.12

Census of Service Industries, 1982: employment, establishments, receipts, and payroll, by SIC 2- to 4-digit kind of business, SMSA, county, and city, State rpt series, 2391–1

Census of Service Industries, 1982: employment, establishments, receipts, and payroll, by SIC 4-digit kind of business and State, preliminary rpt, 2390–2.4

County Business Patterns: establishments, employees, and payrolls, by SIC 4-digit industry and county, 1981, annual State rpt series, 2326–8

County Business Patterns: establishments, employees, and payrolls, by SIC 4-digit industry and county, 1982, annual State rpt series, 2326–6

Employment, earnings, and hours, by SIC 4-digit nonfarm industry, monthly 1974-Feb 1984, annual update, 6744–4

Finances and operations, by SIC 2- to 4-digit industry, 1970s-83 and projected to 1988, annual rpt, 2014–4

FTC budget authority and expenditures for regulatory analysis, by prospective regulation and contractor, 1983, hearings, 21528–56

Income tax returns of sole proprietorships, detailed data by industry div and selected industry group, 1981, annual rpt, 8304–7

Income tax returns of sole proprietorships, receipts, deductions by type, payroll, and net income, by major industry, 1982, annual article, 8302–2.413

Input-output structure of US economy, detailed interindustry transactions for 537 industries, and components of final demand, 1977 benchmark data, 2708–17

Manufacturing census, 1982: financial and operating data, for SIC 4-digit industries by product, preliminary rpt, 2491–1.441

Occupational manpower needs and supply by detailed occupation, and educational and training program enrollees and grads by detailed field, 1982 and 1995, biennial rpt, 6744–3

Price indexes and prices for producers of caskets by detailed type, monthly rpt, 6762–6

Price indexes and prices for producers of caskets by detailed type, monthly 1983, annual supplement, 6764–2

Receipts for selected services, by SIC 2- to 4-digit kind of business, 1983, annual rpt, 2413–8

Workers compensation law provisions of States and Fed Govt, by jurisdiction, as of July 1984, semiannual rpt, 6502–1

see also Military cemeteries and funerals

Census Bureau

see Bureau of Census

Census divisions

see under By Census Division in the "Index by Categories"

Census of Agriculture

Data coding systems for industries used in statistical programs of 6 Federal agencies, comparability, workload, and updating cycles, 1984 rpt, 106–4.5

Data coverage and availability for 1982 Census of Agriculture and related statistics, 1984 guide, 2308–55

Data coverage and availability of Census Bur publications, 1984 annual listing, 2304–2

Data coverage policy for 1982 agriculture and economic censuses, and Federal agency data use, 1984 GAO narrative rpt, 26125–26

Farms, farmland, production and costs, and operator characteristics, 1982 census, preliminary State and county rpt series, 2330–1

Farms, farmland, production, finances, and operator characteristics, by county, 1982 census, final State rpt series, 2331–1

Census of Construction Industries

Data coverage and availability for 1982 economic censuses and related statistics, 1984 guide, 2308–5

Data coverage and availability of Census Bur publications, 1984 annual listing, 2304–2

Financial and operating data, by SIC 4-digit industry and State, 1982 census, final rpt series, 2373–1

Financial and operating data, by SIC 4-digit industry and State, 1982 census, preliminary rpt series, 2371–1

Index by Subjects and Names

Census of Governments

City govt revenues by source, expenditures by function, debt, and assets, by State and city, 1982 census, 2457–4

County govt revenues by source, expenditures by function, debt, and assets, by State and county, 1982 census, 2457–3

Data coverage and availability for 1982 Census of Agriculture and related statistics, 1984 guide, 2308–55

Data coverage and availability of Census Bur publications, 1984 annual listing, 2304–2

Employment, payrolls, and average earnings, by function, level of govt, State, county, population size, and inside-outside SMSAs, 1982 census, 2455–2

Local govt employment by function, payroll, and average earnings, for individual counties, cities, and school and special districts, 1982 census, 2455–1

Properties govt assessed value, sales, and tax rates, by property type, State, SMSA, county, and city, 1982 census, 2453–1

School districts revenues, expenditures, debt, and assets, by district and State, 1982 census, 2457–1

State govt payments to local govts, by program, source of funds, level of govt, and State, 1982 census with trends from 1902, 2460–3

Census of Housing

Data coverage and availability of Census Bur publications, 1984 annual listing, 2304–2

Housing inventory, occupancy, and unit characteristics, changes from 1973 by region and inside-outside SMSAs and central cities, 1980 census, series, 2473–3

Housing occupancy and unit characteristics of SMSAs and central cities, by race, Hispanic origin, and city, 1980 census, State and SMSA rpt series, 2473–1

Housing unit structural, financial, and householder characteristics, by region and State, 1980 census, 2475–4

see also Census of Population and Housing

Census of Manufactures

Data coverage and availability for 1982 economic censuses and related statistics, 1984 guide, 2308–5

Data coverage and availability of Census Bur publications, 1984 annual listing, 2304–2

Financial and operating data, by SIC 2- to 4-digit industry, State, SMSA, and county, 1982 census, preliminary census div rpt series, 2491–3

Financial and operating data, for SIC 4-digit industries by product, 1982 census, preliminary rpt series, 2491–1

Textile mill machinery in place, by machine type and textile industry, 1982 census, special preliminary rpts, 2491–2

Census of Mineral Industries

Data coverage and availability for 1982 economic censuses and related statistics, 1984 guide, 2308–5

Data coverage and availability of Census Bur publications, 1984 annual listing, 2304–2

Financial and operating data, by SIC 2- to 4-digit industry and State, 1982 census, preliminary summary rpts, 2511–2

Index by Subjects and Names

Financial and operating data, including materials consumed, by SIC 4-digit industry and State, 1982 census, preliminary rpt series, 2511–1

Census of Minority-Owned Business Enterprises

see Survey of Minority-Owned Business Enterprises

Census of Outlying Areas

Data coverage and availability for 1982 economic censuses and related statistics, 1984 guide, 2308–5

Virgin Islands economic censuses, 1982: employment, establishments, payroll, and receipts, by SIC 1- to 4-digit industry, island, and city, 2593–1

Census of Population

- Data coverage and availability of Census Bur publications, 1984 annual listing, 2304–2
- Population characteristics, selected and advance data from 1980 census, supplementary rpt series, 2535–1
- Population detailed socioeconomic and demographic characteristics, by age, sex, race, Hispanic origin, and industry, 1980 census, State rpt series, 2531–4
- Population detailed socioeconomic characteristics, by county, city, and inside-outside SMSAs and central cities, 1980 census, State rpt series, 2531–3
- Population socioeconomic characteristics, selected data, 1980 census with trends and projections 1960-2000, young readers pamphlet series, 2326–1

see also Census of Population and Housing

Census of Population and Housing

- Data coverage and availability for 1982 Census of Agriculture and related statistics, 1984 guide, 2308–55
- Data coverage and availability of Census Bur publications, 1984 annual listing, 2304–2
- Data coverage, availability, and uses of 1980 census for urban and transportation planning, 1984 guide, 7558–101
- Mental health facilities needs assessment and program evaluation for small areas, methodology, use of census data, analysis, and sample data, series, 4506–8
- Population and housing detailed characteristics, by county, city, and census tract, 1980 census, State and SMSA rpt series, 2551–2

Census of Retail Trade

- Data coverage and availability for 1982 economic censuses and related statistics, 1984 guide, 2308–5
- Data coverage and availability of Census Bur publications, 1984 annual listing, 2304–2
- Employment, establishments, sales, and payroll, by SIC 2- to 4-digit kind of business, SMSA, and retail district, 1982 census, State rpt series, 2401–1
- Employment, establishments, sales, and payroll, by SIC 2- to 4-digit kind of business, SMSA, county, and city, 1982 census, State rpt series, 2397–1
- Employment, establishments, sales, and payroll, by SIC 4-digit kind of business and State, 1982 census, preliminary rpt series, 2395–1

Census of Service Industries

- Data coverage and availability for 1982 economic censuses and related statistics, 1984 guide, 2308–5
- Data coverage and availability of Census Bur publications, 1984 annual listing, 2304–2
- Employment, establishments, receipts, and payroll, by SIC 2- to 4-digit kind of business, SMSA, city, and county, 1982 census, State rpt series, 2391–1
- Employment, establishments, receipts, and payroll, by SIC 4-digit kind of business and State, 1982 census, preliminary rpt series, 2390–2

Census of Transportation

- Data coverage and availability for transportation industry statistics from Census Bur, 1983 pamphlet, 2326–7.61
- Data coverage and availability for 1982 economic censuses and related statistics, 1984 guide, 2308–5
- Data coverage and availability of Census Bur publications, 1984 annual listing, 2304–2
- Trucks, by detailed characteristics, miles traveled, and type of product carried, 1982 census, State rpt series, 2573–1

see also Nationwide Personal Transportation Study

Census of Wholesale Trade

- Data coverage and availability for 1982 economic censuses and related statistics, 1984 guide, 2308–5
- Data coverage and availability of Census Bur publications, 1984 annual listing, 2304–2
- Employment, establishments, finances, and operations, SIC 2- to 4-digit kind of business, SMSA, county, and city, 1982 census, State rpt series, 2405–1
- Employment, establishments, sales by commodity, and payroll, by SIC 4-digit kind of business and State, 1982 census, preliminary rpt series, 2403–1

Census of Women-Owned Businesses

see Survey of Women-Owned Businesses

Census tracts

- Census of Population and Housing, 1980: detailed population and housing characteristics, by county, city, and census tract, State and SMSA rpt series, 2551–2
- Mental health facilities needs assessment and program evaluation for small areas, methodology, use of census data, analysis, and sample data, series, 4506–8
- NYC population size, demographic characteristics, and rental housing, in 5 neighborhoods by census tract, 1980 with percent change from 1970, article, 9385–1.403

see also Neighborhoods

Centaur Associates, Inc.

"1983 RCS Evaluation Highlights: Cost-Benefit Evaluaton of the Residential Conservation Service Program", 21368–54

Center for Environmental Education

- "Oil Drilling Prohibitions at the Channel Islands and Pt. Reyes-Farallon Islands National Marine Sanctuaries: Some Costs and Benefits", 21448–30.1
- "Outer Continental Shelf, O.C.S. Oil and Gas Leasing, and Marine Sanctuaries: A Comparison of Areas", 21448–30

Centers for Disease Control

Centers for Disease Control

- Cost control proposals for Fed Govt programs and mgmt, 3-year savings by function and agency, and financial and operating data, 1960s-81, 16908–1.7
- Data projects and systems of HHS, by subagency, FY83-84, annual inventory, 4044–3
- Death rates by sex, race, and age for 40 causes, projected for 10-year period, 1982 rpt, 4208–21
- Homicides and homicide rates, by victim characteristics, location, and circumstances, and years of life lost from homicide and other leading causes of death, 1970-78, 4205–38
- Immunization and preventive medicine programs for children in US and Mexico, and disease cases, vaccine reactions, and deaths, 1984 conf papers, 4204–15
- Immunization research publications, 1984 annual listing, 4204–16
- Infectious notifiable diseases and other public health concerns, cases and mortality trends, quarterly rpt articles, 4202–7
- Infectious notifiable diseases, cases and current outbreaks, by region and State, weekly rpt, 4202–1
- Infectious notifiable diseases, cases and incidence, by census div and State, 1982, annual rpt, 4204–1
- Influenza deaths, viruses identified by State and country, epidemiology, and vaccine effects and recommended dosages by age, 1979/80-1980/81, annual rpt, 4205–3
- Malaria cases reported in US, including military personnel and foreign civilians, 1966-82, annual rpt, 4205–4
- Nutrition status of infants and children, blood and height-weight indicators, and low birth weight risk factors, by age, race, and Hispanic origin, 1981, annual rpt, 4205–24
- Public health labs of States, pay scales and job requirements by occupation and State, FY81-83, annual rpt, 4204–7
- Public health labs of States, personnel, finances, workloads, and other activities, by State, FY82, annual rpt, 4204–8
- Rabies cases in animals and humans, for US and Mexico by State and for Canada by Province, 1980-82, annual rpt, 4205–28
- Smoking and tobacco marketing legislation introduced and enacted in State legislatures, by State, 1982, annual rpt, 4204–13
- Tuberculosis cases, deaths, and treatment, by demographic characteristics, State, and city, 1982 and trends from 1953, annual rpt, 4204–2
- Vaccination requirements for intl travel by country, and disease prevention recommendations, 1984 annual rpt, 4204–11
- Venereal disease cases and control activities, annual rpt, suspended, 4204–5
- Venereal disease cases reported and epidemiologic activities, by region, State, and large city, 1982, annual rpt, 4204–14
- Veterans (Vietnam) health condition, methodology for 3 CDC studies on effects of military service and Agent Orange exposure, Nov 1983 rpt, 4208–22

Centers for Disease Control

Waterborne disease outbreaks and cases, by type, source, and location, 1983, annual rpt, 4205–35

see also National Institute for Occupational Safety and Health

CENTO

see Central Treaty Organization

Central African Republic

- AID activities and funding by project and function, FY85, and developing countries summary socioeconomic data, 1970s-83, by country, annual rpt, 9914–3
- AID economic assistance to developing countries, obligations and disbursements by country, quarterly rpt, 9912–4
- *Background Notes,* summary social, political, and economic data, 1983 rpt, 7006–2.2
- Economic conditions and foreign marketing prospects in 46 Sub-Saharan countries, 1983 world region rpt, 2046–5.1
- Economic, social, and political summary data, by country, 1984, annual factbook, 244–11
- Exports of US, detailed Schedule B commodities by country of destination, 1983, annual rpt, 2424–9
- Exports of US, detailed Schedule E commodities by mode of transport and world area and country of destination, 1983, annual rpts, 2424–5
- Imports of US, detailed Schedule A commodities by country and world area of origin, and mode of transport, 1983, annual rpts, 2424–2
- Imports of US, detailed TSUSA commodities by country of origin, 1983, annual rpt, 2424–4
- Loans and grants for economic and military assistance from US and intl agencies, by program and country, FY46-83, annual rpt, 9914–5
- Military aid of US, arms sales, and training programs costs and budget requests by program, world region, and country, FY83-85, annual rpt, 7144–13
- Military spending, arms trade, and armed forces size, with total govt spending and population, by country, 1972-82, annual rpt, 9824–1
- *Minerals Yearbook, 1982,* Vol 3: foreign country reviews of production, trade, and policies, by commodity, annual rpt, 5604–35
- *Minerals Yearbook, 1982,* Vol 3 preprints: foreign country review of production, trade, and policies, by commodity, annual rpt, 5604–17.82
- Oil and gas undiscovered recoverable resources, cumulative production, and identified reserves, as of 1982, preliminary oil basin rpt, 5666–17.13
- Population size and growth rates, and latest available benchmark demographic data, by country, 1950-83, biennial rpt, 2324–4 *see also* under By Foreign Country in the "Index by Categories"

Central America

- Agricultural and food production indexes, and production of selected commodities, by world region and country, 1974-83, annual rpt, 1524–5
- Agricultural exports and imports of US, by detailed commodity and country, FY83 and CY83, semiannual rpts, 1522–4

Agricultural exports of US to Latin America, by commodity, country group, and selected country, FY81-84 and forecast FY85, article, 1522–1.407

- Agricultural situation in Latin America, by country, 1981-83 and outlook for 1984, annual rpt, 1524–4.9
- Agricultural supply/demand, trade, and production, and socioeconomic data, by country, 1950s-77, 1528–179
- AID activities and funding by project and function, FY85, and developing countries summary socioeconomic data, 1970s-83, by country, annual rpt, 9914–3
- AID community dev assistance to local govts in developing countries, program activities and funding, 1960s-80s, 9918–11
- AID economic assistance to 7 Central American countries, by type of aid, FY80-83, GAO rpt, 26123–55
- AID loans authorized, signed, and canceled, by country and world area, monthly rpt, 9912–2
- Budget of US, military and other aid funding, effects of Reagan Admin policy changes, FY85, annual rpt, 104–21
- China economic conditions, agricultural and industrial production, trade, and domestic and foreign investment, 1980-85, 2048–106
- Economic, social, and political conditions in 6 Central America countries, 1960s-83 with trends and projections 1930-2010, 028–19
- Elections in Latin America, votes and share of population voting by country and election type, selected years 1962-83, 7008–42
- Export sales and shipments of US grains, oilseed products, hides, skins, and cotton, by country, weekly rpt, 1922–3
- Exports and imports of OECD, total and for 4 major countries, and US trade by country, by commodity, 1972-82, annual world region rpt, 244–13.3
- Exports and imports of US (waterborne), by type of service, commodity, country, route, and US port, 1982, annual rpt, 7704–2
- Exports and imports of US (waterborne), by type of service, customs district, port, and world area, monthly rpt, 2422–7
- Exports and imports of US, by commodity group, world area, selected country, US coastal area and port, and mode of transport, with seasonal adjustments, monthly rpt, 2422–9
- Exports and imports of US, detailed SIC-based commodities by world area, 1983, annual rpts, 2424–6
- Exports of US, detailed Schedule E commodities by mode of transport and world area and country of destination, 1983, annual rpts, 2424–5
- Food production and needs, and related economic trends and outlook, for 67 developing countries, 1980-86, annual rpt, 1524–6
- Great Lakes trade, by SITC 3-digit commodity, port, vessel type, world area, and country, 1982, annual rpt, 7744–3
- Immigrant and nonimmigrant visas of US issued and refused, and status adjustments, by class and nationality, FY77, annual rpt, 7184–1

Index by Subjects and Names

- Immigration, and alien residents, workers, visitors, deportations, and naturalizations, by country of birth, FY81, annual rpt, 6264–2
- Imports of US, detailed Schedule A commodities by country and world area of origin, and mode of transport, 1983, annual rpts, 2424–2
- Inter-American Foundation activities, grants, and fellowships, by country, FY83, annual rpt, 14424–1
- Inter-American Foundation activities, 1984 narrative semiannual rpt, 14422–2
- Investment (foreign direct) of US, by selected major industry group and world area, 1982-83, annual article, 2702–1.430
- Investment (foreign direct) of US, by world area and country, 1977-83, article, 2702–1.442
- Investment (intl direct) worldwide, and US investment flows by major industry, by world region and country, 1982 and trends from 1950, annual rpt, 2044–25
- Loans and grants for economic and military assistance from US and intl agencies, by program and country, FY46-83, annual rpt, 9914–5
- Military aid of US, arms sales, and training programs costs and budget requests by program, world region, and country, FY83-85, annual rpt, 7144–13
- Military spending, arms trade, and armed forces size, with total govt spending and population, by country, 1972-82, annual rpt, 9824–1
- *Minerals Yearbook, 1982,* Vol 3: foreign country reviews of production, trade, and policies, by commodity, annual rpt, 5604–35
- *Minerals Yearbook, 1982,* Vol 3 preprints: foreign country review of production, trade, and policies, by commodity, annual rpt, 5604–17.86
- Money orders of USPS sent to Latin America, volume and amount by area, 1983 hearings, 21628–55
- Multilateral dev banks economic dev projects, environmental and cultural impacts in developing countries, 1970s-83, hearings, 21248–80
- Natural resources and hazards to resource dev, with data on mineral, energy, and water resources, by Central American country, 1981 with trends from 1977, 5668–71
- Population size and growth rates, and latest available benchmark demographic data, by country, 1950-83, biennial rpt, 2324–4
- R&D Fed Govt funding for foreign performers, by world region and country, FY82-84, annual rpt, 9627–20.2
- Refugee arrivals in US, by world area of origin and processing and nationality, monthly rpt, 7002–4, 7002–5
- Refugee arrivals in US by world area of origin and State of settlement, and Fed Govt intl and domestic assistance costs, FY85, annual rpt, 7004–16
- Refugee migration, settlement status, and assistance, by world area and country of origin and asylum, as of May 1984, annual rpt, 7004–15
- Refugees from Central America by country of origin and asylum, and aid from US and Mexico, FY82-1984, GAO rpt, 26123–70

Index by Subjects and Names

Central cities

Students in US and Soviet bloc training programs, by program type and Latin American country or world region of student origin, selected years 1972-82, GAO rpt, 26123–77

Tide height and time daily at worldwide coastal points, 1985 predictions, annual rpt, 2174–2.1, 2174–2.2

Travel to and from US and travel receipts and payments by world area, and travel to US by country, 1977-83, annual rpt, 2904–10

US policy in Central America, with data on terrorism in El Salvador, Oct 1979-June 1983, human rights certification hearing, 21388–41

USIA info center and reading room operations, by world region, country, and city, FY83, annual rpt, 9854–4

Weather stations of Natl Weather Service, locations and regular observations made, 1984 annual listing, 2184–5

Weather stations of Upper Air Observational Network, by US and foreign location, 1984 annual listing, 2184–6

Women sociodemographic, economic, and fertility characteristics, with comparisons to men, by country, 1960s-85, world region rpt, 2326–15.1

see also Belize
see also Caribbean area
see also Central American Common Market
see also Costa Rica
see also El Salvador
see also Guatemala
see also Honduras
see also Inter-American Development Bank
see also Latin American Free Trade Association
see also Nicaragua
see also Panama
see also under By Foreign Country in the "Index by Categories"

Central American Common Market

Agricultural exports and imports of US, by detailed commodity and country, FY83 and CY83, semiannual rpts, 1522–4

Exports and imports of US, by commodity group, world area, selected country, US coastal area and port, and mode of transport, with seasonal adjustments, monthly rpt, 2422–9

Exports and imports of US, detailed SIC-based commodities by world area, 1983, annual rpts, 2424–6

Exports of US, detailed Schedule E commodities by mode of transport and world area and country of destination, 1983, annual rpts, 2424–5

Imports of US, detailed Schedule A commodities by country and world area of origin, and mode of transport, 1983, annual rpts, 2424–2

Central business districts

Census of Population and Housing, 1980: detailed population and housing characteristics, by county, city, and census tract, State and SMSA rpt series, 2551–2

Census of Population, 1980: detailed socioeconomic and demographic characteristics, by age, sex, race, Hispanic origin, occupation, and industry, State rpt series, 2531–4

Enterprise zone and urban revitalization projects of State and local govts, effect on

business and employment in selected areas, various dates 1972-83, hearing, 21788–140

Retail trade census, 1982: employment, establishments, sales, and payroll, by SIC 2- to 4-digit kind of business, SMSA, and retail district, State rpt series, 2401–1

Central cities

Apartment market absorption rates and characteristics for nonsubsidized privately financed furnished and unfurnished units completed in 1982, annual Current Housing Rpt, 2484–2

Apartment market absorption rates and characteristics for nonsubsidized privately financed units completed in 1983, preliminary annual Current Housing Rpt, 2484–3

Births and birth rates, by detailed demographic characteristics and geographic area, 1979 and trends, US Vital Statistics annual rpt, 4144–1

Census of Housing, 1980: inventory, occupancy, and unit characteristics, changes from 1973 by region and inside-outside SMSAs and central cities, series, 2473–3

Census of Housing, 1980: occupancy and unit characteristics of SMSAs and central cities, by race, Hispanic origin, and city, State and SMSA rpt series, 2473–1

Census of Population and Housing, 1980: detailed population and housing characteristics, by county, city, and census tract, State and SMSA rpt series, 2551–2

Census of Population, 1980: detailed socioeconomic and demographic characteristics, by age, sex, race, Hispanic origin, occupation, and industry, State rpt series, 2531–4

Census of Population, 1980: detailed socioeconomic characteristics, by county, city, and inside-outside SMSAs and central cities, State rpt series, 2531–3

Crime and crime rates, by offense, MSA, and central city, 1983, annual rpt, 6224–2.5

Crime victimization rates by type of offense, and victim and offense characteristics, Natl Crime Survey series, 6066–3

Disability days, injury and illness rates by type, and use of health services and Medicaid, by age, region, metro-nonmetro location, and selected SMSA, 1980-81, 4147–10.146

Employment and unemployment in metro and nonmetro areas, annual averages, 1983, article, 6742–2.403

Employment and unemployment in metro and nonmetro areas, monthly rpt, quarterly data, 6742–2.8

Families and households detailed socioeconomic characteristics, Mar 1982, annual Current Population Rpt, 2546–1.383

Food consumption and nutrient intake by individuals, by food group, source, and socioeconomic characteristics, 1977-78 natl survey, final rpt series, 1356–4

Govt employment and payroll, by function and level of govt in 75 major SMSAs and 69 large counties, Oct 1983, annual rpt, 2466–1.3

Home mortgages (graduated payment) FHA-insured, financial, property, and mortgagor characteristics, for US and selected localities, quarterly rpt, 5142–42

Home mortgages (graduated payment) FHA-insured, financial, property, and mortgagor characteristics, for US and selected States, quarterly rpt, 5142–41

Home mortgages (graduated payment) FHA-insured, financial, property, and mortgagor characteristics, US summary, quarterly rpt, 5142–40

Home mortgages FHA-insured, financial, property, and mortgagor characteristics, for US and selected localities, quarterly rpt, 5142–2

Home mortgages FHA-insured, financial, property, and mortgagor characteristics, for US, selected States, and Puerto Rico, quarterly rpt, 5142–3

Home mortgages FHA-insured, financial, property, and mortgagor characteristics, quarterly rpt, 5142–1

Home mortgages FHA-insured, financial, property, and mortgagor characteristics, 1983, annual rpt, 5144–17

Home mortgages FHA-insured for low-cost homes, financial, construction, property, and mortgagor characteristics, quarterly rpt, 5142–4

Housing and financial characteristics, and unit and neighborhood quality, for 15 SMSAs, 1978, annual survey special supplement, 2485–8

Housing and households characteristics, and low-income housing construction and availability, 1970s-83, hearing, 21968–28.1

Housing and households detailed characteristics, and unit and neighborhood quality, by inside-outside central cities, 1979-82 surveys, SMSA rpt series, 2485–6

Housing and neighborhood quality indicators and attitudes, by occupant and unit characteristics, region, and metro-nonmetro location, 1981, annual survey, 2485–2

Housing energy use, costs, expenditures, and conservation, and household and housing characteristics, survey series, 3166–7

Housing occupancy and unit and household characteristics, by region and metro-nonmetro residence, 1983, biennial survey, 2485–1

Housing units authorized, by public and private ownership, State, and permit-issuing place, 1983, annual rpt, 2384–2

Housing vacancy and occupancy rates, and vacant unit characteristics, by metro-nonmetro location and region, selected years 1960-83, annual rpt, 2484–1.1

Housing vacant unit characteristics and costs, and occupancy and vacancy rates, by region and metro-nonmetro location, quarterly rpt, 2482–1

Income of families and persons, by sociodemographic characteristics, 1983, advance annual Current Population Rpt, 2546–6.41

Local govt finances and population characteristics for cities and suburbs, by region and selected SMSA, selected years 1957-FY83, 10048–61

Mobility of population, detailed data by demographic and socioeconomic characteristics of movers and nonmovers, Mar 1981-82, annual Current Population Rpt, 2546–1.384

Central cities

Older persons by demographic, socioeconomic, and health characteristics, selected years 1900-81 and projected to 2050, Current Population Rpt, 2546–2.125

Population and employment in central cities and suburbs, effect of region, neighborhood, population, and labor characteristics on change, 1970-80, technical paper, 9387–8.89

Population size and change for metro and nonmetro areas and central cities by census div, and growth of areas with large black and aged populations, 1970-82, 2328–47

Poverty status of families and persons, by detailed socioeconomic characteristics, 1982, annual Current Population Rpt, 2546–6.40

see also Central business districts
see also Neighborhoods
see also Urban renewal

Central Intelligence Agency

- Budget of US Appendix, detailed budgets and personnel summaries, by agency, FY85, annual rpt, 104–3
- Budget of US, appropriations, outlays, balances, and budget receipts, by govtl branch and agency, FY83, annual rpt, 8104–2
- China exports and imports, by commodity, world area, and country, quarterly rpt, 242–6
- China exports and imports by SITC 1- to 5-digit commodity, 1970s-82, annual rpt, 244–12
- Communist, OECD, and selected other countries economic statistics, 1960s-83, annual rpt, 244–5
- Cuba economic conditions, agricultural and industrial production and distribution, trade, and intl economic relations, 1970-82 and trends from 1957, 248–40
- Economic indicators and oil use and imports for US and 6 OECD countries, oil production by country, and OPEC prices, biweekly rpt, 242–4
- Energy production by type, and oil prices, trade, and consumption, by country group and selected country, monthly rpt, 242–5
- Foreign economic, social, and political summary data, by country, 1984, annual factbook, 244–11
- Foreign govt Chiefs of State and Cabinet members, by country, monthly listing, 242–7
- OECD trade, total and for 4 major countries, and US trade by country, by commodity, 1972-82, annual world region rpt series, 244–13
- Polygraph lie detection test accuracy, and Fed Govt use by agency, selected years 1947-83, 26358–96
- Soviet Union officials public appearances in and outside of USSR, 1983, annual rpt, 244–8

Central Treaty Organization

Loans and grants for economic and military assistance from US and intl agencies, by program and country, FY46-83, annual rpt, 9914–5

Centrally planned economies
see Communist countries

Ceramics

see Clay industry and products

Cereals

see Grains and grain products

Cerebrovascular diseases

- Death rates for persons 65 and over, by major cause, sex, and age, selected years 1940-80, 4147–3.25
- Deaths and death rates, by cause and age, provisional 1982-83, US Vital Statistics annual rpt, 4144–7
- Deaths and death rates by detailed cause and demographic characteristics, 1979 and selected trends, US Vital Statistics annual rpt, 4144–2.1
- Deaths and death rates, by detailed geographic area, cause, and demographic characteristics, 1979, US Vital Statistics annual rpt, 4144–3
- Deaths and death rates, by selected cause and demographic characteristics, 1981, US Vital Statistics advance rpt, 4146–5.78
- Deaths and death rates, by selected cause and demographic characteristics, 1982, US Vital Statistics advance rpt, 4146–5.81
- Health condition and health care resources, use, and expenditures, 1970s-82 with trends and projections 1900-2000, annual compilation, 4144–11
- Hospital discharges and length of stay, by patient characteristics, facility size, procedure performed, diagnosis, and region, 1982, annual rpt, 4147–13.78
- Natl Heart, Lung, and Blood Inst organization, disease and mortality data, and funds and recipients, FY83 with trends from 1900, annual fact book, 4474–15
- Older persons by demographic, socioeconomic, and health characteristics, selected years 1900-81 and projected to 2050, Current Population Rpt, 2546–2.125
- *see also* under By Disease in the "Index by Categories"

Cerrelli, Ezio C.

- "Alcohol in Fatal Accidents, National Estimates, U.S.A.", 7768–81
- "Large Trucks in Fatal Accidents", 7766–10.10
- "1983 Traffic Fatalities Early Assessment", 7764–14

Certificates of deposit

- Appalachian States, FHLB 5th District member S&Ls financial condition and operations by SMSA, monthly rpt, 9302–8
- Bank certificates of deposit sold and outstanding at large commercial instns, and secondary market rates, monthly rpt, 9365–2.13, 9365–2.14
- Bank deposits in commercial and mutual savings banks and in US branches of foreign banks, by account type, instn, State, SMSA, and county, June 1983, annual rpt, 9295–3
- Bank financial and operating statements, functional cost analysis for Fed Reserve member banks with average and high earnings, by deposit size, 1982, annual rpt, 9364–6
- Brokered certificates of deposit in acquired and closed individual banks and S&Ls, and disposition of instns, 1982-Oct 1983, hearing, 21248–83

Index by Subjects and Names

- Brokered certificates of deposit sold by commercial and mutual savings banks, and issuing instn characteristics, as of Sept 1983, article, 9371–1.412
- Economic indicators and components, current data and annual trends, monthly rpt, 23842–1.5
- Futures trading in selected commodities, foreign currencies, and stock indexes, Chicago and other markets activity, monthly rpt, 11922–1
- Futures trading in selected commodities, foreign currencies, Treasury securities, and stock indexes, NYC, Chicago, and other markets activity, monthly rpt, 11922–5
- Household income, assets, and debt characteristics, sources of credit, and use of financial services, 1983 survey, article, 9362–1.411
- Household income, home value and equity, and financial assets by type, by household characteristics, 1983 survey with trends from 1970, article, 9362–1.406
- Income tax returns of individuals, detailed data, 1982, annual rpt, 8304–2
- North Central States, FHLB 6th District insured S&Ls financial condition and operations by State, monthly rpt, 9302–11
- North Central States, FHLB 6th District insured S&Ls financial condition and operations by State, quarterly rpt, 9302–23
- North Central States, FHLB 8th District member S&Ls financial operations by State and SMSA, monthly rpt, 9302–9
- Savings and loan assn balance sheet items by State and SMSA, and finances of FHLBs, 1983, annual rpt, 9314–3
- Savings and loan assns and FSLIC-insured savings banks and S&Ls, assets, liabilities, and deposit and loan activity, monthly rpt, 9312–4
- South Central States, FHLB 9th District insured S&Ls financial condition and operations by SMSA, monthly rpt, 9302–13
- Southeastern States, Fed Reserve 8th District banking and financial conditions, quarterly rpt, 9391–14
- Southeastern States, FHLB 4th District insured S&Ls financial condition and operations, by SMSA, monthly rpt, 9302–1
- West Central States, FHLB 10th District insured S&Ls finances and operations by SMSA, monthly rpt, 9302–22
- Western States, FHLB 11th District member S&Ls financial operations and housing industry indicators by State, monthly rpt, 9302–17
- Western States, FHLB 12th District member S&Ls financial operations and housing industry indicators by State, monthly rpt, 9302–21

Cervero, Robert

"Intergovernmental Responsibilities for Financing Public Transit Services", 7888–59

Cesium

see Metals and metal industries
see Radioactive materials

Index by Subjects and Names

CETA

see Comprehensive Employment and Training Act

Ceylon

see Sri Lanka

Chad

- Agricultural situation in sub-Saharan Africa, by country, 1982-83 and outlook for 1984, annual rpt, 1524–4.10
- Agricultural supply/demand, trade, and production, and socioeconomic data, by country, 1950s-77, 1528–179
- AID activities and funding by project and function, FY85, and developing countries summary socioeconomic data, 1970s-83, by country, annual rpt, 9914–3
- AID economic assistance to developing countries, obligations and disbursements by country, quarterly rpt, 9912–4
- Economic conditions and foreign marketing prospects in 46 Sub-Saharan countries, 1983 world region rpt, 2046–5.1
- Economic, social, and political summary data, by country, 1984, annual factbook, 244–11
- Economic trends in income, production, prices, employment, finances, and trade, 1984 annual rpt, 2046–4.65
- Exports of US, detailed Schedule B commodities by country of destination, 1983, annual rpt, 2424–9
- Exports of US, detailed Schedule E commodities by mode of transport and world area and country of destination, 1983, annual rpts, 2424–5
- Imports of US, detailed Schedule A commodities by country and world area of origin, and mode of transport, 1983, annual rpts, 2424–2
- Imports of US, detailed TSUSA commodities by country of origin, 1983, annual rpt, 2424–4
- Loans and grants for economic and military assistance from US and intl agencies, by program and country, FY46-83, annual rpt, 9914–5
- Military aid of US, arms sales, and training programs costs and budget requests by program, world region, and country, FY83-85, annual rpt, 7144–13
- Military spending, arms trade, and armed forces size, with total govt spending and population, by country, 1972-82, annual rpt, 9824–1
- *Minerals Yearbook, 1982,* Vol 3: foreign country reviews of production, trade, and policies, by commodity, annual rpt, 5604–35
- *Minerals Yearbook, 1982,* Vol 3 preprints: foreign country review of production, trade, and policies, by commodity, annual rpt, 5604–17.82
- Oil and gas undiscovered recoverable resources, cumulative production, and identified reserves, as of 1982, preliminary oil basin rpt, 5666–17.13
- Population size and growth rates, and latest available benchmark demographic data, by country, 1950-83, biennial rpt, 2324–4
- *see also* under By Foreign Country in the "Index by Categories"

Chall, Daniel E.

"Neighborhood Changes in New York City During the 1970s: Are the 'Gentry' Returning?", 9385–1.403

"Nuclear Power Plant Construction: Paying the Bill", 9385–1.412

Chamberlain, Peter G.

"Gold and Silver Leaching Practices in the U.S.", 5606–6.1

Champaign, Ill.

- Census of Housing, 1980: occupancy and unit characteristics, by race, Hispanic origin, and city, SMSA rpt, 2473–1.113
- Census of Population and Housing, 1980: detailed population and housing characteristics, by county, city, and census tract, SMSA rpt, 2551–2.113
- Housing vacancy rates for single and multifamily units and mobile homes, by county, city, and ZIP code, 1983, annual metro area rpt, 9304–18.1
- Wages by occupation, and benefits for office and plant workers, 1984 labor market area survey rpt, 6785–3.7
- *see also* under By SMSA or MSA in the "Index by Categories"

CHAMPUS

see Civilian Health and Medical Program of the Uniformed Services

Chaney, Elsa M.

"Women of the World: Latin America and the Caribbean", 2326–15.1

Chapman, Brian R.

"Seasonal Abundance and Habitat-Use Patterns of Coastal Bird Populations On Padre and Mustang Island Barrier Beaches", 5508–86

Charity

see Gifts and contributions

see Nonprofit organizations and foundations

Charleston, S.C.

- Census of Housing, 1980: occupancy and unit characteristics, by race, Hispanic origin, and city, SMSA rpt, 2473–1.114
- Census of Population and Housing, 1980: detailed population and housing characteristics, by county, city, and census tract, SMSA rpt, 2551–2.114
- Wages of office and plant workers, by occupation, 1984 labor market area survey rpt, 6785–3.7
- Waterborne commerce of US (domestic and foreign), freight by commodity, traffic, and passengers, by port and waterway, 1982, annual rpt, 3754–3.1
- *see also* under By SMSA or MSA in the "Index by Categories"

Charleston, W.Va.

- Census of Housing, 1980: occupancy and unit characteristics, by race, Hispanic origin, and city, SMSA rpt, 2473–1.115
- Census of Population and Housing, 1980: detailed population and housing characteristics, by county, city, and census tract, SMSA rpt, 2551–2.115
- *see also* under By SMSA or MSA in the "Index by Categories"

Charlotte Amalie, V.I.

Economic Censuses of Virgin Islands, 1982: employment, establishments, payroll, and receipts, by SIC 1- to 4-digit industry, island, and city, 2593–1

Charlotte, N.C.

- Census of Housing, 1980: occupancy and unit characteristics, by race, Hispanic origin, and city, SMSA rpt, 2473–1.116
- Census of Population and Housing, 1980: detailed population and housing characteristics, by county, city, and census tract, SMSA rpt, 2551–2.116

Checking accounts

- Wages by occupation, and benefits for office and plant workers, 1983 labor market area survey rpt, 6785–3.2
- *see also* under By City and By SMSA or MSA in the "Index by Categories"

Charlottesville, Va.

- Census of Housing, 1980: occupancy and unit characteristics, by race, Hispanic origin, and city, SMSA rpt, 2473–1.117
- Census of Population and Housing, 1980: detailed population and housing characteristics, by county, city, and census tract, SMSA rpt, 2551–2.117
- *see also* under By SMSA or MSA in the "Index by Categories"

Chartbooks

- Agricultural production, marketing, trade, supply, food consumption, and food and nutrition programs, 1960s-83, annual chartbook, 1504–3
- Court civil and criminal casloads and activity summary, for Federal district, appeals, and bankruptcy courts, 1975-June 1984, annual chartbook, 18204–9
- Economic indicators and components, and Fed Reserve 4th District business and financial conditions, monthly chartbook, 9377–10
- Economic indicators and labor force characteristics, selected years 1880-1995, chartbook, 6728–30
- Financial and business statistics, historic trends, 1984 annual chartbook, 9364–2
- Financial and business statistics, quarterly chartbook, 9362–2
- Financial data for US and selected foreign countries, including exchange rates, interest rates, gold prices, and security yields, weekly chartbook, 9365–1.5
- Hispanic Americans socioeconomic and demographic characteristics, and compared to non-Hispanics, selected years 1970-83, chartbook, 2328–48
- Military women personnel on active duty, by demographic and service characteristics and service branch, with comparisons to men, FY83, annual chartbook, 3544–26
- Recording industry operations and sales lost from home taping, home taping costs, and material taped by source, 1969-83, hearings with chartbook, 25528–100
- *see also* Maps

Chattanooga, Tenn.

- Census of Housing, 1980: occupancy and unit characteristics, by race, Hispanic origin, and city, SMSA rpt, 2473–1.118
- Census of Population and Housing, 1980: detailed population and housing characteristics, by county, city, and census tract, SMSA rpt, 2551–2.118
- Housing vacancy rates for single and multifamily units and mobile homes, by city and ZIP code, 1984, annual metro area rpt, 9304–27.1
- Wages by occupation, and benefits for office and plant workers, 1984 SMSA survey rpt, 6785–11.9
- *see also* under By City and By SMSA or MSA in the "Index by Categories"

Checking accounts

Bank financial and operating statements, functional cost analysis for Fed Reserve member banks with average and high earnings, by deposit size, 1982, annual rpt, 9364–6

Checking accounts

Clearing of checks, delays in availability of funds deposited, processing volume and costs, and reasons for check returns, 1981-82, press release, 9368–76

Commercial banks holdings of demand deposits of individuals, partnerships, and corporations, monthly rpt, 9362–1.1

Deposits, debits, and deposit turnover at financial instns, 1982, annual rpt, 9364–5.1

Deposits in commercial and mutual savings banks and in US branches of foreign banks, by account type, instn, State, SMSA, and county, June 1983, annual rpt, 9295–3

Economic indicators and components, current data and annual trends, monthly rpt, 23842–1.5

Farm financial assets by type, 1940-84, annual rpt, 1544–16.2

Fed Reserve payments services provided depository instns, financial statements, and costs and revenues by service and district bank, 1983, annual press release, 9364–9

Financial and economic trends, compounded annual rates of change, 1964-83, annual rpt, 9391–9.1

Flow-of-funds accounts, assets and liabilities by type and economic sector, year-end outstandings, 1960-83, annual rpt, 9364–3

Flow-of-funds accounts savings, investments, and credit statements, quarterly rpt, 9365–3.3

Household income, assets, and debt characteristics, sources of credit, and use of financial services, 1983 survey, article, 9362–1.411

Household income, home value and equity, and financial assets by type, by household characteristics, 1983 survey with trends from 1970, article, 9362–1.406

Interest rates (explicit and implicit) on commercial bank deposits, by account type, 1976-82, article, 9387–1.403

Interest rates on bank deposits, deregulation effect on deposits and bank financial performance, 1978-83, hearing, 21248–83

Monetary and Fed Govt budget trends, Fed Reserve Bank of St Louis monthly rpt, 9391–2

New England States financial instn assets and liabilities, Fed Reserve 1st District, monthly rpt, 9373–2.5

Savings and loan assn balance sheet items by State and SMSA, and finances of FHLBs, 1983, annual rpt, 9314–3

Savings and loan assn deregulation impact, financial ratios of S&Ls in 3 States and US, 1980-83, article, 9371–1.426

Southeastern States financial and economic devs, Fed Reserve 6th District, monthly rpt with articles, 9371–1

Transactions by electronic funds transfer and other means, credit card fraud losses, and potential for EFT crime, 1975-82, 6066–19.3

Western States depository instns financial activity by State, and large commercial banks by city, Fed Reserve 10th District, monthly rpt, 9381–11

see also Negotiable orders of withdrawal accounts

Cheese

see Dairy industry and products

Chemical and biological warfare agents

Agent Orange exposure and Vietnam military service effects on veteran health condition, methodology for 3 CDC studies, Nov 1983 rpt, 4208–22

DOD budget, FY85 weapons system requests consistency with US policy and specified treaties, with funding FY83-87, annual rpt, 21384–4

DOD budget justification for R&D programs, and acquisition mgmt, FY83-85, annual rpt, 3504–6

DOD budget justification, programs, and policies, FY85, annual rpt, 3544–2

NATO and US weapons and troop strength compared to Warsaw Pact and USSR, as of Jan 1984, annual rpt, 3564–1

Chemicals and chemical industry

Air pollutant and radiation indoor levels by emissions source, and household exposure and health effects by pollutant type, various periods 1966-83, hearings, 21708–102

Air pollutant emission factors, by detailed source, 3rd edition, 1983-84 supplements, 9198–13

Air pollution abatement equipment shipments by industry, exports, and new and backlog orders, by product, 1983, annual Current Industrial Rpt, 2506–12.5

Air pollution levels for 5 pollutants, by detailed source, State, and Air Quality Control Region, 1981, annual rpt, 9194–7

Arson incidents investigated by Alcohol, Tobacco, and Firearms Bur, and accelerants identified by type, 1982-83, annual rpt, 8484–4.3

Barium chloride from PRC at less than fair value, imports injury to US industry, investigation with background financial and operating data, 1984 rpt, 9886–14.122

Benzenoid chemicals imports by country of origin and product, 1983, annual rpt, 9884–2

Biotechnology commercial uses, R&D funding and output, controls, and industry financial and operating data, for US and 5 countries, 1970s-83 and estimated 1984-85, 26358–98

Biotechnology firms, patents, and trade by country, and effect of industry growth on US drug and chemical trade, selected years 1979-2000, 9886–4.78

Business statistics, detailed data for major industries and economic indicators, *Survey of Current Business,* monthly rpt, 2702–1.9

Calcium hypochlorite from Japan at less than fair value, imports injury to US industry, investigation with background financial and operating data, 1984 rpt, 9886–14.107

Census of Population, 1980: detailed socioeconomic and demographic characteristics, by age, sex, race, Hispanic origin, occupation, and industry, State rpt series, 2531–4

Census of Population, 1980: detailed socioeconomic characteristics, by county, city, and inside-outside SMSAs and central cities, State rpt series, 2531–3

Index by Subjects and Names

China economic conditions, agricultural and industrial production, trade, and domestic and foreign investment, 1980-85, 2048–106

China exports and imports by SITC 1- to 5-digit commodity, 1970s-82, annual rpt, 244–12

Chloropicrin from PRC at less than fair value, imports injury to US industry, investigation with background financial and operating data, 1984 rpt, 9886–14.98

Choline chloride from Canada and UK at less than fair value, imports injury to US industry, investigation with background financial and operating data, 1983 rpt, 9886–14.90

Choline chloride from Canada at less than fair value, imports injury to US industry, investigation with background financial and operating data, 1984 rpt, 9886–14.123

Collective bargaining agreements expiring during year, covered workers by SIC 2-digit industry, firm, and union, with summary of key provisions, 1984, annual rpt, 6784–9

Communist, OECD, and selected other countries consumer and producer goods production, 1960s-83, annual rpt, 244–5.7

Counterfeiting of brand-name products by foreign manufacturers, effects on 6 US industries, investigation with financial and operating data, 1984 rpt, 9886–4.67

County Business Patterns: establishments, employees, and payrolls, by SIC 4-digit industry and county, 1981, annual State rpt series, 2326–8

County Business Patterns: establishments, employees, and payrolls, by SIC 4-digit industry and county, 1982, annual State rpt series, 2326–6

Cuba economic conditions, agricultural and industrial production and distribution, trade, and intl economic relations, 1970-82 and trends from 1957, 248–40

Cyanuric acid and derivatives from Japan, imports injury to US industry, investigation with background financial and operating data, 1984 rpt, 9886–14.102

Earnings by major industry group, and personal income per capita and by source, by region and State, 1929-82, 2708–40

Electric power cogeneration in 5 industries, and fuel use and utility supply/demand effects, by region, 1983-93, 3008–92

Electric power industrial demand model estimates, economic indicators, and supporting data for 5 industries, 1960s-80 with projections to 2000, 3008–87

Employment, earnings, and hours, by selected SIC 1- to 4-digit industry, State, and for 278 major labor areas, 1939-83, annual rpt, 6744–5

Employment, earnings, and hours, by SIC 4-digit nonfarm industry, monthly 1974-Feb 1984, annual update, 6744–4

Energy demand in industry, forecasting model description, detailed technology specifications, and energy use, for 27 SIC 2- to 4-digit industries, 1970s-80 and projected to 2000, 3308–66

Energy producers finances and operations, by energy type for US firms domestic and foreign operations, 1974-82, annual rpt, 3164–44.1

Index by Subjects and Names

Chemicals and chemical industry

Energy use, prices, and conservation and efficiency measures, by fuel type, end-use sector, selected industry, and region, 1960-83, annual rpt, 3164–73

Environmental quality and protection programs, costs, and Fed Govt enforcement, 1983, detailed annual rpt, 484–1

Exports and imports between US and outlying areas, by detailed commodity and mode of transport, monthly rpt, 2422–4

Exports and imports of US, and trade balance, by major commodity group, selected country, and world area, with seasonal adjustments, monthly rpt, 2422–6

Exports and imports of US, by commodity group, world area, selected country, US coastal area and port, and mode of transport, with seasonal adjustments, monthly rpt, 2422–9

Exports and imports of US by country, and trade shifts by commodity, USITC quarterly monitoring rpt, 9882–9

Exports and imports of US, detailed SIC-based commodities by world area, 1983, annual rpts, 2424–6

Exports and imports of US, totals and as percent of domestic production, by SIC 2- to 5-digit commodity, 1981, annual rpt, 2424–3

Exports, imports, tariffs, and industry operating data for chemicals and related products, TSUSA commodity rpt series, 9885–4

Exports of manufactured and agricultural commodities, manufacturing production, and export-related employment, 1960s-82, State rpt series, 2046–3

Exports of US, detailed commodities by country of destination, monthly rpt, 2422–3

Exports of US, detailed Schedule B commodities by country of destination, 1983, annual rpt, 2424–9

Exports of US, detailed Schedule E commodities by mode of transport and world area and country of destination, 1983, annual rpts, 2424–5

Finances and operations, by SIC 2- to 4-digit industry, 1970s-83 and projected to 1988, annual rpt, 2014–4

Financial statements for manufacturing, mining, and trade corporations, by selected SIC 2- to 3-digit industry, quarterly rpt, 2502–1

Foreign direct investment of US, by selected major industry group and world area, 1980-82, annual article, 2702–1.430

Great Lakes trade, by SITC 3-digit commodity, port, vessel type, world area, and country, 1982, annual rpt, 7744–3

Imports of US, detailed Schedule A commodities by country and world area of origin, and mode of transport, 1983, annual rpts, 2424–2

Imports of US, detailed Schedule A commodities by country, monthly rpt, 2422–2

Imports of US, detailed TSUSA commodities by country of origin, 1983, annual rpt, 2424–4

Income tax returns of corporations, detailed income and tax items by industry, 1981, annual rpt, 8304–4

Income tax returns of corporations with foreign tax credit, income and deductions by type, asset size, and selected industry group, 1980, article, 8302–2.415

Income tax returns of foreign subsidiaries of US corporations, income and tax data, by industry and asset size, 1980, article, 8302–2.410

Income tax returns of sole proprietorships, detailed data by industry div and selected industry group, 1981, annual rpt, 8304–7

Income tax returns of sole proprietorships, receipts, deductions by type, payroll, and net income, by major industry, 1982, annual article, 8302–2.413

Injuries and deaths from use of selected consumer products and related activity, by victim age and sex, 1982, annual rpt, 9164–7

Input-output structure of US economy, detailed interindustry transactions for 85 industries, and components of final demand, 1977, article, 2702–1.421

Input-output structure of US economy, detailed interindustry transactions for 537 industries, and components of final demand, 1977 benchmark data, 2708–17

Liquefied petroleum gas sales, by principal use, PAD district, and State, 1981-83, annual rpt, 3164–2

Manufacturing census, 1982: financial and operating data, by SIC 2- to 4-digit industry, State, SMSA, and county, preliminary census div rpt series, 2491–3

Manufacturing census, 1982: financial and operating data, for SIC 4-digit industries by product, preliminary rpt series, 2491–1

Mineral industries census, 1982: financial and operating data, including materials consumed, by SIC 4-digit industry and State, preliminary rpt series, 2511–1

Minority group and women employment, by occupational group and SIC 2- to 3-digit industry, 1981, annual rpt, 9244–1.1

Occupational injury and illness rates, by SIC 2- to 4-digit industry, 1982, annual rpt, 6844–1

Ocean dumping of waste materials, EPA permit program and intl London Dumping Convention activities, 1981-83, annual rpt, 9204–8

OECD trade, total and for 4 major countries, and US trade by country, by commodity, 1972-82, annual world region rpt series, 244–13

Pacific Northwest electricity consumption and prices by end-use sector, and economic and demographic data, 1960s-83 and projected to 2005, annual rpt, 3224–2

Pollution abatement capital and operating costs, by SIC 2- to 4-digit industry, State, and SMSA, 1982, annual Current Industrial Rpt, 2506–3.6

Pollution abatement capital and operating costs under Clean Air and Water Acts, for govts and selected industries, various periods 1970-2000, annual rpt, 9184–11

Pollution abatement expenditures, and effect on economic indicators and industry operations, by major industry, projected under 3 pollution regulation alternatives 1983-95, 9188–84

Potassium chloride from Israel and Spain, imports injury to US industry from foreign subsidized products, investigation with background financial and operating data, 1984 rpt, 9886–15.54

Potassium permanganate from PRC at less than fair value, imports injury to US industry, investigation with background financial and operating data, 1984 rpt, 9886–14.93

Potassium permanganate from Spain at less than fair value, imports injury to US industry, investigation with background financial and operating data, 1984 rpt supplement, 9886–14.92

Producer prices and indexes, by stage of processing and detailed commodity, monthly rpt, 6762–6

Producer prices and indexes, by stage of processing and detailed commodity, monthly 1983, annual supplement, 6764–2

Production, shipments, stocks, and materials used, by detailed chemical product, periodic Current Industrial Rpt series, 2506–8

R&D expenditures of US firms foreign affiliates, by selected industry, 1974-82, 9626–2.131

R&D industry expenditures, total and for 6 leading industries, projected 1984-85 with trends from 1975, 9626–2.145

R&D industry funding and employment of scientists and engineers, by industry group, firm size, and funding source, 1956-82, annual rpt, 9627–21

Scientists, engineers, and technicians employed in private industry, by occupation and industry group, 1980-81, biennial rpt, 9627–23

Scientists, engineers, and technicians employment in transportation, utilities, and retail and wholesale trade, by field of science and industry, 1982, 9628–72

Smoking and health research publications, bimonthly listing, 4042–1

Sulfuric acid production, establishments, and shipments, by census div and State, and trade, 1983, annual Current Industrial Rpt, 2506–8.13

Synthetic organic chemicals production and sales by product, and listing of manufacturers, 1983, annual rpt, 9884–3

Synthetic organic chemicals production, by detailed product, monthly rpt, 9882–1

Tariff Schedules of US, Annotated, classifications and rates of duty for detailed imported commodities, 1985 edition, 9886–13

Transportation census, 1982: trucks, by detailed characteristics, miles traveled, and type of product carried, State rpt series, 2573–1

Water pollution fish kills, by State, location, and pollution source, monthly 1978-80, annual rpt, 9204–3

Waterborne commerce of US (domestic and foreign), freight by commodity, traffic, and passengers, by port and waterway, 1982, annual rpt, 3754–3

Wholesale trade census, 1982: employment, establishments, finances, and operations, by SIC 2- to 4-digit kind of business, SMSA, county, and city, State rpt series, 2405–1

Chemicals and chemical industry

Wholesale trade census, 1982: employment, establishments, sales by commodity, and payroll, by SIC 4-digit kind of business and State, preliminary rpt, 2403–1.35

Wholesale trade sales, inventories, purchases, and gross margins, by SIC 2- to 3-digit kind of business and type of ownership, 1983, annual rpt, 2413–13

see also Chemical and biological warfare agents

see also Drugs

see also Explosives

see also Fertilizers

see also Food additives

see also Gases

see also Gum and wood chemicals

see also Hazardous substances

see also Nonmetallic minerals and mines

see also Paints and varnishes

see also Pesticides

see also Petrochemicals

see also Pharmaceutical industry

see also Plastics and plastics industry

see also Soap and detergent industry

see also Synthetic fibers and fabrics

see also under By Commodity in the "Index by Categories"

see also under By Industry in the "Index by Categories"

Chemistry

- Census of Population, 1980: detailed socioeconomic and demographic characteristics, by age, sex, race, Hispanic origin, occupation, and industry, State rpt series, 2531–4
- DOE R&D projects and funding at natl labs, universities, and other instns, FY84, annual summary rpt, 3004–18.3, 3004–18.5
- High school class of 1982: science and math coursework and assessment, by sociodemographic and school characteristics and educational goal, 4826–2.14
- NSF grant and award recipients, by State, FY83, annual listing, 9624–11
- Nuclear industry nongovt employment by industry segment, occupation, and census div, and DOE and NRC nuclear employment, 1968-83, biennial rpt, 3004–11
- *Occupational Outlook Handbook,* 1984-85 biennial rpt, 6744–1
- Public health labs of States, pay scales and job requirements by occupation and State, FY81-83, annual rpt, 4204–7
- R&D-employed scientists and engineers salaries by degree, type of establishment, age, experience, and field, 1984, annual rpt, 3004–1
- R&D expenditures by higher education instns and federally funded centers, by field, source of funds, instn, and State, FY82, annual rpt, 9627–13
- R&D expenditures by source, and scientists education and employment, detailed data by field, selected years 1953-84, annual rpt, 9624–18
- R&D expenditures of higher education instns, and science and engineering employment and grad students, by field, 1972-83, biennial rpt, 9627–24
- R&D Fed Govt funding for all performers, by field and supporting agency, selected years FY60-84, annual rpt, 9627–20

Science and engineering doctoral degree recipients, by field, sex, race, age, citizenship, postgrad employment and study status, State, and instn, 1960-82, 9626–6.16

- Science and engineering grad enrollment, fields of study, financial support, and other student and instn characteristics, 1975-82, annual survey, 9627–7
- Science and engineering grads of 1980-81, employment characteristics or grad enrollment, by degree level, field, sex, and race, 1982, 9627–25
- Scientists and engineers employed at universities and colleges, by field, sex, State, and instn, Jan 1983 and selected trends from 1967, annual survey, 9627–11
- Scientists and engineers employed in energy-related fields, supply/demand and effects of R&D funding, by energy type, employer type, field, and age, 1962-91, annual rpt, 3004–19
- Scientists, engineers, and technicians employed in private industry, by occupation and industry group, 1980-81, biennial rpt, 9627–23
- Scientists, engineers, and technicians needed in defense and nondefense industries, and supply/demand, by field, 1981-87, 9628–71

see also Chemicals and chemical industry

Chen, Alexander

"Alternative Reverse Mortgages: A Simulation Analysis of Initial Benefits in Baltimore", 9312–7.402

Chen, Nai-Ruenn

"China's Economy and Foreign Trade, 1981-85", 2048–106

Cherries

see Fruit and fruit products

Chesapeake Bay

- Bridges over navigable waters, with type of bridge and use, owner, dimensions, and location, 1984 regional listing, 7406–5.1
- Environmental research findings and water pollution control recommendations of Chesapeake Bay Program, as of 1983, narrative rpt, 9208–121
- Fish landings, employment, gear used, and seafood production, for detailed species by State, 1977, annual rpt, 2164–2.4
- Freight (waterborne domestic and foreign) by commodity, traffic, and passengers, by port and waterway, 1982, annual rpt, 3754–3.1
- Tidal current tables, daily time and velocity by station for US Atlantic coast, 1985, annual rpt, 2174–1.1
- Water supply and quality in streams and lakes, and groundwater levels in wells, by drainage basin, 1980, annual State rpt series, 5666–12
- Water supply and quality in streams and lakes, and groundwater levels in wells, by drainage basin, 1981, annual State rpt series, 5666–16
- Water supply and quality in streams and lakes, and groundwater levels in wells, by drainage basin, 1982, annual State rpt series, 5666–20
- Water supply and quality in streams and lakes, and groundwater levels in wells, by drainage basin, 1983, annual State rpt series, 5666–10

Index by Subjects and Names

Chesapeake, Va.

see also under By City in the "Index by Categories"

Chester, C. V.

"Hazard Mitigation Potential of Earth-Sheltered Residences", 3308–71

Cheyenne, Wyo.

Wages of office and plant workers, by occupation, 1984 labor market area survey rpt, 6785–3.7

Chiang, Shasi W.

"Argentina's Grain Marketing System", 1528–185

Chicago, Ill.

- Air quality and transportation and related energy use, for urban areas and Chicago area, late 1970s-82 and projected under lower auto emission standards to 1995, 3408–31
- Auto dealer repair workers, wages, and benefits, by occupation, size of establishment, and for 24 labor market areas, Nov 1982 survey, 6787–6.202
- Auto emissions control device tampering and fuel-switching incidence in 6 urban areas, 1983, annual rpt, 9194–15
- Census of Population and Housing, 1980: detailed population and housing characteristics, by county, city, and census tract, SMSA rpt, 2551–2.119
- Cheese wholesale prices in selected areas, 1983, annual rpt, 1317–1.3
- CPI by component for US city average, and by region, population size, and for 28 SMSAs, monthly press release, 6762–1
- CPI by detailed component, for US city average, 28 SMSAs, and 4 regions by population size, monthly rpt, 6762–2
- Fruit and vegetable shipments, and arrivals in 23 US and 5 Canada cities, by mode of transport and State or country of origin, 1983, annual rpt, 1311–4.2
- Fruit and vegetable wholesale prices in NYC, Chicago, and selected shipping points, by crop, 1983, annual rpt, 1311–8
- Homeless population and characteristics, and temporary shelter operations, use, and user characteristics, for selected cities, various periods 1979-84, hearing, 21248–85
- Hospital worker wages by sex and occupation, and benefits, for 22 MSAs, Oct 1981 survey, 6787–6.201
- Households and members demographic characteristics, for Chicago Standard Consolidated Area, Mar 1982, annual Current Population Rpt, 2546–1.383
- Housing unit starts and completions authorized by building permits in 20 MSAs, quarterly rpt, 2382–9
- Loan activity of banks in Fed Reserve 7th District and 3 major midwestern cities, monthly rpt, 9375–9
- Office space rental demand methodology using BLS employment data, with results by selected occupation and industry and for Chicago SMSA, 1975-83, article, 6722–1.474
- Population size of top 25 cities, 1980 and 1982, press release, 2328–46
- Radiation and radionuclide concentrations in air, water, and milk, results of EPA and other monitoring programs, by State and site, quarterly rpt, 9232–2.2

Index by Subjects and Names

Radioactivity levels at former AEC and Manhattan Project research and storage sites, 1977/78, 3406–1.35

Radioactivity levels at former AEC and Manhattan Project research and storage sites, 1983, 3406–1.40

Rail high-speed system planned from Chicago, capital and operating costs and profitability by speed class, frequency, and route, 1984 article, 9375–1.406

Repair technicians and apprentices wages and benefits, for 5 types of electrical repair shops in 19 SMSAs, Nov 1981 survey, 6787–6.197

Wages of office and plant workers, by occupation, 1984 SMSA survey rpt, 6785–11.4

Waterborne commerce of US (domestic and foreign), freight by commodity, traffic, and passengers, by port and waterway, 1982, annual rpt, 3754–3.2, 3754–3.3

see also East Chicago, Ind.

see also under By City and By SMSA or MSA in the "Index by Categories"

Chicanos

see Hispanic Americans

see Mexicans in the U.S.

Chickens

see Poultry industry and products

Chico, Calif.

Census of Housing, 1980: occupancy and unit characteristics, by race, Hispanic origin, and city, SMSA rpt, 2473–1.120

Census of Population and Housing, 1980: detailed population and housing characteristics, by county, city, and census tract, SMSA rpt, 2551–2.120

see also under By SMSA or MSA in the "Index by Categories"

Chicopee, Mass.

Census of Housing, 1980: occupancy and unit characteristics, by race, Hispanic origin, and city, SMSA rpt, 2473–1.341

Census of Population and Housing, 1980: detailed population and housing characteristics, by county, city, and census tract, SMSA rpt, 2551–2.341

Housing and financial characteristics, and unit and neighborhood quality, for 15 SMSAs, 1978, annual survey special supplement, 2485–8

Child abuse and neglect

Adolescent abuse, characteristics of victims and abuse, local agencies contacted, drug and alcohol involvement, and reciprocal violence, 1980-81 survey, 4608–18

Fed Govt public welfare programs and tax expenditures benefitting children and youth, participation and funding for 71 programs, FY81-83, 21968–30

HHS aid to each State and local govt or private instn, amount obligated, funding agency, and program, FY83, annual listing, 4004–3

Infant deaths by detailed cause, geographic location, age, race, and sex, 1979, US Vital Statistics annual rpt, 4144–2.2

Kidnapping by parents over intl and interstate boundaries, characteristics of cases referred to State Dept and FBI by State and country, 1979-83, hearing, 25528–95

Violent crimes involving relatives, by victim-offender relationship, circumstances, and victim characteristics, aggregate 1973-81, 6066–19.5

Child day care

Army morale, welfare, and recreation programs, revenue and expenses worldwide by activity and major command, FY82-83, annual rpt, 3704–12

Census of Population, 1980: detailed socioeconomic and demographic characteristics, by age, sex, race, Hispanic origin, occupation, and industry, State rpt series, 2531–4

Census of Population, 1980: labor force, by sex, detailed occupation, and region, with comparison to 1970 census, supplementary rpt, 2535–1.12

Census of Service Industries, 1982: employment, establishments, receipts, and payroll, by SIC 2- to 4-digit kind of business, SMSA, county, and city, State rpt series, 2391–1

Enrollment in preprimary school and child day care services, by age of child and labor force participation of mother, 1980, 6746–1.253

Fed Govt public welfare programs and tax expenditures benefitting children and youth, participation and funding for 71 programs, FY81-83, 21968–30

Food stamp recipient households size and composition, income, and income deductions allowed, Aug 1981, annual rpt, 1364–8

Govt census, 1982: State govt payments to local govts, by program, source of funds, level of govt, and State, with trends from 1902, 2460–3

Income tax returns of corporations, detailed income and tax items by industry, 1981, annual rpt, 8304–4

Income tax returns of individuals, by filing and deduction characteristics and income level, 1983, annual article, 8302–2.414

Input-output structure of US economy, detailed interindustry transactions for 537 industries, and components of final demand, 1977 benchmark data, 2708–17

Occupational manpower needs and supply by detailed occupation, and educational and training program enrollees and grads by detailed field, 1982 and 1995, biennial rpt, 6744–3

State govt social services spending by type and funding source, and admin of Fed Govt block grants, for 13 States, selected years FY80-84, GAO rpt, 26121–76

Tax expenditures, Fed Govt revenues foregone through income tax deductions and exclusions by type, and effect of Deficit Reduction Act, FY84-89, annual rpt, 21784–10

Tax expenditures, Fed Govt revenues foregone through pension and other tax benefit policy changes, FY84-88, and women's labor force and pension participation, 1939-82, hearing, 25368–131

Underground economy, household expenditures and participation by type of goods or service and sociodemographic characteristics, with methodology and bibl, 1981 survey, 8308–27

Women's travel patterns, by employment and sociodemographic characteristics and type of child care used, 1980 survey, 7888–62

Child labor

State labor legislation enacted by 48 States, DC, and Guam, 1983, annual summary article, 6722–1.406

Child support and alimony

AFDC State admin agencies performance measures, caseloads, payments, and costs, by State, FY81, annual rpt, 4704–10

Bankruptcy (personal), filers by debt type and other characteristics, selected years 1978-81, hearing, 25528–97.1

Beneficiaries of noncash public and employer-based transfer programs, by income source and socioeconomic characteristics, 1982, final Current Population Rpt, 2546–6.37

Child Support Enforcement Program cost savings to AFDC, Federal and State govts, and public assistance programs, by State and selected city or county, FY76-85, 4748–37

Child Support Enforcement Program costs, cases, and collections, by State, FY82, semiannual rpt, 4002–5

Child Support Enforcement Program costs, cases, and collections, by State, FY83, annual rpt, 4004–29

Child Support Enforcement Program financial and operating data, FY79-83, annual rpt, 4004–16

Fed Govt programs and mgmt cost control proposals, 3-year savings by function and agency, and financial and operating data, 1960s-81, 16908–1.6

Fed Govt programs under Ways and Means Committee jurisdiction, program operations and financing data for assessing budgetary requirements, by State, FY70s-83, 21788–117

Fed Govt public welfare programs and tax expenditures benefitting children and youth, participation and funding for 71 programs, FY81-83, 21968–30

Govt census, 1982: State govt payments to local govts, by program, source of funds, level of govt, and State, with trends from 1902, 2460–3

Income of households, families, and persons, by detailed socioeconomic characteristics and region, 1982, annual Current Population Rpt, 2546–6.39

Income tax returns of individuals by tax return item, State, and occupation, and income by source and tax owed, by income level, selected years 1916-80, conf papers, 8308–28.1

Income tax returns of individuals, detailed data, 1982, annual rpt, 8304–2

Poverty-level persons and families, by income source, hours of work, earnings, taxes, and family characteristics, various periods 1959-84, 21788–131

Tax expenditures, Fed Govt revenues foregone through pension and other tax benefit policy changes, FY84-88, and women's labor force and pension participation, 1939-82, hearing, 25368–131

Child welfare

Appalachia regional dev spending, by program area and source of funds, FY82, annual rpt, 9084–1

Benefits, beneficiary characteristics, and trust funds of OASDHI, Medicaid, SSI, and other social insurance and public welfare programs, selected years 1937-83, annual rpt, 4744–3

Child welfare

Budget of US, CBO analysis of revenue and spending alternatives and projections of economic indicators, FY85-89, annual rpt, 26304–3.3

Budget of US, effects of Reagan Admin policy changes, by detailed program, FY85, annual rpt, 104–21

Fed Govt aid to State and local govts, expenditures, and direct payments, by program, agency, and State, FY83, annual rpt, 2464–2

Fed Govt programs under Ways and Means Committee jurisdiction, program operations and financing data for assessing budgetary requirements, by State, FY70s-83, 21788–117

Fed Govt public welfare programs and tax expenditures benefitting children and youth, participation and funding for 71 programs, FY81-83, 21968–30

Govt census, 1982: State govt payments to local govts, by program, source of funds, level of govt, and State, with trends from 1902, 2460–3

Govt expenditures for social welfare by program and level of govt, and private expenditures for health care, selected years FY50-82, annual article, 4742–1.425

HHS aid to each State and local govt or private instn, amount obligated, funding agency, and program, FY83, annual listing, 4004–3

Medicaid, OASDHI, SSI, and other social insurance and public welfare programs benefits, beneficiary characteristics, and trust funds, selected years 1937-82, annual rpt, 4744–3.6

Medicaid vendor payments and recipients, by type of service and eligibility category, quarterly rpt, 4652–1.1

Northern Mariana Islands public health payments for off-island Medicaid referrals and prenatal, well-baby, and other clinic and home visits, FY83 and trends, annual rpt, 7004–6.2

OASDHI, Medicaid, SSI, and other social insurance and public welfare programs benefits, beneficiary characteristics, and trust funds, selected years 1937-83, annual rpt, 4744–3.4

Refugee resettlement program activities and funding, arrivals and population by country of origin and State, and employment and other characteristics, FY83, annual rpt, 4704–8

Research and statistical projects and techniques, and evaluation of public welfare programs, 1983 conf papers, 4704–11

Runaway and other homeless youth programs, funding by source, activities, and participant characteristics, FY82, annual rpt, 4604–3

State govt maternal and child health funding, and admin of Fed Govt block grants, by program for 13 States, 1981-83, GAO rpt, 26121–70

State govt social services for youth, coordinating agencies activities, admin, membership, and funding sources, survey, 1984 rpt, 6068–182

State govt social services spending by type and funding source, and admin of Fed Govt block grants, for 13 States, selected years FY80-84, GAO rpt, 26121–76

VA pensions for disability and death not connected with service, by entitlement type and veterans period of service, as of Mar 1984, semiannual rpt, 9922–12

VA programs and activities, monthly rpt, 9922–2

see also Aid to Families with Dependent Children

see also Child abuse and neglect

see also Child day care

see also Child labor

see also Child support and alimony

see also Food assistance

see also Foster home care

see also Head Start Project

see also School lunch and breakfast programs

Childbirth

see Births

see Infant mortality

see Maternity

see Midwives

see Obstetrics and gynecology

Children

Alien children adopted by US citizens, availability of birth records, 1984 annual listing, 4124–7

Blood pressure and heart rate effects of reading aloud, results of study of Baltimore, Md, 5th graders, 1984 article, 4102–1.415

Breast-fed infants, by characteristics of mother and source of prenatal care, various periods 1970-75, article, 4102–1.442

Breast-fed infants, by race and mother's sociodemographic characteristics, 1983 with trends from 1970, article, 4102–1.455

Census of Housing, 1980: inventory, occupancy, and unit characteristics, changes from 1973 by region and inside-outside SMSAs and central cities, series, 2473–3

Census of Housing, 1980: structural, financial, and householder characteristics, by region and State, 2475–4

Census of Population and Housing, 1980: detailed population and housing characteristics, by county, city, and census tract, State and SMSA rpt series, 2551–2

Census of Population, 1980: detailed socioeconomic and demographic characteristics, by age, sex, race, Hispanic origin, occupation, and industry, State rpt series, 2531–4

Census of Population, 1980: detailed socioeconomic characteristics, by county, city, and inside-outside SMSAs and central cities, State rpt series, 2531–3

Costs of raising children, itemized for urban and rural nonfarm areas, by age and region, quarterly rpt, 1702–1

Divorces, and children involved, by race and State, 1979 and trends, US Vital Statistics annual rpt, 4144–4.2

Divorces, and children involved, 1950-81, US Vital Statistics advance rpt, 4146–5.74

Employment status of family members, by occupation, family composition, age of children, and other characteristics, 1983 and trends from 1940, 6746–1.253

Fed Govt civil service retirees and survivors, and monthly benefit, for US territories and foreign countries, and by State, age, and sex, FY81-82, annual rpt, 9844–1.1

Index by Subjects and Names

Fed Govt public welfare programs and tax expenditures benefitting children and youth, participation and funding for 71 programs, FY81-83, 21968–30

Fire (forest) damage and causes, by State and region, 1981, annual rpt, 1204–4

Fires on Forest Service land and acres burned, by cause, forest, and State, 1983, annual rpt, 1204–6

Health condition and health care resources, use, and expenditures, 1970s-82 with trends and projections 1900-2000, annual compilation, 4144–11

Hispanic Americans socioeconomic and demographic characteristics, and compared to non-Hispanics, selected years 1970-83, chartbook, 2328–48

Hospital use by children by Canada Province and US region, and death rates, by diagnosis and sex, selected years 1977-79, 4147–5.1

Household living arrangements, family relationships, and marital status, by age and sex, Mar 1984, advance annual Current Population Rpt, 2546–1.389

Household living arrangements, family relationships, and marital status, by demographic characteristics, Mar 1983, annual Current Population Rpt, 2546–1.388

Households and housing detailed characteristics, and unit and neighborhood quality, by inside-outside central cities, 1979-82 surveys, SMSA rpt series, 2485–6

Households and housing unit characteristics, and employment, housing finance, and social programs data, selected years 1948-83, hearing, 21968–28

Households and housing unit characteristics, by region and metro-nonmetro residence, 1983, biennial survey, 2485–1

Housing and neighborhood quality indicators and attitudes, and occupant characteristics, by urban-rural location and region, 1981, annual survey, 2485–7

Housing and neighborhood quality indicators and attitudes, by occupant and unit characteristics, region, and metro-nonmetro location, 1981, annual survey, 2485–2

Immigrant and nonimmigrant visas issued and refused, and status adjustments, by class and nationality, FY77, annual rpt, 7184–1

Immunization and preventive medicine programs for children in US and Mexico, and disease cases, vaccine reactions, and deaths, 1984 conf papers, 4204–15

Income of households, families, and persons, by detailed socioeconomic characteristics and region, 1982, annual Current Population Rpt, 2546–6.39

Income tax returns of individuals, detailed data, 1982, annual rpt, 8304–2

Injuries and deaths from use of selected consumer products and related activity, by victim age and sex, 1982, annual rpt, 9164–7

Injuries and deaths from use of selected consumer products, by victim age and medical treatment status, 1982, annual rpt, 9164–6

Injuries, deaths, and medical costs from selected consumer products use, by victim age, 1981-83, annual rpt, 9164–2

Index by Subjects and Names

Kidnapping by parents over intl and interstate boundaries, characteristics of cases referred to State Dept and FBI by State and country, 1979-83, hearing, 25528–95

Lead levels in blood by sociodemographic and behavioral characteristics, and potential workplace exposure, 1976-80, 4147–11.201

Married couples with both spouses working, earnings by sociodemographic and employment characteristics and age of children, 1981, Current Population Rpt, 2546–2.120

Massachusetts parents awareness and use of safety measures to protect their children from accidents, for 9 communities by urban-rural location, Sept 1980-June 1982 survey, article, 4102–1.402

Minority language population (Spanish and other), and children with limited English proficiency, by State, 1980, biennial rpt, 4804–14

Mobility of population, detailed data by demographic and socioeconomic characteristics of movers and nonmovers, Mar 1981-82, annual Current Population Rpt, 2546–1.384

Navajo Indians with bacterial meningitis by outcome and bacteria type, and infants with major causative antibody, various periods 1968-80, article, 4102–1.441

Nursing continuing education in maternal and child health at University of Kentucky, course enrollment and student assessment of career value, 1983 article, 4102–1.405

Nutrition status of infants and children, blood and height-weight indicators, and low birth weight risk factors, by age, race, and Hispanic origin, 1981, annual rpt, 4205–24

OASDHI, Medicaid, SSI, and other social insurance and public welfare programs benefits, beneficiary characteristics, and trust funds, selected years 1937-82, annual rpt, 4744–3.12

Obesity and low height-for-age among children aged 1-4 participating in public food programs, by race and Hispanic origin, 1982, article, 4202–7.403

Population demographic and economic characteristics, 1982 with projections of population size to 2050, annual Current Population Rpt, 2546–2.119

Population detailed socioeconomic characteristics, Mar 1982, annual Current Population Rpt, 2546–1.383

Poverty-level persons and families, by income source, hours of work, earnings, taxes, and family characteristics, various periods 1959-84, 21788–131

Poverty population size, effect of counting public noncash transfers as income by recipient characteristics, 1979-83, 2626–2.52

Poverty status of families and persons, by detailed socioeconomic characteristics, 1982, annual Current Population Rpt, 2546–6.40

Research Center for Mothers and Children, activities and funding, as of June 1983, annual rpt, 4474–31

Smoke alarm sound levels by brand, and response time by circumstances and for older and mentally retarded persons, 1983 rpt, 2218–70

Statistical Abstract of US, social, political, and economic data, 1950s-83 and trends, annual rpt, 2324–1.1

Vietnam Amerasian children arriving in US and refugee camps under Orderly Departure Program, monthly rpt, 7002–4

Women in couples with wife as primary earner, socioeconomic and family characteristics, with comparative data for husbands, Mar 1982, 2326–11.9

Women's labor force participation by marital status, and children by parent labor force status, by family composition, race, and Hispanic origin, Mar 1984 and trends from 1970, 6748–78

Women's travel patterns, by employment and sociodemographic characteristics and type of child care used, 1980 survey, 7888–62

see also Abortion
see also Adoption
see also Aid to Families with Dependent Children
see also Birth defects
see also Child abuse and neglect
see also Child day care
see also Child labor
see also Child support and alimony
see also Child welfare
see also Compensatory education
see also Educational tests
see also Elementary and secondary education
see also Fertility
see also Foster home care
see also Handicapped children
see also Head Start Project
see also Illegitimacy
see also Infant mortality
see also Juvenile delinquency
see also Old-Age, Survivors, Disability, and Health Insurance
see also Pediatrics
see also Preschool education
see also School lunch and breakfast programs
see also Special education
see also Students
see also Youth
see also Youth employment
see also under By Age in the "Index by Categories"

Children's Bureau
see Office of Human Development Services

Chile

Agricultural and food production indexes, and production of selected commodities, by world region and country, 1974-83, annual rpt, 1524–5

Agricultural exports of US to Latin America, by commodity, country group, and selected country, FY81-84 and forecast FY85, article, 1522–1.407

Agricultural situation in Latin America, by country, 1981-83 and outlook for 1984, annual rpt, 1524–4.9

Agricultural supply/demand, trade, and production, and socioeconomic data, by country, 1950s-77, 1528–179

AID economic assistance to developing countries, obligations and disbursements by country, quarterly rpt, 9912–4

AID loan repayment status and terms by program and country, and status of predecessor agency loans, quarterly rpt, 9912–3

China, Peoples Republic

Background Notes, summary social, political, and economic data, 1983 rpt, 7006–2.3

Copper production, production costs, prices, wages, and productivity, for US and 3 countries, 1970s-83 and projected to 1989, 21368–55

Economic conditions, income, production, prices, employment, and trade, 1984 semiannual country rpt, 2046–4.108

Economic, social, and political summary data, by country, 1984, annual factbook, 244–11

Economic trends in income, production, prices, employment, finances, and trade, 1984 semiannual rpt, 2046–4.58

Exports and imports of US, by commodity and country, 1972-82, annual world region rpt, 244–13.2

Exports of US, detailed Schedule B commodities by country of destination, 1983, annual rpt, 2424–9

Exports of US, detailed Schedule E commodities by mode of transport and world area and country of destination, 1983, annual rpts, 2424–5

Imports of US, detailed Schedule A commodities by country and world area of origin, and mode of transport, 1983, annual rpts, 2424–2

Imports of US, detailed TSUSA commodities by country of origin, 1983, annual rpt, 2424–4

Loans and grants for economic and military assistance from US and intl agencies, by program and country, FY46-83, annual rpt, 9914–5

Military aid of US, arms sales, and training programs costs and budget requests by program, world region, and country, FY83-85, annual rpt, 7144–13

Military spending, arms trade, and armed forces size, with total govt spending and population, by country, 1972-82, annual rpt, 9824–1

Minerals Yearbook, 1982, Vol 3: foreign country reviews of production, trade, and policies, by commodity, annual rpt, 5604–35

Minerals Yearbook, 1982, Vol 3 preprints: foreign country review of production, trade, and policies, by commodity, annual rpt, 5604–17.15

Population size and growth rates, and latest available benchmark demographic data, by country, 1950-83, biennial rpt, 2324–4

Raisin and dried prune stocks, production, and exports for 4 countries, 1982-83 and forecast 1984, article, 1925–34.416

see also under By Foreign Country in the "Index by Categories"

Chillicothe, Ohio

Wages by occupation, and benefits for office and plant workers, 1984 labor market area survey rpt, 6785–3.7

Chin, E.

"Selected Raw Material Requirements for Japan's Specialty Steel Industry", 5608–144

China, Nationalist
see Taiwan

China, Peoples Republic

Agricultural and food production indexes, and production of selected commodities, by world region and country, 1974-83, annual rpt, 1524–5

China, Peoples Republic

Agricultural exports and imports of US, by detailed commodity and country, FY83 and CY83, semiannual rpts, 1522–4

Agricultural situation in PRC, by commodity, 1983 and outlook for 1984, annual rpt, 1524–4.8

Agricultural supply/demand, consumption per capita, and trade, by world area and country group, 1960s-82, 1528–181

Background Notes, summary social, political, and economic data, 1983 rpt, 7006–2.11

Barium chloride from PRC at less than fair value, imports injury to US industry, investigation with background financial and operating data, 1984 rpt, 9886–14.122

Carbon dioxide emissions from fossil fuel combustion, and growth rates, by country and country group, 1950-80, 3006–7.6

Chloropicrin from PRC at less than fair value, imports injury to US industry, investigation with background financial and operating data, 1984 rpt, 9886–14.98

Cotton and synthetic fiber supply and use, retail clothing sales, and textile mill productivity and equipment, for PRC, 1978-84, article, 1561–1.405

Cotton production, consumption, and trade, selected countries, FAS monthly rpt, 1925–4.2

Cuba economic conditions, agricultural and industrial production and distribution, trade, and intl economic relations, 1970-82 and trends from 1957, 248–40

Economic and business investment conditions in PRC, trade practices, and trade with US by detailed commodity, 1978-82, 2048–72

Economic conditions in Communist and OECD countries, 1982, annual rpt, 7144–11

Economic conditions in Communist, OECD, and selected other countries, 1960s-83, annual rpt, 244–5

Economic conditions in PRC, agricultural and industrial production, trade, and domestic and foreign investment, 1980-85, 2048–106

Economic, social, and political summary data, by country, 1984, annual factbook, 244–11

Economic trends in income, production, prices, employment, finances, and trade, 1984 annual rpt, 2046–4.44

Export licensing and monitoring activities under Export Admin Act, for selected commodities, and for Communist and other countries, FY83, annual rpt, 2044–22

Export sales and shipments of US grains, oilseed products, hides, skins, and cotton, by country, weekly rpt, 1922–3

Exports and imports of NATO countries with PRC, by country, 1980-83, annual rpt, 7144–14

Exports and imports of non-NATO OECD countries with PRC, annual rpt, discontinued, 7144–15

Exports and imports of OECD countries, by country, 1983, annual rpt, 7144–10

Exports and imports of PRC, by commodity, world area, and country, quarterly rpt, 242–6

Exports and imports of PRC, by SITC 1- to 5-digit commodity, 1970s-82, annual rpt, 244–12

Exports and imports of US with Communist countries, by detailed commodity and country, quarterly rpt with articles, 9882–2

Exports of selected textile and leather goods to US from PRC, injury to US industries, and US consumption and producer shipments, 1978-83, 9882–2.401

Exports of US, detailed Schedule B commodities by country of destination, 1983, annual rpt, 2424–9

Exports of US, detailed Schedule E commodities by mode of transport and world area and country of destination, 1983, annual rpts, 2424–5

Imports of US, detailed Schedule A commodities by country and world area of origin, and mode of transport, 1983, annual rpts, 2424–2

Imports of US, detailed TSUSA commodities by country of origin, 1983, annual rpt, 2424–4

Loans and grants for economic and military assistance from US and intl agencies, by program and country, FY46-83, annual rpt, 9914–5

Lumber production, prices, trade, and employment in Northwest US and British Columbia, quarterly rpt, 1202–3

Military spending, arms trade, and armed forces size, with total govt spending and population, by country, 1972-82, annual rpt, 9824–1

Minerals Yearbook, 1982, Vol 3: foreign country reviews of production, trade, and policies, by commodity, annual rpt, 5604–35

Minerals Yearbook, 1982, Vol 3 preprints: foreign country review of production, trade, and policies, by commodity, annual rpt, 5604–17.16

Oil and gas undiscovered recoverable resources, cumulative production, and identified reserves, as of 1983, preliminary oil basin rpt, 5666–17.14

Oil production, and exports by country, for PRC, monthly rpt, 242–5

Oil production by major exporting countries, monthly rpt, 3162–24.10

Population size and growth rates, and latest available benchmark demographic data, by country, 1950-83, biennial rpt, 2324–4

Potassium permanganate from PRC at less than fair value, imports injury to US industry, investigation with background financial and operating data, 1984 rpt, 9886–14.93

Refugee migration, settlement status, and assistance, by world area and country of origin and asylum, as of May 1984, annual rpt, 7004–15

Rice area, yield, and production by crop, 1979/80-1983/84, FAS annual rpt, 1925–2.6

Scientific document exchanges of Albania and PRC with USSR, 1948-61, 2326–9.7

Ships in world merchant fleet, and tonnage, by country of registry, 1982, annual rpt, 7704–3.1

Space launchings attaining Earth orbit or beyond, by country, 1957-83, annual rpt, 9504–9.1

Index by Subjects and Names

Space satellites and other objects launched since 1957, quarterly listing, 9502–2

Tidal current tables, daily time and velocity by station for North America and Asia coasts, 1985, annual rpt, 2174–1.2

Weather conditions and impact assessment, by world area and country, monthly rpt, 2152–9

see also under By Foreign Country in the "Index by Categories"

Chinese Americans

see Asian Americans

Chiropractic and naturopathy

County Business Patterns: establishments, employees, and payrolls, by SIC 4-digit industry and county, 1981, annual State rpt series, 2326–8

County Business Patterns: establishments, employees, and payrolls, by SIC 4-digit industry and county, 1982, annual State rpt series, 2326–6

Degrees conferred in higher education, by race, Hispanic origin, sex, level, and field, selected years 1949/50-1979/80, annual rpt, 4824–2.16

Health care services of selected medical practitioners, use by patient characteristics, 1980 survey with trends from 1963, 4146–12.4

Health condition and health care resources, use, and expenditures, 1970s-82 with trends and projections 1900-2000, annual compilation, 4144–11

Income tax returns of sole proprietorships, detailed data by industry div and selected industry group, 1981, annual rpt, 8304–7

Income tax returns of sole proprietorships, receipts, deductions by type, payroll, and net income, by major industry, 1982, annual article, 8302–2.413

License sanctions of health professionals in 3 States, and subsequent Medicare and Medicaid program participation, by specialty, 1977-82, GAO rpt, 26121–80

Medicare physician charges and reimbursement by enrollee characteristics and carrier, payment limits effects on charges in California, and physician earnings, by specialty, 1950s-84, 25368–127

Occupational manpower needs and supply by detailed occupation, and educational and training program enrollees and grads by detailed field, 1982 and 1995, biennial rpt, 6744–3

Occupational Outlook Handbook, 1984-85 biennial rpt, 6744–1

Service industry census, 1982: employment, establishments, receipts, and payroll, by SIC 2- to 4-digit kind of business, SMSA, county, and city, State rpt series, 2391–1

Chlorine

see Gases

Chocolate

see Cocoa and chocolate

Chojnacky, David C.

"Whole Tree Volume Estimates for the Rocky Mountain States", 1208–200

Chovil, Alan C.

"Occupational Health Services in South Carolina Manufacturing Plants: Results of a Survey", 4102–1.408

Index by Subjects and Names

Citizen lawsuits

Christensen, Lee A.
"Use and Cost of Soil Conservation and Water Quality Practices in the Southeast", 1588–84

Christiansted, V.I.
Economic Censuses of Virgin Islands, 1982: employment, establishments, payroll, and receipts, by SIC 1- to 4-digit industry, island, and city, 2593–1

Christophersen, Gary
"Final Report of the Seattle-Denver Income Maintenance Experiment. Vol. 2: Administration", 4008–64.3

Chromium
see Metals and metal industries

Chronic health conditions
see Diseases and disorders
see Health condition

Chrysler Corp.
Energy economy test results, 1985 model year, annual rpt, 3304–11
Energy use of autos and light trucks, economy standards and manufacturer compliance, and gas prices and taxes, with selected foreign comparisons, FY80-83 and projected to 2000, hearing, 21368–49
Safety of domestic and foreign autos and light trucks, crash test results of selected new models for model year to date, press release series, 7766–7
Sales, prices, and registrations of autos and auto products in US, and trade of 8 countries with US, by make and model, 1964-83, annual rpt, 9884–7

Chrysler Corporation Loan Guarantee Act
Implementation, with related financial and operating data, FY83, last issue of annual rpt, 8004–14

Chrystal, K. Alec
"Dutch Disease or Monetarist Medicine?: The British Economy Under Mrs. Thatcher", 9391–1.414
"International Banking Facilities", 9391–1.409

Church and state
see also Religious liberty

Churches
see Religious organizations

C.I.A.
see Central Intelligence Agency

Cigarettes and cigars
see Smoking
see Tobacco industry and products

Cincinnati, Ohio
Census of Housing, 1980: occupancy and unit characteristics, by race, Hispanic origin, and city, SMSA rpt, 2473–1.121
Census of Population and Housing, 1980: detailed population and housing characteristics, by county, city, and census tract, SMSA rpt, 2551–2.121
CPI by component for US city average, and by region, population size, and for 28 SMSAs, monthly press release, 6762–1
CPI by detailed component, for US city average, 28 SMSAs, and 4 regions by population size, monthly rpt, 6762–2
Fruit and vegetable shipments, and arrivals in 23 US and 5 Canada cities, by mode of transport and State or country of origin, 1983, annual rpt, 1311–4.1
Housing and financial characteristics, and unit and neighborhood quality, for 15 SMSAs, 1978, annual survey special supplement, 2485–8

Housing and households detailed characteristics, and unit and neighborhood quality, by inside-outside central cities, 1982 survey, SMSA rpt, 2485–6.35
Housing unit starts and completions authorized by building permits in 20 MSAs, quarterly rpt, 2382–9
Housing vacancy rates for single and multifamily units and mobile homes, by city and ZIP code, 1984, annual metro area rpt, 9304–27.12
Wages of office and plant workers, by occupation, 1984 SMSA survey rpt, 6785–11.6
see also under By City and By SMSA or MSA in the "Index by Categories"

Cinema
see Motion pictures

Circulatory diseases
Agent Orange exposed Air Force personnel diseases and disorders, by disease type, age, and officer status, 1984 rpt, 3604–3
Deaths and death rates by detailed cause and demographic characteristics, 1979 and selected trends, US Vital Statistics annual rpt, 4144–2.1
Deaths and death rates, by detailed geographic area, cause, and demographic characteristics, 1979, US Vital Statistics annual rpt, 4144–3
Disability Insurance beneficiaries sociodemographic and medical characteristics, 1977-79, annual rpt, 4744–20
Hospital discharges and length of stay, by patient characteristics, facility size, procedure performed, diagnosis, and region, 1982, annual rpt, 4147–13.78
Infant deaths by detailed cause, geographic location, age, race, and sex, 1979, US Vital Statistics annual rpt, 4144–2.2
see also Cardiovascular diseases
see also Cerebrovascular diseases
see also under By Disease in the "Index by Categories"

Cirrhosis of liver
see Digestive diseases

Cities
Census of Housing, 1980: occupancy and unit characteristics of SMSAs and central cities, by race, Hispanic origin, and city, State and SMSA rpt series, 2473–1
Census of Population and Housing, 1980: detailed population and housing characteristics, by county, city, and census tract, State and SMSA rpt series, 2551–2
Census of Population, 1980: detailed socioeconomic characteristics, by county, city, and inside-outside SMSAs and central cities, State rpt series, 2531–3
Community Dev Block Grants to small cities, State admin, project characteristics, and assessments of local officials, 1982, 5188–106
Community dev programs funding and activities, for 5 HUD programs, FY83, annual rpt, 5124–5
County and City Data Book, detailed socioeconomic and demographic data for States, counties, and cities, selected years 1976-82, 2328–1
Crime Index by population size and region, and offenses known to police by large city, Jan-June 1984, semiannual rpt, 6222–1

Crimes, arrests by offender characteristics, and rates, by offense, and law enforcement employees, by population size and jurisdiction, 1970s-83, annual rpt, 6224–2
Economic distress index and components, for 153 cities, 1975 and 1980, article, 9373–1.413
Foreign and US population and land area of major cities and metro areas, for US, France, Japan, and UK, 1940s-82, 26358–97
Housing (rental) unit choice of Pittsburgh, Pa, recent movers related to unit, neighborhood, and town characteristics, 1967 survey, 9306–1.7
Population size, Apr 1980 and July 1982, and per capita income, 1979 and 1981, by county and city, State Current Population Rpt series, 2546–11
Retail trade census, 1982: employment, establishments, sales, and payroll, by SIC 2- to 4-digit kind of business, SMSA, and retail district, State rpt series, 2401–1
Revenue sharing and other Fed Govt grant program alternative allocations, with city govt finances and responses to program cuts, FY79-83, hearings, 25408–86
Revenue sharing payments to States, local govts, Indian tribes, and Alaska Native villages, and entitlement computation data, FY84, series, 8066–1
Service industry census, 1982: employment, establishments, receipts, and payroll, by SIC 2- to 4-digit kind of business, SMSA, county, and city, State rpt series, 2391–1
Transit systems, expenditures by level of govt, and revenues by source, with distribution of commuter trips by mode of transport, 1980-82, article, 10042–1.404
Urban Dev Action Grant awards to local areas, preliminary approvals, with project descriptions, private investment, and jobs and taxes to be created, by city, quarterly press release series, 5002–7
see also Census of Governments
see also Census tracts
see also Central business districts
see also Central cities
see also City and town planning
see also Harbors and ports
see also Local government
see also Metropolitan Statistical Areas
see also Neighborhoods
see also Suburbs
see also Urban areas
see also ZIP codes
see also under By City and By SMSA or MSA in the "Index by Categories"
see also under names of individual cities

Citizen lawsuits
Court of Claims petitions and plaintiffs, FY83, annual rpt, 18224–1
Legal fees awarded private parties in cases against Federal, State, and local govts, by case, selected years 1977-83, 6008–19
US Attorneys civil and criminal case processing in district, appellate, and State courts, by district, FY83, annual rpt, 6004–2

Citizenship

Citizenship

Census of Population, 1980: detailed socioeconomic and demographic characteristics, by age, sex, race, Hispanic origin, occupation, and industry, State rpt series, 2531–4

Census of Population, 1980: detailed socioeconomic characteristics, by county, city, and inside-outside SMSAs and central cities, State rpt series, 2531–3

Certificates of citizenship for US citizens born abroad, availability of records, 1984 annual listing, 4124–7

DOD civilian employment, by service branch and defense agency, with summary military employment data, monthly rpt, 3542–16

Fed Govt civilian employee accessions and separations, by citizenship status and agency for DC metro area and elsewhere, monthly rpt, 9842–1.3

Fed Govt civilian employment abroad, by US citizenship, selected agency, country, and outlying area, 1982, biennial rpt, 9844–8

Health professionals supply and education, by occupation, demographic and professional characteristics, and location, 1950s-83 and projected to 2000, biennial rpt, 4114–8

Immigration, and alien residents, workers, visitors, deportations, and naturalizations, by country of birth, FY81, annual rpt, 6264–2

Peru cocaine addicts and arrested traffickers and users socioeconomic characteristics, and cocaine confiscated, 1974-78, intl conf papers, 7008–40

Physicians of DOD, by pay grade, citizenship, and service branch, FY83, annual rpt, 3544–24.5

Refugee and alien arrivals and resettlements in US, by State, outlying area, country of birth and citizenship, age, sex, and sponsoring agency, monthly rpt, 4702–3

Science and engineering doctoral degree recipients, by field, sex, race, age, citizenship, postgrad employment and study status, State, and instn, 1960-82, 9626–6.16

Science and engineering grad students, by field, type of financial aid, sex, race, Hispanic origin, and citizenship, 1972-83, biennial rpt, 9627–24.3

Statistical Abstract of US, social, political, and economic data, 1950s-83 and trends, annual rpt, 2324–1.1

Citrus fruits

Agricultural Statistics, 1983, annual rpt, 1004–1

Agriculture census, 1982: farms, farmland, production, finances, and operator characteristics, by county, final State rpt series, 2331–1

California farm real estate market values, by use and crop, 1976-84, annual rpt, 1541–8.1

Consumption of food and nutrient intake by individuals, by food group, source, and socioeconomic characteristics, 1977-78 natl survey, final rpt series, 1356–4

Consumption, supply, trade, prices, expenditures, and indexes, by food commodity, 1963-83, annual rpt, 1544–4

Cuba economic conditions, agricultural and industrial production and distribution, trade, and intl economic relations, 1970-82 and trends from 1957, 248–40

Exports (total and to EC) and production of US corn gluten products and citrus pulp, 1960-83, hearing, 25368–135

Exports and imports of US, by agricultural commodity and country, bimonthly rpt with articles, 1522–1

Exports and imports of US, by detailed agricultural commodity and country, FY83 and CY83, semiannual rpts, 1522–4

Exports and imports of US, detailed SIC-based commodities by world area, 1983, annual rpts, 2424–6

Exports and imports of US, totals and as percent of domestic production, by SIC 2- to 5-digit commodity, 1981, annual rpt, 2424–3

Exports of US, detailed commodities by country of destination, monthly rpt, 2422–3

Exports of US, detailed Schedule B commodities by country of destination, 1983, annual rpt, 2424–9

Exports of US, detailed Schedule E commodities by mode of transport and world area and country of destination, 1983, annual rpts, 2424–5

Farm finances, assets, liabilities, income, receipts by commodity and State, and expenses, 1980-83 and trends from 1910, annual rpt, 1544–16

Foreign and US fresh and processed fruit, vegetable, and nut production and trade, FAS monthly rpt with articles, 1925–34

Foreign and US trade of citrus fruit, by country of origin and destination, 1982-83, FAS rpt supplement, 1925–35.2

Fruit fly control, ethylene dibromide fumigation of tropical fruit imports, FY82, and cost of EDB and alternatives for Florida grapefruit and Hawaii papaya, 1984 rpt, 21168–29

Futures trading in selected commodities, foreign currencies, Treasury securities, and stock indexes, NYC, Chicago, and other markets activity, monthly rpt, 11922–5

Imports of US, detailed Schedule A commodities by country and world area of origin, and mode of transport, 1983, annual rpts, 2424–2

Imports of US, detailed Schedule A commodities by country, monthly rpt, 2422–2

Imports of US, detailed TSUSA commodities by country of origin, 1983, annual rpt, 2424–4

Marketing cash receipts of farms, by detailed commodity and State, 1979-82, annual rpt, 1544–18

Orange juice (frozen) futures trading, NYC market activity, monthly rpt, 11922–2

Oranges and frozen juice concentrate production, consumption, and exports of Brazil, 1981-83 and forecast 1983/84, article, 1925–34.420

Prices (farm-retail) for foods, marketing cost components, and industry finances and productivity, selected years 1967-83, annual rpt, 1544–9

Prices (wholesale) for fresh fruit and vegetables in NYC, Chicago, and selected shipping points, by crop, 1983, annual rpt, 1311–8

Prices received by farmers and production value for detailed crops by State, 1981-83, annual rpt, 1621–2

Prices received by farmers for major products, and paid for farm inputs and living items, by commodity and State, monthly rpt, 1629–1

Producer prices and indexes, by stage of processing and detailed commodity, monthly rpt, 6762–6

Producer prices and indexes, by stage of processing and detailed commodity, monthly 1983, annual supplement, 6764–2

Production and use, by crop and producer State, 1977/78-1981/82, 1641–4

Production, farms, acreage, and related data, by selected crop and State, monthly rpt, 1621–1

Production, prices, and use of citrus fruit, by producer State, 1981/82-1983/84, annual rpt, 1621–18.5

Production, prices, trade, stocks, and use, by selected crop, periodic situation rpt with articles, 1561–6

Shipments of fruits and vegetables, and arrivals in 23 US and 5 Canada cities, by mode of transport and State or country of origin, 1983, annual rpt series, 1311–4

see also under By Commodity in the "Index by Categories"

City and town planning

Census of Population and Housing, 1980: data coverage, availability, and uses for urban and transportation planning, 1984 guide, 7558–101

Census of Population, 1980: detailed socioeconomic and demographic characteristics, by age, sex, race, Hispanic origin, occupation, and industry, State rpt series, 2531–4

Census of Population, 1980: labor force, by sex, detailed occupation, and region, with comparison to 1970 census, supplementary rpt, 2535–1.12

Hwy and urban transit systems financing methods of govts and private sector, with case studies for selected metro areas, series, 7556–7

Occupational manpower needs and supply by detailed occupation, and educational and training program enrollees and grads by detailed field, 1982 and 1995, biennial rpt, 6744–3

Occupational Outlook Handbook, 1984-85 biennial rpt, 6744–1

see also New towns

City taxation

see State and local taxes

Civic Service, Inc.

"Attitudes Toward Campaign Financing: A CSI Survey Report", 25688–6

Civil Aeronautics Board

Activities of CAB, and airline industry traffic and financial data by carrier, FY83 with trends from FY73, annual rpt, 9144–1

Airline cash flows for all certificated carriers, quarterly rpt, 9142–34

Airline common stock average price for major carriers, and compared to New York Stock Exchange indexes, quarterly Dec 1977-June 1984, semiannual rpt, 9142–36

Index by Subjects and Names

Civil procedure

Airline financial and operating data for certificated, charter, and cargo carriers, quarterly rpt, 9142–30

Airline financial data, by carrier, carrier group, and for total certificated system, quarterly rpt, 9142–12

Airline income and profitability, by major carrier, 1972-83, annual rpt, 9144–37

Airline income taxes paid, net income, and effective tax rates, by major carrier, 1968-83, annual rpt, 9144–34

Airline intl operations, traffic and financial data for US combination carriers in Atlantic, Pacific, and Latin America regions, quarterly rpt, 9142–41

Airline operating and other costs, itemized for domestic and intl trunk and local service carriers, 1st half 1983, semiannual rpt, 9142–47

Airline operating unit costs for each system major and short-haul natl carrier, quarterly rpt, 9142–37

Airline passenger and cargo traffic, and departures by aircraft type, by airline and US and foreign airport, 1982, annual rpt, 7504–35

Airline passenger traffic and capacity for US and intl operations of major trunk carriers, and seasonal adjustment factors, monthly rpt, 9142–19

Airline passenger traffic, capacity, yields, and load factors, changes for each system major and short-haul natl carrier, periodic rpt, 9142–45

Airline passenger traffic since 1978 deregulation, by major carrier, quarterly rpt, 9142–49

Airline profit margins, for major operators of large aircraft by carrier group and carrier, quarterly rpt, 9142–43

Airline traffic, capacity, and performance, by carrier and type of operation, monthly rpt, 9142–13

Airline traffic, capacity, and performance for medium regionals, by carrier and certification status, quarterly rpt, 9142–44

Budget of US Appendix, detailed budgets and personnel summaries, by agency, FY85, annual rpt, 104–3

Budget of US, appropriations, outlays, balances, and budget receipts, by govtl branch and agency, FY83, annual rpt, 8104–2

Complaints of air passengers and shippers to CAB, by type of complaint and US and foreign air carrier, monthly rpt, 9142–20

Cost control proposals for Fed Govt programs and mgmt, 3-year savings by function and agency, and financial and operating data, 1960s-81, 16908–1.15

Deregulation of airlines in 1978, effect on industry operations and finances, air traffic patterns, and CAB programs, various periods FY76-84, 9148–56

Deregulation of airlines in 1978, resulting traffic and service changes by city, with market shares, fares, and load factors, quarterly rpt, 9142–42

Energy use and costs for domestic and intl operations, by US air carrier group, monthly rpt, 9142–21

Freight yields and revenue ton-miles for major and all cargo domestic air carrier groups, quarterly rpt, 9142–35

Passengers denied confirmed space on commercial flights, by carrier, monthly rpt, 9142–23

Subsidies of Fed Govt paid since 1979 to air carriers serving small communities, by carrier, monthly rpt, 9142–48

Civil aviation

Air pollution levels for 5 pollutants, by detailed source, State, and Air Quality Control Region, 1981, annual rpt, 9194–7

Aviation activity, detailed data on aircraft, air traffic, air carriers, personnel, airports, and FAA operations, 1974-83, annual rpt, 7504–1

Communist, OECD, and selected other countries freight and carrier inventories, by mode of transport, 1960s-83, annual rpt, 244–5.10

FAA aviation medicine research and studies, technical rpt series, 7506–10

Passenger miles and trips, by transport mode, selected years 1929-81, 26358–97

Pilots and nonpilots certified by FAA, by type of certificate, age, sex, region, and State, 1983, annual rpt, 7504–2

Statistical Abstract of US, social, political, and economic data, 1950s-83 and trends, annual rpt, 2324–1.3

Traffic, aircraft operations by type and passenger enplanements, by airport, region, and State, projected FY82-95 and trends from FY76, annual rpt, 7504–7

Traffic, aircraft, pilots, airport activity, and fuel use, forecast FY84-95 with FY79-83 trends, annual rpt, 7504–6

see also Aerospace industry

see also Air cargo

see also Air piracy

see also Air traffic control

see also Aircraft

see also Airlines

see also Airports and airways

see also Aviation accidents and safety

see also General aviation

see also Pilots

Civil defense

Budget of US, effects of Reagan Admin policy changes, by detailed program, FY85, annual rpt, 104–21

Fed Emergency Mgmt Agency activities and funding for disaster and emergency relief, and major disasters, 1983, annual rpt, 9434–2

Fed Emergency Mgmt Agency nuclear attack civil defense plans, funding and operations by component, FY81-84 and projected FY85-89, GAO rpt, 26123–61

Fed Govt aid to State and local govts, expenditures, and direct payments, by program, agency, and State, FY83, annual rpt, 2464–2

Fed Govt financial and nonfinancial domestic aid, 1984 annual comprehensive catalog, 104–5

Govt census, 1982: State govt payments to local govts, by program, source of funds, level of govt, and State, with trends from 1902, 2460–3

Natl Defense Executive reserve members, costs, and training, by agency, annual rpt, suspended, 9434–1

Natl Guard (Army and Air) activities, manpower, and facilities, FY83, annual rpt, 3704–3

see also Fallout shelters

Civil engineering

see Bridges

see Canals

see Dams

see Harbors and ports

see Highways

see Irrigation

see Public works

see Reclamation of land

see Rivers and waterways

Civil liberties

see Civil rights

see Due process of law

see Electronic surveillance

see Habeas corpus

see Right of privacy

see Searches and seizures

Civil-military relations

see also Defense contracts and procurement

see also Defense industries

see also Impacted areas

Civil procedure

Court case filings in State trial courts by case type, and appellate court filings and dispositions by court type, by State, 1978-83, periodic rpt, 6062–2.409

Court caseloads, actions, procedure duration, judges, and jurors, by Federal district and appeals court, 1979-84, annual rpt, 18204–3

Court caseloads for Federal district, appeals, and bankruptcy courts, by type of suit and offense, circuit, and district, quarterly rpt, 18202–1

Court civil and criminal caseloads for Federal district, appeals, and special courts, year ended June 1983 and selected trends from 1940, annual rpt, 18204–8

Court civil and criminal casloads and activity summary, for Federal district, appeals, and bankruptcy courts, 1975-June 1984, annual chartbook, 18204–9

Discrimination against Hispanics and other minorities in employment, Equal Employment Opportunity Commission enforcement activities, personnel, and litigation, 1970s-FY83, 9248–18

FBI undercover operations convictions, fines, recoveries, victim compensation, and status of lawsuits against FBI by operation, FY82, GAO rpt, 26119–67

Judicial Conf semiannual proceedings and findings, 1984 annual rpt, 18204–5

Justice Dept activities, by subagency, FY82, annual rpt, 6004–1

Magistrate case processing duties assigned in Fed Govt district courts, by type of case, duty, and district, 1983 rpt, 18408–24

Patent and trademark litigation, by court, FY83, annual rpt, 2244–1.5

SSA programs, finances, staff, and litigation, FY83, annual rpt, 4704–6

Telephone conference use in civil and criminal hearings, assessment of lawyers and judges in 2 States and Denver, Colo, 1981, 6068–186

US Attorneys civil and criminal case processing in district, appellate, and State courts, by district, FY83, annual rpt, 6004–2

see also Administrative law and procedure

see also Adoption

see also Bankruptcy

Civil procedure

see also Citizen lawsuits
see also Claims
see also Contempt of court
see also Evidence
see also Extradition
see also Habeas corpus
see also Judgments, civil procedure
see also Juries
see also Marriage and divorce
see also Tax protests and appeals
see also Torts
see also Trials

Civil rights

- Budget and staff for civil rights enforcement offices of 6 Federal agencies, FY80-84, 11048–179
- Budget of US, effects of Reagan Admin policy changes, by detailed program, FY85, annual rpt, 104–21
- Budget of US, special analysis of civil rights activities by agency and program, and Fed Govt employment of minorities, FY83-85, annual rpt, 104–1.10
- Central America socioeconomic and political conditions in 6 countries, 1960s-83 with trends and projections 1930-2010, Commission rpt, 028–19.2
- El Salvador terrorist acts against property, casualties, kidnappings, and hostages, Oct 1979-June 1983, human rights certification hearing, 21388–41
- Fed Govt district court magistrates case processing duties, by type of case, duty, and district, 1983 rpt, 18408–24
- Foreign human rights conditions in 162 countries, economic and military aid of US, and economic aid of intl organizations, 1981-83, annual rpt, definitions, 21384–3
- Helsinki Final Act implementation by NATO, Warsaw Pact, and other signatory nations, Dec 1983-Mar 1984, semiannual rpt, 7002–1
- Older persons discrimination in Fed Govt aid programs, Age Discrimination Act enforcement by 28 agencies, FY83, annual rpt, 4004–27
- Revenue sharing entitlements by State, and noncompliance audit cases by type, FY83 and cumulative through FY82, annual rpt, 8064–1.1
- US Attorneys civil case processing and amounts involved, by cause of action, FY83, annual rpt, 6004–2.5
- *see also* Discrimination in education
- *see also* Discrimination in employment
- *see also* Discrimination in housing
- *see also* Due process of law
- *see also* Racial discrimination
- *see also* Right of assembly
- *see also* Right of privacy
- *see also* Right to counsel
- *see also* Sex discrimination

Civil Rights Commission

see Commission on Civil Rights

Civil Service Commission

see Office of Personnel Management

Civil service pensions

- Beneficiaries and taxes collected for social insurance programs since 1940, monthly rpt, 4742–1.1
- Benefits and after-tax salary replacement rates by pension type, and older persons income and income sources, by age and marital status, 1950s-82, conf proceedings, 25408–87

Benefits and beneficiaries of public employee pension plans by eligibility reason, level of govt, and Federal plan, selected years 1954-80, article, 4742–1.403

- Benefits, beneficiary characteristics, and trust funds of OASDHI, Medicaid, SSI, and other social insurance and public welfare programs, selected years 1950-82, annual rpt, 4744–3.9, 4744–3.10
- Benefits for military retirees and compared to US civil and foreign service and foreign countries, and Air Force personnel costs, FY75-84, hearings, 21208–19
- Budget of US Appendix, detailed budgets and personnel summaries, by agency, FY85, annual rpt, 104–3
- Budget of US, CBO analysis and review of FY85 budget by function, annual rpt, 26304–2
- Budget of US, CBO analysis of revenue and spending alternatives and projections of economic indicators, FY85-89, annual rpt, 26304–3.3
- Budget of US, compact budgets by function, agency, and account, FY85 with projections to FY89, annual rpt, 104–2
- Budget of US, effects of Reagan Admin policy changes, by detailed program, FY85, annual rpt, 104–21
- Budget of US, receipts by source and outlays by agency and program, monthly rpt, 8102–3
- Budget of US, receipts by source and outlays by function, FY40-89 estimates revised for consistency with FY85 budget definitions, annual rpt, 104–12
- Budget of US, receipts, outlays, and budget authority, by function and agency, FY84-89 revised estimates, midsession review of FY85 budget, annual rpt, 104–7
- Fed Govt aid to State and local areas, by type of payment, State, and county, FY83, annual rpt, 2464–3.1
- Fed Govt aid to State and local govts, expenditures, and direct payments, by program, agency, and State, FY83, annual rpt, 2464–2
- Fed Govt annuity adjustments, as of Jan 1984 with trends from 1948, 21628–54
- Fed Govt annuity programs actuarial status, by agency and program, as of Sept 1983, annual rpt, 8104–3.4
- Fed Govt cash benefits, and beneficiaries with representative payees by age and relation to payee, by program, as of 1983, GAO rpt, 26121–85
- Fed Govt civil service retirement system actuarial valuation, FY79-83 with projections to FY2060, annual rpt, 9844–34
- Fed Govt civilian and military employee pay, withholdings by type, and income, and special military compensation by type and service branch, 1982-83, GAO rpt, 26123–65
- Fed Govt civilian employee retirement, health, and life insurance benefit plans operations and finances, FY81-82, annual rpt, 9844–1
- Fed Govt consolidated financial statements based on business accounting methods, FY82-83, annual rpt, 8104–5

Index by Subjects and Names

- Fed Govt obligations by function and agency, *Treasury Bulletin,* quarterly rpt, 8002–4.2
- Fed Govt personnel action appeals, decisions of Merit Systems Protection Board, by region, agency, and employee characteristics, FY82, annual rpt, 9494–2
- Fed Govt programs and mgmt cost control proposals, 3-year savings by function and agency, and financial and operating data, 1960s-81, 16908–1
- Fed Govt public welfare programs and tax expenditures benefitting children and youth, participation and funding for 71 programs, FY81-83, 21968–30
- Firefighters death benefits under workers compensation and local pension plans, by State and city, hearing, 21348–94
- Flow-of-funds accounts, assets and liabilities by type and economic sector, year-end outstandings, 1960-83, annual rpt, 9364–3
- Flow-of-funds accounts savings, investments, and credit statements, quarterly rpt, 9365–3.3
- Govt census, 1982: city govt revenues by source, expenditures by function, debt, and assets, by State and city, 2457–4
- Govt census, 1982: county govt revenues by source, expenditures by function, debt, and assets, by State and county, 2457–3
- Govt expenditures for social welfare by program and level of govt, and private expenditures for health care, selected years FY50-82, annual article, 4742–1.425
- Govt finances, by level of govt, State, and for large cities and counties, 1981-83, annual rpt series, 2466–2
- Income (household) and cash and noncash transfer program participation, by sociodemographic characteristics, quarterly rpt, 2542–2
- Income (personal) by source including transfer payments, and social insurance contributions by type, by region, 1929 and 1982, 2708–40
- Income and income sources of older persons, by OASDI beneficiary and poverty status, labor force participation, and demographic characteristics, 1982, biennial rpt, 4744–26
- Income from transfer payments, natl income and product account, *Survey of Current Business,* monthly rpt, monthly and annual tables, 2702–1.23
- Mortgage loan activity, by type of lender, loan, and mortgaged property, monthly rpt, 5142–18
- Mortgage loan originations, purchases, and acquisitions, for 11 lender types, selected years 1960-82, article, 9312–1.407
- Mortgage loan transactions and holdings of State and local govt retirement funds and credit agencies, by type of property and loan, quarterly rpt, 5142–30
- Oregon and Montana earnings by SIC 1- to 3-digit industry and payments to retirees by type, for 4 timber dependent communities, 1970, 1208–196
- Postal Service pension and health benefits subsidized by Fed Govt trust funds, and subsidy reduction plans deficit impact, FY79-84 and projected to FY89, 26306–6.82

State and local govt employee pension plans disclosing finances, and public pension plans operations, funding, and assets, selected years 1974-82, hearing, 21788–142

State and local govt retirement systems, cash and security holdings and finances, quarterly rpt, 2462–2

Tax expenditures from employee benefit plans, for income and payroll tax by benefit type and income, with benefits by industry, 1950-83 and projected to 1988, article, 9373–1.404

see also Foreign Service Retirement and Disability Fund

Civil Service Retirement and Disability Fund *see* Federal trust funds

Civil service system

Fed Govt Equal Opportunity Recruitment Program implementation, and summary employment data, FY83, annual rpt, 9844–33

Fed Govt executive employee performance appraisal system operations, and employee attitudes, 1982 survey, GAO rpt, 26119–61

Fed Govt personnel action appeals, decisions of Merit Systems Protection Board, by region, agency, and employee characteristics, FY82, annual rpt, 9494–2

Fed Govt programs and mgmt cost control proposals, 3-year savings by function and agency, and financial and operating data, 1960s-81, 16908–1.27

Merit system of Office of Personnel Mgmt, implementation and effectiveness, 1982, annual survey, 9494–1

see also Civil service pensions

see also Federal employees

see also Office of Personnel Management

see also State and local employees

Civil War

see War

Civil works

see Public works

Civilian Health and Medical Program of the Uniformed Services

Cost control proposals for Fed Govt programs and mgmt, 3-year savings by function and agency, and financial and operating data, 1960s-81, 16908–1.17

Costs and operations of CHAMPUS, with comparisons to other health care systems, FY83 and trends from FY79, semiannual rpt, 3502–2

Veterans aged 55 and over, socioeconomic characteristics, economic resources, health care and status, and actual and expected use of VA benefits, 1983 survey, 9928–29

Claims

Alaska and Alaska Native corporation claims for Fed Govt land, status and Land Mgmt Bur conveyance problems, various dates 1978-FY84, GAO rpt, 26113–125

Banking and nonbanking firms liabilities to and claims on foreigners, by country, 1981-82, annual rpt, 9364–5.10

Fed Govt contingent liabilities and claims paid on federally insured and guaranteed contracts with foreign obligors, by country and program, periodic rpt, 8002–12

Foreign claims by US banks and nonbanking business enterprises, by type and country, *Treasury Bulletin,* quarterly rpt, 8002–4.12

Foreign govt claims of US natls, by country and type of claim, 1983, annual rpt, 6004–16

see also Insurance

see also under names of specific types of insurance

Clair, Robert T.

"Deposit Insurance, Moral Hazard, and Credit Unions", 9379–1.404

Clapp, Roger B.

"Marine Birds of the Southeastern U.S. and Gulf of Mexico", 5508–72

Clapp-Wincek, Cynthia

"Helmand Valley Project in Afghanistan", 9916–3.18

Clark, Gilbert B.

"Annual Data and Verification Tabulation, Atlantic Tropical Cyclones, 1983", 2184–7

Clark, John P.

"Theft by Employees in Work Organizations, Executive Summary", 6068–178

Clark, Norman

"Dental Malpractice: Baseline Data from Insurance Claims Closed in 1970, with Analysis", 4102–1.416

Clark, Peter B.

"Effects of Fiscal Policy on the U.S. Economy", 9366–1.134

Clark, Phil

"Private Activity Tax-Exempt Bonds, 1983", 8302–2.417

Clark, Robert L.

"Final Report for Inflation and Pension Benefits", 6468–18

Clarksville, Tenn.

Census of Housing, 1980: occupancy and unit characteristics, by race, Hispanic origin, and city, SMSA rpt, 2473–1.122

Census of Population and Housing, 1980: detailed population and housing characteristics, by county, city, and census tract, SMSA rpt, 2551–2.122

Wages of office and plant workers, by occupation, 1984 labor market area survey rpt, 6785–3.4

see also under By SMSA or MSA in the "Index by Categories"

Class actions

see Citizen lawsuits

Classifications

Criminal offense citations manual of US criminal title and section codes, with corresponding detailed offenses and severity levels, 1984, annual rpt, 18204–14

Export and import statistics country classifications, Census Bur codes and designations, revisions to 1981 base edition, 2428–3

Fed Govt standards for data recording, processing, and transfer, and for purchase and use of computer systems, series, 2216–2

Fed Govt supply inventory and automated cataloging system, and DOD mgmt of inventory items for agencies, NATO, and foreign govts, 1970s-83, annual rpt, 21204–1

Health care visits, testing of World Health Organization system to classify reasons people seek care, 1984 article, 4102–1.460

Industry coding systems for statistical programs of 6 Federal agencies, comparability, workload, and updating cycles, 1984 rpt, 106–4.5

Tariff Schedules of US, Annotated, classifications and rates of duty for detailed imported commodities, 1985 edition, 9886–13

Tariff Schedules of US, Annotated, commodity classification revisions under proposed internatl system, 1984 rpt, 9886–4.66

see also "Guide to Selected Standard Classifications" section in ASI Annual

Classified information

see Internal security

Clauson, Annette

"Analyzing Machinery Purchases and Sales by Producers According to Acreage Operated", 1544–19.403

"New Evidence on the Diversity of Agricultural Income and Expense Accounts", 1544–19.401

Clay industry and products

Air pollutant emission factors, by detailed source, 3rd edition, 1983-84 supplements, 9198–13

Business statistics, detailed data for major industries and economic indicators, *Survey of Current Business,* monthly rpt, 2702–1.18

Census of Population, 1980: detailed socioeconomic and demographic characteristics, by age, sex, race, Hispanic origin, occupation, and industry, State rpt series, 2531–4

Ceramic kitchen articles trade, tariffs, and industry operating data, foreign and US, 1978-82, TSUSA commodity rpt supplement, 9885–5.13

County Business Patterns: establishments, employees, and payrolls, by SIC 4-digit industry and county, 1981, annual State rpt series, 2326–8

County Business Patterns: establishments, employees, and payrolls, by SIC 4-digit industry and county, 1982, annual State rpt series, 2326–6

Earnings by major industry group, and personal income per capita and by source, by region and State, 1929-82, 2708–40

Employment, earnings, and hours, by selected SIC 1- to 4-digit industry, State, and for 278 major labor areas, 1939-83, annual rpt, 6744–5

Employment, earnings, and hours, by SIC 4-digit nonfarm industry, monthly 1974-Feb 1984, annual update, 6744–4

Energy use and cost for building materials manufacture, by energy source and industry, 1970s-82, article, 2012–1.401

Exports and imports of US, detailed SIC-based commodities by world area, 1983, annual rpts, 2424–6

Exports and imports of US, totals and as percent of domestic production, by SIC 2- to 5-digit commodity, 1981, annual rpt, 2424–3

Exports of US, detailed commodities by country of destination, monthly rpt, 2422–3

Exports of US, detailed Schedule B commodities by country of destination, 1983, annual rpt, 2424–9

Clay industry and products

- Exports of US, detailed Schedule E commodities by mode of transport and world area and country of destination, 1983, annual rpts, 2424–5
- Foreign minerals production, reserves, and industry role in domestic economy and world supply, country and world region rpt series, 5606–1
- Great Lakes trade, by SITC 3-digit commodity, port, vessel type, world area, and country, 1982, annual rpt, 7744–3
- Imports of US, detailed Schedule A commodities by country and world area of origin, and mode of transport, 1983, annual rpts, 2424–2
- Imports of US, detailed Schedule A commodities by country, monthly rpt, 2422–2
- Imports of US, detailed TSUSA commodities by country of origin, 1983, annual rpt, 2424–4
- Income tax returns of sole proprietorships, detailed data by industry div and selected industry group, 1981, annual rpt, 8304–7
- Input-output structure of US economy, detailed interindustry transactions for 537 industries, and components of final demand, 1977 benchmark data, 2708–17
- Manufacturing census, 1982: financial and operating data, by SIC 2- to 4-digit industry, State, SMSA, and county, preliminary census div rpt series, 2491–3
- Manufacturing census, 1982: financial and operating data, for SIC 4-digit industries by product, preliminary rpt series, 2491–1
- Mineral industries census, 1982: financial and operating data, by SIC 2- to 4-digit industry, preliminary summary rpt, 2511–2.1
- Mineral industries census, 1982: financial and operating data, including materials consumed, by SIC 4-digit industry and State, preliminary rpt series, 2511–1
- Mineral Industry Surveys, commodity review of production, trade, and consumption, 1983, advance annual rpt, 5614–5.11
- *Minerals Yearbook, 1982,* Vol 1: commodity reviews of production, reserves, supply, use, and trade, annual rpt, 5604–33
- *Minerals Yearbook, 1982,* Vol 2 preprints: State reviews of production and sales by commodity, and business activity, annual rpt series, 5604–16
- *Minerals Yearbook, 1982,* Vol 2: State reviews of production, sales, and firms, by commodity, and business activity, annual rpt, 5604–34
- *Minerals Yearbook, 1982,* Vol 3: foreign country reviews of production, trade, and policies, by commodity, annual rpt, 5604–35
- *Minerals Yearbook, 1982,* Vol 3 preprints: foreign country reviews of production, trade, and policies, by commodity, annual rpt series, 5604–17
- *Minerals Yearbook, 1983,* Vol 1 preprints: commodity review of production, reserves, supply, use, and trade, annual rpt, 5604–15.17
- *Minerals Yearbook, 1983,* Vol 3 preprints: foreign country reviews of production, trade, and policies, by commodity, annual rpt series, 5604–23
- Occupational injuries and incidence, nonmetallic mineral mining and related operations, detailed analysis, 1982, annual rpt, 6664–1
- Occupational injury and illness rates, by SIC 2- to 4-digit industry, 1982, annual rpt, 6844–1
- Pollution abatement capital and operating costs, by SIC 2- to 4-digit industry, State, and SMSA, 1982, annual Current Industrial Rpt, 2506–3.6
- Production, prices, trade, use, employment, tariffs, and stockpiling, by mineral commodity, with foreign comparisons, 1979-83, annual rpt, 5604–18
- Production, shipments, PPI, and stocks of building materials, by type, bimonthly rpt, 2012–1.5, 2012–1.6
- Production, shipments, trade, and stocks, by clay product, periodic Current Industrial Rpt series, 2506–9
- Productivity, hours, and employment indexes for selected SIC 3- and 4-digit industries, 1954-82, annual rpt, 6824–1.3
- Scientists, engineers, and technicians employed in private industry, by occupation and industry group, 1980-81, biennial rpt, 9627–23
- Waterborne commerce of US (domestic and foreign), freight by commodity, traffic, and passengers, by port and waterway, 1982, annual rpt, 3754–3
- *see also* under By Commodity in the "Index by Categories"
- *see also* under By Industry in the "Index by Categories"

Clayton, Ronnie

"Estimates of Losses from Short Puts", 9316–1.102

Clayton, Ronnie J.

"Prepayment Implications of Mortgage-Backed Security Prices", 9316–1.106

Clean Air Act

- Abatement capital and operating costs under Clean Air and Water Acts, for govts and selected industries, various periods 1970-2000, annual rpt, 9184–11
- Abatement under Clean Air Act, emissions by source, standards, and effects on auto industry and health, 1970s-83, hearings, 25328–25
- Air quality and transportation and related energy use, for urban areas and Chicago area, late 1970s-82 and projected under lower auto emission standards to 1995, 3408–31
- Steel plant modernization capital investment under Clean Air Act compliance extension program, by firm, 1981-83, GAO rpt, 26113–138

Clean Water Act

Abatement capital and operating costs under Clean Air and Water Acts, for govts and selected industries, various periods 1970-2000, annual rpt, 9184–11

Cleaning services

see Laundry and cleaning services

Clearwater, Fla.

see also under By SMSA or MSA in the "Index by Categories"

Clemency

Executive clemency statistics, FY77-81, annual rpt, 6004–1

Index by Subjects and Names

Clerical workers

- Census of Housing, 1980: structural, financial, and householder characteristics, by region and State, 2475–4
- Census of Population and Housing, 1980: detailed population and housing characteristics, by county, city, and census tract, State and SMSA rpt series, 2551–2
- Census of Population, 1980: detailed socioeconomic and demographic characteristics, by age, sex, race, Hispanic origin, occupation, and industry, State rpt series, 2531–4
- Census of Population, 1980: detailed socioeconomic characteristics, by county, and inside-outside SMSAs and central cities, State rpt series, 2531–3
- Census of Population, 1980: labor force, by sex, detailed occupation, and region, with comparison to 1970 census, supplementary rpt, 2535–1.12
- Employee benefits in private industry, coverage by benefit type and provisions and occupational group, 1983, annual rpt, 6784–19
- Employment and economic conditions, alternative BLS projections to 1995 with selected trends for 1959-82, 6728–29
- Employment by detailed occupation, for 29 SIC 2-digit nonmanufacturing industries, 1981 BLS survey, 6748–60
- Employment, earnings, and hours, monthly press release, 6742–5
- Employment situation, earnings, hours, and other BLS economic indicators, transcripts of BLS Commissioner's monthly testimony, periodic rpt, 23846–4
- Employment, unemployment, and labor force, by demographic and employment characteristics, State, and for 30 metro areas and 11 large cities, 1983, annual rpt, 6744–7
- Fed Govt civilian employment by occupation, total and for 25 agencies, as of Oct 1983, annual article, 9842–1.405
- Fed Govt middle mgmt positions, labor cost savings under alternative grade reduction proposals, FY85-89, 26306–6.84
- Fed Govt minority group and handicapped employment, by race, Hispanic origin, disability, sex, and employment characteristics, as of Sept 1982, biennial rpt, 9844–27
- Fed Govt pay comparability with private industry, and recommended pay rate adjustments, 1983, annual rpt, 104–16
- Foreign women sociodemographic, economic, and fertility characteristics, with comparisons to men, by country, 1960s-85, world region rpt series, 2326–15
- *Handbook of Labor Statistics,* employment, earnings, hours, and labor force characteristics, 1982 and trends, detailed annual rpt, 6724–1
- Hospital worker wages by sex and occupation, and benefits, for 22 MSAs, Oct 1981 survey, 6787–6.201
- Income of households, families, and persons, by detailed socioeconomic characteristics and region, 1982, annual Current Population Rpt, 2546–6.39
- Libraries of colleges and universities, expenditures, holdings by type, use, staff by sex, and Federal grants received, 1979-82, biennial rpt, 4854–1

Index by Subjects and Names

Clinics

Minerals (nonmetallic) mining and related operations injury, employment, and worktime data, 1982, annual rpt, 6664–1

Minority group and women's employment, by occupational group, SIC 2- to 3-digit industry, State, and SMSA, 1981, annual rpt, 9244–1

Nuclear industry nongovt employment by industry segment, occupation, and census div, and DOE and NRC nuclear employment, 1968-83, biennial rpt, 3004–11

Occupational manpower needs and supply by detailed occupation, and educational and training program enrollees and grads by detailed field, 1982 and 1995, biennial rpt, 6744–3

Occupational Outlook Handbook, 1984-85 biennial rpt, 6744–1

Pay ranges for white collar employees, and employees by characteristics of salary policy, by occupation, Mar 1983-84, article, 6722–1.473

Pension plans with postretirement benefit increases, participants and average increase by occupational group and plan characteristics, 1978-81, article, 6722–1.453

Poverty status of families and persons, by detailed socioeconomic characteristics, 1982, annual Current Population Rpt, 2546–6.40

TV and radio industry minority and women employment by occupation, and business owners, by race and State, with revenues and stations, 1971-81, hearing, 21368–45

Wages of white-collar workers, by occupation, work level, and industry div, Mar 1984, annual rpt, 6784–2

Washington State deaths by sex, cause, and detailed occupation, summary data from occupational mortality study, 1950-79, 4248–47

Women's employment and earnings, by labor force and socioeconomic characteristics, and compared to men, 1978-81 and trends from 1940s, 6568–29

see also Area wage surveys

see also Industry wage surveys

see also under By Occupation in the "Index by Categories"

Cleveland, Ohio

Census of Housing, 1980: occupancy and unit characteristics, by race, Hispanic origin, and city, SMSA rpt, 2473–1.123

Census of Population and Housing, 1980: detailed population and housing characteristics, by county, city, and census tract, SMSA rpt, 2551–2.123

CPI by component for US city average, and by region, population size, and for 28 SMSAs, monthly press release, 6762–1

CPI by detailed component, for US city average, 28 SMSAs, and 4 regions by population size, monthly rpt, 6762–2

Hospital worker wages by sex and occupation, and benefits, for 22 MSAs, Oct 1981 survey, 6787–6.201

Population size of top 25 cities, 1980 and 1982, press release, 2328–46

Repair technicians and apprentices wages and benefits, for 5 types of electrical repair shops in 19 SMSAs, Nov 1981 survey, 6787–6.197

Wages of office and plant workers, by occupation, 1984 SMSA survey rpt, 6785–11.10

see also under By City and By SMSA or MSA in the "Index by Categories"

Cleveland, Robert W.

"Earnings in 1981 of Married-Couple Families, by Selected Characteristics of Husbands and Wives", 2546–2.120

Clifton, N.J.

Census of Housing, 1980: occupancy and unit characteristics, by race, Hispanic origin, and city, SMSA rpt, 2473–1.279

Census of Population and Housing, 1980: detailed population and housing characteristics, by county, city, and census tract, SMSA rpt, 2551–2.279

Housing and financial characteristics, and unit and neighborhood quality, for 15 SMSAs, 1978, annual survey special supplement, 2485–8

Housing and households detailed characteristics, and unit and neighborhood quality, by inside-outside central cities, 1982 survey, SMSA rpt, 2485–6.38

Wages by occupation, and benefits for office and plant workers, 1984 SMSA survey rpt, 6785–11.8

see also under By SMSA or MSA in the "Index by Categories"

Climate

see Weather

Clinical laboratory technicians

Census of Population, 1980: labor force, by sex, detailed occupation, and region, with comparison to 1970 census, supplementary rpt, 2535–1.12

DOD medical personnel, trainees, and accessions by source, by occupation, specialty, and service branch, FY83, annual rpt, 3544–24

Health care services of selected medical practitioners, use by patient characteristics, 1980 survey with trends from 1963, 4146–12.4

Hospital employment, vacancies, and vacancy rates, by occupation and by hospital specialty, region, census div, and State, 1980, annual rpt, 4114–12

Hospital worker wages by sex and occupation, and benefits, for 22 MSAs, Oct 1981 survey, 6787–6.201

Occupational manpower needs and supply by detailed occupation, and educational and training program enrollees and grads by detailed field, 1982 and 1995, biennial rpt, 6744–3

Occupational Outlook Handbook, 1984-85 biennial rpt, 6744–1

Public health labs of States, pay scales and job requirements by occupation and State, FY81-83, annual rpt, 4204–7

Public health labs of States, personnel, finances, workloads, and other activities, by State, FY82, annual rpt, 4204–8

Southeastern States health care resource availability, and employment by occupation, by facility type, by State and SMSA in Fed Reserve 6th District, 1970s-81, article, 9371–1.425

VA Medicine and Surgery Dept trainees, by detailed program and city, FY83, annual rpt, 9924–21

Clinics

Abortions (legal), and deaths from abortion and childbirth, by medical and sociodemographic characteristics, 1972-83, hearings, 21368–47

Alaska Native Medical Center visits and ambulatory high use patients by age and sex, and patient deaths, 1972-78, article, 4102–1.440

Army personnel health status, and use of Army medical services in US and abroad by personnel, retirees, and dependents, monthly rpt, 3702–4.1

Breast-fed infants, by characteristics of mother and source of prenatal care, various periods 1970-75, article, 4102–1.442

Construction put in place, private and public nonresidential, by type, region, and census div, 1979-83, monthly rpt, annual tables, 2382–4.3

Family planning and infertility services use by women, by source of service, marital status, age, race, and Hispanic origin, 1982, 4146–8.104

Food aid program of USDA for women, infants, and children, participants, clinics, and costs, by State and Indian agency, FY82, annual table, 1364–12.1

Govt census, 1982: State govt payments to local govts, by program, source of funds, level of govt, and State, with trends from 1902, 2460–3

Health condition and health care resources, use, and expenditures, 1970s-82 with trends and projections 1900-2000, annual compilation, 4144–11

Indian and Alaska Native health program activities, and funding for scholarships, care services, and facilities construction, by city, FY82, annual rpt, 4104–11

Israel health care in rural clinics under prepaid plan, services use and user satisfaction, 1981 survey, article, 4102–1.456

Medicare aged beneficiaries medical care by usual source, and untreated health conditions, by sociodemographic characteristics, 1980, 4146–12.3

Medicare enrollment and bills approved, and reimbursement and Medicaid payments by type of service and beneficiary, quarterly rpt, 4652–1.1

Mental health facilities, services, staff, and patient characteristics, 1970s-82 with trends from 1954, annual rpt, 4504–9

Mental health office and clinic visits, average charges, and total expenditures for services, by type of provider and patient characteristics, 1980, 4146–11.5

Military medical facilities of DOD in US and abroad, admissions, beds, outpatient visits, and live births, by service branch, quarterly rpt, 3542–15

Navy medical facility use by active and retired military personnel, dependents, and others, by facility and type, quarterly rpt, 3802–1

Neighborhood and housing quality indicators and attitudes, and occupant characteristics, by urban-rural location and region, 1981, annual survey, 2485–7

Neighborhood and housing quality indicators and attitudes, by occupant and unit characteristics, region, and metro-nonmetro location, 1981, annual survey, 2485–2

Clinics

New Mexico health clinics staffed by Natl Health Service Corps, income by source and service, and effect of revised system for Federal payback, 1980-83, hearings, 21368–47

NIH Research Resources Div activities, accomplishments, and funding, by program, FY83, annual rpt, 4434–12

NYC health care demonstration project for reorganization of 6 facilities in Brooklyn, Federal and State govt funding by facility, 1979-82, article, 4652–1.419

Pharmacists employment and sociodemographic characteristics, and reasons for not working in field, by State and overseas, as of 1979, 4147–14.28

Service industry census, 1982: employment, establishments, receipts, and payroll, by SIC 2- to 4-digit kind of business, SMSA, county, and city, State rpt series, 2391–1

TTPI budget, vital statistics, and health services data, often by TTPI govt, FY83 and selected trends, annual rpt, 7004–6.1

VA patients in VA and non-VA medical, nursing home, and domiciliary care facilities, FY59-83, annual rpt, 9924–13.3

Veterans health care, patients, visits, costs, and operating beds, by district and individual VA and contract facility, monthly rpt, 9922–5

see also Clinical laboratory technicians

see also Hospitals

see also Laboratories

see also Medical examinations and tests

Clocks

see Instruments and measuring devices

Cloe, William W.

"Selected Occupational Fatalities Related to Oil/Gas Well Drilling and Servicing as Found in Reports of OSHA Fatality/Catastrophe Investigations", 6606–2.11

Cloos, George

"Economic Upheaval in the Midwest", 9375–1.402

Clothing and clothing industry

Business statistics, detailed data for major industries and economic indicators, *Survey of Current Business,* monthly rpt, 2702–1.19

Census of Population, 1980: detailed socioeconomic and demographic characteristics, by age, sex, race, Hispanic origin, occupation, and industry, State rpt series, 2531–4

Census of Population, 1980: labor force, by sex, detailed occupation, and region, with comparison to 1970 census, supplementary rpt, 2535–1.12

China cotton and synthetic fiber supply and use, retail clothing sales, and textile mill productivity and equipment, 1978-84, article, 1561–1.405

China economic conditions, agricultural and industrial production, trade, and domestic and foreign investment, 1980-85, 2048–106

China exports and imports by SITC 1- to 5-digit commodity, 1970s-82, annual rpt, 244–12

China exports to US of selected textile and leather goods harmful to competing US industries, and US consumption and producer shipments, 1978-83, 9882–2.401

Collective bargaining agreements expiring during year, covered workers by SIC 2-digit industry, firm, and union, with summary of key provisions, 1984, annual rpt, 6784–9

Counterfeiting of brand-name products by foreign manufacturers, effects on 6 US industries, investigation with financial and operating data, 1984 rpt, 9886–4.67

County Business Patterns: establishments, employees, and payrolls, by SIC 4-digit industry and county, 1981, annual State rpt series, 2326–8

County Business Patterns: establishments, employees, and payrolls, by SIC 4-digit industry and county, 1982, annual State rpt series, 2326–6

CPI by detailed component, for US city average, 28 SMSAs, and 4 regions by population size, monthly rpt, 6762–2

CPI components relative importance, for selected SMSAs, and US city average by region and population size, 1983, annual rpt, 6884–1

Earnings by major industry group, and personal income per capita and by source, by region and State, 1929-82, 2708–40

Employment, earnings, and hours, by selected SIC 1- to 4-digit industry, State, and for 278 major labor areas, 1939-83, annual rpt, 6744–5

Employment, earnings, and hours, by SIC 4-digit nonfarm industry, monthly 1974-Feb 1984, annual update, 6744–4

Exports and imports of US, by commodity group, world area, selected country, US coastal area and port, and mode of transport, with seasonal adjustments, monthly rpt, 2422–9

Exports and imports of US, detailed SIC-based commodities by world area, 1983, annual rpts, 2424–6

Exports and imports of US, totals and as percent of domestic production, by SIC 2- to 5-digit commodity, 1981, annual rpt, 2424–3

Exports, imports, tariffs, and industry operating data for textile fiber and products, TSUSA commodity rpt series, 9885–3

Exports of manufactured and agricultural commodities, manufacturing production, and export-related employment, 1960s-82, State rpt series, 2046–3

Exports of textiles, by product and country of destination, monthly rpt, 2042–26

Exports of US, detailed commodities by country of destination, monthly rpt, 2422–3

Exports of US, detailed Schedule B commodities by country of destination, 1983, annual rpt, 2424–9

Exports of US, detailed Schedule E commodities by mode of transport and world area and country of destination, 1983, annual rpts, 2424–5

Finances and operations, by SIC 2- to 4-digit industry, 1970s-83 and projected to 1988, annual rpt, 2014–4

Franchise business opportunities, by firm and kind of business, 1984 annual listing, 2044–27

Great Lakes trade, by SITC 3-digit commodity, port, vessel type, world area, and country, 1982, annual rpt, 7744–3

Index by Subjects and Names

Hosiery and footwear industry productivity, hours, and employment indexes, 1954-82, annual rpt, 6824–1.3

Import quotas and tariffs, jobs protected and cost per job for selected products, and foreign trade balance by industry div, various periods 1958-81, article, 9381–1.412

Imports and import limits for textiles under Multifiber Arrangement by product and country, with US exports and use, 1970-83, semiannual rpt, 9882–11

Imports of textiles, by country of origin, monthly rpt, 2042–27

Imports of textiles, by product and country of origin, monthly rpt, 2422–1

Imports of textiles, monthly rpt, 2042–18

Imports of textiles, total and as percents of US production and use, by commodity, 1972-82, annual rpt, 2044–14

Imports of US, detailed Schedule A commodities by country and world area of origin, and mode of transport, 1983, annual rpts, 2424–2

Imports of US, detailed Schedule A commodities by country, monthly rpt, 2422–2

Imports of US, detailed TSUSA commodities by country of origin, 1983, annual rpt, 2424–4

Income tax returns of corporations, detailed income and tax items by industry, 1981, annual rpt, 8304–4

Income tax returns of corporations with foreign tax credit, income and deductions by type, asset size, and selected industry group, 1980, article, 8302–2.415

Income tax returns of partnerships, detailed data by industry, 1981 estimates, annual article, 8302–2.404

Income tax returns of partnerships, receipts by source, deductions by type, and establishments, by selected industry, 1982, annual article, 8302–2.416

Income tax returns of sole proprietorships, detailed data by industry div and selected industry group, 1981, annual rpt, 8304–7

Income tax returns of sole proprietorships, receipts, deductions by type, payroll, and net income, by major industry, 1982, annual article, 8302–2.413

Injuries and deaths from use of selected consumer products and related activity, by victim age and sex, 1982, annual rpt, 9164–7

Injuries and deaths from use of selected consumer products, by victim age and medical treatment status, 1982, annual rpt, 9164–6

Input-output structure of US economy, detailed interindustry transactions for 85 industries, and components of final demand, 1977, article, 2702–1.421

Input-output structure of US economy, detailed interindustry transactions for 537 industries, and components of final demand, 1977 benchmark data, 2708–17

Manufacturing census, 1982: financial and operating data, by SIC 2- to 4-digit industry, State, SMSA, and county, preliminary census div rpt series, 2491–3

Manufacturing census, 1982: financial and operating data, for SIC 4-digit industries by product, preliminary rpt series, 2491–1

Index by Subjects and Names

Minority group and women employment, by occupational group and SIC 2- to 3-digit industry, 1981, annual rpt, 9244–1.1

Occupational injury and illness rates, by SIC 2- to 4-digit industry, 1982, annual rpt, 6844–1

OECD trade, total and for 4 major countries, and US trade by country, by commodity, 1972-82, annual world region rpt series, 244–13

Personal consumption expenditures for clothing and shoes, 1960-83, and percent price change, Dec 1982-Aug 1983, article, 1702–1.403

Personal consumption expenditures, natl income and product account, *Survey of Current Business,* monthly rpt, monthly and annual tables, 2702–1.23

Producer prices and indexes, by stage of processing and detailed commodity, monthly rpt, 6762–6

Producer prices and indexes, by stage of processing and detailed commodity, monthly 1983, annual supplement, 6764–2

Production, shipments, trade, and consumption for apparel industry, by product, periodic Current Industrial Rpt series, 2506–6

Retail clothing business labor productivity, by kind of business, 1967-83, article, 6722–1.463

Retail trade census, 1982: employment, establishments, sales, and payroll, by SIC 2- to 4-digit kind of business, SMSA, and retail district, State rpt series, 2401–1

Retail trade census, 1982: employment, establishments, sales, and payroll, by SIC 2- to 4-digit kind of business, SMSA, county, and city, State rpt series, 2397–1

Retail trade census, 1982: employment, establishments, sales, and payroll, by State, preliminary rpt, 2395–1.16, 2395–1.17

Retail trade productivity, hours, and employment indexes, 1967-82, annual rpt, 6824–1.4

Retail trade sales and inventories, by kind of business, region, census div, and selected State, SMSA, and city, and seasonal adjustments, monthly rpt, 2413–3

Retail trade sales, inventories, purchases, gross margin, and accounts receivable, by SIC 2- to 4-digit kind of business and type of ownership, 1983, annual rpt, 2413–5

Scientists, engineers, and technicians employed in private industry, by occupation and industry group, 1980-81, biennial rpt, 9627–23

Scientists, engineers, and technicians employment in transportation, utilities, and retail and wholesale trade, by field of science and industry, 1982, 9628–72

South Carolina economic indicators, including unemployment rate by county, and textile manufacturing employment, quarterly 1970-83 with estimated unemployment for 1984, article, 9371–1.411

Technological change, impact on productivity and employment in 4 industries, 1960-90, 6828–23

Thefts, and total value of property stolen and recovered, by property type, 1983, annual rpt, 6224–2.1

Virgin Islands economic censuses, 1982: employment, establishments, payroll, and receipts, by SIC 1- to 4-digit industry, island, and city, 2593–1

Wages and benefits of dress industry production and related workers, by occupation, size of establishment, and union status, in 11 market areas, Aug 1982 survey, 6787–6.200

Waterborne commerce of US (domestic and foreign), freight by commodity, traffic, and passengers, by port and waterway, 1982, annual rpt, 3754–3

Wholesale trade census, 1982: employment, establishments, sales by commodity, and payroll, by SIC 4-digit kind of business and State, preliminary rpt series, 2403–1

Wholesale trade sales, inventories, purchases, and gross margins, by SIC 2- to 3-digit kind of business and type of ownership, 1983, annual rpt, 2413–13

see also Shoe industry

see also under By Industry in the "Index by Categories"

Clover

see Seeds

Coakley, George J.

"Mineral Industries of Africa", 5606–1.11

Coal and coal mining

Acid rain causes and effects, air pollutant emissions by source, and control costs, by region and State, selected years 1977-83 and projected to 2000, 26358–104

Acid rain causes and effects, air pollutant emissions by source in US and selected countries, and control costs, 1970s-83 and projected to 2000, 21368–52

Agriculture census, 1982: farms, farmland, production, finances, and operator characteristics, by county, final State rpt series, 2331–1

Air pollutant emission factors, by detailed source, 3rd edition, 1983-84 supplements, 9198–13

Air pollutant sulfur dioxide emissions of coal-fired power plants in eastern US, effect of alternative geographic area limits on power and coal industries, 1983 rpt, 3408–32

Air pollutant sulfur dioxide emissions reduction proposal, effects on polluting industries and coal production by region and State, projected to 2010, 9188–97

Air pollution abatement equipment shipments by industry, exports, and new and backlog orders, by product, 1983, annual Current Industrial Rpt, 2506–12.5

Air pollution levels for 5 pollutants, by detailed source, State, and Air Quality Control Region, 1981, annual rpt, 9194–7

Alaska electric power capacity and generation by fuel type, and marketing, by utility, type of ownership, and location, 1983, annual rpt, 3214–2

Alaska minerals resources, production, claims on wildlife refuges, oil and gas leases, and exploratory wells, with maps and bibl, 1983, annual rpt, 5664–11

Budget of US, effects of Reagan Admin policy changes, by detailed program, FY85, annual rpt, 104–21

Building materials manufacture, energy use and cost by source and industry, 1970s-82, article, 2012–1.401

Coal and coal mining

Buildings (nonresidential) energy use, expenditures, and conservation, by building characteristics, EIA survey series, 3166–8

Business statistics, detailed data for major industries and economic indicators, *Survey of Current Business,* monthly rpt, 2702–1.15

Carbon dioxide atmospheric levels, climatic effects and impacts of fossil and synthetic fuels use, deforestation, and land use patterns, research rpt series, 3406–3

Carbon dioxide emissions, climatic effects, and control costs, projected under alternative emissions controls and energy use restrictions to 2100 with trends 1970s-80, reprint, 9188–88

Carbon dioxide emissions from fossil fuel combustion by fuel type, worldwide estimates based on total and non-oxidized fossil fuel production, 1950-81, 3008–94

Census of Population, 1980: detailed socioeconomic and demographic characteristics, by age, sex, race, Hispanic origin, occupation, and industry, State rpt series, 2531–4

China economic conditions, agricultural and industrial production, trade, and domestic and foreign investment, 1980-85, 2048–106

Collective bargaining agreements expiring during year, covered workers by SIC 2-digit industry, firm, and union, with summary of key provisions, 1984, annual rpt, 6784–9

Communist, OECD, and selected other countries energy reserves, production, and consumption, and oil trade and revenue, 1960s-83, annual rpt, 244–5.5

Consumption, by fuel type, economic sector, and end use, 1983 and 2000, 2006–2.5

Consumption, by fuel type, economic sector, census div, and State, 1960-82, State Energy Data System annual rpt, 3164–39

Consumption of energy, by type of air pollutant source and fuel, and State, 1981, annual rpt, 9194–14

Consumption per capita, and by economic sector, State, and major energy resource, 1960-82, State Energy Data System annual supplement, 3164–55

Consumption, prices, and conservation and efficiency measures, by fuel type, end-use sector, selected industry, and region, 1960-83, annual rpt, 3164–73

County Business Patterns: establishments, employees, and payrolls, by SIC 4-digit industry and county, 1981, annual State rpt series, 2326–8

County Business Patterns: establishments, employees, and payrolls, by SIC 4-digit industry and county, 1982, annual State rpt series, 2326–6

Defense Fuel Supply Center procurement, prices, stocks, transport, and other activities and finances, FY83, annual rpt, 3904–8

DOD electric power plants and major fuel-burning facilities conversion from oil and gas, fuel use data, 1983, annual rpt, 3104–9

DOE in-house energy use, conservation investments, and savings, by type of use and fuel and field office, FY83, annual rpt, 3024–3

Coal and coal mining

Earnings by major industry group, and personal income per capita and by source, by region and State, 1929-82, 2708-40

Electric power plant (coal-fired) capacity addition estimation to forecast coal demand, methodology and input data, series, 3166-11

Electric power plant (coal-fired) capacity, coal demand, and coal supply by mode of transport and region of origin, by State, for units planned 1983-92, 3088-18

Electric power plant (steam) fuel deliveries, costs, and quality, by fuel type, State, and utility, 1983, annual rpt, 3164-42

Electric power plant capacity, production, retail sales, and fuel stocks, use, and costs, by State, 1979-83, annual rpt, 3164-11

Electric power plant capital and operating detailed costs, capacity, and fuel use, by plant, plant type, utility, and State, 1982, annual rpt, 3164-9

Electric power plants and industrial facilities prohibited from oil and gas primary use, and exemption petitions, by facility, with summary fuel use, 1983, annual rpt, 3104-8

Electric power plants, by capacity, fuel used, unit type, region, State, and county, for plants added and retired, 1983 and planned through 1993, annual rpt, 3164-36

Electric utility fuel cost, quality, use, receipts, and stocks, and power plant production, by energy source, State and utility, quarterly rpt, 3162-39

Electric utility production, fuel consumption, stocks, and costs by fuel type, and sales, by State, monthly rpt, 3162-35

Employment by detailed occupation, for 29 SIC 2-digit nonmanufacturing industries, 1981 BLS survey, 6748-60

Employment, earnings, and hours, by selected SIC 1- to 4-digit industry, State, and for 278 major labor areas, 1939-83, annual rpt, 6744-5

Employment, earnings, and hours, by SIC 4-digit nonfarm industry, monthly 1974-Feb 1984, annual update, 6744-4

Environmental quality and protection programs, costs, and Fed Govt enforcement, 1983, detailed annual rpt, 484-1

Excise tax on coal production and other receipts of black lung trust fund, fund disbursements, and benefit claims and benefits by State, 1982, annual rpt, 6504-3

Fed Govt and Indian lands oil, gas, coal, and other mineral production and revenues, by State, 1983 with trends from 1920, annual rpt, 5734-2

Fed Govt coal lands dev plans, environmental and socioeconomic impacts in 12 regions under Fed Coal Mgmt Program, projections to 2000, final statement series, 5726-4

Fed Govt coal lease land dev in Western US, surface and mineral rights by State, and environmental protection adequacy, various periods 1978-85, 26358-103

Fed Govt coal leases, acreage, production, and prices, by State, and legal and mgmt issues, 1970s-83 with production projections to 2000, 11128-1

Fed Govt coal leases and coal supply, by owner, owner industry, and western State, various periods 1950-82 and projected to 2000, hearing, 25318-58

Fed Govt coal leasing activity, acreage, and reserves, by State, coal region, and tract, FY83, annual rpt, 5724-10

Fed Govt coal leasing competitive effects, FY83 annual rpt, 6004-12

Fed Govt coal leasing potential impact on 25 species protected under Migratory Bird Treaty Act, and bird population characteristics, 1900s-82, 5508-88

Fed Govt coal purchases, quality control analyses by mine and location, FY82-83, annual rpt, 3004-15

Fed Govt energy programs proposed budget appropriations, by office or dept and function, FY84-85, annual rpt, 3004-14

Financial statements for manufacturing, mining, and trade corporations, by selected SIC 2- to 3-digit industry, quarterly rpt, 2502-1

Foreign and US coal reserves, production, demand indicators, and trade, by country, selected years 1973-82 and alternative trade projections to 1995, annual rpt, 3164-77

Foreign and US energy production, trade, and reserves, and oil and refined products supply and prices, by country, 1973-83, annual rpt, 3164-50

Foreign minerals production, reserves, and industry role in domestic economy and world supply, country and world region rpt series, 5606-1

Freight shipments by rail, rates and shares of freight and railroad finances and operations, by commodity and railroad, 1970s-82, hearings, 25268-80

Housing census, 1980: inventory, occupancy, and unit characteristics, changes from 1973 by region and inside-outside SMSAs and central cities, series, 2473-3

Housing energy use, costs, expenditures, and conservation, and household and housing characteristics, survey series, 3166-7

Housing occupancy and unit and household characteristics, by region and metro-nonmetro residence, 1983, biennial survey, 2485-1

Housing unit heating fuel, by type, occupant race, Hispanic origin, urban-rural location, and region, 1981, annual survey, 2485-7

Income tax returns of corporations, detailed income and tax items by industry, 1981, annual rpt, 8304-4

Income tax returns of corporations with foreign tax credit, income and deductions by type, asset size, and selected industry group, 1980, article, 8302-2.415

Income tax returns of foreign subsidiaries of US corporations, income and tax data, by industry and asset size, 1980, article, 8302-2.410

Income tax returns of sole proprietorships, detailed data by industry div and selected industry group, 1981, annual rpt, 8304-7

Income tax returns of sole proprietorships, receipts, deductions by type, payroll, and net income, by major industry, 1982, annual article, 8302-2.413

Industrial electric power cogeneration in 5 industries, and fuel use and utility supply/demand effects, by region, 1983-93, 3008-92

Index by Subjects and Names

Industrial energy demand, forecasting model description, detailed technology specifications, and energy use, for 27 SIC 2- to 4-digit industries, 1970s-80 and projected to 2000, 3308-66

Input-output structure of US economy, detailed interindustry transactions for 85 industries, and components of final demand, 1977, article, 2702-1.421

Input-output structure of US economy, detailed interindustry transactions for 537 industries, and components of final demand, 1977 benchmark data, 2708-17

Interior Dept programs, activities, and funding, various periods 1967-84, last issue of annual rpt, 5304-13

Manufacturing census, 1982: financial and operating data, by SIC 2- to 4-digit industry, State, SMSA, and county, preliminary census div rpt series, 2491-3

Manufacturing census, 1982: financial and operating data, for SIC 4-digit industries by product, preliminary rpt, 2491-1.205

Manufacturing energy efficiency progress, and energy use by type, by SIC 2-digit industry, 1982, annual rpt, 3304-8

Mineral industries census, 1982: financial and operating data, by SIC 2- to 4-digit industry, preliminary summary rpt, 2511-2.1

Mineral industries census, 1982: financial and operating data, including materials consumed, by SIC 4-digit industry and State, preliminary rpt series, 2511-1

Mineral Industry Surveys, explosives and blasting agents consumption by type, industry, and State, 1983, annual rpt, 5614-22

Minerals Yearbook, 1982, Vol 3 preprints: foreign country reviews of production, trade, and policies, by commodity, annual rpt series, 5604-17

Minerals Yearbook, 1983, Vol 3 preprints: foreign country reviews of production, trade, and policies, by commodity, annual rpt series, 5604-23

Minority group and women employment, by occupational group and SIC 2- to 3-digit industry, 1981, annual rpt, 9244-1.1

Montana and North Dakota coal production, impact of mining on agricultural land availability and on farm income and production costs, by mining tract, 1982 rpt, 1588-79

Natl Energy Policy Plan, DOE implementation and effect on energy supply/demand, 1983-84, annual rpt, 3024-4

Natl Energy Policy Plan, energy supply, demand, and prices, by fuel and consuming sector, projected 1985-2010, biennial rpt, 3004-13

Pollution abatement capital and operating costs, by SIC 2- to 4-digit industry, State, and SMSA, 1982, annual Current Industrial Rpt, 2506-3.6

Pollution abatement capital and operating costs under Clean Air and Water Acts, for govts and selected industries, various periods 1970-2000, annual rpt, 9184-11

Producers finances and operations, by energy type for US firms domestic and foreign operations, 1974-82, annual rpt, 3164-44

Index by Subjects and Names

Production and mines by county, prices, productivity, miners, reserves, and stocks, by mining method and State, 1982-83, annual rpt, 3164–25

Production and sales of synthetic organic chemicals by product, and listing of manufacturers, 1983, annual rpt, 9884–3

Production and stocks of coal, and electric utility generation, capacity, and coal use, alternative estimates 1977-82, annual rpt, 3164–63

Production and stocks of coal by district, and shipments by district of origin, State of destination, consuming sector, and mode of transport, quarterly rpt, 3162–8

Production by State and region, trade, consumption, and stocks, weekly rpt, 3162–1

Production, dev, and distribution firms revenues and income, quarterly rpt, 3162–38

Production, employment, exports, and finances of coal mines, by district, 1982, 3008–97

Production, reserves, and prices, by fuel type, and selected indicators of energy use, by State, 1982-83 with selected comparisons from 1971, annual rpt, 3164–60

Production, trade, supply, use, conservation, and DOE activities, by energy type, FY83, annual rpt, 3024–2

Production, trade, tariffs, and industry operating data for coal, foreign and US, 1979-83, TSUSA commodity rpt, 9885–5.15

Productivity, hours, and employment indexes for selected SIC 3- and 4-digit industries, 1954-82, annual rpt, 6824–1.2

R&D industry funding and employment of scientists and engineers, by industry group, firm size, and funding source, 1956-82, annual rpt, 9627–21

Research publications on energy of DOE and other sources, monthly listing, 3002–2

Scientists and engineers employed in energy-related fields, supply/demand and effects of R&D funding, by energy type, employer type, field, and age, 1962-91, annual rpt, 3004–19

Scientists, engineers, and technicians employed in private industry, by occupation and industry group, 1980-81, biennial rpt, 9627–23

Ships bunker fuels, oil and coal laden in US on vessels engaged in foreign trade, by port, monthly rpt, 2422–5

Southeastern US water supply and quality, with background socioeconomic data, for 8 States, 1960s-2020 with trends from 1930, 9208–119

Supply/demand and price forecasts, by fuel type, quarterly rpt, 3162–34

Supply/demand and prices, by energy resource and major producing and consuming country and sector, detailed data, monthly rpt, 3162–24

Supply/demand and prices, by energy source and end-use sector and for 7 electric utilities, 1981-2000 with trends from 1960s, 3008–93

Supply/demand and prices, by fuel type and consuming sector with foreign comparisons, 1949-83, annual rpt, 3164–74

Supply/demand and prices, by fuel type, sector, and end use, detailed trends and projections 1973-95, annual rpt, 3164–75

Supply/demand and prices, by fuel type, sector, and end use, with foreign comparisons, 1960-83 and projected to 1995, annual summary rpt, 3164–76

Supply/demand for coal, projected 1983-95 with summary trends from 1865, annual rpt, 3164–68

Supply/demand, prices, trade, and stocks of coal, coke, and breeze, by end-use sector and State, quarterly rpt, 3162–37

Surface mining reclamation costs and Interior Dept regulatory enforcement activities, impacts on industry in 5 States and 3 regions, various periods 1978-82, 6068–177

Transport of coal, environmental impacts by type and mode of transport, methodology for assessing alternative systems, 1983 rpt, 3408–28

Transportation and related energy use, for urban areas, late 1970s-82 and projected under lower auto emission standards to 1995, 3408–31

Transportation finances, operations, vehicles, equipment, accidents, and energy use and transport, by mode of transport, 1955-84, annual rpt, 7304–2

Underground economy, household expenditures and participation by type of goods or service and sociodemographic characteristics, with methodology and bibl, 1981 survey, 8308–27

Wages and benefits of bituminous coal mining production and related workers, by occupation, size of mine, and union status, in 6 States and for Mountain States, July 1982 survey, 6787–6.198

Water pollution from nonpoint sources, source land uses and acreage, and control program funding, by State or region, various periods 1974-FY84, 9208–123

Water supply and quality, and effect of coal mining operations, for selected river basins in Eastern and Interior coal provinces, series, 5666–15

Water supply and quality, and effect of coal mining operations, for selected river basins in Western coal provinces, series, 5666–19

Waterborne commerce of US (domestic and foreign), freight by commodity, traffic, and passengers, by port and waterway, 1982, annual rpt, 3754–3

Western US Fed Govt lands by agency and mining restriction status, and energy resources on potential wilderness areas and other lands, 1970s-81 and projected to 1990, 3308–68

Wholesale trade census, 1982: employment, establishments, sales by commodity, and payroll, by SIC 4-digit kind of business and State, preliminary rpt, 2403–1.7

see also Black lung

see also Coal exports and imports

see also Coal prices

see also Coal reserves

see also Coal stocks

see also Mine accidents and safety

see also under By Commodity in the "Index by Categories"

see also under By Industry in the "Index by Categories"

Coal exports and imports

Coal conservation

see Energy conservation

Coal consumption

see Coal and coal mining

Coal exports and imports

Business statistics, detailed data for major industries and economic indicators, *Survey of Current Business,* monthly rpt, 2702–1.15

China economic conditions, agricultural and industrial production, trade, and domestic and foreign investment, 1980-85, 2048–106

China exports and imports by SITC 1- to 5-digit commodity, 1970s-82, annual rpt, 244–12

Cuba economic conditions, agricultural and industrial production and distribution, trade, and intl economic relations, 1970-82 and trends from 1957, 248–40

Electric utility coal imports, by country of origin and utility, 1979-83, annual rpt, 3164–42

Exports and imports of coal, by country of origin and destination, 1982, annual rpt, 3164–50.6

Exports and imports of US, detailed SIC-based commodities by world area, 1983, annual rpts, 2424–6

Exports and imports of US, totals and as percent of domestic production, by SIC 2- to 5-digit commodity, 1981, annual rpt, 2424–3

Exports, imports, and average price, by country of destination and origin, weekly rpt, monthly data, 3162–1.2

Exports, imports, tariffs, and industry operating data for coal, foreign and US, 1979-83, TSUSA commodity rpt, 9885–5.15

Exports of coal, and export-related employment, by industry, 1981-82, 3008–97

Exports of coal to Canada by mode of transport, and overseas, by district of origin, quarterly rpt, 3162–8

Exports of manufactured and agricultural commodities, manufacturing production, and export-related employment, 1960s-82, State rpt series, 2046–3

Exports of US, detailed commodities by country of destination, monthly rpt, 2422–3

Exports of US, detailed Schedule B commodities by country of destination, 1983, annual rpt, 2424–9

Exports of US, detailed Schedule E commodities by mode of transport and world area and country of destination, 1983, annual rpts, 2424–5

Foreign and US coal reserves, production, demand indicators, and trade, by country, selected years 1973-82 and alternative trade projections to 1995, annual rpt, 3164–77

Great Lakes trade, by SITC 3-digit commodity, port, vessel type, world area, and country, 1982, annual rpt, 7744–3

Imports of US, detailed Schedule A commodities by country and world area of origin, and mode of transport, 1983, annual rpts, 2424–2

Imports of US, detailed Schedule A commodities by country, monthly rpt, 2422–2

Coal exports and imports

Imports of US, detailed TSUSA commodities by country of origin, 1983, annual rpt, 2424–4

Minerals Yearbook, 1982, Vol 3 preprints: foreign country reviews of production, trade, and policies, by commodity, annual rpt series, 5604–17

Minerals Yearbook, 1983, Vol 3 preprints: foreign country reviews of production, trade, and policies, by commodity, annual rpt series, 5604–23

Natl Energy Policy Plan, energy supply, demand, and prices, by fuel and consuming sector, projected 1985-2010, biennial rpt, 3004–13

OECD trade, total and for 4 major countries, and US trade by country, by commodity, 1972-82, annual world region rpt series, 244–13

Port impact on local employment through transport of 5 commodities, by industry for 3 eastern ports, and demand for US coal by country, 1981, 7308 182

Supply/demand and price forecasts, by fuel type, quarterly rpt, 3162–34

Supply/demand and prices, by energy resource and major producing and consuming country and sector, detailed data, monthly rpt, 3162–24

Supply/demand and prices, by fuel type and consuming sector with foreign comparisons, 1949-83, annual rpt, 3164–74

Supply/demand and prices, by fuel type, sector, and end use, detailed trends and projections 1973-95, annual rpt, 3164–75

Supply/demand and prices, by fuel type, sector, and end use, with foreign comparisons, 1960-83 and projected to 1995, annual summary rpt, 3164–76

Supply/demand, prices, trade, and stocks of coal, coke, and breeze, by end-use sector and State, quarterly rpt, 3162–37

Waterborne commerce of US (domestic and foreign), freight by commodity, traffic, and passengers, by port and waterway, 1982, annual rpt, 3754–3

Coal prices

Acid rain causes and effects, air pollutant emissions by source in US and selected countries, and control costs, 1970s-83 and projected to 2000, 21368–52

Business statistics, detailed data for major industries and economic indicators, *Survey of Current Business,* monthly rpt, 2702–1.15

Eastern US coal-fired power plant sulfur dioxide emissions, effect of alternative geographic area limits on power and coal industries, 1983 rpt, 3408–32

Electric power plant (steam) fuel deliveries, costs, and quality, by fuel type, State, and utility, 1983, annual rpt, 3164–42

Electric power plant capacity, production, retail sales, and fuel stocks, use, and costs, by State, 1979-83, annual rpt, 3164–11

Electric power plants (steam), prices paid for fossil fuels, July 1972 and 1982-83, annual rpt, 3084–9

Electric utilities coal receipts, consumption, stocks, and delivered price, by State, and import and export prices, weekly rpt, monthly data, 3162–1.2

Electric utility fuel cost, quality, use, receipts, and stocks, and power plant production, by energy source, State and utility, quarterly rpt, 3162–39

Electric utility production, fuel consumption, stocks, and costs by fuel type, and sales, by State, monthly rpt, 3162–35

Exports of coal by US, and price and demand elasticity, by country, 1981, 7308–182

Fed Govt coal leases, acreage, production, and prices, by State, and legal and mgmt issues, 1970s-83 with production projections to 2000, 11128–1

Natl Energy Policy Plan, energy supply, demand, and prices, by fuel and consuming sector, projected 1985-2010, biennial rpt, 3004–13

OECD energy prices and taxes by energy source and end-use sector, for US and 9 countries, quarterly 1979-83, annual rpt, 3164–71

Pacific Northwest electricity consumption and prices by end-use sector, and economic and demographic data, 1960s-83 and projected to 2005, annual rpt, 3224–2

Pennsylvania electric utility delivered coal prices under sulfur dioxide emissions reduction proposal, projected 1995 and 2000, 9188–97

Prices and expenditures for fuels, by consuming sector, State, and fuel type, 1970-81, annual rpt, 3164–64

Prices and supply/demand, by energy source and end-use sector and for 7 electric utilities, 1981-2000 with trends from 1960s, 3008–93

Prices and supply/demand, by fuel and consuming sector with foreign comparisons, 1949-83, annual rpt, 3164–74

Prices and supply/demand, by fuel, sector, and end use, detailed trends and projections 1973-95, annual rpt, 3164–75

Prices and supply/demand, by fuel, sector, and end use, with foreign comparisons, 1960-83 and projected to 1995, annual summary rpt, 3164–76

Prices and supply/demand, forecast by fuel, quarterly rpt, 3162–34

Prices, productivity, miners, reserves, stocks, and production and mines by county, by mining method and State, 1982-83, annual rpt, 3164–25

Prices, supply/demand, trade, and stocks of coal, coke, and breeze, by end-use sector and State, quarterly rpt, 3162–37

Producer prices and indexes, by stage of processing and detailed commodity, monthly rpt, 6762–6

Producer prices and indexes, by stage of processing and detailed commodity, monthly 1983, annual supplement, 6764–2

Railroad finances, operations, and freight rates and shares, by commodity and railroad, 1970s-82, hearings, 25268–80

Coal reserves

Communist, OECD, and selected other countries energy reserves, production, and consumption, and oil trade and revenue, 1960s-83, annual rpt, 244–5.5

Eastern US coal-fired power plant sulfur dioxide emissions, effect of alternative geographic area limits on power and coal industries, 1983 rpt, 3408–32

Fed Govt coal lands dev plans, environmental and socioeconomic impacts in 12 regions under Fed Coal Mgmt Program, projections to 2000, final statement series, 5726–4

Fed Govt coal leases, acreage, production, and prices, by State, and legal and mgmt issues, 1970s-83 with production projections to 2000, 11128–1

Fed Govt coal leases and coal supply, by owner, owner industry, and western State, various periods 1950-82 and projected to 2000, hearing, 25318–58

Fed Govt coal leasing activity, acreage, and reserves, by State, coal region, and tract, FY83, annual rpt, 5724–10

Foreign and US coal reserves, production, demand indicators, and trade, by country, selected years 1973-82 and alternative trade projections to 1995, annual rpt, 3164–77

Foreign and US energy reserves, by type of fuel and country, as of Jan 1984, annual rpt, 3164–50.7

Minerals Yearbook, 1982, Vol 3 preprints: foreign country reviews of production, trade, and policies, by commodity, annual rpt series, 5604–17

Minerals Yearbook, 1983, Vol 3 preprints: foreign country reviews of production, trade, and policies, by commodity, annual rpt series, 5604–23

Montana and North Dakota coal production, impact of mining on agricultural land availability and on farm income and production costs, by mining tract, 1982 rpt, 1588–79

Reserves, by coal type, region, and State, Jan 1982, annual rpt, 3164–68

Reserves, production, prices, and use, by energy type, and selected indicators of energy use, by State, 1982-83 with selected comparisons from 1971, annual rpt, 3164–60

Reserves, stocks, prices, productivity, miners, and production and mines by county, by mining method and State, 1982-83, annual rpt, 3164–25

Sulfur dioxide content of recoverable coal reserves, by region, 1983 rpt, 3408–27

Supply/demand and prices, by fuel type and consuming sector with foreign comparisons, 1949-83, annual rpt, 3164–74

Supply/demand and prices, by fuel type, sector, and end use, with foreign comparisons, 1960-83 and projected to 1995, annual summary rpt, 3164–76

Western US Fed Govt lands by agency and mining restriction status, and energy resources on potential wilderness areas and other lands, 1970s-81 and projected to 1990, 3308–68

Coal stocks

Business statistics, detailed data for major industries and economic indicators, *Survey of Current Business,* monthly rpt, 2702–1.15

Electric power plant capacity, production, retail sales, and fuel stocks, use, and costs, by State, 1979-83, annual rpt, 3164–11

Electric utilities coal receipts, consumption, stocks, and delivered price, by State, weekly rpt, monthly data, 3162–1.2

Electric utilities, coke plants, and other industry stocks of coal, monthly rpt, 3162–24.6

Index by Subjects and Names

Electric utilities, coke plants, other industrial, producer, and distributor coal stocks, and total coke and breeze stocks, quarterly rpt, 3162–37

Electric utility fuel cost, quality, use, receipts, and stocks, and power plant production, by energy source, State and utility, quarterly rpt, 3162–39

Electric utility production, fuel consumption, stocks, and costs by fuel type, and sales, by State, monthly rpt, 3162–35

Stocks and production of coal, and electric utility generation, capacity, and coal use, alternative estimates 1977-82, annual rpt, 3164–63

Stocks of coal, by district, quarterly rpt, 3162–8

Stocks, prices, productivity, miners, reserves, and production and mines by county, by mining method and State, 1982-83, annual rpt, 3164–25

Supply/demand and price forecasts, by fuel type, quarterly rpt, 3162–34

Supply/demand and prices, by energy resource and major producing and consuming country and sector, detailed data, monthly rpt, 3162–24

Supply/demand and prices, by fuel type and consuming sector with foreign comparisons, 1949-83, annual rpt, 3164–74

Supply/demand and prices, by fuel type, sector, and end use, detailed trends and projections 1973-95, annual rpt, 3164–75

Supply/demand and prices, by fuel type, sector, and end use, with foreign comparisons, 1960-83 and projected to 1995, annual summary rpt, 3164–76

Coalition of Northeastern Governors

"Low-Level Radioactive Waste in the Northeast: Disposal Volume Projections", 25528–93

Coast and Geodetic Survey

see National Ocean Service

Coast Guard

Boat registrations, use, and accident deaths, injuries, and property damage, by detailed cause and State, 1983, annual rpt, 7404–1

Bridges over navigable waters, with type of bridge and use, owner, dimensions, and location, 1984 regional listing series, 7406–5

Budget of US, effects of Reagan Admin policy changes, by detailed program, FY85, annual rpt, 104–21

Cost control proposals for Fed Govt programs and mgmt, 3-year savings by function and agency, and financial and operating data, 1960s-81, 16908–1.11, 16908–1.28, 16908–1.31

Courts-martial cases and actions of DOT General Counsel, FY83, annual rpt, 3504–3

Drug Enforcement Organized Crime Task Forces, funding and staff by agency, region, and city, as of FY83, GAO rpt, 26119–52

Drug enforcement regional task force program investigation activities, funding, and personnel, with nationwide drug abuse data, 1983 annual rpt, 6004–17

Employment at DOT, by subagency, State, and selected personnel characteristics, FY83, annual rpt, 7304–18

Financial statement and safety activities of USCG, FY81, annual rpt, 7304–1

Fraud and abuse in DOT programs, audits and investigations, 1st half FY84, semiannual rpt, 7302–4

Medical facilities of Navy, use by active and retired military personnel, dependents, and others by facility and type, quarterly rpt, 3802–1

Oceanographic research cruise schedules and ship characteristics, by academic instn or Federal agency, 1984, annual rpt, 3804–6

Safety programs, and accidents, injuries, deaths, hazards, and property damage, by mode of transport, 1983, annual rpt, 7304–19

Search and rescue activities of USCG, by district, station, and rescue vessel, FY83 and projected FY88, annual rpt, 7404–2

User fees to recover costs of 7 federally subsidized public service programs, by type of fee, user, and service, FY84-88, 26306–6.68

see also Coast Guard Reserve

see also Service academies

Coast Guard Reserve

Manpower and equipment strengths, readiness, and funding, by reserve component, FY83, annual rpt, 3544–27

Manpower strengths and characteristics, by reserve component, quarterly rpt, 3542–4

Coastal zone

Army Corps of Engineers activities and projects, FY83 and trends from 1800s, annual rpt, 3754–1

Birds (marine) on southeastern US coast, distribution, abundance, and oil spill effects, by species and State, 1820s-1982, 5508–72

Cargo (containerized) carried over principal trade routes, by flag of vessel, port, and US coastal district, 1982, annual rpt, 7704–8

Coast Guard search and rescue activities, by district, station, and rescue vessel, FY83 and projected FY88, annual rpt, 7404–2

Environmental and socioeconomic conditions, and potential impacts of oil and gas OCS leases, final statement series, 5736–1

Environmental characteristics, fish, wildlife, and use, and population socioeconomic data, for individual coastal areas, series, 5506–4

Environmental characteristics, fish, wildlife, uses, and mgmt of individual coastal ecosystems, series, 5506–9

Environmental quality and protection programs, costs, and Fed Govt enforcement, 1983, detailed annual rpt, 484–1

Fish and shellfish landings, life cycles, and environmental needs, for selected species by region, with glossary and bibl, series, 5506–8

Fish catch quotas for US 200 mile zone, allocations by species and country, coastal area rpt series, 7006–5

Fish landings, employment, gear used, and seafood production, for detailed species by State, 1977, annual rpt, 2164–2

Fishery Conservation Zone of US, foreign catch by country and species, 1982-83, annual rpt, 2164–1

Cocoa and chocolate

Marine Fisheries Review, US and foreign fisheries resources, conservation, operations, and research, quarterly rpt articles, 2162–1

Marine Mammal Protection Act admin and populations, strandings, and catch permits by type and applicant, by species and location, Apr 1983-Mar 1984, annual rpt, 2164–11

Ocean dumping and pollution investigations and activities of NOAA, research and monitoring studies funded, and bibl, FY83, annual rpt, 2144–9

Ocean surface temperature by ocean and for US coastal areas, and Bering Sea ice conditions, monthly rpt, 2182–5

Pollution-caused fish kills, by State, location, and pollution source, monthly 1978-80, annual rpt, 9204–3

Tidal current tables, daily time and velocity by station for North America and Asia coasts, 1985, annual rpt, 2174–1

Tide height and time daily at worldwide coastal points, 1985 predictions, annual rpt series, 2174–2

Weather broadcasts for US ships, by major ocean area, as of Jan 1984, biennial rpt, 2184–3

see also Continental shelf

see also Estuaries

see also New York Bight

see also Offshore oil and gas

see also Oil spills

see also Seashores

see also Territorial waters

see also Wetlands

Cobalt

see Metals and metal industries

Cocaine

see Drug abuse and treatment

see Drug and narcotics traffic

Cocoa and chocolate

Agricultural Statistics, 1983, annual rpt, 1004–1

Business statistics, detailed data for major industries and economic indicators, *Survey of Current Business,* monthly rpt, 2702–1.11

Consumption, supply, trade, prices, expenditures, and indexes, by food commodity, 1963-83, annual rpt, 1544–4

County Business Patterns: establishments, employees, and payrolls, by SIC 4-digit industry and county, 1982, annual State rpt series, 2326–6

Exports and imports of US, by agricultural commodity and country, bimonthly rpt with articles, 1522–1

Exports and imports of US, by detailed agricultural commodity and country, FY83 and CY83, semiannual rpts, 1522–4

Exports and imports of US, by detailed agricultural commodity for 8 major commodity groups, monthly rpt, 1922–8

Exports and imports of US, detailed SIC-based commodities by world area, 1983, annual rpts, 2424–6

Exports and imports of US, totals and as percent of domestic production, by SIC 2- to 5-digit commodity, 1981, annual rpt, 2424–3

Exports, imports, tariffs, and industry operating data for cocoa, chocolate, and confectionery products, 1979-83, TSUSA commodity rpt, 9885–1.67

Cocoa and chocolate

Exports of US, detailed commodities by country of destination, monthly rpt, 2422–3

Exports of US, detailed Schedule B commodities by country of destination, 1983, annual rpt, 2424–9

Exports of US, detailed Schedule E commodities by mode of transport and world area and country of destination, 1983, annual rpts, 2424–5

Foreign agricultural production, prices, and trade, by country, 1983 and outlook for 1984/85, annual world region rpt series, 1524–4

Foreign and US agricultural production, trade, and climatic devs, weekly press release, 1922–4

Foreign and US cocoa and cocoa products production, prices, and trade, FAS semiannual circular, 1925–9

Futures trading by commodity and exchange, and Commodity Futures Trading Commission activities, funding, and employment, FY83, annual rpt, 11924–2

Futures trading in selected commodities, foreign currencies, Treasury securities, and stock indexes, NYC, Chicago, and other markets activity, monthly rpt, 11922–5

Futures trading in selected commodities, Treasury securities, and stock indexes, NYC market activity, monthly rpt, 11922–2

Great Lakes trade, by SITC 3-digit commodity, port, vessel type, world area, and country, 1982, annual rpt, 7744–3

Imports of dairy products subject to quota and annual quotas, by commodity and country of origin, FAS monthly circular, 1925–31

Imports of US, detailed Schedule A commodities by country and world area of origin, and mode of transport, 1983, annual rpts, 2424–2

Imports of US, detailed Schedule A commodities by country, monthly rpt, 2422–2

Imports of US, detailed TSUSA commodities by country of origin, 1983, annual rpt, 2424–4

Input-output structure of US economy, detailed interindustry transactions for 537 industries, and components of final demand, 1977 benchmark data, 2708–17

Manufacturing census, 1982: financial and operating data, by SIC 2- to 4-digit industry, State, SMSA, and county, preliminary census div rpt series, 2491–3

Manufacturing census, 1982: financial and operating data, for SIC 4-digit industries by product, preliminary rpt, 2491–1.25

OECD trade, total and for 4 major countries, and US trade by country, by commodity, 1972-82, annual world region rpt series, 244–13

Producer prices and indexes, by stage of processing and detailed commodity, monthly rpt, 6762–6

Producer prices and indexes, by stage of processing and detailed commodity, monthly 1983, annual supplement, 6764–2

Waterborne commerce of US (domestic and foreign), freight by commodity, traffic, and passengers, by port and waterway, 1982, annual rpt, 3754–3

see also Candy and confectionery products *see also* under By Commodity in the "Index by Categories"

Cocoa, Fla.

Census of Housing, 1980: occupancy and unit characteristics, by race, Hispanic origin, and city, SMSA rpt, 2473–1.238

Census of Population and Housing, 1980: detailed population and housing characteristics, by county, city, and census tract, SMSA rpt, 2551–2.238

Coconut oil

see Oils, oilseeds, and fats

Coder, John F.

"Estimates of Poverty Including the Value of Noncash Benefits: 1979-82", 2626–2.50

Coes, Donald V.

"Exchange Market Intervention in Four European Countries", 9373–3.26

Coffee

Acreage, yield, and production of field crops, by State, 1978-82 and preliminary 1983, 1641–7

Agricultural Statistics, 1983, annual rpt, 1004–1

Agriculture census, 1982: farms, farmland, production, finances, and operator characteristics, by municipio, final outlying area rpt, 2331–1.52

Air pollutant emission factors, by detailed source, 3rd edition, 1983-84 supplements, 9198–13

Births by outcome, and mother's sociodemographic, life style, and maternity characteristics, 1980, article, 4102–1.422

Business statistics, detailed data for major industries and economic indicators, *Survey of Current Business,* monthly rpt, 2702–1.11

Consumption of food and nutrient intake by individuals, by food group, source, and socioeconomic characteristics, 1977-78 natl survey, final rpt series, 1356–4

Consumption, supply, trade, prices, expenditures, and indexes, by food commodity, 1963-83, annual rpt, 1544–4

County Business Patterns: establishments, employees, and payrolls, by SIC 4-digit industry and county, 1981, annual State rpt series, 2326–8

County Business Patterns: establishments, employees, and payrolls, by SIC 4-digit industry and county, 1982, annual State rpt series, 2326–6

Cuba economic conditions, agricultural and industrial production and distribution, trade, and intl economic relations, 1970-82 and trends from 1957, 248–40

Eastern Europe agricultural production and trade by commodity, food consumption, and farm inputs, for 6 countries, 1960-80 with projections to 1991, 1528–178

Exports and imports of US, by agricultural commodity and country, bimonthly rpt with articles, 1522–1

Exports and imports of US, by detailed agricultural commodity and country, FY83 and CY83, semiannual rpts, 1522–4

Exports and imports of US, by detailed agricultural commodity for 8 major commodity groups, monthly rpt, 1922–8

Index by Subjects and Names

Exports and imports of US, detailed SIC-based commodities by world area, 1983, annual rpts, 2424–6

Exports and imports of US, totals and as percent of domestic production, by SIC 2- to 5-digit commodity, 1981, annual rpt, 2424–3

Exports of US, detailed commodities by country of destination, monthly rpt, 2422–3

Exports of US, detailed Schedule B commodities by country of destination, 1983, annual rpt, 2424–9

Exports of US, detailed Schedule E commodities by mode of transport and world area and country of destination, 1983, annual rpts, 2424–5

Farm finances, assets, liabilities, income, receipts by commodity and State, and expenses, 1980-83 and trends from 1910, annual rpt, 1544–16

Foreign agricultural production, prices, and trade, by country, 1983 and outlook for 1984/85, annual world region rpt series, 1524–4

Foreign and US agricultural production, trade, and climatic devs, weekly press release, 1922–4

Futures trading by commodity and exchange, and Commodity Futures Trading Commission activities, funding, and employment, FY83, annual rpt, 11924–2

Futures trading in selected commodities, foreign currencies, Treasury securities, and stock indexes, NYC, Chicago, and other markets activity, monthly rpt, 11922–5

Futures trading in selected commodities, Treasury securities, and stock indexes, NYC market activity, monthly rpt, 11922–2

Great Lakes trade, by SITC 3-digit commodity, port, vessel type, world area, and country, 1982, annual rpt, 7744–3

Imports of US, detailed Schedule A commodities by country and world area of origin, and mode of transport, 1983, annual rpts, 2424–2

Imports of US, detailed Schedule A commodities by country, monthly rpt, 2422–2

Imports of US, detailed TSUSA commodities by country of origin, 1983, annual rpt, 2424–4

Input-output structure of US economy, detailed interindustry transactions for 537 industries, and components of final demand, 1977 benchmark data, 2708–17

Manufacturing census, 1982: financial and operating data, by SIC 2- to 4-digit industry, State, SMSA, and county, preliminary census div rpt series, 2491–3

Manufacturing census, 1982: financial and operating data, for SIC 4-digit industries by product, preliminary rpt, 2491–1.40

Marketing cash receipts of farms, by detailed commodity and State, 1979-82, annual rpt, 1544–18

Occupational injury and illness rates, by SIC 2- to 4-digit industry, 1982, annual rpt, 6844–1

OECD trade, total and for 4 major countries, and US trade by country, by commodity, 1972-82, annual world region rpt series, 244–13

Index by Subjects and Names

Prices received by farmers and production value for detailed crops by State, 1981-83, annual rpt, 1621–2

Producer prices and indexes, by stage of processing and detailed commodity, monthly rpt, 6762–6

Producer prices and indexes, by stage of processing and detailed commodity, monthly 1983, annual supplement, 6764–2

Production, farms, acreage, and related data, by selected crop and State, monthly rpt, 1621–1

Production, trade and quotas, and consumption, by country, with US and intl prices, FAS periodic circular, 1925–5

South America and Argentina agricultural exports, and coffee exports of Colombia and Brazil to US and world, market share analysis, 1960-79, 1528–169

Waterborne commerce of US (domestic and foreign), freight by commodity, traffic, and passengers, by port and waterway, 1982, annual rpt, 3754–3

see also under By Commodity in the "Index by Categories"

Coffey, Rosanna M.

"Patients in Public General Hospitals", 4144–11.1

Cogeneration of heat and electricity

Electric power plants, by capacity, fuel used, unit type, region, State, and county, for plants added and retired, 1983 and planned through 1993, annual rpt, 3164–36

Energy demand in industry, forecasting model description, detailed technology specifications, and energy use, for 27 SIC 2- to 4-digit industries, 1970s-80 and projected to 2000, 3308–66

Energy supply/demand and prices, by energy source and end-use sector and for 7 electric utilities, 1981-2000 with trends from 1960s, 3008–93

Industrial electric power cogeneration in 5 industries, and fuel use and utility supply/demand effects, by region, 1983-93, 3008–92

Industrial electric power demand model estimates, economic indicators, and supporting data for 5 industries, 1960s-80 with projections to 2000, 3008–87

Cohen, Darrel

"Effects of Fiscal Policy on the U.S. Economy", 9366–1.134

Cohen, Jacqueline

"Incapacitating Criminals: Recent Research Findings", 6066–20.3

Cohen, Steven B.

"Estimation and Sampling Procedures in the NMCES Insurance Surveys", 4186–4.3

Coins and coinage

China economic conditions, agricultural and industrial production, trade, and domestic and foreign investment, 1980-85, 2048–106

Currency and coin outstanding and in circulation, by type and denomination, *Treasury Bulletin,* quarterly rpt, 8002–4.20

Currency in circulation, denominations, 1982, annual rpt, 9364–5.12

Fed Govt consolidated financial statements based on business accounting methods, FY82-83, annual rpt, 8104–5

Fed Govt programs and mgmt cost control proposals, 3-year savings by function and agency, and financial and operating data, 1960s-81, 16908–1.12

Fed Reserve Bank of Atlanta financial statements, 1982-83, annual rpt, 9371–4

Fed Reserve Bank of Chicago financial statements, 1983, annual rpt, 9375–5

Fed Reserve Bank of Cleveland financial statements, 1982-83, annual rpt, 9377–5

Fed Reserve Bank of Minneapolis financial statements, 1981-82, annual rpt, 9383–2

Fed Reserve Bank of Philadelphia financial statements, 1982-83, annual rpt, 9387–3

Fed Reserve Bank of Richmond financial statements, 1983, annual rpt, 9389–2

Fed Reserve banks financial statements and employees, 1983, annual rpt, 9364–1.1

Fed Reserve payments services provided depository instns, financial statements, and costs and revenues by service and district bank, 1983, annual press release, 9364–9

Imports of US, detailed Schedule A commodities by country, monthly rpt, 2422–2

Injuries and deaths from use of selected consumer products and related activity, by victim age and sex, 1982, annual rpt, 9164–7

Mint Bur activities and finances, production of medals and US and foreign coins, and gold and silver stocks and transactions, by office, FY83, annual rpt, 8204–1

Mint Bur coin production, for US by denomination and mint, and for foreign countries, monthly table, 8202–1

Thefts, and total value of property stolen and recovered, by property type, 1983, annual rpt, 6224–2.1

see also Counterfeiting and forgery

see also Money supply

Coke

see Coal and coal mining

Cold storage and refrigeration

Agricultural Statistics, 1983, annual rpt, 1004–1.2

Capacity of refrigerated warehouses, by State and SMSA, Oct 1983, biennial rpt, 1614–2

CCC dairy inventories, storage and spoilage costs of surplus butter, cheese, and nonfat dry milk, 1982-83, GAO rpt, 26113–120

Construction industries census, 1982: financial and operating data, by SIC 4-digit industry and State, final rpt series, 2373–1

County Business Patterns: establishments, employees, and payrolls, by SIC 4-digit industry and county, 1981, annual State rpt series, 2326–8

County Business Patterns: establishments, employees, and payrolls, by SIC 4-digit industry and county, 1982, annual State rpt series, 2326–6

Dairy products holdings, total and Fed Govt, and USDA purchases, by region, monthly 1983, annual rpt, 1317–1.1

Employment, earnings, and hours, by selected SIC 1- to 4-digit industry, State, and for 278 major labor areas, 1939-83, annual rpt, 6744–5

Employment, earnings, and hours, by SIC 4-digit nonfarm industry, monthly 1974-Feb 1984, annual update, 6744–4

Cold storage and refrigeration

Energy use, by economic sector, end use, and energy source, 1983 and 2000, 2006–2.5

Equipment for cooling and heating, industry productivity trends and technological innovations, 1967-82, article, 6722–1.471

Equipment shipments, trade, and consumption, by product, 1983, annual Current Industrial Rpt, 2506–12.7

Exports and imports of US, detailed SIC-based commodities by world area, 1983, annual rpts, 2424–6

Exports and imports of US, totals and as percent of domestic production, by SIC 2- to 5-digit commodity, 1981, annual rpt, 2424–3

Exports, imports, tariffs, and industry operating data for fans, pumps, compressors, and cooling equipment, 1979-83, TSUSA commodity rpt, 9885–6.83

Exports of air conditioning and refrigeration equipment by world area, and imports, by product, biennial rpt, suspended, 2014–2

Exports of US, detailed commodities by country of destination, monthly rpt, 2422–3

Exports of US, detailed Schedule B commodities by country of destination, 1983, annual rpt, 2424–9

Exports of US, detailed Schedule E commodities by mode of transport and world area and country of destination, 1983, annual rpts, 2424–5

Finances and operations, by SIC 2- to 4-digit industry, 1970s-83 and projected to 1988, annual rpt, 2014–4

Fish (frozen) production by State, 1977, annual rpt, 2164–2

Fish and fish products production by region and State, and trade, by species and product, 1982-83, annual rpt series, 2166–6

Fish and shellfish cold storage holdings, weight by species and form, preliminary data, monthly rpt, 2162–2

Fish and shellfish landings, prices, trade, wholesaler receipts, and market activities at 5 major US ports, weekly rpts, 2162–6

Fish frozen products, weakfish storage stability and potential use of soy proteins in fish sticks, 1983 articles, 2162–1.401

Fishery products cold storage holdings, by species, quarterly 1983, annual rpt, 2164–1.5

Food processing and packaging equipment, foreign market and trade, and user industry operations and demand, country market research rpts, 2045–11

Food stocks in cold storage by commodity and census div, and warehouse cold storage space in use, by State, monthly rpt, 1631–5

Food stocks in cold storage, 77 commodities, by region, 1983, annual rpt, 1631–11

Great Lakes trade, by SITC 3-digit commodity, port, vessel type, world area, and country, 1982, annual rpt, 7744–3

Household energy use, appliances, motor vehicles, and vehicle fuel economy, by census region and urban-rural location, various periods Oct 1980-Mar 1983, annual rpt, 3164–74

Cold storage and refrigeration

Imports of US, detailed Schedule A commodities by country and world area of origin, and mode of transport, 1983, annual rpts, 2424–2

Imports of US, detailed Schedule A commodities by country, monthly rpt, 2422–2

Imports of US, detailed TSUSA commodities by country of origin, 1983, annual rpt, 2424–4

Input-output structure of US economy, detailed interindustry transactions for 537 industries, and components of final demand, 1977 benchmark data, 2708–17

Intermodal containers and equipment owned by US shipping and leasing companies, inventory by type and size, 1983, annual rpt, 7704–10

Japan fish landings, prices, trade by country, cold storage, and market devs, periodic press release, 2162–7

Manufacturing census, 1982: financial and operating data, by SIC 2- to 4-digit industry, State, SMSA, and county, preliminary census div rpt series, 2491–3

Manufacturing census, 1982: financial and operating data, for SIC 4-digit industries by product, preliminary rpt, 2491–1.351

Meat stocks in cold storage, 1970-83, annual rpt, 1564–6.4

Military Sealift Command operations for naval fleet support, and transport of DOD and AID cargo by route, quarterly rpt, 3802–2

Minority group and women employment, by occupational group and SIC 2- to 3-digit industry, 1981, annual rpt, 9244–1.1

Occupational injury and illness rates, by SIC 2- to 4-digit industry, 1982, annual rpt, 6844–1

Occupational Outlook Handbook, 1984-85 biennial rpt, 6744–1

Peanut production, prices, trade by country, and stocks, weekly rpt, 1311–1

Poultry and egg marketing and price data for selected regions, States, and SMSAs, monthly 1983, annual rpt, 1317–2

Producer prices and indexes, by stage of processing and detailed commodity, monthly rpt, 6762–6

Producer prices and indexes, by stage of processing and detailed commodity, monthly 1983, annual supplement, 6764–2

Service industry census, 1982: employment, establishments, receipts, and payroll, by SIC 2- to 4-digit kind of business, SMSA, county, and city, State rpt series, 2391–1

Transportation census, 1982: trucks, by detailed characteristics, miles traveled, and type of product carried, State rpt series, 2573–1

see also Ice, manufactured

Cole, Cheryl

"Changing Composition of the Military and the Effect on Labor Force Data", 6722–1.442

Colella, Cynthia C.

"Federalism in 1983: Mixed Results from Washington", 10042–1.402

Coleman, P. R.

"Population Distribution Analyses for Nuclear Power Plant Siting", 9638–54

Coliform bacteria

see Water pollution

Collective bargaining

see Labor-management relations, general

see Labor-management relations, local and regional

see Labor unions

College Station, Tex.

Census of Housing, 1980: occupancy and unit characteristics, by race, Hispanic origin, and city, SMSA rpt, 2473–1.105

Census of Population and Housing, 1980: detailed population and housing characteristics, by county, city, and census tract, SMSA rpt, 2551–2.105

Housing vacancy rates for single and multifamily units and mobile homes, by city and ZIP code, 1984, annual metro area rpt, 9304–19.17

see also under By SMSA or MSA in the "Index by Categories"

Colleges and universities

see Black colleges

see Federal aid to higher education

see Federal aid to medical education

see Higher education

see Junior colleges

see State aid to higher education

see under By Individual Company or Institution in the "Index by Categories"

Collins, Mark

"Species Profiles: Life Histories and Environmental Requirements of Coastal Fishes and Invertebrates (South Florida), Snook", 5506–8.27

Colombia

Agricultural and food production indexes, and production of selected commodities, by world region and country, 1974-83, annual rpt, 1524–5

Agricultural exports of US to Latin America, by commodity, country group, and selected country, FY81-84 and forecast FY85, article, 1522–1.407

Agricultural situation in Latin America, by country, 1981-83 and outlook for 1984, annual rpt, 1524–4.9

Agricultural supply/demand, trade, and production, and socioeconomic data, by country, 1950s-77, 1528–179

AID economic assistance to developing countries, obligations and disbursements by country, quarterly rpt, 9912–4

AID educational program activities and project impacts in 12 developing countries, 1950s-82, 9916–11.8

AID loan repayment status and terms by program and country, and status of predecessor agency loans, quarterly rpt, 9912–3

Coal imports from US, energy supply/demand, and economic indicators, for 3 countries, selected years 1960-82 and projected to 2000, 3008–97

Coffee exports of Colombia and Brazil to US and world, market share analysis, 1983 rpt, 1528–169

Economic conditions, income, production, prices, employment, and trade, 1984 semiannual country rpt, 2046–4.124

Economic, social, and political summary data, by country, 1984, annual factbook, 244–11

Exports and imports of US, by commodity and country, 1972-82, annual world region rpt, 244–13.2

Index by Subjects and Names

Exports of US, detailed Schedule B commodities by country of destination, 1983, annual rpt, 2424–9

Exports of US, detailed Schedule E commodities by mode of transport and world area and country of destination, 1983, annual rpts, 2424–5

Imports of US, detailed Schedule A commodities by country and world area of origin, and mode of transport, 1983, annual rpts, 2424–2

Imports of US, detailed TSUSA commodities by country of origin, 1983, annual rpt, 2424–4

Loans and grants for economic and military assistance from US and intl agencies, by program and country, FY46-83, annual rpt, 9914–5

Military aid of US, arms sales, and training programs costs and budget requests by program, world region, and country, FY83-85, annual rpt, 7144–13

Military spending, arms trade, and armed forces size, with total govt spending and population, by country, 1972-82, annual rpt, 9824–1

Minerals Yearbook, 1982, Vol 3: foreign country reviews of production, trade, and policies, by commodity, annual rpt, 5604–35

Minerals Yearbook, 1983, Vol 3 preprints: foreign country review of production, trade, and policies, by commodity, annual rpt, 5604–23.17

Population size and growth rates, and latest available benchmark demographic data, by country, 1950-83, biennial rpt, 2324–4

Roses from Colombia at less than fair value, imports injury to US industry, investigation with background financial and operating data, 1984 rpt, 9886–14.118

see also under By Foreign Country in the "Index by Categories"

Colonial Heights, Va.

Census of Housing, 1980: occupancy and unit characteristics, by race, Hispanic origin, and city, SMSA rpt, 2473–1.282

Census of Population and Housing, 1980: detailed population and housing characteristics, by county, city, and census tract, SMSA rpt, 2551–2.282

Colorado

Agriculture census, 1982: farms, farmland, production and costs, and operator characteristics, preliminary State summary and county rpts, 2330–1.8

Agriculture census, 1982: farms, farmland, production, finances, and operator characteristics, by county, final State rpt, 2331–1.6

Bank deposits in commercial and mutual savings banks and in US branches of foreign banks, by account type, instn, State, SMSA, and county, June 1983, annual rpt, 9295–3.15

Census of Housing, 1980: occupancy and unit characteristics of SMSAs and central cities, by race, Hispanic origin, and city, State rpt, 2473–1.7

Census of Population and Housing, 1980: detailed population and housing characteristics, by county, city, and census tract, State rpt, 2551–2.7

Index by Subjects and Names

Columbia River

Census of Population, 1980: detailed socioeconomic and demographic characteristics, by age, sex, race, Hispanic origin, and industry, State rpt, 2531–4.7

Coal dev plans on Fed Govt lease lands, environmental and socioeconomic impacts to 2000, final statement, 5726–4.6

Coal Fed Govt leases, acreage, production, and prices, by State, and legal and mgmt issues, 1970s-83 with production projections to 2000, 11128–1

County Business Patterns: establishments, employees, and payrolls, by SIC 4-digit industry and county, 1982, annual State rpt, 2326–6.7

Court use of telephone conferencing in civil and criminal hearings, assessment of lawyers and judges in 2 States and Denver, Colo, 1981, 6068–186

Employment, earnings, and hours, by selected SIC 1- to 4-digit industry, State, and for 278 major labor areas, 1939-83, annual rpt, 6744–5.1, 6744–5.3

Environmental quality, pollutant discharge by type and source, and EPA protection activities and funding, 1970s-83, biennial regional rpt, 9184–15.8

Exports of manufactured and agricultural commodities, manufacturing production, and export-related employment, 1960s-82, State rpt, 2046–3.6

Farms with sales under $2,500, acreage, finances, operations, and operator characteristics, by region and for 6 States, 1978, 1548–241

Forest biomass in Rocky Mountain States, conversion from volume to dry weight, for softwood and hardwood species, 1977, 1208–200

Forests (natl) below-cost timber sales in Colorado, and volume, costs, revenue, and net loss, by sale and forest, FY81-82, GAO rpt, 26113–131

Foster care children permanent placement, Fed Govt incentive program funding and operations in 7 States, FY80-82, GAO rpt, 26121–81

HHS aid to each State and local govt or private instn, amount obligated, funding agency, and program, FY83, annual listing, 4004–3.8

Hwy and bridge repair projects funded by Fed Govt, and costs, for 7 States, FY81-82, GAO rpt, 26113–121

Income (personal) per capita and by source, and earnings by industry div, by State, MSA, and county, 1977-82, annual regional rpt, 2704–2.8

Manufacturing census, 1982: financial and operating data, by SIC 2- to 4-digit industry, State, SMSA, and county, preliminary census div rpt, 2491–3.8

Medicare beneficiaries in Colorado with partial coverage, use and covered charges by service type or location, and Medicaid coverage status, 1978, article, 4652–1.404

Mineral Industry Surveys, State review of production, 1983, advance annual rpt, 5614–6.6

Minerals Yearbook, 1982, Vol 2 preprints: State review of production and sales by commodity, and business activity, annual rpt, 5604–16.7

Minerals Yearbook, 1982, Vol 2: State reviews of production, sales, and firms, by commodity, and business activity, annual rpt, 5604–34

Occupational health promotion and disease prevention programs by type, and employers interested in programs, 1984 article, 4102–1.453

Oil shale dev projects in Green River area, production goals and cost estimates, as of 1983, article, 9381–1.409

Population, births, deaths, and net migration, by MSA and county, 1980-82, annual State Current Population Rpt, 2546–4.6

Population size, Apr 1980 and July 1982, and per capita income, 1979 and 1981, by county and city, State Current Population Rpt, 2546–11.6

Retail trade census, 1982: employment, establishments, sales, and payroll, by SIC 2- to 4-digit kind of business, SMSA, county, and city, State rpt, 2397–1.6

Savings and loan assns, FHLB 10th District insured members finances and operations by SMSA, monthly rpt, 9302–22

Service industry census, 1982: employment, establishments, receipts, and payroll, by SIC 2- to 4-digit kind of business, SMSA, county, and city, State rpt, 2391–1.6

Timber resources and removals in 9 Rocky Mountain States, and forest and rangeland area, by ownership, forest and tree characteristics, and State, 1977, 1208–201

Water supply and quality, and effect of coal mining operations, for selected river basins in Western coal provinces, 1983 rpt, 5666–19.4, 5666–19.5

Water supply and quality in streams and lakes, and groundwater levels in wells, by drainage basin, 1983, annual State rpt, 5666–10.6

Water supply, and snow survey results, monthly State rpt, 1266–2.3

Wholesale trade census, 1982: employment, establishments, finances, and operations, by SIC 2- to 4-digit kind of business, SMSA, county, and city, State rpt, 2405–1.6

see also Boulder, Colo.

see also Colorado Springs, Colo.

see also Denver, Colo.

see also Denver County, Colo.

see also Fort Collins, Colo.

see also Garland, Colo.

see also Greeley, Colo.

see also Pueblo, Colo.

see also Scioto, Colo.

see also under By State in the "Index by Categories"

Colorado River

Bridges over navigable waters, with type of bridge and use, owner, dimensions, and location, 1984 regional listing, 7406–5.2, 7406–5.4

Reclamation programs of Fed Govt in western US, finances and operations by project and State, 1981-82, annual rpts, 5824–1

Storage project for Colorado River, finances, water resource dev, power production, and other activities in western States, FY83, annual rpt, 5824–3

Water supply and quality in streams and lakes, and groundwater levels in wells, by drainage basin, 1980, annual State rpt series, 5666–12

Water supply and quality in streams and lakes, and groundwater levels in wells, by drainage basin, 1981, annual State rpt series, 5666–16

Water supply and quality in streams and lakes, and groundwater levels in wells, by drainage basin, 1982, annual State rpt series, 5666–20

Water supply and quality in streams and lakes, and groundwater levels in wells, by drainage basin, 1983, annual State rpt series, 5666–10

Colorado Springs, Colo.

Census of Housing, 1980: occupancy and unit characteristics, by race, Hispanic origin, and city, SMSA rpt, 2473–1.124

Census of Population and Housing, 1980: detailed population and housing characteristics, by county, city, and census tract, SMSA rpt, 2551–2.124

Housing and financial characteristics, and unit and neighborhood quality, for 15 SMSAs, 1978, annual survey special supplement, 2485–8

Wages of office and plant workers, by occupation, 1983 labor market area survey rpt, 6785–3.2

see also under By City and By SMSA or MSA in the "Index by Categories"

Coltrane, Robert I.

"Immigration Reform and Agricultural Labor", 1598–192

"Who Gets Rural Jobs?", 1004–16.1

Columbia, Mo.

Census of Housing, 1980: occupancy and unit characteristics, by race, Hispanic origin, and city, SMSA rpt, 2473–1.125

Census of Population and Housing, 1980: detailed population and housing characteristics, by county, city, and census tract, SMSA rpt, 2551–2.125

see also under By SMSA or MSA in the "Index by Categories"

Columbia River

Bonneville Power Admin operations, and Columbia River power system sales and financial statements, FY83, annual rpt, 3224–1

Bridges over navigable waters, with type of bridge and use, owner, dimensions, and location, 1984 regional listing, 7406–5.4

Crab (dungeness) size and leg loss, monthly Jan 1972-Feb 1973, article, 2162–1.403

Fish and shellfish canned and frozen production, imports, landings, and prices, for Alaska and Northwest States, weekly rpt, 2162–6.5

Fish and shellfish landings in Columbia River by Washington State and Oregon fishermen, by type of gear, 1977, annual rpt, 2164–2.7

Freight (waterborne domestic and foreign) by commodity, traffic, and passengers, by port and waterway, 1982, annual rpt, 3754–3.4

Ports, port facilities by type, and inland waterways by size, by location, 1982-83, annual rpt, 7704–16

Reclamation programs of Fed Govt in western US, finances and operations by project and State, 1981-82, annual rpts, 5824–1

Columbia River

Shipping industry impact on local economy, and port dev financing through user fees, by State, other area, industry, and port, 1970s-2020, hearings, 21568–34

Water supply and quality in streams and lakes, and groundwater levels in wells, by drainage basin, 1980, annual State rpt series, 5666–12

Water supply and quality in streams and lakes, and groundwater levels in wells, by drainage basin, 1981, annual State rpt series, 5666–16

Water supply and quality in streams and lakes, and groundwater levels in wells, by drainage basin, 1982, annual State rpt series, 5666–20

Water supply and quality in streams and lakes, and groundwater levels in wells, by drainage basin, 1983, annual State rpt series, 5666–10

Water supply in US and Canada, streamflow, well and reservoir levels, and dissolved solids and temperature in 6 US rivers, by station, monthly rpt, 5662–3

Columbia, S.C.

Census of Housing, 1980: occupancy and unit characteristics, by race, Hispanic origin, and city, SMSA rpt, 2473–1.126

Census of Population and Housing, 1980: detailed population and housing characteristics, by county, city, and census tract, SMSA rpt, 2551–2.126

Fruit and vegetable shipments, and arrivals in 23 US and 5 Canada cities, by mode of transport and State or country of origin, 1983, annual rpt, 1311–4.1

Columbium

see Metals and metal industries

Columbus, Ga.

Census of Housing, 1980: occupancy and unit characteristics, by race, Hispanic origin, and city, SMSA rpt, 2473–1.127

Census of Population and Housing, 1980: detailed population and housing characteristics, by county, city, and census tract, SMSA rpt, 2551–2.127

Wages by occupation, and benefits for office and plant workers, 1984 labor market area survey rpt, 6785–3.5

see also under By City and By SMSA or MSA in the "Index by Categories"

Columbus, Miss.

Wages of office and plant workers, by occupation, 1984 labor market area survey rpt, 6785–3.6

Columbus, Ohio

Census of Housing, 1980: occupancy and unit characteristics, by race, Hispanic origin, and city, SMSA rpt, 2473–1.128

Census of Population and Housing, 1980: detailed population and housing characteristics, by county, city, and census tract, SMSA rpt, 2551–2.128

Housing and financial characteristics, and unit and neighborhood quality, for 15 SMSAs, 1978, annual survey special supplement, 2485–8

Housing and households detailed characteristics, and unit and neighborhood quality, by inside-outside central cities, 1982 survey, SMSA rpt, 2485–6.36

Population size of top 25 cities, 1980 and 1982, press release, 2328–46

Public works capital needs and financing, by project type, level of govt, and selected jurisdiction, 1970s-83 and projected to 2000, hearing, 23848–181

Wages by occupation, and benefits for office and plant workers, 1984 SMSA survey rpt, 6785–11.10

see also under By City and By SMSA or MSA in the "Index by Categories"

Commemorations and memorials

see Monuments and memorials

Commerce

see Foreign trade

see Interstate commerce

Commerce Department

see Department of Commerce

Commercial banking

see Banks and banking

Commercial buildings

Air pollution levels for 5 pollutants, by detailed source, State, and Air Quality Control Region, 1981, annual rpt, 9194–7

Bombing (explosive and incendiary) and arson incidents by target, State, and circumstances, and explosives theft and recovery, 1982-83, annual rpt, 8484–4

Bombing (explosive and incendiary) incidents, damage, injuries, and deaths, by target, State, and circumstances, 1983, annual rpt, 6224–5

Carbon monoxide atmospheric concentrations and levels within buildings and along commuting and residential driving routes, for 4 cities, Jan-Mar 1981, 9198–110

Construction industries census, 1982: financial and operating data, by SIC 4-digit industry and State, final rpt series, 2373–1

Construction industries census, 1982: financial and operating data, by SIC 4-digit industry and State, preliminary rpt series, 2371–1

Construction put in place, permits authorized by region, State, and MSA, and Federal contract awards, by construction type, bimonthly rpt with articles, 2012–1

Construction put in place, value of new public and private structures, by type, monthly rpt, 2382–4

Energy conservation programs of State govts, Fed Govt financial and technical aid, and reported energy savings, by State, 1983, annual rpt, 3304–1

Energy consumption in commercial buildings under alternative heating, cooling, and air conditioning systems and control strategies, for 6 cities, 1983 rpt, 2218–68

Energy supply/demand and prices, by fuel type, sector, and end use, detailed trends and projections 1973-95, annual rpt, 3164–75

Energy use in nonresidential buildings, expenditures, and conservation, by building characteristics, EIA survey series, 3166–8

Energy use, prices, and conservation and efficiency measures, by fuel type, end-use sector, selected industry, and region, 1960-83, annual rpt, 3164–73

Fed Govt programs and mgmt cost control proposals, 3-year savings by function and agency, and financial and operating data, 1960s-81, 16908–1.29

Income tax returns of partnerships, detailed data by industry, 1981 estimates, annual article, 8302–2.404

Index by Subjects and Names

Income tax returns of sole proprietorships, detailed data by industry div and selected industry group, 1981, annual rpt, 8304–7

Mortgage loan activity, by type of lender, loan, and mortgaged property, monthly rpt, 5142–18

Pacific Northwest electricity consumption and prices by end-use sector, and economic and demographic data, 1960s-83 and projected to 2005, annual rpt, 3224–2

Rental office space demand methodology using BLS employment data, with results by selected occupation and industry and for Chicago SMSA, 1975-83, article, 6722–1.474

Southeastern States financial and economic devs, Fed Reserve 6th District, monthly rpt with articles, 9371–1

see also Office furniture and equipment

Commercial education

see Business education

Commercial finance companies

see Finance companies

Commercial law

see also Antitrust law

see also Bankruptcy

see also Interstate commerce

see also Licenses and permits

see also Maritime law

see also Patents

see also Price regulation

see also Trademarks

Commercial treaties

see Trade agreements

Commissaries

see Post exchanges

Commission of Fine Arts

Budget of US Appendix, detailed budgets and personnel summaries, by agency, FY85, annual rpt, 104–3

Budget of US, appropriations, outlays, balances, and budget receipts, by govtl branch and agency, FY83, annual rpt, 8104–2

Commission on Civil Rights

Alabama rural black population, education, employment, health services, and economic status, for 16 counties, selected years 1970-81, 11048–180

Budget and staff for civil rights enforcement offices of 6 Federal agencies, FY80-84, 11048–179

Budget of US Appendix, detailed budgets and personnel summaries, by agency, FY85, annual rpt, 104–3

Budget of US, appropriations, outlays, balances, and budget receipts, by govtl branch and agency, FY83, annual rpt, 8104–2

Minorities and women civil rights progress, Supreme Court decisions, and legislative action, 1957-83, last issue of narrative annual rpt, 11044–3

Commission on Executive, Legislative, and Judicial Salaries

Budget of US, appropriations, outlays, balances, and budget receipts, by govtl branch and agency, FY83, annual rpt, 8104–2

Commission on Fair Market Value Policy for Federal Coal Leasing

Coal Fed Govt leases, acreage, production, and prices, by State, and legal and mgmt issues, 1970s-83 with production projections to 2000, 11128–1

Index by Subjects and Names

Common carriers

Commission on Security and Cooperation in Europe

Budget of US Appendix, detailed budgets and personnel summaries, by agency, FY85, annual rpt, 104–3

Commission on Wartime Relocation and Internment of Civilians

Budget of US, appropriations, outlays, balances, and budget receipts, by govtl branch and agency, FY83, annual rpt, 8104–2

Commissions of the Federal Government

see Federal boards, committees, and commissions

see Federal independent agencies

Committee for Purchase from the Blind and Other Severely Handicapped

Budget of US Appendix, detailed budgets and personnel summaries, by agency, FY85, annual rpt, 104–3

Budget of US, appropriations, outlays, balances, and budget receipts, by govtl branch and agency, FY83, annual rpt, 8104–2

Workshops for blind and handicapped, Fed Govt procurement of goods and services and participating workshops, FY78-82, annual rpt, 11714–1

Committees of Congress

see Congressional committees

Commodities

see Agricultural commodities

see Futures trading

see Manufacturing

see Mines and mineral resources

see Natural resources

see Stockpiling

see Strategic materials

see under By Commodity in the "Index by Categories"

see under names of specific commodities or commodity groups

Commodity Credit Corp.

Agricultural cooperative operating ratios by commodity, and debt financing by source, for 100 largest cooperatives, selected years FY62-83, article, 1122–1.411

Agricultural production, marketing, trade, supply, food consumption, and food and nutrition programs, 1960s-83, annual chartbook, 1504–3

Agricultural Stabilization and Conservation Service programs, annual commodity fact sheet series, 1806–4

Agricultural Statistics, 1983, annual rpt, 1004–1

Agriculture census, 1982: farms, farmland, production, finances, and operator characteristics, by county, final State rpt series, 2331–1

Commodities of CCC for sale, and prices, monthly press release, 1802–4

Commodity inventories of CCC, 1979-83, and borrowing authority appropriations, FY72-83, strategic material stockpile mgmt hearings, 25208–27

Cost control proposals for Fed Govt programs and mgmt, 3-year savings by function and agency, and financial and operating data, 1960s-81, 16908–1.26

Cotton loan rates, and micronaire differentials of CCC, monthly rpt, annual tables, 1309–12.2

Cotton prices at selected spot markets, futures prices at NYC exchange, and CCC loan rates, 1983/84 with some trends from 1920, annual rpt, 1309–2

Cotton prices in 8 spot markets, futures prices at NYC exchange, farm prices, and CCC loan stocks, monthly rpt, 1309–1

Currency (foreign) holdings of US, detailed transactions and balances by program and country, 1st half FY84, semiannual rpt, 8102–7

Dairy inventories of CCC, storage and spoilage costs of surplus butter, cheese, and nonfat dry milk, 1982-83, GAO rpt, 26113–120

Dairy production by State, stocks, prices, and CCC price support activities, by product type, monthly rpt, 1627–3

Dairy products price support purchases, sales, donations, and inventories of CCC, monthly rpt, 1802–2

Dairy products, uncommitted stocks, quarterly situation rpt, 1561–2

Expenditures in natl income and product accounts and in unified budget, *Survey of Current Business,* monthly rpt, annual tables, 2702–1.24

Export credit sales agreement terms, by commodity and country, FY83, annual rpt, 15344–1.11

Exports of CCC commodities in exchange for strategic material imports by world region and country, and strategic material stockpiles, various periods 1950-83, hearings, 21208–20

Exports under Fed Govt-financed programs, by commodity and country, bimonthly rpt, periodic tables, 1522–1.4

Farm finances, assets, expenses, cash flow, receipts, and loans, selected years 1971-85, annual rpt, 1544–13

Farm finances, expenses by type, loans by purpose and source, and credit detail by Fed Reserve District, quarterly rpt, 9365–3.10

Farm non-real estate debt outstanding, by type of lender and district, as of Jan 1983, annual rpt, 9264–4

Farm price support programs for 5 crops, and effects of alternative Fed Govt policies, FY56-83 with projections to FY88, 26306–6.71

Finances and program operations FY83, annual rpt, 1824–1

Grain futures contracts, stocks in deliverable position by type and grade, weekly tables, 11922–4

Honey, CCC loan activity by State, and processing contracts by contractor, weekly rpt, monthly tables, 1311–2

Input-output structure of US economy, detailed interindustry transactions for 537 industries, and components of final demand, 1977 benchmark data, 2708–17

Liabilities (contigent) and claims paid by Fed Govt on federally insured and guaranteed contracts with foreign obligors, by country and program, periodic rpt, 8002–12

Loan activities and operating results of CCC, monthly release, 1802–7

Loans to farmers made and liquidated monthly by commodity, and by State, 1980-83, annual rpt, 1544–16

Loans to farmers outstanding, as of Jan 1978-83, annual rpt, 1544–19

Milk price support alternatives, effects on production, use, prices, and farm receipts, projected 1983/84-1988/89 and actual 1982/83, 1568–246

Milk price supports effect on production, use, prices, and farm receipts, by region and State, 1940s-83 and alternative projections to 1988/89, 1568–245

Rice market activities, prices, inspections, sales, trade, supply, and use, for US and selected foreign markets, weekly rpt, 1313–8

Rice price support loan activity of CCC, 1970-83, semiannual rpt, 1561–8.5

Storage facility and equipment loans to farmers under CCC grain program, by State, FY68-84, annual table, 1804–14

Storage facility and equipment loans to farmers under CCC grain program, by State, monthly table, 1802–9

Tobacco production, trade, consumption, marketing, taxes, and price supports, quarterly situation rpt with articles, 1561–10

Tobacco support program of CCC, itemized costs, adequacy of assessed producer payments, and crop loans and accrued interest, for flue-cured and burley tobacco, various periods 1981-84, GAO rpt, 26113–117

Commodity Exchange Authority

see Commodity Futures Trading Commission

Commodity futures

see Futures trading

Commodity Futures Trading Commission

Activities, funding, and employment of Commission, and futures trading by commodity and exchange, FY83, annual rpt, 11924–2

Budget of US Appendix, detailed budgets and personnel summaries, by agency, FY85, annual rpt, 104–3

Budget of US, appropriations, outlays, balances, and budget receipts, by govtl branch and agency, FY83, annual rpt, 8104–2

Cost control proposals for Fed Govt programs and mgmt, 3-year savings by function and agency, and financial and operating data, 1960s-81, 16908–1.15

Cotton futures unfixed call sales and purchases and open contracts on NYC exchange, weekly rpt, 11922–3

Exchange activity, by exchange for 42 contract commodities, annual rpt, suspended, 11924–3

Futures trading in selected commodities, foreign currencies, and stock indexes, Chicago and other markets activity, monthly rpt, 11922–1

Futures trading in selected commodities, foreign currencies, Treasury securities, and stock indexes, NYC, Chicago, and other markets activity, monthly rpt, 11922–5

Futures trading in selected commodities, Treasury securities, and stock indexes, NYC market activity, monthly rpt, 11922–2

Grain futures contracts, stocks in deliverable position by type and grade, weekly tables, 11922–4

Common carriers

see Airlines

see Buses

see Passenger ships

see Public utilities

see Railroads

see Ships and shipping

Common carriers

see Taxicabs
see Trucks and trucking industry

Common markets and free trade areas

Developing countries free zones, industry financial and operating data by country, with case studies for 5 countries, 1970s-82, 9918–10

Exports and imports, agreement devs, US trade relations, and USITC investigations, 1983, annual rpt, 9884–5

Loans of large US banks to foreigners at all US and foreign offices, by country group and country, quarterly rpt, 13002–1

US foreign trade zones, activities, and value of goods entering and leaving zones, 1973-82, GAO rpt, 26119–56

see also Caribbean Common Market
see also Central American Common Market
see also Council for Mutual Economic Assistance
see also European Community
see also European Free Trade Association
see also International agencies
see also Latin American Free Trade Association

Communicable diseases

see Animal diseases and zoonoses
see Infective and parasitic diseases
see Respiratory diseases
see Venereal diseases

Communications industries

American Samoa minimum wage rates, employment, earnings, and benefits, by establishment and industry, Nov 1983, biennial rpt, 6504–6

Army personnel assigned to critical occupation specialties by skill type, and working outside specialty at 5 installations, as of Mar 1982, GAO rpt, 26123–59

Bombing (explosive and incendiary) incidents, damage, injuries, and deaths, by target, State, and circumstances, 1983, annual rpt, 6224–5

Census of Population, 1980: detailed socioeconomic and demographic characteristics, by age, sex, race, Hispanic origin, occupation, and industry, State rpt series, 2531–4

Census of Population, 1980: detailed socioeconomic characteristics, by county, city, and inside-outside SMSAs and central cities, State rpt series, 2531–3

Census of Population, 1980: labor force, by sex, detailed occupation, and region, with comparison to 1970 census, supplementary rpt, 2535–1.12

Collective bargaining agreements expiring during year, covered workers by SIC 2-digit industry, firm, and union, with summary of key provisions, 1984, annual rpt, 6784–9

Construction industries census, 1982: financial and operating data, by SIC 4-digit industry and State, final rpt series, 2373–1

Construction industries census, 1982: financial and operating data, by SIC 4-digit industry and State, preliminary rpt series, 2371–1

County Business Patterns: establishments, employees, and payrolls, by SIC 4-digit industry and county, 1981, annual State rpt series, 2326–8

County Business Patterns: establishments, employees, and payrolls, by SIC 4-digit industry and county, 1982, annual State rpt series, 2326–6

DOD expenditures for goods and services, by function, 1972-84, article, 2702–1.440

DOD procurement, prime contract awards by detailed procurement category, FY80-83, annual rpt, 3544–18

Earnings by major industry group, and personal income per capita and by source, by region and State, 1929-82, 2708–40

Employment, earnings, and hours, by selected SIC 1- to 4-digit industry, State, and for 278 major labor areas, 1939-83, annual rpt, 6744–5

Employment, earnings, and hours, by SIC 4-digit nonfarm industry, monthly 1974-Feb 1984, annual update, 6744–4

Energy use, by economic sector, end use, and energy source, 1983 and 2000, 2006–2.5

Exports and imports of US, detailed SIC-based commodities by world area, 1983, annual rpts, 2424–6

Exports, imports, tariffs, and industry operating data for microphones, loudspeakers, and sound and visual signaling devices, 1979-83, TSUSA commodity rpt supplement, 9885–6.81

Exports of US, detailed Schedule B commodities by country of destination, 1983, annual rpt, 2424–9

Fed Govt loans, grants, and tax benefits by business, by program and economic sector, projected FY84-88 with effective tax rates for FY80-82, 26306–6.70

Foreign direct investment in US, major investors and investments by SIC 4-digit industry, transaction type and value, and location, 1983, annual rpt, 2044–20

Foreign market and trade for telecommunications equipment, and user industry operations and demand, country market research rpts, 2045–12

Imports of US, detailed TSUSA commodities by country of origin, 1983, annual rpt, 2424–4

Income tax returns of corporations, detailed income and tax items by industry, 1981, annual rpt, 8304–4

Income tax returns of corporations with foreign tax credit, income and deductions by type, asset size, and selected industry group, 1980, article, 8302–2.415

Income tax returns of partnerships, detailed data by industry, 1981 estimates, annual article, 8302–2.404

Income tax returns of partnerships, receipts by source, deductions by type, and establishments, by selected industry, 1982, annual article, 8302–2.416

Income tax returns of sole proprietorships, detailed data by industry div and selected industry group, 1981, annual rpt, 8304–7

Income tax returns of sole proprietorships, receipts, deductions by type, payroll, and net income, by major industry, 1982, annual article, 8302–2.413

Input-output structure of US economy, detailed interindustry transactions for 85 industries, and components of final demand, 1977, article, 2702–1.421

Input-output structure of US economy, detailed interindustry transactions for 537 industries, and components of final demand, 1977 benchmark data, 2708–17

Index by Subjects and Names

Manufacturing census, 1982: financial and operating data, by SIC 2- to 4-digit industry, State, SMSA, and county, preliminary census div rpt series, 2491–3

Minority group and women employment, by occupational group and SIC 2- to 3-digit industry, 1981, annual rpt, 9244–1.1

Natl income and product, comprehensive accounts and components, *Survey of Current Business,* monthly rpt, monthly and annual tables, 2702–1.27

Occupational injury and illness rates, by SIC 2- to 4-digit industry, 1982, annual rpt, 6844–1

Occupational manpower needs and supply by detailed occupation, and educational and training program enrollees and grads by detailed field, 1982 and 1995, biennial rpt, 6744–3

Occupational Outlook Handbook, 1984-85 biennial rpt, 6744- 1

R&D industry funding and employment of scientists and engineers, by industry group, firm size, and funding source, 1956-82, annual rpt, 9627–21

Scientists, engineers, and technicians employment in transportation, utilities, and retail and wholesale trade, by field of science and industry, 1982, 9628–72

Small and minority-owned businesses finances and operations, Federal contracts by agency, and worker characteristics, by industry, race, sex, and State, 1950s-83, annual rpt, 9764–6

Statistical Abstract of US, social, political, and economic data, 1950s-83 and trends, annual rpt, 2324–1.3

see also Books and bookselling
see also Cable television
see also Communications satellites
see also Motion pictures
see also Newspapers
see also Periodicals
see also Phonograph
see also Political broadcasting
see also Printing and publishing industry
see also Public broadcasting
see also Radio
see also Recording industry
see also Telecommunication
see also Telegraph
see also Telephone and telephone industry
see also Television
see also under By Industry in the "Index by Categories"

Communications Satellite Corp.

Financial and operating data, 1981-82, annual rpt, 9284–6.7

Communications satellites

Communications Satellite Corp financial and operating data, 1981-82, annual rpt, 9284–6.7

DOD budget, itemized account of legislative history, FY84, annual rpt, 3504–7

DOD procurement cost estimates for weapons and communications systems, by service branch, quarterly summary rpt, 3502–1

Foreign and US astronautic and aeronautic events, comprehensive chronology, 1976, annual rpt, 9504–2

Foreign economic, social, and political summary data, by country, 1984, annual factbook, 244–11

Index by Subjects and Names

Intl communication satellite systems charges, operations, investment shares by country, and competition impacts, 1964-83 with projections to 2003, hearings, 25388–46

Launchings of satellites and other space objects since 1957, quarterly listing, 9502–2

NASA-launched communications and other satellites, and USSR launches by type, 1957-83, annual rpt, 9504–6.1

NASA project launch schedules and technical descriptions, press release series, 9506–2

Soviet Union and US satellites by mission and vulnerability to attack, and USSR anti-satellite missiles, 1983 and projected to 1989, hearing, 21208–18

Space and aeronautics programs and budgets of Fed Govt by agency, and foreign programs, 1957-FY85, annual rpt, 9504–9

Communism

see Communist countries

see Communist parties

Communist countries

- Agricultural supply/demand, consumption per capita, and trade, by world area and country group, 1960s-82, 1528–181
- Agricultural trade of US, by commodity and country, bimonthly rpt with articles, 1522–1
- China economic conditions, agricultural and industrial production, trade, and domestic and foreign investment, 1980-85, 2048–106
- Cuba economic conditions, agricultural and industrial production and distribution, trade, and intl economic relations, 1970-82 and trends from 1957, 248–40
- Economic conditions in Communist, OECD, and selected other countries, 1960s-83, annual rpt, 244–5
- Economies of Communist countries, special studies series, 2326–9
- Export licensing and monitoring activities under Export Admin Act, for selected commodities, and for Communist and other countries, FY83, annual rpt, 2044–22
- Exports and imports, agreement devs, US trade relations, and USITC investigations, 1983, annual rpt, 9884–5
- Exports and imports of OECD countries, by country, 1983, annual rpt, 7144–10
- Exports and imports of US, by commodity group, world area, selected country, US coastal area and port, and mode of transport, with seasonal adjustments, monthly rpt, 2422–9
- Exports and imports of US, detailed SIC-based commodities by world area, 1983, annual rpts, 2424–6
- Exports and imports of US with Communist countries, by detailed commodity and country, quarterly rpt with articles, 9882–2
- Exports, imports, and economic indicators by country and country group, and US trade policy actions, 1960s-83, annual rpt, 444–1
- Exports of US by selected commodity, and foreign and US economic and employment indicators and balance of payments, by world area and country, 1970s-83, annual rpt, 2044–26

Exports of US, detailed Schedule E commodities by mode of transport and world area and country of destination, 1983, annual rpts, 2424–5

Footwear imports of US, by category, value class, and selected country, monthly rpt, 2042–29

Grenada arms and equipment commitments of USSR and other Communist countries, 1980-85, and arms discovered and personnel evacuated by US, Oct 1983, hearings, 21388–43

Imports from Communist countries, injury to US industries, investigations with background financial and operating data, selected industries and products, series, 9886–12

Military weapons transfers to developing countries from US, USSR, and Europe, by weapon type and world region, 1974-82, 25948–3

Oil and gas production, prices, and trade by country, and consumption, for Communist countries, monthly rpt, 242–5

Oil prices impact on US oil trade and energy-intensive industries, with US and foreign reserves and industry operations, 1950-82 and projected to 2020, 9886–4.69

see also Albania

see also Bulgaria

see also China, Peoples Republic

see also Communist parties

see also Council for Mutual Economic Assistance

see also Cuba

see also Czechoslovakia

see also Eastern Europe

see also Germany, East

see also Hungary

see also Kampuchea

see also Korea, North

see also Poland

see also Romania

see also Soviet Union

see also Vietnam

see also Yugoslavia

see also under By Foreign Country in the "Index by Categories"

Communist parties

- Foreign economic, social, and political summary data, by country, 1984, annual factbook, 244–11
- Soviet Union officials public appearances in and outside of USSR, 1983, annual rpt, 244–8

see also Communist countries

Community action programs

- Community services block grants by type of service provider, State mgmt, and opinions of officials and groups involved, for 13 States, FY81-83, GAO rpt, 26121–84
- Fed Govt aid to State and local govts, expenditures, and direct payments, by program, agency, and State, FY83, annual rpt, 2464–2

Community colleges

see Higher education

see Junior colleges

Community Development Block Grants

Admin, allocation, and family social benefits of Community Dev Block Grants, effect of HUD policy changes to increase local admin responsibility, for 10 cities, 1982, 5188–105

Community development programs

- Budget of US, CBO analysis of revenue and spending alternatives and projections of economic indicators, FY85-89, annual rpt, 26304–3.3
- Budget of US, effects of Reagan Admin policy changes, by detailed program, FY85, annual rpt, 104–21
- Community dev programs funding and activities, for 5 HUD programs, FY83, annual rpt, 5124–5
- Cost control proposals for Fed Govt programs and mgmt, 3-year savings by function and agency, and financial and operating data, 1960s-81, 16908–1.8
- Indian and Alaska Native housing and community dev program operations, FY82 with Community Dev Block Grant funding by tribe and State for FY81, annual rpt, 5004–5
- Rental rehabilitation project, local funding and Section 8 rent supplements for 275 communities and 22 States, May 1984 press release, 5006–3.30
- Small cities program, State admin, project characteristics, and assessments of local officials, 1982, 5188–106

Community development programs

- Agricultural research expenditures and scientist years, by topic, commodity, and performing organization, FY82, annual rpt, 1744–2
- AID activities and funding by project and function, FY85, and developing countries summary socioeconomic data, 1970s-83, by country, annual rpt, 9914–3
- Appalachia regional dev spending, by program area and source of funds, FY82, annual rpt, 9084–1
- Budget of US Appendix, detailed budgets and personnel summaries, by agency, FY85, annual rpt, 104–3
- Budget of US, CBO analysis and review of FY85 budget by function, annual rpt, 26304–2
- Budget of US, CBO analysis of revenue and spending alternatives and projections of economic indicators, FY85-89, annual rpt, 26304–3.3
- Budget of US, compact budgets by function, agency, and account, FY85 with projections to FY89, annual rpt, 104–2
- Budget of US, effects of Reagan Admin policy changes, by detailed program, FY85, annual rpt, 104–21
- Budget of US, receipts by source and outlays by agency and program, monthly rpt, 8102–3
- Budget of US, receipts by source and outlays by function, FY40-89 estimates revised for consistency with FY85 budget definitions, annual rpt, 104–12
- Budget of US, receipts, outlays, and budget authority, by function and agency, FY84-89 revised estimates, midsession review of FY85 budget, annual rpt, 104–7
- Developing countries local govt community dev, AID assistance program activities and funding, 1960s-80s, 9918–11
- Fed Govt aid to State and local govts, expenditures, and direct payments, by program, agency, and State, FY83, annual rpt, 2464–2
- Fed Govt credit assistance costs, policies to improve measurement, with loan and loan

Community development programs

guarantee data by program, and Federal and private credit instns operations, 1970-84, 26306–6.72

Fed Govt financial and nonfinancial domestic aid, 1984 annual comprehensive catalog, 104–5

Fed Govt grants-in-aid for 13 program areas, FY82-84, annual article, 10042–1.402

Fed Govt programs and mgmt cost control proposals, CBO and GAO estimates of savings by function and agency, FY85-89, 26308–45

FmHA loans and grants by program and State, and summary of services, FY83 with trends from FY63, annual rpt, 1184–17

Govt census, 1982: city govt revenues by source, expenditures by function, debt, and assets, by State and city, 2457–4

Govt census, 1982: county govt revenues by source, expenditures by function, debt, and assets, by State and county, 2457–3

Govt census, 1982: employment, payrolls, and average earnings, by function, level of govt, State, county, population size, and inside-outside SMSAs, 2455–2

Govt census, 1982: State govt payments to local govts, by program, source of funds, level of govt, and State, with trends from 1902, 2460–3

HHS aid to each State and local govt or private instn, amount obligated, funding agency, and program, FY83, annual listing, 4004–3

HUD community dev programs funding and activities, for 5 programs, FY83, annual rpt, 5124–5

Puerto Rico organizations in US and Puerto Rico, philanthropic grants received, by foundation, purpose, and recipient, 1979-81, hearings, 21788–137.1

TVA activities, financial and operating data by program and facility, and power sales by customer, FY83, annual rpt, 9804–1

Urban Dev Action Grant awards to local areas, preliminary approvals, with project descriptions, private investment, and jobs and taxes to be created, by city, quarterly press release series, 5002–7

Urban Dev Action Grant program effectiveness, and participation of small cities by State, 1978-82, GAO rpt, 26113–118

see also City and town planning

see also Community Development Block Grants

see also New towns

see also Urban beautification

see also Urban renewal

Community health services

Alabama rural black population, education, employment, health services, and economic status, for 16 counties, selected years 1970-81, 11048–180

Budget of US, effects of Reagan Admin policy changes, by detailed program, FY85, annual rpt, 104–21

Children and youth benefitting from Fed Govt public welfare programs and tax expenditures, participation and funding for 71 programs, FY81-83, 21968–30

DC mental health facilities, services, and costs, and effect of St Elizabeths Hospital operations and finances transfer to DC govt, FY83, GAO rpt, 26121–72

Index by Subjects and Names

Hospital (community) occupancy rates by census div, and percent offering specialized facilities, by bed size, selected years 1978-81, article, 4652–1.418

Preventive health services block grants of Fed Govt, State funding by program, and opinions on State program admin, for 13 States, FY81-84, GAO rpt, 26121–88

Community mental health centers

see Community health services

see Mental health facilities and services

Community Planning and Development, HUD

Community dev programs funding and activities, for 5 HUD programs, FY83, annual rpt, 5124–5

Cost control proposals for Fed Govt programs and mgmt, 3-year savings by function and agency, and financial and operating data, 1960s-81, 16908–1.8

Urban area socioeconomic and fiscal trends and problems, 1950-83 and Fed Govt funding estimates for FY84-87, biennial rpt, 5124–4

Community Relations Service

Activities of Justice Dept, by subagency, FY82, annual rpt, 6004–1

Minority group discrimination disputes, CRS investigation and mediation, FY83, annual rpt, 6004–9

Community treatment centers

see Halfway houses

Commuter air carriers

see Airlines

Commuting

Carbon monoxide atmospheric concentrations and levels within buildings and along commuting and residential driving routes, for 4 cities, Jan-Mar 1981, 9198–110

Census of Housing, 1980: structural, financial, and householder characteristics, by region and State, 2475–4

Census of Population and Housing, 1980: data coverage, availability, and uses for urban and transportation planning, 1984 guide, 7558–101

Census of Population and Housing, 1980: detailed population and housing characteristics, by county, city, and census tract, State and SMSA rpt series, 2551–2

Census of Population, 1980: detailed socioeconomic and demographic characteristics, by age, sex, race, Hispanic origin, occupation, and industry, State rpt series, 2531–4

Census of Population, 1980: detailed socioeconomic characteristics, by county, city, and inside-outside SMSAs and central cities, State rpt series, 2531–3

Chicago area air pollution levels by location, late 1970s-82 and projected under lower auto emission standards to 1995, 3408–31

County and City Data Book, detailed socioeconomic and demographic data for States, counties, and cities, selected years 1976-82, 2328–1

DC metro area Metrorail transit system, effect on commuting patterns, population, business, land use, and environment, series, 7306–8

Energy use in transportation sector by mode, fuel supplies, and demographic and economic determinants of vehicle use, 1970s-83, annual rpt, 3304–5

Environmental quality and protection programs, costs, and Fed Govt enforcement, 1983, detailed annual rpt, 484–1

Fed Govt officials use of Govt chauffeur services for commuting, driver overtime hours and pay by agency, 4th qtr 1982, GAO rpt, 26123–63

Household head principal means of transport to work, distance and travel time, for 15 SMSAs, 1978, annual survey special supplement, 2485–8

Householder principal mode of transport, distance, and travel time to work, by race, Hispanic origin, tenure, urban-rural location, and region, 1981, annual survey, 2485–7

Householders principal means of transport to work, and distance and travel time, by inside-outside central cities, 1979-82 surveys, SMSA rpt series, 2485–6

Housing (rental) unit choice of Pittsburgh, Pa, recent movers related to unit, neighborhood, and town characteristics, 1967 survey, 9306–1.7

New Communities program of HUD, activities, costs, land sales, and community and population characteristics, for 13 communities, 1970s-83, 5188–107

Older persons population characteristics, and needs and costs of social services by type, by metro-nonmetro status, 1970s-82 with trends from 1900, 21148–28

Railroad commuter systems financial and operating data for 7 systems, and public agency cost reimbursement, 1980, 7888–61

Transit services for commuting and other purposes, dev and effects, series, 7306–9

Travel patterns, personal and household characteristics, auto use, and public transport availability, 1977 survey, series, 7556–6

Trips by mode of transport, and transit finances, 1980-82, article, 10042–1.404

Urban travel by purpose, effect of telecommunication advances, land use changes, and alternative work schedules, projected to 2000 with some trends 1950-80, 7888–63

Women's travel patterns, by employment and sociodemographic characteristics and type of child care used, 1980 survey, 7888–62

see also Automobiles

see also Buses

see also High-speed ground transportation

see also Metroliner

see also Pedestrians

see also Subways

see also Urban transportation

Comoros

AID activities and funding by project and function, FY85, and developing countries summary socioeconomic data, 1970s-83, by country, annual rpt, 9914–3

AID economic assistance to developing countries, obligations and disbursements by country, quarterly rpt, 9912–4

Economic, social, and political summary data, by country, 1984, annual factbook, 244–11

Exports of US, detailed Schedule E commodities by mode of transport and world area and country of destination, 1983, annual rpts, 2424–5

Index by Subjects and Names

Competition

Imports of US, detailed TSUSA commodities by country of origin, 1983, annual rpt, 2424–4

Loans and grants for economic and military assistance from US and intl agencies, by program and country, FY46-83, annual rpt, 9914–5

Minerals Yearbook, 1982, Vol 3: foreign country reviews of production, trade, and policies, by commodity, annual rpt, 5604–35

Minerals Yearbook, 1982, Vol 3 preprints: foreign country review of production, trade, and policies, by commodity, annual rpt, 5604–17.83

Population size and growth rates, and latest available benchmark demographic data, by country, 1950-83, biennial rpt, 2324–4

see also under By Foreign Country in the "Index by Categories"

Companies

see Business firms and establishments, number

see Corporations

see under By Individual Company or Institution in the "Index by Categories"

Compensation

see Earnings, general

see Earnings, specific industries

see Federal pay

see Payroll

see State and local employees pay

Compensatory education

Bilingual education programs, teachers, enrollment, and funding, selected years 1976-FY83, biennial rpt, 4804–14

Budget of US, effects of Reagan Admin policy changes, by detailed program, FY85, annual rpt, 104–21

Education Dept financial aid programs for educational instns and individuals, 1984 annual listing, 4804–3

Education Dept programs and activities, FY83, annual rpt, 4804–6

Education Dept programs funding, operations, and effectiveness, FY83, annual rpt, 4804–5

Elementary level Follow Through compensatory education programs beneficiaries, costs, funding, and participant test scores, selected years 1968-82, hearing, 21348–87

Fed Govt education block grants, State allocations by program and selected school district, FY82-84 and trends from FY60, hearing, 21408–75

Fed Govt funding for elementary and secondary education by agency, and Education Dept funding for special education by program, selected years FY60-84, 4808–9.3

Fed Govt public welfare programs and tax expenditures benefitting children and youth, participation and funding for 71 programs, FY81-83, 21968–30

Govt census, 1982: State govt payments to local govts, by program, source of funds, level of govt, and State, with trends from 1902, 2460–3

Indian Education Act, Fed Govt grants and fellowships awarded by State, FY83, and natl advisory council funding, FY73-84, annual rpt, 14874–1

Refugee resettlement program activities and funding, arrivals and population by

country of origin and State, and employment and other characteristics, FY83, annual rpt, 4704–8

Teaching degrees conferred by specialty and State, required credit hours, and instn officials attitudes, by instn type, 1970s-83, hearings, 21348–89

Vocational training bilingual projects, participants, characteristics, and costs, by program, FY82, annual rpt, 4804–26

see also Head Start Project

Competition

Agricultural imports of US, partially competitive and noncompetitive with domestic products, by country, FY83 and CY83, semiannual rpts, 1522–4

Agricultural products trade, tariffs, and industry operating data, 1979-83, TSUSA commodity rpt series, 9885–1

Airline deregulation in 1978, effect on industry operations and finances, air traffic patterns, and CAB programs, various periods FY76-84, 9148–56

Airline deregulation in 1978, traffic and service changes by city, with market shares, fares, and load factors, quarterly rpt, 9142–42

Auto industry finances and operations by manufacturer, foreign competition, and consumer auto expenditures and attitudes toward car buying, selected years 1968-85, annual rpt, 2004–8

Bank holding companies in Florida, profits related to market position, concentration, and deposit growth, 1973-77, article, 9371–1.401

Bank merger antitrust analysis geographic market definition, literature review, 1984 technical paper, 9366–1.138

Chemicals and related products trade, tariffs, and industry operating data, TSUSA commodity rpt series, 9885–4

Coal industry competitive effects of Fed Govt coal leasing, FY83 annual rpt, 6004–12

Communications satellite intl systems charges, operations, investment shares by country, and competition impacts, 1964-83 with projections to 2003, hearings, 25388–46

Export credit program activities of Eximbank and 6 OECD countries, 1982, annual rpt, 9254–3

Fed Govt procurement contract awards, by State, agency, procurement and contractor type, and for top 100 contractors, quarterly rpt, 102–6

Fed Govt programs and mgmt cost control proposals, 3-year savings by function and agency, and financial and operating data, 1960s-81, 16908–1

Financial instn deregulation, interstate banking, and bank performance and risks, 1984 conf papers, 9375–7

FTC investigative activity, litigation, and admin, FY82, annual rpt, 9404–1

Generalized System of Preferences status of 29 commodities, with US production, consumption, tariffs, and trade by country, selected years 1978-87, 9888–17

Import and tariff provisions effect on US industries and products, investigations with background financial and operating data, series, 9886–4

Imports from Communist countries, injury to US industries, investigations with background financial and operating data, selected industries and products, series, 9886–12

Imports injury to price-supported US agricultural industries, investigations with background financial and operating data for selected products, series, 9886–10

Imports injury to US industries from foreign subsidized products and sales in US at less than fair value, investigations with background financial and operating data, series, 9886–19

Imports injury to US industries from foreign subsidized products, investigations with background financial and operating data for selected industries and products, series, 9886–15

Imports injury to US industries from import sales at less than fair value, investigations with background financial and operating data, series, 9886–14

Imports injury to US industries from increased import sales, investigations with background financial and operating data, series, 9886–5

Imports injury to US industries from removal of duties on foreign subsidized products, investigations with background financial and operating data, series, 9886–18

Intl trade position of US and 4 OECD countries, and factors affecting US competition, quarterly pamphlet, 2042–25

Machine tool orders by selected industry, trade, and shipments and Japan share of US market by type of tool, various dates 1972-84, hearing, 25388–48

Manufactured goods relative market shares of largest US and foreign firms by selected industry and firm, 1960, 1970, and 1981, hearing, 21248–79

Manufactured products (miscellaneous) trade, tariffs, and industry operating data, TSUSA commodity rpt series, 9885–7

Metals and metal products trade, tariffs, and industry operating data, TSUSA commodity rpt series, 9885–6

Military procurement competitive, noncompetitive, and formally advertised awards, and awards by statutory authority and pricing provision, FY74-1st half FY84, semiannual rpt, 3542–1.2

Military procurement competitive, noncompetitive, and formally advertised awards, by size, FY83, annual rpt, 3544–19

Minerals (nonmetallic) and mineral products trade, tariffs, and industry operating data, TSUSA commodity rpt series, 9885–5

Mushroom imports injury to US industry, and stocks, production, sales, trade, and consumption, quarterly rpt, 9882–5

NASA procurement contract awards, by type, contractor, State, and country, FY84, semiannual rpt, 9502–6

Navy procurement, by contractor and location of work, FY83, annual rpt, 3804–13

Oil pipeline industry competition, market shares and throughput capacity by firm and market area, as of 1983, 6008–18

Competition

Real estate broker industry structure and practices, sales commissions, and broker and consumer attitudes, selected years 1975-81, 9408–48

Savings and loan assns, FHLB 4th District members financial results related to market competition, regression results, 1973-82, article, 9302–2.402

Semiconductor industry subsidies of Japan govt by program, with financial and operating data by firm, R&D, and comparisons to US industry, 1970s-83, hearings, 21368–46.1

Steel imports of US from EC and other countries, and US industry operating data, for 15 products limited under arrangement with EC, monthly rpt, 9882–10

Textile fiber and products trade, tariffs, and industry operating data, TSUSA commodity rpt series, 9885–3

Trans-Alaska Pipeline System owner companies financial data, and retail gasoline competitive position in 2 States, by company, 1980-83, hearing, 21728–51

Wood, paper, and printed matter trade, tariffs, and industry operating data, TSUSA commodity rpt series, 9885–2

see also Antitrust law

see also Dumping

see also Economic concentration and diversification

Comprehensive Employment and Training Act

Bilingual vocational training projects, participants, characteristics, and costs, by program, FY82, annual rpt, 4804–26

Fraud and abuse in Labor Dept programs, audits and investigations, 1st half FY84, semiannual rpt, 6302–2

Govt census, 1982: State govt payments to local govts, by program, source of funds, level of govt, and State, with trends from 1902, 2460–3

Participants of CETA by sociodemographic characteristics, and Labor Dept activities and staff, FY83, annual rpt, 6304–1

Rural area impact of Job Training Partnership Act, comparison to CETA program, 1973-84, article, 1502–7.403

Comptroller General of the U.S.

see General Accounting Office

Compulsory military service

see Selective service

Computer data file guides

Business Conditions Digest, historical supplement on economic, business, and financial conditions and cyclical fluctuations, with methodology, 1947-82, 2708–31

Census Bur activities, publications, and user services, monthly rpt, 2302–3

Census Bur computer data files, listing with irregular updates, 2302–5

Census Bur data coverage and availability for 1982 economic censuses and related statistics, 1984 guide, 2308–5

Census Bur publications and data files, monthly listing, 2302–6

Census Bur publications data coverage and availability, 1984 annual listing, 2304–2

Census Bur publications, data coverage, and suggested uses, series, 2326–7

Census of Agriculture, 1982: data coverage and availability for agriculture census and related statistics, 1984 guide, 2308–55

Census of Population and Housing, 1980: data coverage, availability, and uses for urban and transportation planning, 1984 guide, 7558–101

Fed Govt computer data files available from NTIS, by subject, 1984 annual listing, 2224–3

Food consumption natl survey, 1977-78, data tape availability, 1356–4.1

Health manpower and facilities data, by county and SMSA, users guide to computerized area resource file, 1983, annual rpt, 4114–11

HHS health data projects and systems, by subagency, FY83-84, annual inventory, 4044–3

High school classes of 1980 and 1982: educational and sociodemographic characteristics and expectations, natl longitudinal study, series, 4826–2

Hispanic Americans socioeconomic and demographic characteristics, and compared to non-Hispanics, selected years 1970-83, chartbook, 2328–48

Housing energy use, costs, expenditures, and conservation, and household and housing characteristics, survey series, 3166–7

Mines Bur publications and patents, monthly listing, 5602–2

NTIS computer data files, by agency, periodic listing, 2222–1

Occupational injuries and illnesses, data available from NTIS, by State, 1981, annual rpt, 6704–2

Computer programmers

see Computer use

Computer sciences

Census of Population, 1980: detailed socioeconomic and demographic characteristics, by age, sex, race, Hispanic origin, occupation, and industry, State rpt series, 2531–4

Computer specialists sociodemographic, educational, and employment characteristics, and Fed Govt support by agency, 1978, biennial Current Population Rpt, 2546–2.124

Degrees conferred in higher education, by race, Hispanic origin, sex, level, and field, selected years 1949/50-1979/80, annual rpt, 4824–2.16

DOT employment by subagency, State, and selected personnel characteristics, FY83, annual rpt, 7304–18

Engineers sociodemographic, educational, and employment characteristics, and Federal support by agency, 1978, Current Population Rpt, 2546–2.121

NSF grant and award recipients, by State, FY83, annual listing, 9624–11

NSF research programs, activities, and funding, FY82-83, annual rpt, 9624–6

Occupational manpower needs and supply by detailed occupation, and educational and training program enrollees and grads by detailed field, 1982 and 1995, biennial rpt, 6744–3

Occupational Outlook Handbook, 1984-85 biennial rpt, 6744–1

R&D and science-related Fed Govt funding and total and federally funded expenditures of universities and colleges, by instn and field of science, FY82, 9626–2.136

Index by Subjects and Names

R&D and science-related Fed Govt funding to higher education and nonprofit instns, by field, instn, agency, and State, FY82, annual rpt, 9627–17

R&D-employed scientists and engineers salaries by degree, type of establishment, age, experience, and field, 1984, annual rpt, 3004–1

R&D equipment at higher education instns, age, cost, funding sources, and users, for computer and physical sciences and engineering, 1982, 9626–2.138

R&D expenditures by higher education instns and federally funded centers, by field, source of funds, instn, and State, FY82, annual rpt, 9627–13

R&D expenditures by source, and scientists education and employment, detailed data by field, selected years 1953-84, annual rpt, 9624–18

R&D expenditures of higher education instns, and science and engineering employment and grad students, by field, 1972-83, biennial rpt, 9627–24

R&D Fed Govt facilities and services available for private sector use, by field of science, 1984 biennial listing, 2224–4

R&D Fed Govt funding for all performers, by field and supporting agency, selected years FY60-84, annual rpt, 9627–20

R&D funding by industry, program, and Federal agency, and high-technology trade performance, selected years 1960-FY84, 26306–6.77

Science and engineering doctoral degree recipients, by field, sex, race, age, citizenship, postgrad employment and study status, State, and instn, 1960-82, 9626–6.16

Science and engineering grad enrollment, fields of study, financial support, and other student and instn characteristics, 1975-82, annual survey, 9627–7

Science and engineering grad program enrollment, by field, degree level, source of financial support, race, and Hispanic origin, 1975-81, 9626–2.134

Science and engineering grad program enrollment by field, sources of financial support, and foreign students, 1975-82, 9626–2.141

Science and engineering grads of 1980-81, employment and median salaries by level and field of degree, 1982, 9626–2.137

Science and engineering grads of 1980-81, employment characteristics or grad enrollment, by degree level, field, sex, and race, 1982, 9627–25

Scientists and engineers employed at universities and colleges, by field, sex, and instn, 1973-82, 9626–2.140

Scientists and engineers employed at universities and colleges, by field, sex, State, and instn, Jan 1983 and selected trends from 1967, annual survey, 9627–11

Scientists and engineers employed in energy-related fields, supply/demand and effects of R&D funding, by energy type, employer type, field, and age, 1962-91, annual rpt, 3004–19

Scientists and engineers employment by sector and activity, and share female, black, and Asian descent, by field, 1982, 9626–2.142

Index by Subjects and Names

Computers

Scientists and engineers supply, employment, and education, by sex, race, Hispanic origin, and field, selected years 1965-83, biennial rpt, 9624–20

Scientists, engineers, and technicians employed in private industry, by occupation and industry group, 1980-81, biennial rpt, 9627–23

Scientists, engineers, and technicians needed in defense and nondefense industries, and supply/demand, by field, 1981-87, 9628–71

Computer software

see Computers

Computer use

- Air Force fiscal mgmt system operations and techniques, info for comptroller personnel, quarterly rpt, 3602–1
- Bank financial and operating statements, functional cost analysis for Fed Reserve member banks with average and high earnings, by deposit size, 1982, annual rpt, 9364–6
- Bank interstate service offices, including S&Ls, bank branches, and nonbank subsidiaries offering financial services, by instn and State, 1981-83, 9371–13
- Census of Population, 1980: detailed socioeconomic and demographic characteristics, by age, sex, race, Hispanic origin, occupation, and industry, State rpt series, 2531–4
- Census of Population, 1980: detailed socioeconomic characteristics, by county, city, and inside-outside SMSAs and central cities, State rpt series, 2531–3
- Census of Population, 1980: labor force, by sex, detailed occupation, and region, with comparison to 1970 census, supplementary rpt, 2535–1.12
- Commerce Dept regional center mgmt assistance operations, assessment, and procurement authority, by subagency, regional rpt series, 2006–4.2
- County Business Patterns: establishments, employees, and payrolls, by SIC 4-digit industry and county, 1982, annual State rpt series, 2326–6
- DOD contract and in-house commercial activities costs and work-years, by service branch, defense agency, State, and installation, FY83, annual rpt, 3544–25
- Employment, earnings, and hours, by SIC 4-digit nonfarm industry, monthly 1974-Feb 1984, annual update, 6744–4
- Employment, unemployment, and labor force, by demographic and employment characteristics, State, and for 30 metro areas and 11 large cities, 1983, annual rpt, 6744–7
- Fed Govt computers and telecommunications systems acquisition plans and obligations, by agency, FY84-89, annual rpt, 104–20
- Fed Govt programs and mgmt cost control proposals, 3-year savings by function and agency, and financial and operating data, 1960s-81, 16908–1
- Fed Govt standards for data recording, processing, and transfer, and for purchase and use of computer systems, series, 2216–2
- Foreign market and trade for computers and computer equipment, and user industry operations and demand, country market research rpts, 2045–1

GAO publications on computers, computer use, and telecommunication, as of 1983, annual listing, 26104–11.1

Graphic presentation of socioeconomic data, use, dev, and standards, 1978 conf papers, 2626–2.51

- GSA computers and automatic data processing systems costs, cost savings, and employment, by activity, subagency, and regional office, FY83-88, 9458–17
- Income tax returns of sole proprietorships, detailed data by industry div and selected industry group, 1981, annual rpt, 8304–7
- Income tax returns of sole proprietorships, receipts, deductions by type, payroll, and net income, by major industry, 1982, annual article, 8302–2.413
- Input-output structure of US economy, detailed interindustry transactions for 537 industries, and components of final demand, 1977 benchmark data, 2708–17
- Metalworking machinery industry computerized automation, by plant characteristics, for 6 industry groups and small plants, 1982 surveys, 23848–179
- Occupational manpower needs and supply by detailed occupation, and educational and training program enrollees and grads by detailed field, 1982 and 1995, biennial rpt, 6744–3
- *Occupational Outlook Handbook,* 1984-85 biennial rpt, 6744–1
- Property tax assessment, local jurisdictions reporting property characteristics, and use of automatic data processing, 1972-82, 1588–81
- Public health labs of States, personnel, finances, workloads, and other activities, by State, FY82, annual rpt, 4204–8
- Regional councils involved in service activities, by type of service and region population size, 1982 survey, hearing, 25408–88
- Schools (elementary and secondary) computer access and use, by region, urban-rural location, and Title I status, spring 1982, 4826–1.10
- Schools (elementary and secondary) computer use, by grade level and type of use, 1983, annual rpt, 4824–1.5
- Schools (elementary and secondary) computer use, by grade level, 1981/82, annual rpt, 4824–2.25
- Scientists, engineers, and technicians employment in transportation, utilities, and retail and wholesale trade, by field of science and industry, 1982, 9628–72
- Scientists, engineers, and technicians needed in defense and nondefense industries, and supply/demand, by field, 1981-87, 9628–71
- Service industry census, 1982: employment, establishments, receipts, and payroll, by SIC 2- to 4-digit kind of business, SMSA, county, and city, State rpt series, 2391–1
- Service industry census, 1982: employment, establishments, receipts, and payroll, by SIC 4-digit kind of business and State, preliminary rpt, 2390–2.7
- Wages of white-collar workers, by occupation, work level, and industry div, Mar 1984, annual rpt, 6784–2

Computers

- Agricultural Stabilization and Conservation Service field offices computer systems, costs and savings by component, FY84-92, GAO rpt, 26125–27
- Commerce Dept regional center mgmt assistance operations, assessment, and procurement authority, by subagency, regional rpt series, 2006–4.2
- County Business Patterns: establishments, employees, and payrolls, by SIC 4-digit industry and county, 1981, annual State rpt series, 2326–8
- County Business Patterns: establishments, employees, and payrolls, by SIC 4-digit industry and county, 1982, annual State rpt series, 2326–6
- Employment, earnings, and hours, by SIC 4-digit nonfarm industry, monthly 1974-Feb 1984, annual update, 6744–4
- Exports and imports of US, detailed SIC-based commodities by world area, 1983, annual rpts, 2424–6
- Exports of equipment with nuclear weapons applications, approvals for shipment to PRC by item and to other foreign markets, July 1981-June 1982, GAO rpt, 26123–76
- Exports of US, detailed commodities by country of destination, monthly rpt, 2422–3
- Exports of US, detailed Schedule B commodities by country of destination, 1983, annual rpt, 2424–9
- Exports of US, detailed Schedule E commodities by mode of transport and world area and country of destination, 1983, annual rpts, 2424–5
- Fed Govt computer software and documentation available from NTIS, by agency and program characteristics, 1984 annual listing, 2224–2
- Fed Govt computer systems and costs, annual chartbook, discontinued, 9454–7
- Fed Govt computer systems and equipment, inventory by manufacturer, type, agency, and location, FY83, last issue of annual rpt, 9454–4
- Fed Govt computers and telecommunications systems acquisition plans and obligations, by agency, FY84-89, annual rpt, 104–20
- Fed Govt programs and mgmt cost control proposals, 3-year savings by function and agency, and financial and operating data, 1960s-81, 16908–1
- Fed Govt standards for data recording, processing, and transfer, and for purchase and use of computer systems, series, 2216–2
- Foreign market and trade for computers and computer equipment, and user industry operations and demand, country market research rpts, 2045–1
- Franchise business opportunities, by firm and kind of business, 1984 annual listing, 2044–27
- GAO publications on computers, computer use, and telecommunication, as of 1983, annual listing, 26104–11.1
- Great Lakes trade, by SITC 3-digit commodity, port, vessel type, world area, and country, 1982, annual rpt, 7744–3
- GSA computers and automatic data processing systems costs, cost savings, and employment, by activity, subagency, and regional office, FY83-88, 9458–17

Computers

- Health Services Research Natl Center grants and contracts, by program area, FY83, annual listing, 4184–2
- House of Representatives salaries, expenses, and contingent fund disbursement, detailed listings, quarterly rpt, 21942–1
- Imports of US, detailed Schedule A commodities by country and world area of origin, and mode of transport, 1983, annual rpts, 2424–2
- Imports of US, detailed Schedule A commodities by country, monthly rpt, 2422–2
- Imports of US, detailed TSUSA commodities by country of origin, 1983, annual rpt, 2424–4
- Industrial process control equipment foreign market and trade, and user industry operations and demand, country market research rpts, 2045–6
- Industry finances and operations, by SIC 2- to 4-digit industry, 1970s-83 and projected to 1988, annual rpt, 2014–4
- Input-output structure of US economy, detailed interindustry transactions for 537 industries, and components of final demand, 1977 benchmark data, 2708–17
- Manufacturing census, 1982: financial and operating data, by SIC 2- to 4-digit industry, State, SMSA, and county, preliminary census div rpt series, 2491–3
- Manufacturing census, 1982: financial and operating data, for SIC 4-digit industries by product, preliminary rpt, 2491–1.345
- Occupational injury and illness rates, by SIC 2- to 4-digit industry, 1982, annual rpt, 6844–1
- OECD trade, total and for 4 major countries, and US trade by country, by commodity, 1972-82, annual world region rpt series, 244–13
- Producer prices and indexes, by stage of processing and detailed commodity, monthly rpt, 6762–6
- Producer prices and indexes, by stage of processing and detailed commodity, monthly 1983, annual supplement, 6764–2
- Robots installed for manufacturing, and jobs displaced and created by occupation, by type of robot use, 1980s-2000, hearings, 21728–54
- Schools (elementary and secondary) computer access and use, by region, urban-rural location, and Title I status, spring 1982, 4826–1.10
- Shipments, trade, and consumption of office computing, accounting, and related machines, by product, 1982-83, annual Current Industrial Rpt, 2506–12.2
- *Statistical Abstract of US,* social, political, and economic data, 1950s-83 and trends, annual rpt, 2324–1.1
- Video games and game software and components, effects of foreign imports on US industry, investigation with background financial and operating data, 1984 rpt, 9886–4.71
- Wholesale trade census, 1982: employment, establishments, sales by commodity, and payroll, by SIC 4-digit kind of business and State, preliminary rpt, 2403–1.12
- *see also* Computer data file guides
- *see also* Computer sciences

see also Computer use
see also Economic and econometric models
see also Information storage and retrieval systems

COMSAT

see Communications Satellite Corp.

COMSIS Corp.

"Transportation Planners' Guide to Using the 1980 Census", 7558–101

Concentration, business

see Economic concentration and diversification

Concord, Calif.

see also under By City in the "Index by Categories"

Concord, N.C.

- Census of Housing, 1980: occupancy and unit characteristics, by race, Hispanic origin, and city, SMSA rpt, 2473–1.316
- Census of Population and Housing, 1980: detailed population and housing characteristics, by county, city, and census tract, SMSA rpt, 2551–2.316

Concrete

see Cement and concrete

Condominiums and cooperatives

- Census of Govts, 1982: properties, govt-assessed value, sales, and tax rates, by property type, State, SMSA, county, and city, 2453–1
- Census of Housing, 1980: inventory, occupancy, and unit characteristics, changes from 1973 by region and inside-outside SMSAs and central cities, series, 2473–3
- Census of Housing, 1980: occupancy and unit characteristics of SMSAs and central cities, by race, Hispanic origin, and city, State and SMSA rpt series, 2473–1
- Florida condominium sales in 3 counties, various periods 1978-83, hearings, 21408–71
- Housing occupancy and unit and household characteristics, by region and metro-nonmetro residence, 1983, biennial survey, 2485–1
- Income tax returns of corporations, detailed income and tax items by industry, 1981, annual rpt, 8304–4
- Market absorption rate and characteristics for nonsubsidized privately financed units completed in 1982, annual Current Housing Rpt, 2484–2
- Market absorption rates and characteristics for nonsubsidized privately financed units completed in 1983, preliminary annual Current Housing Rpt, 2484–3
- Market absorption rates for condominiums, and completions by rent class and sales price, quarterly rpt, 2482–2
- Mortgages FHA-insured, new issues, adjustments, and terminations, by program, quarterly rpt, 5142–6
- New condominiums and townhouses, by intended use, units per structure, tenure, and region, monthly rpt, annual tables, 2382–1
- Vacancy status of condominiums and cooperatives, by occupant race, Hispanic origin, urban-rural location, and region, 1981, annual survey, 2485–7

Confectionery products

see Candy and confectionery products

Index by Subjects and Names

Conferences

- Arms control treaties status, and Arms Control and Disarmament Agency activities, 1983, annual rpt, 9824–2
- Asia developing countries housing finance and low-income housing projects, and activities of 2 countries, 1970s-82, annual conf proceedings, 9914–11
- Auto safety and experimental vehicle designs, 1982, conf proceedings, annual rpt, 7764–3
- Aviation activity forecasts, methodology, data sources, and coverage, Feb 1983 conf papers, annual rpt, 7504–28
- Bonneville Power Admin energy conservation rpts, educational materials, and 1982 conferences, 1983 rpt, 3228–2.2
- Carbon dioxide atmospheric levels, climatic effects and impacts of fossil and synthetic fuels use, deforestation, and land use patterns, research rpt series, 3406–3
- Climatological data mgmt for Antarctic, 1983 workshop proceedings, 2156–18.15
- Cocaine use, user characteristics, medical and botanical research, and South American production and legal policy and enforcement, 1979 intl conf papers, 7008–40
- Crime and criminal justice statistics analysis, methodology, and use in courts, 1983 biennial conf proceedings, 6064–20
- Disabled Hispanic Americans, by disability type and severity and for 5 States, selected years 1970-78, conf proceedings, 16598–5
- Economic time series of Fed Govt, content, design, and methodology, research rpt and conf proceedings series, 2626–7
- Elementary and secondary schools use of tests, teacher and student attitudes, with detail for standardized achievement tests, 1980 conf papers, 4918–15
- Farm finance and credit conditions, forecast 1984, conf papers, annual rpt, 1004–16
- Farm finance and credit conditions, forecast 1984, conf summary, annual rpt, 9264–9
- Financial and monetary studies, Fed Reserve Bank of Boston conf papers and proceedings series, 9373–3
- Financial instn deregulation, interstate banking, and bank performance and risks, 1984 conf papers, 9375–7
- Health survey design and research methods, 1982 biennial conf proceedings, 4184–1
- Immunization and preventive medicine programs for children in US and Mexico, and disease cases, vaccine reactions, and deaths, 1984 conf papers, 4204–15
- IRS and other Fed Govt admin record research methods, data collection and use, 1984 annual conf papers, 8304–17
- Judicial Conf semiannual proceedings and findings, 1984 annual rpt, 18204–5
- Mexico and US range and wildlife characteristics, problems, and research strategies and needs, 1981 conf papers, 1208–197
- Mexico economic indicators, trade, external accounts and debt, oil industry, and relations with US, 1978-83 with trends from 1959, conf proceedings, 21248–82
- NIH intl program activities and funding, by inst and country, FY83, annual rpt, 4474–6

Index by Subjects and Names

NOAA scientific and technical publications, monthly listing, 2142–1

Older persons long-term health care and financing alternatives, including nursing home insurance and use of home equity, 1984 conf papers, 4658–7

Pension and other benefits of private industry, pension plans created and terminated since 1939, and NYC retirement systems assets, 1978-83, conf proceedings, 25408–89

Pension benefits and after-tax salary replacement rates by plan type, and older persons income and income sources, by age and marital status, 1950s-82, conf proceedings, 25408–87

Pension plan investment in Fed Govt mortgage-backed securities, yields by issuer, and fund assets by fund type, 1970s-82, conf papers, 5008–32

Population socioeconomic data graphic presentation use, dev, and standards, 1978 conf papers, 2626–2.51

Productivity of labor and capital, costs, and prices, by selected industry, and compared to 6 OECD countries, selected years 1947-82, 17898–1

Public welfare programs evaluation, and research and statistical projects and techniques, 1983 conf papers, 4704–11

Telecommunications and Info Natl Admin research and engineering rpts, FY83, annual listing, 2804–3

Congenital malformations *see* Birth defects

Conglomerates *see* Business acquisitions and mergers *see* Economic concentration and diversification

Congo

- Agricultural situation in sub-Saharan Africa, by country, 1982-83 and outlook for 1984, annual rpt, 1524–4.10
- AID activities and funding by project and function, FY85, and developing countries summary socioeconomic data, 1970s-83, by country, annual rpt, 9914–3
- AID economic assistance to developing countries, obligations and disbursements by country, quarterly rpt, 9912–4
- Economic conditions and foreign marketing prospects in 46 Sub-Saharan countries, 1983 world region rpt, 2046–5.1
- Economic, social, and political summary data, by country, 1984, annual factbook, 244–11
- Economic trends in income, production, prices, employment, finances, and trade, 1984 annual rpt, 2046–4.20
- Exports of US, detailed Schedule B commodities by country of destination, 1983, annual rpt, 2424–9
- Exports of US, detailed Schedule E commodities by mode of transport and world area and country of destination, 1983, annual rpts, 2424–5
- Imports of US, detailed Schedule A commodities by country and world area of origin, and mode of transport, 1983, annual rpts, 2424–2
- Imports of US, detailed TSUSA commodities by country of origin, 1983, annual rpt, 2424–4
- Loans and grants for economic and military assistance from US and intl agencies, by program and country, FY46-83, annual rpt, 9914–5

Military aid of US, arms sales, and training programs costs and budget requests by program, world region, and country, FY83-85, annual rpt, 7144–13

Military spending, arms trade, and armed forces size, with total govt spending and population, by country, 1972-82, annual rpt, 9824–1

Minerals Yearbook, 1982, Vol 3: foreign country reviews of production, trade, and policies, by commodity, annual rpt, 5604–35

Minerals Yearbook, 1982, Vol 3 preprints: foreign country review of production, trade, and policies, by commodity, annual rpt, 5604–17.82

Population size and growth rates, and latest available benchmark demographic data, by country, 1950-83, biennial rpt, 2324–4

see also under By Foreign Country in the "Index by Categories"

Congress

- Budget of US Appendix, detailed budgets and personnel summaries, by agency, FY85, annual rpt, 104–3
- Budget of US, appropriations, outlays, balances, and budget receipts, by govtl branch and agency, FY83, annual rpt, 8104–2
- Budget of US, effects of Reagan Admin policy changes, by detailed program, FY85, annual rpt, 104–21
- Budget of US, object class analysis of obligations, by branch of Fed Govt and selected depts and agencies, FY85 estimates, annual rpt, 104–9
- Budget of US, receipts by source and outlays by agency and program, monthly rpt, 8102–3
- Fed Govt consolidated financial statements based on business accounting methods, FY82-83, annual rpt, 8104–5
- Financial operations of Fed Govt, detailed data, *Treasury Bulletin,* quarterly rpt, 8002–4
- Immigration and nationality private bills introduced and laws enacted, 77th-97th Congresses, annual rpt, 6264–2
- Mail (franked) USPS operating costs itemized by class of mail, FY83, annual rpt, 9864–4
- Mail (franked) volume and costs, FY83, annual rpt, 9864–2
- Mail (franked) volume and revenue, quarterly rpt, 9862–1
- *Statistical Abstract of US,* social, political, and economic data, 1950s-83 and trends, annual rpt, 2324–1.2
- *see also* Architect of the Capitol
- *see also* Congressional apportionment
- *see also* Congressional Budget Office
- *see also* Congressional committees
- *see also* Congressional districts
- *see also* Congressional employees
- *see also* Congressional-executive relations
- *see also* Congressional investigations
- *see also* Congressional powers
- *see also* Cost Accounting Standards Board
- *see also* General Accounting Office
- *see also* Government Printing Office
- *see also* House of Representatives
- *see also* Library of Congress
- *see also* Office of Technology Assessment
- *see also* Senate

Congressional committees

Congressional apportionment

Statistical Abstract of US, social, political, and economic data, 1950s-83 and trends, annual rpt, 2324–1.2

Congressional Budget Office

- Budget of US Appendix, detailed budgets and personnel summaries, by agency, FY85, annual rpt, 104–3
- Budget of US, appropriations, outlays, balances, and budget receipts, by govtl branch and agency, FY83, annual rpt, 8104–2
- Budget of US, CBO analysis and review of FY85 budget by function, annual rpt, 26304–2
- Budget of US, CBO analysis of revenue and spending alternatives and projections of economic indicators, FY85-89, annual rpt, 26304–3
- Budget of US, CBO analysis of revenue and spending estimation errors in congressional concurrent resolutions, FY80-82, 26308–48
- Cost control proposals for Fed Govt programs and mgmt, CBO and GAO estimates of savings by function and agency, FY85-89, 26308–45
- DOD procurement cost estimate changes for weapons systems, and program delays and mgmt, by system and service branch, 1983, annual rpt, 26304–5
- EPA budget and full-time staff positions by type of activity, and grants to States, by program, FY75-84 and proposed FY85, 26308–47
- Fed Govt agency budget requests and program costs and characteristics, CBO working paper series, 26306–3
- Fed Govt debt by holder, interest rates and costs, and financing mechanisms, projected FY84-89 with data for FY80-83, 26308–50
- Fed Govt programs of congressional legislative interest, objectives, feasibility, benefits, and costs, CBO study series, 26306–6
- Nuclear power plant spent fuel permanent disposal site and transport costs, and Nuclear Waste Fund financing, alternative projections FY83-2037, 26308–49
- Oil and gas finances by firm, and effect of income and excise tax provisions on firms, Fed Govt revenues, and investor tax returns, 1980 and projected to 1992, hearing, 21788–132
- R&D Fed Govt funding, by function, agency, and program, selected years FY80-84 and proposed FY85, 26308–46

Congressional committees

- Cost control proposals for Fed Govt programs and mgmt, CBO and GAO estimates of savings by function and agency, FY85-89, 26308–45
- House of Representatives salaries, expenses, and contingent fund disbursement, detailed listings, quarterly rpt, 21942–1
- Senate committee salaries, expenses, and contingent fund disbursements, by payee, detailed listings, 1st half FY84, semiannual rpt, 25922–1
- *see also* House Administration Committee
- *see also* House Aging Committee, Select
- *see also* House Agriculture Committee
- *see also* House Armed Services Committee

Congressional committees

see also House Banking, Finance and Urban Affairs Committee
see also House Budget Committee
see also House Children, Youth, and Families Committee, Select
see also House Education and Labor Committee
see also House Energy and Commerce Committee
see also House Government Operations Committee
see also House Interior and Insular Affairs Committee
see also House Judiciary Committee
see also House Merchant Marine and Fisheries Committee
see also House Narcotics Abuse and Control Committee, Select
see also House Post Office and Civil Service Committee
see also House Science and Technology Committee
see also House Small Business Committee
see also House Ways and Means Committee
see also Joint Economic Committee
see also Joint Taxation Committee
see also Senate Aging Committee, Special
see also Senate Agriculture, Nutrition, and Forestry Committee
see also Senate Armed Services Committee
see also Senate Banking, Housing, and Urban Affairs Committee
see also Senate Commerce, Science and Transportation Committee
see also Senate Energy and Natural Resources Committee
see also Senate Environment and Public Works Committee
see also Senate Finance Committee
see also Senate Foreign Relations Committee
see also Senate Governmental Affairs Committee
see also Senate Judiciary Committee
see also Senate Rules and Administration Committee
see also Senate Small Business Committee, Select
see also under names of individual subcommittees (starting with Subcommittee)

Congressional districts

Election campaign financial activities of House and Senate candidates for 1984 elections, by State and district, 1983-84, 9276–2.6

Election campaign political action committee funding, by House and Senate candidate, 1978-82 Federal elections, biennial rpt, 9274–4

Energy conservation grants of Fed Govt to public and nonprofit private instns, by building type and State, 1983, annual rpt, 3304–15

Fed Govt aid to State and local areas, by type of payment, State, county, and city, FY83, annual rpt, 2464–3

HHS aid to each State and local govt or private instn, amount obligated, funding agency, and program, FY83, annual listing, 4004–3

Higher education instns, type, location, enrollment, and student charges, by State and congressional district, 1983/84, biennial listing, 4844–11

Schools in federally impacted areas, Fed Govt funding by county and school and congressional district, and eligible pupils, by State, FY83, annual rpt, 4804–10

VA program expenditures, by county and congressional district, FY83, annual rpt, 9924–14

Congressional elections

see Congressional districts
see Elections

Congressional employees

Employment (civilian) of Fed Govt, by location, agency, and pay system, 1982, biennial rpt, 9844–8

Employment, earnings, and hours, by level and branch of govt, and function, monthly 1977-Feb 1984, annual update, 6744–4

GAO workforce composition, and assignments to congressional committees, FY83, annual rpt, 26104–1

House of Representatives salaries, expenses, and contingent fund disbursement, detailed listings, quarterly rpt, 21942–1

Pay rates of Fed Govt civilian employees, by branch of govt, employee category, and pay level, as of 1984 with trends from 1789, 21628–54

Senate salaries, expenses, and contingent fund disbursements, by payee, detailed listings, 1st half FY84, semiannual rpt, 25922–1

Congressional ethics

see Political ethics

Congressional-executive relations

Budget of US, CBO analysis and review of FY85 budget by function, annual rpt, 26304–2

Cost control proposals for Fed Govt programs and mgmt, 3-year savings by function and agency, and financial and operating data, 1960s-81, 16908–1

Info sources and systems of Fed Govt available to Congress, listings, series, 26106–5

see also Executive impoundment of appropriated funds

Congressional investigations

Senate disbursements for inquiries and investigations, detailed listing, 1st half FY84, semiannual rpt, 25922–1

see also General Accounting Office

Congressional joint committees

see also Joint Economic Committee
see also Joint Taxation Committee

Congressional powers

Budget of US, CBO analysis of revenue and spending estimation errors in congressional concurrent resolutions, FY80-82, 26308–48

Cost control proposals for Fed Govt programs and mgmt, 3-year savings by function and agency, and financial and operating data, 1960s-81, 16908–1

Fed Govt expenditures in States and local areas, Census Bur data collection, limitation, contributing agency costs, and opinions of congressional users, 1984

GAO rpt, 26111–20

see also Congressional-executive relations
see also Presidential powers

Congressional Research Service

"Acid Rain: A Survey of Data and Current Analyses", 21368–52

"Comprehensive Federal Crop Insurance: Issues After Two Years", 21168–28

Index by Subjects and Names

"Decline in Competitiveness of the U.S. Copper Industry", 21368–55

"Federal Programs Affecting Children", 21968–30

"Housing: An Overview", 21968–28

"Rental Housing for the Large Family", 21968–28

"Residential Energy Conservation: How Far Have We Progressed and How Much Farther Can We Go?", 21368–48

Conklin, Jonathan E.

"Disease Staging: Implications for Hospital Reimbursement and Management", 4652–1.425

Conley, James R.

"Collective Bargaining Calendar Crowded Again in 1984", 6722–1.402

Connecticut

Agriculture census, 1982: farms, farmland, production and costs, and operator characteristics, preliminary State summary and county rpts, 2330–1.9

Agriculture census, 1982: farms, farmland, production, finances, and operator characteristics, by county, final State rpt, 2331–1.7

Bank deposits in commercial and mutual savings banks and in US branches of foreign banks, by account type, instn, State, SMSA, and county, June 1983, annual rpt, 9295–3.1

Bankruptcy (personal), filings in Connecticut by debt type, whether claiming Federal homestead exemption, and other characteristics, 1980, hearing, 21528–57.1

Cancer cases, incidence, deaths, and death rates, by body site, age, race, Hispanic origin, and sex, for 10 geographic areas, 1973-81, 4478–130

Census of Housing, 1980: occupancy and unit characteristics of SMSAs and central cities, by race, Hispanic origin, and city, State rpt, 2473–1.8

Census of Population and Housing, 1980: detailed population and housing characteristics, by county, city, and census tract, State rpt, 2551–2.8

Census of Population, 1980: detailed socioeconomic and demographic characteristics by age, sex, race, Hispanic origin, and industry, State rpt, 2531–4.8

County Business Patterns: establishments, employees, and payrolls, by SIC 4-digit industry and county, 1982, annual State rpt, 2326–6.8

Economic indicators for New England States, Fed Reserve 1st District, monthly rpt with articles, 9373–2

Employment, earnings, and hours, by selected SIC 1- to 4-digit industry, State, and for 278 major labor areas, 1939-83, annual rpt, 6744–5.1, 6744–5.3

Energy conservation (housing) program of Connecticut utility group, cost effectiveness and characteristics of participants and nonparticipants, 1980-82, 3308–77

Environmental quality, pollutant discharge by type and source, and EPA protection activities and funding, 1970s-83, biennial regional rpt, 9184–15.1

Exports of manufactured and agricultural commodities, manufacturing production, and export-related employment, 1960s-82, State rpt, 2046–3.7

Index by Subjects and Names

HHS aid to each State and local govt or private instn, amount obligated, funding agency, and program, FY83, annual listing, 4004–3.1

Home health agencies costs related to level of medical service and administrative spending, 1981, article, 4652–1.411

Income (personal) per capita and by source, and earnings by industry div, by State, MSA, and county, 1977-82, annual regional rpt, 2704–2.2

Mineral Industry Surveys, State review of production, 1983, advance annual rpt, 5614–6.7

Minerals Yearbook, 1982, Vol 2: State reviews of production, sales, and firms, by commodity, and business activity, annual rpt, 5604–34

Nurses in Connecticut, smoking habits and attitudes on quitting and setting example for others, 1981 with comparisons to nurses nationwide in 1975, article, 4102–1.403

Population size and components of change, by MSA and county, 1980-82, annual State Current Population Rpt, 2546–4.7

Retail trade census, 1982: employment, establishments, sales, and payroll, by SIC 2- to 4-digit kind of business, SMSA, county, and city, State rpt, 2397–1.7

Savings and loan assns, FHLB 1st District member instns financial operations and related economic and housing indicators, monthly rpt, 9302–4

TV and radio industry minority and women employment by occupation, and business owners, by race and State, with revenues and stations, 1971-81, hearing, 21368–45

Wages for 3 occupational groups, relative average levels in 78 labor market areas, 1983, annual press release, 6785–13

Wages of office and plant workers, by occupation, 1984 labor market area survey rpt, 6785–3.9

Wholesale trade census, 1982: employment, establishments, finances, and operations, by SIC 2- to 4-digit kind of business, SMSA, county, and city, State rpt, 2405–1.7

see also Bridgeport, Conn.
see also Bristol, Conn.
see also Danbury, Conn.
see also Hartford, Conn.
see also Meriden, Conn.
see also New Britain, Conn.
see also New Haven, Conn.
see also New London, Conn.
see also Norwalk, Conn.
see also Norwich, Conn.
see also Stamford, Conn.
see also Waterbury, Conn.
see also West Haven, Conn.
see also under By State in the "Index by Categories"

Conrail

see Consolidated Rail Corp.

Conscription

see Selective service

Conservation of natural resources

Agricultural Conservation Program participation and payments, by State, FY83, annual rpt, 1804–7

Agricultural Stabilization and Conservation Service producer payments under 26 programs, monthly rpt, 1802–10

Agricultural Statistics, 1983, annual rpt, 1004–1.2

Budget of US Appendix, detailed budgets and personnel summaries, by agency, FY85, annual rpt, 104–3

Budget of US, compact budgets by function, agency, and account, FY85 with projections to FY89, annual rpt, 104–2

Budget of US, receipts by source and outlays by agency and program, monthly rpt, 8102–3

Budget of US, receipts by source and outlays by function, FY40-89 estimates revised for consistency with FY85 budget definitions, annual rpt, 104–12

Construction industries census, 1982: financial and operating data, by SIC 4-digit industry and State, final rpt, 2373–1.7

Construction industries census, 1982: financial and operating data, by SIC 4-digit industry and State, preliminary rpt series, 2371–1

Construction put in place, permits authorized by region, State, and MSA, and Federal contract awards, by construction type, bimonthly rpt with articles, 2012–1

Construction put in place, value of new public and private structures, by type, monthly rpt, 2382–4

EPA programs fraud and abuse, audits and investigations, 2nd half FY84, semiannual rpt, 9182–10

Fed Govt aid to State and local govts, expenditures, and direct payments, by program, agency, and State, FY83, annual rpt, 2464–2

Fed Govt consolidated financial statements based on business accounting methods, FY82-83, annual rpt, 8104–5

Fed Govt construction grants, loans, and loan guarantees, by program and type of structure, FY80-83 and estimated FY84-85, annual article, 2012–1.404

Fed Govt financial and nonfinancial domestic aid, 1984 annual comprehensive catalog, 104–5

Fed Govt grants-in-aid for 13 program areas, FY82-84, annual article, 10042–1.402

Fish and Wildlife Service conservation and research project descriptions and results, by program, FY83, annual rpt, 5504–20

FmHA loans and grants by program and State, and summary of services, FY83 with trends from FY63, annual rpt, 1184–17

Forest, range, and associated waters use and mgmt assessment, and environmental impacts of Forest Service program options, 1977-2030 and trends from 1920, 1208–24

Forest Service programs and activities, by State and region, FY83, annual rpt, 1204–1

GAO publications on land use, ownership, mgmt, and planning, 1979-83, annual listing, 26104–11.3

Govt census, 1982: city govt revenues by source, expenditures by function, debt, and assets, by State and city, 2457–4

Govt census, 1982: county govt revenues by source, expenditures by function, debt, and assets, by State and county, 2457–3

Consolidated Rail Corp.

Govt census, 1982: employment, payrolls, and average earnings, by function, level of govt, State, county, population size, and inside-outside SMSAs, 2455–2

Govt finances, by level of govt, State, and for large cities and counties, 1981-83, annual rpt series, 2466–2

Govt revenues by source and expenditures by function, natl income and product account, *Survey of Current Business,* monthly rpt, monthly and annual tables, 2702–1.24

Land Mgmt Bur activities and finances, and public land acreage and use, annual State rpt series, 5724–11

Mexico and US range and wildlife characteristics, problems, and research strategies and needs, 1981 conf papers, 1208–197

Occupational manpower needs and supply by detailed occupation, and educational and training program enrollees and grads by detailed field, 1982 and 1995, biennial rpt, 6744–3

Regional councils involved in service activities, by type of service and region population size, 1982 survey, hearing, 25408–88

Statistical Abstract of US, social, political, and economic data, 1950s-83 and trends, annual rpt, 2324–1.1

TVA activities, financial and operating data by program and facility, and power sales by customer, FY83, annual rpt, 9804–1

Water Bank Program agreements, acreage, and Fed Govt payments, by State, monthly rpt, 1802–5

Youth Conservation Corps activities, costs, and participant characteristics, by sponsoring agency, 1982, annual rpt, 5304–12

see also Birds and bird conservation
see also Endangered species
see also Energy conservation
see also Environmental pollution and control
see also Flood control
see also Forests and forestry
see also International cooperation in conservation
see also Land use
see also Marine resources conservation
see also National forests
see also National park system
see also Plants and vegetation
see also Reclamation of land
see also Recycling of waste materials
see also Severance taxes
see also Soils and soil conservation
see also Water resources development
see also Wilderness areas
see also Wildlife and wildlife conservation
see also Wildlife refuges

Considine, Thomas J., Jr.

"Analysis of New York's Timber Resources", 1206–16.7

Consolidated Metropolitan Statistical Areas

see Metropolitan Statistical Areas
see under By SMSA or MSA in the "Index by Categories"

Consolidated Rail Corp.

Finances and operations of railroads, detailed data by firm, class of service, and district, 1983, annual rpt, 9486–6.1

Operations of Conrail and finances and activities of US Railway Assn, FY81-83, annual rpt, 29604–1

Constitutional law

Constitutional law
see also Administrative law and procedure
see also Citizenship
see also Civil rights
see also Congressional-executive relations
see also Congressional powers
see also Due process of law
see also Federal-State relations
see also Habeas corpus
see also Judicial powers
see also Presidential powers

Construction industry

- Air pollutant emission factors, by detailed source, 3rd edition, 1983-84 supplements, 9198–13
- American Samoa minimum wage rates, employment, earnings, and benefits, by establishment and industry, Nov 1983, biennial rpt, 6504–6
- Asbestos workers, exposure levels, cancer incidence, and deaths, by industry and occupation, and asbestos regulation enforcement and costs/benefits, various periods 1940-2027, hearing, 21408–72
- Bombing (explosive and incendiary) incidents, damage, injuries, and deaths, by target, State, and circumstances, 1983, annual rpt, 6224–5
- Business activity indicators (nonfinancial), 1982, annual rpt, 9364–5.9
- Business statistics, detailed data for major industries and economic indicators, *Survey of Current Business,* monthly rpt, 2702–1.3
- Census of Population, 1980: detailed socioeconomic and demographic characteristics, by age, sex, race, Hispanic origin, occupation, and industry, State rpt series, 2531–4
- Census of Population, 1980: detailed socioeconomic characteristics, by county, city, and inside-outside SMSAs and central cities, State rpt series, 2531–3
- Census of Population, 1980: labor force, by sex, detailed occupation, and region, with comparison to 1970 census, supplementary rpt, 2535–1.12
- Collective bargaining agreements expiring during year, covered workers by SIC 2-digit industry, firm, and union, with summary of key provisions, 1984, annual rpt, 6784–9
- Collective bargaining wage and benefit rate changes in labor-mgmt agreements, quarterly press release, 6782–2
- County Business Patterns: establishments, employees, and payrolls, by SIC 4-digit industry and county, 1981, annual State rpt series, 2326–8
- County Business Patterns: establishments, employees, and payrolls, by SIC 4-digit industry and county, 1982, annual State rpt series, 2326–6
- DOD base construction and renovation, budget authorization requests by DOD component, State, country, and project, FY85, annual rpt, 3544–15
- DOD budget, expenditures for each service branch and total defense agencies, by function and State, FY85, annual rpt, 3544–23
- DOD engineering contract awards by function, contract type, and service branch, and oil and port dredging awards by company, 1970s-83, hearings, 21728–53

- DOD outlays and obligations, by function and service branch, quarterly rpt, 3542–3
- DOD prime contract awards to small and total business, for 10 categories and R&D, monthly rpt, 3542–10
- DOD procurement, prime contract awards by category, contract and contractor type, and service branch, FY74-1st half FY84, semiannual rpt, 3542–1
- DOD procurement, prime contract awards by detailed procurement category, FY80-83, annual rpt, 3544–18
- Earnings by industry div, and personal income per capita and by source, by State, MSA, and county, 1977-82, annual regional rpts, 2704–2
- Earnings by major industry group, and personal income per capita and by source, by region and State, 1929-82, 2708–40
- Earnings, weekly averages, monthly rpt, 23842–1.2
- Electric power plant (nuclear and coal-fired) construction itemized cost estimates, and investment per kilowatt for 20 cities, 1980s-95, 9638–52
- Employment and earnings, detailed data, monthly rpt, 6742–2.5
- Employment by detailed occupation, for 29 SIC 2-digit nonmanufacturing industries, 1981 BLS survey, 6748–60
- Employment, earnings, and hours, by selected SIC 1- to 4-digit industry, State, and for 278 major labor areas, 1939-83, annual rpt, 6744–5
- Employment, earnings, and hours, by SIC 4-digit nonfarm industry, monthly 1974-Feb 1984, annual update, 6744–4
- Employment, earnings, and hours, monthly press release, 6742–5
- Employment situation, earnings, hours, and other BLS economic indicators, transcripts of BLS Commissioner's monthly testimony, periodic rpt, 23846–4
- Employment, unemployment, and labor force, by demographic and employment characteristics, State, and for 30 metro areas and 11 large cities, 1983, annual rpt, 6744–7
- Fed Govt loans, grants, and tax benefits to business, by program and economic sector, projected FY84-88 with effective tax rates for FY80-82, 26306–6.70
- Fed Govt procurement contract awards, by State, agency, procurement and contractor type, and for top 100 contractors, quarterly rpt, 102–6
- Fed Govt programs and mgmt cost control proposals, 3-year savings by function and agency, and financial and operating data, 1960s-81, 16908–1.22
- Finances and operations, by SIC 2- to 4-digit industry, 1970s-83 and projected to 1988, annual rpt, 2014–4
- Foreign direct investment in US, major investors and investments by SIC 4-digit industry, transaction type and value, and location, 1983, annual rpt, 2044–20
- Franchise business opportunities, by firm and kind of business, 1984 annual listing, 2044–27
- Franchises of firms engaged in distribution of goods and services by kind of business, establishments by State, and sales, 1982-84, annual rpt, 2014–5

Index by Subjects and Names

- *Handbook of Labor Statistics,* employment, earnings, hours, and labor force characteristics, 1982 and trends, detailed annual rpt, 6724–1
- Hwy construction bids and contracts for Federal-aid interstate and secondary hwys, by State, 1st half 1984, semiannual rpt, 7552–12
- Hwy construction material prices and indexes for Federal-aid system, by type of material and urban-rural location, quarterly rpt, 7552–7
- Hwy receipts by source, and expenditures by function, by level of govt and State, 1983, annual rpt, 7554–1.4
- Income tax returns of corporations, detailed income and tax items by industry, 1981, annual rpt, 8304–4
- Income tax returns of corporations, summary data by industry div, 1981 estimates, annual article, 8302–2.403
- Income tax returns of corporations with foreign tax credit, income and deductions by type, asset size, and selected industry group, 1980, article, 8302–2.415
- Income tax returns of foreign subsidiaries of US corporations, income and tax data, by industry and asset size, 1980, article, 8302–2.410
- Income tax returns of partnerships, detailed data by industry, 1981 estimates, annual article, 8302–2.404
- Income tax returns of partnerships, receipts by source, deductions by type, and establishments, by selected industry, 1982, annual article, 8302–2.416
- Income tax returns of sole proprietorships, detailed data by industry div and selected industry group, 1981, annual rpt, 8304–7
- Income tax returns of sole proprietorships, receipts, deductions by type, payroll, and net income, by major industry, 1982, annual article, 8302–2.413
- Income tax returns with investment credits, for individuals by income, and for sole proprietorships by industry, 1981, article, 8302–2.409
- Industrial construction contracts and housing starts, *Business Conditions Digest,* cyclical indicators, monthly rpt, 2702–3.3
- Industrial construction contracts and housing starts, *Business Conditions Digest,* historical supplement and methodology, 1947-82, 2708–31
- Industry activity, employment, and earnings, and materials prices, by type of construction and region, bimonthly rpt with articles, 2012–1
- Input-output structure of US economy, detailed interindustry transactions for 85 industries, and components of final demand, 1977, article, 2702–1.421
- Input-output structure of US economy, detailed interindustry transactions for 537 industries, and components of final demand, 1977 benchmark data, 2708–17
- Machinery and equipment for construction, shipments and exports by type, quarterly Current Industrial Rpt, 2506–12.3
- Mineral Industry Surveys, explosives and blasting agents consumption by type, industry, and State, 1983, annual rpt, 5614–22
- *Minerals Yearbook, 1982,* Vol 2: State reviews of production, sales, and firms, by commodity, and business activity, annual rpt, 5604–34

Index by Subjects and Names

Minority group and women's employment, by occupational group, SIC 2- to 3-digit industry, State, and SMSA, 1981, annual rpt, 9244–1

Natl income and product, comprehensive accounts and components, *Survey of Current Business,* monthly rpt, monthly and annual tables, 2702–1.27

Natural gas interstate pipeline company detailed financial and operating data, by firm, 1983, annual rpt, 3164–38

New construction (public and private) put in place, value by type, monthly rpt, 2382–4

New construction (publicly and privately owned) activity, and new housing starts, 1929-83, annual rpt, 204–1.3

New England States economic indicators, Fed Reserve 1st District, monthly rpt, 9373–2.3

North Central States economic indicators, Fed Reserve 7th District monthly rpt, 9375–9

Nuclear power plant spent fuel permanent disposal site and transport costs, and Nuclear Waste Fund financing, alternative projections FY83-2037, 26308–49

Occupational injuries, illnesses, and workdays lost, by SIC 2-digit industry, 1982-83, annual press release, 6844–3

Occupational injury and illness rates, by SIC 2- to 4-digit industry, 1982, annual rpt, 6844–1

Occupational manpower needs and supply by detailed occupation, and educational and training program enrollees and grads by detailed field, 1982 and 1995, biennial rpt, 6744–3

Occupational Outlook Handbook, 1984-85 biennial rpt, 6744–1

Pension multiemployer plans in construction, trucking, and entertainment industries, and effect of exemption from withdrawal liability, 1977-81, GAO rpt, 26121–73

Scientists and engineers employed in energy-related fields, supply/demand and effects of R&D funding, by energy type, employer type, field, and age, 1962-91, annual rpt, 3004–19

Scientists, engineers, and technicians employed in private industry, by occupation and industry group, 1980-81, biennial rpt, 9627–23

Services intl transactions, and operations of US multinatl service firms and foreign affiliates, by industry and world region, 1977-82, 2706–5.30

Shipbuilding costs and related employment, by coastal district, 1982, annual rpt, 7704–12

Small and minority-owned businesses finances and operations, Federal contracts by agency, and worker characteristics, by industry, race, sex, and State, 1950s-83, annual rpt, 9764–6

Soil erosion rates for construction sites, by State and region, and water quality effects, 1984 rpt, 9208–123

Southeastern States and 5 SMSAs economic indicators, Fed Reserve 8th District, quarterly rpt, 9391–15

Southeastern States financial and economic devs, Fed Reserve 6th District, monthly rpt with articles, 9371–1

Soviet Union-US science and technology exchange projects, man-hours, and funding, by Fed Govt agency and activity type, FY81-82, 7008–41

Statistical Abstract of US, social, political, and economic data, 1950s-83 and trends, annual rpt, 2324–1.3

Trade assns, professional societies, and labor unions of construction and building materials industries, 1984 listing, article, 2012–1.405

Transportation census, 1982: trucks, by detailed characteristics, miles traveled, and type of product carried, State rpt series, 2573–1

TVA construction projects employment, and impacts on nearby areas, survey rpt series, 9806–7

Virgin Islands economic censuses, 1982: employment, establishments, payroll, and receipts, by SIC 1- to 4-digit industry, island, and city, 2593–1

Wage and benefit changes for construction workers from collective bargaining or employer decisions, quarterly article, 6782–1

Water pollution fish kills, by State, location, and pollution source, monthly 1978-80, annual rpt, 9204–3

Western States economic indicators, Fed Reserve 12th District, quarterly rpt, 9393–1.4

see also Building materials
see also Building permits
see also Cement and concrete
see also Census of Construction Industries
see also Housing construction
see also Housing maintenance and repair
see also Plumbing and heating
see also Wrecking and demolition
see also under By Industry in the "Index by Categories"

Consumer and Marketing Service
see Agricultural Marketing Service
see Animal and Plant Health Inspection Service

Consumer cooperatives
see also Agricultural cooperatives

Consumer credit

Auto and van operating and owning costs by component and vehicle size, for 12 years of operation, 1984 model year, biennial rpt, 7554–21

Auto, mobile home, and bank credit card loans, monthly rpt, 23842–1.5

Auto sales related to usury limits on loans in 2 States, and loans made and outstanding by lender type, various periods 1977-82, article, 9375–1.409

Business Conditions Digest, cyclical indicators, by economic process, monthly rpt, 2702–3.3

Business Conditions Digest, historical supplement on economic, business, and financial conditions and cyclical fluctuations, with methodology, 1947-82, 2708–31

Business statistics, detailed data for major industries and economic indicators, *Survey of Current Business,* monthly rpt, 2702–1.6

Economic growth rates and component economic indicators, selected years 1922-83 and projected under full employment to 1988, hearing, 21348–90

Consumer Price Index

Financial and business detailed statistics, *Fed Reserve Bulletin,* monthly rpt with articles, 9362–1

Financial and business statistics, historic trends, 1984 annual chartbook, 9364–2.11

Financial and business statistics, quarterly chartbook, 9362–2.5

Financial services of nonbank firms and bank holding companies, with financial and operating data by firm, 1981-82 with trends from 1962, technical paper, 9375–11.3

Flow-of-funds accounts, assets and liabilities by type and economic sector, year-end outstandings, 1960-83, annual rpt, 9364–3

Income tax proposals to encourage savings, and personal assets and liabilities by type, 1981, article, 8302–2.407

Installment and noninstallment credit, monthly rpt series, 9365–2

Installment credit extensions and liquidations, 1950-83, annual rpt, 204–1.5

Installment credit outstanding, extensions, and liquidations, monthly rpt, 9362–1.1

Installment credit outstanding, extensions, and liquidations, 1982, annual rpt, 9364–5.7

New England States financial instn assets and liabilities, Fed Reserve 1st District, monthly rpt, 9373–2.5

Savings and loan assn deregulation effect on lending activity, for US and 3 States, as of June 1980-83, article, 9371–1.432

Savings and loan assns and FSLIC-insured savings banks and S&Ls, assets, liabilities, and deposit and loan activity, monthly rpt, 9312–4

Western States economic indicators, Fed Reserve 12th District, quarterly rpt, 9393–1.5

see also Credit cards
see also Credit unions
see also Finance companies
see also Personal debt

Consumer Expenditure Survey

Expenditures and income sources by income, family characteristics, and region, 1980-81, annual rpt, 6724–1.7

Consumer expenditures
see Personal consumption

Consumer income
see Personal and family income

Consumer Price Index

Agricultural and food products prices, monthly rpt, 1502–4

Agricultural production, marketing, trade, supply, food consumption, and food and nutrition programs, 1960s-83, annual chartbook, 1504–3

BLS data collection, analysis, and presentation methods, by program, 1984 handbook, 6888–1

BLS measures of unemployment, labor productivity, and CPI, effects of undisclosed economic activity, with illustrative data, 1958-79, article, 6722–1.401

Budget deficits effect on economic indicators and trade balance of US and 4 countries, model results, various periods 1974-85, technical paper, 9366–7.102

Business statistics, detailed data for major industries and economic indicators, *Survey of Current Business,* monthly rpt, 2702–1.2

Consumer Price Index

Communist, OECD, and selected other countries economic statistics, 1960s-83, annual rpt, 244–5.2

CPI by component for US city average, and by region, population size, and for 28 SMSAs, monthly press release, 6762–1

CPI by detailed component, for US city average, 28 SMSAs, and 4 regions by population size, monthly rpt, 6762–2

CPI components relative importance, for selected SMSAs, and US city average by region and population size, 1983, annual rpt, 6884–1

CPI planned 1987 revisions to urban areas sampled and index publication schedule, 1984 press release, 6888–29

Dairy products CPI for all urban consumers, US city average, monthly rpt, 1317–4.2

Dallas-Fort Worth, Tex, SMSA employment, earnings, hours, and CPI changes, 1983 with trends from 1968, annual rpt, 6964–2

Denver-Boulder, Colo, SMSA employment, earnings, and CPI changes, 1983, annual rpt, 6974–2

Developing countries food supply policies, with farm sector data, tariff income, and prices and imports of 5 grains, for 21 countries, 1960s-81, 1528–168

Developing countries summary socioeconomic data, 1970s-83, and AID activities and funding by project and function, FY82-85, by country, annual rpt, 9914–3

EC social security programs benefits and expenditures, and unemployment rate, and economic indicators growth, 1960-82, article, 4742–1.405

Economic and demographic factors used in OASDI program cost estimates, selected years 1913-82 with alternative projections to 2060, 4706–1.90

Economic and financial trends, natl compounded annual rates of change, 1964-83, annual rpt, 9391–9.2

Economic and population time series data frequently used in statistical demand analyses, 1941-1982, annual rpt, 1544–21

Economic indicators and components, and Fed Reserve 4th District business and financial conditions, monthly chartbook, 9377–10

Economic indicators and components, current data and annual trends, monthly rpt, 23842–1.4

Economic indicators and labor force characteristics, selected years 1880-1995, chartbook, 6728–30

Economic indicators, nonfinancial, monthly rpt, 9362–1.2

Economic indicators, trends and relation to govt revenues and spending by level of govt, selected years 1929-83, annual rpt, 10044–1

Economic performance of US, and Reagan Admin 1984 spending, tax, and monetary policy proposals, with data for 1950s-83 and projected to 1988, press release, 8008–107

Economic trends and projections, 1970s-83, and Budget of US under current fiscal policy and alternatives, FY85-89, annual rpt, 26304–3.1

Economic trends, natl compounded annual rates of change, monthly rpt, 9391–3.1

Index by Subjects and Names

Employment and price changes during recession and recovery, by selected employee characteristics, 1979-Jan 1984, 6728–28

Employment Cost Index wage and salary component changes by occupational group, industry div, and collective bargaining status, and CPI changes, selected periods Sept 1975-Dec 1983, article, 6722–1.430

Financial and business statistics, historic trends, 1984 annual chartbook, 9364–2.6

Financial and business statistics, quarterly chartbook, 9362–2.3

Food price indexes (consumer and producer) and retail prices for selected items, and CPI for 25 cities, 1963-83, annual rpt, 1544–4.5

Footwear production, employment, consumption, prices, and US trade by country, quarterly rpt, 9882–6

Forecasts for selected business activities and natl economic indicators, compilation of representative opinions, 1984, annual rpt, 9389–3

Foreign and US indexes of consumer, producer, and major commodity prices, nonfarm wages, and currency value, US and 4 countries, bimonthly rpt, 2042–11

Foreign and US industrial production indexes and CPI, for US and 6 OECD countries, current data and annual trends, monthly rpt, 23842–1.7

Foreign consumer price indexes, 6 OECD countries and US, *Business Conditions Digest,* historical supplement and methodology, 1947-82, 2708–31

Foreign consumer price indexes, 6 OECD countries and US, *Business Conditions Digest,* monthly rpt, 2702–3.10

Foreign economic and monetary trends, compounded annual rates of change for US and 10 major trading partners, quarterly rpt, 9391–7

Foreign economic indicators and trade by country and country group, and US trade policy actions, 1960s-83, annual rpt, 444–1.4

Foreign economic indicators for 7 OECD countries and US, quarterly rpt, 2042–10

Foreign economic trends and implications for US, annual and semiannual country rpt series, 2046–4

Foreign price indexes, by selected country, 1950-82, annual rpt, 6724–1.10

Health care component of CPI, since 1940, monthly rpt, 4742–1.8

Health condition and health care resources, use, and expenditures, 1970s-82 with trends and projections 1900-2000, annual compilation, 4144–11

Houston, Tex, SMSA employment, earnings, hours, and CPI changes, 1983 with trends from 1968, annual rpt, 6964–1

Inflation rate, money supply growth, and food and energy prices, various periods 1970-2nd qtr 1984, article, 9391–1.420

Kansas City, Mo-Kans, SMSA employment, earnings, and CPI changes, with comparisons to total US, 1983, annual rpt, 6974–1

Mexico economic indicators, trade, external accounts and debt, oil industry, and relations with US, 1978-83 with trends from 1959, conf proceedings, 21248–82

Monthly Labor Review, CPI and PPI current statistics, 6722–1.5

New England States economic indicators, Fed Reserve 1st District, monthly rpt, 9373–2.4

New England States employment, wages, and price conditions by State and selected SMSA, 1983, annual rpt, 6916–7.1

North Central States economic indicators, Fed Reserve 7th District monthly rpt, 9375–9

North Central States farm credit conditions and economic devs, Fed Reserve 7th District, biweekly rpt, 9375–10

Northern Mariana Islands economic, govtl, and population data, 1970s-FY83 and population projections to 1990, annual rpt, 7004–6.2

NYC metro area CPI changes, by major component, 1979-83 with trends from 1916, annual rpt, 6924–2

OECD economic indicators, for US and 6 countries, biweekly rpt, 242–4

Price indexes (consumer and producer) by commodity and service group, and expenditure class, selected years 1929-83, annual rpt, 204–1.4

Price indexes (consumer and producer) changes for selected items, and changes in CPI for selected services, 1982-83, article, 6722–1.429

Price indexes, *Business Conditions Digest,* historical supplement and methodology, 1947-82, 2708–31

Price indexes, *Business Conditions Digest,* monthly rpt, 2702–3.6

Prices and living costs, selected years 1913-82, annual rpt, 6724–1.7

Recession and recovery effect on labor cost and price indexes, changes by index component, various periods 1949-82, article, 6722–1.464

Southeastern States employment, prices, earnings, and union membership in 8 States, Oct 1982-83, annual rpt, 6944–2

Southeastern States financial and economic devs, Fed Reserve 6th District, monthly rpt with articles, 9371–1

St Louis, Mo, SMSA employment, earnings, and CPI changes, 1983, annual rpt, 6974–3

Texas CPI average change by major component, for Dallas-Fort Worth and Houston, with comparisons to South and total US, 1973-82, BLS regional rpt series, 6966–1.12

Western States economic indicators, Fed Reserve 12th District, quarterly rpt, 9393–1.1

Western States housing outlook and economic and demographic trends, FHLB 11th District, urban area rpt series, 9306–2

Consumer Product Safety Commission Activities of CPSC, recalls, and product-related injuries, deaths, and medical costs, by product type and brand, FY83, annual rpt, 9164–2

Budget of US Appendix, detailed budgets and personnel summaries, by agency, FY85, annual rpt, 104–3

Budget of US, appropriations, outlays, balances, and budget receipts, by govtl branch and agency, FY83, annual rpt, 8104–2

Cost control proposals for Fed Govt programs and mgmt, 3-year savings by function and agency, and financial and operating data, 1960s-81, 16908–1.15

Injuries and deaths from use of selected consumer products and related activity, by victim age and sex, 1982, annual rpt, 9164–7

Injuries and deaths from use of selected consumer products, by victim age and medical treatment status, 1982, annual rpt, 9164–6

R&D Fed Govt funding for all performers, by field and supporting agency, selected years FY60-84, annual rpt, 9627–20

Consumer protection

Air passenger and shipper complaints to CAB, by US and foreign air carrier and type of complaint, monthly rpt, 9142–20

Air passengers denied confirmed space on commercial flights, by carrier, monthly rpt, 9142–23

Banking practices, consumer complaints received and Fed Reserve enforcement of FTC regulations, 1983, annual rpt, 9364–1

Budget of US, receipts by source and outlays by function, FY40-89 estimates revised for consistency with FY85 budget definitions, annual rpt, 104–12

Building access for handicapped persons to Fed Govt or federally funded facilities, compliance activities and complaints by agency, FY83, annual rpt, 17614–1

Consumer Product Safety Commission activities, recalls, and product-related injuries, deaths, and medical costs, by product type and brand, FY83, annual rpt, 9164–2

FDA investigation and regulatory activities, quarterly rpt, 4062–3

Fed Govt financial and nonfinancial domestic aid, 1984 annual comprehensive catalog, 104–5

FTC investigative activity, litigation, and admin, FY82, annual rpt, 9404–1

HHS aid to each State and local govt or private instn, amount obligated, funding agency, and program, FY83, annual listing, 4004–3

Imports detained by FDA, by product, shipper or manufacturer, country, and detention reasons, monthly listing, 4062–2

Standards Natl Bur publications, 1983 annual listing, 2214–1

see also Citizen lawsuits

see also Defective products

see also Food additives

see also Food inspection

see also Hazardous substances

see also Labeling

see also Landlord-tenant relations

see also Licenses and permits

see also Motor vehicle safety devices

see also Packaging and containers

see also Product safety

Consumer surveys

Auto industry finances and operations by manufacturer, foreign competition, and consumer auto expenditures and attitudes toward car buying, selected years 1968-85, annual rpt, 2004–8

Consumer sentiment index, *Business Conditions Digest,* historical supplement and methodology, 1947-82, 2708–31

Consumer sentiment index, *Business Conditions Digest,* monthly rpt, 2702–3.3

Food consumer research and marketing devs, and consumption and price trends, quarterly rpt with articles, 1541–7

Real estate broker industry structure and practices, sales commissions, and broker and consumer attitudes, selected years 1975-81, 9408–48

Underground economy, household expenditures and participation by type of goods or service and sociodemographic characteristics, with methodology and bibl, 1981 survey, 8308–27

see also Consumer Expenditure Survey

Consumers

see Boycotts

see Consumer credit

see Consumer Price Index

see Consumer protection

see Consumer surveys

see Cost of living

see Personal and family income

Consumption

see Food consumption

see Personal consumption

see under names of specific commodities or commodity groups

Containerization

DOD shipments of military and personal property, loss claims, passenger traffic, and costs, by mode of transport, quarterly rpt, 3702–1

Foreign trade zones, activities, and value of goods entering and leaving zones, 1973-82, GAO rpt, 26119–56

Fruit and vegetable shipments by mode of transport, arrivals, and imports, by commodity and State and country of origin, weekly rpt, 1311–3

Grain rail and barge loadings, ship and container car availability, ocean freight rates, and export inspections, prices, and sales, weekly rpt, 1272–2

Intermodal containers and equipment owned by US shipping and leasing companies, inventory by type and size, 1983, annual rpt, 7704–10

Merchant ships in US fleet, shipping costs, construction, employment, military availability, and Fed Govt subsidies, 1970s-1984 and projected to 2000, 26306–6.83

Ports, port facilities by type, and inland waterways by size, by location, 1982-83, annual rpt, 7704–16

Transportation census, 1982: trucks, by detailed characteristics, miles traveled, and type of product carried, State rpt series, 2573–1

Waterborne containerized cargo carried over principal trade routes, by flag of vessel, port, and US coastal district, 1982, annual rpt, 7704–8

Containers

see Containerization

see Packaging and containers

Contempt of court

DC criminal cases involving drug users, and user and nonuser rates of detention, pretrial rearrest, and failure to appear in court, 1979-81, 6066–20.7

Pretrial citation release use, cost savings for law enforcement agencies, and failures to appear in court, by offense and selected jurisdiction, 1970s-82, 6068–187

Continental shelf

Budget of US, effects of Reagan Admin policy changes, by detailed program, FY85, annual rpt, 104–21

Environmental characteristics, fish, wildlife, and use, and population socioeconomic data, for individual coastal areas, series, 5506–4

Environmental characteristics, fish, wildlife, uses, and mgmt of individual coastal ecosystems, series, 5506–9

Fed Govt programs and mgmt cost control proposals, 3-year savings by function and agency, and financial and operating data, 1960s-81, 16908–1.9

Marine Fisheries Review, US and foreign fisheries resources, conservation, operations, and research, quarterly rpt articles, 2162–1

Middle Atlantic OCS fishes dietary composition by food item and fish size, for 9 species, fall 1976-winter 1977, 2168–78

Southeastern US OCS, marine vertebrate abundance and seasonal distribution, with oil and gas dev effects and lease status, early 1980s, 5508–85

Workers compensation under Fed Govt-administered programs, coverage, expenditures, and claims and dispositions by district, FY83, annual compilation, 6504–5

see also Coastal zone

see also Offshore mineral resources

see also Offshore oil and gas

see also Territorial waters

Continuing education

see Adult education

Contraband

Customs Service activities, operations, and staff, FY79-83, annual rpt, 8144–1

see also Drug and narcotics traffic

Contraception

see Family planning

Contracts

see Agricultural quotas and price supports

see Defense contracts and procurement

see Futures trading

see Government contracts and procurement

see Labor-management relations, general

see Labor-management relations in government

Contributions

see Gifts and contributions

Convalescent homes

see Nursing homes

Convenience stores

see Food stores

Conventions

see Political conventions

see Treaties and conventions

Convey, John J.

"Color Perception and ATC Job Performance", 7506–10.26

Convictions, criminal

see Sentences, criminal procedure

Conway, Roger K.

"Estimating Retail and Farm Marketing Relationships for U.S. Processed and Fresh Apples", 1561–6.401

"Impossibility of Causality Testing", 1502–3.403

Conzoneri, Matthew B.

Conzoneri, Matthew B.
"Macroeconomic Implications of Labor Contracting with Asymmetric Information", 9366–7.104

Cook Islands
see Oceania

Cook, Philip J.
"Robbery in the U.S.: An Analysis of Recent Trends and Patterns", 6068–180

Cook, Timothy Q.
"Behavior of the Spread Between Treasury Bill Rates and Private Money Market Rates Since 1978", 9389–1.401
"1983 M1 Seasonal Factor Revisions: An Illustration of Problems That May Arise in Using Seasonally Adjusted Data for Policy Purposes", 9389–1.405

Cooper, Brian
"Productivity Trends in Manufacturing in the U.S. and 11 Other Countries", 6722–1.405

Cooper, Richard N.
"Is There a Need for Reform?", 9373–3.28

Cooperative State Research Service
Activities and programs of USDA, by subagency, FY83, annual rpt, 1004–3
Agricultural research expenditures and scientist years, by topic, commodity, and performing organization, FY82, annual rpt, 1744–2
Research grants awarded competitively by USDA for agricultural science, food and nutrition, and energy dev, FY83, annual listing, 1744–1

Cooperatives
Alaska electric power capacity and generation by fuel type, and marketing, by utility, type of ownership, and location, 1983, annual rpt, 3214–2
China economic conditions, agricultural and industrial production, trade, and domestic and foreign investment, 1980-85, 2048–106
Election campaign finances and Fed Election Commission monitoring activities, 1984 Federal elections, biennial rpt series, 9276–2
Election campaign finances, election procedures, and Fed Election Commission monitoring activities, press release series, 9276–1
Election campaign funding and activities of Fed Election Commission, and political action committees funding, 1983, annual rpt, 9274–1
Electric power average bills, by supplier type, consumption level, and State, Jan 1984, annual rpt, 3164–40.3
Electric power sales of Columbia River system by customer, and capital investments by project, FY83, annual rpt, 3224–1
Electric power sales of TVA, by customer, FY83, annual rpt, 9804–1
Electric power wholesale purchases and costs for individual REA borrowers, by supplier and State, 1940-83, annual rpt, 1244–5
Electric utilities privately owned, detailed financial and operating data by company, with summary data for other distributors by type, 1982, annual rpt, 3164–23
Electric utility fuel cost, quality, use, receipts, and stocks, and power plant production, by energy source, State and utility, quarterly rpt, 3162–39

Rural Electrification Admin financed electric power plants, with location, capacity, and owner, as of Jan 1984, annual listing, 1244–6
Rural Electrification Admin loans to power supply and distribution firms, and borrower operating and financial data, by firm and State, 1983, annual rpt, 1244–1
Rural Electrification Program loan activities summary, by State, FY83 and cumulative from 1935, annual rpt, 1244–7
Southwestern Fed Power System financial statements, electric power sales by customer, and project capacity, production, and costs, FY83, annual rpt, 3244–1
Telephone companies borrowing under rural telephone loan program, and financial and operating data, 1983, annual rpt, 1244–2
Telephone operating and financial data by company type, with fixed cost recovery from interstate revenue by Bell company and State, 1981-82 with trends from 1945, 26306–6.79
TVA electric power purchases of municipal and cooperative distributors, and prices and consumption by distributor and consumer sector, monthly rpt, 9802–1
TVA power distributors detailed operating and financial ratios, for individual municipal and cooperative distributors, FY79-83, annual rpt, 9804–19
Western Area Power Admin operations by plant, financial statements, and electric power sales by customer, FY83, annual rpt, 3254–1
see also Agricultural cooperatives
see also Condominiums and cooperatives

Coopers & Lybrand
"Analysis of Tax-Exempt Pollution Control Financing", 21788–135

Copeland, B. J.
"Ecology of Albemarle Sound, North Carolina: An Estuarine Profile", 5506–7.1

Copper and copper industry
Air pollutant emission factors, by detailed source, 3rd edition, 1983-84 supplements, 9198–13
Air pollutant metal levels, by monitoring site, State, and urban-rural location, 1977-79, last issue of annual rpt, 9194–10
Air pollutant sulfur dioxide emissions of 8 copper smelting plants in 2 States, under alternative emission standards, 1981-82, hearings, 25328–25
Business statistics, detailed data for major industries and economic indicators, *Survey of Current Business,* monthly rpt, 2702–1.14
Castings (nonferrous) shipments and unfilled orders, by metal type, monthly Current Industrial Rpt, 2506–10.5
Communist, OECD, and selected other countries minerals and metals production, by commodity, 1960s-83, annual rpt, 244–5.6
County Business Patterns: establishments, employees, and payrolls, by SIC 4-digit industry and county, 1981, annual State rpt series, 2326–8
County Business Patterns: establishments, employees, and payrolls, by SIC 4-digit industry and county, 1982, annual State rpt series, 2326–6

Index by Subjects and Names

Cuba economic conditions, agricultural and industrial production and distribution, trade, and intl economic relations, 1970-82 and trends from 1957, 248–40
Employment, earnings, and hours, by selected SIC 1- to 4-digit industry, State, and for 278 major labor areas, 1939-83, annual rpt, 6744–5
Employment, earnings, and hours, by SIC 4-digit nonfarm industry, monthly 1974-Feb 1984, annual update, 6744–4
Exports and imports of US, detailed SIC-based commodities by world area, 1983, annual rpts, 2424–6
Exports and imports of US, totals and as percent of domestic production, by SIC 2- to 5-digit commodity, 1981, annual rpt, 2424–3
Exports of US, detailed commodities by country of destination, monthly rpt, 2422–3
Exports of US, detailed Schedule B commodities by country of destination, 1983, annual rpt, 2424–9
Exports of US, detailed Schedule E commodities by mode of transport and world area and country of destination, 1983, annual rpts, 2424–5
Finances and operations, by SIC 2- to 4-digit industry, 1970s-83 and projected to 1988, annual rpt, 2014–4
Foreign and US supply under alternative market conditions, reserves, and background industry data, 1983 mineral rpt, 5606–4.11
Foreign minerals production, reserves, and industry role in domestic economy and world supply, country and world region rpt series, 5606–1
Foundry products imports effect on US industry, investigation with background financial and operating data, 1984 rpt, 9886–4.77
Futures trading by commodity and exchange, and Commodity Futures Trading Commission activities, funding, and employment, FY83, annual rpt, 11924–2
Futures trading in selected commodities, foreign currencies, Treasury securities, and stock indexes, NYC, Chicago, and other markets activity, monthly rpt, 11922–5
Futures trading in selected commodities, Treasury securities, and stock indexes, NYC market activity, monthly rpt, 11922–2
Great Lakes trade, by SITC 3-digit commodity, port, vessel type, world area, and country, 1982, annual rpt, 7744–3
Import related unemployment in copper industry, reemployment opportunities, and worker characteristics, trade adjustment assistance investigation, 1980-83, 6406–9.4
Imports of unwrought copper, injury to US industry from increased import sales, investigation with background financial and operating data, 1984 rpt, 9886–5.50
Imports of US, detailed Schedule A commodities by country and world area of origin, and mode of transport, 1983, annual rpts, 2424–2
Imports of US, detailed Schedule A commodities by country, monthly rpt, 2422–2

Index by Subjects and Names

Corn

Imports of US, detailed TSUSA commodities by country of origin, 1983, annual rpt, 2424–4

Input-output structure of US economy, detailed interindustry transactions for 537 industries, and components of final demand, 1977 benchmark data, 2708–17

Manufacturing census, 1982: financial and operating data, by SIC 2- to 4-digit industry, State, SMSA, and county, preliminary census div rpt series, 2491–3

Manufacturing census, 1982: financial and operating data, for SIC 4-digit industries by product, preliminary rpt, 2491–1.260, 2491–1.262

Mexico copper mine expansion in Cananea, effects on US air pollution and copper industry, with US and foreign industry data, 1960s-95, hearing, 21448–31

Mill and foundry copper-base shipments, trade, and consumption, quarterly Current Industrial Rpt, 2506–10.10

Mineral industries census, 1982: financial and operating data, by SIC 2- to 4-digit industry, preliminary summary rpt, 2511–2.1

Mineral industries census, 1982: financial and operating data, including materials consumed, by SIC 4-digit industry and State, preliminary rpt, 2511–1.2

Mineral Industry Surveys, commodity review of production, trade, stocks, and consumption, monthly rpt, 5612–1.6

Minerals Yearbook, 1982, Vol 1: commodity reviews of production, reserves, supply, use, and trade, annual rpt, 5604–33

Minerals Yearbook, 1982, Vol 2 preprints: State reviews of production and sales by commodity, and business activity, annual rpt series, 5604–16

Minerals Yearbook, 1982, Vol 2: State reviews of production, sales, and firms, by commodity, and business activity, annual rpt, 5604–34

Minerals Yearbook, 1982, Vol 3: foreign country reviews of production, trade, and policies, by commodity, annual rpt, 5604–35

Minerals Yearbook, 1982, Vol 3 preprints: foreign country reviews of production, trade, and policies, by commodity, annual rpt series, 5604–17

Minerals Yearbook, 1983, Vol 1 preprints: commodity review of production, reserves, supply, use, and trade, annual rpt, 5604–15.20

Minerals Yearbook, 1983, Vol 3 preprints: foreign country reviews of production, trade, and policies, by commodity, annual rpt series, 5604–23

Occupational injuries and incidence rates at metal mines and related operations, detailed analysis, 1982, annual rpt, 6664–3

Occupational injury and illness rates, by SIC 2- to 4-digit industry, 1982, annual rpt, 6844–1

OECD trade, total and for 4 major countries, and US trade by country, by commodity, 1972-82, annual world region rpt series, 244–13

Producer prices and indexes, by stage of processing and detailed commodity, monthly rpt, 6762–6

Producer prices and indexes, by stage of processing and detailed commodity, monthly 1983, annual supplement, 6764–2

Production, prices, trade, use, employment, tariffs, and stockpiling, by mineral commodity, with foreign comparisons, 1979-83, annual rpt, 5604–18

Production, production costs, prices, wages, and productivity of copper industry, for US and 3 countries, 1970s-83 and projected to 1989, 21368–55

Productivity, hours, and employment indexes for selected SIC 3- and 4-digit industries, 1954-82, annual rpt, 6824–1.2, 6824–1.3

Stockpiling of strategic and critical materials, Fed Govt activities and inventories by commodity, Oct 1983-Mar 1984, semiannual rpt, 9432–1

Stockpiling of strategic materials, inventories, costs, and goals, by commodity, as of June 1984, semiannual rpt, 9452–7

Strategic minerals supply/demand, trade, and foreign and US industry devs by firm and country, by commodity, bimonthly rpt, 5602–4

Telecommunications use of fiber optics and displacement of copper, with Bell System use and copper and fiber optics industry data, 1978-88, 2048–104

Wages and benefits in nonferrous metal manufacturing, by occupation, size of establishment, union status, and metro-nonmetro location, 1981 survey, 6787–6.196

Waterborne commerce of US (domestic and foreign), freight by commodity, traffic, and passengers, by port and waterway, 1982, annual rpt, 3754–3

Wire mill shapes (copper and brass) shipments, inventories, and sales, monthly Current Industrial Rpt, 2506–10.7

see also under By Commodity in the "Index by Categories"

see also under By Industry in the "Index by Categories"

Copyright

Copyright activities of Register of Copyrights, including intl relations, registrations, fees earned, and royalties collected, FY82, annual rpt, 26404–2

Intl agreements of US establishing copyright relations in force, by country, Jan 1984, annual listing, 7004–1

Recording industry operations and sales lost from home taping, home taping costs, and material taped by source, 1969-83, hearings with chartbook, 25528–100

see also Patents

see also Trademarks

Copyright Royalty Tribunal

Budget of US Appendix, detailed budgets and personnel summaries, by agency, FY85, annual rpt, 104–3

Cordage and twine

see Textile industry and fabrics

Corder, Larry S.

"Access to Health Care Among Aged Medicare Beneficiaries", 4146–12.3

Corn

Acreage harvested and cropland area by crop and region, and potential for expansion, 1982-84 with trends from 1949, annual rpt, 1584–4

Acreage planted and harvested, by crop and State, 1982-83 and planned as of June 1984, annual rpt, 1621–23

Acreage planting intended for 19 crops, by State, as of Feb 1984, annual rpt, 1621–22

Acreage reduction payment-in-kind program costs, requirements, producer and diversion payments, and loan interest forgiven, by crop, as of 1983, hearing, 21788–138

Acreage, yield, and production of field crops, by State, 1978-82 and preliminary 1983, 1641–7

Agricultural Statistics, 1983, annual rpt, 1004–1

Agriculture census, 1982: farms, farmland, production and costs, and operator characteristics, preliminary State and county rpt series, 2330–1

Agriculture census, 1982: farms, farmland, production, finances, and operator characteristics, by county, final State rpt series, 2331–1

Agriculture Fact Book of US, compilation of data for 1983 with trends from 1940, annual rpt, 1004–14

Alcohol fuel (ethanol) production in Tennessee Valley, feedstocks, facilities, tax incentives, and related farming data, by State, 1970s-83 and projected to 1992, 9808–69

Alcoholic beverage production, stocks, materials used, and taxable and tax-free removals, for beer and distilled spirits by State, monthly rpt, 8486–1.1, 8486–1.3

Argentina grain and oilseed production, effect of agricultural price regulation, 1947-80, 1528–170

Argentina grain production, exports by firm, storage by facility type and port, and shipments to ports by mode of transport, by grain type, selected years 1954-81, 1528–185

China economic conditions, agricultural and industrial production, trade, and domestic and foreign investment, 1980-85, 2048–106

Consumption, supply, trade, prices, expenditures, and indexes, by food commodity, 1963-83, annual rpt, 1544–4

Cooperatives grain marketing, storage, and shipments by mode of transport, by grain type and region, FY80, 1128–28

County Business Patterns: establishments, employees, and payrolls, by SIC 4-digit industry and county, 1982, annual State rpt series, 2326–6

Developing countries food supply policies, with farm sector data, tariff income, and prices and imports of 5 grains, for 21 countries, 1960s-81, 1528–168

Eastern Europe agricultural production and trade by commodity, food consumption, and farm inputs, for 6 countries, 1960-80 with projections to 1991, 1528–178

Eastern Europe grain production, consumption, and trade, and US farm cooperatives grain and oilseed export potential, for 4 countries, selected years 1960-90, 1128–27

EC food supply/demand and market and support prices, with exchange rates, fertilizer price index, GDP, and population, by country, 1960-83, 1528–173

Corn

Export sales and shipments of US grains, oilseed products, hides, skins, and cotton, by country, weekly rpt, 1922–3

Exports (total and to EC) and production of US corn gluten products and citrus pulp, 1960-83, hearing, 25368–135

Exports and imports of US, by agricultural commodity and country, bimonthly rpt with articles, 1522–1

Exports and imports of US, by detailed agricultural commodity and country, FY83 and CY83, semiannual rpts, 1522–4

Exports and imports of US, by detailed agricultural commodity for 8 major commodity groups, monthly rpt, 1922–8

Exports and imports of US, detailed SIC-based commodities by world area, 1983, annual rpts, 2424–6

Exports and imports of US, totals and as percent of domestic production, by SIC 2- to 5-digit commodity, 1981, annual rpt, 2424–3

Exports of grain, prices and sales by type of grain, weekly rpt, 1272–2

Exports of US, detailed commodities by country of destination, monthly rpt, 2422–3

Exports of US, detailed Schedule B commodities by country of destination, 1983, annual rpt, 2424–9

Exports of US, detailed Schedule E commodities by mode of transport and world area and country of destination, 1983, annual rpts, 2424–5

Exports, stocks, and prices of wheat, corn, and soybeans, effects of appreciated dollar exchange rates, 1980-82 and for hypothetical 20-year period, 1528–174

Exports under PL 480 concessional sales program, by commodity and country, 1955-83, semiannual rpt, 1922–6

Exports under PL 480 concessional sales program, by commodity and country, 1978-83, semiannual rpt, 1922–10

Farm finances, assets, liabilities, income, receipts by commodity and State, and expenses, 1980-83 and trends from 1910, annual rpt, 1544–16

Fertilizer use and acreage of corn and soybeans, for alternative tillage systems by region, 1980 and 1982, article, 1561–16.401

Foreign and US agricultural supply/demand and production data, for selected US and world crops, and for US livestock and dairy products, periodic rpt, 1522–5

Foreign and US grain production, trade, stocks, consumption, and prices, FAS monthly and annual rpt series, 1925–2

Foreign and US production, acreage, and yield for selected crops, forecasts by selected world region and country, FAS monthly rpt, 1925–28

Futures contracts, stocks in deliverable position by type and grade, weekly table, 11922–4.3

Futures trading by commodity and exchange, and Commodity Futures Trading Commission activities, funding, and employment, FY83, annual rpt, 11924–2

Futures trading in selected commodities, foreign currencies, and stock indexes, Chicago and other markets activity, monthly rpt, 11922–1

Futures trading in selected commodities, foreign currencies, Treasury securities, and stock indexes, NYC, Chicago, and other markets activity, monthly rpt, 11922–5

Gasohol production and costs by feedstock, prices, and market penetration rates and excise tax exemption by State, 1983, article, 1561–16.404

Great Lakes trade, by SITC 3-digit commodity, port, vessel type, world area, and country, 1982, annual rpt, 7744–3

Imports of US, detailed Schedule A commodities by country and world area of origin, and mode of transport, 1983, annual rpts, 2424–2

Imports of US, detailed Schedule A commodities by country, monthly rpt, 2422–2

Imports of US, detailed TSUSA commodities by country of origin, 1983, annual rpt, 2424–4

Input-output structure of US economy, detailed interindustry transactions for 537 industries, and components of final demand, 1977 benchmark data, 2708–17

Loan support programs of USDA for grains, activity and status by type of grain and State, monthly rpt, 1802–3

Manufacturing census, 1982: financial and operating data, for SIC 4-digit industries by product, preliminary rpt, 2491–1.17

Marketing cash receipts of farms, by detailed commodity and State, 1979-82, annual rpt, 1544–18

Mill production workers, wages, hours, and benefits, by occupation, mill product, and region, June 1982 survey, 6787–6.204

OECD trade, total and for 4 major countries, and US trade by country, by commodity, 1972-82, annual world region rpt series, 244–13

Oils and fats production, consumption by end use, and stocks, by type, monthly Current Industrial Rpt, 2506–4.4

Oilseed mill production, crushings, and stocks by State, and trade, by oilseed type, monthly Current Industrial Rpt, 2506–4.3

Pesticide (ethylene dibromide) residue in grain and grain foods, and effect of processing and cooking, by selected product, 1984 hearing, 25168–62

Pesticide use effect on corn and soybean production, losses from hypothetical ban on selected pesticides by pest and region, 1984 article, 1561–16.407

Portugal agricultural subsidies, profits, marketing margins, and consumer prices, by commodity or product, and effects of prospective EC membership, 1981, 1528–171

Prices on US farms and for imports at Rotterdam, and EC price supports, by type of grain, weekly press release, 1922–4

Prices received by farmers and production value for detailed crops by State, 1981-83, annual rpt, 1621–2

Prices received by farmers for major products, and paid for farm inputs and living items, by commodity and State, monthly rpt, 1629–1

Producer prices and indexes, by stage of processing and detailed commodity, monthly rpt, 6762–6

Producer prices and indexes, by stage of processing and detailed commodity, monthly 1983, annual supplement, 6764–2

Production, acreage, stocks, use, trade, prices, and price supports, periodic situation rpt with articles, 1561–4

Production and farm finances, expenses by type, and domestic economic impact, selected years 1972-82 and preliminary 1983-84, annual rpt, 1544–19

Production, farms, acreage, and related data, by selected crop and State, monthly rpt, 1621–1

Production itemized costs, receipts, and net returns, for 13 crops, 4 livestock types, and milk, by region, 1981-83, annual rpt, 1544–20

Production, prices, trade, and export inspections by US port and country of destination, by grain type, weekly rpt, 1313–2

Production, prices, trade, and marketing, by commodity, current situation and forecast, monthly rpt, 1502–4

Productivity, hours, and employment indexes for selected SIC 3- and 4-digit industries, 1954-82, annual rpt, 6824–1.3

Southeastern States soil conservation and water pollution reduction participants, costs, and acreage, by conservation method and State, selected years 1973-82, 1588–84

Stocks of grain by region and market city, and grain inspected for export, by type, weekly rpt, 1313–4

Stocks of grain on and off farms and total in all positions, by crop, periodic rpt, 1621–4

Stocks of grains, oilseeds, and hay on and off farms, by State, 1978-83, 1641–17

Supply/demand, prices, and commodity program operations, for selected crops and livestock, 1983 and outlook for 1984, annual article, 9381–1.402

Tillage system effects on corn and soybean yields, itemized production costs, and input use, by region and for 10 States, 1980, 1588–80

Waterborne commerce of US (domestic and foreign), freight by commodity, traffic, and passengers, by port and waterway, 1982, annual rpt, 3754–3

see also under By Commodity in the "Index by Categories"

Coroners

Traffic accidents and casualties detailed direct and indirect costs, by characteristics of persons and vehicles involved, 1979-80, 7768–80

Corporate profits

see Business income and expenses, general

see Business income and expenses, specific industries

Corporation for Public Broadcasting

Budget of US Appendix, detailed budgets and personnel summaries, by agency, FY85, annual rpt, 104–3

Budget of US, appropriations, outlays, balances, and budget receipts, by govtl branch and agency, FY83, annual rpt, 8104–2

Index by Subjects and Names

Corpus Christi, Tex.

Corporations

Agriculture census, 1982: farms, farmland, production and costs, and operator characteristics, preliminary State and county rpt series, 2330–1

Agriculture census, 1982: farms, farmland, production, finances, and operator characteristics, by county, final State rpt series, 2331–1

Aluminum primary production plant ownership, capacity, and type and source of raw material and energy used, by plant, State, and country, June 1984, semiannual listing, 5602–5

Business and financial statistics, historic trends, 1984 annual chartbook, 9364–2.10

Business Conditions Digest, current data on economic, business, and financial conditions and cyclical fluctuations, monthly rpt, 2702–3

Business formation and failures, 1929-83, annual rpt, 204–1.7

Business statistics, detailed data for major industries and economic indicators, *Survey of Current Business,* monthly rpt, 2702–1

California business failures, plant closings, layoffs, and relocations, by plant, industry, county, and city, 1980-83, hearing, 21348–84.1

Capital (fixed), govt and private nonresidential structures and equipment, residential capital, and consumer-owned durable goods by item, 1980-83, annual article, 2702–1.433

Convicted Federal offenders, by offense and district, as of June 1983, annual rpt, 18204–1

Farm business legal organization, finances, operations, tax rates, and State laws restricting farm corporations, 1960s-82, 1548–233

Farm households receiving social security income, farms and amount by characteristics of farm and operator, 1978-82, article, 1702–1.410

Financial and business statistics, quarterly chartbook, 9362–2.5

Financial data, security issues, profits, taxes, and dividends, and nonfinancial corporations assets and liabilities, monthly rpt, 9362–1.1

Financial statements for manufacturing, mining, and trade corporations, by selected SIC 2- to 3-digit industry, quarterly rpt, 2502–1

Flow-of-funds accounts, assets and liabilities by type and economic sector, year-end outstandings, 1960-83, annual rpt, 9364–3

Flow-of-funds accounts savings, investments, and credit statements, quarterly rpt, 9365–3.3

Franchises of firms engaged in distribution of goods and services by kind of business, establishments by State, and sales, 1982-84, annual rpt, 2014–5

Hwy and urban transit systems financing methods of govts and private sector, with case studies for selected metro areas, series, 7556–7

Income (taxable) not reported on individual and corporate returns, and associated Federal revenue losses, by detailed legal and illegal source, 1973-81, 8308–26

Income tax returns filed by type, for US, IRS regions, and service center cities, 1972-82 and projected 1983-90, annual rpt, 8304–9.1

Income tax returns filed for IRS regions, districts, and service centers, 1972-82 and projected to 1990, annual rpt, 8304–8

Income tax returns of corporations, detailed income and tax items by industry, 1981, annual rpt, 8304–4

Income tax returns of corporations with foreign tax credit, income and deductions by type, asset size, and selected industry group, 1980, article, 8302–2.415

Income tax returns, summary data by industry div, 1981 estimates, annual article, 8302–2.403

Income taxes on corporate and personal capital related to capital formation and intl flows, 1984 technical paper, 8006–3.51

Land privately held, acreage and owners by owner characteristics, land use, and region, and purchase and improvement funding, 1978 survey, series, 1506–5

Natl income and product, comprehensive accounts and components, *Survey of Current Business,* monthly rpt, 2702–1.22

Navy procurement, by contractor and location of work, FY83, annual rpt, 3804–13

Nonfinancial corporations labor productivity and costs and profits, preliminary data, quarterly rpt, 6822–2

Nonfinancial corporations labor productivity and costs and profits, revised data, quarterly rpt, 6822–1

Patents (US) granted to US and foreign applicants, by applicant type, firm, State, and country, subject rpt series, 2246–2

Patents (US) granted to US and foreign applicants, by year of grant and application, country, and type of applicant, 1960s-83, annual rpt, 2244–3

Pension plan investment in mortgages and FHLB and Fed Govt mortgage assn mortgage-backed securities, for corporate and union funds, quarterly rpt, 5002–10

Political action committee and other campaign funding, and Fed Election Commission monitoring activities, press release series, 9276–1

Political action committee and other campaign funding, and Fed Election Commission monitoring activities, 1984 Federal elections, biennial series, 9276–2

Political action committee campaign funding, and voting on FTC rules, for individual congressmen, 1978-82, hearings, 25688–6.2

Political action committee campaign funding to individual congressmen, and public opinion on reform proposals and assn influence, 1970s-83, hearings, 21428–7

Political action committee funding to reelect and defeat House and Senate members by candidate, and FEC activities and funding, 1983, annual rpt, 9274–1

Productivity of labor and capital in manufacturing, all nonfarm business, and all private business, indexes and percent change, 1948-83, annual rpt, 6824–2

Profits and securities, 1980-82, annual rpt, 9364–5.5, 9364–5.6

Profits by industry div, profit tax liability, and dividends, monthly rpt, quarterly data, 23842–1.1

Profits by industry, 1929-83, and corporate assets and liabilities, 1939-83, annual rpt, 204–1.7

Retail trade sales, inventories, purchases, gross margin, and accounts receivable, by SIC 2- to 4-digit kind of business and type of ownership, 1983, annual rpt, 2413–5

Service industries receipts, by SIC 2- to 4-digit kind of business, 1983, annual rpt, 2413–8

Small Business Investment Companies finances, funding, licensing, and loan activity, 2nd half FY84, semiannual rpt, 9762–3

Statistical Abstract of US, social, political, and economic data, 1950s-83 and trends, annual rpt, 2324–1.3

Tax collections of State govts, by detailed type of tax and tax rates, by State, FY83, annual rpt, 2466–2.3

Tax expenditures, Fed Govt revenues foregone through income tax deductions and exclusions by type, and effect of Deficit Reduction Act, FY84-89, annual rpt, 21784–10

Tax revenues, by level of govt, type of tax, State, and selected large counties, quarterly rpt, 2462–3

Telephone and telegraph firms intercorporate relationships, 1982, annual rpt, 9284–6.8

Terrorist (intl) incidents, casualties, and attacks on US targets, by attack type and world area, with chronology of events, 1983, annual rpt, 7004–13

Virgin Islands economic censuses, 1982: employment, establishments, payroll, and receipts, by SIC 1- to 4-digit industry, island, and city, 2593–1

Wholesale trade sales, inventories, purchases, and gross margins, by SIC 2- to 3-digit kind of business and type of ownership, 1983, annual rpt, 2413–13

see also Bank holding companies

see also Business acquisitions and mergers

see also Economic concentration and diversification

see also Foreign corporations

see also Government corporations

see also Holding companies

see also Multinational corporations

see also Public utilities

see also under By Individual Company or Institution in the "Index by Categories"

Corps of Engineers

see Army Corps of Engineers

Corpus Christi, Tex.

Census of Housing, 1980: occupancy and unit characteristics, by race, Hispanic origin, and city, SMSA rpt, 2473–1.129

Census of Population and Housing, 1980: detailed population and housing characteristics, by county, city, and census tract, SMSA rpt, 2551–2.129

Housing vacancy rates for single and multifamily units and mobile homes, by city and ZIP code, 1983, annual metro area rpt, 9304–19.1

Wages of office and plant workers, by occupation, 1984 SMSA survey rpt, 6785–11.6

Corpus Christi, Tex.

see also under By City and By SMSA or MSA in the "Index by Categories"

Correctional institutions

- Budget of US, effects of Reagan Admin policy changes, by detailed program, FY85, annual rpt, 104–21
- Census of Population, 1980: detailed socioeconomic and demographic characteristics, by age, sex, race, Hispanic origin, occupation, and industry, State rpt series, 2531–4
- Census of Population, 1980: labor force, by sex, detailed occupation, and region, with comparison to 1970 census, supplementary rpt, 2535–1.12
- Central America socioeconomic and political conditions in 6 countries, 1960s-83 with trends and projections 1930-2010, Commission rpt, 028–19.2
- Crime and criminal justice data, including justice expenditures and employment by level of govt, 1970s-82 with some trends from 1875, 6068–174
- Crime, victimization, offender characteristics, prison population, and other topics, periodic rpt, 6062–2
- Economic indicators relation to measures of social pathology including crime and death rates, various periods 1950-80, 23848–76
- Fed Prison Industries operations and finances, FY83, annual rpt, 6244–3
- Foreign human rights conditions in 162 countries, economic and military aid of US, and economic aid of intl organizations, 1981-83, annual rpt, 21384–3
- Govt census, 1982: city govt revenues by source, expenditures by function, debt, and assets, by State and city, 2457–4
- Govt census, 1982: county govt revenues by source, expenditures by function, debt, and assets, by State and county, 2457–3
- Govt census, 1982: employment, payrolls, and average earnings, by function, level of govt, State, county, population size, and inside-outside SMSAs, 2455–2
- Govt census, 1982: local govt employment by function, payroll, and average earnings, for individual counties, cities, and school and special districts, 2455–1
- Govt census, 1982: State govt payments to local govts, by program, source of funds, level of govt, and State, with trends from 1902, 2460–3
- Govt employment and payroll, by function, level of govt, and jurisdiction, 1983, annual rpt series, 2466–1
- Govt revenues by source and expenditures by function, natl income and product account, *Survey of Current Business,* monthly rpt, monthly and annual tables, 2702–1.24
- Habeas corpus writs filed by State prisoners in Federal district and appeals courts by circuit, and petition disposition, selected years 1961-82, 6066–19.4
- Health services employment at Federal correctional instns, by occupation, instn, and region, monthly rpt, 6242–2
- Jail capacities, conditions, expenditures, and services, and socioeconomic and other characteristics of inmates, various dates 1976-82, 10048–59

Maryland corrections policies, assessments of private citizens and corrections and criminal justice personnel, 1980/81 with prison population trends from 1930, 6068–176

- New Jersey and Maryland prison capacity and population, and New Jersey construction costs by type and funding source, by facility, 1977-82 and projected to 1988, 25528–99
- *Occupational Outlook Handbook,* 1984-85 biennial rpt, 6744–1
- Palau Republic crimes reported, law enforcement staff, and prison capacity and inmates, FY83, annual rpt, 7004–6.2
- Physicians employed in prisons by sociodemographic, employment, and professional characteristics, and compared to all physicians, 1979, article, 4102–1.407
- Prison expansion plans of States, beds and construction costs by region, 1984 survey, 6066–20.6
- Prison mandatory sentencing effects on Crime Index offense rates and prison population, selected years 1960-76, 6066–20.3
- Prison population and capacity by State and individual DC and Federal instn, construction costs, and Fed Govt operating costs, 1983 and projected to 1990, GAO rpt, 26119–59
- Prisoners in Federal and State correctional instns, by sex, region, and State, quarterly release, 6062–3
- Prisoners in Federal correctional instns, by prison, security level, contract facility type, sex, and region, monthly and weekly rpts, 6242–1
- Prisoners in State prisons median sentence, and admissions and releases by prisoner and sentencing characteristics, by offense and State, 1981 and trends from 1926, 6066–19.9
- Prisoners under death sentence, and executions since 1930, by prisoner characteristics, region, and State, 1982, annual rpt, 6065–1
- *Statistical Abstract of US,* social, political, and economic data, 1950s-83 and trends, annual rpt, 2324–1.1
- Witness Security Program costs, participants by arrest record, and prosecutions by offense, offender type, and disposition, various periods FY70-83, GAO rpt, 26119–70
- *see also* Halfway houses
- *see also* Military prisons
- *see also* Parole and probation

Corrigan, E. Gerald

"Economic Prosperity: An Eclectic View", 9383–2

Corruption and bribery

- Govt officials prosecuted and convicted for corruption, by judicial district and level of govt, 1976-83, annual rpt, 6004–13
- Wiretapping authorizations by offense, costs, persons involved, arrests, trials, and convictions, 1983, annual rpt, 18204–7
- *see also* Federal Inspectors General reports

Corundum

see Abrasive materials

Index by Subjects and Names

Cosmetics

- Census of Population, 1980: detailed socioeconomic and demographic characteristics, by age, sex, race, Hispanic origin, occupation, and industry, State rpt series, 2531–4
- County Business Patterns: establishments, employees, and payrolls, by SIC 4-digit industry and county, 1981, annual State rpt series, 2326–8
- County Business Patterns: establishments, employees, and payrolls, by SIC 4-digit industry and county, 1982, annual State rpt series, 2326–6
- CPI by detailed component, for US city average, 28 SMSAs, and 4 regions by population size, monthly rpt, 6762–2
- Exports and imports of US, detailed SIC-based commodities by world area, 1983, annual rpts, 2424–6
- Exports, imports, tariffs, and industry operating data for flavorings, fragrances, perfumes, cosmetics, and toiletries, 1979-83, TSUSA commodity rpt, 9885–4.40
- Exports of US, detailed commodities by country of destination, monthly rpt, 2422–3
- Exports of US, detailed Schedule B commodities by country of destination, 1983, annual rpt, 2424–9
- Exports of US, detailed Schedule E commodities by mode of transport and world area and country of destination, 1983, annual rpts, 2424–5
- FDA investigation and regulatory activities, quarterly rpt, 4062–3
- Franchise business opportunities, by firm and kind of business, 1984 annual listing, 2044–27
- Great Lakes trade, by SITC 3-digit commodity, port, vessel type, world area, and country, 1982, annual rpt, 7744–3
- Imports of US, detailed Schedule A commodities by country and world area of origin, and mode of transport, 1983, annual rpts, 2424–2
- Imports of US, detailed Schedule A commodities by country, monthly rpt, 2422–2
- Imports of US, detailed TSUSA commodities by country of origin, 1983, annual rpt, 2424–4
- Industry finances and operations, by SIC 2- to 4-digit industry, 1970s-83 and projected to 1988, annual rpt, 2014–4
- Industry productivity, hours, and employment indexes, 1958-81, annual rpt, 6824–1.3
- Injuries and deaths from use of selected consumer products, by victim age and medical treatment status, 1982, annual rpt, 9164–6
- Input-output structure of US economy, detailed interindustry transactions for 537 industries, and components of final demand, 1977 benchmark data, 2708–17
- Manufacturing census, 1982: financial and operating data, by SIC 2- to 4-digit industry, State, SMSA, and county, preliminary census div rpt series, 2491–3
- Manufacturing census, 1982: financial and operating data, for SIC 4-digit industries by product, preliminary rpt, 2491–1.188

Index by Subjects and Names

Cotton

OECD trade, total and for 4 major countries, and US trade by country, by commodity, 1972-82, annual world region rpt series, 244–13

Perfume materials and other benzenoid chemical imports by country of origin and product, 1983, annual rpt, 9884–2

Producer prices and indexes, by stage of processing and detailed commodity, monthly rpt, 6762–6

Producer prices and indexes, by stage of processing and detailed commodity, monthly 1983, annual supplement, 6764–2

Production and sales of synthetic organic chemicals by product, and listing of manufacturers, 1983, annual rpt, 9884–3

Wholesale trade census, 1982: employment, establishments, sales by commodity, and payroll, by SIC 4-digit kind of business and State, preliminary rpt, 2403–1.22

Wholesale trade census, 1982: employment, establishments, sales by commodity, and payroll for service industry suppliers, by State, preliminary rpt, 2403–1.17

see also Barber and beauty shops

Cost Accounting Standards Board

Budget of US, compact budgets by function, agency, and account, FY85 with projections to FY89, annual rpt, 104–2

Cost of living

- Agricultural production, marketing, trade, supply, food consumption, and food and nutrition programs, 1960s-83, annual chartbook, 1504–3
- Collective bargaining agreements expiring during year, covered workers by SIC 2-digit industry, firm, and union, with summary of key provisions, 1984, annual rpt, 6784–9
- Consumer goods prices and supplies, family finance, and home economics, quarterly rpt with articles, 1702–1
- Economic indicators and labor force characteristics, selected years 1880-1995, chartbook, 6728–30
- Farmers prices received for major products and paid for farm inputs and living items, by commodity and State, monthly rpt, 1629–1
- Farmers prices received for major products and paid for farm inputs, by commodity and State, 1983, annual rpt, 1629–5
- Food expenditures by selected item, and compared to disposable income and other consumer expenditures, 1963-83, annual rpt, 1544–4.6
- Foreign living costs, State Dept indexes, housing allowances, and hardship differential rates by country and major city, quarterly rpt, 6862–1
- Housing energy use, costs, expenditures, and conservation, and household and housing characteristics, survey series, 3166–7
- Pension plans with postretirement adjustments related to employee and employer characteristics, and effect of inflation on benefit purchasing power, 1973-79, 6468–18
- Pension plans with postretirement benefit increases, for banks and manufacturers by size, 1978-83, hearing, 25368–132
- Prices and living costs, selected years 1913-82, annual rpt, 6724–1.7

Statistical Abstract of US, social, political, and economic data, 1950s-83 and trends, annual rpt, 2324–1.3

Transportation energy use by mode, fuel supplies, and demographic and economic determinants of vehicle use, 1970s-83, annual rpt, 3304–5.1

see also Consumer Price Index

see also Energy prices

see also Escalator clauses

see also Food prices

see also Housing costs and financing

see also Inflation

see also Medical costs

see also Prices

see also Producer Price Index

see also Rent

Cost of production

see Agricultural production costs

see Business income and expenses, general

see Business income and expenses, specific industries

see Energy production costs

see Production costs

Costa Rica

- Agricultural and food production indexes, and production of selected commodities, by world region and country, 1974-83, annual rpt, 1524–5
- Agricultural situation in Latin America, by country, 1981-83 and outlook for 1984, annual rpt, 1524–4.9
- Agricultural supply/demand, trade, and production, and socioeconomic data, by country, 1950s-77, 1528–179
- AID activities and funding by project and function, FY85, and developing countries summary socioeconomic data, 1970s-83, by country, annual rpt, 9914–3
- AID and other foreign assistance, and govt policy, effects on private sector dev and socioeconomic conditions, with case studies for 6 countries, 1960s-80, 9918–12
- AID economic assistance to developing countries, obligations and disbursements by country, quarterly rpt, 9912–4
- AID economic assistance to 7 Central American countries, by type of aid, FY80-83, GAO rpt, 26123–55
- AID loan repayment status and terms by program and country, and status of predecessor agency loans, quarterly rpt, 9912–3
- Economic, social, and political conditions in 6 Central America countries, 1960s-83 with trends and projections 1930-2010, 028–19
- Economic, social, and political summary data, by country, 1984, annual factbook, 244–11
- Economic trends in income, production, prices, employment, finances, and trade, 1984 annual rpt, 2046–4.49
- Employee stock ownership plans in developing countries, and firms finances and operations, with case studies of US and 3 countries, 1970s-82, 9916–3.19
- Exports and imports of US, by commodity and country, 1972-82, annual world region rpt, 244–13.3
- Exports of US, detailed Schedule B commodities by country of destination, 1983, annual rpt, 2424–9

Exports of US, detailed Schedule E commodities by mode of transport and world area and country of destination, 1983, annual rpts, 2424–5

Imports of US, detailed Schedule A commodities by country and world area of origin, and mode of transport, 1983, annual rpts, 2424–2

Imports of US, detailed TSUSA commodities by country of origin, 1983, annual rpt, 2424–4

Loans and grants for economic and military assistance from US and intl agencies, by program and country, FY46-83, annual rpt, 9914–5

Military aid of US, arms sales, and training programs costs and budget requests by program, world region, and country, FY83-85, annual rpt, 7144–13

Military spending, arms trade, and armed forces size, with total govt spending and population, by country, 1972-82, annual rpt, 9824–1

Minerals Yearbook, 1982, Vol 3: foreign country reviews of production, trade, and policies, by commodity, annual rpt, 5604–35

Minerals Yearbook, 1982, Vol 3 preprints: foreign country review of production, trade, and policies, by commodity, annual rpt, 5604–17.86

Natural resources and hazards to resource dev, with data on mineral, energy, and water resources, by Central American country, 1981 with trends from 1977, 5668–71

Population size and growth rates, and latest available benchmark demographic data, by country, 1950-83, biennial rpt, 2324–4

Refugees from Central America by country of origin and asylum, and aid from US and Mexico, FY82-1984, GAO rpt, 26123–70

see also under By Foreign Country in the "Index by Categories"

Cotton

- Acreage harvested and cropland area by crop and region, and potential for expansion, 1982-84 with trends from 1949, annual rpt, 1584–4
- Acreage planted and harvested, by crop and State, 1982-83 and planned as of June 1984, annual rpt, 1621–23
- Acreage planted by State and county, and fiber quality, by cotton variety, 1980-84, annual rpt, 1309–6
- Acreage planting intended for 19 crops, by State, as of Feb 1984, annual rpt, 1621–22
- Acreage, production, prices, stocks, consumption, and trade, US and world, annual rpt, suspended, 1564–10
- Acreage reduction payment-in-kind program costs, requirements, producer and diversion payments, and loan interest forgiven, by crop, as of 1983, hearing, 21788–138
- Acreage, yield, and production of field crops, by State, 1978-82 and preliminary 1983, 1641–7
- Agricultural Stabilization and Conservation Service cotton programs, 1955-84, annual fact sheet, 1806–4.8, 1806–4.11
- Agricultural Stabilization and Conservation Service producer payments under 26 programs, monthly rpt, 1802–10

Cotton

Index by Subjects and Names

Agricultural Statistics, 1983, annual rpt, 1004–1

Agriculture census, 1982: farms, farmland, production and costs, and operator characteristics, preliminary State and county rpt series, 2330–1

Agriculture census, 1982: farms, farmland, production, finances, and operator characteristics, by county, final State rpt series, 2331–1

Agriculture Fact Book of US, compilation of data for 1983 with trends from 1940, annual rpt, 1004–14

Air pollutant emission factors, by detailed source, 3rd edition, 1983-84 supplements, 9198–13

Alcohol fuel (ethanol) production in Tennessee Valley, feedstocks, facilities, tax incentives, and related farming data, by State, 1970s-83 and projected to 1992, 9808–69

Broadwoven fabric production by region and State, inventory, orders, and exports, by product, 1983, annual Current Industrial Rpt, 2506–5.10

Business statistics, detailed data for major industries and economic indicators, *Survey of Current Business,* monthly rpt, 2702–1.19

China economic conditions, agricultural and industrial production, trade, and domestic and foreign investment, 1980-85, 2048–106

Communist, OECD, and selected other countries agricultural production, by commodity, 1960s-83, annual rpt, 244–5.9

Cooperatives finances and operations, aggregate for top 100 assns by principal product and revenue source, FY82, annual rpt, 1124–3

Cooperatives, membership, activities, and finances, by commodity and selected State, 1900-80 with trends from 1863, 1128–30

County Business Patterns: establishments, employees, and payrolls, by SIC 4-digit industry and county, 1981, annual State rpt series, 2326–8

County Business Patterns: establishments, employees, and payrolls, by SIC 4-digit industry and county, 1982, annual State rpt series, 2326–6

Cuba economic conditions, agricultural and industrial production and distribution, trade, and intl economic relations, 1970-82 and trends from 1957, 248–40

Eastern Europe agricultural production and trade by commodity, food consumption, and farm inputs, for 6 countries, 1960-80 with projections to 1991, 1528–178

Employment, earnings, and hours, by selected SIC 1- to 4-digit industry, State, and for 278 major labor areas, 1939-83, annual rpt, 6744–5

Employment, earnings, and hours, by SIC 4-digit nonfarm industry, monthly 1974-Feb 1984, annual update, 6744–4

Export licensing and monitoring activities under Export Admin Act, for selected commodities, and for Communist and other countries, FY83, annual rpt, 2044–22

Export sales and shipments of US grains, oilseed products, hides, skins, and cotton, by country, weekly rpt, 1922–3

Exports and imports of US, by agricultural commodity and country, bimonthly rpt with articles, 1522–1

Exports and imports of US, by detailed agricultural commodity and country, FY83 and CY83, semiannual rpts, 1522–4

Exports and imports of US, by detailed agricultural commodity for 8 major commodity groups, monthly rpt, 1922–8

Exports and imports of US, detailed SIC-based commodities by world area, 1983, annual rpts, 2424–6

Exports and imports of US, totals and as percent of domestic production, by SIC 2- to 5-digit commodity, 1981, annual rpt, 2424–3

Exports and personal expenditures of US and world for selected agricultural commodities, by country, and export share of US farm income, various periods 1926-82, 1528–172

Exports, imports, tariffs, and industry operating data for textile fiber and products, TSUSA commodity rpt series, 9885–3

Exports of manufactured and agricultural commodities, manufacturing production, and export-related employment, 1960s-82, State rpt series, 2046–3

Exports of textiles, by product and country of destination, monthly rpt, 2042–26

Exports of US, detailed commodities by country of destination, monthly rpt, 2422–3

Exports of US, detailed Schedule B commodities by country of destination, 1983, annual rpt, 2424–9

Exports of US, detailed Schedule E commodities by mode of transport and world area and country of destination, 1983, annual rpts, 2424–5

Exports under PL 480 concessional sales program, by commodity and country, 1955-83, semiannual rpt, 1922–6

Exports under PL 480 concessional sales program, by commodity and country, 1978-83, semiannual rpt, 1922–10

Farm finances, assets, liabilities, income, receipts by commodity and State, and expenses, 1980-83 and trends from 1910, annual rpt, 1544–16

Farm production inputs, outputs, and productivity, by region, 1939-82, annual rpt, 1544–17

Fiber and processing test results, by cotton staple, region, State, and production area, seasonal biweekly rpt, 1309–3

Fiber and processing test results, by State, 1983, annual rpt, 1309–4

Fiber grade, staple, and mike, for upland and American Pima cotton by State, monthly rpt, 1309–11

Fiber quality specifications, by State, 1983/84, annual rpt, 1309–7

Fiber quality, supply, disappearance, and carryover, 1983-84, annual rpt, 1309–8

Foreign agricultural production, prices, and trade, by country, 1983 and outlook for 1984/85, annual world region rpt series, 1524–4

Foreign and US agricultural production, prices, trade, and consumption, quarterly rpt with articles, 1522–3

Foreign and US agricultural production, trade, and climatic devs, weekly press release, 1922–4

Foreign and US agricultural supply/demand and production data, for selected US and world crops, and for US livestock and dairy products, periodic rpt, 1522–5

Foreign and US production, acreage, and yield for selected crops, forecasts by selected world region and country, FAS monthly rpt, 1925–28

Foreign and US production and trade of cotton, FAS monthly and annual rpt series, 1925–4

Futures in cotton, unfixed call sales and purchases and open contracts on NYC exchange, weekly rpt, 11922–3

Futures trading by commodity and exchange, and Commodity Futures Trading Commission activities, funding, and employment, FY83, annual rpt, 11924–2

Futures trading in selected commodities, foreign currencies, Treasury securities, and stock indexes, NYC, Chicago, and other markets activity, monthly rpt, 11922–5

Futures trading in selected commodities, Treasury securities, and stock indexes, NYC market activity, monthly rpt, 11922–2

Ginning charges and related data, by State, 1983/84, annual rpt, 1564–3

Ginnings and production for 18 States, by county, 1983 crop, annual rpt, 2344–1

Ginnings, by State and county, seasonal monthly rpt, 2342–2

Ginnings, by State, seasonal semimonthly rpt, 2342–1

Great Lakes trade, by SITC 3-digit commodity, port, vessel type, world area, and country, 1982, annual rpt, 7744–3

Import quotas and imports, by country of origin, monthly rpt, 8146–1.2

Imports and import limits for textiles under Multifiber Arrangement by product and country, with US exports and use, 1970-83, semiannual rpt, 9882–11

Imports of cotton towels from Pakistan, injury to US industry from sales covered by foreign govt grants, investigation with background financial and operating data, 1980-83, 9886–15.48

Imports of textiles, by country of origin, monthly rpt, 2042–27

Imports of textiles, by product and country of origin, monthly rpt, 2422–1

Imports of textiles, by product and country of origin, monthly rpt series, 2046–9

Imports of textiles, by product and country of origin, periodic rpt series, 2046–8

Imports of textiles, monthly rpt, 2042–18

Imports of textiles, total and as percents of US production and use, by commodity, 1972-82, annual rpt, 2044–14

Imports of US, detailed Schedule A commodities by country and world area of origin, and mode of transport, 1983, annual rpts, 2424–2

Imports of US, detailed Schedule A commodities by country, monthly rpt, 2422–2

Imports of US, detailed TSUSA commodities by country of origin, 1983, annual rpt, 2424–4

Index by Subjects and Names

Counties

Input-output structure of US economy, detailed interindustry transactions for 537 industries, and components of final demand, 1977 benchmark data, 2708–17

Linters production, prices, stocks, use, and trade, monthly rpt, 1309–10

Manufacturing census, 1982: financial and operating data, by SIC 2- to 4-digit industry, State, SMSA, and county, preliminary census div rpt series, 2491–3

Manufacturing census, 1982: financial and operating data, for SIC 4-digit industries by product, preliminary rpt series, 2491–1

Manufacturing census, 1982: textile mill machinery in place, by machine type and textile industry, special preliminary rpts, 2491–2

Marketing cash receipts of farms, by detailed commodity and State, 1979-82, annual rpt, 1544–18

Minority group and women employment, by occupational group and SIC 2- to 3-digit industry, 1981, annual rpt, 9244–1.1

OECD trade, total and for 4 major countries, and US trade by country, by commodity, 1972-82, annual world region rpt series, 244–13

PL 480 commodity allocations for long-term credit sales, by country, quarterly press release, 1922–7

Prices at selected spot markets, futures prices at NYC exchange, and CCC loan rates, 1983/84 with some trends from 1920, annual rpt, 1309–2

Prices in selected spot markets, futures prices at NYC exchange, farm prices, and CCC loan stocks, monthly rpt, 1309–1

Prices received by farmers and production value for detailed crops by State, 1981-83, annual rpt, 1621–2

Prices received by farmers for major products, and paid for farm inputs and living items, by commodity and State, monthly rpt, 1629–1

Prices received by farmers for major products, and paid for farm inputs, by commodity and State, 1983, annual rpt, 1629–5

Producer prices and indexes, by stage of processing and detailed commodity, monthly rpt, 6762–6

Producer prices and indexes, by stage of processing and detailed commodity, monthly 1983, annual supplement, 6764–2

Production and farm finances, expenses by type, and domestic economic impact, selected years 1972-82 and preliminary 1983-84, annual rpt, 1544–19

Production, consumption, prices, stocks, and trade, periodic situation rpt with articles, 1561–1

Production, farms, acreage, and related data, by selected crop and State, monthly rpt, 1621–1

Production inputs, land mgmt, and environmental effects, for 4 crops, 1940s-80 and projected to 2010, 9188–94

Production itemized costs, receipts, and net returns, for 13 crops, 4 livestock types, and milk, by region, 1981-83, annual rpt, 1544–20

Production, prices, exports, stocks, and mill consumption of long staple cotton, monthly rpt, 1309–12

Production, prices, trade, and marketing, by commodity, current situation and forecast, monthly rpt, 1502–4

Production, stocks, materials used, and orders, by product and major State, and trade by country, periodic Current Industrial Rpt series, 2506–5

Supply/demand, prices, and commodity program operations, for selected crops and livestock, 1983 and outlook for 1984, annual article, 9381–1.402

Waterborne commerce of US (domestic and foreign), freight by commodity, traffic, and passengers, by port and waterway, 1982, annual rpt, 3754–3

Wholesale trade census, 1982: employment, establishments, sales by commodity, and payroll, by SIC 4-digit kind of business and State, preliminary rpt, 2403–1.23

Yarn (cotton) from Brazil, imports injury to US industry from removal of duties on foreign subsidized products, investigation with selected financial and operating data, 1984 rpt, 9886–18.14

see also under By Commodity in the "Index by Categories"

Cottonseed

see Oils, oilseeds, and fats

Coulehan, John L.

"Epidemiology of Haemophilus Influenzae Type B Disease Among Navajo Indians", 4102–1.441

Council for Inter-American Security

"Revolutionary Terrorism in El Salvador, over 20,000 Victims", 21388–41

Council for Mutual Economic Assistance

Agricultural exports and imports of US, by detailed commodity and country, FY83 and CY83, semiannual rpts, 1522–4

Economic conditions in Communist and OECD countries, 1982, annual rpt, 7144–11

Exports and imports of NATO countries with CEMA Europe members, by country, 1980-83, annual rpt, 7144–5

Exports and imports of non-NATO OECD countries with Europe CMEA members, annual rpt, discontinued, 7144–6

Science and technology dev and transfer between USSR and other members of Council for Mutual Economic Assistance, 1940s-81, 2326–9.7

Council of Economic Advisers

Economic indicators and components, current data and annual trends, monthly rpt, 23842–1

Economic Report of the President for 1984, economic trends from 1929 and Reagan Admin proposals, annual rpt, 204–1

Council of State Housing Agencies

"Council of State Housing Agencies Response to the General Accounting Office Study 'The Costs and Benefits of Mortgage Revenue Bonds: Preliminary Report'", 21788–135

Council on Environmental Quality

Environmental quality and protection programs, costs, and Fed Govt enforcement, 1983, detailed annual rpt, 484–1

Councils of government

see Regional planning

Counterfeiting and forgery

Arrests and arrest rates, by offense, offender characteristics, population size, and State, 1970s-83, annual rpt, 6224–2.2

Court cases, dispositions, convictions, and sentences of Federal criminal defendants, by offense and district, as of June 1983 with trends from 1945, annual rpt, 18204–1

Fed Govt felony court cases, by offense, and characteristics of case processing, sentencing, and offender, 1979-80, periodic rpt, 6062–2.407

Foreign manufacturers counterfeiting of brand-name products, effects on 6 US industries, investigation with financial and operating data, 1984 rpt, 9886–4.67

Income (taxable) not reported, by illegal source, with characteristics of persons involved, methodology, and bibl, 1970s-82, 8008–112

Prisoners in State prisons median sentence, and admissions and releases by prisoner and sentencing characteristics, by offense and State, 1981 and trends from 1926, 6066–19.9

Secret Service investigations in counterfeiting, forgery, protective intelligence, and other matters, FY74-83, annual rpt, 8464–1

Counterinsurgency

see also Guerrilla warfare

Counterintelligence

Polygraph lie detection test accuracy, and Fed Govt use by agency, selected years 1947-83, 26358–96

Counties

Agricultural Conservation Program, counties served by State, FY83, annual rpt, 1804–7

Agriculture census, 1982: farms, farmland, production and costs, and operator characteristics, preliminary State and county rpt series, 2330–1

Agriculture census, 1982: farms, farmland, production, finances, and operator characteristics, by county, final State rpt series, 2331–1

Bank mergers, concentration levels, and market deposits merged, by number of bank organizations in SMSA and county, simulated 1982, technical paper, 9366–1.136

Census of Population and Housing, 1980: detailed population and housing characteristics, by county, city, and census tract, State and SMSA rpt series, 2551–2

Census of Population, 1980: detailed socioeconomic and demographic characteristics, by age, sex, race, Hispanic origin, occupation, and industry, State rpt series, 2531–4

Census of Population, 1980: detailed socioeconomic characteristics, by county, city, and inside-outside SMSAs and central cities, State rpt series, 2531–3

Community Dev Block Grants to small cities, State admin, project characteristics, and assessments of local officials, 1982, 5188–106

Community dev programs funding and activities, for 5 HUD programs, FY83, annual rpt, 5124–5

County and City Data Book, detailed socioeconomic and demographic data for States, counties, and cities, selected years 1976-82, 2328–1

Counties

Crimes, arrests by offender characteristics, and rates, by offense, and law enforcement employees, by population size and jurisdiction, 1970s-83, annual rpt, 6224–2

Farmland (US) owned by foreigners, acreage, value, and use, by State and county, and for 5 leading investor countries, 1983, annual rpt, 1584–3

Income (personal) per capita and by source, and earnings by industry div, by State, MSA, and county, 1977-82, annual regional rpts, 2704–2

Income (personal) per capita and total, by State, MSA, and county, with metro-nonmetro totals, 1980-82, annual article, 2702–1.413

Manufacturing census, 1982: financial and operating data, by SIC 2- to 4-digit industry, State, SMSA, and county, preliminary census div rpt series, 2491–3

Mobility of population, detailed data by demographic and socioeconomic characteristics of movers and nonmovers, Mar 1981-82, annual Current Population Rpt, 2546–1.384

Population size and change for metro and nonmetro areas and central cities by census div, and growth of areas with large black and aged populations, 1970-82, 2328–47

Population size and components of change, by MSA and county, 1980-82, annual State Current Population Rpt series, 2546–4

Population size, Apr 1980 and July 1982, and per capita income, 1979 and 1981, by county and city, State Current Population Rpt series, 2546–11

Revenue sharing payments to States, local govts, Indian tribes, and Alaska Native villages, and entitlement computation data, FY84, series, 8066–1

Service industry census, 1982: employment, establishments, receipts, and payroll, by SIC 2- to 4-digit kind of business, SMSA, county, and city, State rpt series, 2391–1

Soil survey county descriptions and maps of USDA, 1899-1983, annual listing, 1264–11

Transit systems, expenditures by level of govt, and revenues by source, with distribution of commuter trips by mode of transport, 1980-82, article, 10042–1.404

see also Census of Governments

see also County Business Patterns

see also Local government

see also under By County in the "Index by Categories"

County Business Patterns

Employment, establishments, and payrolls, by SIC 4-digit industry and county, 1981, annual State rpt series, 2326–8

Employment, establishments, and payrolls, by SIC 4-digit industry and county, 1982, annual State rpt series, 2326–6

Court of Claims

Budget of US Appendix, detailed budgets and personnel summaries, by agency, FY85, annual rpt, 104–3

Index by Subjects and Names

Budget of US, appropriations, outlays, balances, and budget receipts, by govtl branch and agency, FY83, annual rpt, 8104–2

Caseload statistics of US Court of Claims, FY83, annual rpt, 18224–1

Pay rates of Fed Govt civilian employees, by branch of govt, employee category, and pay level, as of 1984 with trends from 1789, 21628–54

Court of Customs and Patent Appeals

Budget of US Appendix, detailed budgets and personnel summaries, by agency, FY85, annual rpt, 104–3

Court of International Trade

Budget of US Appendix, detailed budgets and personnel summaries, by agency, FY85, annual rpt, 104–3

Budget of US, appropriations, outlays, balances, and budget receipts, by govtl branch and agency, FY83, annual rpt, 8104–2

Caseloads of Court of Intl Trade by type, decisions published, and appeals, FY83-84, annual rpt, 18224–2

Pay rates of Fed Govt civilian employees, by branch of govt, employee category, and pay level, as of 1984 with trends from 1789, 21628–54

Court of Military Appeals

Budget of DOD, itemized account of legislative history, FY84, annual rpt, 3504–7

Cases and court actions, FY83, annual rpt, 3504–3

Courtless, Joan C.

"Recent Trends in Clothing and Textiles", 1702–1.403

Courts

Bankruptcy Courts of US, caseloads by type of estate, Code chapter, circuit, and district, quarterly rpt, 18202–1

Budget of US Appendix, Judicial Branch detailed budgets and personnel summary, FY85, annual rpt, 104–3

Budget of US, appropriations, outlays, balances, and budget receipts, by govtl branch and agency, FY83, annual rpt, 8104–2

Budget of US, compact budgets by function, agency, and account, FY85 with projections to FY89, annual rpt, 104–2

Budget of US, object class analysis of obligations, by branch of Fed Govt and selected depts and agencies, FY85 estimates, annual rpt, 104–9

Budget of US, receipts by source and outlays by agency and program, monthly rpt, 8102–3

Caseloads (civil and criminal) for Federal district, appeals, and special courts, year ended June 1983 and selected trends from 1940, annual rpt, 18204–8

Crime and criminal justice data, including justice expenditures and employment by level of govt, 1970s-82 with some trends from 1875, 6068–174

Crime and criminal justice statistics analysis, methodology, and use in courts, 1983 biennial conf proceedings, 6064–20

Fed Govt civilian employment, by location, agency, and pay system, 1982, biennial rpt, 9844–8

Fed Govt consolidated financial statements based on business accounting methods, FY82-83, annual rpt, 8104–5

Govt census, 1982: State govt payments to local govts, by program, source of funds, level of govt, and State, with trends from 1902, 2460–3

Judicial Conf semiannual proceedings and findings, 1984 annual rpt, 18204–5

Statistical Abstract of US, social, political, and economic data, 1950s-83 and trends, annual rpt, 2324–1.1

see also Administrative Office of the U.S. Courts

see also Civil procedure

see also Contempt of court

see also Court of Claims

see also Court of Customs and Patent Appeals

see also Court of International Trade

see also Court of Military Appeals

see also Courts-martial and courts of inquiry

see also Criminal procedure

see also D.C. courts

see also Federal courts of appeals

see also Federal district courts

see also Federal Judicial Center

see also Judges

see also Judicial powers

see also Judicial reform

see also Juries

see also Juvenile courts

see also Parole and probation

see also Sentences, criminal procedure

see also State courts

see also Supreme Court

see also Tax Court of the U.S.

see also Tax laws and courts

see also Traffic laws and courts

see also Trials

see also Witnesses

Courts-martial and courts of inquiry

Cases and court actions, Court of Military Appeals, Judge Advocates General, and DOT General Counsel, FY83, annual rpt, 3504–3

Drug-related courts martial and other disciplinary actions, by service branch, FY80-84, 3508–19

Navy personnel alcohol and drug abuse, and related deaths, courts-martial, discharges, and treatment program funding and staff, FY83, annual table, 3804–12

Cows

see Dairy industry and products

see Livestock and livestock industry

Cox, W. Michael

"What Is the Rule for Financing Public Debt?", 9379–1.407

Cox, William N.

"Georgia: A Healthy Economy Looks for Solid Growth", 9371–1.405

"In-Store ATMs: Steppingstone to POS", 9371–1.403

"What Distinguishes Larger and More Efficient Credit Unions?", 9371–1.427

Crabs

see Shellfish

Craighead County, Ark.

Housing vacancy rates for single and multifamily units and mobile homes, by city and ZIP code, 1984, annual metro area rpt, 9304–19.11

Index by Subjects and Names

Credit unions

Cranberries
see Fruit and fruit products

Crane, Langdon T.
"Residential Energy Conservation: How Far Have We Progressed and How Much Farther Can We Go?", 21368–48

Craun, Gunther F.
"Waterborne Outbreaks in the U.S., 1971-81", 9208–124

Crawford, Peggy J.
"Effect of the AML Index on the Borrower", 9312–7.403

Creager, James M.
"Affirmative Employment Statistics for Executive Branch Agencies, Sept. 30, 1982", 9842–1.403

Credit

Budget of US, loans and loan guarantees, and Admin proposed limits on credit assistance, by program, FY83-89, annual rpt, 26306–3.65

Budget of US, projected under current fiscal policies, FY85-89, annual rpt, 26304–3.2

Budget of US, special analysis of Fed Govt credit programs and interest subsidy values, FY85, annual rpt, 104–1.6

Business statistics, detailed data for major industries and economic indicators, *Survey of Current Business,* monthly rpt, 2702–1.6

Developing countries govt policy, and AID and other foreign assistance, effects on private sector dev and socioeconomic conditions, with case studies for 6 countries, 1960s-80, 9918–12

Economic indicators and components, current data and annual trends, monthly rpt, 23842–1.5

Economic performance of US, and Reagan Admin 1984 spending, tax, and monetary policy proposals, with data for 1950s-83 and projected to 1988, press release, 8008–107

Fed Govt construction grants, loans, and loan guarantees, by program and type of structure, FY80-83 and estimated FY84-85, annual article, 2012–1.404

Fed Govt industrial dev funding by type, program, and agency, and State govt policies and support, selected years FY75-85, 26306–6.81

Fed Govt loan and loan guarantee liabilities and commitments, as of Sept 1983, annual rpt, 8104–3.4

Fed Govt loan programs, direct and guaranteed loans outstanding by agency and program, *Treasury Bulletin,* quarterly rpt, 8002–4.10

Fed Govt loans and other receivables due, and interest and penalties on delinquencies, by agency, *Treasury Bulletin,* quarterly rpt, 8002–4.16

Fed Govt loans, grants, and tax benefits to business, by program and economic sector, projected FY84-88 with effective tax rates for FY80-82, 26306–6.70

Fed Govt programs and mgmt cost control proposals, 3-year savings by function and agency, and financial and operating data, 1960s-81, 16908–1

Financial and business detailed statistics, *Fed Reserve Bulletin,* monthly rpt with articles, 9362–1

Flow-of-funds accounts, assets and liabilities by type and economic sector, year-end outstandings, 1960-83, annual rpt, 9364–3

Flow-of-funds accounts savings, investments, and credit statements, quarterly rpt, 9365–3.3

Foreign monetary control policy and relation to credit, exchange rates, GNP, and other indicators, US and selected West European countries, various periods 1960-82, conf papers, 9373–3.26

GNP related to M1 and nonfinancial sector debt, and velocity of targets during business expansion, various periods 1958-83, article, 9391–1.416

Inflation and GNP related to growth of money supply and nonfinancial sector debt, various periods 1960-83, article, 9373–1.401

Natl credit market activity indicators, 1974-83, annual rpt, 204–1.5

Small business financing sources and uses of funds, and total and current debt, selected years 1966-80, annual rpt, 9764–6.2

Small business loan and credit activities and assessment, effect of bank deregulation by business characteristics, 1980 and 1982 surveys, hearings, 21728–52.1

see also Agricultural credit

see also Business assets and liabilities, general

see also Business assets and liabilities, specific industries

see also Commodity Credit Corp.

see also Consumer credit

see also Credit cards

see also Credit unions

see also Finance companies

see also International finance

see also Loan delinquency and default

see also Loans

see also Mortgages

see also Public debt

Credit Bureau of Saginaw
"Analysis of Chapter Seven and Eleven Bankruptcies Filed in the Northern Division of Eastern District of Michigan, from Oct. 1979-Feb. 1981", 21528–57.3

Credit cards

Bank financial and operating statements, functional cost analysis for Fed Reserve member banks with average and high earnings, by deposit size, 1982, annual rpt, 9364–6

Bankruptcy (personal), filers by debt type and other characteristics, and impacts in Connecticut and Michigan, various dates 1946-82, hearings, 21528–57

Bankruptcy (personal), filers by debt type and other characteristics, selected years 1978-81, hearing, 25528–97.1

Banks (natl) domestic and intl operations, charters, mergers, and liquidations, by State and instn, and Comptroller of Currency activities, quarterly rpt, 8402–3

Economic indicators and components, current data and annual trends, monthly rpt, 23842–1.5

Financial services of nonbank firms and bank holding companies, with financial and operating data by firm, 1981-82 with trends from 1962, technical paper, 9375–11.3

Financial services offered by bank interstate service offices, including S&Ls, bank branches, and nonbank subsidiaries, by instn and State, 1981-83, 9371–13

Fraud involving credit cards, losses and loss rates, selected years 1975-82, 6066–19.3

Household income, assets, and debt characteristics, sources of credit, and use of financial services, 1983 survey, article, 9362–1.411

Retail trade accounts receivable, by type of account and SIC 2- to 3-digit kind of business, 1983, annual rpt, 2413–5

Statistical Abstract of US, social, political, and economic data, 1950s-83 and trends, annual rpt, 2324–1.3

Credit Research Center
"Consumers' Right to Bankruptcy: Origins and Effects", 21528–57.2

Credit unions

Assets and liabilities of depository instns, monthly rpt, 9362–1.1

Assets and liabilities of savings instns, by type of instn, 1980-82, annual rpt, 9364–5.4

Assets of credit unions, and distribution of assets and liabilities by type, 1976 and 1983, article, 9381–1.410

Auto sales related to usury limits on loans in 2 States, and loans made and outstanding by lender type, various periods 1977-82, article, 9375–1.409

Automated teller machines shared networks by State, and membership and characteristics of top 16 regional and natl networks, Nov 1983, article, 9373–1.403

Bankruptcy (personal), filers by debt type and other characteristics, and impacts in Connecticut and Michigan, various dates 1946-82, hearings, 21528–57

Bankruptcy (personal), filers by debt type and other characteristics, selected years 1978-81, hearing, 25528–97.1

County Business Patterns: establishments, employees, and payrolls, by SIC 4-digit industry and county, 1981, annual State rpt series, 2326–8

County Business Patterns: establishments, employees, and payrolls, by SIC 4-digit industry and county, 1982, annual State rpt series, 2326–6

Farm debt, loans outstanding, and interest rates, by type of lender and State, 1960-83 with trends from 1940, biennial rpt, 1544–2

Financial and membership data for Federal and federally insured State credit unions, with shares, loans, and assets, by State, 1984 annual listing, 9534–6

Financial and membership data for State-chartered credit unions, by State and asset size, annual rpt, discontinued, 9534–2

Financial statements by membership type, region, and State, for Federal and federally insured State credit unions, 1983, annual rpt, 9534–1

Flow-of-funds accounts, assets and liabilities by type and economic sector, year-end outstandings, 1960-83, annual rpt, 9364–3

Flow-of-funds accounts savings, investments, and credit statements, quarterly rpt, 9365–3.3

Household income, assets, and debt characteristics, sources of credit, and use of financial services, 1983 survey, article, 9362–1.411

Credit unions

Income tax returns of corporations, detailed income and tax items by industry, 1981, annual rpt, 8304–4

Income taxes, effective rates, and selected financial data, for financial instns by type and individual firm, with comparisons to other industries, selected years 1960-82, hearing, 25368–129

Installment credit outstanding, by type of financial instn and credit, monthly rpt, 9365–2.6

Insurance (Fed Govt) of deposits related to credit union financial ratios, various periods 1948-82, article, 9379–1.404

Mortgage transactions and holdings, by lender group and type of property and loan, quarterly rpt, 5142–30

Natl Credit Union Admin Central Liquidity Facility, financial performance, quarterly rpt, 9532–4

Natl Credit Union Admin insurance fund financial activity, and insured instns financial and operating data, FY83, annual rpt with semiannual update for 1st qtr FY84, 9534–7

Natl Credit Union Admin operations and chartering activities, annual summary rpt, discontinued, 9534–3

New England States financial instn assets and liabilities, Fed Reserve 1st District, monthly rpt, 9373–2.5

Southeastern States financial and economic devs, Fed Reserve 6th District, monthly rpt with articles, 9371–1

Western States economic indicators, Fed Reserve 12th District, quarterly rpt, 9393–1.5

Creighton, Kathleen P.

"Redesign of the Sample for the Current Population Survey", 6742–2.407

Crime and criminals

Alcohol, tobacco, firearms, and explosives arrests and seizures, by State, FY82, last issue of annual rpt, 8484–1.6

Alcohol use, and health, economic, and social impacts, review of research, 1970s-81, 4488–4

Aliens excluded and deported by cause, 1892-FY81, annual rpt, 6264–2

CETA participants by sociodemographic characteristics, and Labor Dept activities and staff, FY83, annual rpt, 6304–1

Classification codes for US criminal titles and sections, with corresponding detailed offenses and severity levels, 1984, annual rpt, 18204–14

County and City Data Book, detailed socioeconomic and demographic data for States, counties, and cities, selected years 1976-82, 2328–1

Court cases, dispositions, convictions, and sentences of Federal criminal defendants, by offense and district, as of June 1983 with trends from 1945, annual rpt, 18204–1

Crime and criminal justice data, including justice expenditures and employment by level of govt, 1970s-82 with some trends from 1875, 6068–174

Crime and criminal justice research sponsored by Natl Inst of Justice, summary rpt series, 6066–20

Crime and criminal justice statistics analysis, methodology, and use in courts, 1983 biennial conf proceedings, 6064–20

Crime, victimization, offender characteristics, prison population, and other topics, periodic rpt, 6062–2

Crimes, arrests by offender characteristics, and rates, by offense, and law enforcement employees, by population size and jurisdiction, 1970s-83, annual rpt, 6224–2

Criminal justice issues, special rpt series, 6066–19

Drug abuse residential treatment program effectiveness indicators, with data on pre- and post-program characteristics of grads and dropouts, 1970-74 study, 4496–5.18

Economic indicators relation to measures of social pathology including crime and death rates, various periods 1950-80, 23848–76

Electronic funds transfer systems potential for crime, EFT and other transactions, and credit card fraud losses, 1975-82, 6066–19.3

Homeless population and characteristics, and temporary shelter operations, use, and user characteristics, for selected cities, various periods 1979-84, hearing, 21248–85

Income (legal) not reported on Federal income tax returns by source, and legal and illegal underground income, with bibl, 1974-81, article, 2702–1.419

Income (taxable) not reported, by illegal source, with characteristics of persons involved, methodology, and bibl, 1970s-82, 8008–112

Justice Dept activities, by subagency, FY82, annual rpt, 6004–1

Law enforcement officer assaults, murders, and other deaths by circumstances, level of govt, agency, victim and offender characteristics, and location, 1983, annual rpt, 6224–3

NASA programs fraud and abuse, audits and investigations, 2nd half FY84, semiannual rpt, 9502–9

Neighborhood and housing quality indicators and attitudes, and occupant characteristics, by urban-rural location and region, 1981, annual survey, 2485–7

Neighborhood and housing quality indicators and attitudes, by occupant and unit characteristics, region, and metro-nonmetro location, 1981, annual survey, 2485–2

Neighborhood quality, indicators and attitudes by inside-outside central cities, 1979-82 surveys, SMSA rpt series, 2485–6

Prevention of crime, media campaign effects on public attitudes and activities, and socioeconomic characteristics of campaign-exposed group, as of Nov 1981, 6068–183

Public lands trespass cases and collections, FY83, annual rpt, 5724–1.2

School crime, assaults and robberies of secondary students and teachers, 1972-83, 4918–13

School crime, assaults and robberies of teachers and minority and all students, and vandalism incidents, 1976/77, 4808–12

Statistical Abstract of US, social, political, and economic data, 1950s-83 and trends, annual rpt, 2324–1.1

Index by Subjects and Names

TTPI socioeconomic, employment, health, and govtl data, by TTPI govt, FY83 and selected trends, detailed annual rpt, 7004–6.2

Urban area economic distress index and components, for 153 cities, 1975 and 1980, article, 9373–1.413

Victimization rates by type of offense, and victim and offense characteristics, Natl Crime Survey series, 6066–3

Virgin Islands socioeconomic and govtl data, FY81, annual rpt, 5304–4

Wiretapping authorizations by offense, costs, persons involved, arrests, trials, and convictions, 1983, annual rpt, 18204–7

Witness Security Program costs, participants by arrest record, and prosecutions by offense, offender type, and disposition, various periods FY70-83, GAO rpt, 26119–70

see also Air piracy
see also Arrest
see also Arson
see also Assassination
see also Assault
see also Bombs
see also Child abuse and neglect
see also Contraband
see also Correctional institutions
see also Corruption and bribery
see also Counterfeiting and forgery
see also Courts
see also Crime Index
see also Criminal investigations
see also Criminal procedure
see also Detective and protective services
see also Domestic violence
see also Driving while intoxicated
see also Drug and narcotics traffic
see also Fraud
see also Gambling
see also Homicide
see also Hostages
see also Informants
see also Juvenile delinquency
see also Kidnapping
see also Law enforcement
see also Organized crime
see also Parole and probation
see also Pretrial detention and release
see also Prostitution
see also Rape
see also Rehabilitation of criminals
see also Robbery and theft
see also Sentences, criminal procedure
see also Smuggling
see also Terrorism
see also Trials
see also Vandalism

Crime Index

Central cities and suburbs population and employment, effect of region, neighborhood, population, and labor characteristics, 1970-80, technical paper, 9387–8.89

Crimes, arrests by offender characteristics, and rates, by offense, and law enforcement employees, by population size and jurisdiction, 1970s-83, annual rpt, 6224–2

Index by population size and region, and offenses known to police by large city, Jan-June 1984, semiannual rpt, 6222–1

Juvenile arrests for Crime Index offenses, and police assessments, staff, and programs for control of criminal activity by youth gangs in 27 cities, 1980-81, 6068–175

Prison mandatory sentencing effects on Crime Index offense rates and prison population, selected years 1960-76, 6066–20.3

Criminal investigations

Arson investigation and prosecution, by incident characteristics and outcome, motive, and type of evidence, for 4 jurisdictions, 1981, 6068–184

Counterfeiting of currency and forgery of checks and bonds, Secret Service investigations and judicial disposition, FY74-84, annual rpt, 8464–1

Drug Enforcement Admin cases against major drug traffickers by case characteristics, and agents assessment of activities, in 3 cities, 1979-82, GAO rpt, 26119–57

Drug enforcement regional task force program investigation activities, funding, and personnel, with nationwide drug abuse data, 1983 annual rpt, 6004–17

FBI undercover operations convictions, fines, recoveries, victim compensation, and status of lawsuits against FBI by operation, FY82, GAO rpt, 26119–67

Marijuana cultivation control activity of State law enforcement agencies, and aid from Fed Govt and Natl Guard, 1983 survey, GAO rpt, 26119–64

see also Informants

see also Police

Criminal procedure

Alcohol, Tobacco, and Firearms Bur activities nationwide and in 20 cities, funding, and jobs to be transferred to Customs and Secret Service, 1979-82, hearings, 21528–55

Arson investigation and prosecution, by incident characteristics and outcome, motive, and type of evidence, for 4 jurisdictions, 1981, 6068–184

Counterfeiting of currency and forgery of checks and bonds, Secret Service investigations and judicial disposition, FY74-84, annual rpt, 8464–1

Court caseloads, actions, procedure duration, judges, and jurors, by Federal district and appeals court, 1979-84, annual rpt, 18204–3

Court caseloads for Federal district, appeals, and bankruptcy courts, by type of suit and offense, circuit, and district, quarterly rpt, 18202–1

Court cases, dispositions, convictions, and sentences of Federal criminal defendants, by offense and district, as of June 1983 with trends from 1945, annual rpt, 18204–1

Court civil and criminal caseloads for Federal district, appeals, and special courts, year ended June 1983 and selected trends from 1940, annual rpt, 18204–8

Court civil and criminal casloads and activity summary, for Federal district, appeals, and bankruptcy courts, 1975-June 1984, annual chartbook, 18204–9

Court criminal case disposition, effect of victim injury and other factors, and law enforcement official and victim attitudes, 1983 survey, 6068–185

Crime and criminal justice data, including justice expenditures and employment by level of govt, 1970s-82 with some trends from 1875, 6068–174

Crime and criminal justice research sponsored by Natl Inst of Justice, summary rpt series, 6066–20

Crime and criminal justice statistics analysis, methodology, and use in courts, 1983 biennial conf proceedings, 6064–20

Crime, victimization, offender characteristics, prison population, and other topics, periodic rpt, 6062–2

Criminal case processing from arrest to sentencing, series, 6066–22

Criminal justice issues, special rpt series, 6066–19

Criminal justice system local operations and costs, series, 6066–21

Drug enforcement regional task force program investigation activities, funding, and personnel, with nationwide drug abuse data, 1983 annual rpt, 6004–17

FBI undercover operations convictions, fines, recoveries, victim compensation, and status of lawsuits against FBI by operation, FY82, GAO rpt, 26119–67

HUD programs fraud and abuse, audits and investigations, 2nd half FY84, semiannual rpt, 5002–8

Immigration and nationality violations, prosecutions and convictions, and deportation and exclusion cases, FY71-81, annual rpt, 6264–2

Judicial Conf semiannual proceedings and findings, 1984 annual rpt, 18204–5

Justice Dept activities, by subagency, FY82, annual rpt, 6004–1

Juvenile arrests, by disposition and population size, 1983, annual rpt, 6224–2.2

Legal fees awarded private parties in cases against Federal, State, and local govts, by case, selected years 1977-83, 6008–19

Magistrate case processing duties assigned in Fed Govt district courts, by type of case, duty, and district, 1983 rpt, 18408–24

Selective Service activities and staff, nonregistrant prosecution status, and registrants by State, 2nd half FY84, semiannual rpt, 9742–1

South America cocaine traffic legal policy and enforcement, with data on arrests and confiscations in Peru, 1978, intl conf papers, 7008–40

Telephone conference use in civil and criminal hearings, assessment of lawyers and judges in 2 States and Denver, Colo, 1981, 6068–186

US Attorneys civil and criminal case processing in district, appellate, and State courts, by district, FY83, annual rpt, 6004–2

USDA programs fraud and abuse, audits and investigations, 2nd half FY84, semiannual rpt, 1002–4

Witness Security Program costs, participants by arrest record, and prosecutions by offense, offender type, and disposition, various periods FY70-83, GAO rpt, 26119–70

see also Capital punishment

see also Evidence

see also Extradition

see also Habeas corpus

see also Juries

see also Parole and probation

see also Pretrial detention and release

see also Searches and seizures

see also Sentences, criminal procedure

see also Trials

Crom, Richard

"Effects of Simulated Changes in Consumer Preference on the Meat and Poultry Industries", 1502–3.402

Crop insurance

see Agricultural insurance

Crop Reporting Board

Acreage planted and harvested, by crop and State, 1982-83 and planned as of June 1984, annual rpt, 1621–23

Acreage planting intended for 19 crops, by State, as of Feb 1984, annual rpt, 1621–22

Acreage, yield, and production of field crops, by State, 1978-82 and preliminary 1983, 1641–7

Catfish raised on farms, production, inventory, sales, prices, and imports, monthly release, 1631–14

Cattle and calves for beef and milk, inventory and value by State, 1982-84, semiannual press release, 1623–1

Cattle and calves on feed, inventory and marketings by State, monthly release, 1623–2

Celery acreage planted and growing, by major producing State and area, monthly rpt, 1621–14

Chicken and turkey hatchery production, by State, 1983, annual rpt, 1625–8

Cold storage capacity of warehouses, by State and SMSA, Oct 1983, biennial rpt, 1614–2

Cold storage food stocks by commodity and census div, and warehouse cold storage space in use, by State, monthly rpt, 1631–5

Cold storage food stocks of 77 commodities, by region, 1983, annual rpt, 1631–11

Commodity publications, 1984 releases, annual listing, 1614–1

Crop prices and production values, for detailed crops by State, 1981-83, annual rpt, 1621–2

Dairy production by State, stocks, prices, and CCC price support activities, by product type, monthly rpt, 1627–3

Dairy products production by type, and plants, by State, 1983, annual rpt, 1627–5

Egg production and layer inventory, by State, 1982-83, annual rpt, 1625–7

Egg production by type of product, and shell eggs broken under Fed Govt inspection by region, monthly rpt, 1625–2

Farm labor, wages, hours, and perquisites, by State, quarterly rpt, 1631–1

Farm production expenditures, detailed items by farm sales size and region, 1983, annual rpt, 1614–3

Farms, production, acreage, and related data, by selected crop and State, monthly rpt, 1621–1

Fertilizer consumption, by fertilizer type and State, years ended June 1983-84, annual rpt, 1631–13

Crop Reporting Board

Fruit (citrus) production and use, by crop and State, 1977/78-1981/82, 1641–4

Fruit and nut production, prices, and use, 1981-84, annual rpt series, 1621–18

Grain, oilseed, and hay stocks on and off farms, and capacity of off-farm grain storage facilities, by State, 1978-83, 1641–17

Grain production, acreage, and yield, by selected crop and State, 1982-84 with wheat and rye seedings for 1985, annual rpt, 1621–24

Grain stocks on and off farms and total in all positions, by crop, periodic rpt, 1621–4

Hog and pig inventory, value, farrowings, and farms, by State, quarterly release, 1623–3

Hog and pig production, inventory, and farms, by State, 1979-82, 1641–10

Hops stocks held by growers, dealers, and brewers, Sept 1984, semiannual release, 1621–8

Livestock slaughter and meat production, by livestock type and State, monthly rpt, 1623–9

Livestock slaughter by species, meat production, and number of slaughtering plants, by State, 1983, annual rpt, 1623–10

Meat animal production, marketing, slaughter, prices, and producers gross income, by animal type and State, 1982-83, annual rpt, 1623–8

Milk cows, and milk and cream production and marketings, by State, 1981-83, annual rpt, 1627–4

Milk cows and milk production, and grain and other concentrates fed, by State, monthly rpt, 1627–1

Milk of manufacturing grade, fat content and prices received by farmers in Minnesota and Wisconsin, monthly rpt, 1629–6

Milk of manufacturing grade, fat content and prices received by farmers in Minnesota and Wisconsin, 1981-83, annual rpt, 1629–2

Mink and mink pelt production, by State, 1983-84 with trends from 1969, annual rpt, 1631–7

Mushroom production, sales, and prices, by State, 1981/82-1983/84 and planned 1984/85, annual rpt, 1631–9

Peanut stocks, millings, and processing, Feb-July 1984, semiannual rpt, 1621–6

Potato and sweet potato production, stocks, and prices, 1982-83, annual rpt, 1621–11

Potato and sweet potato production, stocks, prices, acreage, and yield, 1978-82 and preliminary 1983, 1641–14

Potato production, stocks, processing, yields, and harvest losses, by State, periodic rpt, 1621–10

Poultry (egg, chicken, and turkey) production and inventories, monthly rpt, 1625–1

Poultry prices received by farmers, for chickens, turkeys, and eggs, by State, monthly and annual average, 1959-78, 1651–3

Poultry production, prices, and producers gross income, by State, 1982-83, annual rpt, 1625–5

Poultry slaughtered under Fed Govt inspection, pounds certified, and condemnations by cause, by State, monthly rpt, 1625–3

Prices received by farmers for major products, and paid for farm inputs and living items, by commodity and State, monthly rpt, 1629–1

Prices received by farmers for major products, and paid for farm inputs, by commodity and State, 1983, annual rpt, 1629–5

Rice stocks on and off farms and total, periodic rpt, 1621–7

Sheep and lambs by State, and goats in Texas, inventories and operations, 1981-84, annual press release, 1623–4

Soybean stocks on and off farms, by State, various dates 1983-84, annual rpt, 1621–5

Sugar production, consumption, supply, and trade, quarterly rpt, 1621–28

Turkey hatcheries incubator egg inventory and poult placements, by region, monthly rpt, 1625–10

Turkey inventories and production, by State, 1981-83 with 1984 breeding intentions, annual release, 1625–6

Vegetable and fruit production, acreage, and prices, for selected fresh and processing crops by State, 1981-84, annual rpts, 1621–25

Vegetable and fruit production, acreage, and yield, current and forecast for selected fresh and processing crops by State, periodic rpt, 1621–12

Wool and mohair production and prices, by State, 1982-83, annual release, 1623–6

Crops

see Agricultural commodities

Cross, Philip K.

"Changes in Rates of Spontaneous Fetal Deaths Reported in Upstate New York Vital Records by Gestational Age, 1968-78", 4102–1.428

Cross, R. L.

"Annual Data and Verification Tabulation, Eastern North Pacific Tropical Storms and Hurricanes, 1983", 2184–8

"Eastern North Pacific Tropical Cyclones, 1983", 2152–8.402

Crosson, Pierre

"Resource and Environmental Impacts of Trends in U.S. Agriculture", 9188–94

CSR, Inc.

"Effect of the Head Start Program on Children's Cognitive Development, Preliminary Report", 4608–20

"Review of Head Start Research Since 1970", 4608–17

Cuba

Agricultural and food production indexes, and production of selected commodities, by world region and country, 1974-83, annual rpt, 1524–5

Agricultural situation in Latin America, by country, 1981-83 and outlook for 1984, annual rpt, 1524–4.9

Deaths in US by State and by outlying area or country of birth, 1979, US Vital Statistics annual rpt, 4144–2.1

Economic conditions in Communist, OECD, and selected other countries, 1960s-83, annual rpt, 244–5

Index by Subjects and Names

Economic conditions in Cuba, agricultural and industrial production and distribution, trade, and intl economic relations, 1970-82 with trends from 1957, 248–40

Economic, social, and political summary data, by country, 1984, annual factbook, 244–11

Exports and imports of US with Communist countries, by detailed commodity and country, quarterly rpt with articles, 9882–2

Exports of US, detailed Schedule E commodities by mode of transport and world area and country of destination, 1983, annual rpts, 2424–5

Hijackings, on-board explosions, other crimes against civil aviation, and circumstances, US and worldwide, 1931-83, annual rpt, 7504–31

Immigration, and alien residents, workers, visitors, deportations, and naturalizations, by country of birth, FY81, annual rpt, 6264–2

Imports of US, detailed Schedule A commodities by country and world area of origin, and mode of transport, 1983, annual rpts, 2424–2

Imports of US, detailed TSUSA commodities by country of origin, 1983, annual rpt, 2424–4

Loans and grants for economic and military assistance from US and intl agencies, by program and country, FY46-83, annual rpt, 9914–5

Military presence of USSR and Cuba by country, and military personnel abroad, as of 1984, 3508–14

Military spending, arms trade, and armed forces size, with total govt spending and population, by country, 1972-82, annual rpt, 9824–1

Minerals Yearbook, 1982, Vol 3: foreign country reviews of production, trade, and policies, by commodity, annual rpt, 5604–35

Minerals Yearbook, 1983, Vol 3 preprints: foreign country review of production, trade, and policies, by commodity, annual rpt, 5604–23.85

Population size and growth rates, and latest available benchmark demographic data, by country, 1950-83, biennial rpt, 2324–4

Refugee resettlement program activities and funding, arrivals and population by country of origin and State, and employment and other characteristics, FY83, annual rpt, 4704–8

Science and technology dev and transfer between USSR and other members of Council for Mutual Economic Assistance, 1940s-81, 2326–9.7

Students in US and Soviet bloc training programs, by program type and Latin American country or world region of student origin, selected years 1972-82, GAO rpt, 26123–77

see also under By Foreign Country in the "Index by Categories"

Cuban Americans

see Hispanic Americans

Cullison, William E.

"Equalizing Regional Differences in Wages: A Study of Wages and Migration in the South and Other Regions", 9389–1.406

Index by Subjects and Names

Culp/Wesner/Culp

"Assessment of Potential Environmental Problems Concerning Water Availability", 9208–125

Cultural relations

see International cooperation in cultural activities

Cumberland, Md.

Census of Housing, 1980: occupancy and unit characteristics, by race, Hispanic origin, and city, SMSA rpt, 2473–1.130

Census of Population and Housing, 1980: detailed population and housing characteristics, by county, city, and census tract, SMSA rpt, 2551–2.130

see also under By SMSA or MSA in the "Index by Categories"

Cummings, K. Michael

"Family Physicians' Beliefs About Screening for Colorectal Cancer Using the Stool Guaiac Slide Test", 4102–1.433

Cummins, David E.

"Cooperative Involvement in Grain Marketing", 1128–31

Cummins, Philip

"Economic Upheaval in the Midwest", 9375–1.402

Cunningham, Charles G.

"Earth and Water Resources and Hazards in Central America", 5668–71

Cunningham, William C.

"Growing Role of Private Security", 6066–20.8

Curlee, T. Randall

"Impacts of Oil Disturbances: Lessons from Experience", 3108–28

Currency

see Coins and coinage

see Flow-of-funds accounts

see Foreign exchange

see Money supply

see Special foreign currency programs

Current Employment Survey

Employment and earnings, detailed data, monthly rpt, 6742–2

Current Population Reports

see Current Population Survey

Current Population Survey

Consumer Income, socioeconomic characteristics of persons, families, and households, detailed cross-tabulations, Current Population Rpt series, 2546–6

Data coverage and availability of Census Bur publications, 1984 annual listing, 2304–2

Employment and earnings, detailed data, monthly rpt, 6742–2

Employment and unemployment current statistics, Monthly Labor Review, 6722–1.1

Employment, unemployment, and labor force, by demographic and employment characteristics, State, and for 30 metro areas and 11 large cities, 1983, annual rpt, 6744–7

Employment, unemployment, and labor force, detailed data by sociodemographic and employment characteristics, and industry, 1940s-83, 6748–72

Farm population, by employment and socioeconomic characteristics, 1983, annual rpt, 2544–1

Income (taxable) not reported, methodology using Current Population Survey labor force data to estimate share of output and nonreporters, 1950s-81, 23848–178

Labor force data series of BLS, Current Population Survey sampling area redesign, Apr 1984-July 1985, article, 6742–2.407

Labor force, revised seasonally adjusted estimates based on 1983 seasonal adjustment factors, monthly 1979-83, article, 6742–2.404

Methodology of CPS and changes since 1959, 1984 narrative article, 6722–1.435

Older persons income and income sources, by OASDI beneficiary and poverty status, labor force participation, and demographic characteristics, 1982, biennial rpt, 4744–26

Population demographic, social, and economic characteristics, Current Population Rpt series, 2546–1

Population demographic subjects, special study series, 2546–2

Population estimates and projections, by region and State, series, 2546–3

Population estimates for civilian, resident, and total population, monthly rpt, 2542–1

Population size, Apr 1980 and July 1982, and per capita income, 1979 and 1981, by county and city, State rpt series, 2546–11

Unemployment duration questions of Current Population Survey, response consistency, and results, 1984 article, 6722–1.421

Unemployment levels and rates, by State and for 240 large SMSAs, monthly press release with Current Population Survey annual benchmark averages, 6742–12

Curricula

Condition of Education, detailed data on enrollment, staff, achievement, finances, curricula, and education effects on employment, 1982-83, annual rpt, 4824–1

Digest of Education Statistics, detailed data on students, staff, finances, and facilities, 1982 and selected trends, annual rpt, 4824–2

DOD Dependents Schools students higher education admissions tests scores by sex and subject, and educational goals and attitudes, 1983, annual rpt, 3504–17

Education highlights, trends in enrollment, expenditures, curricula, and other topics of current interest, periodic press release, 4822–1

Education statistics summary compilation, 1980/81-1982/83 with selected trends from 1869, biennial rpt, 4804–27

High school class of 1982: coursework compared to graduation criteria of natl commission, by student and school characteristics, 4828–16

High school classes of 1980 and 1982: educational and sociodemographic characteristics and expectations, natl longitudinal study, series, 4826–2

High school classes of 1980 and 1982: types od courses taken and years of math and science study, by sex and race, annual rpt, 9624–10.3

Occupational manpower needs and supply by detailed occupation, and educational and training program enrollees and grads by detailed field, 1982 and 1995, biennial rpt, 6744–3

Customs Service

Puerto Rico educational enrollment, finance, completions, curricula, and personnel by instn, and health and vital statistics, selected years 1970-83, hearings, 21348–93

Teaching degrees conferred by specialty and State, required credit hours, and instn officials attitudes, by instn type, 1970s-83, hearings, 21348–89

see also Agricultural education

see also Area studies

see also Arts and the humanities

see also Astronomy

see also Biological sciences

see also Business education

see also Chemistry

see also Earth sciences

see also Economics

see also Environmental sciences

see also Foreign languages

see also Geography

see also Health education

see also History

see also Home economics

see also Industrial arts

see also Journalism

see also Language and literature

see also Legal education

see also Mathematics

see also Medical education

see also Military education

see also Physical education and training

see also Physical sciences

see also Physics

see also Psychology

see also Public administration

see also Scientific education

see also Social sciences

see also Social work

see also Sociology

see also Teacher education

Customs administration

Court of Intl Trade caseloads by type, decisions published, and appeals, FY83-84, annual rpt, 18224–2

Customs Service activities, operations, and staff, FY79-83, annual rpt, 8144–1

Meat and poultry inspection activities and personnel of Federal, State, and foreign govts, FY83, annual rpt, 1374–1

Meat plants inspected and certified for exporting products to US, by country, 1983, annual listing, 1374–2

Plant pests and pathogens found entering US, by country of origin, State, and method of interception, FY82, annual rpt, 1394–16

Ships and tonnage entering and clearing US Customs, by district and port of entry, 1983, annual rpt, 2424–7

Tax collections, refunds, and taxes due IRS, by State and region, and IRS court activity and operating expenses, FY83, annual rpt, 8304–3.3

see also Smuggling

Customs courts

see Court of Customs and Patent Appeals

see Court of International Trade

Customs duties

see Tariffs and foreign trade controls

Customs Service

see U.S. Customs Service

Cutlery

Cutlery
see Household furnishings

Cuyahoga County, Ohio
Arson investigation and prosecution, by incident characteristics and outcome, motive, and type of evidence, for 4 jurisdictions, 1981, 6068–184

Cypress, Beulah K.
- "Health Care of Adolescents by Office-Based Physicians: National Ambulatory Medical Care Survey, 1980-81", 4146–8.100
- "Patterns of Ambulatory Care in Internal Medicine: The National Ambulatory Medical Care Survey, U.S., Jan. 1980-Dec. 1981", 4147–13.80
- "Patterns of Ambulatory Care in Obstetrics and Gynecology: The National Ambulatory Medical Care Survey, U.S., Jan. 1980-Dec. 1981", 4147–13.76
- "Patterns of Ambulatory Care in Office Visits to General Surgeons: The National Ambulatory Medical Care Survey, U.S., Jan. 1980-Dec. 1981", 4147–13.79

Cyprus
- Agricultural and food production indexes, and production of selected commodities, by world region and country, 1974-83, annual rpt, 1524–5
- Agricultural situation in Middle East and North Africa, by country and commodity, 1983 and outlook for 1984, annual rpt, 1524–4.3
- Agricultural supply/demand, trade, and production, and socioeconomic data, by country, 1950s-77, 1528–179
- AID activities and funding by project and function, FY85, and developing countries summary socioeconomic data, 1970s-83, by country, annual rpt, 9914–3
- AID economic assistance to developing countries, obligations and disbursements by country, quarterly rpt, 9912–4
- AID loan repayment status and terms by program and country, and status of predecessor agency loans, quarterly rpt, 9912–3
- Economic, social, and political summary data, by country, 1984, annual factbook, 244–11
- Economic trends in income, production, prices, employment, finances, and trade, 1984 annual rpt, 2046–4.66
- Exports and imports of US with Western Europe, and US market share and export opportunities for selected commodities, by country, 1982-84, 2048–105
- Exports of US, detailed Schedule B commodities by country of destination, 1983, annual rpt, 2424–9
- Exports of US, detailed Schedule E commodities by mode of transport and world area and country of destination, 1983, annual rpts, 2424–5
- Imports of US, detailed Schedule A commodities by country and world area of origin, and mode of transport, 1983, annual rpts, 2424–2
- Imports of US, detailed TSUSA commodities by country of origin, 1983, annual rpt, 2424–4
- Loans and grants for economic and military assistance from US and intl agencies, by program and country, FY46-83, annual rpt, 9914–5

Military aid of US, arms sales, and training programs costs and budget requests by program, world region, and country, FY83-85, annual rpt, 7144–13

Military spending, arms trade, and armed forces size, with total govt spending and population, by country, 1972-82, annual rpt, 9824–1

Minerals Yearbook, 1982, Vol 3: foreign country reviews of production, trade, and policies, by commodity, annual rpt, 5604–35

Minerals Yearbook, 1983, Vol 3 preprints: foreign country review of production, trade, and policies, by commodity, annual rpt, 5604–23.18

Population size and growth rates, and latest available benchmark demographic data, by country, 1950-83, biennial rpt, 2324–4

see also under By Foreign Country in the "Index by Categories"

Czechoslovakia
- Agricultural and food production indexes, and production of selected commodities, by world region and country, 1974-83, annual rpt, 1524–5
- Agricultural production and trade by commodity, food consumption, and farm inputs, for 6 countries, 1960-80 with projections to 1991, 1528–178
- Agricultural situation in Eastern Europe, by country, 1983 and outlook for 1984, annual report, 1524–4.7
- *Background Notes,* summary social, political, and economic data, 1983 rpt, 7006–2.4
- Cuba economic conditions, agricultural and industrial production and distribution, trade, and intl economic relations, 1970-82 and trends from 1957, 248–40
- Economic conditions in Communist, OECD, and selected other countries, 1960s-83, annual rpt, 244–5
- Economic, social, and political summary data, by country, 1984, annual factbook, 244–11
- Export licensing and monitoring activities under Export Admin Act, for selected commodities, and for Communist and other countries, FY83, annual rpt, 2044–22
- Exports and imports of NATO countries with Council for Mutual Economic Assistance Europe members, by country, 1980-83, annual rpt, 7144–5
- Exports and imports of US with Communist countries, by detailed commodity and country, quarterly rpt with articles, 9882–2
- Exports of US, detailed Schedule B commodities by country of destination, 1983, annual rpt, 2424–9
- Exports of US, detailed Schedule E commodities by mode of transport and world area and country of destination, 1983, annual rpts, 2424–5
- Grain production, consumption, and trade, and US farm cooperatives grain and oilseed export potential, for 4 countries, selected years 1960-90, 1128–27
- Imports of US, detailed Schedule A commodities by country and world area of origin, and mode of transport, 1983, annual rpts, 2424–2

Index by Subjects and Names

- Imports of US, detailed TSUSA commodities by country of origin, 1983, annual rpt, 2424–4
- Loans and grants for economic and military assistance from US and intl agencies, by program and country, FY46-83, annual rpt, 9914–5
- Military spending, arms trade, and armed forces size, with total govt spending and population, by country, 1972-82, annual rpt, 9824–1
- *Minerals Yearbook, 1982,* Vol 3: foreign country reviews of production, trade, and policies, by commodity, annual rpt, 5604–35
- *Minerals Yearbook, 1983,* Vol 3 preprints: foreign country review of production, trade, and policies, by commodity, annual rpt, 5604–23.19
- Population size and growth rates, and latest available benchmark demographic data, by country, 1950-83, biennial rpt, 2324–4
- Refugee resettlement program activities and funding, arrivals and population by country of origin and State, and employment and other characteristics, FY83, annual rpt, 4704–8
- Science and technology dev and transfer between USSR and other members of Council for Mutual Economic Assistance, 1940s-81, 2326–9.7
- Space satellites and other objects launched since 1957, quarterly listing, 9502–2
- *see also* under By Foreign Country in the "Index by Categories"

Daberkow, Stan G.
"Distribution of Employment Growth in Nine Kentucky Counties: A Case Study", 1598–194

Dadswell, Michael J.
"Synopsis of Biological Data on Shortnose Sturgeon, Acipenser brevirostrum LeSueur 1818", 2166–16.14

Dahomey
see Benin

Dairy industry and products
- Agricultural Stabilization and Conservation Service dairy programs, 1949-84, annual fact sheet, 1806–4.1
- Agricultural Stabilization and Conservation Service producer payments under 26 programs, monthly rpt, 1802–10
- *Agricultural Statistics, 1983,* annual rpt, 1004–1
- Agriculture census, 1982: farms, farmland, production, finances, and operator characteristics, by county, final State rpt series, 2331–1
- *Agriculture Fact Book of US,* compilation of data for 1983 with trends from 1940, annual rpt, 1004–14
- Business statistics, detailed data for major industries and economic indicators, *Survey of Current Business,* monthly rpt, 2702–1.11
- Candy and confectionery industry sales, shipments, trade, and consumption of selected ingredients, 1983, annual Current Industrial Rpt, 2506–4.5
- Casein trade, tariffs, and industry operating data, foreign and US, 1979-83, TSUSA commodity rpt, 9885–4.38

Index by Subjects and Names

Dairy industry and products

Cattle and calves for beef and milk, inventory and value by State, 1982-84, semiannual press release, 1623–1

CCC dairy inventories, storage and spoilage costs of surplus butter, cheese, and nonfat dry milk, 1982-83, GAO rpt, 26113–120

CCC dairy price support purchases, sales, donations, and inventories, monthly rpt, 1802–2

Census of Population, 1980: detailed socioeconomic and demographic characteristics, by age, sex, race, Hispanic origin, occupation, and industry, State rpt series, 2531–4

Census of Population, 1980: detailed socioeconomic characteristics, by county, city, and inside-outside SMSAs and central cities, State rpt series, 2531–3

China economic conditions, agricultural and industrial production, trade, and domestic and foreign investment, 1980-85, 2048–106

Cold storage food stocks by commodity and census div, and warehouse cold storage space in use, by State, monthly rpt, 1631–5

Cold storage food stocks of 77 commodities, by region, 1983, annual rpt, 1631–11

Communist, OECD, and selected other countries agricultural production, by commodity, 1960s-83, annual rpt, 244–5.9

Consumption of food and nutrient intake by individuals, by food group, source, and socioeconomic characteristics, 1977-78 natl survey, final rpt series, 1356 4

Consumption, supply, trade, prices, expenditures, and indexes, by food commodity, 1963-83, annual rpt, 1544–4

Cooperatives (dairy) sales volume and market shares by commodity, and finances, by region, 1980 with trends from 1957, 1128–29

Cooperatives commercial farmer membership and use, by type and sales size of farm and region, 1980, 1128–32

Cooperatives finances and operations, aggregate for top 100 assns by principal product and revenue source, FY82, annual rpt, 1124–3

Cooperatives itemized costs for manufacturing cheese, butter, and dry milk, plants, and plant capacity, 1981/82, 1128–25

Cooperatives, membership, activities, and finances, by commodity and selected State, 1900-80 with trends from 1863, 1128–30

County Business Patterns: establishments, employees, and payrolls, by SIC 4-digit industry and county, 1981, annual State rpt series, 2326–8

County Business Patterns: establishments, employees, and payrolls, by SIC 4-digit industry and county, 1982, annual State rpt series, 2326–6

CPI by detailed component, for US city average, 28 SMSAs, and 4 regions by population size, monthly rpt, 6762–2

Cuba economic conditions, agricultural and industrial production and distribution, trade, and intl economic relations, 1970-82 and trends from 1957, 248–40

Eastern Europe agricultural production and trade by commodity, food consumption, and farm inputs, for 6 countries, 1960-80 with projections to 1991, 1528–178

EC food supply/demand and market and support prices, with exchange rates, fertilizer price index, GDP, and population, by country, 1960-83, 1528–173

Employment, earnings, and hours, by selected SIC 1- to 4-digit industry, State, and for 278 major labor areas, 1939-83, annual rpt, 6744–5

Employment, earnings, and hours, by SIC 4-digit nonfarm industry, monthly 1974-Feb 1984, annual update, 6744–4

Exports and imports of dairy, livestock, and poultry live animals, meat, and products, by commodity and country of destination, FAS quarterly rpt, 1925–32

Exports and imports of US, by agricultural commodity and country, bimonthly rpt with articles, 1522–1

Exports and imports of US, by detailed agricultural commodity and country, FY83 and CY83, semiannual rpts, 1522–4

Exports and imports of US, by detailed agricultural commodity for 8 major commodity groups, monthly rpt, 1922–8

Exports and imports of US, detailed SIC-based commodities by world area, 1983, annual rpts, 2424–6

Exports and imports of US, totals and as percent of domestic production, by SIC 2- to 5-digit commodity, 1981, annual rpt, 2424–3

Exports of cheese and tobacco by country of origin, various periods 1974-82, strategic material stockpile mgmt hearings, 25208–27

Exports of manufactured and agricultural commodities, manufacturing production, and export-related employment, 1960s-82, State rpt series, 2046–3

Exports of US, detailed commodities by country of destination, monthly rpt, 2422–3

Exports of US, detailed Schedule B commodities by country of destination, 1983, annual rpt, 2424–9

Exports of US, detailed Schedule E commodities by mode of transport and world area and country of destination, 1983, annual rpts, 2424–5

Exports under PL 480 concessional sales program, by commodity and country, 1955-83, semiannual rpt, 1922–6

Farm finances, assets, liabilities, income, receipts by commodity and State, and expenses, 1980-83 and trends from 1910, annual rpt, 1544–16

Farm finances, expenses by type, loans by purpose and source, and credit detail by Fed Reserve District, quarterly rpt, 9365–3.10

Fats, oils, and oilseed production, prices, trade, and consumption, periodic situation rpt with articles, 1561–3

Foreign agricultural production, prices, and trade, by country, 1983 and outlook for 1984/85, annual world region rpt series, 1524–4

Foreign and US agricultural production, trade, and climatic devs, weekly press release, 1922–4

Foreign and US agricultural supply/demand, consumption per capita, and trade, by world area and country group, 1960s-82, 1528–181

Foreign and US dairy products production, consumption, and trade, FAS annual circular series, 1925–10

Foreign and US feed and livestock trade by product and world region, and ocean freight rates between selected countries of origin and destination, selected years 1960-82, 1528–177

Futures trading by commodity and exchange, and Commodity Futures Trading Commission activities, funding, and employment, FY83, annual rpt, 11924–2

Great Lakes trade, by SITC 3-digit commodity, port, vessel type, world area, and country, 1982, annual rpt, 7744–3

Herd Improvement Program activities and research, periodic rpt, 1702–2

Import quotas and imports, by country of origin, monthly rpt, 8146–1.3

Imports of dairy products subject to quota and annual quotas, by commodity and country of origin, FAS monthly circular, 1925–31

Imports of US, detailed Schedule A commodities by country and world area of origin, and mode of transport, 1983, annual rpts, 2424–2

Imports of US, detailed Schedule A commodities by country, monthly rpt, 2422–2

Imports of US, detailed TSUSA commodities by country of origin, 1983, annual rpt, 2424–4

Income tax returns of corporations, detailed income and tax items by industry, 1981, annual rpt, 8304–4

Income tax returns of partnerships, detailed data by industry, 1981 estimates, annual article, 8302–2.404

Income tax returns of partnerships, receipts by source, deductions by type, and establishments, by selected industry, 1982, annual article, 8302–2.416

Income tax returns of sole proprietorships, detailed data by industry div and selected industry group, 1981, annual rpt, 8304–7

Income tax returns of sole proprietorships, receipts, deductions by type, payroll, and net income, by major industry, 1982, annual article, 8302–2.413

Input-output structure of US economy, detailed interindustry transactions for 537 industries, and components of final demand, 1977 benchmark data, 2708–17

Manufactured dairy production by State, stocks, prices, and CCC price support activities, by product type, monthly rpt, 1627–3

Manufactured dairy products production by type, and plants, by State, 1983, annual rpt, 1627–5

Manufacturing census, 1982: financial and operating data, by SIC 2- to 4-digit industry, State, SMSA, and county, preliminary census div rpt series, 2491–3

Manufacturing census, 1982: financial and operating data, for SIC 4-digit industries by product, preliminary rpt series, 2491–1

Marketing and price data for dairy products in selected cities, States, and regions, 1983, annual rpt, 1317–1

Marketing cash receipts of farms, by detailed commodity and State, 1979-82, annual rpt, 1544–18

Dairy industry and products

- Milk and dairy production, prices, consumption, and trade, quarterly situation rpt with articles, 1561–2
- Milk cows, and milk and cream production and marketings, by State, 1981-83, annual rpt, 1627–4
- Milk cows and milk production, and grain and other concentrates fed, by State, monthly rpt, 1627–1
- Milk industry productivity, hours, and employment indexes, 1958-82, annual rpt, 6824–1.3
- Milk of manufacturing grade, fat content and prices received by farmers in Minnesota and Wisconsin, monthly rpt, 1629–6
- Milk of manufacturing grade, fat content and prices received by farmers in Minnesota and Wisconsin, 1981-83, annual rpt, 1629–2
- Milk order market major provisions, summary by Federal marketing area, as of July 1984, annual rpt, 1317–11
- Milk order market prices and detailed operations, by State and market area, monthly 1982-83, annual rpt, 1317–3
- Milk order market prices and detailed operations, monthly rpt with articles, 1317–4
- Milk pasteurized by ultra-high temperature, sales, production, stocks, costs, market shares, and prices, 1980, 1568–247
- Milk price support alternatives, effects on production, use, prices, and farm receipts, projected 1983/84-1988/89 and actual 1982/83, 1568–246
- Milk price supports effect on production, use, prices, and farm receipts, by region and State, 1940s-83 and alternative projections to 1988/89, 1568–245
- Milk processor sales, itemized costs, dealer margins, and production, annual rpt, suspended, 1544–15
- Milk production itemized costs, receipts, and net returns, per cow and per hundredweight, by region, 1981-83, annual rpt, 1544–20
- Minority group and women employment, by occupational group and SIC 2- to 3-digit industry, 1981, annual rpt, 9244–1.1
- Occupational injury and illness rates, by SIC 2- to 4-digit industry, 1982, annual rpt, 6844–1
- OECD trade, total and for 4 major countries, and US trade by country, by commodity, 1972-82, annual world region rpt series, 244–13
- Portugal agricultural subsidies, profits, marketing margins, and consumer prices, by commodity or product, and effects of prospective EC membership, 1981, 1528–171
- Prices (farm-retail) for foods, marketing cost components, and industry finances and productivity, selected years 1967-83, annual rpt, 1544–9
- Prices received by farmers for major products, and paid for farm inputs and living items, by commodity and State, monthly rpt, 1629–1
- Prices received by farmers for major products, and paid for farm inputs, by commodity and State, 1983, annual rpt, 1629–5

Producer prices and indexes, by stage of processing and detailed commodity, monthly rpt, 6762–6

- Producer prices and indexes, by stage of processing and detailed commodity, monthly 1983, annual supplement, 6764–2
- Production and farm finances, expenses by type, and domestic economic impact, selected years 1972-82 and preliminary 1983-84, annual rpt, 1544–19
- Production and supply/demand data, for US livestock and dairy products, and for selected US and world crops, periodic rpt, 1522–5
- Production, prices, trade, and marketing, by commodity, current situation and forecast, monthly rpt, 1502–4
- Radiation and radionuclide concentrations in air, water, and milk, results of EPA and other monitoring programs, by State and site, quarterly rpt, 9232–2
- Radioactive strontium in NYC and San Francisco diet by food item, and in NYC tap water and milk, quarterly 1982 with trends from 1954, annual rpt, 3404–13
- Radionuclide concentrations in air, water, and biota near Nevada and other nuclear test sites, and in milk from western States, by location, 1983, annual rpt, 9234–4
- Underground economy, household expenditures and participation by type of goods or service and sociodemographic characteristics, with methodology and bibl, 1981 survey, 8308–27
- USDA agricultural surplus direct purchase program finances, and purchases and food received by schools by commodity, various periods 1936-83, 1548–243
- Waterborne commerce of US (domestic and foreign), freight by commodity, traffic, and passengers, by port and waterway, 1982, annual rpt, 3754–3
- Wholesale trade census, 1982: employment, establishments, sales by commodity, and payroll, by SIC 4-digit kind of business and State, preliminary rpt, 2403–1.29
- *see also* under By Commodity in the "Index by Categories"

Daley, David M.

"Heavy Rail Transit Safety, 1983 Annual Report", 7884–5

Dallas, Tex.

- Auto dealer repair workers, wages, and benefits, by occupation, size of establishment, and for 24 labor market areas, Nov 1982 survey, 6787–6.202
- Census of Housing, 1980: occupancy and unit characteristics, by race, Hispanic origin, and city, SMSA rpt, 2473–1.131
- Census of Population and Housing, 1980: detailed population and housing characteristics, by county, city, and census tract, SMSA rpt, 2551–2.131
- CPI by component for US city average, and by region, population size, and for 28 SMSAs, monthly press release, 6762–1
- CPI by detailed component, for US city average, 28 SMSAs, and 4 regions by population size, monthly rpt, 6762–2
- CPI by major component, average change for Dallas-Fort Worth and Houston, Tex, with comparisons to South and total US, 1973-82, BLS regional rpt series, 6966–1.12

Index by Subjects and Names

- Dress industry production and related workers, wages, and benefits, by occupation, size of establishment, and union status, for 11 labor market areas, Aug 1982 survey, 6787–6.200
- Employment, earnings, hours, and CPI changes for Dallas-Fort Worth SMSA, 1983 with trends from 1968, annual rpt, 6964–2
- Fruit and vegetable shipments, and arrivals in 23 US and 5 Canada cities, by mode of transport and State or country of origin, 1983, annual rpt, 1311–4.2
- Homeless population and characteristics, and temporary shelter operations, use, and user characteristics, for selected cities, various periods 1979-84, hearing, 21248–85
- Hospital worker wages by sex and occupation, and benefits, for 22 MSAs, Oct 1981 survey, 6787–6.201
- Housing and households detailed characteristics, and unit and neighborhood quality, by inside-outside central cities, 1981 survey, SMSA rpt, 2485–6.21
- Population size of top 25 cities, 1980 and 1982, press release, 2328–46
- Repair technicians and apprentices wages and benefits, for 5 types of electrical repair shops in 19 SMSAs, Nov 1981 survey, 6787–6.197
- Wages by occupation, and benefits for office and plant workers, 1983 SMSA survey rpt, 6785–12.3
- *see also* under By City and By SMSA or MSA in the "Index by Categories"

Dams

- Army Corps of Engineers activities and projects, FY83 and trends from 1800s, annual rpt, 3754–1
- Construction industries census, 1982: financial and operating data, by SIC 4-digit industry and State, preliminary rpt series, 2371–1
- Developing countries economic dev projects funded by multilateral dev banks, environmental and cultural impacts, 1970s-83, hearings, 21248–80
- Fed Govt reclamation projects in western US, electric power capacities and transmission miles, and water storage and carriage facilities, by State, FY81, annual rpt, 5824–1.1
- Foreign and US major dams, reservoirs, and hydroelectric plants, listing with location and characteristics, as of June 1983, 5828–13
- Reclamation Bur water storage and carriage facilities, by type, as of Sept 1983, annual listing, 5824–7
- Tennessee Valley river control and reservoir elevations, storage, flows, and hydroelectric generating capacity use, 1981, annual rpt, 9804–7
- TVA activities, financial and operating data by program and facility, and power sales by customer, FY83, annual rpt, 9804–1
- *see also* Reservoirs

Danbury, Conn.

- Census of Housing, 1980: occupancy and unit characteristics, by race, Hispanic origin, and city, SMSA rpt, 2473–1.132
- Census of Population and Housing, 1980: detailed population and housing characteristics, by county, city, and census tract, SMSA rpt, 2551–2.132

Index by Subjects and Names

see also under By SMSA or MSA in the "Index by Categories"

Dance

Census of Population, 1980: detailed socioeconomic and demographic characteristics, by age, sex, race, Hispanic origin, occupation, and industry, State rpt series, 2531–4

Census of Population, 1980: labor force, by sex, detailed occupation, and region, with comparison to 1970 census, supplementary rpt, 2535–1.12

County Business Patterns: establishments, employees, and payrolls, by SIC 4-digit industry and county, 1981, annual State rpt series, 2326–8

County Business Patterns: establishments, employees, and payrolls, by SIC 4-digit industry and county, 1982, annual State rpt series, 2326–6

Natl Endowment for Arts activities and grants, FY83, annual rpt, 9564–3

Occupational Outlook Handbook, 1984-85 biennial rpt, 6744–1

Service industry census, 1982: employment, establishments, receipts, and payroll, by SIC 2- to 4-digit kind of business, SMSA, county, and city, State rpt series, 2391–1

Danie, Dwight S.

"Species Profiles: Life Histories and Environmental Requirements of Coastal Fishes and Invertebrates (North Atlantic), White Perch", 5506–8.9

Danker, Deborah J.

"Profitability of Insured Commercial Banks in 1983", 9362–1.409

Danville, Va.

Census of Housing, 1980: occupancy and unit characteristics, by race, Hispanic origin, and city, SMSA rpt, 2473–1.133

Census of Population and Housing, 1980: detailed population and housing characteristics, by county, city, and census tract, SMSA rpt, 2551–2.133

see also under By SMSA or MSA in the "Index by Categories"

Danzon, Patricia M.

"Factors Affecting Laboratory Test Use and Prices", 4652–1.415

Darity, William, Jr.

"Kalecki-Keynes Model of World Trade, Finance, and Economic Growth", 9366–7.94

Dark, Shirley J.

"Characteristics of Medically Disqualified Airline Pilots", 7506–10.23

Dart, Richard R.

"Development of Terminal-Based EFT Delivery Systems in the Eighties", 9312–1.409

Data processing

see Computer sciences

see Computers

see Information storage and retrieval systems

Data Resources, Inc.

"Analysis of Tax-Exempt Pollution Control Financing", 21788–135

"Industrial Consequences of Alternative Pollution Regulation Scenarios", 9188–84

"Will Big Deficits Spoil the Recovery?", 21248–79

Davenport, Edgar L.

"Forest Statistics for the Northern Coastal Plain of North Carolina, 1984", 1206–4.6

Davenport, Iowa

Census of Housing, 1980: occupancy and unit characteristics, by race, Hispanic origin, and city, SMSA rpt, 2473–1.134

Census of Population and Housing, 1980: detailed population and housing characteristics, by county, city, and census tract, SMSA rpt, 2551–2.134

Housing vacancy rates for single and multifamily units and mobile homes, by county, city, and ZIP code, 1983, annual metro area rpt, 9304–18.3

Wages of office and plant workers, by occupation, 1984 SMSA survey rpt, 6785–11.4

see also under By City and By SMSA or MSA in the "Index by Categories"

Davidson County, Tenn.

Census of Housing, 1980: occupancy and unit characteristics, by race, Hispanic origin, and city, SMSA rpt, 2473–1.252

Census of Population and Housing, 1980: detailed population and housing characteristics, by county, city, and census tract, SMSA rpt, 2551–2.252

see also under By SMSA or MSA in the "Index by Categories"

Davidson, Donald R.

"Ag Decline Prompts Top 100 To Cut Debt, Prune Assets", 1122–1.410

"Cooperative Vessel Still Afloat; Losses Slashed, Net Margins Tripled", 1122–1.412

"Top 100 Boost Margins Despite Lower Volume", 1122–1.408

"Top 100 Cooperatives, 1982 Financial Profile", 1124–3

"Top 100 Raise Cash Refunds, Retains; Reduce Borrowings from Co-op Banks", 1122–1.411

Davidson, Maria

"Demographic and Socioeconomic Aspects of Aging in the U.S.", 2546–2.125

Davidson, Stephen M.

"Medical Care Advisory Committee for State Medicaid Programs: Current Status and Trends", 4652–1.409

Davila, Alberto E.

"Industrial Diversification, Exchange Rate Shocks, and the Texas-Mexico Border", 9379–1.402

Davis, Cynthia

"Bolivia: A Country Profile", 9916–2.56

Davis, Harvey F., Jr.

"1990 Objectives for the Nation for Injury Prevention: A Progress Review", 4102–1.409

Davis, Mary F.

"Worksite Health Promotion in Colorado", 4102–1.453

Davis, P. Hannah

"Characteristics of Pharmacists, U.S.", 4147–14.28

Day care programs

see Adult day care

see Child day care

Daylight hours

see also Time of day

Dayton, Ohio

Census of Housing, 1980: occupancy and unit characteristics, by race, Hispanic origin, and city, SMSA rpt, 2473–1.135

Census of Population and Housing, 1980: detailed population and housing characteristics, by county, city, and census tract, SMSA rpt, 2551–2.135

D.C.

Wages by occupation, and benefits for office and plant workers, 1983 SMSA survey rpt, 6785–12.3

see also under By City and By SMSA or MSA in the "Index by Categories"

Daytona Beach, Fla.

Census of Housing, 1980: occupancy and unit characteristics, by race, Hispanic origin, and city, SMSA rpt, 2473–1.136

Census of Population and Housing, 1980: detailed population and housing characteristics, by county, city, and census tract, SMSA rpt, 2551–2.136

Wages of office and plant workers, by occupation, 1984 SMSA survey rpt, 6785–11.7

see also under By SMSA or MSA in the "Index by Categories"

D.C.

Airports in DC metro area, financial and operating data, FY82-83, annual rpt, 7504–10

Auto dealer repair workers, wages, and benefits, by occupation, size of establishment, and for 24 labor market areas, Nov 1982 survey, 6787–6.202

Bank deposits in commercial and mutual savings banks and in US branches of foreign banks, by account type, instn, State, SMSA, and county, June 1983, annual rpt, 9295–3.5

Bank income and expenses, Fed Reserve 5th District member banks, by State, 1983, annual rpt, 9389–10

Budget of US, appropriations, outlays, balances, and budget receipts, by govtl branch and agency, FY83, annual rpt, 8104–2

Budget of US, Fed Govt payments and loans to DC, effects of Reagan Admin policy changes, FY85, annual rpt, 104–21

Budget of US, loans and loan guarantees, and Admin proposed limits on credit assistance, by program, FY83-89, annual rpt, 26306–3.65

Census of Housing, 1980: occupancy and unit characteristics, by race, Hispanic origin, and city, SMSA rpt, 2473–1.365

Census of Population and Housing, 1980: detailed population and housing characteristics, by county, city, and census tract, SMSA rpt, 2551–2.365

Census of Population, 1980: detailed socioeconomic and demographic characteristics, by age, sex, race, Hispanic origin, and industry, State rpt, 2531–4.10

County Business Patterns: establishments, employees, and payrolls, by SIC 4-digit industry and county, 1982, annual State rpt, 2326–6.10

CPI by component for US city average, and by region, population size, and for 28 SMSAs, monthly press release, 6762–1

CPI by detailed component, for US city average, 28 SMSAs, and 4 regions by population size, monthly rpt, 6762–2

Criminal cases involving drug users, and user and nonuser rates of detention, pretrial rearrest, and failure to appear in court, for DC, 1979-81, 6066–20.7

DOD military and civilian employment in DC metro area, FY83, and in Pentagon, Apr 1945-Sept 1983, annual rpt, 3544–1.1

D.C.

Economic indicators by State, Fed Reserve 5th District, quarterly rpt, 9389–16

Economic Research Service activities, funding, and staff in DC and other locations, by detailed branch and section, FY83, annual rpt, 1504–7

Economic Research Service activities, funding, and staff in DC and other locations, by detailed branch and section, FY84, annual rpt, 1504–6

Employment, earnings, and hours, by selected SIC 1- to 4-digit industry, State, and for 278 major labor areas, 1939-83, annual rpt, 6744–5.1, 6744–5.3

Environmental quality, pollutant discharge by type and source, and EPA protection activities and funding, 1970s-83, biennial regional rpt, 9184–15.3

Fed Govt civil agency operations, summaries of GAO investigation rpts published 1975-83, annual rpt, 26104–5

Fed Govt civilian employment and payroll, by agency in DC metro area and elsewhere, monthly rpt, 9842–1

Fed Govt payments and loans, Budget of US Appendix, FY85, detailed annual rpt, 104–3

Fruit and vegetable shipments, and arrivals in 23 US and 5 Canada cities, by mode of transport and State or country of origin, 1983, annual rpt, 1311–4.1

HHS aid to each State and local govt or private instn, amount obligated, funding agency, and program, FY83, annual listing, 4004–3.3

Hospital worker wages by sex and occupation, and benefits, for 22 MSAs, Oct 1981 survey, 6787–6.201

Housing and households detailed characteristics, and unit and neighborhood quality, by inside-outside central cities, 1981 survey, SMSA rpt, 2485–6.18

Housing water conservation programs and savings of water and energy, for selected cities and suburbs, 1980-83, 5188–109

Income (personal) per capita and by source, and earnings by industry div, by State, MSA, and county, 1977-82, annual regional rpt, 2704–2.3

Labor unions recognized in Fed Govt, agreements and membership for DC govt employees, Jan 1983, annual listing, 9844–14

Manufacturing census, 1982: financial and operating data, by SIC 2- to 4-digit industry, State, SMSA, and county, preliminary census div rpt, 2491–3.5

Mental health facilities, services, and costs in DC, and effect of St Elizabeths Hospital operations and finances transfer to DC govt, FY83, GAO rpt, 26121–72

Metrorail transit system effect on commuting patterns, population, business, land use, and environment, series, 7306–8

Nutrition and cardiovascular disease consumer education, effectiveness of Natl Heart, Lung, and Blood Inst and Giant Food, Inc, program in DC metro area, 1978-79, 4478–144

Population size of top 25 cities, 1980 and 1982, press release, 2328–46

Prison population and capacity by State and individual DC and Federal instn, construction costs, and Fed Govt operating costs, 1983 and projected to 1990, GAO rpt, 26119–59

Repair technicians and apprentices wages and benefits, for 5 types of electrical repair shops in 19 SMSAs, Nov 1981 survey, 6787–6.197

Retail trade census, 1982: employment, establishments, sales, and payroll, by SIC 2- to 4-digit kind of business, SMSA, county, and city, State rpt, 2397–1.9

Savings and loan assns, FHLB 4th District insured members financial condition and operations, by SMSA, monthly rpt, 9302–1

Transportation census, 1982: trucks, by detailed characteristics, miles traveled, and type of product carried, State rpt, 2573–1.9

Wages by occupation, and benefits for office and plant workers, 1983 SMSA survey rpt, 6785–11.3

Wholesale trade census, 1982: employment, establishments, finances, and operations, by SIC 2- to 4-digit kind of business, SMSA, county, and city, State rpt, 2405–1.9

Workers compensation under Fed Govt-administered programs, coverage, expenditures, and claims and dispositions by district, FY83, annual compilation, 6504–5

see also D.C. courts

see also Washington Metropolitan Area Transit Authority

see also under By City, By SMSA or MSA, and By State in the "Index by Categories"

D.C. courts

Caseloads for Federal district, appeals, and bankruptcy courts, by type of suit and offense, circuit, and district, quarterly rpt, 18202–1

de la Garza, E.

"View from Congress", 1004–16.1

de Leeuw, Frank

"Conflicting Measures of Private Saving", 2702–1.441

"Cyclical Adjustment of the Federal Budget and Federal Debt", 2702–1.403

"Measuring and Analyzing the Cyclically Adjusted Budget", 9373–3.27

De Leon, George

"Therapeutic Community; Study of Effectiveness", 4496–5.18

Deaf

Fed Govt minority group and handicapped employment, by race, Hispanic origin, disability, sex, and employment characteristics, as of Sept 1982, biennial rpt, 9844–27

Handicapped children early education research and service project activities and characteristics, and grants to States for program dev, 1983-84, annual listing, 4804–30

Head Start Project enrollment of handicapped children, by handicap, State, and for Indian and migrant programs, 1982, annual rpt, 4604–1

Special education programs for handicapped children, enrollment, staff, and funding, by handicap, age, and State, 1981/82-1982/83, annual rpt, 4944–4

Vocationally rehabilitated persons under State agency programs, by sociodemographic characteristics and disabling condition, FY79-81, annual rpt, 4944–6

Index by Subjects and Names

Dearborn, Ned W.

"Aggregate Statistics: Accurate or Misleading?", 3162–24.401

Death penalty

see Capital punishment

Deaths

Abortions (legal), and deaths from abortion and childbirth, by medical and sociodemographic characteristics, 1972-83, hearings, 21368–47

Accident deaths by selected cause, 1981 with trends from 1960s and reduction goals for 1990, article, 4102–1.409

Acid rain causes and effects, air pollutant emissions by source, and control costs, by region and State, selected years 1977-83 and projected to 2000, 26358–104

Air pollutant and radiation indoor levels by emissions source, and household exposure and health effects by pollutant type, various periods 1966-83, hearings, 21708–102

Aircraft accident circumstances and severity, by type of flying and aircraft, 1981, annual rpt, 9614–3

Aircraft accidents and deaths for airlines and general aviation, 1983, preliminary annual rpt, 9614–9

Aircraft accidents, deaths, and rates, for airlines and general aviation by type of service, 1974-83, annual rpt, 7504–1.9

Aircraft accidents of commuter carriers and air taxis by seating capacity and cause, and deaths, 1975-82, GAO rpt, 26113–116

Aircraft fatal accidents of commuter airlines, air taxis, and general aviation, alcohol involvement, circumstances, and pilot characteristics, 1975-81, 9618–11

Aircraft hijackings, on-board explosions, other crimes against civil aviation, and circumstances, US and worldwide, 1931-83, annual rpt, 7504–31

Airline and general aviation accident circumstances, severity, and causes, for US operations of domestic and foreign aircraft, periodic rpt, 9612–1

Alaska Native Medical Center visits and ambulatory high use patients by age and sex, and patient deaths, 1972-78, article, 4102–1.440

Alcohol use, and health, economic, and social impacts, review of research, 1970s-81, 4488–4

Army active duty personnel health status and use of Army medical services in US and abroad, by treatment facility, monthly rpt, 3702–4.2

Arson investigation and prosecution, by incident characteristics and outcome, motive, and type of evidence, for 4 jurisdictions, 1981, 6068–184

Asbestos workers, exposure levels, cancer incidence, and deaths, by industry and occupation, and asbestos regulation enforcement and costs/benefits, various periods 1940-2027, hearing, 21408–72

Boat registrations, use, and accident deaths, injuries, and property damage, by detailed cause and State, 1983, annual rpt, 7404–1

Bombing (explosive and incendiary) and arson incidents by target, State, and circumstances, and explosives theft and recovery, 1982-83, annual rpt, 8484–4

Index by Subjects and Names

Deaths

Bombing (explosive and incendiary) incidents, damage, injuries, and deaths, by target, State, and circumstances, 1983, annual rpt, 6224–5

Canada and US hospital use by children by Canada Province and US region, and death rates, by diagnosis and sex, selected years 1977-79, 4147–5.1

Cancer cases, incidence, deaths, and death rates, by body site, age, race, Hispanic origin, and sex, for 10 geographic areas, 1973-81, 4478–130

Cancer deaths and death rates, by body site, race, sex, State, and county, 1950-79, 4478–146

Cancer deaths by age, 1980, and deaths and new cases, 1983, by sex and body site, annual fact book, 4474–13

Cardiovascular disease and other death rates, and hypertension prevalence and control, selected years 1971-82, article, 4102–1.432

Certificates of birth, death, marriage, and divorce, records availability and vital statistics records offices, by State, 1984 annual listing, 4124–7

Child immunization and preventive medicine programs in US and Mexico, disease cases, vaccine reactions, and deaths, 1984 conf papers, 4204–15

Coal mines and related operations, occupational injuries and incidence rates, detailed analysis, 1982, annual rpt, 6664–4

Cold weather and related causes of death, by age, race, State, and city, selected periods 1962-83, 21148–30

Consumer Product Safety Commission activities, recalls, and product-related injuries, deaths, and medical costs, by product type and brand, FY83, annual rpt, 9164–2

Consumer products use and related activity, injuries and deaths by selected product and victim age and sex, quarterly rpt, 9164–7

Consumer products use, injuries and deaths by product, victim age, and medical treatment status, 1982, annual rpt, 9164–6

County and City Data Book, detailed socioeconomic and demographic data for States, counties, and cities, selected years 1976-82, 2328–1

Death rates by age and sex, and persons aged 65 and 80 and older share of population and deaths, selected years 1900-80, article, 4102–1.447

Death rates by sex, race, and age for 40 causes, projected for 10-year period, 1982 rpt, 4208–21

Deaths and death rates, by cause, age, sex, race, and State, provisional 1982-83 with trends from 1950, US Vital Statistics annual rpt, 4144–7

Deaths and death rates, by detailed cause and demographic characteristics, 1979 and summary trends from 1900, US Vital Statistics annual rpt, 4144–2

Deaths and death rates, by detailed geographic area, cause, and demographic characteristics, 1979, US Vital Statistics annual rpt, 4144–3

Deaths and death rates, by selected cause and demographic characteristics, 1981, US Vital Statistics advance rpt, 4146–5.78

Deaths and death rates, by selected cause and demographic characteristics, 1982, US Vital Statistics advance rpt, 4146–5.81

Deaths and death rates from homicide, by location, circumstances, and victim characteristics, and years of life lost from homicide and other leading causes of death, 1970-78, 4205–38

Deaths by cause and life expectancy, by sex and age, 1900-2050, SSA actuarial rpt, 4706–1.89

Deaths by principal or contributing cause, with type of injury reported in accidental, poisoning, and violent deaths, by age, sex, and race, 1978, 4146–5.76

Deaths recorded in 121 cities, weekly rpt, 4202–1

Developing countries govt policy, and AID and other foreign assistance, effects on private sector dev and socioeconomic conditions, with case studies for 6 countries, 1960s-80, 9918–12

Disability Insurance awards, death and recovery termination rates, and life expectancy of disabled, by age and sex, 1965-83 and projected to 2000, 4706–1.93

Diseases causing death, specified notifiable and selected non-notifiable, 1951-82 with trends from 1922, annual rpt, 4204–1

DOE and contractor facility accidents, deaths, illnesses, radiation exposure, and property damage, by facility, 1982, annual rpt, 3004–24

Drug (illegal) supply, use, casualties, treatment program and emergency room admissions in major cities, arrests, and seizures, by drug type, 1982, annual rpt, 15894–1

Earthquake intensity, damage, and deaths, by location for major earthquakes since 1755, and hazard areas and natl reduction program activities, as of 1984, 5668–73

Earthquake intensity, damage, time of origin, and seismic characteristics of all US and major foreign earthquakes, 1981, annual rpt, 5664–13

Economic indicators relation to measures of social pathology including crime and death rates, various periods 1950-80, 23848–76

Fed Govt and total law enforcement officers and firefighters killed, death benefit claims, and non-Fed Govt firefighters death benefits by State and city, 1972-82, hearing, 21348–94

Fed Govt civilian employee occupational injuries, deaths, and illnesses, by agency, 1982, annual rpt, 6604–1

Flood (flash) deaths, by flood circumstances, type of warning, cause of death, and location, Sept 1969-May 1981, article, 4102–1.406

Foreign and US health care resources, use, and per capita public expenditures, and selected population characteristics, for 7 countries, selected years 1975-81, 21148–33

Foreign countries disasters, persons affected, deaths, damage, and aid by US and others, FY83 and trends from FY64, annual rpt, 9914–12

Foreign population size and growth rates, and latest available benchmark demographic data, by country, 1950-83, biennial rpt, 2324–4

Grain handling facility explosions, injuries, deaths, and cause, by company, FY83, annual rpt, 1294–1

Hazardous material transport accidents, casualties, and property damage, by mode of transport, with DOT control activities, 1983, annual rpt, 7304–4

Health condition and health care resources, use, and expenditures, 1970s-82 with trends and projections 1900-2000, annual compilation, 4144–11

Heart attack and cancer incidence and deaths in men aged 35-59, effects of lowering blood cholesterol levels, with background data on other risk factors, 1973-83, 4478–145

Heart, Lung, and Blood Natl Inst activities and funding, with morbidity and mortality data, various periods 1940-88, annual rpt, 4474–22

Heart, Lung, and Blood Natl Inst organization, disease and mortality data, and funds and recipients, FY83 with trends from 1900, annual fact book, 4474–15

Hurricanes and tropical storms in North Atlantic and Caribbean area, paths, surveillance, deaths, property damage, and landfall probabilities by city, 1983, annual rpt, 2184–7

Hurricanes and tropical storms in northeastern Pacific, paths, surveillance, deaths, and property damage, 1983, annual rpt, 2184–8

Indian births, morbidity, and deaths and rates, and health services facilities and use, 1954-83, annual compilation, 4104–7

Infections (hospital-related), drug resistance, and associated deaths, for teaching and non-teaching hospitals, 1980-82, article, 4202–7.401

Influenza deaths, viruses identified by State and country, epidemiology, and vaccine effects and recommended dosages by age, 1979/80-1980/81, annual rpt, 4205–3

Kidney end-stage disease, Medicare dialysis, transplants by facility, donor organ costs, deaths by age, and hospitalization, by region, 1981, annual rpt, 4654–5.2

Kidney end-stage disease Medicare program, new cases by State, total enrollment, and survival and death rates, by age, sex, and race, 1970s-81, article, 4652–1.408

Kidney end-stage disease Medicare reimbursement by treatment, diagnosis, outcome, and patient characteristics, with covered charges for transplants, 1974-79, article, 4652–1.421

Law enforcement officer assaults, murders, and other deaths by circumstances, level of govt, agency, victim and offender characteristics, and location, 1983, annual rpt, 6224–3

Marine-related deaths, and lives saved by Coast Guard search and rescue missions, by district, station, and rescue vessel, FY83, annual rpt, 7404–2

Mental health facilities of States and counties, inpatients, deaths, staff by occupation, and facilities, by State, 1970s-82, 4506–3.13

Metal mines and related operations, occupational injuries and incidence rates, detailed analysis, 1982, annual rpt, 6664–3

Deaths

Minerals (nonmetallic) mining and related operations injury, employment, and worktime data, 1982, annual rpt, 6664–1

Mines (sand and gravel) and related operations, occupational injuries and incidence rates, detailed analysis, 1982, annual rpt, 6664–2

Mines (stone) and related operations, occupational injuries and incidence rates, detailed analysis, 1982, annual rpt, 6664–5

Mines, mills, and quarries occupational injuries, and employees and hours, by State, quarterly rpt, 6662–1

Mobile and manufactured home safety standards, program inspections, enforcement actions, and accidents and casualties by victim characteristics, 1982-83, biennial rpt, 5004–4

Mobile home fires and related deaths, and rates compared to site-built homes, 1960-78, article, 1502–7.402

Natl park system visitor deaths, by park and type of accident, 1973-83, annual rpt, 5544–6

Navy and Marine Corps deaths and death rates, quarterly rpt, annual tables, 3802–1

Navy and Marine Corps disease incidence, medical care, and deaths, by detailed diagnosis, and medical personnel and workloads, 1978-79, annual rpt, 3804–1

OASDI and pension policy, impacts of increased life expectancy, with alternative sociodemographic projections to 2100, hearing, 25368–130

OASDI beneficiary status changes reported late and benefit overpayments, for death, marriage, and leaving school, 1981, GAO rpt, 26121–68

Occupational deaths, by industry div and cause, 1981-82, article, 6722–1.422

Occupational deaths, circumstances and OSHA safety standards violated by type of incident and equipment used, series, 6606–2

Occupational health risks from hazardous substances and radiation, by industry, occupation, age, and sex, with bibl and glossary, 1920s-82, 9638–50

Occupational injuries and illnesses, incidence rates by employment size and industry, workdays lost, and deaths, 1980-81, annual rpt, 6604–2.2

Occupational injury and illness rates, by SIC 2- to 4-digit industry, 1982, annual rpt, 6844–1

Occupational mortality by sex, cause, and detailed occupation, summary data from Washington State study, 1950-79, 4248–47

Oil and gas OCS drilling rigs by country, rig losses, and worker injury and death rates, various periods 1966-83, hearing, 21568–35

Older persons aged 65 and over, death rates by major cause, sex, and age, selected years 1940-80, 4147–3.25

Older persons by demographic, socioeconomic, and health characteristics, selected years 1900-81 and projected to 2050, Current Population Rpt, 2546–2.125

Older persons entitled to both Medicare and Medicaid, demographic characteristics, and health condition and services use, 1980, article, 4652–1.433

Older persons sociodemographic characteristics, and Fed Govt program participation and funding, 1983 with trends and projections 1900-2060, annual rpt, 25144–3.1

Outlying area population size and components of change, by area, 1970-82, Current Population Rpt, 2546–3.127

Pipeline safety regulations enforcement of DOT and States by pipeline type and State, and accidents and commodity losses, selected years 1973-FY84, GAO rpt, 26113–130

Pipelines for natural gas and hazardous liquids, accidents, deaths, and injuries, by cause, 1982, annual rpt, 7304–5

Plague (bubonic and pneumonia-inducing) deaths, and cases by onset date, patient characteristics, and source, 1983 and trends from 1950, article, 4202–7.408

Population size and components of change, by MSA and county, 1980-82, annual State Current Population Rpt series, 2546–4

Population size and components of change, by outlying area, 1980-83, Current Population Rpt, 2546–3.134

Population size and components of change, by region and State, 1970-83, Current Population Rpt, 2546–3.133

Population size and components of change, by region and State, 1970s-83 with projections to 2050, annual Current Population Rpt, 2546–2.119

Population size and components of change, by region, census div, and State, July 1981-83, annual Current Population Rpt, 2546–3.128

Population size and components of change, projected under 3 fertility assumptions, 1982-2080 with trends from 1900, SSA actuarial rpt, 4706–1.92

Population size by single years of age, and components of change, by sex and race, projected 1983-2080, final Current Population Rpt, 2546–3.132

Pregnancy-related deaths and death rates, by age and race, 1974-78, article, 4202–7.406

Puerto Rico educational enrollment, finance, completions, curricula, and personnel by instn, and health and vital statistics, selected years 1970-83, hearings, 21348–93

Railroad accidents, casualties, and property damage, Fed Railroad Admin activities, and safety inspectors by State, 1982, annual rpt, 7604–12

Railroad accidents, circumstances, severity, and railroad involved, quarterly rpt, 9612–3

Railroad accidents investigated by Fed Railroad Admin, casualties, damage, and circumstances, 1982, annual rpt, 7604–3

Railroad-hwy grade crossing accidents, detailed data by State and railroad, 1982, annual rpt, 7604–2

Reye syndrome cases by State, and mortality rate by influenza strain, with patient characteristics, various years 1974-82, article, 4202–7.402

Servicemen's and veterans group life insurance programs, income, expenses, and death rates, as of June 1983, annual rpt, 9924–3

Index by Subjects and Names

Smoking related to chronic obstructive lung disease and deaths, by sociodemographic and smoking characteristics, literature review, 1984 annual Surgeon General rpt, 4044–6

Soviet Union industrial and agricultural production by selected commodity, and demographic trends and projections by Republic, 1950s-2000, hearings, 23848–180

Storm-related deaths from North Atlantic tropical storms, 1983 with trends from 1931, annual article, 2152–8.401

Storms and unusual weather phenomena characteristics, casualties, and property damage, by State and outlying area, monthly listing, 2152–3

Subway accidents, deaths, injuries, and property damage, by type of accident and victim and cause, for 11 systems, 1983, annual rpt, 7884–5

Traffic accidents and casualties detailed direct and indirect costs, by characteristics of persons and vehicles involved, 1979-80, 7768–80

Traffic accidents and deaths by characteristics of persons and vehicles involved and State, and Natl Hwy Traffic Safety Admin activities, 1961-81, annual rpt, 7764–1

Traffic accidents, circumstances, injuries, deaths, and characteristics of persons and vehicles involved, 1982, annual rpt, 7764–13

Traffic accidents, deaths, injuries, and rates, by hwy type and State, 1982, annual rpt, 7554–2

Traffic deaths, accident circumstances, and characteristics of persons and vehicles involved, series, 7766–13

Traffic deaths by region, and death rates for miles traveled, monthly rpt, 7762–7

Traffic deaths, total and alcohol-related, and drunk driver license revocations and other deterrence measures in selected States, 1980-82, 9618–10

Traffic fatal accidents, alcohol levels of drivers and pedestrians by driver age and sex and time of accident, 1980, 7768–81

Traffic fatal accidents, circumstances, and characteristics of persons and vehicles involved, 1983, annual rpt, 7764–14

Traffic fatal accidents detailed circumstances, and characteristics of persons and vehicles involved, 1982, annual rpt, 7764–10

Traffic fatal accidents total and alcohol-related, model results by State, 1976-81, article, 7762–9.405

Traffic safety, accidents, and other data from Natl Statistics and Analysis Center, series, 7766–10

Transit system financial and operating data, by mode, function, fleet size, and individual system, FY82, annual rpt, 7884–4

Transit system operations, tax burden related to ridership, fares, and govt funding, for selected States and cities, 1950s-82, reprint, 7888–59

Transportation accident deaths, by mode, 1982-83, annual summary rpt, 9614–6

Transportation accident investigations and recommendations by Natl Transportation Safety Board, 1983, annual rpt, 9614–1

Index by Subjects and Names

Transportation finances, operations, vehicles, equipment, accidents, and energy use, by mode of transport, 1955-84, annual rpt, 7304–2

Transportation safety programs, and accidents, injuries, deaths, hazards, and property damage, by mode of transport, 1983, annual rpt, 7304–19

Transportation summary data, traffic, accidents, and deaths, FY81, annual rpt, 7304–1

Truck accidents, injuries, deaths, and property damage, by circumstances, carrier type, and driver age and condition, 1983, annual rpt, 7554–9

TTPI budget, vital statistics, and health services data, often by TTPI govt, FY83 and selected trends, annual rpt, 7004–6.1

Tuberculosis cases, deaths, and treatment, by demographic characteristics, State, and city, 1982 and trends from 1953, annual rpt, 4204–2

Uranium ore tailings at active mills, EPA radon and radionuclide emmission standards and US and foreign exposure and health effects, various periods 1957-83, hearings, 21208–17

Veterans disability and deaths not connected with service, pension cases by sex, entitlement type, and period of service, as of Mar 1984, semiannual rpt, 9922–12

Veterans disability by type, and deaths, by period of service, and VA activities, FY83, annual rpt, 9924–1.6

Vital statistics, births, marriages, divorces, and deaths, provisional data, monthly rpt, 4142–1

Weather events socioeconomic impacts and costs, heating and cooling degree days, and housing energy bills, by census div and State, monthly rpt, 2152–12

Workers compensation under Fed Govt-administered programs, coverage, expenditures, and claims and dispositions by district, FY83, annual compilation, 6504–5

see also Autopsies
see also Capital punishment
see also Coroners
see also Fetal deaths
see also Homicide
see also Infant mortality
see also Suicide
see also War casualties

DeBoer, Larry

"Female-Male Unemployment Differential: Effects of Changes in Industry Employment", 6722–1.465

DeBraal, J. Peter

"Foreign Ownership of U.S. Agricultural Land Through Dec. 31, 1983", 1584–2

"Foreign Ownership of U.S. Agricultural Land Through Dec. 31, 1983: County Level Data", 1584–3

Debt

see Agricultural credit
see Business assets and liabilities, general
see Business assets and liabilities, specific industries
see Consumer credit
see Credit
see Foreign debts
see Government securities
see Loans

see Mortgages
see Municipal bonds
see Personal debt
see Public debt
see U.S. savings bonds

Decatur, Ill.

Census of Housing, 1980: occupancy and unit characteristics, by race, Hispanic origin, and city, SMSA rpt, 2473–1.137

Census of Population and Housing, 1980: detailed population and housing characteristics, by county, city, and census tract, SMSA rpt, 2551–2.137

Housing vacancy rates for single and multifamily units and mobile homes, by county, city, and ZIP code, 1984, annual metro area rpt, 9304–18.5

Wages by occupation, and benefits for office and plant workers, 1983 labor market area survey rpt, 6785–3.2

see also under By SMSA or MSA in the "Index by Categories"

Declercq, Eugene R.

"Out-of-Hospital Births, U.S., 1978: Birth Weight and Apgar Score as Measures of Outcome", 4102–1.414

Decontrol of prices

see Price regulation

DeCotiis, Allen R.

"Business Plan for Home Banking", 9371–1.422

Dederick, Robert J.

"Economy", 1004–16.1

Default

see Bankruptcy
see Loan delinquency and default

Defective products

Auto and auto equipment recalls for safety-related defects, by make, quarterly listing, 7762–2

Consumer Product Safety Commission activities, recalls, and product-related injuries, deaths, and medical costs, by product type and brand, FY83, annual rpt, 9164–2

Imports detained by FDA, by product, shipper or manufacturer, country, and detention reasons, monthly listing, 4062–2

Mobile and manufactured home safety standards, program inspections, enforcement actions, and accidents and casualties by victim characteristics, 1982-83, biennial rpt, 5004–4

Motor vehicle safety defect investigations by Natl Hwy Traffic Safety Admin, and recalls, 1981, annual rpt, 7764–1.2

Defectors

see Refugees

Defense

see Civil defense
see Department of Defense
see National defense

Defense agencies

Budget of DOD, expenditures for each service branch and total defense agencies, by function and State, FY85, annual rpt, 3544–23

Budget of DOD, itemized account of legislative history, FY84, annual rpt, 3504–7

Budget of DOD, justification for procurement programs, by equipment type, service branch, and defense agency, FY83-86, annual rpt, 3504–14

Defense budgets and appropriations

Budget of DOD, justification for R&D programs, by item, service branch, and defense agency, FY83-86, annual rpt, 3504–15

Budget of DOD, justification, programs, and policies, FY85, annual rpt, 3544–2

Commercial activities of DOD under contract and performed in-house, costs and work-years, by service branch, defense agency, State, and installation, FY83, annual rpt, 3544–25

Employment (civilian and military) of DOD, by service branch and defense agency, monthly rpt, 3542–14.1

Fraud and abuse in DOD programs, audits and investigations, 1st half FY84, semiannual rpt, 3542–18

Manpower requirements and cost estimates, DOD budget detailed analysis, FY85, annual rpt, 3504–1

Outlays and obligations of DOD, by function and service branch, quarterly rpt, 3542–3

Property, supplies, and equipment inventory of DOD, by service branch, 1983, annual rpt, 3544–6

see also Defense Communications Agency
see also Defense Contract Audit Agency
see also Defense Fuel Supply Center
see also Defense Intelligence Agency
see also Defense Logistics Agency
see also Defense Mapping Agency
see also Defense Nuclear Agency
see also Defense Security Assistance Agency
see also National Security Agency

Defense budgets and appropriations

Air Force fiscal mgmt system operations and techniques, info for comptroller personnel, quarterly rpt, 3602–1

Budget appropriations for defense, actual and requested, FY76-84, article, 2702–1.440

Budget of DOD, itemized account of legislative history, FY84, annual rpt, 3504–7

Budget of DOD, justification for procurement programs, by equipment type, service branch, and defense agency, FY83-86, annual rpt, 3504–14

Budget of DOD, justification for R&D programs, and acquisition mgmt, FY83-85, annual rpt, 3504–6

Budget of DOD, justification for R&D programs, by item, service branch, and defense agency, FY83-86, annual rpt, 3504–15

Budget of DOD, justification, programs, and policies, FY85, annual rpt, 3544–2

Budget of DOD, manpower and cost estimates, detailed analysis, FY85, annual rpt, 3504–1

Budget of DOD, organization, personnel, weapons, and property, by service branch, State, and country, 1984 annual summary rpt, 3504–13

Budget of US Appendix, detailed budgets and personnel summaries, by agency, FY85, annual rpt, 104–3

Budget of US, authority balances in FY85 budget, by agency, FY83-85, annual rpt, 104–8

Budget of US, CBO analysis and review of FY85 budget by function, annual rpt, 26304–2

Defense budgets and appropriations

Budget of US, CBO analysis of revenue and spending alternatives and projections of economic indicators, FY85-89, annual rpt, 26304–3

Budget of US, compact budgets by function, agency, and account, FY85 with projections to FY89, annual rpt, 104–2

Budget of US, loans and loan guarantees, and Admin proposed limits on credit assistance, by program, FY83-89, annual rpt, 26306–3.65

Budget of US, object class analysis of obligations, by branch of Fed Govt and selected depts and agencies, FY85 estimates, annual rpt, 104–9

Budget of US, receipts by source and outlays by agency and program, monthly rpt, 8102–3

Budget of US, receipts by source and outlays by function, FY40-89 estimates revised for consistency with FY85 budget definitions, annual rpt, 104–12

Budget of US, receipts, outlays, and budget authority, by function and agency, FY84-89 revised estimates, midsession review of FY85 budget, annual rpt, 104–7

Budget of US, receipts, outlays, and budget authority, by function and agency, 1st revision of FY85 budget, annual rpt, 104–17

Civilian Health and Medical Program of the Uniformed Services costs and operations, FY83-84, 3502–2

Construction and renovation of military bases, DOD budget authorization requests, by DOD component, State, country, and project, FY85, annual rpt, 3544–15

Cost control proposals for Fed Govt programs and mgmt, 3-year savings by function and agency, and financial and operating data, 1960s-81, 16908–1

Energy programs of Fed Govt proposed budget appropriations, by dept and function, FY84-85, annual rpt, 3004–14

Fed Govt grants-in-aid for 13 program areas, FY82-84, annual article, 10042–1.402

Foreign military aid of US and sales of arms, equipment, and training, by item and country, FY50-83, annual rpt, 3904–3

Foreign military aid of US, arms sales, and training programs costs and budget requests by program, world region, and country, FY83-85, annual rpt, 7144–13

Foreign military and economic aid of US, Reagan Admin budget requests by program and country, FY82-85, annual rpt, 7004–14

Investigations of DOD operations, summaries of GAO rpts published 1979-83, annual rpt, 26104–6

Missile experimental (MX) procurement funding, and contract awards by company, FY84 with procurement projections to FY89, GAO rpt, 26123–75

Natl Guard (Army and Air) activities, manpower, and facilities, FY83, annual rpt, 3704–3

Navy budget and Navy and Marine Corps forces, equipment, and budget summary, planned FY84-85, semiannual pamphlet, 3802–3

Procurement cost unit changes for 96 programs, and DOD total and procurement budget growth, projected FY85-89, hearing, 21268–36

Reserve forces funding by reserve component, and total DOD appropriations, FY75-82 and projected to FY89, annual rpt, 3544–27.3

Space and related R&D program activities and funding of DOD, FY84-85, annual rpt, 3504–9

Statistical Abstract of US, social, political, and economic data, 1950s-83 and trends, annual rpt, 2324–1.2

Training and education programs of DOD, funding, staff, students, and facilities, by service branch and reserve component, FY85, annual rpt, 3504–5

Weapons and support systems costs under multiyear and annual procurement methods for 12 items in FY85 budget, by service branch, 1984 GAO rpt, 26123–83

Weapons budget of DOD, costs of individual weapons or systems, FY83-85, annual rpt, 3504–2

Weapons system procurement cost estimates, DOD methodology for rpts to Congress, with illustrative data and bibl, 1970s-83, GAO rpt, 26123–62

Weapons systems budget of DOD, FY85 requests consistency with US policy and specified treaties, with funding FY83-87, annual rpt, 21384–4

see also Defense expenditures

Defense Communications Agency

Commercial activities of DOD under contract and performed in-house, costs and work-years, by service branch, defense agency, State, and installation, FY83, annual rpt, 3544–25

Construction and renovation of military bases, DOD budget authorization requests, by DOD component, State, country, and project, FY85, annual rpt, 3544–15

Employment (civilian and military) of DOD, by service branch and defense agency, monthly rpt, 3542–14.1

Defense Contract Audit Agency

Employment (civilian and military) of DOD, by service branch and defense agency, monthly rpt, 3542–14.1

Defense contracts and procurement

Accounting mgmt of DOD procurement revolving fund, costs and cost carryovers by cause and activity site, FY82-83, GAO rpt, 26111–22

Aerospace industry sales, and new and backlog orders, for military and nonmilitary customers, quarterly Current Industrial Rpt, 2506–12.22

Air Force B-1B aircraft program procurement and operating costs by component, and personnel, alternative projections FY85-89, GAO rpt, 26123–79

Budget of DOD, justification for procurement programs, by equipment type, service branch, and defense agency, FY83-86, annual rpt, 3504–14

Budget of DOD, organization, personnel, weapons, and property, by service branch, State, and country, 1984 annual summary rpt, 3504–13

Index by Subjects and Names

Budget of US, object class analysis of obligations, by branch of Fed Govt and selected depts and agencies, FY85 estimates, annual rpt, 104–9

Commercial activities of DOD under contract and performed in-house, costs and work-years, by service branch, defense agency, State, and installation, FY83, annual rpt, 3544–25

Commercial activities of Fed Govt, savings from performance under contract over in-house, with DOD costs, employees displaced, and small business awards, by service branch, FY81-82, 108–39

Construction costs and price indexes by type of military facility, and implicit price deflators, 1972-82, article, 2702–1.401

Cost control proposals for Fed Govt programs and mgmt, CBO and GAO estimates of savings by function and agency, FY85-89, 26308–45

Cost control proposals for Fed Govt programs and mgmt, 3-year savings by function and agency, and financial and operating data, 1960s-81, 16908–1

Defense activity indicators, *Business Conditions Digest,* historical supplement and methodology, 1947-82, 2708–31

Defense activity indicators, *Business Conditions Digest,* monthly rpt, 2702–3.8

Defense Fuel Supply Center procurement, prices, stocks, and other activities, FY83, annual rpt, 3904–6

Defense Fuel Supply Center procurement, prices, stocks, transport, and other activities and finances, FY83, annual rpt, 3904–8

Engineering contract awards of DOD by function, contract type, and service branch, and oil and port dredging awards by company, 1970s-83, hearings, 21728–53

Fed Govt aid to State and local areas, by type of payment, State, county, and city, FY83, annual rpt, 2464–3

Fed Govt aid to State and local govts, expenditures, and direct payments, by program, agency, and State, FY83, annual rpt, 2464–2

Fraud and abuse in DOD programs, audits and investigations, 1st half FY84, semiannual rpt, 3542–18

Fuel oil (distillate and residual) and kerosene deliveries, by end use, PAD district, and State, selected years 1978-83, annual rpt, 3164–2

Govt revenues by source and expenditures by function, natl income and product account, *Survey of Current Business,* monthly rpt, monthly and annual tables, 2702–1.24

Input-output structure of US economy, detailed interindustry transactions for 85 industries, and components of final demand, 1977, article, 2702–1.421

Input-output structure of US economy, detailed interindustry transactions for 537 industries, and components of final demand, 1977 benchmark data, 2708–17

Investigations of DOD operations, summaries of GAO rpts published 1979-83, annual rpt, 26104–6

Manufacturers under Fed Govt contract and owned by DOD, operating data by

Index by Subjects and Names

agency, selected SIC 2- to 4-digit industry, State, and SMSA, 1982, annual Current Industrial Rpt, 2506–3.4

Missile experimental (MX) procurement funding, and contract awards by company, FY84 with procurement projections to FY89, GAO rpt, 26123–75

Missile experimental (MX) procurement progress and costs, various dates 1979-83 and projected to 1990, GAO rpt, 26123–74

Natl income and product, comprehensive accounts and components, *Survey of Current Business,* monthly rpt, 2702–1.21

Navy budget and Navy and Marine Corps forces, equipment, and budget summary, planned FY84-85, semiannual pamphlet, 3802–3

Navy F/A-18 weapons tactics trainer costs by trainer type, as of 1984, and demand at 2 locations, projected 1988-94, GAO rpt, 26123–73

Navy procurement, by contractor and location of work, FY83, annual rpt, 3804–13

Outlays and obligations of DOD, by function and service branch, quarterly rpt, 3542–3

Post exchange operations, locations worldwide, sales by type of commodity or service and facility, and employment, FY83, annual rpt, 3504–10

Prime contract awards by DOD, by detailed procurement category and R&D, FY80-83, annual rpt, 3544–18

Prime contract awards by DOD, by size, dept, and type of contract, FY83, annual rpt, 3544–19

Prime contract awards by DOD, by type, service branch and command, and for Defense Logistics Agency, last week compared to total year FY83, 108–38

Prime contract awards by DOD, dollar volume for 100 leading contractors and subsidiaries, FY83, annual rpt, 3544–5

Prime contract awards by DOD for 25 commodity categories and R&D, by State and census div, FY81-83, annual rpt, 3544–11

Prime contract awards by DOD in labor surplus areas, by service branch, State, and area, 1st half FY84, semiannual rpt, 3542–19

Prime contract awards by DOD to small and total business, for 10 categories and R&D, monthly rpt, 3542–10

Prime contract awards of DOD, by category, contract and contractor type, and service branch, FY74-1st half FY84, semiannual rpt, 3542–1

Prime contract awards of DOD, by individual contractor, service branch, State and city, and country, FY83, annual listing, 3544–22

Prime contract awards of DOD for military and civil functions, by service branch and State, 1st half FY83-84, semiannual rpt, 3542–5

Procurement contract awards of Fed Govt, by State, agency, procurement and contractor type, and for top 100 contractors, quarterly rpt, 102–6

Procurement cost unit changes for 96 programs, and DOD total and procurement budget growth, projected FY85-89, hearing, 21268–36

Defense expenditures

Procurement of goods and services by level of govt, *Business Conditions Digest,* historical supplement and methodology, 1947-82, 2708–31

Procurement of identical items from multiple sources by DOD, and price difference by item, by service branch, FY81, GAO rpt, 26123–67

Publications of DOD Directorate for Info Operations and Rpts, FY84, annual listing, 3544–16

R&D prime contract awards of DOD to educational and nonprofit instns and Federal agencies, by instn and location, FY83, annual listing, 3544–17

R&D prime contractors for DOD, top 500 and value of contracts, FY83, annual listing, 3544–4

Small business and minority- and women-owned businesses Federal contracts, by agency, FY81-82, annual rpt, 9764–6.4, 9764–6.5

Statistical Abstract of US, social, political, and economic data, 1950s-83 and trends, annual rpt, 2324–1.2

Subcontract awards by DOD contractors to small and disadvantaged business, by firm and service branch, quarterly listing, 3542–17

Weapons and communications systems cost estimates, by service branch, quarterly summary rpt, 3502–1

Weapons and support systems costs under multiyear and annual procurement methods for 12 items in FY85 budget, by service branch, 1984 GAO rpt, 26123–83

Weapons budget of DOD, costs of individual weapons or systems, FY83-85, annual rpt, 3504–2

Weapons system procurement cost estimate changes, and program delays and mgmt, by system and service branch, 1983, annual rpt, 26304–5

Weapons system procurement cost estimates, DOD methodology for rpts to Congress, with illustrative data and bibl, 1970s-83, GAO rpt, 26123–62

Weapons systems cost underestimation in DOD budget request 5-year plans, and cost change by system, various periods FY79-89, GAO rpt, 26123–68

Western States economic indicators, Fed Reserve 12th District, quarterly rpt, 9393–1.3

Defense Department

see Department of Defense

Defense expenditures

Air Force B-1B aircraft program procurement and operating costs by component, and personnel, alternative projections FY85-89, GAO rpt, 26123–79

Air Force fiscal mgmt system operations and techniques, info for comptroller personnel, quarterly rpt, 3602–1

Base support costs by function, and personnel and acreage by installation, by service branch, FY85, annual rpt, 3504–11

Budget of DOD, expenditures for each service branch and total defense agencies, by function and State, FY85, annual rpt, 3544–23

Commercial activities of DOD under contract and performed in-house, costs

and work-years, by service branch, defense agency, State, and installation, FY83, annual rpt, 3544–25

Communist and and OECD countries economic conditions, 1982, annual rpt, 7144–11

Communist, OECD, and selected other countries economic statistics, 1960s-83, annual rpt, 244–5.2

Cost control proposals for Fed Govt programs and mgmt, CBO and GAO estimates of savings by function and agency, FY85-89, 26308–45

Cost control proposals for Fed Govt programs and mgmt, 3-year savings by function and agency, and financial and operating data, 1960s-81, 16908–1

Defense activity indicators, *Business Conditions Digest,* historical supplement and methodology, 1947-82, 2708–31

Defense activity indicators, *Business Conditions Digest,* monthly rpt, 2702–3.8

Developing countries receiving US economic aid, total govt and defense expenditures, military imports, GNP, and intl reserves by country, 1976-81, annual rpt, 9914–1

Developing countries summary socioeconomic data, 1970s-83, and AID activities and funding by project and function, FY82-85, by country, annual rpt, 9914–3

Economic and financial trends, natl compounded annual rates of change, 1964-83, annual rpt, 9391–9.2

Expenditures for military goods and services, by function, 1972-84, article, 2702–1.440

Fed Govt aid to State and local areas, by type of payment, State, county, and city, FY83, annual rpt, 2464–3

Fed Govt consolidated financial statements based on business accounting methods, FY82-83, annual rpt, 8104–5

Fed Govt revenues by source, expenditures by function, debt, and assets, 1982-83, annual rpt, 2466–2.6

Fed Govt spending by function, with comparisons to State and local govt spending, selected years 1929-83, annual rpt, 10044–1.1

Foreign economic, social, and political summary data, by country, 1984, annual factbook, 244–11

Foreign military, social, and economic summary data by world area and country, 1960s-80s, hearing, 25388–47.1

Foreign military spending, arms trade, and armed forces size, with total govt spending and population, by country, 1972-82, annual rpt, 9824–1

Govt revenues by source and expenditures by function, natl income and product account, *Survey of Current Business,* monthly rpt, monthly and annual tables, 2702–1.24

Investigations of DOD operations, summaries of GAO rpts published 1979-83, annual rpt, 26104–6

Loan programs of Fed Govt, direct and guaranteed loans outstanding by agency and program, *Treasury Bulletin,* quarterly rpt, 8002–4.10

NATO military commitment of US, Europe force strengths by service branch and costs by component, FY82 with trends from FY75, GAO rpt, 26123–71

Defense expenditures

NATO military expenditures, by country, selected years 1971-82, hearing, 21388–42

Navy budget and Navy and Marine Corps forces, equipment, and budget summary, planned FY84-85, semiannual pamphlet, 3802–3

Outlays and obligations of DOD, by function and service branch, quarterly rpt, 3542–3

Public opinion on taxes, tax policy, and intergovtl relations, 1972-84 surveys, annual rpt, 10044–2

Strategic military capability, force strengths, weapons, training, supplies, and requirements, by service branch, FY80-84 and projected to 1990, 3508–19

Training and education programs of DOD, funding, staff, students, and facilities, by service branch and reserve component, FY85, annual rpt, 3504–5

see also Budget of the U.S.

see also Defense budgets and appropriations

see also Defense contracts and procurement

see also Defense research

see also Military pay

Defense Fuel Supply Center

- Procurement, prices, stocks, and other activities of DFSC, FY83, annual rpt, 3904–6
- Procurement, prices, stocks, transport, and other activities and finances of DFSC, FY83, annual rpt, 3904–8

Defense industries

- Aluminum ingot and mill product defense and total shipments, trade, consumption, and inventories, monthly Current Industrial Rpt, 2506–10.9
- Commercial activities of DOD under contract and performed in-house, costs and work-years, by service branch, defense agency, State, and installation, FY83, annual rpt, 3544–25
- Defense activity indicators, *Business Conditions Digest,* historical supplement and methodology, 1947-82, 2708–31
- Defense activity indicators, *Business Conditions Digest,* monthly rpt, 2702–3.8
- Fraud and abuse in DOD programs, audits and investigations, 1st half FY84, semiannual rpt, 3542–18
- Manufacturers under Fed Govt contract and owned by DOD, operating data by agency, selected SIC 2- to 4-digit industry, State, and SMSA, 1982, annual Current Industrial Rpt, 2506–3.4
- Scientists, engineers, and technicians needed in defense and nondefense industries, and supply/demand, by field, 1981-87, 9628–71

see also Arms sales

see also Defense contracts and procurement

see also Defense expenditures

Defense Intelligence Agency

- Commercial activities of DOD under contract and performed in-house, costs and work-years, by service branch, defense agency, State, and installation, FY83, annual rpt, 3544–25
- Construction and renovation of military bases, DOD budget authorization requests, by DOD component, State, country, and project, FY85, annual rpt, 3544–15

Employment (civilian and military) of DOD, by service branch and defense agency, monthly rpt, 3542–14.1

Defense Logistics Agency

- Commercial activities of DOD under contract and performed in-house, costs and work-years, by service branch, defense agency, State, and installation, FY83, annual rpt, 3544–25
- Construction and renovation of military bases, DOD budget authorization requests, by DOD component, State, country, and project, FY85, annual rpt, 3544–15
- Employment (civilian and military) of DOD, by service branch and defense agency, monthly rpt, 3542–14.1
- Engineering contract awards of DOD by function, contract type, and service branch, and oil and port dredging awards by company, 1970s-83, hearings, 21728–53
- Procurement, DOD prime contract awards by category, contract and contractor type, and service branch, FY74-1st half FY84, semiannual rpt, 3542–1
- Procurement, DOD prime contract awards by individual contractor, service branch, State and city, and country, FY83, annual listing, 3544–22
- Procurement, DOD prime contract awards by size, dept, and type of contract, FY83, annual rpt, 3544–19
- Procurement, DOD prime contract awards by type, service branch and command, and for Defense Logistics Agency, last week compared to total year FY83, 108–38
- Procurement, DOD prime contract awards for military and civil functions, by State, 1st half FY84, semiannual rpt, 3542–5
- Procurement, DOD prime contract awards in labor surplus areas, by service branch, State, and area, 1st half FY84, semiannual rpt, 3542–19
- Procurement, DOD prime contract awards to small and total business, for 10 categories and R&D, monthly rpt, 3542–10
- Procurement, subcontract awards by DOD contractors to small and disadvantaged business, by firm and service branch, quarterly listing, 3542–17
- Supply inventory and automated cataloging system of Fed Govt, and DOD mgmt of inventory items for agencies, NATO, and foreign govts, 1970s-83, annual rpt, 21204–1

see also Defense Fuel Supply Center

Defense Mapping Agency

- Commercial activities of DOD under contract and performed in-house, costs and work-years, by service branch, defense agency, State, and installation, FY83, annual rpt, 3544–25
- Construction and renovation of military bases, DOD budget authorization requests, by DOD component, State, country, and project, FY85, annual rpt, 3544–15

Defense Nuclear Agency

- Commercial activities of DOD under contract and performed in-house, costs and work-years, by service branch, defense agency, State, and installation, FY83, annual rpt, 3544–25

Index by Subjects and Names

- Construction and renovation of military bases, DOD budget authorization requests, by DOD component, State, country, and project, FY85, annual rpt, 3544–15
- Employment (civilian and military) of DOD, by service branch and defense agency, monthly rpt, 3542–14.1
- Radiation from 1940s-70s nuclear weapons tests, levels in air and water, and personnel exposure by military unit and job category, series, 3906–1

Defense research

- Budget of DOD, expenditures for each service branch and total defense agencies, by function and State, FY85, annual rpt, 3544–23
- Budget of DOD for weapons systems, FY85 requests consistency with US policy and specified treaties, with funding FY83-87, annual rpt, 21384–4
- Budget of DOD, itemized account of legislative history, FY84, annual rpt, 3504–7
- Budget of DOD, justification for R&D programs, and acquisition mgmt, FY83-85, annual rpt, 3504–6
- Budget of DOD, justification for R&D programs, by item, service branch, and defense agency, FY83-86, annual rpt, 3504–15
- Budget of DOD, justification, programs, and policies, FY85, annual rpt, 3544–2
- Budget of DOD, organization, personnel, weapons, and property, by service branch, State, and country, 1984 annual summary rpt, 3504–13
- Budget of US, effects of Reagan Admin policy changes, by detailed program, FY85, annual rpt, 104–21
- Commercial activities of DOD under contract and performed in-house, costs and work-years, by service branch, defense agency, State, and installation, FY83, annual rpt, 3544–25
- Cost control proposals for Fed Govt programs and mgmt, 3-year savings by function and agency, and financial and operating data, 1960s-81, 16908–1.17
- Cost of DOD base support by function, and personnel and acreage by installation, by service branch, FY85, annual rpt, 3504–11
- Expenditures for military goods and services, by function, 1972-84, article, 2702–1.440
- Expenditures for R&D by source, and scientists education and employment, detailed data by field, selected years 1953-84, annual rpt, 9624–18
- Fed Govt aid to State and local govts, expenditures, and direct payments, by program, agency, and State, FY83, annual rpt, 2464–2
- Fed Govt R&D funding, by function, agency, and program, selected years FY80-84 and proposed FY85, 26308–46
- Fed Govt R&D funding for all performers, by field and supporting agency, selected years FY60-84, annual rpt, 9627–20
- Manufacturers under Fed Govt contract and owned by DOD, operating data by agency, selected SIC 2- to 4-digit industry, State, and SMSA, 1982, annual Current Industrial Rpt, 2506–3.4

Index by Subjects and Names

Delaware

Missile experimental (MX) basing proposals of Reagan Admin, 1984 narrative rpt update, 3508–17

Missile experimental (MX) procurement progress and costs, various dates 1979-83 and projected to 1990, GAO rpt, 26123–74

Nuclear attack civil defense plans of Fed Emergency Mgmt Agency, funding and operations by component, FY81-84 and projected FY85-89, GAO rpt, 26123–61

Nuclear industry nongovt employment by industry segment, occupation, and census div, and DOE and NRC nuclear employment, 1968-83, biennial rpt, 3004–11.1

Nuclear reactors for domestic use and export by function, with owner, operating characteristics, and location, Apr 1984, semiannual listing, 3002–5

Outlays and obligations of DOD, by function and service branch, quarterly rpt, 3542–3

Prime contract awards by DOD, by detailed procurement category and R&D, FY80-83, annual rpt, 3544–18

Prime contract awards by DOD for 25 commodity categories and R&D, by State and census div, FY81-83, annual rpt, 3544–11

Prime contract awards by DOD to small and total business, for 10 categories and R&D, monthly rpt, 3542–10

Prime contract awards of DOD, by category, contract and contractor type, and service branch, FY74-1st half FY84, semiannual rpt, 3542–1

Prime contract awards of DOD for R&D to educational and nonprofit instns and Federal agencies, by instn and location, FY83, annual listing, 3544–17

Prime contractors for DOD, top 500 and value of contracts, FY83, annual listing, 3544–4

Procurement contract awards of Fed Govt, by State, agency, procurement and contractor type, and for top 100 contractors, quarterly rpt, 102–6

Radioactive waste and spent fuel generation, inventory, disposal by site, reprocessing, and characteristics, by source, as of 1983 and projected to 2020, annual rpt, 3364–2

Radioactive wastes from DOE defense facilities, interim storage inventories by site and permanent disposal plan costs, 1982 with projections to 2015, 3358–32

Soviet Union and Warsaw Pact military weapons systems, assistance and presence worldwide, and force strengths, with selected US and NATO comparisons, as of 1984, 3508–14

Space and related R&D program activities and funding of DOD, FY84-85, annual rpt, 3504–9

see also Military science

Defense Security Assistance Agency

Foreign military aid of US and sales of arms, equipment, and training, by item and country, FY50-83, annual rpt, 3904–3

Foreign military training of US, students, costs, and revenue losses from reduced tuition by country, by service branch, FY79-83, GAO rpt, 26123–56

Liabilities (contigent) and claims paid by Fed Govt on federally insured and guaranteed contracts with foreign obligors, by country and program, periodic rpt, 8002–12

Defense Supply Agency

see Defense Logistics Agency

Deficit Reduction Act

AFDC provisions of Act, 1984 narrative article, 4742–1.423

Medicare and Medicaid provisions of Act, 1984 narrative article, 4742–1.422

OASDI and SSI provisions of Act, 1984 narrative article, 4742–1.421

Tax expenditures, Fed Govt revenues foregone through income tax deductions and exclusions by type, and effect of Act, FY84-89, annual rpt, 21784–10

DeFina, Robert H.

"Inflationary Expectations and the Consumer", 9387–8.92

"Union-Nonunion Wage Differentials and the Functional Distribution of Income: Some Simulation Results from a General Equilibrium Model", 9387–8.83

"Unions, Relative Wages, and Economic Efficiency", 9387–8.81

DeFrain, John

"Divorce Process: Developing Educational Programs for Individuals and Families", 1004–16.1

Degrees, educational

see Degrees, higher education

see Educational attainment

see under By Educational Attainment in the "Index by Categories"

Degrees, higher education

Condition of Education, detailed data on enrollment, staff, achievement, finances, curricula, and education effects on employment, 1982-83, annual rpt, 4824–1.2

Degrees conferred in higher education, by detailed field, degree level, sex, and State, annual rpt, suspended, 4844–5

Degrees conferred in higher education, by field and degree level, 1981/82, and occupational manpower and supply, 1982 and 1995, biennial rpt, 6744–3

Degrees conferred in higher education, by race, Hispanic origin, sex, level, and field, selected years 1949/50-1979/80, annual rpt, 4824–2.16

Degrees, highest level offered by individual instns, 1983/84 annual listing, 4844–3

DOD Dependents Schools students higher education admissions tests scores by sex and subject, and educational goals and attitudes, 1983, annual rpt, 3504–17

Education statistics summary compilation, 1980/81-1982/83 with selected trends from 1869, biennial rpt, 4804–27

Educational trends, 1972/73-1992/93, biennial pocket-size card, 4824–3

Health professionals supply and education, by occupation, demographic and professional characteristics, and location, 1950s-83 and projected to 2000, biennial rpt, 4114–8

Health professions employment and training of minorities and women, by field, selected years 1962/63-1983/84, 4118–18

Mental health workers, nursing and social work degrees, psychologists by degree level, and psychiatry residencies, 1950s-81, annual rpt, 4504–9.4

Nuclear engineering student enrollments and degrees granted, by State, instn, and subfield, and placements by sector, 1983, annual rpt, 3004–5

Puerto Rico educational enrollment, finance, completions, curricula, and personnel by instn, and health and vital statistics, selected years 1970-83, hearings, 21348–93

Radiation protection and health physics enrollments and degrees granted by State and instn, and grads employment, 1983, annual rpt, 3004–7

Robotics degrees and courses offered, by State and school level, 1982, 26358–105

Science and engineering doctoral degree recipients and grad students, 1960s-80, 3008–89.2

Science and engineering doctoral degree recipients, by field, sex, race, age, citizenship, postgrad employment and study status, State, and instn, 1960-82, 9626–6.16

Science and engineering enrollment, degrees, and employment, R&D funding, and related topics, highlights series, 9626–2

Science and engineering grads of 1980-81, employment characteristics or grad enrollment, by degree level, field, sex, and race, 1982, 9627–25

Science Indicators, R&D expenditures, innovations, research, and higher education, with foreign comparisons, 1960s- 83, annual rpt, 9624–10

Scientists and engineers employment, salaries, and degrees, by field, type of employer, race, and sex, selected years 1960-81, annual rpt, 9624–18.5

Scientists and engineers supply, employment, and education, by sex, race, Hispanic origin, and field, selected years 1965-83, biennial rpt, 9624–20

Teaching degrees conferred by specialty and State, required credit hours, and instn officials attitudes, by instn type, 1970s-83, hearings, 21348–89

Women awarded degrees in higher education, with comparative data for men, by subject area, biennial rpt, suspended, 4844–9

Women's employment and earnings, by labor force and socioeconomic characteristics, and compared to men, 1978-81 and trends from 1940s, 6568–29

see also under By Educational Attainment in the "Index by Categories"

Delano, Daryl H.

"Employment Outlook for 1984 New England College Graduates", 6916–7.3

Delaware

Agriculture census, 1982: farms, farmland, production, finances, and operator characteristics, by county, final State rpt, 2331–1.8

Bank deposits in commercial and mutual savings banks and in US branches of foreign banks, by account type, instn, State, SMSA, and county, June 1983, annual rpt, 9295–3.4

Census of Housing, 1980: occupancy and unit characteristics of SMSAs and central cities, by race, Hispanic origin, and city, State rpt, 2473–1.9

Census of Population and Housing, 1980: detailed population and housing characteristics, by county, city, and census tract, State rpt, 2551–2.9

ASI Annual Supplement 191

Delaware

Census of Population, 1980: detailed socioeconomic and demographic characteristics, by age, sex, race, Hispanic origin, and industry, State rpt, 2531–4.9

County Business Patterns: establishments, employees, and payrolls, by SIC 4-digit industry and county, 1982, annual State rpt, 2326–6.9

Employment, earnings, and hours, by selected SIC 1- to 4-digit industry, State, and for 278 major labor areas, 1939-83, annual rpt, 6744–5.1, 6744–5.3

Environmental quality, pollutant discharge by type and source, and EPA protection activities and funding, 1970s-83, biennial regional rpt, 9184–15.3

Exports of manufactured and agricultural commodities, manufacturing production, and export-related employment, 1960s-82, State rpt, 2046–3.8

HHS aid to each State and local govt or private instn, amount obligated, funding agency, and program, FY83, annual listing, 4004–3.3

Income (personal) per capita and by source, and earnings by industry div, by State, MSA, and county, 1977-82, annual regional rpt, 2704–2.3

Manufacturing census, 1982: financial and operating data, by SIC 2- to 4-digit industry, State, SMSA, and county, preliminary census div rpt, 2491–3.5

Mineral Industry Surveys, State review of production, 1983, advance annual rpt, 5614–6.8

Minerals Yearbook, 1982, Vol 2 preprints: State review of production and sales by commodity, and business activity, annual rpt, 5604–16.9

Minerals Yearbook, 1982, Vol 2: State reviews of production, sales, and firms, by commodity, and business activity, annual rpt, 5604–34

Population, births, deaths, and net migration, by MSA and county, 1980-82, annual State Current Population Rpt, 2546–4.8

Population size, Apr 1980 and July 1982, and per capita income, 1979 and 1981, by county and city, State Current Population Rpt, 2546–11.8

Retail trade census, 1982: employment, establishments, sales, and payroll, by SIC 2- to 4-digit kind of business, SMSA, county, and city, State rpt, 2397–1.8

Wages of office and plant workers in Lower Eastern Shore, Md-Va-Del, by occupation, 1984 labor market area survey rpt, 6785–3.9

Water supply and quality in streams and lakes, and groundwater levels in wells, by drainage basin, 1983, annual State rpt, 5666–10.19

Wholesale trade census, 1982: employment, establishments, finances, and operations, by SIC 2- to 4-digit kind of business, SMSA, county, and city, State rpt, 2405–1.8

see also Wilmington, Del.

see also under By State in the "Index by Categories"

Delaware River

Bridges over navigable waters, with type of bridge and use, owner, dimensions, and location, 1984 regional listing, 7406–5.1

Freight (waterborne domestic and foreign) by commodity, traffic, and passengers, by port and waterway, 1982, annual rpt, 3754–3.1

Tidal current tables, daily time and velocity by station for US Atlantic coast, 1985, annual rpt, 2174–1.1

Water supply and quality in streams and lakes, and groundwater levels in wells, by drainage basin, 1980, annual State rpt series, 5666–12

Water supply and quality in streams and lakes, and groundwater levels in wells, by drainage basin, 1981, annual State rpt series, 5666–16

Water supply and quality in streams and lakes, and groundwater levels in wells, by drainage basin, 1982, annual State rpt series, 5666–20

Water supply and quality in streams and lakes, and groundwater levels in wells, by drainage basin, 1983, annual State rpt series, 5666–10

Water supply in Northeastern US, precipitation and stream runoff by station, monthly rpt, 2182–3

Water supply in US and Canada, streamflow, well and reservoir levels, and dissolved solids and temperature in 6 US rivers, by station, monthly rpt, 5662–3

Deloney, Julia R.

"Job Attitudes Toward the New Maintenance Concept of the Airway Facilities Service", 7506–10.25

Delray Beach, Fla.

see also under By SMSA or MSA in the "Index by Categories"

Demand deposits

see Checking accounts

see Negotiable orders of withdrawal accounts

Democratic Party

Campaign finances and Fed Election Commission monitoring activities, 1984 Federal elections, biennial rpt series, 9276–2

Campaign finances, election procedures, and Fed Election Commission monitoring activities, press release series, 9276–1

Campaign funding and activities of Fed Election Commission, and political action committees funding, 1983, annual rpt, 9274–1

Campaign funding by political action committee and candidate, proposed candidate spending limits, voting rates by party, and political opinions, by State, 1960-82, hearings, 25688–6

Campaign funding by political action committees to individual congressmen, and public opinion on reform proposals and assn influence, 1970s-83, hearings, 21428–7

Democratic Peoples Republic of Korea

see Korea, North

Demography

see Population characteristics

see Population size

see Vital statistics

see under Demographic Breakdowns in the "Index by Categories"

Demolition

see Wrecking and demolition

Index by Subjects and Names

Demopoulos, George D.

"Do Macroeconomic Policy Decisions Affect the Private Sector Ex Ante?—The EEC Experience with Crowding Out", 9373–3.26

Denison, Tex.

Census of Housing, 1980: occupancy and unit characteristics, by race, Hispanic origin, and city, SMSA rpt, 2473–1.332

Census of Population and Housing, 1980: detailed population and housing characteristics, by county, city, and census tract, SMSA rpt, 2551–2.332

Wages of office and plant workers, by occupation, 1984 labor market area survey rpt, 6785–3.10

see also under By SMSA or MSA in the "Index by Categories"

Denmark

Agricultural and food production indexes, and production of selected commodities, by world region and country, 1974-83, annual rpt, 1524–5

Agricultural situation in Western Europe, by country and commodity, 1983 and outlook for 1984, annual rpt, 1524–4.6

Agricultural supply/demand, trade, and production, and socioeconomic data, by country, 1950s-77, 1528–179

AID loan repayment status and terms by program and country, and status of predecessor agency loans, quarterly rpt, 9912–3

Background Notes, summary social, political, and economic data, 1984 rpt, 7006–2.28

Computers and computer equipment market and trade, and user industry operations and demand, 1983 country market research rpt, 2045–1.42

Economic, social, and political summary data, by country, 1984, annual factbook, 244–11

Economic trends in income, production, prices, employment, finances, and trade, 1984 semiannual rpt, 2046–4.4, 2046–4.67

Exports and imports of NATO countries with Council for Mutual Economic Assistance Europe members, by country, 1980-83, annual rpt, 7144–5

Exports and imports of NATO countries with PRC, by country, 1980-83, annual rpt, 7144–14

Exports and imports of OECD countries, by country, 1983, annual rpt, 7144–10

Exports and imports of US with Western Europe, and US market share and export opportunities for selected commodities, by country, 1982-84, 2048–105

Exports of US, detailed Schedule B commodities by country of destination, 1983, annual rpt, 2424–9

Exports of US, detailed Schedule E commodities by mode of transport and world area and country of destination, 1983, annual rpts, 2424–5

Food supply/demand and market and support prices, with exchange rates, fertilizer price index, GDP, and population, by EC country, 1960-83, 1528–173

Imports of US, detailed Schedule A commodities by country and world area of origin, and mode of transport, 1983, annual rpts, 2424–2

Index by Subjects and Names

Dentists and dentistry

Imports of US, detailed TSUSA commodities by country of origin, 1983, annual rpt, 2424–4

Loans and grants for economic and military assistance from US and intl agencies, by program and country, FY46-83, annual rpt, 9914–5

Manufacturing labor productivity and cost indexes for US and 11 OECD countries, 1960-82, annual article, 6722–1.405

Manufacturing productivity and unit labor cost indexes for US and 11 countries, 1950-82 and preliminary 1983, annual rpt, 6864–1

Military aid of US, arms sales, and training programs costs and budget requests by program, world region, and country, FY83-85, annual rpt, 7144–13

Military spending, arms trade, and armed forces size, with total govt spending and population, by country, 1972-82, annual rpt, 9824–1

Minerals Yearbook, 1982, Vol 3: foreign country reviews of production, trade, and policies, by commodity, annual rpt, 5604–35

Minerals Yearbook, 1982, Vol 3 preprints: foreign country review of production, trade, and policies, by commodity, annual rpt, 5604–17.20

Oil and gas undiscovered recoverable resources, cumulative production, and identified reserves, as of 1982, preliminary oil basin rpt, 5666–17.15

Population size and growth rates, and latest available benchmark demographic data, by country, 1950-83, biennial rpt, 2324–4

Telecommunication equipment market and trade, and user industry operations and demand, 1984 country market research rpt, 2045–12.30

see also under By Foreign Country in the "Index by Categories"

Dentists and dentistry

Census of Population, 1980: detailed socioeconomic and demographic characteristics, by age, sex, race, Hispanic origin, occupation, and industry, State rpt series, 2531–4

Census of Population, 1980: labor force, by sex, detailed occupation, and region, with comparison to 1970 census, supplementary rpt, 2535–1.12

Census of Service Industries, 1982: employment, establishments, receipts, and payroll, by SIC 2- to 4-digit kind of business, SMSA, county, and city, State rpt series, 2391–1

Census of Service Industries, 1982: employment, establishments, receipts, and payroll, by SIC 4-digit kind of business and State, preliminary rpt, 2390–2.15

County and City Data Book, detailed socioeconomic and demographic data for States, counties, and cities, selected years 1976-82, 2328–1

County Business Patterns: establishments, employees, and payrolls, by SIC 4-digit industry and county, 1981, annual State rpt series, 2326–8

County Business Patterns: establishments, employees, and payrolls, by SIC 4-digit industry and county, 1982, annual State rpt series, 2326–6

Degrees conferred in higher education, by race, Hispanic origin, sex, level, and field, selected years 1949/50-1979/80, annual rpt, 4824–2.16

DOD medical personnel, trainees, and accessions by source, by occupation, specialty, and service branch, FY83, annual rpt, 3544–24

Drug prescriptions written by dentists for nonsteroidal anti-inflammatories, 1982, annual rpt, 4064–12

Employment, earnings, and hours, by SIC 4-digit nonfarm industry, monthly 1974-Feb 1984, annual update, 6744–4

Employment in hospitals and nursing homes, total and in selected occupations, by facility bed size, ownership, region, and State, selected years 1969-80, 4147–14.30

Exports of equipment, detailed Schedule B commodities by country of destination, 1983, annual rpt, 2424–9

Franchise business opportunities, by firm and kind of business, 1984 annual listing, 2044–27

Health Care Financing Review, Medicare and Medicaid program activity, health care expenditures, and research, quarterly rpt with articles, 4652–1

Health condition and health care resources, use, and expenditures, 1970s-82 with trends and projections 1900-2000, annual compilation, 4144–11

HHS aid to each State and local govt or private instn, amount obligated, funding agency, and program, FY83, annual listing, 4004–3

Hispanic Americans health services use, illness rates, and disability days, by socieconomic characteristics, and compared to blacks and whites, 1978-80, 4147–10.147

Hospital employment, vacancies, and vacancy rates, by occupation and by hospital specialty, region, census div, and State, 1980, annual rpt, 4114–12

Income tax returns of corporations, detailed income and tax items by industry, 1981, annual rpt, 8304–4

Income tax returns of sole proprietorships, detailed data by industry div and selected industry group, 1981, annual rpt, 8304–7

Income tax returns of sole proprietorships, receipts, deductions by type, payroll, and net income, by major industry, 1982, annual article, 8302–2.413

Income tax returns with investment credits, for individuals by income, and for sole proprietorships by industry, 1981, article, 8302–2.409

Indian births, morbidity, and deaths and rates, and health services facilities and use, 1954-83, annual compilation, 4104–7

Input-output structure of US economy, detailed interindustry transactions for 537 industries, and components of final demand, 1977 benchmark data, 2708–17

License sanctions of health professionals in 3 States, and subsequent Medicare and Medicaid program participation, by specialty, 1977-82, GAO rpt, 26121–80

Malpractice claims for dental procedures, by type, payment amount, region, State, and provider and patient characteristics, 1970, article, 4102–1.416

Manpower supply and education of health professionals, by occupation, demographic and professional characteristics, and location, 1950s-83 and projected to 2000, biennial rpt, 4114–8

Manufacturing census, 1982: financial and operating data, for SIC 4-digit industries by product, preliminary rpt, 2491–1.420

Medicare and Medicaid eligibility, participation, covered services and use, and reimbursements and payments, various periods 1966-82, annual rpt, 4654–1

Military reserve forces medical personnel and wartime requirements by occupation, and medical equipment costs, by reserve component, as of 1983, annual rpt, 3544–27.2

Minority group and women employment and training in health professions, by field, selected years 1962/63-1983/84, 4118–18

Navy and Marine Corps disease incidence, medical care, and deaths, by detailed diagnosis, and medical personnel and workloads, 1978-79, annual rpt, 3804–1

Navy personnel, detailed statistics, quarterly rpt, 3802–4

New York State Medicaid reimbursement of dental costs, evaluation of expedited prior approval process, 1984 article, 4102–1.458

Occupational manpower needs and supply by detailed occupation, and educational and training program enrollees and grads by detailed field, 1982 and 1995, biennial rpt, 6744–3

Occupational Outlook Handbook, 1984-85 biennial rpt, 6744–1

Older persons by demographic, socioeconomic, and health characteristics, selected years 1900-81 and projected to 2050, Current Population Rpt, 2546–2.125

Public Health Service activities, and funding by function and subagency, FY83, annual rpt, 4044–2

R&D-employed scientists and engineers salaries by degree, type of establishment, age, experience, and field, 1984, annual rpt, 3004–1

Receipts for selected services, by SIC 2- to 4-digit kind of business, 1983, annual rpt, 2413–8

Research and training funds awarded by Natl Inst of Dental Research, by recipient instn, FY83, annual listing, 4474–19

Science and engineering grad enrollment, fields of study, financial support, and other student and instn characteristics, 1975-82, annual survey, 9627–7

Southeastern States health care resource availability, and employment by occupation, by facility type, by State and SMSA in Fed Reserve 6th District, 1970s-81, article, 9371–1.425

Statistical Abstract of US, social, political, and economic data, 1950s-83 and trends, annual rpt, 2324–1.1

Supplementary Security Income beneficiary socioeconomic characteristics and health service use, 1970s-83 and SSI program projections to 1995, 25148–29

TTPI budget, vital statistics, and health services data, often by TTPI govt, FY83 and selected trends, annual rpt, 7004–6.1

Dentists and dentistry

VA employment of general and medical personnel, FY59-83, annual rpt, 9924–13.1

VA Medicine and Surgery Dept employment, by medical district and facility, monthly rpt, quarterly data, 9922–5.3

VA Medicine and Surgery Dept trainees, by detailed program and city, FY83, annual rpt, 9924–21

VA physicians, dentists, and nurses, by age, selected employment characteristics, and VA district, quarterly rpt, 9922–11

VA physicians, dentists, and nurses pay rates by grade, Jan 1984, 21628–54

Veterans of Vietnam era, dental outpatient activity, FY70-82, annual rpt, 9924–8.4

Visits to physicians and dentists, by age, metro-nonmetro location, region, and selected SMSA, 1980-81, 4147–10.146

Denver, Colo.

Auto dealer repair workers, wages, and benefits, by occupation, size of establishment, and for 24 labor market areas, Nov 1982 survey, 6787–6.202

Auto emissions control device tampering and fuel-switching incidence in 6 urban areas, 1983, annual rpt, 9194–15

Carbon monoxide atmospheric concentrations and levels within buildings and along commuting and residential driving routes, for 4 cities, Jan-Mar 1981, 9198–110

Census of Housing, 1980: occupancy and unit characteristics, by race, Hispanic origin, and city, SMSA rpt, 2473–1.138

Census of Population and Housing, 1980: detailed population and housing characteristics, by county, city, and census tract, SMSA rpt, 2551–2.138

Court use of telephone conferencing in civil and criminal hearings, assessment of lawyers and judges in 2 States and Denver, Colo, 1981, 6068–186

CPI by component for US city average, and by region, population size, and for 28 SMSAs, monthly press release, 6762–1

CPI by detailed component, for US city average, 28 SMSAs, and 4 regions by population size, monthly rpt, 6762–2

Employment, earnings, and CPI changes in Denver-Boulder, Colo, SMSA, 1983, annual rpt, 6974–2

Fruit and vegetable shipments, and arrivals in 23 US and 5 Canada cities, by mode of transport and State or country of origin, 1983, annual rpt, 1311–4.2

Homeless population and characteristics, and temporary shelter operations, use, and user characteristics, for selected cities, various periods 1979-84, hearing, 21248–85

Hospital worker wages by sex and occupation, and benefits, for 22 MSAs, Oct 1981 survey, 6787–6.201

Housing unit starts and completions authorized by building permits in 20 MSAs, quarterly rpt, 2382–9

Housing vacancy rates for single and multifamily units and mobile homes, by county, city, and ZIP code, 1983, annual SMSA rpt, 9304–22.1

Housing water conservation programs and savings of water and energy, for selected cities and suburbs, 1980-83, 5188–109

Income assistance, effects of experimental negative income tax program on employment, earnings, marital status, and other family characteristics in 2 cities, 1970-75, 4008–64

Population size of top 25 cities, 1980 and 1982, press release, 2328–46

Repair technicians and apprentices wages and benefits, for 5 types of electrical repair shops in 19 SMSAs, Nov 1981 survey, 6787–6.197

Wages by occupation, and benefits for office and plant workers, 1983 SMSA survey rpt, 6785–12.5

see also under By City and By SMSA or MSA in the "Index by Categories"

Denver County, Colo.

Arson investigation and prosecution, by incident characteristics and outcome, motive, and type of evidence, for 4 jurisdictions, 1981, 6068–184

Department of Agriculture

Activities and programs of USDA, by subagency, FY83, annual rpt, 1004–3

Agricultural research and extension program needs, and foreign and US supply/demand indicators by commodity and world area, 1950s-2020, 1008–47

Agricultural Stabilization and Conservation Service payment-in-kind acreage reduction program, ineligible participants and acreage, and estimated incorrect payments, by State and selected county, 1983, 1008–46

Agricultural Statistics, 1983, annual rpt, 1004–1

Agriculture Fact Book of US, compilation of data for 1983 with trends from 1940, annual rpt, 1004–14

Budget of US Appendix, detailed budgets and personnel summaries, by agency, FY85, annual rpt, 104–3

Budget of US, appropriations, outlays, balances, and budget receipts, by govtl branch and agency, FY83, annual rpt, 8104–2

Budget of US, compact budgets by function, agency, and account, FY85 with projections to FY89, annual rpt, 104–2

Budget of US, object class analysis of obligations, by branch of Fed Govt and selected depts and agencies, FY85 estimates, annual rpt, 104–9

Cost control proposals for Fed Govt programs and mgmt, 3-year savings by function and agency, and financial and operating data, 1960s-81, 16908–1, 16908–1.2

Digestive Diseases Interagency Coordinating Committee activities, and related Federal research and funding, by agency, FY79-83, annual rpt, 4434–13

DOD prime contract awards for R&D to educational and nonprofit instns and Federal agencies, by instn and location, FY83, annual listing, 3544–17

Employment (civilian) of Fed Govt, by location, agency, and pay system, 1982, biennial rpt, 9844–8

Farm finance and credit conditions, forecast 1984, conf papers, annual rpt, 1004–16

Foreign cargo shipments and costs of Fed Govt by agency or program and route, and employment and economic impacts of US vessel preference, 1980, GAO rpt, 26117–30

Index by Subjects and Names

Foreign Service positions and union membership by agency, grievances, and pay rates, FY81-83 with ambassador appointments from 1961, GAO rpt, 26123–64

Fraud and abuse in USDA programs, audits and investigations, 2nd half FY84, semiannual rpt, 1002–4

Publications of USDA, annual listing, suspended, 1004–13

R&D and science-related Fed Govt funding to higher education and nonprofit instns, by field, instn, agency, and State, FY82, annual rpt, 9627–17

R&D Fed Govt funding, by function, agency, and program, selected years FY80-84 and proposed FY85, 26308–46

R&D Fed Govt funding for all performers, by field and supporting agency, selected years FY60-84, annual rpt, 9627–20

Space and aeronautics programs and budgets of Fed Govt by agency, and foreign programs, 1957-FY85, annual rpt, 9504–9

Wilderness Preservation Natl System acreage, by natl forest, wilderness and primitive area, and State, 1983, annual rpt, 5304–14

see also Agricultural Cooperative Service

see also Agricultural Marketing Service

see also Agricultural Research Service

see also Agricultural Stabilization and Conservation Service

see also Animal and Plant Health Inspection Service

see also Commodity Credit Corp.

see also Cooperative State Research Service

see also Crop Reporting Board

see also Economic Research Service

see also Farmers Home Administration

see also Federal Crop Insurance Corp.

see also Federal Grain Inspection Service

see also Food and Nutrition Service

see also Food Safety and Inspection Service

see also Foreign Agricultural Service

see also Forest Service

see also Human Nutrition Information Service

see also Office of Transportation, USDA

see also Packers and Stockyards Administration

see also Rural Electrification Administration

see also Soil Conservation Service

see also Statistical Reporting Service

see also under By Federal Agency in the "Index by Categories"

Department of Air Force

Agent Orange exposed Air Force personnel diseases and disorders, by disease type, age, and officer status, 1984 rpt, 3604–3

Aircraft (B-1B) program of Air Force, procurement and operating costs by component, and personnel, alternative projections FY85-89, GAO rpt, 26123–79

Aircraft (C-5 and C-17 cargo) dimensions and operating characteristics, 1983, GAO rpt, 26123–81

Budget of DOD, expenditures for each service branch and total defense agencies, by function and State, FY85, annual rpt, 3544–23

Budget of DOD, itemized account of legislative history, FY84, annual rpt, 3504–7

Index by Subjects and Names

Department of Army

Budget of DOD, justification for procurement programs, by equipment type, service branch, and defense agency, FY83-86, annual rpt, 3504–14

Budget of DOD, justification for R&D programs, by item, service branch, and defense agency, FY83-86, annual rpt, 3504–15

Commercial activities of DOD under contract and performed in-house, costs and work-years, by service branch, defense agency, State, and installation, FY83, annual rpt, 3544–25

Construction and renovation of military bases, DOD budget authorization requests, by DOD component, State, country, and project, FY85, annual rpt, 3544–15

Cost control proposals for Fed Govt programs and mgmt, 3-year savings by function and agency, and financial and operating data, 1960s-81, 16908–1.20

Electric power plants and major fuel-burning facilities of DOD conversion from oil and gas, fuel use data, 1983, annual rpt, 3104–9

Employment (civilian) of DOD, by service branch and defense agency, with summary military employment data, monthly rpt, 3542–16

Employment (civilian) of Fed Govt, by location, agency, and pay system, 1982, biennial rpt, 9844–8

Employment (civilian and military) of DOD, by State, service branch, and major installation, as of Sept 1983, annual rpt, 3544–7

Fiscal mgmt system operations and techniques, info for Air Force Comptroller personnel, quarterly rpt, 3602–1

Foreign military training of US, students, costs, and revenue losses from reduced tuition by country, by service branch, FY79-83, GAO rpt, 26123–56

Judge Advocates General activities, cases and court actions, FY83, annual rpt, 3504–3

Missile experimental (MX) procurement funding, and contract awards by company, FY84 with procurement projections to FY89, GAO rpt, 26123–75

Missile experimental (MX) procurement progress and costs, various dates 1979-83 and projected to 1990, GAO rpt, 26123–74

Outlays and obligations of DOD, by function and service branch, quarterly rpt, 3542–3

Procurement, DOD prime contract awards by category, contract and contractor type, and service branch, FY74-1st half FY84, semiannual rpt, 3542–1

Procurement, DOD prime contract awards by individual contractor, service branch, State and city, and country, FY83, annual listing, 3544–22

Procurement, DOD prime contract awards by size, dept, and type of contract, FY83, annual rpt, 3544–19

Procurement, DOD prime contract awards by type, service branch and command, and for Defense Logistics Agency, last week compared to total year FY83, 108–38

Procurement, DOD prime contract awards for military and civil functions, by State, 1st half FY84, semiannual rpt, 3542–5

Procurement, DOD prime contract awards in labor surplus areas, by service branch, State, and area, 1st half FY84, semiannual rpt, 3542–19

Procurement, DOD prime contract awards to small and total business, for 10 categories and R&D, monthly rpt, 3542–10

Procurement of identical items from multiple sources by DOD, and price difference by item, by service branch, FY81, GAO rpt, 26123–67

Procurement, subcontract awards by DOD contractors to small and disadvantaged business, by firm and service branch, quarterly listing, 3542–17

Property, supplies, and equipment inventory of DOD, by service branch, 1983, annual rpt, 3544–6

Weapons and communications systems cost estimates, by service branch, quarterly summary rpt, 3502–1

Weapons and support systems costs under multiyear and annual procurement methods for 12 items in FY85 budget, by service branch, 1984 GAO rpt, 26123–83

Weapons system procurement cost estimate changes, and program delays and mgmt, by system and service branch, 1983, annual rpt, 26304–5

see also Air Force

see also Service academies

see also terms beginning with Defense and with Military

Department of Army

Budget of DOD, expenditures for each service branch and total defense agencies, by function and State, FY85, annual rpt, 3544–23

Budget of DOD, itemized account of legislative history, FY84, annual rpt, 3504–7

Budget of DOD, justification for procurement programs, by equipment type, service branch, and defense agency, FY83-86, annual rpt, 3504–14

Budget of DOD, justification for R&D programs, by item, service branch, and defense agency, FY83-86, annual rpt, 3504–15

Commercial activities of DOD under contract and performed in-house, costs and work-years, by service branch, defense agency, State, and installation, FY83, annual rpt, 3544–25

Construction and renovation of military bases, DOD budget authorization requests, by DOD component, State, country, and project, FY85, annual rpt, 3544–15

Cost control proposals for Fed Govt programs and mgmt, 3-year savings by function and agency, and financial and operating data, 1960s-81, 16908–1.18

Electric power plants and major fuel-burning facilities of DOD conversion from oil and gas, fuel use data, 1983, annual rpt, 3104–9

Employment (civilian) of DOD, by service branch and defense agency, with summary military employment data, monthly rpt, 3542–16

Employment (civilian) of Fed Govt, by location, agency, and pay system, 1982, biennial rpt, 9844–8

Employment (civilian) wartime needs of Army, status of installation mobilization and staff plans, 1982-83, GAO rpt, 26123–82

Employment (civilian and military) of DOD, by State, service branch, and major installation, as of Sept 1983, annual rpt, 3544–7

Foreign military training of US, students, costs, and revenue losses from reduced tuition by country, by service branch, FY79-83, GAO rpt, 26123–56

Health status of Army personnel, and use of Army medical services in US and abroad by personnel, retirees, and dependents, monthly rpt, 3702–4

Judge Advocates General activities, cases and court actions, FY83, annual rpt, 3504–3

Morale, welfare, and recreation programs, revenue and expenses worldwide, by activity and major command, FY82-83, annual rpt, 3704–12

Natl Guard (Army and Air) activities, manpower, and facilities, FY83, annual rpt, 3704–3

Outlays and obligations of DOD, by function and service branch, quarterly rpt, 3542–3

Procurement, DOD prime contract awards by category, contract and contractor type, and service branch, FY74-1st half FY84, semiannual rpt, 3542–1

Procurement, DOD prime contract awards by individual contractor, service branch, State and city, and country, FY83, annual listing, 3544–22

Procurement, DOD prime contract awards by size, dept, and type of contract, FY83, annual rpt, 3544–19

Procurement, DOD prime contract awards by type, service branch and command, and for Defense Logistics Agency, last week compared to total year FY83, 108–38

Procurement, DOD prime contract awards for military and civil functions, by State, 1st half FY84, semiannual rpt, 3542–5

Procurement, DOD prime contract awards in labor surplus areas, by service branch, State, and area, 1st half FY84, semiannual rpt, 3542–19

Procurement, DOD prime contract awards to small and total business, for 10 categories and R&D, monthly rpt, 3542–10

Procurement of identical items from multiple sources by DOD, and price difference by item, by service branch, FY81, GAO rpt, 26123–67

Procurement, subcontract awards by DOD contractors to small and disadvantaged business, by firm and service branch, quarterly listing, 3542–17

Property, supplies, and equipment inventory of DOD, by service branch, 1983, annual rpt, 3544–6

Shipments by DOD of military and personal property, loss claims, passenger traffic, and costs, by mode of transport, quarterly rpt, 3702–1

Department of Army

War reserve and excess item inventory of Army, 1982, GAO rpt, 26123–58
Weapons and communications systems cost estimates, by service branch, quarterly summary rpt, 3502–1
Weapons and support systems costs under multiyear and annual procurement methods for 12 items in FY85 budget, by service branch, 1984 GAO rpt, 26123–83
Weapons system procurement cost estimate changes, and program delays and mgmt, by system and service branch, 1983, annual rpt, 26304–5
see also Army
see also Army Corps of Engineers
see also National guard
see also Reserve Officers Training Corps
see also Service academies
see also terms beginning with Defense and with Military

Department of Commerce

Auto industry finances and operations by manufacturer, foreign competition, and consumer auto expenditures and attitudes toward car buying, selected years 1968-85, annual rpt, 2004–8
Budget of US Appendix, detailed budgets and personnel summaries, by agency, FY85, annual rpt, 104–3
Budget of US, appropriations, outlays, balances, and budget receipts, by govtl branch and agency, FY83, annual rpt, 8104–2
Budget of US, compact budgets by function, agency, and account, FY85 with projections to FY89, annual rpt, 104–2
Budget of US, object class analysis of obligations, by branch of Fed Govt and selected depts and agencies, FY85 estimates, annual rpt, 104–9
Budgets and permanent staff positions appropriated for Commerce Dept agencies, FY84-85, annual rpt, 2004–6
Cost control proposals for Fed Govt programs and mgmt, 3-year savings by function and agency, and financial and operating data, 1960s-81, 16908–1, 16908–1.3
DOD prime contract awards for R&D to educational and nonprofit instns and Federal agencies, by instn and location, FY83, annual listing, 3544–17
Employment (civilian) of Fed Govt, by location, agency, and pay system, 1982, biennial rpt, 9844–8
Energy supply/demand projections, by energy source and end use, series, 2006–2
Foreign Service positions and union membership by agency, grievances, and pay rates, FY81-83 with ambassador appointments from 1961, GAO rpt, 26123–64
Fraud and abuse in Commerce Dept programs, audits and investigations, 2nd half FY84, semiannual rpt, 2002–5
Mgmt assistance operations of Commerce Dept regional centers, assessment, and procurement authority, by subagency, regional rpt series, 2006–4
Programs, funding, and employment of Commerce Dept agencies, FY83, annual rpt, 2004–1
Publications of Commerce Dept, annual listing, discontinued, 2004–4

Publications of Commerce Dept, with economic indicator performance from 1961, biweekly listing, 2002–1
R&D and science-related Fed Govt funding to higher education and nonprofit instns, by field, instn, agency, and State, FY82, annual rpt, 9627–17
R&D Fed Govt funding, by function, agency, and program, selected years FY80-84 and proposed FY85, 26308–46
R&D Fed Govt funding for all performers, by field and supporting agency, selected years FY60-84, annual rpt, 9627–20
Space and aeronautics programs and budgets of Fed Govt by agency, and foreign programs, 1957-FY85, annual rpt, 9504–9
see also Bureau of Census
see also Bureau of Economic Analysis
see also Bureau of Industrial Economics
see also Economic Development Administration
see also International Trade Administration
see also Minority Business Development Agency
see also National Bureau of Standards
see also National Environmental Satellite, Data, and Information Service
see also National Marine Fisheries Service
see also National Ocean Service
see also National Oceanic and Atmospheric Administration
see also National Technical Information Service
see also National Telecommunications and Information Administration
see also National Weather Service
see also Patent and Trademark Office
see also U.S. Travel and Tourism Administration
see also under By Federal Agency in the "Index by Categories"

Department of Defense

Accounting mgmt of DOD procurement revolving fund, costs and cost carryovers by cause and activity site, FY82-83, GAO rpt, 26111–22
Aides to officers, enlisted personnel authorized and assigned to perform personal services by race and sex, and program costs, by service branch, 1982-83, GAO rpt, 26123–53
Aircraft for DOD noncombat use, costs, Navy and Air Force requirements, and Navy losses, by aircraft type, selected years FY73-86, hearing, 21408–76
Base support costs by function, and personnel and acreage by installation, by service branch, FY85, annual rpt, 3504–11
Budget of DOD, itemized account of legislative history, FY84, annual rpt, 3504–7
Budget of DOD, justification for procurement programs, by equipment type, service branch, and defense agency, FY83-86, annual rpt, 3504–14
Budget of DOD, justification for R&D programs, and acquisition mgmt, FY83-85, annual rpt, 3504–6
Budget of DOD, justification for R&D programs, by item, service branch, and defense agency, FY83-86, annual rpt, 3504–15

Index by Subjects and Names

Budget of DOD, justification, programs, and policies, FY85, annual rpt, 3544–2
Budget of DOD, organization, personnel, weapons, and property, by service branch, State, and country, 1984 annual summary rpt, 3504–13
Budget of US Appendix, detailed budgets and personnel summaries, by agency, FY85, annual rpt, 104–3
Budget of US, appropriations, outlays, balances, and budget receipts, by govtl branch and agency, FY83, annual rpt, 8104–2
Budget of US, compact budgets by function, agency, and account, FY85 with projections to FY89, annual rpt, 104–2
Budget of US, object class analysis of obligations, by branch of Fed Govt and selected depts and agencies, FY85 estimates, annual rpt, 104–9
Civilian Health and Medical Program of the Uniformed Services costs and operations, FY83-84 with trends from FY79, semiannual rpt, 3502–2
Commercial activities of DOD under contract and performed in-house, costs and work-years, by service branch, defense agency, State, and installation, FY83, annual rpt, 3544–25
Commercial activities of Fed Govt, savings from performance under contract over in-house, with DOD costs, employees displaced, and small business awards, by service branch, FY81-82, 108–39
Construction and renovation of military bases, DOD budget authorization requests, by DOD component, State, country, and project, FY85, annual rpt, 3544–15
Cost control proposals for Fed Govt programs and mgmt, 3-year savings by function and agency, and financial and operating data, 1960s-81, 16908–1
Defense activity indicators, *Business Conditions Digest,* historical supplement and methodology, 1947-82, 2708–31
Defense activity indicators, *Business Conditions Digest,* monthly rpt, 2702–3.8
Dependents Schools students higher education admission tests scores by sex and subject, and educational goals and attitudes, 1983, annual rpt, 3504–17
Dependents Schools 1st grader basic skills test scores, by world area and English fluency, fall 1983, annual rpt, 3504–18
Digestive Diseases Interagency Coordinating Committee activities, and related Federal research and funding, by agency, FY79-83, annual rpt, 4434–13
Electric power plants and major fuel-burning facilities of DOD conversion from oil and gas, and fuel use data, 1983, annual rpt, 3104–9
Employment (civilian) of DOD, by service branch and defense agency, with summary military employment data, monthly rpt, 3542–16
Employment (civilian) of Fed Govt, by location, agency, and pay system, 1982, biennial rpt, 9844–8
Employment (civilian and military) of DOD, by State, service branch, and major installation, as of Sept 1983, annual rpt, 3544–7

Index by Subjects and Names

Employment, earnings, and hours, by level and branch of govt, and function, monthly 1977-Feb 1984, annual update, 6744–4

Foreign cargo shipments and costs of Fed Govt by agency or program and route, and employment and economic impacts of US vessel preference, 1980, GAO rpt, 26117–30

Intl exchange and training programs of Fed Govt, participants by world region, and funding, by agency, FY83, annual rpt, 9854–8

Investigations of DOD operations, summaries of GAO rpts published 1979-83, annual rpt, 26104–6

Judge Advocates General activities, cases and court actions, FY83, annual rpt, 3504–3

Latin America students in US and Soviet bloc training programs, by program type and student country, and summary by world region, selected years 1972-82, GAO rpt, 26123–77

Manpower requirements and cost estimates, DOD budget detailed analysis, FY85, annual rpt, 3504–1

Manpower statistics on active duty, civilian, and reserve personnel, by service branch, monthly rpt, 3542–14

Manpower statistics on active duty, civilian, and retired personnel and dependents, FY83 and historical, annual rpt, 3544–1

Manufacturers under Fed Govt contract and owned by DOD, operating data by agency, selected SIC 2- to 4-digit industry, State, and SMSA, 1982, annual Current Industrial Rpt, 2506–3.4

Marijuana cultivation control activity of State law enforcement agencies, and aid from Fed Govt and Natl Guard, 1983 survey, GAO rpt, 26119–64

Medical services for military, potential effects of alternative financing proposals on DOD costs, with service use and out-of-pocket medical costs by type of recipient, FY84-89, 26306–6.74

Military aid of US, arms sales, and training programs costs and budget requests by program, world region, and country, FY83-85, annual rpt, 7144–13

Missile experimental (MX) basing proposals of Reagan Admin, 1984 narrative rpt update, 3508–17

NATO military commitment of US, Europe force strengths by service branch and costs by component, FY82 with trends from FY75, GAO rpt, 26123–71

Post exchange operations, locations worldwide, sales by type of commodity or service and facility, and employment, FY83, annual rpt, 3504–10

Procurement, DOD prime contract awards by category, contract and contractor type, and service branch, FY74-1st half FY84, semiannual rpt, 3542–1

Procurement, DOD prime contract awards by individual contractor, service branch, State and city, and country, FY83, annual listing, 3544–22

Procurement, DOD prime contract awards by type, service branch and command, and for Defense Logistics Agency, last week compared to total year FY83, 108–38

Procurement, DOD prime contract awards for military and civil functions, by State, 1st half FY84, semiannual rpt, 3542–5

Procurement, DOD prime contract awards in labor surplus areas, by service branch, State, and area, 1st half FY84, semiannual rpt, 3542–19

Procurement of identical items from multiple sources by DOD, and price difference by item, by service branch, FY81, GAO rpt, 26123–67

Property, supplies, and equipment inventory of DOD, by service branch, 1983, annual rpt, 3544–6

R&D and science-related Fed Govt funding to higher education and nonprofit instns, by field, instn, agency, and State, FY82, annual rpt, 9627–17

R&D Fed Govt funding, by function, agency, and program, selected years FY80-84 and proposed FY85, 26308–46

R&D Fed Govt funding for all performers, by field and supporting agency, selected years FY60-84, annual rpt, 9627–20

Science and engineering grad enrollment, fields of study, financial support, and other student and instn characteristics, 1975-82, annual survey, 9627–7

Soviet Union and Warsaw Pact military weapons systems, assistance and presence worldwide, and force strengths, with selected US and NATO comparisons, as of 1984, 3508–14

Space and aeronautics programs and budgets of Fed Govt by agency, and foreign programs, 1957-FY85, annual rpt, 9504–9

Space and related R&D program activities and funding of DOD, FY84-85, annual rpt, 3504–9

Strategic military capability, force strengths, weapons, training, supplies, and requirements, by service branch, FY80-84 and projected to 1990, 3508–19

Supply inventory and automated cataloging system of Fed Govt, and DOD mgmt of inventory items for agencies, NATO, and foreign govts, 1970s-83, annual rpt, 21204–1

Training and education programs of DOD, funding, staff, students, and facilities, by service branch and reserve component, FY85, annual rpt, 3504–5

Weapons and communications systems cost estimates, by service branch, quarterly summary rpt, 3502–1

Weapons and support systems costs under multiyear and annual procurement methods for 12 items in FY85 budget, by service branch, 1984 GAO rpt, 26123–83

Weapons budget of DOD, costs of individual weapons or systems, FY83-85, annual rpt, 3504–2

Weapons system procurement cost estimate changes, and program delays and mgmt, by system and service branch, 1983, annual rpt, 26304–5

Weapons system procurement cost estimates, DOD methodology for rpts to Congress, with illustrative data and bibl, 1970s-83, GAO rpt, 26123–62

Weapons systems budget of DOD, FY85 requests consistency with US policy and specified treaties, with funding FY83-87, annual rpt, 21384–4

Department of Education

Weapons systems cost underestimation in DOD budget request 5-year plans, and cost change by system, various periods FY79-89, GAO rpt, 26123–68

see also Armed services
see also Army Corps of Engineers
see also Court of Military Appeals
see also Defense agencies
see also Defense Communications Agency
see also Defense Contract Audit Agency
see also Defense Intelligence Agency
see also Defense Logistics Agency
see also Defense Mapping Agency
see also Defense Nuclear Agency
see also Defense Security Assistance Agency
see also Department of Air Force
see also Department of Army
see also Department of Navy
see also Joint Chiefs of Staff
see also Marine Corps
see also National Security Agency
see also Office of the Secretary of Defense
see also under By Federal Agency in the "Index by Categories"

Department of Education

Bilingual education programs, teachers, enrollment, and funding, selected years 1976-FY83, biennial rpt, 4804–14

Bilingual vocational training projects, participants, characteristics, and costs, by program, FY82, annual rpt, 4804–26

Budget of US Appendix, detailed budgets and personnel summaries, by agency, FY85, annual rpt, 104–3

Budget of US, appropriations, outlays, balances, and budget receipts, by govtl branch and agency, FY83, annual rpt, 8104–2

Budget of US, compact budgets by function, agency, and account, FY85 with projections to FY89, annual rpt, 104–2

Budget of US, object class analysis of obligations, by branch of Fed Govt and selected depts and agencies, FY85 estimates, annual rpt, 104–9

Civil rights enforcement offices funding and staff, for 6 Federal agencies, FY80-84, 11048–179

Cost control proposals for Fed Govt programs and mgmt, 3-year savings by function and agency, and financial and operating data, 1960s-81, 16908–1.5

Education statistics summary compilation, 1980/81-1982/83 with selected trends from 1869, biennial rpt, 4804–27

Elementary and secondary education, factors affecting State expenditures, and tuition tax credits effects on parents choice of public or private school, 1960-82 with some projections to 2000, 4808–9

Employment (civilian) of Fed Govt, by location, agency, and pay system, 1982, biennial rpt, 9844–8

Enrollment and teacher employment in all schools, by grade level and instn control, fall 1983-84, annual press release, 4804–19

Fed Govt educational grants, State allocations by program, type of recipient agency, and State, FY83, annual rpt, 4804–8

Financial aid programs of Education Dept for instns and individuals, 1984 annual listing, 4804–3

Department of Education

Fraud and abuse in Education Dept programs, audits and investigations, 2nd half FY84, semiannual rpt, 4802–1

Handicapped children early education research and service project activities and characteristics, and grants to States for program dev, 1983-84, annual listing, 4804–30

Higher education minority student enrollment, by State, instn, race or ethnic group, and sex, biennial rpt, discontinued, 4804–23

Impacted area schools, Fed Govt funding by county and school and congressional district, and eligible pupils, by State, FY83, annual rpt, 4804–10

Indian Education Act grants to local agencies, Education Dept audit results by region, FY82, annual rpt, 4804–29

Indian education program operations, funding, student progress measures, and opinions of school staff, parents, and students, selected years 1973-83, 4808–13

Intl exchange and training programs of Fed Govt, participants by world region, and funding, by agency, FY83, annual rpt, 9854–8

Library (research) funding of Education Dept, by project, program area, instn, and State, FY84, annual listing, 4804–22

Library and instructional materials acquisitions, and testing and guidance, State expenditures under ESEA Title IV-B, annual rpt, discontinued, 4804–12

Programs and activities of Education Dept, FY83, annual rpt, 4804–6

Programs of Education Dept, funding, operations, and effectiveness, FY83, annual rpt, 4804–5

R&D and science-related Fed Govt funding to higher education and nonprofit instns, by field, instn, agency, and State, FY82, annual rpt, 9627–17

R&D Fed Govt funding for all performers, by field and supporting agency, selected years FY60-84, annual rpt, 9627–20

Refugee resettlement program activities and funding, arrivals and population by country of origin and State, and employment and other characteristics, FY83, annual rpt, 4704–8

School crime, assaults and robberies of teachers and minority and all students, and vandalism incidents, 1976/77, biennial rpt, 4808–12

Student aid basic grant, loan, and work-study awards, Fed Govt share by instn and State, 1984/85, annual rpt, 4804–17

Student aid Federal programs funding and participation, by instn type and control, State, and outlying area, with student loan defaults and collections, FY82, annual rpt, 4804–28

Student aid need-based program funding, and State Student Incentive Grant funding, recipients, and average income and award, by State, FY67-82, GAO rpt, 26121–69

Student aid Pell grants and recipients, by educational costs, family income, instnl type and control, and State, 1981/82, annual rpt, 4804–1

see also National Assessment of Educational Progress

see also National Center for Education Statistics

see also National Institute of Education

see also Office of Special Education and Rehabilitative Services

Department of Energy

Accidents, deaths, illnesses, radiation exposure, and property damage, by DOE and contractor facility, 1982, annual rpt, 3004–24

Air pollutant emission effects of solar and biomass energy use, by region, and projected to 2000, 3408–30

Budget appropriations proposed for Fed Govt energy programs, by office or dept and function, FY84-85, annual rpt, 3004–14

Budget of US Appendix, detailed budgets and personnel summaries, by agency, FY85, annual rpt, 104–3

Budget of US, appropriations, outlays, balances, and budget receipts, by govtl branch and agency, FY83, annual rpt, 8104–2

Budget of US, compact budgets by function, agency, and account, FY85 with projections to FY89, annual rpt, 104–2

Budget of US, object class analysis of obligations, by branch of Fed Govt and selected depts and agencies, FY85 estimates, annual rpt, 104–9

Carbon dioxide emissions from fossil fuel combustion by fuel type, worldwide estimates based on total and non-oxidized fossil fuel production, 1950-81, 3008–94

Coal production, mining employment, exports, and finances, by coal district, 1982, 3008–97

Coal purchases of Fed Govt, quality control analyses by mine and location, FY82-83, annual rpt, 3004–15

Cost control proposals for Fed Govt programs and mgmt, 3-year savings by function and agency, and financial and operating data, 1960s-81, 16908–1, 16908–1.4

Electric power plant capacity, by plant type, age, and DOE region, 1982, and new and replacement capacity trends and projections, 1900-2020, 3008–98

Employment (civilian) of Fed Govt, by location, agency, and pay system, 1982, biennial rpt, 9844–8

Energy supply/demand and prices, by energy source and end-use sector and for 7 electric utilities, 1981-2000 with trends from 1960s, 3008–93

Energy supply/demand, prices, end use, and related technical and socioeconomic data, including impacts of US policy and intl devs, series, 3006–7

Energy use, conservation investments, and savings, for DOE in-house use, by type of use and fuel and field office, FY83, annual rpt, 3024–3

Finances and mgmt of DOE programs, audits and investigations, series, 3006–5

Foreign cargo shipments and costs of Fed Govt by agency or program and route, and employment and economic impacts of US vessel preference, 1980, GAO rpt, 26117–30

Index by Subjects and Names

Fraud and abuse in DOE programs, audits and investigations, 2nd half FY84, semiannual rpt, 3002–12

Industrial electric power cogeneration in 5 industries, and fuel use and utility supply/demand effects, by region, 1983-93, 3008–92

Industrial electric power demand model estimates, economic indicators, and supporting data for 5 industries, 1960s-80 with projections to 2000, 3008–87

Inventions recommended by Natl Bur of Standards for possible DOE support, with DOE evaluation status, 1984, annual listing, 2214–5

Manpower devs and studies for energy-related fields, series, 3006–8

Manufacturers under Fed Govt contract and owned by DOD, operating data by agency, selected SIC 2- to 4-digit industry, State, and SMSA, 1982, annual Current Industrial Rpt, 2506–3.4

Natl Energy Policy Plan, energy supply, demand, and prices, by fuel and consuming sector, projected 1985-2010, biennial rpt, 3004–13

Natural gas prices, reserves, consumption, and production, projected under alternative price controls 1983-95 with market data for various periods 1970-Mar 1984, 3008–96

Natural gas production and trade by State, and underground storage changes, EIA estimates based on alternative data sources, 1980-81, 3008–90

Naval Petroleum and Oil Shale Reserves production, dev, ownership, leasing, sales by purchaser, and Fed Govt revenues, by site, FY83, annual rpt, 3004–22

Nuclear engineering student enrollments and degrees granted, by State, instn, and subfield, and placements by sector, 1983, annual rpt, 3004–5

Nuclear industry nongovt employment by industry segment, occupation, and census div, and DOE and NRC nuclear employment, 1968-83, biennial rpt, 3004–11

Nuclear power and weapons policy, fuel supply/demand, waste disposal and siting, environmental effects of radiation, and public attitudes, 1970s-82 with projections to 2000, 3008–88

Nuclear power plant spent fuel permanent disposal site and transport costs, and Nuclear Waste Fund financing, alternative projections FY83-2037, 26308–49

Nuclear reactors for domestic use and export by function, with owner, operating characteristics, and location, Apr 1984, semiannual listing, 3002–5

Nuclear strategic materials, inventory discrepancies at DOE facilities, 1st half FY83, semiannual rpt, 3002–4

Oil price and allocation regulations enforcement by DOE, and overcharge allegations, settlements, and refunds to States, by company, as of June 1983, hearing, 21368–50

Oil product surveys, lab analyses of aviation, heating, diesel, and gasoline fuel properties, last issues of annual and semiannual rpt series, 3006–2

Procurement and assistance contracts of DOE, by State, contractor type, and 100 top instns, FY83, annual rpt, 3004–21

Index by Subjects and Names

Publications of DOE and other sources, monthly listing, 3002–2

R&D and science and engineering education related to energy, DOE and DOE natl labs aid to selected higher education instns, 1960s-84, 3008–89

R&D and science-related Fed Govt funding to higher education and nonprofit instns, by field, instn, agency, and State, FY82, annual rpt, 9627–17

R&D Fed Govt funding, by function, agency, and program, selected years FY80-84 and proposed FY85, 26308–46

R&D Fed Govt funding for all performers, by field and supporting agency, selected years FY60-84, annual rpt, 9627–20

R&D field facility resources, activities, personnel, and finances, by DOE facility, annual rpt, suspended, 3004–4

R&D projects and funding of DOE at natl labs, universities, and other instns, annual summary rpts, 3004–18

Radiation exposure at DOE-contractor nuclear facilities and for surrounding population, and pollutant releases by type, by site, 1982, annual rpt, 3004–23

Radiation protection and health physics enrollments and degrees granted by State and instn, and grads employment, 1983, annual rpt, 3004–7

Scientists and engineers employed in energy-related fields, supply/demand and effects of R&D funding, by energy type, employer type, field, and age, 1962-91, annual rpt, 3004–19

Scientists and engineers in R&D, salaries by degree, type of establishment, age, experience, and field, 1984, annual rpt, 3004–1

Scientists and engineers in R&D, salary comparisons for DOE labs and non-DOE facilities, Aug 1982-Feb 1984, annual rpt, 3004–9

Scientists and engineers with doctorates engaged in energy-related work, demographic and employment characteristics by field, biennial rpt, suspended, 3004–2

Space and aeronautics programs and budgets of Fed Govt by agency, and foreign programs, 1957-FY85, annual rpt, 9504–9

Strategic Petroleum Reserve activities and funding, by supplier and site, quarterly GAO rpt, 26102–3

Strategic Petroleum Reserve capacity, inventory, fill rate, and finances, quarterly rpt, 3002–13

Strategic Petroleum Reserve operational status, capacities, funding, and costs, by site, 1983, annual rpt, 3004–20

Strategic Petroleum Reserve operational status, funding, and technical evaluation, 1983 rpt, 3008–91

Uranium reserves and mining and milling industries operations and finances, with selected foreign comparisons, various periods 1964-83 and projected to 2000, 3008–95

see also Alaska Power Administration

see also Bonneville Power Administration

see also Department of Energy: Civilian Radioactive Waste Management

see also Department of Energy: Conservation and Renewable Energy

Department of Energy: International Affairs and Energy Emergencies

see also Department of Energy: International Affairs and Energy Emergencies

see also Department of Energy: Nuclear Energy

see also Economic Regulatory Administration

see also Energy Information Administration

see also Federal Energy Regulatory Commission

see also Office of the Secretary of Energy

see also Southeastern Power Administration

see also Southwestern Power Administration

see also Western Area Power Administration

see also under By Federal Agency in the "Index by Categories"

Department of Energy: Civilian Radioactive Waste Management

Idaho Natl Engineering Lab radiation monitoring results, for 4 onsite facilities and nearby areas, 1983, annual rpt, 3354–10

Nuclear Waste Fund obligations by function and receipts, and DOE Civilian Radioactive Mgmt Office activities and staff, quarterly GAO rpt, 26102–4

Radioactive waste mgmt activities and financing of office, FY83-85, annual rpt, 3364–1

Spent fuel and radioactive waste generation, inventory, disposal by site, reprocessing, and characteristics, by source, as of 1983 and projected to 2020, annual rpt, 3364–2

Department of Energy: Conservation and Renewable Energy

Auto engine and power train R&D projects, DOE contracts and funding by recipient, FY83, annual rpt, 3304–17

Auto fuel economy test results for models complying with California emission standards, 1984 model year, annual rpt, 3304–13

Auto fuel economy test results, 1985 model year, annual rpt, 3304–11

Biomass energy from straw- and manure-fed methane generator, research project technical characteristics, annual rpt, discontinued, 3304–14

Connecticut utility group housing energy conservation program, cost effectiveness and characteristics of participants and nonparticipants, 1980-82, 3308–77

Conservation aid of DOE, activities, funding, and grants by State, by program, FY84, annual rpt, 3304–21

Conservation grants of Fed Govt to public and nonprofit private instns, by building type and State, 1983, annual rpt, 3304–15

Energy consumption, prices and price indexes, and efficiency measures, by fuel type and end-use sector, annual rpt, 3304–19

Energy demand in industry, forecasting model description, detailed technology specifications, and energy use, for 27 SIC 2- to 4-digit industries, 1970s-80 and projected to 2000, 3308–66

Energy use and efficiency of Fed Govt, by agency and fuel type, FY83, annual rpt, 3304–22

Gasohol and ethanol plant capacity and production, tax exemptions and sales by State, and prices, 1983, annual rpt, 3304–9

Housing (earth-sheltered) design, energy efficiency, natural and nuclear hazard reduction, and costs, by selected SMSA, 1983 rpt, 3308–71

Housing (multifamily rental) energy use and costs, conservation effect on rental marketing, and effect of utility bill payment methods on conservation efforts, 1970s-80s, 3308–73

Housing electricity and gas costs for 306 cities, by utility, with climatological data, fall 1982, 3308–67

Housing electricity use and savings, methodology for assessment using utility billing data, 1984 rpt, 3308–76

Housing energy conservation devices installation, utility loan program cost effectiveness, and household participation characteristics, Minnesota study, 1980-83, 3308–72

Housing energy conservation programs of utilities, actual and predicted gas savings by conservation measure, Minnesota study, 1980-83, 3308–74

Housing energy conservation programs of utilities, financing, costs, participation, and energy savings, various periods 1981-84, hearing, 21368–54

Housing energy conservation programs of utilities under natl conservation act, cost effectiveness and participating household characteristics, 1980s, 3308–69

Hydrogen energy R&D activities of DOE, and description and funding of 24 projects, FY83, annual rpt, 3304–18

Manufacturing energy efficiency progress, and energy use by type, by SIC 2-digit industry, 1982, annual rpt, 3304–8

Motor vehicles powered by electricity, Fed Govt dev program implementation, with bibl, FY83, annual rpt, 3304–2

Oil refineries financial and operating impacts from auto use of alcohol fuels, projected to 2000 with trends 1964-80, 3308–75

Solar photovoltaic system R&D sponsored by DOE, project descriptions and publications, FY83, annual listing, 3304–20

State govt energy conservation programs, Fed Govt financial and technical aid, and reported energy savings, by State, 1983, annual rpt, 3304–1

Transportation energy use by mode, fuel supplies, and demographic and economic determinants of vehicle use, 1970s-83, annual rpt, 3304–5

Trucks (heavy) energy use, efficiency, and conservation technologies, selected years 1958-82 and projected to 2000, 3308–70

Western US Fed Govt lands by agency and mining restriction status, and energy resources on potential wilderness areas and other lands, 1970s-81 and projected to 1990, 3308–68

Department of Energy: Environmental Protection, Safety and Emergency Preparedness

see Department of Energy

see Department of Energy: International Affairs and Energy Emergencies

Department of Energy: International Affairs and Energy Emergencies

Acid rain causes and effects, air pollutant emissions by source in US and selected countries, control costs, and Fed Govt research funding, 1960s-82, 3408–27

Department of Energy: International Affairs and Energy Emergencies

- Air pollutant sulfur dioxide emissions of coal-fired power plants in eastern US, effect of alternative geographic area limits on power and coal industries, 1983 rpt, 3408–32
- Air quality and transportation and related energy use, for urban areas and Chicago area, late 1970s-82 and projected under lower auto emission standards to 1995, 3408–31
- Carbon dioxide atmospheric levels, climatic effects and impacts of fossil and synthetic fuels use, deforestation, and land use patterns, research rpt series, 3406–3
- Coal transport environmental impacts by type and mode of transport, methodology for assessing alternative systems, 1983 rpt, 3408–28
- Electric power peak demand, generating and interregional transfer capability, and reserve margins, detailed data by region, 1984-93, annual rpt, 3404–6
- Naval Petroleum and Oil Shale Reserves production, dev, ownership, leasing, revenues, and Fed Govt sales revenue by purchaser, by site, annual rpt, 3404–10
- Oil enhanced recovery technologies use and environmental impacts, by oil field, county, and State, 1970s-80 and projected to 2000, 3408–29
- Radiation exposure at DOE and DOE-contractor sites, by facility type and contractor, 1982, annual rpt, 3404–1
- Radioactive contamination of former AEC and Manhattan Project research and storage sites, test results series, 3406–1
- Radioactive strontium fallout, monitoring results for 67 sites worldwide, quarterly 1976-82 with trends from 1958, annual rpt, 3404–12
- Radioactive strontium in NYC and San Francisco diet by food item, and in NYC tap water and milk, quarterly 1982 with trends from 1954, annual rpt, 3404–13
- Uranium reserves, exploration, production, and other industry data, annual rpt, discontinued, 3404–7

Department of Energy National Laboratories

- Budget of US, effects of Reagan Admin policy changes, by detailed program, FY85, annual rpt, 104–21
- Cost control proposals for Fed Govt programs and mgmt, 3-year savings by function and agency, and financial and operating data, 1960s-81, 16908–1.4
- DOD prime contract awards for R&D to educational and nonprofit instns and Federal agencies, by instn and location, FY83, annual listing, 3544–17
- Hydrogen energy R&D activities of DOE, and description and funding of 24 projects, FY83, annual rpt, 3304–18
- Idaho Natl Engineering Lab radiation monitoring results, for 4 onsite facilities and nearby areas, 1983, annual rpt, 3354–10
- Nuclear reactors for domestic use and export by function, with owner, operating characteristics, and location, Apr 1984, semiannual listing, 3002–5
- Nuclear strategic materials, inventory discrepancies at DOE facilities, 1st half FY83, semiannual rpt, 3002–4
- R&D and science and engineering education related to energy, DOE and DOE natl labs aid to selected higher education instns, 1960s-84, 3008–89

R&D and science-related Fed Govt funding to higher education and nonprofit instns, by field, instn, agency, and State, FY82, annual rpt, 9627–17

- R&D expenditures by higher education instns and federally funded centers, by field, source of funds, instn, and State, FY82, annual rpt, 9627–13
- R&D Fed Govt facilities and services available for private sector use, by field of science, 1984 biennial listing, 2224–4
- R&D projects and funding of DOE at natl labs, universities, and other instns, annual summary rpts, 3004–18
- Radiation exposure at DOE-contractor nuclear facilities and for surrounding population, and pollutant releases by type, by site, 1982, annual rpt, 3004–23
- Radioactive wastes from DOE defense facilities, interim storage inventories by site and permanent disposal plan costs, 1982 with projections to 2015, 3358–32
- Scientists and engineers employed at universities and colleges, by field, sex, State, and instn, Jan 1983 and selected trends from 1967, annual survey, 9627–11
- Scientists and engineers employed in energy-related fields, supply/demand and effects of R&D funding, by energy type, employer type, field, and age, 1962-91, annual rpt, 3004–19
- Scientists and engineers in R&D, salary comparisons for DOE labs and non-DOE facilities, Aug 1982-Feb 1984, annual rpt, 3004–9
- Technology transfer of Fed Govt R&D labs to public and private sector, labs complying with requirement, funding, and requests, by agency, FY82, GAO rpt, 26113–141

see also Federally Funded R&D Centers

Department of Energy: Nuclear Energy

- Nuclear power plant capacity, generation, shutdowns, operation status and costs, and fuel, quarterly rpt, 3352–3
- Radioactive wastes from DOE defense facilities, interim storage inventories by site and permanent disposal plan costs, 1982 with projections to 2015, 3358–32
- Reactors at central station power plants, operating status and other characteristics by plant, utility, and State, as of Jan 1984, annual rpt, 3354–11
- Safety standards and research, design, licensing, construction, operation, and finances, for nuclear power plants with data by reactor, bimonthly rpt, 3352–4
- Spent fuel from nuclear power plants and additional storage capacity required, by reactor, projected 1984-93, annual rpt, 3354–2
- Uranium enrichment facilities operations, finances, uranium stocks, and energy use and capital investment by facility, FY83, annual rpt, 3354–7
- Uranium enrichment prices of DOE under alternative TVA power rates, and effects of TVA charges for power not taken, FY84-95, GAO rpt, 26113–114
- Uranium ore tailings at inactive mills and DOE remedial action program activities by site, and program funding, FY84, annual rpt, 3354–9

Index by Subjects and Names

- Uranium resources research publications, 1976-83, listing, 3358–27

Department of Health and Human Services

- Black higher education instns, detailed info on instn characteristics and research, annual listing, discontinued, 4004–28
- Budget of US Appendix, detailed budgets and personnel summaries, by agency, FY85, annual rpt, 104–3
- Budget of US, appropriations, outlays, balances, and budget receipts, by govtl branch and agency, FY83, annual rpt, 8104–2
- Budget of US, compact budgets by function, agency, and account, FY85 with projections to FY89, annual rpt, 104–2
- Budget of US, object class analysis of obligations, by branch of Fed Govt and selected depts and agencies, FY85 estimates, annual rpt, 104–9
- Child Support Enforcement Program costs, cases, and collections, by State, FY82, semiannual rpt, 4002–5
- Child Support Enforcement Program costs, cases, and collections, by State, FY83, annual rpt, 4004–29
- Child Support Enforcement Program financial and operating data, FY79-83, annual rpt, 4004–16
- Civil rights enforcement offices funding and staff, for 6 Federal agencies, FY80-84, 11048–179
- Cost control proposals for Fed Govt programs and mgmt, 3-year savings by function and agency, and financial and operating data, 1960s-81, 16908–1, 16908–1.5
- Data projects and systems of HHS, by subagency, FY83-84, annual inventory, 4044–3
- Digestive Diseases Interagency Coordinating Committee activities, and related Federal research and funding, by agency, FY79-83, annual rpt, 4434–13
- DOD prime contract awards for R&D to educational and nonprofit instns and Federal agencies, by instn and location, FY83, annual listing, 3544–17
- Drug abuse prevalence and health consequences, and Natl Inst on Drug Abuse and other HHS prevention activities, FY82, annual rpt, 4004–26
- Employment (civilian) of Fed Govt, by location, agency, and pay system, 1982, biennial rpt, 9844–8
- Financial assistance to each State and local govt or private instn, amount obligated, funding agency, and program, FY83, annual listing, 4004–3
- Foster care children permanent placement, Fed Govt incentive program funding and operations in 7 States, FY80-82, GAO rpt, 26121–81
- Fraud and abuse in HHS programs, audits and investigations, 2nd half FY84, semiannual rpt, 4002–6
- Freedom of Info Act, requests to HHS received and denied, costs, and fees collected, 1983, annual rpt, 4004–21
- Income assistance, effects of experimental negative income tax program on employment, earnings, marital status, and other family characteristics in 2 cities, 1970-75, 4008–64

Index by Subjects and Names

Intl exchange and training programs of Fed Govt, participants by world region, and funding, by agency, FY83, annual rpt, 9854–8

Older persons discrimination in Fed Govt aid programs, Age Discrimination Act enforcement by 28 agencies, FY83, annual rpt, 4004–27

Poverty status of young adults related to motivation, psychological factors, and family characteristics, by race and sex, 1970s-82, longitudinal studies, 4008–65

Program evaluations and funding of HHS, 1970-83, listing, 4008–60

R&D and science-related Fed Govt funding to higher education and nonprofit instns, by field, instn, agency, and State, FY82, annual rpt, 9627–17

R&D Fed Govt funding, by function, agency, and program, selected years FY80-84 and proposed FY85, 26308–46

R&D Fed Govt funding for all performers, by field and supporting agency, selected years FY60-84, annual rpt, 9627–20

Science and engineering grad enrollment, fields of study, financial support, and other student and instn characteristics, 1975-82, annual survey, 9627–7

see also Alcohol, Drug Abuse and Mental Health Administration

see also Bureau of Health Professions

see also Centers for Disease Control

see also Food and Drug Administration

see also Health Care Financing Administration

see also Health Resources and Services Administration

see also Indian Health Service

see also National Cancer Institute

see also National Center for Health Services Research

see also National Center for Health Statistics

see also National Eye Institute

see also National Heart, Lung, and Blood Institute

see also National Institute for Occupational Safety and Health

see also National Institute of Allergy and Infectious Diseases

see also National Institute of Child Health and Human Development

see also National Institute of General Medical Sciences

see also National Institute of Mental Health

see also National Institute on Alcohol Abuse and Alcoholism

see also National Institute on Drug Abuse

see also National Institutes of Health

see also National Library of Medicine

see also Office of Health Maintenance Organizations

see also Office of Human Development Services

see also Office of Research, Statistics, and International Policy, SSA

see also Office on Smoking and Health

see also Public Health Service

see also Social Security Administration

Department of Health, Education and Welfare

see Department of Education

see Department of Health and Human Services

Department of Housing and Urban Development

Budget of US Appendix, detailed budgets and personnel summaries, by agency, FY85, annual rpt, 104–3

Budget of US, appropriations, outlays, balances, and budget receipts, by govtl branch and agency, FY83, annual rpt, 8104–2

Budget of US, compact budgets by function, agency, and account, FY85 with projections to FY89, annual rpt, 104–2

Budget of US, object class analysis of obligations, by branch of Fed Govt and selected depts and agencies, FY85 estimates, annual rpt, 104–9

Civil rights enforcement offices funding and staff, for 6 Federal agencies, FY80-84, 11048–179

Cost control proposals for Fed Govt programs and mgmt, 3-year savings by function and agency, and financial and operating data, 1960s-81, 16908–1, 16908–1.8

Debt collection plans of HUD, and single-family mortgage foreclosure costs, annual rpt, suspended, 5004–7

Employment (civilian) of Fed Govt, by location, agency, and pay system, 1982, biennial rpt, 9844–8

Finance, construction, and housing improvement programs of HUD, periodic press releases, 5006–3

Fraud and abuse in HUD programs, audits and investigations, 2nd half FY84, semiannual rpt, 5002–8

Housing, new single-family units sold and for sale by price, stage of construction, months on market, and region, and seasonal adjustments, monthly rpt, 2382–3

Indian and Alaska Native housing and community dev program operations, FY82 with Community Dev Block Grant funding by tribe and State for FY81, annual rpt, 5004–5

Interest rate maximums on FHA-insured 1-family mortages, periodic press release, suspended, 5002–6

Mobile and manufactured home safety standards, program inspections, enforcement actions, and accidents and casualties by victim characteristics, 1982-83, biennial rpt, 5004–4

Mortgage and mortgage-related investment of financial instns, by instn type and Fed Govt issuing agency, various dates 1981-84, 5008–33

Mortgage-backed securities of Fed Govt, investment by pension plans, yields by issuer, and fund assets by fund type, 1970s-82, conf papers, 5008–32

Mortgage insurance funds of HUD, financial and property activity, and insurance written, monthly rpt, 5002–9

Mortgage insurance of HUD in force, and property acquisitions and sales, quarterly rpt, 5002–3

Older and handicapped persons housing projects construction and rehabilitation loans of HUD, FY84, annual listing, 5004–6

Pension plan investment in mortgages and FHLB and Fed Govt mortgage assn mortgage-backed securities, for corporate and union funds, quarterly rpt, 5002–10

Department of Interior

R&D Fed Govt funding for all performers, by field and supporting agency, selected years FY60-84, annual rpt, 9627–20

Urban Dev Action Grant awards to local areas, preliminary approvals, with project descriptions, private investment, and jobs and taxes to be created, by city, quarterly press release series, 5002–7

see also Community Planning and Development, HUD

see also Government National Mortgage Association

see also Housing (FHA), HUD

see also Policy Development and Research, HUD

see also under By Federal Agency in the "Index by Categories"

Department of Interior

Assaults, murders, and other deaths of law enforcement officers, by circumstances, level of govt, agency, victim and offender characteristics, and location, 1983, annual rpt, 6224–3

Budget of US Appendix, detailed budgets and personnel summaries, by agency, FY85, annual rpt, 104–3

Budget of US, appropriations, outlays, balances, and budget receipts, by govtl branch and agency, FY83, annual rpt, 8104–2

Budget of US, compact budgets by function, agency, and account, FY85 with projections to FY89, annual rpt, 104–2

Budget of US, object class analysis of obligations, by branch of Fed Govt and selected depts and agencies, FY85 estimates, annual rpt, 104–9

Coal exploration licenses issued by State, and Interior Dept drilling costs and holes drilled, FY76-83, 11128–1

Cost control proposals for Fed Govt programs and mgmt, 3-year savings by function and agency, and financial and operating data, 1960s-81, 16908–1, 16908–1.9

Currency (foreign) holdings of US, detailed transactions and balances by program and country, 1st half FY84, semiannual rpt, 8102–7

Employment (civilian) of Fed Govt, by location, agency, and pay system, 1982, biennial rpt, 9844–8

Fraud and abuse in Interior Dept programs, audits and investigations, 1st half FY84, semiannual rpt, 5302–2

Outlying areas govt financial data and audits by Interior Dept Inspector General, by area, FY83, annual rpt, 5304–15

Programs, activities, and funding of Interior Dept, various periods 1967-84, last issue of annual rpt, 5304–13

R&D and science-related Fed Govt funding to higher education and nonprofit instns, by field, instn, agency, and State, FY82, annual rpt, 9627–17

R&D Fed Govt funding, by function, agency, and program, selected years FY80-84 and proposed FY85, 26308–46

R&D Fed Govt funding for all performers, by field and supporting agency, selected years FY60-84, annual rpt, 9627–20

Space and aeronautics programs and budgets of Fed Govt by agency, and foreign programs, 1957-FY85, annual rpt, 9504–9

Department of Interior

TTPI socioeconomic and political data, annual rpt, discontinued, 5304–3

Virgin Islands govt fiscal condition, FY81, annual rpt, 5304–10

Virgin Islands socioeconomic and govtl data, FY81, annual rpt, 5304–4

Wilderness Preservation Natl System acreage, by natl forest, wilderness and primitive area, and State, 1983, annual rpt, 5304–14

Youth Conservation Corps activities, costs, and participant characteristics, by sponsoring agency, 1982, annual rpt, 5304–12

see also Bureau of Indian Affairs
see also Bureau of Land Management
see also Bureau of Mines
see also Bureau of Reclamation
see also Fish and Wildlife Service
see also Geological Survey
see also Minerals Management Service
see also National Park Service
see also Office of Surface Mining Reclamation and Enforcement
see also Office of Territorial Affairs
see also Office of Water Research and Technology
see also under By Federal Agency in the "Index by Categories"

Department of Justice

Activities of Justice Dept, by subagency, FY82, annual rpt, 6004–1

Assaults, murders, and other deaths of law enforcement officers, by circumstances, level of govt, agency, victim and offender characteristics, and location, 1983, annual rpt, 6224–3

Bankruptcy court cases and admin in districts with and without case trustees, and staff and potential costs of nationwide trustee program, various periods 1979-83, annual rpt, 6004–15

Budget of US Appendix, detailed budgets and personnel summaries, by agency, FY85, annual rpt, 104–3

Budget of US, appropriations, outlays, balances, and budget receipts, by govtl branch and agency, FY83, annual rpt, 8104–2

Budget of US, compact budgets by function, agency, and account, FY85 with projections to FY89, annual rpt, 104–2

Budget of US, object class analysis of obligations, by branch of Fed Govt and selected depts and agencies, FY85 estimates, annual rpt, 104–9

Civil rights enforcement offices funding and staff, for 6 Federal agencies, FY80-84, 11048–179

Claims against foreign govts by US natls, by country and type of claim, 1983, annual rpt, 6004–16

Coal industry competitive effects of Fed Govt coal leasing, FY83 annual rpt, 6004–12

Corrupt govt officials prosecutions and convictions, by judicial district and level of govt, 1976-83, annual rpt, 6004–13

Cost control proposals for Fed Govt programs and mgmt, 3-year savings by function and agency, and financial and operating data, 1960s-81, 16908–1, 16908–1.9

Drug Enforcement Organized Crime Task Forces, funding and staff by agency, region, and city, as of FY83, GAO rpt, 26119–52

Drug enforcement regional task force program investigation activities, funding, and personnel, with nationwide drug abuse data, 1983 annual rpt, 6004–17

Employment (civilian) of Fed Govt, by location, agency, and pay system, 1982, biennial rpt, 9844–8

Legal fees awarded private parties in cases against Federal, State, and local govts, by case, selected years 1977-83, 6008–19

Oil pipeline industry competition, market shares and throughput capacity by firm and market area, as of 1983, 6008–18

Procurement, identical bidding for govt contracts, by bidder, product class, and level of govt, annual rpt, discontinued, 6004–8

R&D Fed Govt funding for all performers, by field and supporting agency, selected years FY60-84, annual rpt, 9627–20

US Attorneys civil and criminal case processing in district, appellate, and State courts, by district, FY83, annual rpt, 6004–2

Witness Security Program costs, participants by arrest record, and prosecutions by offense, offender type, and disposition, various periods FY70-83, GAO rpt, 26119–70

see also Bureau of Prisons
see also Community Relations Service
see also Drug Enforcement Administration
see also Federal Bureau of Investigation
see also Immigration and Naturalization Service
see also Office of Justice Assistance, Research and Statistics
see also U.S. Parole Commission
see also under By Federal Agency in the "Index by Categories"

Department of Labor

Activities and staff of Labor Dept, CETA participant characteristics, and employment service and unemployment insurance activities by State, FY83, annual rpt, 6304–1

Bilingual vocational training projects, participants, characteristics, and costs, by program, FY82, annual rpt, 4804–26

Budget of US Appendix, detailed budgets and personnel summaries, by agency, FY85, annual rpt, 104–3

Budget of US, appropriations, outlays, balances, and budget receipts, by govtl branch and agency, FY83, annual rpt, 8104–2

Budget of US, compact budgets by function, agency, and account, FY85 with projections to FY89, annual rpt, 104–2

Budget of US, object class analysis of obligations, by branch of Fed Govt and selected depts and agencies, FY85 estimates, annual rpt, 104–9

Civil rights enforcement offices funding and staff, for 6 Federal agencies, FY80-84, 11048–179

Cost control proposals for Fed Govt programs and mgmt, 3-year savings by function and agency, and financial and operating data, 1960s-81, 16908–1, 16908–1.3

DOD prime contract awards for R&D to educational and nonprofit instns and Federal agencies, by instn and location, FY83, annual listing, 3544–17

Index by Subjects and Names

Employment (civilian) of Fed Govt, by location, agency, and pay system, 1982, biennial rpt, 9844–8

Fraud and abuse in Labor Dept programs, audits and investigations, 1st half FY84, semiannual rpt, 6302–2

R&D Fed Govt funding for all performers, by field and supporting agency, selected years FY60-84, annual rpt, 9627–20

see also Bureau of International Labor Affairs
see also Bureau of Labor Statistics
see also Employment and Training Administration
see also Employment Standards Administration
see also Labor-Management Services Administration
see also Mine Safety and Health Administration
see also Occupational Safety and Health Administration
see also Women's Bureau
see also under By Federal Agency in the "Index by Categories"

Department of Navy

Alcohol and drug abuse of Navy personnel, and related deaths, courts-martial, discharges, and treatment program funding and staff, FY83, annual table, 3804–12

Budget of DOD, expenditures for each service branch and total defense agencies, by function and State, FY85, annual rpt, 3544–23

Budget of DOD, itemized account of legislative history, FY84, annual rpt, 3504–7

Budget of DOD, justification for procurement programs, by equipment type, service branch, and defense agency, FY83-86, annual rpt, 3504–14

Budget of DOD, justification for R&D programs, by item, service branch, and defense agency, FY83-86, annual rpt, 3504–15

Commercial activities of DOD under contract and performed in-house, costs and work-years, by service branch, defense agency, State, and installation, FY83, annual rpt, 3544–25

Construction and renovation of military bases, DOD budget authorization requests, by DOD component, State, country, and project, FY85, annual rpt, 3544–15

Cost control proposals for Fed Govt programs and mgmt, 3-year savings by function and agency, and financial and operating data, 1960s-81, 16908–1.19

Electric power plants and major fuel-burning facilities of DOD conversion from oil and gas, and fuel use data, 1983, annual rpt, 3104–9

Employment (civilian) of DOD, by service branch and defense agency, with summary military employment data, monthly rpt, 3542–16

Employment (civilian) of Fed Govt, by location, agency, and pay system, 1982, biennial rpt, 9844–8

Employment (civilian and military) of DOD, by State, service branch, and major installation, as of Sept 1983, annual rpt, 3344–7

Index by Subjects and Names

Department of State

Forces, equipment, and budget summary, planned FY84-85, semiannual pamphlet, 3802–3

Foreign govt purchase of Navy vessels, sales prices, fair market value, and Navy costs, for surplus ships sold 1981-82, GAO rpt, 26123–60

Foreign military training of US, students, costs, and revenue losses from reduced tuition by country, by service branch, FY79-83, GAO rpt, 26123–56

Judge Advocates General activities, cases and court actions, FY83, annual rpt, 3504–3

Medical care, disease incidence, and deaths, by detailed diagnosis, and medical personnel and workloads, 1978-79, annual rpt, 3804–1

Medical facilities of Navy, use by active and retired military personnel, dependents, and others by facility and type, quarterly rpt, 3802–1

Oceanographic research cruise schedules and ship characteristics, by academic instn or Federal agency, 1984, annual rpt, 3804–6

Outlays and obligations of DOD, by function and service branch, quarterly rpt, 3542–3

Personnel statistics of Navy, detailed quarterly rpt, 3802–4

Procurement, DOD prime contract awards by category, contract and contractor type, and service branch, FY74-1st half FY84, semiannual rpt, 3542–1

Procurement, DOD prime contract awards by individual contractor, service branch, State and city, and country, FY83, annual listing, 3544–22

Procurement, DOD prime contract awards by size, dept, and type of contract, FY83, annual rpt, 3544–19

Procurement, DOD prime contract awards by type, service branch and command, and for Defense Logistics Agency, last week compared to total year FY83, 108–38

Procurement, DOD prime contract awards for military and civil functions, by State, 1st half FY84, semiannual rpt, 3542–5

Procurement, DOD prime contract awards in labor surplus areas, by service branch, State, and area, 1st half FY84, semiannual rpt, 3542–19

Procurement, DOD prime contract awards to small and total business, for 10 categories and R&D, monthly rpt, 3542–10

Procurement of identical items from multiple sources by DOD, and price difference by item, by service branch, FY81, GAO rpt, 26123–67

Procurement of Navy, by contractor and location of work, FY83, annual rpt, 3804–13

Procurement, subcontract awards by DOD contractors to small and disadvantaged business, by firm and service branch, quarterly listing, 3542–17

Property, supplies, and equipment inventory of DOD, by service branch, 1983, annual rpt, 3544–6

Sealift Military Command operations for naval fleet support, and transport of DOD and AID cargo by route, quarterly rpt, 3802–2

Typhoons in western North Pacific and North Indian Oceans, paths and other characteristics, by mode of surveillance, 1983, annual rpt, 3804–8

Weapons and communications systems cost estimates, by service branch, quarterly summary rpt, 3502–1

Weapons and support systems costs under multiyear and annual procurement methods for 12 items in FY85 budget, by service branch, 1984 GAO rpt, 26123–83

Weapons system procurement cost estimate changes, and program delays and mgmt, by system and service branch, 1983, annual rpt, 26304–5

Weapons tactics trainer (F/A-18) costs by trainer type, as of 1984, and demand at 2 locations, projected 1988-94, GAO rpt, 26123–73

see also Marine Corps

see also Navy

see also Service academies

see also terms beginning with Defense and with Military

Department of State

Budget of US Appendix, detailed budgets and personnel summaries, by agency, FY85, annual rpt, 104–3

Budget of US, appropriations, outlays, balances, and budget receipts, by govtl branch and agency, FY83, annual rpt, 8104–2

Budget of US, compact budgets by function, agency, and account, FY85 with projections to FY89, annual rpt, 104–2

Budget of US, object class analysis of obligations, by branch of Fed Govt and selected depts and agencies, FY85 estimates, annual rpt, 104–9

Cocaine use, user characteristics, medical and botanical research, and South American production and legal policy and enforcement, 1979 intl conf papers, 7008–40

Cost control proposals for Fed Govt programs and mgmt, 3-year savings by function and agency, and financial and operating data, 1960s-81, 16908–1, 16908–1.10

Currency (foreign) holdings of US, detailed transactions and balances by program and country, 1st half FY84, semiannual rpt, 8102–7

Drug and narcotics foreign production, acreage, eradication, and seizures, by substance, with labs destroyed and US aid, by country, 1981-85, annual rpt, 7004–17

Economic and military assistance role in US foreign policy, with aid proposals by world region, FY85 with trends from FY74, 7008–38

El Salvador socioeconomic and political conditions, and US economic and military assistance, 1977-FY84, 7008–39

Employment (civilian) of Fed Govt, by location, agency, and pay system, 1982, biennial rpt, 9844–8

Fish catch quotas for US 200 mile zone, allocations by species and country, coastal area rpt series, 7006–5

Foreign countries *Background Notes,* summary social, political, and economic data, series, 7006–2

Foreign military and economic aid of US, Reagan Admin budget requests by program and country, FY82-85, annual rpt, 7004–14

Foreign Service positions and union membership by agency, grievances, and pay rates, FY81-83 with ambassador appointments from 1961, GAO rpt, 26123–64

Helsinki Final Act implementation by NATO, Warsaw Pact, and other signatory nations, Dec 1983-Mar 1984, semiannual rpt, 7002–1

Human rights conditions in 162 countries, economic and military aid of US, and economic aid of intl organizations, 1981-83, annual rpt, 21384–3

Kidnapping by parents over intl and interstate boundaries, characteristics of cases referred to State Dept and FBI by State and country, 1979-83, hearing, 25528–95

Latin America elections, votes and share of population voting by country and election type, selected years 1962-83, 7008–42

Loan repayment status and terms by program and country, AID and predecessor agencies, quarterly rpt, 9912–3

Minority group and women employment of State Dept and Foreign Service by pay level, and affirmative action plan, FY83, annual rpt, 7004–11

R&D Fed Govt funding for all performers, by field and supporting agency, selected years FY60-84, annual rpt, 9627–20

Refugee arrivals in US, and worldwide Indochinese refugee population and resettlement, by country of origin, monthly rpt, 7002–4

Refugee arrivals in US, by world area of origin and processing and nationality, monthly rpt, 7002–5

Refugee arrivals in US by world area of origin and State of settlement, and Fed Govt intl and domestic assistance costs, FY85, annual rpt, 7004–16

Refugee migration, settlement status, and assistance, by world area and country of origin and asylum, as of May 1984, annual rpt, 7004–15

Refugee resettlement program activities and funding, arrivals and population by country of origin and State, and employment and other characteristics, FY83, annual rpt, 4704–8

Soviet Union-US science and technology exchange projects, man-hours, and funding, by Fed Govt agency and activity type, FY81-82, 7008–41

Space and aeronautics programs and budgets of Fed Govt by agency, and foreign programs, 1957-FY85, annual rpt, 9504–9

Terrorist (intl) incidents, casualties, and attacks on US targets, by attack type and world area, with chronology of events, 1983, annual rpt, 7004–13

Treaties and other bilateral and multilateral agreements of US in force, by country, Jan 1984, annual listing, 7004–1

TTPI socioeconomic, health, and govtl data, by TTPI govt, FY83 and selected trends, detailed annual rpt, 7004–6

Department of State

UN participation of US, and member and nonmember shares of UN budget by country, FY83-85, annual rpt, 7004–5
see also Bureau of Consular Affairs
see also Bureau of Intelligence and Research
see also Diplomatic and consular service
see also U.S. Arms Control and Disarmament Agency
see also under By Federal Agency in the "Index by Categories"

Department of Transportation

- Admin and funding activities of DOT, and transportation traffic and accident data, FY81, annual rpt, 7304–1
- Air travel to and from US on US and foreign flag carriers, by country, world area, and US port, monthly rpt, 7302–2
- Auto fuel economy test results for models complying with California emission standards, 1984 model year, annual rpt, 3304–13
- Auto fuel economy test results, 1985 model year, annual rpt, 3304–11
- Auto industry market, financial, operating, and employment characteristics and prospects, annual rpt, 7304–17
- Auto safety and experimental vehicle designs, 1982, conf proceedings, annual rpt, 7764–3
- Budget of US Appendix, detailed budgets and personnel summaries, by agency, FY85, annual rpt, 104–3
- Budget of US, appropriations, outlays, balances, and budget receipts, by govtl branch and agency, FY83, annual rpt, 8104–2
- Budget of US, compact budgets by function, agency, and account, FY85 with projections to FY89, annual rpt, 104–2
- Budget of US, object class analysis of obligations, by branch of Fed Govt and selected depts and agencies, FY85 estimates, annual rpt, 104–9
- Budget summary of DOT, by subagency and program, FY81-85, annual rpt, 7304–10
- Cost control proposals for Fed Govt programs and mgmt, 3-year savings by function and agency, and financial and operating data, 1960s-81, 16908–1, 16908–1.11
- DC metro area Metrorail transit system, effect on commuting patterns, population, business, land use, and environment, series, 7306–8
- Employment (civilian) of Fed Govt, by location, agency, and pay system, 1982, biennial rpt, 9844–8
- Employment at DOT, by subagency, State, and selected personnel characteristics, FY83, annual rpt, 7304–18
- Fraud and abuse in DOT programs, audits and investigations, 1st half FY84, semiannual rpt, 7302–4
- Govt transportation revenues by source and expenditures, by level of govt and mode of transport, and Fed Govt aid by type, FY77-82, 7308–185
- Grant awards for transportation planning and safety programs, by region, State, and for 35 largest SMSAs, FY83, annual rpt, 7304–7
- Hazardous material transport accidents, casualties, and property damage, by mode of transport, with DOT control activities, 1983, annual rpt, 7304–4

Motor vehicle safety program funding of 4 DOT agencies, FY80, 7768–80

- Natural gas and hazardous liquid pipelines accidents and casualties, and DOT and State govt safety activities, 1982, annual rpt, 7304–5
- Older persons sociodemographic characteristics and transportation needs, selected years 1900-2040, 7308–183
- Pipeline safety regulations enforcement of DOT and States by pipeline type and State, and accidents and commodity losses, selected years 1973-FY84, GAO rpt, 26113–130
- Port impact on local employment through transport of 5 commodities, by industry for 3 eastern ports, and demand for US coal by country, 1981, 7308–182
- R&D Fed Govt funding, by function, agency, and program, selected years FY80-84 and proposed FY85, 26308–46
- R&D Fed Govt funding for all performers, by field and supporting agency, selected years FY60-84, annual rpt, 9627–20
- Railroad accidents, casualties, and property damage, Fed Railroad Admin activities, and safety inspectors by State, annual rpt, issuing agency change, 7304–15
- Safety programs, and accidents, injuries, deaths, hazards, and property damage, by mode of transport, 1983, annual rpt, 7304–19
- Space and aeronautics programs and budgets of Fed Govt by agency, and foreign programs, 1957-FY85, annual rpt, 9504–9
- Transit services for commuting and other purposes, dev and effects, series, 7306–9
- Transit system deficits, effect of cost and service increases and ridership and fare decreases, and govt aid and system operating ratios, 1970-80, 7308–184
- Transportation finances, operations, vehicles, equipment, accidents, and energy use, by mode of transport, 1955-84, annual rpt, 7304–2
- *see also* Coast Guard
- *see also* Coast Guard Reserve
- *see also* Federal Aviation Administration
- *see also* Federal Highway Administration
- *see also* Federal Railroad Administration
- *see also* Maritime Administration
- *see also* National Highway Traffic Safety Administration
- *see also* St. Lawrence Seaway Development Corp.
- *see also* Urban Mass Transportation Administration
- *see also* under By Federal Agency in the "Index by Categories"

Department of Treasury

- Assaults, murders, and other deaths of law enforcement officers, by circumstances, level of govt, agency, victim and offender characteristics, and location, 1983, annual rpt, 6224–3
- Bills with varying maturities, auction results by Fed Reserve district and new offerings, periodic releases, 8002–7
- Budget deficits effect on interest rates, regression results and bibl, various periods 1965-83, 8008–111
- Budget of US Appendix, detailed budgets and personnel summaries, by agency, FY85, annual rpt, 104–3

Index by Subjects and Names

- Budget of US, appropriations, outlays, balances, and budget receipts, by govtl branch and agency, FY83, annual rpt, 8104–2
- Budget of US, compact budgets by function, agency, and account, FY85 with projections to FY89, annual rpt, 104–2
- Budget of US, object class analysis of obligations, by branch of Fed Govt and selected depts and agencies, FY85 estimates, annual rpt, 104–9
- Chrysler Corp Loan Guarantee Act implementation, with related financial and operating data, FY83, last issue of annual rpt, 8004–14
- Cost control proposals for Fed Govt programs and mgmt, 3-year savings by function and agency, and financial and operating data, 1960s-81, 16908–1, 16908–1.12, 16908–1.26
- Debt to US of foreign govts and private obligors, by country and program, periodic rpt, 8002–6
- Drug Enforcement Organized Crime Task Forces, funding and staff by agency, region, and city, as of FY83, GAO rpt, 26119–52
- Drug enforcement regional task force program investigation activities, funding, and personnel, with nationwide drug abuse data, 1983 annual rpt, 6004–17
- Economic performance of US, and Reagan Admin 1984 spending, tax, and monetary policy proposals, with data for 1950s-83 and projected to 1988, press release, 8008–107
- Employment (civilian) of Fed Govt, by location, agency, and pay system, 1982, biennial rpt, 9844–8
- Fed Govt benefit payment by check and direct deposit, costs to agencies and banks, FY81, technical paper, 9366–1.139
- Fed Govt contingent liabilities and claims paid on federally insured and guaranteed contracts with foreign obligors, by country and program, periodic rpt, 8002–12
- Fed Govt financial operations, detailed data, *Treasury Bulletin*, quarterly rpt, 8002–4
- Income tax and social security tax burden of households and effect of indexing by income level, 1982, and Fed Govt revenues by source, FY60-89, press release, 8008–109
- Monetary policy views of Reagan Admin, with data on economic and monetary growth, selected years 1960-83, press release, 8008–108
- Multinatl corporation income reallocation through regulation of intercorporate transactions, by tax item, treaty status, asset size, industry, and tax haven country, 1982, 8008–110
- R&D Fed Govt funding for all performers, by field and supporting agency, selected years FY60-84, annual rpt, 9627–20
- Tax evasion through nonresidents bank claims and deposits, direct investments, income payments, and other transactions in 5 Caribbean countries, 1978-82, 8008–106
- Tax-related economic and fiscal topics, technical research paper series, 8006–3
- Taxable illegal income not reported, by source, with characteristics of persons involved, methodology, and bibl, 19/08-82, 8008–112

Index by Subjects and Names

Depreciation

see also Bureau of Alcohol, Tobacco and Firearms
see also Bureau of Engraving and Printing
see also Bureau of Government Financial Operations
see also Bureau of the Mint
see also Bureau of the Public Debt
see also Federal Financing Bank
see also Federal Open Market Committee
see also Internal Revenue Service
see also Office of Revenue Sharing
see also Office of the Comptroller of Currency
see also U.S. Customs Service
see also U.S. Savings Bonds Division
see also U.S. Secret Service
see also under By Federal Agency in the "Index by Categories"

Department stores

- Census of Population, 1980: detailed socioeconomic and demographic characteristics, by age, sex, race, Hispanic origin, occupation, and industry, State rpt series, 2531–4
- Census of Population, 1980: detailed socioeconomic characteristics, by county, city, and inside-outside SMSAs and central cities, State rpt series, 2531–3
- Census of Retail Trade, 1982: employment, establishments, sales, and payroll, by SIC 2- to 4-digit kind of business, SMSA, and retail district, State rpt series, 2401–1
- Census of Retail Trade, 1982: employment, establishments, sales, and payroll, by SIC 2- to 4-digit kind of business, SMSA, county, and city, State rpt series, 2397–1
- Census of Retail Trade, 1982: employment, establishments, sales, and payroll, by State, preliminary rpt, 2395–1.5, 2395–1.6, 2395–1.7
- Collective bargaining agreements expiring during year, covered workers by SIC 2-digit industry, firm, and union, with summary of key provisions, 1984, annual rpt, 6784–9
- Construction put in place, permits authorized by region, State, and MSA, and Federal contract awards, by construction type, bimonthly rpt with articles, 2012–1
- County Business Patterns: establishments, employees, and payrolls, by SIC 4-digit industry and county, 1981, annual State rpt series, 2326–8
- County Business Patterns: establishments, employees, and payrolls, by SIC 4-digit industry and county, 1982, annual State rpt series, 2326–6
- Employment, earnings, and hours, by selected SIC 1- to 4-digit industry, State, and for 278 major labor areas, 1939-83, annual rpt, 6744–5
- Employment, earnings, and hours, by SIC 4-digit nonfarm industry, monthly 1974-Feb 1984, annual update, 6744–4
- Financial statements for manufacturing, mining, and trade corporations, by selected SIC 2- to 3-digit industry, quarterly rpt, 2502–1
- Franchise business opportunities, by firm and kind of business, 1984 annual listing, 2044–27
- Franchises of firms engaged in distribution of goods and services by kind of business, establishments by State, and sales, 1982-84, annual rpt, 2014–5

Income tax returns of partnerships, detailed data by industry, 1981 estimates, annual article, 8302–2.404

Income tax returns of partnerships, receipts by source, deductions by type, and establishments, by selected industry, 1982, annual article, 8302–2.416

Income tax returns of sole proprietorships, detailed data by industry div and selected industry group, 1981, annual rpt, 8304–7

Income tax returns of sole proprietorships, receipts, deductions by type, payroll, and net income, by major industry, 1982, annual article, 8302–2.413

Inventory price indexes, July 1984, semiannual rpt, 6762–7

Minority group and women employment, by occupational group and SIC 2- to 3-digit industry, 1981, annual rpt, 9244–1.1

Occupational injury and illness rates, by SIC 2- to 4-digit industry, 1982, annual rpt, 6844–1

Sales, inventories, and firms, by region, census div, and selected State, SMSA, and city, monthly rpt, 2413–3

Sales, inventories, purchases, gross margin, and accounts receivable, by type of ownership, 1983, annual rpt, 2413–5

Scientists, engineers, and technicians employment in transportation, utilities, and retail and wholesale trade, by field of science and industry, 1982, 9628–72

Virgin Islands economic censuses, 1982: employment, establishments, payroll, and receipts, by SIC 1- to 4-digit industry, island, and city, 2593–1

Deposits

see Bank deposits
see Certificates of deposit
see Negotiable orders of withdrawal accounts
see Savings

Depreciation

- AID Housing Guaranty Program financial statements, and projects by country, FY83, annual rpt, 9914–4
- Airline financial data, by carrier, carrier group, and for total certificated system, quarterly rpt, 9142–12
- Airline operating and other costs, itemized for domestic and intl trunk and local service carriers, 1st half 1983, semiannual rpt, 9142–47
- Airline operations and passenger, cargo, and mail traffic, by type of service, air carrier, State, and country, 1974-83, annual rpt, 7504–1.6
- Auto and van operating and owning costs by component and vehicle size, for 12 years of operation, 1984 model year, annual rpt, 7304–2.3, 7554–21
- Auto, small airplane, and motorcycle operating costs by component and vehicle size or make, and Fed Govt mileage reimbursement rates, 1983, annual rpt, 9454–13
- Construction industries census, 1982: financial and operating data, by SIC 4-digit industry and State, final rpt series, 2373–1
- Construction industries census, 1982: financial and operating data, by SIC 4-digit industry and State, preliminary rpt series, 2371–1

Corporations profits and capital consumption allowances under alternative depreciation formulas, 1980-83, article, 2702–1.434

Electric utilities privately owned, detailed financial and operating data by company, with summary data for other distributors by type, 1982, annual rpt, 3164–23

Farm Credit System mortgage and other loans, and financial statements, 1982 and selected trends from 1961, annual rpt, 9264–2

Farm finances, assets, liabilities, income, receipts by commodity and State, and expenses, 1980-83 and trends from 1910, annual rpt, 1544–16

Farm finances, production, expenses by type, and domestic economic impact, selected years 1972-82 and preliminary 1983-84, annual rpt, 1544–19

Farm investments, effect of Fed Govt and State tax rates under alternative depreciation methods and inflation rates, 1950-84, 1548–231

Farm production expenses, by type and State, 1979-82, annual rpt, 1544–18

Fed Govt consolidated financial statements based on business accounting methods, FY82-83, annual rpt, 8104–5

Hospital Corp of America capital costs reimbursement from Medicare and Medicaid following acquisition of Hospital Affiliates Intl, 1981-82, GAO rpt, 26121–65

Income tax returns filed by type of filer, selected income items, summary data, quarterly rpt, 8302–2.1

Income tax returns of corporations, detailed income and tax items by industry, 1981, annual rpt, 8304–4

Income tax returns of corporations, summary data by industry div, 1981 estimates, annual article, 8302–2.403

Income tax returns of corporations with foreign tax credit, income and deductions by type, asset size, and selected industry group, 1980, article, 8302–2.415

Income tax returns of individuals, by filing and deduction characteristics and income level, 1983, annual article, 8302–2.414

Income tax returns of partnerships, receipts by source, deductions by type, and establishments, by selected industry, 1982, annual article, 8302–2.416

Income tax returns of sole proprietorships, detailed data by industry div and selected industry group, 1981, annual rpt, 8304–7

Income tax returns of sole proprietorships, receipts, deductions by type, payroll, and net income, by major industry, 1982, annual article, 8302–2.413

Motor vehicle fleet of Fed Govt, costs and operating data by agency, FY83, annual rpt, 9454–9

Natural gas interstate pipeline company detailed financial and operating data, by firm, 1983, annual rpt, 3164–38

Oil and gas companies production and exploration detailed expenditures, revenues, operating ratios, and sales volume, 1982, annual Current Industrial Rpt, 2506–8.11

Oil pipeline in Alaska, owner companies financial data, and retail gasoline competitive position in 2 States, by company, 1980-83, hearing, 21728–51

Depreciation

Partnership finances, tax deductions, and employment, by industry div and size, 1979, article, 8302–2.411

Pollution abatement capital and operating costs, by SIC 2- to 4-digit industry, State, and SMSA, 1982, annual Current Industrial Rpt, 2506–3.6

Railroad finances and operations, detailed data by firm, class of service, and district, 1983, annual rpt, 9486–6.1

Rental housing, effects of Fed Govt tax policies on real estate investment, 1969-81, 5188–104

St Lawrence Seaway Dev Corp finances and activities, and seaway toll charges and cargo tonnage by type of cargo, 1983, annual rpt, 7744–1

Steel industry financial and operating data, steel imports by source, and employment situation at Fairless Hills, Pa, plant, 1970s-90, hearing, 25528–94

Tax expenditures, Fed Govt revenues foregone through income tax deductions and exclusions by type, and effect of Deficit Reduction Act, FY84-89, annual rpt, 21784–10

Telephone and telegraph firms detailed financial, operating, and employment statistics, 1982, annual rpt, 9284–6

Truck transport of fruit and vegetables, costs per vehicle-mile by component for fleets and owner-operator trucks, monthly rpt, 1272–1

TVA activities, financial and operating data by program and facility, and power sales by customer, FY83, annual rpt, 9804–1

TVA power program finances and operations, by plant and distributor, FY83, annual rpt, 9804–23

Depressions

see Business cycles

Deregulation

see Government and business

see Price regulation

Des Moines, Iowa

Census of Housing, 1980: occupancy and unit characteristics, by race, Hispanic origin, and city, SMSA rpt, 2473–1.139

Census of Population and Housing, 1980: detailed population and housing characteristics, by county, city, and census tract, SMSA rpt, 2551–2.139

Wages by occupation, and benefits for office and plant workers, 1984 labor market area survey rpt, 6785–3.6

see also under By City and By SMSA or MSA in the "Index by Categories"

Desegregation of schools

see Discrimination in education

Destroyers

see Naval vessels

Detective and protective services

Assaults, murders, and other deaths of law enforcement officers, by circumstances, level of govt, agency, victim and offender characteristics, and location, 1983, annual rpt, 6224–3

Campus law enforcement personnel and officers, by higher education instn, 1983, annual rpt, 6224–2.3

Census of Housing, 1980: structural, financial, and householder characteristics, by region and State, 2475–4

Census of Population and Housing, 1980: detailed population and housing characteristics, by county, city, and census tract, State and SMSA rpt series, 2551–2

Index by Subjects and Names

Census of Population, 1980: detailed socioeconomic and demographic characteristics, by age, sex, race, Hispanic origin, occupation, and industry, State rpt series, 2531–4

Census of Population, 1980: detailed socioeconomic characteristics, by county, city, and inside-outside SMSAs and central cities, State rpt series, 2531–3

Census of Population, 1980: labor force, by sex, detailed occupation, and region, with comparison to 1970 census, supplementary rpt, 2535–1.12

Census of Service Industries, 1982: employment, establishments, receipts, and payroll, by SIC 2- to 4-digit kind of business, SMSA, county, and city, State rpt series, 2391–1

County Business Patterns: establishments, employees, and payrolls, by SIC 4-digit industry and county, 1981, annual State rpt series, 2326–8

County Business Patterns: establishments, employees, and payrolls, by SIC 4-digit industry and county, 1982, annual State rpt series, 2326–6

Employment, earnings, and hours, by SIC 4-digit nonfarm industry, monthly 1974-Feb 1984, annual update, 6744–4

Employment, unemployment, and labor force, by demographic and employment characteristics, State, and for 30 metro areas and 11 large cities, 1983, annual rpt, 6744–7

Expenditures for security services, by level of govt and for private business by major industry, 1981, 6066–20.8

Fed Reserve payments services provided depository instns, financial statements, and costs and revenues by service and district bank, 1983, annual press release, 9364–9

Fed Reserve System coin and currency transport truck driver and guard wages in 12 cities, effects of locally prevailing wage rate requirements, 1980, article, 9377–1.402

Franchise business opportunities, by firm and kind of business, 1984 annual listing, 2044–27

Govt census, 1982: employment, payrolls, and average earnings, by function, level of govt, State, county, population size, and inside-outside SMSAs, 2455–2

Govt finances, by level of govt, State, and for large cities and counties, 1981-83, annual rpt series, 2466–2

Input-output structure of US economy, detailed interindustry transactions for 537 industries, and components of final demand, 1977 benchmark data, 2708–17

Occupational manpower needs and supply by detailed occupation, and educational and training program enrollees and grads by detailed field, 1982 and 1995, biennial rpt, 6744–3

Occupational Outlook Handbook, 1984-85 biennial rpt, 6744–1

Detention

see Arrest

see Correctional institutions

see Habeas corpus

see Pretrial detention and release

Detergent industry

see Soap and detergent industry

Detroit, Mich.

Auto dealer repair workers, wages, and benefits, by occupation, size of establishment, and for 24 labor market areas, Nov 1982 survey, 6787–6.202

Cancer cases, incidence, deaths, and death rates, by body site, age, race, Hispanic origin, and sex, for 10 geographic areas, 1973-81, 4478–130

Census of Housing, 1980: occupancy and unit characteristics, by race, Hispanic origin, and city, SMSA rpt, 2473–1.140

Census of Population and Housing, 1980: detailed population and housing characteristics, by county, city, and census tract, SMSA rpt, 2551–2.140

CPI by component for US city average, and by region, population size, and for 28 SMSAs, monthly press release, 6762–1

CPI by detailed component, for US city average, 28 SMSAs, and 4 regions by population size, monthly rpt, 6762–2

Employment in traditional and high technology industry by occupation, and wages by industry, for Massachusetts and compared to US and 3 SMSAs, various periods 1976-82, article, 9373–1.416

Fruit and vegetable shipments, and arrivals in 23 US and 5 Canada cities, by mode of transport and State or country of origin, 1983, annual rpt, 1311–4.1

Homeless population and characteristics, and temporary shelter operations, use, and user characteristics, for selected cities, various periods 1979-84, hearing, 21248–85

Hospital worker wages by sex and occupation, and benefits, for 22 MSAs, Oct 1981 survey, 6787–6.201

Housing and households detailed characteristics, and unit and neighborhood quality, by inside-outside central cities, 1981 survey, SMSA rpt, 2485–6.17

Housing unit starts and completions authorized by building permits in 20 MSAs, quarterly rpt, 2382–9

Loan activity of banks in Fed Reserve 7th District and 3 major midwestern cities, monthly rpt, 9375–9

Population size of top 25 cities, 1980 and 1982, press release, 2328–46

Rail high-speed system planned from Chicago, capital and operating costs and profitability by speed class, frequency, and route, 1984 article, 9375–1.406

Visual impairment survey methodology and results by age, in 3 SMSAs, Aug 1981-Dec 1982, 4478–147

Wages of office and plant workers, by occupation, 1984 SMSA survey rpt, 6785–11.4

Waterborne commerce of US (domestic and foreign), freight by commodity, traffic, and passengers, by port and waterway, 1982, annual rpt, 3754–3.3

see also under By City and By SMSA or MSA in the "Index by Categories"

Devaney, F. John

"Urban and Rural Housing Characteristics", 1004–16.1, 1702–1.407

Index by Subjects and Names

Developing countries

Agricultural supply/demand and market for US exports, with socioeconomic indicators, country rpt series, 1526–6

Agricultural supply/demand, consumption per capita, and trade, by world area and country group, 1960s-82, 1528–181

Agricultural trade of US, by commodity and country, bimonthly rpt with articles, 1522–1

AID activities and funding by project and function, FY85, and developing countries summary socioeconomic data, 1970s-83, by country, annual rpt, 9914–3

AID and other foreign assistance, and govt policy, effects on private sector dev and socioeconomic conditions, with case studies for 6 countries, 1960s-80, 9918–12

AID community dev assistance to local govts in developing countries, program activities and funding, 1960s-80s, 9918–11

AID dev assistance activities, evaluation rpt series, 9916–11

AID dev assistance activities, socioeconomic impacts, evaluation rpt series, 9916–1

AID dev assistance activities, special study series, 9916–3

AID economic assistance to developing countries, obligations and disbursements by country, quarterly rpt, 9912–4

AID loan repayment status and terms by program and country, and status of predecessor agency loans, quarterly rpt, 9912–3

AID loans authorized, signed, and canceled, by country and world area, monthly rpt, 9912–2

Auto industry operations, trade, and registrations, foreign and US, selected years 1928-82, domestic content requirement hearings, 21788–134

Carbon dioxide emissions from fossil fuel combustion, and growth rates, by country and country group, 1950-80, 3006–7.6

China economic conditions, agricultural and industrial production, trade, and domestic and foreign investment, 1980-85, 2048–106

China exports and imports, by commodity, world area, and country, quarterly rpt, 242–6

Defense and total govt expenditures, military imports, GNP, and intl reserves of countries receiving US economic aid, by country, 1976-81, annual rpt, 9914–1

Disaster preparedness and summary sociodemographic, political, and economic data, country rpt series, 9916–2

Economic aid of US to developing countries, bilateral and through multilateral dev banks and intl agencies, by world area and country, 1970s-FY83, annual rpts, 9904–1

Economic and military aid of US, Reagan Admin budget requests by program and country, FY82-85, annual rpt, 7004–14

Economic conditions in Communist, OECD, and selected other countries, 1960s-83, annual rpt, 244–5

Eurocurrency syndicated loans, loan fees, and interest rate spread, by country group and selected country, 1981-83, technical paper, 9366–7.105

Exports and imports of US, by commodity group, world area, selected country, US coastal area and port, and mode of transport, with seasonal adjustments, monthly rpt, 2422–9

Exports, imports, and economic indicators by country and country group, and US trade policy actions, 1960s-83, annual rpt, 444–1

Exports of US by selected commodity, and foreign and US economic and employment indicators and balance of payments, by world area and country, 1970s-83, annual rpt, 2044–26

Food production and needs, and related economic trends and outlook, for 67 developing countries, 1980-86, annual rpt, 1524–6

Food supply policies of 21 developing countries, with farm sector data, tariff income, and prices and imports of 5 grains, 1960s-81, 1528–168

Foreign exchange availability effect on economic growth of non-OPEC developing countries, 1960-77, model description, technical paper, 9366–7.106

Free zones in developing countries, industry financial and operating data by country, with case studies for 5 countries, 1970s-82, 9918–10

Generalized System of Preferences status of 29 commodities, with US production, consumption, tariffs, and trade by country, selected years 1978-87, 9888–17

Housing finance and low-income housing projects in Asian developing countries, and activities of 2 countries, 1970s-82, annual conf proceedings, 9914–11

Imports of US given duty-free treatment for value of US materials or parts sent abroad for processing or assembly, by country and commodity, 1979-82, biennial rpt, 9884–14

Inter-American Foundation activities, grants, and fellowships, by country, FY83, annual rpt, 14424–1

Investment (foreign direct) of US, by selected major industry group and world area, 1982-83, annual article, 2702–1.430

Investment (foreign direct) of US, by world area and country, 1977-83, article, 2702–1.442

Investment (intl direct) worldwide, and US investment flows by major industry, by world region and country, 1982 and trends from 1950, annual rpt, 2044–25

Loans and grants for economic and military assistance from US and intl agencies, by program and country, FY46-83, annual rpt, 9914–5

Loans and other funding from intl financial instns by source and disbursements by purpose, by country, with US policy review, FY83, annual rpt, 15344–1

Loans, debts, exchange rates, and intl reserves, for US and selected countries, various periods 1949-84, conf papers, 9373–3.28

Loans from US banks, debt burden, and other economic indicators of non-OPEC developing countries, various periods 1977-84 and loan projections to 1990, article, 9362–1.407

Loans of large US banks to foreigners at all US and foreign offices, by country group and country, quarterly rpt, 13002–1

Development Associates, Inc.

Loans of US banks to developing countries and domestic borrowers, impact of tax policy on investment profits and choice, 1984 technical paper, 9366–7.99

Military aid of US by country and program, and developing countries with advanced weapons systems, FY85, annual rpt, 3544–2

Military, social, and economic summary data, by world area and country, 1960s-80s, hearing, 25388–47.1

Military spending, arms trade, and armed forces size, with total govt spending and population, by country, 1972-82, annual rpt, 9824–1

Military weapons transfers to developing countries from US, USSR, and Europe, by weapon type and world region, 1974-82, 25948–3

Multilateral dev bank economic dev projects, environmental and cultural impacts in developing countries, 1970s-83, hearings, 21248–80

Oil price and demand relationship and real income effects among developed countries and OPEC and non-OPEC developing countries, 1984 technical paper, 9366–7.96

Oil price changes effects on developed countries and on OPEC and non-OPEC developing countries, model description, 1984 technical paper, 9366–7.93

Oil prices impact on US oil trade and energy-intensive industries, with US and foreign reserves and industry operations, 1950-82 and projected to 2020, 9886–4.69

Overseas Private Investment Corp activities, foreign and US project impacts, and list of insured projects and companies, FY83, annual rpt, 9904–3

Overseas Private Investment Corp programs and finances, with list of insured projects and companies, FY83, annual rpt, 9904–2

PL 480 Title I funding and socioeconomic impacts in developing countries, with case studies for 5 countries, 1950s-81, 9918–13

Population demographic data, methodology, and analyses for foreign countries, research rpt series, 2546–10

Soviet Union and Warsaw Pact military weapons systems, assistance and presence worldwide, and force strengths, with selected US and NATO comparisons, as of 1984, 3508–14

Students in US and Soviet bloc training programs, by program type and Latin American country or world region of student origin, selected years 1972-82, GAO rpt, 26123–77

see also under By Foreign Country in the "Index by Categories"

see also under names of individual countries

Development Alternatives, Inc.

"AID Assistance to Local Government: Experience and Issues", 9918–11

Development Associates, Inc.

"Evaluation of the Impact of the Part A Entitlement Program Funded Under Title IV of the Indian Education Act, Final Report", 4808–13

Devens, Richard M., Jr.

Devens, Richard M., Jr.
"Employment in the First Half: Robust Recovery Continues", 6722–1.448

Dewald, William G.
"Deficits and Monetary Growth", 9371–1.402

DeWitt, Rachael
"Species Profiles: Life Histories and Environmental Requirements of Coastal Fishes and Invertebrates (North Atlantic), Hard Clam", 5506–8.23

Di Clemente, John J.
"Bank Mergers Today: New Guidelines, Changing Markets", 9375–1.404

Diabetes
- Deaths and death rates, by cause and age, provisional 1982-83, US Vital Statistics annual rpt, 4144–7
- Deaths and death rates by detailed cause and demographic characteristics, 1979 and selected trends, US Vital Statistics annual rpt, 4144–2.1
- Deaths and death rates, by detailed geographic area, cause, and demographic characteristics, 1979, US Vital Statistics annual rpt, 4144–3
- Deaths and death rates, by selected cause and demographic characteristics, 1981, US Vital Statistics advance rpt, 4146–5.78
- Deaths and death rates, by selected cause and demographic characteristics, 1982, US Vital Statistics advance rpt, 4146–5.81
- Education model program for diabetes outpatients, effect on patient knowledge and clinical test scores, 1983, article, 4102–1.457
- Fed Govt programs and expenditures related to diabetes, by agency and NIH inst, FY84, annual rpt, 4434–8
- Health condition and health care resources, use, and expenditures, 1970s-82 with trends and projections 1900-2000, annual compilation, 4144–11
- Hospital discharges and length of stay, by patient characteristics, facility size, procedure performed, diagnosis, and region, 1982, annual rpt, 4147–13.78
- Indian births, morbidity, and deaths and rates, and health services facilities and use, 1954-83, annual compilation, 4104–7
- Older persons by demographic, socioeconomic, and health characteristics, selected years 1900-81 and projected to 2050, Current Population Rpt, 2546–2.125
- Visual impairment survey methodology and results by age, in 3 SMSAs, Aug 1981-Dec 1982, 4478–147
- *see also* under By Disease in the "Index by Categories"

Diamonds
see Gemstones

Diatomite
see Nonmetallic minerals and mines

Dicer, Gary N.
"Transportation and Agricultural Export Expansion", 1004–16.1

DiCesare, Constance B.
"Our Changing Economy: A BLS Centennial Chartbook", 6728–30

Dickson, Cheryl L.
"Aviation Fuels, 1983", 3006–2.2
"Heating Oils, 1984", 3006–2.4

Dickson, David R.
"Forest Statistics for Maine, 1971 and 1982", 1206–12.7

Dickson, J. C.
"Impacts of Alcohol Fuels on the U.S. Refining Industry", 3308–75

Dictionaries
see Glossaries

Diesel fuel
- Agriculture census, 1982: farms, farmland, production and costs, and operator characteristics, preliminary State and county rpt series, 2330–1
- Agriculture census, 1982: farms, farmland, production, finances, and operator characteristics, by county, final State rpt series, 2331–1
- Alaska electric power capacity and generation by fuel type, and marketing, by utility, type of ownership, and location, 1983, annual rpt, 3214–2
- Arson incidents investigated by Alcohol, Tobacco, and Firearms Bur, and accelerants identified by type, 1982-83, annual rpt, 8484–4.3
- Consumption of energy, by type of air pollutant source and fuel, and State, 1981, annual rpt, 9194–14
- Cuba economic conditions, agricultural and industrial production and distribution, trade, and intl economic relations, 1970-82 and trends from 1957, 248–40
- Defense Fuel Supply Center procurement, prices, stocks, and other activities, FY83, annual rpt, 3904–6
- Farm production expenditures, detailed items by farm sales size and region, 1983, annual rpt, 1614–3
- Farm production inputs supply, use, and prices, periodic situation rpt with articles, 1561–16
- Farmers prices received for major products and paid for farm inputs and living items, by commodity and State, monthly rpt, 1629–1
- Farmers prices received for major products and paid for farm inputs, by commodity and State, 1983, annual rpt, 1629–5
- Foreign and US oil prices, tax, and customs duty, by refined product and major city, July 1983 and Jan 1984, annual rpt, 3164–50.4
- Foreign and US retail gasoline and diesel prices and tax rates, for US and 4 countries, monthly rpt, 242–5
- Injuries and deaths from use of selected consumer products and related activity, by victim age and sex, 1982, annual rpt, 9164–7
- Irrigation system energy use and costs, and irrigated farm acreage by fuel and region, selected years 1974-84 and trends from 1900, article, 1561–16.406
- Mineral industries census, 1982: financial and operating data, including materials consumed, by SIC 4-digit industry and State, preliminary rpt series, 2511–1
- Natl Energy Policy Plan, energy supply, demand, and prices, by fuel and consuming sector, projected 1985-2010, biennial rpt, 3004–13
- OECD energy prices and taxes by energy source and end-use sector, for US and 9 countries, quarterly 1979-83, annual rpt, 3164–71

Index by Subjects and Names

- Price and volume of 13 oil products sold by gas plant operators and refiners, by end-use sector, PAD district, and State, monthly rpt, 3162–11
- Prices and expenditures for fuels, by consuming sector, State, and fuel type, 1970-81, annual rpt, 3164–64
- Prices of wholesale and retail No 2 diesel oil, monthly rpt, 3162–24.9
- Producer prices and indexes, by stage of processing and detailed commodity, monthly rpt, 6762–6
- Producer prices and indexes, by stage of processing and detailed commodity, monthly 1983, annual supplement, 6764–2
- Refinery financial and operating impacts from auto use of alcohol fuels, projected to 2000 with trends 1964-80, 3308–75
- Ships bunker fuels, oil and coal laden in US on vessels engaged in foreign trade, by port, monthly rpt, 2422–5
- Tax (excise) collections of IRS, by source, quarterly press release, 8302–1
- Tax collections, refunds, and taxes due IRS, by State and region, and IRS court activity and operating expenses, FY83, annual rpt, 8304–3.3
- Tax provisions (State) for motor fuel, vehicle registration fees, and disposition of receipts, by State, as of Jan 1984, biennial rpt, 7554–37
- Tax rates for motor fuel, by fuel type and State, monthly rpt, 7552–1
- Tax rates for motor fuel, by State, 1975-83, annual table, 7554–32
- Taxation and revenue systems, by type of tax and system, level of govt, and State, selected years 1958-83, annual rpt, 10044–1.3
- Taxes for hwy use and Trust Fund revenues by tax type, and trucking industry economic effects of tax and size and weight rules, FY82-84 and projected to 1990, GAO rpt, 26117–31
- Taxes for hwy use by tax type, and truck size and weight limits, economic effects on trucking industry, 1982-83 and projected 1984-87, hearings, 25328–24
- Transportation and related energy use, for urban areas, late 1970s-82 and projected under lower auto emission standards to 1995, 3408–31
- Transportation census, 1982: trucks, by detailed characteristics, miles traveled, and type of product carried, State rpt series, 2573–1
- Transportation energy use by mode, fuel supplies, and demographic and economic determinants of vehicle use, 1970s-83, annual rpt, 3304–5
- Transportation finances, operations, vehicles, equipment, accidents, and energy use and transport, by mode of transport, 1955-84, annual rpt, 7304–2
- Trucks (heavy) energy use, efficiency, and conservation technologies, selected years 1958-82 and projected to 2000, 3308–70

Diet
see Nutrition and malnutrition

Dietitians and nutritionists
Census of Population, 1980: detailed socioeconomic and demographic characteristics, by age, sex, race, Hispanic origin, occupation, and industry, State rpt series, 2531–4

Index by Subjects and Names

Directories

Census of Population, 1980: labor force, by sex, detailed occupation, and region, with comparison to 1970 census, supplementary rpt, 2535–1.12

DOD medical personnel, trainees, and accessions by source, by occupation, specialty, and service branch, FY83, annual rpt, 3544–24

Hospital employment, vacancies, and vacancy rates, by occupation and by hospital specialty, region, census div, and State, 1980, annual rpt, 4114–12

Hospital worker wages by sex and occupation, and benefits, for 22 MSAs, Oct 1981 survey, 6787–6.201

Occupational manpower needs and supply by detailed occupation, and educational and training program enrollees and grads by detailed field, 1982 and 1995, biennial rpt, 6744–3

Occupational Outlook Handbook, 1984-85 biennial rpt, 6744–1

Science and engineering doctoral degree recipients, by field, sex, race, age, citizenship, postgrad employment and study status, State, and instn, 1960-82, 9626–6.16

Science and engineering grad enrollment, fields of study, financial support, and other student and instn characteristics, 1975-82, annual survey, 9627–7

VA Medicine and Surgery Dept trainees, by detailed program and city, FY83, annual rpt, 9924–21

Digestive diseases

- Agent Orange exposed Air Force personnel diseases and disorders, by disease type, age, and officer status, 1984 rpt, 3604–3
- Deaths and death rates, by cause and age, provisional 1982-83, US Vital Statistics annual rpt, 4144–7
- Deaths and death rates by detailed cause and demographic characteristics, 1979 and selected trends, US Vital Statistics annual rpt, 4144–2.1
- Deaths and death rates, by detailed geographic area, cause, and demographic characteristics, 1979, US Vital Statistics annual rpt, 4144–3
- Deaths and death rates, by selected cause and demographic characteristics, 1981, US Vital Statistics advance rpt, 4146–5.78
- Deaths and death rates, by selected cause and demographic characteristics, 1982, US Vital Statistics advance rpt, 4146–5.81
- Disability Insurance beneficiaries sociodemographic and medical characteristics, 1977-79, annual rpt, 4744–20
- Economic indicators relation to measures of social pathology including crime and death rates, various periods 1950-80, 23848–76
- Health condition and health care resources, use, and expenditures, 1970s-82 with trends and projections 1900-2000, annual compilation, 4144–11
- Hospital discharges and length of stay, by patient characteristics, facility size, procedure performed, diagnosis, and region, 1982, annual rpt, 4147–13.78
- Indian births, morbidity, and deaths and rates, and health services facilities and use, 1954-83, annual compilation, 4104–7

Infant deaths by detailed cause, geographic location, age, race, and sex, 1979, US Vital Statistics annual rpt, 4144–2.2

Interagency Digestive Diseases Coordinating Committee activities, and related Federal research and funding, by agency, FY79-83, annual rpt, 4434–13

Older persons by demographic, socioeconomic, and health characteristics, selected years 1900-81 and projected to 2050, Current Population Rpt, 2546–2.125

see also Infective and parasitic diseases

see also under By Disease in the "Index by Categories"

Dillard, Fay B.

- "Main Line Natural Gas Sales to Industrial Users, 1982", 3162–4.401
- "Main Line Natural Gas Sales to Industrial Users, 1983", 3162–4.412
- "U.S. Imports and Exports of Natural Gas: 1983", 3162–4.406

Dille, J. R.

"1980 and 1981 Accident Experience of Civil Airmen with Selected Visual Pathology", 7506–10.30

Dion, Mavis J.

"We, the American Women", 2326–1.2

Diphtheria

see Infective and parasitic diseases

Diplomacy

see Diplomatic and consular service

see Foreign relations

Diplomatic and consular service

- AID dev and security assistance, project activities, budget requests, and staff levels, by program and country, FY85, annual rpt, 9914–3
- Cost control proposals for Fed Govt programs and mgmt, 3-year savings by function and agency, and financial and operating data, 1960s-81, 16908–1.10
- Developing countries disaster preparedness and summary sociodemographic, political, and economic data, country rpt series, 9916–2
- Health benefit plans enrollment and premiums, for individual private and employee organization plans, FY81-82, annual rpt, 9844–1.2
- Labor union membership and positions by agency, grievances, and pay rates, for US Foreign Service, FY81-83 with ambassador appointments from 1961, GAO rpt, 26123–64
- Living costs abroad, State Dept indexes, housing allowances, and hardship differential rates by country and major city, quarterly rpt, 6862–1
- Loan programs of Fed Govt, direct and guaranteed loans outstanding by agency and program, *Treasury Bulletin,* quarterly rpt, 8002–4.10
- Minority group and women employment of State Dept and Foreign Service by pay level, and affirmative action plan, FY83, annual rpt, 7004–11
- Pay comparability of Fed Govt with private industry, and recommended pay rate adjustments, 1983, annual rpt, 104–16
- Pay rates of Fed Govt civilian employees, by branch of govt, employee category, and pay level, as of 1984 with trends from 1789, 21628–54

Pension benefits for military retirees and compared to US civil and foreign service and foreign countries, and Air Force personnel costs, FY75-84, hearings, 21208–19

Terrorist (intl) incidents, casualties, and attacks on US targets, by attack type and world area, with chronology of events, 1983, annual rpt, 7004–13

UN participation of US, and member and nonmember shares of UN budget by country, FY83-85, annual rpt, 7004–5

Visas issued and refused to immigrants and nonimmigrants, and status adjustments, by class and nationality, FY77, annual rpt, 7184–1

see also Foreign Service Retirement and Disability Fund

Directories

- AID contracts and grants for technical and support services, by instn, country, and State, FY83, annual listing, 9914–7
- AID contracts and grants to universities for technical assistance to foreign countries and other services, FY83, annual listing, 9914–6
- Airlines (commuter and intrastate) operating in 1978 by region and State, and listing by city, by operation status in 1984, article, 9142–42.404
- Airport planning and dev project grants of Fed Govt, by sponsor, airport, and location, periodic press release series, 7506–8
- Alcohol, Drug Abuse, and Mental Health Admin research grants, awards, and fellowships by recipient, FY83, annual listing, 4044–13
- Allergy and Infectious Diseases Natl Inst activities, grants by instn, State, and country, and disease incidence and costs, FY60s-84, annual rpt, 4474–30
- Aluminum primary production plant ownership, capacity, and type and source of raw material and energy used, by plant, State, and country, June 1984, semiannual listing, 5602–5
- Army Corps of Engineers activities and projects, FY83 and trends from 1800s, annual rpt, 3754–1
- Auto and auto equipment recalls for safety-related defects, by make, quarterly listing, 7762–2
- Bilingual education programs, teachers, enrollment, and funding, selected years 1976-FY83, biennial rpt, 4804–14
- Biotechnology commercial uses, R&D funding and output, controls, and industry financial and operating data, for US and 5 countries, 1970s-83 and estimated 1984-85, 26358–98
- Black higher education instns, detailed info on instn characteristics and research, annual listing, discontinued, 4004–28
- Bridge replacement and rehabilitation program of Fed Govt, funding by bridge and bridge status by State, 1983, annual rpt, 7554–27
- Bridges over navigable waters, with type of bridge and use, owner, dimensions, and location, 1984 regional listing series, 7406–5
- Cancer Natl Inst contracts and grants, by contractor, instn, State, and city, FY83, annual listing, 4474–28

ASI Annual Supplement 209

Directories

Census Bur publications data coverage and availability, 1984 annual listing, 2304–2

Chemicals (synthetic organic) production and sales by product, and listing of manufacturers, 1983, annual rpt, 9884–3

Coal distribution firms and producing districts served, quarterly rpt, annual listing, 3162–8

Computer software and documentation available from NTIS, by agency and program characteristics, 1984 annual listing, 2224–2

Computer systems and equipment of Fed Govt, inventory by manufacturer, type, agency, and location, FY83, last issue of annual rpt, 9454–4

Construction and building materials industries trade assns, professional societies, and labor unions, 1984 listing, article, 2012–1.405

Consumer Product Safety Commission activities, recalls, and product-related injuries, deaths, and medical costs, by product type and brand, FY83, annual rpt, 9164–2

Credit union membership, shares and loans, and asset size, for Federal and federally insured State unions by State, 1984 annual listing, 9534–6

Criminal offense citations manual of US criminal title and section codes, with corresponding detailed offenses and severity levels, 1984, annual rpt, 18204–14

Customs Service headquarters and regional and district offices, FY83, annual rpt, 8144–1

Dams, reservoirs, and hydroelectric plants, listing of major foreign and US structures with location and characteristics, as of June 1983, 5828–13

Dental Research Natl Inst research and training funds awarded, by recipient instn, FY83, annual listing, 4474–19

DOD budget, organization, personnel, weapons, and property, by service branch, State, and country, 1984 annual summary rpt, 3504–13

DOD contractor subcontract awards to small and disadvantaged business, by firm and service branch, quarterly listing, 3542–17

DOD prime contract awards for R&D to educational and nonprofit instns and Federal agencies, by instn and location, FY83, annual listing, 3544–17

DOD procurement, prime contractors for R&D, top 500 and value of contracts, FY83, annual listing, 3544–4

DOE hydrogen energy R&D activities, and description and funding of 24 projects, FY83, annual rpt, 3304–18

DOE R&D projects and funding at natl labs, universities, and other instns, annual summary rpts, 3004–18

Earthquake intensity, damage, and deaths, by location for major earthquakes since 1755, and hazard areas and natl reduction program activities, as of 1984, 5668–73

Economic Dev Admin research grants, by county, FY83 and cumulative FY66-83, annual listing, 2064–2.3

Education Dept financial aid programs for educational instns and individuals, 1984 annual listing, 4804–3

Educational Resources Info Center microfiche, holdings of US and foreign educational and other instns, as of 1983, listing, 4918–14

Electric power plants, by capacity, fuel used, unit type, region, State, and county, for plants added and retired, 1983 and planned through 1993, annual rpt, 3164–36

Electric power wholesale purchases and costs for individual REA borrowers, by supplier and State, 1940-83, annual rpt, 1244–5

Energy conservation aid programs of DOE, with listing of State energy offices, FY84, annual rpt, 3304–21

Energy conservation grants of Fed Govt to public and nonprofit private instns, by building type and State, 1983, annual rpt, 3304–15

Energy-related inventions recommended for possible DOE support by Natl Bur of Standards, with DOE evaluation status, 1984, annual listing, 2214–5

Fed Govt advisory committees, and members, staff, meetings, and costs, by agency, FY83, annual rpt, 9454–18

Fed Govt financial and nonfinancial domestic aid, 1984 annual comprehensive catalog, 104–5

Fed Home Loan Bank System members, with assets of S&Ls, by instn, city, and State, 1983, annual listing, 9314–5

Fed Reserve bank directors, 1983, annual rpt, 9364–1

Fish and eggs for stocking distributed from natl hatcheries, by species, hatchery, and jurisdiction, FY83, annual rpt, 5504–10

Fishery research of State fish and wildlife agencies, federally funded projects and costs by species and State, 1984, annual rpt, 5504–23

Fishery resources mgmt and R&D, Fed Govt grants by project and resulting publications, 1983, annual listing, 2164–3

Foreign govt Chiefs of State and Cabinet members, by country, monthly listing, 242–7

Franchise business opportunities by firm and kind of business, and sources of aid and info, 1984 annual listing, 2044–27

Genetically abnormal human cell cultures available to researchers, and cultures shipped, 1984 annual listing, 4474–23

Handicapped children early education research and service project activities and characteristics, and grants to States for program dev, 1983-84, annual listing, 4804–30

Health Care Financing Admin research activities and grants by research area, as of June 1984, semiannual listing, 4652–8

Health info offices and services of HHS and other Fed Govt agencies, by subject, 1984 listing, 4048–18

Health Services Research Natl Center grants and contracts, by program area, FY83, annual listing, 4184–2

Heart, Lung, and Blood Natl Inst organization, disease and mortality data, and funds and recipients, FY83 with trends from 1900, annual fact book, 4474–15

HHS aid to each State and local govt or private instn, amount obligated, funding agency, and program, FY83, annual listing, 4004–3

Index by Subjects and Names

HHS health data projects and systems, by subagency, FY83-84, annual inventory, 4044–3

HHS program evaluations and funding, 1970-83, listing, 4008–60

Higher education instns, by type, location, and other characteristics, 1983/84 annual listing, 4844–3

Higher education instns, type, location, enrollment, and student charges, by State and congressional district, 1983/84, biennial listing, 4844–11

Higher education tuition and other student charges, for each public and private 2- and 4-year instn, by State, 1983/84, annual listing, 4844–10

Housing projects for older and handicapped persons, construction and rehabilitation loans of HUD, FY84, annual listing, 5004–6

Hydroelectric power small-scale potential generation, site inventory, and costs, by Western Area Power Admin State and county, 1984 rpt, 3258–1

Intermodal containers and equipment owned by US shipping and leasing companies, inventory by type and size, 1983, annual rpt, 7704–10

Investment companies classification, assets, and location, Sept 1982, annual directory, 9734–1

Juvenile Justice and Delinquency Prevention Natl Inst programs and research project funding, FY81-82, annual rpt, 6064–19

Labor Intl Affairs Bur research contracts, by project and contractor, FY73-84, annual listing, 6364–1

Labor surplus areas eligible for preferential Fed Govt contracts, and labor force data for 150 major labor markets, monthly listing, 6402–1

Labor unions recognized in Fed Govt, agreements and membership by agency and office or installation, Jan 1983, annual listing, 9844–14

Labor unions reporting to Labor Dept, parent bodies and locals by State, city, and country, 1983 listing, 6468–17

Libraries, depository for Fed Govt publications, 1983 annual listing, 2214–1

Library (research) funding of Education Dept, by project, program area, instn, and State, FY84, annual listing, 4804–22

Marine mammals research, Fed Govt funding by agency, topic, and performing instn, FY82, annual rpt, 14734–2

Meat plants inspected and certified for exporting products to US, by country, 1983, annual listing, 1374–2

Medicare Supplementary Medical Insurance maximum charges reimbursable for specific services, by State and outlying area, 1983, annual rpt, 4654–4

Military post exchange operations, locations worldwide, sales by type of commodity or service and facility, and employment, FY83, annual rpt, 3504–10

Museum grants of Natl Foundation on Arts and Humanities, by instn, State, and city, FY84, annual rpt series, 9564–6

NASA R&D funding to colleges and universities, by State, field of science, and instn, FY83, annual listing, 9504–7

Natl Endowment for Arts activities and grants, FY83, annual rpt, 9564–3

Index by Subjects and Names

Natl Endowment for Humanities activities and grants, FY83, annual rpt, 9564–2

NIH grants and awards for R&D, training, construction, and medical libraries, by location and recipient, FY83, annual listings, 4434–7

NSF Science Resources Studies Div activities, project descriptions, and 1973-83 publications, 1983 annual listing, 9624–21

Nuclear reactors for domestic use and export by function, with owner, operating characteristics, and location, Apr 1984, semiannual listing, 3002–5

Occupational Outlook Handbook, 1984-85 biennial rpt, 6744–1

Oil and gas fields by State and EIA field code, 1983, annual listing, 3164–70

Overseas Business Reports: economic conditions, investment and export opportunities, and trade practices, annual country market research rpt series, 2046–6

Overseas Private Investment Corp activities, foreign and US project impacts, and list of insured projects and companies, FY83, annual rpt, 9904–3

Park natl system and other areas under Natl Park Service mgmt, acreage by type of area, ownership, and site, as of Sept 1984, semiannual rpt, 5542–1

Pesticide manufacturers listing, 1982, annual rpt, 1804–5

Population and health research funded by 4 private organizations, project listing by topic, with funding data, 1981, annual rpt, 4474–16

Public building construction, alteration, and leasing projects, description and cost by location, Dec 1983, annual listing, 9454–12

R&D Fed Govt facilities and services available for private sector use, by field of science, 1984 biennial listing, 2224–4

Reclamation Bur water storage and carriage facilities, by type, as of Sept 1983, annual listing, 5824–7

Savings and loan assns, FHLB 8th District members, locations, assets, and savings, 1984, annual listing, 9304–9

Savings and loan assns, FHLB 10th District members, locations, assets, and savings, 1984, annual listing, 9304–17

Savings and loan assns, FHLB 11th District member offices, locations, savings balances, and accounts, quarterly listing, 9302–20

Savings instns, FHLB 1st District members, locations, and financial condition, 1984, annual listing, 9304–26

Scientific research and training awards of NSF, recipients by State, FY83, annual listing, 9624–11

Sedimentation control, surveillance, and research activity of Fed Govt, by project, agency, region, and State, 1982, annual rpt, 5664–9

Senate salaries, expenses, and contingent fund disbursements, by payee, detailed listings, 1st half FY84, semiannual rpt, 25922–1

Ships in active US merchant fleet and Natl Defense Reserve Fleet, number and tonnage by name and owner/operator, Jan 1984, semiannual inventory, 7702–2

Ships in world bulk carrier fleet, characteristics by country of registry, 1982, annual rpt, 7704–13

Ships in world tanker fleet, by selected characteristics and country of registry, 1982, annual rpt, 7704–17

Solar collector and photovoltaic module manufacturers, 1983, annual listing, 3164–62

Solar photovoltaic system R&D sponsored by DOE, project descriptions and publications, FY83, annual listing, 3304–20

Standard reference and research materials available from Natl Bur of Standards, 1984-85, biennial catalog, 2214–2

Surety companies authorized to post bonds with Fed Govt, location and bonding limits, as of July 1984, annual listing, 8104–4

Treaties and other bilateral and multilateral agreements of US in force, by country, Jan 1984, annual listing, 7004–1

TV and radio station employment, total and for minorities and women, by full- and part-time status and individual station, 1983, annual rpt, 9284–7

UN participation of US, and member and nonmember shares of UN budget by country, FY83-85, annual rpt, 7004–5

Urban Dev Action Grant awards, private and public investment, and jobs, housing units, and taxes generated, by city and project, FY83, annual rpt, 5124–5

Urban Dev Action Grant awards to local areas, preliminary approvals, with project descriptions, private investment, and jobs and taxes to be created, by city, quarterly press release series, 5002–7

USITC analysts assigned to cover individual commodities, grouped by TSUSA schedule, 1983 listing, 9888–12

VA facilities psychological services, staffing, research, and training programs, 1984 annual listing, 9924–10

VA medical facilities sharing agreement contracts, services, and costs, by region and facility, FY83, annual rpt, 9924–18

Vital statistics records offices and availability of birth, death, marriage, and divorce certificates, by State, 1984 annual listing, 4124–7

Weather broadcasts for US ships, by major ocean area, as of Jan 1984, biennial rpt, 2184–3

Weather stations of Natl Weather Service, locations and regular observations made, 1984 annual listing, 2184–5

Weather stations of Upper Air Observational Network, by US and foreign location, 1984 annual listing, 2184–6

Wildlife and bird research of State fish and wildlife agencies, federally funded projects and costs, by species and State, 1984, annual rpt, 5504–24

Workers compensation advisory committees and study commissions, functions, and interests represented, by State, as of July 1984, annual rpt, 6502–1

see also Bibliographies

see also Computer data file guides

Disability insurance

Employee benefits in private industry, coverage by benefit type and provisions and occupational group, 1983, annual rpt, 6784–19

Disabled and handicapped persons

Employee benefits in private industry, percent of employers providing selected benefits, 1979-82, conf proceedings, 25408–89

Fed Govt civilian employee retirement, health, and life insurance benefit plans operations and finances, FY81-82, annual rpt, 9844–1

Foreign social security programs coverage, funding, eligibility, and benefits, by country, 1983, biennial rpt, 4746–4.58

Income tax returns of individuals, detailed data, 1982, annual rpt, 8304–2

Short-term disability, earnings lost, insurance benefits, sick leave, and work days lost by sex, by type of worker, 1948-81, article, 4742–1.417

Short-term disability insurance laws of States, comparison of provisions, as of Sept 1984, semiannual revision, 6402–2

see also Black lung

see also Old-Age, Survivors, Disability, and Health Insurance

see also Workers compensation

Disability Insurance Trust Fund

see Federal trust funds

Disabled American Veterans

Financial statements of Disabled American Veterans, 1982, GAO rpt, 26111–16

Disabled and handicapped persons

Census of Population and Housing, 1980: detailed population and housing characteristics, by county, city, and census tract, State and SMSA rpt series, 2551–2

Census of Population, 1980: detailed socioeconomic characteristics, by county, city, and inside-outside SMSAs and central cities, State rpt series, 2531–3

CETA participants by sociodemographic characteristics, and Labor Dept activities and staff, FY83, annual rpt, 6304–1

DOT employment by subagency, State, and selected personnel characteristics, FY83, annual rpt, 7304–18.2

Fed Govt civilian employment in selected agencies by handicap status, and worldwide by pay plan and grade, by race, Hispanic origin, and sex, as of Sept 1982, article, 9842–1.403

Fed Govt minority group and handicapped employment, by race, Hispanic origin, disability, sex, and employment characteristics, as of Sept 1982, biennial rpt, 9844–27

Fed Govt noncompetitive temporary hiring of disabled veterans, by pay system, grade, and agency, 2nd half FY82, semiannual rpt, 9842–4

Food stamp recipient households size and composition, income, and income deductions allowed, Aug 1981, annual rpt, 1364–8

Fresno, Calif, economic, population, labor, and housing indicators, various periods 1974-85, hearing, 21248–84

Health Services Research Natl Center grants and contracts, by program area, FY83, annual listing, 4184–2

HHS aid to each State and local govt or private instn, amount obligated, funding agency, and program, FY83, annual listing, 4004–3

High school classes of 1980 and 1982: educational and sociodemographic characteristics and expectations, natl longitudinal study, series, 4826–2

Disabled and handicapped persons

Hispanic Americans with disabilities, by disability type and severity and for 5 States, selected years 1970-78, conf proceedings, 16598-5

Homeless population and characteristics, and temporary shelter operations, use, and user characteristics, for selected cities, various periods 1979-84, hearing, 21248-85

Income (household) and cash and noncash transfer program participation, by sociodemographic characteristics, quarterly rpt, 2542-2

Mail (free) for blind and handicapped, USPS revenue forgone by class of mail, FY83, annual rpt, 9864-5.3

Mail (free) for blind and handicapped, volume and costs, FY83, annual rpt, 9864-2

Mail (free) for blind and handicapped, volume and weight, quarterly rpt, 9862-1

Mail (free) for blind, handicapped, and servicemen, USPS operating costs itemized by class of mail, FY83, annual rpt, 9864-4

Older persons population characteristics, and needs and costs of social services by type, by metro-nonmetro status, 1970s-82 with trends from 1900, 21148-28

Older persons volunteer programs of ACTION, activities and volunteer characteristics, FY82, annual rpt, 9024-2

Pension plans for public employees, benefits and beneficiaries by eligibility reason, level of govt, and Federal plan, selected years 1954-80, article, 4742-1.403

Recreation at outdoor Fed Govt facilities, Golden Age and Golden Access Passports issued, by agency, 1983, annual rpt, 5544-14

Scientists and engineers with disability, by field, race, age, and employment status and type, 1981-82, biennial rpt, 9624-20.1

Treatment and services for developmentally disabled, university-affiliated facility activities, funding, and clients, 1980-FY83, 4608-19

TVA employment of minorities and women, by detailed occupation, pay level, and grade, FY83 and goals for FY84, annual rpt, 9804-17

VA housing aid to paraplegics, monthly rpt, 9922-2

Veteran prisoners of war filing disability claims by period of service, and disability ratings by type and degree, various dates Oct 1981-May 1984, chartbook, 9928-30

Veterans (disabled and nondisabled) Fed Govt appointments and separations, agency, 2nd half FY82, semiannual rpt, 9842-3

Veterans aged 55 and over, socioeconomic characteristics, economic resources, health care and status, and actual and expected use of VA benefits, 1983 survey, 9928-29

Veterans disability and deaths not connected with service, pension cases by sex, entitlement type, and period of service, as of Mar 1984, semiannual rpt, 9922-12

Veterans disability by type, and deaths, by period of service, and VA activities, FY83, annual rpt, 9924-1.6

Veterans disability compensation from VA, cases by sex, type and degree of disability, and period of service, as of Mar 1984, semiannual rpt, 9922-9

Veterans of Vietnam era, compensation cases by degree of impairment, compared with WW II and Korea veterans, FY83, annual rpt, 9924-8.5

Veterans with self-reported disabilities, by age, race, employment status, period of service, and whether applied for VA benefits, 1979, 9926-4.6

Veterans with VA vocational rehabilitation training, employment and other characteristics, and VA employment services, by regional office, as of Aug 1983, GAO rpt, 26121-78

Women with disability, by socioeconomic and demographic characteristics, and compared to nondisabled women and disabled men, 1981, chartbook, 16598-4

see also Adult day care

see also Aid to Permanently and Totally Disabled

see also Blind

see also Deaf

see also Disability insurance

see also Handicapped children

see also Medicare

see also Mental retardation

see also Mobility limitations

see also Old-Age, Survivors, Disability, and Health Insurance

see also Rehabilitation of the disabled

see also Special education

see also Supplemental Security Income

see also Vocational rehabilitation

Disadvantaged

see Compensatory education

see Disabled and handicapped persons

see Discrimination in education

see Discrimination in employment

see Discrimination in housing

see Handicapped children

see Minority groups

see Poverty

Disarmament

see Arms control and disarmament

Disaster relief

Agricultural Conservation Program participation and payments, by State, FY83, annual rpt, 1804-7

Agricultural Stabilization and Conservation Service producer payments under 26 programs, monthly rpt, 1802-10

AID economic assistance to developing countries, obligations and disbursements by country, quarterly rpt, 9912-4

Budget of US Appendix, detailed budgets and personnel summaries, by agency, FY85, annual rpt, 104-3

Budget of US, effects of Reagan Admin policy changes, by detailed program, FY85, annual rpt, 104-21

Budget of US, receipts by source and outlays by function, FY40-89 estimates revised for consistency with FY85 budget definitions, annual rpt, 104-12

Central America economic assistance from AID by type of aid, for 7 countries, FY80-83, GAO rpt, 26123-55

Developing countries disaster preparedness and summary sociodemographic, political, and economic data, country rpt series, 9916-2

Index by Subjects and Names

Farmland restoration from natural disaster, Emergency Conservation Program participation and payments, by practice and State, FY83, annual rpt, 1804-22

Fed Emergency Mgmt Agency activities and funding for disaster and emergency relief, and major disasters, 1983, annual rpt, 9434-2

Fed Govt aid to State and local govts, expenditures, and direct payments, by program, agency, and State, FY83, annual rpt, 2464-2

Fed Govt financial and nonfinancial domestic aid, 1984 annual comprehensive catalog, 104-5

Fed Govt programs and mgmt cost control proposals, 3-year savings by function and agency, and financial and operating data, 1960s-81, 16908-1.13, 16908-1.23

Foreign countries disasters, persons affected, deaths, damage, and aid by US and others, FY83 and trends from FY64, annual rpt, 9914-12

Govt census, 1982: State govt payments to local govts, by program, source of funds, level of govt, and State, with trends from 1902, 2460-3

PL 480 exports by commodity, and recipients, by program, sponsor, and country, FY82 and aggregate from FY55, annual rpt, 1924-7

Red Cross program operations and financial statements, 1982/83, annual rpt, 29254-1

Schools in federally impacted areas, Fed Govt funding by county and school and congressional district, and eligible pupils, by State, FY83, annual rpt, 4804-10

Small Business Admin loan and contract activity by program, and balance sheets, FY83, annual rpt, 9764-1.1

Weather-related disaster programs of Fed Govt, costs by agency, monthly rpt, annual data, 2152-12

see also Agricultural insurance

see also Food assistance

see also International relief

Disasters

Census of Housing, 1980: inventory, occupancy, and unit characteristics, changes from 1973 by region and inside-outside SMSAs and central cities, series, 2473-3

Central America mineral, energy, and water resources, and natural hazards to resource dev, by country, 1981 with trends from 1977, 5668-71

Developing countries disaster preparedness and summary sociodemographic, political, and economic data, country rpt series, 9916-2

Fed Emergency Mgmt Agency activities and funding for disaster and emergency relief, and major disasters, 1983, annual rpt, 9434-2

Foreign countries disasters, persons affected, deaths, damage, and aid by US and others, FY83 and trends from FY64, annual rpt, 9914-12

Housing (earth-sheltered) design, energy efficiency, natural and nuclear hazard reduction, and costs, by selected SMSA, 1983 rpt, 3308-71

Natl Guard (Army and Air) activities, manpower, and facilities, FY83, annual rpt, 3704-3

Index by Subjects and Names

Statistical Abstract of US, social, political, and economic data, 1950s-83 and trends, annual rpt, 2324–1.1

see also Disaster relief
see also Drought
see also Earthquakes
see also Fires and fire prevention
see also Floods
see also Forest fires
see also Storms
see also Volcanoes

Discrimination

see Discrimination in education
see Discrimination in employment
see Discrimination in housing
see Racial discrimination
see Sex discrimination

Discrimination in education

Alabama rural black population, education, employment, health services, and economic status, for 16 counties, selected years 1970-81, 11048–180

Education Dept programs and activities, FY83, annual rpt, 4804–6

Education Dept programs funding, operations, and effectiveness, FY83, annual rpt, 4804–5

Higher education desegregation, Louisiana black instn funding, and Virginia students needed to meet desegregation goals, by instn, late 1970s-85, hearings, 21348–91

Discrimination in employment

Alabama rural black population, education, employment, health services, and economic status, for 16 counties, selected years 1970-81, 11048–180

Budget of US, effects of Reagan Admin policy changes, by detailed program, FY85, annual rpt, 104–21

Fed Govt Equal Opportunity Recruitment Program implementation, and summary employment data, FY83, annual rpt, 9844–33

Hispanic Americans and other minority employment discrimination, Equal Employment Opportunity Commission enforcement activities, personnel, and litigation, 1970s-FY83, 9248–18

Labor legislation enacted by 48 States, DC, and Guam, 1983, annual summary article, 6722–1.406

Minorities and women civil rights progress, Supreme Court decisions, and legislative action, 1957-83, last issue of narrative annual rpt, 11044–3

State Dept and Foreign Service minority and women employment by pay level, and affirmative action plan, FY83, annual rpt, 7004–11

TVA employment of minorities and women, by detailed occupation, pay level, and grade, FY83 and goals for FY84, annual rpt, 9804–17

Discrimination in housing

Children restricted from rental housing, by type of unit, 1980, hearing, 21968–28

Community Dev Block Grants recipients monitored for fair housing practices, and findings, FY82-83, annual rpt, 5124–5

Complaints of housing discrimination collected through HUD-sponsored fair housing study in 9 cities, with nationwide comparisons, 1978/79-1980/81, 5188–102

Fair housing planning program awards to 15 communities, 1984 press release, 5006–3.32

Fair housing programs, HUD grants by community, 1984 press release, 5006–3.34

Minorities and women civil rights progress, Supreme Court decisions, and legislative action, 1957-83, last issue of narrative annual rpt, 11044–3

Diseases and disorders

Agent Orange exposed Air Force personnel diseases and disorders, by disease type, age, and officer status, 1984 rpt, 3604–3

Air pollutant and radiation indoor levels by emissions source, and household exposure and health effects by pollutant type, various periods 1966-83, hearings, 21708–102

Army active duty personnel health status and use of Army medical services in US and abroad, by treatment facility, monthly rpt, 3702–4.2

Cases and incidence of infectious notifiable diseases and other public health concerns, by census div and State, 1982, annual rpt, 4204–1

Cases and mortality trends for infectious notifiable diseases and other public health concerns, quarterly rpt articles, 4202–7

Developing countries disaster preparedness and summary sociodemographic, political, and economic data, country rpt series, 9916–2

Disability Insurance beneficiaries sociodemographic and medical characteristics, 1977-79, annual rpt, 4744–20

HHS aid to each State and local govt or private instn, amount obligated, funding agency, and program, FY83, annual listing, 4004–3

Indian births, morbidity, and deaths and rates, and health services facilities and use, 1954-83, annual compilation, 4104–7

NIH publications, 1983, annual listing, 4434–2

Statistical Abstract of US, social, political, and economic data, 1950s-83 and trends, annual rpt, 2324–1.1

TTPI socioeconomic, health, and govtl data, by TTPI govt, FY83 and selected trends, detailed annual rpt, 7004–6

Vital and Health Statistics series and other NCHS publications, 1979-83, annual listing,, 4124–1

see also Accidents and accident prevention
see also Alcohol use
see also Allergies
see also Animal diseases and zoonoses
see also Birth defects
see also Black lung
see also Blood diseases and disorders
see also Blood pressure
see also Cardiovascular diseases
see also Cerebrovascular diseases
see also Circulatory diseases
see also Diabetes
see also Digestive diseases
see also Drug abuse and treatment
see also Ear diseases and infections
see also Eye diseases and defects
see also Food and waterborne diseases
see also Hearing and hearing disorders

see also Hereditary diseases
see also Infective and parasitic diseases
see also Mental health and illness
see also Mental retardation
see also Metabolic and endocrine diseases
see also Mobility limitations
see also Musculoskeletal diseases
see also Neoplasms
see also Neurological disorders
see also Nutrition and malnutrition
see also Obesity
see also Occupational health and safety
see also Pathology
see also Pneumonia and influenza
see also Poisoning and drug reaction
see also Rabies
see also Respiratory diseases
see also Skin diseases
see also Tuberculosis
see also Urogenital diseases
see also Vaccination and vaccines
see also Venereal diseases
see also under By Disease in the "Index by Categories"

Disposable income

see Personal and family income

Distillate fuels

see Diesel fuel
see Heating oil
see Petroleum and petroleum industry

Distribution of income

see Business income and expenses, general
see Earnings, general
see National income and product accounts
see Personal and family income
see Poverty
see Wealth

District courts

see Federal district courts

District of Columbia

see D.C.

Diversification of business

see Economic concentration and diversification

Division of Health Maintenance Organizations

see Office of Health Maintenance Organizations

Divorce

see Marriage and divorce

Diz, Adolfo C.

"Conditions Attached to Adjustment Financing: Evolution of the IMF Practice", 9373–3.28

Djibouti

Agricultural situation in sub-Saharan Africa, by country, 1982-83 and outlook for 1984, annual rpt, 1524–4.10

AID activities and funding by project and function, FY85, and developing countries summary socioeconomic data, 1970s-83, by country, annual rpt, 9914–3

AID economic assistance to developing countries, obligations and disbursements by country, quarterly rpt, 9912–4

Economic conditions and foreign marketing prospects in 46 Sub-Saharan countries, 1983 world region rpt, 2046–5.1

Economic, social, and political summary data, by country, 1984, annual factbook, 244–11

Exports of US, detailed Schedule B commodities by country of destination, 1983, annual rpt, 2424–9

Djibouti

Exports of US, detailed Schedule E commodities by mode of transport and world area and country of destination, 1983, annual rpts, 2424–5

Imports of US, detailed Schedule A commodities by country and world area of origin, and mode of transport, 1983, annual rpts, 2424–2

Imports of US, detailed TSUSA commodities by country of origin, 1983, annual rpt, 2424–4

Loans and grants for economic and military assistance from US and intl agencies, by program and country, FY46-83, annual rpt, 9914–5

Military aid of US, arms sales, and training programs costs and budget requests by program, world region, and country, FY83-85, annual rpt, 7144–13

Minerals Yearbook, 1982, Vol 3: foreign country reviews of production, trade, and policies, by commodity, annual rpt, 5604–35

Minerals Yearbook, 1982, Vol 3 preprints: foreign country review of production, trade, and policies, by commodity, annual rpt, 5604–17.83

Population size and growth rates, and latest available benchmark demographic data, by country, 1950-83, biennial rpt, 2324–4

see also under By Foreign Country in the "Index by Categories"

Doctors

see Physicians

Documents

see Bibliographies

see Environmental Impact Statements

see Government documents

see Government publications lists

DOD

see Department of Defense

Dolton, David D.

"Mourning Dove Breeding Population Status, 1984", 5504–15

Dombey, Bonita J.

"Analysis of Administration Strategic Arms Reduction and Modernization Proposals", 26306–6.73

Domestic and International Business Administration

see Bureau of Industrial Economics

see International Trade Administration

Domestic International Sales Corporations

Income of multinatl corporations, reallocation through regulation of intercorporate transactions by tax item, treaty status, asset size, industry, and tax haven country, 1982, 8008–110

Income tax returns filed by type of filer, selected income items, summary data, quarterly rpt, 8302–2.1

Income tax returns of corporations, detailed income and tax items by industry, 1981, annual rpt, 8304–4

Income tax returns of corporations with foreign tax credit, income and deductions by type, asset size, and selected industry group, 1980, article, 8302–2.415

Domestic relations

see Child abuse and neglect

see Domestic violence

see Families and households

see Marriage and divorce

Domestic violence

Crimes, arrests by offender characteristics, and rates, by offense, and law enforcement employees, by population size and jurisdiction, 1970s-83, annual rpt, 6224–2

Crimes of violence involving relatives, by victim-offender relationship, circumstances, and victim characteristics, aggregate 1973-81, 6066–19.5

Police dept performance, analyses of police activities effects on neighborhoods and citizens, 1977, compilation of papers, 6068–181

see also Child abuse and neglect

Domestics

see Household workers

Domiciliary care

see Halfway houses

see Home health services

see Homemaker services

see Nursing homes

see Veterans health facilities and services

Dominica

Economic conditions, income, production, prices, employment, and trade, 1984 annual country rpt, 2046–4.101

Economic, social, and political summary data, by country, 1984, annual factbook, 244–11

Imports of US, detailed Schedule A commodities by country and world area of origin, and mode of transport, 1983, annual rpts, 2424–2

Imports of US, detailed TSUSA commodities by country of origin, 1983, annual rpt, 2424–4

Population size and growth rates, and latest available benchmark demographic data, by country, 1950-83, biennial rpt, 2324–4

see also under By Foreign Country in the "Index by Categories"

Dominican Republic

Agricultural and food production indexes, and production of selected commodities, by world region and country, 1974-83, annual rpt, 1524–5

Agricultural situation in Latin America, by country, 1981-83 and outlook for 1984, annual rpt, 1524–4.9

Agricultural supply/demand, trade, and production, and socioeconomic data, by country, 1950s-77, 1528–179

AID activities and funding by project and function, FY85, and developing countries summary socioeconomic data, 1970s-83, by country, annual rpt, 9914–3

AID and other foreign assistance, and govt policy, effects on private sector dev and socioeconomic conditions, with case studies for 6 countries, 1960s-80, 9918–12

AID economic assistance to developing countries, obligations and disbursements by country, quarterly rpt, 9912–4

AID loan repayment status and terms by program and country, and status of predecessor agency loans, quarterly rpt, 9912–3

Disaster preparedness and summary sociodemographic, political, and economic data, 1970s-83, 9916–2.53

Economic, social, and political summary data, by country, 1984, annual factbook, 244–11

Index by Subjects and Names

Exports of US, detailed Schedule B commodities by country of destination, 1983, annual rpt, 2424–9

Exports of US, detailed Schedule E commodities by mode of transport and world area and country of destination, 1983, annual rpts, 2424–5

Food supply policies of 21 developing countries, with farm sector data, tariff income, and prices and imports of 5 grains, 1960s-81, 1528–168

Free zones in developing countries, industry financial and operating data by country, with case studies for 5 countries, 1970s-82, 9918–10

Imports of US, detailed Schedule A commodities by country and world area of origin, and mode of transport, 1983, annual rpts, 2424–2

Imports of US, detailed TSUSA commodities by country of origin, 1983, annual rpt, 2424–4

Loans and grants for economic and military assistance from US and intl agencies, by program and country, FY46-83, annual rpt, 9914–5

Military aid of US, arms sales, and training programs costs and budget requests by program, world region, and country, FY83-85, annual rpt, 7144–13

Military spending, arms trade, and armed forces size, with total govt spending and population, by country, 1972-82, annual rpt, 9824–1

Minerals Yearbook, 1982, Vol 3: foreign country reviews of production, trade, and policies, by commodity, annual rpt, 5604–35

Minerals Yearbook, 1983, Vol 3 preprints: foreign country review of production, trade, and policies, by commodity, annual rpt, 5604–23.85

Population size and growth rates, and latest available benchmark demographic data, by country, 1950-83, biennial rpt, 2324–4

Rum imports (duty-free) of US under Caribbean Basin Initiative, by country, Jan-June 1983-84, annual rpt, 9884–15

see also under By Foreign Country in the "Index by Categories"

Dommel, Paul R.

"Deregulating Community Development", 5188–105

Domowitz, Ian

"Conditional Variance and the Risk Premium in the Foreign Exchange Market", 9381–10.32

"Testing for Serial Correlation in the Presence of Heteroscedasticity with Applications to Exchange Rate Models", 9381–10.31

Donahoe, Gerald F.

"National Income and Product Accounts: Preliminary Revised Estimates, 1977", 2702–1.420

Donahoo, Kathleene K.

"Commercial Bank Investment in Municipal Securities", 9385–1.402

Donald, James R.

"Agricultural Outlook", 1004–16.1

Donkar, Eli N.

"Average Wages for 1982 for Indexing Under the Social Security Act and the Automatic Determinations for 1984", 4706–2.119

Index by Subjects and Names

Donnelly, Dennis M.
"Wood Product Flows and Market Structure in the Rocky Mountain States", 1208–208

Dornan, Daniel L.
"Analysis of Commuter Rail Costs and Cost Allocation Methods", 7888–61

DOT
see Department of Transportation

Dothan, Ala.
see also under By SMSA or MSA in the "Index by Categories"

Dotsey, Michael
"Investigation of Cash Management Practices and Their Effects on the Demand for Money", 9389–1.409

Doulman, David J.
"Recent Developments in Papua New Guinea's Tuna Fishery", 2162–1.402

Douty, H. M.
"Century of Wage Statistics: The BLS Contribution", 6722–1.466

Dover, N.H.
Census of Housing, 1980: occupancy and unit characteristics, by race, Hispanic origin, and city, SMSA rpt, 2473–1.291
Census of Population and Housing, 1980: detailed population and housing characteristics, by county, city, and census tract, SMSA rpt, 2551–2.291
see also under By SMSA or MSA in the "Index by Categories"

Downing, T. E.
"Social Dimensions of Rangeland Management", 1208–197

Drabenstott, Mark
"Better Times Ahead for Agriculture", 9381–1.402
"Fiscal Condition of Tenth District States", 9381–1.403
"Oil Shale in the U.S.: Prospects for Development", 9381–1.409

Draft
see Selective service

Dredging
Army Corps of Engineers activities and projects, FY83 and trends from 1800s, annual rpt, 3754–1
Coastal environmental characteristics, fish, wildlife, and use, and population socioeconomic data, for individual areas, series, 5506–4
Fed Govt programs and mgmt cost control proposals, 3-year savings by function and agency, and financial and operating data, 1960s-81, 16908–1.22
New York Bight pollutant loadings from ocean dumping of municipal wastes by type and source, and concentrations in fish and sediments, 1970s-82, hearings, 21568–36
Ocean dumping and pollution investigations and activities of NOAA, research and monitoring studies funded, and bibl, FY83, annual rpt, 2144–9
Ocean dumping of waste materials, EPA permit program and intl London Dumping Convention activities, 1981-83, annual rpt, 9204–8
Panama Canal dredging operations, FY82, annual rpt, 9664–3.3
Port dev costs and financing through user fees, and shipping industry impact on local economy, by State, other area, industry, commodity, and port, 1970s-2020, hearings, 21568–34

Port dredging hourly labor costs by component and occupation, and Army Corps of Engineers contract awards by region and company, 1970s-83, hearings, 21728–53
Sedimentation control, surveillance, and research activity of Fed Govt, by project, agency, region, and State, 1982, annual rpt, 5664–9
Wetlands environmental characteristics and mgmt, and Army Corps of Engineers projects for discharging dredged material on wetlands, 1950s-80, 26358–102

Drinking places
see Restaurants and restaurant industry

Drinking water
see Water supply and use

Drivers licenses
see Licenses and permits

Driving while intoxicated
Accidents (fatal), alcohol levels of drivers and pedestrians by driver age and sex and time of accident, 1980, 7768–81
Accidents (fatal), circumstances, and characteristics of persons and vehicles involved, detailed data, 1982, annual rpt, ~ 7764–10
Accidents (fatal), circumstances, and characteristics of persons and vehicles involved, 1983, annual rpt, 7764–14
Accidents, circumstances, injuries, deaths, and characteristics of persons and vehicles involved, 1982, annual rpt, 7764–13
Arrests and arrest rates, by offense, offender characteristics, population size, and State, 1970s-83, annual rpt, 6224–2.2
Court cases of Federal criminal defendants, disposition, convictions, and sentences, by offense and district, as of June 1983, annual rpt, 18204–1
Deaths in traffic accidents, total and alcohol-related, and drunk driver license revocations and other deterrence programs in selected States, 1980-82, · 9618–10
Health habits associated with 10 major death causes, prevalence of 8 risk factors in selected States, 1981-83 surveys, article, 4202–7.405
Micronesia Federated States, arrests by type, and traffic and other accidents and deaths, Jan-Aug 1983, annual rpt, 7004–6.2
Natl Hwy Traffic Safety Admin activities and funding, and traffic accident data, 1981, annual rpt, 7764–1.1
Navy personnel alcohol and drug abuse, and related deaths, courts-martial, discharges, and treatment program funding and staff, FY83, annual table, 3804–12
Research on alcoholism, treatment programs, and patient characteristics, quarterly journal, 4482–1
Research projects and traffic safety evaluations, quarterly rpt articles, 7762–9
Research review of alcohol use, and health, economic, and social impacts, 1970s-81, 4488–4
Truck accidents, injuries, deaths, and property damage, by circumstances, carrier type, and driver age and condition, 1983, annual rpt, 7554–9

Dropouts
see School dropouts

Drought
Agricultural water supply, crop moisture, and drought indexes, weekly rpt, seasonal data, 2152–2
Carbon dioxide atmospheric concentration increase effects on hydrologic conditions, projected for 26-35 years, 9188–95
Developing countries disaster preparedness and summary sociodemographic, political, and economic data, country rpt series, 9916–2
Farmland restoration from natural disaster, Emergency Conservation Program participation and payments, by practice and State, FY83, annual rpt, 1804–22
Fed Govt aid to State and local govts, expenditures, and direct payments, by program, agency, and State, FY83, annual rpt, 2464–2
Foreign countries disasters, persons affected, deaths, damage, and aid by US and others, FY83 and trends from FY64, annual rpt, 9914–12
Foreign weather conditions and impact assessment, by world area and country, monthly rpt, 2152–9
Water supply and quality, floods, drought, mudslides, and other hydrologic events, by State, 1983, annual rpt, 5664–12
Weather events socioeconomic impacts and costs, heating and cooling degree days, and housing energy bills, by census div and State, monthly rpt, 2152–12

Drug abuse and treatment

Acquired immune deficiency syndrome (AIDS) cases by sexual preference and intravenous drug use, and drug abusers characteristics, 1979-81, article, 4102–1.427
Adolescent abuse, characteristics of victims and abuse, local agencies contacted, drug and alcohol involvement, and reciprocal violence, 1980-81 survey, 4608–18
Alcohol, Drug Abuse and Mental Health Admin staff, contract awards and grants, by Inst, program, and State, FY83, annual factbook, 4044–1
Aliens excluded and deported by cause, 1892-FY81, annual rpt, 6264–2
Budget of US, effects of Reagan Admin policy changes, by detailed program, FY85, annual rpt, 104–21
Children and youth benefitting from Fed Govt public welfare programs and tax expenditures, participation and funding for 71 programs, FY81-83, 21968–30
Cocaine use, user characteristics, medical and botanical research, and South American production and legal policy and enforcement, 1979 intl conf papers, 7008–40
Crime and criminal justice data, including justice expenditures and employment by level of govt, 1970s-82 with some trends from 1875, 6068–174
Crimes, arrests by offender characteristics, and rates, by offense, and law enforcement employees, by population size and jurisdiction, 1970s-83, annual rpt, 6224–2
DC criminal cases involving drug users, and user and nonuser rates of detention, pretrial rearrest, and failure to appear in court, 1979-81, 6066–20.7

Drug abuse and treatment

- Deaths and death rates by detailed cause and demographic characteristics, 1979 and selected trends, US Vital Statistics annual rpt, 4144–2.1
- Economic indicators relation to measures of social pathology including crime and death rates, various periods 1950-80, 23848–76
- Education Dept programs funding, operations, and effectiveness, FY83, annual rpt, 4804–5
- Employee theft and misconduct in retail, hospital, and manufacturing establishments, by type and frequency of violation, 1978-80, 6068–178
- Fed Govt aid to State and local govts, expenditures, and direct payments, by program, agency, and State, FY83, annual rpt, 2464–2
- Fed Govt plan to reduce drug abuse and trafficking, funding by agency and background data on drug use by substance, selected years FY81-85, biennial rpt, 024–1
- Govt census, 1982: State govt payments to local govts, by program, source of funds, level of govt, and State, with trends from 1902, 2460–3
- HHS aid to each State and local govt or private instn, amount obligated, funding agency, and program, FY83, annual listing, 4004–3
- High school seniors use and assessment of drugs by type, alcohol, and cigarettes, by sex and region, 1975-83 surveys, annual rpt, 4494–4
- High school seniors use of drugs, alcohol, and cigarettes, 1975-82, article, 4102–1.410
- Homeless population and characteristics, and temporary shelter operations, use, and user characteristics, for selected cities, various periods 1979-84, hearing, 21248–85
- Israel and France urban youths use of selected drugs, alcohol, and cigarettes, by age and sex, 1977 and 1979, article, 4102–1.430
- Jail capacities, conditions, expenditures, and services, and socioeconomic and other characteristics of inmates, various dates 1976-82, 10048–59
- Mental health facilities, services, staff, and patient characteristics, 1970s-82 with trends from 1954, annual rpt, 4504–9
- Mental hospitals of States and counties, patients and admissions by diagnosis, age, and State, FY81, annual rpt, 4504–2
- Military personnel drug-related courts martial and other disciplinary actions, by service branch, FY80-84, 3508–19
- Navy personnel alcohol and drug abuse, and related deaths, courts-martial, discharges, and treatment program funding and staff, FY83, annual table, 3804–12
- Organized Crime Drug Enforcement Task Force Program investigation activities, funding, and personnel, with nationwide drug abuse data, 1983 annual rpt, 6004–17
- Research compilations and summaries, bibls, and survey instruments, series, 4496–1
- Research on drug abuse and treatment, highlights of studies by Natl Inst on Drug Abuse grant recipients, periodic rpt, 4492–4

South Carolina manufacturing plants with selected employee health care services, by SIC 2-digit industry, 1982, article, 4102–1.408

- State and local govt officials attitudes toward drug abuse situation, prevention and treatment programs, law enforcement, funding needs, and Fed Govt role, 1983 survey, 21968–27
- State govt alcohol, drug abuse, and mental health treatment funding, and admin of Fed Govt block grants, for 13 States, FY80-84, GAO rpt, 26121–87
- *Statistical Abstract of US,* social, political, and economic data, 1950s-83 and trends, annual rpt, 2324–1.1
- Treatment of alcohol- and drug abuse-related and other mental health disorders, outpatient visits in Baltimore, Md, and visit probability rates, 1981-82, article, 4102–1.449
- Treatment programs, methods, and policy issues, series, 4496–5
- Use, casualties, treatment program and emergency room admissions in major cities, supply, arrests, and seizures, by drug type, 1982, annual rpt, 15894–1
- Use of drugs and health consequences of drug abuse, and Natl Inst on Drug Abuse and other HHS prevention activities, FY82, annual rpt, 4004–26
- *see also* Drug and narcotics traffic
- *see also* Marijuana
- *see also* Methadone treatment

Drug and narcotics traffic

- Aliens excluded and deported by cause, and Immigration and Naturalization Service narcotics activities, 1892-FY81, annual rpt, 6264–2
- Arrests and arrest rates, by offense, offender characteristics, population size, and State, 1970s-83, annual rpt, 6224–2.2
- Cocaine use, user characteristics, medical and botanical research, and South American production and legal policy and enforcement, 1979 intl conf papers, 7008–40
- Convictions, prison sentences, and average sentence lengths, by offense, offender class, and selected State, various periods 1971-84, 6066–19.10
- Court cases, dispositions, convictions, and sentences of Federal criminal defendants, by offense and district, as of June 1983 with trends from 1945, annual rpt, 18204–1
- Criminal case processing from arrest to sentencing, cases and processing time by disposition, dismissal reason, and offense, for 14 cities, 1979, 6066–22.1
- Criminal cases of DEA against leading drug traffickers by case processing characteristics and disposition, and agents assessment of investigative activities, in 3 cities, 1979-82, GAO rpt, 26119–57
- Criminal drug, fraud, and bank robbery Federal defendants, by sociodemographic and case processing characteristics, 1979, 6062–2.403
- Customs Service activities, operations, and staff, FY79-83, annual rpt, 8144–1
- Fed Govt felony court cases, by offense, and characteristics of case processing, sentencing, and offender, 1979-80, periodic rpt, 6062–2.407

Index by Subjects and Names

- Fed Govt plan to reduce drug abuse and trafficking, funding by agency and background data on drug use by substance, selected years FY81-85, biennial rpt, 024–1
- Fed Govt programs and mgmt cost control proposals, 3-year savings by function and agency, and financial and operating data, 1960s-81, 16908–1.9, 16908–1.12
- Fed Govt tax litigation, prosecutions, interpretive law decisions, and operating expenses of IRS, with collections, refunds, and taxes due, by region and State, FY83, annual rpt, 8304–3
- Foreign drug and narcotics production, acreage, eradication, and seizures, by substance, with labs destroyed and US aid, by country, 1981-85, annual rpt, 7004–17
- Income (taxable) not reported, by illegal source, with characteristics of persons involved, methodology, and bibl, 1970s-82, 8008–112
- Income (taxable) not reported on individual and corporate returns, and associated Federal revenue losses, by detailed legal and illegal source, 1973-81, 8308–26
- Justice Dept activities, by subagency, FY82, annual rpt, 6004–1
- Organized Crime Drug Enforcement Task Force Program investigation activities, funding, and personnel, with nationwide drug abuse data, 1983 annual rpt, 6004–17
- Organized Crime Drug Enforcement Task Forces, funding and staff by agency, region, and city, FY83, GAO rpt, 26119–52
- Pretrial citation release use, cost savings for law enforcement agencies, and failures to appear in court, by offense and selected jurisdiction, 1970s-82, 6068–187
- Prison terms actually served by selected State, and Illinois pretrial detention time credited to sentence, by offense, various periods 1977-83, 6066–19.7
- Prisoners in State prisons median sentence, and admissions and releases by prisoner and sentencing characteristics, by offense and State, 1981 and trends from 1926, 6066–19.9
- State and local govt officials attitudes toward drug abuse situation, prevention and treatment programs, law enforcement, funding needs, and Fed Govt role, 1983 survey, 21968–27
- Supply, use, casualties, treatment program and emergency room admissions in major cities, arrests, and seizures, by drug type, 1982, annual rpt, 15894–1
- Wiretapping authorizations by offense, costs, persons involved, arrests, trials, and convictions, 1983, annual rpt, 18204–7

Drug Enforcement Administration

- Activities of DEA, with staff and arrest data, FY82, annual rpt, 6004–1
- Assaults, murders, and other deaths of law enforcement officers, by circumstances, level of govt, agency, victim and offender characteristics, and location, 1983, annual rpt, 6224–3
- Cost control proposals for Fed Govt programs and mgmt, 3-year savings by function and agency, and financial and operating data, 1960s-81, 16908–1.9

Index by Subjects and Names

Criminal cases of DEA against leading drug traffickers by case processing characteristics and disposition, and agents assessment of investigative activities, in 3 cities, 1979-82, GAO rpt, 26119–57

Marijuana cultivation control activity of State law enforcement agencies, and aid from Fed Govt and Natl Guard, 1983 survey, GAO rpt, 26119–64

Drug industry

see Pharmaceutical industry

Drugs

- Allergy and Infectious Diseases Natl Inst activities, grants by instn, State, and country, and disease incidence and costs, FY60s-84, annual rpt, 4474–30
- Analgesic drugs provided during visits to office-based physicians, by patient characteristics, drug brand and type, and physician specialty, 1980-81, 4146–8.99
- Benzenoid chemicals imports by country of origin and product, 1983, annual rpt, 9884–2
- Biotechnology firms, patents, and trade by country, and effect of industry growth on US drug and chemical trade, selected years 1979-2000, 9886–4.78
- China economic conditions, agricultural and industrial production, trade, and domestic and foreign investment, 1980-85, 2048–106
- Costs to pharmacists of brand name prescription drugs, and Medicare maximum allowable costs, by class and manufacturer, July/Aug 1983, 4658–6
- County Business Patterns: establishments, employees, and payrolls, by SIC 4-digit industry and county, 1982, annual State rpt series, 2326–6
- Estrogen prescribed by physicians during menopause, by dosage and physician specialty, 1974 and 1981, article, 4102–1.444
- Exports and imports of US, by agricultural commodity and country, bimonthly rpt with articles, 1522–1
- Exports and imports of US, detailed SIC-based commodities by world area, 1983, annual rpts, 2424–6
- Exports and imports of US, totals and as percent of domestic production, by SIC 2- to 5-digit commodity, 1981, annual rpt, 2424–3
- Exports of US, detailed commodities by country of destination, monthly rpt, 2422–3
- Exports of US, detailed Schedule B commodities by country of destination, 1983, annual rpt, 2424–9
- Exports of US, detailed Schedule E commodities by mode of transport and world area and country of destination, 1983, annual rpts, 2424–5
- FDA investigation and regulatory activities, quarterly rpt, 4062–3
- Great Lakes trade, by SITC 3-digit commodity, port, vessel type, world area, and country, 1982, annual rpt, 7744–3
- *Health Care Financing Review,* Medicare and Medicaid program activity, health care expenditures, and research, quarterly rpt with articles, 4652–1
- Imports of US, detailed Schedule A commodities by country and world area of origin, and mode of transport, 1983, annual rpts, 2424–2

Imports of US, detailed Schedule A commodities by country, monthly rpt, 2422–2

- Imports of US, detailed TSUSA commodities by country of origin, 1983, annual rpt, 2424–4
- Infections (hospital-related), drug resistance, and associated deaths, for teaching and non-teaching hospitals, 1980-82, article, 4202–7.401
- Input-output structure of US economy, detailed interindustry transactions for 85 industries, and components of final demand, 1977, article, 2702–1.421
- Input-output structure of US economy, detailed interindustry transactions for 537 industries, and components of final demand, 1977 benchmark data, 2708–17
- Internist office visits and drugs provided, by characteristics of visit, patient, and physician, and location, 1980-81, 4147–13.80
- Manufacturing census, 1982: financial and operating data, for SIC 4-digit industries by product, preliminary rpt, 2491–1.182, 2491–1.183
- Medicare and Medicaid eligibility, participation, covered services and use, and reimbursements and payments, various periods 1966-82, annual rpt, 4654–1
- Medicare coverage of new medical technologies and reimbursements, and health services use and costs, selected years 1966-82, 26358–106
- Mental health physician office visits, type of by service provided and physician specialty, 1975 and 1980, annual rpt, 4504–9.2
- Obstetrician-gynecologist office visits and drugs used, by visit reason, diagnosis, treatment, and patient and physician characteristics, 1980-81, 4147–13.76
- OECD trade, total and for 4 major countries, and US trade by country, by commodity, 1972-82, annual world region rpt series, 244–13
- Oral contraceptives prescriptions, and market shares by progestin and estrogen content, 1964-80, article, 4102–1.436
- Over-the-counter drug use related to sociodemographic characteristics and perceived need, by drug type, 1975 survey, article, 4102–1.435
- Patent life and FDA approval time for drugs, prices by brand and generic category, and industry R&D costs and finances, selected years 1962-83, hearing, 25528–98
- Physician visits for new pain symptoms, by diagnosis, physician specialty, and patient characteristics, and drugs prescribed or used, 1980-81, 4146–8.97
- Physicians (not office-based) visits by reason, diagnosis, treatment, patient and physician characteristics, and physician primary activity, 1980, 4147–13.77
- Physicians (office-based), drugs prescribed or provided most often, by patient, physician, and drug characteristics, 1981, series, 4146–8
- Plant and animal genetic resource conservation, commercial uses, causes of depletion, and geographic sources, 1984 rpt, 5548–13

Drugstores

- Prescription drug use by outpatient characteristics and generic or brand name, and hospital and drugstore costs by drug class, 1982, annual rpt, 4064–12
- Producer prices and indexes, by stage of processing and detailed commodity, monthly rpt, 6762–6
- Producer prices and indexes, by stage of processing and detailed commodity, monthly 1983, annual supplement, 6764–2
- Production and sales of synthetic organic chemicals by product, and listing of manufacturers, 1983, annual rpt, 9884–3
- Production of synthetic organic chemicals, by detailed product, monthly rpt, 9882–1
- Shipments by region and selected census div and State, trade, and consumption, by product, 1983, annual Current Industrial Rpt, 2506–8.5
- Stockpiling of strategic and critical materials, Fed Govt activities and inventories by commodity, Oct 1983-Mar 1984, semiannual rpt, 9432–1
- Stockpiling of strategic materials, inventories, costs, and goals, by commodity, as of June 1984, semiannual rpt, 9452–7
- Supplementary Security Income beneficiary socioeconomic characteristics and health service use, 1970s-83 and SSI program projections to 1995, 25148–29
- Surgeon office visits and drugs provided, by characteristics of visit, patient, and physician, and location, 1980-81, 4147–13.79
- Tuberculosis cases, deaths, and treatment, by demographic characteristics, State, and city, 1982 and trends from 1953, annual rpt, 4204–2
- Waterborne commerce of US (domestic and foreign), freight by commodity, traffic, and passengers, by port and waterway, 1982, annual rpt, 3754–3

see also Drug abuse and treatment

see also Drug and narcotics traffic

see also Drugstores

see also Marijuana

see also Pharmaceutical industry

see also Poisoning and drug reaction

see also Vaccination and vaccines

see also under By Commodity in the "Index by Categories"

Drugstores

- Census of Population, 1980: detailed socioeconomic and demographic characteristics, by age, sex, race, Hispanic origin, occupation, and industry, State rpt series, 2531–4
- Census of Retail Trade, 1982: employment, establishments, sales, and payroll, by SIC 2- to 4-digit kind of business, SMSA, and retail district, State rpt series, 2401–1
- Census of Retail Trade, 1982: employment, establishments, sales, and payroll, by SIC 2- to 4-digit kind of business, SMSA, county, and city, State rpt series, 2397–1
- Census of Retail Trade, 1982: employment, establishments, sales, and payroll, for drug and proprietary stores, by State, preliminary rpt, 2395–1.26
- County Business Patterns: establishments, employees, and payrolls, by SIC 4-digit industry and county, 1981, annual State rpt series, 2326–8

Drugstores

County Business Patterns: establishments, employees, and payrolls, by SIC 4-digit industry and county, 1982, annual State rpt series, 2326–6

Employment, earnings, and hours, by SIC 4-digit nonfarm industry, monthly 1974-Feb 1984, annual update, 6744–4

Franchise business opportunities, by firm and kind of business, 1984 annual listing, 2044–27

Income tax returns of corporations, detailed income and tax items by industry, 1981, annual rpt, 8304–4

Income tax returns of sole proprietorships, detailed data by industry div and selected industry group, 1981, annual rpt, 8304–7

Income tax returns of sole proprietorships, receipts, deductions by type, payroll, and net income, by major industry, 1982, annual article, 8302–2.413

Minority group and women employment, by occupational group and SIC 2- to 3-digit industry, 1981, annual rpt, 9244–1.1

Pharmacists employment and sociodemographic characteristics, and reasons for not working in field, by State and overseas, as of 1979, 4147–14.28

Prescription drug use by outpatient characteristics and generic or brand name, and hospital and drugstore costs by drug class, 1982, annual rpt, 4064–12

Productivity, hours, and employment indexes for selected SIC 3- and 4-digit industries, 1954-82, annual rpt, 6824–1.4

Sales and inventories, by kind of business, region, census div, and selected State, SMSA, and city, and seasonal adjustments, monthly rpt, 2413–3

Sales, inventories, purchases, gross margin, and accounts receivable, by SIC 2- to 4-digit kind of business and type of ownership, 1983, annual rpt, 2413–5

Scientists, engineers, and technicians employment in transportation, utilities, and retail and wholesale trade, by field of science and industry, 1982, 9628–72

Virgin Islands economic censuses, 1982: employment, establishments, payroll, and receipts, by SIC 1- to 4-digit industry, island, and city, 2593–1

Drunk drivers

see Driving while intoxicated

Drunkenness

see Alcohol use

Dubai

see United Arab Emirates

Dubuque, Iowa

Census of Housing, 1980: occupancy and unit characteristics, by race, Hispanic origin, and city, SMSA rpt, 2473–1.141

Census of Population and Housing, 1980: detailed population and housing characteristics, by county, city, and census tract, SMSA rpt, 2551–2.141

see also under By SMSA or MSA in the "Index by Categories"

Duchin, Faye

"Impacts of Automation on Employment, 1963-2000", 21728–54

Dudley, William

"Comparison of Direct Deposit and Check Payment Costs", 9366–1.139

Index by Subjects and Names

Due process of law

Court civil and criminal caseloads for Federal district, appeals, and special courts, year ended June 1983 and selected trends from 1940, annual rpt, 18204–8

Criminal case processing from arrest to sentencing, series, 6066–22

Foreign human rights conditions in 162 countries, economic and military aid of US, and economic aid of intl organizations, 1981-83, annual rpt, 21384–3

see also Civil procedure

see also Criminal procedure

see also Right to counsel

Duesenberry, James S.

"Political Economy of Central Banking in the U.S. or Quis Custodiet Ipsos Custodes", 9373–3.26

Duewer, Lawrence A.

"Beef and Pork: Capacity of Marketing Services", 1561–7.401

"Changing Trends in the Red Meat Distribution System", 1548–232

Duff, G. Warren

"New York State Police Controlled Access Highway Task Force", 7762–9.403

Duffy, Michael

"Corn and Soybean Fertilizer Use for Alternative Tillage Practices", 1561–16.401

"Pesticide Use and Practices, 1982", 1588–76

"Returns to Corn and Soybean Tillage Practices", 1588–80

Duggan, James E.

"Labor Force Participation of Older Workers", 6886–6.8

Dulles International Airport

Cost control proposals for Fed Govt programs and mgmt, 3-year savings by function and agency, and financial and operating data, 1960s-81, 16908–1.11, 16908–1.28

Financial and operating data for DC metro airports, FY82-83, annual rpt, 7504–10

Duluth, Minn.

Census of Housing, 1980: occupancy and unit characteristics, by race, Hispanic origin, and city, SMSA rpt, 2473–1.142

Census of Population and Housing, 1980: detailed population and housing characteristics, by county, city, and census tract, SMSA rpt, 2551–2.142

Wages of office and plant workers, by occupation, 1984 labor market area survey rpt, 6785–3.6

see also under By SMSA or MSA in the "Index by Categories"

Dumping

Foreign trade and economic indicators by country and country group, and US trade policy actions, 1960s-83, annual rpt, 444–1

Imports injury to US industries from foreign subsidized products and sales in US at less than fair value, investigations with background financial and operating data, series, 9886–19

Imports injury to US industries from foreign subsidized products, investigations with background financial and operating data for selected industries and products, series, 9886–15

Imports injury to US industries from import sales at less than fair value, investigations with background financial and operating data, series, 9886–14

Steel import trigger prices to prevent Japan dumping, and domestic steel prices, employment, and imports, by product and region, various dates 1977-1983, hearings, 21368–51

Dumps

see Refuse and refuse disposal

Duncan, Ann

"Working Data for Demand Analysis", 1544–21

Duncan, Marvin

"Agricultural Policy: Objectives for a New Environment", 9381–1.411

"Better Times Ahead for Agriculture", 9381–1.402

Dunham, Constance

"Interstate Banking: The Drive To Consolidate", 9373–1.409

Dunham, Denis

"Food Cost Review, 1983", 1544–9

Dunkelberg, William C.

"Credit, Banks and Small Business", 21728–52.1

"NFIB Quarterly Economic Report for Small Business, July 1983", 21728–52.2

Dunlop, David W.

"Comparative Analysis of Five PL 480 Title I Impact Evaluation Studies", 9918–13

"Comparative Analysis of Policies and Other Factors Which Affect the Role of the Private Sector in Economic Development", 9918–12

Dunn, John R.

"Co-ops' Production of Crude Oil Down, but Reserve Protection Increased", 1122–1.407

"U.S. Cooperative Involvement in the Petroleum Industry, 1982", 1561–16.403

Durell, Jack

"Preventing Substance Abuse: The State of the Art", 4102–1.410

Durfee, R. C.

"Population Distribution Analyses for Nuclear Power Plant Siting", 9638–54

Durham, N.C.

Census of Housing, 1980: occupancy and unit characteristics, by race, Hispanic origin, and city, SMSA rpt, 2473–1.297

Census of Population and Housing, 1980: detailed population and housing characteristics, by county, city, and census tract, SMSA rpt, 2551–2.297

Wages of office and plant workers, by occupation, 1984 labor market area survey rpt, 6785–3.6

see also under By City and By SMSA or MSA in the "Index by Categories"

Durkin, Joseph T.

"Dungeness Crab Leg Loss in the Columbia River Estuary", 2162–1.403

Duties

see Tariffs and foreign trade controls

Dwyer, Gerald P.

"Is the Dollar Overvalued in Foreign Exchange Markets?", 9371–1.413

Dyes

see Chemicals and chemical industry

Dynatrend, Inc.

"Cost Experience of Automated Guideway Transit Systems, Supplement V Costs and Trends for the Period 1976-82", 7884–6

Index by Subjects and Names

Earnings, general

Ear diseases and infections

Deaths and death rates by detailed cause and demographic characteristics, 1979 and selected trends, US Vital Statistics annual rpt, 4144–2.1

see also under By Disease in the "Index by Categories"

Early, John F.

"Inflation and the Business Cycle During the Postwar Period", 6722–1.464

Earnings, general

- AFDC eligibility under Omnibus Budget Reconciliation Act, effect on caseloads and recipient benefits and living costs, 1981-83, GAO rpt, 26131–11
- Business and financial statistics, historic trends, 1984 annual chartbook, 9364–2.4
- Business and financial statistics, quarterly chartbook, 9362–2.2
- Census of Population and Housing, 1980: detailed population and housing characteristics, by county, city, and census tract, State and SMSA rpt series, 2551–2
- Census of Population, 1980: detailed socioeconomic and demographic characteristics, by age, sex, race, Hispanic origin, occupation, and industry, State rpt series, 2531–4
- Census of Population, 1980: detailed socioeconomic characteristics, by county, city, and inside-outside SMSAs and central cities, State rpt series, 2531–3
- Collective bargaining agreements expiring during year, covered workers by SIC 2-digit industry, firm, and union, with summary of key provisions, 1984, annual rpt, 6784–9
- Collective bargaining contract expirations and wage increases, scheduled and under cost-of-living escalator provisions, by SIC 2-digit industry and selected firm and union, 1984, annual article, 6722–1.402
- Collective bargaining wage adjustments, workers covered, and factors affecting negotiated settlements, selected years 1968-84, article, 9362–1.410
- Collective bargaining wage and benefit rate changes in labor-mgmt agreements, quarterly press release, 6782–2
- Collective bargaining wage and employee benefits changes, by industry group, monthly rpt, 6782–1
- College grads and advanced degree recipients, salary offers, by field, 1978/79-1982/83, annual rpt, 4824–2.23
- Computer specialists sociodemographic, educational, and employment characteristics, and Fed Govt support by agency, 1978, biennial Current Population Rpt, 2546–2.124
- *County and City Data Book,* detailed socioeconomic and demographic data for States, counties, and cities, selected years 1976-82, 2328–1
- Disability (short-term) earnings lost, insurance benefits, sick leave, and work days lost by sex, by type of worker, 1948-81, article, 4742–1.417
- Earnings (real) and compensation indexes, *Business Conditions Digest,* historical supplement and methodology, 1947-82, 2708–31
- Earnings (real) and compensation indexes, *Business Conditions Digest,* monthly rpt, 2702–3.6

Earnings and hours of production or nonsupervisory workers on nonagricultural payrolls, monthly rpt, 6742–2.6

- Earnings by industry div, and personal income per capita and by source, by State, MSA, and county, 1977-82, annual regional rpts, 2704–2
- Earnings by major industry group, and personal income per capita and by source, by region and State, 1929-82, 2708–40
- Earnings by sex and region related to wages in South, with adjustments for job comparability and union membership status, 1978, 1981, and 1983, article, 9389–1.406
- Earnings, hourly and weekly averages and Hourly Earnings Index, by industry div, monthly press release, 6742–3
- Earnings indexes for nonfinancial corporations, preliminary data quarterly rpt, 6822–2
- Earnings indexes for nonfinancial corporations, revised data, quarterly rpt, 6822–1
- Earnings per hour in private economy, natl compounded annual rates of change, monthly rpt, 9391–3.2
- Earnings, revised seasonally adjusted estimates of real average hourly and weekly rates based on 1983 CPI changes, monthly 1964-83, article, 6742–2.405
- Earnings, weekly and hourly, private nonagricultural industries, 1947-83, annual rpt, 204–1.2
- Economic and demographic factors used in OASDI program cost estimates, selected years 1913-82 with alternative projections to 2060, 4706–1.90
- Economic and demographic trends for IRS regions, districts, and service centers, 1972-82 and projected to 1990, annual rpt, 8304–8
- Economic and financial trends, natl compounded annual rates of change, 1964-83, annual rpt, 9391–9.2
- Economic indicators and components, and Fed Reserve 4th District business and financial conditions, monthly chartbook, 9377–10
- Economic indicators and components, current data and annual trends, monthly rpt, 23842–1.2
- Economic performance of US, and Reagan Admin 1984 spending, tax, and monetary policy proposals, with data for 1950s-83 and projected to 1988, press release, 8008–107
- Economic trends and projections, 1970s-83, and Budget of US under current fiscal policy and alternatives, FY85-89, annual rpt, 26304–3.1
- Employment and economic indicators, foreign and US, 1970s-83, annual rpt, 2044–26
- Employment Cost Index and percent change by occupational group, industry div, region, and metro-nonmetro area, quarterly press release, 6782–5
- Employment Cost Index wage and salary component changes by occupational group, industry div, and collective bargaining status, and CPI changes, selected periods Sept 1975-Dec 1983, article, 6722–1.430

Employment, earnings, and hours, by selected SIC 1- to 4-digit industry, State, and for 278 major labor areas, 1939-83, annual rpt, 6744–5

- Employment, earnings, and hours, by SIC 4-digit nonfarm industry, monthly 1974-Feb 1984, annual update, 6744–4
- Employment, earnings, and hours, monthly press release, 6742–5
- Employment situation, earnings, hours, and other BLS economic indicators, transcripts of BLS Commissioner's monthly testimony, periodic rpt, 23846–4
- Engineers sociodemographic, educational, and employment characteristics, and Federal support by agency, 1978, Current Population Rpt, 2546–2.121
- Family earnings by number of earners, and employment status of individual family members, quarterly rpt, 6742–19
- Family earnings by number of earners and members employment status, and earnings of full- and part-time workers, by sociodemographic characteristics, 1982-83, article, 6742–2.406
- Food stamp recipient households size and composition, income, and income deductions allowed, Aug 1981, annual rpt, 1364–8
- High school classes of 1980 and 1982: educational and sociodemographic characteristics and expectations, natl longitudinal study, series, 4826–2
- Hours and earnings of production and nonsupervisory workers, by industry div and major manufacturing group, annual averages, 1980-83, article, 6742–2.403
- Import and tariff provisions effect on US industries and products, investigations with background financial and operating data, series, 9886–4
- Imports injury to US industries from foreign subsidized products and sales in US at less than fair value, investigations with background financial and operating data, series, 9886–19
- Imports injury to US industries from foreign subsidized products, investigations with background financial and operating data for selected industries and products, series, 9886–15
- Imports injury to US industries from import sales at less than fair value, investigations with background financial and operating data, series, 9886–14
- Imports injury to US industries from increased import sales, investigations with background financial and operating data, series, 9886–5
- Imports injury to US industries from removal of duties on foreign subsidized products, investigations with background financial and operating data, series, 9886–18
- Income (household) and cash and noncash transfer program participation, by sociodemographic characteristics, quarterly rpt, 2542–2
- Income (legal) not reported on Federal income tax returns by source, and legal and illegal underground income, with bibl, 1974-81, article, 2702–1.419
- Income (taxable) not reported on individual and corporate returns, and associated Federal revenue losses, by detailed legal and illegal source, 1973-81, 8308–26

Earnings, general

- Income assistance, effects of experimental negative income tax program on employment, earnings, marital status, and other family characteristics in 2 cities, 1970-75, 4008–64
- Income tax returns of elderly, by income statement and tax item and income level, 1981 with trends from 1977, article, 8302–2.412
- Income tax returns of individuals by tax return item, State, and occupation, and income by source and tax owed, by income level, selected years 1916-80, conf papers, 8308–28.1
- Income tax returns of individuals, detailed data, 1982, annual rpt, 8304–2
- Income tax returns of individuals, selected income, deduction, and tax credit data by income, preliminary 1982, annual article, 8302–2.402
- Jail capacities, conditions, expenditures, and services, and socioeconomic and other characteristics of inmates, various dates 1976-82, 10048–59
- Job Training Partnership Act performance standards guide, and CETA job placements, unemployment rates, and average wages, by city or county, FY82, 6408–59.1
- Labor force characteristics and economic indicators, selected years 1880-1995, chartbook, 6728–30
- Labor force experience of men and women by sociodemographic characteristics, and effect on earnings, 1979, Current Population Rpt, 2546–2.123
- Manufacturing census, 1982: financial and operating data, by SIC 2- to 4-digit industry, State, SMSA, and county, preliminary census div rpt series, 2491–3
- Manufacturing census, 1982: financial and operating data, for SIC 4-digit industries by product, preliminary rpt series, 2491–1
- Manufacturing computerized automation dev, R&D, training, and employment impacts, with comparisons to foreign countries, selected years 1960-83, 26358–105
- Manufacturing hours and earnings, by State and selected area, 1981-83, article, 6742–2.408
- Manufacturing plants using bonuses and other employee incentives for exceeding normal production, by incentive type, 1981, article, 6722–1.447
- Manufacturing production workers earnings, by State, with adjustments for industrial mix variations, selected years 1973-82, article, 9373–1.407
- Manufacturing robots installed, and jobs displaced and created by occupation, by type of robot use, 1980s-2000, hearings, 21728–54
- Manufacturing wage growth in US and 2 countries, regression results, 1963-81, technical paper, 9381–10.34
- Manufacturing wage rates in US and 2 countries, by industry, 1975 and 1980, hearing, 21248–79
- Manufacturing wage/price and wage/output adjustment in 6 OECD countries, 1960-81, technical paper, 9381–10.33
- Married couples with both spouses working, to 6 OECD countries, selected years earnings by sociodemographic and

employment characteristics and age of children, 1981, Current Population Rpt, 2546–2.120

- Money supply fluctuation effect on employment and wages, model description, 1984 technical paper, 9366–7.104
- *Monthly Labor Review,* current statistics and articles, 6722–1
- Natl income and product, comprehensive accounts and components, *Survey of Current Business,* monthly rpt, monthly and annual tables, 2702–1.27
- OASDHI and selected social insurance programs, covered workers earnings and characteristics, selected years 1937-82, annual rpt, 4744–3.1, 4744–3.3
- OASDI and pension policy, impacts of increased life expectancy, with alternative sociodemographic projections to 2100, hearing, 25368–130
- OASDI benefit levels under automatic wage indexing, 1984, actuarial note, 4706–2.119
- OASI beneficiaries by income level, and average income, by beneficiary characteristics and income source, before and after receipt of 1st benefit, 1969-77, article, 4742–1.418
- *Occupational Outlook Handbook,* 1984-85 biennial rpt, 6744–1
- Occupational trends and outlook, quarterly rpt, 6742–1
- Older persons by demographic, socioeconomic, and health characteristics, selected years 1900-81 and projected to 2050, Current Population Rpt, 2546–2.125
- Older persons income and income sources, by OASDI beneficiary and poverty status, labor force participation, and demographic characteristics, 1982, biennial rpt, 4744–26
- Older persons income and percent in poverty, by household composition and sex, with comparisons to nonaged, selected years 1950-82, article, 4742–1.413
- Pay comparability of Fed Govt with private industry, and recommended pay rate adjustments, 1983, annual rpt, 104–16
- Personal income and BEA and IRS calculations of adjusted gross income, by source, 1981-82, article, 2702–1.414
- Port dev costs and financing through user fees, and shipping industry impact on local economy, by State, other area, industry, commodity, and port, 1970s-2020, hearings, 21568–34
- Poverty-level persons and families, by income source, hours of work, earnings, taxes, and family characteristics, various periods 1959-84, 21788–131
- Poverty status of young adults related to motivation, psychological factors, and family characteristics, by race and sex, 1970s-82, longitudinal studies, 4008–65
- Production workers hourly and weekly earnings, by industry group and State, 1922-82, annual rpt, 6724–1.3
- Productivity of labor and capital, costs, and prices, by selected industry, and compared to 6 OECD countries, selected years 1947-82, 17898–1

Index by Subjects and Names

- Public and employer-based noncash transfer program recipients, by income source and socioeconomic characteristics, 1982, advance Current Population Rpt, 2546–6.38
- Public and employer-based noncash transfer program recipients, by income source and socioeconomic characteristics, 1982, final Current Population Rpt, 2546–6.37
- Refugee resettlement program activities and funding, arrivals and population by country of origin and State, and employment and other characteristics, FY83, annual rpt, 4704–8
- Science and engineering grads of 1980-81, employment and median salaries by level and field of degree, 1982, 9626–2.137
- Science and engineering grads of 1980-81, employment characteristics or grad enrollment, by degree level, field, sex, and race, 1982, 9627–25
- Scientists and engineers employment, unemployment, and earnings, by field, sex, race, and Hispanic origin, 1970s-82, annual rpt, 9624–10.3
- Scientists and engineers in R&D, median salaries by sex, selected years 1973-81, annual rpt, 9624–18.5
- Scientists and engineers in R&D, salaries by degree, type of establishment, age, experience, and field, 1984, annual rpt, 3004–1
- Scientists and engineers in R&D, salary comparisons for DOE labs and non-DOE facilities, Aug 1982-Feb 1984, annual rpt, 3004–9
- Scientists and engineers supply, employment, and education, by sex, race, Hispanic origin, and field, selected years 1965-83, biennial rpt, 9624–20
- Self-employed, wage and salary, and unpaid family workers, employment, earnings, and hours, by industry div and occupation, 1970-83, article, 6722–1.443
- *Statistical Abstract of US,* social, political, and economic data, 1950s-83 and trends, annual rpt, 2324–1.3
- Supplementary Security Income beneficiary socioeconomic characteristics and health service use, 1970s-83 and SSI program projections to 1995, 25148–29
- Trade adjustment assistance eligibility, reemployment opportunities, and worker characteristics, investigations of industries injured by import competition, series, 6406–9
- Traffic accidents and casualties detailed direct and indirect costs, by characteristics of persons and vehicles involved, 1979-80, 7768–80
- Unemployment and part-time employment, by race, Hispanic origin, sex, family composition, income, and poverty status, 1980-82, annual report, 6744–15
- Unemployment and part-time employment effects on family income, by socioeconomic and labor force characteristics, 1981-82, annual rpt, 6746–1.252
- Unemployment insurance, average annual pay of covered workers by industry div, State, and MSA, 1981-83, annual press releases, 6784–17
- Unemployment insurance, employment and wages of workers covered by State law

Index by Subjects and Names

and Fed Govt employee compensation, by SIC 4-digit industry and State, 1982, annual rpt, 6744–16

Unemployment insurance system finances, claims, payments, and covered employment and wages, by State, 1938-82, 6408–5

Veterans aged 55 and over, socioeconomic characteristics, economic resources, health care and status, and actual and expected use of VA benefits, 1983 survey, 9928–29

Vocationally rehabilitated persons under State agency programs, by sociodemographic characteristics and disabling condition, FY79-81, annual rpt, 4944–6

Wage differential due to unionization, effect on union and nonunion labor income and invested capital return, 1971, technical paper, 9387–8.83

Wage growth and turnover rates related to marital status, sex, age, establishment type, and employer size, 1979/80, article, 9393–8.403

Women and men earnings differential analysis, selected years 1967-83, articles, 6722–1.436, 6722–1.437, 6722–1.438

Women in couples with wife as primary earner, socioeconomic and family characteristics, with comparative data for husbands, Mar 1982, 2326–11.9

Women's employment and earnings, by labor force and socioeconomic characteristics, and compared to men, 1978-81 and trends from 1940s, 6568–29

Women's labor force participation, earnings, and socioeconomic characteristics, 1983, annual fact sheet, 6564–1

see also Agricultural labor
see also Agricultural wages
see also Area wage surveys
see also Earnings, local and regional
see also Earnings, specific industries
see also Employee benefit plans
see also Escalator clauses
see also Farm income
see also Federal pay
see also Foreign labor conditions
see also Industry wage surveys
see also Labor cost indexes
see also Military pay
see also Minimum wage
see also Payroll
see also Personal and family income
see also State and local employees pay
see also Tips and tipping
see also under By Income in the "Index by Categories"

Earnings, local and regional

American Samoa minimum wage rates, employment, earnings, and benefits, by establishment and industry, Nov 1983, biennial rpt, 6504–6

Dallas-Fort Worth, Tex, SMSA employment, earnings, hours, and CPI changes, 1983 with trends from 1968, annual rpt, 6964–2

Denver-Boulder, Colo, SMSA employment, earnings, and CPI changes, 1983, annual rpt, 6974–2

Georgia job expansion in southern rural 10-county area, employment and establishments by worker and industry characteristics, 1976-81, article, 1502–7.401

Houston, Tex, SMSA employment, earnings, hours, and CPI changes, 1983 with trends from 1968, annual rpt, 6964–1

Kansas City, Mo-Kans, SMSA employment, earnings, and CPI changes, with comparisons to total US, 1983, annual rpt, 6974–1

Kentucky employment growth in 9-county rural area, labor force and establishment characteristics, 1979-80, 1598–194

Massachusetts employment in traditional and high technology industry by occupation, and wages by industry, and compared to US and 3 SMSAs, various periods 1976-82, article, 9373–1.416

New England States economic indicators, Fed Reserve 1st District, monthly rpt, 9373–2.2

New England States employment, wages, and price conditions by State and selected SMSA, 1983, annual rpt, 6916–7.1

Northwest US economic impacts of Washington Public Power Supply System nuclear reactors construction, with local power supply/demand, 1980s-2035, hearing, 21448–29

NYC wages by occupation, for office and plant workers, 1983, annual rpt, 6926–1.75

Oregon and Montana earnings by SIC 1- to 3-digit industry and payments to retirees by type, for 4 timber dependent communities, 1970, 1208–196

Pacific coast States and selected areas, impact of shipping industry activities, 1970s-83, hearings, 21568–34

Southeastern region collective bargaining calendar, 1984, annual rpt, 6946–1.68

Southeastern States and 5 SMSAs economic indicators, Fed Reserve 8th District, quarterly rpt, 9391–15

Southeastern States financial and economic devs, Fed Reserve 6th District, monthly rpt with articles, 9371–1

Southeastern States manufacturing production workers average hours and earnings, for 8 States, monthly press release, 6942–7

Southeastern US water supply and quality, with background socioeconomic data, for 8 States, 1960s-2020 with trends from 1930, 9208–119

Southwestern States manufacturing production workers average hours and earnings, for 5 States, monthly rpt, 6962–2

St Louis, Mo, SMSA employment, earnings, and CPI changes, 1983, annual rpt, 6974–3

TTPI socioeconomic, employment, health, and govtl data, by TTPI govt, FY83 and selected trends, detailed annual rpt, 7004–6.2

Western States economic indicators, Fed Reserve 12th District, quarterly rpt, 9393–1.1, 9393–1.2

see also Area wage surveys
see also Industry wage surveys
see also Personal and family income
see also under By Census Division, By City, By County, By Region, By SMSA or MSA, and By State in the "Index by Categories"

Earnings, specific industries

Coal production, mining employment, exports, and finances, by coal district, 1982, 3008–97

Construction industry total and female workers, and construction worker earnings and hours, by selected SIC 2- to 3-digit industry, bimonthly rpt, 2012–1.7

Copper production, production costs, prices, wages, and productivity, for US and 3 countries, 1970s-83 and projected to 1989, 21368–55

Education expenditures for elementary and high school teachers salaries, 1970/71-1981-82, annual rpt, 4824–1.1

Education statistics, detailed data on students, staff, finances, and facilities, 1982 and selected trends, annual rpt, 4824–2

Fed Reserve banks and branch officers and employees, and salaries, 1983, annual rpt, 9364–1.1

Food prices (farm-retail), marketing cost components, and industry finances and productivity, selected years 1967-83, annual rpt, 1544–9.2

Health professionals supply and education, by occupation, demographic and professional characteristics, and location, 1950s-83 and projected to 2000, biennial rpt, 4114–8

Howard University salaries, academic standing, medical research, and library operations, and finances of Howard Inn, selected years 1976-83, GAO rpt, 26121–74

Philanthropic foundations employment and earnings by organization type, and compared to other nonprofit organizations, selected years 1972-82, article, 6722–1.455

Physician earnings, by specialty, 1950s-82, 25368–127

Physician income, 1972-82, and health care expenditures and growth factors, 1950-90, article, 4652–1.407

Physicians employed in prisons by sociodemographic, employment, and professional characteristics, and compared to all physicians, 1979, article, 4102–1.407

Railroad employee earnings, benefits, and hours, by occupation for Class I railroads, 1983, annual rpt, 9484–5

Railroad employees and compensation, by age, sex, occupation, and years of service, 1981, annual rpt, 9704–2.4

Ships in US and OECD merchant fleets, sailors earnings by position, 1983 hearings, 25388–45

Ships in US merchant fleet, shipping costs, construction, employment, military availability, and Fed Govt subsidies, 1970s-1984 and projected to 2000, 26306–6.83

Shipyard employment and earnings, total US and by selected region, 1980-82, annual rpt, 7704–12.2

Steel industry finances and operations under proposed import quota, projected 1985-89 with selected foreign comparisons and trends from 1950, 26306–6.80

Steel industry financial and operating data, steel imports by source, and employment situation at Fairless Hills, Pa, plant, 1970s-90, hearing, 25528–94

Earnings, specific industries

Synthetic Fuels Corp financial statements, activities, and executive staff and salaries, FY83, annual rpt, 29654–1

Textile mill employment and average hours and earnings, for 8 Southeastern States, monthly press release, 6942–1

Timber-based industry hourly earnings, by major industry and selected State, 1972-82, annual rpt, 1204–29

Transportation employment, wages, and average annual earnings, by mode of transport, 1972-82, annual rpt, 7304–2.2

Vending stand concessions operated by blind on Federal and non-Federal property, and income, FY82-83, annual rpt, 4944–2

see also Agricultural labor

see also Agricultural wages

see also Farm income

see also Federal pay

see also Industry wage surveys

see also Payroll

see also State and local employees pay

see also under By Industry in the "Index by Categories"

Earth sciences

- DOE R&D projects and funding at natl labs, universities, and other instns, FY84, annual summary rpt, 3004–18.4
- NASA project launch schedules and technical descriptions, press release series, 9506–2
- NOAA scientific and technical publications, monthly listing, 2142–1
- NSF grant and award recipients, by State, FY83, annual listing, 9624–11
- NSF research programs, activities, and funding, FY82-83, annual rpt, 9624–6
- R&D-employed scientists and engineers salaries by degree, type of establishment, age, experience, and field, 1984, annual rpt, 3004–1
- R&D expenditures by higher education instns and federally funded centers, by field, source of funds, instn, and State, FY82, annual rpt, 9627–13
- R&D expenditures by source, and scientists education and employment, detailed data by field, selected years 1953-84, annual rpt, 9624–18
- R&D expenditures of higher education instns, and science and engineering employment and grad students, by field, 1972-83, biennial rpt, 9627–24
- R&D Fed Govt facilities and services available for private sector use, by field of science, 1984 biennial listing, 2224–4
- R&D Fed Govt funding, by function, agency, and program, selected years FY80-84 and proposed FY85, 26308–46
- R&D Fed Govt funding for all performers, by field and supporting agency, selected years FY60-84, annual rpt, 9627–20
- Science and engineering doctoral degree recipients, by field, sex, race, age, citizenship, postgrad employment and study status, State, and instn, 1960-82, 9626–6.16
- Science and engineering grad enrollment, fields of study, financial support, and other student and instn characteristics, 1975-82, annual survey, 9627–7
- Scientists and engineers employed at universities and colleges, by field, sex, State, and instn, Jan 1983 and selected trends from 1967, annual survey, 9627–11

Scientists and engineers employed in energy-related fields, supply/demand and effects of R&D funding, by energy type, employer type, field, and age, 1962-91, annual rpt, 3004–19

Scientists, engineers, and technicians employed in private industry, by occupation and industry group, 1980-81, biennial rpt, 9627–23

see also Geography

see also Geology

see also Hydrology

see also Oceanography

Earthquakes

- Central America mineral, energy, and water resources, and natural hazards to resource dev, by country, 1981 with trends from 1977, 5668–71
- Developing countries disaster preparedness and summary sociodemographic, political, and economic data, country rpt series, 9916–2
- Fed Emergency Mgmt Agency activities and funding for disaster and emergency relief, and major disasters, 1983, annual rpt, 9434–2
- Foreign countries disasters, persons affected, deaths, damage, and aid by US and others, FY83 and trends from FY64, annual rpt, 9914–12
- Intensity, damage, and deaths, by location for major earthquakes since 1755, and hazard areas and natl reduction program activities, as of 1984, 5668–73
- Intensity, damage, time of origin, and seismic characteristics of all US and major foreign earthquakes, 1981, annual rpt, 5664–13
- Intensity of ground motions measured on USGS Natl Strong-Motion Network by station, and sources of foreign and US info, 1981, annual rpt, 5664–14
- Intensity, time of origin, seismic characteristics, and location of earthquakes, by State, quarterly rpt, 5662–4

East Chicago, Ind.

- Census of Housing, 1980: occupancy and unit characteristics, by race, Hispanic origin, and city, SMSA rpt, 2473–1.169
- Census of Population and Housing, 1980: detailed population and housing characteristics, by county, city, and census tract, SMSA rpt, 2551–2.169
- Wages of office and plant workers, by occupation, 1983 SMSA survey rpt, 6785–12.2

East Lansing, Mich.

- Census of Housing, 1980: occupancy and unit characteristics, by race, Hispanic origin, and city, SMSA rpt, 2473–1.211
- Census of Population and Housing, 1980: detailed population and housing characteristics, by county, city, and census tract, SMSA rpt, 2551–2.211

East Pakistan

see Bangladesh

East-West trade

see under names of individual Communist countries

Eastern Europe

Agricultural and food production indexes, and production of selected commodities, by world region and country, 1974-83, annual rpt, 1524–5

Index by Subjects and Names

- Agricultural exports and imports of US with 7 East European countries, by commodity, 1980-83, article, 1522–1.404
- Agricultural production and trade by commodity, food consumption, and farm inputs, for 6 countries, 1960-80 with projections to 1991, 1528–178
- Agricultural situation in Eastern Europe, by country, 1983 and outlook for 1984, annual report, 1524–4.7
- Agricultural trade of US, by commodity and country, bimonthly rpt with articles, 1522–1
- Carbon dioxide emissions from fossil fuel combustion, and growth rates, by country and country group, 1950-80, 3006–7.6
- China economic conditions, agricultural and industrial production, trade, and domestic and foreign investment, 1980-85, 2048–106
- Cuba economic conditions, agricultural and industrial production and distribution, trade, and intl economic relations, 1970-82 and trends from 1957, 248–40
- Economic conditions in Communist and OECD countries, 1982, annual rpt, 7144–11
- Economic conditions in Communist, OECD, and selected other countries, 1960s-83, annual rpt, 244–5
- Export licensing and monitoring activities under Export Admin Act, for selected commodities, and for Communist and other countries, FY83, annual rpt, 2044–22
- Export sales and shipments of US grains, oilseed products, hides, skins, and cotton, by country, weekly rpt, 1922–3
- Exports and imports of OECD countries, by country, 1983, annual rpt, 7144–10
- Exports and imports of US (waterborne), by type of service, customs district, port, and world area, monthly rpt, 2422–7
- Exports and imports of US, by commodity group, world area, selected country, US coastal area and port, and mode of transport, with seasonal adjustments, monthly rpt, 2422–9
- Exports and imports of US, detailed SIC-based commodities by world area, 1983, annual rpts, 2424–6
- Exports and imports of US with Communist countries, by detailed commodity and country, quarterly rpt with articles, 9882–2
- Grain production, consumption, and trade, and US farm cooperatives grain and oilseed export potential, for 4 countries, selected years 1960-90, 1128–27
- Great Lakes trade, by SITC 3-digit commodity, port, vessel type, world area, and country, 1982, annual rpt, 7744–3
- Helsinki Final Act implementation by NATO, Warsaw Pact, and other signatory nations, Dec 1983-Mar 1984, semiannual rpt, 7002–1
- Loans and grants for economic and military assistance from US and intl agencies, by program and country, FY46-83, annual rpt, 9914–5
- Loans of large US banks to foreigners at all US and foreign offices, by country group and country, quarterly rpt, 13002–1
- Military, social, and economic summary data, by world area and country, 1960s-80s, hearing, 25388–47.1

Index by Subjects and Names

Oil and gas production, consumption, and trade by country, for Communist countries, monthly rpt, 242–5

Population size and growth rates, and latest available benchmark demographic data, by country, 1950-83, biennial rpt, 2324–4

Radio Free Europe and Radio Liberty broadcast and financial data, with comparisons to other intl broadcasters, FY83, annual rpt, 10314–1

Refugee arrivals in US, by world area of origin and processing and nationality, monthly rpt, 7002–4, 7002–5

Refugee arrivals in US by world area of origin and State of settlement, and Fed Govt intl and domestic assistance costs, FY85, annual rpt, 7004–16

Refugee migration, settlement status, and assistance, by world area and country of origin and asylum, as of May 1984, annual rpt, 7004–15

Students in US and Soviet bloc training programs, by program type and Latin American country or world region of student origin, selected years 1972-82, GAO rpt, 26123–77

Terrorist (intl) incidents, casualties, and attacks on US targets, by attack type and world area, with chronology of events, 1983, annual rpt, 7004–13

USIA info center and reading room operations, by world region, country, and city, FY83, annual rpt, 9854–4

see also Albania

see also Bulgaria

see also Council for Mutual Economic Assistance

see also Czechoslovakia

see also Germany, East

see also Hungary

see also Poland

see also Romania

see also Soviet Union

see also Warsaw Pact

see also Yugoslavia

see also under By Foreign Country in the "Index by Categories"

Easton, Pa.

Census of Housing, 1980: occupancy and unit characteristics, by race, Hispanic origin, and city, SMSA rpt, 2473–1.64

Census of Population and Housing, 1980: detailed population and housing characteristics, by county, city, and census tract, SMSA rpt, 2551–2.64

Housing and households detailed characteristics, and unit and neighborhood quality, by inside-outside central cities, 1980 survey, SMSA rpt, 2485–6.7

Eau Claire, Wis.

Census of Housing, 1980: occupancy and unit characteristics, by race, Hispanic origin, and city, SMSA rpt, 2473–1.143

Census of Population and Housing, 1980: detailed population and housing characteristics, by county, city, and census tract, SMSA rpt, 2551–2.143

see also under By SMSA or MSA in the "Index by Categories"

Eavesdropping

see Electronic surveillance

Eck, Alan

"New Occupational Separation Data Improve Estimates of Job Replacement Needs", 6722–1.416

Eckhardt, Kenneth W.

"Analysis of the Reversal in Breast Feeding Trends in the Early 1970s", 4102–1.442

Eckmann, Alex

"Urban Travel Trends: Historical Observations and Future Forecasts, Final Report, May 1984", 7888–63

Ecology

see Conservation of natural resources

see Environmental pollution and control

see Environmental sciences

see Marine pollution

see Marine resources conservation

see Wildlife and wildlife conservation

Economic and econometric models

Agricultural economics technical research, quarterly journal, 1502–3

BLS econometric methodology for measuring prices, labor costs, productivity, and wages, technical paper series, 6886–6

Budget deficits effect on interest rates, regression results and bibl, various periods 1965-83, 8008–111

Budget of US, impacts of deficits on economy, projected FY84-88 with trends and foreign comparisons from 1946, conf papers, 9373–3.27

Computer software and documentation available from NTIS, by agency and program characteristics, 1984 annual listing, 2224–2

Electric power plant (nuclear and coal-fired) construction itemized cost estimates, and investment per kilowatt for 20 cities, 1980s-95, 9638–52

Energy conservation device installation using utility loans, models for predicting household program participation, 1984 rpt, 3308–72

Energy demand in industry, forecasting model description, detailed technology specifications, and energy use, for 27 SIC 2- to 4-digit industries, 1970s-80 and projected to 2000, 3308–66

Energy Info Admin data collection and analysis activities, Jan 1982-Sept 1983, GAO annual rpt, 26104–14

Energy Info Admin surveys, data analysis models, and publications, 1983, annual rpt, 3164–29

Energy supply/demand and prices, by fuel type, sector, and end use, detailed trends and projections 1973-95, annual rpt, 3164–75

Environmental quality and protection programs, costs, and Fed Govt enforcement, 1983, detailed annual rpt, 484–1

Fed Govt budget and debt, cyclically adjusted estimates assuming mid-level unemployment and GNP, and methodology, quarterly 1955-83, 2706–5.31

Fed Govt economic dev assistance generation of jobs by industry div, model methodology and outputs, various periods FY69-78, GAO rpt, 26117–32

Finance (intl) and financial policy, and external factors affecting US economy, technical paper series, 9366–7

Finance (intl) and financial policy, external factors affecting US economy, econometric model methodology and results for US and 4 countries, various periods 1964-75, 9368–78

Economic assistance

Financial and banking devs in southeastern States, research paper series, 9371–10

Financial and economic analysis and forecasting methodology, technical paper series, 9366–6

Financial and economic analysis and forecasting methodology, technical paper series, 9377–9

Financial and economic analysis and methodology, technical paper series, 9375–11

Financial and economic analysis of banking and nonbanking sectors, technical paper series, 9381–10

Financial and monetary research and econometric analyses, series, 9387–8

Financial instn deregulation, interstate banking, and bank performance and risks, 1984 conf papers, 9375–7

Forecasts of economic indicators, predictive value of 5 model types for 7 Texas indicators over 1-6 quarters, 1984 article, 9379–1.403

Housing finance studies, technical paper series, 9316–1

Housing finance studies, technical paper series, 9306–1

Housing finance technical analysis, quarterly rpt articles, 9312–7, 9412–2

Industrial electric power demand model estimates, economic indicators, and supporting data for 5 industries, 1960s-80 with projections to 2000, 3008–87

Money supply and high-employment Fed Govt spending related to nominal GNP, alternative specifications for St Louis equation, 1962-82, article, 9391–1.417

Natural gas price decontrol effect on supply/demand and prices, 1970s-83, 3168–50

OASDHI economic effects, use of models in research, 1984 narrative article, 4742–1.419

Oil refineries financial and operating impacts from auto use of alcohol fuels, projected to 2000 with trends 1964-80, 3308–75

Oil spill off France Brittany coast, cleanup and research costs, marine and tourism industry losses, and recreation losses of tourists and residents, 1971-79, 2178–13

Pollution abatement expenditures, and effect on economic indicators and industry operations, by major industry, projected under 3 pollution regulation alternatives 1983-95, 9188–84

Poverty population by labor force status, and effect of public welfare changes and recession, by family status, FY82, 21788–139

Seasonal adjustment methodology for economic time series, dev and design of Census Bur and other systems, with illustrative data, 1981 conf papers, 2626–7.5

Timber harvest residue recovery for energy, cost-effectiveness of 3 logging systems, 1983 technical paper, 9806–2.37

see also Input-output analysis

Economic assistance

see Economic policy

see Foreign assistance

see Military assistance

Economic censuses

Economic censuses

Data coding systems for industries used in statistical programs of 6 Federal agencies, comparabilty, workload, and updating cycles, 1984 rpt, 106–4.5

Data coverage and availability for 1982 Census of Agriculture and related statistics, 1984 guide, 2308–55

Data coverage and availability for 1982 economic censuses and related statistics, 1984 guide, 2308–5

Data coverage and availability of Census Bur publications, 1984 annual listing, 2304–2

Data coverage policy for 1982 agriculture and economic censuses, and Federal agency data use, 1984 GAO narrative rpt, 26125–26

see also Census of Construction Industries
see also Census of Manufactures
see also Census of Mineral Industries
see also Census of Outlying Areas
see also Census of Retail Trade
see also Census of Service Industries
see also Census of Transportation
see also Census of Wholesale Trade
see also Enterprise Statistics Program
see also Survey of Minority-Owned Business Enterprises
see also Survey of Women-Owned Businesses

Economic concentration and diversification

Airline deregulation in 1978, effect on industry operations and finances, air traffic patterns, and CAB programs, various periods FY76-84, 9148–56

Airline deregulation in 1978, traffic and service changes by city, with market shares, fares, and load factors, quarterly rpt, 9142–42

Auditors of S&Ls, auditing firm concentration ratios by FHLB district, 1976-80, article, 9312–1.403

Bank deposit concentration indicators, by State and for US and 7 OECD countries, various dates 1982-84, article, 9373–1.405

Bank holding companies in Florida, profits related to market position, concentration, and deposit growth, 1973-77, article, 9371–1.401

Bank merger antitrust analysis geographic market definition, literature review, 1984 technical paper, 9366–1.138

Bank merger proposals receiving adverse Justice Dept appraisals, bank deposits, market shares and ratios, and merger disposition, June 1982-Dec 1983, article, 9375–1.404

Bank mergers, concentration levels, and market deposits merged, by number of bank organizations in SMSA and county, simulated 1982, technical paper, 9366–1.136

Banks (commercial) and trust companies, assets and liabilities of 10 largest organizations, by State, 1982, annual rpt, 9364–5.11

Banks (natl) domestic and intl operations, charters, mergers, and liquidations, by State and instn, and Comptroller of Currency activities, quarterly rpt, 8402–3

Cigarette sales, market shares, advertising expenditures and methods, and tar and nicotine content, by cigarette type, selected years 1963-81, annual rpt, 9404–4

Dairy cooperatives and percent share of producers and deliveries, by region, 1982 with trends from 1965, article, 1317–4.403

Electric and gas utility diversification activity by type, and finances and bond ratings by selected firm, various periods 1970-83, hearing, 21368–53

Energy producers finances and operations, by energy type for US firms domestic and foreign operations, 1974-82, annual rpt, 3164–44

Farm business legal organization, finances, operations, tax rates, and State laws restricting farm corporations, 1960s-82, 1548–233

Financial services household use and preferred provider, by respondent age and income, 1982-84 surveys, article, 9371–1.417

Financial services of nonbank firms and bank holding companies, with financial and operating data by firm, 1981-82 with trends from 1962, technical paper, 9375–11.3

Futures trading in selected commodities, foreign currencies, and stock indexes, Chicago and other markets activity, monthly rpt, 11922–1

Futures trading in selected commodities, foreign currencies, Treasury securities, and stock indexes, NYC, Chicago, and other markets activity, monthly rpt, 11922–5

Futures trading in selected commodities, Treasury securities, and stock indexes, NYC market activity, monthly rpt, 11922–2

Imports injury to US industries from import sales at less than fair value, investigations with background financial and operating data, series, 9886–14

Manufactured goods relative market shares of largest US and foreign firms by selected industry and firm, 1960, 1970, and 1981, hearing, 21248–79

Manufacturer-set retail prices under fair-trade law by brand and product, with manufacturers, market concentration, and sales, by industry, selected years 1952-82, 9406–1.38

Manufacturing census, 1982: financial and operating data, for SIC 4-digit industries by product, preliminary rpt series, 2491–1

Oil and gas companies production and exploration detailed expenditures, revenues, operating ratios, and sales volume, 1982, annual Current Industrial Rpt, 2506–8.11

Oil pipeline industry competition, market shares and throughput capacity by firm and market area, as of 1983, 6008–18

Pennsylvania bank, S&L, and savings bank deposit and commercial and industrial loan market shares, and loan activity, 1980-83, article, 9387–1.404

Savings and loan assn acquisitions in Southeastern States related to market concentration and acquired S&L market share, 1974-81, article, 9312–1.401

Small business capital formation under securities law exemptions, effects on stocks offered, issuers, and purchasers, series, 9736–2

Index by Subjects and Names

Stockbroker earnings concentrations, for debt and equity issues, 1970-77 and 1980-82, article, 9371–1.418

Telephone and telegraph firms intercorporate relationships, 1982, annual rpt, 9284–6.8

Tuna fleet, capacity, and processor investment in vessels by investment type, with tuna catch, prices, and imports, selected years 1932-80, 9406–1.39

see also Antitrust law
see also Bank holding companies
see also Business acquisitions and mergers
see also Competition
see also Holding companies
see also Ownership of enterprise

Economic crises and depressions

see Business cycles

Economic development

Agricultural Stabilization and Conservation Service producer payments under 26 programs, monthly rpt, 1802–10

Bond tax-exempt issues by purpose, and Fed Govt mortgage bond revenue losses and borrower characteristics, selected years 1971-85, hearings, 21788–135

Bond tax-exempt issues for private activity, by purpose, face value, major industry, and State, 1983, article, 8302–2.417

Bond tax-exempt issues for public and private purposes, by use of proceeds, 1975-83, article, 9362–1.408

Budget of US Appendix, detailed budgets and personnel summaries, by agency, FY85, annual rpt, 104–3

Budget of US, compact budgets by function, agency, and account, FY85 with projections to FY89, annual rpt, 104–2

Budget of US, receipts by source and outlays by function, FY40-89 estimates revised for consistency with FY85 budget definitions, annual rpt, 104–12

City govt revenue sharing program allocations and use by function, and response to program cuts, by city size and region, 1982 survey, hearings, 25408–86.2

Coastal environmental and socioeconomic conditions, and potential impacts of oil and gas OCS leases, final statement series, 5736–1

Community Dev Block Grants admin, allocation, and family social benefits, effect of policy changes to increase local admin responsibility, for 10 cities, as of 1982, 5188–105

Community Dev Block Grants to small cities, State admin, project characteristics, and assessments of local officials, 1982, 5188–106

Community dev programs funding and activities, for 5 HUD programs, FY83, annual rpt, 5124–5

Economic conditions of US, with some foreign comparisons, 1960s-82 and alternative projections to 1992, hearing, 21248–79

Economic Dev Admin loans and grants, by program, State, county, and project or recipient, FY83 and cumulative FY66-83, annual rpt, 2064–2

Enterprise zone and urban revitalization projects of State and local govts, effect on business and employment in selected areas, various dates 1972-83, hearing, 21788–140

Index by Subjects and Names

Economic indicators

Fed Govt aid to State and local govts, expenditures, and direct payments, by program, agency, and State, FY83, annual rpt, 2464–2

Fed Govt economic dev assistance generation of jobs by industry div, model methodology and outputs, various periods FY69-78, GAO rpt, 26117–32

Fed Govt industrial dev funding by type, program, and agency, and State govt policies and support, selected years FY75-85, 26306–6.81

Foreign and US agricultural supply/demand, trade, and production, and socioeconomic data, by country, 1950s-77, 1528–179

Govt census, 1982: State govt payments to local govts, by program, source of funds, level of govt, and State, with trends from 1902, 2460–3

Govt revenues by source and expenditures by function, natl income and product account, *Survey of Current Business,* monthly rpt, monthly and annual tables, 2702–1.24

Indian and Alaska Native housing and community dev program operations, FY82 with Community Dev Block Grant funding by tribe and State for FY81, annual rpt, 5004–5

Industrial policy dev, economic growth, and labor productivity, 1950s-81 with projections to 1986, 26306–6.69

Intl financial instns funds by source and disbursements by purpose, by country, with US policy review, FY83, annual rpt, 15344–1

NYC South Bronx housing and economic dev, HUD grants to 4 neighborhood organizations, 1984 press release, 5006–3.31

OECD countries GNP and GNP growth, by country, 1973-83, annual rpt, 7144–8

Port impact on local employment through transport of 5 commodities, by industry for 3 eastern ports, and demand for US coal by country, 1981, 7308–182

Regional councils involved in service activities, by type of service and region population size, 1982 survey, hearing, 25408–88

Rural area situation and dev, periodic rpt articles, 1502–7

Saudi Arabia-US Joint Commission on Economic Cooperation project activities and costs, and related contract awards by Fed Govt agency, as of 1983, GAO rpt, 26123–80

Tax expenditures, Fed Govt revenues foregone through income tax deductions and exclusions by type, and effect of Deficit Reduction Act, FY84-89, annual rpt, 21784–10

Technology-intensive industry employment and establishments by industry and selected location, and venture capital investments by source, 1970s-82, 26358–107

Tennessee Valley industrial dev and effects on employment, investment, and TVA power demand, by location and company, 1983, annual rpt, 9804–3

TVA activities, financial and operating data by program and facility, and power sales by customer, FY83, annual rpt, 9804–1

Urban Dev Action Grant awards to local areas, preliminary approvals, with project descriptions, private investment, and jobs and taxes to be created, by city, quarterly press release series, 5002–7

see also Business cycles

see also Developing countries

see also Economic indicators

see also Regional planning

Economic Development Administration

Budgets and permanent staff positions appropriated for Commerce Dept agencies, FY84-85, annual rpt, 2004–6

Cost control proposals for Fed Govt programs and mgmt, 3-year savings by function and agency, and financial and operating data, 1960s-81, 16908–1.3

Programs, funding, and employment of Commerce Dept agencies, FY83, annual rpt, 2004–1

Project grants and loans, by program, State, county, and project or recipient, FY83 and cumulative FY66-83, annual rpt, 2064–2

Economic indicators

AID dev assistance activities, special study series, 9916–3

Banking and financial data, 1982, annual rpt, 9364–5

Budget deficits effect on interest rates and economic indicators, with govt borrowing and saving, for US and 6 OECD countries, 1975-83, technical paper, 9366–7.89

Budget of US, CBO analysis and review of FY85 budget by function, annual rpt, 26304–2

Budget of US, CBO analysis of revenue and spending alternatives and projections of economic indicators, FY85-89, annual rpt, 26304–3

Budget of US, CBO analysis of revenue and spending estimation errors in congressional concurrent resolutions, FY80-82, 26308–48

Budget of US, economic assumptions, FY84-89, midsession review of FY85 budget, annual rpt, 104–7

Budget of US, impacts of deficits on economy, projected FY84-88 with trends and foreign comparisons from 1946, conf papers, 9373–3.27

Budget of US, special analyses of economic and social impact, FY85, annual rpt, 104–1

Business America, foreign and domestic commerce, and US investment and trade opportunities, biweekly rpt articles, 2042–24

Business Conditions Digest, current data on economic, business, and financial conditions and cyclical fluctuations, monthly rpt, 2702–3

Business Conditions Digest, historical supplement on economic, business, and financial conditions and cyclical fluctuations, with methodology, 1947-82, 2708–31

Business statistics, detailed data for major industries and economic indicators, *Survey of Current Business,* monthly rpt, 2702–1

California housing market, and Los Angeles average home price and mortgage rate, 1969-82 with economic indicators projected to 1989, 9306–1.1

China economic conditions, agricultural and industrial production, trade, and domestic and foreign investment, 1980-85, 2048–106

Communist and and OECD countries economic conditions, 1982, annual rpt, 7144–11

Communist, OECD, and selected other countries economic statistics, 1960s-83, annual rpt, 244–5

Developing countries disaster preparedness and summary sociodemographic, political, and economic data, country rpt series, 9916–2

Developing countries govt policy, and AID and other foreign assistance, effects on private sector dev and socioeconomic conditions, with case studies for 6 countries, 1960s-80, 9918–12

Developing countries PL 480 Title I funding and socioeconomic impacts, with case studies for 5 countries, 1950s- 81, 9918–13

Developing countries summary socioeconomic data, 1970s-83, and AID activities and funding by project and function, FY82-85, by country, annual rpt, 9914–3

Economic and population time series data frequently used in statistical demand analyses, 1941-1982, annual rpt, 1544–21

Economic conditions and employment, alternative BLS projections to 1995 with selected trends for 1959-82, 6728–29

Economic conditions of US, with some foreign comparisons, 1960s-82 and alternative projections to 1992, hearing, 21248–79

Economic growth rates and component economic indicators, selected years 1922-83 and projected under full employment to 1988, hearing, 21348–90

Economic indicator performance from 1961, and Commerce Dept publications, biweekly listing, 2002–1

Economic indicators and components, and Fed Reserve 4th District business and financial conditions, monthly chartbook, 9377–10

Economic indicators and components, current data and annual trends, monthly rpt, 23842–1

Economic indicators, and Fed Govt finances and deficits, selected years 1962-83 and projected under cost control proposals to 2000, 16908–1.1

Economic indicators and labor force characteristics, selected years 1880-1995, chartbook, 6728–30

Economic indicators performance for 8 recovery periods, 1949-83, annual article, 6722–1.409

Economic performance of US, and Reagan Admin 1984 spending, tax, and monetary policy proposals, with data for 1950s-83 and projected to 1988, press release, 8008–107

Economic Report of the President for 1984, economic effects of budget proposals, and trends and projections 1950s-89, annual hearings, 23844–4

Economic Report of the President for 1984, economic trends from 1929 and Reagan Admin proposals, annual rpt, 204–1

Economic indicators

Economic Report of the President for 1984, Joint Economic Committee critique and policy recommendations, annual rpt, 23844–2

Economic trends, natl compounded annual rates of change, monthly rpt, 9391–3

El Salvador socioeconomic and political conditions, and US economic and military assistance, 1977-FY84, 7008–39

Energy price increases related to economic indicators, and impact on household energy use by socioeconomic characteristics, selected years 1978-95, 3004–13.3

Energy supply/demand and prices, by fuel type, sector, and end use, detailed trends and projections 1973-95, annual rpt, 3164–75

Farm production, prices, marketing, and trade, by commodity, forecast and current situation, monthly rpt, 1502–4

Fed Govt personal income tax rate, effect of 10% cut on economic indicators, projected 1982-86, model results, technical paper, 9366–1.134

Financial and business detailed statistics, *Fed Reserve Bulletin,* monthly rpt with articles, 9362–1

Financial and business statistics, historic trends, 1984 annual chartbook, 9364–2

Financial and economic devs, Fed Reserve Bank of New York quarterly rpt with articles, 9385–1

Financial and economic trends, natl compounded annual rates of change, 1964-83, annual rpt, 9391–9

Financial and monetary conditions, selected US summary data, weekly rpt, 9391–4

Forecasts for selected business activities and natl economic indicators, and forecasting errors, 1971-84, summary article, 9389–1.404

Forecasts for selected business activities and natl economic indicators, compilation of representative opinions, 1984, annual rpt, 9389–3

Forecasts of economic indicators, predictive value of 5 model types for 7 Texas indicators over 1-6 quarters, 1984 article, 9379–1.403

Foreign and US agricultural supply/demand, trade, and production, and socioeconomic data, by country, 1950s-77, 1528–179

Foreign and US economic and employment indicators and balance of payments, and US exports by selected commodity, by world area and country, 1970s-83, annual rpt, 2044–26

Foreign countries *Background Notes,* summary social, political, and economic data, series, 7006–2

Foreign economic and monetary trends, compounded annual rates of change for US and 10 major trading partners, quarterly rpt, 9391–7

Foreign economic indicators for 7 OECD countries and US, quarterly rpt, 2042–10

Foreign economic, social, and political summary data, by country, 1984, annual factbook, 244–11

Foreign economic trends and implications for US, annual and semiannual country rpt series, 2046–4

Foreign monetary control policy and relation to credit, exchange rates, GNP, and other indicators, US and selected West European countries, various periods 1960-82, conf papers, 9373–3.26

Fresno, Calif, economic, population, labor, and housing indicators, various periods 1974-85, hearing, 21248–84

Industrial electric power demand model estimates, economic indicators, and supporting data for 5 industries, 1960s-80 with projections to 2000, 3008–87

Industrial policy dev, economic growth, and labor productivity, 1950s-81 with projections to 1986, 26306–6.69

Jamaica PL 480 Title I assistance effects on economic dev, with data on govt finance, economic indicators, demography, and dev programs, 1970s-81, 9916–1.51

Mexico economic indicators, trade, external accounts and debt, oil industry, and relations with US, 1978-83 with trends from 1959, conf proceedings, 21248–82

Monetary policy objectives of Fed Reserve, and performance of major economic indicators, July 1984 semiannual rpt, 9362–4

Monetary policy views of Reagan Admin, with data on economic and monetary growth, selected years 1960-83, press release, 8008–108

Natural gas price decontrol alternatives, effect on 9 economic indicators and farm production and income, 1982-90, model results, 1548–239

Natural gas price decontrol effect on prices, Iowa supply/demand, and economic indicators, with US imports from Canada, various periods 1969-95, hearings, 23848–177

New England States economic indicators, Fed Reserve 1st District, monthly rpt with articles, 9373–2

North Central States economic indicators, Fed Reserve 7th District monthly rpt, 9375–9

OECD economic indicators, for US and 6 countries, biweekly rpt, 242–4

Oil (Alaskan) potential exports to Japan, costs and benefits, with background data on oil prices, Pacific Basin supply/demand, and tankers, various periods 1918-99, hearings, 25388–45

Overseas Business Reports: economic conditions, investment and export opportunities, and trade practices, annual country market research rpt series, 2046–6

Overseas Business Reports: economic conditions, investment and export opportunities, and trade practices, world region rpt series, 2046–5

Pacific Basin economic indicators, US and 12 countries, quarterly rpt, 9393–9

Pollution abatement expenditures, and effect on economic indicators and industry operations, by major industry, projected under 3 pollution regulation alternatives 1983-95, 9188–84

Recession and recovery effect on labor cost and productivity indexes, changes by index component, various periods 1948-82, article, 6722–1.470

Seasonal adjustment methodology for economic time series, dev and design of Census Bur and other systems, with illustrative data, 1981 conf papers, 2626–7.5

Index by Subjects and Names

Small business economic conditions, with comparisons to larger businesses, selected years 1979-83, annual rpt, 9764–1.1

Social pathology measures including crime and death rates, relation to selected economic indicators, various periods 1950-80, 23848–76

Southeastern States and 5 SMSAs economic indicators, Fed Reserve 8th District, quarterly rpt, 9391–15

Southeastern States economic indicators, by State, Fed Reserve 5th District, quarterly rpt, 9389–16

Stock price impacts of announced changes in money supply, CPI, economic activity, and Fed Reserve discount rates, 1977-82, technical paper, 9381–10.37

UK economic indicator performance under Thatcher govt, with OECD comparisons, 1970-1983/84, article, 9391–1.414

Western States economic indicators, Fed Reserve 12th District, quarterly rpt, 9393–1

see also Business assets and liabilities, general

see also Business income and expenses, general

see also Business inventories

see also Capital investments, general

see also Consumer Price Index

see also Credit

see also Earnings, general

see also Employment and unemployment, general

see also Flow-of-funds accounts

see also Gross National Product

see also Housing costs and financing

see also Housing sales

see also Industrial capacity and utilization

see also Industrial production

see also Industrial production indexes

see also Industry

see also Job vacancy

see also Labor productivity

see also Labor turnover

see also Money supply

see also National income and product accounts

see also Personal and family income

see also Personal consumption

see also Prices

see also Producer Price Index

Economic policy

Budget of US, CBO analysis of revenue and spending alternatives and projections of economic indicators, FY85-89, annual rpt, 26304–3

Budget of US, economic assumptions, FY84-89, midsession review of FY85 budget, annual rpt, 104–7

Budget of US, effects of Reagan Admin policy changes, by detailed program, FY85, annual rpt, 104–21

Budget of US, impacts of deficits on economy, projected FY84-88 with trends and foreign comparisons from 1946, conf papers, 9373–3.27

Economic growth rates and component economic indicators, selected years 1922-83 and projected under full employment to 1988, hearing, 21348–90

Economic Report of the President for 1984, economic effects of budget proposals, and trends and projections 1950s-89, annual hearings, 23844–4

Index by Subjects and Names

Economic Report of the President for 1984, economic trends from 1929 and Reagan Admin proposals, annual rpt, 204–1

Economic Report of the President for 1984, Joint Economic Committee critique and policy recommendations, annual rpt, 23844–2

Financial and economic devs, Fed Reserve Bank of Atlanta monthly rpt with articles, 9371–1

Financial and economic devs, Fed Reserve Bank of Chicago bimonthly rpt articles, 9375–1

Financial and economic devs, Fed Reserve Bank of Dallas bimonthly rpt articles, 9379–1

Financial and economic devs, Fed Reserve Bank of Kansas City monthly rpt articles, 9381–1

Financial and economic devs, Fed Reserve Bank of Minneapolis quarterly rpt articles, 9383–6

Financial and economic devs, Fed Reserve Bank of New York quarterly rpt with articles, 9385–1

Financial and economic devs, Fed Reserve Bank of Philadelphia bimonthly rpt articles, 9387–1

Financial and economic devs, Fed Reserve Bank of Richmond bimonthly rpt articles, 9389–1

Financial and economic devs, Fed Reserve Bank of San Francisco quarterly rpt articles, 9393–8

Financial and economic devs, Fed Reserve Bank of St Louis monthly rpt articles, 9391–1

Foreign economic trends and implications for US, annual and semiannual country rpt series, 2046–4

Intl Labor Affairs Bur research contracts, by project and contractor, FY73-84, annual listing, 6364–1

Overseas Business Reports: economic conditions, investment and export opportunities, and trade practices, annual country market research rpt series, 2046–6

Overseas Business Reports: economic conditions, investment and export opportunities, and trade practices, world region rpt series, 2046–5

see also Business cycles

see also Defense expenditures

see also Economic development

see also Employment and unemployment, general

see also Fiscal policy

see also Foreign assistance

see also Foreign economic relations

see also Foreign trade

see also Foreign trade promotion

see also Government spending

see also Inflation

see also Interest rates

see also International sanctions

see also Land reform

see also Military assistance

see also Monetary policy

see also Price regulation

see also Prices

see also Subsidies

see also Tariffs and foreign trade controls

see also terms beginning with Federal aid

Economic Regulatory Administration

Budget appropriations proposed for Fed Govt energy programs, by office or dept and function, FY84-85, annual rpt, 3004–14

DOD electric power plants and major fuel-burning facilities conversion from oil and gas, fuel use data, 1983, annual rpt, 3104–9

Electric and gas utility ratemaking and regulatory policy standards, and consumers and sales covered, by type of consumer and utility, 1983, annual rpt, 3104–7

Electric power plants and industrial facilities prohibited from oil and gas primary use, and exemption petitions, by facility, with summary fuel use, 1983, annual rpt, 3104–8

Electric power transactions of US with Canada and Mexico, by utility and US region, 1983, annual rpt, 3104–10

Supply and prices of crude oil and refined products, effects of 3 import disruptions, selected years 1972-82, 3108–28

Economic relations

see Foreign economic relations

Economic Research Service

Acreage harvested and cropland area by crop and region, and potential for expansion, 1982-84 with trends from 1949, annual rpt, 1584–4

Activities and programs of USDA, by subagency, FY83, annual rpt, 1004–3

Activities, funding, and staff in DC and other locations, by detailed ERS branch and section, FY83, annual rpt, 1504–7

Activities, funding, and staff in DC and other locations, by detailed ERS branch and section, FY84, annual rpt, 1504–6

Advertising (generic) for agricultural commodities, activities and funding by source, selected years 1972-83, 1548–242

Agricultural economics technical research, quarterly journal, 1502–3

Agricultural exports and imports, outlook and current situation, quarterly rpt, 1542–4

Agricultural policies of US effect on trade, with US and foreign trade by commodity and grain stocks by world area, various periods 1979-83, 1528–183

Agricultural production, marketing, trade, supply, food consumption, and food and nutrition programs, 1960s-83, annual chartbook, 1504–3

Agricultural situation and farm-related topics, monthly rpt, 1502–6

Agricultural surplus direct purchase program of USDA, finances, and purchases and food received by schools by commodity, various periods 1936-83, 1548–243

Argentina grain and oilseed production, effect of agricultural price regulation, 1947-80, 1528–170

Argentina grain production, exports by firm, storage by facility type and port, and shipments to ports by mode of transport, by grain type, selected years 1954-81, 1528–185

Canada agricultural trade with US, effects of nontariff trade barriers, selected years 1955-81, 1528–175

Canada grain handling and rail transport system financial and operating data, and

Economic Research Service

effects of limited capacity on grain and oilseed exports, selected years 1950-82, 1528–176

Corn and soybean yields, itemized production costs, and input use, effects of alternative tillage systems, by region and for 10 States, 1980, 1588–80

Cotton acreage, production, prices, stocks, consumption, and trade, US and world, annual rpt, suspended, 1564–10

Cotton ginning charges and related data, by State, 1983/84, annual rpt, 1564–3

Cotton, wool, and synthetic fiber production, prices, consumption, and trade, periodic situation rpt with articles, 1561–1

Developing countries agricultural supply/demand and market for US exports, with socioeconomic indicators, country rpt series, 1526–6

Developing countries food production and needs, and related economic trends and outlook, for 67 countries, 1980-86, annual rpt, 1524–6

Developing countries food supply policies, with farm sector data, tariff income, and prices and imports of 5 grains, for 21 countries, 1960s-81, 1528–168

Eastern Europe agricultural production and trade by commodity, food consumption, and farm inputs, for 6 countries, 1960-80 with projections to 1991, 1528–178

EC food supply/demand and market and support prices, with exchange rates, fertilizer price index, GDP, and population, by country, 1960-83, 1528–173

EC fruit and vegetable product trade and tariffs, 1966-78, and effect of Greece, Spain, and Portugal entry into EC, projected to 1986, 1528–182

Economic and population time series data frequently used in statistical demand analyses, 1941-1982, annual rpt, 1544–21

Electric power demand of households in 136 SMSAs and other utility service areas, with fuel prices, family income, and heating degree days, 1975 and projected to 1985, 1588–78

Exports and imports of US, by agricultural commodity and country, bimonthly rpt with articles, 1522–1

Exports and imports of US, by detailed agricultural commodity and country, FY83 and CY83, semiannual rpts, 1522–4

Exports and personal expenditures of US and world for selected agricultural commodities, by country, and export share of US farm income, various periods 1926-82, 1528–172

Farm business legal organization, finances, operations, tax rates, and State laws restricting farm corporations, 1960s-82, 1548–233

Farm debt, loans outstanding, and interest rates, by type of lender and State, 1960-83 with trends from 1940, biennial rpt, 1544–2

Farm finances, assets, expenses, cash flow, receipts, and loans, selected years 1971-85, annual rpt, 1544–13

Farm finances, assets, liabilities, income, receipts by commodity and State, and expenses, 1980-83 and trends from 1910, annual rpt, 1544–16

Economic Research Service

Index by Subjects and Names

Farm finances, production, expenses by type, and domestic economic impact, selected years 1972-82 and preliminary 1983-84, annual rpt, 1544–19

Farm income (gross and net), cash receipts by detailed commodity, and production expenses, by State, 1979-82 and trends from 1950, annual rpt, 1544–18

Farm investments, effect of Fed Govt and State tax rates under alternative depreciation methods and inflation rates, 1950-84, 1548–231

Farm investments, effective rates of Federal/State income and State/local property taxes, by category of structure and equipment, for 7 North Central States, 1981-82, 1548–237

Farm population, by employment and socioeconomic characteristics, 1983, annual rpt, 2544–1

Farm population, by farm type and sales size and selected other characteristics, 1975-80, 1598–144

Farm production inputs, outputs, and productivity, by region, 1939-82, annual rpt, 1544–17

Farm production inputs supply, use, and prices, periodic situation rpt with articles, 1561–16

Farm production itemized costs, receipts, and net returns, for 13 crops, 4 livestock types, and milk, by region, 1981-83, annual rpt, 1544–20

Farm production, prices, marketing, and trade, by commodity, forecast and current situation, monthly rpt, 1502–4

Farm real estate and other debt, by type of lender, 1980 benchmark data with revised estimates for 1970-82, 1548–230

Farm real estate value, sales, financing, taxes, and proposed use after purchase, by State, 1970s-84, annual rpt, 1541–8

Farm sector structure and family farm characteristics, annual rpt, discontinued, 1504–4

Farmland (US) owned by foreigners, acquisitions, dispositions, holdings, and use, by State and type and country of owner, 1983, annual rpt, 1584–2

Farmland (US) owned by foreigners, acreage, value, and use, by State and county, and for 5 leading investor countries, 1983, annual rpt, 1584–3

Farmland acquisitions of foreigners, by State and county, before 1980 and during 1980-82, 1588–77

Farmland eroded by rainfall, acreage by crop, and farm operators by selected characteristics, by soil erosion class, 1977-78, 1588–83

Farms with sales under $2,500, acreage, finances, operations, and operator characteristics, by region and for 6 States, 1978, 1548–241

Fats, oils, and oilseed production, prices, trade, and consumption, periodic situation rpt with articles, 1561–3

Fed Govt policy issues effect on agricultural and food prices, income, and trade, and crop support levels by program, Nov 1984, semiannual rpt, 1542–6

Feed grain production, acreage, stocks, use, trade, prices, and price supports, periodic situation rpt with articles, 1561–4

Fertilizer foreign and US production, prices, trade, and use, annual situation rpt, suspended, 1561–5

Food consumer research and marketing devs, and consumption and price trends, quarterly rpt with articles, 1541–7

Food consumption, supply, trade, prices, expenditures, and indexes, by commodity, 1963-83, annual rpt, 1544–4

Food expenditures for fruit, vegetable, and potato products related to changes in income and other household characteristics, 1977-78, 1548–236

Food industry advertising expenditures by media type, and advertising to sales ratio by selected food item, 1970-79 with some trends from 1955, 1548–234

Food prices (farm-retail), marketing cost components, and industry finances and productivity, selected years 1967-83, annual rpt, 1544–9

Foreign agricultural and food production indexes, and production of selected commodities, by world region and country, 1974-83, annual rpt, 1524–5

Foreign agricultural production, prices, and trade, by country, 1983 and outlook for 1984/85, annual world region rpt series, 1524–4

Foreign and US agricultural production, prices, trade, and consumption, quarterly rpt with articles, 1522–3

Foreign and US agricultural supply/demand and production data, for selected US and world crops, and for US livestock and dairy products, periodic rpt, 1522–5

Foreign and US agricultural supply/demand, consumption per capita, and trade, by world area and country group, 1960s-82, 1528–181

Foreign and US agricultural supply/demand, trade, and production, and socioeconomic data, by country, 1950s-77, 1528–179

Foreign and US cropland per capita, and total arable land area by use, by selected country and world region, selected years 1955-80, 1528–180

Foreign and US feed and livestock trade by product and world region, and ocean freight rates between selected countries of origin and destination, selected years 1960-82, 1528–177

Foreign exchange rate appreciation of dollar, effects on exports, stocks, and prices of wheat, corn, and soybeans, 1980-82 and for hypothetical 20-year period, 1528–174

Fruit and nut production, prices, trade, stocks, and use, by selected crop, periodic situation rpt with articles, 1561–6

Grain ocean freight rates by route, and waterborne trade of grain and selected other commodities worldwide, 1966-82, 1548–235

Grain stocks, supply deviation, and effect on use, trade, and prices, for US and selected countries, various periods 1960-83, 1528–184

Health insurance coverage of farmers, farm population, and managers, by insurance type and selected sociodemographic characteristics, 1976, 1598–191

Hog production, producer characteristics, facilities, and marketing, by type and size of enterprise and region, 1975 and 1980, 1568–248

Housing completions, and new unit sales price, cost per square foot, and heating fuel use, by metro-nonmetro area, 1976-82, 1598–190

Immigrant labor law effects on farm work force, with farm labor, farms, and labor costs, by labor and farm type and State, 1978, 1598–192

Kentucky employment growth in 9-county rural area, labor force and establishment characteristics, 1979-80, 1598–194

Land privately held, acreage and owners by owner characteristics, land use, and region, and purchase and improvement funding, 1978 survey, series, 1506–5

Livestock and meat production, prices, and trade, 1983, annual rpt, 1564–6

Livestock, meat, poultry, and egg production, prices, trade, stocks, and consumption, periodic situation rpt, 1561–7

Meat marketing and distribution establishments, sales, and per capita consumption, 1960s-82 with trends from 1929, 1548–232

Milk and dairy production, prices, consumption, and trade, quarterly situation rpt with articles, 1561–2

Milk pasteurized by ultra-high temperature, sales, production, stocks, costs, market shares, and prices, 1980, 1568–247

Milk price support alternatives, effects on production, use, prices, and farm receipts, projected 1983/84-1988/89 and actual 1982/83, 1568–246

Milk price supports effect on production, use, prices, and farm receipts, by region and State, 1940s-83 and alternative projections to 1988/89, 1568–245

Milk processor sales, itemized costs, dealer margins, and production, annual rpt, suspended, 1544–15

Montana and North Dakota coal production, impact of mining on agricultural land availability and on farm income and production costs, by mining tract, 1982 rpt, 1588–79

Natural gas price changes effect on farm income and fertilizer use, 1980 and projected to 1990, 1548–240

Natural gas price decontrol alternatives effect on farm production by crop, prices, and fertilizer use and costs, 1982-90, model results, 1548–239

Oils, oilseeds, and fats production, prices, trade, stocks, and consumption, annual rpt, suspended, 1564–12

Older persons rural housing condition, selected householder and housing characteristics with comparisons to urban and nonaged population, 1979, 1598–193

Pesticide use and acreage treated, for 12 vegetable and melon crops, by type of pesticide, method of application, and region, 1979, 1588–82

Pesticide use for crops and livestock, acreage treated, application methods, and use of safety equipment and professional services, 1982 survey, 1588–76

Portugal agricultural subsidies, profits, marketing margins, and consumer prices, by commodity or product, and effects of prospective EC membership, 1981, 1528–171

Index by Subjects and Names

Education

Rice production, prices, trade, stocks, and use, 1978-July 1984 and 1984/85 outlook, semiannual situation rpt, 1561–8

Rural area situation and dev, periodic rpt articles, 1502–7

South America and Argentina agricultural exports, and coffee exports of Colombia and Brazil to US and world, market share analysis, 1960-79, 1528–169

Southeastern States soil conservation and water pollution reduction participants, costs, and acreage, by conservation method and State, selected years 1973-82, 1588–84

Sugar and sweeteners production, consumption, prices, supply, and trade, quarterly rpt with articles, 1561–14

Tax assessment, local jurisdictions reporting data on property size, use, location, ownership, and value, 1972-82, 1588–81

Tobacco production, trade, consumption, marketing, taxes, and price supports, quarterly situation rpt with articles, 1561–10

Trucking deregulation effects on marketing food and agricultural commodities, 1976-82, 1548–238

Vegetable production, prices, stocks, and consumption, for selected fresh and processed crops, periodic situation rpt with articles, 1561–11

Wheat and rye foreign and US production, prices, trade, stocks, and use, periodic situation rpt with articles, 1561–12

Economics

Agricultural economics technical research, quarterly journal, 1502–3

Census of Population, 1980: detailed socioeconomic and demographic characteristics, by age, sex, race, Hispanic origin, occupation, and industry, State rpt series, 2531–4

Occupational manpower needs and supply by detailed occupation, and educational and training program enrollees and grads by detailed field, 1982 and 1995, biennial rpt, 6744–3

Occupational Outlook Handbook, 1984-85 biennial rpt, 6744–1

R&D-employed scientists and engineers salaries by degree, type of establishment, age, experience, and field, 1984, annual rpt, 3004–1

R&D expenditures by higher education instns and federally funded centers, by field, source of funds, instn, and State, FY82, annual rpt, 9627–13

R&D expenditures by source, and scientists education and employment, detailed data by field, selected years 1953-84, annual rpt, 9624–18

R&D expenditures of higher education instns, and science and engineering employment and grad students, by field, 1972-83, biennial rpt, 9627–24

R&D Fed Govt funding for all performers, by field and supporting agency, selected years FY60-84, annual rpt, 9627–20

Science and engineering doctoral degree recipients, by field, sex, race, age, citizenship, postgrad employment and study status, State, and instn, 1960-82, 9626–6.16

Science and engineering grad enrollment, fields of study, financial support, and other student and instn characteristics, 1975-82, annual survey, 9627–7

Science and engineering grads of 1980-81, employment characteristics or grad enrollment, by degree level, field, sex, and race, 1982, 9627–25

Scientists and engineers employed at universities and colleges, by field, sex, State, and instn, Jan 1983 and selected trends from 1967, annual survey, 9627–11

Scientists and engineers employed in energy-related fields, supply/demand and effects of R&D funding, by energy type, employer type, field, and age, 1962-91, annual rpt, 3004–19

Scientists, engineers, and technicians employed in private industry, by occupation and industry group, 1980-81, biennial rpt, 9627–23

Scientists, engineers, and technicians needed in defense and nondefense industries, and supply/demand, by field, 1981-87, 9628–71

see also Economic and econometric models *see also* Economic policy

Economics and Statistics Service *see* Economic Research Service *see* Statistical Reporting Service

Ecuador

Agricultural and food production indexes, and production of selected commodities, by world region and country, 1974-83, annual rpt, 1524–5

Agricultural exports of US to Latin America, by commodity, country group, and selected country, FY81-84 and forecast FY85, article, 1522–1.407

Agricultural situation in Latin America, by country, 1981-83 and outlook for 1984, annual rpt, 1524–4.9

Agricultural supply/demand, trade, and production, and socioeconomic data, by country, 1950s-77, 1528–179

AID activities and funding by project and function, FY85, and developing countries summary socioeconomic data, 1970s-83, by country, annual rpt, 9914–3

AID economic assistance to developing countries, obligations and disbursements by country, quarterly rpt, 9912–4

AID educational program activities and project impacts in 12 developing countries, 1950s-82, 9916–11.8

AID loan repayment status and terms by program and country, and status of predecessor agency loans, quarterly rpt, 9912–3

Economic conditions, income, production, prices, employment, and trade, 1984 semiannual country rpt, 2046–4.109

Economic, social, and political summary data, by country, 1984, annual factbook, 244–11

Exports and imports of US, by commodity and country, 1972-82, annual world region rpt, 244–13.2

Exports of US, detailed Schedule B commodities by country of destination, 1983, annual rpt, 2424–9

Exports of US, detailed Schedule E commodities by mode of transport and world area and country of destination, 1983, annual rpts, 2424–5

Imports of US, detailed Schedule A commodities by country and world area of origin, and mode of transport, 1983, annual rpts, 2424–2

Imports of US, detailed TSUSA commodities by country of origin, 1983, annual rpt, 2424–4

Loans and grants for economic and military assistance from US and intl agencies, by program and country, FY46-83, annual rpt, 9914–5

Military aid of US, arms sales, and training programs costs and budget requests by program, world region, and country, FY83-85, annual rpt, 7144–13

Military spending, arms trade, and armed forces size, with total govt spending and population, by country, 1972-82, annual rpt, 9824–1

Minerals Yearbook, 1982, Vol 3: foreign country reviews of production, trade, and policies, by commodity, annual rpt, 5604–35

Minerals Yearbook, 1983, Vol 3 preprints: foreign country review of production, trade, and policies, by commodity, annual rpt, 5604–23.89

Population size and growth rates, and latest available benchmark demographic data, by country, 1950-83, biennial rpt, 2324–4

Weather, effects of El Nino ocean warming off Peru and Ecuador, 1982-83, article, 2152–8.402

see also under By Foreign Country in the "Index by Categories"

Ederer, Fred

"Visual Acuity Impairment Survey Pilot Study", 4478–147

Edgren, John A.

"Implications of Land Contracts for Property Tax Assessment Practices", 9412–2.407

Edinburg, Tex.

Census of Housing, 1980: occupancy and unit characteristics, by race, Hispanic origin, and city, SMSA rpt, 2473–1.236

Census of Population and Housing, 1980: detailed population and housing characteristics, by county, city, and census tract, SMSA rpt, 2551–2.236

Employment and economic impacts on Texas border of Mexican peso devaluation, for 6 counties and 2 SMSAs, 1970s-May 1983, hearing, 21788–133

Housing vacancy rates for single and multifamily units and mobile homes, by city and ZIP code, 1984, annual metro area rpt, 9304–19.23

Wages of office and plant workers, by occupation, 1984 labor market area survey rpt, 6785–3.10

see also under By SMSA or MSA in the "Index by Categories"

Education

Central America socioeconomic and political conditions in 6 countries, 1960s-83 with trends and projections 1930-2010, Commission rpt, 028–19.2

Coastal environmental characteristics, fish, wildlife, and use, and population socioeconomic data, for individual areas, series, 5506–4

Condition of Education, detailed data on enrollment, staff, achievement, finances, curricula, and education effects on employment, 1982-83, annual rpt, 4824–1

Developing countries disaster preparedness and summary sociodemographic, political, and economic data, country rpt series, 9916–2

Education

Digest of Education Statistics, detailed data on students, staff, finances, and facilities, 1982 and selected trends, annual rpt, 4824–2

Foreign human rights conditions in 162 countries, economic and military aid of US, and economic aid of intl organizations, 1981-83, annual rpt, 21384–3

Southeastern States economic dev effect on education, for Fed Reserve 6th District States, selected years 1900-82, article, 9371–1.428

Statistical Abstract of US, social, political, and economic data, 1950s-83 and trends, annual rpt, 2324–1.1

Underground economy, household expenditures and participation by type of goods or service and sociodemographic characteristics, with methodology and bibl, 1981 survey, 8308–27

Virgin Islands socioeconomic and govtl data, FY81, annual rpt, 5304–4

see also Adult education

see also Agricultural education

see also American Schools and Hospitals Abroad

see also Area studies

see also Audiovisual education

see also Business education

see also Compensatory education

see also Curricula

see also Degrees, higher education

see also Discrimination in education

see also Educational attainment

see also Educational broadcasting

see also Educational enrollment

see also Educational exchanges

see also Educational facilities

see also Educational finance

see also Educational materials

see also Educational research

see also Educational retention rates

see also Educational technology

see also Educational tests

see also Elementary and secondary education

see also Federal aid to education

see also Federal aid to higher education

see also Federal aid to medical education

see also Federal aid to vocational education

see also Head Start Project

see also Health education

see also Higher education

see also Legal education

see also Libraries

see also Medical education

see also Military education

see also National Assessment of Educational Progress

see also Physical education and training

see also Preschool education

see also Private schools

see also School administration and staff

see also School busing

see also School districts

see also School dropouts

see also School lunch and breakfast programs

see also Scientific education

see also Special education

see also Student aid

see also Students

see also Teacher education

see also Teachers

see also Vocational education and training

see also Work-study programs

Education Commission of the States

see National Assessment of Educational Progress

Education of handicapped children

see Special education

Educational attainment

Alabama rural black population, education, employment, health services, and economic status, for 16 counties, selected years 1970-81, 11048–180

Census of Housing, 1980: inventory, occupancy, and unit characteristics, changes from 1973 by region and inside-outside SMSAs and central cities, series, 2473–3

Census of Housing, 1980: structural, financial, and householder characteristics, by region and State, 2475–4

Census of Population and Housing, 1980: detailed population and housing characteristics, by county, city, and census tract, State and SMSA rpt series, 2551–2

Census of Population, 1980: detailed socioeconomic and demographic characteristics, by age, sex, race, Hispanic origin, occupation, and industry, State rpt series, 2531–4

Census of Population, 1980: detailed socioeconomic characteristics, by county, city, and inside-outside SMSAs and central cities, State rpt series, 2531–3

Central cities and suburbs population and employment, effect of region, neighborhood, population, and labor characteristics, 1970-80, technical paper, 9387–8.89

Computer specialists sociodemographic, educational, and employment characteristics, and Fed Govt support by agency, 1978, biennial Current Population Rpt, 2546–2.124

Condition of Education, detailed data on enrollment, staff, achievement, finances, curricula, and education effects on employment, 1982-83, annual rpt, 4824–1

County and City Data Book, detailed socioeconomic and demographic data for States, counties, and cities, selected years 1976-82, 2328–1

Digest of Education Statistics, detailed data on students, staff, finances, and facilities, 1982 and selected trends, annual rpt, 4824–2

Education statistics summary compilation, 1980/81-1982/83 with selected trends from 1869, biennial rpt, 4804–27

Educational attainment of population, by sociodemographic characteristics and for large States and SMSAs, 1981 and trends from 1940, biennial Current Population Rpt, 2546–1.390

Elementary and secondary public school districts, schools, enrollment, staff, and finances, by State, 1981/82, annual rpt, 4834–13

Engineers sociodemographic, educational, and employment characteristics, and Federal support by agency, 1978, Current Population Rpt, 2546–2.121

Families and households detailed socioeconomic characteristics, Mar 1982, annual Current Population Rpt, 2546–1.383

Index by Subjects and Names

Foreign and US agricultural supply/demand, trade, and production, and socioeconomic data, by country, 1950s-77, 1528–179

Health professionals supply and education, by occupation, demographic and professional characteristics, and location, 1950s-83 and projected to 2000, biennial rpt, 4114–8

High school classes of 1980 and 1982: educational and sociodemographic characteristics and expectations, natl longitudinal study, series, 4826–2

High school grads and 12th grade enrollment, by State, 1981/82, annual rpt, 4834–12

Housing and neighborhood quality indicators and attitudes, and occupant characteristics, by urban-rural location and region, 1981, annual survey, 2485–7

Income of households, families, and persons, by detailed socioeconomic characteristics and region, 1982, annual Current Population Rpt, 2546–6.39

Labor force educational attainment, by demographic and employment characteristics, 1982-83 with summary trends from 1940, 6746–1.251

Labor force educational attainment, by demographic and employment characteristics, 1983, article, 6722–1.423

Labor force educational attainment, by demographic and employment characteristics, 1984, press release, 6748–79

Labor force, special characteristics, Labor Statistics Handbook, 1947-82, annual rpt, 6724–1.2

Military personnel on active duty, by educational level, 1969-83, annual rpt, 3544–1.2

Military recruits, percent high school grads by sex and service branch, quarterly press release, 3542–7

Occupational manpower needs and supply by detailed occupation, and educational and training program enrollees and grads by detailed field, 1982 and 1995, biennial rpt, 6744–3

Population demographic and economic characteristics, 1982 with projections of population size to 2050, annual Current Population Rpt, 2546–2.119

Poverty status of families and persons, by detailed socioeconomic characteristics, 1982, annual Current Population Rpt, 2546–6.40

Poverty status of young adults related to motivation, psychological factors, and family characteristics, by race and sex, 1970s-82, longitudinal studies, 4008–65

Public health labs of States, pay scales and job requirements by occupation and State, FY81-83, annual rpt, 4204–7

Rural and urban areas comparisons of employment, income, housing, health, and education, 1960s-83, annual chartbook, 1504–3

Science and engineering enrollment, degrees, and employment, R&D funding, and related topics, highlights series, 9626–2

Science Indicators, R&D expenditures, innovations, research, and higher education, with foreign comparisons, 1960s- 83, annual rpt, 9624–10

Index by Subjects and Names

Southeastern States economic dev effect on education, for Fed Reserve 6th District States, selected years 1900-82, article, 9371–1.428

Statistical Abstract of US, social, political, and economic data, 1950s-83 and trends, annual rpt, 2324–1.1

Veterans income and educational attainment compared to nonveterans, by age, 1982-83, annual rpt, 9924–19

Veterans of Vietnam era, educational attainment at separation from armed forces compared with WW II and Korea veterans, and at present, FY83, annual rpt, 9924–8.1, 9924–8.3

Women in couples with wife as primary earner, socioeconomic and family characteristics, with comparative data for husbands, Mar 1982, 2326–11.9

Women's employment and earnings, by labor force and socioeconomic characteristics, and compared to men, 1978-81 and trends from 1940s, 6568–29

Women's labor force participation, earnings, and socioeconomic characteristics, 1983, annual fact sheet, 6564–1

see also Degrees, higher education

see also Illiteracy

see also National Assessment of Educational Progress

see also School dropouts

see also under By Educational Attainment in the "Index by Categories"

Educational broadcasting

Natl Endowment for Arts activities and grants, FY83, annual rpt, 9564–3

Natl Endowment for Humanities activities and grants, FY83, annual rpt, 9564–2

TV and radio stations on the air, by class of operation, monthly press release, 9282–4

TV instructional programs, distribution by grade level, 1980, annual rpt, 4824–2.25

Educational enrollment

AID educational program activities and project impacts in 12 developing countries, 1950s-82, 9916–11.8

Alabama rural black population, education, employment, health services, and economic status, for 16 counties, selected years 1970-81, 11048–180

Bilingual education programs, teachers, enrollment, and funding, selected years 1976-FY83, biennial rpt, 4804–14

Census of Population and Housing, 1980: detailed population and housing characteristics, by county, city, and census tract, State and SMSA rpt series, 2551–2

Census of Population, 1980: detailed socioeconomic and demographic characteristics, by age, sex, race, Hispanic origin, occupation, and industry, State rpt series, 2531–4

Census of Population, 1980: detailed socioeconomic characteristics, by county, city, and inside-outside SMSAs and central cities, State rpt series, 2531–3

Condition of Education, detailed data on enrollment, staff, achievement, finances, curricula, and education effects on employment, 1982-83, annual rpt, 4824–1

County and City Data Book, detailed socioeconomic and demographic data for States, counties, and cities, selected years 1976-82, 2328–1

Educational enrollment

Developing countries govt policy, and AID and other foreign assistance, effects on private sector dev and socioeconomic conditions, with case studies for 6 countries, 1960s-80, 9918–12

Digest of Education Statistics, detailed data on students, staff, finances, and facilities, 1982 and selected trends, annual rpt, 4824–2

Education highlights, trends in enrollment, expenditures, curricula, and other topics of current interest, periodic press release, 4822–1

Education statistics summary compilation, 1980/81-1982/83 with selected trends from 1869, biennial rpt, 4804–27

Educational trends, 1972/73-1992/93, biennial pocket-size card, 4824–3

Elementary and secondary education revenue by level of govt, and change in enrollment, teachers, and expenditures, by State, 1973-83, hearings, 21348–89

Elementary and secondary enrollment, households with children enrolled by school control, householder characteristics, and region, Oct 1982, 4838–13

Elementary and secondary public school districts, schools, enrollment, staff, and finances, by State, 1981/82, annual rpt, 4834–13

Elementary and secondary public school enrollment, by grade level and State, fall 1982, annual rpt, 4834–10

Engineers sociodemographic, educational, and employment characteristics, and Federal support by agency, 1978, Current Population Rpt, 2546–2.121

Enrollment and teacher employment in all schools, by grade level and instn control, fall 1983-84, annual press release, 4804–19

Enrollment of persons aged 3-34, by grade level and student characteristics, Oct 1982, advance annual Current Population Rpt, 2546–1.391

Enrollment of persons aged 3-34, by grade level, instn control, and student characteristics, Oct 1983, advance annual Current Population Rpt, 2546–1.392

Foreign and US agricultural supply/demand, trade, and production, and socioeconomic data, by country, 1950s-77, 1528–179

Foreign and US educational enrollment, average attainment, and public expenditures, and vocational skills test scores, 1960s-76, 26358–105

Foreign military, social, and economic summary data by world area and country, 1960s-80s, hearing, 25388–47.1

Foreign women sociodemographic, economic, and fertility characteristics, with comparisons to men, by country, 1960s-85, world region rpt series, 2326–15

Govt census, 1982: school system total and instructional employment, payroll, and average earnings, by enrollment size and State, 2455–2

Handicapped children public education program enrollment, staff, and funding, by handicap, age, and State, 1981/82-1982/83, annual rpt, 4944–4

Head Start Project enrollment, appropriations, and staff, FY65-84, annual rpt, 4604–8

Head Start Project enrollment of handicapped children, by handicap, State, and for Indian and migrant programs, 1982, annual rpt, 4604–1

Health professionals supply and education, by occupation, demographic and professional characteristics, and location, 1950s-83 and projected to 2000, biennial rpt, 4114–8

Health professions employment and training of minorities and women, by field, selected years 1962/63-1983/84, 4118–18

High school class of 1982: foreign language course enrollment, by language, student and school characteristics, and location, 1984 rpt, 4838–11

High school class of 1982: foreign language coursework, by language, course level, student and school characteristics, and location, 1984 rpt, 4828–17

High school classes of 1980 and 1982: educational and sociodemographic characteristics and expectations, natl longitudinal study, series, 4826–2

High school grads and 12th grade enrollment, by State, 1981/82, annual rpt, 4834–12

Higher education enrollment, by sex and attendance status of students, preliminary annual rpt, suspended, 4844–1

Higher education enrollment, by State and instn, preliminary annual rpt, suspended, 4844–4

Higher education enrollment, by student characteristics, instn type, State, and for 150 instns, fall 1982, annual rpt, 4844–2

Higher education instns, by type, location, and other characteristics, 1983/84 annual listing, 4844–3

Higher education instns, type, location, enrollment, and student charges, by State and congressional district, 1983/84, biennial listing, 4844–11

Higher education minority student enrollment, by State, instn, race or ethnic group, and sex, biennial rpt, discontinued, 4804–23

Impacted area schools, Fed Govt funding by county and school and congressional district, and eligible pupils, by State, FY83, annual rpt, 4804–10

Indian education program operations, funding, student progress measures, and opinions of school staff, parents, and students, selected years 1973-83, 4808–13

Nuclear engineering student enrollments and degrees granted, by State, instn, and subfield, and placements by sector, 1983, annual rpt, 3004–5

Occupational manpower needs and supply by detailed occupation, and educational and training program enrollees and grads by detailed field, 1982 and 1995, biennial rpt, 6744–3

Population demographic and economic characteristics, 1982 with projections of population size to 2050, annual Current Population Rpt, 2546–2.119

Postsecondary enrollment in academic, vocational, and continuing education, by student characteristics, Oct 1982, 4848–16

Educational enrollment

Puerto Rico educational enrollment from 1902, and finance, completions, curricula, and personnel, by instn, selected years 1970-83, hearings, 21348–93

Radiation protection and health physics enrollments and degrees granted by State and instn, and grads employment, 1983, annual rpt, 3004–7

Refugees from Southeast Asia, elementary and secondary enrollment in 12 leading States, FY83, annual rpt, 4704–8

Satellite Landsat system proposed transfer to private sector, uses and product sales by user type, and university programs and personnel by instn, 1973-85, 26358–100

Science and engineering enrollment, degrees, and employment, R&D funding, and related topics, highlights series, 9626–2

Science and engineering grad enrollment, fields of study, financial support, and other student and instn characteristics, 1975-82, annual survey, 9627–7

Science and engineering grad program enrollment, by field, degree level, source of financial support, race, and Hispanic origin, 1975-81, 9626–2.134

Science and engineering grad program enrollment by field, sources of financial support, and foreign students, 1975-82, 9626–2.141

Science and engineering grad students, by field, type of financial aid, sex, race, Hispanic origin, and citizenship, 1972-83, biennial rpt, 9627–24.3

Science and engineering grads of 1980-81, employment characteristics or grad enrollment, by degree level, field, sex, and race, 1982, 9627–25

Science Indicators, R&D expenditures, innovations, research, and higher education, with foreign comparisons, 1960s- 83, annual rpt, 9624–10

Scientists and engineers employed in energy-related fields, supply/demand and effects of R&D funding, by energy type, employer type, field, and age, 1962-91, annual rpt, 3004–19

Southeastern States economic dev effect on education, for Fed Reserve 6th District States, selected years 1900-82, article, 9371–1.428

Statistical Abstract of US, social, political, and economic data, 1950s-83 and trends, annual rpt, 2324–1.1

TTPI socioeconomic, health, and govtl data, by TTPI govt, FY83 and selected trends, detailed annual rpt, 7004–6

TVA construction projects employment, and impacts on nearby areas, survey rpt series, 9806–7

Virginia higher education new enrollment, and students needed to meet desegregation goals, by race and instn, selected years 1978-85, hearings, 21348–91

Women's employment and earnings, by labor force and socioeconomic characteristics, and compared to men, 1978-81 and trends from 1940s, 6568–29

Women's travel patterns, by employment and sociodemographic characteristics and type of child care used, 1980 survey, 7888–62

Youth employment, by high school and college enrollment status, industry div, occupation, and selected demographic characteristics, 1980-82, 6746–1.250

see also Educational retention rates

Educational exchanges

Fed Govt intl exchange and training programs, participants by world region, and funding, by agency, FY83, annual rpt, 9854–8

Fulbright scholarship program lecturers conducting USIA-supported teacher training seminars, by world region and country, FY83, annual rpt, 9854–2

Japan-US Friendship Commission educational and cultural exchange activities, grants, and trust fund status, FY83, annual rpt, 14694–1

Latin America students in US and Soviet bloc training programs, by program type and student country, and summary by world region, selected years 1972-82, GAO rpt, 26123–77

NIH intl program activities and funding, by inst and country, FY83, annual rpt, 4474–6

USIA activities, employment, and funding, FY83-84, annual rpt, 17594–1

Warsaw Pact-US exchange visits under Fulbright-Hays and Intl Exchange Board programs, by country, Dec 1983-Mar 1984, semiannual rpt, 7002–1

see also Exchange of persons programs

Educational facilities

AID educational program activities and project impacts in 12 developing countries, 1950s-82, 9916–11.8

American Samoa minimum wage rates, employment, earnings, and benefits, by establishment and industry, Nov 1983, biennial rpt, 6504–6

Bombing (explosive and incendiary) and arson incidents by target, State, and circumstances, and explosives theft and recovery, 1982-83, annual rpt, 8484–4

Bombing (explosive and incendiary) incidents, damage, injuries, and deaths, by target, State, and circumstances, 1983, annual rpt, 6224–5

Capital (fixed), govt and private nonresidential structures and equipment, residential capital, and consumer-owned durable goods by item, 1980-83, annual article, 2702–1.433

Capital needs and intergovtl financing for public works, by type of project and selected city, various periods 1950-83, 10048–60

Census of Govts, 1982: school districts revenues, expenditures, debt, and assets, by district and State, 2457–1

Census of Govts, 1982: State govt payments to local govts, by program, source of funds, level of govt, and State, with trends from 1902, 2460–3

Construction industries census, 1982: financial and operating data, by SIC 4-digit industry and State, final rpt series, 2373–1

Construction industries census, 1982: financial and operating data, by SIC 4-digit industry and State, preliminary rpt series, 2371–1

Construction put in place, permits authorized by region, State, and MSA, and Federal contract awards, by construction type, bimonthly rpt with articles, 2012–1

Index by Subjects and Names

Construction put in place, value of new public and private structures, by type, monthly rpt, 2382–4

County Business Patterns: establishments, employees, and payrolls, by SIC 4-digit industry and county, 1981, annual State rpt series, 2326–8

County Business Patterns: establishments, employees, and payrolls, by SIC 4-digit industry and county, 1982, annual State rpt series, 2326–6

Digest of Education Statistics, detailed data on students, staff, finances, and facilities, 1982 and selected trends, annual rpt, 4824–2

DOD training and education programs funding, staff, students, and facilities, by service branch and reserve component, FY85, annual rpt, 3504–5

Elementary and secondary public school districts, schools, enrollment, staff, and finances, by State, 1981/82, annual rpt, 4834–13

Energy conservation grants of Fed Govt to public and nonprofit private instns, by building type and State, 1983, annual rpt, 3304–15

Energy use in nonresidential buildings, expenditures, and conservation, by building characteristics, EIA survey series, 3166–8

Finances and operations, by SIC 2- to 4-digit industry, 1970s-83 and projected to 1988, annual rpt, 2014–4

Franchise business opportunities, by firm and kind of business, 1984 annual listing, 2044–27

Head Start Project programs and effect on child dev, literature review with bibl, selected years 1970-83, 4608–17

Impacted area schools, Fed Govt funding by county and school and congressional district, and eligible pupils, by State, FY83, annual rpt, 4804–10

Neighborhood and housing quality indicators and attitudes, and occupant characteristics, by urban-rural location and region, 1981, annual survey, 2485–7

Neighborhood and housing quality indicators and attitudes, by occupant and unit characteristics, region, and metro-nonmetro location, 1981, annual survey, 2485–2

Neighborhood quality, indicators and attitudes by inside-outside central cities, 1979-82 surveys, SMSA rpt series, 2485–6

New Communities program of HUD, activities, costs, land sales, and community and population characteristics, for 13 communities, 1970s-83, 5188–107

Oceanographic research cruise schedules and ship characteristics, by academic instn or Federal agency, 1984, annual rpt, 3804–6

Puerto Rico University enrollment, tuition, construction costs, degrees granted, personnel by sex, and Fed Govt funding of medical research, 1970s-87, hearings, 21348–93

Smoking and tobacco marketing legislation introduced and enacted in State legislatures, by State, 1982, annual rpt, 4204–13

Southeastern States financial and economic devs, Fed Reserve 6th District, monthly rpt with articles, 9371–1

Index by Subjects and Names

Transit system (automated guideway) characteristics and itemized costs, for 16 systems in operation or under construction, 1982, annual rpt, 7884–6

see also Libraries

see also under By Individual Company or Institution in the "Index by Categories"

Educational finance

AID activities and funding by project and function, FY85, and developing countries summary socioeconomic data, 1970s-83, by country, annual rpt, 9914–3

Census of Govts, 1982: city govt revenues by source, expenditures by function, debt, and assets, by State and city, 2457–4

Census of Govts, 1982: county govt revenues by source, expenditures by function, debt, and assets, by State and county, 2457–3

Census of Govts, 1982: employment, payrolls, and average earnings, by function, level of govt, State, county, population size, and inside-outside SMSAs, 2455–2

Census of Govts, 1982: school districts revenues, expenditures, debt, and assets, by district and State, 2457–1

Condition of Education, detailed data on enrollment, staff, achievement, finances, curricula, and education effects on employment, 1982-83, annual rpt, 4824–1

County Business Patterns: establishments, employees, and payrolls, by SIC 4-digit industry and county, 1981, annual State rpt series, 2326–8

County Business Patterns: establishments, employees, and payrolls, by SIC 4-digit industry and county, 1982, annual State rpt series, 2326–6

CPI by detailed component, for US city average, 28 SMSAs, and 4 regions by population size, monthly rpt, 6762–2

Digest of Education Statistics, detailed data on students, staff, finances, and facilities, 1982 and selected trends, annual rpt, 4824–2

Education statistics summary compilation, 1980/81-1982/83 with selected trends from 1869, biennial rpt, 4804–27

Educational trends, 1972/73-1992/93, biennial pocket-size card, 4824–3

Elementary and secondary education, factors affecting State expenditures, and tuition tax credits effects on parents choice of public or private school, 1960-82 with some projections to 2000, 4808–9

Elementary and secondary education revenue by level of govt, and change in enrollment, teachers, and expenditures, by State, 1973-83, hearings, 21348–89

Elementary and secondary public school districts, schools, enrollment, staff, and finances, by State, 1981/82, annual rpt, 4834–13

Elementary and secondary public school systems revenues, by level of govt, selected years 1919/20-1981/82, press release, 4838–12

Expenditures on education and job training, and employment, housing finance, and social programs data, selected years 1948-81, hearing, 21968–28

Finances and operations, by SIC 2- to 4-digit industry, 1970s-83 and projected to 1988, annual rpt, 2014–4

Foreign and US educational enrollment, average attainment, and public expenditures, and vocational skills test scores, 1960s-76, 26358–105

Foreign military, social, and economic summary data by world area and country, 1960s-80s, hearing, 25388–47.1

Govt employment and payrolls, for State and local govts, monthly rpt, 6742–4

Govt expenditures for social welfare by program and level of govt, and private expenditures for health care, selected years FY50-82, annual article, 4742–1.425

Govt finances, by level of govt, State, and for large cities and counties, 1981-83, annual rpt series, 2466–2

Handicapped children public education program enrollment, staff, and funding, by handicap, age, and State, 1981/82-1982/83, annual rpt, 4944–4

Health professionals supply and education, by occupation, demographic and professional characteristics, and location, 1950s-83 and projected to 2000, biennial rpt, 4114–8

Housing (rental) unit choice of Pittsburgh, Pa, recent movers related to unit, neighborhood, and town characteristics, 1967 survey, 9306–1.7

Income tax returns of corporations, detailed income and tax items by industry, 1981, annual rpt, 8304–4

Income tax returns of sole proprietorships, detailed data by industry div and selected industry group, 1981, annual rpt, 8304–7

Income tax returns of sole proprietorships, receipts, deductions by type, payroll, and net income, by major industry, 1982, annual article, 8302–2.413

Indian education program operations, funding, student progress measures, and opinions of school staff, parents, and students, selected years 1973-83, 4808–13

Input-output structure of US economy, detailed interindustry transactions for 85 industries, and components of final demand, 1977, article, 2702–1.421

Input-output structure of US economy, detailed interindustry transactions for 537 industries, and components of final demand, 1977 benchmark data, 2708–17

Japan-US Friendship Commission educational and cultural exchange activities, grants, and trust fund status, FY83, annual rpt, 14694–1

Local govt finances and population characteristics for cities and suburbs, by region and selected SMSA, selected years 1957-FY83, 10048–61

Public opinion on taxes, tax policy, and intergovtl relations, 1972-84 surveys, annual rpt, 10044–2

Puerto Rico organizations in US and Puerto Rico, philanthropic grants received, by foundation, purpose, and recipient, 1979-81, hearings, 21788–137.1

Puerto Rico University enrollment, tuition, construction costs, degrees granted, personnel by sex, and Fed Govt funding of medical research, 1970s-87, hearings, 21348–93

R&D expenditures by higher education instns and federally funded centers, by field, source of funds, instn, and State, FY82, annual rpt, 9627–13

Educational research

Science and engineering grad program enrollment by field, sources of financial support, and foreign students, 1975-82, 9626–2.141

Service industry census, 1982: employment, establishments, receipts, and payroll, by SIC 2- to 4-digit kind of business, SMSA, county, and city, State rpt series, 2391–1

Southeastern States educational finances and indicators of cost burden, for Fed Reserve 6th District States, selected years 1970-83, article, 9371–1.429

Statistical Abstract of US, social, political, and economic data, 1950s-83 and trends, annual rpt, 2324–1.1

Veterans participation in training, rehabilitation, and housing loan programs, Vietnam era compared with WW II and Korea veterans, FY83, annual rpt, 9924–8.6

see also Federal aid to education

see also Federal aid to higher education

see also Federal aid to medical education

see also Federal aid to vocational education

see also State aid to education

see also State aid to higher education

see also Student aid

see also Tuition

Educational materials

Bilingual education programs, teachers, enrollment, and funding, selected years 1976-FY83, biennial rpt, 4804–14

Census of Population, 1980: selected socioeconomic data, with trends and projections 1960-2050, young readers pamphlet series, 2326–1

Franchise business opportunities, by firm and kind of business, 1984 annual listing, 2044–27

Franchises of firms engaged in distribution of goods and services by kind of business, establishments by State, and sales, 1982-84, annual rpt, 2014–5

Govt census, 1982: State govt payments to local govts, by program, source of funds, level of govt, and State, with trends from 1902, 2460–3

Handicapped children early education research and service project activities and characteristics, and grants to States for program dev, 1983-84, annual listing, 4804–30

Health info offices and services of HHS and other Fed Govt agencies, by subject, 1984 listing, 4048–18

Libraries of colleges and universities, expenditures, holdings by type, use, staff by sex, and Federal grants received, 1979-82, biennial rpt, 4854–1

Mail subsidy for USPS revenue forgone, by class of mail, FY83, annual rpt, 9864–5.3

Microfiche from Educational Resources Info Center, holdings of US and foreign educational and other instns, as of 1983, listing, 4918–14

Nutrition and cardiovascular disease consumer education, effectiveness of Natl Heart, Lung, and Blood Inst and Giant Food, Inc, program in DC metro area, 1978-79, 4478–144

see also Audiovisual education

Educational research

Bilingual education programs, teachers, enrollment, and funding, selected years 1976-FY83, biennial rpt, 4804–14

Educational research

Corporate income tax returns, detailed income and tax items by industry, 1981, annual rpt, 8304–4

Education Dept financial aid programs for educational instns and individuals, 1984 annual listing, 4804–3

Education Dept programs and activities, FY83, annual rpt, 4804–6

Education Dept programs funding, operations, and effectiveness, FY83, annual rpt, 4804–5

Education Natl Inst activities and education research grants awarded by recipient, and Education Dept expenditures by function, FY81-82, annual rpt, 4914–4

Fast Response Survey System, current natl estimates for education data, series, 4826–1

Fed Govt procurement contract awards, by State, agency, procurement and contractor type, and for top 100 contractors, quarterly rpt, 102–6

Fed Govt R&D funding for all performers, by field and supporting agency, selected years FY60-84, annual rpt, 9627–20

Handicapped children early education research and service project activities and characteristics, and grants to States for program dev, 1983-84, annual listing, 4804–30

Head Start Project programs effect on child dev, by characteristics of program, child, and family, literature review, selected years 1965-81, 4608–20

Teaching degrees conferred by specialty and State, required credit hours, and instn officials attitudes, by instn type, 1970s-83, hearings, 21348–89

Vocational Education Research Natl Center funding, by purpose and source, selected years 1978-84, GAO rpt, 26121–79

see also National Assessment of Educational Progress

Educational Resources Information Center "Directory of ERIC Microfiche Collections", 4918–14

Educational retention rates

Condition of Education, detailed data on enrollment, staff, achievement, finances, curricula, and education effects on employment, 1982-83, annual rpt, 4824–1

High school classes of 1980 and 1982: educational and sociodemographic characteristics and expectations, natl longitudinal study, series, 4826–2

Indian education program operations, funding, student progress measures, and opinions of school staff, parents, and students, selected years 1973-83, 4808–13

Puerto Rico educational enrollment, finance, completions, curricula, and personnel by instn, and health and vital statistics, selected years 1970-83, hearings, 21348–93

see also School dropouts

Educational technology

Computer access and use in elementary and secondary schools, by region, urban-rural location, and Title I status, spring 1982, 4826–1.10

see also Audiovisual education

Educational television

see Educational broadcasting

Educational tests

Condition of Education, detailed data on enrollment, staff, achievement, finances, curricula, and education effects on employment, 1982-83, annual rpt, 4824–1

Digest of Education Statistics, detailed data on students, staff, finances, and facilities, 1982 and selected trends, annual rpt, 4824–2

DOD Dependents College students higher education admissions tests scores by sex and subject, and educational goals and attitudes, 1983, annual rpt, 3504–17

DOD Dependents Schools 1st grader basic skills test scores, by world area and English fluency, fall 1983, annual rpt, 3504–18

Education Dept programs funding, operations, and effectiveness, FY83, annual rpt, 4804–5

Elementary and secondary schools use of tests, teacher and student attitudes, with detail for standardized achievement tests, 1980 conf papers, 4918–15

Elementary level Follow Through compensatory education programs beneficiaries, costs, funding, and participant test scores, selected years 1968-82, hearing, 21348–87

Foreign and US educational enrollment, average attainment, and public expenditures, and vocational skills test scores, 1960s-76, 26358–105

Govt census, 1982: State govt payments to local govts, by program, source of funds, level of govt, and State, with trends from 1902, 2460–3

Handicapped children early education research and service project activities and characteristics, and grants to States for program dev, 1983-84, annual listing, 4804–30

Head Start Project programs and effect on child dev, literature review with bibl, selected years 1970-83, 4608–17

Head Start Project programs effect on child dev, by characteristics of program, child, and family, literature review, selected years 1965-81, 4608–20

High school classes of 1980 and 1982: educational and sociodemographic characteristics and expectations, natl longitudinal study, series, 4826–2

Indian education program operations, funding, student progress measures, and opinions of school staff, parents, and students, selected years 1973-83, 4808–13

Scholastic Aptitude Test scores of seniors by State, and achievement test scores by sex, by whether planning education major, 1972-82, hearings, 21348–89

Science and engineering test scores, for college-bound seniors and for college students taking Grad Record Exam, 1970s-83, biennial rpt, 9624–20.2

Scientists and engineers Scholastic Aptitude Test and Grad Record Examination scores, by field and sex, 1970s-82, annual rpt, 9624–10.3

Southeastern States economic dev effect on education, for Fed Reserve 6th District States, selected years 1900-82, article, 9371–1.428

Index by Subjects and Names

see also National Assessment of Educational Progress

Edwards, Carolyn

"Driver License Administration Requirements and Fees: Status as of Jan. 1, 1984", 7554–18

Edwards, Clark

"Wheat Price: Past and Future Levels and Volatility", 1502–3.403

EG&G Idaho, Inc.

"Environmental Surveillance for the INEL Radioactive Waste Management Complex and Other Areas, Annual Report, 1983", 3354–10

Eggers, Paul W.

"Medicare Experience with End-Stage Renal Disease: Trends in Incidence, Prevalence, and Survival", 4652–1.408

"Trends in Medicare Reimbursement for End-Stage Renal Disease: 1974-79", 4652–1.421

Eggs

see Poultry industry and products

Egypt

Agricultural and food production indexes, and production of selected commodities, by world region and country, 1974-83, annual rpt, 1524–5

Agricultural situation in Middle East and North Africa, by country and commodity, 1983 and outlook for 1984, annual rpt, 1524–4.3

Agricultural supply/demand, trade, and production, and socioeconomic data, by country, 1950s-77, 1528–179

AID activities and funding by project and function, FY85, and developing countries summary socioeconomic data, 1970s-83, by country, annual rpt, 9914–3

AID community dev assistance to local govts in developing countries, program activities and funding, 1960s-80s, 9918–11

AID economic assistance to developing countries, obligations and disbursements by country, quarterly rpt, 9912–4

AID loan repayment status and terms by program and country, and status of predecessor agency loans, quarterly rpt, 9912–3

Computers and computer equipment market and trade, and user industry operations and demand, 1984 country market research rpt, 2045–1.43

Economic conditions in Communist, OECD, and selected other countries, 1960s-83, annual rpt, 244–5

Economic, social, and political summary data, by country, 1984, annual factbook, 244–11

Economic trends in income, production, prices, employment, finances, and trade, 1984 semiannual rpt, 2046–4.10, 2046–4.80

Exports of US, detailed Schedule B commodities by country of destination, 1983, annual rpt, 2424–9

Exports of US, detailed Schedule E commodities by mode of transport and world area and country of destination, 1983, annual rpts, 2424–5

Imports of US, detailed Schedule A commodities by country and world area of origin, and mode of transport, 1983, annual rpts, 2424–2

Index by Subjects and Names — Elections

Imports of US, detailed TSUSA commodities by country of origin, 1983, annual rpt, 2424–4

Loans and grants for economic and military assistance from US and intl agencies, by program and country, FY46-83, annual rpt, 9914–5

Military aid of US, arms sales, and training programs costs and budget requests by program, world region, and country, FY83-85, annual rpt, 7144–13

Military spending, arms trade, and armed forces size, with total govt spending and population, by country, 1972-82, annual rpt, 9824–1

Minerals Yearbook, 1982, Vol 3: foreign country reviews of production, trade, and policies, by commodity, annual rpt, 5604–35

Nuclear power plant construction and operation status, and capacity, by plant, region, State, and selected country, 1983 and projected to 2020, annual rpt, 3164–57

Oil and gas undiscovered recoverable resources, cumulative production, and identified reserves, as of 1982, preliminary oil basin rpt, 5666–17.13

Oil reserves, production, and resource lifespan under alternative production rates, for 3 countries, 1909-1982 with projections to 2100, 3166–9.8

PL 480 Title I funding and socioeconomic impacts in developing countries, with case studies for 5 countries, 1950s-81, 9918–13

Population size and growth rates, and latest available benchmark demographic data, by country, 1950-83, biennial rpt, 2324–4

see also under By Foreign Country in the "Index by Categories"

Ehlke, Theodore A.

"Hydrology of Area 10, Eastern Coal Province, West Virginia and Virginia", 5666–15.26

Eichers, Theodore R.

"U.S. Fertilizer and Pesticide Outlook and Situation, 1982-84", 1004–16.1

Einhorn, David

"Federal Tax Incentives and Rental Housing", 5188–104

Eisenbeis, Robert A.

"Risk Considerations in Deregulating Bank Activities", 9371–1.416

El Paso, Tex.

Census of Housing, 1980: occupancy and unit characteristics, by race, Hispanic origin, and city, SMSA rpt, 2473–1.144

Census of Population and Housing, 1980: detailed population and housing characteristics, by county, city, and census tract, SMSA rpt, 2551–2.144

Employment and economic impacts on Texas border of Mexican peso devaluation, for 6 counties and 2 SMSAs, 1970s-May 1983, hearing, 21788–133

Employment in Mexico border US-owned plants, and peso devaluation, related to employment in 4 Texas SMSAs, 1978-83, article, 9379–1.402

Housing vacancy rates for single and multifamily units and mobile homes, by city and ZIP code, 1984, annual metro area rpt, 9304–19.25

Wages of office and plant workers, by occupation, 1984 labor market area survey rpt, 6785–3.5

see also under By City and By SMSA or MSA in the "Index by Categories"

El Salvador

Agricultural and food production indexes, and production of selected commodities, by world region and country, 1974-83, annual rpt, 1524–5

Agricultural situation in Latin America, by country, 1981-83 and outlook for 1984, annual rpt, 1524–4.9

Agricultural supply/demand, trade, and production, and socioeconomic data, by country, 1950s-77, 1528–179

AID activities and funding by project and function, FY85, and developing countries summary socioeconomic data, 1970s-83, by country, annual rpt, 9914–3

AID economic assistance to developing countries, obligations and disbursements by country, quarterly rpt, 9912–4

AID economic assistance to 7 Central American countries, by type of aid, FY80-83, GAO rpt, 26123–55

AID loan repayment status and terms by program and country, and status of predecessor agency loans, quarterly rpt, 9912–3

Economic and military assistance of US to El Salvador, and socioeconomic and political conditions, 1977-FY84, 7008–39

Economic conditions, income, production, prices, employment, and trade, 1984 annual country rpt, 2046–4.110

Economic, social, and political conditions in 6 Central America countries, 1960s-83 with trends and projections 1930-2010, 028–19

Economic, social, and political summary data, by country, 1984, annual factbook, 244–11

Economic trends in income, production, prices, employment, finances, and trade, 1984 annual rpt, 2046–4.5

Exports and imports of US, by commodity and country, 1972-82, annual world region rpt, 244–13.3

Exports of US, detailed Schedule B commodities by country of destination, 1983, annual rpt, 2424–9

Exports of US, detailed Schedule E commodities by mode of transport and world area and country of destination, 1983, annual rpts, 2424–5

Imports of US, detailed Schedule A commodities by country and world area of origin, and mode of transport, 1983, annual rpts, 2424–2

Imports of US, detailed TSUSA commodities by country of origin, 1983, annual rpt, 2424–4

Loans and grants for economic and military assistance from US and intl agencies, by program and country, FY46-83, annual rpt, 9914–5

Military aid of US, arms sales, and training programs costs and budget requests by program, world region, and country, FY83-85, annual rpt, 7144–13

Military spending, arms trade, and armed forces size, with total govt spending and population, by country, 1972-82, annual rpt, 9824–1

Minerals Yearbook, 1982, Vol 3: foreign country reviews of production, trade, and policies, by commodity, annual rpt, 5604–35

Minerals Yearbook, 1982, Vol 3 preprints: foreign country review of production, trade, and policies, by commodity, annual rpt, 5604–17.86

Natural resources and hazards to resource dev, with data on mineral, energy, and water resources, by Central American country, 1981 with trends from 1977, 5668–71

Population size and growth rates, and latest available benchmark demographic data, by country, 1950-83, biennial rpt, 2324–4

Refugees from Central America by country of origin and asylum, and aid from US and Mexico, FY82-1984, GAO rpt, 26123–70

Terrorist acts against property, casualties, kidnappings, and hostages, Oct 1979-June 1983, human rights certification hearing, 21388–41

see also under By Foreign Country in the "Index by Categories"

Elam, Emmett W.

"Cross-Hedging Rice Bran and Millfeed", 1561–8.401

Elderly

see Aged and aging

Eldridge, William B.

"District Court Executive Pilot Program: A Report on the Preliminary Experience in Five Federal Courts", 18408–25

Elections

Census of Govts, 1982: State govt payments to local govts, by program, source of funds, level of govt, and State, with trends from 1902, 2460–3

Developing countries disaster preparedness and summary sociodemographic, political, and economic data, country rpt series, 9916–2

Fed Election Commission monitoring activities, campaign finances, and election procedures, press release series, 9276–1

Foreign economic, social, and political summary data, by country, 1984, annual factbook, 244–11

Hispanic Americans socioeconomic and demographic characteristics, and compared to non-Hispanics, selected years 1970-83, chartbook, 2328–48

Labor union representation elections conducted by NLRB, results, monthly rpt, 9582–2

Latin America elections, votes and share of population voting by country and election type, selected years 1962-83, 7008–42

Statistical Abstract of US, social, political, and economic data, 1950s-83 and trends, annual rpt, 2324–1.2

Voting age population, by congressional district, biennial rpt, discontinued, 2544–2

Voting age population for Nov 1984 election, by sex, age, race, Hispanic origin, region, and State, and percent voting during 1930-82, Current Population Rpt, 2546–3.129

Voting age population selected characteristics and participation in presidential elections, 1964-80 with projections to 2000, Current Population Rpt, 2546–2.117

Elections

Voting and registration by party and State, and political opinions, 1980 with trends from 1960, hearings, 25688–6

Voting and registration, by socioeconomic and demographic characteristics, Nov 1982 with trends from 1964, annual Current Population Rpt, 2546–2.119

Voting in 1980 presidential elections, by State and county, *County and City Data Book* , 2328–1

see also Campaign funds

see also Officials

see also Political broadcasting

see also Political conventions

Electric power

- Agriculture census, 1982: farms, farmland, production and costs, and operator characteristics, preliminary State and county rpt series, 2330–1
- Agriculture census, 1982: farms, farmland, production, finances, and operator characteristics, by county, final State rpt series, 2331–1
- Air pollutant emission factors, by detailed source, 3rd edition, 1983-84 supplements, 9198–13
- Alaska electric power capacity and generation by fuel type, and marketing, by utility, type of ownership, and location, 1983, annual rpt, 3214–2
- Alaska Power Admin activities, project operations, and financial statements, annual rpt, suspended, 3214–1
- Bonneville Power Admin operations, and Columbia River power system sales and financial statements, FY83, annual rpt, 3224–1
- Building materials manufacture, energy use and cost by source and industry, 1970s-82, article, 2012–1.401
- Buildings (nonresidential) energy use, expenditures, and conservation, by building characteristics, EIA survey series, 3166–8
- Business statistics, detailed data for major industries and economic indicators, *Survey of Current Business,* monthly rpt, 2702–1.10
- China economic conditions, agricultural and industrial production, trade, and domestic and foreign investment, 1980-85, 2048–106
- China exports and imports by SITC 1- to 5-digit commodity, 1970s-82, annual rpt, 244–12
- Coal production and stocks, and electric utility generation, capacity, and coal use, alternative estimates 1977-82, annual rpt, 3164–63
- Coastal environmental characteristics, fish, wildlife, and use, and population socioeconomic data, for individual areas, series, 5506–4
- Communist, OECD, and selected other countries energy reserves, production, and consumption, and oil trade and revenue, 1960s-83, annual rpt, 244–5.5
- Connecticut utility group housing energy conservation program, cost effectiveness and characteristics of participants and nonparticipants, 1980-82, 3308–77
- Construction put in place, value of new public and private structures, by type, monthly rpt, 2382–4

Consumption by fuel type, and estimated supply from renewable resources, 1977 and projected 2000, hearing, 21448–30

- Consumption, by fuel type, economic sector, and end use, 1983 and 2000, 2006–2.5
- Consumption, by fuel type, economic sector, census div, and State, 1960-82, State Energy Data System annual rpt, 3164–39
- Consumption per capita, and by economic sector, State, and major energy resource, 1960-82, State Energy Data System annual supplement, 3164–55
- Consumption, prices, and conservation and efficiency measures, by fuel type, end-use sector, selected industry, and region, 1960-83, annual rpt, 3164–73
- County Business Patterns: establishments, employees, and payrolls, by SIC 4-digit industry and county, 1981, annual State rpt series, 2326–8
- County Business Patterns: establishments, employees, and payrolls, by SIC 4-digit industry and county, 1982, annual State rpt series, 2326–6
- Cuba economic conditions, agricultural and industrial production and distribution, trade, and intl economic relations, 1970-82 and trends from 1957, 248–40
- Death rates by sex, race, and age for 40 causes, projected for 10-year period, 1982 rpt, 4208–21
- Defense Fuel Supply Center procurement, prices, stocks, transport, and other activities and finances, FY83, annual rpt, 3904–8
- Developing countries disaster preparedness and summary sociodemographic, political, and economic data, country rpt series, 9916–2
- DOE in-house energy use, conservation investments, and savings, by type of use and fuel and field office, FY83, annual rpt, 3024–3
- Employment, earnings, and hours, by SIC 4-digit nonfarm industry, monthly 1974-Feb 1984, annual update, 6744–4
- Environmental quality and protection programs, costs, and Fed Govt enforcement, 1983, detailed annual rpt, 484–1
- Exports and imports of electric power, US transactions with Canada and Mexico by utility and US region, 1983, annual rpt, 3104–10
- Farm finances, assets, liabilities, income, receipts by commodity and State, and expenses, 1980-83 and trends from 1910, annual rpt, 1544–16
- Farm finances, expenses by type, loans by purpose and source, and credit detail by Fed Reserve District, quarterly rpt, 9365–3.10
- Farm finances, production, expenses by type, and domestic economic impact, selected years 1972-82 and preliminary 1983-84, annual rpt, 1544–19
- Farm production expenditures, detailed items by farm sales size and region, 1983, annual rpt, 1614–3
- FERC activities and funding by program, with some natural gas and electric power industry data, FY83, annual rpt, 3084–9
- Foreign countries electric current characteristics, by country and selected city, 1984 rpt, 2018–8

Foreign economic, social, and political summary data, by country, 1984, annual factbook, 244–11

- Foreign economic trends and implications for US, annual and semiannual country rpt series, 2046–4
- Foreign electric power generation and capacity by energy source, for 19 West European countries, Japan, and Canada, 1981, annual rpt, 3164–77
- Fuel oil (distillate and residual) and kerosene deliveries, by end use, PAD district, and State, selected years 1978-83, annual rpt, 3164–2
- Govt census, 1982: city govt revenues by source, expenditures by function, debt, and assets, by State and city, 2457–4
- Govt census, 1982: county govt revenues by source, expenditures by function, debt, and assets, by State and county, 2457–3
- Govt census, 1982: employment, payrolls, and average earnings, by function, level of govt, State, county, population size, and inside-outside SMSAs, 2455–2
- Govt census, 1982: local govt employment by function, payroll, and average earnings, for individual counties, cities, and school and special districts, 2455–1
- Govt employment and payroll, by function, level of govt, and jurisdiction, 1983, annual rpt series, 2466–1
- Household demand for electric power in 136 SMSAs and other utility service areas, with fuel prices, family income, and heating degree days, 1975 and projected to 1985, 1588–78
- Housing (multifamily rental) energy use and costs, conservation effect on rental marketing, and effect of utility bill payment methods on conservation efforts, 1970s-80s, 3308–73
- Housing census, 1980: inventory, occupancy, and unit characteristics, changes from 1973 by region and inside-outside SMSAs and central cities, series, 2473–3
- Housing census, 1980: structural, financial, and householder characteristics, by region and State, 2475–4
- Housing electricity use and savings, methodology for assessment using utility billing data, 1984 rpt, 3308–76
- Housing energy bills and departures from normal by fuel type, and heating and cooling degree days by State, by census div, monthly rpt, 2152–11, 2152–12
- Housing energy conservation programs of utilities, financing, costs, participation, and energy savings, various periods 1981-84, hearing, 21368–54
- Housing energy conservation programs of utilities under natl conservation act, cost effectiveness and participating household characteristics, 1980s, 3308–69
- Housing energy consumption and retail prices, by energy type, region, and for 28 SMSAs and US city average, monthly press release, 6762–8
- Housing energy use, costs, expenditures, and conservation, and household and housing characteristics, survey series, 3166–7
- Housing energy use in SMSAs and central cities, by fuel type, householder race and Hispanic origin, and city, 1980 Census of Housing, State and SMSA rpt series, 2473–1

Index by Subjects and Names

Electric power prices

Housing heating and air conditioning equipment shipments by type of fuel used, monthly rpt, 2012–1.6

Housing occupancy and unit and household characteristics, by region and metro-nonmetro residence, 1983, biennial survey, 2485–1

Housing unit heating fuel, by type, occupant race, Hispanic origin, urban-rural location, and region, 1981, annual survey, 2485–7

Income tax returns of corporations, detailed income and tax items by industry, 1981, annual rpt, 8304–4

Industrial electric power cogeneration in 5 industries, and fuel use and utility supply/demand effects, by region, 1983-93, 3008–92

Industrial electric power demand model estimates, economic indicators, and supporting data for 5 industries, 1960s-80 with projections to 2000, 3008–87

Industrial electric power use indexes, by SIC 2- to 3-digit industry, monthly rpt, 9365–2.10

Industrial energy demand, forecasting model description, detailed technology specifications, and energy use, for 27 SIC 2- to 4-digit industries, 1970s-80 and projected to 2000, 3308–66

Input-output structure of US economy, detailed interindustry transactions for 537 industries, and components of final demand, 1977 benchmark data, 2708–17

Irrigation system energy use and costs, and irrigated farm acreage by fuel and region, selected years 1974-84 and trends from 1900, article, 1561–16.406

Manufacturing energy efficiency progress, and energy use by type, by SIC 2-digit industry, 1982, annual rpt, 3304–8

Meters for electricity, gas, and liquid supply and production, trade, tariffs, and industry operating data, 1979-83, TSUSA commodity rpt supplement, 9885–7.63

Minority group and women employment, by occupational group and SIC 2- to 3-digit industry, 1981, annual rpt, 9244–1.1

Motor vehicles powered by electricity, Fed Govt dev program implementation, with bibl, FY83, annual rpt, 3304–2

Natl Energy Policy Plan, DOE implementation and effect on energy supply/demand, 1983-84, annual rpt, 3024–4

Natl Energy Policy Plan, energy supply, demand, and prices, by fuel and consuming sector, projected 1985-2010, biennial rpt, 3004–13

New England States electricity and gasoline sales, Fed Reserve 1st District, monthly rpt, 9373–2.6

Occupational injury and illness rates, by SIC 2- to 4-digit industry, 1982, annual rpt, 6844–1

OECD trade, total and for 4 major countries, and US trade by country, by commodity, 1972-82, annual world region rpt series, 244–13

Pacific Northwest electricity consumption and prices by end-use sector, and economic and demographic data, 1960s-83 and projected to 2005, annual rpt, 3224–2

Panama Canal electric power generated, purchased, and sold, FY81-82, annual rpt, 9664–3.3

Peak demand, generating and interregional transfer capability, and reserve margins, by region, 1984-93, annual rpt, 3404–6

Photovoltaic modules shipped, and use, with listing of manufacturers, 1983, annual rpt, 3164–62

Production of electric power and fuel use, receipts, cost, quality, and stocks, by energy source, State, and utility, quarterly rpt with articles, 3162–39

Production of electric power, and utility fuel consumption, stocks, and costs by fuel type, and sales, by State, monthly rpt, 3162–35

Production, reserves, and prices, by fuel type, and selected indicators of energy use, by State, 1982-83 with selected comparisons from 1971, annual rpt, 3164–60

Production, retail sales, plant capacity, and fuel supply, use, and costs, by State, 1979-83, annual rpt, 3164–11

Public utility holding company finances, securities issued, and subsidiaries by type, by firm, FY83, annual rpt, 9734–2.6

Regulatory policy standards of electric and gas utilities, and consumers and sales covered, by type of consumer and utility, 1983, annual rpt, 3104–7

Research publications on energy of DOE and other sources, monthly listing, 3002–2

Scientists, engineers, and technicians employment in transportation, utilities, and retail and wholesale trade, by field of science and industry, 1982, 9628–72

Southeastern Power Admin sales by customer, plants, and capacity, and financial statements of Southeastern Fed Power Program, FY83, annual rpt, 3234–1

Southeastern States financial and economic devs, Fed Reserve 6th District, monthly rpt with articles, 9371–1

Southwestern Fed Power System financial statements, electric power sales by customer, and project capacity, production, and costs, FY83, annual rpt, 3244–1

State and local govt productivity measurement, with background data and output indexes for 7 govt services, various periods 1955-82, 6728–27

Supply/demand and price forecasts, by fuel type, quarterly rpt, 3162–34

Supply/demand and prices, by energy resource and major producing and consuming country and sector, detailed data, monthly rpt, 3162–24

Supply/demand and prices, by energy source and end-use sector and for 7 electric utilities, 1981-2000 with trends from 1960s, 3008–93

Supply/demand and prices, by fuel type and consuming sector with foreign comparisons, 1949-83, annual rpt, 3164–74

Supply/demand and prices, by fuel type, sector, and end use, detailed trends and projections 1973-95, annual rpt, 3164–75

Supply/demand and prices, by fuel type, sector, and end use, with foreign comparisons, 1960-83 and projected to 1995, annual summary rpt, 3164–76

Supply/demand, prices, end use, and related technical and socioeconomic data, including impacts of US policy and intl devs, series, 3006–7

Tennessee Valley industrial dev and effects on employment, investment, and TVA power demand, by location and company, 1983, annual rpt, 9804–3

Transportation energy use by mode, fuel supplies, and demographic and economic determinants of vehicle use, 1970s-83, annual rpt, 3304–5

TVA activities, financial and operating data by program and facility, and power sales by customer, FY83, annual rpt, 9804–1

TVA electric power purchases of municipal and cooperative distributors, and prices and consumption by distributor and consumer sector, monthly rpt, 9802–1

TVA power distributors detailed operating and financial ratios, for individual municipal and cooperative distributors, FY79-83, annual rpt, 9804–19

TVA power distributors purchases and resales of TVA power, and rates charged, by consumer class, 1983, annual rpt, 9804–14

Utilities diversification activity by activity type, and finances and bond ratings by selected firm, various periods 1970-83, hearing, 21368–53

Utilities privately owned, capital investment, finances, equity performance, and operating characteristics, 1950-82 with supply estimates to 2010, 3168–87

Utilities privately owned, common stock performance measures for companies with and without nuclear facilities, 1963-82, 3168–88

Utilities privately owned, common stock performance measures, with comparisons to selected industry groups, selected years 1970-82, GAO rpt, 26113–129

Utilities privately owned, detailed financial and operating data by company, with summary data for other distributors by type, 1982, annual rpt, 3164–23

Utilities privately owned, wages and employment by occupation, and benefits, by region, Oct 1982 survey, 6787–6.205

Washington Public Power Supply System nuclear reactors construction financing, with regional economic impacts and power supply/demand, 1980s-2035, hearing, 21448–29

Western Area Power Admin operations by plant, financial statements, and electric power sales by customer, FY83, annual rpt, 3254–1

see also Cogeneration of heat and electricity
see also Electric power prices
see also Electrical machinery and equipment
see also Hydroelectric power
see also Nuclear power
see also Power-generating plants and equipment
see also Rural electrification

Electric power conservation
see Energy conservation

Electric power consumption
see Electric power

Electric power prices

Air pollutant sulfur dioxide emissions reduction proposal, effects on polluting industries and coal production by region and State, projected to 2010, 9188–97

Electric power prices

Alaska electric residential bills, by utility and level of consumption, 1981-83, annual rpt, 3214–2

Bonneville Power Admin sales, revenues, and prices, by class of customer and individual purchaser, 1983, semiannual rpt, 3222–1

Columbia River system electric power sales, by customer, FY83, annual rpt, 3224–1

CPI by detailed component, for US city average, 28 SMSAs, and 4 regions by population size, monthly rpt, 6762–2

Exports and imports of electric power, US transactions with Canada and Mexico by utility and US region, 1983, annual rpt, 3104–10

Farmers electricity use and average monthly bill, monthly rpt, annual table, 1629–1

Household demand for electric power in 136 SMSAs and other utility service areas, with fuel prices, family income, and heating degree days, 1975 and projected to 1985, 1588–78

Housing average electric power bills, State rankings, as of Jan 1983, annual rpt, 1244–1.6

Housing average monthly electric bills, by city, *County and City Data Book,* 1982, 2328–1

Housing electricity and gas costs for 306 cities, by utility, with climatological data, fall 1982, 3308–67

Housing energy use, and savings under alternative conservation strategies, by State, with model methodology and energy prices, selected years 1970-81, 21368–48

Industrial electric power cogeneration in 5 industries, and fuel use and utility supply/demand effects, by region, 1983-93, 3008–92

Natl Energy Policy Plan, energy supply, demand, and prices, by fuel and consuming sector, projected 1985-2010, biennial rpt, 3004–13

Nuclear power accident liability insurance under Price-Anderson Act, effects on industry finances and operations, with insurance coverage, claims, and costs, various periods 1957-82, 9638–49

Nuclear power plant construction cost estimates and electricity first-year price increases, for selected plants, 1984 rpt, 3164–57

Nuclear power plant construction costs and status, capacity, and revenue requirements, by plant and utility, various dates Dec 1983-Mar 1984, article, 9385–1.412

Nuclear power plant licensing 24-month delay, effect on utility financial performance and electric power prices, for plant completed May 1979, 9638–53

OECD energy prices and taxes by energy source and end-use sector, for US and 9 countries, quarterly 1979-83, annual rpt, 3164–71

Pacific Northwest electricity consumption and prices by end-use sector, and economic and demographic data, 1960s-83 and projected to 2005, annual rpt, 3224–2

Prices and expenditures for electricity, by consuming sector, and State, 1970-81, annual rpt, 3164–64

Prices and supply/demand, by energy source and end-use sector and for 7 electric utilities, 1981-2000 with trends from 1960s, 3008–93

Prices and supply/demand, by fuel and consuming sector with foreign comparisons, 1949-83, annual rpt, 3164–74

Prices and supply/demand, by fuel, sector, and end use, detailed trends and projections 1973-95, annual rpt, 3164–75

Prices and supply/demand, by fuel, sector, and end use, with foreign comparisons, 1960-83 and projected to 1995, annual summary rpt, 3164–76

Prices and supply/demand, forecast by fuel, quarterly rpt, 3162–34

Prices, production, use, and reserves, by energy type, and selected indicators of energy use, by State, 1982-83 with selected comparisons from 1971, annual rpt, 3164–60

Prices, supply/demand, end use, and related technical and socioeconomic data, including impacts of US policy and intl devs, series, 3006–7

Prices, use, and conservation and efficiency measures, by fuel type, end-use sector, selected industry, and region, 1960-83, annual rpt, 3164–73

Producer prices and indexes, by stage of processing and detailed commodity, monthly rpt, 6762–6

Producer prices and indexes, by stage of processing and detailed commodity, monthly 1983, annual supplement, 6764–2

Rate minimization from improved electric utility efficiency, proposed FERC incentive program operations and costs, with comparisons to 3 State programs, 1950s-82, 3088–17

Rate schedules by user type, utility, and city, Jan 1984, annual rpt, 3164–40

Ratemaking and regulatory policy standards of electric and gas utilities, and consumers and sales covered, by type of consumer and utility, 1983, annual rpt, 3104–7

Retail electric power prices, by end-use sector in 40 large cities, monthly rpt, 3162–35

Retail electric power prices, by end-use sector in 40 large cities, 1979-83, annual rpt, 3164–11.3

Retail prices for energy and food, and housing fuel consumption, by region, and for 28 SMSAs and US city average, monthly press release, 6762–8

TVA electric power for DOE uranium enrichment, DOE prices under alternative TVA power rates and effects of TVA charges for power not taken, FY84-95, GAO rpt, 26113–114

TVA electric power purchases of municipal and cooperative distributors, and prices and consumption by distributor and consumer sector, monthly rpt, 9802–1

TVA power distributors purchases and resales of TVA power, and rates charged, by consumer class, 1983, annual rpt, 9804–14

TVA power program finances and operations, by plant and distributor, FY83, annual rpt, 9804–23

Index by Subjects and Names

Washington Public Power Supply System nuclear reactors construction financing, with regional economic impacts and power supply/demand, 1980s-2035, hearing, 21448–29

Wholesale purchases and costs for individual REA borrowers, by supplier and State, 1940-83, annual rpt, 1244–5

Electric utilities

see Electric power

see Electric power prices

see Power-generating plants and equipment

see Public utilities

see Rural electrification

Electrical machinery and equipment

Business statistics, detailed data for major industries and economic indicators, *Survey of Current Business,* monthly rpt, 2702–1.14

Census of Population, 1980: detailed socioeconomic and demographic characteristics, by age, sex, race, Hispanic origin, occupation, and industry, State rpt series, 2531–4

Census of Population, 1980: detailed socioeconomic characteristics, by county, city, and inside-outside SMSAs and central cities, State rpt series, 2531–3

China economic conditions, agricultural and industrial production, trade, and domestic and foreign investment, 1980-85, 2048–106

China exports and imports by SITC 1- to 5-digit commodity, 1970s-82, annual rpt, 244–12

Collective bargaining agreements expiring during year, covered workers by SIC 2-digit industry, firm, and union, with summary of key provisions, 1984, annual rpt, 6784–9

Counterfeiting of brand-name products by foreign manufacturers, effects on 6 US industries, investigation with financial and operating data, 1984 rpt, 9886–4.67

County Business Patterns: establishments, employees, and payrolls, by SIC 4-digit industry and county, 1981, annual State rpt series, 2326–8

County Business Patterns: establishments, employees, and payrolls, by SIC 4-digit industry and county, 1982, annual State rpt series, 2326–6

Deaths and death rates from accidents, by place, detailed cause, and demographic characteristics, 1979, US Vital Statistics annual rpt, 4144–2.1, 4144–2.5

DOD shipments of military and personal property, loss claims, passenger traffic, and costs, by mode of transport, quarterly rpt, 3702–1

Earnings by major industry group, and personal income per capita and by source, by region and State, 1929-82, 2708–40

Employment, earnings, and hours, by selected SIC 1- to 4-digit industry, State, and for 278 major labor areas, 1939-83, annual rpt, 6744–5

Employment, earnings, and hours, by SIC 4-digit nonfarm industry, monthly 1974-Feb 1984, annual update, 6744–4

Employment, unemployment, hours, and women's employment, for all durables manufacturing and for 5 metals industries, 1979-82, article, 6722–1.410

Index by Subjects and Names

Electronic funds transfer

Energy use, by economic sector, end use, and energy source, 1983 and 2000, 2006–2.5

Exports and imports of US, detailed SIC-based commodities by world area, 1983, annual rpts, 2424–6

Exports and imports of US, totals and as percent of domestic production, by SIC 2- to 5-digit commodity, 1981, annual rpt, 2424–3

Exports, imports, tariffs, and industry operating data for electric power machinery and equipment, foreign and US, 1979-83, TSUSA commodity rpt supplement, 9885–6.62

Exports of manufactured and agricultural commodities, manufacturing production, and export-related employment, 1960s-82, State rpt series, 2046–3

Exports of US, detailed commodities by country of destination, monthly rpt, 2422–3

Exports of US, detailed Schedule B commodities by country of destination, 1983, annual rpt, 2424–9

Exports of US, detailed Schedule E commodities by mode of transport and world area and country of destination, 1983, annual rpts, 2424–5

Financial statements for manufacturing, mining, and trade corporations, by selected SIC 2- to 3-digit industry, quarterly rpt, 2502–1

Foreign countries electric current characteristics, by country and selected city, 1984 rpt, 2018–8

Foreign direct investment of US, by selected major industry group and world area, 1980-82, annual article, 2702–1.430

Foreign market and trade for electric power systems equipment, and user industry operations and demand, country market research rpts, 2045–15

Great Lakes trade, by SITC 3-digit commodity, port, vessel type, world area, and country, 1982, annual rpt, 7744–3

Imports of US, detailed Schedule A commodities by country and world area of origin, and mode of transport, 1983, annual rpts, 2424–2

Imports of US, detailed Schedule A commodities by country, monthly rpt, 2422–2

Imports of US, detailed TSUSA commodities by country of origin, 1983, annual rpt, 2424–4

Income tax returns of corporations, detailed income and tax items by industry, 1981, annual rpt, 8304–4

Income tax returns of corporations with foreign tax credit, income and deductions by type, asset size, and selected industry group, 1980, article, 8302–2.415

Income tax returns of foreign subsidiaries of US corporations, income and tax data, by industry and asset size, 1980, article, 8302–2.410

Income tax returns of sole proprietorships, detailed data by industry div and selected industry group, 1981, annual rpt, 8304–7

Income tax returns of sole proprietorships, receipts, deductions by type, payroll, and net income, by major industry, 1982, annual article, 8302–2.413

Industry finances and operations, by SIC 2- to 4-digit industry, 1970s-83 and projected to 1988, annual rpt, 2014–4

Input-output structure of US economy, detailed interindustry transactions for 85 industries, and components of final demand, 1977, article, 2702–1.421

Input-output structure of US economy, detailed interindustry transactions for 537 industries, and components of final demand, 1977 benchmark data, 2708–17

Lamps (electric) production, shipments, stocks, trade, and firms, by bulb type, monthly and quarterly Current Industrial Rpts, 2506–12.13

Lamps (fluorescent) production, shipments, trade, and firms, by ballast type, quarterly Current Industrial Rpt, 2506–12.14

Lighting fixture shipments, trade, and consumption, by product, 1983, annual Current Industrial Rpt, 2506–12.19

Manufacturing census, 1982: financial and operating data, by SIC 2- to 4-digit industry, State, SMSA, and county, preliminary census div rpt series, 2491–3

Manufacturing census, 1982: financial and operating data, for SIC 4-digit industries by product, preliminary rpt series, 2491–1

Minority group and women employment, by occupational group and SIC 2- to 3-digit industry, 1981, annual rpt, 9244–1.1

North Central States economic indicators, Fed Reserve 7th District monthly rpt, 9375–9

Occupational injury and illness rates, by SIC 2- to 4-digit industry, 1982, annual rpt, 6844–1

Occupational Outlook Handbook, 1984-85 biennial rpt, 6744–1

OECD trade, total and for 4 major countries, and US trade by country, by commodity, 1972-82, annual world region rpt series, 244–13

Pollution abatement capital and operating costs, by SIC 2- to 4-digit industry, State, and SMSA, 1982, annual Current Industrial Rpt, 2506–3.6

Producer prices and indexes, by stage of processing and detailed commodity, monthly rpt, 6762–6

Producer prices and indexes, by stage of processing and detailed commodity, monthly 1983, annual supplement, 6764–2

Productivity, hours, and employment indexes for selected SIC 3- and 4-digit industries, 1954-82, annual rpt, 6824–1.3

R&D expenditures of US firms foreign affiliates, by selected industry, 1974-82, 9626–2.131

R&D industry expenditures, total and for 6 leading industries, projected 1984-85 with trends from 1975, 9626–2.145

R&D industry funding and employment of scientists and engineers, by industry group, firm size, and funding source, 1956-82, annual rpt, 9627–21

Retail trade census, 1982: employment, establishments, sales, and payroll, for hardware stores by State, preliminary rpt, 2395–1.3

Scientists, engineers, and technicians employed in private industry, by occupation and industry group, 1980-81, biennial rpt, 9627–23

Scientists, engineers, and technicians employment in transportation, utilities, and retail and wholesale trade, by field of science and industry, 1982, 9628–72

Service industry census, 1982: employment, establishments, receipts, and payroll, by SIC 2- to 4-digit kind of business, SMSA, county, and city, State rpt series, 2391–1

Virgin Islands economic censuses, 1982: employment, establishments, payroll, and receipts, by SIC 1- to 4-digit industry, island, and city, 2593–1

Waterborne commerce of US (domestic and foreign), freight by commodity, traffic, and passengers, by port and waterway, 1982, annual rpt, 3754–3

Welding machines and other electric apparatus trade, tariffs, and industry operating data, foreign and US, 1979-83, TSUSA commodity rpt supplement, 9885–6.65

Wholesale trade census, 1982: employment, establishments, sales by commodity, and payroll, by SIC 4-digit kind of business and State, preliminary rpt series, 2403–1

Wholesale trade sales and inventories, by SIC 2- to 3-digit kind of business, monthly rpt, 2413–7

Wholesale trade sales, inventories, purchases, and gross margins, by SIC 2- to 3-digit kind of business and type of ownership, 1983, annual rpt, 2413–13

Wire and cable (insulated) shipments by product, trade, and consumption, 1977-82, annual Current Industrial Rpt, 2506–10.8

Wiring devices and supplies shipments, trade, and firms, by product, 1983, annual Current Industrial Rpt, 2506–12.18

see also Computers

see also Electronics industry and products

see also Household appliances and equipment

see also Power-generating plants and equipment

see also under By Commodity in the "Index by Categories"

see also under By Industry in the "Index by Categories"

Electromagnetic radiation

Radiation from electronic devices, incidents and persons involved by type of device and FDA control program activities, 1983, annual rpt, 4064–13

see also Nuclear radiation

see also Radiology

see also X-rays

Electronic data processing

see Computer sciences

see Computer use

see Computers

see Electronic funds transfer

see Information storage and retrieval systems

Electronic funds transfer

Automated teller machines and point of sale debit card systems offered by retailers, by firm, firm type, and State, 1984 survey, article, 9371–1.421

Automated teller machines installed or planned at southeast US grocery and convenience chain store outlets, and operating characteristics, Aug 1983, article, 9371–1.403

Automated teller machines shared networks by State, and membership and characteristics of top 16 regional and natl networks, Nov 1983, article, 9373–1.403

Electronic funds transfer

Cash mgmt techniques for EFT and short-term investment, effect on money demand, aggregated 1920- 79, article, 9389–1.409

Fed Govt benefit payment by check and direct deposit, costs to agencies and banks, FY81, technical paper, 9366–1.139

Fed Govt programs and mgmt cost control proposals, 3-year savings by function and agency, and financial and operating data, 1960s-81, 16908–1.12, 16908–1.26

Fed Reserve Bank of San Francisco financial statements, 1982-83, annual rpt, 9393–2

Fed Reserve payments services provided depository instns, financial statements, and costs and revenues by service and district bank, 1983, annual press release, 9364–9

In-home banking services, consumer expected use and acceptable costs, 1983 survey, article, 9371–1.422

Interstate EFT networks, by State of origin and Fed Reserve 7th District State served, various dates 1981-83, article, 9375–1.403

Particpation by S&Ls and retailers in EFT, by type of service, 2nd qtr 1983 survey, article, 9312–1.409

Transactions by EFT and other means, credit card fraud losses, and potential for EFT crime, 1975-82, 6066–19.3

Electronic mail

see Postal service

Electronic surveillance

Airport security operations to prevent hijacking, screening results, enforcement actions, and hijacking attempts, 1st half 1984, semiannual rpt, 7502–5

DOD budget, FY85 weapons system requests consistency with US policy and specified treaties, with funding FY83-87, annual rpt, 21384–4

Justice Dept activities, by subagency, FY82, annual rpt, 6004–1

Soviet Union and US satellites by mission and vulnerability to attack, and USSR anti-satellite missiles, 1983 and projected to 1989, hearing, 21208–18

Statistical Abstract of US, social, political, and economic data, 1950s-83 and trends, annual rpt, 2324–1.1

Wiretapping authorizations by offense, costs, persons involved, arrests, trials, and convictions, 1983, annual rpt, 18204–7

see also Radar

Electronics industry and products

Auto industry finances, employment, production, and cost increases to comply with Fed Govt pollution and safety standards, 1970s-83, annual rpt, 3304–5.4

Biotechnology commercial uses, R&D funding and output, controls, and industry financial and operating data, for US and 5 countries, 1970s-83 and estimated 1984-85, 26358–98

Census of Population, 1980: detailed socioeconomic and demographic characteristics, by age, sex, race, Hispanic origin, occupation, and industry, State rpt series, 2531–4

Collective bargaining agreements expiring during year, covered workers by SIC 2-digit industry, firm, and union, with summary of key provisions, 1984, annual rpt, 6784–9

Index by Subjects and Names

Counterfeiting of brand-name products by foreign manufacturers, effects on 6 US industries, investigation with financial and operating data, 1984 rpt, 9886–4.67

County Business Patterns: establishments, employees, and payrolls, by SIC 4-digit industry and county, 1981, annual State rpt series, 2326–8

County Business Patterns: establishments, employees, and payrolls, by SIC 4-digit industry and county, 1982, annual State rpt series, 2326–6

DOD procurement, prime contract awards by category, contract and contractor type, and service branch, FY74-1st half FY84, semiannual rpt, 3542–1

DOD procurement, prime contract awards by detailed procurement category, FY80-83, annual rpt, 3544–18

DOD procurement, prime contract awards for 25 commodity categories and R&D, by State and census div, FY81-83, annual rpt, 3544–11

Earnings by major industry group, and personal income per capita and by source, by region and State, 1929-82, 2708–40

Employment, earnings, and hours, by selected SIC 1- to 4-digit industry, State, and for 278 major labor areas, 1939-83, annual rpt, 6744–5

Employment, earnings, and hours, by SIC 4-digit nonfarm industry, monthly 1974-Feb 1984, annual update, 6744–4

Exports and imports of US, detailed SIC-based commodities by world area, 1983, annual rpts, 2424–6

Exports and imports of US, totals and as percent of domestic production, by SIC 2- to 5-digit commodity, 1981, annual rpt, 2424–3

Exports, imports, tariffs, and industry operating data for consumer electronic products, foreign and US, 1979-83, TSUSA commodity rpt supplement, 9885–6.65

Exports, imports, tariffs, and industry operating data for microphones, loudspeakers, and sound and visual signaling devices, 1979-83, TSUSA commodity rpt supplement, 9885–6.81

Exports of US, detailed commodities by country of destination, monthly rpt, 2422–3

Exports of US, detailed Schedule B commodities by country of destination, 1983, annual rpt, 2424–9

Exports of US, detailed Schedule E commodities by mode of transport and world area and country of destination, 1983, annual rpts, 2424–5

Finances and operations, by SIC 2- to 4-digit industry, 1970s-83 and projected to 1988, annual rpt, 2014–4

Financial statements for manufacturing, mining, and trade corporations, by selected SIC 2- to 3-digit industry, quarterly rpt, 2502–1

Foreign direct investment of US, by selected major industry group and world area, 1980-82, annual article, 2702–1.430

Foreign market and trade for electronic component equipment, and user industry operations and demand, country market research rpts, 2045–4

Foreign market and trade for electronic component manufacturing equipment, and user industry operations and demand, country market research rpts, 2045–5

Great Lakes trade, by SITC 3-digit commodity, port, vessel type, world area, and country, 1982, annual rpt, 7744–3

Imports of US, detailed Schedule A commodities by country and world area of origin, and mode of transport, 1983, annual rpts, 2424–2

Imports of US, detailed Schedule A commodities by country, monthly rpt, 2422–2

Imports of US, detailed TSUSA commodities by country of origin, 1983, annual rpts, 2424–4

Income tax returns of corporations, detailed income and tax items by industry, 1981, annual rpt, 8304–4

Income tax returns of corporations with foreign tax credit, income and deductions by type, asset size, and selected industry group, 1980, annual article, 8302–2.415

Income tax returns of sole proprietorships, detailed data by industry div and selected industry group, 1981, annual rpt, 8304–7

Income tax returns of sole proprietorships, receipts, deductions by type, payroll, and net income, by major industry, 1982, annual article, 8302–2.413

Industrial process control equipment foreign market and trade, and user industry operations and demand, country market research rpts, 2045–6

Injuries and deaths from use of selected consumer products and related activity, by victim age and sex, 1982, annual rpt, 9164–7

Input-output structure of US economy, detailed interindustry transactions for 85 industries, and components of final demand, 1977, article, 2702–1.421

Input-output structure of US economy, detailed interindustry transactions for 537 industries, and components of final demand, 1977 benchmark data, 2708–17

Manufacturing census, 1982: financial and operating data, by SIC 2- to 4-digit industry, State, SMSA, and county, preliminary census div rpt series, 2491–3

Manufacturing census, 1982: financial and operating data, for SIC 4-digit industries by product, preliminary rpt series, 2491–1

Minority group and women employment, by occupational group and SIC 2- to 3-digit industry, 1981, annual rpt, 9244–1.1

Nuclear industry nongovt employment by industry segment, occupation, and census div, and DOE and NRC nuclear employment, 1968-83, biennial rpt, 3004–11

Occupational injury and illness rates, by SIC 2- to 4-digit industry, 1982, annual rpt, 6844–1

Occupational Outlook Handbook, 1984-85 biennial rpt, 6744–1

OECD trade, total and for 4 major countries, and US trade by country, by commodity, 1972-82, annual world region rpt series, 244–13

Patents (US) for telecommunication equipment granted to US and foreign applicants, by applicant type, firm, State, and country, various periods 1963-83, 2246–2.7

Index by Subjects and Names

Elevators

Pollution abatement capital and operating costs, by SIC 2- to 4-digit industry, State, and SMSA, 1982, annual Current Industrial Rpt, 2506–3.6

Producer prices and indexes, by stage of processing and detailed commodity, monthly rpt, 6762–6

Producer prices and indexes, by stage of processing and detailed commodity, monthly 1983, annual supplement, 6764–2

R&D industry funding and employment of scientists and engineers, by industry group, firm size, and funding source, 1956-82, annual rpt, 9627–21

Radiation from electronic devices, incidents and persons involved by type of device and FDA control program activities, 1983, annual rpt, 4064–13

Semiconductor industry subsidies of Japan govt by program, with financial and operating data by firm, R&D, and comparisons to US industry, 1970s-83, hearings, 21368–46.1

Semiconductors trade, tariffs, and industry operating data, foreign and US, 1979-83, TSUSA commodity rpt supplement, 9885–6.67

Service industry census, 1982: employment, establishments, receipts, and payroll, by SIC 2- to 4-digit kind of business, SMSA, county, and city, State rpt series, 2391–1

Shipments, trade, and consumption of electronic equipment and associated products, by product, 1983, annual Current Industrial Rpt, 2506–12.21

Shipments, trade, and consumption of radio, TV, phonograph, and related equipment, by product, 1982-83, annual Current Industrial Rpt, 2506–12.20

Shipments, trade, and consumption of switchgear, switchboard apparatus, relays, and other equipment, by product, 1983, annual Current Industrial Rpt, 2506–12.11

Transformer production, shipments, trade, total capacity, and consumption, by product, 1983, annual Current Industrial Rpt, 2506–12.29

see also Computers

see also Electronic funds transfer

see also Electronic surveillance

see also Lasers

see also Phonograph

see also Radio

see also Recording industry

see also Television

see also under By Commodity in the "Index by Categories"

see also under By Industry in the "Index by Categories"

Elementary and secondary education

Computer access and use in elementary and secondary schools, by region, urban-rural location, and Title I status, spring 1982, 4826–1.10

Computer specialists sociodemographic, educational, and employment characteristics, and Fed Govt support by agency, 1978, biennial Current Population Rpt, 2546–2.124

Condition of Education, detailed data on enrollment, staff, achievement, finances, curricula, and education effects on employment, 1982-83, annual rpt, 4824–1

Crime against students, teachers, and others, by offense, circumstances, and offender sex and race, 1974-76, 6066–20.2

Crime in secondary schools, assaults and robberies of students and teachers, 1972-83, 4918–13

Digest of Education Statistics, detailed data on students, staff, finances, and facilities, 1982 and selected trends, annual rpt, 4824–2

DOD Dependents Schools 1st grader basic skills test scores, by world area and English fluency, fall 1983, annual rpt, 3504–18

Education Dept programs funding, operations, and effectiveness, FY83, annual rpt, 4804–5

Education highlights, trends in enrollment, expenditures, curricula, and other topics of current interest, periodic press release, 4822–1

Education statistics summary compilation, 1980/81-1982/83 with selected trends from 1869, biennial rpt, 4804–27

Educational trends, 1972/73-1992/93, biennial pocket-size card, 4824–3

High school class of 1982: foreign language course enrollment, by language, student and school characteristics, and location, 1984 rpt, 4838–11

High school class of 1982: foreign language coursework, by language, course level, student and school characteristics, and location, 1984 rpt, 4828–17

High school classes of 1980 and 1982: educational and sociodemographic characteristics and expectations, natl longitudinal study, series, 4826–2

Indian Education Act grants to local agencies, Education Dept audit results by region, FY82, annual rpt, 4804–29

Indian education program operations, funding, student progress measures, and opinions of school staff, parents, and students, selected years 1973-83, 4808–13

Southeastern States economic dev effect on education, for Fed Reserve 6th District States, selected years 1900-82, article, 9371–1.428

see also Compensatory education

see also Curricula

see also Discrimination in education

see also Educational attainment

see also Educational broadcasting

see also Educational enrollment

see also Educational exchanges

see also Educational facilities

see also Educational finance

see also Educational materials

see also Educational research

see also Educational technology

see also Educational tests

see also Federal aid to education

see also Head Start Project

see also National Assessment of Educational Progress

see also Preschool education

see also Private schools

see also School administration and staff

see also School districts

see also School lunch and breakfast programs

see also Special education

see also State aid to education

see also Students

see also Teacher education

see also Teachers

see also Vocational education and training

Elementary and Secondary Education Act

Bilingual education programs, teachers, enrollment, and funding, selected years 1976-FY83, biennial rpt, 4804–14

Computer access and use in elementary and secondary schools, by region, urban-rural location, and Title I status, spring 1982, 4826–1.10

Elevators

Census of Housing, 1980: inventory, occupancy, and unit characteristics, changes from 1973 by region and inside-outside SMSAs and central cities, series, 2473–3

Census of Housing, 1980: occupancy and unit characteristics of SMSAs and central cities, by race, Hispanic origin, and city, State and SMSA rpt series, 2473–1

County Business Patterns: establishments, employees, and payrolls, by SIC 4-digit industry and county, 1981, annual State rpt series, 2326–8

County Business Patterns: establishments, employees, and payrolls, by SIC 4-digit industry and county, 1982, annual State rpt series, 2326–6

Exports and imports of US, detailed SIC-based commodities by world area, 1983, annual rpts, 2424–6

Exports and imports of US, totals and as percent of domestic production, by SIC 2- to 5-digit commodity, 1981, annual rpt, 2424–3

Housing and households detailed characteristics, and unit and neighborhood quality, by inside-outside central cities, 1979-82 surveys, SMSA rpt series, 2485–6

Housing and neighborhood quality indicators and attitudes, and occupant characteristics, by urban-rural location and region, 1981, annual survey, 2485–7

Housing and neighborhood quality indicators and attitudes, by occupant and unit characteristics, region, and metro-nonmetro location, 1981, annual survey, 2485–2

Housing occupancy and unit and household characteristics, by region and metro-nonmetro residence, 1983, biennial survey, 2485–1

Injuries and deaths from use of selected consumer products and related activity, by victim age and sex, 1982, annual rpt, 9164–7

Input-output structure of US economy, detailed interindustry transactions for 537 industries, and components of final demand, 1977 benchmark data, 2708–17

Manufacturing census, 1982: financial and operating data, by SIC 2- to 4-digit industry, State, SMSA, and county, preliminary census div rpt series, 2491–3

Manufacturing census, 1982: financial and operating data, for SIC 4-digit industries by product, preliminary rpt, 2491–1.319

Occupational injury and illness rates, by SIC 2- to 4-digit industry, 1982, annual rpt, 6844–1

Elevators

Producer prices and indexes, by stage of processing and detailed commodity, monthly rpt, 6762–6

Producer prices and indexes, by stage of processing and detailed commodity, monthly 1983, annual supplement, 6764–2

Elfring, Chris

"Sustaining Tropical Forest Resources: U.S. and International Institutions", 26358–101.3

Elgin, Ill.

see also under By SMSA or MSA in the "Index by Categories"

Elizabeth, N.J.

Air pollution levels for 28 volatile organic compounds in NYC and New Jersey, by site and urban-rural location, 1979-June 1981, 9198–108

Public works capital needs and intergovtl financing, by type of project and selected city, various periods 1950-83, 10048–60

see also under By City in the "Index by Categories"

Elk City, Okla.

Housing vacancy rates for single and multifamily units and mobile homes, by county, city, and ZIP code, 1984, annual metro area rpt, 9304–22.13

Elkhart, Ind.

Census of Housing, 1980: occupancy and unit characteristics, by race, Hispanic origin, and city, SMSA rpt, 2473–1.145

Census of Population and Housing, 1980: detailed population and housing characteristics, by county, city, and census tract, SMSA rpt, 2551–2.145

see also under By SMSA or MSA in the "Index by Categories"

Ellice Islands

see Tuvalu

Ellson, Richard W.

"South Carolina: A Strong Recovery, but Problems Remain", 9371–1.411

Elmira, N.Y.

Census of Housing, 1980: occupancy and unit characteristics, by race, Hispanic origin, and city, SMSA rpt, 2473–1.146

Census of Population and Housing, 1980: detailed population and housing characteristics, by county, city, and census tract, SMSA rpt, 2551–2.146

see also under By SMSA or MSA in the "Index by Categories"

Elyria, Ohio

Census of Housing, 1980: occupancy and unit characteristics, by race, Hispanic origin, and city, SMSA rpt, 2473–1.225

Census of Population and Housing, 1980: detailed population and housing characteristics, by county, city, and census tract, SMSA rpt, 2551–2.225

see also under By SMSA or MSA in the "Index by Categories"

Embargo

see International sanctions

Embezzlement

see Fraud

Emergency medical service

Ambulances in Fed Govt motor vehicle fleet, cost and operating data by agency, FY83, annual rpt, 9454–9

Drug (illegal) supply, use, casualties, treatment program and emergency room admissions in major cities, arrests, and seizures, by drug type, 1982, annual rpt, 15894–1

Drug abuse prevalence and health consequences, and Natl Inst on Drug Abuse and other HHS prevention activities, FY82, annual rpt, 4004–26

Health care services of selected medical practitioners, use by patient characteristics, 1980 survey with trends from 1963, 4146–12.4

Health Services Research Natl Center grants and contracts, by program area, FY83, annual listing, 4184–2

HHS aid to each State and local govt or private instn, amount obligated, funding agency, and program, FY83, annual listing, 4004–3

Natl Guard (Army and Air) activities, manpower, and facilities, FY83, annual rpt, 3704–3

Occupational manpower needs and supply by detailed occupation, and educational and training program enrollees and grads by detailed field, 1982 and 1995, biennial rpt, 6744–3

Red Cross program operations and financial statements, 1982/83, annual rpt, 29254–1

State govt preventive health services funding by program, Fed Govt block grants, and opinions on State program admin, for 13 States, FY81-84, GAO rpt, 26121–88

Traffic accidents and casualties detailed direct and indirect costs, by characteristics of persons and vehicles involved, 1979-80, 7768–80

Emergency relief

see Disaster relief

Emery

see Abrasive materials

Emery, Richard P., Jr.

"Analysis of the President's Credit Budget for FY85", 26306–3.65

Emigration

see Immigration

see Refugees

Emissions

see Air pollution

see Motor vehicle exhaust

Emminger, Otmar

"Adjustments in World Payments: An Evaluation", 9373–3.28

Emphysema

see Respiratory diseases

Employee benefit plans

Advisory Commission on Intergovtl Relations programs and finances, 1983, annual rpt, 10044–3

Airline operating and other costs, itemized for domestic and intl trunk and local service carriers, 1st half 1983, semiannual rpt, 9142–47

American Samoa minimum wage rates, employment, earnings, and benefits, by establishment and industry, Nov 1983, biennial rpt, 6504–6

Budget of US, CBO analysis of revenue and spending alternatives and projections of economic indicators, FY85-89, annual rpt, 26304–3.3

Budget of US, special analysis of Fed Govt employment and cost of direct compensation and benefits, FY85, annual rpt, 104–1.9

Collective bargaining wage and benefit rate changes in labor-mgmt agreements, quarterly press release, 6782–2

Index by Subjects and Names

Collective bargaining wage and employee benefits changes, by industry group, monthly rpt, 6782–1

Construction industries census, 1982: financial and operating data, by SIC 4-digit industry and State, final rpt series, 2373–1

County Business Patterns: establishments, employees, and payrolls, by SIC 4-digit industry and county, 1981, annual State rpt series, 2326–8

Elementary and secondary public school districts, schools, enrollment, staff, and finances, by State, 1981/82, annual rpt, 4834–13

Employee Retirement Income Security Act admin and enforcement, 1982, annual rpt, 6464–4

Farm labor, wages, hours, and perquisites, by State, quarterly rpt, 1631–1

Farm production expenditures, detailed items by farm sales size and region, 1983, annual rpt, 1614–3

Fed Govt and total law enforcement officers and firefighters killed, death benefit claims, and non-Fed Govt firefighters death benefits by State and city, 1972-82, hearing, 21348–94

Fed Govt civilian and military employee pay, withholdings by type, and income, and special military compensation by type and service branch, 1982-83, GAO rpt, 26123–65

Fed Govt civilian employee retirement, health, and life insurance benefit plans operations and finances, FY81-82, annual rpt, 9844–1

Fed Govt consolidated financial statements based on business accounting methods, FY82-83, annual rpt, 8104–5

Fed Govt employee work-years by work schedule and for overtime and holidays, various periods 1980-82, article, 9842–1.401

Fed Govt programs and mgmt cost control proposals, 3-year savings by function and agency, and financial and operating data, 1960s-81, 16908–1

Fed Govt tax litigation, prosecutions, interpretive law decisions, and operating expenses of IRS, with collections, refunds, and taxes due, by region and State, FY83, annual rpt, 8304–3

Govt finances, by level of govt, State, and for large cities and counties, 1981-83, annual rpt series, 2466–2

Income tax returns filed by type, for US, IRS regions, and service center cities, 1972-82 and projected 1983-90, annual rpt, 8304–9.1

Income tax returns of corporations, detailed income and tax items by industry, 1981, annual rpt, 8304–4

Income tax returns of partnerships, receipts by source, deductions by type, and establishments, by selected industry, 1982, annual article, 8302–2.416

Income tax returns of sole proprietorships, detailed data by industry div and selected industry group, 1981, annual rpt, 8304–7

Income tax returns of sole proprietorships, receipts, deductions by type, payroll, and net income, by major industry, 1982, annual article, 8302–2.413

Index by Subjects and Names

Labor force characteristics and economic indicators, selected years 1880-1995, chartbook, 6728–30

Merchant ships in US fleet, shipping costs, construction, employment, military availability, and Fed Govt subsidies, 1970s-1984 and projected to 2000, 26306–6.83

Michigan bankruptcy filings, by filer type, moving history, income, creditor action, debt and asset type, credit status, exemptions claimed, and county, 1979-81, hearings, 21528–57.3

Misconduct and theft by employees in retail, hospital, and manufacturing establishments, by type and frequency of violation, 1978-80, 6068–178

Natural gas interstate pipeline company detailed financial and operating data, by firm, 1983, annual rpt, 3164–38

NYC metro area small business owners and accountants, assessment of economy, professional activities, and community problems, by county and industry div, 1983 survey, hearings, 21728–52.3

Partnership finances, tax deductions, and employment, by industry div and size, 1979, article, 8302–2.411

Private industry employee benefits, coverage by benefit type and provisions and occupational group, 1983, annual rpt, 6784–19

Private industry pension and other benefits, pension plans created and terminated since 1939, and NYC retirement systems assets, 1978-83, conf proceedings, 25408–89

Railroad employee benefits and beneficiaries by type, and railroad employees and payrolls, FY82, annual rpt, 9704–2

Railroad employee benefits and beneficiaries by type, benefit program finances, and railroad employees and payroll, FY83, annual rpt, 9704–1

Railroad employee earnings, benefits, and hours, by occupation for Class I railroads, 1983, annual rpt, 9484–5

Railroad employee retirement, survivors, unemployment, and sickness insurance programs, monthly rpt, 9702–2

Recreation fees at State outdoor facilities, visits, revenue, costs, and employee salaries, by State, 1982/83, annual rpt, 5544–14.4

Sick leave and insurance benefits for short-term disability, by type of worker, 1948-81, article, 4742–1.417

Small business and all employees sociodemographic characteristics, by industry div and firm size, 1978-1979, annual rpt, 9764–6.3

Statistical Abstract of US, social, political, and economic data, 1950s-83 and trends, annual rpt, 2324–1.3

Stock ownership plans for employees in developing countries, and firms finances and operations, with case studies of US and 3 countries, 1970s-82, 9916–3.19

Tax expenditures, Fed Govt revenues foregone through pension and other tax benefit policy changes, FY84-88, and women's labor force and pension participation, 1939-82, hearing, 25368–131

Tax expenditures from employee benefit plans, for income and payroll tax by benefit type and income, with benefits by industry, 1950-83 and projected to 1988, article, 9373–1.404

Telephone and telegraph company benefit and pension cases and amounts paid, for 61 firms, 1982, annual rpt, 9284–6.4

Traffic accidents and casualties detailed direct and indirect costs, by characteristics of persons and vehicles involved, 1979-80, 7768–80

Transit system financial and operating data, by mode, function, fleet size, and individual system, FY82, annual rpt, 7884–4

Trust assets of banks and trust companies, by type of asset and fund and State, 1983, annual rpt, 13004–1

see also Area wage surveys

see also Civil service pensions

see also Disability insurance

see also Health insurance

see also Health maintenance organizations

see also Industry wage surveys

see also Labor cost indexes

see also Life insurance

see also Pensions

see also Vacations and holidays

Employee Benefit Research Institute "Sources of Economic Security", 25408–87

Employee development

Air Force fiscal mgmt system operations and techniques, info for comptroller personnel, quarterly rpt, 3602–1

Computer specialists sociodemographic, educational, and employment characteristics, and Fed Govt support by agency, 1978, biennial Current Population Rpt, 2546–2.124

Defense Fuel Supply Center procurement, prices, stocks, transport, and other activities and finances, FY83, annual rpt, 3904–8

DOD training and education programs funding, staff, students, and facilities, by service branch and reserve component, FY85, annual rpt, 3504–5

Engineers sociodemographic, educational, and employment characteristics, and Federal support by agency, 1978, Current Population Rpt, 2546–2.121

Fed Govt executive employee dev programs, employee and candidate attitudes in 5 agencies, 1983 survey, GAO rpt, 26119–69

Fed Govt programs and mgmt cost control proposals, 3-year savings by function and agency, and financial and operating data, 1960s-81, 16908–1

Income tax returns of corporations, detailed income and tax items by industry, 1981, annual rpt, 8304–4

Natural gas and hazardous liquid pipelines accidents and casualties, and DOT and State govt safety activities, 1982, annual rpt, 7304–5

Police dept costs and operations, patrol car use, investigations, arrests, and recruit training, by city population size, 1982, 6066–21.1

Transit system mgmt training funded by Urban Mass Transportation Admin, participant characteristics and career impact, 1970-79, 7888–60

Employment and Training Administration

Veterans education assistance program participation and costs under GI Bill and other programs, WW II through Sept 1983, annual rpt, 9924–22

Employee-management relations

see Labor-management relations, general

see Labor-management relations in government

Employee Retirement Income Security Act

IRS determination letters issued on employee benefit plans, FY82-83, annual rpt, 8304–3.3

Older persons retirement income by type, and preretirement income replacement, under alternative inflation rates, various periods 1979-84, article, 9373–1.419

Reporting, disclosure, and enforcement of Act, 1982, annual rpt, 6464–4

Employment and Training Administration

Cost control proposals for Fed Govt programs and mgmt, 3-year savings by function and agency, and financial and operating data, 1960s-81, 16908–1.3

Employment, unemployment, and labor force characteristics, annual rpt, discontinued, 6404–2

Fed Govt employment and training program funding under Job Training Partnership Act, and required matching funds, for 3 programs by State, 1984/85, press release, 6408–58

Fraud and abuse in Labor Dept programs, audits and investigations, 1st half FY84, semiannual rpt, 6302–2

Indian and Alaska Native employment and training program funding allocation under Job Training Partnership Act, by individual tribe and group, FY84, press release, 6408–57

Job Training Partnership Act allotments for migrant and seasonal farm workers retraining assistance, by State and administering organization, as of July 1984, press release, 6408–64

Job Training Partnership Act participants, by program and socieconomic characteristics, Oct 1983-June 1984 with funding to 1985/86, 6408–63

Job Training Partnership Act performance standards guide for States, with data on previous job training programs by State or local area, FY81-82, 6408–59

Older persons community service part-time employment and program funding, by State and outlying area, FY84, press release, 6408–60

Trade adjustment assistance eligibility, reemployment opportunities, and worker characteristics, investigations of industries injured by import competition, series, 6406–9

Trade adjustment assistance for workers, petitions, investigations, and determinations, by major industry group, union, and State, monthly rpt, 6402–13

Unemployed displaced workers training and placement program of Fed Govt, funding and enrollment for 13 States and Guam, June 1984, press release, 6408–61

Unemployment insurance claims, insured unemployment, and exhaustions, by program, weekly rpt, 6402–14

Unemployment insurance laws, comparisons of State provisions, as of Sept 1984, semiannual revision, 6402–2

Employment and Training Administration

Unemployment insurance overpayments detection and recovery from random audit program in selected States, 1975-82 and projected to FY86, GAO rpt, 26121–77

Unemployment insurance State govt program admin, quality appraisal results, FY84, annual rpt, 6404–16

Unemployment insurance State govt program benefits, coverage, and tax provisions, July 1984, semiannual listing, 6402–7

Unemployment insurance system finances, claims, payments, and covered employment and wages, by State, 1938-82, 6408–5

Unemployment, labor surplus areas eligible for preferential Fed Govt contracts, and labor force data for 150 major labor markets, monthly listing, 6402–1

Youth summer job program of Fed Govt, funding and jobs by State and for Indians, summer 1984, press release, 6408–62

Employment and unemployment, general

- AFDC eligibility under Omnibus Budget Reconciliation Act, effect on caseloads and recipient benefits and living costs, 1981-83, GAO rpt, 26131–11
- AFDC foster care and unemployed parent segment, recipients and children, by State and outlying area, quarterly rpt, 4742–6.1
- AFDC recipients including unemployed parents, and emergency assistance, monthly rpt, 4742–2
- Agriculture-related employment by State, 1979, article, 1541–7.403
- Bankruptcy (personal), filers by debt type, employment and financial status, race, and Hispanic origin, 1982 survey, hearings, 21528–57.2
- BLS measures of unemployment, labor productivity, and CPI, effects of undisclosed economic activity, with illustrative data, 1958-79, article, 6722–1.401
- Budget of US, CBO analysis of revenue and spending alternatives and projections of economic indicators, FY85-89, annual rpt, 26304–3
- Budget of US, deficit effect of unemployment and inflation increases and income tax indexing, 1980-83, article, 2702–1.427
- Business activity indicators (nonfinancial), 1982, annual rpt, 9364–5.9
- Business and financial statistics, historic trends, 1984 annual chartbook, 9364–2.4
- Business and financial statistics, quarterly chartbook, 9362–2.2
- *Business Conditions Digest,* current data on economic, business, and financial conditions and cyclical fluctuations, monthly rpt, 2702–3
- *Business Conditions Digest,* historical supplement on economic, business, and financial conditions and cyclical fluctuations, with methodology, 1947-82, 2708–31
- Census of Housing, 1980: structural, financial, and householder characteristics, by region and State, 2475–4
- Census of Population and Housing, 1980: detailed population and housing characteristics, by county, city, and census tract, State and SMSA rpt series, 2551–2

Census of Population, 1980: detailed socioeconomic and demographic characteristics, by age, sex, race, Hispanic origin, occupation, and industry, State rpt series, 2531–4

Census of Population, 1980: detailed socioeconomic characteristics, by county, city, and inside-outside SMSAs and central cities, State rpt series, 2531–3

Census of Population, 1980: labor force, by sex, detailed occupation, and region, with comparison to 1970 census, supplementary rpt, 2535–1.12

Central cities and suburbs population and employment, effect of region, neighborhood, population, and labor characteristics, 1970-80, technical paper, 9387–8.89

City and suburb population characteristics and local govt finances, by region and selected SMSA, 1950s-FY83, 10048–61

Coal dev plans on Fed Govt lease lands in 12 regions under Fed Coal Mgmt Program, environmental and socioeconomic impacts to 2000, final statement series, 5726–4

Coal export-related employment, by industry, 1981-82, 3008–97

Coastal environmental and socioeconomic conditions, and potential impacts of oil and gas OCS leases, final statement series, 5736–1

Coastal environmental characteristics, fish, wildlife, and use, and population socioeconomic data, for individual areas, series, 5506–4

County and City Data Book, detailed socioeconomic and demographic data for States, counties, and cities, selected years 1976-82, 2328–1

County Business Patterns: establishments, employees, and payrolls, by SIC 4-digit industry and county, 1981, annual State rpt series, 2326–8

County Business Patterns: establishments, employees, and payrolls, by SIC 4-digit industry and county, 1982, annual State rpt series, 2326–6

Crime victimization rates by type of offense, and victim and offense characteristics, Natl Crime Survey series, 6066–3

Disabled women, by socioeconomic and demographic characteristics, and compared to nondisabled women and disabled men, 1981, chartbook, 16598–4

DOD prime contract awards in labor surplus areas, by service branch, State, and area, 1st half FY84, semiannual rpt, 3542–19

Drug abuse residential treatment program effectiveness indicators, with data on pre- and post-program characteristics of grads and dropouts, 1970-74 study, 4496–5.18

EC social security programs benefits and expenditures, and unemployment rate, and economic indicators growth, 1960-82, article, 4742–1.405

Economic and demographic factors used in OASDI program cost estimates, selected years 1913-82 with alternative projections to 2060, 4706–1.90

Economic and demographic trends for IRS regions, districts, and service centers, 1972-82 and projected to 1990, annual rpt, 8304–8

Index by Subjects and Names

Economic and financial trends, natl compounded annual rates of change, 1964-83, annual rpt, 9391–9.2

Economic and monetary trends, compounded annual rates of change for US and 10 major trading partners, quarterly rpt, 9391–7

Economic and population time series data frequently used in statistical demand analyses, 1941-1982, annual rpt, 1544–21

Economic conditions of US, with some foreign comparisons, 1960s-82 and alternative projections to 1992, hearing, 21248–79

Economic dev assistance of Fed Govt, generation of jobs by industry div, model methodology and outputs, various periods FY69-78, GAO rpt, 26117–32

Economic growth rates and component economic indicators, selected years 1922-83 and projected under full employment to 1988, hearing, 21348–90

Economic growth, with data on labor force, inflation, and productivity, 1953-83 with inflation and unemployment projections to 1988, article, 9373–1.402

Economic indicators and components, and Fed Reserve 4th District business and financial conditions, monthly chartbook, 9377–10

Economic indicators and components, current data and annual trends, monthly rpt, 23842–1.2

Economic indicators, and Fed Govt finances and deficits, selected years 1962-83 and projected under cost control proposals to 2000, 16908–1.1

Economic indicators and oil use and imports for US and 6 OECD countries, and oil production by country, biweekly rpt, 242–4

Economic indicators, nonfinancial, monthly rpt, 9362–1.2

Economic performance of US, and Reagan Admin 1984 spending, tax, and monetary policy proposals, with data for 1950s-83 and projected to 1988, press release, 8008–107

Economic Report of the President for 1984, Joint Economic Committee critique and policy recommendations, annual rpt, 23844–2

Economic trends, natl compounded annual rates of change, monthly rpt, 9391–3.1

Educational attainment of labor force, by demographic and employment characteristics, 1982-83 with summary trends from 1940, 6746–1.251

Educational attainment of labor force, by demographic and employment characteristics, 1983, article, 6722–1.423

Educational attainment of labor force, by demographic and employment characteristics, 1984, press release, 6748–79

Educational enrollment in postsecondary academic, vocational, and continuing education, by student characteristics, Oct 1982, 4848–16

Employment (nonagricultural) by industry div, manufacturing hours and earnings, labor force, and unemployment, by selected labor market area, 1981-83, article, 6742–2.408

Index by Subjects and Names

Employment and unemployment, general

Employment and earnings, detailed data, monthly rpt, 6742–2

Employment and economic conditions, alternative BLS projections to 1995 with selected trends for 1959-82, 6728–29

Employment and economic indicators, foreign and US, 1970s-83, annual rpt, 2044–26

Employment and price changes during recession and recovery, by selected employee characteristics, 1979-Jan 1984, 6728–28

Employment and unemployment by selected worker characteristics, annual averages, 1983, article, 6742–2.403

Employment by detailed occupation, for 29 SIC 2-digit nonmanufacturing industries, 1981 BLS survey, 6748–60

Employment change over business cycles, by worker characteristics and industry div, quarterly 1982-2nd qtr 1984 with trends from 1948, annual article, 6722–1.448

Employment, earnings, and hours, benchmarks for establishment-based time series, by SIC 2- to 4-digit industry, 1976-83, and seasonal adjustment factors, 1984-85, article, 6742–2.409

Employment, earnings, and hours, by selected SIC 1- to 4-digit industry, State, and for 278 major labor areas, 1939-83, annual rpt, 6744–5

Employment, earnings, and hours, by SIC 4-digit nonfarm industry, monthly 1974-Feb 1984, annual update, 6744–4

Employment, earnings, and hours, monthly press release, 6742–5

Employment-population ratios and unemployment rates, for total and civilian male labor force, by age and race, 1963-82, article, 6722–1.442

Employment situation, earnings, hours, and other BLS economic indicators, transcripts of BLS Commissioner's monthly testimony, periodic rpt, 23846–4

Employment status of family members, by occupation, family composition, age of children, and other characteristics, 1983 and trends from 1940, 6746–1.253

Employment, total and manufacturing, change in metro-nonmetro counties by region and county size, various periods 1951-79, technical paper, 9387–8.90

Employment, unemployment, and labor force, by demographic and employment characteristics, State, and for 30 metro areas and 11 large cities, 1983, annual rpt, 6744–7

Employment, unemployment, and labor force characteristics, annual rpt, discontinued, 6404–2

Employment, unemployment, and labor force, detailed data by sociodemographic and employment characteristics, and industry, 1940s-83, 6748–72

Employment, unemployment, hours, earnings, and productivity, selected years 1929-83, annual rpt, 204–1.2

Energy production, reserves, and prices, by energy type, and selected indicators of energy use, by State, 1982-83 with selected comparisons from 1971, annual rpt, 3164–60

Enterprise zone and urban revitalization projects of State and local govts, effect on business and employment in selected areas, various dates 1972-83, hearing, 21788–140

Exchange rate volatility, effect on employment and production, 1984 technical paper, 9366–7.97

Export-related employment, manufacturing production, and exports of manufactured and agricultural commodities, 1960s-82, State rpt series, 2046–3

Exports and export-related US employment generated by Overseas Private Investment Corp projects, FY83, annual rpt, 9904–3

Exports and imports of US, relative contributions of labor by type and capital to trade balance, selected years 1958-80, technical paper, 9381–10.30

Families and households detailed socioeconomic characteristics, Mar 1982, annual Current Population Rpt, 2546–1.383

Family earnings by number of earners, and employment status of individual family members, quarterly rpt, 6742–19

Family earnings by number of earners and members employment status, and earnings of full- and part-time workers, by sociodemographic characteristics, 1982-83, article, 6742–2.406

Farm population employment by industry div, and unemployment, by region, 1983, annual rpt, 2544–1

Fed Govt aid to State and local govts, expenditures, and direct payments, by program, agency, and State, FY83, annual rpt, 2464–2

Fed Govt budget and debt, cyclically adjusted estimates assuming mid-level unemployment and GNP, and methodology, quarterly 1955-83, 2706–5.31

Fed Govt revenues, deficits, and debt, and GNP and unemployment, cyclically adjusted estimates assuming middle-range unemployment, 1955-3rd qtr 1983, article, 2702–1.403

Forecasts for selected business activities and natl economic indicators, compilation of representative opinions, 1984, annual rpt, 9389–3

Foreign corporation US affiliates, assets and employment by region and State, 1977 and 1981, annual rpt, 2044–25

Foreign direct investment in US by country, and finances, operations, and land ownership, by industry group for businesses acquired and established, 1982-83, annual article, 2702–1.418

Foreign firms US affiliates financial and operating data, by country of parent firm and industry div, 1980-81, article, 2702–1.402

Foreign-owned US multiestablishment firms, employment, and payroll, by country, State, industry group, and foreign ownership share, 1981-82, annual rpt, 2324–6

Franchises of firms engaged in distribution of goods and services, employment by kind of business, 1982, annual rpt, 2014–5.1

GNP growth related to unemployment rate, regression results, various periods 1951-83 and projected to 1989, article, 9393–8.408

Handbook of Labor Statistics, employment, earnings, hours, and labor force characteristics, 1982 and trends, detailed annual rpt, 6724–1

Health care expenditures, natl survey on services use, costs, and sources of payment, by patient and physician characteristics, 1977-78, series, 4186–3

High school and college grads employment status, job opportunities, and income, selected years 1978-83, annual rpt, 4824–2.23

High school classes of 1980 and 1982: educational and sociodemographic characteristics and expectations, natl longitudinal study, series, 4826–2

Hispanic Americans socioeconomic and demographic characteristics, and compared to non-Hispanics, selected years 1970-83, chartbook, 2328–48

Homeless population and characteristics, and temporary shelter operations, use, and user characteristics, by region and selected city, 1983, 5188–108

Homeless population and characteristics, and temporary shelter operations, use, and user characteristics, for selected cities, various periods 1979-84, hearing, 21248–85

Households and housing unit characteristics, and employment, housing finance, and social programs data, selected years 1948-83, hearing, 21968–28

Import and tariff provisions effect on US industries and products, investigations with background financial and operating data, series, 9886–4

Import-sensitive industries employment and wage adjustments, for 25 SIC 3-digit industries, selected years 1960-82, article, 6722–1.439

Imports from Communist countries, injury to US industries, investigations with background financial and operating data, selected industries and products, series, 9886–12

Imports injury to US industries from foreign subsidized products and sales in US at less than fair value, investigations with background financial and operating data, series, 9886–19

Imports injury to US industries from increased import sales, investigations with background financial and operating data, series, 9886–5

Income (household) and cash and noncash transfer program participation, by sociodemographic characteristics, quarterly rpt, 2542–2

Income (taxable) not reported, methodology using Current Population Survey labor force data to estimate share of output and nonreporters, 1950s-81, 23848–178

Income assistance, effects of experimental negative income tax program on employment, earnings, marital status, and other family characteristics in 2 cities, 1970-75, 4008–64

Income of families and persons, by sociodemographic characteristics, 1983, advance annual Current Population Rpt, 2546–6.41

Income of households, families, and persons, by detailed socioeconomic characteristics and region, 1982, annual Current Population Rpt, 2546–6.39

Industry finances and operations, by SIC 2- to 4-digit industry, 1970s-83 and projected to 1988, annual rpt, 2014–4

Employment and unemployment, general

Industry R&D expenditures by funding source, and projected impact on output, employment, and hours of labor, by selected industry, various periods 1953-90, hearings, 25368–133

Jail capacities, conditions, expenditures, and services, and socioeconomic and other characteristics of inmates, various dates 1976-82, 10048–59

Job seeking methods of unemployed jobseekers, by sex, age, and race, monthly rpt, 6742–2.2

Job tenure and occupational mobility of workers, by sociodemographic characteristics and industry div, as of Jan 1983, press release, 6748–76

Kidney end-stage disease patients by patient characteristics and country, and per capita spending for treatment, selected years 1973-81, article, 4102–1.450

Labor force characteristics and economic indicators, selected years 1880-1995, chartbook, 6728–30

Labor force experience of men and women by sociodemographic characteristics, and effect on earnings, 1979, Current Population Rpt, 2546–2.123

Labor force status monthly changes, by selected worker characteristics, 1981-82, biennial rpt, 6744–17

Manufactured products (miscellaneous) trade, tariffs, and industry operating data, TSUSA commodity rpt series, 9885–7

Manufacturers under Fed Govt contract and owned by DOD, operating data by agency, selected SIC 2- to 4-digit industry, State, and SMSA, 1982, annual Current Industrial Rpt, 2506–3.4

Manufacturing census, 1982: financial and operating data, by SIC 2- to 4-digit industry, State, SMSA, and county, preliminary census div rpt series, 2491–3

Manufacturing census, 1982: financial and operating data, for SIC 4-digit industries by product, preliminary rpt series, 2491–1

Manufacturing computerized automation dev, R&D, training, and employment impacts, with comparisons to foreign countries, selected years 1960-83, 26358–105

Manufacturing robots installed, and jobs displaced and created by occupation, by type of robot use, 1980s-2000, hearings, 21728–54

Married couples with both spouses working, earnings by sociodemographic and employment characteristics and age of children, 1981, Current Population Rpt, 2546–2.120

Married women in couples with wife as primary earner, socioeconomic and family characteristics, with comparative data for husbands, Mar 1982, 2326–11.9

Minority business mgmt and financial assistance from federally funded organizations, by region, State, and business characteristics, FY83, annual rpt, 2104–6

Minority group and women's employment, by occupational group, SIC 2- to 3-digit industry, State, and SMSA, 1981, annual rpt, 9244–1

Minority group labor force participation, employment, and unemployment, by race, detailed Hispanic origin, and sex, quarterly rpt, 6742–18

Mobility of population, detailed data by demographic and socioeconomic characteristics of movers and nonmovers, Mar 1981-82, annual Current Population Rpt, 2546–1.384

Money supply fluctuation effect on employment and wages, model description, 1984 technical paper, 9366–7.104

Monthly Labor Review, current statistics and articles, 6722–1

Natl income and product, comprehensive accounts and components, *Survey of Current Business,* monthly rpt, monthly and annual tables, 2702–1.27

New Communities program of HUD, activities, costs, land sales, and community and population characteristics, for 13 communities, 1970s-83, 5188–107

OASDHI and selected social insurance programs, covered workers earnings and characteristics, selected years 1937-82, annual rpt, 4744–3.1, 4744–3.3

Occupational Outlook Handbook, 1984-85 biennial rpt, 6744–1

Occupational trends and outlook, quarterly rpt, 6742–1

Older persons by demographic, socioeconomic, and health characteristics, selected years 1900-81 and projected to 2050, Current Population Rpt, 2546–2.125

Older persons income and income sources, by OASDI beneficiary and poverty status, labor force participation, and demographic characteristics, 1982, biennial rpt, 4744–26

Older persons labor force participation related to age cohort size, income maintenance program participation, and sex, BLS technical paper, 6886–6.8

Older persons population characteristics, and needs and costs of social services by type, by metro-nonmetro status, 1970s-82 with trends from 1900, 21148–28

Older persons sociodemographic characteristics, and Fed Govt program participation and funding, 1983 with trends and projections 1900-2060, annual rpt, 25144–3.1

Older persons sociodemographic characteristics and transportation needs, selected years 1900-2040, 7308–183

Partnership finances, tax deductions, and employment, by industry div and size, 1979, article, 8302–2.411

Pollution abatement expenditures, and effect on economic indicators and industry operations, by major industry, projected under 3 pollution regulation alternatives 1983-95, 9188–84

Pollution abatement labor costs, by SIC 2- to 4-digit industry, State, and SMSA, 1982, annual Current Industrial Rpt, 2506–3.6

Population demographic and economic characteristics, 1982 with projections of population size to 2050, annual Current Population Rpt, 2546–2.119

Port dev costs and financing through user fees, and shipping industry impact on local economy, by State, other area, industry, commodity, and port, 1970s-2020, hearings, 21568–34

Index by Subjects and Names

Port impact on local employment through transport of 5 commodities, by industry for 3 eastern ports, and demand for US coal by country, 1981, 7308–182

Poverty-level persons and families, by income source, hours of work, earnings, taxes, and family characteristics, various periods 1959-84, 21788–131

Poverty population by labor force status, and effect of public welfare changes and recession, by family status, FY82, 21788–139

Poverty population size, effect of counting public noncash transfers as income by recipient characteristics, 1979-83, 2626–2.52

Poverty population size, effects of counting public noncash transfers as income by recipient characteristics, 1979-82, 2626–2.50

Poverty status of families and persons, by detailed socioeconomic characteristics, 1982, annual Current Population Rpt, 2546–6.40

Poverty status of young adults related to motivation, psychological factors, and family characteristics, by race and sex, 1970s-82, longitudinal studies, 4008–65

Productivity, hours, and employment indexes for selected SIC 3- and 4-digit industries, 1954-82, annual rpt, 6824–1

Productivity of labor, economic growth, and industrial policy dev, selected years 1947-82 with some projections to 1986, 26306–6.69

Refugee resettlement program activities and funding, arrivals and population by country of origin and State, and employment and other characteristics, FY83, annual rpt, 4704–8

Retail trade census, 1982: employment, establishments, sales, and payroll, by SIC 2- to 4-digit kind of business, SMSA, and retail district, State rpt series, 2401–1

Retail trade census, 1982: employment, establishments, sales, and payroll, by SIC 2- to 4-digit kind of business, SMSA, county, and city, State rpt series, 2397–1

Retail trade census, 1982: employment, establishments, sales, and payroll, by SIC 4-digit kind of business and State, preliminary rpt series, 2395–1

Seasonal adjustment methodology for economic time series, dev and design of Census Bur and other systems, with illustrative data, 1981 conf papers, 2626–7.5

Service industry census, 1982: employment, establishments, receipts, and payroll, by SIC 2- to 4-digit kind of business, SMSA, county, and city, State rpt series, 2391–1

Service industry census, 1982: employment, establishments, receipts, and payroll, by SIC 4-digit kind of business and State, preliminary rpt series, 2390–2

Services intl transactions, and operations of US multinatl service firms and foreign affiliates, by industry and world region, 1977-82, 2706–5.30

Small and minority-owned businesses finances and operations, Federal contracts by agency, and worker characteristics, by industry, race, sex, and State, 1950s-83, annual rpt, 9764–6

Index by Subjects and Names

Small business capital formation under securities law exemptions, effects on stocks offered, issuers, and purchasers, series, 9736–2

Small business economic conditions, with comparisons to larger businesses, selected years 1979-83, annual rpt, 9764–1.1

Small business employment and receipts size standards for Fed Govt contract awards by industry, and DOD contract awards data, 1970s-83, hearings, 21728–53

Small business loans and credit, operational expectations, and NYC metro area owners economic and professional attitudes, by industry div, 1980-83 surveys, hearings, 21728–52

Social pathology measures including crime and death rates, relation to selected economic indicators, various periods 1950-80, 23848–76

Special Labor Force Reports, series, 6746–1

Statistical Abstract of US, social, political, and economic data, 1950s-83 and trends, annual rpt, 2324–1.3

Supplementary Security Income beneficiary socioeconomic characteristics and health service use, 1970s-83 and SSI program projections to 1995, 25148–29

Taxes, tax policy, and intergovtl relations, public opinion survey results, 1972-84, annual rpt, 10044–2

Technological change, impact on productivity and employment in 4 industries, 1960-90, 6828–23

Technology-intensive and other industry employment, percent change for US, New England States, and Massachusetts, 1975-83, article, 9373–2.404

Technology-intensive industry employment and establishments by industry and selected location, and venture capital investments by source, 1970s-82, 26358–107

Technology-intensive manufacturing employment by selected industry group, 1982, article, 9373–2.402

Trade adjustment assistance eligibility, reemployment opportunities, and worker characteristics, investigations of industries injured by import competition, series, 6406–9

Trade adjustment assistance for workers, petitions, investigations, and determinations, by major industry group, union, and State, monthly rpt, 6402–13

Trade-related employment and production by industry, occupation, and State, and US trade policy actions, 1960s-83, annual rpt, 444–1

Traffic accidents and casualties detailed direct and indirect costs, by characteristics of persons and vehicles involved, 1979-80, 7768–80

Unemployed discouraged workers, by sex, employment history, and job search effort, 1979-83, article, 6722–1.449

Unemployed displaced workers training and placement program of Fed Govt, funding and enrollment for 13 States and Guam, June 1984, press release, 6408–61

Unemployment and part-time employment, by race, Hispanic origin, sex, family composition, income, and poverty status, 1980-82, annual report, 6744–15

Employment and unemployment, local and regional

Unemployment, by duration, work experience during year, sex, race, and Hispanic origin, 1982-83, 6748–77

Unemployment duration and probability of employment or labor force withdrawal, by sex and race, 1982, article, 9373–1.410

Unemployment during business cycles, and by worker age, sex, occupation, industry div, reason, and duration, various periods 1969-82, article, 6722–1.444

Unemployment effect on family income and poverty status, by demographic, employment, and unemployment characteristics, 1981-82, annual article, 6722–1.412

Unemployment insurance, employment and wages of workers covered by State law and Fed Govt employee compensation, by SIC 4-digit industry and State, 1982, annual rpt, 6744–16

Unemployment, labor surplus areas eligible for preferential Fed Govt contracts, and labor force data for 150 major labor markets, monthly listing, 6402–1

Unemployment levels and rates, by State and for 240 large SMSAs, monthly press release with Current Population Survey annual benchmark averages, 6742–12

Unemployment rate and components of change, growth rates for 6 recovery periods 2nd qtr 1954-2nd qtr 1984, and projected unemployment rate for 4th qtr 1985, article, 9373–1.415

Unemployment rate realted to inflation and GNP growth, various periods 1960-83 and projected 1984-89, article, 9385–1.408

Urban area economic distress index and components, for 153 cities, 1975 and 1980, article, 9373–1.413

Urban Dev Action Grant awards to local areas, construction and other jobs to be created, by city, quarterly press release series, 5002–7

Urban Dev Action Grant program effectiveness, and participation of small cities by State, 1978-82, GAO rpt, 26113–118

Urban Dev Action Grant program new and retained permanent jobs for low- and moderate-income persons, by city and project, FY83, annual rpt, 5124–5

Voting age population selected characteristics and participation in presidential elections, 1964-80 with projections to 2000, Current Population Rpt, 2546–2.117

Wage growth and turnover rates related to marital status, sex, age, establishment type, and employer size, 1979/80, article, 9393–8.403

Wholesale trade census, 1982: employment, establishments, finances, and operations, by SIC 2- to 4-digit kind of business, SMSA, county, and city, State rpt series, 2405–1

Wholesale trade census, 1982: employment, establishments, sales by commodity, and payroll, by SIC 4-digit kind of business and State, preliminary rpt series, 2403–1

Widows with minor children receiving OASI survivor benefits, health insurance coverage and health care services and expenses, 1976-78, article, 4742–1.404

see also Absenteeism

see also Agricultural labor

see also Alien workers

see also Area wage surveys

see also Blue collar workers

see also Child labor

see also Clerical workers

see also Discrimination in employment

see also Earnings, general

see also Employee benefit plans

see also Employee development

see also Employment and unemployment, local and regional

see also Employment and unemployment, specific industries

see also Employment services

see also Engineers and engineering

see also Executives

see also Federal employees

see also Foreign labor conditions

see also Health occupations

see also Hours of labor

see also Household workers

see also Industry wage surveys

see also Job vacancy

see also Labor cost indexes

see also Labor law

see also Labor-management relations, general

see also Labor-management relations in government

see also Labor-management relations, local and regional

see also Labor productivity

see also Labor turnover

see also Manpower

see also Manpower training programs

see also Migrant workers

see also Moonlighting

see also Occupational health and safety

see also Occupations

see also Overtime

see also Paraprofessionals

see also Part-time employment

see also Payroll

see also Pensions

see also Professional and technical workers

see also Public service employment

see also Retirement

see also Scientists and technicians

see also Seasonal and summer employment

see also Self-employment

see also State and local employees

see also Unemployment insurance

see also Vacations and holidays

see also Veterans employment

see also Vocational rehabilitation

see also Volunteers

see also Women's employment

see also Work Incentive Program

see also Work stoppages

see also Youth employment

Employment and unemployment, local and regional

Alabama rural black population, education, employment, health services, and economic status, for 16 counties, selected years 1970-81, 11048–180

American Samoa minimum wage rates, employment, earnings, and benefits, by establishment and industry, Nov 1983, biennial rpt, 6504–6

Appalachia population by age and urban-rural location, and employment and net employment change by industry, selected years 1960-90, article, 9088–33

Employment and unemployment, local and regional

California business failures, plant closings, layoffs, and relocations, by plant, industry, county, and city, 1980-83, hearing, 21348–84.1

California housing market, and Los Angeles average home price and mortgage rate, 1969-82 with economic indicators projected to 1989, 9306–1.1

Dallas-Fort Worth, Tex, SMSA employment, earnings, hours, and CPI changes, 1983 with trends from 1968, annual rpt, 6964–2

Denver-Boulder, Colo, SMSA employment, earnings, and CPI changes, 1983, annual rpt, 6974–2

Florida and California elderly migration by selected State of origin or destination, and Florida elderly, by sociodemographic and housing characteristics, 1970 and 1980, 4478–150

Fresno, Calif, economic, population, labor, and housing indicators, various periods 1974-85, hearing, 21248–84

Georgia job expansion in southern rural 10-county area, employment and establishments by worker and industry characteristics, 1976-81, article, 1502–7.401

Georgia small businesses, effect of mgmt counseling on sales, employment, profits, and taxes paid, 1980-81, hearing, 25728–36

Houston, Tex, SMSA employment, earnings, hours, and CPI changes, 1983 with trends from 1968, annual rpt, 6964–1

Kansas City, Mo-Kans, SMSA employment, earnings, and CPI changes, with comparisons to total US, 1983, annual rpt, 6974–1

Kentucky employment growth in 9-county rural area, labor force and establishment characteristics, 1979-80, 1598–194

Massachusetts employment in traditional and high technology industry by occupation, and wages by industry, and compared to US and 3 SMSAs, various periods 1976-82, article, 9373–1.416

Michigan health funding, Blue Cross-Blue Shield and welfare participation, and unemployment, poverty, and food assistance by county, 1979-83, hearing, 21348–86

New England States and Massachusetts technology-intensive and other industry employment, percent change 1975-83, article, 9373–2.404

New England States college grads employment prospects in 1984, annual narrative rpt, 6916–7.3

New England States economic indicators, Fed Reserve 1st District, monthly rpt, 9373–2.2

New England States employment, wages, and price conditions by State and selected SMSA, 1983, annual rpt, 6916–7.1

North Central States manufacturing and total employment, percent change for Fed Reserve 7th District States, various periods 1969-84, article, 9375–1.408

Northeast States timber annual growth, removals, causes of mortality, and products output, and forest ownership and industries, State rpt series, 1206–16

Northwest US and British Columbia forest industry production, prices, trade, and employment, quarterly rpt, 1202–3

Northwest US economic impacts of Washington Public Power Supply System nuclear reactors construction, with local power supply/demand, 1980s-2035, hearing, 21448–29

NYC metro area employment and prices, 1983, annual rpt, 6924–2

NYC metro area employment by industry div, monthly rpt, discontinued coverage, 6922–4

Pacific coast States and selected areas, impact of shipping industry activities, 1970s-83, hearings, 21568–34

Pacific Northwest electricity consumption and prices by end-use sector, and economic and demographic data, 1960s-83 and projected to 2005, annual rpt, 3224–2

Pacific Northwest natl forest sales by bidding method, harvest by company, and effects on local employment by community, 1974-77, 1208–194

Pennsylvania steel plant at Fairless Hills employment situation, US steel imports by source, and steel industry financial and operating data, 1970s-90, hearing, 25528–94

Pittsburgh, Pa, rental housing unit choice of recent movers related to unit, neighborhood, and town characteristics, 1967 survey, 9306–1.7

Southeastern States and 5 SMSAs economic indicators, Fed Reserve 8th District, quarterly rpt, 9391–15

Southeastern States economic indicators, by State, Fed Reserve 5th District, quarterly rpt, 9389–16

Southeastern States employment, prices, earnings, and union membership in 8 States, Oct 1982-83, annual rpt, 6944–2

Southeastern States financial and economic devs, Fed Reserve 6th District, monthly rpt with articles, 9371–1

Southeastern States high technology employment and share of total employment, by State, 1982 and percent change 1975-82, press release, 6948–6

Southeastern States nonagricultural employment by industry div and SMSA, earnings, and hours, for 8 States, monthly press release, 6942–7

Southeastern States personal income and employment growth rates, by State, various periods 1958-82 and forecast to 1984, article, 9389–1.403

Southeastern States textile mill employment and average hours and earnings, for 8 States, monthly press release, 6942–1

Southeastern States textile mill employment, monthly 1951-83, annual summary rpt, 6944–1

Southeastern US water supply and quality, with background socioeconomic data, for 8 States, 1960s-2020 with trends from 1930, 9208–119

Southwestern States employment by major nonagricultural industry, and average hours and earnings of manufacturing production workers, for 5 States, monthly rpt, 6962–2

Southwestern States employment, industrial relations, prices, and economic conditions, regional rpts series, 6966–1

St Louis, Mo, SMSA employment, earnings, and CPI changes, 1983, annual rpt, 6974–3

Index by Subjects and Names

St Louis, Mo, SMSA nonagricultural employment growth rates, with comparisons to US and 4 aggregated SMSAs, 1955-82, article, 9391.405

Tennessee Valley construction projects employment of TVA, and impacts on nearby areas, survey rpt series, 9806–7

Tennessee Valley ethanol production, feedstocks, facilities, tax incentives, and related farming data, by State, 1970s-83 and projected to 1992, 9808–69

Tennessee Valley industrial dev and effects on employment, investment, and TVA power demand, by location and company, 1983, annual rpt, 9804–3

Texas border employment and economic impacts of Mexican peso devaluation, for 6 counties and 2 SMSAs, 1970s-May 1983, hearing, 21788–133

Texas employment in 4 SMSAs related to employment in Mexico border US-owned plants and peso devaluation, 1978-83, article, 9379–1.402

TTPI socioeconomic, employment, health, and govtl data, by TTPI govt, FY83 and selected trends, detailed annual rpt, 7004–6.2

Virgin Islands economic censuses, 1982: employment, establishments, payroll, and receipts, by SIC 1- to 4-digit industry, island, and city, 2593–1

Virgin Islands socioeconomic and govtl data, FY81, annual rpt, 5304–4

Western States economic indicators, Fed Reserve 12th District, quarterly rpt, 9393–1.2

Western States, FHLB 11th District housing, employment, and economic indicators, by SMSA, quarterly rpt, 9302–18

Western States housing outlook and economic and demographic trends, FHLB 11th District, urban area rpt series, 9306–2

see also Earnings, local and regional

see also Industry wage surveys

see also Labor-management relations, local and regional

see also under By Census Division, By City, By County, By Region, By SMSA or MSA, and By State in the "Index by Categories"

Employment and unemployment, specific industries

Airline financial and operating data for certificated, charter, and cargo carriers, quarterly rpt, 9142–30

Alcohol fuel production costs, related employment, and Fed Govt subsidies and impact on farm income, selected years 1978-90, GAO rpt, 26113–140

Asbestos workers, exposure levels, cancer incidence, and deaths, by industry and occupation, and asbestos regulation enforcement and costs/benefits, various periods 1940-2027, hearing, 21408–72

Auto export voluntary restraint of Japan, effect on US auto industry and import sales and prices, 2nd qtr 1981-1st qtr 1984, article, 9377–1.407

Auto industry finances and operations by manufacturer, foreign competition, and consumer auto expenditures and attitudes toward car buying, selected years 1968-85, annual rpt, 2004–8

Index by Subjects and Names

Employment and unemployment, specific industries

Auto industry finances, employment, production, and cost increases to comply with Fed Govt pollution and safety standards, 1970s-83, annual rpt, 3304–5.4

Auto industry operations, and trade by country, monthly rpt, 9882–8

Auto industry operations, trade, and registrations, foreign and US, selected years 1928-82, domestic content requirement hearings, 21788–134

Bus industry collective ratemaking and regulatory reform impacts on operations, finances, and services to older persons and rural areas by State, 1970s-83, 14828–2

Chemicals and related products trade, tariffs, and industry operating data, TSUSA commodity rpt series, 9885–4

Coal employment and economic losses from utility fuel switching to meet emissions standards, with detail for counties in 5 States, 1970s-83 and projected to 1990, 21368–52

Coal miners working daily, mines, and labor productivity, trends and projections, quarterly rpt, 3162–37.4

Coal mines and related operations, injury, employment, worktime, and productivity data, 1982, annual rpt, 6664–4

Coal production and mines by county, prices, productivity, miners, reserves, and stocks, by mining method and State, 1982-83, annual rpt, 3164–25

Coal production, mining employment, exports, and finances, by coal district, 1982, 3008–97

Construction industries census, 1982: financial and operating data, by SIC 4-digit industry and State, final rpt series, 2373–1

Construction industries census, 1982: financial and operating data, by SIC 4-digit industry and State, preliminary rpt series, 2371–1

Construction industry total and female workers, and construction worker earnings and hours, by selected SIC 2- to 3-digit industry, bimonthly rpt, 2012–1.7

Construction jobs to be created by Urban Dev Action Grants to local areas, by city, quarterly press release series, 5002–7

Copper mine expansion in Cananea, Mexico, effects on US air pollution and copper industry, with US and foreign industry data, 1960s-95, hearing, 21448–31

Credit union financial statements by region, State, and type of membership, for Federal and federally insured State unions, 1983, annual rpt, 9534–1

Defense industries employment of scientists, engineers, and technicians, and supply/demand, by field, 1981-87, 9628–71

Electric power plant capital and operating detailed costs, capacity, and fuel use, by plant, plant type, utility, and State, 1982, annual rpt, 3164–9

Electric utilities privately owned, detailed financial and operating data by company, with summary data for other distributors by type, 1982, annual rpt, 3164–23

Energy-related fields manpower devs and studies, series, 3006–8

Fed Reserve banks and branch officers and employees, and salaries, 1983, annual rpt, 9364–1.1

Fishery and fish processing employment, by State, 1977, annual rpt, 2164–2

Fishery and fish processing employment, firms, and vessels, 1950s-83, annual rpt, 2164–1.10

Fishery processed products production and employment, by region and State, 1982, annual rpt, 2166–6.4

Footwear production, employment, consumption, prices, and US trade by country, quarterly rpt, 9882–6

Forest industry establishments, employment, and payroll in Northeast, by SIC 2- to 4-digit industry, State rpt series, 1206–16

Head Start Project enrollment, appropriations, and staff, FY65-84, annual rpt, 4604–8

Libraries of colleges and universities, expenditures, holdings by type, use, staff by sex, and Federal grants received, 1979-82, biennial rpt, 4854–1

Lumber production, prices, trade, and employment in Northwest US and British Columbia, quarterly rpt, 1202–3

Metal mines and related operations, injury, employment, and worktime data, 1982, annual rpt, 6664–3

Metals and metal products trade, tariffs, and industry operating data, TSUSA commodity rpt series, 9885–6

Metals resource recovery through leaching technologies, characteristics of methods and operations, regulation, and research, series, 5606–6

Mineral industries census, 1982: financial and operating data, by SIC 2- to 4-digit industry and State, preliminary summary rpts, 2511–2

Mineral industries census, 1982: financial and operating data, including materials consumed, by SIC 4-digit industry and State, preliminary rpt series, 2511–1

Minerals (nonmetallic) and mineral products trade, tariffs, and industry operating data, TSUSA commodity rpt series, 9885–5

Minerals (nonmetallic) mining and related operations injury, employment, and worktime data, 1982, annual rpt, 6664–1

Minerals (strategic) supply/demand, trade, and foreign and US industry devs by firm and country, by commodity, bimonthly rpt, 5602–4

Minerals production, prices, trade, use, employment, tariffs, and stockpiling, by commodity, with foreign comparisons, 1979-83, annual rpt, 5604–18

Minerals Yearbook, 1982, Vol 2 preprints: State reviews of production and sales by commodity, and business activity, annual rpt series, 5604–16

Mines (sand and gravel) and related operations, injury, employment, and worktime data, 1982, annual rpt, 6664–2

Mines (stone) and related operations, injury, employment, and worktime data, 1982, annual rpt, 6664–5

Mines, mills, and quarries occupational injuries, and employees and hours, by State, quarterly rpt, 6662–1

Motor and rail carriers regulated by ICC, employment and finances by mode of transport, and ICC activities, FY80-83 and trends, annual rpt, 9484–1

Motor carriers (Class I interstate) finances, operations, equipment, employment, and payroll, by district, 1982, annual rpt, 9486–5.3

Motor carriers (Class II) of property financial and operating data, by region, 1982, annual rpt, 9484–10

Motorcycle imports, sales, and inventories of foreign make, and prices and employment for domestic makes, quarterly rpt, 9882–12

Natural gas interstate pipeline company detailed financial and operating data, by firm, 1983, annual rpt, 3164–38

Nuclear industry nongovt employment by industry segment, occupation, and census div, and DOE and NRC nuclear employment, 1968-83, biennial rpt, 3004–11

Nuclear power industry status and outlook, with reactor construction, utility financial and operating data, and foreign comparisons, 1970s-83 with projections to 2010, 26358–99

Nursing home facilities use and characteristics, and nurses employed, by region and State, 1980, 4147–14.29

Oil and gas companies production and exploration detailed expenditures, revenues, operating ratios, and sales volume, 1982, annual Current Industrial Rpt, 2506–8.11

Oil and gas exploratory rigs in operation, wells and footage drilled, and seismic exploration crews, monthly rpt, 3162–24.5

Pest control firms in urban areas, pesticide use by type, employment, and sales, by type of service, 1981 survey, article, 1561–16.408

Philanthropic foundations employment and earnings by organization type, and compared to other nonprofit organizations, selected years 1972-82, article, 6722–1.455

Physicians employed in prisons by sociodemographic, employment, and professional characteristics, and compared to all physicians, 1979, article, 4102–1.407

Prison Industries (Federal) operations and finances, FY83, annual rpt, 6244–3

Railroad employee benefits and beneficiaries by type, benefit program finances, and railroad employees and payroll, FY83, annual rpt, 9704–1

Railroad employee earnings, benefits, and hours, by occupation for Class I railroads, 1983, annual rpt, 9484–5

Railroad employees and compensation, by age, sex, occupation, and years of service, 1981, annual rpt, 9704–2.4

Railroad employment by functional group, for Class I line-haul railroads, monthly rpt, 9482–3

Railroad finances and operations, detailed data by firm, class of service, and district, 1983, annual rpt, 9486–6.1

Recording industry operations and sales lost from home taping, home taping costs, and material taped by source, 1969-83, hearings with chartbook, 25528–100

Rural Electrification Admin loans to power supply and distribution firms, and borrower operating and financial data, by firm and State, 1983, annual rpt, 1244–1

Employment and unemployment, specific industries

Ship-related industries employment, monthly rpt, 7702–1

Shipbuilding and repair facilities, construction capability, number and value of ships under construction, and employment, by shipyard, 1983, annual rpt, 7704–9

Shipbuilding costs and related employment, by coastal district, 1982, annual rpt, 7704–12

Ships in US merchant fleet, shipping costs, construction, employment, military availability, and Fed Govt subsidies, 1970s-1984 and projected to 2000, 26306–6.83

Shipyard, shipboard, and longshore employment, FY82-83, annual rpt, 7704–14.3

Steel (stainless and alloy tool) production, employment, prices, and US importer inventories and unfilled orders, quarterly rpt, 9882–3

Steel import trigger prices to prevent Japan dumping, and domestic steel prices, employment, and imports, by product and region, various dates 1977-1983, hearings, 21368–51

Steel imports of US from EC and other countries, and US industry operating data, for 15 products limited under arrangement with EC, monthly rpt, 9882–10

Steel industry finances and operations under proposed import quota, projected 1985-89 with selected foreign comparisons and trends from 1950, 26306–6.80

Steel industry financial and operating data, steel imports by source, and employment situation at Fairless Hills, Pa, plant, 1970s-90, hearing, 25528–94

Steel plant modernization projects, Urban Dev Action Grant and private funding and jobs created, by plant and city, 1984 press release, 5006–3.37

Synthetic Fuels Corp financial statements, activities, and executive staff and salaries, FY83, annual rpt, 29654–1

Teachers in elementary and secondary schools and colleges, and supply/demand for additional teachers, 1982-83, annual rpt, 4824–1

Telephone and telegraph firms, employment by sex, and employee compensation, 1982, annual rpt, 9284–6

Telephone companies borrowing under rural telephone loan program, and financial and operating data, 1983, annual rpt, 1244–2.3

Textile fiber and products trade, tariffs, and industry operating data, TSUSA commodity rpt series, 9885–3

Textile mill employment and average hours and earnings, for 8 Southeastern States, monthly press release, 6942–1

Transportation employment, wages, and average annual earnings, by mode of transport, 1972-82, annual rpt, 7304–2.2

Truck drivers and guards transporting Fed Reserve System coins and currency, effects on wages of locally prevailing wage rate requirement, for 12 cities, 1980, article, 9377–1.402

TV and radio industry employment, total and for minorities, women, and youth, by job category and State, 1979-83, annual rpt, 9284–16

TV and radio industry minority and women employment by occupation, and business owners, by race and State, with revenues and stations, 1971-81, hearing, 21368–45

TV and radio station employment, total and for minorities and women, by full- and part-time status and individual station, 1983, annual rpt, 9284–7

TVA construction projects employment, and impacts on nearby areas, survey rpt series, 9806–7

TVA employment of minorities and women, by detailed occupation, pay level, and grade, FY83 and goals for FY84, annual rpt, 9804–17

Uranium exploration, land acquisition expenditures, and employment, various periods 1966-83 and planned 1984-85, annual rpt, 3164–65

Uranium mining operations, finances, and costs of alternative methods to meet emissions standards, for industry and selected mines, selected years 1948-90, 9188–96

Uranium prices, deliveries, trade, stocks, secondary marketing, investment, and employment, selected years 1967-83 and for commitments to 2001, annual rpt, 3164–66

Uranium reserves and mining and milling industries operations and finances, with selected foreign comparisons, various periods 1964-83 and projected to 2000, 3008–95

Wood, paper, and printed matter trade, tariffs, and industry operating data, TSUSA commodity rpt series, 9885–2

see also Agricultural labor

see also Earnings, specific industries

see also Federal employees

see also Health occupations

see also Industry wage surveys

see also Payroll

see also State and local employees

see also under By Industry in the "Index by Categories"

see also under By Occupation in the "Index by Categories"

Employment Cost Index

see Labor cost indexes

Employment Service

see Employment and Training Administration

Employment services

Applications and placements of public agencies, Monthly Labor Review, 6722–1.4

Budget of US, effects of Reagan Admin policy changes, by detailed program, FY85, annual rpt, 104–21

Census of Population, 1980: detailed socioeconomic and demographic characteristics, by age, sex, race, Hispanic origin, occupation, and industry, State rpt series, 2531–4

Census of Service Industries, 1982: employment, establishments, receipts, and payroll, by SIC 2- to 4-digit kind of business, SMSA, county, and city, State rpt series, 2391–1

County Business Patterns: establishments, employees, and payrolls, by SIC 4-digit industry and county, 1981, annual State rpt series, 2326–8

Index by Subjects and Names

County Business Patterns: establishments, employees, and payrolls, by SIC 4-digit industry and county, 1982, annual State rpt series, 2326–6

Employment, earnings, and hours, by SIC 4-digit nonfarm industry, monthly 1974-Feb 1984, annual update, 6744–4

Fed Govt aid to State and local govts, expenditures, and direct payments, by program, agency, and State, FY83, annual rpt, 2464–2

Fed Govt employment and training program funding under Job Training Partnership Act, and required matching funds, for 3 programs by State, 1984/85, press release, 6408–58

Fed Govt financial and nonfinancial domestic aid, 1984 annual comprehensive catalog, 104–5

Fed Govt grants-in-aid for 13 program areas, FY82-84, annual article, 10042–1.402

Fed Govt programs and mgmt cost control proposals, 3-year savings by function and agency, and financial and operating data, 1960s-81, 16908–1.27

Franchise business opportunities, by firm and kind of business, 1984 annual listing, 2044–27

Franchises of firms engaged in distribution of goods and services by kind of business, establishments by State, and sales, 1982-84, annual rpt, 2014–5

Homeless population and characteristics, and temporary shelter operations, use, and user characteristics, by region and selected city, 1983, 5188–108

Input-output structure of US economy, detailed interindustry transactions for 537 industries, and components of final demand, 1977 benchmark data, 2708–17

Labor Dept activities and staff, CETA participants characteristics, and employment service and unemployment insurance activities by State, FY83, annual rpt, 6304–1

Labor legislation enacted by 48 States, DC, and Guam, 1983, annual summary article, 6722–1.406

Railroad employee benefits and beneficiaries by type, benefit program finances, and railroad employees and payroll, FY83, annual rpt, 9704–1

State and local govt productivity measurement, with background data and output indexes for 7 govt services, various periods 1955-82, 6728–27

State govt social services spending by type and funding source, and admin of Fed Govt block grants, for 13 States, selected years FY80-84, GAO rpt, 26121–76

Unemployed displaced workers training and placement program of Fed Govt, funding and enrollment for 13 States and Guam, June 1984, press release, 6408–61

VA employment services for disabled veterans with VA vocational rehabilitation training, and veteran characteristics and employment, by regional office, as of 1983, GAO rpt, 26121–78

Employment Standards Administration

American Samoa minimum wage rates, employment, earnings, and benefits, by establishment and industry, Nov 1983, biennial rpt, 6504–6

Index by Subjects and Names

Black lung benefit claims and benefits by State, and trust fund receipts by source and disbursements, 1982, annual rpt, 6504–3

Cost control proposals for Fed Govt programs and mgmt, 3-year savings by function and agency, and financial and operating data, 1960s-81, 16908–1.3

Fraud and abuse in Labor Dept programs, audits and investigations, 1st half FY84, semiannual rpt, 6302–2

Workers compensation law provisions of States and Fed Govt, by jurisdiction, as of July 1984, semiannual rpt, 6502–1

Workers compensation under Fed Govt-administered programs, coverage, expenditures, and claims and dispositions by district, FY83, annual compilation, 6504–5

see also Women's Bureau

Encephalitis

see Infective and parasitic diseases

Endangered species

- Alaska Arctic Natl Wildlife Refuge resources, resident and visitor activities, and environmental impacts of energy exploration, 1983, annual update rpt, 5504–26
- Coastal environmental and wildlife characteristics, use, and mgmt, for individual ecosystems, series, 5506–9
- Coastal environmental characteristics, fish, wildlife, and use, and population socioeconomic data, for individual areas, series, 5506–4
- Environmental quality and protection programs, costs, and Fed Govt enforcement, 1983, detailed annual rpt, 484–1
- Exports and imports of endangered species and plants including reexports of live specimens and products, by purpose, country, and species, 1982, annual rpt, 5504–19
- Fed Govt programs and mgmt cost control proposals, 3-year savings by function and agency, and financial and operating data, 1960s-81, 16908–1.22
- Fish and Wildlife Service conservation and research project descriptions and results, by program, FY83, annual rpt, 5504–20
- Forest, range, and associated waters use and mgmt assessment, and environmental impacts of Forest Service program options, 1977-2030 and trends from 1920, 1208–24
- Genetic resource (plant and animal) conservation, commercial uses, causes of depletion, and geographic sources, 1984 rpt, 5548–13
- Interior Dept programs, activities, and funding, various periods 1967-84, last issue of annual rpt, 5304–13
- Marine Mammal Protection Act admin and populations, strandings, and catch permits by type and applicant, by species and location, Apr 1983-Mar 1984, annual rpt, 2164–11
- Marine mammals protection activities and Fed Govt funding, population status, and research, 1983, annual rpt, 5504–12
- Marine mammals protection, Fed Govt and intl regulatory and research activities, with bibl, 1983, annual rpt, 14734–1

Marine vertebrates off southeastern US coast, abundance and seasonal distribution, with oil and gas dev effects and lease status, early 1980s, 5508–85

Natl Forest System wildlife habitat and fishery improvements, use, and game population and harvest by species and forest, by region, FY83, annual rpt, 1204–31

Endocrine diseases

see Metabolic and endocrine diseases

Energy and Environmental Analysis, Inc.

"Industrial Energy Productivity Project, Final Report", 3308–66

Energy conservation

- Biomass Fuels Program of TVA, technologies and processes dev, costs, and resource requirements, 1970s-90s, series, 9806–9
- Bonneville Power Admin energy conservation program activities and funding data, FY82 and estimated FY83-87, 3228–2
- Budget of US, effects of Reagan Admin policy changes, by detailed program, FY85, annual rpt, 104–21
- Buildings (commercial) energy use under alternative heating, cooling, and air conditioning systems and control strategies, for 6 cities, 1983 rpt, 2218–68
- Buildings (nonresidential) energy use, expenditures, and conservation, by building characteristics, EIA survey series, 3166–8
- Connecticut utility group housing energy conservation program, cost effectiveness and characteristics of participants and nonparticipants, 1980-82, 3308–77
- Conservation and energy efficiency measures, use, and prices, by fuel type, end-use sector, selected industry, and region, 1960-83, annual rpt, 3164–73
- Conservation, use, production, trade, supply, and DOE activities, by energy type, FY83, annual rpt, 3024–2
- DOE energy conservation aid activities, funding, and grants by State, by program, FY84, annual rpt, 3304–21
- DOE in-house energy use, conservation investments, and savings, by type of use and fuel and field office, FY83, annual rpt, 3024–3
- Electric appliance energy efficiency ratios and load control device costs, 1984 rpt, 26358–99
- Electric power plants and industrial facilities prohibited from oil and gas primary use, and exemption petitions, by facility, with summary fuel use, 1983, annual rpt, 3104–8
- Energy supply/demand and prices, by energy source and end-use sector and for 7 electric utilities, 1981-2000 with trends from 1960s, 3008–93
- Fed Govt energy conservation grants to public and nonprofit private instns, by building type and State, 1983, annual rpt, 3304–15
- Fed Govt energy programs proposed budget appropriations, by office or dept and function, FY84-85, annual rpt, 3004–14
- Fed Govt energy use and efficiency, by agency and fuel type, FY83, annual rpt, 3304–22

Energy conservation

- Fed Govt programs and mgmt cost control proposals, 3-year savings by function and agency, and financial and operating data, 1960s-81, 16908–1.29
- Foreign minerals production, reserves, and industry role in domestic economy and world supply, country and world region rpt series, 5606–1
- Govt census, 1982: State govt payments to local govts, by program, source of funds, level of govt, and State, with trends from 1902, 2460–3
- Housing (earth-sheltered) design, energy efficiency, natural and nuclear hazard reduction, and costs, by selected SMSA, 1983 rpt, 3308–71
- Housing (low-income) energy aid of Fed Govt, allocations and average benefits in 13 States, and public interest group assessment, FY81-83, GAO rpt, 26121–75
- Housing (low-income) energy aid of Fed Govt, by income, aid type, and State, FY83, annual rpt, 4744–3.13
- Housing (multifamily rental) energy use and costs, conservation effect on rental marketing, and effect of utility bill payment methods on conservation efforts, 1970s-80s, 3308–73
- Housing electricity use and savings, methodology for assessment using utility billing data, 1984 rpt, 3308–76
- Housing energy bills and departures from normal by fuel type, and heating and cooling degree days by State, by census div, monthly rpt, 2152–11, 2152–12
- Housing energy conservation devices installation, utility loan program cost effectiveness, and household participation characteristics, Minnesota study, 1980-83, 3308–72
- Housing energy conservation programs of utilities, actual and predicted gas savings by conservation measure, Minnesota study, 1980-83, 3308–74
- Housing energy conservation programs of utilities, financing, costs, participation, and energy savings, various periods 1981-84, hearing, 21368–54
- Housing energy conservation programs of utilities under natl conservation act, cost effectiveness and participating household characteristics, 1980s, 3308–69
- Housing energy use, costs, expenditures, and conservation, and household and housing characteristics, survey series, 3166–7
- Housing solar energy and energy conservation projects, HUD grants by State and outlying area, 1984 press release, 5006–3.36
- Income tax returns of corporations, detailed income and tax items by industry, 1981, annual rpt, 8304–4
- Income tax returns of individuals, by filing and deduction characteristics and income level, 1983, annual article, 8302–2.414
- Income tax returns of individuals by tax return item, State, and occupation, and income by source and tax owed, by income level, selected years 1916-80, conf papers, 8308–28.1
- Industrial electric power demand model estimates, economic indicators, and supporting data for 5 industries, 1960s-80 with projections to 2000, 3008–87

Energy conservation

Industrial energy demand, forecasting model description, detailed technology specifications, and energy use, for 27 SIC 2- to 4-digit industries, 1970s-80 and projected to 2000, 3308–66

Manufacturing energy efficiency progress, and energy use by type, by SIC 2-digit industry, 1982, annual rpt, 3304–8

OECD crude oil consumption related to prices, conservation, and real dollar exchange rates, for 7 countries, various periods 1975-83, article, 9379–1.405

Pacific Northwest electricity consumption and prices by end-use sector, and economic and demographic data, 1960s-83 and projected to 2005, annual rpt, 3224–2

R&D industry funding and employment of scientists and engineers, by industry group, firm size, and funding source, 1956-82, annual rpt, 9627–21

Research publications on energy of DOE and other sources, monthly listing, 3002–2

Scientists and engineers employed in energy-related fields, supply/demand and effects of R&D funding, by energy type, employer type, field, and age, 1962-91, annual rpt, 3004–19

State govt energy conservation programs, Fed Govt financial and technical aid, and reported energy savings, by State, 1983, annual rpt, 3304–1

Transportation census, 1982: trucks, by detailed characteristics, miles traveled, and type of product carried, State rpt series, 2573–1

Transportation energy use by mode, fuel supplies, and demographic and economic determinants of vehicle use, 1970s-83, annual rpt, 3304–5

Transportation finances, operations, vehicles, equipment, accidents, and energy use and transport, by mode of transport, 1955-84, annual rpt, 7304–2

Trucks (heavy) energy use, efficiency, and conservation technologies, selected years 1958-82 and projected to 2000, 3308–70

TVA power program finances and operations, by plant and distributor, FY83, annual rpt, 9804–23

see also Fuel allocation

see also Insulation

Energy consumption

see Business energy use

see Energy conservation

see Housing energy use

see Transportation energy use

see Energy resources (for total consumption)

see under names of specific types of energy

Energy exploration and drilling

Aerial survey R&D publications, and sources of natural resource and environmental data gathered by air- and spacecraft, quarterly listing, 9502–7

Alaska Arctic Natl Wildlife Refuge resources, resident and visitor activities, and environmental impacts of energy exploration, 1983, annual update rpt, 5504–26

Alaska minerals resources, production, claims on wildlife refuges, oil and gas leases, and exploratory wells, with maps and bibl, 1983, annual rpt, 5664–11

Alaska potential oil exports to Japan, costs and benefits, with background data on oil prices, Pacific Basin supply/demand, and tankers, various periods 1918-99, hearings, 25388–45

Atlantic Ocean Georges Bank oil and gas drilling on Fed Govt leases, marine pollution problems, 1983 hearings, 21568–36

Census of Population, 1980: detailed socioeconomic and demographic characteristics, by age, sex, race, Hispanic origin, occupation, and industry, State rpt series, 2531–4

Census of Population, 1980: labor force, by sex, detailed occupation, and region, with comparison to 1970 census, supplementary rpt, 2535–1.12

Coal exploration licenses issued by State, and Interior Dept drilling costs and holes drilled, FY76-83, 11128–1

Coastal environmental and wildlife characteristics, use, and mgmt, for individual ecosystems, series, 5506–9

Coastal environmental characteristics, fish, wildlife, and use, and population socioeconomic data, for individual areas, series, 5506–4

Construction industry activity, employment and earnings, prices, Federal aid, and foreign contracts, 1970s-83 with projections to 1988, annual article, 2012–1.402

County Business Patterns: establishments, employees, and payrolls, by SIC 4-digit industry and county, 1981, annual State rpt series, 2326–8

County Business Patterns: establishments, employees, and payrolls, by SIC 4-digit industry and county, 1982, annual State rpt series, 2326–6

DOE R&D projects and funding at natl labs, universities, and other instns, FY84, annual summary rpt, 3004–18.4

Employment by detailed occupation, for 29 SIC 2-digit nonmanufacturing industries, 1981 BLS survey, 6748–60

Employment in regionally concentrated and all industries, and population size, by State, 1970-82, article, 6722–1.413

Energy production, dev, and distribution firms revenues and income, quarterly rpt, 3162–38

Energy R&D and technology publications, quarterly listing, 9502–4

Energy supply/demand and prices, by fuel type and consuming sector with foreign comparisons, 1949-83, annual rpt, 3164–74

Energy supply/demand and prices, by fuel type, sector, and end use, with foreign comparisons, 1960-83 and projected to 1995, annual summary rpt, 3164–76

Foreign oil exploratory and dev wells drilled, historic data, country rpt series, 3166–9

Income tax returns of corporations, detailed income and tax items by industry, 1981, annual rpt, 8304–4

Income tax returns of oil and gas extraction partnerships, detailed data, 1981 estimates, annual article, 8302–2.404

Income tax returns of sole proprietorships, detailed data by industry div and selected industry group, 1981, annual rpt, 8304–7

Index by Subjects and Names

Mineral industries census, 1982: financial and operating data, by SIC 2- to 4-digit industry, preliminary summary rpt, 2511–2.1

Mineral industries census, 1982: financial and operating data, including materials consumed, by SIC 4-digit industry and State, preliminary rpt, 2511–1.7

Natural gas interstate pipeline company detailed financial and operating data, by firm, 1983, annual rpt, 3164–38

Natural gas prices, reserves, consumption, and production, projected under alternative price controls 1983-95 with market data for various periods 1970-Mar 1984, 3008–96

Natural gas production, wells drilled, and contract prices, by Natural Gas Policy Act section, producer and well characteristics, State, and field, selected years 1968-83, 3168–90

Natural gas supply, contract prices, pipeline operations and finances, and residential use, various periods 1966-1983/84, 3168–89

Natural gas well completions, 1975-82, annual rpt, 3084–9

Naval Petroleum and Oil Shale Reserves production, dev, ownership, leasing, sales by purchaser, and Fed Govt revenues, by site, FY83, annual rpt, 3004–22

Oil and gas companies production and exploration detailed expenditures, revenues, operating ratios, and sales volume, 1982, annual Current Industrial Rpt, 2506–8.11

Oil and gas drilling costs and cost indexes for onshore wells and dry holes, by depth and region, 1983-84, annual rpt, 3164–67

Oil and gas drilling equipment imports, effect on US steel industry, investigation with background financial and operating data, 1984 rpt, 9886–4.79

Oil and gas exploratory rigs in operation, wells and footage drilled, and seismic exploration crews, monthly rpt, 3162–24.5

Oil and gas extraction production workers, wages, hours, and benefits, by occupation, region, and for 5 States, June 1982 survey, 6787–6.203

Oil and gas field itemized equipment and operating costs and cost indexes, for 10 producing areas, 1981-83, annual rpt, 3164–45

Oil and gas finances by firm, and effect of income and excise tax provisions on firms, Fed Govt revenues, and investor tax returns, 1980 and projected to 1992, hearing, 21788–132

Oil and gas OCS drilling rigs by country, rig losses, and worker injury and death rates, various periods 1966-83, hearing, 21568–35

Oil and gas OCS reserves of Fed Govt, leasing and exploration activities, production, revenues, and costs, by ocean region, FY83, annual rpt, 5734–4

Oil and gas well drilling and servicing occupational fatalities, circumstances, and OSHA safety standards violated, by type of incident and equipment used, 1977-81, 6606–2.11

Oil and gas 5-year OCS leasing plan and proposed sale off California coast, acreage, costs, and benefits, various periods 1953-2006, hearing, 21448–30

Index by Subjects and Names

Oil enhanced recovery technologies use and environmental impacts, by oil field, county, and State, 1970s-80 and projected to 2000, 3408–29

Oil field equipment from 5 countries, injury to US industry from foreign subsidized imports and less than fair value sales, investigation with background financial and operating data, 1984 rpt, 9886–19.11

Oil, gas, and minerals dev, under Fed Govt OCS leases, with production, revenues, reserves, and oil spills, by State and ocean region, 1950s-82, annual rpt, 5734–3

Producers finances and operations, by energy type for US firms domestic and foreign operations, 1974-82, annual rpt, 3164–44.2

Public land acreage and use, and Land Mgmt Bur activities and finances, annual State rpt series, 5724–11

Public utility holding company finances, securities issued, and subsidiaries by type, by firm, FY83, annual rpt, 9734–2.6

Southeastern US water supply and quality, with background socioeconomic data, for 8 States, 1960s-2020 with trends from 1930, 9208–119

Uranium exploration, land acquisition expenditures, and employment, various periods 1966-83 and planned 1984-85, annual rpt, 3164–65

Uranium prices, deliveries, trade, stocks, secondary marketing, investment, and employment, selected years 1967-83 and for commitments to 2001, annual rpt, 3164–66

Uranium reserves and mining and milling industries operations and finances, with selected foreign comparisons, various periods 1964-83 and projected to 2000, 3008–95

Energy exports and imports

Electric power transactions of US with Canada and Mexico, by utility and US region, 1983, annual rpt, 3104–10

Environmental quality and protection programs, costs, and Fed Govt enforcement, 1983, detailed annual rpt, 484–1

Eximbank credits for energy-related products and services, by country and firm, 1982, annual rpt, 9254–3

Exports and imports of US, and trade balance, by major commodity group, selected country, and world area, with seasonal adjustments, monthly rpt, 2422–6

Exports and imports of US, by commodity group, world area, selected country, US coastal area and port, and mode of transport, with seasonal adjustments, monthly rpt, 2422–9

Exports and imports of US by country, and trade shifts by commodity, USITC quarterly monitoring rpt, 9882–9

Exports and imports of US, totals and as percent of domestic production, by SIC 2- to 5-digit commodity, 1981, annual rpt, 2424–3

Exports of US, detailed commodities by country of destination, monthly rpt, 2422–3

Exports of US, detailed Schedule B commodities by country of destination, 1983, annual rpt, 2424–9

Exports of US, detailed Schedule E commodities by mode of transport and world area and country of destination, 1983, annual rpts, 2424–5

Foreign and US energy production, trade, and reserves, and oil and refined products supply and prices, by country, 1973-83, annual rpt, 3164–50

Foreign minerals production, reserves, and industry role in domestic economy and world supply, country and world region rpt series, 5606–1

Great Lakes trade, by SITC 3-digit commodity, port, vessel type, world area, and country, 1982, annual rpt, 7744–3

Imports of US, detailed Schedule A commodities by country and world area of origin, and mode of transport, 1983, annual rpts, 2424–2

Imports of US, detailed TSUSA commodities by country of origin, 1983, annual rpt, 2424–4

Methanol fuel for autos, regulatory barriers to market dev, with supply/demand and auto fleet use and fuel economy, mid-1970s-82 and projected to 2000, GAO rpt, 26113–112

Minerals Yearbook, 1982, Vol 3 preprints: foreign country reviews of production, trade, and policies, by commodity, annual rpt series, 5604–17

Minerals Yearbook, 1983, Vol 3 preprints: foreign country reviews of production, trade, and policies, by commodity, annual rpt series, 5604–23

OECD trade, total and for 4 major countries, and US trade by country, by commodity, 1972-82, annual world region rpt series, 244–13

Supply/demand and price forecasts, by fuel type, quarterly rpt, 3162–34

Supply/demand and prices, by fuel type and consuming sector with foreign comparisons, 1949-83, annual rpt, 3164–74

Supply/demand and prices, by fuel type, sector, and end use, detailed trends and projections 1973-95, annual rpt, 3164–75

Supply/demand and prices, by fuel type, sector, and end use, with foreign comparisons, 1960-83 and projected to 1995, annual summary rpt, 3164–76

Uranium mining operations, finances, and costs of alternative methods to meet emissions standards, for industry and selected mines, selected years 1948-90, 9188–96

Uranium prices, deliveries, trade, stocks, secondary marketing, investment, and employment, selected years 1967-83 and for commitments to 2001, annual rpt, 3164–66

Uranium production, trade, and reserves, quarterly compilation, 3352–3

Uranium reserves and mining and milling industries operations and finances, with selected foreign comparisons, various periods 1964-83 and projected to 2000, 3008–95

see also Coal exports and imports

see also Natural gas exports and imports

see also Petroleum exports and imports

Energy Information Administration

Energy Information Administration

Budget appropriations proposed for Fed Govt energy programs, by office or dept and function, FY84-85, annual rpt, 3004–14

Coal, coke, and breeze supply/demand, prices, trade, and stocks, by end-use sector and State, quarterly rpt with articles, 3162–37

Coal production and mines by county, prices, productivity, miners, reserves, and stocks, by mining method and State, 1982-83, annual rpt, 3164–25

Coal production and stocks, and electric utility generation, capacity, and coal use, alternative estimates 1977-82, annual rpt, 3164–63

Coal production and stocks by district, and shipments by district of origin, State of destination, consuming sector, and mode of transport, quarterly rpt, 3162–8

Coal production by State and region, trade, consumption, and stocks, weekly rpt, 3162–1

Coal supply/demand, projected 1983-95 with summary trends from 1865, annual rpt, 3164–68

Data collection and analysis of EIA, Jan 1982-Sept 1983, GAO annual rpt, 26104–14

Electric power plant (coal-fired) capacity addition estimation to forecast coal demand, methodology and input data, series, 3166–11

Electric power plant (steam) fuel deliveries, costs, and quality, by fuel type, State, and utility, 1983, annual rpt, 3164–42

Electric power plant capacity, production, retail sales, and fuel stocks, use, and costs, by State, 1979-83, annual rpt, 3164–11

Electric power plant capital and operating detailed costs, capacity, and fuel use, by plant, plant type, utility, and State, 1982, annual rpt, 3164–9

Electric power plants, by capacity, fuel used, unit type, region, State, and county, for plants added and retired, 1983 and planned through 1993, annual rpt, 3164–36

Electric power rate schedules, by user type, utility, and city, Jan 1984, annual rpt, 3164–40

Electric utilities privately owned, capital investment, finances, equity performance, and operating characteristics, 1950-82 with supply estimates to 2010, 3168–87

Electric utilities privately owned, common stock performance measures for companies with and without nuclear facilities, 1963-82, 3168–88

Electric utilities privately owned, detailed financial and operating data by company, with summary data for other distributors by type, 1982, annual rpt, 3164–23

Electric utilities publicly owned, detailed financial and operating data by company, annual rpt, discontinued, 3164–24

Electric utility fuel cost, quality, use, receipts, and stocks, and power plant production, by energy source, State and utility, quarterly rpt, 3162–39

Electric utility production, fuel consumption, stocks, and costs by fuel type, and sales, by State, monthly rpt, 3162–35

Energy Information Administration

Energy Info Admin surveys, data analysis models, and publications, 1983, annual rpt, 3164–29

Energy prices and expenditures for fuels and electricity, by consuming sector, State, and fuel type, 1970-81, annual rpt, 3164–64

Energy producers finances and operations, by energy type for US firms domestic and foreign operations, 1974-82, annual rpt, 3164–44

Energy production, dev, and distribution firms revenues and income, quarterly rpt, 3162–38

Energy production, reserves, and prices, by energy type, and selected indicators of energy use, by State, 1982-83 with selected comparisons from 1971, annual rpt, 3164–60

Energy supply/demand and price forecasts, by fuel type, quarterly rpt, 3162–34

Energy supply/demand and prices, by energy resource and major producing and consuming country and sector, detailed data, monthly rpt, 3162–24

Energy supply/demand and prices, by fuel type and consuming sector with foreign comparisons, 1949-83, annual rpt, 3164–74

Energy supply/demand and prices, by fuel type, sector, and end use, detailed trends and projections 1973-95, annual rpt, 3164–75

Energy supply/demand and prices, by fuel type, sector, and end use, with foreign comparisons, 1960-83 and projected to 1995, annual summary rpt, 3164–76

Energy use, by economic sector, State, census div, and detailed energy resource, 1960-82, State Energy Data System annual rpt, 3164–39

Energy use in nonresidential buildings, expenditures, and conservation, by building characteristics, EIA survey series, 3166–8

Energy use, per capita and by economic sector, State, and major energy resource, 1960-82, State Energy Data System annual supplement, 3164–55

Energy use, prices, and conservation and efficiency measures, by fuel type, end-use sector, selected industry, and region, 1960-83, annual rpt, 3164–73

Foreign and US coal reserves, production, demand indicators, and trade, by country, selected years 1973-82 and alternative trade projections to 1995, annual rpt, 3164–77

Foreign and US energy production, trade, and reserves, and oil and refined products supply and prices, by country, 1973-83, annual rpt, 3164–50

Foreign oil reserves, production, and resource lifespan under alternative production rates, historical and projected, country rpt series, 3166–9

Housing energy use, costs, expenditures, and conservation, and household and housing characteristics, survey series, 3166–7

Hydroelectric power plants construction and production costs, capacities, and hydraulic characteristics, by plant, annual rpt, discontinued, 3164–37

Natural and supplemental gas production, prices, trade, use, reserves, and pipeline company finances, by firm and State, monthly rpt with articles, 3162–4

Natural gas consumer prices, by consumer sector, census div, and State, 1983, preliminary annual rpt, 3164–4

Natural gas interstate pipeline company detailed financial and operating data, by firm, 1983, annual rpt, 3164–38

Natural gas interstate pipeline company supplies, reserves, production, purchases, and contracts, by firm, 1983 with projected deliverability to 2003, annual rpt, 3164–33

Natural gas interstate pipeline sales, total and under minimum fee contract provision, by service type, contract date, and region, 1981, 3168–91

Natural gas price decontrol effect on supply/demand and prices, 1970s-83, 3168–50

Natural gas production and trade by State, and underground storage changes, EIA estimates based on alternative data sources, 1980-81, 3008–90

Natural gas production, wells drilled, and contract prices, by Natural Gas Policy Act section, producer and well characteristics, State, and field, selected years 1968-83, 3168–90

Natural gas supply, contract prices, pipeline operations and finances, and residential use, various periods 1966-1983/84, 3168–89

Nuclear power plant construction and operation status, and capacity, by plant, region, State, and selected country, 1983 and projected to 2020, annual rpt, 3164–57

Nuclear power plant construction costs and status, and capacity, by plant and State, as of Mar 1984, annual rpt, 3164–69

Nuclear power plant spent fuel and demand for uranium and enrichment services, for US and non-Communist country groups, 1983 and projected to 2020, annual rpt, 3164–72

OECD energy prices and taxes by energy source and end-use sector, for US and 9 countries, quarterly 1979-83, annual rpt, 3164–71

Oil and gas drilling costs and cost indexes for onshore wells and dry holes, by depth and region, 1983-84, annual rpt, 3164–67

Oil and gas field itemized equipment and operating costs and cost indexes, for 10 producing areas, 1981-83, annual rpt, 3164–45

Oil and gas fields by State and EIA field code, 1983, annual listing, 3164–70

Oil and refined products and natural gas liquids supply/demand, trade, stocks, and refining, by detailed product, State, and PAD district, monthly rpt with articles, 3162–6

Oil and refined products and natural gas liquids supply/demand, trade, stocks, and refining, by detailed product, State, and PAD district, and refineries in US and territories, 1983 annual rpt, 3164–2

Oil and refined products supply/demand, refinery capacity and use, and OPEC, non-OPEC, and spot market prices, weekly rpt, 3162–32

Oil, gas, and gas liquids reserves and production, by State and selected substate area, 1983, annual rpt, 3164–46

Index by Subjects and Names

Oil production, total and for surveillance fields, by State and inland and Federal offshore area, 1980-82, biennial rpt, 3164–58

Oil refined products sales of gas plant operators, refiners, and resellers, price and volume for 13 products, by end-use sector, PAD district, and State, monthly rpt, 3162–11

Solar collector and photovoltaic module production, sales, and use, with listing of manufacturers, 1983, annual rpt, 3164–62

Uranium exploration, land acquisition expenditures, and employment, various periods 1966-83 and planned 1984-85, annual rpt, 3164–65

Uranium prices, deliveries, trade, stocks, secondary marketing, investment, and employment, selected years 1967-83 and for commitments to 2001, annual rpt, 3164–66

Wood fuel consumption, by end-use sector, SIC 2-digit industry, region, State, and selected industrial and power plant, 1980-83, biennial rpt, 3164–78

Energy prices

Biomass Fuels Program of TVA, technologies and processes dev, costs, and resource requirements, 1970s-90s, series, 9806–9

Buildings (nonresidential) energy use, expenditures, and conservation, by building characteristics, EIA survey series, 3166–8

CPI by detailed component, for US city average, 28 SMSAs, and 4 regions by population size, monthly rpt, 6762–2

CPI components relative importance, for selected SMSAs, and US city average by region and population size, 1983, annual rpt, 6884–1

Electric power plant (steam) fuel deliveries, costs, and quality, by fuel type, State, and utility, 1983, annual rpt, 3164–42

Farm production inputs, land mgmt, and environmental effects, for 4 crops, 1940s-80 and projected to 2010, 9188–94

Farmers prices received for major products and paid for farm inputs and living items, by commodity and State, monthly rpt, 1629–1

Food prices (farm-retail), marketing cost components, and industry finances and productivity, selected years 1967-83, annual rpt, 1544–9

Fossil fuels, prices of imported and domestic oil and wholesale and retail fuels, and dealer margins, monthly rpt, 3162–24.9

Gasohol and ethanol plant capacity and production, tax exemptions and sales by State, and prices, 1983, annual rpt, 3304–9

Gasohol production and costs by feedstock, prices, and market penetration rates and excise tax exemption by State, 1983, article, 1561–16.404

Home heating costs of low-income households, natural gas price decontrol effects, aid programs, and gas supply/demand data, by income level and State, 1970s-95, hearing, 25148–26

Housing energy bills and departures from normal by fuel type, and heating and cooling degree days by State, by census div, monthly rpt, 2152–11, 2152–12

Index by Subjects and Names

Housing energy prices and demand as factors in housing supply, regression results from FHA new-home sales records, 1974-78, 9306–1.2

Housing energy use, costs, expenditures, and conservation, and household and housing characteristics, survey series, 3166–7

Industrial electric power cogeneration in 5 industries, and fuel use and utility supply/demand effects, by region, 1983-93, 3008–92

Industrial electric power demand model estimates, economic indicators, and supporting data for 5 industries, 1960s-80 with projections to 2000, 3008–87

Inflation rate, money supply growth, and food and energy prices, various periods 1970-2nd qtr 1984, article, 9391–1.420

Minerals Yearbook, 1982, Vol 3 preprints: foreign country reviews of production, trade, and policies, by commodity, annual rpt series, 5604–17

Minerals Yearbook, 1983, Vol 3 preprints: foreign country reviews of production, trade, and policies, by commodity, annual rpt series, 5604–23

OECD energy prices and taxes by energy source and end-use sector, for US and 9 countries, quarterly 1979-83, annual rpt, 3164–71

Port dev costs and financing through user fees, and shipping industry impact on local economy, by State, other area, industry, commodity, and port, 1970s-82, hearings, 21568–34.1

Price indexes (consumer and producer) changes for selected items, and changes in CPI for selected services, 1982-83, article, 6722–1.429

Prices and expenditures for fuels and electricity, by consuming sector, State, and fuel type, 1970-81, annual rpt, 3164–64

Prices and supply/demand, by energy source and end-use sector and for 7 electric utilities, 1981-2000 with trends from 1960s, 3008–93

Prices and supply/demand, by fuel and consuming sector with foreign comparisons, 1949-83, annual rpt, 3164–74

Prices and supply/demand, by fuel, sector, and end use, detailed trends and projections 1973-95, annual rpt, 3164–75

Prices and supply/demand, by fuel, sector, and end use, with foreign comparisons, 1960-83 and projected to 1995, annual summary rpt, 3164–76

Prices and supply/demand forecasts, by fuel, quarterly rpt, 3162–34

Prices, production, use, and reserves, by energy type, and selected indicators of energy use, by State, 1982-83 with selected comparisons from 1971, annual rpt, 3164–60

Prices, supply/demand, end use, and related technical and socioeconomic data, including impacts of US policy and intl devs, series, 3006–7

Prices, use, and conservation and efficiency measures, by fuel type, end-use sector, selected industry, and region, 1960-83, annual rpt, 3164–73

Producer Price Index, by major commodity group and subgroup, and processing stage, monthly press release, 6762–5

Producer prices and indexes, by stage of processing and detailed commodity, monthly rpt, 6762–6

Producer prices and indexes, by stage of processing and detailed commodity, monthly 1983, annual supplement, 6764–2

Retail prices for energy and food, and housing fuel consumption, by region, and for 28 SMSAs and US city average, monthly press release, 6762–8

Transportation finances, operations, vehicles, equipment, accidents, and energy use and transport, by mode of transport, 1955-84, annual rpt, 7304–2

Uranium enrichment plants of DOE, production and other costs and selling prices, FY71-83 and projected to FY94, GAO rpt, 26113–137

Uranium mining operations, finances, and costs of alternative methods to meet emissions standards, for industry and selected mines, selected years 1948-90, 9188–96

Uranium prices, deliveries, trade, stocks, secondary marketing, investment, and employment, selected years 1967-83 and for commitments to 2001, annual rpt, 3164–66

Uranium reserves and mining and milling industries operations and finances, with selected foreign comparisons, various periods 1964-83 and projected to 2000, 3008–95

Wood acquired and used for home heating, by household characteristics and wood sources, 1980/81, 1208–204

see also Coal prices
see also Electric power prices
see also Gasoline
see also Natural gas prices
see also Petroleum prices

Energy production

see Energy production costs
see Energy resources (for total production)
see under names of specific types of energy

Energy production costs

Alcohol fuel (ethanol) production in Tennessee Valley, feedstocks, facilities, tax incentives, and related farming data, by State, 1970s-83 and projected to 1992, 9808–69

Alcohol fuel production costs, related employment, and Fed Govt subsidies and impact on farm income, selected years 1978-90, GAO rpt, 26113–140

Biomass Fuels Program of TVA, technologies and processes dev, costs, and resource requirements, 1970s-90s, series, 9806–9

Coal Fed Govt leases, acreage, production, and prices, by State, and legal and mgmt issues, 1970s-83 with production projections to 2000, 11128–1

Electric power plant (nuclear and coal-fired) construction itemized cost estimates, and investment per kilowatt for 20 cities, 1980s-95, 9638–52

Electric power plant capacity, production, retail sales, and fuel stocks, use, and costs, by State, 1979-83, annual rpt, 3164–11

Electric power plant capital and operating detailed costs, capacity, and fuel use, by plant, plant type, utility, and State, 1982, annual rpt, 3164–9

Energy production costs

Electric power plants (steam), delivered cost of coal, residual oil, and natural gas, monthly rpt, 3162–24.9

Electric power rate schedules, by user type, utility, and city, Jan 1984, annual rpt, 3164–40

Electric utilities coal receipts, consumption, stocks, and delivered price, by State, weekly rpt, monthly data, 3162–1.2

Electric utilities privately owned, detailed financial and operating data by company, with summary data for other distributors by type, 1982, annual rpt, 3164–23

Electric utility fuel cost, quality, use, receipts, and stocks, and power plant production, by energy source, State and utility, quarterly rpt, 3162–39

Electric utility production, fuel consumption, stocks, and costs by fuel type, and sales, by State, monthly rpt, 3162–35

Electric utility rate minimization from improved efficiency, proposed FERC incentive program operations and costs, with comparisons to 3 State programs, 1950s-82, 3088–17

Energy supply/demand and prices, by fuel type and consuming sector with foreign comparisons, 1949-83, annual rpt, 3164–74

Energy supply/demand and prices, by fuel type, sector, and end use, with foreign comparisons, 1960-83 and projected to 1995, annual summary rpt, 3164–76

Gasohol production and costs by feedstock, prices, and market penetration rates and excise tax exemption by State, 1983, article, 1561–16.404

Income tax returns of corporations, detailed income and tax items by industry, 1981, annual rpt, 8304–4

Natural gas interstate pipeline company detailed financial and operating data, by firm, 1983, annual rpt, 3164–38

Natural gas pipeline and compressor station construction costs, 1979-82, annual rpt, 3084–3

Nuclear power and weapons policy, fuel supply/demand, waste disposal and siting, environmental effects of radiation, and public attitudes, 1970s-82 with projections to 2000, 3008–88

Nuclear power plant and reactor construction costs, by plant and reactor, for start-up dates 1960-82 and projected to 1995, 3006–7.5

Nuclear power plant capacity, generation, shutdowns, operation status and costs, and fuel, quarterly rpt, 3352–3

Nuclear power plant licensing 24-month delay, effect on utility financial performance and electric power prices, for plant completed May 1979, 9638–53

Oil and gas companies production and exploration detailed expenditures, revenues, operating ratios, and sales volume, 1982, annual Current Industrial Rpt, 2506–8.11

Oil and gas drilling costs and cost indexes for onshore wells and dry holes, by depth and region, 1983-84, annual rpt, 3164–67

Oil and gas field itemized equipment and operating costs and cost indexes, for 10 producing areas, 1981-83, annual rpt, 3164–45

Energy production costs

Oil and gas finances by firm, and effect of income and excise tax provisions on firms, Fed Govt revenues, and investor tax returns, 1980 and projected to 1992, hearing, 21788–132

Oil prices impact on US oil trade and energy-intensive industries, with US and foreign reserves and industry operations, 1950-82 and projected to 2020, 9886–4.69

Oil refineries financial and operating impacts from auto use of alcohol fuels, projected to 2000 with trends 1964-80, 3308–75

OPEC and OECD oil refinery itemized annual costs, under 3 financing assumptions, 1983 hearings, 25368–133.1

Producers finances and operations, by energy type for US firms domestic and foreign operations, 1974-82, annual rpt, 3164–44

Southwestern Fed Power System financial statements, electric power sales by customer, and project capacity, production, and costs, FY83, annual rpt, 3244–1

Uranium enrichment facilities operations, finances, uranium stocks, and energy use and capital investment by facility, FY83, annual rpt, 3354–7

Uranium enrichment plants of DOE, production and other costs and selling prices, FY71-83 and projected to FY94, GAO rpt, 26113–137

Uranium mining operations, finances, and costs of alternative methods to meet emissions standards, for industry and selected mines, selected years 1948-90, 9188–96

Uranium reserves and mining and milling industries operations and finances, with selected foreign comparisons, various periods 1964-83 and projected to 2000, 3008–95

Western Area Power Admin small-scale potential hydroelectric generation, site inventory, characteristics, and costs, by State and county, 1984 rpt, 3258–1

Western States oil shale dev projects in Green River area, production goals and cost estimates, as of 1983, article, 9381–1.409

Energy research and development

Carbon dioxide atmospheric levels, climatic effects and impacts of fossil and synthetic fuels use, deforestation, and land use patterns, research rpt series, 3406–3

Corporate income tax returns, detailed income and tax items by industry, 1981, annual rpt, 8304–4

Electric utilities privately owned, R&D expenditures, by company, 1978-82, annual rpt, 3164–23.2

Energy Info Admin data collection and analysis activities, Jan 1982-Sept 1983, GAO annual rpt, 26104–14

Energy R&D and technology publications, quarterly listing, 9502–4

Expenditures for R&D by source, and scientists education and employment, detailed data by field, selected years 1953-84, annual rpt, 9624–18

Higher education instns aid from DOE and DOE natl labs for energy R&D and scientific and engineering education, 1960s-84, 3008–89

Industry R&D funding and employment of scientists and engineers, by industry group, firm size, and funding source, 1956-82, annual rpt, 9627–21

Minerals Yearbook, 1982, Vol 3 preprints: foreign country reviews of production, trade, and policies, by commodity, annual rpt series, 5604–17

Minerals Yearbook, 1983, Vol 3 preprints: foreign country reviews of production, trade, and policies, by commodity, annual rpt series, 5604–23

Natural gas interstate pipeline company detailed financial and operating data, by firm, 1983, annual rpt, 3164–38

Nuclear industry nongovt employment by industry segment, occupation, and census div, and DOE and NRC nuclear employment, 1968-83, biennial rpt, 3004–11

Nuclear power plant safety standards and research, design, licensing, construction, operation, and finances, with data by reactor, bimonthly rpt, 3352–4

Nuclear reactors for domestic use and export by function, with owner, operating characteristics, and location, Apr 1984, semiannual listing, 3002–5

Nuclear reactors for research, experimental, and testing purposes, by location, monthly rpt, 9632–1.4

Producers finances and operations, by energy type for US firms domestic and foreign operations, 1974-82, annual rpt, 3164–44.2

R&D Fed Govt facilities and services available for private sector use, by field of science, 1984 biennial listing, 2224–4

Radioactive waste and spent fuel generation, inventory, disposal by site, reprocessing, and characteristics, by source, as of 1983 and projected to 2020, annual rpt, 3364–2

Scientists and engineers employed in energy-related fields, supply/demand and effects of R&D funding, by energy type, employer type, field, and age, 1962-91, annual rpt, 3004–19

Scientists and engineers in R&D, salary comparisons for DOE labs and non-DOE facilities, Aug 1982-Feb 1984, annual rpt, 3004–9

Scientists and engineers with doctorates engaged in energy-related work, demographic and employment characteristics by field, biennial rpt, suspended, 3004–2

Solar collector and photovoltaic module production, sales, and use, with listing of manufacturers, 1983, annual rpt, 3164–62

Soviet Union-US science and technology exchange projects, man-hours, and funding, by Fed Govt agency and activity type, FY81-82, 7008–41

TVA activities, financial and operating data by program and facility, and power sales by customer, FY83, annual rpt, 9804–1

Uranium resources research publications, 1976-83, listing, 3358–27

see also Biomass energy

see also Department of Energy National Laboratories

see also Energy exploration and drilling

see also Federal funding for energy programs

Index by Subjects and Names

see also Synthetic fuels

Energy Research and Development Administration

see Department of Energy

Energy reserves

Coastal environmental characteristics, fish, wildlife, and use, and population socioeconomic data, for individual areas, series, 5506–4

Foreign minerals production, reserves, and industry role in domestic economy and world supply, country and world region rpt series, 5606–1

Minerals Yearbook, 1982, Vol 3 preprints: foreign country reviews of production, trade, and policies, by commodity, annual rpt series, 5604–17

Minerals Yearbook, 1983, Vol 3 preprints: foreign country reviews of production, trade, and policies, by commodity, annual rpt series, 5604–23

Reserves, production, prices, and use, by energy type, and selected indicators of energy use, by State, 1982-83 with selected comparisons from 1971, annual rpt, 3164–60

Uranium mining operations, finances, and costs of alternative methods to meet emissions standards, for industry and selected mines, selected years 1948-90, 9188–96

Uranium production, trade, and reserves, quarterly compilation, 3352–3

Uranium reserves and mining and milling industries operations and finances, with selected foreign comparisons, various periods 1964-83 and projected to 2000, 3008–95

Uranium trade, demand, and reserves, 1980s-90, 3008–88

see also Coal reserves

see also Natural gas reserves

see also Petroleum reserves

Energy resources

AID activities and funding by project and function, FY85, and developing countries summary socioeconomic data, 1970s-83, by country, annual rpt, 9914–3

Air pollution levels for 5 pollutants, by detailed source, State, and Air Quality Control Region, 1981, annual rpt, 9194–7

Capacity utilization in 15 manufacturing industries, mining, electric and all utilities, and industrial materials including energy, monthly rpt, 9365–2.19

Central America mineral, energy, and water resources, and natural hazards to resource dev, by country, 1981 with trends from 1977, 5668–71

China economic conditions, agricultural and industrial production, trade, and domestic and foreign investment, 1980-85, 2048–106

Communist, OECD, and selected other countries energy reserves, production, and consumption, and oil trade and revenue, 1960s-83, annual rpt, 244–5.5

Consumption by fuel type, and estimated supply from renewable resources, 1977 and projected 2000, hearing, 21448–30

DOD procurement, prime contract awards by category, contract and contractor type, and service branch, FY74-1st half FY84, semiannual rpt, 3542–1

Index by Subjects and Names

Environmental quality and protection programs, costs, and Fed Govt enforcement, 1983, detailed annual rpt, 484–1

Fed Govt energy use and efficiency, by agency and fuel type, FY83, annual rpt, 3304–22

Fed Govt-owned real property inventory and costs, worldwide summary by location, agency, and use, 1983, annual rpt, 9454–5

Foreign and US energy production, trade, and reserves, and oil and refined products supply and prices, by country, 1973-83, annual rpt, 3164–50

Foreign minerals production, reserves, and industry role in domestic economy and world supply, country and world region rpt series, 5606–1

Manpower devs and studies for energy-related fields, series, 3006–8

Natl Energy Policy Plan, DOE implementation and effect on energy supply/demand, 1983-84, annual rpt, 3024–4

Natl Energy Policy Plan, energy supply, demand, and prices, by fuel and consuming sector, projected 1985-2010, biennial rpt, 3004–13

Pollution abatement capital and operating costs under Clean Air and Water Acts, for govts and selected industries, various periods 1970-2000, annual rpt, 9184–11

Production, reserves, and prices, by fuel type, and selected indicators of energy use, by State, 1982-83 with selected comparisons from 1971, annual rpt, 3164–60

Production, trade, supply, use, conservation, and DOE activities, by energy type, FY83, annual rpt, 3024–2

Research publications on energy of DOE and other sources, monthly listing, 3002–2

Statistical Abstract of US, social, political, and economic data, 1950s-83 and trends, annual rpt, 2324–1.3

Supply/demand and price forecasts, by fuel type, quarterly rpt, 3162–34

Supply/demand and prices, by energy source and end-use sector and for 7 electric utilities, 1981-2000 with trends from 1960s, 3008–93

Supply/demand and prices, by fuel type and consuming sector with foreign comparisons, 1949-83, annual rpt, 3164–74

Supply/demand and prices, by fuel type, sector, and end use, detailed trends and projections 1973-95, annual rpt, 3164–75

Supply/demand and prices, by fuel type, sector, and end use, with foreign comparisons, 1960-83 and projected to 1995, annual summary rpt, 3164–76

Supply/demand projections, by energy source and end use, series, 2006–2

see also Alcohol fuels
see also Aviation fuels
see also Biomass energy
see also Business energy use
see also Coal and coal mining
see also Coal exports and imports
see also Coal prices
see also Coal reserves
see also Coal stocks
see also Cogeneration of heat and electricity
see also Department of Energy National Laboratories
see also Diesel fuel
see also Electric power
see also Electric power prices
see also Energy conservation
see also Energy exploration and drilling
see also Energy exports and imports
see also Energy prices
see also Energy production costs
see also Energy research and development
see also Energy reserves
see also Energy stocks and inventories
see also Federal funding for energy programs
see also Fuel allocation
see also Gasohol
see also Gasoline
see also Geothermal resources
see also Heating oil
see also Housing energy use
see also Hydroelectric power
see also Liquefied petroleum gas
see also Natural gas and gas industry
see also Natural gas exports and imports
see also Natural gas prices
see also Natural gas reserves
see also Nuclear power
see also Offshore oil and gas
see also Oil shale
see also Oil spills
see also Petrochemicals
see also Petroleum and petroleum industry
see also Petroleum exports and imports
see also Petroleum prices
see also Petroleum reserves
see also Petroleum stocks
see also Power-generating plants and equipment
see also Solar energy
see also Synthetic fuels
see also Tar sands
see also Transportation energy use
see also Uranium
see also Water power
see also Wind energy
see also Wood fuel

Energy stocks and inventories

Defense Fuel Supply Center procurement, prices, stocks, and other activities, FY83, annual rpt, 3904–6

Defense Fuel Supply Center procurement, prices, stocks, transport, and other activities and finances, FY83, annual rpt, 3904–8

Electric utilities fuel consumption and end of month stocks, by prime mover and petroleum type, monthly rpt, 3162–24.7

Natl Energy Policy Plan, energy supply, demand, and prices, by fuel and consuming sector, projected 1985-2010, biennial rpt, 3004–13

Natural and supplemental gas production, prices, trade, use, reserves, and pipeline company finances, by firm and State, monthly rpt with articles, 3162–4

Natural gas in underground storage, weekly rpt, 3162–32.2

Natural gas interstate pipeline company detailed financial and operating data, by firm, 1983, annual rpt, 3164–38

Natural gas interstate pipeline company supplies, reserves, production, purchases, and contracts, by firm, 1983 with projected deliverability to 2003, annual rpt, 3164–33

Engineers and engineering

Natural gas liquids supply/demand, trade, stocks, and refining, by detailed product and PAD district, monthly rpt with articles, 3162–6

Natural gas liquids supply/demand, trade, stocks, and refining, by detailed product and PAD district, 1983, annual rpt, 3164–2

Natural gas underground storage injections and withdrawals by operator type, monthly 1976-84 and reservoir capacity by State, Mar 1984, annual article, 3162–4.407

Supply/demand and price forecasts, by fuel type, quarterly rpt, 3162–34

Supply/demand and prices, by fuel type and consuming sector with foreign comparisons, 1949-83, annual rpt, 3164–74

Supply/demand and prices, by fuel type, sector, and end use, detailed trends and projections 1973-95, annual rpt, 3164–75

Supply/demand and prices, by fuel type, sector, and end use, with foreign comparisons, 1960-83 and projected to 1995, annual summary rpt, 3164–76

Uranium enrichment facilities operations, finances, uranium stocks, and energy use and capital investment by facility, FY83, annual rpt, 3354–7

Uranium enrichment plants of DOE, production and other costs and selling prices, FY71-83 and projected to FY94, GAO rpt, 26113–137

Uranium prices, deliveries, trade, stocks, secondary marketing, investment, and employment, selected years 1967-83 and for commitments to 2001, annual rpt, 3164–66

Uranium reserves and mining and milling industries operations and finances, with selected foreign comparisons, various periods 1964-83 and projected to 2000, 3008–95

see also Coal stocks
see also Naval Petroleum Reserves
see also Petroleum stocks
see also Strategic Petroleum Reserve

Energy use

see Business energy use
see Energy conservation
see Housing energy use
see Transportation energy use
see Energy resources (for total consumption)
see under names of specific types of energy

Engels, Richard A.

"Growth in Nonmetropolitan Areas Slows", 2328–47

Engineers and engineering

Army Corps of Engineers activities and projects, FY83 and trends from 1800s, annual rpt, 3754–1

Census of Population, 1980: detailed socioeconomic and demographic characteristics, by age, sex, race, Hispanic origin, occupation, and industry, State rpt series, 2531–4

Census of Population, 1980: detailed socioeconomic characteristics, by county, city, and inside-outside SMSAs and central cities, State rpt series, 2531–3

Census of Population, 1980: labor force, by sex, detailed occupation, and region, with comparison to 1970 census, supplementary rpt, 2535–1.12

Engineers and engineering

Census of Service Industries, 1982: employment, establishments, receipts, and payroll, by SIC 2- to 4-digit kind of business, SMSA, county, and city, State rpt series, 2391–1

Census of Service Industries, 1982: employment, establishments, receipts, and payroll, by SIC 4-digit kind of business and State, preliminary rpt, 2390–2.18

County Business Patterns: establishments, employees, and payrolls, by SIC 4-digit industry and county, 1981, annual State rpt series, 2326–8

County Business Patterns: establishments, employees, and payrolls, by SIC 4-digit industry and county, 1982, annual State rpt series, 2326–6

Degree (doctoral) recipients in science and engineering, by field, sex, race, age, citizenship, postgrad employment and study status, State, and instn, 1960-82, 9626–6.16

Degrees conferred in higher education, by race, Hispanic origin, sex, level, and field, selected years 1949/50-1979/80, annual rpt, 4824–2.16

DOD engineering contract awards by function, contract type, and service branch, and oil and port dredging awards by company, 1970s-83, hearings, 21728–53

DOE construction costs, architect and engineering share for 4 field offices, as of Aug 1984, 3006–5.7

DOT employment by subagency, State, and selected personnel characteristics, FY83, annual rpt, 7304–18

Employment and economic conditions, alternative BLS projections to 1995 with data for selected years 1959-82, 6728–29

Employment characteristics or grad enrollment of science and engineering grads of 1980-81, by degree level, field, sex, and race, 1982, 9627–25

Employment, earnings, and hours, by selected SIC 1- to 4-digit industry, State, and for 278 major labor areas, 1939-83, annual rpt, 6744–5

Employment, earnings, and hours, by SIC 4-digit nonfarm industry, monthly 1974-Feb 1984, annual update, 6744–4

Employment, educational, and sociodemographic characteristics of engineers, 1978, Current Population Rpt, 2546–2.121

Employment, enrollment, and degrees of scientists and engineers, R&D funding, and related topics, highlights series, 9626–2

Employment of scientists and engineers at universities and colleges and federally funded R&D centers, by field, sex, State, and instn, Jan 1983 and selected trends from 1967, annual survey, 9627–11

Employment of scientists, engineers, and technicians in defense and nondefense industries, and supply/demand, by field, 1981-87, 9628–71

Employment of scientists, engineers, and technicians in private industry, by occupation and industry group, 1980-81, biennial rpt, 9627–23

Employment of scientists, engineers, and technicians in transportation, utilities, and retail and wholesale trade, by field of science and industry, 1982, 9628–72

Employment, supply, and education of scientists and engineers, by sex, race, Hispanic origin, and field, selected years 1965-83, biennial rpt, 9624–20

Employment, unemployment, and labor force, by demographic and employment characteristics, State, and for 30 metro areas and 11 large cities, 1983, annual rpt, 6744–7

Energy-related employment of scientists and engineers, supply/demand and effects of R&D funding, by sector, energy type, field, and age, 1962-91, annual rpt, 3004–19

Enrollment in grad science and engineering, fields of study, financial support, and other student and instn characteristics, 1975-82, annual survey, 9627–7

Enrollment in science and engineering grad programs, by field, sex, and instn, 1973-82, 9626–2.141

Exports and imports of US, relative contributions of labor by type and capital to trade balance, selected years 1958-80, technical paper, 9381–10.30

Fed Govt programs and mgmt cost control proposals, 3-year savings by function and agency, and financial and operating data, 1960s-81, 16908–1.22

Flight engineers certified by FAA, by age, sex, region, and State, 1983, annual rpt, 7504–2

Income tax returns of corporations, detailed income and tax items by industry, 1981, annual rpt, 8304–4

Income tax returns of partnerships, detailed data by industry, 1981 estimates, annual article, 8302–2.404

Income tax returns of partnerships, receipts by source, deductions by type, and establishments, by selected industry, 1982, annual article, 8302–2.416

Income tax returns of sole proprietorships, detailed data by industry div and selected industry group, 1981, annual rpt, 8304–7

Income tax returns of sole proprietorships, receipts, deductions by type, payroll, and net income, by major industry, 1982, annual article, 8302–2.413

Industry finances and operations, by SIC 2- to 4-digit industry, 1970s-83 and projected to 1988, annual rpt, 2014–4

Industry R&D funding and employment of scientists and engineers, by industry group, firm size, and funding source, 1956-82, annual rpt, 9627–21

Input-output structure of US economy, detailed interindustry transactions for 537 industries, and components of final demand, 1977 benchmark data, 2708–17

Intl services transactions by type, and sales, assets, and employment of US multinat service firms by industry and world region, 1977-82, 2706–5.30

Minority group and women employment, by occupational group and SIC 2- to 3-digit industry, 1981, annual rpt, 9244–1.1

NASA R&D funding to colleges and universities, by State, field of science, and instn, FY83, annual listing, 9504–7

Navy personnel, detailed statistics, quarterly rpt, 3802–4

NSF grant and award recipients, by State, FY83, annual listing, 9624–11

Index by Subjects and Names

NSF research programs, activities, and funding, FY82-83, annual rpt, 9624–6

NSF Science Resources Studies Div activities, project descriptions, and 1973-83 publications, 1983 annual listing, 9624–21

Nuclear engineering student enrollments and degrees granted, by State, instn, and subfield, and placements by sector, 1983, annual rpt, 3004–5

Nuclear industry nongovt employment by industry segment, occupation, and census div, and DOE and NRC nuclear employment, 1968-83, biennial rpt, 3004–11

Nuclear power plant safety and emergencies, effectiveness of technical advisors, 1983 survey, 9638–55

Nuclear-related employment of scientists and engineers, by field and sector, 1981 and 1983, 3006–8.2

Occupational manpower needs and supply by detailed occupation, and educational and training program enrollees and grads by detailed field, 1982 and 1995, biennial rpt, 6744–3

Occupational Outlook Handbook, 1984-85 biennial rpt, 6744–1

R&D and science-related Fed Govt funding to higher education and nonprofit instns, by field, instn, agency, and State, FY82, annual rpt, 9627–17

R&D equipment at higher education instns, age, cost, funding sources, and users, for computer and physical sciences and engineering, 1982, 9626–2.138

R&D expenditures by higher education instns and federally funded centers, by field, source of funds, instn, and State, FY82, annual rpt, 9627–13

R&D expenditures by source, and scientists education and employment, detailed data by field, selected years 1953-84, annual rpt, 9624–18

R&D expenditures of higher education instns, and science and engineering employment and grad students, by field, 1972-83, biennial rpt, 9627–24

R&D Fed Govt facilities and services available for private sector use, by field of science, 1984 biennial listing, 2224–4

R&D Fed Govt funding, by function, agency, and program, selected years FY80-84 and proposed FY85, 26308–46

R&D Fed Govt funding for all performers, by field and supporting agency, selected years FY60-84, annual rpt, 9627–20

R&D funding by industry, program, and Federal agency, and high-technology trade performance, selected years 1960-FY84, 26306–6.77

Salaries of scientists and engineers in R&D at DOE labs and non-DOE facilities, Aug 1982-Feb 1984, annual rpt, 3004–9

Salaries of scientists and engineers in R&D, by degree, type of establishment, age, experience, and field, 1984, annual rpt, 3004–1

Science Indicators, R&D expenditures, innovations, research, and higher education, with foreign comparisons, 1960s- 83, annual rpt, 9624–10

Statistical Abstract of US, social, political, and economic data, 1950s-83 and trends, annual rpt, 2324–1.3

Index by Subjects and Names

Telecommunications and Info Natl Admin research and engineering rpts, FY83, annual listing, 2804–3

TV and radio industry minority and women employment by occupation, and business owners, by race and State, with revenues and stations, 1971-81, hearing, 21368–45

Virgin Islands economic censuses, 1982: employment, establishments, payroll, and receipts, by SIC 1- to 4-digit industry, island, and city, 2593–1

Wages of white-collar workers, by occupation, work level, and industry div, Mar 1984, annual rpt, 6784–2

see also Architecture

see also Biomedical engineering

see also Technological innovations

see also Traffic engineering

Engines

see Electrical machinery and equipment

see Machines and machinery industry

England

see United Kingdom

English language

see Language and literature

Engsberg, Janice M.

"Cable System Employment, 1980-81: A Report on the Status of Minorities and Women", 21368–45

Enid, Okla.

Census of Housing, 1980: occupancy and unit characteristics, by race, Hispanic origin, and city, SMSA rpt, 2473–1.147

Census of Population and Housing, 1980: detailed population and housing characteristics, by county, city, and census tract, SMSA rpt, 2551–2.147

Housing vacancy rates for single and multifamily units and mobile homes, by county, city, and ZIP code, 1983, annual SMSA rpt, 9304–22.5

see also under By SMSA or MSA in the "Index by Categories"

Enlistment

see Voluntary military service

Enrollment

see Educational enrollment

Enterovirus infections

see Infective and parasitic diseases

Enterprise Statistics Program

Data coverage and availability for 1982 economic censuses and related statistics, 1984 guide, 2308–5

Environmental Data and Information Service

see National Environmental Satellite, Data, and Information Service

Environmental Impact Statements

Coal dev plans on Fed Govt lease lands in 12 regions under Fed Coal Mgmt Program, environmental and socioeconomic impacts to 2000, final statement series, 5726–4

Cost control proposals for Fed Govt programs and mgmt, 3-year savings by function and agency, and financial and operating data, 1960s-81, 16908–1.9, 16908–1.22

Environmental quality and protection programs, costs, and Fed Govt enforcement, 1983, detailed annual rpt, 484–1

Oil and gas OCS leases environmental and socioeconomic impacts and coastal area description, final statement series, 5736–1

Public land acreage and use, and Land Mgmt Bur activities and finances, annual State rpt series, 5724–11

Environmental pollution and control

Abatement capital and operating costs, by SIC 2- to 4-digit industry, State, and SMSA, 1982, annual Current Industrial Rpt, 2506–3.6

Abatement capital and operating costs under Clean Air and Water Acts, for govts and selected industries, various periods 1970-2000, annual rpt, 9184–11

Abatement capital expenditures, by pollution type and selected industry, 1973-84, annual article, 2702–1.423

Abatement expenditures and effect on economic indicators and industry operations, by major industry, projected under 3 pollution regulation alternatives 1983-95, 9188–84

Abatement expenditures by govt, business, and consumers, 1972-82, annual article, 2702–1.407

Abatement R&D industry funding, by pollution type and funding source, 1973-82, annual rpt, 9627–21

Agricultural Conservation Program participation and payments, by State, FY83, annual rpt, 1804–7

Agricultural Statistics, 1983, annual rpt, 1004–1.2

Alaska Arctic Natl Wildlife Refuge resources, resident and visitor activities, and environmental impacts of energy exploration, 1983, annual update rpt, 5504–26

Biotechnology commercial uses, R&D funding and output, controls, and industry financial and operating data, for US and 5 countries, 1970s-83 and estimated 1984-85, 26358–98

Bond tax-exempt issues by purpose, and Fed Govt mortgage bond revenue losses and borrower characteristics, selected years 1971-85, hearings, 21788–135

Bond tax-exempt issues for private activity, by purpose, face value, major industry, and State, 1983, article, 8302–2.417

Bond tax-exempt issues for public and private purposes, by use of proceeds, 1975-83, article, 9362–1.408

Budget of US Appendix, detailed budgets and personnel summaries, by agency, FY85, annual rpt, 104–3

Budget of US, CBO analysis and review of FY85 budget by function, annual rpt, 26304–2

Budget of US, compact budgets by function, agency, and account, FY85 with projections to FY89, annual rpt, 104–2

Budget of US, effects of Reagan Admin policy changes, by detailed program, FY85, annual rpt, 104–21

Budget of US, receipts by source and outlays by agency and program, monthly rpt, 8102–3

Budget of US, receipts by source and outlays by function, FY40-89 estimates revised for consistency with FY85 budget definitions, annual rpt, 104–12

Budget of US, receipts, outlays, and budget authority, by function and agency, FY84-89 revised estimates, midsession review of FY85 budget, annual rpt, 104–7

Environmental pollution and control

Coal dev on Fed Govt lease land in Western US, surface and mineral rights by State, and environmental protection adequacy, various periods 1978-85, 26358–103

Coal transport environmental impacts by type and mode of transport, methodology for assessing alternative systems, 1983 rpt, 3408–28

Corporate income tax returns, detailed income and tax items by industry, 1981, annual rpt, 8304–4

Cost control proposals for Fed Govt programs and mgmt, CBO and GAO estimates of savings by function and agency, FY85-89, 26308–45

Disease related to environmental pollution, Fed Govt research activities and publications, Sept 1982-Aug 1983, annual rpt, 9184–9

Electric utility expenditures for pollution control facilities and operations, by company and type of facility, 1982, annual rpt, 3164–23.2

Environmental quality and protection programs, costs, and Fed Govt enforcement, 1983, detailed annual rpt, 484–1

Environmental quality, pollutant discharge by type, and EPA protection activities, 1970s-83, biennial summary rpt, 9184–16

Environmental quality, pollutant discharge by type and source, and EPA protection activities and funding, 1970s-83, biennial regional rpt series, 9184–15

EPA Office of R&D environmental research plans, and outlays by program, FY84-88, annual rpt, 9184–10

EPA pollution control research and grant assistance program activities, monthly rpt, 9182–8

EPA publications in NTIS collection, quarterly listing, 9182–5

EPA Strategic Planning and Mgmt System activities and progress in meeting mgmt goals, by office and activity, quarterly rpt, 9182–11

Farm production inputs, land mgmt, and environmental effects, for 4 crops, 1940s-80 and projected to 2010, 9188–94

Fed Govt aid to State and local govts, expenditures, and direct payments, by program, agency, and State, FY83, annual rpt, 2464–2

Fed Govt programs and mgmt cost control proposals, 3-year savings by function and agency, and financial and operating data, 1960s-81, 16908–1.22

Fish and Wildlife Service conservation and research project descriptions and results, by program, FY83, annual rpt, 5504–20

Foreign market and trade for pollution control instruments and equipment, and user industry operations and demand, country market research rpts, 2045–17

Forest, range, and associated waters use and mgmt assessment, and environmental impacts of Forest Service program options, 1977-2030 and trends from 1920, 1208–24

Forest research project descriptions and bibl, 1982, annual rpt, 1204–14

GAO publications on land use, ownership, mgmt, and planning, 1979-83, annual listing, 26104–11.3

Environmental pollution and control

Index by Subjects and Names

Govt census, 1982: State govt payments to local govts, by program, source of funds, level of govt, and State, with trends from 1902, 2460–3

- Hazardous waste sites and activities of Fed Govt civil agencies, and EPA data mgmt, by waste location, 1984, GAO rpt, 26113–139
- Industrial plant closings attributed in part to pollution control costs, quarterly rpt, discontinued, 9182–6
- Industry finances and operations, by SIC 2- to 4-digit industry, 1970s-83 and projected to 1988, annual rpt, 2014–4
- Midwestern environmental quality and protection programs in 4 EPA Region 7 States, biennal summary rpt, discontinued, 9184–13
- New England States environmental quality, pollutant levels, and EPA control activities summary, annual rpt, discontinued, 9184–6
- Phosphate rock industry environmental protection costs, by control type and selected State, with background operating data, 1977-81 with cost projections to 1990, 5608–143
- R&D Fed Govt funding, by function, agency, and program, selected years FY80-84 and proposed FY85, 26308–46
- Research publications on energy of DOE and other sources, monthly listing, 3002–2
- *Statistical Abstract of US,* social, political, and economic data, 1950s-83 and trends, annual rpt, 2324–1.1
- Tax (excise) collections of IRS, by source, quarterly press release, 8302–1
- Transit systems research publications, 2nd half FY83, semiannual listing, 7882–1
- TVA activities, financial and operating data by program and facility, and power sales by customer, FY83, annual rpt, 9804–1
- Wildlife refuge revenues from economic and recreational uses, and refuge managers attitudes toward expanded use, FY81-83, GAO rpt, 26113–128

see also Air pollution

see also Citizen lawsuits

see also Electromagnetic radiation

see also Environmental Impact Statements

see also International cooperation in environmental sciences

see also Lead poisoning and pollution

see also Marine pollution

see also Mercury pollution

see also Noise

see also Nuclear radiation

see also Pesticides

see also Radioactive waste

see also Reclamation of land

see also Recycling of waste materials

see also Refuse and refuse disposal

see also Soil pollution

see also Trace metals

see also Water pollution

Environmental Protection Agency

- Activities of EPA Strategic Planning and Mgmt System and progress in meeting mgmt goals, by EPA office and activity, quarterly rpt, 9182–11
- Air pollutant emission factors, by detailed source, 3rd edition, 1983-84 supplements, 9198–13
- Air pollutant metal levels, by monitoring site, State, and urban-rural location, 1977-79, last issue of annual rpt, 9194–10
- Air pollutant nitrate and sulfate emissions, monitoring results by surveillance station, 1979 with trends by urban-rural area from 1971, 9198–107
- Air pollutant sulfur dioxide emissions reduction proposal, effects on polluting industries and coal production by region and State, projected to 2010, 9188–97
- Air pollution control programs, emissions standards dev, monitoring, and enforcement, 1982, annual rpt, 9194–4
- Air pollution levels for 5 pollutants, by detailed source, State, and Air Quality Control Region, 1981, annual rpt, 9194–7
- Air pollution levels for 5 pollutants, by source, 1970- 82 with trends from 1940, annual rpt, 9194–13
- Air pollution levels for 6 pollutants, and measurements exceeding natl standards, by site, 1983, annual rpt, 9194–5
- Air pollution levels for 6 pollutants, by source, region, and for large SMSAs, 1975-82, annual rpt, 9194–1
- Air pollution levels for 132 hazardous organic chemicals, by urban-rural location, city, and for areas with many potential sources, 1970-80, 9198–109
- Air pollution monitoring results for atmospheric turbidity by station and season, with description of model predicting urbanization effects, 1960s-76, 9198–106
- Auto emissions control device tampering and fuel-switching incidence in 6 urban areas, 1983, annual rpt, 9194–15
- Auto fuel economy test results for models complying with California emission standards, 1984 model year, annual rpt, 3304–13
- Auto fuel economy test results, 1985 model year, annual rpt, 3304–11
- Budget and full-time staff positions for EPA by type of activity, and grants to States, by program, FY75-84 and proposed FY85, 26308–47
- Budget of US Appendix, detailed budgets and personnel summaries, by agency, FY85, annual rpt, 104–3
- Budget of US, appropriations, outlays, balances, and budget receipts, by govtl branch and agency, FY83, annual rpt, 8104–2
- Budget of US, compact budgets by function, agency, and account, FY85 with projections to FY89, annual rpt, 104–2
- Budget of US, object class analysis of obligations, by branch of Fed Govt and selected depts and agencies, FY85 estimates, annual rpt, 104–9
- Cancer deaths and death rates, by body site, race, sex, State, and county, 1950-79, 4478–146
- Carbon dioxide atmospheric concentration increase effects on hydrologic conditions, projected for 26-35 years, 9188–95
- Carbon dioxide emissions, climatic effects, and control costs, projected under alternative emissions controls and energy use restrictions to 2100 with trends 1970s-80, reprint, 9188–88

Carbon monoxide atmospheric concentrations and levels within buildings and along commuting and residential driving routes, for 4 cities, Jan-Mar 1981, 9198–110

- Chesapeake Bay Program environmental research findings and water pollution control recommendations, as of 1983, narrative rpt, 9208–121
- Cost control proposals for Fed Govt programs and mgmt, 3-year savings by function and agency, and financial and operating data, 1960s-81, 16908–1, 16908–1.13, 16908–1.31
- Disease related to environmental pollution, Fed Govt research activities and publications, Sept 1982-Aug 1983, annual rpt, 9184–9
- Employment (civilian) of Fed Govt, by location, agency, and pay system, 1982, biennial rpt, 9844–8
- Energy use, by type of air pollutant source and fuel, and State, 1981, annual rpt, 9194–14
- Environmental quality, pollutant discharge by type, and EPA protection activities, 1970s-83, biennial summary rpt, 9184–16
- Environmental quality, pollutant discharge by type and source, and EPA protection activities and funding, 1970s-83, biennial regional rpt series, 9184–15
- Farm production inputs, land mgmt, and environmental effects, for 4 crops, 1940s-80 and projected to 2010, 9188–94
- Fraud and abuse in EPA programs, audits and investigations, 2nd half FY84, semiannual rpt, 9182–10
- Hazardous waste sites and activities of Fed Govt civil agencies, and EPA data mgmt, by waste location, 1984, GAO rpt, 26113–139
- Industrial plant closings attributed in part to pollution control costs, quarterly rpt, discontinued, 9182–6
- Midwestern environmental quality and protection programs in 4 EPA Region 7 States, biennal summary rpt, discontinued, 9184–13
- New England States environmental quality, pollutant levels, and EPA control activities summary, annual rpt, discontinued, 9184–6
- NYC and New Jersey atmospheric levels of 28 volatile organic compounds, by site and urban-rural location, 1979-June 1981, 9198–108
- Ocean dumping of waste materials, EPA permit program and intl London Dumping Convention activities, 1981-83, annual rpt, 9204–8
- Oceanographic research cruise schedules and ship characteristics, by academic instn or Federal agency, 1984, annual rpt, 3804–6
- PCB (polychlorinated biphenyl) concentrations in Great Lakes fish, for 29 species monitored at 24 sites, selected dates 1969-77, 9208–126
- Pollution abatement capital and operating costs under Clean Air and Water Acts, for govts and selected industries, various periods 1970-2000, annual rpt, 9184–11
- Pollution abatement expenditures, and effect on economic indicators and industry operations, by major industry, projected under 3 pollution regulation alternatives 1983-95, 9188–84

Index by Subjects and Names

Pollution control research and grant assistance program activities of EPA, monthly rpt, 9182–8

Publications of EPA in NTIS collection, quarterly listing, 9182–5

R&D and science-related Fed Govt funding to higher education and nonprofit instns, by field, instn, agency, and State, FY82, annual rpt, 9627–17

R&D Fed Govt funding, by function, agency, and program, selected years FY80-84 and proposed FY85, 26308–46

R&D Fed Govt funding for all performers, by field and supporting agency, selected years FY60-84, annual rpt, 9627–20

R&D Office of EPA environmental research plans, and outlays by program, FY84-88, annual rpt, 9184–10

Radiation and radionuclide concentrations in air, water, and milk, results of EPA and other monitoring programs, by State and site, quarterly rpt, 9232–2

Radionuclide concentrations in air, water, and biota near Nevada and other nuclear test sites, and in milk from western States, by location, 1983, annual rpt, 9234–4

Radionuclide concentrations in cattle and wildlife near Nevada nuclear test site, 1957-81, last issue of annual rpt, 9234–5

Southeastern US water supply and quality, with background socioeconomic data, for 8 States, 1960s-2020 with trends from 1930, 9208–119

Uranium mining operations, finances, and costs of alternative methods to meet emissions standards, for industry and selected mines, selected years 1948-90, 9188–96

Uranium ore tailings at active mills, EPA radon and radionuclide emmission standards and US and foreign exposure and health effects, various periods 1957-83, hearings, 21208–17

Water from urban runoff, quality, pollutant concentrations, and control cost-effectiveness, with monitoring sites rainfall and other characteristics, by city and region, 1978-83, 9208–122

Water pollution fish kills, by State, location, and pollution source, monthly 1978-80, annual rpt, 9204–3

Water pollution from nonpoint sources, source land uses and acreage, and control program funding, by State or region, various periods 1974-FY84, 9208–123

Water pollution regulation under EPA wastewater discharge system, operations and funding, various periods FY79-83, GAO rpt, 26113–113

Water quality, pollutant types and sources, and control program compliance, by State, 1982, biennial rpt, 9204–6

Water supply and use in 3 areas with supply problems and total US, and methods to increase supply, selected years 1974-80 and projected to 2010, 9208–125

Water supply contamination by volatile organic chemicals, monitoring results for each State and Puerto Rico, 1981, 9208–120

Waterborne diseases from drinking water, cases and outbreaks, by type and cause, aggregate 1971-80, 9208–124

Environmental sciences

Acid Precipitation Natl Assessment Program activities, and funding by Federal agency, 1983, annual rpt, 14354–1

Carbon dioxide atmospheric levels, climatic effects and impacts of fossil and synthetic fuels use, deforestation, and land use patterns, research rpt series, 3406–3

Census of Population, 1980: detailed socioeconomic and demographic characteristics, by age, sex, race, Hispanic origin, occupation, and industry, State rpt series, 2531–4

DOE R&D projects and funding at natl labs, universities, and other instns, FY83, annual summary rpt, 3004–18.1

Environmental quality and protection programs, costs, and Fed Govt enforcement, 1983, detailed annual rpt, 484–1

Fish and Wildlife Service conservation and research project descriptions and results, by program, FY83, annual rpt, 5504–20

Forests (tropical) status by country and world region, conservation methods, and mgmt role of US, foreign, and intl groups, 1977-80s and projected to 2000, 26358–101.1

NASA R&D funding to colleges and universities, by State, field of science, and instn, FY83, annual listing, 9504–7

NOAA scientific and technical publications, monthly listing, 2142–1

R&D and science-related Fed Govt funding and total and federally funded expenditures of universities and colleges, by instn and field of science, FY82, 9626–2.136

R&D and science-related Fed Govt funding to higher education and nonprofit instns, by field, instn, agency, and State, FY82, annual rpt, 9627–17

R&D expenditures by higher education instns and federally funded centers, by field, source of funds, instn, and State, FY82, annual rpt, 9627–13

R&D expenditures by source, and scientists education and employment, detailed data by field, selected years 1953-84, annual rpt, 9624–18

R&D expenditures of higher education instns, and science and engineering employment and grad students, by field, 1972-83, biennial rpt, 9627–24

R&D Fed Govt facilities and services available for private sector use, by field of science, 1984 biennial listing, 2224–4

R&D Fed Govt funding, by function, agency, and program, selected years FY80-84 and proposed FY85, 26308–46

R&D Fed Govt funding for all performers, by field and supporting agency, selected years FY60-84, annual rpt, 9627–20

R&D funding by industry, program, and Federal agency, and high-technology trade performance, selected years 1960-FY84, 26306–6.77

Satellite Landsat system proposed transfer to private sector, uses and product sales by user type, and university programs and personnel by instn, 1973-85, 26358–100

Science and engineering doctoral degree recipients, by field, sex, race, age, citizenship, postgrad employment and study status, State, and instn, 1960-82, 9626–6.16

Equal Employment Opportunity Commission

Science and engineering grad enrollment, fields of study, financial support, and other student and instn characteristics, 1975-82, annual survey, 9627–7

Science and engineering grad program enrollment, by field, degree level, source of financial support, race, and Hispanic origin, 1975-81, 9626–2.134

Science and engineering grad program enrollment by field, sources of financial support, and foreign students, 1975-82, 9626–2.141

Science and engineering grads of 1980-81, employment and median salaries by level and field of degree, 1982, 9626–2.137

Science and engineering grads of 1980-81, employment characteristics or grad enrollment, by degree level, field, sex, and race, 1982, 9627–25

Scientists and engineers employed at universities and colleges, by field, sex, and instn, 1973-82, 9626–2.140

Scientists and engineers employed at universities and colleges, by field, sex, State, and instn, Jan 1983 and selected trends from 1967, annual survey, 9627–11

Scientists and engineers employed in energy-related fields, supply/demand and effects of R&D funding, by energy type, employer type, field, and age, 1962-91, annual rpt, 3004–19

Scientists and engineers employment by sector and activity, and share female, black, and Asian descent, by field, 1982, 9626–2.142

Scientists and engineers supply, employment, and education, by sex, race, Hispanic origin, and field, selected years 1965-83, biennial rpt, 9624–20

see also Astronomy

see also Atmospheric sciences

see also Earth sciences

see also Energy research and development

see also International cooperation in environmental sciences

see also Meteorology

see also Oceanography

Epidemiology

see Diseases and disorders

see Public health

Epilepsy

see Neurological disorders

Epstein, Marshall S.

"Preliminary Income and Tax Statistics for 1982 Individual Income Tax Returns", 8302–2.402

Equal employment opportunity

see Discrimination in employment

Equal Employment Opportunity Commission

Age Discrimination in Employment Act, Fed Govt compliance activities, annual rpt, discontinued, 9244–8

Apprenticeship of minorities and women in labor-mgmt, employer, and referral union programs, annual rpt, discontinued, 9244–7

Budget of US Appendix, detailed budgets and personnel summaries, by agency, FY85, annual rpt, 104–3

Budget of US, appropriations, outlays, balances, and budget receipts, by govtl branch and agency, FY83, annual rpt, 8104–2

Equal Employment Opportunity Commission

Civil rights enforcement offices funding and staff, for 6 Federal agencies, FY80-84, 11048–179

- Hispanic Americans and other minority employment discrimination, EEOC enforcement activities, personnel, and litigation, 1970s-FY83, 9248–18
- Minority group and women's employment, by occupational group, SIC 2- to 3-digit industry, State, and SMSA, 1981, annual rpt, 9244–1

Equatorial Guinea

- AID activities and funding by project and function, FY85, and developing countries summary socioeconomic data, 1970s-83, by country, annual rpt, 9914–3
- AID economic assistance to developing countries, obligations and disbursements by country, quarterly rpt, 9912–4
- *Background Notes,* summary social, political, and economic data, 1984 rpt, 7006–2.37
- Economic conditions and foreign marketing prospects in 46 Sub-Saharan countries, 1983 world region rpt, 2046–5.1
- Economic, social, and political summary data, by country, 1984, annual factbook, 244–11
- Exports of US, detailed Schedule B commodities by country of destination, 1983, annual rpt, 2424–9
- Exports of US, detailed Schedule E commodities by mode of transport and world area and country of destination, 1983, annual rpts, 2424–5
- Imports of US, detailed Schedule A commodities by country and world area of origin, and mode of transport, 1983, annual rpts, 2424–2
- Imports of US, detailed TSUSA commodities by country of origin, 1983, annual rpt, 2424–4
- Loans and grants for economic and military assistance from US and intl agencies, by program and country, FY46-83, annual rpt, 9914–5
- Military aid of US, arms sales, and training programs costs and budget requests by program, world region, and country, FY83-85, annual rpt, 7144–13
- Military spending, arms trade, and armed forces size, with total govt spending and population, by country, 1972-82, annual rpt, 9824–1
- *Minerals Yearbook, 1982,* Vol 3: foreign country reviews of production, trade, and policies, by commodity, annual rpt, 5604–35
- *Minerals Yearbook, 1982,* Vol 3 preprints: foreign country review of production, trade, and policies, by commodity, annual rpt, 5604–17.82
- Population size and growth rates, and latest available benchmark demographic data, by country, 1950-83, biennial rpt, 2324–4
- *see also* under By Foreign Country in the "Index by Categories"

Erie, Pa.

- Census of Housing, 1980: occupancy and unit characteristics, by race, Hispanic origin, and city, SMSA rpt, 2473–1.148
- Census of Population and Housing, 1980: detailed population and housing characteristics, by county, city, and census tract, SMSA rpt, 2551–2.148

see also under By City and By SMSA or MSA in the "Index by Categories"

Erosion

see Soils and soil conservation

Ershoff, Daniel H.

"Behavioral, Health, and Cost Outcomes of an HMO-Based Prenatal Health Education Program", 4102–1.401

Escalator clauses

- Budget of US, receipts, outlays, and budget authority, by function and agency, FY84-89 revised estimates, midsession review of FY85 budget, annual rpt, 104–7
- Collective bargaining agreements expiring during year, covered workers by SIC 2-digit industry, firm, and union, with summary of key provisions, 1984, annual rpt, 6784–9
- Collective bargaining contract expirations and wage increases, scheduled and under cost-of-living escalator provisions, by SIC 2-digit industry and selected firm and union, 1984, annual article, 6722–1.402
- Collective bargaining wage adjustments, Monthly Labor Review, 6722–1.7
- Collective bargaining wage adjustments, workers covered, and factors affecting negotiated settlements, selected years 1968-84, article, 9362–1.410
- Collective bargaining wage and benefit rate changes in labor-mgmt agreements, quarterly press release, 6782–2
- Fed Govt programs and mgmt cost control proposals, 3-year savings by function and agency, and financial and operating data, 1960s-81, 16908–1.27, 16908–1.34
- Pension plans with postretirement adjustments related to employee and employer characteristics, and effect of inflation on benefit purchasing power, 1973-79, 6468–18
- Pension plans with postretirement benefit increases, for banks and manufacturers by size, 1978-83, hearing, 25368–132
- Pension plans with postretirement benefit increases, participants and average increase by occupational group and plan characteristics, 1978-81, article, 6722–1.453
- Southeastern region collective bargaining calendar, 1984, annual rpt, 6946–1.68
- State and local govt employee wage and benefit changes under collective bargaining, and workers affected, 1979-84, semiannual press release, 6782–6

Eskimos

see Alaska Natives

Essertier, Edward P.

"Federal Offshore Statistics: Leasing, Exploration, Production, Revenue", 5734–3

Estate tax

- Art appraisals accepted and rejected on estate, gift, and income tax returns, and valuation by taxpayers, IRS, and US courts, 1978-82, hearings, 21408–74
- Budget of US, CBO analysis of revenue and spending alternatives and projections of economic indicators, FY85-89, annual rpt, 26304–3
- Budget of US, receipts by source and outlays by agency and program, monthly rpt, 8102–3

Index by Subjects and Names

- Budget of US, receipts by source and outlays by function, FY40-89 estimates revised for consistency with FY85 budget definitions, annual rpt, 104–12
- Budget of US, receipts, outlays, and budget authority, by function and agency, FY84-89 revised estimates, midsession review of FY85 budget, annual rpt, 104–7
- Census of Govts, 1982: State govt payments to local govts, by program, source of funds, level of govt, and State, with trends from 1902, 2460–3
- Fed Govt consolidated financial statements based on business accounting methods, FY82-83, annual rpt, 8104–5
- Fed Govt internal revenue, by type of tax, quarterly rpt, 8302–2.1
- Fed Govt receipts by source and outlays by agency, *Treasury Bulletin,* quarterly rpt, 8002–4.1
- Govt revenues by source and expenditures by function, natl income and product account, *Survey of Current Business,* monthly rpt, monthly and annual tables, 2702–1.24
- Govt revenues, by type, level of govt, and State, selected years 1902-83, annual rpt, 10044–1.2
- Govt tax revenues, by level of govt, type of tax, State, and selected counties, quarterly rpt, 2462–3
- Income tax returns filed by type, for US, IRS regions, and service center cities, 1972-82 and projected 1983-90, annual rpt, 8304–9.1
- IRS collections, by type of tax, region, and State, FY83, annual rpt, 8304–3.3
- IRS collections, FY83, annual rpt, 8104–2.2
- State govt revenues by source, expenditures by function, debt, and holdings by type, FY83, annual rpt, 2466–2.5
- State govt tax collections, by detailed type of tax and tax rates, by State, FY83, annual rpt, 2466–2.3
- *see also* Gift tax

Estrella, Arturo

"Corporate Use of Pension Overfunding", 9385–1.406

Estuaries

- Army Corps of Engineers activities and projects, FY83 and trends from 1800s, annual rpt, 3754–1
- Environmental characteristics, fish, wildlife, and use, and population socioeconomic data, for individual coastal areas, series, 5506–4
- Environmental characteristics, fish, wildlife, uses, and mgmt, for individual estuaries, series, 5506–7
- Environmental characteristics, fish, wildlife, uses, and mgmt of individual coastal ecosystems, series, 5506–9
- Environmental quality and protection programs, costs, and Fed Govt enforcement, 1983, detailed annual rpt, 484–1
- Oil spills in coastal and aquatic wildlife habitats, methodology for cleanup priority rating and listing of wildlife species of concern, 1984 rpt, 5508–87
- Pollution-caused fish kills, by State, location, and pollution source, monthly 1978-80, annual rpt, 9204–3

Index by Subjects and Names

Europe

Sedimentation control, surveillance, and research activity of Fed Govt, by project, agency, region, and State, 1982, annual rpt, 5664–9

see also Wetlands

Ethanol

see Alcohol fuels

Ethics

see also Financial disclosure

see also Judicial ethics

see also Medical ethics

see also Political ethics

Ethiopia

- Agricultural and food production indexes, and production of selected commodities, by world region and country, 1974-83, annual rpt, 1524–5
- Agricultural situation in sub-Saharan Africa, by country, 1982-83 and outlook for 1984, annual rpt, 1524–4.10
- AID economic assistance to developing countries, obligations and disbursements by country, quarterly rpt, 9912–4
- AID loan repayment status and terms by program and country, and status of predecessor agency loans, quarterly rpt, 9912–3
- Economic conditions and foreign marketing prospects in 46 Sub-Saharan countries, 1983 world region rpt, 2046–5.1
- Economic conditions, income, production, prices, employment, and trade, 1984 annual country rpt, 2046–4.111
- Economic, social, and political summary data, by country, 1984, annual factbook, 244–11
- Exports of US, detailed Schedule B commodities by country of destination, 1983, annual rpt, 2424–9
- Exports of US, detailed Schedule E commodities by mode of transport and world area and country of destination, 1983, annual rpts, 2424–5
- Imports of US, detailed Schedule A commodities by country and world area of origin, and mode of transport, 1983, annual rpts, 2424–2
- Imports of US, detailed TSUSA commodities by country of origin, 1983, annual rpt, 2424–4
- Loans and grants for economic and military assistance from US and intl agencies, by program and country, FY46-83, annual rpt, 9914–5
- Military spending, arms trade, and armed forces size, with total govt spending and population, by country, 1972-82, annual rpt, 9824–1
- *Minerals Yearbook, 1982,* Vol 3: foreign country reviews of production, trade, and policies, by commodity, annual rpt, 5604–35
- *Minerals Yearbook, 1982,* Vol 3 preprints: foreign country review of production, trade, and policies, by commodity, annual rpt, 5604–17.83
- Oil and gas undiscovered recoverable resources, cumulative production, and identified reserves, as of 1982, preliminary oil basin rpt, 5666–17.13
- Population size and growth rates, and latest available benchmark demographic data, by country, 1950-83, biennial rpt, 2324–4
- Refugee resettlement program activities and funding, arrivals and population by

country of origin and State, and employment and other characteristics, FY83, annual rpt, 4704–8

see also under By Foreign Country in the "Index by Categories"

Ethnic groups

see Birthplace

see Hispanic Americans

see Minority groups

Etzel, Philip H.

- "Report on the Noncompetitive Employment of 30 Percent or More Disabled Veterans in the Federal Government", 9842–4
- "Veterans Readjustment Appointments in the Federal Government, Apr.-Sept. 1982", 9842–3

Eugene, Oreg.

- Census of Housing, 1980: occupancy and unit characteristics, by race, Hispanic origin, and city, SMSA rpt, 2473–1.149
- Census of Population and Housing, 1980: detailed population and housing characteristics, by county, city, and census tract, SMSA rpt, 2551–2.149
- Housing vacancy rates for single and multifamily units and mobile homes, by city and ZIP code, 1983, annual metro area rpt, 9304–21.6
- *see also* under By City and By SMSA or MSA in the "Index by Categories"

Eurocurrency

- Eurodollar and total market liabilities, dollar liabilities of US bank foreign branches, and Eurodollar deposit rates, quarterly rpt, 9391–7.1
- Eurodollar bond market issues of US corporations, and amount raised and savings relative to domestic market, by company, 1975-82, hearing, 25368–132
- Eurodollar deposit rates, weekly chartbook, 9365–1.5
- Finance (intl) statistics, quarterly chartbook, 9362–2.10
- Foreign loans, debts, exchange rates, and intl reserves, for US and selected countries, various periods 1949-84, conf papers, 9373–3.28
- Forward exchange and interest rate term structure effect on Eurocurrency asset pricing for 2 currencies, various periods 1973-84, technical paper, 9381–10.40
- Futures trading in selected commodities, foreign currencies, and stock indexes, Chicago and other markets activity, monthly rpt, 11922–1
- Futures trading in selected commodities, foreign currencies, Treasury securities, and stock indexes, NYC, Chicago, and other markets activity, monthly rpt, 11922–5
- Loans, loan fees, and interest rate spread for Eurocurrency syndicated loans, by country group and selected country, 1981-83, technical paper, 9366–7.105

Europe

- Acid rain causes and effects, air pollutant emissions by source in US and selected countries, and control costs, 1970s-83 and projected to 2000, 21368–52
- Agricultural and food production indexes, and production of selected commodities, by world region and country, 1974-83, annual rpt, 1524–5
- Agricultural exports and imports of US, by detailed commodity and country, FY83 and CY83, semiannual rpts, 1522–4

- Agricultural situation in Western Europe, by country and commodity, 1983 and outlook for 1984, annual rpt, 1524–4.6
- Agricultural supply/demand, trade, and production, and socioeconomic data, by country, 1950s-77, 1528–179
- Agricultural trade of US, by commodity and country, bimonthly rpt with articles, 1522–1
- AID contracts and grants for technical and support services, by instn, country, and State, FY83, annual listing, 9914–7
- AID economic assistance to developing countries, obligations and disbursements by country, quarterly rpt, 9912–4
- AID loans authorized, signed, and canceled, by country and world area, monthly rpt, 9912–2
- Auto fuel economy measures, for US, Japan, and European makes, 1975 and 1980-83, annual rpt, 3164–73
- Auto industry finances and operations by manufacturer, foreign competition, and consumer auto expenditures and attitudes toward car buying, selected years 1968-85, annual rpt, 2004–8
- Carbon dioxide emissions from fossil fuel combustion, and growth rates, by country and country group, 1950-80, 3006–7.6
- China economic conditions, agricultural and industrial production, trade, and domestic and foreign investment, 1980-85, 2048–106
- Coal reserves, production, demand indicators, and trade, by country, selected years 1973-82 and alternative trade projections to 1995, annual rpt, 3164–77
- Economic conditions in Communist and OECD countries, 1982, annual rpt, 7144–11
- Employment, labor force, and participation and unemployment rates by sex, in US and 9 OECD countries, various periods 1970-3rd qtr 1983, annual article, 6722–1.404
- Energy production by type, and oil prices, trade, and consumption, by country group and selected country, monthly rpt, 242–5
- Export sales and shipments of US grains, oilseed products, hides, skins, and cotton, by country, weekly rpt, 1922–3
- Exports and imports of OECD countries, by country, 1983, annual rpt, 7144–10
- Exports and imports of US (airborne), by world area and US customs district and city, monthly rpt, 2422–8
- Exports and imports of US (waterborne), by type of service, commodity, country, route, and US port, 1982, annual rpt, 7704–2
- Exports and imports of US (waterborne), by type of service, customs district, port, and world area, monthly rpt, 2422–7
- Exports and imports of US, by commodity group, world area, selected country, US coastal area and port, and mode of transport, with seasonal adjustments, monthly rpt, 2422–9
- Exports and imports of US, detailed SIC-based commodities by world area, 1983, annual rpts, 2424–6
- Exports and imports of US with Western Europe, and US market share and export opportunities for selected commodities, by country, 1982-84, 2048–105

Europe

Exports of US, detailed Schedule E commodities by mode of transport and world area and country of destination, 1983, annual rpts, 2424–5

GNP and GNP growth of each OECD member country, 1973-83, annual rpt, 7144–8

Great Lakes trade, by SITC 3-digit commodity, port, vessel type, world area, and country, 1982, annual rpt, 7744–3

Helsinki Final Act implementation by NATO, Warsaw Pact, and other signatory nations, Dec 1983-Mar 1984, semiannual rpt, 7002–1

Immigrant and nonimmigrant visas of US issued and refused, and status adjustments, by class and nationality, FY77, annual rpt, 7184–1

Immigration, and alien residents, workers, visitors, deportations, and naturalizations, by country of birth, FY81, annual rpt, 6264–2

Imports of US, detailed Schedule A commodities by country and world area of origin, and mode of transport, 1983, annual rpts, 2424–2

Investment (foreign direct) in US, by major industry group, world area, and selected country, 1980-83, annual article, 2702–1.439

Investment (foreign direct) of US, by selected major industry group and world area, 1982-83, annual article, 2702–1.430

Investment (foreign direct) of US, by world area and country, 1977-83, article, 2702–1.442

Investment (intl direct) worldwide, and US investment flows by major industry, by world region and country, 1982 and trends from 1950, annual rpt, 2044–25

Loans and grants for economic and military assistance from US and intl agencies, by program and country, FY46-83, annual rpt, 9914–5

Loans of large US banks to foreigners at all US and foreign offices, by country group and country, quarterly rpt, 13002–1

Manufacturing labor productivity and cost indexes for US and 11 OECD countries, 1960-82, annual article, 6722–1.405

Manufacturing productivity and unit labor cost indexes for US and 11 countries, 1950-82 and preliminary 1983, annual rpt, 6864–1

Military aid of US, and sales of arms, equipment, and training, by item and country, FY50-83, annual rpt, 3904–3

Military aid of US, arms sales, and training programs costs and budget requests by program, world region, and country, FY83-85, annual rpt, 7144–13

Military, social, and economic summary data, by world area and country, 1960s-80s, hearing, 25388–47.1

Military spending, arms trade, and armed forces size, with total govt spending and population, by country, 1972-82, annual rpt, 9824–1

Military weapons transfers to developing countries from US, USSR, and Europe, by weapon type and world region, 1974-82, 25948–3

Minerals Yearbook, 1982, Vol 3: foreign country reviews of production, trade, and policies, by commodity, annual rpt, 5604–35

Monetary control policy of US and selected West European countries, and relation to credit, exchange rates, GNP, and other indicators, various periods 1960-82, conf papers, 9373–3.26

Nuclear power plant spent fuel and demand for uranium and enrichment services, for US and non-Communist country groups, 1983 and projected to 2020, annual rpt, 3164–72

Oil and gas undiscovered recoverable resources, cumulative production, and identified reserves, as of 1982, preliminary oil basin rpt, 5666–17.15

Population size and growth rates, and latest available benchmark demographic data, by country, 1950-83, biennial rpt, 2324–4

Precipitation and temperature outlook for US and Northern Hemisphere, and by US and selected foreign weather stations, semimonthly rpt, 2182–1

R&D Fed Govt funding for foreign performers, by world region and country, FY82-84, annual rpt, 9627–20.2

Refugee migration, settlement status, and assistance, by world area and country of origin and asylum, as of May 1984, annual rpt, 7004–15

Ships in US merchant fleet, shipping costs, construction, employment, military availability, and Fed Govt subsidies, 1970s-1984 and projected to 2000, 26306–6.83

Students in US and Soviet bloc training programs, by program type and Latin American country or world region of student origin, selected years 1972-82, GAO rpt, 26123–77

Terrorist (intl) incidents, casualties, and attacks on US targets, by attack type and world area, with chronology of events, 1983, annual rpt, 7004–13

Tide height and time daily at worldwide coastal points, 1985 predictions, annual rpt, 2174–2.3

Travel to and from US and travel receipts and payments by world area, and travel to US by country, 1977-83, annual rpt, 2904–10

Travel to and from US, by world area and selected country, projected 1984-85, annual rpt, 2904–9

Travel to and from US on US and foreign flag air carriers, by country, world area, and US port, monthly rpt, 7302–2

Travel to Europe by US citizens, monthly rpt, 7182–2

Travel to US and receipts by world area and selected country, 1960-83, and US Travel and Tourism Admin activities, 1983, annual rpt, 2904–6

USIA info center and reading room operations, by world region, country, and city, FY83, annual rpt, 9854–4

Weather conditions and effect on agriculture, by US region, State, and city, and world area, weekly rpt, 2152–2

see also Albania
see also Andorra
see also Austria
see also Belgium
see also Bulgaria
see also Central Treaty Organization
see also Cyprus

Index by Subjects and Names

see also Czechoslovakia
see also Denmark
see also Eastern Europe
see also Eurocurrency
see also European Community
see also European Free Trade Association
see also European Space Agency
see also Finland
see also France
see also Germany, East
see also Germany, West
see also Gibraltar
see also Greece
see also Hungary
see also Iceland
see also Ireland
see also Italy
see also Liechtenstein
see also Luxembourg
see also Malta
see also Monaco
see also Netherlands
see also North Atlantic Treaty Organization
see also Norway
see also Poland
see also Portugal
see also Romania
see also San Marino
see also Soviet Union
see also Spain
see also Sweden
see also Switzerland
see also United Kingdom
see also Yugoslavia
see also under By Foreign Country in the "Index by Categories"

European Community

Agricultural exports and imports of US, by detailed commodity and country, FY83 and CY83, semiannual rpts, 1522–4

Agricultural policy changes of EC, effect on price supports by commodity, 1981/82-1984/85, article, 1522–3.402

Agricultural production, acreage, and yield for selected crops, forecasts by selected world region and country, FAS monthly rpt, 1925–28

Agricultural self-sufficiency and trade of EC by selected product, with comparisons to other countries, selected years 1959/60-1983-84, hearing, 25368–135

Agricultural situation in Western Europe, by country and commodity, 1983 and outlook for 1984, annual rpt, 1524–4.6

Agricultural trade of US, by commodity and country, bimonthly rpt with articles, 1522–1

AID loan repayment status and terms by program and country, and status of predecessor agency loans, quarterly rpt, 9912–3

Almond production and trade of US and selected countries, 1982/83-1983/84 and forecast 1985, article, 1925–34.425

Apple imports of EC by country, and France exports by world region, 1981/82-1983/84, article, 1925–34.407

Auto industry operations, trade, and registrations, foreign and US, selected years 1928-82, domestic content requirement hearings, 21788–134

Dairy imports subject to quota by commodity, and meat imports subject to Meat Import Law, by country of origin, FAS monthly circular, 1925–31

Index by Subjects and Names

Evans, Gary F.

Economic conditions in Communist and OECD countries, 1982, annual rpt, 7144–11

Economic conditions in Communist, OECD, and selected other countries, 1960s-83, annual rpt, 244–5

European Monetary System effect on inflation and exchange rates, for 3 member countries, various periods Feb 1974-Mar 1984, technical paper, 9366–7.101

Export sales and shipments of US grains, oilseed products, hides, skins, and cotton, by country, weekly rpt, 1922–3

Exports and imports, agreement devs, US trade relations, and USITC investigations, 1983, annual rpt, 9884–5

Exports and imports of OECD countries, by country, 1983, annual rpt, 7144–10

Exports and imports of US, by commodity group, world area, selected country, US coastal area and port, and mode of transport, with seasonal adjustments, monthly rpt, 2422–9

Exports and imports of US, detailed SIC-based commodities by world area, 1983, annual rpts, 2424–6

Exports and imports of US with EC by country, and total agricultural and nonagricultural trade, selected years 1958-83, annual rpt, 7144–7

Exports and imports of US with Western Europe, and US market share and export opportunities for selected commodities, by country, 1982-84, 2048–105

Exports, imports, and economic indicators by country and country group, and US trade policy actions, 1960s-83, annual rpt, 444–1

Exports, imports, and trade balance of EC, total and excluding intra-EC, quarterly rpt, 2042–10.2

Exports of US by selected commodity, and foreign and US economic and employment indicators and balance of payments, by world area and country, 1970s-83, annual rpt, 2044–26

Exports of US, detailed Schedule E commodities by mode of transport and world area and country of destination, 1983, annual rpts, 2424–5

Filbert production and trade of US and selected countries, 1981/82-1984/85, article, 1925–34.426

Food aid contributions, by commodity group and country, 1975/76-83/84, 1528–181

Food supply/demand and market and support prices, with exchange rates, fertilizer price index, GDP, and population, by EC country, 1960-83, 1528–173

Footwear imports of US, by category, value class, and selected country, monthly rpt, 2042–29

Fruit (deciduous) grower prices and processor net cost and subsidies in 4 countries and EC, 1982/83-1983/84, article, 1925–34.414

Fruit and vegetable product trade and tariffs of EC, 1966-78, and effect of Greece, Spain, and Portugal entry into EC, projected to 1986, 1528–182

GNP and GNP growth of each OECD member country, 1973-83, annual rpt, 7144–8

Grain and soybean import prices at Rotterdam, and EC import levies and supports, by type of grain, weekly press release, 1922–4

Grain production, supply, consumption, and trade, by country or world region, current crop year forecasts and trends, FAS monthly rpt, 1925–2.1

Grain stocks, supply deviation, and effect on use, trade, and prices, for US and selected countries, various periods 1960-83, 1528–184

Human rights conditions in 162 countries, economic and military aid of US, and economic aid of intl organizations, 1981-83, annual rpt, 21384–3

Imports of US, detailed Schedule A commodities by country and world area of origin, and mode of transport, 1983, annual rpts, 2424–2

Investment (foreign direct) in US, by major industry group, world area, and selected country, 1980-83, annual article, 2702–1.439

Investment (foreign direct) of US, by world area and country, 1977-83, article, 2702–1.442

Investment (intl direct) worldwide, and US investment flows by major industry, by world region and country, 1982 and trends from 1950, annual rpt, 2044–25

Loans and grants for economic and military assistance from US and intl agencies, by program and country, FY46-83, annual rpt, 9914–5

Pistachio imports of EC by country, and US exports by world area, 1981-83, article, 1925–34.424

Portugal agricultural subsidies, profits, marketing margins, and consumer prices, by commodity or product, and effects of prospective EC membership, 1981, 1528–171

Prune (dried) production, trade, consumption, and stocks of US and 2 countries, EC subsidies, and US exports by country, 1982/83-1984/85, article, 1925–34.435

Rail high-speed systems and railcar production of US and selected countries, with major cities population and land area, 1940s-82, 26358–97

Seed exports of US, by type of seed, world region, and country, FAS quarterly rpt, 1925–13

Social security programs benefits and expenditures, unemployment rate, and economic indicators growth, for 9 EC countries, 1960-82, article, 4742–1.405

Steel imports of US from EC and other countries, and US industry operating data, for 15 products limited under arrangement with EC, monthly rpt, 9882–10

Steel industry financial and operating data, steel imports by source, and employment situation at Fairless Hills, Pa, plant, 1970s-90, hearing, 25528–94

Steel pipe and tube shipments, imports from EC by country, and exports, by product type, various periods 1978-83 with import duties to 1987, hearing, 25368–134

Tomato processor subsidies and minimum grower prices for Greece and total EC, 1981-83, article, 1925–34.404

Trade promotion policies and industry financing of EC, and effect on competing US industries, 1970s-82, 9886–4.73

Walnut export subsidy of EC, and US imports by EC country, 1981/82-1984/85, article, 1925–34.429

Wheat exports, total and for major producers by world area and country of destination, 1973/74-1983/84, FAS rpt, 1925–2.7

European Free Trade Association

Exports and imports of US with Western Europe, and US market share and export opportunities for selected commodities, by country, 1982-84, 2048–105

European Space Agency

Launchings of satellites and other space objects since 1957, quarterly listing, 9502–2

Eutrophication

Environmental quality, pollutant discharge by type and source, and EPA protection activities and funding, 1970s-83, biennial regional rpt series, 9184–15

Estuary environmental characteristics, fish, wildlife, uses, and mgmt, for individual estuaries, series, 5506–7

Great Lakes basin pollutant discharges by source, and control program activities, 1983 annual rpt, 14644–1

Natl Forest System wildlife habitat and fishery improvements, use, and game population and harvest by species and forest, by region, FY83, annual rpt, 1204–31

New York Bight pollutant loadings from ocean dumping of municipal wastes by type and source, and concentrations in fish and sediments, 1970s-82, hearings, 21568–36

Nonpoint sources of water pollution, source land uses and acreage, and control program funding, by State or region, various periods 1974-FY84, 9208–123

Urban runoff water quality, pollutant concentrations, and control cost-effectiveness, with monitoring sites rainfall and other characteristics, by city and region, 1978-83, 9208–122

Water quality, pollutant types and sources, and control program compliance, by State, 1982, biennial rpt, 9204–6

Water supply and quality, floods, drought, mudslides, and other hydrologic events, by State, 1983, annual rpt, 5664–12

Wetlands environmental characteristics, acreage, uses, and mgmt, by wetland type and region, 1950s-80, 26358–102

Evaluation Technologies, Inc.

"Bolivia: A Country Profile", 9916–2.56

"Cape Verde: A Country Profile", 9916–2.57

"Dominican Republic: A Country Profile", 9916–2.53

"Haiti: A Country Profile", 9916–2.54

"Mauritania: A Country Profile", 9916–2.55

Evans, E. G.

"Air Quality Data for Metals, 1977 Through 1979, from the National Air Surveillance Networks", 9194–10

Evans, Gary F.

"Air Quality Data for Nonmetallic Inorganic Ions: Nitrate and Sulfate for 1979 from the National Air Surveillance Networks", 9198–107

Evans, Robert, Jr.

Evans, Robert, Jr.

"'Lifetime Earnings' in Japan for the Class of 1955", 6722–1.427

"Pay Differentials: The Case of Japan", 6722–1.461

Evansville, Ind.

Census of Housing, 1980: occupancy and unit characteristics, by race, Hispanic origin, and city, SMSA rpt, 2473–1.150

Census of Population and Housing, 1980: detailed population and housing characteristics, by county, city, and census tract, SMSA rpt, 2551–2.150

Economic indicators for Southeastern States and 5 SMSAs, Fed Reserve 8th District, quarterly rpt, 9391–15

see also under By City and By SMSA or MSA in the "Index by Categories"

Everett, Wash.

Census of Housing, 1980: occupancy and unit characteristics, by race, Hispanic origin, and city, SMSA rpt, 2473–1.329

Census of Population and Housing, 1980: detailed population and housing characteristics, by county, city, and census tract, SMSA rpt, 2551–2.329

CPI by component for US city average, and by region, population size, and for 28 SMSAs, monthly press release, 6762–1

CPI by detailed component, for US city average, 28 SMSAs, and 4 regions by population size, monthly rpt, 6762–2

Hospital worker wages by sex and occupation, and benefits, for 22 MSAs, Oct 1981 survey, 6787–6.201

Housing unit starts and completions authorized by building permits in 20 MSAs, quarterly rpt, 2382–9

Wages of office and plant workers, by occupation, 1983 SMSA survey rpt, 6785–12.4

Eversull, E. Eldon

"Co-ops' Production of Crude Oil Down, but Reserve Protection Increased", 1122–1.407

"Sales Programs of Nine Regional Supply Cooperatives", 1128–24

"U.S. Cooperative Involvement in the Petroleum Industry, 1982", 1561–16.403

Evidence

Arson investigation and prosecution, by incident characteristics and outcome, motive, and type of evidence, for 4 jurisdictions, 1981, 6068–184

Crime and criminal justice statistics analysis, methodology, and use in courts, 1983 biennial conf proceedings, 6064–20

Criminal case disposition, effect of victim injury and other factors, and law enforcement official and victim attitudes, 1983 survey, 6068–185

Criminal case processing from arrest to sentencing, cases and processing time by disposition, dismissal reason, and offense, for 14 cities, 1979, 6066–22.1

Polygraph lie detection test accuracy, and Fed Govt use by agency, selected years 1947-83, 26358–96

Exceptional children

see Handicapped children

see Special education

Exchange of persons programs

Fed Govt intl exchange and training programs, participants by world region, and funding, by agency, FY83, annual rpt, 9854–8

Foreign visitors and other nonimmigrants admitted to US, by country of last residence, FY81, annual rpt, 6264–2

Japan-US Friendship Commission educational and cultural exchange activities, grants, and trust fund status, FY83, annual rpt, 14694–1

NIH intl program activities and funding, by inst and country, FY83, annual rpt, 4474–6

Soviet Union-US science and technology exchange projects, man-hours, and funding, by Fed Govt agency and activity type, FY81-82, 7008–41

USIA activities, employment, and funding, FY83-84, annual rpt, 17594–1

see also Educational exchanges

Exchange rates

see Foreign exchange

Excise tax

Alcohol and tobacco production, removals, stocks, and materials used, by State, monthly rpts, 8486–1

Alcohol fuel (ethanol) production in Tennessee Valley, feedstocks, facilities, tax incentives, and related farming data, by State, 1970s-83 and projected to 1992, 9808–69

Alcohol tax collections, by source, FY81-82, last issue of annual rpt, 8484–1.6

Alcohol, Tobacco, and Firearms Bur activities nationwide and in 20 cities, funding, and jobs to be transferred to Customs and Secret Service, 1979-82, hearings, 21528–55

Auto and van operating and owning costs by component and vehicle size, for 12 years of operation, 1984 model year, biennial rpt, 7554–21

Boston, Mass, govt budget and impact of reduced local revenue and Fed Govt aid, and other devs, FY80-86, article, 9373–1.406

Budget of US, CBO analysis of revenue and spending alternatives and projections of economic indicators, FY85-89, annual rpt, 26304–3

Budget of US, receipts by source and outlays by agency and program, monthly rpt, 8102–3

Budget of US, receipts by source and outlays by function, FY40-89 estimates revised for consistency with FY85 budget definitions, annual rpt, 104–12

Budget of US, receipts, outlays, and budget authority, by function and agency, FY84-89 revised estimates, midsession review of FY85 budget, annual rpt, 104–7

Census of Govts, 1982: city govt revenues by source, expenditures by function, debt, and assets, by State and city, 2457–4

Census of Govts, 1982: county govt revenues by source, expenditures by function, debt, and assets, by State and county, 2457–3

Census of Govts, 1982: State govt payments to local govts, by program, source of funds, level of govt, and State, with trends from 1902, 2460–3

Index by Subjects and Names

Coal production excise tax and other receipts of black lung trust fund, fund disbursements, and benefit claims and benefits by State, 1982, annual rpt, 6504–3

Fed Govt collections by IRS, by excise tax source, quarterly press release, 8302–1

Fed Govt consolidated financial statements based on business accounting methods, FY82-83, annual rpt, 8104–5

Fed Govt internal revenue, by type of tax, quarterly rpt, 8302–2.1

Fed Govt programs and mgmt cost control proposals, 3-year savings by function and agency, and financial and operating data, 1960s-81, 16908–1.12, 16908–1.26

Fed Govt receipts by source and outlays by agency, *Treasury Bulletin,* quarterly rpt, 8002–4.1

Foreign and US oil prices, tax, and customs duty, by refined product and major city, July 1983 and Jan 1984, annual rpt, 3164–50.4

Foreign and US retail gasoline and diesel prices and tax rates, for US and 4 countries, monthly rpt, 242–5

Govt finances, by level of govt, State, and for large cities and counties, 1981-83, annual rpt series, 2466–2

Govt revenues by source and expenditures by function, natl income and product account, *Survey of Current Business,* monthly rpt, monthly and annual tables, 2702–1.24

Govt tax revenues, by level of govt, type of tax, State, and selected counties, quarterly rpt, 2462–3

Govt taxation and revenue systems, by type of tax and system, level of govt, and State, selected years 1958-83, annual rpt, 10044–1.3

Hunting and fishing equipment excise tax revenue of Fed Govt fish and wildlife restoration program, by type of equipment, FY84, annual rpt, 5504–13

Hwy Statistics, summary data on traffic, govt finances, fuel use, vehicles, and driver licenses, by State, 1982, annual rpt, 7554–24

Hwy use taxes and Trust Fund revenues by tax type, and tax and truck size and weight limits effects on trucking industry, FY82-84 and projected to 1990, GAO rpt, 26117–31

Hwy use taxes by tax type, and truck size and weight limits, economic effects on trucking industry, 1982-83 and projected 1984-87, hearings, 25328–24

Income tax returns filed by type, for US, IRS regions, and service center cities, 1972-82 and projected 1983-90, annual rpt, 8304–9.1

Income tax returns of individuals, by filing and deduction characteristics and income level, 1983, annual article, 8302–2.414

Income tax returns of individuals, detailed data, 1982, annual rpt, 8304–2

IRS collections, by type of tax, region, and State, FY83, annual rpt, 8304–3.3

IRS collections, FY83, annual rpt, 8104–2.2

IRS tax collections by type of tax, procedures, and interest forgone through processing delay, for selected locations, FY81-82, GAO rpt, 26119–55

Index by Subjects and Names

Local govt spending, reliance on State aid and local taxes by type, and excise tax growth by State, selected years FY57-83, article, 10042–1.403

Motor fuel State tax provisions, motor vehicle registration fees, and disposition of receipts, by State, as of Jan 1984, biennial rpt, 7554–37

Motor fuel State tax rates by fuel type, and Fed Govt and State excise taxes on auto equipment, by State, 1983, annual rpt, 7554–1

Motor fuel tax rates, by State, 1975-83, annual table, 7554–32

Motor fuel taxes and other financing methods of govts and private sector for hwy and urban transit systems, with case studies for selected metro areas, series, 7556–7

Motor fuel taxes in US and selected countries, 1st qtr 1983, hearing, 21368–49

Motorcycle operating costs by component, for 5 makes, and Fed Govt mileage reimbursement rates, 1983, annual rpt, 9454–13.3

OECD energy prices and taxes by energy source and end-use sector, for US and 9 countries, quarterly 1979-83, annual rpt, 3164–71

Oil and gas finances by firm, and effect of income and excise tax provisions on firms, Fed Govt revenues, and investor tax returns, 1980 and projected to 1992, hearing, 21788–132

Oil windfall profits tax admin of IRS and revenues, tax rates, and nonfilers, 1980-86, GAO rpt, 26119–65

Oil windfall profits tax credit or refund and deduction for income tax returns of sole proprietorships, 1982, annual article, 8302–2.413

Oil windfall profits tax liability by tax rate, and exempt oil volume, by price control category, quarterly article, 8302–2.2

Public services subsidized by Fed Govt, user fees to recover costs of 7 programs, by type of fee, user, and service, FY84-88, 26306–6.68

Telephone and telegraph tax accruals and excise taxes collected from users, 1982 annual rpt, 9284–6.1

Tobacco marketing and smoking legislation introduced and enacted in State legislatures, by State, 1982, annual rpt, 4204–13

Tobacco tax collections, by source, FY81-82 with trends from 1880, last issue of annual rpt, 8484–1.5, 8484–1.6

Tobacco tax rates and receipts of Fed Govt and States, FY78-83, annual rpt, 1319–1.4

Tobacco tax revenues of Federal, State, and local govts, quarterly situation rpt with articles, 1561–10

Transportation finances, operations, vehicles, equipment, accidents, and energy use, by mode of transport, 1955-84, annual rpt, 7304–2

Transportation revenues by source and expenditures, by level of govt and mode of transport, and Fed Govt aid by type, FY77-82, 7308–185

see also Sales tax

Exhibitions and trade fairs

see also Tolls

Executive agreements

Bilateral and multilateral agreements of US in force, by country, Jan 1984, annual listing, 7004–1

Executive-congressional relations

see Congressional-executive relations

Executive departments

see Federal executive departments

Executive impoundment of appropriated funds

Budget of US Appendix, detailed budgets and personnel summaries, by agency, FY85, annual rpt, 104–3

Rescissions and deferrals of budget authority, monthly rpt, 102–2

Executive Office of the President

Budget of US Appendix, detailed budgets and personnel summaries, by agency, FY85, annual rpt, 104–3

Budget of US, appropriations, outlays, balances, and budget receipts, by govtl branch and agency, FY83, annual rpt, 8104–2

Budget of US, compact budgets by function, agency, and account, FY85 with projections to FY89, annual rpt, 104–2

Budget of US, object class analysis of obligations, by branch of Fed Govt and selected depts and agencies, FY85 estimates, annual rpt, 104–9

Budget of US, receipts by source and outlays by agency and program, monthly rpt, 8102–3

Central America socioeconomic and political conditions in 6 countries, 1960s-83 with trends and projections 1930-2010, 028–19

Drug abuse and trafficking reduction plan of Fed Govt, funding by agency and background data on drug use by substance, selected years FY81-85, biennial rpt, 024–1

Food aid programs of Fed Govt and others, funding, participant characteristics, and nutrition and poverty data, 1970s-83, 028–20

see also Central Intelligence Agency

see also Council of Economic Advisers

see also Council on Environmental Quality

see also Office of Management and Budget

see also Office of the U.S. Trade Representative

Executives

Census of Population and Housing, 1980: detailed population and housing characteristics, by county, city, and census tract, State and SMSA rpt series, 2551–2

Census of Population, 1980: detailed socioeconomic and demographic characteristics, by age, sex, race, Hispanic origin, occupation, and industry, State rpt series, 2531–4

Census of Population, 1980: detailed socioeconomic characteristics, by county, city, and inside-outside SMSAs and central cities, State rpt series, 2531–3

Census of Population, 1980: labor force, by sex, detailed occupation, and region, with comparison to 1970 census, supplementary rpt, 2535–1.12

Commerce Dept regional center mgmt assistance operations, assessment, and procurement authority, by subagency, regional rpt series, 2006–4

Employment by detailed occupation, for 29 SIC 2-digit nonmanufacturing industries, 1981 BLS survey, 6748–60

Employment, unemployment, and labor force, by demographic and employment characteristics, State, and for 30 metro areas and 11 large cities, 1983, annual rpt, 6744–7

Fed Govt civilian employment of minority groups and women, by grade and agency, 1980 and 1983, 21348–41

Fed Govt civilian pay rates, by branch of govt, employee category, and pay level, as of 1984 with trends from 1789, 21628–54

Fed Govt executive employee dev programs, employee and candidate attitudes in 5 agencies, 1983 survey, GAO rpt, 26119–69

Fed Govt executive employee performance appraisal system operations, and employee attitudes, 1982 survey, GAO rpt, 26119–61

Fed Govt minority group and handicapped employment, by race, Hispanic origin, disability, sex, and employment characteristics, as of Sept 1982, biennial rpt, 9844–27

Fed Govt programs and mgmt cost control proposals, 3-year savings by function and agency, and financial and operating data, 1960s-81, 16908–1.27

Minority group and women's employment, by occupational group, SIC 2- to 3-digit industry, State, and SMSA, 1981, annual rpt, 9244–1

Nuclear industry nongovt employment by industry segment, occupation, and census div, and DOE and NRC nuclear employment, 1968-83, biennial rpt, 3004–11

Occupational manpower needs and supply by detailed occupation, and educational and training program enrollees and grads by detailed field, 1982 and 1995, biennial rpt, 6744–3

Occupational Outlook Handbook, 1984-85 biennial rpt, 6744–1

Small business mgmt counseling by university centers, costs, funding, and businesses served by industry, with detail for 2 States, 1980-83, hearing, 25728–36

Terrorist (intl) incidents, casualties, and attacks on US targets, by attack type and world area, with chronology of events, 1983, annual rpt, 7004–13

TV and radio industry minority and women employment by occupation, and business owners, by race and State, with revenues and stations, 1971-81, hearing, 21368–45

Washington State deaths by sex, cause, and detailed occupation, summary data from occupational mortality study, 1950-79, 4248–47

see also Officials

Exhibitions and trade fairs

Business America, foreign and domestic commerce, and US investment and trade opportunities, biweekly rpt articles, 2042–24

Foreign and US Commercial Service of ITA, overseas staff by category, and trade promotion costs by activity, by country, 1982-83, hearing, 21408–73

Exhibitions and trade fairs

Govt census, 1982: State govt payments to local govts, by program, source of funds, level of govt, and State, with trends from 1902, 2460–3

Eximbank

see Export-Import Bank

Exploration, natural resources

see Energy exploration and drilling

see Natural resources

Explosives

- Air pollutant emission factors, by detailed source, 3rd edition, 1983-84 supplements, 9198–13
- Arrests and seizures involving explosives and firearms, by State, FY82, last issue of annual rpt, 8484–1.6
- Business statistics, detailed data for major industries and economic indicators, *Survey of Current Business,* monthly rpt, 2702–1.9
- China economic conditions, agricultural and industrial production, trade, and domestic and foreign investment, 1980-85, 2048–106
- China exports and imports by SITC 1- to 5-digit commodity, 1970s-82, annual rpt, 244–12
- County Business Patterns: establishments, employees, and payrolls, by SIC 4-digit industry and county, 1981, annual State rpt series, 2326–8
- County Business Patterns: establishments, employees, and payrolls, by SIC 4-digit industry and county, 1982, annual State rpt series, 2326–6
- Deaths and death rates from accidents, by place, detailed cause, and demographic characteristics, 1979, US Vital Statistics annual rpt, 4144–2.1, 4144–2.5
- Exports and imports of US, totals and as percent of domestic production, by SIC 2- to 5-digit commodity, 1981, annual rpt, 2424–3
- Exports of US, detailed commodities by country of destination, monthly rpt, 2422–3
- Exports of US, detailed Schedule B commodities by country of destination, 1983, annual rpt, 2424–9
- Exports of US, detailed Schedule E commodities by mode of transport and world area and country of destination, 1983, annual rpts, 2424–5
- Hwy construction expenditures and contracts awarded for Federal-aid system, by type of material used and State, various periods 1944-83, annual rpt, 7554–29.7
- Hwy construction materials used per $1 million of total expenditures on Federal-aid system, by State, 1980-82, annual rpt, 7554–29.3
- Imports of US, detailed Schedule A commodities by country and world area of origin, and mode of transport, 1983, annual rpts, 2424–2
- Imports of US, detailed Schedule A commodities by country, monthly rpt, 2422–2
- Imports of US, detailed TSUSA commodities by country of origin, 1983, annual rpt, 2424–4
- Input-output structure of US economy, detailed interindustry transactions for 537 industries, and components of final demand, 1977 benchmark data, 2708–17

Law enforcement activities of Alcohol, Tobacco, and Firearms Bur in 20 cities and nationwide, funding, and jobs to be transferred to Customs and Secret Service, 1979-82, hearings, 21528–55

- Manufacturing census, 1982: financial and operating data, for SIC 4-digit industries by product, preliminary rpt, 2491–1.198
- Mineral industries census, 1982: financial and operating data, including materials consumed, by SIC 4-digit industry and State, preliminary rpt series, 2511–1
- Mineral Industry Surveys, explosives and blasting agents consumption by type, industry, and State, 1983, annual rpt, 5614–22
- Minerals industries consumption of explosives, by explosive type, 1977-81, *Minerals Yearbook,* annual rpt, 5604–33.1
- Occupational deaths, by industry div and cause, 1981-82, article, 6722–1.422
- Occupational injury and illness rates, by SIC 2- to 4-digit industry, 1982, annual rpt, 6844–1
- Ocean dumping of waste materials, EPA permit program and intl London Dumping Convention activities, 1981-83, annual rpt, 9204–8
- Producer prices and indexes, by stage of processing and detailed commodity, monthly rpt, 6762–6
- Producer prices and indexes, by stage of processing and detailed commodity, monthly 1983, annual supplement, 6764–2
- Transportation census, 1982: trucks, by detailed characteristics, miles traveled, and type of product carried, State rpt series, 2573–1

see also Ammunition

see also Bombs

see also Nuclear explosives and explosions

Export Administration Act

Customs Service activities, operations, and staff, FY79-83, annual rpt, 8144–1

Export controls

see Tariffs and foreign trade controls

Export-Import Bank

- Agricultural exports under Fed Govt-financed programs, by commodity and country, bimonthly rpt, periodic tables, 1522–1.4
- Budget of US Appendix, detailed budgets and personnel summaries, by agency, FY85, annual rpt, 104–3
- Budget of US, appropriations, outlays, balances, and budget receipts, by govtl branch and agency, FY83, annual rpt, 8104–2
- Budget of US, CBO analysis of revenue and spending alternatives and projections of economic indicators, FY85-89, annual rpt, 26304–3.3
- Budget of US, loans and loan guarantees, and Admin proposed limits on credit assistance, by program, FY83-89, annual rpt, 26306–3.65
- Budget of US, object class analysis of obligations, by branch of Fed Govt and selected depts and agencies, FY85 estimates, annual rpt, 104–9
- Cost control proposals for Fed Govt programs and mgmt, 3-year savings by function and agency, and financial and operating data, 1960s-81, 16908–1.14

Index by Subjects and Names

- Credit assistance costs, policies to improve measurement, with loan and loan guarantee data by program, and Federal and private credit instns operations, 1970-84, 26306–6.72
- Credit programs for export, activities of Eximbank and 6 OECD countries, 1982, annual rpt, 9254–3
- Debt to US of foreign govts and private obligors, by country and program, periodic rpt, 8002–6
- Financial condition, and loan, credit, and insurance authorizations, by country, FY83, annual rpt, 9254–1
- Foreign cargo shipments and costs of Fed Govt by agency or program and route, and employment and economic impacts of US vessel preference, 1980, GAO rpt, 26117–30
- Human rights conditions in 162 countries, economic and military aid of US, and economic aid of intl organizations, 1981-83, annual rpt, 21384–3
- Liabilities (contigent) and claims paid by Fed Govt on federally insured and guaranteed contracts with foreign obligors, by country and program, periodic rpt, 8002–12
- Loans and grants for economic and military assistance from US and intl agencies, by program and country, FY46-83, annual rpt, 9914–5
- Loans, guarantees, and insurance authorizations of Eximbank, by country, FY83, annual rpt, 15344–1.12
- Mexico and Brazil Eximbank loan guarantees and insurance currently provided and needed, and value of worldwide and US trade, 1981-84, hearings, 25248–97

Export Marketing Service

see Foreign Agricultural Service

Export promotion

see Foreign trade promotion

Exports and imports

- *see* Agricultural exports and imports
- *see* Coal exports and imports
- *see* Energy exports and imports
- *see* Foreign trade
- *see* Natural gas exports and imports
- *see* Petroleum exports and imports
- *see* under names of specific commodities or commodity groups

Expositions

see Exhibitions and trade fairs

Expropriation

Claims against foreign govts by US natls, by country and type of claim, 1983, annual rpt, 6004–16

Extension work

see Agricultural extension work

Exterminator services

see Pests and pest control

Extradition

Govt census, 1982: State govt payments to local govts, by program, source of funds, level of govt, and State, with trends from 1902, 2460–3

Eye diseases and defects

- Air traffic controller color blindness exams, comparison of alternative testing methods, 1983 technical rpt, 7506–10.26
- Contact lens price and adverse lens-associated eye conditions related to fitting by ophthalomologists, opticians, and optometrists, 1977-80, 9408–49

Index by Subjects and Names

Deaths and death rates by detailed cause and demographic characteristics, 1979 and selected trends, US Vital Statistics annual rpt, 4144–2.1

Disability Insurance beneficiaries sociodemographic and medical characteristics, 1977-79, annual rpt, 4744–20

Head Start Project enrollment of handicapped children, by handicap, State, and for Indian and migrant programs, 1982, annual rpt, 4604–1

Hospital discharges and length of stay, by patient characteristics, facility size, procedure performed, diagnosis, and region, 1982, annual rpt, 4147–13.78

Indian births, morbidity, and deaths and rates, and health services facilities and use, 1954-83, annual compilation, 4104–7

Pilots with visual defects, hours of flight, and accidents, by defect type and medical certificate class, 1980-81, 7506–10.30

Visual impairment survey methodology and results by age, in 3 SMSAs, Aug 1981-Dec 1982, 4478–147

see also Blind

see also Optometry

see also Vision

see also under By Disease in the "Index by Categories"

FAA

see Federal Aviation Administration

Faber, Joseph F.

"Life Tables for the U.S., 1900-2050", 4706–1.89

Fabrics

see Synthetic fibers and fabrics

see Textile industry and fabrics

Factories

see Industrial plants and equipment

Faculty

see Teachers

Facundo, Blanca

"U.S. Foundations Responsiveness to Puerto Rican Needs and Concerns: Foundation Giving to Puerto Rican Organizations 1979-81", 21788–137.1

Fair employment practices

see Discrimination in employment

Fair housing

see Discrimination in housing

Fair Labor Standards Act

Minimum wage rates under Act, 1938-84, annual rpt, 4744–3.1

Fairfield, Calif.

Census of Population and Housing, 1980: detailed population and housing characteristics, by county, city, and census tract, SMSA rpt, 2551–2.360

Housing vacancy rates for single and multifamily units and mobile homes, by city and ZIP code, 1983, annual metro area rpt, 9304–20.8

Housing vacancy rates for single and multifamily units and mobile homes, by city and ZIP code, 1984, annual metro area rpt, 9304–20.20

see also under By SMSA or MSA in the "Index by Categories"

Fairs

see Exhibitions and trade fairs

Faith

see Religion

Falk, Barry

"Impact of Federally Sponsored Credit Agencies' Policy Instruments on Housing and Credit Markets", 9316–2.45

Falkland Islands

see South America

Fall River, Mass.

Census of Housing, 1980: occupancy and unit characteristics, by race, Hispanic origin, and city, SMSA rpt, 2473–1.151

Census of Population and Housing, 1980: detailed population and housing characteristics, by county, city, and census tract, SMSA rpt, 2551–2.151

Dress industry production and related workers, wages, and benefits, by occupation, size of establishment, and union status, for 11 labor market areas, Aug 1982 survey, 6787–6.200

see also under By SMSA or MSA in the "Index by Categories"

Fallert, Richard F.

"Impacts of Nationwide Adoption of the California Solids Standards for Fluid Milk Product", 1561–2.405

"National and Regional Costs and Returns of Producing Milk", 1561–2.401

Fallout

see Fallout shelters

see Nuclear explosives and explosions

see Nuclear radiation

Fallout shelters

Earth-sheltered housing design, energy efficiency, natural and nuclear hazard reduction, and costs, by selected SMSA, 1983 rpt, 3308–71

Fed Emergency Mgmt Agency nuclear attack civil defense plans, funding and operations by component, FY81-84 and projected FY85-89, GAO rpt, 26123–61

Families and households

Births, fertility rates, expected births, and childless women, by socioeconomic characteristics, June 1982, annual Current Population Rpt, 2546–1.386

Births, fertility rates, expected births, and childless women, by socioeconomic characteristics, June 1983, advance annual Current Population Rpt, 2546–1.385

Births, fertility rates, expected births, and childless women, by socioeconomic characteristics, June 1983, annual Current Population Rpt, 2546–1.393

Census of Housing, 1980: inventory, occupancy, and unit characteristics, changes from 1973 by region and inside-outside SMSAs and central cities, series, 2473–3

Census of Housing, 1980: occupancy and unit characteristics of SMSAs and central cities, by race, Hispanic origin, and city, State and SMSA rpt series, 2473–1

Census of Housing, 1980: structural, financial, and householder characteristics, by region and State, 2475–4

Census of Population and Housing, 1980: detailed population and housing characteristics, by county, city, and census tract, State and SMSA rpt series, 2551–2

Census of Population, 1980: detailed socioeconomic and demographic characteristics, by age, sex, race, Hispanic origin, occupation, and industry, State rpt series, 2531–4

Families and households

Census of Population, 1980: detailed socioeconomic characteristics, by county, city, and inside-outside SMSAs and central cities, State rpt series, 2531–3

Census of Transportation, 1982: trucks, by detailed characteristics, miles traveled, and type of product carried, State rpt series, 2573–1

City and suburb population characteristics and local govt finances, by region and selected SMSA, 1950s-FY83, 10048–61

Community Dev Block Grants admin, allocation, and family social benefits, effect of policy changes to increase local admin responsibility, for 10 cities, as of 1982, 5188–105

Consumer goods prices and supplies, family finance, and home economics, quarterly rpt with articles, 1702–1

Consumer Income, socioeconomic characteristics of persons, families, and households, detailed cross-tabulations, Current Population Rpt series, 2546–6

County and City Data Book, detailed socioeconomic and demographic data for States, counties, and cities, selected years 1976-82, 2328–1

Crime victimization of households, by offense type, race of household head, and family income and urban-rural residence, 1975-83, periodic rpt, 6062–2.404

Crime victimization rates by type of offense, and victim and offense characteristics, Natl Crime Survey series, 6066–3

Dairy products household expenditures, effects of income and other sociodemographic characteristics, modeling results, 1977/78, 1561–2.404

Earnings of couples with both spouses working, by sociodemographic and employment characteristics and age of children, 1981, Current Population Rpt, 2546–2.120

Earnings of families by number of earners, and earnings and employment status of individual family members, quarterly rpt, 6742–19

Earnings of families by number of earners and members employment status, and earnings of full- and part-time workers, by sociodemographic characteristics, 1982-83, article, 6742–2.406

Elementary and secondary enrollment, households with children enrolled by school control, householder characteristics, and region, Oct 1982, 4838–13

Employment and earnings, detailed data, monthly rpt, 6742–2.8

Employment status, by family relationship, monthly rpt, 6742–2.1

Employment status of family members, by occupation, family composition, age of children, and other characteristics, 1983 and trends from 1940, 6746–1.253

Farm population, by employment and socioeconomic characteristics, 1983, annual rpt, 2544–1

Farmers, farm population, and managers health insurance coverage by insurance type and selected sociodemographic characteristics, 1976, 1598–191

Fed Govt cash benefit program beneficiaries with representative payees, by age, relation to payee, and program, as of 1983, GAO rpt, 26121–85

Families and households

- Florida and California elderly migration by selected State of origin or destination, and Florida elderly, by sociodemographic and housing characteristics, 1970 and 1980, 4478–150
- Food expenditures for fruit, vegetable, and potato products related to changes in income and other household characteristics, 1977-78, 1548–236
- Food stamp recipient households size and composition, income, and income deductions allowed, Aug 1981, annual rpt, 1364–8
- Foreign women sociodemographic, economic, and fertility characteristics, with comparisons to men, by country, 1960s-85, world region rpt series, 2326–15
- Head Start Project programs effect on child dev, by characteristics of program, child, and family, literature review, selected years 1965-81, 4608–20
- Health care expenditures, natl survey on services use, costs, and sources of payment, by patient and physician characteristics, 1977-78, series, 4186–3
- High school classes of 1980 and 1982: educational and sociodemographic characteristics and expectations, natl longitudinal study, series, 4826–2
- Hispanic Americans socioeconomic and demographic characteristics, and compared to non-Hispanics, selected years 1970-83, chartbook, 2328–48
- Home mortgages FHA-insured, financial, property, and mortgagor characteristics, quarterly rpt, 5142–1
- Home mortgages FHA-insured, financial, property, and mortgagor characteristics, 1983, annual rpt, 5144–17
- Homeless population and characteristics, and temporary shelter operations, use, and user characteristics, by region and selected city, 1983, 5188–108
- Homeless population and characteristics, and temporary shelter operations, use, and user characteristics, for selected cities, various periods 1979-84, hearing, 21248–85
- Household income, home value and equity, and financial assets by type, by household characteristics, 1983 survey with trends from 1970, article, 9362–1.406
- Household living arrangements, family relationships, and marital status, by age and sex, Mar 1984, advance annual Current Population Rpt, 2546–1.389
- Household living arrangements, family relationships, and marital status, by demographic characteristics, Mar 1983, annual Current Population Rpt, 2546–1.388
- Households and housing detailed characteristics, and unit and neighborhood quality, by inside-outside central cities, 1979-82 surveys, SMSA rpt series, 2485–6
- Households and housing unit characteristics, and employment, housing finance, and social programs data, selected years 1948-83, hearing, 21968–28
- Households and housing unit characteristics, by region and metro-nonmetro residence, 1983, biennial survey, 2485–1
- Households and housing unit selected characteristics, subject rpt series, 2486–1
- Housing (low-income) energy aid of Fed Govt, by income, aid type, and State, FY83, annual rpt, 4744–3.13
- Housing (rental) unit choice of Pittsburgh, Pa, recent movers related to unit, neighborhood, and town characteristics, 1967 survey, 9306–1.7
- Housing and financial characteristics, and unit and neighborhood quality, for 15 SMSAs, 1978, annual survey special supplement, 2485–8
- Housing and neighborhood quality indicators and attitudes, and occupant characteristics, by urban-rural location and region, 1981, annual survey, 2485–7
- Housing and neighborhood quality indicators and attitudes, by occupant and unit characteristics, region, and metro-nonmetro location, 1981, annual survey, 2485–2
- Housing rental assistance, HUD certificates for low-income single parents by community, 1984 press release, 5006–3.35
- Immigrant and nonimmigrant visas issued and refused, and status adjustments, by class and nationality, FY77, annual rpt, 7184–1
- Immigrants admitted under Immigration and Nationality Act, by class of admission, FY78-81, annual rpt, 6264–2
- Income (household) and cash and noncash transfer program participation, by sociodemographic characteristics, quarterly rpt, 2542–2
- Income (household) before and after taxes, by socioeconomic characteristics, type of tax paid, and region, 1981, Current Population Rpt, 2546–2.118
- Income assistance, effects of experimental negative income tax program on employment, earnings, marital status, and other family characteristics in 2 cities, 1970-75, 4008–64
- Labor force, special characteristics, Labor Statistics Handbook, 1947-82, annual rpt, 6724–1.2
- Massachusetts parents awareness and use of safety measures to protect their children from accidents, for 9 communities by urban-rural location, Sept 1980-June 1982 survey, article, 4102–1.402
- Mobility of population, detailed data by demographic and socioeconomic characteristics of movers and nonmovers, Mar 1981-82, annual Current Population Rpt, 2546–1.384
- Natl income and product, comprehensive accounts and components, *Survey of Current Business,* monthly rpt, 2702–1.22
- NYC families caring for aged relatives, preference for social service and financial programs to provide assistance, 1980, article, 4652–1.403
- OASDHI, Medicaid, SSI, and other social insurance and public welfare programs benefits, beneficiary characteristics, and trust funds, selected years 1937-82, annual rpt, 4744–3.6
- Older persons by demographic, socioeconomic, and health characteristics, selected years 1900-81 and projected to 2050, Current Population Rpt, 2546–2.125

Index by Subjects and Names

- Older persons population characteristics, and needs and costs of social services by type, by metro-nonmetro status, 1970s-82 with trends from 1900, 21148–28
- Older persons sociodemographic characteristics, and Fed Govt program participation and funding, 1983 with trends and projections 1900-2060, annual rpt, 25144–3.1
- Older persons sociodemographic characteristics and transportation needs, selected years 1900-2040, 7308–183
- Pacific Northwest electricity consumption and prices by end-use sector, and economic and demographic data, 1960s-83 and projected to 2005, annual rpt, 3224–2
- Population demographic and economic characteristics, 1982 with projections of population size to 2050, annual Current Population Rpt, 2546–2.119
- Population detailed socioeconomic characteristics, Mar 1982, annual Current Population Rpt, 2546–1.383
- Poverty-level persons and families, by income source, hours of work, earnings, taxes, and family characteristics, various periods 1959-84, 21788–131
- Poverty population by labor force status, and effect of public welfare changes and recession, by family status, FY82, 21788–139
- Poverty population size, effect of counting public noncash transfers as income by recipient characteristics, 1979-83, 2626–2.52
- Poverty population size, effects of counting public noncash transfers as income by recipient characteristics, 1979-82, 2626–2.50
- Poverty rate by family composition, and effect of noncash transfers, taxes, unemployment benefits, and business cycles, selected years 1959-82, hearings, 21788–141
- Poverty status of families and persons, by detailed socioeconomic characteristics, 1982, annual Current Population Rpt, 2546–6.40
- Poverty status of families and persons by selected characteristics, public welfare funding, and effect of counting transfer payments as income, selected years 1950-83, 25928–4
- Poverty status of young adults related to motivation, psychological factors, and family characteristics, by race and sex, 1970s-82, longitudinal studies, 4008–65
- Public and employer-based noncash transfer program recipients, by income source and socioeconomic characteristics, 1982, advance Current Population Rpt, 2546–6.38
- Public and employer-based noncash transfer program recipients, by income source and socioeconomic characteristics, 1982, final Current Population Rpt, 2546–6.37
- Public housing under private mgmt, assessment by housing officials and managers, and tenants, with operating costs, crime, and rent delinquency by project type and location, 1982, 5188–103
- School lunch program school and student participation, families eligible, and Federal reimbursement rates, FY79-83, GAO rpt, 26113–123

Index by Subjects and Names

Southeastern US water supply and quality, with background socioeconomic data, for 8 States, 1960s-2020 with trends from 1930, 9208–119

Statistical Abstract of US, social, political, and economic data, 1950s-83 and trends, annual rpt, 2324–1.1

Supplementary Security Income beneficiary socioeconomic characteristics and health service use, 1970s-83 and SSI program projections to 1995, 25148–29

Taxes, tax policy, and intergovtl relations, public opinion survey results, 1972-84, annual rpt, 10044–2

Travel patterns, personal and household characteristics, auto use, and public transport availability, 1977 survey, series, 7556–6

TVA construction projects employment, and impacts on nearby areas, survey rpt series, 9806–7

Underground economy, household expenditures and participation by type of goods or service and sociodemographic characteristics, with methodology and bibl, 1981 survey, 8308–27

Unemployment and part-time employment, by race, Hispanic origin, sex, family composition, income, and poverty status, 1980-82, annual report, 6744–15

Unemployment and part-time employment effects on family income, by socioeconomic and labor force characteristics, 1981-82, annual rpt, 6746–1.252

Urban area socioeconomic and fiscal trends and problems, 1950-83 and Fed Govt funding estimates for FY84-87, biennial rpt, 5124–4

Veterans aged 55 and over, socioeconomic characteristics, economic resources, health care and status, and actual and expected use of VA benefits, 1983 survey, 9928–29

Veterans income and educational attainment compared to nonveterans, by age, 1982-83, annual rpt, 9924–19

Vocationally rehabilitated persons under State agency programs, by sociodemographic characteristics and disabling condition, FY79-81, annual rpt, 4944–6

Warsaw Pact and US citizens divided families, cases pending as of Mar 1984, semiannual rpt, 7002–1

Washington Public Power Supply System nuclear reactors construction financing, with regional economic impacts and power supply/demand, 1980s-2035, hearing, 21448–29

Western States housing outlook and economic and demographic trends, FHLB 11th District, urban area rpt series, 9306–2

Women in couples with wife as primary earner, socioeconomic and family characteristics, with comparative data for husbands, Mar 1982, 2326–11.9

Women's employment and earnings, by labor force and socioeconomic characteristics, and compared to men, 1978-81 and trends from 1940s, 6568–29

Women's labor force participation, by age, race, and family status, quarterly rpt, 6742–17

Women's labor force participation by marital status, and children by parent labor force status, by family composition, race, and Hispanic origin, Mar 1984 and trends from 1970, 6748–78

Women's labor force participation, earnings, and socioeconomic characteristics, 1983, annual fact sheet, 6564–1

Women's travel patterns, by employment and sociodemographic characteristics and type of child care used, 1980 survey, 7888–62

see also Adoption

see also Aid to Families with Dependent Children

see also Child abuse and neglect

see also Child support and alimony

see also Child welfare

see also Children

see also Domestic violence

see also Family planning

see also Housing energy use

see also Illegitimacy

see also Marriage and divorce

see also Men

see also Military dependents

see also Personal and family income

see also Widows and widowers

see also Women

see also Youth

Family budgets

see Cost of living

Family income

see Personal and family income

see under By Income in the "Index by Categories"

Family planning

AID activities and funding by project and function, FY85, and developing countries summary socioeconomic data, 1970s-83, by country, annual rpt, 9914–3

Births, fertility rates, expected births, and childless women, by socioeconomic characteristics, June 1982, annual Current Population Rpt, 2546–1.386

Births, fertility rates, expected births, and childless women, by socioeconomic characteristics, June 1983, advance annual Current Population Rpt, 2546–1.385

Births, fertility rates, expected births, and childless women, by socioeconomic characteristics, June 1983, annual Current Population Rpt, 2546–1.393

Fed Govt public welfare programs and tax expenditures benefitting children and youth, participation and funding for 71 programs, FY81-83, 21968–30

Govt census, 1982: State govt payments to local govts, by program, source of funds, level of govt, and State, with trends from 1902, 2460–3

Health condition and health care resources, use, and expenditures, 1970s-82 with trends and projections 1900-2000, annual compilation, 4144–11

HHS aid to each State and local govt or private instn, amount obligated, funding agency, and program, FY83, annual listing, 4004–3

HHS family planning program activities and funding, annual rpt, suspended, 4044–4

Medicare enrollment and bills approved, and reimbursement and Medicaid payments by type of service and beneficiary, quarterly rpt, 4652–1.1

Farm Credit Administration

Obstetrician-gynecologist office visits and drugs used, by visit reason, diagnosis, treatment, and patient and physician characteristics, 1980-81, 4147–13.76

Oral contraceptives prescriptions, and market shares by progestin and estrogen content, 1964-80, article, 4102–1.436

Population and health research funded by 4 private organizations, project listing by topic, with funding data, 1981, annual rpt, 4474–16

Public Health Service activities, and funding by function and subagency, FY83, annual rpt, 4044–2

State govt maternal and child health funding, and admin of Fed Govt block grants, by program for 13 States, 1981-83, GAO rpt, 26121–70

State govt social services spending by type and funding source, and admin of Fed Govt block grants, for 13 States, selected years FY80-84, GAO rpt, 26121–76

Teenage girls births and sexual experience by race, abortions, and birth control use, by age, 1970s-80 with birth trends from 1920, hearings, 21968–29

Vital and Health Statistics series and other NCHS publications, 1979-83, annual listing,, 4124–1

Women's contraceptives use, by method, marital status, age, and race, 1982, 4146–8.103

Women's family planning and infertility services use, by source of service, marital status, age, race, and Hispanic origin, 1982, 4146–8.104

Youth office visits to physicians by patient and visit characteristics and physician specialty, and drug mentions by brand, 1980-81, 4146–8.100

see also Abortion

see also Sexual sterilization

Farber, Kit D.

"Pollution Abatement and Control Expenditures, 1972-82", 2702–1.407

Fargo, N.Dak.

Census of Housing, 1980: occupancy and unit characteristics, by race, Hispanic origin, and city, SMSA rpt, 2473–1.152

Census of Population and Housing, 1980: detailed population and housing characteristics, by county, city, and census tract, SMSA rpt, 2551–2.152

see also under By SMSA or MSA in the "Index by Categories"

Farley, Pamela J.

"Estimation and Sampling Procedures in the NMCES Insurance Surveys", 4186–4.3

Farm costs

see Agricultural finance

see Agricultural production costs

Farm Credit Administration

Budget of US Appendix, detailed budgets and personnel summaries, by agency, FY85, annual rpt, 104–3

Budget of US, appropriations, outlays, balances, and budget receipts, by govtl branch and agency, FY83, annual rpt, 8104–2

Cost control proposals for Fed Govt programs and mgmt, 3-year savings by function and agency, and financial and operating data, 1960s-81, 16908–1.14

Farm Credit System mortgage and other loans, and financial statements, 1982 and selected trends from 1961, annual rpt, 9264–2

Farm Credit Administration

Farm finance and credit conditions, forecast 1984, conf summary, annual rpt, 9264–9

- Farm mortgage debt outstanding, by type of lender and district, as of Jan 1983, annual rpt, 9264–3
- Farm non-real estate debt outstanding, by type of lender and district, as of Jan 1983, annual rpt, 9264–4
- Federal land banks loan and borrower characteristics, by district, annual rpt, discontinued, 9264–8
- Financial ratios and stock dividends of Student Loan Marketing Assn compared to banks and 4 Fed Govt-sponsored credit assns, 1980-82, GAO rpt, 26121–71
- Financial statements of Farm Credit System banks, Dec 1981-83, annual rpt, 9264–5
- Land privately held, acreage and owners by owner characteristics, land use, and region, and purchase and improvement funding, 1978 survey, series, 1506–5

Farm Credit Banks

see Farm Credit System

Farm Credit System

- Budgets and statements of Fed Govt sponsored enterprises, detailed data, US Budget Appendix, FY85, annual rpt, 104–3.5
- Farm debt, loans outstanding, and interest rates, by type of lender and State, 1960-83 with trends from 1940, biennial rpt, 1544–2
- Farm finances, assets, expenses, cash flow, receipts, and loans, selected years 1971-85, annual rpt, 1544–13
- Farm finances, expenses by type, loans by purpose and source, and credit detail by Fed Reserve District, quarterly rpt, 9365–3.10
- Farm finances, production, expenses by type, and domestic economic impact, selected years 1972-82 and preliminary 1983-84, annual rpt, 1544–19
- Farm mortgage and other loans of Farm Credit System, and financial statements, 1982 and selected trends from 1961, annual rpt, 9264–2
- Farm mortgage debt outstanding, by type of lender and district, as of Jan 1983, annual rpt, 9264–3
- Farm non-real estate debt outstanding, by type of lender and district, as of Jan 1983, annual rpt, 9264–4
- Farm real estate and nonreal estate debt outstanding, by lender, 1940-84, annual rpt, 1544–16.2
- Farm real estate and other debt, by type of lender, 1980 benchmark data with revised estimates for 1970-82, 1548–230
- Farm real estate credit-financed transfers, by type of lender and region, selected years 1945-84, annual rpt, 1541–8.5
- Federal land banks loan and borrower characteristics, by district, annual rpt, discontinued, 9264–8
- Financial statements of Farm Credit System banks, Dec 1981-83, annual rpt, 9264–5
- North Central States farm credit conditions and economic devs, Fed Reserve 7th District, biweekly rpt, 9375–10

Farm debt

see Agricultural credit

see Agricultural finance

Farm income

- Agricultural situation and farm-related topics, monthly rpt, 1502–6
- *Agricultural Statistics, 1983,* annual rpt, 1004–1
- *Agriculture Fact Book of US,* compilation of data for 1983 with trends from 1940, annual rpt, 1004–14
- Alcohol fuel production costs, related employment, and Fed Govt subsidies and impact on farm income, selected years 1978-90, GAO rpt, 26113–140
- Catfish raised on farms, production, inventory, sales, prices, and imports, monthly release, 1631–14
- Census of Agriculture, 1982: farms, farmland, production and costs, and operator characteristics, preliminary State and county rpt series, 2330–1
- Census of Agriculture, 1982: farms, farmland, production, finances, and operator characteristics, by county, final State rpt series, 2331–1
- Census of Population, 1980: detailed socioeconomic and demographic characteristics, by age, sex, race, Hispanic origin, occupation, and industry, State rpt series, 2531–4
- Census of Population, 1980: detailed socioeconomic characteristics, by county, city, and inside-outside SMSAs and central cities, State rpt series, 2531–3
- *County and City Data Book,* detailed socioeconomic and demographic data for States, counties, and cities, selected years 1976-82, 2328–1
- Economic indicators and components, current data and annual trends, monthly rpt, 23842–1.1
- Exports (agricultural) share of farm sales, FY82, State rpt series, 2046–3
- Exports and personal expenditures of US and world for selected agricultural commodities, by country, and export share of US farm income, various periods 1926-82, 1528–172
- Farm business legal organization, finances, operations, tax rates, and State laws restricting farm corporations, 1960s-82, 1548–233
- Farm finance and credit conditions, forecast 1984, conf summary, annual rpt, 9264–9
- Farm finances, assets, expenses, cash flow, receipts, and loans, selected years 1971-85, annual rpt, 1544–13
- Farm finances, assets, liabilities, income, receipts by commodity and State, and expenses, 1980-83 and trends from 1910, annual rpt, 1544–16
- Farm finances, expenses by type, loans by purpose and source, and credit detail by Fed Reserve District, quarterly rpt, 9365–3.10
- Farm finances, production, expenses by type, and domestic economic impact, selected years 1972-82 and preliminary 1983-84, annual rpt, 1544–19
- Farm policies and objectives, farm income, and net family income and net worth per farm, by farm sales class, 1982, article, 9381–1.411
- Farm population, by employment and socioeconomic characteristics, 1983, annual rpt, 2544–1

Index by Subjects and Names

- Farm population, by farm type and sales size and selected other characteristics, 1975-80, 1598–144
- Farm price support programs for 5 crops, and effects of alternative Fed Govt policies, FY56-83 with projections to FY88, 26306–6.71
- Farm production itemized costs, receipts, and net returns, for 13 crops, 4 livestock types, and milk, by region, 1981-83, annual rpt, 1544–20
- Farm production, prices, marketing, and trade, by commodity, forecast and current situation, monthly rpt, 1502–4
- Farm sector financial review, debt outlook, and rural banks condition, 1950s-83, article, 9362–1.401
- Fed Govt policy issues effect on agricultural and food prices, income, and trade, and crop support levels by program, Nov 1984, semiannual rpt, 1542–6
- Hog production, producer characteristics, facilities, and marketing, by type and size of enterprise and region, 1975 and 1980, 1568–248
- Income (legal) not reported on Federal income tax returns by source, and legal and illegal underground income, with bibl, 1974-81, article, 2702–1.419
- Income (personal), and BEA and IRS calculations of adjusted gross income, by source, 1981-82, article, 2702–1.414
- Income (personal) of farm population, and income from farming, 1929-83, annual rpt, 204–1.8
- Income (personal) per capita and by source, and earnings by industry div, by State, MSA, and county, 1977-82, annual regional rpts, 2704–2
- Income (personal) per capita and by source, earnings by major industry group, and social insurance contributions, by region and State, 1929-82, 2708–40
- Income (taxable) not reported on individual and corporate returns, and associated Federal revenue losses, by detailed legal and illegal source, 1973-81, 8308–26
- Income of farm population, prices received and cash receipts by commodity, 1960s-82, annual chartbook, 1504–3
- Income of farms (gross and net), detailed components, by State, 1979-82 and trends from 1950, annual rpt, 1544–18
- Income of households, families, and persons, by detailed socioeconomic characteristics and region, 1982, annual Current Population Rpt, 2546–6.39
- Income tax returns filed by type, for US, IRS regions, and service center cities, 1972-82 and projected 1983-90, annual rpt, 8304–9.1
- Income tax returns of corporations, detailed income and tax items by industry, 1981, annual rpt, 8304–4
- Income tax returns of elderly, by income statement and tax item and income level, 1981 with trends from 1977, article, 8302–2.412
- Income tax returns of individuals, by filing and deduction characteristics and income level, 1983, annual article, 8302–2.414
- Income tax returns of individuals by tax return item, State, and occupation, and income by source and tax owed, by income level, selected years 1916-80, conf papers, 8308–28.1

Index by Subjects and Names

Income tax returns of partnerships, detailed data by industry, 1981 estimates, annual article, 8302–2.404

Income tax returns of partnerships, receipts by source, deductions by type, and establishments, by selected industry, 1982, annual article, 8302–2.416

Income tax returns of sole proprietorships, detailed data by industry div and selected industry group, 1981, annual rpt, 8304–7

Income tax returns of sole proprietorships, receipts, deductions by type, payroll, and net income, by major industry, 1982, annual article, 8302–2.413

Meat animal production, marketing, slaughter, prices, and producers gross income, by animal type and State, 1982-83, annual rpt, 1623–8

Milk cows, and milk and cream production and marketings, by State, 1981-83, annual rpt, 1627–4

Milk price support alternatives, effects on production, use, prices, and farm receipts, projected 1983/84-1988/89 and actual 1982/83, 1568–246

Milk price supports effect on production, use, prices, and farm receipts, by region and State, 1940s-83 and alternative projections to 1988/89, 1568–245

Montana and North Dakota coal production, impact of mining on agricultural land availability and on farm income and production costs, by mining tract, 1982 rpt, 1588–79

Natl income and product, comprehensive accounts and components, *Survey of Current Business,* monthly rpt, 2702–1.21, 2702–1.22

Natural gas price changes effect on farm income and fertilizer use, 1980 and projected to 1990, 1548–240

Natural gas price decontrol alternatives effect on farm production by crop, prices, and fertilizer use and costs, 1982-90, model results, 1548–239

North Central States agricultural credit conditions, earnings, and expenditures, Fed Reserve 9th District, quarterly rpt, 9383–11

North Central States farm credit conditions and economic devs, Fed Reserve 7th District, biweekly rpt, 9375–10

OASDHI income of farm households, farms and amount by characteristics of farm and operator, 1978-82, article, 1702–1.410

Older persons by demographic, socioeconomic, and health characteristics, selected years 1900-81 and projected to 2050, Current Population Rpt, 2546–2.125

Older persons population characteristics, and needs and costs of social services by type, by metro-nonmetro status, 1970s-82 with trends from 1900, 21148–28

Portugal agricultural subsidies, profits, marketing margins, and consumer prices, by commodity or product, and effects of prospective EC membership, 1981, 1528–171

Poultry production, prices, and producers gross income, by State, 1982-83, annual rpt, 1625–5

Poverty-level persons and families, by income source, hours of work, earnings, taxes, and family characteristics, various periods 1959-84, 21788–131

Prices received by farmers for major products, and paid for farm inputs and living items, by commodity and State, monthly rpt, 1629–1

Prices received by farmers for major products, and paid for farm inputs, by commodity and State, 1983, annual rpt, 1629–5

Rural area situation and dev, periodic rpt articles, 1502–7

Small farms with sales under $2,500, acreage, finances, operations, and operator characteristics, by region and for 6 States, 1978, 1548–241

Southeastern States agricultural conditions, Fed Reserve 8th District, quarterly rpt, 9391–13

Southeastern States economic indicators, by State, Fed Reserve 5th District, quarterly rpt, 9389–16

Southeastern States financial and economic devs, Fed Reserve 6th District, monthly rpt with articles, 9371–1

Statistical Abstract of US, social, political, and economic data, 1950s-83 and trends, annual rpt, 2324–1.3

Tennessee farms in TVA mgmt program, and income at start and end of program, 1971-81, 9808–68

Texas farm household income, by income source and substate region, 1979, article, 9379–1.406

Tobacco production, prices, stocks, taxes by State, and trade and foreign production by country, 1983, annual rpt, 1319–1

Western States economic indicators, Fed Reserve 12th District, quarterly rpt, 9393–1.3

see also Agricultural labor

see also Agricultural quotas and price supports

see also Agricultural subsidies

see also Agricultural wages

Farm labor

see Agricultural labor

see Agricultural wages

see Migrant workers

Farm machinery

see Agricultural machinery and equipment

Farm population

Agriculture Fact Book of US, compilation of data for 1983 with trends from 1940, annual rpt, 1004–14

Births, fertility rates, expected births, and childless women, by socioeconomic characteristics, June 1982, annual Current Population Rpt, 2546–1.386

Births, fertility rates, expected births, and childless women, by socioeconomic characteristics, June 1983, annual Current Population Rpt, 2546–1.393

Census of Agriculture, 1982: farms, farmland, production and costs, and operator characteristics, preliminary State and county rpt series, 2330–1

Census of Agriculture, 1982: farms, farmland, production, finances, and operator characteristics, by county, final State rpt series, 2331–1

Census of Population, 1980: detailed socioeconomic and demographic characteristics, by age, sex, race, Hispanic origin, occupation, and industry, State rpt series, 2531–4

Farmers Home Administration

Census of Population, 1980: detailed socioeconomic characteristics, by county, city, and inside-outside SMSAs and central cities, State rpt series, 2531–3

County and City Data Book, detailed socioeconomic and demographic data for States, counties, and cities, selected years 1976-82, 2328–1

Economic and population time series data frequently used in statistical demand analyses, 1941-1982, annual rpt, 1544–21

Farm population and income, 1929-83, annual rpt, 204–1.8

Farm population, by employment and socioeconomic characteristics, 1983, annual rpt, 2544–1

Farm population, by farm type and sales size and selected other characteristics, 1975-80, 1598–144

Foreign and US agricultural supply/demand, trade, and production, and socioeconomic data, by country, 1950s-77, 1528–179

Health insurance coverage of farmers, farm population, and managers, by insurance type and selected sociodemographic characteristics, 1976, 1598–191

Income of families and persons, by sociodemographic characteristics, 1983, advance annual Current Population Rpt, 2546–6.41

OASDHI income of farm households, farms and amount by characteristics of farm and operator, 1978-82, article, 1702–1.410

Population socioeconomic characteristics, and selected rural and urban comparisons, 1960s-82, annual chartbook, 1504–3

Rural area situation and dev, periodic rpt articles, 1502–7

Social security tax liability of farm households, by type of legal organization, 1955-90, article, 1702–1.408

Statistical Abstract of US, social, political, and economic data, 1950s-83 and trends, annual rpt, 2324–1.1

Farm prices

see Agricultural prices

see Food prices

Farmer Cooperative Service

see Agricultural Cooperative Service

Farmers

see Agricultural labor

see Farm population

Farmers Home Administration

Activities and programs of USDA, by subagency, FY83, annual rpt, 1004–3

Borrowers, by loan type, race, Hispanic origin, and State, annual rpt, suspended, 1184–11

Borrowers, by loan type, race, Hispanic origin, and State, quarterly rpt, 1182–5

Cost control proposals for Fed Govt programs and mgmt, 3-year savings by function and agency, and financial and operating data, 1960s-81, 16908–1.2, 16908–1.26

Credit assistance costs, policies to improve measurement, with loan and loan guarantee data by program, and Federal and private credit instns operations, 1970-84, 26306–6.72

Farm debt, loans outstanding, and interest rates, by type of lender and State, 1960-83 with trends from 1940, biennial rpt, 1544–2

Farmers Home Administration

Farm finances, assets, expenses, cash flow, receipts, and loans, selected years 1971-85, annual rpt, 1544–13

Farm finances, expenses by type, loans by purpose and source, and credit detail by Fed Reserve District, quarterly rpt, 9365–3.10

Farm finances, production, expenses by type, and domestic economic impact, selected years 1972-82 and preliminary 1983-84, annual rpt, 1544–19

Farm mortgage debt outstanding, by type of lender and district, as of Jan 1983, annual rpt, 9264–3

Farm non-real estate debt outstanding, by type of lender and district, as of Jan 1983, annual rpt, 9264–4

Farm real estate and nonreal estate debt outstanding, by lender, 1940-84, annual rpt, 1544–16.2

Farm real estate and other debt, by type of lender, 1980 benchmark data with revised estimates for 1970-82, 1548–230

Fraud and abuse in USDA programs, audits and investigations, 2nd half FY84, semiannual rpt, 1002–4

Housing, new single and multifamily unit physical and financial characteristics, by region and metro-nonmetro location, 1979-83, annual rpt, 2384–1

Housing, new single family units sold and sales price by type of financing, monthly rpt, quarterly tables, 2382–3.2

Land privately held, acreage and owners by owner characteristics, land use, and region, and purchase and improvement funding, 1978 survey, series, 1506–5

Loan applications, by loan type, borrower race and Hispanic origin, State, and outlying area, annual rpt, discontinued, 1184–1

Loans (operating), applicant socioeconomic characteristics, and average loan amounts, annual rpt, suspended, 1184–9

Loans (operating), by State and use of funds, annual rpt, suspended, 1184–4

Loans and borrower supervision activities, for FmHA farm and housing programs, by type and State, monthly rpt, 1182–1

Loans and grants of FmHA by program and State, and summary of services, FY83 with trends from FY63, annual rpt, 1184–17

Loans for farm ownership, applicant socioeconomic characteristics, and average loan amounts, annual rpt, suspended, 1184–7

Loans for soil and water projects, applicant socioeconomic characteristics, and average loan amounts, annual rpt, suspended, 1184–8

Loans of FmHA for rural home mortgages, eligibility of current recipients under revised income limit, by State, 1983, GAO rpt, 26113–134

Farming

see Farm income

see Farm population

see Farms and farmland

see Rural electrification

see under Agriculture and terms beginning with Agricultural

see under By Industry in the "Index by Categories"

see under By Occupation in the "Index by Categories"

Farms and farmland

Acreage and owners of privately held land, by owner characteristics, land use, and region, and purchase and improvement funding, 1978 survey, series, 1506–5

Acreage harvested and cropland area by crop and region, and potential for expansion, 1982-84 with trends from 1949, annual rpt, 1584–4

Acreage planted and harvested, by crop and State, 1982-83 and planned as of June 1984, annual rpt, 1621–23

Acreage planting intended for 19 crops, by State, as of Feb 1984, annual rpt, 1621–22

Acreage used, production inputs and outputs, and productivity, by region, 1939-82, annual rpt, 1544–17

Agricultural economics technical research, quarterly journal, 1502–3

Agricultural production, marketing, trade, supply, food consumption, and food and nutrition programs, 1960s-83, annual chartbook, 1504–3

Agricultural Statistics, 1983, annual rpt, 1004–1

Agriculture Fact Book of US, compilation of data for 1983 with trends from 1940, annual rpt, 1004–14

Air pollutant emission factors, by detailed source, 3rd edition, 1983-84 supplements, 9198–13

Bolivia and Peru cocaine producers, area cultivated, and production, 1977-78, intl conf papers, 7008–40

Capital (fixed), govt and private nonresidential structures and equipment, residential capital, and consumer-owned durable goods by item, 1980-83, annual article, 2702–1.433

Census of Agriculture, 1982: farms, farmland, production and costs, and operator characteristics, preliminary State and county rpt series, 2330–1

Census of Agriculture, 1982: farms, farmland, production, finances, and operator characteristics, by county, final State rpt series, 2331–1

Census of Govts, 1982: properties, govt-assessed value, sales, and tax rates, by property type, State, SMSA, county, and city, 2453–1

Coastal environmental characteristics, fish, wildlife, and use, and population socioeconomic data, for individual areas, series, 5506–4

Colorado River Storage Project finances, water resource dev, power production, and other activities in western States, FY83, annual rpt, 5824–3

Conservation practices in rural areas, Agricultural Conservation Program participation and payments, by State, FY83, annual rpt, 1804–7

Construction industries census, 1982: financial and operating data, by SIC 4-digit industry and State, preliminary rpt series, 2371–1

Construction put in place, permits authorized by region, State, and MSA, and Federal contract awards, by construction type, bimonthly rpt with articles, 2012–1

Index by Subjects and Names

Construction put in place, value of new public and private structures, by type, monthly rpt, 2382–4

County and City Data Book, detailed socioeconomic and demographic data for States, counties, and cities, selected years 1976-82, 2328–1

Developing countries agricultural supply/demand and market for US exports, with socioeconomic indicators, country rpt series, 1526–6

Eastern Europe agricultural production and trade by commodity, food consumption, and farm inputs, for 6 countries, 1960-80 with projections to 1991, 1528–178

Emergency Conservation Program participation and payments for farmland restoration from natural disaster, by practice and State, FY83, annual rpt, 1804–22

Energy conservation programs of State govts, Fed Govt financial and technical aid, and reported energy savings, by State, 1983, annual rpt, 3304–1

Environmental quality and protection programs, costs, and Fed Govt enforcement, 1983, detailed annual rpt, 484–1

Erosion of farmland by rainfall, acreage by crop, and farm operators by selected characteristics, by soil erosion class, 1977-78, 1588–83

Farm business legal organization, finances, operations, tax rates, and State laws restricting farm corporations, 1960s-82, 1548–233

Farm finance and credit conditions, forecast 1984, conf papers, annual rpt, 1004–16

Farm finances, assets, liabilities, income, receipts by commodity and State, and expenses, 1980-83 and trends from 1910, annual rpt, 1544–16

Farm finances, expenses by type, loans by purpose and source, and credit detail by Fed Reserve District, quarterly rpt, 9365–3.10

Farm labor, farms, and labor costs, by labor and farm type and State, with immigrant labor law effect on farm work force, 1978, 1598–192

Farm production expenditures, detailed items by farm sales size and region, 1983, annual rpt, 1614–3

Farm production inputs, land mgmt, and environmental effects, for 4 crops, 1940s-80 and projected to 2010, 9188–94

Farm production itemized costs, receipts, and net returns, for 13 crops, 4 livestock types, and milk, by region, 1981-83, annual rpt, 1544–20

Farm production, prices, marketing, and trade, by commodity, forecast and current situation, monthly rpt, 1502–4

Farm sector structure and family farm characteristics, annual rpt, discontinued, 1504–4

Farms, production, acreage, and related data, by selected crop and State, monthly rpt, 1621–1

Fed Govt-owned real property inventory and costs, worldwide summary by location, agency, and use, 1983, annual rpt, 9454–5

Foreign acquisitions of US farmland, by State and county, before 1980 and during 1980-82, 1588–77

Index by Subjects and Names

Foreign and US agricultural supply/demand, consumption per capita, and trade, by world area and country group, 1960s-82, 1528–181

Foreign and US cropland per capita, and total arable land area by use, by selected country and world region, selected years 1955-80, 1528–180

Foreign and US cropland per capita by world region and selected country, and world arable land area by use, selected years 1955-80, summary article, 1522–3.401

Foreign economic, social, and political summary data, by country, 1984, annual factbook, 244–11

Foreign military, social, and economic summary data by world area and country, 1960s-80s, hearing, 25388–47.1

Foreign ownership of US agricultural land, acquisitions, dispositions, holdings, and use, by State and type and country of owner, 1983, annual rpt, 1584–2

Foreign ownership of US agricultural land, acreage, value, and use, by State and county, and for 5 leading investor countries, 1983, annual rpt, 1584–3

Fuel oil (distillate and residual) and kerosene deliveries, by end use, PAD district, and State, selected years 1978-83, annual rpt, 3164–2

Grain loan support programs of USDA, activity and status by type of grain and State, monthly rpt, 1802–3

Hog and pig inventory, value, farrowings, and farms, by State, quarterly release, 1623–3

Hog and pig production, inventory, and farms, by State, 1979-82, 1641–10

Hog production, producer characteristics, facilities, and marketing, by type and size of enterprise and region, 1975 and 1980, 1568–248

Housing and neighborhood quality indicators and attitudes, and occupant characteristics, by urban-rural location and region, 1981, annual survey, 2485–7

Irrigation system energy use and costs, and irrigated farm acreage by fuel and region, selected years 1974-84 and trends from 1900, article, 1561–16.406

Louisiana property tax on forest, agricultural, and marsh lands, impact of change from market to use valuation by parish, 1977-78, 1208–206

Montana and North Dakota coal production, impact of mining on agricultural land availability and on farm income and production costs, by mining tract, 1982 rpt, 1588–79

Pesticide use and acreage treated, for 12 vegetable and melon crops, by type of pesticide, method of application, and region, 1979, 1588–82

Plant and animal genetic resource conservation, commercial uses, causes of depletion, and geographic sources, 1984 rpt, 5548–13

Real estate value, sales, financing, taxes, and proposed use after purchase, by State, 1970s-84, annual rpt, 1541–8

Research (agricultural) expenditures and scientist years, by topic, commodity, and performing organization, FY82, annual rpt, 1744–2

Resources use and mgmt assessment and environmental impacts of Forest Service program options, 1977-2030 and trends from 1920, 1208–24

Rural area situation and dev, periodic rpt articles, 1502–7

Small farms with sales under $2,500, acreage, finances, operations, and operator characteristics, by region and for 6 States, 1978, 1548–241

Southeastern States farm credit conditions and real estate values, Fed Reserve 5th District, quarterly rpt, 9389–17

Southwestern States farm credit conditions and real estate values, Fed Reserve 11th District, quarterly rpt, 9379–11

Statistical Abstract of US, social, political, and economic data, 1950s-83 and trends, annual rpt, 2324–1.3

Storage facility and equipment loans to farmers under CCC grain program, by State, FY68-84, annual table, 1804–14

Storage facility and equipment loans to farmers under CCC grain program, by State, monthly table, 1802–9

Tennessee Valley ethanol production, feedstocks, facilities, tax incentives, and related farming data, by State, 1970s-83 and projected to 1992, 9808–69

Water pollution fish kills, by State, location, and pollution source, monthly 1978-80, annual rpt, 9204–3

Water pollution from nonpoint sources, source land uses and acreage, and control program funding, by State or region, various periods 1974-FY84, 9208–123

Western States farm real estate values, and nonreal estate farm loan trends, monthly rpt, quarterly data, 9381–2

Wetlands environmental characteristics, acreage, uses, and mgmt, by wetland type and region, 1950s-80, 26358–102

see also Agricultural accidents and safety
see also Agricultural commodities
see also Agricultural credit
see also Agricultural education
see also Agricultural exports and imports
see also Agricultural extension work
see also Agricultural finance
see also Agricultural innovations
see also Agricultural insurance
see also Agricultural labor
see also Agricultural machinery and equipment
see also Agricultural marketing
see also Agricultural policies
see also Agricultural prices
see also Agricultural production
see also Agricultural production costs
see also Agricultural productivity
see also Agricultural quotas and price supports
see also Agricultural sciences
see also Agricultural stocks
see also Agricultural subsidies
see also Agricultural surpluses
see also Agricultural wages
see also Farm income
see also Farm population
see also Farmers Home Administration
see also Pasture and rangeland
see also Soil pollution
see also Soils and soil conservation

Fayetteville, N.C.

Farnsworth, Richard L.
"Farmers' Perceptions and Information Sources: A Quantitative Analysis", 1502–3.401

Farrell, John B.
"BLS Establishment Estimates Revised to March 1983 Benchmarks", 6742–2.409

Farrell, Kenneth R.
"Meeting Future Needs for U.S. Food, Fiber, and Forest Products", 1008–47.2

Farrell, Victoria S.
"Effects of Exchange Rate Variability on International Trade and Other Economic Variables: A Review of the Literature", 9366–1.129

Farrell, William
"Administration and Service Delivery in the SSI Program: The First 10 Years", 4742–1.416

Fats and oils
see Oils, oilseeds, and fats

Faucett, Jack, Associates, Inc.
"Effect of U.S. Coal Exports on Domestic Economic Growth and on U.S. National Security", 3008–97

Fay, Clemon W.
"Species Profiles: Life Histories and Environmental Requirements of Coastal Fishes and Invertebrates (Mid-Atlantic), Alewife/Blueback Herring", 5506–8.10

"Species Profiles: Life Histories and Environmental Requirements of Coastal Fishes and Invertebrates (Mid-Atlantic), Atlantic Silverside", 5506–8.11

"Species Profiles: Life Histories and Environmental Requirements of Coastal Fishes and Invertebrates (Mid-Atlantic), Bay Scallop", 5506–8.12

"Species Profiles: Life Histories and Environmental Requirements of Coastal Fishes and Invertebrates (Mid-Atlantic), Striped Bass", 5506–8.13

"Species Profiles: Life Histories and Environmental Requirements of Coastal Fishes and Invertebrates (Mid-Atlantic), Surf Clam", 5506–8.14

Fayette County, Ky.
Census of Housing, 1980: occupancy and unit characteristics, by race, Hispanic origin, and city, SMSA rpt, 2473–1.219

Census of Population and Housing, 1980: detailed population and housing characteristics, by county, city, and census tract, SMSA rpt, 2551–2.219

see also under By City and By SMSA or MSA in the "Index by Categories"

Fayetteville, Ark.
Census of Housing, 1980: occupancy and unit characteristics, by race, Hispanic origin, and city, SMSA rpt, 2473–1.154

Census of Population and Housing, 1980: detailed population and housing characteristics, by county, city, and census tract, SMSA rpt, 2551–2.154

see also under By SMSA or MSA in the "Index by Categories"

Fayetteville, N.C.
Census of Housing, 1980: occupancy and unit characteristics, by race, Hispanic origin, and city, SMSA rpt, 2473–1.153

Census of Population and Housing, 1980: detailed population and housing characteristics, by county, city, and census tract, SMSA rpt, 2551–2.153

Fazio, Antonio

Fazio, Antonio
"Methods of Monetary Control in Italy, 1974-83", 9373–3.26

FBI
see Federal Bureau of Investigation

FCC
see Federal Communications Commission

FDA
see Food and Drug Administration

Federal advisory bodies
see Federal boards, committees, and commissions

Federal agencies
see Federal boards, committees, and commissions
see Federal executive departments
see Federal independent agencies
see under By Federal Agency in the "Index by Categories"

Federal agencies fraud, waste, and abuse investigations
see Federal Inspectors General reports

Federal aid programs
Appalachia regional dev spending, by program area and source of funds, FY82, annual rpt, 9084–1
Budget of US Appendix, detailed budgets and personnel summaries, by agency, FY85, annual rpt, 104–3
Budget of US, brief overview, FY85, annual rpt, 104–6
Budget of US, CBO analysis and review of FY85 budget by function, annual rpt, 26304–2
Budget of US, CBO analysis of revenue and spending alternatives and projections of economic indicators, FY85-89, annual rpt, 26304–3
Budget of US, compact budgets by function, agency, and account, FY85 with projections to FY89, annual rpt, 104–2
Budget of US, effects of Reagan Admin policy changes, by detailed program, FY85, annual rpt, 104–21
Budget of US, loans and loan guarantees, and Admin proposed limits on credit assistance, by program, FY83-89, annual rpt, 26306–3.65
Budget of US, object class analysis of obligations, by branch of Fed Govt and selected depts and agencies, FY85 estimates, annual rpt, 104–9
Budget of US, receipts by source and outlays by agency and program, monthly rpt, 8102–3
Budget of US, receipts by source and outlays by function, FY40-89 estimates revised for consistency with FY85 budget definitions, annual rpt, 104–12
Budget of US, receipts, outlays, and budget authority, by function and agency, FY84-89 revised estimates, midsession review of FY85 budget, annual rpt, 104–7
Budget of US, receipts, outlays, and budget authority, by function and agency, 1st revision of FY85 budget, annual rpt, 104–17
Budget of US, special analyses of economic and social impact, FY85, annual rpt, 104–1
Cost control proposals for Fed Govt programs and mgmt, CBO and GAO estimates of savings by function and agency, FY85-89, 26308–45

Cost control proposals for Fed Govt programs and mgmt, 3-year savings by function and agency, and financial and operating data, 1960s-81, 16908–1
Economic Dev Admin loans and grants, by program, State, county, and project or recipient, FY83 and cumulative FY66-83, annual rpt, 2064–2
Economic Report of the President for 1984, economic effects of budget proposals, and trends and projections 1950s-89, annual hearings, 23844–4
Employment and training program funding under Job Training Partnership Act, and required matching funds, for 3 programs by State, 1984/85, press release, 6408–58
Fed Govt aid to State and local govts, expenditures, and direct payments, by program, agency, and State, FY83, annual rpt, 2464–2
Fed Govt benefit payment by check and direct deposit, costs to agencies and banks, FY81, technical paper, 9366–1.139
Fed Govt consolidated financial statements based on business accounting methods, FY82-83, annual rpt, 8104–5
Fed Govt financial and nonfinancial domestic aid, 1984 annual comprehensive catalog, 104–5
Fed Govt revenues by source, expenditures by function, debt, and assets, 1982-83, annual rpt, 2466–2.6
Govt revenues by source and expenditures by function, natl income and product account, *Survey of Current Business*, monthly rpt, monthly and annual tables, 2702–1.24
Reclamation programs of Fed Govt in western US, finances and operations by project and State, 1981-82, annual rpts, 5824–1
see also Agricultural credit
see also Agricultural quotas and price supports
see also Agricultural subsidies
see also Agricultural surpluses
see also Aid to Families with Dependent Children
see also Child welfare
see also Community Development Block Grants
see also Federal aid to arts and humanities
see also Federal aid to education
see also Federal aid to higher education
see also Federal aid to highways
see also Federal aid to housing
see also Federal aid to law enforcement
see also Federal aid to libraries
see also Federal aid to local areas
see also Federal aid to medical education
see also Federal aid to medicine
see also Federal aid to railroads
see also Federal aid to rural areas
see also Federal aid to States
see also Federal aid to transportation
see also Federal aid to vocational education
see also Federal funding for energy programs
see also Federal funding for research and development
see also Federally Funded R&D Centers
see also Food assistance
see also Food stamp programs
see also Government and business

Index by Subjects and Names

see also Head Start Project
see also Income maintenance
see also Legal aid
see also Medical assistance
see also Medicare
see also Old-Age, Survivors, Disability, and Health Insurance
see also Public housing
see also Public service employment
see also Public welfare programs
see also Rent supplements
see also Revenue sharing
see also School lunch and breakfast programs
see also Shipbuilding and operating subsidies
see also Social security
see also Student aid
see also Subsidies
see also Supplemental Security Income
see also Tax expenditures
see also Unemployment insurance
see also Veterans benefits and pensions
see also Veterans health facilities and services
see also Veterans housing
see also Work Incentive Program

Federal aid to agriculture
see Agricultural credit
see Agricultural quotas and price supports
see Agricultural subsidies
see Agricultural surpluses
see Federal aid to rural areas

Federal aid to arts and humanities
Budget of US, effects of Reagan Admin policy changes, by detailed program, FY85, annual rpt, 104–21
Budget of US, receipts by source and outlays by agency and program, monthly rpt, 8102–3
Education Dept programs funding, operations, and effectiveness, FY83, annual rpt, 4804–5
Fed Govt aid to State and local govts, expenditures, and direct payments, by program, agency, and State, FY83, annual rpt, 2464–2
Fed Govt financial and nonfinancial domestic aid, 1984 annual comprehensive catalog, 104–5
Funding of arts and humanities, by source and State, FY82-83 with trends from FY66, 21408–69
Kennedy Performing Arts Center income and expenses by type, and Fed Govt share of expenses, FY79-83, GAO rpt, 26119–60
Museum grants of Natl Foundation on Arts and Humanities, by instn, State, and city, FY84, annual rpt series, 9564–6
Natl Endowment for Arts activities and grants, FY83, annual rpt, 9564–3
Natl Endowment for Humanities activities and grants, FY83, annual rpt, 9564–2
Smithsonian Instn finances, activities, and visitors, FY83, annual rpt, 9774–3

Federal aid to business
see Government and business
see Subsidies

Federal aid to cities
see Federal aid to local areas

Federal aid to education
Alabama rural black population, education, employment, health services, and economic status, for 16 counties, selected years 1970-81, 11048–180

Index by Subjects and Names

Appalachia regional dev spending, by program area and source of funds, FY82, annual rpt, 9084–1

Bilingual education programs, teachers, enrollment, and funding, selected years 1976-FY83, biennial rpt, 4804–14

Budget of US Appendix, detailed budgets and personnel summaries, by agency, FY85, annual rpt, 104–3

Budget of US, CBO analysis and review of FY85 budget by function, annual rpt, 26304–2

Budget of US, compact budgets by function, agency, and account, FY85 with projections to FY89, annual rpt, 104–2

Budget of US, effects of Reagan Admin policy changes, by detailed program, FY85, annual rpt, 104–21

Budget of US, loans and loan guarantees, and Admin proposed limits on credit assistance, by program, FY83-89, annual rpt, 26306–3.65

Budget of US, receipts by source and outlays by agency and program, monthly rpt, 8102–3

Budget of US, receipts by source and outlays by function, FY40-89 estimates revised for consistency with FY85 budget definitions, annual rpt, 104–12

Budget of US, receipts, outlays, and budget authority, by function and agency, FY84-89 revised estimates, midsession review of FY85 budget, annual rpt, 104–7

Budget of US, receipts, outlays, and budget authority, by function and agency, 1st revision of FY85 budget, annual rpt, 104–17

Census of Govts, 1982: school districts revenues, expenditures, debt, and assets, by district and State, 2457–1

Children and youth benefitting from Fed Govt public welfare programs and tax expenditures, participation and funding for 71 programs, FY81-83, 21968–30

Condition of Education, detailed data on enrollment, staff, achievement, finances, curricula, and education effects on employment, 1982-83, annual rpt, 4824–1.1

Continuing Education Natl Advisory Council activities, 1984 annual narrative rpt, 15214–1

Cost control proposals for Fed Govt programs and mgmt, 3-year savings by function and agency, and financial and operating data, 1960s-81, 16908–1.5

Digest of Education Statistics, detailed data on students, staff, finances, and facilities, 1982 and selected trends, annual rpt, 4824–2

Education Dept financial aid programs for educational instns and individuals, 1984 annual listing, 4804–3

Education Dept programs and activities, FY83, annual rpt, 4804–6

Education Dept programs fraud and abuse, audits and investigations, 2nd half FY84, semiannual rpt, 4802–1

Education Dept programs funding, operations, and effectiveness, FY83, annual rpt, 4804–5

Education Natl Inst activities and education research grants awarded by recipient, and Education Dept expenditures by function, FY81-82, annual rpt, 4914 4.

Elementary and secondary education, factors affecting State expenditures, and tuition tax credits effects on parents choice of public or private school, 1960-82 with some projections to 2000, 4808–9

Elementary and secondary education revenue by level of govt, and change in enrollment, teachers, and expenditures, by State, 1973-83, hearings, 21348–89

Elementary and secondary public school districts, schools, enrollment, staff, and finances, by State, 1981/82, annual rpt, 4834–13

Elementary and secondary public school systems revenues, by level of govt, selected years 1919/20-1981/82, press release, 4838–12

Elementary level Follow Through compensatory education programs beneficiaries, costs, funding, and participant test scores, selected years 1968-82, hearing, 21348–87

Fed Govt aid to State and local govts, expenditures, and direct payments, by program, agency, and State, FY83, annual rpt, 2464–2

Fed Govt education block grants, State allocations by program and selected school district, FY82-84 and trends from FY60, hearing, 21408–75

Fed Govt educational grants, State allocations by program, type of recipient agency, and State, FY83, annual rpt, 4804–8

Fed Govt financial and nonfinancial domestic aid, 1984 annual comprehensive catalog, 104–5

Fed Govt grants-in-aid for 13 program areas, FY82-84, annual article, 10042–1.402

Govt expenditures for public welfare, by level of govt and type of program, selected years FY50-82, 4746–16.1

Govt expenditures for social welfare by program and level of govt, and private expenditures for health care, selected years FY50-82, annual article, 4742–1.425

Govt finances, by level of govt and State, selected years 1929-83, annual rpt, 10044–1

Govt finances, by level of govt, State, and for large cities and counties, 1981-83, annual rpt series, 2466–2

Govt revenues by source and expenditures by function, natl income and product account, *Survey of Current Business,* monthly rpt, monthly and annual tables, 2702–1.24

GSA donations of surplus Federal personal property to State and local agencies and nonprofit instns, by region and State, FY83, annual rpt, 9454–22

Handicapped children early education research and service project activities and characteristics, and grants to States for program dev, 1983-84, annual listing, 4804–30

Handicapped children public education program enrollment, staff, and funding, by handicap, age, and State, 1981/82-1982/83, annual rpt, 4944–4

Impacted area schools, Fed Govt funding by county and school and congressional district, and eligible pupils, by State, FY83, annual rpt, 4804–10

Federal aid to higher education

Indian Education Act, Fed Govt grants and fellowships awarded by State, FY83, and natl advisory council funding, FY73-84, annual rpt, 14874–1

Indian Education Act grants to local agencies, Education Dept audit results by region, FY82, annual rpt, 4804–29

Indian education program operations, funding, student progress measures, and opinions of school staff, parents, and students, selected years 1973-83, 4808–13

Library and instructional materials acquisitions, and testing and guidance, State expenditures under ESEA Title IV-B, annual rpt, discontinued, 4804–12

Loan programs of Fed Govt, direct and guaranteed loans outstanding by agency and program, *Treasury Bulletin,* quarterly rpt, 8002–4.10

Local govt finances and population characteristics for cities and suburbs, by region and selected SMSA, selected years 1957-FY83, 10048–61

Mail subsidy for USPS revenue forgone, by class of mail, FY83, annual rpt, 9864–5.3

Natl Endowment for Arts activities and grants, FY83, annual rpt, 9564–3

Natl Endowment for Humanities activities and grants, FY83, annual rpt, 9564–2

Procurement contract awards of Fed Govt, by State, agency, procurement and contractor type, and for top 100 contractors, quarterly rpt, 102–6

Public opinion on taxes, tax policy, and intergovtl relations, 1972-84 surveys, annual rpt, 10044–2

Refugee resettlement program activities and funding, arrivals and population by country of origin and State, and employment and other characteristics, FY83, annual rpt, 4704–8

Southeastern States educational finances and indicators of cost burden, for Fed Reserve 6th District States, selected years 1970-83, article, 9371–1.429

Statistical Abstract of US, social, political, and economic data, 1950s-83 and trends, annual rpt, 2324–1.1

Tax expenditures, Fed Govt revenues foregone through income tax deductions and exclusions by type, and effect of Deficit Reduction Act, FY84-89, annual rpt, 21784–10

see also Federal aid to higher education
see also Federal aid to medical education
see also Federal aid to vocational education
see also Head Start Project
see also School lunch and breakfast programs
see also Student aid

Federal aid to energy programs
see Federal funding for energy programs

Federal aid to higher education

AID contracts and grants for technical and support services, by instn, country, and State, FY83, annual listing, 9914–7

AID contracts and grants to universities for technical assistance to foreign countries and other services, FY83, annual listing, 9914–6

Alcohol, Drug Abuse, and Mental Health Admin research grants, awards, and fellowships by recipient, FY83, annual listing, 4044–13

Federal aid to higher education

Budget of US, CBO analysis of revenue and spending alternatives and projections of economic indicators, FY85-89, annual rpt, 26304–3.3

Budget of US, compact budgets by function, agency, and account, FY85 with projections to FY89, annual rpt, 104–2

Budget of US, effects of Reagan Admin policy changes, by detailed program, FY85, annual rpt, 104–21

Budget of US, receipts by source and outlays by function, FY40-89 estimates revised for consistency with FY85 budget definitions, annual rpt, 104–12

Census of Govts, 1982: school districts revenues, expenditures, debt, and assets, by district and State, 2457–1

Condition of Education, detailed data on enrollment, staff, achievement, finances, curricula, and education effects on employment, 1982-83, annual rpt, 4824–1.2

Cost control proposals for Fed Govt programs and mgmt, 3-year savings by function and agency, and financial and operating data, 1960s-81, 16908–1.30

DOD prime contract awards for R&D to educational and nonprofit instns and Federal agencies, by instn and location, FY83, annual listing, 3544–17

DOD procurement, prime contract awards for 25 commodity categories and R&D, by State and census div, FY81-83, annual rpt, 3544–11

DOD procurement, prime contractors for R&D, top 500 and value of contracts, FY83, annual listing, 3544–4

DOE procurement and assistance contracts, by State, contractor type, and top 100 instns, FY83, annual rpt, 3004–21

DOE R&D projects and funding at natl labs, universities, and other instns, annual summary rpts, 3004–18

Education Dept financial aid programs for educational instns and individuals, 1984 annual listing, 4804–3

Education Dept programs and activities, FY83, annual rpt, 4804–6

Education Dept programs funding, operations, and effectiveness, FY83, annual rpt, 4804–5

Energy R&D and science and engineering education, DOE and DOE natl labs aid to selected higher education instns, 1960s-84, 3008–89.2

Fed Govt aid to State and local govts, expenditures, and direct payments, by program, agency, and State, FY83, annual rpt, 2464–2

Fed Govt educational grants, State allocations by program, type of recipient agency, and State, FY83, annual rpt, 4804–8

Fed Govt financial and nonfinancial domestic aid, 1984 annual comprehensive catalog, 104–5

Fed Govt funding for education, by agency, program, and State, selected years FY79-85, annual rpt, 4824–2.22

Fish and eggs for stocking distributed from natl hatcheries, by species, hatchery, and jurisdiction, FY83, annual rpt, 5504–10

HHS aid to each State and local govt or private instn, amount obligated, funding agency, and program, FY83, annual listing, 4004–3

Index by Subjects and Names

Library (research) funding of Education Dept, by project, program area, instn, and State, FY84, annual listing, 4804–22

NASA procurement contract awards, by type, contractor, State, and country, FY84, semiannual rpt, 9502–6

Natl Endowment for Humanities activities and grants, FY83, annual rpt, 9564–2

NIH extramural grant and contract awards for research, R&D, and construction, FY72-83, annual rpt, 4434–9

NIH grants, awards, and obligations by State and type of recipient, and full-time personnel, by inst, FY83, annual rpt, 4434–3

NSF grant and award recipients, by State, FY83, annual listing, 9624–11

NSF research programs, activities, and funding, FY82-83, annual rpt, 9624–6

R&D and science-related Fed Govt funding to higher education and nonprofit instns, by field, instn, agency, and State, FY82, annual rpt, 9627–17

R&D expenditures by higher education instns and federally funded centers, by field, source of funds, instn, and State, FY82, annual rpt, 9627–13

R&D expenditures by source, and scientists education and employment, detailed data by field, selected years 1953-84, annual rpt, 9624–18

R&D Fed Govt funding for all performers, by field and supporting agency, selected years FY60-84, annual rpt, 9627–20

Satellite Landsat system proposed transfer to private sector, uses and product sales by user type, and university programs and personnel by instn, 1973-85, 26358–100

Science and engineering enrollment, degrees, and employment, R&D funding, and related topics, highlights series, 9626–2

Science Indicators, R&D expenditures, innovations, research, and higher education, with foreign comparisons, 1960s- 83, annual rpt, 9624–10

Urban Mass Transportation Admin grants to higher education instns for research and training, by project, FY84, annual rpt, 7884–7

see also Federal aid to medical education
see also Student aid
see also Work-study programs

Federal aid to highways

Appalachia hwy system and access roads funding and completion status, by State, quarterly tables, 9082–1

Appalachia regional dev spending, by program area and source of funds, FY82, annual rpt, 9084–1

Bridge replacement and rehabilitation program of Fed Govt, funding by bridge and bridge status by State, 1983, annual rpt, 7554–27

Budget of US, CBO analysis of revenue and spending alternatives and projections of economic indicators, FY85-89, annual rpt, 26304–3.3

Budget of US, effects of Reagan Admin policy changes, by detailed program, FY85, annual rpt, 104–21

Construction bids and contracts for Federal-aid interstate and secondary hwys, by State, 1st half 1984, semiannual rpt, 7552–12

Construction expenditures and contracts awarded for Federal-aid hwy system, by type of material used and State, various periods 1944-83, annual rpts, 7554–29

Construction grants, loans, and loan guarantees of Fed Govt, by program and type of structure, FY80-83 and estimated FY84-85, annual article, 2012–1.404

Construction material prices and indexes for Federal-aid hwy system, by type of material and urban-rural location, quarterly rpt, 7552–7

Cost control proposals for Fed Govt programs and mgmt, 3-year savings by function and agency, and financial and operating data, 1960s-81, 16908–1.11, 16908–1.22, 16908–1.31

DOT grant awards for transportation planning and safety programs, by region, State, and for 35 largest SMSAs, FY83, annual rpt, 7304–7

Fed Govt aid to State and local govts, expenditures, and direct payments, by program, agency, and State, FY83, annual rpt, 2464–2

Fed Govt aid to transportation by type, and govt transportation finances by level of govt and mode of transport, FY77-82, 7308–185

Fed Govt financial and nonfinancial domestic aid, 1984 annual comprehensive catalog, 104–5

Fed Govt revenues by source, expenditures by function, debt, and assets, 1982-83, annual rpt, 2466–2.6

Fed Hwy Admin activities, grants, and special studies, press release series, 7556–3

Govt finances, by level of govt and State, selected years 1929-83, annual rpt, 10044–1

Hwy and urban transit systems financing methods of govts and private sector, with case studies for selected metro areas, series, 7556–7

Hwy expenditures by level of govt, 1972-82, annual rpt, 7304–2

Hwy funding provisions of Fed Govt by agency and program, and State motor fuel tax provisions and vehicle registration fees, as of Jan 1984, biennial rpt, 7554–37

Hwy safety program Fed Govt appropriations, by State and program, quarterly rpt, 7552–9

Hwy Statistics, detailed data on traffic, govt finances, fuel use, vehicles, driver licenses, and hwy characteristics, by State, 1983, annual rpt, 7554–1

Hwy Statistics, summary data on traffic, govt finances, fuel use, vehicles, and driver licenses, by State, 1982, annual rpt, 7554–24

Hwy Trust Fund receipts, expenditures, assets, and liabilities, monthly rpt, 8102–9.7

Industrial dev Fed Govt funding by type, program, and agency, and State govt policies and support, selected years FY75-85, 26306–6.81

Public works capital needs and financing, by project type, level of govt, and selected jurisdiction, 1970s-83 and projected to 2000, hearing, 23848–181

Index by Subjects and Names

Public works capital needs and intergovtl financing, by type of project and selected city, various periods 1950-83, 10048–60

R&D for hwy design and construction, quarterly journal, 7552–3

R&D projects funded by Fed Hwy Admin, FY83, annual summary rpt, 7554–14

Repair projects for hwys and bridges funded by Fed Govt, and costs, for 7 States, FY81-82, GAO rpt, 26113–121

Safety improvement programs federally funded, implementation by State, FY83, annual rpt, 7554–26

State govt revenues by source, expenditures by function, debt, and holdings by type, FY83, annual rpt, 2466–2.5

see also Federal aid to transportation

Federal aid to housing

- Appalachia regional dev spending, by program area and source of funds, FY82, annual rpt, 9084–1
- Budget of US Appendix, detailed budgets and personnel summaries, by agency, FY85, annual rpt, 104–3
- Budget of US, compact budgets by function, agency, and account, FY85 with projections to FY89, annual rpt, 104–2
- Budget of US, effects of Reagan Admin policy changes, by detailed program, FY85, annual rpt, 104–21
- Budget of US, loans and loan guarantees, and Admin proposed limits on credit assistance, by program, FY83-89, annual rpt, 26306–3.65
- Budget of US, receipts by source and outlays by agency and program, monthly rpt, 8102–3
- Budget of US, receipts by source and outlays by function, FY40-89 estimates revised for consistency with FY85 budget definitions, annual rpt, 104–12
- Budget of US, receipts, outlays, and budget authority, by function and agency, FY84-89 revised estimates, midsession review of FY85 budget, annual rpt, 104–7
- Budget of US, receipts, outlays, and budget authority, by function and agency, 1st revision of FY85 budget, annual rpt, 104–17
- Children and youth benefitting from Fed Govt public welfare programs and tax expenditures, participation and funding for 71 programs, FY81-83, 21968–30
- Community Dev Block Grants admin, allocation, and family social benefits, effect of policy changes to increase local admin responsibility, for 10 cities, as of 1982, 5188–105
- Community Dev Block Grants to small cities, State admin, project characteristics, and assessments of local officials, 1982, 5188–106
- Community dev programs funding and activities, for 5 HUD programs, FY83, annual rpt, 5124–5
- Construction grants, loans, and loan guarantees of Fed Govt, by program and type of structure, FY80-83 and estimated FY84-85, annual article, 2012–1.404
- Cost control proposals for Fed Govt programs and mgmt, 3-year savings by function and agency, and financial and operating data, 1960s-81, 16908–1.8, 16908–1.22, 16908–1.23

Farm debt, loans outstanding, and interest rates, by type of lender and State, 1960-83 with trends from 1940, biennial rpt, 1544–2

- Fed Govt aid to State and local govts, expenditures, and direct payments, by program, agency, and State, FY83, annual rpt, 2464–2
- Fed Govt financial and nonfinancial domestic aid, 1984 annual comprehensive catalog, 104–5
- Govt expenditures for public welfare, by level of govt and type of program, selected years FY50-82, 4746–16.1
- Govt finances, by level of govt and State, selected years 1929-83, annual rpt, 10044–1
- Govt finances, by level of govt, State, and for large cities and counties, 1981-83, annual rpt series, 2466–2
- Govt Natl Mortgage Assn financial statements, and mortgage-backed securities program, FY82-83, annual rpt, 5144–6
- Govt revenues by source and expenditures by function, natl income and product account, *Survey of Current Business,* monthly rpt, monthly and annual tables, 2702–1.24
- HUD New Communities program, activities, costs, land sales, and community and population characteristics, for 13 communities, 1970s-83, 5188–107
- HUD programs for housing finance, construction, and improvement, periodic press releases, 5006–3
- Indian and Alaska Native housing and community dev program operations, FY82 with Community Dev Block Grant funding by tribe and State for FY81, annual rpt, 5004–5
- Industrial dev Fed Govt funding by type, program, and agency, and State govt policies and support, selected years FY75-85, 26306–6.81
- Loan programs of Fed Govt, direct and guaranteed loans outstanding by agency and program, *Treasury Bulletin,* quarterly rpt, 8002–4.10
- Older and handicapped persons housing projects construction and rehabilitation loans of HUD, FY84, annual listing, 5004–6
- Older persons sociodemographic characteristics, and Fed Govt program participation and funding, 1983 with trends and projections 1900-2060, annual rpt, 25144–3.1
- Property improvement and mobile home loans FHA-insured, by State and county, 1983 and cumulative from 1934, annual rpt, 5144–16
- Rental housing, effects of Fed Govt tax policies on real estate investment, 1969-81, 5188–104
- Tax expenditures, Fed Govt revenues foregone through income tax deductions and exclusions by type, and effect of Deficit Reduction Act, FY84-89, annual rpt, 21784–10
- Urban Dev Action Grant awards to local areas, preliminary approvals, with project descriptions, private investment, and jobs and taxes to be created, by city, quarterly press release series, 5002–7

Federal aid to law enforcement

see also Farmers Home Administration

see also Mortgages

see also Public housing

see also Rent supplements

see also Veterans housing

Federal aid to law enforcement

- Budget of US Appendix, detailed budgets and personnel summaries, by agency, FY85, annual rpt, 104–3
- Budget of US, compact budgets by function, agency, and account, FY85 with projections to FY89, annual rpt, 104–2
- Budget of US, effects of Reagan Admin policy changes, by detailed program, FY85, annual rpt, 104–21
- Budget of US, receipts by source and outlays by agency and program, monthly rpt, 8102–3
- Budget of US, receipts by source and outlays by function, FY40-89 estimates revised for consistency with FY85 budget definitions, annual rpt, 104–12
- Budget of US, receipts, outlays, and budget authority, by function and agency, FY84-89 revised estimates, midsession review of FY85 budget, annual rpt, 104–7
- Budget of US, receipts, outlays, and budget authority, by function and agency, 1st revision of FY85 budget, annual rpt, 104–17
- Crime and criminal justice data, including justice expenditures and employment by level of govt, 1970s-82 with some trends from 1875, 6068–174
- Drug abuse and trafficking reduction plan of Fed Govt, funding by agency and background data on drug use by substance, selected years FY81-85, biennial rpt, 024–1
- Drug Enforcement Organized Crime Task Forces, funding and staff by agency, region, and city, as of FY83, GAO rpt, 26119–52
- Drug enforcement regional task force program investigation activities, funding, and personnel, with nationwide drug abuse data, 1983 annual rpt, 6004–17
- Fed Govt aid to State and local govts, expenditures, and direct payments, by program, agency, and State, FY83, annual rpt, 2464–2
- Fed Govt financial and nonfinancial domestic aid, 1984 annual comprehensive catalog, 104–5
- Fed Govt grants-in-aid for 13 program areas, FY82-84, annual article, 10042–1.402
- Govt revenues by source and expenditures by function, natl income and product account, *Survey of Current Business,* monthly rpt, monthly and annual tables, 2702–1.24
- Jail capacities, conditions, expenditures, and services, and socioeconomic and other characteristics of inmates, various dates 1976-82, 10048–59
- Juvenile delinquency prevention, Fed Govt programs funding by Federal agency and block grant, FY82, annual rpt, 6064–11
- Juvenile Justice and Delinquency Prevention Natl Inst programs and research project funding, FY81-82, annual rpt, 6064–19
- Marijuana cultivation control activity of State law enforcement agencies, and aid from Fed Govt and Natl Guard, 1983 survey, GAO rpt, 26119–64

Federal aid to law enforcement

Prison population and capacity by State and individual DC and Federal instn, construction costs, and Fed Govt operating costs, 1983 and projected to 1990, GAO rpt, 26119–59

Public and community defender grants, FY85, Judicial Conf semiannual proceedings, annual rpt, 18204–5

Witness Security Program costs, participants by arrest record, and prosecutions by offense, offender type, and disposition, various periods FY70-83, GAO rpt, 26119–70

Federal aid to libraries

- Budget of US, CBO analysis of revenue and spending alternatives and projections of economic indicators, FY85-89, annual rpt, 26304–3.3
- Budget of US, compact budgets by function, agency, and account, FY85 with projections to FY89, annual rpt, 104–2
- Budget of US, effects of Reagan Admin policy changes, by detailed program, FY85, annual rpt, 104–21
- Education Dept financial aid programs for educational instns and individuals, 1984 annual listing, 4804–3
- Education Dept programs funding, operations, and effectiveness, FY83, annual rpt, 4804–5
- Fed Govt aid to State and local govts, expenditures, and direct payments, by program, agency, and State, FY83, annual rpt, 2464–2
- Fed Govt educational grants, State allocations by program, type of recipient agency, and State, FY83, annual rpt, 4804–8
- Fed Govt financial and nonfinancial domestic aid, 1984 annual comprehensive catalog, 104–5
- HHS aid to each State and local govt or private instn, amount obligated, funding agency, and program, FY83, annual listing, 4004–3
- Higher education instns libraries expenditures, holdings by type, use, staff by sex, and Federal grants received, 1979-82, biennial rpt, 4854–1
- Mail subsidy for USPS revenue forgone, by class of mail, FY83, annual rpt, 9864–5.3
- Medicine Natl Library activities, collections, and grants, FY81-83, annual rpt, 4464–1
- Natl Commission on Libraries and Info Science activities, funding, expenditures, and publications lists, FY83, annual rpt, 15634–1
- Natl Endowment for Humanities activities and grants, FY83, annual rpt, 9564–2
- NIH grants and awards for R&D, training, construction, and medical libraries, by location and recipient, FY83, annual listings, 4434–7
- NIH newly announced grants and awards, quarterly listing, 4432–1
- Research library funding of Education Dept, by project, program area, instn, and State, FY84, annual listing, 4804–22

Federal aid to local areas

- Airline deregulation in 1978, effect on industry operations and finances, air traffic patterns, and CAB programs, various periods FY76-84, 9148–56
- Appalachia regional dev spending, by program area and source of funds, FY82, annual rpt, 9084–1

Index by Subjects and Names

- Bonneville Power Admin energy conservation program activities and funding data, FY82 and estimated FY83-87, 3228–2
- Boston, Mass, govt budget and impact of reduced local revenue and Fed Govt aid, and other devs, FY80-86, article, 9373–1.406
- Budget of US Appendix, detailed budgets and personnel summaries, by agency, FY85, annual rpt, 104–3
- Budget of US, CBO analysis of revenue and spending alternatives and projections of economic indicators, FY85-89, annual rpt, 26304–3.3
- Budget of US, compact budgets by function, agency, and account, FY85 with projections to FY89, annual rpt, 104–2
- Budget of US, effects of Reagan Admin policy changes, by detailed program, FY85, annual rpt, 104–21
- Budget of US, loans and loan guarantees, and Admin proposed limits on credit assistance, by program, FY83-89, annual rpt, 26306–3.65
- Budget of US, receipts by source and outlays by function, FY40-89 estimates revised for consistency with FY85 budget definitions, annual rpt, 104–12
- Budget of US, receipts, outlays, and budget authority, by function and agency, FY84-89 revised estimates, midsession review of FY85 budget, annual rpt, 104–7
- Budget of US, receipts, outlays, and budget authority, by function and agency, 1st revision of FY85 budget, annual rpt, 104–17
- Budget of US, special analysis of grants-in-aid outlays, by agency, function, and region, FY83-87, annual rpt, 104–1.8
- Census of Govts, 1982: city govt revenues by source, expenditures by function, debt, and assets, by State and city, 2457–4
- Census of Govts, 1982: county govt revenues by source, expenditures by function, debt, and assets, by State and county, 2457–3
- Community dev programs funding and activities, for 5 HUD programs, FY83, annual rpt, 5124–5
- Community services block grants by type of service provider, State mgmt, and opinions of officials and groups involved, for 13 States, FY81-83, GAO rpt, 26121–84
- Cost control proposals for Fed Govt programs and mgmt, 3-year savings by function and agency, and financial and operating data, 1960s-81, 16908–1.22
- DOE procurement and assistance contracts, by State, contractor type, and top 100 instns, FY83, annual rpt, 3004–21
- DOT grant awards for transportation planning and safety programs, by region, State, and for 35 largest SMSAs, FY83, annual rpt, 7304–7
- Drug abuse situation, prevention and treatment programs, law enforcement, funding needs, and Fed Govt role, attitudes of State and local officials, 1983 survey, 21968–27
- Economic Dev Admin loans and grants, by program, State, county, and project or recipient, FY83 and cumulative FY66-83, annual rpt, 2064–2

- Economic dev assistance of Fed Govt, generation of jobs by industry div, model methodology and outputs, various periods FY69-78, GAO rpt, 26117–32
- Energy conservation aid of DOE, activities, funding, and grants by State, by program, FY84, annual rpt, 3304–21
- Environmental quality and protection programs, costs, and Fed Govt enforcement, 1983, detailed annual rpt, 484–1
- EPA pollution control research and grant assistance program activities, monthly rpt, 9182–8
- Fed Govt aid to State and local areas, by type of payment, State, county, and city, FY83, annual rpt, 2464–3
- Fed Govt aid to State and local govts, expenditures, and direct payments, by program, agency, and State, FY83, annual rpt, 2464–2
- Fed Govt financial and nonfinancial domestic aid, 1984 annual comprehensive catalog, 104–5
- Fed Govt grants-in-aid for 13 program areas, FY82-84, annual article, 10042–1.402
- Fed Govt grants to State and local govts, cumulative for fiscal year, annual trends, and quarterly data, monthly rpt, 23842–1.6
- Fed Govt grants to State and local govts, various periods 1948-83, article, 9385–1.401
- Fed Govt revenue sharing and other grant program alternative allocations, with city govt finances and responses to program cuts, FY79-83, hearings, 25408–86
- Financial and business statistics, historic trends, 1984 annual chartbook, 9364–2.9
- Fish and eggs for stocking distributed from natl hatcheries, by species, hatchery, and jurisdiction, FY83, annual rpt, 5504–10
- Forestry activities on State and private lands, Fed Govt and State funding by project and State, FY83, annual tables, 1204–32
- Govt finances, by level of govt and State, selected years 1929-83, annual rpt, 10044–1
- Govt finances, by level of govt, State, and for large cities and counties, 1981-83, annual rpt series, 2466–2
- Govt revenues by source and expenditures by function, natl income and product account, *Survey of Current Business*, monthly rpt, monthly and annual tables, 2702–1.24
- GSA donations of surplus Federal personal property to State and local agencies and nonprofit instns, by region and State, FY83, annual rpt, 9454–22
- HHS aid to each State and local govt or private instn, amount obligated, funding agency, and program, FY83, annual listing, 4004–3
- HUD New Communities program, activities, costs, land sales, and community and population characteristics, for 13 communities, 1970s-83, 5188–107
- Interior Dept programs, activities, and funding, various periods 1967-84, last issue of annual rpt, 5304–13
- Labor surplus areas eligible for preferential Fed Govt contracts, and labor force data for 150 major labor markets, monthly listing, 6402–1

Index by Subjects and Names

Federal aid to medicine

Loan programs of Fed Govt, direct and guaranteed loans outstanding by agency and program, *Treasury Bulletin,* quarterly rpt, 8002–4.10

Local govt finances and population characteristics for cities and suburbs, by region and selected SMSA, selected years 1957-FY83, 10048–61

NYC health care demonstration project for reorganization of 6 facilities in Brooklyn, Federal and State govt funding by facility, 1979-82, article, 4652–1.419

Outlying areas govt financial data and audits by Interior Dept Inspector General, by area, FY83, annual rpt, 5304–15

Pollution abatement expenditures of govt, business, and consumers, 1972-82, annual article, 2702–1.407

Public lands, Fed Govt payments to local govts in lieu of property taxes by State, FY84, annual press release, 5724–9

Public opinion on taxes, tax policy, and intergovtl relations, 1972-84 surveys, annual rpt, 10044–2

Public works capital needs and financing, by project type, level of govt, and selected jurisdiction, 1970s-83 and projected to 2000, hearing, 23848–181

Public works capital needs and intergovtl financing, by type of project and selected city, various periods 1950-83, 10048–60

R&D Fed Govt funding by type of performer, and funding for industrial dev by type, program, and agency, selected years FY75-85, 26306–6.81

R&D Fed Govt labs required technology transfer to public and private sector, labs complying, funding, and requests, by agency, FY82, GAO rpt, 26113–141

Recreation outdoor area dev, Interior Dept Land and Water Conservation Fund grants by State, FY85, annual press release, 5544–15

Regulatory growth of Fed Govt effect on local compliance costs and funding, local officials assessment, and comparisons to State govt regulations, 1970s-82 with trends from 1900, 10048–58

Schools in federally impacted areas, Fed Govt funding by county and school and congressional district, and eligible pupils, by State, FY83, annual rpt, 4804–10

Transit system financial and operating data, by mode, function, fleet size, and individual system, FY82, annual rpt, 7884–4

Urban area socioeconomic and fiscal trends and problems, 1950-83 and Fed Govt funding estimates for FY84-87, biennial rpt, 5124–4

Urban Dev Action Grant awards to local areas, preliminary approvals, with project descriptions, private investment, and jobs and taxes to be created, by city, quarterly press release series, 5002–7

Urban Dev Action Grant program effectiveness, and participation of small cities by State, 1978-82, GAO rpt, 26113–118

Virgin Islands govt fiscal condition, FY81, annual rpt, 5304–10

Virgin Islands socioeconomic and govtl data, FY81, annual rpt, 5304–4

see also Community Development Block Grants

see also Federal aid to rural areas

see also Revenue sharing

Federal aid to medical education

Alcohol, Drug Abuse and Mental Health Admin staff, contract awards, and grants, by Inst, program, and State, FY83, annual factbook, 4044–1

Allergy and Infectious Diseases Natl Inst activities, grants by instn, State, and country, and disease incidence and costs, FY60s-84, annual rpt, 4474–30

Budget of US, effects of Reagan Admin policy changes, by detailed program, FY85, annual rpt, 104–21

Cancer Natl Inst contracts and grants, by contractor, instn, State, and city, FY83, annual listing, 4474–28

Cost control proposals for Fed Govt programs and mgmt, 3-year savings by function and agency, and financial and operating data, 1960s-81, 16908–1.7

Dental Research Natl Inst research and training funds awarded, by recipient instn, FY83, annual listing, 4474–19

Digestive Diseases Interagency Coordinating Committee activities, and related Federal research and funding, by agency, FY79-83, annual rpt, 4434–13

Fed Govt financial and nonfinancial domestic aid, 1984 annual comprehensive catalog, 104–5

General Medical Sciences Natl Inst research programs and funding, FY83, annual rpt, 4474–12

Health professionals supply and education, by occupation, demographic and professional characteristics, and location, 1950s-83 and projected to 2000, biennial rpt, 4114–8

Heart, Lung, and Blood Natl Inst activities and funding, with morbidity and mortality data, various periods 1940-88, annual rpt, 4474–22

Heart, Lung, and Blood Natl Inst organization, disease and mortality data, and funds and recipients, FY83 with trends from 1900, annual fact book, 4474–15

HHS aid to each State and local govt or private instn, amount obligated, funding agency, and program, FY83, annual listing, 4004–3

NIH activities, staff, funding, and facilities, historical data, 1984 annual rpt, 4434–1

NIH extramural grant and contract awards for research, R&D, and construction, FY72-83, annual rpt, 4434–9

NIH grants and awards for R&D, training, construction, and medical libraries, by location and recipient, FY83, annual listings, 4434–7

NIH grants, awards, and obligations by State and type of recipient, and full-time personnel, by inst, FY83, annual rpt, 4434–3

NIH Research Resources Div activities, accomplishments, and funding, by program, FY83, annual rpt, 4434–12

NIMH mental health clinical training funding, by program and field, FY80-83, GAO rpt, 26121–86

Science and engineering grad enrollment, fields of study, financial support, and other student and instn characteristics, 1975-82, annual survey, 9627–7

Federal aid to medicine

Acquired immune deficiency syndrome (AIDS) cases, and research funding and activities, monthly rpt, 4042–2

Acquired immune deficiency syndrome (AIDS) research expenditures in 3 areas, by NIH inst, FY82, 4102–1.404

Alabama rural black population, education, employment, health services, and economic status, for 16 counties, selected years 1970-81, 11048–180

Alcohol, Drug Abuse, and Mental Health Admin research grants, awards, and fellowships by recipient, FY83, annual listing, 4044–13

Alcohol, Drug Abuse and Mental Health Admin staff, contract awards, and grants, by Inst, program, and State, FY83, annual factbook, 4044–1

Alcoholism research, treatment programs, and patient characteristics, quarterly journal, 4482–1

Allergy and Infectious Diseases Natl Inst activities, grants by instn, State, and country, and disease incidence and costs, FY60s-84, annual rpt, 4474–30

Appalachia regional dev spending, by program area and source of funds, FY82, annual rpt, 9084–1

Budget of US Appendix, detailed budgets and personnel summaries, by agency, FY85, annual rpt, 104–3

Budget of US, CBO analysis and review of FY85 budget by function, annual rpt, 26304–2

Budget of US, CBO analysis of revenue and spending alternatives and projections of economic indicators, FY85-89, annual rpt, 26304–3.3

Budget of US, compact budgets by function, agency, and account, FY85 with projections to FY89, annual rpt, 104–2

Budget of US, loans and loan guarantees, and Admin proposed limits on credit assistance, by program, FY83-89, annual rpt, 26306–3.65

Budget of US, receipts by source and outlays by agency and program, monthly rpt, 8102–3

Budget of US, receipts by source and outlays by function, FY40-89 estimates revised for consistency with FY85 budget definitions, annual rpt, 104–12

Budget of US, receipts, outlays, and budget authority, by function and agency, FY84-89 revised estimates, midsession review of FY85 budget, annual rpt, 104–7

Budget of US, receipts, outlays, and budget authority, by function and agency, 1st revision of FY85 budget, annual rpt, 104–17

Cancer Natl Inst contracts and grants, by contractor, instn, State, and city, FY83, annual listing, 4474–28

Cancer Natl Inst epidemiology and biometry activities, staff, budget, and contract awards by project and recipient instn, FY83, annual rpt, 4474–29

Cancer Natl Inst programs, organization, and budget, FY83, with cancer deaths by body site, 1980 and 1983, annual fact book, 4474–13

Construction grants, loans, and loan guarantees of Fed Govt, by program and type of structure, FY80-83 and estimated FY84-85, annual article, 2012–1.404

Federal aid to medicine

Cost control proposals for Fed Govt programs and mgmt, 3-year savings by function and agency, and financial and operating data, 1960s-81, 16908–1

Dental Research Natl Inst research and training funds awarded, by recipient instn, FY83, annual listing, 4474–19

Diabetes programs and expenditures of Fed Govt, by agency and NIH inst, FY84, annual rpt, 4434–8

Digestive Diseases Interagency Coordinating Committee activities, and related Federal research and funding, by agency, FY79-83, annual rpt, 4434–13

Drug abuse and trafficking reduction plan of Fed Govt, funding by agency and background data on drug use by substance, selected years FY81-85, biennial rpt, 024–1

Fed Govt aid to State and local govts, expenditures, and direct payments, by program, agency, and State, FY83, annual rpt, 2464–2

Fed Govt financial and nonfinancial domestic aid, 1984 annual comprehensive catalog, 104–5

General Medical Sciences Natl Inst research programs and funding, FY83, annual rpt, 4474–12

Govt expenditures for social welfare by program and level of govt, and private expenditures for health care, selected years FY50-82, annual article, 4742–1.425

Govt finances, by level of govt, State, and for large cities and counties, 1981-83, annual rpt series, 2466–2

Govt revenues by source and expenditures by function, natl income and product account, *Survey of Current Business,* monthly rpt, monthly and annual tables, 2702–1.24

GSA donations of surplus Federal personal property to State and local agencies and nonprofit instns, by region and State, FY83, annual rpt, 9454–22

Health care expenditures, growth factors, medical equipment and drugs trade, and physician income, 1950-90, article, 4652–1.407

Health care expenditures, natl and personal total and per capita amounts, by type of service and source of funds, 1983 and trends from 1929, annual article, 4652–1.429

Health Care Financing Admin research activities and grants by research area, as of June 1984, semiannual listing, 4652–8

Health condition and health care resources, use, and expenditures, 1970s-82 with trends and projections 1900-2000, annual compilation, 4144–11

Health maintenance organizations and prepaid health plans enrollment, use, and Fed Govt aid, FY83, annual rpt, 4104–8

Health Services Research Natl Center grants and contracts, by program area, FY83, annual listing, 4184–2

Heart, Lung, and Blood Natl Inst activities and funding, with morbidity and mortality data, various periods 1940-88, annual rpt, 4474–22

Heart, Lung, and Blood Natl Inst, Advisory Council recommended programs and budget, FY85-89, annual rpt, 4474–11

Heart, Lung, and Blood Natl Inst organization, disease and mortality data, and funds and recipients, FY83 with trends from 1900, annual fact book, 4474–15

HHS aid to each State and local govt or private instn, amount obligated, funding agency, and program, FY83, annual listing, 4004–3

HHS programs fraud and abuse, audits and investigations, 2nd half FY84, semiannual rpt, 4002–6

Indian and Alaska Native health program activities, and funding for scholarships, care services, and facilities construction, by city, FY82, annual rpt, 4104–11

Industry R&D funding and employment of scientists and engineers, by industry group, firm size, and funding source, 1956-82, annual rpt, 9627–21

Loan programs of Fed Govt, direct and guaranteed loans outstanding by agency and program, *Treasury Bulletin,* quarterly rpt, 8002–4.10

Maternal and child health, State govt spending and admin of Fed Govt block grants, by program for 13 States, 1981-83, GAO rpt, 26121–70

Mental health facilities of States and counties, inpatients, deaths, staff by occupation, and facilities, by State, 1970s-82, 4506–3.13

Mental health facilities, services, and costs in DC, and effect of St Elizabeths Hospital operations and finances transfer to DC govt, FY83, GAO rpt, 26121–72

Mothers and Children Research Center activities and funding, as of June 1983, annual rpt, 4474–31

NASA R&D funding to colleges and universities, by State, field of science, and instn, FY83, annual listing, 9504–7

NIH activities, staff, funding, and facilities, historical data, 1984 annual rpt, 4434–1

NIH extramural grant and contract awards for research, R&D, and construction, FY72-83, annual rpt, 4434–9

NIH grants and awards for R&D, training, construction, and medical libraries, by location and recipient, FY83, annual listings, 4434–7

NIH grants, awards, and obligations by State and type of recipient, and full-time personnel, by inst, FY83, annual rpt, 4434–3

NIH intl program activities and funding, by inst and country, FY83, annual rpt, 4474–6

NIH Library of Medicine activities, holdings, and grants, FY80-82, annual rpt, 4464–1

NIH newly announced grants and awards, quarterly listing, 4432–1

NIH Research Resources Div activities, accomplishments, and funding, by program, FY83, annual rpt, 4434–12

NYC health care demonstration project for reorganization of 6 facilities in Brooklyn, Federal and State govt funding by facility, 1979-82, article, 4652–1.419

Preventive health services block grants of Fed Govt, State funding by program, and opinions on State program admin, for 13 States, FY81-84, GAO rpt, 26121–88

Index by Subjects and Names

Public health labs of States, personnel, finances, workloads, and other activities, by State, FY82, annual rpt, 4204–8

Public Health Service activities, funding by function and subagency, and loans to HMOs, FY83, annual rpt, 4044–2

Puerto Rico University enrollment, tuition, construction costs, degrees granted, personnel by sex, and Fed Govt funding of medical research, 1970s-87, hearings, 21348–93

R&D expenditures of higher education instns, by source, field of science, census div, and State, 1972-83, biennial rpt, 9627–24.1

R&D Fed Govt funding, by function, agency, and program, selected years FY80-84 and proposed FY85, 26308–46

R&D Fed Govt funding for all performers, by field and supporting agency, selected years FY60-84, annual rpt, 9627–20

R&D funding by industry, program, and Federal agency, and high-technology trade performance, selected years 1960-FY84, 26306–6.77

Radiation from electronic devices, incidents and persons involved by type of device and FDA control program activities, 1983, annual rpt, 4064–13

Tax expenditures, Fed Govt revenues foregone through income tax deductions and exclusions by type, and effect of Deficit Reduction Act, FY84-89, annual rpt, 21784–10

TTPI socioeconomic, health, and govtl data, by TTPI govt, FY83 and selected trends, detailed annual rpt, 7004–6

see also Civilian Health and Medical Program of the Uniformed Services

see also Federal aid to medical education

see also Medicaid

see also Medicare

see also Veterans health facilities and services

Federal aid to railroads

Budget of US, effects of Reagan Admin policy changes, by detailed program, FY85, annual rpt, 104–21

Conrail operations and US Railway Assn finances and activities, FY81-83, annual rpt, 29604–1

Cost control proposals for Fed Govt programs and mgmt, 3-year savings by function and agency, and financial and operating data, 1960s-81, 16908–1.11

Credit assistance costs, policies to improve measurement, with loan and loan guarantee data by program, and Federal and private credit instns operations, 1970-84, 26306–6.72

DOT programs fraud and abuse, audits and investigations, 1st half FY84, semiannual rpt, 7302–4

Fed Govt aid to transportation by type, and govt transportation finances by level of govt and mode of transport, FY77-82, 7308–185

Fed Govt financial and nonfinancial domestic aid, 1984 annual comprehensive catalog, 104–5

Fed Hwy Admin allocations for hwys and bridges, by project and State, FY85, 7556–3.2

Land grants by Fed Govt to railroads, 1850-FY83, annual rpt, 5724–1.1

Index by Subjects and Names

Federal aid to States

Northeast Corridor rail improvement project goals, funding, and progress, and Amtrak finances and operations, FY83, annual rpt, 7604–9

Rail equipment commitments of Fed Govt, by type of vehicle, FY65-82, 26358–97

Federal aid to research and development *see* Federal funding for research and development

Federal aid to rural areas

Agricultural Stabilization and Conservation Service producer payments under 26 programs, monthly rpt, 1802–10

Agricultural Statistics, 1983, annual rpt, 1004–1

Alabama rural black population, education, employment, health services, and economic status, for 16 counties, selected years 1970-81, 11048–180

Appalachia hwy system and access roads funding and completion status, by State, quarterly tables, 9082–1

Appalachia regional dev spending, by program area and source of funds, FY82, annual rpt, 9084–1

Budget of US, CBO analysis of revenue and spending alternatives and projections of economic indicators, FY85-89, annual rpt, 26304–3.3

Budget of US, effects of Reagan Admin policy changes, by detailed program, FY85, annual rpt, 104–21

Budget of US, receipts by source and outlays by agency and program, monthly rpt, 8102–3

Cherokee Indians Eastern Band of North Carolina, financial and operating data for Bur of Indian Affairs assistance programs, FY83, annual rpt, 5704–4

Conservation practices in rural areas, Agricultural Conservation Program participation and payments, by State, FY83, annual rpt, 1804–7

Emergency Conservation Program participation and payments for farmland restoration from natural disaster, by practice and State, FY83, annual rpt, 1804–22

Farm debt, loans outstanding, and interest rates, by type of lender and State, 1960-83 with trends from 1940, biennial rpt, 1544–2

Farm finances, assets, liabilities, income, receipts by commodity and State, and expenses, 1980-83 and trends from 1910, annual rpt, 1544–16

Fed Govt aid to State and local govts, expenditures, and direct payments, by program, agency, and State, FY83, annual rpt, 2464–2

Fed Govt financial and nonfinancial domestic aid, 1984 annual comprehensive catalog, 104–5

Fish hatchery production, deliveries, and operating costs, and fishery assistance, by region, hatchery, and Fed Govt assistance station, FY82, annual rpt, 5504–9

FmHA loans for rural home mortgages, eligibility of current recipients under revised income limit, by State, 1983, GAO rpt, 26113–134

Forestry Incentives Program, Fed Govt cost-sharing funds for private timberland improvement, by region and State, monthly rpt, 1802–11

HHS aid to each State and local govt or private instn, amount obligated, funding agency, and program, FY83, annual listing, 4004–3

Rural area situation and dev, periodic rpt articles, 1502–7

Transit service aid of Fed Govt for older and handicapped persons and rural areas, and impacts of regulatory reform on bus industry, by State, 1970s-83, 14828–2.2

see also Agricultural quotas and price supports

see also Agricultural subsidies

see also Farm Credit Administration

see also Farm Credit System

see also Farmers Home Administration

see also Rural Electrification Administration

see also Rural Telephone Bank

Federal aid to States

AFDC recipients and payments, applications by disposition, payment discontinuances by reason, and hearings by outcome, by State, quarterly rpt, 4742–6

Agricultural research funding from Fed Govt and States, by region, State, and outlying area, FY78-82, GAO rpt, 26113–111

Bonneville Power Admin energy conservation program activities and funding data, FY82 and estimated FY83-87, 3228–2

Budget of US Appendix, detailed budgets and personnel summaries, by agency, FY85, annual rpt, 104–3

Budget of US, CBO analysis of revenue and spending alternatives and projections of economic indicators, FY85-89, annual rpt, 26304–3.3

Budget of US, compact budgets by function, agency, and account, FY85 with projections to FY89, annual rpt, 104–2

Budget of US, effects of Reagan Admin policy changes, by detailed program, FY85, annual rpt, 104–21

Budget of US, receipts by source and outlays by function, FY40-89 estimates revised for consistency with FY85 budget definitions, annual rpt, 104–12

Budget of US, special analysis of grants-in-aid outlays, by agency, function, and region, FY83-87, annual rpt, 104–1.8

Census of Govts, 1982: State govt payments to local govts, by program, source of funds, level of govt, and State, with trends from 1902, 2460–3

Child Support Enforcement Program admin, Fed Govt incentive payments to States, FY79-83, annual rpt, 4004–16.2

Child Support Enforcement Program cost savings to AFDC, Federal and State govts, and public assistance programs, by State and selected city or county, FY76-85, 4748–37

Child Support Enforcement Program costs, cases, and collections, by State, FY82, semiannual rpt, 4002–5

Child Support Enforcement Program costs, cases, and collections, by State, FY83, annual rpt, 4004–29

Community services block grants by type of service provider, State mgmt, and opinions of officials and groups involved, for 13 States, FY81-83, GAO rpt, 26121–84

Cost control proposals for Fed Govt programs and mgmt, 3-year savings by function and agency, and financial and operating data, 1960s-81, 16908–1

DOE procurement and assistance contracts, by State, contractor type, and top 100 instns, FY83, annual rpt, 3004–21

DOT grant awards for transportation planning and safety programs, by region, State, and for 35 largest SMSAs, FY83, annual rpt, 7304–7

Drug abuse situation, prevention and treatment programs, law enforcement, funding needs, and Fed Govt role, attitudes of State and local officials, 1983 survey, 21968–27

Economic Dev Admin loans and grants, by program, State, county, and project or recipient, FY83 and cumulative FY66-83, annual rpt, 2064–2

Economic dev assistance of Fed Govt, generation of jobs by industry div, model methodology and outputs, various periods FY69-78, GAO rpt, 26117–32

Education block grants of Fed Govt, State allocations by program and selected school district, FY82- 84 and trends from FY60, hearing, 21408–75

Education grants of Fed Govt, State allocations by program, type of recipient agency, and State, FY83, annual rpt, 4804–8

Energy conservation aid of DOE, activities, funding, and grants by State, by program, FY84, annual rpt, 3304–21

Energy conservation programs of State govts, Fed Govt financial and technical aid, and reported energy savings, by State, 1983, annual rpt, 3304–1

Environmental quality and protection programs, costs, and Fed Govt enforcement, 1983, detailed annual rpt, 484–1

EPA budget and full-time staff positions by type of activity, and grants to States, by program, FY75-84 and proposed FY85, 26308–47

EPA environmental protection activities and funding, and environmental quality, 1970s-83, biennial regional rpt series, 9184–15

EPA pollution control research and grant assistance program activities, monthly rpt, 9182–8

Fed Govt aid to State and local areas, by type of payment, State, county, and city, FY83, annual rpt, 2464–3

Fed Govt aid to State and local govt public service programs, annual rpt, discontinued, 8104–1

Fed Govt aid to State and local govts, expenditures, and direct payments, by program, agency, and State, FY83, annual rpt, 2464–2

Fed Govt financial and nonfinancial domestic aid, 1984 annual comprehensive catalog, 104–5

Fed Govt grants-in-aid for 13 program areas, FY82-84, annual article, 10042–1.402

Fed Govt grants to State and local govts, cumulative for fiscal year, annual trends, and quarterly data, monthly rpt, 23842–1.6

Federal aid to States

Fed Govt grants to State and local govts, various periods 1948-83, article, 9385–1.401

Fed Govt revenue sharing and other grant program alternative allocations, with city govt finances and responses to program cuts, FY79-83, hearings, 25408–86

Financial and business statistics, historic trends, 1984 annual chartbook, 9364–2.9

Fish and eggs for stocking distributed from natl hatcheries, by species, hatchery, and jurisdiction, FY83, annual rpt, 5504–10

Fish and Wildlife Service restoration programs, including new sites, funding, and research, by State, FY81, annual rpt, 5504–1

Fishery research of State fish and wildlife agencies, federally funded projects and costs by species and State, 1984, annual rpt, 5504–23

Fishery resources mgmt and R&D, Fed Govt grants by project and resulting publications, 1983, annual listing, 2164–3

Forestry activities on State and private lands, Fed Govt and State funding by project and State, FY83, annual tables, 1204–32

Foster care children permanent placement, Fed Govt incentive program funding and operations in 7 States, FY80-82, GAO rpt, 26121–81

Govt finances, by level of govt and State, selected years 1929-83, annual rpt, 10044–1

Govt finances, by level of govt, State, and for large cities and counties, 1981-83, annual rpt series, 2466–2

Govt revenues by source and expenditures by function, natl income and product account, *Survey of Current Business,* monthly rpt, monthly and annual tables, 2702–1.24

GSA donations of surplus Federal personal property to State and local agencies and nonprofit instns, by region and State, FY83, annual rpt, 9454–22

Handicapped children early education research and service project activities and characteristics, and grants to States for program dev, 1983-84, annual listing, 4804–30

HHS aid to each State and local govt or private instn, amount obligated, funding agency, and program, FY83, annual listing, 4004–3

Historic Preservation Fund grants, by State, FY85, annual press release, 5544–9

Housing (low-income) energy aid of Fed Govt, allocations and average benefits in 13 States, and public interest group assessment, FY81-83, GAO rpt, 26121–75

Hwy Statistics, detailed data on traffic, govt finances, fuel use, vehicles, driver licenses, and hwy characteristics, by State, 1983, annual rpt, 7554–1

Indian Education Act, Fed Govt grants and fellowships awarded by State, FY83, and natl advisory council funding, FY73-84, annual rpt, 14874–1

Industrial dev Fed Govt funding by type, program, and agency, and State govt policies and support, selected years FY75-85, 26306–6.81

Interior Dept programs, activities, and funding, various periods 1967-84, last issue of annual rpt, 5304–13

Maternal and child health, State govt spending and admin of Fed Govt block grants, by program for 13 States, 1981-83, GAO rpt, 26121–70

Medicaid medical vendor payment expenditures of Federal, State, and local govt, with Medicare and Medicaid program data, various periods 1966-82, annual rpt, 4654–1

Mental health and drug and alcohol abuse treatment funding of State govts, and admin of Fed Govt block grants, for 13 States, FY80-84, GAO rpt, 26121–87

Michigan health funding, Blue Cross-Blue Shield and welfare participation, and unemployment, poverty, and food assistance by county, 1979-83, hearing, 21348–86

Natural gas and hazardous liquid pipelines accidents and casualties, and DOT and State govt safety activities, 1982, annual rpt, 7304–5

Nuclear Waste Fund obligations by function and receipts, and DOE Civilian Radioactive Mgmt Office activities and staff, quarterly GAO rpt, 26102–4

Older persons community service part-time employment and program funding, by State and outlying area, FY84, press release, 6408–60

Older persons sociodemographic characteristics, and Fed Govt program participation and funding by agency, 1983 with trends and projections 1900-2080, annual rpt, 25144–3

Pipeline safety regulations enforcement of DOT and States by pipeline type and State, and accidents and commodity losses, selected years 1973-FY84, GAO rpt, 26113–130

Pollution abatement expenditures of govt, business, and consumers, 1972-82, annual article, 2702–1.407

Preventive health services block grants of Fed Govt, State funding by program, and opinions on State program admin, for 13 States, FY81-84, GAO rpt, 26121–88

Public lands receipts, Fed Govt allocations to States, 1803-FY83, annual rpt, 5724–1.4

Public opinion on taxes, tax policy, and intergovtl relations, 1972-84 surveys, annual rpt, 10044–2

Public works capital needs and financing, by project type, level of govt, and selected jurisdiction, 1970s-83 and projected to 2000, hearing, 23848–181

Public works capital needs and intergovtl financing, by type of project and selected city, various periods 1950-83, 10048–60

R&D Fed Govt funding for all performers, by field and supporting agency, selected years FY60-84, annual rpt, 9627–20

R&D Fed Govt labs required technology transfer to public and private sector, labs complying, funding, and requests, by agency, FY82, GAO rpt, 26113–141

Radioactive materials transport surveillance program activities, results, and Fed Govt funding, by State, 1984 summary rpt, 9636–1.23

Index by Subjects and Names

Recreation outdoor area dev, Interior Dept Land and Water Conservation Fund grants by State, FY85, annual press release, 5544–15

Refugee resettlement program activities and funding, arrivals and population by country of origin and State, and employment and other characteristics, FY83, annual rpt, 4704–8

Social service spending of State govts by service type and funding source, and admin of Fed Govt block grants, for 13 States, selected years FY80-84, GAO rpt, 26121–76

Traffic accidents and casualties detailed direct and indirect costs, by characteristics of persons and vehicles involved, 1979-80, 7768–80

Unemployed displaced workers training and placement program of Fed Govt, funding and enrollment for 13 States and Guam, June 1984, press release, 6408–61

Unemployment insurance system finances, claims, payments, and covered employment and wages, by State, 1938-82, 6408–5

Urban area socioeconomic and fiscal trends and problems, 1950-83 and Fed Govt funding estimates for FY84-87, biennial rpt, 5124–4

Vocational rehabilitation State agency expenditures, caseloads, rehabilitations, and staff, under Section 110 of the Rehabilitation Act, by State, FY82, annual rpt, 4944–9

Water Bank Program agreements, acreage, and Fed Govt payments, by State, FY72-83, annual rpt, 1804–21

Wildlife and bird research of State fish and wildlife agencies, federally funded projects and costs, by species and State, 1984, annual rpt, 5504–24

Youth social services of State govts, coordinating agencies activities, admin, membership, and funding sources, survey, 1984 rpt, 6068–182

Youth summer job program of Fed Govt, funding and jobs by State and for Indians, summer 1984, press release, 6408–62

see also Revenue sharing

see also Supplemental Security Income

Federal aid to transportation

Air traffic control and airway facilities and services, operations, and finances, FY83, annual rpt, 7504–37

Airline deregulation in 1978, effect on industry operations and finances, air traffic patterns, and CAB programs, various periods FY76-84, 9148–56

Airline financial and operating data for certificated, charter, and cargo carriers, quarterly rpt, 9142–30

Airline subsidies of Fed Govt paid since 1979 to air carriers serving small communities, by carrier, monthly rpt, 9142–48

Airport and inland waterways trust funds receipts, expenditures, assets, and liabilities, monthly rpt, 8102–9.5, 8102–9.8

Airport dev program grants and projects, by FAA region and State, FY83, annual rpt, 7504–1.3

Airport financing by source, bond issues by region, and airport operations, by airport and operator type, FY75-83 and projected to FY93, 26306–6.75

Index by Subjects and Names

Airport improvement program grants and activities, by State and airport, FY83, annual rpt, 7504–38

Airport planning and dev project grants of Fed Govt, by sponsor, airport, and location, periodic press release series, 7506–8

Budget of US Appendix, detailed budgets and personnel summaries, by agency, FY85, annual rpt, 104–3

Budget of US, CBO analysis and review of FY85 budget by function, annual rpt, 26304–2

Budget of US, CBO analysis of revenue and spending alternatives and projections of economic indicators, FY85-89, annual rpt, 26304–3.3

Budget of US, compact budgets by function, agency, and account, FY85 with projections to FY89, annual rpt, 104–2

Budget of US, effects of Reagan Admin policy changes, by detailed program, FY85, annual rpt, 104–21

Budget of US, loans and loan guarantees, and Admin proposed limits on credit assistance, by program, FY83-89, annual rpt, 26306–3.65

Budget of US, receipts by source and outlays by agency and program, monthly rpt, 8102–3

Budget of US, receipts by source and outlays by function, FY40-89 estimates revised for consistency with FY85 budget definitions, annual rpt, 104–12

Budget of US, receipts, outlays, and budget authority, by function and agency, FY84-89 revised estimates, midsession review of FY85 budget, annual rpt, 104–7

Budget of US, receipts, outlays, and budget authority, by function and agency, 1st revision of FY85 budget, annual rpt, 104–17

Budget summary of DOT, by subagency and program, FY81-85, annual rpt, 7304–10

Bus industry collective ratemaking and regulatory reform impacts on operations, finances, and services to older persons and rural areas by State, 1970s-83, 14828–2

Cost control proposals for Fed Govt programs and mgmt, CBO and GAO estimates of savings by function and agency, FY85-89, 26308–45

Cost control proposals for Fed Govt programs and mgmt, 3-year savings by function and agency, and financial and operating data, 1960s-81, 16908–1.11, 16908–1.22

DOT grant awards for transportation planning and safety programs, by region, State, and for 35 largest SMSAs, FY83, annual rpt, 7304–7

DOT programs fraud and abuse, audits and investigations, 1st half FY84, semiannual rpt, 7302–4

FAA activities and finances, and employees by region, FY82-83, annual rpt, 7504–10

Fed Govt aid to State and local govts, expenditures, and direct payments, by program, agency, and State, FY83, annual rpt, 2464–2

Fed Govt aid to transportation by type, and govt transportation finances by level of govt and mode of transport, FY77-82, 7308–185

Fed Govt financial and nonfinancial domestic aid, 1984 annual comprehensive catalog, 104–5

Fed Govt grants-in-aid for 13 program areas, FY82-84, annual article, 10042–1.402

Fed Govt loans, grants, and tax benefits to business, by program and economic sector, projected FY84-88 with effective tax rates for FY80-82, 26306–6.70

Govt revenues by source and expenditures by function, natl income and product account, *Survey of Current Business,* monthly rpt, monthly and annual tables, 2702–1.24

Industrial dev Fed Govt funding by type, program, and agency, and State govt policies and support, selected years FY75-85, 26306–6.81

Loan programs of Fed Govt, direct and guaranteed loans outstanding by agency and program, *Treasury Bulletin,* quarterly rpt, 8002–4.10

Motor vehicle safety program funding of 4 DOT agencies, FY80, 7768–80

Motor vehicles powered by electricity, Fed Govt dev program implementation, with bibl, FY83, annual rpt, 3304–2

Older persons sociodemographic characteristics, and Fed Govt program participation and funding, 1983 with trends and projections 1900-2060, annual rpt, 25144–3.1

Pipelines for natural gas and hazardous liquids, accidents and casualties, and DOT and State govts safety activities, 1982, annual rpt, 7304–5

Public works capital needs and intergovtl financing, by type of project and selected city, various periods 1950-83, 10048–60

R&D Fed Govt funding, by function, agency, and program, selected years FY80-84 and proposed FY85, 26308–46

Tax expenditures, Fed Govt revenues foregone through income tax deductions and exclusions by type, and effect of Deficit Reduction Act, FY84-89, annual rpt, 21784–10

Transit services for commuting and other purposes, dev and effects, series, 7306–9

Transit system deficits, effect of cost and service increases and ridership and fare decreases, and govt aid and system operating ratios, 1970-80, 7308–184

Transit system financial and operating data, by mode, function, fleet size, and individual system, FY82, annual rpt, 7884–4

Transit system mgmt training funded by Urban Mass Transportation Admin, participant characteristics and career impact, 1970-79, 7888–60

Transit system operations, tax burden related to ridership, fares, and govt funding, for selected States and cities, 1950s-82, reprint, 7888–59

Transit systems, expenditures by level of govt, and revenues by source, with distribution of commuter trips by mode of transport, 1980-82, article, 10042–1.404

Transit systems research publications, 2nd half FY83, semiannual listing, 7882–1

Urban Mass Transportation Admin grants to higher education instns for research and training, by project, FY84, annual rpt, 7884–7

Federal aid to vocational education

Urban mass transportation capital grants, by type, FY71-81, annual rpt, 7304–1

Urban transit and hwy systems financing methods of govts and private sector, with case studies for selected metro areas, series, 7556–7

User fees to recover costs of 7 federally subsidized public service programs, by type of fee, user, and service, FY84-88, 26306–6.68

see also Federal aid to highways

see also Federal aid to railroads

see also Shipbuilding and operating subsidies

Federal aid to vocational education

Appalachia regional dev spending, by program area and source of funds, FY82, annual rpt, 9084–1

Bilingual vocational training projects, participants, characteristics, and costs, by program, FY82, annual rpt, 4804–26

Budget of US Appendix, detailed budgets and personnel summaries, by agency, FY85, annual rpt, 104–3

Budget of US, CBO analysis of revenue and spending alternatives and projections of economic indicators, FY85-89, annual rpt, 26304–3.3

Budget of US, compact budgets by function, agency, and account, FY85 with projections to FY89, annual rpt, 104–2

Budget of US, effects of Reagan Admin policy changes, by detailed program, FY85, annual rpt, 104–21

Budget of US, receipts by source and outlays by function, FY40-89 estimates revised for consistency with FY85 budget definitions, annual rpt, 104–12

Children and youth benefitting from Fed Govt public welfare programs and tax expenditures, participation and funding for 71 programs, FY81-83, 21968–30

Education Dept financial aid programs for educational instns and individuals, 1984 annual listing, 4804–3

Education Dept programs and activities, FY83, annual rpt, 4804–6

Fed Govt aid to State and local govts, expenditures, and direct payments, by program, agency, and State, FY83, annual rpt, 2464–2

Fed Govt education block grants, State allocations by program and selected school district, FY82-84 and trends from FY60, hearing, 21408–75

Fed Govt educational grants, State allocations by program, type of recipient agency, and State, FY83, annual rpt, 4804–8

Fed Govt financial and nonfinancial domestic aid, 1984 annual comprehensive catalog, 104–5

Fed Govt funding for education, by agency, program, and State, selected years FY79-85, annual rpt, 4824–2.22

HHS aid to each State and local govt or private instn, amount obligated, funding agency, and program, FY83, annual listing, 4004–3

Natl Center for Research in Vocational Education funding, by purpose and source, selected years 1978-84, GAO rpt, 26121–79

Veterans education assistance program participation and costs under GI Bill and other programs, WW II through Sept 1983, annual rpt, 9924–22

Federal aid to vocational education

Vocational rehabilitation State agency expenditures, caseloads, rehabilitations, and staff, under Section 110 of the Rehabilitation Act, by State, FY82, annual rpt, 4944–9

Federal Aviation Administration

- Activities and finances of FAA, and employees by region, FY82-83, annual rpt, 7504–10
- Air passenger traffic, and aircraft operations by type, by airport, region, and State, projected FY82-95 and trends from FY76, annual rpt, 7504–7
- Air traffic control and airway facilities and equipment, FAA improvement activities and R&D under Natl Airspace System Plan, 1982-2000, annual rpt, 7504–12
- Air traffic control and airway facilities and services, operations, and finances, FY83, annual rpt, 7504–37
- Air traffic levels at FAA-operated control facilities, including instrument operations, by airport and State, FY83, annual rpt, 7504–27
- Aircraft collisions, and near collisions by circumstances and State, by type of aircraft, various periods 1980-84, 7508–61
- Aircraft registered with FAA, by type and characteristics of aircraft, carrier, make, State, and county, 1983, annual rpt, 7504–3
- Airport improvement program grants and activities, by State and airport, FY83, annual rpt, 7504–38
- Airport inspector workloads by region, and review of FAA regulations, 1984 rpt, 9618–12
- Airport planning and dev project grants of Fed Govt, by sponsor, airport, and location, periodic press release series, 7506–8
- Airport security operations to prevent hijacking, screening results, enforcement actions, and hijacking attempts, 1st half 1984, semiannual rpt, 7502–5
- Aviation activity, detailed data on aircraft, air traffic, air carriers, personnel, airports, and FAA operations, 1974-83, annual rpt, 7504–1
- Aviation activity forecasts, methodology, data sources, and coverage, Feb 1983 conf papers, annual rpt, 7504–28
- Aviation medicine research and studies, FAA technical rpt series, 7506–10
- Aviation traffic, aircraft, pilots, airport activity, and fuel use, forecast FY84-95 with FY79-83 trends, annual rpt, 7504–6
- Cost control proposals for Fed Govt programs and mgmt, 3-year savings by function and agency, and financial and operating data, 1960s-81, 16908–1.11, 16908–1.28
- Employment at DOT, by subagency, State, and selected personnel characteristics, FY83, annual rpt, 7304–18
- Flight and engine hours, and shutdown rates, by aircraft and engine model for each air carrier, monthly rpt, 7502–13
- Fraud and abuse in DOT programs, audits and investigations, 1st half FY84, semiannual rpt, 7302–4
- General aviation aircraft, hours flown, and equipment, by type, use, and model of aircraft, region, and State, 1982, annual rpt, 7504–29

General aviation violations of FAA flight operations and maintenance standards, and FAA enforcement actions, annual rpt, discontinued, 7504–25

- Hijackings, on-board explosions, other crimes against civil aviation, and circumstances, US and worldwide, 1931-83, annual rpt, 7504–31
- Instrument flight rule aircraft handled, by user type, FAA traffic control center, and region, FY69-83 and forecast to FY95, annual rpt, 7504–15
- Pilots and nonpilots certified by FAA, by type of certificate, age, sex, region, and State, 1983, annual rpt, 7504–2
- Traffic (passenger and cargo) and departures by aircraft type, by airline and US and foreign airport, 1982, annual rpt, 7504–35

Federal boards, committees, and commissions

- Advisory committees of Fed Govt, and members, staff, meetings, and costs, by agency, FY83, annual rpt, 9454–18
- Army Corps of Engineers and associated commissions activities and projects, FY83 and trends from 1800s, annual rpt, 3754–1
- Audit activities, funding, and staff of Fed Govt agencies without inspectors general, by agency, FY83, GAO rpt, 26111–23
- Budget of US Appendix, detailed budgets and personnel summaries, by agency, FY85, annual rpt, 104–3
- Budget of US, appropriations, outlays, balances, and budget receipts, by govtl branch and agency, FY83, annual rpt, 8104–2
- Budget of US, compact budgets by function, agency, and account, FY85 with projections to FY89, annual rpt, 104–2
- Budget of US, effects of Reagan Admin policy changes, by detailed program, FY85, annual rpt, 104–21
- Budget of US, receipts by source and outlays by agency and program, monthly rpt, 8102–3
- Budget of US, special analyses of economic and social impact, FY85, annual rpt, 104–1
- Cost control proposals for Fed Govt programs and mgmt, CBO and GAO estimates of savings by function and agency, FY85-89, 26308–45
- Cost control proposals for Fed Govt programs and mgmt, 3-year savings by function and agency, and financial and operating data, 1960s-81, 16908–1
- Employment (civilian) of Fed Govt, by location, agency, and pay system, 1982, biennial rpt, 9844–8
- Employment and payroll (civilian) of Fed Govt, by agency in DC metro area, total US, and abroad, monthly rpt, 9842–1
- Financial operations of Fed Govt, detailed data, *Treasury Bulletin,* quarterly rpt, 8002–4
- Labor unions recognized in Fed Govt, agreements and membership by agency and office or installation, Jan 1983, annual listing, 9844–14
- Property (real) of Fed Govt, inventory and costs, worldwide summary by location, agency, and use, 1983, annual rpt, 9454–5

Index by Subjects and Names

- Property (real) of Fed Govt, leased property inventory and rental costs, worldwide summary by location and agency, Sept 1983, annual rpt, 9454–10
- Radio frequency assignments for Federal agency use, 2nd half 1983, semiannual rpt, 2802–1
- Saudi Arabia-US Joint Commission on Economic Cooperation project activities and costs, and related contract awards by Fed Govt agency, as of 1983, GAO rpt, 26123–80
- *see also* Advisory Commission on Intergovernmental Relations
- *see also* Advisory Committee on Federal Pay
- *see also* Advisory Council on Social Security
- *see also* Board for International Broadcasting
- *see also* Commission on Civil Rights
- *see also* Commission on Executive, Legislative, and Judicial Salaries
- *see also* Commission on Fair Market Value Policy for Federal Coal Leasing
- *see also* Commission on Wartime Relocation and Internment of Civilians
- *see also* Committee for Purchase from the Blind and Other Severely Handicapped
- *see also* Commodity Futures Trading Commission
- *see also* Federal Committee on Statistical Methodology
- *see also* Federal Election Commission
- *see also* Federal Financial Institutions Examination Council
- *see also* Federal independent agencies
- *see also* Federal Labor Relations Authority
- *see also* Federal Mine Safety and Health Review Commission
- *see also* Inter-American Foundation
- *see also* Interdepartment Radio Advisory Committee
- *see also* International Boundary and Water Commission, U.S. and Mexico
- *see also* International Joint Commission, U.S. and Canada
- *see also* Japan-U.S. Friendship Commission
- *see also* Marine Mammal Commission
- *see also* Motor Carrier Ratemaking Study Commission
- *see also* National Advisory Committee on Oceans and Atmosphere
- *see also* National Advisory Council on Continuing Education
- *see also* National Advisory Council on Indian Education
- *see also* National Advisory Council on International Monetary and Financial Policies
- *see also* National Capital Planning Commission
- *see also* National Commission on Air Quality
- *see also* National Commission on Excellence in Education
- *see also* National Commission on Libraries and Information Science
- *see also* National Commission on Social Security Reform
- *see also* National Commission on Student Financial Assistance
- *see also* National Council on Educational Research
- *see also* National Narcotics Intelligence Consumers Committee

Index by Subjects and Names

see also National Transportation Policy Study Commission

see also Pennsylvania Avenue Development Corp.

see also President's Commission for the Study of Ethical Problems in Medicine and Biomedical and Behavioral Research

see also President's Commission on Pension Policy

see also President's Committee on Employment of the Handicapped

see also President's Private Sector Survey on Cost Control

see also Select Commission on Immigration and Refugee Policy

see also Truman, Harry S., Scholarship Foundation

see also U.S. Advisory Commission on Public Diplomacy

see also U.S. Architectural and Transportation Barriers Compliance Board

see also Water Resources Council

see also White House Conference on Productivity

see also under By Federal Agency in the "Index by Categories"

Federal budget

see Budget of the U.S.

Federal buildings

see Public buildings

Federal Bureau of Investigation

Assaults, murders, and other deaths of law enforcement officers, by circumstances, level of govt, agency, victim and offender characteristics, and location, 1983, annual rpt, 6224–3

Bombing (explosive and incendiary) incidents, damage, injuries, and deaths, by target, State, and circumstances, 1983, annual rpt, 6224–5

Crime Index by population size and region, and offenses known to police by large city, Jan-June 1984, semiannual rpt, 6222–1

Crimes, arrests by offender characteristics, and rates, by offense, and law enforcement employees, by population size and jurisdiction, 1970s-83, annual rpt, 6224–2

Justice Dept activities, by subagency, FY82, annual rpt, 6004–1

Kidnapping by parents over intl and interstate boundaries, characteristics of cases referred to State Dept and FBI by State and country, 1979-83, hearing, 25528–95

Undercover operations of FBI, convictions, fines, recoveries, victim compensation, and status of lawsuits against FBI by operation, FY82, GAO rpt, 26119–67

Federal Bureau of Prisons

see Bureau of Prisons

Federal Committee on Statistical Methodology

Fed Govt statistical policies relating to technical operation of programs, methodology, and use of Federal data, working paper series, 106–4

Federal Communications Commission

Budget of US Appendix, detailed budgets and personnel summaries, by agency, FY85, annual rpt, 104–3

Budget of US, appropriations, outlays, balances, and budget receipts, by govtl branch and agency, FY83, annual rpt, 8104–2

Cost control proposals for Fed Govt programs and mgmt, 3-year savings by function and agency, and financial and operating data, 1960s-81, 16908–1.15, 16908–1.31

R&D Fed Govt funding for all performers, by field and supporting agency, selected years FY60-84, annual rpt, 9627–20

Space and aeronautics programs and budgets of Fed Govt by agency, and foreign programs, 1957-FY85, annual rpt, 9504–9

Telegraph carriers financial and operating data, for 7 firms, quarterly rpt, 9282–1

Telephone and telegraph firms detailed financial, operating, and employment statistics, 1982, annual rpt, 9284–6

Telephone carriers financial and operating data, quarterly rpt, discontinued, 9282–2

TV (cable) industry financial and operating data, by region and State, annual rpt, discontinued, 9284–15

TV and radio industry employment, total and for minorities, women, and youth, by job category and State, 1979-83, annual rpt, 9284–16

TV and radio station employment, total and for minorities and women, by full- and part-time status and individual station, 1983, annual rpt, 9284–7

TV and radio stations on the air, by class of operation, monthly press release, 9282–4

TV channels allocation and licensing status, for commercial and noncommercial UHF and VHF TV by market and community, as of Dec 1983, semiannual rpt, 9282–6

Federal contracts

see Government contracts and procurement

Federal corporations

see Government corporations

Federal courts

see Administrative Office of the U.S. Courts

see Court of Claims

see Court of Customs and Patent Appeals

see Court of International Trade

see Court of Military Appeals

see Courts

see Federal courts of appeals

see Federal district courts

see Supreme Court

see Tax Court of the U.S.

Federal courts of appeals

Budget of US Appendix, detailed budgets and personnel summaries, by agency, FY85, annual rpt, 104–3

Budget of US, effects of Reagan Admin policy changes, by detailed program, FY85, annual rpt, 104–21

Caseloads (civil and criminal) and activity summary, 1975-June 1984, annual chartbook, 18204–9

Caseloads (civil and criminal), year ended June 1983 and selected trends from 1940, annual rpt, 18204–8

Caseloads, actions, procedure duration, judges, and jurors, by Federal district and appeals court, 1979-84, annual rpt, 18204–3

Caseloads for Federal district, appeals, and bankruptcy courts, by type of suit and offense, circuit, and district, quarterly rpt, 18202–1

Caseloads of Court of Intl Trade by type, decisions published, and appeals, FY83-84, annual rpt, 18224–2

Federal district courts

Habeas corpus writs filed by State prisoners in Federal district and appeals courts by circuit, and petition disposition, selected years 1961-82, 6066–19.4

Judgeships recommended for Federal district and appeals courts, by circuit, Judicial Conf semiannual proceedings, 1984 annual rpt, 18204–5

Pay rates of Fed Govt civilian employees, by branch of govt, employee category, and pay level, as of 1984 with trends from 1789, 21628–54

Statistical Abstract of US, social, political, and economic data, 1950s-83 and trends, annual rpt, 2324–1.1

US Attorneys civil and criminal case processing in district, appellate, and State courts, by district, FY83, annual rpt, 6004–2

Federal Crop Insurance Corp.

Activities and costs of FCIC, and FCIC and private insurance company gains and losses, 1980-84 with some trends from 1948, GAO rpt, 26113–119

Activities and programs of USDA, by subagency, FY83, annual rpt, 1004–3

Cost control proposals for Fed Govt programs and mgmt, 3-year savings by function and agency, and financial and operating data, 1960s-81, 16908–1.15

Crop insurance participation and operations in 2 States by crop, and Fed Crop Insurance Corp finances, 1980-84, GAO rpt, 26113–132

Finances and operations of FCIC, for FCIC policies and private policies reinsured by FCIC, 1970s-84 with some trends from 1948, hearing, 21168–28

Fraud and abuse in USDA programs, audits and investigations, 2nd half FY84, semiannual rpt, 1002–4

Federal Deposit Insurance Corp.

Bank examination activities and supervisory actions of FDIC, 1983, annual rpt, 9294–1

Budget of US Appendix, detailed budgets and personnel summaries, by agency, FY85, annual rpt, 104–3

Budget of US, appropriations, outlays, balances, and budget receipts, by govtl branch and agency, FY83, annual rpt, 8104–2

Budget of US, object class analysis of obligations, by branch of Fed Govt and selected depts and agencies, FY85 estimates, annual rpt, 104–9

Cost control proposals for Fed Govt programs and mgmt, 3-year savings by function and agency, and financial and operating data, 1960s-81, 16908–1.14

Deposits in commercial and mutual savings banks and in US branches of foreign banks, by account type, instn, State, SMSA, and county, June 1983, annual rpt, 9295–3

Insurance payoff and assumption cases and fund net loss, 1965-83, and FDIC balance sheet, 1982, article, 9393–8.407

Federal district courts

Bankruptcy caseloads in Federal district courts and new judges needed, by circuit and district, and characteristics of bankruptcy filers, 1978-83, hearing, 25528–97

Federal district courts

Budget of US Appendix, detailed budgets and personnel summaries, by agency, FY85, annual rpt, 104–3

Budget of US, effects of Reagan Admin policy changes, by detailed program, FY85, annual rpt, 104–21

Caseloads (civil and criminal) and activity summary, 1975-June 1984, annual chartbook, 18204–9

Caseloads (civil and criminal), year ended June 1983 and selected trends from 1940, annual rpt, 18204–8

Caseloads (criminal), dispositions, convictions, and sentences of Federal defendants, by offense and district, as of June 1983 with trends from 1945, annual rpt, 18204–1

Caseloads, actions, procedure duration, judges, and jurors, by Federal district and appeals court, 1979-84, annual rpt, 18204–3

Caseloads for Federal district, appeals, and bankruptcy courts, by type of suit and offense, circuit, and district, quarterly rpt, 18202–1

Corrupt govt officials prosecutions and convictions, by judicial district and level of govt, 1976-83, annual rpt, 6004–13

Habeas corpus writs filed by State prisoners in Federal district and appeals courts by circuit, and petition disposition, selected years 1961-82, 6066–19.4

Judgeships recommended for Federal district and appeals courts, by circuit, Judicial Conf semiannual proceedings, 1984 annual rpt, 18204–5

Juror (grand and petit) usage and costs, trials, and trial days, by Federal district court, years ended June 1980-84, annual rpt, 18204–4

Magistrate case processing duties assigned in Fed Govt district courts, by type of case, duty, and district, 1983 rpt, 18408–24

Marijuana cultivation control activity of State law enforcement agencies, and aid from Fed Govt and Natl Guard, 1983 survey, GAO rpt, 26119–64

Pay rates of Fed Govt civilian employees, by branch of govt, employee category, and pay level, as of 1984 with trends from 1789, 21628–54

Staff by position in Federal district courts, and visiting judges, visits, and visit days, by large district, various dates 1982-84, 18408–25

Statistical Abstract of US, social, political, and economic data, 1950s-83 and trends, annual rpt, 2324–1.1

US Attorneys civil and criminal case processing in district, appellate, and State courts, by district, FY83, annual rpt, 6004–2

Wiretapping authorizations by offense, costs, persons involved, arrests, trials, and convictions, 1983, annual rpt, 18204–7

Federal Election Commission

Budget of US Appendix, detailed budgets and personnel summaries, by agency, FY85, annual rpt, 104–3

Budget of US, appropriations, outlays, balances, and budget receipts, by govtl branch and agency, FY83, annual rpt, 8104–2

Campaign finances and Fed Election Commission monitoring activities, 1984 Federal elections, biennial rpt series, 9276–2

Campaign finances, election procedures, and FEC monitoring activities, press release series, 9276–1

Campaign funding and activities of Fed Election Commission, and political action committees funding, 1983, annual rpt, 9274–1

Political action committee campaign funding, by House and Senate candidate, 1978-82 Federal elections, biennial rpt, 9274–4

Federal Emergency Management Agency

Budget of US Appendix, detailed budgets and personnel summaries, by agency, FY85, annual rpt, 104–3

Budget of US, appropriations, outlays, balances, and budget receipts, by govtl branch and agency, FY83, annual rpt, 8104–2

Cost control proposals for Fed Govt programs and mgmt, 3-year savings by function and agency, and financial and operating data, 1960s-81, 16908–1.13

Disaster and emergency relief activities and funding, and major disasters, 1983, annual rpt, 9434–2

Flood insurance program of Fed Govt, average premiums, premium income, and program costs, selected years FY68-84, hearing, 21248–81

Natl Defense Executive reserve members, costs, and training, by agency, annual rpt, suspended, 9434–1

Nuclear attack civil defense plans of Fed Emergency Mgmt Agency, funding and operations by component, FY81-84 and projected FY85-89, GAO rpt, 26123–61

Publications of FEMA, annual listing, suspended, 9434–5

R&D Fed Govt funding for all performers, by field and supporting agency, selected years FY60-84, annual rpt, 9627–20

Strategic and critical materials stockpiling activities and inventories of Fed Govt, by commodity, as of Mar 1984, semiannual rpt, 9432–1

Federal employees

Advisory committees of Fed Govt, and members, staff, meetings, and costs, by agency, FY83, annual rpt, 9454–18

Assaults, murders, and other deaths of law enforcement officers, by circumstances, level of govt, agency, victim and offender characteristics, and location, 1983, annual rpt, 6224–3

Audit activities, funding, and staff of Fed Govt agencies without inspectors general, by agency, FY83, GAO rpt, 26111–23

Benefits for Federal civilian employees, retirement, health, and life insurance programs operations and finances, FY81-82, annual rpt, 9844–1

Budget of US, CBO analysis of revenue and spending alternatives and projections of economic indicators, FY85-89, annual rpt, 26304–3.3

Budget of US, effects of Reagan Admin policy changes, by detailed program, FY85, annual rpt, 104–21

Budget of US, special analysis of civil rights activities by agency and program, and Fed Govt employment of minorities, FY83-85, annual rpt, 104–1.10

Budget of US, special analysis of Fed Govt employment and cost of direct compensation and benefits, FY85, annual rpt, 104–1.9

Index by Subjects and Names

Census of Govts, 1982: employment, payrolls, and average earnings, by function, level of govt, State, county, population size, and inside-outside SMSAs, 2455–2

Census of Population and Housing, 1980: detailed population and housing characteristics, by county, city, and census tract, State and SMSA rpt series, 2551–2

Census of Population, 1980: detailed socioeconomic and demographic characteristics, by age, sex, race, Hispanic origin, occupation, and industry, State rpt series, 2531–4

Census of Population, 1980: detailed socioeconomic characteristics, by county, city, and inside-outside SMSAs and central cities, State rpt series, 2531–3

Charity contributions of Fed Govt employees to Combined Federal Campaign, funds by type of recipient, 1982 and trends from 1973, GAO rpt, 26119–66

Civil rights enforcement offices funding and staff, for 6 Federal agencies, FY80-84, 11048–179

Computer specialists sociodemographic, educational, and employment characteristics, and Fed Govt support by agency, 1978, biennial Current Population Rpt, 2546–2.124

Corrupt govt officials prosecutions and convictions, by judicial district and level of govt, 1976-83, annual rpt, 6004–13

Cost control proposals for Fed Govt programs and mgmt, CBO and GAO estimates of savings by function and agency, FY85-89, 26308–45

Cost control proposals for Fed Govt programs and mgmt, 3-year savings by function and agency, and financial and operating data, 1960s-81, 16908–1

County and City Data Book, detailed socioeconomic and demographic data for States, counties, and cities, selected years 1976-82, 2328–1

County Business Patterns: establishments, employees, and payrolls, by SIC 4-digit industry and county, 1981, annual State rpt series, 2326–8

County Business Patterns: establishments, employees, and payrolls, by SIC 4-digit industry and county, 1982, annual State rpt series, 2326–6

Crime and criminal justice data, including justice expenditures and employment by level of govt, 1970s-82 with some trends from 1875, 6068–174

Criminal justice employment by job category and level of govt, and arrests for serious crimes in 5 States by disposition, Dec 1983 rpt, 6062–2.401

Disability (short-term) earnings lost, insurance benefits, sick leave, and work days lost by sex, by type of worker, 1948-81, article, 4742–1.417

Drug enforcement regional task force program investigation activities, funding, and personnel, with nationwide drug abuse data, 1983 annual rpt, 6004–17

Employment (civilian) in executive branch agencies, FY82-86, annual brief budget overview, 104–6

Employment (civilian) in executive branch depts and major agencies, FY85 Budget of US, annual rpt, 104–2

Index by Subjects and Names

Employment (civilian) of Fed Govt, by location, agency, and pay system, 1982, biennial rpt, 9844–8

Employment and earnings, by level of govt and State, selected years 1929-82, annual rpt, 10044–1.5

Employment and earnings, detailed data, monthly rpt, 6742–2.5

Employment and payroll (civilian) of Fed Govt, by agency in DC metro area, total US, and abroad, monthly rpt, 9842–1

Employment and wages of workers covered by State unemployment insurance laws and Fed Govt unemployment compensation, by SIC 4-digit industry and State, 1982, annual rpt, 6744–16

Employment, earnings, and hours, by level and branch of govt, and function, monthly 1977-Feb 1984, annual update, 6744–4

Employment, earnings, and hours, by selected SIC 1- to 4-digit industry, State, and for 278 major labor areas, 1939-83, annual rpt, 6744–5

Employment of Federal and State/local workers, monthly press release, 6742–5

Employment situation, earnings, hours, and other BLS economic indicators, transcripts of BLS Commissioner's monthly testimony, periodic rpt, 23846–4

Engineers sociodemographic, educational, and employment characteristics, and Federal support by agency, 1978, Current Population Rpt, 2546–2.121

Equal Opportunity Recruitment Program implementation, and summary employment data, FY83, annual rpt, 9844–33

Executive employee dev programs of Fed Govt, employee and candidate attitudes in 5 agencies, 1983 survey, GAO rpt, 26119–69

Executive employee performance appraisal system of Fed Govt, operations and employee attitudes, 1982 survey, GAO rpt, 26119–61

Handicapped persons employed by Fed Govt, annual rpt, suspended, 9844–23

Health benefits program of Fed Govt, finances, benefit reductions, and rate increases, by plan, 1981-82, GAO rpt, 26121–67

Health maintenance organizations and prepaid health plans enrollment, use, and Fed Govt aid, FY83, annual rpt, 4104–8

Health professionals supply and education, by occupation, demographic and professional characteristics, and location, 1950s-83 and projected to 2000, biennial rpt, 4114–8

Immigrants admitted under Immigration and Nationality Act, by class of admission, FY78-81, annual rpt, 6264–2

Info security clearances of Fed Govt and contractor employees, polygraph use, and prepublication reviews, by agency, 1979-83, GAO rpt, 26123–66

Judges (administrative law), by Fed Govt agency and grade, various dates 1947-82, hearings, 25528–96

Mail (franked and penalty), USPS subsidy for revenue forgone by class of mail, FY83, annual rpt, 9864–5.3

Meat and poultry inspection activities and personnel of Federal, State, and foreign govts, FY83, annual rpt, 1374–1

Minority group and handicapped employment of Fed Govt, by race, Hispanic origin, disability, sex, and employment characteristics, as of Sept 1982, biennial rpt, 9844–27

Minority group and women civilian employment of Fed Govt, by grade and agency, 1980 and 1983, 21348–41

Minority group and women civilian employment of Fed Govt, by pay system and grade level, preliminary annual rpt, discontinued, 9844–13

Minority group and women civilian employment of Fed Govt, by pay system and occupation, annual press release, discontinued, 9844–29

New England States economic indicators, Fed Reserve 1st District, monthly rpt, 9373–2.2

Occupational injuries, deaths, and illnesses, by agency, 1982, annual rpt, 6604–1

Occupational Outlook Handbook, 1984-85 biennial rpt, 6744–1

Physicians (not office-based) visits by reason, diagnosis, treatment, patient and physician characteristics, and physician primary activity, 1980, 4147–13.77

Polygraph lie detection test accuracy, and Fed Govt use by agency, selected years 1947-83, 26358–96

Productivity of labor and capital, costs, and prices, by selected industry, and compared to 6 OECD countries, selected years 1947-82, 17898–1

Science and engineering grads of 1980-81, employment characteristics or grad enrollment, by degree level, field, sex, and race, 1982, 9627–25

Scientists and engineers employment by sector and activity, and share female, black, and Asian descent, by field, 1982, 9626–2.142

Scientists and engineers in nuclear-related industry, by field and sector, 1981 and 1983, 3006–8.2

Senior Executive Service of Fed Govt, employee admin, and program status and effectiveness, by agency and by executive and job characteristics, July 1979-Sept 1983, GAO rpt, 26119–51

Southwestern States nonagricultural employment, including Federal and State/local govts, monthly rpt, 6962–2

Statistical Abstract of US, social, political, and economic data, 1950s-83 and trends, annual rpt, 2324–1.2

Traffic accidents and casualties detailed direct and indirect costs, by characteristics of persons and vehicles involved, 1979-80, 7768–80

Travel expenses of Fed Govt employees on official business, and reimbursement rates, for high rate cities, 1983, annual rpt, 9454–16

Travel expenses of Fed Govt employees, operating costs for private autos, airplanes, and motorcycles and reimbursement rates for business use, 1983, annual rpt, 9454–13

Unemployment insurance benefits and claims, by program, Monthly Labor Review, 6722–1.4

Unemployment insurance claims, insured unemployment, and exhaustions, by program, weekly rpt, 6402–14

Federal Energy Regulatory Commission

Veterans (disabled and nondisabled) Fed Govt appointments and separations, agency, 2nd half FY82, semiannual rpt, 9842–3

Veterans with disability hired by Fed Govt under noncompetitive temporary hiring authority, by pay system, grade, and agency, 2nd half FY82, semiannual rpt, 9842–4

Vietnam Orderly Departure Program, former Fed Govt employees arrivals in US and refugee camps, monthly rpt, 7002–4

Weather operations personnel of Fed Govt, by function, FY84-85, annual rpt, 2144–2

Women's employment and earnings, by labor force and socioeconomic characteristics, and compared to men, 1978-81 and trends from 1940s, 6568–29

Workers compensation coverage by State, benefits, degree of disability, employer costs, and insurance industry finances, 1939-80, article, 4742–1.414

Workers compensation law provisions of States and Fed Govt, by jurisdiction, as of July 1984, semiannual rpt, 6502–1

Workers compensation under Fed Govt-administered programs, coverage, expenditures, and claims and dispositions by district, FY83, annual compilation, 6504–5

see also Civil service pensions

see also Civil service system

see also Congressional employees

see also Diplomatic and consular service

see also Federal pay

see also Financial disclosure

see also Labor-management relations in government

see also Military pay

see also Military pensions

see also Military personnel

see also Officials

see also Postal employees

see also Presidential appointments

see also under names of individual Federal departments and agencies

Federal Energy Administration

see Department of Energy

Federal Energy Regulatory Commission

Budget appropriations proposed for Fed Govt energy programs, by office or dept and function, FY84-85, annual rpt, 3004–14

Cost control proposals for Fed Govt programs and mgmt, 3-year savings by function and agency, and financial and operating data, 1960s-81, 16908–1.4, 16908–1.31

Electric power plant (coal-fired) capacity, coal demand, and coal supply by mode of transport and region of origin, by State, for units planned 1983-92, 3088–18

Electric utility rate minimization from improved efficiency, proposed FERC incentive program operations and costs, with comparisons to 3 State programs, 1950s-82, 3088–17

Natural gas pipeline and compressor station construction costs, 1979-82, annual rpt, 3084–3

Program activities and funding of FERC, with some natural gas and electric power industry data, FY83, annual rpt, 3084–9

Federal executive departments

Federal executive departments

Budget of US Appendix, detailed budgets and personnel summaries, by agency, FY85, annual rpt, 104–3

Budget of US, appropriations, outlays, balances, and budget receipts, by govtl branch and agency, FY83, annual rpt, 8104–2

Budget of US, authority balances in FY85 budget, by agency, FY83-85, annual rpt, 104–8

Budget of US, compact budgets by function, agency, and account, FY85 with projections to FY89, annual rpt, 104–2

Budget of US, effects of Reagan Admin policy changes, by detailed program, FY85, annual rpt, 104–21

Budget of US, receipts by source and outlays by agency and program, monthly rpt, 8102–3

Budget of US, receipts by source and outlays by function, FY40-89 estimates revised for consistency with FY85 budget definitions, annual rpt, 104–12

Budget of US, receipts, outlays, and budget authority, by function and agency, FY84-89 revised estimates, midsession review of FY85 budget, annual rpt, 104–7

Budget of US, special analyses of economic and social impact, FY85, annual rpt, 104–1

Building construction, acquisition, and alteration proposals for historic and other Fed Govt projects, costs and tenure by city and project, as of 1983, hearings, 25328–23

Collective bargaining agreements of Federal employees, unions involved, and employees covered, by agency for agreements expiring July 1984-June 1985, annual listing, 9847–1

Collective bargaining multi-unit agreements of Federal employees, by labor union and agency, as of July 1983, annual listing, 9847–4

Computer systems and equipment of Fed Govt, inventory by manufacturer, type, agency, and location, FY83, last issue of annual rpt, 9454–4

Computers and telecommunications systems major acquisition plans and obligations of Fed Govt, by agency, FY84-89, annual listing, 104–20

Cost control proposals for Fed Govt programs and mgmt, CBO and GAO estimates of savings by function and agency, FY85-89, 26308–45

Cost control proposals for Fed Govt programs and mgmt, 3-year savings by function and agency, and financial and operating data, 1960s-81, 16908–1

Employment (civilian) of Fed Govt, by location, agency, and pay system, 1982, biennial rpt, 9844–8

Employment and payroll (civilian) of Fed Govt, by agency in DC metro area, total US, and abroad, monthly rpt, 9842–1

Employment, earnings, and hours, by level and branch of govt, and function, monthly 1977-Feb 1984, annual update, 6744–4

Energy use and efficiency of Fed Govt, by agency and fuel type, FY83, annual rpt, 3304–22

Fed Govt aid to State and local govts, expenditures, and direct payments, by program, agency, and State, FY83, annual rpt, 2464–2

Fed Govt consolidated financial statements based on business accounting methods, FY82-83, annual rpt, 8104–5

Financial operations of Fed Govt, detailed data, *Treasury Bulletin,* quarterly rpt, 8002–4

GAO evaluations of Federal programs, 1984 listing, 26106–5.1

Investigations of Fed Govt civil agencies operations, summaries of GAO rpts published 1975-83, annual rpt, 26104–5

Labor unions recognized in Fed Govt, agreements and membership by agency and office or installation, Jan 1983, annual listing, 9844–14

Liabilities and other financial commitments, by Federal agency, as of Sept 1983, annual rpt, 8104–3

Minority business Fed Govt funding, procurement, and subsidies, and deposits in minority-owned banks, by agency, FY69-83, annual rpt, 2104–5

Older persons programs, funding and participation by agency, FY83 with trends from FY79, annual rpt, 25144–3.2

Pacific Northwest electricity consumption and prices by end-use sector, and economic and demographic data, 1960s-83 and projected to 2005, annual rpt, 3224–2

Property (real) of Fed Govt, inventory and costs, worldwide summary by location, agency, and use, 1983, annual rpt, 9454–5

Property (real) of Fed Govt, leased property inventory and rental costs, worldwide summary by location and agency, Sept 1983, annual rpt, 9454–10

R&D Fed Govt funding for all performers, by field and supporting agency, selected years FY60-84, annual rpt, 9627–20

Radio frequency assignments for Federal agency use, 2nd half 1983, semiannual rpt, 2802–1

Veterans (disabled and nondisabled) Fed Govt appointments and separations, agency, 2nd half FY82, semiannual rpt, 9842–3

see also Federal boards, committees, and commissions

see also Federal independent agencies

see also under By Federal Agency in the "Index by Categories"

see also under names of individual Federal departments and agencies

Federal expenditures

see Budget of the U.S.

see Defense expenditures

see Government spending

Federal Financial Institutions Examination Council

Cost control proposals for Fed Govt programs and mgmt, 3-year savings by function and agency, and financial and operating data, 1960s-81, 16908–1.14

Financial statements of Fed Financial Instns Examination Council, 1982-83, with summary data on financial instns by type, year ended June 1983, annual rpt, 13004–2

Index by Subjects and Names

Foreign lending of large US banks at all US and foreign offices, by country group and country, quarterly rpt, 13002–1

Trust assets of banks and trust companies, by type of asset and fund and State, 1983, annual rpt, 13004–1

Federal Financing Bank

Budget of US, appropriations, outlays, balances, and budget receipts, by govtl branch and agency, FY83, annual rpt, 8104–2

Budget of US, effects of Reagan Admin policy changes, by detailed program, FY85, annual rpt, 104–21

Budget of US, loans and loan guarantees, and Admin proposed limits on credit assistance, by program, FY83-89, annual rpt, 26306–3.65

Cost control proposals for Fed Govt programs and mgmt, 3-year savings by function and agency, and financial and operating data, 1960s-81, 16908–1.8, 16908–1.26

Credit assistance costs, policies to improve measurement, with loan and loan guarantee data by program, and Federal and private credit instns operations, 1970-84, 26306–6.72

Fed Govt off-budget outlays, by function FY62-89, and by entity FY73-89, annual rpt, 104–12

Fed Govt programs under Ways and Means Committee jurisdiction, program operations and financing data for assessing budgetary requirements, by State, FY70s-83, 21788–117

Finances of Federal off-budget entities, US Budget Appendix, FY85, detailed annual rpt, 104–3.3

Holdings and transactions of Fed Financing Bank, monthly press release, 9322–1

Holdings of Fed Financing Bank, as of Sept 1983, and Fed Govt debt, interest, and financing mechanisms, FY80-83 and projected FY84-89, 26308–50

Liabilities (contigent) and claims paid by Fed Govt on federally insured and guaranteed contracts with foreign obligors, by country and program, periodic rpt, 8002–12

Small Business Investment Companies finances, funding, licensing, and loan activity, 2nd half FY84, semiannual rpt, 9762–3

Federal funding for energy programs

Agricultural science, food and nutrition, and energy dev research grants awarded by USDA, FY83, annual listing, 1744–1

Auto engine and power train R&D projects, DOE contracts and funding by recipient, FY83, annual rpt, 3304–17

Bonneville Power Admin energy conservation program activities and funding data, FY82 and estimated FY83-87, 3228–2

Budget appropriations proposed for Fed Govt energy programs, by office or dept and function, FY84-85, annual rpt, 3004–14

Budget of US Appendix, detailed budgets and personnel summaries, by agency, FY85, annual rpt, 104–3

Budget of US, CBO analysis and review of FY85 budget by function, annual rpt, 26304–2

Index by Subjects and Names

Budget of US, CBO analysis of revenue and spending alternatives and projections of economic indicators, FY85-89, annual rpt, 26304–3.3

Budget of US, compact budgets by function, agency, and account, FY85 with projections to FY89, annual rpt, 104–2

Budget of US, effects of Reagan Admin policy changes, by detailed program, FY85, annual rpt, 104–21

Budget of US, loans and loan guarantees, and Admin proposed limits on credit assistance, by program, FY83-89, annual rpt, 26306–3.65

Budget of US, receipts by source and outlays by agency and program, monthly rpt, 8102–3

Budget of US, receipts by source and outlays by function, FY40-89 estimates revised for consistency with FY85 budget definitions, annual rpt, 104–12

Budget of US, receipts, outlays, and budget authority, by function and agency, FY84-89 revised estimates, midsession review of FY85 budget, annual rpt, 104–7

Budget of US, receipts, outlays, and budget authority, by function and agency, 1st revision of FY85 budget, annual rpt, 104–17

Commerce Dept budgets and permanent staff positions appropriated, by activity, FY84-85, annual rpt, 2004–6

Conservation aid of DOE, activities, funding, and grants by State, by program, FY84, annual rpt, 3304–21

Conservation grants of Fed Govt to public and nonprofit private instns, by building type and State, 1983, annual rpt, 3304–15

Conservation programs of State govts, Fed Govt financial and technical aid, and reported energy savings, by State, 1983, annual rpt, 3304–1

Conservation programs of utilities, financing, costs, participation, and energy savings, various periods 1981-84, hearing, 21368–54

Cost control proposals for Fed Govt programs and mgmt, CBO and GAO estimates of savings by function and agency, FY85-89, 26308–45

Cost control proposals for Fed Govt programs and mgmt, 3-year savings by function and agency, and financial and operating data, 1960s-81, 16908–1.4, 16908–1.23

DOE procurement and assistance contracts, by State, contractor type, and top 100 instns, FY83, annual rpt, 3004–21

DOE programs finances and mgmt, audits and investigations, series, 3006–5

Energy production, trade, supply, use, conservation, and DOE activities, by energy type, FY83, annual rpt, 3024–2

Fed Govt financial and nonfinancial domestic aid, 1984 annual comprehensive catalog, 104–5

Fed Govt grants-in-aid for 13 program areas, FY82-84, annual article, 10042–1.402

Fed Govt programs under Ways and Means Committee jurisdiction, program operations and financing data for assessing budgetary requirements, by State, FY70s-83, 21788–117

Federal funding for research and development

Govt revenues by source and expenditures by function, natl income and product account, *Survey of Current Business,* monthly rpt, monthly and annual tables, 2702–1.24

Home heating costs of low-income households, natural gas price decontrol effects, aid programs, and gas supply/demand data, by income level and State, 1970s-95, hearing, 25148–26

Household income and cash and noncash transfer program participation, by sociodemographic characteristics, quarterly rpt, 2542–2

Housing (low-income) energy aid of Fed Govt, allocations and average benefits in 13 States, and public interest group assessment, FY81-83, GAO rpt, 26121–75

Housing (low-income) energy aid of Fed Govt, by income, aid type, and State, FY83, annual rpt, 4744–3.13

Hydrogen energy R&D activities of DOE, and description and funding of 24 projects, FY83, annual rpt, 3304–18

Industry R&D funding and employment of scientists and engineers, by industry group, firm size, and funding source, 1956-82, annual rpt, 9627–21

Inventions recommended by Natl Bur of Standards for possible DOE support, with DOE evaluation status, 1984, annual listing, 2214–5

Loan programs of Fed Govt, direct and guaranteed loans outstanding by agency and program, *Treasury Bulletin,* quarterly rpt, 8002–4.10

Natural gas and hazardous liquid pipelines accidents and casualties, and DOT and State govt safety activities, 1982, annual rpt, 7304–5

Naval Petroleum and Oil Shale Reserves production, dev, ownership, leasing, sales by purchaser, and Fed Govt revenues, by site, FY83, annual rpt, 3004–22

Nuclear power plant safety standards and research, design, licensing, construction, operation, and finances, with data by reactor, bimonthly rpt, 3352–4

Nuclear power plant spent fuel permanent disposal site and transport costs, and Nuclear Waste Fund financing, alternative projections FY83-2037, 26308–49

Nuclear Regulatory Commission budget appropriations, personnel, and workloads, by program, FY83-85, annual rpt, 9634–9

Nuclear-related employment of scientists and engineers, by field and sector, 1981 and 1983, 3006–8.2

Nuclear Waste Fund obligations by function and receipts, and DOE Civilian Radioactive Mgmt Office activities and staff, quarterly GAO rpt, 26102–4

Older persons sociodemographic characteristics, and Fed Govt program participation and funding, 1983 with trends and projections 1900-2060, annual rpt, 25144–3.1

Procurement contract awards of Fed Govt, by State, agency, procurement and contractor type, and for top 100 contractors, quarterly rpt, 102–6

R&D and science and engineering education related to energy, DOE and DOE natl labs aid to selected higher education instns, 1960s-84, 3008–89

R&D Fed Govt funding, by function, agency, and program, selected years FY80-84 and proposed FY85, 26308–46

R&D Fed Govt funding for all performers, by field and supporting agency, selected years FY60-84, annual rpt, 9627–20

R&D field facility resources, activities, personnel, and finances, by DOE facility, annual rpt, suspended, 3004–4

R&D Office of EPA environmental research plans, and outlays by program, FY84-88, annual rpt, 9184–10

R&D projects and funding of DOE at natl labs, universities, and other instns, annual summary rpts, 3004–18

Rural Electrification Admin loans to power supply and distribution firms, and borrower operating and financial data, by firm and State, 1983, annual rpt, 1244–1

Scientists and engineers employed in energy-related fields, supply/demand and effects of R&D funding, by energy type, employer type, field, and age, 1962-91, annual rpt, 3004–19

Solar photovoltaic system R&D sponsored by DOE, project descriptions and publications, FY83, annual listing, 3304–20

Southeastern Power Admin sales by customer, plants, and capacity, and financial statements of Southeastern Fed Power Program, FY83, annual rpt, 3234–1

Strategic Petroleum Reserve capacity, inventory, fill rate, and finances, quarterly rpt, 3002–13

Synthetic Fuels Corp financial statements, activities, and executive staff and salaries, FY83, annual rpt, 29654–1

Tax expenditures, Fed Govt revenues foregone through income tax deductions and exclusions by type, and effect of Deficit Reduction Act, FY84-89, annual rpt, 21784–10

Uranium enrichment plants of DOE, production and other costs and selling prices, FY71-83 and projected to FY94, GAO rpt, 26113–137

Uranium ore tailings at inactive mills and DOE remedial action program activities by site, and program funding, FY84, annual rpt, 3354–9

Washington Public Power Supply System nuclear reactors construction financing, with regional economic impacts and power supply/demand, 1980s-2035, hearing, 21448–29

see also Department of Energy National Laboratories

Federal funding for research and development

Acid Precipitation Natl Assessment Program activities, and funding by Federal agency, 1983, annual rpt, 14354–1

Acid rain causes and effects, air pollutant emissions by source in US and selected countries, control costs, and Fed Govt research funding, 1960s-82, 3408–27

Agricultural research and extension program needs, and foreign and US supply/demand indicators by commodity and world area, 1950s-2020, 1008–47

Agricultural research expenditures and scientist years, by topic, commodity, and performing organization, FY82, annual rpt, 1744–2

Federal funding for research and development

Agricultural research funding from Fed Govt and States, by region, State, and outlying area, FY78-82, GAO rpt, 26113-111

Agricultural science, food and nutrition, and energy dev research competitive grants awarded by USDA, FY83, annual listing, 1744-1

AID contracts and grants for technical and support services, by instn, country, and State, FY83, annual listing, 9914-7

AID contracts and grants to universities for technical assistance to foreign countries and other services, FY83, annual listing, 9914-6

Air traffic control and airway facilities and equipment, FAA improvement activities and R&D under Natl Airspace System Plan, 1982-2000, annual rpt, 7504-12

Alcohol, Drug Abuse, and Mental Health Admin research grants, awards, and fellowships by recipient, FY83, annual listing, 4044-13

Appalachia regional dev spending, by program area and source of funds, FY82, annual rpt, 9084-1

Biotechnology commercial uses, R&D funding and output, controls, and industry financial and operating data, for US and 5 countries, 1970s-83 and estimated 1984-85, 26358-98

Budget of US Appendix, detailed budgets and personnel summaries, by agency, FY85, annual rpt, 104-3

Budget of US, CBO analysis and review of FY85 budget by function, annual rpt, 26304-2

Budget of US, CBO analysis of revenue and spending alternatives and projections of economic indicators, FY85-89, annual rpt, 26304-3.3

Budget of US, compact budgets by function, agency, and account, FY85 with projections to FY89, annual rpt, 104-2

Budget of US, effects of Reagan Admin policy changes, by detailed program, FY85, annual rpt, 104-21

Budget of US, loans and loan guarantees, and Admin proposed limits on credit assistance, by program, FY83-89, annual rpt, 26306-3.65

Budget of US, receipts by source and outlays by agency and program, monthly rpt, 8102-3

Budget of US, receipts by source and outlays by function, FY40-89 estimates revised for consistency with FY85 budget definitions, annual rpt, 104-12

Budget of US, receipts, outlays, and budget authority, by function and agency, 1st revision of FY85 budget, annual rpt, 104-17

Budget of US, special analyses of economic and social impact, FY85, annual rpt, 104-1

Computer specialists sociodemographic, educational, and employment characteristics, and Fed Govt support by agency, 1978, biennial Current Population Rpt, 2546-2.124

Cost control proposals for Fed Govt programs and mgmt, CBO and GAO estimates of savings by function and agency, FY85-89, 26308-45

Index by Subjects and Names

Cost control proposals for Fed Govt programs and mgmt, 3-year savings by function and agency, and financial and operating data, 1960s-81, 16908-1

Digestive Diseases Interagency Coordinating Committee activities, and related Federal research and funding, by agency, FY79-83, annual rpt, 4434-13

DOD budget, expenditures for each service branch and total defense agencies, by function and State, FY85, annual rpt, 3544-23

DOD outlays and obligations, by function and service branch, quarterly rpt, 3542-3

DOD prime contract awards by category, contract and contractor type, and service branch, FY74-1st half FY84, semiannual rpt, 3542-1

DOD prime contract awards for R&D to educational and nonprofit instns and Federal agencies, by instn and location, FY83, annual listing, 3544-17

DOD prime contract awards to small and total business, for 10 categories and R&D, monthly rpt, 3542-10

DOD procurement, prime contract awards for 25 commodity categories and R&D, by State and census div, FY81-83, annual rpt, 3544-11

DOD procurement, prime contractors for R&D, top 500 and value of contracts, FY83, annual listing, 3544-4

DOD space and related R&D program activities and funding, FY84-85, annual rpt, 3504-9

DOT grant awards for transportation planning and safety programs, by region, State, and for 35 largest SMSAs, FY83, annual rpt, 7304-7

DOT programs fraud and abuse, audits and investigations, 1st half FY84, semiannual rpt, 7302-4

Economic Dev Admin research grants, by county, FY83 and cumulative FY66-83, annual listing, 2064-2.3

Education Natl Inst activities and education research grants awarded by recipient, and Education Dept expenditures by function, FY81-82, annual rpt, 4914-4

Engineers sociodemographic, educational, and employment characteristics, and Federal support by agency, 1978, Current Population Rpt, 2546-2.121

Environmental quality and protection programs, costs, and Fed Govt enforcement, 1983, detailed annual rpt, 484-1

EPA budget and full-time staff positions by type of activity, and grants to States, by program, FY75-84 and proposed FY85, 26308-47

EPA Office of R&D environmental research plans, and outlays by program, FY84-88, annual rpt, 9184-10

EPA pollution control research and grant assistance program activities, monthly rpt, 9182-8

Fed Govt aid to State and local govts, expenditures, and direct payments, by program, agency, and State, FY83, annual rpt, 2464-2

Fed Govt financial and nonfinancial domestic aid, 1984 annual comprehensive catalog, 104-5

Fed Govt funding for basic research and R&D, by performer and field, FY81 and estimated FY82-83, annual rpt, 4824-2.22

Fed Govt loans, grants, and tax benefits to business, by program and economic sector, projected FY84-88 with effective tax rates for FY80-82, 26306-6.70

Fish and eggs for stocking distributed from natl hatcheries, by species, hatchery, and jurisdiction, FY83, annual rpt, 5504-10

Fish and Wildlife Service conservation and research project descriptions and results, by program, FY83, annual rpt, 5504-20

Fish and Wildlife Service restoration programs, including new sites, funding, and research, by State, FY81, annual rpt, 5504-1

Fishery research of State fish and wildlife agencies, federally funded projects and costs by species and State, 1984, annual rpt, 5504-23

Fishery resources mgmt and R&D, Fed Govt grants by project and resulting publications, 1983, annual listing, 2164-3

Fishing (ocean sport) effort and catch, and Natl Marine Fisheries Service tagging and research activity, by species and location, 1983, annual rpt, 2164-7

Higher education instns R&D expenditures, by funding source, science and engineering field, and location, 1972-83, biennial rpt, 9627-24.1

Higher education R&D and science-related Fed Govt funding, and total and federally funded expenditures, by instn, FY82, 9626-2.135, 9626-2.136

Hwy design and construction R&D, quarterly journal, 7552-3

Hwy R&D projects funded by Federal Hwy Admin, FY83, annual summary rpt, 7554-14

Industrial dev Fed Govt funding by type, program, and agency, and State govt policies and support, selected years FY75-85, 26306-6.81

Industry R&D expenditures by funding source, and projected impact on output, employment, and hours of labor, by selected industry, various periods 1953-90, hearings, 25368-133

Industry R&D funding and employment of scientists and engineers, by industry group, firm size, and funding source, 1956-82, annual rpt, 9627-21

Juvenile Justice and Delinquency Prevention Natl Inst programs and research project funding, FY81-82, annual rpt, 6064-19

Labor Intl Affairs Bur research contracts, by project and contractor, FY73-84, annual listing, 6364-1

MarAd shipbuilding and operating subsidies and other activities, and world merchant fleets operations, FY83, annual rpt, 7704-14

Marine mammals protection activities and Fed Govt funding, population status, and research, 1983, annual rpt, 5504-12

Marine mammals research, Fed Govt funding by agency, topic, and performing instn, FY82, annual rpt, 14734-2

Meteorological services and research of Fed Govt, programs and funding by agency, FY84-85, annual rpt, 2144-2

Index by Subjects and Names

Minerals depletion allowance of foreign countries and US, and financial assistance for exploration and R&D, for 87 commodities, 1983, annual rpt, 5604–18

Motor vehicle safety research and funding of Natl Hwy Traffic Safety Admin and Federal Hwy Admin, 1981, annual rpt, 7764–1

Motor vehicles powered by electricity, Fed Govt dev program implementation, with bibl, FY83, annual rpt, 3304–2

NASA procurement contract awards, by type, contractor, State, and country, FY84, semiannual rpt, 9502–6

NASA R&D funding to colleges and universities, by State, field of science, and instn, FY83, annual listing, 9504–7

NASA R&D spending and employment data, FY59-83, annual rpt, 9504–6.2

NIH newly announced grants and awards, quarterly listing, 4432–1

NSF grant and award recipients, by State, FY83, annual listing, 9624–11

NSF research programs, activities, and funding, FY82-83, annual rpt, 9624–6

Ocean dumping and pollution investigations and activities of NOAA, research and monitoring studies funded, and bibl, FY83, annual rpt, 2144–9

Office of Technology Assessment activities, programs, and publications list, 1983, annual rpt, 26354–3

Procurement contract awards of Fed Govt, by State, agency, procurement and contractor type, and for top 100 contractors, quarterly rpt, 102–6

R&D expenditures by higher education instns and federally funded centers, by field, source of funds, instn, and State, FY82, annual rpt, 9627–13

R&D expenditures by source, and scientists education and employment, detailed data by field, selected years 1953-84, annual rpt, 9624–18

R&D Fed Govt funding, by agency and performer, FY83-84, 9626–2.132

R&D Fed Govt funding, by function, agency, and program, selected years FY80-84 and proposed FY85, 26308–46

R&D Fed Govt funding for all performers, by field and supporting agency, selected years FY60-84, annual rpt, 9627–20

R&D funding by industry, program, and Federal agency, and high-technology trade performance, selected years 1960-FY84, 26306–6.77

Robots for industrial use, R&D, training, and employment impacts, US with comparisons to foreign countries, 1980s with projections to 1992, 26358–105

Science and engineering enrollment, degrees, and employment, R&D funding, and related topics, highlights series, 9626–2

Science Indicators, R&D expenditures, innovations, research, and higher education, with foreign comparisons, 1960s- 83, annual rpt, 9624–10

Science-related and R&D Fed Govt funding for higher education and nonprofit instns, by field, instn, agency, and State, FY82, annual rpt, 9627–17

Sedimentation control, surveillance, and research activity of Fed Govt, by project, agency, region, and State, 1982, annual rpt, 5664–9

Small Business Admin loan and contract activity by program, and balance sheets, FY83, annual rpt, 9764–1.1

Soviet Union-US science and technology exchange projects, man-hours, and funding, by Fed Govt agency and activity type, FY81-82, 7008–41

Space and aeronautics programs and budgets of Fed Govt by agency, and foreign programs, 1957-FY85, annual rpt, 9504–9

Tax expenditures, Fed Govt revenues foregone through income tax deductions and exclusions by type, and effect of Deficit Reduction Act, FY84-89, annual rpt, 21784–10

Telecommunications and Info Natl Admin research and engineering rpts, FY83, annual listing, 2804–3

Urban Mass Transportation Admin grants to higher education instns for research and training, by project, FY84, annual rpt, 7884–7

Vocational Education Research Natl Center funding, by purpose and source, selected years 1978-84, GAO rpt, 26121–79

Wildlife and bird research of State fish and wildlife agencies, federally funded projects and costs, by species and State, 1984, annual rpt, 5504–24

see also Department of Energy National Laboratories

see also Federal aid to medicine

see also Federal funding for energy programs

see also Federally Funded R&D Centers

Federal Grain Inspection Service

Activities and finances by program, foreign complaint investigations by country, and grain handling facility explosions, FY83, annual rpt, 1294–1

Fraud and abuse in USDA programs, audits and investigations, 2nd half FY84, semiannual rpt, 1002–4

Federal grants

see terms beginning with Federal aid

Federal Highway Administration

Activities, grants, and special studies of FHwA, press release series, 7556–3

Auto and van operating and owning costs by component and vehicle size, for 12 years of operation, 1984 model year, biennial rpt, 7554–21

Bridge replacement and rehabilitation program of Fed Govt, funding by bridge and bridge status by State, 1983, annual rpt, 7554–27

Census of Population and Housing, 1980: data coverage, availability, and uses for urban and transportation planning, 1984 guide, 7558–101

Construction bids and contracts for Federal-aid interstate and secondary hwys, by State, 1st half 1984, semiannual rpt, 7552–12

Construction expenditures and contracts awarded for Federal-aid hwy system, by type of material used and State, various periods 1944-83, annual rpts, 7554–29

Construction material prices and indexes for Federal-aid hwy system, by type of material and urban-rural location, quarterly rpt, 7552–7

Cost control proposals for Fed Govt programs and mgmt, 3-year savings by function and agency, and financial and operating data, 1960s-81, 16908–1.11

Federal Highway Administration

Drivers license requirements and admin, by State and Canada Province, 1984, biennial rpt, 7554–18

Drivers licensed by age and sex, and licensing policies, by State, 1982, annual rpt, 7554–16

Fraud and abuse in DOT programs, audits and investigations, 1st half FY84, semiannual rpt, 7302–4

Gasoline and gasohol consumption, and motor fuel tax rates by fuel type, by State, monthly rpt, 7552–1

Hwy and bridge repair projects funded by Fed Govt, and costs, for 7 States, FY81-82, GAO rpt, 26113–121

Hwy and urban transit systems financing methods of govts and private sector, with case studies for selected metro areas, series, 7556–7

Hwy Statistics, detailed data on traffic, govt finances, fuel use, vehicles, driver licenses, and hwy characteristics, by State, 1983, annual rpt, 7554–1

Hwy Statistics, summary data on traffic, govt finances, fuel use, vehicles, and driver licenses, by State, 1982, annual rpt, 7554–24

Motor fuel State tax provisions, motor vehicle registration fees, and disposition of receipts, by State, as of Jan 1984, biennial rpt, 7554–37

Motor fuel tax rates, by State, 1975-83, annual table, 7554–32

Motor vehicle safety program funding of 4 DOT agencies, FY80, 7768–80

R&D for hwy design and construction, quarterly journal, 7552–3

R&D projects funded by FHwA, FY83, annual summary rpt, 7554–14

Safety improvement programs federally funded, implementation by State, FY83, annual rpt, 7554–26

Safety inspections of motor carriers by FHwA, audits of driver qualification and vehicle operation records, and violations cited, 1982, annual rpt, 7554–38

Safety inspections of motor carriers on interstate hwys, violations cited, and vehicles and drivers ordered out of service, 1982, annual rpt, 7554–35

Safety inspections of motor carriers on interstate hwys, violations cited, and vehicles and drivers ordered out of service, May 1983, semiannual rpt, 7552–15

Safety program Fed Govt appropriations, by State and program, quarterly rpt, 7552–9

Sedimentation control, surveillance, and research activity of Fed Govt, by project, agency, region, and State, 1982, annual rpt, 5664–9

Speed averages and vehicles exceeding 55 mph, by State, quarterly rpt, 7552–14

Traffic accidents, deaths, injuries, and rates, by hwy type and State, 1982, annual rpt, 7554–2

Traffic volume on rural roads and city streets, by region, monthly rpt, 7552–8

Travel patterns, personal and household characteristics, auto use, and public transport availability, 1977 survey, series, 7556–6

Truck accidents, injuries, deaths, and property damage, by circumstances, carrier type, and driver age and condition, 1983, annual rpt, 7554–9

Federal Home Loan Bank Board

Federal Home Loan Bank Board

- Budget of US Appendix, detailed budgets and personnel summaries, by agency, FY85, annual rpt, 104–3
- Budget of US, appropriations, outlays, balances, and budget receipts, by govtl branch and agency, FY83, annual rpt, 8104–2
- Budget of US, object class analysis of obligations, by branch of Fed Govt and selected depts and agencies, FY85 estimates, annual rpt, 104–9
- Cost control proposals for Fed Govt programs and mgmt, 3-year savings by function and agency, and financial and operating data, 1960s-81, 16908–1.14
- Financial condition and mortgage loan activities of FHLBs and S&Ls, monthly rpt with articles, 9312–1
- Financial ratios and stock dividends of Student Loan Marketing Assn compared to banks and 4 Fed Govt-sponsored credit assns, 1980-82, GAO rpt, 26121–71
- Home mortgage (conventional) terms on loans closed, and commitment rates, by type of loan and lender and for 32 SMSAs, monthly rpt, 9312–2
- Housing finance studies, technical paper series, 9316–1
- Housing finance studies, technical paper series, 9316–2
- Housing finance technical analysis, quarterly rpt articles, 9312–7
- Housing financing of S&Ls and others, mortgage terms and debt outstanding, and balance sheets of S&Ls and FHLBs, 1983, annual rpt, 9314–3
- Members of FHLB System, with assets of S&Ls, by instn, city, and State, 1983, annual listing, 9314–5
- R&D Fed Govt funding for all performers, by field and supporting agency, selected years FY60-84, annual rpt, 9627–20
- Savings and loan assns and FSLIC-insured savings banks and S&Ls, assets, liabilities, and deposit and loan activity, monthly rpt, 9312–4
- Savings and loan assns assets and liabilities, by FHLB district and State, selected years 1955-82, annual rpt, 9314–1
- Savings instns FSLIC- insured, income, expenses, and financial ratios, 2nd half 1983, semiannual rpt, 9312–6
- Savings instns FSLIC-insured, offices, and savings deposits, by State, SMSA, and county, 1983, annual rpt, 9314–4

Federal Home Loan Bank of Atlanta

- Financial statements of Bank, 1982-83, annual rpt, 9304–1
- Savings and loan assns, FHLB 4th District insured members financial condition and operations, by SMSA, monthly rpt, 9302–1
- Savings and loan assns, FHLB 4th District members financial ratios and mortgage portfolios by State, 2nd half 1983, semiannual rpt, 9302–3
- Savings and loan industry review, periodic rpt articles, 9302–2

Federal Home Loan Bank of Boston

- Banks and thrift instns in New England, financial statements by type of instn and State, 1972 and 1982, annual rpt, 9304–3
- Financial statements of bank, 1983, annual rpt, 9304–2

Savings and loan assns, FHLB 1st District member instns financial operations and related economic and housing indicators, monthly rpt, 9302–4

Savings instns, FHLB 1st District members, locations, and financial condition, 1984, annual listing, 9304–26

Federal Home Loan Bank of Chicago

- Financial statements of Bank, 1982-83, annual rpt, 9304–4
- Housing vacancy rates for single and multifamily units and mobile homes in FHLB 7th District, by ZIP code, annual metro area rpt series, 9304–18
- Mortgage interest fixed and adjustable rates and fees offered by Illinois S&Ls, monthly rpt, 9302–6
- Mortgage interest fixed and adjustable rates and fees offered by Wisconsin S&Ls, monthly rpt, 9302–7
- Savings and loan assns, FHLB 7th District insured members cost of funds, and savings flows and mortgage loans closed by SMSA, monthly rpt, 9302–5

Federal Home Loan Bank of Cincinnati

- Financial statements of Bank, 1982-83, annual rpt, 9304–6
- Housing vacancy rates for single and multifamily units and mobile homes in FHLB 5th District, by ZIP code, annual metro area rpt series, 9304–27
- Savings and loan assns, FHLB 5th District members financial condition and operations by SMSA, monthly rpt, 9302–8

Federal Home Loan Bank of Dallas

- Financial statements of Bank, 1982-83, annual rpt, 9304–11
- Housing vacancy rates for single and multifamily units and mobile homes in FHLB 9th District, by ZIP code, annual metro area rpt series, 9304–19
- Savings and loan assns, FHLB 9th District insured members financial condition and operations by SMSA, monthly rpt, 9302–13

Federal Home Loan Bank of Des Moines

- Financial statements of Bank, 1982-83, annual rpt, 9304–7
- Savings and loan assns, FHLB 8th District members financial operations by State and SMSA, monthly rpt, 9302–9
- Savings and loan assns, FHLB 8th District members, locations, assets, and savings, 1984, annual listing, 9304–9

Federal Home Loan Bank of Indianapolis

- Financial statements of Bank, 1982-83, annual rpt, 9304–10
- Savings and loan assns, FHLB 6th District insured members financial condition and operations by State, monthly rpt, 9302–11
- Savings and loan assns, FHLB 6th District insured members financial condition and operations by State, quarterly rpt, 9302–23

Federal Home Loan Bank of Little Rock *see* Federal Home Loan Bank of Dallas

Federal Home Loan Bank of New York

- Financial statements of Bank, 1982-83, annual rpt, 9304–12
- Savings instns, FHLB 2nd District members financial operations, by State, monthly rpt, 9302–14

Index by Subjects and Names

Federal Home Loan Bank of Pittsburgh

- Financial statements of Bank, 1982-83, annual rpt, 9304–13
- Savings and loan assns, FHLB 3rd District members financial operations and housing industry indicators, by SMSA, monthly rpt, suspended, 9302–16

Federal Home Loan Bank of San Francisco

- Financial statements of Bank, 1982-83, annual rpt, 9304–14
- Housing, employment, and economic indicators in FHLB 11th District, by SMSA, quarterly rpt, 9302–18
- Housing finance studies, technical paper series, 9306–1
- Housing outlook and economic and demographic trends, FHLB 11th District, urban area rpt series, 9306–2
- Housing vacancy rates for single and multifamily units and mobile homes in FHLB 11th District, by ZIP code, annual metro area rpt series, 9304–20
- Savings and loan assns, FHLB 11th District member offices, locations, savings balances, and accounts, quarterly listing, 9302–20
- Savings and loan assns, FHLB 11th District members financial condition and operations by State, quarterly rpt, 9302–19
- Savings and loan assns, FHLB 11th District members financial operations and housing industry indicators by State, monthly rpt, 9302–17

Federal Home Loan Bank of Seattle

- Financial statements of Bank, 1982-83, annual rpt, 9304–15
- Housing vacancy rates for single and multifamily units and mobile homes in FHLB 12th District, by ZIP code, annual metro area rpt series, 9304–21
- Savings and loan assns, FHLB 12th District members financial operations and housing industry indicators by State, monthly rpt, 9302–21

Federal Home Loan Bank of Topeka

- Financial statements of Bank, 1982-83, annual rpt, 9304–16
- Housing vacancy rates for single and multifamily units and mobile homes in FHLB 10th District, by ZIP code, annual metro area rpt series, 9304–22
- Savings and loan assns, FHLB 10th District insured members finances and operations by SMSA, monthly rpt, 9302–22
- Savings and loan assns, FHLB 10th District members, locations, assets, and savings, 1984, annual listing, 9304–17

Federal Home Loan Banks

- Budgets and statements of Fed Govt sponsored enterprises, detailed data, US Budget Appendix, FY85, annual rpt, 104–3.5
- Cost control proposals for Fed Govt programs and mgmt, 3-year savings by function and agency, and financial and operating data, 1960s-81, 16908–1.14
- Finances of FHLBs, assets, liabilities, and loans outstanding, 1930s-83, annual rpt, 9314–3.1
- Financial condition and mortgage loan activity, monthly rpt with articles, 9312–1
- Flow-of-funds accounts, assets and liabilities by type and economic sector, year-end outstandings, 1960-83, annual rpt, 9364–3

Index by Subjects and Names

Federal independent agencies

Mortgage and mortgage-related investment of financial instns, by instn type and Fed Govt issuing agency, various dates 1981-84, 5008–33

Pension plan investment in mortgages and FHLB and Fed Govt mortgage assn mortgage-backed securities, for corporate and union funds, quarterly rpt, 5002–10

see also Federal Home Loan Bank Board

see also Federal Home Loan Bank of Atlanta

see also Federal Home Loan Bank of Boston

see also Federal Home Loan Bank of Chicago

see also Federal Home Loan Bank of Cincinnati

see also Federal Home Loan Bank of Dallas

see also Federal Home Loan Bank of Des Moines

see also Federal Home Loan Bank of Indianapolis

see also Federal Home Loan Bank of New York

see also Federal Home Loan Bank of Pittsburgh

see also Federal Home Loan Bank of San Francisco

see also Federal Home Loan Bank of Seattle

see also Federal Home Loan Bank of Topeka

Federal Home Loan Mortgage Corp.

Budgets and statements of Fed Govt sponsored enterprises, detailed data, US Budget Appendix, FY85, annual rpt, 104–3.5

Cost control proposals for Fed Govt programs and mgmt, 3-year savings by function and agency, and financial and operating data, 1960s-81, 16908–1.14

Credit assistance costs, policies to improve measurement, with loan and loan guarantee data by program, and Federal and private credit instns operations, 1970-84, 26306–6.72

Financial ratios and stock dividends of Student Loan Marketing Assn compared to banks and 4 Fed Govt-sponsored credit assns, 1980-82, GAO rpt, 26121–71

Financial statements and activities of FHLMC, 1983, annual rpt, 9414–1

Home mortgage market activity and debt outstanding, 1979-82, annual rpt, 9364–5.7

Home mortgage terms on conventional loans by eligibility for Fed Govt secondary purchase, 1983, and alternative eligibility limits for 28 cities, 1984, GAO rpt, 26113–135

Housing finance technical analysis, quarterly rpt articles, 9412–2

Mortgage and mortgage-related investment of financial instns, by instn type and Fed Govt issuing agency, various dates 1981-84, 5008–33

Pension plan investment in mortgages and FHLB and Fed Govt mortgage assn mortgage-backed securities, for corporate and union funds, quarterly rpt, 5002–10

Federal Housing Administration

see Housing (FHA), HUD

Federal independent agencies

Audit activities, funding, and staff of Fed Govt agencies without inspectors general, by agency, FY83, GAO rpt, 26111–23

Budget of US Appendix, detailed budgets and personnel summaries, by agency, FY85, annual rpt, 104–3

Budget of US, appropriations, outlays, balances, and budget receipts, by govtl branch and agency, FY83, annual rpt, 8104–2

Budget of US, authority balances in FY85 budget, by agency, FY83-85, annual rpt, 104–8

Budget of US, compact budgets by function, agency, and account, FY85 with projections to FY89, annual rpt, 104–2

Budget of US, effects of Reagan Admin policy changes, by detailed program, FY85, annual rpt, 104–21

Budget of US, receipts by source and outlays by agency and program, monthly rpt, 8102–3

Budget of US, receipts by source and outlays by function, FY40-89 estimates revised for consistency with FY85 budget definitions, annual rpt, 104–12

Budget of US, receipts, outlays, and budget authority, by function and agency, FY84-89 revised estimates, midsession review of FY85 budget, annual rpt, 104–7

Budget of US, special analyses of economic and social impact, FY85, annual rpt, 104–1

Building construction, acquisition, and alteration proposals for historic and other Fed Govt projects, costs and tenure by city and project, as of 1983, hearings, 25328–23

Collective bargaining agreements of Federal employees, unions involved, and employees covered, by agency for agreements expiring July 1984-June 1985, annual listing, 9847–1

Collective bargaining multi-unit agreements of Federal employees, by labor union and agency, as of July 1983, annual listing, 9847–4

Computer systems and equipment of Fed Govt, inventory by manufacturer, type, agency, and location, FY83, last issue of annual rpt, 9454–4

Computers and telecommunications systems major acquisition plans and obligations of Fed Govt, by agency, FY84-89, annual listing, 104–20

Cost control proposals for Fed Govt programs and mgmt, CBO and GAO estimates of savings by function and agency, FY85-89, 26308–45

Cost control proposals for Fed Govt programs and mgmt, 3-year savings by function and agency, and financial and operating data, 1960s-81, 16908–1

Employment (civilian) of Fed Govt, by location, agency, and pay system, 1982, biennial rpt, 9844–8

Employment and payroll (civilian) of Fed Govt, by agency in DC metro area, total US, and abroad, monthly rpt, 9842–1

Energy use and efficiency of Fed Govt, by agency and fuel type, FY83, annual rpt, 3304–22

Fed Govt aid to State and local govts, expenditures, and direct payments, by program, agency, and State, FY83, annual rpt, 2464–2

Fed Govt consolidated financial statements based on business accounting methods, FY82-83, annual rpt, 8104–5

Financial operations of Fed Govt, detailed data, *Treasury Bulletin,* quarterly rpt, 8002–4

Flow-of-funds accounts savings, investments, and credit statements, quarterly rpt, 9365–3.3

GAO evaluations of Federal programs, 1984 listing, 26106–5.1

Investigations of Fed Govt civil agencies operations, summaries of GAO rpts published 1975-83, annual rpt, 26104–5

Labor unions recognized in Fed Govt, agreements and membership by agency and office or installation, Jan 1983, annual listing, 9844–14

Liabilities and other financial commitments, by Federal agency, as of Sept 1983, annual rpt, 8104–3

Minority business Fed Govt funding, procurement, and subsidies, and deposits in minority-owned banks, by agency, FY69-83, annual rpt, 2104–5

Older persons programs, funding and participation by agency, FY83 with trends from FY79, annual rpt, 25144–3.2

Property (real) of Fed Govt, inventory and costs, worldwide summary by location, agency, and use, 1983, annual rpt, 9454–5

Property (real) of Fed Govt, leased property inventory and rental costs, worldwide summary by location and agency, Sept 1983, annual rpt, 9454–10

R&D Fed Govt funding for all performers, by field and supporting agency, selected years FY60-84, annual rpt, 9627–20

Radio frequency assignments for Federal agency use, 2nd half 1983, semiannual rpt, 2802–1

Veterans (disabled and nondisabled) Fed Govt appointments and separations, by agency, 2nd half FY82, semiannual rpt, 9842–3

see also ACTION

see also Administrative Conference of the U.S.

see also Advisory Council on Historic Preservation

see also American Battle Monuments Commission

see also Appalachian Regional Commission

see also Atomic Energy Commission

see also Civil Aeronautics Board

see also Commission of Fine Arts

see also Consumer Product Safety Commission

see also Environmental Protection Agency

see also Equal Employment Opportunity Commission

see also Export-Import Bank

see also Farm Credit Administration

see also Federal boards, committees, and commissions

see also Federal Communications Commission

see also Federal Deposit Insurance Corp.

see also Federal Emergency Management Agency

see also Federal Financing Bank

see also Federal Home Loan Bank Board

see also Federal Maritime Commission

Federal independent agencies

see also Federal Mediation and Conciliation Service
see also Federal Reserve System
see also Federal Trade Commission
see also Foreign Claims Settlement Commission
see also General Services Administration
see also Government corporations
see also Interstate Commerce Commission
see also Merit Systems Protection Board
see also National Aeronautics and Space Administration
see also National Credit Union Administration
see also National Foundation on the Arts and the Humanities
see also National Labor Relations Board
see also National Mediation Board
see also National Science Foundation
see also National Transportation Safety Board
see also Nuclear Regulatory Commission
see also Occupational Safety and Health Review Commission
see also Office of Personnel Management
see also Panama Canal Commission
see also Peace Corps
see also Postal Rate Commission
see also Railroad Retirement Board
see also Securities and Exchange Commission
see also Selective Service System
see also Small Business Administration
see also Smithsonian Institution
see also Tennessee Valley Authority
see also U.S. Arms Control and Disarmament Agency
see also U.S. Information Agency
see also U.S. International Development Cooperation Agency
see also U.S. International Trade Commission
see also U.S. Postal Service
see also Veterans Administration
see also under By Federal Agency in the "Index by Categories"

Federal Inspectors General reports

- Activities of Inspectors General, and audits and investigations of Fed Govt fraud and abuse, by agency, 1st half FY84, semiannual rpt, 102–5
- Agricultural Stabilization and Conservation Service payment-in-kind acreage reduction program, ineligible participants and acreage, and estimated incorrect payments, by State and selected county, 1983, 1008–46
- Commerce Dept programs fraud and abuse, audits and investigations, 2nd half FY84, semiannual rpt, 2002–5
- DOD programs fraud and abuse, audits and investigations, 1st half FY84, semiannual rpt, 3542–18
- DOE programs finances and mgmt, audits and investigations, series, 3006–5
- DOE programs fraud and abuse, audits and investigations, 2nd half FY84, semiannual rpt, 3002–12
- DOT programs fraud and abuse, audits and investigations, 1st half FY84, semiannual rpt, 7302–4
- Education Dept programs fraud and abuse, audits and investigations, 2nd half FY84, semiannual rpt, 4802–1

EPA programs fraud and abuse, audits and investigations, 2nd half FY84, semiannual rpt, 9182–10

- GSA programs fraud and abuse, audits and investigations, 2nd half FY84, semiannual rpt, 9452–8
- HHS programs fraud and abuse, audits and investigations, 2nd half FY84, semiannual rpt, 4002–6
- HUD programs fraud and abuse, audits and investigations, 2nd half FY84, semiannual rpt, 5002–8
- Interior Dept programs fraud and abuse, audits and investigations, 1st half FY84, semiannual rpt, 5302–2
- Labor Dept programs fraud and abuse, audits and investigations, 1st half FY84, semiannual rpt, 6302–2
- NASA programs fraud and abuse, audits and investigations, 2nd half FY84, semiannual rpt, 9502–9
- Outlying areas govt financial data and audits by Interior Dept Inspector General, by area, FY83, annual rpt, 5304–15
- Small Business Admin programs fraud and abuse, audits and investigations, 1st half FY84, semiannual rpt, 9762–5
- USDA programs fraud and abuse, audits and investigations, 2nd half FY84, semiannual rpt, 1002–4
- VA programs fraud and abuse, audits and investigations, 2nd half FY84, semiannual rpt, 9922–13
- Virgin Islands govt fiscal condition, FY81, annual rpt, 5304–10

Federal Intermediate Credit Banks

see Farm Credit System

Federal Judicial Center

- Budget of US Appendix, detailed budgets and personnel summaries, by agency, FY85, annual rpt, 104–3
- Budget of US, appropriations, outlays, balances, and budget receipts, by govtl branch and agency, FY83, annual rpt, 8104–2
- Federal district court staff by position, and visiting judges, visits, and visit days, by large district, various dates 1982-84, 18408–25
- Magistrate case processing duties assigned in Fed Govt district courts, by type of case, duty, and district, 1983 rpt, 18408–24

Federal Labor Relations Authority

- Activities of FLRA and Fed Service Impasses Panel, and cases by region, union, and agency, FY79-83, annual rpt, 13364–1
- Budget of US Appendix, detailed budgets and personnel summaries, by agency, FY85, annual rpt, 104–3
- Budget of US, appropriations, outlays, balances, and budget receipts, by govtl branch and agency, FY83, annual rpt, 8104–2

Federal land banks

see Farm Credit System

Federal lands

see Government property
see Military bases, posts, and reservations
see Public lands

Federal-local relations

Army Corps of Engineers activities and projects, FY83 and trends from 1800s, annual rpt, 3754–1

Index by Subjects and Names

Community Dev Block Grants admin, allocation, and family social benefits, effect of policy changes to increase local admin responsibility, for 10 cities, as of 1982, 5188–105

- Regulatory growth of Fed Govt effect on local compliance costs and funding, local officials assessment, and comparisons to State govt regulations, 1970s-82 with trends from 1900, 10048–58

see also Federal aid to local areas
see also Federal-State relations
see also Intergovernmental relations
see also Revenue sharing

Federal Maritime Commission

- Budget of US Appendix, detailed budgets and personnel summaries, by agency, FY85, annual rpt, 104–3
- Budget of US, appropriations, outlays, balances, and budget receipts, by govtl branch and agency, FY83, annual rpt, 8104–2
- Cost control proposals for Fed Govt programs and mgmt, 3-year savings by function and agency, and financial and operating data, 1960s-81, 16908–1.15
- Mgmt and enforcement activities, filings by type and disposition, and civil penalties by shipper, FY83, annual rpt, 9334–1

Federal Mediation and Conciliation Service

- Budget of US Appendix, detailed budgets and personnel summaries, by agency, FY85, annual rpt, 104–3
- Budget of US, appropriations, outlays, balances, and budget receipts, by govtl branch and agency, FY83, annual rpt, 8104–2

Federal Mine Safety and Health Review Commission

- Budget of US Appendix, detailed budgets and personnel summaries, by agency, FY85, annual rpt, 104–3
- Budget of US, appropriations, outlays, balances, and budget receipts, by govtl branch and agency, FY83, annual rpt, 8104–2
- Cost control proposals for Fed Govt programs and mgmt, 3-year savings by function and agency, and financial and operating data, 1960s-81, 16908–1.15

Federal National Mortgage Association

- Budgets and statements of Fed Govt sponsored enterprises, detailed data, US Budget Appendix, FY85, annual rpt, 104–3.5
- Cost control proposals for Fed Govt programs and mgmt, 3-year savings by function and agency, and financial and operating data, 1960s-81, 16908–1.14
- Credit assistance costs, policies to improve measurement, with loan and loan guarantee data by program, and Federal and private credit instns operations, 1970-84, 26306–6.72
- Financial ratios and stock dividends of Student Loan Marketing Assn compared to banks and 4 Fed Govt-sponsored credit assns, 1980-82, GAO rpt, 26121–71
- Home mortgage market activity and debt outstanding, 1979-82, annual rpt, 9364–5.7
- Home mortgage terms on conventional loans by eligibility for Fed Govt secondary purchase, 1983, and alternative eligibility limits for 28 cities, 1984, GAO rpt, 26113–135

Index by Subjects and Names

Mortgage and mortgage-related investment of financial instns, by instn type and Fed Govt issuing agency, various dates 1981-84, 5008–33

Pension plan investment in mortgages and FHLB and Fed Govt mortgage assn mortgage-backed securities, for corporate and union funds, quarterly rpt, 5002–10

Federal officials

see Officials

Federal Open Market Committee

Monetary aggregates growth and related devs, and Fed Open Market Committee activity, various dates 1959-83, annual article, 9385–1.407

Policies and transactions, *Fed Reserve Bulletin,* monthly rpt with articles, 9362–1

Federal Parent Locator Service

Child Support Enforcement Program costs, cases, and collections, by State, FY82, semiannual rpt, 4002–5

Child Support Enforcement Program costs, cases, and collections, by State, FY83, annual rpt, 4004–29

Child Support Enforcement Program financial and operating data, FY79-83, annual rpt, 4004–16

Federal pay

Advisory Commission on Intergovtl Relations programs and finances, 1983, annual rpt, 10044–3

Advisory committees of Fed Govt, and members, staff, meetings, and costs, by agency, FY83, annual rpt, 9454–18

Budget of US Appendix, total and average compensation by agency, FY85, detailed annual rpt, 104–3

Budget of US, CBO analysis and review of FY85 budget by function, annual rpt, 26304–2

Budget of US, CBO analysis of revenue and spending alternatives and projections of economic indicators, FY85-89, annual rpt, 26304–3.3

Budget of US, object class analysis of obligations, by branch of Fed Govt and selected depts and agencies, FY85 estimates, annual rpt, 104–9

Budget of US, receipts, outlays, and budget authority, by function and agency, FY84-89 revised estimates, midsession review of FY85 budget, annual rpt, 104–7

Budget of US, special analysis of Fed Govt employment and cost of direct compensation and benefits, FY85, annual rpt, 104–1.9

Census of Govts, 1982: employment, payrolls, and average earnings, by function, level of govt, State, county, population size, and inside-outside SMSAs, 2455–2

Chauffeur services of Fed Govt used by officials for commuting, driver overtime hours and pay by agency, 4th qtr 1982, GAO rpt, 26123–63

Cost control proposals for Fed Govt programs and mgmt, CBO and GAO estimates of savings by function and agency, FY85-89, 26308–45

Cost control proposals for Fed Govt programs and mgmt, 3-year savings by function and agency, and financial and operating data, 1960s-81, 16908–1

County and City Data Book, detailed socioeconomic and demographic data for States, counties, and cities, selected years 1976-82, 2328–1

County Business Patterns: establishments, employees, and payrolls, by SIC 4-digit industry and county, 1981, annual State rpt series, 2326–8

County Business Patterns: establishments, employees, and payrolls, by SIC 4-digit industry and county, 1982, annual State rpt series, 2326–6

Crime and criminal justice data, including justice expenditures and employment by level of govt, 1970s-82 with some trends from 1875, 6068–174

Disability (short-term) earnings lost, insurance benefits, sick leave, and work days lost by sex, by type of worker, 1948-81, article, 4742–1.417

DOD-owned manufacturing and R&D facilities, operating data by selected SIC 2- to 3-digit industry, State, and SMSA, 1982, annual Current Industrial Rpt, 2506–3.4

Earnings by industry div, and personal income per capita and by source, by State, MSA, and county, 1977-82, annual regional rpts, 2704–2

Earnings by major industry group, and personal income per capita and by source, by region and State, 1929-82, 2708–40

Employment and payroll (civilian) of Fed Govt, by agency in DC metro area, total US, and abroad, monthly rpt, 9842–1

Employment and wages of workers covered by State unemployment insurance laws and Fed Govt unemployment compensation, by SIC 4-digit industry and State, 1982, annual rpt, 6744–16

Employment, earnings, and hours, by level and branch of govt, and function, monthly 1977-Feb 1984, annual update, 6744–4

Fed Employees Health Benefits Program finances, benefit reductions, and rate increases, by plan, 1981-82, GAO rpt, 26121–67

Fed Govt aid to State and local areas, by type of payment, State, and county, FY83, annual rpt, 2464–3.1

Fed Govt aid to State and local govts, expenditures, and direct payments, by program, agency, and State, FY83, annual rpt, 2464–2

Fed Govt consolidated financial statements based on business accounting methods, FY82-83, annual rpt, 8104–5

Fed Govt obligations by function and agency, *Treasury Bulletin,* quarterly rpt, 8002–4.2

Foreign Service positions and union membership by agency, grievances, and pay rates, FY81-83 with ambassador appointments from 1961, GAO rpt, 26123–64

Govt finances, by level of govt and State, selected years 1929-83, annual rpt, 10044–1

Income of households, families, and persons, by detailed socioeconomic characteristics and region, 1982, annual Current Population Rpt, 2546–6.39

Income, pay, and withholdings by type for Fed civilian and military employees, and special military compensation by type and service branch, 1982-83, GAO rpt, 26123–65

Federal Railroad Administration

Middle mgmt positions, labor cost savings under alternative grade reduction proposals, FY85-89, 26306–6.84

Minority group and handicapped employment of Fed Govt, by race, Hispanic origin, disability, sex, and employment characteristics, as of Sept 1982, biennial rpt, 9844–27

Nuclear attack civil defense plans of Fed Emergency Mgmt Agency, funding and operations by component, FY81-84 and projected FY85-89, GAO rpt, 26123–61

Occupational Outlook Handbook, 1984-85 biennial rpt, 6744–1

Pay comparability of Fed Govt with private industry, and recommended and actual pay increase, various dates 1971-84, annual rpt, 10104–1

Pay comparability of Fed Govt with private industry, and recommended pay rate adjustments, 1983, annual rpt, 104–16

Pay rates of Fed Govt civilian employees, by branch of govt, employee category, and pay level, as of 1984 with trends from 1789, 21628–54

Postal employees gross hourly earnings, with comparisons to 9 private industries, 1983, annual rpt, 9864–5.1

Postal Service operating costs, itemized by class of mail, FY83, annual rpt, 9864–4

R&D personnel costs for intramural programs, by agency, FY82-84, annual rpt, 9627–20.2

Science and engineering grads of 1980-81, employment characteristics or grad enrollment, by degree level, field, sex, and race, 1982, 9627–25

Scientists and engineers in R&D, salary comparisons for DOE labs and non-DOE facilities, Aug 1982-Feb 1984, annual rpt, 3004–9

Senior Executive Service of Fed Govt, employee admin, and program status and effectiveness, by agency and by executive and job characteristics, July 1979-Sept 1983, GAO rpt, 26119–51

Statistical Abstract of US, social, political, and economic data, 1950s-83 and trends, annual rpt, 2324–1.2

see also Civil service pensions

see also Military pay

see also Military pensions

Federal Power Commission

see Department of Energy

Federal Prison Industries

Cost control proposals for Fed Govt programs and mgmt, 3-year savings by function and agency, and financial and operating data, 1960s-81, 16908–1.9

Operations and finances, FY83, annual rpt, 6244–3

Federal prisons

see Correctional institutions

Federal publications lists

see Government publications lists

Federal Railroad Administration

Accidents, casualties, and property damage, FRA activities, and safety inspectors by State, 1982, annual rpt, 7604–12

Accidents investigated by FRA, casualties, damage, and circumstances, 1982, annual rpt, 7604–3

Cost control proposals for Fed Govt programs and mgmt, 3-year savings by function and agency, and financial and operating data, 1960s-81, 16908–1.11

Federal Railroad Administration

Employment at DOT, by subagency, State, and selected personnel characteristics, FY83, annual rpt, 7304–18

Fraud and abuse in DOT programs, audits and investigations, 1st half FY84, semiannual rpt, 7302–4

Freight volume and revenues of railroads, by commodity and region of origin and destination, 1982, annual rpt, 7604–6

Hwy-railroad grade-crossing accidents, detailed data by State and railroad, 1982, annual rpt, 7604–2

Northeast Corridor rail improvement project goals, funding, and progress, and Amtrak finances and operations, FY83, annual rpt, 7604–9

Safety law violations, claims settled FY83, annual rpt, 7604–10

Federal Republic of Germany

see Germany, West

Federal Reserve Bank of Atlanta

Bank interstate service offices, including S&Ls, bank branches, and nonbank subsidiaries offering financial services, by instn and State, 1981-83, 9371–13

Financial and banking devs in southeastern States, research paper series, 9371–10

Financial and economic devs, monthly rpt with articles, 9371–1

Financial statements of Bank, 1982-83, annual rpt, 9371–4

Federal Reserve Bank of Boston

Economic indicators for New England States, Fed Reserve 1st District, monthly rpt with articles, 9373–2

Financial and economic devs, bimonthly rpt articles, 9373–1

Financial and monetary studies, conf papers and proceedings series, 9373–3

Federal Reserve Bank of Chicago

Economic indicators, Fed Reserve 7th District monthly rpt, 9375–9

Economic issues affecting North Central States, Fed Reserve 7th District, working paper series, 9375–13

Farm credit conditions and economic devs, Fed Reserve 7th District, biweekly rpt, 9375–10

Farm finances, expenses by type, loans by purpose and source, and credit detail by Fed Reserve District, quarterly rpt, 9365–3.10

Financial and economic analysis and methodology, technical paper series, 9375–11

Financial and economic devs, bimonthly rpt articles, 9375–1

Financial instn deregulation, interstate banking, and bank performance and risks, 1984 conf papers, 9375–7

Financial statements of Bank, 1983, annual rpt, 9375–5

Federal Reserve Bank of Cleveland

Economic indicators and components, and Fed Reserve 4th District business and financial conditions, monthly chartbook, 9377–10

Financial and economic analysis and forecasting methodology, technical paper series, 9377–9

Financial and economic devs, quarterly rpt articles, 9377–1

Financial statements of Bank, 1982-83, annual rpt, 9377–5

Manufacturing activity diffusion indexes, Fed Reserve 4th District 10-year summary charts, monthly rpt, 9377–4

Federal Reserve Bank of Dallas

Farm credit conditions and real estate values, Fed Reserve 11th District, quarterly rpt, 9379–11

Financial and economic devs, bimonthly rpt articles, 9379–1

Financial statements of Bank, 1982-83, annual rpt, 9379–2

Federal Reserve Bank of Kansas City

Bank deposits, loans, investments, and borrowings, Fed Reserve 10th District depository instns, monthly rpt, 9381–2

Bank financial activity, Fed Reserve 10th District depository instns by State, and large commercial banks by city, monthly rpt, 9381–11

Farm finances, expenses by type, loans by purpose and source, and credit detail by Fed Reserve District, quarterly rpt, 9365–3.10

Financial and economic analysis of banking and nonbanking sectors, technical paper series, 9381–10

Financial and economic devs, monthly rpt articles, 9381–1

Financial statements of Bank, 1982-83, annual rpt, 9381–3

Federal Reserve Bank of Minneapolis

Farm credit conditions, earnings, and expenditures, Fed Reserve 9th District, quarterly rpt, 9383–11

Farm finances, expenses by type, loans by purpose and source, and credit detail by Fed Reserve District, quarterly rpt, 9365–3.10

Financial and economic devs, quarterly rpt articles, 9383–6

Financial statements of Bank, 1982-83, annual rpt, 9383–2

Federal Reserve Bank of New York

Argentina debt financing, effect on income of 7 US bank holding companies, actual and in event of interest nonpayment, 1st qtr 1984, press release, 9368–77

Financial and economic devs, quarterly rpt with articles, 9385–1

Financial statements of Bank, 1982-83, annual rpt, 9385–2

Federal Reserve Bank of Philadelphia

Financial and economic devs, bimonthly rpt articles, 9387–1

Financial and monetary research and econometric analyses, series, 9387–8

Financial statements of Bank, 1982-83, annual rpt, 9387–3

Federal Reserve Bank of Richmond

Bank income and expenses, Fed Reserve 5th District member banks, by State, 1983, annual rpt, 9389–10

Business and natl economic forecasts, compilation of representative opinions, 1983, annual rpt, 9389–3

Economic indicators by State, Fed Reserve 5th District, quarterly rpt, 9389–16

Farm credit conditions and real estate values, Fed Reserve 5th District, quarterly rpt, 9389–17

Farm finances, expenses by type, loans by purpose and source, and credit detail by Fed Reserve District, quarterly rpt, 9365–3.10

Index by Subjects and Names

Financial and economic devs, bimonthly rpt articles, 9389–1

Financial statements of Bank, 1983, annual rpt, 9389–2

Federal Reserve Bank of San Francisco

Economic indicators, Fed Reserve 12th District, quarterly rpt, 9393–1

Financial and economic devs, quarterly rpt articles, 9393–8

Financial statements of Bank, 1982-83, annual rpt, 9393–2

Pacific Basin economic indicators, US and 12 countries, quarterly rpt, 9393–9

Federal Reserve Bank of St. Louis

Agricultural conditions in Southeastern States, Fed Reserve 8th District, quarterly rpt, 9391–13

Banking and financial conditions, Fed Reserve 8th District, quarterly rpt, 9391–14

Economic indicators for Southeastern States and 5 SMSAs, Fed Reserve 8th District, quarterly rpt, 9391–15

Economic trends, natl compounded annual rates of change, monthly rpt, 9391–3

Financial and economic devs, monthly rpt articles, 9391–1

Financial and economic trends, natl compounded annual rates of change, 1964-83, annual rpt, 9391–9

Financial and monetary conditions, selected US summary data, weekly rpt, 9391–4

Intl transactions of US, and economic and monetary trends for US and 10 major trading partners, quarterly rpt, 9391–7

Monetary and Fed Govt budget trends, monthly rpt, 9391–2

Federal Reserve Board of Governors

Banking and financial data, 1982, annual rpt, 9364–5

Banking practices and economic policy, Fed Reserve staff study series, 9366–1

Check clearing, delays in availability of funds deposited, processing volume and costs, and reasons for check returns, 1981-82, press release, 9368–76

Credit, interest rates, banking activity, and industrial production, monthly rpt series, 9365–2

Data concordance for monthly *Federal Reserve Bulletin* and *Annual Statistical Digest,* 1983, annual rpt, 9364–8

Finance (intl) and financial policy, and external factors affecting US economy, technical paper series, 9366–7

Finance (intl) and financial policy, external factors affecting US economy, econometric model methodology and results for US and 4 countries, various periods 1964-75, 9368–78

Finances of Federal off-budget entities, US Budget Appendix, FY85, detailed annual rpt, 104–3.3

Financial and business detailed statistics, *Fed Reserve Bulletin,* monthly rpt with articles, 9362–1

Financial and business statistics, historic trends, 1984 annual chartbook, 9364–2

Financial and business statistics, quarterly chartbook, 9362–2

Financial and economic analysis and forecasting methodology, technical paper series, 9366–6

Financial and operating statements, functional cost analysis for Fed Reserve

Index by Subjects and Names

member banks with average and high earnings, by deposit size, 1982, annual rpt, 9364–6

Financial, banking, and mortgage market activity, weekly release series, 9365–1

Financial statements and employees of Fed Reserve Board and Reserve banks, and review of monetary policy and economic devs, 1983, annual rpt, 9364–1

Flow-of-funds accounts, assets and liabilities by type and economic sector, year-end outstandings, 1960-83, annual rpt, 9364–3

Flow-of-funds accounts, assets and liabilities of foreign branches of US banks, and agricultural finance, quarterly rpt series, 9365–3

Monetary control procedures of Fed Reserve, impact on interest rate volatility, Nov 1977-Dec 1983, technical paper, 9387–8.93

Monetary policy objectives of Fed Reserve, and performance of major economic indicators, July 1984 semiannual rpt, 9362–4

Negotiable orders of withdrawal accounts authorized and offered at industrial banks, S&Ls, and savings banks, and instns and deposits, by State, as of Dec 1983, press release, 9368–75

Payments services of Fed Reserve provided depository instns, financial statements, and costs and revenues by service and district bank, 1983, annual press release, 9364–9

Federal Reserve System

Banking and financial data, 1982, annual rpt, 9364–5

Check processing volume and costs of Fed Reserve System, 1981-82, press release, 9368–76

Cost control proposals for Fed Govt programs and mgmt, 3-year savings by function and agency, and financial and operating data, 1960s-81, 16908–1.14

County Business Patterns: establishments, employees, and payrolls, by SIC 4-digit industry and county, 1981, annual State rpt series, 2326–8

County Business Patterns: establishments, employees, and payrolls, by SIC 4-digit industry and county, 1982, annual State rpt series, 2326–6

Credit and reserves of member banks, 1929-83, and deposits, 1959-83, annual rpt, 204–1.5

Earnings of Fed Reserve System deposited with Treasury, Budget of US estimates revised for consistency with FY85 budget definitions, FY40-89, annual rpt, 104–12

Employment, earnings, and hours, by SIC 4-digit nonfarm industry, monthly 1974-Feb 1984, annual update, 6744–4

Fed Govt benefit payment by check and direct deposit, costs to agencies and banks, FY81, technical paper, 9366–1.139

Fed Govt debt by holder, interest rates and costs, and financing mechanisms, projected FY84-89 with data for FY80-83, 26308–50

Financial activity of Fed Reserve 10th District depository instns by State, and large commercial banks by city, monthly rpt, 9381–11

Financial and business statistics, historic trends, 1984 annual chartbook, 9364–2

Financial and operating statements, functional cost analysis for Fed Reserve member banks with average and high earnings, by deposit size, 1982, annual rpt, 9364–6

Financial, banking, and mortgage market activity, weekly release series, 9365–1

Financial instn deregulation, interstate banking, and bank performance and risks, 1984 conf papers, 9375–7

Financial operations of Fed Govt, detailed data, *Treasury Bulletin,* quarterly rpt, 8002–4

Financial statements and employees of Fed Reserve Board and Reserve banks, and review of monetary policy and economic devs, 1983, annual rpt, 9364–1

Payments services of Fed Reserve provided depository instns, financial statements, and costs and revenues by service and district bank, 1983, annual press release, 9364–9

Receipts, outlays, and debt account transactions of Fed Govt, daily statement, 8102–4

Reserve requirements before and after Monetary Control Act of 1980, by deposit type, 1984 article, 9381–1.408

Reserve requirements of Fed Reserve, effect on depository instn demand for excess reserves, July 1981-Sept 1984, article, 9385–1.414

Reserve requirements of Fed Reserve, effect on volatility of M1 and interest rates, various periods 1979-84, article, 9391–1.422

Reserve requirements of Fed Reserve System contemporaneous accounting system, effects on methodology for calculating of adjusted monetary base, 1984 narrative article, 9391–1.407

Reserves and borrowings of all member banks, monthly rpt, 23842–1.5

Reserves of depository instns, reserve and margin requirements, and borrowings from Fed Reserve, monthly rpt, 9362–1.1

Statistical Abstract of US, social, political, and economic data, 1950s-83 and trends, annual rpt, 2324–1.3

Stock in banks, ownership changes, monthly rpt, 9365–2.15

Truck drivers and guards transporting Fed Reserve System coins and currency, effects on wages of locally prevailing wage rate requirement, for 12 cities, 1980, article, 9377–1.402

see also Federal Open Market Committee

see also Federal Reserve Bank of Atlanta

see also Federal Reserve Bank of Boston

see also Federal Reserve Bank of Chicago

see also Federal Reserve Bank of Cleveland

see also Federal Reserve Bank of Dallas

see also Federal Reserve Bank of Kansas City

see also Federal Reserve Bank of Minneapolis

see also Federal Reserve Bank of New York

see also Federal Reserve Bank of Philadelphia

see also Federal Reserve Bank of Richmond

see also Federal Reserve Bank of San Francisco

Federal Trade Commission

see also Federal Reserve Bank of St. Louis

see also Federal Reserve Board of Governors

Federal Savings and Loan Insurance Corp.

Assets and liabilities of S&Ls insured by FSLIC, by FHLB district and State, selected years 1955-82, annual rpt, 9314–1

Cost control proposals for Fed Govt programs and mgmt, 3-year savings by function and agency, and financial and operating data, 1960s-81, 16908–1.14

Deposits in FSLIC-insured instns, and offices, by State, SMSA, and county, 1983, annual rpt, 9314–4

Financial ratios, income, and expenses of FSLIC-insured savings instns, 2nd half 1983, semiannual rpt, 9312–6

Federal Service Impasses Panel

see Federal Labor Relations Authority

Federal-State relations

Cattle brucellosis eradication, and testing of goats and swine, cooperative Federal-State program activities, by State, FY83, annual rpt, 1394–6

Cattle tuberculosis eradication and surveillance, cooperative Federal-State program activities, by State, FY83, annual rpt, 1394–13

Consumer Product Safety Commission activities, recalls, and product-related injuries, deaths, and medical costs, by product type and brand, FY83, annual rpt, 9164–2

Cost control proposals for Fed Govt programs and mgmt, 3-year savings by function and agency, and financial and operating data, 1960s-81, 16908–1

EPA Strategic Planning and Mgmt System activities and progress in meeting mgmt goals, by office and activity, quarterly rpt, 9182–11

Land grants by Fed Govt to individual States, by purpose, 1803-FY83, annual rpt, 5724–1.1

Meat and poultry inspection activities and personnel of Federal, State, and foreign govts, FY83, annual rpt, 1374–1

Natural gas and hazardous liquid pipelines accidents and casualties, and DOT and State govt safety activities, 1982, annual rpt, 7304–5

see also Federal aid to States

see also Federal-local relations

see also Intergovernmental relations

Federal stockpiles

see Stockpiling

Federal Trade Commission

Budget authority and expenditures of FTC for regulatory analysis contracts, by prospective regulation and contractor, 1983, hearings, 21528–56

Budget of US Appendix, detailed budgets and personnel summaries, by agency, FY85, annual rpt, 104–3

Budget of US, appropriations, outlays, balances, and budget receipts, by govtl branch and agency, FY83, annual rpt, 8104–2

Cigarette sales, market shares, advertising expenditures and methods, and tar and nicotine content, by cigarette type, selected years 1963-81, annual rpt, 9404–4

Cigarette tar, nicotine, and carbon monoxide content in 207 varieties, 1982, periodic rpt, 9402–2

Federal Trade Commission

Contact lens price and adverse lens-associated eye conditions related to fitting by ophthalomologists, opticians, and optometrists, 1977-80, 9408–49

Cost control proposals for Fed Govt programs and mgmt, 3-year savings by function and agency, and financial and operating data, 1960s-81, 16908–1.15

Election campaign funding by political action committees and voting on FTC rules, for individual congressmen, 1978-82, hearings, 21428–7.2, 25688–6.2

Industry coding systems for statistical programs of 6 Federal agencies, comparability, workload, and updating cycles, 1984 rpt, 106–4.5

Industry structure, conduct, and performance, effects on competition, series, 9406–1

Investigative activities, litigation, and admin, FY82, annual rpt, 9404–1

Manufacturing corporation sales, costs, and assets by detailed product line, FTC annual survey, suspended, 9404–5

R&D Fed Govt funding for all performers, by field and supporting agency, selected years FY60-84, annual rpt, 9627–20

Real estate broker industry structure and practices, sales commissions, and broker and consumer attitudes, selected years 1975-81, 9408–48

Federal trust funds

Airport and airway trust fund income, outlays, and balance, FY83, annual rpt, 7504–37

Airport and airway trust fund receipts and outlays, FY82-83, annual rpt, 7504–10

Army Medical/Life, Central Insurance, and Central Retirement Fund financial statements, FY83, annual rpt, 3704–12

Black Lung Disability Trust Fund receipts by source, disbursements, and benefit claims and benefits by State, 1982, annual rpt, 6504–3

Budget of US Appendix, detailed budgets and personnel summaries, by agency, FY85, annual rpt, 104–3

Budget of US, appropriations, outlays, balances, and budget receipts, by govtl branch and agency, FY83, annual rpt, 8104–2

Budget of US, authority balances in FY85 budget, by agency, FY83-85, annual rpt, 104–8

Budget of US, compact budgets by function, agency, and account, FY85 with projections to FY89, annual rpt, 104–2

Budget of US, effects of Reagan Admin policy changes, by detailed program, FY85, annual rpt, 104–21

Budget of US, object class analysis of obligations, by branch of Fed Govt and selected depts and agencies, FY85 estimates, annual rpt, 104–9

Budget of US, receipts by source and outlays by agency and program, monthly rpt, 8102–3

Budget of US, receipts by source and outlays by function, FY40-89 estimates revised for consistency with FY85 budget definitions, annual rpt, 104–12

Budget of US, receipts, outlays, and budget authority, by function and agency, FY84-89 revised estimates, midsession review of FY85 budget, annual rpt, 104–7

Budget of US, special analysis of trust fund receipts and outlays, by fund, FY83-85, annual rpt, 104–1.3

Civil Service Retirement Fund income by source, projected 1983-92, conf proceedings, 25408–87

Civil service retirement system actuarial valuation, FY79-83 with projections to FY2060, annual rpt, 9844–34

Cost control proposals for Fed Govt programs and mgmt, 3-year savings by function and agency, and financial and operating data, 1960s-81, 16908–1

Currency (foreign) accounts owned by US under AID admin and by foreign govts with joint AID control, status by program and country, quarterly rpt, 9912–1

Deposit Insurance Trust Fund payoff and assumption cases and fund net loss, 1965-83, and FDIC balance sheet, 1982, article, 9393–8.407

DOD budget, itemized account of legislative history, FY84, annual rpt, 3504–7

DOD outlays and obligations, by function and service branch, quarterly rpt, 3542–3

Fed Govt aid to State and local govts, expenditures, and direct payments, by program, agency, and State, FY83, annual rpt, 2464–2

Fed Govt civilian employee retirement, health, and life insurance benefit plans operations and finances, FY81-82, annual rpt, 9844–1

Fed Govt consolidated financial statements based on business accounting methods, FY82-83, annual rpt, 8104–5

Fed Govt debt by holder, interest rates and costs, and financing mechanisms, projected FY84-89 with data for FY80-83, 26308–50

Fed Govt programs under Ways and Means Committee jurisdiction, program operations and financing data for assessing budgetary requirements, by State, FY70s-83, 21788–117

Fed Govt revenues by source, expenditures by function, debt, and assets, 1982-83, annual rpt, 2466–2.6

Flow-of-funds accounts, assets and liabilities by type and economic sector, year-end outstandings, 1960-83, annual rpt, 9364–3

Helium (US-produced) market demand and Bur of Mines production, sales, and helium program financial statement, FY83, annual rpt, 5604–32

Historic Preservation Fund grants, by State, FY85, annual press release, 5544–9

HUD mortgage insurance funds, insurance in force, and property acquisitions and sales, quarterly rpt, 5002–3

Hwy Trust Fund receipts by source, and apportionments, by State, 1983, annual rpt, 7554–1.3

Hwy Trust Fund revenues and use taxes by tax type, and tax and truck size and weight limits effects on trucking industry, FY82-84 and projected to 1990, GAO rpt, 26117–31

Hwy Trust Fund status and net revenues, FY57-83, annual summary rpt, 7554–24

Labor Dept activities and staff, CETA participants characteristics, and employment service and unemployment insurance activities by State, FY83, annual rpt, 6304–1

Index by Subjects and Names

Land and Water Conservation Fund grants for outdoor recreation area dev, by State, FY85, annual press release, 5544–15

Liabilities and other financial commitments, by Federal agency, as of Sept 1983, annual rpt, 8104–3

Life insurance for veterans and servicemen, actuarial analysis of 5 VA programs, 1982, annual rpt, 9924–16

Medicare Hospital Insurance (HI) and Supplementary Medical Insurance trust fund operations, and HI trust fund financing, 1970-82 with projections to 1996, article, 4652–1.401

Medicare Hospital Insurance and Supplementary Medical Insurance Trust Fund operations, and Medicare and Medicaid program data, various periods 1966-82, annual rpt, 4654–1

Medicare Hospital Insurance Trust Fund and Medicare program operations, Advisory Council on Social Security recommendations, 1982 quadrennial rpt, 10178–1

Medicare Hospital Insurance Trust Fund financial operations and payroll taxes, FY83 and selected years 1966-2005, annual rpt, 4704–5

Medicare Supplementary Medical Insurance Trust Fund financial operations, FY83 and selected years 1966-87, annual rpt, 4704–3

Medicare trust funds financial operations and payroll taxes, annual summary of 1984 trustees rpts, 4654–8

Nuclear power plant spent fuel permanent disposal site and transport costs, and Nuclear Waste Fund financing, alternative projections FY83-2037, 26308–49

Nuclear Waste Fund finances, FY83-85, annual rpt, 3364–1

OASDHI and Supplementary Medical Insurance trust fund financial status summary, as of 1983 with projections to 2000, articles, 4742–1.410, 4742–1.411

OASDHI and Supplementary Medical Insurance trust funds receipts and expenditures including benefits paid, selected years 1937-83, annual rpt, 4744–3.2

OASDHI trust fund assets, total and tax income, and outlays, alternative projections to 2060, 4706–2.120

OASDHI trust funds receipts, expenditures, and assets since 1940, monthly rpt, 4742–1.2

OASDI trust fund financial status, and Fed Govt budget balance adjusted for OASDI, various periods 1946-83, article, 9373–1.414

OASDI trust funds financial operations, FY83 and selected years 1940s-2060, annual rpt, 4704–4

Pension fund assets, for public and private funds, 1971-82, annual rpt, 9364–5.12

Pension insurance trust funds operating and program data for OASDI, military, and railroad retirement, 1984-2060 with trends from 1937, annual rpt, 25144–3.1

Postal Service pension and health benefits subsidized by Fed Govt trust funds, and subsidy reduction plans deficit impact, FY79-84 and projected to FY89, 26306–6.82

Index by Subjects and Names — Fertility

Public debt issued, redeemed, and outstanding, by individual issue and source, monthly rpt, 8242–2

Railroad employee benefits and beneficiaries by type, benefit program finances, and railroad employees and payroll, FY83, annual rpt, 9704–1

Railroad retirement and unemployment insurance accounts status, and interchange with OASDHI fund, FY82, annual rpt, 9704–2.1

Receipts, expenditures, assets, and liabilities of 9 Federal trust funds, periodic rpt series, 8102–9

Receipts, outlays, debt, and assets, by fund, *Treasury Bulletin*, quarterly rpt, 8002–4.1, 8002–4.4, 8002–4.18

Reclamation fund, amounts credited from public land and timber sales, 1901-FY83, annual rpt, 5724–1.4

Reclamation programs of Fed Govt in western US, trust funds financial status, FY81, annual rpt, 5824–1.1

Revenue sharing and antirecession fiscal assistance program admin and trust funds status, FY83, annual rpt, 8064–1.2

Small Business Admin loan and contract activity by program, and balance sheets, FY83, annual rpt, 9764–1.1

Smithsonian Instn finances, activities, and visitors, FY83, annual rpt, 9774–3

SSA programs, finances, staff, and litigation, FY83, annual rpt, 4704–6

Transportation revenues by source and expenditures, by level of govt and mode of transport, and Fed Govt aid by type, FY77-82, 7308–185

Truman, Harry S, Scholarship Fund receipts by source, transfers, and investment holdings and transactions, monthly rpt, 14312–1

VA life insurance for veterans and servicemen, finances and coverage of 8 programs, 1983, annual rpt, 9924–2

Federally Funded R&D Centers

Cost control proposals for Fed Govt programs and mgmt, 3-year savings by function and agency, and financial and operating data, 1960s-81, 16908–1.4, 16908–1.30

Energy R&D and science and engineering education, DOE and DOE natl labs aid to selected higher education instns, 1960s-84, 3008–89

Expenditures for R&D by higher education instns and federally funded centers, by field, source of funds, instn, and State, FY82, annual rpt, 9627–13

Expenditures for R&D by source, and scientists education and employment, detailed data by field, selected years 1953-84, annual rpt, 9624–18

Industry R&D funding and employment of scientists and engineers, by industry group, firm size, and funding source, 1956-82, annual rpt, 9627–21

Inventory and costs of Fed Govt-owned real property, worldwide summary by location, agency, and use, 1983, annual rpt, 9454–5

NASA procurement contract awards, by type, contractor, State, and country, FY84, semiannual rpt, 9502–6

R&D and science-related Fed Govt funding to higher education and nonprofit instns, by field, instn, agency, and State, FY82, annual rpt, 9627–17

R&D Fed Govt facilities and services available for private sector use, by field of science, 1984 biennial listing, 2224–4

R&D Fed Govt funding, by agency and performer, FY83-84, 9626–2.132

R&D Fed Govt funding by agency and State, and expenditures by subject, for Federal research centers, 1972-81, annual rpt, 9624–10.5

R&D Fed Govt funding by type of performer, and funding for industrial dev by type, program, and agency, selected years FY75-85, 26306–6.81

R&D Fed Govt funding for all performers, by field and supporting agency, selected years FY60-84, annual rpt, 9627–20

Radiation exposure at DOE-contractor nuclear facilities and for surrounding population, and pollutant releases by type, by site, 1982, annual rpt, 3004–23

Scientists and engineers employed at universities and colleges, by field, sex, State, and instn, Jan 1983 and selected trends from 1967, annual survey, 9627–11

Scientists and engineers in R&D, salaries by degree, type of establishment, age, experience, and field, 1984, annual rpt, 3004–1

Scientists and engineers in R&D, salary comparisons for DOE labs and non-DOE facilities, Aug 1982-Feb 1984, annual rpt, 3004–9

Technology transfer of Fed Govt R&D labs to public and private sector, labs complying with requirement, funding, and requests, by agency, FY82, GAO rpt, 26113–141

see also Department of Energy National Laboratories

Federally impacted areas *see* Impacted areas

Feeds *see* Animal feed

Feedstocks, petrochemical *see* Petrochemicals

Feitz, Robert H. "Data on Female Veterans, FY83", 9924–24

Feldman, Angela M.

"After-Tax Money Income Estimates of Households: 1981", 2546–2.118

"After-Tax Money Income Estimates of Households: 1982", 2546–2.122

"Characteristics of Households and Persons Receiving Selected Noncash Benefits: 1982", 2546–6.37

"Characteristics of Households Receiving Noncash Benefits: 1982 (Advance Data from the Mar. 1983 Current Population Survey)", 2546–6.38

Feldman, Margaret "Family Caregiving for the Elderly", 1004–16.1

Feldman, Stanley J. "Industrial Consequences of Alternative Pollution Regulation Scenarios", 9188–84

Feldspar *see* Nonmetallic minerals and mines

Felgran, Steven D. "Bank Entry into Securities Brokerage: Competitive and Legal Aspects", 9373–1.417

"Shared ATM Networks: Market Structure and Public Policy", 9373–1.403

Feller, Barbara A. "Need for Care Among the Noninstitutionalized Elderly", 4144–11.1

Fellowships *see* Student aid

Felt, Dorothy G.

"Forest Area and Timber Resource Statistics for State and Private Lands in New Mexico, 1980", 1206–23.7

"Forest Area and Timber Resource Statistics for State and Private Lands in Southwestern Montana, 1978", 1206–25.6

Fendler, Carol

"Characteristics of the Population Below the Poverty Level: 1982", 2546–6.40

"Estimates of Poverty Including the Value of Noncash Benefits: 1983", 2626–2.52

"Money Income and Poverty Status of Families and Persons in the U.S.: 1983 (Advance Data from the Mar. 1984 Current Population Survey)", 2546–6.41

Ferguson, Robert

"Some Aspects of the Work Environment and Subsequent Disability Among Working-Age Men", 4746–5.43

Ferguson, Walter L. "1979 Pesticide Use on Vegetables in Five Regions", 1588–82

Fernandez, Rosa M.

"College Costs: Basic Student Charges, 2-Year and 4-Year Institutions, 1983-84", 4844–10

"1983-84 Education Directory, Colleges and Universities", 4844–3

Ferreira, Eurico J. "Assumable Loan Value in Creative Financing", 9412–2.404

Ferries

Finances and operations of transit systems, by mode of transport, function, fleet size, and system, FY82, annual rpt, 7884–4

Finances, operations, vehicles, equipment, accidents, and energy use, by mode of transport, 1955-84, annual rpt, 7304–2

Ferroalloys *see* Iron and steel industry

Ferrosilicon *see* Metals and metal industries

Fertility

Agent Orange exposed Air Force personnel diseases and disorders, by disease type, age, and officer status, 1984 rpt, 3604–3

Births and birth and fertility rates, by State, provisional 1982-83, US Vital Statistics annual rpt, 4144–7

Births and birth rates, by demographic and birth characteristics, 1981 with trends from 1940, US Vital Statistics advance rpt, 4146–5.73

Births and birth rates, by parent and birth characteristics and infant condition at birth, 1982 and trends from 1940, US Vital Statistics annual advance rpt, 4146–5.79

Births, and birth rates for unmarried and all women, by race of child, age and Hispanic origin of mother, and State, 1980, 4147–21.42

Births and fertility rates, by detailed demographic characteristics and geographic area, 1979 and trends, US Vital Statistics annual rpt, 4144–1.1

Births, fertility rates, expected births, and childless women, by socioeconomic characteristics, June 1982, annual Current Population Rpt, 2546–1.386

Fertility

Births, fertility rates, expected births, and childless women, by socioeconomic characteristics, June 1983, advance annual Current Population Rpt, 2546–1.385

Births, fertility rates, expected births, and childless women, by socioeconomic characteristics, June 1983, annual Current Population Rpt, 2546–1.393

Census of Population and Housing, 1980: detailed population and housing characteristics, by county, city, and census tract, State and SMSA rpt series, 2551–2

Census of Population, 1980: detailed socioeconomic and demographic characteristics, by age, sex, race, Hispanic origin, occupation, and industry, State rpt series, 2531–4

Census of Population, 1980: detailed socioeconomic characteristics, by county, city, and inside-outside SMSAs and central cities, State rpt series, 2531–3

Central America socioeconomic and political conditions in 6 countries, 1960s-83 with trends and projections 1930-2010, Commission rpt, 028–19.2

Developing countries govt policy, and AID and other foreign assistance, effects on private sector dev and socioeconomic conditions, with case studies for 6 countries, 1960s-80, 9918–12

Developing countries PL 480 Title I funding and socioeconomic impacts, with case studies for 5 countries, 1950s- 81, 9918–13

Farm population, by employment and socioeconomic characteristics, 1983, annual rpt, 2544–1

Foreign women sociodemographic, economic, and fertility characteristics, with comparisons to men, by country, 1960s-85, world region rpt series, 2326–15

Health condition and health care resources, use, and expenditures, 1970s-82 with trends and projections 1900-2000, annual compilation, 4144–11

High school classes of 1980 and 1982: educational and sociodemographic characteristics and expectations, natl longitudinal study, series, 4826–2

Hispanic Americans births and birth and fertility rates, by detailed Hispanic origin, characteristics of mother, birth, and prenatal care, and for 22 States, 1981, 4146–5.80

Income assistance, effects of experimental negative income tax program on employment, earnings, marital status, and other family characteristics in 2 cities, 1970-75, 4008–64

OASDI and pension policy, impacts of increased life expectancy, with alternative sociodemographic projections to 2100, hearing, 25368–130

Population and health research funded by 4 private organizations, project listing by topic, with funding data, 1981, annual rpt, 4474–16

Population demographic and economic characteristics, 1982 with projections of population size to 2050, annual Current Population Rpt, 2546–2.119

Population size and components of change, projected under 3 fertility assumptions, 1982-2080 with trends from 1900, SSA actuarial rpt, 4706–1.92

Population size by single years of age, and components of change, by sex and race, projected 1983-2080, final Current Population Rpt, 2546–3.132

Soviet Union industrial and agricultural production by selected commodity, and demographic trends and projections by Republic, 1950s-2000, hearings, 23848–180

see also Abortion

see also Births

see also Family planning

see also Population size

Fertilizers

Agricultural production, marketing, trade, supply, food consumption, and food and nutrition programs, 1960s-83, annual chartbook, 1504–3

Agricultural Statistics, 1983, annual rpt, 1004–1.2

Agriculture census, 1982: farms, farmland, production and costs, and operator characteristics, preliminary State and county rpt series, 2330–1

Agriculture census, 1982: farms, farmland, production, finances, and operator characteristics, by county, final State rpt series, 2331–1

Air pollutant emission factors, by detailed source, 3rd edition, 1983-84 supplements, 9198–13

Biotechnology firms, patents, and trade by country, and effect of industry growth on US drug and chemical trade, selected years 1979-2000, 9886–4.78

Business statistics, detailed data for major industries and economic indicators, *Survey of Current Business,* monthly rpt, 2702–1.9

Census of Population, 1980: detailed socioeconomic and demographic characteristics, by age, sex, race, Hispanic origin, occupation, and industry, State rpt series, 2531–4

China economic conditions, agricultural and industrial production, trade, and domestic and foreign investment, 1980-85, 2048–106

China exports and imports by SITC 1- to 5-digit commodity, 1970s-82, annual rpt, 244–12

Communist, OECD, and selected other countries fertilizer production and consumption, 1960s-83, annual rpt, 244–5.7, 244–5.9

Consumption of fertilizer, by fertilizer type and State, 1984, annual rpt, 1631–13

Cooperatives farm supply sales programs, services offered, inventory mgmt and marketing methods, and sales force and compensation system, for 4 products, 1982, 1128–24

Cooperatives, membership, activities, and finances, by commodity and selected State, 1900-80 with trends from 1863, 1128–30

County Business Patterns: establishments, employees, and payrolls, by SIC 4-digit industry and county, 1981, annual State rpt series, 2326–8

County Business Patterns: establishments, employees, and payrolls, by SIC 4-digit industry and county, 1982, annual State rpt series, 2326–6

Index by Subjects and Names

Cuba economic conditions, agricultural and industrial production and distribution, trade, and intl economic relations, 1970-82 and trends from 1957, 248–40

Eastern Europe agricultural production and trade by commodity, food consumption, and farm inputs, for 6 countries, 1960-80 with projections to 1991, 1528–178

EC food supply/demand and market and support prices, with exchange rates, fertilizer price index, GDP, and population, by country, 1960-83, 1528–173

Employment, earnings, and hours, by selected SIC 1- to 4-digit industry, State, and for 278 major labor areas, 1939-83, annual rpt, 6744–5

Employment, earnings, and hours, by SIC 4-digit nonfarm industry, monthly 1974-Feb 1984, annual update, 6744–4

Exports and imports of US, by agricultural commodity and country, bimonthly rpt with articles, 1522–1

Exports and imports of US, detailed SIC-based commodities by world area, 1983, annual rpts, 2424–6

Exports and imports of US, totals and as percent of domestic production, by SIC 2- to 5-digit commodity, 1981, annual rpt, 2424–3

Exports, imports, tariffs, and industry operating data for fertilizers, 1979-83, TSUSA commodity rpt, 9885–4.44

Exports of US, detailed commodities by country of destination, monthly rpt, 2422–3

Exports of US, detailed Schedule B commodities by country of destination, 1983, annual rpt, 2424–9

Exports of US, detailed Schedule E commodities by mode of transport and world area and country of destination, 1983, annual rpts, 2424–5

Farm finances, assets, liabilities, income, receipts by commodity and State, and expenses, 1980-83 and trends from 1910, annual rpt, 1544–16

Farm finances, expenses by type, loans by purpose and source, and credit detail by Fed Reserve District, quarterly rpt, 9365–3.10

Farm finances, production, expenses by type, and domestic economic impact, selected years 1972-82 and preliminary 1983-84, annual rpt, 1544–19

Farm production expenditures, detailed items by farm sales size and region, 1983, annual rpt, 1614–3

Farm production expenses, by type and State, 1979-82, annual rpt, 1544–18

Farm production inputs, land mgmt, and environmental effects, for 4 crops, 1940s-80 and projected to 2010, 9188–94

Farm production inputs, outputs, and productivity, by region, 1939-82, annual rpt, 1544–17

Farm production inputs supply, use, and prices, periodic situation rpt with articles, 1561–16

Farm production itemized costs, receipts, and net returns, for 13 crops, 4 livestock types, and milk, by region, 1981-83, annual rpt, 1544–20

Farm production, prices, marketing, and trade, by commodity, forecast and current situation, monthly rpt, 1502–4

Index by Subjects and Names

Fetters, William B.

Farmers prices received for major products and paid for farm inputs and living items, by commodity and State, monthly rpt, 1629–1

Farmers prices received for major products and paid for farm inputs, by commodity and State, 1983, annual rpt, 1629–5

Foreign agricultural production, prices, and trade, by country, 1983 and outlook for 1984/85, annual world region rpt series, 1524–4

Foreign and US agricultural supply/demand, consumption per capita, and trade, by world area and country group, 1960s-82, 1528–181

Foreign and US agricultural supply/demand, trade, and production, and socioeconomic data, by country, 1950s-77, 1528–179

Foreign and US production, and potential requirements for selected carbon dioxide sequestering forests, by fertilizer type, 1970s-80, reprint, 9188–88

Foreign and US production, prices, trade, and use, annual situation rpt, suspended, 1561–5

Great Lakes trade, by SITC 3-digit commodity, port, vessel type, world area, and country, 1982, annual rpt, 7744–3

Imports of US, detailed Schedule A commodities by country and world area of origin, and mode of transport, 1983, annual rpts, 2424–2

Imports of US, detailed Schedule A commodities by country, monthly rpt, 2422–2

Imports of US, detailed TSUSA commodities by country of origin, 1983, annual rpt, 2424–4

Income tax returns of corporations, detailed income and tax items by industry, 1981, annual rpt, 8304–4

Industry finances and operations, by SIC 2- to 4-digit industry, 1970s-83 and projected to 1988, annual rpt, 2014–4

Inorganic fertilizers and related products production, shipments, stocks, trade, and consumption, monthly Current Industrial Rpt, 2506–8.2

Input-output structure of US economy, detailed interindustry transactions for 537 industries, and components of final demand, 1977 benchmark data, 2708–17

Korea (South) agricultural services projects of AID and Korea govt, economic impacts, 1950s-83, 9916–1.52

Manufacturing census, 1982: financial and operating data, by SIC 2- to 4-digit industry, State, SMSA, and county, preliminary census div rpt series, 2491–3

Manufacturing census, 1982: financial and operating data, for SIC 4-digit industries by product, preliminary rpt, 2491–1.193, 2491–1.194, 2491–1.195

Mineral industries census, 1982: financial and operating data, by SIC 2- to 4-digit industry, preliminary summary rpt, 2511–2.1

Mineral industries census, 1982: financial and operating data, including materials consumed, by SIC 4-digit industry and State, preliminary rpt, 2511–1.11

Mineral Industry Surveys, commodity review of production, trade, and consumption, 1983, advance annual rpt, 5614–5.1

Mineral Industry Surveys, commodity review of production, trade, stocks, and consumption, monthly rpt, 5612–1.30

Mineral Industry Surveys, phosphate rock production, sales, exports, and use, 1984 crop year, annual rpt, 5614–20

Minerals Yearbook, 1982, Vol 1: commodity reviews of production, reserves, supply, use, and trade, annual rpt, 5604–33

Minerals Yearbook, 1982, Vol 2 preprints: State reviews of production and sales by commodity, and business activity, annual rpt series, 5604–16

Minerals Yearbook, 1982, Vol 3: foreign country reviews of production, trade, and policies, by commodity, annual rpt, 5604–35

Minerals Yearbook, 1982, Vol 3 preprints: foreign country reviews of production, trade, and policies, by commodity, annual rpt series, 5604–17

Minerals Yearbook, 1983, Vol 1 preprints: commodity reviews of production, reserves, supply, use, and trade, annual rpt series, 5604–15

Minerals Yearbook, 1983, Vol 3 preprints: foreign country reviews of production, trade, and policies, by commodity, annual rpt series, 5604–23

Natural gas price changes effect on farm income and fertilizer use, 1980 and projected to 1990, 1548–240

Natural gas price decontrol alternatives effect on farm production by crop, prices, and fertilizer use and costs, 1982-90, model results, 1548–239

Occupational injuries and incidence, nonmetallic mineral mining and related operations, detailed analysis, 1982, annual rpt, 6664–1

Occupational injury and illness rates, by SIC 2- to 4-digit industry, 1982, annual rpt, 6844–1

OECD trade, total and for 4 major countries, and US trade by country, by commodity, 1972-82, annual world region rpt series, 244–13

Phosphate rock industry environmental protection costs, by control type and selected State, with background operating data, 1977-81 with cost projections to 1990, 5608–143

Phosphate rock reserves in southeastern and northwestern US, by location, 1984 rpt, 5668–74

Portugal agricultural subsidies, profits, marketing margins, and consumer prices, by commodity or product, and effects of prospective EC membership, 1981, 1528–171

Potassium chloride from 4 countries, imports injury to US industry from foreign subsidized products, investigation with background financial and operating data, 1984 rpt, 9886–15.52

Producer prices and indexes, by stage of processing and detailed commodity, monthly rpt, 6762–6

Producer prices and indexes, by stage of processing and detailed commodity, monthly 1983, annual supplement, 6764–2

Production and trade, and consumption by region and State, 1983, annual rpt, 1804–6

Production, prices, trade, use, employment, tariffs, and stockpiling, by mineral commodity, with foreign comparisons, 1979-83, annual rpt, 5604–18

TVA agricultural dev program fertilizer shipments by fertilizer type, and farms participating, 1935-60, 9808–68

TVA fertilizer dev expenses, FY83, annual rpt, 9804–23.2

TVA fertilizer distribution in farmer education programs by State, dev costs, and shipments by type and purpose, FY83, annual rpt, 9804–1.2

Water pollution fish kills, by State, location, and pollution source, monthly 1978-80, annual rpt, 9204–3

Waterborne commerce of US (domestic and foreign), freight by commodity, traffic, and passengers, by port and waterway, 1982, annual rpt, 3754–3

see also under By Commodity in the "Index by Categories"

Fescue

see Seeds

Fesharaki, Fereidun

"Hydrocarbon Processing in OPEC Countries: Excess Capacities and Readjustment Pains in the World Refining Industry", 25368–133.1

Fetal deaths

Agent Orange exposed Air Force personnel diseases and disorders, by disease type, age, and officer status, 1984 rpt, 3604–3

Births (live) weighing 2,500 grams or less, by outcome of last pregnancy including fetal deaths, 1979, US Vital Statistics annual rpt, 4144–1.1

Deaths and death rates, by detailed geographic area, cause, and demographic characteristics, 1979, US Vital Statistics annual rpt, 4144–3

Fetal deaths and rates, by gestation period, birth weight and order, race, age of mother, and geographic area, 1979, US Vital Statistics annual rpt, 4144–2.3

Health characteristics of infants, by mother's sociodemographic, lifestyle, and maternity characteristics, 1980, article, 4102–1.418, 4102–1.422, 4102–1.424

Health condition and health care resources, use, and expenditures, 1970s-82 with trends and projections 1900-2000, annual compilation, 4144–11

Infant and fetal deaths, and women with no prenatal care during 1st trimester, by race and Hispanic origin, 1960-80 and reduction goals for 1990, article, 4102–1.425

New York State spontaneous fetal death rates, by period of gestation, 1968-78, article, 4102–1.428

Perinatal deaths and death rates, by State, urban-rural location, sex, and race, 1979, US Vital Statistics annual rpt, 4144–2.4

Pregnancy health counseling effect on smoking, diet, delivery costs, and birth weight, by sociodemographic characteristics and pregnancy history, 1983 article, 4102–1.401

see also Abortion

see also Infant mortality

Fetters, William B.

"High School and Beyond Tabulation: Foreign Language Course Taking by 1980 High School Sophomores Who Graduated in 1982", 4828–17

Fetters, William B.

"High School Seniors: A Comparative Study of the Classes of 1972 and 1980", 4826–2.15

"Quality of Responses of High School Students to Questionniare Items", 4826–2.22

Ffolliott, P. F.

"Social Dimensions of Rangeland Management", 1208–197

FHA

see Housing (FHA), HUD

FHwA

see Federal Highway Administration

Fibers

Agricultural Statistics, 1983, annual rpt, 1004–1

Brooms (broomcorn) shipments, trade, and apparent consumption data for USITC import quota determination, 1983, annual rpt, 9884–6

Business statistics, detailed data for major industries and economic indicators, *Survey of Current Business,* monthly rpt, 2702–1.19

China economic conditions, agricultural and industrial production, trade, and domestic and foreign investment, 1980-85, 2048–106

Employment in farm and nonfarm food and fiber sectors, and costs in food marketing bill, 1973-82, annual rpt, 1544–19

Exports and imports of US, by agricultural commodity and country, bimonthly rpt with articles, 1522–1

Exports and imports of US, by detailed agricultural commodity and country, FY83 and CY83, semiannual rpts, 1522–4

Exports and imports of US, detailed SIC-based commodities by world area, 1983, annual rpts, 2424–6

Exports and imports of US, totals and as percent of domestic production, by SIC 2- to 5-digit commodity, 1981, annual rpt, 2424–3

Exports, imports, tariffs, and industry operating data for textile fiber and products, TSUSA commodity rpt series, 9885–3

Exports of textiles, by product and country of destination, monthly rpt, 2042–26

Exports of US, detailed commodities by country of destination, monthly rpt, 2422–3

Exports of US, detailed Schedule B commodities by country of destination, 1983, annual rpt, 2424–9

Exports of US, detailed Schedule E commodities by mode of transport and world area and country of destination, 1983, annual rpts, 2424–5

Foreign agricultural production, prices, and trade, by country, 1983 and outlook for 1984/85, annual world region rpt series, 1524–4

Foreign and US agricultural production, trade, and climatic devs, weekly press release, 1922–4

Glass (fibrous) production and shipments, by product, 1983, annual Current Industrial Rpt, 2506–9.5

Great Lakes trade, by SITC 3-digit commodity, port, vessel type, world area, and country, 1982, annual rpt, 7744–3

Imports and import limits for textiles under Multifiber Arrangement by product and country, with US exports and use, 1970-83, semiannual rpt, 9882–11

Imports of textiles, by country of origin, monthly rpt, 2042–27

Imports of textiles, by product and country of origin, monthly rpt series, 2046–9

Imports of textiles, by product and country of origin, periodic rpt series, 2046–8

Imports of textiles, monthly rpt, 2042–18

Imports of textiles, total and as percents of US production and use, by commodity, 1972-82, annual rpt, 2044–14

Imports of US, detailed Schedule A commodities by country and world area of origin, and mode of transport, 1983, annual rpts, 2424–2

Imports of US, detailed Schedule A commodities by country, monthly rpt, 2422–2

Imports of US, detailed TSUSA commodities by country of origin, 1983, annual rpt, 2424–4

Manufacturing census, 1982: financial and operating data, for SIC 4-digit industries by product, preliminary rpt series, 2491–1

OECD trade, total and for 4 major countries, and US trade by country, by commodity, 1972-82, annual world region rpt series, 244–13

Production, consumption, prices, and trade of cotton, wool, and synthetic fibers, periodic situation rpt with articles, 1561–1

Production, stocks, materials used, and orders, by product and major State, and trade by country, periodic Current Industrial Rpt series, 2506–5

Stockpiling of strategic and critical materials, Fed Govt activities and inventories by commodity, Oct 1983-Mar 1984, semiannual rpt, 9432–1

Stockpiling of strategic materials, inventories, costs, and goals, by commodity, as of June 1984, semiannual rpt, 9452–7

Waterborne commerce of US (domestic and foreign), freight by commodity, traffic, and passengers, by port and waterway, 1982, annual rpt, 3754–3

see also Cotton

see also Paper and paper products

see also Silk

see also Synthetic fibers and fabrics

see also Wool and wool trade

see also under By Commodity in the "Index by Categories"

FICA

see Social security

see Social security tax

Field seeds

see Seeds

Fieleke, Norman S.

"Budget Deficit: Are the International Consequences Unfavorable?", 9373–1.408

"Price Behavior During Balance of Payments Adjustment", 9373–1.418

Fiji

AID economic assistance to developing countries, obligations and disbursements by country, quarterly rpt, 9912–4

Economic, social, and political summary data, by country, 1984, annual factbook, 244–11

Index by Subjects and Names

Imports of US, detailed TSUSA commodities by country of origin, 1983, annual rpt, 2424–4

Military aid of US, arms sales, and training programs costs and budget requests by program, world region, and country, FY83-85, annual rpt, 7144–13

Military spending, arms trade, and armed forces size, with total govt spending and population, by country, 1972-82, annual rpt, 9824–1

Minerals Yearbook, 1982, Vol 3: foreign country reviews of production, trade, and policies, by commodity, annual rpt, 5604–35

Minerals Yearbook, 1982, Vol 3 preprints: foreign country review of production, trade, and policies, by commodity, annual rpt, 5604–17.90

Minerals Yearbook, 1983, Vol 3 preprints: foreign country review of production, trade, and policies, by commodity, annual rpt, 5604–23.90

Population size and growth rates, and latest available benchmark demographic data, by country, 1950-83, biennial rpt, 2324–4

Filipino Americans

see Asian Americans

Films

see Motion pictures

Fimmano, Anthony V.

"Wages in New York City, May 1983", 6926–1.75

Finance

Fed Govt financial operations, detailed data, *Treasury Bulletin,* quarterly rpt, 8002–4

Federal Reserve Bulletin, detailed financial statistics, monthly rpt with articles, 9362–1

Financial and banking devs in southeastern States, research paper series, 9371–10

Financial and business statistics, historic trends, 1984 annual chartbook, 9364–2

Financial and business statistics, quarterly chartbook, 9362–2

Financial and economic analysis and forecasting methodology, technical paper series, 9377–9

Financial and economic analysis of banking and nonbanking sectors, technical paper series, 9381–10

Financial and economic devs, Fed Reserve Bank of Atlanta monthly rpt with articles, 9371–1

Financial and economic devs, Fed Reserve Bank of Chicago bimonthly rpt articles, 9375–1

Financial and economic devs, Fed Reserve Bank of Cleveland quarterly rpt articles, 9377–1

Financial and economic devs, Fed Reserve Bank of Dallas bimonthly rpt articles, 9379–1

Financial and economic devs, Fed Reserve Bank of Kansas City monthly rpt articles, 9381–1

Financial and economic devs, Fed Reserve Bank of Minneapolis quarterly rpt articles, 9383–6

Financial and economic devs, Fed Reserve Bank of New York quarterly rpt with articles, 9385–1

Financial and economic devs, Fed Reserve Bank of Philadelphia bimonthly rpt articles, 9387–1

Index by Subjects and Names

Financial institutions

Financial and economic devs, Fed Reserve Bank of Richmond bimonthly rpt articles, 9389–1

Financial and economic devs, Fed Reserve Bank of San Francisco quarterly rpt articles, 9393–8

Financial and economic devs, Fed Reserve Bank of St Louis monthly rpt articles, 9391–1

Financial and monetary research and econometric analyses, series, 9387–8

Financial and monetary studies, Fed Reserve Bank of Boston conf papers and proceedings series, 9373–3

Statistical Abstract of US, social, political, and economic data, 1950s-83 and trends, annual rpt, 2324–1.3

see also Agricultural credit

see also Agricultural finance

see also Bankruptcy

see also Banks and banking

see also Certificates of deposit

see also Consumer credit

see also Credit

see also Educational finance

see also Financial institutions

see also Fiscal policy

see also Flow-of-funds accounts

see also Foreign exchange

see also Government securities

see also Gross National Product

see also Housing costs and financing

see also Individual retirement arrangements

see also Inflation

see also Input-output analysis

see also Insurance

see also Interest rates

see also International finance

see also Investments

see also Loans

see also Monetary policy

see also Money supply

see also Municipal bonds

see also National income and product accounts

see also New York Stock Exchange

see also Prices

see also Securities

see also Stock exchanges

Finance companies

Assets, liabilities, and business credit, 1982, annual rpt, 9364–5.7

Assets, liabilities, and credit activities, monthly rpt series, 9365–2

Auto sales related to usury limits on loans in 2 States, and loans made and outstanding by lender type, various periods 1977-82, article, 9375–1.409

Bank interstate service offices, including S&Ls, bank branches, and nonbank subsidiaries offering financial services, by instn and State, 1981-83, 9371–13

Bankruptcy (personal), filers by debt type and other characteristics, selected years 1978-81, hearing, 25528–97.1

Connecticut personal bankruptcy filings, by debt type, whether claiming Federal homestead exemption, and other characteristics, 1980, hearing, 21528–57.1

Financial and business statistics, historic trends, 1984 annual chartbook, 9364–2.14

Flow-of-funds accounts, assets and liabilities by type and economic sector, year-end outstandings, 1960-83, annual rpt, 9364–3

Flow-of-funds accounts savings, investments, and credit statements, quarterly rpt, 9365–3.3

Franchises of firms engaged in distribution of goods and services by kind of business, establishments by State, and sales, 1982-84, annual rpt, 2014–5

Income tax returns of corporations with foreign tax credit, income and deductions by type, asset size, and selected industry group, 1980, article, 8302–2.415

Income tax returns of partnerships, receipts by source, deductions by type, and establishments, by selected industry, 1982, annual article, 8302–2.416

Income tax returns of sole proprietorships, receipts, deductions by type, payroll, and net income, by major industry, 1982, annual article, 8302–2.413

Input-output structure of US economy, detailed interindustry transactions for 537 industries, and components of final demand, 1977 benchmark data, 2708–17

Minority group and women employment, by occupational group and SIC 2- to 3-digit industry, 1981, annual rpt, 9244–1.1

Mortgage loan activity, by type of lender, loan, and mortgaged property, monthly rpt, 5142–18

Mortgage transactions and holdings, by lender group and type of property and loan, quarterly rpt, 5142–30

Statistical Abstract of US, social, political, and economic data, 1950s-83 and trends, annual rpt, 2324–1.3

Financial crises and depressions

see Business cycles

Financial disclosure

Election campaign finances and Fed Election Commission monitoring activities, 1984 Federal elections, biennial rpt series, 9276–2

Election campaign funding and activities of Fed Election Commission, and political action committees funding, 1983, annual rpt, 9274–1

Financial institutions

AID loan repayment status and terms by program and country, and status of predecessor agency loans, quarterly rpt, 9912–3

American Samoa minimum wage rates, employment, earnings, and benefits, by establishment and industry, Nov 1983, biennial rpt, 6504–6

Census of Population, 1980: detailed socioeconomic and demographic characteristics, by age, sex, race, Hispanic origin, occupation, and industry, State rpt series, 2531–4

Census of Population, 1980: detailed socioeconomic characteristics, by county, city, and inside-outside SMSAs and central cities, State rpt series, 2531–3

County Business Patterns: establishments, employees, and payrolls, by SIC 4-digit industry and county, 1981, annual State rpt series, 2326–8

County Business Patterns: establishments, employees, and payrolls, by SIC 4-digit industry and county, 1982, annual State rpt series, 2326–6

Crimes against financial instns, by State, semiannual article, 9312–1

Deposit insurance of Fed Govt, regulatory control of insured instn risk-taking, narrative analysis, 1984 technical paper, 9316–1.107

Deregulation of financial instns, interstate banking, and bank performance and risks, 1984 conf papers, 9375–7

Developing countries govt policy, and AID and other foreign assistance, effects on private sector dev and socioeconomic conditions, with case studies for 6 countries, 1960s-80, 9918–12

Earnings by industry div, and personal income per capita and by source, by State, MSA, and county, 1977-82, annual regional rpts, 2704–2

Earnings by major industry group, and personal income per capita and by source, by region and State, 1929-82, 2708–40

Employment and earnings, detailed data, monthly rpt, 6742–2.5

Employment by detailed occupation, for 29 SIC 2-digit nonmanufacturing industries, 1981 BLS survey, 6748–60

Employment, earnings, and hours, by selected SIC 1- to 4-digit industry, State, and for 278 major labor areas, 1939-83, annual rpt, 6744–5

Employment, earnings, and hours, by SIC 4-digit nonfarm industry, monthly 1974-Feb 1984, annual update, 6744–4

Employment, unemployment, and labor force, by demographic and employment characteristics, State, and for 30 metro areas and 11 large cities, 1983, annual rpt, 6744–7

Fed Govt loans, grants, and tax benefits to business, by program and economic sector, projected FY84-88 with effective tax rates for FY80-82, 26306–6.70

Finances, firms, and SEC registrations and terminations, by type of investment firm, as of FY83, annual rpt, 9734–2.2

Financial and business statistics, historic trends, 1984 annual chartbook, 9364–2

Financial and business statistics, quarterly chartbook, 9362–2.7

Financial and economic analysis and methodology, technical paper series, 9375–11

Financial and economic analysis of banking and nonbanking sectors, technical paper series, 9381–10

Financial services of nonbank firms and bank holding companies, with financial and operating data by firm, 1981-82 with trends from 1962, technical paper, 9375–11.3

Flow-of-funds accounts, assets and liabilities by type and economic sector, year-end outstandings, 1960-83, annual rpt, 9364–3

Foreign direct investment in US, major investors and investments by SIC 4-digit industry, transaction type and value, and location, 1983, annual rpt, 2044–20

Foreign direct investment of US, by selected major industry group and world area, 1980-82, annual article, 2702–1.430

Foreign exchange bank and nonbank activity, and foreign exchange turnover in US and 3 foreign markets, Mar 1980 and Apr 1983, article, 9385–1.411

Handbook of Labor Statistics, employment, earnings, hours, and labor force characteristics, 1982 and trends, detailed annual rpt, 6724–1

Financial institutions

Household income, assets, and debt characteristics, sources of credit, and use of financial services, 1983 survey, article, 9362–1.411

- Housing low-rent project financing notes sold by local authorities, terms and individual issuers and purchasers, monthly listing, 5142–43
- Housing low-rent project financing notes sold by local authorities, terms and individual purchasers, monthly press release, 5142–37
- Income tax returns of corporations, detailed income and tax items by industry, 1981, annual rpt, 8304–4
- Income tax returns of corporations, summary data by industry div, 1981 estimates, annual article, 8302–2.403
- Income tax returns of corporations with foreign tax credit, income and deductions by type, asset size, and selected industry group, 1980, article, 8302–2.415
- Income tax returns of foreign subsidiaries of US corporations, income and tax data, by industry and asset size, 1980, article, 8302–2.410
- Income tax returns of partnerships, detailed data by industry, 1981 estimates, annual article, 8302–2.404
- Income tax returns of partnerships, receipts by source, deductions by type, and establishments, by selected industry, 1982, annual article, 8302–2.416
- Income tax returns of sole proprietorships, detailed data by industry div and selected industry group, 1981, annual rpt, 8304–7
- Income tax returns of sole proprietorships, receipts, deductions by type, payroll, and net income, by major industry, 1982, annual article, 8302–2.413
- Income tax returns with investment credits, for individuals by income, and for sole proprietorships by industry, 1981, article, 8302–2.409
- Input-output structure of US economy, detailed interindustry transactions for 85 industries, and components of final demand, 1977, article, 2702–1.421
- Input-output structure of US economy, detailed interindustry transactions for 537 industries, and components of final demand, 1977 benchmark data, 2708–17
- Investment companies classification, assets, and location, Sept 1982, annual directory, 9734–1
- Minority group and women's employment, by occupational group, SIC 2- to 3-digit industry, State, and SMSA, 1981, annual rpt, 9244–1
- Natl income and product, comprehensive accounts and components, *Survey of Current Business,* monthly rpt, monthly and annual tables, 2702–1.27
- Occupational injuries, illnesses, and workdays lost, by SIC 2-digit industry, 1982-83, annual press release, 6844–3
- Occupational injury and illness rates, by SIC 2- to 4-digit industry, 1982, annual rpt, 6844–1
- Occupational manpower needs and supply by detailed occupation, and educational and training program enrollees and grads by detailed field, 1982 and 1995, biennial rpt, 6744–3

Scientists, engineers, and technicians employed in private industry, by occupation and industry group, 1980-81, biennial rpt, 9627–23

- Small and minority-owned businesses finances and operations, Federal contracts by agency, and worker characteristics, by industry, race, sex, and State, 1950s-83, annual rpt, 9764–6
- Small business capital formation, sources, needs, and tax and other investment incentives and barriers, 1983 annual conf rpt, 9734–4
- *Statistical Abstract of US,* social, political, and economic data, 1950s-83 and trends, annual rpt, 2324–1.3
- Trade policy of Fed Govt, with data on US industry foreign trade and revenues, and Japan semiconductor industry subsidies, 1970s-83, hearings, 21368–46
- *see also* Bank holding companies
- *see also* Banks and banking
- *see also* Credit unions
- *see also* Farm Credit System
- *see also* Federal Reserve System
- *see also* Finance companies
- *see also* Insurance industry
- *see also* Mutual funds
- *see also* Savings and loan associations
- *see also* Savings banks
- *see also* Stockbrokers
- *see also* under By Industry in the "Index by Categories"

Financial ratios

see Operating ratios

Financial statements

- *see* Business assets and liabilities, general
- *see* Business assets and liabilities, specific industries
- *see* Business income and expenses, general
- *see* Business income and expenses, specific industries
- *see* Operating ratios

Fine arts

- *see* Art
- *see* Arts and the humanities

Fines

- *see* Administrative law and procedure
- *see* Judgments, civil procedure
- *see* Sentences, criminal procedure

Fingerhut, Lois A.

"Changes in Mortality Among the Elderly: U.S., 1940-78. Supplement to 1980", 4147–3.25

Finland

- Agricultural and food production indexes, and production of selected commodities, by world region and country, 1974-83, annual rpt, 1524–5
- Agricultural imports of 3 countries, by commodity and country of origin, 1981-FY84, article, 1925–34.431
- Agricultural situation in Western Europe, by country and commodity, 1983 and outlook for 1984, annual rpt, 1524–4.6
- Agricultural supply/demand, trade, and production, and socioeconomic data, by country, 1950s-77, 1528–179
- AID loan repayment status and terms by program and country, and status of predecessor agency loans, quarterly rpt, 9912–3
- Economic, social, and political summary data, by country, 1984, annual factbook, 244–11

Index by Subjects and Names

- Economic trends in income, production, prices, employment, finances, and trade, 1984 annual rpt, 2046–4.68
- Exports and imports of OECD countries, by country, 1983, annual rpt, 7144–10
- Exports and imports of US with Western Europe, and US market share and export opportunities for selected commodities, by country, 1982-84, 2048–105
- Exports of US, detailed Schedule B commodities by country of destination, 1983, annual rpt, 2424–9
- Exports of US, detailed Schedule E commodities by mode of transport and world area and country of destination, 1983, annual rpts, 2424–5
- Imports of US, detailed Schedule A commodities by country and world area of origin, and mode of transport, 1983, annual rpts, 2424–2
- Imports of US, detailed TSUSA commodities by country of origin, 1983, annual rpt, 2424–4
- Loans and grants for economic and military assistance from US and intl agencies, by program and country, FY46-83, annual rpt, 9914–5
- Military aid of US, arms sales, and training programs costs and budget requests by program, world region, and country, FY83-85, annual rpt, 7144–13
- Military spending, arms trade, and armed forces size, with total govt spending and population, by country, 1972-82, annual rpt, 9824–1
- *Minerals Yearbook, 1982,* Vol 3: foreign country reviews of production, trade, and policies, by commodity, annual rpt, 5604–35
- *Minerals Yearbook, 1982,* Vol 3 preprints: foreign country review of production, trade, and policies, by commodity, annual rpt, 5604–17.22
- Nuclear power generation in US and 18 non-Communist countries, monthly rpt, 3162–24.10
- Nuclear power plant construction and operation status, and capacity, by plant, region, State, and selected country, 1983 and projected to 2020, annual rpt, 3164–57
- Population size and growth rates, and latest available benchmark demographic data, by country, 1950-83, biennial rpt, 2324–4
- Steel from 5 countries, injury to US industry from foreign subsidized products and sales at less than fair value, investigation with background financial and operating data, 1984 rpt, 9886–19.8
- *see also* under By Foreign Country in the "Index by Categories"

Fire departments

- Bombing (explosive and incendiary) incidents, damage, injuries, and deaths, by target, State, and circumstances, 1983, annual rpt, 6224–5
- Census of Govts, 1982: city govt revenues by source, expenditures by function, debt, and assets, by State and city, 2457–4
- Census of Govts, 1982: county govt revenues by source, expenditures by function, debt, and assets, by State and county, 2457–3
- Census of Govts, 1982: employment, payrolls, and average earnings, by

Index by Subjects and Names

function, level of govt, State, county, population size, and inside-outside SMSAs, 2455–2

- Census of Govts, 1982: local govt employment by function, payroll, and average earnings, for individual counties, cities, and school and special districts, 2455–1
- Census of Govts, 1982: State govt payments to local govts, by program, source of funds, level of govt, and State, with trends from 1902, 2460–3
- Census of Population, 1980: detailed socioeconomic and demographic characteristics, by age, sex, race, Hispanic origin, occupation, and industry, State rpt series, 2531–4
- Census of Population, 1980: detailed socioeconomic characteristics, by county, city, and inside-outside SMSAs and central cities, State rpt series, 2531–3
- Census of Population, 1980: labor force, by sex, detailed occupation, and region, with comparison to 1970 census, supplementary rpt, 2535–1.12
- Employment and payroll, by function and level of govt, 1983, annual rpt series, 2466–1
- Fed Govt and total law enforcement officers and firefighters killed, death benefit claims, and non-Fed Govt firefighters death benefits by State and city, 1972-82, hearing, 21348–94
- Govt finances, by level of govt, State, and for large cities and counties, 1981-83, annual rpt series, 2466–2
- Govt revenues by source and expenditures by function, natl income and product account, *Survey of Current Business,* monthly rpt, monthly and annual tables, 2702–1.24
- Local govt per capita expenditures, by function and State, 1981-82, annual rpt, 10044–1.7
- Neighborhood quality, indicators and attitudes by inside-outside central cities, 1979-82 surveys, SMSA rpt series, 2485–6
- Occupational manpower needs and supply by detailed occupation, and educational and training program enrollees and grads by detailed field, 1982 and 1995, biennial rpt, 6744–3
- *Occupational Outlook Handbook,* 1984-85 biennial rpt, 6744–1
- Public opinion on taxes, tax policy, and intergovtl relations, 1972-84 surveys, annual rpt, 10044–2
- Traffic accidents and casualties detailed direct and indirect costs, by characteristics of persons and vehicles involved, 1979-80, 7768–80

Firearms

- Aircraft hijackings, on-board explosions, other crimes against civil aviation, and circumstances, US and worldwide, 1931-83, annual rpt, 7504–31
- Airport security operations to prevent hijacking, screening results, enforcement actions, and hijacking attempts, 1st half 1984, semiannual rpt, 7502–5
- Assaults, murders, and other deaths of law enforcement officers, by circumstances, level of govt, agency, victim and offender characteristics, and location, 1983, annual rpt, 6224–3
- County Business Patterns: establishments, employees, and payrolls, by SIC 4-digit industry and county, 1981, annual State rpt series, 2326–8
- County Business Patterns: establishments, employees, and payrolls, by SIC 4-digit industry and county, 1982, annual State rpt series, 2326–6
- Crime victimization rates by type of offense, and victim and offense characteristics, Natl Crime Survey series, 6066–3
- Crimes, arrests by offender characteristics, and rates, by offense, and law enforcement employees, by population size and jurisdiction, 1970s-83, annual rpt, 6224–2
- Crimes of violence involving relatives, by victim-offender relationship, circumstances, and victim characteristics, aggregate 1973-81, 6066–19.5
- Criminal case processing from arrest to sentencing, cases and processing time by disposition, dismissal reason, and offense, for 14 cities, 1979, 6066–22.1
- Criminal cases of Federal defendants, disposition, convictions, and sentences, by offense and district, as of June 1983 with trends from 1961, annual rpt, 18204–1
- Death rates by sex, race, and age for 40 causes, projected for 10-year period, 1982 rpt, 4208–21
- Deaths and death rates from accidents, by place, detailed cause, and demographic characteristics, 1979, US Vital Statistics annual rpt, 4144–2.1, 4144–2.5
- Exports and imports of US, detailed SIC-based commodities by world area, 1983, annual rpts, 2424–6
- Exports and imports of US, totals and as percent of domestic production, by SIC 2- to 5-digit commodity, 1981, annual rpt, 2424–3
- Exports, imports, tariffs, and industry operating data for small arms and parts, foreign and US, 1978-82, TSUSA commodity rpt supplement, 9885–7.53
- Exports of US, detailed commodities by country of destination, monthly rpt, 2422–3
- Exports of US, detailed Schedule B commodities by country of destination, 1983, annual rpt, 2424–9
- Exports of US, detailed Schedule E commodities by mode of transport and world area and country of destination, 1983, annual rpts, 2424–5
- Foreign market and trade for sporting goods and recreational equipment and vehicles, country market research rpts, 2045–14
- Homicide and suicide rates for youth, by sex, race, and circumstances, selected years 1970-79, and stress and violent behavior reduction goals for 1990, 4102–1.437
- Imports of US, detailed Schedule A commodities by country and world area of origin, and mode of transport, 1983, annual rpts, 2424–2
- Imports of US, detailed Schedule A commodities by country, monthly rpt, 2422–2
- Imports of US, detailed TSUSA commodities by country of origin, 1983, annual rpt, 2424–4

Fires and fire prevention

- Injuries and deaths from use of selected consumer products and related activity, by victim age and sex, 1982, annual rpt, 9164–7
- Injuries and deaths from use of selected consumer products, by victim age and medical treatment status, 1982, annual rpt, 9164–6
- Law enforcement activities of Alcohol, Tobacco, and Firearms Bur in 20 cities and nationwide, funding, and jobs to be transferred to Customs and Secret Service, 1979-82, hearings, 21528–55
- Manufacturing census, 1982: financial and operating data, for SIC 4-digit industries by product, preliminary rpt, 2491–1.303
- OECD trade, total and for 4 major countries, and US trade by country, by commodity, 1972-82, annual world region rpt series, 244–13
- Pretrial citation release use, cost savings for law enforcement agencies, and failures to appear in court, by offense and selected jurisdiction, 1970s-82, 6068–187
- Producer prices and indexes, by stage of processing and detailed commodity, monthly rpt, 6762–6
- Producer prices and indexes, by stage of processing and detailed commodity, monthly 1983, annual supplement, 6764–2
- Production, imports, and seizures and arrests by State, FY82 with trends from 1968, last issue of annual rpt, 8484–1.6
- Robbery rates and circumstances, medical costs and property losses of victims, and offender and victim characteristics, 1960s-81, 6068–180
- Tax (excise) collections of IRS, by source, quarterly press release, 8302–1
- Tax (excise) on hunting and fishing equipment, revenue of Fed Govt fish and wildlife restoration program by type of equipment, FY84, annual rpt, 5504–13
- Tax collections, refunds, and taxes due IRS, by State and region, and IRS court activity and operating expenses, FY83, annual rpt, 8304–3.3
- *see also* Ammunition
- *see also* Military weapons

Fires and fire prevention

- Air pollution levels for 5 pollutants, by detailed source, State, and Air Quality Control Region, 1981, annual rpt, 9194–7
- Air pollution levels for 5 pollutants, by source, 1970- 82 with trends from 1940, annual rpt, 9194–13
- Aircraft accidents in general aviation by State, circumstances, and pilots involved by age and blood alcohol level, 1981, annual rpt, 9614–3.1
- Airline and general aviation accident circumstances, severity, and causes, for US operations of domestic and foreign aircraft, periodic rpt, 9612–1
- Airport size and safety, and accidents at or near airports by circumstance, for total and selected airports, various periods 1964-81, 9618–12
- Alcohol use, and health, economic, and social impacts, review of research, 1970s-81, 4488–4
- Death rates by sex, race, and age for 40 causes, projected for 10-year period, 1982 rpt, 4208–21

Fires and fire prevention

Deaths and death rates from accidents, by place, detailed cause, and demographic characteristics, 1979, US Vital Statistics annual rpt, 4144–2.1, 4144–2.5

Deaths due to cold weather and related causes, by age, race, State, and city, selected periods 1962-83, 21148–30

Deaths from accidents by selected cause, 1981 with trends from 1960s and reduction goals for 1990, article, 4102–1.409

DOE and contractor facility accidents, deaths, illnesses, radiation exposure, and property damage, by facility, 1982, annual rpt, 3004–24

Fed Govt aid to State and local govts, expenditures, and direct payments, by program, agency, and State, FY83, annual rpt, 2464–2

Foreign countries disasters, persons affected, deaths, damage, and aid by US and others, FY83 and trends from FY64, annual rpt, 9914–12

Govt census, 1982: State govt payments to local govts, by program, source of funds, level of govt, and State, with trends from 1902, 2460–3

Housing electrical fires in 10 cities, by type of wiring and equipment involved and circumstances, 1980-81, 2218–71

Injuries and deaths from use of selected consumer products, by victim age and medical treatment status, 1982, annual rpt, 9164–6

Mobile and manufactured home safety standards, program inspections, enforcement actions, and accidents and casualties by victim characteristics, 1982-83, biennial rpt, 5004–4

Mobile home fires and related deaths, and rates compared to site-built homes, 1960-78, article, 1502–7.402

Occupational deaths, by industry div and cause, 1981-82, article, 6722–1.422

Panama Canal fires and property loss, FY81-82, annual rpt, 9664–3.3

Price indexes and prices for producers of fire extinguishers, monthly rpt, 6762–6

Price indexes and prices for producers of fire extinguishers, monthly 1983, annual supplement, 6764–2

Public lands fires, area burned, and protection costs, 1982-83, annual rpt, 5724–1.2

Smoke alarm sound levels by brand, and response time by circumstances and for older and mentally retarded persons, 1983 rpt, 2218–70

Sprinkler system brass components from Italy at less than fair value, imports injury to US industry, investigation with background financial and operating data, 1984 rpt, 9886–14.100

see also Arson

see also Fire departments

see also Forest fires

Fiscal policy

Budget of US, CBO analysis of revenue and spending alternatives and projections of economic indicators, FY85-89, annual rpt, 26304–3

Economic policy and banking practices, Fed Reserve staff study series, 9366–1

Economic Report of the President for 1984, economic effects of budget proposals, and trends and projections 1950s-89, annual hearings, 23844–4

Economic Report of the President for 1984, economic trends from 1929 and Reagan Admin proposals, annual rpt, 204–1

Economic Report of the President for 1984, Joint Economic Committee critique and policy recommendations, annual rpt, 23844–2

Fed Govt consolidated financial statements based on business accounting methods, FY82-83, annual rpt, 8104–5

Fed Govt credit assistance costs, policies to improve measurement, with loan and loan guarantee data by program, and Federal and private credit instns operations, 1970-84, 26306–6.72

Fed Govt deficits and fiscal policy, with expenditures by level of govt, selected years 1929-83, article, 10042–1.401

Fed Govt financial operations, detailed data, *Treasury Bulletin,* quarterly rpt, 8002–4

Fed Govt programs and mgmt cost control proposals, CBO and GAO estimates of savings by function and agency, FY85-89, 26308–45

Fed Govt programs and mgmt cost control proposals, 3-year savings by function and agency, and financial and operating data, 1960s-81, 16908–1

Financial and economic analysis of banking and nonbanking sectors, technical paper series, 9381–10

Govt finances, by level of govt, State, and for large cities and counties, 1981-83, annual rpt series, 2466–2

Intl finance and financial policy, external factors affecting US economy, econometric model methodology and results for US and 4 countries, various periods 1964-75, 9368–78

Statistical Abstract of US, social, political, and economic data, 1950s-83 and trends, annual rpt, 2324–1.2

Tax-related economic and fiscal topics, technical research paper series, 8006–3

see also Budget of the U.S.

see also Business cycles

see also Credit

see also Government spending

see also Income taxes

see also Inflation

see also Monetary policy

see also Prices

see also Public debt

see also Subsidies

see also Tax incentives and shelters

see also Taxation

see also terms beginning with Federal aid

Fish and fishing industry

Acid rain causes and effects, air pollutant emissions by source in US and selected countries, control costs, and Fed Govt research funding, 1960s-82, 3408–27

Agricultural Statistics, 1983, annual rpt, 1004–1.2

Air pollutant emission factors, by detailed source, 3rd edition, 1983-84 supplements, 9198–13

Air pollution and acid rain environmental effects, and methods of neutralizing acidified water bodies, summary research rpt series, 5506–5

Alaska Arctic Natl Wildlife Refuge resources, resident and visitor activities, and environmental impacts of energy exploration, 1983, annual update rpt, 5504–26

Index by Subjects and Names

Atlantic Ocean sport and commercial landings and allowable and potential catch of US and Canada, for 34 species, 1983, annual rpt, 2164–14

Budget of US, effects of Reagan Admin policy changes, by detailed program, FY85, annual rpt, 104–21

Business statistics, detailed data for major industries and economic indicators, *Survey of Current Business,* monthly rpt, 2702–1.11

California marine resources and environmental effects of proposed oil and gas dev, for 2 sanctuaries off central and northern coasts, 1970s-2006, hearing, 21448–30

Caribbean area fish larvae abundance and distribution, by fish species or group, summer 1972 and winter 1973, 2168–80

Census of Population and Housing, 1980: detailed population and housing characteristics, by county, city, and census tract, State and SMSA rpt series, 2551–2

Census of Population, 1980: detailed socioeconomic and demographic characteristics, by age, sex, race, Hispanic origin, occupation, and industry, State rpt series, 2531–4

Census of Population, 1980: detailed socioeconomic characteristics, by county, city, and inside-outside SMSAs and central cities, State rpt series, 2531–3

Census of Population, 1980: labor force, by sex, detailed occupation, and region, with comparison to 1970 census, supplementary rpt, 2535–1.12

China economic conditions, agricultural and industrial production, trade, and domestic and foreign investment, 1980-85, 2048–106

China exports and imports by SITC 1- to 5-digit commodity, 1970s-82, annual rpt, 244–12

Coastal environmental and socioeconomic conditions, and potential impacts of oil and gas OCS leases, final statement series, 5736–1

Coastal environmental and wildlife characteristics, use, and mgmt, for individual ecosystems, series, 5506–9

Coastal environmental characteristics, fish, wildlife, and use, and population socioeconomic data, for individual areas, series, 5506–4

Coastal fish and shellfish landings, life cycles, and environmental needs, for selected species by region, with glossary and bibl, series, 5506–8

Codfish (dried salted) from Canada at less than fair value, imports injury to US industry, investigation with background financial and operating data, 1984 rpt, 9886–14.115

Cold storage holdings of fish and shellfish products, weight by species and form, preliminary data, monthly rpt, 2162–2

Communist, OECD, and selected other countries fish catch and fishing fleets, selected years 1960-83, annual rpt, 244–5.9, 244–5.10

Consumption of food and nutrient intake by individuals, by food group, source, and socioeconomic characteristics, 1977-78 natl survey, final rpt series, 1356–4

Index by Subjects and Names

Fish and fishing industry

Consumption, supply, trade, prices, expenditures, and indexes, by food commodity, 1963-83, annual rpt, 1544–4

County Business Patterns: establishments, employees, and payrolls, by SIC 4-digit industry and county, 1981, annual State rpt series, 2326–8

County Business Patterns: establishments, employees, and payrolls, by SIC 4-digit industry and county, 1982, annual State rpt series, 2326–6

CPI by detailed component, for US city average, 28 SMSAs, and 4 regions by population size, monthly rpt, 6762–2

Cuba economic conditions, agricultural and industrial production and distribution, trade, and intl economic relations, 1970-82 and trends from 1957, 248–40

Earnings by major industry group, and personal income per capita and by source, by region and State, 1929-82, 2708–40

Employment, earnings, and hours, by selected SIC 1- to 4-digit industry, State, and for 278 major labor areas, 1939-83, annual rpt, 6744–5

Environmental quality and protection programs, costs, and Fed Govt enforcement, 1983, detailed annual rpt, 484–1

Environmental quality, pollutant discharge by type, and EPA protection activities, 1970s-83, biennial summary rpt, 9184–16

Environmental quality, pollutant discharge by type and source, and EPA protection activities and funding, 1970s-83, biennial regional rpt series, 9184–15

Estuary environmental characteristics, fish, wildlife, uses, and mgmt, for individual estuaries, series, 5506–7

Europe (Western) fish and shellfish wholesale prices and market activity in 8 countries, weekly rpt, 2162–8

Exports and imports of US, by agricultural commodity and country, bimonthly rpt with articles, 1522–1

Exports and imports of US, by commodity group, world area, selected country, US coastal area and port, and mode of transport, with seasonal adjustments, monthly rpt, 2422–9

Exports and imports of US, detailed SIC-based commodities by world area, 1983, annual rpts, 2424–6

Exports and imports of US, totals and as percent of domestic production, by SIC 2- to 5-digit commodity, 1981, annual rpt, 2424–3

Exports of US, detailed commodities by country of destination, monthly rpt, 2422–3

Exports of US, detailed Schedule B commodities by country of destination, 1983, annual rpt, 2424–9

Exports of US, detailed Schedule E commodities by mode of transport and world area and country of destination, 1983, annual rpts, 2424–5

Fed Govt fish and wildlife restoration programs, including new sites, funding, and research, by State, FY81, annual rpt, 5504–1

Fish and fish products production by region and State, and trade, by species and product, 1982-83, annual rpt series, 2166–6

Fish and shellfish of economic importance, biological, fishery, and mgmt data, literature review series, 2166–16

Fish and Wildlife Service conservation and research project descriptions and results, by program, FY83, annual rpt, 5504–20

Fish meal and oil, production and trade, monthly rpt, 2162–3

Fishery Conservation Zone admin, annual rpt, discontinued, 2164–12

Foreign and US production and trade of fats, oils, and meals, FAS monthly and annual circular series, 1925–1

Foreign economic, social, and political summary data, by country, 1984, annual factbook, 244–11

France Brittany coast oil spill cleanup and research costs, marine and tourism industry losses, and recreation losses of tourists and residents, 1971-79, 2178–13

Genetic resource (plant and animal) conservation, commercial uses, causes of depletion, and geographic sources, 1984 rpt, 5548–13

Great Lakes basin pollutant discharges by source, and control program activities, 1983 annual rpt, 14644–1

Great Lakes trade, by SITC 3-digit commodity, port, vessel type, world area, and country, 1982, annual rpt, 7744–3

Hatchery (natl) distribution of fish and eggs for stocking, by species, hatchery, and jurisdiction, FY83, annual rpt, 5504–10

Hatchery production, deliveries, and operating costs, and fishery assistance, by region, hatchery, and Fed Govt assistance station, FY82, annual rpt, 5504–9

Imports of US, detailed Schedule A commodities by country and world area of origin, and mode of transport, 1983, annual rpts, 2424–2

Imports of US, detailed Schedule A commodities by country, monthly rpt, 2422–2

Imports of US, detailed TSUSA commodities by country of origin, 1983, annual rpt, 2424–4

Income tax returns of corporations, summary data by industry div, 1981 estimates, annual article, 8302–2.403

Income tax returns of partnerships, detailed data by industry, 1981 estimates, annual article, 8302–2.404

Income tax returns of sole proprietorships, detailed data by industry div and selected industry group, 1981, annual rpt, 8304–7

Income tax returns of sole proprietorships, receipts, deductions by type, payroll, and net income, by major industry, 1982, annual article, 8302–2.413

Input-output structure of US economy, detailed interindustry transactions for 85 industries, and components of final demand, 1977, article, 2702–1.421

Input-output structure of US economy, detailed interindustry transactions for 537 industries, and components of final demand, 1977 benchmark data, 2708–17

Japan fish landings, prices, trade by country, cold storage, and market devs, periodic press release, 2162–7

Landings, employment, gear used, and seafood production, for detailed species by State, 1977, annual rpt, 2164–2

Landings, prices, trade, consumption, and industry operating data, for US with foreign comparisons, 1982-83, annual rpt, 2164–1

Landings, prices, trade, wholesaler receipts, and market activities at 5 major US ports, weekly rpts, 2162–6

Manufacturing census, 1982: financial and operating data, for SIC 4-digit industries by product, preliminary rpt, 2491–1.38, 2491–1.39

Marine Fisheries Review, US and foreign fisheries resources, conservation, operations, and research, quarterly rpt articles, 2162–1

Middle Atlantic OCS fishes dietary composition by food item and fish size, for 9 species, fall 1976-winter 1977, 2168–78

Nets (fishing), trade, tariffs, and industry operating data, foreign and US, 1979-83, TSUSA commodity rpt supplement, 9885–3.44

New York Bight pollutant loadings from ocean dumping of municipal wastes by type and source, and concentrations in fish and sediments, 1970s-82, hearings, 21568–36

NOAA scientific and technical publications, monthly listing, 2142–1

OECD trade, total and for 4 major countries, and US trade by country, by commodity, 1972-82, annual world region rpt series, 244–13

Oils from fish and animals, trade, tariffs, and industry operating data, foreign and US, 1978-82, TSUSA commodity rpt, 9885–1.62

PCB (polychlorinated biphenyl) concentrations in Great Lakes fish, for 29 species monitored at 24 sites, selected dates 1969-77, 9208–126

Permits and quotas for commercial fishing incidental take of marine mammals, by applicant and species, 1984, annual rpt, 2164–11

Pesticide and metal residues and industrial contaminants in domestic and imported fish, by species, annual rpt, discontinued, 4064–8

Pollution-caused fish kills, by State, location, and pollution source, monthly 1978-80, annual rpt, 9204–3

Producer prices and indexes, by stage of processing and detailed commodity, monthly rpt, 6762–6

Producer prices and indexes, by stage of processing and detailed commodity, monthly 1983, annual supplement, 6764–2

Public lands commercial fish spawned and harvested, FY83, annual rpt, 5724–1.2

Quotas for US 200 mile fishing zone, allocations by species and country, coastal area rpt series, 7006–5

R&D and mgmt of fishery resources, Fed Govt grants by project and resulting publications, 1983, annual listing, 2164–3

Research of State fish and wildlife agencies, federally funded fishery projects and costs by species and State, 1984, annual rpt, 5504–23

Small and minority-owned businesses finances and operations, Federal contracts by agency, and worker characteristics, by industry, race, sex, and State, 1950s-83, annual rpt, 9764–6

Fish and fishing industry

Statistical Abstract of US, social, political, and economic data, 1950s-83 and trends, annual rpt, 2324–1.3

TTPI socioeconomic, health, and govtl data, by TTPI govt, FY83 and selected trends, detailed annual rpt, 7004–6

Tuna fish (canned) import related unemployment, reemployment opportunities, and worker characteristics, trade adjustment assistance investigation, 1980-83, 6406–9.6

Tuna fish (canned) imports injury to US industry from increased import sales, investigation with background financial and operating data, 1984 rpt, 9886–5.52

Tuna fishery porpoise kill and injury, and Fed Govt and intl marine mammal protection activity, with bibl, 1983, annual rpt, 14734–1

Tuna fleet, capacity, and processor investment in vessels by investment type, with tuna catch, prices, and imports, selected years 1932-80, 9406–1.39

Tuna imports of US by country, and American Samoa tuna industry production, employment, and minimum wage rates by establishment, 1970-83, biennial rpt, 6504–6

User fees to recover costs of 7 federally subsidized public service programs, by type of fee, user, and service, FY84-88, 26306–6.68

Waterborne commerce of US (domestic and foreign), freight by commodity, traffic, and passengers, by port and waterway, 1982, annual rpt, 3754–3

Wetlands environmental characteristics, acreage, uses, and mgmt, by wetland type and region, 1950s-80, 26358–102

Wildlife refuge revenues from economic and recreational uses, and refuge managers attitudes toward expanded use, FY81-83, GAO rpt, 26113–128

see also Aquaculture

see also Fishing, sport

see also Marine mammals

see also Marine resources conservation

see also Shellfish

see also under By Commodity in the "Index by Categories"

see also under By Industry in the "Index by Categories"

Fish and Wildlife Service

Air pollution and acid rain environmental effects, and methods of neutralizing acidified water bodies, summary research rpt series, 5506–5

Alaska Arctic Natl Wildlife Refuge resources, resident and visitor activities, and environmental impacts of energy exploration, 1983, annual update rpt, 5504–26

Birds (marine) on southeastern US coast, distribution, abundance, and oil spill effects, by species and State, 1820s-1982, 5508–72

Birds (shore) on Padre and Mustang Islands, Texas, distribution, abundance, and oil spill effects, by species, 1979-81, 5508–86

Birds protected under Migratory Bird Treaty Act, population characteristics and potential impact of Fed Govt coal leasing, for 25 species, 1900s-82, 5508–88

Coastal environmental and wildlife characteristics, use, and mgmt, for individual ecosystems, series, 5506–9

Coastal environmental characteristics, fish, wildlife, and use, and population socioeconomic data, for individual areas, series, 5506–4

Conservation and research projects of FWS, descriptions and results by program, FY83, annual rpt, 5504–20

Cost control proposals for Fed Govt programs and mgmt, 3-year savings by function and agency, and financial and operating data, 1960s-81, 16908–1.9, 16908–1.31

Duck hunting stamp sales, with philatelic data and reproductions, 1983/84, annual fact sheet, 5504–25

Endangered animals and plants foreign trade including reexports of live specimens and products, by purpose, country, and species, 1982, annual rpt, 5504–19

Estuary environmental characteristics, fish, wildlife, uses, and mgmt, for individual estuaries, series, 5506–7

Fed Govt fish and wildlife restoration programs, including new sites, funding, and research, by State, FY81, annual rpt, 5504–1

Fish and eggs for stocking distributed from natl hatcheries, by species, hatchery, and jurisdiction, FY83, annual rpt, 5504–10

Fish and shellfish landings, life cycles, and environmental needs, for selected species by region, with glossary and bibl, series, 5506–8

Fish and wildlife restoration program of Fed Govt, finances, funding by State, and hunting and fishing equipment excise tax revenue, FY84, annual rpt, 5504–13

Fish hatchery production, deliveries, and operating costs, and fishery assistance, by region, hatchery, and Fed Govt assistance station, FY82, annual rpt, 5504–9

Licenses for fishing and hunting issued and gross cost to sportsmen, by State, FY83, annual rpt, 5504–16

Marine mammals protection activities and Fed Govt funding, population status, and research, 1983, annual rpt, 5504–12

Marine vertebrates off southeastern US coast, abundance and seasonal distribution, with oil and gas dev effects and lease status, early 1980s, 5508–85

Mourning dove population, by region and hunting and nonhunting State, 1984, annual rpt, 5504–15

Oil spills in coastal and aquatic wildlife habitats, methodology for cleanup priority rating and listing of wildlife species of concern, 1984 rpt, 5508–87

Recreation fees and collection costs, visitors, and capacity of outdoor Fed Govt, State, and private facilities, by managing agency and State, 1983, annual rpt, 5544–14

Research of State fish and wildlife agencies, federally funded fishery projects and costs by species and State, 1984, annual rpt, 5504–23

Research of State fish and wildlife agencies, federally funded wildlife and bird projects and costs, by species and State, 1984, annual rpt, 5504–24

Waterfowl harvested during hunting season, by species, State, and county, annual average for 1971-80, decennial rpt, 5508–18

Index by Subjects and Names

Wetlands acreage and losses, by wetland type and location, 1970s-83, 5508–89

Woodcock population and hunter harvest, by region and State, 1984 and trends from 1966, annual rpt, 5504–11

Youth Conservation Corps activities, costs, and participant characteristics, by sponsoring agency, 1982, annual rpt, 5304–12

Fisheries

see Fish and fishing industry

Fishing, sport

Acid rain causes and effects, air pollutant emissions by source, and control costs, by region and State, selected years 1977-83 and projected to 2000, 26358–104

Alaska Arctic Natl Wildlife Refuge resources, resident and visitor activities, and environmental impacts of energy exploration, 1983, annual update rpt, 5504–26

Army Corps of Engineers water resources dev projects, recreation activities by district and project, 1982, annual rpt, 3754–5

Atlantic Ocean sport and commercial landings and allowable and potential catch of US and Canada, for 34 species, 1983, annual rpt, 2164–14

California (southern) marlin catch and mean weight, for 2 angling clubs, July-Nov of selected years 1945-80, article, 2162–1.401

California marine resources and environmental effects of proposed oil and gas dev, for 2 sanctuaries off central and northern coasts, 1980s and projected to 2006, hearing, 21448–30.1

Coastal environmental characteristics, fish, wildlife, and use, and population socioeconomic data, for individual areas, series, 5506–4

Coastal fish and shellfish landings, life cycles, and environmental needs, for selected species by region, with glossary and bibl, series, 5506–8

Colorado River Storage Project finances, water resource dev, power production, and other activities in western States, FY83, annual rpt, 5824–3

Estuary environmental characteristics, fish, wildlife, uses, and mgmt, for individual estuaries, series, 5506–7

Fed Govt fish and wildlife restoration program finances, funding by State, and hunting and fishing equipment excise tax revenue, FY84, annual rpt, 5504–13

Fed Govt fish and wildlife restoration programs, including new sites, funding, and research, by State, FY81, annual rpt, 5504–1

Fish and shellfish of economic importance, biological, fishery, and mgmt data, literature review series, 2166–16

Foreign market and trade for sporting goods and recreational equipment and vehicles, country market research rpts, 2045–14

Forest, range, and associated waters use and mgmt assessment, and environmental impacts of Forest Service program options, 1977-2030 and trends from 1920, 1208–24

Hatchery (natl) distribution of fish and eggs for stocking, by species, hatchery, and jurisdiction, FY83, annual rpt, 5504–10

Index by Subjects and Names — Floods

Hatchery production, deliveries, and operating costs, and fishery assistance, by region, hatchery, and Fed Govt assistance station, FY82, annual rpt, 5504–9

Injuries and deaths from use of selected consumer products and related activity, by victim age and sex, 1982, annual rpt, 9164–7

Land Mgmt Bur activities and finances, and public land acreage and use, annual State rpt series, 5724–11

Landings of US recreational fishermen, by ocean subregion and species, 1979-80, annual rpt, 2164–1.2

Licenses for fishing and hunting issued and gross cost to sportsmen, by State, FY83, annual rpt, 5504–16

Natl Forest System wildlife habitat and fishery improvements, use, and game population and harvest by species and forest, by region, FY83, annual rpt, 1204–31

Natl forests recreational use, visitor-days by State and activity, FY79-83, annual rpt, 1204–1.1

Natl forests recreational use, visitor-days by type of activity, forest, and State, FY83 with trends from 1924, annual rpt series, 1204–17

New York State Adirondack fishing waters, economic value of fisheries, and potential losses from acid rain, 1980, 21368–52

Ocean sport fishermen, fishing activities, and catch by species, by fisherman characteristics, State, and coastal region, series, 2166–17

Ocean sport fishing effort and catch, and Natl Marine Fisheries Service tagging and research activity, by species and location, 1983, annual rpt, 2164–7

Public lands, miles of fishing streams, by State, FY83, annual rpt, 5724–1.2

Research of State fish and wildlife agencies, federally funded fishery projects and costs by species and State, 1984, annual rpt, 5504–23

Tax collections of State govts, by detailed type of tax and tax rates, by State, FY83, annual rpt, 2466–2.3

TVA activities, financial and operating data by program and facility, and power sales by customer, FY83, annual rpt, 9804–1

Wetlands environmental characteristics, acreage, uses, and mgmt, by wetland type and region, 1950s-80, 26358–102

see also Fish and fishing industry

Fisk, Donald M.

"Measuring Productivity in State and Local Government", 6728–27

Fissionable materials

see Nuclear radiation

see Uranium

Fitchburg, Mass.

Census of Housing, 1980: occupancy and unit characteristics, by race, Hispanic origin, and city, SMSA rpt, 2473–1.155

Census of Population and Housing, 1980: detailed population and housing characteristics, by county, city, and census tract, SMSA rpt, 2551–2.155

see also under By SMSA or MSA in the "Index by Categories"

Fitzgerald, E. V.

"Kalecki-Keynes Model of World Trade, Finance, and Economic Growth", 9366–7.94

Fixed investment

see Capital investments, general

see Capital investments, specific industries

Flaim, Paul O.

"Discouraged Workers: How Strong Are Their Links to the Job Market?", 6722–1.449

"Unemployment in 1982: The Cost to Workers and Their Families", 6722–1.412

"Work Experience of the Population in 1981-82", 6746–1.252

Flannery, Mark J.

"Market Evidence on the Effective Maturity of Bank Assets and Liabilities", 9387–8.82

Flaxseed

see Oils, oilseeds, and fats

Fleischman, Robert

"Average Bankrupt: A Description and Analysis of 753 Personal Bankruptcy Filings in Nine States", 25528–97.1

Flint, Mich.

Census of Housing, 1980: occupancy and unit characteristics, by race, Hispanic origin, and city, SMSA rpt, 2473–1.156

Census of Population and Housing, 1980: detailed population and housing characteristics, by county, city, and census tract, SMSA rpt, 2551–2.156

see also under By City and By SMSA or MSA in the "Index by Categories"

Flood control

Army Corps of Engineers activities and projects, FY83 and trends from 1800s, annual rpt, 3754–1

Colorado River Storage Project finances, water resource dev, power production, and other activities in western States, FY83, annual rpt, 5824–3

Developing countries disaster preparedness and summary sociodemographic, political, and economic data, country rpt series, 9916–2

Fed Govt aid to State and local govts, expenditures, and direct payments, by program, agency, and State, FY83, annual rpt, 2464–2

Fed Govt-owned real property inventory and costs, worldwide summary by location, agency, and use, 1983, annual rpt, 9454–5

Fed Govt programs and mgmt cost control proposals, 3-year savings by function and agency, and financial and operating data, 1960s-81, 16908–1.22

Fed Govt reclamation programs in western US, finances and operations by project and State, 1981-82, annual rpts, 5824–1

FmHA loans and grants by program and State, and summary of services, FY83 with trends from FY63, annual rpt, 1184–17

Reclamation Bur water storage and carriage facilities, by type, as of Sept 1983, annual listing, 5824–7

Tennessee Valley river control and reservoir elevations, storage, flows, and hydroelectric generating capacity use, 1981, annual rpt, 9804–7

TVA activities, financial and operating data by program and facility, and power sales by customer, FY83, annual rpt, 9804–1

Water supply and quality in streams and lakes, and groundwater levels in wells, by drainage basin, 1980, annual State rpt series, 5666–12

Water supply and quality in streams and lakes, and groundwater levels in wells, by drainage basin, 1981, annual State rpt series, 5666–16

Water supply and quality in streams and lakes, and groundwater levels in wells, by drainage basin, 1982, annual State rpt series, 5666–20

Water supply and quality in streams and lakes, and groundwater levels in wells, by drainage basin, 1983, annual State rpt series, 5666–10

see also Dams

see also Dredging

see also Reservoirs

see also Watershed projects

Floods

Central America mineral, energy, and water resources, and natural hazards to resource dev, by country, 1981 with trends from 1977, 5668–71

Coastal environmental characteristics, fish, wildlife, and use, and population socioeconomic data, for individual areas, series, 5506–4

Deaths from flash floods, by flood circumstances, type of warning, cause of death, and location, Sept 1969-May 1981, article, 4102–1.406

Developing countries disaster preparedness and summary sociodemographic, political, and economic data, country rpt series, 9916–2

Farmland restoration from natural disaster, Emergency Conservation Program participation and payments, by practice and State, FY83, annual rpt, 1804–22

Fed Emergency Mgmt Agency activities and funding for disaster and emergency relief, and major disasters, 1983, annual rpt, 9434–2

Fed Govt flood insurance program average premiums, premium income, and program costs, selected years FY68-84, hearing, 21248–81

Forecast methodology, accuracy, and applications, technical rpt series, 2186–4

Foreign countries disasters, persons affected, deaths, damage, and aid by US and others, FY83 and trends from FY64, annual rpt, 9914–12

Foreign weather conditions and impact assessment, by world area and country, monthly rpt, 2152–9

Mount St Helens, Wash, volcanic eruptions, effects on water quality and other environmental characteristics of Washington and Oregon watersheds, series, 5666–14

Utah Salt Lake surface level, land coverage, water budget, salinity, and effects of human activity, various periods 1847-1983, 5668–70

Water supply and quality, and effect of coal mining operations, for selected river basins in Eastern and Interior coal provinces, series, 5666–15

ods

ater supply and quality, and effect of coal mining operations, for selected river basins in Western coal provinces, series, 5666–19

Water supply and quality, floods, drought, mudslides, and other hydrologic events, by State, 1983, annual rpt, 5664–12

Water supply in US and Canada, streamflow, well and reservoir levels, and dissolved solids and temperature in 6 US rivers, by station, monthly rpt, 5662–3

Weather events socioeconomic impacts and costs, heating and cooling degree days, and housing energy bills, by census div and State, monthly rpt, 2152–12

see also Flood control

Florence, Ala.

Census of Housing, 1980: occupancy and unit characteristics, by race, Hispanic origin, and city, SMSA rpt, 2473–1.157

Census of Population and Housing, 1980: detailed population and housing characteristics, by county, city, and census tract, SMSA rpt, 2551–2.157

see also under By SMSA or MSA in the "Index by Categories"

Florence, S.C.

Census of Housing, 1980: occupancy and unit characteristics, by race, Hispanic origin, and city, SMSA rpt, 2473–1.158

Census of Population and Housing, 1980: detailed population and housing characteristics, by county, city, and census tract, SMSA rpt, 2551–2.158

see also under By SMSA or MSA in the "Index by Categories"

Florida

Agriculture census, 1982: farms, farmland, production and costs, and operator characteristics, preliminary State summary and county rpts, 2330–1.12

Agriculture census, 1982: farms, farmland, production, finances, and operator characteristics, by county, final State rpt, 2331–1.9

Bank deposits in commercial and mutual savings banks and in US branches of foreign banks, by account type, instn, State, SMSA, and county, June 1983, annual rpt, 9295–3.8

Bank holding companies in Florida, profits related to market position, concentration, and deposit growth, 1973-77, article, 9371–1.401

Biomass Fuels Program of TVA, technologies and processes dev, costs, and resource requirements, 1970s-90s, series, 9806–9

Celery acreage planted and growing, by major producing State and area, monthly rpt, 1621–14

Census of Housing, 1980: occupancy and unit characteristics of SMSAs and central cities, by race, Hispanic origin, and city, State rpt, 2473–1.11

Census of Population and Housing, 1980: detailed population and housing characteristics, by county, city, and census tract, State rpt, 2551–2.11

Census of Population, 1980: detailed socioeconomic and demographic characteristics, by age, sex, race, Hispanic origin, and industry, State rpt, 2531–4.11

Coastal environmental and wildlife characteristics, use, and mgmt, for individual ecosystems, 1970s-83, 5506–9.3, 5506–9.8

Coastal environmental characteristics, fish, wildlife, and use, and population socioeconomic data, for individual areas, 1983 rpt, 5506–4.8, 5506–4.9

Collective bargaining calendar for Southeast US, 1984, annual rpt, 6946–1.68

County Business Patterns: establishments, employees, and payrolls, by SIC 4-digit industry and county, 1982, annual State rpt, 2326–6.11

Economic indicators in Florida, including residential and nonresidential construction by SMSA, various periods 1970s-84, article, 9371–1.404

Employment (nonagricultural) by industry div and SMSA, earnings, and hours, for 8 southeastern States, monthly press release, 6942–7

Employment, earnings, and hours, by selected SIC 1- to 4-digit industry, State, and for 278 major labor areas, 1939-83, annual rpt, 6744–5.1, 6744–5.3

Employment, prices, earnings, and union membership in 8 southeastern States, Oct 1982-83, annual rpt, 6944–2

Energy conservation programs in Florida, activities and cost effectiveness by program and utility, as of 2nd quarter 1983, hearing, 21368–54

Environmental quality, pollutant discharge by type and source, and EPA protection activities and funding, 1970s-83, biennial regional rpt, 9184–15.4

Exports of manufactured and agricultural commodities, manufacturing production, and export-related employment, 1960s-82, State rpt, 2046–3.9

Financial and economic devs, Fed Reserve Bank of Atlanta monthly rpt with articles, 9371–1

Fish and shellfish landings, prices, and cannery production, for Gulf States and North Carolina, by area, weekly rpt, 2162–6.3

Fruit (citrus) production and use, by crop and State, 1977/78-1981/82, 1641–4

Fruit fly control, ethylene dibromide fumigation of tropical fruit imports, FY82, and cost of EDB and alternatives for Florida grapefruit and Hawaii papaya, 1984 rpt, 21168–29

HHS aid to each State and local govt or private instn, amount obligated, funding agency, and program, FY83, annual listing, 4004–3.4

Income (personal) per capita and by source, and earnings by industry div, by State, MSA, and county, 1977-82, annual regional rpt, 2704–2.6

Manufacturing census, 1982: financial and operating data, by SIC 2- to 4-digit industry, State, SMSA, and county, preliminary census div rpt, 2491–3.5

Mineral Industry Surveys, phosphate rock production, sales, exports, and use, 1984 crop year, annual rpt, 5614–20

Mineral Industry Surveys, State review of production, 1983, advance annual rpt, 5614–6.9

Minerals Yearbook, 1982, Vol 2 preprints: State review of production and sales by commodity, and business activity, annual rpt, 5604–16.10

Minerals Yearbook, 1982, Vol 2: State reviews of production, sales, and firms, by commodity, and business activity, annual rpt, 5604–34

Index by Subjects and Names

Older persons migrating to and from Florida and California by selected State of origin or destination, and Florida elderly, by sociodemographic and housing characteristics, 1970-80, 4478–150

Peach production, marketing, and prices in 4 Southeastern States and Appalachia, 1983, annual rpt, 1311–12

Phosphate rock reserves in southeastern and northwestern US, by location, 1984 rpt, 5668–74

Population, births, deaths, and net migration, by MSA and county, 1980-82, annual State Current Population Rpt, 2546–4.9

Population size, Apr 1980 and July 1982, and per capita income, 1979 and 1981, by county and city, State Current Population Rpt, 2546–11.9

Retail trade census, 1982: employment, establishments, sales, and payroll, by SIC 2- to 4-digit kind of business, SMSA, county, and city, State rpt, 2397–1.10

Savings and loan assn deregulation effect on lending activity, for US and 3 States, as of June 1980-83, article, 9371–1.432

Savings and loan assn deregulation impact, financial ratios of S&Ls in 3 States and US, 1980-83, article, 9371–1.426

Savings and loan assns, FHLB 4th District insured members financial condition and operations, by SMSA, monthly rpt, 9302–1

Service industry census, 1982: employment, establishments, receipts, and payroll, by SIC 2- to 4-digit kind of business, SMSA, county, and city, State rpt, 2391–1.10

Textile mill employment and average hours and earnings, for 8 Southeastern States, monthly press release, 6942–1

Water supply and quality in streams and lakes, and groundwater levels in wells, by drainage basin, 1982, annual State rpt, 5666–20.8

Water supply and quality in 8 southeastern States, with background socioeconomic data, 1960s-2020 with trends from 1930, 9208–119

see also Boca Raton, Fla.

see also Bradenton, Fla.

see also Broward County, Fla.

see also Cape Coral, Fla.

see also Cocoa, Fla.

see also Daytona Beach, Fla.

see also Fort Lauderdale, Fla.

see also Fort Myers, Fla.

see also Fort Walton Beach, Fla.

see also Gainesville, Fla.

see also Hollywood, Fla.

see also Jacksonville, Fla.

see also Lakeland, Fla.

see also Melbourne, Fla.

see also Miami, Fla.

see also Ocala, Fla.

see also Orlando, Fla.

see also Panama City, Fla.

see also Pensacola, Fla.

see also Pinellas County, Fla.

see also Sarasota, Fla.

see also St. Petersburg, Fla.

see also Tallahassee, Fla.

see also Tampa, Fla.

see also Titusville, Fla.

see also West Palm Beach, Fla.

see also Winter Haven, Fla.
see also under By State in the "Index by Categories"

Florists
see Flowers and nursery products

Flour
see Baking and bakery products
see Grains and grain products

Flow-of-funds accounts
Assets and liabilities in flow-of-funds accounts, by type and economic sector, year-end outstandings, 1960-83, annual rpt, 9364–3
Business Conditions Digest, cyclical indicators, by economic process, monthly rpt, 2702–3.3
Business Conditions Digest, historical supplement on economic, business, and financial conditions and cyclical fluctuations, with methodology, 1947-82, 2708–31
Credit market debt outstanding, and sector statements of financial assets and liabilities, 1971-82, annual rpt, 9364–5.8
Credit markets, direct and indirect sources of funds, monthly rpt, 9362–1.1
Current account deficits, and financing by source, for US and 5 OECD countries, selected years 1973-1st qtr 1984, article, 9385–1.409
Fed Govt consolidated financial statements based on business accounting methods, FY82-83, annual rpt, 8104–5
Flow-of-funds accounts savings, investments, and credit statements, quarterly rpt, 9365–3.3
Foreign direct investment in US, by major industry group, world area, and selected country, 1980-83, annual article, 2702–1.439
Foreign direct investment of US, by selected major industry group and world area, 1980-82, annual article, 2702–1.430
Foreign direct investment of US, by world area and country, 1977-83, article, 2702–1.442
Foreign sector in flow-of-funds and natl income and product accounts, data reconciliation, 1984 technical paper, 9366–7.95
Funds raised and borrowings, quarterly chartbook, 9362–2.4
Intl investment position of US, net change by component, investment type, and world region, and for 2 countries, 1982-83, annual article, 2702–1.424
Intl investment position of US, US assets abroad and foreign assets in US, 1970-82, annual rpt, 204–1.9
Savings (personal) measures from natl income and product and flow-of-funds accounts, 1977 and 1982, article, 2702–1.441
Statistical Abstract of US, social, political, and economic data, 1950s-83 and trends, annual rpt, 2324–1.3

Flowers and nursery products
Agricultural Statistics, 1983, annual rpt, 1004–1
Agriculture census, 1982: farms, farmland, production and costs, and operator characteristics, preliminary State and county rpt series, 2330–1
Agriculture census, 1982: farms, farmland, production, finances, and operator characteristics, by county, final State rpt series, 2331–1

Census of Population, 1980: detailed socioeconomic and demographic characteristics, by age, sex, race, Hispanic origin, occupation, and industry, State rpt series, 2531–4
County Business Patterns: establishments, employees, and payrolls, by SIC 4-digit industry and county, 1981, annual State rpt series, 2326–8
County Business Patterns: establishments, employees, and payrolls, by SIC 4-digit industry and county, 1982, annual State rpt series, 2326–6
Exports and imports of US, by agricultural commodity and country, bimonthly rpt with articles, 1522–1
Exports and imports of US, by detailed agricultural commodity and country, FY83 and CY83, semiannual rpts, 1522–4
Exports and imports of US, by detailed agricultural commodity for 8 major commodity groups, monthly rpt, 1922–8
Exports and imports of US, detailed SIC-based commodities by world area, 1983, annual rpts, 2424–6
Exports and imports of US, totals and as percent of domestic production, by SIC 2- to 5-digit commodity, 1981, annual rpt, 2424–3
Exports of US, detailed commodities by country of destination, monthly rpt, 2422–3
Exports of US, detailed Schedule B commodities by country of destination, 1983, annual rpt, 2424–9
Exports of US, detailed Schedule E commodities by mode of transport and world area and country of destination, 1983, annual rpts, 2424–5
Exports of US nursery stock and live ornamental plants, by world and country, 1982-83, article, 1925–34.417
Farm finances, assets, liabilities, income, receipts by commodity and State, and expenses, 1980-83 and trends from 1910, annual rpt, 1544–16
Franchise business opportunities, by firm and kind of business, 1984 annual listing, 2044–27
Imports of cut flowers, by type and country, FAS monthly rpt with articles, 1925–34
Imports of US, detailed Schedule A commodities by country and world area of origin, and mode of transport, 1983, annual rpts, 2424–2
Imports of US, detailed Schedule A commodities by country, monthly rpt, 2422–2
Imports of US, detailed TSUSA commodities by country of origin, 1983, annual rpt, 2424–4
Income tax returns of partnerships, detailed data by industry, 1981 estimates, annual article, 8302–2.404
Income tax returns of sole proprietorships, detailed data by industry div and selected industry group, 1981, annual rpt, 8304–7
Income tax returns of sole proprietorships, receipts, deductions by type, payroll, and net income, by major industry, 1982, annual article, 8302–2.413
Industry finances and operations, by SIC 2- to 4-digit industry, 1970s-83 and projected to 1988, annual rpt, 2014–4

Input-output structure of US economy, detailed interindustry transactions for 537 industries, and components of final demand, 1977 benchmark data, 2708–17
Marketing cash receipts of farms, by detailed commodity and State, 1979-82, annual rpt, 1544–18
Retail trade census, 1982: employment, establishments, sales, and payroll, for florists by State, preliminary rpt, 2395–1.38
Retail trade census, 1982: employment, establishments, sales, and payroll, by SIC 2- to 4-digit kind of business, SMSA, and retail district, State rpt series, 2401–1
Roses from Colombia at less than fair value, imports injury to US industry, investigation with background financial and operating data, 1984 rpt, 9886–14.118
Shipments of domestic and imported cut flowers and decorative greens, by State or country of origin, weekly rpt, 1311–3
see also Seeds
see also under By Commodity in the "Index by Categories"

Flu
see Pneumonia and influenza

Fluoridation
see Water fluoridation

Fluorine
see Gases

Fluorocarbons
see Chemicals and chemical industry

Fluorspar
see Nonmetallic minerals and mines

Flynn, K. F.
"Post-Remedial-Action Radiological Survey of the Westinghouse Advanced Reactors Division, Plutonium Fuel Laboratories, Cheswick, Pa., Oct. 1-8, 1981", 3406–1.38

Flynn, Patricia M.
"Lowell: A High Technology Success Story", 9373–1.416

FNMA
see Federal National Mortgage Association

Fogarty International Center for Advanced Study in the Health Sciences
Intl programs of NIH, activities and funding, by inst and country, FY83, annual rpt, 4474–6

Food additives
Biotechnology commercial uses, R&D funding and output, controls, and industry financial and operating data, for US and 5 countries, 1970s-83 and estimated 1984-85, 26358–98
Exports and imports of US, detailed SIC-based commodities by world area, 1983, annual rpts, 2424–6
Exports, imports, tariffs, and industry operating data for flavorings, fragrances, perfumes, cosmetics, and toiletries, 1979-83, TSUSA commodity rpt, 9885–4.40
Exports of US, detailed commodities by country of destination, monthly rpt, 2422–3
Exports of US, detailed Schedule B commodities by country of destination, 1983, annual rpt, 2424–9
Flavoring materials and other benzenoid chemical imports by country of origin and product, 1983, annual rpt, 9884–2

Food additives

Imports of US, detailed Schedule A commodities by country, monthly rpt, 2422–2

Imports of US, detailed TSUSA commodities by country of origin, 1983, annual rpt, 2424–4

Producer prices and indexes, by stage of processing and detailed commodity, monthly rpt, 6762–6

Producer prices and indexes, by stage of processing and detailed commodity, monthly 1983, annual supplement, 6764–2

Production and sales of synthetic organic chemicals by product, and listing of manufacturers, 1983, annual rpt, 9884–3

Food and Drug Administration

Cost control proposals for Fed Govt programs and mgmt, 3-year savings by function and agency, and financial and operating data, 1960s-81, 16908–1.7

Data projects and systems of HHS, by subagency, FY83-84, annual inventory, 4044–3

Drug (prescription) use by outpatient characteristics and generic or brand name, and hospital and drugstore costs by drug class, 1982, annual rpt, 4064–12

Fish pesticide and metal residue and industrial contaminant levels, for domestic and imported fish by species, annual rpt, discontinued, 4064–8

Imports detained by FDA, by product, shipper or manufacturer, country, and detention reasons, monthly listing, 4062–2

Investigation and regulatory activities of FDA, quarterly rpt, 4062–3

Investigatory and regulatory activities and funding of FDA, by program, annual rpt, discontinued, 4064–2

Radiation control program activities, State and local expenditures, personnel, and NRC licenses, by State, FY80-82, annual rpt, 4064–3

Radiation from electronic devices, incidents and persons involved by type of device and FDA control program activities, 1983, annual rpt, 4064–13

State govt food, drugs, and cosmetics control programs, expenditures, personnel, and labs, biennial rpt, suspended, 4064–11

Food and food industry

Advertising expenditures by media type, and advertising to sales ratio, by selected food item, 1970-79 with some trends from 1955, 1548–234

Agricultural cooperatives, membership, activities, and finances, by commodity and selected State, 1900-80 with trends from 1863, 1128–30

Agricultural Statistics, 1983, annual rpt, 1004–1

Agriculture Fact Book of US, compilation of data for 1983 with trends from 1940, annual rpt, 1004–14

Air pollutant emission factors, by detailed source, 3rd edition, 1983-84 supplements, 9198–13

Air pollution levels for 5 pollutants, by detailed source, State, and Air Quality Control Region, 1981, annual rpt, 9194–7

Army morale, welfare, and recreation programs, revenue and expenses worldwide by activity and major command, FY82-83, annual rpt, 3704–12

Business statistics, detailed data for major industries and economic indicators, *Survey of Current Business,* monthly rpt, 2702–1.11

Census of Population, 1980: detailed socioeconomic and demographic characteristics, by age, sex, race, Hispanic origin, occupation, and industry, State rpt series, 2531–4

Census of Population, 1980: detailed socioeconomic characteristics, by county, city, and inside-outside SMSAs and central cities, State rpt series, 2531–3

Census of Population, 1980: labor force, by sex, detailed occupation, and region, with comparison to 1970 census, supplementary rpt, 2535–1.12

China exports and imports by SITC 1- to 5-digit commodity, 1970s-82, annual rpt, 244–12

Collective bargaining agreements expiring during year, covered workers by SIC 2-digit industry, firm, and union, with summary of key provisions, 1984, annual rpt, 6784–9

Consumer research and marketing devs, and consumption and price trends, quarterly rpt with articles, 1541–7

County Business Patterns: establishments, employees, and payrolls, by SIC 4-digit industry and county, 1981, annual State rpt series, 2326–8

County Business Patterns: establishments, employees, and payrolls, by SIC 4-digit industry and county, 1982, annual State rpt series, 2326–6

Cuba economic conditions, agricultural and industrial production and distribution, trade, and intl economic relations, 1970-82 and trends from 1957, 248–40

Earnings by major industry group, and personal income per capita and by source, by region and State, 1929-82, 2708–40

Electric power cogeneration in 5 industries, and fuel use and utility supply/demand effects, by region, 1983-93, 3008–92

Electric power industrial demand model estimates, economic indicators, and supporting data for 5 industries, 1960s-80 with projections to 2000, 3008–87

Employment, earnings, and hours, by selected SIC 1- to 4-digit industry, State, and for 278 major labor areas, 1939-83, annual rpt, 6744–5

Employment, earnings, and hours, by SIC 4-digit nonfarm industry, monthly 1974-Feb 1984, annual update, 6744–4

Employment in farm and nonfarm food and fiber sectors, and costs in food marketing bill, 1973-82, annual rpt, 1544–19

Employment, unemployment, and labor force, by demographic and employment characteristics, State, and for 30 metro areas and 11 large cities, 1983, annual rpt, 6744–7

Exports and imports between US and outlying areas, by detailed commodity and mode of transport, monthly rpt, 2422–4

Exports and imports of US, by commodity group, world area, selected country, US coastal area and port, and mode of transport, with seasonal adjustments, monthly rpt, 2422–9

Exports and imports of US, by detailed agricultural commodity and country, FY83 and CY83, semiannual rpts, 1522–4

Exports and imports of US, detailed SIC-based commodities by world area, 1983, annual rpts, 2424–6

Exports and imports of US, totals and as percent of domestic production, by SIC 2- to 5-digit commodity, 1981, annual rpt, 2424–3

Exports and personal expenditures of US and world for selected agricultural commodities, by country, and export share of US farm income, various periods 1926-82, 1528–172

Exports of manufactured and agricultural commodities, manufacturing production, and export-related employment, 1960s-82, State rpt series, 2046–3

Exports of US, detailed Schedule E commodities by mode of transport and world area and country of destination, 1983, annual rpts, 2424–5

Fed Govt programs and mgmt cost control proposals, 3-year savings by function and agency, and financial and operating data, 1960s-81, 16908–1.23

Finances and operations, by SIC 2- to 4-digit industry, 1970s-83 and projected to 1988, annual rpt, 2014–4

Financial statements for manufacturing, mining, and trade corporations, by selected SIC 2- to 3-digit industry, quarterly rpt, 2502–1

Foreign agricultural and food production indexes, and production of selected commodities, by world region and country, 1974-83, annual rpt, 1524–5

Foreign Agriculture, production, consumption, and policies, and US export dev and promotion, monthly rpt, 1922–2

Foreign direct investment of US, by selected major industry group and world area, 1980-82, annual article, 2702–1.430

Foreign food processing and packaging equipment market and trade, and user industry operations and demand, country market research rpts, 2045–11

GAO publications on food, agriculture, and nutrition, 1981-83, annual listing, 26104–11.2

Great Lakes trade, by SITC 3-digit commodity, port, vessel type, world area, and country, 1982, annual rpt, 7744–3

Imports of US, detailed Schedule A commodities by country and world area of origin, and mode of transport, 1983, annual rpts, 2424–2

Imports of US, detailed Schedule A commodities by country, monthly rpt, 2422–2

Imports of US, detailed TSUSA commodities by country of origin, 1983, annual rpt, 2424–4

Income tax returns of corporations, detailed income and tax items by industry, 1981, annual rpt, 8304–4

Income tax returns of corporations with foreign tax credit, income and deductions by type, asset size, and selected industry group, 1980, article, 8302–2.415

Income tax returns of foreign subsidiaries of US corporations, income and tax data, by industry and asset size, 1980, article, 8302–2.410

Index by Subjects and Names

Income tax returns of sole proprietorships, detailed data by industry div and selected industry group, 1981, annual rpt, 8304–7

Income tax returns of sole proprietorships, receipts, deductions by type, payroll, and net income, by major industry, 1982, annual article, 8302–2.413

Input-output structure of US economy, detailed interindustry transactions for 85 industries, and components of final demand, 1977, article, 2702–1.421

Input-output structure of US economy, detailed interindustry transactions for 537 industries, and components of final demand, 1977 benchmark data, 2708–17

Manufacturing census, 1982: financial and operating data, by SIC 2- to 4-digit industry, State, SMSA, and county, preliminary census div rpt series, 2491–3

Manufacturing census, 1982: financial and operating data, for SIC 4-digit industries by product, preliminary rpt series, 2491–1

Marketing cost components, farm-retail food prices, and industry finances and productivity, selected years 1967-83, annual rpt, 1544–9

Minority group and women employment, by occupational group and SIC 2- to 3-digit industry, 1981, annual rpt, 9244–1.1

Occupational injury and illness rates, by SIC 2- to 4-digit industry, 1982, annual rpt, 6844–1

Occupational manpower needs and supply by detailed occupation, and educational and training program enrollees and grads by detailed field, 1982 and 1995, biennial rpt, 6744–3

OECD trade, total and for 4 major countries, and US trade by country, by commodity, 1972-82, annual world region rpt series, 244–13

Pacific Northwest electricity consumption and prices by end-use sector, and economic and demographic data, 1960s-83 and projected to 2005, annual rpt, 3224–2

Pollution abatement capital and operating costs, by SIC 2- to 4-digit industry, State, and SMSA, 1982, annual Current Industrial Rpt, 2506–3.6

Portugal agricultural subsidies, profits, marketing margins, and consumer prices, by commodity or product, and effects of prospective EC membership, 1981, 1528–171

Processed foods production and stocks by State, shipments, exports, materials used, and consumption, by product, periodic Current Industrial Rpt series, 2506–4

Productivity, hours, and employment indexes for selected SIC 3- and 4-digit industries, 1954-82, annual rpt, 6824–1.3

R&D expenditures of US firms foreign affiliates, by selected industry, 1974-82, 9626–2.131

R&D industry funding and employment of scientists and engineers, by industry group, firm size, and funding source, 1956-82, annual rpt, 9627–21

Radioactive strontium in NYC and San Francisco diet by food item, and in NYC tap water and milk, quarterly 1982 with trends from 1954, annual rpt, 3404–13

Research grants awarded competitively by USDA for agricultural science, food and nutrition, and energy dev, FY83, annual listing, 1744–1

Retail trade census, 1982: employment, establishments, sales, and payroll, for direct selling establishments, by State, preliminary rpt, 2395–1.35

Scientists, engineers, and technicians employed in private industry, by occupation and industry group, 1980-81, biennial rpt, 9627–23

Scientists, engineers and technicians employment in transportation, utilities, and retail and wholesale trade, by field of science and industry, 1982, 9628–72

Supply, consumption, trade, prices, expenditures, and indexes, by food commodity, 1963-83, annual rpt, 1544–4

Transportation census, 1982: trucks, by detailed characteristics, miles traveled, and type of product carried, State rpt series, 2573–1

Underground economy, household expenditures and participation by type of goods or service and sociodemographic characteristics, with methodology and bibl, 1981 survey, 8308–27

Virgin Islands economic censuses, 1982: employment, establishments, payroll, and receipts, by SIC 1- to 4-digit industry, island, and city, 2593–1

Water pollution fish kills, by State, location, and pollution source, monthly 1978-80, annual rpt, 9204–3

Waterborne commerce of US (domestic and foreign), freight by commodity, traffic, and passengers, by port and waterway, 1982, annual rpt, 3754–3

Wholesale trade census, 1982: employment, establishments, finances, and operations, by SIC 2- to 4-digit kind of business, SMSA, county, and city, State rpt series, 2405–1

Wholesale trade census, 1982: employment, establishments, sales by commodity, and payroll, by SIC 4-digit kind of business and State, preliminary rpt series, 2403–1

Wholesale trade sales and inventories, by SIC 2- to 3-digit kind of business, monthly rpt, 2413–7

Wholesale trade sales, inventories, purchases, and gross margins, by SIC 2- to 3-digit kind of business and type of ownership, 1983, annual rpt, 2413–13

see also Animal feed
see also Aquaculture
see also Baking and bakery products
see also Beer and breweries
see also Beverages
see also Candy and confectionery products
see also Cocoa and chocolate
see also Coffee
see also Cold storage and refrigeration
see also Dairy industry and products
see also Fish and fishing industry
see also Food additives
see also Food and waterborne diseases
see also Food assistance
see also Food consumption
see also Food inspection
see also Food prices
see also Food stamp programs
see also Food stores

Food and waterborne diseases

see also Food supply
see also Fruit and fruit products
see also Grains and grain products
see also Honey and beekeeping
see also Ice, manufactured
see also Liquor industry
see also Livestock and livestock industry
see also Meat and meat products
see also Nuts
see also Oils, oilseeds, and fats
see also Packaging and containers
see also Poultry industry and products
see also Restaurants and restaurant industry
see also Shellfish
see also Soft drink industry
see also Spices and herbs
see also Sugar industry and products
see also Syrups and sweeteners
see also Tea
see also Vegetables and vegetable products
see also Wine and winemaking
see also under By Commodity in the "Index by Categories"
see also under By Industry in the "Index by Categories"

Food and Nutrition Service

Activities and programs of USDA, by subagency, FY83, annual rpt, 1004–3

Child nutrition programs of USDA, activities and finances, FY79-83, annual rpt, 1364–14

Food aid programs of USDA, participants and costs by program and region, monthly rpt, 1362–14

Food aid programs of USDA, participants, monthly press release, 1362–13

Food stamp program participation and coupons distributed, by region, State, and project area, quarterly rpt, 1362–6

Food stamp recipient households size and composition, income, and income deductions allowed, Aug 1981, annual rpt, 1364–8

Fraud and abuse in USDA programs, audits and investigations, 2nd half FY84, semiannual rpt, 1002–4

Indian reservations and TTPI food distribution program participants, irregular rpt, 1362–15

School breakfast and other USDA child nutrition programs, participation and finances, by region and State, annual rpt series, 1364–13

School lunch program school and student participation, families eligible, and Federal reimbursement rates, FY79-83, GAO rpt, 26113–123

Women, infants, and children food aid program of USDA, participants and costs by State and Indian agency, FY82 and trends from FY74, annual tables, 1364–12

Food and waterborne diseases

Cases and incidence of infectious notifiable diseases and other public health concerns, by census div and State, 1982, annual rpt, 4204–1

Cases and outbreaks of waterborne disease, by type, source, and location, 1983, annual rpt, 4205–35

Cases and outbreaks of waterborne diseases from drinking water, by type and cause, aggregate 1971-80, 9208–124

Cases of notifiable infectious diseases and current outbreaks, by region and State, weekly rpt, 4202–1

Food and waterborne diseases

Ciguatera incidence in Caribbean area, by island, 1984 article, 2162–1.403

Deaths and death rates by detailed cause and demographic characteristics, 1979 and selected trends, US Vital Statistics annual rpt, 4144–2.1

Environmental quality, pollutant discharge by type and source, and EPA protection activities and funding, 1970s-83, biennial regional rpt series, 9184–15

Foreign travel vaccination requirements by country, and disease prevention recommendations, 1984 annual rpt, 4204–11

Southeastern US water supply and quality, with background socioeconomic data, for 8 States, 1960s-2020 with trends from 1930, 9208–119

Water supply and quality in streams and lakes, and groundwater levels in wells, by drainage basin, 1980, annual State rpt series, 5666–12

Water supply and quality in streams and lakes, and groundwater levels in wells, by drainage basin, 1981, annual State rpt series, 5666–16

Water supply and quality in streams and lakes, and groundwater levels in wells, by drainage basin, 1982, annual State rpt series, 5666–20

Water supply and quality in streams and lakes, and groundwater levels in wells, by drainage basin, 1983, annual State rpt series, 5666–10

see also Food inspection

see also under By Disease in the "Index by Categories"

Food assistance

Agricultural production, marketing, trade, supply, food consumption, and food and nutrition programs, 1960s-83, annual chartbook, 1504–3

Agricultural Statistics, 1983, annual rpt, 1004–1.2

AID activities and funding by project and function, FY85, and developing countries summary socioeconomic data, 1970s-83, by country, annual rpt, 9914–3

Budget of US, effects of Reagan Admin policy changes, by detailed program, FY85, annual rpt, 104–21

CCC dairy price support program foreign donations and domestic donations to poor, schools, Prisons Bur, DOD, and VA, monthly rpt, 1802–2

CCC finances and program operations, FY83, annual rpt, 1824–1

Child nutrition programs of USDA, activities and finances, FY79-83, annual rpt, 1364–14

Child obesity and low height-for-age, for public food program participants aged 1-4, by race and Hispanic origin, 1982, article, 4202–7.403

Children and youth benefitting from Fed Govt public welfare programs and tax expenditures, participation and funding for 71 programs, FY81-83, 21968–30

Debt to US of foreign govts and private obligors, by country and program, periodic rpt, 8002–6

Developing countries food production and needs, and related economic trends and outlook, for 67 countries, 1980-86, annual rpt, 1524–6

Exports of US, detailed Schedule B commodities by country of destination, 1983, annual rpt, 2424–9

Exports under Fed Govt-financed programs, by commodity and country, bimonthly rpt, periodic tables, 1522–1.4

Fed Govt aid to State and local govts, expenditures, and direct payments, by program, agency, and State, FY83, annual rpt, 2464–2

Fed Govt and other food aid programs, funding, participant characteristics, and nutrition and poverty data, 1970s-83, 028–20

Fed Govt financial and nonfinancial domestic aid, 1984 annual comprehensive catalog, 104–5

Fed Govt policy issues effect on agricultural and food prices, income, and trade, and crop support levels by program, Nov 1984, semiannual rpt, 1542–6

Fed Govt programs and mgmt cost control proposals, 3-year savings by function and agency, and financial and operating data, 1960s-81, 16908–1

Foreign and US food aid contributions, by commodity group and country, 1975/76-83/84, 1528–181

Foreign human rights conditions in 162 countries, economic and military aid of US, and economic aid of intl organizations, 1981-83, annual rpt, 21384–3

Govt census, 1982: State govt payments to local govts, by program, source of funds, level of govt, and State, with trends from 1902, 2460–3

Govt expenditures for social welfare by program and level of govt, and private expenditures for health care, selected years FY50-82, annual article, 4742–1.425

Income (household) and cash and noncash transfer program participation, by sociodemographic characteristics, quarterly rpt, 2542–2

Indian reservations and TTPI food distribution program participants, irregular rpt, 1362–15

Michigan health funding, Blue Cross-Blue Shield and welfare participation, and unemployment, poverty, and food assistance by county, 1979-83, hearing, 21348–86

Milk price supports effect on production, use, prices, and farm receipts, by region and State, 1940s-83 and alternative projections to 1988/89, 1568–245

Older persons nutrition services program operations and assessment, and participant sociodemographic, health, and diet characteristics, 1976 and 1982, 4608–16

Older persons population characteristics, and needs and costs of social services by type, by metro-nonmetro status, 1970s-82 with trends from 1900, 21148–28

Philippines dev and military assistance funding from US, FY78-84 and proposed FY85-89, GAO rpt, 26123–54

Public noncash transfers counted as income, effect on poverty population size by selected recipient characteristics, 1979-83, 2626–2.52

Purchases of food for domestic aid programs, by commodity, firm, and shipping point or destination, weekly rpt, 1302–3

Index by Subjects and Names

Statistical Abstract of US, social, political, and economic data, 1950s-83 and trends, annual rpt, 2324–1.1

USDA food aid programs participants and costs, by program and region, monthly rpt, 1362–14

USDA funding for school lunch, milk, other food assistance, and nutrition education programs, by State and outlying area, FY82, annual rpt, 4824–2.22

USDA programs participants, monthly press release, 1362–13

Women, infants, and children food aid program of USDA, participants and costs by State and Indian agency, FY82 and trends from FY74, annual tables, 1364–12

Women, infants, and children special supplemental food program effectiveness, and participants characteristics, 1973-82, GAO rpt, 26131–10

see also Food stamp programs

see also Public Law 480

see also School lunch and breakfast programs

Food consumption

AFDC eligibility under Omnibus Budget Reconciliation Act, effect on caseloads and recipient benefits and living costs, 1981-83, GAO rpt, 26131–11

Agricultural production, marketing, trade, supply, food consumption, and food and nutrition programs, 1960s-83, annual chartbook, 1504–3

Agricultural Statistics, 1983, annual rpt, 1004–1.2

Consumer research and marketing devs, and consumption and price trends, quarterly rpt with articles, 1541–7

Consumption of food and nutrient intake by households, adjustments for meals eaten at home and nutritional requirements of household members, 1977/78, article, 1502–3.401

Consumption of food and nutrient intake by individuals, by food group, source, and socioeconomic characteristics, 1977-78 natl survey, final rpt series, 1356–4

Consumption, supply, trade, prices, expenditures, and indexes, by food commodity, 1963-83, annual rpt, 1544–4

Dairy products foreign and US production, consumption, and trade, FAS annual circular series, 1925–10

Developing countries agricultural supply/demand and market for US exports, with socioeconomic indicators, country rpt series, 1526–6

Developing countries disaster preparedness and summary sociodemographic, political, and economic data, country rpt series, 9916–2

Developing countries food production and needs, and related economic trends and outlook, for 67 countries, 1980-86, annual rpt, 1524–6

Eastern Europe agricultural production and trade by commodity, food consumption, and farm inputs, for 6 countries, 1960-80 with projections to 1991, 1528–178

Economic and population time series data frequently used in statistical demand analyses, 1941-1982, annual rpt, 1544–21

Expenditures for food by consumers, 1972-83, annual rpt, 1544–9

Index by Subjects and Names

Food prices

Expenditures for fruit, vegetable, and potato products related to income and other household characteristics, 1977-78, 1548–236

Expenditures for tips and meals at eating places, and visits to eating places, 1982, article, 8302–2.406

Farm finance and credit conditions, forecast 1984, conf papers, annual rpt, 1004–16

Farm households consumption of agricultural commodities, by State, 1980-83, annual rpt, 1544–16

Farm production, prices, marketing, and trade, by commodity, forecast and current situation, monthly rpt, 1502–4

Fats, oils, and oilseed production, prices, trade, and consumption, periodic situation rpt with articles, 1561–3

Fish and fish products per capita consumption for US 1909-83, and by country, average 1975-77, annual rpt, 2164–1.9

Foreign agricultural production, prices, and trade, by country, 1983 and outlook for 1984/85, annual world region rpt series, 1524–4

Foreign and US agricultural supply/demand and production data, for selected US and world crops, and for US livestock and dairy products, periodic rpt, 1522–5

Foreign and US agricultural supply/demand, consumption per capita, and trade, by world area and country group, 1960s-82, 1528–181

Foreign and US agricultural supply/demand indicators by commodity and world area, and related research and extension program needs, 1950s-2020, 1008–47

Fruit and nut production, prices, trade, stocks, and use, by selected crop, periodic situation rpt with articles, 1561–6

Household weekly food allowances recommended under USDA thrifty food plan, by age and sex, 1983 with comparisons to 1975, article, 1702–1.402

Imports injury to price-supported US agricultural industries, investigations with background financial and operating data for selected products, series, 9886–10

Input-output structure of US economy, detailed interindustry transactions for 537 industries, and components of final demand, 1977 benchmark data, 2708–17

Livestock, poultry, and products foreign and US production, consumption, and trade, FAS semiannual circular, 1925–33

Meat and poultry consumption, impact of hypothetical consumer demand changes on price structure and industry performance, model, 1982-91, article, 1502–3.402

Meat consumption by type, total and per capita civilian and military, quarterly 1970-83, annual rpt, 1564–6.2

Meat marketing and distribution establishments, sales, and per capita consumption, 1950s-82 with trends from 1929, 1548–232

Meat, poultry, and egg consumption per capita, periodic situation rpt, 1561–7

Milk and dairy production, prices, consumption, and trade, quarterly situation rpt with articles, 1561–2

Milk price support alternatives, effects on production, use, prices, and farm receipts, projected 1983/84-1988/89 and actual 1982/83, 1568–246

Milk price supports effect on production, use, prices, and farm receipts, by region and State, 1940s-83 and alternative projections to 1988/89, 1568–245

Mushroom imports injury to US industry, and stocks, production, sales, trade, and consumption, quarterly rpt, 9882–5

Natl income and product, comprehensive accounts and components, *Survey of Current Business,* monthly rpt, 2702–1.21

Older persons nutrition services program operations and assessment, and participant sociodemographic, health, and diet characteristics, 1976 and 1982, 4608–16

Personal consumption expenditures, natl income and product account, *Survey of Current Business,* monthly rpt, monthly and annual tables, 2702–1.23

Research (agricultural) expenditures and scientist years, by topic, commodity, and performing organization, FY82, annual rpt, 1744–2

Sugar and sweeteners production, consumption, prices, supply, and trade, quarterly rpt with articles, 1561–14

Sugar, molasses, and honey foreign and US production, trade, and consumption, FAS annual rpt series, 1925–14

Sugar production, consumption, supply, and trade, quarterly rpt, 1621–28

Vegetable production, prices, stocks, and consumption, for selected fresh and processed crops, periodic situation rpt with articles, 1561–11

Wheat and rye foreign and US production, prices, trade, stocks, and use, periodic situation rpt with articles, 1561–12

see also Food assistance

see also Nutrition and malnutrition

Food for Peace Program

see Public Law 480

Food inspection

Budget of US, effects of Reagan Admin policy changes, by detailed program, FY85, annual rpt, 104–21

Cattle tuberculosis eradication and surveillance, cooperative Federal-State program activities, by State, FY83, annual rpt, 1394–13

Census of Population, 1980: detailed socioeconomic and demographic characteristics, by age, sex, race, Hispanic origin, occupation, and industry, State rpt series, 2531–4

Egg production by type of product, and shell eggs broken under Fed Govt inspection by region, monthly rpt, 1625–2

FDA investigation and regulatory activities, quarterly rpt, 4062–3

FDA investigatory and regulatory activities and funding, by program, annual rpt, discontinued, 4064–2

Fed Govt aid to State and local govts, expenditures, and direct payments, by program, agency, and State, FY83, annual rpt, 2464–2

Fed Govt programs and mgmt cost control proposals, 3-year savings by function and agency, and financial and operating data, 1960s-81, 16908–1.2, 16908–1.31

Federal Grain Inspection Service activities and finances by program, and foreign complaint investigations by country, FY83, annual rpt, 1294–1

Fishery products and establishments inspected, 1983, annual rpt, 2164–1.10

Foreign meat plants inspected and certified for exporting products to US, 1983, annual listing, 1374–2

Grain production, prices, trade, and export inspections by US port and country of destination, by grain type, weekly rpt, 1313–2

Grain rail and barge loadings, ship and container car availability, ocean freight rates, and export inspections, prices, and sales, weekly rpt, 1272–2

Grains inspected for export, weekly rpt, 1313–4

Imports detained by FDA, by product, shipper or manufacturer, country, and detention reasons, monthly listing, 4062–2

Livestock inspected by Fed Govt, by type, weekly rpt, 1315–1

Livestock slaughter and meat and meat products prepared under Federal inspection, by type, monthly 1970-83, annual rpt, 1564–6.2, 1564–6.4

Livestock slaughter by species, meat production, and number of slaughtering plants, by State, 1983, annual rpt, 1623–10

Livestock slaughter under Fed Govt inspection, by livestock type and region, monthly rpt, 1623–9

Meat and poultry inspection activities and personnel of Federal, State, and foreign govts, FY83, annual rpt, 1374–1

Meat and poultry inspection by Food Safety and Inspection Service, FY83, annual rpt, 1374–3

Occupational Outlook Handbook, 1984-85 biennial rpt, 6744–1

Peanut production, prices, stocks, exports, use, inspection, and quality, by region and State, selected crop years 1974-83, annual rpt, 1311–5

Poultry and egg marketing and price data for selected regions, States, and SMSAs, monthly 1983, annual rpt, 1317–2

Poultry slaughtered under Fed Govt inspection, pounds certified, and condemnations by cause, by State, monthly rpt, 1625–3

Rice market activities, prices, inspections, sales, trade, supply, and use, for US and selected foreign markets, weekly rpt, 1313–8

see also Food and waterborne diseases

Food poisoning

see Food and waterborne diseases

Food prices

Agricultural production, marketing, trade, supply, food consumption, and food and nutrition programs, 1960s-83, annual chartbook, 1504–3

Agricultural Statistics, 1983, annual rpt, 1004–1

Agriculture Fact Book of US, compilation of data for 1983 with trends from 1940, annual rpt, 1004–14

Business and financial statistics, historic trends, 1984 annual chartbook, 9364–2.6

Business and financial statistics, quarterly chartbook, 9362–2.3

Consumer goods prices and supplies, family finance, and home economics, quarterly rpt with articles, 1702–1

Food prices

Consumer research and marketing devs, and consumption and price trends, quarterly rpt with articles, 1541–7

CPI by detailed component, for US city average, 28 SMSAs, and 4 regions by population size, monthly rpt, 6762–2

CPI components relative importance, for selected SMSAs, and US city average by region and population size, 1983, annual rpt, 6884–1

Dairy marketing and price data for selected cities, States, and regions, 1983, annual rpt, 1317–1

Dairy production by State, stocks, prices, and CCC price support activities, by product type, monthly rpt, 1627–3

Developing countries food supply policies, with farm sector data, tariff income, and prices and imports of 5 grains, for 21 countries, 1960s-81, 1528–168

EC food supply/demand and market and support prices, with exchange rates, fertilizer price index, GDP, and population, by country, 1960-83, 1528–173

Economic and population time series data frequently used in statistical demand analyses, 1941-1982, annual rpt, 1544–21

Economic indicators and labor force characteristics, selected years 1880-1995, chartbook, 6728–30

Export and import price indexes for food and manufactured products, quarterly press release, 6762–13

Farm finance and credit conditions, forecast 1984, conf summary, annual rpt, 9264–9

Farm finances, production, expenses by type, and domestic economic impact, selected years 1972-82 and preliminary 1983-84, annual rpt, 1544–19

Farm production, prices, marketing, and trade, by commodity, forecast and current situation, monthly rpt, 1502–4

Farm-retail food prices, marketing cost components, and industry finances and productivity, selected years 1967-83, annual rpt, 1544–9

Fish and shellfish landings, prices, trade, wholesaler receipts, and market activities at 5 major US ports, weekly rpts, 2162–6

Fish prices, exvessel 1978-83, and wholesale and retail 1983, annual rpt, 2164–1.8

Fishing diesel and sail-assisted boats in Hawaiian waters, fuel use, earnings, and operating costs, with fuel and fish price indexes, various periods 1967-81, article, 2162–1.401

Food purchases for domestic aid programs, by commodity, firm, and shipping point or destination, weekly rpt, 1302–3

Foreign and US food prices for 15 items in DC and 15 foreign capital cities, weekly press release, periodic table, 1922–4

Foreign and US indexes of consumer, producer, and major commodity prices, nonfarm wages, and currency value, US and 4 countries, bimonthly rpt, 2042–11

Fruit (noncitrus) and nut production, prices, and use, by crop and State, 1981-83, annual rpt, 1621–18.1, 1621–18.3

Fruit and nut production, prices, trade, stocks, and use, by selected crop, periodic situation rpt with articles, 1561–6

Fruit and vegetable wholesale prices in NYC, Chicago, and selected shipping points, by crop, 1983, annual rpt, 1311–8

Inflation rate, money supply growth, and food and energy prices, various periods 1970-2nd qtr 1984, article, 9391–1.420

Meat and poultry consumption, impact of hypothetical consumer demand changes on price structure and industry performance, model, 1982-91, article, 1502–3.402

Meat, poultry, and egg production, prices, trade, stocks, and consumption, periodic situation rpt, 1561–7

Meat prices (wholesale and retail) for beef, pork, veal, and lamb, 1967-83, annual rpt, 1564–6.3

Milk and dairy production, prices, consumption, and trade, quarterly situation rpt with articles, 1561–2

Milk pasteurized by ultra-high temperature, sales, production, stocks, costs, market shares, and prices, 1980, 1568–247

North Central States farm credit conditions and economic devs, Fed Reserve 7th District, biweekly rpt, 9375–10

OECD economic indicators, for US and 6 countries, biweekly rpt, 242–4

Portugal agricultural subsidies, profits, marketing margins, and consumer prices, by commodity or product, and effects of prospective EC membership, 1981, 1528–171

Poultry and egg marketing and price data for selected regions, States, and SMSAs, monthly 1983, annual rpt, 1317–2

Price indexes (consumer and producer) and retail prices for selected food items, and CPI for 25 cities, 1963-83, annual rpt, 1544–4.5

Price indexes (consumer and producer) changes for selected items, and changes in CPI for selected services, 1982-83, article, 6722–1.429

Producer Price Index, by major commodity group and subgroup, and processing stage, monthly press release, 6762–5

Producer prices and indexes, by stage of processing and detailed commodity, monthly rpt, 6762–6

Producer prices and indexes, by stage of processing and detailed commodity, monthly 1983, annual supplement, 6764–2

Retail prices for energy and food, and housing fuel consumption, by region, and for 28 SMSAs and US city average, monthly press release, 6762–8

Sugar and sweeteners production, consumption, prices, supply, and trade, quarterly rpt with articles, 1561–14

Tuna fleet, capacity, and processor investment in vessels by investment type, with tuna catch, prices, and imports, selected years 1932-80, 9406–1.39

Vegetable production, prices, stocks, and consumption, for selected fresh and processed crops, periodic situation rpt with articles, 1561–11

Wheat, rye, and white pan bread prices, price indexes, and farm-retail spreads, periodic situation rpt with articles, 1561–12

see also Agricultural prices

Food Safety and Inspection Service

Activities and programs of USDA, by subagency, FY83, annual rpt, 1004–3

Index by Subjects and Names

Foreign meat plants inspected and certified for exporting products to US, 1983, annual listing, 1374–2

Fraud and abuse in USDA programs, audits and investigations, 2nd half FY84, semiannual rpt, 1002–4

Meat and poultry inspection activities and personnel of Federal, State, and foreign govts, FY83, annual rpt, 1374–1

Meat and poultry inspection by Food Safety and Inspection Service, FY83, annual rpt, 1374–3

Food Safety and Quality Service

see Food Safety and Inspection Service

Food shortage

see Food supply

see Nutrition and malnutrition

Food stamp programs

AFDC eligibility under Omnibus Budget Reconciliation Act, effect on caseloads and recipient benefits and living costs, 1981-83, GAO rpt, 26131–11

Agricultural production, marketing, trade, supply, food consumption, and food and nutrition programs, 1960s-83, annual chartbook, 1504–3

Alabama rural black population, education, employment, health services, and economic status, for 16 counties, selected years 1970-81, 11048–180

Beneficiaries of noncash public and employer-based transfer programs, by income source and socioeconomic characteristics, 1982, advance Current Population Rpt, 2546–6.38

Beneficiaries of noncash public and employer-based transfer programs, by income source and socioeconomic characteristics, 1982, final Current Population Rpt, 2546–6.37

Beneficiary households size and composition, income, and income deductions allowed, Aug 1981, annual rpt, 1364–8

Benefit overpayments, payment error rates, and sanctions imposed, for food stamp, AFDC, and SSI programs, by State, various dates 1980-82, GAO rpt, 26113–136

Benefits and beneficiary characteristics of OASDHI, Medicaid, SSI, and other social insurance and public welfare programs, selected years 1937-82, annual rpt, 4744–3.13

Budget of US, CBO analysis of revenue and spending alternatives and projections of economic indicators, FY85-89, annual rpt, 26304–3.3

Budget of US, effects of Reagan Admin policy changes, by detailed program, FY85, annual rpt, 104–21

Children and youth benefitting from Fed Govt public welfare programs and tax expenditures, participation and funding for 71 programs, FY81-83, 21968–30

Consumer research and marketing devs, and consumption and price trends, quarterly rpt with articles, 1541–7

Cost control proposals for Fed Govt programs and mgmt, 3-year savings by function and agency, and financial and operating data, 1960s-81, 16908–1.2, 16908–1.23

Costs and productivity of AFDC and food stamp programs in 8 States, 1973-82, GAO rpt, 26111–18

Index by Subjects and Names

Food stores

Criminal cases of Federal defendants, disposition, convictions, and sentences, by offense and district, as of June 1983, annual rpt, 18204–1

Fed Govt aid to State and local govts, expenditures, and direct payments, by program, agency, and State, FY83, annual rpt, 2464–2

Fed Govt and other food aid programs, funding, participant characteristics, and nutrition and poverty data, 1970s-83, 028–20

Fed Govt programs under Ways and Means Committee jurisdiction, program operations and financing data for assessing budgetary requirements, by State, FY70s-83, 21788–117

Food expenditures for fruit, vegetable, and potato products related to changes in income and other household characteristics, 1977-78, 1548–236

Fraud in Fed Govt benefit programs and other unreported taxable income from illegal activities, with methodology and bibl, 1970s-82, 8008–112

Fresno, Calif, economic, population, labor, and housing indicators, various periods 1974-85, hearing, 21248–84

Govt census, 1982: State govt payments to local govts, by program, source of funds, level of govt, and State, with trends from 1902, 2460–3

Hispanic Americans socioeconomic and demographic characteristics, and compared to non-Hispanics, selected years 1970-83, chartbook, 2328–48

Income (household) and cash and noncash transfer program participation, by sociodemographic characteristics, quarterly rpt, 2542–2

Income (personal) by source including transfer payments, and social insurance contributions by type, by region, 1982, 2708–40

Michigan health funding, Blue Cross-Blue Shield and welfare participation, and unemployment, poverty, and food assistance by county, 1979-83, hearing, 21348–86

NYC families caring for aged relatives, preference for social service and financial programs to provide assistance, 1980, article, 4652–1.403

Older persons Fed Govt pension and health spending, by program and as percents of budget and GNP, 1965-85 with projections to 2040, 25148–28

Older persons nutrition services program operations and assessment, and participant sociodemographic, health, and diet characteristics, 1976 and 1982, 4608–16

Older persons sociodemographic characteristics, and Fed Govt program participation and funding, 1983 with trends and projections 1900-2060, annual rpt, 25144–3.1

Participation and costs of USDA food aid programs, by program, region, and State, monthly rpt, 1362–14

Participation and coupons distributed, by region, State, and project area, quarterly rpt, 1362–6

Participation of USDA food aid programs, monthly rpt, 1362–13

Poverty-level persons and families, by income source, hours of work, earnings, taxes, and family characteristics, various periods 1959-84, 21788–131

Public noncash transfers counted as income, effects on poverty population size by recipient characteristics, 1979-82, 2626–2.50

Refugee arrivals in US by world area of origin and State of settlement, and Fed Govt intl and domestic assistance costs, FY85, annual rpt, 7004–16

Research and statistical projects and techniques, and evaluation of public welfare programs, 1983 conf papers, 4704–11

Supplementary Security Income beneficiary socioeconomic characteristics and health service use, 1970s-83 and SSI program projections to 1995, 25148–29

Traffic accidents and casualties detailed direct and indirect costs, by characteristics of persons and vehicles involved, 1979-80, 7768–80

Wisconsin public welfare programs caseloads, selected vital statistics, and households in poverty, 1970s-83, hearings, 21788–141

Food stocks
see Agricultural stocks
see Food supply

Food stores

Advertising expenditures by media type, and advertising to sales ratio, by selected food item, 1970-79 with some trends from 1955, 1548–234

Automated teller machines and point of sale debit card systems offered by retailers, by firm, firm type, and State, 1984 survey, article, 9371–1.421

Automated teller machines installed or planned at southeast US grocery and convenience chain store outlets, and operating characteristics, Aug 1983, article, 9371–1.403

Campground facilities privately owned, and financial and operating data, by region, 1982, annual rpt, 5544–14.5

Census of Population, 1980: detailed socioeconomic and demographic characteristics, by age, sex, race, Hispanic origin, occupation, and industry, State rpt series, 2531–4

Census of Population, 1980: detailed socioeconomic characteristics, by county, city, and inside-outside SMSAs and central cities, State rpt series, 2531–3

Census of Retail Trade, 1982: employment, establishments, sales, and payroll, by SIC 2- to 4-digit kind of business, SMSA, and retail district, State rpt series, 2401–1

Census of Retail Trade, 1982: employment, establishments, sales, and payroll, by SIC 2- to 4-digit kind of business, SMSA, county, and city, State rpt series, 2397–1

Census of Retail Trade, 1982: employment, establishments, sales, and payroll, for grocery stores, by State, preliminary rpt, 2395–1.8

Collective bargaining agreements expiring during year, covered workers by SIC 2-digit industry, firm, and union, with summary of key provisions, 1984, annual rpt, 6784–9

Consumer research and marketing devs, and consumption and price trends, quarterly rpt with articles, 1541–7

County Business Patterns: establishments, employees, and payrolls, by SIC 4-digit industry and county, 1981, annual State rpt series, 2326–8

County Business Patterns: establishments, employees, and payrolls, by SIC 4-digit industry and county, 1982, annual State rpt series, 2326–6

Dairy cooperatives sales volume and market shares by commodity, and finances, by region, 1980 with trends from 1957, 1128–29

Employment, earnings, and hours, by selected SIC 1- to 4-digit industry, State, and for 278 major labor areas, 1939-83, annual rpt, 6744–5

Employment, earnings, and hours, by SIC 4-digit nonfarm industry, monthly 1974-Feb 1984, annual update, 6744–4

Finances and operations, by SIC 2- to 4-digit industry, 1970s-83 and projected to 1988, annual rpt, 2014–4

Financial statements for manufacturing, mining, and trade corporations, by selected SIC 2- to 3-digit industry, quarterly rpt, 2502–1

Franchise business opportunities, by firm and kind of business, 1984 annual listing, 2044–27

Franchises of firms engaged in distribution of goods and services by kind of business, establishments by State, and sales, 1982-84, annual rpt, 2014–5

Income tax returns of corporations, detailed income and tax items by industry, 1981, annual rpt, 8304–4

Income tax returns of corporations with foreign tax credit, income and deductions by type, asset size, and selected industry group, 1980, article, 8302–2.415

Income tax returns of partnerships, detailed data by industry, 1981 estimates, annual article, 8302–2.404

Income tax returns of partnerships, receipts by source, deductions by type, and establishments, by selected industry, 1982, annual article, 8302–2.416

Income tax returns of sole proprietorships, detailed data by industry div and selected industry group, 1981, annual rpt, 8304–7

Income tax returns of sole proprietorships, receipts, deductions by type, payroll, and net income, by major industry, 1982, annual article, 8302–2.413

Income tax returns with investment credits, for individuals by income, and for sole proprietorships by industry, 1981, article, 8302–2.409

Meat marketing and distribution establishments, sales, and per capita consumption, 1950s-82 with trends from 1929, 1548–232

Minority group and women employment, by occupational group and SIC 2- to 3-digit industry, 1981, annual rpt, 9244–1.1

Nutrition and cardiovascular disease consumer education, effectiveness of Natl Heart, Lung, and Blood Inst and Giant Food, Inc, program in DC metro area, 1978-79, 4478–144

Occupational injury and illness rates, by SIC 2- to 4-digit industry, 1982, annual rpt, 6844–1

Food stores

Prices (farm-retail) for foods, marketing cost components, and industry finances and productivity, selected years 1967-83, annual rpt, 1544–9

Productivity, hours, and employment indexes for selected SIC 3- and 4-digit industries, 1954-82, annual rpt, 6824–1.4

Robberies, by type of premises, population size, and region, 1983, annual rpt, 6224–2.1

Sales and inventories, by kind of business, region, census div, and selected State, SMSA, and city, and seasonal adjustments, monthly rpt, 2413–3

Sales, inventories, purchases, gross margin, and accounts receivable, by SIC 2- to 4-digit kind of business and type of ownership, 1983, annual rpt, 2413–5

Scientists, engineers, and technicians employment in transportation, utilities, and retail and wholesale trade, by field of science and industry, 1982, 9628–72

UK retail food outlets by type, 1970s-82, and US agricultural exports to UK by commodity, FY81-83, article, 1925–34.406

Virgin Islands economic censuses, 1982: employment, establishments, payroll, and receipts, by SIC 1- to 4-digit industry, island, and city, 2593–1

Watermelon grower-to-retailer handling costs and time, by handling phase and method, 1982, 1308–18

Food supply

Agricultural Statistics, 1983, annual rpt, 1004–1

Cuba economic conditions, agricultural and industrial production and distribution, trade, and intl economic relations, 1970-82 and trends from 1957, 248–40

Developing countries agricultural supply/demand and market for US exports, with socioeconomic indicators, country rpt series, 1526–6

Developing countries disaster preparedness and summary sociodemographic, political, and economic data, country rpt series, 9916–2

Developing countries food production and needs, and related economic trends and outlook, for 67 countries, 1980-86, annual rpt, 1524–6

Farm finance and credit conditions, forecast 1984, conf papers, annual rpt, 1004–16

Farm production, prices, marketing, and trade, by commodity, forecast and current situation, monthly rpt, 1502–4

Foreign agricultural and food production indexes, and production of selected commodities, by world region and country, 1974-83, annual rpt, 1524–5

Foreign agricultural production, prices, and trade, by country, 1983 and outlook for 1984/85, annual world region rpt series, 1524–4

Foreign and US agricultural supply/demand and production data, for selected US and world crops, and for US livestock and dairy products, periodic rpt, 1522–5

Foreign and US agricultural supply/demand indicators by commodity and world area, and related research and extension program needs, 1950s-2020, 1008–47

Plant and animal genetic resource conservation, commercial uses, causes of depletion, and geographic sources, 1984 rpt, 5548–13

Research (agricultural) expenditures and scientist years, by topic, commodity, and performing organization, FY82, annual rpt, 1744–2

Supply, consumption, trade, prices, expenditures, and indexes, by food commodity, 1963-83, annual rpt, 1544–4

see also Agricultural production

see also Agricultural stocks

see also Nutrition and malnutrition

see also under names of specific agricultural commodities (for production and stocks data)

Foot health and diseases

see Podiatry

Football

Injuries and deaths from use of selected consumer products and related activity, by victim age and sex, 1982, annual rpt, 9164–7

Forage

see Animal feed

see Pasture and rangeland

Ford Foundation

Population and health research funded by 4 private organizations, project listing by topic, with funding data, 1981, annual rpt, 4474–16

Ford, Harold D.

"Money Market Account Competition", 9371–1.431

Ford Motor Co.

Energy economy test results, 1985 model year, annual rpt, 3304–11

Energy use of autos and light trucks, economy standards and manufacturer compliance, and gas prices and taxes, with selected foreign comparisons, FY80-83 and projected to 2000, hearing, 21368–49

Safety of domestic and foreign autos and light trucks, crash test results of selected new models for model year to date, press release series, 7766–7

Sales, prices, and registrations of autos and auto products in US, and trade of 8 countries with US, by make and model, 1964-83, annual rpt, 9884–7

Forecasts

see Projections

Foreign affairs

see Foreign relations

Foreign Agricultural Service

Activities and programs of USDA, by subagency, FY83, annual rpt, 1004–3

Cocoa and cocoa products, foreign and US production, prices, and trade, FAS semiannual circular, 1925–9

Coffee production, trade and quotas, and consumption, by country, with US and intl prices, FAS periodic circular, 1925–5

Cotton production and trade, foreign and US, FAS monthly and annual rpt series, 1925–4

Dairy imports subject to quota by commodity, and meat imports subject to Meat Import Law, by country of origin, FAS monthly circular, 1925–31

Dairy products foreign and US production, consumption, and trade, FAS annual circular series, 1925–10

Export sales and shipments of US grains, oilseed products, hides, skins, and cotton, by country, weekly rpt, 1922–3

Index by Subjects and Names

Exports and imports of US, by detailed agricultural commodity for 8 major commodity groups, monthly rpt, 1922–8

Fats, oils, and related products foreign and US production and trade, FAS monthly and annual circular series, 1925–1

Foreign Agriculture, production, consumption, and policies, and US export dev and promotion, monthly rpt, 1922–2

Fraud and abuse in USDA programs, audits and investigations, 2nd half FY84, semiannual rpt, 1002–4

Fruits, vegetables, and nuts (fresh and processed) foreign and US production and trade, FAS monthly rpt with articles, 1925–34

Fruits, vegetables, and nuts (fresh and processed) foreign and US production and trade, FAS rpt supplement series, 1925–35

Grain production, trade, stocks, and prices, foreign and US, FAS monthly and annual rpt series, 1925–2

Livestock, poultry, and dairy live animals, meat, and products trade, by commodity and country of destination, FAS quarterly rpt, 1925–32

Livestock, poultry, and products foreign and US production, consumption, and trade, FAS semiannual circular, 1925–33

Lumber and wood products exports of US, by commodity and country, FAS quarterly rpt, 1925–36

PL 480 commodity allocations for long-term credit sales, by country, quarterly press release, 1922–7

PL 480 concessional sales agreements, market value and date signed, and shipping costs, by country, 1954-83, annual rpt, 1924–6

PL 480 concessional sales program, exports by commodity and country, 1955-83, semiannual rpt, 1922–6

PL 480 concessional sales program, exports by commodity and country, 1978-83, semiannual rpt, 1922–10

PL 480 exports by commodity, and recipients, by program, sponsor, and country, FY82 and aggregate from FY55, annual rpt, 1924–7

Production, acreage, and yield for selected crops, forecasts by selected world region and country, FAS monthly rpt, 1925–28

Production, trade, and climatic devs, foreign and US, weekly press release, 1922–4

Publications of FAS, annual listing, discontinued, 1924–1

Seed exports of US, by type of seed, world region, and country, FAS quarterly rpt, 1925–13

Spice, essential oil, and tea foreign and US production, prices, and trade, FAS annual rpt series, 1925–15

Sugar and specialty sugar imports of US under quota, by country, weekly rpt, 1922–9

Sugar, molasses, and honey foreign and US production, trade, and consumption, FAS annual rpt series, 1925–14

Tobacco products foreign and US production, prices, trade, and acreage, FAS monthly rpt with articles, 1925–16

Index by Subjects and Names

Foreign agriculture

Agricultural policies of US effect on trade, with US and foreign trade by commodity and grain stocks by world area, various periods 1979-83, 1528–183

Agricultural production, marketing, trade, supply, food consumption, and food and nutrition programs, 1960s-83, annual chartbook, 1504–3

Agricultural Statistics, 1983, annual rpt, 1004–1

Agricultural supply/demand, consumption per capita, and trade, by world area and country group, 1960s-82, 1528–181

AID activities and funding by project and function, FY85, and developing countries summary socioeconomic data, 1970s-83, by country, annual rpt, 9914–3

AID dev assistance activities, evaluation rpt series, 9916–11

AID dev assistance activities, socioeconomic impacts, evaluation rpt series, 9916–1

Animal disease outbreaks in US and foreign countries, quarterly rpt, 1392–3

Background Notes, foreign countries summary social, political, and economic data, series, 7006–2

Bean (dried) prices by State, and foreign and US production, use, stocks, and trade, weekly rpt, 1311–17

Cocoa and cocoa products, foreign and US production, prices, and trade, FAS semiannual circular, 1925–9

Coffee production, trade and quotas, and consumption, by country, with US and intl prices, FAS periodic circular, 1925–5

Communist, OECD, and selected other countries agricultural production and labor, and average commodity prices, 1960s-83, annual rpt, 244–5.2, 244–5.9

Cotton production and trade, foreign and US, FAS monthly and annual rpt series, 1925–4

Cotton, wool, and synthetic fiber production, prices, consumption, and trade, periodic situation rpt with articles, 1561–1

Cuba economic conditions, agricultural and industrial production and distribution, trade, and intl economic relations, 1970-82 and trends from 1957, 248–40

Dairy products foreign and US production, consumption, and trade, FAS annual circular series, 1925–10

Developing countries disaster preparedness and summary sociodemographic, political, and economic data, country rpt series, 9916–2

Developing countries food production and needs, and related economic trends and outlook, for 67 countries, 1980-86, annual rpt, 1524–6

Developing countries govt policy, and AID and other foreign assistance, effects on private sector dev and socioeconomic conditions, with case studies for 6 countries, 1960s-80, 9918–12

Developing countries PL 480 Title I funding and socioeconomic impacts, with case studies for 5 countries, 1950s- 81, 9918–13

Drug and narcotics foreign production, acreage, eradication, and seizures, by substance, with labs destroyed and US aid, by country, 1981-85, annual rpt, 7004–17

Eastern Europe grain production, consumption, and trade, and US farm cooperatives grain and oilseed export potential, for 4 countries, selected years 1960-90, 1128–27

EC agricultural self-sufficiency and trade by selected product, with comparisons to other countries, selected years 1959/60-1983/84, hearing, 25368–135

Economic, social, and political summary data, by country, 1984, annual factbook, 244–11

Economic trends in foreign countries and implications for US, annual and semiannual country rpt series, 2046–4

Farm production, prices, marketing, and trade, by commodity, forecast and current situation, monthly rpt, 1502–4

Fats, oils, and related products foreign and US production and trade, FAS monthly and annual circular series, 1925–1

Fertilizer production and consumption, by type and country group, periodic situation rpt with articles, 1561–16

Foreign Agricultural Service publications, annual listing, discontinued, 1924–1

Fruits, vegetables, and nuts (fresh and processed) foreign and US production and trade, FAS monthly rpt with articles, 1925–34

Fruits, vegetables, and nuts (fresh and processed) foreign and US production and trade, FAS rpt supplement series, 1925–35

Grain production, trade, stocks, and prices, foreign and US, FAS monthly and annual rpt series, 1925–2

Grain stocks, supply deviation, and effect on use, trade, and prices, for US and selected countries, various periods 1960-83, 1528–184

Imports injury to price-supported US agricultural industries, investigations with background financial and operating data for selected products, series, 9886–10

Livestock, poultry, and products foreign and US production, consumption, and trade, FAS semiannual circular, 1925–33

Meat and poultry inspection activities and personnel of Federal, State, and foreign govts, FY83, annual rpt, 1374–1

Overseas Business Reports: economic conditions, investment and export opportunities, and trade practices, annual country market research rpt series, 2046–6

Peanut and peanut oil exports of US, and foreign peanut production, by country, crop years 1979-83, annual rpt, 1311–5.2

Production, acreage, and yield for selected crops, forecasts by selected world region and country, FAS monthly rpt, 1925–28

Production and supply/demand data, for selected foreign and US crops, and for US livestock and dairy products, periodic rpt, 1522–5

Production, consumption, and policies for selected countries, and US export dev and promotion, monthly rpt, 1922–2

Production indexes and production of selected commodities, by world region and country, 1974-83, annual rpt, 1524–5

Production, prices, and trade of agricultural commodities, by country, 1983 and outlook for 1984/85, annual world region rpt series, 1524–4

Foreign assistance

Production, prices, trade, and consumption, foreign and US, quarterly rpt with articles, 1522–3

Production, trade, and climatic devs, foreign and US, weekly press release, 1922–4

Production, trade, and supply/demand, with socioeconomic data, by country, 1950s-77, 1528–179

Research (agricultural) expenditures and scientist years, by topic, commodity, and performing organization, FY82, annual rpt, 1744–2

Rice market activities, prices, inspections, sales, trade, supply, and use, for US and selected foreign markets, weekly rpt, 1313–8

Rice production and trade, for selected countries and world regions, 1980/81-1983/84, semiannual rpt, 1561–8.4

Spice, essential oil, and tea foreign and US production, prices, and trade, FAS annual rpt series, 1925–15

Sugar, molasses, and honey foreign and US production, trade, and consumption, FAS annual rpt series, 1925–14

Tobacco acreage and production in selected countries, 1979-83, annual rpt, 1319–1.6

Tobacco production and trade, by country, quarterly situation rpt with articles, 1561–10

Tobacco products foreign and US production, prices, trade, and acreage, FAS monthly rpt with articles, 1925–16

Weather conditions and effect on agriculture, by US region, State, and city, and world area, weekly rpt, 2152–2

Weather conditions and impact assessment, by world area and country, monthly rpt, 2152–9

Wheat and rye foreign and US production, prices, trade, stocks, and use, periodic situation rpt with articles, 1561–12

see also under names of specific countries or world regions

Foreign area studies

see Area studies

Foreign assistance

AID activities and funding by project and function, FY85, and developing countries summary socioeconomic data, 1970s-83, by country, annual rpt, 9914–3

AID community dev assistance to local govts in developing countries, program activities and funding, 1960s-80s, 9918–11

AID contracts and grants for technical and support services, by instn, country, and State, FY83, annual listing, 9914–7

AID contracts and grants to universities for technical assistance to foreign countries and other services, FY83, annual listing, 9914–6

AID dev assistance activities, evaluation rpt series, 9916–11

AID dev assistance activities, socioeconomic impacts, evaluation rpt series, 9916–1

AID dev assistance activities, special study series, 9916–3

AID economic assistance to developing countries, obligations and disbursements by country, quarterly rpt, 9912–4

AID Housing Guaranty Program financial statements, and projects by country, FY83, annual rpt, 9914–4

Foreign assistance

AID loan repayment status and terms by program and country, and status of predecessor agency loans, quarterly rpt, 9912–3

AID loans authorized, signed, and canceled, by country and world area, monthly rpt, 9912–2

Background Notes, foreign countries summary social, political, and economic data, series, 7006–2

Banks (multilateral dev) economic dev projects, environmental and cultural impacts in developing countries, 1970s-83, hearings, 21248–80

Budget of US Appendix, detailed budgets and personnel summaries, by agency, FY85, annual rpt, 104–3

Budget of US, CBO analysis and review of FY85 budget by function, annual rpt, 26304–2

Budget of US, CBO analysis of revenue and spending alternatives and projections of economic indicators, FY85-89, annual rpt, 26304–3.3

Budget of US, compact budgets by function, agency, and account, FY85 with projections to FY89, annual rpt, 104–2

Budget of US, effects of Reagan Admin policy changes, by detailed program, FY85, annual rpt, 104–21

Budget of US, loans and loan guarantees, and Admin proposed limits on credit assistance, by program, FY83-89, annual rpt, 26306–3.65

Budget of US, Reagan Admin funding requests for foreign economic and military aid by program and country, FY82-85, annual rpt, 7004–14

Budget of US, receipts by source and outlays by agency and program, monthly rpt, 8102–3

Budget of US, receipts by source and outlays by function, FY40-89 estimates revised for consistency with FY85 budget definitions, annual rpt, 104–12

Budget of US, receipts, outlays, and budget authority, by function and agency, 1st revision of FY85 budget, annual rpt, 104–17

Central America economic assistance from AID by type of aid, for 7 countries, FY80-83, GAO rpt, 26123–55

Central America socioeconomic and political conditions in 6 countries, 1960s-83 with trends and projections 1930-2010, 028–19

Cost control proposals for Fed Govt programs and mgmt, CBO and GAO estimates of savings by function and agency, FY85-89, 26308–45

Cost control proposals for Fed Govt programs and mgmt, 3-year savings by function and agency, and financial and operating data, 1960s-81, 16908–1.10

Cuba economic conditions, agricultural and industrial production and distribution, trade, and intl economic relations, 1970-82 and trends from 1957, 248–40

Currency (foreign) accounts owned by US under AID admin and by foreign govts with joint AID control, status by program and country, quarterly rpt, 9912–1

Debt to US of foreign govts and private obligors, by country and program, periodic rpt, 8002–6

Developing countries economic aid of US, bilateral and through multilateral dev banks and intl agencies, by world area and country, 1970s-FY83, annual rpts, 9904–1

Developing countries economic and military aid from US, Communist, and selected other countries, 1954-83, annual rpt, 244–5.4

Developing countries govt policy, and AID and other foreign assistance, effects on private sector dev and socioeconomic conditions, with case studies for 6 countries, 1960s-80, 9918–12

Developing countries receiving US economic aid, total govt and defense expenditures, military imports, GNP, and intl reserves by country, 1976-81, annual rpt, 9914–1

Drug and narcotics foreign production, acreage, eradication, and seizures, by substance, with labs destroyed and US aid, by country, 1981-85, annual rpt, 7004–17

Economic and military assistance loans and grants from US and intl agencies, by program and country, FY46-83, annual rpt, 9914–5

Economic and military assistance role in US foreign policy, with aid proposals by world region, FY85 with trends from FY74, 7008–38

Economic, social, and political summaries, by country, 1984, annual rpt, 244–11

El Salvador socioeconomic and political conditions, and US economic and military assistance, 1977-FY84, 7008–39

Fed Govt contingent liabilities and claims paid on federally insured and guaranteed contracts with foreign obligors, by country and program, periodic rpt, 8002–12

Fed Govt economic and military aid, by program and country, selected years 1940-82, annual rpt, 15344–1.1

Financial instns funds by source and disbursements by purpose, by country, with US policy review, FY83, annual rpt, 15344–1

Foreign military, social, and economic summary data by world area and country, 1960s-80s, hearing, 25388–47.1

Forests (tropical) status by country and world region, conservation methods, and mgmt role of US, foreign, and intl groups, 1977-81 and projected to 2000, 26358–101

Govt revenues by source and expenditures by function, natl income and product account, *Survey of Current Business,* monthly rpt, monthly and annual tables, 2702–1.24

Human rights conditions in 162 countries, economic and military aid of US, and economic aid of intl organizations, 1981-83, annual rpt, 21384–3

Inter-American Foundation activities, grants, and fellowships, by country, FY83, annual rpt, 14424–1

Latin America students in US and Soviet bloc training programs, by program type and student country, and summary by world region, selected years 1972-82, GAO rpt, 26123–77

Loan programs of Fed Govt, direct and guaranteed loans outstanding by agency and program, *Treasury Bulletin,* quarterly rpt, 8002–4.10

Index by Subjects and Names

Philippines dev and military assistance funding from US, FY78-84 and proposed FY85-89, GAO rpt, 26123–54

Statistical Abstract of US, selected social, political, and economic data, by country, 1945-83 and trends, annual rpt, 2324–1.4

USIA English teaching programs and teacher seminars, by world region and country, FY83, annual rpt, 9854–2

Voluntary agencies overseas foreign aid programs funding and expenditures, by agency, 1982/83, annual rpt, 9914–9

see also Export-Import Bank

see also Food assistance

see also International relief

see also Military assistance

see also Public Law 480

see also War relief

Foreign budgets

Biotechnology commercial uses, R&D funding and output, controls, and industry financial and operating data, for US and 5 countries, 1970s-83 and estimated 1984-85, 26358–98

Cuba economic conditions, agricultural and industrial production and distribution, trade, and intl economic relations, 1970-82 and trends from 1957, 248–40

Current account balance related to budget balances, for US and 58 countries, various periods 1948-82, article, 9379–1.401

Deficit and economic indicators, with US/foreign comparisons, 1973-83, conf papers, 9373–3.27

Deficits effect on interest rates and economic indicators, with govt borrowing and saving, for US and 6 OECD countries, 1975-83, technical paper, 9366–7.89

Developing countries govt policy, and AID and other foreign assistance, effects on private sector dev and socioeconomic conditions, with case studies for 6 countries, 1960s-80, 9918–12

Developing countries PL 480 Title I funding and socioeconomic impacts, with case studies for 5 countries, 1950s- 81, 9918–13

Developing countries receiving US economic aid, total govt and defense expenditures, military imports, GNP, and intl reserves by country, 1976-81, annual rpt, 9914–1

Developing countries summary socioeconomic data, 1970s-83, and AID activities and funding by project and function, FY82-85, by country, annual rpt, 9914–3

Economic, social, and political summary data, by country, 1984, annual factbook, 244–11

Economic trends in foreign countries and implications for US, annual and semiannual country rpt series, 2046–4

Interest rates and budget balances of US and 6 OECD countries, 1973-83, annual rpt, 26304–3.1

Israel health care natl expenditures, with comparisons to other budget sectors and expenditures of other countries, 1950s-83, article, 4102–1.446

Jamaica PL 480 Title I assistance effects on economic dev, with data on govt finance, economic indicators, demography, and dev programs, 1970s-81, 9916–1.51

Index by Subjects and Names

Foreign countries

Mexico economic indicators, trade, external accounts and debt, oil industry, and relations with US, 1978-83 with trends from 1959, conf proceedings, 21248–82

Military spending, arms trade, and armed forces size, with total govt spending and population, by country, 1972-82, annual rpt, 9824–1

Overseas Business Reports: economic conditions, investment and export opportunities, and trade practices, annual country market research rpt series, 2046–6

Overseas Business Reports: economic conditions, investment and export opportunities, and trade practices, world region rpt series, 2046–5

Papua New Guinea tuna landings by species, and fishery operating data and govt revenues generated, 1979-81, article, 2162–1.402

Foreign Claims Settlement Commission Activities of Justice Dept, by subagency, FY82, annual rpt, 6004–1

Foreign corporations

- Aluminum primary production plant ownership, capacity, and type and source of raw material and energy used, by plant, State, and country, June 1984, semiannual listing, 5602–5
- Argentina grain production, exports by firm, storage by facility type and port, and shipments to ports by mode of transport, by grain type, selected years 1954-81, 1528–185
- *Background Notes,* foreign countries summary social, political, and economic data, series, 7006–2
- Bank and nonbank foreign exchange activity, and foreign exchange turnover in US and 3 foreign markets, Mar 1980 and Apr 1983, article, 9385–1.411
- Bank branches and agencies of foreign banks, assets and liabilities, monthly rpt, 9362–1.1
- Biotechnology commercial uses, R&D funding and output, controls, and industry financial and operating data, for US and 5 countries, 1970s-83 and estimated 1984-85, 26358–98
- Biotechnology firms, patents, and trade by country, and effect of industry growth on US drug and chemical trade, selected years 1979-2000, 9886–4.78
- *Business America,* foreign and domestic commerce, and US investment and trade opportunities, biweekly rpt articles, 2042–24
- Developing countries free zones, industry financial and operating data by country, with case studies for 5 countries, 1970s-82, 9918–10
- DOD procurement, prime contractors for R&D, top 500 and value of contracts, FY83, annual listing, 3544–4
- Employee stock ownership plans in developing countries, and firms finances and operations, with case studies of US and 3 countries, 1970s-82, 9916–3.19
- Import and tariff provisions effect on US industries and products, investigations with background financial and operating data, series, 9886–4
- Income tax returns of corporations, detailed income and tax items by industry, 1981, annual rpt, 8304–4

Manufactured goods relative market shares of largest US and foreign firms by selected industry and firm, 1960, 1970, and 1981, hearing, 21248–79

Minerals (nonfuel) foreign and US supply under alternative market conditions, reserves, and background industry data, series, 5606–4

Minerals (strategic) supply/demand, trade, and foreign and US industry devs by firm and country, by commodity, bimonthly rpt, 5602–4

Navy procurement, by contractor and location of work, FY83, annual rpt, 3804–13

Nuclear power plant construction and operation status, and capacity, by plant, region, State, and selected country, 1983 and projected to 2020, annual rpt, 3164–57

Overseas Business Reports: economic conditions, investment and export opportunities, and trade practices, annual country market research rpt series, 2046–6

Patents (US) granted to US and foreign applicants, by applicant type, firm, State, and country, subject rpt series, 2246–2

Patents (US) granted to US and foreign applicants, by year of grant and application, country, and type of applicant, 1960s-83, annual rpt, 2244–3

see also Multinational corporations

Foreign countries

- Abortions performed in 12 States and NYC, by State of residence and for non-US residents by selected area, 1980, US Vital Statistics final rpt, 4146–5.72
- Acid rain causes and effects, air pollutant emissions by source in US and selected countries, control costs, and Fed Govt research funding, 1960s-82, 3408–27
- Aircraft hijackings, on-board explosions, other crimes against civil aviation, and circumstances, US and worldwide, 1931-83, annual rpt, 7504–31
- Animal disease outbreaks in US and foreign countries, quarterly rpt, 1392–3
- *Background Notes,* foreign countries summary social, political, and economic data, series, 7006–2
- Cement (portland) shipments from plants in US and Puerto Rico, by destination, bimonthly rpt, 2012–1.6
- Chiefs of State and Cabinet members, by country, monthly listing, 242–7
- Classification codes for countries for Census Bur foreign trade statistics, revisions to 1981 base edition, 2428–3
- Coin production of US Mint Bur for foreign countries, FY83, annual rpt, 8204–1
- DOD base support costs by function, and personnel and acreage by installation, by service branch, FY85, annual rpt, 3504–11
- DOD medical facilities in US and abroad, admissions, beds, outpatient visits, and live births, by service branch, quarterly rpt, 3542–15
- DOD prime contract awards for R&D to educational and nonprofit instns and Federal agencies, by instn and location, FY83, annual listing, 3544–17
- DOT employment by subagency, State, and selected personnel characteristics, FY83, annual rpt, 7304–18.1

Drug Enforcement Admin cases against major drug traffickers by case characteristics, and agents assessment of activities, in 3 cities, 1979-82, GAO rpt, 26119–57

Education summary statistics by world area and country, and foreign students enrolled in US higher education instns, 1982 with trends, annual rpt, 4824–2.24

Energy supply/demand and prices, by fuel type and consuming sector with foreign comparisons, 1949-83, annual rpt, 3164–74

Energy supply/demand and prices, by fuel type, sector, and end use, with foreign comparisons, 1960-83 and projected to 1995, annual summary rpt, 3164–76

Fish and shellfish landings, prices, trade, consumption, and industry operating data, for US with foreign comparisons, 1982-83, annual rpt, 2164–1

Glaciology intl research summaries, methodology, and bibls, series, 2156–18

Medicare facilities and services use, covered charges, and reimbursements, by beneficiary type and area of residence, series, 4656–1

Minerals (nonfuel) foreign and US supply under alternative market conditions, reserves, and background industry data, series, 5606–4

Navy vessels sold to foreign govts, sales prices, fair market value, and Navy costs, for surplus ships sold 1981-82, GAO rpt, 26123–60

Nuclear power and weapons policy, fuel supply/demand, waste disposal and siting, environmental effects of radiation, and public attitudes, 1970s-82 with projections to 2000, 3008–88

Nuclear power plant fuel assembly performance and failures, by fuel vendor for US and some foreign reactors, 1982, annual rpt, 9634–8

Nuclear power plant spent fuel and demand for uranium and enrichment services, for US and non-Communist country groups, 1983 and projected to 2020, annual rpt, 3164–72

OASDHI, Medicaid, SSI, and other social insurance and public welfare programs benefits, beneficiary characteristics, and trust funds, selected years 1937-82, annual rpt, 4744–3.6, 4744–3.9

Overseas Business Reports: economic conditions, investment and export opportunities, and trade practices, annual country market research rpt series, 2046–6

Overseas Business Reports: economic conditions, investment and export opportunities, and trade practices, world region rpt series, 2046–5

Pharmacists employment and sociodemographic characteristics, and reasons for not working in field, by State and overseas, as of 1979, 4147–14.28

Population and housing census, 1980: birthplace and 1975 residence abroad, and population by ancestral origin, by census tract, State and SMSA rpt series, 2551–2

Population demographic data, methodology, and analyses for foreign countries, research rpt series, 2546–10

Foreign countries

R&D Fed Govt funding by type of performer, and funding for industrial dev by type, program, and agency, selected years FY75-85, 26306–6.81

Science Indicators, R&D expenditures, innovations, research, and higher education, with foreign comparisons, 1960s- 83, annual rpt, 9624–10

Smoking related to chronic obstructive lung disease and deaths, by sociodemographic and smoking characteristics, literature review, 1984 annual Surgeon General rpt, 4044–6

Tariff Schedules of US, Annotated, classifications and rates of duty for detailed imported commodities, and codes for ports and foreign countries, 1985 edition, 9886–13

US citizens birthplace abroad, 1980 Census of Population, State rpt series, 2531–4

US govt civil service retirees and survivors, and monthly benefit, for foreign countries, by age and sex, FY81-82, annual rpt, 9844–1.1

US govt civilian employment and payrolls abroad, by agency, monthly rpt, 9842–1

US military draft registrants residing in foreign countries, 2nd half FY84, semiannual rpt, 9742–1

US military personnel abroad, by age, sex, and race, as of July 1982, Current Population Rpt, 2546–3.132

Vaccination requirements for intl travel by country, and disease prevention recommendations, 1984 annual rpt, 4204–11

Vital and Health Statistics series: foreign and US comparisons, analytical studies, 4147–5

see also Africa

see also Asia

see also Caribbean area

see also Central America

see also Communist countries

see also Developing countries

see also Eastern Europe

see also Europe

see also Foreign agriculture

see also Foreign assistance

see also Foreign budgets

see also Foreign corporations

see also Foreign debts

see also Foreign economic relations

see also Foreign exchange

see also Foreign investments

see also Foreign labor conditions

see also Foreign languages

see also Foreign medical graduates

see also Foreign relations

see also Foreign students

see also Foreign trade

see also Foreign trade promotion

see also International cooperation in conservation

see also International cooperation in cultural activities

see also International cooperation in environmental sciences

see also International cooperation in science and technology

see also International finance

see also International military forces

see also International relief

see also International sanctions

Index by Subjects and Names

see also International transactions

see also Middle East

see also North America

see also Oceania

see also South America

see also Southeast Asia

see also under By Foreign Country in the "Index by Categories"

see also under names of individual countries

Foreign currency programs

see Special foreign currency programs

Foreign debts

- AID loan repayment status and terms by program and country, and status of predecessor agency loans, quarterly rpt, 9912–3
- AID loans authorized, signed, and canceled, by country and world area, monthly rpt, 9912–2
- Argentina debt financing, effect on income of 7 US bank holding companies, actual and in event of interest nonpayment, 1st qtr 1984, press release, 9368–77
- Bank and nonbank liabilities to and claims on foreigners, by type and world area, monthly rpt, 9362–1.3
- Banking and nonbanking firms liabilities to and claims on foreigners, by country, 1981-82, annual rpt, 9364–5.10
- Central America socioeconomic and political conditions in 6 countries, 1960s-83 with trends and projections 1930-2010, Commission rpt, 028–19.2
- Claims against foreign govts by US natls, by country and type of claim, 1983, annual rpt, 6004–16
- Cuba economic conditions, agricultural and industrial production and distribution, trade, and intl economic relations, 1970-82 and trends from 1957, 248–40
- Currency (foreign) positions of US firms and foreign branches or affiliates, *Treasury Bulletin,* quarterly rpt, 8002–4.13
- Developing countries (non-OPEC) loans from US banks, debt burden, and other economic indicators, various periods 1977-84 and loan projections to 1990, article, 9362–1.407
- Developing countries economic aid of US, bilateral and through multilateral dev banks and intl agencies, by world area and country, 1970s-FY83, annual rpts, 9904–1
- Developing countries food production and needs, and related economic trends and outlook, for 67 countries, 1980-86, annual rpt, 1524–6.2
- Developing countries receiving US economic aid, total govt and defense expenditures, military imports, GNP, and intl reserves by country, 1976-81, annual rpt, 9914–1
- Developing countries summary socioeconomic data, 1970s-83, and AID activities and funding by project and function, FY82-85, by country, annual rpt, 9914–3
- Eastern Europe and USSR gross and net hard currency debt to western countries, and USSR balance of payments, 1960s-83, annual rpt, 244–5.2, 244–5.3
- Eurocurrency syndicated loans, loan fees, and interest rate spread, by country group and selected country, 1981-83, technical paper, 9366–7.105

Finance (intl) statistics, quarterly chartbook, 9362–2.9

Financial and business statistics, historic trends, 1984 annual chartbook, 9364–2.17

- Foreign military, social, and economic summary data by world area and country, 1960s-80s, hearing, 25388–47.1
- Intl investment position of US, net change by component, investment type, and world region, and for 2 countries, 1982-83, annual article, 2702–1.424
- Loans, debts, exchange rates, and intl reserves, for US and selected countries, various periods 1949-84, conf papers, 9373–3.28
- Loans of large US banks to foreigners at all US and foreign offices, by country group and country, quarterly rpt, 13002–1
- Mexico copper mine expansion in Cananea, loans from US banks, 1983, hearing, 21448–31
- Mexico economic indicators, trade, external accounts and debt, oil industry, and relations with US, 1978-83 with trends from 1959, conf proceedings, 21248–82
- Outstanding debt on US credit, by program, world area, and country, selected years 1940-82, annual rpt, 15344–1.1
- Outstanding debt to US of foreign govts and private obligors, by country and program, periodic rpt, 8002–6
- *Overseas Business Reports:* economic conditions, investment and export opportunities, and trade practices, world region rpt series, 2046–5
- Pacific Basin economic indicators, US and 12 countries, quarterly rpt, 9393–9
- US govt contingent liabilities and claims paid on federally insured and guaranteed contracts with foreign obligors, by country and program, periodic rpt, 8002–12
- US liabilities to foreigners and foreign official instns, *Treasury Bulletin,* quarterly rpt, 8002–4.11

see also International transactions

see also Public debt

Foreign Economic Development Service

see Economic Research Service

Foreign economic relations

- *Background Notes,* foreign countries summary social, political, and economic data, series, 7006–2
- Communist, OECD, and selected other countries economic statistics, 1960s-83, annual rpt, 244–5
- Copyright activities of Register of Copyrights, including intl relations, registrations, fees earned, and royalties collected, FY82, annual rpt, 26404–2
- Cuba economic conditions, agricultural and industrial production and distribution, trade, and intl economic relations, 1970-82 and trends from 1957, 248–40
- Economic indicators and currency exchange rates, by world area and selected country, mid-1960s-83, annual rpt, 204–1.9
- Economic trends in foreign countries and implications for US, annual and semiannual country rpt series, 2046–4
- Helsinki Final Act implementation by NATO, Warsaw Pact, and other signatory nations, Dec 1983-Mar 1984, semiannual rpt, 7002–1

Index by Subjects and Names

Foreign exchange

Mexico economic indicators, trade, external accounts and debt, oil industry, and relations with US, 1978-83 with trends from 1959, conf proceedings, 21248–82

Overseas Business Reports: economic conditions, investment and export opportunities, and trade practices, annual country market research rpt series, 2046–6

Overseas Business Reports: economic conditions, investment and export opportunities, and trade practices, world region rpt series, 2046–5

Research contracts of Bur of Intl Labor Affairs, by project and contractor, FY73-84, annual listing, 6364–1

see also Agricultural exports and imports
see also Arms sales
see also Dumping
see also Foreign assistance
see also Foreign corporations
see also Foreign debts
see also Foreign exchange
see also Foreign investments
see also Foreign trade
see also Foreign trade promotion
see also International finance
see also International transactions
see also Military assistance
see also Multinational corporations
see also Tariffs and foreign trade controls
see also Trade agreements
see also Treaties and conventions

Foreign exchange

Bank and nonbank foreign exchange activity, and foreign exchange turnover in US and 3 foreign markets, Mar 1980 and Apr 1983, article, 9385–1.411

China economic conditions, agricultural and industrial production, trade, and domestic and foreign investment, 1980-85, 2048–106

Communist and and OECD countries economic conditions, 1982, annual rpt, 7144–11

Communist, OECD, and selected other countries economic statistics, 1960s-83, annual rpt, 244–5

Cuba economic conditions, agricultural and industrial production and distribution, trade, and intl economic relations, 1970-82 and trends from 1957, 248–40

Currency (foreign) accounts owned by US under AID admin and by foreign govts with joint AID control, status by program and country, quarterly rpt, 9912–1

Currency (foreign) holdings of US, detailed transactions and balances by program and country, 1st half FY84, semiannual rpt, 8102–7

Currency (foreign) positions of US firms and foreign branches or affiliates, *Treasury Bulletin*, quarterly rpt, 8002–4.13

Currency (foreign) purchases by US with dollars, by country, Oct 1983-Mar 1984, semiannual rpt, 8102–5

Currency (foreign) transactions of US banks, and combined Fed Reserve-Treasury purchases and sales, various periods 1977-83, article, 9391–1.413

Developing countries disaster preparedness and summary sociodemographic, political, and economic data, country rpt series, 9916–2

Developing countries food production and needs, and related economic trends and outlook, for 67 countries, 1980-86, annual rpt, 1524–6.2

Dollar appreciation effects on exports, stocks, and prices of wheat, corn, and soybeans, 1980-82 and for hypothetical 20-year period, 1528–174

Dollar exchange and money rates, for 39 countries, 1982, annual rpt, 9364–5.10

Dollar exchange rate and selected price indexes, US and 4 countries, bimonthly rpt, 2042–11

Dollar exchange rate and US agricultural exports, percent change for 12 countries, 1981-83, article, 9391–1.421

Dollar exchange rate changes, weighted averages, *Treasury Bulletin*, quarterly rpt, 8002–4.11

Dollar exchange rate indexes with Canada, Japan, and 9 West European countries, 1950-82, annual rpt, 6864–1

Dollar exchange rate indexes with 7 OECD countries, quarterly rpt, 2042–10.4

Dollar exchange rate indexes with 10 countries, *Survey of Current Business*, monthly rpt, quarterly tables, 2702–1.31

Dollar exchange rate with German mark, intervention by Fed Reserve, model results, Nov 1978-Oct 1979, technical paper, 9377–9.12

Dollar exchange rate with mark, daily and monthly variability, various periods June 1973-Apr 1984, article, 9381–1.413

Dollar exchange rates, and State Dept indexes of living costs abroad and allowances, by country and major city, quarterly rpt, 6862–1

Dollar exchange rates, general data, *Statistical Abstract of US*, 1983 annual rpt, 2324–1.4

Dollar exchange rates of 5 currencies, average current and 3-month forward rates, 1983, article, 9371–1.413

Dollar exchange rates of 5 OECD countries, bimonthly rpt with articles, 1522–1.1

Dollar exchange rates of 10 major currencies, and trade-weighted value of US dollar, 1967-83, annual rpt, 204–1.9

Dollar exchange rates of 35 countries, monthly rpt, 9362–1.3

Dollar exchange rates of 35 countries, weekly release, 9365–1.5

Dollar exchange rates offered by US disbursing offices, by country, quarterly rpt, 8102–6

Dollar holdings rate of return related to domestic real money stock for 5 OECD countries, regression results, various periods 1966-84, article, 9391–1.418

Dollar spot and forward exchange rates for UK, France, and West Germany, serial correlation analysis, 1973-82, technical paper, 9381–10.31

EC food supply/demand and market and support prices, with exchange rates, fertilizer price index, GDP, and population, by country, 1960-83, 1528–173

Economic and employment indicators, balance of payments, and US exports by selected commodity, by world area and country, 1970s-83, annual rpt, 2044–26

Economic indicators and components, and Fed Reserve 4th District business and financial conditions, monthly chartbook, 9377–10

Economic indicators and trade by country and country group, and US trade policy actions, 1960s-83, annual rpt, 444–1.4

Economic policy and banking practices, Fed Reserve staff study series, 9366–1

Economic, social, and political summary data, by country, 1984, annual factbook, 244–11

Economic trends in foreign countries and implications for US, annual and semiannual country rpt series, 2046–4

Exchange rate changes of US and 10 major trading partners, quarterly rpt, 9391–7

Exchange rate multicountry simulation model, 1983 technical paper, 9387–8.84

Exchange rate uncertainty related to exports and imports of manufactured goods by West Germany and US, regression results, 1974-81, article, 9385–1.405

Exchange rates correlation with price and trade indicators, for 14 countries, 1977-83, article, 9373–1.418

Exchange rates related to domestic/foreign price ratios, correlation analysis using prices and currencies of 4 OECD countries, 1920s-84, technical paper, 9381–10.36

Exchange rates with yen for US and 2 countries, and measures of manufacturing competitiveness, 1983 with 1974-80 and 1979-80 averages, article, 9385–1.404

Exchange Stabilization Fund balance sheet and income and expenses, *Treasury Bulletin*, quarterly rpt, 8002–4.14

Exports and imports, intl position of US and 4 OECD countries, and factors affecting US competition, quarterly pamphlet, 2042–25

Fed Govt programs and mgmt cost control proposals, 3-year savings by function and agency, and financial and operating data, 1960s-81, 16908–1.10, 16908–1.37

Finance (intl) and financial policy, and external factors affecting US economy, technical paper series, 9366–7

Finance (intl) and financial policy, external factors affecting US economy, econometric model methodology and results for US and 4 countries, various periods 1964-75, 9368–78

Finance (intl), loans, debts, exchange rates, and intl reserves, for US and selected countries, various periods 1949-84, conf papers, 9373–3.28

Finance (intl) statistics, quarterly chartbook, 9362–2.10

Financial and business statistics, historic trends, 1984 annual chartbook, 9364–2.17

Flow-of-funds accounts, assets and liabilities by type and economic sector, year-end outstandings, 1960-83, annual rpt, 9364–3

Flow-of-funds accounts savings, investments, and credit statements, quarterly rpt, 9365–3.3

Forward exchange and interest rate term structure effect on Eurocurrency asset pricing for 2 currencies, various periods 1973-84, technical paper, 9381–10.40

Futures trading in selected commodities, foreign currencies, and stock indexes, Chicago and other markets activity, monthly rpt, 11922–1

Foreign exchange

Futures trading in selected commodities, foreign currencies, Treasury securities, and stock indexes, NYC, Chicago, and other markets activity, monthly rpt, 11922–5

Futures trading in selected foreign currencies on Chicago Intl Monetary Market, total and as percent of interbank transfers and foreign trade volume, various periods 1977-83, article, 9375–1.401

Futures trading summary data by type of investment, and Commodity Futures Trading Commission activities, funding, and employment, FY83, annual rpt, 11924–2

Investment (intl) position of US, net change by component, investment type, and world region, and for 2 countries, 1982-83, annual article, 2702–1.424

Jamaica PL 480 Title I assistance effects on economic dev, with data on govt finance, economic indicators, demography, and dev programs, 1970s-81, 9916–1.51

Japan yen/dollar exchange rate, 2-country model of sterilized intervention and effect of fiscal balance and private savings, 1973-82, article, 9393–8.405

Massachusetts (Colonial era) prices, foreign exchange rate, and per capita money supply, and compared to other New England colonies, 1720-70, article, 9383–6.402

Mexico border employment in US-owned plants and peso devaluation, related to employment in 4 Texas SMSAs, 1978-83, article, 9379–1.402

Mexico economic indicators, trade, external accounts and debt, oil industry, and relations with US, 1978-83 with trends from 1959, conf proceedings, 21248–82

Monetary control policy of US and selected West European countries, and relation to credit, exchange rates, GNP, and other indicators, various periods 1960-82, conf papers, 9373–3.26

OECD crude oil consumption related to prices, conservation, and real dollar exchange rates, for 7 countries, various periods 1975-83, article, 9379–1.405

Overseas Private Investment Corp activities, foreign and US project impacts, and list of insured projects and companies, FY83, annual rpt, 9904–3

Pacific Basin economic indicators, US and 12 countries, quarterly rpt, 9393–9

Risk premium in foreign exchange markets, model description, 1983 technical paper, 9381–10.32

Treasury and Fed Reserve foreign exchange operations, final and interim rpts, *Fed Reserve Bulletin,* monthly rpt, quarterly article, 9362–1

Treasury and Fed Reserve foreign exchange operations, semiannual article, 9385–1

UK economic indicator performance under Thatcher govt, with OECD comparisons, 1970-1983/84, article, 9391–1.414

see also Eurocurrency

see also International transactions

Foreign investments

Banking and nonbanking firms liabilities to and claims on foreigners, by country, 1981-82, annual rpt, 9364–5.10

Business America, foreign and domestic commerce, and US investment and trade opportunities, biweekly rpt articles, 2042–24

Business and financial statistics, historic trends, 1984 annual chartbook, 9364–2.17

Capital expenditures of multinatl US firms foreign affiliates, by major industry group and country, 1977-85, semiannual article, 2702–1.437

Capital expenditures of multinatl US firms foreign affiliates, by major industry group and country, 1978-84, semiannual article, 2702–1.410

Capital movements among countries, effect on economic stability and monetary policy, 2-country simulation model, 1983 technical paper, 9387–8.85

China economic and business investment conditions, trade practices, and trade with US by detailed commodity, 1978-82, 2048–72

China economic conditions, agricultural and industrial production, trade, and domestic and foreign investment, 1980-85, 2048–106

Corporate and govt securities of US, foreign transactions, monthly rpt, 9362–1.3

Currency (foreign) positions of US firms and foreign branches or affiliates, *Treasury Bulletin,* quarterly rpt, 8002–4.13

Developing countries free zones, industry financial and operating data by country, with case studies for 5 countries, 1970s-82, 9918–10

Direct foreign investment in and by US, by industry group and for selected countries and world regions, 1977 and 1980, article, 9373–1.411

Direct foreign investment in US by country, and finances, operations, and land owned, by industry group for businesses acquired and established, 1982-83, annual article, 2702–1.418

Direct foreign investment in US, by major industry group, world area, and selected country, 1980-83, annual article, 2702–1.439

Direct foreign investment in US, major investors and investments by SIC 4-digit industry, transaction type and value, and location, 1983, annual rpt, 2044–20

Direct foreign investment in US, US investment abroad, and net position, 1974-82, annual rpt, 2044–26

Direct foreign investment, net capital flows, for 7 OECD countries and US, quarterly rpt, 2042–10.4

Direct foreign investment of US, by selected major industry group and world area, 1982-83, annual article, 2702–1.430

Direct foreign investment of US, by world area and country, 1977-83, article, 2702–1.442

Direct foreign investment worldwide, and US investment flows by major industry, by world region and country, 1982 and trends from 1950, annual rpt, 2044–25

Economic trends and projections, 1970s-83, and Budget of US under current fiscal policy and alternatives, FY85-89, annual rpt, 26304–3.1

Energy producers finances and operations, by energy type for US firms domestic and foreign operations, 1974-82, annual rpt, 3164–44

Eurodollar bond market issues of US corporations, and amount raised and savings relative to domestic market, by company, 1975-82, hearing, 25368–132

Index by Subjects and Names

Exports and imports, intl position of US and 4 OECD countries, and factors affecting US competition, quarterly pamphlet, 2042–25

Farmland (US) owned by foreigners, acquisitions, dispositions, holdings, and use, by State and type and country of owner, 1983, annual rpt, 1584–2

Farmland (US) owned by foreigners, acreage, value, and use, by State and county, and for 5 leading investor countries, 1983, annual rpt, 1584–3

Farmland acquisitions of foreigners, by State and county, before 1980 and during 1980-82, 1588–77

Finance (intl) statistics, quarterly chartbook, 9362–2.9

Flow-of-funds accounts, assets and liabilities by type and economic sector, year-end outstandings, 1960-83, annual rpt, 9364–3

Flow-of-funds accounts savings, investments, and credit statements, quarterly rpt, 9365–3.3

Income on US investments abroad and foreign investments in US, *Business Conditions Digest,* historical supplement and methodology, 1947-82, 2708–31

Income on US investments abroad and foreign investments in US, *Business Conditions Digest,* monthly rpt, 2702–3.9

Income tax returns filed by type of filer, selected income items, summary data, quarterly rpt, 8302–2.1

Income tax returns of corporations, detailed income and tax items by industry, 1981, annual rpt, 8304–4

Income tax returns of corporations with foreign tax credit, income and deductions by type, asset size, and selected industry group, 1980, article, 8302–2.415

Income tax returns of individuals, by filing and deduction characteristics and income level, 1983, annual article, 8302–2.414

Income tax returns of individuals, detailed data, 1982, annual rpt, 8304–2

Intl finance, loans, debts, exchange rates, and intl reserves, for US and selected countries, various periods 1949-84, conf papers, 9373–3.28

Intl investment position, and service industry trade balance and agreements, for US and foreign countries, various periods 1970-82, 448–1

Intl investment position of US, US assets abroad and foreign assets in US, 1970-82, annual rpt, 204–1.9

Investment (intl) position of US, net change by component, investment type, and world region, and for 2 countries, 1982-83, annual article, 2702–1.424

Jamaica PL 480 Title I assistance effects on economic dev, with data on govt finance, economic indicators, demography, and dev programs, 1970s-81, 9916–1.51

Liabilities (contigent) and claims paid by Fed Govt on federally insured and guaranteed contracts with foreign obligors, by country and program, periodic rpt, 8002–12

Minerals industries direct foreign investment of US, 1978-81, *Minerals Yearbook,* annual rpt, 5604–35.1

Index by Subjects and Names

Foreign labor conditions

Natl income and product, comprehensive accounts and components, *Survey of Current Business,* monthly rpt, monthly and annual tables, 2702–1.25

Oil sources of US, foreign direct investment of OPEC and other countries, 1974-82, annual rpt, 3024–2

OPEC direct investment in US, major direct investors and investments, by country and SIC 2- to 3-digit industry, annual listing, suspended, 2044–23

Overseas Business Reports: economic conditions, investment and export opportunities, and trade practices, annual country market research rpt series, 2046–6

Overseas Business Reports: economic conditions, investment and export opportunities, and trade practices, world region rpt series, 2046–5

Overseas Private Investment Corp activities, foreign and US project impacts, and list of insured projects and companies, FY83, annual rpt, 9904–3

Overseas Private Investment Corp programs and finances, with list of insured projects and companies, FY83, annual rpt, 9904–2

Research contracts of Bur of Intl Labor Affairs, by project and contractor, FY73-84, annual listing, 6364–1

Tax evasion through nonresidents bank claims and deposits, direct investments, income payments, and other transactions in 5 Caribbean countries, 1978-82, 8008–106

Tax expenditures, Fed Govt revenues foregone through income tax deductions and exclusions by type, and effect of Deficit Reduction Act, FY84-89, annual rpt, 21784–10

Trust assets of banks and trust companies, by type of asset and fund and State, 1983, annual rpt, 13004–1

see also Expropriation

see also Foreign corporations

see also International transactions

see also Multinational corporations

Foreign labor conditions

Agricultural supply/demand, trade, and production, and socioeconomic data, by country, 1950s-77, 1528–179

Australia and US youth unemployment rates, by sex and age, Mar 1983 and trends from 1960s, article, 6722–1.462

Central America socioeconomic and political conditions in 6 countries, 1960s-83 with trends and projections 1930-2010, Commission rpt, 028–19.2

China economic and business investment conditions, trade practices, and trade with US by detailed commodity, 1978-82, 2048–72

Communist, OECD, and selected other countries economic statistics, 1960s-83, annual rpt, 244–5.2

Computers and computer equipment foreign market and trade, and user industry operations and demand, country market research rpts, 2045–1

Cooperative labor-mgmt experiments in US with comparisons to other countries, 1800s-1940s, narrative article, 6722–1.433

Copper production, production costs, prices, wages, and productivity, for US and 3 countries, 1970s-83 and projected to 1989, 21368–55

Cuba economic conditions, agricultural and industrial production and distribution, trade, and intl economic relations, 1970-82 and trends from 1957, 248–40

Developing countries free zones, industry financial and operating data by country, with case studies for 5 countries, 1970s-82, 9918–10

Developing countries govt policy, and AID and other foreign assistance, effects on private sector dev and socioeconomic conditions, with case studies for 6 countries, 1960s-80, 9918–12

Developing countries PL 480 Title I funding and socioeconomic impacts, with case studies for 5 countries, 1950s- 81, 9918–13

Economic and monetary trends, compounded annual rates of change for US and 10 major trading partners, quarterly rpt, 9391–7

Economic indicators and currency exchange rates, by world area and selected country, mid-1960s-83, annual rpt, 204–1.9

Economic indicators and trade by country and country group, and US trade policy actions, 1960s-83, annual rpt, 444–1.4

Economic indicators for 7 OECD countries and US, quarterly rpt, 2042–10.5

Economic, social, and political summary data, by country, 1984, annual factbook, 244–11

Economic trends in foreign countries and implications for US, annual and semiannual country rpt series, 2046–4

Electronic component equipment foreign market and trade, and user industry operations and demand, country market research rpts, 2045–4

Electronic component manufacturing equipment foreign market and trade, and user industry operations and demand, country market research rpts, 2045–5

Employee stock ownership plans in developing countries, and firms finances and operations, with case studies of US and 3 countries, 1970s-82, 9916–3.19

Employment and economic indicators, foreign and US, 1970s-83, annual rpt, 2044–26

Employment and unemployment current statistics and articles, Monthly Labor Review, 6722–1

Employment, labor force, and participation and unemployment rates by sex, in US and 9 OECD countries, various periods 1970-3rd qtr 1983, annual article, 6722–1.404

Farm machinery and equipment foreign market and trade, and user industry operations and demand, country market research rpts, 2045–13

Food processing and packaging equipment, foreign market and trade, and user industry operations and demand, country market research rpts, 2045–11

France Brittany coast oil spill cleanup and research costs, marine and tourism industry losses, and recreation losses of tourists and residents, 1971-79, 2178–13

Graphic industries equipment foreign market and trade, and user industry operations and demand, country market research rpts, 2045–3

Industrial process control equipment foreign market and trade, and user industry operations and demand, country market research rpts, 2045–6

Jamaica PL 480 Title I assistance effects on economic dev, with data on govt finance, economic indicators, demography, and dev programs, 1970s-81, 9916–1.51

Japan unemployment rates, official and adjusted to US concepts, with alternative measures for US and Japan, 1970s-82, article, 6722–1.418

Japan worker earnings, by years of service and other characteristics, selected years 1955-80, article, 6722–1.427

Japan workers wages in smaller firms relative to wages in larger firms, by worker characteristics, firm size, and industry div, 1950s-81, article, 6722–1.461

Lab instruments foreign market and trade, and user industry operations and demand, country market research rpts, 2045–10

Labor force output and earnings, price indexes, and work stoppages, by selected country, 1950-82, annual rpt, 6724–1.10

Manufacturing competitiveness measures, and exchange rates with yen for US and 2 countries, 1983 with 1974-80 and 1979-80 averages, article, 9385–1.404

Manufacturing computerized automation dev, R&D, training, and employment impacts, with comparisons to foreign countries, selected years 1960-83, 26358–105

Manufacturing labor productivity and cost indexes for US and 11 OECD countries, 1960-82, annual article, 6722–1.405

Manufacturing productivity and unit labor cost indexes for US and 11 countries, 1950-82 and preliminary 1983, annual rpt, 6864–1

Manufacturing wage growth in US and 2 countries, regression results, 1963-81, technical paper, 9381–10.34

Manufacturing wage rates in US and 2 countries, by industry, 1975 and 1980, hearing, 21248–79

Manufacturing wage/price and wage/output adjustment in 6 OECD countries, 1960-81, technical paper, 9381–10.33

Medical and health care equipment foreign market and trade, and user industry operations and demand, country market research rpts, 2045–2

Mexico border employment in US-owned plants and peso devaluation, related to employment in 4 Texas SMSAs, 1978-83, article, 9379–1.402

Mexico economic indicators, trade, external accounts and debt, oil industry, and relations with US, 1978-83 with trends from 1959, conf proceedings, 21248–82

Minerals (strategic) supply/demand, trade, and foreign and US industry devs by firm and country, by commodity, bimonthly rpt, 5602–4

Minerals production, reserves, and industry role in domestic economy and world supply, country and world region rpt series, 5606–1

Foreign labor conditions

OECD economic indicators, for US and 6 countries, biweekly rpt, 242–4

- Older persons characteristics, with related health care data and vital statistics, by world area and selected country, 1950-80 and projected to 2020, 2546–10.12
- *Overseas Business Reports:* economic conditions, investment and export opportunities, and trade practices, annual country market research rpt series, 2046–6
- *Overseas Business Reports:* economic conditions, investment and export opportunities, and trade practices, world region rpt series, 2046–5
- Overseas Private Investment Corp activities, foreign and US project impacts, and list of insured projects and companies, FY83, annual rpt, 9904–3
- R&D expenditures and employment in science and technology, for US and 4 countries, selected years 1953-84, annual rpt, 9624–18.1
- Research contracts of Bur of Intl Labor Affairs, by project and contractor, FY73-84, annual listing, 6364–1
- *Science Indicators,* R&D expenditures, innovations, research, and higher education, with foreign comparisons, 1960s- 83, annual rpt, 9624–10.1
- Services intl transactions, and operations of US multinatl service firms and foreign affiliates, by industry and world region, 1977-82, 2706–5.30
- Telecommunication equipment foreign market and trade, and user industry operations and demand, country market research rpts, 2045–12
- UK economic indicator performance under Thatcher govt, with OECD comparisons, 1970-1983/84, article, 9391–1.414
- Uranium ore tailings at active mills, EPA radon and radionuclide emmission standards and US and foreign exposure and health effects, various periods 1957-83, hearings, 21208–17
- US Govt civilian employment abroad, by US citizenship, selected agency, and country, 1982, biennial rpt, 9844–8
- Women sociodemographic, economic, and fertility characteristics, with comparisons to men, by country, 1960s-85, world region rpt series, 2326–15
- Worker participation in mgmt decisions, experience in US and 2 countries, 1983 narrative article, 6722–1.457

Foreign languages

- Census of Population, 1980: detailed socioeconomic and demographic characteristics, by age, sex, race, Hispanic origin, occupation, and industry, State rpt series, 2531–4
- Census of Population, 1980: detailed socioeconomic characteristics, by county, city, and inside-outside SMSAs and central cities, State rpt series, 2531–3
- Degrees conferred in higher education, by race, Hispanic origin, sex, level, and field, selected years 1949/50-1979/80, annual rpt, 4824–2.16
- Developing countries disaster preparedness and summary sociodemographic, political, and economic data, country rpt series, 9916–2

Florida and California elderly migration by selected State of origin or destination, and Florida elderly, by sociodemographic and housing characteristics, 1970 and 1980, 4478–150

- Foreign economic, social, and political summary data, by country, 1984, annual factbook, 244–11
- Health care services for elderly, knowledge, use, and factors affecting service quality, by race and Hispanic origin, 1984 article, 4652–1.406
- High school class of 1982: foreign language course enrollment, by language, student and school characteristics, and location, 1984 rpt, 4838–11
- High school class of 1982: foreign language coursework, by language, course level, student and school characteristics, and location, 1984 rpt, 4828–17
- High school classes of 1980 and 1982: educational and sociodemographic characteristics and expectations, natl longitudinal study, series, 4826–2
- High school enrollment in foreign language classes, by language, 1965-78, annual rpt, 4824–2.7
- Hispanic Americans socioeconomic and demographic characteristics, and compared to non-Hispanics, selected years 1970-83, chartbook, 2328–48
- Japan-US Friendship Commission educational and cultural exchange activities, grants, and trust fund status, FY83, annual rpt, 14694–1
- Minority language population (Spanish and other), and children with limited English proficiency, by State, 1980, biennial rpt, 4804–14
- Minority-language population under and over 18 years old, by State, Apr 1980, annual rpt, 4824–1
- Radio weather broadcasts for US ships by major ocean area, foreign language broadcasts where English unavailable, as of Jan 1984, biennial rpt, 2184–3
- Refugee resettlement program activities and funding, arrivals and population by country of origin and State, and employment and other characteristics, FY83, annual rpt, 4704–8
- *Statistical Abstract of US,* social, political, and economic data, 1950s-83 and trends, annual rpt, 2324–1.1
- Vocational training bilingual projects, participants, characteristics, and costs, by program, FY82, annual rpt, 4804–26

Foreign loans

see Export-Import Bank

see Foreign assistance

see Military assistance

Foreign medical graduates

- Developing countries disaster preparedness and summary sociodemographic, political, and economic data, country rpt series, 9916–2
- Developing countries population/physician ratios, by country, 1970s, annual rpt, 9914–3
- DOD physicians, by pay grade, citizenship, and service branch, FY83, annual rpt, 3544–24.5
- Foreign military, social, and economic summary data by world area and country, 1960s-80s, hearing, 25388–47.1

Index by Subjects and Names

- Health care resources, use, and per capita public expenditures, and selected population characteristics, for US and 6 countries, selected years 1975-81, 21148–33
- Health professionals supply and education, by occupation, demographic and professional characteristics, and location, 1950s-83 and projected to 2000, biennial rpt, 4114–8
- Prison physicians by sociodemographic, employment, and professional characteristics, and compared to all physicians, 1979, article, 4102–1.407
- Psychiatry residencies as percent of all residencies and percent foreign medical graduates, 1961-81, annual rpt, 4504–9.4

Foreign military sales

see Arms sales

see Military assistance

Foreign relations

- *Background Notes,* foreign countries summary social, political, and economic data, series, 7006–2
- Budget of US Appendix, detailed budgets and personnel summaries, by agency, FY85, annual rpt, 104–3
- Budget of US, compact budgets by function, agency, and account, FY85 with projections to FY89, annual rpt, 104–2
- Budget of US, receipts by source and outlays by function, FY40-89 estimates revised for consistency with FY85 budget definitions, annual rpt, 104–12
- Budget of US, receipts, outlays, and budget authority, by function and agency, FY84-89 revised estimates, midsession review of FY85 budget, annual rpt, 104–7
- Budget of US, receipts, outlays, and budget authority, by function and agency, 1st revision of FY85 budget, annual rpt, 104–17
- Central America socioeconomic and political conditions in 6 countries, 1960s-83 with trends and projections 1930-2010, 028–19
- Economic and military assistance role in US foreign policy, with aid proposals by world region, FY85 with trends from FY74, 7008–38
- Fed Govt consolidated financial statements based on business accounting methods, FY82-83, annual rpt, 8104–5
- Helsinki Final Act implementation by NATO, Warsaw Pact, and other signatory nations, Dec 1983-Mar 1984, semiannual rpt, 7002–1
- Soviet Union-US relations, and summary military, social, and economic data by country and world region, 1960s-80s, hearing, 25388–47
- USIA activities, employment, and funding, FY83-84, annual rpt, 17594–1
- *see also* Arms sales
- *see also* Diplomatic and consular service
- *see also* Educational exchanges
- *see also* Exchange of persons programs
- *see also* Executive agreements
- *see also* Food assistance
- *see also* Foreign assistance
- *see also* Foreign countries
- *see also* Foreign debts
- *see also* Foreign economic relations

see also Foreign students
see also Foreign trade
see also Foreign trade promotion
see also International cooperation in conservation
see also International cooperation in cultural activities
see also International cooperation in environmental sciences
see also International cooperation in science and technology
see also Military assistance
see also Treaties and conventions
see also War

Foreign Service

see Diplomatic and consular service

Foreign Service Retirement and Disability Fund

Benefits, and beneficiaries with representative payees by age and relation to payee, by Fed Govt cash program, as of 1983, GAO rpt, 26121–85

Cost control proposals for Fed Govt programs and mgmt, 3-year savings by function and agency, and financial and operating data, 1960s-81, 16908–1.10

Foreign students

Digest of Education Statistics, detailed data on students, staff, finances, and facilities, 1982 and selected trends, annual rpt, 4824–2

Education Dept programs fraud and abuse, audits and investigations, 2nd half FY84, semiannual rpt, 4802–1

Education statistics summary compilation, 1980/81-1982/83 with selected trends from 1869, biennial rpt, 4804–27

Foreign visitors and other nonimmigrants admitted to US, by country of last residence, FY81, annual rpt, 6264–2

Health professionals supply and education, by occupation, demographic and professional characteristics, and location, 1950s-83 and projected to 2000, biennial rpt, 4114–8

Higher education enrollment, by student characteristics, instn type, State, and for 150 instns, fall 1982, annual rpt, 4844–2

Higher education enrollment of non-resident aliens, full- and part-time teaching staff, and average undergrad tuition, by instn type, selected years 1970/71-1992/93, annual rpt, 4824–1.2

Inter-American Foundation activities, grants, and fellowships, by country, FY83, annual rpt, 14424–1

Latin America students in US and Soviet bloc training programs, by program type and student country, and summary by world region, selected years 1972-82, GAO rpt, 26123–77

Military training of US for foreign govts, students, costs, and revenue losses from reduced tuition by country, by service branch, FY79-83, GAO rpt, 26123–56

Nuclear engineering student enrollments and degrees granted, by State, instn, and subfield, and placements by sector, 1983, annual rpt, 3004–5

Radiation protection and health physics enrollments and degrees granted by State and instn, and grads employment, 1983, annual rpt, 3004–7

Science and engineering doctoral degree recipients, by field, sex, race, age,

citizenship, postgrad employment and study status, State, and instn, 1960-82, 9626–6.16

Science and engineering doctoral degrees of women and foreign students, and median years to degree attainment by sex, 1983 with trends from 1960, 9626–2.144

Science and engineering grad enrollment, fields of study, financial support, and other student and instn characteristics, 1975-82, annual survey, 9627–7

Science and engineering grad program enrollment by field, sources of financial support, and foreign students, 1975-82, 9626–2.141

Science and engineering grad students, by field, type of financial aid, sex, race, Hispanic origin, and citizenship, 1972-83, biennial rpt, 9627–24.3

Science Indicators, R&D expenditures, innovations, research, and higher education, with foreign comparisons, 1960s- 83, annual rpt, 9624–10

Travel to US, by characteristics of visit and traveler, country, and State of destination, quarterly rpt, 2902–1

Visas issued and refused to immigrants and nonimmigrants, and status adjustments, by class and nationality, FY77, annual rpt, 7184–1

see also Foreign medical graduates

Foreign trade

Airborne exports and imports of US, by world area and US customs district and city, monthly rpt, 2422–8

Background Notes, foreign countries summary social, political, and economic data, series, 7006–2

Business America, foreign and domestic commerce, and US investment and trade opportunities, biweekly rpt articles, 2042–24

Business statistics, detailed data for major industries and economic indicators, *Survey of Current Business,* monthly rpt, 2702–1

Census Bur publications data coverage and availability, 1984 annual listing, 2304–2

Central America socioeconomic and political conditions in 6 countries, 1960s-83 with trends and projections 1930-2010, Commission rpt, 028–19.2

China economic conditions, agricultural and industrial production, trade, and domestic and foreign investment, 1980-85, 2048–106

China exports and imports, by commodity, world area, and country, quarterly rpt, 242–6

China exports and imports by SITC 1- to 5-digit commodity, 1970s-82, annual rpt, 244–12

Classification codes for countries for Census Bur foreign trade statistics, revisions to 1981 base edition, 2428–3

Communist and and OECD countries economic conditions, 1982, annual rpt, 7144–11

Communist country trade with US, by detailed commodity and country, quarterly rpt with articles, 9882–2

Communist, OECD, and selected other countries trade value and direction, 1960s-83, annual rpt, 244–5.4

Containerized cargo carried over principal trade routes, by flag of vessel, port, and US coastal district, 1982, annual rpt, 7704–8

County Business Patterns: establishments, employees, and payrolls, by SIC 4-digit industry and county, 1982, annual State rpt series, 2326–6

Cuba economic conditions, agricultural and industrial production and distribution, trade, and intl economic relations, 1970-82 and trends from 1957, 248–40

Developing countries disaster preparedness and summary sociodemographic, political, and economic data, country rpt series, 9916–2

Developing countries food production and needs, and related economic trends and outlook, for 67 countries, 1980-86, annual rpt, 1524–6.2

Developing countries govt policy, and AID and other foreign assistance, effects on private sector dev and socioeconomic conditions, with case studies for 6 countries, 1960s-80, 9918–12

Developing countries receiving US economic aid, total govt and defense expenditures, military imports, GNP, and intl reserves by country, 1976-81, annual rpt, 9914–1

Developing countries summary socioeconomic data, 1970s-83, and AID activities and funding by project and function, FY82-85, by country, annual rpt, 9914–3

EC trade with US by country, and total agricultural and nonagricultural trade, selected years 1958-83, annual rpt, 7144–7

Economic conditions and employment, alternative BLS projections to 1995 with selected trends for 1959-82, 6728–29

Economic indicators and components, and Fed Reserve 4th District business and financial conditions, monthly chartbook, 9377–10

Economic indicators and components, current data and annual trends, monthly rpt, 23842–1.7

Economic indicators and labor force characteristics, selected years 1880-1995, chartbook, 6728–30

Economic, social, and political summary data, by country, 1984, annual factbook, 244–11

Economic trends in foreign countries and implications for US, annual and semiannual country rpt series, 2046–4

Europe (Western) trade with US, and US market share and export opportunities for selected commodities, by country, 1982-84, 2048–105

Export licensing and monitoring activities under Export Admin Act, for selected commodities, and for Communist and other countries, FY83, annual rpt, 2044–22

Exports and export-related US employment generated by Overseas Private Investment Corp projects, FY83, annual rpt, 9904–3

Exports and imports, agreement devs, US trade relations, and USITC investigations, 1983, annual rpt, 9884–5

Exports and imports, and indexes of export prices, dollar exchange, and US and foreign industrial production, annual rpt, discontinued, 2044–17

Foreign trade

Exports and imports, *Business Conditions Digest,* historical supplement and methodology, 1947-82, 2708–31

Exports and imports, *Business Conditions Digest,* monthly rpt, 2702–3.5

- Exports and imports of manufactured goods by West Germany and US related to exchange rate uncertainty, regression results, 1974-81, article, 9385–1.405
- Exports and imports of US and selected foreign countries, various years 1946-83, annual rpt, 204–1.9
- Exports and imports of US, and trade balance, by major commodity group, selected country, and world area, with seasonal adjustments, monthly rpt, 2422–6
- Exports and imports of US, by commodity group, world area, selected country, US coastal area and port, and mode of transport, with seasonal adjustments, monthly rpt, 2422–9
- Exports and imports of US by country, and trade shifts by commodity, USITC quarterly monitoring rpt, 9882–9
- Exports and imports of US, detailed SIC-based commodities by world area, 1983, annual rpts, 2424–6
- Exports and imports of US, price indexes by selected commodity groups, 1975-82, annual rpt, 6724–1.7
- Exports and imports of US, totals and as percent of domestic production, by SIC 2- to 5-digit commodity, 1981, annual rpt, 2424–3
- Exports, imports, and economic indicators by country and country group, and US trade policy actions, 1960s-83, annual rpt, 444–1
- Exports, imports, and tariffs, USITC investigation publications issued, 1960-83, annual listing, 9884–12
- Exports, imports, and tariffs, USITC investigations, publications, and other activities, FY83, annual rpt, 9884–1
- Exports, imports, and trade balances, monthly rpt, 9362–1.3
- Exports of manufactured and agricultural commodities, manufacturing production, and export-related employment, 1960s-82, State rpt series, 2046–3
- Exports of US by selected commodity, and foreign and US economic and employment indicators and balance of payments, by world area and country, 1970s-83, annual rpt, 2044–26
- Exports of US, detailed commodities by country of destination, monthly rpt, 2422–3
- Exports of US, detailed Schedule B commodities by country of destination, 1983, annual rpt, 2424–9
- Exports of US, detailed Schedule E commodities by mode of transport and world area and country of destination, 1983, annual rpts, 2424–5
- FDA-detained imports, by product, shipper or manufacturer, country, and detention reasons, monthly listing, 4062–2
- Fed Govt foreign cargo shipments and costs by agency or program and route, and employment and economic impacts of US vessel preference, 1980, GAO rpt, 26117–30

Fed Govt trade policy, with data on US industry foreign trade and revenues, and Japan semiconductor industry subsidies, 1970s-83, hearings, 21368–46

- Finance (intl) and financial policy, and external factors affecting US economy, technical paper series, 9366–7
- Finance (intl) and financial policy, external factors affecting US economy, econometric model methodology and results for US and 4 countries, various periods 1964-75, 9368–78
- Finance (intl) statistics, quarterly chartbook, 9362–2.9
- Financial and business statistics, historic trends, 1984 annual chartbook, 9364–2.17
- Forecasts for selected business activities and natl economic indicators, compilation of representative opinions, 1984, annual rpt, 9389–3
- Foreign economic indicators for 7 OECD countries and US, quarterly rpt, 2042–10
- Foreign exchange rates correlation with price and trade indicators, for 14 countries, 1977-83, article, 9373–1.418
- Foreign exchange rates for currencies of US and 2 countries with yen, and measures of manufacturing competitiveness, 1983 with 1974-80 and 1979-80 averages, article, 9385–1.404
- Foreign firms US affiliates financial and operating data, by country of parent firm and industry div, 1980-81, article, 2702–1.402
- Foreign trade balance of US, by commodity group, FY80-83, annual rpt, 26304–3.1
- Generalized System of Preferences status of 29 commodities, with US production, consumption, tariffs, and trade by country, selected years 1978-87, 9888–17
- Great Lakes trade, by SITC 3-digit commodity, port, vessel type, world area, and country, 1982, annual rpt, 7744–3
- Import and tariff provisions effect on US industries and products, investigations with background financial and operating data, series, 9886–4
- Import quotas and imports for selected commodities, by country of origin, monthly rpt, 8146–1
- Import quotas and tariffs, jobs protected and cost per job for selected products, and foreign trade balance by industry div, various periods 1958-81, article, 9381–1.412
- Imports from Communist countries, injury to US industries, investigations with background financial and operating data, selected industries and products, series, 9886–12
- Imports injury to US industries from foreign subsidized products, investigations with background financial and operating data for selected industries and products, series, 9886–15
- Imports injury to US industries from import sales at less than fair value, investigations with background financial and operating data, series, 9886–14
- Imports injury to US industries from increased import sales, investigations with background financial and operating data, series, 9886–5

Index by Subjects and Names

- Imports injury to US industries from removal of duties on foreign subsidized products, investigations with background financial and operating data, series, 9886–18
- Imports of US, detailed Schedule A commodities by country and world area of origin, and mode of transport, 1983, annual rpts, 2424–2
- Imports of US, detailed Schedule A commodities by country, monthly rpt, 2422–2
- Imports of US, detailed TSUSA commodities by country of origin, 1983, annual rpt, 2424–4
- Imports of US given duty-free treatment for value of US materials or parts sent abroad for processing or assembly, by country and commodity, 1979-82, biennial rpt, 9884–14
- Industrial policy dev, economic growth, and labor productivity, 1950s-81 with projections to 1986, 26306–6.69
- Industry finances and operations, by SIC 2- to 4-digit industry, 1970s-83 and projected to 1988, annual rpt, 2014–4
- Input-output structure of US economy, detailed interindustry transactions for 85 industries, and components of final demand, 1977, article, 2702–1.421
- Input-output structure of US economy, detailed interindustry transactions for 537 industries, and components of final demand, 1977 benchmark data, 2708–17
- Intl trade position of US and 4 OECD countries, and factors affecting US competition, quarterly pamphlet, 2042–25
- Jamaica PL 480 Title I assistance effects on economic dev, with data on govt finance, economic indicators, demography, and dev programs, 1970s-81, 9916–1.51
- Manufactured and total exports and imports of US, relative contributions of labor by type and capital to trade balance, selected years 1958-80, technical paper, 9381–10.30
- Manufacturing operating and financial data, 1980-81 Annual Survey of Manufactures rpt reprints, hardbound vol, 2504–1
- Mexico and Brazil Eximbank loan guarantees and insurance currently provided and needed, and value of worldwide and US trade, 1981-84, hearings, 25248–97
- Mexico economic indicators, trade, external accounts and debt, oil industry, and relations with US, 1978-83 with trends from 1959, conf proceedings, 21248–82
- Natl income and product, comprehensive accounts and components, *Survey of Current Business,* monthly rpt, 2702–1.21
- Natl income and product, comprehensive accounts and components, *Survey of Current Business,* monthly rpt, monthly and annual tables, 2702–1.25
- NATO countries trade with Council for Mutual Economic Assistance Europe members, by country, 1980-83, annual rpt, 7144–5
- NATO countries trade with PRC, by country, 1983, annual rpt, 7144–14
- OECD economic indicators, for US and 6 countries, biweekly rpt, 242–4

Index by Subjects and Names

OECD non-NATO countries trade with Europe Council for Mutual Economic Assistance members, annual rpt, discontinued, 7144–6

OECD non-NATO countries trade with PRC, annual rpt, discontinued, 7144–15

OECD trade, by country, 1983, annual rpt, 7144–10

OECD trade, total and for 4 major countries, and US trade by country, by commodity, 1972-82, annual world region rpt series, 244–13

Overseas Business Reports: economic conditions, investment and export opportunities, and trade practices, annual country market research rpt series, 2046–6

Overseas Business Reports: economic conditions, investment and export opportunities, and trade practices, world region rpt series, 2046–5

Pacific Basin economic indicators, US and 12 countries, quarterly rpt, 9393–9

Panama Canal commerce, by commodity, flag of vessel, and trade routes, FY82, annual rpt, 9664–3.2

Price indexes (export and import) for selected commodities, 1st half 1984, semiannual article, 6722–1.459

Price indexes for consumer and producer goods, major commodities, exports, imports, nonfarm wages, and currency value, US and 4 countries, bimonthly rpt, 2042–11

Price indexes for exports and imports of selected commodities, 1983, semiannual article, 6722–1.424

Price indexes for food and manufactured exports and imports, quarterly press release, 6762–13

Puerto Rico and US possessions, trade with US, by detailed commodity and mode of transport, monthly rpt, 2422–4

Research contracts of Bur of Intl Labor Affairs, by project and contractor, FY73-84, annual listing, 6364–1

Services trade regulation proposals of US, with agreements, goods and services trade, intl investment, and GDP, by country, various periods 1970-82, 448–1

Shipping and shipbuilding subsidies and aid, and summary fleet, trade, and GNP data, for US and 47 countries, 1979-80, biennial rpt, 7704–18

Soviet Union hard currency trade by commodity, and balance of payments, 1970s-83, annual rpt, 244–5.3

Statistical Abstract of US, selected social, political, and economic data, by country, 1945-83 and trends, annual rpt, 2324–1.4

Technology-intensive products and patents, US trade balance, 1960s-80 with trends, annual rpt, 9624–10.1

Technology-intensive products trade performance, selected years 1960-FY84, 26306–6.77

TTPI socioeconomic, employment, health, and govtl data, by TTPI govt, FY83 and selected trends, detailed annual rpt, 7004–6.2

UK economic indicator performance under Thatcher govt, with OECD comparisons, 1970-1983/84, article, 9391–1.414

Vancouver, Canada, nonagricultural exports, by commodity, 1970-80, 1528–176

Waterborne commerce of US (domestic and foreign), freight by commodity, traffic, and passengers, by port and waterway, 1982, annual rpt, 3754–3

Waterborne exports and imports of US, by type of service, customs district, port, and world area, monthly rpt, 2422–7

Waterborne trade of US, and Fed Govt sponsored cargo by agency, total and US-flag share by vessel type, selected years 1973-82, annual rpt, 7704–14.2, 7704–14.3

Waterborne trade of US, by type of service, commodity, country, route, and US port, 1982, annual rpt, 7704–2

Western States economic indicators, Fed Reserve 12th District, quarterly rpt, 9393–1.1

see also Agricultural exports and imports
see also Arms sales
see also Cartels
see also Coal exports and imports
see also Common markets and free trade areas
see also Contraband
see also Customs administration
see also Domestic International Sales Corporations
see also Dumping
see also Energy exports and imports
see also Export-Import Bank
see also Foreign assistance
see also Foreign exchange
see also Foreign investments
see also Foreign trade promotion
see also International transactions
see also Maritime law
see also Military assistance
see also Multinational corporations
see also Natural gas exports and imports
see also Petroleum exports and imports
see also Ships and shipping
see also Tariffs and foreign trade controls
see also Trade adjustment assistance
see also Trade agreements
see also under names of specific commodities or commodity groups

Foreign trade promotion

Agricultural commodities generic advertising, activities and funding by source, selected years 1972-82, 1548–242

Agricultural research expenditures and scientist years, by topic, commodity, and performing organization, FY82, annual rpt, 1744–2

AID activities and funding by project and function, FY85, and developing countries summary socioeconomic data, 1970s-83, by country, annual rpt, 9914–3

Budget of US, effects of Reagan Admin policy changes, by detailed program, FY85, annual rpt, 104–21

Business America, foreign and domestic commerce, and US investment and trade opportunities, biweekly rpt articles, 2042–24

CCC finances and program operations, FY83, annual rpt, 1824–1

China economic and business investment conditions, trade practices, and trade with US by detailed commodity, 1978-82, 2048–72

Computers and computer equipment foreign market and trade, and user industry operations and demand, country market research rpts, 2045–1

Electric power systems equipment foreign market and trade, and user industry operations and demand, country market research rpts, 2045–15

Electronic component equipment foreign market and trade, and user industry operations and demand, country market research rpts, 2045–4

Electronic component manufacturing equipment foreign market and trade, and user industry operations and demand, country market research rpts, 2045–5

Europe (Western) trade with US, and US market share and export opportunities for selected commodities, by country, 1982-84, 2048–105

Export credit program activities of Eximbank and 6 OECD countries, 1982, annual rpt, 9254–3

Farm machinery and equipment foreign market and trade, and user industry operations and demand, country market research rpts, 2045–13

Fed Govt contingent liabilities and claims paid on federally insured and guaranteed contracts with foreign obligors, by country and program, periodic rpt, 8002–12

Fed Govt programs and mgmt cost control proposals, 3-year savings by function and agency, and financial and operating data, 1960s-81, 16908–1.3

Food processing and packaging equipment, foreign market and trade, and user industry operations and demand, country market research rpts, 2045–11

Foreign Agriculture, production, consumption, and policies, and US export dev and promotion, monthly rpt, 1922–2

Foreign trade zones operations and economic effects, with data on merchandise shipments, value added, employment, hours, and customs revenue, 1978-83, 9886–4.70

Graphic industries equipment foreign market and trade, and user industry operations and demand, country market research rpts, 2045–3

Helsinki Final Act implementation by NATO, Warsaw Pact, and other signatory nations, Dec 1983-Mar 1984, semiannual rpt, 7002–1

Industrial process control equipment foreign market and trade, and user industry operations and demand, country market research rpts, 2045–6

ITA foreign and US Commercial Service, overseas staff by category, and trade promotion costs by activity, by country, 1982-83, hearing, 21408–73

Lab instruments foreign market and trade, and user industry operations and demand, country market research rpts, 2045–10

Machine tools and equipment foreign market and trade, and user industry operations and demand, country market research rpts, 2045–9

Medical and health care equipment foreign market and trade, and user industry operations and demand, country market research rpts, 2045–2

Mining industry equipment foreign market and trade, and user industry operations and demand, country market research rpts, 2045–16

Foreign trade promotion

Overseas Business Reports: economic conditions, investment and export opportunities, and trade practices, annual country market research rpt series, 2046–6

Overseas Business Reports: economic conditions, investment and export opportunities, and trade practices, world region rpt series, 2046–5

Pollution control instruments and equipment foreign market and trade, and user industry operations and demand, country market research rpts, 2045–17

Services trade regulation proposals of US, with agreements, goods and services trade, intl investment, and GDP, by country, various periods 1970-82, 448–1

Sporting goods and recreational equipment and vehicles foreign market and trade, country market research rpts, 2045–14

Telecommunication equipment foreign market and trade, and user industry operations and demand, country market research rpts, 2045–12

see also Exhibitions and trade fairs

Forest fires

- Air pollutant emission factors, by detailed source, 3rd edition, 1983-84 supplements, 9198–13
- Air pollution levels for 5 pollutants, by detailed source, State, and Air Quality Control Region, 1981, annual rpt, 9194–7
- Air pollution levels for 5 pollutants, by source, 1970- 82 with trends from 1940, annual rpt, 9194–13
- Control expenditures of Federal and State govts, annual rpt, discontinued, 1204–10
- Developing countries disaster preparedness and summary sociodemographic, political, and economic data, country rpt series, 9916–2
- Forest Service land, fires and acres burned by cause, forest, and State, 1983, annual rpt, 1204–6
- Forestry activities on State and private lands, Fed Govt and State funding by project and State, FY83, annual tables, 1204–32
- Govt census, 1982: State govt payments to local govts, by program, source of funds, level of govt, and State, with trends from 1902, 2460–3
- Land Mgmt Bur activities and finances, and public land acreage and use, annual State rpt series, 5724–11
- Land Mgmt Bur public lands admin and program activities in western States, FY82-84, annual rpt, 5724–13
- Public lands fires, area burned, and protection costs, 1982-83, annual rpt, 5724–1.2
- Research project descriptions and bibl for forestry, 1982, annual rpt, 1204–14
- Wildfires damage and causes, by State and region, 1981, annual rpt, 1204–4
- Wildfires on State and private lands protected under Cooperative Forestry Assistance Act, number and acres protected and burned, by State, 1982, annual rpt, 1204–1.2
- Wisconsin forest fires damage to timber, crops, game, waterfowl, and recreation sites, economic effects by county, 1980-82, 1208–198

Index by Subjects and Names

Forest Service

- Activities and programs of USDA, by subagency, FY83, annual rpt, 1004–3
- Alaska timber acreage and resources, by species, ownership class, and inventory unit, 1967-74, series, 1206–9
- Biomass timber in Rocky Mountain States, conversion from volume to dry weight, for softwood and hardwood species, 1977, 1208–200
- Colorado natl forest below-cost timber sales, and volume, costs, revenue, and net loss, by sale and forest, FY81-82, GAO rpt, 26113–131
- Cost control proposals for Fed Govt programs and mgmt, 3-year savings by function and agency, and financial and operating data, 1960s-81, 16908–1.2, 16908–1.31
- Fire (forest) damage and causes, by State and region, 1981, annual rpt, 1204–4
- Fire control cooperative expenditures of Federal and and State govts, annual rpt, discontinued, 1204–10
- Fires on Forest Service land and acres burned, by cause, forest, and State, 1983, annual rpt, 1204–6
- Forest and windbarrier planting and seeding, by State, FY83, annual rpt, 1204–7
- Forest, range, and associated waters use and mgmt assessment, and environmental impacts of Forest Service program options, 1977-2030 and trends from 1920, 1208–24
- Forestry activities on State and private lands, Fed Govt and State funding by project and State, FY83, annual tables, 1204–32
- Forests (natl) and other lands under Forest Service mgmt, by forest and location, Sept 1983, annual rpt, 1204–2
- Fraud and abuse in USDA programs, audits and investigations, 2nd half FY84, semiannual rpt, 1002–4
- Georgia timber resources and removals, by species, ownership class, and county, 1981-83, series, 1206–26
- Horse and burro wild herd areas in western States, population, adoption, and protection and mgmt costs, as of 1984, biennial rpt, 5724–8
- Idaho and Montana recreation sites of Forest Service, itemized operating and maintenance costs by type of site, 1980, 1208–202
- Insect and disease incidence and damage in forests, 1983, annual regional rpt series, 1206–11
- Insect and disease incidence in forests, by region or State, 1983, annual rpt, 1204–8
- Livestock grazing on Natl Forest System lands, and losses from predators, poisonous plants, and other causes, by region and State, FY83, annual rpt, 1204–5
- Louisiana property tax on forest, agricultural, and marsh lands, impact of change from market to use valuation by parish, 1977-78, 1208–206
- Lumber and wood product production, consumption by end use, shipments, exports, and market channels, for Rocky Mountain States, 1974-76, 1208–208
- Mexico and US range and wildlife characteristics, problems, and research strategies and needs, 1981 conf papers, 1208–197

Michigan timber acreage and yield, 1979-80 with projections to 2010, 1208–193

- Michigan timber acreage by ownership, county, and forest and tree characteristics, 1980, 1208–192
- Minnesota timber acreage, resources, and removals, by species, county, and ownership class, series, 1206–24
- Montana timber acreage, resources, and mortality, by species and ownership class, 1976-80, series, 1206–25
- Natl Forest System wildlife habitat and fishery improvements, use, and game population and harvest by species and forest, by region, FY83, annual rpt, 1204–31
- New Mexico timber acreage and resources, by species, ownership class, and county, 1977-80, series, 1206–23
- North Carolina timber acreage and resources, by species, ownership class, and county, 1982-83, series, 1206–4
- North Central States pulpwood production by county, imports, and individual mill capacity, by species, 1982, annual rpt, 1204–19
- North Central States timber removals, and mill receipts and production, by species, product, and county, series, 1206–10
- North Central States veneer log production, mill receipts, and use, biennial rpt, discontinued, 1204–24
- Northeast and North Central regions biomass timber, green weight by biomass component and State, 1981, 1208–207
- Northeast States forest land owner characteristics, owners and acreage, series, 1206–7
- Northeast States timber annual growth, removals, causes of mortality, and products output, and forest ownership and industries, State rpt series, 1206–16
- Northeastern region timber resources and removals, by species, ownership, and county, State rpt series, 1206–12
- Northwest US and British Columbia forest industry production, prices, trade, and employment, quarterly rpt, 1202–3
- Northwest US natl forest timber sales contract operations by forest and firm, and lumber supply/demand, FY76-1983, hearings, 25318–57
- Oregon and Montana earnings by SIC 1- to 3-digit industry and payments to retirees by type, for 4 timber dependent communities, 1970, 1208–196
- Pacific Northwest natl forest sales by bidding method, harvest by company, and effects on local employment by community, 1974-77, 1208–194
- Programs and activities, by State and region, FY83, annual rpt, 1204–1
- Public lands sales of Land Mgmt Bur, prices of Nevada and California acreage, and effect on Forest Service land acquisition program, 1983, GAO rpt, 26113–122
- Puerto Rico wood and wood product shipments from US by type, and from selected foreign sources, 1971-81, 1208–205
- Pulpwood prices, expenditures, and transportation modes in Southeast, 1981-82, annual rpt, 1204–22
- Recreation (outdoor) participation, by type of activity, projected 1985-2030, 1208–195

Index by Subjects and Names

Forests and forestry

Recreation fees and collection costs, visitors, and capacity of outdoor Fed Govt, State, and private facilities, by managing agency and State, 1983, annual rpt, 5544–14

Recreational sites in natl forests, area, and capacity, by type of activity, 1983, annual rpt, 1204–28

Recreational use of natl forests, visitor-days and visits by type of activity, forest, and State, FY83 with trends from 1924, annual rpt series, 1204–17

Research project descriptions and bibl, 1982, annual rpt, 1204–14

Rocky Mountain forest and rangeland area, and timber resources and removals, by ownership, forest and tree characteristics, and State, 1977, 1208–201

Sedimentation control, surveillance, and research activity of Fed Govt, by project, agency, region, and State, 1982, annual rpt, 5664–9

South Carolina industrial roundwood production and residue volume, by species, product type, State region, and county, 1977-81, 1208–203

Southeast region biomass timber, trees, volume, and green weight by species, site and diameter class, and stand age, 1982, 1208–199

Southeastern States timber resources and removals, for 5 States, interim rpt series, 1206–32

Timber production, prices by region and State, trade by country, and consumption, by species and product, with industry earnings, 1950-83, annual rpt, 1204–29

Timber stumpage prices, for sawtimber sold from natl forests by species and region, quarterly rpt, 1202–1

Utah timber acreage and resources, by species, ownership class, and stand size, and forest recreation, 1978, series, 1206–22

Washington State timber acreage and resources, by species, ownership class, and county, 1980, and harvest, 1950-81, series, 1206–28

Western regions natl forests below-cost timber sales and revenue by forest, and volume, average price by species, and costs by region, FY80-1982, GAO rpt, 26113–126

Wisconsin forest fires damage to timber, crops, game, waterfowl, and recreation sites, economic effects by county, 1980-82, 1208–198

Wood acquired and used for home heating, by household characteristics and wood sources, 1980/81, 1208–204

Wood fuel removal program itemized costs to Service in 3 central Appalachia natl forests, 1981, 1208–191

Wood used in manufacturing, by type of wood, end use, and SIC 4-digit industry, 1977 with summary trends from 1928, 1208–3

Forests and forestry

Acid rain causes and effects, air pollutant emissions by source, and control costs, by region and State, selected years 1977-83 and projected to 2000, 26358–104

Acid rain causes and effects, air pollutant emissions by source in US and selected countries, and control costs, 1970s-83 and projected to 2000, 21368–52

Acreage harvested and cropland area by crop and region, and potential for expansion, 1982-84 with trends from 1949, annual rpt, 1584–4

Aerial survey R&D publications, and sources of natural resource and environmental data gathered by air- and spacecraft, quarterly listing, 9502–7

Agricultural Conservation Program participation and payments, by State, FY83, annual rpt, 1804–7

Agricultural Stabilization and Conservation Service producer payments under 26 programs, monthly rpt, 1802–10

Agricultural Statistics, 1983, annual rpt, 1004–1.2

Agriculture census, 1982: farms, farmland, production and costs, and operator characteristics, preliminary State and county rpt series, 2330–1

Agriculture census, 1982: farms, farmland, production, finances, and operator characteristics, by county, final State rpt series, 2331–1

Alaska timber acreage and resources, by species, ownership class, and inventory unit, 1967-74, series, 1206–9

Biomass Fuels Program of TVA, technologies and processes dev, costs, and resource requirements, 1970s-90s, series, 9806–9

Carbon dioxide atmospheric levels, climatic effects and impacts of fossil and synthetic fuels use, deforestation, and land use patterns, research rpt series, 3406–3

Census of Population and Housing, 1980: detailed population and housing characteristics, by county, city, and census tract, State and SMSA rpt series, 2551–2

Census of Population, 1980: detailed socioeconomic and demographic characteristics, by age, sex, race, Hispanic origin, occupation, and industry, State rpt series, 2531–4

Census of Population, 1980: detailed socioeconomic characteristics, by county, city, and inside-outside SMSAs and central cities, State rpt series, 2531–3

Census of Population, 1980: labor force, by sex, detailed occupation, and region, with comparison to 1970 census, supplementary rpt, 2535–1.12

Cherokee Indians Eastern Band of North Carolina, financial and operating data for Bur of Indian Affairs assistance programs, FY83, annual rpt, 5704–4

Colorado natl forest below-cost timber sales, and volume, costs, revenue, and net loss, by sale and forest, FY81-82, GAO rpt, 26113–131

County Business Patterns: establishments, employees, and payrolls, by SIC 4-digit industry and county, 1981, annual State rpt series, 2326–8

County Business Patterns: establishments, employees, and payrolls, by SIC 4-digit industry and county, 1982, annual State rpt series, 2326–6

Developing countries agricultural supply/demand and market for US exports, with socioeconomic indicators, country rpt series, 1526–6

Developing countries economic dev projects funded by multilateral dev banks, environmental and cultural impacts, 1970s-83, hearings, 21248–80

DOE R&D projects and funding at natl labs, universities, and other instns, FY83, annual summary rpt, 3004–18.1

Earnings by major industry group, and personal income per capita and by source, by region and State, 1929-82, 2708–40

Environmental quality and protection programs, costs, and Fed Govt enforcement, 1983, detailed annual rpt, 484–1

Exports and imports of US, by commodity group, world area, selected country, US coastal area and port, and mode of transport, with seasonal adjustments, monthly rpt, 2422–9

Farm improvement, acreage and owners by improvement type, funding source, land use, and region, 1978 survey, 1506–5.20

Farm real estate transfers, by proposed use of property, region, and State, 1982-83, annual rpt, 1541–8.4

Fed Govt aid to State and local govts, expenditures, and direct payments, by program, agency, and State, FY83, annual rpt, 2464–2

Fed Govt and State funding of forestry activities on State and private lands, by project and State, FY83, annual tables, 1204–32

Fed Govt-owned real property inventory and costs, worldwide summary by location, agency, and use, 1983, annual rpt, 9454–5

Fed Govt Reforestation Trust Fund receipts, expenditures, assets, and liabilities, monthly rpt, 8102–9.9

Foreign and US agricultural supply/demand, consumption per capita, and trade, by world area and country group, 1960s-82, 1528–181

Foreign and US agricultural supply/demand indicators by commodity and world area, and related research and extension program needs, 1950s-2020, 1008–47

Foreign and US cropland per capita, and total arable land area by use, by selected country and world region, selected years 1955-80, 1528–180

Foreign and US cropland per capita by world region and selected country, and world arable land area by use, selected years 1955-80, summary article, 1522–3.401

Foreign and US tropical forests status by country and world region, conservation methods, and mgmt role of US, foreign, and intl groups, 1977-81 and projected to 2000, 26358–101, 26358–101.1

Foreign economic, social, and political summary data, by country, 1984, annual factbook, 244–11

Foreign ownership of US agricultural land, acquisitions, dispositions, holdings, and use, by State and type and country of owner, 1983, annual rpt, 1584–2

Foreign ownership of US agricultural land, acreage, value, and use, by State and county, and for 5 leading investor countries, 1983, annual rpt, 1584–3

Forest Service programs and activities, by State and region, FY83, annual rpt, 1204–1

Forestry Incentives Program, Fed Govt cost-sharing funds for private timberland improvement, by region and State, monthly rpt, 1802–11

Forests and forestry

Genetic resource (plant and animal) conservation, commercial uses, causes of depletion, and geographic sources, 1984 rpt, 5548–13

Georgia timber resources and removals, by species, ownership class, and county, 1981-83, series, 1206–26

Govt census, 1982: State govt payments to local govts, by program, source of funds, level of govt, and State, with trends from 1902, 2460–3

Income tax returns of corporations, summary data by industry div, 1981 estimates, annual article, 8302–2.403

Income tax returns of partnerships, detailed data by industry, 1981 estimates, annual article, 8302–2.404

Income tax returns of sole proprietorships, detailed data by industry div and selected industry group, 1981, annual rpt, 8304–7

Income tax returns of sole proprietorships, receipts, deductions by type, payroll, and net income, by major industry, 1982, annual article, 8302–2.413

Input-output structure of US economy, detailed interindustry transactions for 85 industries, and components of final demand, 1977, article, 2702–1.421

Input-output structure of US economy, detailed interindustry transactions for 537 industries, and components of final demand, 1977 benchmark data, 2708–17

Insect and disease incidence and damage in forests, 1983, annual regional rpt series, 1206–11

Insect and disease incidence in forests, by region or State, 1983, annual rpt, 1204–8

Land owner characteristics for Northeast States, owners and acreage, series, 1206–7

Louisiana property tax on forest, agricultural, and marsh lands, impact of change from market to use valuation by parish, 1977-78, 1208–206

Marketing cash receipts of farms, by detailed commodity and State, 1979-82, annual rpt, 1544–18

Meteorological services and research of Fed Govt, programs and funding by agency, FY84-85, annual rpt, 2144–2

Michigan timber acreage and yield, 1979-80 with projections to 2010, 1208–193

Michigan timber acreage by ownership, county, and forest and tree characteristics, 1980, 1208–192

Michigan timber acreage, volume, growth, removals, and production, by ownership, county, and forest and tree characteristics, 1980, series, 1206–31

Minnesota timber acreage, resources, and removals, by species, county, and ownership class, series, 1206–24

Montana timber acreage, resources, and mortality, by species and ownership class, 1976-80, series, 1206–25

New Mexico timber acreage and resources, by species, ownership class, and county, 1977-80, series, 1206–23

North Carolina timber acreage and resources, by species, ownership class, and county, 1982-83, series, 1206–4

North Central States timber removals, and mill receipts and production, by species, product, and county, series, 1206–10

Northeast and North Central regions biomass timber, green weight by biomass component and State, 1981, 1208–207

Northeast States timber annual growth, removals, causes of mortality, and products output, and forest ownership and industries, State rpt series, 1206–16

Northeastern region timber resources and removals, by species, ownership, and county, State rpt series, 1206–12

Northwest US and British Columbia forest industry production, prices, trade, and employment, quarterly rpt, 1202–3

Northwest US natl forest timber sales contract operations by forest and firm, and lumber supply/demand, FY76-1983, hearings, 25318–57

Occupational injury and illness rates, by SIC 2- to 4-digit industry, 1982, annual rpt, 6844–1

Occupational manpower needs and supply by detailed occupation, and educational and training program enrollees and grads by detailed field, 1982 and 1995, biennial rpt, 6744–3

Occupational Outlook Handbook, 1984-85 biennial rpt, 6744–1

Planting and seeding for forests and windbarriers, by State, FY83, annual rpt, 1204–7

Public lands timber sales, FY83, annual rpt, 5724–1.2

Research (agricultural) expenditures and scientist years, by topic, commodity, and performing organization, FY82, annual rpt, 1744–2

Research project descriptions and bibl for forestry, 1982, annual rpt, 1204–14

Resources use and mgmt assessment and environmental impacts of Forest Service program options, 1977-2030 and trends from 1920, 1208–24

Rocky Mountain forest and rangeland area, and timber resources and removals, by ownership, forest and tree characteristics, and State, 1977, 1208–201

Rocky Mountain States forest biomass, conversion from volume to dry weight, for softwood and hardwood species, 1977, 1208–200

Science and engineering doctoral degree recipients, by field, sex, race, age, citizenship, postgrad employment and study status, State, and instn, 1960-82, 9626–6.16

Small and minority-owned businesses finances and operations, Federal contracts by agency, and worker characteristics, by industry, race, sex, and State, 1950s-83, annual rpt, 9764–6

Southeast region biomass timber, trees, volume, and green weight by species, site and diameter class, and stand age, 1982, 1208–199

Southeastern States timber resources and removals, for 5 States, interim rpt series, 1206–32

Statistical Abstract of US, social, political, and economic data, 1950s-83 and trends, annual rpt, 2324–1.3

Tennessee Valley ethanol production, feedstocks, facilities, tax incentives, and related farming data, by State, 1970s-83 and projected to 1992, 9808–69

Index by Subjects and Names

Timber production, prices by region and State, trade by country, and consumption, by species and product, with industry earnings, 1950-83, annual rpt, 1204–29

Transportation census, 1982: trucks, by detailed characteristics, miles traveled, and type of product carried, State rpt series, 2573–1

TVA activities, financial and operating data by program and facility, and power sales by customer, FY83, annual rpt, 9804–1

Utah timber acreage and resources, by species, ownership class, and stand size, and forest recreation, 1978, series, 1206–22

Washington State timber acreage and resources, by species, ownership class, and county, 1980, and harvest, 1950-81, series, 1206–28

Water pollution from nonpoint sources, source land uses and acreage, and control program funding, by State or region, various periods 1974-FY84, 9208–123

Wildlife refuge revenues from economic and recreational uses, and refuge managers attitudes toward expanded use, FY81-83, GAO rpt, 26113–128

see also Forest fires

see also Gum and wood chemicals

see also Lumber industry and products

see also National forests

see also National park system

see also under By Industry in the "Index by Categories"

Forgery

see Counterfeiting and forgery

Forst, Brian

"Criminal Justice System Response to Victim Harm", 6068–185.1

Forstall, Richard L.

"Growth in Nonmetropolitan Areas Slows", 2328–47

Fort Arthur, Tex.

Housing vacancy rates for single and multifamily units and mobile homes, by city and ZIP code, 1984, annual metro area rpt, 9304–19.15

Fort Collins, Colo.

Census of Housing, 1980: occupancy and unit characteristics, by race, Hispanic origin, and city, SMSA rpt, 2473–1.159

Census of Population and Housing, 1980: detailed population and housing characteristics, by county, city, and census tract, SMSA rpt, 2551–2.159

Housing vacancy rates for single and multifamily units and mobile homes, by ZIP code, 1983, annual SMSA rpt, 9304–22.3

see also By SMSA or MSA in the "Index by Categories"

Fort Lauderdale, Fla.

Census of Housing, 1980: occupancy and unit characteristics, by race, Hispanic origin, and city, SMSA rpt, 2473–1.160

Census of Population and Housing, 1980: detailed population and housing characteristics, by county, city, and census tract, SMSA rpt, 2551–2.160

Wages by occupation, and benefits for office and plant workers, 1984 labor market area survey rpt, 6785–3.3

Index by Subjects and Names

Fort Myers, Fla.
Census of Population and Housing, 1980: detailed population and housing characteristics, by county, city, and census tract, SMSA rpt, 2551–2.161
see also under By SMSA or MSA in the "Index by Categories"

Fort Pierce, Fla.
see also under By SMSA or MSA in the "Index by Categories"

Fort Riley, Kans.
Wages of office and plant workers, by occupation, 1984 labor market area survey rpt, 6785–3.9

Fort Smith, Ark.
Census of Housing, 1980: occupancy and unit characteristics, by race, Hispanic origin, and city, SMSA rpt, 2473–1.162
Census of Population and Housing, 1980: detailed population and housing characteristics, by county, city, and census tract, SMSA rpt, 2551–2.162
Housing vacancy rates for single and multifamily units and mobile homes, by city and ZIP code, 1984, annual metro area rpt, 9304–19.19
Wages by occupation, and benefits for office and plant workers, 1983 labor market area survey rpt, 6785–3.2
see also under By SMSA or MSA in the "Index by Categories"

Fort Walton Beach, Fla.
Census of Housing, 1980: occupancy and unit characteristics, by race, Hispanic origin, and city, SMSA rpt, 2473–1.163
Census of Population and Housing, 1980: detailed population and housing characteristics, by county, city, and census tract, SMSA rpt, 2551–2.163
see also under By SMSA or MSA in the "Index by Categories"

Fort Wayne, Ind.
Census of Housing, 1980: occupancy and unit characteristics, by race, Hispanic origin, and city, SMSA rpt, 2473–1.164
Census of Population and Housing, 1980: detailed population and housing characteristics, by county, city, and census tract, SMSA rpt, 2551–2.164
Wages of office and plant workers, by occupation, 1984 labor market area survey rpt, 6785–3.7
see also under By City and By SMSA or MSA in the "Index by Categories"

Fort Worth, Tex.
Auto dealer repair workers, wages, and benefits, by occupation, size of establishment, and for 24 labor market areas, Nov 1982 survey, 6787–6.202
Census of Housing, 1980: occupancy and unit characteristics, by race, Hispanic origin, and city, SMSA rpt, 2473–1.131
Census of Population and Housing, 1980: detailed population and housing characteristics, by county, city, and census tract, SMSA rpt, 2551–2.131
CPI by component for US city average, and by region, population size, and for 28 SMSAs, monthly press release, 6762–1
CPI by detailed component, for US city average, 28 SMSAs, and 4 regions by population size, monthly rpt, 6762–2
CPI by major component, average change for Dallas-Fort Worth and Houston, Tex, with comparisons to South and total US, 1973-82, BLS regional rpt series, 6966–1.12

Dress industry production and related workers, wages, and benefits, by occupation, size of establishment, and union status, for 11 labor market areas, Aug 1982 survey, 6787–6.200
Employment, earnings, hours, and CPI changes for Dallas-Fort Worth SMSA, 1983 with trends from 1968, annual rpt, 6964–2
Homeless population and characteristics, and temporary shelter operations, use, and user characteristics, for selected cities, various periods 1979-84, hearing, 21248–85
Hospital worker wages by sex and occupation, and benefits, for 22 MSAs, Oct 1981 survey, 6787–6.201
Housing and households detailed characteristics, and unit and neighborhood quality, by inside-outside central cities, 1981 survey, SMSA rpt, 2485–6.22
Repair technicians and apprentices wages and benefits, for 5 types of electrical repair shops in 19 SMSAs, Nov 1981 survey, 6787–6.197
Wages by occupation, and benefits for office and plant workers, 1983 SMSA survey rpt, 6785–12.3
see also under By SMSA or MSA in the "Index by Categories"

Fortier, Diana A.
"Bank Mergers Today: New Guidelines, Changing Markets", 9375–1.404

Fosse, E. Ray
"Global Perspective for Crop Insurance in 1984", 1004–16.1

Foster home care
AFDC foster care and unemployed parent segment, recipients and children, by State and outlying area, quarterly rpt, 4742–6.1
AFDC recipient families and children, by State, monthly rpt, 4742–1.5
Benefits per child for AFDC and foster home care, for selected States, 1974 and 1982, hearing, 21968–28
Budget of US, effects of Reagan Admin policy changes, by detailed program, FY85, annual rpt, 104–21
Fed Govt incentives to States for permanent placement of foster children, program funding and operations in 7 States, FY80-82, GAO rpt, 26121–81
Fed Govt programs under Ways and Means Committee jurisdiction, program operations and financing data for assessing budgetary requirements, by State, FY70s-83, 21788–117
Fed Govt public welfare programs and tax expenditures benefitting children and youth, participation and funding for 71 programs, FY81-83, 21968–30
Govt census, 1982: State govt payments to local govts, by program, source of funds, level of govt, and State, with trends from 1902, 2460–3
State govt social services spending by type and funding source, and admin of Fed Govt block grants, for 13 States, selected years FY80-84, GAO rpt, 26121–76

Foundations
see Nonprofit organizations and foundations

Foundries
see Metals and metal industries

Fowler, Dean L.
"Species Profiles: Life Histories and Environmental Requirements of Coastal Fishes and Invertebrates (South Atlantic), Blue Crab", 5506–8.24

Fox, Alan
"Income Changes at and After Social Security Benefit Receipt: Evidence from the Retirement History Study", 4742–1.418

Fox, Daphne D.
"Analyses of Natural Gases, 1983", 5604–2

Fox, Douglas R.
"Motor Vehicles, Model Year 1984", 2702–1.438

France
Agricultural and food production indexes, and production of selected commodities, by world region and country, 1974-83, annual rpt, 1524–5
Agricultural situation in Western Europe, by country and commodity, 1983 and outlook for 1984, annual rpt, 1524–4.6
Agricultural supply/demand, trade, and production, and socioeconomic data, by country, 1950s-77, 1528–179
AID loan repayment status and terms by program and country, and status of predecessor agency loans, quarterly rpt, 9912–3
Apple imports of EC by country, and France exports by world region, 1981/82-1983/84, article, 1925–34.407
Auto and auto products sales, prices, and registrations in US, and trade of 8 countries with US, by make and model, 1964-83, annual rpt, 9884–7
Auto safety and experimental vehicle designs, 1982, conf proceedings, annual rpt, 7764–3
Background Notes, summary social, political, and economic data, 1984 rpt, 7006–2.17
Biotechnology commercial uses, R&D funding and output, controls, and industry financial and operating data, for US and 5 countries, 1970s-83 and estimated 1984-85, 26358–98
Current account deficits, and financing by source, for US and 5 OECD countries, selected years 1973-1st qtr 1984, article, 9385–1.409
Dollar holdings rate of return related to domestic real money stock for 5 OECD countries, regression results, various periods 1966-84, article, 9391–1.418
Drug, alcohol, and cigarette use among urban youths in Israel and France, by substance type, age, and sex, 1977 and 1979, article, 4102–1.430
Economic and monetary trends, compounded annual rates of change for US and 10 major trading partners, quarterly rpt, 9391–7
Economic conditions, consumer and stock prices and production indexes, 6 OECD countries and US, *Business Conditions Digest,* monthly rpt, 2702–3.10, 2708–31
Economic conditions in Communist, OECD, and selected other countries, 1960s-83, annual rpt, 244–5

France

Economic conditions, investment and export opportunities, and trade practices, 1984 country market research rpt, 2046–6.5

Economic indicators and oil use and imports for US and 6 OECD countries, and oil production by country, biweekly rpt, 242–4

Economic indicators for 7 OECD countries and US, quarterly rpt, 2042–10

Economic, social, and political summary data, by country, 1984, annual factbook, 244–11

Economic trends in income, production, prices, employment, finances, and trade, 1984 semiannual rpt, 2046–4.50

Employment, labor force, and participation and unemployment rates by sex, in US and 9 OECD countries, various periods 1970-3rd qtr 1983, annual article, 6722–1.404

Energy prices and taxes by energy source and end-use sector, for US and 9 OECD countries, quarterly 1979-83, annual rpt, 3164–71

Energy production by type, and oil prices, trade, and consumption, by country group and selected country, monthly rpt, 242–5

European Monetary System effect on inflation and exchange rates, for 3 member countries, various periods Feb 1974-Mar 1984, technical paper, 9366–7.101

Export credit program activities of Eximbank and 6 OECD countries, 1982, annual rpt, 9254–3

Exports and imports, intl position of US and 4 OECD countries, and factors affecting US competition, quarterly pamphlet, 2042–25

Exports and imports of NATO countries with Council for Mutual Economic Assistance Europe members, by country, 1980-83, annual rpt, 7144–5

Exports and imports of NATO countries with PRC, by country, 1980-83, annual rpt, 7144–14

Exports and imports of OECD countries, by country, 1983, annual rpt, 7144–10

Exports and imports of OECD, total and for 4 major countries, and US trade by commodity, 1972-82, annual world region rpt series, 244–13

Exports and imports of US with Western Europe, and US market share and export opportunities for selected commodities, by country, 1982-84, 2048–105

Exports of US, detailed Schedule B commodities by country of destination, 1983, annual rpt, 2424–9

Exports of US, detailed Schedule E commodities by mode of transport and world area and country of destination, 1983, annual rpts, 2424–5

Fish and shellfish wholesale prices and market activity in 8 West Europe countries, weekly rpt, 2162–8

Food processing and packaging equipment market and trade, and user industry operations and demand, 1983 market research rpt, 2045–11.25

Food supply/demand and market and support prices, with exchange rates, fertilizer price index, GDP, and population, by EC country, 1960-83, 1528–173

Foreign exchange rates for currencies of US and 2 countries with yen, and measures of manufacturing competitiveness, 1983 with 1974-80 and 1979-80 averages, article, 9385–1.404

Imports of US, detailed Schedule A commodities by country and world area of origin, and mode of transport, 1983, annual rpts, 2424–2

Imports of US, detailed TSUSA commodities by country of origin, 1983, annual rpt, 2424–4

Industrial process control equipment market and trade, and user industry operations and demand, 1984 country market research rpt, 2045–6.40

Industrial production indexes of 7 OECD countries and US, biweekly rpt, periodic article, 2042–24

Interest rates and budget balances of US and 6 OECD countries, 1973-83, annual rpt, 26304–3.1

Intl transactions of US with 10 countries, 1981-83, *Survey of Current Business*, monthly rpt, annual table, 2702–1.31

Investment (foreign direct) in US, major investors and investments by SIC 4-digit industry, transaction type and value, and location, 1983, annual rpt, 2044–20

Loans and grants for economic and military assistance from US and intl agencies, by program and country, FY46-83, annual rpt, 9914–5

Manufacturing labor productivity and cost indexes for US and 11 OECD countries, 1960-82, annual article, 6722–1.405

Manufacturing productivity and unit labor cost indexes for US and 11 countries, 1950-82 and preliminary 1983, annual rpt, 6864–1

Manufacturing wage/price and wage/output adjustment in 6 OECD countries, 1960-81, technical paper, 9381–10.33

Military aid of US, arms sales, and training programs costs and budget requests by program, world region, and country, FY83-85, annual rpt, 7144–13

Military pension lifetime earnings in US and 7 countries, as of 1983, 26306–6.76

Military spending, arms trade, and armed forces size, with total govt spending and population, by country, 1972-82, annual rpt, 9824–1

Military weapons transfers to developing countries from US, USSR, and Europe, by weapon type and world region, 1974-82, 25948–3

Minerals Yearbook, 1982, Vol 3: foreign country reviews of production, trade, and policies, by commodity, annual rpt, 5604–35

Minerals Yearbook, 1982, Vol 3 preprints: foreign country review of production, trade, and policies, by commodity, annual rpt, 5604–17.23

Monetary control policy of US and selected West European countries, and relation to credit, exchange rates, GNP, and other indicators, various periods 1960-82, conf papers, 9373–3.26

Nuclear power generation in US and 18 non-Communist countries, monthly rpt, 3162–24.10

Nuclear power plant construction and operation status, and capacity, by plant,

Index by Subjects and Names

region, State, and selected country, 1983 and projected to 2020, annual rpt, 3164–57

Oil consumption and stocks for major consuming countries, monthly rpt, 3162–24.10

Oil spill off Brittany coast, cleanup and research costs, marine and tourism industry losses, and recreation losses of tourists and residents, 1971-79, 2178–13

Population size and growth rates, and latest available benchmark demographic data, by country, 1950-83, biennial rpt, 2324–4

Price indexes for consumer and producer goods, major commodities, exports, imports, nonfarm wages, and currency value, US and 4 countries, bimonthly rpt, 2042–11

Prune (dried) production, trade, consumption, and stocks of US and 2 countries, EC subsidies, and US exports by country, 1982/83-1984/85, article, 1925–34.435

R&D expenditures and employment in science and technology, for US and 4 countries, selected years 1953-84, annual rpt, 9624–18.1

Rail high-speed systems and railcar production of US and selected countries, with major cities population and land area, 1940s-82, 26358–97

Science Indicators, R&D expenditures, innovations, research, and higher education, with foreign comparisons, 1960s- 83, annual rpt, 9624–10.1

Ships in world merchant fleet, and tonnage, by country of registry, 1982, annual rpt, 7704–3.1

Space launchings attaining Earth orbit or beyond, by country, 1957-83, annual rpt, 9504–9.1

Space satellites and other objects launched since 1957, quarterly listing, 9502–2

Steel imports of US from EC and other countries, and US industry operating data, for 15 products limited under arrangement with EC, monthly rpt, 9882–10

Trade promotion policies and industry financing of EC, and effect on competing US industries, 1970s-82, 9886–4.73

Travel to and from US, by world area and selected country, projected 1984-85, annual rpt, 2904–9

Walnut production, stocks, use, and exports of US and 4 countries, and EC export subsidy, selected years 1977-1984/85, article, 1925–34.429

Wine from France and Italy, imports injury to US industry from sales covered by foreign govt grants, investigation with background financial and operating data, 1984 rpt, 9886–19.9

see also French Guiana

see also Monaco

see also under By Foreign Country in the "Index by Categories"

Franchises

Auto dealer franchise productivity, hours, and employment indexes, 1958-82, annual rpt, 6824–1.4

Business opportunities for franchises by firm and kind of business, and sources of aid and info, 1984 annual listing, 2044–27

Enterprise zone and urban revitalization projects of State and local govts, effect on

Index by Subjects and Names

business and employment in selected areas, various dates 1972-83, hearing, 21788–140

Establishments and sales of firms with franchises engaged in distribution of goods and services, by State and kind of business, 1982-84, annual rpt, 2014–5

Finances and operations, by SIC 2- to 4-digit industry, 1970s-83 and projected to 1988, annual rpt, 2014–4

Food consumer research and marketing devs, and consumption and price trends, quarterly rpt with articles, 1541–7

Pharmacists employment and sociodemographic characteristics, and reasons for not working in field, by State and overseas, as of 1979, 4147–14.28

Statistical Abstract of US, social, political, and economic data, 1950s-83 and trends, annual rpt, 2324–1.3

Frankel, Allen B.

"Federal Taxation and the Domestic-Foreign Asset Choice of a U.S. Bank", 9366–7.99

Frankena, Mark W.

"Economic Analysis of Taxicab Regulation", 9406–1.37

Fraser, James E.

"Liming of Acidified Waters: A Review of Methods and Effects on Aquatic Ecosystems", 5506–5.13

Fratoe, Frank A.

"Job Training Partnership Act, CETA, and Rural Communities", 1502–7.403

Fraud

Arrests and arrest rates, by offense, offender characteristics, population size, and State, 1970s-83, annual rpt, 6224–2.2

Arson investigation and prosecution, by incident characteristics and outcome, motive, and type of evidence, for 4 jurisdictions, 1981, 6068–184

Bombing (explosive and incendiary) and arson incidents by target, State, and circumstances, and explosives theft and recovery, 1982-83, annual rpt, 8484–4

Court cases, dispositions, convictions, and sentences of Federal criminal defendants, by offense and district, as of June 1983 with trends from 1945, annual rpt, 18204–1

Credit card fraud losses, transactions by electronic funds transfer and other means, and potential for EFT crime, 1975-82, 6066–19.3

Criminal drug, fraud, and bank robbery Federal defendants, by sociodemographic and case processing characteristics, 1979, 6062–2.403

Customs Service activities, operations, and staff, FY79-83, annual rpt, 8144–1

DOD Civilian Health and Medical Program of the Uniformed Services fraud and abuse cases and referrals, FY83-84, semiannual rpt, 3502–2.4

Economic indicators relation to measures of social pathology including crime and death rates, various periods 1950-80, 23848–76

Employee theft and misconduct in retail, hospital, and manufacturing establishments, by type and frequency of violation, 1978-80, 6068–178

Fed Govt felony court cases, by offense, and characteristics of case processing, sentencing, and offender, 1979-80, periodic rpt, 6062–2.407

Freight

Income (taxable) not reported, by illegal source, with characteristics of persons involved, methodology, and bibl, 1970s-82, 8008–112

Income (taxable) not reported on individual and corporate returns, and associated Federal revenue losses, by detailed legal and illegal source, 1973-81, 8308–26

Medicaid fraud and abuse investigations and overpayments by State and outlying area, and Medicaid and Medicare program data, various periods 1966-82, annual rpt, 4654–1

Prisoners in State prisons median sentence, and admissions and releases by prisoner and sentencing characteristics, by offense and State, 1981 and trends from 1926, 6066–19.9

SEC securities law enforcement activities, FY83, annual rpt, 9734–2.5

Social security representative payee system, SSI fraud cases and convictions, and OASDI funds misused and recovered, various periods FY74-81, GAO rpt, 26121–85

Unemployment insurance overpayments detection and recovery from random audit program in selected States, 1975-82 and projected to FY86, GAO rpt, 26121–77

US Attorneys civil case processing and amounts involved, by cause of action, FY83, annual rpt, 6004–2.5

see also Counterfeiting and forgery

see also Federal Inspectors General reports

Frederick, Md.

Cancer-related resources directory for Frederick County, Md, evaluation of accuracy and usefulness, 1984 article, 4102–1.459

Frederiksted, V.I.

Economic Censuses of Virgin Islands, 1982: employment, establishments, payroll, and receipts, by SIC 1- to 4-digit industry, island, and city, 2593–1

Freedom of Information Act

Cost control proposals for Fed Govt programs and mgmt, 3-year savings by function and agency, and financial and operating data, 1960s-81, 16908–1.31

HHS activities, requests received and denied, costs, and fees collected, 1983, annual rpt, 4004–21

IRS prosecutions, litigations, and interpretive law decisions, FY83 with comparisons to FY82, annual rpt, 8304–3.2

USDA Inspector General FOIA requests and processing, 2nd half 1984, semiannual rpt, 1002–4

Freedom of the press

Foreign human rights conditions in 162 countries, economic and military aid of US, and economic aid of intl organizations, 1981-83, annual rpt, 21384–3

Freeland, Mark S.

"Health Spending in the 1980s: Integration of Clinical Practice Patterns with Management", 4652–1.407

Freeways

see Highways

Freight

Argentina grain production, exports by firm, storage by facility type and port, and shipments to ports by mode of transport, by grain type, selected years 1954-81, 1528–185

Canada grain handling and rail transport system financial and operating data, and effects of limited capacity on grain and oilseed exports, selected years 1950-82, 1528–176

China economic conditions, agricultural and industrial production, trade, and domestic and foreign investment, 1980-85, 2048–106

Coal-fired electric power plants, capacity, coal demand, and coal supply by mode of transport and region of origin, by State, for units planned 1983-92, annual rpt, 3088–18

Coal production and stocks by district, and shipments by district of origin, State of destination, consuming sector, and mode of transport, quarterly rpt, 3162–8

Coal transport environmental impacts by type and mode of transport, methodology for assessing alternative systems, 1983 rpt, 3408–28

Coastal environmental characteristics, fish, wildlife, and use, and population socioeconomic data, for individual areas, series, 5506–4

Communist, OECD, and selected other countries freight and carrier inventories, by mode of transport, 1960s-83, annual rpt, 244–5.10

County Business Patterns: establishments, employees, and payrolls, by SIC 4-digit industry and county, 1981, annual State rpt series, 2326–8

County Business Patterns: establishments, employees, and payrolls, by SIC 4-digit industry and county, 1982, annual State rpt series, 2326–6

Cuba economic conditions, agricultural and industrial production and distribution, trade, and intl economic relations, 1970-82 and trends from 1957, 248–40

Defense Fuel Supply Center procurement, prices, stocks, transport, and other activities and finances, FY83, annual rpt, 3904–8

DOD shipments of military and personal property, loss claims, passenger traffic, and costs, by mode of transport, quarterly rpt, 3702–1

Employment and finances of ICC-regulated carriers by mode of transport, and ICC activities, FY80-83 and trends, annual rpt, 9484–1

Employment, earnings, and hours, by SIC 4-digit nonfarm industry, monthly 1974-Feb 1984, annual update, 6744–4

Energy use in transportation sector by mode, fuel supplies, and demographic and economic determinants of vehicle use, 1970s-83, annual rpt, 3304–5

Exports of US, detailed Schedule E commodities by mode of transport and world area and country of destination, 1983, annual rpts, 2424–5

Farm, food, and all products rail freight index, monthly rpt, 1502–4

Fed Govt foreign cargo shipments and costs by agency or program and route, and employment and economic impacts of US vessel preference, 1980, GAO rpt, 26117–30

Fed Govt programs and mgmt cost control proposals, 3-year savings by function and agency, and financial and operating data, 1960s-81, 16908–1

Freight

Food prices (farm-retail), marketing cost components, and industry finances and productivity, selected years 1967-83, annual rpt, 1544–9

Foreign and US feed and livestock trade by product and world region, and ocean freight rates between selected countries of origin and destination, selected years 1960-82, 1528–177

Fruit and vegetable shipments, and arrivals in 23 US and 5 Canada cities, by mode of transport and State or country of origin, 1983, annual rpt series, 1311–4

Fruit and vegetable shipments by mode of transport, arrivals, and imports, by commodity and State and country of origin, weekly rpt, 1311–3

Fruit and vegetable truck freight rates to 6 major markets, weekly by commodity and region, with monthly truck-mile costs, 1983, annual rpt, 1311–15

Grain cooperatives marketing, storage, and shipments by mode of transport, by grain type and region, FY80, 1128–28

Grain ocean freight rates by route, and waterborne trade of grain and selected other commodities worldwide, 1966-82, 1548–235

Grain rail and barge loadings, ship and container car availability, ocean freight rates, and export inspections, prices, and sales, weekly rpt, 1272–2

Great Lakes trade, by SITC 3-digit commodity, port, vessel type, world area, and country, 1982, annual rpt, 7744–3

Hazardous material transport accidents, casualties, and property damage, by mode of transport, with DOT control activities, 1983, annual rpt, 7304–4

Household goods carriers (Class I) operating revenues, net income, and revenue tons, by firm, quarterly rpt, 9482–14

Income tax returns of sole proprietorships, detailed data by industry div and selected industry group, 1981, annual rpt, 8304–7

Income tax returns of sole proprietorships, receipts, deductions by type, payroll, and net income, by major industry, 1982, annual article, 8302–2.413

Input-output structure of US economy, detailed interindustry transactions for 85 industries, and components of final demand, 1977, article, 2702–1.421

Input-output structure of US economy, detailed interindustry transactions for 537 industries, and components of final demand, 1977 benchmark data, 2708–17

Intercity freight ton-miles and energy consumption rates, by mode of transport, 1970-82, annual rpt, 3164–73

Intl services transactions by type, and sales, assets, and employment of US multinatl service firms by industry and world region, 1977-82, 2706–5.30

Motor carriers (Class I) of property financial and operating data, by region and firm, quarterly rpt, 9482–5

Motor carriers (Class I interstate) finances, operations, equipment, employment, and payroll, by district, 1982, annual rpt, 9486–5.3

Motor carriers (Class II) of property financial and operating data, by region, 1982, annual rpt, 9484–10

Nuclear power plant spent fuel permanent disposal site and transport costs, and Nuclear Waste Fund financing, alternative projections FY83-2037, 26308–49

Oil (Alaskan) potential exports to Japan, costs and benefits, with background data on oil prices, Pacific Basin supply/demand, and tankers, various periods 1918-99, hearings, 25388–45

Ports, port facilities by type, and inland waterways by size, by location, 1982-83, annual rpt, 7704–16

Pulpwood prices, expenditures, and transportation modes in Southeast, 1981-82, annual rpt, 1204–22

Radioactive materials transport surveillance program activities and results, State survey rpt series, 9636–1

Radioactive waste and spent fuel generation, inventory, disposal by site, reprocessing, and characteristics, by source, as of 1983 and projected to 2020, annual rpt, 3364–2

Railroad finances and operations, detailed data by firm, class of service, and district, 1983, annual rpt, 9486–6.1

Railroad finances, operations, and freight rates and shares, by commodity and railroad, 1970s-82, hearings, 25268–80

Railroad freight producer price indexes, monthly 1983, annual supplement, 6762–6, 6764–2

Railroad freight volume and revenues, by commodity and region of origin and destination, 1982, annual rpt, 7604–6

Railroad revenue, income, freight, and rate of return, by Class I freight railroad and district, quarterly rpt, 9482–2

Scientists, engineers, and technicians employment in transportation, utilities, and retail and wholesale trade, by field of science and industry, 1982, 9628–72

Ships in world merchant fleet, and tonnage, by country of registry, 1982, annual rpt, 7704–3

St Lawrence Seaway ships, cargo and passenger volumes, and toll revenues, 1981-82 and trends from 1959, annual rpt, 7744–2

Statistical Abstract of US, social, political, and economic data, 1950s-83 and trends, annual rpt, 2324–1.3

Transportation census, 1982: trucks, by detailed characteristics, miles traveled, and type of product carried, State rpt series, 2573–1

Transportation finances, operations, vehicles, equipment, accidents, and energy use, by mode of transport, 1955-84, annual rpt, 7304–2

Waterborne commerce of US (domestic and foreign), freight by commodity, traffic, and passengers, by port and waterway, 1982, annual rpt, 3754–3

Waterborne trade of US, and Fed Govt sponsored cargo by agency, total and US-flag share by vessel type, selected years 1973-82, annual rpt, 7704–14.2, 7704–14.3

Waterborne trade of US, by type of service, commodity, country, route, and US port, 1982, annual rpt, 7704–2

Watermelon grower-to-retailer handling costs and time, by handling phase and method, 1982, 1308–18

Index by Subjects and Names

Western States economic indicators, Fed Reserve 12th District, quarterly rpt, 9393–1.1

see also Air cargo

see also Containerization

Fremont, Calif.

see also under By City in the "Index by Categories"

French Antilles

see Caribbean area

French, Carol L.

"Hydroelectric Power: 1983 Was a Record Year", 3162–39.401

French Guiana

Background Notes, summary social, political, and economic data, 1983 rpt, 7006–2.12

Economic, social, and political summary data, by country, 1984, annual factbook, 244–11

Exports of US, detailed Schedule B commodities by country of destination, 1983, annual rpt, 2424–9

Exports of US, detailed Schedule E commodities by mode of transport and world area and country of destination, 1983, annual rpts, 2424–5

Imports of US, detailed Schedule A commodities by country and world area of origin, and mode of transport, 1983, annual rpts, 2424–2

Imports of US, detailed TSUSA commodities by country of origin, 1983, annual rpt, 2424–4

Minerals Yearbook, 1982, Vol 3: foreign country reviews of production, trade, and policies, by commodity, annual rpt, 5604–35

Minerals Yearbook, 1983, Vol 3 preprints: foreign country review of production, trade, and policies, by commodity, annual rpt, 5604–23.89

Population size and growth rates, and latest available benchmark demographic data, by country, 1950-83, biennial rpt, 2324–4

see also under By Foreign Country in the "Index by Categories"

French, Jean

"Mortality from Flash Floods: A Review of National Weather Service Reports, 1969-81", 4102–1.406

French Polynesia

see Oceania

French West Indies

see Caribbean area

Fresno, Calif.

Census of Housing, 1980: occupancy and unit characteristics, by race, Hispanic origin, and city, SMSA rpt, 2473–1.165

Census of Population and Housing, 1980: detailed population and housing characteristics, by county, city, and census tract, SMSA rpt, 2551–2.165

Economic conditions in Fresno, Calif, and population, labor, and housing indicators, various periods 1974-85, hearing, 21248–84

Wages of office and plant workers, by occupation, 1984 SMSA survey rpt, 6785–11.6

see also under By City and By SMSA or MSA in the "Index by Categories"

Index by Subjects and Names

Fruit and fruit products

Fresno County, Calif.

Economic conditions in Fresno, Calif, and population, labor, and housing indicators, various periods 1974-85, hearing, 21248–84

Fried, Joel

"Government Loan and Guarantee Programs", 9391–1.403

Friedenberg, Howard

"Regional Nonfarm Wages and Salaries Thus Far in the Recovery", 2702–1.412

"Regional Shifts in Personal Income by Industrial Component, 1959-83", 2702–1.443

Friedman, Benjamin M.

"Implications of the Government Deficit for U.S. Capital Formation", 9373–3.27

Friedman, Brian

"Apparel Stores Display Above-Average Productivity", 6722–1.463

Friedman, Edward A.

"Consumer Spending: Recovery and Beyond", 1004–16.1

Fringe benefits

see Employee benefit plans

Frisbee, Pamela

"Bankers' Banks: An Institution Whose Time Has Come?", 9371–1.415

Fritts, Thomas H.

"Turtles, Birds, and Mammals in the Northern Gulf of Mexico and Nearby Atlantic Waters: An Overview Based on Aerial Surveys of OCS Areas, with Emphasis on Oil and Gas Effects", 5508–85

Fruit and fruit products

Agricultural Statistics, 1983, annual rpt, 1004–1

Agriculture census, 1982: farms, farmland, production and costs, and operator characteristics, preliminary State and county rpt series, 2330–1

Agriculture census, 1982: farms, farmland, production, finances, and operator characteristics, by county, final State rpt series, 2331–1

Apple production, marketing, and prices in 4 Appalachian States, 1983/84 crop year, annual rpt, 1311–13

California farm real estate market values, by use and crop, 1976-84, annual rpt, 1541–8.1

Canned and preserved fruits industries, productivity, hours, and employment indexes, 1954-81, annual rpt, 6824–1.3

Census of Population, 1980: detailed socioeconomic and demographic characteristics, by age, sex, race, Hispanic origin, occupation, and industry, State rpt series, 2531–4

Cherry production, prices, and use, by producer State, 1981-83, annual rpt, 1621–18.6

Cherry production, prices, and use, by producer State, 1982-84, annual rpt, 1621–18.2

China economic conditions, agricultural and industrial production, trade, and domestic and foreign investment, 1980-85, 2048–106

Cold storage capacity of warehouses, by State and SMSA, Oct 1983, biennial rpt, 1614–2

Cold storage food stocks by commodity and census div, and warehouse cold storage space in use, by State, monthly rpt, 1631–5

Cold storage food stocks of 77 commodities, by region, 1983, annual rpt, 1631–11

Consumer expenditures for fruit, vegetable, and potato products related to changes in income and other household characteristics, 1977-78, 1548–236

Consumption of food and nutrient intake by individuals, by food group, source, and socioeconomic characteristics, 1977-78 natl survey, final rpt series, 1356–4

Consumption, supply, trade, prices, expenditures, and indexes, by food commodity, 1963-83, annual rpt, 1544–4

Cooperatives finances and operations, aggregate for top 100 assns by principal product and revenue source, FY82, annual rpt, 1124–3

Cooperatives, membership, activities, and finances, by commodity and selected State, 1900-80 with trends from 1863, 1128–30

County Business Patterns: establishments, employees, and payrolls, by SIC 4-digit industry and county, 1981, annual State rpt series, 2326–8

County Business Patterns: establishments, employees, and payrolls, by SIC 4-digit industry and county, 1982, annual State rpt series, 2326–6

CPI by detailed component, for US city average, 28 SMSAs, and 4 regions by population size, monthly rpt, 6762–2

Cranberry production, prices, area, and yield, for 5 States, 1982-83 and forecast 1984, annual rpt, 1621–18.4

Cuba economic conditions, agricultural and industrial production and distribution, trade, and intl economic relations, 1970-82 and trends from 1957, 248–40

Eastern Europe agricultural production and trade by commodity, food consumption, and farm inputs, for 6 countries, 1960-80 with projections to 1991, 1528–178

EC fruit and vegetable product trade and tariffs, 1966-78, and effect of Greece, Spain, and Portugal entry into EC, projected to 1986, 1528–182

Employment, earnings, and hours, by selected SIC 1- to 4-digit industry, State, and for 278 major labor areas, 1939-83, annual rpt, 6744–5

Employment, earnings, and hours, by SIC 4-digit nonfarm industry, monthly 1974-Feb 1984, annual update, 6744–4

Exports and imports of US, by agricultural commodity and country, bimonthly rpt with articles, 1522–1

Exports and imports of US, by detailed agricultural commodity and country, FY83 and CY83, semiannual rpts, 1522–4

Exports and imports of US, by detailed agricultural commodity for 8 major commodity groups, monthly rpt, 1922–8

Exports and imports of US, detailed SIC-based commodities by world area, 1983, annual rpts, 2424–6

Exports and imports of US, totals and as percent of domestic production, by SIC 2- to 5-digit commodity, 1981, annual rpt, 2424–3

Exports of manufactured and agricultural commodities, manufacturing production, and export-related employment, 1960s-82, State rpt series, 2046–3

Exports of US, detailed commodities by country of destination, monthly rpt, 2422–3

Exports of US, detailed Schedule B commodities by country of destination, 1983, annual rpt, 2424–9

Exports of US, detailed Schedule E commodities by mode of transport and world area and country of destination, 1983, annual rpts, 2424–5

Exports under PL 480 concessional sales program, by commodity and country, 1955-83, semiannual rpt, 1922–6

Farm finances, assets, liabilities, income, receipts by commodity and State, and expenses, 1980-83 and trends from 1910, annual rpt, 1544–16

Farm production inputs, outputs, and productivity, by region, 1939-82, annual rpt, 1544–17

Finances and operations, by SIC 2- to 4-digit industry, 1970s-83 and projected to 1988, annual rpt, 2014–4

Foreign agricultural production, prices, and trade, by country, 1983 and outlook for 1984/85, annual world region rpt series, 1524–4

Foreign and US agricultural production, trade, and climatic devs, weekly press release, 1922–4

Foreign and US fresh and processed fruit, vegetable, and nut production and trade, FAS monthly rpt with articles, 1925–34

Foreign and US trade of fresh and processed tropical fruit, by country, 1981-82, FAS rpt supplement, 1925–35.1

Fruit fly control, ethylene dibromide fumigation of tropical fruit imports, FY82, and cost of EDB and alternatives for Florida grapefruit and Hawaii papaya, 1984 rpt, 21168–29

Futures trading by commodity and exchange, and Commodity Futures Trading Commission activities, funding, and employment, FY83, annual rpt, 11924–2

Genetic resource (plant and animal) conservation, commercial uses, causes of depletion, and geographic sources, 1984 rpt, 5548–13

Great Lakes trade, by SITC 3-digit commodity, port, vessel type, world area, and country, 1982, annual rpt, 7744–3

Imports of US, detailed Schedule A commodities by country and world area of origin, and mode of transport, 1983, annual rpts, 2424–2

Imports of US, detailed Schedule A commodities by country, monthly rpt, 2422–2

Imports of US, detailed TSUSA commodities by country of origin, 1983, annual rpt, 2424–4

Income tax returns of corporations, detailed income and tax items by industry, 1981, annual rpt, 8304–4

Income tax returns of partnerships, detailed data by industry, 1981 estimates, annual article, 8302–2.404

Income tax returns of partnerships, receipts by source, deductions by type, and establishments, by selected industry, 1982, annual article, 8302–2.416

Income tax returns of sole proprietorships, detailed data by industry div and selected industry group, 1981, annual rpt, 8304–7

Fruit and fruit products

Income tax returns of sole proprietorships, receipts, deductions by type, payroll, and net income, by major industry, 1982, annual article, 8302–2.413

Input-output structure of US economy, detailed interindustry transactions for 537 industries, and components of final demand, 1977 benchmark data, 2708–17

Juice (fruit) trade, tariffs, and industry operating data, 1979-83, TSUSA commodity rpt, 9885–1.70

Kiwifruit exports of New Zealand, by country of destination, 1977-83, article, 1925–34.410

Liquor production, stocks, and materials used, by type and State, FY81-82, last issue of annual rpt, 8484–1.2

Liquor production, stocks, materials used, and taxable and tax-free removals, by State, monthly rpt, 8486–1.3

Manufacturing census, 1982: financial and operating data, by SIC 2- to 4-digit industry, State, SMSA, and county, preliminary census div rpt series, 2491–3

Manufacturing census, 1982: financial and operating data, for SIC 4-digit industries by product, preliminary rpt, 2491–1.9, 2491–1.10, 2491–1.12

Marketing cash receipts of farms, by detailed commodity and State, 1979-82, annual rpt, 1544–18

Melon production, prices, stocks, and consumption, periodic situation rpt with articles, 1561–11

Minority group and women employment, by occupational group and SIC 2- to 3-digit industry, 1981, annual rpt, 9244–1.1

Occupational injury and illness rates, by SIC 2- to 4-digit industry, 1982, annual rpt, 6844–1

OECD trade, total and for 4 major countries, and US trade by country, by commodity, 1972-82, annual world region rpt series, 244–13

Peach production, marketing, and prices in 4 Southeastern States and Appalachia, 1983, annual rpt, 1311–12

Pesticide use and acreage treated, for 12 vegetable and melon crops, by type of pesticide, method of application, and region, 1979, 1588–82

Pineapple production, processing, and trade, by country, 1982-84, article, 1925–34.415

Prices (farm-retail) for foods, marketing cost components, and industry finances and productivity, selected years 1967-83, annual rpt, 1544–9

Prices (wholesale) for fresh fruit and vegetables in NYC, Chicago, and selected shipping points, by crop, 1983, annual rpt, 1311–8

Prices received by farmers and production value for detailed crops by State, 1981-83, annual rpt, 1621–2

Prices received by farmers for major products, and paid for farm inputs and living items, by commodity and State, monthly rpt, 1629–1

Prices received by farmers for major products, and paid for farm inputs, by commodity and State, 1983, annual rpt, 1629–5

Producer prices and indexes, by stage of processing and detailed commodity, monthly rpt, 6762–6

Producer prices and indexes, by stage of processing and detailed commodity, monthly 1983, annual supplement, 6764–2

Production, acreage, and prices, for melons and strawberries, by State, 1981-84, annual rpts, 1621–25

Production, acreage, and yield, current and forecast for melons and strawberries by State, periodic rpt, 1621–12

Production and farm finances, expenses by type, and domestic economic impact, selected years 1972-82 and preliminary 1983-84, annual rpt, 1544–19

Production, farms, acreage, and related data, by selected crop and State, monthly rpt, 1621–1

Production, prices, and use, 1981-84, annual rpt series, 1621–18

Production, prices, trade, and marketing, by commodity, current situation and forecast, monthly rpt, 1502–4

Production, prices, trade, stocks, and use, by selected crop, periodic situation rpt with articles, 1561–6

Prune (dried) production, trade, consumption, and stocks of US and 2 countries, EC subsidies, and US exports by country, 1982/83-1984/85, article, 1925–34.435

Raisin production, trade, consumption, and stocks of US and 3 countries, and US exports by country, various periods 1982/83-1984/85, article, 1925–34.434

Raspberries from Canada at less than fair value, imports injury to US industry, investigation with background financial and operating data, 1984 rpt, 9886–14.112

Shipments by mode of transport, arrivals, and imports, for fruit and vegetables by commodity and State and country of origin, weekly rpt, 1311–3

Shipments of fruits and vegetables, and arrivals in 23 US and 5 Canada cities, by mode of transport and State or country of origin, 1983, annual rpt series, 1311–4

Truck transport of fruit and vegetables, costs per vehicle-mile by component for fleets and owner-operator trucks, monthly rpt, 1272–1

Truck transport of fruit and vegetables to 6 major markets, weekly rates by commodity and region, and monthly truck-mile costs, 1983 annual rpt, 1311–15

Underground economy, household expenditures and participation by type of goods or service and sociodemographic characteristics, with methodology and bibl, 1981 survey, 8308–27

USDA agricultural surplus direct purchase program finances, and purchases and food received by schools by commodity, various periods 1936-83, 1548–243

Virgin Islands economic censuses, 1982: employment, establishments, payroll, and receipts, by SIC 1- to 4-digit industry, island, and city, 2593–1

Waterborne commerce of US (domestic and foreign), freight by commodity, traffic, and passengers, by port and waterway, 1982, annual rpt, 3754–3

Watermelon grower-to-retailer handling costs and time, by handling phase and method, 1982, 1308–18

Index by Subjects and Names

Wholesale trade census, 1982: employment, establishments, sales by commodity, and payroll, by SIC 4-digit kind of business and State, preliminary rpt, 2403–1.32

Wine production, withdrawals, and stocks, and materials used by type, by State, FY81-82, last issue of annual rpt, 8484–1.4

see also Citrus fruits

see also Nuts

see also under By Commodity in the "Index by Categories"

Ft. Lauderdale, Fla.

see also under By City and By SMSA or MSA in the "Index by Categories"

FTC

see Federal Trade Commission

FTC Communications

Financial and operating data for 7 major telegraph carriers, quarterly rpt, 9282–1

Fuel

see terms listed under Energy resources

Fuel allocation

Regulation of oil prices and allocation, DOE enforcement, and overcharge allegations, settlements, and refunds to States, by company, as of June 1983, hearing, 21368–50

Fujairah

see United Arab Emirates

Fulco, Lawrence J.

"Strong Post-Recession Gain in Productivity Contributes to Slow Growth in Labor Costs", 6722–1.470

Fullerton, Calif.

see also under By City in the "Index by Categories"

Fullerton, Howard N., Jr.

"1995 Labor Force: A Second Look", 6728–29

Funerals

see Cemeteries and funerals

see Military cemeteries and funerals

Fungicides

see Pesticides

Funk, Velton T.

"Costs and Indexes for Domestic Oil and Gas Field Equipment and Production Operations, 1983", 3164–45

"Indexes and Estimates of Domestic Well Drilling Costs, 1983 and 1984", 3164–67

Furniture

see Household furnishings

see Office furniture and equipment

Furs and fur industry

Agriculture census, 1982: farms, farmland, production, finances, and operator characteristics, by county, final State rpt series, 2331–1

County Business Patterns: establishments, employees, and payrolls, by SIC 4-digit industry and county, 1981, annual State rpt series, 2326–8

County Business Patterns: establishments, employees, and payrolls, by SIC 4-digit industry and county, 1982, annual State rpt series, 2326–6

Endangered animals and plants foreign trade including reexports of live specimens and products, by purpose, country, and species, 1982, annual rpt, 5504–19

Exports and imports of dairy, livestock, and poultry live animals, meat, and products, by commodity and country of destination, FAS quarterly rpt, 1925–32

Index by Subjects and Names

Gainesville, Fla.

Exports and imports of US, by agricultural commodity and country, bimonthly rpt with articles, 1522–1

Exports and imports of US, by detailed agricultural commodity and country, FY83 and CY83, semiannual rpts, 1522–4

Exports and imports of US, detailed SIC-based commodities by world area, 1983, annual rpts, 2424–6

Exports and imports of US, totals and as percent of domestic production, by SIC 2- to 5-digit commodity, 1981, annual rpt, 2424–3

Exports of US, detailed commodities by country of destination, monthly rpt, 2422–3

Exports of US, detailed Schedule B commodities by country of destination, 1983, annual rpt, 2424–9

Exports of US, detailed Schedule E commodities by mode of transport and world area and country of destination, 1983, annual rpts, 2424–5

Imports of US, detailed Schedule A commodities by country, monthly rpt, 2422–2

Imports of US, detailed TSUSA commodities by country of origin, 1983, annual rpt, 2424–4

Income tax returns of sole proprietorships, detailed data by industry div and selected industry group, 1981, annual rpt, 8304–7

Income tax returns of sole proprietorships, receipts, deductions by type, payroll, and net income, by major industry, 1982, annual article, 8302–2.413

Manufacturing census, 1982: financial and operating data, by SIC 2- to 4-digit industry, State, SMSA, and county, preliminary census div rpt series, 2491–3

Manufacturing census, 1982: financial and operating data, for SIC 4-digit industries by product, preliminary rpt, 2491–1.96

Mink and mink pelt production, by State, 1983-84 with trends from 1969, annual rpt, 1631–7

Thefts, and total value of property stolen and recovered, by property type, 1983, annual rpt, 6224–2.1

see also Hides and skins

see also under By Commodity in the "Index by Categories"

see also under By Industry in the "Index by Categories"

Future

see Projections

Futures Group

"Central America: The Effects of Population on Economic and Social Development", 028–19.2

Futures trading

Agricultural Statistics, 1983, annual rpt, 1004–1.2

Cocoa bean futures prices at NYC exchange, FAS semiannual circular, 1925–9

Cotton futures unfixed call sales and purchases and open contracts on NYC exchange, weekly rpt, 11922–3

Cotton prices at selected spot markets, futures prices at NYC exchange, and CCC loan rates, 1983/84 with some trends from 1920, annual rpt, 1309–2

Cotton prices in 8 spot markets, futures prices at NYC exchange, farm prices, and CCC loan stocks, monthly rpt, 1309–1

Dairy marketing and price data for selected cities, States, and regions, 1983, annual rpt, 1317–1

Employment by detailed occupation, for 29 SIC 2-digit nonmanufacturing industries, 1981 BLS survey, 6748–60

Exchange activity by commodity, and Commodities Futures Trading Commission oversight, FY83, annual rpt, 11924–2

Exchange activity, by exchange for 42 contract commodities, annual rpt, suspended, 11924–3

Exchange activity in selected commodities, foreign currencies, and stock indexes, Chicago and other markets, monthly rpt, 11922–1

Exchange activity in selected commodities, Treasury securities, and stock indexes, NYC, Chicago, and other markets, monthly rpt, 11922–5

Exchange activity in selected commodities, Treasury securities, and stock indexes, NYC market, monthly rpt, 11922–2

Foreign currency futures trading on Chicago Intl Monetary Market, total and as percent of interbank transfers and foreign trade volume, various periods 1977-83, article, 9375–1.401

Foreign currency futures turnover at Intl Monetary Market, by currency, Mar 1980 and Apr 1983, article, 9385–1.411

Futures market efficiency tests for Treasury bills, 1984 technical paper, 9316–1.105

Gold and silver production, stocks, consumption, prices, and futures trading, Mineral Industry survey, monthly rpt, 5612–1.10

Grain futures contracts, stocks in deliverable position by type and grade, weekly tables, 11922–4

Grain futures settlement prices, by commodity and exchange, weekly rpt, 1313–2

Income tax returns of sole proprietorships, detailed data by industry div and selected industry group, 1981, annual rpt, 8304–7

North Central States, FHLB 6th District insured S&Ls financial condition and operations by State, quarterly rpt, 9302–23

Rice market activities, prices, inspections, sales, trade, supply, and use, for US and selected foreign markets, weekly rpt, 1313–8

Rice, sunflower seed, and soybean futures market hedging and price forecasting efficiency, 1980-83, article, 1502–3.404

Treasury bill spot and futures market investments, relative rates of return, 1978-82, technical paper, 9387–8.88

Treasury bond futures options pricing measures, for 53 call options traded Oct 1982-Apr 1983, article, 9391–1.404

Treasury securities put options trading, hypothetical thrift instn losses, 1983 technical paper, 9316–1.102

Gabon

Economic conditions and foreign marketing prospects in 46 Sub-Saharan countries, 1983 world region rpt, 2046–5.1

Economic, social, and political summary data, by country, 1984, annual factbook, 244–11

Economic trends in income, production, prices, employment, finances, and trade, 1984 semiannual rpt, 2046–4.11

Exports and imports of US, by commodity and country, 1972-82, annual world region rpt, 244–13.4

Exports of US, detailed Schedule B commodities by country of destination, 1983, annual rpt, 2424–9

Exports of US, detailed Schedule E commodities by mode of transport and world area and country of destination, 1983, annual rpts, 2424–5

Imports of US, detailed Schedule A commodities by country and world area of origin, and mode of transport, 1983, annual rpts, 2424–2

Imports of US, detailed TSUSA commodities by country of origin, 1983, annual rpt, 2424–4

Loans and grants for economic and military assistance from US and intl agencies, by program and country, FY46-83, annual rpt, 9914–5

Military aid of US, arms sales, and training programs costs and budget requests by program, world region, and country, FY83-85, annual rpt, 7144–13

Military spending, arms trade, and armed forces size, with total govt spending and population, by country, 1972-82, annual rpt, 9824–1

Minerals Yearbook, 1982, Vol 3: foreign country reviews of production, trade, and policies, by commodity, annual rpt, 5604–35

Minerals Yearbook, 1983, Vol 3 preprints: foreign country review of production, trade, and policies, by commodity, annual rpt, 5604–23.24

Population size and growth rates, and latest available benchmark demographic data, by country, 1950-83, biennial rpt, 2324–4

see also under By Foreign Country in the "Index by Categories"

Gabriel, Stephen C.

"Agricultural Finance Situation and Outlook", 1004–16.1

"Non-Real Estate and Real Estate Farm Debt Held by Individuals and Others: 1980 Benchmark and Revisions, 1972-82", 1548–230

Gadsden, Ala.

Census of Housing, 1980: occupancy and unit characteristics, by race, Hispanic origin, and city, SMSA rpt, 2473–1.166

Census of Population and Housing, 1980: detailed population and housing characteristics, by county, city, and census tract, SMSA rpt, 2551–2.166

see also under By SMSA or MSA in the "Index by Categories"

Gainesville, Fla.

Census of Housing, 1980: occupancy and unit characteristics, by race, Hispanic origin, and city, SMSA rpt, 2473–1.167

Census of Population and Housing, 1980: detailed population and housing characteristics, by county, city, and census tract, SMSA rpt, 2551–2.167

Wages of office and plant workers, by occupation, 1984 SMSA survey rpt, 6785–11.9

Gainesville, Fla.

see also under By SMSA or MSA in the "Index by Categories"

Galbraith, Karl D.
"National Defense Spending: A Review of Appropriations and Real Purchases", 2702–1.440

Gallager, John L.
"Ecology of Tidal Marshes of the Pacific Northwest Coast: A Community Profile", 5506–9.11

Gallaway, Benny J.
"Ecology of Petroleum Platforms in the Northwestern Gulf of Mexico: A Community Profile", 5506–9.7

Gallick, Edward C.
"Exclusive Dealing and Vertical Integration: The Efficiency of Contracts in the Tuna Industry", 9406–1.39

Gallipolis, Ohio
Wages by occupation, and benefits for office and plant workers, 1984 labor market area survey rpt, 6785–3.7

Gallium
see Metals and metal industries

Gallo, Anthony E.
"Advertising and Promotion in Food Marketing", 1548–234

Galper, Harvey
"Tax Incentives for Saving", 8302–2.407

Galveston, Tex.
Census of Housing, 1980: occupancy and unit characteristics, by race, Hispanic origin, and city, SMSA rpt, 2473–1.168
Census of Population and Housing, 1980: detailed population and housing characteristics, by county, city, and census tract, SMSA rpt, 2551–2.168
Waterborne commerce of US (domestic and foreign), freight by commodity, traffic, and passengers, by port and waterway, 1982, annual rpt, 3754–3.2
see also under By SMSA or MSA in the "Index by Categories"

Gambia
Agricultural situation in sub-Saharan Africa, by country, 1982-83 and outlook for 1984, annual rpt, 1524 4.10
AID activities and funding by project and function, FY85, and developing countries summary socioeconomic data, 1970s-83, by country, annual rpt, 9914–3
AID economic assistance to developing countries, obligations and disbursements by country, quarterly rpt, 9912–4
Economic conditions and foreign marketing prospects in 46 Sub-Saharan countries, 1983 world region rpt, 2046–5.1
Economic, social, and political summary data, by country, 1984, annual factbook, 244–11
Exports of US, detailed Schedule B commodities by country of destination, 1983, annual rpt, 2424–9
Exports of US, detailed Schedule E commodities by mode of transport and world area and country of destination, 1983, annual rpts, 2424–5
Imports of US, detailed Schedule A commodities by country and world area of origin, and mode of transport, 1983, annual rpts, 2424–2
Imports of US, detailed TSUSA commodities by country of origin, 1983, annual rpt, 2424–4

Loans and grants for economic and military assistance from US and intl agencies, by program and country, FY46-83, annual rpt, 9914–5
Military aid of US, arms sales, and training programs costs and budget requests by program, world region, and country, FY83-85, annual rpt, 7144–13
Military spending, arms trade, and armed forces size, with total govt spending and population, by country, 1972-82, annual rpt, 9824–1
Minerals Yearbook, 1982, Vol 3: foreign country reviews of production, trade, and policies, by commodity, annual rpt, 5604–35
Minerals Yearbook, 1982, Vol 3 preprints: foreign country review of production, trade, and policies, by commodity, annual rpt, 5604–17.84
Population size and growth rates, and latest available benchmark demographic data, by country, 1950-83, biennial rpt, 2324–4
see also under By Foreign Country in the "Index by Categories"

Gambling
Arrests and arrest rates, by offense, offender characteristics, population size, and State, 1970s-83, annual rpt, 6224–2.2
Court cases, dispositions, convictions, and sentences of Federal criminal defendants by offense and district, as of June 1983 with trends from 1945, annual rpt, 18204–1
Govt census, 1982: State govt payments to local govts, by program, source of funds, level of govt, and State, with trends from 1902, 2460–3
Income (taxable) not reported, by illegal source, with characteristics of persons involved, methodology, and bibl, 1970s-82, 8008–112
Income (taxable) not reported on individual and corporate returns, and associated Federal revenue losses, by detailed legal and illegal source, 1973-81, 8308 26
Pretrial citation release use, cost savings for law enforcement agencies, and failures to appear in court, by offense and selected jurisdiction, 1970s-82, 6068–187
Tax (excise) collections of IRS, by source, quarterly press release, 8302–1
Tax collections of State govts, by detailed type of tax and tax rates, by State, FY83, annual rpt, 2466–2.3
Tax collections, refunds, and taxes due IRS, by State and region, and IRS court activity and operating expenses, FY83, annual rpt, 8304–3.3
Taxation and revenue systems, by type of tax and system, level of govt, and State, selected years 1958-83, annual rpt, 10044–1.3
Wiretapping authorizations by offense, costs, persons involved, arrests, trials, and convictions, 1983, annual rpt, 18204–7
see also Horse racing
see also Lotteries

Game
see Birds and bird conservation
see Hunting and trapping
see Wildlife and wildlife conservation

Index by Subjects and Names

Gannon, Martin J.
"Preferences of Temporary Workers: Time, Variety, and Flexibility", 6722–1.452

GAO
see General Accounting Office

Garbage
see Refuse and refuse disposal

Garcia, Gillian
"Discriminant Analysis of S&L Accounting Profits: 1976-81", 9316–2.47
"Right Rabbit: Which Intermediate Target Should the Fed Pursue?", 9375–1.405

Garden Grove, Calif.
Census of Housing, 1980: occupancy and unit characteristics, by race, Hispanic origin, and city, SMSA rpt, 2473–1.67
Census of Population and Housing, 1980: detailed population and housing characteristics, by county, city, and census tract, SMSA rpt, 2551–2.67
Housing and households detailed characteristics, and unit and neighborhood quality, by inside-outside central cities, 1981 survey, SMSA rpt, 2485–6.19
Housing unit starts and completions authorized by building permits in 20 MSAs, quarterly rpt, 2382–9
Housing vacancy rates for single and multifamily units and mobile homes, by city and ZIP code, 1983, annual metro area rpt, 9304–20.7
Wages of office and plant workers, by occupation, 1983 SMSA survey rpt, 6785–12.2
see also under By City in the "Index by Categories"

Gardening
see Flowers and nursery products
see Horticulture

Gardocki, Gloria J.
"National Ambulatory Medical Care Complement Survey: U.S., 1980", 4147–13.77

Garland, Colo.
Housing vacancy rates for single and multifamily units and mobile homes, by county, city, and ZIP code, 1984, annual metro area rpt, 9304–22.8

Garland, Tex.
see also under By City in the "Index by Categories"

Garment industry
see Clothing and clothing industry

Gary, Ind.
Census of Housing, 1980: occupancy and unit characteristics, by race, Hispanic origin, and city, SMSA rpt, 2473–1.169
Census of Population and Housing, 1980: detailed population and housing characteristics, by county, city, and census tract, SMSA rpt, 2551–2.169
Wages of office and plant workers, by occupation, 1983 SMSA survey rpt, 6785–12.2
see also under By City and By SMSA or MSA in the "Index by Categories"

Gas appliances
see Household appliances and equipment

Gas utilities
see Natural gas and gas industry

Gas wells
see Energy exploration and drilling

Index by Subjects and Names

Gases

- Business statistics, detailed data for major industries and economic indicators, *Survey of Current Business,* monthly rpt, 2702–1.9
- County Business Patterns: establishments, employees, and payrolls, by SIC 4-digit industry and county, 1981, annual State rpt series, 2326–8
- County Business Patterns: establishments, employees, and payrolls, by SIC 4-digit industry and county, 1982, annual State rpt series, 2326–6
- Deaths and death rates from accidents, by place, detailed cause, and demographic characteristics, 1979, US Vital Statistics annual rpt, 4144–2.1, 4144–2.5
- Exports and imports of US, detailed SIC-based commodities by world area, 1983, annual rpts, 2424–6
- Exports of US, detailed commodities by country of destination, monthly rpt, 2422–3
- Exports of US, detailed Schedule B commodities by country of destination, 1983, annual rpt, 2424–9
- Exports of US, detailed Schedule E commodities by mode of transport and world area and country of destination, 1983, annual rpts, 2424–5
- Foreign minerals production, reserves, and industry role in domestic economy and world supply, country and world region rpt series, 5606–1
- Great Lakes trade, by SITC 3-digit commodity, port, vessel type, world area, and country, 1982, annual rpt, 7744–3
- Helium (US-produced) market demand and Bur of Mines production, sales, and helium program financial statement, FY83, annual rpt, 5604–32
- Helium and other components of natural gas, analyses of samples from individual wells and pipelines in 26 States and 2 countries, 1983, annual survey, 5604–2
- Hydrogen energy R&D activities of DOE, and description and funding of 24 projects, FY83, annual rpt, 3304–18
- Imports of US, detailed TSUSA commodities by country of origin, 1983, annual rpt, 2424–4
- Industrial gases production, by product, monthly Current Industrial Rpt, 2506–8.3
- Manufacturing census, 1982: financial and operating data, for SIC 4-digit industries by product, preliminary rpt, 2491–1.175
- *Minerals Yearbook, 1982,* Vol 1: commodity reviews of production, reserves, supply, use, and trade, annual rpt, 5604–33
- *Minerals Yearbook, 1982,* Vol 2 preprints: State reviews of production and sales by commodity, and business activity, annual rpt series, 5604–16
- *Minerals Yearbook, 1982,* Vol 2: State reviews of production, sales, and firms, by commodity, and business activity, annual rpt, 5604–34
- *Minerals Yearbook, 1982,* Vol 3: foreign country reviews of production, trade, and policies, by commodity, annual rpt, 5604–35
- *Minerals Yearbook, 1982,* Vol 3 preprints: foreign country reviews of production, trade, and policies, by commodity, annual rpt series, 5604–17
- *Minerals Yearbook, 1983,* Vol 1 preprints: commodity reviews of production, reserves, supply, use, and trade, annual rpt series, 5604–15
- *Minerals Yearbook, 1983,* Vol 3 preprints: foreign country reviews of production, trade, and policies, by commodity, annual rpt series, 5604–23
- Producer prices and indexes, by stage of processing and detailed commodity, monthly rpt, 6762–6
- Producer prices and indexes, by stage of processing and detailed commodity, monthly 1983, annual supplement, 6764–2
- Production, prices, trade, use, employment, tariffs, and stockpiling, by mineral commodity, with foreign comparisons, 1979-83, annual rpt, 5604–18
- *see also* Air pollution
- *see also* Liquefied petroleum gas
- *see also* Natural gas and gas industry
- *see also* under By Commodity in the "Index by Categories"

Gasohol

- Agriculture census, 1982: farms, farmland, production, finances, and operator characteristics, by county, final State rpt series, 2331–1
- Consumption of gasohol, by State, 1983, annual rpt, 7554–1.1
- Consumption of gasoline and gasohol, and motor fuel tax rates by fuel type, by State, monthly rpt, 7552–1
- Defense Fuel Supply Center procurement, prices, stocks, transport, and other activities and finances, FY83, annual rpt, 3904–8
- Production and costs of gasohol by feedstock type, prices, and market penetration rates and excise tax exemption by State, 1983, article, 1561–16.404
- Production of gasohol and ethanol fuels, plant capacity, tax exemptions and sales by State, and prices, 1983, annual rpt, 3304–9
- Refinery financial and operating impacts from auto use of alcohol fuels, projected to 2000 with trends 1964-80, 3308–75
- Supply/demand, trade, stocks, and refining of oil and natural gas liquids, by detailed product, State, and PAD district, and refineries in US and territories, 1983 annual rpt, 3164–2
- Tax provisions (State) for motor fuel, vehicle registration fees, and disposition of receipts, by State, as of Jan 1984, biennial rpt, 7554–37
- Tennessee Valley ethanol production, feedstocks, facilities, tax incentives, and related farming data, by State, 1970s-83 and projected to 1992, 9808–69

Gasoline

- Agriculture census, 1982: farms, farmland, production and costs, and operator characteristics, preliminary State and county rpt series, 2330–1
- Agriculture census, 1982: farms, farmland, production, finances, and operator characteristics, by county, final State rpt series, 2331–1
- Air pollutant emission factors, by detailed source, 3rd edition, 1983-84 supplements, 9198–13

Gasoline

- Arson incidents investigated by Alcohol, Tobacco, and Firearms Bur, and accelerants identified by type, 1982-83, annual rpt, 8484–4.3
- Auto and light truck fuel economy performance by make, and standards, 1978-85 model years, annual rpt, 7764–9
- Auto and van operating and owning costs by component and vehicle size, for 12 years of operation, 1984 model year, biennial rpt, 7554–21
- Auto emissions control device tampering and fuel-switching incidence in 6 urban areas, 1983, annual rpt, 9194–15
- Auto fuel economy test results for models complying with California emission standards, 1984 model year, annual rpt, 3304–13
- Auto fuel economy test results, 1985 model year, annual rpt, 3304–11
- Auto, small airplane, and motorcycle operating costs by component and vehicle size or make, and Fed Govt mileage reimbursement rates, 1983, annual rpt, 9454–13
- Business statistics, detailed data for major industries and economic indicators, *Survey of Current Business,* monthly rpt, 2702–1.15
- China economic conditions, agricultural and industrial production, trade, and domestic and foreign investment, 1980-85, 2048–106
- Consumption, by fuel type, economic sector, and end use, 1983 and 2000, 2006–2.5
- Consumption, by fuel type, economic sector, census div, and State, 1960-82, State Energy Data System annual rpt, 3164–39
- Consumption, by State, 1982-83, annual summary rpt, 7554–24
- Consumption of energy, by type of air pollutant source and fuel, and State, 1981, annual rpt, 9194–14
- Consumption of gasoline and gasohol, and motor fuel tax rates by fuel type, by State, monthly rpt, 7552–1
- Consumption of motor fuel, by consuming sector, hwy-nonhwy use, and State, 1983, annual rpt, 7554–1.1
- Consumption, prices, and conservation and efficiency measures, by fuel type, end-use sector, selected industry, and region, 1960-83, annual rpt, 3164–73
- Cuba economic conditions, agricultural and industrial production and distribution, trade, and intl economic relations, 1970-82 and trends from 1957, 248–40
- Defense Fuel Supply Center procurement, prices, stocks, and other activities, FY83, annual rpt, 3904–6
- Defense Fuel Supply Center procurement, prices, stocks, transport, and other activities and finances, FY83, annual rpt, 3904–8
- DOE in-house energy use, conservation investments, and savings, by type of use and fuel and field office, FY83, annual rpt, 3024–3
- Exports and imports of US, detailed SIC-based commodities by world area, 1983, annual rpts, 2424–6
- Exports of US, detailed commodities by country of destination, monthly rpt, 2422–3

Gasoline

Exports of US, detailed Schedule B commodities by country of destination, 1983, annual rpt, 2424–9

Exports of US, detailed Schedule E commodities by mode of transport and world area and country of destination, 1983, annual rpts, 2424–5

Farm finances, assets, liabilities, income, receipts by commodity and State, and expenses, 1980-83 and trends from 1910, annual rpt, 1544–16

Farm finances, production, expenses by type, and domestic economic impact, selected years 1972-82 and preliminary 1983-84, annual rpt, 1544–19

Farm production expenditures, detailed items by farm sales size and region, 1983, annual rpt, 1614–3

Farm production inputs supply, use, and prices, periodic situation rpt with articles, 1561–16

Farmers prices received for major products and paid for farm inputs and living items, by commodity and State, monthly rpt, 1629–1

Farmers prices received for major products and paid for farm inputs, by commodity and State, 1983, annual rpt, 1629–5

Fed Govt motor vehicle fleet costs and operating data, by agency, FY83, annual rpt, 9454–9

Foreign and US oil production, trade, stocks, and prices in major cities, by refined product and country, various dates 1982-84, annual rpt, 3164–50.3, 3164–50.4

Foreign and US retail gasoline and diesel prices and tax rates, for US and 4 countries, monthly rpt, 242–5

Futures trading by commodity and exchange, and Commodity Futures Trading Commission activities, funding, and employment, FY83, annual rpt, 11924–2

Futures trading in selected commodities, foreign currencies, and stock indexes, Chicago and other markets activity, monthly rpt, 11922–1

Futures trading in selected commodities, foreign currencies, Treasury securities, and stock indexes, NYC, Chicago, and other markets activity, monthly rpt, 11922–5

Futures trading in selected commodities, Treasury securities, and stock indexes, NYC market activity, monthly rpt, 11922–2

Imports of US, detailed Schedule A commodities by country and world area of origin, and mode of transport, 1983, annual rpts, 2424–2

Imports of US, detailed Schedule A commodities by country, monthly rpt, 2422–2

Imports of US, detailed TSUSA commodities by country of origin, 1983, annual rpt, 2424–4

Injuries and deaths from use of selected consumer products and related activity, by victim age and sex, 1982, annual rpt, 9164–7

Irrigation system energy use and costs, and irrigated farm acreage by fuel and region, selected years 1974-84 and trends from 1900, article, 1561–16.406

Manufacturing energy efficiency progress, and energy use by type, by SIC 2-digit industry, 1982, annual rpt, 3304–8

Mineral industries census, 1982: financial and operating data, including materials consumed, by SIC 4-digit industry and State, preliminary rpt series, 2511–1

Natl Energy Policy Plan, energy supply, demand, and prices, by fuel and consuming sector, projected 1985-2010, biennial rpt, 3004–13

New England States electricity and gasoline sales, Fed Reserve 1st District, monthly rpt, 9373–2.6

OECD energy prices and taxes by energy source and end-use sector, for US and 9 countries, quarterly 1979-83, annual rpt, 3164–71

Price and volume of 13 oil products sold by gas plant operators, refiners, and resellers, by end-use sector, PAD district, and State, monthly rpt, 3162–11

Prices (retail), by type of fuel, region, and for 28 SMSAs and US city average, monthly press release, 6762–8

Prices and expenditures for fuels, by consuming sector, State, and fuel type, 1970-81, annual rpt, 3164–64

Prices, average retail, for selected US cities, 1979-80, hearings, 25388–45

Producer prices and indexes, by stage of processing and detailed commodity, monthly rpt, 6762–6

Producer prices and indexes, by stage of processing and detailed commodity, monthly 1983, annual supplement, 6764–2

Producers finances and operations, by energy type for US firms domestic and foreign operations, 1974-82, annual rpt, 3164–44

Production, reserves, and prices, by fuel type, and selected indicators of energy use, by State, 1982-83 with selected comparisons from 1971, annual rpt, 3164–60

Properties of gasoline, lab analysis, 1983, last issue of semiannual rpt, 3006–2.1, 3006–2.3

Refinery financial and operating impacts from auto use of alcohol fuels, projected to 2000 with trends 1964-80, 3308–75

Statistical Abstract of US, social, political, and economic data, 1950s-83 and trends, annual rpt, 2324–1.3

Supply/demand and price forecasts, by fuel type, quarterly rpt, 3162–34

Supply/demand and prices, by energy resource and major producing and consuming country and sector, detailed data, monthly rpt, 3162–24

Supply/demand and prices, by fuel type and consuming sector with foreign comparisons, 1949-83, annual rpt, 3164–74

Supply/demand and prices, by fuel type, sector, and end use, detailed trends and projections 1973-95, annual rpt, 3164–75

Supply/demand and prices, by fuel type, sector, and end use, with foreign comparisons, 1960-83 and projected to 1995, annual summary rpt, 3164–76

Supply/demand of oil and refined products, refinery capacity and use, and OPEC, non-OPEC, and spot market prices, weekly rpt, 3162–32

Index by Subjects and Names

Supply/demand, trade, stocks, and refining of oil and natural gas liquids, by detailed product, State, and PAD district, with fuel oil sulfur content, monthly rpt with articles, 3162–6

Supply/demand, trade, stocks, and refining of oil and natural gas liquids, by detailed product, State, and PAD district, and refineries in US and territories, 1983 annual rpt, 3164–2

Tax (excise) collections of IRS, by source, quarterly press release, 8302–1

Tax (excise) revenue of local govts, by excise type and State, average annual growth FY72-82, article, 10042–1.403

Tax collections of State govts, by detailed type of tax and tax rates, by State, FY83, annual rpt, 2466–2.3

Tax provisions (State) for motor fuel, vehicle registration fees, and disposition of receipts, by State, as of Jan 1984, biennial rpt, 7554–37

Tax rates for motor fuel, by State, 1975-83, annual table, 7554–32

Taxation and revenue systems, by type of tax and system, level of govt, and State, selected years 1958-83, annual rpt, 10044–1.3

Taxes for hwy use and Trust Fund revenues by tax type, and trucking industry economic effects of tax and size and weight rules, FY82-84 and projected to 1990, GAO rpt, 26117–31

Taxes for hwy use by tax type, and truck size and weight limits, economic effects on trucking industry, 1982-83 and projected 1984-87, hearings, 25328–24

Trans-Alaska Pipeline System owner companies financial data, and retail gasoline competitive position in 2 States, by company, 1980-83, hearing, 21728–51

Transportation and related energy use, for urban areas, late 1970s-82 and projected under lower auto emission standards to 1995, 3408–31

Transportation census, 1982: trucks, by detailed characteristics, miles traveled, and type of product carried, State rpt series, 2573–1

Transportation energy use by mode, fuel supplies, and demographic and economic determinants of vehicle use, 1970s-83, annual rpt, 3304–5

Transportation finances, operations, vehicles, equipment, accidents, and energy use and transport, by mode of transport, 1955-84, annual rpt, 7304–2

Trucks (heavy) energy use, efficiency, and conservation technologies, selected years 1958-82 and projected to 2000, 3308–70

Waterborne commerce of US (domestic and foreign), freight by commodity, traffic, and passengers, by port and waterway, 1982, annual rpt, 3754–3

Wholesale trade census, 1982: employment, establishments, sales by commodity, and payroll, by SIC 4-digit kind of business and State, preliminary rpt, 2403–1.36

see also Aviation fuels

see also Diesel fuel

see also Gasohol

see also Gasoline service stations

see also Petroleum and petroleum industry

Index by Subjects and Names

Gasoline service stations

- Automated teller machines and point of sale debit card systems offered by retailers, by firm, firm type, and State, 1984 survey, article, 9371–1.421
- Census of Population, 1980: detailed socioeconomic and demographic characteristics, by age, sex, race, Hispanic origin, occupation, and industry, State rpt series, 2531–4
- Census of Population, 1980: detailed socioeconomic characteristics, by county, city, and inside-outside SMSAs and central cities, State rpt series, 2531–3
- Census of Retail Trade, 1982: employment, establishments, sales, and payroll, by SIC 2- to 4-digit kind of business, SMSA, and retail district, State rpt series, 2401–1
- Census of Retail Trade, 1982: employment, establishments, sales, and payroll, by SIC 2- to 4-digit kind of business, SMSA, county, and city, State rpt series, 2397–1
- Census of Retail Trade, 1982: employment, establishments, sales, and payroll, for gasoline service stations, by State, preliminary rpt, 2395–1.12
- Collective bargaining agreements expiring during year, covered workers by SIC 2-digit industry, firm, and union, with summary of key provisions, 1984, annual rpt, 6784–9
- Construction industries census, 1982: financial and operating data, by SIC 4-digit industry and State, final rpt series, 2373–1
- Construction industries census, 1982: financial and operating data, by SIC 4-digit industry and State, preliminary rpt series, 2371–1
- Construction put in place, permits authorized by region, State, and MSA, and Federal contract awards, by construction type, bimonthly rpt with articles, 2012–1
- County Business Patterns: establishments, employees, and payrolls, by SIC 4-digit industry and county, 1981, annual State rpt series, 2326–8
- County Business Patterns: establishments, employees, and payrolls, by SIC 4-digit industry and county, 1982, annual State rpt series, 2326–6
- Employment, earnings, and hours, by selected SIC 1- to 4-digit industry, State, and for 278 major labor areas, 1939-83, annual rpt, 6744–5
- Employment, earnings, and hours, by SIC 4-digit nonfarm industry, monthly 1974-Feb 1984, annual update, 6744–4
- Energy use in nonresidential buildings, expenditures, and conservation, by building characteristics, EIA survey series, 3166–8
- Franchises of firms engaged in distribution of goods and services by kind of business, establishments by State, and sales, 1982-84, annual rpt, 2014–5
- Income tax returns of corporations, detailed income and tax items by industry, 1981, annual rpt, 8304–4
- Income tax returns of corporations with foreign tax credit, income and deductions by type, asset size, and selected industry group, 1980, article, 8302–2.415

Income tax returns of partnerships, detailed data by industry, 1981 estimates, annual article, 8302–2.404

- Income tax returns of partnerships, receipts by source, deductions by type, and establishments, by selected industry, 1982, annual article, 8302–2.416
- Income tax returns of sole proprietorships, detailed data by industry div and selected industry group, 1981, annual rpt, 8304–7
- Income tax returns of sole proprietorships, receipts, deductions by type, payroll, and net income, by major industry, 1982, annual article, 8302–2.413
- Income tax returns with investment credits, for individuals by income, and for sole proprietorships by industry, 1981, article, 8302–2.409
- Minority group and women employment, by occupational group and SIC 2- to 3-digit industry, 1981, annual rpt, 9244–1.1
- Occupational injury and illness rates, by SIC 2- to 4-digit industry, 1982, annual rpt, 6844–1
- Productivity, hours, and employment indexes for selected SIC 3- and 4-digit industries, 1954-82, annual rpt, 6824–1.4
- Robberies, by type of premises, population size, and region, 1983, annual rpt, 6224–2.1
- Sales and inventories, by kind of business, region, census div, and selected State, SMSA, and city, and seasonal adjustments, monthly rpt, 2413–3
- Sales, inventories, purchases, gross margin, and accounts receivable, by SIC 2- to 4-digit kind of business and type of ownership, 1983, annual rpt, 2413–5
- Scientists, engineers, and technicians employment in transportation, utilities, and retail and wholesale trade, by field of science and industry, 1982, 9628–72
- Tax provisions (State) for motor fuel, vehicle registration fees, and disposition of receipts, by State, as of Jan 1984, biennial rpt, 7554–37
- Virgin Islands economic censuses, 1982: employment, establishments, payroll, and receipts, by SIC 1- to 4-digit industry, island, and city, 2593–1

see also Automobile repair

Gasoline tax

see Excise tax

Gastonia, N.C.

- Census of Housing, 1980: occupancy and unit characteristics, by race, Hispanic origin, and city, SMSA rpt, 2473–1.116
- Census of Population and Housing, 1980: detailed population and housing characteristics, by county, city, and census tract, SMSA rpt, 2551–2.116
- Wages by occupation, and benefits for office and plant workers, 1983 labor market area survey rpt, 6785–3.2

see also under By SMSA or MSA in the "Index by Categories"

Gastrointestinal diseases

see Digestive diseases

Gavin, William T.

- "Forecasting the Money Supply in Time Series Models", 9377–9.8
- "Reflections on Money and Inflation", 9377–1.403
- "Velocity: A Multivariate Time-Series Approach", 9377–9.13

Gemstones

Gay, Robert S.

"Union Settlements and Aggregate Wage Behavior in the 1980s", 9362–1.410

Gayer, Peter D.

"Use Valuation of Louisiana's Rural Lands: Short-Run Fiscal Impacts", 1208–206

GCA Corp.

"Acid Rain Information Book, Second Edition", 3408–27

Geller, E. Scott

"Development of Corporate Incentive Programs for Motivating Safety Belt Use: A Review", 7762–9.409

Gemstones

- Exports and imports of US, detailed SIC-based commodities by world area, 1983, annual rpts, 2424–6
- Exports of US, detailed commodities by country of destination, monthly rpt, 2422–3
- Exports of US, detailed Schedule B commodities by country of destination, 1983, annual rpt, 2424–9
- Exports of US, detailed Schedule E commodities by mode of transport and world area and country of destination, 1983, annual rpts, 2424–5
- Foreign minerals production, reserves, and industry role in domestic economy and world supply, country and world region rpt series, 5606–1
- Great Lakes trade, by SITC 3-digit commodity, port, vessel type, world area, and country, 1982, annual rpt, 7744–3
- Imports of US, detailed Schedule A commodities by country and world area of origin, and mode of transport, 1983, annual rpts, 2424–2
- Imports of US, detailed Schedule A commodities by country, monthly rpt, 2422–2
- Imports of US, detailed TSUSA commodities by country of origin, 1983, annual rpt, 2424–4
- *Minerals Yearbook, 1982,* Vol 1: commodity reviews of production, reserves, supply, use, and trade, annual rpt, 5604–33
- *Minerals Yearbook, 1982,* Vol 2 preprints: State reviews of production and sales by commodity, and business activity, annual rpt series, 5604–16
- *Minerals Yearbook, 1982,* Vol 2: State reviews of production, sales, and firms, by commodity, and business activity, annual rpt, 5604–34
- *Minerals Yearbook, 1982,* Vol 3: foreign country reviews of production, trade, and policies, by commodity, annual rpt, 5604–35
- *Minerals Yearbook, 1982,* Vol 3 preprints: foreign country reviews of production, trade, and policies, by commodity, annual rpt series, 5604–17
- *Minerals Yearbook, 1983,* Vol 1 preprints: commodity review of production, reserves, supply, use, and trade, annual rpt, 5604–15.26
- *Minerals Yearbook, 1983,* Vol 3 preprints: foreign country reviews of production, trade, and policies, by commodity, annual rpt series, 5604–23
- Occupational injuries and incidence, nonmetallic mineral mining and related operations, detailed analysis, 1982, annual rpt, 6664–1

Gemstones

Production, prices, trade, use, employment, tariffs, and stockpiling, by mineral commodity, with foreign comparisons, 1979-83, annual rpt, 5604–18

Retail trade census, 1982: employment, establishments, sales, and payroll, for jewelry stores, by State, preliminary rpt, 2395–1.30

Stockpiling of strategic and critical materials, Fed Govt activities and inventories by commodity, Oct 1983-Mar 1984, semiannual rpt, 9432–1

Stockpiling of strategic materials, inventories, costs, and goals, by commodity, as of June 1984, semiannual rpt, 9452–7

Wholesale trade census, 1982: employment, establishments, sales by commodity, and payroll, by SIC 4-digit kind of business and State, preliminary rpt, 2403–1.19

see also Jewelry

see also under By Commodity in the "Index by Categories"

Gendreau, Brian C.

"Carrying Costs and Treasury Bill Futures", 9387–8.88

General Accounting Office

- Activities and operations of GAO, and resulting Fed Govt savings, FY83, annual rpt, 26104–1
- AFDC and food stamp program costs and productivity in 8 States, 1973-82, GAO rpt, 26111–18
- AFDC eligibility under Omnibus Budget Reconciliation Act, effect on caseloads and recipient benefits and living costs, 1981-83, GAO rpt, 26131–11
- AFDC, food stamp, and SSI overpayments, payment error rates, and sanctions imposed, by State, various dates 1980-82, GAO rpt, 26113–136
- AFDC workfare program participation and requirements in 16 States, Feb 1983, GAO rpt, 26131–9
- Agricultural research funding from Fed Govt and States, by region, State, and outlying area, FY78-82, GAO rpt, 26113–111
- Agricultural Stabilization and Conservation Service field offices computer systems, costs and savings by component, FY84-92, GAO rpt, 26125–27
- AID economic assistance to 7 Central American countries, by type of aid, FY80-83, GAO rpt, 26123–55
- Air Force B-1B aircraft program procurement and operating costs by component, and personnel, alternative projections FY85-89, GAO rpt, 26123–79
- Air Force C-5 and C-17 cargo aircraft dimensions and operating characteristics, 1983, GAO rpt, 26123–81
- Aircraft accidents of commuter carriers and air taxis by seating capacity and cause, and deaths, 1975-82, GAO rpt, 26113–116
- Alaska and Alaska Native corporation claims for Fed Govt land, status and Land Mgmt Bur conveyance problems, various dates 1978-FY84, GAO rpt, 26113–125
- Alcohol fuel production costs, related employment, and Fed Govt subsidies and impact on farm income, selected years 1978-90, GAO rpt, 26113–140

Index by Subjects and Names

- Army civilian employment wartime needs, status of installation mobilization and staff plans, 1982-83, GAO rpt, 26123–82
- Army personnel assigned to critical occupation specialties by skill type, and working outside specialty at 5 installations, as of Mar 1982, GAO rpt, 26123–59
- Army Reserve and Natl Guard manpower strengths and mobilization alert system efficiency, for selected units, 1982-83 survey, GAO rpt, 26123–57
- Army war reserve and excess item inventory, 1982, GAO rpt, 26123–58
- Budget of US Appendix, detailed budgets and personnel summaries, by agency, FY85, annual rpt, 104–3
- Budget of US, appropriations, outlays, balances, and budget receipts, by govtl branch and agency, FY83, annual rpt, 8104–2
- Budget of US, compact budgets by function, agency, and account, FY85 with projections to FY89, annual rpt, 104–2
- CCC dairy inventories, storage and spoilage costs of surplus butter, cheese, and nonfat dry milk, 1982-83, GAO rpt, 26113–120
- CCC tobacco support program itemized costs, adequacy of assessed producer payments, and crop loans and accrued interest, for flue-cured and burley tobacco, various periods 1981-84, GAO rpt, 26113–117
- Census Bur data coverage policy for agriculture and economic censuses, and Federal agency data use, 1984 GAO narrative rpt, 26125–26
- Charity contributions of Fed Govt employees to Combined Federal Campaign, funds by type of recipient, 1982 and trends from 1973, GAO rpt, 26119–66
- Community services block grants by type of service provider, State mgmt, and opinions of officials and groups involved, for 13 States, FY81-83, GAO rpt, 26121–84
- Computers and other equipment with nuclear weapons applications, approvals for export to PRC by item and to other foreign markets, July 1981-June 1982, GAO rpt, 26123–76
- Cost control proposals for Fed Govt programs and mgmt, CBO and GAO estimates of savings by function and agency, FY85-89, 26308–45
- Cost control proposals for Fed Govt programs and mgmt, 3-year savings by function and agency, and financial and operating data, 1960s-81, 16908–1
- Disabled American Veterans financial statements, 1982, GAO rpt, 26111–16
- DOD operations, summaries of GAO investigation rpts published 1979-83, annual rpt, 26104–6
- DOD procurement of identical items from multiple sources, and price difference by item, by service branch, FY81, GAO rpt, 26123–67
- DOD procurement revolving fund accounting mgmt, costs and cost carryovers by cause and activity site, FY82-83, GAO rpt, 26111–22
- DOD weapons and support systems costs under multiyear and annual procurement methods for 12 items in FY85 budget, by service branch, 1984 GAO rpt, 26123–83

- DOD weapons system procurement cost underestimation in budget request 5-year plans, and cost change by system, various periods FY79-89, GAO rpt, 26123–68
- DOD weapons systems cost estimates, methodology for rpts to Congress, with illustrative data and bibl, 1970s-83, GAO rpt, 26123–62
- Drug Enforcement Admin cases against major drug traffickers by case characteristics, and agents assessment of activities, in 3 cities, 1979-82, GAO rpt, 26119–57
- Drug Enforcement Organized Crime Task Forces, funding and staff by agency, region, and city, as of FY83, GAO rpt, 26119–52
- Economic dev assistance of Fed Govt, generation of jobs by industry div, model methodology and outputs, various periods FY69-78, GAO rpt, 26117–32
- Electric utilities privately owned, common stock performance measures, with comparisons to selected industry groups, selected years 1970-82, GAO rpt, 26113–129
- Energy Info Admin data collection and analysis activities, Jan 1982-Sept 1983, GAO annual rpt, 26104–14
- Executive employee performance appraisal system of Fed Govt, operations and employee attitudes, 1982 survey, GAO rpt, 26119–61
- FBI undercover operations convictions, fines, recoveries, victim compensation, and status of lawsuits against FBI by operation, FY82, GAO rpt, 26119–67
- Fed Crop Insurance Corp finances, and insurance participation and operations in 2 States by crop, 1980-84, GAO rpt, 26113–132
- Fed Crop Insurance Corp program activities and costs, and FCIC and private insurance company gains and losses, 1980-84 with some trends from 1948, GAO rpt, 26113–119
- Fed Emergency Mgmt Agency nuclear attack civil defense plans, funding and operations by component, FY81-84 and projected FY85-89, GAO rpt, 26123–61
- Fed Employees Health Benefits Program finances, benefit reductions, and rate increases, by plan, 1981-82, GAO rpt, 26121–67
- Fed Govt agencies internal audits and resolution of questioned costs, by selected agency, FY81-83, GAO rpt, 26111–24
- Fed Govt agencies without inspectors general, internal audit activities, funding, and staff, by agency, FY83, GAO rpt, 26111–23
- Fed Govt cash benefits and beneficiaries with representative payees by program, and OASDI and SSI fraud and misuse, various periods FY74-81, GAO rpt, 26121–85
- Fed Govt civil agency operations, summaries of GAO investigation rpts published 1975-83, annual rpt, 26104–5
- Fed Govt civilian and military employee pay, withholdings by type, and income, and special military compensation by type and service branch, 1982-83, GAO rpt, 26123–65

Index by Subjects and Names

General Accounting Office

Fed Govt classified info security clearances of Govt and contractor employees, polygraph use, and prepublication reviews, by agency, 1979-83, GAO rpt, 26123–66

Fed Govt employees labor contract negotiations, costs, time spent, and negotiator attitudes, 1983 survey, GAO rpt, 26119–62

Fed Govt executive employee dev programs, employee and candidate attitudes in 5 agencies, 1983 survey, GAO rpt, 26119–69

Fed Govt expenditures in States and local areas, Census Bur data collection, limitation, contributing agency costs, and opinions of congressional users, 1984 GAO rpt, 26111–20

Fed Govt officials use of Govt chauffeur services for commuting, driver overtime hours and pay by agency, 4th qtr 1982, GAO rpt, 26123–63

FmHA loans for rural home mortgages, eligibility of current recipients under revised income limit, by State, 1983, GAO rpt, 26113–134

Food aid special supplemental program for women, infants, and children, effectiveness and participant characteristics, 1973-82, GAO rpt, 26131–10

Foreign Service positions and union membership by agency, grievances, and pay rates, FY81-83 with ambassador appointments from 1961, GAO rpt, 26123–64

Foreign trade zones, activities, and value of goods entering and leaving zones, 1973-82, GAO rpt, 26119–56

Forests (natl) below-cost timber sales and revenue by western forest, and volume, average price by species, and costs by western region, FY80-1982, GAO rpt, 26113–126

Forests (natl) below-cost timber sales in Colorado, and volume, costs, revenue, and net loss, by sale and forest, FY81-82, GAO rpt, 26113–131

Foster care children permanent placement, Fed Govt incentive program funding and operations in 7 States, FY80-82, GAO rpt, 26121–81

GPO depository library program quality and mgmt, opinions of librarians, 1983 survey, GAO rpt, 26111–19

GPO document sales program mgmt and finances, and bookstore operations by location, FY78-82, GAO rpt, 26111–17

Hazardous waste generation and disposal taxes in 3 States, and effects on waste mgmt, 1981-83, with assessment of 3 Fed Govt tax proposals, GAO rpt, 26113–124

Hazardous waste sites and activities of Fed Govt civil agencies, and EPA data mgmt, by waste location, 1984, GAO rpt, 26113–139

Health professionals license sanctions in 3 States, and subsequent Medicare and Medicaid program participation, by specialty, 1977-82, GAO rpt, 26121–80

Home mortgage terms on conventional loans by eligibility for Fed Govt secondary purchase, 1983, and alternative eligibility limits for 28 cities, 1984, GAO rpt, 26113–135

Hospital Corp of America capital costs reimbursement from Medicare and Medicaid following acquisition of Hospital Affiliates Intl, 1981-82, GAO rpt, 26121–65

Housing (low-income) energy aid of Fed Govt, allocations and average benefits in 13 States, and public interest group assessment, FY81-83, GAO rpt, 26121–75

Howard University salaries, academic standing, medical research, and library operations, and finances of Howard Inn, selected years 1976-83, GAO rpt, 26121–74

Hwy and bridge repair projects funded by Fed Govt, and costs, for 7 States, FY81-82, GAO rpt, 26113–121

ICC enforcement of motor carrier regulations, staff by position, and caseload by violation type, by ICC region, selected years FY80-85, GAO rpt, 26113–133

Info sources and systems of Fed Govt available to Congress, listings, series, 26106–5

IRS tax collections by type of tax, procedures, and interest forgone through processing delay, for selected locations, FY81-82, GAO rpt, 26119–55

IRS taxpayer assistance program operations and use, and users evaluation, selected years 1979-82, GAO rpt, 26119–58

Kennedy Performing Arts Center income and expenses by type, and Fed Govt share of expenses, FY79-83, GAO rpt, 26119–60

Land Mgmt Bur public lands sales, prices of Nevada and California acreage, and effect on Forest Service land acquisition program, 1983, GAO rpt, 26113–122

Latin America students in US and Soviet bloc training programs, by program type and student country, and summary by world region, selected years 1972-82, GAO rpt, 26123–77

Mail postage ratemaking and classification cases, processing, and participant costs and attitudes, 1970s-84, GAO rpt, 26119–63

Marijuana cultivation control activity of State law enforcement agencies, and aid from Fed Govt and Natl Guard, 1983 survey, GAO rpt, 26119–64

Maternal and child health, State govt spending and admin of Fed Govt block grants, by program for 13 States, 1981-83, GAO rpt, 26121–70

Medicare reimbursement rates in Massachusetts, and rates used and physicians not certified in designated specialty by selected carrier, various periods 1981-82, GAO rpt, 26121–82

Mental health and drug and alcohol abuse treatment funding of State govts, and admin of Fed Govt block grants, for 13 States, FY80-84, GAO rpt, 26121–87

Mental health clinical training funding by NIMH, by program and field, FY80-83, GAO rpt, 26121–86

Methanol fuel for autos, regulatory barriers to market dev, with supply/demand and auto fleet use and fuel economy, mid-1970s-82 and projected to 2000, GAO rpt, 26113–112

Military officers aides, enlisted personnel authorized and assigned to perform personal services by race and sex, and program costs, by service branch, 1982-83, GAO rpt, 26123–53

Military training of US for foreign govts, students, costs, and revenue losses from reduced tuition by country, by service branch, FY79-83, GAO rpt, 26123–56

Missile experimental (MX) procurement funding, and contract awards by company, FY84 with procurement projections to FY89, GAO rpt, 26123–75

Missile experimental (MX) procurement progress and costs, various dates 1979-83 and projected to 1990, GAO rpt, 26123–74

Mortgage (home) subsidy bonds Fed Govt costs, and loans, mortgage value, and borrowers by jurisdiction, by borrower income, Dec 1981-July 1982, GAO rpt, 26113–127

NATO military commitment of US, Europe force strengths by service branch and costs by component, FY82 with trends from FY75, GAO rpt, 26123–71

Navy F/A-18 weapons tactics trainer costs by trainer type, as of 1984, and demand at 2 locations, projected 1988-94, GAO rpt, 26123–73

Navy personnel by grade and length of service, reenlistment rate, and need for petty officers, FY72-83 and projected to FY88, GAO rpt, 26123–69

Navy vessels sold to foreign govts, sales prices, fair market value, and Navy costs, for surplus ships sold 1981-82, GAO rpt, 26123–60

Nuclear Waste Fund obligations by function and receipts, and DOE Civilian Radioactive Mgmt Office activities and staff, quarterly GAO rpt, 26102–4

OASDI beneficiary status changes reported late and benefit overpayments, for death, marriage, and leaving school, 1981, GAO rpt, 26121–68

Oil windfall profits tax admin of IRS and revenues, tax rates, and nonfilers, 1980-86, GAO rpt, 26119–65

Pension multiemployer plans in construction, trucking, and entertainment industries, and effect of exemption from withdrawal liability, 1977-81, GAO rpt, 26121–73

Pension multiemployer plans lacking complete participant data for actuarial valuations, 1982-83 survey, GAO rpt, 26121–83

Philanthropic foundations detailed financial and operating data, and stock holdings by instn, 1979 with selected trends from 1920, GAO rpt, 26119–53

Philippines dev and military assistance funding from US, FY78-84 and proposed FY85-89, GAO rpt, 26123–54

Pipeline safety regulations enforcement of DOT and States by pipeline type and State, and accidents and commodity losses, selected years 1973-FY84, GAO rpt, 26113–130

Preventive health services block grants of Fed Govt, State funding by program, and opinions on State program admin, for 13 States, FY81-84, GAO rpt, 26121–88

General Accounting Office

Prison population and capacity by State and individual DC and Federal instn, construction costs, and Fed Govt operating costs, 1983 and projected to 1990, GAO rpt, 26119-59

Public service job creation program of Fed Govt for unemployed, funding by agency, as of June 1983, GAO rpt, 26115-51

Publications of GAO on automatic data processing, food, health, and land use, annual listing series, 26104-11

Publications of GAO, 2nd half 1983, semiannual listing, 26102-1

R&D Fed Govt labs required technology transfer to public and private sector, labs complying, funding, and requests, by agency, FY82, GAO rpt, 26113-141

Recreation construction for water resources dev projects of Army Corps of Engineers and Reclamation Bur, unfunded costs by project, FY82, GAO rpt, 26113-115

Refugees from Central America by country of origin and asylum, and aid from US and Mexico, FY82-1984, GAO rpt, 26123-70

Saudi Arabia-US Joint Commission on Economic Cooperation project activities and costs, and related contract awards by Fed Govt agency, as of 1983, GAO rpt, 26123-80

School lunch program school and student participation, families eligible, and Federal reimbursement rates, FY79-83, GAO rpt, 26113-123

Senior Executive Service of Fed Govt, employee admin, and program status and effectiveness, by agency and by executive and job characteristics, July 1979-Sept 1983, GAO rpt, 26119-51

Shipping costs and foreign cargo shipments of Fed Govt by agency or program and route, and employment and economic impacts of US vessel preference, 1980, GAO rpt, 26117-30

Space shuttle launch guests by type, and itemized Fed Govt costs by agency, Apr 1981-Nov 1983, GAO rpt, 26123-78

St Elizabeths Hospital operations and finances transfer to DC govt, and DC mental health facilities, services, and costs, FY83, GAO rpt, 26121-72

State govt social services spending by type and funding source, and admin of Fed Govt block grants, for 13 States, selected years FY80-84, GAO rpt, 26121-76

Statistical agencies of Fed Govt missions and appropriations, and effect of budget cuts on principal programs, FY80-84, GAO rpt, 26125-28

Steel plant modernization capital investment under Clean Air Act compliance extension program, by firm, 1981-83, GAO rpt, 26113-138

Strategic Petroleum Reserve activities and funding, by supplier and site, quarterly GAO rpt, 26102-3

Student aid need-based program funding, and State Student Incentive Grant funding, recipients, and average income and award, by State, FY67-82, GAO rpt, 26121-69

Student Loan Marketing Assn activities, and financial ratios and stock dividends compared to banks and 4 Fed Govt-sponsored credit assns, 1980-82, GAO rpt, 26121-71

Index by Subjects and Names

Tax penalty abatements of IRS, 1978-83, and estimated error rates by category of taxpayer excuse, FY81, GAO rpt, 26119-68

Trucking industry economic effects of tax and size and weight rules, and hwy use taxes and Trust Fund revenues by tax type, FY82-84 and projected to 1990, GAO rpt, 26117-31

TTPI and American Samoa off-island medical referrals, costs, and potential savings, by govt, FY83 and comparisons from FY78, GAO rpt, 26123-72

Unemployment insurance overpayments detection and recovery from random audit program in selected States, 1975-82 and projected to FY86, GAO rpt, 26121-77

Uranium enrichment plants of DOE, production and other costs and selling prices, FY71-83 and projected to FY94, GAO rpt, 26113-137

Uranium enrichment prices of DOE under alternative TVA power rates, and effects of TVA charges for power not taken, FY84-95, GAO rpt, 26113-114

Urban Dev Action Grant program effectiveness, and participation of small cities by State, 1978-82, GAO rpt, 26113-118

VA employment services for disabled veterans with VA vocational rehabilitation training, and veteran characteristics and employment, by regional office, as of 1983, GAO rpt, 26121-78

VA medical care costs, and amount recovered through billings, by facility, 1982, GAO rpt, 26121-66

Vietnam Veterans Memorial Fund receipts by source, and disbursements by item and payee, Apr 1979-Mar 1984, GAO rpt, 26111-21

Virgin Islands import duty collections, and reimbursement of US Customs Service collections expenses, FY81-83, GAO rpt, 26119-54

Vocational Education Research Natl Center funding, by purpose and source, selected years 1978-84, GAO rpt, 26121-79

Water pollution regulation under EPA wastewater discharge system, operations and funding, various periods FY79-83, GAO rpt, 26113-113

Wildlife refuge revenues from economic and recreational uses, and refuge managers attitudes toward expanded use, FY81-83, GAO rpt, 26113-128

Witness Security Program costs, participants by arrest record, and prosecutions by offense, offender type, and disposition, various periods FY70-83, GAO rpt, 26119-70

General aviation

Accident circumstances and severity, by type of flying and aircraft, 1981, annual rpt, 9614-3

Accident circumstances, severity, and causes, for domestic and foreign air carriers in US operations, periodic rpt, 9612-1

Accidents and deaths for airlines and general aviation, 1983, preliminary annual rpt, 9614-9

Accidents of commuter airlines, air taxies, and general aviation, alcohol-related fatal accidents by pilot characteristics and circumstances, 1975-81, 9618-11

Air traffic control and airway facilities and equipment, FAA improvement activities and R&D under Natl Airspace System Plan, 1982-2000, annual rpt, 7504-12

Aircraft (general aviation), hours flown, and equipment, by type, use, and model of aircraft, region, and State, 1982, annual rpt, 7504-29

Aircraft collisions, and near collisions by circumstances and State, by type of aircraft, various periods 1980-84, 7508-61

Aircraft registered with FAA, by type and characteristics of aircraft, carrier, make, State, and county, 1983, annual rpt, 7504-3

Airport financing by source, bond issues by region, and airport operations, by airport and operator type, FY75-83 and projected to FY93, 26306-6.75

Aviation activity, detailed data on aircraft, air traffic, air carriers, personnel, airports, and FAA operations, 1974-83, annual rpt, 7504-1

Aviation activity forecasts, methodology, data sources, and coverage, Feb 1983 conf papers, annual rpt, 7504-28

FAA aviation medicine research and studies, technical rpt series, 7506-10

Finances, operations, vehicles, equipment, accidents, and energy use, by mode of transport, 1955-84, annual rpt, 7304-2

Hijacking attempts and airport security operations, screening results, and enforcement actions, 1st half 1984, semiannual rpt, 7502-5

Hijackings, on-board explosions, other crimes against civil aviation, and circumstances, US and worldwide, 1931-83, annual rpt, 7504-31

Instrument flight rule aircraft handled, by user type, FAA traffic control center, and region, FY69-83 and forecast to FY95, annual rpt, 7504-15

Pilots and nonpilots certified by FAA, by type of certificate, age, sex, region, and State, 1983, annual rpt, 7504-2

Traffic, aircraft operations by type and passenger enplanements, by airport, region, and State, projected FY82-95 and trends from FY76, annual rpt, 7504-7

Traffic, aircraft, pilots, airport activity, and fuel use, forecast FY84-95 with FY79-83 trends, annual rpt, 7504-6

Traffic levels, accidents, and deaths for airlines and general aviation, 1970-80, annual rpt, 7304-1

Traffic levels at FAA air traffic control facilities, by airport and State, FY83, annual rpt, 7504-27

General Motors Corp.

Energy economy test results, 1985 model year, annual rpt, 3304-11

Energy use of autos and light trucks, economy standards and manufacturer compliance, and gas prices and taxes, with selected foreign comparisons, FY80-83 and projected to 2000, hearing, 21368-49

Safety of domestic and foreign autos and light trucks, crash test results of selected new models for model year to date, press release series, 7766-7

Sales, prices, and registrations of autos and auto products in US, and trade of 8 countries with US, by make and model, 1964-83, annual rpt, 9884-7

Index by Subjects and Names

General Research Corp.

"Liming of Acidified Waters: A Review of Methods and Effects on Aquatic Ecosystems", 5506–5.13

General Services Administration

Activities and finances of GSA, FY78-83, annual rpt, 9454–23

Advisory committees of Fed Govt, and members, staff, meetings, and costs, by agency, FY83, annual rpt, 9454–18

Auto, small airplane, and motorcycle operating costs by component and vehicle size or make, and Fed Govt mileage reimbursement rates, 1983, annual rpt, 9454–13

Budget of US Appendix, detailed budgets and personnel summaries, by agency, FY85, annual rpt, 104–3

Budget of US, appropriations, outlays, balances, and budget receipts, by govtl branch and agency, FY83, annual rpt, 8104–2

Budget of US, compact budgets by function, agency, and account, FY85 with projections to FY89, annual rpt, 104–2

Budget of US, object class analysis of obligations, by branch of Fed Govt and selected depts and agencies, FY85 estimates, annual rpt, 104–9

Building construction, acquisition, and alteration proposals for historic and other Fed Govt projects, costs and tenure by city and project, as of 1983, hearings, 25328–23

Computer systems and costs of Fed Govt, annual chartbook, discontinued, 9454–7

Computer systems and equipment of Fed Govt, inventory by manufacturer, type, agency, and location, FY83, last issue of annual rpt, 9454–4

Computers and automatic data processing systems of GSA, costs, cost savings, and employment, by activity, subagency, and regional office, FY83-88, 9458–17

Cost control proposals for Fed Govt programs and mgmt, 3-year savings by function and agency, and financial and operating data, 1960s-81, 16908–1

DOD prime contract awards for R&D to educational and nonprofit instns and Federal agencies, by instn and location, FY83, annual listing, 3544–17

Employment (civilian) of Fed Govt, by location, agency, and pay system, 1982, biennial rpt, 9844–8

Fraud and abuse in GSA programs, audits and investigations, 2nd half FY84, semiannual rpt, 9452–8

Info Security Oversight Office monitoring of Fed Govt classified info security measures and classification actions, FY83, annual rpt, 9454–21

Motor vehicle fleet of Fed Govt, costs and operating data by agency, FY83, annual rpt, 9454–9

Operations of GSA, by dept, annual rpt, discontinued, 9454–1

Property (real) of Fed Govt, inventory and costs, worldwide summary by location, agency, and use, 1983, annual rpt, 9454–5

Property (real) of Fed Govt, leased property inventory and rental costs, worldwide summary by location and agency, Sept 1983, annual rpt, 9454–10

Property (surplus personal) of Fed Govt donated to State and local agencies and nonprofit instns, by region and State, FY83, annual rpt, 9454–22

Public building construction, alteration, and leasing projects, description and cost by location, Dec 1983, annual listing, 9454–12

R&D Fed Govt funding for all performers, by field and supporting agency, selected years FY60-84, annual rpt, 9627–20

Strategic materials stockpile inventories, costs, and goals, by commodity, as of June 1984, semiannual rpt, 9452–7

Travel expenses of Fed Govt employees on official business, and reimbursement rates, for high rate cities, 1983, annual rpt, 9454–16

see also National Archives and Records Service

Generating plants

see Power-generating plants and equipment

Genetics

Abnormal (genetically) human cell cultures available to researchers, and cultures shipped, 1984 annual listing, 4474–23

Biotechnology commercial uses, R&D funding and output, controls, and industry financial and operating data, for US and 5 countries, 1970s-83 and estimated 1984-85, 26358–98

Conservation of plant and animal genetic resources, commercial uses, causes of depletion, and geographic sources, 1984 rpt, 5548–13

Dairy Herd Improvement Program activities and research, periodic rpt, 1702–2

General Medical Sciences Natl Inst research programs and funding, FY83, annual rpt, 4474–12

Science and engineering doctoral degree recipients, by field, sex, race, age, citizenship, postgrad employment and study status, State, and instn, 1960-82, 9626–6.16

Science and engineering grad enrollment, fields of study, financial support, and other student and instn characteristics, 1975-82, annual survey, 9627–7

State govt maternal and child health funding, and admin of Fed Govt block grants, by program for 13 States, 1981-83, GAO rpt, 26121–70

see also Hereditary diseases

Genito-urinary diseases

see Urogenital diseases

Geoghegan, Glenda E.

"Health Characteristics of Male Veterans and Nonveterans, Health Interview Surveys, 1971-81", 9926–1.18

Geography

Census Bur activities, publications, and user services, monthly rpt, 2302–3

Developing countries disaster preparedness and summary sociodemographic, political, and economic data, country rpt series, 9916–2

Foreign countries *Background Notes,* summary social, political, and economic data, series, 7006–2

Foreign economic, social, and political summary data, by country, 1984, annual factbook, 244–11

Science and engineering doctoral degree recipients, by field, sex, race, age,

Geological Survey

citizenship, postgrad employment and study status, State, and instn, 1960-82, 9626–6.16

Science and engineering grad enrollment, fields of study, financial support, and other student and instn characteristics, 1975-82, annual survey, 9627–7

Statistical Abstract of US, social, political, and economic data, 1950s-83 and trends, annual rpt, 2324–1.1

see also Cartography

Geological phenomena

see Earthquakes

see Volcanoes

Geological Survey

Alaska minerals resources, production, claims on wildlife refuges, oil and gas leases, and exploratory wells, with maps and bibl, 1983, annual rpt, 5664–11

Central America mineral, energy, and water resources, and natural hazards to resource dev, by country, 1981 with trends from 1977, 5668–71

Cost control proposals for Fed Govt programs and mgmt, 3-year savings by function and agency, and financial and operating data, 1960s-81, 16908–1.9

Earthquake and other ground motion intensity measured on USGS Natl Strong-Motion Network by station, and sources of foreign and US info, 1981, annual rpt, 5664–14

Earthquake intensity, damage, and deaths, by location for major earthquakes since 1755, and hazard areas and natl reduction program activities, as of 1984, 5668–73

Earthquake intensity, damage, time of origin, and seismic characteristics of all US and major foreign earthquakes, 1981, annual rpt, 5664–13

Earthquake intensity, time of origin, seismic characteristics, and location, by State, quarterly rpt, 5662–4

Foreign oil and gas undiscovered recoverable resources, cumulative production, and identified reserves, final oil basin rpt series, 5666–18

Foreign oil and gas undiscovered recoverable resources, cumulative production, and identified reserves, preliminary oil basin rpt series, 5666–17

Foreign oil reserves, production, and resource lifespan under alternative production rates, historical and projected, country rpt series, 3166–9

Mount St Helens, Wash, volcanic eruptions, effects on water quality and other environmental characteristics of Washington and Oregon watersheds, series, 5666–14

Oceanographic research cruise schedules and ship characteristics, by academic instn or Federal agency, 1984, annual rpt, 3804–6

Oil and gas potential reserves in Western States wilderness areas, for 11 States, 1982-83, compilation of papers, 5668–69

Oil, gas, coal, and other mineral production and royalties from Fed Govt and Indian lands, by State and commodity, annual rpt, discontinued, 5664–3

Oil identified and undiscovered reserves, by country and oil type, and cumulative production, as of 1981 and 1983, 5668–72

Geological Survey

Phosphate rock reserves in southeastern and northwestern US, by location, 1984 rpt, 5668–74

Programs and funding, FY78-83, annual rpt, 5664–8

Publications of USGS, monthly listing, 5662–1

Publications of USGS, 1983, annual listing, 5664–4

Sedimentation control, surveillance, and research activity of Fed Govt, by project, agency, region, and State, 1982, annual rpt, 5664–9

Utah Salt Lake surface level, land coverage, water budget, salinity, and effects of human activity, various periods 1847-1983, 5668–70

Water supply and quality, and effect of coal mining operations, for selected river basins in Eastern and Interior coal provinces, series, 5666–15

Water supply and quality, and effect of coal mining operations, for selected river basins in Western coal provinces, series, 5666–19

Water supply and quality, floods, drought, mudslides, and other hydrologic events, by State, 1983, annual rpt, 5664–12

Water supply and quality in streams and lakes, and groundwater levels in wells, by drainage basin, 1980, annual State rpt series, 5666–12

Water supply and quality in streams and lakes, and groundwater levels in wells, by drainage basin, 1981, annual State rpt series, 5666–16

Water supply and quality in streams and lakes, and groundwater levels in wells, by drainage basin, 1982, annual State rpt series, 5666–20

Water supply and quality in streams and lakes, and groundwater levels in wells, by drainage basin, 1983, annual State rpt series, 5666–10

Water supply in US and Canada, streamflow, well and reservoir levels, and dissolved solids and temperature in 6 US rivers, by station, monthly rpt, 5662–3

Geology

Census of Population, 1980: detailed socioeconomic and demographic characteristics, by age, sex, race, Hispanic origin, occupation, and industry, State rpt series, 2531–4

Coal mining effect on water supply and quality in selected river basins of Eastern and Interior coal provinces, 1970s, series, 5666–15

Coal mining effect on water supply and quality in selected river basins of Western coal provinces, series, 5666–19

Coastal environmental and socioeconomic conditions, and potential impacts of oil and gas OCS leases, final statement series, 5736–1

Coastal environmental and wildlife characteristics, use, and mgmt, for individual ecosystems, series, 5506–9

Coastal environmental characteristics, fish, wildlife, and use, and population socioeconomic data, for individual areas, series, 5506–4

Earthquake and other ground motion intensity measured on USGS Natl Strong-Motion Network by station, and sources of foreign and US info, 1981, annual rpt, 5664–14

Estuary environmental characteristics, fish, wildlife, uses, and mgmt, for individual estuaries, series, 5506–7

Geological Survey and other publications, 1983, annual listing, 5664–4

Geological Survey programs and funding, FY78-83, annual rpt, 5664–8

High school class of 1982: science and math coursework and assessment, by sociodemographic and school characteristics and educational goal, 4826–2.14

Nuclear industry nongovt employment by industry segment, occupation, and census div, and DOE and NRC nuclear employment, 1968-83, biennial rpt, 3004–11

Nuclear power and weapons policy, fuel supply/demand, waste disposal and siting, environmental effects of radiation, and public attitudes, 1970s-82 with projections to 2000, 3008–88

Occupational Outlook Handbook, 1984-85 biennial rpt, 6744–1

Oceanographic data, stations and cruises recording data for World Data Center A by country, ship, and type of data, 1983, annual rpt, 2144–15

R&D Fed Govt funding for all performers, by field and supporting agency, selected years FY60-84, annual rpt, 9627–20

Science and engineering doctoral degree recipients, by field, sex, race, age, citizenship, postgrad employment and study status, State, and instn, 1960-82, 9626–6.16

Scientists, engineers, and technicians needed in defense and nondefense industries, and supply/demand, by field, 1981-87, 9628–71

Georgia

Agriculture census, 1982: farms, farmland, production and costs, and operator characteristics, preliminary State summary and county rpts, 2330–1.13

Agriculture census, 1982: farms, farmland, production, finances, and operator characteristics, by county, final State rpt, 2331–1.10

Alcohol fuel (ethanol) production in Tennessee Valley, feedstocks, facilities, tax incentives, and related farming data, by State, 1970s-83 and projected to 1992, 9808–69

Bank deposits in commercial and mutual savings banks and in US branches of foreign banks, by account type, instn, State, SMSA, and county, June 1983, annual rpt, 9295–3.8

Biomass Fuels Program of TVA, technologies and processes dev, costs, and resource requirements, 1970s-90s, series, 9806–9

Census of Housing, 1980: occupancy and unit characteristics of SMSAs and central cities, by race, Hispanic origin, and city, State rpt, 2473–1.12

Census of Population and Housing, 1980: detailed population and housing characteristics, by county, city, and census tract, State rpt, 2551–2.12

Census of Population, 1980: detailed socioeconomic and demographic characteristics, by age, sex, race, Hispanic origin, and industry, State rpt, 2531–4.12

Index by Subjects and Names

Collective bargaining calendar for Southeast US, 1984, annual rpt, 6946–1.68

County Business Patterns: establishments, employees, and payrolls, by SIC 4-digit industry and county, 1982, annual State rpt, 2326–6.12

Credit unions in Georgia, operating and financial ratios and other performance indicators for 53 large instns, as of Dec 1983, article, 9371–1.427

Employment (nonagricultural) by industry div and SMSA, earnings, and hours, for 8 southeastern States, monthly press release, 6942–7

Employment, earnings, and hours, by selected SIC 1- to 4-digit industry, State, and for 278 major labor areas, 1939-83, annual rpt, 6744–5.1, 6744–5.3

Employment, prices, earnings, and union membership in 8 southeastern States, Oct 1982-83, annual rpt, 6944–2

Environmental quality, pollutant discharge by type and source, and EPA protection activities and funding, 1970s-83, biennial rpt, 9184–15.4

Exports of manufactured and agricultural commodities, manufacturing production, and export-related employment, 1960s-82, State rpt, 2046–3.10

Financial and economic devs, Fed Reserve Bank of Atlanta monthly rpt with articles, 9371–1

HHS aid to each State and local govt or private instn, amount obligated, funding agency, and program, FY83, annual listing, 4004–3.4

Hwy and bridge repair projects funded by Fed Govt, and costs, for 7 States, FY81-82, GAO rpt, 26113–121

Income (personal) per capita and by source, and earnings by industry div, by State, MSA, and county, 1977-82, annual regional rpt, 2704–2.6

Income per capita and total personal income in 10 highest- and 10 lowest-income Georgia counties, 1980 with selected State economic data for 1970s-83, article, 9371–1.405

Job expansion in southern Georgia 10-county rural area, employment and establishments by worker and industry characteristics, 1976-81, article, 1502–7.401

Manufacturing census, 1982: financial and operating data, by SIC 2- to 4-digit industry, State, SMSA, and county, preliminary census div rpt, 2491–3.5

Mineral Industry Surveys, State review of production, 1983, advance annual rpt, 5614–6.10

Minerals Yearbook, 1982, Vol 2 preprints: State review of production and sales by commodity, and business activity, annual rpt, 5604–16.11

Minerals Yearbook, 1982, Vol 2: State reviews of production, sales, and firms, by commodity, and business activity, annual rpt, 5604–34

Peach production, marketing, and prices in 4 Southeastern States and Appalachia, 1983, annual rpt, 1311–12

Phosphate rock reserves in southeastern and northwestern US, by location, 1984 rpt, 5668–74

Index by Subjects and Names

Germany, West

Population size, Apr 1980 and July 1982, and per capita income, 1979 and 1981, by county and city, State Current Population Rpt, 2546–11.10

Retail trade census, 1982: employment, establishments, sales, and payroll, by SIC 2- to 4-digit kind of business, SMSA, county, and city, State rpt, 2397–1.11

Savings and loan assns, FHLB 4th District insured members financial condition and operations, by SMSA, monthly rpt, 9302–1

Small business mgmt counseling by university centers, costs, funding, and businesses served by industry, with detail for 2 States, 1980-83, hearing, 25728–36

Textile mill employment and average hours and earnings, for 8 Southeastern States, monthly press release, 6942–1

Timber resources and removals in Georgia, by species, ownership class, and county, 1981-83, series, 1206–26

Water supply and quality, and effect of coal mining operations, for selected river basins in Eastern and Interior coal provinces, 1983 rpt, 5666–15.23

Water supply and quality in 8 southeastern States, with background socioeconomic data, 1960s-2020 with trends from 1930, 9208–119

Wood residue production and use in TVA region, by tree species group and residue type, for 44 counties, 1979, technical paper, 9806–2.36

see also Albany, Ga.

see also Athens, Ga.

see also Atlanta, Ga.

see also Augusta, Ga.

see also Brunswick, Ga.

see also Columbus, Ga.

see also Macon, Ga.

see also Savannah, Ga.

see also under By State in the "Index by Categories"

Geothermal resources

Alaska minerals resources, production, claims on wildlife refuges, oil and gas leases, and exploratory wells, with maps and bibl, 1983, annual rpt, 5664–11

Budget of US, effects of Reagan Admin policy changes, by detailed program, FY85, annual rpt, 104–21

Consumption, by fuel type, economic sector, and end use, 1983 and 2000, 2006–2.5

Consumption, by fuel type, economic sector, census div, and State, 1960-82, State Energy Data System annual rpt, 3164–39

Electric power plants, by capacity, fuel used, unit type, region, State, and county, for plants added and retired, 1983 and planned through 1993, annual rpt, 3164–36

Fed Govt energy programs proposed budget appropriations, by office or dept and function, FY84-85, annual rpt, 3004–14

Interior Dept programs, activities, and funding, various periods 1967-84, last issue of annual rpt, 5304–13

Land Mgmt Bur public lands admin and program activities in western States, FY82-84, annual rpt, 5724–13

Natl Energy Policy Plan, energy supply, demand, and prices, by fuel and consuming sector, projected 1985-2010, biennial rpt, 3004–13

Producers finances and operations, by energy type for US firms domestic and foreign operations, 1974-82, annual rpt, 3164–44.2

Production, trade, supply, use, conservation, and DOE activities, by energy type, FY83, annual rpt, 3024–2

R&D industry funding and employment of scientists and engineers, by industry group, firm size, and funding source, 1956-82, annual rpt, 9627–21

Research publications on energy of DOE and other sources, monthly listing, 3002–2

Supply/demand and prices, by energy source and end-use sector and for 7 electric utilities, 1981-2000 with trends from 1960s, 3008–93

Supply/demand and prices, by fuel type and consuming sector with foreign comparisons, 1949-83, annual rpt, 3164–74

Western US Fed Govt lands by agency and mining restriction status, and energy resources on potential wilderness areas and other lands, 1970s-81 and projected to 1990, 3308–68

German Democratic Republic

see Germany, East

Germanium

see Metals and metal industries

Germany, East

Agricultural and food production indexes, and production of selected commodities, by world region and country, 1974-83, annual rpt, 1524–5

Agricultural production and trade by commodity, food consumption, and farm inputs, for 6 countries, 1960-80 with projections to 1991, 1528–178

Agricultural situation in Eastern Europe, by country, 1983 and outlook for 1984, annual report, 1524–4.7

Cuba economic conditions, agricultural and industrial production and distribution, trade, and intl economic relations, 1970-82 and trends from 1957, 248–40

Economic conditions in Communist, OECD, and selected other countries, 1960s-83, annual rpt, 244–5

Economic, social, and political summary data, by country, 1984, annual factbook, 244–11

Economic trends in income, production, prices, employment, finances, and trade, 1984 annual rpt, 2046–4.22

Export licensing and monitoring activities under Export Admin Act, for selected commodities, and for Communist and other countries, FY83, annual rpt, 2044–22

Exports and imports of NATO countries with Council for Mutual Economic Assistance Europe members, by country, 1980-83, annual rpt, 7144–5

Exports and imports of US with Communist countries, by detailed commodity and country, quarterly rpt with articles, 9882–2

Exports of US, detailed Schedule B commodities by country of destination, 1983, annual rpt, 2424–9

Exports of US, detailed Schedule E commodities by mode of transport and world area and country of destination, 1983, annual rpts, 2424–5

Grain production, consumption, and trade, and US farm cooperatives grain and oilseed export potential, for 4 countries, selected years 1960-90, 1128–27

Imports of US, detailed Schedule A commodities by country and world area of origin, and mode of transport, 1983, annual rpts, 2424–2

Imports of US, detailed TSUSA commodities by country of origin, 1983, annual rpt, 2424–4

Loans and grants for economic and military assistance from US and intl agencies, by program and country, FY46-83, annual rpt, 9914–5

Military spending, arms trade, and armed forces size, with total govt spending and population, by country, 1972-82, annual rpt, 9824–1

Minerals Yearbook, 1982, Vol 3: foreign country reviews of production, trade, and policies, by commodity, annual rpt, 5604–35

Minerals Yearbook, 1982, Vol 3 preprints: foreign country review of production, trade, and policies, by commodity, annual rpt, 5604–17.25

Population size and growth rates, and latest available benchmark demographic data, by country, 1950-83, biennial rpt, 2324–4

Potassium chloride from 4 countries, imports injury to US industry from foreign subsidized products, investigation with background financial and operating data, 1984 rpt, 9886–15.52

Science and technology dev and transfer between USSR and other members of Council for Mutual Economic Assistance, 1940s-81, 2326–9.7

Steel (carbon) wire rod from East Germany at less than fair value, imports injury to US industry, investigation with background financial and operating data, 1984 rpt, 9886–14.127

see also under By Foreign Country in the "Index by Categories"

Germany, West

Agricultural and food production indexes, and production of selected commodities, by world region and country, 1974-83, annual rpt, 1524–5

Agricultural situation in Western Europe, by country and commodity, 1983 and outlook for 1984, annual rpt, 1524–4.6

Agricultural supply/demand, trade, and production, and socioeconomic data, by country, 1950s-77, 1528–179

AID loan repayment status and terms by program and country, and status of predecessor agency loans, quarterly rpt, 9912–3

Auto and auto products sales, prices, and registrations in US, and trade of 8 countries with US, by make and model, 1964-83, annual rpt, 9884–7

Auto safety and experimental vehicle designs, 1982, conf proceedings, annual rpt, 7764–3

Biotechnology commercial uses, R&D funding and output, controls, and industry financial and operating data, for US and 5 countries, 1970s-83 and estimated 1984-85, 26358–98

Capital formation and steel industry employment costs in US and OECD countries, 1960s-82, 26306–6.69

Germany, West

China exports and imports, by commodity, world area, and country, quarterly rpt, 242–6

China trade and trade balances with world and major trading partners, by selected commodity, quarterly rpt, 242–6.1

Current account balances of US, Japan, and West Germany, effects of business cycles, modeling results, 1970s-82 and projected 1983-86, technical paper, 9366–7.92

Current account deficits, and financing by source, for US and 5 OECD countries, selected years 1973-1st qtr 1984, article, 9385–1.409

Dollar holdings rate of return related to domestic real money stock for 5 OECD countries, regression results, various periods 1966-84, article, 9391–1.418

Drug (animal) approval of govts, months to approval in US and 2 countries by drug brand and manufacturer, selected years 1965-83, hearing, 25528–98

Economic and monetary trends, compounded annual rates of change for US and 10 major trading partners, quarterly rpt, 9391–7

Economic conditions, consumer and stock prices and production indexes, 6 OECD countries and US, *Business Conditions Digest,* monthly rpt, 2702–3.10, 2708–31

Economic conditions in Communist, OECD, and selected other countries, 1960s-83, annual rpt, 244–5

Economic conditions, income, production, prices, employment, and trade, 1984 semiannual country rpt, 2046–4.102

Economic indicators and oil use and imports for US and 6 OECD countries, and oil production by country, biweekly rpt, 242–4

Economic indicators and trade balance of US and 4 countries, effect of US budget deficits, model results, various periods 1974-85, technical paper, 9366–7.102

Economic indicators for 7 OECD countries and US, quarterly rpt, 2042–10

Economic, social, and political summary data, by country, 1984, annual factbook, 244–11

Economic trends in income, production, prices, employment, finances, and trade, 1984 semiannual rpt, 2046–4.21

Employment, labor force, and participation and unemployment rates by sex, in US and 9 OECD countries, various periods 1970-3rd qtr 1983, annual article, 6722–1.404

Energy prices and taxes by energy source and end-use sector, for US and 9 OECD countries, quarterly 1979-83, annual rpt, 3164–71

Energy production by type, and oil prices, trade, and consumption, by country group and selected country, monthly rpt, 242–5

European Monetary System effect on inflation and exchange rates, for 3 member countries, various periods Feb 1974-Mar 1984, technical paper, 9366–7.101

Export credit program activities of Eximbank and 6 OECD countries, 1982, annual rpt, 9254–3

Exports and imports, intl position of US and 4 OECD countries, and factors affecting US competition, quarterly pamphlet, 2042–25

Exports and imports of manufactured goods by West Germany and US related to exchange rate uncertainty, regression results, 1974-81, article, 9385–1.405

Exports and imports of NATO countries with Council for Mutual Economic Assistance Europe members, by country, 1980-83, annual rpt, 7144–5

Exports and imports of NATO countries with PRC, by country, 1980-83, annual rpt, 7144–14

Exports and imports of OECD countries, by country, 1983, annual rpt, 7144–10

Exports and imports of OECD, total and for 4 major countries, and US trade by country, by commodity, 1972-82, annual world region rpt series, 244–13

Exports and imports of US, by commodity group, world area, selected country, US coastal area and port, and mode of transport, with seasonal adjustments, monthly rpt, 2422–9

Exports and imports of US, detailed SIC-based commodities by world area, 1983, annual rpts, 2424–6

Exports and imports of US with Western Europe, and US market share and export opportunities for selected commodities, by country, 1982-84, 2048–105

Exports of US, detailed Schedule B commodities by country of destination, 1983, annual rpt, 2424–9

Exports of US, detailed Schedule E commodities by mode of transport and world area and country of destination, 1983, annual rpts, 2424–5

Farmland (US) owned by foreigners, acreage, value, and use, by State and county, and for 5 leading investor countries, 1983, annual rpt, 1584–3

Finance (intl) and financial policy, external factors affecting US economy, econometric model methodology and results for US and 4 countries, various periods 1964-75, 9368–78

Fish and shellfish wholesale prices and market activity in 8 West Europe countries, weekly rpt, 2162–8

Food supply/demand and market and support prices, with exchange rates, fertilizer price index, GDP, and population, by EC country, 1960-83, 1528–173

Foreign exchange rate intervention in dollar-mark market by Fed Reserve, model results, Nov 1978-Oct 1979, technical paper, 9377–9.12

Foreign exchange rate intervention in dollar-mark market by Fed Reserve, various periods Oct 1974-Sept 1981, technical paper, 9366–1.127, 9366–1.128

Foreign exchange rate intervention in 3 currency markets by Fed Reserve, various periods Sept 1977-Dec 1979, technical paper, 9366–1.140

Foreign exchange rate of dollar with mark, daily and monthly variability, various periods June 1973-Apr 1984, article, 9381–1.413

Foreign exchange rates for currencies of US and 2 countries with yen, and measures of manufacturing competitiveness, 1983 with 1974-80 and 1979-80 averages, article, 9385–1.404

Index by Subjects and Names

Graphic industries equipment market and trade, and user industry operations and demand, 1984 country market research rpt, 2045–3.31

Health care resources, use, and per capita public expenditures, and selected population characteristics, for US and 6 countries, selected years 1975-81, 21148–33

Housing units completed by type, and housing activity financial indicators, for Germany, selected 1950-81, article, 9312–1.405

Imports of US, detailed Schedule A commodities by country and world area of origin, and mode of transport, 1983, annual rpts, 2424–2

Imports of US, detailed TSUSA commodities by country of origin, 1983, annual rpt, 2424–4

Industrial process control equipment market and trade, and user industry operations and demand, 1982 country market research rpt, 2045–6.39

Industrial production indexes of 7 OECD countries and US, biweekly rpt, periodic article, 2042–24

Interest rate term structure in West Germany and Canada related to short-term US rates, 1973-82, article, 9393–8.401

Interest rates and budget balances of US and 6 OECD countries, 1973-83, annual rpt, 26304–3.1

Intl transactions of US with 10 countries, 1981-83, *Survey of Current Business,* monthly rpt, annual table, 2702–1.31

Investment (foreign direct) in US, major investors and investments by SIC 4-digit industry, transaction type and value, and location, 1983, annual rpt, 2044–20

Loans and grants for economic and military assistance from US and intl agencies, by program and country, FY46-83, annual rpt, 9914–5

Manufacturing labor productivity and cost indexes for US and 11 OFCD countries, 1960-82, annual article, 6722–1.405

Manufacturing productivity and unit labor cost indexes for US and 11 countries, 1950-82 and preliminary 1983, annual rpt, 6864–1

Manufacturing wage rates in US and 2 countries, by industry, 1975 and 1980, hearing, 21248–79

Manufacturing wage/price and wage/output adjustment in 6 OECD countries, 1960-81, technical paper, 9381–10.33

Military aid of US, arms sales, and training programs costs and budget requests by program, world region, and country, FY83-85, annual rpt, 7144–13

Military pension lifetime earnings in US and 7 countries, as of 1983, 26306–6.76

Military spending, arms trade, and armed forces size, with total govt spending and population, by country, 1972-82, annual rpt, 9824–1

Military weapons transfers to developing countries from US, USSR, and Europe, by weapon type and world region, 1974-82, 25948–3

Minerals Yearbook, 1982, Vol 3: foreign country reviews of production, trade, and policies, by commodity, annual rpt, 5604–35

Index by Subjects and Names

Gift tax

Minerals Yearbook, 1982, Vol 3 preprints: foreign country review of production, trade, and policies, by commodity, annual rpt, 5604–17.26

Monetary control policy of US and selected West European countries, and relation to credit, exchange rates, GNP, and other indicators, various periods 1960-82, conf papers, 9373–3.26

Nuclear power generation in US and 18 non-Communist countries, monthly rpt, 3162–24.10

Nuclear power plant construction and operation status, and capacity, by plant, region, State, and selected country, 1983 and projected to 2020, annual rpt, 3164–57

Oil and gas undiscovered recoverable resources, cumulative production, and identified reserves, as of 1982, preliminary oil basin rpt, 5666–17.15

Oil consumption and stocks for major consuming countries, monthly rpt, 3162–24.10

Population size and growth rates, and latest available benchmark demographic data, by country, 1950-83, biennial rpt, 2324–4

Price indexes for consumer and producer goods, major commodities, exports, imports, nonfarm wages, and currency value, US and 4 countries, bimonthly rpt, 2042–11

R&D expenditures and employment in science and technology, for US and 4 countries, selected years 1953-84, annual rpt, 9624–18.1

Science Indicators, R&D expenditures, innovations, research, and higher education, with foreign comparisons, 1960s- 83, annual rpt, 9624–10.1

Ships in world merchant fleet, and tonnage, by country of registry, 1982, annual rpt, 7704–3.1

Space satellites and other objects launched since 1957, quarterly listing, 9502–2

Steel imports of US from EC and other countries, and US industry operating data, for 15 products limited under arrangement with EC, monthly rpt, 9882–10

Steel plate from West Germany at less than fair value, imports injury to US industry, investigation with background financial and operating data, 1984 rpt, 9886–14.108

Trade promotion policies and industry financing of EC, and effect on competing US industries, 1970s-82, 9886–4.73

Travel to and from US, by world area and selected country, projected 1984-85, annual rpt, 2904–9

Work-sharing effect on labor productivity, for US and compared to West Germany, 1930s-82, narrative article, 6722–1.458

Worker participation in mgmt decisions, experience in US and 2 countries, 1983 narrative article, 6722–1.457

see also under By Foreign Country in the "Index by Categories"

Gerrish, Harold P.

"North Atlantic Tropical Cyclones, 1983", 2152–8.401

Gettinger, Stephen

"Assessing Criminal Justice Needs", 6066–20.4

Ghana

Agricultural and food production indexes, and production of selected commodities, by world region and country, 1974-83, annual rpt, 1524–5

Agricultural situation in sub-Saharan Africa, by country, 1982-83 and outlook for 1984, annual rpt, 1524–4.10

AID activities and funding by project and function, FY85, and developing countries summary socioeconomic data, 1970s-83, by country, annual rpt, 9914–3

AID economic assistance to developing countries, obligations and disbursements by country, quarterly rpt, 9912–4

AID loan repayment status and terms by program and country, and status of predecessor agency loans, quarterly rpt, 9912–3

Economic conditions and foreign marketing prospects in 46 Sub-Saharan countries, 1983 world region rpt, 2046–5.1

Economic, social, and political summary data, by country, 1984, annual factbook, 244–11

Exports of US, detailed Schedule B commodities by country of destination, 1983, annual rpt, 2424–9

Exports of US, detailed Schedule E commodities by mode of transport and world area and country of destination, 1983, annual rpts, 2424–5

Imports of US, detailed Schedule A commodities by country and world area of origin, and mode of transport, 1983, annual rpts, 2424–2

Imports of US, detailed TSUSA commodities by country of origin, 1983, annual rpt, 2424–4

Loans and grants for economic and military assistance from US and intl agencies, by program and country, FY46-83, annual rpt, 9914–5

Military aid of US, arms sales, and training programs costs and budget requests by program, world region, and country, FY83-85, annual rpt, 7144–13

Military spending, arms trade, and armed forces size, with total govt spending and population, by country, 1972-82, annual rpt, 9824–1

Minerals Yearbook, 1982, Vol 3: foreign country reviews of production, trade, and policies, by commodity, annual rpt, 5604–35

Minerals Yearbook, 1983, Vol 3 preprints: foreign country review of production, trade, and policies, by commodity, annual rpt, 5604–23.27

Population size and growth rates, and latest available benchmark demographic data, by country, 1950-83, biennial rpt, 2324–4

see also under By Foreign Country in the "Index by Categories"

GI Bill

see Veterans benefits and pensions

Gianelos, Arthur

"Controlled Foreign Corporations, 1980", 8302–2.410

Giant Food, Inc.

Nutrition and cardiovascular disease consumer education, effectiveness of Natl Heart, Lung, and Blood Inst and Giant Food, Inc, program in DC metro area, 1978-79, 4478–144

Gibbard, Kathy

"Survey of U.S. Uranium Exploration Activity, 1983", 3164–65

Gibbons, J. Whitfield

"Ecology of Southeastern Shrub Bogs (Pocosins) and Carolina Bays: A Community Profile", 5506–9.9

Gibbs, Kenneth C.

"Costs of Developed Recreation Sites in the Northern Region, USDA Forest Service", 1208–202

Gibraltar

Economic, social, and political summary data, by country, 1984, annual factbook, 244–11

Exports of US, detailed Schedule B commodities by country of destination, 1983, annual rpt, 2424–9

Exports of US, detailed Schedule E commodities by mode of transport and world area and country of destination, 1983, annual rpts, 2424–5

Imports of US, detailed Schedule A commodities by country and world area of origin, and mode of transport, 1983, annual rpts, 2424–2

Imports of US, detailed TSUSA commodities by country of origin, 1983, annual rpt, 2424–4

Population size and growth rates, and latest available benchmark demographic data, by country, 1950-83, biennial rpt, 2324–4

see also under By Foreign Country in the "Index by Categories"

Gibson, David

"End-Stage Renal Disease: A Profile of Facilities Furnishing Treatment", 4652–1.434

Gibson, J. H.

"Rocky Mountain Acidification Study", 5506–5.17

Gibson, Robert M.

"National Health Expenditures, 1983", 4652–1.429

Gielecki, Mark

"Commercial Nuclear Power, 1984: Prospects for the U.S. and the World", 3164–57

Gift tax

Art appraisals accepted and rejected on estate, gift, and income tax returns, and valuation by taxpayers, IRS, and US courts, 1978-82, hearings, 21408–74

Budget of US, CBO analysis of revenue and spending alternatives and projections of economic indicators, FY85-89, annual rpt, 26304–3

Budget of US, receipts by source and outlays by agency and program, monthly rpt, 8102–3

Budget of US, receipts by source and outlays by function, FY40-89 estimates revised for consistency with FY85 budget definitions, annual rpt, 104–12

Budget of US, receipts, outlays, and budget authority, by function and agency, FY84-89 revised estimates, midsession review of FY85 budget, annual rpt, 104–7

Fed Govt internal revenue, by type of tax, quarterly rpt, 8302–2.1

Fed Govt receipts by source and outlays by agency, *Treasury Bulletin,* quarterly rpt, 8002–4.1

Gift tax

Govt revenues, by type, level of govt, and State, selected years 1902-83, annual rpt, 10044–1.2

Govt tax revenues, by level of govt, type of tax, State, and selected counties, quarterly rpt, 2462–3

Income tax returns filed by type, for US, IRS regions, and service center cities, 1972-82 and projected 1983-90, annual rpt, 8304–9.1

IRS collections, by type of tax, region, and State, FY83, annual rpt, 8304–3.3

IRS collections, FY83, annual rpt, 8104–2.2

State govt revenues by source, expenditures by function, debt, and holdings by type, FY83, annual rpt, 2466–2.5

State govt tax collections, by detailed type of tax and tax rates, by State, FY83, annual rpt, 2466–2.3

Gifts and contributions

Arts and humanities funding, by source and State, FY82-83 with trends from FY66, 21408–69

Fed Govt employees charity contributions to Combined Federal Campaign, funds by type of recipient, 1982 and trends from 1973, GAO rpt, 26119–66

Fed Govt receipts, tax and other, FY83, annual rpt, 8104–2.2

Fed Govt surplus personal property donations to State and local agencies and nonprofit instns, by region and State, FY83, annual rpt, 9454–22

Foreign aid programs of private voluntary agencies, funding and expenditures, by agency, 1982/83, annual rpt, 9914–9

Handicapped children early education research and service project activities and characteristics, and grants to States for program dev, 1983-84, annual listing, 4804–30

Income (personal) by source including transfer payments, and social insurance contributions by type, by region, 1929 and 1982, 2708–40

Income tax returns of corporations, detailed income and tax items by industry, 1981, annual rpt, 8304–4

Income tax returns of elderly, by income statement and tax item and income level, 1981 with trends from 1977, article, 8302–2.412

Income tax returns of individuals, by filing and deduction characteristics and income level, 1983, annual article, 8302–2.414

Income tax returns of individuals by tax return item, State, and occupation, and income by source and tax owed, by income level, selected years 1916-80, conf papers, 8308–28.1

Income tax returns of individuals, detailed data, 1982, annual rpt, 8304–2

Income tax returns of individuals, selected income, deduction, and tax credit data by income, preliminary 1982, annual article, 8302–2.402

Kennedy Performing Arts Center income and expenses by type, and Fed Govt share of expenses, FY79-83, GAO rpt, 26119–60

Natl Endowment for Arts activities and grants, FY83, annual rpt, 9564–3

Natl Endowment for Humanities activities and grants, FY83, annual rpt, 9564–2

Nutrition services for elderly, program operations and assessment, and participant sociodemographic, health, and diet characteristics, 1976 and 1982, 4608–16

Philanthropic foundations assets and grants for 50 largest foundations, and for selected foundations by recipient, selected years 1975-82, hearings, 21788–137

Philanthropic foundations detailed financial and operating data, and stock holdings by instn, 1979 with selected trends from 1920, GAO rpt, 26119–53

Red Cross program operations and financial statements, 1982/83, annual rpt, 29254–1

Smithsonian Instn finances, activities, and visitors, FY83, annual rpt, 9774–3

Statistical Abstract of US, social, political, and economic data, 1950s-83 and trends, annual rpt, 2324–1.3

Tax expenditures, Fed Govt revenues foregone through income tax deductions and exclusions by type, and effect of Deficit Reduction Act, FY84-89, annual rpt, 21784–10

Tax return art appraisals accepted and rejected on estate, gift, and income tax cases, and valuation by taxpayers, IRS, and US courts, 1978-82, hearings, 21408–74

Truman, Harry S, Scholarship Fund receipts by source, transfers, and investment holdings and transactions, monthly rpt, 14312–1

Vietnam Veterans Memorial Fund receipts by source, and disbursements by item and payee, Apr 1979-Mar 1984, GAO rpt, 26111–21

Youth social services of State govts, coordinating agencies activities, admin, membership, and funding sources, survey, 1984 rpt, 6068–182

see also Campaign funds

see also Gift tax

Gilbert Islands

see Kiribati

Gilbert, R. Alton

"Calculating the Adjusted Monetary Base Under Contemporaneous Reserve Requirements", 9391–1.407

"Has the Deregulation of Deposit Interest Rates Raised Mortgage Rates?", 9391–1.412

Gill, Mohinder

"Alcohol Fuels in the U.S.: Status and Prospects", 1561–16.404

Ginzburg, Harold M.

"Intravenous Drug Users and the Acquired Immune Deficiency Syndrome", 4102–1.427

Glaciers

Mount St Helens, Wash, volcanic eruptions, effects on water quality and other environmental characteristics of Washington and Oregon watersheds, series, 5666–14

Research (intl) in glaciology, summaries, methodology, and bibls, series, 2156–18

see also Ice conditions

Glade, Edward H.

"Cotton Ginning Charges, Harvesting Practices, and Selected Marketing Costs, 1983/84 Season", 1564–3

Index by Subjects and Names

"Utilization and Ownership of U.S. Cotton Storage Capacity", 1561–1.406

Glahn, Harry R.

"Trends in Skill and Accuracy of National Weather Service POP Forecasts", 2188–17

Glass and glass industry

Air pollutant emission factors, by detailed source, 3rd edition, 1983-84 supplements, 9198–13

Business statistics, detailed data for major industries and economic indicators, *Survey of Current Business,* monthly rpt, 2702–1.18

Census of Population, 1980: detailed socioeconomic and demographic characteristics, by age, sex, race, Hispanic origin, occupation, and industry, State rpt series, 2531–4

China economic conditions, agricultural and industrial production, trade, and domestic and foreign investment, 1980-85, 2048–106

Collective bargaining agreements expiring during year, covered workers by SIC 2-digit industry, firm, and union, with summary of key provisions, 1984, annual rpt, 6784–9

Container industry productivity, hours, and employment indexes, 1954-82, annual rpt, 6824–1.3

Containers of glass trade, tariffs, and industry operating data, foreign and US, 1978-82, TSUSA commodity rpt supplement, 9885–5.14

County Business Patterns: establishments, employees, and payrolls, by SIC 4-digit industry and county, 1981, annual State rpt series, 2326–8

County Business Patterns: establishments, employees, and payrolls, by SIC 4-digit industry and county, 1982, annual State rpt series, 2326–6

Earnings by major industry group, and personal income per capita and by source, by region and State, 1929-82, 2708–40

Employment, earnings, and hours, by selected SIC 1- to 4-digit industry, State, and for 278 major labor areas, 1939-83, annual rpt, 6744–5

Employment, earnings, and hours, by SIC 4-digit nonfarm industry, monthly 1974-Feb 1984, annual update, 6744–4

Energy use and cost for building materials manufacture, by energy source and industry, 1970s-82, article, 2012–1.401

Exports and imports of US, detailed SIC-based commodities by world area, 1983, annual rpts, 2424–6

Exports and imports of US, totals and as percent of domestic production, by SIC 2- to 5-digit commodity, 1981, annual rpt, 2424–3

Exports, imports, tariffs, and industry operating data for household glassware, 1979-83, TSUSA commodity rpt supplement, 9885–5.18

Exports of US, detailed commodities by country of destination, monthly rpt, 2422–3

Exports of US, detailed Schedule B commodities by country of destination, 1983, annual rpt, 2424–9

Index by Subjects and Names

Gold

Exports of US, detailed Schedule E commodities by mode of transport and world area and country of destination, 1983, annual rpts, 2424–5

Fiber optics displacement of copper in telecommunications, with Bell System use and copper and fiber optics industry data, 1978-88, 2048–104

Finances and operations, by SIC 2- to 4-digit industry, 1970s-83 and projected to 1988, annual rpt, 2014–4

Great Lakes trade, by SITC 3-digit commodity, port, vessel type, world area, and country, 1982, annual rpt, 7744–3

Imports of US, detailed Schedule A commodities by country and world area of origin, and mode of transport, 1983, annual rpts, 2424–2

Imports of US, detailed Schedule A commodities by country, monthly rpt, 2422–2

Imports of US, detailed TSUSA commodities by country of origin, 1983, annual rpt, 2424–4

Income tax returns of corporations, detailed income and tax items by industry, 1981, annual rpt, 8304–4

Income tax returns of sole proprietorships, detailed data by industry div and selected industry group, 1981, annual rpt, 8304–7

Input-output structure of US economy, detailed interindustry transactions for 85 industries, and components of final demand, 1977, article, 2702–1.421

Input-output structure of US economy, detailed interindustry transactions for 537 industries, and components of final demand, 1977 benchmark data, 2708–17

Manufacturing census, 1982: financial and operating data, by SIC 2- to 4-digit industry, State, SMSA, and county, preliminary census div rpt series, 2491–3

Manufacturing census, 1982: financial and operating data, for SIC 4-digit industries by product, preliminary rpt series, 2491–1

Minority group and women employment, by occupational group and SIC 2- to 3-digit industry, 1981, annual rpt, 9244–1.1

Occupational health risks from hazardous substances and radiation, by industry, occupation, age, and sex, with bibl and glossary, 1920s-82, 9638–50

Occupational injury and illness rates, by SIC 2- to 4-digit industry, 1982, annual rpt, 6844–1

OECD trade, total and for 4 major countries, and US trade by country, by commodity, 1972-82, annual world region rpt series, 244–13

Pollution abatement capital and operating costs, by SIC 2- to 4-digit industry, State, and SMSA, 1982, annual Current Industrial Rpt, 2506–3.6

Producer prices and indexes, by stage of processing and detailed commodity, monthly rpt, 6762–6

Producer prices and indexes, by stage of processing and detailed commodity, monthly 1983, annual supplement, 6764–2

Production, shipments, PPI, and stocks of building materials, by type, bimonthly rpt, 2012–1.5

Production, shipments, trade, and stocks, by glass product, periodic Current Industrial Rpt series, 2506–9

Scientists, engineers, and technicians employed in private industry, by occupation and industry group, 1980-81, biennial rpt, 9627–23

Waterborne commerce of US (domestic and foreign), freight by commodity, traffic, and passengers, by port and waterway, 1982, annual rpt, 3754–3

Window shipments and prices by market sector, and installation by unit type and State, for wood and aluminum frames, selected years 1967-82, article, 2012–1.403

see also under By Commodity in the "Index by Categories"

see also under By Industry in the "Index by Categories"

Glendale, Calif.

see also under By City in the "Index by Categories"

Glens Falls, N.Y.

Census of Housing, 1980: occupancy and unit characteristics, by race, Hispanic origin, and city, SMSA rpt, 2473–1.170

Census of Population and Housing, 1980: detailed population and housing characteristics, by county, city, and census tract, SMSA rpt, 2551–2.170

see also under By SMSA or MSA in the "Index by Categories"

Glossaries

Agriculture Fact Book of US, compilation of data for 1983 with trends from 1940, annual rpt, 1004–14

Biotechnology commercial uses, R&D funding and output, controls, and industry financial and operating data, for US and 5 countries, 1970s-83 and estimated 1984-85, 26358–98

Computer systems purchase and use, and data recording, processing, and transfer, Fed Govt standards, series, 2216–2

Earthquake intensity, damage, and deaths, by location for major earthquakes since 1755, and hazard areas and natl reduction program activities, as of 1984, 5668–73

Energy producers finances and operations, by energy type for US firms domestic and foreign operations, 1974-82, annual rpt, 3164–44

Energy supply/demand and prices, by fuel type, sector, and end use, detailed trends and projections 1973-95, annual rpt, 3164–75

FERC activities and funding by program, with some natural gas and electric power industry data, FY83, annual rpt, 3084–9

Fish and shellfish landings, life cycles, and environmental needs, for selected species by region, with glossary and bibl, series, 5506–8

Forests (tropical) status by country and world region, conservation methods, and mgmt role of US, foreign, and intl groups, 1977-80s and projected to 2000, 26358–101.1

Futures trading by commodity and exchange, and Commodity Futures Trading Commission activities, funding, and employment, FY83, annual rpt, 11924–2

Genetic resource (plant and animal) conservation, commercial uses, causes of depletion, and geographic sources, 1984 rpt, 5548–13

Housing energy use, costs, expenditures, and conservation, and household and housing characteristics, survey series, 3166–7

Info processing systems dictionary, ordering info, 1983 rpt, 2216–2.125

Natural and supplemental gas production, prices, trade, use, reserves, and pipeline company finances, by firm and State, monthly rpt with articles, 3162–4

Nuclear power industry status and outlook, with reactor construction, utility financial and operating data, and foreign comparisons, 1970s-83 with projections to 2010, 26358–99

OASDHI, Medicaid, SSI, and other social insurance and public welfare programs benefits, beneficiary characteristics, and trust funds, selected years 1937-83, annual rpt, 4744–3

Occupational health risks from hazardous substances and radiation, by industry, occupation, age, and sex, with bibl and glossary, 1920s-82, 9638–50

Oil, gas, and minerals dev, under Fed Govt OCS leases, with production, revenues, reserves, and oil spills, by State and ocean region, 1950s-82, annual rpt, 5734–3

Ports, port facilities by type, and inland waterways by size, by location, 1982-83, annual rpt, 7704–16

Tidal current tables, daily time and velocity by station for North America and Asia coasts, 1985, annual rpt, 2174–1

Water pollution from nonpoint sources, source land uses and acreage, and control program funding, by State or region, various periods 1974-FY84, 9208–123

Wetlands environmental characteristics, acreage, uses, and mgmt, by wetland type and region, 1950s-80, 26358–102

Gloucester, Mass.

Fish and shellfish landings and prices at Boston and other New England ports, and total New England cold storage holdings, weekly rpt, 2162–6.2

see also under By SMSA or MSA in the "Index by Categories"

Gloves and mittens

see Clothing and clothing industry

GNMA

see Government National Mortgage Association

GNP

see Gross National Product

Goeltz, Richard

"Comparison of Actual and Predicted Energy Savings in Minnesota Gas-Heated Single-Family Homes", 3308–74

Gold

Alaska minerals resources, production, claims on wildlife refuges, oil and gas leases, and exploratory wells, with maps and bibl, 1983, annual rpt, 5664–11

Business statistics, detailed data for major industries and economic indicators, *Survey of Current Business,* monthly rpt, 2702–1.6

China economic conditions, agricultural and industrial production, trade, and domestic and foreign investment, 1980-85, 2048–106

Gold

Communist, OECD, and selected other countries minerals and metals production, by commodity, 1960s-83, annual rpt, 244–5.6

County Business Patterns: establishments, employees, and payrolls, by SIC 4-digit industry and county, 1982, annual State rpt series, 2326–6

Exports and imports of US, detailed SIC-based commodities by world area, 1983, annual rpts, 2424–6

Exports of US, detailed commodities by country of destination, monthly rpt, 2422–3

Exports of US, detailed Schedule B commodities by country of destination, 1983, annual rpt, 2424–9

Fed Reserve Bank of Atlanta financial statements, 1982-83, annual rpt, 9371–4

Fed Reserve Bank of Chicago financial statements, 1983, annual rpt, 9375–5

Fed Reserve Bank of Cleveland financial statements, 1982-83, annual rpt, 9377–5

Fed Reserve Bank of Kansas City financial statements, 1982-83, annual rpt, 9381–3

Fed Reserve Bank of Minneapolis financial statements, 1981-82, annual rpt, 9383–2

Fed Reserve Bank of New York financial statements, 1982-83, annual rpt, 9385–2

Fed Reserve Bank of Philadelphia financial statements, 1982-83, annual rpt, 9387–3

Fed Reserve Bank of Richmond financial statements, 1983, annual rpt, 9389–2

Fed Reserve Bank of San Francisco financial statements, 1982-83, annual rpt, 9393–2

Fed Reserve banks financial statements and employees, 1983, annual rpt, 9364–1.1

Financial and business statistics, historic trends, 1984 annual chartbook, 9364–2.17

Flow-of-funds accounts, assets and liabilities by type and economic sector, year-end outstandings, 1960-83, annual rpt, 9364–3

Flow-of-funds accounts savings, investments, and credit statements, quarterly rpt, 9365–3.3

Foreign economic trends and implications for US, annual and semiannual country rpt series, 2046–4

Foreign loans, debts, exchange rates, and intl reserves, for US and selected countries, various periods 1949-84, conf papers, 9373–3.28

Foreign minerals production, reserves, and industry role in domestic economy and world supply, country and world region rpt series, 5606–1

Futures trading by commodity and exchange, and Commodity Futures Trading Commission activities, funding, and employment, FY83, annual rpt, 11924–2

Futures trading in selected commodities, foreign currencies, and stock indexes, Chicago and other markets activity, monthly rpt, 11922–1

Futures trading in selected commodities, foreign currencies, Treasury securities, and stock indexes, NYC, Chicago, and other markets activity, monthly rpt, 11922–5

Futures trading in selected commodities, Treasury securities, and stock indexes, NYC market activity, monthly rpt, 11922–2

Imports of US, detailed Schedule A commodities by country and world area of origin, and mode of transport, 1983, annual rpts, 2424–2

Imports of US, detailed Schedule A commodities by country, monthly rpt, 2422–2

Imports of US, detailed TSUSA commodities by country of origin, 1983, annual rpt, 2424–4

Investment (intl) position of US, net change by component, investment type, and world region, and for 2 countries, 1982-83, annual article, 2702–1.424

Mineral industries census, 1982: financial and operating data, by SIC 2- to 4-digit industry, preliminary summary rpt, 2511–2.1

Mineral industries census, 1982: financial and operating data, including materials consumed, by SIC 4-digit industry and State, preliminary rpt, 2511–1.2

Mineral Industry Surveys, commodity review of production, trade, stocks, and consumption, monthly rpt, 5612–1.10

Minerals Yearbook, 1982, Vol 1: commodity reviews of production, reserves, supply, use, and trade, annual rpt, 5604–33

Minerals Yearbook, 1982, Vol 2 preprints: State reviews of production and sales by commodity, and business activity, annual rpt series, 5604–16

Minerals Yearbook, 1982, Vol 2: State reviews of production, sales, and firms, by commodity, and business activity, annual rpt, 5604–34

Minerals Yearbook, 1982, Vol 3: foreign country reviews of production, trade, and policies, by commodity, annual rpt, 5604–35

Minerals Yearbook, 1982, Vol 3 preprints: foreign country reviews of production, trade, and policies, by commodity, annual rpt series, 5604–17

Minerals Yearbook, 1983, Vol 1 preprints: commodity review of production, reserves, supply, use, and trade, annual rpt, 5604–15.27

Minerals Yearbook, 1983, Vol 3 preprints: foreign country reviews of production, trade, and policies, by commodity, annual rpt series, 5604–23

Mint Bur activities and finances, production of medals and US and foreign coins, and gold and silver stocks and transactions, by office, FY83, annual rpt, 8204–1

Occupational injuries and incidence rates at metal mines and related operations, detailed analysis, 1982, annual rpt, 6664–3

Prices in London, current and 4-year trends, weekly chartbook, 9365–1.5

Producer prices and indexes, by stage of processing and detailed commodity, monthly rpt, 6762–6

Producer prices and indexes, by stage of processing and detailed commodity, monthly 1983, annual supplement, 6764–2

Production, prices, trade, use, employment, tariffs, and stockpiling, by mineral commodity, with foreign comparisons, 1979-83, annual rpt, 5604–18

Index by Subjects and Names

Recovery of metal resources through leaching technologies, characteristics of methods and operations, as of 1984, 5606–6.1

Reserve assets of US by type, *Treasury Bulletin,* quarterly rpt, 8002–4.11

Reserve assets of US, monthly rpt, 9362–1.3

Soviet Union production and reserves, 1965-83, annual rpt, 244–5.3

see also Coins and coinage

see also under By Commodity in the "Index by Categories"

Goldberg, Michael

"Science Base Underlying Research on Acquired Immune Deficiency Syndrome", 4102–1.404

Goldfarb, Marsha G.

"Who Receives Cesareans: Patient and Hospital Characteristics", 4186–6.4

Goldmark, Susan

"Capitalizing Workers: The Impact of Employee Stock Ownership Plans in Selected Developing Countries", 9916–3.19

Goldsmith, Harold F.

"Health Demographic Profile System's Inventory of Small Area Social Indicators", 4506–8.4

Goldstein, Henry N.

"Foreign Currency Futures: Some Further Aspects", 9375–1.401

Goldstein, Steven J.

"Prepayment Implications of Mortgage-Backed Security Prices", 9316–1.106

Golf

Army morale, welfare, and recreation programs, revenue and expenses worldwide by activity and major command, FY82-83, annual rpt, 3704–12

County Business Patterns: establishments, employees, and payrolls, by SIC 4-digit industry and county, 1981, annual State rpt series, 2326–8

County Business Patterns: establishments, employees, and payrolls, by SIC 4-digit industry and county, 1982, annual State rpt series, 2326–6

Foreign market and trade for sporting goods and recreational equipment and vehicles, country market research rpts, 2045–14

Injuries and deaths from use of selected consumer products and related activity, by victim age and sex, 1982, annual rpt, 9164–7

Recreation fees at State outdoor facilities, visits, revenue, costs, and employee salaries, by State, 1982/83, annual rpt, 5544–14.4

Service industry census, 1982: employment, establishments, receipts, and payroll, by SIC 2- to 4-digit kind of business, SMSA, county, and city, State rpt series, 2391–1

Gonorrhea

see Venereal diseases

Goodloe, Carol A.

"Global Stocks of Grain: Implications for U.S. Policy", 1528–184

Goodman, Allen C.

"Studies in Port Facilities and Urban Economic Development", 7308–182

Index by Subjects and Names

Gordon, Douglas
"Performance of Thin Futures Markets: Rice and Sunflower Seed Futures", 1502–3.404
"Stockpiling U.S. Agricultural Commodities with Volatile World Markets: The Case of Soybeans", 1502–3.402

Gordon, Scott
"Generation of Behavioral Lags for ISTUM2", 3308–66.8

Gornick, Marian
"Dually Entitled Elderly Medicare and Medicaid Population Living in the Community", 4652–1.433

Gorte, Ross W.
"Fire Effects Appraisal System for Wisconsin", 1208–198

Goshen, Ind.
see also under By SMSA or MSA in the "Index by Categories"

Goss, Stephen C.
"Long-Range Estimates of the Financial Status of the Old-Age, Survivors, and Disability Insurance Program, 1983", 4706–1.91

Gottfredson, Stephen D.
"Correctional Crisis: Prison Populations and Public Policy", 6068–176

Goudreau, Robert E.
"S&L Use of New Powers: A Comparative Study of State- and Federal-Chartered Associations", 9371–1.426
"S&L Use of New Powers: Consumer and Commercial Loan Expansion", 9371–1.432

Gough, Robert A.
"Will Big Deficits Spoil the Recovery?", 21248–79

Gould, Julia A.
"Merging of the Savings and Loan Industry", 9312–1.402

Goulden, Darrell R.
"Bibliography on Shift Work Research: 1950-82", 7506–10.29

Government agencies
see Government corporations
see Local government
see State government
see under By Federal Agency in the "Index by Categories"
see under Federal boards, committees, and commissions
see under Federal executive departments
see under Federal independent agencies

Government and business

Bank deposit interest rate deregulation, effect on bank deposits and bank financial performance, 1978-83, hearing, 21248–83
Budget of US Appendix, detailed budgets and personnel summaries, by agency, FY85, annual rpt, 104–3
Budget of US, compact budgets by function, agency, and account, FY85 with projections to FY89, annual rpt, 104–2
Budget of US, effects of Reagan Admin policy changes, by detailed program, FY85, annual rpt, 104–21
Budget of US, loans and loan guarantees, and Admin proposed limits on credit assistance, by program, FY83-89, annual rpt, 26306–3.65
Budget of US, receipts by source and outlays by agency and program, monthly rpt, 8102–3

Budget of US, receipts by source and outlays by function, FY40-89 estimates revised for consistency with FY85 budget definitions, annual rpt, 104–12
Budget of US, receipts, outlays, and budget authority, by function and agency, FY84-89 revised estimates, midsession review of FY85 budget, annual rpt, 104–7
Budget of US, receipts, outlays, and budget authority, by function and agency, 1st revision of FY85 budget, annual rpt, 104–17
Budget of US, special analysis of Fed Govt credit programs and interest subsidy values, FY85, annual rpt, 104–1.6
Chrysler Corp Loan Guarantee Act implementation, with related financial and operating data, FY83, last issue of annual rpt, 8004–14
Construction grants, loans, and loan guarantees of Fed Govt, by program and type of structure, FY80-83 and estimated FY84-85, annual article, 2012–1.404
Construction industry activity, employment and earnings, prices, Federal aid, and foreign contracts, 1970s-83 with projections to 1988, annual article, 2012–1.402
Data recording, processing, and transfer, and purchase and use of computer systems, Fed Govt standards, series, 2216–2
DC metro area Metrorail transit system, land use planning dev and impacts, 1984 narrative rpt, 7306–8.3
Deposit insurance of Fed Govt, regulatory control of insured instn risk-taking, narrative analysis, 1984 technical paper, 9316–1.107
Developing countries free zones, industry financial and operating data by country, with case studies for 5 countries, 1970s-82, 9918–10
Developing countries govt policy, and AID and other foreign assistance, effects on private sector dev and socioeconomic conditions, with case studies for 6 countries, 1960s-80, 9918–12
EC trade promotion policies and financing by industry, and effect on competing US industries, 1970s-82, 9886–4.73
Economic Dev Admin loans and grants, by program, State, county, and project or recipient, FY83 and cumulative FY66-83, annual rpt, 2064–2
Economic Report of the President for 1984, economic trends from 1929 and Reagan Admin proposals, annual rpt, 204–1
Electric power plants and industrial facilities prohibited from oil and gas primary use, and exemption petitions, by facility, with summary fuel use, 1983, annual rpt, 3104–8
Export credit program activities of Eximbank and 6 OECD countries, 1982, annual rpt, 9254–3
Farm business legal organization, finances, operations, tax rates, and State laws restricting farm corporations, 1960s-82, 1548–233
Fed Govt aid to State and local govts, expenditures, and direct payments, by program, agency, and State, FY83, annual rpt, 2464–2

Fed Govt financial and nonfinancial domestic aid, 1984 annual comprehensive catalog, 104–5
Fed Govt industrial dev funding by type, program, and agency, and State govt policies and support, selected years FY75-85, 26306–6.81
Fed Govt programs and mgmt cost control proposals, CBO and GAO estimates of savings by function and agency, FY85-89, 26308–45
Fed Govt programs and mgmt cost control proposals, 3-year savings by function and agency, and financial and operating data, 1960s-81, 16908–1
Financial instn deregulation, interstate banking, and bank performance and risks, 1984 conf papers, 9375–7
Fish and eggs for stocking distributed from natl hatcheries, by species, hatchery, and jurisdiction, FY83, annual rpt, 5504–10
Forests (natl) timber sales contract operations in Northwest US by forest and firm, and lumber supply/demand, FY76-1983 with trends from 1913, hearings, 25318–57
Franchise business opportunities by firm and kind of business, and sources of aid and info, 1984 annual listing, 2044–27
Govt revenues by source and expenditures by function, natl income and product account, *Survey of Current Business,* monthly rpt, monthly and annual tables, 2702–1.24
Livestock grazing on Natl Forest System lands, and losses from predators, poisonous plants, and other causes, by region and State, FY83, annual rpt, 1204–5
Loan and loan guarantee liabilities and commitments of Fed Govt, as of Sept 1983, annual rpt, 8104–3.4
Loan programs of Fed Govt, direct and guaranteed loans outstanding by agency and program, *Treasury Bulletin,* quarterly rpt, 8002–4.10
Loans and loan guarantees of Fed Govt issued and outstanding, by agency, off-budget entity, or program, FY82, article, 9391–1.403
Loans, grants, and tax benefits of Fed Govt to business, by program and economic sector, projected FY84-88 with effective tax rates FY80-82, 26306–6.70
Metals resource recovery through leaching technologies, characteristics of methods and operations, regulation, and research, series, 5606–6
Methanol fuel for autos, regulatory barriers to market dev, with supply/demand and auto fleet use and fuel economy, mid-1970s-82 and projected to 2000, GAO rpt, 26113–112
Minority business Fed Govt funding, procurement, and subsidies, and deposits in minority-owned banks, by agency, FY69-83, annual rpt, 2104–5
Motor carrier safety inspections by Fed Hwy Admin, audits of driver qualification and vehicle operation records, and violations cited, 1982, annual rpt, 7554–38
Motor carrier safety inspections on interstate hwys, violations cited, and vehicles and drivers ordered out of service, 1982, annual rpt, 7554–35

Government and business

Motor carrier safety inspections on interstate hwys, violations cited, and vehicles and drivers ordered out of service, May 1983, semiannual rpt, 7552–15

NASA-launched communications and other satellites, and USSR launches by type, 1957-83, annual rpt, 9504–6.1

Natural gas and hazardous liquid pipelines accidents and casualties, and DOT and State govt safety activities, 1982, annual rpt, 7304–5

Nuclear power plant licensing 24-month delay, effect on utility financial performance and electric power prices, for plant completed May 1979, 9638–53

Paperwork requirements of Fed Govt, small business perceived burden, and burden for 4 Fed Govt agencies, FY83, 9768–14

Pollution abatement capital and operating costs under Clean Air and Water Acts, for govts and selected industries, various periods 1970-2000, annual rpt, 9184–11

Pollution abatement expenditures, and effect on economic indicators and industry operations, by major industry, projected under 3 pollution regulation alternatives 1983-95, 9188–84

Pollution abatement payments to govt for public sewage use and solid waste disposal, by SIC 2- to 4-digit industry, State, and SMSA, 1982, annual Current Industrial Rpt, 2506–3.6

R&D Fed Govt facilities and services available for private sector use, by field of science, 1984 biennial listing, 2224–4

R&D Fed Govt labs required technology transfer to public and private sector, labs complying, funding, and requests, by agency, FY82, GAO rpt, 26113–141

Real estate broker govt certification requirements, licenses, and exam results, by State and Canada Province, 1977-78, 9408–48

Satellite Landsat system proposed transfer to private sector, uses and product sales by user type, and university programs and personnel by instn, 1973-85, 26358–100

Satellite systems (foreign and US) for civil observation, data product revenue, and proposed transfer of Fed Govt system to private sector, selected years 1978-FY84, 2148–47

Small and minority-owned businesses finances and operations, Federal contracts by agency, and worker characteristics, by industry, race, sex, and State, 1950s-83, annual rpt, 9764–6

Small Business Admin activities, balance sheets, and loans and contracts by firm, with small business economic conditions, FY83, annual rpt, 9764–1

Small business capital formation, sources, needs, and tax and other investment incentives and barriers, 1983 annual conf rpt, 9734–4

Small business capital formation under securities law exemptions, effects on stocks offered, issuers, and purchasers, series, 9736–2

Small business loans and credit, operational expectations, and NYC metro area owners economic and professional attitudes, by industry div, 1980-83 surveys, hearings, 21728–52

Small business mgmt counseling by university centers, costs, funding, and businesses served by industry, with detail for 2 States, 1980-83, hearing, 25728–36

Smoking and tobacco marketing legislation introduced and enacted in State legislatures, by State, 1982, annual rpt, 4204–13

Steel plant modernization capital investment under Clean Air Act compliance extension program, by firm, 1981-83, GAO rpt, 26113–138

Taxicab licenses, density, fares, license prices, and deregulation effects, by selected city, various dates 1970-84, 9406–1.37

Trade policy of Fed Govt, with data on US industry foreign trade and revenues, and Japan semiconductor industry subsidies, 1970s-83, hearings, 21368–46

Trucking industry economic effects of size and weight limits, and hwy use taxes by tax type, 1982-83 and projected 1984-87, hearings, 25328–24

Trucking industry economic effects of tax and size and weight rules, and hwy use taxes and Trust Fund revenues by tax type, FY82-84 and projected to 1990, GAO rpt, 26117–31

Urban Dev Action Grant awards to local areas, preliminary approvals, with project descriptions, private investment, and jobs and taxes to be created, by city, quarterly press release series, 5002–7

see also Administrative law and procedure

see also Agricultural subsidies

see also Defense contracts and procurement

see also Defense industries

see also Federal aid to railroads

see also Foreign assistance

see also Fuel allocation

see also Government contracts and procurement

see also Government corporations

see also Lobbying

see also Military assistance

see also Mineral leases

see also Oil and gas leases

see also Price regulation

see also Subsidies

see also Tax exempt securities

see also Tax expenditures

see also Tax incentives and shelters

see also Trade adjustment assistance

see also under names of individual Federal agencies and commissions

Government and the press

see also Government information

Government bonds

see Government securities

see Municipal bonds

see Tax exempt securities

see U.S. savings bonds

Government buildings

see Public buildings

Government census

see Census of Governments

Government contracts and procurement

Aerospace industry sales, and new and backlog orders, for military and nonmilitary customers, quarterly Current Industrial Rpt, 2506–12.22

AID contracts and grants for technical and support services, by instn, country, and State, FY83, annual listing, 9914–7

Index by Subjects and Names

AID contracts and grants to universities for technical assistance to foreign countries and other services, FY83, annual listing, 9914–6

AID Housing Guaranty Program financial statements, and projects by country, FY83, annual rpt, 9914–4

Astronautic and aeronautic events, foreign and US, comprehensive chronology, 1976, annual rpt, 9504–2

Blind and handicapped workshops, Fed Govt procurement of goods and services and participating workshops, FY78-82, annual rpt, 11714–1

Budget of US, CBO analysis of revenue and spending alternatives and projections of economic indicators, FY85-89, annual rpt, 26304–3.3

Budget of US, object class analysis of obligations, by branch of Fed Govt and selected depts and agencies, FY85 estimates, annual rpt, 104–9

Budget of US, special analyses of economic and social impact, FY85, annual rpt, 104–1

Building construction, acquisition, and alteration proposals for historic and other Fed Govt projects, costs and tenure by city and project, as of 1983, hearings, 25328–23

Cancer Natl Inst contracts and grants, by contractor, instn, State, and city, FY83, annual listing, 4474–28

Capitol Architect detailed expenditures for buildings and grounds, salaries, supplies, and services, 1st half FY84, semiannual rpt, 25922–2

Civil case processing of US Attorneys and amounts involved, by cause of action, FY83, annual rpt, 6004–2.5

Coal purchases of Fed Govt, quality control analyses by mine and location, FY82-83, annual rpt, 3004–15

Commerce Dept programs fraud and abuse, audits and investigations, 2nd half FY84, semiannual rpt, 2002–5

Commerce Dept regional center mgmt assistance operations, assessment, and procurement authority, by subagency, regional rpt series, 2006–4

Commercial activities of Fed Govt, savings from performance under contract over in-house, with DOD costs, employees displaced, and small business awards, by service branch, FY81-82, 108–39

Computers and telecommunications systems major acquisition plans and obligations of Fed Govt, by agency, FY84-89, annual listing, 104–20

Construction grants, loans, and loan guarantees of Fed Govt, by program and type of structure, FY80-83 and estimated FY84-85, annual article, 2012–1.404

Construction put in place, permits authorized by region, State, and MSA, and Federal contract awards, by construction type, bimonthly rpt with articles, 2012–1

Cost control proposals for Fed Govt programs and mgmt, CBO and GAO estimates of savings by function and agency, FY85-89, 26308–45

Cost control proposals for Fed Govt programs and mgmt, 3-year savings by function and agency, and financial and operating data, 1960s-81, 16908–1

Index by Subjects and Names

Government contracts and procurement

DOE and contractor facility accidents, deaths, illnesses, radiation exposure, and property damage, by facility, 1982, annual rpt, 3004–24

DOE procurement and assistance contracts, by State, contractor type, and top 100 instns, FY83, annual rpt, 3004–21

DOE programs finances and mgmt, audits and investigations, series, 3006–5

DOE programs fraud and abuse, audits and investigations, 2nd half FY84, semiannual rpt, 3002–12

DOT programs fraud and abuse, audits and investigations, 1st half FY84, semiannual rpt, 7302–4

EC trade promotion policies and financing by industry, and effect on competing US industries, 1970s-82, 9886–4.73

Economic trends, natl compounded annual rates of change, monthly rpt, 9391–3.2

Education Dept programs and activities, FY83, annual rpt, 4804–6

EPA programs fraud and abuse, audits and investigations, 2nd half FY84, semiannual rpt, 9182–10

Fed Govt agencies fraud and abuse, Inspectors General investigations and audits by agency, 1st half FY84, semiannual rpt, 102–5

Fed Govt aid to State and local areas, by type of payment, State, county, and city, FY83, annual rpt, 2464–3

Fed Govt aid to State and local govts, expenditures, and direct payments, by program, agency, and State, FY83, annual rpt, 2464–2

Fed Govt civil agency operations, summaries of GAO investigation rpts published 1975-83, annual rpt, 26104–5

Fed Govt consolidated financial statements based on business accounting methods, FY82-83, annual rpt, 8104–5

Fed Govt obligations by function and agency, *Treasury Bulletin,* quarterly rpt, 8002–4.2

Fed Govt per capita expenditures, by State, FY82, annual rpt, 10044–1.4

Fed Reserve System coin and currency transport truck driver and guard wages in 12 cities, effects of locally prevailing wage rate requirements, 1980, article, 9377–1.402

Financial and business statistics, quarterly chartbook, 9362–2.2

Forecasts for selected business activities and natl economic indicators, compilation of representative opinions, 1984, annual rpt, 9389–3

FTC budget authority and expenditures for regulatory analysis, by prospective regulation and contractor, 1983, hearings, 21528–56

Govt revenues by source and expenditures by function, natl income and product account, *Survey of Current Business,* monthly rpt, monthly and annual tables, 2702–1.24

GSA mgmt activities and finances, FY78-83, annual rpt, 9454–23

GSA programs fraud and abuse, audits and investigations, 2nd half FY84, semiannual rpt, 9452–8

HHS programs fraud and abuse, audits and investigations, 2nd half FY84, semiannual rpt, 4002–6

Housing units authorized, by public and private ownership, by region, div, State, selected MSA, and 4,700 permit-issuing places, monthly rpt, 2382–5

Housing units authorized, by public and private ownership, State, and permit-issuing place, 1983, annual rpt, 2384–2

HUD programs fraud and abuse, audits and investigations, 2nd half FY84, semiannual rpt, 5002–8

Hwy construction bids and contracts for Federal-aid interstate and secondary hwys, by State, 1st half 1984, semiannual rpt, 7552–12

Hwy construction expenditures and contracts awarded for Federal-aid system, by type of material used and State, various periods 1944-83, annual rpts, 7554–29

Input-output structure of US economy, detailed interindustry transactions for 85 industries, and components of final demand, 1977, article, 2702–1.421

Input-output structure of US economy, detailed interindustry transactions for 537 industries, and components of final demand, 1977 benchmark data, 2708–17

Interior Dept programs fraud and abuse, audits and investigations, 1st half FY84, semiannual rpt, 5302–2

Labor surplus areas eligible for preferential Fed Govt contracts, and labor force data for 150 major labor markets, monthly listing, 6402–1

Liabilities and other financial commitments, by Federal agency, as of Sept 1983, annual rpt, 8104–3

Manufacturers under Fed Govt contract and owned by DOD, operating data by agency, selected SIC 2- to 4-digit industry, State, and SMSA, 1982, annual Current Industrial Rpt, 2506–3.4

Minority business Fed Govt funding, procurement, and subsidies, and deposits in minority-owned banks, by agency, FY69-83, annual rpt, 2104–5

Minority business mgmt and financial assistance from federally funded organizations, by region, State, and business characteristics, FY83, annual rpt, 2104–6

Motor vehicle fleet of Fed Govt, costs and operating data by agency, FY83, annual rpt, 9454–9

NASA contract awards, by State, FY83, annual rpt, 9504–6.2

NASA procurement contract awards, by type, contractor, State, and country, FY84, semiannual rpt, 9502–6

NASA programs fraud and abuse, audits and investigations, 2nd half FY84, semiannual rpt, 9502–9

Natl income and product, comprehensive accounts and components, *Survey of Current Business,* monthly rpt, 2702–1.21

NIH extramural grant and contract awards for research, R&D, and construction, FY72-83, annual rpt, 4434–9

Nuclear reactor components and other atomic energy products and services, orders, total and Fed Govt shipments, and exports, 1983, annual Current Industrial Rpt, 2506–12.27

Overseas Business Reports: economic conditions, investment and export opportunities, and trade practices, annual country market research rpt series, 2046–6

Paperwork requirements of Fed Govt, small business perceived burden, and burden for 4 Fed Govt agencies, FY83, 9768–14

Prison Industries (Federal) operations and finances, FY83, annual rpt, 6244–3

Procurement contract awards of Fed Govt, by State, agency, procurement and contractor type, and for top 100 contractors, quarterly rpt, 102–6

Procurement, identical bidding for govt contracts, by bidder, product class, and level of govt, annual rpt, discontinued, 6004–8

Procurement of goods and services by level of govt, *Business Conditions Digest,* historical supplement and methodology, 1947-82, 2708–31

Procurement of goods and services by level of govt, *Business Conditions Digest,* monthly rpt, 2702–3.5

Rail equipment commitments of Fed Govt, by type of vehicle, FY65-82, 26358–97

Saudi Arabia-US Joint Commission on Economic Cooperation project activities and costs, and related contract awards by Fed Govt agency, as of 1983, GAO rpt, 26123–80

Security clearances of Fed Govt and contractor employees, polygraph use, and prepublication reviews, by agency, 1979-83, GAO rpt, 26123–66

Shipbuilding contracts awarded under Merchant Marine Act, 1971-81, annual rpt, 7704–12.1

Small Business Admin activities, balance sheets, and loans and contracts by firm, with small business economic conditions, FY83, annual rpt, 9764–1

Small Business Admin programs fraud and abuse, audits and investigations, 1st half FY84, semiannual rpt, 9762–5

Small business and minority- and women-owned businesses Federal contracts, by agency, FY81-82, annual rpt, 9764–6.4, 9764–6.5

Small business employment and receipts size standards for Fed Govt contract awards by industry, and DOD contract awards data, 1970s-83, hearings, 21728–53

Strategic Petroleum Reserve activities and funding, by supplier and site, quarterly GAO rpt, 26102–3

Strategic Petroleum Reserve capacity, inventory, fill rate, and finances, quarterly rpt, 3002–13

Survey contracts procedure of Federal agencies, 1983 narrative rpt, 106–4.3

TVA activities, financial and operating data by program and facility, and power sales by customer, FY83, annual rpt, 9804–1

USDA programs fraud and abuse, audits and investigations, 2nd half FY84, semiannual rpt, 1002–4

VA medical facilities sharing agreement contracts, services, and costs, by region and facility, FY83, annual rpt, 9924–18

VA programs fraud and abuse, audits and investigations, 2nd half FY84, semiannual rpt, 9922–13

Government contracts and procurement

see also Defense contracts and procurement
see also Federal funding for energy programs
see also Federal funding for research and development

Government corporations

Budget of US Appendix, detailed budgets and personnel summaries, by agency, FY85, annual rpt, 104–3

Budget of US, compact budgets by function, agency, and account, FY85 with projections to FY89, annual rpt, 104–2

Budget of US, effects of Reagan Admin policy changes, by detailed program, FY85, annual rpt, 104–21

Budget of US, receipts by source and outlays by agency and program, monthly rpt, 8102–3

Budget of US, receipts, outlays, and budget authority, by function and agency, FY84-89 revised estimates, midsession review of FY85 budget, annual rpt, 104–7

Budget of US, special analyses of economic and social impact, FY85, annual rpt, 104–1

China economic conditions, agricultural and industrial production, trade, and domestic and foreign investment, 1980-85, 2048–106

Cost control proposals for Fed Govt programs and mgmt, CBO and GAO estimates of savings by function and agency, FY85-89, 26308–45

Cost control proposals for Fed Govt programs and mgmt, 3-year savings by function and agency, and financial and operating data, 1960s-81, 16908–1

Fed Govt consolidated financial statements based on business accounting methods, FY82-83, annual rpt, 8104–5

Financial operations of Fed Govt, detailed data, *Treasury Bulletin,* quarterly rpt, 8002–4

Input-output structure of US economy, detailed interindustry transactions for 85 industries, and components of final demand, 1977, article, 2702–1.421

Input-output structure of US economy, detailed interindustry transactions for 537 industries, and components of final demand, 1977 benchmark data, 2708–17

Investigations of Fed Govt civil agencies operations, summaries of GAO rpts published 1975-83, annual rpt, 26104–5

Kentucky Higher Education Student Loan Corp student loans, loan purchases and defaults by instn, and revenue bonds status, various dates 1979-84, hearing, 21348–92

Mortgage loan activity, by type of lender, loan, and mortgaged property, monthly rpt, 5142–18

Mortgage loan originations, purchases, and acquisitions, for 11 lender types, selected years 1960-82, article, 9312–1.407

Natl income and product, comprehensive accounts and components, *Survey of Current Business,* monthly rpt, 2702–1.22

Natl income and product, comprehensive accounts and components, *Survey of Current Business,* monthly rpt, monthly and annual tables, 2702–1.27

see also Commodity Credit Corp.

see also Communications Satellite Corp.
see also Corporation for Public Broadcasting
see also Export-Import Bank
see also Federal Crop Insurance Corp.
see also Federal Deposit Insurance Corp.
see also Federal Home Loan Mortgage Corp.
see also Federal National Mortgage Association
see also Federal Prison Industries
see also Federal Savings and Loan Insurance Corp.
see also Government National Mortgage Association
see also Inter-American Foundation
see also Legal Services Corp.
see also National Railroad Passenger Corp.
see also Overseas Private Investment Corp.
see also Pennsylvania Avenue Development Corp.
see also Pension Benefit Guaranty Corp.
see also Rural Telephone Bank
see also Smithsonian Institution
see also St. Lawrence Seaway Development Corp.
see also Tennessee Valley Authority
see also U.S. Postal Service
see also U.S. Synthetic Fuels Corp.

Government debt

see Public debt

Government documents

Census Bur activities, publications, and user services, monthly rpt, 2302–3

Census Bur publications, data coverage, and suggested uses, series, 2326–7

Fed Govt programs and mgmt cost control proposals, 3-year savings by function and agency, and financial and operating data, 1960s-81, 16908–1

GPO activities, finances, and production, FY83, annual rpt, 26204–1

GPO depository library program quality and mgmt, opinions of librarians, 1983 survey, GAO rpt, 26111–19

GPO document sales program mgmt and finances, and bookstore operations by location, FY78-82, GAO rpt, 26111–17

GSA mgmt activities and finances, FY78-83, annual rpt, 9454–23

Libraries of colleges and universities, expenditures, holdings by type, use, staff by sex, and Federal grants received, 1979-82, biennial rpt, 4854–1

see also Environmental Impact Statements
see also Government publications lists

Government efficiency

AFDC and food stamp program costs and productivity in 8 States, 1973-82, GAO rpt, 26111–18

AFDC, food stamp, and SSI overpayments, payment error rates, and sanctions imposed, by State, various dates 1980-82, GAO rpt, 26113–136

AFDC State admin agencies performance measures, caseloads, payments, and costs, by State, FY81, annual rpt, 4704–10

AID dev assistance activities, evaluation rpt series, 9916–11

Air Force fiscal mgmt system operations and techniques, info for comptroller personnel, quarterly rpt, 3602–1

Budget of US, effects of Reagan Admin policy changes, by detailed program, FY85, annual rpt, 104–21

Child Support Enforcement Program cost savings to AFDC, Federal and State

Index by Subjects and Names

govts, and public assistance programs, by State and selected city or county, FY76-85, 4748–37

Commerce Dept regional center mgmt assistance operations, assessment, and procurement authority, by subagency, regional rpt series, 2006–4

Community Dev Block Grants reductions in respondent paperwork burden, FY81-83, annual rpt, 5124–5

Court caseloads, actions, procedure duration, judges, and jurors, by Federal district and appeals court, 1979-84, annual rpt, 18204–3

DOD Directorate for Info Operations and Rpts publications, FY84, annual listing, 3544–16

DOD operations, summaries of GAO investigation rpts published 1979-83, annual rpt, 26104–6

DOD procurement, prime contract awards by type, service branch and command, and for Defense Logistics Agency, last week compared to total year FY83, 108–38

DOD weapons system procurement cost underestimation in budget request 5-year plans, and cost change by system, various periods FY79-89, GAO rpt, 26123–68

DOE in-house energy use, conservation investments, and savings, by type of use and fuel and field office, FY83, annual rpt, 3024–3

EPA Strategic Planning and Mgmt System activities and progress in meeting mgmt goals, by office and activity, quarterly rpt, 9182–11

Fed Govt benefit payment by check and direct deposit, costs to agencies and banks, FY81, technical paper, 9366–1.139

Fed Govt civil agency operations, summaries of GAO investigation rpts published 1975-83, annual rpt, 26104–5

Fed Govt executive employee performance appraisal system operations, and employee attitudes, 1982 survey, GAO rpt, 26119–61

Fed Govt programs and mgmt cost control proposals, CBO and GAO estimates of savings by function and agency, FY85-89, 26308–45

Fed Govt programs and mgmt cost control proposals, 3-year savings by function and agency, and financial and operating data, 1960s-81, 16908–1

GAO activities and operations, and resulting Fed Govt cost savings, FY83, annual rpt, 26104–1

GAO evaluations of Federal programs, 1984 listing, 26106–5.1

GSA mgmt activities and finances, FY78-83, annual rpt, 9454–23

Industry coding systems for statistical programs of 6 Federal agencies, comparability, workload, and updating cycles, 1984 rpt, 106–4.5

IRS taxpayer assistance program operations and use, and users evaluation, selected years 1979-82, GAO rpt, 26119–58

Medicare program operations and admin efficiency, Blue Shield participants, and end-stage renal disease program activity, FY81, annual rpt, 4654–5

Index by Subjects and Names

Merit system of Office of Personnel Mgmt, implementation and effectiveness, 1982, annual survey, 9494–1

Natl Weather Service, effects of proposed reorganization and technological improvement on staff and expenditures, FY82 and projected to 2000, 2188–16

Occupational health and safety State govt program staffing requirements, and occupational injury data, for selected States, selected years 1973-81, hearings, 21348–88

Paperwork Reduction Act effects on Fed Govt info collection requirements and respondent burden, by agency, FY80-84, annual rpt, 104–19

Paperwork requirements of Fed Govt, small business perceived burden, and burden for 4 Fed Govt agencies, FY83, 9768–14

Police dept performance, analyses of police activities effects on neighborhoods and citizens, 1977, compilation of papers, 6068–181

Postal ratemaking and classification cases, processing, and participant attitudes, 1970s-84, GAO rpt, 26119–63

Postal Service operations, employment, productivity, and financial statements, FY79-83, annual rpt, 9864–1

Postal Service operations, finances, and employee productivity, performance, and compensation, FY83 with projections to FY85, annual rpt, 9864–5

Productivity in Fed Govt FY71-81, and in private sectors 1947-82, annual rpt, 6724–1.5

Productivity of labor and capital, costs, and prices, by selected industry, and compared to 6 OECD countries, selected years 1947-82, 17898–1

Public opinion on taxes, tax policy, and intergovtl relations, 1972-84 surveys, annual rpt, 10044–2

Public welfare programs evaluation, and research and statistical projects and techniques, 1983 conf papers, 4704–11

Regulatory growth of Fed Govt effect on local compliance costs and funding, local officials assessment, and comparisons to State govt regulations, 1970s-82 with trends from 1900, 10048–58

State and local govt productivity measurement, with background data and output indexes for 7 govt services, various periods 1955-82, 6728–27

State govt social services for youth, coordinating agencies activities, admin, membership, and funding sources, survey, 1984 rpt, 6068–182

Supplementary Security Income claims processing, disability awards, and payment error by reason, various dates 1974-83, article, 4742–1.416

Unemployment insurance State govt program admin, quality appraisal results, FY84, annual rpt, 6404–16

VA workloads and productivity at each Dept of Veterans Benefits field office, with regional summaries, quarterly rpt, 9922–7

see also Federal Inspectors General reports

Government employees

see Congressional employees

see Federal employees

see Military personnel

see Postal employees

see State and local employees

Government grants

see Community Development Block Grants

see Federal aid programs

see Federal funding for research and development

see Revenue sharing

see terms beginning with Federal aid

see terms beginning with State aid

Government housing

see Public housing

Government information

Advisory committees of Fed Govt, open and closed meetings, FY83, annual rpt, 9454–18

Census Bur publications, data coverage, and suggested uses, series, 2326–7

Commerce Dept budgets and permanent staff positions appropriated, by activity, FY84-85, annual rpt, 2004–6

Earthquake and other ground motion intensity measured on USGS Natl Strong-Motion Network by station, and sources of foreign and US info, 1981, annual rpt, 5664–14

Election campaign funding and activities of Fed Election Commission, and political action committees funding, 1983, annual rpt, 9274–1

Employee Retirement Income Security Act admin and enforcement, 1982, annual rpt, 6464–4

Fed Govt financial and nonfinancial domestic aid, 1984 annual comprehensive catalog, 104–5

Fed Govt info sources and systems available to Congress, listings, series, 26106–5

Fed Govt programs and mgmt cost control proposals, 3-year savings by function and agency, and financial and operating data, 1960s-81, 16908–1

Fed Reserve, concordance of data in monthly *Federal Reserve Bulletin* and *Annual Statistical Digest,* 1983, annual rpt, 9364–8

Franchise business opportunities by firm and kind of business, and sources of aid and info, 1984 annual listing, 2044–27

Freedom of Info Act, requests to HHS received and denied, costs, and fees collected, 1983, annual rpt, 4004–21

Geological Survey programs and funding, FY78-83, annual rpt, 5664–8

GSA programs fraud and abuse, audits and investigations, 2nd half FY84, semiannual rpt, 9452–8

Health info offices and services of HHS and other Fed Govt agencies, by subject, 1984 listing, 4048–18

HHS health data projects and systems, by subagency, FY83-84, annual inventory, 4044–3

Info Security Oversight Office monitoring of Fed Govt classified info security measures and classification actions, FY83, annual rpt, 9454–21

Land Mgmt Bur activities and finances, and public land acreage and use, annual State rpt series, 5724–11

NSF Science Resources Studies Div activities, project descriptions, and 1973-83 publications, 1983 annual listing, 9624–21

Government investigations

Nuclear Regulatory Commission activities, employment, and finances, and operations of individual power plants by State, FY83, annual rpt, 9634–2

Occupational injuries and illnesses, data available from NTIS, by State, 1981, annual rpt, 6704–2

Paperwork Reduction Act effects on Fed Govt info collection requirements and respondent burden, by agency, FY80-84, annual rpt, 104–19

Paperwork requirements of Fed Govt, small business perceived burden, and burden for 4 Fed Govt agencies, FY83, 9768–14

R&D Fed Govt facilities and services available for private sector use, by field of science, 1984 biennial listing, 2224–4

Satellite systems (foreign and US) for civil observation, data product revenue, and proposed transfer of Fed Govt system to private sector, selected years 1978-FY84, 2148–47

Security clearances of Fed Govt and contractor employees, polygraph use, and prepublication reviews, by agency, 1979-83, GAO rpt, 26123–66

USITC trade and tariff investigations, publications, and other activities, FY83, annual rpt, 9884–1

Vital statistics records offices and availability of birth, death, marriage, and divorce certificates, by State, 1984 annual listing, 4124–7

Water supply and quality, and effect of coal mining operations, for selected river basins in Eastern and Interior coal provinces, series, 5666–15

Water supply and quality, and effect of coal mining operations, for selected river basins in Western coal provinces, series, 5666–19

see also Bibliographies

see also Computer data file guides

see also Government documents

see also Government publications lists

see also Statistical programs and activities

Government investigations

Coal surface mining reclamation costs and Interior Dept regulatory enforcement activities, impacts on industry in 5 States and 3 regions, various periods 1978-82, 6068–177

Community Relations Service investigation and mediation of minority discrimination disputes, FY83, annual rpt, 6004–9

Cost control proposals for Fed Govt programs and mgmt, 3-year savings by function and agency, and financial and operating data, 1960s-81, 16908–1.25

Employee Retirement Income Security Act admin and enforcement, 1982, annual rpt, 6464–4

EPA environmental protection activities and funding, and environmental quality, 1970s-83, biennial regional rpt series, 9184–15

Exports and imports, agreement devs, US trade relations, and USITC investigations, 1983, annual rpt, 9884–5

Fed Govt agencies without inspectors general, internal audit activities, funding, and staff, by agency, FY83, GAO rpt, 26111–23

Foreign trade and economic indicators by country and country group, and US trade policy actions, 1960s-83, annual rpt, 444–1

Government investigations

Generalized System of Preferences status of 29 commodities, with US production, consumption, tariffs, and trade by country, selected years 1978-87, 9888–17

Hazardous material transport accidents, casualties, and property damage, by mode of transport, with DOT control activities, 1983, annual rpt, 7304–4

HHS program evaluations and funding, 1970-83, listing, 4008–60

Import and tariff provisions effect on US industries and products, investigations with background financial and operating data, series, 9886–4

Imports from Communist countries, injury to US industries, investigations with background financial and operating data, selected industries and products, series, 9886–12

Imports injury to price-supported US agricultural industries, investigations with background financial and operating data for selected products, series, 9886–10

Imports injury to US industries from foreign subsidized products and sales in US at less than fair value, investigations with background financial and operating data, series, 9886–19

Imports injury to US industries from foreign subsidized products, investigations with background financial and operating data for selected industries and products, series, 9886–15

Imports injury to US industries from import sales at less than fair value, investigations with background financial and operating data, series, 9886–14

Imports injury to US industries from increased import sales, investigations with background financial and operating data, series, 9886–5

Imports injury to US industries from removal of duties on foreign subsidized products, investigations with background financial and operating data, series, 9886–18

Maritime Commission mgmt and enforcement activities, filings by type and disposition, and civil penalties by shipper, FY83, annual rpt, 9334–1

Mobile and manufactured home safety standards, program inspections, enforcement actions, and accidents and casualties by victim characteristics, 1982-83, biennial rpt, 5004–4

Motor vehicle safety defect investigations by Natl Hwy Traffic Safety Admin, and recalls, 1981, annual rpt, 7764–1.2

Oil price and allocation regulations enforcement by DOE, and overcharge allegations, settlements, and refunds to States, by company, as of June 1983, hearing, 21368–50

Railroad accidents investigated by Fed Railroad Admin, casualties, damage, and circumstances, 1982, annual rpt, 7604–3

Secret Service investigations in counterfeiting, forgery, protective intelligence, and other matters, FY74-83, annual rpt, 8464–1

Security clearances of Fed Govt and contractor employees, polygraph use, and prepublication reviews, by agency, 1979-83, GAO rpt, 26123–66

Trade adjustment assistance eligibility, reemployment opportunities, and worker characteristics, investigations of industries injured by import competition, series, 6406–9

Transportation accident investigations and recommendations by Natl Transportation Safety Board, 1983, annual rpt, 9614–1

USITC trade and tariff investigation publications issued, 1960-83, annual listing, 9884–12

USITC trade and tariff investigations, publications, and other activities, FY83, annual rpt, 9884–1

see also Congressional investigations

see also Criminal investigations

see also Federal Inspectors General reports

see also General Accounting Office

Government lands

see Public lands

Government loans

see Federal aid programs

see Federal funding for research and development

see terms beginning with Federal aid

see terms beginning with State aid

Government National Mortgage Association

Budget of US, loans and loan guarantees, and Admin proposed limits on credit assistance, by program, FY83-89, annual rpt, 26306–3.65

Cost control proposals for Fed Govt programs and mgmt, 3-year savings by function and agency, and financial and operating data, 1960s-81, 16908–1.8, 16908–1.14

Credit assistance costs, policies to improve measurement, with loan and loan guarantee data by program, and Federal and private credit instns operations, 1970-84, 26306–6.72

Financial statements and mortgage-backed securities program, FY82-83, annual rpt, 5144–6

Futures trading in selected commodities, foreign currencies, and stock indexes, Chicago and other markets activity, monthly rpt, 11922–1

Futures trading in selected commodities, foreign currencies, Treasury securities, and stock indexes, NYC, Chicago, and other markets activity, monthly rpt, 11922–5

Mortgage and mortgage-related investment of financial instns, by instn type and Fed Govt issuing agency, various dates 1981-84, 5008–33

Pension plan investment in mortgages and FHLB and Fed Govt mortgage assn mortgage-backed securities, for corporate and union funds, quarterly rpt, 5002–10

Government ownership

Agriculture census, 1982: farms, farmland, production, finances, and operator characteristics, by county, final State rpt series, 2331–1

Aluminum primary production plant ownership, capacity, and type and source of raw material and energy used, by plant, State, and country, June 1984, semiannual listing, 5602–5

Argentina grain production, exports by firm, storage by facility type and port, and shipments to ports by mode of transport, by grain type, selected years 1954-81, 1528–185

Index by Subjects and Names

China economic conditions, agricultural and industrial production, trade, and domestic and foreign investment, 1980-85, 2048–106

Construction put in place, value of new public and private structures, by type, monthly rpt, 2382–4

Developing countries govt policy, and AID and other foreign assistance, effects on private sector dev and socioeconomic conditions, with case studies for 6 countries, 1960s-80, 9918–12

Electric utilities privately owned, detailed financial and operating data by company, with summary data for other distributors by type, 1982, annual rpt, 3164–23

Electric utilities revenues and income, by census div, quarterly rpt, 3162–38

Electric utility fuel cost, quality, use, receipts, and stocks, and power plant production, by energy source, State and utility, quarterly rpt, 3162–39

GSA mgmt activities and finances, FY78-83, annual rpt, 9454–23

Shipping and shipbuilding subsidies and aid, and summary fleet, trade, and GNP data, for US and 47 countries, 1979-80, biennial rpt, 7704–18

Statistical Abstract of US, social, political, and economic data, 1950s-83 and trends, annual rpt, 2324–1.2

see also Government corporations

see also Government property

see also Military bases, posts, and reservations

see also Military hospitals

see also Military supplies and property

see also Public buildings

see also Public lands

see also Surplus government property

see also Veterans health facilities and services

Government price control

see Price regulation

Government Printing Office

Activities, finances, and production, FY83, annual rpt, 26204–1

Budget of US Appendix, detailed budgets and personnel summaries, by agency, FY85, annual rpt, 104–3

Budget of US, appropriations, outlays, balances, and budget receipts, by govtl branch and agency, FY83, annual rpt, 8104–2

Budget of US, compact budgets by function, agency, and account, FY85 with projections to FY89, annual rpt, 104–2

Cost control proposals for Fed Govt programs and mgmt, 3-year savings by function and agency, and financial and operating data, 1960s-81, 16908–1.32

Depository library program of GPO, opinions of librarians on quality and mgmt, 1983 survey, GAO rpt, 26111–19

Document sales program mgmt and finances, and bookstore operations by location, FY78-82, GAO rpt, 26111–17

Government property

Alaska electric power capacity and generation by fuel type, and marketing, by utility, type of ownership, and location, 1983, annual rpt, 3214–2

Auto fleet size, trip characteristics, and energy use, by fleet type, 1970s-83, annual rpt, 3304–5.2

Index by Subjects and Names

Bombing (explosive and incendiary) and arson incidents by target, State, and circumstances, and explosives theft and recovery, 1982-83, annual rpt, 8484–4

Bombing (explosive and incendiary) incidents, damage, injuries, and deaths, by target, State, and circumstances, 1983, annual rpt, 6224–5

Bridges over navigable waters, with type of bridge and use, owner, dimensions, and location, 1984 regional listing series, 7406–5

Budget of US, CBO analysis of revenue and spending alternatives and projections of economic indicators, FY85-89, annual rpt, 26304–3.3

Budget of US, effects of Reagan Admin policy changes, by detailed program, FY85, annual rpt, 104–21

Capital (fixed), govt and private nonresidential structures and equipment, residential capital, and consumer-owned durable goods by item, 1980-83, annual article, 2702–1.433

Coal Fed Govt leases, acreage, production, and prices, by State, and legal and mgmt issues, 1970s-83 with production projections to 2000, 11128–1

Colorado River Storage Project finances, water resource dev, power production, and other activities in western States, FY83, annual rpt, 5824–3

Computer systems and equipment of Fed Govt, inventory by manufacturer, type, agency, and location, FY83, last issue of annual rpt, 9454–4

Construction put in place, value of new public and private structures, by type, monthly rpt, 2382–4

Cost control proposals for Fed Govt programs and mgmt, CBO and GAO estimates of savings by function and agency, FY85-89, 26308–45

Cost control proposals for Fed Govt programs and mgmt, 3-year savings by function and agency, and financial and operating data, 1960s-81, 16908–1

DOE and contractor facility accidents, deaths, illnesses, radiation exposure, and property damage, by facility, 1982, annual rpt, 3004–24

DOE in-house energy use, conservation investments, and savings, by type of use and fuel and field office, FY83, annual rpt, 3024–3

Farm Credit System property acquisitions and disposals, by State, as of Dec 1982, annual rpt, 9264–2

Fed Govt consolidated financial statements based on business accounting methods, FY82-83, annual rpt, 8104–5

Fed Govt obligations by function and agency, *Treasury Bulletin,* quarterly rpt, 8002–4.2

GSA mgmt activities and finances, FY78-83, annual rpt, 9454–23

GSA programs fraud and abuse, audits and investigations, 2nd half FY84, semiannual rpt, 9452–8

HUD-acquired single family homes through mortgage default, and disposition, by city, monthly rpt, 5142–31

HUD New Communities program, activities, costs, land sales, and community and population characteristics, for 13 communities, 1970s-83, 5188–107

Government publications lists

Inventory and automated cataloging system of Fed Govt supplies, and DOD mgmt of inventory items for agencies, NATO, and foreign govts, 1970s-83, annual rpt, 21204–1

Loan programs of Fed Govt, direct and guaranteed loans outstanding by agency and program, *Treasury Bulletin,* quarterly rpt, 8002–4.10

Motor vehicle fleet of Fed Govt, auto and light truck fuel use by agency, FY77-83, hearing, 21368–49

Motor vehicle fleet of Fed Govt, costs and operating data by agency, FY83, annual rpt, 9454–9

Motor vehicle registrations, by public and private ownership, vehicle type, and State, 1983, annual rpt, 7554–1.2

Patents (US) granted to US and foreign applicants, by applicant type, firm, State, and country, subject rpt series, 2246–2

Patents (US) granted to US and foreign applicants, by year of grant and application, country, and type of applicant, 1960s-83, annual rpt, 2244–3

Real property leased by Fed Govt, inventory and rental costs, worldwide summary by location and agency, 1983, annual rpt, 9454–10

Real property own-to-lease ratio for Fed Govt, by State and for 25 SMSAs, as of 1983, hearings, 25328–23

Real property owned by Fed Govt, inventory and costs, worldwide summary by location, agency, and use, 1983, annual rpt, 9454–5

Satellite systems (foreign and US) for civil observation, data product revenue, and proposed transfer of Fed Govt system to private sector, selected years 1978-FY84, 2148–47

Ships and tonnage of Fed Govt merchant fleet, by type of vessel and whether active, monthly rpt, 7702–1

Ships in US merchant fleet, by selected characteristics and private-govt ownership, as of Jan 1983, annual rpt, 7704–1

Terrorist (intl) incidents, casualties, and attacks on US targets, by attack type and world area, with chronology of events, 1983, annual rpt, 7004–13

VA-acquired defaulted properties, FY59-83, annual rpt, 9924–13.3

Virgin Islands socioeconomic and govtl data, FY81, annual rpt, 5304–4

Waterborne commerce of US (domestic and foreign), freight by commodity, traffic, and passengers, by port and waterway, 1982, annual rpt, 3754–3

see also Military bases, posts, and reservations

see also Military supplies and property

see also Public buildings

see also Public lands

see also Surplus government property

Government publications

see Government documents

see Government publications lists

Government publications lists

Agricultural publications of USDA, annual listing, suspended, 1004–13

Agriculture Fact Book of US, compilation of data for 1983 with trends from 1940, annual rpt, 1004–14

Alaska minerals resources, production, claims on wildlife refuges, oil and gas leases, and exploratory wells, with maps and bibl, 1983, annual rpt, 5664–11

Aviation medicine research and studies, FAA technical rpt series, 7506–10

Background Notes, foreign countries summary social, political, and economic data, 1984 index, 7006–2.22

BLS major statistical and analytical programs and publications, annual listing, suspended, 6704–1

Bonneville Power Admin energy conservation rpts, educational materials, and 1982 conferences, 1983 rpt, 3228–2.2

Census Bur publications and data files, monthly listing, 2302–6

Census Bur publications data coverage and availability, 1984 annual listing, 2304–2

Census Bur publications, data coverage, and suggested uses, series, 2326–7

Census of Agriculture, 1982: data coverage and availability for agriculture census and related statistics, 1984 guide, 2308–55

Census of Population and Housing, 1980: data coverage, availability, and uses for urban and transportation planning, 1984 guide, 7558–101

Commerce Dept publications, annual listing, discontinued, 2004–4

Commerce Dept publications, biweekly listing, 2002–1

Computer software and documentation available from NTIS, by agency and program characteristics, 1984 annual listing, 2224–2

Crime and criminal justice data, including justice expenditures and employment by level of govt, 1970s-82 with some trends from 1875, 6068–174

Crop Reporting Board commodity publications, 1984 releases, annual listing, 1614–1

DOD Directorate for Info Operations and Rpts publications, FY84, annual listing, 3544–16

Energy Info Admin surveys, data analysis models, and publications, 1983, annual rpt, 3164–29

EPA publications in NTIS collection, quarterly listing, 9182–5

Fed Emergency Mgmt Agency publications, annual listing, suspended, 9434–5

Fed Information Processing Standards publications, 1968-83, listing, 2216–2.121

Fish and Wildlife Service conservation and research project descriptions and results, by program, FY83, annual rpt, 5504–20

Foreign Agricultural Service publications, annual listing, discontinued, 1924–1

GAO activities and operations, and resulting Fed Govt cost savings, FY83, annual rpt, 26104–1

GAO evaluations of Federal programs, 1984 listing, 26106–5.1

GAO publications issued, 2nd half 1983, semiannual listing, 26102–1

GAO publications on automatic data processing, food, health, and land use, annual listing series, 26104–11

Geological Survey and other publications, 1983, annual listing, 5664–4

Geological Survey publications, monthly listing, 5662–1

Government publications lists

Health info offices and services of HHS and other Fed Govt agencies, by subject, 1984 listing, 4048–18

Health Statistics Natl Center publications, quarterly listing, 4122–2

HHS program evaluations and funding, 1970-83, listing, 4008–60

Housing energy use, costs, expenditures, and conservation, and household and housing characteristics, survey series, 3166–7

Hwy design and construction R&D, quarterly journal, 7552–3

Intl Trade Admin publications, biweekly rpt, annual listing, 2042–24

Investigations of DOD operations, summaries of GAO rpts published 1979-83, annual rpt, 26104–6

Investigations of Fed Govt civil agencies operations, summaries of GAO rpts published 1975-83, annual rpt, 26104–5

Justice Natl Inst publications, annual listing, suspended, 6064–8

Libraries and Info Science Natl Commission, activities, funding, expenditures, and publications lists, FY83, annual rpt, 15634–1

MarAd shipbuilding and operating subsidies and other activities, and world merchant fleets operations, FY83, annual rpt, 7704–14

Medicine Natl Library activities, collections, and grants, FY81-83, annual rpt, 4464–1

Mines Bur publications and other material, 1982, annual listing, 5604–40

Mines Bur publications and patents, monthly listing, 5602–2

Natl Center for Health Statistics publications, 1979-83, annual listing, 4124–1

NIH publications, 1983, annual listing, 4434–2

NOAA scientific and technical publications, monthly listing, 2142–1

NSF Science Resources Studies Div activities, project descriptions, and 1973-83 publications, 1983 annual listing, 9624–21

Radioactive materials transport surveillance program activities, results, and Fed Govt funding, by State, 1984 summary rpt, 9636–1.23

Research publications on energy of DOE and other sources, monthly listing, 3002–2

Senate Aging Committee, Special, publications, 1961-83, annual listing, 25144–3.1

Smithsonian Instn finances, activities, and visitors, FY83, annual rpt, 9774–3

Soil survey county descriptions and maps of USDA, 1899-1983, annual listing, 1264–11

Standards Natl Bur publications, 1983 annual listing, 2214–1

Technology Assessment Office activities, programs, and publications list, 1983, annual rpt, 26354–3

Telecommunications and Info Natl Admin research and engineering rpts, FY83, annual listing, 2804–3

Uranium resources research publications, 1976-83, listing, 3358–27

USITC trade and tariff investigation publications issued, 1960-83, annual listing, 9884–12

USITC trade and tariff investigations, publications, and other activities, FY83, annual rpt, 9884–1

see also Federal Inspectors General reports

Government regulation

see Administrative law and procedure

see Antitrust law

see Government and business

see Interstate commerce

see Licenses and permits

see Price regulation

Government reorganization

Budget of US, effects of Reagan Admin policy changes, by detailed program, FY85, annual rpt, 104–21

FAA airport maintenance employees attitudes toward reorganization of field offices and automation of facilities, 1980 survey, 7506–10.25

Fed Govt programs and mgmt cost control proposals, 3-year savings by function and agency, and financial and operating data, 1960s-81, 16908–1

Law enforcement activities of Alcohol, Tobacco, and Firearms Bur in 20 cities and nationwide, funding, and jobs to be transferred to Customs and Secret Service, 1979-82, hearings, 21528–55

Natl Weather Service, effects of proposed reorganization and technological improvement on staff and expenditures, FY82 and projected to 2000, 2188–16

Government revenues

Boston, Mass, govt budget and impact of reduced local revenue and Fed Govt aid, and other devs, FY80-86, article, 9373–1.406

Business Conditions Digest, historical supplement on economic, business, and financial conditions and cyclical fluctuations, with methodology, 1947-82, 2708–31

Census of Govts, 1982: city govt revenues by source, expenditures by function, debt, and assets, by State and city, 2457–4

Census of Govts, 1982: county govt revenues by source, expenditures by function, debt, and assets, by State and county, 2457–3

Census of Govts, 1982: school districts revenues, expenditures, debt, and assets, by district and State, 2457–1

City govt fiscal condition, revenue sharing program allocations, and responses to program cuts, FY81-83, surveys, hearings, 25408–86

Copyright activities of Register of Copyrights, including intl relations, registrations, fees earned, and royalties collected, FY82, annual rpt, 26404–2

County and City Data Book, detailed socioeconomic and demographic data for States, counties, and cities, selected years 1976-82, 2328–1

Economic conditions of US, with some foreign comparisons, 1960s-82 and alternative projections to 1992, hearing, 21248–79

Economic performance of US, and Reagan Admin 1984 spending, tax, and monetary policy proposals, with data for 1950s-83 and projected to 1988, press release, 8008–107

Economic Report of the President for 1984, economic effects of budget proposals, and trends and projections 1950s-89, annual hearings, 23844–4

Index by Subjects and Names

EPA Superfund revenues by source, and disbursements by purpose, FY81-84 and proposed FY85, 26308–47

Fed Govt consolidated financial statements based on business accounting methods, FY82-83, annual rpt, 8104–5

Fed Govt programs and mgmt cost control proposals, 3-year savings by function and agency, and financial and operating data, 1960s-81, 16908–1

Fed Govt programs under Ways and Means Committee jurisdiction, program operations and financing data for assessing budgetary requirements, by State, FY70s-83, 21788–117

Fed Govt receipts by source and outlays by agency, *Treasury Bulletin,* quarterly rpt, 8002–4.1

Fed Govt receipts, outlays, and debt account transactions, daily statement, 8102–4

Fed Govt receipts, tax and other, FY83, annual rpt, 8104–2.2

Fed Govt revenues by source, FY60-89, and income and social security tax burden of households and effect of indexing by income level, 1982, press release, 8008–109

Fed Govt revenues, deficits, and debt, and GNP and unemployment, cyclically adjusted estimates assuming middle-range unemployment, 1955-3rd qtr 1983, article, 2702–1.403

Foreign economic trends and implications for US, annual and semiannual country rpt series, 2046–4

Forests (natl) below-cost timber sales and revenue by western forest, and volume, average price by species, and costs by western region, FY80-1982, GAO rpt, 26113–126

Forests (natl) below-cost timber sales in Colorado, and volume, costs, revenue, and net loss, by sale and forest, FY81-82, GAO rpt, 26113–131

Govt finances, by level of govt and State, selected years 1929-83, annual rpt, 10044–1

Govt finances, by level of govt, State, and for large cities and counties, 1981-83, annual rpt series, 2466–2

Govt revenue and expenditures, surplus/deficit, and tax capacity and effort indexes, for US and 7 western States, selected years 1967-82, article, 9381–1.403

Govt revenues and expenditures by level of govt, natl income and product accounts, selected years 1929-83, annual rpt, 204–1.6

Govt revenues by source and expenditures by function, natl income and product account, *Survey of Current Business,* monthly rpt, monthly and annual tables, 2702–1.24

HUD mortgage insurance funds financial and property activity, and insurance written, monthly rpt, 5002–9

HUD mortgage insurance funds, insurance in force, and property acquisitions and sales, quarterly rpt, 5002–3

Hwy and urban transit systems financing methods of govts and private sector, with case studies for selected metro areas, series, 7556–7

Index by Subjects and Names

Government securities

Hwy receipts by source, and expenditures by function, by level of govt and State, 1983, annual rpt, 7554–1.3

Local govt spending, reliance on State aid and local taxes by type, and excise tax growth by State, selected years FY57-83, article, 10042–1.403

Natl income and product, comprehensive accounts and components, *Survey of Current Business,* monthly rpt, 2702–1.21

Naval Petroleum and Oil Shale Reserves production, dev, ownership, leasing, sales by purchaser, and Fed Govt revenues, by site, FY83, annual rpt, 3004–22

New England State govts revenues, expenditures, and year-end closing balances, for 6 States, FY83 and projected FY84, article, 9373–2.401

Oil (Alaskan) potential exports to Japan, costs and benefits, with background data on oil prices, Pacific Basin supply/demand, and tankers, various periods 1918-99, hearings, 25388–45

Outlying areas govt financial data and audits by Interior Dept Inspector General, by area, FY83, annual rpt, 5304–15

Public health labs of States, personnel, finances, workloads, and other activities, by State, FY82, annual rpt, 4204–8

Public lands sales of Land Mgmt Bur, prices of Nevada and California acreage, and effect on Forest Service land acquisition program, 1983, GAO rpt, 26113–122

Satellite systems (foreign and US) for civil observation, data product revenue, and proposed transfer of Fed Govt system to private sector, selected years 1978-FY84, 2148–47

State and local govt revenue and spending growth rates, and bond offerings by purpose, various periods 1948-84, article, 9362–1.408

State and local govt revenue by source and expenditures by function, 1980-83, article, 2702–1.436

State and local govt revenues by source and expenditures by type, 1978-83, annual article, 2702–1.405

State govt motor fuel tax provisions, motor vehicle registration fees, and disposition of receipts, by State, as of Jan 1984, biennial rpt, 7554–37

Statistical Abstract of US, social, political, and economic data, 1950s-83 and trends, annual rpt, 2324–1.2

Transportation revenues by source and expenditures, by level of govt and mode of transport, and Fed Govt aid by type, FY77-82, 7308–185

TTPI socioeconomic, health, and govtl data, by TTPI govt, FY83 and selected trends, detailed annual rpt, 7004–6

Virgin Islands govt fiscal condition, FY81, annual rpt, 5304–10

Virgin Islands socioeconomic and govtl data, FY81, annual rpt, 5304–4

Wildlife refuge revenues from economic and recreational uses, and refuge managers attitudes toward expanded use, FY81-83, GAO rpt, 26113–128

see also Budget of the U.S.

see also Estate tax

see also Excise tax

see also Foreign budgets

see also Gift tax

see also Income taxes

see also Mineral leases

see also Oil and gas leases

see also Property tax

see also Sales tax

see also Severance taxes

see also Social security tax

see also State and local taxes

see also Tariffs and foreign trade controls

see also Tax expenditures

see also Taxation

see also Tolls

see also Unemployment insurance tax

see also User fees

Government securities

Banks (natl) domestic and intl operations, charters, mergers, and liquidations, by State and instn, and Comptroller of Currency activities, quarterly rpt, 8402–3

Budget of US, effects of Reagan Admin policy changes, by detailed program, FY85, annual rpt, 104–21

Budget of US, special analysis of Federal agencies investment in Fed Govt securities, FY85, annual rpt, 104–1.5

Business statistics, detailed data for major industries and economic indicators, *Survey of Current Business,* monthly rpt, 2702–1.6

Census of Govts, 1982: city govt revenues by source, expenditures by function, debt, and assets, by State and city, 2457–4

Census of Govts, 1982: county govt revenues by source, expenditures by function, debt, and assets, by State and county, 2457–3

Conrail operations and US Railway Assn finances and activities, FY81-83, annual rpt, 29604–1

Economic trends and projections, 1970s-83, and Budget of US under current fiscal policy and alternatives, FY85-89, annual rpt, 26304–3.1

Eximbank financial condition, and loan, credit, and insurance authorizations, by country, FY83, annual rpt, 9254–1

Farm Credit System mortgage and other loans, and financial statements, 1982 and selected trends from 1961, annual rpt, 9264–2

FDIC officials and operations, 1983, annual rpt, 9294–1.2

Fed Govt agencies transactions and balances, monthly rpt, 8102–3

Fed Govt consolidated financial statements based on business accounting methods, FY82-83, annual rpt, 8104–5

Fed Govt debt by holder, interest rates and costs, and financing mechanisms, projected FY84-89 with data for FY80-83, 26308–50

Fed Govt programs and mgmt cost control proposals, 3-year savings by function and agency, and financial and operating data, 1960s-81, 16908–1

Fed Govt programs under Ways and Means Committee jurisdiction, program operations and financing data for assessing budgetary requirements, by State, FY70s-83, 21788–117

Fed Govt securities issued, and held as investments, FY82-83, annual rpt, 8104–2.1

Fed Govt trust fund receipts, expenditures, assets, and liabilities, for 9 funds, periodic rpt series, 8102–9

Fed Home Loan Mortgage Corp activities and financial statements, 1983, annual rpt, 9414–1

Fed Reserve Bank of Atlanta financial statements, 1982-83, annual rpt, 9371–4

Fed Reserve Bank of Chicago financial statements, 1983, annual rpt, 9375–5

Fed Reserve Bank of Cleveland financial statements, 1982-83, annual rpt, 9377–5

Fed Reserve Bank of Kansas City financial statements, 1982-83, annual rpt, 9381–3

Fed Reserve Bank of Minneapolis financial statements, 1981-82, annual rpt, 9383–2

Fed Reserve Bank of New York financial statements, 1982-83, annual rpt, 9385–2

Fed Reserve Bank of Philadelphia financial statements, 1982-83, annual rpt, 9387–3

Fed Reserve Bank of Richmond financial statements, 1983, annual rpt, 9389–2

Fed Reserve Bank of San Francisco financial statements, 1982-83, annual rpt, 9393–2

Fed Reserve banks financial statements and employees, 1983, annual rpt, 9364–1.1

Financial and business detailed statistics, *Fed Reserve Bulletin,* monthly rpt with articles, 9362–1

Financial and business statistics, historic trends, 1984 annual chartbook, 9364–2.8, 9364–2.9

Financial operations of Fed Govt, detailed data, *Treasury Bulletin,* quarterly rpt, 8002–4

Flow-of-funds accounts, assets and liabilities by type and economic sector, year-end outstandings, 1960-83, annual rpt, 9364–3

Flow-of-funds accounts savings, investments, and credit statements, quarterly rpt, 9365–3.3

Forecasts for selected business activities and natl economic indicators, compilation of representative opinions, 1984, annual rpt, 9389–3

Foreign industrial stock indices and long-term government bond yields, US and 7 foreign countries, weekly chartbook, 9365–1.5

Foreign official assets and liabilities, and transactions in securities, monthly rpt, 9362–1.3

Forgery investigations of Secret Service, case closure, and bond value, FY79-83, annual rpt, 8464–1

Futures trading in selected commodities, foreign currencies, and stock indexes, Chicago and other markets activity, monthly rpt, 11922–1

Futures trading in selected commodities, foreign currencies, Treasury securities, and stock indexes, NYC, Chicago, and other markets activity, monthly rpt, 11922–5

Futures trading in selected commodities, Treasury securities, and stock indexes, NYC market activity, monthly rpt, 11922–2

Futures trading summary data by type of investment, and Commodity Futures Trading Commission activities, funding, and employment, FY83, annual rpt, 11924–2

Govt finances, by level of govt, State, and for large cities and counties, 1981-83, annual rpt series, 2466–2

Government securities

Govt finances, quarterly chartbook, 9362–2.4

Govt Natl Mortgage Assn mortgage-backed securities program, FY82-83, annual rpt, 5144–6

Hwy receipts by source, and expenditures by function, by level of govt and State, 1983, annual rpt, 7554–1.3, 7554–1.4

Income tax proposals to encourage savings, and personal assets and liabilities by type, 1981, article, 8302–2.407

Intl investment position of US, net position and components, selected years 1897-1982, annual rpt, 2044–25

Investment (intl) position of US, net change by component, investment type, and world region, and for 2 countries, 1982-83, annual article, 2702–1.424

Kentucky Higher Education Student Loan Corp student loans, loan purchases and defaults by instn, and revenue bonds status, various dates 1979-84, hearing, 21348–92

Liabilities and other financial commitments, by Federal agency, as of Sept 1983, annual rpt, 8104–3

Medicare Hospital Insurance Trust Fund financial operations and payroll taxes, FY83 and selected years 1966-2005, annual rpt, 4704–5

Medicare Supplementary Medical Insurance Trust Fund financial operations, FY83 and selected years 1966-87, annual rpt, 4704–3

Mortgage and mortgage-related investment of financial instns, by instn type and Fed Govt issuing agency, various dates 1981-84, 5008–33

Mortgage-backed securities of FHLB and 3 Fed Govt mortgage assns, investment by corporate and union pension funds, quarterly rpt, 5002–10

Mortgages (home) and mortgage pool participation by lender type, and FHA mortgage yields, various periods 1950-84 with trends from 1900, technical paper, 9375–11.4

Note and bond new issues delivered by Bur of Engraving and Printing, annual rpt, discontinued, 8164–1

OASDI trust funds financial operations, FY83 and selected years 1940s-2060, annual rpt, 4704–4

Ownership of govt securities, dealer transactions and financing sources, and new State and local issues, monthly rpt, 9362–1.1

Ownership of govt securities, dealer transactions and financing sources, and new State and local issues, 1982, annual rpt, 9364–5.5, 9364–5.10

Pension plan investment in Fed Govt mortgage-backed securities, yields by issuer, and fund assets by fund type, 1970s-82, conf papers, 5008–32

Public debt account transactions for Fed Govt, daily statement, 8102–4

Public debt issued, redeemed, and outstanding, by individual issue and source, monthly rpt, 8242–2

Public debt securities, types, ownership, and maturity, 1976-83, annual rpt, 204–1.6

Savings and loan assn balance sheet items by State and SMSA, and finances of FHLBs, 1983, annual rpt, 9314–3

Small Business Admin loan and contract activity by program, and balance sheets, FY83, annual rpt, 9764–1.1

Southeastern States banks by asset size, finances, and loans and deposits by type, Fed Reserve 5th District, various dates 1979-83, annual article, 9389–1.408

State and local govt retirement systems, cash and security holdings and finances, quarterly rpt, 2462–2

State, municipal, and corporate security offerings, 1934-83, and common stock prices and earnings, 1949-83, annual rpt, 204–1.7

Statistical Abstract of US, social, political, and economic data, 1950s-83 and trends, annual rpt, 2324–1.2

Student Loan Marketing Assn activities, and financial ratios and stock dividends compared to banks and 4 Fed Govt-sponsored credit assns, 1980-82, GAO rpt, 26121–71

Treasury bill futures market efficiency tests, 1984 technical paper, 9316–1.105

Treasury bill offerings and auction results, by Fed Reserve district and term to maturity, periodic releases, 8002–7

Treasury bill spot and futures market investments, relative rates of return, 1978-82, technical paper, 9387–8.88

Treasury bond futures options pricing measures, for 53 call options traded Oct 1982-Apr 1983, article, 9391–1.404

Treasury securities put options trading, hypothetical thrift instn losses, 1983 technical paper, 9316–1.102

Truman, Harry S, Scholarship Fund receipts by source, transfers, and investment holdings and transactions, monthly rpt, 14312–1

Trust assets of banks and trust companies, by type of asset and fund and State, 1983, annual rpt, 13004–1

Virgin Islands govt fiscal condition, FY81, annual rpt, 5304–10

Western States depository instns financial activity by State, and large commercial banks by city, Fed Reserve 10th District, monthly rpt, 9381–11

Western States economic indicators, Fed Reserve 12th District, quarterly rpt, 9393–1.5

Yields and interest rates, *Business Conditions Digest,* cyclical indicators, monthly rpt, 2702–3.3

Yields and interest rates, *Business Conditions Digest,* historical supplement and methodology, 1947-82, 2708–31

Yields and interest rates for Treasury bills and US and municipal bonds, monthly rpt, 23842–1.5

Yields and interest rates, govt and private issues, weekly rpt, 9391–4

Yields and interest rates on public and private securities, 1929-83, annual rpt, 204–1.5

Yields, interest rates, and bond prices, for commercial paper and govt securities, monthly rpt, 9365–2.14

see also Federal Financing Bank

see also Municipal bonds

see also Tax exempt securities

see also U.S. savings bonds

Government spending

Advisory committees of Fed Govt, and members, staff, meetings, and costs, by agency, FY83, annual rpt, 9454–18

Arts and humanities funding, by source and State, FY82-83 with trends from FY66, 21408–69

Bankruptcy court cases and admin in districts with and without case trustees, and staff and potential costs of nationwide trustee program, various periods 1979-83, annual rpt, 6004–15

Boston, Mass, govt budget and impact of reduced local revenue and Fed Govt aid, and other devs, FY80-86, article, 9373–1.406

Business Conditions Digest, historical supplement on economic, business, and financial conditions and cyclical fluctuations, with methodology, 1947-82, 2708–31

Business statistics, detailed data for major industries and economic indicators, *Survey of Current Business,* monthly rpt, 2702–1.6

Census of Govts, 1982: city govt revenues by source, expenditures by function, debt, and assets, by State and city, 2457–4

Census of Govts, 1982: county govt revenues by source, expenditures by function, debt, and assets, by State and county, 2457–3

Census of Govts, 1982: school districts revenues, expenditures, debt, and assets, by district and State, 2457–1

Child Support Enforcement Program cost savings to AFDC, Federal and State govts, and public assistance programs, by State and selected city or county, FY76-85, 4748–37

City govt fiscal condition, revenue sharing program allocations, and responses to program cuts, FY81-83, surveys, hearings, 25408–86

Colorado River Storage Project finances, water resource dev, power production, and other activities in western States, FY83, annual rpt, 5824–3

County and City Data Book, detailed socioeconomic and demographic data for States, counties, and cities, selected years 1976-82, 2328–1

Crime and criminal justice data, including justice expenditures and employment by level of govt, 1970s-82 with some trends from 1875, 6068–174

Criminal justice system local operations and costs, series, 6066–21

Economic and financial trends, natl compounded annual rates of change, 1964-83, annual rpt, 9391–9.2

Economic growth rates and component economic indicators, selected years 1922-83 and projected under full employment to 1988, hearing, 21348–90

Economic indicators and components, cumulative for fiscal year, annual trends, and quarterly data, monthly rpt, 23842–1.6

Economic performance of US, and Reagan Admin 1984 spending, tax, and monetary policy proposals, with data for 1950s-83 and projected to 1988, press release, 8008–107

Index by Subjects and Names

Government spending

Economic Report of the President for 1984, economic effects of budget proposals, and trends and projections 1950s-89, annual hearings, 23844–4

Energy conservation programs of utilities, financing, costs, participation, and energy savings, various periods 1981-84, hearing, 21368–54

Environmental quality and protection programs, costs, and Fed Govt enforcement, 1983, detailed annual rpt, 484–1

Fed Govt civil agency operations, summaries of GAO investigation rpts published 1975-83, annual rpt, 26104–5

Fed Govt consolidated financial statements based on business accounting methods, FY82-83, annual rpt, 8104–5

Fed Govt deficits and fiscal policy, with expenditures by level of govt, selected years 1929-83, article, 10042–1.401

Fed Govt expenditures in States and local areas, Census Bur data collection, limitation, contributing agency costs, and opinions of congressional users, 1984 GAO rpt, 26111–20

Fed Govt financial operations, detailed data, *Treasury Bulletin,* quarterly rpt, 8002–4

Fed Govt liabilities and other financial commitments, by agency, as of Sept 1983, annual rpt, 8104–3

Fed Govt programs and mgmt cost control proposals, 3-year savings by function and agency, and financial and operating data, 1960s-81, 16908–1

Fed Govt receipts, outlays, and debt account transactions, daily statement, 8102–4

Fed Govt revenues, deficits, and debt, and GNP and unemployment, cyclically adjusted estimates assuming middle-range unemployment, 1955-3rd qtr 1983, article, 2702–1.403

Financial and business statistics, historic trends, 1984 annual chartbook, 9364–2.2, 9364–2.8, 9364–2.9

Flow-of-funds accounts savings, investments, and credit statements, quarterly rpt, 9365–3.3

Food aid programs of Fed Govt and others, funding, participant characteristics, and nutrition and poverty data, 1970s-83, 028–20

Foreign countries disasters, persons affected, deaths, damage, and aid by US and others, FY83 and trends from FY64, annual rpt, 9914–12

Foreign economic trends and implications for US, annual and semiannual country rpt series, 2046–4

Govt finances, by level of govt and State, selected years 1929-83, annual rpt, 10044–1

Govt finances, by level of govt, State, and for large cities and counties, 1981-83, annual rpt series, 2466–2

Govt revenue and expenditures, surplus/deficit, and tax capacity and effort indexes, for US and 7 western States, selected years 1967-82, article, 9381–1.403

Govt revenues and expenditures by level of govt, natl income and product accounts, selected years 1929-83, annual rpt, 204–1.6

Govt revenues by source and expenditures by function, natl income and product account, *Survey of Current Business,* monthly rpt, monthly and annual tables, 2702–1.24

Great Lakes basin pollutant discharges by source, and control program activities, 1983 annual rpt, 14644–1

Health care expenditures by type and source, and govt aid to health R&D by level of govt and Federal agency, 1970s-83, annual compilation, 4144–11.5

Housing (rental) unit choice of Pittsburgh, Pa, recent movers related to unit, neighborhood, and town characteristics, 1967 survey, 9306–1.7

Hwy and urban transit systems financing methods of govts and private sector, with case studies for selected metro areas, series, 7556–7

Hwy expenditures and aid per capita related to local area characteristics, for 10 eastern counties, annual averages 1965-76, technical paper, 9377–9.9

Hwy expenditures by level of govt, 1972-82, annual rpt, 7304–2

Input-output structure of US economy, detailed interindustry transactions for 537 industries, and components of final demand, 1977 benchmark data, 2708–17

Intl exchange and training programs of Fed Govt, participants by world region, and funding, by agency, FY83, annual rpt, 9854–8

Jail capacities, conditions, expenditures, and services, and socioeconomic and other characteristics of inmates, various dates 1976-82, 10048–59

Local govt finances and population characteristics for cities and suburbs, by region and selected SMSA, selected years 1957-FY83, 10048–61

Mental health facilities of States and counties, inpatients, deaths, staff by occupation, and facilities, by State, 1970s-82, 4506–3.13

Money supply and high-employment Fed Govt spending related to nominal GNP, alternative specifications for St Louis equation, 1962-82, article, 9391–1.417

Natl income and product, comprehensive accounts and components, *Survey of Current Business,* monthly rpt, 2702–1.21

Natl Weather Service, effects of proposed reorganization and technological improvement on staff and expenditures, FY82 and projected to 2000, 2188–16

Natural gas and hazardous liquid pipelines accidents and casualties, and DOT and State govt safety activities, 1982, annual rpt, 7304–5

Natural gas interstate pipeline company detailed financial and operating data, by firm, 1983, annual rpt, 3164–38

New England State govts revenues, expenditures, and year-end closing balances, for 6 States, FY83 and projected FY84, article, 9373–2.401

NYC ocean dumping of municipal wastes, and sewage production and disposal barge capacity and operating costs, 1970s-82 and projected to 2000, hearings, 21568–36

Outlying areas govt financial data and audits by Interior Dept Inspector General, by area, FY83, annual rpt, 5304–15

Police services expenditures, by level of govt, 1981, 6066–20.8

Pollution abatement capital and operating costs under Clean Air and Water Acts, for govts and selected industries, various periods 1970-2000, annual rpt, 9184–11

Pollution abatement expenditures of govt, business, and consumers, 1972-82, annual article, 2702–1.407

Preventive health services block grants of Fed Govt, State funding by program, and opinions on State program admin, for 13 States, FY81-84, GAO rpt, 26121–88

Prison expansion plans of States, beds and construction costs by region, 1984 survey, 6066–20.6

Prison population and capacity by State and individual DC and Federal instn, construction costs, and Fed Govt operating costs, 1983 and projected to 1990, GAO rpt, 26119–59

Public defender systems, costs, cases, and expenditures by level of govt and State, with system characteristics and lawyer fee ranges, 1981, 6066–19.8

Public health labs of States, personnel, finances, workloads, and other activities, by State, FY82, annual rpt, 4204–8

Public opinion on taxes, tax policy, and intergovtl relations, 1972-84 surveys, annual rpt, 10044–2

Public works capital needs and financing, by project type, level of govt, and selected jurisdiction, 1970s-83 and projected to 2000, hearing, 23848–181

Public works capital needs and intergovtl financing, by type of project and selected city, various periods 1950-83, 10048–60

R&D expenditures of higher education instns, by source, field of science, census div, and State, 1972-83, biennial rpt, 9627–24.1

Railroad commuter systems financial and operating data for 7 systems, and public agency cost reimbursement, 1980, 7888–61

Recreation fees at State outdoor facilities, visits, revenue, costs, and employee salaries, by State, 1982/83, annual rpt, 5544–14.4

Regulatory growth of Fed Govt effect on local compliance costs and funding, local officials assessment, and comparisons to State govt regulations, 1970s-82 with trends from 1900, 10048–58

Revenues and expenditures, by level of govt, *Business Conditions Digest,* monthly rpt, 2702–3.8

Satellite Landsat system proposed transfer to private sector, uses and product sales by user type, and university programs and personnel by instn, 1973-85, 26358–100

Senate salaries, expenses, and contingent fund disbursements, by payee, detailed listings, 1st half FY84, semiannual rpt, 25922–1

Social welfare expenditures by program and level of govt, and private expenditures for health care, selected years FY50-82, annual article, 4742–1.425

Space and aeronautics programs and budgets of Fed Govt by agency, and foreign programs, 1957-FY85, annual rpt, 9504–9

Government spending

Space shuttle launch guests by type, and itemized Fed Govt costs by agency, Apr 1981-Nov 1983, GAO rpt, 26123–78

State and local govt fiscal position on national income and product basis, 1976-83, article, 2702–1.409

State and local govt grants from Fed Govt, expenditures by function, and business cycle effects on spending, various periods 1948-83, article, 9385–1.401

State and local govt revenue and spending growth rates, and bond offerings by purpose, various periods 1948-84, article, 9362–1.408

State and local govt revenue by source and expenditures by function, 1980-83, article, 2702–1.436

State and local govt revenues by source and expenditures by type, 1978-83, annual article, 2702–1.405

State govt motor fuel tax provisions, motor vehicle registration fees, and disposition of receipts, by State, as of Jan 1984, biennial rpt, 7554–37

Statistical Abstract of US, social, political, and economic data, 1950s-83 and trends, annual rpt, 2324–1.2

Transit systems, expenditures by level of govt, and revenues by source, with distribution of commuter trips by mode of transport, 1980-82, article, 10042–1.404

Transportation revenues by source and expenditures, by level of govt and mode of transport, and Fed Govt aid by type, FY77-82, 7308–185

Travel expenses of Fed Govt employees on official business, and reimbursement rates, for high rate cities, 1983, annual rpt, 9454–16

TTPI socioeconomic, health, and govtl data, by TTPI govt, FY83 and selected trends, detailed annual rpt, 7004–6

UN participation of US, and member and nonmember shares of UN budget by country, FY83-85, annual rpt, 7004–5

Virgin Islands govt fiscal condition, FY81, annual rpt, 5304–10

Virgin Islands socioeconomic and govtl data, FY81, annual rpt, 5304–4

Water from urban runoff, quality, pollutant concentrations, and control cost-effectiveness, with monitoring sites rainfall and other characteristics, by city and region, 1978-83, 9208–122

Water pollution from nonpoint sources, source land uses and acreage, and control program funding, by State or region, various periods 1974-FY84, 9208–123

Youth Conservation Corps activities, costs, and participant characteristics, by sponsoring agency, 1982, annual rpt, 5304–12

see also Agricultural quotas and price supports

see also Agricultural subsidies

see also Budget of the U.S.

see also Defense expenditures

see also Economic indicators

see also Executive impoundment of appropriated funds

see also Federal aid programs

see also Federal aid to arts and humanities

see also Federal aid to education

see also Federal aid to higher education

see also Federal aid to highways

see also Federal aid to housing

see also Federal aid to law enforcement

see also Federal aid to libraries

see also Federal aid to local areas

see also Federal aid to medical education

see also Federal aid to medicine

see also Federal aid to railroads

see also Federal aid to rural areas

see also Federal aid to States

see also Federal aid to transportation

see also Federal aid to vocational education

see also Federal funding for energy programs

see also Federal funding for research and development

see also Federal pay

see also Foreign budgets

see also Government contracts and procurement

see also Nonappropriated funds

see also Public welfare programs

see also Revenue sharing

see also State aid to education

see also State aid to higher education

see also State aid to local areas

see also State and local employees pay

see also Subsidies

see also under names of individual Federal departments and agencies

Government workers

see Congressional employees

see Federal employees

see Military personnel

see Postal employees

see State and local employees

Grabowski, Henry G.

"Studies on Drug Substitution, Patent Policy and Innovation in the Pharmaceutical Industry", 25528–98

Grace Commission

see President's Private Sector Survey on Cost Control

Grad, Susan

"Income of the Population 55 and Over, 1982", 4744–26

"Incomes of the Aged and Nonaged, 1950-82", 4742–1.413

Graduates

see Degrees, higher education

see Educational attainment

Graham, Avy

"Surviving Spouse's Benefits in Private Pension Plans", 6722–1.426

Graham, Harry

"Are Unions Facing a Crisis? Labor Officials Are Divided", 6722–1.451

Grains and grain products

Acreage harvested and cropland area by crop and region, and potential for expansion, 1982-84 with trends from 1949, annual rpt, 1584–4

Acreage planted and harvested, by crop and State, 1982-83 and planned as of June 1984, annual rpt, 1621–23

Acreage planting intended for 19 crops, by State, as of Feb 1984, annual rpt, 1621–22

Acreage reduction payment-in-kind program costs, requirements, producer and diversion payments, and loan interest forgiven, by crop, as of 1983, hearing, 21788–138

Acreage, yield, and production of field crops, by State, 1978-82 and preliminary 1983, 1641–7

Index by Subjects and Names

Agricultural policies of US effect on trade, with US and foreign trade by commodity and grain stocks by world area, various periods 1979-83, 1528–183

Agricultural Stabilization and Conservation Service rye programs, 1955-84, annual fact sheet, 1806–4.5

Agricultural Statistics, 1983, annual rpt, 1004–1

Agriculture census, 1982: farms, farmland, production and costs, and operator characteristics, preliminary State and county rpt series, 2330–1

Agriculture census, 1982: farms, farmland, production, finances, and operator characteristics, by county, final State rpt series, 2331–1

Air pollutant emission factors, by detailed source, 3rd edition, 1983-84 supplements, 9198–13

Air pollution abatement equipment shipments by industry, exports, and new and backlog orders, by product, 1983, annual Current Industrial Rpt, 2506–12.5

Alcoholic beverage production, stocks, materials used, and taxable and tax-free removals, for beer and distilled spirits by State, monthly rpt, 8486–1.1, 8486–1.3

Argentina grain production, exports by firm, storage by facility type and port, and shipments to ports by mode of transport, by grain type, selected years 1954-81, 1528–185

Beer and cereal beverages production, removals, and stocks, by State, FY81-82, last issue of annual rpt, 8484–1.3

Business statistics, detailed data for major industries and economic indicators, *Survey of Current Business,* monthly rpt, 2702–1.11

Canada grain handling and rail transport system financial and operating data, and effects of limited capacity on grain and oilseed exports, selected years 1950-82, 1528–176

Census of Population, 1980: detailed socioeconomic and demographic characteristics, by age, sex, race, Hispanic origin, occupation, and industry, State rpt series, 2531–4

China economic conditions, agricultural and industrial production, trade, and domestic and foreign investment, 1980-85, 2048–106

China exports and imports by SITC 1- to 5-digit commodity, 1970s-82, annual rpt, 244–12

Communist, OECD, and selected other countries agricultural production, by commodity, 1960s-83, annual rpt, 244–5.9

Consumption of food and nutrient intake by individuals, by food group, source, and socioeconomic characteristics, 1977-78 natl survey, final rpt series, 1356–4

Consumption, supply, trade, prices, expenditures, and indexes, by food commodity, 1963-83, annual rpt, 1544–4

Cooperatives commercial farmer membership and use, by type and sales size of farm and region, 1980, 1128–32

Cooperatives finances and operations, aggregate for top 100 assns by principal product and revenue source, FY82, annual rpt, 1124–3

Index by Subjects and Names

Grains and grain products

Cooperatives for grain, storage and handling facilities, sales, exports, and financial condition, selected years 1974-82, 1128–31

Cooperatives grain marketing, storage, and shipments by mode of transport, by grain type and region, FY80, 1128–28

Cooperatives, membership, activities, and finances, by commodity and selected State, 1900-80 with trends from 1863, 1128–30

County Business Patterns: establishments, employees, and payrolls, by SIC 4-digit industry and county, 1981, annual State rpt series, 2326–8

County Business Patterns: establishments, employees, and payrolls, by SIC 4-digit industry and county, 1982, annual State rpt series, 2326–6

Developing countries food production and needs, and related economic trends and outlook, for 67 countries, 1980-86, annual rpt, 1524–6

Developing countries food supply policies, with farm sector data, tariff income, and prices and imports of 5 grains, for 21 countries, 1960s-81, 1528–168

Eastern Europe agricultural production and trade by commodity, food consumption, and farm inputs, for 6 countries, 1960-80 with projections to 1991, 1528–178

Eastern Europe grain production, consumption, and trade, and US farm cooperatives grain and oilseed export potential, for 4 countries, selected years 1960-90, 1128–27

EC food supply/demand and market and support prices, with exchange rates, fertilizer price index, GDP, and population, by country, 1960-83, 1528–173

Employment, earnings, and hours, by selected SIC 1- to 4-digit industry, State, and for 278 major labor areas, 1939-83, annual rpt, 6744–5

Employment, earnings, and hours, by SIC 4-digit nonfarm industry, monthly 1974-Feb 1984, annual update, 6744–4

Export licensing and monitoring activities under Export Admin Act, for selected commodities, and for Communist and other countries, FY83, annual rpt, 2044–22

Export sales and shipments of US grains, oilseed products, hides, skins, and cotton, by country, weekly rpt, 1922–3

Exports and imports of US, by agricultural commodity and country, bimonthly rpt with articles, 1522–1

Exports and imports of US, by detailed agricultural commodity and country, FY83 and CY83, semiannual rpts, 1522–4

Exports and imports of US, by detailed agricultural commodity for 8 major commodity groups, monthly rpt, 1922–8

Exports and imports of US, detailed SIC-based commodities by world area, 1983, annual rpts, 2424–6

Exports and imports of US, totals and as percent of domestic production, by SIC 2- to 5-digit commodity, 1981, annual rpt, 2424–3

Exports and personal expenditures of US and world for selected agricultural

commodities, by country, and export share of US farm income, various periods 1926-82, 1528–172

Exports, imports, tariffs, and industry operating data for grains and grain products, 1979-83, TSUSA commodity rpt, 9885–1.68

Exports of manufactured and agricultural commodities, manufacturing production, and export-related employment, 1960s-82, State rpt series, 2046–3

Exports of US, detailed commodities by country of destination, monthly rpt, 2422–3

Exports of US, detailed Schedule B commodities by country of destination, 1983, annual rpt, 2424–9

Exports of US, detailed Schedule E commodities by mode of transport and world area and country of destination, 1983, annual rpts, 2424–5

Exports under PL 480 concessional sales program, by commodity and country, 1955-83, semiannual rpt, 1922–6

Exports under PL 480 concessional sales program, by commodity and country, 1978-83, semiannual rpt, 1922–10

Farm finances, assets, liabilities, income, receipts by commodity and State, and expenses, 1980-83 and trends from 1910, annual rpt, 1544–16

Farm production inputs, outputs, and productivity, by region, 1939-82, annual rpt, 1544–17

Federal Grain Inspection Service activities and finances by program, and foreign complaint investigations by country, FY83, annual rpt, 1294–1

Flour milling production by census div and State, daily capacity, and exports by country, monthly Current Industrial Rpt, 2506–4.1

Foreign agricultural production, prices, and trade, by country, 1983 and outlook for 1984/85, annual world region rpt series, 1524–4

Foreign and US agricultural production, prices, trade, and consumption, quarterly rpt with articles, 1522–3

Foreign and US agricultural production, trade, and climatic devs, with US and Rotterdam prices and EC supports by type of grain, weekly press release, 1922–4

Foreign and US agricultural supply/demand and production data, for selected US and world crops, and for US livestock and dairy products, periodic rpt, 1522–5

Foreign and US agricultural supply/demand, consumption per capita, and trade, by world area and country group, 1960s-82, 1528–181

Foreign and US grain production, trade, stocks, consumption, and prices, FAS monthly and annual rpt series, 1925–2

Foreign and US grain stocks, supply deviation, and effect on use, trade, and prices, by selected country, various periods 1960-83, 1528–184

Foreign and US production, acreage, and yield for selected crops, forecasts by selected world region and country, FAS monthly rpt, 1925–28

Foreign and US rye production, prices, trade, stocks, and use, periodic situation rpt with articles, 1561–12

Freight shipments by rail, rates and shares of freight and railroad finances and operations, by commodity and railroad, 1970s-82, hearings, 25268–80

Futures contracts, stocks in deliverable position by type and grade, weekly tables, 11922–4

Futures trading by commodity and exchange, and Commodity Futures Trading Commission activities, funding, and employment, FY83, annual rpt, 11924–2

Futures trading in selected commodities, foreign currencies, and stock indexes, Chicago and other markets activity, monthly rpt, 11922–1

Futures trading in selected commodities, foreign currencies, Treasury securities, and stock indexes, NYC, Chicago, and other markets activity, monthly rpt, 11922–5

Genetic resource (plant and animal) conservation, commercial uses, causes of depletion, and geographic sources, 1984 rpt, 5548–13

Great Lakes trade, by SITC 3-digit commodity, port, vessel type, world area, and country, 1982, annual rpt, 7744–3

Imports of US, detailed Schedule A commodities by country and world area of origin, and mode of transport, 1983, annual rpts, 2424–2

Imports of US, detailed Schedule A commodities by country, monthly rpt, 2422–2

Imports of US, detailed TSUSA commodities by country of origin, 1983, annual rpt, 2424–4

Income tax returns of corporations, detailed income and tax items by industry, 1981, annual rpt, 8304–4

Input-output structure of US economy, detailed interindustry transactions for 537 industries, and components of final demand, 1977 benchmark data, 2708–17

Loan support programs of USDA for grains, activity and status by type of grain and State, monthly rpt, 1802–3

Manufacturing census, 1982: financial and operating data, by SIC 2- to 4-digit industry, State, SMSA, and county, preliminary census div rpt series, 2491–3

Manufacturing census, 1982: financial and operating data, for SIC 4-digit industries by product, preliminary rpt, 2491–1.33

Manufacturing census, 1982: financial and operating data, for SIC 4-digit industries by product, preliminary rpt series, 2491–1

Marketing cash receipts of farms, by detailed commodity and State, 1979-82, annual rpt, 1544–18

Mill production workers, wages, hours, and benefits, by occupation, mill product, and region, June 1982 survey, 6787–6.204

Minority group and women employment, by occupational group and SIC 2- to 3-digit industry, 1981, annual rpt, 9244–1.1

Montana and North Dakota coal production, impact of mining on agricultural land availability and on farm income and production costs, by mining tract, 1982 rpt, 1588–79

Occupational injury and illness rates, by SIC 2- to 4-digit industry, 1982, annual rpt, 6844–1

Grains and grain products

OECD trade, total and for 4 major countries, and US trade by country, by commodity, 1972-82, annual world region rpt series, 244–13

Pesticide (ethylene dibromide) residue in grain and grain foods, and effect of processing and cooking, by selected product, 1984 hearing, 25168–62

Prices (farm-retail) for foods, marketing cost components, and industry finances and productivity, selected years 1967-83, annual rpt, 1544–9

Prices received by farmers and production value for detailed crops by State, 1981-83, annual rpt, 1621–2

Prices received by farmers for major products, and paid for farm inputs and living items, by commodity and State, monthly rpt, 1629–1

Prices received by farmers for major products, and paid for farm inputs, by commodity and State, 1983, annual rpt, 1629–5

Producer prices and indexes, by stage of processing and detailed commodity, monthly rpt, 6762–6

Producer prices and indexes, by stage of processing and detailed commodity, monthly 1983, annual supplement, 6764–2

Production, acreage, and yield, for selected grains by State, 1982-84 with wheat and rye seedings for 1985, annual rpt, 1621–24

Production and farm finances, expenses by type, and domestic economic impact, selected years 1972-82 and preliminary 1983-84, annual rpt, 1544–19

Production, farms, acreage, and related data, by selected crop and State, monthly rpt, 1621–1

Production itemized costs, receipts, and net returns, for 13 crops, 4 livestock types, and milk, by region, 1981-83, annual rpt, 1544–20

Production, prices, trade, and export inspections by US port and country of destination, by grain type, weekly rpt, 1313–2

Production, prices, trade, and marketing, by commodity, current situation and forecast, monthly rpt, 1502–4

Productivity, hours, and employment indexes for selected SIC 3- and 4-digit industries, 1954-82, annual rpt, 6824–1.3

Seed exports of US, by type of seed, world region, and country, FAS quarterly rpt, 1925–13

Shipments, rail and barge loadings, ship and container car availability, ocean freight rates, and export inspections, prices, and sales, weekly rpt, 1272–2

Soviet Union grain area, yield, production, trade, supply, and use forecasts, FAS monthly rpt, 1925–2.3

Stocks of grain by region and market city, and grain inspected for export, by type, weekly rpt, 1313–4

Stocks of grain on and off farms and total in all positions, by crop, periodic rpt, 1621–4

Stocks of grains, oilseeds, and hay on and off farms, and capacity of off-farm grain storage facilities, by State, 1978-83, 1641–17

Storage facility and equipment loans to farmers under CCC grain program, by State, FY68-84, annual table, 1804–14

Storage facility and equipment loans to farmers under CCC grain program, by State, monthly table, 1802–9

Supply/demand, prices, and commodity program operations, for selected crops and livestock, 1983 and outlook for 1984, annual article, 9381–1.402

Waterborne commerce of US (domestic and foreign), freight by commodity, traffic, and passengers, by port and waterway, 1982, annual rpt, 3754–3

Waterborne trade of grain and selected other commodities worldwide, and grain ocean freight rates by route, 1966-82, 1548–235

Whiskey and other distilled spirits production, stocks, and materials used, by type and State, FY81-82, last issue of annual rpt, 8484–1.2

Wholesale trade census, 1982: employment, establishments, sales by commodity, and payroll, by SIC 4-digit kind of business and State, preliminary rpt, 2403–1.33

see also Animal feed

see also Baking and bakery products

see also Corn

see also Gasohol

see also Hops

see also Rice

see also Soybeans

see also Wheat

see also under By Commodity in the "Index by Categories"

Grand Forks, N.Dak.

Census of Housing, 1980: occupancy and unit characteristics, by race, Hispanic origin, and city, SMSA rpt, 2473–1.171

Census of Population and Housing, 1980: detailed population and housing characteristics, by county, city, and census tract, SMSA rpt, 2551–2.171

see also under By SMSA or MSA in the "Index by Categories"

Grand Island, Nebr.

Wages by occupation, and benefits for office and plant workers, 1984 labor market area survey rpt, 6785–3.9

Grand Rapids, Mich.

Census of Housing, 1980: occupancy and unit characteristics, by race, Hispanic origin, and city, SMSA rpt, 2473–1.172

Census of Population and Housing, 1980: detailed population and housing characteristics, by county, city, and census tract, SMSA rpt, 2551–2.172

Housing and households detailed characteristics, and unit and neighborhood quality, by inside-outside central cities, 1980 survey, SMSA rpt, 2485–6.9

see also under By City and By SMSA or MSA in the "Index by Categories"

Grand Trunk Western Railroad

Finances and operations of 7 commuter rail systems, and public agency cost reimbursement, 1980, 7888–61

Granite City, Ill.

see also under By SMSA or MSA in the "Index by Categories"

Grant, W. R.

"Economic Impacts of Increased Price Variability: A Case Study with Rice", 1502–3.404

Index by Subjects and Names

Grant, W. Vance

"Digest of Education Statistics, 1983-84", 4824–2

Grants and grants-in-aid

see State aid to local areas

see terms beginning with Federal aid

Granville Corp.

"Public Housing Authority Experience with Private Management", 5188–103

Grapefruit

see Citrus fruits

Grapes

see Fruit and fruit products

Graphics

see Advertising

see Art

see Audiovisual education

see Chartbooks

see Photography

see Printing and publishing industry

Graphite

see Nonmetallic minerals and mines

Gravel

see Quarries and stone products

Graves, Edmund J.

"CAT Scan Use in Short-Stay Non-Federal Hospitals: U.S., 1979-82", 4146–8.102

"Utilization of Short-Stay Hospitals, U.S., 1982 Annual Summary", 4147–13.78

"1983 Summary: National Hospital Discharge Survey", 4146–8.101

Gray, Fred

"U.S. Outlook for Sweeteners and Tropical Products", 1004–16.1

Grayson, Paul E.

"Life Cycle of Individual Income Tax Returns", 8302–2.408

Grazing

see Pasture and rangeland

Great Britain

see United Kingdom

Great Falls, Mont.

Census of Housing, 1980: occupancy and unit characteristics, by race, Hispanic origin, and city, SMSA rpt, 2473–1.173

Census of Population and Housing, 1980: detailed population and housing characteristics, by county, city, and census tract, SMSA rpt, 2551–2.173

see also under By SMSA or MSA in the "Index by Categories"

Great Lakes

Coal production and stocks by district, and shipments by district of origin, State of destination, consuming sector, and mode of transport, quarterly rpt, 3162–8

Conservation and research projects of Fish and Wildlife Service, descriptions and results by program, FY83, annual rpt, 5504–20

Construction and conversion costs for merchant ships by owner and builder, fleet size, and employment, monthly rpt, 7702–1

Environmental quality, pollutant discharge by type and source, and EPA protection activities and funding, 1970s-83, biennial regional rpt, 9184–15.5

Exports and imports, by SITC 3-digit commodity, Great Lakes port, vessel type, world are, and country, 1982, annual rpt, 7744–3

Exports and imports of US (waterborne), by type of service, commodity, country, route, and US port, 1982, annual rpt, 7704–2

Index by Subjects and Names

Fish and eggs for stocking distributed from natl hatcheries, by species, hatchery, and jurisdiction, FY83, annual rpt, 5504–10

Fish landings, employment, gear used, and seafood production, for detailed species by State, 1977, annual rpt, 2164–2.8

PCB (polychlorinated biphenyl) concentrations in Great Lakes fish, for 29 species monitored at 24 sites, selected dates 1969-77, 9208–126

Pollution control programs and discharges in Great Lakes basin, 1983 annual rpt, 14644–1

Ports, port facilities by type, and inland waterways by size, by location, 1982-83, annual rpt, 7704–16

Shipboard jobs in Great Lakes, by license status, monthly rpt, 7702–1

Shipbuilding costs and related employment, by coastal district, 1982, annual rpt, 7704–12

Ships in Great Lakes fleet, and tonnage, by activity status and vessel type, FY83, annual rpt, 7704–14.2

Ships in US merchant fleet, shipping costs, construction, employment, military availability, and Fed Govt subsidies, 1970s-1984 and projected to 2000, 26306–6.83

St Lawrence Seaway Dev Corp finances and activities, and seaway toll charges and cargo tonnage by type of cargo, 1983, annual rpt, 7744–1

Transportation finances, operations, vehicles, equipment, accidents, and energy use and transport, by mode of transport, 1955-84, annual rpt, 7304–2

Water levels in Great Lakes, daily and monthly averages by station, 1982 and with summary 1900-82, annual rpt, 2174–3

Water levels of Great Lakes and connecting channels, recorded and expected, biweekly rpt, 3752–2

Water levels of Great Lakes, trends and projections, monthly rpt, 3752–1

Water levels, surface and drainage area, depth, and volume, and connecting and outlet channel flows, various periods 1900-83, 3758–6

Water supply and quality in streams and lakes, and groundwater levels in wells, by drainage basin, 1980, annual State rpt series, 5666–12

Water supply and quality in streams and lakes, and groundwater levels in wells, by drainage basin, 1981, annual State rpt series, 5666–16

Water supply and quality in streams and lakes, and groundwater levels in wells, by drainage basin, 1982, annual State rpt series, 5666–20

Water supply and quality in streams and lakes, and groundwater levels in wells, by drainage basin, 1983, annual State rpt series, 5666–10

Waterborne commerce of US (domestic and foreign), freight by commodity, traffic, and passengers, by port and waterway, 1982, annual rpt, 3754–3.3

Weather and navigation conditions of Great Lakes, 1983 with trends from 1900, annual article, 2152–8.403

Weather broadcasts for US ships, by major ocean area, as of Jan 1984, biennial rpt, 2184–3

Great Plains

see North Central States

Greditor, Allan

"HFCS Competition: A Year of Transition", 1004–16.1

Greece

Agricultural and food production indexes, and production of selected commodities, by world region and country, 1974-83, annual rpt, 1524–5

Agricultural situation in Western Europe, by country and commodity, 1983 and outlook for 1984, annual rpt, 1524–4.6

Agricultural supply/demand, trade, and production, and socioeconomic data, by country, 1950s-77, 1528–179

AID loan repayment status and terms by program and country, and status of predecessor agency loans, quarterly rpt, 9912–3

Economic, social, and political summary data, by country, 1984, annual factbook, 244–11

Economic trends in income, production, prices, employment, finances, and trade, 1984 semiannual rpt, 2046–4.23

Exports and imports of NATO countries with Council for Mutual Economic Assistance Europe members, by country, 1980-83, annual rpt, 7144–5

Exports and imports of NATO countries with PRC, by country, 1980-83, annual rpt, 7144–14

Exports and imports of OECD countries, by country, 1983, annual rpt, 7144–10

Exports and imports of US with Western Europe, and US market share and export opportunities for selected commodities, by country, 1982-84, 2048–105

Exports of US, detailed Schedule B commodities by country of destination, 1983, annual rpt, 2424–9

Exports of US, detailed Schedule E commodities by mode of transport and world area and country of destination, 1983, annual rpts, 2424–5

Fruit (deciduous) grower prices and processor net cost and subsidies in 4 countries and EC, 1982/83-1983/84, article, 1925–34.414

Fruit and vegetable product trade and tariffs of EC, 1966-78, and effect of Greece, Spain, and Portugal entry into EC, projected to 1986, 1528–182

Imports of US, detailed Schedule A commodities by country and world area of origin, and mode of transport, 1983, annual rpts, 2424–2

Imports of US, detailed TSUSA commodities by country of origin, 1983, annual rpt, 2424–4

Loans and grants for economic and military assistance from US and intl agencies, by program and country, FY46-83, annual rpt, 9914–5

Military aid of US, arms sales, and training programs costs and budget requests by program, world region, and country, FY83-85, annual rpt, 7144–13

Military spending, arms trade, and armed forces size, with total govt spending and population, by country, 1972-82, annual rpt, 9824–1

Minerals Yearbook, 1982, Vol 3: foreign country reviews of production, trade, and policies, by commodity, annual rpt, 5604–35

Greene, Margaret L.

Minerals Yearbook, 1982, Vol 3 preprints: foreign country review of production, trade, and policies, by commodity, annual rpt, 5604–17.28

Nuclear power plant construction and operation status, and capacity, by plant, region, State, and selected country, 1983 and projected to 2020, annual rpt, 3164–57

Population size and growth rates, and latest available benchmark demographic data, by country, 1950-83, biennial rpt, 2324–4

Raisin production, trade, consumption, and stocks of US and 3 countries, and US exports by country, various periods 1982/83-1984/85, article, 1925–34.434

Ships in world merchant fleet, and tonnage, by country of registry, 1982, annual rpt, 7704–3.1

Tomato processor subsidies and minimum grower prices for Greece and total EC, 1981-83, article, 1925–34.404

Tomato products from Greece, imports injury to US industry from removal of duties on foreign subsidized products, investigation with financial and operating data, 1984 rpt, 9886–18.16

see also under By Foreign Country in the "Index by Categories"

Greeley, Colo.

Census of Housing, 1980: occupancy and unit characteristics, by race, Hispanic origin, and city, SMSA rpt, 2473–1.174

Census of Population and Housing, 1980: detailed population and housing characteristics, by county, city, and census tract, SMSA rpt, 2551–2.174

see also under By SMSA or MSA in the "Index by Categories"

Green, Alan W.

"Forest Resources of the Rocky Mountain States", 1208–201

"Utah's Forest Resources, 1978", 1206–22.6

Green Bay, Wis.

Census of Housing, 1980: occupancy and unit characteristics, by race, Hispanic origin, and city, SMSA rpt, 2473–1.175

Census of Population and Housing, 1980: detailed population and housing characteristics, by county, city, and census tract, SMSA rpt, 2551–2.175

Wages by occupation, and benefits for office and plant workers, 1984 SMSA survey rpt, 6785–11.8

see also under By SMSA or MSA in the "Index by Categories"

Green, Jerry

"Effect of Interest Rates on Mortgage Prepayments", 9306–1.6

Green, John W.

"Coal from the Nation: Household Demand for Electricity", 1588–78

Greenbelts

see Open space land programs

Greene, David L.

"Trends in Heavy Truck Energy Use and Efficiency", 3308–70

Greene, Margaret L.

"U.S. Experience with Exchange Market Intervention: Jan.-Mar. 1975", 9366–1.127

"U.S. Experience with Exchange Market Intervention: Sept. 1977-Dec. 1979", 9366–1.140

Greene, Margaret L.

"U.S. Experience with Exchange Market Intervention: Oct. 1980-Sept. 1981", 9366–1.128

Greene, Vernon L.

"Premature Institutionalization Among the Rural Elderly in Arizona", 4102–1.413

Greenhouse effect

see Air pollution

Greenia, Nick

"Partnership Employment and Payroll, 1979", 8302–2.411

Greenland

- Economic, social, and political summary data, by country, 1984, annual factbook, 244–11
- Exports of US, detailed Schedule B commodities by country of destination, 1983, annual rpt, 2424–9
- Exports of US, detailed Schedule E commodities by mode of transport and world area and country of destination, 1983, annual rpts, 2424–5
- Imports of US, detailed Schedule A commodities by country and world area of origin, and mode of transport, 1983, annual rpts, 2424–2
- Imports of US, detailed TSUSA commodities by country of origin, 1983, annual rpt, 2424–4
- *Minerals Yearbook, 1982,* Vol 3: foreign country reviews of production, trade, and policies, by commodity, annual rpt, 5604–35
- *Minerals Yearbook, 1982,* Vol 3 preprints: foreign country review of production, trade, and policies, by commodity, annual rpt, 5604–17.20
- Population size and growth rates, and latest available benchmark demographic data, by country, 1950-83, biennial rpt, 2324–4
- Tide height and time daily at worldwide coastal points, 1985 predictions, annual rpt, 2174–2.2
- *see also* under By Foreign Country in the "Index by Categories"

Greensboro, N.C.

- Census of Housing, 1980: occupancy and unit characteristics, by race, Hispanic origin, and city, SMSA rpt, 2473–1.176
- Census of Population and Housing, 1980: detailed population and housing characteristics, by county, city, and census tract, SMSA rpt, 2551–2.176
- Wages of office and plant workers, by occupation, 1984 SMSA survey rpt, 6785–11.8
- *see also* under By City and By SMSA or MSA in the "Index by Categories"

Greenville, S.C.

- Census of Housing, 1980: occupancy and unit characteristics, by race, Hispanic origin, and city, SMSA rpt, 2473–1.177
- Census of Population and Housing, 1980: detailed population and housing characteristics, by county, city, and census tract, SMSA rpt, 2551–2.177
- Wages of office and plant workers, by occupation, 1984 SMSA survey rpt, 6785–11.6
- *see also* under By SMSA or MSA in the "Index by Categories"

Greeting cards

see Printing and publishing industry

Grefe, Edward A.

"Information Explosion", 1004–16.1

Gregg, William P., Jr.

"National Park Service Scientific Activities in the Southwestern U.S.", 1208–197

Gregorash, Sue F.

"Midwest Prepares for Interstate Banking", 9375–1.403

Gregory, Thomas H.

"Are Options on Treasury Bond Futures Priced Efficiently?", 9391–1.404

Grenada

- AID activities and funding by project and function, FY85, and developing countries summary socioeconomic data, 1970s-83, by country, annual rpt, 9914–3
- AID economic assistance to developing countries, obligations and disbursements by country, quarterly rpt, 9912–4
- *Background Notes,* summary social, political, and economic data, 1984 rpt, 7006–2.18
- Economic, social, and political summary data, by country, 1984, annual factbook, 244–11
- Military arms and equipment commitments of USSR and other Communist countries to Grenada, 1980-85, and arms discovered and personnel evacuated by US, Oct 1983, hearings, 21388–43
- Nutmeg and mace production, 1975/76-1982/83, FAS annual rpt, 1925–15.1
- Population size and growth rates, and latest available benchmark demographic data, by country, 1950-83, biennial rpt, 2324–4
- *see also* under By Foreign Country in the "Index by Categories"

Greyhound Corp.

- Bus industry collective ratemaking regulatory reform impacts on operations, finances, and services to older persons and rural areas by State, 1970s-83, 14828–2
- Finances, operations, equipment, passengers, employment, and payroll for Class I interstate motor carriers, by district, 1982, annual rpt, 9486–5.3

Grichar, James S.

"Mergers in the Nonfuel Minerals Industry: Trends and Motives", 5608–145

Grinnell, Gerald

"Groundwater Contamination from Underground Fuel Tanks", 1561–16.405

Grise, Verner N.

- "Costs of Producing and Selling Flue-Cured Tobacco: 1982, Preliminary 1983, and Projected 1984", 1561–10.402
- "Costs of Producing Burley Tobacco: 1982 and 1983 and Projected 1984", 1561–10.401
- "1984 Outlook for Tobacco", 1004–16.1

Grocery stores

see Food stores

Gross National Product

- BLS projections of employment by industry and GNP by component, analysis of projections to 1980 made selected years 1970-76, article, 6722–1.450
- Budget deficits effect on economic indicators and trade balance of US and 4 countries, model results, various periods 1974-85, technical paper, 9366–7.102
- Budget of US, CBO analysis of revenue and spending alternatives and projections of economic indicators, FY85-89, annual rpt, 26304–3

Index by Subjects and Names

- Budget of US estimates revised for consistency with FY85 budget definitions, receipts and outlays as percent of GNP, FY40-89, annual rpt, 104–12
- Business activity indicators (nonfinancial), 1982, annual rpt, 9364–5.9
- Business and financial statistics, historic trends, 1984 annual chartbook, 9364–2.2
- Business and financial statistics, quarterly chartbook, 9362–2.2
- *Business Conditions Digest,* current data on economic, business, and financial conditions and cyclical fluctuations, monthly rpt, 2702–3
- *Business Conditions Digest,* historical supplement on economic, business, and financial conditions and cyclical fluctuations, with methodology, 1947-82, 2708–31
- Business statistics, detailed data for major industries and economic indicators, *Survey of Current Business,* monthly rpt, 2702–1
- Central America mineral, energy, and water resources, and natural hazards to resource dev, by country, 1981 with trends from 1977, 5668–71
- China economic conditions, agricultural and industrial production, trade, and domestic and foreign investment, 1980-85, 2048–106
- Communist and and OECD countries economic conditions, 1982, annual rpt, 7144–11
- Communist, OECD, and selected other countries economic statistics, 1960s-83, annual rpt, 244–5
- Cuba economic conditions, agricultural and industrial production and distribution, trade, and intl economic relations, 1970-82 and trends from 1957, 248–40
- Current account balance related to Fed Govt budget deficit, with balance for 14 OECD countries, various periods 1952-83, article, 9373–1.408
- Developing countries agricultural supply/demand and market for US exports, with socioeconomic indicators, country rpt series, 1526–6
- Developing countries disaster preparedness and summary sociodemographic, political, and economic data, country rpt series, 9916–2
- Developing countries food supply policies, with farm sector data, tariff income, and prices and imports of 5 grains, for 21 countries, 1960s-81, 1528–168
- Developing countries govt policy, and AID and other foreign assistance, effects on private sector dev and socioeconomic conditions, with case studies for 6 countries, 1960s-80, 9918–12
- Developing countries PL 480 Title I funding and socioeconomic impacts, with case studies for 5 countries, 1950s- 81, 9918–13
- Developing countries receiving US economic aid, total govt and defense expenditures, military imports, GNP, and intl reserves by country, 1976-81, annual rpt, 9914–1
- Developing countries summary socioeconomic data, 1970s-83, and AID activities and funding by project and function, FY82-85, by country, annual rpt, 9914–3

Index by Subjects and Names

Gross National Product

EC food supply/demand and market and support prices, with exchange rates, fertilizer price index, GDP, and population, by country, 1960-83, 1528–173

EC social security programs benefits and expenditures, and unemployment rate, and economic indicators growth, 1960-82, article, 4742–1.405

Economic and demographic factors used in OASDI program cost estimates, selected years 1913-82 with alternative projections to 2060, 4706–1.90

Economic and financial trends, natl compounded annual rates of change, 1964-83, annual rpt, 9391–9.2

Economic and population time series data frequently used in statistical demand analyses, 1941-1982, annual rpt, 1544–21

Economic conditions and employment, alternative BLS projections to 1995 with selected trends for 1959-82, 6728–29

Economic growth rates and component economic indicators, selected years 1922-83 and projected under full employment to 1988, hearing, 21348–90

Economic indicators and components, and Fed Reserve 4th District business and financial conditions, monthly chartbook, 9377–10

Economic indicators and components, current data and annual trends, monthly rpt, 23842–1.1

Economic indicators, and Fed Govt finances and deficits, selected years 1962-83 and projected under cost control proposals to 2000, 16908–1.1

Economic indicators, nonfinancial, monthly rpt, 9362–1.2

Economic indicators, trends and relation to govt revenues and spending by level of govt, selected years 1929-83, annual rpt, 10044–1

Economic performance of US, and Reagan Admin 1984 spending, tax, and monetary policy proposals, with data for 1950s-83 and projected to 1988, press release, 8008–107

Economic trends, natl compounded annual rates of change, monthly rpt, 9391–3.2

Fed Govt budget and debt, cyclically adjusted estimates assuming mid-level unemployment and GNP, and methodology, quarterly 1955-83, 2706–5.31

Fed Govt receipts, outlays, and debt shares of GNP, and tax expenditures as percentage of outlays and revenue, FY66-83 and projected FY84-87, article, 9383–2

Fed Govt receipts, outlays, and debt shares of GNP, FY66-87, annual rpt, 104–2

Fed Govt revenues, deficits, and debt, and GNP and unemployment, cyclically adjusted estimates assuming middle-range unemployment, 1955-3rd qtr 1983, article, 2702–1.403

Forecasts for selected business activities and natl economic indicators, compilation of representative opinions, 1984, annual rpt, 9389–3

Foreign aged population characteristics, with related health care data and vital statistics, by world area and selected country, 1950-80 and projected to 2020, 2546–10.12

Foreign and US agricultural supply/demand indicators by commodity and world area, and related research and extension program needs, 1950s-2020, 1008–47

Foreign and US economic and employment indicators and balance of payments, and US exports by selected commodity, by world area and country, 1970s-83, annual rpt, 2044–26

Foreign and US services trade agreements, goods and services trade, intl investment, and GDP, by country, and US regulatory proposals, various periods 1970-82, 448–1

Foreign and US shipping and shipbuilding subsidies and aid, with summary fleet, trade, and GNP data, for 48 countries, 1979-80, biennial rpt, 7704–18

Foreign countries *Background Notes,* summary social, political, and economic data, series, 7006–2

Foreign economic and monetary trends, compounded annual rates of change for US and 10 major trading partners, quarterly rpt, 9391–7

Foreign economic indicators and currency exchange rates, by world area and selected country, mid-1960s-83, annual rpt, 204–1.9

Foreign economic indicators and trade by country and country group, and US trade policy actions, 1960s-83, annual rpt, 444–1.4

Foreign economic indicators for 7 OECD countries and US, quarterly rpt, 2042–10

Foreign economic, social, and political summary data, by country, 1984, annual factbook, 244–11

Foreign economic trends and implications for US, annual and semiannual country rpt series, 2046–4

Foreign military, social, and economic summary data by world area and country, 1960s-80s, hearing, 25388–47.1

Foreign military spending, arms trade, and armed forces size, with total govt spending and population, by country, 1972-82, annual rpt, 9824–1

Foreign money supply and velocity, prices, and real GNP, growth rates for 4 OECD countries and US, various periods 1954-81, article, 9391–1.401

GNP (potential) related to actual GNP, effects of data revisions and noninflationary unemployment rate, 1952-76, article, 9377–1.404

GNP growth related to inflation and unemployment rate, various periods 1960-83 and projected 1984-89, article, 9385–1.408

GNP in current and constant dollars, and implicit price deflators, by industry div, 1981-83, article, 2702–1.416

GNP in current and constant dollars, by product and sector, and implicit price deflators, selected years 1929-83, annual rpt, 204–1.1

Health care expenditures, growth factors, medical equipment and drugs trade, and physician income, 1950-90, article, 4652–1.407

Health condition and health care resources, use, and expenditures, 1970s-82 with trends and projections 1900-2000, annual compilation, 4144–11

Income (taxable) not reported, methodology using Current Population Survey labor force data to estimate share of output and nonreporters, 1950s-81, 23848–178

Industrial electric power demand model estimates, economic indicators, and supporting data for 5 industries, 1960s-80 with projections to 2000, 3008–87

Interest rates (real) and other credit terms, related to GNP growth, various periods 1952-82, article, 9381–1.405

Jamaica PL 480 Title I assistance effects on economic dev, with data on govt finance, economic indicators, demography, and dev programs, 1970s-81, 9916–1.51

Money supply and high-employment Fed Govt spending related to nominal GNP, alternative specifications for St Louis equation, 1962-82, article, 9391–1.417

Money supply and nonfinancial sector debt related to GNP, and velocity of targets during business expansion, various periods 1958-83, article, 9391–1.416

Money supply and nonfinancial sector debt related to inflation and GNP, various periods 1960-83, article, 9373–1.401

Money supply growth rate variability related to GNP, regression analysis, various periods 1962-83, article, 9391–1.411

Money supply, negotiable orders of withdrawal accounts and other M1 components changes related to growth of GNP components, various periods 1948-84, article, 9385–1.413

Natl income and product, comprehensive accounts and components, *Survey of Current Business,* monthly rpt, 2702–1.21, 2702–1.22

New England States gross product by industry sector and State, and compared to GNP, 1981-82, annual article, 9373–2.403

OECD countries GNP and GNP growth, by country, 1973-83, annual rpt, 7144–8

OECD countries natl savings and current account balance ratios to GDP, by country, various periods 1963-81, technical paper, 9366–7.100

OECD economic indicators, for US and 6 countries, biweekly rpt, 242–4

Older persons Fed Govt pension and health spending, by program and as percents of budget and GNP, 1965-85 with projections to 2040, 25148–28

Overseas Business Reports: economic conditions, investment and export opportunities, and trade practices, annual country market research rpt series, 2046–6

Overseas Business Reports: economic conditions, investment and export opportunities, and trade practices, world region rpt series, 2046–5

Pacific Basin economic indicators, US and 12 countries, quarterly rpt, 9393–9

Productivity of labor and capital, costs, and prices, by selected industry, and compared to 6 OECD countries, selected years 1947-82, 17898–1

Productivity of labor, economic growth, and industrial policy dev, selected years 1947-82 with some projections to 1986, 26306–6.69

Statistical Abstract of US, social, political, and economic data, 1950s-83 and trends, annual rpt, 2324–1.3

Gross National Product

Transportation energy use by mode, fuel supplies, and demographic and economic determinants of vehicle use, 1970s-83, annual rpt, 3304–5.1

Underground economic activity, estimates of unreported income based on monetary statistics, various periods 1950-82, article, 9362–1.402

Unemployment rate related to GNP growth, regression results, various periods 1951-83 and projected to 1989, article, 9393–8.408

Groundwater

see Hydrology

see Rivers and waterways

see Water supply and use

Group health

see Blue Cross-Blue Shield

see Health insurance

see Health maintenance organizations

Grubert, Harry

"Corporate and Personal Taxation of Capital Income in an Open Economy", 8006–3.51

Gruenstein, John M.

"Targeting High Tech in the Delaware Valley", 9387–1.401

GSA

see General Services Administration

Guadeloupe

see Caribbean area

Guam

- Agriculture census, 1982: farms, farmland, production, finances, and operator characteristics, by election district, final outlying area rpt, 2331–1.53
- Bank deposits in commercial and mutual savings banks and in US branches of foreign banks, by account type, instn, State, SMSA, and county, June 1983, annual rpt, 9295–3.18
- Births (live) by selected demographic characteristics, for 3 outlying areas, 1979, US Vital Statistics annual rpt, 4144–1.3
- DOD budget, expenditures for each service branch and total defense agencies, by function and State, FY85, annual rpt, 3544–23
- Environmental quality, pollutant discharge by type and source, and EPA protection activities and funding, 1970s-83, biennial regional rpt, 9184–15.9
- Exports and imports between US and outlying areas, by detailed commodity and mode of transport, monthly rpt, 2422–4
- Fed Home Loan Bank System members, with assets of S&Ls, by instn, city, and State, 1983, annual listing, 9314–5
- Fishery cooperatives in US, Puerto Rico, and Guam, 1983, annual rpt, 2164–1.10
- Forest fire damage and causes, by State and region, 1981, annual rpt, 1204–4
- Govt census, 1982: properties, govt-assessed value, sales, and tax rates, by property type, State, SMSA, county, and city, 2453–1
- Govt financial data, audits of Interior Dept Inspector General, FY83, annual rpt, 5304–15.6
- HHS aid to each State and local govt or private instn, amount obligated, funding agency, and program, FY83, annual listing, 4004–3.9
- *Hwy Statistics,* detailed data on traffic, govt finances, fuel use, vehicles, driver licenses, and hwy characteristics, 1983, annual rpt, 7554–1.6

Labor legislation enacted by 48 States, DC, and Guam, 1983, annual summary article, 6722–1.406

- Medicare Supplementary Medical Insurance maximum charges reimbursable for specific services, by State and outlying area, 1983, annual rpt, 4654–4
- *Minerals Yearbook, 1982,* Vol 2: State reviews of production, sales, and firms, by commodity, and business activity, annual rpt, 5604–34
- NIH grants, awards, and obligations by State and type of recipient, and full-time personnel, by inst, FY83, annual rpt, 4434–3
- NSF grant and award recipients, by State, FY83, annual listing, 9624–11
- Population size and components of change, by outlying area, 1970-82, Current Population Rpt, 2546–3.127
- Population size and components of change, by outlying area, 1980-83, Current Population Rpt, 2546–3.134
- Population size and growth rates, and latest available benchmark demographic data, by country, 1950-83, biennial rpt, 2324–4
- Port dev costs and financing through user fees, and shipping industry impact on local economy, by State, other area, industry, commodity, and port, 1970s-82, hearings, 21568–34.1
- Savings and loan assns assets and liabilities, by FHLB district and State, selected years 1955-82, annual rpt, 9314–1
- Savings and loan assns, FHLB 12th District members financial operations and housing industry indicators by State, monthly rpt, 9302–21
- Telephone companies borrowing under rural telephone loan program, and financial and operating data, 1983, annual rpt, 1244–2.3
- Unemployed displaced workers training and placement program of Fed Govt, funding and enrollment for 13 States and Guam, June 1984, press release, 6408–61
- US Attorneys civil and criminal case processing in district, appellate, and State courts, by district, FY83, annual rpt, 6004–2
- Wages for 3 occupational groups, relative average levels in 78 labor market areas, 1983, annual press release, 6785–13
- Water supply and quality in streams and lakes, and groundwater levels in wells, by drainage basin, 1983, annual State rpt, 5666–10.10

see also under By Outlying Area in the "Index by Categories"

Guaranteed income

see Income maintenance

Guaranteed Student Loan Program

see Student aid

Guarantees and warranties

see also Surety bonds

Guatemala

- Agricultural and food production indexes, and production of selected commodities, by world region and country, 1974-83, annual rpt, 1524–5
- Agricultural situation in Latin America, by country, 1981-83 and outlook for 1984, annual rpt, 1524–4.9
- AID activities and funding by project and function, FY85, and developing countries summary socioeconomic data, 1970s-83, by country, annual rpt, 9914–3

Index by Subjects and Names

- AID economic assistance to developing countries, obligations and disbursements by country, quarterly rpt, 9912–4
- AID economic assistance to 7 Central American countries, by type of aid, FY80-83, GAO rpt, 26123–55
- AID loan repayment status and terms by program and country, and status of predecessor agency loans, quarterly rpt, 9912–3
- Economic, social, and political conditions in 6 Central America countries, 1960s-83 with trends and projections 1930-2010, 028–19
- Economic, social, and political summary data, by country, 1984, annual factbook, 244–11
- Economic trends in income, production, prices, employment, finances, and trade, 1984 annual rpt, 2046–4.45
- Exports and imports of US, by commodity and country, 1972-82, annual world region rpt, 244–13.3
- Exports of US, detailed Schedule B commodities by country of destination, 1983, annual rpt, 2424–9
- Exports of US, detailed Schedule E commodities by mode of transport and world area and country of destination, 1983, annual rpts, 2424–5
- Food supply policies of 21 developing countries, with farm sector data, tariff income, and prices and imports of 5 grains, 1960s-81, 1528–168
- Imports of US, detailed Schedule A commodities by country and world area of origin, and mode of transport, 1983, annual rpts, 2424–2
- Imports of US, detailed TSUSA commodities by country of origin, 1983, annual rpt, 2424–4
- Loans and grants for economic and military assistance from US and intl agencies, by program and country, FY46-83, annual rpt, 9914–5
- Military aid of US, arms sales, and training programs costs and budget requests by program, world region, and country, FY83-85, annual rpt, 7144–13
- Military spending, arms trade, and armed forces size, with total govt spending and population, by country, 1972-82, annual rpt, 9824–1
- *Minerals Yearbook, 1982,* Vol 3: foreign country reviews of production, trade, and policies, by commodity, annual rpt, 5604–35
- *Minerals Yearbook, 1982,* Vol 3 preprints: foreign country review of production, trade, and policies, by commodity, annual rpt, 5604–17.86
- Natural resources and hazards to resource dev, with data on mineral, energy, and water resources, by Central American country, 1981 with trends from 1977, 5668–71
- Oil and gas undiscovered recoverable resources, cumulative production, and identified reserves, as of 1981, final world oil basin rpt, 5666–18.4
- Population size and growth rates, and latest available benchmark demographic data, by country, 1950-83, biennial rpt, 2324–4
- Refugees from Central America by country of origin and asylum, and aid from US and Mexico, FY82-1984, GAO rpt, 26123–70

Index by Subjects and Names

see also under By Foreign Country in the "Index by Categories"

Gubler, Duane J.

"Dengue in the U.S., 1982", 4202–7.407

Guerrilla warfare

El Salvador socioeconomic and political conditions, and US economic and military assistance, 1977-FY84, 7008–39

Guinea

- Agricultural and food production indexes, and production of selected commodities, by world region and country, 1974-83, annual rpt, 1524–5
- Agricultural situation in sub-Saharan Africa, by country, 1982-83 and outlook for 1984, annual rpt, 1524–4.10
- AID activities and funding by project and function, FY85, and developing countries summary socioeconomic data, 1970s-83, by country, annual rpt, 9914–3
- AID economic assistance to developing countries, obligations and disbursements by country, quarterly rpt, 9912–4
- AID loan repayment status and terms by program and country, and status of predecessor agency loans, quarterly rpt, 9912–3
- Economic conditions and foreign marketing prospects in 46 Sub-Saharan countries, 1983 world region rpt, 2046–5.1
- Economic, social, and political summary data, by country, 1984, annual factbook, 244–11
- Exports of US, detailed Schedule B commodities by country of destination, 1983, annual rpt, 2424–9
- Exports of US, detailed Schedule E commodities by mode of transport and world area and country of destination, 1983, annual rpts, 2424–5
- Imports of US, detailed Schedule A commodities by country and world area of origin, and mode of transport, 1983, annual rpts, 2424–2
- Imports of US, detailed TSUSA commodities by country of origin, 1983, annual rpt, 2424–4
- Loans and grants for economic and military assistance from US and intl agencies, by program and country, FY46-83, annual rpt, 9914–5
- Military aid of US, arms sales, and training programs costs and budget requests by program, world region, and country, FY83-85, annual rpt, 7144–13
- Military spending, arms trade, and armed forces size, with total govt spending and population, by country, 1972-82, annual rpt, 9824–1
- *Minerals Yearbook, 1983,* Vol 3 preprints: foreign country review of production, trade, and policies, by commodity, annual rpt, 5604–23.92
- Population size and growth rates, and latest available benchmark demographic data, by country, 1950-83, biennial rpt, 2324–4
- *see also* under By Foreign Country in the "Index by Categories"

Guinea-Bissau

- AID activities and funding by project and function, FY85, and developing countries summary socioeconomic data, 1970s-83, by country, annual rpt, 9914–3
- AID economic assistance to developing countries, obligations and disbursements by country, quarterly rpt, 9912–4

Economic conditions and foreign marketing prospects in 46 Sub-Saharan countries, 1983 world region rpt, 2046–5.1

- Economic, social, and political summary data, by country, 1984, annual factbook, 244–11
- Imports of US, detailed TSUSA commodities by country of origin, 1983, annual rpt, 2424–4
- Loans and grants for economic and military assistance from US and intl agencies, by program and country, FY46-83, annual rpt, 9914–5
- Military aid of US, arms sales, and training programs costs and budget requests by program, world region, and country, FY83-85, annual rpt, 7144–13
- Military spending, arms trade, and armed forces size, with total govt spending and population, by country, 1972-82, annual rpt, 9824–1
- *Minerals Yearbook, 1982,* Vol 3: foreign country reviews of production, trade, and policies, by commodity, annual rpt, 5604–35
- *Minerals Yearbook, 1982,* Vol 3 preprints: foreign country review of production, trade, and policies, by commodity, annual rpt, 5604–17.84
- Population size and growth rates, and latest available benchmark demographic data, by country, 1950-83, biennial rpt, 2324–4
- *see also* under By Foreign Country in the "Index by Categories"

Gulf of Alaska

- Fish and shellfish landings, prices, trade, consumption, and industry operating data, for US with foreign comparisons, 1982-83, annual rpt, 2164–1
- Fish catch quotas for US 200 mile zone, allocations by species and country, 1984 coastal area rpt, 7006–5.1
- Oil and gas OCS reserves of Fed Govt, leasing and exploration activities, production, revenues, and costs, by ocean region, FY83, annual rpt, 5734–4

Gulf of Mexico

- Birds (marine) on southeastern US coast, distribution, abundance, and oil spill effects, by species and State, 1820s-1982, 5508–72
- Birds (shore) on Padre and Mustang Islands, Texas, distribution, abundance, and oil spill effects, by species, 1979-81, 5508–86
- Coastal environmental and socioeconomic conditions, and potential impacts of oil and gas OCS leases, final statement series, 5736–1
- Coastal environmental and wildlife characteristics, use, and mgmt, for individual ecosystems, series, 5506–9
- Coastal environmental characteristics, fish, wildlife, and use, and population socioeconomic data, for individual areas, series, 5506–4
- Dumping of waste materials, EPA permit program and intl London Dumping Convention activities, 1981-83, annual rpt, 9204–8
- Fish and eggs for stocking distributed from natl hatcheries, by species, hatchery, and jurisdiction, FY83, annual rpt, 5504–10
- Fish and shellfish landings, life cycles, and environmental needs, for selected species by region, with glossary and bibl, series, 5506–8

Gum and wood chemicals

- Fish and shellfish landings, prices, and cannery production, for Gulf States and North Carolina, by area, weekly rpt, 2162–6.3
- Fish and shellfish landings, prices, trade, consumption, and industry operating data, for US with foreign comparisons, 1982-83, annual rpt, 2164–1
- Fish landings, employment, gear used, and seafood production, for detailed species by State, 1977, annual rpt, 2164–2.6
- Fishermen (ocean sport), fishing activities, and catch by species, by fisherman characteristics and State, for Atlantic and Gulf of Mexico coasts, 1979-80, 2166–17.2
- Fishing (ocean sport) effort and catch, and Natl Marine Fisheries Service tagging and research activity, by species and location, 1983, annual rpt, 2164–7
- Hurricanes and tropical storms in North Atlantic and Caribbean area, paths, surveillance, deaths, property damage, and landfall probabilities by city, 1983, annual rpt, 2184–7
- Mineral industries census, 1982: financial and operating data, by State and for 4 offshore regions, preliminary summary rpt, 2511–2.2
- Oil and gas field itemized equipment and operating costs and cost indexes, for 10 producing areas, 1981-83, annual rpt, 3164–45
- Oil and gas OCS reserves of Fed Govt, leasing and exploration activities, production, revenues, and costs, by ocean region, FY83, annual rpt, 5734–4
- Oil, gas, and minerals dev, under Fed Govt OCS leases, with production, revenues, reserves, and oil spills, by State and ocean region, 1950s-82, annual rpt, 5734–3
- Oil spill risk analyses for OCS proposed lease sale areas, series, 5736–2
- Temperature of sea surface by ocean and for US coastal areas, and Bering Sea ice conditions, monthly rpt, 2182–5
- Tide height and time daily at worldwide coastal points, 1985 predictions, annual rpt, 2174–2.2
- Vertebrates (marine) abundance and seasonal distribution off southeastern US coast, with oil and gas dev effects and lease status, early 1980s, 5508–85
- Weather broadcasts for US ships, by major ocean area, as of Jan 1984, biennial rpt, 2184–3

Gulfport, Miss.

- Census of Housing, 1980: occupancy and unit characteristics, by race, Hispanic origin, and city, SMSA rpt, 2473–1.91
- Census of Population and Housing, 1980: detailed population and housing characteristics, by county, city, and census tract, SMSA rpt, 2551–2.91
- Wages of office and plant workers, by occupation, 1984 labor market area survey rpt, 6785–3.9
- *see also* under By SMSA or MSA in the "Index by Categories"

Gum and wood chemicals

County Business Patterns: establishments, employees, and payrolls, by SIC 4-digit industry and county, 1982, annual State rpt series, 2326–6

Gum and wood chemicals

Employment, earnings, and hours, by SIC 4-digit nonfarm industry, monthly 1974-Feb 1984, annual update, 6744–4

Exports and imports of US, by detailed agricultural commodity and country, FY83 and CY83, semiannual rpts, 1522–4

Exports and imports of US, detailed SIC-based commodities by world area, 1983, annual rpts, 2424–6

Exports and imports of US, totals and as percent of domestic production, by SIC 2- to 5-digit commodity, 1981, annual rpt, 2424–3

Exports, imports, tariffs, and industry operating data for fatty substances, natural chemicals, and radioactive materials, foreign and US, 1979-83, TSUSA commodity rpt, 9885–4.38

Exports, imports, tariffs, and industry operating data for naval stores (turpentine, rosin, and pine gum), foreign and US, 1978-82, TSUSA commodity rpt supplement, 9885–1.59

Exports of US, detailed commodities by country of destination, monthly rpt, 2422–3

Exports of US, detailed Schedule B commodities by country of destination, 1983, annual rpt, 2424–9

Exports of US, detailed Schedule E commodities by mode of transport and world area and country of destination, 1983, annual rpts, 2424–5

Glue, gelatin, and related products trade, tariffs, and industry operating data, 1979-83, TSUSA commodity rpt supplement, 9885–4.48

Imports of US, detailed Schedule A commodities by country and world area of origin, and mode of transport, 1983, annual rpts, 2424–2

Imports of US, detailed Schedule A commodities by country, monthly rpt, 2422–2

Imports of US, detailed TSUSA commodities by country of origin, 1983, annual rpt, 2424–4

Input-output structure of US economy, detailed interindustry transactions for 537 industries, and components of final demand, 1977 benchmark data, 2708–17

Manufacturing census, 1982: financial and operating data, for SIC 4-digit industries by product, preliminary rpt, 2491–1.190

Occupational injury and illness rates, by SIC 2- to 4-digit industry, 1982, annual rpt, 6844–1

Waterborne commerce of US (domestic and foreign), freight by commodity, traffic, and passengers, by port and waterway, 1982, annual rpt, 3754–3

see also under By Commodity in the "Index by Categories"

see also under By Industry in the "Index by Categories"

Guns

see Firearms

see Military weapons

Gunther, Emil B.

"Annual Data and Verification Tabulation, Eastern North Pacific Tropical Storms and Hurricanes, 1983", 2184–8

"Eastern North Pacific Tropical Cyclones, 1983", 2152–8.402

Gurin, Gerald

"Longitudinal Study of Black Youth: Issues, Scope and Findings. Part II, Final Report of the Project: Motivation and Economic Mobility of the Poor", 4008–65.2

Gurwitz, Aaron S.

"Nuclear Power Plant Construction: Paying the Bill", 9385–1.412

Gustaferro, Joseph F.

"U.S. Energy for the Rest of the Century, 1984 Edition", 2006–2.5

Gustafson, David H.

"Assessment of Level of Care: Implications of Interrater Reliability on Health Policy", 4652–1.431

Gustafson, Ronald A.

"Red Meats Outlook", 1004–16.1

Gustman, Alan L.

"Modeling the Retirement Process for Policy Evaluation and Research", 6722–1.445

Guyana

Agricultural and food production indexes, and production of selected commodities, by world region and country, 1974-83, annual rpt, 1524–5

Agricultural situation in Latin America, by country, 1981-83 and outlook for 1984, annual rpt, 1524–4.9

Agricultural supply/demand, trade, and production, and socioeconomic data, by country, 1950s-77, 1528–179

AID economic assistance to developing countries, obligations and disbursements by country, quarterly rpt, 9912–4

AID loan repayment status and terms by program and country, and status of predecessor agency loans, quarterly rpt, 9912–3

Economic conditions, income, production, prices, employment, and trade, 1984 annual country rpt, 2046–4.103

Economic, social, and political summary data, by country, 1984, annual factbook, 244–11

Exports of US, detailed Schedule B commodities by country of destination, 1983, annual rpt, 2424–9

Exports of US, detailed Schedule E commodities by mode of transport and world area and country of destination, 1983, annual rpts, 2424–5

Imports of US, detailed Schedule A commodities by country and world area of origin, and mode of transport, 1983, annual rpts, 2424–2

Imports of US, detailed TSUSA commodities by country of origin, 1983, annual rpt, 2424–4

Loans and grants for economic and military assistance from US and intl agencies, by program and country, FY46-83, annual rpt, 9914–5

Military aid of US, arms sales, and training programs costs and budget requests by program, world region, and country, FY83-85, annual rpt, 7144–13

Military spending, arms trade, and armed forces size, with total govt spending and population, by country, 1972-82, annual rpt, 9824–1

Minerals Yearbook, 1982, Vol 3: foreign country reviews of production, trade, and policies, by commodity, annual rpt, 5604–35

Index by Subjects and Names

Minerals Yearbook, 1983, Vol 3 preprints: foreign country review of production, trade, and policies, by commodity, annual rpt, 5604–23.89

Population size and growth rates, and latest available benchmark demographic data, by country, 1950-83, biennial rpt, 2324–4

see also under By Foreign Country in the "Index by Categories"

Guzda, Henry P.

"Industrial Democracy: Made in the U.S.A.", 6722–1.433

Gypsum

see Nonmetallic minerals and mines

Haas, Ellen

"Food Prices and Marketing", 1004–16.1

Haas, Richard D.

"Alternative Financial Strategies: The Results of Some Policy Simulations with the Multi-Country Model", 9366–7.90

Habeas corpus

Deportation and exclusion cases, writs of habeas corpus, judicial review, and declaratory judgments, 1976-81, annual rpt, 6264–2

Fed Govt district court magistrates case processing duties, by type of case, duty, and district, 1983 rpt, 18408–24

Foreign human rights conditions in 162 countries, economic and military aid of US, and economic aid of intl organizations, 1981-83, annual rpt, 21384–3

Prisoner petitions filed in Federal courts of appeals and district courts, by type of petition, circuit, and district, quarterly rpt, 18202–1

Prisoner writs filed in Federal district and appeals courts by circuit, and petition disposition, selected years 1961-82, 6066–19.4

US Attorneys civil case processing and amounts involved, by cause of action, FY83, annual rpt, 6004–2.5

see also Pretrial detention and release

Habegger, Loren

"Environmental Implications of Solar and Biomass Energy Growth", 3408–30

Haber, Shraga

"Epidemiology, Health Policy, and Resource Allocation: The Israeli Perspective", 4102–1.446

Hacklander, Duane

"Marketing Methods, Pricing Arrangements, and Marketing Channels Used by Southern Soybean Producers in 1982/83", 1561–3.402

Hafer, R. W.

"Currency Substitution: A Test of Its Importance", 9391–1.418

"Examining the Recent Behavior of Inflation", 9391–1.420

"Money, Debt and Economic Activity", 9391–1.416

"Money-GNP Link: Assessing Alternative Transaction Measures", 9391–1.408

Hafnium

see Metals and metal industries

Hagerstown, Md.

Census of Housing, 1980: occupancy and unit characteristics, by race, Hispanic origin, and city, SMSA rpt, 2473–1.178

Index by Subjects and Names — Hand tools

Census of Population and Housing, 1980: detailed population and housing characteristics, by county, city, and census tract, SMSA rpt, 2551–2.178

see also under By SMSA or MSA in the "Index by Categories"

Hahn, Jerold T.

"Michigan's Fourth Forest Inventory: Timber Volumes and Projections of Timber Supply", 1206–31.6

Hailey, Gary D.

"Comparative Analysis of Cosmetic Contact Lens Fitting by Ophthalmologists, Optometrists, and Opticians", 9408–49

Haines, Terry A.

"Regional Survey of the Chemistry of Headwater Lakes and Streams in New England: Vulnerability to Acidification", 5506–5.15

Hair, Dwight

"Longrun Timber Supply and Demand", 1004–16.1

Haiti

- Agricultural and food production indexes, and production of selected commodities, by world region and country, 1974-83, annual rpt, 1524–5
- Agricultural situation in Latin America, by country, 1981-83 and outlook for 1984, annual rpt, 1524–4.9
- AID activities and funding by project and function, FY85, and developing countries summary socioeconomic data, 1970s-83, by country, annual rpt, 9914–3
- AID economic assistance to developing countries, obligations and disbursements by country, quarterly rpt, 9912–4
- AID loan repayment status and terms by program and country, and status of predecessor agency loans, quarterly rpt, 9912–3
- *Background Notes,* summary social, political, and economic data, 1984 rpt, 7006–2.38
- Disaster preparedness and summary sociodemographic, political, and economic data, 1970s-83, 9916–2.54
- Economic, social, and political summary data, by country, 1984, annual factbook, 244–11
- Exports of US, detailed Schedule B commodities by country of destination, 1983, annual rpt, 2424–9
- Exports of US, detailed Schedule E commodities by mode of transport and world area and country of destination, 1983, annual rpts, 2424–5
- Food supply policies of 21 developing countries, with farm sector data, tariff income, and prices and imports of 5 grains, 1960s-81, 1528–168
- Imports of US, detailed Schedule A commodities by country and world area of origin, and mode of transport, 1983, annual rpts, 2424–2
- Imports of US, detailed TSUSA commodities by country of origin, 1983, annual rpt, 2424–4
- Loans and grants for economic and military assistance from US and intl agencies, by program and country, FY46-83, annual rpt, 9914–5
- Military aid of US, arms sales, and training programs costs and budget requests by program, world region, and country, FY83-85, annual rpt, 7144–13

Military spending, arms trade, and armed forces size, with total govt spending and population, by country, 1972-82, annual rpt, 9824–1

Minerals Yearbook, 1982, Vol 3: foreign country reviews of production, trade, and policies, by commodity, annual rpt, 5604–35

Minerals Yearbook, 1983, Vol 3 preprints: foreign country review of production, trade, and policies, by commodity, annual rpt, 5604–23.85

Population size and growth rates, and latest available benchmark demographic data, by country, 1950-83, biennial rpt, 2324–4

Rum imports (duty-free) of US under Caribbean Basin Initiative, by country, Jan-June 1983-84, annual rpt, 9884–15

see also under By Foreign Country in the "Index by Categories"

Hakkio, Craig S.

- "Conditional Variance and the Risk Premium in the Foreign Exchange Market", 9381–10.32
- "Exchange Rate Volatility and Federal Reserve Policy", 9381–1.413
- "Intertemporal Asset Pricing and the Term Structure of Exchange and Interest Rates: The Eurocurrency Market", 9381–10.40
- "Reexamination of Purchasing Power Parity: A Multi-Country and Multi-Period Study", 9381–10.36
- "Testing for Serial Correlation in the Presence of Heteroscedasticity with Applications to Exchange Rate Models", 9381–10.31
- "Vector Autoregressions: A User's Guide", 9381–10.41

Hale, Malcolm B.

"Proximate Chemical Composition and Fatty Acids of Three Small Coastal Pelagic Species", 2162–1.403

Halfway houses

Prisoners in Federal correctional instns, by prison, security level, contract facility type, sex, and region, monthly and weekly rpts, 6242–1

Hall, Arden R.

"Recent Trends in Adjustable and Other Mortgage Lending: A Survey of the Eleventh District", 9306–1.5

Hall, John R., Jr.

"Analysis of Electrical Fire Investigations in Ten Cities", 2218–71

Halperin, Sharon F.

"Knowledge of Accident Prevention Among Parents of Young Children in Nine Massachusetts Towns", 4102–1.402

Hambor, John C.

"Econometric Models and the Study of the Economic Effects of Social Security", 4742–1.419

Hamdani, Kausar

"CRR and Excess Reserves: An Early Appraisal", 9385–1.414

Hamilton, Ohio

- Census of Housing, 1980: occupancy and unit characteristics, by race, Hispanic origin, and city, SMSA rpt, 2473–1.179
- Census of Population and Housing, 1980: detailed population and housing characteristics, by county, city, and census tract, SMSA rpt, 2551–2.179

see also under By SMSA or MSA in the "Index by Categories"

Hamilton, Peggy M.

"Radiation Procedures Performed on U.S. Women During Pregnancy: Findings from Two 1980 Surveys", 4102–1.421

Hammond, Ind.

- Census of Housing, 1980: occupancy and unit characteristics, by race, Hispanic origin, and city, SMSA rpt, 2473–1.169
- Census of Population and Housing, 1980: detailed population and housing characteristics, by county, city, and census tract, SMSA rpt, 2551–2.169
- Wages of office and plant workers, by occupation, 1983 SMSA survey rpt, 6785–12.2

see also under By SMSA or MSA in the "Index by Categories"

Hampton, Va.

- Census of Housing, 1980: occupancy and unit characteristics, by race, Hispanic origin, and city, SMSA rpt, 2473–1.264
- Census of Population and Housing, 1980: detailed population and housing characteristics, by county, city, and census tract, SMSA rpt, 2551–2.264
- Housing and financial characteristics, and unit and neighborhood quality, for 15 SMSAs, 1978, annual survey special supplement, 2485–8

see also under By City in the "Index by Categories"

Hand, Jed S.

"Dental Record Documentation in Selected Ambulatory Care Facilities", 4102–1.458

Hand tools

- Census of Population, 1980: detailed socioeconomic and demographic characteristics, by age, sex, race, Hispanic origin, occupation, and industry, State rpt series, 2531–4
- Counterfeiting of brand-name products by foreign manufacturers, effects on 6 US industries, investigation with financial and operating data, 1984 rpt, 9886–4.67
- County Business Patterns: establishments, employees, and payrolls, by SIC 4-digit industry and county, 1981, annual State rpt series, 2326–8
- County Business Patterns: establishments, employees, and payrolls, by SIC 4-digit industry and county, 1982, annual State rpt series, 2326–6
- Employment, earnings, and hours, by selected SIC 1- to 4-digit industry, State, and for 278 major labor areas, 1939-83, annual rpt, 6744–5
- Employment, earnings, and hours, by SIC 4-digit nonfarm industry, monthly 1974-Feb 1984, annual update, 6744–4
- Exports and imports of US, detailed SIC-based commodities by world area, 1983, annual rpts, 2424–6
- Exports and imports of US, totals and as percent of domestic production, by SIC 2- to 5-digit commodity, 1981, annual rpt, 2424–3
- Exports, imports, tariffs, and industry operating data for hand-controlled power tools, 1979-83, TSUSA commodity rpt, 9885–6.79
- Exports, imports, tariffs, and industry operating data for miscellaneous wood products, foreign and US, 1979-83, TSUSA commodity rpt, 9885–2.30

Hand tools

Exports of US, detailed commodities by country of destination, monthly rpt, 2422–3

Exports of US, detailed Schedule B commodities by country of destination, 1983, annual rpt, 2424–9

Exports of US, detailed Schedule E commodities by mode of transport and world area and country of destination, 1983, annual rpts, 2424–5

Franchise business opportunities, by firm and kind of business, 1984 annual listing, 2044–27

Great Lakes trade, by SITC 3-digit commodity, port, vessel type, world area, and country, 1982, annual rpt, 7744–3

Imports of nonpowered hand tools, effects on US industry, investigation with background financial and operating data, 1984 rpt, 9886–4.68

Imports of US, detailed Schedule A commodities by country and world area of origin, and mode of transport, 1983, annual rpts, 2424–2

Imports of US, detailed Schedule A commodities by country, monthly rpt, 2422–2

Imports of US, detailed TSUSA commodities by country of origin, 1983, annual rpt, 2424–4

Income tax returns of corporations, detailed income and tax items by industry, 1981, annual rpt, 8304–4

Injuries and deaths from use of selected consumer products and related activity, by victim age and sex, 1982, annual rpt, 9164–7

Injuries and deaths from use of selected consumer products, by victim age and medical treatment status, 1982, annual rpt, 9164–6

Injuries, deaths, and medical costs from consumer products use, and Consumer Product Safety Commission activities and recalls, by product type and brand, FY83, annual rpt, 9164–2

Input-output structure of US economy, detailed interindustry transactions for 537 industries, and components of final demand, 1977 benchmark data, 2708–17

Manufacturing census, 1982: financial and operating data, by SIC 2- to 4-digit industry, State, SMSA, and county, preliminary census div rpt series, 2491–3

Minority group and women employment, by occupational group and SIC 2- to 3-digit industry, 1981, annual rpt, 9244–1.1

Occupational injury and illness rates, by SIC 2- to 4-digit industry, 1982, annual rpt, 6844–1

OECD trade, total and for 4 major countries, and US trade by country, by commodity, 1972-82, annual world region rpt series, 244–13

Producer prices and indexes, by stage of processing and detailed commodity, monthly rpt, 6762–6

Producer prices and indexes, by stage of processing and detailed commodity, monthly 1983, annual supplement, 6764–2

Retail trade census, 1982: employment, establishments, sales, and payroll, for hardware stores by State, preliminary rpt, 2395–1.3

Scissors and shears from Brazil, imports injury to US industry from removal of duties, investigation with background financial and operating data, 1983 rpt, 9886–18.12

Wholesale trade census, 1982: employment, establishments, sales by commodity, and payroll, by SIC 4-digit kind of business and State, preliminary rpt, 2403–1.10

see also Hardware

Handbags

see Leather industry and products

Handicapped

see Blind

see Deaf

see Disabled and handicapped persons

see Handicapped children

see Mental retardation

see Mobility limitations

see Rehabilitation of the disabled

Handicapped children

- Fed Govt public welfare programs and tax expenditures benefitting children and youth, participation and funding for 71 programs, FY81-83, 21968–30
- Govt census, 1982: State govt payments to local govts, by program, source of funds, level of govt, and State, with trends from 1902, 2460–3
- Head Start Project enrollment, appropriations, and staff, FY65-84, annual rpt, 4604–8
- Head Start Project enrollment of handicapped children, by handicap, State, and for Indian and migrant programs, 1982, annual rpt, 4604–1
- Head Start Project programs and effect on child dev, literature review with bibl, selected years 1970-83, 4608–17
- Health condition and health care resources, use, and expenditures, 1970s-82 with trends and projections 1900-2000, annual compilation, 4144–11
- HHS aid to each State and local govt or private instn, amount obligated, funding agency, and program, FY83, annual listing, 4004–3
- Medicaid, OASDHI, SSI, and other social insurance and public welfare programs benefits, beneficiary characteristics, and trust funds, selected years 1937-82, annual rpt, 4744–3.6
- Mental health facilities, beds, and bed/population ratios, by facility type, region, and State, 1982 with trends from 1972, 4506–3.14
- Mental health facilities of States and counties, inpatients, deaths, staff by occupation, and facilities, by State, 1970s-82, 4506–3.13
- Mental hospitals of States and counties, patients and admissions by diagnosis, age, and State, FY81, annual rpt, 4504–2
- OASDHI, Medicaid, SSI, and other social insurance and public welfare programs benefits, beneficiary characteristics, and trust funds, selected years 1937-82, annual rpt, 4744–3.12
- State govt maternal and child health funding, and admin of Fed Govt block grants, by program for 13 States, 1981-83, GAO rpt, 26121–70
- Treatment and services for developmentally disabled, university-affiliated facility activities, funding, and clients, 1980-FY83, 4608–19

Index by Subjects and Names

see also Birth defects

see also Old-Age, Survivors, Disability, and Health Insurance

see also Special education

see also Supplemental Security Income

Hanford Engineering Development Laboratory

see also Department of Energy National Laboratories

Hanrahan, Charles E.

"Longrun Changes in World Food Supply and Demand: Implications for Development Assistance Policy", 1528–181

Hansen, Kristin A.

"Geographical Mobility: Mar. 1981 to Mar. 1982", 2546–1.384

Hanthorn, Michael

"Corn and Soybean Fertilizer Use for Alternative Tillage Practices", 1561–16.401

"Returns to Corn and Soybean Tillage Practices", 1588–80

Harbeson, John W.

"Area Development in Liberia: Toward Integration and Participation", 9916–1.53

Harbors and ports

- Argentina grain production, exports by firm, storage by facility type and port, and shipments to ports by mode of transport, by grain type, selected years 1954-81, 1528–185
- Army Corps of Engineers activities and projects, FY83 and trends from 1800s, annual rpt, 3754–1
- Bond tax-exempt issues for private activity, by purpose, face value, major industry, and State, 1983, article, 8302–2.417
- Bridges over navigable waters, with type of bridge and use, owner, dimensions, and location, 1984 regional listing series, 7406–5
- Bunker fuels, oil, and coal laden in US on vessels engaged in foreign trade, by port, monthly rpt, 2422–5
- Coal production and stocks by district, and shipments by district of origin, State of destination, consuming sector, and mode of transport, quarterly rpt, 3162–8
- Coastal environmental characteristics, fish, wildlife, and use, and population socioeconomic data, for individual areas, series, 5506–4
- Construction industries census, 1982: financial and operating data, by SIC 4-digit industry and State, final rpt, 2373–1.7
- Construction industries census, 1982: financial and operating data, by SIC 4-digit industry and State, preliminary rpt series, 2371–1
- Containerized cargo carried over principal trade routes, by flag of vessel, port, and US coastal district, 1982, annual rpt, 7704–8
- County Business Patterns: establishments, employees, and payrolls, by SIC 4-digit industry and county, 1982, annual State rpt series, 2326–6
- Customs collections of 15 largest collection districts, by port, quarterly rpt, 8142–1
- Developing countries disaster preparedness and summary sociodemographic, political, and economic data, country rpt series, 9916–2

Index by Subjects and Names

Hardware

DOD shipments of military and personal property, loss claims, passenger traffic, and costs, by mode of transport, quarterly rpt, 3702–1

Exports and imports of US (waterborne), by type of service, commodity, country, route, and US port, 1982, annual rpt, 7704–2

Exports and imports of US (waterborne), by type of service, customs district, port, and world area, monthly rpt, 2422–7

Exports and imports of US, by commodity group, world area, selected country, US coastal area and port, and mode of transport, with seasonal adjustments, monthly rpt, 2422–9

Fed Govt-owned real property inventory and costs, worldwide summary by location, agency, and use, 1983, annual rpt, 9454–5

Fed Govt programs and mgmt cost control proposals, 3-year savings by function and agency, and financial and operating data, 1960s-81, 16908–1.11

Fish and shellfish landings, prices, trade, wholesaler receipts, and market activities at 5 major US ports, weekly rpts, 2162–6

Fish landings by species and State, and value at leading ports and disposition, 1970s-83, annual rpt, 2164–1.1

Foreign and US coal reserves, production, demand indicators, and trade, by country, selected years 1973-82 and alternative trade projections to 1995, annual rpt, 3164–77

Foreign economic, social, and political summary data, by country, 1984, annual factbook, 244–11

Foreign offloading ports accessible to tankers of 200,000 deadweight tons and larger, by country, Jan 1984, annual rpt, 244–5.10

Freight (waterborne domestic and foreign) by commodity, traffic, and passengers, by port and waterway, 1982, annual rpt, 3754–3

Govt census, 1982: State govt payments to local govts, by program, source of funds, level of govt, and State, with trends from 1902, 2460–3

Govt employment and payroll, by function, level of govt, and jurisdiction, 1983, annual rpt series, 2466–1

Great Lakes trade, by SITC 3-digit commodity, port, vessel type, world area, and country, 1982, annual rpt, 7744–3

Immigration, and alien residents, workers, visitors, deportations, and naturalizations, by country of birth, FY81, annual rpt, 6264–2

Oil spills from US OCS platforms and pipelines, and from tankers at sea and in port worldwide, various periods 1964-80, 5738–1

Port dev costs and financing through user fees, and shipping industry impact on local economy, by State, other area, industry, commodity, and port, 1970s-2020, hearings, 21568–34

Port impact on local employment through transport of 5 commodities, by industry for 3 eastern ports, and demand for US coal by country, 1981, 7308–182

Ports, port facilities by type, and inland waterways by size, by location, 1982-83, annual rpt, 7704–16

Services intl transactions, and operations of US multinatl service firms and foreign affiliates, by industry and world region, 1977-82, 2706–5.30

Ships and tonnage entering and clearing US Customs, by district and port of entry, 1983, annual rpt, 2424–7

St Lawrence Seaway ships, cargo and passenger volumes, and toll revenues, 1981-82 and trends from 1959, annual rpt, 7744–2

Tariff Schedules of US, Annotated, classifications and rates of duty for detailed imported commodities, and codes for ports and foreign countries, 1985 edition, 9886–13

Tidal current tables, daily time and velocity by station for North America and Asia coasts, 1985, annual rpt, 2174–1

Tide height and time daily at worldwide coastal points, 1985 predictions, annual rpt series, 2174–2

User fees to recover costs of 7 federally subsidized public service programs, by type of fee, user, and service, FY84-88, 26306–6.68

Workers compensation for employees of private contractors under Fed Govt-administered programs, cases and dispositions by district, FY79-83, annual compilation, 6504–5

see also Dredging

Hardin, Clifford M.

"Farm Programs and the Congressional Subcommittees", 1004–16.1

Harding, Christina M.

"Social Desirability of Preventive Health Behavior", 4102–1.438

Hardware

Census of Population, 1980: detailed socioeconomic and demographic characteristics, by age, sex, race, Hispanic origin, occupation, and industry, State rpt series, 2531–4

County Business Patterns: establishments, employees, and payrolls, by SIC 4-digit industry and county, 1981, annual State rpt series, 2326–8

County Business Patterns: establishments, employees, and payrolls, by SIC 4-digit industry and county, 1982, annual State rpt series, 2326–6

Employment, earnings, and hours, by selected SIC 1- to 4-digit industry, State, and for 278 major labor areas, 1939-83, annual rpt, 6744–5

Employment, earnings, and hours, by SIC 4-digit nonfarm industry, monthly 1974-Feb 1984, annual update, 6744–4

Exports and imports of US, detailed SIC-based commodities by world area, 1983, annual rpts, 2424–6

Exports and imports of US, totals and as percent of domestic production, by SIC 2- to 5-digit commodity, 1981, annual rpt, 2424–3

Exports, imports, tariffs, and industry operating data for fasteners and hardware, 1979-83, TSUSA commodity rpt supplement, 9885–6.82

Exports of US, detailed commodities by country of destination, monthly rpt, 2422–3

Exports of US, detailed Schedule B commodities by country of destination, 1983, annual rpt, 2424–9

Exports of US, detailed Schedule E commodities by mode of transport and world area and country of destination, 1983, annual rpts, 2424–5

Franchise business opportunities, by firm and kind of business, 1984 annual listing, 2044–27

Great Lakes trade, by SITC 3-digit commodity, port, vessel type, world area, and country, 1982, annual rpt, 7744–3

Imports of US, detailed Schedule A commodities by country and world area of origin, and mode of transport, 1983, annual rpts, 2424–2

Imports of US, detailed Schedule A commodities by country, monthly rpt, 2422–2

Imports of US, detailed TSUSA commodities by country of origin, 1983, annual rpt, 2424–4

Income tax returns of corporations, detailed income and tax items by industry, 1981, annual rpt, 8304–4

Income tax returns of partnerships, detailed data by industry, 1981 estimates, annual article, 8302–2.404

Income tax returns of sole proprietorships, detailed data by industry div and selected industry group, 1981, annual rpt, 8304–7

Income tax returns of sole proprietorships, receipts, deductions by type, payroll, and net income, by major industry, 1982, annual article, 8302–2.413

Industry finances and operations, by SIC 2- to 4-digit industry, 1970s-83 and projected to 1988, annual rpt, 2014–4

Injuries and deaths from use of selected consumer products and related activity, by victim age and sex, 1982, annual rpt, 9164–7

Input-output structure of US economy, detailed interindustry transactions for 85 industries, and components of final demand, 1977, article, 2702–1.421

Input-output structure of US economy, detailed interindustry transactions for 537 industries, and components of final demand, 1977 benchmark data, 2708–17

Manufacturing census, 1982: financial and operating data, by SIC 2- to 4-digit industry, State, SMSA, and county, preliminary census div rpt series, 2491–3

Manufacturing census, 1982: financial and operating data, for SIC 4-digit industries by product, preliminary rpt series, 2491–1

Minority group and women employment, by occupational group and SIC 2- to 3-digit industry, 1981, annual rpt, 9244–1.1

Occupational injury and illness rates, by SIC 2- to 4-digit industry, 1982, annual rpt, 6844–1

Producer prices and indexes, by stage of processing and detailed commodity, monthly rpt, 6762–6

Producer prices and indexes, by stage of processing and detailed commodity, monthly 1983, annual supplement, 6764–2

Production, shipments, PPI, and stocks of building materials, by type, bimonthly rpt, 2012–1.5

Retail trade census, 1982: employment, establishments, sales, and payroll, by SIC 2- to 4-digit kind of business, SMSA, and retail district, State rpt series, 2401–1

Hardware

Retail trade census, 1982: employment, establishments, sales, and payroll, for hardware stores by State, preliminary rpt, 2395–1.3

Retail trade sales and inventories, by kind of business, region, census div, and selected State, SMSA, and city, and seasonal adjustments, monthly rpt, 2413–3

Retail trade sales, inventories, purchases, gross margin, and accounts receivable, by SIC 2- to 4-digit kind of business and type of ownership, 1983, annual rpt, 2413–5

Transportation census, 1982: trucks, by detailed characteristics, miles traveled, and type of product carried, State rpt series, 2573–1

Virgin Islands economic censuses, 1982: employment, establishments, payroll, and receipts, by SIC 1- to 4-digit industry, island, and city, 2593–1

Wholesale trade census, 1982: employment, establishments, finances, and operations, by SIC 2- to 4-digit kind of business, SMSA, county, and city, State rpt series, 2405–1

Wholesale trade census, 1982: employment, establishments, sales by commodity, and payroll, by SIC 4-digit kind of business and State, preliminary rpt, 2403–1.10

Wholesale trade sales and inventories, by SIC 2- to 3-digit kind of business, monthly rpt, 2413–7

Wholesale trade sales, inventories, purchases, and gross margins, by SIC 2- to 3-digit kind of business and type of ownership, 1983, annual rpt, 2413–13

see also Hand tools

Harless, Caroline T.

"Brokered Deposits: Issues and Alternatives", 9371–1.412

Harlingen, Tex.

Census of Housing, 1980: occupancy and unit characteristics, by race, Hispanic origin, and city, SMSA rpt, 2473–1.104

Census of Population and Housing, 1980: detailed population and housing characteristics, by county, city, and census tract, SMSA rpt, 2551–2.104

Employment and economic impacts on Texas border of Mexican peso devaluation, for 6 counties and 2 SMSAs, 1970s-May 1983, hearing, 21788–133

Wages of office and plant workers, by occupation, 1984 labor market area survey rpt, 6785–3.10

see also under By SMSA or MSA in the "Index by Categories"

Harper, Charles P.

"Effect of the AML Index on the Borrower", 9312–7.403

Harrell, Adele

"Effect of the Head Start Program on Children's Cognitive Development, Preliminary Report", 4608–20

Harrington, Charlene

"Medicaid Nursing Home Reimbursement Policies, Rates, and Expenditures", 4652–1.422

Harris, J. Michael

"Ocean Fleet Shipping Rates, Capacity, and Utilization for Grains", 1548–235

Harris, Ruth D.

"Educational Programs for Other Cultured Families", 1004–16.1

Harrisburg, Pa.

Census of Housing, 1980: occupancy and unit characteristics, by race, Hispanic origin, and city, SMSA rpt, 2473–1.180

Census of Population and Housing, 1980: detailed population and housing characteristics, by county, city, and census tract, SMSA rpt, 2551–2.180

Wages by occupation, and benefits for office and plant workers, 1983 labor market area survey rpt, 6785–3.2

see also under By SMSA or MSA in the "Index by Categories"

Harry S. Truman Scholarship Foundation

see Truman, Harry S., Scholarship Foundation

Hartford, Conn.

Census of Housing, 1980: occupancy and unit characteristics, by race, Hispanic origin, and city, SMSA rpt, 2473–1.181

Census of Population and Housing, 1980: detailed population and housing characteristics, by county, city, and census tract, SMSA rpt, 2551–2.181

Wages of office and plant workers, by occupation, 1984 SMSA survey rpt, 6785–11.8

see also under By City and By SMSA or MSA in the "Index by Categories"

Hartzog, Jerry

"Asset/Liability Management: An Overview", 9306–1.4

Hasha, Gene

"Recent CAP Changes: Will They Reduce Subsidized Exports?", 1522–3.402

Hastings, Nebr.

Wages by occupation, and benefits for office and plant workers, 1984 labor market area survey rpt, 6785–3.9

Hathaway, Dale E.

"Agricultural Trade: 1984 and Beyond", 1004–16.1

Hattiesburg, Miss.

Housing vacancy rates for single and multifamily units and mobile homes, by city and ZIP code, 1984, annual metro area rpt, 9304–19.13

Haupt, Barbara

"1982 Summary: National Hospital Discharge Survey", 4146–8.96

Haverhill, Mass.

Census of Housing, 1980: occupancy and unit characteristics, by race, Hispanic origin, and city, SMSA rpt, 2473–1.216

Census of Population and Housing, 1980: detailed population and housing characteristics, by county, city, and census tract, SMSA rpt, 2551–2.216

see also under By SMSA or MSA in the "Index by Categories"

Hawaii

Agriculture census, 1982: farms, farmland, production and costs, and operator characteristics, preliminary State summary and county rpts, 2330–1.15

Agriculture census, 1982: farms, farmland, production, finances, and operator characteristics, by county, final State rpt, 2331–1.11

Airline departures and seats scheduled weekly from Hawaii, by city, Apr 1978 and 1984, article, 9142–42.406

Index by Subjects and Names

Army Corps of Engineers activities and projects, FY83 and trends from 1800s, annual rpt, 3754–1

Bank deposits in commercial and mutual savings banks and in US branches of foreign banks, by account type, instn, State, SMSA, and county, June 1983, annual rpt, 9295–3.18

Cancer cases, incidence, deaths, and death rates, by body site, age, race, Hispanic origin, and sex, for 10 geographic areas, 1973-81, 4478–130

Census of Housing, 1980: occupancy and unit characteristics of SMSAs and central cities, by race, Hispanic origin, and city, State rpt, 2473–1.13

Census of Population and Housing, 1980: detailed population and housing characteristics, by county, city, and census tract, State rpt, 2551–2.13

Census of Population, 1980: detailed socioeconomic and demographic characteristics, by age, sex, race, Hispanic origin, and industry, State rpt, 2531–4.13

County Business Patterns: establishments, employees, and payrolls, by SIC 4-digit industry and county, 1982, annual State rpt, 2326–6.13

Employment, earnings, and hours, by selected SIC 1- to 4-digit industry, State, and for 278 major labor areas, 1939-83, annual rpt, 6744–5.1, 6744–5.3

Environmental quality, pollutant discharge by type and source, and EPA protection activities and funding, 1970s-83, biennial regional rpt, 9184–15.9

Exports of manufactured and agricultural commodities, manufacturing production, and export-related employment, 1960s-82, State rpt, 2046–3.11

Fishing diesel and sail-assisted boats in Hawaiian waters, fuel use, earnings, and operating costs, with fuel and fish price indexes, various periods 1967-81, article, 2162–1.401

Fruit fly control, ethylene dibromide fumigation of tropical fruit imports, FY82, and cost of EDB and alternatives for Florida grapefruit and Hawaii papaya, 1984 rpt, 21168–29

HHS aid to each State and local govt or private instn, amount obligated, funding agency, and program, FY83, annual listing, 4004–3.9

Income (personal) per capita and by source, and earnings by industry div, by State, MSA, and county, 1977-82, annual regional rpt, 2704–2.9

Manufacturing census, 1982: financial and operating data, by SIC 2- to 4-digit industry, State, SMSA, and county, preliminary census div rpt, 2491–3.9

Mineral Industry Surveys, State review of production, 1983, advance annual rpt, 5614–6.11

Minerals Yearbook, 1982, Vol 2: State reviews of production, sales, and firms, by commodity, and business activity, annual rpt, 5604–34

Population size, Apr 1980 and July 1982, and per capita income, 1979 and 1981, by county and city, State Current Population Rpt, 2546–11.11

Port dev costs and financing through user fees, and shipping industry impact on

Index by Subjects and Names

Hazardous substances

local economy, by State, other area, industry, commodity, and port, 1970s-82, hearings, 21568–34.1

Retail trade census, 1982: employment, establishments, sales, and payroll, by SIC 2- to 4-digit kind of business, SMSA, and retail district, State rpt, 2401–1.12

Retail trade census, 1982: employment, establishments, sales, and payroll, by SIC 2- to 4-digit kind of business, SMSA, county, and city, State rpt, 2397–1.12

Savings and loan assns, FHLB 12th District members financial operations and housing industry indicators by State, monthly rpt, 9302–21

Service industry census, 1982: employment, establishments, receipts, and payroll, by SIC 2- to 4-digit kind of business, SMSA, county, and city, State rpt, 2391–1.12

Sugar production, consumption, supply, and trade, quarterly rpt, 1621–28

Tide height and time daily at worldwide coastal points, 1985 predictions, annual rpt, 2174–2.1

Water supply and quality in streams and lakes, and groundwater levels in wells, by drainage basin, 1983, annual State rpt, 5666–10.10

Waterborne commerce of US (domestic and foreign), freight by commodity, traffic, and passengers, by port and waterway, 1982, annual rpt, 3754–3.4

Weather broadcasts for US ships, by major ocean area, as of Jan 1984, biennial rpt, 2184–3

Wholesale trade census, 1982: employment, establishments, finances, and operations, by SIC 2- to 4-digit kind of business, SMSA, county, and city, State rpt, 2405–1.12

see also Honolulu, Hawaii

see also under By State in the "Index by Categories"

Hawkins, Bert W.

"Protecting American Agriculture: APHIS", 1004–16.1

Hawley, K. A.

"Summary of Environmental Reports, Department of Energy Sites", 3004–23

Hay

see Animal feed

see Pasture and rangeland

Hay, Joel W.

"Home Health Care Cost-Function Analysis", 4652–1.411

Hayes, Samuel L., III

"Investment Banking: Commercial Banks' Inroads", 9371–1.418

Hayghe, Howard

"Educational Attainment of Workers, Mar. 1982-83", 6746–1.251

"Married Couples: Work and Income Patterns", 6746–1.253

"More U.S. Workers Are College Graduates", 6722–1.423

Hayworth, Steven C.

"Implications of Land Contracts for Property Tax Assessment Practices", 9412–2.407

Hazardous Liquid Pipeline Safety Act

Enforcement, funding, and training activities of DOT and State govts, and pipeline accidents and casualties, 1982, annual rpt, 7304–5

Hazardous substances

Alcohol auto fuels health effects and safety review, as of 1983, 3308–75

Asbestos workers, exposure levels, cancer incidence, and deaths, by industry and occupation, and asbestos regulation enforcement and costs/benefits, various periods 1940-2027, hearing, 21408–72

Cigarette sales, market shares, advertising expenditures and methods, and tar and nicotine content, by cigarette type, selected years 1963-81, annual rpt, 9404–4

Cigarette tar, nicotine, and carbon monoxide content in 207 varieties, 1982, periodic rpt, 9402–2

Deaths and death rates from accidents, by place, detailed cause, and demographic characteristics, 1979, US Vital Statistics annual rpt, 4144–2.1, 4144–2.5

Environmental quality and protection programs, costs, and Fed Govt enforcement, 1983, detailed annual rpt, 484–1

Environmental quality, pollutant discharge by type, and EPA protection activities, 1970s-83, biennial summary rpt, 9184–16

Environmental quality, pollutant discharge by type and source, and EPA protection activities and funding, 1970s-83, biennial regional rpt series, 9184–15

EPA budget and full-time staff positions by type of activity, and grants to States, by program, FY75-84 and proposed FY85, 26308–47

EPA Office of R&D environmental research plans, and outlays by program, FY84-88, annual rpt, 9184–10

EPA pollution control research and grant assistance program activities, monthly rpt, 9182–8

Fed Govt civil agency hazardous waste sites and activities, and EPA data mgmt, by agency and waste location, 1984, GAO rpt, 26113–139

Fed Govt Hazardous Substance Response Trust Fund receipts, expenditures, assets, and liabilities, monthly rpt, 8102–9.6

Injuries and deaths from use of selected consumer products and related activity, by victim age and sex, 1982, annual rpt, 9164–7

Injuries and deaths from use of selected consumer products, by victim age and medical treatment status, 1982, annual rpt, 9164–6

Injuries, deaths, and medical costs from consumer products use, and Consumer Product Safety Commission activities and recalls, by product type and brand, FY83, annual rpt, 9164–2

Motor carrier safety inspections on interstate hwys, violations cited, and vehicles and drivers ordered out of service, 1982, annual rpt, 7554–35

Motor carrier safety inspections on interstate hwys, violations cited, and vehicles and drivers ordered out of service, May 1983, semiannual rpt, 7552–15

Occupational health risks from hazardous substances and radiation, by industry, occupation, age, and sex, with bibl and glossary, 1920s-82, 9638–50

PCB (polychlorinated biphenyl) concentrations in Great Lakes fish, for 29 species monitored at 24 sites, selected dates 1969-77, 9208–126

Pipeline safety regulations enforcement of DOT and States by pipeline type and State, and accidents and commodity losses, selected years 1973-FY84, GAO rpt, 26113–130

Pipelines for natural gas and hazardous liquids, accidents and casualties, and DOT and State govts safety activities, 1982, annual rpt, 7304–5

Pollution abatement expenditures, and effect on economic indicators and industry operations, by major industry, projected under 3 pollution regulation alternatives 1983-95, 9188–84

Railroad accidents, casualties, and property damage, Fed Railroad Admin activities, and safety inspectors by State, 1982, annual rpt, 7604–12

Railroad accidents, circumstances, severity, and railroad involved, quarterly rpt, 9612–3

Railroad freight volume and revenues, by commodity and region of origin and destination, 1982, annual rpt, 7604–6

Railroad safety law violations, claims settled FY83, annual rpt, 7604–10

Smoking and health research, article abstracts and indexes, 1983, annual rpt, 4044–8

Southeastern US water supply and quality, with background socioeconomic data, for 8 States, 1960s-2020 with trends from 1930, 9208–119

Taxes on hazardous waste generation and disposal in 3 States, and effects on waste mgmt, 1981-83, with assessment of 3 Fed Govt tax proposals, GAO rpt, 26113–124

Transport of hazardous material, accidents, casualties, and property damage, by mode of transport, with DOT control activities, 1983, annual rpt, 7304–4

Transportation accident investigations and recommendations by Natl Transportation Safety Board, 1983, annual rpt, 9614–1

Transportation census, 1982: trucks, by detailed characteristics, miles traveled, and type of product carried, State rpt series, 2573–1

Transportation safety programs, and accidents, injuries, deaths, hazards, and property damage, by mode of transport, 1983, annual rpt, 7304–19

Truck accidents, injuries, deaths, and property damage, by circumstances, carrier type, and driver age and condition, 1983, annual rpt, 7554–9

see also Air pollution

see also Carcinogens

see also Electromagnetic radiation

see also Lead poisoning and pollution

see also Mercury pollution

see also Motor vehicle exhaust

see also Nuclear radiation

see also Pesticides

see also Poisoning and drug reaction

see also Product safety

see also Radioactive materials

see also Soil pollution

see also Trace metals

Hazardous substances

see also Water pollution

Hazelton, Pa.

Dress industry production and related workers, wages, and benefits, by occupation, size of establishment, and union status, for 11 labor market areas, Aug 1982 survey, 6787–6.200

Head Start Project

Budget of US, effects of Reagan Admin policy changes, by detailed program, FY85, annual rpt, 104–21

Child dev effects of Head Start Project programs, by characteristics of program, child, and family, literature review, selected years 1965-81, 4608–20

Enrollment, appropriations, and staff of Head Start programs, FY65-84, annual rpt, 4604–8

Fed Govt public welfare programs and tax expenditures benefitting children and youth, participation and funding for 71 programs, FY81-83, 21968–30

Handicapped children enrollment in Head Start, by handicap, State, and for Indian Start, and migrant programs, 1982, annual rpt, 4604–1

HHS aid to each State and local govt or private instn, amount obligated, funding agency, and program, FY83, annual listing, 4004–3

Programs and effect on child dev, literature review with bibl, selected years 1970-83, 4608–17

Health care costs

see Medical costs

Health Care Financing Administration

- Abortions funded by Medicaid by justification, and expenditures, by State, FY78-83, annual rpt, 4654–9
- Cost control proposals for Fed Govt programs and mgmt, 3-year savings by function and agency, and financial and operating data, 1960s-81, 16908–1.7
- Data projects and systems of HHS, by subagency, FY83-84, annual inventory, 4044–3
- Drugs (prescription) invoice costs to pharmacists, and Medicare maximum allowable costs, by drug class and manufacturer, July/Aug 1983, 4658–6
- Fraud and abuse in HHS programs, audits and investigations, 2nd half FY84, semiannual rpt, 4002–6
- *Health Care Financing Review,* Medicare and Medicaid program activity, health care expenditures, and research, quarterly rpt with articles, 4652–1
- Kidney end-stage disease, Medicare program costs and enrollment, and participants dialysis, transplants, and deaths, by region and facility, annual rpt, discontinued, 4654–7
- Medicaid benefits and beneficiaries, by type of service and payment, basis for eligibility, and recipient age, sex, and race, annual rpt, discontinued, 4657–10
- Medicare aged and disabled enrollees short-stay hospital use, charges, and reimbursements, annual rpt, discontinued, 4657–9
- Medicare and Medicaid eligibility, participation, covered services and use, and reimbursements and payments, various periods 1966-82, annual rpt, 4654–1

Medicare disabled enrollees use of hospital services, charges, and reimbursements, by demographic characteristics, biennial rpt, discontinued, 4657–7

- Medicare enrollment, reimbursement, and use and covered charges by type of service, by State and census div, 1978-82, 4658–8
- Medicare facilities and services use, covered charges, and reimbursements, by beneficiary type and area of residence, series, 4656–1
- Medicare program operations and admin efficiency, Blue Shield participants, and end-stage renal disease program activity, FY81, annual rpt, 4654–5
- Medicare Supplementary Medical Insurance maximum charges reimbursable for specific services, by State and outlying area, 1983, annual rpt, 4654–4
- Medicare trust funds financial operations and payroll taxes, annual summary of 1984 trustees rpts, 4654–8
- Older persons long-term health care and financing alternatives, including nursing home insurance and use of home equity, 1984 conf papers, 4658–7
- Research activities and grants of HCFA by research area, as of June 1984, semiannual listing, 4652–8

Health Care Financing Study Group

"Uses and Impacts of Hospital Tax-Exempt Financing", 21788–135

Health condition

- Acid rain causes and effects, air pollutant emissions by source, and control costs, by region and State, selected years 1977-83 and projected to 2000, 26358–104
- Army personnel health status, and use of Army medical services in US and abroad by personnel, retirees, and dependents, monthly rpt, 3702–4
- Asian and Pacific Islands Americans births by ethnic origin and sociodemographic and birth characteristics, with comparisons to blacks and whites, 1978-80, 4146–5.75
- Aviation medicine research and studies, FAA technical rpt series, 7506–10
- Births and birth rates, by parent and birth characteristics and infant condition at birth, 1982 and trends from 1940, US Vital Statistics annual advance rpt, 4146–5.79
- Chicago area air pollution levels by location, and population sensitive to pollution, late 1970s-82 and projected under lower auto emission standards to 1995, 3408–31
- County and SMSA health manpower and facilities data, users guide to computerized area resource file, 1983, annual rpt, 4114–11
- Health and Nutrition Examination Natl Survey, health and dental condition and body measurements by age, sex, and race, Vital and Health Statistics series, 4147–11
- Health care expenditures, natl survey on services use, costs, and sources of payment, by patient and physician characteristics, 1977-78, series, 4186–3
- Health care use and expenditures, methodology and findings of natl survey of households, Medicare records, and Medicaid records in 4 States, 1980, series, 4146–12

Index by Subjects and Names

- Health condition and health care resources, use, and expenditures, 1970s-82 with trends and projections 1900-2000, annual compilation, 4144–11
- Health condition, hospitalization, disability, and medical costs, by demographic characteristics, Vital and Health Statistics series, 4147–10
- Health habits of adults, including physical activity, smoking, alcohol use, hypertension, and seat belt use, by age and sex, 1982, annual rpt, 4204–1.3
- Homeless population and characteristics, and temporary shelter operations, use, and user characteristics, for selected cities, various periods 1979-84, hearing, 21248–85
- Indian births, morbidity, and deaths and rates, and health services facilities and use, 1954-83, annual compilation, 4104–7
- Infants condition at birth, by race, 1981, US Vital Statistics advance rpt, 4146–5.73
- Medical Care Utilization and Expenditure Natl Survey results, series, 4146–11
- Older persons by demographic, socioeconomic, and health characteristics, selected years 1900-81 and projected to 2050, Current Population Rpt, 2546–2.125
- Older persons health status, health services use and expenditures by type, Medicare enrollment and reimbursement, and private insurance coverage, 1977-84, article, 4652–1.420
- Older persons nutrition services program operations and assessment, and participant sociodemographic, health, and diet characteristics, 1976 and 1982, 4608–16
- Older persons population characteristics, and needs and costs of social services by type, by metro-nonmetro status, 1970s-82 with trends from 1900, 21148–28
- *Public Health Reports,* articles and special studies rpts, bimonthly journal, 4102–1
- Research methods and design of health surveys, 1982 biennial conf proceedings, 4184–1
- *Statistical Abstract of US,* social, political, and economic data, 1950s-83 and trends, annual rpt, 2324–1.1
- Teenage girls births and rates, and distribution of births with low birth weight and Apgar scores, by mother and infant characteristics, 1970-81, 4147–21.41
- Veterans aged 55 and over, socioeconomic characteristics, economic resources, health care and status, and actual and expected use of VA benefits, 1983 survey, 9928–29
- Vital and Health Statistics series: advance data rpts, 4146–8
- Vital and Health Statistics series: analytical studies, 4147–3
- Vital and Health Statistics series and other NCHS publications, 1979-83, annual listing,, 4124–1
- Vital and Health Statistics series: foreign and US comparisons, analytical studies, 4147–5
- Widows with minor children receiving OASI survivor benefits, health insurance coverage and health care services and expenses, 1976-78, article, 4742–1.404

see also Absenteeism

see also Blind
see also Deaf
see also Disabled and handicapped persons
see also Diseases and disorders
see also Handicapped children
see also Hospitalization
see also Medical examinations and tests
see also Mental health and illness
see also Mobility limitations
see also Nutrition and malnutrition
see also Obesity
see also Occupational health and safety
see also Vital statistics

Health education

- Cancer-related resources directory for Frederick County, Md, evaluation of accuracy and usefulness, 1984 article, 4102–1.459
- Census of Population, 1980: detailed socioeconomic and demographic characteristics, by age, sex, race, Hispanic origin, occupation, and industry, State rpt series, 2531–4
- Census of Population, 1980: labor force, by sex, detailed occupation, and region, with comparison to 1970 census, supplementary rpt, 2535–1.12
- Diabetes outpatient health education model program, effect on patient knowledge and clinical test scores, 1983, article, 4102–1.457
- Fed Govt health info offices and services of HHS and other agencies, by subject, 1984 listing, 4048–18
- Heart, Lung, and Blood Natl Inst activities and funding, with morbidity and mortality data, various periods 1940-88, annual rpt, 4474–22
- Indian and Alaska Native health program activities, and funding for scholarships, care services, and facilities construction, by city, FY82, annual rpt, 4104–11
- Medicine Natl Library activities, collections, and grants, FY81-83, annual rpt, 4464–1
- Nursing continuing education in maternal and child health at University of Kentucky, course enrollment and student assessment of career value, 1983 article, 4102–1.405
- Nutrition services for elderly, program operations and assessment, and participant sociodemographic, health, and diet characteristics, 1976 and 1982, 4608–16
- Preventive health services block grants of Fed Govt, State funding by program, and opinions on State program admin, for 13 States, FY81-84, GAO rpt, 26121–88
- Public Health Service activities, and funding by function and subagency, FY83, annual rpt, 4044–2
- Red Cross program operations and financial statements, 1982/83, annual rpt, 29254–1
- Smoking and health research, article abstracts and indexes, 1983, annual rpt, 4044–8
- Teaching degrees conferred by specialty and State, required credit hours, and instn officials attitudes, by instn type, 1970s-83, hearings, 21348–89

Health, Education and Welfare Department

see Department of Education
see Department of Health and Human Services

Health facilities administration

- Census of Population, 1980: detailed socioeconomic and demographic characteristics, by age, sex, race, Hispanic origin, occupation, and industry, State rpt series, 2531–4
- Census of Population, 1980: labor force, by sex, detailed occupation, and region, with comparison to 1970 census, supplementary rpt, 2535–1.12
- DOD medical personnel, trainees, and accessions by source, by occupation, specialty, and service branch, FY83, annual rpt, 3544–24
- Fed Govt programs and mgmt cost control proposals, 3-year savings by function and agency, and financial and operating data, 1960s-81, 16908–1.24
- Govt employment and payroll, by function, level of govt, and jurisdiction, 1983, annual rpt series, 2466–1
- Health care expenditures, growth factors, medical equipment and drugs trade, and physician income, 1950-90, article, 4652–1.407
- Health care expenditures, natl and personal total and per capita amounts, by type of service and source of funds, 1983 and trends from 1929, annual article, 4652–1.429
- Hospital costs and use, data compilation project analyses, series, 4186–6
- Hospital employment, vacancies, and vacancy rates, by occupation and by hospital specialty, region, census div, and State, 1980, annual rpt, 4114–12
- Labs (public health) of States, pay scales and job requirements by occupation and State, FY81-83, annual rpt, 4204–7
- Manpower supply and education of health professionals, by occupation, demographic and professional characteristics, and location, 1950s-83 and projected to 2000, biennial rpt, 4114–8
- Mental health facilities info systems needs, implementation, uses, and costs, series, 4506–2
- Mental health facilities, services, staff, and patient characteristics, *Statistical Notes* series, 4506–3
- NYC health care demonstration project for reorganization of 6 facilities in Brooklyn, Federal and State govt funding by facility, 1979-82, article, 4652–1.419
- *Occupational Outlook Handbook,* 1984-85 biennial rpt, 6744–1
- Physicians (not office-based) visits by reason, diagnosis, treatment, patient and physician characteristics, and physician primary activity, 1980, 4147–13.77
- St Elizabeths Hospital operations and finances transfer to DC govt, and DC mental health facilities, services, and costs, FY83, GAO rpt, 26121–72
- VA Medicine and Surgery Dept trainees, by detailed program and city, FY83, annual rpt, 9924–21

see also Health planning and evaluation

Health facilities and services

- AFDC eligibility under Omnibus Budget Reconciliation Act, effect on caseloads and recipient benefits and living costs, 1981-83, GAO rpt, 26131–11
- AID activities and funding by project and function, FY85, and developing countries summary socioeconomic data, 1970s-83, by country, annual rpt, 9914–3

Health facilities and services

- Alabama rural black population, education, employment, health services, and economic status, for 16 counties, selected years 1970-81, 11048–180
- Bombing (explosive and incendiary) incidents, damage, injuries, and deaths, by target, State, and circumstances, 1983, annual rpt, 6224–5
- Budget of US, effects of Reagan Admin policy changes, by detailed program, FY85, annual rpt, 104–21
- Census of Population, 1980: detailed socioeconomic and demographic characteristics, by age, sex, race, Hispanic origin, occupation, and industry, State rpt series, 2531–4
- Census of Population, 1980: detailed socioeconomic characteristics, by county, city, and inside-outside SMSAs and central cities, State rpt series, 2531–3
- Census of Service Industries, 1982: employment, establishments, receipts, and payroll, by SIC 2- to 4-digit kind of business, SMSA, county, and city, State rpt series, 2391–1
- Coastal environmental characteristics, fish, wildlife, and use, and population socioeconomic data, for individual areas, series, 5506–4
- Collective bargaining agreements expiring during year, covered workers by SIC 2-digit industry, firm, and union, with summary of key provisions, 1984, annual rpt, 6784–9
- County and SMSA health manpower and facilities data, users guide to computerized area resource file, 1983, annual rpt, 4114–11
- County Business Patterns: establishments, employees, and payrolls, by SIC 4-digit industry and county, 1981, annual State rpt series, 2326–8
- County Business Patterns: establishments, employees, and payrolls, by SIC 4-digit industry and county, 1982, annual State rpt series, 2326–6
- Developing countries disaster preparedness and summary sociodemographic, political, and economic data, country rpt series, 9916–2
- Earnings by major industry group, and personal income per capita and by source, by region and State, 1929-82, 2708–40
- Employment by detailed occupation, for 29 SIC 2-digit nonmanufacturing industries, 1981 BLS survey, 6748–60
- Employment, earnings, and hours, by selected SIC 1- to 4-digit industry, State, and for 278 major labor areas, 1939-83, annual rpt, 6744–5
- Employment, earnings, and hours, by SIC 4-digit nonfarm industry, monthly 1974-Feb 1984, annual update, 6744–4
- Fed Govt aid to State and local govts, expenditures, and direct payments, by program, agency, and State, FY83, annual rpt, 2464–2
- Finances and operations, by SIC 2- to 4-digit industry, 1970s-83 and projected to 1988, annual rpt, 2014–4
- Foreign aged population characteristics, with related health care data and vital statistics, by world area and selected country, 1950-80 and projected to 2020, 2546–10.12

Health facilities and services

Foreign and US health care resources, use, and per capita public expenditures, and selected population characteristics, for 7 countries, selected years 1975-81, 21148–33

Foreign human rights conditions in 162 countries, economic and military aid of US, and economic aid of intl organizations, 1981-83, annual rpt, 21384–3

Foreign market and trade for medical and health care equipment, and user industry operations and demand, country market research rpts, 2045–2

Franchise business opportunities, by firm and kind of business, 1984 annual listing, 2044–27

Govt employment and payroll, by function, level of govt, and jurisdiction, 1983, annual rpt series, 2466–1

Govt finances, by level of govt and State, selected years 1929-83, annual rpt, 10044–1

Govt finances, by level of govt, State, and for large cities and counties, 1981-83, annual rpt series, 2466–2

Health and vital statistics collection, and use in program planning and evaluation, Public Health Conf papers, 1983, biennial rpt, 4164–2

Health care expenditures, natl survey on services use, costs, and sources of payment, by patient and physician characteristics, 1977-78, series, 4186–3

Health Care Financing Review, Medicare and Medicaid program activity, health care expenditures, and research, quarterly rpt with articles, 4652–1

Health care use and expenditures, methodology and findings of natl survey of households, Medicare records, and Medicaid records in 4 States, 1980, series, 4146–12

Health info offices and services of HHS and other Fed Govt agencies, by subject, 1984 listing, 4048–18

Health services delivery and related topics, Natl Center for Health Services Research rpts, series, 4186–2

Health Services Research Natl Center grants and contracts, by program area, FY83, annual listing, 4184–2

HHS aid to each State and local govt or private instn, amount obligated, funding agency, and program, FY83, annual listing, 4004–3

HHS health data projects and systems, by subagency, FY83-84, annual inventory, 4044–3

Income tax returns of corporations, detailed income and tax items by industry, 1981, annual rpt, 8304–4

Income tax returns of partnerships, detailed data by industry, 1981 estimates, annual article, 8302–2.404

Income tax returns of partnerships, receipts by source, deductions by type, and establishments, by selected industry, 1982, annual article, 8302–2.416

Income tax returns of sole proprietorships, detailed data by industry div and selected industry group, 1981, annual rpt, 8304–7

Income tax returns of sole proprietorships, receipts, deductions by type, payroll, and net income, by major industry, 1982, annual article, 8302–2.413

Income tax returns with investment credits, for individuals by income, and for sole proprietorships by industry, 1981, article, 8302–2.409

Indian and Alaska Native health program activities, and funding for scholarships, care services, and facilities construction, by city, FY82, annual rpt, 4104–11

Indian births, morbidity, and deaths and rates, and health services facilities and use, 1954-83, annual compilation, 4104–7

Input-output structure of US economy, detailed interindustry transactions for 537 industries, and components of final demand, 1977 benchmark data, 2708–17

Jail capacities, conditions, expenditures, and services, and socioeconomic and other characteristics of inmates, various dates 1976-82, 10048–59

Medical Care Utilization and Expenditure Natl Survey results, series, 4146–11

Medical technologies coverage and reimbursements of Medicare, and health services use and costs, selected years 1966-82, 26358–106

Medicare and Medicaid eligibility, participation, covered services and use, and reimbursements and payments, various periods 1966-82, annual rpt, 4654–1

Medicare coverage of new medical technologies and reimbursements, and health services use and costs, selected years 1966-82, 26358–106

Medicare end-stage renal disease dialysis, transplants by facility, donor organ costs, deaths by age, and hospitalization, by region, 1981, annual rpt, 4654–5.2

Medicare facilities and services use, covered charges, and reimbursements, by beneficiary type and area of residence, series, 4656–1

Mentally retarded and developmentally disabled treatment and services, university-affiliated facility funding, activities, and clients, 1980-FY83, 4608–19

Minority group and women employment, by occupational group and SIC 2- to 3-digit industry, 1981, annual rpt, 9244–1.1

Navy and Marine Corps disease incidence, medical care, and deaths, by detailed diagnosis, and medical personnel and workloads, 1978-79, annual rpt, 3804–1

Neighborhood quality, indicators and attitudes by inside-outside central cities, 1979-82 surveys, SMSA rpt series, 2485–6

New Mexico health clinics staffed by Natl Health Service Corps, income by source and service, and effect of revised system for Federal payback, 1980-83, hearings, 21368–47

NIH activities, staff, funding, and facilities, historical data, 1984 annual rpt, 4434–1

NIH grants and awards for R&D, training, construction, and medical libraries, by location and recipient, FY83, annual listings, 4434–7

Occupational injury and illness rates, by SIC 2- to 4-digit industry, 1982, annual rpt, 6844–1

Older persons population characteristics, and needs and costs of social services by type, by metro-nonmetro status, 1970s-82 with trends from 1900, 21148–28

Index by Subjects and Names

Older persons sociodemographic characteristics, and Fed Govt program participation and funding, 1983 with trends and projections 1900-2060, annual rpt, 25144–3.1

Public Health Reports, articles and special studies rpts, bimonthly journal, 4102–1

Public Health Service activities, and funding by function and subagency, FY83, annual rpt, 4044–2

Publications of NCHS, quarterly listing, 4122–2

Publications of NCHS, 1979-83, annual listing, 4124–1

Puerto Rico educational enrollment, finance, completions, curricula, and personnel by instn, and health and vital statistics, selected years 1970-83, hearings, 21348–93

Receipts for selected services, by SIC 2- to 4-digit kind of business, 1983, annual rpt, 2413–8

Red Cross program operations and financial statements, 1982/83, annual rpt, 29254–1

Rural and urban areas comparisons of employment, income, housing, health, and education, 1960s-83, annual chartbook, 1504–3

Senegal rural health care projects of AID, mgmt and effectiveness, 1978-83, 9916–3.20

Statistical Abstract of US, social, political, and economic data, 1950s-83 and trends, annual rpt, 2324–1.1

Traffic accidents and casualties detailed direct and indirect costs, by characteristics of persons and vehicles involved, 1979-80, 7768–80

TTPI and American Samoa off-island medical referrals, costs, and potential savings, by govt, FY83 and comparisons from FY78, GAO rpt, 26123–72

TTPI socioeconomic, health, and govtl data, by TTPI govt, FY83 and selected trends, detailed annual rpt, 7004–6

Use of health facilities and manpower, by patient and facility characteristics, Vital and Health Statistics series, 4147–13

VA medical facilities sharing agreement contracts, services, and costs, by region and facility, FY83, annual rpt, 9924–18

Vital and Health Statistics series: foreign and US comparisons, analytical studies, 4147–5

Vital and Health Statistics series: manpower and facilities resources, 4147–14

see also Adult day care

see also Civilian Health and Medical Program of the Uniformed Services

see also Clinics

see also Community health services

see also Emergency medical service

see also Halfway houses

see also Health facilities administration

see also Health insurance

see also Health maintenance organizations

see also Health occupations

see also Health planning and evaluation

see also Home health services

see also Hospitalization

see also Hospitals

see also Laboratories

see also Medical examinations and tests

Index by Subjects and Names

Health insurance

see also Medical supplies and equipment
see also Mental health facilities and services
see also Military hospitals
see also Nursing homes
see also Public health
see also Regional medical programs
see also Vaccination and vaccines
see also Veterans health facilities and services

see also terms listed under Health occupations
see also under By Industry in the "Index by Categories"
see also under Medicine and terms beginning with Medical

Health insurance

- AFDC eligibility under Omnibus Budget Reconciliation Act, effect on caseloads and recipient benefits and living costs, 1981-83, GAO rpt, 26131–11
- Army Medical/Life, Central Insurance, and Central Retirement Fund financial statements, FY83, annual rpt, 3704–12
- Beneficiaries of noncash public and employer-based transfer programs, by income source and socioeconomic characteristics, 1982, advance Current Population Rpt, 2546–6.38
- Beneficiaries of noncash public and employer-based transfer programs, by income source and socioeconomic characteristics, 1982, final Current Population Rpt, 2546–6.37
- Births (cesarean and total) in hospitals affiliated and not affiliated with medical schools, by characteristics of mother, birth, and hospital, 1977, 4186–6.4
- Budget of US, CBO analysis of revenue and spending alternatives and projections of economic indicators, FY85-89, annual rpt, 26304–3.3
- Canada and US hospital use by children by Canada Province and US region, and death rates, by diagnosis and sex, selected years 1977-79, 4147–5.1
- County Business Patterns: establishments, employees, and payrolls, by SIC 4-digit industry and county, 1981, annual State rpt series, 2326–8
- County Business Patterns: establishments, employees, and payrolls, by SIC 4-digit industry and county, 1982, annual State rpt series, 2326–6
- Crime victimization rates by type of offense, and victim and offense characteristics, Natl Crime Survey series, 6066–3
- DOD Civilian Health and Medical Program of the Uniformed Services costs and operations, FY83-84 with trends from FY79, semiannual rpt, 3502–2
- Employee benefits in private industry, coverage by benefit type and provisions and occupational group, 1983, annual rpt, 6784–19
- Employee benefits in private industry, percent of employers providing selected benefits, 1979-82, conf proceedings, 25408–89
- Farmers, farm population, and managers health insurance coverage by insurance type and selected sociodemographic characteristics, 1976, 1598–191
- Fed Employees Health Benefits Program finances, benefit reductions, and rate increases, by plan, 1981-82, GAO rpt, 26121–67

Fed Govt civilian employee retirement, health, and life insurance benefit plans operations and finances, FY81-82, annual rpt, 9844–1

- Fed Govt programs and mgmt cost control proposals, 3-year savings by function and agency, and financial and operating data, 1960s-81, 16908–1.27
- Foreign social security programs coverage, funding, eligibility, and benefits, by country, 1983, biennial rpt, 4746–4.58
- Health care expenditures, growth factors, medical equipment and drugs trade, and physician income, 1950-90, article, 4652–1.407
- Health care expenditures, methodology of natl survey of households, physicians, health insurance firms, and employers, 1977-79, series, 4186–4
- Health care expenditures, natl and personal total and per capita amounts, by type of service and source of funds, 1983 and trends from 1929, annual article, 4652–1.429
- Health care expenditures, natl survey on services use, costs, and sources of payment, by patient and physician characteristics, 1977-78, series, 4186–3
- Health care services for elderly, knowledge, use, and factors affecting service quality, by race and Hispanic origin, 1984 article, 4652–1.406
- Health care use and expenditures, methodology and findings of natl survey of households, Medicare records, and Medicaid records in 4 States, 1980, series, 4146–12
- Health condition and health care resources, use, and expenditures, 1970s-82 with trends and projections 1900-2000, annual compilation, 4144–11
- Health Services Research Natl Center grants and contracts, by program area, FY83, annual listing, 4184–2
- Hospital and physician reimbursement by patient disease type and severity category, and patients in 2 or more categories by coverage type, FY80-83, article, 4652–1.426
- Laboratory tests ordered by physicians, number and costs related to health insurance type, coverage, and reimbursement, 1975-76, article, 4652–1.415
- Michigan bankruptcy filings, by filer type, moving history, income, creditor action, debt and asset type, credit status, exemptions claimed, and county, 1979-81, hearings, 21528–57.3
- Military medical services, potential effects of alternative financing proposals on DOD costs, with service use and out-of-pocket medical costs by type of recipient, FY84-89, 26306–6.74
- Minority group and women employment, by occupational group and SIC 2- to 3-digit industry, 1981, annual rpt, 9244–1.1
- New Mexico health clinics staffed by Natl Health Service Corps, income by source and service, and effect of revised system for Federal payback, 1980-83, hearings, 21368–47
- Occupational injury and illness rates, by SIC 2- to 4-digit industry, 1982, annual rpt, 6844–1

Older persons health care expenditures, costs, and insurance, and effects of proposed Medicare cost share increase, selected years 1965-81, 25148–27

- Older persons health care total and out-of-pocket expenditures, by sociodemographic characteristics, poverty and health status, and degree of functional limitation, 1980, 4146–11.4
- Older persons health status, health services use and expenditures by type, Medicare enrollment and reimbursement, and private insurance coverage, 1977-84, article, 4652–1.420
- Older persons long-term health care and financing alternatives, including nursing home insurance and use of home equity, 1984 conf papers, 4658–7
- Older persons population characteristics, and needs and costs of social services by type, by metro-nonmetro status, 1970s-82 with trends from 1900, 21148–28
- Personal consumption expenditures, natl income and product account, *Survey of Current Business,* monthly rpt, monthly and annual tables, 2702–1.23
- Postal Service pension and health benefits subsidized by Fed Govt trust funds, and subsidy reduction plans deficit impact, FY79-84 and projected to FY89, 26306–6.82
- Poverty-level persons and families, by income source, hours of work, earnings, taxes, and family characteristics, various periods 1959-84, 21788–131
- Prepaid health plans and HMOs enrollment, use, and Fed Govt aid, FY83, annual rpt, 4104–8
- Private health insurance premiums, and benefits by type of administering insurer and insurer at risk, 1983 and trends from 1965, article, 4652–1.430
- Railroad employees sickness benefits and beneficiaries, by age, occupation, and sickness type, 1981/82, annual rpt, 9704–2.3
- Research methods and design of health surveys, 1982 biennial conf proceedings, 4184–1
- Rhode Island State health insurance claims and benefit-cost ratio by income and Medicare eligibility status, various periods 1975-79, article, 4652–1.423
- School employees health insurance plans in 7 cities, as of 1980, hearing, 21788–136
- *Statistical Abstract of US,* social, political, and economic data, 1950s-83 and trends, annual rpt, 2324–1.1
- Supplementary Security Income beneficiary socioeconomic characteristics and health service use, 1970s-83 and SSI program projections to 1995, 25148–29
- Tax expenditures from employee benefit plans, for income and payroll tax by benefit type and income, with benefits by industry, 1950-83 and projected to 1988, article, 9373–1.404
- Traffic accidents and casualties detailed direct and indirect costs, by characteristics of persons and vehicles involved, 1979-80, 7768–80
- Veterans aged 55 and over, socioeconomic characteristics, economic resources, health care and status, and actual and expected use of VA benefits, 1983 survey, 9928–29

Health insurance

Vital and Health Statistics series and other NCHS publications, 1979-83, annual listing,, 4124–1

Widows with minor children receiving OASI survivor benefits, health insurance coverage and health care services and expenses, 1976-78, article, 4742–1.404

see also Area wage surveys

see also Blue Cross-Blue Shield

see also Civilian Health and Medical Program of the Uniformed Services

see also Disability insurance

see also Health maintenance organizations

see also Industry wage surveys

see also Labor cost indexes

see also Medicaid

see also Medicare

see also Old-Age, Survivors, Disability, and Health Insurance

see also Workers compensation

Health Maintenance Organization Service *see* Office of Health Maintenance Organizations

Health maintenance organizations

Employee benefits in private industry, coverage by benefit type and provisions and occupational group, 1983, annual rpt, 6784–19

Employer attitudes toward HMOs for employee health insurance, enrollment, premiums, and coverage, by region and industry div, 1982, 4108–32

Enrollment (total, Medicare, and Medicaid), finances, use, Fed Govt qualification status, and PHS loan activity, by HMO, FY83, annual rpt, 4044–2

Enrollment, use, and Fed Govt aid for HMOs and prepaid health plans, FY83, annual rpt, 4104–8

Fed Employees Health Benefits Program finances, benefit reductions, and rate increases, by plan, 1981-82, GAO rpt, 26121–67

Fed Govt civilian health benefit plans enrollment and premiums, for individual private and employee organization plans, FY81-82, annual rpt, 9844–1.2

Fed Govt credit assistance costs, policies to improve measurement, with loan and loan guarantee data by program, and Federal and private credit instns operations, 1970-84, 26306–6.72

Health insurance (private) premiums, and benefits by type of administering insurer and insurer at risk, 1983 and trends from 1965, article, 4652–1.430

HHS aid to each State and local govt or private instn, amount obligated, funding agency, and program, FY83, annual listing, 4004–3

Israel health care in rural clinics under prepaid plan, services use and user satisfaction, 1981 survey, article, 4102–1.456

Medicare beneficiaries HMO enrollment, and Medicare and Medicaid program data, various periods 1966-82, annual rpt, 4654–1

Health occupations

Census of Population, 1980: detailed socioeconomic and demographic characteristics, by age, sex, race, Hispanic origin, occupation, and industry, State rpt series, 2531–4

Census of Population, 1980: detailed socioeconomic characteristics, by county, city, and inside-outside SMSAs and central cities, State rpt series, 2531–3

Census of Population, 1980: labor force, by sex, detailed occupation, and region, with comparison to 1970 census, supplementary rpt, 2535–1.12

Correctional instns (Federal) health services employment, by occupation, instn, and region, monthly rpt, 6242–2

County and SMSA health manpower and facilities data, users guide to computerized area resource file, 1983, annual rpt, 4114–11

County Business Patterns: establishments, employees, and payrolls, by SIC 4-digit industry and county, 1981, annual State rpt series, 2326–8

County Business Patterns: establishments, employees, and payrolls, by SIC 4-digit industry and county, 1982, annual State rpt series, 2326–6

Degrees conferred in higher education, by race, Hispanic origin, sex, level, and field, selected years 1949/50-1979/80, annual rpt, 4824–2.16

DOD medical personnel, trainees, and accessions by source, by occupation, specialty, and service branch, FY83, annual rpt, 3544–24

Employment and economic conditions, alternative BLS projections to 1995 with selected trends for 1959-82, 6728–29

Employment by detailed occupation, for 29 SIC 2-digit nonmanufacturing industries, 1981 BLS survey, 6748–60

Employment in hospitals and nursing homes, total and in selected occupations, by facility bed size, ownership, region, and State, selected years 1969-80, 4147–14.30

Employment, unemployment, and labor force, by demographic and employment characteristics, State, and for 30 metro areas and 11 large cities, 1983, annual rpt, 6744–7

Foreign market and trade for medical and health care equipment, and user industry operations and demand, country market research rpts, 2045–2

Govt census, 1982: employment, payrolls, and average earnings, by function, level of govt, State, county, population size, and inside-outside SMSAs, 2455–2

Govt census, 1982: local govt employment by function, payroll, and average earnings, for individual counties, cities, and school and special districts, 2455–1

Health condition and health care resources, use, and expenditures, 1970s-82 with trends and projections 1900-2000, annual compilation, 4144–11

Health facilities and manpower use, by patient and facility characteristics, Vital and Health Statistics series, 4147–13

Health Services Research Natl Center grants and contracts, by program area, FY83, annual listing, 4184–2

Hospital employment, vacancies, and vacancy rates, by occupation and by hospital specialty, region, census div, and State, 1980, annual rpt, 4114–12

Manpower supply and education of health professionals, by occupation, demographic

Index by Subjects and Names

and professional characteristics, and location, 1950s-83 and projected to 2000, biennial rpt, 4114–8

Mental health clinical training funding by NIMH, by program and field, FY80-83, GAO rpt, 26121–86

Mental health facilities, services, and costs in DC, and effect of St Elizabeths Hospital operations and finances transfer to DC govt, FY83, GAO rpt, 26121–72

Mental health facilities staffing, by discipline and selected characteristics of health services personnel, selected years 1954-81, annual rpt, 4504–9.4

Military reserve forces medical personnel and wartime requirements by occupation and medical equipment costs, by reserve component, as of 1983, annual rpt, 3544–27.2

Minority group and women employment and training in health professions, by field, selected years 1962/63-1983/84, 4118–18

Natl Guard (Army and Air) activities, manpower, and facilities, FY83, annual rpt, 3704–3

Nuclear industry nongovt employment by industry segment, occupation, and census div, and DOE and NRC nuclear employment, 1968-83, biennial rpt, 3004–11

Occupational manpower needs and supply by detailed occupation, and educational and training program enrollees and grads by detailed field, 1982 and 1995, biennial rpt, 6744–3

Occupational Outlook Handbook, 1984-85 biennial rpt, 6744–1

Puerto Rico educational enrollment, finance, completions, curricula, and personnel by instn, and health and vital statistics, selected years 1970-83, hearings, 21348–93

Radiation protection and health physics enrollments and degrees granted by State and instn, and grads employment, 1983, annual rpt, 3004–7

Southeastern States health care resource availability, and employment by occupation, by facility type, by State and SMSA in Fed Reserve 6th District, 1970s-81, article, 9371–1.425

Training and research grants and contract awards of Health Professions Bur, annual listing, suspended, 4114–1

TTPI socioeconomic, health, and govtl data, by TTPI govt, FY83 and selected trends, detailed annual rpt, 7004–6

VA pay rates recommended to provide comparability to private sector, 1983, annual rpt, 104–16

Vital and Health Statistics series and other NCHS publications, 1979-83, annual listing,, 4124–1

Vital and Health Statistics series: manpower and facilities resources, 4147–14

Wages of hospital workers by sex and occupation, and benefits, for 22 MSAs, Oct 1981 survey, 6787–6.201

see also Allied health personnel

see also Biomedical engineering

see also Chiropractic and naturopathy

see also Clinical laboratory technicians

see also Coroners

Index by Subjects and Names

see also Dentists and dentistry
see also Dietitians and nutritionists
see also Health facilities administration
see also Medical education
see also Midwives
see also Nurses and nursing
see also Obstetrics and gynecology
see also Occupational therapy
see also Optometry
see also Orthopedics
see also Osteopathy
see also Pathology
see also Pediatrics
see also Pharmacists and pharmacy
see also Physical therapy
see also Physicians
see also Podiatry
see also Psychiatry
see also Psychology
see also Radiology
see also Social work
see also Speech pathology and audiology
see also Surgeons and surgery
see also Veterinary medicine
see also under Medicine and terms beginning with Medical

Health of workers
see Absenteeism
see Occupational health and safety

Health planning and evaluation

- County and SMSA health manpower and facilities data, users guide to computerized area resource file, 1983, annual rpt, 4114–11
- Digestive Diseases Interagency Coordinating Committee activities, and related Federal research and funding, by agency, FY79-83, annual rpt, 4434–13
- Drug abuse prevalence and health consequences, and Natl Inst on Drug Abuse and other HHS prevention activities, FY82, annual rpt, 4004–26
- Foreign aged population characteristics, with related health care data and vital statistics, by world area and selected country, 1950-80 and projected to 2020, 2546–10.12
- Health and vital statistics collection, and use in program planning and evaluation, Public Health Conf papers, 1983, biennial rpt, 4164–2
- Health care visits, testing of World Health Organization system to classify reasons people seek care, 1984 article, 4102–1.460
- Health info offices and services of HHS and other Fed Govt agencies, by subject, 1984 listing, 4048–18
- Health professions data collection needs and activities, as of May 1984, biennial rpt, 4114–8
- Health services delivery and related topics, Natl Center for Health Services Research rpts, series, 4186–2
- Health Services Research Natl Center grants and contracts, by program area, FY83, annual listing, 4184–2
- HHS aid to each State and local govt or private instn, amount obligated, funding agency, and program, FY83, annual listing, 4004–3
- HHS health data projects and systems, by subagency, FY83-84, annual inventory, 4044–3

HHS program evaluations and funding, 1970-83, listing, 4008–60

- Medicaid advisory committees members by type, and operating characteristics, 1979, article, 4652–1.409
- Mental health facilities info systems needs, implementation, uses, and costs, series, 4506–2
- Mental health facilities needs assessment and program evaluation for small areas, methodology, use of census data, analysis, and sample data, series, 4506–8
- *Public Health Reports,* articles and special studies rpts, bimonthly journal, 4102–1
- Public Health Service activities, and funding by function and subagency, FY83, annual rpt, 4044–2
- Research methods and design of health surveys, 1982 biennial conf proceedings, 4184–1
- Smoking and health research, article abstracts and indexes, 1983, annual rpt, 4044–8
- Vital and Health Statistics series and other NCHS publications, 1979-83, annual listing,, 4124–1

Health Resources Administration
see Health Resources and Services Administration

Health Resources and Services Administration

- Cost control proposals for Fed Govt programs and mgmt, 3-year savings by function and agency, and financial and operating data, 1960s-81, 16908–1.7
- Data projects and systems of HHS, by subagency, FY83-84, annual inventory, 4044–3
- *Public Health Reports,* articles and special studies rpts, bimonthly journal, 4102–1
- *see also* Bureau of Health Professions
- *see also* Indian Health Service
- *see also* National Health Service Corps
- *see also* Office of Health Maintenance Organizations

Health Services Administration
see Health Resources and Services Administration

Health surveys
see under names of individual surveys (listed under Surveys)

Hearing and hearing disorders

- Fed Govt minority group and handicapped employment, by race, Hispanic origin, disability, sex, and employment characteristics, as of Sept 1982, biennial rpt, 9844–27
- Handicapped children early education research and service project activities and characteristics, and grants to States for program dev, 1983-84, annual listing, 4804–30
- Head Start Project enrollment of handicapped children, by handicap, State, and for Indian and migrant programs, 1982, annual rpt, 4604–1
- Hearing aid performance evaluation, by model and manufacturer, 1984, annual rpt, 9924–5
- Older persons nutrition services program operations and assessment, and participant sociodemographic, health, and diet characteristics, 1976 and 1982, 4608–16
- Veterans aged 55 and over, socioeconomic characteristics, economic resources, health

Heating oil

care and status, and actual and expected use of VA benefits, 1983 survey, 9928–29

see also Deaf
see also Ear diseases and infections
see also Speech pathology and audiology
see also under By Disease in the "Index by Categories"

Heart diseases
see Cardiovascular diseases

Heart transplantation
see Medical transplants

Heating
see Plumbing and heating

Heating oil

- Air pollutant emission factors, by detailed source, 3rd edition, 1983-84 supplements, 9198–13
- Air pollution levels for 5 pollutants, by detailed source, State, and Air Quality Control Region, 1981, annual rpt, 9194–7
- Buildings (nonresidential) energy use, expenditures, and conservation, by building characteristics, EIA survey series, 3166–8
- Connecticut utility group housing energy conservation program, cost effectiveness and characteristics of participants and nonparticipants, 1980-82, 3308–77
- Consumption, by fuel type, economic sector, and end use, 1983 and 2000, 2006–2.5
- Consumption, by fuel type, economic sector, census div, and State, 1960-82, State Energy Data System annual rpt, 3164–39
- DOE in-house energy use, conservation investments, and savings, by type of use and fuel and field office, FY83, annual rpt, 3024–3
- Environmental quality and protection programs, costs, and Fed Govt enforcement, 1983, detailed annual rpt, 484–1
- Farm production expenditures, detailed items by farm sales size and region, 1983, annual rpt, 1614–3
- Foreign and US oil prices, tax, and customs duty, by refined product and major city, July 1983 and Jan 1984, annual rpt, 3164–50.4
- Futures trading by commodity and exchange, and Commodity Futures Trading Commission activities, funding, and employment, FY83, annual rpt, 11924–2
- Futures trading in selected commodities, foreign currencies, and stock indexes, Chicago and other markets activity, monthly rpt, 11922–1
- Futures trading in selected commodities, foreign currencies, Treasury securities, and stock indexes, NYC, Chicago, and other markets activity, monthly rpt, 11922–5
- Futures trading in selected commodities, Treasury securities, and stock indexes, NYC market activity, monthly rpt, 11922–2
- Housing census, 1980: inventory, occupancy, and unit characteristics, changes from 1973 by region and inside-outside SMSAs and central cities, series, 2473–3
- Housing census, 1980: structural, financial, and householder characteristics, by region and State, 2475–4

Heating oil

Housing completions, and new unit sales price, cost per square foot, and heating fuel use, by metro-nonmetro area, 1976-82, 1598–190

Housing energy bills and departures from normal by fuel type, and heating and cooling degree days by State, by census div, monthly rpt, 2152–11, 2152–12

Housing energy use, by fuel type, county, city, and census tract, 1980 Census of Population and Housing, State and SMSA rpt series, 2551–2

Housing energy use, costs, expenditures, and conservation, and household and housing characteristics, survey series, 3166–7

Housing heating and air conditioning equipment shipments by type of fuel used, monthly rpt, 2012–1.6

Housing occupancy and unit and household characteristics, by region and metro-nonmetro residence, 1983, biennial survey, 2485–1

Housing unit heating fuel, by type, occupant race, Hispanic origin, urban-rural location, and region, 1981, annual survey, 2485–7

Imports of US, detailed Schedule A commodities by country, monthly rpt, 2422–2

Income tax returns of sole proprietorships, detailed data by industry div and selected industry group, 1981, annual rpt, 8304–7

Manufacturing energy efficiency progress, and energy use by type, by SIC 2-digit industry, 1982, annual rpt, 3304–8

OECD energy prices and taxes by energy source and end-use sector, for US and 9 countries, quarterly 1979-83, annual rpt, 3164–71

Pacific Northwest electricity consumption and prices by end-use sector, and economic and demographic data, 1960s-83 and projected to 2005, annual rpt, 3224–2

Price and volume of 13 oil products sold by gas plant operators and refiners, by end-use sector, PAD district, and State, monthly rpt, 3162–11

Prices (retail) and housing consumption, by energy type, region, and for 28 SMSAs and US city average, monthly press release, 6762–8

Prices and expenditures for fuels, by consuming sector, State, and fuel type, 1970-81, annual rpt, 3164–64

Properties of heating oil, lab analysis, 1984, last issue of annual rpt, 3006–2.4

Refinery financial and operating impacts from auto use of alcohol fuels, projected to 2000 with trends 1964-80, 3308–75

Retail trade census, 1982: employment, establishments, sales, and payroll, for fuel dealers, by State, preliminary rpt, 2395–1.36

Supply/demand and price forecasts, by fuel type, quarterly rpt, 3162–34

Supply/demand and prices, by energy resource and major producing and consuming country and sector, detailed data, monthly rpt, 3162–24

Supply/demand and prices, by fuel type and consuming sector with foreign comparisons, 1949-83, annual rpt, 3164–74

Supply/demand and prices, by fuel type, sector, and end use, detailed trends and projections 1973-95, annual rpt, 3164–75

Supply/demand and prices, by fuel type, sector, and end use, with foreign comparisons, 1960-83 and projected to 1995, annual summary rpt, 3164–76

Supply/demand of oil and refined products, refinery capacity and use, and OPEC, non-OPEC, and spot market prices, weekly rpt, 3162–32

Supply/demand, trade, stocks, and refining of oil and natural gas liquids, by detailed product, State, and PAD district, with fuel oil sulfur content, monthly rpt with articles, 3162–6

Supply/demand, trade, stocks, and refining of oil and natural gas liquids, by detailed product, State, and PAD district, and refineries in US and territories, 1983 annual rpt, 3164–2

Waterborne commerce of US (domestic and foreign), freight by commodity, traffic, and passengers, by port and waterway, 1982, annual rpt, 3754–3

Hedging

see Futures trading

Hefferan, Colien

"Economic Outlook for Families, 1984", 1004–16.1, 1702–1.404

"New Savings and Transaction Instruments", 1702–1.401

Hegg, Karl M.

"Timber Resource Statistics for the Upper Tanana Block, Tanana Inventory Unit, Alaska, 1974", 1206–9.9

Heifner, Richard

"Review of Existing and Alternative Federal Dairy Programs", 1568–245

Height

see Body measurements

Heimlich, Ralph E.

"Assessing Erosion on U.S. Cropland, Land Management and Physical Features", 1588–83

Helbing, Charles

"Medicare: Use and Reimbursement for Aged Persons by Survival Status, 1979", 4656–1.17

Helicopters

Accident circumstances and severity, by type of flying and aircraft, 1981, annual rpt, 9614–3

Accident circumstances, severity, and causes, for domestic and foreign air carriers in US operations, periodic rpt, 9612–1

Air traffic control and airway facilities and equipment, FAA improvement activities and R&D under Natl Airspace System Plan, 1982-2000, annual rpt, 7504–12

Aviation activity, detailed data on aircraft, air traffic, air carriers, personnel, airports, and FAA operations, 1974-83, annual rpt, 7504–1

Aviation activity forecasts, methodology, data sources, and coverage, Feb 1983 conf papers, annual rpt, 7504–28

Developing countries arms transfers from US, USSR, and Europe, by weapon type and world region, 1974-82, 25948–3

DOD budget, costs of individual weapons or weapons systems, FY83-85, annual rpt, 3504–2

DOD budget, itemized account of legislative history, FY84, annual rpt, 3504–7

DOD budget justification, programs, and policies, FY85, annual rpt, 3544–2

Index by Subjects and Names

DOD procurement cost estimates for weapons and communications systems, by service branch, quarterly summary rpt, 3502–1

FAA-registered aircraft, by type and characteristics of aircraft, carrier, make, State, and county, 1983, annual rpt, 7504–3

Fed Govt programs and mgmt cost control proposals, 3-year savings by function and agency, and financial and operating data, 1960s-81, 16908–1.19

Financial data for airlines, by carrier, carrier group, and for total certificated system, quarterly rpt, 9142–12

Flight and engine hours, and shutdown rates, by aircraft and engine model for each air carrier, monthly rpt, 7502–13

Foreign military spending, arms trade, and armed forces size, with total govt spending and population, by country, 1972-82, annual rpt, 9824–1

Forest fires on Forest Service land and acres burned, by cause, forest, and State, 1983, annual rpt, 1204–6

General aviation aircraft, hours flown, and equipment, by type, use, and model of aircraft, region, and State, 1982, annual rpt, 7504–29

Manufacturing census, 1982: financial and operating data, for SIC 4-digit industries by product, preliminary rpt, 2491–1.398, 2491–1.400

Marijuana cultivation control activity of State law enforcement agencies, and aid from Fed Govt and Natl Guard, 1983 survey, GAO rpt, 26119–64

Navy budget and Navy and Marine Corps forces, equipment, and budget summary, planned FY84-85, semiannual pamphlet, 3802–3

Pilots and nonpilots certified by FAA, by type of certificate, age, sex, region, and State, 1983, annual rpt, 7504–2

Shipments, trade, consumption, and firms, by type of aircraft and aircraft engine, monthly Current Industrial Rpt, 2506–12.24

Soviet Union and Warsaw Pact military weapons systems, assistance and presence worldwide, and force strengths, with selected US and NATO comparisons, as of 1984, 3508–14

Traffic, aircraft, pilots, airport activity, and fuel use, forecast FY84-95 with FY79-83 trends, annual rpt, 7504–6

Helium

see Gases

Helmick, Sandra A.

"Microcomputer as Home Equipment: A Role for Home Economists", 1004–16.1

Helms, William F.

"Protecting American Agriculture: The PPQ Role", 1004–16.1

Hemel, Eric

"Federal Deposit Insurance as a Call Option: Implications for Depository Institution and Insurer Behavior", 9316–1.107

Hendershot, Gerry E.

"Analysis of the Reversal in Breast Feeding Trends in the Early 1970s", 4102–1.442

"Infant Health Consequences of Childbearing by Teenagers and Older Mothers", 4102–1.420

Index by Subjects and Names

Henderson, Dale W.
"Definition and Measurement of Exchange Market Intervention", 9366–1.126

Hendrickson, Bruce H.
"Maritime Subsidies", 7704–18

Henson, Mary F.
"Earnings in 1981 of Married-Couple Families, by Selected Characteristics of Husbands and Wives", 2546–2.120
"Money Income of Households, Families, and Persons in the U.S.: 1982", 2546–6.39

Henson, William L.
"Differences Between the 9-City and 12-City Broiler Price Reports", 1561–7.404

Hepatitis
see Infective and parasitic diseases

Herb, William J.
"Hydrology of Area 1, Eastern Coal Province, Pennsylvania", 5666–15.24
"Hydrology of Area 2, Eastern Coal Province, Pennsylvania and New York", 5666–15.25

Herbert, John
"Recent Residential Sales of Natural Gas in the North Central U.S.", 3162–4.402

Herbicides
see Pesticides

Herbs
see Spices and herbs

Hereditary diseases
Deaths and death rates by detailed cause and demographic characteristics, 1979 and selected trends, US Vital Statistics annual rpt, 4144–2.1
Genetically abnormal human cell cultures available to researchers, and cultures shipped, 1984 annual listing, 4474–23
Infant deaths by detailed cause, geographic location, age, race, and sex, 1979, US Vital Statistics annual rpt, 4144–2.2
see also Birth defects

Heritage Conservation and Recreation Service
see National Park Service

Herlihy, M.
"EC Grains, Oilseeds, and Livestock: Selected Statistics, 1960-80", 1528–173

Herman, Arthur S.
"Productivity Declined in 1982 in a Majority of Industries Measured", 6722–1.408
"Productivity Growth in the Switchgear Industry Slows After 1973", 6722–1.420

Hernon, Jolene C.
"Criminal Justice System Response to Victim Harm", 6068–185.1

Heroin
see Drug abuse and treatment
see Drug and narcotics traffic
see Drugs
see Methadone treatment

Herr, William M.
"Private Sector Financing of Family Farms", 1004–16.1

Herrick, Samuel F., Jr.
"U.S. Tuna Trade Summary, 1982", 2162–1.403

Hertweck, Floyd R., Jr.
"Analyses of Natural Gases, 1983", 5604–2

Heshizer, Brian
"Are Unions Facing a Crisis? Labor Officials Are Divided", 6722–1.451

Hess, Alison
"Sustaining Tropical Forest Resources: Reforestation of Degraded Lands", 26358–101.2

Hession, John C.
"Safety Standards for Mobile Homes Make a Difference", 1502–7.402

HEW
see Department of Education
see Department of Health and Human Services

Hewlett, James G.
"Investor Perceptions of Nuclear Power", 3168–88

Hialeah, Fla.
see also under By City and By SMSA or MSA in the "Index by Categories"

Hickman, Clifford A.
"Use Valuation of Louisiana's Rural Lands: Short-Run Fiscal Impacts", 1208–206

Hickory, N.C.
Census of Population and Housing, 1980: detailed population and housing characteristics, by county, city, and census tract, SMSA rpt, 2551–2.182
see also under By SMSA or MSA in the "Index by Categories"

Hides and skins
Agricultural Statistics, 1983, annual rpt, 1004–1
Agriculture census, 1982: farms, farmland, production, finances, and operator characteristics, by county, final State rpt series, 2331–1
Animal and plant genetic resource conservation, commercial uses, causes of depletion, and geographic sources, 1984 rpt, 5548–13
China economic conditions, agricultural and industrial production, trade, and domestic and foreign investment, 1980-85, 2048–106
China exports and imports by SITC 1- to 5-digit commodity, 1970s-82, annual rpt, 244–12
County Business Patterns: establishments, employees, and payrolls, by SIC 4-digit industry and county, 1981, annual State rpt series, 2326–8
Endangered animals and plants foreign trade including reexports of live specimens and products, by purpose, country, and species, 1982, annual rpt, 5504–19
Export sales and shipments of US grains, oilseed products, hides, skins, and cotton, by country, weekly rpt, 1922–3
Exports and imports of dairy, livestock, and poultry live animals, meat, and products, by commodity and country of destination, FAS quarterly rpt, 1925–32
Exports and imports of US, by agricultural commodity and country, bimonthly rpt with articles, 1522–1
Exports and imports of US, by detailed agricultural commodity and country, FY83 and CY83, semiannual rpts, 1522–4
Exports and imports of US, detailed SIC-based commodities by world area, 1983, annual rpts, 2424–6
Exports and imports of US, totals and as percent of domestic production, by SIC 2- to 5-digit commodity, 1981, annual rpt, 2424–3

High School and Beyond Survey

Exports and personal expenditures of US and world for selected agricultural commodities, by country, and export share of US farm income, various periods 1926-82, 1528–172
Exports of manufactured and agricultural commodities, manufacturing production, and export-related employment, 1960s-82, State rpt series, 2046–3
Exports of US, detailed commodities by country of destination, monthly rpt, 2422–3
Exports of US, detailed Schedule B commodities by country of destination, 1983, annual rpt, 2424–9
Exports of US, detailed Schedule E commodities by mode of transport and world area and country of destination, 1983, annual rpts, 2424–5
Foreign agricultural production, prices, and trade, by country, 1983 and outlook for 1984/85, annual world region rpt series, 1524–4
Great Lakes trade, by SITC 3-digit commodity, port, vessel type, world area, and country, 1982, annual rpt, 7744–3
Imports of US, detailed Schedule A commodities by country and world area of origin, and mode of transport, 1983, annual rpts, 2424–2
Imports of US, detailed Schedule A commodities by country, monthly rpt, 2422–2
Imports of US, detailed TSUSA commodities by country of origin, 1983, annual rpt, 2424–4
Market news summary statistics for livestock, meat, and wool, by animal type and market, weekly rpt, 1315–1
OECD trade, total and for 4 major countries, and US trade by country, by commodity, 1972-82, annual world region rpt series, 244–13
Producer prices and indexes, by stage of processing and detailed commodity, monthly rpt, 6762–6
Producer prices and indexes, by stage of processing and detailed commodity, monthly 1983, annual supplement, 6764–2
Seal harvest, mgmt, and skins taken and rejected for northern fur seals of Pribilof Islands, Alaska, various dates 1786-1981, 2168–79
see also Furs and fur industry
see also Leather industry and products
see also under By Commodity in the "Index by Categories"

High Point, N.C.
Census of Housing, 1980: occupancy and unit characteristics, by race, Hispanic origin, and city, SMSA rpt, 2473–1.176
Census of Population and Housing, 1980: detailed population and housing characteristics, by county, city, and census tract, SMSA rpt, 2551–2.176
Wages of office and plant workers, by occupation, 1984 SMSA survey rpt, 6785–11.8
see also under By SMSA or MSA in the "Index by Categories"

High School and Beyond Survey
High school class of 1982: coursework compared to graduation criteria of natl commission, by student and school characteristics, 4828–16

High School and Beyond Survey

High school class of 1982: foreign language coursework, by language, course level, student and school characteristics, and location, 1984 rpt, 4828–17

Student aid and earnings used to pay higher education costs of 1980 high school seniors, by instn type and family income, 1980-82, 4848–15

High schools

see Elementary and secondary education

High-speed ground transportation

- Foreign and US rail high-speed systems and railcar production, and proposed US projects costs and funding, with population and land area for selected foreign cities, 1940s-82, 26358–97
- Midwest high-speed rail system planned from Chicago, capital and operating costs and profitability by speed class, frequency, and route, 1984 article, 9375–1.406
- Research publications on public transit, 2nd half FY83, semiannual listing, 7882–1

see also Metroliner

Higher education

- Census of Population, 1980: detailed socioeconomic and demographic characteristics, by age, sex, race, Hispanic origin, occupation, and industry, State rpt series, 2531–4
- Census of Population, 1980: detailed socioeconomic characteristics, by county, city, and inside-outside SMSAs and central cities, State rpt series, 2531–3
- Computer specialists sociodemographic, educational, and employment characteristics, and Fed Govt support by agency, 1978, biennial Current Population Rpt, 2546–2.124
- *Condition of Education,* detailed data on enrollment, staff, achievement, finances, curricula, and education effects on employment, 1982-83, annual rpt, 4824–1.2
- Crime and crime rates at higher education instns by offense, and law enforcement employees, by instn, 1983, annual rpt, 6224–2
- Desegregation in higher education, Louisiana black instn funding, and Virginia students needed to meet desegregation goals, by instn, late 1970s-85, hearings, 21348–91
- *Digest of Education Statistics,* detailed data on students, staff, finances, and facilities, 1982 and selected trends, annual rpt, 4824–2
- Education Dept programs funding, operations, and effectiveness, FY83, annual rpt, 4804–5
- Education highlights, trends in enrollment, expenditures, curricula, and other topics of current interest, periodic press release, 4822–1
- Education statistics summary compilation, 1980/81-1982/83 with selected trends from 1869, biennial rpt, 4804–27
- Educational trends, 1972/73-1992/93, biennial pocket-size card, 4824–3
- Finances of higher education instns, revenues and expenditures, endowments, and physical plant assets and debt, by State and region, annual rpt, suspended, 4844–6
- Florida and California elderly migration by selected State of origin or destination, and

Florida elderly, by sociodemographic and housing characteristics, 1970 and 1980, 4478–150

- Foreign women sociodemographic, economic, and fertility characteristics, with comparisons to men, by country, 1960s-85, world region rpt series, 2326–15
- High school class of 1980: use of student aid and earnings to pay higher education costs, by instn type and family income, 1980-82, 4848–15
- High school classes of 1980 and 1982: educational and sociodemographic characteristics and expectations, natl longitudinal study, series, 4826–2
- Higher education instns, by type, location, and other characteristics, 1983/84 annual listing, 4844–3
- Higher education instns, type, location, enrollment, and student charges, by State and congressional district, 1983/84, biennial listing, 4844–11
- Howard University salaries, academic standing, medical research, and library operations, and finances of Howard Inn, selected years 1976-83, GAO rpt, 26121–74
- Indian education program operations, funding, student progress measures, and opinions of school staff, parents, and students, selected years 1973-83, 4808–13
- Libraries of colleges and universities, expenditures, holdings by type, use, staff by sex, and Federal grants received, 1979-82, biennial rpt, 4854–1
- Mentally retarded and developmentally disabled treatment and services, university-affiliated facility funding, activities, and clients, 1980-FY83, 4608–19
- Microfiche from Educational Resources Info Center, holdings of US and foreign educational and other instns, as of 1983, listing, 4918–14
- NASA R&D funding to colleges and universities, by State, field of science, and instn, FY83, annual listing, 9504–7
- Nuclear reactors for domestic use and export by function, with owner, operating characteristics, and location, Apr 1984, semiannual listing, 3002–5
- Patents (US) granted to US and foreign applicants, by year of grant and application, country, and type of applicant, 1960s-83, annual rpt, 2244–3
- Puerto Rico educational enrollment, finance, completions, curricula, and personnel by instn, and health and vital statistics, selected years 1970-83, hearings, 21348–93
- R&D and science-related Fed Govt funding and total and federally funded expenditures of universities and colleges, by instn and field of science, FY82, 9626–2.135, 9626–2.136
- R&D expenditures by higher education instns and federally funded centers, by field, source of funds, instn, and State, FY82, annual rpt, 9627–13
- R&D Fed Govt funding, by agency and performer, FY83-84, 9626–2.132
- R&D Fed Govt funding by type of performer, and funding for industrial dev by type, program, and agency, selected years FY75-85, 26306–6.81

Index by Subjects and Names

- R&D higher education expenditures, funding sources, and science and engineering staff, by field, late 1960s-83, annual rpt, 9624–18.4
- *Science Indicators,* R&D expenditures, innovations, research, and higher education, with foreign comparisons, 1960s- 83, annual rpt, 9624–10
- Scientists and engineers employed at universities and colleges, by field, sex, and instn, 1973-82, 9626–2.140
- Scientists and engineers employed in energy-related fields, supply/demand and effects of R&D funding, by energy type, employer type, field, and age, 1962-91, annual rpt, 3004–19
- Scientists and engineers in R&D, salaries by type of establishment, age, degree, type of experience, and field, 1984, annual rpt, 3004–1
- Scientists and engineers in R&D, salary comparisons for DOE labs and non-DOE facilities, Aug 1982-Feb 1984, annual rpt, 3004–9
- Small business mgmt counseling by university centers, costs, funding, and businesses served by industry, with detail for 2 States, 1980-83, hearing, 25728–36
- Southeastern States economic dev effect on education, for Fed Reserve 6th District States, selected years 1900-82, article, 9371–1.428
- TTPI socioeconomic, health, and govtl data, by TTPI govt, FY83 and selected trends, detailed annual rpt, 7004–6
- Tuition and other student charges at each public and private 2- and 4-year higher education instn, by State, 1983/84, annual listing, 4844–10

see also Adult education

see also Agricultural education

see also Area studies

see also Black colleges

see also Business education

see also Curricula

see also Degrees, higher education

see also Educational attainment

see also Educational broadcasting

see also Educational enrollment

see also Educational exchanges

see also Educational facilities

see also Educational finance

see also Educational materials

see also Educational research

see also Educational technology

see also Educational tests

see also Federal aid to higher education

see also Federal aid to medical education

see also Junior colleges

see also Legal education

see also Medical education

see also Reserve Officers Training Corps

see also School administration and staff

see also Scientific education

see also Service academies

see also State aid to higher education

see also Student aid

see also Students

see also Teacher education

see also Teachers

see also Vocational education and training

see also Work-study programs

Index by Subjects and Names

Hildebrand, Diane M.

Highway Trust Fund
see Federal trust funds

Highways

Air pollutant emission factors, by detailed source, 3rd edition, 1983-84 supplements, 9198–13

Appalachia hwy system and access roads funding and completion status, by State, quarterly tables, 9082–1

Appalachia regional dev spending, by program area and source of funds, FY82, annual rpt, 9084–1

Bridge replacement and rehabilitation program of Fed Govt, funding by bridge and bridge status by State, 1983, annual rpt, 7554–27

Bridges over navigable waters, with type of bridge and use, owner, dimensions, and location, 1984 regional listing series, 7406–5

Capital (fixed), govt and private nonresidential structures and equipment, residential capital, and consumer-owned durable goods by item, 1980-83, annual article, 2702–1.433

Capital needs and financing for public works, by project type, level of govt, and selected jurisdiction, 1970s-83 and projected to 2000, hearing, 23848–181

Capital needs and intergovtl financing for public works, by type of project and selected city, various periods 1950-83, 10048–60

China economic conditions, agricultural and industrial production, trade, and domestic and foreign investment, 1980-85, 2048–106

Coal dev plans on Fed Govt lease lands in 12 regions under Fed Coal Mgmt Program, environmental and socioeconomic impacts to 2000, final statement series, 5726–4

Coastal environmental characteristics, fish, wildlife, and use, and population socioeconomic data, for individual areas, series, 5506–4

Colorado River Storage Project finances, water resource dev, power production, and other activities in western States, FY83, annual rpt, 5824–3

Construction bids and contracts for Federal-aid interstate and secondary hwys, by State, 1st half 1984, semiannual rpt, 7552–12

Construction expenditures and contracts awarded for Federal-aid hwy system, by type of material used and State, various periods 1944-83, annual rpts, 7554–29

Construction industries census, 1982: financial and operating data, by SIC 4-digit industry and State, final rpt series, 2373–1

Construction industries census, 1982: financial and operating data, by SIC 4-digit industry and State, preliminary rpt series, 2371–1

Construction material prices and indexes for Federal-aid hwy system, by type of material and urban-rural location, quarterly rpt, 7552–7

Construction of hwys and other transportation energy use, for urban areas, late 1970s-82 and projected under lower auto emission standards to 1995, 3408–31

Construction put in place, permits authorized by region, State, and MSA, and Federal contract awards, by construction type, bimonthly rpt with articles, 2012–1

Construction put in place, value of new public and private structures, by type, monthly rpt, 2382–4

County Business Patterns: establishments, employees, and payrolls, by SIC 4-digit industry and county, 1981, annual State rpt series, 2326–8

County Business Patterns: establishments, employees, and payrolls, by SIC 4-digit industry and county, 1982, annual State rpt series, 2326–6

Developing countries disaster preparedness and summary sociodemographic, political, and economic data, country rpt series, 9916–2

Eastern US local govt hwy expenditures, per capita aid, and bridges by condition, by selected county and city, various periods 1965-80, article, 9377–1.405

Employment, earnings, and hours, by selected SIC 1- to 4-digit industry, State, and for 278 major labor areas, 1939-83, annual rpt, 6744–5

Energy use in transportation sector by mode, fuel supplies, and demographic and economic determinants of vehicle use, 1970s-83, annual rpt, 3304–5

Fed Hwy Admin activities, grants, and special studies, press release series, 7556–3

Finances, operations, vehicles, equipment, accidents, and energy use, by mode of transport, 1955-84, annual rpt, 7304–2

Financing methods of govts and private sector for hwy and urban transit systems, with case studies for selected metro areas, series, 7556–7

Foreign economic, social, and political summary data, by country, 1984, annual factbook, 244–11

Forests (natl) timber sales contract operations in Northwest US by forest and firm, and lumber supply/demand, FY76-1983 with trends from 1913, hearings, 25318–57

Govt census, 1982: city govt revenues by source, expenditures by function, debt, and assets, by State and city, 2457–4

Govt census, 1982: county govt revenues by source, expenditures by function, debt, and assets, by State and county, 2457–3

Govt census, 1982: employment, payrolls, and average earnings, by function, level of govt, State, county, population size, and inside-outside SMSAs, 2455–2

Govt census, 1982: local govt employment by function, payroll, and average earnings, for individual counties, cities, and school and special districts, 2455–1

Govt census, 1982: State govt payments to local govts, by program, source of funds, level of govt, and State, with trends from 1902, 2460–3

Govt employment and payroll, by function, level of govt, and jurisdiction, 1983, annual rpt series, 2466–1

Govt finances, by level of govt and State, selected years 1929-83, annual rpt, 10044–1

Govt finances, by level of govt, State, and for large cities and counties, 1981-83, annual rpt series, 2466–2

Govt transportation revenues by source and expenditures, by level of govt and mode of transport, and Fed Govt aid by type, FY77-82, 7308–185

Hwy Statistics, detailed data on traffic, govt finances, fuel use, vehicles, driver licenses, and hwy characteristics, by State, 1983, annual rpt, 7554–1

Hwy Statistics, summary data on traffic, govt finances, fuel use, vehicles, and driver licenses, by State, 1982, annual rpt, 7554–24

Income tax returns of sole proprietorships, detailed data by industry div and selected industry group, 1981, annual rpt, 8304–7

Local govt hwy expenditures and aid per capita related to area characteristics, for 10 eastern counties, annual averages 1965-76, technical paper, 9377–9.9

Local govt spending, reliance on State aid and local taxes by type, and excise tax growth by State, selected years FY57-83, article, 10042–1.403

Natl Hwy Traffic Safety Admin activities and funding, and traffic accident data, 1981, annual rpt, 7764–1

New Communities program of HUD, activities, costs, land sales, and community and population characteristics, for 13 communities, 1970s-83, 5188–107

Public land acreage and use, and Land Mgmt Bur activities and finances, annual State rpt series, 5724–11

R&D for hwy design and construction, quarterly journal, 7552–3

R&D projects funded by Fed Hwy Admin, FY83, annual summary rpt, 7554–14

Robberies, by type of premises, population size, and region, 1983, annual rpt, 6224–2.1

Speed averages and vehicles exceeding 55 mph, by State, quarterly rpt, 7552–14

State govt motor fuel tax provisions, motor vehicle registration fees, and disposition of receipts, by State, as of Jan 1984, biennial rpt, 7554–37

Statistical Abstract of US, social, political, and economic data, 1950s-83 and trends, annual rpt, 2324–1.3

Traffic volume on rural roads and city streets, by region, monthly rpt, 7552–8

User fees and other taxes and Trust Fund revenues by tax type, and trucking industry economic effects of tax and size and weight rules, FY82-84 and projected to 1990, GAO rpt, 26117–31

User fees and other taxes by tax type, and truck size and weight limits, economic effects on trucking industry, 1982-84 and projected 1984-87, hearings, 25328–24

see also Federal aid to highways

see also Traffic accidents and safety

see also Traffic engineering

Hijacking of aircraft

see Air piracy

Hildebrand, Diane M.

"Forest Insect and Disease Conditions in the Rocky Mountain Region, 1983", 1206–11.1

Hilgert, Cecelia

Hilgert, Cecelia
"70th Year of Individual Income and Tax Statistics, 1913-82", 8302–2.401

Hilgert, Ronald J.
"Air Service in Alaska: An Update", 9142–42.405
"Air Service in Hawaii", 9142–42.406
"Capacity Shares at the Medium Hubs, 1978-84", 9142–42.408
"Changes in Air Traffic Hub Classifications, 1978-1982", 9142–42.401
"Changes in Scheduled Airline Flights by Number of Intermediate Stops, Dec. 1978 to Dec. 1983", 9142–42.403
"Changes in the Number of Carriers Serving Domestic Points, Dec. 1983 vs. Dec. 1978", 9142–42.402
"Commuter Airline Industry Since Deregulation", 9142–42.404
"Hourly Flight Operations at 32 Selected Airports, Sept. 1984", 9142–42.411
"Jet and Non-Jet Service in the 48 States, June 1978-June 1984", 9142–42.409
"Rankings of Air Carriers by Number of Stations Served, New Stations Added and Stations Closed in the Past Year", 9142–42.410
"Route Strategies at the Large Hubs, 1978-84", 9142–42.407

Hill, Diane
"How Social Security Payments Affect Private Pensions", 6722–1.431

Hill, Lawrence J.
"Effects of Delaying the Operation of a Nuclear Power Plant", 9638–53

Hill, Martha S.
"Final Report of the Project: Motivation and Economic Mobility of the Poor, Part I", 4008–65.1

Hill, O. F.
"Nuclear Fact Book", 3008–88

Hill, Susan
"Participants in Postsecondary Education: Oct. 1982", 4848–16

Hilton, R. Spence
"Effects of Exchange Rate Uncertainty on German and U.S. Trade", 9385–1.405

Hires
see Labor turnover

Hirst, Eric
"Comparison of Actual and Predicted Energy Savings in Minnesota Gas-Heated Single-Family Homes", 3308–74
"Evaluation of Utility Home Energy Audit (RCS) Programs", 3308–69
"Residential Conservation Service in Connecticut: Evaluation of the CONN SAVE Program", 3308–77
"Use of Electricity Billing Data To Determine Household Energy Use 'Fingerprints'", 3308–76

Hispanic Americans
Agriculture census, 1982: farms, farmland, production, finances, and operator characteristics, by county, final State rpt series, 2331–1
Bankruptcy (personal), filers by debt type, employment and financial status, race, and Hispanic origin, 1982 survey, hearings, 21528–57.2
Births and birth and fertility rates, by detailed Hispanic origin, characteristics of mother, birth, and prenatal care, and for 22 States, 1981, 4146–5.80

Cancer cases, incidence, deaths, and death rates, by body site, age, race, Hispanic origin, and sex, for 10 geographic areas, 1973-81, 4478–130
Census of Housing, 1980: inventory, occupancy, and unit characteristics, changes from 1973 by region and inside-outside SMSAs and central cities, series, 2473–3
Census of Housing, 1980: occupancy and unit characteristics of SMSAs and central cities, by race, Hispanic origin, and city, State and SMSA rpt series, 2473–1
Census of Population and Housing, 1980: detailed population and housing characteristics, by county, city, and census tract, State and SMSA rpt series, 2551–2
Census of Population, 1980: detailed socioeconomic and demographic characteristics, by age, sex, race, Hispanic origin, occupation, and industry, State rpt series, 2531–4
Census of Population, 1980: detailed socioeconomic characteristics, by county, city, and inside-outside SMSAs and central cities, State rpt series, 2531–3
Census of Population, 1980: migration since 1975, by county and selected demographic characteristics, supplementary rpt, 2535–1.14
Census of Population, 1980: migration since 1975, by State and selected demographic characteristics, supplementary rpt, 2535–1.13
County and City Data Book, detailed socioeconomic and demographic data for States, counties, and cities, selected years 1976-82, 2328–1
Dallas-Fort Worth, Tex, SMSA employment, earnings, hours, and CPI changes, 1983 with trends from 1968, annual rpt, 6964–2
Disabled Hispanic Americans, by disability type and severity and for 5 States, selected years 1970-78, conf proceedings, 16598–5
Earnings of full- and part-time workers, and of families by number of earners, quarterly rpt, 6742–19
Employment and labor force statistics by major industry group and demographic characteristics, *Survey of Current Business,* monthly rpt, 2702–1.5
Employment and unemployment current statistics and articles, Monthly Labor *Review,* 6722–1
Employment discrimination against Hispanics and other minorities, Equal Employment Opportunity Commission enforcement activities, personnel, and litigation, 1970s-FY83, 9248–18
Employment, unemployment, and labor force, by demographic and employment characteristics, State, and for 30 metro areas and 11 large cities, 1983, annual rpt, 6744–7
Employment, unemployment, and labor force, detailed data by sociodemographic and employment characteristics, and industry, 1940s-83, 6748–72
Employment, unemployment, and labor force participation, by detailed Hispanic origin, race, and sex, quarterly rpt, 6742–18

Florida and California elderly migration by selected State of origin or destination, and Florida elderly, by sociodemographic and housing characteristics, 1970 and 1980, 4478–150
Fresno, Calif, economic, population, labor, and housing indicators, various periods 1974-85, hearing, 21248–8
Handbook of Labor Statistics, employment, earnings, hours, and labor force characteristics, 1982 and trends, detailed annual rpt, 6724–1
Health care services for elderly, knowledge, use, and factors affecting service quality, by race and Hispanic origin, 1984 article, 4652–1.406
Health insurance and Medicaid coverage, by Hispanic origin group and by race for non-Hispanics, annual average 1978-80, article, 4144–11.1
Health services use, illness rates, and disability days of Hispanics, by socioeconomic characteristics, and compared to blacks and whites, 1978-80, 4147–10.147
Homeless population and characteristics, and temporary shelter operations, use, and user characteristics, for selected cities, various periods 1979-84, hearing, 21248–85
Houston, Tex, SMSA employment, earnings, hours, and CPI changes, 1983 with trends from 1968, annual rpt, 6964–1
Income (household) and cash and noncash transfer program participation, by sociodemographic characteristics, quarterly rpt, 2542–2
Income and socioeconomic characteristics of persons, families, and households, detailed cross-tabulations, Current Population Rpt series, 2546–6
Medical residents by specialty and race, and minority medical faculty by race and Hispanic origin, selected years 1980-83, 4102–1.412
Minority language population (Spanish and other), and children with limited English proficiency, by State, 1980, biennial rpt, 4804–14
Population demographic, social, and economic characteristics, Current Population Rpt series, 2546–1
Population socioeconomic and demographic characteristics of Hispanics, and compared to non-Hispanics, selected years 1970-83, chartbook, 2328–48
Poverty population size, effect of counting public noncash transfers as income by recipient characteristics, 1979-83, 2626–2.52
Puerto Rico educational enrollment, finance, completions, curricula, and personnel by instn, and health and vital statistics, selected years 1970-83, hearings, 21348–93
Statistical Abstract of US, social, political, and economic data, 1950s-83 and trends, annual rpt, 2324–1.1, 2324–1.3
Vocational training bilingual projects, participants, characteristics, and costs, by program, FY82, annual rpt, 4804–26

Historic sites
Alteration, construction, and acquisition proposals for historic and other Fed Govt building projects, costs and tenure by city and project, as of 1983, hearings, 25328–23

Index by Subjects and Names

Home economics

Budget of US, effects of Reagan Admin policy changes, by detailed program, FY85, annual rpt, 104–21

Coal dev plans on Fed Govt lease lands in 12 regions under Fed Coal Mgmt Program, environmental and socioeconomic impacts to 2000, final statement series, 5726–4

Coastal environmental characteristics, fish, wildlife, and use, and population socioeconomic data, for individual areas, series, 5506–4

Environmental quality and protection programs, costs, and Fed Govt enforcement, 1983, detailed annual rpt, 484–1

Fed Govt aid to State and local govts, expenditures, and direct payments, by program, agency, and State, FY83, annual rpt, 2464–2

Fed Govt-owned real property inventory and costs, worldwide summary by location, agency, and use, 1983, annual rpt, 9454–5

Fed Govt programs and mgmt cost control proposals, 3-year savings by function and agency, and financial and operating data, 1960s-81, 16908–1.22

Govt census, 1982: State govt payments to local govts, by program, source of funds, level of govt, and State, with trends from 1902, 2460–3

Natl forests recreational use, visitor-days by type of activity, forest, and State, FY83 with trends from 1924, annual rpt series, 1204–17

Preservation Historic Fund grants, by State, FY85, annual press release, 5544–9

State outdoor recreation units and acreage, by State, 1982/83, annual rpt, 5544–14.4

see also Monuments and memorials

see also National park system

History

Census of Population, 1980: detailed socioeconomic and demographic characteristics, by age, sex, race, Hispanic origin, occupation, and industry, State rpt series, 2531–4

R&D expenditures of higher education instns, and science and engineering employment and grad students, by field, 1972-83, biennial rpt, 9627–24

see also Archeology

Hoar, Gay S.

"Economic Crisis in Mexico", 21248–82

Hodgman, Donald R.

"Determinants of Monetary Policy in France, The Federal Republic of Germany, Italy and the UK: A Comparative Analysis", 9373–3.26

Hodgson, Thomas A.

"Health Care Expenditures for Major Diseases", 4144–11.1

"Health Care Expenditures for Major Diseases in 1980", 4652–1.413

Hoehn, James G.

"Regional Economic Forecasting Procedure Applied to Texas", 9377–9.10

"Time Series Forecasting Models of the Texas Economy: A Comparison", 9379–1.403

Hof, John G.

"Projections of Future Forest Recreation Use", 1208–195

Hoff, Frederic L.

"Sugarbeet and Sugarcane Grower Receipts, Production Costs, and Net Returns, 1981-83 Crops", 1561–14.403

"Sugarbeet and Sugarcane Production and Processing Costs: 1982 Crop", 1561–14.402

Hoffman, Larry G.

"Environmental Surveillance for the INEL Radioactive Waste Management Complex and Other Areas, Annual Report, 1983", 3354–10

Hoffman, Peter B.

"Burnout: Age at Release from Prison and Recidivism", 6006–2.31

"Reliability in Guideline Application: Initial Hearings, 1982", 6006–2.33

Hog cholera

see Animal diseases and zoonoses

Hogs

see Livestock and livestock industry

Holahan, John

"Paying for Physician Services in State Medicaid Programs", 4652–1.410

Holcomb, Mary C.

"Transportation Energy Data Book: Edition 7", 3304–5

Holder, David L.

"Electronic Marketing Developments", 1004–16.1

Holder, Russ R.

"Residential Energy Costs for SOLCOST Data Bank Cities, Winter 1982-83", 3308–67

Holding companies

County Business Patterns: establishments, employees, and payrolls, by SIC 4-digit industry and county, 1982, annual State rpt series, 2326–6

Employment by detailed occupation, for 29 SIC 2-digit nonmanufacturing industries, 1981 BLS survey, 6748–60

Employment, earnings, and hours, by SIC 4-digit nonfarm industry, monthly 1974-Feb 1984, annual update, 6744–4

Income tax returns of corporations with foreign tax credit, income and deductions by type, asset size, and selected industry group, 1980, article, 8302–2.415

Income tax returns of partnerships, detailed data by industry, 1981 estimates, annual article, 8302–2.404

Income tax returns of partnerships, receipts by source, deductions by type, and establishments, by selected industry, 1982, annual article, 8302–2.416

Philanthropic foundations detailed financial and operating data, and stock holdings by instn, 1979 with selected trends from 1920, GAO rpt, 26119–53

Public utility holding company finances, securities issued, and subsidiaries by type, by firm, FY83, annual rpt, 9734–2.6

Telephone and telegraph firms intercorporate relationships, 1982, annual rpt, 9284–6.8

see also Bank holding companies

Holidays

see Vacations and holidays

Holik, Dan

"Taxpayers Age 65 or Over, 1977-81", 8302–2.412

Holland

see Netherlands

Holland, A. Steven

"Does Higher Inflation Lead to More Uncertain Inflation?", 9391–1.406

"Has the Deregulation of Deposit Interest Rates Raised Mortgage Rates?", 9391–1.412

Holland, David G.

"Forest Insect and Disease Conditions, Intermountain Region, 1983", 1206–11.3

Holliday, Mark C.

"Marine Recreational Fishery Statistics Survey, Pacific Coast, 1979-80", 2166–17.1

Hollinger, Richard C.

"Theft by Employees in Work Organizations, Executive Summary", 6068–178

Holloway, Thomas M.

"Cyclical Adjustment of the Federal Budget and Federal Debt", 2702–1.403

"Cyclical Adjustment of the Federal Budget and Federal Debt: Detailed Methodology and Estimates", 2706–5.31

"Economy and the Federal Budget: Guides to the Automatic Effects", 2702–1.427

"Measuring and Analyzing the Cyclically Adjusted Budget", 9373–3.27

Hollywood, Fla.

Census of Housing, 1980: occupancy and unit characteristics, by race, Hispanic origin, and city, SMSA rpt, 2473–1.160

Census of Population and Housing, 1980: detailed population and housing characteristics, by county, city, and census tract, SMSA rpt, 2551–2.160

Wages by occupation, and benefits for office and plant workers, 1984 labor market area survey rpt, 6785–3.3

see also under By City and By SMSA or MSA in the "Index by Categories"

Holmes, Douglas

"Differences Among Black, Hispanic, and White People in Knowledge About Long-Term Care Services", 4652–1.406

Holyoke, Mass.

Census of Housing, 1980: occupancy and unit characteristics, by race, Hispanic origin, and city, SMSA rpt, 2473–1.341

Census of Population and Housing, 1980: detailed population and housing characteristics, by county, city, and census tract, SMSA rpt, 2551–2.341

Housing and financial characteristics, and unit and neighborhood quality, for 15 SMSAs, 1978, annual survey special supplement, 2485–8

Home economics

Consumer goods prices and supplies, family finance, and home economics, quarterly rpt with articles, 1702–1

Degrees conferred in higher education, by race, Hispanic origin, sex, level, and field, selected years 1949/50-1979/80, annual rpt, 4824–2.16

Fed Govt educational grants, State allocations by program, type of recipient agency, and State, FY83, annual rpt, 4804–8

Teaching degrees conferred by specialty and State, required credit hours, and instn officials attitudes, by instn type, 1970s-83, hearings, 21348–89

Home health services

Home health services

Births attended by midwives and in nonhospital settings, by mother's sociodemographic and prenatal care characteristics and infant race and birthweight, 1978-79 with trends from 1935, 4147–21.40

Births, by birth weight, Apgar score, infant and mother characteristics, birthplace, and attendant, 1978, article, 4102–1.414

Govt census, 1982: State govt payments to local govts, by program, source of funds, level of govt, and State, with trends from 1902, 2460–3

Health Care Financing Review, Medicare and Medicaid program activity, health care expenditures, and research, quarterly rpt with articles, 4652–1

Israel, Tel Aviv Medical Center services and use, by patient age and condition, selected years 1976-83, article, 4102–1.445

Medicare admissions to hospitals and other facilities, and enrollee reimbursement claims, by beneficiary type, 1966-83, annual rpt, 4744–3.7

Medicare and Medicaid eligibility, participation, covered services and use, and reimbursements and payments, various periods 1966-82, annual rpt, 4654–1

Medicare claims approved, total charges, and reimbursements by type of service, from 1974, monthly rpt, quarterly data, 4742–1.11

Medicare end-stage renal disease dialysis, transplants by facility, donor organ costs, deaths by age, and hospitalization, by region, 1981, annual rpt, 4654–5.2

Medicare enrollment, reimbursement, and use and covered charges by type of service, by State and census div, 1978-82, 4658–8

Medicare facilities and services use, covered charges, and reimbursements, by beneficiary type and area of residence, series, 4656–1

Traffic accidents and casualties detailed direct and indirect costs, by characteristics of persons and vehicles involved, 1979-80, 7768–80

Veterans aged 55 and over, socioeconomic characteristics, economic resources, health care and status, and actual and expected use of VA benefits, 1983 survey, 9928–29

Home ownership

see Housing sales

see Housing tenure

Homemaker services

Employment, earnings, and hours, by SIC 4-digit nonfarm industry, monthly 1974-Feb 1984, annual update, 6744–4

Health care services for elderly, knowledge, use, and factors affecting service quality, by race and Hispanic origin, 1984 article, 4652–1.406

Older persons population characteristics, and needs and costs of social services by type, by metro-nonmetro status, 1970s-82 with trends from 1900, 21148–28

State govt social services spending by type and funding source, and admin of Fed Govt block grants, for 13 States, selected years FY80-84, GAO rpt, 26121–76

Temporary health care employees, reasons for desiring temporary and part-time work, and preferences for work time, by skill level, survey, 1984 article, 6722–1.452

Homesteads

HUD-acquired single family homes through mortgage default, and disposition, by city, monthly rpt, 5142–31

Public lands homestead entries and acreage, by State, FY83 and historical from 1862, annual rpt, 5724–1.2

Urban Homesteading Demonstration Program financing, and homesteading properties characteristics, by locality, FY83, annual rpt, 5124–5

Homicide

Bombing (explosive and incendiary) and arson incidents by target, State, and circumstances, and explosives theft and recovery, 1982-83, annual rpt, 8484–4

Central America socioeconomic and political conditions in 6 countries, 1960s-83 with trends and projections 1930-2010, Commission rpt, 028–19.2

Convictions, prison sentences, and average sentence lengths, by offense, offender class, and selected State, various periods 1971-84, 6066–19.10

Court cases, dispositions, convictions, and sentences of Federal criminal defendants, by offense and district, as of June 1983 with trends from 1945, annual rpt, 18204–1

Court criminal case disposition, effect of victim injury and other factors, and law enforcement official and victim attitudes, 1983 survey, 6068–185

Crime and criminal justice data, including justice expenditures and employment by level of govt, 1970s-82 with some trends from 1875, 6068–174

Crime Index by population size and region, and offenses known to police by large city, Jan-June 1984, semiannual rpt, 6222–1

Crimes, arrests by offender characteristics, and rates, by offense, and law enforcement employees, by population size and jurisdiction, 1970s-83, annual rpt, 6224–2

Criminal case processing from arrest to sentencing, cases and processing time by disposition, dismissal reason, and offense, for 14 cities, 1979, 6066–22.1

Death rates by sex, race, and age for 40 causes, projected for 10-year period, 1982 rpt, 4208–21

Deaths and death rates, by cause and age, provisional 1982-83, US Vital Statistics annual rpt, 4144–7

Deaths and death rates by detailed cause and demographic characteristics, 1979 and selected trends, US Vital Statistics annual rpt, 4144–2.1

Deaths and death rates, by detailed geographic area, cause, and demographic characteristics, 1979, US Vital Statistics annual rpt, 4144–3

Deaths and death rates, by selected cause and demographic characteristics, 1981, US Vital Statistics advance rpt, 4146–5.78

Deaths and death rates, by selected cause and demographic characteristics, 1982, US Vital Statistics advance rpt, 4146–5.81

Deaths and death rates from homicide, by location, circumstances, and victim characteristics, and years of life lost from homicide and other leading causes of death, 1970-78, 4205–38

Deaths by principal or contributing cause, with type of injury reported in accidental, poisoning, and violent deaths, by age, sex, and race, 1978, 4146–5.76

Economic indicators relation to measures of social pathology including crime and death rates, various periods 1950-80, 23848–76

El Salvador socioeconomic and political conditions, and US economic and military assistance, 1977-FY84, 7008–39

El Salvador terrorist acts against property, casualties, kidnappings, and hostages, Oct 1979-June 1983, human rights certification hearing, 21388–41

Executions since 1930, and prisoners under death sentence, by prisoner characteristics, region, and State, 1982, annual rpt, 6065–1

Health condition and health care resources, use, and expenditures, 1970s-82 with trends and projections 1900-2000, annual compilation, 4144–11

Homicides, by victim-offender relationship, 1982, 6066–19.5

Indian births, morbidity, and deaths and rates, and health services facilities and use, 1954-83, annual compilation, 4104–7

Infant deaths by detailed cause, geographic location, age, race, and sex, 1979, US Vital Statistics annual rpt, 4144–2.2

Law enforcement officer assaults, murders, and other deaths by circumstances, level of govt, agency, victim and offender characteristics, and location, 1983, annual rpt, 6224–3

Minnesota crime sentencing guidelines by type and severity of offense, 1982, 10048–59

Prison terms actually served by selected State, and Illinois pretrial detention time credited to sentence, by offense, various periods 1977-83, 6066–19.7

Prisoners in State prisons median sentence, and admissions and releases by prisoner and sentencing characteristics, by offense and State, 1981 and trends from 1926, 6066–19.9

Robbery rates and circumstances, medical costs and property losses of victims, and offender and victim characteristics, 1960s-81, 6068–180

Statistical Abstract of US, social, political, and economic data, 1950s-83 and trends, annual rpt, 2324–1.1

Terrorist (intl) incidents, casualties, and attacks on US targets, by attack type and world area, with chronology of events, 1983, annual rpt, 7004–13

Wiretapping authorizations by offense, costs, persons involved, arrests, trials, and convictions, 1983, annual rpt, 18204–7

Youth homicide and suicide rates, by sex, race, and circumstances, selected years 1970-79, and stress and violent behavior reduction goals for 1990, 4102–1.437

Honduras

Agricultural and food production indexes, and production of selected commodities, by world region and country, 1974-83, annual rpt, 1524–5

Index by Subjects and Names

Hong Kong

Agricultural situation in Latin America, by country, 1981-83 and outlook for 1984, annual rpt, 1524–4.9

Agricultural supply/demand and market for US exports, with socioeconomic indicators, selected years 1969-82 and projected to 1990, country rpt, 1526–6.3

Agricultural supply/demand, trade, and production, and socioeconomic data, by country, 1950s-77, 1528–179

AID activities and funding by project and function, FY85, and developing countries summary socioeconomic data, 1970s-83, by country, annual rpt, 9914–3

AID economic assistance to developing countries, obligations and disbursements by country, quarterly rpt, 9912–4

AID economic assistance to 7 Central American countries, by type of aid, FY80-83, GAO rpt, 26123–55

AID loan repayment status and terms by program and country, and status of predecessor agency loans, quarterly rpt, 9912–3

Background Notes, summary social, political, and economic data, 1984 rpt, 7006–2.57

Economic, social, and political conditions in 6 Central America countries, 1960s-83 with trends and projections 1930-2010, 028–19

Economic, social, and political summary data, by country, 1984, annual factbook, 244–11

Economic trends in income, production, prices, employment, finances, and trade, 1984 annual rpt, 2046–4.12, 2046–4.96

Exports of US, detailed Schedule B commodities by country of destination, 1983, annual rpt, 2424–9

Exports of US, detailed Schedule E commodities by mode of transport and world area and country of destination, 1983, annual rpts, 2424–5

Imports of US, detailed Schedule A commodities by country and world area of origin, and mode of transport, 1983, annual rpts, 2424–2

Imports of US, detailed TSUSA commodities by country of origin, 1983, annual rpt, 2424–4

Loans and grants for economic and military assistance from US and intl agencies, by program and country, FY46-83, annual rpt, 9914–5

Military aid of US, arms sales, and training programs costs and budget requests by program, world region, and country, FY83-85, annual rpt, 7144–13

Military spending, arms trade, and armed forces size, with total govt spending and population, by country, 1972-82, annual rpt, 9824–1

Minerals Yearbook, 1982, Vol 3: foreign country reviews of production, trade, and policies, by commodity, annual rpt, 5604–35

Minerals Yearbook, 1982, Vol 3 preprints: foreign country review of production, trade, and policies, by commodity, annual rpt, 5604–17.86

Natural resources and hazards to resource dev, with data on mineral, energy, and water resources, by Central American country, 1981 with trends from 1977, 5668–71

Population size and growth rates, and latest available benchmark demographic data, by country, 1950-83, biennial rpt, 2324–4

Refugees from Central America by country of origin and asylum, and aid from US and Mexico, FY82-1984, GAO rpt, 26123–70

see also under By Foreign Country in the "Index by Categories"

Honey and beekeeping

Agricultural Stabilization and Conservation Service honey program, 1950-84, annual fact sheet, 1806–4.7

Agricultural Statistics, 1983, annual rpt, 1004–1

Agriculture census, 1982: farms, farmland, production, finances, and operator characteristics, by county, final State rpt series, 2331–1

China economic conditions, agricultural and industrial production, trade, and domestic and foreign investment, 1980-85, 2048–106

Exports and imports of US, by detailed agricultural commodity and country, FY83 and CY83, semiannual rpts, 1522–4

Exports and imports of US, detailed SIC-based commodities by world area, 1983, annual rpts, 2424–6

Exports and imports of US, totals and as percent of domestic production, by SIC 2- to 5-digit commodity, 1981, annual rpt, 2424–3

Exports, imports, tariffs, and industry operating data for sugar, syrups, and honey, 1979-83, TSUSA commodity rpt, 9885–1.71

Exports of US, detailed commodities by country of destination, monthly rpt, 2422–3

Exports of US, detailed Schedule B commodities by country of destination, 1983, annual rpt, 2424–9

Exports of US, detailed Schedule E commodities by mode of transport and world area and country of destination, 1983, annual rpts, 2424–5

Foreign and US production, trade, and consumption, by country, FAS annual rpt series, 1925–14

Great Lakes trade, by SITC 3-digit commodity, port, vessel type, world area, and country, 1982, annual rpt, 7744–3

Imports of US, detailed Schedule A commodities by country and world area of origin, and mode of transport, 1983, annual rpts, 2424–2

Imports of US, detailed Schedule A commodities by country, monthly rpt, 2422–2

Imports of US, detailed TSUSA commodities by country of origin, 1983, annual rpt, 2424–4

Marketing cash receipts of farms, by detailed commodity and State, 1979-82, annual rpt, 1544–18

Production, prices, imports, and use, quarterly rpt, 1561–14.2

Production, prices, trade, stocks, and marketing of honey, and CCC loan activity and processing awards, weekly rpt, 1311–2

see also under By Commodity in the "Index by Categories"

Hong Kong

Agricultural imports of Hong Kong from US by detailed commodity, and import duties on wine and champagne, 1979-84, article, 1925–34.408

Agricultural situation in 4 East Asian countries, by commodity, 1983 and outlook for 1984, annual rpt, 1524–4.2

AID economic assistance to developing countries, obligations and disbursements by country, quarterly rpt, 9912–4

Background Notes, summary social, political, and economic data, 1983 rpt, 7006–2.5

China exports and imports, by commodity, world area, and country, quarterly rpt, 242–6

China trade and trade balances with world and major trading partners, and exports of selected commodities through Hong Kong by country of destination, quarterly rpt, 242–6.1

Computers and computer equipment market and trade, and user industry operations and demand, 1984 country market research rpt, 2045–1.44

Economic indicators of 12 Pacific Basin countries or areas and US, quarterly rpt, 9393–9

Economic, social, and political summary data, by country, 1984, annual factbook, 244–11

Economic trends in income, production, prices, employment, finances, and trade, 1984 semiannual rpt, 2046–4.24, 2046–4.81

Electronic component manufacturing equipment market and trade, and user industry operations and demand, 1979 country market research rpt, 2045–5.16

Exports and imports of US, by commodity and country, 1972-82, annual world region rpt, 244–13.5

Exports of US, detailed Schedule B commodities by country of destination, 1983, annual rpt, 2424–9

Exports of US, detailed Schedule E commodities by mode of transport and world area and country of destination, 1983, annual rpts, 2424–5

Farmland (US) owned by foreigners, acreage, value, and use, by State and county, and for 5 leading investor countries, 1983, annual rpt, 1584–3

Imports of US, detailed Schedule A commodities by country and world area of origin, and mode of transport, 1983, annual rpts, 2424–2

Imports of US, detailed TSUSA commodities by country of origin, 1983, annual rpt, 2424–4

Loans and grants for economic and military assistance from US and intl agencies, by program and country, FY46-83, annual rpt, 9914–5

Medical and health care equipment market and trade, and user industry operations and demand, 1984 country market research rpt, 2045–2.48

Minerals Yearbook, 1982, Vol 3: foreign country reviews of production, trade, and policies, by commodity, annual rpt, 5604–35

Minerals Yearbook, 1982, Vol 3 preprints: foreign country review of production, trade, and policies, by commodity, annual rpt, 5604–17.87

Hong Kong

Population size and growth rates, and latest available benchmark demographic data, by country, 1950-83, biennial rpt, 2324–4

see also under By Foreign Country in the "Index by Categories"

Honolulu, Hawaii

- Census of Housing, 1980: occupancy and unit characteristics, by race, Hispanic origin, and city, SMSA rpt, 2473–1.183
- Census of Population and Housing, 1980: detailed population and housing characteristics, by county, city, and census tract, SMSA rpt, 2551–2.183
- CPI by component for US city average, and by region, population size, and for 28 SMSAs, monthly press release, 6762–1
- CPI by detailed component, for US city average, 28 SMSAs, and 4 regions by population size, monthly rpt, 6762–2
- Housing and households detailed characteristics, and unit and neighborhood quality, by inside-outside central cities, 1979 survey, SMSA rpt, 2485–6.1
- Population size of top 25 cities, 1980 and 1982, press release, 2328–46
- *see also* under By City and By SMSA or MSA in the "Index by Categories"

Hooper, Peter

- "Current Account of the U.S., Japan, and Germany: A Cyclical Analysis", 9366–7.92
- "International Repercussions of the U.S. Budget Deficit", 9366–7.102

Hoover, Sally L.

"International Trends and Perspectives: Aging", 2546–10.12

Hopewell, Va.

- Census of Housing, 1980: occupancy and unit characteristics, by race, Hispanic origin, and city, SMSA rpt, 2473–1.282
- Census of Population and Housing, 1980: detailed population and housing characteristics, by county, city, and census tract, SMSA rpt, 2551–2.282

Hopkinsville, Ky.

- Census of Housing, 1980: occupancy and unit characteristics, by race, Hispanic origin, and city, SMSA rpt, 2473–1.122
- Census of Population and Housing, 1980: detailed population and housing characteristics, by county, city, and census tract, SMSA rpt, 2551–2.122
- Wages of office and plant workers, by occupation, 1984 labor market area survey rpt, 6785–3.4
- *see also* under By SMSA or MSA in the "Index by Categories"

Hops

- Acreage, yield, and production of field crops, by State, 1978-82 and preliminary 1983, 1641–7
- *Agricultural Statistics, 1983,* annual rpt, 1004–1
- Beer production, stocks, materials used, tax-free removals, and taxable removals by State, monthly rpt, 8486–1.1
- Exports and imports of US, by agricultural commodity and country, bimonthly rpt with articles, 1522–1
- Exports and imports of US, totals and as percent of domestic production, by SIC 2- to 5-digit commodity, 1981, annual rpt, 2424–3

Exports of US, detailed Schedule B commodities by country of destination, 1983, annual rpt, 2424–9

- Exports of US, detailed Schedule E commodities by mode of transport and world area and country of destination, 1983, annual rpts, 2424–5
- Farm finances, assets, liabilities, income, receipts by commodity and State, and expenses, 1980-83 and trends from 1910, annual rpt, 1544–16
- Foreign and US fresh and processed fruit, vegetable, and nut production and trade, FAS monthly rpt with articles, 1925–34
- Marketing cash receipts of farms, by detailed commodity and State, 1979-82, annual rpt, 1544–18
- Prices received by farmers and production value for detailed crops by State, 1981-83, annual rpt, 1621–2
- Production and farm finances, expenses by type, and domestic economic impact, selected years 1972-82 and preliminary 1983-84, annual rpt, 1544–19
- Production, farms, acreage, and related data, by selected crop and State, monthly rpt, 1621–1
- Production, stocks, and use of hops, and US trade by country, monthly rpt, 1313–7
- Stocks held by growers, dealers, and brewers, Sept 1984, semiannual release, 1621–8
- *see also* under By Commodity in the "Index by Categories"

Horn, Marjorie C.

"Use of Services for Family Planning and Infertility: U.S., 1982", 4146–8.104

Horowitz, Amy

"Social and Economic Incentives for Family Caregivers", 4652–1.403

Horrigan, Brian

- "Pitfalls in Analyzing Deficits and Inflation", 9387–8.86
- "Sizing Up the Deficit: An Efficient Tax Perspective", 9387–1.402

Horse racing

- County Business Patterns: establishments, employees, and payrolls, by SIC 4-digit industry and county, 1981, annual State rpt series, 2326–8
- County Business Patterns: establishments, employees, and payrolls, by SIC 4-digit industry and county, 1982, annual State rpt series, 2326–6
- Govt census, 1982: State govt payments to local govts, by program, source of funds, level of govt, and State, with trends from 1902, 2460–3
- Income (taxable) not reported, by illegal source, with characteristics of persons involved, methodology, and bibl, 1970s-82, 8008–112
- Income (taxable) not reported on individual and corporate returns, and associated Federal revenue losses, by detailed legal and illegal source, 1973-81, 8308–26
- Income tax returns of sole proprietorships, detailed data by industry div and selected industry group, 1981, annual rpt, 8304–7
- Income tax returns of sole proprietorships, receipts, deductions by type, payroll, and net income, by major industry, 1982, annual article, 8302–2.413
- Input-output structure of US economy, detailed interindustry transactions for 537 industries, and components of final demand, 1977 benchmark data, 2708–17

Index by Subjects and Names

- Service industry census, 1982: employment, establishments, receipts, and payroll, by SIC 2- to 4-digit kind of business, SMSA, county, and city, State rpt series, 2391–1
- State govt revenues by source, expenditures by function, debt, and holdings by type, FY83, annual rpt, 2466–2.5
- Taxation and revenue systems, by type of tax and system, level of govt, and State, selected years 1958-83, annual rpt, 10044–1.3

Horses

see Animals

see Horse racing

see Livestock and livestock industry

Horst, Thomas

"Consequences of Imposing the U.S. 30 Percent Withholding Tax on Interest Paid to or by Netherlands Antilles Finance Subsidiaries of U.S. Corporations", 21408–71

Horticulture

- Census of Population, 1980: detailed socioeconomic and demographic characteristics, by age, sex, race, Hispanic origin, occupation, and industry, State rpt series, 2531–4
- County Business Patterns: establishments, employees, and payrolls, by SIC 4-digit industry and county, 1981, annual State rpt series, 2326–8
- County Business Patterns: establishments, employees, and payrolls, by SIC 4-digit industry and county, 1982, annual State rpt series, 2326–6
- Imports of equipment, detailed TSUSA commodities by country of origin, 1983, annual rpt, 2424–4
- Income tax returns of sole proprietorships, detailed data by industry div and selected industry group, 1981, annual rpt, 8304–7
- R&D in botany and other plant sciences at higher education instns, funding by source, grad students, and staff, 1983, 9626–2.143
- Science and engineering doctoral degree recipients, by field, sex, race, age, citizenship, postgrad employment and study status, State, and instn, 1960-82, 9626–6.16
- *see also* Flowers and nursery products

Hosiery

see Clothing and clothing industry

Hoskin, Roger

"Domestic Soybean Outlook", 1004–16.1

Hospital administration and staff

see Health facilities administration

Hospital Insurance Trust Fund

see Federal trust funds

Hospitalization

- Alcohol-related hospital discharges, by diagnosis and patient age, for Indian Health Service facilities and total US, 1981, 4488–4
- Army personnel health status, and use of Army medical services in US and abroad by personnel, retirees, and dependents, monthly rpt, 3702–4
- Births and birth rates, by demographic and birth characteristics, 1981 with trends from 1940, US Vital Statistics advance rpt, 4146–5.73
- Births and birth rates, by parent and birth characteristics and infant condition at birth, 1982 and trends from 1940, US Vital Statistics annual advance rpt, 4146–5.79

Index by Subjects and Names

Hospitalization

Births attended by midwives and in nonhospital settings, by mother's sociodemographic and prenatal care characteristics and infant race and birthweight, 1978-79 with trends from 1935, 4147–21.40

Births, proportion inside-outside hospital and with physician or midwife attending, 1940-79, US Vital Statistics annual rpt, 4144–1

Canada and US hospital use by children by Canada Province and US region, and death rates, by diagnosis and sex, selected years 1977-79, 4147–5.1

Cancer incidence, deaths, patient median age and 5-year survival rates, and 1st stay hospital days, by body site, selected years 1945-83, article, 4102–1.448

Consumer products use and related activity, injuries and deaths by selected product and victim age and sex, quarterly rpt, 9164–7

Consumer products use, injuries and deaths by product, victim age, and medical treatment status, 1982, annual rpt, 9164–6

Costs and use of hospitals, data compilation project analyses, series, 4186–6

Crime victimization rates by type of offense, and victim and offense characteristics, Natl Crime Survey series, 6066–3

Criminal case disposition, effect of victim injury and other factors, and law enforcement official and victim attitudes, 1983 survey, 6068–185

Discharges and length of hospital stay of aged and non-aged persons, by region, facility size, and diagnosis, 1981, 4146–8.98

Discharges and length of stay, by patient age and sex, facility size and ownership, procedure performed, and region, 1983, 4146–8.101

Discharges and length of stay, by patient characteristics, facility size, procedure performed, diagnosis, and region, 1982, annual rpt, 4147–13.78

Discharges from hospitals and length of stay, by patient age and sex, facility size and ownership, procedure performed, and region, 1982, 4146–8.96

DOD Civilian Health and Medical Program of the Uniformed Services costs and operations, FY83-84 with trends from FY79, semiannual rpt, 3502–2

Foreign and US health care resources, use, and per capita public expenditures, and selected population characteristics, for 7 countries, selected years 1975-81, 21148–33

Health Care Financing Review, Medicare and Medicaid program activity, health care expenditures, and research, quarterly rpt with articles, 4652–1

Health condition and health care resources, use, and expenditures, 1970s-82 with trends and projections 1900-2000, annual compilation, 4144–11

Health maintenance organizations and prepaid health plans enrollment, use, and Fed Govt aid, FY83, annual rpt, 4104–8

Health maintenance organizations enrollment (total, Medicare, and Medicaid), finances, Fed Govt qualification status, and PHS loan activity, by HMO, FY83, annual rpt, 4044–2

Heart, Lung, and Blood Natl Inst activities and funding, with morbidity and mortality data, various periods 1940-88, annual rpt, 4474–22

Hispanic Americans births and birth and fertility rates, by detailed Hispanic origin, characteristics of mother, birth, and prenatal care, and for 22 States, 1981, 4146–5.80

Hispanic Americans health services use, illness rates, and disability days, by socieconomic characteristics, and compared to blacks and whites, 1978-80, 4147–10.147

Hospitals and nursing homes, employees, and use, by ownership, bed size, region, and State, selected years 1969-80, 4147–14.30

Indian births, morbidity, and deaths and rates, and health services facilities and use, 1954-83, annual compilation, 4104–7

Indian Health Service hospital admissions, discharges, births, total and occupied beds, length of stay, and outpatient visits, by area and facility, quarterly rpt, 4102–3

Inpatient episodes and bed days per capita, by age, metro-nonmetro location, region, and selected SMSA, 1980-81, 4147–10.146

Israel, Tel Aviv Medical Center services and use, by patient age and condition, selected years 1976-83, article, 4102–1.445

Medicare admissions to hospitals and other facilities, and enrollee reimbursement claims, by beneficiary type, 1966-83, annual rpt, 4744–3.7

Medicare and Medicaid eligibility, participation, covered services and use, and reimbursements and payments, various periods 1966-82, annual rpt, 4654–1

Medicare claims approved, total charges, and reimbursements by type of service, from 1974, monthly rpt, quarterly data, 4742–1.11

Medicare coverage of new medical technologies and reimbursements, and health services use and costs, selected years 1966-82, 26358–106

Medicare end-stage renal disease dialysis, transplants by facility, donor organ costs, deaths by age, and hospitalization, by region, 1981, annual rpt, 4654–5.2

Medicare enrollment, reimbursement, and use and covered charges by type of service, by State and census div, 1978-82, 4658–8

Medicare facilities and services use, covered charges, and reimbursements, by beneficiary type and area of residence, series, 4656–1

Mental health facilities, services, and costs in DC, and effect of St Elizabeths Hospital operations and finances transfer to DC govt, FY83, GAO rpt, 26121–72

Mental health facilities, services, staff, and patient characteristics, *Statistical Notes* series, 4506–3

Mental health facilities, services, staff, and patient characteristics, 1970s-82 with trends from 1954, annual rpt, 4504–9

Mental hospitals of States and counties, patients and admissions by diagnosis, age, and State, FY81, annual rpt, 4504–2

Military medical facilities of DOD in US and abroad, admissions, beds, outpatient visits, and live births, by service branch, quarterly rpt, 3542–15

Navy and Marine Corps disease incidence, medical care, and deaths, by detailed diagnosis, and medical personnel and workloads, 1978-79, annual rpt, 3804–1

Navy medical facility use by active and retired military personnel, dependents, and others, by facility and type, quarterly rpt, 3802–1

Older persons by demographic, socioeconomic, and health characteristics, selected years 1900-81 and projected to 2050, Current Population Rpt, 2546–2.125

Older persons nutrition services program operations and assessment, and participant sociodemographic, health, and diet characteristics, 1976 and 1982, 4608–16

Older persons sociodemographic characteristics, and Fed Govt program participation and funding, 1983 with trends and projections 1900-2060, annual rpt, 25144–3.1

Robbery rates and circumstances, medical costs and property losses of victims, and offender and victim characteristics, 1960s-81, 6068–180

Supplementary Security Income beneficiary socioeconomic characteristics and health service use, 1970s-83 and SSI program projections to 1995, 25148–29

Traffic accidents and casualties detailed direct and indirect costs, by characteristics of persons and vehicles involved, 1979-80, 7768–80

Traffic accidents, circumstances, injuries, deaths, and characteristics of persons and vehicles involved, 1982, annual rpt, 7764–13

TTPI socioeconomic, health, and govtl data, by TTPI govt, FY83 and selected trends, detailed annual rpt, 7004–6

Tuberculosis cases, deaths, and treatment, by demographic characteristics, State, and city, 1982 and trends from 1953, annual rpt, 4204–2

VA patients in VA and non-VA medical, nursing home, and domiciliary care facilities, FY59-83, annual rpt, 9924–13.3

VA programs and activities, and veterans characteristics, FY83, annual rpt, 9924–1

Veterans aged 55 and over, socioeconomic characteristics, economic resources, health care and status, and actual and expected use of VA benefits, 1983 survey, 9928–29

Veterans and nonveterans health condition, and veteran use of VA and non-VA hospitals by disease, by age, race, income, and metro-nonmetro location, various periods 1971-81, 9926–1.18

Veterans health care, patients, visits, costs, and operating beds, by district and individual VA and contract facility, monthly rpt, 9922–5

Veterans of Vietnam era in VA hospitals, various periods FY68-83, annual rpt, 9924–8.4

Workers compensation benefits under each State and Federal program by payment source, and State and black lung benefits by type, 1979-81, article, 4742–1.409

Hospitalization insurance

Hospitalization insurance
see Health insurance

Hospitals

- Abortions (legal), and deaths from abortion and childbirth, by medical and sociodemographic characteristics, 1972-83, hearings, 21368–47
- Alcohol, Drug Abuse, and Mental Health Admin research grants, awards, and fellowships by recipient, FY83, annual listing, 4044–13
- Allergy and Infectious Diseases Natl Inst activities, grants by instn, State, and country, and disease incidence and costs, FY60s-84, annual rpt, 4474–30
- American Samoa minimum wage rates, employment, earnings, and benefits, by establishment and industry, Nov 1983, biennial rpt, 6504–6
- Arizona hospitals and nursing homes, finances and operations for specified facilities, and itemized expenses for selected cases, 1978-83, hearing, 21148–29
- Births, by birth weight, Apgar score, infant and mother characteristics, birthplace, and attendant, 1978, article, 4102–1.414
- Bond tax-exempt issues by purpose, and Fed Govt mortgage bond revenue losses and borrower characteristics, selected years 1971-85, hearings, 21788–135
- Bond tax-exempt issues for public and private purposes, by use of proceeds, 1975-83, article, 9362–1.408
- Capital (fixed), govt and private nonresidential structures and equipment, residential capital, and consumer-owned durable goods by item, 1980-83, annual article, 2702–1.433
- Capital needs and intergovtl financing for public works, by type of project and selected city, various periods 1950-83, 10048–60
- Census of Population, 1980: detailed socioeconomic and demographic characteristics, by age, sex, race, Hispanic origin, occupation, and industry, State rpt series, 2531–4
- Census of Population, 1980: detailed socioeconomic characteristics, by county, city, and inside-outside SMSAs and central cities, State rpt series, 2531–3
- Coastal environmental characteristics, fish, wildlife, and use, and population socioeconomic data, for individual areas, series, 5506–4
- Computer specialists sociodemographic, educational, and employment characteristics, and Fed Govt support by agency, 1978, biennial Current Population Rpt, 2546–2.124
- Construction grants, loans, and loan guarantees of Fed Govt, by program and type of structure, FY80-83 and estimated FY84-85, annual article, 2012–1.404
- Construction industries census, 1982: financial and operating data, by SIC 4-digit industry and State, final rpt series, 2373–1
- Construction industries census, 1982: financial and operating data, by SIC 4-digit industry and State, preliminary rpt series, 2371–1
- Construction put in place, permits authorized by region, State, and MSA,

and Federal contract awards, by construction type, bimonthly rpt with articles, 2012–1

- Construction put in place, value of new public and private structures, by type, monthly rpt, 2382–4
- Cost measurement for hospital reimbursement, alternative methods including classification of disease severity, 1984 articles, 4652–1.425, 4652–1.426, 4652–1.427, 4652–1.428
- Costs and use of hospitals, data compilation project analyses, series, 4186–6
- *County and City Data Book,* detailed socioeconomic and demographic data for States, counties, and cities, selected years 1976-82, 2328–1
- County Business Patterns: establishments, employees, and payrolls, by SIC 4-digit industry and county, 1981, annual State rpt series, 2326–8
- County Business Patterns: establishments, employees, and payrolls, by SIC 4-digit industry and county, 1982, annual State rpt series, 2326–6
- Dental Research Natl Inst research and training funds awarded, by recipient instn, FY83, annual listing, 4474–19
- Discharges from hospitals and nursing homes, by age, sex, marital status, and selected diagnosis, 1976 and 1979, article, 4102–1.443
- DOD Civilian Health and Medical Program of the Uniformed Services costs and operations, FY83-84 with trends from FY79, semiannual rpt, 3502–2
- Drug (prescription) use by outpatient characteristics and generic or brand name, and hospital and drugstore costs by drug class, 1982, annual rpt, 4064–12
- Employee theft and misconduct in retail, hospital, and manufacturing establishments, by type and frequency of violation, 1978-80, 6068–178
- Employment and earnings in philanthropic organizations by organization type, and compared to other nonprofit organizations, selected years 1972-82, article, 6722–1.455
- Employment by detailed occupation, for 29 SIC 2-digit nonmanufacturing industries, 1981 BLS survey, 6748–60
- Employment, earnings, and hours, by selected SIC 1- to 4-digit industry, State, and for 278 major labor areas, 1939-83, annual rpt, 6744–5
- Employment, earnings, and hours, by SIC 4-digit nonfarm industry, monthly 1974-Feb 1984, annual update, 6744–4
- Employment, vacancies, and vacancy rates, by occupation and by hospital specialty, region, census div, and State, 1980, annual rpt, 4114–12
- Energy conservation grants of Fed Govt to public and nonprofit private instns, by building type and State, 1983, annual rpt, 3304–15
- Energy use in nonresidential buildings, expenditures, and conservation, by building characteristics, EIA survey series, 3166–8
- Facilities, employees, and use of general and specialty hospitals and nursing homes, by ownership, bed size, region, and State, selected years 1969-80, 4147–14.30

Index by Subjects and Names

- Fed Govt programs and mgmt cost control proposals, 3-year savings by function and agency, and financial and operating data, 1960s-81, 16908–1.7, 16908–1.24
- Govt census, 1982: city govt revenues by source, expenditures by function, debt, and assets, by State and city, 2457–4
- Govt census, 1982: county govt revenues by source, expenditures by function, debt, and assets, by State and county, 2457–3
- Govt census, 1982: employment, payrolls, and average earnings, by function, level of govt, State, county, population size, and inside-outside SMSAs, 2455–2
- Govt census, 1982: local govt employment by function, payroll, and average earnings, for individual counties, cities, and school and special districts, 2455–1
- Govt employment and payroll, by function, level of govt, and jurisdiction, 1983, annual rpt series, 2466–1
- Govt finances, by level of govt and State, selected years 1929-83, annual rpt, 10044–1
- Govt finances, by level of govt, State, and for large cities and counties, 1981-83, annual rpt series, 2466–2
- *Health Care Financing Review,* Medicare and Medicaid program activity, health care expenditures, and research, quarterly rpt with articles, 4652–1
- Health condition and health care resources, use, and expenditures, 1970s-82 with trends and projections 1900-2000, annual compilation, 4144–11
- Health facilities and manpower use, by patient and facility characteristics, Vital and Health Statistics series, 4147–13
- Income tax returns of corporations, detailed income and tax items by industry, 1981, annual rpt, 8304–4
- Income tax returns of sole proprietorships, detailed data by industry div and selected industry group, 1981, annual rpt, 8304–7
- Income tax returns of sole proprietorships, receipts, deductions by type, payroll, and net income, by major industry, 1982, annual article, 8302–2.413
- Indian and Alaska Native health program activities, and funding for scholarships, care services, and facilities construction, by city, FY82, annual rpt, 4104–11
- Indian births, morbidity, and deaths and rates, and health services facilities and use, 1954-83, annual compilation, 4104–7
- Indian Health Service hospital admissions, discharges, births, total and occupied beds, length of stay, and outpatient visits, by area and facility, quarterly rpt, 4102–3
- Infections (hospital-related), drug resistance, and associated deaths, for teaching and non-teaching hospitals, 1980-82, article, 4202–7.401
- Input-output structure of US economy, detailed interindustry transactions for 537 industries, and components of final demand, 1977 benchmark data, 2708–17
- Israel, Tel Aviv Medical Center services and use, by patient age and condition, selected years 1976-83, article, 4102–1.445
- Manpower supply and education of health professionals, by occupation, demographic and professional characteristics, and location, 1950s-83 and projected to 2000, biennial rpt, 4114–8

Index by Subjects and Names

Hotels and motels

Medicare admissions to hospitals and other facilities, and enrollee reimbursement claims, by beneficiary type, 1966-83, annual rpt, 4744–3.7

Medicare and Medicaid capital cost reimbursements to Hospital Corp of America following acquisition of Hospital Affiliates Intl, 1981-82, GAO rpt, 26121–65

Medicare enrollment, reimbursement, and use and covered charges by type of service, by State and census div, 1978-82, 4658–8

Medicare-participating facilities by control, beds, and terminated facilities, by facility type, region, and State, 1975-81, 4656–1.19

Minority group and women employment, by occupational group and SIC 2- to 3-digit industry, 1981, annual rpt, 9244–1.1

Neighborhood and housing quality indicators and attitudes, and occupant characteristics, by urban-rural location and region, 1981, annual survey, 2485–7

Neighborhood and housing quality indicators and attitudes, by occupant and unit characteristics, region, and metro-nonmetro location, 1981, annual survey, 2485–2

NIH grants and awards for R&D, training, construction, and medical libraries, by location and recipient, FY83, annual listings, 4434–7

Occupational injury and illness rates, by SIC 2- to 4-digit industry, 1982, annual rpt, 6844–1

Pharmacists employment and sociodemographic characteristics, and reasons for not working in field, by State and overseas, as of 1979, 4147–14.28

Physicians (not office-based) visits by reason, diagnosis, treatment, patient and physician characteristics, and physician primary activity, 1980, 4147–13.77

R&D and science-related Fed Govt funding to higher education and nonprofit instns, by field, instn, agency, and State, FY82, annual rpt, 9627–17

Research activities and grants of HCFA by research area, as of June 1984, semiannual listing, 4652–8

Southeastern States financial and economic devs, Fed Reserve 6th District, monthly rpt with articles, 9371–1

Southeastern States health care resource availability, and employment by occupation, by facility type, by State and SMSA in Fed Reserve 6th District, 1970s-81, article, 9371–1.425

Transit system (automated guideway) characteristics and itemized costs, for 16 systems in operation or under construction, 1982, annual rpt, 7884–6

TTPI socioeconomic, health, and govtl data, by TTPI govt, FY83 and selected trends, detailed annual rpt, 7004–6

Wages of hospital workers by sex and occupation, and benefits, for 22 MSAs, Oct 1981 survey, 6787–6.201

see also American Schools and Hospitals Abroad

see also Clinics

see also Emergency medical service

see also Health facilities administration

see also Health maintenance organizations

see also Hospitalization

see also Mental health facilities and services

see also Military hospitals

see also Nurses and nursing

see also Nursing homes

see also Veterans health facilities and services

Hostages

El Salvador terrorist acts against property, casualties, kidnappings, and hostages, Oct 1979-June 1983, human rights certification hearing, 21388–41

Terrorist (intl) incidents, casualties, and attacks on US targets, by attack type and world area, with chronology of events, 1983, annual rpt, 7004–13

Hostetler, John

"Energy and Irrigation", 1561–16.406

Hotels and motels

American Samoa minimum wage rates, employment, earnings, and benefits, by establishment and industry, Nov 1983, biennial rpt, 6504–6

Army morale, welfare, and recreation programs, revenue and expenses worldwide by activity and major command, FY82-83, annual rpt, 3704–12

Bombing (explosive and incendiary) incidents, damage, injuries, and deaths, by target, State, and circumstances, 1983, annual rpt, 6224–5

Business statistics, detailed data for major industries and economic indicators, *Survey of Current Business,* monthly rpt, 2702–1.8

Census of Population, 1980: detailed socioeconomic and demographic characteristics, by age, sex, race, Hispanic origin, occupation, and industry, State rpt series, 2531–4

Census of Service Industries, 1982: employment, establishments, receipts, and payroll, by SIC 2- to 4-digit kind of business, SMSA, county, and city, State rpt series, 2391–1

Census of Service Industries, 1982: employment, establishments, receipts, and payroll, by SIC 4-digit kind of business and State, preliminary rpt, 2390–2.1

Collective bargaining agreements expiring during year, covered workers by SIC 2-digit industry, firm, and union, with summary of key provisions, 1984, annual rpt, 6784–9

Construction put in place, permits authorized by region, State, and MSA, and Federal contract awards, by construction type, bimonthly rpt with articles, 2012–1

County Business Patterns: establishments, employees, and payrolls, by SIC 4-digit industry and county, 1981, annual State rpt series, 2326–8

County Business Patterns: establishments, employees, and payrolls, by SIC 4-digit industry and county, 1982, annual State rpt series, 2326–6

Earnings by major industry group, and personal income per capita and by source, by region and State, 1929-82, 2708–40

Employment by detailed occupation, for 29 SIC 2-digit nonmanufacturing industries, 1981 BLS survey, 6748–60

Employment, earnings, and hours, by selected SIC 1- to 4-digit industry, State, and for 278 major labor areas, 1939-83, annual rpt, 6744–5

Employment, earnings, and hours, by SIC 4-digit nonfarm industry, monthly 1974-Feb 1984, annual update, 6744–4

Energy use in nonresidential buildings, expenditures, and conservation, by building characteristics, EIA survey series, 3166–8

Fed Govt employee travel expenses for official business trips, and reimbursement rates, for high rate cities, 1983, annual rpt, 9454–16

Finances and operations, by SIC 2- to 4-digit industry, 1970s-83 and projected to 1988, annual rpt, 2014–4

France Brittany coast oil spill cleanup and research costs, marine and tourism industry losses, and recreation losses of tourists and residents, 1971-79, 2178–13

Franchise business opportunities, by firm and kind of business, 1984 annual listing, 2044–27

Franchises of firms engaged in distribution of goods and services by kind of business, establishments by State, and sales, 1982-84, annual rpt, 2014–5

Howard Inn owned by Howard University, expenditures, revenues, and deficit, June 1982-83, GAO rpt, 26121–74

Income tax returns of corporations, detailed income and tax items by industry, 1981, annual rpt, 8304–4

Income tax returns of corporations with foreign tax credit, income and deductions by type, asset size, and selected industry group, 1980, article, 8302–2.415

Income tax returns of partnerships, detailed data by industry, 1981 estimates, annual article, 8302–2.404

Income tax returns of partnerships, receipts by source, deductions by type, and establishments, by selected industry, 1982, annual article, 8302–2.416

Income tax returns of sole proprietorships, detailed data by industry div and selected industry group, 1981, annual rpt, 8304–7

Income tax returns of sole proprietorships, receipts, deductions by type, payroll, and net income, by major industry, 1982, annual article, 8302–2.413

Income tax returns with investment credits, for individuals by income, and for sole proprietorships by industry, 1981, article, 8302–2.409

Input-output structure of US economy, detailed interindustry transactions for 85 industries, and components of final demand, 1977, article, 2702–1.421

Input-output structure of US economy, detailed interindustry transactions for 537 industries, and components of final demand, 1977 benchmark data, 2708–17

Minority group and women employment, by occupational group and SIC 2- to 3-digit industry, 1981, annual rpt, 9244–1.1

Occupational injury and illness rates, by SIC 2- to 4-digit industry, 1982, annual rpt, 6844–1

Occupational manpower needs and supply by detailed occupation, and educational and training program enrollees and grads by detailed field, 1982 and 1995, biennial rpt, 6744–3

Hotels and motels

Occupational Outlook Handbook, 1984-85 biennial rpt, 6744–1

Productivity, hours, and employment indexes for selected SIC 3- and 4-digit industries, 1954-82, annual rpt, 6824–1.4

Receipts for selected services, by SIC 2- to 4-digit kind of business, 1983, annual rpt, 2413–8

Recreation fees at State outdoor facilities, visits, revenue, costs, and employee salaries, by State, 1982/83, annual rpt, 5544–14.4

Tax evasion through tax haven countries, with income, investments, and taxes withheld by country, various periods 1975- 83, hearings, 21408–71

Virgin Islands economic censuses, 1982: employment, establishments, payroll, and receipts, by SIC 1- to 4-digit industry, island, and city, 2593–1

Waterborne disease outbreaks and cases, by type, source, and location, 1983, annual rpt, 4205–35

see also under By Industry in the "Index by Categories"

Houma, La.

Housing vacancy rates for single and multifamily units and mobile homes, by city and ZIP code, 1984, annual metro area rpt, 9304–19.20

see also under By SMSA or MSA in the "Index by Categories"

Hours of labor

- AFDC eligibility under Omnibus Budget Reconciliation Act, effect on caseloads and recipient benefits and living costs, 1981-83, GAO rpt, 26131–11
- Agriculture census, 1982: farms, farmland, production, finances, and operator characteristics, by county, final State rpt series, 2331–1
- Auto export voluntary restraint of Japan, effect on US auto industry and import sales and prices, 2nd qtr 1981-1st qtr 1984, article, 9377–1.407
- Business and financial statistics, historic trends, 1984 annual chartbook, 9364–2.2
- *Business Conditions Digest,* cyclical indicators, by economic process, monthly rpt, 2702–3.3
- *Business Conditions Digest,* historical supplement on economic, business, and financial conditions and cyclical fluctuations, with methodology, 1947-82, 2708–31
- Census of Population, 1980: detailed socioeconomic and demographic characteristics, by age, sex, race, Hispanic origin, occupation, and industry, State rpt series, 2531–4
- Coal mines and related operations, injury, employment, worktime, and productivity data, 1982, annual rpt, 6664–4
- Construction industries census, 1982: financial and operating data, by SIC 4-digit industry and State, final rpt series, 2373–1
- Construction industries census, 1982: financial and operating data, by SIC 4-digit industry and State, preliminary rpt series, 2371–1
- Construction industry total and female workers, and construction worker earnings and hours, by selected SIC 2- to 3-digit industry, bimonthly rpt, 2012–1.7

Index by Subjects and Names

Cooling and heating equipment industry productivity trends and technological innovations, 1967-82, article, 6722–1.471

Dallas-Fort Worth, Tex, SMSA employment, earnings, hours, and CPI changes, 1983 with trends from 1968, annual rpt, 6964–2

Denver-Boulder, Colo, SMSA employment, earnings, and CPI changes, 1983, annual rpt, 6974–2

DOD contract and in-house commercial activities costs and work-years, by service branch, defense agency, State, and installation, FY83, annual rpt, 3544–25

DOD-owned manufacturing and R&D facilities, operating data by selected SIC 2- to 3-digit industry, State, and SMSA, 1982, annual Current Industrial Rpt, 2506–3.4

Economic indicators and components, current data and annual trends, monthly rpt, 23842–1.2

Employee benefits in private industry, coverage by benefit type and provisions and occupational group, 1983, annual rpt, 6784–19

Employment and earnings, detailed data, monthly rpt, 6742–2.3, 6742–2.6

Employment and economic conditions, alternative BLS projections to 1995 with selected trends for 1959-82, 6728–29

Employment and labor force statistics by major industry group and demographic characteristics, *Survey of Current Business,* monthly rpt, 2702–1.5

Employment, earnings, and hours, by selected SIC 1- to 4-digit industry, State, and for 278 major labor areas, 1939-83, annual rpt, 6744–5

Employment, earnings, and hours, by SIC 4-digit nonfarm industry, monthly 1974-Feb 1984, annual update, 6744–4

Employment, earnings, and hours, monthly press release, 6742–5

Employment situation, earnings, hours, and other BLS economic indicators, transcripts of BLS Commissioner's monthly testimony, periodic rpt, 23846–4

Farm labor, wages, hours, and perquisites, by State, quarterly rpt, 1631–1

Farm production inputs, outputs, and productivity, by region, 1939-82, annual rpt, 1544–17

Fed Govt classified info security clearances of Govt and contractor employees, polygraph use, and prepublication reviews, by agency, 1979-83, GAO rpt, 26123–66

Fed Govt employees labor contract negotiations, costs, time spent, and negotiator attitudes, 1983 survey, GAO rpt, 26119–62

Fed Govt programs and mgmt cost control proposals, 3-year savings by function and agency, and financial and operating data, 1960s-81, 16908–1

Foreign manufacturing labor productivity and unit cost indexes for US and 11 OECD countries, 1960-82, annual article, 6722–1.405

Foreign trade zones operations and economic effects, with data on merchandise shipments, value added, employment, hours, and customs revenue, 1978-83, 9886–4.70

Health and productivity effects of rotating work schedules, 1983 bibl, 7506–10.29

High school classes of 1980 and 1982: educational and sociodemographic characteristics and expectations, natl longitudinal study, series, 4826–2

Hours and earnings, by industry div and major manufacturing group, Monthly Labor Review, 6722–1.3

Hours and earnings, selected nonfarm industries, 1947-83, annual rpt, 204–1.2

Hours at work and hours paid ratios and impacts on productivity measures, by firm size and major industry group, with survey methodology, 1981-82, article, 6722–1.434

Hours, by industry div, major industry group, and State, selected years 1932-82, annual rpt, 6724–1.3

Houston, Tex, SMSA employment, earnings, hours, and CPI changes, 1983 with trends from 1968, annual rpt, 6964–1

Import and tariff provisions effect on US industries and products, investigations with background financial and operating data, series, 9886–4

Imports from Communist countries, injury to US industries, investigations with background financial and operating data, selected industries and products, series, 9886–12

Imports injury to US industries from foreign subsidized products and sales in US at less than fair value, investigations with background financial and operating data, series, 9886–19

Imports injury to US industries from foreign subsidized products, investigations with background financial and operating data for selected industries and products, series, 9886–15

Imports injury to US industries from import sales at less than fair value, investigations with background financial and operating data, series, 9886–14

Imports injury to US industries from increased import sales, investigations with background financial and operating data, series, 9886–5

Imports injury to US industries from removal of duties on foreign subsidized products, investigations with background financial and operating data, series, 9886–18

Income assistance, effects of experimental negative income tax program on employment, earnings, marital status, and other family characteristics in 2 cities, 1970-75, 4008–64

Income of households, families, and persons, by detailed socioeconomic characteristics and region, 1982, annual Current Population Rpt, 2546–6.39

Industry R&D expenditures by funding source, and projected impact on output, employment, and hours of labor, by selected industry, various periods 1953-90, hearings, 25368–133

Kansas City, Mo-Kans, SMSA employment, earnings, and CPI changes, with comparisons to total US, 1983, annual rpt, 6974–1

Libraries of colleges and universities, expenditures, holdings by type, use, staff by sex, and Federal grants received, 1979-82, biennial rpt, 4854–1

Index by Subjects and Names

Hours of labor

Manufacturing census, 1982: financial and operating data, by SIC 2- to 4-digit industry, State, SMSA, and county, preliminary census div rpt series, 2491–3

Manufacturing census, 1982: financial and operating data, for SIC 4-digit industries by product, preliminary rpt series, 2491–1

Manufacturing computerized automation dev, R&D, training, and employment impacts, with comparisons to foreign countries, selected years 1960-83, 26358–105

Manufacturing employment, unemployment, hours, and women's employment, for all durables and for 5 metals industries, 1979-82, article, 6722–1.410

Manufacturing hours and earnings, by State and selected area, 1981-83, article, 6742–2.408

Meatpacking and prepared meats industry productivity trends and technological innovations, 1967-82, article, 6722–1.428

Metal mines and related operations, injury, employment, and worktime data, 1982, annual rpt, 6664–3

Mineral industries census, 1982: financial and operating data, by SIC 2- to 4-digit industry and State, preliminary summary rpts, 2511–2

Mineral industries census, 1982: financial and operating data, including materials consumed, by SIC 4-digit industry and State, preliminary rpt series, 2511–1

Minerals (nonmetallic) mining and related operations injury, employment, and worktime data, 1982, annual rpt, 6664–1

Mines (sand and gravel) and related operations, injury, employment, and worktime data, 1982, annual rpt, 6664–2

Mines (stone) and related operations, injury, employment, and worktime data, 1982, annual rpt, 6664–5

Mines, mills, and quarries occupational injuries, and employees and hours, by State, quarterly rpt, 6662–1

Misconduct and theft by employees in retail, hospital, and manufacturing establishments, by type and frequency of violation, 1978-80, 6068–178

Motor carrier safety inspections by Fed Hwy Admin, audits of driver qualification and vehicle operation records, and violations cited, 1982, annual rpt, 7554–38.2

Motor carrier safety inspections on interstate hwys, violations cited, and vehicles and drivers ordered out of service, 1982, annual rpt, 7554–35

Motor carrier safety inspections on interstate hwys, violations cited, and vehicles and drivers ordered out of service, May 1983, semiannual rpt, 7552–15

Motorcycle imports, sales, and inventories of foreign make, and prices and employment for domestic makes, quarterly rpt, 9882–12

New England States economic indicators, Fed Reserve 1st District, monthly rpt, 9373–2.2

New England States employment, wages, and price conditions by State and selected SMSA, 1983, annual rpt, 6916–7.1

NYC metro area small business owners and accountants, assessment of economy, professional activities, and community problems, by county and industry div, 1983 survey, hearings, 21728–52.3

Occupational injuries and illnesses, incidence rates by employment size and industry, workdays lost, and deaths, 1980-81, annual rpt, 6604–2.2

Pharmacists employment and sociodemographic characteristics, and reasons for not working in field, by State and overseas, as of 1979, 4147–14.28

Physicians employed in prisons by sociodemographic, employment, and professional characteristics, and compared to all physicians, 1979, article, 4102–1.407

Poverty-level persons and families, by income source, hours of work, earnings, taxes, and family characteristics, various periods 1959-84, 21788–131

Poverty status of families and persons, by detailed socioeconomic characteristics, 1982, annual Current Population Rpt, 2546–6.40

Poverty status of young adults related to motivation, psychological factors, and family characteristics, by race and sex, 1970s-82, longitudinal studies, 4008–65

Productivity and costs of labor for private, nonfarm business, and manufacturing sectors, preliminary data, quarterly rpt, 6822–1

Productivity and costs of labor for private, nonfarm business, and manufacturing sectors, revised data, quarterly rpt, 6822–2

Productivity, hours, and employment indexes for selected SIC 3- and 4-digit industries, 1954-82, annual rpt, 6824–1

Productivity of labor and capital in manufacturing, all nonfarm business, and all private business, indexes and percent change, 1948-83, annual rpt, 6824–2

Productivity related to changes in capital and hours of labor inputs, 1984 technical paper, 9381–10.35

Psychologists in health service provision by degree level, employment and service setting, services provided, and weekly hours worked, 1978, annual rpt, 4504–9.4

Railroad employee earnings, benefits, and hours, by occupation for Class I railroads, 1983, annual rpt, 9484–5

Recession and recovery effect on labor cost and productivity indexes, changes by index component, various periods 1948-82, article, 6722–1.470

Retail clothing business labor productivity, by kind of business, 1967-83, article, 6722–1.463

Self-employed, wage and salary, and unpaid family workers, employment, earnings, and hours, by industry div and occupation, 1970-83, article, 6722–1.443

Small business and all employees sociodemographic characteristics, by industry div and firm size, 1978-1979, annual rpt, 9764–6.3

Southeastern States financial and economic devs, Fed Reserve 6th District, monthly rpt with articles, 9371–1

Southeastern States manufacturing production workers average hours and earnings, for 8 States, monthly press release, 6942–7

Southwestern States manufacturing production workers average hours and earnings, for 5 States, monthly rpt, 6962–2

St Louis, Mo, SMSA employment, earnings, and CPI changes, 1983, annual rpt, 6974–3

State labor legislation enacted by 48 States, DC, and Guam, 1983, annual summary article, 6722–1.406

Steel (stainless and alloy tool) production, employment, prices, and US importer inventories and unfilled orders, quarterly rpt, 9882–3

Steel industry financial and operating data, steel imports by source, and employment situation at Fairless Hills, Pa, plant, 1970s-90, hearing, 25528–94

Strategic Petroleum Reserve activities and funding, by supplier and site, quarterly GAO rpt, 26102–3

Switchgear industry labor productivity trends and technological innovations, 1963-82, article, 6722–1.420

Teachers in public elementary and secondary schools, demographic and employment characteristics, 1961-81, annual rpt, 4824–2.8

Textile mill employment and average hours and earnings, for 8 Southeastern States, monthly press release, 6942–1

Transit system (automated guideway) characteristics and itemized costs, for 16 systems in operation or under construction, 1982, annual rpt, 7884–6

Unemployment rate and components of change, growth rates for 6 recovery periods 2nd qtr 1954-2nd qtr 1984, and projected unemployment rate for 4th qtr 1985, article, 9373–1.415

Uranium mining operations, finances, and costs of alternative methods to meet emissions standards, for industry and selected mines, selected years 1948-90, 9188–96

Urban travel by purpose, effect of telecommunication advances, land use changes, and alternative work schedules, projected to 2000 with some trends 1950-80, 7888–63

US Attorneys hours of work in court, by district, FY83, annual rpt, 6004–2.6

Watermelon grower-to-retailer handling costs and time, by handling phase and method, 1982, 1308–18

White-collar workers average weekly hours, by industry div and occupation, Mar 1984, annual rpt, 6784–2

Women in couples with wife as primary earner, socioeconomic and family characteristics, with comparative data for husbands, Mar 1982, 2326–11.9

Youth Conservation Corps activities, costs, and participant characteristics, by sponsoring agency, 1982, annual rpt, 5304–12

Youth employment and hours worked, by high school and college enrollment status, sex, race, and Hispanic origin, 1982-83, annual article, 6722–1.446

Hours of labor

see also Absenteeism
see also Area wage surveys
see also Earnings, general
see also Earnings, local and regional
see also Industry wage surveys
see also Moonlighting
see also Overtime
see also Part-time employment

House Administration Committee

Election campaign funding by political action committees to individual congressmen, and public opinion on reform proposals and assn influence, 1970s-83, hearings, 21428–7

House Aging Committee, Select

- Airline pilots terminated for medical reasons and reinstated by carrier, and aircraft accidents by age of flight crew, selected years 1960-81, hearing, 21148–34
- California (southern) housing demand by county, prices and sales, and costs after homeowner tax deductions, 1970s-80, hearing, 21148–31
- Deaths due to cold weather and related causes, by age, race, State, and city, selected periods 1962-83, 21148–30
- Foreign and US health care resources, use, and per capita public expenditures, and selected population characteristics, for 7 countries, selected years 1975-81, 21148–33
- Hospitals and nursing homes in Arizona, finances and operations for specified facilities, and itemized expenses for selected cases, 1978-83, hearing, 21148–29
- Older persons population characteristics, and needs and costs of social services by type, by metro-nonmetro status, 1970s-82 with trends from 1900, 21148–28
- Washington State telephone rates including govt long-distance access charges, by company, 1983-89, hearing, 21148–32

House Agriculture Committee

- Fed Crop Insurance Corp program operations and finances, for FCIC policies and private policies reinsured by FCIC, 1970s-84 with trends from 1948, hearing, 21168–28
- Fruit fly control, ethylene dibromide fumigation of tropical fruit imports, FY82, and cost of EDB and alternatives for Florida grapefruit and Hawaii papaya, 1984 rpt, 21168–29

House Armed Services Committee

- Fed Govt supply inventory and automated cataloging system, and DOD mgmt of inventory items for agencies, NATO, and foreign govts, 1970s-83, annual rpt, 21204–1
- Pension benefits for military retirees and compared to US civil and foreign service compared to US civil and foreign service and foreign countries, and Air Force personnel costs, FY75-84, hearings, 21208–19
- Soviet Union and US satellites by mission and vulnerability to attack, and USSR anti-satellite missiles, 1983 and projected to 1989, hearing, 21208–18
- Strategic materials stockpiles, and imports in exchange for CCC commodity exports by world region and country, various periods 1950-83, hearings, 21208–20
- Uranium ore tailings at active mills, EPA radon and radionuclide emmission

standards and US and foreign exposure and health effects, various periods 1957-83, hearings, 21208–17

House Banking, Currency and Housing Committee

see House Banking, Finance and Urban Affairs Committee

House Banking, Finance and Urban Affairs Committee

- Bank deposit interest rate deregulation, effect on bank deposits and bank financial performance, 1978-83, hearing, 21248–83
- Economic conditions of US, with some foreign comparisons, 1960s-82 and alternative projections to 1992, hearing, 21248–79
- Flood insurance program of Fed Govt, average premiums, premium income, and program costs, selected years FY68-84, hearing, 21248–81
- Fresno, Calif, economic, population, labor, and housing indicators, various periods 1974-85, hearing, 21248–84
- Homeless population and characteristics, and temporary shelter operations, use, and user characteristics, for selected cities, various periods 1979-84, hearing, 21248–85
- Mexico economic indicators, trade, external accounts and debt, oil industry, and relations with US, 1978-83 with trends from 1959, conf proceedings, 21248–82
- Multilateral dev banks economic dev projects, environmental and cultural impacts in developing countries, 1970s-83, hearings, 21248–80

House Budget Committee

DOD procurement cost unit changes for 96 programs, and total and procurement budget growth, projected FY85-89, hearing, 21268–36

House Children, Youth, and Families Committee, Select

- Fed Govt public welfare programs and tax expenditures benefitting children and youth, participation and funding for 71 programs, FY81-83, 21968–30
- Households and housing unit characteristics, and employment, housing finance, and social programs data, selected years 1948-83, hearing, 21968–28
- Teenage girls births and sexual experience by race, abortions, and birth control use, by age, 1970s-80 with birth trends from 1920, hearings, 21968–29

House Education and Labor Committee

- Asbestos-related occupational disease compensation paid and defendant and plaintiff litigation costs, with comparisons to other tort suits, selected years 1968-82, hearings, 21348–85
- Business failures, plant closings, layoffs, and relocations, for California by industry, individual plant, county, and city, 1980-83, hearing, 21348–84
- Economic growth rates and component economic indicators, selected years 1922-83 and projected under full employment to 1988, hearing, 21348–90
- Education of teachers, teaching degrees and salaries, high school seniors achievement test scores, and school enrollment and finances, 1970s-83, hearings, 21348–89
- Elementary level Follow Through compensatory education programs

Index by Subjects and Names

beneficiaries, costs, funding, and participant test scores, selected years 1968-82, hearing, 21348–87

- Fed Govt and total law enforcement officers and firefighters killed, death benefit claims, and non-Fed Govt firefighters death benefits by State and city, 1972-82, hearing, 21348–94
- Fed Govt civilian employment of minority groups and women, by grade and agency, 1980 and 1983, 21348–41
- Higher education desegregation, Louisiana black instn funding, and Virginia students needed to meet desegregation goals, by instn, late 1970s-85, hearings, 21348–91
- Kentucky Higher Education Student Loan Corp student loans, loan purchases and defaults by instn, and revenue bonds status, various dates 1979-84, hearing, 21348–92
- Michigan health funding, Blue Cross-Blue Shield and welfare participation, and unemployment, poverty, and food assistance by county, 1979-83, hearing, 21348–86
- Occupational health and safety State govt program staffing requirements, and occupational injury data, for selected States, selected years 1973-81, hearings, 21348–88
- Pension plan funding, assets, benefits, and participants for private and public systems, and State and local plans disclosing finances, selected years 1974-82, hearing, 21788–142
- Puerto Rico educational enrollment, finance, completions, curricula, and personnel by instn, and health and vital statistics, selected years 1970-83, hearings, 21348–93

House Energy and Commerce Committee

- Abortions (legal), and deaths from abortion and childbirth, by medical and sociodemographic characteristics, and New Mexico health clinics financial data, 1972-83, hearings, 21368–47
- Acid rain causes and effects, air pollutant emissions by source in US and selected countries, and control costs, 1970s-83 and projected to 2000, 21368–52
- Auto and light truck fuel use, economy standards and manufacturer compliance, and gas prices and taxes, with selected foreign comparisons, FY80-83 and projected to 2000, hearing, 21368–49
- Copper production, production costs, prices, wages, and productivity, for US and 3 countries, 1970s-83 and projected to 1989, 21368–55
- Electric and gas utility diversification activity by type, and finances and bond ratings by selected firm, various periods 1970-83, hearing, 21368–53
- Energy conservation programs of utilities, financing, costs, participation, and energy savings, various periods 1981-84, hearing, 21368–54
- Housing energy use, and savings under alternative conservation strategies, by State, with model methodology and energy prices, selected years 1970-81, 21368–48
- Medicare physician charges and reimbursement by enrollee characteristics and carrier, payment limits effects on

charges in California, and physician earnings, by specialty, 1950s-84, 25368–127

Oil price and allocation regulations enforcement by DOE, and overcharge allegations, settlements, and refunds to States, by company, as of June 1983, hearing, 21368–50

Steel import trigger prices to prevent Japan dumping, and domestic steel prices, employment, and imports, by product and region, various dates 1977-1983, hearings, 21368–51

Trade policy of Fed Govt, with data on US industry foreign trade and revenues, and Japan semiconductor industry subsidies, 1970s-83, hearings, 21368–46

TV and radio industry minority and women employment by occupation, and business owners, by race and State, with revenues and stations, 1971-81, hearing, 21368–45

House Foreign Affairs Committee

DOD budget, FY85 weapons system requests consistency with US policy and specified treaties, with funding FY83-87, annual rpt, 21384–4

El Salvador terrorist acts against property, casualties, kidnappings, and hostages, Oct 1979-June 1983, human rights certification hearing, 21388–41

Grenada arms and equipment commitments of USSR and other Communist countries, 1980-85, and arms discovered and personnel evacuated by US, Oct 1983, hearings, 21388–43

Human rights conditions in 162 countries, economic and military aid of US, and economic aid of intl organizations, 1981-83, annual rpt, 21384–3

Mexico economic indicators, trade, external accounts and debt, oil industry, and relations with US, 1978-83 with trends from 1959, conf proceedings, 21248–82

NATO military expenditures, by country, selected years 1971-82, hearing, 21388–42

Soviet Union industrial and agricultural production by selected commodity, and demographic trends and projections by Republic, 1950s-2000, hearings, 23848–180

House Government Operations Committee

Art appraisals accepted and rejected on estate, gift, and income tax returns, and valuation by taxpayers, IRS, and US courts, 1978-82, hearings, 21408–74

Arts and humanities funding, by source and State, FY82-83 with trends from FY66, 21408–69

Asbestos workers, exposure levels, cancer incidence, and deaths, by industry and occupation, and asbestos regulation enforcement and costs/benefits, various periods 1940-2027, hearing, 21408–72

DOD aircraft for noncombat use, costs, Navy and Air Force requirements, and Navy losses, by aircraft type, selected years FY73-86, hearing, 21408–76

Education block grants of Fed Govt, State allocations by program and selected school district, FY82-84 and trends from FY60, hearing, 21408–75

Foreign and US Commercial Service of ITA, overseas staff by category, and trade promotion costs by activity, by country, 1982-83, hearing, 21408–73

Mail electronic system message volume and profitability under USPS proposed rate and service increases, FY82 and projected to FY87, 21408–70

Tax evasion through tax haven countries, with income, investments, and taxes withheld by country, various periods 1975- 83, hearings, 21408–71

House Interior and Insular Affairs Committee

Copper mine expansion in Cananea, Mexico, effects on US air pollution and copper industry, with US and foreign industry data, 1960s-95, hearing, 21448–31

Nuclear power plants construction financing of Washington Public Power Supply System, with regional economic impacts and power supply/demand, 1980s-2035, hearing, 21448–29

Oil and gas 5-year OCS leasing plan and proposed sale off California coast, acreage, costs, and benefits, various periods 1953-2006, hearing, 21448–30

House International Relations Committee see House Foreign Affairs Committee

House Interstate and Foreign Commerce Committee see House Energy and Commerce Committee

House Judiciary Committee

Alcohol, Tobacco, and Firearms Bur activities nationwide and in 20 cities, funding, and jobs to be transferred to Customs and Secret Service, 1979-82, hearings, 21528–55

Bankruptcy (personal), filers by debt type and other characteristics, and impacts in Connecticut and Michigan, various dates 1946-82, hearings, 21528–57

FTC budget authority and expenditures for regulatory analysis, by prospective regulation and contractor, 1983, hearings, 21528–56

Higher education desegregation, Louisiana black instn funding, and Virginia students needed to meet desegregation goals, by instn, late 1970s-85, hearings, 21348–91

House Merchant Marine and Fisheries Committee

Marine pollution problems from municipal waste dumping in New York Bight, oil and gas drilling on Georges Bank, and radioactive waste disposal in oceans, 1970s-82, hearings, 21568–36

Oil and gas OCS drilling rigs by country, rig losses, and worker injury and death rates, various periods 1966-83, hearing, 21568–35

Port dev costs and financing through user fees, and shipping industry impact on local economy, by State, other area, industry, commodity, and port, 1970s-2020, hearings, 21568–34

House Narcotics Abuse and Control Committee, Select

Drug abuse situation, prevention and treatment programs, law enforcement, funding needs, and Fed Govt role, attitudes of State and local officials, 1983 survey, 21968–27

House of Representatives

Budget of US Appendix, detailed budgets and personnel summaries, by agency, FY85, annual rpt, 104–3

Budget of US, appropriations, outlays, balances, and budget receipts, by govtl branch and agency, FY83, annual rpt, 8104–2

House Small Business Committee

Budget of US, compact budgets by function, agency, and account, FY85 with projections to FY89, annual rpt, 104–2

Campaign finances and Fed Election Commission monitoring activities, 1984 Federal elections, biennial rpt series, 9276–2

Campaign finances, election procedures, and Fed Election Commission monitoring activities, press release series, 9276–1

Campaign funding by political action committee and candidate, proposed candidate spending limits, voting rates by party, and political opinions, by State, 1960-82, hearings, 25688–6

Campaign funding by political action committees to individual congressmen, and public opinion on reform proposals and assn influence, 1970s-83, hearings, 21428–7

Campaign funding by political action committees to reelect and defeat House and Senate members by candidate, and FEC activities and funding, 1983, annual rpt, 9274–1

Election campaign political action committee funding, by House and Senate candidate, 1978-82 Federal elections, biennial rpt, 9274–4

Salaries, expenses, and contingent fund disbursement, detailed listings, quarterly rpt, 21942–1

see also House Special Publications

see also under names of individual committees (starting with House or Joint)

see also under names of individual subcommittees (starting with Subcommittee)

House Post Office and Civil Service Committee

Pay rates of Fed Govt civilian employees, by branch of govt, employee category, and pay level, as of 1984 with trends from 1789, 21628–54

Postal Service operations, revenues by source, and employee characteristics, 1970s-83, and electronic mail promotion costs, FY82-87, hearings, 21628–55

House Science and Technology Committee

Air pollutant and radiation indoor levels by emissions source, and household exposure and health effects by pollutant type, various periods 1966-83, hearings, 21708–102

House Small Business Committee

Robots installed for manufacturing, and jobs displaced and created by occupation, by type of robot use, 1980s-2000, hearings, 21728–54

Small business employment and receipts size standards for Fed Govt contract awards by industry, and DOD contract awards data, 1970s-83, hearings, 21728–53

Small business loans and credit, operational expectations, and NYC metro area owners economic and professional attitudes, by industry div, 1980-83 surveys, hearings, 21728–52

Trans-Alaska Pipeline System owner companies financial data, and retail gasoline competitive position in 2 States, by company, 1980-83, hearing, 21728–51

House Special Publications

House Special Publications

House of Representatives salaries, expenses, and contingent fund disbursement, detailed listings, quarterly rpt, 21942–1

House trailers

see Mobile homes

House Ways and Means Committee

- Auto industry operations, trade, and registrations, foreign and US, selected years 1928-82, domestic content requirement hearings, 21788–134
- Bond tax-exempt issues by purpose, and Fed Govt mortgage bond revenue losses and borrower characteristics, selected years 1971-85, hearings, 21788–135
- Crop acreage reduction payment-in-kind program costs, requirements, producer and diversion payments, and loan interest forgiven, by crop, as of 1983, hearing, 21788–138
- Election campaign funding by political action committees and voting on FTC rules, for individual congressmen, 1978-82, hearings, 21428–7.2, 25688–6.2
- Enterprise zone and urban revitalization projects of State and local govts, effect on business and employment in selected areas, various dates 1972-83, hearing, 21788–140
- Fed Govt programs under Ways and Means Committee jurisdiction, program operations and financing data for assessing budgetary requirements, by State, FY70s-83, 21788–117
- Medicare physician charges and reimbursement by enrollee characteristics and carrier, payment limits effects on charges in California, and physician earnings, by specialty, 1950s-84, 25368–127
- Oil and gas finances by firm, and effect of income and excise tax provisions on firms, Fed Govt revenues, and investor tax returns, 1980 and projected to 1992, hearing, 21788–132
- Pension plan funding, assets, benefits, and participants for private and public systems, and State and local plans disclosing finances, selected years 1974-82, hearing, 21788–142
- Philanthropic foundations assets and grants for 50 largest foundations, and for selected foundations by recipient, selected years 1975-82, hearings, 21788–137
- Poverty-level persons and families, by income source, hours of work, earnings, taxes, and family characteristics, various periods 1959-84, 21788–131
- Poverty population by labor force status, and effect of public welfare changes and recession, by family status, FY82, 21788–139
- Poverty rate by family composition, and effect of noncash transfers, taxes, unemployment benefits, and business cycles, selected years 1959-82, hearings, 21788–141
- Tax expenditures, Fed Govt revenues foregone through income tax deductions and exclusions by type, and effect of Deficit Reduction Act, FY84-89, annual rpt, 21784–10
- Teachers salaries in schools and colleges by State, 1982/83, and school employees health insurance plans in 7 cities, as of 1980, hearing, 21788–136

Texas border employment and economic impacts of Mexican peso devaluation, for 6 counties and 2 SMSAs, 1970s-May 1983, hearing, 21788–133

Household appliances and equipment

- Air pollutant and radiation indoor levels by emissions source, and household exposure and health effects by pollutant type, various periods 1966-83, hearings, 21708–102
- Air pollutant emission factors, by detailed source, 3rd edition, 1983-84 supplements, 9198–13
- Brooms (broomcorn) shipments, trade, and apparent consumption data for USITC import quota determination, 1983, annual rpt, 9884–6
- Business statistics, detailed data for major industries and economic indicators, *Survey of Current Business,* monthly rpt, 2702–1.14
- Census of Housing, 1980: inventory, occupancy, and unit characteristics, changes from 1973 by region and inside-outside SMSAs and central cities, series, 2473–3
- Census of Population and Housing, 1980: detailed population and housing characteristics, by county, city, and census tract, State and SMSA rpt series, 2551–2
- Census of Population, 1980: detailed socioeconomic and demographic characteristics, by age, sex, race, Hispanic origin, occupation, and industry, State rpt series, 2531–4
- China economic conditions, agricultural and industrial production, trade, and domestic and foreign investment, 1980-85, 2048–106
- Collective bargaining agreements expiring during year, covered workers by SIC 2-digit industry, firm, and union, with summary of key provisions, 1984, annual rpt, 6784–9
- County Business Patterns: establishments, employees, and payrolls, by SIC 4-digit industry and county, 1981, annual State rpt series, 2326–8
- County Business Patterns: establishments, employees, and payrolls, by SIC 4-digit industry and county, 1982, annual State rpt series, 2326–6
- Cuba economic conditions, agricultural and industrial production and distribution, trade, and intl economic relations, 1970-82 and trends from 1957, 248–40
- Electric and gas appliances, by census region and urban-rural location, Nov 1982, annual rpt, 3164–74
- Electric housewares and fans shipments, trade, and consumption, by product, 1983, annual Current Industrial Rpt, 2506–12.15
- Employment, earnings, and hours, by selected SIC 1- to 4-digit industry, State, and for 278 major labor areas, 1939-83, annual rpt, 6744–5
- Employment, earnings, and hours, by SIC 4-digit nonfarm industry, monthly 1974-Feb 1984, annual update, 6744–4
- Energy efficiency ratios for selected household appliances, and load control device costs, 1984 rpt, 26358–99
- Energy supply/demand and prices, by fuel type, sector, and end use, with foreign comparisons, 1960-83 and projected to 1995, annual summary rpt, 3164–76

Index by Subjects and Names

- Energy use and costs in multifamily rental housing, conservation effect on rental marketing, and effect of utility bill payment methods on conservation efforts, 1970s-80s, 3308–73
- Energy use, costs, expenditures, and conservation, and household and housing characteristics, EIA survey series, 3166–7
- Energy use in housing, and savings under alternative conservation strategies, by State, with model methodology and energy prices, selected years 1970-81, 21368–48
- Exports and imports between US and outlying areas, by detailed commodity and mode of transport, monthly rpt, 2422–4
- Exports and imports of US, detailed SIC-based commodities by world area, 1983, annual rpts, 2424–6
- Exports and imports of US, totals and as percent of domestic production, by SIC 2- to 5-digit commodity, 1981, annual rpt, 2424–3
- Exports of US, detailed commodities by country of destination, monthly rpt, 2422–3
- Exports of US, detailed Schedule B commodities by country of destination, 1983, annual rpt, 2424–9
- Exports of US, detailed Schedule E commodities by mode of transport and world area and country of destination, 1983, annual rpts, 2424–5
- Fires (housing electrical) in 10 cities, by type of wiring and equipment involved and circumstances, 1980-81, 2218–71
- Garden and lawn equipment shipments, trade, and consumption, by product, 1982-83, annual Current Industrial Rpt, 2506–12.1
- Great Lakes trade, by SITC 3-digit commodity, port, vessel type, world area, and country, 1982, annual rpt, 7744–3
- Home mortgages (graduated payment) FHA-insured, financial, property, and mortgagor characteristics, US summary, quarterly rpt, 5142–40
- Home mortgages FHA-insured, financial, property, and mortgagor characteristics, for US and selected localities, quarterly rpt, 5142–2
- Home mortgages FHA-insured, financial, property, and mortgagor characteristics, for US, selected States, and Puerto Rico, quarterly rpt, 5142–3
- Home mortgages FHA-insured, financial, property, and mortgagor characteristics, quarterly rpt, 5142–1
- Home mortgages FHA-insured, financial, property, and mortgagor characteristics, 1983, annual rpt, 5144–17
- Home mortgages FHA-insured for low-cost homes, financial, construction, property, and mortgagor characteristics, quarterly rpt, 5142–4
- Housing and households detailed characteristics, and unit and neighborhood quality, by inside-outside central cities, 1979-82 surveys, SMSA rpt series, 2485–6
- Housing, new single and multifamily unit physical and financial characteristics, by region and metro-nonmetro location, 1979-83, annual rpt, 2384–1

Index by Subjects and Names

Household furnishings

Housing occupancy and unit and household characteristics, by region and metro-nonmetro residence, 1983, biennial survey, 2485–1

Imports of US, detailed Schedule A commodities by country and world area of origin, and mode of transport, 1983, annual rpts, 2424–2

Imports of US, detailed Schedule A commodities by country, monthly rpt, 2422–2

Imports of US, detailed TSUSA commodities by country of origin, 1983, annual rpt, 2424–4

Income tax returns of corporations, detailed income and tax items by industry, 1981, annual rpt, 8304–4

Income tax returns of partnerships, detailed data by industry, 1981 estimates, annual article, 8302–2.404

Income tax returns of sole proprietorships, detailed data by industry div and selected industry group, 1981, annual rpt, 8304–7

Income tax returns of sole proprietorships, receipts, deductions by type, payroll, and net income, by major industry, 1982, annual article, 8302–2.413

Industry finances and operations, by SIC 2- to 4-digit industry, 1970s-83 and projected to 1988, annual rpt, 2014–4

Injuries and deaths from use of selected consumer products and related activity, by victim age and sex, 1982, annual rpt, 9164–7

Injuries and deaths from use of selected consumer products, by victim age and medical treatment status, 1982, annual rpt, 9164–6

Injuries, deaths, and medical costs from consumer products use, and Consumer Product Safety Commission activities and recalls, by product type and brand, FY83, annual rpt, 9164–2

Input-output structure of US economy, detailed interindustry transactions for 85 industries, and components of final demand, 1977, article, 2702–1.421

Input-output structure of US economy, detailed interindustry transactions for 537 industries, and components of final demand, 1977 benchmark data, 2708–17

Lamps (electric) production, shipments, stocks, trade, and firms, by bulb type, monthly and quarterly Current Industrial Rpts, 2506–12.13

Lamps (fluorescent) production, shipments, trade, and firms, by ballast type, quarterly Current Industrial Rpt, 2506–12.14

Lighting fixture shipments, trade, and consumption, by product, 1983, annual Current Industrial Rpt, 2506–12.19

Manufacturing census, 1982: financial and operating data, by SIC 2- to 4-digit industry, State, SMSA, and county, preliminary census div rpt series, 2491–3

Manufacturing census, 1982: financial and operating data, for SIC 4-digit industries by product, preliminary rpt series, 2491–1

Minority group and women employment, by occupational group and SIC 2- to 3-digit industry, 1981, annual rpt, 9244–1.1

Natural gas utility marketing and servicing of household appliances and conservation equipment in US and Canada, by firm and product, 1978, hearing, 21368–54

Occupational injury and illness rates, by SIC 2- to 4-digit industry, 1982, annual rpt, 6844–1

OECD trade, total and for 4 major countries, and US trade by country, by commodity, 1972-82, annual world region rpt series, 244–13

Pacific Northwest electricity consumption and prices by end-use sector, and economic and demographic data, 1960s-83 and projected to 2005, annual rpt, 3224–2

Personal stocks of durable goods, by type, in current and constant dollars, 1980-83, annual article, 2702–1.433

Pollution abatement capital and operating costs, by SIC 2- to 4-digit industry, State, and SMSA, 1982, annual Current Industrial Rpt, 2506–3.6

Producer prices and indexes, by stage of processing and detailed commodity, monthly rpt, 6762–6

Producer prices and indexes, by stage of processing and detailed commodity, monthly 1983, annual supplement, 6764–2

Production, shipments, PPI, and stocks of building materials, by type, bimonthly rpt, 2012–1.6

Productivity, hours, and employment indexes for selected SIC 3- and 4-digit industries, 1954-82, annual rpt, 6824–1.3

Quality of housing and neighborhoods, indicators and attitudes, and occupant characteristics, by urban-rural location and region, 1981, annual survey, 2485–7

Quality of housing and neighborhoods, indicators and attitudes, by occupant and unit characteristics, region, and metro-nonmetro location, 1981, annual survey, 2485–2

Repair technicians and apprentices wages and benefits, for 5 types of electrical repair shops in 19 SMSAs, Nov 1981 survey, 6787–6.197

Retail trade census, 1982: employment, establishments, sales, and payroll, for direct selling establishments, by State, preliminary rpt, 2395–1.35

Retail trade census, 1982: employment, establishments, sales, and payroll, by SIC 2- to 4-digit kind of business, SMSA, and retail district, State rpt series, 2401–1

Retail trade census, 1982: employment, establishments, sales, and payroll, by SIC 2- to 4-digit kind of business, SMSA, county, and city, State rpt series, 2397–1

Retail trade census, 1982: employment, establishments, sales, and payroll, for household appliance stores, by State, preliminary rpt, 2395–1.21

Retail trade sales and inventories, by kind of business, region, census div, and selected State, SMSA, and city, and seasonal adjustments, monthly rpt, 2413–3

Retail trade sales, inventories, purchases, gross margin, and accounts receivable, by SIC 2- to 4-digit kind of business and type of ownership, 1983, annual rpt, 2413–5

Scientists, engineers and technicians employment in transportation, utilities, and retail and wholesale trade, by field of science and industry, 1982, 9628–72

Sewing machines trade, tariffs, and industry operating data, foreign and US, 1979-83, TSUSA commodity rpt supplement, 9885–6.66

Shipments, trade, consumption, and firms, by product, 1982-83, annual Current Industrial Rpt, 2506–12.16

Solar collector and photovoltaic module production, sales, and use, with listing of manufacturers, 1983, annual rpt, 3164–62

Soviet Union refrigerators and washing machines in use compared to US, 1960s-83, annual rpt, 244–5.1

Thefts, and total value of property stolen and recovered, by property type, 1983, annual rpt, 6224–2.1

Transportation census, 1982: trucks, by detailed characteristics, miles traveled, and type of product carried, State rpt series, 2573–1

Underground economy, household expenditures and participation by type of goods or service and sociodemographic characteristics, with methodology and bibl, 1981 survey, 8308–27

Virgin Islands economic censuses, 1982: employment, establishments, payroll, and receipts, by SIC 1- to 4-digit industry, island, and city, 2593–1

Wholesale trade census, 1982: employment, establishments, finances, and operations, by SIC 2- to 4-digit kind of business, SMSA, county, and city, State rpt series, 2405–1

Wholesale trade census, 1982: employment, establishments, sales by commodity, and payroll, by SIC 4-digit kind of business and State, preliminary rpt series, 2403–1

see also Air conditioning

see also Hand tools

see also Hardware

see also Insulation

see also Phonograph

see also Plumbing and heating

see also Radio

see also Television

see also under By Commodity in the "Index by Categories"

see also under By Industry in the "Index by Categories"

Household furnishings

Apartment market absorption rates and characteristics for nonsubsidized privately financed furnished and unfurnished units completed in 1982, annual Current Housing Rpt, 2484–2

Census of Population, 1980: detailed socioeconomic and demographic characteristics, by age, sex, race, Hispanic origin, occupation, and industry, State rpt series, 2531–4

Census of Population, 1980: detailed socioeconomic characteristics, by county, city, and inside-outside SMSAs and central cities, State rpt series, 2531–3

Ceramic kitchen articles trade, tariffs, and industry operating data, foreign and US, 1978-82, TSUSA commodity rpt supplement, 9885–5.13

Chairs (metal stacking) from Italy and Taiwan at less than fair value, imports injury to US industry, investigation with background financial and operating data, 1984 rpt, 9886–14.121

Household furnishings

China economic conditions, agricultural and industrial production, trade, and domestic and foreign investment, 1980-85, 2048–106

China exports and imports by SITC 1- to 5-digit commodity, 1970s-82, annual rpt, 244–12

Collective bargaining agreements expiring during year, covered workers by SIC 2-digit industry, firm, and union, with summary of key provisions, 1984, annual rpt, 6784–9

County Business Patterns: establishments, employees, and payrolls, by SIC 4-digit industry and county, 1981, annual State rpt series, 2326–8

County Business Patterns: establishments, employees, and payrolls, by SIC 4-digit industry and county, 1982, annual State rpt series, 2326–6

CPI by detailed component, for US city average, 28 SMSAs, and 4 regions by population size, monthly rpt, 6762–2

DOD shipments of military and personal property, loss claims, passenger traffic, and costs, by mode of transport, quarterly rpt, 3702–1

Earnings by major industry group, and personal income per capita and by source, by region and State, 1929-82, 2708–40

Employment, earnings, and hours, by selected SIC 1- to 4-digit industry, State, and for 278 major labor areas, 1939-83, annual rpt, 6744–5

Employment, earnings, and hours, by SIC 4-digit nonfarm industry, monthly 1974-Feb 1984, annual update, 6744–4

Exports and imports between US and outlying areas, by detailed commodity and mode of transport, monthly rpt, 2422–4

Exports and imports of US, by commodity group, world area, selected country, US coastal area and port, and mode of transport, with seasonal adjustments, monthly rpt, 2422–9

Exports and imports of US, detailed SIC-based commodities by world area, 1983, annual rpts, 2424–6

Exports and imports of US, totals and as percent of domestic production, by SIC 2- to 5-digit commodity, 1981, annual rpt, 2424–3

Exports, imports, tariffs, and industry operating data for bedroom furnishings and nontextile floor coverings, 1979-83, TSUSA commodity rpt supplement, 9885–7.61

Exports, imports, tariffs, and industry operating data for furniture, 1979-83, TSUSA commodity rpt supplement, 9885–7.62

Exports of manufactured and agricultural commodities, manufacturing production, and export-related employment, 1960s-82, State rpt series, 2046–3

Exports of US, detailed commodities by country of destination, monthly rpt, 2422–3

Exports of US, detailed Schedule B commodities by country of destination, 1983, annual rpt, 2424–9

Exports of US, detailed Schedule E commodities by mode of transport and world area and country of destination, 1983, annual rpts, 2424–5

Index by Subjects and Names

Flatware of stainless steel, imports injury to US industry from increased import sales, investigation with selected financial and operating data, 1984 rpt, 9886–5.48

Franchise business opportunities, by firm and kind of business, 1984 annual listing, 2044–27

Furniture (household) imports effect on US industry, investigation with background financial and operating data, 1984 rpt, 9886–4.74

Glassware (household), trade, tariffs, and industry operating data, 1979-83, TSUSA commodity rpt supplement, 9885–5.18

Glassware shipments, trade, and consumption, by product, 1983, annual Current Industrial Rpt, 2506–9.3

Great Lakes trade, by SITC 3-digit commodity, port, vessel type, world area, and country, 1982, annual rpt, 7744–3

Imports of US, detailed Schedule A commodities by country and world area of origin, and mode of transport, 1983, annual rpts, 2424–2

Imports of US, detailed Schedule A commodities by country, monthly rpt, 2422–2

Imports of US, detailed TSUSA commodities by country of origin, 1983, annual rpt, 2424–4

Income tax returns of corporations, detailed income and tax items by industry, 1981, annual rpt, 8304–4

Income tax returns of corporations with foreign tax credit, income and deductions by type, asset size, and selected industry group, 1980, article, 8302–2.415

Income tax returns of partnerships, detailed data by industry, 1981 estimates, annual article, 8302–2.404

Income tax returns of partnerships, receipts by source, deductions by type, and establishments, by selected industry, 1982, annual article, 8302–2.416

Income tax returns of sole proprietorships, detailed data by industry div and selected industry group, 1981, annual rpt, 8304–7

Income tax returns of sole proprietorships, receipts, deductions by type, payroll, and net income, by major industry, 1982, annual article, 8302–2.413

Industry finances and operations, by SIC 2- to 4-digit industry, 1970s-83 and projected to 1988, annual rpt, 2014–4

Injuries and deaths from use of selected consumer products and related activity, by victim age and sex, 1982, annual rpt, 9164–7

Injuries and deaths from use of selected consumer products, by victim age and medical treatment status, 1982, annual rpt, 9164–6

Injuries, deaths, and medical costs from consumer products use, and Consumer Product Safety Commission activities and recalls, by product type and brand, FY83, annual rpt, 9164–2

Input-output structure of US economy, detailed interindustry transactions for 85 industries, and components of final demand, 1977, article, 2702–1.421

Input-output structure of US economy, detailed interindustry transactions for 537 industries, and components of final demand, 1977 benchmark data, 2708–17

Linens and other textile imports, by product and country of origin, monthly rpt, 2422–1

Linens production, shipments, trade, inventories, and consumption, quarterly Current Industrial Rpt, 2506–6.6

Manufacturing census, 1982: financial and operating data, by SIC 2- to 4-digit industry, State, SMSA, and county, preliminary census div rpt series, 2491–3

Manufacturing census, 1982: financial and operating data, for SIC 4-digit industries by product, preliminary rpt series, 2491–1

Manufacturing census, 1982: textile mill machinery in place, by machine type and textile industry, special preliminary rpts, 2491–2

Michigan bankruptcy filings, by filer type, moving history, income, creditor action, debt and asset type, credit status, exemptions claimed, and county, 1979-81, hearings, 21528–57.3

Military Sealift Command operations for naval fleet support, and transport of DOD and AID cargo by route, quarterly rpt, 3802–2

Minority group and women employment, by occupational group and SIC 2- to 3-digit industry, 1981, annual rpt, 9244–1.1

Motor carriers (Class I) of household goods operating revenues, net income, and revenue tons, by firm, quarterly rpt, 9482–14

Natl income and product, comprehensive accounts and components, *Survey of Current Business,* monthly rpt, 2702–1.21

Occupational injury and illness rates, by SIC 2- to 4-digit industry, 1982, annual rpt, 6844–1

Occupational manpower needs and supply by detailed occupation, and educational and training program enrollees and grads by detailed field, 1982 and 1995, biennial rpt, 6744–3

Occupational Outlook Handbook, 1984-85 biennial rpt, 6744–1

OECD trade, total and for 4 major countries, and US trade by country, by commodity, 1972-82, annual world region rpt series, 244–13

Personal consumption expenditures, natl income and product account, *Survey of Current Business,* monthly rpt, monthly and annual tables, 2702–1.23

Personal stocks of durable goods, by type, in current and constant dollars, 1980-83, annual article, 2702–1.433

Pollution abatement capital and operating costs, by SIC 2- to 4-digit industry, State, and SMSA, 1982, annual Current Industrial Rpt, 2506–3.6

Producer prices and indexes, by stage of processing and detailed commodity, monthly rpt, 6762–6

Producer prices and indexes, by stage of processing and detailed commodity, monthly 1983, annual supplement, 6764–2

Productivity, hours, and employment indexes for selected SIC 3- and 4-digit industries, 1954-82, annual rpt, 6824–1.3

Retail trade census, 1982: employment, establishments, sales, and payroll, by SIC 2- to 4-digit kind of business, SMSA, and retail district, State rpt series, 2401–1

Index by Subjects and Names

Retail trade census, 1982: employment, establishments, sales, and payroll, by SIC 2- to 4-digit kind of business, SMSA, county, and city, State rpt series, 2397–1

Retail trade census, 1982: employment, establishments, sales, and payroll, for floor covering stores by State, preliminary rpt, 2395–1.20

Retail trade census, 1982: employment, establishments, sales, and payroll, for furniture stores, by State, preliminary rpt, 2395–1.19

Retail trade sales and inventories, by kind of business, region, census div, and selected State, SMSA, and city, and seasonal adjustments, monthly rpt, 2413–3

Retail trade sales, inventories, purchases, gross margin, and accounts receivable, by SIC 2- to 4-digit kind of business and type of ownership, 1983, annual rpt, 2413–5

Rug and carpet shipments, trade, and consumption, by product, quarterly Current Industrial Rpt, 2506–5.9

Scientists, engineers, and technicians employed in private industry, by occupation and industry group, 1980-81, biennial rpt, 9627–23

Scientists, engineers, and technicians employment in transportation, utilities, and retail and wholesale trade, by field of science and industry, 1982, 9628–72

Service industry census, 1982: employment, establishments, receipts, and payroll, by SIC 2- to 4-digit kind of business, SMSA, county, and city, State rpt series, 2391–1

Thefts, and total value of property stolen and recovered, by property type, 1983, annual rpt, 6224–2.1

Transportation census, 1982: trucks, by detailed characteristics, miles traveled, and type of product carried, State rpt series, 2573–1

Underground economy, household expenditures and participation by type of goods or service and sociodemographic characteristics, with methodology and bibl, 1981 survey, 8308–27

Virgin Islands economic censuses, 1982: employment, establishments, payroll, and receipts, by SIC 1- to 4-digit industry, island, and city, 2593–1

Waterborne commerce of US (domestic and foreign), freight by commodity, traffic, and passengers, by port and waterway, 1982, annual rpt, 3754–3

Wholesale trade census, 1982: employment, establishments, finances, and operations, by SIC 2- to 4-digit kind of business, SMSA, county, and city, State rpt series, 2405–1

Wholesale trade census, 1982: employment, establishments, sales by commodity, and payroll, by SIC 4-digit kind of business and State, preliminary rpt, 2403–1.3

Wholesale trade sales and inventories, by SIC 2- to 3-digit kind of business, monthly rpt, 2413–7

Wholesale trade sales, inventories, purchases, and gross margins, by SIC 2- to 3-digit kind of business and type of ownership, 1983, annual rpt, 2413–13

see also Antiques

see also Household appliances and equipment

see also under By Commodity in the "Index by Categories"

see also under By Industry in the "Index by Categories"

Household workers

Census of Housing, 1980: structural, financial, and householder characteristics, by region and State, 2475–4

Census of Population and Housing, 1980: detailed population and housing characteristics, by county, city, and census tract, State and SMSA rpt series, 2551–2

Census of Population, 1980: detailed socioeconomic and demographic characteristics, by age, sex, race, Hispanic origin, occupation, and industry, State rpt series, 2531–4

Census of Population, 1980: detailed socioeconomic characteristics, by county, city, and inside-outside SMSAs and central cities, State rpt series, 2531–3

Census of Population, 1980: labor force, by sex, detailed occupation, and region, with comparison to 1970 census, supplementary rpt, 2535–1.12

Census of Service Industries, 1982: employment, establishments, receipts, and payroll, by SIC 4-digit kind of business and State, preliminary rpt, 2390–2.6

Earnings by major industry group, and personal income per capita and by source, by region and State, 1929-82, 2708–40

Employment and earnings, detailed data, monthly rpt, 6742–2.3, 6742–2.4, 6742–2.8

Employment and economic conditions, alternative BLS projections to 1995 with selected trends for 1959-82, 6728–29

Employment, unemployment, and labor force, by demographic and employment characteristics, State, and for 30 metro areas and 11 large cities, 1983, annual rpt, 6744–7

Income of households, families, and persons, by detailed socioeconomic characteristics and region, 1982, annual Current Population Rpt, 2546–6.39

Military officers aides, enlisted personnel authorized and assigned to perform personal services by race and sex, and program costs, by service branch, 1982-83, GAO rpt, 26123–53

Occupational manpower needs and supply by detailed occupation, and educational and training program enrollees and grads by detailed field, 1982 and 1995, biennial rpt, 6744–3

Personal consumption expenditures, natl income and product account, *Survey of Current Business,* monthly rpt, monthly and annual tables, 2702–1.23

Poverty status of families and persons, by detailed socioeconomic characteristics, 1982, annual Current Population Rpt, 2546–6.40

Underground economy, household expenditures and participation by type of goods or service and sociodemographic characteristics, with methodology and bibl, 1981 survey, 8308–27

Workers compensation law provisions of States and Fed Govt, by jurisdiction, as of July 1984, semiannual rpt, 6502–1

Housing (FHA), HUD

Households

see Families and households

Housewares

see Household appliances and equipment

see Household furnishings

Housing

see Apartment houses

see Condominiums and cooperatives

see Discrimination in housing

see Halfway houses

see Homesteads

see Household appliances and equipment

see Household furnishings

see Housing condition and occupancy ✓

see Housing construction

see Housing costs and financing

see Housing energy use

see Housing maintenance and repair

see Housing sales

see Housing tenure

see Insulation

see Low-income housing

see Military housing

see Mobile homes

see Mortgages

see Prefabricated buildings

see Public housing

see Real estate business

see Relocation

see Rooming and boarding houses

see Transient housing

see Urban renewal

see Veterans housing

see Wrecking and demolition

Housing (FHA), HUD

Budget of US, loans and loan guarantees, and Admin proposed limits on credit assistance, by program, FY83-89, annual rpt, 26306–3.65

Cost control proposals for Fed Govt programs and mgmt, 3-year savings by function and agency, and financial and operating data, 1960s-81, 16908–1.8

Credit assistance costs, policies to improve measurement, with loan and loan guarantee data by program, and Federal and private credit instns operations, 1970-84, 26306–6.72

Defaulted mortgages, single family homes acquired by HUD and disposition by city, monthly rpt, 5142–31

Govt Natl Mortgage Assn financial statements, and mortgage-backed securities program, FY82-83, annual rpt, 5144–6

Home and condominium mortgages FHA-insured, new issues, adjustments, and terminations, by program, quarterly rpt, 5142–6

Home mortgage applications for 1- to 4-family homes, commitments, insurance, starts, and units readied, quarterly rpt, 5142–5

Home mortgage loan originations, by State and for Puerto Rico, 1978-83, press release, 5148–6

Home mortgages (graduated payment) FHA-insured, financial, property, and mortgagor characteristics, for US and selected localities, quarterly rpt, 5142–42

Home mortgages (graduated payment) FHA-insured, financial, property, and mortgagor characteristics, for US and selected States, quarterly rpt, 5142–41

Housing (FHA), HUD

Home mortgages (graduated payment) FHA-insured, financial, property, and mortgagor characteristics, US summary, quarterly rpt, 5142-40

Home mortgages and mortgage pool participation by lender type, and FHA mortgage yields, various periods 1950-84 with trends from 1900, technical paper, 9375-11.4

Home mortgages FHA-insured, claims, and foreclosures, for low- and moderate-income rental housing and 1- to 4-family homes, periodic rpt, suspended, 5142-27

Home mortgages FHA-insured, financial, property, and mortgagor characteristics, for US and selected localities, quarterly rpt, 5142-2

Home mortgages FHA-insured, financial, property, and mortgagor characteristics, for US, selected States, and Puerto Rico, quarterly rpt, 5142-3

Home mortgages FHA-insured, financial, property, and mortgagor characteristics, quarterly rpt, 5142-1

Home mortgages FHA-insured, financial, property, and mortgagor characteristics, 1983, annual rpt, 5144-17

Home mortgages FHA-insured for low-cost homes, financial, construction, property, and mortgagor characteristics, quarterly rpt, 5142-4

Home mortgages FHA-insured, secondary market prices and interest rates on conventional loans, by region, monthly press release, 5142-20

Home mortgages insured by private companies, for 1- to 4-family units, monthly press release, 5142-38

Housing, new single and multifamily unit physical and financial characteristics, by region and metro-nonmetro location, 1979-83, annual rpt, 2384-1

Housing, new single family units sold and sales price by type of financing, monthly rpt, quarterly tables, 2382-3.2

Land privately held, acreage and owners by owner characteristics, land use, and region, and purchase and improvement funding, 1978 survey, series, 1506-5

Low-rent housing project financing notes sold by local authorities, terms and individual issuers and purchasers, monthly listing, 5142-43

Low-rent housing project financing notes sold by local authorities, terms and individual purchasers, monthly press release, 5142-37

Mortgage and mortgage-related investment of financial instns, by instn type and Fed Govt issuing agency, various dates 1981-84, 5008-33

Mortgage holdings, transactions, and commitments, monthly rpt, 9312-1.1

Mortgage insurance funds of HUD, financial and property activity, and insurance written, monthly rpt, 5002-9

Mortgage insurance of FHA and VA for new housing, bimonthly rpt, 2012-1.2

Mortgage loan activity, by type of lender, loan, and mortgaged property, monthly rpt, 5142-18

Mortgage transactions and holdings, by lender group and type of property and loan, quarterly rpt, 5142-30

Property improvement and mobile home loans FHA-insured, and claims paid, quarterly rpt, 5142-9

Property improvement and mobile home loans FHA-insured, by State and county, 1983 and cumulative from 1934, annual rpt, 5144-16

Property improvement and mobile home loans, FHA-insured, monthly rpt, suspended, 5142-10

Urban renewal project financing notes sold by local authorities, monthly press release, suspended, 5142-36

Housing and Urban Development Department *see* Department of Housing and Urban Development

Housing census *see* Census of Housing *see* Census of Population and Housing

Housing condition and occupancy

Apartment market absorption rates and characteristics for nonsubsidized privately financed furnished and unfurnished units completed in 1982, annual Current Housing Rpt, 2484-2

Apartment market absorption rates and characteristics for nonsubsidized privately financed units completed in 1983, preliminary annual Current Housing Rpt, 2484-3

Appalachian States, FHLB 5th District housing vacancy rates for single and multifamily units and mobile homes, by ZIP code, annual metro area rpt series, 9304-27

Arson incidents by occupancy of structure, average property value, and arrest rates, by type of property, 1983, annual rpt, 6224-2.1

Asia developing countries housing finance and low-income housing projects, and activities of 2 countries, 1970s-82, annual conf proceedings, 9914-11

Bombing (explosive and incendiary) and arson incidents by target, State, and circumstances, and explosives theft and recovery, 1982-83, annual rpt, 8484-4

Bombing (explosive and incendiary) incidents, damage, injuries, and deaths, by target, State, and circumstances, 1983, annual rpt, 6224-5

Census of Housing, 1980: inventory, occupancy, and unit characteristics, changes from 1973 by region and inside-outside SMSAs and central cities, series, 2473-3

Census of Housing, 1980: occupancy and unit characteristics of SMSAs and central cities, by race, Hispanic origin, and city, State and SMSA rpt series, 2473-1

Census of Housing, 1980: structural, financial, and householder characteristics, by region and State, 2475-4

Census of Population and Housing, 1980: detailed population and housing characteristics, by county, city, and census tract, State and SMSA rpt series, 2551-2

Census of Population, 1980: Indian and Alaska Native population and housing occupancy, by reservation, Alaska Native village, and other Indian area, supplementary rpt, 2535-1.16

Coastal environmental characteristics, fish, wildlife, and use, and population socioeconomic data, for individual areas, series, 5506-4

Index by Subjects and Names

Community dev programs funding and activities, for 5 HUD programs, FY83, annual rpt, 5124-5

County and City Data Book, detailed socioeconomic and demographic data for States, counties, and cities, selected years 1976-82, 2328-1

Crime victimization rates by type of offense, and victim and offense characteristics, Natl Crime Survey series, 6066-3

Developing countries disaster preparedness and summary sociodemographic, political, and economic data, country rpt series, 9916-2

Economic indicators and components, current data and annual trends, monthly rpt, 23842-1.3

Energy conservation programs of utilities under natl conservation act, cost effectiveness and participating household characteristics, 1980s, 3308-69

Energy supply/demand and prices, by fuel type, sector, and end use, detailed trends and projections 1973-95, annual rpt, 3164-75

Energy use, costs, expenditures, and conservation, and household and housing characteristics, EIA survey series, 3166-7

Fires (housing electrical) in 10 cities, by type of wiring and equipment involved and circumstances, 1980-81, 2218-71

Florida and California elderly migration by selected State of origin or destination, and Florida elderly, by sociodemographic and housing characteristics, 1970 and 1980, 4478-150

Foreign human rights conditions in 162 countries, economic and military aid of US, and economic aid of intl organizations, 1981-83, annual rpt, 21384-3

Fresno, Calif, economic, population, labor, and housing indicators, various periods 1974-85, hearing, 21248-84

Home mortgages (graduated payment) FHA-insured, financial, property, and mortgaor characteristics, for US and selected localities, quarterly rpt, 5142-42

Home mortgages (graduated payment) FHA-insured, financial, property, and mortgagor characteristics, for US and selected States, quarterly rpt, 5142-41

Home mortgages (graduated payment) FHA-insured, financial, property, and mortgagor characteristics, US summary, quarterly rpt, 5142-40

Home mortgages FHA-insured, financial, property, and mortgagor characteristics, for US and selected localities, quarterly rpt, 5142-2

Home mortgages FHA-insured, financial, property, and mortgagor characteristics, for US, selected States, and Puerto Rico, quarterly rpt, 5142-3

Home mortgages FHA-insured, financial, property, and mortgagor characteristics, quarterly rpt, 5142-1

Home mortgages FHA-insured, financial, property, and mortgagor characteristics, 1983, annual rpt, 5144-17

Home mortgages FHA-insured for low-cost homes, financial, construction, property, and mortgagor characteristics, quarterly rpt, 5142-4

Index by Subjects and Names

Housing construction

Housing (rental) unit choice of Pittsburgh, Pa, recent movers related to unit, neighborhood, and town characteristics, 1967 survey, 9306–1.7

Housing activity indicators, private housing starts, unsold homes, and rental vacancy rates, monthly rpt with articles, 9312–1.1

Housing and households characteristics, and employment, housing finance, and social programs data, selected years 1948-83, hearing, 21968–28

Housing and households detailed characteristics, and unit and neighborhood quality, by inside-outside central cities, 1979-82 surveys, SMSA rpt series, 2485–6

Housing occupancy and unit and household characteristics, by region and metro-nonmetro residence, 1983, biennial survey, 2485–1

Indian and Alaska Native housing and community dev program operations, FY82 with Community Dev Block Grant funding by tribe and State for FY81, annual rpt, 5004–5

Korea (South) housing situation and govt policy, selected years 1975-82, article, 9312–1.404

New single and multifamily housing physical and financial characteristics, by region and metro-nonmetro location, 1979-83, annual rpt, 2384–1

North Central States, FHLB 7th District housing vacancy rates for single and multifamily units and mobile homes, by ZIP code, annual metro area rpt series, 9304–18

Older persons population characteristics, and needs and costs of social services by type, by metro-nonmetro status, 1970s-82 with trends from 1900, 21148–28

Older persons rural housing condition, selected householder and housing characteristics with comparisons to urban and nonaged population, 1979, 1598–193

Pacific Northwest electricity consumption and prices by end-use sector, and economic and demographic data, 1960s-83 and projected to 2005, annual rpt, 3224–2

Poverty status of families and persons, by detailed socioeconomic characteristics, 1982, annual Current Population Rpt, 2546–6.40

Public housing under private mgmt, assessment by housing officials and managers, and tenants, with operating costs, crime, and rent delinquency by project type and location, 1982, 5188–103

Quality of housing and neighborhoods, indicators and attitudes, and occupant characteristics, by urban-rural location and region, 1981, annual survey, 2485–7

Quality of housing and neighborhoods, indicators and attitudes, by occupant and unit characteristics, region, and metro-nonmetro location, 1981, annual survey, 2485–2

Quality of housing and neighborhoods, indicators and attitudes for 15 SMSAs, 1978, annual survey special supplement, 2485–8

Rural and urban areas comparisons of employment, income, housing, health, and education, 1960s-83, annual chartbook, 1504–3

South Central States, FHLB 9th District housing vacancy rates for single and multifamily units and mobile homes by ZIP code, annual metro area rpt series, 9304–19

Uranium ore tailings at active mills, EPA radon and radionuclide emmission standards and US and foreign exposure and health effects, various periods 1957-83, hearings, 21208–17

Urban and rural housing, home ownership rates and unit age, by region, 1980, article, 1702–1.407

Urban area economic distress index and components, for 153 cities, 1975 and 1980, article, 9373–1.413

Urban area socioeconomic and fiscal trends and problems, 1950-83 and Fed Govt funding estimates for FY84-87, biennial rpt, 5124–4

Vacancy and occupancy rates, and vacant housing characteristics, by region and metro-nonmetro location, selected years 1960-83, annual rpt, 2484–1

Vacant housing characteristics and costs, and occupancy and vacancy rates, by region and metro-nonmetro location, quarterly rpt, 2482–1

West Central States, FHLB 10th District housing vacancy rates for single and multifamily units and mobile homes, by ZIP code, annual metro area rpt series, 9304–22

Western States economic indicators, Fed Reserve 12th District, quarterly rpt, 9393–1.4

Western States, FHLB 11th District housing, employment, and economic indicators, by SMSA, quarterly rpt, 9302–18

Western States, FHLB 11th District housing vacancy rates for single and multifamily units and mobile homes, by ZIP code, annual metro area rpt series, 9304–20

Western States, FHLB 12th District housing vacancy rates for single and multifamily units and mobile homes, by ZIP code, annual metro area rpt series, 9304–21

Western States housing outlook and economic and demographic trends, FHLB 11th District, urban area rpt series, 9306–2

see also Abandoned buildings

see also Families and households

see also Household appliances and equipment

see also Household furnishings

see also Housing maintenance and repair

see also Housing tenure

see also Insulation

see also Landlord-tenant relations

see also Plumbing and heating

see also Rent

see also Rent supplements

see also Transient housing

Housing construction

Apartment and condominium completions by rent class and sales price, and market absorption rates, quarterly rpt, 2482–2

Apartment market absorption rates and characteristics for nonsubsidized privately financed furnished and unfurnished units completed in 1982, annual Current Housing Rpt, 2484–2

Apartment market absorption rates and characteristics for nonsubsidized privately financed units completed in 1983, preliminary annual Current Housing Rpt, 2484–3

Appalachian States, FHLB 5th District housing vacancy rates for single and multifamily units and mobile homes, by ZIP code, annual metro area rpt series, 9304–27

Asia developing countries housing finance and low-income housing projects, and activities of 2 countries, 1970s-82, annual conf proceedings, 9914–11

Business Conditions Digest, current data on economic, business, and financial conditions and cyclical fluctuations, monthly rpt, 2702–3

Business Conditions Digest, historical supplement on economic, business, and financial conditions and cyclical fluctuations, with methodology, 1947-82, 2708–31

Business statistics, detailed data for major industries and economic indicators, *Survey of Current Business,* monthly rpt, 2702–1.3

California housing market, and Los Angeles average home price and mortgage rate, 1969-82 with economic indicators projected to 1989, 9306–1.1

Census of Construction Industries, 1982: financial and operating data, by SIC 4-digit industry and State, final rpt series, 2373–1

Census of Construction Industries, 1982: financial and operating data, by SIC 4-digit industry and State, preliminary rpt series, 2371–1

Census of Housing, 1980: inventory, occupancy, and unit characteristics, changes from 1973 by region and inside-outside SMSAs and central cities, series, 2473–3

Coastal environmental characteristics, fish, wildlife, and use, and population socioeconomic data, for individual areas, series, 5506–4

Communist, OECD, and selected other countries consumer and producer goods production, 1960s-83, annual rpt, 244–5.8

Community dev programs funding and activities, for 5 HUD programs, FY83, annual rpt, 5124–5

County and City Data Book, detailed socioeconomic and demographic data for States, counties, and cities, selected years 1976-82, 2328–1

Economic indicators and components, and Fed Reserve 4th District business and financial conditions, monthly chartbook, 9377–10

Economic indicators and components, current data and annual trends, monthly rpt, 23842–1.3

Economic indicators, and Fed Govt finances and deficits, selected years 1962-83 and projected under cost control proposals to 2000, 16908–1.1

Economic indicators, nonfinancial, monthly rpt, 9362–1.2

Employment, earnings, and hours, by SIC 4-digit nonfarm industry, monthly 1974-Feb 1984, annual update, 6744–4

Housing construction

Energy supply/demand and prices, by fuel type, sector, and end use, detailed trends and projections 1973-95, annual rpt, 3164–75

Farm real estate transfers, by proposed use of property, region, and State, 1982-83, annual rpt, 1541–8.4

Financial and business statistics, historic trends, 1984 annual chartbook, 9364–2.12

Financial and business statistics, quarterly chartbook, 9362–2.6

Fires and related deaths in mobile homes, and rates compared to site-built homes, 1960-78, article, 1502–7.402

Forecasts for selected business activities and natl economic indicators, compilation of representative opinions, 1984, annual rpt, 9389–3

Fresno, Calif, economic, population, labor, and housing indicators, various periods 1974-85, hearing, 21248–84

Germany (West) housing units completed by type, and housing activity financial indicators, selected years 1950-81, article, 9312–1.405

Housing activity indicators, private housing starts, unsold homes, and rental vacancy rates, monthly rpt with articles, 9312–1.1

Housing and householder selected characteristics, by urban-rural location, 1981, annual survey, 2485–7.1

Housing occupancy and unit and household characteristics, by region and metro-nonmetro residence, 1983, biennial survey, 2485–1

Income tax returns of sole proprietorships, detailed data by industry div and selected industry group, 1981, annual rpt, 8304–7

Indian and Alaska Native housing and community dev program operations, FY82 with Community Dev Block Grant funding by tribe and State for FY81, annual rpt, 5004–5

Input-output structure of US economy, detailed interindustry transactions for 537 industries, and components of final demand, 1977 benchmark data, 2708–17

Korea (South) housing situation and govt policy, selected years 1975-82, article, 9312–1.404

Korea (South) housing units completed and home loans and loan value by instn, cumulative 1967-75 and 1976-82, article, 9312–1.406

Natl income and product, comprehensive accounts and components, *Survey of Current Business,* monthly rpt, 2702–1.22

New Communities program of HUD, activities, costs, land sales, and community and population characteristics, for 13 communities, 1970s-83, 5188–107

New construction (public and private) put in place, value by type, monthly rpt, 2382–4

New England States economic indicators, Fed Reserve 1st District, monthly rpt, 9373–2.3

New England States, FHLB 1st District member instns financial operations and housing industry indicators, monthly rpt, 9302–4

New housing completions, sales price, cost per square foot, and heating fuel use, by metro-nonmetro area, 1976-82, 1598–190

New housing starts, 1959-83, annual rpt, 204–1.3

New housing unit starts and completions authorized by building permits in 20 MSAs, quarterly rpt, 2382–9

New housing unit starts, and FHA 1- to 4-family home mortgage applications, commitments, and insurance, quarterly rpt, 5142–5

New housing unit starts, by units per structure and metro-nonmetro location, and mobile home placements and sales price, by region, monthly rpt, 2382–1

New housing units authorized, by public and private ownership, by region, div, State, selected MSA, and 4,700 permit-issuing places, monthly rpt, 2382–5

New housing units authorized, by public and private ownership, State, and permit-issuing place, 1983, annual rpt, 2384–2

New housing units completed and under construction, by units per structure, region, and inside-outside SMSAs, monthly rpt, 2382–2

New housing units, permits, and Fed Govt contracts, by type of construction and region, bimonthly rpt with articles, 2012–1

New single-family homes sold and for sale, by price, stage of construction, months on market, and region, and seasonal adjustments, monthly rpt, 2382–3

North Central States, FHLB 7th District housing vacancy rates for single and multifamily units and mobile homes, by ZIP code, annual metro area rpt series, 9304–18

Occupational injury and illness rates, by SIC 2- to 4-digit industry, 1982, annual rpt, 6844–1

Older and handicapped persons housing projects construction and rehabilitation loans of HUD, FY84, annual listing, 5004–6

Pacific Northwest electricity consumption and prices by end-use sector, and economic and demographic data, 1960s-83 and projected to 2005, annual rpt, 3224–2

Public and subsidized rental housing construction starts and completions, 1975-84, hearing, 21968–28

Seasonal adjustment methodology for economic time series, dev and design of Census Bur and other systems, with illustrative data, 1981 conf papers, 2626–7.5

South Central States, FHLB 9th District housing vacancy rates for single and multifamily units and mobile homes by ZIP code, annual metro area rpt series, 9304–19

Southeastern States and 5 SMSAs economic indicators, Fed Reserve 8th District, quarterly rpt, 9391–15

Southeastern States financial and economic devs, Fed Reserve 6th District, monthly rpt with articles, 9371–1

Statistical Abstract of US, social, political, and economic data, 1950s-83 and trends, annual rpt, 2324–1.3

West Central States, FHLB 10th District housing vacancy rates for single and multifamily units and mobile homes, by ZIP code, annual metro area rpt series, 9304–22

Index by Subjects and Names

Western States economic indicators, Fed Reserve 12th District, quarterly rpt, 9393–1.4

Western States, FHLB 11th District housing, employment, and economic indicators, by SMSA, quarterly rpt, 9302–18

Western States, FHLB 11th District housing vacancy rates for single and multifamily units and mobile homes, by ZIP code, annual metro area rpt series, 9304–20

Western States, FHLB 11th District member S&Ls financial operations and housing industry indicators by State, monthly rpt, 9302–17

Western States, FHLB 12th District housing vacancy rates for single and multifamily units and mobile homes, by ZIP code, annual metro area rpt series, 9304–21

Window shipments and prices by market sector, and installation by unit type and State, for wood and aluminum frames, selected years 1967-82, article, 2012–1.403

see also Building materials
see also Federal aid to housing
see also Housing condition and occupancy
see also Housing costs and financing
see also Housing maintenance and repair
see also Housing tenure
see also Insulation
see also Low-income housing
see also Mortgages
see also Prefabricated buildings
see also Property value
see also Public housing
see also Wrecking and demolition

Housing costs and financing

AID activities and funding by project and function, FY85, and developing countries summary socioeconomic data, 1970s-83, by country, annual rpt, 9914–3

Alteration and repair expenditures for residential property, by characteristics of property and region, 1983, annual rpt, 2384–4

Asia developing countries housing finance and low-income housing projects, and activities of 2 countries, 1970s-82, annual conf proceedings, 9914–11

Bond tax-exempt issues by purpose, and Fed Govt mortgage bond revenue losses and borrower characteristics, selected years 1971-85, hearings, 21788–135

Bond tax-exempt issues for private activity, by purpose, face value, major industry, and State, 1983, article, 8302–2.417

Bond tax-exempt issues for public and private purposes, by use of proceeds, 1975-83, article, 9362–1.408

Bonds for home mortgage subsidy, purchase price limit for tax-exempt status, by State and MSA, 1984 annual press release, 8304–16.2

California (southern) housing demand by county, prices and sales, and costs after homeowner tax deductions, 1970s-80, hearing, 21148–31

Census of Govts, 1982: properties, govt-assessed value, sales, and tax rates, by property type, State, SMSA, county, and city, 2453–1

Census of Housing, 1980: inventory, occupancy, and unit characteristics, changes from 1973 by region and inside-outside SMSAs and central cities, series, 2473–3

Index by Subjects and Names

Housing costs and financing

Census of Housing, 1980: occupancy and unit characteristics of SMSAs and central cities, by race, Hispanic origin, and city, State and SMSA rpt series, 2473–1

Census of Housing, 1980: structural, financial, and householder characteristics, by region and State, 2475–4

Census of Population and Housing, 1980: detailed population and housing characteristics, by county, city, and census tract, State and SMSA rpt series, 2551–2

Community dev programs funding and activities, for 5 HUD programs, FY83, annual rpt, 5124–5

Condominium completions by rent class and sales price, and market absorption rates, quarterly rpt, 2482–2

Condominium market absorption rates and characteristics for nonsubsidized privately financed units completed in 1983, preliminary annual Current Housing Rpt, 2484–3

County and City Data Book, detailed socioeconomic and demographic data for States, counties, and cities, selected years 1976-82, 2328–1

CPI by detailed component, for US city average, 28 SMSAs, and 4 regions by population size, monthly rpt, 6762–2

CPI components relative importance, for selected SMSAs, and US city average by region and population size, 1983, annual rpt, 6884–1

Developing countries Housing Guaranty Program of AID, financial statements, and projects by country, FY83, annual rpt, 9914–4

Earth-sheltered housing design, energy efficiency, natural and nuclear hazard reduction, and costs, by selected SMSA, 1983 rpt, 3308–71

Economic indicators and components, and Fed Reserve 4th District business and financial conditions, monthly chartbook, 9377–10

Economic indicators and components, current data and annual trends, monthly rpt, 23842–1.3

Economic indicators and labor force characteristics, selected years 1880-1995, chartbook, 6728–30

Energy supply/demand and prices, by energy resource and major producing and consuming country and sector, detailed data, monthly rpt, 3162–24

Energy use, costs, expenditures, and conservation, and household and housing characteristics, EIA survey series, 3166–7

Farm debt, loans outstanding, and interest rates, by type of lender and State, 1960-83 with trends from 1940, biennial rpt, 1544–2

Financial and business statistics, quarterly chartbook, 9362–2.6

FmHA loans and borrower supervision activities in farm and housing programs, by type and State, monthly rpt, 1182–1

FmHA loans and grants by program and State, and summary of services, FY83 with trends from FY63, annual rpt, 1184–17

FmHA rural housing loans, by race, Hispanic origin, and State, quarterly rpt, 1182–5

Food stamp recipient households size and composition, income, and income deductions allowed, Aug 1981, annual rpt, 1364–8

Germany (West) housing units completed by type, and housing activity financial indicators, selected years 1950-81, article, 9312–1.405

Home mortgages (graduated payment) FHA-insured, financial, property, and mortgagor characteristics, for US and selected localities, quarterly rpt, 5142–42

Home mortgages (graduated payment) FHA-insured, financial, property, and mortgagor characteristics, for US and selected States, quarterly rpt, 5142–41

Home mortgages (graduated payment) FHA-insured, financial, property, and mortgagor characteristics, US summary, quarterly rpt, 5142–40

Home mortgages FHA-insured, financial, property, and mortgagor characteristics, for US and selected localities, quarterly rpt, 5142–2

Home mortgages FHA-insured, financial, property, and mortgagor characteristics, for US, selected States, and Puerto Rico, quarterly rpt, 5142–3

Home mortgages FHA-insured, financial, property, and mortgagor characteristics, quarterly rpt, 5142–1

Home mortgages FHA-insured, financial, property, and mortgagor characteristics, 1983, annual rpt, 5144–17

Home mortgages FHA-insured for low-cost homes, financial, construction, property, and mortgagor characteristics, quarterly rpt, 5142–4

Household income, home value and equity, and financial assets by type, by household characteristics, 1983 survey with trends from 1970, article, 9362–1.406

Housing adequacy, quality, and affordability by condition and age of unit, rent paid or owner expense and share of income, and metro-nonmetro location, 1980, article, 1702–1.406

Housing and financial characteristics, and unit and neighborhood quality, for 15 SMSAs, 1978, annual survey special supplement, 2485–8

Housing and households characteristics, and employment, housing finance, and social programs data, selected years 1948-83, hearing, 21968–28

Housing and households detailed characteristics, and unit and neighborhood quality, by inside-outside central cities, 1979-82 surveys, SMSA rpt series, 2485–6

Housing finance studies, technical paper series, 9316–1

Housing finance studies, technical paper series, 9316–2

Housing finance studies, technical paper series, 9306–1

Housing finance technical analysis, quarterly rpt articles, 9312–7, 9412–2

Housing occupancy and unit and household characteristics, by region and metro-nonmetro residence, 1983, biennial survey, 2485–1

Housing tenure related to housing price uncertainty and changes in home-owner tax shelters, 1984 technical paper, 8006–3.50

Indian and Alaska Native housing and community dev program operations, FY82 with Community Dev Block Grant funding by tribe and State for FY81, annual rpt, 5004–5

Low-rent housing project financing notes sold by local authorities, terms and individual purchasers, monthly press release, 5142–37

Mobile homes placed, average sales price, and dealer inventories, by region, monthly rpt, 2382–1

Natl income and product, comprehensive accounts and components, *Survey of Current Business,* monthly rpt, 2702–1.21

New Communities program of HUD, activities, costs, land sales, and community and population characteristics, for 13 communities, 1970s-83, 5188–107

New construction (public and private) put in place, value by type, monthly rpt, 2382–4

New England States, FHLB 1st District member instns financial operations and housing industry indicators, monthly rpt, 9302–4

New housing completions, sales price, cost per square foot, and heating fuel use, by metro-nonmetro area, 1976-82, 1598–190

New housing starts and completions by number of units and inside-outside MSA, new and existing home sales, and new home prices, by region, bimonthly rpt, 2012–1.2

New single and multifamily housing physical and financial characteristics, by region and metro-nonmetro location, 1979-83, annual rpt, 2384–1

New single-family homes sold and for sale, by price, stage of construction, months on market, and region, and seasonal adjustments, monthly rpt, 2382–3

New single-family houses sold, prices and price index by region, quarterly rpt, 2382–8

Older and handicapped persons housing projects construction and rehabilitation loans of HUD, FY84, annual listing, 5004–6

Personal consumption expenditures, natl income and product account, *Survey of Current Business,* monthly rpt, monthly and annual tables, 2702–1.23

Property improvement and mobile home loans FHA-insured, and claims paid, quarterly rpt, 5142–9

Property improvement and mobile home loans FHA-insured, by State and county, 1983 and cumulative from 1934, annual rpt, 5144–16

Quality of housing and neighborhoods, indicators and attitudes, and occupant characteristics, by urban-rural location and region, 1981, annual survey, 2485–7

Real estate broker industry structure and practices, sales commissions, and broker and consumer attitudes, selected years 1975-81, 9408–48

Savings and loan assns and other home financing, 1983, annual rpt, 9314–3

Statistical Abstract of US, social, political, and economic data, 1950s-83 and trends, annual rpt, 2324–1.3

Housing costs and financing

Urban renewal project financing notes sold by local authorities, monthly press release, suspended, 5142–36

Vacant housing characteristics and costs, and occupancy and vacancy rates, by region and metro-nonmetro location, quarterly rpt, 2482–1

Vacant housing characteristics and rent or sales price asked, by metro-nonmetro location, selected years 1960-83, annual rpt, 2484–1.2

Western States economic indicators, Fed Reserve 12th District, quarterly rpt, 9393–1.4

Western States housing outlook and economic and demographic trends, FHLB 11th District, urban area rpt series, 9306–2

see also Federal aid to housing
see also Housing sales
see also Mortgages
see also Property value
see also Rent

Housing energy conservation
see Housing energy use
see Insulation

Housing energy use

- Air pollutant emission factors, by detailed source, 3rd edition, 1983-84 supplements, 9198–13
- Air pollution levels for 5 pollutants, by detailed source, State, and Air Quality Control Region, 1981, annual rpt, 9194–7
- Air pollution levels for 5 pollutants, by source, 1970- 82 with trends from 1940, annual rpt, 9194–13
- Alaska electric power capacity and generation by fuel type, and marketing, by utility, type of ownership, and location, 1983, annual rpt, 3214–2
- Bonneville Power Admin energy conservation program activities and funding data, FY82 and estimated FY83-87, 3228–2
- Bonneville Power Admin sales, revenues, and prices, by class of customer and individual purchaser, 1983, semiannual rpt, 3222–1
- Census of Govts, 1982: State govt payments to local govts, by program, source of funds, level of govt, and State, with trends from 1902, 2460–3
- Census of Housing, 1980: inventory, occupancy, and unit characteristics, changes from 1973 by region and inside-outside SMSAs and central cities, series, 2473–3
- Census of Housing, 1980: occupancy and unit characteristics of SMSAs and central cities, by race, Hispanic origin, and city, State and SMSA rpt series, 2473–1
- Census of Housing, 1980: structural, financial, and householder characteristics, by region and State, 2475–4
- Census of Population and Housing, 1980: detailed population and housing characteristics, by county, city, and census tract, State and SMSA rpt series, 2551–2
- Coal, coke, and breeze supply/demand, prices, trade, and stocks, by end-use sector and State, quarterly rpt with articles, 3162–37
- Coal production and stocks by district, and shipments by district of origin, State of destination, consuming sector, and mode of transport, quarterly rpt, 3162–8

Connecticut utility group housing energy conservation program, cost effectiveness and characteristics of participants and nonparticipants, 1980-82, 3308–77

- Conservation devices installation, utility loan program cost effectiveness, and household participation characteristics, Minnesota study, 1980-83, 3308–72
- Conservation in housing energy use and savings under alternative conservation strategies, by State, with model methodology and energy prices, selected years 1970-81, 21368–48
- Conservation programs of utilities, actual and predicted gas savings by conservation measure, Minnesota study, 1980-83, 3308–74
- Conservation programs of utilities, financing, costs, participation, and energy savings, various periods 1981-84, hearing, 21368–54
- Conservation programs of utilities under natl conservation act, cost effectiveness and participating household characteristics, 1980s, 3308–69
- *County and City Data Book,* detailed socioeconomic and demographic data for States, counties, and cities, selected years 1976-82, 2328–1
- Earth-sheltered housing design, energy efficiency, natural and nuclear hazard reduction, and costs, by selected SMSA, 1983 rpt, 3308–71
- Electric and gas utility ratemaking and regulatory policy standards, and consumers and sales covered, by type of consumer and utility, 1983, annual rpt, 3104–7
- Electric power demand of households in 136 SMSAs and other utility service areas, with fuel prices, family income, and heating degree days, 1975 and projected to 1985, 1588–78
- Electric power rate schedules, by user type, utility, and city, Jan 1984, annual rpt, 3164–40
- Electric utilities privately owned, sales revenues by company and consuming sector, with summary data for other distributors by type, 1982, annual rpt, 3164–23
- Electric utility production, fuel consumption, stocks, and costs by fuel type, and sales, by State, monthly rpt, 3162–35
- Electric utility sales, by consuming sector, census div, and State, 1979-83, annual rpt, 3164–11.3
- Electricity and gas costs for residential use in 306 cities, by utility, with climatological data, fall 1982, 3308–67
- Electricity use and savings of households, methodology for assessment using utility billing data, 1984 rpt, 3308–76
- Energy bills of housing and departures from normal by fuel type, and heating and cooling degree days by State, by census div, monthly rpt, 2152–11, 2152–12
- Energy Info Admin survey of household energy use, costs, expenditures, and conservation, and household and housing characteristics, series, 3166–7
- Energy prices and demand as factors in housing supply, regression results from FHA new-home sales records, 1974-78, 9306–1.2

Index by Subjects and Names

- Energy prices and expenditures for fuels and electricity, by consuming sector, State, and fuel type, 1970-81, annual rpt, 3164–64
- Energy production, reserves, and prices, by energy type, and selected indicators of energy use, by State, 1982-83 with selected comparisons from 1971, annual rpt, 3164–60
- Energy supply/demand and prices, by energy resource and major producing and consuming country and sector, detailed data, monthly rpt, 3162–24
- Energy supply/demand and prices, by energy source and end-use sector and for 7 electric utilities, 1981-2000 with trends from 1960s, 3008–93
- Energy supply/demand and prices, by fuel type and consuming sector with foreign comparisons, 1949-83, annual rpt, 3164–74
- Energy supply/demand and prices, by fuel type, sector, and end use, detailed trends and projections 1973-95, annual rpt, 3164–75
- Energy supply/demand and prices, by fuel type, sector, and end use, with foreign comparisons, 1960-83 and projected to 1995, annual summary rpt, 3164–76
- Energy supply/demand, prices, end use, and related technical and socioeconomic data, including impacts of US policy and intl devs, series, 3006–7
- Energy use, by economic sector, end use, and energy source, 1983 and 2000, 2006–2.5
- Energy use, by economic sector, State, census div, and detailed energy resource, 1960-82, State Energy Data System annual rpt, 3164–39
- Energy use, by type of air pollutant source and fuel, and State, 1981, annual rpt, 9194–14
- Energy use in transportation and other sectors, by fuel, selected years 1970-83, annual rpt, 3304–5
- Energy use, per capita and by economic sector, State, and major energy resource, 1960-82, State Energy Data System annual supplement, 3164–55
- Energy use, prices, and conservation and efficiency measures, by fuel type, end-use sector, selected industry, and region, 1960-83, annual rpt, 3164–73
- Environmental quality and protection programs, costs, and Fed Govt enforcement, 1983, detailed annual rpt, 484–1
- Fuel oil (distillate and residual) and kerosene deliveries, by end use, PAD district, and State, selected years 1978-83, annual rpt, 3164–2
- Heating fuel use, for new housing units, by metro-nonmetro area, 1976-82, 1598–190
- Housing and households detailed characteristics, and unit and neighborhood quality, by inside-outside central cities, 1979-82 surveys, SMSA rpt series, 2485–6
- Housing and neighborhood quality indicators and attitudes, and occupant characteristics, by urban-rural location and region, 1981, annual survey, 2485–7
- Housing, new single and multifamily unit physical and financial characteristics, by region and metro-nonmetro location, 1979-83, annual rpt, 2384–1

Index by Subjects and Names

Housing occupancy and unit and household characteristics, by region and metro-nonmetro residence, 1983, biennial survey, 2485–1

Input-output structure of US economy, detailed interindustry transactions for 537 industries, and components of final demand, 1977 benchmark data, 2708–17

Low-income households energy aid of Fed Govt, allocations and average benefits in 13 States, and public interest group assessment, FY81-83, GAO rpt, 26121–75

Low-income households energy aid of Fed Govt, by income, aid type, and State, FY83, annual rpt, 4744–3.13

Natl Energy Policy Plan, energy supply, demand, and prices, by fuel and consuming sector, projected 1985-2010, biennial rpt, 3004–13

Natl income and product, comprehensive accounts and components, *Survey of Current Business,* monthly rpt, 2702–1.21

Natural and supplemental gas production, prices, trade, use, reserves, and pipeline company finances, by firm and State, monthly rpt with articles, 3162–4

Natural gas consumer prices, by consumer sector, census div, and State, 1983, preliminary annual rpt, 3164–4

Natural gas interstate pipeline company detailed financial and operating data, by firm, 1983, annual rpt, 3164–38

Natural gas price decontrol alternatives effect on supply/demand, prices, and home heating costs of low-income households, 1970s-95, hearing, 25148–26

Natural gas prices, reserves, consumption, and production, projected under alternative price controls 1983-95 with market data for various periods 1970-Mar 1984, 3008–96

Natural gas supply, contract prices, pipeline operations and finances, and residential use, various periods 1966-1983/84, 3168–89

New England States electricity and gasoline sales, Fed Reserve 1st District, monthly rpt, 9373–2.6

North Central States natural gas supply/demand, and percent of residential heating with natural gas, by Fed Reserve 7th district State and for total US, 1970s-82, 9375–13.3

OECD energy prices and taxes by energy source and end-use sector, for US and 9 countries, quarterly 1979-83, annual rpt, 3164–71

Oil refined products sales of gas plant operators, refiners, and resellers, price and volume for 13 products, by end-use sector, PAD district, and State, monthly rpt, 3162–11

Older persons Fed Govt pension and health spending, by program and as percents of budget and GNP, 1965-85 with projections to 2040, 25148–28

Older persons sociodemographic characteristics, and Fed Govt program participation and funding, 1983 with trends and projections 1900-2060, annual rpt, 25144–3.1

Pacific Northwest electricity consumption and prices by end-use sector, and

economic and demographic data, 1960s-83 and projected to 2005, annual rpt, 3224–2

Personal consumption expenditures, natl income and product account, *Survey of Current Business,* monthly rpt, monthly and annual tables, 2702–1.23

Prices (retail) and housing consumption, by energy type, region, and for 28 SMSAs and US city average, monthly press release, 6762–8

Rental multifamily housing energy use and costs, conservation effect on rental marketing, and effect of utility bill payment methods on conservation efforts, 1970s-80s, 3308–73

Solar collector and photovoltaic module production, sales, and use, with listing of manufacturers, 1983, annual rpt, 3164–62

Statistical Abstract of US, social, political, and economic data, 1950s-83 and trends, annual rpt, 2324–1.3

TVA electric power purchases of municipal and cooperative distributors, and prices and consumption by distributor and consumer sector, monthly rpt, 9802–1

TVA power program finances and operations, by plant and distributor, FY83, annual rpt, 9804–23

Water conservation, residential programs and savings of water and energy for selected cities and suburbs, 1980-83, 5188–109

Wood acquired and used for home heating, by household characteristics and wood sources, 1980/81, 1208–204

Wood fuel consumption, by end-use sector, SIC 2-digit industry, region, State, and selected industrial and power plant, 1980-83, biennial rpt, 3164–78

Housing insulation

see Insulation

Housing maintenance and repair

Census of Construction Industries, 1982: financial and operating data, by SIC 4-digit industry and State, final rpt series, 2373–1

Census of Construction Industries, 1982: financial and operating data, by SIC 4-digit industry and State, preliminary rpt series, 2371–1

Census of Population, 1980: labor force, by sex, detailed occupation, and region, with comparison to 1970 census, supplementary rpt, 2535–1.12

Community Dev Block Grants to small cities, State admin, project characteristics, and assessments of local officials, 1982, 5188–106

CPI by detailed component, for US city average, 28 SMSAs, and 4 regions by population size, monthly rpt, 6762–2

Employment, earnings, and hours, by SIC 4-digit nonfarm industry, monthly 1974-Feb 1984, annual update, 6744–4

Energy conservation devices installation, utility loan program cost effectiveness, and household participation characteristics, Minnesota study, 1980-83, 3308–72

Energy conservation programs of utilities, actual and predicted gas savings by conservation measure, Minnesota study, 1980-83, 3308–74

Housing maintenance and repair

Expenditures for housing alteration and repair, by type and property size, various periods 1963-83, article, 2012–1.406

Expenditures for residential alteration and repair, by characteristics of property and region, 1983, annual rpt, 2384–4

Expenditures for residential alterations and repair, quarterly rpt, 2382–7

Farm finances, assets, liabilities, income, receipts by commodity and State, and expenses, 1980-83 and trends from 1910, annual rpt, 1544–16

FmHA loans and grants by program and State, and summary of services, FY83 with trends from FY63, annual rpt, 1184–17

Franchise business opportunities, by firm and kind of business, 1984 annual listing, 2044–27

Franchises of firms engaged in distribution of goods and services by kind of business, establishments by State, and sales, 1982-84, annual rpt, 2014–5

Fresno, Calif, economic, population, labor, and housing indicators, various periods 1974-85, hearing, 21248–84

Home mortgages (graduated payment) FHA-insured, financial, property, and mortgagor characteristics, for US and selected localities, quarterly rpt, 5142–42

Home mortgages (graduated payment) FHA-insured, financial, property, and mortgagor characteristics, for US and selected States, quarterly rpt, 5142–41

Home mortgages (graduated payment) FHA-insured, financial, property, and mortgagor characteristics, US summary, quarterly rpt, 5142–40

Home mortgages FHA-insured, financial, property, and mortgagor characteristics, for US and selected localities, quarterly rpt, 5142–2

Home mortgages FHA-insured, financial, property, and mortgagor characteristics, for US, selected States, and Puerto Rico, quarterly rpt, 5142–3

Home mortgages FHA-insured, financial, property, and mortgagor characteristics, quarterly rpt, 5142–1

Home mortgages FHA-insured, financial, property, and mortgagor characteristics, 1983, annual rpt, 5144–17

Home mortgages FHA-insured for low-cost homes, financial, construction, property, and mortgagor characteristics, quarterly rpt, 5142–4

HUD rental rehabilitation grants for low- and moderate-income housing, by community, 1984 press release, 5006–3.33

HUD rental rehabilitation program allocations, by State, county, and city, FY85, press release, 5006–3.39

HUD rental rehabilitation projects, local funding and Section 8 rent supplements for 22 States and 275 communities, 1984 press release, 5006–3.30

HUD rental rehabilitation projects, owner minority status, funding, assisted units, and location for 141 projects, 1984 press release, 5006–3.38

Indian and Alaska Native housing and community dev program operations, FY82 with Community Dev Block Grant funding by tribe and State for FY81, annual rpt, 5004–5

Housing maintenance and repair

Input-output structure of US economy, detailed interindustry transactions for 85 industries, and components of final demand, 1977, article, 2702–1.421

Input-output structure of US economy, detailed interindustry transactions for 537 industries, and components of final demand, 1977 benchmark data, 2708–17

Loans (FHA-insured) for property improvement and mobile homes, by State and county, 1983 and cumulative from 1934, annual rpt, 5144–16

Older and handicapped persons housing projects construction and rehabilitation loans of HUD, FY84, annual listing, 5004–6

Property improvement and mobile home loans FHA-insured, and claims paid, quarterly rpt, 5142–9

Property improvement and mobile home loans, FHA-insured, monthly rpt, suspended, 5142–10

Public housing under private mgmt, assessment by housing officials and managers, and tenants, with operating costs, crime, and rent delinquency by project type and location, 1982, 5188–103

Quality of housing and neighborhoods, indicators and attitudes, and occupant characteristics, by urban-rural location and region, 1981, annual survey, 2485–7

Quality of housing and neighborhoods, indicators and attitudes, by occupant and unit characteristics, region, and metro-nonmetro location, 1981, annual survey, 2485–2

Quality of housing and neighborhoods, indicators and attitudes for 15 SMSAs, 1978, annual survey special supplement, 2485–8

Rental multifamily housing energy use and costs, conservation effect on rental marketing, and effect of utility bill payment methods on conservation efforts, 1970s-80s, 3308–73

Underground economy, household expenditures and participation by type of goods or service and sociodemographic characteristics, with methodology and bibl, 1981 survey, 8308–27

Value of private residential additions and alterations, monthly rpt, 2382–4

Window shipments and prices by market sector, and installation by unit type and State, for wood and aluminum frames, selected years 1967-82, article, 2012–1.403

see also Insulation

Housing rehabilitation

see Housing maintenance and repair

see Urban renewal

Housing sales

California (southern) housing demand by county, prices and sales, and costs after homeowner tax deductions, 1970s-80, hearing, 21148–31

Census of Govts, 1982: properties, govt-assessed value, sales, and tax rates, by property type, State, SMSA, county, and city, 2453–1

Existing single-family home sales, by price and region, 1982, hearing, 21788–135

Housing and households characteristics, and employment, housing finance, and social programs data, selected years 1948-83, hearing, 21968–28

HUD mortgage insurance funds financial and property activity, and insurance written, monthly rpt, 5002–9

Income tax returns of individuals, by filing and deduction characteristics and income level, 1983, annual article, 8302–2.414

New England States, FHLB 1st District member instns financial operations and housing industry indicators, monthly rpt, 9302–4

New housing completions, sales price, cost per square foot, and heating fuel use, by metro-nonmetro area, 1976-82, 1598–190

New housing starts and completions by number of units and inside-outside MSA, new and existing home sales, and new home prices, by region, bimonthly rpt, 2012–1.2

New single and multifamily housing physical and financial characteristics, by region and metro-nonmetro location, 1979-83, annual rpt, 2384–1

New single-family homes sold and for sale, by price, stage of construction, months on market, and region, and seasonal adjustments, monthly rpt, 2382–3

New single-family houses sold, prices and price index by region, quarterly rpt, ◇ 2382–8

Real estate broker industry structure and practices, sales commissions, and broker and consumer attitudes, selected years 1975-81, 9408–48

Statistical Abstract of US, social, political, and economic data, 1950s-83 and trends, annual rpt, 2324–1.3

Western States economic indicators, Fed Reserve 12th District, quarterly rpt, 9393–1.4

Housing tenure

Bankruptcy (personal), filers by debt type and other characteristics, selected years 1978-81, hearing, 25528–97.1

Capital (fixed), govt and private nonresidential structures and equipment, residential capital, and consumer-owned durable goods by item, 1980-83, annual article, 2702–1.433

Census of Housing, 1980: inventory, occupancy, and unit characteristics, changes from 1973 by region and inside-outside SMSAs and central cities, series, 2473–3

Census of Housing, 1980: occupancy and unit characteristics of SMSAs and central cities, by race, Hispanic origin, and city, State and SMSA rpt series, 2473–1

Census of Housing, 1980: structural, financial, and householder characteristics, by region and State, 2475–4

Census of Population and Housing, 1980: detailed population and housing characteristics, by county, city, and census tract, State and SMSA rpt series, 2551–2

City and suburb population characteristics and local govt finances, by region and selected SMSA, 1950s-FY83, 10048–61

Coastal environmental characteristics, fish, wildlife, and use, and population socioeconomic data, for individual areas, series, 5506–4

Community dev programs funding and activities, for 5 HUD programs, FY83, annual rpt, 5124–5

Index by Subjects and Names

Connecticut personal bankruptcy filings, by debt type, whether claiming Federal homestead exemption, and other characteristics, 1980, hearing, 21528–57.1

County and City Data Book, detailed socioeconomic and demographic data for States, counties, and cities, selected years 1976-82, 2328–1

Crime victimization rates by type of offense, and victim and offense characteristics, Natl Crime Survey series, 6066–3

Energy conservation programs of utilities under natl conservation act, cost effectiveness and participating household characteristics, 1980s, 3308–69

Families and households detailed socioeconomic characteristics, Mar 1982, annual Current Population Rpt, 2546–1.383

Farm hired workers, sociodemographic characteristics, and farm/nonfarm income and workdays, by whether worked in Mar 1981, article, 6722–1.440

Florida and California elderly migration by selected State of origin or destination, and Florida elderly, by sociodemographic and housing characteristics, 1970 and 1980, 4478–150

High school classes of 1980 and 1982: educational and sociodemographic characteristics and expectations, natl longitudinal study, series, 4826–2

Hispanic Americans socioeconomic and demographic characteristics, and compared to non-Hispanics, selected years 1970-83, chartbook, 2328–48

Home ownership rates, and households and household formation by tenure, selected years 1940-83, 2486–1.6

Household income, assets, and debt characteristics, sources of credit, and use of financial services, 1983 survey, article, 9362–1.411

Household income, home value and equity, and financial assets by type, by household characteristics, 1983 survey with trends from 1970, article, 9362–1.406

Housing (rental) unit choice of Pittsburgh, Pa, recent movers related to unit, neighborhood, and town characteristics, 1967 survey, 9306–1.7

Housing adequacy, quality, and affordability by condition and age of unit, rent paid or owner expense and share of income, and metro-nonmetro location, 1980, article, 1702–1.406

Housing alteration and repair expenditures by characteristics of property and region, 1983, annual rpt, 2384–4

Housing and financial characteristics, and unit and neighborhood quality, for 15 SMSAs, 1978, annual survey special supplement, 2485–8

Housing and households characteristics, and employment, housing finance, and social programs data, selected years 1948-83, hearing, 21968–28

Housing and households detailed characteristics, and unit and neighborhood quality, by inside-outside central cities, 1979-82 surveys, SMSA rpt series, 2485–6

Housing energy use, costs, expenditures, and conservation, and household and housing characteristics, survey series, 3166–7

Housing occupancy and unit and household characteristics, by region and metro-nonmetro residence, 1983, biennial survey, 2485–1

Income (household) before and after taxes, by socioeconomic characteristics, type of tax paid, and region, 1981, Current Population Rpt, 2546–2.118

Income (household) before and after taxes, by socioeconomic characteristics, type of tax paid, and region, 1982, annual Current Population Rpt, 2546–2.122

Income of households, families, and persons, by detailed socioeconomic characteristics and region, 1982, annual Current Population Rpt, 2546–6.39

Older persons population characteristics, and needs and costs of social services by type, by metro-nonmetro status, 1970s-82 with trends from 1900, 21148–28

Older persons rural housing condition, selected householder and housing characteristics with comparisons to urban and nonaged population, 1979, 1598–193

Poverty-level persons and families, by income source, hours of work, earnings, taxes, and family characteristics, various periods 1959-84, 21788–131

Poverty status of families and persons, by detailed socioeconomic characteristics, 1982, annual Current Population Rpt, 2546–6.40

Quality of housing and neighborhoods, indicators and attitudes, and occupant characteristics, by urban-rural location and region, 1981, annual survey, 2485–7

Quality of housing and neighborhoods, indicators and attitudes, by occupant and unit characteristics, region, and metro-nonmetro location, 1981, annual survey, 2485–2

Rental housing, effects of Fed Govt tax policies on real estate investment, 1969-81, 5188–104

Supplemental Security Income payments, and recipients by other income source, eligibility type, and other characteristics, by State, 1982, annual rpt, 4744–16

Tax assessment, local jurisdictions reporting data on property size, use, location, ownership, and value, 1972-82, 1588–81

Tax shelter changes for homeowners, and housing price uncertainty, related to housing tenure, 1984 technical paper, 8006–3.50

Taxes, tax policy, and intergovtl relations, public opinion survey results, 1972-84, annual rpt, 10044–2

TVA construction projects employment, and impacts on nearby areas, survey rpt series, 9806–7

Urban and rural housing, home ownership rates and unit age, by region, 1980, article, 1702–1.407

Vacancy and occupancy rates, and vacant housing characteristics, by region and metro-nonmetro location, selected years 1960-83, annual rpt, 2484–1

Western States housing outlook and economic and demographic trends, FHLB 11th District, urban area rpt series, 9306–2

Women in couples with wife as primary earner, socioeconomic and family characteristics, with comparative data for husbands, Mar 1982, 2326–11.9

Wood acquired and used for home heating, by household characteristics and wood sources, 1980/81, 1208–204

see also Apartment houses

see also Condominiums and cooperatives

see also Housing sales

see also Rent

Houston Endowment Inc.

Philanthropic foundations assets and grants for 50 largest foundations, and for selected foundations by recipient, selected years 1975-82, hearings, 21788–137

Houston, Tex.

Auto dealer repair workers, wages, and benefits, by occupation, size of establishment, and for 24 labor market areas, Nov 1982 survey, 6787–6.202

Auto emissions control device tampering and fuel-switching incidence in 6 urban areas, 1983, annual rpt, 9194–15

Census of Housing, 1980: occupancy and unit characteristics, by race, Hispanic origin, and city, SMSA rpt, 2473–1.184

Census of Population and Housing, 1980: detailed population and housing characteristics, by county, city, and census tract, SMSA rpt, 2551–2.184

CPI by component for US city average, and by region, population size, and for 28 SMSAs, monthly press release, 6762–1

CPI by detailed component, for US city average, 28 SMSAs, and 4 regions by population size, monthly rpt, 6762–2

CPI by major component, average change for Dallas-Fort Worth and Houston, Tex, with comparisons to South and total US, 1973-82, BLS regional rpt series, 6966–1.12

Employment, earnings, hours, and CPI changes for Houston SMSA, 1983 with trends from 1968, annual rpt, 6964–1

Homeless population and characteristics, and temporary shelter operations, use, and user characteristics, for selected cities, various periods 1979-84, hearing, 21248–85

Hospital worker wages by sex and occupation, and benefits, for 22 MSAs, Oct 1981 survey, 6787–6.201

Population size of top 25 cities, 1980 and 1982, press release, 2328–46

Wages of office and plant workers, by occupation, 1984 SMSA survey rpt, 6785–11.5

see also under By City and By SMSA or MSA in the "Index by Categories"

Howard, David H.

"Domestic Saving, Current Accounts, and International Capital Mobility", 9366–7.100

Howard University

Salaries, academic standing, medical research, and library operations, and finances of Howard Inn, selected years 1976-83, GAO rpt, 26121–74

Howell, Craig

"Inflation Remained Low in 1983 in Face of Strong Recovery", 6722–1.429

"Producer Price Trends Continue Moderate in the Third Quarter", 6722–1.407

Howenstine, Ned G.

"U.S. Affiliates of Foreign Companies: Operations in 1981", 2702–1.402

"U.S. Direct Investment Abroad in 1983", 2702–1.430

Howland, Kenneth E.

"World Tobacco Outlook", 1004–16.1

Huang, Ben W.

"Outlook for Fruit and Tree Nuts", 1004–16.1

Hubbell, Ruth

"Review of Head Start Research Since 1970", 4608–17

HUD

see Department of Housing and Urban Development

Hudson, C. R., II

"Age and Capacity Profile of Electric Generation Plants in the U.S.", 3008–98

Hudson River

Bridges over navigable waters, with type of bridge and use, owner, dimensions, and location, 1984 regional listing, 7406–5.1

Freight (waterborne domestic and foreign) by commodity, traffic, and passengers, by port and waterway, 1982, annual rpt, 3754–3.1

Pollutant concentrations in sediments and fish and shellfish species, by pollutant type, late 1970s-82, hearings, 21568–36

Water supply and quality in streams and lakes, and groundwater levels in wells, by drainage basin, 1980, annual State rpt series, 5666–12

Water supply and quality in streams and lakes, and groundwater levels in wells, by drainage basin, 1981, annual State rpt series, 5666–16

Water supply and quality in streams and lakes, and groundwater levels in wells, by drainage basin, 1983, annual State rpt series, 5666–10

Water supply in Northeastern US, precipitation and stream runoff by station, monthly rpt, 2182–3

Huffstutler, Clyde

"Productivity in Making Air Conditioners, Refrigeration Equipment, and Furnaces", 6722–1.471

Hughes, James M.

"Nosocomial Infection Surveillance, 1980-82", 4202–7.401

Hughes, Vergie

"Producer Milk Marketed Under Federal Milk Orders by State of Origin", 1317–4.405

Hull, David B.

"Factors Affecting Domestic Soybean Meal Use", 1561–3.401

"Factors Affecting Quarterly Domestic Feed Demand for Corn", 1561–4.403

Human Genetic Mutant Cell Repository

Genetically abnormal human cell cultures available to researchers, and cultures shipped, 1984 annual listing, 4474–23

Human Nutrition Information Service

Activities and programs of USDA, by subagency, FY83, annual rpt, 1004–3

Food consumption and nutrient intake by individuals, by food group, source, and socioeconomic characteristics, 1977-78 natl survey, final rpt series, 1356–4

Human rights

see Civil rights

Humanities

see Arts and the humanities

Humpage, Owen F.

"Dollar Intervention and the Deutschemark-Dollar Exchange Rate: A Daily Time-Series Model", 9377–9.12

Humpage, Owen F.

"Voluntary Export Restraints: The Cost of Building Walls", 9377–1.407

Humphrey, Joseph F.

"Changing Asset/Liability Structure of Savings Institutions in a Deregulated Environment", 9306–1.3

Hungary

- Agricultural and food production indexes, and production of selected commodities, by world region and country, 1974-83, annual rpt, 1524–5
- Agricultural production and trade by commodity, food consumption, and farm inputs, for 6 countries, 1960-80 with projections to 1991, 1528–178
- Agricultural situation in Eastern Europe, by country, 1983 and outlook for 1984, annual report, 1524–4.7
- Cuba economic conditions, agricultural and industrial production and distribution, trade, and intl economic relations, 1970-82 and trends from 1957, 248–40
- Economic conditions in Communist, OECD, and selected other countries, 1960s-83, annual rpt, 244–5
- Economic conditions, income, production, prices, employment, and trade, 1984 annual country rpt, 2046–4.104
- Economic, social, and political summary data, by country, 1984, annual factbook, 244–11
- Economic trends in income, production, prices, employment, finances, and trade, 1984 annual rpt, 2046–4.25
- Export licensing and monitoring activities under Export Admin Act, for selected commodities, and for Communist and other countries, FY83, annual rpt, 2044–22
- Exports and imports of NATO countries with Council for Mutual Economic Assistance Europe members, by country, 1980-83, annual rpt, 7144–5
- Exports and imports of US with Communist countries, by detailed commodity and country, quarterly rpt with articles, 9882–2
- Exports of US, detailed Schedule B commodities by country of destination, 1983, annual rpt, 2424–9
- Exports of US, detailed Schedule E commodities by mode of transport and world area and country of destination, 1983, annual rpts, 2424–5
- Grain production, consumption, and trade, and US farm cooperatives grain and oilseed export potential, for 4 countries, selected years 1960-90, 1128–27
- Imports of US, detailed Schedule A commodities by country and world area of origin, and mode of transport, 1983, annual rpts, 2424–2
- Imports of US, detailed TSUSA commodities by country of origin, 1983, annual rpt, 2424–4
- Loans and grants for economic and military assistance from US and intl agencies, by program and country, FY46-83, annual rpt, 9914–5
- Military spending, arms trade, and armed forces size, with total govt spending and population, by country, 1972-82, annual rpt, 9824–1
- *Minerals Yearbook, 1982,* Vol 3: foreign country reviews of production, trade, and policies, by commodity, annual rpt, 5604–35

Minerals Yearbook, 1982, Vol 3 preprints: foreign country review of production, trade, and policies, by commodity, annual rpt, 5604–17.29

- Population size and growth rates, and latest available benchmark demographic data, by country, 1950-83, biennial rpt, 2324–4
- Refugee resettlement program activities and funding, arrivals and population by country of origin and State, and employment and other characteristics, FY83, annual rpt, 4704–8
- Science and technology dev and transfer between USSR and other members of Council for Mutual Economic Assistance, 1940s-81, 2326–9.7
- *see also* under By Foreign Country in the "Index by Categories"

Hunger

- *see* Food assistance
- *see* Food supply
- *see* Nutrition and malnutrition

Hunley, Charles

"Marketing and Transportation of Grain by Local Cooperatives", 1128–28

Hunterdon County, N.J.

see also under By SMSA or MSA in the "Index by Categories"

Hunting and trapping

- Alaska Arctic Natl Wildlife Refuge resources, resident and visitor activities, and environmental impacts of energy exploration, 1983, annual update rpt, 5504–26
- Animal and plant genetic resource conservation, commercial uses, causes of depletion, and geographic sources, 1984 rpt, 5548–13
- Army Corps of Engineers water resources dev projects, recreation activities by district and project, 1982, annual rpt, 3754–5
- Army morale, welfare, and recreation programs, revenue and expenses worldwide by activity and major command, FY82-83, annual rpt, 3704–12
- Census of Population, 1980: detailed socioeconomic and demographic characteristics, by age, sex, race, Hispanic origin, occupation, and industry, State rpt series, 2531–4
- Census of Population, 1980: labor force, by sex, detailed occupation, and region, with comparison to 1970 census, supplementary rpt, 2535–1.12
- Coastal environmental characteristics, fish, wildlife, and use, and population socioeconomic data, for individual areas, series, 5506–4
- County Business Patterns: establishments, employees, and payrolls, by SIC 4-digit industry and county, 1981, annual State rpt series, 2326–8
- County Business Patterns: establishments, employees, and payrolls, by SIC 4-digit industry and county, 1982, annual State rpt series, 2326–6
- Duck hunting stamp sales, with philatelic data and reproductions, 1983/84, annual fact sheet, 5504–25
- Fed Govt fish and wildlife restoration program finances, funding by State, and hunting and fishing equipment excise tax revenue, FY84, annual rpt, 5504–13

Index by Subjects and Names

- Foreign market and trade for sporting goods and recreational equipment and vehicles, country market research rpts, 2045–14
- Forest, range, and associated waters use and mgmt assessment, and environmental impacts of Forest Service program options, 1977-2030 and trends from 1920, 1208–24
- Income tax returns of sole proprietorships, detailed data by industry div and selected industry group, 1981, annual rpt, 8304–7
- Licenses for fishing and hunting issued and gross cost to sportsmen, by State, FY83, annual rpt, 5504–16
- Marine mammals protection activities and Fed Govt funding, population status, and research, 1983, annual rpt, 5504–12
- Mourning dove population, by region and hunting and nonhunting State, 1984, annual rpt, 5504–15
- Natl Forest System wildlife habitat and fishery improvements, use, and game population and harvest by species and forest, by region, FY83, annual rpt, 1204–31
- Natl forests recreational use, visitor-days by State and activity, FY79-83, annual rpt, 1204–1.1
- Natl forests recreational use, visitor-days by type of activity, forest, and State, FY83 with trends from 1924, annual rpt series, 1204–17
- Research of State fish and wildlife agencies, federally funded wildlife and bird projects and costs, by species and State, 1984, annual rpt, 5504–24
- Seal harvest, mgmt, and skins taken and rejected for northern fur seals of Pribilof Islands, Alaska, various dates 1786-1981, 2168–79
- Tax collections of State govts, by detailed type of tax and tax rates, by State, FY83, annual rpt, 2466–2.3
- Waterfowl harvested during hunting season, by species, State, and county, annual average for 1971-80, decennial rpt, 5508–18
- Wetlands environmental characteristics, acreage, uses, and mgmt, by wetland type and region, 1950s-80, 26358–102
- Wildlife refuge revenues from economic and recreational uses, and refuge managers attitudes toward expanded use, FY81-83, GAO rpt, 26113–128
- Woodcock population and hunter harvest, by region and State, 1984 and trends from 1966, annual rpt, 5504–11

Huntington Beach, Calif.

see also under By City in the "Index by Categories"

Huntington, W.Va.

- Census of Housing, 1980: occupancy and unit characteristics, by race, Hispanic origin, and city, SMSA rpt, 2473–1.185
- Census of Population and Housing, 1980: detailed population and housing characteristics, by county, city, and census tract, SMSA rpt, 2551–2.185
- Housing vacancy rates for single and multifamily units and mobile homes, by city and ZIP code, 1984, annual metro area rpt, 9304–27.10
- Waterborne commerce of US (domestic and foreign), freight by commodity, traffic, and passengers, by port and waterway, 1982, annual rpt, 3754–3.2

Index by Subjects and Names

see also under By SMSA or MSA in the "Index by Categories"

Huntsville, Ala.

Census of Housing, 1980: occupancy and unit characteristics, by race, Hispanic origin, and city, SMSA rpt, 2473–1.186

Census of Population and Housing, 1980: detailed population and housing characteristics, by county, city, and census tract, SMSA rpt, 2551–2.186

Wages of office and plant workers, by occupation, 1984 SMSA survey rpt, 6785–11.3

see also under By City and By SMSA or MSA in the "Index by Categories"

Hurricanes

see Storms

Hutchins, Cecil C., Jr.

"Pulpwood Prices in the Southeast, 1982", 1204–22

Hutchins, Vince

"Trends in Maternal and Infant Health Factors Associated with Low Infant Birth Weight, U.S., 1972 and 1980", 4102–1.423

Hutchinson, T. Q.

"Implications of the Motor Carrier Act of 1980", 1548–238

Hutchison, Michael M.

"Intervention, Deficit Finance and Real Exchange Rates: The Case of Japan", 9393–8.405

Hydrocarbons

see Petrochemicals

Hydroelectric power

Alaska electric power capacity and generation by fuel type, and marketing, by utility, type of ownership, and location, 1983, annual rpt, 3214–2

Army Corps of Engineers activities and projects, FY83 and trends from 1800s, annual rpt, 3754–1

Bonneville Power Admin sales, revenues, and prices, by class of customer and individual purchaser, 1983, semiannual rpt, 3222–1

China economic conditions, agricultural and industrial production, trade, and domestic and foreign investment, 1980-85, 2048–106

Colorado River Storage Project finances, water resource dev, power production, and other activities in western States, FY83, annual rpt, 5824–3

Consumption by fuel type, and estimated supply from renewable resources, 1977 and projected 2000, hearing, 21448–30

Consumption, by fuel type, economic sector, and end use, 1983 and 2000, 2006–2.5

Consumption, by fuel type, economic sector, census div, and State, 1960-82, State Energy Data System annual rpt, 3164–39

Consumption per capita, and by economic sector, State, and major energy resource, 1960-82, State Energy Data System annual supplement, 3164–55

Cuba economic conditions, agricultural and industrial production and distribution, trade, and intl economic relations, 1970-82 and trends from 1957, 248–40

Electric utilities privately owned, detailed financial and operating data by company, with summary data for other distributors by type, 1982, annual rpt, 3164–23

Electric utilities production, plant capacity, and fuel use, by prime mover, census div, and State, 1979-83, annual rpt, 3164–11.1

Electric utility fuel cost, quality, use, receipts, and stocks, and power plant production, by energy source, State and utility, quarterly rpt, 3162–39

Electric utility production, fuel consumption, stocks, and costs by fuel type, and sales, by State, monthly rpt, 3162–35

Fed Govt energy programs proposed budget appropriations, by office or dept and function, FY84-85, annual rpt, 3004–14

Fed Govt reclamation projects in western US, electric power capacities and transmission miles, and water storage and carriage facilities, by State, FY81, annual rpt, 5824–1.1

FERC activities and funding by program, with some natural gas and electric power industry data, FY83, annual rpt, 3084–9

Foreign and US energy production, by energy type and country, 1973-83, annual rpt, 3164–50.1, 3164–50.2

Natl Energy Policy Plan, energy supply, demand, and prices, by fuel and consuming sector, projected 1985-2010, biennial rpt, 3004–13

Production, reserves, and prices, by fuel type, and selected indicators of energy use, by State, 1982-83 with selected comparisons from 1971, annual rpt, 3164–60

Production, trade, supply, use, conservation, and DOE activities, by energy type, FY83, annual rpt, 3024–2

Reclamation Bur water storage and carriage facilities, by type, as of Sept 1983, annual listing, 5824–7

Research publications on energy of DOE and other sources, monthly listing, 3002–2

Southwestern Fed Power System financial statements, electric power sales by customer, and project capacity, production, and costs, FY83, annual rpt, 3244–1

Supply/demand and price forecasts, by fuel type, quarterly rpt, 3162–34

Supply/demand and prices, by energy resource and major producing and consuming country and sector, detailed data, monthly rpt, 3162–24

Supply/demand and prices, by energy source and end-use sector and for 7 electric utilities, 1981-2000 with trends from 1960s, 3008–93

Supply/demand and prices, by fuel type and consuming sector with foreign comparisons, 1949-83, annual rpt, 3164–74

Supply/demand and prices, by fuel type, sector, and end use, detailed trends and projections 1973-95, annual rpt, 3164–75

Supply/demand and prices, by fuel type, sector, and end use, with foreign comparisons, 1960-83 and projected to 1995, annual summary rpt, 3164–76

Transportation and related energy use, for urban areas, late 1970s-82 and projected under lower auto emission standards to 1995, 3408–31

TVA activities, financial and operating data by program and facility, and power sales by customer, FY83, annual rpt, 9804–1

Hydrology

Western Area Power Admin operations by plant, financial statements, and electric power sales by customer, FY83, annual rpt, 3254–1

Western Area Power Admin small-scale potential hydroelectric generation, site inventory, characteristics, and costs, by State and county, 1984 rpt, 3258–1

Western US Fed Govt lands by agency and mining restriction status, and energy resources on potential wilderness areas and other lands, 1970s-81 and projected to 1990, 3308–68

see also Electric power

see also Electric power prices

see also Power-generating plants and equipment

Hydrogen

see Gases

Hydrology

Carbon dioxide atmospheric concentration increase effects on hydrologic conditions, projected for 26-35 years, 9188–95

Classifications for US and outlying area hydrologic units, ordering info, 1983 rpt, 2216–2.126

Coal mining effect on water supply and quality in selected river basins of Eastern and Interior coal provinces, 1970s, series, 5666–15

Coal mining effect on water supply and quality in selected river basins of Western coal provinces, series, 5666–19

Coastal environmental and wildlife characteristics, use, and mgmt, for individual ecosystems, series, 5506–9

Coastal environmental characteristics, fish, wildlife, and use, and population socioeconomic data, for individual areas, series, 5506–4

DOE R&D projects and funding at natl labs, universities, and other instns, FY83, annual summary rpt, 3004–18.1

DOE R&D projects and funding at natl labs, universities, and other instns, FY84, annual summary rpt, 3004–18.4

Estuary environmental characteristics, fish, wildlife, uses, and mgmt, for individual estuaries, series, 5506–7

Geological Survey and other publications, 1983, annual listing, 5664–4

Great Lakes water levels, surface and drainage area, depth, and volume, and connecting and outlet channel flows, various periods 1900-83, 3758–6

NOAA scientific and technical publications, monthly listing, 2142–1

Science and engineering doctoral degree recipients, by field, sex, race, age, citizenship, postgrad employment and study status, State, and instn, 1960-82, 9626–6.16

Sedimentation control, surveillance, and research activity of Fed Govt, by project, agency, region, and State, 1982, annual rpt, 5664–9

Urban runoff water quality, pollutant concentrations, and control cost-effectiveness, with monitoring sites rainfall and other characteristics, by city and region, 1978-83, 9208–122

see also Oceanography

see also Water pollution

see also Water power

Hydrology

see also Water resources development
see also Water supply and use
see also Watershed projects

Hydrothermal power
see Geothermal resources

Hypertension
see Blood pressure

IBRD
see International Bank for Reconstruction and Development

ICC
see Interstate Commerce Commission

Ice conditions
- Bering Sea and Alaska north coast ice conditions, monthly rpt, 2182–5
- Forecast methodology, accuracy, and applications, technical rpt series, 2186–4
- Foreign weather conditions and impact assessment, by world area and country, monthly rpt, 2152–9
- *see also* Glaciers

Ice, manufactured
- Census of Population, 1980: detailed socioeconomic and demographic characteristics, by age, sex, race, Hispanic origin, occupation, and industry, State rpt series, 2531–4
- County Business Patterns: establishments, employees, and payrolls, by SIC 4-digit industry and county, 1981, annual State rpt series, 2326–8
- County Business Patterns: establishments, employees, and payrolls, by SIC 4-digit industry and county, 1982, annual State rpt series, 2326–6
- Income tax returns of sole proprietorships, detailed data by industry div and selected industry group, 1981, annual rpt, 8304–7
- Income tax returns of sole proprietorships, receipts, deductions by type, payroll, and net income, by major industry, 1982, annual article, 8302–2.413
- Input-output structure of US economy, detailed interindustry transactions for 537 industries, and components of final demand, 1977 benchmark data, 2708–17
- Manufacturing census, 1982: financial and operating data, for SIC 4-digit industries by product, preliminary rpt, 2491–1.41
- Occupational injury and illness rates, by SIC 2- to 4-digit industry, 1982, annual rpt, 6844–1
- *see also* under By Commodity in the "Index by Categories"

Icebreakers
- DOD budget, itemized account of legislative history, FY84, annual rpt, 3504–7

Iceland
- Agricultural supply/demand, trade, and production, and socioeconomic data, by country, 1950s-77, 1528–179
- AID loan repayment status and terms by program and country, and status of predecessor agency loans, quarterly rpt, 9912–3
- *Background Notes,* summary social, political, and economic data, 1984 rpt, 7006–2.46
- Economic, social, and political summary data, by country, 1984, annual factbook, 244–11
- Economic trends in income, production, prices, employment, finances, and trade, 1984 annual rpt, 2046–4.26

Exports and imports of NATO countries with Council for Mutual Economic Assistance Europe members, by country, 1980-83, annual rpt, 7144–5

Exports and imports of NATO countries with PRC, by country, 1980-83, annual rpt, 7144–14

Exports and imports of OECD countries, by country, 1983, annual rpt, 7144–10

Exports and imports of US with Western Europe, and US market share and export opportunities for selected commodities, by country, 1982-84, 2048–105

Exports of US, detailed Schedule B commodities by country of destination, 1983, annual rpt, 2424–9

Exports of US, detailed Schedule E commodities by mode of transport and world area and country of destination, 1983, annual rpts, 2424–5

Imports of US, detailed Schedule A commodities by country and world area of origin, and mode of transport, 1983, annual rpts, 2424–2

Imports of US, detailed TSUSA commodities by country of origin, 1983, annual rpt, 2424–4

Loans and grants for economic and military assistance from US and intl agencies, by program and country, FY46-83, annual rpt, 9914–5

Military aid of US, arms sales, and training programs costs and budget requests by program, world region, and country, FY83-85, annual rpt, 7144–13

Military spending, arms trade, and armed forces size, with total govt spending and population, by country, 1972-82, annual rpt, 9824–1

Minerals Yearbook, 1982, Vol 3: foreign country reviews of production, trade, and policies, by commodity, annual rpt, 5604–35

Minerals Yearbook, 1983, Vol 3 preprints: foreign country review of production, trade, and policies, by commodity, annual rpt, 5604–23.30

Population size and growth rates, and latest available benchmark demographic data, by country, 1950-83, biennial rpt, 2324–4

see also under By Foreign Country in the "Index by Categories"

ICF Incorporated
- "Analysis of a Senate Emission Reduction Bill (S-3041)", 9188–97
- "Summary of Acid Rain Analyses Undertaken by ICF for the Edison Electric Institute, National Wildlife Federation and Environmental Protection Agency", 21368–52

Idaho
- Agriculture census, 1982: farms, farmland, production and costs, and operator characteristics, preliminary State summary and county rpts, 2330–1.16
- Agriculture census, 1982: farms, farmland, production, finances, and operator characteristics, by county, final State rpt, 2331–1.12
- Bank deposits in commercial and mutual savings banks and in US branches of foreign banks, by account type, instn, State, SMSA, and county, June 1983, annual rpt, 9295–3.17

Index by Subjects and Names

- Census of Housing, 1980: occupancy and unit characteristics of SMSAs and central cities, by race, Hispanic origin, and city, State rpt, 2473–1.14
- Census of Population and Housing, 1980: detailed population and housing characteristics, by county, city, and census tract, State rpt, 2551–2.14
- Census of Population, 1980: detailed socioeconomic and demographic characteristics, by age, sex, race, Hispanic origin, and industry, State rpt, 2531–4.14
- County Business Patterns: establishments, employees, and payrolls, by SIC 4-digit industry and county, 1982, annual State rpt, 2326–6.14
- Employment, earnings, and hours, by selected SIC 1- to 4-digit industry, State, and for 278 major labor areas, 1939-83, annual rpt, 6744–5.1, 6744–5.3
- Environmental quality, pollutant discharge by type and source, and EPA protection activities and funding, 1970s-83, biennial regional rpt, 9184–15.10
- Exports of manufactured and agricultural commodities, manufacturing production, and export-related employment, 1960s-82, State rpt, 2046–3.12
- Forest biomass in Rocky Mountain States, conversion from volume to dry weight, for softwood and hardwood species, 1977, 1208–200
- Forests (natl) timber sales contract operations in Northwest US by forest and firm, and lumber supply/demand, FY76-1983 with trends from 1913, hearings, 25318–57
- Grizzly bears in and around Yellowstone Natl Park, population, physical characteristics, diet, and movements, 1982, annual rpt, 5544–4
- HHS aid to each State and local govt or private instn, amount obligated, funding agency, and program, FY83, annual listing, 4004–3.10
- Income (personal) per capita and by source, and earnings by industry div, by State, MSA, and county, 1977-82, annual regional rpt, 2704–2.8
- Lumber production, prices, trade, and employment in Northwest US and British Columbia, quarterly rpt, 1202–3
- Manufacturing census, 1982: financial and operating data, by SIC 2- to 4-digit industry, State, SMSA, and county, preliminary census div rpt, 2491–3.8
- Mineral Industry Surveys, State review of production, 1983, advance annual rpt, 5614–6.12
- *Minerals Yearbook, 1982,* Vol 2 preprints: State review of production and sales by commodity, and business activity, annual rpt, 5604–16.13
- *Minerals Yearbook, 1982,* Vol 2: State reviews of production, sales, and firms, by commodity, and business activity, annual rpt, 5604–34
- Phosphate rock reserves in southeastern and northwestern US, by location, 1984 rpt, 5668–74
- Population size and components of change, by MSA and county, 1980-82, annual State Current Population Rpt, 2546–4.12
- Population size, Apr 1980 and July 1982, and per capita income, 1979 and 1981, by county and city, State Current Population Rpt, 2546–11.12

Index by Subjects and Names

Illinois

Radiation monitoring results of Idaho Natl Engineering Lab, for 4 onsite facilities and nearby areas, 1983, annual rpt, 3354–10

Recreation sites of Forest Service in northern Idaho and Montana, itemized operating and maintenance costs by type of site, 1980, 1208–202

Retail trade census, 1982: employment, establishments, sales, and payroll, by SIC 2- to 4-digit kind of business, SMSA, and retail district, State rpt, 2401–1.13

Savings and loan assns, FHLB 12th District members financial operations and housing industry indicators by State, monthly rpt, 9302–21

Service industry census, 1982: employment, establishments, receipts, and payroll, by SIC 2- to 4-digit kind of business, SMSA, county, and city, State rpt, 2391–1.13

Timber resources and removals in 9 Rocky Mountain States, and forest and rangeland area, by ownership, forest and tree characteristics, and State, 1977, 1208–201

Traffic accidents alcohol-related in 3 Idaho counties, effect of reduction program, model results, 1970-80, article, 7762–9.404

Water supply, and snow survey results, monthly State rpt, 1266–2.4

Wholesale trade census, 1982: employment, establishments, finances, and operations, by SIC 2- to 4-digit kind of business, SMSA, county, and city, State rpt, 2405–1.13

see also Boise, Idaho

see also Twin Falls, Idaho

see also under By State in the "Index by Categories"

Idaho National Engineering Laboratory

see also Department of Energy National Laboratories

Illegitimacy

Asian and Pacific Islands Americans births by ethnic origin and sociodemographic and birth characteristics, with comparisons to blacks and whites, 1978-80, 4146–5.75

Births and birth rates, by demographic and birth characteristics, 1981 with trends from 1940, US Vital Statistics advance rpt, 4146–5.73

Births and birth rates, by detailed demographic characteristics and geographic area, 1979 and trends, US Vital Statistics annual rpt, 4144–1

Births and birth rates, by parent and birth characteristics and infant condition at birth, 1982 and trends from 1940, US Vital Statistics annual advance rpt, 4146–5.79

Births, and birth rates for unmarried and all women, by race of child, age and Hispanic origin of mother, and State, 1980, 4147–21.42

Births by outcome, and mother's sociodemographic, life style, and maternity characteristics, 1980, article, 4102–1.420

Births, fertility rates, expected births, and childless women, by socioeconomic characteristics, June 1982, annual Current Population Rpt, 2546–1.386

Births, fertility rates, expected births, and childless women, by socioeconomic characteristics, June 1983, advance annual Current Population Rpt, 2546–1.385

Births, fertility rates, expected births, and childless women, by socioeconomic characteristics, June 1983, annual Current Population Rpt, 2546–1.393

Birthspacing by period of woman's birth and marriage, period of child's birth, and sociodemographic characteristics, June 1980, Current Population Rpt, 2546–1.387

Fertility rates for single women, by age, race, and Hispanic origin, June 1982, Current Population Rpt, 2546–2.119

Fetal deaths and rates, by gestation period, birth weight and order, race, age of mother, and geographic area, 1979, US Vital Statistics annual rpt, 4144–2.3

Teenage girls births and rates, and distribution of births with low birth weight and Apgar scores, by mother and infant characteristics, 1970-81, 4147–21.41

Teenage girls births and sexual experience by race, abortions, and birth control use, by age, 1970s-80 with birth trends from 1920, hearings, 21968–29

Illinois

Agricultural cooperatives, membership, activities, and finances, by commodity and selected State, 1900-80 with trends from 1863, 1128–30

Agriculture census, 1982: farms, farmland, production, finances, and operator characteristics, by county, final State rpt, 2331–1.13

Arts and humanities funding, by source and State, FY82-83 with trends from FY66, 21408–69

Bank deposits in commercial and mutual savings banks and in US branches of foreign banks, by account type, instn, State, SMSA, and county, June 1983, annual rpt, 9295–3.13

Census of Housing, 1980: occupancy and unit characteristics of SMSAs and central cities, by race, Hispanic origin, and city, State rpt, 2473–1.15

Census of Population and Housing, 1980: detailed population and housing characteristics, by county, city, and census tract, State rpt, 2551–2.15

Census of Population, 1980: detailed socioeconomic and demographic characteristics, by age, sex, race, Hispanic origin, and industry, State rpt, 2531–4.15

Coal (bituminous) mining production and related workers, wages by occupation, and benefits, by size of mine and union status, in 6 States and aggregate for Rocky Mountain States, July 1982 survey, 6787–6.198

Coal employment and economic losses from utility fuel switching to meet emissions standards, with detail for counties in 5 States, 1970s-83 and projected to 1990, 21368–52

County Business Patterns: establishments, employees, and payrolls, by SIC 4-digit industry and county, 1982, annual State rpt, 2326–6.15

Criminal pretrial detention time credited to prison terms in Illinois, by offense, for prisoners released 1978-82, 6066–19.7

Employment, earnings, and hours, by selected SIC 1- to 4-digit industry, State, and for 278 major labor areas, 1939-83, annual rpt, 6744–5.1, 6744–5.3

Environmental quality, pollutant discharge by type and source, and EPA protection activities and funding, 1970s-83, biennial regional rpt, 9184–15.5

Exports of manufactured and agricultural commodities, manufacturing production, and export-related employment, 1960s-82, State rpt, 2046–3.13

Farm investments, effective rates of Federal/State income and State/local property taxes, by category of structure and equipment, for 7 North Central States, 1981-82, 1548–237

Farms with sales under $2,500, acreage, finances, operations, and operator characteristics, by region and for 6 States, 1978, 1548–241

HHS aid to each State and local govt or private instn, amount obligated, funding agency, and program, FY83, annual listing, 4004–3.5

Home mortgages originated by S&Ls in Wisconsin and Illinois, effects of usury ceiling and market interest rates on supply and loan-to-price ratios, 1978-80, article, 9312–7.404

Homeless population and characteristics, and temporary shelter operations, use, and user characteristics, for selected cities, various periods 1979-84, hearing, 21248–85

Housing vacancy rates for single and multifamily units and mobile homes in FHLB 7th District, by ZIP code, annual metro area rpt series, 9304–18

Hwy and bridge repair projects funded by Fed Govt, and costs, for 7 States, FY81-82, GAO rpt, 26113–121

Income (personal) per capita and by source, and earnings by industry div, by State, MSA, and county, 1977-82, annual regional rpt, 2704–2.4

Manufacturing census, 1982: financial and operating data, by SIC 2- to 4-digit industry, State, SMSA, and county, preliminary census div rpt, 2491–3.3

Mineral Industry Surveys, State review of production, 1983, advance annual rpt, 5614–6.13

Minerals Yearbook, 1982, Vol 2 preprints: State review of production and sales by commodity, and business activity, annual rpt, 5604–16.14

Minerals Yearbook, 1982, Vol 2: State reviews of production, sales, and firms, by commodity, and business activity, annual rpt, 5604–34

Mortgage interest fixed and adjustable rates and fees offered by Illinois S&Ls, monthly rpt, 9302–6

Population, births, deaths, and net migration, by MSA and county, 1980-82, annual State Current Population Rpt, 2546–4.13

Pulpwood production by county, imports, and individual mill capacity, by species for 7 North Central States, 1982, annual rpt, 1204–19

Retail trade census, 1982: employment, establishments, sales, and payroll, by SIC 2- to 4-digit kind of business, SMSA, county, and city, State rpt, 2397–1.14

Savings and loan assns, FHLB 7th District insured members cost of funds, and savings flows and mortgage loans closed by SMSA, monthly rpt, 9302–5

Illinois

Transportation census, 1982: trucks, by detailed characteristics, miles traveled, and type of product carried, State rpt, 2573–1.14

Water supply and quality in streams and lakes, and groundwater levels in wells, by drainage basin, 1982, annual State rpt, 5666–20.12

Water supply and quality in streams and lakes, and groundwater levels in wells, by drainage basin, 1983, annual State rpt, 5666–10.12

see also Bloomington, Ill.
see also Champaign, Ill.
see also Chicago, Ill.
see also Decatur, Ill.
see also Joliet, Ill.
see also Kankakee, Ill.
see also Moline, Ill.
see also Normal, Ill.
see also Peoria, Ill.
see also Rantoul, Ill.
see also Rock Island, Ill.
see also Rockford, Ill.
see also Springfield, Ill.
see also Urbana, Ill.
see also under By State in the "Index by Categories"

Illinois River

Freight (waterborne domestic and foreign) by commodity, traffic, and passengers, by port and waterway, 1982, annual rpt, 3754–3.2, 3754–3.3

Water supply and quality in streams and lakes, and groundwater levels in wells, by drainage basin, 1980, annual State rpt series, 5666–12

Water supply and quality in streams and lakes, and groundwater levels in wells, by drainage basin, 1981, annual State rpt series, 5666–16

Water supply and quality in streams and lakes, and groundwater levels in wells, by drainage basin, 1983, annual State rpt series, 5666–10

Illiteracy

Aliens excluded and deported by cause, 1892-FY81, annual rpt, 6264–2

Communist, OECD, and selected other countries living standards and commodity production, 1960s-83, annual rpt, 244–5.1

Developing countries disaster preparedness and summary sociodemographic, political, and economic data, country rpt series, 9916–2

Developing countries govt policy, and AID and other foreign assistance, effects on private sector dev and socioeconomic conditions, with case studies for 6 countries, 1960s-80, 9918–12

Developing countries PL 480 Title I funding and socioeconomic impacts, with case studies for 5 countries, 1950s- 81, 9918–13

Developing countries summary socioeconomic data, 1970s-83, and AID activities and funding by project and function, FY82-85, by country, annual rpt, 9914–3

Digest of Education Statistics, detailed data on students, staff, finances, and facilities, 1982 and selected trends, annual rpt, 4824–2

Foreign and US agricultural supply/demand, trade, and production, and socioeconomic data, by country, 1950s-77, 1528–179

Foreign economic, social, and political summary data, by country, 1984, annual factbook, 244–11

Foreign human rights conditions in 162 countries, economic and military aid of US, and economic aid of intl organizations, 1981-83, annual rpt, 21384–3

Foreign military, social, and economic summary data by world area and country, 1960s-80s, hearing, 25388–47.1

Foreign population size and growth rates, and latest available benchmark demographic data, by country, 1950-83, biennial rpt, 2324–4

Foreign women sociodemographic, economic, and fertility characteristics, with comparisons to men, by country, 1960s-85, world region rpt series, 2326–15

Jamaica PL 480 Title I assistance effects on economic dev, with data on govt finance, economic indicators, demography, and dev programs, 1970s-81, 9916–1.51

Older persons by demographic, socioeconomic, and health characteristics, selected years 1900-81 and projected to 2050, Current Population Rpt, 2546–2.125

Southeastern States economic dev effect on education, for Fed Reserve 6th District States, selected years 1900-82, article, 9371–1.428

Statistical Abstract of US, social, political, and economic data, 1950s-83 and trends, annual rpt, 2324–1.1

Illness

see Disabled and handicapped persons
see Diseases and disorders
see Hospitalization

Immigration

Census of Population, 1980: detailed socioeconomic and demographic characteristics, by age, sex, race, Hispanic origin, occupation, and industry, State rpt series, 2531–4

Census of Population, 1980: detailed socioeconomic characteristics, by county, city, and inside-outside SMSAs and central cities, State rpt series, 2531–3

Central America socioeconomic and political conditions in 6 countries, 1960s-83 with trends and projections 1930-2010, Commission rpt, 028–19.2

Criminal cases of Federal defendants, disposition, convictions, and sentences, by offense and district, as of June 1983 with trends from 1961, annual rpt, 18204–1

Fed Govt programs and mgmt cost control proposals, 3-year savings by function and agency, and financial and operating data, 1960s-81, 16908–1.9

Foreign human rights conditions in 162 countries, economic and military aid of US, and economic aid of intl organizations, 1981-83, annual rpt, 21384–3

Foreign population and recent immigrants, by State, Apr 1970 and 1980, annual rpt, 4824–1.4

Hispanic Americans socioeconomic and demographic characteristics, and compared to non-Hispanics, selected years 1970-83, chartbook, 2328–48

Index by Subjects and Names

Immigration, and alien residents, workers, visitors, deportations, and naturalizations, by country of birth, FY81, annual rpt, 6264–2

Jamaica PL 480 Title I assistance effects on economic dev, with data on govt finance, economic indicators, demography, and dev programs, 1970s-81, 9916–1.51

Mobility of population, detailed data by demographic and socioeconomic characteristics of movers and nonmovers, Mar 1981-82, annual Current Population Rpt, 2546–1.384

OASDI and pension policy, impacts of increased life expectancy, with alternative sociodemographic projections to 2100, hearing, 25368–130

Population and housing census, 1980: birthplace and 1975 residence abroad, and population by ancestral origin, by census tract, State and SMSA rpt series, 2551–2

Population size and components of change, projected under 3 fertility assumptions, 1982-2080 with trends from 1900, SSA actuarial rpt, 4706–1.92

Population size by single years of age, and components of change, by sex and race, projected 1983-2080, final Current Population Rpt, 2546–3.132

Professional, technical, and kindred workers and total students admitted to US, by detailed occupation and country of origin, annual rpt, suspended, 6264–1

Scientists, engineers, and technicians needed in defense and nondefense industries, and supply/demand, by field, 1981-87, 9628–71

Statistical Abstract of US, social, political, and economic data, 1950s-83 and trends, annual rpt, 2324–1.1

Visas issued and refused to immigrants and nonimmigrants, and status adjustments, by class and nationality, FY77, annual rpt, 7184–1

see also Alien workers
see also Aliens
see also Foreign medical graduates
see also Refugees

Immigration and Naturalization Service

Activities of Justice Dept, by subagency, FY82, annual rpt, 6004–1

Assaults, murders, and other deaths of law enforcement officers, by circumstances, level of govt, agency, victim and offender characteristics, and location, 1983, annual rpt, 6224–3

Cost control proposals for Fed Govt programs and mgmt, 3-year savings by function and agency, and financial and operating data, 1960s-81, 16908–1.9

Immigrants admitted to US as professional, technical, and kindred workers, and total students, by detailed occupation and country of origin, annual rpt, suspended, 6264–1

Immigration, and alien residents, workers, visitors, deportations, and naturalizations, by country of birth, FY81, annual rpt, 6264–2

Refugee resettlement program activities and funding, arrivals and population by country of origin and State, and employment and other characteristics, FY83, annual rpt, 4704–8

Index by Subjects and Names

Immunology

see Vaccination and vaccines

Impacted areas

Children and youth benefitting from Fed Govt public welfare programs and tax expenditures, participation and funding for 71 programs, FY81-83, 21968–30

Education Dept programs funding, operations, and effectiveness, FY83, annual rpt, 4804–5

Fed Govt aid to State and local govts, expenditures, and direct payments, by program, agency, and State, FY83, annual rpt, 2464–2

Schools in federally impacted areas, Fed Govt funding by county and school and congressional district, and eligible pupils, by State, FY83, annual rpt, 4804–10

TVA construction projects employment, and impacts on nearby areas, survey rpt series, 9806–7

Import restrictions

see Tariffs and foreign trade controls

Imports

see Agricultural exports and imports
see Coal exports and imports
see Energy exports and imports
see Foreign trade
see Natural gas exports and imports
see Petroleum exports and imports

Impoundment

see Executive impoundment of appropriated funds

Income

see Business income and expenses, general
see Business income and expenses, specific industries
see Earnings, general
see Earnings, local and regional
see Farm income
see Income maintenance
see Income taxes
see National income and product accounts
see Personal and family income
see Poverty
see Tips and tipping
see under By Income in the "Index by Categories"

Income maintenance

Benefits and beneficiaries of SSI and other income maintenance programs, by State, monthly rpt, 4742–2

Benefits and beneficiaries with representative payees by Fed Govt cash benefit program, and OASDI and SSI fraud and misuse, various periods FY74-81, GAO rpt, 26121–85

Budget of US Appendix, detailed budgets and personnel summaries, by agency, FY85, annual rpt, 104–3

Budget of US, CBO analysis and review of FY85 budget by function, annual rpt, 26304–2

Budget of US, CBO analysis of revenue and spending alternatives and projections of economic indicators, FY85-89, annual rpt, 26304–3.3

Budget of US, compact budgets by function, agency, and account, FY85 with projections to FY89, annual rpt, 104–2

Budget of US, effects of Reagan Admin policy changes, by detailed program, FY85, annual rpt, 104–21

Budget of US, loans and loan guarantees, and Admin proposed limits on credit assistance, by program, FY83-89, annual rpt, 26306–3.65

Budget of US, receipts by source and outlays by function, FY40-89 estimates revised for consistency with FY85 budget definitions, annual rpt, 104–12

Budget of US, receipts, outlays, and budget authority, by function and agency, FY84-89 revised estimates, midsession review of FY85 budget, annual rpt, 104–7

Budget of US, receipts, outlays, and budget authority, by function and agency, 1st revision of FY85 budget, annual rpt, 104–17

Budget of US, special analyses of economic and social impact, FY85, annual rpt, 104–1

Census of Population, 1980: detailed socioeconomic and demographic characteristics, by age, sex, race, Hispanic origin, occupation, and industry, State rpt series, 2531–4

Census of Population, 1980: detailed socioeconomic characteristics, by county, city, and inside-outside SMSAs and central cities, State rpt series, 2531–3

Fed Govt aid to State and local areas, by type of payment, State, and county, FY83, annual rpt, 2464–3.1

Fed Govt aid to State and local govts, expenditures, and direct payments, by program, agency, and State, FY83, annual rpt, 2464–2

Fed Govt financial and nonfinancial domestic aid, 1984 annual comprehensive catalog, 104–5

Fed Govt grants-in-aid for 13 program areas, FY82-84, annual article, 10042–1.402

Fed Govt programs and mgmt cost control proposals, CBO and GAO estimates of savings by function and agency, FY85-89, 26308–45

Fed Govt programs and mgmt cost control proposals, 3-year savings by function and agency, and financial and operating data, 1960s-81, 16908–1

Fed Govt programs under Ways and Means Committee jurisdiction, program operations and financing data for assessing budgetary requirements, by State, FY70s-83, 21788–117

Govt census, 1982: city govt revenues by source, expenditures by function, debt, and assets, by State and city, 2457–4

Govt census, 1982: county govt revenues by source, expenditures by function, debt, and assets, by State and county, 2457–3

Govt census, 1982: employment, payrolls, and average earnings, by function, level of govt, State, county, population size, and inside-outside SMSAs, 2455–2

Govt census, 1982: State govt payments to local govts, by program, source of funds, level of govt, and State, with trends from 1902, 2460–3

Govt expenditures for public welfare, by level of govt and type of program, selected years FY50-82, 4746–16.1

Income (household) and cash and noncash transfer program participation, by sociodemographic characteristics, quarterly rpt, 2542–2

Income (personal) per capita and by source, and earnings by industry div, by State, MSA, and county, 1977-82, annual regional rpts, 2704–2

Income (personal) per capita and by source, earnings by major industry group, and social insurance contributions, by region and State, 1929-82, 2708–40

Negative income tax experimental program, effects on employment, earnings, marital status, and other family characteristics in 2 cities, 1970-75, 4008–64

OASDHI, Medicaid, SSI, and other social insurance and public welfare programs benefits, beneficiary characteristics, and trust funds, selected years 1937-83, annual rpt, 4744–3

Older persons Fed Govt pension and health spending, by program and as percents of budget and GNP, 1965-85 with projections to 2040, 25148–28

Older persons sociodemographic characteristics, and Fed Govt program participation and funding, 1983 with trends and projections 1900-2060, annual rpt, 25144–3.1

Poverty-level persons and families, by income source, hours of work, earnings, taxes, and family characteristics, various periods 1959-84, 21788–131

Poverty status of families and persons by selected characteristics, public welfare funding, and effect of counting transfer payments as income, selected years 1950-83, 25928–4

Poverty status of young adults related to motivation, psychological factors, and family characteristics, by race and sex, 1970s-82, longitudinal studies, 4008–65

Public noncash transfers counted as income, effect on poverty population size by selected recipient characteristics, 1979-83, 2626–2.52

Public noncash transfers counted as income, effects on poverty population size by recipient characteristics, 1979-82, 2626–2.50

Public opinion on taxes, tax policy, and intergovtl relations, 1972-84 surveys, annual rpt, 10044–2

Research and statistical projects and techniques, and evaluation of public welfare programs, 1983 conf papers, 4704–11

Statistical Abstract of US, social, political, and economic data, 1950s-83 and trends, annual rpt, 2324–1.2

Tax expenditures, Fed Govt revenues foregone through income tax deductions and exclusions by type, and effect of Deficit Reduction Act, FY84-89, annual rpt, 21784–10

see also Aid to Families with Dependent Children
see also Disability insurance
see also Food stamp programs
see also Medicaid
see also Medicare
see also Old-Age, Survivors, Disability, and Health Insurance
see also Public welfare programs
see also Rent supplements
see also Social security
see also Supplemental Security Income
see also Unemployment insurance
see also Workers compensation

Income taxes

Index by Subjects and Names

Income taxes

Agricultural cooperative finances and operations, aggregate for top 100 assns by principal product and revenue source, FY82, annual rpt, 1124–3

Airline income taxes paid, net income, and effective tax rates, by major carrier, 1968-83, annual rpt, 9144–34

Assistance program of IRS for taxpayers, operations and use, and users evaluation, selected years 1979-82, GAO rpt, 26119–58

Bankruptcy (personal), filers by debt type and other characteristics, selected years 1978-81, hearing, 25528–97.1

Banks (US) foreign and domestic lending, impact of tax policy favoring developing countries on investment profits and spending alternatives for revenue and choice, 1984 technical paper, 9366–7.99

Budget of US, CBO analysis of revenue and spending alternatives and projections of economic indicators, FY85-89, annual rpt, 26304–3

Budget of US, deficit effect of unemployment and inflation increases and income tax indexing, 1980-83, article, 2702–1.427

Budget of US, receipts by source and outlays by agency and program, monthly rpt, 8102–3

Budget of US, receipts, outlays, and budget authority, by function and agency, FY84-89 revised estimates, midsession review of FY85 budget, annual rpt, 104–7

Business Conditions Digest, historical supplement on economic, business, and financial conditions and cyclical fluctuations, with methodology, 1947-82, 2708–31

Capital formation and intl flows related to corporate and personal capital income taxes, 1984 technical paper, 8006–3.51

Capital investment net costs for 35 types of structures and equipment, under 1980-82 tax laws, article, 9387–1.405

Census of Govts, 1982: city govt revenues by source, expenditures by function, debt, and assets, by State and city, 2457–4

Census of Govts, 1982: county govt revenues by source, expenditures by function, debt, and assets, by State and county, 2457–3

Census of Govts, 1982: State govt payments to local govts, by program, source of funds, level of govt, and State, with trends from 1902, 2460–3

Child support overdue payments deducted from income tax refunds and unemployment benefits, by State, FY83, annual rpt, 4004–16.3

Coal production, mining employment, exports, and finances, by coal district, 1982, 3008–97

Coal taxes for surface and underground mines, by type of tax and State, 1984 rpt, 11128–1

Corporate and individual income taxes, Budget of US estimates revised for consistency with FY85 budget definitions, FY40-89, annual rpt, 104–12

Corporate and individual income taxes, cumulative for fiscal year, annual trends, and quarterly data, monthly rpt, 23842–1.6

Corporate effective tax rates by economic sector, FY80-82, 26306–6.70

Corporate income tax returns, detailed income and tax items by industry, 1981, annual rpt, 8304–4

Corporate income tax returns, summary data by industry div, 1981 estimates, annual article, 8302–2.403

Corporate taxes and effective rates on US, foreign, and worldwide income, by major industry group, and share of Fed Govt receipts, 1980-82, 23868–14

Economic indicators, and Fed Govt finances and deficits, selected years 1962-83 and projected under cost control proposals to 2000, 16908–1.1

Economic Report of the President for 1984, Joint Economic Committee critique and policy recommendations, annual rpt, 23844–2

Electric utilities privately owned, detailed financial and operating data by company, with summary data for other distributors by type, 1982, annual rpt, 3164–23

Employee benefit plans effects on income and payroll tax revenue by benefit type and income, with benefits by industry, 1950-83 and projected to 1988, article, 9373–1.404

Energy producers finances and operations, by energy type for US firms domestic and foreign operations, 1974-82, annual rpt, 3164–44

Farm business legal organization, finances, operations, tax rates, and State laws restricting farm corporations, 1960s-82, 1548–233

Farm finances, assets, liabilities, income, receipts by commodity and State, and expenses, 1980-83 and trends from 1910, annual rpt, 1544–16

Farm finances, production, expenses by type, and domestic economic impact, selected years 1972-82 and preliminary 1983-84, annual rpt, 1544–19

Farm investments, effect of Fed Govt and State tax rates under alternative depreciation methods and inflation rates, 1950-84, 1548–231

Fed Govt civilian and military employee pay, withholdings by type, and income, and special military compensation by type and service branch, 1982-83, GAO rpt, 26123–65

Fed Govt consolidated financial statements based on business accounting methods, FY82-83, annual rpt, 8104–5

Fed Govt internal revenue, by type of tax, quarterly rpt, 8302–2.1

Fed Govt internal revenue from personal taxes under current tax law and 3 flat-rate proposals, and consumption tax characteristics, 1984 article, 9381–1.415

Fed Govt personal income tax rate, effect of 10% cut on economic indicators, projected 1982-86, model results, technical paper, 9366–1.134

Fed Govt receipts by source and outlays by agency, *Treasury Bulletin,* quarterly rpt, 8002–4.1

Financial and business statistics, historic trends, 1984 annual chartbook, 9364–2.8

Financial instns income taxes, effective rates, and selected financial data, by instn type and firm, with comparisons to other industries, selected years 1960-82, hearing, 25368–129

Georgia small businesses, effect of mgmt counseling on sales, employment, profits, and taxes paid, 1980-81, hearing, 25728–36

Govt finances, by level of govt and State, selected years 1929-83, annual rpt, 10044–1

Govt finances, by level of govt, State, and for large cities and counties, 1981-83, annual rpt series, 2466–2

Govt revenues by source and expenditures by function, natl income and product account, *Survey of Current Business,* monthly rpt, monthly and annual tables, 2702–1.24

Govt tax revenues, by level of govt, type of tax, State, and selected counties, quarterly rpt, 2462–3

Household income and social security tax burden and effect of indexing by income level, 1982, and Fed Govt revenues by source, FY60-89, press release, 8008–109

Household income before and after taxes, by socioeconomic characteristics, type of tax paid, and region, 1981, Current Population Rpt, 2546–2.118

Household income before and after taxes, by socioeconomic characteristics, type of tax paid, and region, 1982, annual Current Population Rpt, 2546–2.122

Illegal taxable income not reported, by source, with characteristics of persons involved, methodology, and bibl, 1970s-82, 8008–112

Income (taxable) not reported on individual and corporate returns, and associated Federal revenue losses, by detailed legal and illegal source, 1973-81, 8308–26

Income received through life insurance companies, taxation measurement, allocation, and accounting methods, 1984 technical paper, 8006–3.49

Individual income tax liabilities and payments to Fed Govt, and total and taxable personal income, quarterly 1980-82, annual article, 2702–1.415

Individual income tax returns, detailed data, 1982, annual rpt, 8304–2

Individual income tax returns, income, and tax, 1913-82, article, 8302–2.401

Individual income tax returns, selected income, deduction, and tax credit data by income group, preliminary 1982, annual article, 8302–2.402

Insurance industry (property and casualty) financial and operating data, investments, and tax liability, various periods 1951-82, hearing, 25368–128

Interest rates related to income taxes, 1952-83, article, 9389–1.407

IRS and other Fed Govt admin record research methods, data collection and use, 1984 compilation of papers, 8308–28

IRS collections, by type of tax, region, and State, FY83, annual rpt, 8304–3

IRS collections, FY83, annual rpt, 8104–2.2

IRS tax collections by type of tax, procedures, and interest forgone through processing delay, for selected locations, FY81-82, GAO rpt, 26119–55

Local govt spending, reliance on State aid and local taxes by type, and excise tax growth by State, selected years FY57-83, article, 10042–1.403

Index by Subjects and Names

India

Michigan bankruptcy filings, by filer type, moving history, income, creditor action, debt and asset type, credit status, exemptions claimed, and county, 1979-81, hearings, 21528-57.3

Motor carriers (Class I interstate) finances, operations, equipment, employment, and payroll, by district, 1982, annual rpt, 9486-5.3

Motor carriers (Class II) of property financial and operating data, by region, 1982, annual rpt, 9484-10

Multinatl and multistate corporations income under alternative State income tax treatment methods, by major industry, 1977, article, 9373-1.412

Multinatl corporation income reallocation through regulation of intercorporate transactions, by tax item, treaty status, asset size, industry, and tax haven country, 1982, 8008-110

Natl income and product, comprehensive accounts and components, *Survey of Current Business,* monthly rpt, 2702-1.21

Natl income and product revised estimates, adjustment for misreporting of income tax returns info, 1977, article, 2702-1.422

Natural gas interstate pipeline company detailed financial and operating data, by firm, 1983, annual rpt, 3164-38

North Central States farm investments, effective rates of Federal/State income and State/local property taxes, by category of structure and equipment and State, 1981-82, 1548-237

North Central States, FHLB 6th District insured S&Ls financial condition and operations by State, monthly rpt, 9302-11

North Central States, FHLB 6th District insured S&Ls financial condition and operations by State, quarterly rpt, 9302-23

Oil and gas finances by firm, and effect of income and excise tax provisions on firms, Fed Govt revenues, and investor tax returns, 1980 and projected to 1992, hearing, 21788-132

Oil pipeline in Alaska, owner companies financial data, and retail gasoline competitive position in 2 States, by company, 1980-83, hearing, 21728-51

Poverty-level persons and families, by income source, hours of work, earnings, taxes, and family characteristics, various periods 1959-84, 21788-131

Poverty rate by family composition, and effect of noncash transfers, taxes, unemployment benefits, and business cycles, selected years 1959-82, hearings, 21788-141

Public opinion on taxes, tax policy, and intergovtl relations, 1972-84 surveys, annual rpt, 10044-2

Returns filed and collections, for IRS regions, districts, and service centers, 1972-82 and projections to 1990, annual rpt, 8304-8

Returns filed, by type of filer, detailed preliminary and supplementary data, quarterly rpt with articles, 8302-2

Returns filed, by type of return, 1972-82 and projected 1983-90, annual rpt, 8304-9

Revenue sharing payments to States, local govts, Indian tribes, and Alaska Native villages, and entitlement computation data, FY84, series, 8066-1

Small business capital formation, sources, needs, and tax and other investment incentives and barriers, 1983 annual conf rpt, 9734-4

Sole proprietorships income tax returns, detailed data by industry div and selected industry group, 1981, annual rpt, 8304-7

State and local tax rates by selected jurisdiction, and average family tax burden by income level and selected city, by type of tax, 1982, 10046-8.2

Statistical Abstract of US, social, political, and economic data, 1950s-83 and trends, annual rpt, 2324-1.2

Stock ownership plans for employees in developing countries, and firms finances and operations, with case studies of US and 3 countries, 1970s-82, 9916-3.19

Tax evasion through nonresidents bank claims and deposits, direct investments, income payments, and other transactions in 5 Caribbean countries, 1978-82, 8008-106

Tax expenditures, Fed Govt revenues foregone through income tax deductions and exclusions by type, and effect of Deficit Reduction Act, FY84-89, annual rpt, 21784-10

Tax preparation service franchises, establishments by State, and sales, 1982-84, annual rpt, 2014-5

see also Tax incentives and shelters

see also Tax protests and appeals

Independence, Mo.

see also under By City in the "Index by Categories"

Independent agencies

see Federal independent agencies

Indexes

see Bibliographies

see Consumer Price Index

see Cost of living

see Crime Index

see Directories

see Government publications lists

see Industrial production indexes

see Labor cost indexes

see Producer Price Index

India

Agricultural and food production indexes, and production of selected commodities, by world region and country, 1974-83, annual rpt, 1524-5

Agricultural situation in 5 South Asia countries, by commodity, 1970s-1983/84 and outlook for 1984/85, annual rpt, 1524-4.11

Agricultural supply/demand, trade, and production, and socioeconomic data, by country, 1950s-77, 1528-179

AID activities and funding by project and function, FY85, and developing countries summary socioeconomic data, 1970s-83, by country, annual rpt, 9914-3

AID economic assistance to developing countries, obligations and disbursements by country, quarterly rpt, 9912-4

AID loan repayment status and terms by program and country, and status of predecessor agency loans, quarterly rpt, 9912-3

Economic conditions in Communist, OECD, and selected other countries, 1960s-83, annual rpt, 244-5

Economic, social, and political summary data, by country, 1984, annual factbook, 244-11

Economic trends in income, production, prices, employment, finances, and trade, 1984 semiannual rpt, 2046-4.27, 2046-4.82

Export sales and shipments of US grains, oilseed products, hides, skins, and cotton, by country, weekly rpt, 1922-3

Exports and imports of US, by commodity and country, 1972-82, annual world region rpt, 244-13.5

Exports of US, detailed Schedule B commodities by country of destination, 1983, annual rpt, 2424-9

Exports of US, detailed Schedule E commodities by mode of transport and world area and country of destination, 1983, annual rpts, 2424-5

Food supply policies of 21 developing countries, with farm sector data, tariff income, and prices and imports of 5 grains, 1960s-81, 1528-168

Imports of US, detailed Schedule A commodities by country and world area of origin, and mode of transport, 1983, annual rpts, 2424-2

Imports of US, detailed TSUSA commodities by country of origin, 1983, annual rpt, 2424-4

Loans and grants for economic and military assistance from US and intl agencies, by program and country, FY46-83, annual rpt, 9914-5

Military aid of US, arms sales, and training programs costs and budget requests by program, world region, and country, FY83-85, annual rpt, 7144-13

Military spending, arms trade, and armed forces size, with total govt spending and population, by country, 1972-82, annual rpt, 9824-1

Minerals Yearbook, 1982, Vol 3: foreign country reviews of production, trade, and policies, by commodity, annual rpt, 5604-35

Minerals Yearbook, 1982, Vol 3 preprints: foreign country review of production, trade, and policies, by commodity, annual rpt, 5604-17.31

Mining industry equipment market and trade, and user industry operations and demand, 1984 country market research rpt, 2045-16.3

Nuclear power generation in US and 18 non-Communist countries, monthly rpt, 3162-24.10

Nuclear power plant construction and operation status, and capacity, by plant, region, State, and selected country, 1983 and projected to 2020, annual rpt, 3164-57

Population size and growth rates, and latest available benchmark demographic data, by country, 1950-83, biennial rpt, 2324-4

Space launchings attaining Earth orbit or beyond, by country, 1957-83, annual rpt, 9504-9.1

Space satellites and other objects launched since 1957, quarterly listing, 9502-2

India

Tea exports of 3 Asian countries, by country of destination, 1982-83, FAS annual rpt, 1925–15.3

Walnut production, stocks, use, and exports of US and 4 countries, and EC export subsidy, selected years 1977-1984/85, article, 1925–34.429

see also under By Foreign Country in the "Index by Categories"

Indian Health Service

- Alcohol-related hospital discharges, by diagnosis and patient age, for IHS facilities and total US, 1981, 4488–4
- Cost control proposals for Fed Govt programs and mgmt, 3-year savings by function and agency, and financial and operating data, 1960s-81, 16908–1.7, 16908–1.24
- Health condition of Indians, births, morbidity, and deaths and rates, and health services facilities and use, 1954-83, annual compilation, 4104–7
- Health programs for Indians and Alaska Natives, activities and funding for scholarships, care services, and facilities construction, by city, FY82, annual rpt, 4104–11
- Hospitals of IHS, admissions, discharges, births, total and occupied beds, length of stay, and outpatient visits, by area and facility, quarterly rpt, 4102–3
- Hospitals of IHS, discharge rates by age and primary diagnosis, biennial rpt, suspended, 4104–9

Indian Ocean

- Temperature of sea surface by ocean and for US coastal areas, and Bering Sea ice conditions, monthly rpt, 2182–5
- Tide height and time daily at worldwide coastal points, 1985 predictions, annual rpt, 2174–2.4
- Typhoons in western North Pacific and North Indian Oceans, paths and other characteristics, by mode of surveillance, 1983, annual rpt, 3804–8
- Weather and tropical cyclones, quarterly journal with articles, 2152–8
- Weather broadcasts for US ships, by major ocean area, as of Jan 1984, biennial rpt, 2184–3

Indian wars

see War

Indiana

- Agricultural cooperatives, membership, activities, and finances, by commodity and selected State, 1900-80 with trends from 1863, 1128–30
- Agriculture census, 1982: farms, farmland, production, finances, and operator characteristics, by county, final State rpt, 2331–1.14
- Bank deposits in commercial and mutual savings banks and in US branches of foreign banks, by account type, instn, State, SMSA, and county, June 1983, annual rpt, 9295–3.10
- Census of Housing, 1980: occupancy and unit characteristics of SMSAs and central cities, by race, Hispanic origin, and city, State rpt, 2473–1.16
- Census of Population and Housing, 1980: detailed population and housing characteristics, by county, city, and census tract, State rpt, 2551–2.16

Census of Population, 1980: detailed socioeconomic and demographic characteristics, by age, sex, race, Hispanic origin, and industry, State rpt, 2531–4.16

- Coal employment and economic losses from utility fuel switching to meet emissions standards, with detail for counties in 5 States, 1970s-83 and projected to 1990, 21368–52
- County Business Patterns: establishments, employees, and payrolls, by SIC 4-digit industry and county, 1982, annual State rpt, 2326–6.16
- Employment, earnings, and hours, by selected SIC 1- to 4-digit industry, State, and for 278 major labor areas, 1939-83, annual rpt, 6744–5.1, 6744–5.3
- Environmental quality, pollutant discharge by type and source, and EPA protection activities and funding, 1970s-83, biennial regional rpt, 9184–15.5
- Exports of manufactured and agricultural commodities, manufacturing production, and export-related employment, 1960s-82, State rpt, 2046–3.14
- HHS aid to each State and local govt or private instn, amount obligated, funding agency, and program, FY83, annual listing, 4004–3.5
- Income (personal) per capita and by source, and earnings by industry div, by State, MSA, and county, 1977-82, annual regional rpt, 2704–2.4
- Manufacturing census, 1982: financial and operating data, by SIC 2- to 4-digit industry, State, SMSA, and county, preliminary census div rpt, 2491–3.3
- Mineral Industry Surveys, State review of production, 1983, advance annual rpt, 5614–6.14
- *Minerals Yearbook, 1982,* Vol 2 preprints: State review of production and sales by commodity, and business activity, annual rpt, 5604–16.15
- *Minerals Yearbook, 1982,* Vol 2: State reviews of production, sales, and firms, by commodity, and business activity, annual rpt, 5604–34
- Population, births, deaths, and net migration, by MSA and county, 1980-82, annual State Current Population Rpt, 2546–4.14
- Population size, Apr 1980 and July 1982, and per capita income, 1979 and 1981, by county and city, State Current Population Rpt, 2546–11.14
- Pulpwood production by county, imports, and individual mill capacity, by species for 7 North Central States, 1982, annual rpt, 1204–19
- Radiation and radionuclide concentrations in air, water, and milk, results of EPA and other monitoring programs, by State and site, quarterly rpt, 9232–2.2
- Retail trade census, 1982: employment, establishments, sales, and payroll, by SIC 2- to 4-digit kind of business, SMSA, county, and city, State rpt, 2397–1.15
- Savings and loan assns, FHLB 6th District insured members financial condition and operations by State, monthly rpt, 9302–11
- Savings and loan assns, FHLB 6th District insured members financial condition and operations by State, quarterly rpt, 9302–23

Water supply and quality in streams and lakes, and groundwater levels in wells, by drainage basin, 1983, annual State rpt, 5666–10.13

see also Anderson, Ind.
see also Bloomington, Ind.
see also East Chicago, Ind.
see also Elkhart, Ind.
see also Evansville, Ind.
see also Fort Wayne, Ind.
see also Gary, Ind.
see also Hammond, Ind.
see also Indianapolis, Ind.
see also Kokomo, Ind.
see also Lafayette, Ind.
see also Logansport, Ind.
see also Muncie, Ind.
see also Peru, Ind.
see also South Bend, Ind.
see also Terre Haute, Ind.
see also Vincennes, Ind.
see also West Lafayette, Ind.
see also under By State in the "Index by Categories"

Indianapolis, Ind.

- Auto dealer repair workers, wages, and benefits, by occupation, size of establishment, and for 24 labor market areas, Nov 1982 survey, 6787–6.202
- Census of Housing, 1980: occupancy and unit characteristics, by race, Hispanic origin, and city, SMSA rpt, 2473–1.187
- Census of Population and Housing, 1980: detailed population and housing characteristics, by county, city, and census tract, SMSA rpt, 2551–2.187
- Housing and households detailed characteristics, and unit and neighborhood quality, by inside-outside central cities, 1980 survey, SMSA rpt, 2485–6.10
- Loan activity of banks in Fed Reserve 7th District and 3 major midwestern cities, monthly rpt, 9375–9
- Population size of top 25 cities, 1980 and 1982, press release, 2328–46
- Wages by occupation, and benefits for office and plant workers, 1984 SMSA survey rpt, 6785–11.10
- Wages of office and plant workers, by occupation, 1983 SMSA survey rpt, 6785–12.1

see also under By City and By SMSA or MSA in the "Index by Categories"

Indians

- Agriculture census, 1982: farms, farmland, production, finances, and operator characteristics, by county, final State rpt series, 2331–1
- Budget of US, effects of Reagan Admin policy changes, by detailed program, FY85, annual rpt, 104–21
- Cancer cases, incidence, deaths, and death rates, by body site, age, race, Hispanic origin, and sex, for 10 geographic areas, 1973-81, 4478–130
- Census of Housing, 1980: occupancy and unit characteristics of SMSAs and central cities, by race, Hispanic origin, and city, State and SMSA rpt series, 2473–1
- Census of Population and Housing, 1980: detailed population and housing characteristics, by county, city, and census tract, State and SMSA rpt series, 2551–2
- Census of Population, 1980: detailed socioeconomic and demographic

Index by Subjects and Names

characteristics, by age, sex, race, Hispanic origin, occupation, and industry, State rpt series, 2531–4

Census of Population, 1980: detailed socioeconomic characteristics, by county, city, and inside-outside SMSAs and central cities, State rpt series, 2531–3

Census of Population, 1980: Indian and Alaska Native population and housing occupancy, by reservation, Alaska Native village, and other Indian area, supplementary rpt, 2535–1.16

Census of Population, 1980: migration since 1975, by State and selected demographic characteristics, supplementary rpt, 2535–1.13

Cherokee Indians Eastern Band of North Carolina, financial and operating data for Bur of Indian Affairs assistance programs, FY83, annual rpt, 5704–4

Children and youth benefitting from Fed Govt public welfare programs and tax expenditures, participation and funding for 71 programs, FY81-83, 21968–30

Colorado River Storage Project finances, water resource dev, power production, and other activities in western States, FY83, annual rpt, 5824–3

Community services block grants by type of service provider, State mgmt, and opinions of officials and groups involved, for 13 States, FY81-83, GAO rpt, 26121–84

County and City Data Book, detailed socioeconomic and demographic data for States, counties, and cities, selected years 1976-82, 2328–1

Economic Dev Admin loans and grants, by program, State, county, and project or recipient, FY83 and cumulative FY66-83, annual rpt, 2064–2

Education Dept grants to local agencies under Indian Education Act, audit results by region, FY82, annual rpt, 4804–29

Education Dept programs funding, operations, and effectiveness, FY83, annual rpt, 4804–5

Education, Fed Govt Indian Education Act grants and fellowships awarded by State, FY83, and natl advisory council funding, FY73-84, annual rpt, 14874–1

Education program for Indians, operations, funding, student progress measures, and opinions of school staff, parents, and students, selected years 1973-83, 4808–13

Employment and training programs for Indians and Alaska Natives, funding allocation under Job Training Partnership Act, by individual tribe and group, FY84, press release, 6408–57

Fed Govt aid to State and local govts, expenditures, and direct payments, by program, agency, and State, FY83, annual rpt, 2464–2

Fed Govt employment and training program funding under Job Training Partnership Act, and required matching funds, for 3 programs by State, 1984/85, press release, 6408–58

Fed Govt financial and nonfinancial domestic aid, 1984 annual comprehensive catalog, 104–5

Fed Govt programs and mgmt cost control proposals, 3-year savings by function and agency, and financial and operating data, 1960s-81, 16908–1.9

Individual retirement arrangements

Fish and eggs for stocking distributed from natl hatcheries, by species, hatchery, and jurisdiction, FY83, annual rpt, 5504–10

FmHA loans and grants by program and State, and summary of services, FY83 with trends from FY63, annual rpt, 1184–17

Food aid program of USDA for women, infants, and children, participants, clinics, and costs, by State and Indian agency, FY82, annual table, 1364–12.1

Food aid programs of USDA, participants and costs by program and region, monthly rpt, 1362–14

Food aid programs of USDA, participants, monthly press release, 1362–13

Food distribution program participants on individual Indian reservations and in TTPI, irregular rpt, 1362–15

Govt census, 1982: State govt payments to local govts, by program, source of funds, level of govt, and State, with trends from 1902, 2460–3

Handicapped children public education program enrollment, staff, and funding, by handicap, age, and State, 1981/82-1982/83, annual rpt, 4944–4

Head Start Project enrollment of handicapped children, by handicap, State, and for Indian and migrant programs, 1982, annual rpt, 4604–1

Health condition of Indians, births, morbidity, and deaths and rates, and health services facilities and use, 1954-83, annual compilation, 4104–7

Health programs for Indians and Alaska Natives, activities and funding for scholarships, care services, and facilities construction, by city, FY82, annual rpt, 4104–11

HHS aid to each State and local govt or private instn, amount obligated, funding agency, and program, FY83, annual listing, 4004–3

Hospitals of Indian Health Service admissions, discharges, births, total and occupied beds, length of stay, and outpatient visits, by area and facility, quarterly rpt, 4102–3

Hospitals of Indian Health Service, discharge rates by age and primary diagnosis, biennial rpt, suspended, 4104–9

Housing and community dev program operations for Indians and Alaska Natives, FY82 with Community Dev Block Grant funding by tribe and State for FY81, annual rpt, 5004–5

Infant and fetal deaths, and women with no prenatal care during 1st trimester, by race and Hispanic origin, 1960-80 and reduction goals for 1990, article, 4102–1.425

Interior Dept programs, activities, and funding, various periods 1967-84, last issue of annual rpt, 5304–13

Navajo Indians with bacterial meningitis by outcome and bacteria type, and infants with major causative antibody, various periods 1968-80, article, 4102–1.441

Oil, gas, coal, and other mineral production and revenues from Fed Govt and Indian lands, by State, 1983 with trends from 1920, annual rpt, 5734–2

Plague (bubonic and pneumonia-inducing) deaths, and cases by onset date, patient characteristics, and source, 1983 and trends from 1950, article, 4202–7.408

Revenue sharing payments to States, local govts, Indian tribes, and Alaska Native villages, and entitlement computation data, FY84, series, 8066–1

Schools in federally impacted areas, Fed Govt funding by county and school and congressional district, and eligible pupils, by State, FY83, annual rpt, 4804–10

Statistical Abstract of US, social, political, and economic data, 1950s-83 and trends, annual rpt, 2324–1.1

Uranium mining operations, finances, and costs of alternative methods to meet emissions standards, for industry and selected mines, selected years 1948-90, 9188–96

Vocational training bilingual projects, participants, characteristics, and costs, by program, FY82, annual rpt, 4804–26

Youth summer job program of Fed Govt, funding and jobs by State and for Indians, summer 1984, press release, 6408–62

Indigent defense

see Legal aid

Individual retirement arrangements

Bank financial and operating statements, functional cost analysis for Fed Reserve member banks with average and high earnings, by deposit size, 1982, annual rpt, 9364–6

Household income, assets, and debt characteristics, sources of credit, and use of financial services, 1983 survey, article, 9362–1.411

Household income, home value and equity, and financial assets by type, by household characteristics, 1983 survey with trends from 1970, article, 9362–1.406

Income tax returns of individuals, by filing and deduction characteristics and income level, 1983, annual article, 8302–2.414

Income tax returns of individuals by tax return item, State, and occupation, and income by source and tax owed, by income level, selected years 1916-80, conf papers, 8308–28.1

Income tax returns of individuals, detailed data, 1982, annual rpt, 8304–2

Income tax returns of individuals, selected income, deduction, and tax credit data by income, preliminary 1982, annual article, 8302–2.402

Older persons retirement income by type, and preretirement income replacement, under alternative inflation rates, various periods 1979-84, article, 9373–1.419

Older persons sociodemographic characteristics, and Fed Govt program participation and funding, 1983 with trends and projections 1900-2060, annual rpt, 25144–3.1

Tax expenditures, Fed Govt revenues foregone through pension and other tax benefit policy changes, FY84-88, and women's labor force and pension participation, 1939-82, hearing, 25368–131

Trust assets of banks and trust companies, by type of asset and fund and State, 1983, annual rpt, 13004–1

Indochina

Indochina
see Kampuchea
see Laos
see Southeast Asia
see Vietnam

Indonesia

- Agricultural and food production indexes, and production of selected commodities, by world region and country, 1974-83, annual rpt, 1524–5
- Agricultural situation in Southeast Asia, by country and commodity, 1983 and outlook for 1984, annual rpt, 1524–4.5
- Agricultural supply/demand, trade, and production, and socioeconomic data, by country, 1950s-77, 1528–179
- AID activities and funding by project and function, FY85, and developing countries summary socioeconomic data, 1970s-83, by country, annual rpt, 9914–3
- AID economic assistance to developing countries, obligations and disbursements by country, quarterly rpt, 9912–4
- AID loan repayment status and terms by program and country, and status of predecessor agency loans, quarterly rpt, 9912–3
- Economic indicators of 12 Pacific Basin countries or areas and US, quarterly rpt, 9393–9
- Economic, social, and political summary data, by country, 1984, annual factbook, 244–11
- Economic trends in income, production, prices, employment, finances, and trade, 1984 semiannual rpt, 2046–4.28, 2046–4.83
- Electric power systems equipment market and trade, and user industry operations and demand, 1983 country market research rpt, 2045–15.3
- Exports and imports of US, by commodity and country, 1972-82, annual world region rpt, 244–13.5
- Exports of US, detailed Schedule B commodities by country of destination, 1983, annual rpt, 2424–9
- Exports of US, detailed Schedule E commodities by mode of transport and world area and country of destination, 1983, annual rpts, 2424–5
- Food supply policies of 21 developing countries, with farm sector data, tariff income, and prices and imports of 5 grains, 1960s-81, 1528–168
- Housing finance and low-income housing projects in Asian developing countries, and activities of 2 countries, 1970s-82, annual conf proceedings, 9914–11
- Imports of US, detailed Schedule A commodities by country and world area of origin, and mode of transport, 1983, annual rpts, 2424–2
- Imports of US, detailed TSUSA commodities by country of origin, 1983, annual rpt, 2424–4
- Loans and grants for economic and military assistance from US and intl agencies, by program and country, FY46-83, annual rpt, 9914–5
- Medical and health care equipment market and trade, and user industry operations and demand, 1977 country market research rpt, 2045–2.50

Military aid of US, arms sales, and training programs costs and budget requests by program, world region, and country, FY83-85, annual rpt, 7144–13

- Military spending, arms trade, and armed forces size, with total govt spending and population, by country, 1972-82, annual rpt, 9824–1
- *Minerals Yearbook, 1982,* Vol 3: foreign country reviews of production, trade, and policies, by commodity, annual rpt, 5604–35
- *Minerals Yearbook, 1982,* Vol 3 preprints: foreign country review of production, trade, and policies, by commodity, annual rpt, 5604–17.32
- Oil production, and exports and prices to US, by major exporting country, detailed data, monthly rpt, 3162–24
- Oil reserves, production, and resource lifespan under alternative production rates, for 4 Asian countries, late 1800s-1982 and projected to 2030, 3166–9.9
- Population size and growth rates, and latest available benchmark demographic data, by country, 1950-83, biennial rpt, 2324–4
- Refugee migration, settlement status, and assistance, by world area and country of origin and asylum, as of May 1984, annual rpt, 7004–15
- Space satellites and other objects launched since 1957, quarterly listing, 9502–2
- Tea exports of 3 Asian countries, by country of destination, 1982-83, FAS annual rpt, 1925–15.3
- *see also* under By Foreign Country in the "Index by Categories"

Industrial accidents and safety
see Hazardous substances
see Mine accidents and safety
see Occupational health and safety
see Railroad accidents and safety

Industrial arts

- Teaching degrees conferred by specialty and State, required credit hours, and instn officials attitudes, by instn type, 1970s-83, hearings, 21348–89
- Vocational education, detailed data on enrollment, achievement, curricula, and effects on employment, selected years 1980-82, annual rpt, 4824–1.3

Industrial capacity and utilization

- Business activity indicators (nonfinancial), 1982, annual rpt, 9364–5.9
- Business and financial statistics, historic trends, 1984 annual chartbook, 9364–2.5
- Business and financial statistics, quarterly chartbook, 9362–2.3
- *Business Conditions Digest,* current data on economic, business, and financial conditions and cyclical fluctuations, monthly rpt, 2702–3
- *Business Conditions Digest,* historical supplement on economic, business, and financial conditions and cyclical fluctuations, with methodology, 1947-82, 2708–31
- Capacity utilization in 15 manufacturing industries, mining, electric and all utilities, and industrial materials including energy, monthly rpt, 9365–2.19
- China cotton and synthetic fiber supply and use, retail clothing sales, and textile mill productivity and equipment, 1978-84, article, 1561–1.405

Index by Subjects and Names

- Coal Fed Govt leases, acreage, production, and prices, by State, and legal and mgmt issues, 1970s-83 with production projections to 2000, 11128–1
- Copper mine expansion in Cananea, Mexico, effects on US air pollution and copper industry, with US and foreign industry data, 1960s-95, hearing, 21448–31
- Dairy cooperatives itemized costs for manufacturing cheese, butter, and dry milk, plants, and plant capacity, 1981/82, 1128–25
- Economic indicators and components, and Fed Reserve 4th District business and financial conditions, monthly chartbook, 9377–10
- Economic indicators and components, current data and annual trends, monthly rpt, 23842–1.3
- Economic indicators, nonfinancial, monthly rpt, 9362–1.2
- Electric power peak demand, generating and interregional transfer capability, and reserve margins, detailed data by region, 1984-93, annual rpt, 3404–6
- Electric power plant capacity, production, retail sales, and fuel stocks, use, and costs, by State, 1979-83, annual rpt, 3164–11
- Energy supply/demand and prices, by fuel type, sector, and end use, with foreign comparisons, 1960-83 and projected to 1995, annual summary rpt, 3164–76
- Foreign economic indicators for 7 OECD countries and US, quarterly rpt, 2042–10
- Import and tariff provisions effect on US industries and products, investigations with background financial and operating data, series, 9886–4
- Imports injury to US industries from foreign subsidized products, investigations with background financial and operating data for selected industries and products, series, 9886–15
- Imports injury to US industries from import sales at less than fair value, investigations with background financial and operating data, series, 9886–14
- Manufacturers capacity utilization rates and production indexes, sales, inventories, shipments, and orders, 1947-83, annual rpt, 204–1.3
- Manufacturing capacity utilization, by SIC 2- to 4-digit industry, 1983, annual Current Industrial Rpt, 2506–3.7
- Minerals (strategic) supply/demand, trade, and foreign and US industry devs by firm and country, by commodity, bimonthly rpt, 5602–4
- Nuclear power and weapons policy, fuel supply/demand, waste disposal and siting, environmental effects of radiation, and public attitudes, 1970s-82 with projections to 2000, 3008–88
- Nuclear power industry status and outlook, with reactor construction, utility financial and operating data, and foreign comparisons, 1970s-83 with projections to 2010, 26358–99
- Nuclear power plant capacity, generation, shutdowns, operation status and costs, and fuel, quarterly rpt, 3352–3
- Nuclear power plant construction and operation status, and capacity, by plant, region, State, and selected country, 1983 and projected to 2020, annual rpt, 3164–57

Index by Subjects and Names

Nuclear power plant generation, capacity, and capacity utilization, monthly rpt, 3162–24.8

Nuclear power plant operating and safety data, by plant, 1981, annual rpt, 9634–6

Nuclear power plant safety standards and research, design, licensing, construction, operation, and finances, with data by reactor, bimonthly rpt, 3352–4

Nuclear power plants construction financing of Washington Public Power Supply System, with regional economic impacts and power supply/demand, 1980s-2035, hearing, 21448–29

Nuclear reactor operating and inspection data for individual commercial facilities, monthly rpt, 9632–1

Oil companies energy production and imports by type, and financial data, 1975-81, annual rpt, 3164–74

Oil industry refining capacity utilization, 1981-82, annual rpt, 3164–44.3

Oil prices impact on US oil trade and energy-intensive industries, with US and foreign reserves and industry operations, 1950-82 and projected to 2020, 9886–4.69

Oil refineries financial and operating impacts from auto use of alcohol fuels, projected to 2000 with trends 1964-80, 3308–75

Oil refinery capacity and use, weekly rpt, 3162–32

Oil refinery locations and capacities in US and territories, by company, Jan 1983, annual rpt, 3164–2

OPEC oil production and capacity, by member, monthly rpt, 242–5

OPEC oil refining capacity and production by city, and oil use and exports, by member, with comparisons to other countries, projected 1985-90, hearings, 25368–133.1

Southwestern Fed Power System financial statements, electric power sales by customer, and project capacity, production, and costs, FY83, annual rpt, 3244–1

Steel imports of US from EC and other countries, and US industry operating data, for 15 products limited under arrangement with EC, monthly rpt, 9882–10

Steel industry finances and operations under proposed import quota, projected 1985-89 with selected foreign comparisons and trends from 1950, 26306–6.80

Sugarcane and beet processing capacity and sugar production, 1970s-83, article, 1561–14.401

Tennessee Valley river control and reservoir elevations, storage, flows, and hydroelectric generating capacity use, 1981, annual rpt, 9804–7

Uranium mining operations, finances, and costs of alternative methods to meet emissions standards, for industry and selected mines, selected years 1948-90, 9188–96

Uranium reserves and mining and milling industries operations and finances, with selected foreign comparisons, various periods 1964-83 and projected to 2000, 3008–95

Western Area Power Admin small-scale potential hydroelectric generation, site inventory, characteristics, and costs, by State and county, 1984 rpt, 3258–1

Industrial controls

see Electrical machinery and equipment

see Instruments and measuring devices

see Quality control and testing

Industrial location

see Industrial siting

Industrial management

Census of Housing, 1980: structural, financial, and householder characteristics, by region and State, 2475–4

Census of Population, 1980: detailed socioeconomic and demographic characteristics, by age, sex, race, Hispanic origin, occupation, and industry, State rpt series, 2531–4

Census of Population, 1980: labor force, by sex, detailed occupation, and region, with comparison to 1970 census, supplementary rpt, 2535–1.12

County Business Patterns: establishments, employees, and payrolls, by SIC 4-digit industry and county, 1981, annual State rpt series, 2326–8

County Business Patterns: establishments, employees, and payrolls, by SIC 4-digit industry and county, 1982, annual State rpt series, 2326–6

Foreign women sociodemographic, economic, and fertility characteristics, with comparisons to men, by country, 1960s-85, world region rpt series, 2326–15

Income tax returns of sole proprietorships, detailed data by industry div and selected industry group, 1981, annual rpt, 8304–7

Input-output structure of US economy, detailed interindustry transactions for 537 industries, and components of final demand, 1977 benchmark data, 2708–17

Minority business mgmt and financial assistance from federally funded organizations, by region, State, and business characteristics, FY83, annual rpt, 2104–6

Natural gas interstate pipeline company detailed financial and operating data, by firm, 1983, annual rpt, 3164–38

Service industry census, 1982: employment, establishments, receipts, and payroll, by SIC 2- to 4-digit kind of business, SMSA, county, and city, State rpt series, 2391–1

see also Executives

see also Industrial siting

see also Labor-management relations, general

see also Labor-management relations, local and regional

Industrial parks

Bond tax-exempt issues for private activity, by purpose, face value, major industry, and State, 1983, article, 8302–2.417

Industrial plants and equipment

Acid rain causes and effects, air pollutant emissions by source in US and selected countries, control costs, and Fed Govt research funding, 1960s-82, 3408–27

Air pollutant emission factors, by detailed source, 3rd edition, 1983-84 supplements, 9198–13

Air pollutant emissions, control costs, and acid rain causes and effects, selected years 1977-83 and projected to 2000, 26358–104

Air pollutant emissions in US and selected countries, control costs, and acid rain causes and effects, 1970s-83 and projected to 2000, 21368–52

Industrial plants and equipment

Air pollutant sulfur dioxide emissions reduction proposal, effects on polluting industries and coal production by region and State, projected to 2010, 9188–97

Air pollution abatement under Clean Air Act, emissions by source, standards, and effects on auto industry and health, 1970s-83, hearings, 25328–25

Air pollution levels for 5 pollutants, by detailed source, State, and Air Quality Control Region, 1981, annual rpt, 9194–7

Alcohol fuel (ethanol) production in Tennessee Valley, feedstocks, facilities, tax incentives, and related farming data, by State, 1970s-83 and projected to 1992, 9808–69

Aluminum primary production plant ownership, capacity, and type and source of raw material and energy used, by plant, State, and country, June 1984, semiannual listing, 5602–5

Arson incidents by occupancy of structure, average property value, and arrest rates, by type of property, 1983, annual rpt, 6224–2.1

Bonneville Power Admin energy conservation program activities and funding data, FY82 and estimated FY83-87, 3228–2

Business Conditions Digest, historical supplement on economic, business, and financial conditions and cyclical fluctuations, with methodology, 1947-82, 2708–31

Business statistics, detailed data for major industries and economic indicators, *Survey of Current Business,* monthly rpt, 2702–1.14

California business failures, plant closings, layoffs, and relocations, by plant, industry, county, and city, 1980-83, hearing, 21348–84.1

Capital (fixed), govt and private nonresidential structures and equipment, residential capital, and consumer-owned durable goods by item, 1980-83, annual article, 2702–1.433

Census of Construction Industries, 1982: financial and operating data, by SIC 4-digit industry and State, final rpt series, 2373–1

Census of Construction Industries, 1982: financial and operating data, by SIC 4-digit industry and State, preliminary rpt series, 2371–1

China cotton and synthetic fiber supply and use, retail clothing sales, and textile mill productivity and equipment, 1978-84, article, 1561–1.405

China economic conditions, agricultural and industrial production, trade, and domestic and foreign investment, 1980-85, 2048–106

Coastal environmental characteristics, fish, wildlife, and use, and population socioeconomic data, for individual areas, series, 5506–4

Construction put in place, permits authorized by region, State, and MSA, and Federal contract awards, by construction type, bimonthly rpt with articles, 2012–1

Construction put in place, value of new public and private structures, by type, monthly rpt, 2382–4

Industrial plants and equipment

Copper mine expansion in Cananea, Mexico, effects on US air pollution and copper industry, with US and foreign industry data, 1960s-95, hearing, 21448–31

County Business Patterns: establishments, employees, and payrolls, by SIC 4-digit industry and county, 1981, annual State rpt series, 2326–8

County Business Patterns: establishments, employees, and payrolls, by SIC 4-digit industry and county, 1982, annual State rpt series, 2326–6

Economic indicators and components, and Fed Reserve 4th District business and financial conditions, monthly chartbook, 9377–10

Economic indicators and components, current data and annual trends, monthly rpt, 23842–1.1

Employment, earnings, and hours, by SIC 4-digit nonfarm industry, monthly 1974-Feb 1984, annual update, 6744–4

Energy use in nonresidential buildings, expenditures, and conservation, by building characteristics, EIA survey series, 3166–8

Exports and imports of US, totals and as percent of domestic production, by SIC 2- to 5-digit commodity, 1981, annual rpt, 2424–3

Exports, imports, tariffs, and industry operating data for metals and metal products, TSUSA commodity rpt series, 9885–6

Exports of US, detailed commodities by country of destination, monthly rpt, 2422–3

Fabric (narrow) machinery in place, 1983, annual Current Industrial Rpt, 2506–5.6

Food processing and packaging equipment, foreign market and trade, and user industry operations and demand, country market research rpts, 2045–11

Foreign direct investment in US, major investors and investments by SIC 4-digit industry, transaction type and value, and location, 1983, annual rpt, 2044–20

Foreign firms US affiliates financial and operating data, by country of parent firm and industry div, 1980-81, article, 2702–1.402

Foreign market and trade for machine tools and equipment, and user industry operations and demand, country market research rpts, 2045–9

Foreign market and trade for pollution control instruments and equipment, and user industry operations and demand, country market research rpts, 2045–17

Foreign meat plants inspected and certified for exporting products to US, 1983, annual listing, 1374–2

Gasohol and ethanol plant capacity and production, tax exemptions and sales by State, and prices, 1983, annual rpt, 3304–9

Great Lakes trade, by SITC 3-digit commodity, port, vessel type, world area, and country, 1982, annual rpt, 7744–3

Heat treatment equipment trade, tariffs, and industry operating data, 1979-83, TSUSA commodity rpt, 9885–6.72

Imports of US, detailed Schedule A commodities by country and world area of origin, and mode of transport, 1983, annual rpts, 2424–2

Index by Subjects and Names

Imports of US, detailed Schedule A commodities by country, monthly rpt, 2422–2

Industrial process control equipment foreign market and trade, and user industry operations and demand, country market research rpts, 2045–6

Industry finances and operations, by SIC 2- to 4-digit industry, 1970s-83 and projected to 1988, annual rpt, 2014–4

Injuries, detailed accident circumstances and safety data, by body part injured, type of equipment used, or industry, series, 6846–1

Input-output structure of US economy, detailed interindustry transactions for 537 industries, and components of final demand, 1977 benchmark data, 2708–17

Livestock slaughtering plants, total and federally inspected, by State, 1983, annual rpt, 1623–10.2

Manufacturing census, 1982: financial and operating data, by SIC 2- to 4-digit industry, State, SMSA, and county, preliminary census div rpt series, 2491–3

Manufacturing census, 1982: financial and operating data, for SIC 4-digit industries by product, preliminary rpt series, 2491–1

Manufacturing census, 1982: textile mill machinery in place, by machine type and textile industry, special preliminary rpts, 2491–2

Mineral industries census, 1982: financial and operating data, including materials consumed, by SIC 4-digit industry and State, preliminary rpt series, 2511–1

Minerals (strategic) supply/demand, trade, and foreign and US industry devs by firm and country, by commodity, bimonthly rpt, 5602–4

Minerals Yearbook, 1982, Vol 1: commodity reviews of industry economic conditions, supply/demand, and trade, annual rpt, 5604–33.3

Minority group and women employment, by occupational group and SIC 2- to 3-digit industry, 1981, annual rpt, 9244–1.1

Molds (industrial) from Canada, effect on competing US industry, investigation with background financial and operating data, 1979-83, 9886–4.72

Natural gas interstate pipeline company detailed financial and operating data, by firm, 1983, annual rpt, 3164–38

Natural gas pipeline and compressor station construction costs, 1979-82, annual rpt, 3084–3

Nuclear power and weapons policy, fuel supply/demand, waste disposal and siting, environmental effects of radiation, and public attitudes, 1970s-82 with projections to 2000, 3008–88

Occupational deaths, circumstances and OSHA safety standards violated by type of incident and equipment used, series, 6606–2

Oil and gas field equipment detailed specifications for a west Texas site, by depth, 1983, annual rpt, 3164–45

Oil and gas OCS drilling rigs by country, rig losses, and worker injury and death rates, various periods 1966-83, hearing, 21568–35

Oil field equipment from 5 countries, injury to US industry from foreign subsidized imports and less than fair value sales, investigation with background financial and operating data, 1984 rpt, 9886–19.11

Oil refineries in operation, and refineries bought and sold by company, by capacity, various dates 1980-85, article, 3162–6.401

Oil refinery locations and capacities in US and territories, by company, Jan 1983, annual rpt, 3164–2

Pacific Northwest electricity consumption and prices by end-use sector, and economic and demographic data, 1960s-83 and projected to 2005, annual rpt, 3224–2

Producer prices and indexes, by stage of processing and detailed commodity, monthly rpt, 6762–6

Producer prices and indexes, by stage of processing and detailed commodity, monthly 1983, annual supplement, 6764–2

Shipbuilding and repair facilities, construction capability, number and value of ships under construction, and employment, by shipyard, 1983, annual rpt, 7704–9

Soviet Union gross fixed capital investment and capital stock, by sector, 1960s-83, annual rpt, 244–5.3

Telephone and telegraph firms detailed financial, operating, and employment statistics, 1982, annual rpt, 9284–6

Tennessee Valley industrial dev and effects on employment, investment, and TVA power demand, by location and company, 1983, annual rpt, 9804–3

Timber harvest residue recovery for energy, cost-effectiveness of 3 logging systems, 1983 technical paper, 9806–2.37

Uranium enrichment facilities operations, finances, uranium stocks, and energy use and capital investment by facility, FY83, annual rpt, 3354–7

Uranium ore tailings at inactive mills and DOE remedial action program activities by site, and program funding, FY84, annual rpt, 3354–9

Virgin Islands economic censuses, 1982: employment, establishments, payroll, and receipts, by SIC 1- to 4-digit industry, island, and city, 2593–1

Water pollution regulation under EPA wastewater discharge system, operations and funding, various periods FY79-83, GAO rpt, 26113–113

Wholesale trade census, 1982: employment, establishments, finances, and operations, by SIC 2- to 4-digit kind of business, SMSA, county, and city, State rpt series, 2405–1

Wholesale trade census, 1982: employment, establishments, sales by commodity, and payroll, by SIC 4-digit kind of business and State, preliminary rpt series, 2403–1

see also Business firms and establishments, number

see also Capital investments, general

see also Capital investments, specific industries

see also Depreciation

see also Industrial capacity and utilization

Index by Subjects and Names

see also Industrial siting
see also Office furniture and equipment
see also Power-generating plants and equipment
see also Railroad equipment and vehicles
see also Warehouses

Industrial pollution

see Air pollution
see Environmental pollution and control
see Lead poisoning and pollution
see Marine pollution
see Noise
see Nuclear radiation
see Refuse and refuse disposal
see Water pollution

Industrial production

Business and financial statistics, historic trends, 1984 annual chartbook, 9364–2.2, 9364–2.5

Business and financial statistics, quarterly chartbook, 9362–2.2, 9362–2.3

Business Conditions Digest, current data on economic, business, and financial conditions and cyclical fluctuations, monthly rpt, 2702–3

Business Conditions Digest, historical supplement on economic, business, and financial conditions and cyclical fluctuations, with methodology, 1947-82, 2708–31

Business statistics, detailed data for major industries and economic indicators, *Survey of Current Business,* monthly rpt, 2702–1

China economic conditions, agricultural and industrial production, trade, and domestic and foreign investment, 1980-85, 2048–106

Communist and and OECD countries economic conditions, 1982, annual rpt, 7144–11

Communist, OECD, and selected other countries economic statistics, 1960s-83, annual rpt, 244–5

Cuba economic conditions, agricultural and industrial production and distribution, trade, and intl economic relations, 1970-82 and trends from 1957, 248–40

Economic and financial trends, natl compounded annual rates of change, 1964-83, annual rpt, 9391–9.2

Economic conditions and employment, alternative BLS projections to 1995 with selected trends for 1959-82, 6728–29

Economic conditions of US, with some foreign comparisons, 1960s-82 and alternative projections to 1992, hearing, 21248–79

Economic indicators and components, and Fed Reserve 4th District business and financial conditions, monthly chartbook, 9377–10

Economic indicators and components, current data and annual trends, monthly rpt, 23842–1.3

Economic indicators, and Fed Govt finances and deficits, selected years 1962-83 and projected under cost control proposals to 2000, 16908–1.1

Economic indicators, nonfinancial, monthly rpt, 9362–1.2

Exchange rate volatility, effect on employment and production, 1984 technical paper, 9366–7.97

Exports and imports of US, totals and as percent of domestic production, by SIC 2- to 5-digit commodity, 1981, annual rpt, 2424–3

Fed Govt contractors and DOD-owned facilities, operating data by agency, selected SIC 2- to 4-digit industry, State, and SMSA, 1982, annual Current Industrial Rpt, 2506–3.4

Foreign economic and monetary trends, compounded annual rates of change for US and 10 major trading partners, quarterly rpt, 9391–7

Foreign economic indicators and currency exchange rates, by world area and selected country, mid-1960s-83, annual rpt, 204–1.9

Foreign economic indicators for 7 OECD countries and US, quarterly rpt, 2042–10

Foreign economic trends and implications for US, annual and semiannual country rpt series, 2046–4

Fresno, Calif, economic, population, labor, and housing indicators, various periods 1974-85, hearing, 21248–84

Generalized System of Preferences status of 29 commodities, with US production, consumption, tariffs, and trade by country, selected years 1978-87, 9888–17

Import and tariff provisions effect on US industries and products, investigations with background financial and operating data, series, 9886–4

Imports from Communist countries, injury to US industries, investigations with background financial and operating data, selected industries and products, series, 9886–12

Imports injury to US industries from foreign subsidized products, investigations with background financial and operating data for selected industries and products, series, 9886–15

Imports injury to US industries from import sales at less than fair value, investigations with background financial and operating data, series, 9886–14

Imports injury to US industries from increased import sales, investigations with background financial and operating data, series, 9886–5

Imports injury to US industries from removal of duties on foreign subsidized products, investigations with background financial and operating data, series, 9886–18

Industry finances and operations, by SIC 2- to 4-digit industry, 1970s-83 and projected to 1988, annual rpt, 2014–4

Input-output structure of US economy, detailed interindustry transactions for 85 industries, and components of final demand, 1977, article, 2702–1.421

Input-output structure of US economy, detailed interindustry transactions for 537 industries, and components of final demand, 1977 benchmark data, 2708–17

Intl trade position of US and 4 OECD countries, and factors affecting US competition, quarterly pamphlet, 2042–25

Manufacturers shipments, inventories, and orders, by industry, monthly Current Industrial Rpt, 2506–3.1

Industrial production indexes

Manufacturing census, 1982: financial and operating data, for SIC 4-digit industries by product, preliminary rpt series, 2491–1

Manufacturing production, export-related employment, and exports of manufactured and agricultural commodities, 1960s-82, State rpt series, 2046–3

North Central States economic indicators, Fed Reserve 7th District monthly rpt, 9375–9

Overseas Business Reports: economic conditions, investment and export opportunities, and trade practices, annual country market research rpt series, 2046–6

Overseas Business Reports: economic conditions, investment and export opportunities, and trade practices, world region rpt series, 2046–5

Pacific Basin economic indicators, US and 12 countries, quarterly rpt, 9393–9

Pollution abatement expenditures, and effect on economic indicators and industry operations, by major industry, projected under 3 pollution regulation alternatives 1983-95, 9188–84

Production, shipments, PPI, and stocks of building materials, by type, bimonthly rpt, 2012–1.6

Seasonal adjustment methodology for economic time series, dev and design of Census Bur and other systems, with illustrative data, 1981 conf papers, 2626–7.5

Soviet Union industrial and agricultural production by selected commodity, and demographic trends and projections by Republic, 1950s-2000, hearings, 23848–180

Statistical Abstract of US, social, political, and economic data, 1950s-83 and trends, annual rpt, 2324–1.3

UK economic indicator performance under Thatcher govt, with OECD comparisons, 1970-1983/84, article, 9391–1.414

see also Business inventories
see also Business orders
see also Industrial capacity and utilization
see also Industrial production indexes
see also Labor productivity
see also Production costs
see also Productivity
see also under names of specific industries or industry groups

Industrial production indexes

Business activity indicators (nonfinancial), 1982, annual rpt, 9364–5.9

Business Conditions Digest, current data on economic, business, and financial conditions and cyclical fluctuations, monthly rpt, 2702–3

Business Conditions Digest, historical supplement on economic, business, and financial conditions and cyclical fluctuations, with methodology, 1947-82, 2708–31

Business statistics, detailed data for major industries and economic indicators, *Survey of Current Business,* monthly rpt, 2702–1.1

Communist, OECD, and selected other countries economic statistics, 1960s-83, annual rpt, 244–5.2

Industrial production indexes

Economic indicators and components, current data and annual trends, monthly rpt, 23842–1.3

Economic indicators, nonfinancial, monthly rpt, 9362–1.2

Economic trends, natl compounded annual rates of change, monthly rpt, 9391–3.1

Energy supply/demand, prices, end use, and related technical and socioeconomic data, including impacts of US policy and intl devs, series, 3006–7

Forecasts for selected business activities and natl economic indicators, compilation of representative opinions, 1984, annual rpt, 9389–3

Foreign and US industrial production indexes and CPI, for US and 6 OECD countries, current data and annual trends, monthly rpt, 23842–1.7

Foreign economic indicators for 7 OECD countries and US, quarterly rpt, 2042–10

Foreign economic trends and implications for US, annual and semiannual country rpt series, 2046–4

Foreign industrial production indexes of 7 OECD countries and US, biweekly rpt, periodic article, 2042–24

Foreign production indexes, 6 OECD countries and US, *Business Conditions Digest,* historical supplement and methodology, 1947-82, 2708–31

Foreign production indexes, 6 OECD countries and US, *Business Conditions Digest,* monthly rpt, 2702–3.10

Industrial electric power demand model estimates, economic indicators, and supporting data for 5 industries, 1960s-80 with projections to 2000, 3008–87

Manufacturers indexes for selected product and market groups, 1947-83 with trends for major industry divs from 1929, annual rpt, 204–1.3

Minerals (strategic) supply/demand, trade, and foreign and US industry devs by firm and country, by commodity, bimonthly rpt, 5602–4

New England States economic indicators, Fed Reserve 1st District, monthly rpt, 9373–2.1

North Central States manufacturing activity diffusion indexes, Fed Reserve 4th District 10-year summary charts, monthly rpt, 9377–4

OECD economic indicators, for US and 6 countries, biweekly rpt, 242–4

Production indexes, by SIC 2- to 4-digit industry, monthly rpt, 9365–2.10

Productivity of labor and capital in manufacturing, all nonfarm business, and all private business, indexes and percent change, 1948-83, annual rpt, 6824–2

Western States economic indicators, Fed Reserve 12th District, quarterly rpt, 9393–1.3

Industrial relations

see Labor-management relations, general

see Labor-management relations, local and regional

see Work stoppages

Industrial revenue bonds

see Tax exempt securities

Industrial siting

California business failures, plant closings, layoffs, and relocations, by plant, industry, county, and city, 1980-83, hearing, 21348–84.1

Census of Govts, 1982: properties, govt-assessed value, sales, and tax rates, by property type, State, SMSA, county, and city, 2453–1

Closings of plants attributed in part to pollution control costs, quarterly rpt, discontinued, 9182–6

Closings of plants, Fed Govt and State law provisions, corporate policies, collective bargaining agreements, and job loss in California and total US, 1982, article, 9377–1.401

Farm real estate transfers, by proposed use of property, region, and State, 1982-83, annual rpt, 1541–8.4

Gasohol and ethanol plant capacity and production, tax exemptions and sales by State, and prices, 1983, annual rpt, 3304–9

Georgia total and per capita personal income in 10 highest- and 10 lowest-income counties, 1980 with selected economic data for 1970s-83, article, 9371–1.405

New Communities program of HUD, activities, costs, land sales, and community and population characteristics, for 13 communities, 1970s-83, 5188–107

Nuclear power and weapons policy, fuel supply/demand, waste disposal and siting, environmental effects of radiation, and public attitudes, 1970s-82 with projections to 2000, 3008–88

Nuclear power plant capacity, generation, shutdowns, operation status and costs, and fuel, quarterly rpt, 3352–3

Nuclear power plant safety standards and research, design, licensing, construction, operation, and finances, with data by reactor, bimonthly rpt, 3352–4

Nuclear power plant siting population criteria and estimated compliance of selected regions and sites, 1983 rpt, 9638–54

NYC metro area small business owners and accountants, assessment of economy, professional activities, and community problems, by county and industry div, 1983 survey, hearings, 21728–52.3

Oil refinery locations and capacities in US and territories, by company, Jan 1983, annual rpt, 3164–2

Tax incentives to attract and hold industry, 1977 public opinion survey, annual rpt, 10044–2.2

Technology-intensive industry employment and establishments by industry and selected location, and venture capital investments by source, 1970s-82, 26358–107

Technology-intensive industry plant location factors and assessment for Philadelphia SMSA, 1984 narrative article, 9387–1.401

Tennessee Valley industrial dev and effects on employment, investment, and TVA power demand, by location and company, 1983, annual rpt, 9804–3

TVA construction projects employment, and impacts on nearby areas, survey rpt series, 9806–7

Western Area Power Admin small-scale potential hydroelectric generation, site inventory, characteristics, and costs, by State and county, 1984 rpt, 3258–1

Index by Subjects and Names

see also Industrial parks

Industrial standards

FTC budget authority and expenditures for regulatory analysis, by prospective regulation and contractor, 1983, hearings, 21528–56

Natl Bur of Standards standard reference and research materials available, 1984-85, biennial catalog, 2214–2

Natl Standards Bur publications, 1983 annual listing, 2214–1

Nuclear power plant safety standards and research, design, licensing, construction, operation, and finances, with data by reactor, bimonthly rpt, 3352–4

Small business employment and receipts size standards for Fed Govt contract awards by industry, and DOD contract awards data, 1970s-83, hearings, 21728–53

see also Quality control and testing

see also Weights and measures

Industry

Business America, foreign and domestic commerce, and US investment and trade opportunities, biweekly rpt articles, 2042–24

Business Conditions Digest, current data on economic, business, and financial conditions and cyclical fluctuations, monthly rpt, 2702–3

Business Conditions Digest, historical supplement on economic, business, and financial conditions and cyclical fluctuations, with methodology, 1947-82, 2708–31

Business statistics, detailed data for major industries and economic indicators, *Survey of Current Business,* monthly rpt, 2702–1

Economic conditions of US, with some foreign comparisons, 1960s-82 and alternative projections to 1992, hearing, 21248–79

Finances and operations, by SIC 2- to 4-digit industry, 1970s-83 and projected to 1988, annual rpt, 2014–4

Overseas Business Reports: economic conditions, investment and export opportunities, and trade practices, world region rpt series, 2046–5

R&D expenditures by higher education instns and federally funded centers, by field, source of funds, instn, and State, FY82, annual rpt, 9627–13

R&D Fed Govt funding, by agency and performer, FY83-84, 9626–2.132

R&D Fed Govt funding by type of performer, and funding for industrial dev by type, program, and agency, selected years FY75-85, 26306–6.81

Science Indicators, R&D expenditures, innovations, research, and higher education, with foreign comparisons, 1960s- 83, annual rpt, 9624–10

Scientists and engineers employment by sector and activity, and share female, black, and Asian descent, by field, 1982, 9626–2.142

Statistical Abstract of US, social, political, and economic data, 1950s-83 and trends, annual rpt, 2324–1.3

Statistical programs of 6 Federal agencies, industry coding system comparability, workload, and updating cycles, 1984 rpt, 106–4.5

Index by Subjects and Names

see also Agriculture
see also Area wage surveys
see also Automation
see also Banks and banking
see also Business acquisitions and mergers
see also Business assets and liabilities, general
see also Business assets and liabilities, specific industries
see also Business cycles
see also Business education
see also Business energy use
see also Business firms and establishments, number
see also Business income and expenses, general
see also Business income and expenses, specific industries
see also Business orders
see also Capital investments, general
see also Capital investments, specific industries
see also Commercial buildings
see also Communications industries
see also Competition
see also Construction industry
see also Corporations
see also Credit
see also Defense industries
see also Earnings, general
see also Earnings, local and regional
see also Earnings, specific industries
see also Economic concentration and diversification
see also Employee benefit plans
see also Employment and unemployment, general
see also Employment and unemployment, local and regional
see also Employment and unemployment, specific industries
see also Executives
see also Financial institutions
see also Fish and fishing industry
see also Foreign corporations
see also Forests and forestry
see also Franchises
see also Government and business
see also Hours of labor
see also Industrial arts
see also Industrial capacity and utilization
see also Industrial management
see also Industrial parks
see also Industrial plants and equipment
see also Industrial production
see also Industrial production indexes
see also Industrial siting
see also Industrial standards
see also Industry wage surveys
see also Input-output analysis
see also Insurance industry
see also Labor law
see also Labor-management relations, general
see also Labor-management relations, local and regional
see also Labor mobility
see also Labor productivity
see also Labor turnover
see also Labor unions
see also Manpower
see also Manufacturing
see also Marketing
see also Mines and mineral resources

see also Minority businesses
see also Multinational corporations
see also Occupational health and safety
see also Occupations
see also Ownership of enterprise
see also Power-generating plants and equipment
see also Printing and publishing industry
see also Production costs
see also Productivity
see also Public administration
see also Public utilities
see also Real estate business
see also Repair industries
see also Retail trade
see also Service industries
see also Small business
see also Trade adjustment assistance
see also Trademarks
see also Transportation and transportation equipment
see also Wholesale trade
see also under By Industry in the "Index by Categories"
see also under names of specific industries or industry groups

Industry and Trade Administration

see Bureau of Industrial Economics
see International Trade Administration

Industry wage surveys

- Auto dealer repair workers, wages, and benefits, by occupation, size of establishment, and for 24 labor market areas, Nov 1982 survey, 6787–6.202
- Coal (bituminous) mining production and related workers, wages by occupation, and benefits, by size of mine and union status, in 6 States and aggregate for Rocky Mountain States, July 1982 survey, 6787–6.198
- Dress industry production and related workers, wages, and benefits, by occupation, size of establishment, and union status, for 11 labor market areas, Aug 1982 survey, 6787–6.200
- Electric and gas privately owned utilities, wages and employment by occupation, and benefits, by region, Oct 1982 survey, 6787–6.205
- Grain mill production workers, wages, hours, and benefits, by occupation, mill product, and region, June 1982 survey, 6787–6.204
- Hospital worker wages by sex and occupation, and benefits, for 22 MSAs, Oct 1981 survey, 6787–6.201
- Iron and steel production workers and wages by occupation, and benefits, by region, Aug 1983 survey, 6787–6.206
- Metal (nonferrous) manufacturing wages and benefits, by occupation, size of establishment, and for metro-nonmetro areas, 1981 survey, 6787–6.196
- Oil and gas extraction production workers, wages, hours, and benefits, by occupation, region, and for 5 States, June 1982 survey, 6787–6.203
- Repair technicians and apprentices wages and benefits, for 5 types of electrical repair shops in 19 SMSAs, Nov 1981 survey, 6787–6.197
- Telephone and telegraph industry employment and wages, by occupation and sex, 1981, annual survey, 6787–6.199

Infant mortality

- Wages, hours, benefits, and employment, by occupation and selected geographic areas, industry surveys series, 6787–6
- *see also* Area wage surveys

Infant health

see Pediatrics

Infant mortality

- Agent Orange exposed Air Force personnel diseases and disorders, by disease type, age, and officer status, 1984 rpt, 3604–3
- Alabama rural black population, education, employment, health services, and economic status, for 16 counties, selected years 1970-81, 11048–180
- Canada and US hospital use by children by Canada Province and US region, and death rates, by diagnosis and sex, selected years 1977-79, 4147–5.1
- Deaths and death rates, by cause, age, sex, race, and State, provisional 1982-83 with trends from 1979, US Vital Statistics annual rpt, 4144–7
- Deaths and death rates, by detailed geographic area, cause, and demographic characteristics, 1979, US Vital Statistics annual rpt, 4144–3
- Deaths and death rates, by selected cause and demographic characteristics, 1981, US Vital Statistics advance rpt, 4146–5.78
- Deaths and death rates, by selected cause and demographic characteristics, 1982, US Vital Statistics advance rpt, 4146–5.81
- Deaths by principal or contributing cause, with type of injury reported in accidental, poisoning, and violent deaths, by age, sex, and race, 1978, 4146–5.76
- Deaths recorded in 121 cities, by age group and for infants, weekly rpt, 4202–1
- Developing countries summary socioeconomic data, 1970s-83, and AID activities and funding by project and function, FY82-85, by country, annual rpt, 9914–3
- Food aid special supplemental program for women, infants, and children, effectiveness and participant characteristics, 1973-82, GAO rpt, 26131–10
- Foreign and US health care resources, use, and per capita public expenditures, and selected population characteristics, for 7 countries, selected years 1975-81, 21148–33
- Foreign military, social, and economic summary data by world area and country, 1960s-80s, hearing, 25388–47.1
- Foreign population size and growth rates, and latest available benchmark demographic data, by country, 1950-83, biennial rpt, 2324–4
- Foreign women sociodemographic, economic, and fertility characteristics, with comparisons to men, by country, 1960s-85, world region rpt series, 2326–15
- Health condition and health care resources, use, and expenditures, 1970s-82 with trends and projections 1900-2000, annual compilation, 4144–11
- HHS aid to each State and local govt or private instn, amount obligated, funding agency, and program, FY83, annual listing, 4004–3
- Indian births, morbidity, and deaths and rates, and health services facilities and use, 1954-83, annual compilation, 4104–7

Infant mortality

Infant and fetal deaths, and women with no prenatal care during 1st trimester, by race and Hispanic origin, 1960-80 and reduction goals for 1990, article, 4102–1.425

Infant death rates, by race and for 22 cities, 1980, 028–20

Infant, neonatal, and postneonatal deaths, by detailed cause and age, with geographic detail, 1979, US Vital Statistics annual rpt, 4144–2.2

Jamaica PL 480 Title I assistance effects on economic dev, with data on govt finance, economic indicators, demography, and dev programs, 1970s-81, 9916–1.51

Perinatal deaths and death rates, by State, urban-rural location, sex, and race, 1979, US Vital Statistics annual rpt, 4144–2.4

Puerto Rico educational enrollment, finance, completions, curricula, and personnel by instn, and health and vital statistics, selected years 1970-83, hearings, 21348–93

State govt maternal and child health funding, and admin of Fed Govt block grants, by program for 13 States, 1981-83, GAO rpt, 26121–70

TTPI budget, vital statistics, and health services data, often by TTPI govt, FY83 and selected trends, annual rpt, 7004–6.1

Vital statistics, births, marriages, divorces, and deaths, provisional data, monthly rpt, 4142–1

see also Fetal deaths

Infective and parasitic diseases

Acquired immune deficiency syndrome (AIDS) cases, and research funding and activities, monthly rpt, 4042–2

Acquired immune deficiency syndrome (AIDS) cases by patient sexual preference, 1979-83, and tuberculosis death rates in NYC, UK, and Prussia, 1860s-1920, article, 4102–1.431

Acquired immune deficiency syndrome (AIDS) cases by sexual preference and intravenous drug use, and drug abusers characteristics, 1979-81, article, 4102–1.427

Acquired immune deficiency syndrome (AIDS) inpatients at New York Hospital, by mental health and other characteristics, 1981-83, article, 4102–1.426

Acquired immune deficiency syndrome (AIDS) research expenditures in 3 areas, by NIH inst, FY82, 4102–1.404

Brazil malaria cases, by State and proximity to water resource dev project, 1983 hearings, 21248–80

Cases and incidence of infectious notifiable diseases and other public health concerns, by census div and State, 1982, annual rpt, 4204–1

Cases and mortality trends for infectious notifiable diseases and other public health concerns, quarterly rpt articles, 4202–7

Cases of notifiable infectious diseases and current outbreaks, by region and State, weekly rpt, 4202–1

Child immunization and preventive medicine programs in US and Mexico, disease cases, vaccine reactions, and deaths, 1984 conf papers, 4204–15

Coxsackie B virus cases, by isolate, associated clinical syndrome and patient age and sex, US and Nassau County, NY, 1970-79, article, 4102–1.452

Deaths and death rates, by cause and age, provisional 1982-83, US Vital Statistics annual rpt, 4144–7

Deaths and death rates by detailed cause and demographic characteristics, 1979 and selected trends, US Vital Statistics annual rpt, 4144–2.1

Deaths and death rates, by detailed geographic area, cause, and demographic characteristics, 1979, US Vital Statistics annual rpt, 4144–3

Deaths and death rates, by selected cause and demographic characteristics, 1981, US Vital Statistics advance rpt, 4146–5.78

Deaths and death rates, by selected cause and demographic characteristics, 1982, US Vital Statistics advance rpt, 4146–5.81

Dengue and dengue-like illness cases reported and confirmed in Puerto Rico by month or week of onset, and cases by State, 1982, article, 4202–7.407

Disability Insurance beneficiaries sociodemographic and medical characteristics, 1977-79, annual rpt, 4744–20

Foreign travel vaccination requirements by country, and disease prevention recommendations, 1984 annual rpt, 4204–11

Health condition and health care resources, use, and expenditures, 1970s-82 with trends and projections 1900-2000, annual compilation, 4144–11

Hospital discharges and length of stay, by patient characteristics, facility size, procedure performed, diagnosis, and region, 1982, annual rpt, 4147–13.78

Indian births, morbidity, and deaths and rates, and health services facilities and use, 1954-83, annual compilation, 4104–7

Infant deaths by detailed cause, geographic location, age, race, and sex, 1979, US Vital Statistics annual rpt, 4144–2.2

Malaria cases reported in US, including military personnel and foreign civilians, 1966-82, annual rpt, 4205–4

Measles immunization, natural immunity, and incidence rates in Israel, by age, 1965-83 and projected to 1990, article, 4102–1.429

Natl Inst of Allergy and Infectious Diseases activities, grants by instn, State, and country, and disease incidence and costs, FY60s-84, annual rpt, 4474–30

Navajo Indians with bacterial meningitis by outcome and bacteria type, and infants with major causative antibody, various periods 1968-80, article, 4102–1.441

Older persons by demographic, socioeconomic, and health characteristics, selected years 1900-81 and projected to 2050, Current Population Rpt, 2546–2.125

Pests (plant) and pathogens found entering US, by country of origin, State, and method of interception, FY82, annual rpt, 1394–16

Plague (bubonic and pneumonia-inducing) deaths, and cases by onset date, patient characteristics, and source, 1983 and trends from 1950, article, 4202–7.408

Reporting of communicable diseases to public health depts, physician reasons for underreporting, 1982 survey, article, 4102–1.411

Index by Subjects and Names

Senegal rural health care projects of AID, mgmt and effectiveness, 1978-83, 9916–3.20

see also Animal diseases and zoonoses

see also Food and waterborne diseases

see also Pneumonia and influenza

see also Rabies

see also Tuberculosis

see also Vaccination and vaccines

see also Venereal diseases

see also under By Disease in the "Index by Categories"

Inflation

Budget of US, CBO analysis of revenue and spending alternatives and projections of economic indicators, FY85-89, annual rpt, 26304–3

Budget of US, deficit effect of unemployment and inflation increases and income tax indexing, 1980-83, article, 2702–1.427

Budget of US, deficit effect on inflation, and debt outstanding by holder, Reagan Admin mid-1983 outlook for FY83-84 with supporting data from 1949, article, 9371–1.402

Central America socioeconomic and political conditions in 6 countries, 1960s-83 with trends and projections 1930-2010, Commission rpt, 028–19.2

Consumption related to inflation expectations, regression results, 1st qtr 1960-1st qtr 1978, technical paper, 9387–8.92

CPI and Personal Consumption Expenditures Index measures of inflation, effects of differences in weights and housing treatment, 1977-2nd qtr 1984, article, 6762–2.401

Economic growth, with data on labor force, inflation, and productivity, 1953-83 with inflation and unemployment projections to 1988, article, 9373–1.402

Economic indicators and labor force characteristics, selected years 1880-1995, chartbook, 6728–30

Economic indicators, trends and relation to govt revenues and spending by level of govt, selected years 1929-83, annual rpt, 10044–1

Economic performance of US, and Reagan Admin 1984 spending, tax, and monetary policy proposals, with data for 1950s-83 and projected to 1988, press release, 8008–107

Economic Report of the President for 1984, economic trends from 1929 and Reagan Admin proposals, annual rpt, 204–1

Economic Report of the President for 1984, Joint Economic Committee critique and policy recommendations, annual rpt, 23844–2

European Monetary System effect on inflation and exchange rates, for 3 member countries, various periods Feb 1974-Mar 1984, technical paper, 9366–7.101

Farm investments, effect of Fed Govt and State tax rates under alternative depreciation methods and inflation rates, 1950-84, 1548–231

Fed Govt finances and deficits, and economic indicators, selected years 1962-83 and projected under cost control proposals to 2000, 16908–1.1

Index by Subjects and Names

Forecast errors in inflation predictions, effects of anticipated energy price rise, 1954-83, article, 9391–1.406

Forecasts for selected business activities and natl economic indicators, compilation of representative opinions, 1984, annual rpt, 9389–3

Foreign economic and monetary trends, compounded annual rates of change for US and 10 major trading partners, quarterly rpt, 9391–7

Foreign economic indicators for 7 OECD countries and US, quarterly rpt, 2042–10

Foreign money supply and velocity, prices, and real GNP, growth rates for 4 OECD countries and US, various periods 1954-81, article, 9391–1.401

GNP (potential) related to actual GNP, effects of data revisions and noninflationary unemployment rate, 1952-76, article, 9377–1.404

GNP growth related to inflation and unemployment rate, various periods 1960-83 and projected 1984-89, article, 9385–1.408

GNP implicit price deflator and other prices, natl compounded annual rates of change, 1964-83, annual rpt, 9391–9.2

GNP implicit price deflator, natl compounded annual rates of change, monthly rpt, 9391–3.2

GNP implicit price deflators, monthly rpt, quarterly data, 23842–1.1

GNP implicit price deflators, total and major components, quarterly data with benchmark revisions for 1980-2nd qtr 1984, *Survey of Current Business,* monthly rpt, 2702–1.28

GNP implicit price deflators, total and major components, *Survey of Current Business,* monthly rpt, 2702–1.21

GNP in current and constant dollars, and implicit price deflators, by industry div, 1981-83, article, 2702–1.416

Health care expenditures, growth factors, medical equipment and drugs trade, and physician income, 1950-90, article, 4652–1.407

Inflation rate, money supply growth, and food and energy prices, various periods 1970-2nd qtr 1984, article, 9391–1.420

Interest rates (medium- and long-term real) and expected inflation rates related to other forward rates, regression results, various periods 1976-82, article, 9393–8.406

Massachusetts (Colonial era) prices, foreign exchange rate, and per capita money supply, and compared to other New England colonies, 1720-70, article, 9383–6.402

Mexico economic indicators, trade, external accounts and debt, oil industry, and relations with US, 1978-83 with trends from 1959, conf proceedings, 21248–82

Military construction costs and price indexes by type of facility, and implicit price deflators, 1972-82, article, 2702–1.401

Money supply and nonfinancial sector debt related to inflation and GNP, various periods 1960-83, article, 9373–1.401

Money supply growth related to inflation, wage growth, and corporate bond and real interest rates, 1960-83, article, 9377–1.403

Information storage and retrieval systems

Older persons retirement income by type, and preretirement income replacement, under alternative inflation rates, various periods 1979-84, article, 9373–1.419

Pension plans with postretirement adjustments related to employee and employer characteristics, and effect of inflation on benefit purchasing power, 1973-79, 6468–18

Recession and recovery effect on labor cost and price indexes, changes by index component, various periods 1949-82, article, 6722–1.464

UK economic indicator performance under Thatcher govt, with OECD comparisons, 1970-1983/84, article, 9391–1.414

UK money supply growth and inflation rates related public and private monetary control, 1694-1913, article, 9391–1.410

Weapons system procurement cost estimate changes, and program delays and mgmt, by system and service branch, 1983, annual rpt, 26304–5

see also Consumer Price Index
see also Cost of living
see also Economic indicators
see also Food prices
see also Interest rates
see also Monetary policy
see also Money supply
see also Price regulation
see also Prices
see also Producer Price Index

Influenza

see Pneumonia and influenza

Informants

Drug Enforcement Admin cases against major drug traffickers by case characteristics, and agents assessment of activities, in 3 cities, 1979-82, GAO rpt, 26119–57

Marijuana cultivation control activity of State law enforcement agencies, and aid from Fed Govt and Natl Guard, 1983 survey, GAO rpt, 26119–64

Protection under Witness Security Program, costs, participants by arrest record, and prosecutions by offense, offender type, and disposition, various periods FY70-83, GAO rpt, 26119–70

Information services

Census of Population, 1980: detailed socioeconomic and demographic characteristics, by age, sex, race, Hispanic origin, occupation, and industry, State rpt series, 2531–4

Census of Service Industries, 1982: employment, establishments, receipts, and payroll, by SIC 2- to 4-digit kind of business, SMSA, county, and city, State rpt series, 2391–1

Finances and operations, by SIC 2- to 4-digit industry, 1970s-83 and projected to 1988, annual rpt, 2014–4

see also Government information
see also Information storage and retrieval systems
see also Libraries
see also Research
see also under By Industry in the "Index by Categories"

Information storage and retrieval systems

Aerial survey R&D publications, and sources of natural resource and environmental data gathered by air- and spacecraft, quarterly listing, 9502–7

Agricultural Stabilization and Conservation Service field offices computer systems, costs and savings by component, FY84-92, GAO rpt, 26125–27

Air Force fiscal mgmt system operations and techniques, info for comptroller personnel, quarterly rpt, 3602–1

Counterfeiting of brand-name products by foreign manufacturers, effects on 6 US industries, investigation with financial and operating data, 1984 rpt, 9886–4.67

County Business Patterns: establishments, employees, and payrolls, by SIC 4-digit industry and county, 1981, annual State rpt series, 2326–8

County Business Patterns: establishments, employees, and payrolls, by SIC 4-digit industry and county, 1982, annual State rpt series, 2326–6

DOD procurement cost estimates for weapons and communications systems, by service branch, quarterly summary rpt, 3502–1

Fed Govt computers and telecommunications systems acquisition plans and obligations, by agency, FY84-89, annual rpt, 104–20

Fed Govt programs and mgmt cost control proposals, 3-year savings by function and agency, and financial and operating data, 1960s-81, 16908–1

Fed Govt standards for data recording, processing, and transfer, and for purchase and use of computer systems, series, 2216–2

Fed Govt supply inventory and automated cataloging system, and DOD mgmt of inventory items for agencies, NATO, and foreign govts, 1970s-83, annual rpt, 21204–1

GAO publications on computers, computer use, and telecommunication, as of 1983, annual listing, 26104–11.1

Glaciology intl research summaries, methodology, and bibls, series, 2156–18

GSA computers and automatic data processing systems costs, cost savings, and employment, by activity, subagency, and regional office, FY83-88, 9458–17

GSA mgmt activities and finances, FY78-83, annual rpt, 9454–23

Health and vital statistics collection, and use in program planning and evaluation, Public Health Conf papers, 1983, biennial rpt, 4164–2

Health info offices and services of HHS and other Fed Govt agencies, by subject, 1984 listing, 4048–18

Health manpower and facilities data, by county and SMSA, users guide to computerized area resource file, 1983, annual rpt, 4114–11

Hwy Traffic Safety Natl Admin data collection and analysis activities, 1981, annual rpt, 7764–1

Medical info on-line and data bank services of Natl Library of Medicine, FY81-83, annual rpt, 4464–1

Mental health facilities info systems needs, implementation, uses, and costs, series, 4506–2

New York State home health care program info system on public assistance benefits and services received by program participants, 1984 article, 4652–1.402

Information storage and retrieval systems

R&D Fed Govt facilities and services available for private sector use, by field of science, 1984 biennial listing, 2224–4

- Water supply and quality, and effect of coal mining operations, for selected river basins in Eastern and Interior coal provinces, series, 5666–15
- Water supply and quality, and effect of coal mining operations, for selected river basins in Western coal provinces, series, 5666–19
- *see also* Computer data file guides
- *see also* Computers
- *see also* Microforms
- *see also* Statistical programs and activities

Inheritance tax

see Estate tax

Injuries

- *see* Accidents and accident prevention
- *see* Agricultural accidents and safety
- *see* Aviation accidents and safety
- *see* Marine accidents and safety
- *see* Mine accidents and safety
- *see* Occupational health and safety
- *see* Railroad accidents and safety
- *see* Traffic accidents and safety

Inland water transportation

- Army Corps of Engineers activities and projects, FY83 and trends from 1800s, annual rpt, 3754–1
- China economic conditions, agricultural and industrial production, trade, and domestic and foreign investment, 1980-85, 2048–106
- Coal production and stocks by district, and shipments by district of origin, State of destination, consuming sector, and mode of transport, quarterly rpt, 3162–8
- Communist, OECD, and selected other countries freight and carrier inventories, by mode of transport, 1960s-83, annual rpt, 244–5.10
- County Business Patterns: establishments, employees, and payrolls, by SIC 4-digit industry and county, 1981, annual State rpt series, 2326–8
- County Business Patterns: establishments, employees, and payrolls, by SIC 4-digit industry and county, 1982, annual State rpt series, 2326–6
- Developing countries disaster preparedness and summary sociodemographic, political, and economic data, country rpt series, 9916–2
- DOD shipments of military and personal property, loss claims, passenger traffic, and costs, by mode of transport, quarterly rpt, 3702–1
- Energy use in transportation sector by mode, fuel supplies, and demographic and economic determinants of vehicle use, 1970s-83, annual rpt, 3304–5
- Exports and imports of US (waterborne), by type of service, customs district, port, and world area, monthly rpt, 2422–7
- Fed Govt Inland Waterways Trust Fund receipts, expenditures, assets, and liabilities, monthly rpt, 8102–9.8
- Fed Govt programs and mgmt cost control proposals, 3-year savings by function and agency, and financial and operating data, 1960s-81, 16908–1.11, 16908–1.31
- Finances and operations, by SIC 2- to 4-digit industry, 1970s-83 and projected to 1988, annual rpt, 2014–4

Finances, operations, vehicles, equipment, accidents, and energy use, by mode of transport, 1955-84, annual rpt, 7304–2

- Foreign economic, social, and political summary data, by country, 1984, annual factbook, 244–11
- Freight (waterborne domestic and foreign) by commodity, traffic, and passengers, by port and waterway, 1982, annual rpt, 3754–3
- Govt census, 1982: employment, payrolls, and average earnings, by function, level of govt, State, county, population size, and inside-outside SMSAs, 2455–2
- Govt employment and payroll, by function, level of govt, and jurisdiction, 1983, annual rpt series, 2466–1
- Govt finances, by level of govt, State, and for large cities and counties, 1981-83, annual rpt series, 2466–2
- Govt transportation revenues by source and expenditures, by level of govt and mode of transport, and Fed Govt aid by type, FY77-82, 7308–185
- Occupational injury and illness rates, by SIC 2- to 4-digit industry, 1982, annual rpt, 6844–1
- Passenger miles and trips, by transport mode, selected years 1929-81, 26358–97
- Ports, port facilities by type, and inland waterways by size, by location, 1982-83, annual rpt, 7704–16
- Scientists, engineers, and technicians employment in transportation, utilities, and retail and wholesale trade, by field of science and industry, 1982, 9628–72
- St Lawrence Seaway Dev Corp finances and activities, and seaway toll charges and cargo tonnage by type of cargo, 1983, annual rpt, 7744–1
- St Lawrence Seaway ships, cargo and passenger volumes, and toll revenues, 1981-82 and trends from 1959, annual rpt, 7744–2
- *Statistical Abstract of US,* social, political, and economic data, 1950s-83 and trends, annual rpt, 2324–1.3
- TVA activities, financial and operating data by program and facility, and power sales by customer, FY83, annual rpt, 9804–1
- User fees to recover costs of 7 federally subsidized public service programs, by type of fee, user, and service, FY84-88, 26306–6.68
- *see also* Barges
- *see also* Dredging
- *see also* Rivers and waterways

Inner cities

see Central cities

Inoculation

see Vaccination and vaccines

Inorganic chemicals

see Chemicals and chemical industry

Input-output analysis

- Foreign input-output tables construction methods using incomplete economic data, 1984 narrative rpt, 2546–10.13
- Input-output structure of US economy, detailed interindustry transactions for 85 industries, and components of final demand, 1977, article, 2702–1.421
- Input-output structure of US economy, detailed interindustry transactions for 537 industries, and components of final demand, 1977 benchmark data, 2708–17

Index by Subjects and Names

Insecticides

see Pesticides

Insects

- *see* Animal diseases and zoonoses
- *see* Honey and beekeeping
- *see* Infective and parasitic diseases
- *see* Pests and pest control

INSLAW, Inc.

"Criminal Justice System Response to Victim Harm", 6068–185.1

Inspection of industrial products

see Quality control and testing

Inspectors General reports

see Federal Inspectors General reports

Installment credit

see Consumer credit

Institute for Civil Justice

"Costs of Asbestos Litigation", 21348–85

Institute for Energy Analysis

"Research Memoranda", 3006–7

Institute for Research on Poverty

"Poverty in the U.S.: Where Do We Stand Now?", 25928–4

Institute for Social Research

"Motivation and Economic Mobility of the Poor, Final Report of the Project", 4008–65

Instructional materials

see Educational materials

Instruments and measuring devices

- Aerial survey R&D publications, and sources of natural resource and environmental data gathered by air- and spacecraft, quarterly listing, 9502–7
- Air passenger traffic, and aircraft operations by type, by airport, region, and State, projected FY82-95 and trends from FY76, annual rpt, 7504–7
- Air traffic levels at FAA-operated control facilities, including instrument operations, by airport and State, FY83, annual rpt, 7504–27
- Aircraft (general aviation), hours flown, and equipment, by type, use, and model of aircraft, region, and State, 1982, annual rpt, 7504–29
- Aircraft accident circumstances and severity, by type of flying and aircraft, 1981, annual rpt, 9614–3
- Aircraft collisions, and near collisions by circumstances and State, by type of aircraft, various periods 1980-84, 7508–61
- Aircraft handled by instrument flight rule, by user type, FAA traffic control center, and region, FY69-83 and forecast to FY95, annual rpt, 7504–15
- Aircraft pilot instrument ratings, by type of certificate and region, 1983, annual rpt, 7504–2
- Census of Population, 1980: detailed socioeconomic and demographic characteristics, by age, sex, race, Hispanic origin, occupation, and industry, State rpt series, 2531–4
- Centrifuges and filtering and purifying equipment and parts, trade, tariffs, and industry operating data, foreign and US, 1978-82, TSUSA commodity rpt, 9885–6.60
- China economic conditions, agricultural and industrial production, trade, and domestic and foreign investment, 1980-85, 2048–106

Index by Subjects and Names

Instruments and measuring devices

China exports and imports by SITC 1- to 5-digit commodity, 1970s-82, annual rpt, 244–12

Collective bargaining agreements expiring during year, covered workers by SIC 2-digit industry, firm, and union, with summary of key provisions, 1984, annual rpt, 6784–9

County Business Patterns: establishments, employees, and payrolls, by SIC 4-digit industry and county, 1981, annual State rpt series, 2326–8

County Business Patterns: establishments, employees, and payrolls, by SIC 4-digit industry and county, 1982, annual State rpt series, 2326–6

Earnings by major industry group, and personal income per capita and by source, by region and State, 1929-82, 2708–40

Employment, earnings, and hours, by selected SIC 1- to 4-digit industry, State, and for 278 major labor areas, 1939-83, annual rpt, 6744–5

Employment, earnings, and hours, by SIC 4-digit nonfarm industry, monthly 1974-Feb 1984, annual update, 6744–4

Exports and imports of measuring and controlling instruments, watches and clocks, and photographic supplies, by world area, 1983, annual rpt, 2424–6

Exports and imports of US, by commodity group, world area, selected country, US coastal area and port, and mode of transport, with seasonal adjustments, monthly rpt, 2422–9

Exports and imports of US, totals and as percent of domestic production, by SIC 2- to 5-digit commodity, 1981, annual rpt, 2424–3

Exports, imports, tariffs, and industry operating data for microphones, loudspeakers, and sound and visual signaling devices, 1979-83, TSUSA commodity rpt supplement, 9885–6.81

Exports of equipment with nuclear weapons applications, approvals for shipment to PRC by item and to other foreign markets, July 1981-June 1982, GAO rpt, 26123–76

Exports of manufactured and agricultural commodities, manufacturing production, and export-related employment, 1960s-82, State rpt series, 2046–3

Exports of measuring and controlling instruments, watches, and clocks, by mode of transport and world area and country of destination, 1983, annual rpts, 2424–5

Exports of US, detailed commodities by country of destination, monthly rpt, 2422–3

Exports of US, detailed Schedule B commodities by country of destination, 1983, annual rpt, 2424–9

Financial statements for manufacturing, mining, and trade corporations, by selected SIC 2- to 3-digit industry, quarterly rpt, 2502–1

Foreign market and trade for telecommunications equipment, and user industry operations and demand, country market research rpts, 2045–12

Great Lakes trade, by SITC 3-digit commodity, port, vessel type, world area, and country, 1982, annual rpt, 7744–3

Imports of measuring and controlling instruments, watches, and clocks, by country and world area, and method of transport, 1983, annual rpts, 2424–2

Imports of US, detailed Schedule A commodities by country, monthly rpt, 2422–2

Imports of US, detailed TSUSA commodities by country of origin, 1983, annual rpt, 2424–4

Income tax returns of corporations, detailed income and tax items by industry, 1981, annual rpt, 8304–4

Income tax returns of corporations with foreign tax credit, income and deductions by type, asset size, and selected industry group, 1980, article, 8302–2.415

Industrial process control equipment foreign market and trade, and user industry operations and demand, country market research rpts, 2045–6

Industry finances and operations, by SIC 2- to 4-digit industry, 1970s-83 and projected to 1988, annual rpt, 2014–4

Injuries and deaths from use of selected consumer products and related activity, by victim age and sex, 1982, annual rpt, 9164–7

Input-output structure of US economy, detailed interindustry transactions for 85 industries, and components of final demand, 1977, article, 2702–1.421

Input-output structure of US economy, detailed interindustry transactions for 537 industries, and components of final demand, 1977 benchmark data, 2708–17

Lab instruments foreign market and trade, and user industry operations and demand, country market research rpts, 2045–10

Manufacturing census, 1982: financial and operating data, by SIC 2- to 4-digit industry, State, SMSA, and county, preliminary census div rpt series, 2491–3

Manufacturing census, 1982: financial and operating data, for SIC 4-digit industries by product, preliminary rpt series, 2491–1

Meters effect on residential water use, for selected cities and suburbs, 1980-83, 5188–109.2

Meters for electricity, gas, and liquid supply and production, trade, tariffs, and industry operating data, 1979-83, TSUSA commodity rpt supplement, 9885–7.63

Minority group and women employment, by occupational group and SIC 2- to 3-digit industry, 1981, annual rpt, 9244–1.1

Natl Bur of Standards standard reference and research materials available, 1984-85, biennial catalog, 2214–2

Natural gas interstate pipeline company detailed financial and operating data, by firm, 1983, annual rpt, 3164–38

Nuclear attack civil defense plans of Fed Emergency Mgmt Agency, funding and operations by component, FY81-84 and projected FY85-89, GAO rpt, 26123–61

Nuclear industry nongovt employment by industry segment, occupation, and census div, and DOE and NRC nuclear employment, 1968-83, biennial rpt, 3004–11.1

Occupational injury and illness rates, by SIC 2- to 4-digit industry, 1982, annual rpt, 6844–1

OECD trade, total and for 4 major countries, and US trade by country, by commodity, 1972-82, annual world region rpt series, 244–13

Patents (US) for telecommunication equipment granted to US and foreign applicants, by applicant type, firm, State, and country, various periods 1963-83, 2246–2.7

Pollution abatement capital and operating costs, by SIC 2- to 4-digit industry, State, and SMSA, 1982, annual Current Industrial Rpt, 2506–3.6

Polygraph lie detection test accuracy, and Fed Govt use by agency, selected years 1947-83, 26358–96

Producer prices and indexes, by stage of processing and detailed commodity, monthly rpt, 6762–6

Producer prices and indexes, by stage of processing and detailed commodity, monthly 1983, annual supplement, 6764–2

Productivity, hours, and employment indexes for selected SIC 3- and 4-digit industries, 1954-82, annual rpt, 6824–1.3

R&D expenditures of US firms foreign affiliates, by selected industry, 1974-82, 9626–2.131

R&D industry expenditures, total and for 6 leading industries, projected 1984-85 with trends from 1975, 9626–2.145

R&D industry funding and employment of scientists and engineers, by industry group, firm size, and funding source, 1956-82, annual rpt, 9627–21

Scientific equipment in academic instns, age and use, by field, 1981, annual rpt, 9624–10.5

Scientists, engineers, and technicians employed in private industry, by occupation and industry group, 1980-81, biennial rpt, 9627–23

Service industry census, 1982: employment, establishments, receipts, and payroll, by SIC 2- to 4-digit kind of business, SMSA, county, and city, State rpt series, 2391–1

Shipments, trade, and consumption of electronic equipment and associated products, by product, 1983, annual Current Industrial Rpt, 2506–12.21

Shipments, trade, and consumption of industrial control and other equipment, by product, 1983, annual Current Industrial Rpt, 2506–12.11

Shipments, trade, and consumption of instruments and related products, by product, 1981-82, annual Current Industrial Rpt, 2506–12.26

Virgin Islands economic censuses, 1982: employment, establishments, payroll, and receipts, by SIC 1- to 4-digit industry, island, and city, 2593–1

Watches and parts shipments, consumption, and trade data for USITC import quota determination, annual rpt, suspended, 9884–6

Waterborne commerce of US (domestic and foreign), freight by commodity, traffic, and passengers, by port and waterway, 1982, annual rpt, 3754–3

Wholesale trade census, 1982: employment, establishments, sales by commodity, and payroll, by SIC 4-digit kind of business and State, preliminary rpt, 2403–1.19

Instruments and measuring devices

see also Medical supplies and equipment
see also Radar
see also under By Commodity in the "Index by Categories"
see also under By Industry in the "Index by Categories"

Instruments, musical
see Musical instruments

Insulation

- Asbestos workers, exposure levels, cancer incidence, and deaths, by industry and occupation, and asbestos regulation enforcement and costs/benefits, various periods 1940-2027, hearing, 21408–72
- Buildings (nonresidential) energy use, expenditures, and conservation, by building characteristics, EIA survey series, 3166–8
- Connecticut utility group housing energy conservation program, cost effectiveness and characteristics of participants and nonparticants, 1980-82, 3308–77
- Construction industries census, 1982: financial and operating data, by SIC 4-digit industry and State, preliminary rpt, 2371–1.14
- Energy conservation devices installation, utility loan program cost effectiveness, and household participation characteristics, Minnesota study, 1980-83, 3308–72
- Energy conservation programs of utilities, actual and predicted gas savings by conservation measure, Minnesota study, 1980-83, 3308–74
- Energy use, prices, and conservation and efficiency measures, by fuel type, end-use sector, selected industry, and region, 1960-83, annual rpt, 3164–73
- Exports of US, detailed commodities by country of destination, monthly rpt, 2422–3
- Exports of US, detailed Schedule B commodities by country of destination, 1983, annual rpt, 2424–9
- Housing (multifamily rental) energy use and costs, conservation effect on rental marketing, and effect of utility bill payment methods on conservation efforts, 1970s-80s, 3308–73
- Housing and financial characteristics, and unit and neighborhood quality, for 15 SMSAs, 1978, annual survey special supplement, 2485–8
- Housing energy conservation programs of utilities, financing, costs, participation, and energy savings, various periods 1981-84, hearing, 21368–54
- Housing energy use, and savings under alternative conservation strategies, by State, with model methodology and energy prices, selected years 1970-81, 21368–48
- Housing energy use, costs, expenditures, and conservation, and household and housing characteristics, survey series, 3166–7
- Manufacturing census, 1982: financial and operating data, for SIC 4-digit industries by product, preliminary rpt, 2491–1.247
- Production, shipments, PPI, and stocks of building materials, by type, bimonthly rpt, 2012–1.5

Insurance

- Aircraft operating costs by component for privately owned small planes, and Fed Govt mileage reimbursement rates, 1983, annual rpt, 9454–13.2
- Airline operating and other costs, itemized for domestic and intl trunk and local service carriers, 1st half 1983, semiannual rpt, 9142–47
- Bank interstate service offices, including S&Ls, bank branches, and nonbank subsidiaries offering financial services, by instn and State, 1981-83, 9371–13
- Bombing (explosive and incendiary) and arson incidents by target, State, and circumstances, and explosives theft and recovery, 1982-83, annual rpt, 8484–4
- Budget of US, effects of Reagan Admin policy changes, by detailed program, FY85, annual rpt, 104–21
- CPI by detailed component, for US city average, 28 SMSAs, and 4 regions by population size, monthly rpt, 6762–2
- Credit union financial ratios related to Federal deposit insurance status, various periods 1948-82, article, 9379–1.404
- Dental malpractice claims, by amount, procedure type, region, State, and provider and patient characteristics, 1970, article, 4102–1.416
- Deposit insurance of Fed Govt, regulatory control of insured instn risk-taking, narrative analysis, 1984 technical paper, 9316–1.107
- Export credit program activities of Eximbank and 6 OECD countries, 1982, annual rpt, 9254–3
- Fed Emergency Mgmt Agency activities and funding for disaster and emergency relief, and major disasters, 1983, annual rpt, 9434–2
- Fed Govt aid to State and local areas, by type of payment, State, county, and city, FY83, annual rpt, 2464–3
- Fed Govt aid to State and local govts, expenditures, and direct payments, by program, agency, and State, FY83, annual rpt, 2464–2
- Fed Govt insurance commitments, by agency and program, as of Sept 1983, annual rpt, 8104–3.4
- Fed Govt programs and mgmt cost control proposals, 3-year savings by function and agency, and financial and operating data, 1960s-81, 16908–1
- Flood insurance program of Fed Govt, average premiums, premium income, and program costs, selected years FY68-84, hearing, 21248–81
- Home mortgage applications for 1- to 4-family homes, commitments, insurance, starts, and units readied, quarterly rpt, 5142–5
- Home mortgages (graduated payment) FHA-insured, financial, property, and mortgagor characteristics, for US and selected localities, quarterly rpt, 5142–42
- Home mortgages (graduated payment) FHA-insured, financial, property, and mortgagor characteristics, for US and selected States, quarterly rpt, 5142–41
- Home mortgages (graduated payment) FHA-insured, financial, property, and mortgagor characteristics, US summary, quarterly rpt, 5142–40

Index by Subjects and Names

- Home mortgages FHA-insured, financial, property, and mortgagor characteristics, for US and selected localities, quarterly rpt, 5142–2
- Home mortgages FHA-insured, financial, property, and mortgagor characteristics, for US, selected States, and Puerto Rico, quarterly rpt, 5142–3
- Home mortgages FHA-insured, financial, property, and mortgagor characteristics, quarterly rpt, 5142–1
- Home mortgages FHA-insured, financial, property, and mortgagor characteristics, 1983, annual rpt, 5144–17
- Home mortgages FHA-insured for low-cost homes, financial, construction, property, and mortgagor characteristics, quarterly rpt, 5142–4
- Home mortgages insured by private companies, for 1- to 4-family units, monthly press release, 5142–38
- Housing and households detailed characteristics, and unit and neighborhood quality, by inside-outside central cities, 1979-82 surveys, SMSA rpt series, 2485–6
- Marine and war-risk insurance approved for US and foreign vessels, FY83, annual rpt, 7704–14.4
- Michigan bankruptcy filings, by filer type, moving history, income, creditor action, debt and asset type, credit status, exemptions claimed, and county, 1979-81, hearings, 21528–57.3
- Mortgage insurance of HUD in force, and property acquisitions and sales, quarterly rpt, 5002–3
- Natural gas interstate pipeline company detailed financial and operating data, by firm, 1983, annual rpt, 3164–38
- Nuclear power accident liability insurance under Price-Anderson Act, effects on industry finances and operations, with insurance coverage, claims, and costs, various periods 1957-82, 9638–49
- Nuclear power industry status and outlook, with reactor construction, utility financial and operating data, and foreign comparisons, 1970s-83 with projections to 2010, 26358–99
- Political risk insurance and other programs and finances of Overseas Private Investment Corp, including list of insured projects and companies, FY83, annual rpt, 9904–2
- Postal Service revenue and mail volume by class, and special service transactions, quarterly rpt, 9862–1
- Smoking and tobacco marketing legislation introduced and enacted in State legislatures, by State, 1982, annual rpt, 4204–13
- *Statistical Abstract of US,* social, political, and economic data, 1950s-83 and trends, annual rpt, 2324–1.3
- Truck transport of fruit and vegetables, costs per vehicle-mile by component for fleets and owner-operator trucks, monthly rpt, 1272–1

see also Agricultural insurance
see also Automobile insurance
see also Disability insurance
see also Employee benefit plans
see also Federal Deposit Insurance Corp.

Index by Subjects and Names

see also Federal Savings and Loan Insurance Corp.

see also Health insurance

see also Insurance industry

see also Life insurance

see also Medicare

see also Old-Age, Survivors, Disability, and Health Insurance

see also Servicemen's life insurance programs

see also Surety bonds

see also Unemployment insurance

see also Workers compensation

Insurance industry

- Agricultural cooperative operating ratios by commodity, and debt financing by source, for 100 largest cooperatives, selected years FY62-83, article, 1122–1.411
- Airline indebtedness by type of holder, and debt shares of major holders, by carrier, as of Dec 1982, annual rpt, 9144–1.4
- American Samoa minimum wage rates, employment, earnings, and benefits, by establishment and industry, Nov 1983, biennial rpt, 6504–6
- Census of Population, 1980: detailed socioeconomic and demographic characteristics, by age, sex, race, Hispanic origin, occupation, and industry, State rpt series, 2531–4
- Census of Population, 1980: detailed socioeconomic characteristics, by county, city, and inside-outside SMSAs and central cities, State rpt series, 2531–3
- Census of Population, 1980: labor force, by sex, detailed occupation, and region, with comparison to 1970 census, supplementary rpt, 2535–1.12
- Collective bargaining agreements expiring during year, covered workers by SIC 2-digit industry, firm, and union, with summary of key provisions, 1984, annual rpt, 6784–9
- County Business Patterns: establishments, employees, and payrolls, by SIC 4-digit industry and county, 1981, annual State rpt series, 2326–8
- County Business Patterns: establishments, employees, and payrolls, by SIC 4-digit industry and county, 1982, annual State rpt series, 2326–6
- Employment and earnings, detailed data, monthly rpt, 6742–2.5
- Employment by detailed occupation, for 29 SIC 2-digit nonmanufacturing industries, 1981 BLS survey, 6748–60
- Employment, earnings, and hours, by selected SIC 1- to 4-digit industry, State, and for 278 major labor areas, 1939-83, annual rpt, 6744–5
- Employment, earnings, and hours, by SIC 4-digit nonfarm industry, monthly 1974-Feb 1984, annual update, 6744–4
- Farm debt, loans outstanding, and interest rates, by type of lender and State, 1960-83 with trends from 1940, biennial rpt, 1544–2
- Farm finances, expenses by type, loans by purpose and source, and credit detail by Fed Reserve District, quarterly rpt, 9365–3.10
- Farm finances, production, expenses by type, and domestic economic impact, selected years 1972-82 and preliminary 1983-84, annual rpt, 1544–19

Farm mortgage debt outstanding, by type of lender and district, as of Jan 1983, annual rpt, 9264–3

- Farm real estate and nonreal estate debt outstanding, by lender, 1940-84, annual rpt, 1544–16.2
- Farm real estate and other debt, by type of lender, 1980 benchmark data with revised estimates for 1970-82, 1548–230
- Farm real estate credit-financed transfers, by type of lender and region, selected years 1945-84, annual rpt, 1541–8.5
- Fed Govt loans, grants, and tax benefits to business, by program and economic sector, projected FY84-88 with effective tax rates for FY80-82, 26306–6.70
- Fed Home Loan Bank System members, with assets of S&Ls, by instn, city, and State, 1983, annual listing, 9314–5
- Finances and operations, by SIC 2- to 4-digit industry, 1970s-83 and projected to 1988, annual rpt, 2014–4
- Financial and business statistics, historic trends, 1984 annual chartbook, 9364–2.14
- Financial and business statistics, quarterly chartbook, 9362–2.7
- Financial services of nonbank firms and bank holding companies, with financial and operating data by firm, 1981-82 with trends from 1962, technical paper, 9375–11.3
- Flow-of-funds accounts, assets and liabilities by type and economic sector, year-end outstandings, 1960-83, annual rpt, 9364–3
- Flow-of-funds accounts savings, investments, and credit statements, quarterly rpt, 9365–3.3
- Foreign direct investment in US, major investors and investments by SIC 4-digit industry, transaction type and value, and location, 1983, annual rpt, 2044–20
- Franchise business opportunities, by firm and kind of business, 1984 annual listing, 2044–27
- Income received through life insurance companies, taxation measurement, allocation, and accounting methods, 1984 technical paper, 8006–3.49
- Income tax returns of corporations, detailed income and tax items by industry, 1981, annual rpt, 8304–4
- Income tax returns of corporations, summary data by industry div, 1981 estimates, annual article, 8302–2.403
- Income tax returns of corporations with foreign tax credit, income and deductions by type, asset size, and selected industry group, 1980, article, 8302–2.415
- Income tax returns of foreign subsidiaries of US corporations, income and tax data, by industry and asset size, 1980, article, 8302–2.410
- Income tax returns of partnerships, detailed data by industry, 1981 estimates, annual article, 8302–2.404
- Income tax returns of partnerships, receipts by source, deductions by type, and establishments, by selected industry, 1982, annual article, 8302–2.416
- Income tax returns of sole proprietorships, detailed data by industry div and selected industry group, 1981, annual rpt, 8304–7

Income tax returns of sole proprietorships, receipts, deductions by type, payroll, and net income, by major industry, 1982, annual article, 8302–2.413

Insurance industry

- Input-output structure of US economy, detailed interindustry transactions for 85 industries, and components of final demand, 1977, article, 2702–1.421
- Input-output structure of US economy, detailed interindustry transactions for 537 industries, and components of final demand, 1977 benchmark data, 2708–17
- Intl services transactions by type, and sales, assets, and employment of US multinatl service firms by industry and world region, 1977-82, 2706–5.30
- Land privately held, acreage and owners by owner characteristics, land use, and region, and purchase and improvement funding, 1978 survey, series, 1506–5
- Life insurance companies assets and liabilities, monthly rpt, 9362–1.1
- Life insurance companies assets and liabilities, 1981-82, annual rpt, 9364–5.4
- Minority group and women employment, by occupational group and SIC 2- to 3-digit industry, 1981, annual rpt, 9244–1.1
- Mortgage and mortgage-related investment of financial instns, by instn type and Fed Govt issuing agency, various dates 1981-84, 5008–33
- Mortgage loan originations, purchases, and acquisitions, for 11 lender types, selected years 1960-82, article, 9312–1.407
- Mortgage transactions and holdings, by lender group and type of property and loan, quarterly rpt, 5142–30
- Mortgages (home) and mortgage pool participation by lender type, and FHA mortgage yields, various periods 1950-84 with trends from 1900, technical paper, 9375–11.4
- Occupational injury and illness rates, by SIC 2- to 4-digit industry, 1982, annual rpt, 6844–1
- Occupational manpower needs and supply by detailed occupation, and educational and training program enrollees and grads by detailed field, 1982 and 1995, biennial rpt, 6744–3
- *Occupational Outlook Handbook,* 1984-85 biennial rpt, 6744–1
- Property and casualty insurance firms financial and operating data, investments, and estimated tax liability, various periods 1951-82, hearing, 25368–128
- Scientists, engineers, and technicians employed in private industry, by occupation and industry group, 1980-81, biennial rpt, 9627–23
- Small and minority-owned businesses finances and operations, Federal contracts by agency, and worker characteristics, by industry, race, sex, and State, 1950s-83, annual rpt, 9764–6
- *Statistical Abstract of US,* social, political, and economic data, 1950s-83 and trends, annual rpt, 2324–1.3
- Surety companies authorized to post bonds with Fed Govt, location and bonding limits, as of July 1984, annual listing, 8104–4
- Tax collections of State govts, by detailed type of tax and tax rates, by State, FY83, annual rpt, 2466–2.3

Insurance industry

Workers compensation benefits under State programs, by benefit type, insurance source, and State, and Fed Govt black lung program payments, 1980-82, article, 4742–1.424

Workers compensation coverage by State, benefits, degree of disability, employer costs, and insurance industry finances, 1939-80, article, 4742–1.414

see also under By Industry in the "Index by Categories"

Insurgency

see also Guerrilla warfare

Intelligence services

Budget of US, appropriations, outlays, balances, and budget receipts, by govtl branch and agency, FY83, annual rpt, 8104–2

see also Bureau of Intelligence and Research *see also* Central Intelligence Agency *see also* Counterintelligence *see also* Detective and protective services *see also* Military intelligence

Inter-American Development Bank

Environmental and cultural impacts of multilateral dev banks economic dev projects in developing countries, 1970s-83, hearings, 21248–80

Human rights conditions in 162 countries, economic and military aid of US, and economic aid of intl organizations, 1981-83, annual rpt, 21384–3

Loan activity by purpose and country, and funds by source, FY83, annual rpt, 15344–1.7

Loans and grants for economic and military assistance from US and intl agencies, by program and country, FY46-83, annual rpt, 9914–5

Inter-American Foundation

Activities, grants, and fellowships, by region and country, FY83, annual rpt, 14424–1

Activities of Foundation, 1984 narrative semiannual rpt, 14422–2

Budget of US Appendix, detailed budgets and personnel summaries, by agency, FY85, annual rpt, 104–3

Interagency Task Force on Acid Precipitation

Acid Precipitation Natl Assessment Program activities, and funding by Federal agency, 1983, annual rpt, 14354–1

Interdepartment Radio Advisory Committee

Radio frequency assignments for Federal agency use, 2nd half 1983, semiannual rpt, 2802–1

Interest groups

see Lobbying

see Nonprofit organizations and foundations

Interest rates

AID loan repayment status and terms by program and country, and status of predecessor agency loans, quarterly rpt, 9912–3

Auto sales related to usury limits on loans in 2 States, and loans made and outstanding by lender type, various periods 1977-82, article, 9375–1.409

Bank deposit explicit and implicit interest rates, by type of account, 1976-82, article, 9387–1.403

Bank deposit interest rate deregulation, effect on bank deposits and bank financial performance, 1978-83, hearing, 21248–83

Bank profitability, finances, loans and terms, intl earnings, and operating ratios for insured commercial instns, 1980-83, annual article, 9362–1.409

Banking and financial data, 1982, annual rpt, 9364–5

Bond yields and interest rates on public and private securities, 1929-83, annual rpt, 204–1.5

Budget deficit-interest rate relationship, and deficit cyclical and structural components, various periods 1955-83 and projected FY84-89, article, 9391–1.415

Budget deficits effect on economic indicators and trade balance of US and 4 countries, model results, various periods 1974-85, technical paper, 9366–7.102

Budget deficits effect on interest rates and economic indicators, with govt borrowing and saving, for US and 6 OECD countries, 1975-83, technical paper, 9366–7.89

Budget deficits effect on interest rates, regression results and bibl, various periods 1965-83, 8008–111

Budget of US, CBO analysis of revenue and spending alternatives and projections of economic indicators, FY85-89, annual rpt, 26304–3

Budget of US, special analysis of Fed Govt credit programs and interest subsidy values, FY85, annual rpt, 104–1.6

Business Conditions Digest, cyclical indicators, by economic process, monthly rpt, 2702–3.3

Business Conditions Digest, historical supplement on economic, business, and financial conditions and cyclical fluctuations, with methodology, 1947-82, 2708–31

Business statistics, detailed data for major industries and economic indicators, *Survey of Current Business,* monthly rpt, 2702–1.6

California (southern) housing demand by county, prices and sales, and costs after homeowner tax deductions, 1970s-80, hearing, 21148–31

Canada and West Germany interest rate term structure related to US short-term rates, 1973-82, article, 9393–8.401

Census of Govts, 1982: properties, govt-assessed value, sales, and tax rates, by property type, State, SMSA, county, and city, 2453–1

Commercial paper and govt security yields, interest rates, and bond prices, monthly rpt, 9365–2.14

Credit unions in Georgia, operating and financial ratios and other performance indicators for 53 large instns, as of Dec 1983, article, 9371–1.427

Developing countries govt policy, and AID and other foreign assistance, effects on private sector dev and socioeconomic conditions, with case studies for 6 countries, 1960s-80, 9918–12

Economic indicators and components, and Fed Reserve 4th District business and financial conditions, monthly chartbook, 9377–10

Economic indicators and components, current data and annual trends, monthly rpt, 23842–1.5

Economic performance of US, and Reagan Admin 1984 spending, tax, and monetary policy proposals, with data for 1950s-83 and projected to 1988, press release, 8008–107

Index by Subjects and Names

Eurocurrency syndicated loans, loan fees, and interest rate spread, by country group and selected country, 1981-83, technical paper, 9366–7.105

Eurodollar and total market liabilities, dollar liabilities of US bank foreign branches, and Eurodollar deposit rates, quarterly rpt, 9391–7.1

Eurodollar deposit rates, interest arbitrage, and other short-term rates, current and 4-year trends, weekly chartbook, 9365–1.5

Export credit program activities of Eximbank and 6 OECD countries, 1982, annual rpt, 9254–3

Farm credit conditions, earnings, and expenditures, Fed Reserve 9th District, quarterly rpt, 9383–11

Farm Credit System mortgage and other loans, and financial statements, 1982 and selected trends from 1961, annual rpt, 9264–2

Farm debt, loans outstanding, and interest rates, by type of lender and State, 1960-83 with trends from 1940, biennial rpt, 1544–2

Farm finances, expenses by type, loans by purpose and source, and credit detail by Fed Reserve District, quarterly rpt, 9365–3.10

Farm finances, production, expenses by type, and domestic economic impact, selected years 1972-82 and preliminary 1983-84, annual rpt, 1544–19

Fed Financing Bank holdings and transactions, monthly press release, 9322–1

Fed Govt debt by holder, interest rates and costs, and financing mechanisms, projected FY84-89 with data for FY80-83, 26308–50

Fed Govt debt from foreign govts and private obligors, by country and program, periodic rpt, 8002–6

Fed Govt financial operations, detailed data, *Treasury Bulletin,* quarterly rpt, 8002–4

Fed Home Loan Bank of Atlanta financial statements, 1982-83, annual rpt, 9304–1

Fed Home Loan Bank of Chicago financial statements, 1982-83, annual rpt, 9304–4

Fed Home Loan Bank of Cincinnati financial statements, 1982-83, annual rpt, 9304–6

Fed Home Loan Bank of Dallas financial statements, 1982-83, annual rpt, 9304–11

Fed Home Loan Bank of Des Moines financial statements, 1982-83, annual rpt, 9304–7

Fed Home Loan Bank of Indianapolis financial statements, 1982-83, annual rpt, 9304–10

Fed Home Loan Bank of Pittsburgh financial statements, 1982-83, annual rpt, 9304–13

Fed Home Loan Bank of San Francisco financial statements, 1982-83, annual rpt, 9304–14

Fed Home Loan Bank of Seattle financial statements, 1982-83, annual rpt, 9304–15

Fed Home Loan Bank of Topeka financial statements, 1982-83, annual rpt, 9304–16

Fed Reserve bank interest rates, maximum rates payable on deposits, and bank prime rates, monthly rpt, 9362–1.1

Index by Subjects and Names

Interest rates

Fed Reserve banks interest rates, Dec 1983, annual rpt, 9364–1.1

Fed Reserve monetary control procedures and money supply announcements impacts on interest rate volatility, Nov 1977-Dec 1983, technical paper, 9387–8.93

Fed Reserve reserve requirements effect on volatility of M1 and interest rates, various periods 1979-84, article, 9391–1.422

Federal funds and other govt and private interest rates, weekly release, 9365–1.6

Finance (intl) statistics, quarterly chartbook, 9362–2.10

Financial and business statistics, historic trends, 1984 annual chartbook, 9364–2.16

Financial and business statistics, quarterly chartbook, 9362–2.8

Financial and economic analysis of banking and nonbanking sectors, technical paper series, 9381–10

Financial and monetary conditions, selected US summary data, weekly rpt, 9391–4

Forecasts for selected business activities and natl economic indicators, compilation of representative opinions, 1984, annual rpt, 9389–3

Foreign and US economic and employment indicators and balance of payments, and US exports by selected commodity, by world area and country, 1970s-83, annual rpt, 2044–26

Foreign central banks discount and short-term interest rates, monthly rpt, 9362–1.3

Foreign countries interest and exchange rate differentials, model description, 1984 technical paper, 9366–7.91

Foreign economic trends and implications for US, annual and semiannual country rpt series, 2046–4

Foreign loans of US banks to non-OPEC developing countries, with terms and capital exposure, various periods 1977-83 and projected to 1990, article, 9362–1.407

Foreign monetary control policy and relation to credit, exchange rates, GNP, and other indicators, US and selected West European countries, various periods 1960-82, conf papers, 9373–3.26

GNP growth related to real interest rates and other credit terms, various periods 1952-82, article, 9381–1.405

Home mortgage (conventional) terms on loans closed, and commitment rates, by type of loan and lender and for 32 SMSAs, monthly rpt, 9312–2

Home mortgage adjustable rate loan indexes, Treasury bill yields, FHLBB average rate and cost of funds, and FHLB 8th District cost of funds, monthly rpt, 9302–9

Home mortgage commitment and closing interest rates, and yields on Govt Natl Mortgage Assn securities and 10-year Fed Govt bonds, 1963-82, article, 9312–1.408

Home mortgage interest rates, effect of deposit interest rate ceiling deregulation, various periods Apr 1975-Mar 1984, article, 9391–1.412

Home mortgage loan rates for conventional first mortgages on new and existing homes, by region, monthly press release, 5142–20

Home mortgage prepayments, effect of rising interest rates, 1975-82, for California mortgages issued 1947-76, 9306–1.6

Home mortgage terms on conventional loans by eligibility for Fed Govt secondary purchase, 1983, and alternative eligibility limits for 28 cities, 1984, GAO rpt, 26113–135

Home mortgage terms on single and multifamily dwellings, and mortgage debt outstanding, by selected SMSA, 1960s-83, annual rpt, 9314–3.3

Home mortgages (adjustable rate) regulation, and characteristics of 24 unidentified ARM programs, Sept 1983 survey, technical paper, 9316–1.104

Home mortgages originated by S&Ls in Wisconsin and Illinois, effects of usury ceiling and market interest rates on supply and loan-to-price ratios, 1978-80, article, 9312–7.404

Housing and households characteristics, and employment, housing finance, and social programs data, selected years 1948-83, hearing, 21968–28

Housing low-rent project financing notes sold by local authorities, terms and individual issuers and purchasers, monthly listing, 5142–43

Illinois S&Ls, mortgage interest fixed and adjustable rates and fees offered, monthly rpt, 9302–6

Income taxes related to interest rates, 1952-83, article, 9389–1.407

Monetary and Fed Govt budget trends, Fed Reserve Bank of St Louis monthly rpt, 9391–2

Money market mutual funds and deposit accounts, and super negotiable orders of withdrawal accounts, interest rates, monthly Dec 1982-Sept 1983, article, 1702–1.401

Money market mutual funds and deposit accounts balances, and correlation results for interest rates and flows by type of fund, various periods Dec 1982-June 1984, article, 9371–1.431

Money supply control based on interest rate targeting, for US and Canada, 1975-79, technical paper, 9381–10.38

Money supply targeting, effects of deregulated interest rates on M1 growth, 1984 article, 9393–8.402

Money supply targeting, effects of inflation expectations and interest rates on M1 velocity, 1922-83, article, 9393–8.409

Mortgage, bond, and bank loan interest rates, bimonthly rpt, 2012–1.5

Natural gas interstate pipeline company detailed financial and operating data, by firm, 1983, annual rpt, 3164–38

New England States, FHLB 1st District member instns financial operations and housing industry indicators, monthly rpt, 9302–4

New England States mortgage interest rates in selected SMSAs, Fed Reserve 1st District, monthly rpt, 9373–2.5

North Central States farm credit conditions and economic devs, Fed Reserve 7th District, biweekly rpt, 9375–10

North Central States, FHLB 6th District insured S&Ls financial condition and operations by State, monthly rpt, 9302–11

North Central States, FHLB 7th District insured S&Ls cost of funds, and savings flows and mortgage loans closed by SMSA, monthly rpt, 9302–5

North Central States tax exempt industrial revenue bonds issued by local govts, by Fed Reserve 7th District State, county, and city, with interest rate spread, 1975-80, 9375–13.2

Postal Service interest expense on bonds, notes, and mortgages, borrowing and repayment schedule, and rates, FY82-85, annual rpt, 9864–5.3

Public debt, net interest paid by Fed Govt, cumulative for fiscal year, annual trends, and quarterly data, monthly rpt, 23842–1.6

Public debt, rate on interest and non-interest bearing securities, monthly rpt, 8242–2

Real and nominal interest rate term structure premium associated with uncertainty, model description, 1983 technical paper, 9387–8.91

Real medium- and long-term interest and expected inflation rates related to other forward rates, regression results, various periods 1976-82, article, 9393–8.406

Recession, M1 and interest rates performance as leading indicators, various periods 1949-83, article, 9385–1.410

Risk exposure of banks related to bank stock prices and balance sheet data, Jan 1976-Nov 1981, technical paper, 9387–8.82

Savings and loan assns (FSLIC-insured), financial ratios of profitable and unprofitable S&Ls, selected years 1965-82, technical paper, 9316–2.47

Savings and loan assns (FSLIC-insured) interest and dividend rates paid and return on mortgages, by FHLB district, monthly rpt with articles, 9312–1

Savings and time deposits, maximum rates payable at federally insured instns, Dec 1983, annual rpt, 9364–1.2

Seasonal adjustment methodology for economic time series, dev and design of Census Bur and other systems, with illustrative data, 1981 conf papers, 2626–7.5

Small Business Investment Companies finances, funding, licensing, and loan activity, 2nd half FY84, semiannual rpt, 9762–3

Small business loans and credit, operational expectations, and NYC metro area owners economic and professional attitudes, by industry div, 1980-83 surveys, hearings, 21728–52

South Central States, FHLB 9th District insured S&Ls financial condition and operations by SMSA, monthly rpt, 9302–13

Southeastern States farm credit conditions and real estate values, Fed Reserve 5th District, quarterly rpt, 9389–17

Southeastern States, Fed Reserve 8th District banking and financial conditions, quarterly rpt, 9391–14

Southwestern States farm credit conditions and real estate values, Fed Reserve 11th District, quarterly rpt, 9379–11

Stock price index changes related to corporate bond rate, regression results, 1961-83, article, 9391–1.419

Interest rates

Treasury bill and private money market interest rate spread related to risk, State tax rates, and Treasury bill supply, 1979-mid 1983, article, 9389–1.401

Treasury bills, notes, and bonds market bid yields at constant maturities, Treasury Bulletin quarterly rpt, 8002–4.8

Wisconsin S&Ls, mortgage interest fixed and adjustable rates and fees offered, monthly rpt, 9302–7

Intergovernmental relations

- Advisory Commission on Intergovtl Relations programs and finances, 1983, annual rpt, 10044–3
- Federal, State, and local govt finances, policy, and intergovtl relations, series, 10046–8
- Govt finances, by level of govt and State, selected years 1929-83, annual rpt, 10044–1
- *Intergovernmental Perspective,* quarterly rpt, 10042–1
- Public opinion on taxes, tax policy, and intergovtl relations, 1972-84 surveys, annual rpt, 10044–2
- Regional councils involved in service activities, by type of service and region population size, 1982 survey, hearing, 25408–88
- *see also* Federal-local relations
- *see also* Federal-State relations
- *see also* State-local relations

Intergovernmental tax relations

see Revenue sharing

see State and local taxes

Interindustry transactions

see Input-output analysis

Interior Department

see Department of Interior

Internal combustion engines

see Machines and machinery industry

Internal Revenue Service

- Alcohol and tobacco tax refund claims, FY81-82, last issue of annual rpt, 8484–1.6
- Art appraisals accepted and rejected on estate, gift, and income tax returns, and valuation by taxpayers, IRS, and US courts, 1978-82, hearings, 21408–74
- Assaults, murders, and other deaths of law enforcement officers, by circumstances, level of govt, agency, victim and offender characteristics, and location, 1983, annual rpt, 6224–3
- Assistance program of IRS for taxpayers, operations and use, and users evaluation, selected years 1979-82, GAO rpt, 26119–58
- Bond tax-exempt issues for home mortgage subsidy, issuance and purchase price limits for tax-exempt status, by State and MSA, 1984 annual press releases, 8304–16
- Collections of IRS, by State and district, FY83, annual rpt, 8104–2.2
- Collections of IRS by type of tax, procedures, and interest foregone through processing delay, for selected locations, FY81-82, GAO rpt, 26119–55
- Corporate income tax returns, detailed income and tax data by industry, 1981, annual rpt, 8304–4
- Cost control proposals for Fed Govt programs and mgmt, 3-year savings by function and agency, and financial and operating data, 1960s-81, 16908–1.12

Data collection and use, IRS and other Fed Govt admin record research methods, 1984 annual conf papers, 8304–17

- Data collection and use, IRS and other Fed Govt admin record research methods, 1984 compilation of papers, 8308–28
- Data collection programs, missions, and appropriations of Fed Govt statistical agencies, and effect of budget cuts, FY80-84, GAO rpt, 26125–28
- Excise tax collections of IRS, by source, quarterly press release, 8302–1
- Income (taxable) not reported on individual and corporate returns, and associated Federal revenue losses, by detailed legal and illegal source, 1973-81, 8308–26
- Individual income tax returns, detailed data, 1982, annual rpt, 8304–2
- Industry coding systems for statistical programs of 6 Federal agencies, comparability, workload, and updating cycles, 1984 rpt, 106–4.5
- Oil windfall profits tax admin of IRS and revenues, tax rates, and nonfilers, 1980-86, GAO rpt, 26119–65
- Penalty abatements of IRS, 1978-83, and estimated error rates by category of taxpayer excuse, FY81, GAO rpt, 26119–68
- Prosecutions and litigations of IRS, and cases received, amounts in dispute, and disposition, FY83, annual rpt, 8304–3
- Returns and collections and economic and demographic trends for IRS regions, districts, and service centers, 1972-82 and projected to 1990, annual rpt, 8304–8
- Returns filed, by type of filer, detailed preliminary and supplementary data, quarterly rpt with articles, 8302–2
- Returns filed, by type of return, 1972-82 and projected 1983-90, annual rpt, 8304–9
- Sole proprietorships income tax returns, detailed data by industry div and selected industry group, 1981, annual rpt, 8304–7
- Underground economy, household expenditures and participation by type of goods or service and sociodemographic characteristics, with methodology and bibl, 1981 survey, 8308–27

Internal security

- Aliens excluded and deported by cause, 1892-FY81, annual rpt, 6264–2
- Fed Govt programs and mgmt cost control proposals, 3-year savings by function and agency, and financial and operating data, 1960s-81, 16908–1
- Info security clearances of Fed Govt and contractor employees, polygraph use, and prepublication reviews, 1979-83, GAO rpt, 26123–66
- Info Security Oversight Office monitoring of Fed Govt classified info security measures and classification actions, FY83, annual rpt, 9454–21
- Polygraph lie detection test accuracy, and Fed Govt use by agency, selected years 1947-83, 26358–96
- *see also* Underground movements

International agencies

AID activities and funding by project and function, FY85, and developing countries summary socioeconomic data, 1970s-83, by country, annual rpt, 9914–3

Index by Subjects and Names

- AID economic assistance to developing countries, obligations and disbursements by country, quarterly rpt, 9912–4
- AID loan repayment status and terms by program and country, and status of predecessor agency loans, quarterly rpt, 9912–3
- Bombing (explosive and incendiary) incidents, damage, injuries, and deaths, by target, State, and circumstances, 1983, annual rpt, 6224–5
- Budget of US, effects of Reagan Admin policy changes, by detailed program, FY85, annual rpt, 104–21
- Developing countries disaster preparedness and summary sociodemographic, political, and economic data, country rpt series, 9916–2
- Developing countries economic aid of US, bilateral and through multilateral dev banks and intl agencies, by world area and country, 1970s-FY83, annual rpts, 9904–1
- Financial instns (intl) funds by source and disbursements by purpose, by country, with US policy review, FY83, annual rpt, 15344–1
- Foreign economic, social, and political summary data, by country, 1984, annual factbook, 244–11
- Human rights conditions in 162 countries, economic and military aid of US, and economic aid of intl organizations, 1981-83, annual rpt, 21384–3
- Loans and grants for economic and military assistance from US and intl agencies, by program and country, FY46-83, annual rpt, 9914–5
- Loans of large US banks to foreigners at all US and foreign offices, by country group and country, quarterly rpt, 13002–1
- NIH intl research grants, by inst and recipient country and agency, historical data, 1984 annual rpt, 4434–1
- PL 480 exports by commodity, and recipients, by program, sponsor, and country, FY82 and aggregate from FY55, annual rpt, 1924–7
- R&D Fed Govt funding for foreign performers, by world region and country, FY82-84, annual rpt, 9627–20.2
- Refugee arrivals in US by world area of origin and State of settlement, and Fed Govt intl and domestic assistance costs, FY85, annual rpt, 7004–16
- Treaties and other bilateral and multilateral agreements of US in force, by country, Jan 1984, annual listing, 7004–1
- US Budget Appendix, detailed budgets and personnel summaries, by agency, FY85, annual rpt, 104–3
- US commitments to intl agencies and funds, as of Sept 1983, annual rpt, 8104–3.4
- *see also* African Development Bank
- *see also* African Development Fund
- *see also* Asian Development Bank
- *see also* Association of South East Asian Nations
- *see also* Central Treaty Organization
- *see also* Common markets and free trade areas
- *see also* European Space Agency
- *see also* Inter-American Development Bank
- *see also* International Atomic Energy Agency

Index by Subjects and Names

see also International Bank for Reconstruction and Development
see also International Development Association
see also International employees
see also International Energy Agency
see also International Finance Corp.
see also International Monetary Fund
see also North Atlantic Treaty Organization
see also Organization for Economic Cooperation and Development
see also United Nations
see also Warsaw Pact

International agreements
see Executive agreements
see Trade agreements
see Treaties and conventions

International Atomic Energy Agency
AID activities and funding by project and function, FY85, and developing countries summary socioeconomic data, 1970s-83, by country, annual rpt, 9914–3

International Bank for Reconstruction and Development

Environmental and cultural impacts of multilateral dev banks economic dev projects in developing countries, 1970s-83, hearings, 21248–80

Human rights conditions in 162 countries, economic and military aid of US, and economic aid of intl organizations, 1981-83, annual rpt, 21384–3

Loan activity by purpose and country, and funds by source, FY83, annual rpt, 15344–1.4

Loans and grants for economic and military assistance from US and intl agencies, by program and country, FY46-83, annual rpt, 9914–5

see also International Development Association

see also International Finance Corp.

International Boundary and Water Commission, U.S. and Mexico

Hydroelectric power generating capacity and plant characteristics, for Western States, FY83, annual rpt, 3254–1

International Communication Agency
see U.S. Information Agency

International conferences, congresses and conventions
see Conferences

International cooperation in conservation

Fish and eggs for stocking distributed from natl hatcheries, by species, hatchery, and jurisdiction, FY83, annual rpt, 5504–10

Forests (tropical) status by country and world region, conservation methods, and mgmt role of US, foreign, and intl groups, 1977-81 and projected to 2000, 26358–101

Marine Mammal Protection Act admin and populations, strandings, and catch permits by type and applicant, by species and location, Apr 1983-Mar 1984, annual rpt, 2164–11

Marine mammals protection, Fed Govt and intl regulatory and research activities, with bibl, 1983, annual rpt, 14734–1

Soviet Union-US science and technology exchange projects, man-hours, and funding, by Fed Govt agency and activity type, FY81-82, 7008–41

Treaties and other bilateral and multilateral agreements of US in force, by country, Jan 1984, annual listing, 7004–1

see also International cooperation in environmental sciences

International cooperation in cultural activities

English teaching programs and teacher seminars supported by USIA, by world region and country, FY83, annual rpt, 9854–2

Helsinki Final Act implementation by NATO, Warsaw Pact, and other signatory nations, Dec 1983-Mar 1984, semiannual rpt, 7002–1

Japan-US Friendship Commission educational and cultural exchange activities, grants, and trust fund status, FY83, annual rpt, 14694–1

Treaties and other bilateral and multilateral agreements of US in force, by country, Jan 1984, annual listing, 7004–1

USIA info center and reading room operations, by world region, country, and city, FY83, annual rpt, 9854–4

see also Educational exchanges
see also Exchange of persons programs

International cooperation in environmental sciences

Acid Precipitation Natl Assessment Program activities, and funding by Federal agency, 1983, annual rpt, 14354–1

Acid rain causes and effects, air pollutant emissions by source in US and selected countries, control costs, and Fed Govt research funding, 1960s-82, 3408–27

Earthquake and other ground motion intensity measured on USGS Natl Strong-Motion Network by station, and sources of foreign and US info, 1981, annual rpt, 5664–14

Environmental quality and protection programs, costs, and Fed Govt enforcement, 1983, detailed annual rpt, 484–1

EPA pollution control research and grant assistance program activities, monthly rpt, 9182–8

Forests (tropical) status by country and world region, conservation methods, and mgmt role of US, foreign, and intl groups, 1977-81 and projected to 2000, 26358–101

Glaciology intl research summaries, methodology, and bibls, series, 2156–18

Ocean dumping of waste materials, EPA permit program and intl London Dumping Convention activities, 1981-83, annual rpt, 9204–8

Oceanographic data, stations and cruises recording data for World Data Center A by country, ship, and type of data, 1983, annual rpt, 2144–15

Oil spill off France Brittany coast, cleanup and research costs, marine and tourism industry losses, and recreation losses of tourists and residents, 1971-79, 2178–13

Soviet Union-US science and technology exchange projects, man-hours, and funding, by Fed Govt agency and activity type, FY81-82, 7008–41

Treaties and other bilateral and multilateral agreements of US in force, by country, Jan 1984, annual listing, 7004–1

Weather stations of Upper Air Observational Network, by US and foreign location, 1984 annual listing, 2184–6

World Weather Program, Fed Govt funding by agency, FY83-85, annual rpt, 2144–2

International crime

International cooperation in science and technology

AID activities and funding by project and function, FY85, and developing countries summary socioeconomic data, 1970s-83, by country, annual rpt, 9914–3

Allergy and Infectious Diseases Natl Inst activities, grants by instn, State, and country, and disease incidence and costs, FY60s-84, annual rpt, 4474–30

Auto safety and experimental vehicle designs, 1982, conf proceedings, annual rpt, 7764–3

Cancer Natl Inst foreign research grants and contracts, FY83, annual fact book, 4474–13

Council for Mutual Economic Assistance science and technology dev and transfer between USSR and other member countries, 1940s-81, 2326–9.7

Dental Research Natl Inst research and training funds awarded, by recipient instn, FY83, annual listing, 4474–19

Fed Govt intl exchange and training programs, participants by world region, and funding, by agency, FY83, annual rpt, 9854–8

Heart, Lung, and Blood Natl Inst foreign visiting scientists and grants and contracts, by country, aggregate 1972-81, annual rpt, 4474–22.6

Helsinki Final Act implementation by NATO, Warsaw Pact, and other signatory nations, Dec 1983-Mar 1984, semiannual rpt, 7002–1

NIH intl program activities and funding, by inst and country, FY83, annual rpt, 4474–6

NIH intl research grants, by inst and recipient country and agency, historical data, 1984 annual rpt, 4434–1

NSF grant and award recipients, by State, FY83, annual listing, 9624–11

NSF research programs, activities, and funding, FY82-83, annual rpt, 9624–6

Nuclear Regulatory Commission activities, employment, and finances, and operations of individual power plants by State, FY83, annual rpt, 9634–2

R&D Fed Govt funding, by function, agency, and program, selected years FY80-84 and proposed FY85, 26308–46

Science Indicators, R&D expenditures, innovations, research, and higher education, with foreign comparisons, 1960s- 83, annual rpt, 9624–10.1

Soviet Union-US science and technology exchange projects, man-hours, and funding, by Fed Govt agency and activity type, FY81-82, 7008–41

Treaties and other bilateral and multilateral agreements of US in force, by country, Jan 1984, annual listing, 7004–1

see also European Space Agency
see also International cooperation in environmental sciences
see also Technology transfer

International corporations
see Foreign corporations
see Multinational corporations

International crime
see Air piracy
see Drug and narcotics traffic
see Smuggling

International crime

see Terrorism

International debts

see Foreign debts

International Development Association

Human rights conditions in 162 countries, economic and military aid of US, and economic aid of intl organizations, 1981-83, annual rpt, 21384–3

Loan activity by purpose and country, and funds by source, FY83, annual rpt, 15344–1.5

Loans and grants for economic and military assistance from US and intl agencies, by program and country, FY46-83, annual rpt, 9914–5

International Development Cooperation Agency

see U.S. International Development Cooperation Agency

International economic relations

see Foreign debts

see Foreign economic relations

see Foreign investments

see Foreign trade

see International finance

see International transactions

see Multinational corporations

International employees

Computer specialists sociodemographic, educational, and employment characteristics, and Fed Govt support by agency, 1978, biennial Current Population Rpt, 2546–2.124

Foreign visitors and other nonimmigrants admitted to US, by country of last residence, FY81, annual rpt, 6264–2

International Energy Agency

Oil consumption for major consuming countries, monthly rpt, 3162–24.10

International finance

Bank balance sheet statements by Fed Reserve District, for major banks in NYC, and for US branches and agencies of foreign banks, weekly release, 9365–1.3

Banking intl facilities by State and ownership, and aggregate assets and liabilities, various dates 1981-83, article, 9391–1.409

Banking intl facilities of foreign and US banks in New York State and total US, assets and liabilities, monthly rpt, 9365–2.22

Budget of US, effects of Reagan Admin policy changes, by detailed program, FY85, annual rpt, 104–21

Capital movements between US and foreign countries, *Treasury Bulletin,* quarterly rpt, 8002–4.12

Developing countries food production and needs, and related economic trends and outlook, for 67 countries, 1980-86, annual rpt, 1524–6.2

Developing countries receiving US economic aid, total govt and defense expenditures, military imports, GNP, and intl reserves by country, 1976-81, annual rpt, 9914–1

Export credit program activities of Eximbank and 6 OECD countries, 1982, annual rpt, 9254–3

Financial and business statistics, historic trends, 1984 annual chartbook, 9364–2.17

Foreign and US intl financial statistics: transactions, debt and security holdings, interest and exchange rates, and US reserve assets, monthly rpt, 9362–1.3

Foreign economic indicators for 7 OECD countries and US, quarterly rpt, 2042–10

Foreign lending of large US banks at all US and foreign offices, by country group and country, quarterly rpt, 13002–1

Foreign loans, debts, exchange rates, and intl reserves, for US and selected countries, various periods 1949-84, conf papers, 9373–3.28

Intl financial instns funds by source and disbursements by purpose, by country, with US policy review, FY83, annual rpt, 15344–1

Pacific Basin economic indicators, US and 12 countries, quarterly rpt, 9393–9

see also African Development Bank

see also African Development Fund

see also Asian Development Bank

see also Eurocurrency

see also Export-Import Bank

see also Foreign debts

see also Foreign economic relations

see also Foreign exchange

see also Foreign investments

see also Inter-American Development Bank

see also Inter-American Foundation

see also International Bank for Reconstruction and Development

see also International Development Association

see also International Monetary Fund

see also International transactions

see also Multinational corporations

see also Organization for Economic Cooperation and Development

see also Special Drawing Rights

International Finance Corp.

Human rights conditions in 162 countries, economic and military aid of US, and economic aid of intl organizations, 1981-83, annual rpt, 21384–3

Loan activity by purpose and country, and funds by source, FY83, annual rpt, 15344–1.6

Loans and grants for economic and military assistance from US and intl agencies, by program and country, FY46-83, annual rpt, 9914–5

International Joint Commission, U.S. and Canada

Air pollution levels in Detroit-Windsor and Port Huron-Sarnia areas of US-Canadian border, annual rpt, discontinued, 14644–5

Great Lakes basin pollutant discharges by source, and control program activities, 1983 annual rpt, 14644–1

International labor

see Foreign labor conditions

International law

see also Air piracy

see also Aliens

see also Citizenship

see also Diplomatic and consular service

see also Executive agreements

see also Expropriation

see also Extradition

see also International military forces

see also International sanctions

see also Maritime law

see also Passports and visas

see also Territorial waters

see also Treaties and conventions

International military forces

Budget of US, Reagan Admin funding requests for foreign economic and military aid by program and country, FY82-85, annual rpt, 7004–14

NATO and US weapons and troop strength compared to Warsaw Pact and USSR, and US participation in intl peacekeeping operations, as of Jan 1984, annual rpt, 3564–1

International Monetary Fund

Assets of IMF, official Treasury Dept figures, FY82-83, annual rpt, 8104–2.1

Currency transactions and Special Drawing Rights positions of IMF, by country, FY83, annual rpt, 15344–1.3

Fed Govt receipts by source and outlays by agency, *Treasury Bulletin,* quarterly rpt, 8002–4.1

Investment (intl) position of US, net change by component, investment type, and world region, and for 2 countries, 1982-83, annual article, 2702–1.424

Loans, debts, exchange rates, and intl reserves, for US and selected countries, various periods 1949-84, conf papers, 9373–3.28

Reserve assets of US by type, *Treasury Bulletin,* quarterly rpt, 8002–4.11

International relations

see Foreign economic relations

see Foreign relations

see International military forces

see International sanctions

see United Nations

International relief

AID activities and funding by project and function, FY85, and developing countries summary socioeconomic data, 1970s-83, by country, annual rpt, 9914–3

Foreign countries disasters, persons affected, deaths, damage, and aid by US and others, FY83 and trends from FY64, annual rpt, 9914–12

Funding of US, by program and country, selected years 1940-82, annual rpt, 15344–1.1

Human rights conditions in 162 countries, economic and military aid of US, and economic aid of intl organizations, 1981-83, annual rpt, 21384–3

PL 480 exports by commodity, and recipients, by program, sponsor, and country, FY82 and aggregate from FY55, annual rpt, 1924–7

Red Cross program operations and financial statements, 1982/83, annual rpt, 29254–1

Voluntary agencies overseas foreign aid programs funding and expenditures, by agency, 1982/83, annual rpt, 9914–9

see also Disaster relief

see also Refugees

see also War relief

International sanctions

Arab OPEC members 1973-74 embargo on oil exports to US, effect on electric utility oil use, 1973-83, article, 3162–39.402

see also Boycotts

International Security and Development Cooperation Act

El Salvador terrorist acts against property, casualties, kidnappings, and hostages, Oct 1979-June 1983, human rights certification hearing, 21388–41

Index by Subjects and Names

International Telecommunications Satellite Organization

Communications satellite intl systems charges, operations, investment shares by country, and competition impacts, 1964-83 with projections to 2003, hearings, 25388–46

Launchings of satellites and other space objects since 1957, quarterly listing, 9502–2

NASA project launch schedules and technical descriptions, press release series, 9506–2

International trade

see Foreign exchange
see Foreign investments
see Foreign trade
see International transactions
see Maritime law
see Multinational corporations
see Ships and shipping
see Trade agreements

International Trade Administration

- Budgets and permanent staff positions appropriated for Commerce Dept agencies, FY84-85, annual rpt, 2004–6
- *Business America,* foreign and domestic commerce, and US investment and trade opportunities, biweekly rpt articles, 2042–24
- China economic and business investment conditions, trade practices, and trade with US by detailed commodity, 1978-82, 2048–72
- China economic conditions, agricultural and industrial production, trade, and domestic and foreign investment, 1980-85, 2048–106
- Computers and computer equipment foreign market and trade, and user industry operations and demand, country market research rpts, 2045–1
- Copper displacement by fiber optics in telecommunications, with Bell System use and copper and fiber optics industry data, 1978-88, 2048–104
- Cost control proposals for Fed Govt programs and mgmt, 3-year savings by function and agency, and financial and operating data, 1960s-81, 16908–1.3
- Electric power systems equipment foreign market and trade, and user industry operations and demand, country market research rpts, 2045–15
- Electronic component equipment foreign market and trade, and user industry operations and demand, country market research rpts, 2045–4
- Electronic component manufacturing equipment foreign market and trade, and user industry operations and demand, country market research rpts, 2045–5
- Europe (Western) trade with US, and US market share and export opportunities for selected commodities, by country, 1982-84, 2048–105
- Export licensing and monitoring activities under Export Admin Act, for selected commodities, and for Communist and other countries, FY83, annual rpt, 2044–22
- Exports and imports, and indexes of export prices, dollar exchange, and US and foreign industrial production, annual rpt, discontinued, 2044–17

Exports of manufactured and agricultural commodities, manufacturing production, and export-related employment, 1960s-82, State rpt series, 2046–3

- Exports of US by selected commodity, and foreign and US economic and employment indicators and balance of payments, by world area and country, 1970s-83, annual rpt, 2044–26
- Farm machinery and equipment foreign market and trade, and user industry operations and demand, country market research rpts, 2045–13
- Food processing and packaging equipment, foreign market and trade, and user industry operations and demand, country market research rpts, 2045–11
- Footwear imports of US, by category, value class, and selected country, monthly rpt, 2042–29
- Foreign and US Commercial Service of ITA, overseas staff by category, and trade promotion costs by activity, by country, 1982-83, hearing, 21408–73
- Foreign direct investment in US, major investors and investments by SIC 4-digit industry, transaction type and value, and location, 1983, annual rpt, 2044–20
- Foreign direct investment worldwide, and US investment flows by major industry, by world region and country, 1982 and trends from 1950, annual rpt, 2044–25
- Foreign economic indicators for 7 OECD countries and US, quarterly rpt, 2042–10
- Foreign economic trends and implications for US, annual and semiannual country rpt series, 2046–4
- Franchise business opportunities by firm and kind of business, and sources of aid and info, 1984 annual listing, 2044–27
- Graphic industries equipment foreign market and trade, and user industry operations and demand, country market research rpts, 2045–3
- Industrial process control equipment foreign market and trade, and user industry operations and demand, country market research rpts, 2045–6
- Intl trade position of US and 4 OECD countries, and factors affecting US competition, quarterly pamphlet, 2042–25
- Lab instruments foreign market and trade, and user industry operations and demand, country market research rpts, 2045–10
- Machine tools and equipment foreign market and trade, and user industry operations and demand, country market research rpts, 2045–9
- Medical and health care equipment foreign market and trade, and user industry operations and demand, country market research rpts, 2045–2
- Mining industry equipment foreign market and trade, and user industry operations and demand, country market research rpts, 2045–16
- OPEC direct investment in US, major direct investors and investments, by country and SIC 2- to 3-digit industry, annual listing, suspended, 2044–23
- *Overseas Business Reports:* economic conditions, investment and export opportunities, and trade practices, annual country market research rpt series, 2046–6

International transactions

- *Overseas Business Reports:* economic conditions, investment and export opportunities, and trade practices, world region rpt series, 2046–5
- Pollution control instruments and equipment foreign market and trade, and user industry operations and demand, country market research rpts, 2045–17
- Price indexes for consumer and producer goods, major commodities, exports, imports, nonfarm wages, and currency value, US and 4 countries, bimonthly rpt, 2042–11
- Programs, funding, and employment of Commerce Dept agencies, FY83, annual rpt, 2004–1
- Publications of Commerce Dept, biweekly listing, 2002–1
- Sporting goods and recreational equipment and vehicles foreign market and trade, country market research rpts, 2045–14
- Technology-intensive industry employment, cpaital expenditures, trade, and shipments, for 22 industries, quarterly rpt, suspended, 2042–28
- Telecommunication equipment foreign market and trade, and user industry operations and demand, country market research rpts, 2045–12
- Textile exports, by product and country of destination, monthly rpt, 2042–26
- Textile imports, by country of origin, monthly rpt, 2042–27
- Textile imports, by product and country of origin, monthly rpt series, 2046–9
- Textile imports, by product and country of origin, periodic rpt series, 2046–8
- Textile imports, monthly rpt, 2042–18
- Textile imports, total and as percents of US domestic production and use, by commodity, 1972-82, annual rpt, 2044–14
- Trade adjustment assistance, operations of centers to help firms apply for ITA aid, annual rpt, suspended, 2044–24

International Trade Commission

see U.S. International Trade Commission

International transactions

- Accounts and component transactions, *Survey of Current Business,* monthly rpt, quarterly tables, 2702–1.31
- Banking and nonbanking firms liabilities to and claims on foreigners, by country, 1981-82, annual rpt, 9364–5.10
- Business cycles effects on current account balances of Japan, West Germany, and US, modeling results, 1970s-82 and projected 1983-86, technical paper, 9366–7.92
- Capital movements between US and foreign countries, *Treasury Bulletin,* quarterly rpt, 8002–4.12
- China hard currency balance of payments, and intl lines of credit, quarterly rpt, 242–6.1
- Communist, OECD, and selected other countries economic statistics, 1960s-83, annual rpt, 244–5
- Cuba economic conditions, agricultural and industrial production and distribution, trade, and intl economic relations, 1970-82 and trends from 1957, 248–40
- Current account balance related to Fed Govt budget deficit, with balance for 14 OECD countries, various periods 1952-83, article, 9373–1.408

International transactions

Current account deficits, and financing by source, for US and 5 OECD countries, selected years 1973-1st qtr 1984, article, 9385–1.409

Developing countries (non-OPEC) loans from US banks, debt burden, and other economic indicators, various periods 1977-84 and loan projections to 1990, article, 9362–1.407

Developing countries agricultural supply/demand and market for US exports, with socioeconomic indicators, country rpt series, 1526–6

Developing countries summary socioeconomic data, 1970s-83, and AID activities and funding by project and function, FY82-85, by country, annual rpt, 9914–3

Economic indicators and components, current data and annual trends, monthly rpt, 23842–1.7

Economic indicators and trade balance of US and 4 countries, effect of US budget deficits, model results, various periods 1974-85, technical paper, 9366–7.102

Fed Govt consolidated financial statements based on business accounting methods, FY82-83, annual rpt, 8104–5

Fed Govt financial operations, detailed data, *Treasury Bulletin,* quarterly rpt, 8002–4

Finance (intl) and financial policy, external factors affecting US economy, econometric model methodology and results for US and 4 countries, various periods 1964-75, 9368–78

Finance (intl) statistics, quarterly chartbook, 9362–2.9

Financial and business statistics, historic trends, 1984 annual chartbook, 9364–2.17

Flow-of-funds accounts, assets and liabilities by type and economic sector, year-end outstandings, 1960-83, annual rpt, 9364–3

Foreign and US current account balance related to budget balances, for 59 countries, various periods 1948-82, article, 9379–1.401

Foreign and US economic and employment indicators and balance of payments, and US exports by selected commodity, by world area and country, 1970s-83, annual rpt, 2044–26

Foreign economic indicators for 7 OECD countries and US, quarterly rpt, 2042–10

Foreign economic trends and implications for US, annual and semiannual country rpt series, 2046–4

Foreign exchange rates correlation with price and trade indicators, for 14 countries, 1977-83, article, 9373–1.418

Foreign loans, debts, exchange rates, and intl reserves, for US and selected countries, various periods 1949-84, conf papers, 9373–3.28

GNP in current and constant dollars, by product and sector, and implicit price deflators, selected years 1929-83, annual rpt, 204–1.1

Intl dev lending instns disbursements, impact on US balance of payments by sector, FY83, annual rpt, 15344–1

Intl trade position of US and 4 OECD countries, and factors affecting US competition, quarterly pamphlet, 2042–25

Intl transactions, *Business Conditions Digest,* historical supplement and methodology, 1947-82, 2708–31

Intl transactions, *Business Conditions Digest,* monthly rpt, 2702–3.9

Intl transactions of US, and economic and monetary trends for US and 10 major trading partners, quarterly rpt, 9391–7

Intl transactions summary, monthly rpt, 9362–1.3

Investment (intl) position of US, net change by component, investment type, and world region, and for 2 countries, 1982-83, annual article, 2702–1.424

Investment (intl direct) worldwide, and US investment flows by major industry, by world region and country, 1982 and trends from 1950, annual rpt, 2044–25

Investment income of US from foreign activities, 1946-83, annual rpt, 204–1.9

Mexico economic indicators, trade, external accounts and debt, oil industry, and relations with US, 1978-83 with trends from 1959, conf proceedings, 21248–82

Natl income and product, comprehensive accounts and components, *Survey of Current Business,* monthly rpt, 2702–1.21

Natl income and product, comprehensive accounts and components, *Survey of Current Business,* monthly rpt, monthly and annual tables, 2702–1.25

OECD economic indicators, for US and 6 countries, biweekly rpt, 242–4

Overseas Business Reports: economic conditions, investment and export opportunities, and trade practices, annual country market research rpt series, 2046–6

Overseas Business Reports: economic conditions, investment and export opportunities, and trade practices, world region rpt series, 2046–5

Services intl transactions, and operations of US multinatl service firms and foreign affiliates, by industry and world region, 1977-82, 2706–5.30

Steel industry finances and operations under proposed import quota, projected 1985-89 with selected foreign comparisons and trends from 1950, 26306–6.80

Tax evasion through nonresidents bank claims and deposits, direct investments, income payments, and other transactions in 5 Caribbean countries, 1978-82, 8008–106

Travel to and from US and travel receipts and payments by world area, and travel to US by country, 1977-83, annual rpt, 2904–10

Travel to and from US, receipts and expenditures by world area and country, 1979-83, annual article, 2702–1.417

Travel to US and receipts by world area and selected country, 1960-83, and US Travel and Tourism Admin activities, 1983, annual rpt, 2904–6

see also Foreign debts
see also Foreign exchange
see also Foreign investments
see also Foreign trade

International trusteeships

see also Trust Territory of the Pacific Islands

Index by Subjects and Names

Interstate commerce

Bank holding company interstate service applications, and New England acquisitions and mergers effect on assets, by firm, Dec 1974-Sept 1983, article, 9373–1.409

Bank interstate service offices, including S&Ls, bank branches, and nonbank subsidiaries offering financial services, by instn and State, 1981-83, 9371–13

County Business Patterns: establishments, employees, and payrolls, by SIC 4-digit industry and county, 1982, annual State rpt series, 2326–6

Fed Govt programs and mgmt cost control proposals, 3-year savings by function and agency, and financial and operating data, 1960s-81, 16908–1.15

Motor and rail carriers regulated by ICC, employment and finances by mode of transport, and ICC activities, FY80-83 and trends, annual rpt, 9484–1

Transportation finances and operations, detailed statistics on rail and motor carriers, 1982, annual rpt series, 9486–5

Transportation finances and operations, detailed statistics on rail and motor carriers, 1983, annual rpt series, 9486–6

see also Antitrust law
see also Buses
see also Contraband
see also Freight
see also Inland water transportation
see also Pipelines
see also Railroads
see also Ships and shipping
see also Transportation and transportation equipment
see also Trucks and trucking industry

Interstate Commerce Commission

Budget of US Appendix, detailed budgets and personnel summaries, by agency, FY85, annual rpt, 104–3

Budget of US, appropriations, outlays, balances, and budget receipts, by govtl branch and agency, FY83, annual rpt, 8104–2

Bus industry collective ratemaking and regulatory reform impacts on operations, finances, and services to older persons and rural areas by State, 1970s-83, 14828–2

Cost control proposals for Fed Govt programs and mgmt, 3-year savings by function and agency, and financial and operating data, 1960s-81, 16908–1.15

Motor and rail carriers regulated by ICC, employment and finances by mode of transport, and ICC activities, FY80-83 and trends, annual rpt, 9484–1

Motor carrier passengers and selected revenue data, for individual large Class I motor carriers, quarterly rpt, 9482–13

Motor carrier regulation enforcement of ICC, staff by position, and caseload by violation type, by ICC region, selected years FY80-85, GAO rpt, 26113–133

Motor carriers (Class I) of household goods operating revenues, net income, and revenue tons, by firm, quarterly rpt, 9482–14

Motor carriers (Class I) of property financial and operating data, by region and firm, quarterly rpt, 9482–5

Index by Subjects and Names

Investments

Motor carriers (Class II) of property financial and operating data, by region, 1982, annual rpt, 9484–10

Railroad employee earnings, benefits, and hours, by occupation for Class I railroads, 1983, annual rpt, 9484–5

Railroad employment by functional group, for Class I line-haul railroads, monthly rpt, 9482–3

Railroad finances, operations, and freight rates and shares, by commodity and railroad, 1970s-82, hearings, 25268–80

Railroad revenue, income, freight, and rate of return, by Class I freight railroad and district, quarterly rpt, 9482–2

Transportation finances and operations, detailed statistics on rail and motor carriers, 1982, annual rpt series, 9486–5

Transportation finances and operations, detailed statistics on rail and motor carriers, 1983, annual rpt series, 9486–6

Interstate highways *see* Highways

Interstate relations *see also* Regional planning

Inventions

- Energy-related inventions recommended for possible DOE support by Natl Bur of Standards, with DOE evaluation status, 1984, annual listing, 2214–5
- NSF-supported activities, number of resulting patents and inventions, FY83, annual rpt, 9624–6
- *see also* Automation
- *see also* Patents
- *see also* Technological innovations
- *see also* Technology transfer

Inventories

- *see* Agricultural stocks
- *see* Agricultural surpluses
- *see* Business inventories
- *see* Energy stocks and inventories
- *see* Stockpiling

Investigations

- *see* Congressional investigations
- *see* Criminal investigations
- *see* Government investigations

Investments

- Airline cash flows for all certificated carriers, quarterly rpt, 9142–34
- Airline financial data, by carrier, carrier group, and for total certificated system, quarterly rpt, 9142–12
- Army morale, welfare, and recreation programs, revenue and expenses worldwide by activity and major command, FY82-83, annual rpt, 3704–12
- Bank holding company ratios of financial involvement in nonbank subsidiaries and subsidiary performance, by holding company size, various periods 1978-82, article, 9377–1.406
- Bank loans and investments of commercial banks, 1939-83, annual rpt, 204–1.5
- Banking and financial data, 1982, annual rpt, 9364–5
- Banks (natl) domestic and intl operations, charters, mergers, and liquidations, by State and instn, and Comptroller of Currency activities, quarterly rpt, 8402–3
- *Business Conditions Digest,* current data on economic, business, and financial conditions and cyclical fluctuations, monthly rpt, 2702–3

Business Conditions Digest, historical supplement on economic, business, and financial conditions and cyclical fluctuations, with methodology, 1947-82, 2708–31

- Cash mgmt techniques for electronic funds transfer and short-term investment, effect on money demand, aggregated 1920-79, article, 9389–1.409
- China economic conditions, agricultural and industrial production, trade, and domestic and foreign investment, 1980-85, 2048–106
- Colorado River Storage Project finances, water resource dev, power production, and other activities in western States, FY83, annual rpt, 5824–3
- County Business Patterns: establishments, employees, and payrolls, by SIC 4-digit industry and county, 1982, annual State rpt series, 2326–6
- Credit union financial statements by region, State, and type of membership, for Federal and federally insured State unions, 1983, annual rpt, 9534–1
- Credit Union Natl Admin insurance fund financial activity, and insured instns financial and operating data, FY83, annual rpt with semiannual update for 1st qtr FY84, 9534–7
- Economic indicators and components, and Fed Reserve 4th District business and financial conditions, monthly chartbook, 9377–10
- Economic indicators and components, current data and annual trends, monthly rpt, 23842–1.5
- Economic indicators, and Fed Govt finances and deficits, selected years 1962-83 and projected under cost control proposals to 2000, 16908–1.1
- Economic trends, natl compounded annual rates of change, monthly rpt, 9391–3.2
- Farm Credit System banks financial statements, Dec 1979-83, annual rpt, 9264–5
- Farm Credit System mortgage and other loans, and financial statements, 1982 and selected trends from 1961, annual rpt, 9264–2
- Farm finances, expenses by type, loans by purpose and source, and credit detail by Fed Reserve District, quarterly rpt, 9365–3.10
- Fed Govt budget deficit related to current account balance, with balance for 14 OECD countries, various periods 1952-83, article, 9373–1.408
- Fed Govt receipts by source and outlays by agency, *Treasury Bulletin,* quarterly rpt, 8002–4.1
- Fed Home Loan Bank of Atlanta financial statements, 1982-83, annual rpt, 9304–1
- Fed Reserve banks financial statements and employees, 1983, annual rpt, 9364–1.1
- Financial and business statistics, historic trends, 1984 annual chartbook, 9364–2.13
- Financial and business statistics, quarterly chartbook, 9362–2.2, 9362–2.7
- Financial and economic trends, compounded annual rates of change, 1964-83, annual rpt, 9391–9.1
- Flow-of-funds accounts, assets and liabilities by type and economic sector, year-end outstandings, 1960-83, annual rpt, 9364–3

Flow-of-funds accounts savings, investments, and credit statements, quarterly rpt, 9365–3.3

- Income (personal) per capita and by source, and earnings by industry div, by State, MSA, and county, 1977-82, annual regional rpts, 2704–2
- Income (personal) per capita and by source, earnings by major industry group, and social insurance contributions, by region and State, 1929-82, 2708–40
- Income tax returns of corporations with foreign tax credit, income and deductions by type, asset size, and selected industry group, 1980, article, 8302–2.415
- Income tax returns of elderly, by income statement and tax item and income level, 1981 with trends from 1977, article, 8302–2.412
- Income tax returns of individuals, by filing and deduction characteristics and income level, 1983, annual article, 8302–2.414
- Income tax returns of individuals, detailed data, 1982, annual rpt, 8304–2
- Income tax returns of individuals, selected income, deduction, and tax credit data by income, preliminary 1982, annual article, 8302–2.402
- Income tax returns of partnerships, receipts by source, deductions by type, and establishments, by selected industry, 1982, annual article, 8302–2.416
- Input-output structure of US economy, detailed interindustry transactions for 85 industries, and components of final demand, 1977, article, 2702–1.421
- Insurance industry (property and casualty) financial and operating data, investments, and tax liability, various periods 1951-82, hearing, 25368–128
- Investment companies classification, assets, and location, Sept 1982, annual directory, 9734–1
- Monetary and Fed Govt budget trends, Fed Reserve Bank of St Louis monthly rpt, 9391–2
- Motor carrier rates of return for Class I carriers of property, by region and firm, quarterly rpt, 9482–5
- Multinatl corporation income reallocation through regulation of intercorporate transactions, by tax item, treaty status, asset size, industry, and tax haven country, 1982, 8008–110
- Natl income and product, comprehensive accounts and components, *Survey of Current Business,* monthly rpt, 2702–1.21
- Natural gas interstate pipeline company detailed financial and operating data, by firm, 1983, annual rpt, 3164–38
- New England States, FHLB 1st District member savings instns, locations, and financial condition, 1984, annual listing, 9304–26
- North Central States, FHLB 6th District insured S&Ls financial condition and operations by State, quarterly rpt, 9302–23
- North Central States, FHLB 8th District member S&Ls financial operations by State and SMSA, monthly rpt, 9302–9
- OASI beneficiaries by income level, and average income, by beneficiary characteristics and income source, before and after receipt of 1st benefit, 1969-77, article, 4742–1.418

Investments

Older persons income and income sources, by OASDI beneficiary and poverty status, labor force participation, and demographic characteristics, 1982, biennial rpt, 4744–26

- Older persons sociodemographic characteristics, and Fed Govt program participation and funding, 1983 with trends and projections 1900-2060, annual rpt, 25144–3.1
- Pension plan investment in Fed Govt mortgage-backed securities, yields by issuer, and fund assets by fund type, 1970s-82, conf papers, 5008–32
- Personal income and BEA and IRS calculations of adjusted gross income, by source, 1981-82, article, 2702–1.414
- Philanthropic foundations detailed financial and operating data, and stock holdings by instn, 1979 with selected trends from 1920, GAO rpt, 26119–53
- Private domestic gross investment, 1929-83, annual rpt, 204–1.1
- Railroad finances and operations, detailed data by firm, class of service, and district, 1983, annual rpt, 9486–6.1
- Savings and loan assn deregulation impact, financial ratios of S&Ls in 3 States and US, 1980-83, article, 9371–1.426
- Small Business Admin loan and contract activity by program, and balance sheets, FY83, annual rpt, 9764–1.1
- Southeastern States banks by asset size, finances, and loans and deposits by type, Fed Reserve 5th District, various dates 1979-83, annual article, 9389–1.408
- Southeastern States, FHLB 4th District insured S&Ls financial condition and operations, by SMSA, monthly rpt, 9302–1
- State and local govt retirement systems, cash and security holdings and finances, quarterly rpt, 2462–2
- Steel plant modernization projects, Urban Dev Action Grant and private funding and jobs created, by plant and city, 1984 press release, 5006–3.37
- Tax expenditures, Fed Govt revenues foregone through income tax deductions and exclusions by type, and effect of Deficit Reduction Act, FY84-89, annual rpt, 21784–10
- Technology-intensive industry employment and establishments by industry and selected location, and venture capital investments by source, 1970s-82, 26358–107
- Texas farm household income, by income source and substate region, 1979, article, 9379–1.406
- Trust assets of banks and trust companies, by type of asset and fund and State, 1983, annual rpt, 13004–1
- Tuna fleet, capacity, and processor investment in vessels by investment type, with tuna catch, prices, and imports, selected years 1932-80, 9406–1.39
- TVA power program finances and operations, by plant and distributor, FY83, annual rpt, 9804–23
- Urban Dev Action Grant awards, private and public investment, and jobs, housing units, and taxes generated, by city and project, FY83, annual rpt, 5124–5

Urban Dev Action Grant awards to local areas, preliminary approvals, with project descriptions, private investment, and jobs and taxes to be created, by city, quarterly press release series, 5002–7

- Urban Dev Action Grant program effectiveness, and participation of small cities by State, 1978-82, GAO rpt, 26113–118
- Veterans aged 55 and over, socioeconomic characteristics, economic resources, health care and status, and actual and expected use of VA benefits, 1983 survey, 9928–29
- Western States depository instns financial activity by State, and large commercial banks by city, Fed Reserve 10th District, monthly rpt, 9381–11
- Western States economic indicators, Fed Reserve 12th District, quarterly rpt, 9393–1.5
- Western States, FHLB 11th District member S&Ls financial condition and operations by State, quarterly rpt, 9302–19
- Western States, FHLB 11th District member S&Ls financial operations and housing industry indicators by State, monthly rpt, 9302–17

see also Capital investments, general

see also Capital investments, specific industries

see also Foreign investments

see also Futures trading

see also Government securities

see also Loans

see also Mortgages

see also Mutual funds

see also New York Stock Exchange

see also Securities

see also Stock exchanges

Iodine

see Nonmetallic minerals and mines

Iowa

- Agriculture census, 1982: farms, farmland, production and costs, and operator characteristics, preliminary State summary and county rpts, 2330–1.19
- Agriculture census, 1982: farms, farmland, production, finances, and operator characteristics, by county, final State rpt, 2331–1.15
- Bank deposits in commercial and mutual savings banks and in US branches of foreign banks, by account type, instn, State, SMSA, and county, June 1983, annual rpt, 9295–3.12
- Cancer cases, incidence, deaths, and death rates, by body site, age, race, Hispanic origin, and sex, for 10 geographic areas, 1973-81, 4478–130
- Census of Housing, 1980: occupancy and unit characteristics of SMSAs and central cities, by race, Hispanic origin, and city, State rpt, 2473–1.17
- Census of Population and Housing, 1980: detailed population and housing characteristics, by county, city, and census tract, State rpt, 2551–2.17
- Census of Population, 1980: detailed socioeconomic and demographic characteristics, by age, sex, race, Hispanic origin, and industry, State rpt, 2531–4.17
- County Business Patterns: establishments, employees, and payrolls, by SIC 4-digit industry and county, 1982, annual State rpt, 2326–6.17

Index by Subjects and Names

- Crop insurance participation and operations in 2 states by crop, and Fed Crop Insurance Corp finances, 1980-84, GAO rpt, 26113–132
- Democratic Party of Iowa, income by source and expenditures by type, 1980-82, hearings, 21428–7
- Employment, earnings, and hours, by selected SIC 1- to 4-digit industry, State, and for 278 major labor areas, 1939-83, annual rpt, 6744–5.1, 6744–5.3
- Environmental quality, pollutant discharge by type and source, and EPA protection activities and funding, 1970s-83, biennial regional rpt, 9184–15.7
- Exports of manufactured and agricultural commodities, manufacturing production, and export-related employment, 1960s-82, State rpt, 2046–3.15
- HHS aid to each State and local govt or private instn, amount obligated, funding agency, and program, FY83, annual listing, 4004–3.7
- Income (personal) per capita and by source, and earnings by industry div, by State, MSA, and county, 1977-82, annual regional rpt, 2704–2.5
- Manufacturing census, 1982: financial and operating data, by SIC 2- to 4-digit industry, State, SMSA, and county, preliminary census div rpt, 2491–3.4
- Mineral Industry Surveys, State review of production, 1983, advance annual rpt, 5614–6.15
- *Minerals Yearbook, 1982,* Vol 2 preprints: State review of production and sales by commodity, and business activity, annual rpt, 5604–16.16
- *Minerals Yearbook, 1982,* Vol 2: State reviews of production, sales, and firms, by commodity, and business activity, annual rpt, 5604–34
- Natural gas utilities and pipelines in Iowa, financial and operating data, selected years 1969-81, hearings, 23848–177
- Population, births, deaths, and net migration, by MSA and county, 1980-82, annual State Current Population Rpt, 2546–4.15
- Population size, Apr 1980 and July 1982, and per capita income, 1979 and 1981, by county and city, State Current Population Rpt, 2546–11.15
- Pulpwood production by county, imports, and individual mill capacity, by species for 7 North Central States, 1982, annual rpt, 1204–19
- Radiation and radionuclide concentrations in air, water, and milk, results of EPA and other monitoring programs, by State and site, quarterly rpt, 9232–2.2
- Retail trade census, 1982: employment, establishments, sales, and payroll, by SIC 2- to 4-digit kind of business, SMSA, county, and city, State rpt, 2397–1.16
- Savings and loan assns, FHLB 8th District members financial operations by State and SMSA, monthly rpt, 9302–9
- Water supply and quality in streams and lakes, and groundwater levels in wells, by drainage basin, 1983, annual State rpt, 5666–10.14

see also Cedar Falls, Iowa

see also Cedar Rapids, Iowa

Index by Subjects and Names

Ireland

see also Davenport, Iowa
see also Des Moines, Iowa
see also Dubuque, Iowa
see also Iowa City, Iowa
see also Sioux City, Iowa
see also Waterloo, Iowa
see also under By State in the "Index by Categories"

Iowa City, Iowa

Census of Housing, 1980: occupancy and unit characteristics, by race, Hispanic origin, and city, SMSA rpt, 2473–1.188
Census of Population and Housing, 1980: detailed population and housing characteristics, by county, city, and census tract, SMSA rpt, 2551–2.188
see also under By SMSA or MSA in the "Index by Categories"

Iran

Agricultural and food production indexes, and production of selected commodities, by world region and country, 1974-83, annual rpt, 1524–5
Agricultural situation in Middle East and North Africa, by country and commodity, 1983 and outlook for 1984, annual rpt, 1524–4.3
Agricultural supply/demand, trade, and production, and socioeconomic data, by country, 1950s-77, 1528–179
AID loan repayment status and terms by program and country, and status of predecessor agency loans, quarterly rpt, 9912–3
Economic conditions in Communist, OECD, and selected other countries, 1960s-83, annual rpt, 244–5
Economic, social, and political summary data, by country, 1984, annual factbook, 244–11
Exports and imports of US, by commodity and country, 1972-82, annual world region rpt, 244–13.1
Exports of US, detailed Schedule B commodities by country of destination, 1983, annual rpt, 2424–9
Exports of US, detailed Schedule E commodities by mode of transport and world area and country of destination, 1983, annual rpts, 2424–5
Imports of US, detailed Schedule A commodities by country and world area of origin, and mode of transport, 1983, annual rpts, 2424–2
Imports of US, detailed TSUSA commodities by country of origin, 1983, annual rpt, 2424–4
Loans and grants for economic and military assistance from US and intl agencies, by program and country, FY46-83, annual rpt, 9914–5
Military spending, arms trade, and armed forces size, with total govt spending and population, by country, 1972-82, annual rpt, 9824–1
Minerals Yearbook, 1982, Vol 3: foreign country reviews of production, trade, and policies, by commodity, annual rpt, 5604–35
Minerals Yearbook, 1983, Vol 3 preprints: foreign country review of production, trade, and policies, by commodity, annual rpt, 5604–23.33
Oil production, and exports and prices to US, by major exporting country, detailed data, monthly rpt, 3162–24

Population size and growth rates, and latest available benchmark demographic data, by country, 1950-83, biennial rpt, 2324–4
Refugee resettlement program activities and funding, arrivals and population by country of origin and State, and employment and other characteristics, FY83, annual rpt, 4704–8
see also under By Foreign Country in the "Index by Categories"

Iraq

Agricultural and food production indexes, and production of selected commodities, by world region and country, 1974-83, annual rpt, 1524–5
Agricultural situation in Middle East and North Africa, by country and commodity, 1983 and outlook for 1984, annual rpt, 1524–4.3
Agricultural supply/demand, trade, and production, and socioeconomic data, by country, 1950s-77, 1528–179
Economic, social, and political summary data, by country, 1984, annual factbook, 244–11
Economic trends in income, production, prices, employment, finances, and trade, 1984 annual rpt, 2046–4.46
Exports and imports of US, by commodity and country, 1972-82, annual world region rpt, 244–13.1
Exports of US, detailed Schedule B commodities by country of destination, 1983, annual rpt, 2424–9
Exports of US, detailed Schedule E commodities by mode of transport and world area and country of destination, 1983, annual rpts, 2424–5
Imports of US, detailed Schedule A commodities by country and world area of origin, and mode of transport, 1983, annual rpts, 2424–2
Imports of US, detailed TSUSA commodities by country of origin, 1983, annual rpt, 2424–4
Loans and grants for economic and military assistance from US and intl agencies, by program and country, FY46-83, annual rpt, 9914–5
Military spending, arms trade, and armed forces size, with total govt spending and population, by country, 1972-82, annual rpt, 9824–1
Minerals Yearbook, 1982, Vol 3: foreign country reviews of production, trade, and policies, by commodity, annual rpt, 5604–35
Minerals Yearbook, 1983, Vol 3 preprints: foreign country review of production, trade, and policies, by commodity, annual rpt, 5604–23.34
Oil production by major exporting countries, monthly rpt, 3162–24.10
Population size and growth rates, and latest available benchmark demographic data, by country, 1950-83, biennial rpt, 2324–4
Refugee resettlement program activities and funding, arrivals and population by country of origin and State, and employment and other characteristics, FY83, annual rpt, 4704–8
see also under By Foreign Country in the "Index by Categories"

Ireland

Agricultural and food production indexes, and production of selected commodities, by world region and country, 1974-83, annual rpt, 1524–5
Agricultural situation in Western Europe, by country and commodity, 1983 and outlook for 1984, annual rpt, 1524–4.6
Agricultural supply/demand, trade, and production, and socioeconomic data, by country, 1950s-77, 1528–179
AID loan repayment status and terms by program and country, and status of predecessor agency loans, quarterly rpt, 9912–3
Background Notes, summary social, political, and economic data, 1984 rpt, 7006–2.29
Economic, social, and political summary data, by country, 1984, annual factbook, 244–11
Economic trends in income, production, prices, employment, finances, and trade, 1984 annual rpt, 2046–4.59
Exports and imports of OECD countries, by country, 1983, annual rpt, 7144–10
Exports and imports of US with Western Europe, and US market share and export opportunities for selected commodities, by country, 1982-84, 2048–105
Exports of US, detailed Schedule B commodities by country of destination, 1983, annual rpt, 2424–9
Exports of US, detailed Schedule E commodities by mode of transport and world area and country of destination, 1983, annual rpts, 2424–5
Food supply/demand and market and support prices, with exchange rates, fertilizer price index, GDP, and population, by EC country, 1960-83, 1528–173
Imports of US, detailed Schedule A commodities by country and world area of origin, and mode of transport, 1983, annual rpts, 2424–2
Imports of US, detailed TSUSA commodities by country of origin, 1983, annual rpt, 2424–4
Loans and grants for economic and military assistance from US and intl agencies, by program and country, FY46-83, annual rpt, 9914–5
Military aid of US, arms sales, and training programs costs and budget requests by program, world region, and country, FY83-85, annual rpt, 7144–13
Military spending, arms trade, and armed forces size, with total govt spending and population, by country, 1972-82, annual rpt, 9824–1
Minerals Yearbook, 1982, Vol 3: foreign country reviews of production, trade, and policies, by commodity, annual rpt, 5604–35
Minerals Yearbook, 1982, Vol 3 preprints: foreign country review of production, trade, and policies, by commodity, annual rpt, 5604–17.35
Oil and gas undiscovered recoverable resources, cumulative production, and identified reserves, as of 1982, preliminary oil basin rpt, 5666–17.15
Population size and growth rates, and latest available benchmark demographic data, by country, 1950-83, biennial rpt, 2324–4

Ireland

see also under By Foreign Country in the "Index by Categories"

Iron and steel industry

- Air pollutant emission factors, by detailed source, 3rd edition, 1983-84 supplements, 9198–13
- Air pollutant metal levels, by monitoring site, State, and urban-rural location, 1977-79, last issue of annual rpt, 9194–10
- Air pollution abatement equipment shipments by industry, exports, and new and backlog orders, by product, 1983, annual Current Industrial Rpt, 2506–12.5
- Business statistics, detailed data for major industries and economic indicators, *Survey of Current Business,* monthly rpt, 2702–1.14
- Census of Population, 1980: detailed socioeconomic and demographic characteristics, by age, sex, race, Hispanic origin, occupation, and industry, State rpt series, 2531–4
- China economic conditions, agricultural and industrial production, trade, and domestic and foreign investment, 1980-85, 2048–106
- China exports and imports by SITC 1- to 5-digit commodity, 1970s-82, annual rpt, 244–12
- Communist, OECD, and selected other countries minerals and metals production, by commodity, 1960s-83, annual rpt, 244–5.6
- County Business Patterns: establishments, employees, and payrolls, by SIC 4-digit industry and county, 1981, annual State rpt series, 2326–8
- County Business Patterns: establishments, employees, and payrolls, by SIC 4-digit industry and county, 1982, annual State rpt series, 2326–6
- Cuba economic conditions, agricultural and industrial production and distribution, trade, and intl economic relations, 1970-82 and trends from 1957, 248–40
- DOD shipments of military and personal property, loss claims, passenger traffic, and costs, by mode of transport, quarterly rpt, 3702–1
- Drums and pails (steel shipping) shipments, trade, consumption, and firms, quarterly Current Industrial Rpt, 2506–11.5
- Electric power cogeneration in 5 industries, and fuel use and utility supply/demand effects, by region, 1983-93, 3008–92
- Electric power industrial demand model estimates, economic indicators, and supporting data for 5 industries, 1960s-80 with projections to 2000, 3008–87
- Employment, earnings, and hours, by selected SIC 1- to 4-digit industry, State, and for 278 major labor areas, 1939-83, annual rpt, 6744–5
- Employment, earnings, and hours, by SIC 4-digit nonfarm industry, monthly 1974-Feb 1984, annual update, 6744–4
- Energy demand in industry, forecasting model description, detailed technology specifications, and energy use, for 27 SIC 2- to 4-digit industries, 1970s-80 and projected to 2000, 3308–66
- Energy use, prices, and conservation and efficiency measures, by fuel type, end-use sector, selected industry, and region, 1960-83, annual rpt, 3164–73

- Exports and imports of metal ores, scrap, and manufactured products, by world area, 1983, annual rpt, 2424–6
- Exports and imports of US, totals and as percent of domestic production, by SIC 2- to 5-digit commodity, 1981, annual rpt, 2424–3
- Exports of US, detailed commodities by country of destination, monthly rpt, 2422–3
- Exports of US, detailed Schedule B commodities by country of destination, 1983, annual rpt, 2424–9
- Exports of US, detailed Schedule E commodities by mode of transport and world area and country of destination, 1983, annual rpts, 2424–5
- Ferrosilicon from USSR, injury to US industry, investigation with background financial and operating data, 1965-82, 9886–12.8
- Finances and operations, by SIC 2- to 4-digit industry, 1970s-83 and projected to 1988, annual rpt, 2014–4
- Financial and operating data, steel imports by source, and employment situation at Fairless Hills, Pa, plant, 1970s-90, hearing, 25528–94
- Financial statements for manufacturing, mining, and trade corporations, by selected SIC 2- to 3-digit industry, quarterly rpt, 2502–1
- Foreign and US coal reserves, production, demand indicators, and trade, by country, selected years 1973-82 and alternative trade projections to 1995, annual rpt, 3164–77
- Foreign and US hourly employment costs for steel industry in selected OECD countries, selected years 1969-82, 26306–6.69
- Foreign economic, social, and political summary data, by country, 1984, annual factbook, 244–11
- Foreign minerals production, reserves, and industry role in domestic economy and world supply, country and world region rpt series, 5606–1
- Foundry products imports effect on US industry, investigation with background financial and operating data, 1984 rpt, 9886–4.77
- Great Lakes trade, by SITC 3-digit commodity, port, vessel type, world area, and country, 1982, annual rpt, 7744–3
- Hwy construction expenditures and contracts awarded for Federal-aid system, by type of material used and State, various periods 1944-83, annual rpt, 7554–29.8
- Hwy construction material prices and indexes for Federal-aid system, by type of material and urban-rural location, quarterly rpt, 7552–7
- Hwy construction materials prices on Federal-aid hwy system, 3rd qtr 1984, 7556–3.3
- Hwy construction materials used per $1 million of total expenditures on Federal-aid system, by State, 1980-82, annual rpt, 7554–29.4
- Import quotas and tariffs, jobs protected and cost per job for selected products, and foreign trade balance by industry div, various periods 1958-81, article, 9381–1.412

Index by Subjects and Names

- Import related unemployment in carbon and alloy steel industry, reemployment opportunities, and worker characteristics, trade adjustment assistance investigation, 1979-83, 6406–9.5
- Import trigger prices to prevent Japan dumping, and domestic steel prices, employment, and imports, by product and region, various dates 1977-1983, hearings, 21368–51
- Imports injury to US industries from foreign subsidized products, investigations with background financial and operating data for selected industries and products, series, 9886–15
- Imports injury to US industries from import sales at less than fair value, investigations with background financial and operating data, series, 9886–14
- Imports injury to US industry from foreign subsidized products and imports at less than fair value, investigations with background financial and operating data, series, 9886–19
- Imports of carbon and alloy steel products, injury to US industry from increased import sales, investigation with background financial and operating data, 1984 rpt, 9886–5.51
- Imports of steel from EC and other countries, and US industry operating data, for 15 products limited under arrangement with EC, monthly rpt, 9882–10
- Imports of structural steel, effect on US industry, investigation with background financial and operating data, 1984 rpt, 9886–4.79
- Imports of US, detailed Schedule A commodities by country and world area of origin, and mode of transport, 1983, annual rpts, 2424–2
- Imports of US, detailed Schedule A commodities by country, monthly rpt, 2422–2
- Imports of US, detailed TSUSA commodities by country of origin, 1983, annual rpt, 2424–4
- Income tax returns of corporations, detailed income and tax items by industry, 1981, annual rpt, 8304–4
- Input-output structure of US economy, detailed interindustry transactions for 85 industries, and components of final demand, 1977, article, 2702–1.421
- Input-output structure of US economy, detailed interindustry transactions for 537 industries, and components of final demand, 1977 benchmark data, 2708–17
- Japan specialty steel and ferroalloy raw material supply/demand, with industry market and manufacturing data, selected years 1970-81, 5608–144
- Manufacturing census, 1982: financial and operating data, by SIC 2- to 4-digit industry, State, SMSA, and county, preliminary census div rpt series, 2491–3
- Manufacturing census, 1982: financial and operating data, for SIC 4-digit industries by product, preliminary rpt series, 2491–1
- Mineral industries census, 1982: financial and operating data, by SIC 2- to 4-digit industry, preliminary summary rpt, 2511–2.1

Index by Subjects and Names — Irrigation

Mineral industries census, 1982: financial and operating data, including materials consumed, by SIC 4-digit industry and State, preliminary rpt series, 2511–1

Mineral Industry Surveys, commodity review of production, trade, stocks, and consumption, monthly rpt, 5612–1.11, 5612–1.12

Minerals Yearbook, 1982, Vol 1: commodity reviews of production, reserves, supply, use, and trade, annual rpt, 5604–33

Minerals Yearbook, 1982, Vol 2 preprints: State reviews of production and sales by commodity, and business activity, annual rpt series, 5604–16

Minerals Yearbook, 1982, Vol 2: State reviews of production, sales, and firms, by commodity, and business activity, annual rpt, 5604–34

Minerals Yearbook, 1982, Vol 3: foreign country reviews of production, trade, and policies, by commodity, annual rpt, 5604–35

Minerals Yearbook, 1982, Vol 3 preprints: foreign country reviews of production, trade, and policies, by commodity, annual rpt series, 5604–17

Minerals Yearbook, 1983, Vol 1 preprints: commodity reviews of production, reserves, supply, use, and trade, annual rpt series, 5604–15

Minerals Yearbook, 1983, Vol 3 preprints: foreign country reviews of production, trade, and policies, by commodity, annual rpt series, 5604–23

Minority group and women employment, by occupational group and SIC 2- to 3-digit industry, 1981, annual rpt, 9244–1.1

Modernization of steel plants, capital investment under Clean Air Act compliance extension program by firm, 1981-83, GAO rpt, 26113–138

Modernization of steel plants, Urban Dev Action Grant and private funding and jobs created, by plant and city, 1984 press release, 5006–3.37

North Central States economic indicators, Fed Reserve 7th District monthly rpt, 9375–9

Occupational injuries and incidence rates at metal mines and related operations, detailed analysis, 1982, annual rpt, 6664–3

Occupational injury and illness rates, by SIC 2- to 4-digit industry, 1982, annual rpt, 6844–1

OECD trade, total and for 4 major countries, and US trade by country, by commodity, 1972-82, annual world region rpt series, 244–13

Pollution abatement expenditures, and effect on economic indicators and industry operations, by major industry, projected under 3 pollution regulation alternatives 1983-95, 9188–84

Producer prices and indexes, by stage of processing and detailed commodity, monthly rpt, 6762–6

Producer prices and indexes, by stage of processing and detailed commodity, monthly 1983, annual supplement, 6764–2

Production, prices, trade, use, employment, tariffs, and stockpiling, by mineral commodity, with foreign comparisons, 1979-83, annual rpt, 5604–18

Production, shipments, trade, inventories, and unfilled orders, for primary metal products, periodic Current Industrial Rpt series, 2506–10

Productivity, hours, and employment indexes for selected SIC 3- and 4-digit industries, 1954-82, annual rpt, 6824–1.2, 6824–1.3

R&D industry funding and employment of scientists and engineers, by industry group, firm size, and funding source, 1956-82, annual rpt, 9627–21

Stainless and alloy tool steel production, employment, prices, and US importer inventories and unfilled orders, quarterly rpt, 9882–3

Statistical Abstract of US, social, political, and economic data, 1950s-83 and trends, annual rpt, 2324–1.3

Steel industry finances and operations under proposed import quota, projected 1985-89 with selected foreign comparisons and trends from 1950, 26306–6.80

Steel pipe and tube shipments, imports from EC by country, and exports, by product type, various periods 1978-83 with import duties to 1987, hearing, 25368–134

Strategic minerals supply/demand, trade, and foreign and US industry devs by firm and country, by commodity, bimonthly rpt, 5602–4

Wages and production workers by occupation, and benefits, by region, Aug 1983 survey, 6787–6.206

Waterborne commerce of US (domestic and foreign), freight by commodity, traffic, and passengers, by port and waterway, 1982, annual rpt, 3754–3

see also under By Commodity in the "Index by Categories"

see also under By Industry in the "Index by Categories"

Irregular warfare

see Guerrilla warfare

Irrigation

Afghanistan irrigation and rural dev in Helmand Valley, funding and effectiveness of AID-sponsored projects, 1949-79, 9916–3.18

Agricultural Conservation Program participation and payments, by State, FY83, annual rpt, 1804–7

Agricultural Statistics, 1983, annual rpt, 1004–1.2

Agriculture Fact Book of US, compilation of data for 1983 with trends from 1940, annual rpt, 1004–14

Army Corps of Engineers activities and projects, FY83 and trends from 1800s, annual rpt, 3754–1

Budget of US, CBO analysis of revenue and spending alternatives and projections of economic indicators, FY85-89, annual rpt, 26304–3.3

Census of Agriculture, 1982: farms, farmland, production and costs, and operator characteristics, preliminary State and county rpt series, 2330–1

Census of Agriculture, 1982: farms, farmland, production, finances, and operator characteristics, by county, final State rpt series, 2331–1

Census of Population, 1980: detailed socioeconomic and demographic characteristics, by age, sex, race, Hispanic origin, occupation, and industry, State rpt series, 2531–4

Colorado River Storage Project finances, water resource dev, power production, and other activities in western States, FY83, annual rpt, 5824–3

County Business Patterns: establishments, employees, and payrolls, by SIC 4-digit industry and county, 1981, annual State rpt series, 2326–8

County Business Patterns: establishments, employees, and payrolls, by SIC 4-digit industry and county, 1982, annual State rpt series, 2326–6

Developing countries agricultural supply/demand and market for US exports, with socioeconomic indicators, country rpt series, 1526–6

Eastern Europe agricultural production and trade by commodity, food consumption, and farm inputs, for 6 countries, 1960-80 with projections to 1991, 1528–178

Energy use and costs, and acreage, for farm irrigation systems by fuel and region, selected years 1974-84 and trends from 1900, article, 1561–16.406

Farm finances, expenses by type, loans by purpose and source, and credit detail by Fed Reserve District, quarterly rpt, 9365–3.10

Farm improvement, acreage and owners by improvement type, funding source, land use, and region, 1978 survey, 1506–5.20

Farm production expenditures, detailed items by farm sales size and region, 1983, annual rpt, 1614–3

Farm production inputs, land mgmt, and environmental effects, for 4 crops, 1940s-80 and projected to 2010, 9188–94

Farm production itemized costs, receipts, and net returns, for 13 crops, 4 livestock types, and milk, by region, 1981-83, annual rpt, 1544–20

Farm real estate value, sales, financing, taxes, and proposed use after purchase, by State, 1970s-84, annual rpt, 1541–8

Fed Govt-owned real property inventory and costs, worldwide summary by location, agency, and use, 1983, annual rpt, 9454–5

FmHA loans and grants by program and State, and summary of services, FY83 with trends from FY63, annual rpt, 1184–17

Foreign and US agricultural supply/demand, consumption per capita, and trade, by world area and country group, 1960s-82, 1528–181

Pacific Northwest electricity consumption and prices by end-use sector, and economic and demographic data, 1960s-83 and projected to 2005, annual rpt, 3224–2

Reclamation Bur water storage and carriage facilities, by type, as of Sept 1983, annual listing, 5824–7

Reclamation programs of Fed Govt in western US, finances and operations by project and State, 1981-82, annual rpts, 5824–1

Research (agricultural) expenditures and scientist years, by topic, commodity, and performing organization, FY82, annual rpt, 1744–2

User fees to recover costs of 7 federally subsidized public service programs, by type of fee, user, and service, FY84-88, 26306–6.68

Irrigation

Water supply and use in 3 areas with supply problems and total US, and methods to increase supply, selected years 1974-80 and projected to 2010, 9208–125

Western Area Power Admin operations by plant, financial statements, and electric power sales by customer, FY83, annual rpt, 3254–1

see also Dams

see also Reservoirs

see also Watershed projects

IRS

see Internal Revenue Service

Irving, Tex.

see also under By City in the "Index by Categories"

Isaak, David T.

"Hydrocarbon Processing in OPEC Countries: Excess Capacities and Readjustment Pains in the World Refining Industry", 25368–133.1

Isard, Peter

"U.S. International Transactions in 1983", 9362–1.403

Islam, Shafiqul

"Currency Misalignments: The Case of the Dollar and the Yen", 9385–1.404

Israel

- Agricultural and food production indexes, and production of selected commodities, by world region and country, 1974-83, annual rpt, 1524–5
- Agricultural situation in Middle East and North Africa, by country and commodity, 1983 and outlook for 1984, annual rpt, 1524–4.3
- Agricultural supply/demand, trade, and production, and socioeconomic data, by country, 1950s-77, 1528–179
- AID economic assistance to developing countries, obligations and disbursements by country, quarterly rpt, 9912–4
- AID loan repayment status and terms by program and country, and status of predecessor agency loans, quarterly rpt, 9912–3
- AID projects and funding by function, with West Bank and Gaza dev and support, FY82-85, and developing countries socioeconomic data, 1970s-83, by country, annual rpt, 9914–3
- Drug, alcohol, and cigarette use among urban youths in Israel and France, by substance type, age, and sex, 1977 and 1979, article, 4102–1.430
- Economic, social, and political summary data, by country, 1984, annual factbook, 244–11
- Economic trends in income, production, prices, employment, finances, and trade, 1984 annual rpt, 2046–4.84
- Exports of US, detailed Schedule B commodities by country of destination, 1983, annual rpt, 2424–9
- Exports of US, detailed Schedule E commodities by mode of transport and world area and country of destination, 1983, annual rpts, 2424–5
- Health care in rural clinics under prepaid plan, services use and user satisfaction, 1981 survey, article, 4102–1.456
- Health care natl expenditures in Israel, with comparisons to other budget sectors and expenditures of other countries, 1950s-83, article, 4102–1.446

Health services and use at Tel Aviv Medical Center, by patient age and condition, selected years 1976-83, article, 4102–1.445

- Imports of US, detailed Schedule A commodities by country and world area of origin, and mode of transport, 1983, annual rpts, 2424–2
- Imports of US, detailed TSUSA commodities by country of origin, 1983, annual rpt, 2424–4
- Loans and grants for economic and military assistance from US and intl agencies, by program and country, FY46-83, annual rpt, 9914–5
- Measles immunization, natural immunity, and incidence rates in Israel, by age, 1965-83 and projected to 1990, article, 4102–1.429
- Military aid of US, arms sales, and training programs costs and budget requests by program, world region, and country, FY83-85, annual rpt, 7144–13
- Military pension lifetime earnings in US and 7 countries, as of 1983, 26306–6.76
- Military spending, arms trade, and armed forces size, with total govt spending and population, by country, 1972-82, annual rpt, 9824–1
- *Minerals Yearbook, 1982,* Vol 3: foreign country reviews of production, trade, and policies, by commodity, annual rpt, 5604–35
- *Minerals Yearbook, 1983,* Vol 3 preprints: foreign country review of production, trade, and policies, by commodity, annual rpt, 5604–23.36
- Nuclear power plant construction and operation status, and capacity, by plant, region, State, and selected country, 1983 and projected to 2020, annual rpt, 3164–57
- Population size and growth rates, and latest available benchmark demographic data, by country, 1950-83, biennial rpt, 2324–4
- Potassium chloride from Israel and Spain, imports injury to US industry from foreign subsidized products, investigation with background financial and operating data, 1984 rpt, 9886–15.54
- Potassium chloride from 4 countries, imports injury to US industry from foreign subsidized products, investigation with background financial and operating data, 1984 rpt, 9886–15.52

see also under By Foreign Country in the "Index by Categories"

Italy

- Agricultural and food production indexes, and production of selected commodities, by world region and country, 1974-83, annual rpt, 1524–5
- Agricultural situation in Western Europe, by country and commodity, 1983 and outlook for 1984, annual rpt, 1524–4.6
- Agricultural supply/demand, trade, and production, and socioeconomic data, by country, 1950s-77, 1528–179
- AID economic assistance to developing countries, obligations and disbursements by country, quarterly rpt, 9912–4
- AID loan repayment status and terms by program and country, and status of predecessor agency loans, quarterly rpt, 9912–3

Index by Subjects and Names

- Almond production and trade of US and selected countries, 1982/83-1983/84 and forecast 1985, article, 1925–34.425
- Auto and auto products sales, prices, and registrations in US, and trade of 8 countries with US, by make and model, 1964-83, annual rpt, 9884–7
- Auto safety and experimental vehicle designs, 1982, conf proceedings, annual rpt, 7764–3
- *Background Notes,* summary social, political, and economic data, 1984 rpt, 7006–2.47
- Bearings (roller) for rail vehicles from Italy and Japan at less than fair value, imports injury to US industry, investigation with background financial and operating data, 1984 rpt, 9886–14.96
- Chairs (metal stacking) from Italy and Taiwan at less than fair value, imports injury to US industry, investigation with background financial and operating data, 1984 rpt, 9886–14.121
- Coal imports from US, energy supply/demand, and economic indicators, for 3 countries, selected years 1960-82 and projected to 2000, 3008–97
- Current account deficits, and financing by source, for US and 5 OECD countries, selected years 1973-1st qtr 1984, article, 9385–1.409
- Economic and monetary trends, compounded annual rates of change for US and 10 major trading partners, quarterly rpt, 9391–7
- Economic conditions, consumer and stock prices and production indexes, 6 OECD countries and US, *Business Conditions Digest,* monthly rpt, 2702–3.10, 2708–31
- Economic conditions in Communist, OECD, and selected other countries, 1960s-83, annual rpt, 244–5
- Economic indicators and oil use and imports for US and 6 OECD countries, and oil production by country, biweekly rpt, 242–4
- Economic indicators for 7 OECD countries and US, quarterly rpt, 2042–10
- Economic, social, and political summary data, by country, 1984, annual factbook, 244–11
- Economic trends in income, production, prices, employment, finances, and trade, 1984 semiannual rpt, 2046–4.60
- Employment, labor force, and participation and unemployment rates by sex, in US and 9 OECD countries, various periods 1970-3rd qtr 1983, annual article, 6722–1.404
- Energy prices and taxes by energy source and end-use sector, for US and 9 OECD countries, quarterly 1979-83, annual rpt, 3164–71
- Energy production by type, and oil prices, trade, and consumption, by country group and selected country, monthly rpt, 242–5
- European Monetary System effect on inflation and exchange rates, for 3 member countries, various periods Feb 1974-Mar 1984, technical paper, 9366–7.101
- Export credit program activities of Eximbank and 6 OECD countries, 1982, annual rpt, 9254–3

Index by Subjects and Names

Ivory Coast

Exports and imports of NATO countries with Council for Mutual Economic Assistance Europe members, by country, 1980-83, annual rpt, 7144–5

Exports and imports of NATO countries with PRC, by country, 1980-83, annual rpt, 7144–14

Exports and imports of OECD countries, by country, 1983, annual rpt, 7144–10

Exports and imports of US with Western Europe, and US market share and export opportunities for selected commodities, by country, 1982-84, 2048–105

Exports of US, detailed Schedule B commodities by country of destination, 1983, annual rpt, 2424–9

Exports of US, detailed Schedule E commodities by mode of transport and world area and country of destination, 1983, annual rpts, 2424–5

Filbert production and trade of US and selected countries, 1981/82-1984/85, article, 1925–34.426

Fish and shellfish wholesale prices and market activity in 8 West Europe countries, weekly rpt, 2162–8

Food supply/demand and market and support prices, with exchange rates, fertilizer price index, GDP, and population, by EC country, 1960-83, 1528–173

Fruit (deciduous) grower prices and processor net cost and subsidies in 4 countries and EC, 1982/83-1983/84, article, 1925–34.414

Imports of US, detailed Schedule A commodities by country and world area of origin, and mode of transport, 1983, annual rpts, 2424–2

Imports of US, detailed TSUSA commodities by country of origin, 1983, annual rpt, 2424–4

Industrial production indexes of 7 OECD countries and US, biweekly rpt, periodic article, 2042–24

Interest rates and budget balances of US and 6 OECD countries, 1973-83, annual rpt, 26304–3.1

Intl transactions of US with 10 countries, 1981-83, *Survey of Current Business,* monthly rpt, annual table, 2702–1.31

Loans and grants for economic and military assistance from US and intl agencies, by program and country, FY46-83, annual rpt, 9914–5

Machinery undercarriage components from Italy, imports injury to US industry from sales covered by foreign govt grants, investigation with background financial and operating data, 1980-83, 9886–15.46

Manufacturing labor productivity and cost indexes for US and 11 OECD countries, 1960-82, annual article, 6722–1.405

Manufacturing productivity and unit labor cost indexes for US and 11 countries, 1950-82 and preliminary 1983, annual rpt, 6864–1

Manufacturing wage/price and wage/output adjustment in 6 OECD countries, 1960-81, technical paper, 9381–10.33

Military aid of US, arms sales, and training programs costs and budget requests by program, world region, and country, FY83-85, annual rpt, 7144–13

Military spending, arms trade, and armed forces size, with total govt spending and population, by country, 1972-82, annual rpt, 9824–1

Military weapons transfers to developing countries from US, USSR, and Europe, by weapon type and world region, 1974-82, 25948–3

Minerals Yearbook, 1982, Vol 3: foreign country reviews of production, trade, and policies, by commodity, annual rpt, 5604–35

Minerals Yearbook, 1982, Vol 3 preprints: foreign country review of production, trade, and policies, by commodity, annual rpt, 5604–17.37

Minerals Yearbook, 1983, Vol 3 preprints: foreign country review of production, trade, and policies, by commodity, annual rpt, 5604–23.37

Monetary control policy of US and selected West European countries, and relation to credit, exchange rates, GNP, and other indicators, various periods 1960-82, conf papers, 9373–3.26

Nuclear power generation in US and 18 non-Communist countries, monthly rpt, 3162–24.10

Nuclear power plant construction and operation status, and capacity, by plant, region, State, and selected country, 1983 and projected to 2020, annual rpt, 3164–57

Oil consumption and stocks for major consuming countries, monthly rpt, 3162–24.10

Population size and growth rates, and latest available benchmark demographic data, by country, 1950-83, biennial rpt, 2324–4

Ships in world merchant fleet, and tonnage, by country of registry, 1982, annual rpt, 7704–3.1

Space launchings attaining Earth orbit or beyond, by country, 1957-83, annual rpt, 9504–9.1

Space satellites and other objects launched since 1957, quarterly listing, 9502–2

Sprinkler system brass components from Italy at less than fair value, imports injury to US industry, investigation with background financial and operating data, 1984 rpt, 9886–14.100

Steel imports of US from EC and other countries, and US industry operating data, for 15 products limited under arrangement with EC, monthly rpt, 9882–10

Walnut production, stocks, use, and exports of US and 4 countries, and EC export subsidy, selected years 1977-1984/85, article, 1925–34.429

Wine from France and Italy, imports injury to US industry from sales covered by foreign govt grants, investigation with background financial and operating data, 1984 rpt, 9886–19.9

Woodwind instrument key pads from Italy at less than fair value, imports injury to US industry, investigation with background financial and operating data, 1984 rpt, 9886–14.114

Woodwind instrument key pads from Italy, injury to US industry from foreign subsidized and less than fair value imports, investigation with background financial and operating data, 1980-83, 9886–19.6

see also San Marino

see also Vatican City

see also under By Foreign Country in the "Index by Categories"

ITT World Communications

Financial and operating data for 7 major telegraph carriers, quarterly rpt, 9282–1

Ivory Coast

Agricultural and food production indexes, and production of selected commodities, by world region and country, 1974-83, annual rpt, 1524–5

Agricultural situation in sub-Saharan Africa, by country, 1982-83 and outlook for 1984, annual rpt, 1524–4.10

Agricultural supply/demand, trade, and production, and socioeconomic data, by country, 1950s-77, 1528–179

AID economic assistance to developing countries, obligations and disbursements by country, quarterly rpt, 9912–4

AID loan repayment status and terms by program and country, and status of predecessor agency loans, quarterly rpt, 9912–3

Economic conditions and foreign marketing prospects in 46 Sub-Saharan countries, 1983 world region rpt, 2046–5.1

Economic conditions, income, production, prices, employment, and trade, 1984 annual country rpt, 2046–4.112

Economic, social, and political summary data, by country, 1984, annual factbook, 244–11

Exports and imports of US, by commodity and country, 1972-82, annual world region rpt, 244–13.4

Exports of US, detailed Schedule B commodities by country of destination, 1983, annual rpt, 2424–9

Exports of US, detailed Schedule E commodities by mode of transport and world area and country of destination, 1983, annual rpts, 2424–5

Imports of US, detailed Schedule A commodities by country and world area of origin, and mode of transport, 1983, annual rpts, 2424–2

Imports of US, detailed TSUSA commodities by country of origin, 1983, annual rpt, 2424–4

Loans and grants for economic and military assistance from US and intl agencies, by program and country, FY46-83, annual rpt, 9914–5

Military aid of US, arms sales, and training programs costs and budget requests by program, world region, and country, FY83-85, annual rpt, 7144–13

Military spending, arms trade, and armed forces size, with total govt spending and population, by country, 1972-82, annual rpt, 9824–1

Minerals Yearbook, 1982, Vol 3: foreign country reviews of production, trade, and policies, by commodity, annual rpt, 5604–35

Minerals Yearbook, 1982, Vol 3 preprints: foreign country review of production, trade, and policies, by commodity, annual rpt, 5604–17.84

Population size and growth rates, and latest available benchmark demographic data, by country, 1950-83, biennial rpt, 2324–4

Ivory Coast

see also under By Foreign Country in the "Index by Categories"

Jackson, Mich.

Census of Housing, 1980: occupancy and unit characteristics, by race, Hispanic origin, and city, SMSA rpt, 2473–1.189

Census of Population and Housing, 1980: detailed population and housing characteristics, by county, city, and census tract, SMSA rpt, 2551–2.189

Jackson, Miss.

Census of Housing, 1980: occupancy and unit characteristics, by race, Hispanic origin, and city, SMSA rpt, 2473–1.190

Census of Population and Housing, 1980: detailed population and housing characteristics, by county, city, and census tract, SMSA rpt, 2551–2.190

Housing vacancy rates for single and multifamily units and mobile homes, by city and ZIP code, 1983, annual metro area rpt, 9304–19.4

Wages of office and plant workers, by occupation, 1984 SMSA survey rpt, 6785–11.1

see also under By City and By SMSA or MSA in the "Index by Categories"

Jacksonville, Fla.

Census of Housing, 1980: occupancy and unit characteristics, by race, Hispanic origin, and city, SMSA rpt, 2473–1.191

Census of Population and Housing, 1980: detailed population and housing characteristics, by county, city, and census tract, SMSA rpt, 2551–2.191

Population size of top 25 cities, 1980 and 1982, press release, 2328–46

Wages of office and plant workers, by occupation, 1983 SMSA survey rpt, 6785–12.2

Waterborne commerce of US (domestic and foreign), freight by commodity, traffic, and passengers, by port and waterway, 1982, annual rpt, 3754–3.1, 3754–3.2

see also under By City and By SMSA or MSA in the "Index by Categories"

Jacksonville, N.C.

Census of Housing, 1980: occupancy and unit characteristics, by race, Hispanic origin, and city, SMSA rpt, 2473–1.192

Census of Population and Housing, 1980: detailed population and housing characteristics, by county, city, and census tract, SMSA rpt, 2551–2.192

see also under By SMSA or MSA in the "Index by Categories"

Jacobs, Bruce

"Home Equity Financing of Long-Term Care for the Elderly", 4658–7

Jacobson, Laurence R.

"Calculations of Profitability for U.S. Dollar-Deutsche Mark Intervention", 9366–1.130

Jaffee, Dwight M.

"Creative Finance: Measures, Sources, and Tests", 9412–2.401

Jager, Gil

"Satellite Indicators of Rapid Cyclogenesis", 2152–8.401

Jahr, Dale

"Economic Issues of a Changing Telecommunications Industry", 23848–176

Jails

see Correctional institutions

Jakes, Pamela J.

"Michigan's Predicted Timber Yields, 1981-2010", 1208–193

Jamaica

Agricultural and food production indexes, and production of selected commodities, by world region and country, 1974-83, annual rpt, 1524–5

Agricultural situation in Latin America, by country, 1981-83 and outlook for 1984, annual rpt, 1524–4.9

Agricultural supply/demand, trade, and production, and socioeconomic data, by country, 1950s-77, 1528–179

AID activities and funding by project and function, FY85, and developing countries summary socioeconomic data, 1970s-83, by country, annual rpt, 9914–3

AID economic assistance to developing countries, obligations and disbursements by country, quarterly rpt, 9912–4

AID loan repayment status and terms by program and country, and status of predecessor agency loans, quarterly rpt, 9912–3

Economic conditions, income, production, prices, employment, and trade, 1984 annual country rpt, 2046–4.105

Economic, social, and political summary data, by country, 1984, annual factbook, 244–11

Economic trends in income, production, prices, employment, finances, and trade, 1984 annual rpt, 2046–4.6

Exports of US, detailed Schedule B commodities by country of destination, 1983, annual rpt, 2424–9

Exports of US, detailed Schedule E commodities by mode of transport and world area and country of destination, 1983, annual rpts, 2424–5

Food supply policies of 21 developing countries, with farm sector data, tariff income, and prices and imports of 5 grains, 1960s-81, 1528–168

Imports of US, detailed Schedule A commodities by country and world area of origin, and mode of transport, 1983, annual rpts, 2424–2

Imports of US, detailed TSUSA commodities by country of origin, 1983, annual rpt, 2424–4

Loans and grants for economic and military assistance from US and intl agencies, by program and country, FY46-83, annual rpt, 9914–5

Military aid of US, arms sales, and training programs costs and budget requests by program, world region, and country, FY83-85, annual rpt, 7144–13

Military spending, arms trade, and armed forces size, with total govt spending and population, by country, 1972-82, annual rpt, 9824–1

Minerals Yearbook, 1982, Vol 3: foreign country reviews of production, trade, and policies, by commodity, annual rpt, 5604–35

Minerals Yearbook, 1983, Vol 3 preprints: foreign country review of production, trade, and policies, by commodity, annual rpt, 5604–23.85

Index by Subjects and Names

PL 480 Title I assistance effects on economic dev, with data on govt finance, economic indicators, demography, and dev programs, 1970s-81, 9916–1.51

PL 480 Title I funding and socioeconomic impacts in developing countries, with case studies for 5 countries, 1950s-81, 9918–13

Population size and growth rates, and latest available benchmark demographic data, by country, 1950-83, biennial rpt, 2324–4

Rum imports (duty-free) of US under Caribbean Basin Initiative, by country, Jan-June 1983-84, annual rpt, 9884–15

see also under By Foreign Country in the "Index by Categories"

James, Christopher

"Market Evidence on the Effective Maturity of Bank Assets and Liabilities", 9387–8.82

Janesville, Wis.

Census of Housing, 1980: occupancy and unit characteristics, by race, Hispanic origin, and city, SMSA rpt, 2473–1.193

Census of Population and Housing, 1980: detailed population and housing characteristics, by county, city, and census tract, SMSA rpt, 2551–2.193

see also under By SMSA or MSA in the "Index by Categories"

Japan

Agricultural and food production indexes, and production of selected commodities, by world region and country, 1974-83, annual rpt, 1524–5

Agricultural exports and imports of US, by detailed commodity and country, FY83 and CY83, semiannual rpts, 1522–4

Agricultural imports from US, by detailed commodity, 1974-83, article, 1925–34.421

Agricultural situation in 4 East Asian countries, by commodity, 1983 and outlook for 1984, annual rpt, 1524–4.2

Agricultural supply/demand, trade, and production, and socioeconomic data, by country, 1950s-77, 1528–179

AID loan repayment status and terms by program and country, and status of predecessor agency loans, quarterly rpt, 9912–3

Almond production and trade of US and selected countries, 1982/83-1983/84 and forecast 1985, article, 1925–34.425

Auto and auto products sales, prices, and registrations in US, and trade of 8 countries with US, by make and model, 1964-83, annual rpt, 9884–7

Auto export voluntary restraint of Japan, effect on US auto industry and import sales and prices, 2nd qtr 1981-1st qtr 1984, article, 9377–1.407

Auto fuel economy measures, for US, Japan, and European makes, 1975 and 1980-83, annual rpt, 3164–73

Auto industry finances and operations by manufacturer, foreign competition, and consumer auto expenditures and attitudes toward car buying, selected years 1968-85, annual rpt, 2004–8

Auto industry operations, trade, and registrations, foreign and US, selected years 1928-82, domestic content requirement hearings, 21788–134

Index by Subjects and Names

Japan

Auto manufacturers suggested retail prices of selected US and Japan models by firm, and US auto industry operating and trade data, monthly rpt, 9882–8

Auto safety and experimental vehicle designs, 1982, conf proceedings, annual rpt, 7764–3

Bearings (roller) for rail vehicles from Italy and Japan at less than fair value, imports injury to US industry, investigation with background financial and operating data, 1984 rpt, 9886–14.96

Biotechnology commercial uses, R&D funding and output, controls, and industry financial and operating data, for US and 5 countries, 1970s-83 and estimated 1984-85, 26358–98

Calcium hypochlorite from Japan at less than fair value, imports injury to US industry, investigation with background financial and operating data, 1984 rpt, 9886–14.107

Capital formation and steel industry employment costs in US and OECD countries, 1960s-82, 26306–6.69

Cellular telephones and parts from Japan at less than fair value, imports injury to US industry, investigation with background financial and operating data, 1984 rpt, 9886–14.130

China exports and imports, by commodity, world area, and country, quarterly rpt, 242–6

China trade and trade balances with world and major trading partners, by selected commodity, quarterly rpt, 242–6.1

Coal reserves, production, demand indicators, and trade, by country, selected years 1973-82 and alternative trade projections to 1995, annual rpt, 3164–77

Current account balances of US, Japan, and West Germany, effects of business cycles, modeling results, 1970s-82 and projected 1983-86, technical paper, 9366–7.92

Current account deficits, and financing by source, for US and 5 OECD countries, selected years 1973-1st qtr 1984, article, 9385–1.409

Cyanuric acid and derivatives from Japan, imports injury to US industry, investigation with background financial and operating data, 1984 rpt, 9886–14.102

Earnings of workers in Japan, by years of service and other characteristics, selected years 1955-80, article, 6722–1.427

Earnings of workers in Japan for smaller firms relative to wages in larger firms, by worker characteristics, firm size, and industry div, 1950s-81, article, 6722–1.461

Economic and monetary trends, compounded annual rates of change for US and 10 major trading partners, quarterly rpt, 9391–7

Economic conditions, consumer and stock prices and production indexes, 6 OECD countries and US, *Business Conditions Digest,* monthly rpt, 2702–3.10, 2708–31

Economic conditions in Communist and OECD countries, 1982, annual rpt, 7144–11

Economic conditions in Communist, OECD, and selected other countries, 1960s-83, annual rpt, 244–5

Economic indicators and oil use and imports for US and 6 OECD countries, and oil production by country, biweekly rpt, 242–4

Economic indicators and trade balance of US and 4 countries, effect of US budget deficits, model results, various periods 1974-85, technical paper, 9366–7.102

Economic indicators for 7 OECD countries and US, quarterly rpt, 2042–10

Economic indicators of 12 Pacific Basin countries or areas and US, quarterly rpt, 9393–9

Economic, social, and political summary data, by country, 1984, annual factbook, 244–11

Economic trends in income, production, prices, employment, finances, and trade, 1984 semiannual rpt, 2046–4.13, 2046–4.51

Electronic component equipment market and trade, and user industry operations and demand, 1983 country market research rpt, 2045–4.23

Employment, labor force, and participation and unemployment rates by sex, in US and 9 OECD countries, various periods 1970-3rd qtr 1983, annual article, 6722–1.404

Energy prices and taxes by energy source and end-use sector, for US and 9 OECD countries, quarterly 1979-83, annual rpt, 3164–71

Energy production by type, and oil prices, trade, and consumption, by country group and selected country, monthly rpt, 242–5

Export credit program activities of Eximbank and 6 OECD countries, 1982, annual rpt, 9254–3

Export sales and shipments of US grains, oilseed products, hides, skins, and cotton, by country, weekly rpt, 1922–3

Exports and imports, agreement devs, US trade relations, and USITC investigations, 1983, annual rpt, 9884–5

Exports and imports, intl position of US and 4 OECD countries, and factors affecting US competition, quarterly pamphlet, 2042–25

Exports and imports of OECD countries, by country, 1983, annual rpt, 7144–10

Exports and imports of OECD, total and for 4 major countries, and US trade by country, by commodity, 1972-82, annual world region rpt series, 244–13

Exports and imports of US, by commodity group, world area, selected country, US coastal area and port, and mode of transport, with seasonal adjustments, monthly rpt, 2422–9

Exports and imports of US, detailed SIC-based commodities by world area, 1983, annual rpts, 2424–6

Exports of US by selected commodity, and foreign and US economic and employment indicators and balance of payments, by world area and country, 1970s-83, annual rpt, 2044–26

Exports of US, detailed Schedule B commodities by country of destination, 1983, annual rpt, 2424–9

Exports of US, detailed Schedule E commodities by mode of transport and world area and country of destination, 1983, annual rpts, 2424–5

Fabric and neoprene laminate from Japan at less than fair value, imports injury to US industry, investigation with background financial and operating data, 1984 rpt, 9886–14.128

Finance (intl) and financial policy, external factors affecting US economy, econometric model methodology and results for US and 4 countries, various periods 1964-75, 9368–78

Fish landings, prices, trade by country, stocks, and market devs, for Japan, periodic press release, 2162–7

Foreign exchange bank and nonbank activity, and currency futures turnover in US and 3 foreign markets, Mar 1980 and Apr 1983, article, 9385–1.411

Foreign exchange rate intervention in 3 currency markets by Fed Reserve, various periods Sept 1977-Dec 1979, technical paper, 9366–1.140

Foreign exchange rates for currencies of US and 2 countries with yen, and measures of manufacturing competitiveness, 1983 with 1974-80 and 1979-80 averages, article, 9385–1.404

Foreign exchange 2-country model of yen/dollar sterilized intervention, and effect of fiscal balance and private savings, 1972-82, article, 9393–8.405

Graphic industries equipment market and trade, and user industry operations and demand, 1984 country market research rpt, 2045–3.29

Health care resources, use, and per capita public expenditures, and selected population characteristics, for US and 6 countries, selected years 1975-81, 21148–33

Imports of US, detailed Schedule A commodities by country and world area of origin, and mode of transport, 1983, annual rpts, 2424–2

Imports of US, detailed TSUSA commodities by country of origin, 1983, annual rpt, 2424–4

Industrial production indexes of 7 OECD countries and US, biweekly rpt, periodic article, 2042–24

Interest rates and budget balances of US and 6 OECD countries, 1973-83, annual rpt, 26304–3.1

Investment (foreign direct) in US, by major industry group, world area, and selected country, 1980-83, annual article, 2702–1.439

Investment (foreign direct) in US, major investors and investments by SIC 4-digit industry, transaction type and value, and location, 1983, annual rpt, 2044–20

Investment (foreign direct) of US, by world area and country, 1977-83, article, 2702–1.442

Investment (intl) position of US, net change by component, investment type, and world region, and for 2 countries, 1982-83, annual article, 2702–1.424

Lab instruments market and trade, and user industry operations and demand, 1984 country market research rpt, 2045–10.19

Loans and grants for economic and military assistance from US and intl agencies, by program and country, FY46-83, annual rpt, 9914–5

Japan

Lumber production, prices, trade, and employment in Northwest US and British Columbia, quarterly rpt, 1202–3

Machine tool orders by selected industry, trade, and shipments and Japan share of US market by type of tool, various dates 1972-84, hearing, 25388–48

Manufacturing computerized automation dev, R&D, training, and employment impacts, with comparisons to foreign countries, selected years 1960-83, 26358–105

Manufacturing labor productivity and cost indexes for US and 11 OECD countries, 1960-82, annual article, 6722–1.405

Manufacturing productivity and unit labor cost indexes for US and 11 countries, 1950-82 and preliminary 1983, annual rpt, 6864–1

Manufacturing wage growth in US and 2 countries, regression results, 1963-81, technical paper, 9381–10.34

Manufacturing wage rates in US and 2 countries, by industry, 1975 and 1980, hearing, 21248–79

Manufacturing wage/price and wage/output adjustment in 6 OECD countries, 1960-81, technical paper, 9381–10.33

Medical and health care equipment market and trade, and user industry operations and demand, 1984 country market research rpt, 2045–2.49

Military aid of US, arms sales, and training programs costs and budget requests by program, world region, and country, FY83-85, annual rpt, 7144–13

Military spending, arms trade, and armed forces, size, with total govt spending and population, by country, 1972-82, annual rpt, 9824–1

Military weapons of USSR, Warsaw Pact, and NATO/Japan, selected years 1974-83, annual rpt, 3544–2

Minerals Yearbook, 1982, Vol 3: foreign country reviews of production, trade, and policies, by commodity, annual rpt, 5604–35

Minerals Yearbook, 1982, Vol 3 preprints: foreign country review of production, trade, and policies, by commodity, annual rpt, 5604–17.38

Natural gas and liquefied natural gas trade of US with 4 countries, by US pipeline company, 1982-83, annual article, 3162–4.406

Natural gas and liquefied natural gas transported, by State and country of origin and destination, 1982, article, 3162–4.409

Natural gas exports of US to Canada, Mexico, and Japan, 1980-83, annual rpt, 3024–2

Nuclear power generation in US and 18 non-Communist countries, monthly rpt, 3162–24.10

Nuclear power plant construction and operation status, and capacity, by plant, region, State, and selected country, 1983 and projected to 2020, annual rpt, 3164–57

Oil (Alaskan) potential exports to Japan, costs and benefits, with background data on oil prices, Pacific Basin supply/demand, and tankers, various periods 1918-99, hearings, 25388–45

Oil consumption and stocks for major consuming countries, monthly rpt, 3162–24.10

Population size and growth rates, and latest available benchmark demographic data, by country, 1950-83, biennial rpt, 2324–4

Price indexes for consumer and producer goods, major commodities, exports, imports, nonfarm wages, and currency value, US and 4 countries, bimonthly rpt, 2042–11

R&D expenditures and employment in science and technology, for US and 4 countries, selected years 1953-84, annual rpt, 9624–18.1

Radio (mobile) cellular transceivers and parts from Japan at less than fair value, imports injury to US industry, investigation with background financial and operating data, 1984 rpt, 9886–14.95

Rail high-speed systems and railcar production of US and selected countries, with major cities population and land area, 1940s-82, 26358–97

Science Indicators, R&D expenditures, innovations, research, and higher education, with foreign comparisons, 1960s- 83, annual rpt, 9624–10.1

Semiconductor industry subsidies of Japan govt by program, with financial and operating data by firm, R&D, and comparisons to US industry, 1970s-83, hearings, 21368–46.1

Ships in world merchant fleet, and tonnage, by country of registry, 1982, annual rpt, 7704–3.1

Space launchings attaining Earth orbit or beyond, by country, 1957-83, annual rpt, 9504–9.1

Space satellites and other objects launched since 1957, quarterly listing, 9502–2

Sporting goods and recreational equipment and vehicles market and trade, 1982 country market research rpt, 2045–14.10

Steel (specialty) and ferroalloy production in Japan and raw material supply/demand, with industry market and manufacturing data, selected years 1970-81, 5608–144

Steel import trigger prices to prevent Japan dumping, and domestic steel prices, employment, and imports, by product and region, various dates 1977-1983, hearings, 21368–51

Steel imports of US from EC and other countries, and US industry operating data, for 15 products limited under arrangement with EC, monthly rpt, 9882–10

Steel products from Japan at less than fair value, imports injury to US industry, investigation with background financial and operating data, 1984 rpt, 9886–14.109, 9886–14.110

Tidal current tables, daily time and velocity by station for North America and Asia coasts, 1985, annual rpt, 2174–1.2

Titanium sponge from Japan and UK at less than fair value, imports injury to US industry, investigation with background financial and operating data, 1984 rpt, 9886–14.94, 9886–14.129

Travel to and from US, by world area and selected country, projected 1984-85, annual rpt, 2904–9

Unemployment rates in Japan, official and adjusted to US concepts, with alternative measures for US and Japan, 1970s-82, article, 6722–1.418

Index by Subjects and Names

US-Japan Friendship Commission educational and cultural exchange activities, grants, and trust fund status, FY83, annual rpt, 14694–1

Worker participation in mgmt decisions, experience in US and 2 countries, 1983 narrative article, 6722–1.457

see also under By Foreign Country in the "Index by Categories"

Japan-U.S. Friendship Commission

Budget of US Appendix, detailed budgets and personnel summaries, by agency, FY85, annual rpt, 104–3

Budget of US, appropriations, outlays, balances, and budget receipts, by govtl branch and agency, FY83, annual rpt, 8104–2

Educational and cultural exchange activities of Commission, grants, and trust fund status, FY83, annual rpt, 14694–1

Japanese Americans

see Asian Americans

Jarvinen, Denise M.

"New England State Governments—Looking Ahead to a Better Fiscal Year", 9373–2.401

Jensen, Helen H.

"Farm People's Health Insurance Coverage", 1598–191

Jeremias, Ronald A.

"Combined Effective Income and Property Tax Rates for Farm Capital", 1548–237

"Effective Income Tax Rates for Farm Capital, 1950-84", 1548–231

"Trends in the Real After-Tax Cost of Farm Machinery, 1960-83", 1561–16.402

Jeri, F. R.

"Further Experience with the Syndromes Produced by Coca Paste Smoking", 7008–40

Jersey City, N.J.

Census of Housing, 1980: occupancy and unit characteristics, by race, Hispanic origin, and city, SMSA rpt, 2473–1.194

Census of Population and Housing, 1980: detailed population and housing characteristics, by county, city, and census tract, SMSA rpt, 2551–2.194

Dress industry production and related workers, wages, and benefits, by occupation, size of establishment, and union status, for 11 labor market areas, Aug 1982 survey, 6787–6.200

Public works capital needs and intergovtl financing, by type of project and selected city, various periods 1950-83, 10048–60

see also under By City and By SMSA or MSA in the "Index by Categories"

Jet fuel

see Aviation fuels

Jet Propulsion Laboratory

"Photovoltaic Energy Systems: Program Summary, FY83", 3304–20

Jewelry

Census of Population, 1980: detailed socioeconomic and demographic characteristics, by age, sex, race, Hispanic origin, occupation, and industry, State rpt series, 2531–4

County Business Patterns: establishments, employees, and payrolls, by SIC 4-digit industry and county, 1981, annual State rpt series, 2326–8

Index by Subjects and Names

Job vacancy

County Business Patterns: establishments, employees, and payrolls, by SIC 4-digit industry and county, 1982, annual State rpt series, 2326–6

Employment, earnings, and hours, by selected SIC 1- to 4-digit industry, State, and for 278 major labor areas, 1939-83, annual rpt, 6744–5

Employment, earnings, and hours, by SIC 4-digit nonfarm industry, monthly 1974-Feb 1984, annual update, 6744–4

Exports and imports of US, detailed SIC-based commodities by world area, 1983, annual rpts, 2424–6

Exports and imports of US, totals and as percent of domestic production, by SIC 2- to 5-digit commodity, 1981, annual rpt, 2424–3

Exports of US, detailed commodities by country of destination, monthly rpt, 2422–3

Exports of US, detailed Schedule B commodities by country of destination, 1983, annual rpt, 2424–9

Exports of US, detailed Schedule E commodities by mode of transport and world area and country of destination, 1983, annual rpts, 2424–5

Great Lakes trade, by SITC 3-digit commodity, port, vessel type, world area, and country, 1982, annual rpt, 7744–3

Imports of ivory carvings and jewelry, 1982, annual rpt, 5504–19

Imports of US, detailed Schedule A commodities by country and world area of origin, and mode of transport, 1983, annual rpts, 2424–2

Imports of US, detailed Schedule A commodities by country, monthly rpt, 2422–2

Imports of US, detailed TSUSA commodities by country of origin, 1983, annual rpt, 2424–4

Income tax returns of sole proprietorships, detailed data by industry div and selected industry group, 1981, annual rpt, 8304–7

Income tax returns of sole proprietorships, receipts, deductions by type, payroll, and net income, by major industry, 1982, annual article, 8302–2.413

Industry finances and operations, by SIC 2- to 4- digit industry, 1970s-83 and projected to 1988, annual rpt, 2014–4

Injuries and deaths from use of selected consumer products and related activity, by victim age and sex, 1982, annual rpt, 9164–7

Input-output structure of US economy, detailed interindustry transactions for 537 industries, and components of final demand, 1977 benchmark data, 2708–17

Manufacturing census, 1982: financial and operating data, by SIC 2- to 4-digit industry, State, SMSA, and county, preliminary census div rpt series, 2491–3

Manufacturing census, 1982: financial and operating data, for SIC 4-digit industries by product, preliminary rpt, 2491–1.424, 2491–1.426, 2491–1.435

Occupational injury and illness rates, by SIC 2- to 4-digit industry, 1982, annual rpt, 6844–1

Occupational manpower needs and supply by detailed occupation, and educational and training program enrollees and grads by detailed field, 1982 and 1995, biennial rpt, 6744–3

Occupational Outlook Handbook, 1984-85 biennial rpt, 6744–1

OECD trade, total and for 4 major countries, and US trade by country, by commodity, 1972-82, annual world region rpt series, 244–13

Personal stocks of durable goods, by type, in current and constant dollars, 1980-83, annual article, 2702–1.433

Producer prices and indexes, by stage of processing and detailed commodity, monthly rpt, 6762–6

Producer prices and indexes, by stage of processing and detailed commodity, monthly 1983, annual supplement, 6764–2

Retail trade census, 1982: employment, establishments, sales, and payroll, by SIC 2- to 4-digit kind of business, SMSA, and retail district, State rpt series, 2401–1

Retail trade census, 1982: employment, establishments, sales, and payroll, for jewelry stores, by State, preliminary rpt, 2395–1.30

Retail trade sales and inventories, by kind of business, region, census div, and selected State, SMSA, and city, and seasonal adjustments, monthly rpt, 2413–3

Retail trade sales, inventories, purchases, gross margin, and accounts receivable, by SIC 2- to 4-digit kind of business and type of ownership, 1983, annual rpt, 2413–5

Service industry census, 1982: employment, establishments, receipts, and payroll, by SIC 2- to 4-digit kind of business, SMSA, county, and city, State rpt series, 2391–1

Thefts, and total value of property stolen and recovered, by property type, 1983, annual rpt, 6224–2.1

Virgin Islands economic censuses, 1982: employment, establishments, payroll, and receipts, by SIC 1- to 4-digit industry, island, and city, 2593–1

Wholesale trade census, 1982: employment, establishments, sales by commodity, and payroll, by SIC 4-digit kind of business and State, preliminary rpt, 2403–1.19

see also Gemstones

Job Corps

Bilingual vocational training projects, participants, characteristics, and costs, by program, FY82, annual rpt, 4804–26

Budget of US, effects of Reagan Admin policy changes, by detailed program, FY85, annual rpt, 104–21

Children and youth benefitting from Fed Govt public welfare programs and tax expenditures, participation and funding for 71 programs, FY81-83, 21968–30

Forest Service programs and activities, by State and region, FY83, annual rpt, 1204–1

Job discrimination

see Discrimination in employment

Job placement

see Employment services

Job Training Partnership Act

Fed Govt employment and training program funding under Job Training Partnership Act, and required matching funds, for 3 programs by State, 1984/85, press release, 6408–58

Fed Govt industrial dev funding by type, program, and agency, and State govt policies and support, selected years FY75-85, 26306–6.81

Indian and Alaska Native employment and training program funding allocation under Job Training Partnership Act, by individual tribe and group, FY84, press release, 6408–57

Migrant and seasonal farm workers retraining assistance, Job Training Partnership Act allotments by State and administering organization, as of July 1984, press release, 6408–64

Participants, by program and socieconomic characteristics, Oct 1983-June 1984 with funding to 1985/86, 6408–63

Performance standards guide for States, with data on previous programs by State or local area, FY81-82, 6408–59

Rural area impact of Job Training Partnership Act, comparison to CETA program, 1973-84, article, 1502–7.403

Unemployed displaced workers training and placement program of Fed Govt, funding and enrollment for 13 States and Guam, June 1984, press release, 6408–61

Youth summer job program of Fed Govt, funding and jobs by State and for Indians, summer 1984, press release, 6408–62

Job vacancy

Business Conditions Digest, cyclical indicators, by economic process, monthly rpt, 2702–3.3

Business Conditions Digest, historical supplement on economic, business, and financial conditions and cyclical fluctuations, with methodology, 1947-82, 2708–31

Employment and labor force statistics by major industry group and demographic characteristics, *Survey of Current Business,* monthly rpt, 2702–1.5

Hospital employment, vacancies, and vacancy rates, by occupation and by hospital specialty, region, census div, and State, 1980, annual rpt, 4114–12

Income tax returns of corporations, detailed income and tax items by industry, 1981, annual rpt, 8304–4

Income tax returns of corporations with foreign tax credit, income and deductions by type, asset size, and selected industry group, 1980, article, 8302–2.415

Income tax returns of individuals by tax return item, State, and occupation, and income by source and tax owed, by income level, selected years 1916-80, conf papers, 8308–28.1

Income tax returns of individuals, new job credit items and other detailed data, 1982, annual rpt, 8304–2

Income tax returns of sole proprietorships, receipts, deductions by type, payroll, and net income, by major industry, 1982, annual article, 8302–2.413

Kentucky employment growth in 9-county rural area, labor force and establishment characteristics, 1979-80, 1598–194

New England States economic indicators, Fed Reserve 1st District, monthly rpt, 9373–2.2

New England States, FHLB 1st District member instns financial operations and housing industry indicators, monthly rpt, 9302–4

NYC metro area small business owners and accountants, assessment of economy, professional activities, and community problems, by county and industry div, 1983 survey, hearings, 21728–52.3

Job vacancy

Small business owners expectations of operations, expansion opportunity, and loan availability during coming quarter, July 1983 survey, hearings, 21728–52.2

Texas border employment and economic impacts of Mexican peso devaluation, for 6 counties and 2 SMSAs, 1970s-May 1983, hearing, 21788–133

TTPI socioeconomic, employment, health, and govtl data, by TTPI govt, FY83 and selected trends, detailed annual rpt, 7004–6.2

see also Labor turnover

Jobs

see Employment and unemployment, general

see Employment and unemployment, local and regional

see Employment and unemployment, specific industries

see Job vacancy

see Labor turnover

see Occupations

see Seasonal and summer employment

see Veterans employment

see Women's employment

see Youth employment

see under By Occupation in the "Index by Categories"

Johannsen, Paula

"Tennessee: Continuing the Momentum of Recovery", 9371–1.406

Johnson, Beverly L.

"Most Women Who Maintain Families Receive Poor Labor Market Returns", 6746–1.253

Johnson City, Tenn.

Census of Housing, 1980: occupancy and unit characteristics, by race, Hispanic origin, and city, SMSA rpt, 2473–1.195

Census of Population and Housing, 1980: detailed population and housing characteristics, by county, city, and census tract, SMSA rpt, 2551–2.195

see also under By SMSA or MSA in the "Index by Categories"

Johnson, D. Gale

"Future Food Imports of the Soviet Union and Other Centrally Planned Economies", 1004–16.1

Johnson, Delmas M.

"Classification and Estimation of Alcohol Involvement in Fatalities", 7762–9.405

Johnson, Donald G.

"Current Status of the Natural Resources in the Northwest of Mexico", 1208–197

Johnson, James

"Farm Income Situation and Outlook", 1004–16.1

"New Evidence on the Diversity of Agricultural Income and Expense Accounts", 1544–19.401

Johnson, Justine

"Survey of Nuclear Power Plant Construction Costs, 1984", 3164–69

Johnson, Lawrence, and Associates, Inc.

"Study of Demographic, Situational, and Motivational Factors Affecting Restraint Usage in Automobiles", 7768–82

Johnson, Mae D.

"Cotton Ginning Charges, Harvesting Practices, and Selected Marketing Costs, 1983/84 Season", 1564–3

Johnson, Mark J.

"Effects of Strong Dollar, Economic Recovery Apparent in First-Half Import and Export Prices", 6722–1.459

"Robust Growth and the Strong Dollar Set Pattern for 1983 Import and Export Prices", 6722–1.424

Johnson, Martha

"Residential Energy Consumption Survey. Consumption and Expenditures by End Use for 1978, 1980, and 1981", 3166–7.21

Johnson, Melvin E.

"Petroleum Consumption by Electric Utilities: 10 Years After the Arab Oil Embargo", 3162–39.402

Johnston, Lloyd D.

"Highlights from Drugs and American High-School Students, 1975-83", 4494–4

Johnstown, Pa.

Census of Housing, 1980: occupancy and unit characteristics, by race, Hispanic origin, and city, SMSA rpt, 2473–1.196

Census of Population and Housing, 1980: detailed population and housing characteristics, by county, city, and census tract, SMSA rpt, 2551–2.196

see also under By SMSA or MSA in the "Index by Categories"

Joint Center for Urban Mobility Research

"Financing Urban Transportation Improvements, Report 3: A Guide to Alternative Financing Mechanisms for Urban Highways", 7556–7.3

Joint Chiefs of Staff

Military weapons and troop strength of US and NATO compared to USSR and Warsaw Pact, as of Jan 1984, annual rpt, 3564–1

Joint Economic Committee

Economic indicators and components, current data and annual trends, monthly rpt, 23842–1

Economic Report of the President for 1984, economic effects of budget proposals, and trends and projections 1950s-89, annual hearings, 23844–4

Economic Report of the President for 1984, Joint Economic Committee critique and policy recommendations, annual rpt, 23844–2

Employment situation, earnings, hours, and other BLS economic indicators, transcripts of BLS Commissioner's monthly testimony, periodic rpt, 23846–4

Income (taxable) not reported, methodology using Current Population Survey labor force data to estimate share of output and nonreporters, 1950s-81, 23848–178

Metalworking machinery industry computerized automation, by plant characteristics, for 6 industry groups and small plants, 1982 surveys, 23848–179

Natural gas price decontrol effect on prices, Iowa supply/demand, and economic indicators, with US imports from Canada, various periods 1969-95, hearings, 23848–177

Public works capital needs and financing, by project type, level of govt, and selected jurisdiction, 1970s-83 and projected to 2000, hearing, 23848–181

Social pathology measures including crime and death rates, relation to selected economic indicators, various periods 1950-80, 23848–76

Index by Subjects and Names

Soviet Union industrial and agricultural production by selected commodity, and demographic trends and projections by Republic, 1950s-2000, hearings, 23848–180

Telephone operating data, costs, and billings for American Telephone and Telegraph Co local and long distance lines, by State, 1980-82 with trends from 1970, 23848–176

Joint Taxation Committee

Corporate taxes and effective rates on US, foreign, and worldwide income, by major industry group, and share of Fed Govt receipts, 1980-82, 23868–14

Tax expenditures, Fed Govt revenues foregone through income tax deductions and exclusions by type, and effect of Deficit Reduction Act, FY84-89, annual rpt, 21784–10

Joliet, Ill.

Radioactivity levels at former AEC and Manhattan Project research and storage sites, 1978, 3406–1.36

see also under By SMSA or MSA in the "Index by Categories"

Jones, Calvin

"High School and Beyond Course Offerings and Course Enrollments Survey (1982), Data File User's Manual", 4826–2.17

"High School and Beyond Transcripts Survey (1982), Data File User's Manual", 4826–2.16

Jones, Harold B., Jr.

"Recent Shifts in the Location of U.S. Egg Production", 1561–7.403

Joplin, Mo.

Census of Housing, 1980: occupancy and unit characteristics, by race, Hispanic origin, and city, SMSA rpt, 2473–1.197

Census of Population and Housing, 1980: detailed population and housing characteristics, by county, city, and census tract, SMSA rpt, 2551–2.197

see also under By SMSA or MSA in the "Index by Categories"

Jordan

Agricultural and food production indexes, and production of selected commodities, by world region and country, 1974-83, annual rpt, 1524–5

Agricultural situation in Middle East and North Africa, by country and commodity, 1983 and outlook for 1984, annual rpt, 1524–4.3

AID activities and funding by project and function, FY85, and developing countries summary socioeconomic data, 1970s-83, by country, annual rpt, 9914–3

AID economic assistance to developing countries, obligations and disbursements by country, quarterly rpt, 9912–4

AID educational program activities and project impacts in 12 developing countries, 1950s-82, 9916–11.8

AID loan repayment status and terms by program and country, and status of predecessor agency loans, quarterly rpt, 9912–3

Economic, social, and political summary data, by country, 1984, annual factbook, 244–11

Economic trends in income, production, prices, employment, finances, and trade, 1984 annual rpt, 2046–4.85

Index by Subjects and Names

Exports of US, detailed Schedule B commodities by country of destination, 1983, annual rpt, 2424–9

Exports of US, detailed Schedule E commodities by mode of transport and world area and country of destination, 1983, annual rpts, 2424–5

Imports of US, detailed Schedule A commodities by country and world area of origin, and mode of transport, 1983, annual rpts, 2424–2

Imports of US, detailed TSUSA commodities by country of origin, 1983, annual rpt, 2424–4

Loans and grants for economic and military assistance from US and intl agencies, by program and country, FY46-83, annual rpt, 9914–5

Military aid of US, arms sales, and training programs costs and budget requests by program, world region, and country, FY83-85, annual rpt, 7144–13

Military spending, arms trade, and armed forces size, with total govt spending and population, by country, 1972-82, annual rpt, 9824–1

Minerals Yearbook, 1982, Vol 3: foreign country reviews of production, trade, and policies, by commodity, annual rpt, 5604–35

Minerals Yearbook, 1983, Vol 3 preprints: foreign country review of production, trade, and policies, by commodity, annual rpt, 5604–23.91

Population size and growth rates, and latest available benchmark demographic data, by country, 1950-83, biennial rpt, 2324–4

see also under By Foreign Country in the "Index by Categories"

Josling, Timothy E.

"Agricultural Subsidies in Portugal: Their Impact on Farm Income and Consumer Cost in the Context of Accession to the European Community", 1528–171

Josselyn, Michael

"Ecology of San Francisco Bay Tidal Marshes: A Community Profile", 5506–9.10

Journalism

Census of Population, 1980: detailed socioeconomic and demographic characteristics, by age, sex, race, Hispanic origin, occupation, and industry, State rpt series, 2531–4

Census of Population, 1980: labor force, by sex, detailed occupation, and region, with comparison to 1970 census, supplementary rpt, 2535–1.12

Occupational Outlook Handbook, 1984-85 biennial rpt, 6744–1

see also Newspapers

Judd, John P.

"Deregulated Deposit Rates and Monetary Policy", 9393–8.402

"'Great Velocity Decline' of 1982-83: A Comparative Analysis of M1 and M2", 9393–8.410

Judges

Assaults, murders, and other deaths of law enforcement officers, by circumstances, level of govt, agency, victim and offender characteristics, and location, 1983, annual rpt, 6224–3

Census of Population, 1980: detailed socioeconomic and demographic

characteristics, by age, sex, race, Hispanic origin, occupation, and industry, State rpt series, 2531–4

Census of Population, 1980: labor force, by sex, detailed occupation, and region, with comparison to 1970 census, supplementary rpt, 2535–1.12

Criminal case disposition, effect of victim injury and other factors, and law enforcement official and victim attitudes, 1983 survey, 6068–185

Fed Govt administrative law judges by agency and grade, various dates 1947-82, and New Jersey administrative law cases, FY80-84, hearings, 25528–96

Fed Govt civilian pay rates, by branch of govt, employee category, and pay level, as of 1984 with trends from 1789, 21628–54

Federal district and appeals court caseloads, actions, procedure duration, judges, and jurors, by court, 1979-84, annual rpt, 18204–3

Federal district and appeals court recommended judgeships, by circuit, Judicial Conf semiannual proceedings, 1984 annual rpt, 18204–5

Federal district, appeals, and bankruptcy courts, civil and criminal caseloads and activity summary, 1975-June 1984, annual chartbook, 18204–9

Federal district court staff by position, and visiting judges, visits, and visit days, by large district, various dates 1982-84, 18408–25

Federal district courts new judges needed and court bankruptcy caseloads, by circuit and district, various dates 1982-83, hearing, 25528–97

Govt census, 1982: State govt payments to local govts, by program, source of funds, level of govt, and State, with trends from 1902, 2460–3

Magistrate case processing duties assigned in Fed Govt district courts, by type of case, duty, and district, 1983 rpt, 18408–24

Occupational manpower needs and supply by detailed occupation, and educational and training program enrollees and grads by detailed field, 1982 and 1995, biennial rpt, 6744–3

Pension systems of State and local govts finances, membership, beneficiaries, and benefits, by system, 1982-83, annual rpt, 2466–2.4

Telephone conference use in civil and criminal hearings, assessment of lawyers and judges in 2 States and Denver, Colo, 1981, 6068–186

Wiretapping authorizations by offense, costs, persons involved, arrests, trials, and convictions, 1983, annual rpt, 18204–7

see also Judicial ethics

see also Judicial powers

see also Judicial reform

Judgments, civil procedure

Airport security operations to prevent hijacking, screening results, enforcement actions, and hijacking attempts, 1st half 1984, semiannual rpt, 7502–5

Asbestos workers, exposure levels, cancer incidence, and deaths, by industry and occupation, and asbestos regulation enforcement and costs/benefits, various periods 1940-2027, hearing, 21408–72

Judgments, civil procedure

Discrimination against Hispanics and other minorities in employment, Equal Employment Opportunity Commission enforcement activities, personnel, and litigation, 1970s-FY83, 9248–18

DOT programs fraud and abuse, audits and investigations, 1st half FY84, semiannual rpt, 7302–4

Education Dept programs fraud and abuse, audits and investigations, 2nd half FY84, semiannual rpt, 4802–1

EPA programs fraud and abuse, audits and investigations, 2nd half FY84, semiannual rpt, 9182–10

Export Admin Act antiboycott provisions, violations and fines by company, and boycotts by firm type and country, FY83, annual rpt, 2044–22

FBI undercover operations convictions, fines, recoveries, victim compensation, and status of lawsuits against FBI by operation, FY82, GAO rpt, 26119–67

Fed Govt agencies fraud and abuse, Inspectors General investigations and audits by agency, 1st half FY84, semiannual rpt, 102–5

Federal district, appeals, and bankruptcy courts, civil cases terminated by circuit and district, quarterly rpt, 18202–1

HUD programs fraud and abuse, audits and investigations, 2nd half FY84, semiannual rpt, 5002–8

Legal fees awarded private parties in cases against Federal, State, and local govts, by case, selected years 1977-83, 6008–19

Magistrate case processing duties assigned in Fed Govt district courts, by type of case, duty, and district, 1983 rpt, 18408–24

Maritime Commission mgmt and enforcement activities, filings by type and disposition, and civil penalties by shipper, FY83, annual rpt, 9334–1

Motor fuel State tax provisions, motor vehicle registration fees, and disposition of receipts, by State, as of Jan 1984, biennial rpt, 7554–37

NASA programs fraud and abuse, audits and investigations, 2nd half FY84, semiannual rpt, 9502–9

Nuclear Regulatory Commission activities, employment, and finances, and operations of individual power plants by State, FY83, annual rpt, 9634–2

Oil price and allocation regulations enforcement by DOE, and overcharge allegations, settlements, and refunds to States, by company, as of June 1983, hearing, 21368–50

Railroad safety law violations, claims settled FY83, annual rpt, 7604–10

Small Business Admin programs fraud and abuse, audits and investigations, 1st half FY84, semiannual rpt, 9762–5

Tax prosecutions and litigations of IRS, and cases received, amounts in dispute, and disposition, FY83, annual rpt, 8304–3

Telephone conference use in civil and criminal hearings, assessment of lawyers and judges in 2 States and Denver, Colo, 1981, 6068–186

US Attorneys civil and criminal case processing in district, appellate, and State courts, by district, FY83, annual rpt, 6004–2

Judgments, civil procedure

VA programs fraud and abuse, audits and investigations, 2nd half FY84, semiannual rpt, 9922–13

Judicial Branch

see Administrative Office of the U.S. Courts
see Court of Claims
see Court of Customs and Patent Appeals
see Court of International Trade
see Court of Military Appeals
see Federal courts of appeals
see Federal district courts
see Federal Judicial Center
see Supreme Court

Judicial Conference of the U.S.

Proceedings and findings of semiannual meeting, 1984 annual rpt, 18204–5
Proceedings of Mar and Sept 1983 confs, annual rpt, 18204–8

Judicial ethics

Judicial Conf semiannual proceedings and findings, 1984 annual rpt, 18204–5

Judicial powers

Judicial Conf semiannual proceedings and findings, 1984 annual rpt, 18204–5

Judicial reform

Federal district court staff by position, and visiting judges, visits, and visit days, by large district, various dates 1982-84, 18408–25
Judicial Conf semiannual proceedings and findings, 1984 annual rpt, 18204–5

Junction City, Kans.

Wages of office and plant workers, by occupation, 1984 labor market area survey rpt, 6785–3.9

Junior colleges

Condition of Education, detailed data on enrollment, staff, achievement, finances, curricula, and education effects on employment, 1982-83, annual rpt, 4824–1.2
Digest of Education Statistics, detailed data on students, staff, finances, and facilities, 1982 and selected trends, annual rpt, 4824–2
Enrollment in higher education, by student characteristics, instn type, State, and for 150 instns, fall 1982, annual rpt, 4844–2
Govt census, 1982: State govt payments to local govts, by program, source of funds, level of govt, and State, with trends from 1902, 2460–3
High school class of 1980: use of student aid and earnings to pay higher education costs, by instn type and family income, 1980-82, 4848–15
Higher education instns, by type, location, and other characteristics, 1983/84 annual listing, 4844–3
Higher education instns, type, location, enrollment, and student charges, by State and congressional district, 1983/84, biennial listing, 4844–11
Kentucky Higher Education Student Loan Corp student loans, loan purchases and defaults by instn, and revenue bonds status, various dates 1979-84, hearing, 21348–92
Occupational manpower needs and supply by detailed occupation, and educational and training program enrollees and grads by detailed field, 1982 and 1995, biennial rpt, 6744–3
R&D and science-related Fed Govt funding to higher education and nonprofit instns, by field, instn, agency, and State, FY82, annual rpt, 9627–17

Index by Subjects and Names

Science and engineering employment in higher education instns, by sex, field of science, and instn type, 1972-83, biennial rpt, 9627–24.2
Student aid Federal programs funding and participation, by instn type and control, State, and outlying area, with student loan defaults and collections, FY82, annual rpt, 4804–28
Student aid Pell grants and recipients, by educational costs, family income, instnl type and control, and State, 1981/82, annual rpt, 4804–1
Teachers salaries in schools and colleges by State, 1982/83, and school employees health insurance plans in 7 cities, as of 1980, hearing, 21788–136
Teaching degrees conferred by specialty and State, required credit hours, and instn officials attitudes, by instn type, 1970s-83, hearings, 21348–89
Virginia higher education new enrollment, and students needed to meet desegregation goals, by race and instn, selected years 1978-85, hearings, 21348–91

Juries

Crime and criminal justice data, including justice expenditures and employment by level of govt, 1970s-82 with some trends from 1875, 6068–174
Federal district and appeals court caseloads, actions, procedure duration, judges, and jurors, by court, 1979-84, annual rpt, 18204–3
Federal district, appeals, and bankruptcy courts, civil and criminal caseloads and activity summary, 1975-June 1984, annual chartbook, 18204–9
Federal district court grand and petit juror use and costs, trials, and trial days, by court, years ended June 1980-84, annual rpt, 18204–4
Federal district courts grand and petit juror use, by circuit and district, quarterly rpt, annual tables, 18202–1
Judicial Conf semiannual proceedings and findings, 1984 annual rpt, 18204–5

Jurisdiction

see Administration of justice
see Administrative law and procedure
see Courts
see Law

Justice Department

see Department of Justice

Jute

see Fibers

Juvenile courts

Case filings in State trial courts by case type, and appellate court filings and dispositions by court type, by State, 1978-83, periodic rpt, 6062–2.409
Crime and criminal justice data, including justice expenditures and employment by level of govt, 1970s-82 with some trends from 1875, 6068–174

Juvenile delinquency

Arrests and arrest rates by offense, offender characteristics, and State, and juvenile arrests by disposition, by population size, 1970s-83, annual rpt, 6224–2.2
Arrests of juvenile status offenders, and other police dept operations, by city population size, 1982, 6066–21.1

Budget of US, CBO analysis of revenue and spending alternatives and projections of economic indicators, FY85-89, annual rpt, 26304–3.3
Convictions, prison sentences, and average sentence lengths, by offense, offender class, and selected State, various periods 1971-84, 6066–19.10
Correction of serious, violent, and chronic juvenile delinquents, Fed Govt program activities, 1975-80, narrative rpt, 6068–179
Court cases, dispositions, convictions, and sentences of Federal criminal defendants, by offense and district, as of June 1983 with trends from 1945, annual rpt, 18204–1
Crime and criminal justice data, including justice expenditures and employment by level of govt, 1970s-82 with some trends from 1875, 6068–174
Education Dept programs funding, operations, and effectiveness, FY83, annual rpt, 4804–5
Education grants of Fed Govt, State allocations by program, type of recipient agency, and State, FY83, annual rpt, 4804–8
Fed Govt juvenile delinquency prevention programs funding, by Federal agency and under block grants, FY82, annual rpt, 6064–11
Fed Govt public welfare programs and tax expenditures benefitting children and youth, participation and funding for 71 programs, FY81-83, 21968–30
Govt census, 1982: State govt payments to local govts, by program, source of funds, level of govt, and State, with trends from 1902, 2460–3
Jail capacities, conditions, expenditures, and services, and socioeconomic and other characteristics of inmates, various dates 1976-82, 10048–59
Natl Inst for Juvenile Justice and Delinquency Prevention programs and research project funding, FY81-82, annual rpt, 6064–19
Runaway and other homeless youth programs, funding by source, activities, and participant characteristics, FY82, annual rpt, 4604–3
Social services of State govts for youth, coordinating agencies activities, admin, membership, and funding sources, survey, 1984 rpt, 6068–182
Statistical Abstract of US, social, political, and economic data, 1950s-83 and trends, annual rpt, 2324–1.1
Youth gang criminal activity control, police assessments, staff, and programs in 27 cities, with juvenile arrests nationwide for Crime Index offenses, 1980-81, 6068–175
see also Juvenile courts

Juvenile Justice and Delinquency Prevention Act

Correction of serious, violent, and chronic juvenile delinquents, Fed Govt program activities, 1975-80, narrative rpt, 6068–179

Index by Subjects and Names

Kansas City, Kans.

Kabat, Hugh F.
"Nigerians' Use of Native and Western Medicine for the Same Illness", 4102–1.417

Kahley, William J.
"Louisiana: Hopes Ride on World Trade, Energy and World's Fair", 9371–1.407
"Robot Corps in Southeastern Industry", 9371–1.423
"Southeast's Occupational Employment Outlook", 9371–1.430

Kahn, Arthur L.
"Program and Demographic Characteristics of Supplemental Security Income Beneficiaries, Dec. 1982", 4744–16

Kahn, George A.
"International Differences in Wage Behavior: Real, Nominal, or Exaggerated?", 9381–10.34
"Nominal and Real Wage Stickiness in Six Large OECD Countries", 9381–10.33

Kaiser, H. Fred
"Projections of Future Forest Recreation Use", 1208–195

Kaiser, Wilson
"Agricultural Finance Statistics, 1960-83", 1544–2

Kakalik, James S.
"Costs of Asbestos Litigation", 21348–85

Kalamazoo, Mich.
Census of Housing, 1980: occupancy and unit characteristics, by race, Hispanic origin, and city, SMSA rpt, 2473–1.198
Census of Population and Housing, 1980: detailed population and housing characteristics, by county, city, and census tract, SMSA rpt, 2551–2.198
see also under By SMSA or MSA in the "Index by Categories"

Kaman Tempo
"Operation CROSSROADS, 1946", 3906–1.42
"Operation SANDSTONE, 1948", 3906–1.41

Kamerman, Sheila B.
"Child-Care Services: A National Picture", 6746–1.253

Kampuchea
Agricultural situation in Southeast Asia, by country and commodity, 1983 and outlook for 1984, annual rpt, 1524–4.5
Background Notes, summary social, political, and economic data, 1984 rpt, 7006–2.33
Economic, social, and political summary data, by country, 1984, annual factbook, 244–11
Exports of US, detailed Schedule B commodities by country of destination, 1983, annual rpt, 2424–9
Exports of US, detailed Schedule E commodities by mode of transport and world area and country of destination, 1983, annual rpts, 2424–5
Imports of US, detailed Schedule A commodities by country and world area of origin, and mode of transport, 1983, annual rpts, 2424–2
Imports of US, detailed TSUSA commodities by country of origin, 1983, annual rpt, 2424–4
Loans and grants for economic and military assistance from US and intl agencies, by program and country, FY46-83, annual rpt, 9914–5

Military spending, arms trade, and armed forces size, with total govt spending and population, by country, 1972-82, annual rpt, 9824–1
Minerals Yearbook, 1982, Vol 3: foreign country reviews of production, trade, and policies, by commodity, annual rpt, 5604–35
Minerals Yearbook, 1982, Vol 3 preprints: foreign country review of production, trade, and policies, by commodity, annual rpt, 5604–17.87
Population size and growth rates, and latest available benchmark demographic data, by country, 1950-83, biennial rpt, 2324–4
Refugee Indochinese population, arrivals, and departures, by country of origin and resettlement, camp, and ethnicity, monthly rpt, 7002–4
Refugee migration, settlement status, and assistance, by world area and country of origin and asylum, as of May 1984, annual rpt, 7004–15
Refugee resettlement program activities and funding, arrivals and population by country of origin and State, and employment and other characteristics, FY83, annual rpt, 4704–8
see also under By Foreign Country in the "Index by Categories"

Kandel, Denise
"Substance Abuse by Adolescents in Israel and France: A Cross-Cultural Perspective", 4102–1.430

Kanhouwa, Suraj P.
"Historical Financial Analysis of the Investor-Owned Electric Utility Industry", 3168–87

Kankakee, Ill.
Census of Housing, 1980: occupancy and unit characteristics, by race, Hispanic origin, and city, SMSA rpt, 2473–1.199
Census of Population and Housing, 1980: detailed population and housing characteristics, by county, city, and census tract, SMSA rpt, 2551–2.199
see also under By SMSA or MSA in the "Index by Categories"

Kansas
Agricultural cooperatives, membership, activities, and finances, by commodity and selected State, 1900-80 with trends from 1863, 1128–30
Agriculture census, 1982: farms, farmland, production and costs, and operator characteristics, preliminary State summary and county rpts, 2330–1.20
Agriculture census, 1982: farms, farmland, production, finances, and operator characteristics, by county, final State rpt, 2331–1.16
Bank deposits in commercial and mutual savings banks and in US branches of foreign banks, by account type, instn, State, SMSA, and county, June 1983, annual rpt, 9295–3.14
Census of Housing, 1980: occupancy and unit characteristics of SMSAs and central cities, by race, Hispanic origin, and city, State rpt, 2473–1.18
Census of Population and Housing, 1980: detailed population and housing characteristics, by county, city, and census tract, State rpt, 2551–2.18

Census of Population, 1980: detailed socioeconomic and demographic characteristics, by age, sex, race, Hispanic origin, and industry, State rpt, 2531–4.18
County Business Patterns: establishments, employees, and payrolls, by SIC 4-digit industry and county, 1982, annual State rpt, 2326–6.18
Employment, earnings, and hours, by selected SIC 1- to 4-digit industry, State, and for 278 major labor areas, 1939-83, annual rpt, 6744–5.1, 6744–5.3
Environmental quality, pollutant discharge by type and source, and EPA protection activities and funding, 1970s-83, biennial regional rpt, 9184–15.7
Exports of manufactured and agricultural commodities, manufacturing production, and export-related employment, 1960s-82, State rpt, 2046–3.16
Hay prices in 10 market areas, for baled alfalfa and prairie hay, weekly rpt, 1313–5
HHS aid to each State and local govt or private instn, amount obligated, funding agency, and program, FY83, annual listing, 4004–3.7
Income (personal) per capita and by source, and earnings by industry div, by State, MSA, and county, 1977-82, annual regional rpt, 2704–2.5
Manufacturing census, 1982: financial and operating data, by SIC 2- to 4-digit industry, State, SMSA, and county, preliminary census div rpt, 2491–3.4
Mineral Industry Surveys, State review of production, 1983, advance annual rpt, 5614–6.16
Minerals Yearbook, 1982, Vol 2 preprints: State review of production and sales by commodity, and business activity, annual rpt, 5604–16.17
Minerals Yearbook, 1982, Vol 2: State reviews of production, sales, and firms, by commodity, and business activity, annual rpt, 5604–34
Population size and components of change, by MSA and county, 1980-82, annual State Current Population Rpt, 2546–4.16
Population size, Apr 1980 and July 1982, and per capita income, 1979 and 1981, by county and city, State Current Population Rpt, 2546–11.16
Retail trade census, 1982: employment, establishments, sales, and payroll, by SIC 2- to 4-digit kind of business, SMSA, county, and city, State rpt, 2397–1.17
Savings and loan assns, FHLB 10th District insured members finances and operations by SMSA, monthly rpt, 9302–22
see also Fort Riley, Kans.
see also Junction City, Kans.
see also Kansas City, Kans.
see also Lawrence, Kans.
see also Salina, Kans.
see also Topeka, Kans.
see also Wichita, Kans.
see also under By State in the "Index by Categories"

Kansas City, Kans.
Auto dealer repair workers, wages, and benefits, by occupation, size of establishment, and for 24 labor market areas, Nov 1982 survey, 6787–6.202

Kansas City, Kans.

Census of Housing, 1980: occupancy and unit characteristics, by race, Hispanic origin, and city, SMSA rpt, 2473–1.200

Census of Population and Housing, 1980: detailed population and housing characteristics, by county, city, and census tract, SMSA rpt, 2551–2.200

CPI by component for US city average, and by region, population size, and for 28 SMSAs, monthly press release, 6762–1

CPI by detailed component, for US city average, 28 SMSAs, and 4 regions by population size, monthly rpt, 6762–2

Employment, earnings, and CPI changes, with comparisons to total US, 1983, annual rpt, 6974–1

Hospital worker wages by sex and occupation, and benefits, for 22 MSAs, Oct 1981 survey, 6787–6.201

Housing and financial characteristics, and unit and neighborhood quality, for 15 SMSAs, 1978, annual survey special supplement, 2485–8

Repair technicians and apprentices wages and benefits, for 5 types of electrical repair shops in 19 SMSAs, Nov 1981 survey, 6787–6.197

Wages of office and plant workers, by occupation, 1984 SMSA survey rpt, 6785–11.10

see also under By City and By SMSA or MSA in the "Index by Categories"

Kansas City, Mo.

Auto dealer repair workers, wages, and benefits, by occupation, size of establishment, and for 24 labor market areas, Nov 1982 survey, 6787–6.202

Census of Housing, 1980: occupancy and unit characteristics, by race, Hispanic origin, and city, SMSA rpt, 2473–1.200

Census of Population and Housing, 1980: detailed population and housing characteristics, by county, city, and census tract, SMSA rpt, 2551–2.200

CPI by component for US city average, and by region, population size, and for 28 SMSAs, monthly press release, 6762–1

CPI by detailed component, for US city average, 28 SMSAs, and 4 regions by population size, monthly rpt, 6762–2

Employment, earnings, and CPI changes, with comparisons to total US, 1983, annual rpt, 6974–1

Hospital worker wages by sex and occupation, and benefits, for 22 MSAs, Oct 1981 survey, 6787–6.201

Housing and financial characteristics, and unit and neighborhood quality, for 15 SMSAs, 1978, annual survey special supplement, 2485–8

Housing and households detailed characteristics, and unit and neighborhood quality, by inside-outside central cities, 1982 survey, SMSA rpt, 2485–6.37

Public works capital needs and financing, by project type, level of govt, and selected jurisdiction, 1970s-83 and projected to 2000, hearing, 23848–181

Repair technicians and apprentices wages and benefits, for 5 types of electrical repair shops in 19 SMSAs, Nov 1981 survey, 6787–6.197

Wages of office and plant workers, by occupation, 1984 SMSA survey rpt, 6785–11.10

see also under By City and By SMSA or MSA in the "Index by Categories"

Kao, James Y.

"Strategies for Energy Conservation for a Large Office Building", 2218–68

Kapantais, G. Gloria

"Characteristics of Pharmacists, U.S.", 4147–14.28

"Trends in Health Personnel", 4144–11.1

Kaplan, E.

"Assessment of Environmental Problems Associated with Increased Enhanced Oil Recovery in the U.S.: 1980-2000", 3408–29

Kaplan, Sherri

"Curtailing Indirect Federal Subsidies to the U.S. Postal Service", 26306–6.82

Kapplin, Steven D.

"Economic Implications of Alternative Home Financing", 9412–2.406

Kashyap, A. K.

"Estimating Distributed Lag Relationships Using Near-Minimax Procedures", 9366–6.79

Katz, Elliott L.

"Underground Storage of Large Volumes of Crude Oil: The U.S. Strategic Petroleum Reserve Program", 3008–91

Kaufman, George G.

"Role of Traditional Mortgage Lenders in Future Mortgage Lending: Problems and Prospects", 9375–11.4

Kaunitz, Andrew M.

"Maternal Mortality Surveillance, 1974-78", 4202–7.406

Kawecki Associates

"Sulfur Oxides and Public Health: Evidence of Greater Risks", 25328–25

Kebbekus, Barbara B.

"Volatile Organic Compounds in the Ambient Atmosphere of the New Jersey, New York Area", 9198–108

Keeley, Michael C.

"Economics of Firm Size: Implications from Labor-Market Studies", 9393–8.403

Kelley, William B.

"Disabled-Worker Projections for OASDI Cost Estimates, 1984", 4706–1.93

Kelly, Karen

"Natural Gas Overview: Winter 1984-85", 3162–4.411

Kelsey, Shara L.

"Extending Driver Licenses by Mail: A 36-Month Follow-Up", 7762–9.401

Kennedy, John F., Center for the Performing Arts, D.C.

Income and expenses of Kennedy Performing Arts Center by type, and Fed Govt share of expenses, FY79-83, GAO rpt, 26119–60

Kennewick, Wash.

Census of Housing, 1980: occupancy and unit characteristics, by race, Hispanic origin, and city; SMSA rpt, 2473–1.301

Census of Population and Housing, 1980: detailed population and housing characteristics, by county, city, and census tract, SMSA rpt, 2551–2.301

Wages of office and plant workers, by occupation, 1984 labor market area survey rpt, 6785–3.9

see also under By SMSA or MSA in the "Index by Categories"

Index by Subjects and Names

Kenosha, Wis.

Census of Housing, 1980: occupancy and unit characteristics, by race, Hispanic origin, and city, SMSA rpt, 2473–1.201

Census of Population and Housing, 1980: detailed population and housing characteristics, by county, city, and census tract, SMSA rpt, 2551–2.201

see also under By SMSA or MSA in the "Index by Categories"

Kentucky

Agriculture census, 1982: farms, farmland, production and costs, and operator characteristics, preliminary State summary and county rpts, 2330–1.21

Agriculture census, 1982: farms, farmland, production, finances, and operator characteristics, by county, final State rpt, 2331–1.17

Alcohol fuel (ethanol) production in Tennessee Valley, feedstocks, facilities, tax incentives, and related farming data, by State, 1970s-83 and projected to 1992, 9808–69

Bank deposits in commercial and mutual savings banks and in US branches of foreign banks, by account type, instn, State, SMSA, and county, June 1983, annual rpt, 9295–3.6

Biomass Fuels Program of TVA, technologies and processes dev, costs, and resource requirements, 1970s-90s, series, 9806–9

Census of Housing, 1980: occupancy and unit characteristics of SMSAs and central cities, by race, Hispanic origin, and city, State rpt, 2473–1.19

Census of Population and Housing, 1980: detailed population and housing characteristics, by county, city, and census tract, State rpt, 2551–2.19

Census of Population, 1980: detailed socioeconomic and demographic characteristics, by age, sex, race, Hispanic origin, and industry, State rpt, 2531–4.19

Coal (bituminous) mining production and related workers, wages by occupation, and benefits, by size of mine and union status, in 6 States and aggregate for Rocky Mountain States, July 1982 survey, 6787–6.198

Coal employment and economic losses from utility fuel switching to meet emissions standards, with detail for counties in 5 States, 1970s-83 and projected to 1990, 21368–52

Collective bargaining calendar for Southeast US, 1984, annual rpt, 6946–1.68

County Business Patterns: establishments, employees, and payrolls, by SIC 4-digit industry and county, 1982, annual State rpt, 2326–6.19

Employment (nonagricultural) by industry div and SMSA, earnings, and hours, for 8 southeastern States, monthly press release, 6942–7

Employment, earnings, and hours, by selected SIC 1- to 4-digit industry, State, and for 278 major labor areas, 1939-83, annual rpt, 6744–5.1, 6744–5.3

Employment growth in Kentucky 9-county rural area, labor force and establishment characteristics, 1979-80, 1598–194

Employment, prices, earnings, and union membership in 8 southeastern States, Oct 1982-83, annual rpt, 6944–2

Index by Subjects and Names

Environmental quality, pollutant discharge by type and source, and EPA protection activities and funding, 1970s-83, biennial regional rpt, 9184–15.4

Exports of manufactured and agricultural commodities, manufacturing production, and export-related employment, 1960s-82, State rpt, 2046–3.17

HHS aid to each State and local govt or private instn, amount obligated, funding agency, and program, FY83, annual listing, 4004–3.4

Income (personal) per capita and by source, and earnings by industry div, by State, MSA, and county, 1977-82, annual regional rpt, 2704–2.6

Manufacturing census, 1982: financial and operating data, by SIC 2- to 4-digit industry, State, SMSA, and county, preliminary census div rpt, 2491–3.6

Mineral Industry Surveys, State review of production, 1983, advance annual rpt, 5614–6.17

Minerals Yearbook, 1982, Vol 2 preprints: State review of production and sales by commodity, and business activity, annual rpt, 5604–16.18

Minerals Yearbook, 1982, Vol 2: State reviews of production, sales, and firms, by commodity, and business activity, annual rpt, 5604–34

Population, births, deaths, and net migration, by MSA and county, 1980-82, annual State Current Population Rpt, 2546–4.17

Population size, Apr 1980 and July 1982, and per capita income, 1979 and 1981, by county and city, State Current Population Rpt, 2546–11.17

Public works capital needs and financing, by project type, level of govt, and selected jurisdiction, 1970s-83 and projected to 2000, hearing, 23848–181

Retail trade census, 1982: employment, establishments, sales, and payroll, by SIC 2- to 4-digit kind of business, SMSA, county, and city, State rpt, 2397–1.18

Savings and loan assns, FHLB 5th District members financial condition and operations by SMSA, monthly rpt, 9302–8

Student loans, loan purchases and defaults by instn, and revenue bonds status, for Kentucky Higher Education Student Loan Corp, various dates 1979-84, hearing, 21348–92

Textile mill employment and average hours and earnings, for 8 Southeastern States, monthly press release, 6942–1

Transportation census, 1982: trucks, by detailed characteristics, miles traveled, and type of product carried, State rpt, 2573–1.18

Water supply and quality, and effect of coal mining operations, for selected river basins in Eastern and Interior coal provinces, 1983 rpt, 5666–15.22

Water supply and quality in streams and lakes, and groundwater levels in wells, by drainage basin, 1982, annual State rpt, 5666–20.16

Water supply and quality in streams and lakes, and groundwater levels in wells, by drainage basin, 1983, annual State rpt, 5666–10.16

Water supply and quality in 8 southeastern States, with background socioeconomic data, 1960s-2020 with trends from 1930, 9208–119

Wood residue production and use in TVA region, by tree species group and residue type, for 44 counties, 1979, technical paper, 9806–2.36

see also Ashland, Ky.

see also Hopkinsville, Ky.

see also Lexington, Ky.

see also Louisville, Ky.

see also Owensboro, Ky.

see also Paducah, Ky.

see also under By State in the "Index by Categories"

Kentucky Higher Education Student Loan Corp.

Student loans, loan purchases and defaults by instn, and revenue bonds status, for Kentucky Higher Education Student Loan Corp, various dates 1979-84, hearing, 21348–92

Kenya

Agricultural and food production indexes, and production of selected commodities, by world region and country, 1974-83, annual rpt, 1524–5

Agricultural situation in sub-Saharan Africa, by country, 1982-83 and outlook for 1984, annual rpt, 1524–4.10

Agricultural supply/demand, trade, and production, and socioeconomic data, by country, 1950s-77, 1528–179

AID activities and funding by project and function, FY85, and developing countries summary socioeconomic data, 1970s-83, by country, annual rpt, 9914–3

AID economic assistance to developing countries, obligations and disbursements by country, quarterly rpt, 9912–4

AID educational program activities and project impacts in 12 developing countries, 1950s-82, 9916–11.8

AID loan repayment status and terms by program and country, and status of predecessor agency loans, quarterly rpt, 9912–3

Economic conditions and foreign marketing prospects in 46 Sub-Saharan countries, 1983 world region rpt, 2046–5.1

Economic, social, and political summary data, by country, 1984, annual factbook, 244–11

Economic trends in income, production, prices, employment, finances, and trade, 1984 annual rpt, 2046–4.29

Exports and imports of US, by commodity and country, 1972-82, annual world region rpt, 244–13.4

Exports of US, detailed Schedule B commodities by country of destination, 1983, annual rpt, 2424–9

Exports of US, detailed Schedule E commodities by mode of transport and world area and country of destination, 1983, annual rpts, 2424–5

Food supply policies of 21 developing countries, with farm sector data, tariff income, and prices and imports of 5 grains, 1960s-81, 1528–168

Imports of US, detailed Schedule A commodities by country and world area of origin, and mode of transport, 1983, annual rpts, 2424–2

Kiedrowski, Julian

Imports of US, detailed TSUSA commodities by country of origin, 1983, annual rpt, 2424–4

Loans and grants for economic and military assistance from US and intl agencies, by program and country, FY46-83, annual rpt, 9914–5

Military aid of US, arms sales, and training programs costs and budget requests by program, world region, and country, FY83-85, annual rpt, 7144–13

Military spending, arms trade, and armed forces size, with total govt spending and population, by country, 1972-82, annual rpt, 9824–1

Minerals Yearbook, 1982, Vol 3: foreign country reviews of production, trade, and policies, by commodity, annual rpt, 5604–35

Population size and growth rates, and latest available benchmark demographic data, by country, 1950-83, biennial rpt, 2324–4

see also under By Foreign Country in the "Index by Categories"

Keogh plan

see Individual retirement arrangements

Keppel, Kenneth G.

"Social and Clinical Correlates of Postpartum Sterilization in the U.S., 1972 and 1980", 4102–1.419

Keran, Michael W.

"Velocity and Inflation Expectations: 1922-1983", 9393–8.409

Kerr, Richard L.

"USDA 1983 Thrifty Food Plan", 1702–1.402

Keyes, Dale

"Can We Delay a Greenhouse Warming? The Effectiveness and Feasibility of Options To Slow a Build-Up of Carbon Dioxide in the Atmosphere", 9188–88

Kickback

see Corruption and bribery

Kidnapping

Aircraft hijackings, on-board explosions, other crimes against civil aviation, and circumstances, US and worldwide, 1931-83, annual rpt, 7504–31

Central America socioeconomic and political conditions in 6 countries, 1960s-83 with trends and projections 1930-2010, Commission rpt, 028–19.2

El Salvador terrorist acts against property, casualties, kidnappings, and hostages, Oct 1979-June 1983, human rights certification hearing, 21388–41

Executions since 1930, and prisoners under death sentence, by prisoner characteristics, region, and State, 1982, annual rpt, 6065–1

Parental kidnapping over intl and interstate boundaries, characteristics of cases referred to State Dept and FBI by State and country, 1979-83, hearing, 25528–95

Terrorist (intl) incidents, casualties, and attacks on US targets, by attack type and world area, with chronology of events, 1983, annual rpt, 7004–13

see also Hostages

Kidney diseases

see Urogenital diseases

Kiedrowski, Julian

"Underground Natural Gas Storage in the U.S., 1983-84 Heating Year (Apr. 1983-Mar. 1984)", 3162–4.407

Kiesler, Jay

Kiesler, Jay
"Hydrology of Area 13, Eastern Coal Province, Kentucky, Virginia, and West Virginia", 5666–15.22

Kilgore, Catherine C.
"Lead and Zinc Availability, Domestic: A Minerals Availability Program Appraisal", 5606–4.10

Killeen, Tex.
Census of Housing, 1980: occupancy and unit characteristics, by race, Hispanic origin, and city, SMSA rpt, 2473–1.202
Census of Population and Housing, 1980: detailed population and housing characteristics, by county, city, and census tract, SMSA rpt, 2551–2.202
Housing vacancy rates for single and multifamily units and mobile homes, by city and ZIP code, 1984, annual metro area rpt, 9304–19.31
Wages of office and plant workers, by occupation, 1984 labor market area survey rpt, 6785–3.7
see also under By SMSA or MSA in the "Index by Categories"

Kimbell, Charles L.
"Minerals in the World Economy", 5604–35.1

Kimley-Horn and Associates, Inc.
"Financing Urban Transportation Improvements, Report 2: Use of Private Funds for Highway Improvements", 7556–7.2

Kindergarten
see Preschool education

Kingsport, Tenn.
Census of Housing, 1980: occupancy and unit characteristics, by race, Hispanic origin, and city, SMSA rpt, 2473–1.195
Census of Population and Housing, 1980: detailed population and housing characteristics, by county, city, and census tract, SMSA rpt, 2551–2.195
TVA construction project employment, and impacts on nearby area, 1981 survey rpt, 9806–7.1
TVA construction project employment, and impacts on nearby area, 1982 survey rpt, 9806–7.2
see also under By SMSA or MSA in the "Index by Categories"

Kingston, N.Y.
Wages by occupation, and benefits for office and plant workers, 1983 SMSA survey rpt, 6785–12.2

Kirby, Michael P.
"Drug Use and Pretrial Crime in the District of Columbia", 6066–20.7

Kiribati
Economic, social, and political summary data, by country, 1984, annual factbook, 244–11
Export and import statistics country classifications, Census Bur codes and designations, 1984 revisions, 2428–3.3, 2428–3.4
Imports of US, detailed Schedule A commodities by country and world area of origin, and mode of transport, 1983, annual rpts, 2424–2
Minerals Yearbook, 1982, Vol 3 preprints: foreign country review of production, trade, and policies, by commodity, annual rpt, 5604–17.90

Index by Subjects and Names

Minerals Yearbook, 1983, Vol 3 preprints: foreign country review of production, trade, and policies, by commodity, annual rpt, 5604–23.90
Population size and growth rates, and latest available benchmark demographic data, by country, 1950-83, biennial rpt, 2324–4
see also under By Foreign Country in the "Index by Categories"

Kirkpatrick, Rickey C.
"North Carolina: Impressive Growth, Long-Term Questions", 9371–1.410

Kirschner Associates, Inc.
"Evaluation of the Nutrition Services for the Elderly", 4608–16

Kitchen utensils and appliances
see Household appliances and equipment

Klaus, Patsy A.
"Economic Cost of Crime to Victims", 6066–19.6
"Family Violence", 6066–19.5

Klein, Deborah P.
"Occupational Employment Statistics for 1972-82", 6742–2.402
"Trends in Employment and Unemployment in Families", 6746–1.253

Klein, John M.
"Some Chemical Effects of the Mount St. Helens Eruption on Selected Streams in the State of Washington", 5666–14.9

Klein, L. R.
"Deficit and the Fiscal and Monetary Policy Mix", 9373–3.27

Klein, Robert E.
"Personal Income and Educational Attainment of Male War Veterans and Nonveterans, Mar. 1983", 9924–19

Kleinman, Joel
"Variation in Use of Obstetric Technology", 4144–11.1

Klemme, H. Douglas
"Assessment of Undiscovered Conventionally Recoverable Petroleum Resources of the Northwest European Assessment Region", 5666–17.15

Kluender, Richard A.
"Evaluation of Logging Systems Designed To Recover Harvesting Residues for Energy", 9806–2.37

Klusek, C. S.
"Strontium-90 in the U.S. Diet, 1982", 3404–13

Knapp, Deanne E.
"Utilization of Analgesic Drugs in Office-Based Ambulatory Care: National Ambulatory Medical Care Survey, 1980-81", 4146–8.99

Knapp, Dee A.
"Management of New Pain in Office-Based Ambulatory Care: National Ambulatory Medical Care Survey, 1980 and 1981", 4146–8.97

Knight, Herbert A.
"Empirical Yields of Timber and Forest Biomass in the Southeast", 1208–199
"Georgia's Forests", 1206–26.7

Knight, Richard R.
"Yellowstone Grizzly Bear Investigations, Report of the Interagency Study Team, 1982", 5544–4

Knit fabrics
see Textile industry and fabrics

Knobf, M. K.
"Comparison of Nurses' Smoking Habits: The 1975 DHEW Survey and Connecticut Nurses, 1981", 4102–1.403

Knoxville, Tenn.
Census of Housing, 1980: occupancy and unit characteristics, by race, Hispanic origin, and city, SMSA rpt, 2473–1.203
Census of Population and Housing, 1980: detailed population and housing characteristics, by county, city, and census tract, SMSA rpt, 2551–2.203
Wages by occupation, and benefits for office and plant workers, 1983 labor market area survey rpt, 6785–3.2
see also under By City and By SMSA or MSA in the "Index by Categories"

Koch, Donald L.
"Florida: Expecting a Boom", 9371–1.404
"High-Performance Companies in the Southeast: What Can They Teach Us?", 9371–1.414

Koch, Hugo
"Management of New Pain in Office-Based Ambulatory Care: National Ambulatory Medical Care Survey, 1980 and 1981", 4146–8.97
"Utilization of Analgesic Drugs in Office-Based Ambulatory Care: National Ambulatory Medical Care Survey, 1980-81", 4146–8.99

Koelling, Gordon W.
"Average Price of Natural Gas Delivered to Consumers, 1983 (Preliminary Data Report)", 3164–4
"Average Price of Natural Gas Delivered to Consumers, 1983 (Preliminary)", 3162–4.413
"Natural Gas Production and Wellhead Price, 1983 (Preliminary)", 3162–4.410
"Underground Natural Gas Storage in the U.S., 1983-84 Heating Year (Apr. 1983-Mar. 1984)", 3162–4.407

Kokomo, Ind.
Census of Housing, 1980: occupancy and unit characteristics, by race, Hispanic origin, and city, SMSA rpt, 2473–1.204
Census of Population and Housing, 1980: detailed population and housing characteristics, by county, city, and census tract, SMSA rpt, 2551–2.204
see also under By SMSA or MSA in the "Index by Categories"

Kominski, Gerald F.
"Unrecognized Redistributions of Revenue in Diagnosis-Related Group-Based Prospective Payment Systems", 4652–1.428

Konowitz, Paul M.
"Underreporting of Disease and Physicians' Knowledge of Reporting Requirements", 4102–1.411

Koontz, Ann M.
"Pregnancy and Infant Health: Progress Toward the 1990 Objectives", 4102–1.425

Koop, C. Everett
"Breast Feeding—the Community Norm. Report of a Workshop", 4102–1.455

Kopcke, Richard W.
"Inflation and the Choice of 'Monetary' Guidelines", 9373–1.401
"Will Big Deficits Spoil the Recovery?", 9373–3.27

Index by Subjects and Names

Koppel, Herbert

"Sentencing Practices in 13 States", 6066–19.10

"Time Served in Prison", 6066–19.7

Kopstein, Andrea N.

"Health Care Expenditures for Major Diseases", 4144–11.1

"Health Care Expenditures for Major Diseases in 1980", 4652–1.413

Korea, North

Background Notes, summary social, political, and economic data, 1984 rpt, 7006–2.23

Cuba economic conditions, agricultural and industrial production and distribution, trade, and intl economic relations, 1970-82 and trends from 1957, 248–40

Economic conditions in Communist, OECD, and selected other countries, 1960s-83, annual rpt, 244–5

Economic, social, and political summary data, by country, 1984, annual factbook, 244–11

Exports and imports of US with Communist countries, by detailed commodity and country, quarterly rpt with articles, 9882–2

Exports of US, detailed Schedule E commodities by mode of transport and world area and country of destination, 1983, annual rpts, 2424–5

Imports of US, detailed Schedule A commodities by country and world area of origin, and mode of transport, 1983, annual rpts, 2424–2

Military spending, arms trade, and armed forces size, with total govt spending and population, by country, 1972-82, annual rpt, 9824–1

Minerals Yearbook, 1982, Vol 3: foreign country reviews of production, trade, and policies, by commodity, annual rpt, 5604–35

Minerals Yearbook, 1982, Vol 3 preprints: foreign country review of production, trade, and policies, by commodity, annual rpt, 5604–17.87

Population size and growth rates, and latest available benchmark demographic data, by country, 1950-83, biennial rpt, 2324–4

Science and technology dev and transfer between USSR and other members of Council for Mutual Economic Assistance, 1940s-81, 2326–9.7

see also under By Foreign Country in the "Index by Categories"

Korea, South

Agricultural and food production indexes, and production of selected commodities, by world region and country, 1974-83, annual rpt, 1524–5

Agricultural situation in 4 East Asian countries, by commodity, 1983 and outlook for 1984, annual rpt, 1524–4.2

Agricultural supply/demand, trade, and production, and socioeconomic data, by country, 1950s-77, 1528–179

AID and Korea govt agricultural services projects economic impacts, 1950s-83, 9916–1.52

AID educational program activities and project impacts in 12 developing countries, 1950s-82, 9916–11.8

AID loan repayment status and terms by program and country, and status of predecessor agency loans, quarterly rpt, 9912–3

Background Notes, summary social, political, and economic data, 1983 rpt, 7006–2.6

Coal imports from US, energy supply/demand, and economic indicators, for 3 countries, selected years 1960-82 and projected to 2000, 3008–97

Economic conditions in Communist, OECD, and selected other countries, 1960s-83, annual rpt, 244–5

Economic conditions, income, production, prices, employment, and trade, 1984 semiannual country rpt, 2046–4.113

Economic indicators of 12 Pacific Basin countries or areas and US, quarterly rpt, 9393–9

Economic, social, and political summary data, by country, 1984, annual factbook, 244–11

Economic trends in income, production, prices, employment, finances, and trade, 1984 semiannual rpt, 2046–4.30, 2046–4.69

Exports and imports of US, by commodity and country, 1972-82, annual world region rpt, 244–13.5

Exports of US, detailed Schedule B commodities by country of destination, 1983, annual rpt, 2424–9

Exports of US, detailed Schedule E commodities by mode of transport and world area and country of destination, 1983, annual rpts, 2424–5

Food processing and packaging equipment market and trade, and user industry operations and demand, 1984 market research rpt, 2045–11.21

Free zones in developing countries, industry financial and operating data by country, with case studies for 5 countries, 1970s-82, 9918–10

Housing situation and govt policy in Korea, selected years 1975-82, article, 9312–1.404

Housing units completed and home loans and loan value by instn, for Korea, cumulative 1967-75 and 1976-82, article, 9312–1.406

Imports of US, detailed Schedule A commodities by country and world area of origin, and mode of transport, 1983, annual rpts, 2424–2

Imports of US, detailed TSUSA commodities by country of origin, 1983, annual rpt, 2424–4

Industrial process control equipment market and trade, and user industry operations and demand, 1984 country market research rpt, 2045–6.35

Loans and grants for economic and military assistance from US and intl agencies, by program and country, FY46-83, annual rpt, 9914–5

Medical and health care equipment market and trade, and user industry operations and demand, 1984 country market research rpt, 2045–2.51

Military aid of US, arms sales, and training programs costs and budget requests by program, world region, and country, FY83-85, annual rpt, 7144–13

Military spending, arms trade, and armed forces size, with total govt spending and population, by country, 1972-82, annual rpt, 9824–1

Kowalewski, K.J.

Minerals Yearbook, 1982, Vol 3: foreign country reviews of production, trade, and policies, by commodity, annual rpt, 5604–35

Minerals Yearbook, 1982, Vol 3 preprints: foreign country review of production, trade, and policies, by commodity, annual rpt, 5604–17.40

Nuclear power generation in US and 18 non-Communist countries, monthly rpt, 3162–24.10

Nuclear power plant construction and operation status, and capacity, by plant, region, State, and selected country, 1983 and projected to 2020, annual rpt, 3164–57

Oil field equipment from 5 countries, injury to US industry from foreign subsidized imports and less than fair value sales, investigation with background financial and operating data, 1984 rpt, 9886–19.11

Pianos from South Korea at less than fair value, imports injury to US industry, investigation with background financial and operating data, 1984 rpt, 9886–14.124

Population size and growth rates, and latest available benchmark demographic data, by country, 1950-83, biennial rpt, 2324–4

Steel imports of US from EC and other countries, and US industry operating data, for 15 products limited under arrangement with EC, monthly rpt, 9882–10

Steel pipes and tubes from South Korea and Taiwan at less than fair value, imports injury to US industry, investigation with background financial and operating data, 1984 rpt, 9886–14.104

Steel plate (hot-rolled) from South Korea at less than fair value, imports injury to US industry, investigation with background financial and operating data, 1983 rpt, 9886–14.91

Steel products from South Korea at less than fair value, imports injury to US industry, investigation with background financial and operating data, 1984 rpt, 9886–14.111

Steel sheet and structural shapes from South Korea, imports injury to US industry from foreign subsidized products, investigation with background financial and operating data, 1984 rpt, 9886–15.51

Tire imports from South Korea at less than fair value, injury to US industry, investigation with background financial and operating data, 1984 rpt, 9886–14.117

TVs (color) from South Korea and Taiwan at less than fair value, imports injury to US industry, investigation with background financial and operating data, 1984 rpt, 9886–14.101

see also under By Foreign Country in the "Index by Categories"

Korean War

see War

Kovar, Mary G.

"Expenditures for the Medical Care of Elderly People Living in the Community Throughout 1980", 4146–11.4

Kowalewski, K.J.

"Outlook for Inflation", 9377–1.404

Kozak, Lola J.

Kozak, Lola J.
"Hospital Use by Children in the U.S. and Canada", 4147–5.1

Kozielec, John
"Taxpayers Age 65 or Over, 1977-81", 8302–2.412

Kozlow, Ralph
"Capital Expenditures by Majority-Owned Foreign Affiliates of U.S. Companies, 1984", 2702–1.410
"Capital Expenditures by Majority-Owned Foreign Affiliates of U.S. Companies, 1984 and 1985", 2702–1.437

Kraenzle, Charles A.
"Nation's Commercial Farmers Find Supply, Marketing Co-ops Useful", 1122–1.401

Krause, Kenneth R.
"Corporate Farming: Importance, Incentives, and State Restrictions", 1548–233

Krause, Richard M.
"Koch's Postulates and the Search for the AIDS Agent", 4102–1.431

Kristiansen, Connie M.
"Social Desirability of Preventive Health Behavior", 4102–1.438

Krueger, Dean E.
"Visual Acuity Impairment Survey Pilot Study", 4478–147

Krugman, Paul
"International Aspects of U.S. Monetary and Fiscal Policy", 9373–3.27

Kubarych, Roger M.
"Financing the U.S. Current Account Deficit", 9385–1.409

Kuchler, Fred
"Corn and Soybean Production Losses from Potential Pesticide Regulatory Actions", 1561–16.407

Kuczynski, Pedro-Pablo
"International Emergency Lending Facilities—Are They Adequate?", 9373–3.28

Kuhn, Gerhard
"Hydrology of Area 54, Northern Great Plains, and Rocky Mountain Coal Provinces, Colorado, and Wyoming", 5666–19.4

Kunkel, Lawrence R.
"Effect of Illinois and Wisconsin Usury Laws on the Supply and Quality of Mortgage Credit Offered", 9312–7.404

Kunze, Kent
"New BLS Survey Measures the Ratio of Hours Worked to Hours Paid", 6722–1.434

Kuprianov, Anatoli
"Economic Outlook for Fifth District States in 1984: Forecasts from Vector Autoregression Models", 9389–1.403

Kutner, Mark A.
"Federal Education Policies and Programs: Intergovernmental Issues in Their Design, Operation, and Effects", 4808–9.3

Kuwait
Agricultural situation in Middle East and North Africa, by country and commodity, 1983 and outlook for 1984, annual rpt, 1524–4.3
Computers and computer equipment market and trade, and user industry operations and demand, 1984 country market research rpt, 2045–1.48
Economic, social, and political summary data, by country, 1984, annual factbook, 244–11

Economic trends in income, production, prices, employment, finances, and trade, 1984 annual rpt, 2046–4.61
Exports and imports of US, by commodity and country, 1972-82, annual world region rpt, 244–13.1
Exports of US, detailed Schedule B commodities by country of destination, 1983, annual rpt, 2424–9
Exports of US, detailed Schedule E commodities by mode of transport and world area and country of destination, 1983, annual rpts, 2424–5
Imports of US, detailed Schedule A commodities by country and world area of origin, and mode of transport, 1983, annual rpts, 2424–2
Imports of US, detailed TSUSA commodities by country of origin, 1983, annual rpt, 2424–4
Loans and grants for economic and military assistance from US and intl agencies, by program and country, FY46-83, annual rpt, 9914–5
Military aid of US, arms sales, and training programs costs and budget requests by program, world region, and country, FY83-85, annual rpt, 7144–13
Military spending, arms trade, and armed forces size, with total govt spending and population, by country, 1972-82, annual rpt, 9824–1
Minerals Yearbook, 1982, Vol 3: foreign country reviews of production, trade, and policies, by commodity, annual rpt, 5604–35
Minerals Yearbook, 1983, Vol 3 preprints: foreign country review of production, trade, and policies, by commodity, annual rpt, 5604–23.42
Oil production by major exporting countries, monthly rpt, 3162–24.10
Population size and growth rates, and latest available benchmark demographic data, by country, 1950-83, biennial rpt, 2324–4
Telecommunication equipment market and trade, and user industry operations and demand, 1982 country market research rpt, 2045–12.32
see also under By Foreign Country in the "Index by Categories"

Kuypers-Denlinger, Corrinne
"Society's Coming New Age", 1004–16.1

Kyanite
see Nonmetallic minerals and mines

La Crosse, Wis.
Census of Housing, 1980: occupancy and unit characteristics, by race, Hispanic origin, and city, SMSA rpt, 2473–1.205
Census of Population and Housing, 1980: detailed population and housing characteristics, by county, city, and census tract, SMSA rpt, 2551–2.205
Housing vacancy rates for single and multifamily units and mobile homes, by county, city, and ZIP code, 1984, annual metro area rpt, 9304–18.7
see also under By SMSA or MSA in the "Index by Categories"

LaBau, Vernon J.
"Timber Resource Statistics for the Petersburg/Wrangell Inventory Unit, Alaska, 1972", 1206–9.11

Index by Subjects and Names

"Timber Resource Statistics for the Prince of Wales Inventory Unit, Alaska, 1973", 1206–9.12
"Timber Resource Statistics for the Sitka Inventory Unit, Alaska, 1971", 1206–9.10
"Timber Resource Statistics for the Yakutat Inventory Unit, Alaska, 1975", 1206–9.15

Labeling
Alcohol label activity of Fed Govt, certificates for distilled spirits, wines, and malt beverages approved, exempted, and disapproved, FY82, last issue of annual rpt, 8484–1.6
Imports detained by FDA, by product, shipper or manufacturer, country, and detention reasons, monthly listing, 4062–2
Meat and poultry inspection activities and personnel of Federal, State, and foreign govts, FY83, annual rpt, 1374–1
see also Trademarks

LaBelle, Robert P.
"Oilspill Risk Analysis for the Gulf of Alaska/Cook Inlet Lease Offering (Oct. 1984)", 5736–2.7

Labor
see Agricultural labor
see Employment and unemployment, general
see Employment and unemployment, local and regional
see Employment and unemployment, specific industries
see Foreign labor conditions
see Labor cost indexes
see Labor law
see Labor-management relations, general
see Labor-management relations, local and regional
see Labor mobility
see Labor productivity
see Labor turnover
see Labor unions
see Manpower

Labor cost indexes
Business Conditions Digest, cyclical indicators, by economic process, monthly rpt, 2702–3.3, 2702–3.6
Business Conditions Digest, historical supplement on economic, business, and financial conditions and cyclical fluctuations, with methodology, 1947-82, 2708–31
Copper production, production costs, prices, wages, and productivity, for US and 3 countries, 1970s-83 and projected to 1989, 21368–55
Electric power plant (nuclear and coal-fired) construction itemized cost estimates, and investment per kilowatt for 20 cities, 1980s-95, 9638–52
Employment and earnings, detailed data, monthly rpt, 6742–2.6
Employment and labor force statistics by major industry group and demographic characteristics, *Survey of Current Business,* monthly rpt, 2702–1.5
Employment Cost Index and percent change, by industry, occupational group, region, and union status, 1975-83, annual rpt, 6724–1.6
Employment Cost Index and percent change by occupational group, industry div, region, and metro-nonmetro area, quarterly press release, 6782–5

Index by Subjects and Names

Employment Cost Index changes for nonfarm workers, by occupation, industry div, region, and bargaining status, monthly rpt, 6782–1

Employment Cost Index wage and salary component changes by occupational group, industry div, and collective bargaining status, and CPI changes, selected periods Sept 1975-Dec 1983, article, 6722–1.430

Employment, earnings, and hours, monthly press release, 6742–5

Foreign and US indexes of consumer, producer, and major commodity prices, nonfarm wages, and currency value, US and 4 countries, bimonthly rpt, 2042–11

Foreign economic indicators for 7 OECD countries and US, quarterly rpt, 2042–10

Foreign exchange rates for currencies of US and 2 countries with yen, and measures of manufacturing competitiveness, 1983 with 1974-80 and 1979-80 averages, article, 9385–1.404

Foreign manufacturing labor productivity and unit cost indexes for US and 11 OECD countries, 1960-82, annual article, 6722–1.405

Foreign manufacturing productivity and unit labor cost indexes for US and 11 countries, 1950-82 and preliminary 1983, annual rpt, 6864–1

Import-sensitive industries employment and wage adjustments, for 25 SIC 3-digit industries, selected years 1960-82, article, 6722–1.439

Labor force characteristics and economic indicators, selected years 1880-1995, chartbook, 6728–30

Monthly labor Review, output, compensation, labor and nonlabor unit costs, and indexes, 6722–1.6, 6722–1.7

New England States employment, wages, and price conditions by State and selected SMSA, 1983, annual rpt, 6916–7.1

Output and unit labor costs of Fed Govt FY71-81, and of private sectors 1947-82, annual rpt, 6724–1.5

Port dredging hourly labor costs by component and occupation, and Army Corps of Engineers contract awards by region and company, 1970s-83, hearings, 21728–53

Private, nonfarm business, and manufacturing sectors, labor productivity and costs, preliminary data, quarterly rpt, 6822–1

Private, nonfarm business, and manufacturing sectors, labor productivity and costs, revised data, quarterly rpt, 6822–2

Productivity of labor and capital, costs, and prices, by selected industry, and compared to 6 OECD countries, selected years 1947-82, 17898–1

Recession and recovery effect on labor cost and price indexes, changes by index component, various periods 1949-82, article, 6722–1.464

Recession and recovery effect on labor cost and productivity indexes, changes by index component, various periods 1948-82, article, 6722–1.470

Labor costs

see Labor cost indexes

see Labor productivity

see Payroll

Labor Department

see Department of Labor

Labor force

see Employment and unemployment, general

see Employment and unemployment, local and regional

see Employment and unemployment, specific industries

see Foreign labor conditions

Labor law

- Asbestos-related occupational disease compensation paid by defendant and plaintiff litigation costs, with comparisons to other tort suits, selected years 1968-82, hearings, 21348–85
- Black lung benefit claims and benefits by State, and trust fund receipts by source and disbursements, 1982, annual rpt, 6504–3
- Collective bargaining devs, negotiated wage increases and concessions, legislation, and court decisions, 1983, annual narrative article, 6722–1.403
- Disability (short-term) earnings lost, insurance benefits, sick leave, and work days lost by sex, by type of worker, 1948-81, article, 4742–1.417
- Employee Retirement Income Security Act admin and enforcement, 1982, annual rpt, 6464–4
- Fed Govt programs and mgmt cost control proposals, 3-year savings by function and agency, and financial and operating data, 1960s-81, 16908–1.3, 16908–1.33
- Fed Labor Relations Authority and Fed Service Impasses Panel activities, and cases by region, union, and agency, FY79-82, annual rpt, 13364–1
- Immigrant labor law effects on farm work force, with farm labor, farms, and labor costs, by labor and farm type and State, 1978, 1598–192
- Industrial relations devs and collective bargaining agreements expiring during month, Monthly Labor Review, 6722–1
- Occupational Safety and Health Admin enforcement activities and funding, State programs and staff, and illnesses and injuries by industry div, 1980-82 with FY83-84 estimates, annual rpt, 6604–2
- Plant closing provisions of Fed Govt and State law, corporate policies, collective bargaining agreements, and job loss in California and total US, 1982, article, 9377–1.401
- State labor legislation enacted by 48 States, DC, and Guam, 1983, annual summary article, 6722–1.406
- Unemployment insurance laws, changes in coverage, benefits, and tax rates, for 43 States and DC, 1983, annual article, 6722–1.414
- Unemployment insurance laws, comparisons of State provisions, as of Sept 1984, semiannual revision, 6402–2
- Women, laws affecting employment and working conditions, 1983 rpt, 6568–29
- Workers compensation law provisions of States and Fed Govt, by jurisdiction, as of July 1984, semiannual rpt, 6502–1

Labor-management relations, general

- Workers compensation laws, changes in coverage, benefits, and premium rates, for 49 States, DC, and Virgin Islands, 1983, annual article, 6722–1.415
- *see also* Minimum wage

Labor-management relations, general

- Agreement coverage of plant and office workers, by industry div and SMSA, 1981-83, area wage survey annual rpt, 6785–1.3
- Agreements expiring and wage increases, scheduled and under cost-of-living escalator provisions, by SIC 2-digit industry and selected firm and union, 1984, annual article, 6722–1.402
- Agreements expiring during month, and industrial relations devs, current statistics and articles, Monthly Labor Review, 6722–1
- Agreements expiring during year, covered workers by SIC 2-digit industry, firm, and union, with summary of key provisions, 1984, annual rpt, 6784–9
- American Telephone and Telegraph Co cooperative labor-mgmt program for policy dev, 1984 narrative article, 6722–1.419
- Bombing (explosive and incendiary) and arson incidents by target, State, and circumstances, and explosives theft and recovery, 1982-83, annual rpt, 8484–4
- Census of Population, 1980: detailed socioeconomic and demographic characteristics, by age, sex, race, Hispanic origin, occupation, and industry, State rpt series, 2531–4
- Collective bargaining wage and benefit rate changes in labor-mgmt agreements, quarterly press release, 6782–2
- Cooperative labor-mgmt experiments in US with comparisons to other countries, 1800s-1940s, narrative article, 6722–1.433
- Employee Retirement Income Security Act admin and enforcement, 1982, annual rpt, 6464–4
- Foreign labor conditions in selected OECD countries, 1950-82, annual rpt, 6724–1.10
- Labor legislation enacted by 48 States, DC, and Guam, 1983, annual summary article, 6722–1.406
- Misconduct and theft by employees in retail, hospital, and manufacturing establishments, by type and frequency of violation, 1978-80, 6068–178
- *Occupational Outlook Handbook,* 1984-85 biennial rpt, 6744–1
- Plant closing provisions of Fed Govt and State law, corporate policies, collective bargaining agreements, and job loss in California and total US, 1982, article, 9377–1.401
- Representation elections conducted by NLRB, results, monthly rpt, 9582–2
- Wage adjustments in collective bargaining, workers covered, and factors affecting negotiated settlements, selected years 1968-84, article, 9362–1.410
- Wage and benefit changes from collective bargaining or employer decisions, by industry group, monthly rpt, 6782–1
- Wage-benefit negotiated decisions, annual rates of change, *Business Conditions Digest,* monthly rpt, 2702–3.6

Labor-management relations, general

Wage-benefit negotiated decisions, average rates of change, *Business Conditions Digest,* historical supplement and methodology, 1947-82, 2708–31

Wage changes in major collective bargaining situations, 1954-82, annual rpt, 6724–1.6

Wage increases and concessions, legislation, court decisions, and other collective bargaining devs, 1983, annual narrative article, 6722–1.403

Worker participation in mgmt decisions, experience in US and 2 countries, 1983 narrative article, 6722–1.457

see also Absenteeism

see also Employee benefit plans

see also Escalator clauses

see also Labor-management relations in government

see also Labor-management relations, local and regional

see also Labor unions

see also Pensions

see also Work stoppages

Labor-management relations in government

Collective bargaining multi-unit agreements of Federal employees, by labor union and agency, as of July 1983, annual listing, 9847–4

Fed Govt employee collective bargaining agreements, unions involved, and employees covered, by agency for agreements expiring July 1984-June 1985, annual listing, 9847–1

Fed Govt employees labor contract negotiations, costs, time spent, and negotiator attitudes, 1983 survey, GAO rpt, 26119–62

Fed Govt programs and mgmt cost control proposals, 3-year savings by function and agency, and financial and operating data, 1960s-81, 16908–1

Fed Labor Relations Authority and Fed Service Impasses Panel activities, and cases by region, union, and agency, FY79-82, annual rpt, 13364–1

Foreign Service positions and union membership by agency, grievances, and pay rates, FY81-83 with ambassador appointments from 1961, GAO rpt, 26123–64

Labor unions recognized in Fed Govt, agreements and membership by agency and office or installation, Jan 1983, annual listing, 9844–14

Labor unions recognized in Fed Govt, membership by agency and union, as of Jan 1983, annual rpt, 9844–17

Merit Systems Protection Board decisions on appeals of Fed Govt personnel actions, by region, agency, and employee characteristics, FY82, annual rpt, 9494–2

State and local employees collective bargaining wage and compensation changes, periodic article, 6782–1

State and local govt employee wage and benefit changes under collective bargaining, and workers affected, 1979-84, semiannual press release, 6782–6

Wage increases and concessions, legislation, court decisions, and other collective bargaining devs, 1983, annual narrative article, 6722–1.403

Labor-management relations, local and regional

New England States collective bargaining contract terminations and workers covered, by industry and firm, 1984, annual rpt, 6916–7.2

New England States employment, wages, and price conditions by State and selected SMSA, 1983, annual rpt, 6916–7.1

Southeastern region collective bargaining calendar, 1984, annual rpt, 6946–1.68

Southwestern States employment, industrial relations, prices, and economic conditions, regional rpts series, 6966–1

see also under By Census Division, By City, By County, By Region, By SMSA or MSA, and By State in the "Index by Categories"

Labor-Management Services Administration

Cost control proposals for Fed Govt programs and mgmt, 3-year savings by function and agency, and financial and operating data, 1960s-81, 16908–1.3

Employee Retirement Income Security Act admin and enforcement, 1982, annual rpt, 6464–4

Fraud and abuse in Labor Dept programs, audits and investigations, 1st half FY84, semiannual rpt, 6302–2

Labor-Mgmt Reporting and Disclosure Act compliance, enforcement, and reporting, annual rpt, suspended, 6464–2

Labor unions reporting to Labor Dept, parent bodies and locals by State, city, and country, 1983 listing, 6468–17

Pension plans with postretirement adjustments related to employee and employer characteristics, and effect of inflation on benefit purchasing power, 1973-79, 6468–18

Labor mobility

Farm population movement, 1960s-82, annual chartbook, 1504–3

Fed Govt employment and training program funding under Job Training Partnership Act, and required matching funds, for 3 programs by State, 1984/85, press release, 6408–58

Job tenure and occupational mobility of workers, by sociodemographic characteristics and industry div, as of Jan 1983, press release, 6748–76

Job tenure and occupational mobility of workers, by sociodemographic characteristics and occupation, as of Jan 1983, article, 6722–1.460

Scientists, engineers, and technicians needed in defense and nondefense industries, and supply/demand, by field, 1981-87, 9628–71

TVA construction projects employment, and impacts on nearby areas, survey rpt series, 9806–7

see also Labor turnover

see also Migrant workers

see also Migration

Labor productivity

Alcohol use, and health, economic, and social impacts, review of research, 1970s-81, 4488–4

Auto industry finances and operations by manufacturer, foreign competition, and consumer auto expenditures and attitudes toward car buying, selected years 1968-85, annual rpt, 2004–8

Index by Subjects and Names

BLS measures of unemployment, labor productivity, and CPI, effects of undisclosed economic activity, with illustrative data, 1958-79, article, 6722–1.401

Business and financial statistics, historic trends, 1984 annual chartbook, 9364–2.2, 9364–2.4

China cotton and synthetic fiber supply and use, retail clothing sales, and textile mill productivity and equipment, 1978-84, article, 1561–1.405

China economic conditions, agricultural and industrial production, trade, and domestic and foreign investment, 1980-85, 2048–106

Coal miners working daily, mines, and labor productivity, trends and projections, quarterly rpt, 3162–37.4

Coal mines and related operations, injury, employment, worktime, and productivity data, 1982, annual rpt, 6664–4

Coal mining production per man-day, 1949-83, annual rpt, 3164–74.5

Coal production and mines by county, prices, productivity, miners, reserves, and stocks, by mining method and State, 1982-83, annual rpt, 3164–25

Cooling and heating equipment industry productivity trends and technological innovations, 1967-82, article, 6722–1.471

Copper production, production costs, prices, wages, and productivity, for US and 3 countries, 1970s-83 and projected to 1989, 21368–55

Developing countries PL 480 Title I funding and socioeconomic impacts, with case studies for 5 countries, 1950s- 81, 9918–13

Economic and demographic factors used in OASDI program cost estimates, selected years 1913-82 with alternative projections to 2060, 4706–1.90

Economic and financial trends, natl compounded annual rates of change, 1964-83, annual rpt, 9391–9.2

Economic conditions and employment, alternative BLS projections to 1995 with selected trends for 1959-82, 6728–29

Economic growth, with data on labor force, inflation, and productivity, 1953-83 with inflation and unemployment projections to 1988, article, 9373–1.402

Economic indicators and components, current data and annual trends, monthly rpt, 23842–1.2

Economic performance of US, and Reagan Admin 1984 spending, tax, and monetary policy proposals, with data for 1950s-83 and projected to 1988, press release, 8008–107

Economic trends, natl compounded annual rates of change, monthly rpt, 9391–3.2

Food prices (farm-retail), marketing cost components, and industry finances and productivity, selected years 1967-83, annual rpt, 1544–9.2

Foreign and US economic and employment indicators and balance of payments, and US exports by selected commodity, by world area and country, 1970s-83, annual rpt, 2044–26

Foreign economic indicators for 7 OECD countries and US, quarterly rpt, 2042–10

Index by Subjects and Names

Labor turnover

Foreign labor conditions in selected OECD countries, 1950-82, annual rpt, 6724–1.10

Foreign manufacturing labor productivity and unit cost indexes for US and 11 OECD countries, 1960·82, annual article, 6722–1.405

Foreign manufacturing productivity and unit labor cost indexes for US and 11 countries, 1950-82 and preliminary 1983, annual rpt, 6864–1

Hours at work and hours paid ratios and impacts on productivity measures, by firm size and major industry group, with survey methodology, 1981-82, article, 6722–1.434

Industry R&D expenditures by funding source, and projected impact on output, employment, and hours of labor, by selected industry, various periods 1953-90, hearings, 25368–133

Labor force characteristics and economic indicators, selected years 1880-1995, chartbook, 6728–30

Manufacturing plants using bonuses and other employee incentives for exceeding normal production, by incentive type, 1981, article, 6722–1.447

Manufacturing productivity, by selected country, 1960-82, annual rpt, 9624–10.1

Meatpacking and prepared meats industry productivity trends and technological innovations, 1967-82, article, 6722–1.428

Mines (stone) and related operations, injury, employment, and worktime data, 1982, annual rpt, 6664–5

Misconduct and theft by employees in retail, hospital, and manufacturing establishments, by type and frequency of violation, 1978-80, 6068–178

Output and unit labor costs of Fed Govt FY71-81, and of private sectors 1947-82, annual rpt, 6724–1.5

Output, compensation, labor and nonlabor unit costs, and indexes, Monthly Labor Review, 6722–1.6

Output indexes and labor costs, *Business Conditions Digest,* historical supplement and methodology of business indicators, 1947-82, 2708–31

Output indexes and labor costs, *Business Conditions Digest,* monthly rpt, 2702–3.3, 2702–3.6

Output levels and changes, 1947-83, annual rpt, 204–1.2

Output per hour, compensation and unit labor costs, percent change, monthly rpt, 6742–2.6

Private, nonfarm business, and manufacturing sectors, labor productivity and costs, preliminary data, quarterly rpt, 6822–1

Private, nonfarm business, and manufacturing sectors, labor productivity and costs, revised data, quarterly rpt, 6822–2

Productivity growth adjusted for wage and price controls of early 1970s, and regression results, by industry, 1948-81, article, 9381–1.407

Productivity, hours, and employment indexes for selected SIC 3- and 4-digit industries, 1954-82, annual rpt, 6824–1

Productivity indexes for 128 SIC 2- to 4-digit industries, 1977-82, article, 6722–1.408

Productivity of labor and capital, costs, and prices, by selected industry, and compared to 6 OECD countries, selected years 1947-82, 17898–1

Productivity of labor and capital, growth by SIC 1- to 2-digit industry, and measurement methods and bibl, various periods 1948-78 with trends from 1800, 2218–69

Productivity of labor and capital in manufacturing, all nonfarm business, and all private business, indexes and percent change, 1948-83, annual rpt, 6824–2

Productivity of labor, economic growth, and industrial policy dev, selected years 1947-82 with some projections to 1986, 26306–6.69

Productivity related to changes in capital and hours of labor inputs, 1984 technical paper, 9381–10.35

Recession and recovery effect on labor cost and productivity indexes, changes by index component, various periods 1948-82, article, 6722–1.470

Retail clothing business labor productivity, by kind of business, 1967-83, article, 6722–1.463

Shift work, effects of rotating schedules on productivity and health, 1983 bibl, 7506–10.29

Statistical Abstract of US, social, political, and economic data, 1950s-83 and trends, annual rpt, 2324–1.3

Switchgear industry labor productivity trends and technological innovations, 1963-82, article, 6722–1.420

Technological change, impact on productivity and employment in 4 industries, 1960-90, 6828–23

Traffic accidents and casualties detailed direct and indirect costs, by characteristics of persons and vehicles involved, 1979-80, 7768–80

Unemployment rate and components of change, growth rates for 6 recovery periods 2nd qtr 1954-2nd qtr 1984, and projected unemployment rate for 4th qtr 1985, article, 9373–1.415

Uranium mining operations, finances, and costs of alternative methods to meet emissions standards, for industry and selected mines, selected years 1948-90, 9188–96

Wage differential due to unionization, effect on production and prices by industry div, 1971, technical paper, 9387–8.81

Watermelon grower-to-retailer handling costs and time, by handling phase and method, 1982, 1308–18

Work-sharing effect on labor productivity, for US and compared to West Germany, 1930s-82, narrative article, 6722–1.458

Worker participation in mgmt decisions, experience in US and 2 countries, 1983 narrative article, 6722–1.457

see also Agricultural productivity

see also Government efficiency

see also Industrial production indexes

see also Production costs

Labor turnover

Auto industry operations, trade, and registrations, foreign and US, selected years 1928-82, domestic content requirement hearings, 21788–134

Botany and other plant science R&D at higher education instns, funding by source, grad students, and staff, 1983, 9626–2.143

Business Conditions Digest, historical supplement on economic, business, and financial conditions and cyclical fluctuations, with methodology, 1947-82, 2708–31

California business failures, plant closings, layoffs, and relocations, by plant, industry, county, and city, 1980-83, hearing, 21348–84.1

City govt fiscal condition, revenue sharing program allocations, and responses to program cuts, FY81-83, surveys, hearings, 25408–86

Computer specialists sociodemographic, educational, and employment characteristics, and Fed Govt support by agency, 1978, biennial Current Population Rpt, 2546–2.124

DOT employment by subagency, State, and selected personnel characteristics, FY83, annual rpt, 7304–18.3

Engineers sociodemographic, educational, and employment characteristics, and Federal support by agency, 1978, Current Population Rpt, 2546–2.121

Fed Govt appointments and separations of disabled and nondisabled veterans, by agency, 2nd half FY82, semiannual rpt, 9842–3

Fed Govt civilian employee accessions and separations, by citizenship status and agency for DC metro area and elsewhere, monthly rpt, 9842–1.3

Fed Govt jobs of Alcohol, Tobacco, and Firearms Bur to be eliminated or transferred to Customs and Secret Service, by job category, 1981, hearings, 21528–55

Fed Govt personnel action appeals, decisions of Merit Systems Protection Board, by region, agency, and employee characteristics, FY82, annual rpt, 9494–2

Fed Govt programs and mgmt cost control proposals, 3-year savings by function and agency, and financial and operating data, 1960s-81, 16908–1

Job tenure and occupational mobility of workers, by sociodemographic characteristics and industry div, as of Jan 1983, press release, 6748–76

Job tenure and occupational mobility of workers, by sociodemographic characteristics and occupation, as of Jan 1983, article, 6722–1.460

Kentucky employment growth in 9-county rural area, labor force and establishment characteristics, 1979-80, 1598–194

Labor force not at work on day of survey, employed part-time, or unemployed, by reason, sex, race, Hispanic origin, region, and State, 1983, annual rpt, 6744–7

Manufacturing labor turnover rates, by major industry group, selected years 1930-81, annual rpt, 6724–1.3

Manufacturing robots installed, and jobs displaced and created by occupation, by type of robot use, 1980s-2000, hearings, 21728–54

Military active duty strength, recruits, and reenlistment, by race, Hispanic origin, sex, and service branch, quarterly press release, 3542–7

Labor turnover

Military personnel enlistments and reenlistment rates, by service branch, monthly rpt, 3542–14.4

Military personnel enlistments and reenlistment rates, FY75-83, annual rpt, 3544–1.2

Military women personnel on active duty, by demographic and service characteristics and service branch, with comparisons to men, FY83, annual chartbook, 3544–26

Minerals (strategic) supply/demand, trade, and foreign and US industry devs by firm and country, by commodity, bimonthly rpt, 5602–4

Natl Weather Service, effects of proposed reorganization and technological improvement on staff and expenditures, FY82 and projected to 2000, 2188–16

Occupational separation rates by worker characteristics, and replacement rates, 1980-81 with projections to 1990, article, 6722–1.416

Plant closing provisions of Fed Govt and State law, corporate policies, collective bargaining agreements, and job loss in California and total US, 1982, article, 9377–1.401

Pollution control costs, related industrial plant closings, quarterly rpt, discontinued, 9182–6

Small business and all employees sociodemographic characteristics, by industry div and firm size, 1978-1979, annual rpt, 9764–6.3

Statistical Abstract of US, social, political, and economic data, 1950s-83 and trends, annual rpt, 2324–1.3

Steel imports of US from EC and other countries, and US industry operating data, for 15 products limited under arrangement with EC, monthly rpt, 9882–10

Trade adjustment assistance eligibility, reemployment opportunities, and worker characteristics, investigations of industries injured by import competition, series, 6406–9

Unemployment, by duration, selected demographic characteristics, industry div, and reason for job loss, various periods 1979-June 1983, article, 6722–1.411

Unemployment by reason, detailed data, monthly rpt, 6742–2

Unemployment by reason, monthly press release, 6742–5

Wage growth and turnover rates related to marital status, sex, age, establishment type, and employer size, 1979/80, article, 9393–8.403

see also Job vacancy

Labor unions

American Samoa minimum wage rates, employment, earnings, and benefits, by establishment and industry, Nov 1983, biennial rpt, 6504–6

California business and plant closings, relocations, and layoffs, with union represented, by county, city, and plant, 1980-83, hearing, 21348–84.1

Central cities and suburbs population and employment, effect of region, neighborhood, population, and labor characteristics, 1970-80, technical paper, 9387–8.89

Coal (bituminous) mining production and related workers, wages by occupation, and

benefits, by size of mine and union status, in 6 States and aggregate for Rocky Mountain States, July 1982 survey, 6787–6.198

Collective bargaining agreements expiring during year, covered workers by SIC 2-digit industry, firm, and union, with summary of key provisions, 1984, annual rpt, 6784–9

Construction and building materials industries trade assns, professional societies, and labor unions, 1984 listing, article, 2012–1.405

County Business Patterns: establishments, employees, and payrolls, by SIC 4-digit industry and county, 1981, annual State rpt series, 2326–8

County Business Patterns: establishments, employees, and payrolls, by SIC 4-digit industry and county, 1982, annual State rpt series, 2326–6

Dress industry production and related workers, wages, and benefits, by occupation, size of establishment, and union status, for 11 labor market areas, Aug 1982 survey, 6787–6.200

Election campaign funding of maritime and other labor unions for congressional campaigns, by party, 1981-82, hearings, 25388–45

Employment Cost Index wage and salary component changes by occupational group, industry div, and collective bargaining status, and CPI changes, selected periods Sept 1975-Dec 1983, article, 6722–1.430

Employment, earnings, and hours, by SIC 4-digit nonfarm industry, monthly 1974-Feb 1984, annual update, 6744–4

Fed Govt labor unions recognized, agreements and membership by agency and office or installation, Jan 1983, annual listing, 9844–14

Fed Govt labor unions recognized, membership by agency and union, as of Jan 1983, annual rpt, 9844–17

Fed Labor Relations Authority and Fed Service Impasses Panel activities, and cases by region, union, and agency, FY79-82, annual rpt, 13364–1

Foreign economic, social, and political summary data, by country, 1984, annual factbook, 244–11

Input-output structure of US economy, detailed interindustry transactions for 537 industries, and components of final demand, 1977 benchmark data, 2708–17

Labor force characteristics and economic indicators, selected years 1880-1995, chartbook, 6728–30

Labor-Mgmt Reporting and Disclosure Act compliance, enforcement, and reporting, annual rpt, suspended, 6464–2

Labor union leaders attitudes toward labor movement, 1963 and 1983, article, 6722–1.451

Labor unions reporting to Labor Dept, parent bodies and locals by State, city, and country, 1983 listing, 6468–17

Mergers of labor organizations, and affiliation and membership at time of merger, Jan 1979-Apr 1984, article, 6722–1.456

Metal (nonferrous) manufacturing wages and benefits, by occupation, size of establishment, and for metro-nonmetro areas, 1981 survey, 6787–6.196

Index by Subjects and Names

Metalworking machinery industry computerized automation, by plant characteristics, for 6 industry groups and small plants, 1982 surveys, 23848–179

Pension fund and other financial instn mortgage and mortgage-related investments, by instn type and Fed Govt issuing agency, various dates 1981-84, 5008–33

Pension plan investment in mortgages and FHLB and Fed Govt mortgage assn mortgage-backed securities, for corporate and union funds, quarterly rpt, 5002–10

Pension plans with postretirement adjustments related to employee and employer characteristics, and effect of inflation on benefit purchasing power, 1973-79, 6468–18

Political action committee and other campaign funding, and Fed Election Commission monitoring activities, press release series, 9276–1

Political action committee and other campaign funding, and Fed Election Commission monitoring activities, 1984 Federal elections, biennial series, 9276–2

Political action committee and TV influence on govtl action and public opinion, surveys, various dates 1977-83, hearings, 21428–7.1

Political action committee funding to reelect and defeat House and Senate members by candidate, and FEC activities and funding, 1983, annual rpt, 9274–1

Private pension plans integrated with OASI benefits, and salary replacement rates, by formula type, salary level, and firm collective bargaining status, 1981, article, 6722–1.431

Representation elections conducted by NLRB, results, monthly rpt, 9582–2

Small business and all employees sociodemographic characteristics, by industry div and firm size, 1978-1979, annual rpt, 9764–6.3

Southeastern States employment, prices, earnings, and union membership in 8 States, Oct 1982-83 with union members covered by agreements expiring in 1984, annual rpt, 6944–2

Statistical Abstract of US, social, political, and economic data, 1950s-83 and trends, annual rpt, 2324–1.3

Trade adjustment assistance eligibility and certification of workers and companies, by industry and labor union, 1975-83, annual rpt, 444–1.2

Trade adjustment assistance for workers, petitions, investigations, and determinations, by major industry group, union, and State, monthly rpt, 6402–13

Wage differential due to unionization, effect on production and prices by industry div, 1971, technical paper, 9387–8.81

Wage differential due to unionization, effect on union and nonunion labor income and invested capital return, 1971, technical paper, 9387–8.83

Witness Security Program costs, participants by arrest record, and prosecutions by offense, offender type, and disposition, various periods FY70-83, GAO rpt, 26119–70

Women's employment and earnings, by labor force and socioeconomic characteristics, and compared to men, 1978-81 and trends from 1940s, 6568–29

Index by Subjects and Names

Lakes and lakeshores

Work stoppages involving 6 workers or more, workers and days idle by major issue, industry, and State, selected years 1930-82, annual rpt, 6724–1.8

see also Industry wage surveys

see also Labor-management relations, general

see also Labor-management relations in government

see also Labor-management relations, local and regional

Laboratories

- County Business Patterns: establishments, employees, and payrolls, by SIC 4-digit industry and county, 1981, annual State rpt series, 2326–8
- County Business Patterns: establishments, employees, and payrolls, by SIC 4-digit industry and county, 1982, annual State rpt series, 2326–6
- Dental labs receipts, 1983, annual rpt, 2413–8
- DOE R&D projects and funding at natl labs, universities, and other instns, annual summary rpts, 3004–18
- Drug and narcotics foreign production, acreage, eradication, and seizures, by substance, with labs destroyed and US aid, by country, 1981-85, annual rpt, 7004–17
- Employment, earnings, and hours, by SIC 4-digit nonfarm industry, monthly 1974-Feb 1984, annual update, 6744–4
- Fed Govt programs and mgmt cost control proposals, 3-year savings by function and agency, and financial and operating data, 1960s-81, 16908–1
- Fed Govt R&D labs required technology transfer to public and private sector, labs complying, funding, and requests, by agency, FY82, GAO rpt, 26113–141
- Foreign market and trade for lab instruments, and user industry operations and demand, country market research rpts, 2045–10
- Income tax returns of corporations, detailed income and tax items by industry, 1981, annual rpt, 8304–4
- Income tax returns of sole proprietorships, detailed data by industry div and selected industry group, 1981, annual rpt, 8304–7
- Income tax returns of sole proprietorships, receipts, deductions by type, payroll, and net income, by major industry, 1982, annual article, 8302–2.413
- Medicaid advisory committees members by type, and operating characteristics, 1979, article, 4652–1.409
- Medicare admissions to hospitals and other facilities, and enrollee reimbursement claims, by beneficiary type, 1966-83, annual rpt, 4744–3.7
- Medicare claims approved, total charges, and reimbursements by type of service, from 1974, monthly rpt, quarterly data, 4742–1.11
- Medicare enrollment and bills approved, and reimbursement and Medicaid payments by type of service and beneficiary, quarterly rpt, 4652–1.1
- Medicare enrollment, reimbursement, and use and covered charges by type of service, by State and census div, 1978-82, 4658–8

Medicare kidney end-stage program, reimbursement by treatment, diagnosis, outcome, and patient characteristics, with covered charges for transplants, 1974-79, article, 4652–1.421

- Medicare-participating facilities by control, beds, and terminated facilities, by facility type, region, and State, 1975-81, 4656–1.19
- NIH grants and awards for R&D, training, construction, and medical libraries, by location and recipient, FY83, annual listings, 4434–7
- Occupational injury and illness rates, by SIC 2- to 4-digit industry, 1982, annual rpt, 6844–1
- Public health labs of States, pay scales and job requirements by occupation and State, FY81-83, annual rpt, 4204–7
- Public health labs of States, personnel, finances, workloads, and other activities, by State, FY82, annual rpt, 4204–8
- R&D equipment at higher education instns, age, cost, funding sources, and users, for computer and physical sciences and engineering, 1982, 9626–2.138
- R&D Fed Govt facilities and services available for private sector use, by field of science, 1984 biennial listing, 2224–4
- Service industry census, 1982: employment, establishments, receipts, and payroll, by SIC 2- to 4-digit kind of business, SMSA, county, and city, State rpt series, 2391–1
- Southeastern States health care resource availability, and employment by occupation, by facility type, by State and SMSA in Fed Reserve 6th District, 1970s-81, article, 9371–1.425

see also Clinical laboratory technicians

see also Department of Energy National Laboratories

Lacombe, John J., II

"Collective Bargaining Calendar Crowded Again in 1984", 6722–1.402

Lafayette, Ind.

- Census of Housing, 1980: occupancy and unit characteristics, by race, Hispanic origin, and city, SMSA rpt, 2473–1.207
- Census of Population and Housing, 1980: detailed population and housing characteristics, by county, city, and census tract, SMSA rpt, 2551–2.207
- *see also* under By SMSA or MSA in the "Index by Categories"

Lafayette, La.

- Census of Housing, 1980: occupancy and unit characteristics, by race, Hispanic origin, and city, SMSA rpt, 2473–1.206
- Census of Population and Housing, 1980: detailed population and housing characteristics, by county, city, and census tract, SMSA rpt, 2551–2.206
- *see also* under By SMSA or MSA in the "Index by Categories"

Lake Charles, La.

- Census of Housing, 1980: occupancy and unit characteristics, by race, Hispanic origin, and city, SMSA rpt, 2473–1.208
- Census of Population and Housing, 1980: detailed population and housing characteristics, by county, city, and census tract, SMSA rpt, 2551–2.208
- Housing vacancy rates for single and multifamily units and mobile homes, by city and ZIP code, 1984, annual metro area rpt, 9304–19.30

Wages of office and plant workers, by occupation, 1984 labor market area survey rpt, 6785–3.6

see also under By SMSA or MSA in the "Index by Categories"

Lake County, Ill.

see also under By SMSA or MSA in the "Index by Categories"

Lakeland, Fla.

- Census of Population and Housing, 1980: detailed population and housing characteristics, by county, city, and census tract, SMSA rpt, 2551–2.209
- *see also* under By SMSA or MSA in the "Index by Categories"

Lakes and lakeshores

- Acid rain causes and effects, air pollutant emissions by source, and control costs, by region and State, selected years 1977-83 and projected to 2000, 26358–104
- Acid rain causes and effects, air pollutant emissions by source in US and selected countries, and control costs, 1970s-83 and projected to 2000, 21368–52
- Agricultural Stabilization and Conservation Service producer payments under 26 programs, monthly rpt, 1802–10
- Air pollution and acid rain environmental effects, and methods of neutralizing acidified water bodies, summary research rpt series, 5506–5
- Army Corps of Engineers activities and projects, FY83 and trends from 1800s, annual rpt, 3754–1
- Bridges over navigable waters, with type of bridge and use, owner, dimensions, and location, 1984 regional listing series, 7406–5
- Developing countries disaster preparedness and summary sociodemographic, political, and economic data, country rpt series, 9916–2
- Fish and eggs for stocking distributed from natl hatcheries, by species, hatchery, and jurisdiction, FY83, annual rpt, 5504–10
- Fish and Wildlife Service restoration programs, including new sites, funding, and research, by State, FY81, annual rpt, 5504–1
- Freight (waterborne domestic and foreign) by commodity, traffic, and passengers, by port and waterway, 1982, annual rpt, 3754–3
- Mount St Helens, Wash, volcanic eruptions, effects on water quality and other environmental characteristics of Washington and Oregon watersheds, series, 5666–14
- Natl Forest System wildlife habitat and fishery improvements, use, and game population and harvest by species and forest, by region, FY83, annual rpt, 1204–31
- Natl forests recreational use, visitor-days by type of activity, forest, and State, FY83 with trends from 1924, annual rpt series, 1204–17
- Natl park system and other areas under Natl Park Service mgmt, acreage by type of area, ownership, and site, as of Sept 1984, semiannual rpt, 5542–1
- Pollution-caused fish kills, by State, location, and pollution source, monthly 1978-80, annual rpt, 9204–3

Lakes and lakeshores

Sedimentation control, surveillance, and research activity of Fed Govt, by project, agency, region, and State, 1982, annual rpt, 5664–9

Utah Salt Lake surface level, land coverage, water budget, salinity, and effects of human activity, various periods 1847-1983, 5668–70

Water supply and quality in streams and lakes, and groundwater levels in wells, by drainage basin, 1980, annual State rpt series, 5666–12

Water supply and quality in streams and lakes, and groundwater levels in wells, by drainage basin, 1981, annual State rpt series, 5666–16

Water supply and quality in streams and lakes, and groundwater levels in wells, by drainage basin, 1982, annual State rpt series, 5666–20

Water supply and quality in streams and lakes, and groundwater levels in wells, by drainage basin, 1983, annual State rpt series, 5666–10

Water supply in US and Canada, streamflow, well and reservoir levels, and dissolved solids and temperature in 6 US rivers, by station, monthly rpt, 5662–3

Waterborne disease outbreaks and cases, by type, source, and location, 1983, annual rpt, 4205–35

see also Dredging
see also Great Lakes
see also National park system
see also Reservoirs
see also Water resources development
see also Water supply and use
see also Wetlands

Lakewood, Colo.

see also under By City in the "Index by Categories"

Lalich, Nina R.

"Employment Characteristics of Mothers During Pregnancy", 4144–11.1

"Maternal Occupation and Industry and the Pregnancy Outcome of U.S. Married Women, 1980", 4102–1.422

Lambert, Drexel B.

"HFCS Competition: A Year of Transition", 1004–16.1

Lamberts, Henk

"Classification of Reasons Why Persons Seek Primary Care: Pilot Study of a New System", 4102–1.460

Lamps, electric

see Household appliances and equipment

Lancaster, Pa.

Census of Housing, 1980: occupancy and unit characteristics, by race, Hispanic origin, and city, SMSA rpt, 2473–1.210

Census of Population and Housing, 1980: detailed population and housing characteristics, by county, city, and census tract, SMSA rpt, 2551–2.210

see also under By SMSA or MSA in the "Index by Categories"

Land

see Farms and farmland
see Forests and forestry
see Homesteads
see Land area
see Land ownership
see Land reform

see Land use
see Open space land programs
see Pasture and rangeland
see Public lands
see Real estate business
see Reclamation of land
see Soil pollution
see Soils and soil conservation

Land area

Alaska timber acreage and resources, by species, ownership class, and inventory unit, 1967-74, series, 1206–9

Biomass Fuels Program of TVA, technologies and processes dev, costs, and resource requirements, 1970s-90s, series, 9806–9

City and suburb population characteristics and local govt finances, by region and selected SMSA, 1950s-FY83, 10048–61

Coal dev on Fed Govt lease land in Western US, surface and mineral rights by State, and environmental protection adequacy, various periods 1978-85, 26358–103

Coal Fed Govt leases, acreage, production, and prices, by State, and legal and mgmt issues, 1970s-83 with production projections to 2000, 11128–1

Coal lands of Fed Govt leasing activity, acreage, and reserves, by State, coal region, and tract, FY83, annual rpt, 5724–10

Coastal environmental characteristics, fish, wildlife, and use, and population socioeconomic data, for individual areas, series, 5506–4

County and City Data Book, detailed socioeconomic and demographic data for States, counties, and cities, selected years 1976-82, 2328–1

Developing countries agricultural supply/demand and market for US exports, with socioeconomic indicators, country rpt series, 1526–6

Developing countries disaster preparedness and summary sociodemographic, political, and economic data, country rpt series, 9916–2

Developing countries economic dev projects funded by multilateral dev banks, environmental and cultural impacts, 1970s-83, hearings, 21248–80

DOD base support costs by function, and personnel and acreage by installation, by service branch, FY85, annual rpt, 3504–11

Energy production, reserves, and prices, by energy type, and selected indicators of energy use, by State, 1982-83 with selected comparisons from 1971, annual rpt, 3164–60

Foreign and US cropland per capita, and total arable land area by use, by selected country and world region, selected years 1955-80, 1528–180

Foreign and US cropland per capita by world region and selected country, and world arable land area by use, selected years 1955-80, summary article, 1522–3.401

Foreign and US rail high-speed systems and railcar production, and proposed US projects costs and funding, with population and land area for selected foreign cities, 1940s-82, 26358–97

Index by Subjects and Names

Foreign economic, social, and political summary data, by country, 1984, annual factbook, 244–11

Forest and windbarrier planting and seeding, by State, FY83, annual rpt, 1204–7

Forest Natl System wildlife habitat and fishery improvements, use, and game population and harvest by species and forest, by region, FY83, annual rpt, 1204–31

Forest, range, and associated waters use and mgmt assessment, and environmental impacts of Forest Service program options, 1977-2030 and trends from 1920, 1208–24

Georgia timber resources and removals, by species, ownership class, and county, 1981-83, series, 1206–26

Great Lakes water levels, surface and drainage area, depth, and volume, and connecting and outlet channel flows, various periods 1900-83, 3758–6

Jamaica PL 480 Title I assistance effects on economic dev, with data on govt finance, economic indicators, demography, and dev programs, 1970s-81, 9916–1.51

Michigan timber acreage, volume, growth, removals, and production, by ownership, county, and forest and tree characteristics, 1980, series, 1206–31

Minnesota timber acreage, resources, and removals, by species, county, and ownership class, series, 1206–24

Montana and North Dakota coal production, impact of mining on agricultural land availability and on farm income and production costs, by mining tract, 1982 rpt, 1588–79

Montana timber acreage, resources, and mortality, by species and ownership class, 1976-80, series, 1206–25

Natl forests and other lands under Forest Service mgmt, by forest and location, Sept 1983, annual rpt, 1204–2

New Mexico timber acreage and resources, by species, ownership class, and county, 1977-80, series, 1206–23

North Carolina timber acreage and resources, by species, ownership class, and county, 1982-83, series, 1206–4

Northeastern region timber resources and removals, by species, ownership, and county, State rpt series, 1206–12

Nuclear power plant siting population criteria and estimated compliance of selected regions and sites, 1983 rpt, 9638–54

Park natl system and other areas under Natl Park Service mgmt, acreage by type of area, ownership, and site, as of Sept 1984, semiannual rpt, 5542–1

Privately held land, acreage and owners by owner characteristics, land use, and region, and purchase and improvement funding, 1978 survey, series, 1506–5

Public land acreage and use, and Land Mgmt Bur activities and finances, annual State rpt series, 5724–11

Public lands mgmt, grants, sales, and use, by State, FY83 and historical, annual rpt, 5724–1

Rocky Mountain forest and rangeland area, and timber resources and removals, by ownership, forest and tree characteristics, and State, 1977, 1208–201

Index by Subjects and Names

Land use

Rocky Mountain States forest biomass, conversion from volume to dry weight, for softwood and hardwood species, 1977, 1208–200

Soil Conservation Service activities, services, and acreage covered, by program, FY83, annual rpt, 1264–2

Southeastern States timber resources and removals, for 5 States, interim rpt series, 1206–32

Southeastern US water supply and quality, with background socioeconomic data, for 8 States, 1960s-2020 with trends from 1930, 9208–119

Star position tables for land surveying use, 1984 annual rpt, 5724–7

Statistical Abstract of US, social, political, and economic data, 1950s-83 and trends, annual rpt, 2324–1.1

Tennessee Valley ethanol production, feedstocks, facilities, tax incentives, and related farming data, by State, 1970s-83 and projected to 1992, 9808–69

Utah timber acreage and resources, by species, ownership class, and stand size, and forest recreation, 1978, series, 1206–22

Washington State timber acreage and resources, by species, ownership class, and county, 1980, and harvest, 1950-81, series, 1206–28

Water Bank Program agreements, acreage, and Fed Govt payments, by State, FY72-83, annual rpt, 1804–21

Wetlands acreage and losses, by wetland type and location, 1970s-83, 5508–89

Wetlands environmental characteristics, acreage, uses, and mgmt, by wetland type and region, 1950s-80, 26358–102

Wilderness Preservation Natl System acreage, by natl forest, wilderness and primitive area, and State, 1983, annual rpt, 5304–14

see also Farms and farmland

see also Land ownership

see also Land use

Land claims

see Claims

Land ownership

Agricultural production, marketing, trade, supply, food consumption, and food and nutrition programs, 1960s-83, annual chartbook, 1504–3

Alaska timber acreage and resources, by species, ownership class, and inventory unit, 1967-74, series, 1206–9

Coal Fed Govt leases, acreage, production, and prices, by State, and legal and mgmt issues, 1970s-83 with production projections to 2000, 11128–1

Coal mining effect on water supply and quality in selected river basins of Eastern and Interior coal provinces, 1970s, series, 5666–15

Coal mining effect on water supply and quality in selected river basins of Western coal provinces, series, 5666–19

Environmental quality and protection programs, costs, and Fed Govt enforcement, 1983, detailed annual rpt, 484–1

Farm real estate transfers, by type of buyer and seller, region, and State, 1982-83, annual rpt, 1541–8.3

Farmland (US) owned by foreigners, acquisitions, dispositions, holdings, and use, by State and type and country of owner, 1983, annual rpt, 1584–2

Farmland acquisitions of foreigners, by State and county, before 1980 and during 1980-82, 1588–77

Foreign direct investment in US by country, and finances, operations, and land ownership, by industry group for businesses acquired and established, 1982-83, annual article, 2702–1.418

Foreign direct investment in US, major investors and investments by SIC 4-digit industry, transaction type and value, and location, 1983, annual rpt, 2044–20

Foreign firms US affiliates financial and operating data, by country of parent firm and industry div, 1980-81, article, 2702–1.402

Foreign ownership of US agricultural land, acreage, value, and use, by State and county, and for 5 leading investor countries, 1983, annual rpt, 1584–3

Forest, range, and associated waters use and mgmt assessment, and environmental impacts of Forest Service program options, 1977-2030 and trends from 1920, 1208–24

Georgia timber resources and removals, by species, ownership class, and county, 1981-83, series, 1206–26

Guam acreage owned privately, and by US and Guam govts, 1984 rpt, 26358–101.1

Michigan timber acreage by ownership, county, and forest and tree characteristics, 1980, 1208–192

Michigan timber acreage, volume, growth, removals, and production, by ownership, county, and forest and tree characteristics, 1980, series, 1206–31

Minnesota timber acreage, resources, and removals, by species, county, and ownership class, series, 1206–24

Montana timber acreage, resources, and mortality, by species and ownership class, 1976-80, series, 1206–25

New Mexico timber acreage and resources, by species, ownership class, and county, 1977-80, series, 1206–23

North Carolina timber acreage and resources, by species, ownership class, and county, 1982-83, series, 1206–4

Northeast States forest land owner characteristics, owners and acreage, series, 1206–7

Northeastern region timber resources and removals, by species, ownership, and county, State rpt series, 1206–12

Park natl system and other areas under Natl Park Service mgmt, acreage by type of area, ownership, and site, as of Sept 1984, semiannual rpt, 5542–1

Privately held land, acreage and owners by owner characteristics, land use, and region, and purchase and improvement funding, 1978 survey, series, 1506–5

Rocky Mountain forest and rangeland area, and timber resources and removals, by ownership, forest and tree characteristics, and State, 1977, 1208–201

Rocky Mountain States forest biomass, conversion from volume to dry weight, for softwood and hardwood species, 1977, 1208–200

Southeastern States timber resources and removals, for 5 States, interim rpt series, 1206–32

Tax assessment, local jurisdictions reporting data on property size, use, location, ownership, and value, 1972-82, 1588–81

Uranium mining operations, finances, and costs of alternative methods to meet emissions standards, for industry and selected mines, selected years 1948-90, 9188–96

Utah timber acreage and resources, by species, ownership class, and stand size, and forest recreation, 1978, series, 1206–22

Washington State timber acreage and resources, by species, ownership class, and county, 1980, and harvest, 1950-81, series, 1206–28

Western Area Power Admin small-scale potential hydroelectric generation, site inventory, characteristics, and costs, by State and county, 1984 rpt, 3258–1

see also Government property

see also Homesteads

see also Public lands

see also Real estate business

Land reclamation

see Reclamation of land

Land reform

El Salvador socioeconomic and political conditions, and US economic and military assistance, 1977-FY84, 7008–39

Foreign and US tropical forests status by country and world region, conservation methods, and mgmt role of US, foreign, and intl groups, 1977-81 and projected to 2000, 26358–101

Land surveying

see Land area

Land tax

see Property tax

Land use

Aerial survey R&D publications, and sources of natural resource and environmental data gathered by air- and spacecraft, quarterly listing, 9502–7

Agricultural and rural area dev research, scientist years and funds expended, FY82, annual rpt, 1744–2

Alaska and Alaska Native corporation claims for Fed Govt land, status and Land Mgmt Bur conveyance problems, various dates 1978-FY84, GAO rpt, 26113–125

Biomass Fuels Program of TVA, technologies and processes dev, costs, and resource requirements, 1970s-90s, series, 9806–9

Census of Govts, 1982: properties, govt-assessed value, sales, and tax rates, by property type, State, SMSA, county, and city, 2453–1

Coal dev plans on Fed Govt lease lands in 12 regions under Fed Coal Mgmt Program, environmental and socioeconomic impacts to 2000, final statement series, 5726–4

Coal mining effect on water supply and quality in selected river basins of Eastern and Interior coal provinces, 1970s, series, 5666–15

Coal mining effect on water supply and quality in selected river basins of Western coal provinces, series, 5666–19

Land use

Coastal environmental and socioeconomic conditions, and potential impacts of oil and gas OCS leases, final statement series, 5736–1

Coastal environmental characteristics, fish, wildlife, and use, and population socioeconomic data, for individual areas, series, 5506–4

Condemnation case and tract processing of US Attorneys, by district, FY83, annual rpt, 6004–2.6

Developing countries agricultural supply/demand and market for US exports, with socioeconomic indicators, country rpt series, 1526–6

Developing countries disaster preparedness and summary sociodemographic, political, and economic data, country rpt series, 9916–2

Environmental quality and protection programs, costs, and Fed Govt enforcement, 1983, detailed annual rpt, 484–1

Estuary environmental characteristics, fish, wildlife, uses, and mgmt, for individual estuaries, series, 5506–7

Farm real estate transfers, by proposed use of property, region, and State, 1982-83, annual rpt, 1541–8.4

Foreign and US cropland per capita, and total arable land area by use, by selected country and world region, selected years 1955-80, 1528–180

Foreign and US cropland per capita by world region and selected country, and world arable land area by use, selected years 1955-80, summary article, 1522–3.401

Foreign economic, social, and political summary data, by country, 1984, annual factbook, 244–11

Foreign ownership of US agricultural land, acquisitions, dispositions, holdings, and use, by State and type and country of owner, 1983, annual rpt, 1584–2

Foreign ownership of US agricultural land, acreage, value, and use, by State and county, and for 5 leading investor countries, 1983, annual rpt, 1584–3

GAO publications on land use, ownership, mgmt, and planning, 1979-83, annual listing, 26104–11.3

Geological Survey and other publications, 1983, annual listing, 5664–4

Geological Survey programs and funding, FY78-83, annual rpt, 5664–8

Louisiana property tax on forest, agricultural, and marsh lands, impact of change from market to use valuation by parish, 1977-78, 1208–206

Montana and North Dakota coal production, impact of mining on agricultural land availability and on farm income and production costs, by mining tract, 1982 rpt, 1588–79

New Communities program of HUD, activities, costs, land sales, and community and population characteristics, for 13 communities, 1970s-83, 5188–107

North and South Carolina Yadkin-Pee Dee River basin, acreage by land use, projected to 2010, 9208–125

Privately held land, acreage and owners by owner characteristics, land use, and region, and purchase and improvement funding, 1978 survey, series, 1506–5

Satellite Landsat system proposed transfer to private sector, uses and product sales by user type, and university programs and personnel by instn, 1973-85, 26358–100

Soil survey county descriptions and maps of USDA, 1899-1983, annual listing, 1264–11

Statistical Abstract of US, social, political, and economic data, 1950s-83 and trends, annual rpt, 2324–1.1

Tax assessment, local jurisdictions reporting data on property size, use, location, ownership, and value, 1972-82, 1588–81

Transit systems research publications, 2nd half FY83, semiannual listing, 7882–1

Uranium mining operations, finances, and costs of alternative methods to meet emissions standards, for industry and selected mines, selected years 1948-90, 9188–96

Urban runoff water quality, pollutant concentrations, and control cost-effectiveness, with monitoring sites rainfall and other characteristics, by city and region, 1978-83, 9208–122

Urban travel by purpose, effect of telecommunication advances, land use changes, and alternative work schedules, projected to 2000 with some trends 1950-80, 7888–63

Water pollution from nonpoint sources, source land uses and acreage, and control program funding, by State or region, various periods 1974-FY84, 9208–123

Wetlands environmental characteristics, acreage, uses, and mgmt, by wetland type and region, 1950s-80, 26358–102

see also Farms and farmland

see also Forests and forestry

see also Industrial siting

see also Land ownership

see also Land reform

see also Mines and mineral resources

see also Pasture and rangeland

see also Public lands

see also Reclamation of land

see also Regional planning

see also Zoning and zoning laws

Landefeld, J. Steven

"Plant and Equipment Expenditures, 1984", 2702–1.404

Landfills

see Refuse and refuse disposal

Landlord-tenant relations

Public housing under private mgmt, assessment by housing officials and managers, and tenants, with operating costs, crime, and rent delinquency by project type and location, 1982, 5188–103

Landscape protection

see Environmental pollution and control

see Land use

see Open space land programs

Laney, Leroy O.

"Strong Dollar, the Current Account, and Federal Deficits: Cause and Effect", 9379–1.401

Lanfear, Kenneth J.

"Reexamination of Occurrence Rates for Accidental Oil Spills on the U.S. Outer Continental Shelf", 5738–1

Index by Subjects and Names

Langberg, Robert

"Work Experience and Income of Male Veterans and Nonveterans in 1981", 9924–23

Langley, Ann

"Medicare and the Health Costs of Older Americans: The Extent and Effects of Cost Sharing", 25148–27

Language and literature

Census of Population and Housing, 1980: detailed population and housing characteristics, by county, city, and census tract, State and SMSA rpt series, 2551–2

Census of Population, 1980: detailed socioeconomic and demographic characteristics, by age, sex, race, Hispanic origin, occupation, and industry, State rpt series, 2531–4

Census of Population, 1980: detailed socioeconomic characteristics, by county, city, and inside-outside SMSAs and central cities, State rpt series, 2531–3

Condition of Education, detailed data on enrollment, staff, achievement, finances, curricula, and education effects on employment, 1982-83, annual rpt, 4824–1

Degrees conferred in higher education, by race, Hispanic origin, sex, level, and field, selected years 1949/50-1979/80, annual rpt, 4824–2.16

DOD Dependents Schools 1st grader basic skills test scores, by world area and English fluency, fall 1983, annual rpt, 3504–18

English teaching programs and teacher seminars supported by USIA, by world region and country, FY83, annual rpt, 9854–2

High school classes of 1980 and 1982: educational and sociodemographic characteristics and expectations, natl longitudinal study, series, 4826–2

Natl Endowment for Arts activities and grants, FY83, annual rpt, 9564–3

Older persons by demographic, socioeconomic, and health characteristics, selected years 1900-81 and projected to 2050, Current Population Rpt, 2546–2.125

Science and engineering doctoral degree recipients, by field, sex, race, age, citizenship, postgrad employment and study status, State, and instn, 1960-82, 9626–6.16

Science and engineering grad enrollment, fields of study, financial support, and other student and instn characteristics, 1975-82, annual survey, 9627–7

Statistical Abstract of US, social, political, and economic data, 1950s-83 and trends, annual rpt, 2324–1.1

see also Area studies

see also Foreign languages

see also Reading ability and habits

Lanier, William P.

"Ecology of Intertidal Oyster Reefs of the South Atlantic Coast: A Community Profile", 5506–9.2

Lansing, Mich.

Census of Housing, 1980: occupancy and unit characteristics, by race, Hispanic origin, and city, SMSA rpt, 2473–1.211

Census of Population and Housing, 1980: detailed population and housing characteristics, by county, city, and census tract, SMSA rpt, 2551–2.211

Index by Subjects and Names

see also under By City and By SMSA or MSA in the "Index by Categories"

Laos

- Agricultural situation in Southeast Asia, by country and commodity, 1983 and outlook for 1984, annual rpt, 1524–4.5
- AID loan repayment status and terms by program and country, and status of predecessor agency loans, quarterly rpt, 9912–3
- *Background Notes,* summary social, political, and economic data, 1984 rpt, 7006–2.24
- Economic, social, and political summary data, by country, 1984, annual factbook, 244–11
- Exports of US, detailed Schedule E commodities by mode of transport and world area and country of destination, 1983, annual rpts, 2424–5
- Imports of US, detailed Schedule A commodities by country and world area of origin, and mode of transport, 1983, annual rpts, 2424–2
- Imports of US, detailed TSUSA commodities by country of origin, 1983, annual rpt, 2424–4
- Loans and grants for economic and military assistance from US and intl agencies, by program and country, FY46-83, annual rpt, 9914–5
- Military spending, arms trade, and armed forces size, with total govt spending and population, by country, 1972-82, annual rpt, 9824–1
- *Minerals Yearbook,* 1982, Vol 3: foreign country reviews of production, trade, and policies, by commodity, annual rpt, 5604–35
- *Minerals Yearbook,* 1982, Vol 3 preprints: foreign country review of production, trade, and policies, by commodity, annual rpt, 5604–17.87
- Population size and growth rates, and latest available benchmark demographic data, by country, 1950-83, biennial rpt, 2324–4
- Refugee Indochinese population, arrivals, and departures, by country of origin and resettlement, camp, and ethnicity, monthly rpt, 7002–4
- Refugee migration, settlement status, and assistance, by world area and country of origin and asylum, as of May 1984, annual rpt, 7004–15
- Refugee resettlement program activities and funding, arrivals and population by country of origin and State, and employment and other characteristics, FY83, annual rpt, 4704–8
- *see also* under By Foreign Country in the "Index by Categories"

Lapan, Harvey E.

"Exchange Rate Determination and Real Interest Rate Differentials Under Uncertainty", 9366–7.91

Larbi, E. B.

"Population Attributable Risk of Hypertension from Heavy Alcohol Consumption", 4102–1.434

Larceny

see Robbery and theft

Lard

see Oils, oilseeds, and fats

Laredo, Tex.

- Census of Housing, 1980: occupancy and unit characteristics, by race, Hispanic origin, and city, SMSA rpt, 2473–1.212
- Census of Population and Housing, 1980: detailed population and housing characteristics, by county, city, and census tract, SMSA rpt, 2551–2.212
- Employment and economic impacts on Texas border of Mexican peso devaluation, for 6 counties and 2 SMSAs, 1970s-May 1983, hearing, 21788–133
- Employment in Mexico border US-owned plants, and peso devaluation, related to employment in 4 Texas SMSAs, 1978-83, article, 9379–1.402
- Housing vacancy rates for single and multifamily units and mobile homes, by city and ZIP code, 1984, annual metro area rpt, 9304–19.27
- Wages of office and plant workers, by occupation, 1984 labor market area survey rpt, 6785–3.9
- *see also* under By SMSA or MSA in the "Index by Categories"

Larsen, Richard J.

"Worldwide Deposition of Strontium-90 Through 1982", 3404–12

Las Cruces, N.Mex.

- Census of Housing, 1980: occupancy and unit characteristics, by race, Hispanic origin, and city, SMSA rpt, 2473–1.213
- Census of Population and Housing, 1980: detailed population and housing characteristics, by county, city, and census tract, SMSA rpt, 2551–2.213
- Wages of office and plant workers, by occupation, 1984 labor market area survey rpt, 6785–3.5
- *see also* under By SMSA or MSA in the "Index by Categories"

Las Vegas, Nev.

- Census of Housing, 1980: occupancy and unit characteristics, by race, Hispanic origin, and city, SMSA rpt, 2473–1.214
- Census of Population and Housing, 1980: detailed population and housing characteristics, by county, city, and census tract, SMSA rpt, 2551–2.214
- Housing unit starts and completions authorized by building permits in 20 MSAs, quarterly rpt, 2382–9
- Land Mgmt Bur public lands sales, prices of Nevada and California acreage, and effect on Forest Service land acquisition program, 1983, GAO rpt, 26113–122
- *see also* under By City and By SMSA or MSA in the "Index by Categories"

Lasers

- DOD budget, FY85 weapons system requests consistency with US policy and specified treaties, with funding FY83-87, annual rpt, 21384–4
- Patents (US) for telecommunication equipment granted to US and foreign applicants, by applicant type, firm, State, and country, various periods 1963-83, 2246–2.7

Lasley, Floyd A.

"Economic Impacts of the Avian Influenza Outbreak", 1561–7.402

Lassuy, Dennis R.

"Species Profiles: Life Histories and Environmental Requirements of Coastal Fishes and Invertebrates (Gulf of Mexico), Atlantic Croaker", 5506–8.16

Laundry and cleaning services

- "Species Profiles: Life Histories and Environmental Requirements of Coastal Fishes and Invertebrates (Gulf of Mexico), Brown Shrimp", 5506–8.18
- "Species Profiles: Life Histories and Environmental Requirements of Coastal Fishes and Invertebrates (Gulf of Mexico), Gulf Menhaden", 5506–8.19
- "Species Profiles: Life Histories and Environmental Requirements of Coastal Fishes and Invertebrates (Gulf of Mexico), Spotted Seatrout", 5506–8.21

Lathrop, George D.

"Project Ranch Hand II: An Epidemiologic Investigation of Health Effects in Air Force Personnel Following Exposure to Herbicides, Baseline Morbidity Study Results", 3604–3

Latin America

- *see* Caribbean area
- *see* Central America
- *see* Central American Common Market
- *see* Inter-American Development Bank
- *see* Latin American Free Trade Association
- *see* Mexico
- *see* South America
- *see* under By Foreign Country in the "Index by Categories"

Latin American Free Trade Association

- Agricultural exports and imports of US, by detailed commodity and country, FY83 and CY83, semiannual rpts, 1522–4
- Exports and imports of US, by commodity group, world area, selected country, US coastal area and port, and mode of transport, with seasonal adjustments, monthly rpt, 2422–9
- Exports and imports of US, detailed SIC-based commodities by world area, 1983, annual rpts, 2424–6
- Exports of US by selected commodity, and foreign and US economic and employment indicators and balance of payments, by world area and country, 1970s-83, annual rpt, 2044–26
- Exports of US, detailed Schedule E commodities by mode of transport and world area and country of destination, 1983, annual rpts, 2424–5
- Imports of US, detailed Schedule A commodities by country and world area of origin, and mode of transport, 1983, annual rpts, 2424–2

Laundry and cleaning services

- Air pollutant emission factors, by detailed source, 3rd edition, 1983-84 supplements, 9198–13
- Census of Population, 1980: detailed socioeconomic and demographic characteristics, by age, sex, race, Hispanic origin, occupation, and industry, State rpt series, 2531–4
- Census of Population, 1980: labor force, by sex, detailed occupation, and region, with comparison to 1970 census, supplementary rpt, 2535–1.12
- Census of Service Industries, 1982: employment, establishments, receipts, and payroll, by SIC 2- to 4-digit kind of business, SMSA, county, and city, State rpt series, 2391–1
- Census of Service Industries, 1982: employment, establishments, receipts, and payroll, by SIC 4-digit kind of business and State, preliminary rpt, 2390–2.2, 2390–2.6

Laundry and cleaning services

County Business Patterns: establishments, employees, and payrolls, by SIC 4-digit industry and county, 1981, annual State rpt series, 2326–8

County Business Patterns: establishments, employees, and payrolls, by SIC 4-digit industry and county, 1982, annual State rpt series, 2326–6

Employment, earnings, and hours, by selected SIC 1- to 4-digit industry, State, and for 278 major labor areas, 1939-83, annual rpt, 6744–5

Employment, earnings, and hours, by SIC 4-digit nonfarm industry, monthly 1974-Feb 1984, annual update, 6744–4

Employment, unemployment, and labor force, by demographic and employment characteristics, State, and for 30 metro areas and 11 large cities, 1983, annual rpt, 6744–7

Fed Govt programs and mgmt cost control proposals, 3-year savings by function and agency, and financial and operating data, 1960s-81, 16908–1.29

Franchise business opportunities, by firm and kind of business, 1984 annual listing, 2044–27

Franchises of firms engaged in distribution of goods and services by kind of business, establishments by State, and sales, 1982-84, annual rpt, 2014–5

Hospital worker wages by sex and occupation, and benefits, for 22 MSAs, Oct 1981 survey, 6787–6.201

Income tax returns of sole proprietorships, detailed data by industry div and selected industry group, 1981, annual rpt, 8304–7

Income tax returns of sole proprietorships, receipts, deductions by type, payroll, and net income, by major industry, 1982, annual article, 8302–2.413

Input-output structure of US economy, detailed interindustry transactions for 537 industries, and components of final demand, 1977 benchmark data, 2708–17

Minority group and women employment, by occupational group and SIC 2- to 3-digit industry, 1981, annual rpt, 9244–1.1

Occupational injury and illness rates, by SIC 2- to 4-digit industry, 1982, annual rpt, 6844–1

Occupational manpower needs and supply by detailed occupation, and educational and training program enrollees and grads by detailed field, 1982 and 1995, biennial rpt, 6744–3

Occupational Outlook Handbook, 1984-85 biennial rpt, 6744–1

Price indexes and prices for producers of laundry and cleaning equipment by detailed type, monthly 1983, annual supplement, 6762–6, 6764–2

Productivity, hours, and employment indexes for selected SIC 3- and 4-digit industries, 1954-82, annual rpt, 6824–1.4

Receipts for selected services, by SIC 2- to 4-digit kind of business, 1983, annual rpt, 2413–8

Technological change, impact on productivity and employment in 4 industries, 1960-90, 6828–23

Underground economy, household expenditures and participation by type of goods or service and sociodemographic characteristics, with methodology and bibl, 1981 survey, 8308–27

Index by Subjects and Names

Virgin Islands economic censuses, 1982: employment, establishments, payroll, and receipts, by SIC 1- to 4-digit industry, island, and city, 2593–1

Wholesale trade census, 1982: employment, establishments, sales by commodity, and payroll for service industry suppliers, by State, preliminary rpt, 2403–1.17

see also under By Industry in the "Index by Categories"

Lave, Roy E.

"Study of the Careers of Participants in UMTA's Transit Management Programs (Section 10)", 7888–60

Law

Death penalty legal status, listing of statutes by State, 1982, annual rpt, 6065–1

Foreign economic, social, and political summary data, by country, 1984, annual factbook, 244–11

Judicial Conf semiannual proceedings and findings, 1984 annual rpt, 18204–5

see also Administration of justice

see also Administrative law and procedure

see also Antitrust law

see also Building permits

see also Citizen lawsuits

see also Courts

see also Due process of law

see also Labor law

see also Law enforcement

see also Lawyers

see also Legal education

see also Maritime law

see also Military law

see also U.S. statutes

see also Zoning and zoning laws

Law enforcement

Assaults, murders, and other deaths of law enforcement officers, by circumstances, level of govt, agency, victim and offender characteristics, and location, 1983, annual rpt, 6224–3

Crimes, arrests by offender characteristics, and rates, by offense, and law enforcement employees, by population size and jurisdiction, 1970s-83, annual rpt, 6224–2

Drug abuse situation, prevention and treatment programs, law enforcement, funding needs, and Fed Govt role, attitudes of State and local officials, 1983 survey, 21968–27

Drug enforcement regional task force program investigation activities, funding, and personnel, with nationwide drug abuse data, 1983 annual rpt, 6004–17

Fed Govt and total law enforcement officers and firefighters killed, death benefit claims, and non-Fed Govt firefighters death benefits by State and city, 1972-82, hearing, 21348–94

Govt census, 1982: local govt employment by function, payroll, and average earnings, for individual counties, cities, and school and special districts, 2455–1

Govt census, 1982: State govt payments to local govts, by program, source of funds, level of govt, and State, with trends from 1902, 2460–3

Justice Dept activities, by subagency, FY82, annual rpt, 6004–1

Land Mgmt Bur public lands admin and program activities in western States, FY82-84, annual rpt, 5724–13

South America cocaine traffic legal policy and enforcement, with data on arrests and confiscations in Peru, 1978, intl conf papers, 7008–40

TTPI socioeconomic, health, and govtl data, by TTPI govt, FY83 and selected trends, detailed annual rpt, 7004–6

see also Administration of justice

see also Administrative law and procedure

see also Arrest

see also Correctional institutions

see also Courts

see also Crime and criminals

see also Criminal investigations

see also Criminal procedure

see also Electronic surveillance

see also Federal aid to law enforcement

see also Juvenile delinquency

see also Organized crime

see also Police

see also Pretrial detention and release

see also Riots and disorders

see also Searches and seizures

see also Traffic laws and courts

Law Enforcement Assistance Administration

see Office of Justice Assistance, Research and Statistics

Law of the sea

see Maritime law

Law schools

see Legal education

Lawler, Thomas A.

"Behavior of the Spread Between Treasury Bill Rates and Private Money Market Rates Since 1978", 9389–1.401

Lawn and garden equipment

see Household appliances and equipment

Lawrence Berkeley Laboratory

see also Department of Energy National Laboratories

Lawrence, Kans.

Census of Housing, 1980: occupancy and unit characteristics, by race, Hispanic origin, and city, SMSA rpt, 2473–1.215

Census of Population and Housing, 1980: detailed population and housing characteristics, by county, city, and census tract, SMSA rpt, 2551–2.215

Housing vacancy rates for single and multifamily units and mobile homes, by county, city, and ZIP code, 1984, annual metro area rpt, 9304–22.15

Housing vacancy rates for single and multifamily units and mobile homes, by ZIP code, 1983, annual SMSA rpt, 9304–22.4

see also under By SMSA or MSA in the "Index by Categories"

Lawrence Livermore Laboratory

see also Department of Energy National Laboratories

Lawrence, Mass.

Census of Housing, 1980: occupancy and unit characteristics, by race, Hispanic origin, and city, SMSA rpt, 2473–1.216

Census of Population and Housing, 1980: detailed population and housing characteristics, by county, city, and census tract, SMSA rpt, 2551–2.216

see also under By SMSA or MSA in the "Index by Categories"

Lawrence, Michael S.

"Coal-Fired Capacity Additions System: Evaluation and Testing", 3166–11.1

Index by Subjects and Names

Lead and lead industry

Lawson, Michael W.

"Significant Features of Fiscal Federalism, 1982-83 Edition", 10044–1

"Tax Burdens for Families Residing in the Largest City in Each State, 1982", 10046–8.2

Lawton, Okla.

Census of Housing, 1980: occupancy and unit characteristics, by race, Hispanic origin, and city, SMSA rpt, 2473–1.217

Census of Population and Housing, 1980: detailed population and housing characteristics, by county, city, and census tract, SMSA rpt, 2551–2.217

Housing vacancy rates for single and multifamily units and mobile homes, by county, city, and ZIP code, 1984, annual metro area rpt, 9304–22.12

see also under By SMSA or MSA in the "Index by Categories"

Lawyers

Asbestos-related occupational disease compensation paid and defendant and plaintiff litigation costs, with comparisons to other tort suits, selected years 1968-82, hearings, 21348–85

Bankruptcy (personal), filers by debt type and other characteristics, selected years 1978-81, hearing, 25528–97.1

Census of Population, 1980: detailed socioeconomic and demographic characteristics, by age, sex, race, Hispanic origin, occupation, and industry, State rpt series, 2531–4

Census of Population, 1980: labor force, by sex, detailed occupation, and region, with comparison to 1970 census, supplementary rpt, 2535–1.12

Census of Service Industries, 1982: employment, establishments, receipts, and payroll, by SIC 2- to 4-digit kind of business, SMSA, county, and city, State rpt series, 2391–1

Census of Service Industries, 1982: employment, establishments, receipts, and payroll, by SIC 4-digit kind of business and State, preliminary rpt, 2390–2.17

County Business Patterns: establishments, employees, and payrolls, by SIC 4-digit industry and county, 1981, annual State rpt series, 2326–8

County Business Patterns: establishments, employees, and payrolls, by SIC 4-digit industry and county, 1982, annual State rpt series, 2326–6

Criminal case disposition, effect of victim injury and other factors, and law enforcement official and victim attitudes, 1983 survey, 6068–185

Drug enforcement regional task force program investigation activities, funding, and personnel, with nationwide drug abuse data, 1983 annual rpt, 6004–17

Earnings by major industry group, and personal income per capita and by source, by region and State, 1929-82, 2708–40

Employment by detailed occupation, for 29 SIC 2-digit nonmanufacturing industries, 1981 BLS survey, 6748–60

Employment, earnings, and hours, by selected SIC 1- to 4-digit industry, State, and for 278 major labor areas, 1939-83, annual rpt, 6744–5

Employment, earnings, and hours, by SIC 4-digit nonfarm industry, monthly 1974-Feb 1984, annual update, 6744–4

Fed Govt programs and mgmt cost control proposals, 3-year savings by function and agency, and financial and operating data, 1960s-81, 16908–1

Fees (legal) awarded private parties in cases against Federal, State, and local govts, by case, selected years 1977-83, 6008–19

Income tax returns of corporations, detailed income and tax items by industry, 1981, annual rpt, 8304–4

Income tax returns of partnerships, detailed data by industry, 1981 estimates, annual article, 8302–2.404

Income tax returns of partnerships, receipts by source, deductions by type, and establishments, by selected industry, 1982, annual article, 8302–2.416

Income tax returns of sole proprietorships, detailed data by industry div and selected industry group, 1981, annual rpt, 8304–7

Income tax returns of sole proprietorships, receipts, deductions by type, payroll, and net income, by major industry, 1982, annual article, 8302–2.413

Income tax returns with investment credits, for individuals by income, and for sole proprietorships by industry, 1981, article, 8302–2.409

Input-output structure of US economy, detailed interindustry transactions for 537 industries, and components of final demand, 1977 benchmark data, 2708–17

Minority group and women employment, by occupational group and SIC 2- to 3-digit industry, 1981, annual rpt, 9244–1.1

Occupational manpower needs and supply by detailed occupation, and educational and training program enrollees and grads by detailed field, 1982 and 1995, biennial rpt, 6744–3

Occupational Outlook Handbook, 1984-85 biennial rpt, 6744–1

Parole examiner workloads and decisions, and hearings with legal representation for inmate, FY80-82, 6006–2.32

Receipts for selected services, by SIC 2- to 4-digit kind of business, 1983, annual rpt, 2413–8

Statistical Abstract of US, social, political, and economic data, 1950s-83 and trends, annual rpt, 2324–1.1

Telephone conference use in civil and criminal hearings, assessment of lawyers and judges in 2 States and Denver, Colo, 1981, 6068–186

US Attorneys civil and criminal case processing in district, appellate, and State courts, by district, FY83, annual rpt, 6004–2

Virgin Islands economic censuses, 1982: employment, establishments, payroll, and receipts, by SIC 1- to 4-digit industry, island, and city, 2593–1

Wages of white-collar workers, by occupation, work level, and industry div, Mar 1984, annual rpt, 6784–2

Wiretapping authorizations by offense, costs, persons involved, arrests, trials, and convictions, 1983, annual rpt, 18204–7

Workers compensation law provisions of States and Fed Govt, by jurisdiction, as of July 1984, semiannual rpt, 6502–1

see also Judges

see also Legal aid

see also Legal education

see also Right to counsel

see also under By Industry in the "Index by Categories"

Layoffs

see Labor turnover

Lazenby, Helen C.

"Demographic Characteristics and Health Care Use and Expenditures by the Aged in the U.S.: 1977-84", 4652–1.420

Lead and lead industry

Business statistics, detailed data for major industries and economic indicators, *Survey of Current Business,* monthly rpt, 2702–1.14

Castings (nonferrous) shipments and unfilled orders, by metal type, monthly Current Industrial Rpt, 2506–10.5

Communist, OECD, and selected other countries minerals and metals production, by commodity, 1960s-83, annual rpt, 244–5.6

County Business Patterns: establishments, employees, and payrolls, by SIC 4-digit industry and county, 1981, annual State rpt series, 2326–8

County Business Patterns: establishments, employees, and payrolls, by SIC 4-digit industry and county, 1982, annual State rpt series, 2326–6

Exports and imports of US, detailed SIC-based commodities by world area, 1983, annual rpts, 2424–6

Exports and imports of US, totals and as percent of domestic production, by SIC 2- to 5-digit commodity, 1981, annual rpt, 2424–3

Exports of US, detailed commodities by country of destination, monthly rpt, 2422–3

Exports of US, detailed Schedule B commodities by country of destination, 1983, annual rpt, 2424–9

Exports of US, detailed Schedule E commodities by mode of transport and world area and country of destination, 1983, annual rpts, 2424–5

Foreign and US supply under alternative market conditions, reserves, and background industry data, 1983 mineral rpt, 5606–4.10

Foreign minerals production, reserves, and industry role in domestic economy and world supply, country and world region rpt series, 5606–1

Great Lakes trade, by SITC 3-digit commodity, port, vessel type, world area, and country, 1982, annual rpt, 7744–3

Imports of US, detailed Schedule A commodities by country and world area of origin, and mode of transport, 1983, annual rpts, 2424–2

Imports of US, detailed Schedule A commodities by country, monthly rpt, 2422–2

Imports of US, detailed TSUSA commodities by country of origin, 1983, annual rpt, 2424–4

Input-output structure of US economy, detailed interindustry transactions for 537 industries, and components of final demand, 1977 benchmark data, 2708–17

Manufacturing census, 1982: financial and operating data, for SIC 4-digit industries by product, preliminary rpt, 2491–1.263

Lead and lead industry

Mineral industries census, 1982: financial and operating data, by SIC 2- to 4-digit industry, preliminary summary rpt, 2511–2.1

Mineral industries census, 1982: financial and operating data, including materials consumed, by SIC 4-digit industry and State, preliminary rpt, 2511–1.2

Mineral Industry Surveys, commodity review of production, trade, stocks, and consumption, monthly rpt, 5612–1.13

Minerals Yearbook, 1982, Vol 1: commodity reviews of production, reserves, supply, use, and trade, annual rpt, 5604–33

Minerals Yearbook, 1982, Vol 2 preprints: State reviews of production and sales by commodity, and business activity, annual rpt series, 5604–16

Minerals Yearbook, 1982, Vol 2: State reviews of production, sales, and firms, by commodity, and business activity, annual rpt, 5604–34

Minerals Yearbook, 1982, Vol 3: foreign country reviews of production, trade, and policies, by commodity, annual rpt, 5604–35

Minerals Yearbook, 1982, Vol 3 preprints: foreign country reviews of production, trade, and policies, by commodity, annual rpt series, 5604–17

Minerals Yearbook, 1983, Vol 1 preprints: commodity review of production, reserves, supply, use, and trade, annual rpt, 5604–15.37

Minerals Yearbook, 1983, Vol 3 preprints: foreign country reviews of production, trade, and policies, by commodity, annual rpt series, 5604–23

Occupational injuries and incidence rates at metal mines and related operations, detailed analysis, 1982, annual rpt, 6664–3

Occupational injury and illness rates, by SIC 2- to 4-digit industry, 1982, annual rpt, 6844–1

Producer prices and indexes, by stage of processing and detailed commodity, monthly rpt, 6762–6

Producer prices and indexes, by stage of processing and detailed commodity, monthly 1983, annual supplement, 6764–2

Production, prices, trade, use, employment, tariffs, and stockpiling, by mineral commodity, with foreign comparisons, 1979-83, annual rpt, 5604–18

Stockpiling of strategic and critical materials, Fed Govt activities and inventories by commodity, Oct 1983-Mar 1984, semiannual rpt, 9432–1

Stockpiling of strategic materials, inventories, costs, and goals, by commodity, as of June 1984, semiannual rpt, 9452–7

Strategic minerals supply/demand, trade, and foreign and US industry devs by firm and country, by commodity, bimonthly rpt, 5602–4

Waterborne commerce of US (domestic and foreign), freight by commodity, traffic, and passengers, by port and waterway, 1982, annual rpt, 3754–3

see also Lead poisoning and pollution

see also under By Commodity in the "Index by Categories"

see also under By Industry in the "Index by Categories"

Lead poisoning and pollution

Air pollutant and radiation indoor levels by emissions source, and household exposure and health effects by pollutant type, various periods 1966-83, hearings, 21708–102

Air pollutant emission factors, by detailed source, 3rd edition, 1983-84 supplements, 9198–13

Air pollutant metal levels, by monitoring site, State, and urban-rural location, 1977-79, last issue of annual rpt, 9194–10

Air pollution levels for 6 pollutants, and measurements exceeding natl standards, by site, 1983, annual rpt, 9194–5

Air pollution levels for 6 pollutants, by source, region, and for large SMSAs, 1975-82, annual rpt, 9194–1

Blood lead levels by sociodemographic and behavioral characteristics, and potential workplace exposure, 1976-80, 4147–11.201

Children screened for lead toxicity and results, by region, Oct 1981-Sept 1982, annual rpt, 4204–1.3

Environmental quality, pollutant discharge by type, and EPA protection activities, 1970s-83, biennial summary rpt, 9184–16

Environmental quality, pollutant discharge by type and source, and EPA protection activities and funding, 1970s-83, biennial regional rpt series, 9184–15

New York Bight pollutant loadings from ocean dumping of municipal wastes by type and source, and concentrations in fish and sediments, 1970s-82, hearings, 21568–36

Occupational health risks from hazardous substances and radiation, by industry, occupation, age, and sex, with bibl and glossary, 1920s-82, 9638–50

State govt maternal and child health funding, and admin of Fed Govt block grants, by program for 13 States, 1981-83, GAO rpt, 26121–70

Water from urban runoff, quality, pollutant concentrations, and control cost-effectiveness, with monitoring sites rainfall and other characteristics, by city and region, 1978-83, 9208–122

Water supply and quality in streams and lakes, and groundwater levels in wells, by drainage basin, 1980, annual State rpt series, 5666–12

Water supply and quality in streams and lakes, and groundwater levels in wells, by drainage basin, 1981, annual State rpt series, 5666–16

Water supply and quality in streams and lakes, and groundwater levels in wells, by drainage basin, 1982, annual State rpt series, 5666–20

Water supply and quality in streams and lakes, and groundwater levels in wells, by drainage basin, 1983, annual State rpt series, 5666–10

Leading indicators

see Economic indicators

Index by Subjects and Names

Leasing

see Mineral leases

see Oil and gas leases

see Rental industries

Leath, Mack

"Marketing Methods, Pricing Arrangements, and Marketing Channels Used by Southern Soybean Producers in 1982/83", 1561–3.402

Leather industry and products

Business statistics, detailed data for major industries and economic indicators, *Survey of Current Business,* monthly rpt, 2702–1.12

Census of Population, 1980: detailed socioeconomic and demographic characteristics, by age, sex, race, Hispanic origin, occupation, and industry, State rpt series, 2531–4

China economic conditions, agricultural and industrial production, trade, and domestic and foreign investment, 1980-85, 2048–106

China exports and imports by SITC 1- to 5-digit commodity, 1970s-82, annual rpt, 244–12

China exports to US of selected textile and leather goods harmful to competing US industries, and US consumption and producer shipments, 1978-83, 9882–2.401

Collective bargaining agreements expiring during year, covered workers by SIC 2-digit industry, firm, and union, with summary of key provisions, 1984, annual rpt, 6784–9

County Business Patterns: establishments, employees, and payrolls, by SIC 4-digit industry and county, 1981, annual State rpt series, 2326–8

County Business Patterns: establishments, employees, and payrolls, by SIC 4-digit industry and county, 1982, annual State rpt series, 2326–6

Earnings by major industry group, and personal income per capita and by source, by region and State, 1929-82, 2708–40

Employment, earnings, and hours, by selected SIC 1- to 4-digit industry, State, and for 278 major labor areas, 1939-83, annual rpt, 6744–5

Employment, earnings, and hours, by SIC 4-digit nonfarm industry, monthly 1974-Feb 1984, annual update, 6744–4

Endangered animals and plants foreign trade including reexports of live specimens and products, by purpose, country, and species, 1982, annual rpt, 5504–19

Exports and imports of dairy, livestock, and poultry live animals, meat, and products, by commodity and country of destination, FAS quarterly rpt, 1925–32

Exports and imports of US, by commodity group, world area, selected country, US coastal area and port, and mode of transport, with seasonal adjustments, monthly rpt, 2422–9

Exports and imports of US, detailed SIC-based commodities by world area, 1983, annual rpts, 2424–6

Exports and imports of US, totals and as percent of domestic production, by SIC 2- to 5-digit commodity, 1981, annual rpt, 2424–3

Index by Subjects and Names

Legal aid

Exports of manufactured and agricultural commodities, manufacturing production, and export-related employment, 1960s-82, State rpt series, 2046–3

Exports of US, detailed commodities by country of destination, monthly rpt, 2422–3

Exports of US, detailed Schedule B commodities by country of destination, 1983, annual rpt, 2424–9

Exports of US, detailed Schedule E commodities by mode of transport and world area and country of destination, 1983, annual rpts, 2424–5

Finances and operations, by SIC 2- to 4-digit industry, 1970s-83 and projected to 1988, annual rpt, 2014–4

Great Lakes trade, by SITC 3-digit commodity, port, vessel type, world area, and country, 1982, annual rpt, 7744–3

Handbags trade, tariffs, and industry operating data, 1979-83, TSUSA commodity rpt supplement, 9885–7.60

Imports of textile manufactures other than cotton, wool, or man-made fibers, by product and country of origin, June 1984, semiannual rpt, 2046–8.5

Imports of US, detailed Schedule A commodities by country and world area of origin, and mode of transport, 1983, annual rpts, 2424–2

Imports of US, detailed Schedule A commodities by country, monthly rpt, 2422–2

Imports of US, detailed TSUSA commodities by country of origin, 1983, annual rpt, 2424–4

Income tax returns of corporations, detailed income and tax items by industry, 1981, annual rpt, 8304–4

Income tax returns of corporations with foreign tax credit, income and deductions by type, asset size, and selected industry group, 1980, article, 8302–2.415

Income tax returns of sole proprietorships, detailed data by industry div and selected industry group, 1981, annual rpt, 8304–7

Income tax returns of sole proprietorships, receipts, deductions by type, payroll, and net income, by major industry, 1982, annual article, 8302–2.413

Input-output structure of US economy, detailed interindustry transactions for 85 industries, and components of final demand, 1977, article, 2702–1.421

Input-output structure of US economy, detailed interindustry transactions for 537 industries, and components of final demand, 1977 benchmark data, 2708–17

Manufacturing census, 1982: financial and operating data, by SIC 2- to 4-digit industry, State, SMSA, and county, preliminary census div rpt series, 2491–3

Manufacturing census, 1982: financial and operating data, for SIC 4-digit industries by product, preliminary rpt series, 2491–1

Minority group and women employment, by occupational group and SIC 2- to 3-digit industry, 1981, annual rpt, 9244–1.1

Occupational injury and illness rates, by SIC 2- to 4-digit industry, 1982, annual rpt, 6844–1

OECD trade, total and for 4 major countries, and US trade by country, by commodity, 1972-82, annual world region rpt series, 244–13

Pollution abatement capital and operating costs, by SIC 2- to 4-digit industry, State, and SMSA, 1982, annual Current Industrial Rpt, 2506–3.6

Producer prices and indexes, by stage of processing and detailed commodity, monthly rpt, 6762–6

Producer prices and indexes, by stage of processing and detailed commodity, monthly 1983, annual supplement, 6764–2

Scientists, engineers, and technicians employed in private industry, by occupation and industry group, 1980-81, biennial rpt, 9627–23

Waterborne commerce of US (domestic and foreign), freight by commodity, traffic, and passengers, by port and waterway, 1982, annual rpt, 3754–3

see also Hides and skins

see also Shoe industry

see also under By Commodity in the "Index by Categories"

see also under By Industry in the "Index by Categories"

Lebanon

Agricultural and food production indexes, and production of selected commodities, by world region and country, 1974-83, annual rpt, 1524–5

Agricultural situation in Middle East and North Africa, by country and commodity, 1983 and outlook for 1984, annual rpt, 1524–4.3

AID activities and funding by project and function, FY85, and developing countries summary socioeconomic data, 1970s-83, by country, annual rpt, 9914–3

AID economic assistance to developing countries, obligations and disbursements by country, quarterly rpt, 9912–4

AID loan repayment status and terms by program and country, and status of predecessor agency loans, quarterly rpt, 9912–3

Economic, social, and political summary data, by country, 1984, annual factbook, 244–11

Exports of US, detailed Schedule B commodities by country of destination, 1983, annual rpt, 2424–9

Exports of US, detailed Schedule E commodities by mode of transport and world area and country of destination, 1983, annual rpts, 2424–5

Imports of US, detailed Schedule A commodities by country and world area of origin, and mode of transport, 1983, annual rpts, 2424–2

Imports of US, detailed TSUSA commodities by country of origin, 1983, annual rpt, 2424–4

Loans and grants for economic and military assistance from US and intl agencies, by program and country, FY46-83, annual rpt, 9914–5

Military aid of US, arms sales, and training programs costs and budget requests by program, world region, and country, FY83-85, annual rpt, 7144–13

Military spending, arms trade, and armed forces size, with total govt spending and population, by country, 1972-82, annual rpt, 9824–1

Minerals Yearbook, 1982, Vol 3: foreign country reviews of production, trade, and policies, by commodity, annual rpt, 5604–35

Minerals Yearbook, 1982, Vol 3 preprints: foreign country review of production, trade, and policies, by commodity, annual rpt, 5604–17.88

Population size and growth rates, and latest available benchmark demographic data, by country, 1950-83, biennial rpt, 2324–4

see also under By Foreign Country in the "Index by Categories"

Lebanon, Pa.

Wages by occupation, and benefits for office and plant workers, 1983 labor market area survey rpt, 6785–3.2

see also under By SMSA or MSA in the "Index by Categories"

LeBlanc, Michael

"Agricultural Implications of Natural Gas Deregulation", 1548–239

"Effects of Natural Gas Decontrol on Farming Costs and Income", 1548–240

Lebo, Dennis E.

"Public/Private Cooperation in Rural Roadway Improvements", 1004–16.1

Lee County, Miss.

Housing vacancy rates for single and multifamily units and mobile homes, by city and ZIP code, 1984, annual metro area rpt, 9304–19.29

Lee, Jeffrey

"China's Economy and Foreign Trade, 1981-85", 2048–106

Lee, John E., Jr.

"Forces Shaping the Future of U.S. Agriculture", 1004–16.1

Lee, Myung-Hoon

"Plant Closings and Worker Dislocation", 9377–1.401

Lee, Rose E.

"Report on the Noncompetitive Employment of 30 Percent or More Disabled Veterans in the Federal Government", 9842–4

"Veterans Readjustment Appointments in the Federal Government, Apr.-Sept. 1982", 9842–3

Leeward and Windward Islands

see Caribbean area

Legal aid

Bank robbery court cases by case processing, sentencing, and offender characteristics, and compared to other Fed Govt felony cases, 1979-80, periodic rpt, 6062–2.407

Budget of US, CBO analysis of revenue and spending alternatives and projections of economic indicators, FY85-89, annual rpt, 26304–3.3

Census of Population, 1980: detailed socioeconomic and demographic characteristics, by age, sex, race, Hispanic origin, occupation, and industry, State rpt series, 2531–4

Census of Service Industries, 1982: employment, establishments, receipts, and payroll, by SIC 2- to 4-digit kind of business, SMSA, county, and city, State rpt series, 2391–1

Court civil and criminal casloads and activity summary, for Federal district, appeals, and bankruptcy courts, 1975-June 1984, annual chartbook, 18204–9

Legal aid

Fed Govt financial and nonfinancial domestic aid, 1984 annual comprehensive catalog, 104–5

Federal district court public defender caseloads, by district, quarterly rpt, annual tables, 18202–1

Govt census, 1982: State govt payments to local govts, by program, source of funds, level of govt, and State, with trends from 1902, 2460–3

Older persons population characteristics, and needs and costs of social services by type, by metro-nonmetro status, 1970s-82 with trends from 1900, 21148–28

Public and community defender grants, FY85, Judicial Conf semiannual proceedings, annual rpt, 18204–5

Public defender systems, costs, cases, and expenditures by level of govt and State, with system characteristics and lawyer fee ranges, 1981, 6066–19.8

Puerto Rico organizations in US and Puerto Rico, philanthropic grants received, by foundation, purpose, and recipient, 1979-81, hearings, 21788–137.1

Traffic accidents and casualties detailed direct and indirect costs, by characteristics of persons and vehicles involved, 1979-80, 7768–80

see also Lawyers

Legal education

Census of Population, 1980: labor force, by sex, detailed occupation, and region, with comparison to 1970 census, supplementary rpt, 2535–1.12

Degrees conferred in higher education, by race, Hispanic origin, sex, level, and field, selected years 1949/50-1979/80, annual rpt, 4824–2.16

Education Dept programs funding, operations, and effectiveness, FY83, annual rpt, 4804–5

Howard University salaries, academic standing, medical research, and library operations, and finances of Howard Inn, selected years 1976-83, GAO rpt, 26121–74

Student aid Federal programs funding and participation, by instn type and control, State, and outlying area, with student loan defaults and collections, FY82, annual rpt, 4804–28

Legal ethics

see also Judicial ethics

Legal profession

see Lawyers

Legal services

see Lawyers

see Legal aid

see Legal Services Corp.

Legal Services Corp.

Budget of US Appendix, detailed budgets and personnel summaries, by agency, FY85, annual rpt, 104–3

Budget of US, appropriations, outlays, balances, and budget receipts, by govtl branch and agency, FY83, annual rpt, 8104–2

Legislative bodies

see Congress

see House of Representatives

see Senate

see State legislatures

Leiderman, Leonardo

"Intertemporal Asset Pricing and the Term Structure of Exchange and Interest Rates: The Eurocurrency Market", 9381–10.40

Leisure activities

see Recreation

Lemons

see Citrus fruits

Lentils

see Vegetables and vegetable products

Leominster, Mass.

Census of Housing, 1980: occupancy and unit characteristics, by race, Hispanic origin, and city, SMSA rpt, 2473–1.155

Census of Population and Housing, 1980: detailed population and housing characteristics, by county, city, and census tract, SMSA rpt, 2551–2.155

see also under By SMSA or MSA in the "Index by Categories"

Leon, Carol B.

"Working for Uncle Sam: A Look at Members of the Armed Forces", 6722–1.441

Leontief, Wassily

"Impacts of Automation on Employment, 1963-2000", 21728–54

Leprosy

see Infective and parasitic diseases

Leptospirosis

see Animal diseases and zoonoses

Lerner, Philip R.

"Social Security Beneficiaries by State and County, Dec. 1982", 4748–38

Lesotho

Agricultural situation in sub-Saharan Africa, by country, 1982-83 and outlook for 1984, annual rpt, 1524–4.10

AID activities and funding by project and function, FY85, and developing countries summary socioeconomic data, 1970s-83, by country, annual rpt, 9914–3

AID economic assistance to developing countries, obligations and disbursements by country, quarterly rpt, 9912–4

Background Notes, summary social, political, and economic data, 1984 rpt, 7006–2.48

Economic conditions and foreign marketing prospects in 46 Sub-Saharan countries, 1983 world region rpt, 2046–5.1

Economic, social, and political summary data, by country, 1984, annual factbook, 244–11

Exports of US, detailed Schedule B commodities by country of destination, 1983, annual rpt, 2424–9

Exports of US, detailed Schedule E commodities by mode of transport and world area and country of destination, 1983, annual rpts, 2424–5

Imports of US, detailed Schedule A commodities by country and world area of origin, and mode of transport, 1983, annual rpts, 2424–2

Imports of US, detailed TSUSA commodities by country of origin, 1983, annual rpt, 2424–4

Loans and grants for economic and military assistance from US and intl agencies, by program and country, FY46-83, annual rpt, 9914–5

Military spending, arms trade, and armed forces size, with total govt spending and population, by country, 1972-82, annual rpt, 9824–1

Index by Subjects and Names

Minerals Yearbook, 1982, Vol 3: foreign country reviews of production, trade, and policies, by commodity, annual rpt, 5604–35

Minerals Yearbook, 1982, Vol 3 preprints: foreign country review of production, trade, and policies, by commodity, annual rpt, 5604–17.83

Population size and growth rates, and latest available benchmark demographic data, by country, 1950-83, biennial rpt, 2324–4

see also under By Foreign Country in the "Index by Categories"

Letter carriers

see Postal employees

Lettuce

see Vegetables and vegetable products

Leukemia

see Neoplasms

Level of education

see Degrees, higher education

see Educational attainment

see School dropouts

Levin, David J.

"Receipts and Expenditures of State Governments and of Local Governments, 1980-83", 2702–1.436

"State and Local Government Fiscal Position: An Alternative Measure", 2702–1.409

"State and Local Government Fiscal Position in 1983", 2702–1.405

Levitan, Sar A.

"Worker Participation and Productivity Change", 6722–1.457

Lewbel, George S.

"Ecology of Petroleum Platforms in the Northwestern Gulf of Mexico: A Community Profile", 5506–9.7

Lewis, David

"Financing U.S. Airports in the 1980s", 26306–6.75

Lewis, Douglas

"Improving U.S. Farmland", 1506–5.20

Lewis, John B.

"International Pesticide Outlook", 1004–16.1

Lewis, W. Frank

"Marital Status and Its Relation to the Use of Short-Stay Hospitals and Nursing Homes", 4102–1.443

Lewiston, Maine

Census of Housing, 1980: occupancy and unit characteristics, by race, Hispanic origin, and city, SMSA rpt, 2473–1.218

Census of Population and Housing, 1980: detailed population and housing characteristics, by county, city, and census tract, SMSA rpt, 2551–2.218

see also under By SMSA or MSA in the "Index by Categories"

Lexington, Ky.

Census of Housing, 1980: occupancy and unit characteristics, by race, Hispanic origin, and city, SMSA rpt, 2473–1.219

Census of Population and Housing, 1980: detailed population and housing characteristics, by county, city, and census tract, SMSA rpt, 2551–2.219

see also under By City and By SMSA or MSA in the "Index by Categories"

Liberia

Agricultural and food production indexes, and production of selected commodities, by world region and country, 1974-83, annual rpt, 1524–5

Index by Subjects and Names

Libya

Agricultural situation in sub-Saharan Africa, by country, 1982-83 and outlook for 1984, annual rpt, 1524–4.10

Agricultural supply/demand, trade, and production, and socioeconomic data, by country, 1950s-77, 1528–179

AID activities and funding by project and function, FY85, and developing countries summary socioeconomic data, 1970s-83, by country, annual rpt, 9914–3

AID economic assistance to developing countries, obligations and disbursements by country, quarterly rpt, 9912–4

AID loan repayment status and terms by program and country, and status of predecessor agency loans, quarterly rpt, 9912–3

AID program for rural dev assistance in Liberia, socioeconomic impacts, 1976-77, 9916–1.53

Background Notes, summary social, political, and economic data, 1984 rpt, 7006–2.39

Economic conditions and foreign marketing prospects in 46 Sub-Saharan countries, 1983 world region rpt, 2046–5.1

Economic conditions, income, production, prices, employment, and trade, 1984 annual country rpt, 2046–4.125

Economic, social, and political summary data, by country, 1984, annual factbook, 244–11

Economic trends in income, production, prices, employment, finances, and trade, 1984 annual rpt, 2046–4.31

Exports and imports of US, by commodity and country, 1972-82, annual world region rpt, 244–13.4

Exports of US, detailed Schedule B commodities by country of destination, 1983, annual rpt, 2424–9

Exports of US, detailed Schedule E commodities by mode of transport and world area and country of destination, 1983, annual rpts, 2424–5

Imports of US, detailed Schedule A commodities by country and world area of origin, and mode of transport, 1983, annual rpts, 2424–2

Imports of US, detailed TSUSA commodities by country of origin, 1983, annual rpt, 2424–4

Loans and grants for economic and military assistance from US and intl agencies, by program and country, FY46-83, annual rpt, 9914–5

Military aid of US, arms sales, and training programs costs and budget requests by program, world region, and country, FY83-85, annual rpt, 7144–13

Military spending, arms trade, and armed forces size, with total govt spending and population, by country, 1972-82, annual rpt, 9824–1

Minerals Yearbook, 1982, Vol 3: foreign country reviews of production, trade, and policies, by commodity, annual rpt, 5604–35

Minerals Yearbook, 1983, Vol 3 preprints: foreign country review of production, trade, and policies, by commodity, annual rpt, 5604–23.43

Population size and growth rates, and latest available benchmark demographic data, by country, 1950-83, biennial rpt, 2324–4

Ships in world merchant fleet, and tonnage, by country of registry, 1982, annual rpt, 7704–3.1

see also under By Foreign Country in the "Index by Categories"

Librarians

Census of Population, 1980: detailed socioeconomic and demographic characteristics, by age, sex, race, Hispanic origin, occupation, and industry, State rpt series, 2531–4

Census of Population, 1980: detailed socioeconomic characteristics, by county, city, and inside-outside SMSAs and central cities, State rpt series, 2531–3

Census of Population, 1980: labor force, by sex, detailed occupation, and region, with comparison to 1970 census, supplementary rpt, 2535–1.12

Degrees conferred in higher education, by race, Hispanic origin, sex, level, and field, selected years 1949/50-1979/80, annual rpt, 4824–2.16

Depository library program of GPO, opinions of librarians on quality and mgmt, 1983 survey, GAO rpt, 26111–19

Govt census, 1982: employment, payrolls, and average earnings, by function, level of govt, State, county, population size, and inside-outside SMSAs, 2455–2

Govt census, 1982: local govt employment by function, payroll, and average earnings, for individual counties, cities, and school and special districts, 2455–1

Govt employment and payroll, by function, level of govt, and jurisdiction, 1983, annual rpt series, 2466–1

Higher education instns libraries expenditures, holdings by type, use, staff by sex, and Federal grants received, 1979-82, biennial rpt, 4854–1

Hospital worker wages by sex and occupation, and benefits, for 22 MSAs, Oct 1981 survey, 6787–6.201

Occupational manpower needs and supply by detailed occupation, and educational and training program enrollees and grads by detailed field, 1982 and 1995, biennial rpt, 6744–3

Occupational Outlook Handbook, 1984-85 biennial rpt, 6744–1

Libraries

Army morale, welfare, and recreation programs, revenue and expenses worldwide by activity and major command, FY82-83, annual rpt, 3704–12

Census Bur publications data coverage and availability, 1984 annual listing, 2304–2

Census of Service Industries, 1982: employment, establishments, receipts, and payroll, by SIC 2- to 4-digit kind of business, SMSA, county, and city, State rpt series, 2391–1

County Business Patterns: establishments, employees, and payrolls, by SIC 4-digit industry and county, 1981, annual State rpt series, 2326–8

County Business Patterns: establishments, employees, and payrolls, by SIC 4-digit industry and county, 1982, annual State rpt series, 2326–6

Depository libraries for Fed Govt publications, 1983 annual listing, 2214–1

Depository library program of GPO, opinions of librarians on quality and mgmt, 1983 survey, GAO rpt, 26111–19

Geological Survey programs and funding, FY78-83, annual rpt, 5664–8

Govt census, 1982: city govt revenues by source, expenditures by function, debt, and assets, by State and city, 2457–4

Govt census, 1982: county govt revenues by source, expenditures by function, debt, and assets, by State and county, 2457–3

Govt census, 1982: State govt payments to local govts, by program, source of funds, level of govt, and State, with trends from 1902, 2460–3

Govt finances, by level of govt, State, and for large cities and counties, 1981-83, annual rpt series, 2466–2

Higher education instns libraries expenditures, holdings by type, use, staff by sex, and Federal grants received, 1979-82, biennial rpt, 4854–1

Howard University salaries, academic standing, medical research, and library operations, and finances of Howard Inn, selected years 1976-83, GAO rpt, 26121–74

Japan-US Friendship Commission educational and cultural exchange activities, grants, and trust fund status, FY83, annual rpt, 14694–1

Microfiche from Educational Resources Info Center, holdings of US and foreign educational and other instns, as of 1983, listing, 4918–14

Natl Agricultural Library activities and programs, FY83, annual rpt, 1004–3

Public, public school, and higher education instn libraries, selected data, 1973-82, annual rpt, 4824–2.25

Statistical Abstract of US, social, political, and economic data, 1950s-83 and trends, annual rpt, 2324–1.1

USIA info center and reading room operations, by world region, country, and city, FY83, annual rpt, 9854–4

see also Federal aid to libraries

see also Librarians

see also Library of Congress

see also Medical libraries

Library of Congress

Budget of US Appendix, detailed budgets and personnel summaries, by agency, FY85, annual rpt, 104–3

Budget of US, appropriations, outlays, balances, and budget receipts, by govtl branch and agency, FY83, annual rpt, 8104–2

Budget of US, compact budgets by function, agency, and account, FY85 with projections to FY89, annual rpt, 104–2

Capitol Architect detailed expenditures for buildings and grounds, salaries, supplies, and services, 1st half FY84, semiannual rpt, 25922–2

Copyright activities of Register of Copyrights, including intl relations, registrations, fees earned, and royalties collected, FY82, annual rpt, 26404–2

R&D Fed Govt funding for all performers, by field and supporting agency, selected years FY60-84, annual rpt, 9627–20

see also Congressional Research Service

Libya

Agricultural and food production indexes, and production of selected commodities, by world region and country, 1974-83, annual rpt, 1524–5

Libya

Agricultural situation in Middle East and North Africa, by country and commodity, 1983 and outlook for 1984, annual rpt, 1524–4.3

Agricultural supply/demand, trade, and production, and socioeconomic data, by country, 1950s-77, 1528–179

AID loan repayment status and terms by program and country, and status of predecessor agency loans, quarterly rpt, 9912–3

Economic, social, and political summary data, by country, 1984, annual factbook, 244–11

Exports of US, detailed Schedule B commodities by country of destination, 1983, annual rpt, 2424–9

Exports of US, detailed Schedule E commodities by mode of transport and world area and country of destination, 1983, annual rpts, 2424–5

Imports of US, detailed Schedule A commodities by country and world area of origin, and mode of transport, 1983, annual rpts, 2424–2

Imports of US, detailed TSUSA commodities by country of origin, 1983, annual rpt, 2424–4

Loans and grants for economic and military assistance from US and intl agencies, by program and country, FY46-83, annual rpt, 9914–5

Military spending, arms trade, and armed forces size, with total govt spending and population, by country, 1972-82, annual rpt, 9824–1

Minerals Yearbook, 1982, Vol 3: foreign country reviews of production, trade, and policies, by commodity, annual rpt, 5604–35

Minerals Yearbook, 1983, Vol 3 preprints: foreign country review of production, trade, and policies, by commodity, annual rpt, 5604–23.44

Oil production and exports, by major exporting country, detailed data, monthly rpt, 3162–24

Oil reserves, production, and resource lifespan under alternative production rates, for 3 countries, 1909-1982 with projections to 2100, 3166–9.8

Population size and growth rates, and latest available benchmark demographic data, by country, 1950-83, biennial rpt, 2324–4

see also under By Foreign Country in the "Index by Categories"

Licenses and permits

Alcohol and tobacco operations permits, FY82, last issue of annual rpt, 8484–1.1

Alcohol, Tobacco, and Firearms Bur activities nationwide and in 20 cities, funding, and jobs to be transferred to Customs and Secret Service, 1979-82, hearings, 21528–55

Animal protection, licensing, and inspection activities of USDA, and animals used in research, by State, FY83, annual rpt, 1394–10

Auto and van operating and owning costs by component and vehicle size, for 12 years of operation, 1984 model year, annual rpt, 7304–2, 7304–2.3, 7554–21

Auto operating costs by component and vehicle size, and Fed Govt mileage reimbursement rates, 1983, annual rpt, 9454–13.1

Index by Subjects and Names

Boat registrations, by State, class, propulsion type, and hull material, 1983, annual rpt, 7404–1.1

Coal exploration licenses issued by State, and Interior Dept drilling costs and holes drilled, FY76-83, 11128–1

Coal lands of Fed Govt leasing activity, acreage, and reserves, by State, coal region, and tract, FY83, annual rpt, 5724–10

Coastal environmental characteristics, fish, wildlife, and use, and population socioeconomic data, for individual areas, series, 5506–4

Copyright royalty fees collected for secondary cable TV transmissions and jukeboxes, FY82, annual rpt, 26404–2

Day care (child) in underground economy, households using services by provider licensing status and annual expenditure, 1981 survey, 8308–27

Drivers license requirements and admin, by State and Canada Province, 1984, biennial rpt, 7554–18

Drivers license revocation and other drunk driving deterrence measures in selected States, and total and alcohol-related traffic deaths, 1980-82, 9618–10

Drivers licensed and travel patterns, 1977 survey, series, 7556–6

Drivers licensed by age and sex, and licensing policies, by State, 1982, annual rpt, 7554–16

Drivers licenses by age and sex, 1961-81, annual rpt, 7764–1

Drivers licenses in force, by age, sex, and State, 1982-83, annual summary rpt, 7554–24

Drivers licenses in force by license type, sex, and age, and revenues, by State, 1983, annual rpt, 7554–1.2, 7554–1.4

Electric power transactions of US with Canada and Mexico, by utility and US region, 1983, annual rpt, 3104–10

Energy production, reserves, and prices, by energy type, and selected indicators of energy use, by State, 1982-83 with selected comparisons from 1971, annual rpt, 3164–60

Export licensing and monitoring activities under Export Admin Act, for selected commodities, and for Communist and other countries, FY83, annual rpt, 2044–22

Farm production expenditures, detailed items by farm sales size and region, 1983, annual rpt, 1614–3

FERC activities and funding by program, with some natural gas and electric power industry data, FY83, annual rpt, 3084–9

Fishing and hunting licenses, by State, FY84, annual rpt, 5504–13

Fishing and hunting licenses issued and gross cost to sportsmen, by State, FY83, annual rpt, 5504–16

Govt census, 1982: city govt revenues by source, expenditures by function, debt, and assets, by State and city, 2457–4

Govt census, 1982: county govt revenues by source, expenditures by function, debt, and assets, by State and county, 2457–3

Govt census, 1982: State govt payments to local govts, by program, source of funds, level of govt, and State, with trends from 1902, 2460–3

Govt finances, by level of govt, State, and for large cities and counties, 1981-83, annual rpt series, 2466–2

Govt revenues, by type, level of govt, and State, selected years 1902-83, annual rpt, 10044–1.2

Grazing of livestock on Natl Forest System lands, and losses from predators, poisonous plants, and other causes, by region and State, FY83, annual rpt, 1204–5

Health professionals license sanctions in 3 States, and subsequent Medicare and Medicaid program participation, by specialty, 1977-82, GAO rpt, 26121–80

Hunting for migratory birds, duck stamp sales, with philatelic data and reproductions, 1983/84, annual fact sheet, 5504–25

Income tax returns of corporations with foreign tax credit, income and deductions by type, asset size, and selected industry group, 1980, article, 8302–2.415

Land Mgmt Bur activities and finances, and public land acreage and use, annual State rpt series, 5724–11

Land Mgmt Bur public lands admin and program activities in western States, FY82-84, annual rpt, 5724–13

Land Mgmt Bur public lands receipts from mineral leases, licenses, and permits, FY83, annual rpt, 5724–1.4

Marine Mammal Protection Act admin and populations, strandings, and catch permits by type and applicant, by species and location, Apr 1983-Mar 1984, annual rpt, 2164–11

Marine mammals protection activities and Fed Govt funding, population status, and research, 1983, annual rpt, 5504–12

Meat plants inspected and certified for exporting products to US, by country, 1983, annual listing, 1374–2

Motor fuel State tax provisions, motor vehicle registration fees, and disposition of receipts, by State, as of Jan 1984, biennial rpt, 7554–37

Motor vehicle and operators taxes, State and local revenues, quarterly rpt, 2462–3

Nuclear fuel facilities inventory discrepancies, 2nd half 1983, semiannual rpt, 9632–3

Nuclear power and weapons policy, fuel supply/demand, waste disposal and siting, environmental effects of radiation, and public attitudes, 1970s-82 with projections to 2000, 3008–88

Nuclear power plant capacity, generation, shutdowns, operation status and costs, and fuel, quarterly rpt, 3352–3

Nuclear power plant construction and operation status, and capacity, by plant, region, State, and selected country, 1983 and projected to 2020, annual rpt, 3164–57

Nuclear power plant licensing actions and status, by action type and plant, monthly rpt, 9632–5

Nuclear power plant licensing 24-month delay, effect on utility financial performance and electric power prices, for plant completed May 1979, 9638–53

Nuclear power plant safety standards and research, design, licensing, construction, operation, and finances, with data by reactor, bimonthly rpt, 3352–4

Index by Subjects and Names

Nuclear power plants licensed for operation, construction permits granted and pending, and plants ordered and announced, monthly rpt, 3162–24.8

Nuclear reactor operating and inspection data for individual commercial facilities, monthly rpt, 9632–1

Nuclear Regulatory Commission activities, employment, and finances, and operations of individual power plants by State, FY83, annual rpt, 9634–2

Ocean dumping of waste materials, EPA permit program and intl London Dumping Convention activities, 1981-83, annual rpt, 9204–8

Physicians initial licensure in US, for US, Canada, and other foreign medical grads, 1950-81, biennial rpt, 4114–8

Pilot and nonpilot certificates held and issued, by type of certificate, region, State, and for women, 1983, annual rpt, 7504–1.7

Pilots and nonpilots certified by FAA, by type of certificate, age, sex, region, and State, 1983, annual rpt, 7504–2

Radiation control program activities, State and local expenditures, personnel, and NRC licenses, by State, FY80-82, annual rpt, 4064–3

Real estate broker govt certification requirements, licenses, and exam results, by State and Canada Province, 1977-78, 9408–48

Small Business Investment Companies finances, funding, licensing, and loan activity, 2nd half FY84, semiannual rpt, 9762–3

Taxicab licenses, density, fares, license prices, and deregulation effects, by selected city, various dates 1970-84, 9406–1.37

Traffic fatal accidents detailed circumstances, and characteristics of persons and vehicles involved, 1982, annual rpt, 7764–10

Traffic safety projects research and evaluation, quarterly rpt articles, 7762–9

Transportation revenues by source and expenditures, by level of govt and mode of transport, and Fed Govt aid by type, FY77-82, 7308–185

Truck transport of fruit and vegetables, costs per vehicle-mile by component for fleets and owner-operator trucks, monthly rpt, 1272–1

TV channels allocation and licensing status, for commercial and noncommercial UHF and VHF TV by market and community, as of Dec 1983, semiannual rpt, 9282–6

Water pollution regulation under EPA wastewater discharge system, operations and funding, various periods FY79-83, GAO rpt, 26113–113

Wood fuel removal program itemized costs to Forest Service in 3 central Appalachia natl forests, 1981, 1208–191

see also Building permits

see also Motor vehicle registrations

see also Severance taxes

see also Tariffs and foreign trade controls

Lichtenstein, Richard L.

"Licensed Physicians Who Work in Prisons: A Profile", 4102–1.407

Liechtenstein

Economic, social, and political summary data, by country, 1984, annual factbook, 244–11

Imports of US, detailed TSUSA commodities by country of origin, 1983, annual rpt, 2424–4

Population size and growth rates, and latest available benchmark demographic data, by country, 1950-83, biennial rpt, 2324–4

see also under By Foreign Country in the "Index by Categories"

Life expectancy

Communist, OECD, and selected other countries living standards and commodity production, 1960s-83, annual rpt, 244–5.1

Developing countries disaster preparedness and summary sociodemographic, political, and economic data, country rpt series, 9916–2

Developing countries govt policy, and AID and other foreign assistance, effects on private sector dev and socioeconomic conditions, with case studies for 6 countries, 1960s-80, 9918–12

Developing countries PL 480 Title I funding and socioeconomic impacts, with case studies for 5 countries, 1950s- 81, 9918–13

Developing countries summary socioeconomic data, 1970s-83, and AID activities and funding by project and function, FY82-85, by country, annual rpt, 9914–3

Disability Insurance awards, death and recovery termination rates, and life expectancy of disabled, by age and sex, 1965-83 and projected to 2000, 4706–1.93

Foreign aged population characteristics, with related health care data and vital statistics, by world area and selected country, 1950-80 and projected to 2020, 2546–10.12

Foreign and US life expectancy by sex, for 7 countries, selected years 1975-81, 21148–33

Foreign military, social, and economic summary data by world area and country, 1960s-80s, hearing, 25388–47.1

Foreign population size and growth rates, and latest available benchmark demographic data, by country, 1950-83, biennial rpt, 2324–4

Foreign women sociodemographic, economic, and fertility characteristics, with comparisons to men, by country, 1960s-85, world region rpt series, 2326–15

Health condition and health care resources, use, and expenditures, 1970s-82 with trends and projections 1900-2000, annual compilation, 4144–11

Life expectancy, and deaths by cause, by sex and age, 1900-2050, SSA actuarial rpt, 4706–1.89

Life tables, abridged, 1981, US Vital Statistics advance rpt, 4146–5.78

Life tables, abridged, 1982, US Vital Statistics advance rpt, 4146–5.81

Life tables, 1979 and trends from 1900, US Vital Statistics annual rpt, 4144–2.6

Life tables, 1980 and trends from 1900, US Vital Statistics annual rpt, 4144–5

Life insurance

Life tables, 1983, and life expectancy by race and sex, selected years 1950-83, US Vital Statistics annual rpt, 4144–7

OASDI and pension policy, impacts of increased life expectancy, with alternative sociodemographic projections to 2100, hearing, 25368–130

Occupational health risks from hazardous substances and radiation, by industry, occupation, age, and sex, with bibl and glossary, 1920s-82, 9638–50

Older persons by demographic, socioeconomic, and health characteristics, selected years 1900-81 and projected to 2050, Current Population Rpt, 2546–2.125

Older persons sociodemographic characteristics, and Fed Govt program participation and funding, 1983 with trends and projections 1900-2060, annual rpt, 25144–3.1

Older persons sociodemographic characteristics and transportation needs, selected years 1900-2040, 7308–183

Population size and components of change, projected under 3 fertility assumptions, 1982-2080 with trends from 1900, SSA actuarial rpt, 4706–1.92

Population size by single years of age, and components of change, by sex and race, projected 1983-2080, final Current Population Rpt, 2546–3.132

Puerto Rico educational enrollment, finance, completions, curricula, and personnel by instn, and health and vital statistics, selected years 1970-83, hearings, 21348–93

Retirement ages for OASDI, proposed revisions based on increased life expectancy, by sex under 4 measurement methods, selected years 1940-2050, article, 4742–1.406

Soviet Union industrial and agricultural production by selected commodity, and demographic trends and projections by Republic, 1950s-2000, hearings, 23848–180

Life insurance

County Business Patterns: establishments, employees, and payrolls, by SIC 4-digit industry and county, 1982, annual State rpt series, 2326–6

Employee benefits in private industry, coverage by benefit type and provisions and occupational group, 1983, annual rpt, 6784–19

Employee benefits in private industry, percent of employers providing selected benefits, 1979-82, conf proceedings, 25408–89

Farm finances, assets, expenses, cash flow, receipts, and loans, selected years 1971-85, annual rpt, 1544–13

Fed Govt civilian employee retirement, health, and life insurance benefit plans operations and finances, FY81-82, annual rpt, 9844–1

Fed Govt programs and mgmt cost control proposals, 3-year savings by function and agency, and financial and operating data, 1960s-81, 16908–1.27

Financial and business statistics, historic trends, 1984 annual chartbook, 9364–2.14

Life insurance

Flow-of-funds accounts, assets and liabilities by type and economic sector, year-end outstandings, 1960-83, annual rpt, 9364–3

Income received through life insurance companies, taxation measurement, allocation, and accounting methods, 1984 technical paper, 8006–3.49

Income tax returns of corporations, detailed income and tax items by industry, 1981, annual rpt, 8304–4

Minority group and women employment, by occupational group and SIC 2- to 3-digit industry, 1981, annual rpt, 9244–1.1

Mortgage loan activity, by type of lender, loan, and mortgaged property, monthly rpt, 5142–18

Tax expenditures, Fed Govt revenues foregone through income tax deductions and exclusions by type, and effect of Deficit Reduction Act, FY84-89, annual rpt, 21784–10

Tax expenditures from employee benefit plans, for income and payroll tax by benefit type and income, with benefits by industry, 1950-83 and projected to 1988, article, 9373–1.404

Traffic accidents and casualties detailed direct and indirect costs, by characteristics of persons and vehicles involved, 1979-80, 7768–80

Veterans aged 55 and over, socioeconomic characteristics, economic resources, health care and status, and actual and expected use of VA benefits, 1983 survey, 9928–29

see also Area wage surveys

see also Old-Age, Survivors, Disability, and Health Insurance

see also Servicemen's life insurance programs

Life insurance companies

see Insurance industry

Light

see also Lasers

Lighthouses and lightships

Census of Population, 1980: detailed socioeconomic and demographic characteristics, by age, sex, race, Hispanic origin, occupation, and industry, State rpt series, 2531–4

Lighting equipment

see Electrical machinery and equipment

Lima, Ohio

Census of Housing, 1980: occupancy and unit characteristics, by race, Hispanic origin, and city, SMSA rpt, 2473–1.220

Census of Population and Housing, 1980: detailed population and housing characteristics, by county, city, and census tract, SMSA rpt, 2551–2.220

Housing vacancy rates for single and multifamily units and mobile homes, by city and ZIP code, 1984, annual metro area rpt, 9304–27.7

Wages of office and plant workers, by occupation, 1984 labor market area survey rpt, 6785–3.9

see also under By SMSA or MSA in the "Index by Categories"

Lime

see Fertilizers

see Nonmetallic minerals and mines

Lincoln, Nebr.

Census of Housing, 1980: occupancy and unit characteristics, by race, Hispanic origin, and city, SMSA rpt, 2473–1.221

Census of Population and Housing, 1980: detailed population and housing characteristics, by county, city, and census tract, SMSA rpt, 2551–2.221

see also under By City and By SMSA or MSA in the "Index by Categories"

Lindberg, William J.

"Species Profiles: Life Histories and Environmental Requirements of Coastal Fishes and Invertebrates (South Florida), Stone Crab", 5506–8.28

Linens

see Household furnishings

Ling, K. Charles

"Dairy Product Manufacturing Costs at Cooperative Plants", 1128–25

Link, Albert N.

"Measurement and Analysis of Productivity Growth: A Synthesis of Thought", 2218–69

Linnane, James P.

"Annual Southwestern Region Pest Conditions Report, 1983", 1206–11.2

Linseed

see Oils, oilseeds, and fats

Liquefied natural gas

see Natural gas and gas industry

Liquefied petroleum gas

Agriculture census, 1982: farms, farmland, production, finances, and operator characteristics, by county, final State rpt series, 2331–1

Air pollutant emission factors, by detailed source, 3rd edition, 1983-84 supplements, 9198–13

Air pollution levels for 5 pollutants, by detailed source, State, and Air Quality Control Region, 1981, annual rpt, 9194–7

Buildings (nonresidential) energy use, expenditures, and conservation, by building characteristics, EIA survey series, 3166–8

Consumption, by fuel type, economic sector, and end use, 1983 and 2000, 2006–2.5

Consumption, by fuel type, economic sector, census div, and State, 1960-82, State Energy Data System annual rpt, 3164–39

Consumption of energy, by type of air pollutant source and fuel, and State, 1981, annual rpt, 9194–14

DOE in-house energy use, conservation investments, and savings, by type of use and fuel and field office, FY83, annual rpt, 3024–3

Farm production expenditures, detailed items by farm sales size and region, 1983, annual rpt, 1614–3

Farm production inputs supply, use, and prices, periodic situation rpt with articles, 1561–16

Farmers prices received for major products and paid for farm inputs and living items, by commodity and State, monthly rpt, 1629–1

Farmers prices received for major products and paid for farm inputs, by commodity and State, 1983, annual rpt, 1629–5

Foreign and US oil prices, tax, and customs duty, by refined product and major city, July 1983 and Jan 1984, annual rpt, 3164–50.4

Index by Subjects and Names

Futures trading in selected commodities, foreign currencies, Treasury securities, and stock indexes, NYC, Chicago, and other markets activity, monthly rpt, 11922–5

Futures trading in selected commodities, Treasury securities, and stock indexes, NYC market activity, monthly rpt, 11922–2

Housing census, 1980: inventory, occupancy, and unit characteristics, changes from 1973 by region and inside-outside SMSAs and central cities, series, 2473–3

Housing census, 1980: structural, financial, and householder characteristics, by region and State, 2475–4

Housing energy use, by fuel type, county, city, and census tract, 1980 Census of Population and Housing, State and SMSA rpt series, 2551–2

Housing energy use, costs, expenditures, and conservation, and household and housing characteristics, survey series, 3166–7

Housing energy use in SMSAs and central cities, by fuel type, householder race and Hispanic origin, and city, 1980 Census of Housing, State and SMSA rpt series, 2473–1

Income tax returns of sole proprietorships, detailed data by industry div and selected industry group, 1981, annual rpt, 8304–7

Income tax returns of sole proprietorships, receipts, deductions by type, payroll, and net income, by major industry, 1982, annual article, 8302–2.413

Irrigation system energy use and costs, and irrigated farm acreage by fuel and region, selected years 1974-84 and trends from 1900, article, 1561–16.406

Manufacturing energy efficiency progress, and energy use by type, by SIC 2-digit industry, 1982, annual rpt, 3304–8

Mineral industries census, 1982: financial and operating data, including materials consumed, by SIC 4-digit industry and State, preliminary rpt series, 2511–1

Naval Petroleum and Oil Shale Reserves production, dev, ownership, leasing, sales by purchaser, and Fed Govt revenues, by site, FY83, annual rpt, 3004–22

Prices and expenditures for fuels, by consuming sector, State, and fuel type, 1970-81, annual rpt, 3164–64

Producer prices and indexes, by stage of processing and detailed commodity, monthly rpt, 6762–6

Producer prices and indexes, by stage of processing and detailed commodity, monthly 1983, annual supplement, 6764–2

Producers finances and operations, by energy type for US firms domestic and foreign operations, 1974-82, annual rpt, 3164–44

Refinery financial and operating impacts from auto use of alcohol fuels, projected to 2000 with trends 1964-80, 3308–75

Retail trade census, 1982: employment, establishments, sales, and payroll, for liquefied petroleum gas (bottled gas) dealers, by State, preliminary rpt, 2395–1.37

Supply/demand and prices, by energy resource and major producing and consuming country and sector, detailed data, monthly rpt, 3162–24

Index by Subjects and Names

Liquor industry

Supply/demand and prices, by fuel type and consuming sector with foreign comparisons, 1949-83, annual rpt, 3164–74

Supply/demand and prices, by fuel type, sector, and end use, detailed trends and projections 1973-95, annual rpt, 3164–75

Supply/demand and prices, by fuel type, sector, and end use, with foreign comparisons, 1960-83 and projected to 1995, annual summary rpt, 3164–76

Supply/demand, trade, stocks, and refining of oil and natural gas liquids, by detailed product, State, and PAD district, with fuel oil sulfur content, monthly rpt with articles, 3162–6

Supply/demand, trade, stocks, and refining of oil and natural gas liquids, by detailed product, State, and PAD district, and refineries in US and territories, 1983 annual rpt, 3164–2

Tax provisions (State) for motor fuel, vehicle registration fees, and disposition of receipts, by State, as of Jan 1984, biennial rpt, 7554–37

Tax rates for motor fuel, by fuel type and State, monthly rpt, 7552–1

Tax rates for motor fuel, by State, 1975-83, annual table, 7554–32

Transportation census, 1982: trucks, by detailed characteristics, miles traveled, and type of product carried, State rpt series, 2573–1

Transportation energy use by mode, fuel supplies, and demographic and economic determinants of vehicle use, 1970s-83, annual rpt, 3304–5

Waterborne commerce of US (domestic and foreign), freight by commodity, traffic, and passengers, by port and waterway, 1982, annual rpt, 3754–3

Liquor industry

Air pollutant emission factors, by detailed source, 3rd edition, 1983-84 supplements, 9198–13

American Samoa govt owned liquor stores minimum wage rates, employment, earnings, and benefits, Nov 1983, biennial rpt, 6504–6

Army morale, welfare, and recreation programs, revenue and expenses worldwide by activity and major command, FY82-83, annual rpt, 3704–12

Business statistics, detailed data for major industries and economic indicators, *Survey of Current Business,* monthly rpt, 2702–1.11

Census of Population, 1980: detailed socioeconomic and demographic characteristics, by age, sex, race, Hispanic origin, occupation, and industry, State rpt series, 2531–4

Consumption, supply, trade, prices, expenditures, and indexes, by food commodity, 1963-83, annual rpt, 1544–4

County Business Patterns: establishments, employees, and payrolls, by SIC 4-digit industry and county, 1981, annual State rpt series, 2326–8

County Business Patterns: establishments, employees, and payrolls, by SIC 4-digit industry and county, 1982, annual State rpt series, 2326–6

CPI by detailed component, for US city average, 28 SMSAs, and 4 regions by population size, monthly rpt, 6762–2

Employment, earnings, and hours, by selected SIC 1- to 4-digit industry, State, and for 278 major labor areas, 1939-83, annual rpt, 6744–5

Employment, earnings, and hours, by SIC 4-digit nonfarm industry, monthly 1974-Feb 1984, annual update, 6744–4

Exports and imports of US, by detailed agricultural commodity for 8 major commodity groups, monthly rpt, 1922–8

Exports and imports of US, detailed SIC-based commodities by world area, 1983, annual rpts, 2424–6

Exports and imports of US, totals and as percent of domestic production, by SIC 2- to 5-digit commodity, 1981, annual rpt, 2424–3

Exports, imports, tariffs, and industry operating data for selected alcoholic beverages, 1979-83, TSUSA commodity rpt, 9885–1.72

Exports of US, detailed commodities by country of destination, monthly rpt, 2422–3

Exports of US, detailed Schedule B commodities by country of destination, 1983, annual rpt, 2424–9

Exports of US, detailed Schedule E commodities by mode of transport and world area and country of destination, 1983, annual rpts, 2424–5

Finances and operations, by SIC 2- to 4-digit industry, 1970s-83 and projected to 1988, annual rpt, 2014–4

Govt census, 1982: city govt revenues by source, expenditures by function, debt, and assets, by State and city, 2457–4

Govt census, 1982: county govt revenues by source, expenditures by function, debt, and assets, by State and county, 2457–3

Govt census, 1982: employment, payrolls, and average earnings, by function, level of govt, State, county, population size, and inside-outside SMSAs, 2455–2

Govt finances, by level of govt, State, and for large cities and counties, 1981-83, annual rpt series, 2466–2

Great Lakes trade, by SITC 3-digit commodity, port, vessel type, world area, and country, 1982, annual rpt, 7744–3

Imports of US, detailed Schedule A commodities by country and world area of origin, and mode of transport, 1983, annual rpts, 2424–2

Imports of US, detailed Schedule A commodities by country, monthly rpt, 2422–2

Imports of US, detailed TSUSA commodities by country of origin, 1983, annual rpt, 2424–4

Income tax returns of corporations, detailed income and tax items by industry, 1981, annual rpt, 8304–4

Income tax returns of partnerships, detailed data by industry, 1981 estimates, annual article, 8302–2.404

Income tax returns of partnerships, receipts by source, deductions by type, and establishments, by selected industry, 1982, annual article, 8302–2.416

Income tax returns of sole proprietorships, detailed data by industry div and selected industry group, 1981, annual rpt, 8304–7

Income tax returns of sole proprietorships, receipts, deductions by type, payroll, and net income, by major industry, 1982, annual article, 8302–2.413

Input-output structure of US economy, detailed interindustry transactions for 537 industries, and components of final demand, 1977 benchmark data, 2708–17

Internal revenue violations, Federal court cases disposition, convictions, and sentences, by district, asof June 1983 with trends from 1961, annual rpt, 18204–1

Law enforcement activities of Alcohol, Tobacco, and Firearms Bur in 20 cities and nationwide, funding, and jobs to be transferred to Customs and Secret Service, 1979-82, hearings, 21528–55

Occupational injury and illness rates, by SIC 2- to 4-digit industry, 1982, annual rpt, 6844–1

Producer prices and indexes, by stage of processing and detailed commodity, monthly rpt, 6762–6

Producer prices and indexes, by stage of processing and detailed commodity, monthly 1983, annual supplement, 6764–2

Production, stocks, and Fed Govt tax and enforcement activities, by State, FY81-82, last issue of annual rpt, 8484–1

Retail trade census, 1982: employment, establishments, sales, and payroll, by SIC 2- to 4-digit kind of business, SMSA, and retail district, State rpt series, 2401–1

Retail trade census, 1982: employment, establishments, sales, and payroll, for liquor stores, by State, preliminary rpt, 2395–1.27

Retail trade sales and inventories, by kind of business, region, census div, and selected State, SMSA, and city, and seasonal adjustments, monthly rpt, 2413–3

Retail trade sales, inventories, purchases, gross margin, and accounts receivable, by SIC 2- to 4-digit kind of business and type of ownership, 1983, annual rpt, 2413–5

Rum production, trade by selected country, consumption, and shipments from Puerto Rico and Virgin Islands, Jan-June 1983-84, annual rpt, 9884–15

Scientists, engineers, and technicians employment in transportation, utilities, and retail and wholesale trade, by field of science and industry, 1982, 9628–72

State and local govt productivity measurement, with background data and output indexes for 7 govt services, various periods 1955-82, 6728–27

Tax (excise) collections of IRS, by source, quarterly press release, 8302–1

Tax (excise) revenue of local govts, by excise type and State, average annual growth FY72-82, article, 10042–1.403

Tax collections of State govts, by detailed type of tax and tax rates, by State, FY83, annual rpt, 2466–2.3

Tax collections, refunds, and taxes due IRS, by State and region, and IRS court activity and operating expenses, FY83, annual rpt, 8304–3.3

Tax revenues, by level of govt, type of tax, State, and selected large counties, quarterly rpt, 2462–3

Taxation and revenue systems, by type of tax and system, level of govt, and State, selected years 1958-83, annual rpt, 10044–1.3

Liquor industry

Virgin Islands economic censuses, 1982: employment, establishments, payroll, and receipts, by SIC 1- to 4-digit industry, island, and city, 2593–1

Waterborne commerce of US (domestic and foreign), freight by commodity, traffic, and passengers, by port and waterway, 1982, annual rpt, 3754–3

Whiskey and other distilled spirits production, stocks, materials used, and taxable and tax-free removals, by State, monthly rpt, 8486–1.3

Wholesale trade census, 1982: employment, establishments, finances, and operations, by SIC 2- to 4-digit kind of business, SMSA, county, and city, State rpt series, 2405–1

Wholesale trade sales and inventories, by SIC 2- to 3-digit kind of business, monthly rpt, 2413–7

Wholesale trade sales, inventories, purchases, and gross margins, by SIC 2- to 3-digit kind of business and type of ownership, 1983, annual rpt, 2413–13

see also Beer and breweries

see also Wine and winemaking

see also under By Industry in the "Index by Categories"

Lister, C. Kendall

"Forest Insect and Disease Conditions in the Rocky Mountain Region, 1983", 1206–11.1

Listerosis

see Animal diseases and zoonoses

Literature

see Language and literature

Lithium

see Metals and metal industries

Litter

see Refuse and refuse disposal

Little, Jane S.

"Industrial Composition of Foreign Direct Investment in the U.S. and Abroad: A Preliminary Look", 9373–1.411

Little Rock, Ark.

- Census of Housing, 1980: occupancy and unit characteristics, by race, Hispanic origin, and city, SMSA rpt, 2473–1.222
- Census of Population and Housing, 1980: detailed population and housing characteristics, by county, city, and census tract, SMSA rpt, 2551–2.222
- Economic indicators for Southeastern States and 5 SMSAs, Fed Reserve 8th District, quarterly rpt, 9391–15
- Housing vacancy rates for single and multifamily units and mobile homes, by city and ZIP code, 1983, annual metro area rpt, 9304–19.2
- Wages by occupation, and benefits for office and plant workers, 1984 labor market area survey rpt, 6785–3.8
- Waterborne commerce of US (domestic and foreign), freight by commodity, traffic, and passengers, by port and waterway, 1982, annual rpt, 3754–3.2
- *see also* under By City and By SMSA or MSA in the "Index by Categories"

Littman, Daniel A.

"Plant Closings and Worker Dislocation", 9377–1.401

Liu, Lillian

"Social Security Problems in Western European Countries", 4742–1.405

Liver diseases

see Digestive diseases

Livestock and livestock industry

- Agricultural cooperative livestock producer members, and patronage for marketing and supplies purchase, by region and farm sales size, 1980, 1128–26
- *Agricultural Statistics, 1983,* annual rpt, 1004–1
- Agriculture census, 1982: farms, farmland, production and costs, and operator characteristics, preliminary State and county rpt series, 2330–1
- Agriculture census, 1982: farms, farmland, production, finances, and operator characteristics, by county, final State rpt series, 2331–1
- *Agriculture Fact Book of US,* compilation of data for 1983 with trends from 1940, annual rpt, 1004–14
- Biotechnology commercial uses, R&D funding and output, controls, and industry financial and operating data, for US and 5 countries, 1970s-83 and estimated 1984-85, 26358–98
- Business statistics, detailed data for major industries and economic indicators, *Survey of Current Business,* monthly rpt, 2702–1.11
- Cattle and calves for beef and milk, inventory and value by State, 1982-84, semiannual press release, 1623–1
- Cattle and calves on feed, inventory and marketings by State, monthly release, 1623–2
- Census of Population, 1980: detailed socioeconomic and demographic characteristics, by age, sex, race, Hispanic origin, occupation, and industry, State rpt series, 2531–4
- China exports and imports by SITC 1- to 5-digit commodity, 1970s-82, annual rpt, 244–12
- Communist, OECD, and selected other countries agricultural production, by commodity, 1960s-83, annual rpt, 244–5.9
- Cooperatives commercial farmer membership and use, by type and sales size of farm and region, 1980, 1128–32
- Cooperatives, membership, activities, and finances, by commodity and selected State, 1900-80 with trends from 1863, 1128–30
- County Business Patterns: establishments, employees, and payrolls, by SIC 4-digit industry and county, 1981, annual State rpt series, 2326–8
- County Business Patterns: establishments, employees, and payrolls, by SIC 4-digit industry and county, 1982, annual State rpt series, 2326–6
- Cuba economic conditions, agricultural and industrial production and distribution, trade, and intl economic relations, 1970-82 and trends from 1957, 248–40
- Eastern Europe agricultural production and trade by commodity, food consumption, and farm inputs, for 6 countries, 1960-80 with projections to 1991, 1528–178
- EC food supply/demand and market and support prices, with exchange rates, fertilizer price index, GDP, and population, by country, 1960-83, 1528–173

Index by Subjects and Names

- Exports and imports of dairy, livestock, and poultry live animals, meat, and products, by commodity and country of destination, FAS quarterly rpt, 1925–32
- Exports and imports of US, by agricultural commodity and country, bimonthly rpt with articles, 1522–1
- Exports and imports of US, by commodity group, world area, selected country, US coastal area and port, and mode of transport, with seasonal adjustments, monthly rpt, 2422–9
- Exports and imports of US, by detailed agricultural commodity and country, FY83 and CY83, semiannual rpts, 1522–4
- Exports and imports of US, by detailed agricultural commodity for 8 major commodity groups, monthly rpt, 1922–8
- Exports and imports of US, detailed SIC-based commodities by world area, 1983, annual rpts, 2424–6
- Exports and imports of US, totals and as percent of domestic production, by SIC 2- to 5-digit commodity, 1981, annual rpt, 2424–3
- Exports and personal expenditures of US and world for selected agricultural commodities, by country, and export share of US farm income, various periods 1926-82, 1528–172
- Exports of US, detailed commodities by country of destination, monthly rpt, 2422–3
- Exports of US, detailed Schedule B commodities by country of destination, 1983, annual rpt, 2424–9
- Exports of US, detailed Schedule E commodities by mode of transport and world area and country of destination, 1983, annual rpts, 2424–5
- Farm finances, assets, liabilities, income, receipts by commodity and State, and expenses, 1980-83 and trends from 1910, annual rpt, 1544–16
- Farm finances, expenses by type, loans by purpose and source, and credit detail by Fed Reserve District, quarterly rpt, 9365–3.10
- Farm production inputs, outputs, and productivity, by region, 1939-82, annual rpt, 1544–17
- Foreign agricultural production, prices, and trade, by country, 1983 and outlook for 1984/85, annual world region rpt series, 1524–4
- Foreign and US agricultural production, trade, and climatic devs, weekly press release, 1922–4
- Foreign and US feed and livestock trade by product and world region, and ocean freight rates between selected countries of origin and destination, selected years 1960-82, 1528–177
- Foreign and US livestock, poultry, and products production, consumption, and trade, FAS semiannual circular, 1925–33
- Futures trading by commodity and exchange, and Commodity Futures Trading Commission activities, funding, and employment, FY83, annual rpt, 11924–2
- Futures trading in selected commodities, foreign currencies, and stock indexes, Chicago and other markets activity, monthly rpt, 11922–1

Index by Subjects and Names

Futures trading in selected commodities, foreign currencies, Treasury securities, and stock indexes, NYC, Chicago, and other markets activity, monthly rpt, 11922–5

Genetic resource (plant and animal) conservation, commercial uses, causes of depletion, and geographic sources, 1984 rpt, 5548–13

Hog and pig inventory, value, farrowings, and farms, by State, quarterly release, 1623–3

Hog and pig production, inventory, and farms, by State, 1979-82, 1641–10

Hog production, producer characteristics, facilities, and marketing, by type and size of enterprise and region, 1975 and 1980, 1568–248

Hogs and pigs fed garbage, monthly rpt, discontinued, 1392–5

Hogs and pork from Canada, effect on US industry, investigation with background financial and operating data, 1984 rpt, 9886–4.80

Imports of US, detailed Schedule A commodities by country and world area of origin, and mode of transport, 1983, annual rpts, 2424–2

Imports of US, detailed Schedule A commodities by country, monthly rpt, 2422–2

Imports of US, detailed TSUSA commodities by country of origin, 1983, annual rpt, 2424–4

Income tax returns of partnerships, detailed data by industry, 1981 estimates, annual article, 8302–2.404

Income tax returns of partnerships, receipts by source, deductions by type, and establishments, by selected industry, 1982, annual article, 8302–2.416

Income tax returns of sole proprietorships, detailed data by industry div and selected industry group, 1981, annual rpt, 8304–7

Income tax returns of sole proprietorships, receipts, deductions by type, payroll, and net income, by major industry, 1982, annual article, 8302–2.413

Input-output structure of US economy, detailed interindustry transactions for 85 industries, and components of final demand, 1977, article, 2702–1.421

Input-output structure of US economy, detailed interindustry transactions for 537 industries, and components of final demand, 1977 benchmark data, 2708–17

Land Mgmt Bur public lands admin and program activities in western States, FY82-84, annual rpt, 5724–13

Market news summary statistics for livestock, meat, and wool, by animal type and market, weekly rpt, 1315–1

Marketing cash receipts of farms, by detailed commodity and State, 1979-82, annual rpt, 1544–18

Mexico and US range and wildlife characteristics, problems, and research strategies and needs, 1981 conf papers, 1208–197

Montana and North Dakota coal production, impact of mining on agricultural land availability and on farm income and production costs, by mining tract, 1982 rpt, 1588–79

Natl Forest System lands livestock grazing, and losses from predators, poisonous plants, and other causes, by region and State, FY83, annual rpt, 1204–5

North Central States economic indicators, Fed Reserve 7th District monthly rpt, 9375–9

Occupational injury and illness rates, by SIC 2- to 4-digit industry, 1982, annual rpt, 6844–1

Packers purchases and feeding, and livestock markets, dealers, and sales, by region and State, 1981-82, annual rpt, 1384–1

Pesticide use for crops and livestock, acreage treated, application methods, and use of safety equipment and professional services, 1982 survey, 1588–76

Portugal agricultural subsidies, profits, marketing margins, and consumer prices, by commodity or product, and effects of prospective EC membership, 1981, 1528–171

Prices received by farmers for major products, and paid for farm inputs and living items, by commodity and State, monthly rpt, 1629–1

Prices received by farmers for major products, and paid for farm inputs, by commodity and State, 1983, annual rpt, 1629–5

Production and farm finances, expenses by type, and domestic economic impact, selected years 1972-82 and preliminary 1983-84, annual rpt, 1544–19

Production and supply/demand data, for US livestock and dairy products, and for selected US and world crops, periodic rpt, 1522–5

Production expenditures, detailed items by farm sales size and region, 1983, annual rpt, 1614–3

Production itemized costs, receipts, and net returns, for 13 crops, 4 livestock types, and milk, by region, 1981-83, annual rpt, 1544–20

Production, marketing, slaughter, prices, and producers gross income, for meat animals by animal type and State, 1982-83, annual rpt, 1623–8

Production, prices, and trade of livestock and meat, 1983, annual rpt, 1564–6

Production, prices, trade, and marketing, by commodity, current situation and forecast, monthly rpt, 1502–4

Production, prices, trade, stocks, and consumption, periodic situation rpt, 1561–7

Radionuclide concentrations in cattle and wildlife near Nevada nuclear test site, 1957-81, last issue of annual rpt, 9234–5

Sheep and lambs by State, and goats in Texas, inventories and operations, 1981-84, annual press release, 1623–4

Slaughter and meat production, by livestock type and State, monthly rpt, 1623–9

Slaughter by species, meat production, and number of slaughtering plants, by State, 1983, annual rpt, 1623–10

Small farms with sales under $2,500, acreage, finances, operations, and operator characteristics, by region and for 6 States, 1978, 1548–241

Soviet Union livestock and poultry stocks, and hog and cattle slaughter, FAS monthly rpt, 1925–2.3

Supply/demand, prices, and commodity program operations, for selected crops and livestock, 1983 and outlook for 1984, annual article, 9381–1.402

Loan delinquency and default

Thefts, and total value of property stolen and recovered, by property type, 1983, annual rpt, 6224–2.1

TTPI socioeconomic, health, and govtl data, by TTPI govt, FY83 and selected trends, detailed annual rpt, 7004–6

Waterborne commerce of US (domestic and foreign), freight by commodity, traffic, and passengers, by port and waterway, 1982, annual rpt, 3754–3

Wholesale trade census, 1982: employment, establishments, sales by commodity, and payroll, by SIC 4-digit kind of business and State, preliminary rpt series, 2403–1

see also Animal diseases and zoonoses

see also Animal feed

see also Dairy industry and products

see also Food and waterborne diseases

see also Hides and skins

see also Meat and meat products

see also Pasture and rangeland

see also Poultry industry and products

see also Veterinary medicine

see also under By Commodity in the "Index by Categories"

Living standard

see Cost of living

see Personal and family income

see Quality of life

Livonia, Mich.

see also under By City in the "Index by Categories"

Loan delinquency and default

AID Housing Guaranty Program financial statements, and projects by country, FY83, annual rpt, 9914–4

AID loan repayment status and terms by program and country, and status of predecessor agency loans, quarterly rpt, 9912–3

Banks (natl) domestic and intl operations, charters, mergers, and liquidations, by State and instn, and Comptroller of Currency activities, quarterly rpt, 8402–3

Business Conditions Digest, current data on economic, business, and financial conditions and cyclical fluctuations, monthly rpt, 2702–3

Business Conditions Digest, historical supplement on economic, business, and financial conditions and cyclical fluctuations, with methodology, 1947-82, 2708–31

Credit union financial statements by region, State, and type of membership, for Federal and federally insured State unions, 1983, annual rpt, 9534–1

Credit unions in Georgia, operating and financial ratios and other performance indicators for 53 large instns, as of Dec 1983, article, 9371–1.427

Education Dept programs fraud and abuse, audits and investigations, 2nd half FY84, semiannual rpt, 4802–1

EPA programs fraud and abuse, audits and investigations, 2nd half FY84, semiannual rpt, 9182–10

Farm Credit System mortgage and other loans, and financial statements, 1982 and selected trends from 1961, annual rpt, 9264–2

Farm finance and credit conditions, forecast 1984, conf summary, annual rpt, 9264–9

Farm finances, assets, expenses, cash flow, receipts, and loans, selected years 1971-85, annual rpt, 1544–13

Loan delinquency and default

Fed Govt consolidated financial statements based on business accounting methods, FY82-83, annual rpt, 8104–5

Fed Govt loans and other receivables due, and interest and penalties on delinquencies, by agency, *Treasury Bulletin,* quarterly rpt, 8002–4.16

Fed Govt programs and mgmt cost control proposals, 3-year savings by function and agency, and financial and operating data, 1960s-81, 16908–1

Fed Home Loan Mortgage Corp activities and financial statements, 1983, annual rpt, 9414–1

FmHA loans and borrower supervision activities in farm and housing programs, by type and State, monthly rpt, 1182–1

FmHA loans and grants by program and State, and summary of services, FY83 with trends from FY63, annual rpt, 1184–17

Health maintenance organizations enrollment (total, Medicare, and Medicaid), finances, Fed Govt qualification status, and PHS loan activity, by HMO, FY83, annual rpt, 4044–2

HHS programs fraud and abuse, audits and investigations, 2nd half FY84, semiannual rpt, 4002–6

Home and condominium mortgages FHA-insured, new issues, adjustments, and terminations, by program, quarterly rpt, 5142–6

Home mortgage defaults, single family homes acquired by HUD and disposition by city, monthly rpt, 5142–31

Housing financing of S&Ls and others, mortgage terms and debt outstanding, and balance sheets of S&Ls and FHLBs, 1983, annual rpt, 9314–3

HUD programs fraud and abuse, audits and investigations, 2nd half FY84, semiannual rpt, 5002–8

HUD Section 312 loan program activities for rehabilitation of housing and nonresidential property, and recipient locality characteristics, FY83, annual rpt, 5124–5

Income (personal) by source including transfer payments, and social insurance contributions by type, by region, 1929 and 1982, 2708–40

Kentucky Higher Education Student Loan Corp student loans, loan purchases and defaults by instn, and revenue bonds status, various dates 1979-84, hearing, 21348–92

Natural gas interstate pipeline company detailed financial and operating data, by firm, 1983, annual rpt, 3164–38

North Central States, FHLB 6th District insured S&Ls financial condition and operations by State, monthly rpt, 9302–11

North Central States, FHLB 6th District insured S&Ls financial condition and operations by State, quarterly rpt, 9302–23

Savings and loan assns and FSLIC-insured savings banks and S&Ls, assets, liabilities, and deposit and loan activity, monthly rpt, 9312–4

Small Business Admin programs fraud and abuse, audits and investigations, 1st half FY84, semiannual rpt, 9762–5

Student aid Federal programs funding and participation, by instn type and control, State, and outlying area, with student loan defaults and collections, FY82, annual rpt, 4804–28

USDA programs fraud and abuse, audits and investigations, 2nd half FY84, semiannual rpt, 1002–4

VA mortgage loan guarantee and life insurance programs, activities and enrollees, FY59-83, annual rpt, 9924–13.3

VA programs fraud and abuse, audits and investigations, 2nd half FY84, semiannual rpt, 9922–13

Loans

Agricultural cooperative operating ratios by commodity, and debt financing by source, for 100 largest cooperatives, selected years FY62-83, article, 1122–1.411

Airline indebtedness by type of holder, and debt shares of major holders, by carrier, as of Dec 1982, annual rpt, 9144–1.4

Appalachian States, FHLB 5th District member S&Ls financial condition and operations by SMSA, monthly rpt, 9302–8

Bank financial and operating statements, functional cost analysis for Fed Reserve member banks with average and high earnings, by deposit size, 1982, annual rpt, 9364–6

Bank interstate service offices, including S&Ls, bank branches, and nonbank subsidiaries offering financial services, by instn and State, 1981-83, 9371–13

Bank loan amounts outstanding, for commercial and Fed Reserve banks, monthly rpt, 9362–1.1

Bank loans and investments of commercial banks, 1939-83, annual rpt, 204–1.5

Bank loans by selected major industry group, and deposits, 1982, annual rpt, 9364–5.2

Bank profitability, finances, loans and terms, intl earnings, and operating ratios for insured commercial instns, 1980-83, annual article, 9362–1.409

Banking activity, consumer credit, and interest rates, monthly rpt series, 9365–2

Bankruptcy (personal), filers by debt type and other characteristics, and impacts in Connecticut and Michigan, various dates 1946-82, hearings, 21528–57

Bankruptcy (personal), filers by debt type and other characteristics, selected years 1978-81, hearing, 25528–97.1

Banks (natl) domestic and intl operations, charters, mergers, and liquidations, by State and instn, and Comptroller of Currency activities, quarterly rpt, 8402–3

Budget of US, CBO analysis of revenue and spending alternatives and projections of economic indicators, FY85-89, annual rpt, 26304–3

Business Conditions Digest, cyclical indicators, by economic process, monthly rpt, 2702–3.3

Business Conditions Digest, historical supplement on economic, business, and financial conditions and cyclical fluctuations, with methodology, 1947-82, 2708–31

Business loans by large commercial banks, weekly rpt, 9391–4

Index by Subjects and Names

Business short-term loans at all and small banks, by loan size and interest rate, various dates 1980-83, hearing, 21248–83

Business statistics, detailed data for major industries and economic indicators, *Survey of Current Business,* monthly rpt, 2702–1.6

Chrysler Corp Loan Guarantee Act implementation, with related financial and operating data, FY83, last issue of annual rpt, 8004–14

Commercial and industrial unused loan commitments and outstanding loans at selected large banks, monthly rpt, 9365–2.18

Community dev programs funding and activities, for 5 HUD programs, FY83, annual rpt, 5124–5

DOD programs fraud and abuse, audits and investigations, 1st half FY84, semiannual rpt, 3542–18

Energy conservation devices installation, utility loan program cost effectiveness, and household participation characteristics, Minnesota study, 1980-83, 3308–72

Fed Financing Bank holdings and transactions, monthly press release, 9322–1

Fed Govt financial operations, detailed data, *Treasury Bulletin,* quarterly rpt, 8002–4

Fed Govt programs and mgmt cost control proposals, 3-year savings by function and agency, and financial and operating data, 1960s-81, 16908–1

Fed Home Loan Bank of Des Moines financial statements, 1982-83, annual rpt, 9304–7

Fed Reserve Bank of Chicago financial statements, 1983, annual rpt, 9375–5

Fed Reserve Bank of Cleveland financial statements, 1982-83, annual rpt, 9377–5

Fed Reserve Bank of Kansas City financial statements, 1982-83, annual rpt, 9381–3

Fed Reserve Bank of Minneapolis financial statements, 1981-82, annual rpt, 9383–2

Fed Reserve Bank of New York financial statements, 1982-83, annual rpt, 9385–2

Fed Reserve Bank of Philadelphia financial statements, 1982-83, annual rpt, 9387–3

Fed Reserve Bank of Richmond financial statements, 1983, annual rpt, 9389–2

Fed Reserve Bank of San Francisco financial statements, 1982-83, annual rpt, 9393–2

Fed Reserve banks financial statements and employees, 1983, annual rpt, 9364–1.1

Financial and business statistics, historic trends, 1984 annual chartbook, 9364–2.13

Financial and business statistics, quarterly chartbook, 9362–2.5, 9362–2.7

Financial, banking, and mortgage market activity, weekly release series, 9365–1

Financial services of nonbank firms and bank holding companies, with financial and operating data by firm, 1981-82 with trends from 1962, technical paper, 9375–11.3

Flow-of-funds accounts, assets and liabilities by type and economic sector, year-end outstandings, 1960-83, annual rpt, 9364–3

Foreign lending of large US banks at all US and foreign offices, by country group and country, quarterly rpt, 13002–1

Index by Subjects and Names

Income tax returns of corporations, detailed income and tax items by industry, 1981, annual rpt, 8304–4

Income tax returns of foreign subsidiaries of US corporations, income and tax data, by industry and asset size, 1980, article, 8302–2.410

Land privately held, acreage and owners by owner characteristics, land use, and region, and purchase and improvement funding, 1978 survey, series, 1506–5

Minority business mgmt and financial assistance from federally funded organizations, by region, State, and business characteristics, FY83, annual rpt, 2104–6

Monetary and Fed Govt budget trends, Fed Reserve Bank of St Louis monthly rpt, 9391–2

New England States, FHLB 1st District member savings instns, locations, and financial condition, 1984, annual listing, 9304–26

New England States financial instn assets and liabilities, Fed Reserve 1st District, monthly rpt, 9373–2.5

North Central States, bank loan activity of Fed Reserve 7th District and 3 major midwestern cities, monthly rpt, 9375–9

North Central States, FHLB 6th District insured S&Ls financial condition and operations by State, monthly rpt, 9302–11

North Central States, FHLB 6th District insured S&Ls financial condition and operations by State, quarterly rpt, 9302–23

North Central States, FHLB 8th District member S&Ls financial operations by State and SMSA, monthly rpt, 9302–9

Pennsylvania bank, S&L, and savings bank deposit and commercial and industrial loan market shares, and loan activity, 1980-83, article, 9387–1.404

Postal Service interest expense on bonds, notes, and mortgages, borrowing and repayment schedule, and rates, FY82-85, annual rpt, 9864–5.3

Red Cross program operations and financial statements, 1982/83, annual rpt, 29254–1

Savings and loan assn deregulation effect on lending activity, for US and 3 States, as of June 1980-83, article, 9371–1.432

Savings and loan assn deregulation impact, financial ratios of S&Ls in 3 States and US, 1980-83, article, 9371–1.426

Savings and loan assns and FSLIC-insured savings banks and S&Ls, assets, liabilities, and deposit and loan activity, monthly rpt, 9312–4

Savings and loan assns assets and liabilities, by FHLB district and State, selected years 1955-82, annual rpt, 9314–1

Shipping and shipbuilding subsidies and aid, and summary fleet, trade, and GNP data, for US and 47 countries, 1979-80, biennial rpt, 7704–18

Small Business Investment Companies finances, funding, licensing, and loan activity, 2nd half FY84, semiannual rpt, 9762–3

Small business loans and credit, operational expectations, and NYC metro area owners' economic and professional attitudes, by industry div, 1980-83 surveys, hearings, 21728–52

South Central States, FHLB 9th District insured S&Ls financial condition and operations by SMSA, monthly rpt, 9302–13

Southeastern States banks by asset size, finances, and loans and deposits by type, Fed Reserve 5th District, various dates 1979-83, annual article, 9389–1.408

Southeastern States economic indicators, by State, Fed Reserve 5th District, quarterly rpt, 9389–16

Southeastern States, Fed Reserve 8th District banking and financial conditions, quarterly rpt, 9391–14

Southeastern States, FHLB 4th District insured S&Ls financial condition and operations, by SMSA, monthly rpt, 9302–1

Statistical Abstract of US, social, political, and economic data, 1950s-83 and trends, annual rpt, 2324–1.3

West Central States, FHLB 10th District insured S&Ls finances and operations by SMSA, monthly rpt, 9302–22

Western States depository instns financial activity by State, and large commercial banks by city, Fed Reserve 10th District, monthly rpt, 9381–11

Western States economic indicators, Fed Reserve 12th District, quarterly rpt, 9393–1.5

Western States, Fed Reserve 10th District depository instns deposits, loans, investments, and borrowings, monthly rpt, 9381–2

Western States, FHLB 11th District member S&Ls financial condition and operations by State, quarterly rpt, 9302–19

Western States, FHLB 12th District member S&Ls financial operations and housing industry indicators by State, monthly rpt, 9302–21

see also Agricultural credit
see also Consumer credit
see also Credit
see also Credit unions
see also Export-Import Bank
see also Federal aid programs
see also Federal aid to arts and humanities
see also Federal aid to education
see also Federal aid to higher education
see also Federal aid to highways
see also Federal aid to housing
see also Federal aid to law enforcement
see also Federal aid to libraries
see also Federal aid to local areas
see also Federal aid to medical education
see also Federal aid to medicine
see also Federal aid to railroads
see also Federal aid to rural areas
see also Federal aid to States
see also Federal aid to transportation
see also Federal aid to vocational education
see also Federal funding for energy programs
see also Federal funding for research and development
see also Finance companies
see also Foreign assistance
see also Foreign debts
see also Government and business
see also Interest rates
see also Loan delinquency and default
see also Military assistance
see also Mortgages

Local government

see also Public debt
see also Student aid
see also Veterans benefits and pensions
see also Veterans housing

Lobbying

Election campaign finances and Fed Election Commission monitoring activities, 1984 Federal elections, biennial rpt series, 9276–2

Election campaign finances, election procedures, and Fed Election Commission monitoring activities, press release series, 9276–1

Election campaign funding by political action committees, and voting on FTC rules, for individual congressmen, 1978-82, hearings, 25688–6.2

Election campaign funding by political action committees to individual congressmen, and public opinion on reform proposals and assn influence, 1970s-83, hearings, 21428–7

Public opinion on taxes, tax policy, and intergovtl relations, 1972-84 surveys, annual rpt, 10044–2

Lobsters

see Shellfish

Local-Federal relations

see Federal-local relations

Local government

Airport financing by source, bond issues by region, and airport operations, by airport and operator type, FY75-83 and projected to FY93, 26306–6.75

Alabama rural black population, education, employment, health services, and economic status, for 16 counties, selected years 1970-81, 11048–180

Boston, Mass, govt budget and impact of reduced local revenue and Fed Govt aid, and other devs, FY80-86, article, 9373–1.406

City and suburb population characteristics and local govt finances, by region and selected SMSA, 1950s-FY83, 10048–61

City govt fiscal condition, revenue sharing program allocations, and responses to program cuts, FY81-83, surveys, hearings, 25408–86

Community services block grants by type of service provider, State mgmt, and opinions of officials and groups involved, for 13 States, FY81-83, GAO rpt, 26121–84

Construction put in place, value of new public and private structures, by type, monthly rpt, 2382–4

County and City Data Book, detailed socioeconomic and demographic data for States, counties, and cities, selected years 1976-82, 2328–1

Criminal justice system local operations and costs, series, 6066–21

Developing countries local govt community dev, AID assistance program activities and funding, 1960s-80s, 9918–11

Eastern US local govt hwy expenditures, per capita aid, and bridges by condition, by selected county and city, various periods 1965-80, article, 9377–1.405

Education programs for handicapped children, funding, enrollment, and staff, by handicap, age, and State, 1981/82-1982/83, annual rpt, 4944–4

Local government

Educational expenditures of State and local govt, per capita and as percent of personal income, by State, 1980/81, annual rpt, 4824–2.5

Electric power sales of Columbia River system by customer, and capital investments by project, FY83, annual rpt, 3224–1

Electric power sales of TVA, by customer, FY83, annual rpt, 9804–1

Electric power sales, revenues, and prices of Bonneville Power Admin, by class of customer and individual purchaser, 1983, semiannual rpt, 3222–1

Electric utilities privately owned, detailed financial and operating data by company, with summary data for other distributors by type, 1982, annual rpt, 3164–23

Electric utilities privately owned, sales revenues by company and consuming sector, 1982, annual rpt, 3164–23

Financial and business statistics, historic trends, 1984 annual chartbook, 9364–2.9

Flow-of-funds accounts, assets and liabilities by type and economic sector, year-end outstandings, 1960-83, annual rpt, 9364–3

Flow-of-funds accounts savings, investments, and credit statements, quarterly rpt, 9365–3.3

Govt expenditures for social welfare by program and level of govt, and private expenditures for health care, selected years FY50-82, annual article, 4742–1.425

Govt finances, by level of govt and State, selected years 1929-83, annual rpt, 10044–1

Govt finances, by level of govt, State, and for large cities and counties, 1981-83, annual rpt series, 2466–2

Govt finances, policy, and intergovtl relations of Federal, State, and local govts, series, 10046–8

Govt finances, quarterly chartbook, 9362–2.4

Govt revenue and spending growth rates, and bond offerings by purpose, for State and local govts, various periods 1948-84, article, 9362–1.408

Govt revenue by source and expenditures by function, for State and local govts, 1980-83, article, 2702–1.436

Govt revenues and expenditures, State and local govt, selected years FY27-82, annual rpt, 204–1.6

Govt revenues by source and expenditures by function, natl income and product account, *Survey of Current Business,* monthly rpt, 2702–1.21, 2702–1.24

Govt revenues by source and expenditures by type, for State and local govts, 1978-83, annual article, 2702–1.405

Hwy expenditures and aid per capita related to local area characteristics, for 10 eastern counties, annual averages 1965-76, technical paper, 9377–9.9

Hwy Statistics, detailed data on traffic, govt finances, fuel use, vehicles, driver licenses, and hwy characteristics, by State, 1983, annual rpt, 7554–1

Input-output structure of US economy, detailed interindustry transactions for 85 industries, and components of final demand, 1977, article, 2702–1.421

Index by Subjects and Names

Input-output structure of US economy, detailed interindustry transactions for 537 industries, and components of final demand, 1977 benchmark data, 2708–17

Jail capacities, conditions, expenditures, and services, and socioeconomic and other characteristics of inmates, various dates 1976-82, 10048–59

Legal fees awarded private parties in cases against Federal, State, and local govts, by case, selected years 1977-83, 6008–19

Mortgage loan activity, by type of lender, loan, and mortgaged property, monthly rpt, 5142–18

Mortgage loan transactions and holdings of State and local govt retirement funds and credit agencies, by type of property and loan, quarterly rpt, 5142–30

Nuclear attack civil defense plans of Fed Emergency Mgmt Agency, funding and operations by component, FY81-84 and projected FY85-89, GAO rpt, 26123–61

NYC metro area small business owners and accountants, assessment of economy, professional activities, and community problems, by county and industry div, 1983 survey, hearings, 21728–52.3

Pollution abatement capital and operating costs under Clean Air and Water Acts, for govts and selected industries, various periods 1970-2000, annual rpt, 9184–11

Procurement of goods and services, and budget surplus and deficit, by level of govt, *Business Conditions Digest,* historical supplement and methodology, 1947-82, 2708–31

Procurement of goods and services by level of govt, *Business Conditions Digest,* monthly rpt, 2702–3.5

Productivity measurement of State and local govt, with background data and output indexes for 7 govt services, various periods 1955-82, 6728–27

Public defender systems, costs, cases, and expenditures by level of govt and State, with system characteristics and lawyer fee ranges, 1981, 6066–19.8

Public welfare expenditures by level of govt and program type, selected years FY50-82, 4746–16.1

Public works capital needs and financing, by project type, level of govt, and selected jurisdiction, 1970s-83 and projected to 2000, hearing, 23848–181

R&D expenditures by higher education instns and federally funded centers, by field, source of funds, instn, and State, FY82, annual rpt, 9627–13

R&D Fed Govt funding, by agency and performer, FY83-84, 9626–2.132

R&D Fed Govt funding for all performers, by field and supporting agency, selected years FY60-84, annual rpt, 9627–20

Radiation control program activities, State and local expenditures, personnel, and NRC licenses, by State, FY80-82, annual rpt, 4064–3

Retirement systems of State and local govts, cash and security holdings and finances, quarterly rpt, 2462–2

Revenue reliance of local govts on State aid and local taxes by type, spending, and excise tax growth by State, selected years FY57-83, article, 10042–1.403

Revenue sharing payments to States, local govts, Indian tribes, and Alaska Native villages, and entitlement computation data, FY84, series, 8066–1

Runaway and other homeless youth programs, funding by source, activities, and participant characteristics, FY82, annual rpt, 4604–3

Rural and urban areas comparisons of employment, income, housing, health, and education, 1960s-83, annual chartbook, 1504–3

Security issues of State and local govts and corporations, 1982, annual rpt, 9364–5.5

Statistical Abstract of US, social, political, and economic data, 1950s-83 and trends, annual rpt, 2324–1.2

Transit system operations, tax burden related to ridership, fares, and govt funding, for selected States and cities, 1950s-82, reprint, 7888–59

Transit systems, expenditures by level of govt, and revenues by source, with distribution of commuter trips by mode of transport, 1980-82, article, 10042–1.404

TVA power distributors purchases and resales of TVA power, and rates charged, by consumer class, 1983, annual rpt, 9804–14

Urban Dev Action Grant awards to local areas, preliminary approvals, with project descriptions, private investment, and jobs and taxes to be created, by city, quarterly press release series, 5002–7

Virgin Islands govt fiscal condition, FY81, annual rpt, 5304–10

see also Census of Governments

see also Federal aid to local areas

see also Federal-local relations

see also Fire departments

see also Police

see also School districts

see also Special districts

see also State aid to local areas

see also State and local employees

see also State and local employees pay

see also State-local relations

see also Urban areas

Local taxation

see State and local taxes

Location of industries

see Industrial siting

Lockouts

see Labor-management relations, general

see Labor-management relations, local and regional

Lodging

see Hotels and motels

Loeys, Jan G.

"Market Perceptions of Monetary Policy and the Weekly M1 Announcements", 9387–8.93

Logan County, Ohio

Housing vacancy rates for single and multifamily units and mobile homes, by city and ZIP code, 1984, annual metro area rpt, 9304–27.3

Logansport, Ind.

Wages of office and plant workers, by occupation, 1984 labor market area survey rpt, 6785–3.5

Logistics

DOD budget, itemized account of legislative history, FY84, annual rpt, 3504–7

DOD budget justification, programs, and policies, FY85, annual rpt, 3544–2

DOD Directorate for Info Operations and Rpts publications, FY84, annual listing, 3544–16

DOD shipments of military and personal property, loss claims, passenger traffic, and costs, by mode of transport, quarterly rpt, 3702–1

DOD strategic capability, force strengths, weapons, training, supplies, and requirements, by service branch, FY80-84 and projected to 1990, 3508–19

Fed Govt programs and mgmt cost control proposals, 3-year savings by function and agency, and financial and operating data, 1960s-81, 16908–1

Sealift Military Command operations for naval fleet support, and transport of DOD and AID cargo by route, quarterly rpt, 3802–2

Soviet Union and Warsaw Pact military weapons systems, assistance and presence worldwide, and force strengths, with selected US and NATO comparisons, as of 1984, 3508–14

Supply inventory and automated cataloging system of Fed Govt, and DOD mgmt of inventory items for agencies, NATO, and foreign govts, 1970s-83, annual rpt, 21204–1

see also Military supplies and property

Lombra, Raymond E.

"Changing Role of Real and Nominal Interest Rates", 9381–1.405

Lompoc, Calif.

- Census of Housing, 1980: occupancy and unit characteristics, by race, Hispanic origin, and city, SMSA rpt, 2473–1.324
- Census of Population and Housing, 1980: detailed population and housing characteristics, by county, city, and census tract, SMSA rpt, 2551–2.324
- Wages of office and plant workers, by occupation, 1984 labor market area survey rpt, 6785–3.7
- *see also* under By SMSA or MSA in the "Index by Categories"

Long Beach, Calif.

- Auto dealer repair workers, wages, and benefits, by occupation, size of establishment, and for 24 labor market areas, Nov 1982 survey, 6787–6.202
- Census of Housing, 1980: occupancy and unit characteristics, by race, Hispanic origin, and city, SMSA rpt, 2473–1.226
- Census of Population and Housing, 1980: detailed population and housing characteristics, by county, city, and census tract, SMSA rpt, 2551–2.226
- CPI by component for US city average, and by region, population size, and for 28 SMSAs, monthly press release, 6762–1
- CPI by detailed component, for US city average, 28 SMSAs, and 4 regions by population size, monthly rpt, 6762–2
- Dress industry production and related workers, wages, and benefits, by occupation, size of establishment, and union status, for 11 labor market areas, Aug 1982 survey, 6787–6.200
- Hospital worker wages by sex and occupation, and benefits, for 22 MSAs, Oct 1981 survey, 6787–6.201

Housing and households detailed characteristics, and unit and neighborhood quality, by inside-outside central cities, 1980 survey, SMSA rpt, 2485–6.3

- Housing unit starts and completions authorized by building permits in 20 MSAs, quarterly rpt, 2382–9
- Housing vacancy rates for single and multifamily units and mobile homes, by city and ZIP code, 1983, annual metro area rpt, 9304–20.2
- Repair technicians and apprentices wages and benefits, for 5 types of electrical repair shops in 19 SMSAs, Nov 1981 survey, 6787–6.197
- Shipping industry impact on local economy, and port dev financing through user fees, by State, other area, industry, and port, 1970s-2020, hearings, 21568–34
- Wages of office and plant workers, by occupation, 1983 SMSA survey rpt, 6785–12.1
- *see also* under By City and By SMSA or MSA in the "Index by Categories"

Long Branch, N.J.

- Census of Housing, 1980: occupancy and unit characteristics, by race, Hispanic origin, and city, SMSA rpt, 2473–1.223
- Census of Population and Housing, 1980: detailed population and housing characteristics, by county, city, and census tract, SMSA rpt, 2551–2.223

Long Island Railroad

Finances and operations of 7 commuter rail systems, and public agency cost reimbursement, 1980, 7888–61

Longino, Charles F., Jr.

"Statistical Profile of Older Floridians, For State and Area Agency Planners", 4478–150

Longmire, Jim

- "Long-Term Developments in Trade in Feeds and Livestock Products", 1528–177
- "Strong Dollar Dampens Demand for U.S. Farm Exports", 1528–174

Longmont, Colo.

see also under By SMSA or MSA in the "Index by Categories"

Longshoremen

- Census of Population, 1980: detailed socioeconomic and demographic characteristics, by age, sex, race, Hispanic origin, occupation, and industry, State rpt series, 2531–4
- Employment shipboard, shipyard, and longshore, FY82-83, annual rpt, 7704–14.3
- Manpower supply in 4 coastal regions, monthly rpt, 7702–1
- Merchant ships in US fleet, shipping costs, construction, employment, military availability, and Fed Govt subsidies, 1970s-1984 and projected to 2000, 26306–6.83
- Workers compensation law provisions of States and Fed Govt, by jurisdiction, as of July 1984, semiannual rpt, 6502–1
- Workers compensation under Fed Govt-administered programs, coverage, expenditures, and claims and dispositions by district, FY83, annual compilation, 6504–5

Longview, Tex.

- Census of Housing, 1980: occupancy and unit characteristics, by race, Hispanic origin, and city, SMSA rpt, 2473–1.224
- Census of Population and Housing, 1980: detailed population and housing characteristics, by county, city, and census tract, SMSA rpt, 2551–2.224
- *see also* under By SMSA or MSA in the "Index by Categories"

Loopesko, Bonnie E.

"Relationships Among Exchange Rates, Intervention, and Interest Rates: An Empirical Investigation", 9366–1.132

Lopez, Esperanza

"Disabled-Worker Projections for OASDI Cost Estimates, 1984", 4706–1.93

Lorain, Ohio

- Census of Housing, 1980: occupancy and unit characteristics, by race, Hispanic origin, and city, SMSA rpt, 2473–1.225
- Census of Population and Housing, 1980: detailed population and housing characteristics, by county, city, and census tract, SMSA rpt, 2551–2.225
- *see also* under By SMSA or MSA in the "Index by Categories"

Lord, Blair M.

"Distributional Assessment of Rhode Island's Catastrophic Health Insurance Plan (CHIP)", 4652–1.423

Los Alamos National Laboratory

see also Department of Energy National Laboratories

Los Angeles, Calif.

- Auto dealer repair workers, wages, and benefits, by occupation, size of establishment, and for 24 labor market areas, Nov 1982 survey, 6787–6.202
- Auto emissions control device tampering and fuel-switching incidence in 6 urban areas, 1983, annual rpt, 9194–15
- Carbon monoxide atmospheric concentrations and levels within buildings and along commuting and residential driving routes, for 4 cities, Jan-Mar 1981, 9198–110
- Census of Housing, 1980: occupancy and unit characteristics, by race, Hispanic origin, and city, SMSA rpt, 2473–1.226
- Census of Population and Housing, 1980: detailed population and housing characteristics, by county, city, and census tract, SMSA rpt, 2551–2.226
- CPI by component for US city average, and by region, population size, and for 28 SMSAs, monthly press release, 6762–1
- CPI by detailed component, for US city average, 28 SMSAs, and 4 regions by population size, monthly rpt, 6762–2
- Dress industry production and related workers, wages, and benefits, by occupation, size of establishment, and union status, for 11 labor market areas, Aug 1982 survey, 6787–6.200
- Fruit and vegetable shipments, and arrivals in 23 US and 5 Canada cities, by mode of transport and State or country of origin, 1983, annual rpt, 1311–4.2
- Hospital worker wages by sex and occupation, and benefits, for 22 MSAs, Oct 1981 survey, 6787–6.201
- Households and members demographic characteristics, for Los Angeles SMSA, Mar 1982, annual Current Population Rpt, 2546–1.383

Los Angeles, Calif.

Housing and households detailed characteristics, and unit and neighborhood quality, by inside-outside central cities, 1980 survey, SMSA rpt, 2485–6.3

Housing market in California, and Los Angeles average home price and mortgage rate, 1969-82 with economic indicators projected to 1989, 9306–1.1

Housing unit starts and completions authorized by building permits in 20 MSAs, quarterly rpt, 2382–9

Housing vacancy rates for single and multifamily units and mobile homes, by city and ZIP code, 1983, annual metro area rpt, 9304–20.2

Housing water conservation programs and savings of water and energy, for selected cities and suburbs, 1980-83, 5188–109

Population size of top 25 cities, 1980 and 1982, press release, 2328–46

Repair technicians and apprentices wages and benefits, for 5 types of electrical repair shops in 19 SMSAs, Nov 1981 survey, 6787–6.197

Shipping industry impact on local economy, and port dev financing through user fees, by State, other area, industry, and port, 1970s-2020, hearings, 21568–34

Wages of office and plant workers, by occupation, 1983 SMSA survey rpt, 6785–12.1

Waterborne commerce of US (domestic and foreign), freight by commodity, traffic, and passengers, by port and waterway, 1982, annual rpt, 3754–3.4

see also under By City and By SMSA or MSA in the "Index by Categories"

Losey, Robert L.

"Determinants of Stock Savings and Loan Value", 9316–2.46

Lotteries

Govt census, 1982: State govt payments to local govts, by program, source of funds, level of govt, and State, with trends from 1902, 2460–3

Income (taxable) not reported on individual and corporate returns, and associated Federal revenue losses, by detailed legal and illegal source, 1973-81, 8308–26

Taxation and revenue systems, by type of tax and system, level of govt, and State, selected years 1958-83, annual rpt, 10044–1.3

Virgin Islands economic censuses, 1982: employment, establishments, payroll, and receipts, by SIC 1- to 4-digit industry, island, and city, 2593–1

Virgin Islands socioeconomic and govtl data, FY81, annual rpt, 5304–4

Loughlin, Thomas R.

"Incidental Catch of Marine Mammals by Foreign Fishing Vessels, 1978-81", 2162–1.401

Louisiana

Agriculture census, 1982: farms, farmland, production and costs, and operator characteristics, preliminary State summary and county rpts, 2330–1.22

Agriculture census, 1982: farms, farmland, production, finances, and operator characteristics, by county, final State rpt, 2331–1.18

Alcohol fuel (ethanol) production in Tennessee Valley, feedstocks, facilities, tax incentives, and related farming data, by State, 1970s-83 and projected to 1992, 9808–69

Bank deposits in commercial and mutual savings banks and in US branches of foreign banks, by account type, instn, State, SMSA, and county, June 1983, annual rpt, 9295–3.9

Biomass Fuels Program of TVA, technologies and processes dev, costs, and resource requirements, 1970s-90s, series, 9806–9

Black higher education instns in Louisiana, State funding for desegregation by purpose and instn, 1982/83-1983/84, hearings, 21348–91

Census of Housing, 1980: occupancy and unit characteristics of SMSAs and central cities, by race, Hispanic origin, and city, State rpt, 2473–1.20

Census of Population and Housing, 1980: detailed population and housing characteristics, by county, city, and census tract, State rpt, 2551–2.20

Census of Population, 1980: detailed socioeconomic and demographic characteristics, by age, sex, race, Hispanic origin, and industry, State rpt, 2531–4.20

Coastal environmental characteristics, fish, wildlife, and use, and population socioeconomic data, for individual areas, 1983 rpt, 5506–4.2

County Business Patterns: establishments, employees, and payrolls, by SIC 4-digit industry and county, 1982, annual State rpt, 2326–6.20

Employment and unemployment in Louisiana, by SMSA and major manufacturing industry group, 1970s-83, article, 9371–1.407

Employment by major nonagricultural industry, and average hours and earnings of manufacturing production workers, for 5 southwestern States, monthly rpt, 6962–2

Employment, earnings, and hours, by selected SIC 1- to 4-digit industry, State, and for 278 major labor areas, 1939-83, annual rpt, 6744–5.1, 6744–5.3

Employment, industrial relations, prices, and economic conditions in 5 Southwestern States, regional rpts series, 6966–1

Environmental quality, pollutant discharge by type and source, and EPA protection activities and funding, 1970s-83, biennial regional rpt, 9184–15.6

Exports of manufactured and agricultural commodities, manufacturing production, and export-related employment, 1960s-82, State rpt, 2046–3.18

Financial and economic devs, Fed Reserve Bank of Atlanta monthly rpt with articles, 9371–1

Fish and shellfish landings, prices, and cannery production, for Gulf States and North Carolina, by area, weekly rpt, 2162–6.3

HHS aid to each State and local govt or private instn, amount obligated, funding agency, and program, FY83, annual listing, 4004–3.6

Income (personal) per capita and by source, and earnings by industry div, by State, MSA, and county, 1977-82, annual regional rpt, 2704–2.6

Mineral Industry Surveys, State review of production, 1983, advance annual rpt, 5614–6.18

Index by Subjects and Names

Minerals Yearbook, 1982, Vol 2 preprints: State review of production and sales by commodity, and business activity, annual rpt, 5604–16.19

Minerals Yearbook, 1982, Vol 2: State reviews of production, sales, and firms, by commodity, and business activity, annual rpt, 5604–34

Oil and gas extraction production workers, wages, hours, and benefits, by occupation, region, and for 5 States, June 1982 survey, 6787–6.203

Oil and gas field itemized equipment and operating costs and cost indexes, for 10 producing areas, 1981-83, annual rpt, 3164–45

Oil spills in coastal and aquatic wildlife habitats, methodology for cleanup priority rating and listing of wildlife species of concern, 1984 rpt, 5508–87

Population size and components of change, by MSA and county, 1980-82, annual State Current Population Rpt, 2546–4.18

Population size, Apr 1980 and July 1982, and per capita income, 1979 and 1981, by county and city, State Current Population Rpt, 2546–11.18

Property tax on forest, agricultural, and marsh lands, impact of change from market to use valuation by parish, 1977-78, 1208–206

Retail trade census, 1982: employment, establishments, sales, and payroll, by SIC 2- to 4-digit kind of business, SMSA, county, and city, State rpt, 2397–1.19

Rice market activities, prices, inspections, sales, trade, supply, and use, for US and selected foreign markets, weekly rpt, 1313–8

Rice stocks on and off farms and total, periodic rpt, 1621–7

Savings and loan assns, FHLB 9th District, insured members financial condition and operations by SMSA, monthly rpt, 9302–13

Service industry census, 1982: employment, establishments, receipts, and payroll, by SIC 2- to 4-digit kind of business, SMSA, county, and city, State rpt, 2391–1.19

Water supply and quality in streams and lakes, and groundwater levels in wells, by drainage basin, 1982, annual State rpt, 5666–20.17

Water supply and quality in streams and lakes, and groundwater levels in wells, by drainage basin, 1983, annual State rpt, 5666–10.17

Wholesale trade census, 1982: employment, establishments, finances, and operations, by SIC 2- to 4-digit kind of business, SMSA, county, and city, State rpt, 2405–1.19

see also Alexandria, La.
see also Baton Rouge, La.
see also Houma, La.
see also Lafayette, La.
see also Lake Charles, La.
see also Monroe, La.
see also New Orleans, La.
see also Shreveport, La.
see also Thibodaux, La.
see also Vernon Parish, La.
see also under By State in the "Index by Categories"

Index by Subjects and Names

Lumber industry and products

Louisville, Ky.

Census of Housing, 1980: occupancy and unit characteristics, by race, Hispanic origin, and city, SMSA rpt, 2473–1.227

Census of Population and Housing, 1980: detailed population and housing characteristics, by county, city, and census tract, SMSA rpt, 2551–2.227

Economic indicators for Southeastern States and 5 SMSAs, Fed Reserve 8th District, quarterly rpt, 9391–15

Housing and households detailed characteristics, and unit and neighborhood quality, by inside-outside central cities, 1980 survey, SMSA rpt, 2485–6.11

Wages by occupation, and benefits for office and plant workers, 1983 SMSA survey rpt, 6785–12.1

Waterborne commerce of US (domestic and foreign), freight by commodity, traffic, and passengers, by port and waterway, 1982, annual rpt, 3754–3.2

see also under By City and By SMSA or MSA in the "Index by Categories"

Lousiana

Manufacturing census, 1982: financial and operating data, by SIC 2- to 4-digit industry, State, SMSA, and county, preliminary census div rpt, 2491–3.7

Loveland, Colo

see also under By SMSA or MSA in the "Index by Categories"

Low-income housing

- Asia developing countries housing finance and low-income housing projects, and activities of 2 countries, 1970s-82, annual conf proceedings, 9914–11
- Budget of US, effects of Reagan Admin policy changes, by detailed program, FY85, annual rpt, 104–21
- Community dev programs funding and activities, for 5 HUD programs, FY83, annual rpt, 5124–5
- Corporate income tax returns, detailed income and tax items by industry, 1981, annual rpt, 8304–4
- Energy aid of Fed Govt for low-income households, allocations and average benefits in 13 States, and public interest group assessment, FY81-83, GAO rpt, 26121–75
- Energy aid of Fed Govt for low-income households, by income, aid type, and State, FY83, annual rpt, 4744–3.13
- Financing notes sold by local authorities for low-rent housing projects, with terms and purchaser, by project, monthly listing, 5142–43
- Financing project notes sold by local authorities, terms and individual purchasers, monthly press release, 5142–37
- FmHA loans and borrower supervision activities in farm and housing programs, by type and State, monthly rpt, 1182–1
- FmHA loans and grants by program and State, and summary of services, FY83 with trends from FY63, annual rpt, 1184–17
- Govt Natl Mortgage Assn financial statements, and mortgage-backed securities program, FY82-83, annual rpt, 5144–6
- Home mortgages FHA-insured for low-cost homes, financial, construction, property, and mortgagor characteristics, quarterly rpt, 5142–4

Housing and households characteristics, and employment, housing finance, and social programs data, selected years 1948-83, hearing, 21968–28

Housing value or rent, and household income groups, by housing and household characteristics, and inside-outside central cities, 1979-82 surveys, SMSA rpt series, 2485–6

HUD rental rehabilitation projects, local funding and Section 8 rent supplements for 22 States and 275 communities, 1984 press release, 5006–3.30

Income assistance, effects of experimental negative income tax program on employment, earnings, marital status, and other family characteristics in 2 cities, 1970-75, 4008–64

Natural gas price decontrol alternatives effect on supply/demand, prices, and home heating costs of low-income households, 1970s-95, hearing, 25148–26

see also Public housing

see also Rent supplements

Lowell, Mass.

Census of Housing, 1980: occupancy and unit characteristics, by race, Hispanic origin, and city, SMSA rpt, 2473–1.228

Census of Population and Housing, 1980: detailed population and housing characteristics, by county, city, and census tract, SMSA rpt, 2551–2.228

Employment in traditional and high technology industry by occupation, and wages by industry, for Massachusetts and compared to US and 3 SMSAs, various periods 1976-82, article, 9373–1.416

see also under By SMSA or MSA in the "Index by Categories"

Lownes County, Miss.

Housing vacancy rates for single and multifamily units and mobile homes, by city and ZIP code, 1984, annual metro area rpt, 9304–19.12

LPG

see Liquefied petroleum gas

Lubbock, Tex.

Census of Population and Housing, 1980: detailed population and housing characteristics, by county, city, and census tract, SMSA rpt, 2551–2.229

see also under By City and By SMSA or MSA in the "Index by Categories"

Lubitz, James

"Use and Costs of Medicare Services in the Last Years of Life", 4144–11.1

"Use and Costs of Medicare Services in the Last 2 Years of Life", 4652–1.412

Lucier, Gary

"Farm Income Situation and Outlook", 1004–16.1

Lucke, Robert

"Analysis of Special Tax Provisions Affecting Independent Oil and Gas Producers, Special Study", 21788–132

Luggage

see Leather industry and products

Lumber industry and products

Agricultural Statistics, 1983, annual rpt, 1004–1.2

Air pollutant emission factors, by detailed source, 3rd edition, 1983-84 supplements, 9198–13

Air pollution levels for 5 pollutants, by detailed source, State, and Air Quality Control Region, 1981, annual rpt, 9194–7

Buildings (nonresidential) energy use, expenditures, and conservation, by building characteristics, EIA survey series, 3166–8

Business statistics, detailed data for major industries and economic indicators, *Survey of Current Business,* monthly rpt, 2702–1.13

Carbon dioxide atmospheric levels, climatic effects and impacts of fossil and synthetic fuels use, deforestation, and land use patterns, research rpt series, 3406–3

Census of Population, 1980: detailed socioeconomic and demographic characteristics, by age, sex, race, Hispanic origin, occupation, and industry, State rpt series, 2531–4

Census of Population, 1980: detailed socioeconomic characteristics, by county, city, and inside-outside SMSAs and central cities, State rpt series, 2531–3

Census of Population, 1980: labor force, by sex, detailed occupation, and region, with comparison to 1970 census, supplementary rpt, 2535–1.12

China economic conditions, agricultural and industrial production, trade, and domestic and foreign investment, 1980-85, 2048–106

China exports and imports by SITC 1- to 5-digit commodity, 1970s-82, annual rpt, 244–12

Coastal environmental characteristics, fish, wildlife, and use, and population socioeconomic data, for individual areas, series, 5506–4

Collective bargaining agreements expiring during year, covered workers by SIC 2-digit industry, firm, and union, with summary of key provisions, 1984, annual rpt, 6784–9

Colorado natl forest below-cost timber sales, and volume, costs, revenue, and net loss, by sale and forest, FY81-82, GAO rpt, 26113–131

Communist, OECD, and selected other countries consumer and producer goods production, 1960s-83, annual rpt, 244–5.8

County Business Patterns: establishments, employees, and payrolls, by SIC 4-digit industry and county, 1981, annual State rpt series, 2326–8

County Business Patterns: establishments, employees, and payrolls, by SIC 4-digit industry and county, 1982, annual State rpt series, 2326–6

Cuba economic conditions, agricultural and industrial production and distribution, trade, and intl economic relations, 1970-82 and trends from 1957, 248–40

Earnings by major industry group, and personal income per capita and by source, by region and State, 1929-82, 2708–40

Employment, earnings, and hours, by selected SIC 1- to 4-digit industry, State, and for 278 major labor areas, 1939-83, annual rpt, 6744–5

Employment, earnings, and hours, by SIC 4-digit nonfarm industry, monthly 1974-Feb 1984, annual update, 6744–4

Employment in regionally concentrated and all industries, and population size, by State, 1970-82, article, 6722–1.413

Lumber industry and products

Energy use and cost for building materials manufacture, by energy source and industry, 1970s-82, article, 2012–1.401

Exports and imports between US and outlying areas, by detailed commodity and mode of transport, monthly rpt, 2422–4

Exports and imports of US, by commodity group, world area, selected country, US coastal area and port, and mode of transport, with seasonal adjustments, monthly rpt, 2422–9

Exports and imports of US by country, and trade shifts by commodity, USITC quarterly monitoring rpt, 9882–9

Exports and imports of US, detailed SIC-based commodities by world area, 1983, annual rpts, 2424–6

Exports and imports of US, totals and as percent of domestic production, by SIC 2- to 5-digit commodity, 1981, annual rpt, 2424–3

Exports, imports, tariffs, and industry operating data for wood, paper, and printed matter, TSUSA commodity rpt series, 9885–2

Exports of manufactured and agricultural commodities, manufacturing production, and export-related employment, 1960s-82, State rpt series, 2046–3

Exports of US, detailed commodities by country of destination, monthly rpt, 2422–3

Exports of US, detailed Schedule B commodities by country of destination, 1983, annual rpt, 2424–9

Exports of US, detailed Schedule E commodities by mode of transport and world area and country of destination, 1983, annual rpts, 2424–5

Exports of US lumber and wood products, by commodity and country, FAS quarterly rpt, 1925–36

Fed Govt programs and mgmt cost control proposals, 3-year savings by function and agency, and financial and operating data, 1960s-81, 16908–1.2

Finances and operations, by SIC 2- to 4-digit industry, 1970s-83 and projected to 1988, annual rpt, 2014–4

Foreign and US agricultural production, trade, and climatic devs, weekly press release, 1922–4

Foreign and US agricultural supply/demand indicators by commodity and world area, and related research and extension program needs, 1950s-2020, 1008–47

Foreign and US tropical forests status by country and world region, conservation methods, and mgmt role of US, foreign, and intl groups, 1977-81 and projected to 2000, 26358–101.1

Foreign tropical hardwood exports, by world region and country, selected years 1955-79, hearings, 21248–80

Futures trading by commodity and exchange, and Commodity Futures Trading Commission activities, funding, and employment, FY83, annual rpt, 11924–2

Futures trading in selected commodities, foreign currencies, and stock indexes, Chicago and other markets activity, monthly rpt, 11922–1

Futures trading in selected commodities, foreign currencies, Treasury securities, and stock indexes, NYC, Chicago, and other markets activity, monthly rpt, 11922–5

Index by Subjects and Names

Great Lakes trade, by SITC 3-digit commodity, port, vessel type, world area, and country, 1982, annual rpt, 7744–3

Hwy construction expenditures and contracts awarded for Federal-aid system, by type of material used and State, various periods 1944-83, annual rpt, 7554–29.7

Hwy construction materials used per $1 million of total expenditures on Federal-aid system, by State, 1980-82, annual rpt, 7554–29.3

Imports of US, detailed Schedule A commodities by country and world area of origin, and mode of transport, 1983, annual rpts, 2424–2

Imports of US, detailed Schedule A commodities by country, monthly rpt, 2422–2

Imports of US, detailed TSUSA commodities by country of origin, 1983, annual rpt, 2424–4

Income tax returns of corporations, detailed income and tax items by industry, 1981, annual rpt, 8304–4

Income tax returns of corporations with foreign tax credit, income and deductions by type, asset size, and selected industry group, 1980, article, 8302–2.415

Income tax returns of sole proprietorships, detailed data by industry div and selected industry group, 1981, annual rpt, 8304–7

Income tax returns of sole proprietorships, receipts, deductions by type, payroll, and net income, by major industry, 1982, annual article, 8302–2.413

Input-output structure of US economy, detailed interindustry transactions for 85 industries, and components of final demand, 1977, article, 2702–1.421

Input-output structure of US economy, detailed interindustry transactions for 537 industries, and components of final demand, 1977 benchmark data, 2708–17

Land Mgmt Bur activities and finances, and public land acreage and use, annual State rpt series, 5724–11

Land Mgmt Bur public lands admin and program activities in western States, FY82-84, annual rpt, 5724–13

Manufacturing census, 1982: financial and operating data, by SIC 2- to 4-digit industry, State, SMSA, and county, preliminary census div rpt series, 2491–3

Manufacturing census, 1982: financial and operating data, for SIC 4-digit industries by product, preliminary rpt series, 2491–1

Manufacturing use of wood, by type of wood, end use, and SIC 4-digit industry, 1977 with summary trends from 1928, 1208–3

Marketing cash receipts of farms, by detailed commodity and State, 1979-82, annual rpt, 1544–18

Michigan timber acreage, volume, growth, removals, and production, by ownership, county, and forest and tree characteristics, 1980, series, 1206–31

Minority group and women employment, by occupational group and SIC 2- to 3-digit industry, 1981, annual rpt, 9244–1.1

Natl forest timber sold and harvested by State, FY83, annual rpt, 1204–1

North Central States pulpwood production by county, imports, and individual mill capacity, by species, 1982, annual rpt, 1204–19

North Central States timber removals, and mill receipts and production, by species, product, and county, series, 1206–10

Northeast pulpwood production and yield per acre, for 14 States, by county, 1981, TVA technical paper, 9806–2.38

Northeast States timber annual growth, removals, causes of mortality, and products output, and forest ownership and industries, State rpt series, 1206–16

Northeastern region timber resources and removals, by species, ownership, and county, State rpt series, 1206–12

Northwest US and British Columbia forest industry production, prices, trade, and employment, quarterly rpt, 1202–3

Northwest US natl forest timber sales contract operations by forest and firm, and lumber supply/demand, FY76-1983, hearings, 25318–57

Occupational injuries in logging, by accident circumstances, characteristics of persons and equipment involved, and body part injured, Apr-June 1983, 6846–1.14

Occupational injury and illness rates, by SIC 2- to 4-digit industry, 1982, annual rpt, 6844–1

OECD trade, total and for 4 major countries, and US trade by country, by commodity, 1972-82, annual world region rpt series, 244–13

Oregon and Montana earnings by SIC 1- to 3-digit industry and payments to retirees by type, for 4 timber dependent communities, 1970, 1208–196

Pacific Northwest electricity consumption and prices by end-use sector, and economic and demographic data, 1960s-83 and projected to 2005, annual rpt, 3224–2

Pacific Northwest natl forest sales by bidding method, harvest by company, and effects on local employment by community, 1974-77, 1208–194

Plant and animal genetic resource conservation, commercial uses, causes of depletion, and geographic sources, 1984 rpt, 5548–13

Pollution abatement capital and operating costs, by SIC 2- to 4-digit industry, State, and SMSA, 1982, annual Current Industrial Rpt, 2506–3.6

Pollution abatement capital and operating costs under Clean Air and Water Acts, for govts and selected industries, various periods 1970-2000, annual rpt, 9184–11

Prices (stumpage) for sawtimber sold from natl forests, by species and region, quarterly rpt, 1202–1

Producer prices and indexes, by stage of processing and detailed commodity, monthly rpt, 6762–6

Producer prices and indexes, by stage of processing and detailed commodity, monthly 1983, annual supplement, 6764–2

Production and shipments by region and State, inventories, trade, and consumption, by detailed lumber product, periodic Current Industrial Rpt series, 2506–7

Index by Subjects and Names

Luxembourg

Production, prices by region and State, trade by country, and consumption, for timber by species and product, with industry earnings, 1950-83, annual rpt, 1204–29

Production, shipments, PPI, and stocks of building materials, by type, bimonthly rpt, 2012–1.5, 2012–1.6

Productivity, hours, and employment indexes for selected SIC 3- and 4-digit industries, 1954-82, annual rpt, 6824–1.3

Puerto Rico wood and wood product shipments from US by type, and from selected foreign sources, 1971-81, 1208–205

R&D industry funding and employment of scientists and engineers, by industry group, firm size, and funding source, 1956-82, annual rpt, 9627–21

Research project descriptions and bibl for forestry, 1982, annual rpt, 1204–14

Retail trade census, 1982: employment, establishments, sales, and payroll, for lumber yards, by State, preliminary rpt, 2395–1.1

Rocky Mountain forest and rangeland area, and timber resources and removals, by ownership, forest and tree characteristics, and State, 1977, 1208–201

Rocky Mountain States lumber and wood product production, consumption by end use, shipments, exports, and market channels, 1974-76, 1208–208

Scientists, engineers, and technicians employed in private industry, by occupation and industry group, 1980-81, biennial rpt, 9627–23

Scientists, engineers, and technicians employment in transportation, utilities, and retail and wholesale trade, by field of science and industry, 1982, 9628–72

South Carolina industrial roundwood production and residue volume, by species, product type, State region, and county, 1977-81, 1208–203

Southeastern States pulpwood prices, expenditures, and transport modes, 1980-81, annual rpt, 1204–22

Southeastern States timber resources and removals, for 5 States, interim rpt series, 1206–32

Statistical Abstract of US, social, political, and economic data, 1950s-83 and trends, annual rpt, 2324–1.3

Supply/demand, prices, and volume of timber, 1977 and projected to 2030, 1208–24.4

Tariff Schedules of US, Annotated, classifications and rates of duty for detailed imported commodities, 1985 edition, 9886–13

Timber harvest residue recovery for energy, cost-effectiveness of 3 logging systems, 1983 technical paper, 9806–2.37

Transportation census, 1982: trucks, by detailed characteristics, miles traveled, and type of product carried, State rpt series, 2573–1

TTPI socioeconomic, health, and govtl data, by TTPI govt, FY83 and selected trends, detailed annual rpt, 7004–6

TVA region wood residue production and use, by tree species group and wood residue type, for 44 counties, 1979, technical paper, 9806–2.36

Utah timber acreage and resources, by species, ownership class, and stand size, and forest recreation, 1978, series, 1206–22

Veneer log production, mill receipts, and use, North Central States, biennial rpt, discontinued, 1204–24

Virgin Islands economic censuses, 1982: employment, establishments, payroll, and receipts, by SIC 1- to 4-digit industry, island, and city, 2593–1

Water pollution fish kills, by State, location, and pollution source, monthly 1978-80, annual rpt, 9204–3

Waterborne commerce of US (domestic and foreign), freight by commodity, traffic, and passengers, by port and waterway, 1982, annual rpt, 3754–3

Western regions natl forests below-cost timber sales and revenue by forest, and volume, average price by species, and costs by region, FY80-1982, GAO rpt, 26113–126

Wholesale trade census, 1982: employment, establishments, finances, and operations, by SIC 2- to 4-digit kind of business, SMSA, county, and city, State rpt series, 2405–1

Wholesale trade census, 1982: employment, establishments, sales by commodity, and payroll, by SIC 4-digit kind of business and State, preliminary rpt, 2403–1.4

see also Forests and forestry

see also Gum and wood chemicals

see also Paper and paper products

see also Wood fuel

see also under By Commodity in the "Index by Categories"

see also under By Industry in the "Index by Categories"

Lundahl, Sandra L.

"Development and Evaluation of a Community Cancer Resource Directory", 4102–1.459

Lundine, Ronald L.

"Weather and Crop Prospects, 1984", 1004–16.1

Lunenfeld, Bruno

"Epidemiology, Health Policy, and Resource Allocation: The Israeli Perspective", 4102–1.446

Lung diseases

see Black lung

see Pneumonia and influenza

see Respiratory diseases

see Tuberculosis

Lupoletti, William

"Economic Outlook for Fifth District States in 1984: Forecasts from Vector Autoregression Models", 9389–1.403

Lutton, Thomas

"Elasticity of Substitution and Land Use in Agricultural Production: A Cause for Optimism?", 1502–3.403

Luxembourg

Agricultural and food production indexes, and production of selected commodities, by world region and country, 1974-83, annual rpt, 1524–5

Agricultural situation in Western Europe, by country and commodity, 1983 and outlook for 1984, annual rpt, 1524–4.6

Agricultural supply/demand, trade, and production, and socioeconomic data, by country, 1950s-77, 1528–179

AID loan repayment status and terms by program and country, and status of predecessor agency loans, quarterly rpt, 9912–3

Background Notes, summary social, political, and economic data, 1984 rpt, 7006–2.58

Economic, social, and political summary data, by country, 1984, annual factbook, 244–11

Economic trends in income, production, prices, employment, finances, and trade, 1984 annual rpt, 2046–4.86

Exports and imports of NATO countries with Council for Mutual Economic Assistance Europe members, by country, 1980-83, annual rpt, 7144–5

Exports and imports of NATO countries with PRC, by country, 1980-83, annual rpt, 7144–14

Exports and imports of OECD countries, by country, 1983, annual rpt, 7144–10

Exports and imports of US with Western Europe, and US market share and export opportunities for selected commodities, by country, 1982-84, 2048–105

Exports of US, detailed Schedule B commodities by country of destination, 1983, annual rpt, 2424–9

Exports of US, detailed Schedule E commodities by mode of transport and world area and country of destination, 1983, annual rpts, 2424–5

Food supply/demand and market and support prices, with exchange rates, fertilizer price index, GDP, and population, by EC country, 1960-83, 1528–173

Imports of US, detailed Schedule A commodities by country and world area of origin, and mode of transport, 1983, annual rpts, 2424–2

Imports of US, detailed TSUSA commodities by country of origin, 1983, annual rpt, 2424–4

Intl transactions of US with 10 countries, 1981-83, *Survey of Current Business,* monthly rpt, annual table, 2702–1.31

Loans and grants for economic and military assistance from US and intl agencies, by program and country, FY46-83, annual rpt, 9914–5

Military aid of US, arms sales, and training programs costs and budget requests by program, world region, and country, FY83-85, annual rpt, 7144–13

Military spending, arms trade, and armed forces size, with total govt spending and population, by country, 1972-82, annual rpt, 9824–1

Minerals Yearbook, 1982, Vol 3: foreign country reviews of production, trade, and policies, by commodity, annual rpt, 5604–35

Minerals Yearbook, 1983, Vol 3 preprints: foreign country review of production, trade, and policies, by commodity, annual rpt, 5604–23.8

Population size and growth rates, and latest available benchmark demographic data, by country, 1950-83, biennial rpt, 2324–4

Steel imports of US from EC and other countries, and US industry operating data, for 15 products limited under arrangement with EC, monthly rpt, 9882–10

Luytjes, Jan

Luytjes, Jan
"Can Interstate Banking Increase Competitive Market Performance? An Empirical Test", 9371–1.401

Lynchburg, Va.

Census of Housing, 1980: occupancy and unit characteristics, by race, Hispanic origin, and city, SMSA rpt, 2473–1.230

Census of Population and Housing, 1980: detailed population and housing characteristics, by county, city, and census tract, SMSA rpt, 2551–2.230

see also under By SMSA or MSA in the "Index by Categories"

Macao

Economic, social, and political summary data, by country, 1984, annual factbook, 244–11

Exports of US, detailed Schedule B commodities by country of destination, 1983, annual rpt, 2424–9

Imports of US, detailed Schedule A commodities by country and world area of origin, and mode of transport, 1983, annual rpts, 2424–2

Imports of US, detailed TSUSA commodities by country of origin, 1983, annual rpt, 2424–4

Population size and growth rates, and latest available benchmark demographic data, by country, 1950-83, biennial rpt, 2324–4

see also under By Foreign Country in the "Index by Categories"

MacArthur Foundation

Philanthropic foundations assets and grants for 50 largest foundations, and for selected foundations by recipient, selected years 1975-82, hearings, 21788–137

MacAuley, Patrick H.
"Federal Construction-Related Expenditures, 1980-85", 2012–1.404

Maccini, Louis J.
"Joint Production, Quasi-Fixed Factors of Production and Investment in Finished Goods Inventories", 9387–8.79

Maccoby, Michael
"Helping Labor and Management Set Up a Quality-of-Worklife Program", 6722–1.419

Machine-readable data file guides
see Computer data file guides

Machine tools
see Machines and machinery industry

Machines and machinery industry

Air pollutant emission factors, by detailed source, 3rd edition, 1983-84 supplements, 9198–13

Business Conditions Digest, historical supplement on economic, business, and financial conditions and cyclical fluctuations, with methodology, 1947-82, 2708–31

Business statistics, detailed data for major industries and economic indicators, *Survey of Current Business,* monthly rpt, 2702–1.14

Census of Population, 1980: detailed socioeconomic and demographic characteristics, by age, sex, race, Hispanic origin, occupation, and industry, State rpt series, 2531–4

Census of Population, 1980: detailed socioeconomic characteristics, by county, city, and inside-outside SMSAs and central cities, State rpt series, 2531–3

Index by Subjects and Names

Census of Population, 1980: labor force, by sex, detailed occupation, and region, with comparison to 1970 census, supplementary rpt, 2535–1.12

China economic conditions, agricultural and industrial production, trade, and domestic and foreign investment, 1980-85, 2048–106

China exports and imports by SITC 1- to 5-digit commodity, 1970s-82, annual rpt, 244–12

Collective bargaining agreements expiring during year, covered workers by SIC 2-digit industry, firm, and union, with summary of key provisions, 1984, annual rpt, 6784–9

Communist, OECD, and selected other countries consumer and producer goods production, 1960s-83, annual rpt, 244–5.8

Construction industries census, 1982: financial and operating data, by SIC 4-digit industry and State, final rpt series, 2373–1

Construction industries census, 1982: financial and operating data, by SIC 4-digit industry and State, preliminary rpt series, 2371–1

Construction machinery and metal cutting and forming tools industries, productivity, hours, and employment indexes, 1958-82, annual rpt, 6824–1.3

Counterfeiting of brand-name products by foreign manufacturers, effects on 6 US industries, investigation with financial and operating data, 1984 rpt, 9886–4.67

County Business Patterns: establishments, employees, and payrolls, by SIC 4-digit industry and county, 1981, annual State rpt series, 2326–8

County Business Patterns: establishments, employees, and payrolls, by SIC 4-digit industry and county, 1982, annual State rpt series, 2326–6

DOD procurement, prime contract awards by detailed procurement category, FY80-83, annual rpt, 3544–18

DOD shipments of military and personal property, loss claims, passenger traffic, and costs, by mode of transport, quarterly rpt, 3702–1

Earnings by major industry group, and personal income per capita and by source, by region and State, 1929-82, 2708–40

Earnings for selected industries and occupations, and interarea pay comparisons, 1945-82, annual rpt, 6724–1.6

Employment, earnings, and hours, by selected SIC 1- to 4-digit industry, State, and for 278 major labor areas, 1939-83, annual rpt, 6744–5

Employment, earnings, and hours, by SIC 4-digit nonfarm industry, monthly 1974-Feb 1984, annual update, 6744–4

Employment, unemployment, hours, and women's employment, for all durables manufacturing and for 5 metals industries, 1979-82, article, 6722–1.410

Exports and imports between US and outlying areas, by detailed commodity and mode of transport, monthly rpt, 2422–4

Exports and imports of US, and trade balance, by major commodity group, selected country, and world area, with seasonal adjustments, monthly rpt, 2422–6

Exports and imports of US, by commodity group, world area, selected country, US coastal area and port, and mode of transport, with seasonal adjustments, monthly rpt, 2422–9

Exports and imports of US by country, and trade shifts by commodity, USITC quarterly monitoring rpt, 9882–9

Exports and imports of US, detailed SIC-based commodities by world area, 1983, annual rpts, 2424–6

Exports and imports of US, totals and as percent of domestic production, by SIC 2- to 5-digit commodity, 1981, annual rpt, 2424–3

Exports, imports, tariffs, and industry operating data for machines for rubber and plastic molding, foreign and US, 1979-83, TSUSA commodity rpt, 9885–6.61

Exports, imports, tariffs, and industry operating data for metals and metal products, TSUSA commodity rpt series, 9885–6

Exports of agricultural products and nonelectrical machinery, *Business Conditions Digest,* monthly rpt, 2702–3.9

Exports of manufactured and agricultural commodities, manufacturing production, and export-related employment, 1960s-82, State rpt series, 2046–3

Exports of US, detailed commodities by country of destination, monthly rpt, 2422–3

Exports of US, detailed Schedule B commodities by country of destination, 1983, annual rpt, 2424–9

Exports of US, detailed Schedule E commodities by mode of transport and world area and country of destination, 1983, annual rpts, 2424–5

Finances and operations, by SIC 2- to 4-digit industry, 1970s-83 and projected to 1988, annual rpt, 2014–4

Financial statements for manufacturing, mining, and trade corporations, by selected SIC 2- to 3-digit industry, quarterly rpt, 2502–1

Fishing for squid off Washington State with jig devices, catch and mean squid length, selected dates May-Sept 1981, article, 2162–1.401

Foreign direct investment of US, by selected major industry group and world area, 1980-82, annual article, 2702–1.430

Foreign market and trade for machine tools and equipment, and user industry operations and demand, country market research rpts, 2045–9

Great Lakes trade, by SITC 3-digit commodity, port, vessel type, world area, and country, 1982, annual rpt, 7744–3

Imports of machinery undercarriage components from Italy, injury to US industry from sales covered by foreign govt grants, investigation with background financial and operating data, 1983 rpt, 9886–15.46

Imports of US, detailed Schedule A commodities by country and world area of origin, and mode of transport, 1983, annual rpts, 2424–2

Imports of US, detailed Schedule A commodities by country, monthly rpt, 2422–2

Index by Subjects and Names

Imports of US, detailed TSUSA commodities by country of origin, 1983, annual rpt, 2424–4

Income tax returns of corporations, detailed income and tax items by industry, 1981, annual rpt, 8304–4

Income tax returns of corporations with foreign tax credit, income and deductions by type, asset size, and selected industry group, 1980, article, 8302–2.415

Income tax returns of foreign subsidiaries of US corporations, income and tax data, by industry and asset size, 1980, article, 8302–2.410

Income tax returns of sole proprietorships, detailed data by industry div and selected industry group, 1981, annual rpt, 8304–7

Income tax returns of sole proprietorships, receipts, deductions by type, payroll, and net income, by major industry, 1982, annual article, 8302–2.413

Input-output structure of US economy, detailed interindustry transactions for 85 industries, and components of final demand, 1977, article, 2702–1.421

Input-output structure of US economy, detailed interindustry transactions for 537 industries, and components of final demand, 1977 benchmark data, 2708–17

Liquefied petroleum gas sales, by principal use, PAD district, and State, 1981-83, annual rpt, 3164–2

Machine tool orders by selected industry, trade, and shipments and Japan share of US market by type of tool, various dates 1972-84, hearing, 25388–48

Manufacturing census, 1982: financial and operating data, by SIC 2- to 4-digit industry, State, SMSA, and county, preliminary census div rpt series, 2491–3

Manufacturing census, 1982: financial and operating data, for SIC 4-digit industries by product, preliminary rpt series, 2491–1

Metalworking machinery industry computerized automation, by plant characteristics, for 6 industry groups and small plants, 1982 surveys, 23848–179

Mineral industries census, 1982: financial and operating data, including materials consumed, by SIC 4-digit industry and State, preliminary rpt series, 2511–1

Minority group and women employment, by occupational group and SIC 2- to 3-digit industry, 1981, annual rpt, 9244–1.1

North Central States economic indicators, Fed Reserve 7th District monthly rpt, 9375–9

Occupational deaths, circumstances and OSHA safety standards violated by type of incident and equipment used, series, 6606–2

Occupational injury and illness rates, by SIC 2- to 4-digit industry, 1982, annual rpt, 6844–1

Occupational Outlook Handbook, 1984-85 biennial rpt, 6744–1

OECD trade, total and for 4 major countries, and US trade by country, by commodity, 1972-82, annual world region rpt series, 244–13

Pollution abatement capital and operating costs, by SIC 2- to 4-digit industry, State, and SMSA, 1982, annual Current Industrial Rpt, 2506–3.6

Producer prices and indexes, by stage of processing and detailed commodity, monthly rpt, 6762–6

Producer prices and indexes, by stage of processing and detailed commodity, monthly 1983, annual supplement, 6764–2

Production, shipments, trade, stocks, consumption, and orders of machinery and equipment, and firms, by product, periodic Current Industrial Rpts series, 2506–12

R&D expenditures of US firms foreign affiliates, by selected industry, 1974-82, 9626–2.131

R&D industry expenditures, total and for 6 leading industries, projected 1984-85 with trends from 1975, 9626–2.145

R&D industry funding and employment of scientists and engineers, by industry group, firm size, and funding source, 1956-82, annual rpt, 9627–21

Scientists, engineers, and technicians employed in private industry, by occupation and industry group, 1980-81, biennial rpt, 9627–23

Scientists, engineers, and technicians employment in transportation, utilities, and retail and wholesale trade, by field of science and industry, 1982, 9628–72

Sewing machines trade, tariffs, and industry operating data, foreign and US, 1979-83, TSUSA commodity rpt supplement, 9885–6.66

Transportation census, 1982: trucks, by detailed characteristics, miles traveled, and type of product carried, State rpt series, 2573–1

Virgin Islands economic censuses, 1982: employment, establishments, payroll, and receipts, by SIC 1- to 4-digit industry, island, and city, 2593–1

Waterborne commerce of US (domestic and foreign), freight by commodity, traffic, and passengers, by port and waterway, 1982, annual rpt, 3754–3

Wholesale trade census, 1982: employment, establishments, finances, and operations, by SIC 2- to 4-digit kind of business, SMSA, county, and city, State rpt series, 2405–1

Wholesale trade census, 1982: employment, establishments, sales by commodity, and payroll, by SIC 4-digit kind of business and State, preliminary rpt series, 2403–1

Wholesale trade sales and inventories, by SIC 2- to 3-digit kind of business, monthly rpt, 2413–7

Wholesale trade sales, inventories, purchases, and gross margins, by SIC 2- to 3-digit kind of business and type of ownership, 1983, annual rpt, 2413–13

see also Agricultural machinery and equipment

see also Electrical machinery and equipment

see also Hand tools

see also Hardware

see also Industrial plants and equipment

see also Power-generating plants and equipment

see also Vending machines and stands

see also under By Commodity in the "Index by Categories"

see also under By Industry in the "Index by Categories"

Madagascar

Mack, Juanita

"Statistics of Interstate Natural Gas Pipeline Companies, 1983", 3164–38

Mackie, Arthur B.

"U.S. Farmer and World Market Development", 1528–172

Macon, Ga.

Census of Housing, 1980: occupancy and unit characteristics, by race, Hispanic origin, and city, SMSA rpt, 2473–1.231

Census of Population and Housing, 1980: detailed population and housing characteristics, by county, city, and census tract, SMSA rpt, 2551–2.231

see also under By City and By SMSA or MSA in the "Index by Categories"

Macon, Janet

"BLS' 1982 Survey of Work-Related Deaths", 6722–1.422

Madagascar

Agricultural and food production indexes, and production of selected commodities, by world region and country, 1974-83, annual rpt, 1524–5

Agricultural situation in sub-Saharan Africa, by country, 1982-83 and outlook for 1984, annual rpt, 1524–4.10

Agricultural supply/demand, trade, and production, and socioeconomic data, by country, 1950s-77, 1528–179

AID activities and funding by project and function, FY85, and developing countries summary socioeconomic data, 1970s-83, by country, annual rpt, 9914–3

AID economic assistance to developing countries, obligations and disbursements by country, quarterly rpt, 9912–4

AID loan repayment status and terms by program and country, and status of predecessor agency loans, quarterly rpt, 9912–3

Economic conditions and foreign marketing prospects in 46 Sub-Saharan countries, 1983 world region rpt, 2046–5.1

Economic conditions, income, production, prices, employment, and trade, 1984 annual country rpt, 2046–4.126

Economic, social, and political summary data, by country, 1984, annual factbook, 244–11

Economic trends in income, production, prices, employment, finances, and trade, 1984 annual rpt, 2046–4.62

Exports of US, detailed Schedule B commodities by country of destination, 1983, annual rpt, 2424–9

Exports of US, detailed Schedule E commodities by mode of transport and world area and country of destination, 1983, annual rpts, 2424–5

Imports of US, detailed Schedule A commodities by country and world area of origin, and mode of transport, 1983, annual rpts, 2424–2

Imports of US, detailed TSUSA commodities by country of origin, 1983, annual rpt, 2424–4

Loans and grants for economic and military assistance from US and intl agencies, by program and country, FY46-83, annual rpt, 9914–5

Military aid of US, arms sales, and training programs costs and budget requests by program, world region, and country, FY83-85, annual rpt, 7144–13

Madagascar

Military spending, arms trade, and armed forces size, with total govt spending and population, by country, 1972-82, annual rpt, 9824–1

Minerals Yearbook, 1982, Vol 3: foreign country reviews of production, trade, and policies, by commodity, annual rpt, 5604–35

Minerals Yearbook, 1983, Vol 3 preprints: foreign country review of production, trade, and policies, by commodity, annual rpt, 5604–23.45

Population size and growth rates, and latest available benchmark demographic data, by country, 1950-83, biennial rpt, 2324–4

see also under By Foreign Country in the "Index by Categories"

Madewell, Carl E.

"Agricultural Fuel Crops, 201-County Tennessee Valley Region", 9808–69

Madison, Wis.

Census of Housing, 1980: occupancy and unit characteristics, by race, Hispanic origin, and city, SMSA rpt, 2473–1.232

Census of Population and Housing, 1980: detailed population and housing characteristics, by county, city, and census tract, SMSA rpt, 2551–2.232

Housing and households detailed characteristics, and unit and neighborhood quality, by inside-outside central cities, 1981 survey, SMSA rpt, 2485–6.20

Housing vacancy rates for single and multifamily units and mobile homes, by county, city, and ZIP code, 1983, annual metro area rpt, 9304–18.4

see also under By City and By SMSA or MSA in the "Index by Categories"

Mafia

see Organized crime

Magazines

see Periodicals

Magistrates

see Judges

Magnesium

see Metals and metal industries

Mahaffey, Kathryn

"Blood Lead Levels for Persons Ages 6 Months-74 Years, U.S., 1976-80", 4147–11.201

Maiden, Jon

"Investment Tax Credit for Individual Taxpayers, 1981", 8302–2.409

Mail

see Postal service

see U.S. Postal Service

Maine

Agriculture census, 1982: farms, farmland, production and costs, and operator characteristics, preliminary State summary and county rpts, 2330–1.23

Agriculture census, 1982: farms, farmland, production, finances, and operator characteristics, by county, final State rpt, 2331–1.19

Bank deposits in commercial and mutual savings banks and in US branches of foreign banks, by account type, instn, State, SMSA, and county, June 1983, annual rpt, 9295–3.1

Census of Housing, 1980: occupancy and unit characteristics of SMSAs and central cities, by race, Hispanic origin, and city, State rpt, 2473–1.21

Census of Population and Housing, 1980: detailed population and housing characteristics, by county, city, and census tract, State rpt, 2551–2.21

County Business Patterns: establishments, employees, and payrolls, by SIC 4-digit industry and county, 1982, annual State rpt, 2326–6.21

Economic indicators for New England States, Fed Reserve 1st District, monthly rpt with articles, 9373–2

Employment, earnings, and hours, by selected SIC 1- to 4-digit industry, State, and for 278 major labor areas, 1939-83, annual rpt, 6744–5.1, 6744–5.3

Environmental quality, pollutant discharge by type and source, and EPA protection activities and funding, 1970s-83, biennial regional rpt, 9184–15.1

Exports of manufactured and agricultural commodities, manufacturing production, and export-related employment, 1960s-82, State rpt, 2046–3.19

Farms with sales under $2,500, acreage, finances, operations, and operator characteristics, by region and for 6 States, 1978, 1548–241

Fish and shellfish landings and prices at Boston and other New England ports, and total New England cold storage holdings, weekly rpt, 2162–6.2

Foster care children permanent placement, Fed Govt incentive program funding and operations in 7 States, FY80-82, GAO rpt, 26121–81

HHS aid to each State and local govt or private instn, amount obligated, funding agency, and program, FY83, annual listing, 4004–3.1

Income (personal) per capita and by source, and earnings by industry div, by State, MSA, and county, 1977-82, annual regional rpt, 2704–2.2

Mineral Industry Surveys, State review of production, 1983, advance annual rpt, 5614–6.19

Minerals Yearbook, 1982, Vol 2 preprints: State review of production and sales by commodity, and business activity, annual rpt, 5604–16.20

Minerals Yearbook, 1982, Vol 2: State reviews of production, sales, and firms, by commodity, and business activity, annual rpt, 5604–34

Population, births, deaths, and net migration, by MSA and county, 1980-82, annual State Current Population Rpt, 2546–4.19

Population size, Apr 1980 and July 1982, and per capita income, 1979 and 1981, by county and city, State Current Population Rpt, 2546–11.19

Retail trade census, 1982: employment, establishments, sales, and payroll, by SIC 2- to 4-digit kind of business, SMSA, county, and city, State rpt, 2397–1.20

Savings and loan assn deregulation effect on lending activity, for US and 3 States, as of June 1980-83, article, 9371–1.432

Savings and loan assn deregulation impact, financial ratios of S&Ls in 3 States and US, 1980-83, article, 9371–1.426

Savings and loan assns, FHLB 1st District member instns financial operations and related economic and housing indicators, monthly rpt, 9302–4

Index by Subjects and Names

Service industry census, 1982: employment, establishments, receipts, and payroll, by SIC 2- to 4-digit kind of business, SMSA, county, and city, State rpt, 2391–1.20

Timber resources and removals, by species, ownership class, and county, 1971 and 1982, 1206–12.7

Transportation census, 1982: trucks, by detailed characteristics, miles traveled, and type of product carried, State rpt, 2573–1.20

Water supply and quality in streams and lakes, and groundwater levels in wells, by drainage basin, 1983, annual State rpt, 5666–10.18

Wholesale trade census, 1982: employment, establishments, finances, and operations, by SIC 2- to 4-digit kind of business, SMSA, county, and city, State rpt, 2405–1.20

see also Auburn, Maine

see also Bangor, Maine

see also Lewiston, Maine

see also Portland, Maine

see also under By State in the "Index by Categories"

Majchrowicz, T. Alexander

"Comparing Distributions of Foreign Investment in U.S. Agricultural Land", 1588–77

"Foreign Ownership of U.S. Agricultural Land Through Dec. 31, 1983", 1584–2

"Foreign Ownership of U.S. Agricultural Land Through Dec. 31, 1983: County Level Data", 1584–3

"Information Contained in Local Assessment Records, 1972 to 1982", 1588–81

Maki, Hidero

"U.S.-Japan Agricultural Relations", 1004–16.1

Makuc, Diane

"Employment Characteristics of Mothers During Pregnancy", 4144–11.1

Malagasy Republic

see Madagascar

Malaria

see Infective and parasitic diseases

Malawi

Agricultural and food production indexes, and production of selected commodities, by world region and country, 1974-83, annual rpt, 1524–5

Agricultural situation in sub-Saharan Africa, by country, 1982-83 and outlook for 1984, annual rpt, 1524–4.10

Agricultural supply/demand, trade, and production, and socioeconomic data, by country, 1950s-77, 1528–179

AID activities and funding by project and function, FY85, and developing countries summary socioeconomic data, 1970s-83, by country, annual rpt, 9914–3

AID and other foreign assistance, and govt policy, effects on private sector dev and socioeconomic conditions, with case studies for 6 countries, 1960s-80, 9918–12

AID economic assistance to developing countries, obligations and disbursements by country, quarterly rpt, 9912–4

AID loan repayment status and terms by program and country, and status of predecessor agency loans, quarterly rpt, 9912–3

Index by Subjects and Names

Malnutrition

Economic conditions and foreign marketing prospects in 46 Sub-Saharan countries, 1983 world region rpt, 2046–5.1

Economic, social, and political summary data, by country, 1984, annual factbook, 244–11

Economic trends in income, production, prices, employment, finances, and trade, 1984 annual rpt, 2046–4.63

Exports of US, detailed Schedule B commodities by country of destination, 1983, annual rpt, 2424–9

Exports of US, detailed Schedule E commodities by mode of transport and world area and country of destination, 1983, annual rpts, 2424–5

Imports of US, detailed Schedule A commodities by country and world area of origin, and mode of transport, 1983, annual rpts, 2424–2

Imports of US, detailed TSUSA commodities by country of origin, 1983, annual rpt, 2424–4

Loans and grants for economic and military assistance from US and intl agencies, by program and country, FY46-83, annual rpt, 9914–5

Military aid of US, arms sales, and training programs costs and budget requests by program, world region, and country, FY83-85, annual rpt, 7144–13

Military spending, arms trade, and armed forces size, with total govt spending and population, by country, 1972-82, annual rpt, 9824–1

Minerals Yearbook, 1982, Vol 3: foreign country reviews of production, trade, and policies, by commodity, annual rpt, 5604–35

Minerals Yearbook, 1982, Vol 3 preprints: foreign country review of production, trade, and policies, by commodity, annual rpt, 5604–17.83

Population size and growth rates, and latest available benchmark demographic data, by country, 1950-83, biennial rpt, 2324–4

see also under By Foreign Country in the "Index by Categories"

Malaysia

Agricultural and food production indexes, and production of selected commodities, by world region and country, 1974-83, annual rpt, 1524–5

Agricultural situation in Southeast Asia, by country and commodity, 1983 and outlook for 1984, annual rpt, 1524–4.5

Agricultural supply/demand, trade, and production, and socioeconomic data, by country, 1950s-77, 1528–179

AID loan repayment status and terms by program and country, and status of predecessor agency loans, quarterly rpt, 9912–3

Background Notes, summary social, political, and economic data, 1983 rpt, 7006–2.8

Economic indicators of 12 Pacific Basin countries or areas and US, quarterly rpt, 9393–9

Economic, social, and political summary data, by country, 1984, annual factbook, 244–11

Economic trends in income, production, prices, employment, finances, and trade, 1984 semiannual rpt, 2046–4.47

Exports and imports of US, by commodity and country, 1972-82, annual world region rpt, 244–13.5

Exports of US, detailed Schedule B commodities by country of destination, 1983, annual rpt, 2424–9

Exports of US, detailed Schedule E commodities by mode of transport and world area and country of destination, 1983, annual rpts, 2424–5

Imports of US, detailed Schedule A commodities by country and world area of origin, and mode of transport, 1983, annual rpts, 2424–2

Imports of US, detailed TSUSA commodities by country of origin, 1983, annual rpt, 2424–4

Loans and grants for economic and military assistance from US and intl agencies, by program and country, FY46-83, annual rpt, 9914–5

Military aid of US, arms sales, and training programs costs and budget requests by program, world region, and country, FY83-85, annual rpt, 7144–13

Military spending, arms trade, and armed forces size, with total govt spending and population, by country, 1972-82, annual rpt, 9824–1

Minerals Yearbook, 1982, Vol 3: foreign country reviews of production, trade, and policies, by commodity, annual rpt, 5604–35

Minerals Yearbook, 1982, Vol 3 preprints: foreign country review of production, trade, and policies, by commodity, annual rpt, 5604–17.45

Oil reserves, production, and resource lifespan under alternative production rates, for 4 Asian countries, late 1800s-1982 and projected to 2030, 3166–9.9

Population size and growth rates, and latest available benchmark demographic data, by country, 1950-83, biennial rpt, 2324–4

see also under By Foreign Country in the "Index by Categories"

Maldives

Background Notes, summary social, political, and economic data, 1984 rpt, 7006–2.34

Economic, social, and political summary data, by country, 1984, annual factbook, 244–11

Exports of US, detailed Schedule B commodities by country of destination, 1983, annual rpt, 2424–9

Imports of US, detailed Schedule A commodities by country and world area of origin, and mode of transport, 1983, annual rpts, 2424–2

Imports of US, detailed TSUSA commodities by country of origin, 1983, annual rpt, 2424–4

Military aid of US, arms sales, and training programs costs and budget requests by program, world region, and country, FY83-85, annual rpt, 7144–13

Population size and growth rates, and latest available benchmark demographic data, by country, 1950-83, biennial rpt, 2324–4

Mali

Agricultural and food production indexes, and production of selected commodities, by world region and country, 1974-83, annual rpt, 1524–5

Agricultural situation in sub-Saharan Africa, by country, 1982-83 and outlook for 1984, annual rpt, 1524–4.10

AID activities and funding by project and function, FY85, and developing countries summary socioeconomic data, 1970s-83, by country, annual rpt, 9914–3

AID economic assistance to developing countries, obligations and disbursements by country, quarterly rpt, 9912–4

AID loan repayment status and terms by program and country, and status of predecessor agency loans, quarterly rpt, 9912–3

Background Notes, summary social, political, and economic data, 1984 rpt, 7006–2.19

Economic conditions and foreign marketing prospects in 46 Sub-Saharan countries, 1983 world region rpt, 2046–5.1

Economic, social, and political summary data, by country, 1984, annual factbook, 244–11

Exports of US, detailed Schedule B commodities by country of destination, 1983, annual rpt, 2424–9

Exports of US, detailed Schedule E commodities by mode of transport and world area and country of destination, 1983, annual rpts, 2424–5

Food supply policies of 21 developing countries, with farm sector data, tariff income, and prices and imports of 5 grains, 1960s-81, 1528–168

Imports of US, detailed Schedule A commodities by country and world area of origin, and mode of transport, 1983, annual rpts, 2424–2

Imports of US, detailed TSUSA commodities by country of origin, 1983, annual rpt, 2424–4

Loans and grants for economic and military assistance from US and intl agencies, by program and country, FY46-83, annual rpt, 9914–5

Military aid of US, arms sales, and training programs costs and budget requests by program, world region, and country, FY83-85, annual rpt, 7144–13

Military spending, arms trade, and armed forces size, with total govt spending and population, by country, 1972-82, annual rpt, 9824–1

Minerals Yearbook, 1982, Vol 3: foreign country reviews of production, trade, and policies, by commodity, annual rpt, 5604–35

Minerals Yearbook, 1982, Vol 3 preprints: foreign country review of production, trade, and policies, by commodity, annual rpt, 5604–17.84

Oil and gas undiscovered recoverable resources, cumulative production, and identified reserves, as of 1982, preliminary oil basin rpt, 5666–17.13

Population size and growth rates, and latest available benchmark demographic data, by country, 1950-83, biennial rpt, 2324–4

see also under By Foreign Country in the "Index by Categories"

Malnutrition

see Nutrition and malnutrition

Malt

Malt

see Grains and grain products

Malta

- AID loan repayment status and terms by program and country, and status of predecessor agency loans, quarterly rpt, 9912–3
- Economic, social, and political summary data, by country, 1984, annual factbook, 244–11
- Economic trends in income, production, prices, employment, finances, and trade, 1984 annual rpt, 2046–4.87
- Exports and imports of US with Western Europe, and US market share and export opportunities for selected commodities, by country, 1982-84, 2048–105
- Exports of US, detailed Schedule B commodities by country of destination, 1983, annual rpt, 2424–9
- Exports of US, detailed Schedule E commodities by mode of transport and world area and country of destination, 1983, annual rpts, 2424–5
- Imports of US, detailed Schedule A commodities by country and world area of origin, and mode of transport, 1983, annual rpts, 2424–2
- Imports of US, detailed TSUSA commodities by country of origin, 1983, annual rpt, 2424–4
- Loans and grants for economic and military assistance from US and intl agencies, by program and country, FY46-83, annual rpt, 9914–5
- Military spending, arms trade, and armed forces size, with total govt spending and population, by country, 1972-82, annual rpt, 9824–1
- *Minerals Yearbook, 1982,* Vol 3: foreign country reviews of production, trade, and policies, by commodity, annual rpt, 5604–35
- *Minerals Yearbook, 1983,* Vol 3 preprints: foreign country review of production, trade, and policies, by commodity, annual rpt, 5604–23.47
- Population size and growth rates, and latest available benchmark demographic data, by country, 1950-83, biennial rpt, 2324–4

see also under By Foreign Country in the "Index by Categories"

Malvinas Islands

see South America

Management

see Executives

see Government efficiency

see Industrial management

see Labor-management relations, general

see Labor-management relations in government

see Labor-management relations, local and regional

Manchester, Joyce

"Evidence on Possible Default and the Tilt Problem Under Three Mortgage Contracts", 9381–10.39

Manchester, N.H.

- Census of Housing, 1980: occupancy and unit characteristics, by race, Hispanic origin, and city, SMSA rpt, 2473–1.233
- Census of Population and Housing, 1980: detailed population and housing characteristics, by county, city, and census tract, SMSA rpt, 2551–2.233

see also under By SMSA or MSA in the "Index by Categories"

Mandes, George

"Home Health Care Cost-Function Analysis", 4652–1.411

Manfredi, Eileen M.

"World Food Grain Outlook", 1004–16.1

Manganese

see Metals and metal industries

Mango, Cecily

"Cape Verde: A Country Profile", 9916–2.57

Manned space flight

see Astronauts

see Space programs

Manpower

- Economic indicators and components, current data and annual trends, monthly rpt, 23842–1.2
- Employment and labor force statistics by major industry group and demographic characteristics, *Survey of Current Business,* monthly rpt, 2702–1.5
- *Handbook of Labor Statistics,* employment, earnings, hours, and labor force characteristics, 1982 and trends, detailed annual rpt, 6724–1
- Labor force employment and earnings, detailed data, monthly rpt, 6742–2
- Labor force, revised seasonally adjusted estimates based on 1983 seasonal adjustment factors, monthly 1979-83, article, 6742–2.404
- *Monthly Labor Review,* current statistics and articles, 6722–1
- New England States economic indicators, Fed Reserve 1st District, monthly rpt, 9373–2.2
- Nuclear attack civil defense plans of Fed Emergency Mgmt Agency, funding and operations by component, FY81-84 and projected FY85-89, GAO rpt, 26123–61
- *Statistical Abstract of US,* social, political, and economic data, 1950s-83 and trends, annual rpt, 2324–1.3

see also Absenteeism

see also Agricultural labor

see also Alien workers

see also Blue collar workers

see also Child labor

see also Clerical workers

see also Employee benefit plans

see also Employee development

see also Employment and unemployment, general

see also Employment and unemployment, specific industries

see also Federal employees

see also Foreign labor conditions

see also Health occupations

see also Hours of labor

see also Job vacancy

see also Labor law

see also Labor-management relations, general

see also Labor-management relations, local and regional

see also Labor mobility

see also Labor productivity

see also Labor turnover

see also Labor unions

see also Manpower training programs

see also Merchant seamen

see also Migrant workers

Index by Subjects and Names

see also Occupational health and safety

see also Occupations

see also Old-Age, Survivors, Disability, and Health Insurance

see also Pensions

see also Professional and technical workers

see also Retirement

see also Sales workers

see also Seasonal and summer employment

see also State and local employees

see also Unemployment insurance

see also Vacations and holidays

see also Veterans employment

see also Women's employment

see also Youth employment

see also under names of specific occupations

Manpower Administration

see Employment and Training Administration

Manpower training programs

- AFDC workfare program participation and requirements in 16 States, Feb 1983, GAO rpt, 26131–9
- Asia developing countries housing finance and low-income housing projects, and activities of 2 countries, 1970s-82, annual conf proceedings, 9914–11
- Black young adults economic status and educational attainment related to motivation, goals, family characteristics, and social factors, 1982, longitudinal study, 4008–65.2
- Budget of US Appendix, detailed budgets and personnel summaries, by agency, FY85, annual rpt, 104–3
- Budget of US, CBO analysis of revenue and spending alternatives and projections of economic indicators, FY85-89, annual rpt, 26304–3.3
- Budget of US, compact budgets by function, agency, and account, FY85 with projections to FY89, annual rpt, 104–2
- Budget of US, effects of Reagan Admin policy changes, by detailed program, FY85, annual rpt, 104–21
- Budget of US, receipts by source and outlays by function, FY40-89 estimates revised for consistency with FY85 budget definitions, annual rpt, 104–12
- Budget of US, receipts, outlays, and budget authority, by function and agency, FY84-89 revised estimates, midsession review of FY85 budget, annual rpt, 104–7
- Budget of US, receipts, outlays, and budget authority, by function and agency, 1st revision of FY85 budget, annual rpt, 104–17
- Children and youth benefitting from Fed Govt public welfare programs and tax expenditures, participation and funding for 71 programs, FY81-83, 21968–30
- EPA pollution control research and grant assistance program activities, monthly rpt, 9182–8
- Expenditures on education and job training, and employment, housing finance, and social programs data, selected years 1948-81, hearing, 21968–28
- Fed Govt aid to State and local govts, expenditures, and direct payments, by program, agency, and State, FY83, annual rpt, 2464–2
- Fed Govt employment and training program funding under Job Training Partnership

Index by Subjects and Names

Manufacturing

Act, and required matching funds, for 3 programs by State, 1984/85, press release, 6408–58

Fed Govt financial and nonfinancial domestic aid, 1984 annual comprehensive catalog, 104–5

Fed Govt industrial dev funding by type, program, and agency, and State govt policies and support, selected years FY75-85, 26306–6.81

Fed Govt procurement contract awards, by State, agency, procurement and contractor type, and for top 100 contractors, quarterly rpt, 102–6

Govt census, 1982: State govt payments to local govts, by program, source of funds, level of govt, and State, with trends from 1902, 2460–3

Govt revenues by source and expenditures by function, natl income and product account, *Survey of Current Business,* monthly rpt, monthly and annual tables, 2702–1.24

HHS aid to each State and local govt or private instn, amount obligated, funding agency, and program, FY83, annual listing, 4004–3

Indian and Alaska Native employment and training program funding allocation under Job Training Partnership Act, by individual tribe and group, FY84, press release, 6408–57

Input-output structure of US economy, detailed interindustry transactions for 537 industries, and components of final demand, 1977 benchmark data, 2708–17

Job Training Partnership Act participants, by program and socioeconomic characteristics, Oct 1983-June 1984 with funding to 1985/86, 6408–63

Job Training Partnership Act performance standards guide for States, with data on previous job training programs by State or local area, FY81-82, 6408–59

Occupational manpower needs and supply by detailed occupation, and educational and training program enrollees and grads by detailed field, 1982 and 1995, biennial rpt, 6744–3

Rural area impact of Job Training Partnership Act, comparison to CETA program, 1973-84, article, 1502–7.403

Service industry census, 1982: employment, establishments, receipts, and payroll, by SIC 2- to 4-digit kind of business, SMSA, county, and city, State rpt series, 2391–1

Unemployed displaced workers training and placement program of Fed Govt, funding and enrollment for 13 States and Guam, June 1984, press release, 6408–61

Wage growth and turnover rates related to marital status, sex, age, establishment type, and employer size, 1979/80, article, 9393–8.403

see also Apprenticeship

see also Employee development

see also Military training

see also Vocational education and training

see also Vocational rehabilitation

see also Work Incentive Program

see also Youth Conservation Corps

Mansfield, Ohio

Census of Housing, 1980: occupancy and unit characteristics, by race, Hispanic origin, and city, SMSA rpt, 2473–1.234

Census of Population and Housing, 1980: detailed population and housing characteristics, by county, city, and census tract, SMSA rpt, 2551–2.234

Wages by occupation, and benefits for office and plant workers, 1983 labor market area survey rpt, 6785–3.1

see also under By SMSA or MSA in the "Index by Categories"

Manufacturing

Air pollutant emission factors, by detailed source, 3rd edition, 1983-84 supplements, 9198–13

Annual Survey of Manufactures, 1980-81: operating and financial data, rpt reprints, hardbound vol, 2504–1

Asbestos workers, exposure levels, cancer incidence, and deaths, by industry and occupation, and asbestos regulation enforcement and costs/benefits, various periods 1940-2027, hearing, 21408–72

Business and financial statistics, historic trends, 1984 annual chartbook, 9364–2.3

Business Conditions Digest, current data on economic, business, and financial conditions and cyclical fluctuations, monthly rpt, 2702–3

Business Conditions Digest, historical supplement on economic, business, and financial conditions and cyclical fluctuations, with methodology, 1947-82, 2708–31

California business failures, plant closings, layoffs, and relocations, by plant, industry, county, and city, 1980-83, hearing, 21348–84.1

Capital (fixed), govt and private nonresidential structures and equipment, residential capital, and consumer-owned durable goods by item, 1980-83, annual article, 2702–1.433

Capital expenditures and prices for plant and equipment, actual and expected, by major industry group, 1981-84, annual article, 2702–1.404

Capital expenditures for new plants and equipment, by industry div, monthly rpt, quarterly data, 23842–1.1

Census of Construction Industries, 1982: financial and operating data, by SIC 4-digit industry and State, final rpt series, 2373–1

Census of Population and Housing, 1980: detailed population and housing characteristics, by county, city, and census tract, State and SMSA rpt series, 2551–2

Census of Population, 1980: detailed socioeconomic and demographic characteristics, by age, sex, race, Hispanic origin, occupation, and industry, State rpt series, 2531–4

Census of Population, 1980: detailed socioeconomic characteristics, by county, city, and inside-outside SMSAs and central cities, State rpt series, 2531–3

Census of Transportation, 1982: trucks, by detailed characteristics, miles traveled, and type of product carried, State rpt series, 2573–1

Central cities and suburbs population and employment, effect of region, neighborhood, population, and labor characteristics, 1970-80, technical paper, 9387–8.89

China economic conditions, agricultural and industrial production, trade, and domestic and foreign investment, 1980-85, 2048–106

China exports and imports by SITC 1- to 5-digit commodity, 1970s-82, annual rpt, 244–12

Coal consumption, average prices, and stocks at manufacturing plants, by SIC 2-digit industry, quarterly rpt, 3162–37.2

Counterfeiting of brand-name products by foreign manufacturers, effects on 6 US industries, investigation with financial and operating data, 1984 rpt, 9886–4.67

County and City Data Book, detailed socioeconomic and demographic data for States, counties, and cities, selected years 1976-82, 2328–1

County Business Patterns: establishments, employees, and payrolls, by SIC 4-digit industry and county, 1981, annual State rpt series, 2326–8

County Business Patterns: establishments, employees, and payrolls, by SIC 4-digit industry and county, 1982, annual State rpt series, 2326–6

Developing countries govt policy, and AID and other foreign assistance, effects on private sector dev and socioeconomic conditions, with case studies for 6 countries, 1960s-80, 9918–12

Developing countries PL 480 Title I funding and socioeconomic impacts, with case studies for 5 countries, 1950s- 81, 9918–13

DOD procurement, prime contract awards by detailed procurement category, FY80-83, annual rpt, 3544–18

Earnings and hours, by industry div and major manufacturing group, Monthly Labor Review, 6722–1.3

Earnings and hours of work, weekly averages, monthly rpt, 23842–1.2

Earnings by industry div, and personal income per capita and by source, by State, MSA, and county, 1977-82, annual regional rpts, 2704–2

Earnings by major industry group, and personal income per capita and by source, by region and State, 1929-82, 2708–40

Earnings of manufacturing production workers, by State, with adjustments for industrial mix variations, selected years 1973-82, article, 9373–1.407

Economic conditions of US, with some foreign comparisons, 1960s-82 and alternative projections to 1992, hearing, 21248–79

Electric power cogeneration in 5 industries, and fuel use and utility supply/demand effects, by region, 1983-93, 3008–92

Electric power industrial demand model estimates, economic indicators, and supporting data for 5 industries, 1960s-80 with projections to 2000, 3008–87

Employee theft and misconduct in retail, hospital, and manufacturing establishments, by type and frequency of violation, 1978-80, 6068–178

Employment and earnings, detailed data, monthly rpt, 6742–2.5, 6742–2.6

Employment by industry div, major manufacturing group, and State, Monthly Labor Review, 6722–1.2

Manufacturing

Index by Subjects and Names

Employment, by sector, major industry group, and sex, selected years 1850-1982, article, 6722–1.425

Employment, earnings, and hours, by selected SIC 1- to 4-digit industry, State, and for 278 major labor areas, 1939-83, annual rpt, 6744–5

Employment, earnings, and hours, by SIC 4-digit nonfarm industry, monthly 1974-Feb 1984, annual update, 6744–4

Employment, earnings, and hours, monthly press release, 6742–5

Employment situation, earnings, hours, and other BLS economic indicators, transcripts of BLS Commissioner's monthly testimony, periodic rpt, 23846–4

Employment, total and manufacturing, change in metro-nonmetro counties by region and county size, various periods 1951-79, technical paper, 9387–8.90

Employment, unemployment, and labor force, by demographic and employment characteristics, State, and for 30 metro areas and 11 large cities, 1983, annual rpt, 6744–7

Employment, unemployment, hours, and women's employment, for all durables manufacturing and for 5 metals industries, 1979-82, article, 6722–1.410

Energy demand growth for fuel and electricity, and price elasticities, input data and model estimates by SIC 2-digit manufacturing industry, 1958-78, 3006–7.4

Energy demand in industry, forecasting model description, detailed technology specifications, and energy use, for 27 SIC 2- to 4-digit industries, 1970s-80 and projected to 2000, 3308–66

Energy efficiency progress, and energy use by type, by SIC 2-digit manufacturing industry, 1982, annual rpt, 3304–8

Energy use in nonresidential buildings, expenditures, and conservation, by building characteristics, EIA survey series, 3166–8

Export and import price indexes for food and manufactured products, quarterly press release, 6762–13

Exports and imports between US and outlying areas, by detailed commodity and mode of transport, monthly rpt, 2422–4

Exports and imports of manufactured goods by West Germany and US related to exchange rate uncertainty, regression results, 1974-81, article, 9385–1.405

Exports and imports of US, and trade balance, by major commodity group, selected country, and world area, with seasonal adjustments, monthly rpt, 2422–6

Exports and imports of US by country, and trade shifts by commodity, USITC quarterly monitoring rpt, 9882–9

Exports and imports of US, detailed SIC-based commodities by world area, 1983, annual rpts, 2424–6

Exports and imports of US, relative contributions of labor by type and capital to trade balance, selected years 1958-80, technical paper, 9381–10.30

Exports and imports of US, totals and as percent of domestic production, by SIC 2- to 5-digit commodity, 1981, annual rpt, 2424–3

Exports, imports, and economic indicators by country and country group, and US trade policy actions, 1960s-83, annual rpt, 444–1

Exports, imports, tariffs, and industry operating data for miscellaneous manufactured products, TSUSA commodity rpt series, 9885–7

Exports of manufactured and agricultural commodities, manufacturing production, and export-related employment, 1960s-82, State rpt series, 2046–3

Exports of US by selected commodity, and foreign and US economic and employment indicators and balance of payments, by world area and country, 1970s-83, annual rpt, 2044–26

Exports of US, detailed Schedule B commodities by country of destination, 1983, annual rpt, 2424–9

Exports of US, detailed Schedule E commodities by mode of transport and world area and country of destination, 1983, annual rpts, 2424–5

Fed Govt loans, grants, and tax benefits to business, by program and economic sector, projected FY84-88 with effective tax rates for FY80-82, 26306–6.70

Finances and operations, by SIC 2- to 4-digit industry, 1970s-83 and projected to 1988, annual rpt, 2014–4

Financial statements for manufacturing, mining, and trade corporations, by selected SIC 2- to 3-digit industry, quarterly rpt, 2502–1

Foreign direct investment in US, major investors and investments by SIC 4-digit industry, transaction type and value, and location, 1983, annual rpt, 2044–20

Foreign direct investment of US, by selected major industry group and world area, 1980-82, annual article, 2702–1.430

Foreign economic, social, and political summary data, by country, 1984, annual factbook, 244–11

Foreign exchange rates for currencies of US and 2 countries with yen, and measures of manufacturing competitiveness, 1983 with 1974-80 and 1979-80 averages, article, 9385–1.404

Foreign labor conditions in selected OECD countries, 1950-82, annual rpt, 6724–1.10

Foreign manufacturing labor productivity and unit cost indexes for US and 11 OECD countries, 1960-82, annual article, 6722–1.405

Foreign manufacturing productivity and unit labor cost indexes for US and 11 countries, 1950-82 and preliminary 1983, annual rpt, 6864–1

Foreign trade zones, activities, and value of goods entering and leaving zones, 1973-82, GAO rpt, 26119–56

Fresno, Calif, economic, population, labor, and housing indicators, various periods 1974-85, hearing, 21248–84

Great Lakes trade, by SITC 3-digit commodity, port, vessel type, world area, and country, 1982, annual rpt, 7744–3

Handbook of Labor Statistics, employment, earnings, hours, and labor force characteristics, 1982 and trends, detailed annual rpt, 6724–1

Imports of US, detailed Schedule A commodities by country and world area of origin, and mode of transport, 1983, annual rpts, 2424–2

Imports of US, detailed Schedule A commodities by country, monthly rpt, 2422–2

Imports of US, detailed TSUSA commodities by country of origin, 1983, annual rpt, 2424–4

Income tax returns of corporations, detailed income and tax items by industry, 1981, annual rpt, 8304–4

Income tax returns of corporations, summary data by industry div, 1981 estimates, annual article, 8302–2.403

Income tax returns of corporations with foreign tax credit, income and deductions by type, asset size, and selected industry group, 1980, article, 8302–2.415

Income tax returns of foreign subsidiaries of US corporations, income and tax data, by industry and asset size, 1980, article, 8302–2.410

Income tax returns of partnerships, detailed data by industry, 1981 estimates, annual article, 8302–2.404

Income tax returns of partnerships, receipts by source, deductions by type, and establishments, by selected industry, 1982, annual article, 8302–2.416

Income tax returns of sole proprietorships, detailed data by industry div and selected industry group, 1981, annual rpt, 8304–7

Income tax returns of sole proprietorships, receipts, deductions by type, payroll, and net income, by major industry, 1982, annual article, 8302–2.413

Income tax returns with investment credits, for individuals by income, and for sole proprietorships by industry, 1981, article, 8302–2.409

Input-output structure of US economy, detailed interindustry transactions for 85 industries, and components of final demand, 1977, article, 2702–1.421

Input-output structure of US economy, detailed interindustry transactions for 537 industries, and components of final demand, 1977 benchmark data, 2708–17

Inventories, sales, and inventory/sales ratios for manufacturing and trade, quarterly article, 2702–1.34

Liquefied petroleum gas sales, by principal use, PAD district, and State, 1981-83, annual rpt, 3164–2

Minority group and women's employment, by occupational group, SIC 2- to 3-digit industry, State, and SMSA, 1981, annual rpt, 9244–1

Molds (industrial) from Canada, effect on competing US industry, investigation with background financial and operating data, 1979-83, 9886–4.72

Natl income and product, comprehensive accounts and components, *Survey of Current Business,* monthly rpt, monthly and annual tables, 2702–1.27

North Central States employment in durable goods manufacturing by industry group and State, and Fed Govt outlays, for Fed Reserve 7th District, 1978-FY82, article, 9375–1.402

North Central States manufacturing activity diffusion indexes, Fed Reserve 4th District 10-year summary charts, monthly rpt, 9377–4

North Central States manufacturing and total employment, percent change for Fed Reserve 7th District States, various periods 1969-84, article, 9375–1.408

Index by Subjects and Names

Occupational health risks from hazardous substances and radiation, by industry, occupation, age, and sex, with bibl and glossary, 1920s-82, 9638–50

Occupational injuries, illnesses, and workdays lost, by SIC 2-digit industry, 1982-83, annual press release, 6844–3

Occupational injury and illness rates, by SIC 2- to 4-digit industry, 1982, annual rpt, 6844–1

Occupational manpower needs and supply by detailed occupation, and educational and training program enrollees and grads by detailed field, 1982 and 1995, biennial rpt, 6744–3

Occupational Outlook Handbook, 1984-85 biennial rpt, 6744–1

Pacific Basin economic indicators, US and 12 countries, quarterly rpt, 9393–9

Pacific Northwest electricity consumption and prices by end-use sector, and economic and demographic data, 1960s-83 and projected to 2005, annual rpt, 3224–2

Pollution abatement capital and operating costs under Clean Air and Water Acts, for govts and selected industries, various periods 1970-2000, annual rpt, 9184–11

Producer prices and indexes, by stage of processing and detailed commodity, monthly rpt, 6762–6

Producer prices and indexes, by stage of processing and detailed commodity, monthly 1983, annual supplement, 6764–2

Production, shipments, inventories, and new orders, monthly rpt, 23842–1.3

Production, shipments, inventories, orders, and pollution control expenses of manufacturers, periodic Current Industrial Rpt series, 2506–3

Productivity and costs of labor for private, nonfarm business, and manufacturing sectors, preliminary data, quarterly rpt, 6822–1

Productivity and costs of labor for private, nonfarm business, and manufacturing sectors, revised data, quarterly rpt, 6822–2

Productivity growth adjusted for wage and price controls of early 1970s, and regression results, by industry, 1948-81, article, 9381–1.407

Productivity of labor and capital, growth by SIC 1- to 2-digit industry, and measurement methods and bibl, various periods 1948-78 with trends from 1800, 2218–69

Productivity of labor and capital in manufacturing, all nonfarm business, and all private business, indexes and percent change, 1948-83, annual rpt, 6824–2

Productivity of labor, economic growth, and industrial policy dev, selected years 1947-82 with some projections to 1986, 26306–6.69

Productivity of labor in manufacturing, by selected country, 1960-82, annual rpt, 9624–10.1

R&D expenditures of industry by funding source, and projected impact on output, employment, and hours of labor, by selected industry, various periods 1953-90, hearings, 25368–133

R&D Fed Govt facilities and services available for private sector use, by field of science, 1984 biennial listing, 2224–4

R&D funding by industry, program, and Federal agency, and high-technology trade performance, selected years 1960-FY84, 26306–6.77

R&D industry funding and employment of scientists and engineers, by industry group, firm size, and funding source, 1956-82, annual rpt, 9627–21

Retail prices set by manufacturers under fair-trade law by brand and product, with manufacturers, market concentration, and sales, by industry, selected years 1952-82, 9406–1.38

Sales, costs, assets, and specialization ratios of manufacturing corporations, by detailed product line, FTC annual survey, suspended, 9404–5

Scientists, engineers, and technicians employed in private industry, by occupation and industry group, 1980-81, biennial rpt, 9627–23

Seasonal adjustment methodology for economic time series, dev and design of Census Bur and other systems, with illustrative data, 1981 conf papers, 2626–7.5

Shipments, sales, production indexes, profits, and stockholder equity, 1929-83, annual rpt, 204–1.3, 204–1.7

Small and minority-owned businesses finances and operations, Federal contracts by agency, and worker characteristics, by industry, race, sex, and State, 1950s-83, annual rpt, 9764–6

South Carolina manufacturing plants with selected employee health care services, by SIC 2-digit industry, 1982, article, 4102–1.408

Southeastern States and 5 SMSAs economic indicators, Fed Reserve 8th District, quarterly rpt, 9391–15

Statistical Abstract of US, social, political, and economic data, 1950s-83 and trends, annual rpt, 2324–1.3

Tariff Schedules of US, Annotated, classifications and rates of duty for detailed imported commodities, 1985 edition, 9886–13

Trade policy of Fed Govt, with data on US industry foreign trade and revenues, and Japan semiconductor industry subsidies, 1970s-83, hearings, 21368–46

Unemployment rate and components of change, growth rates for 6 recovery periods 2nd qtr 1954-2nd qtr 1984, and projected unemployment rate for 4th qtr 1985, article, 9373–1.415

Virgin Islands economic censuses, 1982: employment, establishments, payroll, and receipts, by SIC 1- to 4-digit industry, island, and city, 2593–1

Wage and benefit changes for manufacturing workers from collective bargaining or employer decisions, quarterly article, 6782–1

Wages by occupation, and benefits for office and plant workers in 70 SMSAs, 1983, annual rpt, 6785–1

Wages by occupation, and benefits for office and plant workers, 1983, annual SMSA survey rpt series, 6785–12

Maps

Wages by occupation, and benefits for office and plant workers, 1984, annual SMSA survey rpt series, 6785–11

Water pollution fish kills, by State, location, and pollution source, monthly 1978-80, annual rpt, 9204–3

see also Aerospace industry

see also Aircraft

see also Aluminum and aluminum industry

see also Cement and concrete

see also Census of Manufactures

see also Chemicals and chemical industry

see also Clay industry and products

see also Clothing and clothing industry

see also Copper and copper industry

see also Electrical machinery and equipment

see also Electronics industry and products

see also Food and food industry

see also Furs and fur industry

see also Glass and glass industry

see also Gum and wood chemicals

see also Household appliances and equipment

see also Household furnishings

see also Ice, manufactured

see also Industrial capacity and utilization

see also Industrial production

see also Instruments and measuring devices

see also Iron and steel industry

see also Leather industry and products

see also Lumber industry and products

see also Machines and machinery industry

see also Metals and metal industries

see also Motor vehicle industry

see also Musical instruments

see also Office furniture and equipment

see also Paints and varnishes

see also Paper and paper products

see also Petroleum and petroleum industry

see also Pharmaceutical industry

see also Plastics and plastics industry

see also Printing and publishing industry

see also Quarries and stone products

see also Rubber and rubber industry

see also Ships and shipping

see also Sporting goods

see also Textile industry and fabrics

see also Tires and tire industry

see also Tobacco industry and products

see also Toys and toy industry

see also Transportation and transportation equipment

see also Zinc and zinc industry

see also under By Commodity in the "Index by Categories"

see also under By Industry in the "Index by Categories"

Maps

Aerial survey R&D publications, and sources of natural resource and environmental data gathered by air- and spacecraft, quarterly listing, 9502–7

Alaska Arctic Natl Wildlife Refuge resources, resident and visitor activities, and environmental impacts of energy exploration, 1983, annual update rpt, 5504–26

Alaska minerals resources, production, claims on wildlife refuges, oil and gas leases, and exploratory wells, with maps and bibl, 1983, annual rpt, 5664–11

Census Bur publications data coverage and availability, 1984 annual listing, 2304–2

Coastal environmental and socioeconomic conditions, and potential impacts of oil and gas OCS leases, final statement series, 5736–1

Maps

Coastal environmental and wildlife characteristics, use, and mgmt, for individual ecosystems, series, 5506–9

- Coastal environmental characteristics, fish, wildlife, and use, and population socioeconomic data, for individual areas, series, 5506–4
- Earthquake intensity, damage, and deaths, by location for major earthquakes since 1755, and hazard areas and natl reduction program activities, as of 1984, 5668–73
- Earthquake intensity, time of origin, seismic characteristics, and location, by State, quarterly rpt, 5662–4
- Exports of US, detailed commodities by country of destination, monthly rpt, 2422–3
- Forest fires on Forest Service land and acres burned, by cause, forest, and State, 1983, annual rpt, 1204–6
- Geological Survey and other publications, 1983, annual listing, 5664–4
- Geological Survey publications, monthly listing, 5662–1
- Glaciology intl research summaries, methodology, and bibls, series, 2156–18
- Heating and cooling degree days by State, and housing energy bills and departures from normal by fuel type, by census div, monthly rpt, 2152–11
- Housing energy use, costs, expenditures, and conservation, and household and housing characteristics, survey series, 3166–7
- Marine weather and tropical cyclones, quarterly journal with articles, 2152–8
- Northeast pulpwood production and yield per acre, for 14 States, by county, 1981, TVA technical paper, 9806–2.38
- Nuclear power plant siting population criteria and estimated compliance of selected regions and sites, 1983 rpt, 9638–54
- Oil and gas potential reserves in Western States wilderness areas, for 11 States, 1982-83, compilation of papers, 5668–69
- Precipitation and temperature outlook for US and Northern Hemisphere, and by US and selected foreign weather stations, semimonthly rpt, 2182–1
- Soil survey county descriptions and maps of USDA, 1899-1983, annual listing, 1264–11
- Uranium mining operations, finances, and costs of alternative methods to meet emissions standards, for industry and selected mines, selected years 1948-90, 9188–96
- Uranium resources research publications, 1976-83, listing, 3358–27
- Weather conditions and effect on agriculture, by US region, State, and city, and world area, weekly rpt, 2152–2
- Weather conditions and impact assessment, by world area and country, monthly rpt, 2152–9
- Weather events socioeconomic impacts and costs, heating and cooling degree days, and housing energy bills, by census div and State, monthly rpt, 2152–12

see also Cartography

Maravall, Agustin

"Transmission of Data Noise into Policy Noise in Monetary Control", 9366–6.74

Marble

see Quarries and stone products

Margarine

see Oils, oilseeds, and fats

Mariana Islands

see Guam

see Northern Mariana Islands

Marietta, Ohio

- Census of Housing, 1980: occupancy and unit characteristics, by race, Hispanic origin, and city, SMSA rpt, 2473–1.277
- Census of Population and Housing, 1980: detailed population and housing characteristics, by county, city, and census tract, SMSA rpt, 2551–2.277

see also under By SMSA or MSA in the "Index by Categories"

Marijuana

- Arrests and arrest rates, by offense, offender characteristics, population size, and State, 1970s-83, annual rpt, 6224–2.2
- Court cases, dispositions, convictions, and sentences of Federal criminal defendants, by offense and district, as of June 1983 with trends from 1945, annual rpt, 18204–1
- Cultivation of marijuana, State law enforcement agency control activity and aid from Fed Govt and Natl Guard, 1983 survey, GAO rpt, 26119–64
- Customs Service activities, operations, and staff, FY79-83, annual rpt, 8144–1
- Drug Enforcement Admin cases against major drug traffickers by case characteristics, and agents assessment of activities, in 3 cities, 1979-82, GAO rpt, 26119–57
- Drug enforcement regional task force program investigation activities, funding, and personnel, with nationwide drug abuse data, 1983 annual rpt, 6004–17
- Fed Govt plan to reduce drug abuse and trafficking, funding by agency and background data on drug use by substance, selected years FY81-85, biennial rpt, 024–1
- Foreign drug and narcotics production, acreage, eradication, and seizures, by substance, with labs destroyed and US aid, by country, 1981-85, annual rpt, 7004–17
- Health condition and health care resources, use, and expenditures, 1970s-82 with trends and projections 1900-2000, annual compilation, 4144–11
- High school classes of 1980 and 1982: educational and sociodemographic characteristics and expectations, natl longitudinal study, series, 4826–2
- High school seniors use and assessment of drugs by type, alcohol, and cigarettes, by sex and region, 1975-83 surveys, annual rpt, 4494–4
- Income (taxable) not reported, by illegal source, with characteristics of persons involved, methodology, and bibl, 1970s-82, 8008–112
- Israel and France urban youths use of selected drugs, alcohol, and cigarettes, by age and sex, 1977 and 1979, article, 4102–1.430
- Jail capacities, conditions, expenditures, and services, and socioeconomic and other characteristics of inmates, various dates 1976-82, 10048–59

Index by Subjects and Names

- Research compilations and summaries, bibls, and survey instruments, series, 4496–1
- Supply, use, casualties, treatment program and emergency room admissions in major cities, arrests, and seizures, by drug type, 1982, annual rpt, 15894–1
- Use of drugs and health consequences of drug abuse, and Natl Inst on Drug Abuse and other HHS prevention activities, FY82, annual rpt, 4004–26
- Use of marijuana and health consequences of marijuana abuse, annual research review, discontinued, 4494–1

see also Drug and narcotics traffic

Marin County, Calif.

Housing vacancy rates for single and multifamily units and mobile homes, by city and ZIP code, 1983, annual metro area rpt, 9304–20.11

Marine accidents and safety

- Accident investigations and recommendations by Natl Transportation Safety Board, 1983, annual rpt, 9614–1
- Accidents and deaths in transportation, by mode of transport, 1972-82, annual rpt, 7304–2
- Boat registrations, use, and accident deaths, injuries, and property damage, by detailed cause and State, 1983, annual rpt, 7404–1
- Coast Guard search and rescue activities, by district, station, and rescue vessel, FY83 and projected FY88, annual rpt, 7404–2
- Death rates by sex, race, and age for 40 causes, projected for 10-year period, 1982 rpt, 4208–21
- Deaths and death rates by detailed cause and demographic characteristics, 1979 and selected trends, US Vital Statistics annual rpt, 4144–2.1
- Deaths in transportation accidents, by mode, 1982-83, annual summary rpt, 9614–6
- DOT grant awards for transportation planning and safety programs, by region, State, and for 35 largest SMSAs, FY83, annual rpt, 7304–7
- Fed Govt aid to State and local govts, expenditures, and direct payments, by program, agency, and State, FY83, annual rpt, 2464–2
- Fed Govt programs and mgmt cost control proposals, 3-year savings by function and agency, and financial and operating data, 1960s-81, 16908–1.11, 16908–1.31
- Hazardous material transport accidents, casualties, and property damage, by mode of transport, with DOT control activities, 1983, annual rpt, 7304–4
- Oil and gas OCS drilling rigs by country, rig losses, and worker injury and death rates, various periods 1966-83, hearing, 21568–35
- Safety programs, and accidents, injuries, deaths, hazards, and property damage, by mode of transport, 1983, annual rpt, 7304–19
- User fees to recover costs of 7 federally subsidized public service programs, by type of fee, user, and service, FY84-88, 26306–6.68

see also Oil spills

Marine bases

see Military bases, posts, and reservations

Index by Subjects and Names

Marine Corps

- Aides to officers, enlisted personnel authorized and assigned to perform personal services by race and sex, and program costs, by service branch, 1982-83, GAO rpt, 26123–53
- Base support costs by function, and personnel and acreage by installation, by service branch, FY85, annual rpt, 3504–11
- Budget of DOD, itemized account of legislative history, FY84, annual rpt, 3504–7
- Commercial activities of DOD under contract and performed in-house, costs and work-years, by service branch, defense agency, State, and installation, FY83, annual rpt, 3544–25
- Construction and renovation of military bases, DOD budget authorization requests, by DOD component, State, country, and project, FY85, annual rpt, 3544–15
- Manpower active duty strength, recruits, and reenlistment, by race, Hispanic origin, sex, and service branch, quarterly press release, 3542–7
- Manpower, equipment, and budget summary, planned FY84-85, semiannual pamphlet, 3802–3
- Manpower of DOD, and organization, budget, weapons, and property, by service branch, State, and country, 1984 annual summary rpt, 3504–13
- Manpower requirements and cost estimates, DOD budget detailed analysis, FY85, annual rpt, 3504–1
- Manpower statistics on active duty, civilian, and reserve personnel, by service branch, monthly rpt, 3542–14
- Manpower statistics on active duty, civilian, and retired personnel and dependents, FY83 and historical, annual rpt, 3544–1
- Manpower strengths, and military pension earnings and program costs, under alternative policies, selected years FY71-2020, 26306–6.76
- Manpower strengths in US and abroad, by service branch, world area, and country, quarterly news release, 3542–9
- Manpower strengths of active duty, reserve, and civilian personnel, by service branch, selected years FY68-89, annual rpt, 3544–2
- Manpower strengths, summary by service branch, monthly press release, 3542–2
- Medical care, disease incidence, and deaths, by detailed diagnosis, and medical personnel and workloads, 1978-79, annual rpt, 3804–1
- Medical facilities of DOD in US and abroad, beds, admissions, outpatient visits, and live births by service branch, quarterly rpt, 3542–15
- Medical facilities of Navy, use by active and retired military personnel, dependents, and others by facility and type, quarterly rpt, 3802–1
- NATO military commitment of US, Europe force strengths by service branch and costs by component, FY82 with trends from FY75, GAO rpt, 26123–71
- Procurement of Navy, by contractor and location of work, FY83, annual rpt, 3804–13
- Property, supplies, and equipment inventory of DOD, by service branch, 1983, annual rpt, 3544–6
- Reserve forces manpower and equipment strengths, readiness, and funding, by reserve component, FY83, annual rpt, 3544–27
- Reserve forces manpower strengths and characteristics, by component, quarterly rpt, 3542–4
- Strategic military capability, force strengths, weapons, training, supplies, and requirements, by service branch, FY80-84 and projected to 1990, 3508–19
- Training and education programs of DOD, funding, staff, students, and facilities, by service branch and reserve component, FY85, annual rpt, 3504–5
- Women military personnel on active duty, by demographic and service characteristics and service branch, with comparisons to men, FY83, annual chartbook, 3544–26

Marine Mammal Commission

- Budget of US Appendix, detailed budgets and personnel summaries, by agency, FY85, annual rpt, 104–3
- Budget of US, appropriations, outlays, balances, and budget receipts, by govtl branch and agency, FY83, annual rpt, 8104–2
- Protection of marine mammals, Fed Govt and intl regulatory and research activities, with bibl, 1983, annual rpt, 14734–1
- Research on marine mammals, Fed Govt funding by agency, topic, and performing instn, FY70-82, annual rpt, 14734–2

Marine Mammal Protection Act

- Marine mammals population, strandings, and catch permits by type and applicant, by species and location, and admin of Act, Apr 1983-Mar 1984, annual rpt, 2164–11

Marine mammals

- Alaska Arctic Natl Wildlife Refuge resources, resident and visitor activities, and environmental impacts of energy exploration, 1983, annual update rpt, 5504–26
- California marine resources and environmental effects of proposed oil and gas dev, for 2 sanctuaries off central and northern coasts, 1970s-2006, hearing, 21448–30
- Coastal environmental and wildlife characteristics, use, and mgmt, for individual ecosystems, series, 5506–9
- Environmental quality and protection programs, costs, and Fed Govt enforcement, 1983, detailed annual rpt, 484–1
- Genetic resource (plant and animal) conservation, commercial uses, causes of depletion, and geographic sources, 1984 rpt, 5548–13
- Landings of marine mammals taken incidentally with fish catch of foreign vessels, by species and country of vessel origin, 1978-81, article, 2162–1.401
- Protection Act admin and populations, strandings, and catch permits by type and applicant, by species and location, Apr 1983-Mar 1984, annual rpt, 2164–11
- Protection activities and Fed Govt funding, population status, and research, 1983, annual rpt, 5504–12

Marine pollution

- Protection of marine mammals, Fed Govt and intl regulatory and research activities, with bibl, 1983, annual rpt, 14734–1
- Research on marine mammals, Fed Govt funding by agency, topic, and performing instn, FY70-82, annual rpt, 14734–2
- Seal harvest, mgmt, and skins taken and rejected for northern fur seals of Pribilof Islands, Alaska, various dates 1786-1981, 2168–79
- Southeastern US OCS, marine vertebrate abundance and seasonal distribution, with oil and gas dev effects and lease status, early 1980s, 5508–85

Marine pollution

- Coastal environmental and wildlife characteristics, use, and mgmt, for individual ecosystems, series, 5506–9
- Coastal environmental characteristics, fish, wildlife, and use, and population socioeconomic data, for individual areas, series, 5506–4
- Environmental quality and protection programs, costs, and Fed Govt enforcement, 1983, detailed annual rpt, 484–1
- Environmental quality, pollutant discharge by type and source, and EPA protection activities and funding, 1970s-83, biennial regional rpt series, 9184–15
- Fed Govt programs and mgmt cost control proposals, 3-year savings by function and agency, and financial and operating data, 1960s-81, 16908–1.31
- Fish and shellfish landings, life cycles, and environmental needs, for selected species by region, with glossary and bibl, series, 5506–8
- Fish and shellfish of economic importance, biological, fishery, and mgmt data, literature review series, 2166–16
- Fish kills from water pollution, by State, location, and pollution source, monthly 1978-80, annual rpt, 9204–3
- NOAA scientific and technical publications, monthly listing, 2142–1
- Ocean dumping and pollution investigations and activities of NOAA, research and monitoring studies funded, and bibl, FY83, annual rpt, 2144–9
- Ocean dumping of waste materials, EPA permit program and intl London Dumping Convention activities, 1981-83, annual rpt, 9204–8
- Oceanographic data, stations and cruises recording data for World Data Center A by country, ship, and type of data, 1983, annual rpt, 2144–15
- Pollution problems from municipal waste dumping in New York Bight, oil and gas drilling on Georges Bank, and radioactive waste disposal in oceans, 1970s-82, hearings, 21568–36
- Radioactive waste and spent fuel generation, inventory, disposal by site, reprocessing, and characteristics, by source, as of 1983 and projected to 2020, annual rpt, 3364–2
- User fees to recover costs of 7 federally subsidized public service programs, by type of fee, user, and service, FY84-88, 26306–6.68
- *see also* Offshore oil and gas
- *see also* Oil spills

Marine resources

Marine resources

Aerial survey R&D publications, and sources of natural resource and environmental data gathered by air- and spacecraft, quarterly listing, 9502–7

California marine resources and environmental effects of proposed oil and gas dev, for 2 sanctuaries off central and northern coasts, 1980s and projected to 2006, hearing, 21448–30.1

Coastal environmental and socioeconomic conditions, and potential impacts of oil and gas OCS leases, final statement series, 5736–1

France Brittany coast oil spill cleanup and research costs, marine and tourism industry losses, and recreation losses of tourists and residents, 1971-79, 2178–13

NOAA scientific and technical publications, monthly listing, 2142–1

see also Coastal zone

see also Continental shelf

see also Fish and fishing industry

see also Marine mammals

see also Marine pollution

see also Marine resources conservation

see also Offshore mineral resources

see also Offshore oil and gas

see also Oil spills

see also Shellfish

see also Water resources development

Marine resources conservation

California marine resources and environmental effects of proposed oil and gas dev, for 2 sanctuaries off central and northern coasts, 1970s-2006, hearing, 21448–30

Coastal environmental and wildlife characteristics, use, and mgmt, for individual ecosystems, series, 5506–9

Coastal environmental characteristics, fish, wildlife, and use, and population socioeconomic data, for individual areas, series, 5506–4

Estuary environmental characteristics, fish, wildlife, uses, and mgmt, for individual estuaries, series, 5506–7

Fish and shellfish landings, life cycles, and environmental needs, for selected species by region, with glossary and bibl, series, 5506–8

Fish and Wildlife Service conservation and research project descriptions and results, by program, FY83, annual rpt, 5504–20

Fishery resources mgmt and R&D, Fed Govt grants by project and resulting publications, 1983, annual listing, 2164–3

Marine Fisheries Review, US and foreign fisheries resources, conservation, operations, and research, quarterly rpt articles, 2162–1

NOAA scientific and technical publications, monthly listing, 2142–1

Oil spill risk analyses for OCS proposed lease sale areas, series, 5736–2

Southeastern US OCS, marine vertebrate abundance and seasonal distribution, with oil and gas dev effects and lease status, early 1980s, 5508–85

see also Marine mammals

see also Marine pollution

Marine safety

see Marine accidents and safety

Marion County, Ohio

Housing vacancy rates for single and multifamily units and mobile homes, by city and ZIP code, 1984, annual metro area rpt, 9304–27.5

Marital status

see Marriage and divorce

see Widows and widowers

see under By Marital Status in the "Index by Categories"

Maritime academies

see Service academies

Maritime Administration

Bulk carrier ships in world fleet, characteristics by country of registry, 1982, annual rpt, 7704–13

Construction and conversion costs for merchant ships by owner and builder, fleet size, and employment, monthly rpt, 7702–1

Containerized cargo carried over principal trade routes, by flag of vessel, port, and US coastal district, 1982, annual rpt, 7704–8

Cost control proposals for Fed Govt programs and mgmt, 3-year savings by function and agency, and financial and operating data, 1960s-81, 16908–1.11

Employment at DOT, by subagency, State, and selected personnel characteristics, FY83, annual rpt, 7304–18

Exports and imports of US (waterborne), by type of service, commodity, country, route, and US port, 1982, annual rpt, 7704–2

Foreign and US shipping and shipbuilding subsidies and aid, with summary fleet, trade, and GNP data, for 48 countries, 1979-80, biennial rpt, 7704–18

Fraud and abuse in DOT programs, audits and investigations, 1st half FY84, semiannual rpt, 7302–4

Intermodal containers and equipment owned by US shipping and leasing companies, inventory by type and size, 1983, annual rpt, 7704–10

Merchant fleets operations, and MarAd shipbuilding and operating subsidies and other activities, and FY83, annual rpt, 7704–14

Merchant ships in active US fleet and Natl Defense Reserve Fleet, number and tonnage by owner/operator, Jan 1984, semiannual inventory, 7702–2

Merchant ships in world fleet, and tonnage, by country of registry, 1982, annual rpt, 7704–3

Merchant ships in world fleet, by selected characteristics and country of registry, as of Jan 1983, annual rpt, 7704–1

Ports, port facilities by type, and inland waterways by size, by location, 1982-83, annual rpt, 7704–16

Shipbuilding and deliveries, by type and by country of construction and registry, 1982, annual rpt, 7704–4

Shipbuilding and repair facilities, construction capability, number and value of ships under construction, and employment, by shipyard, 1983, annual rpt, 7704–9

Shipbuilding costs and related employment, by coastal district, 1982, annual rpt, 7704–12

Index by Subjects and Names

Tanker ships in the world fleet, by selected characteristics and country of registry, 1982, annual rpt, 7704–17

Maritime industry

see Shipbuilding and operating subsidies

see Ships and shipping

Maritime law

Japan fish landings, prices, trade by country, cold storage, and market devs, periodic press release, 2162–7

Marine Mammal Protection Act admin and populations, strandings, and catch permits by type and applicant, by species and location, Apr 1983-Mar 1984, annual rpt, 2164–11

Marine mammals protection activities and Fed Govt funding, population status, and research, 1983, annual rpt, 5504–12

Maritime Commission mgmt and enforcement activities, filings by type and disposition, and civil penalties by shipper, FY83, annual rpt, 9334–1

US Attorneys civil case processing and amounts involved, by cause of action, FY83, annual rpt, 6004–2.5

Market research

Business America, foreign and domestic commerce, and US investment and trade opportunities, biweekly rpt articles, 2042–24

Computers and computer equipment foreign market and trade, and user industry operations and demand, country market research rpts, 2045–1

Electric power systems equipment foreign market and trade, and user industry operations and demand, country market research rpts, 2045–15

Electronic component equipment foreign market and trade, and user industry operations and demand, country market research rpts, 2045–4

Electronic component manufacturing equipment foreign market and trade, and user industry operations and demand, country market research rpts, 2045–5

Farm machinery and equipment foreign market and trade, and user industry operations and demand, country market research rpts, 2045–13

Fish marketability, perceived importance of selected fish characteristics, 1976, article, 2162–1.401

Food processing and packaging equipment, foreign market and trade, and user industry operations and demand, country market research rpts, 2045–11

Graphic industries equipment foreign market and trade, and user industry operations and demand, country market research rpts, 2045–3

Industrial process control equipment foreign market and trade, and user industry operations and demand, country market research rpts, 2045–6

Lab instruments foreign market and trade, and user industry operations and demand, country market research rpts, 2045–10

Machine tools and equipment foreign market and trade, and user industry operations and demand, country market research rpts, 2045–9

Medical and health care equipment foreign market and trade, and user industry operations and demand, country market research rpts, 2045–2

Index by Subjects and Names

Maryland

Mining industry equipment foreign market and trade, and user industry operations and demand, country market research rpts, 2045–16

Overseas Business Reports: economic conditions, investment and export opportunities, and trade practices, annual country market research rpt series, 2046–6

Overseas Business Reports: economic conditions, investment and export opportunities, and trade practices, world region rpt series, 2046–5

Pollution control instruments and equipment foreign market and trade, and user industry operations and demand, country market research rpts, 2045–17

Sporting goods and recreational equipment and vehicles foreign market and trade, country market research rpts, 2045–14

Telecommunication equipment foreign market and trade, and user industry operations and demand, country market research rpts, 2045–12

see also Consumer surveys

Market shares

see Economic concentration and diversification

Marketing

Census of Population, 1980: detailed socioeconomic and demographic characteristics, by age, sex, race, Hispanic origin, occupation, and industry, State rpt series, 2531–4

see also Advertising

see also Agricultural marketing

see also Competition

see also Consumer credit

see also Consumer protection

see also Consumer surveys

see also Credit

see also Economic concentration and diversification

see also Foreign trade promotion

see also Labeling

see also Market research

see also Packaging and containers

see also Price regulation

see also Prices

see also Retail trade

see also Sales promotion

see also Sales workers

see also Shopping centers

see also Wholesale trade

see also under names of specific commodities or commodity groups

Marketing quotas

see Agricultural quotas and price supports

Marks, Denton

"Incomplete Experience Rating in State Unemployment Insurance", 6722–1.469

Marland, Gregg

"Carbon Dioxide Emissions from Fossil Fuels: A Procedure for Estimation and Results for 1950-81", 3008–94

Marquez, Jaime

"Currency Substitution, Duality, and Exchange Rate Indeterminancy: An Empirical Analysis of the Venezuelan Experience", 9366–7.98

"Foreign Exchange Constraints and Growth Possibilities in LDCs", 9366–7.106

"Oil Price Effects in Theory and Practice", 9366–7.93

"Oil Prices, Welfare Tradeoffs, and International Policy Coordination in a Three Region World Model: An Optimizing Approach", 9366–7.96

Marriage and divorce

Census of Housing, 1980: inventory, occupancy, and unit characteristics, changes from 1973 by region and inside-outside SMSAs and central cities, series, 2473–3

Census of Housing, 1980: structural, financial, and householder characteristics, by region and State, 2475–4

Census of Population and Housing, 1980: detailed population and housing characteristics, by county, city, and census tract, State and SMSA rpt series, 2551–2

Census of Population, 1980: detailed socioeconomic and demographic characteristics, by age, sex, race, Hispanic origin, occupation, and industry, State rpt series, 2531–4

Census of Population, 1980: detailed socioeconomic characteristics, by county, city, and inside-outside SMSAs and central cities, State rpt series, 2531–3

Certificates of birth, death, marriage, and divorce, records availability and vital statistics records offices, by State, 1984 annual listing, 4124–7

County and City Data Book, detailed socioeconomic and demographic data for States, counties, and cities, selected years 1976-82, 2328–1

Crimes of violence involving relatives, by victim-offender relationship, circumstances, and victim characteristics, aggregate 1973-81, 6066–19.5

Divorces, divorce rates, and characteristics, by region and State, 1981, US Vital Statistics advance rpt, 4146–5.74

Employment, unemployment, and labor force, by demographic and employment characteristics, State, and for 30 metro areas and 11 large cities, 1983, annual rpt, 6744–7

Foreign women sociodemographic, economic, and fertility characteristics, with comparisons to men, by country, 1960s-85, world region rpt series, 2326–15

Immigrant and nonimmigrant visas issued and refused, and status adjustments, by class and nationality, FY77, annual rpt, 7184–1

Income assistance, effects of experimental negative income tax program on employment, earnings, marital status, and other family characteristics in 2 cities, 1970-75, 4008–64

Marital status, living arrangements, and family relationships, by age and sex, Mar 1984, advance annual Current Population Rpt, 2546–1.389

Marital status, living arrangements, and family relationships, by demographic characteristics, Mar 1983 annual Current Population Rpt, 2546–1.388

Marriages and marriage rates by State, and bride and groom characteristics, 1981, advance annual US Vital Statistics rpt, 4146–5.77

Marriages, divorces, and rates, by detailed demographic and geographic characteristics, 1979 and trends, US Vital Statistics annual rpt, 4144–4

Marriages, divorces, and rates, by State, provisional 1982-83 with trends from 1975, US Vital Statistics annual rpt, 4144–7

OASDI beneficiary status changes reported late and benefit overpayments, for death, marriage, and leaving school, 1981, GAO rpt, 26121–68

Population size and components of change, projected under 3 fertility assumptions, 1982-2080 with trends from 1900, SSA actuarial rpt, 4706–1.92

Statistical Abstract of US, social, political, and economic data, 1950s-83 and trends, annual rpt, 2324–1.1

Vital statistics, births, marriages, divorces, and deaths, provisional data, monthly rpt, 4142–1

Warsaw Pact and US citizens binatl marriage problem cases pending as of Mar 1984, semiannual rpt, 7002–1

see also Child support and alimony

see also Families and households

see also Illegitimacy

see also Widows and widowers

see also under By Marital Status in the "Index by Categories"

Marshall, Michael J.

"Species Profiles: Life Histories and Environmental Requirements of Coastal Fishes and Invertebrates (South Florida), Stone Crab", 5506–8.28

Marshall, Patricia B.

"Evaluation of the Bonneville County DUI Accident Prevention Program (Project Safety)", 7762–9.404

Marshall, Tex.

Census of Housing, 1980: occupancy and unit characteristics, by race, Hispanic origin, and city, SMSA rpt, 2473–1.224

Census of Population and Housing, 1980: detailed population and housing characteristics, by county, city, and census tract, SMSA rpt, 2551–2.224

see also under By SMSA or MSA in the "Index by Categories"

Marshes

see Wetlands

Marten, John F.

"Future Farm Program Needs", 1004–16.1

Martens, David G.

"Wood Used in U.S. Manufacturing Industries, 1977", 1208–3

Martin, David K.

"Microcomputer Program for the Calculation of a Trawlnet Section Taper", 2162–1.402

Martin, Randolph C.

"South Carolina: A Strong Recovery, but Problems Remain", 9371–1.411

Martin, Roy E.

"Toward an Improved Seafood Nomenclature System", 2162–1.401

Martinique

see Caribbean area

Maryland

Agriculture census, 1982: farms, farmland, production, finances, and operator characteristics, by county, final State rpt, 2331–1.20

Apple production, marketing, and prices in 4 Appalachian States, 1983/84 crop year, annual rpt, 1311–13

Bank deposits in commercial and mutual savings banks and in US branches of

Maryland

foreign banks, by account type, instn, State, SMSA, and county, June 1983, annual rpt, 9295–3.5

Bank income and expenses, Fed Reserve 5th District member banks, by State, 1983, annual rpt, 9389–10

Census of Housing, 1980: occupancy and unit characteristics of SMSAs and central cities, by race, Hispanic origin, and city, State rpt, 2473–1.22

Census of Population and Housing, 1980: detailed population and housing characteristics, by county, city, and census tract, State rpt, 2551–2.22

Census of Population, 1980: detailed socioeconomic and demographic characteristics, by age, sex, race, Hispanic origin, and industry, State rpt, 2531–4.22

Corrections policies in Maryland, assessments of private citizens and corrections and criminal justice personnel, 1980-81 with prison population trends from 1930, 6068–176

County Business Patterns: establishments, employees, and payrolls, by SIC 4-digit industry and county, 1982, annual State rpt, 2326–6.22

Economic indicators by State, Fed Reserve 5th District, quarterly rpt, 9389–16

Employment, earnings, and hours, by selected SIC 1- to 4-digit industry, State, and for 278 major labor areas, 1939-83, annual rpt, 6744–5.1, 6744–5.3

Environmental quality, pollutant discharge by type and source, and EPA protection activities and funding, 1970s-83, biennial regional rpt, 9184–15.3

Exports of manufactured and agricultural commodities, manufacturing production, and export-related employment, 1960s-82, State rpt, 2046–3.20

Foster care children permanent placement, Fed Govt incentive program funding and operations in 7 States, FY80-82, GAO rpt, 26121–81

HHS aid to each State and local govt or private instn, amount obligated, funding agency, and program, FY83, annual listing, 4004–3.3

Income (personal) per capita and by source, and earnings by industry div, by State, MSA, and county, 1977-82, annual regional rpt, 2704–2.3

Lower Eastern Shore wages of office and plant workers, by occupation, 1984 labor market area survey rpt, 6785–3.9

Manufacturing census, 1982: financial and operating data, by SIC 2- to 4-digit industry, State, SMSA, and county, preliminary census div rpt, 2491–3.5

Mineral Industry Surveys, State review of production, 1983, advance annual rpt, 5614–6.20

Minerals Yearbook, 1982, Vol 2 preprints: State review of production and sales by commodity, and business activity, annual rpt, 5604–16.21

Minerals Yearbook, 1982, Vol 2: State reviews of production, sales, and firms, by commodity, and business activity, annual rpt, 5604–34

Population, births, deaths, and net migration, by MSA and county, 1980-82, annual State Current Population Rpt, 2546–4.20

Population size, Apr 1980 and July 1982, and per capita income, 1979 and 1981, by county and city, State Current Population Rpt, 2546–11.20

Prison capacity and population, by facility for 2 States, various periods 1977-82 with projections to 1988, 25528–99

Retail trade census, 1982: employment, establishments, sales, and payroll, by SIC 2- to 4-digit kind of business, SMSA, county, and city, State rpt, 2397–1.21

Savings and loan assns, FHLB 4th District insured members financial condition and operations, by SMSA, monthly rpt, 9302–1

Transportation census, 1982: trucks, by detailed characteristics, miles traveled, and type of product carried, State rpt, 2573–1.21

Water supply and quality in streams and lakes, and groundwater levels in wells, by drainage basin, 1983, annual State rpt, 5666–10.19

Wholesale trade census, 1982: employment, establishments, finances, and operations, by SIC 2- to 4-digit kind of business, SMSA, county, and city, State rpt, 2405–1.21

see also Baltimore, Md.

see also Cumberland, Md.

see also Frederick, Md.

see also Hagerstown, Md.

see also under By State in the "Index by Categories"

Maskus, Keith E.

"Changes in the Factor Requirements of U.S. Foreign Trade", 9381–10.30

"Rising Protectionism and U.S. International Trade Policy", 9381–1.412

Mass media

Statistical Abstract of US, social, political, and economic data, 1950s-83 and trends, annual rpt, 2324–1.3

see also Advertising

see also Motion pictures

see also Newspapers

see also Periodicals

see also Public broadcasting

see also Radio

see also Television

Mass transit

see Airlines

see Buses

see Metroliner

see National Railroad Passenger Corp.

see Railroads

see Subways

see Urban transportation

Massachusetts

Agriculture census, 1982: farms, farmland, production, finances, and operator characteristics, by county, final State rpt, 2331–1.21

Bank deposits in commercial and mutual savings banks and in US branches of foreign banks, by account type, instn, State, SMSA, and county, June 1983, annual rpt, 9295–3.1

Census of Housing, 1980: occupancy and unit characteristics of SMSAs and central cities, by race, Hispanic origin, and city, State rpt, 2473–1.23

Census of Population and Housing, 1980: detailed population and housing characteristics, by county, city, and census tract, State rpt, 2551–2.23

Index by Subjects and Names

Census of Population, 1980: detailed socioeconomic and demographic characteristics, by age, sex, race, Hispanic origin, and industry, State rpt, 2531–4.23

Children's accident prevention, parents awareness and use of safety measures in 9 Massachusetts communities, by urban-rural location, Sept 1980-June 1982 survey, article, 4102–1.402

County Business Patterns: establishments, employees, and payrolls, by SIC 4-digit industry and county, 1982, annual State rpt, 2326–6.23

Cranberry production, prices, area, and yield, for 5 States, 1982-83 and forecast 1984, annual rpt, 1621–18.4

Economic indicators for New England States, Fed Reserve 1st District, monthly rpt with articles, 9373–2

Employment, earnings, and hours, by selected SIC 1- to 4-digit industry, State, and for 278 major labor areas, 1939-83, annual rpt, 6744–5.1, 6744–5.3

Employment in traditional and high technology industry by occupation, and wages by industry, for Massachusetts compared to US and 3 SMSAs, various periods 1976-82, article, 9373–1.416

Environmental quality, pollutant discharge by type and source, and EPA protection activities and funding, 1970s-83, biennial regional rpt, 9184–15.1

Exports of manufactured and agricultural commodities, manufacturing production, and export-related employment, 1960s-82, State rpt, 2046–3.21

Fish and shellfish landings and prices at Boston and other New England ports, and total New England cold storage holdings, weekly rpt, 2162–6.2

Gasoline retail sales in Massachusetts, and Trans-Alaska Pipeline owner companies financial data, by company, 1981-83, hearing, 21728–51

HHS aid to each State and local govt or private instn, amount obligated, funding agency, and program, FY83, annual listing, 4004–3.1

Income (personal) per capita and by source, and earnings by industry div, by State, MSA, and county, 1977-82, annual regional rpt, 2704–2.2

Medicare reimbursement rates in Massachusetts, by procedure and physician specialty, July 1981-June 1982, GAO rpt, 26121–82

Mineral Industry Surveys, State review of production, 1983, advance annual rpt, 5614–6.21

Minerals Yearbook, 1982, Vol 2 preprints: State review of production and sales by commodity, and business activity, annual rpt, 5604–16.22

Minerals Yearbook, 1982, Vol 2: State reviews of production, sales, and firms, by commodity, and business activity, annual rpt, 5604–34

Population estimates and components of change, by MSA and county, 1980-82, annual State Current Population Rpt, 2546–4.21

Population size, Apr 1980 and July 1982, and per capita income, 1979 and 1981, by county and city, State Current Population Rpt, 2546–11.21

Index by Subjects and Names

Maternity

Prices, foreign exchange rate, and per capita money supply in Colonial era Massachusetts, and compared to other New England colonies, 1720-70, article, 9383–6.402

Retail trade census, 1982: employment, establishments, sales, and payroll, by SIC 2- to 4-digit kind of business, SMSA, county, and city, State rpt, 2397–1.22

Savings and loan assns, FHLB 1st District member instns financial operations and related economic and housing indicators, monthly rpt, 9302–4

Service industry census, 1982: employment, establishments, receipts, and payroll, by SIC 2- to 4-digit kind of business, SMSA, county, and city, State rpt, 2391–1.22

Wages of office and plant workers, in southeastern Massachusetts, 1983 labor market area survey rpt, 6785–3.5

Water supply and quality in streams and lakes, and groundwater levels in wells, by drainage basin, 1982, annual State rpt, 5666–20.20

Wholesale trade census, 1982: employment, establishments, finances, and operations, by SIC 2- to 4-digit kind of business, SMSA, county, and city, State rpt, 2405–1.22

see also Boston, Mass.
see also Brockton, Mass.
see also Chicopee, Mass.
see also Fall River, Mass.
see also Fitchburg, Mass.
see also Haverhill, Mass.
see also Holyoke, Mass.
see also Lawrence, Mass.
see also Leominster, Mass.
see also Lowell, Mass.
see also New Bedford, Mass.
see also Pittsfield, Mass.
see also Springfield, Mass.
see also Worcester, Mass.
see also under By State in the "Index by Categories"

Masters, Charles D.

"Assessment of Undiscovered Conventionally Recoverable Petroleum Resources of the Northwest European Assessment Region", 5666–17.15

"Distribution and Quantitative Assessment of World Crude-Oil Reserves and Resources", 5668–72

MATCH Institution

"Urban Travel Trends: Historical Observations and Future Forecasts, Final Report, May 1984", 7888–63

Maternity

Abortions, by patient sociodemographic characteristics, pregnancy history, and procedure, 1980, US Vital Statistics final rpt, 4146–5.72

Alcohol use, and health, economic, and social impacts, review of research, 1970s-81, 4488–4

Asian and Pacific Islands Americans births by ethnic origin and sociodemographic and birth characteristics, with comparisons to blacks and whites, 1978-80, 4146–5.75

Births, fertility rates, expected births, and childless women, by socioeconomic characteristics, June 1982, annual Current Population Rpt, 2546–1.386

Births, fertility rates, expected births, and childless women, by socioeconomic characteristics, June 1983, advance annual Current Population Rpt, 2546–1.385

Births, fertility rates, expected births, and childless women, by socioeconomic characteristics, June 1983, annual Current Population Rpt, 2546–1.393

Birthspacing by period of woman's birth and marriage, period of child's birth, and sociodemographic characteristics, June 1980, Current Population Rpt, 2546–1.387

Breast-fed infants, by characteristics of mother and source of prenatal care, various periods 1970-75, article, 4102–1.442

Breast-fed infants, by race and mother's sociodemographic characteristics, 1983 with trends from 1970, article, 4102–1.455

Census of Population and Housing, 1980: detailed population and housing characteristics, by county, city, and census tract, State and SMSA rpt series, 2551–2

Deaths (maternal and infant) from pregnancy and childbirth complications, by detailed cause and age, with geographic detail, 1979, US Vital Statistics annual rpt, 4144–2.1, 4144–2.2

Deaths and death rates, by cause and age, provisional 1982-83, US Vital Statistics annual rpt, 4144–7

Deaths and death rates, by detailed geographic area, cause, and demographic characteristics, 1979, US Vital Statistics annual rpt, 4144–3

Deaths and death rates related to pregnancy, by age and race, 1974-78, article, 4202–7.406

Deaths and death rates related to pregnancy, 1981, US Vital Statistics advance rpt, 4146–5.78

Deaths and death rates related to pregnancy, 1982, US Vital Statistics advance rpt, 4146–5.81

Deaths by principal or contributing cause, with type of injury reported in accidental, poisoning, and violent deaths, by age, sex, and race, 1978, 4146–5.76

Deaths from childbirth, and legal abortion deaths by procedure, location, and type of pre-existing medical condition, by age and sex, 1972-80, hearings, 21368–47

DOD Civilian Health and Medical Program of the Uniformed Services costs and operations, FY83-84 with trends from FY79, semiannual rpt, 3502–2

Fed Govt public welfare programs and tax expenditures benefitting children and youth, participation and funding for 71 programs, FY81-83, 21968–30

Food aid special supplemental program for women, infants, and children, effectiveness and participant characteristics, 1973-82, GAO rpt, 26131–10

Foreign women sociodemographic, economic, and fertility characteristics, with comparisons to men, by country, 1960s-85, world region rpt series, 2326–15

Health characteristics of infants, by mother's sociodemographic, lifestyle, and maternity characteristics, 1980, article, 4102–1.418, 4102–1.421, 4102–1.422

Health condition and health care resources, use, and expenditures, 1970s-82 with trends and projections 1900-2000, annual compilation, 4144–11

Health counseling during pregnancy, effect on smoking, diet, delivery costs, and birth weight, by sociodemographic characteristics and pregnancy history, 1983 article, 4102–1.401

HHS aid to each State and local govt or private instn, amount obligated, funding agency, and program, FY83, annual listing, 4004–3

Hospital discharges and length of stay, by patient characteristics, facility size, procedure performed, diagnosis, and region, 1982, annual rpt, 4147–13.78

Immunization and preventable disease elimination programs for children and pregnant women, 1983 conf papers, 4204–15

Navy and Marine Corps disease incidence, medical care, and deaths, by detailed diagnosis, and medical personnel and workloads, 1978-79, annual rpt, 3804–1

Northern Mariana Islands public health payments for off-island Medicaid referrals and prenatal, well-baby, and other clinic and home visits, FY83 and trends, annual rpt, 7004–6.2

Nursing continuing education in maternal and child health at University of Kentucky, course enrollment and student assessment of career value, 1983 article, 4102–1.405

Nutrition status of infants and children, blood and height-weight indicators, and low birth weight risk factors, by age, race, and Hispanic origin, 1981, annual rpt, 4205–24

Obstetrician-gynecologist office visits and drugs used, by visit reason, diagnosis, treatment, and patient and physician characteristics, 1980-81, 4147–13.76

Prenatal care during 1st trimester, by race and Hispanic origin and for teenage mothers, selected years 1970-80, and goals for 1990, article, 4102–1.420, 4102–1.425

Prenatal care visits and month begun, by mother's characteristics and State, 1979, US Vital Statistics annual rpt, 4144–1

Research Center for Mothers and Children, activities and funding, as of June 1983, annual rpt, 4474–31

Smoking and health research, article abstracts and indexes, 1983, annual rpt, 4044–8

Smoking and health research publications, bimonthly listing, 4042–1

State govt maternal and child health funding, and admin of Fed Govt block grants, by program for 13 States, 1981-83, GAO rpt, 26121–70

Statistical Abstract of US, social, political, and economic data, 1950s-83 and trends, annual rpt, 2324–1.1

Teenage girls births and rates, and distribution of births with low birth weight and Apgar scores, by mother and infant characteristics, 1970-81, 4147–21.41

Teenage girls births and sexual experience by race, abortions, and birth control use, by age, 1970s-80 with birth trends from 1920, hearings, 21968–29

see also Birth defects
see also Births
see also Family planning

Maternity

see also Fertility
see also Fetal deaths
see also Illegitimacy
see also Infant mortality
see also Midwives
see also Obstetrics and gynecology

Mathematica Policy Research, Inc.

- "Effects of the Omnibus Budget Reconciliation Act of 1981 (OBRA) Welfare Changes and the Recession on Poverty", 21788–139
- "Final Report of the Seattle-Denver Income Maintenance Experiment. Vol. 2: Administration", 4008–64.3

Mathematics

- Census of Population, 1980: detailed socioeconomic and demographic characteristics, by age, sex, race, Hispanic origin, occupation, and industry, State rpt series, 2531–4
- Census of Population, 1980: labor force, by sex, detailed occupation, and region, with comparison to 1970 census, supplementary rpt, 2535–1.12
- *Condition of Education,* detailed data on enrollment, staff, achievement, finances, curricula, and education effects on employment, 1982-83, annual rpt, 4824–1
- Degrees conferred in higher education, by race, Hispanic origin, sex, level, and field, selected years 1949/50-1979/80, annual rpt, 4824–2.16
- DOD Dependents Schools students higher education admissions tests scores by sex and subject, and educational goals and attitudes, 1983, annual rpt, 3504–17
- DOD Dependents Schools 1st grader basic skills test scores, by world area and English fluency, fall 1983, annual rpt, 3504–18
- Educational progress, natl assessment summary data for 7 learning areas, by characteristics of participants, selected years 1971-82, annual rpt, 4824–2.6
- High school classes of 1980 and 1982: educational and sociodemographic characteristics and expectations, natl longitudinal study, series, 4826–2
- Indian education program operations, funding, student progress measures, and opinions of school staff, parents, and students, selected years 1973-83, 4808–13
- NASA R&D funding to colleges and universities, by State, field of science, and instn, FY83, annual listing, 9504–7
- NSF grant and award recipients, by State, FY83, annual listing, 9624–11
- NSF research programs, activities, and funding, FY82-83, annual rpt, 9624–6
- Nuclear industry nongovt employment by industry segment, occupation, and census div, and DOE and NRC nuclear employment, 1968-83, biennial rpt, 3004–11
- Occupational manpower needs and supply by detailed occupation, and educational and training program enrollees and grads by detailed field, 1982 and 1995, biennial rpt, 6744–3
- *Occupational Outlook Handbook,* 1984-85 biennial rpt, 6744–1

R&D and science-related Fed Govt funding and total and federally funded expenditures of universities and colleges, by instn and field of science, FY82, 9626–2.136

- R&D and science-related Fed Govt funding to higher education and nonprofit instns, by field, instn, agency, and State, FY82, annual rpt, 9627–17
- R&D-employed scientists and engineers salaries by degree, type of establishment, age, experience, and field, 1984, annual rpt, 3004–1
- R&D expenditures by higher education instns and federally funded centers, by field, source of funds, instn, and State, FY82, annual rpt, 9627–13
- R&D expenditures by source, and scientists education and employment, detailed data by field, selected years 1953-84, annual rpt, 9624–18
- R&D expenditures of higher education instns, and science and engineering employment and grad students, by field, 1972-83, biennial rpt, 9627–24
- R&D Fed Govt funding for all performers, by field and supporting agency, selected years FY60-84, annual rpt, 9627–20
- R&D industry funding and employment of scientists and engineers, by industry group, firm size, and funding source, 1956-82, annual rpt, 9627–21
- Science and engineering doctoral degree recipients, by field, sex, race, age, citizenship, postgrad employment and study status, State, and instn, 1960-82, 9626–6.16
- Science and engineering grad enrollment, fields of study, financial support, and other student and instn characteristics, 1975-82, annual survey, 9627–7
- Science and engineering grad program enrollment, by field, degree level, source of financial support, race, and Hispanic origin, 1975-81, 9626–2.134
- Science and engineering grad program enrollment by field, sources of financial support, and foreign students, 1975-82, 9626–2.141
- Science and engineering grads of 1980-81, employment and median salaries by level and field of degree, 1982, 9626–2.137
- Science and engineering grads of 1980-81, employment characteristics or grad enrollment, by degree level, field, sex, and race, 1982, 9627–25
- Scientists and engineers employed at universities and colleges, by field, sex, and instn, 1973-82, 9626–2.140
- Scientists and engineers employed at universities and colleges, by field, sex, State, and instn, Jan 1983 and selected trends from 1967, annual survey, 9627–11
- Scientists and engineers employed in energy-related fields, supply/demand and effects of R&D funding, by energy type, employer type, field, and age, 1962-91, annual rpt, 3004–19
- Scientists and engineers employment by sector and activity, and share female, black, and Asian descent, by field, 1982, 9626–2.142
- Scientists and engineers supply, employment, and education, by sex, race, Hispanic origin, and field, selected years 1965-83, biennial rpt, 9624–20

Index by Subjects and Names

- Scientists, engineers, and technicians employed in private industry, by occupation and industry group, 1980-81, biennial rpt, 9627–23
- Scientists, engineers, and technicians needed in defense and nondefense industries, and supply/demand, by field, 1981-87, 9628–71
- Teaching degrees conferred by specialty and State, required credit hours, and instn officials attitudes, by instn type, 1970s-83, hearings, 21348–89
- *see also* Computer sciences
- *see also* Statisticians

Mathtech, Inc.

"Assessment of Factors Affecting Industrial Electricity Demand", 3008–87

Matsumoto Walter M.

"Synopsis of Biological Data on Skipjack Tuna", 2166–16.12

Mattresses

see Household furnishings

Mattson, David R.

"10-Year Review of the Supplemental Security Income Program", 4742–1.402

Mauritania

- Agricultural situation in sub-Saharan Africa, by country, 1982-83 and outlook for 1984, annual rpt, 1524–4.10
- AID activities and funding by project and function, FY85, and developing countries summary socioeconomic data, 1970s-83, by country, annual rpt, 9914–3
- AID economic assistance to developing countries, obligations and disbursements by country, quarterly rpt, 9912–4
- Disaster preparedness and summary sociodemographic, political, and economic data, 1970s-83, 9916–2.55
- Economic conditions and foreign marketing prospects in 46 Sub-Saharan countries, 1983 world region rpt, 2046–5.1
- Economic, social, and political summary data, by country, 1984, annual factbook, 244–11
- Economic trends in income, production, prices, employment, finances, and trade, 1984 annual rpt, 2046–4.32
- Exports of US, detailed Schedule B commodities by country of destination, 1983, annual rpt, 2424–9
- Exports of US, detailed Schedule E commodities by mode of transport and world area and country of destination, 1983, annual rpts, 2424–5
- Imports of US, detailed Schedule A commodities by country and world area of origin, and mode of transport, 1983, annual rpts, 2424–2
- Imports of US, detailed TSUSA commodities by country of origin, 1983, annual rpt, 2424–4
- Loans and grants for economic and military assistance from US and intl agencies, by program and country, FY46-83, annual rpt, 9914–5
- Military aid of US, arms sales, and training programs costs and budget requests by program, world region, and country, FY83-85, annual rpt, 7144–13
- Military spending, arms trade, and armed forces size, with total govt spending and population, by country, 1972-82, annual rpt, 9824–1

Index by Subjects and Names

Minerals Yearbook, 1982, Vol 3: foreign country reviews of production, trade, and policies, by commodity, annual rpt, 5604–35

Minerals Yearbook, 1983, Vol 3 preprints: foreign country review of production, trade, and policies, by commodity, annual rpt, 5604–23.48

Oil and gas undiscovered recoverable resources, cumulative production, and identified reserves, as of 1982, preliminary oil basin rpt, 5666–17.13

Population size and growth rates, and latest available benchmark demographic data, by country, 1950-83, biennial rpt, 2324–4

see also under By Foreign Country in the "Index by Categories"

Mauritius

- Agricultural situation in sub-Saharan Africa, by country, 1982-83 and outlook for 1984, annual rpt, 1524–4.10
- Agricultural supply/demand, trade, and production, and socioeconomic data, by country, 1950s-77, 1528–179
- AID activities and funding by project and function, FY85, and developing countries summary socioeconomic data, 1970s-83, by country, annual rpt, 9914–3
- AID economic assistance to developing countries, obligations and disbursements by country, quarterly rpt, 9912–4
- Economic conditions and foreign marketing prospects in 46 Sub-Saharan countries, 1983 world region rpt, 2046–5.1
- Economic, social, and political summary data, by country, 1984, annual factbook, 244–11
- Exports of US, detailed Schedule B commodities by country of destination, 1983, annual rpt, 2424–9
- Exports of US, detailed Schedule E commodities by mode of transport and world area and country of destination, 1983, annual rpts, 2424–5
- Imports of US, detailed Schedule A commodities by country and world area of origin, and mode of transport, 1983, annual rpts, 2424–2
- Imports of US, detailed TSUSA commodities by country of origin, 1983, annual rpt, 2424–4
- Loans and grants for economic and military assistance from US and intl agencies, by program and country, FY46-83, annual rpt, 9914–5
- Military aid of US, arms sales, and training programs costs and budget requests by program, world region, and country, FY83-85, annual rpt, 7144–13
- Military spending, arms trade, and armed forces size, with total govt spending and population, by country, 1972-82, annual rpt, 9824–1
- *Minerals Yearbook, 1982,* Vol 3: foreign country reviews of production, trade, and policies, by commodity, annual rpt, 5604–35
- *Minerals Yearbook, 1982,* Vol 3 preprints: foreign country review of production, trade, and policies, by commodity, annual rpt, 5604–17.83
- Population size and growth rates, and latest available benchmark demographic data, by country, 1950-83, biennial rpt, 2324–4

see also under By Foreign Country in the "Index by Categories"

Maximus, Inc.

"Evaluation of the Child Support Enforcement Program, Final Report", 4748–37

May, V. Jeff

"Hydrology of Area 21, Eastern Coal Province, Tennessee, Alabama and Georgia", 5666–15.23

Mayaguez, P.R.

see also under By SMSA or MSA in the "Index by Categories"

Mayas, J. M.

"Study of Demographic, Situational, and Motivational Factors Affecting Restraint Usage in Automobiles", 7768–82

Mayengon, Rene

"Warm Core Cyclones in the Mediterranean", 2152–8.401

Mays, G. T.

"Nuclear Power Plant Operating Experience, 1981", 9634–6

McAllen, Tex.

- Census of Housing, 1980: occupancy and unit characteristics, by race, Hispanic origin, and city, SMSA rpt, 2473–1.236
- Census of Population and Housing, 1980: detailed population and housing characteristics, by county, city, and census tract, SMSA rpt, 2551–2.236
- Employment and economic impacts on Texas border of Mexican peso devaluation, for 6 counties and 2 SMSAs, 1970s-May 1983, hearing, 21788–133
- Employment in Mexico border US-owned plants, and peso devaluation, related to employment in 4 Texas SMSAs, 1978-83, article, 9379–1.402
- Housing vacancy rates for single and multifamily units and mobile homes, by city and ZIP code, 1984, annual metro area rpt, 9304–19.23
- Wages of office and plant workers, by occupation, 1984 labor market area survey rpt, 6785–3.10

see also under By SMSA or MSA in the "Index by Categories"

McCall, Nelda

"Utilization of Medicare Services by Beneficiaries Having Partial Medicare Coverage", 4652–1.404

McCarthy, Eileen

"Hospital Use by Children in the U.S. and Canada", 4147–5.1

McCarthy, F. Ward, Jr.

"Evolution of the Bank Regulatory Structure: A Reappraisal", 9389–2

"Review of Bank Performance in the Fifth District, 1983", 9389–1.408

McCarthy, Mary A.

"Federal Civilian Leave Data for the Executive Branch, Leave Year 1981", 9842–1.402

"Federal Civilian Work Years and Personnel Costs in the Executive Branch for FY82", 9842–1.401

"Full-Time Civilian Employment and Salary Statistics, Mar. 31, 1984", 9842–1.404

McClelland, Lou

"Tenant-Paid Energy Costs in Multifamily Rental Housing: Effects on Energy Use, Owner Investment, and the Market Value of Energy", 3308–73

McMullan, Michael

McClure, Joe P.

"Empirical Yields of Timber and Forest Biomass in the Southeast", 1208–199

McCollom, Steven R.

"Data on Female Veterans, FY83", 9924–24

McCrackin, Bobbie H.

"Dynamics of Growth and Change in the Health-Care Industry", 9371–1.425

"Financing Education in the Southeast", 9371–1.429

"Tennessee: Continuing the Momentum of Recovery", 9371–1.406

McCrohan, Kevin F.

"Estimates of Tip Income in Eating Places, 1982", 8302–2.406

McDonald, Margaret R.

"Average Price of Natural Gas Delivered to Consumers, 1983 (Preliminary Data Report)", 3164–4

"Average Price of Natural Gas Delivered to Consumers, 1983 (Preliminary)", 3162–4.413

"Interstate Movements of Natural Gas, 1982", 3162–4.409

McDonald, Richard J.

"The 'Underground Economy' and BLS Statistical Data", 6722–1.401

McDonald, Thomas

"Improving U.S. Farmland", 1506–5.20

McDonnell, Richard T.

"World Oilseeds Outlook", 1004–16.1

McDowell, Bruce D.

"Governmental Actors and Factors in Mass Transit", 10042–1.404

McGill, Dan M.

"Defined Benefit Plans", 25408–87

McGinnis, J. Michael

"Nutrition Monitoring and Research in the Department of Health and Human Services", 4102–1.454

McIntire, Robert J.

"New Seasonal Adjustment Factors for Household Data Series", 6742–2.411

"Revision of Seasonally Adjusted Labor Force Series", 6742–2.401

McKean, John R.

"Coal from the Nation: Household Demand for Electricity", 1588–78

McKee, Richard

"1983 Promotional Activities Under Federal Milk Orders", 1317–4.406

McKeever, David B.

"Wood Used in U.S. Manufacturing Industries, 1977", 1208–3

McKenzie, Joseph A.

"Affordability of Alternative Mortgage Instruments: A Household Analysis", 9312–7.401

McLaughlin, Mary M.

"Profitability of Insured Commercial Banks in 1983", 9362–1.409

McMillan, Alma

"Dually Entitled Elderly Medicare and Medicaid Population Living in the Community", 4652–1.433

McMillen, Marilyn M.

"Sex-Specific Equivalent Retirement Ages: 1940-2050", 4742–1.406

McMullan, Michael

"End-Stage Renal Disease: A Profile of Facilities Furnishing Treatment", 4652–1.434

McNees, Stephen K.

McNees, Stephen K.
"Economic Growth: How Much Is Too Much?", 9373–1.402

McNeil, John M.
"Lifetime Work Experience and Its Effect on Earnings: Retrospective Data from the 1979 Income Survey Development Program", 2546–2.123

McNulty, James E.
"Secondary Mortgage Markets: Recent Trends and Research Results", 9312–1.408

McWilliams, Ruth T.
"Public/Private Cooperation in Rural Roadway Improvements", 1004–16.1

Mears, Leon G.
"World Cotton Outlook", 1004–16.1

Measles
see Infective and parasitic diseases

Measures
see Industrial standards
see Instruments and measuring devices
see Weights and measures

Meat and meat products
- *Agricultural Statistics, 1983,* annual rpt, 1004–1
- Agriculture census, 1982: farms, farmland, production and costs, and operator characteristics, preliminary State and county rpt series, 2330–1
- Agriculture census, 1982: farms, farmland, production, finances, and operator characteristics, by county, final State rpt series, 2331–1
- Beef labeling by grade at supermarkets, and consumer demand for lean pork, 1967-83, article, 1541–7.403
- Business statistics, detailed data for major industries and economic indicators, *Survey of Current Business,* monthly rpt, 2702–1.11
- Census of Population, 1980: detailed socioeconomic and demographic characteristics, by age, sex, race, Hispanic origin, occupation, and industry, State rpt series, 2531–4
- Central America beef exports to US, by country, 1973-82, hearings, 21248–80
- China economic conditions, agricultural and industrial production, trade, and domestic and foreign investment, 1980-85, 2048–106
- China exports and imports by SITC 1- to 5-digit commodity, 1970s-82, annual rpt, 244–12
- Cold storage food stocks by commodity and census div, and warehouse cold storage space in use, by State, monthly rpt, 1631–5
- Cold storage food stocks of 77 commodities, by region, 1983, annual rpt, 1631–11
- Communist, OECD, and selected other countries agricultural production, by commodity, 1960s-83, annual rpt, 244–5.9
- Consumption of food and nutrient intake by individuals, by food group, source, and socioeconomic characteristics, 1977-78 natl survey, final rpt series, 1356–4
- Consumption of meat and poultry, impact of hypothetical consumer demand changes in price structure and industry performance, model, 1982-91, article, 1502–3.402
- Consumption, supply, trade, prices, expenditures, and indexes, by food commodity, 1963-83, annual rpt, 1544–4
- County Business Patterns: establishments, employees, and payrolls, by SIC 4-digit industry and county, 1981, annual State rpt series, 2326–8
- County Business Patterns: establishments, employees, and payrolls, by SIC 4-digit industry and county, 1982, annual State rpt series, 2326–6
- CPI by detailed component, for US city average, 28 SMSAs, and 4 regions by population size, monthly rpt, 6762–2
- Cuba economic conditions, agricultural and industrial production and distribution, trade, and intl economic relations, 1970-82 and trends from 1957, 248–40
- Eastern Europe agricultural production and trade by commodity, food consumption, and farm inputs, for 6 countries, 1960-80 with projections to 1991, 1528–178
- Eastern Europe meat consumption, and meat exports to US, for 4 countries, selected years 1960-82, 1128–27
- EC food supply/demand and market and support prices, with exchange rates, fertilizer price index, GDP, and population, by country, 1960-83, 1528–173
- Employment, earnings, and hours, by selected SIC 1- to 4-digit industry, State, and for 278 major labor areas, 1939-83, annual rpt, 6744–5
- Employment, earnings, and hours, by SIC 4-digit nonfarm industry, monthly 1974-Feb 1984, annual update, 6744–4
- Exports and imports of dairy, livestock, and poultry live animals, meat, and products, by commodity and country of destination, FAS quarterly rpt, 1925–32
- Exports and imports of US, by agricultural commodity and country, bimonthly rpt with articles, 1522–1
- Exports and imports of US, by detailed agricultural commodity and country, FY83 and CY83, semiannual rpts, 1522–4
- Exports and imports of US, by detailed agricultural commodity for 8 major commodity groups, monthly rpt, 1922–8
- Exports and imports of US, detailed SIC-based commodities by world area, 1983, annual rpts, 2424–6
- Exports and imports of US, totals and as percent of domestic production, by SIC 2- to 5-digit commodity, 1981, annual rpt, 2424–3
- Exports of manufactured and agricultural commodities, manufacturing production, and export-related employment, 1960s-82, State rpt series, 2046–3
- Exports of US, detailed commodities by country of destination, monthly rpt, 2422–3
- Exports of US, detailed Schedule B commodities by country of destination, 1983, annual rpt, 2424–9
- Exports of US, detailed Schedule E commodities by mode of transport and world area and country of destination, 1983, annual rpts, 2424–5
- Exports under PL 480 concessional sales program, by commodity and country, 1955-83, semiannual rpt, 1922–6
- Fed Govt cost control through ground meat soy-extenders in feeding programs, proposed 3-year savings, and background data, FY70s-83, 16908–1.23

Index by Subjects and Names

- Food consumer research and marketing devs, and consumption and price trends, quarterly rpt with articles, 1541–7
- Foreign agricultural production, prices, and trade, by country, 1983 and outlook for 1984/85, annual world region rpt series, 1524–4
- Foreign and US agricultural production, prices, trade, and consumption, quarterly rpt with articles, 1522–3
- Foreign and US agricultural production, trade, and climatic devs, weekly press release, 1922·4
- Foreign and US agricultural supply/demand, consumption per capita, and trade, by world area and country group, 1960s-82, 1528–181
- Foreign and US feed and livestock trade by product and world region, and ocean freight rates between selected countries of origin and destination, selected years 1960-82, 1528–177
- Foreign and US livestock, poultry, and products production, consumption, and trade, FAS semiannual circular, 1925–33
- Foreign meat plants inspected and certified for exporting products to US, 1983, annual listing, 1374–2
- Futures trading by commodity and exchange, and Commodity Futures Trading Commission activities, funding, and employment, FY83, annual rpt, 11924–2
- Great Lakes trade, by SITC 3-digit commodity, port, vessel type, world area, and country, 1982, annual rpt, 7744–3
- Hog production, producer characteristics, facilities, and marketing, by type and size of enterprise and region, 1975 and 1980, 1568–248
- Imports of meat subject to Meat Import Law, by country of origin, FAS monthly circular, 1925–31
- Imports of US, detailed Schedule A commodities by country and world area of origin, and mode of transport, 1983, annual rpts, 2424–2
- Imports of US, detailed Schedule A commodities by country, monthly rpt, 2422–2
- Imports of US, detailed TSUSA commodities by country of origin, 1983, annual rpt, 2424–4
- Income tax returns of corporations, detailed income and tax items by industry, 1981, annual rpt, 8304–4
- Income tax returns of sole proprietorships, detailed data by industry div and selected industry group, 1981, annual rpt, 8304–7
- Income tax returns of sole proprietorships, receipts, deductions by type, payroll, and net income, by major industry, 1982, annual article, 8302–2.413
- Industry finances and operations, by SIC 2- to 4-digit industry, 1970s-83 and projected to 1988, annual rpt, 2014–4
- Input-output structure of US economy, detailed interindustry transactions for 537 industries, and components of final demand, 1977 benchmark data, 2708–17
- Inspection of meat and poultry by Food Safety and Inspection Service, FY83, annual rpt, 1374–3
- Inspection of meat and poultry, Federal aid to State and local programs by agency and State, FY83, annual rpt, 2464–2

Index by Subjects and Names

Medicaid

Inspection of meat and poultry, Federal, State, and foreign govts activities and personnel, FY83, annual rpt, 1374–1

Lamb meat from New Zealand, injury to US industry from foreign subsidized products and sales at less than fair value, investigation with selected financial and operating data, 1984 rpt, 9886–19.10

Manufacturing census, 1982: financial and operating data, by SIC 2- to 4-digit industry, State, SMSA, and county, preliminary census div rpt series, 2491–3

Manufacturing census, 1982: financial and operating data, for SIC 4-digit industries by product, preliminary rpt, 2491–1.1

Market news summary statistics for livestock, meat, and wool, by animal type and market, weekly rpt, 1315–1

Marketing and distribution of meat, establishments, sales, and per capita consumption, 1950s-82 with trends from 1929, 1548–232

Minority group and women employment, by occupational group and SIC 2- to 3-digit industry, 1981, annual rpt, 9244–1.1

Occupational injury and illness rates, by SIC 2- to 4-digit industry, 1982, annual rpt, 6844–1

Occupational Outlook Handbook, 1984-85 biennial rpt, 6744–1

OECD trade, total and for 4 major countries, and US trade by country, by commodity, 1972-82, annual world region rpt series, 244–13

Pork and hogs from Canada, effect on US industry, investigation with background financial and operating data, 1984 rpt, 9886–4.80

Prices (farm-retail) for foods, marketing cost components, and industry finances and productivity, selected years 1967-83, annual rpt, 1544–9

Producer prices and indexes, by stage of processing and detailed commodity, monthly rpt, 6762–6

Producer prices and indexes, by stage of processing and detailed commodity, monthly 1983, annual supplement, 6764–2

Production and supply/demand data, for US livestock and dairy products, and for selected US and world crops, periodic rpt, 1522–5

Production itemized costs, receipts, and net returns, for 13 crops, 4 livestock types, and milk, by region, 1981-83, annual rpt, 1544–20

Production, marketing, slaughter, prices, and producers gross income, for meat animals by animal type and State, 1982-83, annual rpt, 1623–8

Production of meat and lard, by State, 1983, annual rpt, 1623–10

Production of meat and livestock slaughter, by livestock type and State, monthly rpt, 1623–9

Production, prices, and trade of livestock and meat, 1983, annual rpt, 1564–6

Production, prices, trade, and marketing, by commodity, current situation and forecast, monthly rpt, 1502–4

Production, prices, trade, stocks, and consumption, periodic situation rpt, 1561–7

Productivity, hours, and employment indexes for selected SIC 3- and 4-digit industries, 1954-82, annual rpt, 6824–1.3

Productivity trends and technological innovations in the meatpacking and prepared meats industry, 1967-82, article, 6722–1.428

Sausage potential use of fish, with fish supply, cost effectiveness, and nutritional value, various periods 1977-82, article, 2162–1.401

Underground economy, household expenditures and participation by type of goods or service and sociodemographic characteristics, with methodology and bibl, 1981 survey, 8308–27

USDA agricultural surplus direct purchase program finances, and purchases and food received by schools by commodity, various periods 1936-83, 1548–243

Waterborne commerce of US (domestic and foreign), freight by commodity, traffic, and passengers, by port and waterway, 1982, annual rpt, 3754–3

Wholesale trade census, 1982: employment, establishments, sales by commodity, and payroll, by SIC 4-digit kind of business and State, preliminary rpt, 2403–1.31

see also Food and waterborne diseases

see also Oils, oilseeds, and fats

see also under By Commodity in the "Index by Categories"

Medals

see Awards, medals, and prizes

see Military awards, decorations, and medals

Medford, Oreg.

Census of Housing, 1980: occupancy and unit characteristics, by race, Hispanic origin, and city, SMSA rpt, 2473–1.237

Census of Population and Housing, 1980: detailed population and housing characteristics, by county, city, and census tract, SMSA rpt, 2551–2.237

see also under By SMSA or MSA in the "Index by Categories"

Media

see Mass media

Medicaid

Abortions funded by Medicaid by justification, and expenditures, by State, FY78-83, annual rpt, 4654–9

AFDC eligibility under Omnibus Budget Reconciliation Act, effect on caseloads and recipient benefits and living costs, 1981-83, GAO rpt, 26131–11

Alabama rural black population, education, employment, health services, and economic status, for 16 counties, selected years 1970-81, 11048–180

Beneficiaries of noncash public and employer-based transfer programs, by income source and socioeconomic characteristics, 1982, final Current Population Rpt, 2546–6.37

Benefits and beneficiaries, by type of service and payment, basis for eligibility, and recipient age, sex, and race, annual rpt, discontinued, 4657–10

Benefits and beneficiary characteristics of OASDHI, Medicaid, SSI, and other social insurance and public welfare programs, selected years 1937-82, annual rpt, 4744–3.8

Births (cesarean and total) in hospitals affiliated and not affiliated with medical schools, by characteristics of mother, birth, and hospital, 1977, 4186–6.4

Budget of US Appendix, detailed budgets and personnel summaries, by agency, FY85, annual rpt, 104–3

Budget of US, CBO analysis and review of FY85 budget by function, annual rpt, 26304–2

Budget of US, CBO analysis of revenue and spending alternatives and projections of economic indicators, FY85-89, annual rpt, 26304–3.3

Budget of US, compact budgets by function, agency, and account, FY85 with projections to FY89, annual rpt, 104–2

Budget of US, effects of Reagan Admin policy changes, by detailed program, FY85, annual rpt, 104–21

Budget of US, receipts by source and outlays by agency and program, monthly rpt, 8102–3

Cost control proposals for Fed Govt programs and mgmt, 3-year savings by function and agency, and financial and operating data, 1960s-81, 16908–1.6, 16908–1.23

Deficit Reduction Act provisions related to Medicare and Medicaid, 1984 narrative article, 4742–1.422

Eligibility, participation, covered services and use, and payments and reimbursements, for Medicare and Medicaid, various periods 1966-82, annual rpt, 4654–1

Fed Govt aid to State and local govts, expenditures, and direct payments, by program, agency, and State, FY83, annual rpt, 2464–2

Fed Govt pension and health spending for older persons, by program and as percents of budget and GNP, 1965-85 with projections to 2040, 25148–28

Fed Govt programs under Ways and Means Committee jurisdiction, program operations and financing data for assessing budgetary requirements, by State, FY70s-83, 21788–117

Fraud in Fed Govt benefit programs and other unreported taxable income from illegal activities, with methodology and bibl, 1970s-82, 8008–112

Health and vital statistics collection, and use in program planning and evaluation, Public Health Conf papers, 1983, biennial rpt, 4164–2

Health care expenditures, natl survey on services use, costs, and sources of payment, by patient and physician characteristics, 1977-78, series, 4186–3

Health Care Financing Admin research activities and grants by research area, as of June 1984, semiannual listing, 4652–8

Health Care Financing Review, Medicare and Medicaid program activity, health care expenditures, and research, quarterly rpt with articles, 4652–1

Health care use and expenditures, methodology and findings of natl survey of households, Medicare records, and Medicaid records in 4 States, 1980, series, 4146–12

Health condition and health care resources, use, and expenditures, 1970s-82 with trends and projections 1900-2000, annual compilation, 4144–11

Health condition and Medicaid coverage and use, by age, metro-nonmetro location, region, and selected SMSA, 1980-81, 4147–10.146

Medicaid

Health maintenance organizations and prepaid health plans enrollment, use, and Fed Govt aid, FY83, annual rpt, 4104–8

- Health maintenance organizations enrollment (total, Medicare, and Medicaid), finances, Fed Govt qualification status, and PHS loan activity, by HMO, FY83, annual rpt, 4044–2
- Health professionals license sanctions in 3 States, and subsequent Medicare and Medicaid program participation, by specialty, 1977-82, GAO rpt, 26121–80
- HHS aid to each State and local govt or private instn, amount obligated, funding agency, and program, FY83, annual listing, 4004–3
- Hispanic Americans socioeconomic and demographic characteristics, and compared to non-Hispanics, selected years 1970-83, chartbook, 2328–48
- Hospital Corp of America capital costs reimbursement from Medicare and Medicaid following acquisition of Hospital Affiliates Intl, 1981-82, GAO rpt, 26121–65
- Income (household) and cash and noncash transfer program participation, by sociodemographic characteristics, quarterly rpt, 2542–2
- Income (taxable) not reported, by illegal source, with characteristics of persons involved, methodology, and bibl, 1970s-82, 8008–112
- Indian and Alaska Native health program activities, and funding for scholarships, care services, and facilities construction, by city, FY82, annual rpt, 4104–11
- Mental health facilities, services, and costs in DC, and effect of St Elizabeths Hospital operations and finances transfer to DC govt, FY83, GAO rpt, 26121–72
- Michigan health funding, Blue Cross-Blue Shield and welfare participation, and unemployment, poverty, and food assistance by county, 1979-83, hearing, 21348–86
- New Mexico health clinics staffed by Natl Health Service Corps, income by source and service, and effect of revised system for Federal payback, 1980-83, hearings, 21368–47
- New York State Medicaid reimbursement of dental costs, evaluation of expedited prior approval process, 1984 article, 4102–1.458
- Northern Mariana Islands public health payments for off-island Medicaid referrals and prenatal, well-baby, and other clinic and home visits, FY83 and trends, annual rpt, 7004–6.2
- Older persons health care expenditures, costs, and insurance, and effects of proposed Medicare cost share increase, selected years 1965-81, 25148–27
- Older persons nutrition services program operations and assessment, and participant sociodemographic, health, and diet characteristics, 1976 and 1982, 4608–16
- Older persons population characteristics, and needs and costs of social services by type, by metro-nonmetro status, 1970s-82 with trends from 1900, 21148–28
- Payment limits of Medicare and Medicaid, effects on physician charges in California, by specialty, 1950s-82, 25368–127

Poverty rate by family composition, and effect of noncash transfers, taxes, unemployment benefits, and business cycles, selected years 1959-82, hearings, 21788–141

- Public noncash transfers counted as income, effects on poverty population size by recipient characteristics, 1979-82, 2626–2.50
- Refugee arrivals in US by world area of origin and State of settlement, and Fed Govt intl and domestic assistance costs, FY85, annual rpt, 7004–16
- Research and statistical projects and techniques, and evaluation of public welfare programs, 1983 conf papers, 4704–11
- Supplementary Security Income beneficiary socioeconomic characteristics and health service use, 1970s-83 and SSI program projections to 1995, 25148–29
- Traffic accidents and casualties detailed direct and indirect costs, by characteristics of persons and vehicles involved, 1979-80, 7768–80
- Veterans aged 55 and over, socioeconomic characteristics, economic resources, health care and status, and actual and expected use of VA benefits, 1983 survey, 9928–29
- Widows with minor children receiving OASI survivor benefits, health insurance coverage and health care services and expenses, 1976-78, article, 4742–1.404

Medical assistance

- AID activities and funding by project and function, FY85, and developing countries summary socioeconomic data, 1970s-83, by country, annual rpt, 9914–3
- Arizona Health Care Cost-Containment System care to medically indigent, persons eligible and per capita costs, for 4 providers, 1982, article, 4652–1.414
- Beneficiaries of noncash public and employer-based transfer programs, by income source and socioeconomic characteristics, 1982, advance Current Population Rpt, 2546–6.38
- Budget of US, receipts by source and outlays by function, FY40-89 estimates revised for consistency with FY85 budget definitions, annual rpt, 104–12
- Budget of US, receipts, outlays, and budget authority, by function and agency, FY84-89 revised estimates, midsession review of FY85 budget, annual rpt, 104–7
- Budget of US, receipts, outlays, and budget authority, by function and agency, 1st revision of FY85 budget, annual rpt, 104–17
- Cost control proposals for Fed Govt programs and mgmt, 3-year savings by function and agency, and financial and operating data, 1960s-81, 16908–1.6, 16908–1.7
- Fed Govt financial and nonfinancial domestic aid, 1984 annual comprehensive catalog, 104–5
- Fed Govt grants-in-aid for 13 program areas, FY82-84, annual article, 10042–1.402
- Govt census, 1982: city govt revenues by source, expenditures by function, debt, and assets, by State and city, 2457–4

Index by Subjects and Names

- Govt census, 1982: county govt revenues by source, expenditures by function, debt, and assets, by State and county, 2457–3
- Govt census, 1982: State govt payments to local govts, by program, source of funds, level of govt, and State, with trends from 1902, 2460–3
- Govt expenditures for public welfare, by level of govt and type of program, selected years FY50-82, 4746–16.1
- Govt expenditures for social welfare by program and level of govt, and private expenditures for health care, selected years FY50-82, annual article, 4742–1.425
- HHS health data projects and systems, by subagency, FY83-84, annual inventory, 4044–3
- Public noncash transfers counted as income, effect on poverty population size by selected recipient characteristics, 1979-83, 2626–2.52
- *Statistical Abstract of US,* social, political, and economic data, 1950s-83 and trends, annual rpt, 2324–1.2
- Wisconsin public welfare programs caseloads, selected vital statistics, and households in poverty, 1970s-83, hearings, 21788–141
- *see also* Medicaid
- *see also* Medicare

Medical centers

- *see* Hospitals
- *see* Military hospitals
- *see* Veterans health facilities and services

Medical costs

- Alcohol use, and health, economic, and social impacts, review of research, 1970s-81, 4488–4
- Allergy and Infectious Diseases Natl Inst activities, grants by instn, State, and country, and disease incidence and costs, FY60s-84, annual rpt, 4474–30
- Arizona hospitals and nursing homes, finances and operations for specified facilities, and itemized expenses for selected cases, 1978-83, hearing, 21148–29
- Bankruptcy (personal), filers by debt type and other characteristics, and impacts in Connecticut and Michigan, various dates 1946-82, hearings, 21528–57
- Bankruptcy (personal), filers by debt type and other characteristics, selected years 1978-81, hearing, 25528–97.1
- Blood pressure screening and hypertension treatment itemized costs at 9 worksites, 1978-80, 4478–148
- Blood program collection, production, and distribution activities, technical services, research, and processing fees, 1982/83, annual rpt, 29254–3
- Consumer Product Safety Commission activities, recalls, and product-related injuries, deaths, and medical costs, by product type and brand, FY83, annual rpt, 9164–2
- CPI by detailed component, for US city average, 28 SMSAs, and 4 regions by population size, monthly rpt, 6762–2
- CPI components relative importance, for selected SMSAs, and US city average by region and population size, 1983, annual rpt, 6884–1

Index by Subjects and Names

Medical education

CPI health care component, since 1940, monthly rpt, 4742–1.8

Crime victim medical expenses and property loss, and median loss by victim characteristics, by offense type, 1975-81, 6066–19.6

Crime victimization rates by type of offense, and victim and offense characteristics, Natl Crime Survey series, 6066–3

Diseases direct and indirect costs, by diagnosis, 1981, annual fact book, 4474–15

DOD Civilian Health and Medical Program of the Uniformed Services costs and operations, FY83-84 with trends from FY79, semiannual rpt, 3502–2

Drugs (prescription) invoice costs to pharmacists, and Medicare maximum allowable costs, by drug class and manufacturer, July/Aug 1983, 4658–6

Economic indicators and labor force characteristics, selected years 1880-1995, chartbook, 6728–30

Fed Govt programs and mgmt cost control proposals, 3-year savings by function and agency, and financial and operating data, 1960s-81, 16908–1

Food stamp recipient households size and composition, income, and income deductions allowed, Aug 1981, annual rpt, 1364–8

Govt expenditures for social welfare by program and level of govt, and private expenditures for health care, selected years FY50-82, annual article, 4742–1.425

Health and vital statistics collection, and use in program planning and evaluation, Public Health Conf papers, 1983, biennial rpt, 4164–2

Health care expenditures, methodology of natl survey of households, physicians, health insurance firms, and employers, 1977-79, series, 4186–4

Health care expenditures, natl survey on services use, costs, and sources of payment, by patient and physician characteristics, 1977-78, series, 4186–3

Health Care Financing Review, Medicare and Medicaid program activity, health care expenditures, and research, quarterly rpt with articles, 4652–1

Health care services use and costs, and Medicare coverage of new medical technologies and reimbursements selected years 1966-82, 26358–106

Health care use and expenditures, methodology and findings of natl survey of households, Medicare records, and Medicaid records in 4 States, 1980, series, 4146–12

Health condition and health care resources, use, and expenditures, 1970s-82 with trends and projections 1900-2000, annual compilation, 4144–11

Health Services Research Natl Center grants and contracts, by program area, FY83, annual listing, 4184–2

Heart, Lung, and Blood Natl Inst activities and funding, with morbidity and mortality data, various periods 1940-88, annual rpt, 4474–22

Hospital costs and use, data compilation project analyses, series, 4186–6

Income tax returns of elderly, by income statement and tax item and income level, 1981 with trends from 1977, article, 8302–2.412

Income tax returns of individuals by tax return item, State, and occupation, and income by source and tax owed, by income level, selected years 1916-80, conf papers, 8308–28.1

Income tax returns of individuals, detailed data, 1982, annual rpt, 8304–2

Income tax returns of individuals, selected income, deduction, and tax credit data by income, preliminary 1982, annual article, 8302–2.402

Israel health care natl expenditures, with comparisons to other budget sectors and expenditures of other countries, 1950s-83, article, 4102–1.446

Mental health facilities of States and counties, inpatients, deaths, staff by occupation, and facilities, by State, 1970s-82, 4506–3.13

Mental health facilities, services, and costs in DC, and effect of St Elizabeths Hospital operations and finances transfer to DC govt, FY83, GAO rpt, 26121–72

Mental health facilities, services, staff, and patient characteristics, 1970s-82 with trends from 1954, annual rpt, 4504–9

Mental health office and clinic visits, average charges, and total expenditures for services, by type of provider and patient characteristics, 1980, 4146–11.5

Military medical services, potential effects of alternative financing proposals on DOD costs, with service use and out-of-pocket medical costs by type of recipient, FY84-89, 26306–6.74

Older persons by demographic, socioeconomic, and health characteristics, selected years 1900-81 and projected to 2050, Current Population Rpt, 2546–2.125

Older persons health care expenditures, costs, and insurance, and effects of proposed Medicare cost share increase, selected years 1965-81, 25148–27

Older persons health care total and out-of-pocket expenditures, by sociodemographic characteristics, poverty and health status, and degree of functional limitation, 1980, 4146–11.4

Older persons long-term health care and financing alternatives, including nursing home insurance and use of home equity, 1984 conf papers, 4658–7

Older persons physician visits by age group, projected 1980-2050, and health care expenditures by type, 1981, annual rpt, 25144–3.1

Personal consumption expenditures, natl income and product account, *Survey of Current Business,* monthly rpt, monthly and annual tables, 2702–1.23

Research activities and grants of HCFA by research area, as of June 1984, semiannual listing, 4652–8

Research methods and design of health surveys, 1982 biennial conf proceedings, 4184–1

Robbery rates and circumstances, medical costs and property losses of victims, and offender and victim characteristics, 1960s-81, 6068–180

Supplementary Security Income beneficiary socioeconomic characteristics and health service use, 1970s-83 and SSI program projections to 1995, 25148–29

Tax expenditures, Fed Govt revenues foregone through income tax deductions and exclusions by type, and effect of Deficit Reduction Act, FY84-89, annual rpt, 21784–10

Traffic accidents and casualties detailed direct and indirect costs, by characteristics of persons and vehicles involved, 1979-80, 7768–80

TTPI and American Samoa off-island medical referrals, costs, and potential savings, by govt, FY83 and comparisons from FY78, GAO rpt, 26123–72

VA expenditures for medical benefits programs and operating costs, FY59-83, annual rpt, 9924–13.1

VA medical care costs, and amount recovered through billings, by facility, 1982, GAO rpt, 26121–66

VA medical facilities sharing agreement contracts, services, and costs, by region and facility, FY83, annual rpt, 9924–18

Veterans aged 55 and over, socioeconomic characteristics, economic resources, health care and status, and actual and expected use of VA benefits, 1983 survey, 9928–29

Veterans inpatient care in VA hospitals by diagnosis, facilities operating costs, and other VA activities, FY83, annual rpt, 9924–1.3

Veterans medical care costs, patients, and capacity of VA and non-VA facilties, by service type and patient age, 1970s-83 and projected to 2030, 26306–6.78

Widows with minor children receiving OASI survivor benefits, health insurance coverage and health care services and expenses, 1976-78, article, 4742–1.404

Workers compensation benefits under State programs, by benefit type, insurance source, and State, and Fed Govt black lung program payments, 1980-82, article, 4742–1.424

Workers compensation coverage by State, benefits, degree of disability, employer costs, and insurance industry finances, 1939-80, article, 4742–1.414

see also Health insurance

see also Medicaid

see also Medical assistance

see also Medicare

Medical education

Births (cesarean and total) in hospitals affiliated and not affiliated with medical schools, by characteristics of mother, birth, and hospital, 1977, 4186–6.4

Black medical residents by specialty, and minority medical faculty by race and Hispanic origin, selected years 1980-83, article, 4102–1.412

Census of Population, 1980: labor force, by sex, detailed occupation, and region, with comparison to 1970 census, supplementary rpt, 2535–1.12

Computer specialists sociodemographic, educational, and employment characteristics, and Fed Govt support by agency, 1978, biennial Current Population Rpt, 2546–2.124

Medical education

Degrees conferred in higher education, by race, Hispanic origin, sex, level, and field, selected years 1949/50-1979/80, annual rpt, 4824–2.16

DOD medical personnel, trainees, and accessions by source, by occupation, specialty, and service branch, FY83, annual rpt, 3544–24

Enrollment in grad science and engineering, fields of study, financial support, and other student and instn characteristics, 1975-82, annual survey, 9627–7

Health condition and health care resources, use, and expenditures, 1970s-82 with trends and projections 1900-2000, annual compilation, 4144–11

Health professionals supply and education, by occupation, demographic and professional characteristics, and location, 1950s-83 and projected to 2000, biennial rpt, 4114–8

Indian and Alaska Native health program activities, and funding for scholarships, care services, and facilities construction, by city, FY82, annual rpt, 4104–11

Labs (public health) of States, pay scales and job requirements by occupation and State, FY81-83, annual rpt, 4204–7

Mental health workers, nursing and social work degrees, psychologists by degree level, and psychiatry residencies, 1950s-81, annual rpt, 4504–9.4

Minority group and women employment and training in health professions, by field, selected years 1962/63-1983/84, 4118–18

Nursing continuing education in maternal and child health at University of Kentucky, course enrollment and student assessment of career value, 1983 article, 4102–1.405

Pharmacists employment and sociodemographic characteristics, and reasons for not working in field, by State and overseas, as of 1979, 4147–14.28

Radiation protection and health physics enrollments and degrees granted by State and instn, and grads employment, 1983, annual rpt, 3004–7

Scientists and engineers employed at universities and colleges, by field, sex, State, and instn, Jan 1983 and selected trends from 1967, annual survey, 9627–11

TTPI socioeconomic, health, and govtl data, by TTPI govt, FY83 and selected trends, detailed annual rpt, 7004–6

VA facilities psychological services, staffing, research, and training programs, 1984 annual listing, 9924–10

VA Medicine and Surgery Dept trainees, by detailed program and city, FY83, annual rpt, 9924–21

see also Federal aid to medical education
see also Foreign medical graduates
see also Medical research
see also Regional medical programs

Medical equipment

see Medical supplies and equipment

Medical ethics

License sanctions of health professionals in 3 States, and subsequent Medicare and Medicaid program participation, by specialty, 1977-82, GAO rpt, 26121–80

Medical examinations and tests

Army personnel health status, and use of Army medical services in US and abroad by personnel, retirees, and dependents, monthly rpt, 3702–4.1

Births and birth rates, by parent and birth characteristics and infant condition at birth, 1982 and trends from 1940, US Vital Statistics annual advance rpt, 4146–5.79

Births by outcome, and mother's sociodemographic, life style, and maternity characteristics, 1980, article, 4102–1.421, 4102–1.424

Cancer (colorectal) screening, family physicians attitudes toward use of guaiac slide test, 1982 New York State survey, article, 4102–1.433

Health condition and health care resources, use, and expenditures, 1970s-82 with trends and projections 1900-2000, annual compilation, 4144–11

Hospital discharges and length of stay, by patient age and sex, facility size and ownership, procedure performed, and region, 1983, 4146–8.101

Hospital discharges and length of stay, by patient characteristics, facility size, procedure performed, diagnosis, and region, 1982, annual rpt, 4147–13.78

Infants condition at birth, by race, 1981, US Vital Statistics advance rpt, 4146–5.73

Internist office visits and drugs provided, by characteristics of visit, patient, and physician, and location, 1980-81, 4147–13.80

Laboratory tests ordered by physicians, number and costs related to health insurance type, coverage, and reimbursement, 1975-76, article, 4652–1.415

Medicare and Medicaid eligibility, participation, covered services and use, and reimbursements and payments, various periods 1966-82, annual rpt, 4654–1

Medicare coverage of new medical technologies and reimbursements, and health services use and costs, selected years 1966-82, 26358–106

Medicare fee assignments, physician acceptance rates for selected services related to professional characteristics, FY76-78, article, 4652–1.416

Medicare Supplementary Medical Insurance maximum charges reimbursable for specific services, by State and outlying area, 1983, annual rpt, 4654–4

Motor carrier safety inspections by Fed Hwy Admin, audits of driver qualification and vehicle operation records, and violations cited, 1982, annual rpt, 7554–38.1

Navy personnel alcohol and drug abuse, and related deaths, courts-martial, discharges, and treatment program funding and staff, FY83, annual table, 3804–12

Neonatal screenings for treatable metabolic disorders, and States with programs, 1984 article, 4102–1.425

Obstetrician-gynecologist office visits and drugs used, by visit reason, diagnosis, treatment, and patient and physician characteristics, 1980-81, 4147–13.76

Index by Subjects and Names

Physicians (not office-based) visits by reason, diagnosis, treatment, patient and physician characteristics, and physician primary activity, 1980, 4147–13.77

South Carolina manufacturing plants with selected employee health care services, by SIC 2-digit industry, 1982, article, 4102–1.408

Surgeon office visits and drugs provided, by characteristics of visit, patient, and physician, and location, 1980-81, 4147–13.79

Tuberculosis cases, deaths, and treatment, by demographic characteristics, State, and city, 1982 and trends from 1953, annual rpt, 4204–2

Veterans aged 55 and over, socioeconomic characteristics, economic resources, health care and status, and actual and expected use of VA benefits, 1983 survey, 9928–29

Youth office visits to physicians by patient and visit characteristics and physician specialty, and drug mentions by brand, 1980-81, 4146–8.100

see also Autopsies

see also X-rays

Medical facilities and services

see Health facilities and services

Medical instruments

see Medical supplies and equipment

Medical insurance

see Blue Cross-Blue Shield

see Health insurance

see Health maintenance organizations

Medical libraries

NIH grants and awards for R&D, training, construction, and medical libraries, by location and recipient, FY83, annual listings, 4434–7

NIH Library of Medicine activities, holdings, and grants, FY81-83, annual rpt, 4464–1

Medical personnel

see Health occupations

Medical research

Acquired immune deficiency syndrome (AIDS) cases, and research funding and activities, monthly rpt, 4042–2

Acquired immune deficiency syndrome (AIDS) research expenditures in 3 areas, by NIH inst, FY82, 4102–1.404

Alcoholism research, treatment programs, and patient characteristics, quarterly journal, 4482–1

Allergy and Infectious Diseases Natl Inst activities, grants by instn, State, and country, and disease incidence and costs, FY60s-84, annual rpt, 4474–30

Animals used in research, by State, FY83, annual rpt, 1394–10

Aviation medicine research and studies, FAA technical rpt series, 7506–10

Cancer Natl Inst contracts and grants, by contractor, instn, State, and city, FY83, annual listing, 4474–28

Cancer Natl Inst epidemiology and biometry activities, staff, budget, and contract awards by project and recipient instn, FY83, annual rpt, 4474–29

Cancer Natl Inst programs, organization, and budget, FY83, with cancer deaths by body site, 1980 and 1983, annual fact book, 4474–13

Index by Subjects and Names

Medical supplies and equipment

Cocaine use, user characteristics, medical and botanical research, and South American production and legal policy and enforcement, 1979 intl conf papers, 7008–40

Dental Research Natl Inst research and training funds awarded, by recipient instn, FY83, annual listing, 4474–19

Diabetes programs and expenditures of Fed Govt, by agency and NIH inst, FY84, annual rpt, 4434–8

Digestive Diseases Interagency Coordinating Committee activities, and related Federal research and funding, by agency, FY79-83, annual rpt, 4434–13

DOD medical personnel, trainees, and accessions by source, by occupation, specialty, and service branch, FY83, annual rpt, 3544–24

Drug abuse and treatment research, highlights of studies by Natl Inst on Drug Abuse grant recipients, periodic rpt, 4492–4

Drugs nonmedical use and effects, research compilations and summaries, bibls, and survey instruments, series, 4496–1

Environmental pollution-related disease research activities and publications, Sept 1982-Aug 1983, annual rpt, 9184–9

Expenditures for R&D by higher education instns and federally funded centers, by field, source of funds, instn, and State, FY82, annual rpt, 9627–13

Expenditures for R&D by source, and scientists education and employment, detailed data by field, selected years 1953-84, annual rpt, 9624–18

Fed Govt procurement contract awards, by State, agency, procurement and contractor type, and for top 100 contractors, quarterly rpt, 102–6

Fed Govt R&D funding for all performers, by field and supporting agency, selected years FY60-84, annual rpt, 9627–20

General Medical Sciences Natl Inst research programs and funding, FY83, annual rpt, 4474–12

Govt expenditures for social welfare by program and level of govt, and private expenditures for health care, selected years FY50-82, annual article, 4742–1.425

Health and population research funded by 4 private organizations, project listing by topic, with funding data, 1981, annual rpt, 4474–16

Health care expenditures, growth factors, medical equipment and drugs trade, and physician income, 1950-90, article, 4652–1.407

Health care expenditures, natl and personal total and per capita amounts, by type of service and source of funds, 1983 and trends from 1929, annual article, 4652–1.429

Health condition and health care resources, use, and expenditures, 1970s-82 with trends and projections 1900-2000, annual compilation, 4144–11

Health Services Research Natl Center grants and contracts, by program area, FY83, annual listing, 4184–2

Heart attack and cancer incidence and deaths in men aged 35-59, effects of lowering blood cholesterol levels, with background data on other risk factors, 1973-83, 4478–145

Heart, Lung, and Blood Natl Inst activities and funding, with morbidity and mortality data, various periods 1940-88, annual rpt, 4474–22

Heart, Lung, and Blood Natl Inst, Advisory Council recommended programs and budget, FY85-89, annual rpt, 4474–11

Heart, Lung, and Blood Natl Inst organization, disease and mortality data, and funds and recipients, FY83 with trends from 1900, annual fact book, 4474–15

HHS aid to each State and local govt or private instn, amount obligated, funding agency, and program, FY83, annual listing, 4004–3

HHS health data projects and systems, by subagency, FY83-84, annual inventory, 4044–3

Higher education instns R&D expenditures, and science and engineering employment and grad students, by field, 1972-83, biennial rpt, 9627–24

Howard University salaries, academic standing, medical research, and library operations, and finances of Howard Inn, selected years 1976-83, GAO rpt, 26121–74

Industry R&D funding and employment of scientists and engineers, by industry group, firm size, and funding source, 1956-82, annual rpt, 9627–21

Manpower supply and education of health professionals, by occupation, demographic and professional characteristics, and location, 1950s-83 and projected to 2000, biennial rpt, 4114–8

Mothers and Children Research Center activities and funding, as of June 1983, annual rpt, 4474–31

NIH activities, staff, funding, and facilities, historical data, 1984 annual rpt, 4434–1

NIH extramural grant and contract awards for research, R&D, and construction, FY72-83, annual rpt, 4434–9

NIH grants and awards for R&D, training, construction, and medical libraries, by location and recipient, FY83, annual listings, 4434–7

NIH intl program activities and funding, by inst and country, FY83, annual rpt, 4474–6

NIH newly announced grants and awards, quarterly listing, 4432–1

NIH publications, 1983, annual listing, 4434–2

NIH Research Resources Div activities, accomplishments, and funding, by program, FY83, annual rpt, 4434–12

Nuclear industry nongovt employment by industry segment, occupation, and census div, and DOE and NRC nuclear employment, 1968-83, biennial rpt, 3004–11.1

Physicians (not office-based) visits by reason, diagnosis, treatment, patient and physician characteristics, and physician primary activity, 1980, 4147–13.77

Public Health Service activities, and funding by function and subagency, FY83, annual rpt, 4044–2

R&D Fed Govt facilities and services available for private sector use, by field of science, 1984 biennial listing, 2224–4

Red Cross blood program collection, production, distribution activities, technical services, research, and processing fees, 1982/83, annual rpt, 29254–3

Research methods and design of health surveys, 1982 biennial conf proceedings, 4184–1

Scientists and engineers employed at universities and colleges, by field, sex, State, and instn, Jan 1983 and selected trends from 1967, annual survey, 9627–11

Smoking and health research, article abstracts and indexes, 1983, annual rpt, 4044–8

Smoking and health research publications, bimonthly listing, 4042–1

Smoking related to chronic obstructive lung disease and deaths, by sociodemographic and smoking characteristics, literature review, 1984 annual Surgeon General rpt, 4044–6

Soviet Union-US science and technology exchange projects, man-hours, and funding, by Fed Govt agency and activity type, FY81-82, 7008–41

VA facilities psychological services, staffing, research, and training programs, 1984 annual listing, 9924–10

VA Medicine and Surgery Dept employment, by medical district and facility, monthly rpt, quarterly data, 9922–5.3

Veterans (Vietnam) health condition, methodology for 3 CDC studies on effects of military service and Agent Orange exposure, Nov 1983 rpt, 4208–22

see also Genetics

see also Laboratories

see also Regional medical programs

Medical Services Administration

see Health Care Financing Administration

Medical supplies and equipment

Contact lens price and adverse lens-associated eye conditions related to fitting by ophthalomologists, opticians, and optometrists, 1977-80, 9408–49

County Business Patterns: establishments, employees, and payrolls, by SIC 4-digit industry and county, 1981, annual State rpt series, 2326–8

County Business Patterns: establishments, employees, and payrolls, by SIC 4-digit industry and county, 1982, annual State rpt series, 2326–6

DOD procurement, prime contract awards by category, contract and contractor type, and service branch, FY74-1st half FY84, semiannual rpt, 3542–1

Employment, earnings, and hours, by selected SIC 1- to 4-digit industry, State, and for 278 major labor areas, 1939-83, annual rpt, 6744–5

Employment, earnings, and hours, by SIC 4-digit nonfarm industry, monthly 1974-Feb 1984, annual update, 6744–4

Exports and imports of US, detailed SIC-based commodities by world area, 1983, annual rpts, 2424–6

Exports and imports of US, totals and as percent of domestic production, by SIC 2- to 5-digit commodity, 1981, annual rpt, 2424–3

Medical supplies and equipment

Exports of US, detailed commodities by country of destination, monthly rpt, 2422–3

Exports of US, detailed Schedule B commodities by country of destination, 1983, annual rpt, 2424–9

Exports of US, detailed Schedule E commodities by mode of transport and world area and country of destination, 1983, annual rpts, 2424–5

FDA investigation and regulatory activities, quarterly rpt, 4062–3

Fed Govt programs and mgmt cost control proposals, 3-year savings by function and agency, and financial and operating data, 1960s-81, 16908–1.24

Foreign market and trade for medical and health care equipment, and user industry operations and demand, country market research rpts, 2045–2

Franchise business opportunities, by firm and kind of business, 1984 annual listing, 2044–27

Genetically abnormal human cell cultures available to researchers, and cultures shipped, 1984 annual listing, 4474–23

Great Lakes trade, by SITC 3-digit commodity, port, vessel type, world area, and country, 1982, annual rpt, 7744–3

Health care expenditures, growth factors, medical equipment and drugs trade, and physician income, 1950-90, article, 4652–1.407

Health care expenditures, natl and personal total and per capita amounts, by type of service and source of funds, 1983 and trends from 1929, annual article, 4652–1.429

Health condition and health care resources, use, and expenditures, 1970s-82 with trends and projections 1900-2000, annual compilation, 4144–11

Hearing aid performance evaluation, by model and manufacturer, 1984, annual rpt, 9924–5

Imports of US, detailed Schedule A commodities by country and world area of origin, and mode of transport, 1983, annual rpts, 2424–2

Imports of US, detailed Schedule A commodities by country, monthly rpt, 2422–2

Imports of US, detailed TSUSA commodities by country of origin, 1983, annual rpt, 2424–4

Income tax returns of corporations, detailed income and tax items by industry, 1981, annual rpt, 8304–4

Industry finances and operations, by SIC 2- to 4-digit industry, 1970s-83 and projected to 1988, annual rpt, 2014–4

Input-output structure of US economy, detailed interindustry transactions for 85 industries, and components of final demand, 1977, article, 2702–1.421

Input-output structure of US economy, detailed interindustry transactions for 537 industries, and components of final demand, 1977 benchmark data, 2708–17

Lenses (unmounted ophthalmic), trade, tariffs, and industry operating data, foreign and US, 1979-83, TSUSA commodity rpt supplement, 9885–7.57

Manufacturing census, 1982: financial and operating data, by SIC 2- to 4-digit industry, State, SMSA, and county, preliminary census div rpt series, 2491–3

Manufacturing census, 1982: financial and operating data, for SIC 4-digit industries by product, preliminary rpt, 2491–1.418, 2491–1.419, 2491–1.421

Manufacturing census, 1982: financial and operating data, for SIC 4-digit industries by product, preliminary rpt series, 2491–1

Medicare coverage of new medical technologies and reimbursements, and health services use and costs, selected years 1966-82, 26358–106

Medicare kidney end-stage program, reimbursement by treatment, diagnosis, outcome, and patient characteristics, with covered charges for transplants, 1974-79, article, 4652–1.421

Medicare Supplementary Medical Insurance maximum charges reimbursable for specific services, by State and outlying area, 1983, annual rpt, 4654–4

Military reserve forces medical personnel and wartime requirements by occupation, and medical equipment costs, by reserve component, as of 1983, annual rpt, 3544–27.2

Minority group and women employment, by occupational group and SIC 2- to 3-digit industry, 1981, annual rpt, 9244–1.1

NIH extramural grant and contract awards for research, R&D, and construction, FY72-83, annual rpt, 4434–9

Occupational injury and illness rates, by SIC 2- to 4-digit industry, 1982, annual rpt, 6844–1

OECD trade, total and for 4 major countries, and US trade by country, by commodity, 1972-82, annual world region rpt series, 244–13

Older persons health status, health services use and expenditures by type, Medicare enrollment and reimbursement, and private insurance coverage, 1977-84, article, 4652–1.420

Personal stocks of durable goods, by type, in current and constant dollars, 1980-83, annual article, 2702–1.433

Producer prices and indexes, by stage of processing and detailed commodity, monthly rpt, 6762–6

Producer prices and indexes, by stage of processing and detailed commodity, monthly 1983, annual supplement, 6764–2

Retail trade census, 1982: employment, establishments, sales, and payroll, for optical goods stores, by State, preliminary rpt, 2395–1.39

Southeastern States health care resource availability, and employment by occupation, by facility type, by State and SMSA in Fed Reserve 6th District, 1970s-81, article, 9371–1.425

Supplementary Security Income beneficiary socioeconomic characteristics and health service use, 1970s-83 and SSI program projections to 1995, 25148–29

VA medical facilities sharing agreement contracts, services, and costs, by region and facility, FY83, annual rpt, 9924–18

see also Drugs

see also Prosthetics and orthotics

Index by Subjects and Names

Medical technicians

see Allied health personnel

see Clinical laboratory technicians

see Health occupations

Medical transplants

Kidney end-stage disease Medicare certified facilities, by facility type, service type, and region, 1980-83, article, 4652–1.434

Kidney end-stage disease, Medicare dialysis, transplants by facility, donor organ costs, deaths by age, and hospitalization, by region, 1981, annual rpt, 4654–5.2

Kidney end-stage disease Medicare reimbursement by treatment, diagnosis, outcome, and patient characteristics, with covered charges for transplants, 1974-79, article, 4652–1.421

Medicare coverage of new medical technologies and reimbursements, and health services use and costs, selected years 1966-82, 26358–106

Medicare

Actuarial studies, Medicare and OASDI future cost estimates and past experience analyses, series, 4706–1

Advisory Council on Social Security Medicare recommendations, and trust fund and program operations, 1982 quadrennial rpt, 10178–1

Beneficiaries of noncash public and employer-based transfer programs, by income source and socioeconomic characteristics, 1982, advance Current Population Rpt, 2546–6.38

Beneficiaries of noncash public and employer-based transfer programs, by income source and socioeconomic characteristics, 1982, final Current Population Rpt, 2546–6.37

Benefits and beneficiary characteristics of OASDHI, Medicaid, SSI, and other social insurance and public welfare programs, selected years 1937-82, annual rpt, 4744–3.7

Budget of US Appendix, detailed budgets and personnel summaries, by agency, FY85, annual rpt, 104–3

Budget of US, CBO analysis and review of FY85 budget by function, annual rpt, 26304–2

Budget of US, CBO analysis of revenue and spending alternatives and projections of economic indicators, FY85-89, annual rpt, 26304–3.3

Budget of US, compact budgets by function, agency, and account, FY85 with projections to FY89, annual rpt, 104–2

Budget of US, effects of Reagan Admin policy changes, by detailed program, FY85, annual rpt, 104–21

Budget of US, receipts by source and outlays by agency and program, monthly rpt, 8102–3

Claims approved, total changes, and amount reimbursements by type of service, from 1974, monthly rpt, quarterly data, 4742–1.11

Cost control proposals for Fed Govt programs and mgmt, 3-year savings by function and agency, and financial and operating data, 1960s-81, 16908–1.7, 16908–1.23

County and City Data Book, detailed socioeconomic and demographic data for States, counties, and cities, selected years 1976-82, 2328–1

Index by Subjects and Names

Medicine

Deficit Reduction Act provisions related to Medicare and Medicaid, 1984 narrative article, 4742–1.422

Disabled enrollees use of hospital services, charges, and reimbursements, by demographic characteristics, biennial rpt, discontinued, 4657–7

Drugs (prescription) invoice costs to pharmacists, and Medicare maximum allowable costs, by drug class and manufacturer, July/Aug 1983, 4658–6

Eligibility, participation, covered services and use, and payments and reimbursements, for Medicare and Medicaid, various periods 1966-82, annual rpt, 4654–1

Enrollment and reimbursement for Medicare, and use and covered charges by type of service, by State and census div, 1978-82, 4658–8

Fed Govt aid to State and local govts, expenditures, and direct payments, by program, agency, and State, FY83, annual rpt, 2464–2

Fed Govt civilian and military employee pay, withholdings by type, and income, and special military compensation by type and service branch, 1982-83, GAO rpt, 26123–65

Fed Govt pension and health spending for older persons, by program and as percents of budget and GNP, 1965-85 with projections to 2040, 25148–28

Fed Govt programs under Ways and Means Committee jurisdiction, program operations and financing data for assessing budgetary requirements, by State, FY70s-83, 21788–117

Finances of Medicare trust fund, receipts, expenditures, and assets since 1966, monthly rpt, 4742–1.2

Fraud in Fed Govt benefit programs and other unreported taxable income from illegal activities, with methodology and bibl, 1970s-82, 8008–112

Health and vital statistics collection, and use in program planning and evaluation, Public Health Conf papers, 1983, biennial rpt, 4164–2

Health care expenditures, natl survey on services use, costs, and sources of payment, by patient and physician characteristics, 1977-78, series, 4186–3

Health Care Financing Admin research activities and grants by research area, as of June 1984, semiannual listing, 4652–8

Health Care Financing Review, Medicare and Medicaid program activity, health care expenditures, and research, quarterly rpt with articles, 4652–1

Health care use and expenditures, methodology and findings of natl survey of households, Medicare records, and Medicaid records in 4 States, 1980, series, 4146–12

Health condition and health care resources, use, and expenditures, 1970s-82 with trends and projections 1900-2000, annual compilation, 4144–11

Health data projects and systems of HHS, by subagency, FY83-84, annual inventory, 4044–3

Health facilities and services use, covered charges, and reimbursements, by beneficiary type and area of residence, series, 4656–1

Health maintenance organizations and prepaid health plans enrollment, use, and Fed Govt aid, FY83, annual rpt, 4104–8

Health maintenance organizations enrollment (total, Medicare, and Medicaid), finances, Fed Govt qualification status, and PHS loan activity, by HMO, FY83, annual rpt, 4044–2

Health professionals license sanctions in 3 States, and subsequent Medicare and Medicaid program participation, by specialty, 1977-82, GAO rpt, 26121–80

HHS aid to each State and local govt or private instn, amount obligated, funding agency, and program, FY83, annual listing, 4004–3

Hospital Corp of America capital costs reimbursement from Medicare and Medicaid following acquisition of Hospital Affiliates Intl, 1981-82, GAO rpt, 26121–65

Hospital Insurance and Supplementary Medical Insurance trust funds operations and payroll taxes, 1974-2008, annual summary of 1984 trustees rpts, 4654–8

Hospital Insurance Trust Fund financial operations and payroll taxes, FY83 and selected years 1966-2005, annual rpt, 4704–5

Hospitalization (short-stay) for aged and disabled enrollees, and charges and reimbursements, annual rpt, discontinued, 4657–9

Income (household) and cash and noncash transfer program participation, by sociodemographic characteristics, quarterly rpt, 2542–2

Income (personal) by source including transfer payments, and social insurance contributions by type, by region, 1982, 2708–40

Income (taxable) not reported, by illegal source, with characteristics of persons involved, methodology, and bibl, 1970s-82, 8008–112

Indian and Alaska Native health program activities, and funding for scholarships, care services, and facilities construction, by city, FY82, annual rpt, 4104–11

Kidney end-stage disease patients by patient characteristics and country, and per capita spending for treatment, selected years 1973-81, article, 4102–1.450

Medical technologies coverage and reimbursements of Medicare, and health services use and costs, selected years 1966-82, 26358–106

New Mexico health clinics staffed by Natl Health Service Corps, income by source and service, and effect of revised system for Federal payback, 1980-83, hearings, 21368–47

Older persons health care expenditures, costs, and insurance, and effects of proposed Medicare cost share increase, selected years 1965-81, 25148–27

Older persons population characteristics, and needs and costs of social services by type, by metro-nonmetro status, 1970s-82 with trends from 1900, 21148–28

Older persons sociodemographic characteristics, and Fed Govt program participation and funding, 1983 with trends and projections 1900-2060, annual rpt, 25144–3.1

Physician charges and reimbursement by Medicare enrollee characteristics and carrier, payment limits effects on charges in California, and physician earnings, by specialty, 1950s-82, 25368–127

Physician reimbursement rates in Massachusetts, and rates used and physicians not certified in designated specialty by selected carrier, various periods 1981-82, GAO rpt, 26121–82

Program operations and admin efficiency of Medicare, Blue Shield participants, and end-stage renal disease program activities, FY81, annual rpt, 4654–5

Public noncash transfers counted as income, effects on poverty population size by recipient characteristics, 1979-82, 2626–2.50

SSA programs, finances, staff, and litigation, FY83, annual rpt, 4704–6

Supplementary Medical Insurance maximum charges reimbursable for specific services, by State and outlying area, 1983, annual rpt, 4654–4

Supplementary Medical Insurance Trust Fund financial statements, FY83 and selected years 1966-87, annual rpt, 4704–3

Supplementary Medical Insurance Trust Fund receipts, expenditures, assets, and liabilities, monthly rpt, 8102–9.3

Supplementary Security Income beneficiary socioeconomic characteristics and health service use, 1970s-83 and SSI program projections to 1995, 25148–29

Traffic accidents and casualties detailed direct and indirect costs, by characteristics of persons and vehicles involved, 1979-80, 7768–80

Veterans aged 55 and over, socioeconomic characteristics, economic resources, health care and status, and actual and expected use of VA benefits, 1983 survey, 9928–29

see also Old-Age, Survivors, Disability, and Health Insurance

Medicine

Statistical Abstract of US, social, political, and economic data, 1950s-83 and trends, annual rpt, 2324–1.1

see also Aviation medicine

see also Biomedical engineering

see also Chiropractic and naturopathy

see also Dentists and dentistry

see also Diseases and disorders

see also Drugs

see also Federal aid to medical education

see also Federal aid to medicine

see also Health condition

see also Health education

see also Health facilities administration

see also Health facilities and services

see also Health insurance

see also Health maintenance organizations

see also Health occupations

see also Hospitals

see also Medicaid

see also Medical assistance

see also Medical costs

see also Medical education

see also Medical ethics

see also Medical examinations and tests

see also Medical libraries

see also Medical research

Medicine

see also Medical supplies and equipment
see also Medical transplants
see also Medicare
see also Nurses and nursing
see also Nursing homes
see also Optometry
see also Osteopathy
see also Pathology
see also Pediatrics
see also Pharmaceutical industry
see also Pharmacists and pharmacy
see also Physicians
see also Physiology
see also Podiatry
see also Preventive medicine
see also Psychiatry
see also Public health
see also Regional medical programs
see also Space medicine
see also Surgeons and surgery
see also Vaccination and vaccines
see also Veterinary medicine

Medina-Lopez, Fausto

"Constant Market Share Analysis of Latin America's Agricultural Export Growth", 1528–169

Mediterranean Sea

- Cyclones over Sea, weather conditions and sea-surface temperature for selected warm core cyclones, 1982-83, article, 2152–8.401
- Exports and imports of US (waterborne), by type of service, commodity, country, route, and US port, 1982, annual rpt, 7704–2
- Tide height and time daily at worldwide coastal points, 1985 predictions, annual rpt, 2174–2.3
- Weather broadcasts for US ships, by major ocean area, as of Jan 1984, biennial rpt, 2184–3

Meeks, Carol B.

"Housing Quality and Affordability", 1702–1.406

"Housing Quality and Affordability, 1980", 1004–16.1

Mehra, Yash

"Tax Effect, and the Recent Behaviour of the After-Tax Real Rate: Is It Too High?", 9389–1.407

Meiners, Mark R.

"State of the Art in Long-Term Care Insurance", 4658–7

Meinke, Wilmon W.

"Composition, Nutritive Value, and Sensory Attributes of Fish Sticks Prepared from Minced Fish Flesh Fortified with Textured Soy Proteins", 2162–1.401

Meisner, Laurence J.

"Financing Urban Transportation Improvements, Report 2: Use of Private Funds for Highway Improvements", 7556–7.2

Melber, B. D.

"Experience with the Shift Technical Advisor Position: Interviews with Personnel from Nine Plants", 9638–55

Melbourne, Fla.

- Census of Housing, 1980: occupancy and unit characteristics, by race, Hispanic origin, and city, SMSA rpt, 2473–1.238
- Census of Population and Housing, 1980: detailed population and housing characteristics, by county, city, and census tract, SMSA rpt, 2551–2.238

see also under By SMSA or MSA in the "Index by Categories"

Melichar, Emanuel

"Financial Perspective on Agriculture", 9362–1.401

Mellon Foundation

Population and health research funded by 4 private organizations, project listing by topic, with funding data, 1981, annual rpt, 4474–16

Mellon Institute

"Industrial Energy Productivity Project, Final Report", 3308–66

Mellor, Earl F.

"Investigating the Differences in Weekly Earnings of Women and Men", 6722–1.437

Melons

see Fruit and fruit products

Membership organizations

see Associations
see Nonprofit organizations and foundations

Memorials

see Monuments and memorials

Memphis, Ark.

see also under By SMSA or MSA in the "Index by Categories"

Memphis, Tenn.

- Auto dealer repair workers, wages, and benefits, by occupation, size of establishment, and for 24 labor market areas, Nov 1982 survey, 6787–6.202
- Census of Housing, 1980: occupancy and unit characteristics, by race, Hispanic origin, and city, SMSA rpt, 2473–1.239
- Census of Population and Housing, 1980: detailed population and housing characteristics, by county, city, and census tract, SMSA rpt, 2551–2.239
- Economic indicators for Southeastern States and 5 SMSAs, Fed Reserve 8th District, quarterly rpt, 9391–15
- Housing and households detailed characteristics, and unit and neighborhood quality, by inside-outside central cities, 1980 survey, SMSA rpt, 2485–6.4
- Housing vacancy rates for single and multifamily units and mobile homes, by city and ZIP code, 1984, annual metro area rpt, 9304–19.22
- Population size of top 25 cities, 1980 and 1982, press release, 2328–46
- Repair technicians and apprentices wages and benefits, for 5 types of electrical repair shops in 19 SMSAs, Nov 1981 survey, 6787–6.197
- Wages of office and plant workers, by occupation, 1983 SMSA survey rpt, 6785–12.1
- Waterborne commerce of US (domestic and foreign), freight by commodity, traffic, and passengers, by port and waterway, 1982, annual rpt, 3754–3.2
- *see also* under By City and By SMSA or MSA in the "Index by Categories"

Men

- Census of Housing, 1980: inventory, occupancy, and unit characteristics, changes from 1973 by region and inside-outside SMSAs and central cities, series, 2473–3
- Census of Housing, 1980: occupancy and unit characteristics of SMSAs and central cities, by race, Hispanic origin, and city, State and SMSA rpt series, 2473–1

Index by Subjects and Names

- Census of Population, 1980: detailed socioeconomic and demographic characteristics, by age, sex, race, Hispanic origin, occupation, and industry, State rpt series, 2531–4
- Census of Population, 1980: detailed socioeconomic characteristics, by county, city, and inside-outside SMSAs and central cities, State rpt series, 2531–3
- Disability (work-related), incidence among men aged 22-64 related to sociodemographic and employment characteristics and to self-evaluated mental stress, 1972-74, 4746–5.43
- Earnings of families by number of earners, and earnings and employment status of individual family members, quarterly rpt, 6742–19
- Earnings of women and men, analysis of differential, selected years 1967-83, articles, 6722–1.436, 6722–1.438
- Employment-population ratios and unemployment rates, for total and civilian male labor force, by age and race, 1963-82, article, 6722–1.442
- Foreign population size and growth rates, and latest available benchmark demographic data, by country, 1950-83, biennial rpt, 2324–4
- Haiti men at 2 US immigration processing centers, incidence of breast enlargement, Dec 1981-May 1982, article, 4102–1.451
- Health condition and health care resources, use, and expenditures, 1970s-82 with trends and projections 1900-2000, annual compilation, 4144–11
- Income and educational attainment of veterans compared to nonveterans, by age, 1982-83, annual rpt, 9924–19
- Soviet Union industrial and agricultural production by selected commodity, and demographic trends and projections by Republic, 1950s-2000, hearings, 23848–180
- *Statistical Abstract of US,* social, political, and economic data, 1950s-83 and trends, annual rpt, 2324–1.1
- Veterans income and employment status, by age and war or peacetime service, with comparisons to nonveterans, 1981, annual rpt, 9924–23
- *see also* Families and households
- *see also* under By Sex in the "Index by Categories"

Menchik, Mark D.

"Financing Public Physical Infrastructure", 10048–60

Meningitis, aseptic

see Infective and parasitic diseases

Mental health and illness

- Acquired immune deficiency syndrome (AIDS) inpatients at New York Hospital, by mental health and other characteristics, 1981-83, article, 4102–1.426
- Agent Orange exposed Air Force personnel diseases and disorders, by disease type, age, and officer status, 1984 rpt, 3604–3
- Airline pilots terminated for medical reasons and reinstated by carrier, and aircraft accidents by age of flight crew, selected years 1960-81, hearing, 21148–34
- Alcohol, Drug Abuse and Mental Health Admin staff, contract awards, and grants, by Inst, program, and State, FY83, annual factbook, 4044–1

Index by Subjects and Names

Cocaine use, user characteristics, medical and botanical research, and South American production and legal policy and enforcement, 1979 intl conf papers, 7008–40

Criminal (mentally disordered) admissions to instns by legal mcntal status, 1978, and arrest rate for released New York State patients by arrest record, 1975, 6066–20.5

Criminal case disposition, effect of victim injury and other factors, and law enforcement official and victim attitudes, 1983 survey, 6068–185

Deaths and death rates by detailed cause and demographic characteristics, 1979 and selected trends, US Vital Statistics annual rpt, 4144–2.1

Disability (work-related), incidence among men aged 22-64 related to sociodemographic and employment characteristics and to self-evaluated mental stress, 1972-74, 4746–5.43

Disability Insurance beneficiaries sociodemographic and medical characteristics, 1977-79, annual rpt, 4744–20

Drug abuse residential treatment program effectiveness indicators, with data on pre- and post-program characteristics of grads and dropouts, 1970-74 study, 4496–5.18

Economic indicators relation to measures of social pathology including crime and death rates, various periods 1950-80, 23848–76

Head Start Project enrollment of handicapped children, by handicap, State, and for Indian and migrant programs, 1982, annual rpt, 4604–1

Homeless population and characteristics, and temporary shelter operations, use, and user characteristics, by region and selected city, 1983, 5188–108

Homeless population and characteristics, and temporary shelter operations, use, and user characteristics, for selected cities, various periods 1979-84, hearing, 21248–85

Hospital discharges and length of stay, by patient characteristics, facility size, procedure performed, diagnosis, and region, 1982, annual rpt, 4147–13.78

Older persons nutrition services program operations and assessment, and participant sociodemographic, health, and diet characteristics, 1976 and 1982, 4608–16

Patient, facility, services, and staff characteristics, 1970s-82 with trends from 1954, annual rpt, 4504–9

Patients and admissions of State and county mental hospitals, by diagnosis, age, and State, FY80, annual rpt, 4504–2

Research grants, awards, and fellowships of ADAMHA, by recipient, FY82, annual listing, 4044–13

Special education programs for handicapped children, enrollment, staff, and funding, by handicap, age, and State, 1981/82-1982/83, annual rpt, 4944–4

Statistics on mental health, natl reporting program historical overview, 1840-1983, narrative rpt, 4508–5

Treatment of alcohol- and drug abuse-related and other mental health disorders, outpatient visits in Baltimore, Md, and visit probability rates, 1981-82, article, 4102–1.449

Veterans aged 55 and over, socioeconomic characteristics, economic resources, health care and status, and actual and expected use of VA benefits, 1983 survey, 9928–29

Veterans medical care costs, patients, and capacity of VA and non-VA facilties, by service type and patient age, 1970s-83 and projected to 2030, 26306–6.78

Veterans of Vietnam era, compensation cases by degree of impairment, compared with WW II and Korea veterans, FY83, annual rpt, 9924–8.5

Vital and Health Statistics series and other NCHS publications, 1979-83, annual listing,, 4124–1

Vocationally rehabilitated persons under State agency programs, by sociodemographic characteristics and disabling condition, FY79-81, annual rpt, 4944–6

see also Mental health facilities and services *see also* Mental retardation *see also* Neurological disorders *see also* Psychiatry *see also* Psychology *see also* under By Disease in the "Index by Categories"

Mental health facilities and services

Aircraft hijackers committed to mental instns, 1961-82, annual rpt, 7504–31.5

Alcohol, Drug Abuse, and Mental Health Admin research grants, awards, and fellowships by recipient, FY83, annual listing, 4044–13

Alcohol, Drug Abuse and Mental Health Admin staff, contract awards, and grants, by Inst, program, and State, FY83, annual factbook, 4044–1

Budget of US, effects of Reagan Admin policy changes, by detailed program, FY85, annual rpt, 104–21

Census of Population, 1980: detailed socioeconomic and demographic characteristics, by age, sex, race, Hispanic origin, occupation, and industry, State rpt series, 2531–4

Census of Population, 1980: detailed socioeconomic characteristics, by county, city, and inside-outside SMSAs and central cities, State rpt series, 2531–3

Community mental health centers federally funded, staff, expenditures, funding sources, and patient characteristics, annual rpt, suspended, 4504–5

Crime and criminal justice data, including justice expenditures and employment by level of govt, 1970s-82 with some trends from 1875, 6068–174

Criminal (mentally disordered) admissions to instns by legal mental status, 1978, and arrest rate for released New York State patients by arrest record, 1975, 6066–20.5

DC mental health facilities, services, and costs, and effect of St Elizabeths Hospital operations and finances transfer to DC govt, FY83, GAO rpt, 26121–72

DOD Civilian Health and Medical Program of the Uniformed Services costs and operations, FY83-84 with trends from FY79, semiannual rpt, 3502–2

Fed Govt aid to State and local govts, expenditures, and direct payments, by program, agency, and State, FY83, annual rpt, 2464–2

Mental health facilities and services

Govt census, 1982: State govt payments to local govts, by program, source of funds, level of govt, and State, with trends from 1902, 2460–3

Health condition and health care resources, use, and expenditures, 1970s-82 with trends and projections 1900-2000, annual compilation, 4144–11

HHS aid to each State and local govt or private instn, amount obligated, funding agency, and program, FY83, annual listing, 4004–3

Homeless population and characteristics, and temporary shelter operations, use, and user characteristics, for selected cities, various periods 1979-84, hearing, 21248–85

Hospital employment, vacancies, and vacancy rates, by occupation and by hospital specialty, region, census div, and State, 1980, annual rpt, 4114–12

Info systems needs of mental health facilities, and system implementation, uses, and costs, series, 4506–2

Medicare admissions to hospitals and other facilities, and enrollee reimbursement claims, by beneficiary type, 1966-83, annual rpt, 4744–3.7

Medicare and Medicaid eligibility, participation, covered services and use, and reimbursements and payments, various periods 1966-82, annual rpt, 4654–1

Medicare enrollment and bills approved, and reimbursement and Medicaid payments by type of service and beneficiary, quarterly rpt, 4652–1.1

Medicare-participating facilities by control, beds, and terminated facilities, by facility type, region, and State, 1975-81, 4656–1.19

Mental health facilities needs assessment and program evaluation for small areas, methodology, use of census data, analysis, and sample data, series, 4506–8

Mental health facilities, services, staff, and patient characteristics, 1970s-82 with trends from 1954, annual rpt, 4504–9

NIH grants and awards for R&D, training, construction, and medical libraries, by location and recipient, FY83, annual listings, 4434–7

NIMH mental health clinical training funding, by program and field, FY80-83, GAO rpt, 26121–86

Outpatient office and clinic visits, average charges, and total expenditures for services, by type of provider and patient characteristics, 1980, 4146–11.5

Outpatient visits for treatment of alcohol- and drug abuse-related and other mental health disorders in Baltimore, Md, and visit probability rates, 1981-82, article, 4102–1.449

Patient, facility, services, and staff characteristics, *Statistical Notes* series, 4506–3

Patients and admissions of State and county mental hospitals, by diagnosis, age, and State, FY81, annual rpt, 4504–2

State govt alcohol, drug abuse, and mental health treatment funding, and admin of Fed Govt block grants, for 13 States, FY80-84, GAO rpt, 26121–87

Mental health facilities and services

Statistics on mental health, natl reporting program historical overview, 1840-1983, narrative rpt, 4508–5

- VA facilities psychological services, staffing, research, and training programs, 1984 annual listing, 9924–10
- Veterans health care, patients, visits, costs, and operating beds, by district and individual VA and contract facility, monthly rpt, 9922–5

Mental retardation

- Food aid special supplemental program for women, infants, and children, effectiveness and participant characteristics, 1973-82, GAO rpt, 26131–10
- Handicapped children early education research and service project activities and characteristics, and grants to States for program dev, 1983-84, annual listing, 4804–30
- Head Start Project enrollment of handicapped children, by handicap, State, and for Indian and migrant programs, 1982, annual rpt, 4604–1
- HHS aid to each State and local govt or private instn, amount obligated, funding agency, and program, FY83, annual listing, 4004–3
- Medicare and Medicaid eligibility, participation, covered services and use, and reimbursements and payments, various periods 1966-82, annual rpt, 4654–1
- Mental health facilities, services, staff, and patient characteristics, 1970s-82 with trends from 1954, annual rpt, 4504–9
- Patients and admissions of State and county mental hospitals, by diagnosis, age, and State, FY81, annual rpt, 4504–2
- Research methods and design of health surveys, 1982 biennial conf proceedings, 4184–1
- Smoke alarm sound levels by brand, and response time by circumstances and for older and mentally retarded persons, 1983 rpt, 2218–70
- Special education programs for handicapped children, enrollment, staff, and funding, by handicap, age, and State, 1981/82-1982/83, annual rpt, 4944–4
- Statistics on mental health, natl reporting program historical overview, 1840-1983, narrative rpt, 4508–5
- Treatment and services for developmentally disabled, university-affiliated facility activities, funding, and clients, 1980-FY83, 4608–19
- Vocationally rehabilitated persons under State agency programs, by sociodemographic characteristics and disabling condition, FY79-81, annual rpt, 4944–6

Menz, Fredric C.

"Acidification Impact on Fisheries: Substitution and the Valuation of Recreation Resources", 21368–52

Menzie, Elmer L.

"Barriers to Trade in Agricultural Products Between Canada and the U.S.", 1528–175

Mercer, Roger W.

"Experimental Squid Jigging Off the Washington Coast", 2162–1.401

Merchant marine

see Merchant seamen

see Ships and shipping

Merchant seamen

- Budget of US, effects of Reagan Admin policy changes, by detailed program, FY85, annual rpt, 104–21
- Census of Population, 1980: detailed socioeconomic and demographic characteristics, by age, sex, race, Hispanic origin, occupation, and industry, State rpt series, 2531–4
- Employment, by type and ownership of vessel and license status of seaman, monthly rpt, 7702–1
- Employment shipboard, shipyard, and longshore, FY82-83, annual rpt, 7704–14.3
- Fed Govt foreign cargo shipments and costs by agency or program and route, and employment and economic impacts of US vessel preference, 1980, GAO rpt, 26117–30
- Merchant ships in US fleet, shipping costs, construction, employment, military availability, and Fed Govt subsidies, 1970s-1984 and projected to 2000, 26306–6.83

Mercury

see Mercury pollution

see Metals and metal industries

Mercury pollution

- Air pollutant and radiation indoor levels by emissions source, and household exposure and health effects by pollutant type, various periods 1966-83, hearings, 21708–102
- Environmental quality, pollutant discharge by type and source, and EPA protection activities and funding, 1970s-83, biennial regional rpt series, 9184–15
- Great Lakes basin pollutant discharges by source, and control program activities, 1983 annual rpt, 14644–1
- New York Bight pollutant loadings from ocean dumping of municipal wastes by type and source, and concentrations in fish and sediments, 1970s-82, hearings, 21568–36
- Water supply and quality in streams and lakes, and groundwater levels in wells, by drainage basin, 1980, annual State rpt series, 5666–12
- Water supply and quality in streams and lakes, and groundwater levels in wells, by drainage basin, 1981, annual State rpt series, 5666–16
- Water supply and quality in streams and lakes, and groundwater levels in wells, by drainage basin, 1982, annual State rpt series, 5666–20
- Water supply and quality in streams and lakes, and groundwater levels in wells, by drainage basin, 1983, annual State rpt series, 5666–10

Mergers

see Business acquisitions and mergers

Meriden, Conn.

- Census of Housing, 1980: occupancy and unit characteristics, by race, Hispanic origin, and city, SMSA rpt, 2473–1.240
- Census of Population and Housing, 1980: detailed population and housing characteristics, by county, city, and census tract, SMSA rpt, 2551–2.240

Index by Subjects and Names

see also under By SMSA or MSA in the "Index by Categories"

Meridian, Miss.

Wages of office and plant workers, by occupation, 1984 labor market area survey rpt, 6785–3.9

Merit Systems Protection Board

- Appeals decisions on Fed Govt personnel actions, by region, agency, and employee characteristics, FY82, annual rpt, 9494–2
- Budget of US Appendix, detailed budgets and personnel summaries, by agency, FY85, annual rpt, 104–3
- Budget of US, appropriations, outlays, balances, and budget receipts, by govtl branch and agency, FY83, annual rpt, 8104–2
- Office of Personnel Mgmt merit system, implementation and effectiveness, 1982, annual survey, 9494–1

Mertens, H. W.

"Age, Altitude, and Workload Effects on Complex Performance", 7506–10.27

Mertz, Walter

"Importance of Nutrient Data", 1004–16.1

Mesa, Ariz.

see also under By City in the "Index by Categories"

Messick, Samuel

"National Assessment of Educational Progress Reconsidered: A New Design for a New Era", 4898–15

Metabolic and endocrine diseases

- Agent Orange exposed Air Force personnel diseases and disorders, by disease type, age, and officer status, 1984 rpt, 3604–3
- Breast enlargement incidence among Haitian men at 2 US immigration processing centers, Dec 1981-May 1982, article, 4102–1.451
- Deaths and death rates by detailed cause and demographic characteristics, 1979 and selected trends, US Vital Statistics annual rpt, 4144–2.1
- Disability Insurance beneficiaries sociodemographic and medical characteristics, 1977-79, annual rpt, 4744–20
- Hospital discharges and length of stay, by patient characteristics, facility size, procedure performed, diagnosis, and region, 1982, annual rpt, 4147–13.78
- *see also* Diabetes
- *see also* Nutrition and malnutrition
- *see also* under By Disease in the "Index by Categories"

Metals and metal industries

- Air pollutant emission factors, by detailed source, 3rd edition, 1983-84 supplements, 9198–13
- Air pollution abatement equipment shipments by industry, exports, and new and backlog orders, by product, 1983, annual Current Industrial Rpt, 2506–12.5
- Air pollution levels for 5 pollutants, by detailed source, State, and Air Quality Control Region, 1981, annual rpt, 9194–7
- Alaska minerals resources, production, claims on wildlife refuges, oil and gas leases, and exploratory wells, with maps and bibl, 1983, annual rpt, 5664–11
- Business statistics, detailed data for major industries and economic indicators, *Survey of Current Business,* monthly rpt, 2702–1.14

Index by Subjects and Names

Metals and metal industries

Census of Population, 1980: detailed socioeconomic and demographic characteristics, by age, sex, race, Hispanic origin, occupation, and industry, State rpt series, 2531–4

Census of Population, 1980: detailed socioeconomic characteristics, by county, city, and inside-outside SMSAs and central cities, State rpt series, 2531–3

Central America mineral, energy, and water resources, and natural hazards to resource dev, by country, 1981 with trends from 1977, 5668–71

China economic conditions, agricultural and industrial production, trade, and domestic and foreign investment, 1980-85, 2048–106

China exports and imports by SITC 1- to 5-digit commodity, 1970s-82, annual rpt, 244–12

Cobalt consumption by end use, and stockpile inventories and quality, selected years 1950-82, hearings, 25208–27

Collective bargaining agreements expiring during year, covered workers by SIC 2-digit industry, firm, and union, with summary of key provisions, 1984, annual rpt, 6784–9

Communist, OECD, and selected other countries minerals and metals production, by commodity, 1960s-83, annual rpt, 244–5.6

Computerized automation in metalworking machinery industry, by plant characteristics, for 6 industry groups and small plants, 1982 surveys, 23848–179

County Business Patterns: establishments, employees, and payrolls, by SIC 4-digit industry and county, 1981, annual State rpt series, 2326–8

County Business Patterns: establishments, employees, and payrolls, by SIC 4-digit industry and county, 1982, annual State rpt series, 2326–6

Cuba economic conditions, agricultural and industrial production and distribution, trade, and intl economic relations, 1970-82 and trends from 1957, 248–40

DOE R&D projects and funding at natl labs, universities, and other instns, FY84, annual summary rpt, 3004–18.3

Earnings by major industry group, and personal income per capita and by source, by region and State, 1929-82, 2708–40

Employment by detailed occupation, for 29 SIC 2-digit nonmanufacturing industries, 1981 BLS survey, 6748–60

Employment, earnings, and hours, by selected SIC 1- to 4-digit industry, State, and for 278 major labor areas, 1939-83, annual rpt, 6744–5

Employment, earnings, and hours, by SIC 4-digit nonfarm industry, monthly 1974-Feb 1984, annual update, 6744–4

Employment, unemployment, hours, and women's employment, for all durables manufacturing and for 5 metals industries, 1979-82, article, 6722–1.410

Energy use and cost for building materials manufacture, by energy source and industry, 1970s-82, article, 2012–1.401

Energy use, prices, and conservation and efficiency measures, by fuel type, end-use sector, selected industry, and region, 1960-83, annual rpt, 3164–73

Environmental quality and protection programs, costs, and Fed Govt enforcement, 1983, detailed annual rpt, 484–1

Exports and imports of metal ores, scrap, and manufactured products, by world area, 1983, annual rpt, 2424–6

Exports and imports of US, by commodity group, world area, selected country, US coastal area and port, and mode of transport, with seasonal adjustments, monthly rpt, 2422–9

Exports and imports of US, totals and as percent of domestic production, by SIC 2- to 5-digit commodity, 1981, annual rpt, 2424–3

Exports, imports, tariffs, and industry operating data for metals and metal products, TSUSA commodity rpt series, 9885–6

Exports of manufactured and agricultural commodities, manufacturing production, and export-related employment, 1960s-82, State rpt series, 2046–3

Exports of US, detailed commodities by country of destination, monthly rpt, 2422–3

Exports of US, detailed Schedule B commodities by country of destination, 1983, annual rpt, 2424–9

Exports of US, detailed Schedule E commodities by mode of transport and world area and country of destination, 1983, annual rpts, 2424–5

Fiber optics displacement of copper in telecommunications, with Bell System use and copper and fiber optics industry data, 1978-88, 2048–104

Finances and operations, by SIC 2- to 4-digit industry, 1970s-83 and projected to 1988, annual rpt, 2014–4

Financial statements for manufacturing, mining, and trade corporations, by selected SIC 2- to 3-digit industry, quarterly rpt, 2502–1

Foreign and US nonfuel minerals supply under alternative market conditions, reserves, and background industry data, series, 5606–4

Foreign direct investment of US, by selected major industry group and world area, 1980-82, annual article, 2702–1.430

Foreign minerals production, reserves, and industry role in domestic economy and world supply, country and world region rpt series, 5606–1

Foundry construction receipts, 1982 Census of Construction Industries, final rpt series, 2373–1

Foundry construction receipts, 1982 Census of Construction Industries, preliminary rpt series, 2371–1

Foundry products imports effect on US industry, investigation with background financial and operating data, 1984 rpt, 9886–4.77

Futures trading by commodity and exchange, and Commodity Futures Trading Commission activities, funding, and employment, FY83, annual rpt, 11924–2

Futures trading in selected commodities, foreign currencies, Treasury securities, and stock indexes, NYC, Chicago, and other markets activity, monthly rpt, 11922–5

Futures trading in selected commodities, Treasury securities, and stock indexes, NYC market activity, monthly rpt, 11922–2

Geological Survey and other publications, 1983, annual listing, 5664–4

Great Lakes trade, by SITC 3-digit commodity, port, vessel type, world area, and country, 1982, annual rpt, 7744–3

Imports of US, detailed Schedule A commodities by country and world area of origin, and mode of transport, 1983, annual rpts, 2424–2

Imports of US, detailed Schedule A commodities by country, monthly rpt, 2422–2

Imports of US, detailed TSUSA commodities by country of origin, 1983, annual rpt, 2424–4

Income tax returns of corporations, detailed income and tax items by industry, 1981, annual rpt, 8304–4

Income tax returns of corporations with foreign tax credit, income and deductions by type, asset size, and selected industry group, 1980, article, 8302–2.415

Income tax returns of partnerships, detailed data by industry, 1981 estimates, annual article, 8302–2.404

Income tax returns of partnerships, receipts by source, deductions by type, and establishments, by selected industry, 1982, annual article, 8302–2.416

Income tax returns of sole proprietorships, detailed data by industry div and selected industry group, 1981, annual rpt, 8304–7

Income tax returns of sole proprietorships, receipts, deductions by type, payroll, and net income, by major industry, 1982, annual article, 8302–2.413

Input-output structure of US economy, detailed interindustry transactions for 537 industries, and components of final demand, 1977 benchmark data, 2708–17

Japan specialty steel and ferroalloy raw material supply/demand, with industry market and manufacturing data, selected years 1970-81, 5608–144

Machinery for metalworking, shipments, unfilled orders, trade, and consumption, quarterly Current Industrial Rpt, 2506–12.12

Manufacturing census, 1982: financial and operating data, by SIC 2- to 4-digit industry, State, SMSA, and county, preliminary census div rpt series, 2491–3

Manufacturing census, 1982: financial and operating data, for SIC 4-digit industries by product, preliminary rpt series, 2491–1

Marine nonfuel minerals demand, by mineral type, selected years 1978-83 with projections to 2000, 15048–4

Mergers of nonfuel minerals companies by SIC 1- to 4-digit industry of acquired and acquiring firm, and asset and earnings measures, various periods 1960-79, 5608–145

Mineral industries census, 1982: financial and operating data, by SIC 2- to 4-digit industry, preliminary summary rpt, 2511–2.1

Mineral industries census, 1982: financial and operating data, including materials consumed, by SIC 4-digit industry and State, preliminary rpt series, 2511–1

Metals and metal industries

Mineral Industry Surveys, commodity reviews of production, trade, and consumption, advance annual rpt series, 5614–5

Mineral Industry Surveys, commodity reviews of production, trade, stocks, and consumption, monthly rpt series, 5612–1

Mineral Industry Surveys, commodity reviews of production, trade, stocks, and consumption, quarterly rpt series, 5612–2

Mineral Industry Surveys, explosives and blasting agents consumption by type, industry, and State, 1983, annual rpt, 5614–22

Mineral Industry Surveys, State reviews of production, 1983, advance annual rpt series, 5614–6

Minerals Yearbook, 1982, Vol 1: commodity reviews of production, reserves, supply, use, and trade, annual rpt, 5604–33

Minerals Yearbook, 1982, Vol 2 preprints: State reviews of production and sales by commodity, and business activity, annual rpt series, 5604–16

Minerals Yearbook, 1982, Vol 2: State reviews of production, sales, and firms, by commodity, and business activity, annual rpt, 5604–34

Minerals Yearbook, 1982, Vol 3: foreign country reviews of production, trade, and policies, by commodity, annual rpt, 5604–35

Minerals Yearbook, 1982, Vol 3 preprints: foreign country reviews of production, trade, and policies, by commodity, annual rpt series, 5604–17

Minerals Yearbook, 1983, Vol 1 preprints: commodity reviews of production, reserves, supply, use, and trade, annual rpt series, 5604–15

Minerals Yearbook, 1983, Vol 3 preprints: foreign country reviews of production, trade, and policies, by commodity, annual rpt series, 5604–23

Minority group and women employment, by occupational group and SIC 2- to 3-digit industry, 1981, annual rpt, 9244–1.1

Occupational health risks from hazardous substances and radiation, by industry, occupation, age, and sex, with bibl and glossary, 1920s-82, 9638–50

Occupational injuries, and employees and hours, of mines, mills, and quarries, by State, quarterly rpt, 6662–1

Occupational injuries and incidence rates at metal mines and related operations, detailed analysis, 1982, annual rpt, 6664–3

Occupational injury and illness rates, by SIC 2- to 4-digit industry, 1982, annual rpt, 6844–1

Occupational manpower needs and supply by detailed occupation, and educational and training program enrollees and grads by detailed field, 1982 and 1995, biennial rpt, 6744–3

OECD trade, total and for 4 major countries, and US trade by country, by commodity, 1972-82, annual world region rpt series, 244–13

Pacific Northwest electricity consumption and prices by end-use sector, and economic and demographic data, 1960s-83 and projected to 2005, annual rpt, 3224–2

Pollution abatement capital and operating costs, by SIC 2- to 4-digit industry, State, and SMSA, 1982, annual Current Industrial Rpt, 2506–3.6

Pollution abatement capital and operating costs under Clean Air and Water Acts, for govts and selected industries, various periods 1970-2000, annual rpt, 9184–11

Pollution abatement expenditures, and effect on economic indicators and industry operations, by major industry, projected under 3 pollution regulation alternatives 1983-95, 9188–84

Prices of nonferrous metals in US, UK, and Canada, by commodity, 1978-81 and monthly 1982, *Minerals Yearbook,* annual rpt, 5604–35.1

Producer prices and indexes, by stage of processing and detailed commodity, monthly rpt, 6762–6

Producer prices and indexes, by stage of processing and detailed commodity, monthly 1983, annual supplement, 6764–2

Production, prices, trade, use, employment, tariffs, and stockpiling, by mineral commodity, with foreign comparisons, 1979-83, annual rpt, 5604–18

Production, shipments, trade, inventories, and unfilled orders, for primary metal products, periodic Current Industrial Rpt series, 2506–10

Productivity, hours, and employment indexes for selected SIC 3- and 4-digit industries, 1954-82, annual rpt, 6824–1.3

R&D expenditures of US firms foreign affiliates, by selected industry, 1974-82, 9626–2.131

R&D industry funding and employment of scientists and engineers, by industry group, firm size, and funding source, 1956-82, annual rpt, 9627–21

Recovery of metal resources through leaching technologies, characteristics of methods and operations, regulation, and research, series, 5606–6

Scientists, engineers, and technicians employed in private industry, by occupation and industry group, 1980-81, biennial rpt, 9627–23

Scientists, engineers, and technicians employment in transportation, utilities, and retail and wholesale trade, by field of science and industry, 1982, 9628–72

Shipments, trade, and inventories of intermediate metal products, periodic Current Industrial Rpt series, 2506–11

Statistical Abstract of US, social, political, and economic data, 1950s-83 and trends, annual rpt, 2324–1.3

Tariff Schedules of US, Annotated, classifications and rates of duty for detailed imported commodities, 1985 edition, 9886–13

Titanium sponge from Japan and UK at less than fair value, imports injury to US industry, investigation with background financial and operating data, 1984 rpt, 9886–14.94, 9886–14.129

Transportation census, 1982: trucks, by detailed characteristics, miles traveled, and type of product carried, State rpt series, 2573–1

Wages and benefits in nonferrous metal manufacturing, by occupation, size of

Index by Subjects and Names

establishment, union status, and metro-nonmetro location, 1981 survey, 6787–6.196

Water pollution fish kills, by State, location, and pollution source, monthly 1978-80, annual rpt, 9204–3

Waterborne commerce of US (domestic and foreign), freight by commodity, traffic, and passengers, by port and waterway, 1982, annual rpt, 3754–3

Wholesale trade sales, inventories, purchases, and gross margins, by SIC 2- to 3-digit kind of business and type of ownership, 1983, annual rpt, 2413–13

see also Abrasive materials
see also Aluminum and aluminum industry
see also Copper and copper industry
see also Gold
see also Hardware
see also Iron and steel industry
see also Lead and lead industry
see also Lead poisoning and pollution
see also Mercury pollution
see also Offshore mineral resources
see also Scrap metals
see also Silver
see also Stockpiling
see also Strategic materials
see also Tin and tin industry
see also Trace metals
see also Uranium
see also Zinc and zinc industry
see also under By Commodity in the "Index by Categories"
see also under By Industry in the "Index by Categories"

Meteorological satellites

Cyclone satellite images for cyclone off California, Nov 1981, article, 2152–8.401

Foreign and US astronautic and aeronautic events, comprehensive chronology, 1976, annual rpt, 9504–2

Foreign and US satellite systems for civil observation, data product revenue, and proposed transfer of Fed Govt system to private sector, selected years 1978-FY84, 2148–47

Glaciology intl research summaries, methodology, and bibls, series, 2156–18

Hurricanes and tropical storms in North Atlantic and Caribbean area, paths, surveillance, deaths, property damage, and landfall probabilities by city, 1983, annual rpt, 2184–7

Hurricanes and tropical storms in northeastern Pacific, paths, surveillance, deaths, and property damage, 1983, annual rpt, 2184–8

Launchings of satellites and other space objects since 1957, quarterly listing, 9502–2

NASA-launched communications and other satellites, and USSR launches by type, 1957-83, annual rpt, 9504–6.1

NASA project launch schedules and technical descriptions, press release series, 9506–2

Natl Weather Service, effects of proposed reorganization and technological improvement on staff and expenditures, FY82 and projected to 2000, 2188–16

Soviet Union and US satellites by mission and vulnerability to attack, and USSR anti-satellite missiles, 1983 and projected to 1989, hearing, 21208–18

Index by Subjects and Names

Methodology

Space and aeronautics programs and budgets of Fed Govt by agency, and foreign programs, 1957-FY85, annual rpt, 9504–9

Typhoons in western North Pacific and North Indian Oceans, paths and other characteristics, by mode of surveillance, 1983, annual rpt, 3804–8

Weather satellite program costs, by function, FY84-85, and satellite launch schedule, FY84-89, annual rpt, 2144–2

Meteorology

Carbon dioxide atmospheric concentration increase effects on hydrologic conditions, projected for 26-35 years, 9188–95

DOE R&D projects and funding at natl labs, universities, and other instns, FY83, annual summary rpt, 3004–18.1

Fed Govt programs and mgmt cost control proposals, 3-year savings by function and agency, and financial and operating data, 1960s-81, 16908–1.3

Fed Govt services and research programs and funding, by agency, FY84-85, annual rpt, 2144–2

Forecast methodology, accuracy, and applications, technical rpt series, 2186–4

Natl Weather Service program and service descriptions, with maps of areas covered, annual rpt, suspended, 2184–1

Natl Weather Service station locations and regular observations made, 1984 annual listing, 2184–5

NOAA scientific and technical publications, monthly listing, 2142–1

Occupational Outlook Handbook, 1984-85 biennial rpt, 6744–1

Oceanographic data, stations and cruises recording data for World Data Center A by country, ship, and type of data, 1983, annual rpt, 2144–15

Precipitation forecast accuracy, by season, forecast period, and region, various periods 1966-82, technical memorandum, 2188–17

Science and engineering doctoral degree recipients, by field, sex, race, age, citizenship, postgrad employment and study status, State, and instn, 1960-82, 9626–6.16

Scientists, engineers, and technicians employed in private industry, by occupation and industry group, 1980-81, biennial rpt, 9627–23

Weather stations of Upper Air Observational Network, by US and foreign location, 1984 annual listing, 2184–6

see also Meteorological satellites

see also Stratosphere

see also Weather

see also Weather control

Methadone treatment

Research on drug abuse and treatment, highlights of studies by Natl Inst on Drug Abuse grant recipients, periodic rpt, 4492–4

Methanol

see Alcohol fuels

Methodology

Agricultural economics technical research, quarterly journal, 1502–3

Air pollution and acid rain environmental effects, and methods of neutralizing acidified water bodies, summary research rpt series, 5506–5

Air pollution monitoring results for atmospheric turbidity by station and season, with description of model predicting urbanization effects, 1960s-76, 9198–106

Auto emissions control device tampering and fuel-switching incidence in 6 urban areas, 1983, annual rpt, 9194–15

Aviation activity forecasts, methodology, data sources, and coverage, Feb 1983 conf papers, annual rpt, 7504–28

Aviation medicine research and studies, FAA technical rpt series, 7506–10

BLS data collection, analysis, and presentation methods, by program, 1984 handbook, 6888–1

Body measurements of women, methodology and summary results, 1983 technical rpt, 7506–10.28

Business Conditions Digest, historical supplement on economic, business, and financial conditions and cyclical fluctuations, with methodology, 1947-82, 2708–31

Carbon dioxide emissions from fossil fuel combustion by fuel type, worldwide estimates based on total and non-oxidized fossil fuel production, 1950-81, 3008–94

Census Bur data collection methodology, programs, and measurement techniques, technical paper series, 2626–2

Census of Population and Housing, 1980: data coverage, availability, and uses for urban and transportation planning, 1984 guide, 7558–101

Coal production and stocks, and electric utility generation, capacity, and coal use, alternative estimates 1977-82, annual rpt, 3164–63

Coal transport environmental impacts by type and mode of transport, methodology for assessing alternative systems, 1983 rpt, 3408–28

Coastal environmental characteristics, fish, wildlife, and use, and population socioeconomic data, for individual areas, series, 5506–4

CPI components relative importance, for selected SMSAs, and US city average by region and population size, 1983, annual rpt, 6884–1

Crime and criminal justice statistics analysis, methodology, and use in courts, 1983 biennial conf proceedings, 6064–20

Current Population Survey methodology and changes since 1959, 1984 narrative article, 6722–1.435

Current Population Survey unemployment duration questions, response consistency, and results, 1984 article, 6722–1.421

DOD budget, manpower and cost estimates, detailed analysis, FY85, annual rpt, 3504–1

DOD weapons systems cost estimates, methodology for rpts to Congress, with illustrative data and bibl, 1970s-83, GAO rpt, 26123–62

Economic time series of Fed Govt, content, design, and methodology, research rpt and conf proceedings series, 2626–7

Educational progress, methodology changes in natl assessment sampling, data collection, and tabulation, 1983, 4898–15

Electric power plant (coal-fired) capacity addition estimation to forecast coal demand, methodology and input data, series, 3166–11

Electric utilities privately owned, common stock performance measures for companies with and without nuclear facilities, 1963-82, 3168–88

Electricity use and savings of households, methodology for assessment using utility billing data, 1984 rpt, 3308–76

Employment Cost Index methodology, occupational definitions, and coverage, quarterly press release, 6782–5

Employment, earnings, and hours, benchmarks for establishment-based time series, by SIC 2- to 4-digit industry, 1976-83, and seasonal adjustment factors, 1984-85, article, 6742–2.409

Energy Info Admin data on residential fuel use and prices, State variations, 1980-81, article, 3162–24.401

Energy Natl Policy Plan, energy supply, demand, and prices, by fuel and sector, projected 1985-2010, biennial rpt, 3004–13

Energy supply/demand and prices, by energy source and end-use sector and for 7 electric utilities, 1981-2000 with trends from 1960s, 3008–93

Energy supply/demand and prices, by fuel type, sector, and end use, detailed trends and projections 1973-95, annual rpt, 3164–75

Energy supply/demand, prices, end use, and related technical and socioeconomic data, including impacts of US policy and intl devs, series, 3006–7

Farm financial data of USDA Farm Production Expenditure Survey, 1980-82, articles, 1544–19

Fed Govt expenditures in States and local areas, Census Bur data collection, limitation, contributing agency costs, and opinions of congressional users, 1984 GAO rpt, 26111–20

Fed Govt standards for data recording, processing, and transfer, and for purchase and use of computer systems, series, 2216–2

Fed Govt statistical policies relating to technical operation of programs, methodology, and use of Federal data, working paper series, 106–4

Finance (intl) and financial policy, and external factors affecting US economy, technical paper series, 9366–7

Financial and economic analysis and forecasting methodology, technical paper series, 9366–6

Financial and economic analysis and forecasting methodology, technical paper series, 9377–9

Financial and economic analysis of banking and nonbanking sectors, technical paper series, 9381–10

Fishing trawlnets, model and computer program for designing tapered nets, 1984 articles, 2162–1.402

Foreign countries population demographic data, methodology, and analyses, research rpt series, 2546–10

Glaciology intl research summaries, methodology, and bibls, series, 2156–18

Health and vital statistics collection, and use in program planning and evaluation, Public Health Conf papers, 1983, biennial rpt, 4164–2

Methodology

Health care expenditures, methodology of natl survey of households, physicians, health insurance firms, and employers, 1977-79, series, 4186-4

Health care use and expenditures, methodology and findings of natl survey of households, Medicare records, and Medicaid records in 4 States, 1980, series, 4146-12

Health condition of Vietnam veterans, methodology for 3 CDC studies on effects of military service and Agent Orange exposure, Nov 1983 rpt, 4208-22

Health survey design and research methods, 1982 biennial conf proceedings, 4184-1

High school classes of 1980 and 1982: educational and sociodemographic characteristics and expectations, natl longitudinal study, series, 4826-2

Hours at work and hours paid ratios and impacts on productivity measures, by firm size and major industry group, with survey methodology, 1981-82, article, 6722-1.434

Housing energy use, and savings under alternative conservation strategies, by State, with model methodology and energy prices, selected years 1970-81, 21368-48

Housing energy use, costs, expenditures, and conservation, and household and housing characteristics, survey series, 3166-7

Hwy and urban transit systems financing methods of govts and private sector, with case studies for selected metro areas, series, 7556-7

Income (taxable) not reported, by illegal source, with characteristics of persons involved, methodology, and bibl, 1970s-82, 8008-112

Income (taxable) not reported, methodology using Current Population Survey labor force data to estimate share of output and nonreporters, 1950s-81, 23848-178

Inflation measures of CPI and Personal Consumption Expenditures Index, effects of differences in weights and housing treatment, 1977-2nd quarter 1984 article, 6762-2.401

IRS and other Fed Govt admin record research methods, data collection and use, 1984 annual conf papers, 8304-17

IRS and other Fed Govt admin record research methods, data collection and use, 1984 compilation of papers, 8308-28

IRS income tax return projections, methodology and base period used, annual rpt, discontinued, 8304-9.2

Marriages, divorces, and rates, by detailed demographic and geographic characteristics, 1979 and trends, US Vital Statistics annual rpt, 4144-4

Mental health facilities needs assessment and program evaluation for small areas, methodology, use of census data, analysis, and sample data, series, 4506-8

Meteorological forecast methodology, accuracy, and applications, technical rpt series, 2186-4

Milk order market data collection methodology of USDA, selected years 1947-83, annual article, 1317-4.402

Natl income and product accounts 1983 revisions, methodology and data sources, 1984 article, 2702-1.425

Nuclear power plant construction and operation status, and capacity, by plant, region, State, and selected country, 1983 and projected to 2020, annual rpt, 3164-57

Nuclear power plant siting population criteria and estimated compliance of selected regions and sites, 1983 rpt, 9638-54

Office space rental demand methodology using BLS employment data, with results by selected occupation and industry and for Chicago SMSA, 1975-83, article, 6722-1.474

Oil spills in coastal and aquatic wildlife habitats, methodology for cleanup priority rating and listing of wildlife species of concern, 1984 rpt, 5508-87

Parole decisions guidelines validation and hearing examiner workloads, Parole Commission research rpt series, 6006-2

Precipitation forecast accuracy, by season, forecast period, and region, various periods 1966-82, technical memorandum, 2188-17

Productivity of labor and capital, growth by SIC 1- to 2-digit industry, and measurement methods and bibl, various periods 1948-78 with trends from 1800, 2218-69

Public welfare programs evaluation, and research and statistical projects and techniques, 1983 conf papers, 4704-11

Retirement ages for OASDI, proposed revisions based on increased life expectancy, by sex under 4 measurement methods, selected years 1940-2050, article, 4742-1.406

Savings (personal) measures from natl income and product and flow-of-funds accounts, 1977 and 1982, article, 2702-1.441

Savings and loan assns, FHLB 4th District members financial results related to market competition, regression results, 1973-82, article, 9302-2.402

State and local govt productivity measurement, with background data and output indexes for 7 govt services, various periods 1955-82, 6728-27

Traffic safety projects research and evaluation, quarterly rpt articles, 7762-9

Underground economy, household expenditures and participation by type of goods or service and sociodemographic characteristics, with methodology and bibl, 1981 survey, 8308-27

Visual impairment survey methodology and results by age, in 3 SMSAs, Aug 1981-Dec 1982, 4478-147

Water from urban runoff, quality, pollutant concentrations, and control cost-effectiveness, with monitoring sites rainfall and other characteristics, by city and region, 1978-83, 9208-122

see also Classifications

see also Economic and econometric models

see also Seasonal adjustment factors

Metrication

see Weights and measures

Metroliner

Northeast Corridor rail improvement project goals, funding, and progress, and Amtrak finances and operations, FY83, annual rpt, 7604-9

Index by Subjects and Names

Metropolitan areas

see Central cities

see Metropolitan Statistical Areas

see Suburbs

see Urban areas

see under By City, By SMSA or MSA, and By Urban-Rural and Metro-Nonmetro in the "Index by Categories"

Metropolitan Statistical Areas

- Air pollution levels for 6 pollutants, by source, region, and for large SMSAs, 1975-82, annual rpt, 9194-1
- Apartment market absorption rates and characteristics for nonsubsidized privately financed furnished and unfurnished units completed in 1982, annual Current Housing Rpt, 2484-2
- Bank mergers, concentration levels, and market deposits merged, by number of bank organizations in SMSA and county, simulated 1982, technical paper, 9366-1.136
- Births and birth rates, by selected demographic characteristics and geographic area, 1979 and trends, US Vital Statistics annual rpt, 4144-1.1
- Bonds for home mortgage subsidy, purchase price limit for tax-exempt status, by State and MSA, 1984 annual press release, 8304-16.2
- Census of Govts, 1982: properties, govt-assessed value, sales, and tax rates, by property type, State, SMSA, county, and city, 2453-1
- Census of Housing, 1980: inventory, occupancy, and unit characteristics, changes from 1973 by region and inside-outside SMSAs and central cities, series, 2473-3
- Census of Housing, 1980: occupancy and unit characteristics of SMSAs and central cities, by race, Hispanic origin, and city, State and SMSA rpt series, 2473-1
- Census of Population and Housing, 1980: detailed population and housing characteristics, by county, city, and census tract, State and SMSA rpt series, 2551-2
- Census of Population, 1980: detailed socioeconomic and demographic characteristics, by age, sex, race, Hispanic origin, occupation, and industry, State rpt series, 2531-4
- Census of Population, 1980: detailed socioeconomic characteristics, by county, city, and inside-outside SMSAs and central cities, State rpt series, 2531-3
- Crimes, arrests by offender characteristics, and rates, by offense, and law enforcement employees, by population size and jurisdiction, 1970s-83, annual rpt, 6224-2
- Disability days, injury and illness rates by type, and use of health services and Medicaid, by age, region, metro-nonmetro location, and selected SMSA, 1980-81, 4147-10.146
- Govt census, 1982: employment, payrolls, and average earnings, by function, level of govt, State, county, population size, and inside-outside SMSAs, 2455-2
- Govt employment and payroll, by function and level of govt in 75 major SMSAs and 69 large counties, Oct 1983, annual rpt, 2466-1.3

Index by Subjects and Names

Mexico

Housing and households detailed characteristics, and unit and neighborhood quality, by inside-outside central cities, 1979-82 surveys, SMSA rpt series, 2485–6

Housing and neighborhood quality indicators and attitudes, and occupant characteristics, by urban-rural location and region, 1981, annual survey, 2485–7

Housing and neighborhood quality indicators and attitudes, by occupant and unit characteristics, region, and metro-nonmetro location, 1981, annual survey, 2485–2

Housing occupancy and unit and household characteristics, by region and metro-nonmetro residence, 1983, biennial survey, 2485–1

Housing unit starts and completions authorized by building permits in 20 MSAs, quarterly rpt, 2382–9

Housing vacancy and occupancy rates, and vacant unit characteristics, by metro-nonmetro location and region, selected years 1960-83, annual rpt, 2484–1

Housing vacant unit characteristics and costs, and occupancy and vacancy rates, by region and metro-nonmetro location, quarterly rpt, 2482–1

Income (personal) per capita and by source, and earnings by industry div, by State, MSA, and county, 1977-82, annual regional rpts, 2704–2

Income (personal) per capita and total, by State, MSA, and county, with metro-nonmetro totals, 1980-82, annual article, 2702–1.413

Local govt finances and population characteristics for cities and suburbs, by region and selected SMSA, selected years 1957-FY83, 10048–61

Manufacturing census, 1982: financial and operating data, by SIC 2- to 4-digit industry, State, SMSA, and county, preliminary census div rpt series, 2491–3

Mobility of population, detailed data by demographic and socioeconomic characteristics of movers and nonmovers, Mar 1981-82, annual Current Population Rpt, 2546–1.384

Population size and change for metro and nonmetro areas and central cities by census div, and growth of areas with large black and aged populations, 1970-82, 2328–47

Population size and components of change, by MSA and county, 1980-82, annual State Current Population Rpt series, 2546–4

Retail trade census, 1982: employment, establishments, sales, and payroll, by SIC 2- to 4-digit kind of business, SMSA, and retail district, State rpt series, 2401–1

Service industry census, 1982: employment, establishments, receipts, and payroll, by SIC 2- to 4-digit kind of business, SMSA, county, and city, State rpt series, 2391–1

Unemployment levels and rates, by State and for 240 large SMSAs, monthly press release with Current Population Survey annual benchmark averages, 6742–12

Wages of white-collar workers, by occupation, work level, and industry div, Mar 1984, annual rpt, 6784–2

Wages of workers covered by unemployment insurance, by MSA, 1982-83, annual press release, 6784–17.3

see also Area wage surveys

see also Central business districts

see also Central cities

see also under By SMSA or MSA in the "Index by Categories"

Metropolitan Washington Council of Governments

"Metrorail Before-and-After Study Reports", 7306–8

Mexican Americans

see Hispanic Americans

see Mexicans in the U.S.

Mexicans in the U.S.

Births, by birth weight, Apgar score, infant and mother characteristics, birthplace, and attendant, 1978, article, 4102–1.414

Census of Population, 1980: detailed socioeconomic characteristics, by county, city, and inside-outside SMSAs and central cities, State rpt series, 2531–3

Deaths in US by State and by outlying area or country of birth, 1979, US Vital Statistics annual rpt, 4144–2.1

Hispanic Americans socioeconomic and demographic characteristics, and compared to non-Hispanics, selected years 1970-83, chartbook, 2328–48

Immigration, and alien residents, workers, visitors, deportations, and naturalizations, by country of birth, FY81, annual rpt, 6264–2

see also Hispanic Americans

Mexico

Agricultural and food production indexes, and production of selected commodities, by world region and country, 1974-83, annual rpt, 1524–5

Agricultural exports of US to Latin America, by commodity, country group, and selected country, FY81-84 and forecast FY85, article, 1522–1.407

Agricultural situation in Latin America, by country, 1981-83 and outlook for 1984, annual rpt, 1524–4.9

Agricultural supply/demand, trade, and production, and socioeconomic data, by country, 1950s-77, 1528–179

AID economic assistance to developing countries, obligations and disbursements by country, quarterly rpt, 9912–4

AID loan repayment status and terms by program and country, and status of predecessor agency loans, quarterly rpt, 9912–3

Citrus fruit production of Mexico by State, and exports and processing, by type of fruit, 1980/81-1983/84, article, 1925–34.405

Copper mine expansion in Cananea, Mexico, effects on US air pollution and copper industry, with US and foreign industry data, 1960s-95, hearing, 21448–31

Economic and monetary trends, compounded annual rates of change for US and 13 trading partners, quarterly rpt annual supplement, 9391–7

Economic conditions in Communist, OECD, and selected other countries, 1960s-83, annual rpt, 244–5

Economic conditions, income, production, prices, employment, and trade, 1984 semiannual country rpt, 2046–4.114

Economic indicators, trade, external accounts and debt, oil industry, and US-Mexico relations, 1978-83 with trends from 1959, conf proceedings, 21248–82

Economic, social, and political summary data, by country, 1984, annual factbook, 244–11

Economic trends in income, production, prices, employment, finances, and trade, 1984 semiannual rpt, 2046–4.33

Electric power transactions of US with Canada and Mexico, by utility and US region, 1983, annual rpt, 3104–10

Employment in Mexico border US-owned plants, and peso devaluation, related to employment in 4 Texas SMSAs, 1978-83, article, 9379–1.402

Eximbank loan guarantees and insurance currently provided and needed by Mexico and Brazil, and value of worldwide and US trade, 1981-84, hearings, 25248–97

Exports and imports, agreement devs, US trade relations, and USITC investigations, 1983, annual rpt, 9884–5

Exports and imports of US, by commodity and country, 1972-82, annual world region rpt, 244–13.3

Exports of US, detailed Schedule B commodities by country of destination, 1983, annual rpt, 2424–9

Exports of US, detailed Schedule E commodities by mode of transport and world area and country of destination, 1983, annual rpts, 2424–5

Graphic industries equipment market and trade, and user industry operations and demand, 1984 country market research rpt, 2045–3.28

Health care resources, use, and per capita public expenditures, and selected population characteristics, for US and 6 countries, selected years 1975-81, 21148–33

Immigration, and alien residents, workers, visitors, deportations, and naturalizations, by country of birth, FY81, annual rpt, 6264–2

Immunization and preventive medicine programs for children in US and Mexico, and disease cases, vaccine reactions, and deaths, 1984 conf papers, 4204–15

Imports of US, detailed Schedule A commodities by country and world area of origin, and mode of transport, 1983, annual rpts, 2424–2

Imports of US, detailed TSUSA commodities by country of origin, 1983, annual rpt, 2424–4

Intl transactions of US with 10 countries, 1981-83, *Survey of Current Business,* monthly rpt, annual table, 2702–1.31

Loans and grants for economic and military assistance from US and intl agencies, by program and country, FY46-83, annual rpt, 9914–5

Military aid of US, arms sales, and training programs costs and budget requests by program, world region, and country, FY83-85, annual rpt, 7144–13

Military spending, arms trade, and armed forces size, with total govt spending and population, by country, 1972-82, annual rpt, 9824–1

Minerals Yearbook, 1982, Vol 3: foreign country reviews of production, trade, and policies, by commodity, annual rpt, 5604–35

Mexico

Minerals Yearbook, 1982, Vol 3 preprints: foreign country review of production, trade, and policies, by commodity, annual rpt, 5604–17.48

Natural gas and liquefied natural gas trade of US with 4 countries, by US pipeline company, 1982-83, annual article, 3162–4.406

Natural gas and liquefied natural gas transported, by State and country of origin and destination, 1982, article, 3162–4.409

Natural gas exports of US to Canada, Mexico, and Japan, 1980-83, annual rpt, 3024–2

Natural gas imports and contracted supply from Canada and Mexico, by US pipeline firm, 1982-83, annual rpt, 3164–33.6

Nuclear power plant construction and operation status, and capacity, by plant, region, State, and selected country, 1983 and projected to 2020, annual rpt, 3164–57

Oil and gas undiscovered recoverable resources, cumulative production, and identified reserves, as of 1981, final world oil basin rpt, 5666–18.4

Oil field equipment from 5 countries, injury to US industry from foreign subsidized imports and less than fair value sales, investigation with background financial and operating data, 1984 rpt, 9886–19.11

Oil production, and exports and prices to US, by major exporting country, detailed data, monthly rpt, 3162–24

Population size and growth rates, and latest available benchmark demographic data, by country, 1950-83, biennial rpt, 2324–4

R&D Fed Govt funding for foreign performers, by world region and country, FY82-84, annual rpt, 9627–20.2

Raisin production, trade, consumption, and stocks of US and 3 countries, and US exports by country, various periods 1982/83-1984/85, article, 1925–34.434

Range and wildlife characteristics, problems, and research strategies and needs, northern Mexico and southwestern US, 1981 conf papers, 1208–197

Refugees from Central America by country of origin and asylum, and aid from US and Mexico, FY82-1984, GAO rpt, 26123–70

Sporting goods and recreational equipment and vehicles market and trade, 1983 country market research rpt, 2045–14.11

Steel wire rod from 4 countries, imports injury to US industry from sales covered by foreign govt grants, investigation with background financial and operating data, 1980-83, 9886–15.47

Travel to and from US and travel receipts and payments by world area, and travel to US by country, 1977-83, annual rpt, 2904–10

Travel to and from US, by world area and selected country, projected 1984-85, annual rpt, 2904–9

Weather conditions and effect on agriculture, by US region, State, and city, and world area, weekly rpt, 2152–2

Weather stations of Natl Weather Service, locations and regular observations made, 1984 annual listing, 2184–5

Weather stations of Upper Air Observational Network, by US and foreign location, 1984 annual listing, 2184–6

see also Gulf of Mexico

see also Mexicans in the U.S.

see also under By Foreign Country in the "Index by Categories"

Meyer, Stephen A.

"Tax Policy Effects on Investment: The 1981 and 1982 Tax Acts", 9387–1.405

Miami, Fla.

Auto dealer repair workers, wages, and benefits, by occupation, size of establishment, and for 24 labor market areas, Nov 1982 survey, 6787–6.202

Census of Housing, 1980: occupancy and unit characteristics, by race, Hispanic origin, and city, SMSA rpt, 2473–1.241

Census of Population and Housing, 1980: detailed population and housing characteristics, by county, city, and census tract, SMSA rpt, 2551–2.241

CPI by component for US city average, and by region, population size, and for 28 SMSAs, monthly press release, 6762–1

CPI by detailed component, for US city average, 28 SMSAs, and 4 regions by population size, monthly rpt, 6762–2

Dress industry production and related workers, wages, and benefits, by occupation, size of establishment, and union status, for 11 labor market areas, Aug 1982 survey, 6787–6.200

Housing unit starts and completions authorized by building permits in 20 MSAs, quarterly rpt, 2382–9

Repair technicians and apprentices wages and benefits, for 5 types of electrical repair shops in 19 SMSAs, Nov 1981 survey, 6787–6.197

Wages by occupation, and benefits for office and plant workers, 1984 SMSA survey rpt, 6785–11.10

see also under By City and By SMSA or MSA in the "Index by Categories"

Mica

see Nonmetallic minerals and mines

Michaeli, D.

"Aging of the Population of a City and Its Implications for Hospital-Based services: The Example of Tel Aviv-Yaffo", 4102–1.445

Michelson, William

"Impact of Changing Women's Roles on Transportation Needs and Usage, Final Report", 7888–62

Michigan

Agricultural cooperatives, membership, activities, and finances, by commodity and selected State, 1900-80 with trends from 1863, 1128–30

Agriculture census, 1982: farms, farmland, production and costs, and operator characteristics, preliminary State summary and county rpts, 2330–1.26

Agriculture census, 1982: farms, farmland, production, finances, and operator characteristics, by county, final State rpt, 2331–1.22

Bank deposits in commercial and mutual savings banks and in US branches of foreign banks, by account type, instn, State, SMSA, and county, June 1983, annual rpt, 9295–3.11

Index by Subjects and Names

Bankruptcy filings in Michigan, by filer type, moving history, income, creditor action, debt and asset type, credit status, exemptions claimed, and county, 1979-81, hearings, 21528–57.3

Celery acreage planted and growing, by major producing State and area, monthly rpt, 1621–14

Census of Population and Housing, 1980: detailed population and housing characteristics, by county, city, and census tract, State rpt, 2551–2.24

Census of Population, 1980: detailed socioeconomic and demographic characteristics, by age, sex, race, Hispanic origin, and industry, State rpt, 2531–4.24

County Business Patterns: establishments, employees, and payrolls, by SIC 4-digit industry and county, 1982, annual State rpt, 2326–6.24

Employment, earnings, and hours, by selected SIC 1- to 4-digit industry, State, and for 278 major labor areas, 1939-83, annual rpt, 6744–5.1, 6744–5.3

Environmental quality, pollutant discharge by type and source, and EPA protection activities and funding, 1970s-83, biennial regional rpt, 9184–15.5

Exports of manufactured and agricultural commodities, manufacturing production, and export-related employment, 1960s-82, State rpt, 2046–3.22

Farm investments, effective rates of Federal/State income and State/local property taxes, by category of structure and equipment, for 7 North Central States, 1981-82, 1548–237

Health professionals license sanctions in 3 States, and subsequent Medicare and Medicaid program participation, by specialty, 1977-82, GAO rpt, 26121–80

HHS aid to each State and local govt or private instn, amount obligated, funding agency, and program, FY83, annual listing, 4004–3.5

Income (personal) per capita and by source, and earnings by industry div, by State, MSA, and county, 1977-82, annual regional rpt, 2704–2.4

Manufacturing census, 1982: financial and operating data, by SIC 2- to 4-digit industry, State, SMSA, and county, preliminary census div rpt, 2491–3.3

Mineral Industry Surveys, State review of production, 1983, advance annual rpt, 5614–6.22

Minerals Yearbook, 1982, Vol 2 preprints: State review of production and sales by commodity, and business activity, annual rpt, 5604–16.23

Minerals Yearbook, 1982, Vol 2: State reviews of production, sales, and firms, by commodity, and business activity, annual rpt, 5604–34

Population size, Apr 1980 and July 1982, and per capita income, 1979 and 1981, by county and city, State Current Population Rpt, 2546–11.22

Pulpwood production by county, imports, and individual mill capacity, by species for 7 North Central States, 1982, annual rpt, 1204–19

Retail trade census, 1982: employment, establishments, sales, and payroll, by SIC 2- to 4-digit kind of business, SMSA, county, and city, State rpt, 2397–1.23

Index by Subjects and Names

Middle East

Savings and loan assns, FHLB 6th District insured members financial condition and operations by State, monthly rpt, 9302–11

Savings and loan assns, FHLB 6th District insured members financial condition and operations by State, quarterly rpt, 9302–23

Timber acreage and yield in Michigan, 1979-80 with projections to 2010, 1208–193

Timber acreage in Michigan, by ownership, county, and forest and tree characteristics, 1980, 1208–192

Timber acreage, volume, growth, removals, and production in Michigan, by ownership, county, and forest and tree characteristics, 1980, series, 1206–31

Unemployment, poverty, and food assistance by Michigan county, public health funding, and Blue Cross-Blue Shield and welfare participation, 1979-83, hearing, 21348–86

Upper Peninsula wages of office and plant workers, by occupation, 1984 labor market area survey rpt, 6785–3.9

Water supply and quality in streams and lakes, and groundwater levels in wells, by drainage basin, 1983, annual State rpt, 5666–10.21

see also Alpena, Mich.
see also Ann Arbor, Mich.
see also Battle Creek, Mich.
see also Bay City, Mich.
see also Benton Harbor, Mich.
see also Detroit, Mich.
see also East Lansing, Mich.
see also Flint, Mich.
see also Grand Rapids, Mich.
see also Jackson, Mich.
see also Kalamazoo, Mich.
see also Lansing, Mich.
see also Muskegon Heights, Mich.
see also Muskegon, Mich.
see also Norton Shores, Mich.
see also Portage, Mich.
see also Saginaw, Mich.
see also Standish, Mich.
see also Tawas City, Mich.
see also under By State in the "Index by Categories"

Microforms

Census Bur activities, publications, and user services, monthly rpt, 2302–3

Census Bur data coverage and availability for 1982 economic censuses and related statistics, 1984 guide, 2308–5

Census Bur publications and data files, monthly listing, 2302–6

Census Bur publications data coverage and availability, 1984 annual listing, 2304–2

Census Bur publications, data coverage, and suggested uses, series, 2326–7

Census of Agriculture, 1982: data coverage and availability for agriculture census and related statistics, 1984 guide, 2308–55

Census of Population and Housing, 1980: data coverage, availability, and uses for urban and transportation planning, 1984 guide, 7558–101

Educational Resources Info Center microfiche, holdings of US and foreign educational and other instns, as of 1983, listing, 4918–14

Fed Govt standards for data recording, processing, and transfer, and for purchase and use of computer systems, series, 2216–2

GPO depository library program quality and mgmt, opinions of librarians, 1983 survey, GAO rpt, 26111–19

Libraries of colleges and universities, expenditures, holdings by type, use, staff by sex, and Federal grants received, 1979-82, biennial rpt, 4854–1

Micronesia

Minerals Yearbook, 1982, Vol 3: foreign country reviews of production, trade, and policies, by commodity, annual rpt, 5604–35

Population size and growth rates, and latest available benchmark demographic data, by country, 1950-83, biennial rpt, 2324–4

Water supply and quality in streams and lakes, and groundwater levels in wells, by drainage basin, 1983, annual State rpt, 5666–10.10

see also American Samoa
see also Guam
see also Kiribati
see also Northern Mariana Islands
see also Trust Territory of the Pacific Islands

Micronesian Claims Commission
see Foreign Claims Settlement Commission

Microscopes
see Instruments and measuring devices

Middle Atlantic States

Army Corps of Engineers activities and projects, FY83 and trends from 1800s, annual rpt, 3754–1

Bridges over navigable waters, with type of bridge and use, owner, dimensions, and location, 1984 regional listing, 7406–5.1, 7406–5.2, 7406–5.3

Census of Population, 1980: detailed socioeconomic and demographic characteristics, by age, sex, race, Hispanic origin, occupation, and industry, US summary rpt, 2531–4.1

Electric and gas privately owned utilities, wages and employment by occupation, and benefits, by region, Oct 1982 survey, 6787–6.205

Employment and price conditions for Middle Atlantic region, series, 6926–1

Environmental quality and protection programs, costs, and Fed Govt enforcement, 1983, detailed annual rpt, 484–1

Environmental quality, pollutant discharge by type and source, and EPA protection activities and funding, 1970s-83, biennial regional rpt, 9184–15.2, 9184–15.3

Farm production inputs, outputs, and productivity, by region, 1939-82, annual rpt, 1544–17

Financial and economic devs, Fed Reserve Bank of Philadelphia bimonthly rpt articles, 9387–1

Financial and economic devs, Fed Reserve Bank of Richmond bimonthly rpt articles, 9389–1

Fish and shellfish landings, life cycles, and environmental needs, for selected species by region, with glossary and bibl, series, 5506–8

Fish landings, employment, gear used, and seafood production, for detailed species by State, 1977, annual rpt, 2164–2.3, 2164–2.4

Fishes from Middle Atlantic OCS, dietary composition by food item and fish size, for 9 species, fall 1976-winter 1977, 2168–78

Fishing (ocean sport and commercial) landings and allowable and potential catch of US and Canada, for 34 species in North Atlantic, 1983, annual rpt, 2164–14

Fruit and vegetable shipments, and arrivals in 23 US and 5 Canada cities, by mode of transport and State or country of origin, 1983, annual rpt, 1311–4.1

Govt census, 1982: city govt revenues by source, expenditures by function, debt, and assets, by State and city, 2457–4

Grain mill production workers, wages, hours, and benefits, by occupation, mill product, and region, June 1982 survey, 6787–6.204

HHS aid to each State and local govt or private instn, amount obligated, funding agency, and program, FY83, annual listing, 4004–3

Income (personal) by industry group and region, percent change 1959-79 and 1979-83, article, 2702–1.443

Income (personal) per capita and by source, and earnings by industry div, by State, MSA, and county, 1977-82, annual regional rpt, 2704–2.3

Income (personal) per capita and by source, earnings by major industry group, and social insurance contributions, by region and State, 1929-82, 2708–40

Manufacturing census, 1982: financial and operating data, by SIC 2- to 4-digit industry, State, SMSA, and county, preliminary census div rpt, 2491–3.2, 2491–3.5

Oil and gas extraction production workers, wages, hours, and benefits, by occupation, region, and for 5 States, June 1982 survey, 6787–6.203

Pulpwood production and yield per acre, for 14 northeastern States, by county, 1981, TVA technical paper, 9806–2.38

Savings instns, FHLB 2nd District members financial operations, by State, monthly rpt, 9302–14

Shipbuilding costs and related employment, by coastal district, 1982, annual rpt, 7704–12

Tide height and time daily at worldwide coastal points, 1985 predictions, annual rpt, 2174–2.2

Waterborne commerce of US (domestic and foreign), freight by commodity, traffic, and passengers, by port and waterway, 1982, annual rpt, 3754–3.1

see also Appalachia
see also under By Region in the "Index by Categories"
see also under names of individual States

Middle East

Agricultural and food production indexes, and production of selected commodities, by world region and country, 1974-83, annual rpt, 1524–5

Agricultural situation in Middle East and North Africa, by country and commodity, 1983 and outlook for 1984, annual rpt, 1524–4.3

Agricultural supply/demand, trade, and production, and socioeconomic data, by country, 1950s-77, 1528–179

Middle East

Agricultural trade of US, by commodity and country, bimonthly rpt with articles, 1522–1

AID activities and funding by project and function, FY85, and developing countries summary socioeconomic data, 1970s-83, by country, annual rpt, 9914–3

AID community dev assistance to local govts in developing countries, program activities and funding, 1960s-80s, 9918–11

AID contracts and grants for technical and support services, by instn, country, and State, FY83, annual listing, 9914–7

AID economic assistance to developing countries, obligations and disbursements by country, quarterly rpt, 9912–4

AID Housing Guaranty Program financial statements, and projects by country, FY83, annual rpt, 9914–4

AID loan repayment status and terms by program and country, and status of predecessor agency loans, quarterly rpt, 9912–3

AID loans authorized, signed, and canceled, by country and world area, monthly rpt, 9912–2

China economic conditions, agricultural and industrial production, trade, and domestic and foreign investment, 1980-85, 2048–106

Defense and total govt expenditures, military imports, GNP, and intl reserves of countries receiving US economic aid, by country, 1976-81, annual rpt, 9914–1

Energy production by type, and oil prices, trade, and consumption, by country group and selected country, monthly rpt, 242–5

Exports and imports of OECD, total and for 4 major countries, and US trade by country, by commodity, 1972-82, annual world region rpt, 244–13.1

Exports and imports of US (waterborne), by type of service, commodity, country, route, and US port, 1982, annual rpt, 7704–2

Exports of US, detailed Schedule E commodities by mode of transport and world area and country of destination, 1983, annual rpts, 2424–5

Food production and needs, and related economic trends and outlook, for 67 developing countries, 1980-86, annual rpt, 1524–6

Great Lakes trade, by SITC 3-digit commodity, port, vessel type, world area, and country, 1982, annual rpt, 7744–3

Investment (foreign direct) in US, by major industry group, world area, and selected country, 1980-83, annual article, 2702–1.439

Investment (foreign direct) of US, by world area and country, 1977-83, article, 2702–1.442

Investment (intl direct) worldwide, and US investment flows by major industry, by world region and country, 1982 and trends from 1950, annual rpt, 2044–25

Loans and grants for economic and military assistance from US and intl agencies, by program and country, FY46-83, annual rpt, 9914–5

Military aid of US, and sales of arms, equipment, and training, by item and country, FY50-83, annual rpt, 3904–3

Military aid of US, arms sales, and training programs costs and budget requests by program, world region, and country, FY83-85, annual rpt, 7144–13

Military, social, and economic summary data, by world area and country, 1960s-80s, hearing, 25388–47.1

Military spending, arms trade, and armed forces size, with total govt spending and population, by country, 1972-82, annual rpt, 9824–1

Minerals Yearbook, 1982, Vol 3: foreign country reviews of production, trade, and policies, by commodity, annual rpt, 5604–35

Minerals Yearbook, 1982, Vol 3 preprints: foreign country review of production, trade, and policies, by commodity, annual rpt, 5604–17.88

Population size and growth rates, and latest available benchmark demographic data, by country, 1950-83, biennial rpt, 2324–4

Precipitation and temperature outlook for US and Northern Hemisphere, and by US and selected foreign weather stations, semimonthly rpt, 2182–1

R&D Fed Govt funding for foreign performers, by world region and country, FY82-84, annual rpt, 9627–20.2

Refugee arrivals in US, by world area of origin and processing and nationality, monthly rpt, 7002–4, 7002–5

Refugee arrivals in US by world area of origin and State of settlement, and Fed Govt intl and domestic assistance costs, FY85, annual rpt, 7004–16

Refugee migration, settlement status, and assistance, by world area and country of origin and asylum, as of May 1984, annual rpt, 7004–15

Students in US and Soviet bloc training programs, by program type and Latin American country or world region of student origin, selected years 1972-82, GAO rpt, 26123–77

Telecommunication equipment market and trade, and user industry operations and demand, 1982 country market research rpt, 2045–12.32

Terrorist (intl) incidents, casualties, and attacks on US targets, by attack type and world area, with chronology of events, 1983, annual rpt, 7004–13

Travel to US and receipts by world area and selected country, 1960-83, and US Travel and Tourism Admin activities, 1983, annual rpt, 2904–6

USIA info center and reading room operations, by world region, country, and city, FY83, annual rpt, 9854–4

see also Bahrain

see also Central Treaty Organization

see also Cyprus

see also Egypt

see also Iran

see also Iraq

see also Israel

see also Jordan

see also Kuwait

see also Lebanon

see also Mediterranean Sea

see also Oman

see also Organization of Petroleum Exporting Countries

see also Qatar

see also Saudi Arabia

see also Syria

see also Turkey

see also United Arab Emirates

see also Yemen, North

see also Yemen, South

see also under By Foreign Country in the "Index by Categories"

Middlesex County, N.J.

Wages of office and plant workers, by occupation, 1983 labor market area survey rpt, 6785–3.3

see also under By SMSA or MSA in the "Index by Categories"

Middletown, Conn.

see also under By SMSA or MSA in the "Index by Categories"

Middletown, N.Y.

Census of Housing, 1980: occupancy and unit characteristics, by race, Hispanic origin, and city, SMSA rpt, 2473–1.263

Census of Population and Housing, 1980: detailed population and housing characteristics, by county, city, and census tract, SMSA rpt, 2551–2.263

Middletown, Ohio

Census of Housing, 1980: occupancy and unit characteristics, by race, Hispanic origin, and city, SMSA rpt, 2473–1.179

Census of Population and Housing, 1980: detailed population and housing characteristics, by county, city, and census tract, SMSA rpt, 2551–2.179

see also under By SMSA or MSA in the "Index by Categories"

Midland, Mich.

see also under By SMSA or MSA in the "Index by Categories"

Midland, Tex.

Census of Housing, 1980: occupancy and unit characteristics, by race, Hispanic origin, and city, SMSA rpt, 2473–1.242

Census of Population and Housing, 1980: detailed population and housing characteristics, by county, city, and census tract, SMSA rpt, 2551–2.242

see also under By SMSA or MSA in the "Index by Categories"

Midwestern States

see North Central States

Midwives

Births (nonhospital) attended by midwives, by race and State, 1979, US Vital Statistics annual rpt, 4144–1.2

Births and birth rates, by demographic and birth characteristics, 1981 with trends from 1940, US Vital Statistics advance rpt, 4146–5.73

Births and birth rates, by parent and birth characteristics and infant condition at birth, 1982 and trends from 1940, US Vital Statistics annual advance rpt, 4146–5.79

Births attended by midwives and in nonhospital settings, by mother's sociodemographic and prenatal care characteristics and infant race and birthweight, 1978-79 with trends from 1935, 4147–21.40

Births, by birth weight, Apgar score, infant and mother characteristics, birthplace, and attendant, 1978, article, 4102–1.414

Births, proportion inside-outside hospital and with physician or midwife attending, and prenatal care, 1940-79, US Vital Statistics annual rpt, 4144–1

Index by Subjects and Names

Foreign and US health care resources, use, and per capita public expenditures, and selected population characteristics, for 7 countries, selected years 1975-81, 21148–33

Hispanic Americans births and birth and fertility rates, by detailed Hispanic origin, characteristics of mother, birth, and prenatal care, and for 22 States, 1981, 4146–5.80

Senegal rural health care projects of AID, mgmt and effectiveness, 1978-83, 9916–3.20

Mielke, Myles J.

"Brazil: An Export Market Profile", 1526–6.4

Migrant workers

- CETA participants by sociodemographic characteristics, and Labor Dept activities and staff, FY83, annual rpt, 6304–1
- Children and youth benefitting from Fed Govt public welfare programs and tax expenditures, participation and funding for 71 programs, FY81-83, 21968–30
- Community services block grants by type of service provider, State mgmt, and opinions of officials and groups involved, for 13 States, FY81-83, GAO rpt, 26121–84
- Education Dept programs funding, operations, and effectiveness, FY83, annual rpt, 4804–5
- Education grants of Fed Govt, State allocations by program, type of recipient agency, and State, FY83, annual rpt, 4804–8
- Farm labor, farms, and labor costs, by labor and farm type and State, with immigrant labor law effect on farm work force, 1978, 1598–192
- Head Start Project enrollment of handicapped children, by handicap, State, and for Indian and migrant programs, 1982, annual rpt, 4604–1
- HHS aid to each State and local govt or private instn, amount obligated, funding agency, and program, FY83, annual listing, 4004–3
- Job Training Partnership Act allotments for migrant and seasonal farm workers retraining assistance, by State and administering organization, as of July 1984, press release, 6408–64

Migration

- Census of Housing, 1980: inventory, occupancy, and unit characteristics, changes from 1973 by region and inside-outside SMSAs and central cities, series, 2473–3
- Census of Population and Housing, 1980: detailed population and housing characteristics, by county, city, and census tract, State and SMSA rpt series, 2551–2
- Census of Population, 1980: detailed socioeconomic and demographic characteristics, by age, sex, race, Hispanic origin, occupation, and industry, State rpt series, 2531–4
- Census of Population, 1980: detailed socioeconomic characteristics, by county, city, and inside-outside SMSAs and central cities, State rpt series, 2531–3
- Census of Population, 1980: migration since 1975, by county and selected demographic characteristics, supplementary rpt, 2535–1.14

Census of Population, 1980: migration since 1975, by State and selected demographic characteristics, supplementary rpt, 2535–1.13

- Central America socioeconomic and political conditions in 6 countries, 1960s-83 with trends and projections 1930-2010, Commission rpt, 028–19.2
- City and suburb population characteristics and local govt finances, by region and selected SMSA, 1950s-FY83, 10048–61
- *County and City Data Book,* detailed socioeconomic and demographic data for States, counties, and cities, selected years 1976-82, 2328–1
- Farm population movement, 1960s-82, annual chartbook, 1504–3
- Florida and California elderly migration by selected State of origin or destination, and Florida elderly, by sociodemographic and housing characteristics, 1970 and 1980, 4478–150
- Foreign women sociodemographic, economic, and fertility characteristics, with comparisons to men, by country, 1960s-85, world region rpt series, 2326–15
- Higher education, residence and migration in and out of State for new students, by State, fall 1981, annual rpt, 4824–2.13
- Homeless population and characteristics, and temporary shelter operations, use, and user characteristics, for selected cities, various periods 1979-84, hearing, 21248–85
- Housing and financial characteristics of recent movers, for 15 SMSAs, 1978, annual survey special supplement, 2485–8
- Housing and householder selected characteristics, by urban-rural location, 1981, annual survey, 2485–7.1
- Housing characteristics of recent movers for new and previous unit, and household characteristics, by inside-outside central cities, 1979-82 surveys, SMSA rpt series, 2485–6
- Income assistance, effects of experimental negative income tax program on employment, earnings, marital status, and other family characteristics in 2 cities, 1970-75, 4008–64
- Income of households, families, and persons, by detailed socioeconomic characteristics and region, 1982, annual Current Population Rpt, 2546–6.39
- Kentucky employment growth in 9-county rural area, labor force and establishment characteristics, 1979-80, 1598–194
- Michigan bankruptcy filings, by filer type, moving history, income, creditor action, debt and asset type, credit status, exemptions claimed, and county, 1979-81, hearings, 21528–57.3
- Mobility of population, detailed data by demographic and socioeconomic characteristics of movers and nonmovers, Mar 1981-82, annual Current Population Rpt, 2546–1.384
- NYC population size, demographic characteristics, and rental housing, in 5 neighborhoods by census tract, 1980 with percent change from 1970, article, 9385–1.403

Military aircraft

- Older persons by demographic, socioeconomic, and health characteristics, selected years 1900-81 and projected to 2050, Current Population Rpt, 2546–2.125
- Older persons population characteristics, and needs and costs of social services by type, by metro-nonmetro status, 1970s-82 with trends from 1900, 21148–28
- Older persons sociodemographic characteristics and transportation needs, selected years 1900-2040, 7308–183
- Outlying area population size and components of change, by area, 1970-82, Current Population Rpt, 2546–3.127
- Pacific Northwest electricity consumption and prices by end-use sector, and economic and demographic data, 1960s-83 and projected to 2005, annual rpt, 3224–2
- Population and health research funded by 4 private organizations, project listing by topic, with funding data, 1981, annual rpt, 4474–16
- Population size and components of change, by MSA and county, 1980-82, annual State Current Population Rpt series, 2546–4
- Population size and components of change, by outlying area, 1980-83, Current Population Rpt, 2546–3.134
- Population size and components of change, by region and State, 1970-83, Current Population Rpt, 2546–3.133
- Population size and components of change, by region, census div, and State, July 1981-83, annual Current Population Rpt, 2546–3.128
- Population size and components of change, by region, census div, and State, 1970s-83 with projections to 2050, annual Current Population Rpt, 2546–2.119
- Poverty status of families and persons, by detailed socioeconomic characteristics, 1982, annual Current Population Rpt, 2546–6.40
- Veteran population and ratio to civilians, by census div and for 10 States with largest change, 1970 and 1980, 9926–4.7
- *see also* Labor mobility
- *see also* Migrant workers
- *see also* Refugees

Milford, Conn.

see also under By SMSA or MSA in the "Index by Categories"

Milham, Samuel, Jr.

"Occupational Mortality in Washington State, 1950-79", 4248–47

Military aircraft

- Air Force B-1B aircraft program procurement and operating costs by component, and personnel, alternative projections FY85-89, GAO rpt, 26123–79
- Air Force C-5 and C-17 cargo aircraft dimensions and operating characteristics, 1983, GAO rpt, 26123–81
- Air pollution levels for 5 pollutants, by detailed source, State, and Air Quality Control Region, 1981, annual rpt, 9194–7
- Budget justification for DOD aircraft for noncombat use, costs, Navy and Air Force requirements, and Navy losses, by aircraft type, selected years FY73-86, hearing, 21408–76

Military aircraft

Budget of DOD, costs of individual weapons or weapon systems, FY83-85, annual rpt, 3504–2

Budget of DOD for weapons systems, FY85 requests consistency with US policy and specified treaties, with funding FY83-87, annual rpt, 21384–4

Budget of DOD, itemized account of legislative history, FY84, annual rpt, 3504–7

Budget of DOD, justification for procurement programs, by equipment type, service branch, and defense agency, FY83-86, annual rpt, 3504–14

Budget of DOD, justification, programs, and policies, FY85, annual rpt, 3544–2

Budget of DOD, organization, personnel, weapons, and property, by service branch, State, and country, 1984 annual summary rpt, 3504–13

Collisions of aircraft, and near collisions by circumstances and State, by type of aircraft, various periods 1980-84, 7508–61

Cost control proposals for Fed Govt programs and mgmt, 3-year savings by function and agency, and financial and operating data, 1960s-81, 16908–1.19, 16908–1.20

Developing countries arms transfers from US, USSR, and Europe, by weapon type and world region, 1974-82, 25948–3

Expenditures for military goods and services, by function, 1972-84, article, 2702–1.440

Exports of US, detailed commodities by country of destination, monthly rpt, 2422–3

Exports of US, detailed Schedule B commodities by country of destination, 1983, annual rpt, 2424–9

Foreign military aid of US and sales of arms, equipment, and training, by item, FY50-83, annual rpt, 3904–3

Foreign military spending, arms trade, and armed forces size, with total govt spending and population, by country, 1972-82, annual rpt, 9824–1

Manufacturing census, 1982: financial and operating data, for SIC 4-digit industries by product, preliminary rpt, 2491–1.398, 2491–1.399, 2491–1.400

Natl Guard (Army and Air) activities, manpower, and facilities, FY83, annual rpt, 3704–3

NATO and US weapons and troop strength compared to Warsaw Pact and USSR, as of Jan 1984, annual rpt, 3564–1

Navy budget and Navy and Marine Corps forces, equipment, and budget summary, planned FY84-85, semiannual pamphlet, 3802–3

Outlays and obligations of DOD, by function and service branch, quarterly rpt, 3542–3

Procurement cost estimate changes for weapons systems, and program delays and mgmt, by system and service branch, 1983, annual rpt, 26304–5

Procurement cost estimates for weapons and communications systems, by service branch, quarterly summary rpt, 3502–1

Procurement, DOD prime contract awards by category, contract and contractor type, and service branch, FY74-1st half FY84, semiannual rpt, 3542–1

Procurement, DOD prime contract awards by detailed procurement category, FY80-83, annual rpt, 3544–18

Procurement, DOD prime contract awards for 25 commodity categories and R&D, by State and census div, FY81-83, annual rpt, 3544–11

Procurement, DOD prime contract awards to small and total business, for 10 categories and R&D, monthly rpt, 3542–10

Propeller shipments and exports, 1983, annual Current Industrial Rpt, 2506–12.23

Sealift Military Command operations for naval fleet support, and transport of DOD and AID cargo by route, quarterly rpt, 3802–2

Soviet Union and Warsaw Pact military weapons systems, assistance and presence worldwide, and force strengths, with selected US and NATO comparisons, as of 1984, 3508–14

Strategic military capability, force strengths, weapons, training, supplies, and requirements, by service branch, FY80-84 and projected to 1990, 3508–19

Strategic nuclear weapon forces of US and USSR under Strategic Arms Reduction Talks and alternative proposals and counting methods, by weapon and system, FY84-96, 26306–6.73

see also Helicopters

Military airlift

Air Force C-5 and C-17 cargo aircraft dimensions and operating characteristics, 1983, GAO rpt, 26123–81

Cost control proposals for Fed Govt programs and mgmt, 3-year savings by function and agency, and financial and operating data, 1960s-81, 16908–1.20, 16908–1.32

Shipments by DOD of military and personal property, loss claims, passenger traffic, and costs, by mode of transport, quarterly rpt, 3702–1

Military appropriations

see Defense budgets and appropriations

Military assistance

AID activities and funding by project and function, FY85, and developing countries summary socioeconomic data, 1970s-83, by country, annual rpt, 9914–3

Budget of DOD, itemized account of legislative history, FY84, annual rpt, 3504–7

Budget of DOD, justification, programs, and policies, FY85, annual rpt, 3544–2

Budget of US Appendix, detailed budgets and personnel summaries, by agency, FY85, annual rpt, 104–3

Budget of US, CBO analysis and review of FY85 budget by function, annual rpt, 26304–2

Budget of US, effects of Reagan Admin policy changes, by detailed program, FY85, annual rpt, 104–21

Budget of US, Reagan Admin funding requests for foreign economic and military aid by program and country, FY82-85, annual rpt, 7004–14

Budget of US, receipts by source and outlays by agency and program, monthly rpt, 8102–3

Index by Subjects and Names

Budget of US, receipts by source and outlays by function, FY40-89 estimates revised for consistency with FY85 budget definitions, annual rpt, 104–12

Central America socioeconomic and political conditions in 6 countries, 1960s-83 with trends and projections 1930-2010, 028–19

Cost of DOD base support by function, and personnel and acreage by installation, by service branch, FY85, annual rpt, 3504–11

Credit assistance costs, policies to improve measurement, with loan and loan guarantee data by program, and Federal and private credit instns operations, 1970-84, 26306–6.72

Debt to US of foreign govts and private obligors, by country and program, periodic rpt, 8002–6

Defense activity indicators, *Business Conditions Digest,* historical supplement and methodology, 1947-82, 2708–31

Defense activity indicators, *Business Conditions Digest,* monthly rpt, 2702–3.8

Developing countries economic and military aid from US, Communist, and selected other countries, 1954-83, annual rpt, 244–5.4

DOD Military Assistance Program Grant-Aid shipments, monthly rpt, 2422–6, 2422–9

Economic indicators and components, current data and annual trends, monthly rpt, 23842–1.7

El Salvador socioeconomic and political conditions, and US economic and military assistance, 1977-FY84, 7008–39

Exports of US by selected commodity, and foreign and US economic and employment indicators and balance of payments, by world area and country, 1970s-83, annual rpt, 2044–26

Foreign economic and military assistance role in US foreign policy, with aid proposals by world region, FY85 with trends from FY74, 7008–38

Foreign military aid of US, arms sales, and training programs costs and budget requests by program, world region, and country, FY83-85, annual rpt, 7144–13

Foreign military and economic aid of US, by program and country, selected years 1940-82, annual rpt, 15344–1.1

Foreign military, social, and economic summary data by world area and country, 1960s-80s, hearing, 25388–47.1

Foreign military spending, arms trade, and armed forces size, with total govt spending and population, by country, 1972-82, annual rpt, 9824–1

Foreign military training of US, students, costs, and revenue losses from reduced tuition by country, by service branch, FY79-83, GAO rpt, 26123–56

Grenada arms and equipment commitments of USSR and other Communist countries, 1980-85, and arms discovered and personnel evacuated by US, Oct 1983, hearings, 21388–43

Human rights conditions in 162 countries, economic and military aid of US, and economic aid of intl organizations, 1981-83, annual rpt, 21384–3

Index by Subjects and Names

Intl economic and military assistance loans and grants from US and intl agencies, by program and country, FY46-83, annual rpt, 9914–5

Latin America students in US and Soviet bloc training programs, by program type and student country, and summary by world region, selected years 1972-82, GAO rpt, 26123–77

Loan programs of Fed Govt, direct and guaranteed loans outstanding by agency and program, *Treasury Bulletin*, quarterly rpt, 8002–4.10

NATO and US weapons and troop strength compared to Warsaw Pact and USSR, as of Jan 1984, annual rpt, 3564–1

Navy vessels sold to foreign govts, sales prices, fair market value, and Navy costs, for surplus ships sold 1981-82, GAO rpt, 26123–60

Philippines dev and military assistance funding from US, FY78-84 and proposed FY85-89, GAO rpt, 26123–54

Soviet Union and Warsaw Pact military weapons systems, assistance and presence worldwide, and force strengths, with selected US and NATO comparisons, as of 1984, 3508–14

Treaties and other bilateral and multilateral agreements of US in force, by country, Jan 1984, annual listing, 7004–1

Treaties on arms control status, and Arms Control and Disarmament Agency activities, 1983, annual rpt, 9824–2

see also Arms sales

see also War relief

Military aviation

- Air traffic control and airway facilities and equipment, FAA improvement activities and R&D under Natl Airspace System Plan, 1982-2000, annual rpt, 7504–12
- Air traffic controller trainees test scores and failure rates, by level of experience and military branch served, 1977-81, 7506–10.24
- Airline traffic, capacity, and performance, by carrier and type of operation, monthly rpt, 9142–13
- Aviation activity, detailed data on aircraft, air traffic, air carriers, personnel, airports, and FAA operations, 1974-83, annual rpt, 7504–1
- Cost control proposals for Fed Govt programs and mgmt, 3-year savings by function and agency, and financial and operating data, 1960s-81, 16908–1.17
- FAA air traffic control facilities traffic levels, by airport and State, FY83, annual rpt, 7504–27
- Instrument flight rule aircraft handled, by user type, FAA traffic control center, and region, FY69-83 and forecast to FY95, annual rpt, 7504–15
- Inventory and costs of Fed Govt-owned real property, worldwide summary by location, agency, and use, 1983, annual rpt, 9454–5
- Meteorological services and research of Fed Govt, programs and funding by agency, FY84-85, annual rpt, 2144–2
- Navy F/A-18 weapons tactics trainer costs by trainer type, as of 1984, and demand at 2 locations, projected 1988-94, GAO rpt, 26123–73

Navy personnel, detailed statistics, quarterly rpt, 3802–4

- Traffic, aircraft operations by type and passenger enplanements, by airport, region, and State, projected FY82-95 and trends from FY76, annual rpt, 7504–7
- Traffic, aircraft, pilots, airport activity, and fuel use, forecast FY84-95 with FY79-83 trends, annual rpt, 7504–6
- Training and education programs of DOD, funding, staff, students, and facilities, by service branch and reserve component, FY85, annual rpt, 3504–5
- Typhoons in western North Pacific and North Indian Oceans, paths and other characteristics, by mode of surveillance, 1983, annual rpt, 3804–8

see also Military aircraft

see also Military airlift

Military awards, decorations, and medals

- Mint Bur activities and finances, production of medals and US and foreign coins, and gold and silver stocks and transactions, by office, FY83, annual rpt, 8204–1
- Natl Guard (Army and Air) activities, manpower, and facilities, FY83, annual rpt, 3704–3

Military bases, posts, and reservations

- Acreage of natl park system and other areas under Natl Park System mgmt, by type of area, ownership, and site, as of Sept 1984, semiannual rpt, 5542–1
- Army personnel assigned to critical occupation specialties by skill type, and working outside specialty at 5 installations, as of Mar 1982, GAO rpt, 26123–59
- Bombing (explosive and incendiary) and arson incidents by target, State, and circumstances, and explosives theft and recovery, 1982-83, annual rpt, 8484–4
- Bombing (explosive and incendiary) incidents, damage, injuries, and deaths, by target, State, and circumstances, 1983, annual rpt, 6224–5
- Budget of DOD, itemized account of legislative history, FY84, annual rpt, 3504–7
- Budget of DOD, organization, personnel, weapons, and property, by service branch, State, and country, 1984 annual summary rpt, 3504–13
- Commercial activities of DOD under contract and performed in-house, costs and work-years, by service branch, defense agency, State, and installation, FY83, annual rpt, 3544–25
- Construction and renovation of military bases, DOD budget authorization requests, by DOD component, State, country, and project, FY85, annual rpt, 3544–15
- Construction costs and price indexes by type of military facility, and implicit price deflators, 1972-82, article, 2702–1.401
- Construction grants, loans, and loan guarantees of Fed Govt, by program and type of structure, FY80-83 and estimated FY84-85, annual article, 2012–1.404
- Construction put in place, permits authorized by region, State, and MSA, and Federal contract awards, by construction type, bimonthly rpt with articles, 2012–1

Military bases, posts, and reservations

- Construction put in place, value of new public and private structures, by type, monthly rpt, 2382–4
- Cost control proposals for Fed Govt programs and mgmt, 3-year savings by function and agency, and financial and operating data, 1960s-81, 16908–1
- Cost of DOD base support by function, and personnel and acreage by installation, by service branch, FY85, annual rpt, 3504–11
- Employment (civilian and military) of DOD, by State, service branch, and major installation, as of Sept 1983, annual rpt, 3544–7
- Expenditures for military goods and services, by function, 1972-84, article, 2702–1.440
- Fed Govt aid to State and local govts, expenditures, and direct payments, by program, agency, and State, FY83, annual rpt, 2464–2
- Fish and eggs for stocking distributed from natl hatcheries, by species, hatchery, and jurisdiction, FY83, annual rpt, 5504–10
- Foreign military, social, and economic summary data by world area and country, 1960s-80s, hearing, 25388–47.1
- High school class of 1982: foreign language coursework, by language, course level, student and school characteristics, and location, 1984 rpt, 4828–17
- Inventory and costs of Fed Govt-owned real property, worldwide summary by location, agency, and use, 1983, annual rpt, 9454–5
- Natl Guard (Army and Air) activities, manpower, and facilities, FY83, annual rpt, 3704–3
- Navy budget and Navy and Marine Corps forces, equipment, and budget summary, planned FY84-85, semiannual pamphlet, 3802–3
- Pentagon personnel, Apr 1945-Sept 1983, annual rpt, 3544–1.1
- Radioactive contamination of former AEC and Manhattan Project research and storage sites, test results series, 3406–1
- Schools in federally impacted areas, Fed Govt funding by county and school and congressional district, and eligible pupils, by State, FY83, annual rpt, 4804–10
- Soviet Union and Warsaw Pact military weapons systems, assistance and presence worldwide, and force strengths, with selected US and NATO comparisons, as of 1984, 3508–14
- Strategic military capability, force strengths, weapons, training, supplies, and requirements, by service branch, FY80-84 and projected to 1990, 3508–19
- Terrorist (intl) incidents, casualties, and attacks on US targets, by attack type and world area, with chronology of events, 1983, annual rpt, 7004–13
- Training and education programs of DOD, funding, staff, students, and facilities, by service branch and reserve component, FY85, annual rpt, 3504–5
- Workers compensation for employees of private contractors under Fed Govt-administered programs, cases and dispositions by district, FY79-83, annual compilation, 6504–5

ASI Annual Supplement 531

Military bases, posts, and reservations

see also Military clubs and messes
see also Military housing
see also Missile bases
see also Post exchanges

Military cemeteries and funerals

- Acreage of natl park system and other areas under Natl Park System mgmt, by type of area, ownership, and site, as of Sept 1984, semiannual rpt, 5542–1
- Natl cemetery interments, and applications and orders for headstones and markers, monthly rpt, 9922–2
- Natl cemetery projects status, interments, and status of gravesites, and other VA activities, FY83, annual rpt, 9924–1
- Veterans aged 55 and over, socioeconomic characteristics, economic resources, health care and status, and actual and expected use of VA benefits, 1983 survey, 9928–29

Military clubs and messes

- Army morale, welfare, and recreation programs, revenue and expenses worldwide by activity and major command, FY82-83, annual rpt, 3704–12
- Cost control proposals for Fed Govt programs and mgmt, 3-year savings by function and agency, and financial and operating data, 1960s-81, 16908–1.17, 16908–1.23

Military contracts and procurement

see Defense contracts and procurement

Military courts

see Court of Military Appeals
see Courts-martial and courts of inquiry

Military dependents

- Army personnel health status, and use of Army medical services in US and abroad by personnel, retirees, and dependents, monthly rpt, 3702–4.1
- Budget of DOD, itemized account of legislative history, FY84, annual rpt, 3504–7
- Children and youth benefitting from Fed Govt public welfare programs and tax expenditures, participatic \ and funding for 71 programs, FY81-83, 21968–30
- Civilian Health and Medical Program of the Uniformed Services costs and operations, FY83-84 with trends from FY79, semiannual rpt, 3502–2
- Dependents of DOD military and civilian personnel, FY83, annual rpt, 3544–1
- Educational assistance program participation and costs, under GI Bill and other veterans programs, WW II through Sept 1983, annual rpt, 9924–22
- Medical facilities of DOD in US and abroad, beds, admissions, outpatient visits, and live births by service branch, quarterly rpt, 3542–15
- Medical services for military, potential effects of alternative financing proposals on DOD costs, with service use and out-of-pocket medical costs by type of recipient, FY84-89, 26306–6.74
- Navy medical facility use by active and retired military personnel, dependents, and others, by facility and type, quarterly rpt, 3802–1
- Students in DOD Dependents Schools, higher education admission tests scores by sex and subject, and educational goals and attitudes, 1983, annual rpt, 3504–17

Students in DOD Dependents Schools, 1st grader basic skills test scores, by world area and English fluency, fall 1983, annual rpt, 3504–18

see also Civilian Health and Medical Program of the Uniformed Services

Military education

- Budget of US, effects of Reagan Admin policy changes, by detailed program, FY85, annual rpt, 104–21
- Commercial activities of DOD under contract and performed in-house, costs and work-years, by service branch, defense agency, State, and installation, FY83, annual rpt, 3544–25
- Degrees conferred in higher education, by race, Hispanic origin, sex, level, and field, selected years 1949/50-1979/80, annual rpt, 4824–2.16
- Funding, staff, students, and facilities for DOD training and education programs, by service branch and reserve component, FY85, annual rpt, 3504–5
- Medical personnel, trainees, and accessions by source, by occupation, specialty, and service branch, FY83, annual rpt, 3544–24
- Navy personnel, detailed statistics, quarterly rpt, 3802–4
- *see also* Military training
- *see also* Reserve Officers Training Corps
- *see also* Service academies

Military expenditures

see Defense expenditures
see Military assistance

Military funerals

see Military cemeteries and funerals

Military hospitals

- Admissions, beds, outpatient visits, and live births in DOD medical facilities in US and abroad, by service branch, quarterly rpt, 3542–15
- Army personnel health status, and use of Army medical services in US and abroad by personnel, retirees, and dependents, monthly rpt, 3702–4
- Budget of DOD, itemized account of legislative history, FY84, annual rpt, 3504–7
- Budget of US, CBO analysis of revenue and spending alternatives and projections of economic indicators, FY85-89, annual rpt, 26304–3.3
- Commercial activities of DOD under contract and performed in-house, costs and work-years, by service branch, defense agency, State, and installation, FY83, annual rpt, 3544–25
- Cost control proposals for Fed Govt programs and mgmt, 3-year savings by function and agency, and financial and operating data, 1960s-81, 16908–1.17, 16908–1.24
- Medical personnel, trainees, and accessions by source, by occupation, specialty, and service branch, FY83, annual rpt, 3544–24
- Medical services for military, potential effects of alternative financing proposals on DOD costs, with service use and out-of-pocket medical costs by type of recipient, FY84-89, 26306–6.74
- Navy and Marine Corps disease incidence, medical care, and deaths, by detailed diagnosis, and medical personnel and workloads, 1978-79, annual rpt, 3804–1

Index by Subjects and Names

- Navy medical facility use by active and retired military personnel, dependents, and others, by facility and type, quarterly rpt, 3802–1
- Navy personnel alcohol and drug abuse, and related deaths, courts-martial, discharges, and treatment program funding and staff, FY83, annual table, 3804–12
- *see also* Veterans health facilities and services

Military housing

- Army morale, welfare, and recreation programs, revenue and expenses worldwide by activity and major command, FY82-83, annual rpt, 3704–12
- Budget of DOD, itemized account of legislative history, FY84, annual rpt, 3504–7
- Census of Population, 1980: detailed socioeconomic and demographic characteristics, by age, sex, race, Hispanic origin, occupation, and industry, State rpt series, 2531–4
- Construction and renovation of military bases, DOD budget authorization requests, by DOD component, State, country, and project, FY85, annual rpt, 3544–15
- Construction put in place, permits authorized by region, State, and MSA, and Federal contract awards, by construction type, bimonthly rpt with articles, 2012–1
- Cost control proposals for Fed Govt programs and mgmt, 3-year savings by function and agency, and financial and operating data, 1960s-81, 16908–1.29
- Outlays and obligations of DOD, by function and service branch, quarterly rpt, 3542–3

Military intelligence

- Army personnel assigned to critical occupation specialties by skill type, and working outside specialty at 5 installations, as of Mar 1982, GAO rpt, 26123–59
- Budget of DOD, itemized account of legislative history, FY84, annual rpt, 3504–7
- Budget of DOD, justification for R&D programs, and acquisition mgmt, FY83-85, annual rpt, 3504–6
- Budget of DOD, justification for R&D programs, by item, service branch, and defense agency, FY83-86, annual rpt, 3504–15
- Budget of DOD, justification, programs, and policies, FY85, annual rpt, 3544–2
- Polygraph lie detection test accuracy, and Fed Govt use by agency, selected years 1947-83, 26358–96
- *see also* Defense Intelligence Agency

Military law

- Budget of DOD, itemized account of legislative history, FY84, annual rpt, 3504–7
- Cases and court actions, Court of Military Appeals and Judge Advocates General, FY83, annual rpt, 3504–3
- Drug-related courts martial and other disciplinary actions, by service branch, FY80-84, 3508–19
- Navy personnel, detailed statistics, quarterly rpt, 3802–4

Index by Subjects and Names

see also Court of Military Appeals
see also Courts-martial and courts of inquiry

Military pay

Air Force B-1B aircraft program procurement and operating costs by component, and personnel, alternative projections FY85-89, GAO rpt, 26123–79

Air Force enlisted men and pilots lifetime earnings and retirement benefits, and comparisons to similar civilian jobs, as of 1983, hearings, 21208–19

Budget of DOD, expenditures for each service branch and total defense agencies, by function and State, FY85, annual rpt, 3544–23

Budget of DOD, itemized account of legislative history, FY84, annual rpt, 3504–7

Budget of DOD, manpower and cost estimates, detailed analysis, FY85, annual rpt, 3504–1

Budget of US, CBO analysis of revenue and spending alternatives and projections of economic indicators, FY85-89, annual rpt, 26304–3.3

Census of Govts, 1982: employment, payrolls, and average earnings, by function, level of govt, State, county, population size, and inside-outside SMSAs, 2455–2

Cost control proposals for Fed Govt programs and mgmt, 3-year savings by function and agency, and financial and operating data, 1960s-81, 16908–1

Earnings by industry div, and personal income per capita and by source, by State, MSA, and county, 1977-82, annual regional rpts, 2704–2

Earnings by major industry group, and personal income per capita and by source, by region and State, 1929-82, 2708–40

Employment, earnings, and hours, by level and branch of govt, and function, monthly 1977-Feb 1984, annual update, 6744–4

Expenditures for military goods and services, by function, 1972-84, article, 2702–1.440

Fed Govt aid to State and local areas, by type of payment, State, and county, FY83, annual rpt, 2464–3.1

Income, pay, and withholdings by type for Fed Govt civilian and military employees, and special military compensation by type and service branch, 1982-83, GAO rpt, 26123–65

Manpower of DOD, and organization, budget, weapons, and property, by service branch, State, and country, 1984 annual summary rpt, 3504–13

Outlays and obligations of DOD, by function and service branch, quarterly rpt, 3542–3

Pay comparability of Fed Govt with private industry, and recommended and actual pay increase, various dates 1971-84, annual rpt, 10104–1

Reserve forces manpower strengths and characteristics, by component, quarterly rpt, 3542–4

Tax expenditures, Fed Govt revenues foregone through income tax deductions and exclusions by type, and effect of Deficit Reduction Act, FY84-89, annual rpt, 21784–10

Military pensions

Air Force B-1B aircraft program procurement and operating costs by component, and personnel, alternative projections FY85-89, GAO rpt, 26123–79

Annuitants, DOD retired military personnel, FY50-83, annual rpt, 3544–1.4

Army Medical/Life, Central Insurance, and Central Retirement Fund financial statements, FY83, annual rpt, 3704–12

Benefits and after-tax salary replacement rates by pension type, and older persons income and income sources, by age and marital status, 1950s-82, conf proceedings, 25408–87

Benefits and beneficiaries of public employee pension plans by eligibility reason, level of govt, and Federal plan, selected years 1954-80, article, 4742–1.403

Benefits, and beneficiaries with representative payees by age and relation to payee, by Fed Govt cash program, as of 1983, GAO rpt, 26121–85

Benefits for military retirees and compared to US civil and foreign service and foreign countries, and Air Force personnel costs, FY75-84, hearings, 21208–19

Budget of DOD, expenditures for each service branch and total defense agencies, by function and State, FY85, annual rpt, 3544–23

Budget of DOD, itemized account of legislative history, FY84, annual rpt, 3504–7

Budget of US, CBO analysis of revenue and spending alternatives and projections of economic indicators, FY85-89, annual rpt, 26304–3.3

Budget of US, effects of Reagan Admin policy changes, by detailed program, FY85, annual rpt, 104–21

Cost control proposals for Fed Govt programs and mgmt, 3-year savings by function and agency, and financial and operating data, 1960s-81, 16908–1

Costs of pension programs, and pension earnings and force strengths, under alternative policies, FY70s-2020, and lifetime pension earnings in 7 countries, 1983, 26306–6.76

Fed Govt aid to State and local areas, by type of payment, State, and county, FY83, annual rpt, 2464–3.1

Fed Govt aid to State and local govts, expenditures, and direct payments, by program, agency, and State, FY83, annual rpt, 2464–2

Fed Govt consolidated financial statements based on business accounting methods, FY82-83, annual rpt, 8104–5

Income (household) and cash and noncash transfer program participation, by sociodemographic characteristics, quarterly rpt, 2542–2

Income and income sources of older persons, by OASDI beneficiary and poverty status, labor force participation, and demographic characteristics, 1982, biennial rpt, 4744–26

Oregon and Montana earnings by SIC 1- to 3-digit industry and payments to retirees by type, for 4 timber dependent communities, 1970, 1208–196

Military personnel

Outlays and obligations of DOD, by function and service branch, quarterly rpt, 3542–3

Tax expenditures, Fed Govt revenues foregone through income tax deductions and exclusions by type, and effect of Deficit Reduction Act, FY84-89, annual rpt, 21784–10

see also Veterans benefits and pensions

Military personnel

Agent Orange exposed Air Force personnel diseases and disorders, by disease type, age, and officer status, 1984 rpt, 3604–3

Aides to officers, enlisted personnel authorized and assigned to perform personal services by race and sex, and program costs, by service branch, 1982-83, GAO rpt, 26123–53

Air Force B-1B aircraft program procurement and operating costs by component, and personnel, alternative projections FY85-89, GAO rpt, 26123–79

Air Force fiscal mgmt system operations and techniques, info for comptroller personnel, quarterly rpt, 3602–1

Army civilian employment wartime needs, status of installation mobilization and staff plans, 1982-83, GAO rpt, 26123–82

Army personnel assigned to critical occupation specialties by skill type, and working outside specialty at 5 installations, as of Mar 1982, GAO rpt, 26123–59

Army personnel health status, and use of Army medical services in US and abroad by personnel, retirees, and dependents, monthly rpt, 3702–4

Base support costs by function, and personnel and acreage by installation, by service branch, FY85, annual rpt, 3504–11

Budget of DOD, itemized account of legislative history, FY84, annual rpt, 3504–7

Budget of DOD, justification, programs, and policies, FY85, annual rpt, 3544–2

Budget of DOD, manpower and cost estimates, detailed analysis, FY85, annual rpt, 3504–1

Budget of US, CBO analysis of revenue and spending alternatives and projections of economic indicators, FY85-89, annual rpt, 26304–3

Census of Govts, 1982: employment, payrolls, and average earnings, by function, level of govt, State, county, population size, and inside-outside SMSAs, 2455–2

Census of Housing, 1980: structural, financial, and householder characteristics, by region and State, 2475–4

Census of Population, 1980: detailed socioeconomic and demographic characteristics, by age, sex, race, Hispanic origin, occupation, and industry, State rpt series, 2531–4

Census of Population, 1980: detailed socioeconomic characteristics, by county, city, and inside-outside SMSAs and central cities, State rpt series, 2531–3

Census of Population, 1980: migration since 1975, by county and selected demographic characteristics, supplementary rpt, 2535–1.14

Military personnel

Census of Population, 1980: migration since 1975, by State and selected demographic characteristics, supplementary rpt, 2535–1.13

Computer specialists sociodemographic, educational, and employment characteristics, and Fed Govt support by agency, 1978, biennial Current Population Rpt, 2546–2.124

Cost control proposals for Fed Govt programs and mgmt, 3-year savings by function and agency, and financial and operating data, 1960s-81, 16908–1

Defense activity indicators, *Business Conditions Digest,* historical supplement and methodology, 1947-82, 2708–31

Defense activity indicators, *Business Conditions Digest,* monthly rpt, 2702–3.8

Defense Fuel Supply Center procurement, prices, stocks, and other activities, FY83, annual rpt, 3904–6

Defense Fuel Supply Center procurement, prices, stocks, transport, and other activities and finances, FY83, annual rpt, 3904–8

Economic indicators and components, current data and annual trends, monthly rpt, 23842–1.2

Educational assistance program participation and costs, under GI Bill and other veterans programs, WW II through Sept 1983, annual rpt, 9924–22

El Salvador socioeconomic and political conditions, and US economic and military assistance, 1977-FY84, 7008–39

Employment (civilian) of DOD, by service branch and defense agency, with summary military employment data, monthly rpt, 3542–16

Employment, earnings, and hours, by level and branch of govt, and function, monthly 1977-Feb 1984, annual update, 6744–4

Employment-population ratios and unemployment rates, for total and civilian male labor force, by age and race, 1963-82, article, 6722–1.442

Employment status of population, including Armed Forces in the US, Monthly Labor Review, 6722–1.1

Employment status of population, including Armed Forces in US, by sex, monthly press release, 6742–5

Employment status of population, including Armed Forces in US, monthly rpt, 6742–2.4

Employment, unemployment, and labor force, including Armed Forces in the US, detailed seasonally adjusted data, by sex, 1950-83, 6748–72.3

Foreign economic, social, and political summary data, by country, 1984, annual factbook, 244–11

Foreign military, social, and economic summary data by world area and country, 1960s-80s, hearing, 25388–47.1

Fraud and abuse in DOD programs, audits and investigations, 1st half FY84, semiannual rpt, 3542–18

Grenada arms and equipment commitments of USSR and other Communist countries, 1980-85, and arms discovered and personnel evacuated by US, Oct 1983, hearings, 21388–43

Index by Subjects and Names

Health professionals supply and education, by occupation, demographic and professional characteristics, and location, 1950s-83 and projected to 2000, biennial rpt, 4114–8

High school classes of 1980 and 1982: educational and sociodemographic characteristics and expectations, natl longitudinal study, series, 4826–2

Jail capacities, conditions, expenditures, and services, and socioeconomic and other characteristics of inmates, various dates 1976-82, 10048–59

Mail (free) for blind, handicapped, and servicemen, USPS operating costs itemized by class of mail, FY83, annual rpt, 9864–4

Malaria cases reported in US, including military personnel and foreign civilians, 1966-82, annual rpt, 4205–4

Manpower active duty strength, recruits, and reenlistment, by race, Hispanic origin, sex, and service branch, quarterly press release, 3542–7

Manpower levels in US, and civilian employment, by age, sex, occupation, and educational attainment, 1982 and summary trends from 1950, article, 6722–1.441

Manpower levels, recruits, reenlistment, desertion, and drug-related disciplinary action, by service branch, FY80-84 and projected to 1990, 3508–19

Manpower of DOD, and organization, budget, weapons, and property, by service branch, State, and country, 1984 annual summary rpt, 3504–13

Manpower of DOD, by State, service branch, and major installation, as of Sept 1983, annual rpt, 3544–7

Manpower statistics on active duty, civilian, and reserve personnel, by service branch, monthly rpt, 3542–14

Manpower statistics on active duty, civilian, and retired personnel and dependents, FY83 and historical, annual rpt, 3544–1

Manpower strengths, and military pension earnings and program costs, under alternative policies, selected years FY71-2020, 26306–6.76

Manpower strengths in US and abroad, by service branch, world area, and country, quarterly news release, 3542–9

Manpower strengths, summary by service branch, monthly press release, 3542–2

Meat consumption by type, total and per capita civilian and military, quarterly 1970-83, annual rpt, 1564–6.2

Medical facilities of DOD in US and abroad, beds, admissions, outpatient visits, and live births by service branch, quarterly rpt, 3542–15

Medical personnel, trainees, and accessions by source, by occupation, specialty, and service branch, FY83, annual rpt, 3544–24

Medical services for military, potential effects of alternative financing proposals on DOD costs, with service use and out-of-pocket medical costs by type of recipient, FY84-89, 26306–6.74

Mobility of population, detailed data by demographic and socioeconomic characteristics of movers and nonmovers, Mar 1981-82, annual Current Population Rpt, 2546–1.384

Natl Guard (Army and Air) activities, manpower, and facilities, FY83, annual rpt, 3704–3

NATO and US weapons and troop strength compared to Warsaw Pact and USSR, as of Jan 1984, annual rpt, 3564–1

NATO military commitment of US, Europe force strengths by service branch and costs by component, FY82 with trends from FY75, GAO rpt, 26123–71

Navy and Marine Corps disease incidence, medical care, and deaths, by detailed diagnosis, and medical personnel and workloads, 1978-79, annual rpt, 3804–1

Navy budget and Navy and Marine Corps forces, equipment, and budget summary, planned FY84-85, semiannual pamphlet, 3802–3

Navy medical facility use by active and retired military personnel, dependents, and others, by facility and type, quarterly rpt, 3802–1

Navy personnel alcohol and drug abuse, and related deaths, courts-martial, discharges, and treatment program funding and staff, FY83, annual table, 3804–12

Navy personnel by grade and length of service, reenlistment rate, and need for petty officers, FY72-83 and projected to FY88, GAO rpt, 26123–69

Navy personnel, detailed statistics, quarterly rpt, 3802–4

Occupational distribution of DOD enlisted personnel, Sept 1982, biennial rpt, 6744–3

Patents issued to US residents including military personnel, FY76-83, annual rpt, 2244–1.2

Population estimates for civilian, resident, and total population, monthly Current Population Rpt, 2542–1

Population of military, total and abroad, by age, sex, and race, as of July 1982, Current Population Rpt, 2546–3.132

Publications of DOD Directorate for Info Operations and Rpts, FY84, annual listing, 3544–16

Radiation from 1940s-70s nuclear weapons tests, levels in air and water, and personnel exposure by military unit and job category, series, 3906–1

Red Cross program operations and financial statements, 1982/83, annual rpt, 29254–1

Reserve forces manpower and equipment strengths, readiness, and funding, by reserve component, FY83, annual rpt, 3544–27

Reserve forces manpower strengths and characteristics, by component, quarterly rpt, 3542–4

Reserve forces manpower strengths and mobilization alert system efficiency, for selected Army Reserve and Natl Guard units, 1982-83 survey, GAO rpt, 26123–57

Sealift Military Command operations for naval fleet support, and transport of DOD and AID cargo by route, quarterly rpt, 3802–2

Soviet Union and Warsaw Pact military weapons systems, assistance and presence worldwide, and force strengths, with selected US and NATO comparisons, as of 1984, 3508–14

Index by Subjects and Names

Statistical Abstract of US, social, political, and economic data, 1950s-83 and trends, annual rpt, 2324–1.2

Terrorist (intl) incidents, casualties, and attacks on US targets, by attack type and world area, with chronology of events, 1983, annual rpt, 7004–13

Training and education programs of DOD, funding, staff, students, and facilities, by service branch and reserve component, FY85, annual rpt, 3504–5

Transport of personnel by DOD, and costs, by mode of transport, quarterly rpt, 3702–1

Venereal disease cases diagnosed and reported by military, 1981-82, annual rpt, 4204–14.1

Vietnam era veterans separated from armed forces, by age at time of discharge, FY65-83, annual rpt, 9924–8.1

War participants, deaths, veterans living, and compensation and pension recipients, for each US war, 1775-1983, semiannual rpt, 9922–8

Women military personnel on active duty, by demographic and service characteristics and service branch, with comparisons to men, FY83, annual chartbook, 3544–26

Women's employment and earnings, by labor force and socioeconomic characteristics, and compared to men, 1978-81 and trends from 1940s, 6568–29

see also Coast Guard
see also Military dependents
see also Military pay
see also Military pensions
see also Retired military personnel
see also Selective service
see also Servicemen's life insurance programs
see also Veterans
see also Voluntary military service

Military policy
see Arms sales
see Defense budgets and appropriations
see Military assistance
see Military strategy
see National defense

Military prisons

Prisoners in Federal correctional instns, by prison, security level, contract facility type, sex, and region, monthly and weekly rpts, 6242–1

Military research
see Defense research

Military reserves
see Armed services reserves

Military science

Army personnel assigned to critical occupation specialties by skill type, and working outside specialty at 5 installations, as of Mar 1982, GAO rpt, 26123–59

Budget of DOD, itemized account of legislative history, FY84, annual rpt, 3504–7

see also Arms control and disarmament
see also Civil defense
see also Defense research
see also Guerrilla warfare
see also Logistics
see also Military strategy

Military service
see Selective service
see Voluntary military service

Military service academies
see Service academies

Military services
see Armed services

Military strategy

Budget of DOD, justification for R&D programs, by item, service branch, and defense agency, FY83-86, annual rpt, 3504–15

Budget of DOD, justification, programs, and policies, FY85, annual rpt, 3544–2

Cost of DOD base support by function, and personnel and acreage by installation, by service branch, FY85, annual rpt, 3504–11

Deployment of forces and manpower requirements, DOD budget detailed analysis, FY85, annual rpt, 3504–1

DOD budget, FY85 weapons system requests consistency with US policy and specified treaties, with funding FY83-87, annual rpt, 21384–4

Missile experimental (MX) basing proposals of Reagan Admin, 1984 narrative rpt update, 3508–17

NATO and US weapons and troop strength compared to Warsaw Pact and USSR, as of Jan 1984, annual rpt, 3564–1

Reserve forces manpower and equipment strengths, readiness, and funding, by reserve component, FY83, annual rpt, 3544–27

Soviet Union and Warsaw Pact military weapons systems, assistance and presence worldwide, and force strengths, with selected US and NATO comparisons, as of 1984, 3508–14

Strategic military capability, force strengths, weapons, training, supplies, and requirements, by service branch, FY80-84 and projected to 1990, 3508–19

Military supplies and property

Air pollutant emission factors, by detailed source, 3rd edition, 1983-84 supplements, 9198–13

Alaska electric power capacity and generation by fuel type, and marketing, by utility, type of ownership, and location, 1983, annual rpt, 3214–2

Army morale, welfare, and recreation programs, revenue and expenses worldwide by activity and major command, FY82-83, annual rpt, 3704–12

Army personnel assigned to critical occupation specialties by skill type, and working outside specialty at 5 installations, as of Mar 1982, GAO rpt, 26123–59

Army war reserve and excess item inventory, 1982, GAO rpt, 26123–58

Budget of DOD, costs of individual weapons or weapon systems, FY83-85, annual rpt, 3504–2

Budget of DOD, itemized account of legislative history, FY84, annual rpt, 3504–7

Budget of DOD, justification for procurement programs, by equipment type, service branch, and defense agency, FY83-86, annual rpt, 3504–14

Budget of DOD, justification, programs, and policies, FY85, annual rpt, 3544–2

Military supplies and property

Capital (fixed), govt and private nonresidential structures and equipment, residential capital, and consumer-owned durable goods by item, 1980-83, annual article, 2702–1.433

China exports and imports by SITC 1- to 5-digit commodity, 1970s-82, annual rpt, 244–12

Commercial activities of DOD under contract and performed in-house, costs and work-years, by service branch, defense agency, State, and installation, FY83, annual rpt, 3544–25

Computer systems and equipment of Fed Govt, inventory by manufacturer, type, agency, and location, FY83, last issue of annual rpt, 9454–4

Cost control proposals for Fed Govt programs and mgmt, 3-year savings by function and agency, and financial and operating data, 1960s-81, 16908–1

Cost of DOD base support by function, and personnel and acreage by installation, by service branch, FY85, annual rpt, 3504–11

Defense Fuel Supply Center procurement, prices, stocks, and other activities, FY83, annual rpt, 3904–6

Defense Fuel Supply Center procurement, prices, stocks, transport, and other activities and finances, FY83, annual rpt, 3904–8

Electric power plants and major fuel-burning facilities of DOD conversion from oil and gas, fuel use data, 1983, annual rpt, 3104–9

Expenditures for military goods and services, by function, 1972-84, article, 2702–1.440

Exports of US, detailed commodities by country of destination, monthly rpt, 2422–3

Fed Govt consolidated financial statements based on business accounting methods, FY82-83, annual rpt, 8104–5

Food supply, trade, and use, by commodity, 1963-83, annual rpt, 1544–4.4

Foreign military aid of US and sales of arms, equipment, and training, by item and country, FY50-83, annual rpt, 3904–3

Foreign military aid of US, arms sales, and training programs costs and budget requests by program, world region, and country, FY83-85, annual rpt, 7144–13

Fraud and abuse in DOD programs, audits and investigations, 1st half FY84, semiannual rpt, 3542–18

Grenada arms and equipment commitments of USSR and other Communist countries, 1980-85, and arms discovered and personnel evacuated by US, Oct 1983, hearings, 21388–43

Imports of US, detailed Schedule A commodities by country, monthly rpt, 2422–2

Inventory and automated cataloging system of Fed Govt supplies, and DOD mgmt of inventory items for agencies, NATO, and foreign govts, 1970s-83, annul rpt, 21204–1

Inventory of DOD property, supplies, and equipment, by service branch, 1983, annual rpt, 3544–6

Military supplies and property

Navy budget and Navy and Marine Corps forces, equipment, and budget summary, planned FY84-85, semiannual pamphlet, 3802–3

Occupational injury and illness rates, by SIC 2- to 4-digit industry, 1982, annual rpt, 6844–1

Outlays and obligations of DOD, by function and service branch, quarterly rpt, 3542–3

Reserve forces manpower and equipment strengths, readiness, and funding, by reserve component, FY83, annual rpt, 3544–27

Sealift Military Command operations for naval fleet support, and transport of DOD and AID cargo by route, quarterly rpt, 3802–2

Shipments by DOD of military and personal property, loss claims, passenger traffic, and costs, by mode of transport, quarterly rpt, 3702–1

Soviet Union and Warsaw Pact military weapons systems, assistance and presence worldwide, and force strengths, with selected US and NATO comparisons, as of 1984, 3508–14

Strategic military capability, force strengths, weapons, training, supplies, and requirements, by service branch, FY80-84 and projected to 1990, 3508–19

Waterborne commerce of US (domestic and foreign), freight by commodity, traffic, and passengers, by port and waterway, 1982, annual rpt, 3754–3

see also Ammunition

see also Arms sales

see also Defense contracts and procurement

see also Logistics

see also Military assistance

see also Military bases, posts, and reservations

see also Military vehicles

see also Military weapons

Military training

Air Force B-1B aircraft program procurement and operating costs by component, and personnel, alternative projections FY85-89, GAO rpt, 26123–79

Aircraft for DOD noncombat use, costs, Navy and Air Force requirements, and Navy losses, by aircraft type, selected years FY73-86, hearing, 21408–76

Budget of DOD, itemized account of legislative history, FY84, annual rpt, 3504–7

Budget of US, effects of Reagan Admin policy changes, by detailed program, FY85, annual rpt, 104–21

Commercial activities of DOD under contract and performed in-house, costs and work-years, by service branch, defense agency, State, and installation, FY83, annual rpt, 3544–25

Computer specialists sociodemographic, educational, and employment characteristics, and Fed Govt support by agency, 1978, biennial Current Population Rpt, 2546–2.124

Cost control proposals for Fed Govt programs and mgmt, 3-year savings by function and agency, and financial and operating data, 1960s-81, 16908–1

Cost of DOD base support by function, and personnel and acreage by installation, by service branch, FY85, annual rpt, 3504–11

Foreign military aid of US and sales of arms, equipment, and training, by item and country, FY50-83, annual rpt, 3904–3

Foreign military aid of US, arms sales, and training programs costs and budget requests by program, world region, and country, FY83-85, annual rpt, 7144–13

Foreign military training of US, students, costs, and revenue losses from reduced tuition by country, by service branch, FY79-83, GAO rpt, 26123–56

Funding, staff, students, and facilities for DOD training and education programs, by service branch and reserve component, FY85, annual rpt, 3504–5

Latin America students in US and Soviet bloc training programs, by program type and student country, and summary by world region, selected years 1972-82, GAO rpt, 26123–77

Manpower of DOD, and organization, budget, weapons, and property, by service branch, State, and country, 1984 annual summary rpt, 3504–13

Medical personnel, trainees, and accessions by source, by occupation, specialty, and service branch, FY83, annual rpt, 3544–24

Natl Guard (Army and Air) activities, manpower, and facilities, FY83, annual rpt, 3704–3

Navy F/A-18 weapons tactics trainer costs by trainer type, as of 1984, and demand at 2 locations, projected 1988-94, GAO rpt, 26123–73

Navy personnel, detailed statistics, quarterly rpt, 3802–4

Reserve forces manpower and equipment strengths, readiness, and funding, by reserve component, FY83, annual rpt, 3544–27

Strategic military capability, force strengths, weapons, training, supplies, and requirements, by service branch, FY80-84 and projected to 1990, 3508–19

see also Military education

see also Reserve Officers Training Corps

see also Service academies

Military tribunals

see Courts-martial and courts of inquiry

Military vehicles

Budget of DOD, costs of individual weapons or weapon systems, FY83-85, annual rpt, 3504–2

Budget of DOD, itemized account of legislative history, FY84, annual rpt, 3504–7

Budget of DOD, justification for procurement programs, by equipment type, service branch, and defense agency, FY83-86, annual rpt, 3504–14

Budget of DOD, justification, programs, and policies, FY85, annual rpt, 3544–2

Cost control proposals for Fed Govt programs and mgmt, 3-year savings by function and agency, and financial and operating data, 1960s-81, 16908–1

County Business Patterns: establishments, employees, and payrolls, by SIC 4-digit industry and county, 1982, annual State rpt series, 2326–6

Index by Subjects and Names

Developing countries arms transfers from US, USSR, and Europe, by weapon type and world region, 1974-82, 25948–3

Energy use in transportation sector by mode, fuel supplies, and demographic and economic determinants of vehicle use, 1970s-83, annual rpt, 3304–5

Expenditures for military goods and services, by function, 1972-84, article, 2702–1.440

Exports and imports of US, detailed SIC-based commodities by world area, 1983, annual rpts, 2424–6

Exports, imports, tariffs, and industry operating data for military and special-purpose vehicles, 1979-83, TSUSA commodity rpt, 9885–6.78

Exports of US, detailed commodities by country of destination, monthly rpt, 2422–3

Exports of US, detailed Schedule E commodities by mode of transport and world area and country of destination, 1983, annual rpts, 2424–5

Foreign military aid of US and sales of arms, equipment, and training, by item, FY50-83, annual rpt, 3904–3

Foreign military spending, arms trade, and armed forces size, with total govt spending and population, by country, 1972-82, annual rpt, 9824–1

Great Lakes trade, by SITC 3-digit commodity, port, vessel type, world area, and country, 1982, annual rpt, 7744–3

Imports of US, detailed Schedule A commodities by country and world area of origin, and mode of transport, 1983, annual rpts, 2424–2

Imports of US, detailed Schedule A commodities by country, monthly rpt, 2422–2

Input-output structure of US economy, detailed interindustry transactions for 537 industries, and components of final demand, 1977 benchmark data, 2708–17

Manufacturing census, 1982: financial and operating data, for SIC 4-digit industries by product, preliminary rpt, 2491–1.393, 2491–1.409

Procurement cost estimate changes for weapons systems, and program delays and mgmt, by system and service branch, 1983, annual rpt, 26304–5

Procurement, DOD prime contract awards by category, contract and contractor type, and service branch, FY74-1st half FY84, semiannual rpt, 3542–1

Procurement, DOD prime contract awards by detailed procurement category, FY80-83, annual rpt, 3544–18

Procurement, DOD prime contract awards for 25 commodity categories and R&D, by State and census div, FY81-83, annual rpt, 3544–11

Reserve forces manpower and equipment strengths, readiness, and funding, by reserve component, FY83, annual rpt, 3544–27

Shipments by DOD of military and personal property, loss claims, passenger traffic, and costs, by mode of transport, quarterly rpt, 3702–1

Soviet Union and Warsaw Pact military weapons systems, assistance and presence worldwide, and force strengths, with selected US and NATO comparisons, as of 1984, 3508–14

Index by Subjects and Names

Military weapons

Budget of DOD, costs of individual weapons or weapon systems, FY83-85, annual rpt, 3504–2

Budget of DOD for weapons systems, FY85 requests consistency with US policy and specified treaties, with funding FY83-87, annual rpt, 21384–4

Budget of DOD, itemized account of legislative history, FY84, annual rpt, 3504–7

Budget of DOD, justification for procurement programs, by equipment type, service branch, and defense agency, FY83-86, annual rpt, 3504–14

Budget of DOD, justification for R&D programs, and acquisition mgmt, FY83-85, annual rpt, 3504–6

Budget of DOD, justification for R&D programs, by item, service branch, and defense agency, FY83-86, annual rpt, 3504–15

Budget of DOD, justification, programs, and policies, FY85, annual rpt, 3544–2

Budget of DOD, organization, personnel, weapons, and property, by service branch, State, and country, 1984 annual summary rpt, 3504–13

Budget of US, effects of Reagan Admin policy changes, by detailed program, FY85, annual rpt, 104–21

China economic conditions, agricultural and industrial production, trade, and domestic and foreign investment, 1980-85, 2048–106

Cost control proposals for Fed Govt programs and mgmt, 3-year savings by function and agency, and financial and operating data, 1960s-81, 16908–1

Cost estimate changes for weapons procurement, and program delays and mgmt, by service branch and system, 1983, annual rpt, 26304–5

Cost estimates for weapons and communications systems, by service branch, quarterly summary rpt, 3502–1

Cost estimates for weapons systems, DOD methodology for rpts to Congress, with illustrative data and bibl, 1970s-83, GAO rpt, 26123–62

Exports and imports of US, detailed SIC-based commodities by world area, 1983, annual rpts, 2424–6

Exports and imports of US, totals and as percent of domestic production, by SIC 2- to 5-digit commodity, 1981, annual rpt, 2424–3

Exports of US, detailed commodities by country of destination, monthly rpt, 2422–3

Exports of US, detailed Schedule E commodities by mode of transport and world area and country of destination, 1983, annual rpts, 2424–5

Foreign military aid of US, arms sales, and training programs costs and budget requests by program, world region, and country, FY83-85, annual rpt, 7144–13

Foreign military spending, arms trade, and armed forces size, with total govt spending and population, by country, 1972-82, annual rpt, 9824–1

Great Lakes trade, by SITC 3-digit commodity, port, vessel type, world area, and country, 1982, annual rpt, 7744–3

Imports of US, detailed Schedule A commodities by country and world area of origin, and mode of transport, 1983, annual rpts, 2424–2

Manufacturing census, 1982: financial and operating data, for SIC 4-digit industries by product, preliminary rpt, 2491–1.304

NATO and US weapons and troop strength compared to Warsaw Pact and USSR, as of Jan 1984, annual rpt, 3564–1

Outlays and obligations of DOD, by function and service branch, quarterly rpt, 3542–3

Radioactive wastes from DOE defense facilities, interim storage inventories by site and permanent disposal plan costs, 1982 with projections to 2015, 3358–32

Shipments by DOD of military and personal property, loss claims, passenger traffic, and costs, by mode of transport, quarterly rpt, 3702–1

Soviet Union and Warsaw Pact military weapons systems, assistance and presence worldwide, and force strengths, with selected US and NATO comparisons, as of 1984, 3508–14

Strategic military capability, force strengths, weapons, training, supplies, and requirements, by service branch, FY80-84 and projected to 1990, 3508–19

see also Ammunition

see also Arms sales

see also Chemical and biological warfare agents

see also Defense contracts and procurement

see also Defense expenditures

see also Military aircraft

see also Military assistance

see also Military vehicles

see also Missiles and rockets

see also Naval vessels

see also Nuclear weapons

see also Torpedoes

Milk and milk products

see Dairy industry and products

Miller, Glenn H., Jr.

"Alternatives to the Current Individual Income Tax", 9381–1.415

"U.S. Economy and Monetary Policy in 1983", 9381–1.401

Miller, James J.

"Impact of Ultra-High Temperature Milk on the U.S. Dairy Industry", 1568–247

"Participation in the Milk Diversion Program", 1561–2.402

Miller, Louisa

"Estimates of the Population of the U.S., by Age, Sex, and Race: 1980-83", 2546–3.130

Miller, Preston J.

"Budget Deficit Mythology", 9383–6.401

Millikin, Mark R.

"Synopsis of Biological Data on the Blue Crab, Callinectes sapidus Rathbun", 2166–16.13

Millionaires

see Wealth

Mills, Edwin S.

"Metropolitan Central City Population and Employment Growth During the 1970's", 9387–8.89

Mills, Rodney H.

"Determination of Front-End Fees on Syndicated Eurocurrency Credits", 9366–7.105

Mine accidents and safety

Millville, N.J.

Census of Housing, 1980: occupancy and unit characteristics, by race, Hispanic origin, and city, SMSA rpt, 2473–1.362

Census of Population and Housing, 1980: detailed population and housing characteristics, by county, city, and census tract, SMSA rpt, 2551–2.362

see also under By SMSA or MSA in the "Index by Categories"

Milwaukee, Wis.

Auto dealer repair workers, wages, and benefits, by occupation, size of establishment, and for 24 labor market areas, Nov 1982 survey, 6787–6.202

Census of Housing, 1980: occupancy and unit characteristics, by race, Hispanic origin, and city, SMSA rpt, 2473–1.243

Census of Population and Housing, 1980: detailed population and housing characteristics, by county, city, and census tract, SMSA rpt, 2551–2.243

CPI by component for US city average, and by region, population size, and for 28 SMSAs, monthly press release, 6762–1

CPI by detailed component, for US city average, 28 SMSAs, and 4 regions by population size, monthly rpt, 6762–2

Homeless population and characteristics, and temporary shelter operations, use, and user characteristics, for selected cities, various periods 1979-84, hearing, 21248–85

Population size of top 25 cities, 1980 and 1982, press release, 2328–46

Rail high-speed system planned from Chicago, capital and operating costs and profitability by speed class, frequency, and route, 1984 article, 9375–1.406

Wages by occupation, and benefits for office and plant workers, 1984 SMSA survey rpt, 6785–11.6

see also under By City and By SMSA or MSA in the "Index by Categories"

Mine accidents and safety

Coal miners black lung exams and incidence, and health and safety NIOSH research activities, annual rpt, suspended, 4244–1

Coal mines and related operations, occupational injuries and incidence rates, detailed analysis, 1982, annual rpt, 6664–4

Deaths at metal and nonmetallic mines and mills, by cause, State, and victim occupation, annual rpt, suspended, 6664–7

Fed Govt aid to State and local govts, expenditures, and direct payments, by program, agency, and State, FY83, annual rpt, 2464–2

Fed Govt programs and mgmt cost control proposals, 3-year savings by function and agency, and financial and operating data, 1960s-81, 16908–1.15

Foreign countries disasters, persons affected, deaths, damage, and aid by US and others, FY83 and trends from FY64, annual rpt, 9914–12

Injuries, illnesses, and workdays lost, by SIC 2-digit industry, 1982-83, annual press release, 6844–3

Injury and illness rates and causes, by SIC 2- to 4-digit industry, 1982, annual rpt, 6844–1

Mine accidents and safety

Metal mines and related operations, occupational injuries and incidence rates, detailed analysis, 1982, annual rpt, 6664–3

Nonmetallic mineral mining and related operations, occupational injuries and incidence, detailed analysis, 1982, annual rpt, 6664–1

Occupational injuries, employment, and hours in mines and quarries, with coal production, by State, quarterly rpt, 6662–1

Sand and gravel mines and related operations, occupational injuries and incidence rates, detailed analysis, 1982, annual rpt, 6664–2

Stone mines and related operations, occupational injuries and incidence rates, detailed analysis, 1982, annual rpt, 6664–5

Mine Safety and Health Administration

Coal mines and related operations, occupational injuries and incidence rates, detailed analysis, 1982, annual rpt, 6664–4

Cost control proposals for Fed Govt programs and mgmt, 3-year savings by function and agency, and financial and operating data, 1960s-81, 16908–1.3

Deaths at metal and nonmetallic mines and mills, by cause, State, and victim occupation, annual rpt, suspended, 6664–7

Metal mines and related operations, occupational injuries and incidence rates, detailed analysis, 1982, annual rpt, 6664–3

Mines, mills, and quarries occupational injuries, and employees and hours, by State, quarterly rpt, 6662–1

Nonmetallic mineral mining and related operations, occupational injuries and incidence, detailed analysis, 1982, annual rpt, 6664–1

Sand and gravel mines and related operations, occupational injuries and incidence rates, detailed analysis, 1982, annual rpt, 6664–2

Stone mines and related operations, occupational injuries and incidence rates, detailed analysis, 1982, annual rpt, 6664–5

Mineral Industry Surveys

Explosives and blasting agents consumption by type, industry, and State, 1983, annual rpt, 5614–22

Phosphate rock production, sales, exports, and use, 1984 crop year, annual rpt, 5614–20

Production of minerals, 1983, advance annual State rpt series, 5614–6

Production, trade, and consumption of minerals, commodity reviews, advance annual rpt series, 5614–5

Production, trade, stocks, and consumption, commodity reviews, monthly rpt series, 5612–1

Production, trade, stocks, and consumption, quarterly commodity rpt series, 5612–2

Mineral leases

Coal dev on Fed Govt lease land in Western US, surface and mineral rights by State, and environmental protection adequacy, various periods 1978-85, 26358–103

Coal Fed Govt leases, acreage, production, and prices, by State, and legal and mgmt issues, 1970s-83 with production projections to 2000, 11128–1

Coal industry competitive effects of Fed Govt coal leasing, FY83 annual rpt, 6004–12

Coal lands of Fed Govt leasing activity, acreage, and reserves, by State, coal region, and tract, FY83, annual rpt, 5724–10

Coal leasing of Fed Govt, potential impact on 25 species protected under Migratory Bird Treaty Act, and bird population characteristics, 1900s-82, 5508–88

Coal supply and Fed Govt coal leases, by owner, owner industry, and western State, various periods 1950-82 and projected to 2000, hearing, 25318–58

Coastal environmental characteristics, fish, wildlife, and use, and population socioeconomic data, for individual areas, series, 5506–4

Cost control proposals for Fed Govt programs and mgmt, 3-year savings by function and agency, and financial and operating data, 1960s-81, 16908–1.9, 16908–1.29

Fed Govt aid to State and local govts, expenditures, and direct payments, by program, agency, and State, FY83, annual rpt, 2464–2

Fed Govt receipts by source and outlays by agency, *Treasury Bulletin,* quarterly rpt, 8002–4.1

Foreign firms US affiliates financial and operating data, by country of parent firm and industry div, 1980-81, article, 2702–1.402

GAO publications on land use, ownership, mgmt, and planning, 1979-83, annual listing, 26104–11.3

Interior Dept programs, activities, and funding, various periods 1967-84, last issue of annual rpt, 5304–13

Land Mgmt Bur activities and finances, and public land acreage and use, annual State rpt series, 5724–11

Land Mgmt Bur public lands admin and program activities in western States, FY82-84, annual rpt, 5724–13

Offshore rent and royalty revenue of Fed Govt, and interest on OCS escrow account, midsession review of FY85 budget, annual rpt, 104–7

Production and revenues from oil, gas, coal, and other minerals on Fed Govt and Indian lands, by State, 1983 with trends from 1920, annual rpt, 5734–2

Production and royalties from oil, gas, coal, and other minerals on Fed Govt and Indian lands, by State and commodity, annual rpt, discontinued, 5664–3

Production, leases, licenses, patents, and Fed Govt receipts for minerals from public lands, FY83, annual rpt, 5724–1.2, 5724–1.4

Production of fossil fuels from Fed Govt administered lands, and percent of US total, 1949-82, annual rpt, 3164–74.1

Production, revenues, and reserves of oil, gas, and minerals from Fed Govt OCS leases, by State and ocean region, 1950s-82, annual rpt, 5734–3

Index by Subjects and Names

State govt taxes on mineral production, severance tax and royalty revenue by selected State, selected years FY73-83, article, 9375–1.407

Wildlife refuge revenues from economic and recreational uses, and refuge managers attitudes toward expanded use, FY81-83, GAO rpt, 26113–128

see also Oil and gas leases

Mineral resources

see Mines and mineral resources

Minerals Management Service

Cost control proposals for Fed Govt programs and mgmt, 3-year savings by function and agency, and financial and operating data, 1960s-81, 16908–1.9

Land Mgmt Bur accounts, Minerals Mgmt Service receipts deposited, FY83, annual rpt, 5724–1.4

Oil and gas OCS leases environmental and socioeconomic impacts and coastal area description, final statement series, 5736–1

Oil and gas OCS reserves of Fed Govt, leasing and exploration activities, production, revenues, and costs, by ocean region, FY83, annual rpt, 5734–4

Oil and gas production, royalties and other revenues, and inspections of leased Federal and Indian lands, annual rpt, discontinued, 5734–1

Oil, gas, and minerals dev, under Fed Govt OCS leases, with production, revenues, reserves, and oil spills, by State and ocean region, 1950s-82, annual rpt, 5734–3

Oil, gas, coal, and other mineral production and revenues from Fed Govt and Indian lands, by State, 1983 with trends from 1920, annual rpt, 5734–2

Oil spill risk analyses for OCS proposed lease sale areas, series, 5736–2

Oil spills from US OCS platforms and pipelines, and from tankers at sea and in port worldwide, various periods 1964-80, 5738–1

Mines and mineral resources

Aerial survey R&D publications, and sources of natural resource and environmental data gathered by air- and spacecraft, quarterly listing, 9502–7

Air pollutant emission factors, by detailed source, 3rd edition, 1983-84 supplements, 9198–13

Air pollution levels for 5 pollutants, by detailed source, State, and Air Quality Control Region, 1981, annual rpt, 9194–7

Alaska minerals resources, production, claims on wildlife refuges, oil and gas leases, and exploratory wells, with maps and bibl, 1983, annual rpt, 5664–11

Biotechnology commercial uses, R&D funding and output, controls, and industry financial and operating data, for US and 5 countries, 1970s-83 and estimated 1984-85, 26358–98

Capacity utilization in 15 manufacturing industries, mining, electric and all utilities, and industrial materials including energy, monthly rpt, 9365–2.19

Capital expenditures for new plants and equipment, by industry div, monthly rpt, quarterly data, 23842–1.1

Census of Population, 1980: detailed socioeconomic and demographic

Index by Subjects and Names

Mines and mineral resources

characteristics, by age, sex, race, Hispanic origin, occupation, and industry, State rpt series, 2531–4

Census of Population, 1980: detailed socioeconomic characteristics, by county, city, and inside-outside SMSAs and central cities, State rpt series, 2531–3

Census of Population, 1980: labor force, by sex, detailed occupation, and region, with comparison to 1970 census, supplementary rpt, 2535–1.12

Central America mineral, energy, and water resources, and natural hazards to resource dev, by country, 1981 with trends from 1977, 5668–71

China economic conditions, agricultural and industrial production, trade, and domestic and foreign investment, 1980-85, 2048–106

Collective bargaining agreements expiring during year, covered workers by SIC 2-digit industry, firm, and union, with summary of key provisions, 1984, annual rpt, 6784–9

Communist, OECD, and selected other countries minerals and metals production, by commodity, 1960s-83, annual rpt, 244–5.6

Construction industry activity, employment and earnings, prices, Federal aid, and foreign contracts, 1970s-83 with projections to 1988, annual article, 2012–1.402

County Business Patterns: establishments, employees, and payrolls, by SIC 4-digit industry and county, 1981, annual State rpt series, 2326–8

County Business Patterns: establishments, employees, and payrolls, by SIC 4-digit industry and county, 1982, annual State rpt series, 2326–6

Developing countries govt policy, and AID and other foreign assistance, effects on private sector dev and socioeconomic conditions, with case studies for 6 countries, 1960s-80, 9918–12

Earnings by industry div, and personal income per capita and by source, by State, MSA, and county, 1977-82, annual regional rpts, 2704–2

Earnings by major industry group, and personal income per capita and by source, by region and State, 1929-82, 2708–40

Employment and earnings, detailed data, monthly rpt, 6742–2.5

Employment by detailed occupation, for 29 SIC 2-digit nonmanufacturing industries, 1981 BLS survey, 6748–60

Employment, earnings, and hours, by selected SIC 1- to 4-digit industry, State, and for 278 major labor areas, 1939-83, annual rpt, 6744–5

Employment, earnings, and hours, by SIC 4-digit nonfarm industry, monthly 1974-Feb 1984, annual update, 6744–4

Employment, earnings, and hours, monthly press release, 6742–5

Employment in regionally concentrated and all industries, and population size, by State, 1970-82, article, 6722–1.413

Employment situation, earnings, hours, and other BLS economic indicators, transcripts of BLS Commissioner's monthly testimony, periodic rpt, 23846–4

Employment, unemployment, and labor force, by demographic and employment characteristics, State, and for 30 metro areas and 11 large cities, 1983, annual rpt, 6744–7

Environmental quality and protection programs, costs, and Fed Govt enforcement, 1983, detailed annual rpt, 484–1

Exports and imports between US and outlying areas, by detailed commodity and mode of transport, monthly rpt, 2422–4

Exports and imports of US, by commodity group, world area, selected country, US coastal area and port, and mode of transport, with seasonal adjustments, monthly rpt, 2422–9

Exports and imports of US by country, and trade shifts by commodity, USITC quarterly monitoring rpt, 9882–9

Exports and imports of US, detailed SIC-based commodities by world area, 1983, annual rpts, 2424–6

Exports and imports of US, totals and as percent of domestic production, by SIC 2- to 5-digit commodity, 1981, annual rpt, 2424–3

Exports of US, detailed Schedule B commodities by country of destination, 1983, annual rpt, 2424–9

Exports of US, detailed Schedule E commodities by mode of transport and world area and country of destination, 1983, annual rpts, 2424–5

Farm real estate transfers, by proposed use of property, region, and State, 1982-83, annual rpt, 1541–8.4

Fed Govt loans, grants, and tax benefits to business, by program and economic sector, projected FY84-88 with effective tax rates for FY80-82, 26306–6.70

Finances and operations, by SIC 2- to 4-digit industry, 1970s-83 and projected to 1988, annual rpt, 2014–4

Financial statements for manufacturing, mining, and trade corporations, by selected SIC 2- to 3-digit industry, quarterly rpt, 2502–1

Foreign direct investment in US, major investors and investments by SIC 4-digit industry, transaction type and value, and location, 1983, annual rpt, 2044–20

Foreign direct investment of US, by selected major industry group and world area, 1980-82, annual article, 2702–1.430

Foreign market and trade for mining industry equipment, and user industry operations, country market research rpts, 2045–16

Foreign minerals production, reserves, and industry role in domestic economy and world supply, country and world region rpt series, 5606–1

Forest, range, and associated waters use and mgmt assessment, and environmental impacts of Forest Service program options, 1977-2030 and trends from 1920, 1208–24

Geological Survey and other publications, 1983, annual listing, 5664–4

Geological Survey programs and funding, FY78-83, annual rpt, 5664–8

Great Lakes trade, by SITC 3-digit commodity, port, vessel type, world area, and country, 1982, annual rpt, 7744–3

Handbook of Labor Statistics, employment, earnings, hours, and labor force characteristics, 1982 and trends, detailed annual rpt, 6724–1

Imports of US, detailed Schedule A commodities by country and world area of origin, and mode of transport, 1983, annual rpts, 2424–2

Imports of US, detailed Schedule A commodities by country, monthly rpt, 2422–2

Imports of US, detailed TSUSA commodities by country of origin, 1983, annual rpt, 2424–4

Income tax returns of corporations, detailed income and tax items by industry, 1981, annual rpt, 8304–4

Income tax returns of corporations, summary data by industry div, 1981 estimates, annual article, 8302–2.403

Income tax returns of corporations with foreign tax credit, income and deductions by type, asset size, and selected industry group, 1980, article, 8302–2.415

Income tax returns of foreign subsidiaries of US corporations, income and tax data, by industry and asset size, 1980, article, 8302–2.410

Income tax returns of partnerships, detailed data by industry, 1981 estimates, annual article, 8302–2.404

Income tax returns of partnerships, receipts by source, deductions by type, and establishments, by selected industry, 1982, annual article, 8302–2.416

Income tax returns of sole proprietorships, detailed data by industry div and selected industry group, 1981, annual rpt, 8304–7

Income tax returns of sole proprietorships, receipts, deductions by type, payroll, and net income, by major industry, 1982, annual article, 8302–2.413

Income tax returns with investment credits, for individuals by income, and for sole proprietorships by industry, 1981, article, 8302–2.409

Input-output structure of US economy, detailed interindustry transactions for 85 industries, and components of final demand, 1977, article, 2702–1.421

Input-output structure of US economy, detailed interindustry transactions for 537 industries, and components of final demand, 1977 benchmark data, 2708–17

Machinery and equipment shipments and exports, by product, 1982-83, annual Current Industrial Rpt, 2506–12.4

Manufacturing census, 1982: financial and operating data, for SIC 4-digit industries by product, preliminary rpt series, 2491–1

Marine nonfuel minerals demand, by mineral type, selected years 1978-83 with projections to 2000, 15048–4

Mineral Industry Surveys, commodity reviews of production, trade, and consumption, advance annual rpt series, 5614–5

Mineral Industry Surveys, commodity reviews of production, trade, stocks, and consumption, monthly rpt series, 5612–1

Mineral Industry Surveys, commodity reviews of production, trade, stocks, and consumption, quarterly rpt series, 5612–2

Mines and mineral resources

Mineral Industry Surveys, explosives and blasting agents consumption by type, industry, and State, 1983, annual rpt, 5614–22

Mineral Industry Surveys, State reviews of production, 1983, advance annual rpt series, 5614–6

Minerals Yearbook, 1982, Vol 1: commodity reviews of production, reserves, supply, use, and trade, annual rpt, 5604–33

Minerals Yearbook, 1982, Vol 2 preprints: State reviews of production and sales by commodity, and business activity, annual rpt series, 5604–16

Minerals Yearbook, 1982, Vol 2: State reviews of production, sales, and firms, by commodity, and business activity, annual rpt, 5604–34

Minerals Yearbook, 1982, Vol 3: foreign country reviews of production, trade, and policies, by commodity, annual rpt, 5604–35

Minerals Yearbook, 1982, Vol 3 preprints: foreign country reviews of production, trade, and policies, by commodity, annual rpt series, 5604–17

Minerals Yearbook, 1983, Vol 1 preprints: commodity reviews of production, reserves, supply, use, and trade, annual rpt series, 5604–15

Minerals Yearbook, 1983, Vol 3 preprints: foreign country reviews of production, trade, and policies, by commodity, annual rpt series, 5604–23

Minority group and women's employment, by occupational group, SIC 2- to 3-digit industry, State, and SMSA, 1981, annual rpt, 9244–1

Natl Forest System wildlife habitat and fishery improvements, use, and game population and harvest by species and forest, by region, FY83, annual rpt, 1204–31

Natl income and product, comprehensive accounts and components, *Survey of Current Business,* monthly rpt, monthly and annual tables, 2702–1.27

Nonfuel minerals company mergers by SIC 1- to 4-digit industry of acquired and acquiring firm, assets, and earnings measures, various periods 1960-79, 5608–145

Nonfuel minerals foreign and US supply under alternative market conditions, reserves, and background industry data, series, 5606–4

Occupational manpower needs and supply by detailed occupation, and educational and training program enrollees and grads by detailed field, 1982 and 1995, biennial rpt, 6744–3

OECD trade, total and for 4 major countries, and US trade by country, by commodity, 1972-82, annual world region rpt series, 244–13

Pollution abatement capital and operating costs under Clean Air and Water Acts, for govts and selected industries, various periods 1970-2000, annual rpt, 9184–11

Producer prices and indexes, by stage of processing and detailed commodity, monthly rpt, 6762–6

Producer prices and indexes, by stage of processing and detailed commodity, monthly 1983, annual supplement, 6764–2

Production, prices, trade, use, employment, tariffs, and stockpiling, by mineral commodity, with foreign comparisons, 1979-83, annual rpt, 5604–18

Productivity, hours, and employment indexes for selected SIC 3- and 4-digit industries, 1954-82, annual rpt, 6824–1.2

Public lands mgmt activities of Land Mgmt Bur in western States, FY82-84, annual rpt, 5724–13

Publications and other material of Mines Bur, 1982, annual listing, 5604–40

Publications and patents of Mines Bur, monthly listing, 5602–2

R&D Fed Govt facilities and services available for private sector use, by field of science, 1984 biennial listing, 2224–4

Scientists, engineers, and technicians employed in private industry, by occupation and industry group, 1980-81, biennial rpt, 9627–23

Small and minority-owned businesses finances and operations, Federal contracts by agency, and worker characteristics, by industry, race, sex, and State, 1950s-83, annual rpt, 9764–6

Southeastern US water supply and quality, with background socioeconomic data, for 8 States, 1960s-2020 with trends from 1930, 9208–119

Statistical Abstract of US, social, political, and economic data, 1950s-83 and trends, annual rpt, 2324–1.3

Transportation census, 1982: trucks, by detailed characteristics, miles traveled, and type of product carried, State rpt series, 2573–1

Water pollution fish kills, by State, location, and pollution source, monthly 1978-80, annual rpt, 9204–3

Water pollution from nonpoint sources, source land uses and acreage, and control program funding, by State or region, various periods 1974-FY84, 9208–123

Water supply and quality, floods, drought, mudslides, and other hydrologic events, by State, 1983, annual rpt, 5664–12

Western States industrial production indexes, Fed Reserve 12th District, quarterly rpt, 9393–1.3

Western US Fed Govt lands by agency and mining restriction status, and energy resources on potential wilderness areas and other lands, 1970s-81 and projected to 1990, 3308–68

Wholesale trade census, 1982: employment, establishments, finances, and operations, by SIC 2- to 4-digit kind of business, SMSA, county, and city, State rpt series, 2405–1

Wholesale trade sales and inventories, by SIC 2- to 3-digit kind of business, monthly rpt, 2413–7

Wholesale trade sales, inventories, purchases, and gross margins, by SIC 2- to 3-digit kind of business and type of ownership, 1983, annual rpt, 2413–13

see also Aluminum and aluminum industry
see also Cement and concrete
see also Census of Mineral Industries
see also Clay industry and products
see also Coal and coal mining
see also Copper and copper industry
see also Gases

Index by Subjects and Names

see also Gemstones
see also Gold
see also Iron and steel industry
see also Lead and lead industry
see also Metals and metal industries
see also Mine accidents and safety
see also Mineral leases
see also Natural gas and gas industry
see also Nonmetallic minerals and mines
see also Offshore mineral resources
see also Offshore oil and gas
see also Oil shale
see also Petroleum and petroleum industry
see also Quarries and stone products
see also Severance taxes
see also Silver
see also Stockpiling
see also Strategic materials
see also Tar sands
see also Tin and tin industry
see also Uranium
see also Zinc and zinc industry
see also under By Commodity in the "Index by Categories"
see also under By Industry in the "Index by Categories"

Minimum income

see Income maintenance

Minimum wage

American Samoa minimum wage rates, employment, earnings, and benefits, by establishment and industry, Nov 1983, biennial rpt, 6504–6

Fair Labor Standards Act minimum wages for farm and nonfarm workers, 1938-84, annual rpt, 4744–3.1

Fed Govt programs and mgmt cost control proposals, 3-year savings by function and agency, and financial and operating data, 1960s-81, 16908–1.3, 16908–1.33

Labor legislation enacted by 48 States, DC, and Guam, 1983, annual summary article, 6722–1.406

Mining

see Mines and mineral resources

Mining Enforcement and Safety Administration

see Mine Safety and Health Administration

Minneapolis, Minn.

Auto dealer repair workers, wages, and benefits, by occupation, size of establishment, and for 24 labor market areas, Nov 1982 survey, 6787–6.202

Census of Housing, 1980: occupancy and unit characteristics, by race, Hispanic origin, and city, SMSA rpt, 2473–1.244

Census of Population and Housing, 1980: detailed population and housing characteristics, by county, city, and census tract, SMSA rpt, 2551–2.244

CPI by component for US city average, and by region, population size, and for 28 SMSAs, monthly press release, 6762–1

CPI by detailed component, for US city average, 28 SMSAs, and 4 regions by population size, monthly rpt, 6762–2

Hospital worker wages by sex and occupation, and benefits, for 22 MSAs, Oct 1981 survey, 6787–6.201

Housing and households detailed characteristics, and unit and neighborhood quality, by inside-outside central cities, 1981 survey, SMSA rpt, 2485–6.29

Repair technicians and apprentices wages and benefits, for 5 types of electrical repair shops in 19 SMSAs, Nov 1981 survey, 6787–6.197

Index by Subjects and Names

Visual impairment survey methodology and results by age, in 3 SMSAs, Aug 1981-Dec 1982, 4478–147

Wages by occupation, and benefits for office and plant workers, 1984 SMSA survey rpt, 6785–11.1

see also under By City and By SMSA or MSA in the "Index by Categories"

Minnesota

- Agricultural cooperatives, membership, activities, and finances, by commodity and selected State, 1900-80 with trends from 1863, 1128–30
- Agriculture census, 1982: farms, farmland, production and costs, and operator characteristics, preliminary State summary and county rpts, 2330–1.27
- Bank deposits in commercial and mutual savings banks and in US branches of foreign banks, by account type, instn, State, SMSA, and county, June 1983, annual rpt, 9295–3.12
- Census of Housing, 1980: occupancy and unit characteristics of SMSAs and central cities, by race, Hispanic origin, and city, State rpt, 2473–1.25
- Census of Population and Housing, 1980: detailed population and housing characteristics, by county, city, and census tract, State rpt, 2551–2.25
- Census of Population, 1980: detailed socioeconomic and demographic characteristics, by age, sex, race, Hispanic origin, and industry, State rpt, 2531–4.25
- County Business Patterns: establishments, employees, and payrolls, by SIC 4-digit industry and county, 1982, annual State rpt, 2326–6.25
- Crime sentencing guidelines for Minnesota by type and severity of offense, 1982, 10048–59
- Employment, earnings, and hours, by selected SIC 1- to 4-digit industry, State, and for 278 major labor areas, 1939-83, annual rpt, 6744–5.1, 6744–5.3
- Energy conservation programs of utilities, actual and predicted gas savings by conservation measure, Minnesota study, 1980-83, 3308–74
- Environmental quality, pollutant discharge by type and source, and EPA protection activities and funding, 1970s-83, biennial regional rpt, 9184–15.5
- Exports of manufactured and agricultural commodities, manufacturing production, and export-related employment, 1960s-82, State rpt, 2046–3.23
- Farm investments, effective rates of Federal/State income and State/local property taxes, by category of structure and equipment, for 7 North Central States, 1981-82, 1548–237
- HHS aid to each State and local govt or private instn, amount obligated, funding agency, and program, FY83, annual listing, 4004–3.5
- Income (personal) per capita and by source, and earnings by industry div, by State, MSA, and county, 1977-82, annual regional rpt, 2704–2.5
- Manufacturing census, 1982: financial and operating data, by SIC 2- to 4-digit industry, State, SMSA, and county, preliminary census div rpt, 2491–3.4

Minority businesses

- Mineral Industry Surveys, State review of production, 1983, advance annual rpt, 5614–6.23
- *Minerals Yearbook, 1982,* Vol 2 preprints: State review of production and sales by commodity, and business activity, annual rpt, 5604–16.24
- *Minerals Yearbook, 1982,* Vol 2: State reviews of production, sales, and firms, by commodity, and business activity, annual rpt, 5604–34
- Population, births, deaths, and net migration, by MSA and county, 1980-82, annual State Current Population Rpt, 2546–4.23
- Population size, Apr 1980 and July 1982, and per capita income, 1979 and 1981, by county and city, State Current Population Rpt, 2546–11.23
- Pulpwood production by county, imports, and individual mill capacity, by species for 7 North Central States, 1982, annual rpt, 1204–19
- Retail trade census, 1982: employment, establishments, sales, and payroll, by SIC 2- to 4-digit kind of business, SMSA, county, and city, State rpt, 2397–1.24
- Savings and loan assns, FHLB 8th District members financial operations by State and SMSA, monthly rpt, 9302–9
- Timber acreage, resources, and removals in Minnesota, by species, county, and ownership class, series, 1206–24
- Transportation census, 1982: trucks, by detailed characteristics, miles traveled, and type of product carried, State rpt, 2573–1.24
- Water supply and quality in streams and lakes, and groundwater levels in wells, by drainage basin, 1982, annual State rpt, 5666–20.22
- *see also* Duluth, Minn.
- *see also* Minneapolis, Minn.
- *see also* Moorhead, Minn.
- *see also* Rochester, Minn.
- *see also* St. Cloud, Minn.
- *see also* St. Paul, Minn.
- *see also* under By State in the "Index by Categories"

Minority Business Development Agency

- Budgets and permanent staff positions appropriated for Commerce Dept agencies, FY84-85, annual rpt, 2004–6
- Fed Govt funding, procurement, and subsidies for minority business, and deposits in minority-owned banks, by agency, FY69-83, annual rpt, 2104–5
- Mgmt and financial assistance through federally funded organizations for minority business, by region, State, and business characteristics, FY83, annual rpt, 2104–6
- Programs, funding, and employment of Commerce Dept agencies, FY83, annual rpt, 2004–1

Minority businesses

- Agriculture census, 1982: farms, farmland, production, finances, and operator characteristics, by county, final State rpt series, 2331–1
- Alabama rural black population, education, employment, health services, and economic status, for 16 counties, selected years 1970-81, 11048–180

Banks minority-owned, selected assets and liabilities, 1982, annual rpt, 9364–5.11

- Defense Fuel Supply Center procurement, prices, stocks, and other activities, FY83, annual rpt, 3904–6
- Defense Fuel Supply Center procurement, prices, stocks, transport, and other activities and finances, FY83, annual rpt, 3904–8
- DOD contractor subcontract awards to small and disadvantaged business, by firm and service branch, quarterly listing, 3542–17
- DOD engineering contract awards by function, contract type, and service branch, and oil and port dredging awards by company, 1970s-83, hearings, 21728–53
- DOE procurement and assistance contracts, by State, contractor type, and top 100 instns, FY83, annual rpt, 3004–21
- Fed Govt aid to State and local govts, expenditures, and direct payments, by program, agency, and State, FY83, annual rpt, 2464–2
- Fed Govt funding, procurement, and subsidies for minority business, and deposits in minority-owned banks, by agency, FY69-83, annual rpt, 2104–5
- Fed Govt procurement contract awards, by State, agency, procurement and contractor type, and for top 100 contractors, quarterly rpt, 102–6
- Franchise businesses minority-owned, by kind of business, 1982, annual rpt, 2014–5.1
- Hispanic Americans socioeconomic and demographic characteristics, and compared to non-Hispanics, selected years 1970-83, chartbook, 2328–48
- Mgmt and financial assistance through federally funded organizations for minority business, by region, State, and business characteristics, FY83, annual rpt, 2104–6
- Mgmt counseling of small business by university centers, costs, funding, and businesses served by industry, with detail for 2 States, 1980-83, hearing, 25728–36
- NASA procurement contract awards, by type, contractor, State, and country, FY84, semiannual rpt, 9502–6
- Navy procurement awards to disadvantaged and women-owned businesses, FY83, annual rpt, 3804–13.3
- Small Business Admin loan and contract activity by program, and balance sheets, FY83, annual rpt, 9764–1.1
- Small Business Investment Companies finances, funding, licensing, and loan activity, 2nd half FY84, semiannual rpt, 9762–3
- Small businesses owned by minorities and women, firms and receipts, owner characteristics, and Federal contracts by agency, by product or service, 1970s-82, annual rpt, 9764–6.4
- Travel agency financial and operating data, and airline ticket sales by type of distributor, 1970s-82, hearing, 25268–81
- TV and radio industry minority and women employment by occupation, and business owners, by race and State, with revenues and stations, 1971-81, hearing, 21368 45

Minority businesses

see also Survey of Minority-Owned Business Enterprises

Minority Enterprise Small Business Investment Companies

see Small Business Investment Companies

Minority groups

- Apprenticeship of minorities and women in labor-mgmt, employer, and referral union programs, annual rpt, discontinued, 9244–7
- Cancer deaths and death rates, by body site, race, sex, State, and county, 1950-79, 4478–146
- Census of Housing, 1980: inventory, occupancy, and unit characteristics, changes from 1973 by region and inside-outside SMSAs and central cities, series, 2473–3
- Census of Housing, 1980: occupancy and unit characteristics of SMSAs and central cities, by race, Hispanic origin, and city, State and SMSA rpt series, 2473–1
- Census of Population and Housing, 1980: detailed population and housing characteristics, by county, city, and census tract, State and SMSA rpt series, 2551–2
- Census of Population, 1980: detailed socioeconomic and demographic characteristics, by age, sex, race, Hispanic origin, occupation, and industry, State rpt series, 2531–4
- Census of Population, 1980: detailed socioeconomic characteristics, by county, city, and inside-outside SMSAs and central cities, State rpt series, 2531–3
- Community dev programs funding and activities, for 5 HUD programs, FY83, annual rpt, 5124–5
- Crime in public schools, assaults and robberies of teachers and minority and other students, and vandalism incidents, 1976/77, 4808–12
- Defense Fuel Supply Center procurement, prices, stocks, transport, and other activities and finances, FY83, annual rpt, 3904–8
- Developing countries disaster preparedness and summary sociodemographic, political, and economic data, country rpt series, 9916–2
- Developing countries economic dev projects funded by multilateral dev banks, environmental and cultural impacts, 1970s-83, hearings, 21248–80
- DOT employment of minorities and women full-time, 1971-81, annual rpt, 7304–1
- Economic Dev Admin loans and grants, by program, State, county, and project or recipient, FY83 and cumulative FY66-83, annual rpt, 2064–2
- Employment of minorities and and women, by occupational group, SIC 2- to 3-digit industry, State, and SMSA, 1981, annual rpt, 9244–1
- Fed Govt civilian employment of minority groups and women, by grade and agency, 1980 and 1983, 21348–41
- Fed Govt minority group and handicapped employment, by race, Hispanic origin, disability, sex, and employment characteristics, as of Sept 1982, biennial rpt, 9844–27
- Foreign economic, social, and political summary data, by country, 1984, annual factbook, 244–11

Head Start Project programs effect on child dev, by characteristics of program, child, and family, literature review, selected years 1965-81, 4608–20

- Health professionals supply and education, by occupation, demographic and professional characteristics, and location, 1950s-83 and projected to 2000, biennial rpt, 4114–8
- Health professions employment and training of minorities and women, by field, selected years 1962/63-1983/84, 4118–18
- Health Services Research Natl Center grants and contracts, by program area, FY83, annual listing, 4184–2
- Homeless population and characteristics, and temporary shelter operations, use, and user characteristics, by region and selected city, 1983, 5188–108
- Housing (rental) rehabilitation projects of HUD, owner minority status, funding, assisted units, and location for 141 projects, 1984 press release, 5006–3.38
- Job Training Partnership Act participants, by program and socieconomic characteristics, Oct 1983-June 1984 with funding to 1985/86, 6408–63
- Medical residents by specialty and race, and minority medical faculty by race and Hispanic origin, selected years 1980-83, 4102–1.412
- Medical Sciences Natl Inst research programs and funding, FY83, annual rpt, 4474–12
- New Communities program of HUD, activities, costs, land sales, and community and population characteristics, for 13 communities, 1970s-83, 5188–107
- NIH Research Resources Div activities, accomplishments, and funding, by program, FY83, annual rpt, 4434–12
- Nuclear engineering student enrollments and degrees granted, by State, instn, and subfield, and placements by sector, 1983, annual rpt, 3004–5
- Older persons population characteristics, and needs and costs of social services by type, by metro-nonmetro status, 1970s-82 with trends from 1900, 21148–28
- Radiation protection and health physics enrollments and degrees granted by State and instn, and grads employment, 1983, annual rpt, 3004–7
- Scientists and engineers employment, salaries, and degrees, by field, type of employer, race, and sex, selected years 1960-81, annual rpt, 9624–18.5
- State Dept and Foreign Service minority and women employment by pay level, and affirmative action plan, FY83, annual rpt, 7004–11
- *Statistical Abstract of US,* social, political, and economic data, 1950s-83 and trends, annual rpt, 2324–1.1
- TV and radio industry employment, total and for minorities, women, and youth, by job category and State, 1979-83, annual rpt, 9284–16
- TV and radio industry minority and women employment by occupation, and business owners, by race and State, with revenues and stations, 1971-81, hearing, 21368–45
- TV and radio station employment, total and for minorities and women, by full- and part-time status and individual station, 1983, annual rpt, 9284–7

Index by Subjects and Names

- TVA employment of minorities and women, by detailed occupation, pay level, and grade, FY83 and goals for FY84, annual rpt, 9804–17
- *see also* Alaska Natives
- *see also* Asian Americans
- *see also* Black Americans
- *see also* Civil rights
- *see also* Hispanic Americans
- *see also* Indians
- *see also* Minority businesses
- *see also* Pacific Islands Americans
- *see also* Racial discrimination
- *see also* Survey of Minority-Owned Business Enterprises
- *see also* under By Race in the "Index by Categories"

Minority-Owned Business Enterprise Survey

see Survey of Minority-Owned Business Enterprises

Mint

see Spices and herbs

Mint Bureau

see Bureau of the Mint

Miscarriage

see Fetal deaths

Mishawaka, Ind.

see also under By SMSA or MSA in the "Index by Categories"

Missile bases

- Construction put in place, permits authorized by region, State, and MSA, and Federal contract awards, by construction type, bimonthly rpt with articles, 2012–1
- MX missile basing proposals of Reagan Admin, 1984 narrative rpt update, 3508–17

Missiles and rockets

- Army personnel assigned to critical occupation specialties by skill type, and working outside specialty at 5 installations, as of Mar 1982, GAO rpt, 26123–59
- Census of Population, 1980: detailed socioeconomic and demographic characteristics, by age, sex, race, Hispanic origin, occupation, and industry, State rpt series, 2531–4
- County Business Patterns: establishments, employees, and payrolls, by SIC 4-digit industry and county, 1981, annual State rpt series, 2326–8
- County Business Patterns: establishments, employees, and payrolls, by SIC 4-digit industry and county, 1982, annual State rpt series, 2326–6
- Developing countries arms transfers from US, USSR, and Europe, by weapon type and world region, 1974-82, 25948–3
- DOD budget, costs of individual weapons or weapons systems, FY83-85, annual rpt, 3504–2
- DOD budget, FY85 weapons system requests consistency with US policy and specified treaties, with funding FY83-87, annual rpt, 21384–4
- DOD budget, itemized account of legislative history, FY84, annual rpt, 3504–7
- DOD budget justification for procurement programs, by equipment type, service branch, and defense agency, FY83-86, annual rpt, 3504–14
- DOD budget justification, programs, and policies, FY85, annual rpt, 3544–2

Index by Subjects and Names

Mississippi

DOD budget, organization, personnel, weapons, and property, by service branch, State, and country, 1984 annual summary rpt, 3504–13

DOD expenditures for goods and services, by function, 1972-84, article, 2702–1.440

DOD outlays and obligations, by function and service branch, quarterly rpt, 3542–3

DOD procurement cost estimate changes for weapons systems, and program delays and mgmt, by system and service branch, 1983, annual rpt, 26304–5

DOD procurement cost estimates for weapons and communications systems, by service branch, quarterly summary rpt, 3502–1

DOD procurement, prime contract awards by category, contract and contractor type, and service branch, FY74-1st half FY84, semiannual rpt, 3542–1

DOD procurement, prime contract awards by detailed procurement category, FY80-83, annual rpt, 3544–18

DOD procurement, prime contract awards for 25 commodity categories and R&D, by State and census div, FY81-83, annual rpt, 3544–11

Employment, earnings, and hours, by selected SIC 1- to 4-digit industry, State, and for 278 major labor areas, 1939-83, annual rpt, 6744–5

Employment, earnings, and hours, by SIC 4-digit nonfarm industry, monthly 1974-Feb 1984, annual update, 6744–4

Exports and imports of US, detailed SIC-based commodities by world area, 1983, annual rpts, 2424–6

Exports and imports of US, totals and as percent of domestic production, by SIC 2- to 5-digit commodity, 1981, annual rpt, 2424–3

Foreign and US astronautic and aeronautic events, comprehensive chronology, 1976, annual rpt, 9504–2

Foreign military aid of US and sales of arms, equipment, and training, by item, FY50-83, annual rpt, 3904–3

Foreign military spending, arms trade, and armed forces size, with total govt spending and population, by country, 1972-82, annual rpt, 9824–1

Income tax returns of corporations, detailed income and tax items by industry, 1981, annual rpt, 8304–4

Input-output structure of US economy, detailed interindustry transactions for 537 industries, and components of final demand, 1977 benchmark data, 2708–17

Manufacturing census, 1982: financial and operating data, by SIC 2- to 4-digit industry, State, SMSA, and county, preliminary census div rpt series, 2491–3

Manufacturing census, 1982: financial and operating data, for SIC 4-digit industries by product, preliminary rpt, 2491–1.401, 2491–1.402, 2491–1.403

MX missile basing proposals of Reagan Admin, 1984 narrative rpt update, 3508–17

MX missile procurement funding, and contract awards by company, FY84 with procurement projections to FY89, GAO rpt, 26123–75

MX missile procurement progress and costs, various dates 1979-83 and projected to 1990, GAO rpt, 26123–74

NASA project launch schedules and technical descriptions, press release series, 9506–2

NATO and US weapons and troop strength compared to Warsaw Pact and USSR, as of Jan 1984, annual rpt, 3564–1

Navy budget and Navy and Marine Corps forces, equipment, and budget summary, planned FY84-85, semiannual pamphlet, 3802–3

Nuclear reactors for domestic use and export by function, with owner, operating characteristics, and location, Apr 1984, semiannual listing, 3002–5

Nuclear weapon forces of US and USSR under Strategic Arms Reduction Talks and alternative proposals and counting methods, by weapon and system, FY84-96, 26306–6.73

Occupational injury and illness rates, by SIC 2- to 4-digit industry, 1982, annual rpt, 6844–1

Procurement, DOD prime contract awards to small and total business, for 10 categories and R&D, monthly rpt, 3542–10

Sales, and new and backlog orders for military and nonmilitary customers, quarterly Current Industrial Rpt, 2506–12.22

Soviet Union and US satellites by mission and vulnerability to attack, and USSR anti-satellite missiles, 1983 and projected to 1989, hearing, 21208–18

Soviet Union and US space flights, and NASA financial and employment data, 1957-83, annual rpt, 9504–6

Soviet Union and Warsaw Pact military weapons systems, assistance and presence worldwide, and force strengths, with selected US and NATO comparisons, as of 1984, 3508–14

Soviet Union propaganda campaign against NATO nuclear missile deployment, and USSR and NATO nuclear arms and aircraft in place, 1977-83, narrative rpt, 9828–25

Space and aeronautics programs and budgets of Fed Govt by agency, and foreign programs, 1957-FY85, annual rpt, 9504–9

see also Missile bases

Mission, Tex.

Housing vacancy rates for single and multifamily units and mobile homes, by city and ZIP code, 1984, annual metro area rpt, 9304–19.23

see also under By SMSA or MSA in the "Index by Categories"

Mississippi

Agriculture census, 1982: farms, farmland, production, finances, and operator characteristics, by county, final State rpt, 2331–1.24

Alcohol fuel (ethanol) production in Tennessee Valley, feedstocks, facilities, tax incentives, and related farming data, by State, 1970s-83 and projected to 1992, 9808–69

Bank deposits in commercial and mutual savings banks and in US branches of foreign banks, by account type, instn, State, SMSA, and county, June 1983, annual rpt, 9295–3.9

Biomass Fuels Program of TVA, technologies and processes dev, costs, and resource requirements, 1970s-90s, series, 9806–9

Census of Housing, 1980: occupancy and unit characteristics of SMSAs and central cities, by race, Hispanic origin, and city, State rpt, 2473–1.26

Census of Population and Housing, 1980: detailed population and housing characteristics, by county, city, and census tract, State rpt, 2551–2.26

Census of Population, 1980: detailed socioeconomic and demographic characteristics, by age, sex, race, Hispanic origin, and industry, State rpt, 2531–4.26

Coastal environmental characteristics, fish, wildlife, and use, and population socioeconomic data, for individual areas, 1983 rpt, 5506–4.2

Collective bargaining calendar for Southeast US, 1984, annual rpt, 6946–1.68

County Business Patterns: establishments, employees, and payrolls, by SIC 4-digit industry and county, 1982, annual State rpt, 2326–6.26

Employment (nonagricultural) by industry div and SMSA, earnings, and hours, for 8 southeastern States, monthly press release, 6942–7

Employment, earnings, and hours, by selected SIC 1- to 4-digit industry, State, and for 278 major labor areas, 1939-83, annual rpt, 6744–5.1, 6744–5.3

Employment, prices, earnings, and union membership in 8 southeastern States, Oct 1982-83, annual rpt, 6944–2

Employment, unemployment, farm cash receipts, and residential building permits, for Mississippi, various periods 1968-83, article, 9371–1.409

Environmental quality, pollutant discharge by type and source, and EPA protection activities and funding, 1970s-83, biennial regional rpt, 9184–15.4

Exports of manufactured and agricultural commodities, manufacturing production, and export-related employment, 1960s-82, State rpt, 2046–3.24

Financial and economic devs, Fed Reserve Bank of Atlanta monthly rpt with articles, 9371–1

Fish and shellfish landings, prices, and cannery production, for Gulf States and North Carolina, by area, weekly rpt, 2162–6.3

HHS aid to each State and local govt or private instn, amount obligated, funding agency, and program, FY83, annual listing, 4004–3.4

Income (personal) per capita and by source, and earnings by industry div, by State, MSA, and county, 1977-82, annual regional rpt, 2704–2.6

Manufacturing census, 1982: financial and operating data, by SIC 2- to 4-digit industry, State, SMSA, and county, preliminary census div rpt, 2491–3.6

Mineral Industry Surveys, State review of production, 1983, advance annual rpt, 5614–6.24

Minerals Yearbook, 1982, Vol 2 preprints: State review of production and sales by commodity, and business activity, annual rpt, 5604–16.25

Mississippi

Minerals Yearbook, 1982, Vol 2: State reviews of production, sales, and firms, by commodity, and business activity, annual rpt, 5604–34

- Population, births, deaths, and net migration, by MSA and county, 1980-82, annual State Current Population Rpt, 2546–4.24
- Population size, Apr 1980 and July 1982, and per capita income, 1979 and 1981, by county and city, State Current Population Rpt, 2546–11.24
- Retail trade census, 1982: employment, establishments, sales, and payroll, by SIC 2- to 4-digit kind of business, SMSA, county, and city, State rpt, 2397–1.25
- Rice stocks on and off farms and total, periodic rpt, 1621–7
- Savings and loan assns, FHLB 9th District insured members financial condition and operations by SMSA, monthly rpt, 9302–13
- Service industry census, 1982: employment, establishments, receipts, and payroll, by SIC 2- to 4-digit kind of business, SMSA, county, and city, State rpt, 2391–1.25
- Textile mill employment and average hours and earnings, for 8 Southeastern States, monthly press release, 6942–1
- Water supply and quality in streams and lakes, and groundwater levels in wells, by drainage basin, 1982, annual State rpt, 5666–20.23
- Water supply and quality in 8 southeastern States, with background socioeconomic data, 1960s-2020 with trends from 1930, 9208–119
- Wood residue production and use in TVA region, by tree species group and residue type, for 44 counties, 1979, technical paper, 9806–2.36
- *see also* Biloxi, Miss.
- *see also* Columbus, Miss.
- *see also* Gulfport, Miss.
- *see also* Hattiesburg, Miss.
- *see also* Jackson, Miss.
- *see also* Lownes County, Miss.
- *see also* Meridian, Miss.
- *see also* Moss Point, Miss.
- *see also* Pascagoula, Miss.
- *see also* Vicksburg, Miss.
- *see also* under By State in the "Index by Categories"

Mississippi River

- Bridges over navigable waters, with type of bridge and use, owner, dimensions, and location, 1984 regional listing, 7406–5.2
- Fish landings, employment, gear used, and seafood production, for detailed species by State, 1977, annual rpt, 2164–2.9
- Freight (waterborne domestic and foreign) by commodity, traffic, and passengers, by port and waterway, 1982, annual rpt, 3754–3.2
- Ports, port facilities by type, and inland waterways by size, by location, 1982-83, annual rpt, 7704–16
- Water supply and quality in streams and lakes, and groundwater levels in wells, by drainage basin, 1980, annual State rpt series, 5666–12
- Water supply and quality in streams and lakes, and groundwater levels in wells, by drainage basin, 1981, annual State rpt series, 5666–16

Water supply and quality in streams and lakes, and groundwater levels in wells, by drainage basin, 1982, annual State rpt series, 5666–20

- Water supply and quality in streams and lakes, and groundwater levels in wells, by drainage basin, 1983, annual State rpt series, 5666–10
- Water supply in US and Canada, streamflow, well and reservoir levels, and dissolved solids and temperature in 6 US rivers, by station, monthly rpt, 5662–3

Missouri

- Agricultural cooperatives, membership, activities, and finances, by commodity and selected State, 1900-80 with trends from 1863, 1128–30
- Agriculture census, 1982: farms, farmland, production and costs, and operator characteristics, preliminary State summary and county rpts, 2330–1.29
- Agriculture census, 1982: farms, farmland, production, finances, and operator characteristics, by county, final State rpt, 2331–1.25
- Bank deposits in commercial and mutual savings banks and in US branches of foreign banks, by account type, instn, State, SMSA, and county, June 1983, annual rpt, 9295–3.13
- Census of Housing, 1980: occupancy and unit characteristics of SMSAs and central cities, by race, Hispanic origin, and city, State rpt, 2473–1.27
- Census of Population and Housing, 1980: detailed population and housing characteristics, by county, city, and census tract, State rpt, 2551–2.27
- Census of Population, 1980: detailed socioeconomic and demographic characteristics, by age, sex, race, Hispanic origin, and industry, State rpt, 2531–4.27
- County Business Patterns: establishments, employees, and payrolls, by SIC 4-digit industry and county, 1982, annual State rpt, 2326–6.27
- Employment, earnings, and hours, by selected SIC 1- to 4-digit industry, State, and for 278 major labor areas, 1939-83, annual rpt, 6744–5.1, 6744–5.3
- Environmental quality, pollutant discharge by type and source, and EPA protection activities and funding, 1970s-83, biennial regional rpt, 9184–15.7
- Exports of manufactured and agricultural commodities, manufacturing production, and export-related employment, 1960s-82, State rpt, 2046–3.25
- HHS aid to each State and local govt or private instn, amount obligated, funding agency, and program, FY83, annual listing, 4004–3.7
- Income (personal) per capita and by source, and earnings by industry div, by State, MSA, and county, 1977-82, annual regional rpt, 2704–2.5
- Manufacturing census, 1982: financial and operating data, by SIC 2- to 4-digit industry, State, SMSA, and county, preliminary census div rpt, 2491–3.4
- Mineral Industry Surveys, State review of production, 1983, advance annual rpt, 5614–6.25
- *Minerals Yearbook, 1982,* Vol 2 preprints: State review of production and sales by commodity, and business activity, annual rpt, 5604–16.26

Index by Subjects and Names

- *Minerals Yearbook, 1982,* Vol 2: State reviews of production, sales, and firms, by commodity, and business activity, annual rpt, 5604–34
- Population size and components of change, by MSA and county, 1980-82, annual State Current Population Rpt, 2546–4.25
- Population size, Apr 1980 and July 1982, and per capita income, 1979 and 1981, by county and city, State Current Population Rpt, 2546–11.25
- Pulpwood production by county, imports, and individual mill capacity, by species for 7 North Central States, 1982, annual rpt, 1204–19
- Retail trade census, 1982: employment, establishments, sales, and payroll, by SIC 2- to 4-digit kind of business, SMSA, county, and city, State rpt, 2397–1.26
- Rice stocks on and off farms and total, periodic rpt, 1621–7
- Savings and loan assns, FHLB 8th District members financial operations by State and SMSA, monthly rpt, 9302–9
- Timber production in Missouri, by species, product, and inventory unit, 1980, with trends from 1946, 1206–10.6
- Water supply and quality in streams and lakes, and groundwater levels in wells, by drainage basin, 1980, annual State rpt, 5666–12.24
- *see also* Columbia, Mo.
- *see also* Joplin, Mo.
- *see also* Kansas City, Mo.
- *see also* Springfield, Mo.
- *see also* St. Joseph, Mo.
- *see also* St. Louis, Mo.
- *see also* under By State in the "Index by Categories"

Missouri River

- Bridges over navigable waters, with type of bridge and use, owner, dimensions, and location, 1984 regional listing, 7406–5.2, 7406–5.4
- Freight (waterborne domestic and foreign) by commodity, traffic, and passengers, by port and waterway, 1982, annual rpt, 3754–3.2
- Reclamation programs of Fed Govt in western US, finances and operations by project and State, 1981-82, annual rpts, 5824–1
- Water supply and quality in streams and lakes, and groundwater levels in wells, by drainage basin, 1980, annual State rpt series, 5666–12
- Water supply and quality in streams and lakes, and groundwater levels in wells, by drainage basin, 1981, annual State rpt series, 5666–16
- Water supply and quality in streams and lakes, and groundwater levels in wells, by drainage basin, 1982, annual State rpt series, 5666–20
- Water supply and quality in streams and lakes, and groundwater levels in wells, by drainage basin, 1983, annual State rpt series, 5666–10
- Water supply in US and Canada, streamflow, well and reservoir levels, and dissolved solids and temperature in 6 US rivers, by station, monthly rpt, 5662–3

Index by Subjects and Names

Mobility limitations

Mitchell, Karlyn

"Interest Rate Uncertainty and Corporate Debt Maturity", 9381–10.29

Mobile, Ala.

- Census of Housing, 1980: occupancy and unit characteristics, by race, Hispanic origin, and city, SMSA rpt, 2473–1.245
- Census of Population and Housing, 1980: detailed population and housing characteristics, by county, city, and census tract, SMSA rpt, 2551–2.245
- Wages by occupation, and benefits for office and plant workers, 1984 labor market area survey rpt, 6785–3.9
- Waterborne commerce of US (domestic and foreign), freight by commodity, traffic, and passengers, by port and waterway, 1982, annual rpt, 3754–3.2

see also under By City and By SMSA or MSA in the "Index by Categories"

Mobile homes

- Appalachian States, FHLB 5th District housing vacancy rates for single and multifamily units and mobile homes, by ZIP code, annual metro area rpt series, 9304–27
- California housing market, and Los Angeles average home price and mortgage rate, 1969-82 with economic indicators projected to 1989, 9306–1.1
- California mobile home sales, monthly rpt, 9302–17
- Census of Housing, 1980: inventory, occupancy, and unit characteristics, changes from 1973 by region and inside-outside SMSAs and central cities, series, 2473–3
- Census of Housing, 1980: occupancy and unit characteristics of SMSAs and central cities, by race, Hispanic origin, and city, State and SMSA rpt series, 2473–1
- Census of Housing, 1980: structural, financial, and householder characteristics, by region and State, 2475–4
- Census of Population and Housing, 1980: detailed population and housing characteristics, by county, city, and census tract, State and SMSA rpt series, 2551–2
- Census of Population, 1980: detailed socioeconomic and demographic characteristics, by age, sex, race, Hispanic origin, occupation, and industry, State rpt series, 2531–4
- County Business Patterns: establishments, employees, and payrolls, by SIC 4-digit industry and county, 1981, annual State rpt series, 2326–8
- County Business Patterns: establishments, employees, and payrolls, by SIC 4-digit industry and county, 1982, annual State rpt series, 2326–6
- Employment, earnings, and hours, by selected SIC 1- to 4-digit industry, State, and for 278 major labor areas, 1939-83, annual rpt, 6744–5
- Employment, earnings, and hours, by SIC 4-digit nonfarm industry, monthly 1974-Feb 1984, annual update, 6744–4
- Energy use, costs, expenditures, and conservation, and household and housing characteristics, EIA survey series, 3166–7
- Exports and imports of US, detailed SIC-based commodities by world area, 1983, annual rpts, 2424–6

Exports of US, detailed commodities by country of destination, monthly rpt, 2422–3

- Fed Govt programs and mgmt cost control proposals, 3-year savings by function and agency, and financial and operating data, 1960s-81, 16908–1.31
- Fires and related deaths in mobile homes, and rates compared to site-built homes, 1960-78, article, 1502–7.402
- Florida and California elderly migration by selected State of origin or destination, and Florida elderly, by sociodemographic and housing characteristics, 1970 and 1980, 4478–150
- Housing and households detailed characteristics, and unit and neighborhood quality, by inside-outside central cities, 1979-82 surveys, SMSA rpt series, 2485–6
- Housing and households selected characteristics, by urban-rural location, 1981, annual survey, 2485–7.1
- Housing occupancy and unit and household characteristics, by region and metro-nonmetro residence, 1983, biennial survey, 2485–1
- Income tax returns of corporations, detailed income and tax items by industry, 1981, annual rpt, 8304–4
- Income tax returns of sole proprietorships, detailed data by industry div and selected industry group, 1981, annual rpt, 8304–7
- Income tax returns of sole proprietorships, receipts, deductions by type, payroll, and net income, by major industry, 1982, annual article, 8302–2.413
- Input-output structure of US economy, detailed interindustry transactions for 537 industries, and components of final demand, 1977 benchmark data, 2708–17
- Installment credit outstanding, by type of financial instn and credit, monthly rpt, 9365–2.6, 9365–2.7
- Loans (FHA-insured) for property improvement and mobile homes, by State and county, 1983 and cumulative from 1972, annual rpt, 5144–16
- Loans for property improvement and mobile homes, FHA-insured and claims paid, quarterly rpt, 5142–9
- Loans for property improvement and mobile homes, FHA-insured, monthly rpt, suspended, 5142–10
- Manufacturing census, 1982: financial and operating data, by SIC 2- to 4-digit industry, State, SMSA, and county, preliminary census div rpt series, 2491–3
- Manufacturing census, 1982: financial and operating data, for SIC 4-digit industries by product, preliminary rpt, 2491–1.126
- North Central States, FHLB 7th District housing vacancy rates for single and multifamily units and mobile homes, by ZIP code, annual metro area rpt series, 9304–18
- Pacific Northwest electricity consumption and prices by end-use sector, and economic and demographic data, 1960s-83 and projected to 2005, annual rpt, 3224–2
- Producer prices and indexes, by stage of processing and detailed commodity, monthly rpt, 6762–6

Producer prices and indexes, by stage of processing and detailed commodity, monthly 1983, annual supplement, 6764–2

- Residential placements, average sales price, and dealer inventories, by region, monthly rpt, 2382–1
- Retail trade census, 1982: employment, establishments, sales, and payroll, for mobile home dealers, by State, preliminary rpt, 2395–1.4
- Retail trade sales, inventories, purchases, gross margin, and accounts receivable, by SIC 2- to 4-digit kind of business and type of ownership, 1983, annual rpt, 2413–5
- Safety standards, program inspections, enforcement actions, and accidents and casualties in mobile homes by victim characteristics, 1982-83 biennial rpt, 5004–4
- Shipments by manufacturers, bimonthly rpt, 2012–1.2
- Shipments by manufacturers, *Survey of Current Business,* monthly rpt, 2702–1.3
- Shipments from manufacturers, by State, monthly rpt, periodic table, 2382–5
- Shipments of mobile homes, by State, 1981-83, annual rpt, 2384–2
- South Central States, FHLB 9th District housing vacancy rates for single and multifamily units and mobile homes by ZIP code, annual metro area rpt series, 9304–19
- VA loan guarantee operations, monthly rpt, 9922–1
- VA programs and activities, monthly rpt, 9922–2
- Virgin Islands economic censuses, 1982: employment, establishments, payroll, and receipts, by SIC 1- to 4-digit industry, island, and city, 2593–1
- West Central States, FHLB 10th District housing vacancy rates for single and multifamily units and mobile homes, by ZIP code, annual metro area rpt series, 9304–22
- Western States, FHLB 11th District housing vacancy rates for single and multifamily units and mobile homes, by ZIP code, annual metro area rpt series, 9304–20
- Western States, FHLB 12th District housing vacancy rates for single and multifamily units and mobile homes, by ZIP code, annual metro area rpt series, 9304–21
- Western States housing outlook and economic and demographic trends, FHLB 11th District, urban area rpt series, 9306–2

Mobility

see Labor mobility

see Migration

see Mobility limitations

Mobility limitations

- Arizona nursing home patients aged 55 and older in urban and rural areas, impairment levels for specified functions, 1980, article, 4102–1.413
- Building access for handicapped persons to Fed Govt or federally funded facilities, compliance activities and complaints by agency, FY83, annual rpt, 17614–1
- Bus industry collective ratemaking and regulatory reform impacts on operations, finances, and services to older persons and rural areas by State, 1970s-83, 14828–2

Mobility limitations

Canada and US hospital use by children by Canada Province and US region, and death rates, by diagnosis and sex, selected years 1977-79, 4147–5.1

Census of Population and Housing, 1980: detailed population and housing characteristics, by county, city, and census tract, State and SMSA rpt series, 2551–2

Census of Population, 1980: detailed socioeconomic characteristics, by county, city, and inside-outside SMSAs and central cities, State rpt series, 2531–3

Children with disability, early education research and service project activities and characteristics, and grants to States for program dev, 1983-84, annual listing, 4804–30

Disability Insurance beneficiaries sociodemographic and medical characteristics, 1977-79, annual rpt, 4744–20

Fed Govt minority group and handicapped employment, by race, Hispanic origin, disability, sex, and employment characteristics, as of Sept 1982, biennial rpt, 9844–27

Florida and California elderly migration by selected State of origin or destination, and Florida elderly, by sociodemographic and housing characteristics, 1970 and 1980, 4478–150

Head Start Project enrollment of handicapped children, by handicap, State, and for Indian and migrant programs, 1982, annual rpt, 4604–1

Health condition and health care resources, use, and expenditures, 1970s-82 with trends and projections 1900-2000, annual compilation, 4144–11

Health insurance coverage and health services use, for persons with and without activity limitation, 1977 survey, 4186–3.19

Hispanic Americans health services use, illness rates, and disability days, by socieconomic characteristics, and compared to blacks and whites, 1978-80, 4147–10.147

Housing projects for older and handicapped persons, construction and rehabilitation loans of HUD, FY84, annual listing, 5004–6

Older persons by demographic, socioeconomic, and health characteristics, selected years 1900-81 and projected to 2050, Current Population Rpt, 2546–2.125

Older persons entitled to both Medicare and Medicaid, demographic characteristics, and health condition and services use, 1980, article, 4652–1.433

Older persons health care total and out-of-pocket expenditures, by sociodemographic characteristics, poverty and health status, and degree of functional limitation, 1980, 4146–11.4

Older persons health status, health services use and expenditures by type, Medicare enrollment and reimbursement, and private insurance coverage, 1977-84, article, 4652–1.420

Older persons nutrition services program operations and assessment, and participant sociodemographic, health, and diet characteristics, 1976 and 1982, 4608–16

Older persons population characteristics, and needs and costs of social services by type, by metro-nonmetro status, 1970s-82 with trends from 1900, 21148–28

Transit services ridership, by service type, 1983 rpt, 7306–9.6

Transit systems research publications, 2nd half FY83, semiannual listing, 7882–1

Vital and Health Statistics series and other NCHS publications, 1979-83, annual listing,, 4124–1

Vocationally rehabilitated persons under State agency programs, by sociodemographic characteristics and disabling condition, FY79-81, annual rpt, 4944–6

see also Disabled and handicapped persons

Mobs

see Riots and disorders

Model cities programs

see Community Development Block Grants

Models

see Economic and econometric models

Modesto, Calif.

Census of Housing, 1980: occupancy and unit characteristics, by race, Hispanic origin, and city, SMSA rpt, 2473–1.246

Census of Population and Housing, 1980: detailed population and housing characteristics, by county, city, and census tract, SMSA rpt, 2551–2.246

Housing vacancy rates for single and multifamily units and mobile homes, by city and ZIP code, 1983, annual metro area rpt, 9304–20.1

see also under By City and By SMSA or MSA in the "Index by Categories"

Moffatt, Ronald E.

"Oceanographic Data Exchange, 1983", 2144–15

Moffitt, L. Joe

"Farmers' Perceptions and Information Sources: A Quantitative Analysis", 1502–3.401

Mohair

see Wool and wool trade

Mohler, Stanley R.

"Civil Pilot Taxonomy: Implications for Flight Safety", 21148–34

Molasses

see Sugar industry and products

Moles, Oliver C.

"Trends in Interpersonal Crimes in Schools", 4918–13

Moline, Ill.

Census of Housing, 1980: occupancy and unit characteristics, by race, Hispanic origin, and city, SMSA rpt, 2473–1.134

Census of Population and Housing, 1980: detailed population and housing characteristics, by county, city, and census tract, SMSA rpt, 2551–2.134

Housing vacancy rates for single and multifamily units and mobile homes, by county, city, and ZIP code, 1983, annual metro area rpt, 9304–18.3

Wages of office and plant workers, by occupation, 1984 SMSA survey rpt, 6785–11.4

see also under By SMSA or MSA in the "Index by Categories"

Molybdenum

see Metals and metal industries

Index by Subjects and Names

Monaco

Economic, social, and political summary data, by country, 1984, annual factbook, 244–11

Exports of US, detailed Schedule B commodities by country of destination, 1983, annual rpt, 2424–9

Imports of US, detailed TSUSA commodities by country of origin, 1983, annual rpt, 2424–4

Population size and growth rates, and latest available benchmark demographic data, by country, 1950-83, biennial rpt, 2324–4

see also under By Foreign Country in the "Index by Categories"

Monahan, John

"Crime and Mental Disorder", 6066–20.5

Monder, Harvey

"Child Support Enforcement Statistics, FY83", 4004–29

Monetary Control Act

Reserve requirements before and after Monetary Control Act of 1980, by deposit type, 1984 article, 9381–1.408

Monetary policy

Capital movements among countries, effect on economic stability and monetary policy, 2-country simulation model, 1983 technical paper, 9387–8.85

Economic performance of US, and Reagan Admin 1984 spending, tax, and monetary policy proposals, with data for 1950s-83 and projected to 1988, press release, 8008–107

Economic policy and banking practices, Fed Reserve staff study series, 9366–1

Economic Report of the President for 1984, economic trends from 1929 and Reagan Admin proposals, annual rpt, 204–1

Economic Report of the President for 1984, Joint Economic Committee critique and policy recommendations, annual rpt, 23844–2

Fed Reserve Board and Reserve banks financial statements and employees, and review of monetary policy and economic devs, 1983, annual rpt, 9364–1

Fed Reserve lagged and contemporaneous reserve requirements accounting, and monetary policy operating procedures, effects on discount window borrowing, 1983 technical paper, 9387–8.87

Fed Reserve monetary control, evaluation of reserve-oriented operating procedures, Oct 1979-Oct 1982, technical paper, 9366–6.78

Fed Reserve monetary control procedures and money supply announcements impacts on interest rate volatility, Nov 1977-Dec 1983, technical paper, 9387–8.93

Fed Reserve monetary policy, intermediate target preference among economists and financial analysts, 1983 surveys, article, 9375–1.405

Fed Reserve monetary policy objectives, and performance of major economic indicators, July 1984, semiannual rpt, 9362–4

Fed Reserve monetary policy, with debt, GNP, and M1 velocity growth, and interest rates, 1980-82 and monthly 1983, annual article, 9381–1.401

Fed Reserve reserve requirements before and after Monetary Control Act of 1980, by deposit type, 1984 article, 9381–1.408

Index by Subjects and Names

Money supply

Financial and economic analysis of banking and nonbanking sectors, technical paper series, 9381–10

Financial and economic devs, Fed Reserve Bank of Dallas bimonthly rpt articles, 9379–1

Financial and economic devs, Fed Reserve Bank of Minneapolis quarterly rpt articles, 9383–6

Financial and economic devs, Fed Reserve Bank of New York quarterly rpt with articles, 9385–1

Financial and economic devs, Fed Reserve Bank of Philadelphia bimonthly rpt articles, 9387–1

Financial and economic devs, Fed Reserve Bank of St Louis monthly rpt articles, 9391–1

Foreign monetary control policy and relation to credit, exchange rates, GNP, and other indicators, US and selected West European countries, various periods 1960-82, conf papers, 9373–3.26

Intl finance and financial policy, external factors affecting US economy, econometric model methodology and results for US and 4 countries, various periods 1964-75, 9368–78

Monetary aggregates, targeted and actual growth of M1, 1980-84, and velocity of M1 over business cycles, 1954-82, article, 9381–1.406

Monetary policy views of Reagan Admin, with data on economic and monetary growth, selected years 1960-83, press release, 8008–108

see also Credit
see also Fiscal policy
see also Foreign exchange
see also Inflation
see also Money supply

Money market funds
see Mutual funds

Money supply

Budget deficits effect on economic indicators and trade balance of US and 4 countries, model results, various periods 1974-85, technical paper, 9366–7.102

Budget of US, deficit effect on inflation, and debt outstanding by holder, Reagan Admin mid-1983 outlook for FY83-84 with supporting data from 1949, article, 9371–1.402

Business Conditions Digest, cyclical indicators, by economic process, monthly rpt, 2702–3.3

Business Conditions Digest, historical supplement on economic, business, and financial conditions and cyclical fluctuations, with methodology, 1947-82, 2708–31

Business statistics, detailed data for major industries and economic indicators, *Survey of Current Business,* monthly rpt, 2702–1.6

Cash mgmt techniques for electronic funds transfer and short-term investment, effect on money demand, aggregated 1920-79, article, 9389–1.409

Currency and coin outstanding and in circulation, by type and denomination, *Treasury Bulletin,* quarterly rpt, 8002–4.20

Currency and other products delivered by Bur of Engraving and Printing, annual rpt, discontinued, 8164–1

Economic and population time series data frequently used in statistical demand analyses, 1941-1982, annual rpt, 1544–21

Economic indicators and components, and Fed Reserve 4th District business and financial conditions, monthly chartbook, 9377–10

Economic indicators and components, current data and annual trends, monthly rpt, 23842–1.5

Economic performance of US, and Reagan Admin 1984 spending, tax, and monetary policy proposals, with data for 1950s-83 and projected to 1988, press release, 8008–107

Employment and wages, effect of money supply fluctuation, model description, 1984 technical paper, 9366–7.104

Fed Reserve lagged and contemporaneous reserve requirements accounting, and monetary policy operating procedures, effects on discount window borrowing, 1983 technical paper, 9387–8.87

Fed Reserve monetary control procedures and money supply announcements impacts on interest rate volatility, Nov 1977-Dec 1983, technical paper, 9387–8.93

Fed Reserve monetary policy objectives, and performance of major economic indicators, July 1984, semiannual rpt, 9362–4

Financial and business statistics, historic trends, 1984 annual chartbook, 9364–2.1

Financial and business statistics, quarterly chartbook, 9362–2.1

Financial and economic analysis and forecasting methodology, technical paper series, 9366–6

Financial and economic devs, Fed Reserve Bank of St Louis monthly rpt articles, 9391–1

Financial and economic trends, compounded annual rates of change, 1964-83, annual rpt, 9391–9.1

Financial and monetary conditions, selected US summary data, weekly rpt, 9391–4

Foreign economic and monetary trends, compounded annual rates of change for US and 10 major trading partners, quarterly rpt, 9391–7

Foreign economic indicators and currency exchange rates, by world area and selected country, mid-1960s-83, annual rpt, 204–1.9

Foreign economic indicators for 7 OECD countries and US, quarterly rpt, 2042–10

Foreign economic trends and implications for US, annual and semiannual country rpt series, 2046–4

Foreign monetary control policy and relation to credit, exchange rates, GNP, and other indicators, US and selected West European countries, various periods 1960-82, conf papers, 9373–3.26

Foreign money supply and velocity, prices, and real GNP, growth rates for 4 OECD countries and US, various periods 1954-81, article, 9391–1.401

GNP components growth related to changes in negotiable orders of withdrawal accounts and other M1 components, various periods 1948-84, article, 9385–1.413

GNP related to money supply growth rate variability, regression analysis, various periods 1962-83, article, 9391–1.411

GNP related to M1 with and without interest-bearing checkable deposits, 1960-83, regression results, article, 9391–1.408

Inflation and GNP related to growth of money supply and nonfinancial sector debt, various periods 1960-83, article, 9373–1.401

Inflation related to money supply growth, wage growth, and corporate bond and real interest rates, 1960-83, article, 9377–1.403

Interest rates as targets for money supply control, for US and Canada, 1975-79, technical paper, 9381–10.38

Massachusetts (Colonial era) prices, foreign exchange rate, and per capita money supply, and compared to other New England colonies, 1720-70, article, 9383–6.402

Monetary aggregates and money stock, 1979-82, annual rpt, 9364–5.1

Monetary aggregates, demand for M1 and M2, quarterly 1982-83, article, 9393–8.410

Monetary aggregates, domestic nonfinancial debt, GNP, and interest rates, regression analysis of interrelationships, 1954-1982, article, 9389–1.402

Monetary aggregates growth and related devs, and Fed Open Market Committee activity, various dates 1959-83, annual article, 9385–1.407

Monetary aggregates, money stock measures and components, monthly rpt, 9362–1.1

Monetary aggregates, targeted and actual growth of M1, 1980-84, and velocity of M1 over business cycles, 1954-82, article, 9381–1.406

Monetary aggregates velocity under 3 forecasting models, 2nd qtr 1959-2nd qtr 1984, technical paper, 9377–9.13

Monetary and Fed Govt budget trends, Fed Reserve Bank of St Louis monthly rpt, 9391–2

Monetary growth rates, revisions to M1, M2, and M3, and effects of seasonal and benchmark adjustments, various periods 1978-84, article, 9362–1.404

Monetary policy views of Reagan Admin, with data on economic and monetary growth, selected years 1960-83, press release, 8008–108

Monetary targets, effects of deregulated interest rates on M1 growth, 1984 article, 9393–8.402

Monetary targets, effects of inflation expectations and interest rates on M1 velocity, 1984 article, 9393–8.409

Money demand and actual money balances, alternative dynamic adjustment models, various periods Oct 1976-Oct 1983, article, 9393–8.404

Money market mutual funds exclusion from M1, assessment based on activity of 1 fund, 1982-June 1983, article, 9383–6.403

Money stock, 1959-83, annual rpt, 204–1.5

OECD economic indicators, for US and 6 countries, biweekly rpt, 242–4

Pacific Basin economic indicators, US and 12 countries, quarterly rpt, 9393–9

Money supply

Recession, M1 and interest rates performance as leading indicators, various periods 1949-83, article, 9385–1.410

Reserve requirements of Fed Reserve System contemporaneous accounting system, effects on methodology for calculating of adjusted monetary base, 1984 narrative article, 9391–1.407

Seasonal adjustment methodology for economic time series, dev and design of Census Bur and other systems, with illustrative data, 1981 conf papers, 2626–7.5

Seasonal adjustments to monetary growth rates, accuracy assessment and behavior of various M1 components, Aug 1973-Feb 1984, article, 9389–1.405

UK money supply growth and inflation rates related public and private monetary control, 1694-1913, article, 9391–1.410

Underground economic activity, estimates of unreported income based on monetary statistics, various periods 1950-82, article, 9362–1.402

see also Coins and coinage

see also Counterfeiting and forgery

see also Credit

see also Eurocurrency

see also Flow-of-funds accounts

see also Foreign exchange

see also Monetary policy

see also Special foreign currency programs

Mongelli, Robert C.

"Costs of Watermelon Handling from Grower to Retailer", 1308–18

Mongolia

Background Notes, summary social, political, and economic data, 1983 rpt, 7006–2.13

Cuba economic conditions, agricultural and industrial production and distribution, trade, and intl economic relations, 1970-82 and trends from 1957, 248–40

Economic, social, and political summary data, by country, 1984, annual factbook, 244–11

Export licensing and monitoring activities under Export Admin Act, for selected commodities, and for Communist and other countries, FY83, annual rpt, 2044–22

Exports and imports of US with Communist countries, by detailed commodity and country, quarterly rpt with articles, 9882–2

Exports of US, detailed Schedule B commodities by country of destination, 1983, annual rpt, 2424–9

Exports of US, detailed Schedule E commodities by mode of transport and world area and country of destination, 1983, annual rpts, 2424–5

Imports of US, detailed Schedule A commodities by country and world area of origin, and mode of transport, 1983, annual rpts, 2424–2

Imports of US, detailed TSUSA commodities by country of origin, 1983, annual rpt, 2424–4

Military spending, arms trade, and armed forces size, with total govt spending and population, by country, 1972-82, annual rpt, 9824–1

Minerals Yearbook, 1982, Vol 3: foreign country reviews of production, trade, and policies, by commodity, annual rpt, 5604–35

Minerals Yearbook, 1982, Vol 3 preprints: foreign country review of production, trade, and policies, by commodity, annual rpt, 5604–17.87

Population size and growth rates, and latest available benchmark demographic data, by country, 1950-83, biennial rpt, 2324–4

Science and technology dev and transfer between USSR and other members of Council for Mutual Economic Assistance, 1940s-81, 2326–9.7

see also under By Foreign Country in the "Index by Categories"

Monmouth County, N.J.

Wages of office and plant workers, by occupation, 1983 labor market area survey rpt, 6785–3.3

see also under By SMSA or MSA in the "Index by Categories"

Monopolies

see also Antitrust law

see also Cartels

see also Competition

see also Economic concentration and diversification

Monroe, La.

Census of Housing, 1980: occupancy and unit characteristics, by race, Hispanic origin, and city, SMSA rpt, 2473–1.247

Census of Population and Housing, 1980: detailed population and housing characteristics, by county, city, and census tract, SMSA rpt, 2551–2.247

see also under By SMSA or MSA in the "Index by Categories"

Montana

Agriculture census, 1982: farms, farmland, production and costs, and operator characteristics, preliminary State summary and county rpts, 2330–1.30

Agriculture census, 1982: farms, farmland, production, finances, and operator characteristics, by county, final State rpt, 2331–1.26

Bank deposits in commercial and mutual savings banks and in US branches of foreign banks, by account type, instn, State, SMSA, and county, June 1983, annual rpt, 9295–3.15

Census of Housing, 1980: occupancy and unit characteristics of SMSAs and central cities, by race, Hispanic origin, and city, State rpt, 2473–1.28

Census of Population and Housing, 1980: detailed population and housing characteristics, by county, city, and census tract, State rpt, 2551–2.28

Coal Fed Govt leases, acreage, production, and prices, by State, and legal and mgmt issues, 1970s-83 with production projections to 2000, 11128–1

Coal production in Montana and North Dakota impact of mining on agricultural land availability and on farm income and production costs, by mining tract, 1982 rpt, 1588–79

County Business Patterns: establishments, employees, and payrolls, by SIC 4-digit industry and county, 1982, annual State rpt, 2326–6.28

Earnings by SIC 1- to 3-digit industry and payments to retirees by type, for 4 timber dependent communities in Oregon and Montana, 1970 and 1978, 1208–196

Index by Subjects and Names

Employment, earnings, and hours, by selected SIC 1- to 4-digit industry, State, and for 278 major labor areas, 1939-83, annual rpt, 6744–5.1, 6744–5.3

Environmental quality, pollutant discharge by type and source, and EPA protection activities and funding, 1970s-83, biennial regional rpt, 9184–15.8

Exports of manufactured and agricultural commodities, manufacturing production, and export-related employment, 1960s-82, State rpt, 2046–3.26

Forest biomass in Rocky Mountain States, conversion from volume to dry weight, for softwood and hardwood species, 1977, 1208–200

Grizzly bears in and around Yellowstone Natl Park, population, physical characteristics, diet, and movements, 1982, annual rpt, 5544–4

HHS aid to each State and local govt or private instn, amount obligated, funding agency, and program, FY83, annual listing, 4004–3.8

Hwy and bridge repair projects funded by Fed Govt, and costs, for 7 States, FY81-82, GAO rpt, 26113–121

Income (personal) per capita and by source, and earnings by industry div, by State, MSA, and county, 1977-82, annual regional rpt, 2704–2.8

Lumber production, prices, trade, and employment in Northwest US and British Columbia, quarterly rpt, 1202–3

Manufacturing census, 1982: financial and operating data, by SIC 2- to 4-digit industry, State, SMSA, and county, preliminary census div rpt, 2491–3.8

Mineral Industry Surveys, State review of production, 1983, advance annual rpt, 5614–6.26

Minerals Yearbook, 1982, Vol 2 preprints: State review of production and sales by commodity, and business activity, annual rpt, 5604–16.27

Minerals Yearbook, 1982, Vol 2: State reviews of production, sales, and firms, by commodity, and business activity, annual rpt, 5604–34

Phosphate rock reserves in southeastern and northwestern US, by location, 1984 rpt, 5668–74

Population size and components of change, by MSA and county, 1980-82, annual State Current Population Rpt, 2546–4.26

Population size, Apr 1980 and July 1982, and per capita income, 1979 and 1981, by county and city, State Current Population Rpt, 2546–11.26

Recreation sites of Forest Service in northern Idaho and Montana, itemized operating and maintenance costs by type of site, 1980, 1208–202

Retail trade census, 1982: employment, establishments, sales, and payroll, by SIC 2- to 4-digit kind of business, SMSA, and retail district, State rpt, 2401–1.27

Retail trade census, 1982: employment, establishments, sales, and payroll, by SIC 2- to 4-digit kind of business, SMSA, county, and city, State rpt, 2397–1.27

Savings and loan assns, FHLB 12th District members financial operations and housing industry indicators by State, monthly rpt, 9302–21

Index by Subjects and Names

Morocco

Service industry census, 1982: employment, establishments, receipts, and payroll, by SIC 2- to 4-digit kind of business, SMSA, county, and city, State rpt, 2391–1.27

Timber acreage, resources, and mortality in Montana, by species and ownership class, 1976-80, series, 1206–25

Timber resources and removals in 9 Rocky Mountain States, and forest and rangeland area, by ownership, forest and tree characteristics, and State, 1977, 1208–201

Wages for 3 occupational groups, relative average levels in 78 labor market areas, 1983, annual press release, 6785–13

Wages of office and plant workers, by occupation, 1984 labor market area survey rpt, 6785–3.9

Water supply and quality in streams and lakes, and groundwater levels in wells, by drainage basin, 1983, annual State rpt, 5666–10.25

Water supply, and snow survey results, monthly State rpt, 1266–2.5

Water supply in Montana, snow water accumulations and reservoir storage, annual rpt, suspended, 1264–7

Wholesale trade census, 1982: employment, establishments, finances, and operations, by SIC 2- to 4-digit kind of business, SMSA, county, and city, State rpt, 2405–1.27

see also Billings, Mont.

see also Great Falls, Mont.

see also under By State in the "Index by Categories"

Monterey, Calif.

Census of Housing, 1980: occupancy and unit characteristics, by race, Hispanic origin, and city, SMSA rpt, 2473–1.315

Census of Population and Housing, 1980: detailed population and housing characteristics, by county, city, and census tract, SMSA rpt, 2551–2.315

Housing vacancy rates for single and multifamily units and mobile homes, by city and ZIP code, 1983, annual metro area rpt, 9304–20.6

see also under By SMSA or MSA in the "Index by Categories"

Montgomery, Ala.

Census of Housing, 1980: occupancy and unit characteristics, by race, Hispanic origin, and city, SMSA rpt, 2473–1.248

Census of Population and Housing, 1980: detailed population and housing characteristics, by county, city, and census tract, SMSA rpt, 2551–2.248

see also under By City and By SMSA or MSA in the "Index by Categories"

Montreal, Canada

Fruit and vegetable shipments, and arrivals in 23 US and 5 Canada cities, by mode of transport and State or country of origin, 1983, annual rpt, 1311–4.1

Monuments and memorials

Acid rain causes and effects, air pollutant emissions by source in US and selected countries, and control costs, 1970s-83 and projected to 2000, 21368–52

Fed Govt-owned real property inventory and costs, worldwide summary by location, agency, and use, 1983, annual rpt, 9454–5

Natl park area visits and overnight stays, visitors, and vehicles, by State and park, 1983, annual rpt, 5544–12

Natl park system and other areas under Natl Park Service mgmt, acreage by type of area, ownership, and site, as of Sept 1984, semiannual rpt, 5542–1

Preservation Historic Fund grants, by State, FY85, annual press release, 5544–9

Vietnam Veterans Memorial Fund receipts by source, and disbursements by item and payee, Apr 1979-Mar 1984, GAO rpt, 26111–21

Moonlighting

Labor force, special characteristics, Labor Statistics Handbook, 1947-82, annual rpt, 6724–1.2

Women's employment and earnings, by labor force and socioeconomic characteristics, and compared to men, 1978-81 and trends from 1940s, 6568–29

Moore, Jesse F.

"Changing Technology in Cotton Classing", 1004–16.1

Moore, Melinda

"Epidemiologic, Clinical, and Laboratory Features of Coxsackie B1-B5 Infections in the U.S., 1970-79", 4102–1.452

Moorhead, Minn.

Census of Housing, 1980: occupancy and unit characteristics, by race, Hispanic origin, and city, SMSA rpt, 2473–1.152

Census of Population and Housing, 1980: detailed population and housing characteristics, by county, city, and census tract, SMSA rpt, 2551–2.152

see also under By SMSA or MSA in the "Index by Categories"

Moorhead, Muriel B.

"Petroleum Consumption by Electric Utilities: 10 Years After the Arab Oil Embargo", 3162–39.402

Mopeds

Commuting to work, householder principal mode of transport, distance, and travel time, by race, Hispanic origin, tenure, urban-rural location, and region, 1981, annual survey, 2485–7

Energy use in transportation sector by mode, fuel supplies, and demographic and economic determinants of vehicle use, 1970s-83, annual rpt, 3304–5

Exports of US, detailed Schedule B commodities by country of destination, 1983, annual rpt, 2424–9

Injuries and deaths from use of selected consumer products and related activity, by victim age and sex, 1982, annual rpt, 9164–7

Traffic accidents and occupant and non-occupant deaths, 1972-82, annual rpt, 7304–2

Moran, Michael J.

"Recent Financing Activity of Nonfinancial Corporations", 9362–1.405

Morbidity

see Diseases and disorders

Morey, Art

"Strong Dollar Dampens Demand for U.S. Farm Exports", 1528–174

Morocco

Agricultural and food production indexes, and production of selected commodities, by world region and country, 1974-83, annual rpt, 1524–5

Agricultural situation in Middle East and North Africa, by country and commodity, 1983 and outlook for 1984, annual rpt, 1524–4.3

Agricultural supply/demand, trade, and production, and socioeconomic data, by country, 1950s-77, 1528–179

AID activities and funding by project and function, FY85, and developing countries summary socioeconomic data, 1970s-83, by country, annual rpt, 9914–3

AID economic assistance to developing countries, obligations and disbursements by country, quarterly rpt, 9912–4

AID loan repayment status and terms by program and country, and status of predecessor agency loans, quarterly rpt, 9912–3

Almond production and trade of US and selected countries, 1982/83-1983/84 and forecast 1985, article, 1925–34.425

Economic conditions, income, production, prices, employment, and trade, 1984 annual country rpt, 2046–4.106

Economic, social, and political summary data, by country, 1984, annual factbook, 244–11

Exports of US, detailed Schedule B commodities by country of destination, 1983, annual rpt, 2424–9

Exports of US, detailed Schedule E commodities by mode of transport and world area and country of destination, 1983, annual rpts, 2424–5

Food supply policies of 21 developing countries, with farm sector data, tariff income, and prices and imports of 5 grains, 1960s-81, 1528–168

Imports of US, detailed Schedule A commodities by country and world area of origin, and mode of transport, 1983, annual rpts, 2424–2

Imports of US, detailed TSUSA commodities by country of origin, 1983, annual rpt, 2424–4

Loans and grants for economic and military assistance from US and intl agencies, by program and country, FY46-83, annual rpt, 9914–5

Military aid of US, arms sales, and training programs costs and budget requests by program, world region, and country, FY83-85, annual rpt, 7144–13

Military spending, arms trade, and armed forces size, with total govt spending and population, by country, 1972-82, annual rpt, 9824–1

Minerals Yearbook, 1982, Vol 3: foreign country reviews of production, trade, and policies, by commodity, annual rpt, 5604–35

Minerals Yearbook, 1983, Vol 3 preprints: foreign country review of production, trade, and policies, by commodity, annual rpt, 5604–23.49

Oil and gas undiscovered recoverable resources, cumulative production, and identified reserves, as of 1982, preliminary oil basin rpt, 5666–17.13

Phosphate rock exports of Morocco by country of destination, Mineral Industry Surveys, monthly rpt, periodic table, 5612–1.30

Population size and growth rates, and latest available benchmark demographic data, by country, 1950-83, biennial rpt, 2324–4

Morocco

see also under By Foreign Country in the "Index by Categories"

Moroney, Rita L.

"History of the U.S. Postal Service, 1775-1982", 9864–6

Morra, Marion E.

"Comparison of Nurses' Smoking Habits: The 1975 DHEW Survey and Connecticut Nurses, 1981", 4102–1.403

Morris, Charles S.

"Cyclical Productivity and the Returns to Labor: A Vector Autoregressive Analysis", 9381–10.35

"Productivity 'Slowdown': A Sectoral Analysis", 9381–1.407

"Vector Autoregressions: A User's Guide", 9381–10.41

Morrison, Rosanna M.

"Generic Advertising of Farm Products", 1548–242

Mortality

see Deaths

see Fetal deaths

see Homicide

see Infant mortality

see Life expectancy

see Suicide

see Vital statistics

Mortgages

- Adjustable rate mortgage (ARM) regulation, and characteristics of 24 unidentified ARM programs, Sept 1983 survey, technical paper, 9316–1.104
- AFDC eligibility under Omnibus Budget Reconciliation Act, effect on caseloads and recipient benefits and living costs, 1981-83, GAO rpt, 26131–11
- Appalachian States, FHLB 5th District member S&Ls financial condition and operations by SMSA, monthly rpt, 9302–8
- Bank financial and operating statements, functional cost analysis for Fed Reserve member banks with average and high earnings, by deposit size, 1982, annual rpt, 9364–6
- Bank interstate service offices, including S&Ls, bank branches, and nonbank subsidiaries offering financial services, by instn and State, 1981-83, 9371–13
- Bankruptcy (personal), filers by debt type, employment and financial status, race, and Hispanic origin, 1982 survey, hearings, 21528–57.2
- Bond tax-exempt issues by purpose, and Fed Govt mortgage bond revenue losses and borrower characteristics, selected years 1971-85, hearings, 21788–135
- Bond tax-exempt issues for home mortgage subsidy, Fed Govt costs, and loans, mortgage value, and borrowers by jurisdiction, by borrower income, Dec 1981-July 1982, GAO rpt, 26113–127
- Bond tax-exempt issues for home mortgage subsidy, issuance and purchase price limits for tax-exempt status, by State and MSA, 1984 annual press releases, 8304–16
- Bond tax-exempt issues for public and private purposes, by use of proceeds, 1975-83, article, 9362–1.408
- Budget of US, effects of Reagan Admin policy changes, by detailed program, FY85, annual rpt, 104–21
- *Business Conditions Digest,* cyclical indicators, by economic process, monthly rpt, 2702–3.3

Business Conditions Digest, historical supplement on economic, business, and financial conditions and cyclical fluctuations, with methodology, 1947-82, 2708–31

- Business statistics, detailed data for major industries and economic indicators, *Survey of Current Business,* monthly rpt, 2702–1.3
- California (southern) housing demand by county, prices and sales, and costs after homeowner tax deductions, 1970s-80, hearing, 21148–31
- California housing market, and Los Angeles average home price and mortgage rate, 1969-82 with economic indicators projected to 1989, 9306–1.1
- Census of Govts, 1982: properties, govt-assessed value, sales, and tax rates, by property type, State, SMSA, county, and city, 2453–1
- Census of Housing, 1980: inventory, occupancy, and unit characteristics, changes from 1973 by region and inside-outside SMSAs and central cities, series, 2473–3
- Census of Housing, 1980: occupancy and unit characteristics of SMSAs and central cities, by race, Hispanic origin, and city, State and SMSA rpt series, 2473–1
- Census of Housing, 1980: structural, financial, and householder characteristics, by region and State, 2475–4
- Census of Population and Housing, 1980: detailed population and housing characteristics, by county, city, and census tract, State and SMSA rpt series, 2551–2
- Debt outstanding, by type of property and holder, 1939-83, annual rpt, 204–1.5
- Defaulted mortgages, single family homes acquired by HUD and disposition by city, monthly rpt, 5142–31
- Economic trends and projections, 1970s-83, and Budget of US under current fiscal policy and alternatives, FY85-89, annual rpt, 26304–3.1
- Fed Govt aid to State and local govts, expenditures, and direct payments, by program, agency, and State, FY83, annual rpt, 2464–2
- Fed Govt mortgage insurance of FHA and VA for new housing, bimonthly rpt, 2012–1.2
- Fed Govt programs and mgmt cost control proposals, 3-year savings by function and agency, and financial and operating data, 1960s-81, 16908–1.8
- Fed Home Loan Banks and S&Ls, financial condition and mortgage loan activity, monthly rpt with articles, 9312–1
- Fed Home Loan Mortgage Corp activities and financial statements, 1983, annual rpt, 9414–1
- Financial and business statistics, historic trends, 1984 annual chartbook, 9364–2.11, 9364–2.12
- Financial and business statistics, quarterly chartbook, 9362–2.6
- Financial instn mortgage and mortgage-related investments, by instn type and Fed Govt issuing agency, various dates 1981-84, 5008–33
- Financial instns income taxes, effective rates, and selected financial data, by instn type and firm, with comparisons to other industries, selected years 1960-82, hearing, 25368–129

Index by Subjects and Names

- Financial services of nonbank firms and bank holding companies, with financial and operating data by firm, 1981-82 with trends from 1962, technical paper, 9375–11.3
- Flow-of-funds accounts, assets and liabilities by type and economic sector, year-end outstandings, 1960-83, annual rpt, 9364–3
- Flow-of-funds accounts savings, investments, and credit statements, quarterly rpt, 9365–3.3
- FmHA loans for rural home mortgages, eligibility of current recipients under revised income limit, by State, 1983, GAO rpt, 26113–134
- Govt Natl Mortgage Assn financial statements, and mortgage-backed securities program, FY82-83, annual rpt, 5144–6
- Govt Natl Mortgage Assn futures trading, traders open interest contracts on Chicago markets, monthly rpt, 11922–1, 11922–5
- Home and condominium mortgages FHA-insured, new issues, adjustments, and terminations, by program, quarterly rpt, 5142–6
- Home mortgage (conventional) terms on loans closed, and commitment rates, by type of loan and lender and for 32 SMSAs, monthly rpt, 9312–2
- Home mortgage applications for 1- to 4-family homes, commitments, insurance, starts, and units readied, quarterly rpt, 5142–5
- Home mortgage-backed securities prepayment rates and duration, July 1983-June 1984, technical paper, 9316–1.106
- Home mortgage default prospects by mortgage type and borrower characteristics, various periods 1967-82, technical paper, 9381–10.39
- Home mortgage interest rates, effect of deposit interest rate ceiling deregulation, various periods Apr 1975-Mar 1984, article, 9391–1.412
- Home mortgage loan originations, by State and for Puerto Rico, 1978-83, press release, 5148–6
- Home mortgage market activity and debt outstanding, 1979-82, annual rpt, 9364–5.7
- Home mortgage terms on conventional loans by eligibility for Fed Govt secondary purchase, 1983, and alternative eligibility limits for 28 cities, 1984, GAO rpt, 26113–135
- Home mortgage yields of FHLBB for new homes, monthly rpt, 23842–1.5
- Home mortgages (graduated payment) FHA-insured, financial, property, and mortgagor characteristics, for US and selected localities, quarterly rpt, 5142–42
- Home mortgages (graduated payment) FHA-insured, financial, property, and mortgagor characteristics, for US and selected States, quarterly rpt, 5142–41
- Home mortgages (graduated payment) FHA-insured, financial, property, and mortgagor characteristics, US summary, quarterly rpt, 5142–40
- Home mortgages and mortgage pool participation by lender type, and FHA

Index by Subjects and Names

Mortgages

mortgage yields, various periods 1950-84 with trends from 1900, technical paper, 9375–11.4

- Home mortgages FHA-insured, claims, and foreclosures, for low- and moderate-income rental housing and 1- to 4-family homes, periodic rpt, suspended, 5142–27
- Home mortgages FHA-insured, financial, property, and mortgagor characteristics, for US and selected localities, quarterly rpt, 5142–2
- Home mortgages FHA-insured, financial, property, and mortgagor characteristics, for US, selected States, and Puerto Rico, quarterly rpt, 5142–3
- Home mortgages FHA-insured, financial, property, and mortgagor characteristics, quarterly rpt, 5142–1
- Home mortgages FHA-insured, financial, property, and mortgagor characteristics, 1983, annual rpt, 5144–17
- Home mortgages FHA-insured for low-cost homes, financial, construction, property, and mortgagor characteristics, quarterly rpt, 5142–4
- Home mortgages FHA-insured, secondary market prices and interest rates on conventional loans, by region, monthly press release, 5142–20
- Home mortgages insured by private companies, for 1- to 4-family units, monthly press release, 5142–38
- Household income, assets, and debt characteristics, sources of credit, and use of financial services, 1983 survey, article, 9362–1.411
- Housing and households characteristics, and employment, housing finance, and social programs data, selected years 1948-83, hearing, 21968–28
- Housing and households detailed characteristics, and unit and neighborhood quality, by inside-outside central cities, 1979-82 surveys, SMSA rpt series, 2485–6
- Housing and neighborhood quality indicators and attitudes, and occupant characteristics, by urban-rural location and region, 1981, annual survey, 2485–7
- Housing finance studies, technical paper series, 9306–1
- Housing finance technical analysis, quarterly rpt articles, 9312–7, 9412–2
- Housing financing of S&Ls and others, mortgage terms and debt outstanding, and balance sheets of S&Ls and FHLBs, 1983, annual rpt, 9314–3
- Housing, new single and multifamily unit physical and financial characteristics, by region and metro-nonmetro location, 1979-83, annual rpt, 2384–1
- Housing occupancy and unit and household characteristics, by region and metro-nonmetro residence, 1983, biennial survey, 2485–1
- HUD debt collection plans, and single family mortgage foreclosure costs, annual rpt, suspended, 5004–7
- HUD mortgage insurance funds financial and property activity, and insurance written, monthly rpt, 5002–9
- HUD mortgage insurance funds, insurance in force, and property acquisitions and sales, quarterly rpt, 5002–3

HUD programs fraud and abuse, audits and investigations, 2nd half FY84, semiannual rpt, 5002–8

- Illinois S&Ls, mortgage interest fixed and adjustable rates and fees offered, monthly rpt, 9302–6
- Income tax proposals to encourage savings, and personal assets and liabilities by type, 1981, article, 8302–2.407
- Income tax returns of corporations, detailed income and tax items by industry, 1981, annual rpt, 8304–4
- Income tax returns of elderly, by income statement and tax item and income level, 1981 with trends from 1977, article, 8302–2.412
- Income tax returns of individuals, detailed data, 1982, annual rpt, 8304–2
- Interest rate maximums on FHA-insured 1-family mortages, periodic press release, suspended, 5002–6
- Korea (South) housing units completed and home loans and loan value by instn, cumulative 1967-75 and 1976-82, article, 9312–1.406
- Land privately held, acreage and owners by owner characteristics, land use, and region, and purchase and improvement funding, 1978 survey, series, 1506–5
- Life insurance companies commitments for income property mortgages, 1980-82, annual rpt, 9364–5.13
- Loan activity for mortgages, by type of lender, loan, and mortgaged property, monthly rpt, 5142–18
- Loan transactions and holdings, by lender group and type of property and loan, quarterly rpt, 5142–30
- Middle Atlantic States, FHLB 2nd District member savings instns financial operations, by State, monthly rpt, 9302–14
- New England States, FHLB 1st District member instns financial operations and housing industry indicators, monthly rpt, 9302–4
- New England States, FHLB 1st District member savings instns, locations, and financial condition, 1984, annual listing, 9304–26
- New England States financial instn assets and liabilities, Fed Reserve 1st District, monthly rpt, 9373–2.5
- New England States thrift and commercial banking instns financial statements, by type of instn and State, 1972 and 1982, annual rpt, 9304–3
- North Central States, FHLB 6th District insured S&Ls financial condition and operations by State, monthly rpt, 9302–11
- North Central States, FHLB 6th District insured S&Ls financial condition and operations by State, quarterly rpt, 9302–23
- North Central States, FHLB 7th District insured S&Ls cost of funds, and savings flows and mortgage loans closed by SMSA, monthly rpt, 9302–5
- North Central States, FHLB 8th District member S&Ls financial operations by State and SMSA, monthly rpt, 9302–9
- Pension plan investment in Fed Govt mortgage-backed securities, yields by issuer, and fund assets by fund type, 1970s-82, conf papers, 5008–32

Pension plan investment in mortgages and FHLB and Fed Govt mortgage assn mortgage-backed securities, for corporate and union funds, quarterly rpt, 5002–10

- Pension systems of State and local govts finances, membership, beneficiaries, and benefits, by system, 1982-83, annual rpt, 2466–2.4
- Savings and loan assn deregulation impact, financial ratios of S&Ls in 3 States and US, 1980-83, article, 9371–1.426
- Savings and loan assns and FSLIC-insured savings banks and S&Ls, assets, liabilities, and deposit and loan activity, monthly rpt, 9312–4
- Savings and loan assns assets and liabilities, by FHLB district and State, selected years 1955-82, annual rpt, 9314–1
- South Central States, FHLB 9th District insured S&Ls financial condition and operations by SMSA, monthly rpt, 9302–13
- Southeastern States banks by asset size, finances, and loans and deposits by type, Fed Reserve 5th District, various dates 1979-83, annual article, 9389–1.408
- Southeastern States economic indicators, by State, Fed Reserve 5th District, quarterly rpt, 9389–16
- Southeastern States, FHLB 4th District insured S&Ls financial condition and operations, by SMSA, monthly rpt, 9302–1
- Southeastern States, FHLB 4th District member S&Ls financial ratios and mortgage portfolios by State, 2nd half 1983, semiannual rpt, 9302–3
- Southeastern States financial and economic devs, Fed Reserve 6th District, monthly rpt with articles, 9371–1
- Southeastern States S&Ls adjustable- and fixed-rate, and other home mortgages issued, by State and asset size, 4th qtr 1983, survey results, article, 9302–2.401
- Southeastern States S&Ls adjustable rate and other home mortgage terms offered, 4th qtr 1983 and 2nd qtr 1984, article, 9302–2.403
- State and local govt retirement systems, cash and security holdings and finances, quarterly rpt, 2462–2
- Tax expenditures, Fed Govt revenues foregone through income tax deductions and exclusions by type, and effect of Deficit Reduction Act, FY84-89, annual rpt, 21784–10
- Terms, yields, and debt outstanding, monthly rpt, 9362–1.1
- Trust assets of banks and trust companies, by type of asset and fund and State, 1983, annual rpt, 13004–1
- West Central States, FHLB 10th District insured S&Ls finances and operations by SMSA, monthly rpt, 9302–22
- Western States, FHLB 11th District member S&Ls financial condition and operations by State, quarterly rpt, 9302–19
- Western States, FHLB 11th District member S&Ls financial operations and housing industry indicators by State, monthly rpt, 9302–17
- Western States, FHLB 12th District member S&Ls financial operations and housing industry indicators by State, monthly rpt, 9302–21

ASI Annual Supplement 551

Mortgages

Western States housing outlook and economic and demographic trends, FHLB 11th District, urban area rpt series, 9306–2

Wisconsin S&Ls, mortgage interest fixed and adjustable rates and fees offered, monthly rpt, 9302–7

see also Agricultural credit

see also Farm Credit System

see also Veterans housing

Morticians

see Cemeteries and funerals

Morton, Andrew S.

"Crop Price-Support Programs: Policy Options for Contemporary Agriculture", 26306–6.71

Mosher, William D.

"Social and Clinical Correlates of Postpartum Sterilization in the U.S., 1972 and 1980", 4102–1.419

"Use of Contraception in the U.S., 1982", 4146–8.103

"Use of Services for Family Planning and Infertility: U.S., 1982", 4146–8.104

Moss, Abigail J.

"Health Indicators for Hispanic, Black, and White Americans", 4147–10.147

"Health Insurance Coverage and Physician Visits Among Hispanic and Non-Hispanic People", 4144–11.1

Moss Point, Miss.

Census of Housing, 1980: occupancy and unit characteristics, by race, Hispanic origin, and city, SMSA rpt, 2473–1.278

Census of Population and Housing, 1980: detailed population and housing characteristics, by county, city, and census tract, SMSA rpt, 2551–2.278

Wages of office and plant workers, by occupation, 1984 labor market area survey rpt, 6785–3.9

Motels

see Hotels and motels

Mothers

see Aid to Families with Dependent Children

see Births

see Child day care

see Families and households

see Fertility

see Maternity

see Women

Motion pictures

Bombing (explosive and incendiary) incidents, damage, injuries, and deaths, by target, State, and circumstances, 1983, annual rpt, 6224–5

Census of Population, 1980: detailed socioeconomic and demographic characteristics, by age, sex, race, Hispanic origin, occupation, and industry, State rpt series, 2531–4

Census of Population, 1980: labor force, by sex, detailed occupation, and region, with comparison to 1970 census, supplementary rpt, 2535–1.12

Collective bargaining agreements expiring during year, covered workers by SIC 2-digit industry, firm, and union, with summary of key provisions, 1984, annual rpt, 6784–9

County Business Patterns: establishments, employees, and payrolls, by SIC 4-digit industry and county, 1981, annual State rpt series, 2326–8

County Business Patterns: establishments, employees, and payrolls, by SIC 4-digit industry and county, 1982, annual State rpt series, 2326–6

Earnings by major industry group, and personal income per capita and by source, by region and State, 1929-82, 2708–40

Employment by detailed occupation, for 29 SIC 2-digit nonmanufacturing industries, 1981 BLS survey, 6748–60

Employment, earnings, and hours, by selected SIC 1- to 4-digit industry, State, and for 278 major labor areas, 1939-83, annual rpt, 6744–5

Employment, earnings, and hours, by SIC 4-digit nonfarm industry, monthly 1974-Feb 1984, annual update, 6744–4

Exports and imports of US, detailed SIC-based commodities by world area, 1983, annual rpts, 2424–6

Exports of US, detailed Schedule B commodities by country of destination, 1983, annual rpt, 2424–9

Finances and operations, by SIC 2- to 4-digit industry, 1970s-83 and projected to 1988, annual rpt, 2014–4

Income tax returns of corporations, detailed income and tax items by industry, 1981, annual rpt, 8304–4

Income tax returns of partnerships, detailed data by industry, 1981 estimates, annual article, 8302–2.404

Income tax returns of sole proprietorships, detailed data by industry div and selected industry group, 1981, annual rpt, 8304–7

Income tax returns of sole proprietorships, receipts, deductions by type, payroll, and net income, by major industry, 1982, annual article, 8302–2.413

Input-output structure of US economy, detailed interindustry transactions for 537 industries, and components of final demand, 1977 benchmark data, 2708–17

Minority group and women employment, by occupational group and SIC 2- to 3-digit industry, 1981, annual rpt, 9244–1.1

Natl Endowment for Arts activities and grants, FY83, annual rpt, 9564–3

Occupational injury and illness rates, by SIC 2- to 4-digit industry, 1982, annual rpt, 6844–1

Receipts for selected services, by SIC 2- to 4-digit kind of business, 1983, annual rpt, 2413–8

Service industry census, 1982: employment, establishments, receipts, and payroll, by SIC 2- to 4-digit kind of business, SMSA, county, and city, State rpt series, 2391–1

Service industry census, 1982: employment, establishments, receipts, and payroll, by SIC 4-digit kind of business and State, preliminary rpt, 2390–2.12

see also under By Industry in the "Index by Categories"

Motley, Brian

"Dynamic Adjustment in Money Demand", 9393–8.404

"'Great Velocity Decline' of 1982-83: A Comparative Analysis of M1 and M2", 9393–8.410

"How Soon Will the U.S. Reach Full Employment? An Assessment Based on Okun's Law", 9393–8.408

Index by Subjects and Names

Motor Carrier Ratemaking Study Commission

Budget of US, appropriations, outlays, balances, and budget receipts, by govt branch and agency, FY83, annual rpt, 8104–2

Bus industry collective ratemaking and regulatory reform impacts on operations, finances, and services to older persons and rural areas by State, 1970s-83, 14828–2

Motor fuels

see Diesel fuel

see Gasohol

see Gasoline

Motor transportation

see Automobiles

see Buses

see Motor vehicle industry

see Motorcycles

see Taxicabs

see Traffic accidents and safety

see Trucks and trucking industry

Motor vehicle exhaust

Abatement programs, emissions standards dev, monitoring, and enforcement, 1982, annual rpt, 9194–4

Abatement under Clean Air Act, emissions by source, standards, and effects on auto industry and health, 1970s-83, hearings, 25328–25

Acid rain causes and effects, air pollutant emissions by source, and control costs, by region and State, selected years 1977-83 and projected to 2000, 26358–104

Acid rain causes and effects, air pollutant emissions by source in US and selected countries, and control costs, 1970s-83 and projected to 2000, 21368–52

Air quality and transportation and related energy use, for urban areas and Chicago area, late 1970s-82 and projected under lower auto emission standards to 1995, 3408–31

Emission factors, by detailed source, 3rd edition, 1983-84 supplements, 9198–13

Emissions control device tampering and fuel-switching incidence in 6 urban areas, 1983, annual rpt, 9194–15

Emissions levels for 5 pollutants, by detailed source, State, and Air Quality Control Region, 1981, annual rpt, 9194–7

Emissions levels for 5 pollutants, by source, 1970-82 with trends from 1940, annual rpt, 9194–13

Emissions levels for 6 pollutants, by source, region, and for large SMSAs, 1975-82, annual rpt, 9194–1

Emissions standards by vehicle type, and compliance capital and operating costs for auto industry, various periods 1970-90, annual rpt, 9184–11.1

Energy economy test results for autos complying with California emission standards, 1984 model year, annual rpt, 3304–13

Energy use in transportation sector by mode, fuel supplies, and demographic and economic determinants of vehicle use, 1970s-83, annual rpt, 3304–5

Environmental quality and protection programs, costs, and Fed Govt enforcement, 1983, detailed annual rpt, 484–1

Transit system operations, tax burden related to ridership, fares, and govt funding, for selected States and cities, 1950s-82, reprint, 7888–59

Index by Subjects and Names

Motor vehicle industry

see also Air pollution

Motor vehicle industry

- Air pollutant emission factors, by detailed source, 3rd edition, 1983-84 supplements, 9198–13
- Air pollutant emissions control and safety required equipment costs, emissions standards, and diesel car sales by make, 1970s-83, hearings, 25328–25
- Business statistics, detailed data for major industries and economic indicators, *Survey of Current Business,* monthly rpt, 2702–1.20
- Census of Population, 1980: detailed socioeconomic and demographic characteristics, by age, sex, race, Hispanic origin, occupation, and industry, State rpt series, 2531–4
- Census of Population, 1980: detailed socioeconomic characteristics, by county, city, and inside-outside SMSAs and central cities, State rpt series, 2531–3
- China economic conditions, agricultural and industrial production, trade, and domestic and foreign investment, 1980-85, 2048–106
- Collective bargaining agreements expiring during year, covered workers by SIC 2-digit industry, firm, and union, with summary of key provisions, 1984, annual rpt, 6784–9
- Communist, OECD, and selected other countries consumer and producer goods production, 1960s-83, annual rpt, 244–5.8
- County Business Patterns: establishments, employees, and payrolls, by SIC 4-digit industry and county, 1981, annual State rpt series, 2326–8
- County Business Patterns: establishments, employees, and payrolls, by SIC 4-digit industry and county, 1982, annual State rpt series, 2326–6
- Cuba economic conditions, agricultural and industrial production and distribution, trade, and intl economic relations, 1970-82 and trends from 1957, 248–40
- Earnings by major industry group, and personal income per capita and by source, by region and State, 1929-82, 2708–40
- Economic indicators and components, and Fed Reserve 4th District business and financial conditions, monthly chartbook, 9377–10
- Electric-powered vehicles, Fed Govt dev program implementation, FY83, annual rpt, 3304–2
- Employment by detailed occupation, for 29 SIC 2-digit nonmanufacturing industries, 1981 BLS survey, 6748–60
- Employment, earnings, and hours, by selected SIC 1- to 4-digit industry, State, and for 278 major labor areas, 1939-83, annual rpt, 6744–5
- Employment, earnings, and hours, by SIC 4-digit nonfarm industry, monthly 1974-Feb 1984, annual update, 6744–4
- Employment generated by motor vehicle demand, by industry group, and foreign trade zones operations, 1981, 9886–4.70
- Employment in regionally concentrated and all industries, and population size, by State, 1970-82, article, 6722–1.413
- Energy use of autos and light trucks, economy standards and manufacturer

compliance, and gas prices and taxes, with selected foreign comparisons, FY80-83 and projected to 2000, hearing, 21368–49

- Engine production and shipments, by type and size of internal combustion engine, 1982-83, annual Current Industrial Rpt, 2506–12.6
- Experimental vehicle designs and auto safety, 1982, conf proceedings, annual rpt, 7764–3
- Exports and imports of US, detailed SIC-based commodities by world area, 1983, annual rpts, 2424–6
- Exports and imports of US, totals and as percent of domestic production, by SIC 2- to 5-digit commodity, 1981, annual rpt, 2424–3
- Exports, imports, tariffs, and industry operating data for motor vehicles and bodies and chassis, foreign and US, 1979-83, TSUSA commodity rpt, 9885–6.63
- Exports of US, detailed commodities by country of destination, monthly rpt, 2422–3
- Exports of US, detailed Schedule E commodities by mode of transport and world area and country of destination, 1983, annual rpts, 2424–5
- Farmers prices received for major products and paid for farm inputs and living items, by commodity and State, monthly rpt, 1629–1
- Farmers prices received for major products and paid for farm inputs, by commodity and State, 1983, annual rpt, 1629–5
- Fed Govt motor vehicle fleet costs and operating data, by agency, FY83, annual rpt, 9454–9
- Finances and operations, by SIC 2- to 4-digit industry, 1970s-83 and projected to 1988, annual rpt, 2014–4
- Finances, employment, production, and cost increases to comply with Fed Govt pollution and safety standards, 1970s-83, annual rpt, 3304–5.4
- Financial statements for manufacturing, mining, and trade corporations, by selected SIC 2- to 3-digit industry, quarterly rpt, 2502–1
- Foreign and US auto industry operations, trade, and registrations, selected years 1928-82, domestic content requirement hearings, 21788–134
- Franchise business opportunities, by firm and kind of business, 1984 annual listing, 2044–27
- Franchise new car dealers productivity, hours, and employment indexes, 1958-82, annual rpt, 6824–1.4
- Franchises of firms engaged in distribution of goods and services by kind of business, establishments by State, and sales, 1982-84, annual rpt, 2014–5
- FTC budget authority and expenditures for regulatory analysis, by prospective regulation and contractor, 1983, hearings, 21528–56
- Great Lakes trade, by SITC 3-digit commodity, port, vessel type, world area, and country, 1982, annual rpt, 7744–3
- Import quotas and tariffs, jobs protected and cost per job for selected products, and foreign trade balance by industry div, various periods 1958-81, article, 9381–1.412

- Imports of US, detailed Schedule A commodities by country and world area of origin, and mode of transport, 1983, annual rpts, 2424–2
- Income tax returns of corporations, detailed income and tax items by industry, 1981, annual rpt, 8304–4
- Income tax returns of corporations with foreign tax credit, income and deductions by type, asset size, and selected industry group, 1980, article, 8302–2.415
- Income tax returns of foreign subsidiaries of US corporations, income and tax data, by industry and asset size, 1980, article, 8302–2.410
- Income tax returns of partnerships, detailed data by industry, 1981 estimates, annual article, 8302–2.404
- Income tax returns of partnerships, receipts by source, deductions by type, and establishments, by selected industry, 1982, annual article, 8302–2.416
- Income tax returns of sole proprietorships, detailed data by industry div and selected industry group, 1981, annual rpt, 8304–7
- Income tax returns of sole proprietorships, receipts, deductions by type, payroll, and net income, by major industry, 1982, annual article, 8302–2.413
- Industry finances and operations by auto manufacturer, foreign competition, and consumer auto expenditures and attitudes toward car buying, selected years 1968-85, annual rpt, 2004–8
- Industry selected operations, and trade data by country, monthly rpt, 9882–8
- Input-output structure of US economy, detailed interindustry transactions for 85 industries, and components of final demand, 1977, article, 2702–1.421
- Input-output structure of US economy, detailed interindustry transactions for 537 industries, and components of final demand, 1977 benchmark data, 2708–17
- Japan auto export voluntary restraint, effect on US auto industry and import sales and prices, 2nd qtr 1981-1st qtr 1984, article, 9377–1.407
- Manufacturing census, 1982: financial and operating data, by SIC 2- to 4-digit industry, State, SMSA, and county, preliminary census div rpt series, 2491–3
- Manufacturing census, 1982: financial and operating data, for SIC 4-digit industries by product, preliminary rpt series, 2491–1
- Minority group and women employment, by occupational group and SIC 2- to 3-digit industry, 1981, annual rpt, 9244–1.1
- Natl income and product, comprehensive accounts and components, *Survey of Current Business,* monthly rpt, 2702–1.22
- North Central States economic indicators, Fed Reserve 7th District monthly rpt, 9375–9
- Occupational injury and illness rates, by SIC 2- to 4-digit industry, 1982, annual rpt, 6844–1
- OECD trade, total and for 4 major countries, and US trade by country, by commodity, 1972-82, annual world region rpt series, 244–13
- Producer prices and indexes, by stage of processing and detailed commodity, monthly rpt, 6762–6

Motor vehicle industry

Producer prices and indexes, by stage of processing and detailed commodity, monthly 1983, annual supplement, 6764–2

Productivity, hours, and employment indexes for selected SIC 3- and 4-digit industries, 1954-82, annual rpt, 6824–1.3

R&D expenditures of US firms foreign affiliates, by selected industry, 1974-82, 9626–2.131

R&D industry expenditures, total and for 6 leading industries, projected 1984-85 with trends from 1975, 9626–2.145

R&D industry funding and employment of scientists and engineers, by industry group, firm size, and funding source, 1956-82, annual rpt, 9627–21

Recalls of motor vehicles and equipment with safety-related defects, by make, quarterly listing, 7762–2

Retail trade census, 1982: employment, establishments, sales, and payroll, by SIC 2- to 4-digit kind of business, SMSA, and retail district, State rpt series, 2401–1

Retail trade census, 1982: employment, establishments, sales, and payroll, by SIC 2- to 4-digit kind of business, SMSA, county, and city, State rpt series, 2397–1

Retail trade census, 1982: employment, establishments, sales, and payroll, for tire, battery, and auto accessory dealers by State, preliminary rpt, 2395–1.11

Retail trade sales and inventories, by kind of business, region, census div, and selected State, SMSA, and city, and seasonal adjustments, monthly rpt, 2413–3

Robots installed for manufacturing, and jobs displaced and created by occupation, by type of robot use, 1980s-2000, hearings, 21728–54

Sales of domestic and imported new autos and trucks, and US auto production and inventories, 1983-84, annual article, 2702–1.438

Sales, prices, and registrations of autos and auto products in US, and trade of 8 countries with US, by make and model, 1964-83, annual rpt, 9884–7

Scientists, engineers, and technicians employment in transportation, utilities, and retail and wholesale trade, by field of science and industry, 1982, 9628–72

Statistical Abstract of US, social, political, and economic data, 1950s-83 and trends, annual rpt, 2324–1.3

Transportation summary data, traffic, accidents, and deaths, FY81, annual rpt, 7304–1

Virgin Islands economic censuses, 1982: employment, establishments, payroll, and receipts, by SIC 1- to 4-digit industry, island, and city, 2593–1

Wholesale trade census, 1982: employment, establishments, finances, and operations, by SIC 2- to 4-digit kind of business, SMSA, county, and city, State rpt series, 2405–1

Wholesale trade census, 1982: employment, establishments, sales by commodity, and payroll, by SIC 4-digit kind of business and State, preliminary rpt series, 2403–1

Wholesale trade sales and inventories, by SIC 2- to 3-digit kind of business, monthly rpt, 2413–7

Wholesale trade sales, inventories, purchases, and gross margins, by SIC 2- to 3-digit kind of business and type of ownership, 1983, annual rpt, 2413–13

see also American Motors Corp.
see also Automobile repair
see also Automobiles
see also Buses
see also Chrysler Corp.
see also Ford Motor Co.
see also General Motors Corp.
see also Motor vehicle exhaust
see also Motor vehicle registrations
see also Motor vehicle safety devices
see also Motorcycles
see also Recreational vehicles
see also Rubber and rubber industry
see also Tires and tire industry
see also Trucks and trucking industry
see also under By Industry in the "Index by Categories"

Motor vehicle registrations

Communist, OECD, and selected other countries auto registrations, 1983, annual rpt, 244–5.1

Costs of operating and owning autos and vans by component and vehicle size, for 12 years of operation, 1984 model year, annual rpt, 7304–2, 7304–2.3, 7554–21

Costs of operating autos and motorcycles by component and vehicle size or make, and Fed Govt mileage reimbursement rates, 1983, annual rpt, 9454–13

Energy production, reserves, and prices, by energy type, and selected indicators of energy use, by State, 1982-83 with selected comparisons from 1971, annual rpt, 3164–60

Energy use in transportation sector by mode, fuel supplies, and demographic and economic determinants of vehicle use, 1970s-83, annual rpt, 3304–5

Farm production expenditures, detailed items by farm sales size and region, 1983, annual rpt, 1614–3

Foreign and US auto registrations, 1928-81, hearings, 21788–134

Govt census, 1982: State govt payments to local govts, by program, source of funds, level of govt, and State, with trends from 1902, 2460–3

Govt revenues, by type, level of govt, and State, selected years 1902-83, annual rpt, 10044–1.2

Registration fees by type of vehicle, motor fuel tax provisions, and disposition of tax receipts, by State, as of Jan 1984, biennial rpt, 7554–37

Registrations and fuel economy, by type of vehicle, 1960-83, annual rpt, 3164–74.3

Registrations by public and private ownership and vehicle type, and revenues, by State, 1983, annual rpt, 7554–1.2, 7554–1.4

Registrations of motor vehicles, by State and type of vehicle, 1982-83, annual summary rpt, 7554–24

Registrations of new cars, US-made and imports, by region and State, 1964-83, annual rpt, 9884–7.4

Registrations, total and per capita, selected years 1961-81, annual rpt, 7764–1

Tax collections of State govts, by detailed type of tax and tax rates, by State, FY83, annual rpt, 2466–2.3

Index by Subjects and Names

Motor vehicle safety

see Motor vehicle safety devices
see Traffic accidents and safety

Motor vehicle safety devices

Costs of required emissions control and safety devices, 1970s-83, hearings, 25328–25

Experimental vehicle designs and auto safety, 1982, conf proceedings, annual rpt, 7764–3

Fed Govt pollution and safety standards, production cost increases to auto industry, 1970s-83, annual rpt, 3304–5.4

Natl Hwy Traffic Safety Admin activities and funding, and traffic accident data, 1981, annual rpt, 7764–1

Seat belt nonuse and 7 other risk factors associated with 10 major death causes, prevalence in selected States, 1981-83 surveys, article, 4202–7.405

Seat belt use and injury rates, and motorcycle helmet use in all and fatal accidents, 1982, annual rpt, 7764–13

Seat belt use and other health habits of adults, including physical activity, smoking, alcohol use, and hypertension, by age and sex, 1982, annual rpt, 4204–1.3

Seat belt use by blue and white collar workers, results of Virginia projects to increase use, 1983, article, 7762–9.409

Seat belt use by race and sex, results of North Carolina projects to increase use, 1981-84, article, 7762–9.408

Seat belt use, effects of driving circumstances and driver characteristics and attitudes, 1981 survey, 7768–82

Traffic fatal accidents, circumstances, and characteristics of persons and vehicles involved, 1983, annual rpt, 7764–14

Traffic fatal accidents detailed circumstances, and characteristics of persons and vehicles involved, 1982, annual rpt, 7764–10

Motorcycles

Accident deaths in transportation, by mode, 1982-83, annual summary rpt, 9614–6

Accidents (fatal), circumstances, and characteristics of persons and vehicles involved, detailed data, 1982, annual rpt, 7764–10

Accidents (fatal), circumstances, and characteristics of persons and vehicles involved, 1983, annual rpt, 7764–14

Accidents and casualties detailed direct and indirect costs, by characteristics of persons and vehicles involved, 1979-80, 7768–80

Accidents, circumstances, injuries, deaths, and characteristics of persons and vehicles involved, 1982, annual rpt, 7764–13

Accidents, deaths, circumstances, and characteristics of persons and vehicles involved, series, 7766–13

Census of Housing, 1980: structural, financial, and householder characteristics, by region and State, 2475–4

Census of Population, 1980: detailed socioeconomic and demographic characteristics, by age, sex, race, Hispanic origin, occupation, and industry, State rpt series, 2531–4

Census of Population, 1980: detailed socioeconomic characteristics, by county, city, and inside-outside SMSAs and central cities, State rpt series, 2531–3

Index by Subjects and Names

Commuting to work, householder principal mode of transport, distance, and travel time, by race, Hispanic origin, tenure, urban-rural location, and region, 1981, annual survey, 2485–7

Costs of operating motorcycles by component, for 5 makes, and Fed Govt mileage reimbursement rates, 1983, annual rpt, 9454–13.3

County Business Patterns: establishments, employees, and payrolls, by SIC 4-digit industry and county, 1981, annual State rpt series, 2326–8

County Business Patterns: establishments, employees, and payrolls, by SIC 4-digit industry and county, 1982, annual State rpt series, 2326–6

Energy economy and registrations, by type of vehicle, 1960-83, annual rpt, 3164–74.3

Energy use in transportation sector by mode, fuel supplies, and demographic and economic determinants of vehicle use, 1970s-83, annual rpt, 3304–5

Exports and imports of US, detailed SIC-based commodities by world area, 1983, annual rpts, 2424–6

Exports and imports of US, totals and as percent of domestic production, by SIC 2- to 5-digit commodity, 1981, annual rpt, 2424–3

Exports, imports, tariffs, and industry operating data for motorcycles, 1979-83, TSUSA commodity rpt supplement, 9885–6.76

Exports of US, detailed commodities by country of destination, monthly rpt, 2422–3

Exports of US, detailed Schedule B commodities by country of destination, 1983, annual rpt, 2424–9

Exports of US, detailed Schedule E commodities by mode of transport and world area and country of destination, 1983, annual rpts, 2424–5

Great Lakes trade, by SITC 3-digit commodity, port, vessel type, world area, and country, 1982, annual rpt, 7744–3

Hwy-railroad grade-crossing accidents, detailed data by State and railroad, 1982, annual rpt, 7604–2

Hwy safety, accident, and traffic data from Natl Statistics and Analysis Center, series, 7766–10

Hwy Statistics, detailed data on traffic, govt finances, fuel use, vehicles, driver licenses, and hwy characteristics, by State, 1983, annual rpt, 7554–1

Imports of US, detailed Schedule A commodities by country and world area of origin, and mode of transport, 1983, annual rpts, 2424–2

Imports of US, detailed Schedule A commodities by country, monthly rpt, 2422–2

Imports of US, detailed TSUSA commodities by country of origin, 1983, annual rpt, 2424–4

Imports, sales, and inventories of foreign make motorcycles, and prices and employment for domestic makes, quarterly rpt, 9882–12

Income tax returns of sole proprietorships, detailed data by industry div and selected industry group, 1981, annual rpt, 8304–7

Income tax returns of sole proprietorships, receipts, deductions by type, payroll, and net income, by major industry, 1982, annual article, 8302–2.413

Industry finances and operations, by SIC 2- to 4-digit industry, 1970s-83 and projected to 1988, annual rpt, 2014–4

Injuries and deaths from use of selected consumer products and related activity, by victim age and sex, 1982, annual rpt, 9164–7

Input-output structure of US economy, detailed interindustry transactions for 537 industries, and components of final demand, 1977 benchmark data, 2708–17

Manufacturing census, 1982: financial and operating data, for SIC 4-digit industries by product, preliminary rpt, 2491–1.407

OECD trade, total and for 4 major countries, and US trade by country, by commodity, 1972-82, annual world region rpt series, 244–13

Recalls of motor vehicles and equipment with safety-related defects, by make, quarterly listing, 7762–2

Registrations of motor vehicles, by State and type of vehicle, 1982-83, annual summary rpt, 7554–24

Safety programs, and accidents, injuries, deaths, hazards, and property damage, by mode of transport, 1983, annual rpt, 7304–19

Traffic accidents and deaths by characteristics of persons and vehicles involved and State, and Natl Hwy Traffic Safety Admin activities, 1961-81, annual rpt, 7764–1

Traffic accidents, and licensing test results and costs, for 3 California motorcycle licensing programs, 1976-78, article, 7762–9.402

Traffic deaths and death rates, by victim and demographic characteristics, 1979, US Vital Statistics annual rpt, 4144–2.1, 4144–2.5

Transportation finances, operations, vehicles, equipment, accidents, and energy use, by mode of transport, 1955-84, annual rpt, 7304–2

see also Mopeds

see also Motor vehicle exhaust

Motors

see Electrical machinery and equipment

see Machines and machinery industry

see Motor vehicle industry

see Power-generating plants and equipment

Moulton, Janice M.

"Antitrust Implications of Thrifts' Expanded Commercial Loan Powers", 9387–1.404

Mount St. Helens, Wash.

Volcanic eruptions of Mount St Helens, effects on water quality and other environmental characteristics of Oregon and Washington watersheds, series, 5666–14

Mountain-Plains States

see Western States

see under By Region in the "Index by Categories"

Movie industry

see Motion pictures

Moy, Joyanna

"Recent Labor Market Developments in the U.S. and Nine Other Countries", 6722–1.404

Mullen, John K.

Mozambique

Agricultural and food production indexes, and production of selected commodities, by world region and country, 1974-83, annual rpt, 1524–5

Agricultural situation in sub-Saharan Africa, by country, 1982-83 and outlook for 1984, annual rpt, 1524–4.10

AID economic assistance to developing countries, obligations and disbursements by country, quarterly rpt, 9912–4

Economic conditions and foreign marketing prospects in 46 Sub-Saharan countries, 1983 world region rpt, 2046–5.1

Economic, social, and political summary data, by country, 1984, annual factbook, 244–11

Economic trends in income, production, prices, employment, finances, and trade, 1984 annual rpt, 2046–4.70

Exports of US, detailed Schedule B commodities by country of destination, 1983, annual rpt, 2424–9

Exports of US, detailed Schedule E commodities by mode of transport and world area and country of destination, 1983, annual rpts, 2424–5

Imports of US, detailed Schedule A commodities by country and world area of origin, and mode of transport, 1983, annual rpts, 2424–2

Imports of US, detailed TSUSA commodities by country of origin, 1983, annual rpt, 2424–4

Loans and grants for economic and military assistance from US and intl agencies, by program and country, FY46-83, annual rpt, 9914–5

Military spending, arms trade, and armed forces size, with total govt spending and population, by country, 1972-82, annual rpt, 9824–1

Minerals Yearbook, 1982, Vol 3: foreign country reviews of production, trade, and policies, by commodity, annual rpt, 5604–35

Minerals Yearbook, 1982, Vol 3 preprints: foreign country review of production, trade, and policies, by commodity, annual rpt, 5604–17.83

Population size and growth rates, and latest available benchmark demographic data, by country, 1950-83, biennial rpt, 2324–4

see also under By Foreign Country in the "Index by Categories"

MSA

see Metropolitan Statistical Areas

see under By SMSA or MSA in the "Index by Categories"

Mudge, Richard R.

"Charging for Federal Services", 26306–6.68

Mugge, Robert H.

"Persons Receiving Care from Selected Health Care Practitioners: U.S., 1980", 4146–12.4

"Visits to Physicians and Other Health Care Practitioners", 4144–11.1

Mullen, Joan

"Corrections and the Private Sector", 6066–20.6

Mullen, John K.

"Acidification Impact on Fisheries: Substitution and the Valuation of Recreation Resources", 21368–52

Multi-Systems, Inc.

Multi-Systems, Inc.
"Paratransit: Options for the Future. The Overview Report", 7306–9.6

Multilateral development banks
see African Development Bank
see Asian Development Bank
see Inter-American Development Bank
see International Bank for Reconstruction and Development

Multinational corporations
- Bank balance sheet statements by Fed Reserve District, for major banks in NYC, and for US branches and agencies of foreign banks, weekly release, 9365–1.3
- Bank deposits in commercial and mutual savings banks and in US branches of foreign banks, by account type, instn, State, SMSA, and county, June 1983, annual rpt, 9295–3
- Bank interstate service offices, including S&Ls, bank branches, and nonbank subsidiaries offering financial services, by instn and State, 1981-83, 9371–13
- Banking intl facilities by State and ownership, and aggregate assets and liabilities, various dates 1981-83, article, 9391–1.409
- Banking intl facilities of foreign and US banks in New York State and total US, assets and liabilities, monthly rpt, 9365–2.22
- Banks (natl) domestic and intl operations, charters, mergers, and liquidations, by State and instn, and Comptroller of Currency activities, quarterly rpt, 8402–3
- Banks (US) foreign branches assets and liabilities, by world region and country, quarterly rpt, 9365–3.7
- Banks (US) foreign branches assets, liabilities, and intl earnings, 1982-83, annual article, 9362–1.409
- Banks (US) foreign lending at all US and foreign offices, by country group and country, quarterly rpt, 13002–1
- Biotechnology commercial uses, R&D funding and output, controls, and industry financial and operating data, for US and 5 countries, 1970s-83 and estimated 1984-85, 26358–98
- Capital expenditures of multinatl US firms foreign affiliates, by major industry group and country, 1977-85, semiannual article, 2702–1.437
- Capital expenditures of multinatl US firms foreign affiliates, by major industry group and country, 1978-84, semiannual article, 2702–1.410
- Communications satellite intl systems charges, operations, investment shares by country, and competition impacts, 1964-83 with projections to 2003, hearings, 25388–46
- Currency (foreign) positions of US firms and foreign branches or affiliates, *Treasury Bulletin,* quarterly rpt, 8002–4.13
- Eurodollar bond market issues of US corporations, and amount raised and savings relative to domestic market, by company, 1975-82, hearing, 25368–132
- Farmland (US) owned by foreigners, acquisitions, dispositions, holdings, and use, by State and type and country of owner, 1983, annual rpt, 1584–2
- Financial and operating data for US affiliates of foreign firms by country of parent and industry div, 1980-81, article, 2702–1.402

Financial services of nonbank firms and bank holding companies, with financial and operating data by firm, 1981-82 with trends from 1962, technical paper, 9375–11.3

- Foreign corporation US affiliates, assets and employment by region and State, 1977 and 1981, annual rpt, 2044–25
- Foreign direct investment in US, by major industry group, world area, and selected country, 1980-83, annual article, 2702–1.439
- Foreign direct investment in US, major investors and investments by SIC 4-digit industry, transaction type and value, and location, 1983, annual rpt, 2044–20
- Foreign direct investment of US, by selected major industry group and world area, 1980-82, annual article, 2702–1.430
- Foreign direct investment of US, by world area and country, 1977-83, article, 2702–1.442
- Foreign-owned US multiestablishment firms, employment, and payroll, by country, State, industry group, and foreign ownership share, 1981-82, annual rpt, 2324–6
- Forests (tropical) conservation, mgmt role of public and private US, foreign, and intl groups, 1983 rpt, 26358–101.3
- Franchises of US firms engaged in distribution of goods and services, by country, 1982, annual rpt, 2014–5.1
- Income of multinatl and multistate corporations under alternative State income tax treatment methods, by major industry, 1977, article, 9373–1.412
- Income of multinatl corporations, reallocation through regulation of intercorporate transactions by tax item, treaty status, asset size, industry, and tax haven country, 1982, 8008–110
- Income tax returns of corporations with foreign tax credit, income and deductions by type, asset size, and selected industry group, 1980, article, 8302–2.415
- Income tax returns of foreign subsidiaries of US corporations, income and tax data, by industry and asset size, 1980, article, 8302–2.410
- Income tax returns of US corporations, summary data by industry div, 1981 estimates, annual article, 8302–2.403
- Income taxes and effective rates on corporate US, foreign, and worldwide income, by major industry group, and share of Fed Govt receipts, 1980-82, 23868–14
- Oil and gas production and refinery operations and gasoline sales for foreign-affiliated US firms, 1978-82, annual rpt, 3024–2
- R&D expenditures of US firms foreign affiliates, by selected industry, 1974-82, 9626–2.131
- *Science Indicators,* R&D expenditures, innovations, research, and higher education, with foreign comparisons, 1960s- 83, annual rpt, 9624–10
- Services intl transactions, and operations of US multinatl service firms and foreign affiliates, by industry and world region, 1977-82, 2706–5.30
- *Statistical Abstract of US,* social, political, and economic data, 1950s-83 and trends, annual rpt, 2324–1.3

Tax evasion through tax haven countries, with income, investments, and taxes withheld by country, various periods 1975- 83, hearings, 21408–71

- Trade policy of Fed Govt, with data on US industry foreign trade and revenues, and Japan semiconductor industry subsidies, 1970s-83, hearings, 21368–46
- Uranium exploration, land acquisition expenditures, and employment, various periods 1966-83 and planned 1984-85, annual rpt, 3164–65

Multnomah County, Oreg.
- Homeless population and characteristics, and temporary shelter operations, use, and user characteristics, for selected cities, various periods 1979-84, hearing, 21248–85

Muncie, Ind.
- Census of Housing, 1980: occupancy and unit characteristics, by race, Hispanic origin, and city, SMSA rpt, 2473–1.249
- Census of Population and Housing, 1980: detailed population and housing characteristics, by county, city, and census tract, SMSA rpt, 2551–2.249
- *see also* under By SMSA or MSA in the "Index by Categories"

Muncy, Robert J.
"Species Profiles: Life Histories and Environmental Requirements of Coastal Fishes and Invertebrates (Gulf of Mexico), Sea Catfish and Gafftopsail Catfish", 5506–8.20

Municipal bonds
- Bank investment returns on capital assets for leasing, and municipal bond holdings, for 16 States, 1982, article, 9385–1.402
- Business statistics, detailed data for major industries and economic indicators, *Survey of Current Business,* monthly rpt, 2702–1.6
- Financial and business statistics, historic trends, 1984 annual chartbook, 9364–2.9
- Govt finances, by level of govt, State, and for large cities and counties, 1981-83, annual rpt series, 2466–2
- Govt fiscal condition, plans to raise or lower taxes and city employment, and use of municipal bonds, FY81-83, survey, hearings, 25408–86.1
- Housing low-rent project financing notes sold by local authorities, terms and individual issuers and purchasers, monthly listing, 5142–43
- Housing low-rent project financing notes sold by local authorities, terms and individual purchasers, monthly press release, 5142–37
- Hwy receipts by source, and expenditures by function, by level of govt and State, 1983, annual rpt, 7554–1.3, 7554–1.4
- Industrial dev Fed Govt funding by type, program, and agency, and State govt policies and support, selected years FY75-85, 26306–6.81
- New Jersey and Maryland prison capacity and population, and New Jersey construction costs by type and funding source, by facility, 1977-82 and projected to 1988, 25528–99
- NYC metro area small business owners and accountants, assessment of economy, professional activities, and community problems, by county and industry div, 1983 survey, hearings, 21728–52.3

Index by Subjects and Names

NYC retirement systems assets, by type for 6 systems, selected years 1978-83, conf proceedings, 25408–89

Offerings of State and municipal bonds, by purpose, 1975-83, article, 9362–1.408

Offerings of State, municipal, and corporate securities, 1934-83, and common stock prices and earnings, 1949-83, annual rpt, 204–1.7

State and local govt retirement systems, cash and security holdings and finances, quarterly rpt, 2462–2

Stockbroker firms by type of organization and State, finances, and SEC applications and registrations, 1978-FY83, annual rpt, 9734–2.1

Trust assets of banks and trust companies, by type of asset and fund and State, 1983, annual rpt, 13004–1

Yields and interest rates, *Business Conditions Digest,* cyclical indicators, monthly rpt, 2702–3.3

Yields and interest rates, *Business Conditions Digest,* historical supplement and methodology, 1947-82, 2708–31

Yields and issues of municipal bonds, 1972-83, hearing, 21788–135

Yields, interest rates, and bond prices, for commercial paper and govt securities, monthly rpt, 9365–2.14

Yields of Treasury, corporate, and municipal long-term bonds, *Treasury Bulletin,* quarterly rpt, 8002–4.9

Municipal government *see* Local government

Municipal taxation *see* State and local taxes

Municipal transportation *see* Urban transportation

Munnell, Alicia H.

"Do We Want Large Social Security Surpluses?", 9373–1.414

"Employee Benefits and the Tax Base", 9373–1.404

"ERISA—The First Decade: Was the Legislation Consistent with Other National Goals?", 9373–1.419

Murder *see* Homicide

Musculoskeletal diseases

- Deaths and death rates by detailed cause and demographic characteristics, 1979 and selected trends, US Vital Statistics annual rpt, 4144–2.1
- Deaths and death rates, by selected cause and demographic characteristics, 1981, US Vital Statistics advance rpt, 4146–5.78
- Deaths and death rates, by selected cause and demographic characteristics, 1982, US Vital Statistics advance rpt, 4146–5.81
- Dental Research Natl Inst research and training funds awarded, by recipient instn, FY83, annual listing, 4474–19
- Disability Insurance beneficiaries sociodemographic and medical characteristics, 1977-79, annual rpt, 4744–20
- Hospital discharges and length of stay, by patient characteristics, facility size, procedure performed, diagnosis, and region, 1982, annual rpt, 4147–13.78
- Infant deaths by detailed cause, geographic location, age, race, and sex, 1979, US Vital Statistics annual rpt, 4144–2.2

Older persons by demographic, socioeconomic, and health characteristics, selected years 1900-81 and projected to 2050, Current Population Rpt, 2546–2.125

see also Mobility limitations

see also Podiatry

see also under By Disease in the "Index by Categories"

Musell, R. Mark

"Reducing Grades of the General Schedule Work Force", 26306–6.84

Museums

Army morale, welfare, and recreation programs, revenue and expenses worldwide by activity and major command, FY82-83, annual rpt, 3704–12

Census of Population, 1980: detailed socioeconomic and demographic characteristics, by age, sex, race, Hispanic origin, occupation, and industry, State rpt series, 2531–4

Census of Population, 1980: labor force, by sex, detailed occupation, and region, with comparison to 1970 census, supplementary rpt, 2535–1.12

Census of Service Industries, 1982: employment, establishments, receipts, and payroll, by SIC 2- to 4-digit kind of business, SMSA, county, and city, State rpt series, 2391–1

County Business Patterns: establishments, employees, and payrolls, by SIC 4-digit industry and county, 1981, annual State rpt series, 2326–8

County Business Patterns: establishments, employees, and payrolls, by SIC 4-digit industry and county, 1982, annual State rpt series, 2326–6

Earnings by major industry group, and personal income per capita and by source, by region and State, 1929-82, 2708–40

Employment by detailed occupation, for 29 SIC 2-digit nonmanufacturing industries, 1981 BLS survey, 6748–60

Employment, earnings, and hours, by selected SIC 1- to 4-digit industry, State, and for 278 major labor areas, 1939-83, annual rpt, 6744–5

Employment, earnings, and hours, by SIC 4-digit nonfarm industry, monthly 1974-Feb 1984, annual update, 6744–4

Endangered animals and plants foreign trade including reexports of live specimens and products, by purpose, country, and species, 1982, annual rpt, 5504–19

Library (research) funding of Education Dept, by project, program area, instn, and State, FY84, annual listing, 4804–22

Minority group and women employment, by occupational group and SIC 2- to 3-digit industry, 1981, annual rpt, 9244–1.1

Natl Endowment for Arts activities and grants, FY83, annual rpt, 9564–3

Natl Endowment for Humanities activities and grants, FY83, annual rpt, 9564–2

Natl Foundation on Arts and Humanities grants to museums, by instn, State, and city, FY84, annual rpt series, 9564–6

Occupational injury and illness rates, by SIC 2- to 4-digit industry, 1982, annual rpt, 6844–1

Statistical Abstract of US, social, political, and economic data, 1950s-83 and trends, annual rpt, 2324–1.1

Musical instruments

Musgrave, John C.

"Fixed Reproducible Tangible Wealth in the U.S., 1980-83", 2702–1.433

Mushrooms

see Vegetables and vegetable products

Music

Army morale, welfare, and recreation programs, revenue and expenses worldwide by activity and major command, FY82-83, annual rpt, 3704–12

Census of Population, 1980: detailed socioeconomic and demographic characteristics, by age, sex, race, Hispanic origin, occupation, and industry, State rpt series, 2531–4

Census of Population, 1980: labor force, by sex, detailed occupation, and region, with comparison to 1970 census, supplementary rpt, 2535–1.12

County Business Patterns: establishments, employees, and payrolls, by SIC 4-digit industry and county, 1981, annual State rpt series, 2326–8

Educational progress, natl assessment summary data for 7 learning areas, by characteristics of participants, selected years 1971-82, annual rpt, 4824–2.6

Educational services in underground economy, household expenditures and participation by type of instruction, 1981 survey, 8308–27

Exports and imports of sheet music, by world area, 1983, annual rpt, 2424–6

Exports of sheet music, by country of destination, 1983, annual rpt, 2424–9

Exports of US, detailed commodities by country of destination, monthly rpt, 2422–3

Imports of sheet music, by country of origin, 1983, annual rpt, 2424–4

Imports of US, detailed Schedule A commodities by country, monthly rpt, 2422–2

Income tax returns of sole proprietorships, detailed data by industry div and selected industry group, 1981, annual rpt, 8304–7

Income tax returns of sole proprietorships, receipts, deductions by type, payroll, and net income, by major industry, 1982, annual article, 8302–2.413

Natl Endowment for Arts activities and grants, FY83, annual rpt, 9564–3

Occupational Outlook Handbook, 1984-85 biennial rpt, 6744–1

Recording industry operations and sales lost from home taping, home taping costs, and material taped by source, 1969-83, hearings with chartbook, 25528–100

Teaching degrees conferred by specialty and State, required credit hours, and instn officials attitudes, by instn type, 1970s-83, hearings, 21348–89

Musical instruments

County Business Patterns: establishments, employees, and payrolls, by SIC 4-digit industry and county, 1981, annual State rpt series, 2326–8

County Business Patterns: establishments, employees, and payrolls, by SIC 4-digit industry and county, 1982, annual State rpt series, 2326–6

Employment, earnings, and hours, by SIC 4-digit nonfarm industry, monthly 1974-Feb 1984, annual update, 6744–4

Musical instruments

Exports and imports of US, detailed SIC-based commodities by world area, 1983, annual rpts, 2424–6

Exports and imports of US, totals and as percent of domestic production, by SIC 2- to 5-digit commodity, 1981, annual rpt, 2424–3

Exports of US, detailed commodities by country of destination, monthly rpt, 2422–3

Exports of US, detailed Schedule B commodities by country of destination, 1983, annual rpt, 2424–9

Exports of US, detailed Schedule E commodities by mode of transport and world area and country of destination, 1983, annual rpts, 2424–5

Great Lakes trade, by SITC 3-digit commodity, port, vessel type, world area, and country, 1982, annual rpt, 7744–3

Imports of US, detailed Schedule A commodities by country and world area of origin, and mode of transport, 1983, annual rpts, 2424–2

Imports of US, detailed Schedule A commodities by country, monthly rpt, 2422–2

Imports of US, detailed TSUSA commodities by country of origin, 1983, annual rpt, 2424–4

Income tax returns of sole proprietorships, detailed data by industry div and selected industry group, 1981, annual rpt, 8304–7

Input-output structure of US economy, detailed interindustry transactions for 537 industries, and components of final demand, 1977 benchmark data, 2708–17

Manufacturing census, 1982: financial and operating data, by SIC 2- to 4-digit industry, State, SMSA, and county, preliminary census div rpt series, 2491–3

Manufacturing census, 1982: financial and operating data, for SIC 4-digit industries by product, preliminary rpt, 2491–1.427

Occupational injury and illness rates, by SIC 2- to 4-digit industry, 1982, annual rpt, 6844–1

Occupational Outlook Handbook, 1984-85 biennial rpt, 6744–1

Pianos from South Korea at less than fair value, imports injury to US industry, investigation with background financial and operating data, 1984 rpt, 9886–14.124

Pianos trade, tariffs, and industry operating data, foreign and US, 1979-83, TSUSA commodity rpt supplement, 9885–7.55

Producer prices and indexes, by stage of processing and detailed commodity, monthly rpt, 6762–6

Producer prices and indexes, by stage of processing and detailed commodity, monthly 1983, annual supplement, 6764–2

Woodwind instrument key pads from Italy at less than fair value, imports injury to US industry, investigation with background financial and operating data, 1984 rpt, 9886–14.114

Woodwind instrument key pads from Italy, injury to US industry from foreign subsidized and less than fair value imports, investigation with background financial and operating data, 1980-83, 9886–19.6

Muskegon Heights, Mich.

Census of Housing, 1980: occupancy and unit characteristics, by race, Hispanic origin, and city, SMSA rpt, 2473–1.250

Census of Population and Housing, 1980: detailed population and housing characteristics, by county, city, and census tract, SMSA rpt, 2551–2.250

Muskegon, Mich.

Census of Housing, 1980: occupancy and unit characteristics, by race, Hispanic origin, and city, SMSA rpt, 2473–1.250

Census of Population and Housing, 1980: detailed population and housing characteristics, by county, city, and census tract, SMSA rpt, 2551–2.250

see also under By SMSA or MSA in the "Index by Categories"

Muskingum County, Ohio

Housing vacancy rates for single and multifamily units and mobile homes, by city and ZIP code, 1984, annual metro area rpt, 9304–27.6

Mussey, Sol

"Actuarial Status of the HI and SMI Trust Funds", 4742–1.411

Mutti, John

"Corporate and Personal Taxation of Capital Income in an Open Economy", 8006–3.51

Mutual funds

Finances, firms, and SEC registrations and terminations, by type of investment firm, as of FY83, annual rpt, 9734–2.2

Financial and monetary conditions, selected US summary data, weekly rpt, 9391–4

Flow-of-funds accounts, assets and liabilities by type and economic sector, year-end outstandings, 1960-83, annual rpt, 9364–3

Household income, assets, and debt characteristics, sources of credit, and use of financial services, 1983 survey, article, 9362–1.411

Household income, home value and equity, and financial assets by type, by household characteristics, 1983 survey with trends from 1970, article, 9362–1.406

Investment companies classification, assets, and location, Sept 1982, annual directory, 9734–1

Money market assets of 10 nonbank instns, Dec 1982 and June 1983, technical paper, 9375–11.3

Money market mutual funds and deposit accounts, and super negotiable orders of withdrawal accounts, interest rates, monthly Dec 1982-Sept 1983, article, 1702–1.401

Money market mutual funds and deposit accounts balances, and correlation results for interest rates and flows by type of fund, various periods Dec 1982-June 1984, article, 9371–1.431

Money market mutual funds exclusion from M1, assessment based on activity of 1 fund, 1982-June 1983, article, 9383–6.403

OECD economic indicators, for US and 6 countries, biweekly rpt, 242–4

Savings and loan assns and FSLIC-insured savings banks and S&Ls, assets, liabilities, and deposit and loan activity, monthly rpt, 9312–4

Index by Subjects and Names

Transactions volume and proceeds and new issue registrations, for US registered exchanges, SEC monthly rpt, 9732–1

Mutual savings banks *see* Savings banks

Mycoses *see* Infective and parasitic diseases

Myers, Peter C.

"Promising Outlook for Soil and Water Conservation", 1004–16.1

Namibia

Economic conditions and foreign marketing prospects in 46 Sub-Saharan countries, 1983 world region rpt, 2046–5.1

Economic, social, and political summary data, by country, 1984, annual factbook, 244–11

Exports of US, detailed Schedule B commodities by country of destination, 1983, annual rpt, 2424–9

Exports of US, detailed Schedule E commodities by mode of transport and world area and country of destination, 1983, annual rpts, 2424–5

Imports of US, detailed Schedule A commodities by country and world area of origin, and mode of transport, 1983, annual rpts, 2424–2

Imports of US, detailed TSUSA commodities by country of origin, 1983, annual rpt, 2424–4

Minerals Yearbook, 1982, Vol 3: foreign country reviews of production, trade, and policies, by commodity, annual rpt, 5604–35

Population size and growth rates, and latest available benchmark demographic data, by country, 1950-83, biennial rpt, 2324–4

see also under By Foreign Country in the "Index by Categories"

Napa, Calif.

Census of Population and Housing, 1980: detailed population and housing characteristics, by county, city, and census tract, SMSA rpt, 2551–2.360

Housing vacancy rates for single and multifamily units and mobile homes, by city and ZIP code, 1983, annual metro area rpt, 9304–20.8

Housing vacancy rates for single and multifamily units and mobile homes, by city and ZIP code, 1984, annual metro area rpt, 9304–20.20

see also under By SMSA or MSA in the "Index by Categories"

Narcotics

see Drug abuse and treatment *see* Drug and narcotics traffic *see* Drugs

NASA

see National Aeronautics and Space Administration

NASA Goddard Space Flight Center

"Potential Climatic Impacts of Increasing Atmospheric Carbon Dioxide With Emphasis on Water Availability and Hydrology in the U.S.", 9188–95

Nashua, N.H.

Census of Housing, 1980: occupancy and unit characteristics, by race, Hispanic origin, and city, SMSA rpt, 2473–1.251

Census of Population and Housing, 1980: detailed population and housing characteristics, by county, city, and census tract, SMSA rpt, 2551–2.251

Index by Subjects and Names

see also under By SMSA or MSA in the "Index by Categories"

Nashville, Tenn.

Census of Housing, 1980: occupancy and unit characteristics, by race, Hispanic origin, and city, SMSA rpt, 2473–1.252

Census of Population and Housing, 1980: detailed population and housing characteristics, by county, city, and census tract, SMSA rpt, 2551–2.252

Waterborne commerce of US (domestic and foreign), freight by commodity, traffic, and passengers, by port and waterway, 1982, annual rpt, 3754–3.2

see also under By City and By SMSA or MSA in the "Index by Categories"

Nassau County, N.Y.

Auto dealer repair workers, wages, and benefits, by occupation, size of establishment, and for 24 labor market areas, Nov 1982 survey, 6787–6.202

Census of Housing, 1980: occupancy and unit characteristics, by race, Hispanic origin, and city, SMSA rpt, 2473–1.253

Census of Population and Housing, 1980: detailed population and housing characteristics, by county, city, and census tract, SMSA rpt, 2551–2.253

Coxsackie B virus cases, by isolate, associated clinical syndrome and patient age and sex, US and Nassau County, NY, 1970-79, article, 4102–1.452

Repair technicians and apprentices wages and benefits, for 5 types of electrical repair shops in 19 SMSAs, Nov 1981 survey, 6787–6.197

Wages by occupation, and benefits for office and plant workers, 1984 SMSA survey rpt, 6785–11.9

see also under By SMSA or MSA in the "Index by Categories"

National Advisory Committee on Oceans and Atmosphere

Minerals (nonfuel) from marine sources, demand by mineral type, selected years 1978-83 with projections to 2000, 15048–4

National Advisory Council on Continuing Education

Activities of Council, 1984 annual narrative rpt, 15214–1

National Advisory Council on Indian Education

Indian Education Act, Fed Govt grants and fellowships awarded by State, FY83, and natl advisory council funding, FY73-84, annual rpt, 14874–1

National Advisory Council on International Monetary and Financial Policies

Intl financial instns funds by source and disbursements by purpose, by country, with US policy review, FY83, annual rpt, 15344–1

National Aeronautics and Space Administration

Aerial survey R&D publications, and sources of natural resource and environmental data gathered by air- and spacecraft, quarterly listing, 9502–7

Budget of US Appendix, detailed budgets and personnel summaries, by agency, FY85, annual rpt, 104–3

Budget of US, appropriations, outlays, balances, and budget receipts, by govtl branch and agency, FY83, annual rpt, 8104–2

Budget of US, compact budgets by function, agency, and account, FY85 with projections to FY89, annual rpt, 104–2

Budget of US, object class analysis of obligations, by branch of Fed Govt and selected depts and agencies, FY85 estimates, annual rpt, 104–9

Building size, value, employees, costs of GSA rental and services, and construction budget, by NASA facility, FY82-88, hearings, 25328–23

Cost control proposals for Fed Govt programs and mgmt, 3-year savings by function and agency, and financial and operating data, 1960s-81, 16908–1.28, 16908–1.30

DOD prime contract awards for R&D to educational and nonprofit instns and Federal agencies, by instn and location, FY83, annual listing, 3544–17

Employment (civilian) of Fed Govt, by location, agency, and pay system, 1982, biennial rpt, 9844–8

Energy R&D and technology publications, quarterly listing, 9502–4

Foreign and US astronautic and aeronautic events, comprehensive chronology, 1976, annual rpt, 9504–2

Fraud and abuse in NASA programs, audits and investigations, 2nd half FY84, semiannual rpt, 9502–9

Launch schedules and technical descriptions of NASA projects, press release series, 9506–2

Manufacturers under Fed Govt contract and owned by DOD, operating data by agency, selected SIC 2- to 4-digit industry, State, and SMSA, 1982, annual Current Industrial Rpt, 2506–3.4

Procurement awards in Western States, Fed Reserve 12th District, quarterly rpt, 9393–1.3

Procurement contract awards of NASA, by type, contractor, State, and country, FY84, semiannual rpt, 9502–6

Programs and budgets of Fed Govt by agency, and foreign programs, 1957-FY85, annual rpt, 9504–9

R&D and science-related Fed Govt funding to higher education and nonprofit instns, by field, instn, agency, and State, FY82, annual rpt, 9627–17

R&D Fed Govt funding, by function, agency, and program, selected years FY80-84 and proposed FY85, 26308–46

R&D Fed Govt funding for all performers, by field and supporting agency, selected years FY60-84, annual rpt, 9627–20

R&D funding to colleges and universities, by State, field of science, and instn, FY83, annual listing, 9504–7

Space flights of US and USSR, and NASA financial and employment data, 1957-83, annual rpt, 9504–6

Space satellites and other objects launched since 1957, quarterly listing, 9502–2

Space shuttle launch guests by type, and itemized Fed Govt costs by agency, Apr 1981-Nov 1983, GAO rpt, 26123–78

National Ambulatory Medical Care Complement Survey

Health facilities and manpower use, by patient and facility characteristics, Vital and Health Statistics series, 4147–13

National Bureau of Standards

National Ambulatory Medical Care Survey

Drugs prescribed or provided by office-based physicians most often, by brand or generic name and therapeutic category, 1981, 4146–8.99

Health facilities and manpower use, by patient and facility characteristics, Vital and Health Statistics series, 4147–13

Publications of NCHS, quarterly listing, 4122–2

Youth office visits to physicians by patient and visit characteristics and physician specialty, and drug mentions by brand, 1980-81, 4146–8.100

National Archives and Records Service

Computers and automatic data processing systems of GSA, costs, cost savings, and employment, by activity, subagency, and regional office, FY83-88, 9458–17

Cost control proposals for Fed Govt programs and mgmt, 3-year savings by function and agency, and financial and operating data, 1960s-81, 16908–1.29

Fraud and abuse in GSA programs, audits and investigations, 2nd half FY84, semiannual rpt, 9452–8

GSA mgmt activities and finances, FY78-83, annual rpt, 9454–23

National Assessment of Educational Progress

Condition of Education, detailed data on enrollment, staff, achievement, finances, curricula, and education effects on employment, 1982-83, annual rpt, 4824–1

Methodology changes in natl assessment sampling, data collection, and tabulation, 1983, 4898–15

Results, by selected participant characteristics, summary data for 7 learning areas, selected years 1971-82, annual rpt, 4824–2.6

Results, work in progress, and other activities, quarterly newsletter, 4892–1

National Association of Blue Shield Plans *see* Blue Cross-Blue Shield

National Association of Manufacturers "U.S. Trade: Record of the 1970s—Challenge of the 1980s", 21368–46

National Association of Regional Councils "Survey Results: Profile of 1983 Regional Council Activities", 25408–88.1

National Association of Social Workers Membership and membership/population ratio, 1960-81, annual rpt, 4504–9.4

National Automobile Dealers Association Election campaign funding by political action committees and voting on FTC rules, for individual congressmen, 1978-82, hearings, 21428–7.2, 25688–6.2

National Bipartisan Commission on Central America

Economic, social, and political conditions in 6 Central America countries, 1960s-83 with trends and projections 1930-2010, 028–19

National Bureau of Standards

Budgets and permanent staff positions appropriated for Commerce Dept agencies, FY84-85, annual rpt, 2004–6

Cost control proposals for Fed Govt programs and mgmt, 3-year savings by function and agency, and financial and operating data, 1960s-81, 16908–1.3, 16908–1.31

National Bureau of Standards

Energy consumption in commercial buildings under alternative heating, cooling, and air conditioning systems and control strategies, for 6 cities, 1983 rpt, 2218–68

Energy-related inventions recommended for possible DOE support by Natl Bur of Standards, with DOE evaluation status, 1984, annual listing, 2214–5

Fed Govt standards for data recording, processing, and transfer, and for purchase and use of computer systems, series, 2216–2

Fires (housing electrical) in 10 cities, by type of wiring and equipment involved and circumstances, 1980-81, 2218–71

Hearing aid performance evaluation, by model and manufacturer, 1984, annual rpt, 9924–5

Productivity of labor and capital, growth by SIC 1- to 2-digit industry, and measurement methods and bibl, various periods 1948-78 with trends from 1800, 2218–69

Programs, funding, and employment of Commerce Dept agencies, FY83, annual rpt, 2004–1

Publications of Commerce Dept, biweekly listing, 2002–1

Publications of NBS, 1983 annual listing, 2214–1

R&D Fed Govt funding, by function, agency, and program, selected years FY80-84 and proposed FY85, 26308–46

Smoke alarm sound levels by brand, and response time by circumstances and for older and mentally retarded persons, 1983 rpt, 2218–70

Standard reference and research materials available from Natl Bur of Standards, 1984-85, biennial catalog, 2214–2

National Cancer Institute

Cancer cases, incidence, deaths, and death rates, by body site, age, race, Hispanic origin, and sex, for 10 geographic areas, 1973-81, 4478–130

Cancer deaths and death rates, by body site, race, sex, State, and county, 1950-79, 4478–146

Cancer Natl Inst epidemiology and biometry activities, staff, budget, and contract awards by project and recipient instn, FY83, annual rpt, 4474–29

Contracts and grants of Natl Cancer Inst, by contractor, instn, State, and city, FY83, annual listing, 4474–28

Programs, organization, and budget, FY83, with cancer deaths by body site, 1980 and 1983, annual fact book, 4474–13

Public knowledge, attitudes, and behavior regarding cancer prevention and risk, 1983 survey, 4478–149

National Capital Planning Commission

Budget of US Appendix, detailed budgets and personnel summaries, by agency, FY85, annual rpt, 104–3

Budget of US, appropriations, outlays, balances, and budget receipts, by govtl branch and agency, FY83, annual rpt, 8104–2

National Center for Education Statistics

Adult basic and secondary education programs, students, staff, and facilities, annual summary rpt, suspended, 4864–4

Index by Subjects and Names

Condition of Education, detailed data on enrollment, staff, achievement, finances, curricula, and education effects on employment, 1982-83, annual rpt, 4824–1

Data collection programs, missions, and appropriations of Fed Govt statistical agencies, and effect of budget cuts, FY80-84, GAO rpt, 26125–28

Degrees conferred to women in higher education, with comparative data for men, by subject area, biennial rpt, suspended, 4844–9

Digest of Education Statistics, detailed data on students, staff, finances, and facilities, 1982 and selected trends, annual rpt, 4824–2

Education Dept programs and activities, FY83, annual rpt, 4804–6

Education highlights, trends in enrollment, expenditures, curricula, and other topics of current interest, periodic press release, 4822–1

Educational trends, 1972/73-1992/93, biennial pocket-size card, 4824–3

Elementary and secondary enrollment, households with children enrolled by school control, householder characteristics, and region, Oct 1982, 4838–13

Elementary and secondary public school districts, schools, enrollment, staff, and finances, by State, 1981/82, annual rpt, 4834–13

Elementary and secondary public school enrollment, by grade level and State, fall 1982, annual rpt, 4834–10

Elementary and secondary public school systems, annual listing, discontinued, 4834–1

Elementary and secondary public school systems revenues, by level of govt, selected years 1919/20-1981/82, press release, 4838–12

Elementary and secondary public schools by type, enrollment by grade, and staff, for 10-20 largest cities, annual rpt, discontinued, 4834–11

Fast Response Survey System, current natl estimates for education data, series, 4826–1

High school class of 1980: use of student aid and earnings to pay higher education costs, by instn type and family income, 1980-82, 4848–15

High school class of 1982: coursework compared to graduation criteria of natl commission, by student and school characteristics, 4828–16

High school class of 1982: foreign language course enrollment, by language, student and school characteristics, and location, 1984 rpt, 4838–11

High school class of 1982: foreign language coursework, by language, course level, student and school characteristics, and location, 1984 rpt, 4828–17

High school classes of 1980 and 1982: educational and sociodemographic characteristics and expectations, natl longitudinal study, series, 4826–2

High school grads and 12th grade enrollment, by State, 1981/82, annual rpt, 4834–12

Higher education degrees conferred, by detailed field, degree level, sex, and State, annual rpt, suspended, 4844–5

Higher education enrollment, by sex and attendance status of students, preliminary annual rpt, suspended, 4844–1

Higher education enrollment, by State and instn, preliminary annual rpt, suspended, 4844–4

Higher education enrollment, by student characteristics, instn type, State, and for 150 instns, fall 1982, annual rpt, 4844–2

Higher education instn revenues, expenditures, endowments, and physical plant assets and debt, by State and region, annual rpt, suspended, 4844–6

Higher education instns, by type, location, and other characteristics, 1983/84 annual listing, 4844–3

Higher education instns, type, location, enrollment, and student charges, by State and congressional district, 1983/84, biennial listing, 4844–11

Higher education tuition and other student charges, for each public and private 2- and 4-year instn, by State, 1983/84, annual listing, 4844–10

Kindergarten and nursery school enrollment, by sociodemographic characteristics of child and mother or household head, annual rpt, suspended, 4834–7

Libraries of colleges and universities, expenditures, holdings by type, use, staff by sex, and Federal grants received, 1979-82, biennial rpt, 4854–1

Postsecondary enrollment in academic, vocational, and continuing education, by student characteristics, Oct 1982, 4848–16

Vocational education enrollment and staff, annual rpt, suspended, 4864–8

Vocational education enrollment, annual rpt, suspended, 4864–6

Vocational education expenditures of Federal, State, and local govts, annual rpt, discontinued, 4864–7

Vocational education program staff, by State, program area, instn type, and employment status, annual rpt, suspended, 4864–5

National Center for Health Services Research

Grants and contracts, by program area, FY83, annual listing, 4184–2

Health care expenditures, methodology of natl survey of households, physicians, health insurance firms, and employers, 1977-79, series, 4186–4

Health care expenditures, natl survey on services use, costs, and sources of payment, by patient and physician characteristics, 1977-78, series, 4186–3

Health services delivery and related topics, Natl Center for Health Services Research rpts, series, 4186–2

Health survey design and research methods, 1982 biennial conf proceedings, 4184–1

Hospital costs and use, data compilation project analyses, series, 4186–6

National Center for Health Statistics

Births and birth rates, by detailed demographic characteristics and geographic area, 1979 and trends, US Vital Statistics annual rpt, 4144–1

Data collection programs, missions, and appropriations of Fed Govt statistical agencies, and effect of budget cuts, FY80-84, GAO rpt, 26125–28

Index by Subjects and Names

Deaths and death rates, by detailed cause and demographic characteristics, 1979 and summary trends from 1900, US Vital Statistics annual rpt, 4144–2

Deaths and death rates, by detailed geographic area, cause, and demographic characteristics, 1979, US Vital Statistics annual rpt, 4144–3

Health and vital statistics collection, and use in program planning and evaluation, Public Health Conf papers, 1983, biennial rpt, 4164–2

Health care use and expenditures, methodology and findings of natl survey of households, Medicare records, and Medicaid records in 4 States, 1980, series, 4146–12

Health condition and health care resources, use, and expenditures, 1970s-82 with trends and projections 1900-2000, annual compilation, 4144–11

Health status measurement methodology, confs, and publications, quarterly listing, suspended, 4122–1

Life tables, 1980 and trends from 1900, US Vital Statistics annual rpt, 4144–5

Marriages, divorces, and rates, by detailed demographic and geographic characteristics, 1979 and trends, US Vital Statistics annual rpt, 4144–4

Medical Care Utilization and Expenditure Natl Survey results, series, 4146–11

Publications of NCHS, quarterly listing, 4122–2

Publications of NCHS, 1979-83, annual listing, 4124–1

Vital and Health Statistics series: advance data rpts, 4146–8

Vital and Health Statistics series: analytical studies, 4147–3

Vital and Health Statistics series: foreign and US comparisons, analytical studies, 4147–5

Vital and Health Statistics series: health condition, hospitalization, disability, and medical costs, by demographic characteristics, 4147–10

Vital and Health Statistics series: manpower and facilities resources, 4147–14

Vital and Health Statistics series: medical and physical data from Natl Health and Nutrition Examination Survey, 4147–11

Vital and Health Statistics series: natality, marriage, and divorce trends, 4147–21

Vital and Health Statistics series: use of health manpower and facilities, 4147–13

Vital statistics, births, marriages, divorces, and deaths, provisional data, monthly rpt, 4142–1

Vital statistics, provisional 1982-83 with trends from 1950, annual rpt, 4144–7

Vital statistics records offices and availability of birth, death, marriage, and divorce certificates, by State, 1984 annual listing, 4124–7

Vital statistics, supplements to monthly rpts, series, 4146–5

National Center for Research in Vocational Education

Funding of Center by purpose and source, selected years 1978-84, GAO rpt, 26121–79

National Center for Social Statistics

see Health Care Financing Administration

see Office of Human Development Services

see Office of Research, Statistics, and International Policy, SSA

National Clearinghouse for Smoking and Health

see Office on Smoking and Health

National Commission on Air Quality

Budget of US, appropriations, outlays, balances, and budget receipts, by govtl branch and agency, FY83, annual rpt, 8104–2

National Commission on Excellence in Education

High school class of 1982: coursework compared to graduation criteria of natl commission, by student and school characteristics, 4828–16

High school dropout rate and reasons, educational goals and achievement, and required and recommended curricula, by school control, selected years 1972-83, annual rpt, 4824–1.5

National Commission on International Year of the Child

Budget of US, appropriations, outlays, balances, and budget receipts, by govtl branch and agency, FY83, annual rpt, 8104–2

National Commission on Libraries and Information Science

Activities, funding, expenditures, and publications lists, FY83, annual rpt, 15634–1

Budget of US Appendix, detailed budgets and personnel summaries, by agency, FY85, annual rpt, 104–3

Budget of US, appropriations, outlays, balances, and budget receipts, by govtl branch and agency, FY83, annual rpt, 8104–2

National Commission on Social Security Reform

Budget of US, appropriations, outlays, balances, and budget receipts, by govtl branch and agency, FY83, annual rpt, 8104–2

National Commission on Student Financial Assistance

Budget of US, appropriations, outlays, balances, and budget receipts, by govtl branch and agency, FY83, annual rpt, 8104–2

National commissions

see Federal boards, committees, and commissions

see Federal independent agencies

National Conservative Political Action Committee

Campaign funding by political action committee and candidate, proposed candidate spending limits, voting rates by party, and political opinions, by State, 1960-82, hearings, 25688–6

National Council on Educational Research

Education Natl Inst activities and education research grants awarded by recipient, and Education Dept expenditures by function, FY81-82, annual rpt, 4914–4

National Credit Union Administration

Budget of US Appendix, detailed budgets and personnel summaries, by agency, FY85, annual rpt, 104–3

National defense

Budget of US, appropriations, outlays, balances, and budget receipts, by govtl branch and agency, FY83, annual rpt, 8104–2

Cost control proposals for Fed Govt programs and mgmt, 3-year savings by function and agency, and financial and operating data, 1960s-81, 16908–1.14

Financial activity of Natl Credit Union Admin insurance fund, and insured instns financial and operating data, FY83, annual rpt with semiannual update for 1st qtr 1984, 9534–7

Financial and membership data for Federal and federally insured State credit unions, with shares, loans, and assets, by State, 1984 annual listing, 9534–6

Financial and membership data for State-chartered credit unions, by State and asset size, annual rpt, discontinued, 9534–2

Financial performance of Natl Credit Union Admin Central Liquidity Facility, quarterly rpt, 9532–4

Financial statements by membership type, region, and State, for Federal and federally insured State credit unions, 1983, annual rpt, 9534–1

Operations and chartering activities, annual summary rpt, discontinued, 9534–3

National Crime Survey

Crime victimization rates by type of offense, and victim and offense characteristics, Natl Crime Survey series, 6066–3

National debt

see Public debt

National defense

Central America socioeconomic and political conditions in 6 countries, 1960s-83 with trends and projections 1930-2010, 028–19

Foreign economic, social, and political summary data, by country, 1984, annual factbook, 244–11

Foreign military, social, and economic summary data by world area and country, 1960s-80s, hearing, 25388–47.1

Foreign military spending, arms trade, and armed forces size, with total govt spending and population, by country, 1972-82, annual rpt, 9824–1

Military weapons and troop strength of US and NATO compared to USSR and Warsaw Pact, as of Jan 1984, annual rpt, 3564–1

Soviet Union and Warsaw Pact military weapons systems, assistance and presence worldwide, and force strengths, with selected US and NATO comparisons, as of 1984, 3508–14

Statistical Abstract of US, social, political, and economic data, 1950s-83 and trends, annual rpt, 2324–1.2

see also Armed services

see also Armed services reserves

see also Arms control and disarmament

see also Civil defense

see also Defense agencies

see also Defense budgets and appropriations

see also Defense contracts and procurement

see also Defense expenditures

see also Defense industries

see also Defense research

see also Department of Defense

National defense

see also Foreign relations
see also Logistics
see also Military aircraft
see also Military airlift
see also Military assistance
see also Military aviation
see also Military awards, decorations, and medals
see also Military bases, posts, and reservations
see also Military education
see also Military hospitals
see also Military housing
see also Military intelligence
see also Military law
see also Military pay
see also Military personnel
see also Military prisons
see also Military science
see also Military strategy
see also Military supplies and property
see also Military training
see also Military vehicles
see also Military weapons
see also National guard
see also Naval vessels
see also Service academies
see also Strategic materials

National Endowment for the Arts
see National Foundation on the Arts and the Humanities

National Endowment for the Humanities
see National Foundation on the Arts and the Humanities

National Environmental Satellite, Data, and Information Service
Climatological data by census div and State, and departures from long-term mean, from 1895, series, 2156–17
Climatological data for surface and upper air, averages by foreign and US station, monthly rpt, 2152–4
Climatological data for 284 US and outlying stations, for period of record through 1982, annual rpt, 2154–8
Glaciology intl research summaries, methodology, and bibls, series, 2156–18
Heating and cooling degree days by State, and housing energy bills and departures from normal by fuel type, by census div, monthly rpt, 2152–11
Heating and cooling degree days weighted by population, by census div and State, with area-weighted temperature and precipitation, monthly rpt, 2152–13
Marine weather and tropical cyclones, quarterly journal with articles, 2152–8
Storms and unusual weather phenomena characteristics, casualties, and property damage, by State and outlying area, monthly listing, 2152–3
Weather conditions and effect on agriculture, by US region, State, and city, and world area, weekly rpt, 2152–2
Weather conditions and impact assessment, by world area and country, monthly rpt, 2152–9
Weather events socioeconomic impacts and costs, heating and cooling degree days, and housing energy bills, by census div and State, monthly rpt, 2152–12
see also National Weather Service

National Eye Institute
Visual impairment survey methodology and results by age, in 3 SMSAs, Aug 1981-Dec 1982, 4478–147

National Fire Prevention and Control Administration
see Federal Emergency Management Agency

National forests
Agricultural Statistics, 1983, annual rpt, 1004–1.2
Area under Forest Service mgmt, by forest and location, Sept 1983, annual rpt, 1204–2
Colorado natl forest below-cost timber sales, and volume, costs, revenue, and net loss, by sale and forest, FY81-82, GAO rpt, 26113–131
Cost control proposals for Fed Govt programs and mgmt, 3-year savings by function and agency, and financial and operating data, 1960s-81, 16908–1.31
Environmental quality and protection programs, costs, and Fed Govt enforcement, 1983, detailed annual rpt, 484–1
Fed Govt aid to State and local govts, expenditures, and direct payments, by program, agency, and State, FY83, annual rpt, 2464–2
Fire (forest) damage and causes, by State and region, 1981, annual rpt, 1204–4
Fires on Forest Service land and acres burned, by cause, forest, and State, 1983, annual rpt, 1204–6
Forest, range, and associated waters use and mgmt assessment, and environmental impacts of Forest Service program options, 1977-2030 and trends from 1920, 1208–24
Forest Service programs and activities, by State and region, FY83, annual rpt, 1204–1
Georgia timber resources and removals, by species, ownership class, and county, 1981-83, series, 1206–26
Govt census, 1982: State govt payments to local govts, by program, source of funds, level of govt, and State, with trends from 1902, 2460–3
Horse and burro wild herd areas in western States, population, adoption, and protection and mgmt costs, as of 1984, biennial rpt, 5724–8
Hwy and bridge Fed Hwy Admin allocations, by project and State, FY85, 7556–3.2
Land area of natl forests, by State, FY83, annual rpt, 5724–1.1
Land Mgmt Bur activities and finances, and public land acreage and use, annual State rpt series, 5724–11
Land Mgmt Bur public lands admin and program activities in western States, FY82-84, annual rpt, 5724–13
Livestock grazing on Natl Forest System lands, and losses from predators, poisonous plants, and other causes, by region and State, FY83, annual rpt, 1204–5
Michigan timber acreage, volume, growth, removals, and production, by ownership, county, and forest and tree characteristics, 1980, series, 1206–31
Minnesota timber acreage, resources, and removals, by species, county, and ownership class, series, 1206–24

Index by Subjects and Names

Northeast States timber annual growth, removals, causes of mortality, and products output, and forest ownership and industries, State rpt series, 1206–16
Northeastern region timber resources and removals, by species, ownership, and county, State rpt series, 1206–12
Northwest US and British Columbia forest industry production, prices, trade, and employment, quarterly rpt, 1202–3
Northwest US natl forest timber sales contract operations by forest and firm, and lumber supply/demand, FY76-1983, hearings, 25318–57
Pacific Northwest natl forest sales by bidding method, harvest by company, and effects on local employment by community, 1974-77, 1208–194
Planting and seeding for forests and windbarriers, by State, FY83, annual rpt, 1204–7
Recreational sites in natl forests, area, and capacity, by type of activity, 1983, annual rpt, 1204–28
Recreational use of natl forests, visitor-days and visits by type of activity, forest, and State, FY83 with trends from 1924, annual rpt series, 1204–17
Rocky Mountain forest and rangeland area, and timber resources and removals, by ownership, forest and tree characteristics, and State, 1977, 1208–201
Rocky Mountain States forest biomass, conversion from volume to dry weight, for softwood and hardwood species, 1977, 1208–200
Schools in federally impacted areas, Fed Govt funding by county and school and congressional district, and eligible pupils, by State, FY83, annual rpt, 4804–10
Southeast region biomass timber, trees, volume, and green weight by species, site and diameter class, and stand age, 1982, 1208–199
Timber production, prices by region and State, trade by country, and consumption, by species and product, with industry earnings, 1950-83, annual rpt, 1204–29
Timber stumpage prices, for sawtimber sold from natl forests by species and region, quarterly rpt, 1202–1
Utah timber acreage and resources, and forest recreational use and big game population by species, 1977-78, 1206–22.6
Washington State timber acreage and resources, by species, ownership class, and county, 1980, and harvest, 1950-81, series, 1206–28
Western regions natl forests below-cost timber sales and revenue by forest, and volume, average price by species, and costs by region, FY80-1982, GAO rpt, 26113–126
Wildlife habitat and fishery improvements, use, and game population and harvest by species and forest, for Natl Forest System by region, FY83, annual rpt, 1204–31
Wood acquired and used for home heating, by household characteristics and wood sources, 1980/81, 1208–204
Wood fuel removal program itemized costs to Forest Service in 3 central Appalachia natl forests, 1981, 1208–191

Index by Subjects and Names

see also Wilderness areas

National Foundation on the Arts and the Humanities

- Activities and grants of Natl Endowment for Arts, FY83, annual rpt, 9564–3
- Activities and grants of Natl Endowment for Humanities, FY83, annual rpt, 9564–2
- Budget of US Appendix, detailed budgets and personnel summaries, by agency, FY85, annual rpt, 104–3
- Budget of US, appropriations, outlays, balances, and budget receipts, by govtl branch and agency, FY83, annual rpt, 8104–2
- Funding of arts and humanities, by source and State, FY82-83 with trends from FY66, 21408–69
- Museum grants, by instn, State, and city, FY84, annual rpt series, 9564–6

National grasslands

- Area under Forest Service mgmt, by location, Sept 1983, annual rpt, 1204–2
- Cost control proposals for Fed Govt programs and mgmt, 3-year savings by function and agency, and financial and operating data, 1960s-81, 16908–1.9, 16908–1.31
- Fed Govt aid to State and local govts, expenditures, and direct payments, by program, agency, and State, FY83, annual rpt, 2464–2
- Govt census, 1982: State govt payments to local govts, by program, source of funds, level of govt, and State, with trends from 1902, 2460–3
- Land Mgmt Bur activities and finances, and public land acreage and use, annual State rpt series, 5724–11
- Land Mgmt Bur public lands admin and program activities in western States, FY82-84, annual rpt, 5724–13
- Livestock grazing on Natl Forest System lands, and losses from predators, poisonous plants, and other causes, by region and State, FY83, annual rpt, 1204–5
- Wildlife habitat and fishery improvements, use, and game population and harvest by species and forest, for Natl Forest System by region, FY83, annual rpt, 1204–31

National Guard

- Activities, manpower, and facilities of Army and Air Natl Guard, FY83, annual rpt, 3704–3
- Budget of DOD, itemized account of legislative history, FY84, annual rpt, 3504–7
- Construction and renovation of military bases, DOD budget authorization requests, by DOD component, State, country, and project, FY85, annual rpt, 3544–15
- Manpower active duty strength, recruits, and reenlistment, by race, Hispanic origin, sex, and service branch, quarterly press release, 3542–7
- Manpower and equipment strengths, readiness, and funding, by reserve component, FY83, annual rpt, 3544–27
- Manpower strengths and characteristics, by reserve component, quarterly rpt, 3542–4
- Manpower strengths and mobilization alert system efficiency, for selected Army Reserve and Natl Guard units, 1982-83 survey, GAO rpt, 26123–57

Marijuana cultivation control activity of State law enforcement agencies, and aid from Fed Govt and Natl Guard, 1983 survey, GAO rpt, 26119–64

Training and education programs of DOD, funding, staff, students, and facilities, by service branch and reserve component, FY85, annual rpt, 3504–5

National Health and Nutrition Examination Survey

- Health and dental condition and body measurements, by age, sex, and race, Vital and Health Statistics series, 4147–11
- Publications of NCHS, quarterly listing, 4122–2

National Health Examination Survey *see* National Health and Nutrition Examination Survey

National Health Interview Survey

- Design and research methods for health surveys, 1982 biennial conf proceedings, 4184–1
- Health condition, hospitalization, disability, and medical costs, by demographic characteristics, Vital and Health Statistics series, 4147–10
- Publications of NCHS, quarterly listing, 4122–2
- Visual impairment survey methodology and results by age, in 3 SMSAs, Aug 1981-Dec 1982, 4478–147

National Health Service Corps

New Mexico health clinics staffed by Natl Health Service Corps, income by source and service, and effect of revised system for Federal payback, 1980-83, hearings, 21368–47

National Health Survey

see under names of individual survey components

National Heart, Lung, and Blood Institute

- Activities and funding of Inst, with morbidity and mortality data, various periods 1940-88, annual rpt, 4474–22
- Blood pressure screening and hypertension treatment itemized costs at 9 worksites, 1978-80, 4478–148
- Heart attack and cancer incidence and deaths in men aged 35-59, effects of lowering blood cholesterol levels, with background data on other risk factors, 1973-83, 4478–145
- Hypertension prevalence and control, and change in death rates from all causes and cardiovascular disease, selected years 1971-82, article, 4102–1.432
- Nutrition and cardiovascular disease consumer education, effectiveness of Natl Heart, Lung, and Blood Inst and Giant Food, Inc, program in DC metro area, 1978-79, 4478–144
- Organization, disease and mortality data, and funds and recipients, FY83 with trends from 1900, annual fact book, 4474–15
- Programs and budget recommended by Advisory Council, FY85-89, annual rpt, 4474–11

National Highway Traffic Safety Administration

- Accidents (fatal), circumstances, and characteristics of persons and vehicles involved, detailed data, 1982, annual rpt, 7764–10

Accidents (fatal), circumstances, and characteristics of persons and vehicles involved, 1983, annual rpt, 7764–14

- Accidents and casualties detailed direct and indirect costs, by characteristics of persons and vehicles involved, with DOT safety program funding, 1979-80, 7768–80
- Accidents and deaths by characteristics of persons and vehicles involved and State, and Natl Hwy Traffic Safety Admin activities, 1961-81, annual rpt, 7764–1
- Accidents, circumstances, injuries, deaths, and characteristics of persons and vehicles involved, 1982, annual rpt, 7764–13
- Accidents, deaths, circumstances, and characteristics of persons and vehicles involved, series, 7766–13
- Auto and light truck fuel economy performance by make, and standards, 1978-85 model years, annual rpt, 7764–9
- Auto and light truck safety, crash test results of selected new domestic and foreign models for model year to date, press release series, 7766–7
- Auto safety and experimental vehicle designs, 1982, conf proceedings, annual rpt, 7764–3
- Cost control proposals for Fed Govt programs and mgmt, 3-year savings by function and agency, and financial and operating data, 1960s-81, 16908–1.11
- Deaths in traffic accidents by region, and death rates for miles traveled, monthly rpt, 7762–7
- Employment at DOT, by subagency, State, and selected personnel characteristics, FY83, annual rpt, 7304–18
- Employment in NHTSA fuel economy programs, by office, FY80-83, hearing, 21368–49
- Fraud and abuse in DOT programs, audits and investigations, 1st half FY84, semiannual rpt, 7302–4
- Hwy safety, accident, and traffic data from Natl Statistics and Analysis Center, series, 7766–10
- Recalls of motor vehicles and equipment with safety-related defects, by make, quarterly listing, 7762–2
- Seat belt use, effects of driving circumstances and driver characteristics and attitudes, 1981 survey, 7768–82
- Traffic fatal accidents, alcohol levels of drivers and pedestrians by driver age and sex and time of accident, 1980, 7768–81
- Traffic safety projects research and evaluation, quarterly rpt articles, 7762–9

National Hospital Discharge Survey

- Health facilities and manpower use, by patient and facility characteristics, Vital and Health Statistics series, 4147–13
- Hospital discharges and length of stay of aged and nonaged persons, by region, facility size, and diagnosis, 1981, 4146–8.98
- Publications of NCHS, quarterly listing, 4122–2

National Hurricane Center

"Annual Data and Verification Tabulation, Atlantic Tropical Cyclones, 1983", 2184–7

National income and product accounts

National income and product accounts

Budget of US, compact budgets by function, agency, and account, FY85 with projections to FY89, annual rpt, 104–2

Budget of US, projected under current fiscal policies, FY85-89, annual rpt, 26304–3.2

Budget of US, special analysis of Fed Govt transactions in natl income accounts, FY85, annual rpt, 104–1.2

Business Conditions Digest, current data on economic, business, and financial conditions and cyclical fluctuations, monthly rpt, 2702–3

Business Conditions Digest, historical supplement on economic, business, and financial conditions and cyclical fluctuations, with methodology, 1947-82, 2708–31

Business statistics, detailed data for major industries and economic indicators, *Survey of Current Business,* monthly rpt, 2702–1

Flow-of-funds accounts savings, investments, and credit statements, quarterly rpt, 9365–3.3

Foreign sector in flow-of-funds and natl income and product accounts, data reconciliation, 1984 technical paper, 9366–7.95

Govt revenues and expenditures by level of govt, natl income and product accounts, selected years 1929-83, annual rpt, 204–1.6

Natl income and product accounts 1983 revisions, methodology and data sources, 1984 article, 2702–1.425

Natl income and product, comprehensive accounts and components, benchmark revisions, 1929-76, errata, 2702–1.426

Natl income and product, comprehensive accounts and components, *Survey of Current Business,* monthly rpt, 2702–1.21

Savings (personal) measures from natl income and product and flow-of-funds accounts, 1977 and 1982, article, 2702–1.441

Statistical Abstract of US, social, political, and economic data, 1950s-83 and trends, annual rpt, 2324–1.2, 2324–1.3

see also Gross National Product

National Institute for Occupational Safety and Health

Coal miners black lung exams and incidence, and health and safety NIOSH research activities, annual rpt, suspended, 4244–1

Hazardous substances and radiation effects on workers health, by industry, occupation, age, and sex, with bibl and glossary, 1920s-82, 9638–50

Occupational safety and health projects supported by NIOSH, by region and State, annual listing, suspended, 4244–2

Washington State deaths by sex, cause, and detailed occupation, summary data from occupational mortality study, 1950-79, 4248–47

National Institute of Allergy and Infectious Diseases

Activities of Inst, grants by instn, State, and country, and disease incidence and costs, FY60s-84, annual rpt, 4474–30

National Institute of Child Health and Human Development

Head Start Project programs effect on child dev, by characteristics of program, child, and family, literature review, selected years 1965-81, 4608–20

Population and health research funded by 4 private organizations, project listing by topic, with funding data, 1981, annual rpt, 4474–16

Research Center for Mothers and Children, activities and funding, as of June 1983, annual rpt, 4474–31

National Institute of Dental Research

Research and training funds awarded by Natl Inst of Dental Research, by recipient instn, FY83, annual listing, 4474–19

National Institute of Education

Activities of NIE and education research grants awarded by recipient, FY81-82, annual rpt, 4914–4

Education Dept programs and activities, FY83, annual rpt, 4804–6

Microfiche from Educational Resources Info Center, holdings of US and foreign educational and other instns, as of 1983, listing, 4918–14

School crime, assaults and robberies of secondary students and teachers, 1972-83, 4918–13

Testing in elementary and secondary schools, teacher and student attitudes, with detail for standardized achievement tests, 1980 conf papers, 4918–15

National Institute of General Medical Sciences

Genetically abnormal human cell cultures available to researchers, and cultures shipped, 1984 annual listing, 4474–23

Research programs and funding, FY83, annual rpt, 4474–12

National Institute of Justice

see Office of Justice Assistance, Research and Statistics

National Institute of Mental Health

Community mental health centers federally funded, staff, expenditures, funding sources, and patient characteristics, annual rpt, suspended, 4504–5

Contract awards, grants, and staff of ADAMHA, by Inst, program, and State, FY83, annual factbook, 4044–1

Info systems needs of mental health facilities, and system implementation, uses, and costs, series, 4506–2

Mental health clinical training funding by NIMH, by program and field, FY80-83, GAO rpt, 26121–86

Mental health facilities needs assessment and program evaluation for small areas, methodology, use of census data, analysis, and sample data, series, 4506–8

Mental health facilities, services, staff, and patient characteristics, *Statistical Notes* series, 4506–3

Mental health facilities, services, staff, and patient characteristics, 1970s-82 with trends from 1954, annual rpt, 4504–9

Mental health statistics, natl reporting program historical overview, 1840-1983, narrative rpt, 4508–5

Patients and admissions of State and county mental hospitals, by diagnosis, age, and State, FY81, annual rpt, 4504–2

Index by Subjects and Names

National Institute on Aging

Florida and California elderly migration by selected State of origin or destination, and Florida elderly, by sociodemographic and housing characteristics, 1970 and 1980, 4478–150

Genetically abnormal human cell cultures available to researchers, and cultures shipped, 1984 annual listing, 4474–23

National Institute on Alcohol Abuse and Alcoholism

Contract awards, grants, and staff of ADAMHA, by Inst, program, and State, FY83, annual factbook, 4044–1

Research on alcoholism, treatment programs, and patient characteristics, quarterly journal, 4482–1

Research review of alcohol use, and health, economic, and social impacts, 1970s-81, 4488–4

National Institute on Drug Abuse

Contract awards, grants, and staff of ADAMHA, by Inst, program, and State, FY83, annual factbook, 4044–1

Drugs nonmedical use and effects, research compilations and summaries, bibls, and survey instruments, series, 4496–1

High school seniors use and assessment of drugs by type, alcohol, and cigarettes, by sex and region, 1975-83 surveys, annual rpt, 4494–4

Marijuana health consequences and use, annual research review, discontinued, 4494–1

Research on drug abuse and treatment, highlights of studies by Natl Inst on Drug Abuse grant recipients, periodic rpt, 4492–4

Treatment programs for drug abuse, methods, and policy issues, series, 4496–5

National Institutes of Health

Acquired immune deficiency syndrome (AIDS) research expenditures in 3 areas, by NIH inst, FY82, 4102–1.404

Activities, staff, funding, and facilities of NIH, historical data, 1984 annual rpt, 4434–1

Cost control proposals for Fed Govt programs and mgmt, 3-year savings by function and agency, and financial and operating data, 1960s-81, 16908–1.7

Data projects and systems of HHS, by subagency, FY83-84, annual inventory, 4044–3

Diabetes programs and expenditures of Fed Govt, by agency and NIH inst, FY84, annual rpt, 4434–8

Digestive Diseases Interagency Coordinating Committee activities, and related Federal research and funding, by agency, FY79-83, annual rpt, 4434–13

Grant and contract extramural awards of NIH for research, R&D, training, and construction, FY72-83, annual rpt, 4434–9

Grants and awards for R&D, training, construction, and medical libraries, by location and recipient, FY83, annual listings, 4434–7

Grants, awards, and obligations by State and type of recipient, and full-time personnel, by NIH inst, FY83, annual rpt, 4434–3

Intl programs of NIH, activities and funding, by inst and country, FY83, annual rpt, 4474–6

Index by Subjects and Names

Program activities, accomplishments, and funding of NIH Research Resources Div, by program, FY83, annual rpt, 4434–12

Publications of NIH, 1983, annual listing, 4434–2

R&D Fed Govt funding for all performers, by field and supporting agency, selected years FY60-84, annual rpt, 9627–20

Radioactive waste volume by disposal method, and shipments by form, 1982, hearing, 25528–93

Research grants and awards, quarterly listing, 4432–1

Science and engineering grad enrollment, fields of study, financial support, and other student and instn characteristics, 1975-82, annual survey, 9627–7

see also Fogarty International Center for Advanced Study in the Health Sciences

see also National Cancer Institute

see also National Eye Institute

see also National Heart, Lung, and Blood Institute

see also National Institute of Allergy and Infectious Diseases

see also National Institute of Child Health and Human Development

see also National Institute of Dental Research

see also National Institute of General Medical Sciences

see also National Institute on Aging

see also National Library of Medicine

National Labor Relations Board

Budget of US Appendix, detailed budgets and personnel summaries, by agency, FY85, annual rpt, 104–3

Budget of US, appropriations, outlays, balances, and budget receipts, by govtl branch and agency, FY83, annual rpt, 8104–2

Representation elections conducted by NLRB, results, monthly rpt, 9582–2

National League of Cities

"City Fiscal Conditions in FY83: Dark Clouds on the Horizon", 25408–86.1

"Importance of GRS Continues and the Need for Renewal Increases", 25408–86.2

National Library of Medicine

Activities, collections, and grants, FY81-83, annual rpt, 4464–1

National Marine Fisheries Service

Atlantic Ocean sport and commercial landings and allowable and potential catch of US and Canada, for 34 species, 1983, annual rpt, 2164–14

Cold storage holdings of fish and shellfish products, weight by species and form, preliminary data, monthly rpt, 2162–2

Europe (Western) fish and shellfish wholesale prices and market activity in 8 countries, weekly rpt, 2162–8

Fish and fish products production by region and State, and trade, by species and product, 1982-83, annual rpt series, 2166–6

Fish and shellfish landings, prices, trade, consumption, and industry operating data, for US with foreign comparisons, 1982-83, annual rpt, 2164–1

Fish and shellfish landings, prices, trade, wholesaler receipts, and market activities at 5 major US ports, weekly rpts, 2162–6

National Oceanic and Atmospheric Administration

Fish and shellfish of economic importance, biological, fishery, and mgmt data, literature review series, 2166–16

Fish landings, employment, gear used, and seafood production, for detailed species by State, 1977, annual rpt, 2164–2

Fish larvae abundance and distribution in Caribbean area, by fish species or group, summer 1972 and winter 1973, 2168–80

Fish meal and oil, production and trade, monthly rpt, 2162–3

Fishermen (ocean sport), fishing activities, and catch by species, by fisherman characteristics, State, and coastal region, series, 2166–17

Fishery Conservation Zone admin, annual rpt, discontinued, 2164–12

Fishing (ocean sport) effort and catch, and Natl Marine Fisheries Service tagging and research activity, by species and location, 1983, annual rpt, 2164–7

Japan fish landings, prices, trade by country, cold storage, and market devs, periodic press release, 2162–7

Marine Fisheries Review, US and foreign fisheries resources, conservation, operations, and research, quarterly rpt articles, 2162–1

Marine Mammal Protection Act admin and populations, strandings, and catch permits by type and applicant, by species and location, Apr 1983-Mar 1984, annual rpt, 2164–11

Middle Atlantic OCS fishes dietary composition by food item and fish size, for 9 species, fall 1976-winter 1977, 2168–78

R&D and mgmt of fishery resources, Fed Govt grants by project and resulting publications, 1983, annual listing, 2164–3

Seal harvest, mgmt, and skins taken and rejected for northern fur seals of Pribilof Islands, Alaska, various dates 1786-1981, 2168–79

National Master Facility Inventory Survey

Hospitals and nursing homes, employees, and use, by ownership, bed size, region, and State, selected years 1969-80, 4147–14.30

Nursing home facilities use and characteristics, and nurses employed, by region and State, 1980, 4147–14.29

National Mediation Board

Budget of US Appendix, detailed budgets and personnel summaries, by agency, FY85, annual rpt, 104–3

Budget of US, appropriations, outlays, balances, and budget receipts, by govtl branch and agency, FY83, annual rpt, 8104–2

National Medical Care Expenditure Survey

Design and research methods for health surveys, 1982 biennial conf proceedings, 4184–1

Health care expenditures, natl survey on services use, costs, and sources of payment, by patient and physician characteristics, 1977-78, series, 4186–3

Methodology of natl survey of households, physicians, health insurance firms, and employers, series, 4186–4

National Medical Care Utilization and Expenditure Survey

Health and vital statistics collection, and use in program planning and evaluation, Public Health Conf papers, 1983, biennial rpt, 4164–2

Health care facility and services use and expenditures, survey results, series, 4146–11

Methodology and findings of natl survey of households, Medicare records, and Medicaid records in 4 States, 1980, series, 4146–12

Publications of NCHS, quarterly listing, 4122–2

National monuments

see Monuments and memorials

National Narcotics Intelligence Consumers Committee

Drug (illegal) supply, use, casualties, treatment program and emergency room admissions in major cities, arrests, and seizures, by drug type, 1982, annual rpt, 15894–1

National Nursing Home Survey

Health facilities and manpower use, by patient and facility characteristics, Vital and Health Statistics series, 4147–13

Publications of NCHS, quarterly listing, 4122–2

National Ocean Service

France Brittany coast oil spill cleanup and research costs, marine and tourism industry losses, and recreation losses of tourists and residents, 1971-79, 2178–13

Great Lakes water levels, daily and monthly averages by station, 1982 and summary 1900-82, annual rpt, 2174–3

Tidal current tables, daily time and velocity by station for North America and Asia coasts, 1985, annual rpt, 2174–1

Tide height and time daily at worldwide coastal points, 1985 predictions, annual rpt series, 2174–2

National Ocean Survey

see National Ocean Service

National Oceanic and Atmospheric Administration

Budgets and permanent staff positions appropriated for Commerce Dept agencies, FY84-85, annual rpt, 2004–6

Cost control proposals for Fed Govt programs and mgmt, 3-year savings by function and agency, and financial and operating data, 1960s-81, 16908–1.3

Earthquake intensity, damage, time of origin, and seismic characteristics of all US and major foreign earthquakes, 1981, annual rpt, 5664–13

Medical facilities of Navy, use by active and retired military personnel, dependents, and others by facility and type, quarterly rpt, 3802–1

Meteorological services and research of Fed Govt, programs and funding by agency, FY84-85, annual rpt, 2144–2

Ocean dumping and pollution investigations and activities of NOAA, research and monitoring studies funded, and bibl, FY83, annual rpt, 2144–9

Oceanographic data, stations and cruises recording data for World Data Center A by country, ship, and type of data, 1983, annual rpt, 2144–15

Oceanographic research cruise schedules and ship characteristics, by academic instn or Federal agency, 1984, annual rpt, 3804–6

Programs, funding, and employment of Commerce Dept agencies, FY83, annual rpt, 2004–1

National Oceanic and Atmospheric Administration

Publications of Commerce Dept, biweekly listing, 2002–1

R&D Fed Govt funding, by function, agency, and program, selected years FY80-84 and proposed FY85, 26308–46

Satellite systems (foreign and US) for civil observation, data product revenue, and proposed transfer of Fed Govt system to private sector, selected years 1978-FY84, 2148–47

Scientific and technical publications of NOAA, monthly listing, 2142–1

Weather modification activity rpts and summary, annual rpt, suspended, 2144–8

see also National Environmental Satellite, Data, and Information Service

see also National Marine Fisheries Service

see also National Ocean Service

see also National Weather Service

National Opinion Research Center

"High School and Beyond Course Offerings and Course Enrollments Survey (1982), Data File User's Manual", 4826–2.17

"High School and Beyond Transcripts Survey (1982), Data File User's Manual", 4826–2.16

National Park Service

- Acreage of natl park system and other areas under NPS mgmt, by type of area, ownership, and site, as of Sept 1984, semiannual rpt, 5542–1
- Assaults, murders, and other deaths of law enforcement officers, by circumstances, level of govt, agency, victim and offender characteristics, and location, 1983, annual rpt, 6224–3
- Cost control proposals for Fed Govt programs and mgmt, 3-year savings by function and agency, and financial and operating data, 1960s-81, 16908–1.9, 16908–1.31
- Genetic resource (plant and animal) conservation, commercial uses, causes of depletion, and geographic sources, 1984 rpt, 5548–13
- Grizzly bears in and around Yellowstone Natl Park, population, physical characteristics, diet, and movements, 1982, annual rpt, 5544–4
- Historic Preservation Fund grants, by State, FY85, annual press release, 5544–9
- Kennedy Performing Arts Center income and expenses by type, and Fed Govt share of expenses, FY79-83, GAO rpt, 26119–60
- Recreation fees and collection costs, visitors, and capacity of outdoor Fed Govt, State, and private facilities, by managing agency and State, 1983, annual rpt, 5544–14
- Recreation outdoor area dev, Interior Dept Land and Water Conservation Fund grants by State, FY85, annual press release, 5544–15
- Visitor deaths, by park and type of accident, 1973-83, annual rpt, 5544–6
- Visits and overnight stays, visitors, and vehicles, by State and park, 1983, annual rpt, 5544–12
- Youth Conservation Corps activities, costs, and participant characteristics, by sponsoring agency, 1982, annual rpt, 5304–12

National park system

- Acid rain causes and effects, air pollutant emissions by source in US and selected countries, and control costs, 1970s-83 and projected to 2000, 21368–52
- Acid rain effects on water quality, fish populations, and soils in Rocky Mountain and Yellowstone natl parks, as of 1983, summary research rpt, 5506–5.17
- Acreage of natl park system and other areas under Natl Park Service mgmt, by type of area, ownership, and site, as of Sept 1984, semiannual rpt, 5542–1
- Air pollutant metal levels, by monitoring site, State, and urban-rural location, 1977-79, last issue of annual rpt, 9194–10
- Air quality protection classification of natl parks, acreage covered and recommended for redesignation by park, as of 1983, hearings, 25328–25
- Cost control proposals for Fed Govt programs and mgmt, 3-year savings by function and agency, and financial and operating data, 1960s-81, 16908–1.9, 16908–1.31
- Environmental quality and protection programs, costs, and Fed Govt enforcement, 1983, detailed annual rpt, 484–1
- Interior Dept programs, activities, and funding, various periods 1967-84, last issue of annual rpt, 5304–13
- Inventory and costs of Fed Govt-owned real property, worldwide summary by location, agency, and use, 1983, annual rpt, 9454–5
- Recreation fees and collection costs, visitors, and capacity of outdoor Fed Govt, State, and private facilities, by managing agency and State, 1983, annual rpt, 5544–14
- Visitor deaths, by park and type of accident, 1973-83, annual rpt, 5544–6
- Visits and overnight stays, visitors, and vehicles, by State and park, 1983, annual rpt, 5544–12

see also National forests

see also Parks

see also Wilderness areas

see also Wildlife refuges

see also Yellowstone National Park

National planning

see Economic policy

see Fiscal policy

National Railroad Passenger Corp.

- Energy use in transportation sector by mode, fuel supplies, and demographic and economic determinants of vehicle use, 1970s-83, annual rpt, 3304–5
- Finances, operations, vehicles, equipment, accidents, and energy use, by mode of transport, 1955-84, annual rpt, 7304–2
- Northeast Corridor rail improvement project goals, funding, and progress, and Amtrak finances and operations, FY83, annual rpt, 7604–9
- Revenue, cost, and ridership data for Amtrak, summary data FY72-81, annual rpt, 7304–1

see also Metroliner

National Reporting System for Family Planning Services

Health facilities and manpower use, by patient and facility characteristics, Vital and Health Statistics series, 4147–13

Index by Subjects and Names

Publications of NCHS, quarterly listing, 4122–2

National school lunch and breakfast programs

see School lunch and breakfast programs

National Science Foundation

- Budget of US Appendix, detailed budgets and personnel summaries, by agency, FY85, annual rpt, 104–3
- Budget of US, appropriations, outlays, balances, and budget receipts, by govtl branch and agency, FY83, annual rpt, 8104–2
- DOD prime contract awards for R&D to educational and nonprofit instns and Federal agencies, by instn and location, FY83, annual listing, 3544–17
- Grants and awards of NSF, recipients by State, FY83, annual listing, 9624–11
- Intl exchange and training programs of Fed Govt, participants by world region, and funding, by agency, FY83, annual rpt, 9854–8
- Oceanographic research cruise schedules and ship characteristics, by academic instn or Federal agency, 1984, annual rpt, 3804–6
- R&D and science-related Fed Govt funding to higher education and nonprofit instns, by field, instn, agency, and State, FY82, annual rpt, 9627–17
- R&D expenditures by higher education instns and federally funded centers, by field, source of funds, instn, and State, FY82, annual rpt, 9627–13
- R&D expenditures by source, and scientists education and employment, detailed data by field, selected years 1953-84, annual rpt, 9624–18
- R&D expenditures of higher education instns, and science and engineering employment and grad students, by field, 1972-83, biennial rpt, 9627–24
- R&D Fed Govt funding, by function, agency, and program, selected years FY80-84 and proposed FY85, 26308–46
- R&D Fed Govt funding for all performers, by field and supporting agency, selected years FY60-84, annual rpt, 9627–20
- R&D industry funding and employment of scientists and engineers, by industry group, firm size, and funding source, 1956-82, annual rpt, 9627–21
- Research programs, activities, and funding of NSF, FY82-83, annual rpt, 9624–6
- Science and engineering enrollment, degrees, and employment, R&D funding, and related topics, highlights series, 9626–2
- Science and engineering grad enrollment, fields of study, financial support, and other student and instn characteristics, 1975-82, annual survey, 9627–7
- Science and engineering grads of 1980-81, employment characteristics or grad enrollment, by degree level, field, sex, and race, 1982, 9627–25
- *Science Indicators,* R&D expenditures, innovations, research, and higher education, with foreign comparisons, 1960s- 83, annual rpt, 9624–10
- Science resources, special rpts series, 9626–6
- Science Resources Studies Div of NSF, activities, project descriptions, and 1973-83 publications, 1983 annual listing, 9624–21

Index by Subjects and Names

Scientists and engineers employed at universities and colleges, by field, sex, State, and instn, Jan 1983 and selected trends from 1967, annual survey, 9627–11

Scientists and engineers supply, employment, and education, by sex, race, Hispanic origin, and field, selected years 1965-83, biennial rpt, 9624–20

Scientists, engineers, and technicians employed in private industry, by occupation and industry group, 1980-81, biennial rpt, 9627–23

Scientists, engineers, and technicians employment in transportation, utilities, and retail and wholesale trade, by field of science and industry, 1982, 9628–72

Scientists, engineers, and technicians needed in defense and nondefense industries, and supply/demand, by field, 1981-87, 9628–71

Space and aeronautics programs and budgets of Fed Govt by agency, and foreign programs, 1957-FY85, annual rpt, 9504–9

National security *see* Internal security *see* National defense

National Security Agency

Construction and renovation of military bases, DOD budget authorization requests, by DOD component, State, country, and project, FY85, annual rpt, 3544–15

National Service Life Insurance Fund *see* Federal trust funds

National stockpiles *see* Stockpiling

National Survey of Family Growth Publications of NCHS, quarterly listing, 4122–2

National Survey of Professional, Administrative, Technical and Clerical Pay

Wages of white-collar workers, by occupation, work level, and industry div, Mar 1984, annual rpt, 6784–2

National Technical Information Service

Computer data files available from NTIS, by subject, 1984 annual listing, 2224–3

Computer data files of NTIS, by agency, periodic listing, 2222–1

Computer software and documentation available from NTIS, by agency and program characteristics, 1984 annual listing, 2224–2

Cost control proposals for Fed Govt programs and mgmt, 3-year savings by function and agency, and financial and operating data, 1960s-81, 16908–1.30

EPA publications in NTIS collection, quarterly listing, 9182–5

Occupational injuries and illnesses, data available from NTIS, by State, 1981, annual rpt, 6704–2

Programs, funding, and employment of Commerce Dept agencies, FY83, annual rpt, 2004–1

Publications of Commerce Dept, biweekly listing, 2002–1

R&D Fed Govt facilities and services available for private sector use, by field of science, 1984 biennial listing, 2224–4

National Telecommunications and Information Administration

Budgets and permanent staff positions appropriated for Commerce Dept agencies, FY84-85, annual rpt, 2004–6

Programs, funding, and employment of Commerce Dept agencies, FY83, annual rpt, 2004–1

Publications of Commerce Dept, biweekly listing, 2002–1

Radio frequency assignments for Federal agency use, 2nd half 1983, semiannual rpt, 2802–1

Research and engineering rpts of NTIA, FY83, annual listing, 2804–3

National Transportation Policy Study Commission

Budget of US, appropriations, outlays, balances, and budget receipts, by govtl branch and agency, FY83, annual rpt, 8104–2

National Transportation Safety Board

Accident investigations and recommendations by NTSB, 1983, annual rpt, 9614–1

Aircraft accident circumstances and severity, by type of flying and aircraft, 1981, annual rpt, 9614–3

Aircraft accidents and deaths for airlines and general aviation, 1983, preliminary annual rpt, 9614–9

Aircraft fatal accidents of commuter airlines, air taxis, and general aviation, alcohol involvement, circumstances, and pilot characteristics, 1975-81, 9618–11

Airline and general aviation accident circumstances, severity, and causes, for US operations of domestic and foreign aircraft, periodic rpt, 9612–1

Airport size and safety, and accidents at or near airports by circumstance, for total and selected airports, various periods 1964-81, 9618–12

Alcohol-related and total traffic deaths, and drunk driver license revocations and other deterrence measures in selected States, 1980-82, 9618–10

Budget of US Appendix, detailed budgets and personnel summaries, by agency, FY85, annual rpt, 104–3

Budget of US, appropriations, outlays, balances, and budget receipts, by govtl branch and agency, FY83, annual rpt, 8104–2

Deaths in transportation accidents, by mode, 1982-83, annual summary rpt, 9614–6

Railroad accidents, circumstances, severity, and railroad involved, quarterly rpt, 9612–3

National Weather Service

Cost control proposals for Fed Govt programs and mgmt, 3-year savings by function and agency, and financial and operating data, 1960s-81, 16908–1.3

Flood (flash) deaths, by flood circumstances, type of warning, cause of death, and location, Sept 1969-May 1981, article, 4102–1.406

Forecast methodology, accuracy, and applications, technical rpt series, 2186–4

Hurricanes and tropical storms in North Atlantic and Caribbean area, paths, surveillance, deaths, property damage, and landfall probabilities by city, 1983, annual rpt, 2184–7

Nationwide Personal Transportation Study

Hurricanes and tropical storms in northeastern Pacific, paths, surveillance, deaths, and property damage, 1983, annual rpt, 2184–8

Marine weather broadcasts for US ships, by major ocean area, as of Jan 1984, biennial rpt, 2184–3

New York State area snow depth and water equivalent, by site, winter 1982/83, annual rpt, 2184–2

Northeastern US water supply, precipitation and stream runoff by station, monthly rpt, 2182–3

Ocean surface temperature by ocean and for US coastal areas, and Bering Sea ice conditions, monthly rpt, 2182–5

Precipitation and temperature outlook for US and Northern Hemisphere, and by US and selected foreign weather stations, semimonthly rpt, 2182–1

Precipitation forecast accuracy, by season, forecast period, and region, various periods 1966-82, technical memorandum, 2188–17

Program and service descriptions, with maps of areas covered, annual rpt, suspended, 2184–1

Reorganization and technological improvement proposal, effects on NWS staff and expenditures, FY82 and projected to 2000, 2188–16

Station locations and regular observations made, 1984 annual list, 2184–5

Stations of Upper Air Observational Network, by US and foreign location, 1984, annual listing, 2184–6

Western US water supply, streamflow and reservoir storage forecasts by stream and station, Jan-May monthly rpt, 1262–1

see also National Environmental Satellite, Data, and Information Service

National Wildlife Federation "Scientists' Acid Deposition Survey", 25328–25

National Wildlife Refuge System *see* Wildlife refuges

Nationality *see* Citizenship

Nationalization *see* Government ownership

Nationalization of alien property *see* Expropriation

Nationwide Food Consumption Survey

Dairy products household expenditures, effects of income and other sociodemographic characteristics, modeling results, 1977/78, 1561–2.404

Expenditures for fruit, vegetable, and potato products related to income and other household characteristics, 1977-78, 1548–236

Food consumption and nutrient intake by individuals, by food group, source, and socioeconomic characteristics, 1977-78 natl survey, final rpt series, 1356–4

Food consumption expenditures and nutrient intake of low-income households, by food stamp program participation and race, 1979-80, article, 1541–7.402

Nationwide Personal Transportation Study

Data coverage and availability for transportation industry statistics from Census Bur, 1983 pamphlet, 2326–7.61

Travel patterns, personal and household characteristics, auto use, and public transport availability, 1977 survey, series, 7556–6

Nativity

Nativity
see Birthplace

NATO
see North Atlantic Treaty Organization

Natural disasters
see Disasters
see Drought
see Earthquakes
see Floods
see Forest fires
see Glaciers
see Storms
see Volcanoes

Natural gas and gas industry

- Agricultural cooperatives oil and gas production, supply, and reserves, 1979 and 1982, article, 1561–16.403
- Agricultural cooperatives oil and gas production, supply, and reserves, 1982 with comparisons to 1979, article, 1122–1.407
- Agriculture census, 1982: farms, farmland, production, finances, and operator characteristics, by county, final State rpt series, 2331–1
- Air pollutant emission factors, by detailed source, 3rd edition, 1983-84 supplements, 9198–13
- Air pollutant sulfur dioxide emissions reduction proposal, effects on polluting industries and coal production by region and State, projected to 2010, 9188–97
- Air pollution levels for 5 pollutants, by detailed source, State, and Air Quality Control Region, 1981, annual rpt, 9194–7
- Alaska electric power capacity and generation by fuel type, and marketing, by utility, type of ownership, and location, 1983, annual rpt, 3214–2
- Alaska minerals resources, production, claims on wildlife refuges, oil and gas leases, and exploratory wells, with maps and bibl, 1983, annual rpt, 5664–11
- Budget of US, effects of Reagan Admin policy changes, by detailed program, FY85, annual rpt, 104–21
- Building materials manufacture, energy use and cost by source and industry, 1970s-82, article, 2012–1.401
- Buildings (nonresidential) energy use, expenditures, and conservation, by building characteristics, EIA survey series, 3166–8
- Business statistics, detailed data for major industries and economic indicators, *Survey of Current Business,* monthly rpt, 2702–1.10
- Carbon dioxide atmospheric levels, climatic effects and impacts of fossil and synthetic fuels use, deforestation, and land use patterns, research rpt series, 3406–3
- Carbon dioxide emissions from fossil fuel combustion by fuel type, worldwide estimates based on total and non-oxidized fossil fuel production, 1950-81, 3008–94
- China economic conditions, agricultural and industrial production, trade, and domestic and foreign investment, 1980-85, 2048–106
- Coastal environmental characteristics, fish, wildlife, and use, and population socioeconomic data, for individual areas, series, 5506–4

Communist, OECD, and selected other countries energy reserves, production, and consumption, and oil trade and revenue, 1960s-83, annual rpt, 244–5.5

- Connecticut utility group housing energy conservation program, cost effectiveness and characteristics of participants and nonparticipants, 1980-82, 3308–77
- Construction put in place, value of new public and private structures, by type, monthly rpt, 2382–4
- Consumption, by fuel type, economic sector, and end use, 1983 and 2000, 2006–2.5
- Consumption, by fuel type, economic sector, census div, and State, 1960-82, State Energy Data System annual rpt, 3164–39
- Consumption of energy, by type of air pollutant source and fuel, and State, 1981, annual rpt, 9194–14
- Consumption per capita, and by economic sector, State, and major energy resource, 1960-82, State Energy Data System annual supplement, 3164–55
- Consumption, prices, and conservation and efficiency measures, by fuel type, end-use sector, selected industry, and region, 1960-83, annual rpt, 3164–73
- County Business Patterns: establishments, employees, and payrolls, by SIC 4-digit industry and county, 1981, annual State rpt series, 2326–8
- County Business Patterns: establishments, employees, and payrolls, by SIC 4-digit industry and county, 1982, annual State rpt series, 2326–6
- Cuba economic conditions, agricultural and industrial production and distribution, trade, and intl economic relations, 1970-82 and trends from 1957, 248–40
- Defense Fuel Supply Center procurement, prices, stocks, transport, and other activities and finances, FY83, annual rpt, 3904–8
- DOD electric power plants and major fuel-burning facilities conversion from oil and gas, fuel use data, 1983, annual rpt, 3104–9
- DOE in-house energy use, conservation investments, and savings, by type of use and fuel and field office, FY83, annual rpt, 3024–3
- Earnings by major industry group, and personal income per capita and by source, by region and State, 1929-82, 2708–40
- Electric power plant (steam) fuel deliveries, costs, and quality, by fuel type, State, and utility, 1983, annual rpt, 3164–42
- Electric power plant capacity, production, retail sales, and fuel stocks, use, and costs, by State, 1979-83, annual rpt, 3164–11
- Electric power plant capital and operating detailed costs, capacity, and fuel use, by plant, plant type, utility, and State, 1982, annual rpt, 3164–9
- Electric power plants and industrial facilities prohibited from oil and gas primary use, and exemption petitions, by facility, with summary fuel use, 1983, annual rpt, 3104–8
- Electric power plants, by capacity, fuel used, unit type, region, State, and county, for plants added and retired, 1983 and planned through 1993, annual rpt, 3164–36

Index by Subjects and Names

- Electric utility fuel cost, quality, use, receipts, and stocks, and power plant production, by energy source, State and utility, quarterly rpt, 3162–39
- Electric utility production, fuel consumption, stocks, and costs by fuel type, and sales, by State, monthly rpt, 3162–35
- Employment by detailed occupation, for 29 SIC 2-digit nonmanufacturing industries, 1981 BLS survey, 6748–60
- Employment, earnings, and hours, by selected SIC 1- to 4-digit industry, State, and for 278 major labor areas, 1939-83, annual rpt, 6744–5
- Employment, earnings, and hours, by SIC 4-digit nonfarm industry, monthly 1974-Feb 1984, annual update, 6744–4
- Employment, wages, benefits, and hours of oil and gas extraction production workers, by occupation, region, and for 5 States, June 1982 survey, 6787–6.203
- Energy Info Admin natural gas supply estimates based on alternative data sources, for production and trade by State, and underground storage changes, 1980-81, 3008–90
- Farm production expenditures, detailed items by farm sales size and region, 1983, annual rpt, 1614–3
- Fed Govt energy programs proposed budget appropriations, by office or dept and function, FY84-85, annual rpt, 3004–14
- FERC activities and funding by program, with some natural gas and electric power industry data, FY83, annual rpt, 3084–9
- Finances and operations, by SIC 2- to 4-digit industry, 1970s-83 and projected to 1988, annual rpt, 2014–4
- Finances by firm, and effect of income and excise tax provisions on firms, Fed Govt revenues, and investor tax returns, 1980 and projected to 1992, hearing, 21788–132
- Foreign and US energy production, trade, and reserves, and oil and refined products supply and prices, by country, 1973-83, annual rpt, 3164–50
- Foreign and US natural gas production, by non-Communist country, monthly rpt, 242–5
- Foreign minerals production, reserves, and industry role in domestic economy and world supply, country and world region rpt series, 5606–1
- Foreign oil and gas undiscovered recoverable resources, cumulative production, and identified reserves, final oil basin rpt series, 5666–18
- Foreign oil and gas undiscovered recoverable resources, cumulative production, and identified reserves, preliminary oil basin rpt series, 5666–17
- Govt census, 1982: city govt revenues by source, expenditures by function, debt, and assets, by State and city, 2457–4
- Govt census, 1982: county govt revenues by source, expenditures by function, debt, and assets, by State and county, 2457–3
- Govt census, 1982: employment, payrolls, and average earnings, by function, level of govt, State, county, population size, and inside-outside SMSAs, 2455–2
- Govt census, 1982: local govt employment by function, payroll, and average earnings, for individual counties, cities, and school and special districts, 2455–1

Index by Subjects and Names

Natural gas and gas industry

Govt employment and payroll, by function, level of govt, and jurisdiction, 1983, annual rpt series, 2466–1

Helium and other components of natural gas, analyses of samples from individual wells and pipelines in 26 States and 2 countries, 1983, annual survey, 5604–2

Home heating costs of low-income households, natural gas price decontrol effects, aid programs, and gas supply/demand data, by income level and State, 1970s-95, hearing, 25148–26

Housing census, 1980: inventory, occupancy, and unit characteristics, changes from 1973 by region and inside-outside SMSAs and central cities, series, 2473–3

Housing census, 1980: structural, financial, and householder characteristics, by region and State, 2475–4

Housing energy bills and departures from normal by fuel type, and heating and cooling degree days by State, by census div, monthly rpt, 2152–11, 2152–12

Housing energy conservation programs of utilities, actual and predicted gas savings by conservation measure, Minnesota study, 1980-83, 3308–74

Housing energy conservation programs of utilities, financing, costs, participation, and energy savings, various periods 1981-84, hearing, 21368–54

Housing energy conservation programs of utilities under natl conservation act, cost effectiveness and participating household characteristics, 1980s, 3308–69

Housing energy consumption and retail prices, by energy type, region, and for 28 SMSAs and US city average, monthly press release, 6762–8

Housing energy use, by fuel type, county, city, and census tract, 1980 Census of Population and Housing, State and SMSA rpt series, 2551–2

Housing energy use, costs, expenditures, and conservation, and household and housing characteristics, survey series, 3166–7

Housing energy use in SMSAs and central cities, by fuel type, householder race and Hispanic origin, and city, 1980 Census of Housing, State and SMSA rpt series, 2473–1

Housing heating and air conditioning equipment shipments by type of fuel used, monthly rpt, 2012–1.6

Housing occupancy and unit and household characteristics, by region and metro-nonmetro residence, 1983, biennial survey, 2485–1

Housing unit heating fuel, by type, occupant race, Hispanic origin, urban-rural location, and region, 1981, annual survey, 2485–7

Income tax returns of corporations, detailed income and tax items by industry, 1981, annual rpt, 8304–4

Income tax returns of corporations with foreign tax credit, income and deductions by type, asset size, and selected industry group, 1980, article, 8302–2.415

Income tax returns of partnerships, receipts by source, deductions by type, and establishments, by selected industry, 1982, annual article, 8302–2.416

Income tax returns of sole proprietorships, receipts, deductions by type, payroll, and net income, by major industry, 1982, annual article, 8302–2.413

Industrial electric power cogeneration in 5 industries, and fuel use and utility supply/demand effects, by region, 1983-93, 3008–92

Industrial energy demand, forecasting model description, detailed technology specifications, and energy use, for 27 SIC 2- to 4-digit industries, 1970s-80 and projected to 2000, 3308–66

Input-output structure of US economy, detailed interindustry transactions for 85 industries, and components of final demand, 1977, article, 2702–1.421

Input-output structure of US economy, detailed interindustry transactions for 537 industries, and components of final demand, 1977 benchmark data, 2708–17

Irrigation system energy use and costs, and irrigated farm acreage by fuel and region, selected years 1974-84 and trends from 1900, article, 1561–16.406

Liquids (natural gas), supply/demand, trade, stocks, and refining, by detailed product and PAD district, monthly rpt with articles, 3162–6

Liquids (natural gas), supply/demand, trade, stocks, and refining, by detailed product and PAD district, 1983, annual rpt, 3164–2

Manufacturing energy efficiency progress, and energy use by type, by SIC 2-digit industry, 1982, annual rpt, 3304–8

Meters for electricity, gas, and liquid supply and production, trade, tariffs, and industry operating data, 1979-83, TSUSA commodity rpt supplement, 9885–7.63

Methane gas from straw- and manure-fed methane generator, research project technical characteristics, annual rpt, discontinued, 3304–14

Mineral industries census, 1982: financial and operating data, by SIC 2- to 4-digit industry, preliminary summary rpt, 2511–2.1

Mineral industries census, 1982: financial and operating data, including materials consumed, by SIC 4-digit industry and State, preliminary rpt series, 2511–1

Minerals Yearbook, 1982, Vol 3 preprints: foreign country reviews of production, trade, and policies, by commodity, annual rpt series, 5604–17

Minerals Yearbook, 1983, Vol 3 preprints: foreign country reviews of production, trade, and policies, by commodity, annual rpt series, 5604–23

Minority group and women employment, by occupational group and SIC 2- to 3-digit industry, 1981, annual rpt, 9244–1.1

Natl Energy Policy Plan, DOE implementation and effect on energy supply/demand, 1983-84, annual rpt, 3024–4

Natl Energy Policy Plan, energy supply, demand, and prices, by fuel and consuming sector, projected 1985-2010, biennial rpt, 3004–13

North Central States natural gas supply/demand, and percent of residential heating with natural gas, by Fed Reserve 7th district State and for total US, 1970s-82, 9375–13.3

Occupational injury and illness rates, by SIC 2- to 4-digit industry, 1982, annual rpt, 6844–1

Pacific Northwest electricity consumption and prices by end-use sector, and economic and demographic data, 1960s-83 and projected to 2005, annual rpt, 3224–2

Pipeline and compressor station costs, 1979-82, annual rpt, 3084–3

Pollution abatement capital and operating costs under Clean Air and Water Acts, for govts and selected industries, various periods 1970-2000, annual rpt, 9184–11

Producers finances and operations, by energy type for US firms domestic and foreign operations, 1974-82, annual rpt, 3164–44

Production and exploration expenditures and revenues, and sales volume, 1982, annual Current Industrial Rpt, 2506–8.11

Production and reserves of oil, gas, and gas liquids, by State and selected substrate area, 1983, annual rpt, 3164–46

Production, contract prices, and wells drilled, by Natural Gas Policy Act section, producer and well characteristics, State, and field, selected years 1968-83, 3168–90

Production, dev, and distribution firms revenues and income, quarterly rpt, 3162–38

Production equipment and operating costs and cost indexes, itemized, for oil and gas fields in 10 producing areas, 1981-83, annual rpt, 3164–45

Production, prices, reserves, and consumption, projected under alternative price controls 1983-95 with market data for various periods 1970-Mar 1984, 3008–96

Production, prices, trade, use, reserves, pipeline finances, and wells classified, for natural and supplemental gas, by firm and State, monthly rpt with articles, 3162–4

Production, reserves, and prices, by fuel type, and selected indicators of energy use, by State, 1982-83 with selected comparisons from 1971, annual rpt, 3164–60

Production, trade, supply, use, conservation, and DOE activities, by energy type, FY83, annual rpt, 3024–2

Public utility holding company finances, securities issued, and subsidiaries by type, by firm, FY83, annual rpt, 9734–2.6

R&D industry funding and employment of scientists and engineers, by industry group, firm size, and funding source, 1956-82, annual rpt, 9627–21

Regulatory policy standards of electric and gas utilities, and consumers and sales covered, by type of consumer and utility, 1983, annual rpt, 3104–7

Research publications on energy of DOE and other sources, monthly listing, 3002–2

Scientists and engineers employed in energy-related fields, supply/demand and effects of R&D funding, by energy type, employer type, field, and age, 1962-91, annual rpt, 3004–19

Scientists, engineers, and technicians employment in transportation, utilities, and retail and wholesale trade, by field of science and industry, 1982, 9628–72

Supply, contract prices, pipeline operations and finances, and residential use, various periods 1966-1983/84, 3168–89

Natural gas and gas industry

Supply/demand and price forecasts, by fuel type, quarterly rpt, 3162–34

Supply/demand and prices, by energy resource and major producing and consuming country and sector, detailed data, monthly rpt, 3162–24

Supply/demand and prices, by energy source and end-use sector and for 7 electric utilities, 1981-2000 with trends from 1960s, 3008–93

Supply/demand and prices, by fuel type and consuming sector with foreign comparisons, 1949-83, annual rpt, 3164–74

Supply/demand and prices, by fuel type, sector, and end use, detailed trends and projections 1973-95, annual rpt, 3164–75

Supply/demand and prices, by fuel type, sector, and end use, with foreign comparisons, 1960-83 and projected to 1995, annual summary rpt, 3164–76

Supply/demand and prices, effect of price decontrol, 1970s-83, 3168–50

Supply/demand, prices, end use, and related technical and socioeconomic data, including impacts of US policy and anti devs, series, 3006–7

Transportation and related energy use, for urban areas, late 1970s-82 and projected under lower auto emission standards to 1995, 3408–31

Transportation energy use by mode, fuel supplies, and demographic and economic determinants of vehicle use, 1970s-83, annual rpt, 3304–5

Transportation finances, operations, vehicles, equipment, accidents, and energy use and transport, by mode of transport, 1955-84, annual rpt, 7304–2

Utilities diversification activity by activity type, and finances and bond ratings by selected firm, various periods 1970-83, hearing, 21368–53

Utilities privately owned, detailed financial and operating data, by company, 1982, annual rpt, 3164–23

Utilities privately owned, wages and employment by occupation, and benefits, by region, Oct 1982 survey, 6787–6.205

Utilities productivity, hours, and employment indexes, 1954-82, annual rpt, 6824–1.4

Waterborne commerce of US (domestic and foreign), freight by commodity, traffic, and passengers, by port and waterway, 1982, annual rpt, 3754–3

Western US Fed Govt lands by agency and mining restriction status, and energy resources on potential wilderness areas and other lands, 1970s-81 and projected to 1990, 3308–68

see also Energy exploration and drilling

see also Liquefied petroleum gas

see also Natural gas exports and imports

see also Natural gas prices

see also Natural gas reserves

see also Offshore oil and gas

see also Oil and gas leases

see also Pipelines

see also under By Commodity in the "Index by Categories"

see also under By Industry in the "Index by Categories"

Natural gas conservation

see Energy conservation

Natural gas consumption

see Natural gas and gas industry

Natural gas exports and imports

- Canada natural gas exports to US, by importing company and Canada supplier, actual 1981 and projected maximum under contract, hearings, 23848–177
- China economic conditions, agricultural and industrial production, trade, and domestic and foreign investment, 1980-85, 2048–106
- China exports and imports by SITC 1- to 5-digit commodity, 1970s-82, annual rpt, 244–12
- Eastern Europe and USSR natural gas trade, by country, monthly rpt, 242–5
- Energy Info Admin natural gas supply estimates based on alternative data sources, for production and trade by State, and underground storage changes, 1980-81, 3008–90
- Exports and imports of natural gas, by country of origin and destination, 1982, annual rpt, 3164–50.5
- Exports and imports of US, detailed SIC-based commodities by world area, 1983, annual rpts, 2424–6
- Exports and imports of US, totals and as percent of domestic production, by SIC 2- to 5-digit commodity, 1981, annual rpt, 2424–3
- Exports, imports, production, prices, use, reserves, and pipeline finances, for natural gas, by firm and State, monthly rpt with articles, 3162–4
- Exports of US, detailed commodities by country of destination, monthly rpt, 2422–3
- Exports of US, detailed Schedule B commodities by country of destination, 1983, annual rpt, 2424–9
- Exports of US, detailed Schedule E commodities by mode of transport and world area and country of destination, 1983, annual rpts, 2424–5
- Exports of US natural gas to Canada, Mexico, and Japan, 1980-83, annual rpt, 3024–2
- Great Lakes trade, by SITC 3-digit commodity, port, vessel type, world area, and country, 1982, annual rpt, 7744–3
- Imports and contracted supply of natural gas from Canada and Mexico, by US pipeline firm, 1982-83, annual rpt, 3164–33.6
- Imports of US, detailed Schedule A commodities by country and world area of origin, and mode of transport, 1983, annual rpts, 2424–2
- Imports of US, detailed Schedule A commodities by country, monthly rpt, 2422–2
- Imports of US, detailed TSUSA commodities by country of origin, 1983, annual rpt, 2424–4
- Input-output structure of US economy, detailed interindustry transactions for 537 industries, and components of final demand, 1977 benchmark data, 2708–17
- Liquids (natural gas), supply/demand, trade, stocks, and refining, by detailed product and PAD district, monthly rpt with articles, 3162–6

Index by Subjects and Names

- Liquids (natural gas), supply/demand, trade, stocks, and refining, by detailed product and PAD district, 1983, annual rpt, 3164–2
- *Minerals Yearbook, 1982,* Vol 3 preprints: foreign country reviews of production, trade, and policies, by commodity, annual rpt series, 5604–17
- *Minerals Yearbook, 1983,* Vol 3 preprints: foreign country reviews of production, trade, and policies, by commodity, annual rpt series, 5604–23
- Natl Energy Policy Plan, energy supply, demand, and prices, by fuel and consuming sector, projected 1985-2010, biennial rpt, 3004–13
- OECD trade, total and for 4 major countries, and US trade by country, by commodity, 1972-82, annual world region rpt series, 244–13
- Pipelines interstate company natural gas production, purchases, sales, prices, and deliveries, for 20 firms, various periods 1978-83, 3168–50.5
- Prices, reserves, consumption, and production, projected under alternative price controls 1983-95 with market data for various periods 1970-Mar 1984, 3008–96
- Supply/demand and price forecasts, by fuel type, quarterly rpt, 3162–34
- Supply/demand and prices, by energy resource and major producing and consuming country and sector, detailed data, monthly rpt, 3162–24
- Supply/demand and prices, by fuel type and consuming sector with foreign comparisons, 1949-83, annual rpt, 3164–74
- Supply/demand and prices, by fuel type, sector, and end use, detailed trends and projections 1973-95, annual rpt, 3164–75
- Supply/demand and prices, by fuel type, sector, and end use, with foreign comparisons, 1960-83 and projected to 1995, annual summary rpt, 3164–76
- Supply/demand and prices, effect of price decontrol alternatives on natural gas prices, 1970s-95, hearing, 25148–26
- Waterborne commerce of US (domestic and foreign), freight by commodity, traffic, and passengers, by port and waterway, 1982, annual rpt, 3754–3

Natural gas liquids

see Natural gas and gas industry

Natural Gas Pipeline Safety Act

Enforcement, funding, and training activities of DOT and State govts, and pipeline accidents and casualties, 1982, annual rpt, 7304–5

Natural Gas Policy Act

Contract prices, production, and wells drilled, by Natural Gas Policy Act section, producer and well characteristics, State, and field, selected years 1968-83, 3168–90

Decontrol alternatives effects on prices, reserves, consumption, and production, projected 1983-95 with market data for various periods 1970-Mar 1984, 3008–96

Decontrol under Act, effect on gas prices, Iowa supply/demand, and economic indicators, various periods 1969-55, hearings, 23848–177

Index by Subjects and Names

Natural gas reserves

Decontrol under Act, effect on supply/demand and prices, 1970s-83, 3168–50

Home heating costs of low-income households, natural gas price decontrol effects, aid programs, and gas supply/demand data, by income level and State, 1970s-95, hearing, 25148–26

Natural gas prices

Consumer prices of natural gas, by consumer sector, census div, and State, 1983, preliminary annual rpt, 3164–4

Contract prices, production, and wells drilled, by Natural Gas Policy Act section, producer and well characteristics, State, and field, selected years 1968-83, 3168–90

Contract prices, supply, pipeline operations and finances, and residential use, various periods 1966-1983/84, 3168–89

CPI by detailed component, for US city average, 28 SMSAs, and 4 regions by population size, monthly rpt, 6762–2

Decontrol alternatives effect on supply/demand, prices, and home heating costs of low-income households, 1970s-95, hearing, 25148–26

Decontrol alternatives effects on prices, reserves, consumption, and production, projected 1983-95 with market data for various periods 1970-Mar 1984, 3008–96

Decontrol effect on gas prices, Iowa supply/demand, and economic indicators, various periods 1969-95, hearings, 23848–177

Decontrol effect on supply/demand and prices, 1970s-83, 3168–50

Electric power plant (steam) fuel deliveries, costs, and quality, by fuel type, State, and utility, 1983, annual rpt, 3164–42

Electric power plant capacity, production, retail sales, and fuel stocks, use, and costs, by State, 1979-83, annual rpt, 3164–11

Electric power plants (steam), prices paid for fossil fuels, July 1972 and 1982-83, annual rpt, 3084–9

Electric utility fuel cost, quality, use, receipts, and stocks, and power plant production, by energy source, State and utility, quarterly rpt, 3162–39

Electric utility production, fuel consumption, stocks, and costs by fuel type, and sales, by State, monthly rpt, 3162–35

Farm income and fertilizer use, effect of natural gas price changes, 1980 and projected to 1990, 1548–240

Farm production by crop, prices, and fertilizer use and costs, effect of natural gas price decontrol alternatives, 1982-90, model results, 1548–239

Household demand for electric power in 136 SMSAs and other utility service areas, with fuel prices, family income, and heating degree days, 1975 and projected to 1985, 1588–78

Housing electricity and gas costs for 306 cities, by utility, with climatological data, fall 1982, 3308–67

Housing energy use, and savings under alternative conservation strategies, by State, with model methodology and energy prices, selected years 1970-81, 21368–48

Natl Energy Policy Plan, energy supply, demand, and prices, by fuel and consuming sector, projected 1985-2010, biennial rpt, 3004–13

OECD energy prices and taxes by energy source and end-use sector, for US and 9 countries, quarterly 1979-83, annual rpt, 3164–71

Pacific Northwest electricity consumption and prices by end-use sector, and economic and demographic data, 1960s-83 and projected to 2005, annual rpt, 3224–2

Pipeline interstate company sales, total and under minimum fee contract provision, by service type, contract date, and region, 1981, 3168–91

Prices and expenditures for fuels, by consuming sector, State, and fuel type, 1970-81, annual rpt, 3164–64

Prices and supply/demand, by energy source and end-use sector and for 7 electric utilities, 1981-2000 with trends from 1960s, 3008–93

Prices and supply/demand, by fuel and consuming sector with foreign comparisons, 1949-83, annual rpt, 3164–74

Prices and supply/demand, by fuel, sector, and end use, detailed trends and projections 1973-95, annual rpt, 3164–75

Prices and supply/demand, by fuel, sector, and end use, with foreign comparisons, 1960-83 and projected to 1995, annual summary rpt, 3164–76

Prices and supply/demand forecasts, by fuel, quarterly rpt, 3162–34

Prices, production, trade, use, reserves, and pipeline company finances, for natural gas, by firm and State, monthly rpt with articles, 3162–4

Prices, supply/demand, end use, and related technical and socioeconomic data, including impacts of US policy and intl devs, series, 3006–7

Prices, use, and conservation and efficiency measures, by fuel type, end-use sector, selected industry, and region, 1960-83, annual rpt, 3164–73

Producer prices and indexes, by stage of processing and detailed commodity, monthly rpt, 6762–6

Producer prices and indexes, by stage of processing and detailed commodity, monthly 1983, annual supplement, 6764–2

Ratemaking and regulatory policy standards of electric and gas utilities, and consumers and sales covered, by type of consumer and utility, 1983, annual rpt, 3104–7

Retail prices for energy and food, and housing fuel consumption, by region, and for 28 SMSAs and US city average, monthly press release, 6762–8

Wholesale and wellhead prices to electric plants, and prices to residential customers, monthly rpt, 3162–24.9

Natural gas reserves

Agricultural cooperatives oil and gas production, supply, and reserves, 1979 and 1982, article, 1122–1.407 1561–16.403

Coastal environmental characteristics, fish, wildlife, and use, and population socioeconomic data, for individual areas, series, 5506–4

Communist, OECD, and selected other countries energy reserves, production, and consumption, and oil trade and revenue, 1960s-83, annual rpt, 244–5.5

Energy Info Admin natural gas supply estimates based on alternative data sources, for production and trade by State, and underground storage changes, 1980-81, 3008–90

Fed Govt OCS oil and gas reserves, leasing and exploration activities, production, revenues, and costs, by ocean region, FY83, annual rpt, 5734–4

Fed Govt OCS oil, gas, and mineral production, revenues, and reserves, by State and ocean region, 1950s-82, annual rpt, 5734–3

Foreign and US energy reserves, by type of fuel and country, as of Jan 1984, annual rpt, 3164–50.7

Foreign minerals production, reserves, and industry role in domestic economy and world supply, country and world region rpt series, 5606–1

Foreign oil and gas undiscovered recoverable resources, cumulative production, and identified reserves, final oil basin rpt series, 5666–18

Foreign oil and gas undiscovered recoverable resources, cumulative production, and identified reserves, preliminary oil basin rpt series, 5666–17

Minerals Yearbook, 1982, Vol 3 preprints: foreign country reviews of production, trade, and policies, by commodity, annual rpt series, 5604–17

Minerals Yearbook, 1983, Vol 3 preprints: foreign country reviews of production, trade, and policies, by commodity, annual rpt series, 5604–23

Pipeline interstate company natural gas supplies, reserves, production, purchases, and contracts, by firm, 1983 with projected deliverability to 2003, annual rpt, 3164–33

Producers finances and operations, by energy type for US firms domestic and foreign operations, 1974- 82, annual rpt, 3164–44.2

Reserve fields by State and EIA field code, 1983, annual listing, 3164–70

Reserves and production of oil, gas, and gas liquids, by State and selected substate area, 1983, annual rpt, 3164–46

Reserves, consumption, production, and prices, projected under alternative price controls 1983-95 with market data for various periods 1970-Mar 1984, 3008–96

Reserves, production, prices, and use, by energy type, and selected indicators of energy use, by State, 1982-83 with selected comparisons from 1971, annual rpt, 3164–60

Reserves, production, prices, trade, use, reserves, and pipeline finances, for natural and supplemental gas, by firm and State, monthly rpt with articles, 3162–4

Storage of natural gas underground, weekly rpt, 3162–32.2

Supply/demand and prices, by fuel type and consuming sector with foreign comparisons, 1949-83, annual rpt, 3164–74

Supply/demand and prices, by fuel type, sector, and end use, with foreign comparisons, 1960-83 and projected to 1995, annual summary rpt, 3164–76

Natural gas reserves

Supply/demand and prices, effect of price decontrol alternatives on natural gas prices, 1970s-95, hearing, 25148–26 Western States wilderness areas potential oil and natural gas reserves, for 11 States, 1982-83, compilation of papers, 5668–69 Western US Fed Govt lands by agency and mining restriction status, and energy resources on potential wilderness areas and other lands, 1970s-81 and projected to 1990, 3308–68

Natural resources

- Aerial survey R&D publications, and sources of natural resource and environmental data gathered by air- and spacecraft, quarterly listing, 9502–7
- Budget of US, CBO analysis and review of FY85 budget by function, annual rpt, 26304–2
- Budget of US, loans and loan guarantees, and Admin proposed limits on credit assistance, by program, FY83-89, annual rpt, 26306–3.65
- Budget of US, receipts, outlays, and budget authority, by function and agency, FY84-89 revised estimates, midsession review of FY85 budget, annual rpt, 104–7
- Budget of US, receipts, outlays, and budget authority, by function and agency, 1st revision of FY85 budget, annual rpt, 104–17
- China economic and business investment conditions, trade practices, and trade with US by detailed commodity, 1978-82, 2048–72
- Geological Survey and other publications, 1983, annual listing, 5664–4
- *Overseas Business Reports*: economic conditions, investment and export opportunities, and trade practices, annual country market research rpt series, 2046–6
- *Overseas Business Reports*: economic conditions, investment and export opportunities, and trade practices, world region rpt series, 2046–5
- *Statistical Abstract of US*, social, political, and economic data, 1950s-83 and trends, annual rpt, 2324–1.1
- Tax expenditures, Fed Govt revenues foregone through income tax deductions and exclusions by type, and effect of Deficit Reduction Act, FY84-89, annual rpt, 21784–10
- *see also* Conservation of natural resources
- *see also* Energy resources
- *see also* Fish and fishing industry
- *see also* Forests and forestry
- *see also* Geothermal resources
- *see also* Marine resources
- *see also* Mines and mineral resources
- *see also* Plants and vegetation
- *see also* Reclamation of land
- *see also* Severance taxes
- *see also* Strategic materials
- *see also* Water power
- *see also* Water resources development
- *see also* Water supply and use

Naturalization

see Citizenship

Naturopathy

see Chiropractic and naturopathy

Nauru

- Economic, social, and political summary data, by country, 1984, annual factbook, 244–11
- Exports of US, detailed Schedule B commodities by country of destination, 1983, annual rpt, 2424–9
- Imports of US, detailed Schedule A commodities by country and world area of origin, and mode of transport, 1983, annual rpts, 2424–2
- Imports of US, detailed TSUSA commodities by country of origin, 1983, annual rpt, 2424–4
- *Minerals Yearbook, 1982*, Vol 3: foreign country reviews of production, trade, and policies, by commodity, annual rpt, 5604–35
- *Minerals Yearbook, 1982*, Vol 3 preprints: foreign country review of production, trade, and policies, by commodity, annual rpt, 5604–17.90
- *Minerals Yearbook, 1983*, Vol 3 preprints: foreign country review of production, trade, and policies, by commodity, annual rpt, 5604–23.90
- Population size and growth rates, and latest available benchmark demographic data, by country, 1950-83, biennial rpt, 2324–4
- *see also* under By Foreign Country in the "Index by Categories"

Navajo and Hopi Indian Relocation Commission

Budget of US, appropriations, outlays, balances, and budget receipts, by govtl branch and agency, FY83, annual rpt, 8104–2

Naval Academy

see Service academies

Naval bases

see Military bases, posts, and reservations

Naval contracts and procurement

see Defense contracts and procurement

Naval Petroleum Reserves

- Budget appropriations proposed for Fed Govt energy programs, by office or dept and function, FY84-85, annual rpt, 3004–14
- Budget of US, effects of Reagan Admin policy changes, by detailed program, FY85, annual rpt, 104–21
- Defense Fuel Supply Center procurement, prices, stocks, and other activities, FY83, annual rpt, 3904–6
- Defense Fuel Supply Center procurement, prices, stocks, transport, and other activities and finances, FY83, annual rpt, 3904–8
- Production, dev, ownership, leasing, sales by purchaser, and Fed Govt revenues, by site, FY83, annual rpt, 3004–22

Naval science

see also Navigation

Naval stores

see Gum and wood chemicals

Naval vessels

- Budget of DOD, costs of individual weapons or weapon systems, FY83-85, annual rpt, 3504–2
- Budget of DOD, itemized account of legislative history, FY84, annual rpt, 3504–7
- Budget of DOD, justification for procurement programs, by equipment type, service branch, and defense agency, FY83-86, annual rpt, 3504–14

Index by Subjects and Names

- Budget of DOD, justification, programs, and policies, FY85, annual rpt, 3544–2
- Budget of DOD, organization, personnel, weapons, and property, by service branch, State, and country, 1984 annual summary rpt, 3504–13
- Developing countries arms transfers from US, USSR, and Europe, by weapon type and world region, 1974-82, 25948–3
- Engineering contract awards by function, contract type, and service branch, and oil and port dredging awards by company, 1970s-83, hearings, 21728–53
- Expenditures for military goods and services, by function, 1972-84, article, 2702–1.440
- Forces, equipment, and budget summary, planned FY84-85, semiannual pamphlet, 3802–3
- Foreign govt purchase of Navy vessels, sales prices, fair market value, and Navy costs, for surplus ships sold 1981-82, GAO rpt, 26123–60
- Foreign military aid of US and sales of arms, equipment, and training, by item, FY50-83, annual rpt, 3904–3
- Foreign military spending, arms trade, and armed forces size, with total govt spending and population, by country, 1972-82, annual rpt, 9824–1
- Medical facilities of Navy, use by active and retired military personnel, dependents, and others by facility and type, quarterly rpt, 3802–1
- Merchant ships in US fleet, shipping costs, construction, employment, military availability, and Fed Govt subsidies, 1970s-1984 and projected to 2000, 26306–6.83
- Military Sealift Command operations for naval fleet support, and transport of DOD and AID cargo by route, quarterly rpt, 3802–2
- Natl Defense Reserve Fleet inventory from FY45, and ships and tonnage by vessel type, with location, FY83, annual rpt, 7704–14.2, 7704–14.4
- Natl Defense Reserve Fleet inventory, Jan 1984, semiannual rpt, 7702–2
- NATO and US weapons and troop strength compared to Warsaw Pact and USSR, as of Jan 1984, annual rpt, 3564–1
- Outlays and obligations of DOD, by function and service branch, quarterly rpt, 3542–3
- Procurement cost estimate changes for weapons systems, and program delays and mgmt, by system and service branch, 1983, annual rpt, 26304–5
- Procurement cost estimates for weapons and communications systems, by service branch, quarterly summary rpt, 3502–1
- Procurement, DOD prime contract awards by category, contract and contractor type, and service branch, FY74-1st half FY84, semiannual rpt, 3542–1
- Procurement, DOD prime contract awards by detailed procurement category, FY80-83, annual rpt, 3544–18
- Procurement, DOD prime contract awards for 25 commodity categories and R&D, by State and census div, FY81-83, annual rpt, 3544–11
- Procurement, DOD prime contract awards to small and total business, for 10 categories and R&D, monthly rpt, 3542–10

Index by Subjects and Names

Nebraska

Soviet Union and Warsaw Pact military weapons systems, assistance and presence worldwide, and force strengths, with selected US and NATO comparisons, as of 1984, 3508–14

Strategic military capability, force strengths, weapons, training, supplies, and requirements, by service branch, FY80-84 and projected to 1990, 3508–19

see also Icebreakers

see also Nuclear-powered ships

see also Submarines

Navigation

Meteorological services and research of Fed Govt, programs and funding by agency, FY84-85, annual rpt, 2144–2

NOAA scientific and technical publications, monthly listing, 2142–1

User fees to recover costs of 7 federally subsidized public service programs, by type of fee, user, and service, FY84-88, 26306–6.68

Weather and tropical cyclones, quarterly journal with articles, 2152–8

Weather broadcasts for US ships, by major ocean area, as of Jan 1984, biennial rpt, 2184–3

see also Aeronautical navigation

see also Lighthouses and lightships

see also Marine accidents and safety

see also Radar

Navratil, Frank J.

"Estimation of Mortgage Prepayment Rates", 9316–1.103

Navy

Aides to officers, enlisted personnel authorized and assigned to perform personal services by race and sex, and program costs, by service branch, 1982-83, GAO rpt, 26123–53

Aircraft for DOD noncombat use, costs, Navy and Air Force requirements, and Navy losses, by aircraft type, selected years FY73-86, hearing, 21408–76

Alcohol and drug abuse of Navy personnel, and related deaths, courts-martial, discharges, and treatment program funding and staff, FY83, annual table, 3804–12

Base support costs by function, and personnel and acreage by installation, by service branch, FY85, annual rpt, 3504–11

Cost control proposals for Fed Govt programs and mgmt, 3-year savings by function and agency, and financial and operating data, 1960s-81, 16908–1.19

Manpower active duty strength, recruits, and reenlistment, by race, Hispanic origin, sex, and service branch, quarterly press release, 3542–7

Manpower by grade and length of service, reenlistment rate, and need for petty officers, FY72-83 and projected to FY88, GAO rpt, 26123–69

Manpower, equipment, and budget summary, planned FY84-85, semiannual pamphlet, 3802–3

Manpower of DOD, and organization, budget, weapons, and property, by service branch, State, and country, 1984 annual summary rpt, 3504–13

Manpower of DOD, by State, service branch, and major installation, as of Sept 1983, annual rpt, 3544–7

Manpower requirements and cost estimates, DOD budget detailed analysis, FY85, annual rpt, 3504–1

Manpower statistics of Navy, detailed quarterly rpt, 3802–4

Manpower statistics on active duty, civilian, and reserve personnel, by service branch, monthly rpt, 3542–14

Manpower statistics on active duty, civilian, and retired personnel and dependents, FY83 and historical, annual rpt, 3544–1

Manpower strengths, and military pension earnings and program costs, under alternative policies, selected years FY71-2020, 26306–6.76

Manpower strengths in US and abroad, by service branch, world area, and country, quarterly news release, 3542–9

Manpower strengths of active duty, reserve, and civilian personnel, by service branch, selected years FY68-89, annual rpt, 3544–2

Manpower strengths, summary by service branch, monthly press release, 3542–2

Medical facilities of DOD in US and abroad, beds, admissions, outpatient visits, and live births by service branch, quarterly rpt, 3542–15

Medical facilities of Navy, use by active and retired military personnel, dependents, and others by facility and type, quarterly rpt, 3802–1

Medical personnel, trainees, and accessions by source, by occupation, specialty, and service branch, FY83, annual rpt, 3544–24

Military weapons and troop strength of US and NATO compared to USSR and Warsaw Pact, as of Jan 1984, annual rpt, 3564–1

NATO military commitment of US, Europe force strengths by service branch and costs by component, FY82 with trends from FY75, GAO rpt, 26123–71

Radiation from 1940s-70s nuclear weapons tests, levels in air and water, and personnel exposure by military unit and job category, series, 3906–1

Reserve forces manpower and equipment strengths, readiness, and funding, by reserve component, FY83, annual rpt, 3544–27

Reserve forces manpower strengths and characteristics, by component, quarterly rpt, 3542–4

Sealift Military Command operations for naval fleet support, and transport of DOD and AID cargo by route, quarterly rpt, 3802–2

Strategic military capability, force strengths, weapons, training, supplies, and requirements, by service branch, FY80-84 and projected to 1990, 3508–19

Training and education programs of DOD, funding, staff, students, and facilities, by service branch and reserve component, FY85, annual rpt, 3504–5

Weapons tactics trainer (F/A-18) costs by trainer type, as of 1984, and demand at 2 locations, projected 1988-94, GAO rpt, 26123–73

Women military personnel on active duty, by demographic and service characteristics and service branch, with comparisons to men, FY83, annual chartbook, 3544–26

see also Department of Navy

see also Marine Corps

see also Naval Petroleum Reserves

see also Naval vessels

Nealer, Kevin G.

"Unconventional Arms Policy: Selling Ourselves Short. Promotion of Military Sales to the Developing World Under the Reagan Administration", 25948–3

Near East

see Middle East

Nebraska

Agricultural cooperatives, membership, activities, and finances, by commodity and selected State, 1900-80 with trends from 1863, 1128–30

Agriculture census, 1982: farms, farmland, production and costs, and operator characteristics, preliminary State summary and county rpts, 2330–1.31

Agriculture census, 1982: farms, farmland, production, finances, and operator characteristics, by county, final State rpt, 2331–1.27

Bank deposits in commercial and mutual savings banks and in US branches of foreign banks, by account type, instn, State, SMSA, and county, June 1983, annual rpt, 9295–3.14

Census of Housing, 1980: occupancy and unit characteristics of SMSAs and central cities, by race, Hispanic origin, and city, State rpt, 2473–1.29

Census of Population and Housing, 1980: detailed population and housing characteristics, by county, city, and census tract, State rpt, 2551–2.29

Census of Population, 1980: detailed socioeconomic and demographic characteristics, by age, sex, race, Hispanic origin, and industry, State rpt, 2531–4.29

County Business Patterns: establishments, employees, and payrolls, by SIC 4-digit industry and county, 1982, annual State rpt, 2326–6.29

Employment, earnings, and hours, by selected SIC 1- to 4-digit industry, State, and for 278 major labor areas, 1939-83, annual rpt, 6744–5.1, 6744–5.3

Environmental quality, pollutant discharge by type and source, and EPA protection activities and funding, 1970s-83, biennial regional rpt, 9184–15.7

Exports of manufactured and agricultural commodities, manufacturing production, and export-related employment, 1960s-82, State rpt, 2046–3.27

Hay prices in 10 market areas, for baled alfalfa and prairie hay, weekly rpt, 1313–5

HHS aid to each State and local govt or private instn, amount obligated, funding agency, and program, FY83, annual listing, 4004–3.7

Income (personal) per capita and by source, and earnings by industry div, by State, MSA, and county, 1977-82, annual regional rpt, 2704–2.5

Land Mgmt Bur activities and finances, and public land acreage and use, 1984 annual State rpt, 5724–11.1

Manufacturing census, 1982: financial and operating data, by SIC 2- to 4-digit industry, State, SMSA, and county, preliminary census div rpt, 2491–3.4

Nebraska

Mineral Industry Surveys, State review of production, 1983, advance annual rpt, 5614–6.27

Minerals Yearbook, 1982, Vol 2 preprints: State review of production and sales by commodity, and business activity, annual rpt, 5604–16.28

Minerals Yearbook, 1982, Vol 2: State reviews of production, sales, and firms, by commodity, and business activity, annual rpt, 5604–34

- Population size and components of change, by MSA and county, 1980-82, annual State Current Population Rpt, 2546–4.27
- Population size, Apr 1980 and July 1982, and per capita income, 1979 and 1981, by county and city, State Current Population Rpt, 2546–11.27
- Retail trade census, 1982: employment, establishments, sales, and payroll, by SIC 2- to 4-digit kind of business, SMSA, county, and city, State rpt, 2397–1.28
- Savings and loan assns, FHLB 10th District insured members finances and operations by SMSA, monthly rpt, 9302–22
- Service industry census, 1982: employment, establishments, receipts, and payroll, by SIC 2- to 4-digit kind of business, SMSA, county, and city, State rpt, 2391–1.28
- Transportation census, 1982: trucks, by detailed characteristics, miles traveled, and type of product carried, State rpt, 2573–1.28
- Water supply and quality in streams and lakes, and groundwater levels in wells, by drainage basin, 1982, annual State rpt, 5666–20.26
- Wholesale trade census, 1982: employment, establishments, finances, and operations, by SIC 2- to 4-digit kind of business, SMSA, county, and city, State rpt, 2405–1.28

see also Grand Island, Nebr.

see also Hastings, Nebr.

see also Lincoln, Nebr.

see also Omaha, Nebr.

see also under By State in the "Index by Categories"

Needle, Jerome A.

"Police Handling of Youth Gangs", 6068–175

Neenah, Wis.

see also under By SMSA or MSA in the "Index by Categories"

Negotiable orders of withdrawal accounts

- Authorizations and offerings of NOW accounts at industrial banks, S&Ls, and savings banks, by State, as of Dec 1983, press release, 9368–75
- Commercial bank debits, deposits, and deposit turnover, by type of account, monthly rpt, 9365–2.5
- Financial and monetary conditions, selected US summary data, weekly rpt, 9391–4
- GNP components growth related to changes in NOW accounts and other M1 components, various periods 1948-84, article, 9385–1.413
- Interest rates (explicit and implicit) on commercial bank deposits, by account type, 1976-82, article, 9387–1.403
- Interest rates on bank deposits, deregulation effect on deposits and bank financial performance, 1978-83, hearing, 21248–83

Interest rates on money market mutual funds and deposit accounts, and super NOW accounts, monthly Dec 1982-Sept 1983, article, 1702–1.401

- Savings and loan assn deregulation effect on lending activity and noninterest NOW accounts, for US and 3 States, as of June 1980-83, article, 9371–1.432
- Savings and loan assn deregulation impact, financial ratios of S&Ls in 3 States and US, 1980-83, article, 9371–1.426
- Savings and loan assns and FSLIC-insured savings banks and S&Ls, assets, liabilities, and deposit and loan activity, monthly rpt, 9312–4
- Southeastern States banks by asset size, finances, and loans and deposits by type, Fed Reserve 5th District, various dates 1979-83, annual article, 9389–1.408
- Southeastern States, Fed Reserve 8th District banking and financial conditions, quarterly rpt, 9391–14
- Southeastern States financial and economic devs, Fed Reserve 6th District, monthly rpt with articles, 9371–1
- Super NOW and other mutual funds accounts, correlation results for interest rates and flows by type of fund, various periods Dec 1982-June 1984, article, 9371–1.431

Negotiations

see also Strategic Arms Limitation Treaties

see also Strategic Arms Reduction Talks

see also Treaties and conventions

Negroes

see Black Americans

Nehrt, Roy C.

"Public Elementary and Secondary Education in the U.S., 1981-82: A Statistical Compendium", 4834–13

Neighborhood action programs

see Community action programs

Neighborhood Reinvestment Corp.

- Budget of US Appendix, detailed budgets and personnel summaries, by agency, FY85, annual rpt, 104–3
- Budget of US, appropriations, outlays, balances, and budget receipts, by govtl branch and agency, FY83, annual rpt, 8104–2

Neighborhoods

- Black young adults economic status and educational attainment related to motivation, goals, family characteristics, and social factors, 1982, longitudinal study, 4008–65.2
- Carbon monoxide atmospheric concentrations and levels within buildings and along commuting and residential driving routes, for 4 cities, Jan-Mar 1981, 9198–110
- Community dev programs funding and activities, for 5 HUD programs, FY83, annual rpt, 5124–5
- Home mortgages FHA-insured, financial, property, and mortgagor characteristics, 1983, annual rpt, 5144–17
- Housing (rental) unit choice of Pittsburgh, Pa, recent movers related to unit, neighborhood, and town characteristics, 1967 survey, 9306–1.7
- NYC metro area small business owners and accountants, assessment of economy, professional activities, and community problems, by county and industry div, 1983 survey, hearings, 21728–52.3

Index by Subjects and Names

- NYC population size, demographic characteristics, and rental housing, in 5 neighborhoods by census tract, 1980 with percent change from 1970, article, 9385–1.403
- NYC South Bronx housing and economic dev, HUD grants to 4 neighborhood organizations, 1984 press release, 5006–3.31
- Police dept performance, analyses of police activities effects on neighborhoods and citizens, 1977, compilation of papers, 6068–181
- Quality of housing and neighborhoods, indicators and attitudes, and occupant characteristics, by urban-rural location and region, 1981, annual survey, 2485–7
- Quality of housing and neighborhoods, indicators and attitudes, by occupant and unit characteristics, region, and metro-nonmetro location, 1981, annual survey, 2485–2
- Quality of housing and neighborhoods, indicators and attitudes for 15 SMSAs, 1978, annual survey special supplement, 2485–8
- Urban Dev Action Grant awards to local areas, preliminary approvals, with project descriptions, private investment, and jobs and taxes to be created, by city, quarterly press release series, 5002–7

Nelson, Charles T.

- "After-Tax Money Income Estimates of Households: 1981", 2546–2.118
- "After-Tax Money Income Estimates of Households: 1982", 2546–2.122
- "Characteristics of Households Receiving Noncash Benefits: 1982 (Advance Data from the Mar. 1983 Current Population Survey)", 2546–6.38

Nelson, Gary

"Crop Quality Differences and Estimates of Corn for Feed Use", 1561–4.405

Nelson, Kenneth E.

"U.S. Hog Industry", 1568–248

Nelson, Richard R.

"State Labor Legislation Enacted in 1983", 6722–1.406

Nelson, William J., Jr.

"Changing the Method for Calculating Quarters of Coverage: The Impact on Workers Insured Status", 4742–1.408

Nemirow, Martin

"Work-Sharing Approaches: Past and Present", 6722–1.458

Neoplasms

- Agent Orange exposed Air Force personnel diseases and disorders, by disease type, age, and officer status, 1984 rpt, 3604–3
- Air pollutant and radiation indoor levels by emissions source, and household exposure and health effects by pollutant type, various periods 1966-83, hearings, 21708–102
- Asbestos workers, exposure levels, cancer incidence, and deaths, by industry and occupation, and asbestos regulation enforcement and costs/benefits, various periods 1940-2027, hearing, 21408–72
- Cancer incidence, deaths, patient median age and 5-year survival rates, and 1st stay hospital days, by body site, selected years 1945-83, article, 4102–1.448
- Cancer-related resources directory for Frederick County, Md, evaluation of accuracy and usefulness, 1984 article, 4102–1.459

Index by Subjects and Names

Netherlands

Cholesterol blood levels, effects of lowering levels on heart attack and cancer incidence and deaths in men aged 35-59, with background data on other risk factors, 1973-83, 4478–145

Colorectal cancer screening, family physicians attitudes toward use of guaiac slide test, 1982 New York State survey, article, 4102–1.433

Death rates for persons 65 and over, by major cause, sex, and age, selected years 1940-80, 4147–3.25

Deaths and death rates, by cause and age, provisional 1982-83, US Vital Statistics annual rpt, 4144–7

Deaths and death rates by detailed cause and demographic characteristics, 1979 and selected trends, US Vital Statistics annual rpt, 4144–2.1

Deaths and death rates, by detailed geographic area, cause, and demographic characteristics, 1979, US Vital Statistics annual rpt, 4144–3

Deaths and death rates, by selected cause and demographic characteristics, 1981, US Vital Statistics advance rpt, 4146–5.78

Deaths and death rates, by selected cause and demographic characteristics, 1982, US Vital Statistics advance rpt, 4146–5.81

Deaths and death rates for cancer, for 35 body sites, by race, sex, State, and county, 1950-79, 4478–146

Digestive Diseases Interagency Coordinating Committee activities, and related Federal research and funding, by agency, FY79-83, annual rpt, 4434–13

Disability Insurance beneficiaries sociodemographic and medical characteristics, 1977-79, annual rpt, 4744–20

Environmental pollution-related disease research activities and publications, Sept 1982-Aug 1983, annual rpt, 9184–9

Health condition and health care resources, use, and expenditures, 1970s-82 with trends and projections 1900-2000, annual compilation, 4144–11

HHS aid to each State and local govt or private instn, amount obligated, funding agency, and program, FY83, annual listing, 4004–3

Hospital discharges and length of stay, by patient characteristics, facility size, procedure performed, diagnosis, and region, 1982, annual rpt, 4147–13.78

Incidence, cases, deaths, and death rates for cancer, by body site, age, race, Hispanic origin, and sex, for 10 geographic areas, 1973-81, 4478–130

Infant deaths by detailed cause, geographic location, age, race, and sex, 1979, US Vital Statistics annual rpt, 4144–2.2

Natl Cancer Inst contracts and grants, by contractor, instn, State, and city, FY83, annual listing, 4474–28

Natl Cancer Inst epidemiology and biometry activities, budget, and contract awards by project and recipient instn, FY83, annual rpt, 4474–29

Natl Cancer Inst programs, organization, and budget, FY83, with cancer deaths by body site, 1980 and 1983, annual fact book, 4474–13

Occupational health risks from hazardous substances and radiation, by industry, occupation, age, and sex, with bibl and glossary, 1920s-82, 9638–50

Older persons by demographic, socioeconomic, and health characteristics, selected years 1900-81 and projected to 2050, Current Population Rpt, 2546–2.125

Public knowledge, attitudes, and behavior regarding cancer prevention and risk, 1983 survey, 4478–149

Research methods and design of health surveys, 1982 biennial conf proceedings, 4184–1

Smoking and health research publications, bimonthly listing, 4042–1

Soviet Union industrial and agricultural production by selected commodity, and demographic trends and projections by Republic, 1950s-2000, hearings, 23848–180

Uranium ore tailings at active mills, EPA radon and radionuclide emmission standards and US and foreign exposure and health effects, various periods 1957-83, hearings, 21208–17

Venereal cancer cases and rates, by region, State, and city, 1977-82, annual rpt, 4204–14.1

Veterans (Vietnam) health condition, methodology for 3 CDC studies on effects of military service and Agent Orange exposure, Nov 1983 rpt, 4208–22

Veterans aged 55 and over, socioeconomic characteristics, economic resources, health care and status, and actual and expected use of VA benefits, 1983 survey, 9928–29

see also Carcinogens

see also under By Disease in the "Index by Categories"

Nepal

Agricultural situation in 5 South Asia countries, by commodity, 1970s-1983/84 and outlook for 1984/85, annual rpt, 1524–4.11

AID activities and funding by project and function, FY85, and developing countries summary socioeconomic data, 1970s-83, by country, annual rpt, 9914–3

AID economic assistance to developing countries, obligations and disbursements by country, quarterly rpt, 9912–4

AID educational program activities and project impacts in 12 developing countries, 1950s-82, 9916–11.8

AID loan repayment status and terms by program and country, and status of predecessor agency loans, quarterly rpt, 9912–3

Background Notes, summary social, political, and economic data, 1984 rpt, 7006–2.59

Economic, social, and political summary data, by country, 1984, annual factbook, 244–11

Economic trends in income, production, prices, employment, finances, and trade, 1984 annual rpt, 2046–4.7

Exports of US, detailed Schedule B commodities by country of destination, 1983, annual rpt, 2424–9

Exports of US, detailed Schedule E commodities by mode of transport and world area and country of destination, 1983, annual rpts, 2424–5

Imports of US, detailed Schedule A commodities by country and world area of origin, and mode of transport, 1983, annual rpts, 2424–2

Imports of US, detailed TSUSA commodities by country of origin, 1983, annual rpt, 2424–4

Loans and grants for economic and military assistance from US and intl agencies, by program and country, FY46-83, annual rpt, 9914–5

Military aid of US, arms sales, and training programs costs and budget requests by program, world region, and country, FY83-85, annual rpt, 7144–13

Military spending, arms trade, and armed forces size, with total govt spending and population, by country, 1972-82, annual rpt, 9824–1

Minerals Yearbook, 1982, Vol 3: foreign country reviews of production, trade, and policies, by commodity, annual rpt, 5604–35

Minerals Yearbook, 1982, Vol 3 preprints: foreign country review of production, trade, and policies, by commodity, annual rpt, 5604–17.87

Population size and growth rates, and latest available benchmark demographic data, by country, 1950-83, biennial rpt, 2324–4

see also under By Foreign Country in the "Index by Categories"

Nervous system

see Neurological disorders

Netherlands

Agricultural and food production indexes, and production of selected commodities, by world region and country, 1974-83, annual rpt, 1524–5

Agricultural situation in Western Europe, by country and commodity, 1983 and outlook for 1984, annual rpt, 1524–4.6

Agricultural supply/demand, trade, and production, and socioeconomic data, by country, 1950s-77, 1528–179

AID loan repayment status and terms by program and country, and status of predecessor agency loans, quarterly rpt, 9912–3

Auto safety and experimental vehicle designs, 1982, conf proceedings, annual rpt, 7764–3

Dollar holdings rate of return related to domestic real money stock for 5 OECD countries, regression results, various periods 1966-84, article, 9391–1.418

Economic and monetary trends, compounded annual rates of change for US and 10 major trading partners, quarterly rpt, 9391–7

Economic conditions in Communist, OECD, and selected other countries, 1960s-83, annual rpt, 244–5

Economic indicators for 7 OECD countries and US, quarterly rpt, 2042–10

Economic, social, and political summary data, by country, 1984, annual factbook, 244–11

Economic trends in income, production, prices, employment, finances, and trade, 1984 semiannual rpt, 2046–4.34, 2046–4.88

Electronic component equipment market and trade, and user industry operations and demand, 1983 country market research rpt, 2045–4.24

Employment, labor force, and participation and unemployment rates by sex, in US and 9 OECD countries, various periods 1970-3rd qtr 1983, annual article, 6722–1.404

Netherlands

Energy prices and taxes by energy source and end-use sector, for US and 9 OECD countries, quarterly 1979-83, annual rpt, 3164–71

Exports and imports of NATO countries with Council for Mutual Economic Assistance Europe members, by country, 1980-83, annual rpt, 7144–5

Exports and imports of NATO countries with PRC, by country, 1980-83, annual rpt, 7144–14

Exports and imports of OECD countries, by country, 1983, annual rpt, 7144–10

Exports and imports of US with Western Europe, and US market share and export opportunities for selected commodities, by country, 1982-84, 2048–105

Exports of US, detailed Schedule B commodities by country of destination, 1983, annual rpt, 2424–9

Exports of US, detailed Schedule E commodities by mode of transport and world area and country of destination, 1983, annual rpts, 2424–5

Fish and shellfish wholesale prices and market activity in 8 West Europe countries, weekly rpt, 2162–8

Food supply/demand and market and support prices, with exchange rates, fertilizer price index, GDP, and population, by EC country, 1960-83, 1528–173

Graphic industries equipment market and trade, and user industry operations and demand, 1984 country market research rpt, 2045–3.30

Imports of US, detailed Schedule A commodities by country and world area of origin, and mode of transport, 1983, annual rpts, 2424–2

Imports of US, detailed TSUSA commodities by country of origin, 1983, annual rpt, 2424–4

Industrial production indexes of 7 OECD countries and US, biweekly rpt, periodic article, 2042–24

Intl transactions of US with 10 countries, 1981-83, *Survey of Current Business,* monthly rpt, annual table, 2702–1.31

Investment (foreign direct) in US, major investors and investments by SIC 4-digit industry, transaction type and value, and location, 1983, annual rpt, 2044–20

Loans and grants for economic and military assistance from US and intl agencies, by program and country, FY46-83, annual rpt, 9914–5

Manufacturing labor productivity and cost indexes for US and 11 OECD countries, 1960-82, annual article, 6722–1.405

Manufacturing productivity and unit labor cost indexes for US and 11 countries, 1950-82 and preliminary 1983, annual rpt, 6864–1

Military aid of US, arms sales, and training programs costs and budget requests by program, world region, and country, FY83-85, annual rpt, 7144–13

Military spending, arms trade, and armed forces size, with total govt spending and population, by country, 1972-82, annual rpt, 9824–1

Minerals Yearbook, 1982, Vol 3: foreign country reviews of production, trade, and policies, by commodity, annual rpt, 5604–35

Minerals Yearbook, 1983, Vol 3 preprints: foreign country review of production, trade, and policies, by commodity, annual rpt, 5604–23.52

Nuclear power generation in US and 18 non-Communist countries, monthly rpt, 3162–24.10

Nuclear power plant construction and operation status, and capacity, by plant, region, State, and selected country, 1983 and projected to 2020, annual rpt, 3164–57

Oil and gas undiscovered recoverable resources, cumulative production, and identified reserves, as of 1982, preliminary oil basin rpt, 5666–17.15

Population size and growth rates, and latest available benchmark demographic data, by country, 1950-83, biennial rpt, 2324–4

Space satellites and other objects launched since 1957, quarterly listing, 9502–2

Steel imports of US from EC and other countries, and US industry operating data, for 15 products limited under arrangement with EC, monthly rpt, 9882–10

see also under By Foreign Country in the "Index by Categories"

Netherlands Antilles

see Caribbean area

Netting, fish

see Fish and fishing industry

Networks

see Information storage and retrieval systems

see Public broadcasting

see Radio

see Television

Neubig, Thomas

"Taxation of Income Flowing Through Life Insurance Companies", 8006–3.49

Neubig, Tom

"Private Activity Tax-Exempt Bonds, 1983", 8302–2.417

Neurological disorders

Agent Orange exposed Air Force personnel diseases and disorders, by disease type, age, and officer status, 1984 rpt, 3604–3

Cases and incidence of infectious notifiable diseases and other public health concerns, by census div and State, 1982, annual rpt, 4204–1

Cases of notifiable infectious diseases and current outbreaks, by region and State, weekly rpt, 4202–1

Deaths and death rates by detailed cause and demographic characteristics, 1979 and selected trends, US Vital Statistics annual rpt, 4144–2.1

Disability Insurance beneficiaries sociodemographic and medical characteristics, 1977-79, annual rpt, 4744–20

HHS aid to each State and local govt or private instn, amount obligated, funding agency, and program, FY83, annual listing, 4004–3

Hospital discharges and length of stay, by patient characteristics, facility size, procedure performed, diagnosis, and region, 1982, annual rpt, 4147–13.78

Mental hospitals of States and counties, patients and admissions by diagnosis, age, and State, FY81, annual rpt, 4504–2

Research methods and design of health surveys, 1982 biennial conf proceedings, 4184–1

Index by Subjects and Names

Veterans of Vietnam era, compensation cases by degree of impairment, compared with WW II and Korea veterans, FY83, annual rpt, 9924–8.5

see also Mental health and illness

see also Rabies

see also under By Disease in the "Index by Categories"

Nevada

- Agriculture census, 1982: farms, farmland, production and costs, and operator characteristics, preliminary State summary and county rpts, 2330–1.32
- Agriculture census, 1982: farms, farmland, production, finances, and operator characteristics, by county, final State rpt, 2331–1.28
- Bank deposits in commercial and mutual savings banks and in US branches of foreign banks, by account type, instn, State, SMSA, and county, June 1983, annual rpt, 9295–3.17
- Census of Housing, 1980: occupancy and unit characteristics of SMSAs and central cities, by race, Hispanic origin, and city, State rpt, 2473–1.30
- Census of Population and Housing, 1980: detailed population and housing characteristics, by county, city, and census tract, State rpt, 2551–2.30
- Census of Population, 1980: detailed socioeconomic and demographic characteristics, by age, sex, race, Hispanic origin, and industry, State rpt, 2531–4.30
- Copper smelting sulfur dioxide emissions of 8 plants in 2 States, under alternative emission standards, 1981-82, hearings, 25328–25
- County Business Patterns: establishments, employees, and payrolls, by SIC 4-digit industry and county, 1982, annual State rpt, 2326–6.30
- Employment, earnings, and hours, by selected SIC 1- to 4-digit industry, State, and for 278 major labor areas, 1939-83, annual rpt, 6744–5.1, 6744–5.3
- Environmental quality, pollutant discharge by type and source, and EPA protection activities and funding, 1970s-83, biennial regional rpt, 9184–15.9
- Exports of manufactured and agricultural commodities, manufacturing production, and export-related employment, 1960s-82, State rpt, 2046–3.28
- Forest biomass in Rocky Mountain States, conversion from volume to dry weight, for softwood and hardwood species, 1977, 1208–200
- HHS aid to each State and local govt or private instn, amount obligated, funding agency, and program, FY83, annual listing, 4004–3.9
- Income (personal) per capita and by source, and earnings by industry div, by State, MSA, and county, 1977-82, annual regional rpt, 2704–2.9
- Land Mgmt Bur public lands sales, prices of Nevada and California acreage, and effect on Forest Service land acquisition program, 1983, GAO rpt, 26113–122
- Manufacturing census, 1982: financial and operating data, by SIC 2- to 4-digit industry, State, SMSA, and county, preliminary census div rpt, 2491–3.8

Index by Subjects and Names

New Haven, Conn.

Mineral Industry Surveys, State review of production, 1983, advance annual rpt, 5614–6.28

Minerals Yearbook, 1982, Vol 2 preprints: State review of production and sales by commodity, and business activity, annual rpt, 5604–16.29

Minerals Yearbook, 1982, Vol 2: State reviews of production, sales, and firms, by commodity, and business activity, annual rpt, 5604–34

Population size and components of change, by MSA and county, 1980-82, annual State Current Population Rpt, 2546–4.28

Population size, Apr 1980 and July 1982, and per capita income, 1979 and 1981, by county and city, State Current Population Rpt, 2546–11.28

Radiation from 1940s-70s nuclear weapons tests, levels in air and water, and personnel exposure by military unit and job category, series, 3906–1

Radionuclide concentrations in air, water, and biota near Nevada and other nuclear test sites, and in milk from western States, by location, 1983, annual rpt, 9234–4

Radionuclide concentrations in cattle and wildlife near Nevada nuclear test site, 1957-81, last issue of annual rpt, 9234–5

Retail trade census, 1982: employment, establishments, sales, and payroll, by SIC 2- to 4-digit kind of business, SMSA, and retail district, State rpt, 2401–1.29

Retail trade census, 1982: employment, establishments, sales, and payroll, by SIC 2- to 4-digit kind of business, SMSA, county, and city, State rpt, 2397–1.29

Savings and loan assns, FHLB 11th District members financial condition and operations by State, quarterly rpt, 9302–19

Savings and loan assns, FHLB 11th District members financial operations and housing industry indicators by State, monthly rpt, 9302–17

Service industry census, 1982: employment, establishments, receipts, and payroll, by SIC 2- to 4-digit kind of business, SMSA, county, and city, State rpt, 2391–1.29

Timber resources and removals in 9 Rocky Mountain States, and forest and rangeland area, by ownership, forest and tree characteristics, and State, 1977, 1208–201

Water supply, and snow survey results, monthly State rpt, 1266–2.6

Water supply in Nevada, streamflow, reservoir storage, and precipitation, 1984 water year, annual rpt, 1264–8

Wholesale trade census, 1982: employment, establishments, finances, and operations, by SIC 2- to 4-digit kind of business, SMSA, county, and city, State rpt, 2405–1.29

see also Las Vegas, Nev.

see also Reno, Nev.

see also under By State in the "Index by Categories"

New Bedford, Mass.

Census of Housing, 1980: occupancy and unit characteristics, by race, Hispanic origin, and city, SMSA rpt, 2473–1.254

Census of Population and Housing, 1980: detailed population and housing characteristics, by county, city, and census tract, SMSA rpt, 2551–2.254

Dress industry production and related workers, wages, and benefits, by occupation, size of establishment, and union status, for 11 labor market areas, Aug 1982 survey, 6787–6.200

Fish and shellfish landings and prices at Boston and other New England ports, and total New England cold storage holdings, weekly rpt, 2162–6.2

see also under By SMSA or MSA in the "Index by Categories"

New Britain, Conn.

Census of Housing, 1980: occupancy and unit characteristics, by race, Hispanic origin, and city, SMSA rpt, 2473–1.255

Census of Population and Housing, 1980: detailed population and housing characteristics, by county, city, and census tract, SMSA rpt, 2551–2.255

see also under By SMSA or MSA in the "Index by Categories"

New Brunswick, N.J.

Census of Housing, 1980: occupancy and unit characteristics, by race, Hispanic origin, and city, SMSA rpt, 2473–1.256

Census of Population and Housing, 1980: detailed population and housing characteristics, by county, city, and census tract, SMSA rpt, 2551–2.256

New Caledonia

see Oceania

New England

see Northeast States

New Guinea

see Papua New Guinea

New Hampshire

Agriculture census, 1982: farms, farmland, production and costs, and operator characteristics, preliminary State summary and county rpts, 2330–1.33

Agriculture census, 1982: farms, farmland, production, finances, and operator characteristics, by county, final State rpt, 2331–1.29

Bank deposits in commercial and mutual savings banks and in US branches of foreign banks, by account type, instn, State, SMSA, and county, June 1983, annual rpt, 9295–3.1

Census of Housing, 1980: occupancy and unit characteristics of SMSAs and central cities, by race, Hispanic origin, and city, State rpt, 2473–1.31

Census of Population and Housing, 1980: detailed population and housing characteristics, by county, city, and census tract, State rpt, 2551–2.31

Census of Population, 1980: detailed socioeconomic and demographic characteristics, by age, sex, race, Hispanic origin, and industry, State rpt, 2531–4.31

County Business Patterns: establishments, employees, and payrolls, by SIC 4-digit industry and county, 1982, annual State rpt, 2326–6.31

Economic indicators for New England States, Fed Reserve 1st District, monthly rpt with articles, 9373–2

Employment, earnings, and hours, by selected SIC 1- to 4-digit industry, State, and for 278 major labor areas, 1939-83, annual rpt, 6744–5.2, 6744–5.3

Environmental quality, pollutant discharge by type and source, and EPA protection activities and funding, 1970s-83, biennial regional rpt, 9184–15.1

Exports of manufactured and agricultural commodities, manufacturing production, and export-related employment, 1960s-82, State rpt, 2046–3.29

Hazardous waste generation and disposal taxes in 3 States, and effects on waste mgmt, 1981-83, with assessment of 3 Fed Govt tax proposals, GAO rpt, 26113–124

HHS aid to each State and local govt or private instn, amount obligated, funding agency, and program, FY83, annual listing, 4004–3.1

Income (personal) per capita and by source, and earnings by industry div, by State, MSA, and county, 1977-82, annual regional rpt, 2704–2.2

Mineral Industry Surveys, State review of production, 1983, advance annual rpt, 5614–6.29

Minerals Yearbook, 1982, Vol 2 preprints: State review of production and sales by commodity, and business activity, annual rpt, 5604–16.30

Minerals Yearbook, 1982, Vol 2: State reviews of production, sales, and firms, by commodity, and business activity, annual rpt, 5604–34

Population, births, deaths, and net migration, by MSA and county, 1980-82, annual State Current Population Rpt, 2546–4.29

Population size, Apr 1980 and July 1982, and per capita income, 1979 and 1981, by county and city, State Current Population Rpt, 2546–11.29

Retail trade census, 1982: employment, establishments, sales, and payroll, by SIC 2- to 4-digit kind of business, SMSA, county, and city, State rpt, 2397–1.30

Savings and loan assns, FHLB 1st District member instns financial operations and related economic and housing indicators, monthly rpt, 9302–4

Service industry census, 1982: employment, establishments, receipts, and payroll, by SIC 2- to 4-digit kind of business, SMSA, county, and city, State rpt, 2391–1.30

Wages for 3 occupational groups, relative average levels in 78 labor market areas, 1983, annual press release, 6785–13

Wages of office and plant workers, by occupation, 1983 labor market area survey rpt, 6785–3.1

Water supply and quality in streams and lakes, and groundwater levels in wells, by drainage basin, 1982, annual State rpt, 5666–20.28

Wholesale trade census, 1982: employment, establishments, finances, and operations, by SIC 2- to 4-digit kind of business, SMSA, county, and city, State rpt, 2405–1.30

see also Dover, N.H.

see also Manchester, N.H.

see also Nashua, N.H.

see also Portsmouth, N.H.

see also Rochester, N.H.

see also under By State in the "Index by Categories"

New Haven, Conn.

Census of Housing, 1980: occupancy and unit characteristics, by race, Hispanic origin, and city, SMSA rpt, 2473–1.257

New Haven, Conn.

Census of Population and Housing, 1980: detailed population and housing characteristics, by county, city, and census tract, SMSA rpt, 2551-2.257

see also under By City and By SMSA or MSA in the "Index by Categories"

New Hebrides

see Vanuatu

New Jersey

- Administrative law cases, disposition, and processing time, by New Jersey govt agency, selected years FY80-84, hearings, 25528-96
- Agriculture census, 1982: farms, farmland, production, finances, and operator characteristics, by county, final State rpt, 2331-1.30
- Air pollution levels for 28 volatile organic compounds in NYC and New Jersey, by site and urban-rural location, 1979-June 1981, 9198-108
- Bank deposits in commercial and mutual savings banks and in US branches of foreign banks, by account type, instn, State, SMSA, and county, June 1983, annual rpt, 9295-3.4
- Census of Housing, 1980: occupancy and unit characteristics of SMSAs and central cities, by race, Hispanic origin, and city, State rpt, 2473-1.32
- Census of Population and Housing, 1980: detailed population and housing characteristics, by county, city, and census tract, State rpt, 2551-2.32
- Census of Population, 1980: detailed socioeconomic and demographic characteristics, by age, sex, race, Hispanic origin, and industry, State rpt, 2531-4.32
- County Business Patterns: establishments, employees, and payrolls, by SIC 4-digit industry and county, 1982, annual State rpt, 2326-6.32
- Court use of telephone conferencing in civil and criminal hearings, assessment of lawyers and judges in 2 States and Denver, Colo, 1981, 6068-186
- Cranberry production, prices, area, and yield, for 5 States, 1982-83 and forecast 1984, annual rpt, 1621-18.4
- Employment and prices in NYC metro area, 1983, annual rpt, 6924-2
- Employment, earnings, and hours, by selected SIC 1- to 4-digit industry, State, and for 278 major labor areas, 1939-83, annual rpt, 6744-5.2, 6744-5.3
- Environmental quality, pollutant discharge by type and source, and EPA protection activities and funding, 1970s-83, biennial regional rpt, 9184-15.2
- Exports of manufactured and agricultural commodities, manufacturing production, and export-related employment, 1960s-82, State rpt, 2046-3.30
- HHS aid to each State and local govt or private instn, amount obligated, funding agency, and program, FY83, annual listing, 4004-3.2
- Hwy and bridge repair projects funded by Fed Govt, and costs, for 7 States, FY81-82, GAO rpt, 26113-121
- Income (personal) per capita and by source, and earnings by industry div, by State, MSA, and county, 1977-82, annual regional rpt, 2704-2.3

Manufacturing census, 1982: financial and operating data, by SIC 2- to 4-digit industry, State, SMSA, and county, preliminary census div rpt, 2491-3.2

- Mineral Industry Surveys, State review of production, 1983, advance annual rpt, 5614-6.30
- *Minerals Yearbook, 1982,* Vol 2 preprints: State review of production and sales by commodity, and business activity, annual rpt, 5604-16.31
- *Minerals Yearbook, 1982,* Vol 2: State reviews of production, sales, and firms, by commodity, and business activity, annual rpt, 5604-34
- New York Bight pollutant loadings from ocean dumping of municipal wastes by type and source, and concentrations in fish and sediments, 1970s-82, hearings, 21568-36
- Nursing care in New Jersey by nursing unit type, level of care related to length of stay, and costs by diagnosis under 2 allocation methods, as of 1981, article, 4652-1.424
- Population, births, deaths, and net migration, by MSA and county, 1980-82, annual State Current Population Rpt, 2546-4.30
- Population size, Apr 1980 and July 1982, and per capita income, 1979 and 1981, by county and city, State Current Population Rpt, 2546-11.30
- Prison capacity and population for 2 States, and New Jersey construction costs by type and funding source, by facility, 1977-82 with projections to 1988, 25528-99
- Retail trade census, 1982: employment, establishments, sales, and payroll, by SIC 2- to 4-digit kind of business, SMSA, county, and city, State rpt, 2397-1.31
- Savings instns, FHLB 2nd District members financial operations, by State, monthly rpt, 9302-14
- Water supply and quality in streams and lakes, and groundwater levels in wells, by drainage basin, 1980, annual State rpt, 5666-12.29
- Water supply and quality in streams and lakes, and groundwater levels in wells, by drainage basin, 1981, annual State rpt, 5666-16.29
- Water supply and quality in streams and lakes, and groundwater levels in wells, by drainage basin, 1983, annual State rpt, 5666-10.29
- Wholesale trade census, 1982: employment, establishments, finances, and operations, by SIC 2- to 4-digit kind of business, SMSA, county, and city, State rpt, 2405-1.31

see also Asbury Park, N.J.

see also Atlantic City, N.J.

see also Bridgeton, N.J.

see also Camden, N.J.

see also Clifton, N.J.

see also Elizabeth, N.J.

see also Jersey City, N.J.

see also Long Branch, N.J.

see also Middlesex County, N.J.

see also Millville, N.J.

see also Monmouth County, N.J.

see also New Brunswick, N.J.

Index by Subjects and Names

see also Newark, N.J.

see also Ocean County, N.J.

see also Passaic, N.J.

see also Paterson, N.J.

see also Perth Amboy, N.J.

see also Sayreville, N.J.

see also Trenton, N.J.

see also Vineland, N.J.

see also under By State in the "Index by Categories"

New London, Conn.

- Census of Housing, 1980: occupancy and unit characteristics, by race, Hispanic origin, and city, SMSA rpt, 2473-1.258
- Census of Population and Housing, 1980: detailed population and housing characteristics, by county, city, and census tract, SMSA rpt, 2551-2.258

see also under By SMSA or MSA in the "Index by Categories"

New Mexico

- Agriculture census, 1982: farms, farmland, production and costs, and operator characteristics, preliminary State summary and county rpts, 2330-1.35
- Agriculture census, 1982: farms, farmland, production, finances, and operator characteristics, by county, final State rpt, 2331-1.31
- Bank deposits in commercial and mutual savings banks and in US branches of foreign banks, by account type, instn, State, SMSA, and county, June 1983, annual rpt, 9295-3.17
- Cancer cases, incidence, deaths, and death rates, by body site, age, race, Hispanic origin, and sex, for 10 geographic areas, 1973-81, 4478-130
- Census of Housing, 1980: occupancy and unit characteristics of SMSAs and central cities, by race, Hispanic origin, and city, State rpt, 2473-1.33
- Census of Population and Housing, 1980: detailed population and housing characteristics, by county, city, and census tract, State rpt, 2551-2.33
- Census of Population, 1980: detailed socioeconomic and demographic characteristics, by age, sex, race, Hispanic origin, and industry, State rpt, 2531-4.33
- Coal dev plans on Fed Govt lease lands, environmental and socioeconomic impacts to 2000, final statement, 5726-4.7
- Coal Fed Govt leases, acreage, production, and prices, by State, and legal and mgmt issues, 1970s-83 with production projections to 2000, 11128-1
- County Business Patterns: establishments, employees, and payrolls, by SIC 4-digit industry and county, 1982, annual State rpt, 2326-6.33
- Employment by major nonagricultural industry, and average hours and earnings of manufacturing production workers, for 5 southwestern States, monthly rpt, 6962-2
- Employment, earnings, and hours, by selected SIC 1- to 4-digit industry, State, and for 278 major labor areas, 1939-83, annual rpt, 6744-5.2, 6744-5.3
- Employment, industrial relations, prices, and economic conditions in 5 Southwestern States, regional rpts series, 6966-1
- Environmental quality, pollutant discharge by type and source, and EPA protection activities and funding, 1970s-83, biennial regional rpt, 9184-15.6

Index by Subjects and Names

New York City

Exports of manufactured and agricultural commodities, manufacturing production, and export-related employment, 1960s-82, State rpt, 2046–3.31

Forest biomass in Rocky Mountain States, conversion from volume to dry weight, for softwood and hardwood species, 1977, 1208–200

Health clinics staffed by Natl Health Service Corps in New Mexico, income sources, and effect of revised system for Federal payback, 1980-83, hearings, 21368–47

HHS aid to each State and local govt or private instn, amount obligated, funding agency, and program, FY83, annual listing, 4004–3.6

Income (personal) per capita and by source, and earnings by industry div, by State, MSA, and county, 1977-82, annual regional rpt, 2704–2.7

Manufacturing census, 1982: financial and operating data, by SIC 2- to 4-digit industry, State, SMSA, and county, preliminary census div rpt, 2491–3.8

Mineral Industry Surveys, State review of production, 1983, advance annual rpt, 5614–6.31

Minerals Yearbook, 1982, Vol 2 preprints: State review of production and sales by commodity, and business activity, annual rpt, 5604–16.32

Minerals Yearbook, 1982, Vol 2: State reviews of production, sales, and firms, by commodity, and business activity, annual rpt, 5604–34

Population size and components of change, by MSA and county, 1980-82, annual State Current Population Rpt, 2546–4.31

Population size, Apr 1980 and July 1982, and per capita income, 1979 and 1981, by county and city, State Current Population Rpt, 2546–11.31

Retail trade census, 1982: employment, establishments, sales, and payroll, by SIC 2- to 4-digit kind of business, SMSA, county, and city, State rpt, 2397–1.32

Savings and loan assns, FHLB 9th District insured members financial condition and operations by SMSA, monthly rpt, 9302–13

Service industry census, 1982: employment, establishments, receipts, and payroll, by SIC 2- to 4-digit kind of business, SMSA, county, and city, State rpt, 2391–1.32

Timber acreage and resources in New Mexico, by species, ownership class, and county 1977-80, series, 1206–23

Timber resources and removals in 9 Rocky Mountain States, and forest and rangeland area, by ownership, forest and tree characteristics, and State, 1977, 1208–201

Water supply and quality, and effect of coal mining operations, for selected river basins in western coal provinces, 1983 rpt, 5666–19.5

Water supply, and snow survey results, monthly State rpt, 1266–2.3

Wholesale trade census, 1982: employment, establishments, finances, and operations, by SIC 2- to 4-digit kind of business, SMSA, county, and city, State rpt, 2405–1.32

see also Alamogordo, N.Mex.

see also Albuquerque, N.Mex.

see also Las Cruces, N.Mex.

see also under By State in the "Index by Categories"

New Orleans, La.

Census of Housing, 1980: occupancy and unit characteristics, by race, Hispanic origin, and city, SMSA rpt, 2473–1.259

Census of Population and Housing, 1980: detailed population and housing characteristics, by county, city, and census tract, SMSA rpt, 2551–2.259

Fish and shellfish landings, prices, and cannery production, for Gulf States and North Carolina, by area, weekly rpt, 2162–6.3

Fruit and vegetable shipments, and arrivals in 23 US and 5 Canada cities, by mode of transport and State or country of origin, 1983, annual rpt, 1311–4.2

Housing and financial characteristics, and unit and neighborhood quality, for 15 SMSAs, 1978, annual survey special supplement, 2485–8

Housing and households detailed characteristics, and unit and neighborhood quality, by inside-outside central cities, 1982 survey, SMSA rpt, 2485–6.43

Housing unit starts and completions authorized by building permits in 20 MSAs, quarterly rpt, 2382–9

Housing vacancy rates for single and multifamily units and mobile homes, by city and ZIP code, 1983, annual metro area rpt, 9304–19.5

Population size of top 25 cities, 1980 and 1982, press release, 2328–46

Wages by occupation, and benefits for office and plant workers, 1984 SMSA survey rpt, 6785–11.10

Waterborne commerce of US (domestic and foreign), freight by commodity, traffic, and passengers, by port and waterway, 1982, annual rpt, 3754–3.2

see also under By City and By SMSA or MSA in the "Index by Categories"

New towns

New Communities program of HUD, activities, costs, land sales, and community and population characteristics, for 13 communities, 1970s-83, 5188–107

New York Bight

Freight (waterborne domestic and foreign) by commodity, traffic, and passengers, by port and waterway, 1982, annual rpt, 3754–3.1

Pollutant loadings from ocean dumping of municipal wastes by type and source, and concentrations in fish and sediments, 1970s-82, hearings, 21568–36

New York City

Abortions, by patient sociodemographic characteristics, pregnancy history, and procedure, 1980, US Vital Statistics final rpt, 4146–5.72

Air pollution levels for 28 volatile organic compounds in NYC and New Jersey, by site and urban-rural location, 1979-June 1981, 9198–108

Arson investigation and prosecution, by incident characteristics and outcome, motive, and type of evidence, for 4 jurisdictions, 1981, 6068–184

Auto dealer repair workers, wages, and benefits, by occupation, size of establishment, and for 24 labor market areas, Nov 1982 survey, 6787–6.202

Bank balance sheet statements by Fed Reserve District, for major banks in NYC, and for US branches and agencies of foreign banks, weekly release, 9365–1.3

Banks (commercial) debits to demand deposits, and demand deposits and turnover, monthly rpt, 9365–2.5

Census of Housing, 1980: occupancy and unit characteristics, by race, Hispanic origin, and city, SMSA rpt, 2473–1.260

Census of Population and Housing, 1980: detailed population and housing characteristics, by county, city, and census tract, SMSA rpt, 2551–2.260

CPI by component for US city average, and by region, population size, and for 28 SMSAs, monthly press release, 6762–1

CPI by detailed component, for US city average, 28 SMSAs, and 4 regions by population size, monthly rpt, 6762–2

Diseases (infectious notifiable) cases and incidence, by census div and State, 1981, annual rpt, 4204–1

Dress industry production and related workers, wages, and benefits, by occupation, size of establishment, and union status, for 11 labor market areas, Aug 1982 survey, 6787–6.200

Employment and earnings, detailed data, monthly rpt, 6742–2.5, 6742–2.6

Employment and prices in NYC metro area, 1983, annual rpt, 6924–2

Fish and shellfish receipts, wholesale prices, and market activities at NYC, weekly rpt, 2162–6.1

Fruit and vegetable shipments, and arrivals in 23 US and 5 Canada cities, by mode of transport and State or country of origin, 1983, annual rpt, 1311–4.1

Fruit and vegetable wholesale prices in NYC, Chicago, and selected shipping points, by crop, 1983, annual rpt, 1311–8

Health care demonstration project for reorganization of 6 facilities in Brooklyn, Federal and State govt funding by facility, 1979-82, article, 4652–1.419

Homeless population and characteristics, and temporary shelter operations, use, and user characteristics, for selected cities, various periods 1979-84, hearing, 21248–85

Hospital worker wages by sex and occupation, and benefits, for 22 MSAs, Oct 1981 survey, 6787–6.201

Households and members, NYC Standard Consolidated Area, Mar 1982, annual Current Population Rpt, 2546–1.383

Housing and economic dev in South Bronx, HUD grants to 4 neighborhood organizations, June 1984 press release, 5006–3.31

Housing and households detailed characteristics, and unit and neighborhood quality, by inside-outside central cities, 1980 survey, SMSA rpt, 2485–6.12

Housing unit starts and completions authorized by building permits in 20 MSAs, quarterly rpt, 2382–9

Infectious notifiable diseases, cases and current outbreaks, by region and State, weekly rpt, 4202–1

Mail (1st class), performance ratings for stamped and metered overnight mail in NYC and Northeast US, FY82-83, annual rpt, 9864–5.2

New York City

Ocean dumping of municipal wastes, and sewage production and disposal barge capacity and operating costs, 1970s-82 and projected to 2000, hearings, 21568–36

Population census, 1980: migration since 1975, by county and selected demographic characteristics, and for New York City, supplementary rpt, 2535–1.14

Population size, demographic characteristics, and rental housing, in 5 NYC neighborhoods by census tract, 1980 with percent change from 1970, article, 9385–1.403

Population size of top 25 cities, 1980 and 1982, press release, 2328–46

Public works capital needs and financing, by project type, level of govt, and selected jurisdiction, 1970s-83 and projected to 2000, hearing, 23848–181

Public works capital needs and intergovtl financing, by type of project and selected city, various periods 1950-83, 10048–60

Radioactive strontium in NYC and San Francisco diet by food item, and in NYC tap water and milk, quarterly 1982 with trends from 1954, annual rpt, 3404–13

Repair technicians and apprentices wages and benefits, for 5 types of electrical repair shops in 19 SMSAs, Nov 1981 survey, 6787–6.197

Retirement systems of NYC, assets by type for 6 systems, selected years 1978-83, conf proceedings, 25408–89

Small business owners and accountants, assessment of economy, professional activities, and community problems, by county and industry div, 1983 surveys, hearings, 21728–52.3

Tuberculosis death rates in NYC, UK, and Prussia, selected years 1865-1920, article, 4102–1.431

TV and radio industry minority and women employment by occupation, and business owners, by race and State, with revenues and stations, 1971-81, hearing, 21368–45

Vital statistics, births, marriages, divorces, and deaths, provisional data, monthly rpt, 4142–1

Wages by occupation, and benefits for office and plant workers, 1984 SMSA survey rpt, 6785–11.7

Wages by occupation for NYC office and plant workers, 1983, annual rpt, 6926–1.75

Waterborne commerce of US (domestic and foreign), freight by commodity, traffic, and passengers, by port and waterway, 1982, annual rpt, 3754–3.1

see also New York Stock Exchange

see also under By City and By SMSA or MSA in the "Index by Categories"

New York State

Agricultural cooperatives, membership, activities, and finances, by commodity and selected State, 1900-80 with trends from 1863, 1128–30

Agriculture census, 1982: farms, farmland, production and costs, and operator characteristics, preliminary State summary and county rpts, 2330–1.36

Agriculture census, 1982: farms, farmland, production, finances, and operator characteristics, by county, final State rpt, 2331–1.32

Arrest rate for released New York State mental patients, by arrest record, 1975, 6066–20.5

Bank deposits in commercial and mutual savings banks and in US branches of foreign banks, by account type, instn, State, SMSA, and county, June 1983, annual rpt, 9295–3.2

Banking intl facilities of foreign and US banks in New York State and total US, assets and liabilities, monthly rpt, 9365–2.22

Celery acreage planted and growing, by major producing State and area, monthly rpt, 1621–14

Census of Housing, 1980: occupancy and unit characteristics of SMSAs and central cities, by race, Hispanic origin, and city, State rpt, 2473–1.34

Census of Population and Housing, 1980: detailed population and housing characteristics, by county, city, and census tract, State rpt, 2551–2.34

Census of Population, 1980: detailed socioeconomic and demographic characteristics, by age, sex, race, Hispanic origin, and industry, State rpt, 2531–4.34

County Business Patterns: establishments, employees, and payrolls, by SIC 4-digit industry and county, 1982, annual State rpt, 2326–6.34

Dental cost Medicaid reimbursement in New York State, evaluation of expedited prior approval process, 1984 article, 4102–1.458

Employment, earnings, and hours, by selected SIC 1- to 4-digit industry, State, and for 278 major labor areas, 1939-83, annual rpt, 6744–5.2, 6744–5.3

Environmental quality, pollutant discharge by type and source, and EPA protection activities and funding, 1970s-83, biennial regional rpt, 9184–15.2

Exports of manufactured and agricultural commodities, manufacturing production, and export-related employment, 1960s-82, State rpt, 2046–3.32

Families in NYC caring for aged relatives, preference for financial and social services programs to provide assistance, 1980, article, 4652–1.403

Forest land owner characteristics, owners and acreage, 1980, 1206–7.10

Hazardous waste generation and disposal taxes in 3 States, and effects on waste mgmt, 1981-83, with assessment of 3 Fed Govt tax proposals, GAO rpt, 26113–124

HHS aid to each State and local govt or private instn, amount obligated, funding agency, and program, FY83, annual listing, 4004–3.2

Home health care program in New York State, info system on public assistance benefits and services received by program participants, 1984 article, 4652–1.402

Hwy and bridge repair projects funded by Fed Govt, and costs, for 7 States, FY81-82, GAO rpt, 26113–121

Hwy speeding and accident rates related to use of marked and unmarked New York State patrol cars, 1977-79, article, 7762–9.403

Income (personal) per capita and by source, and earnings by industry div, by State, MSA, and county, 1977-82, annual regional rpt, 2704–2.3

Index by Subjects and Names

Manufacturing census, 1982: financial and operating data, by SIC 2- to 4-digit industry, State, SMSA, and county, preliminary census div rpt, 2491–3.2

Mineral Industry Surveys, State review of production, 1983, advance annual rpt, 5614–6.32

Minerals Yearbook, 1982, Vol 2 preprints: State review of production and sales by commodity, and business activity, annual rpt, 5604–16.33

Minerals Yearbook, 1982, Vol 2: State reviews of production, sales, and firms, by commodity, and business activity, annual rpt, 5604–34

Northern New York State wages of office and plant workers, by occupation, 1984 labor market area survey rpt, 6785–3.9

Philanthropic grants of Altman Foundation in New York by recipient, and Foundation income and expenses, selected years 1913-82, hearings, 21788–137

Population estimates and components of change, by MSA and county, 1980-82, annual State Current Population Rpt, 2546–4.32

Population size, Apr 1980 and July 1982, and per capita income, 1979 and 1981, by county and city, State Current Population Rpt, 2546–11.32

Public works capital needs and financing, by project type, level of govt, and selected jurisdiction, 1970s-83 and projected to 2000, hearing, 23848–181

Retail trade census, 1982: employment, establishments, sales, and payroll, by SIC 2- to 4-digit kind of business, SMSA, county, and city, State rpt, 2397–1.33

Savings instns, FHLB 2nd District members financial operations, by State, monthly rpt, 9302–14

Snow depth and water equivalent in New York State area, by site, winter 1982/83, annual rpt, 2184–2

Timber annual growth, removals, products output, and forest ownership and industries, 1980, State rpt, 1206–16.7

Transportation census, 1982: trucks, by detailed characteristics, miles traveled, and type of product carried, State rpt, 2573–1.33

Water supply and quality, and effect of coal mining operations, for selected river basins in Eastern and Interior coal provinces, 1983 rpt, 5666–15.25

Water supply and quality in streams and lakes, and groundwater levels in wells, by drainage basin, 1983, annual State rpt, 5666–10.31

Wholesale trade census, 1982: employment, establishments, finances, and operations, by SIC 2- to 4-digit kind of business, SMSA, county, and city, State rpt, 2405–1.33

see also Albany, N.Y.

see also Binghamton, N.Y.

see also Buffalo, N.Y.

see also Elmira, N.Y.

see also Glens Falls, N.Y.

see also Kingston, N.Y.

see also Middletown, N.Y.

see also Nassau County, N.Y.

see also New York Bight

see also New York City

Index by Subjects and Names

see also Newburgh, N.Y.
see also Poughkeepsie, N.Y.
see also Rochester, N.Y.
see also Rome, N.Y.
see also Schenectady, N.Y.
see also Suffolk County, N.Y.
see also Syracuse, N.Y.
see also Troy, N.Y.
see also Utica, N.Y.
see also under By State in the "Index by Categories"

New York Stock Exchange

Trading volume on New York and American Stock Exchanges, monthly rpt, 9362–1.1

Trading volume, securities listed by type, and exchange finances, by stock exchange, selected years 1935-82, annual rpt, 9734–2.1, 9734–2.3

Transactions volume and proceeds and new issue registrations, for US registered exchanges, SEC monthly rpt, 9732–1

Transportation and composite NYSE indexes, and compared to average airline common stock prices, quarterly Dec 1977-June 1984, semiannual rpt, 9142–36

see also Stock exchanges
see also Stockbrokers

New Zealand

Agricultural and food production indexes, and production of selected commodities, by world region and country, 1974-83, annual rpt, 1524–5

Agricultural imports from US by detailed commodity, and from other countries by selected fruit, 1980-FY83, article, 1925–34.402

Agricultural situation in North America and Oceania, by country and commodity, 1983 and outlook for 1984, annual rpt, 1524–4.1

Agricultural supply/demand, trade, and production, and socioeconomic data, by country, 1950s-77, 1528–179

Background Notes, summary social, political, and economic data, 1984 rpt, 7006–2.49

Economic conditions in Communist and OECD countries, 1982, annual rpt, 7144–11

Economic indicators of 12 Pacific Basin countries or areas and US, quarterly rpt, 9393–9

Economic, social, and political summary data, by country, 1984, annual factbook, 244–11

Exports and imports of OECD countries, by country, 1983, annual rpt, 7144–10

Exports of US, detailed Schedule B commodities by country of destination, 1983, annual rpt, 2424–9

Exports of US, detailed Schedule E commodities by mode of transport and world area and country of destination, 1983, annual rpts, 2424–5

Imports of US, detailed Schedule A commodities by country and world area of origin, and mode of transport, 1983, annual rpts, 2424–2

Imports of US, detailed TSUSA commodities by country of origin, 1983, annual rpt, 2424–4

Kiwifruit exports of New Zealand, by country of destination, 1977-83, article, 1925–34.410

Lamb meat from New Zealand, injury to US industry from foreign subsidized products and sales at less than fair value, investigation with selected financial and operating data, 1984 rpt, 9886–19.10

Loans and grants for economic and military assistance from US and intl agencies, by program and country, FY46-83, annual rpt, 9914–5

Military aid of US, arms sales, and training programs costs and budget requests by program, world region, and country, FY83-85, annual rpt, 7144–13

Military spending, arms trade, and armed forces size, with total govt spending and population, by country, 1972-82, annual rpt, 9824–1

Minerals Yearbook, 1982, Vol 3: foreign country reviews of production, trade, and policies, by commodity, annual rpt, 5604–35

Minerals Yearbook, 1982, Vol 3 preprints: foreign country review of production, trade, and policies, by commodity, annual rpt, 5604–17.53

Population size and growth rates, and latest available benchmark demographic data, by country, 1950-83, biennial rpt, 2324–4

R&D Fed Govt funding for foreign performers, by world region and country, FY82-84, annual rpt, 9627–20.2

see also under By Foreign Country in the "Index by Categories"

Newark, N.J.

Air pollution levels for 28 volatile organic compounds in NYC and New Jersey, by site and urban-rural location, 1979-June 1981, 9198–108

Census of Housing, 1980: occupancy and unit characteristics, by race, Hispanic origin, and city, SMSA rpt, 2473–1.261

Census of Population and Housing, 1980: detailed population and housing characteristics, by county, city, and census tract, SMSA rpt, 2551–2.261

Dress industry production and related workers, wages, and benefits, by occupation, size of establishment, and union status, for 11 labor market areas, Aug 1982 survey, 6787–6.200

Fruit and vegetable shipments, and arrivals in 23 US and 5 Canada cities, by mode of transport and State or country of origin, 1983, annual rpt, 1311–4.1

Housing and households detailed characteristics, and unit and neighborhood quality, by inside-outside central cities, 1981 survey, SMSA rpt, 2485–6.31

Public works capital needs and intergovtl financing, by type of project and selected city, various periods 1950-83, 10048–60

Repair technicians and apprentices wages and benefits, for 5 types of electrical repair shops in 19 SMSAs, Nov 1981 survey, 6787–6.197

Wages of office and plant workers, by occupation, 1984 SMSA survey rpt, 6785–11.2

see also under By City and By SMSA or MSA in the "Index by Categories"

Newark, Ohio

Census of Housing, 1980: occupancy and unit characteristics, by race, Hispanic origin, and city, SMSA rpt, 2473–1.262

Newspapers

Census of Population and Housing, 1980: detailed population and housing characteristics, by county, city, and census tract, SMSA rpt, 2551–2.262

Newburgh, N.Y.

Census of Housing, 1980: occupancy and unit characteristics, by race, Hispanic origin, and city, SMSA rpt, 2473–1.263

Census of Population and Housing, 1980: detailed population and housing characteristics, by county, city, and census tract, SMSA rpt, 2551–2.263

Wages by occupation, and benefits for office and plant workers, 1983 SMSA survey rpt, 6785–12.2

Newman, Jeanne S.

"Women of the World: Sub-Saharan Africa", 2326–15.2

Newport News, Va.

Census of Housing, 1980: occupancy and unit characteristics, by race, Hispanic origin, and city, SMSA rpt, 2473–1.264

Census of Population and Housing, 1980: detailed population and housing characteristics, by county, city, and census tract, SMSA rpt, 2551–2.264

Housing and financial characteristics, and unit and neighborhood quality, for 15 SMSAs, 1978, annual survey special supplement, 2485–8

see also under By City and By SMSA or MSA in the "Index by Categories"

Newspapers

Bombing (explosive and incendiary) incidents, damage, injuries, and deaths, by target, State, and circumstances, 1983, annual rpt, 6224–5

Census of Population, 1980: detailed socioeconomic and demographic characteristics, by age, sex, race, Hispanic origin, occupation, and industry, State rpt series, 2531–4

County Business Patterns: establishments, employees, and payrolls, by SIC 4-digit industry and county, 1981, annual State rpt series, 2326–8

County Business Patterns: establishments, employees, and payrolls, by SIC 4-digit industry and county, 1982, annual State rpt series, 2326–6

Employment, earnings, and hours, by selected SIC 1- to 4-digit industry, State, and for 278 major labor areas, 1939-83, annual rpt, 6744–5

Employment, earnings, and hours, by SIC 4-digit nonfarm industry, monthly 1974-Feb 1984, annual update, 6744–4

Exports and imports of US, detailed SIC-based commodities by world area, 1983, annual rpts, 2424–6

Exports and imports of US, totals and as percent of domestic production, by SIC 2- to 5-digit commodity, 1981, annual rpt, 2424–3

Exports, imports, tariffs, and industry operating data for books, magazines, newspapers, and other printed matter, foreign and US, 1978-82, TSUSA commodity rpt, 9885–2.28

Exports of US, detailed commodities by country of destination, monthly rpt, 2422–3

Exports of US, detailed Schedule B commodities by country of destination, 1983, annual rpt, 2424–9

Newspapers

Exports of US, detailed Schedule E commodities by mode of transport and world area and country of destination, 1983, annual rpts, 2424–5

Food industry advertising expenditures by media type, and advertising to sales ratio by selected food item, 1970-79 with some trends from 1955, 1548–234

Imports of US, detailed Schedule A commodities by country, monthly rpt, 2422–2

Imports of US, detailed TSUSA commodities by country of origin, 1983, annual rpt, 2424–4

Income tax returns of corporations, detailed income and tax items by industry, 1981, annual rpt, 8304–4

Income tax returns of sole proprietorships, detailed data by industry div and selected industry group, 1981, annual rpt, 8304–7

Income tax returns of sole proprietorships, receipts, deductions by type, payroll, and net income, by major industry, 1982, annual article, 8302–2.413

Input-output structure of US economy, detailed interindustry transactions for 537 industries, and components of final demand, 1977 benchmark data, 2708–17

Manufacturing census, 1982: financial and operating data, by SIC 2- to 4-digit industry, State, SMSA, and county, preliminary census div rpt series, 2491–3

Manufacturing census, 1982: financial and operating data, for SIC 4-digit industries by product, preliminary rpt, 2491–1.158

Minority group and women employment, by occupational group and SIC 2- to 3-digit industry, 1981, annual rpt, 9244–1.1

Occupational injury and illness rates, by SIC 2- to 4-digit industry, 1982, annual rpt, 6844–1

Producer prices and indexes, by stage of processing and detailed commodity, monthly rpt, 6762–6

Producer prices and indexes, by stage of processing and detailed commodity, monthly 1983, annual supplement, 6764–2

see also Freedom of the press

see also Journalism

Niagara Falls, N.Y.

see also under By SMSA or MSA in the "Index by Categories"

Nicaragua

Agricultural and food production indexes, and production of selected commodities, by world region and country, 1974-83, annual rpt, 1524–5

Agricultural situation in Latin America, by country, 1981-83 and outlook for 1984, annual rpt, 1524–4.9

Agricultural supply/demand, trade, and production, and socioeconomic data, by country, 1950s-77, 1528–179

AID economic assistance to developing countries, obligations and disbursements by country, quarterly rpt, 9912–4

AID economic assistance to 7 Central American countries, by type of aid, FY80-83, GAO rpt, 26123–55

AID loan repayment status and terms by program and country, and status of predecessor agency loans, quarterly rpt, 9912–3

Index by Subjects and Names

Economic, social, and political conditions in 6 Central America countries, 1960s-83 with trends and projections 1930-2010, 028–19

Economic, social, and political summary data, by country, 1984, annual factbook, 244–11

Economic trends in income, production, prices, employment, finances, and trade, 1984 annual rpt, 2046–4.14

Exports of US, detailed Schedule B commodities by country of destination, 1983, annual rpt, 2424–9

Exports of US, detailed Schedule E commodities by mode of transport and world area and country of destination, 1983, annual rpts, 2424–5

Imports of US, detailed Schedule A commodities by country and world area of origin, and mode of transport, 1983, annual rpts, 2424–2

Imports of US, detailed TSUSA commodities by country of origin, 1983, annual rpt, 2424–4

Loans and grants for economic and military assistance from US and intl agencies, by program and country, FY46-83, annual rpt, 9914–5

Military spending, arms trade, and armed forces size, with total govt spending and population, by country, 1972-82, annual rpt, 9824–1

Minerals Yearbook, 1982, Vol 3: foreign country reviews of production, trade, and policies, by commodity, annual rpt, 5604–35

Minerals Yearbook, 1982, Vol 3 preprints: foreign country review of production, trade, and policies, by commodity, annual rpt, 5604–17.86

Natural resources and hazards to resource dev, with data on mineral, energy, and water resources, by Central American country, 1981 with trends from 1977, 5668–71

Population size and growth rates, and latest available benchmark demographic data, by country, 1950-83, biennial rpt, 2324–4

Refugees from Central America by country of origin and asylum, and aid from US and Mexico, FY82-1984, GAO rpt, 26123–70

see also under By Foreign Country in the "Index by Categories"

Nicholson, William J.

"Occupational Exposure to Asbestos: Population at Risk and Projected Mortality, 1980-2030", 21408–72

Nickel

see Metals and metal industries

Niger

Agricultural and food production indexes, and production of selected commodities, by world region and country, 1974-83, annual rpt, 1524–5

Agricultural situation in sub-Saharan Africa, by country, 1982-83 and outlook for 1984, annual rpt, 1524–4.10

Agricultural supply/demand, trade, and production, and socioeconomic data, by country, 1950s-77, 1528–179

AID activities and funding by project and function, FY85, and developing countries summary socioeconomic data, 1970s-83, by country, annual rpt, 9914–3

AID economic assistance to developing countries, obligations and disbursements by country, quarterly rpt, 9912–4

AID loan repayment status and terms by program and country, and status of predecessor agency loans, quarterly rpt, 9912–3

Economic conditions and foreign marketing prospects in 46 Sub-Saharan countries, 1983 world region rpt, 2046–5.1

Economic, social, and political summary data, by country, 1984, annual factbook, 244–11

Exports of US, detailed Schedule B commodities by country of destination, 1983, annual rpt, 2424–9

Exports of US, detailed Schedule E commodities by mode of transport and world area and country of destination, 1983, annual rpts, 2424–5

Imports of US, detailed Schedule A commodities by country and world area of origin, and mode of transport, 1983, annual rpts, 2424–2

Imports of US, detailed TSUSA commodities by country of origin, 1983, annual rpt, 2424–4

Loans and grants for economic and military assistance from US and intl agencies, by program and country, FY46-83, annual rpt, 9914–5

Military aid of US, arms sales, and training programs costs and budget requests by program, world region, and country, FY83-85, annual rpt, 7144–13

Military spending, arms trade, and armed forces size, with total govt spending and population, by country, 1972-82, annual rpt, 9824–1

Minerals Yearbook, 1982, Vol 3: foreign country reviews of production, trade, and policies, by commodity, annual rpt, 5604–35

Minerals Yearbook, 1982, Vol 3 preprints: foreign country review of production, trade, and policies, by commodity, annual rpt, 5604–17.84

Oil and gas undiscovered recoverable resources, cumulative production, and identified reserves, as of 1982, preliminary oil basin rpt, 5666–17.13

Population size and growth rates, and latest available benchmark demographic data, by country, 1950-83, biennial rpt, 2324–4

see also under By Foreign Country in the "Index by Categories"

Nigeria

Agricultural and food production indexes, and production of selected commodities, by world region and country, 1974-83, annual rpt, 1524–5

Agricultural exports of US to South Africa, Nigeria, and total sub-Saharan Africa, 1981-83, and forecast 1984, article, 1522–1.401

Agricultural situation in sub-Saharan Africa, by country, 1982-83 and outlook for 1984, annual rpt, 1524–4.10

Agricultural supply/demand, trade, and production, and socioeconomic data, by country, 1950s-77, 1528–179

AID economic assistance to developing countries, obligations and disbursements by country, quarterly rpt, 9912–4

Index by Subjects and Names

AID educational program activities and project impacts in 12 developing countries, 1950s-82, 9916–11.8

AID loan repayment status and terms by program and country, and status of predecessor agency loans, quarterly rpt, 9912–3

Background Notes, summary social, political, and economic data, 1984 rpt, 7006–2.60

Economic conditions and foreign marketing prospects in 46 Sub-Saharan countries, 1983 world region rpt, 2046–5.1

Economic conditions in Communist, OECD, and selected other countries, 1960s-83, annual rpt, 244–5

Economic, social, and political summary data, by country, 1984, annual factbook, 244–11

Economic trends in income, production, prices, employment, finances, and trade, 1984 semiannual rpt, 2046–4.89

Electric power systems equipment market and trade, and user industry operations and demand, 1984 country market research rpt, 2045–15.6

Exports and imports of US, by commodity and country, 1972-82, annual world region rpt, 244–13.4

Exports of US, detailed Schedule B commodities by country of destination, 1983, annual rpt, 2424–9

Exports of US, detailed Schedule E commodities by mode of transport and world area and country of destination, 1983, annual rpts, 2424–5

Food supply policies of 21 developing countries, with farm sector data, tariff income, and prices and imports of 5 grains, 1960s-81, 1528–168

Health care from native and Western systems by Nigerians in 3 tribes, by sociodemographic characteristics, 1984 article, 4102–1.417

Imports of US, detailed Schedule A commodities by country and world area of origin, and mode of transport, 1983, annual rpts, 2424–2

Imports of US, detailed TSUSA commodities by country of origin, 1983, annual rpt, 2424–4

Loans and grants for economic and military assistance from US and intl agencies, by program and country, FY46-83, annual rpt, 9914–5

Military aid of US, arms sales, and training programs costs and budget requests by program, world region, and country, FY83-85, annual rpt, 7144–13

Military spending, arms trade, and armed forces size, with total govt spending and population, by country, 1972-82, annual rpt, 9824–1

Minerals Yearbook, 1982, Vol 3: foreign country reviews of production, trade, and policies, by commodity, annual rpt, 5604–35

Minerals Yearbook, 1982, Vol 3 preprints: foreign country review of production, trade, and policies, by commodity, annual rpt, 5604–17.54

Oil and gas undiscovered recoverable resources, cumulative production, and identified reserves, as of 1982, preliminary oil basin rpt, 5666–17.13

Oil production, and exports and prices to US, by major exporting country, detailed data, monthly rpt, 3162–24

Population size and growth rates, and latest available benchmark demographic data, by country, 1950-83, biennial rpt, 2324–4

Telecommunication equipment market and trade, and user industry operations and demand, 1982 country market research rpt, 2045–12.35

see also under By Foreign Country in the "Index by Categories"

Nighswander, Thomas S.

"High Utilizers of Ambulatory Care Services: 6-Year Followup at Alaska Native Medical Center", 4102–1.440

NIH

see National Institutes of Health

Nilsen, Diane M.

"Employment in Durable Goods Anything but Durable in 1979-82", 6722–1.410

Nilsen, Peggy M.

"Nonmetro Areas Gain in New Housing Market", 1598–190

Nilsen, Sigurd R.

"Job Training Partnership Act, CETA, and Rural Communities", 1502–7.403

"Recessionary Impacts on the Unemployment of Men and Women", 6722–1.432

NIMH

see National Institute of Mental Health

Nitrocellulose

see Chemicals and chemical industry

Nitrogen

see Gases

Nitrogen oxides

see Air pollution

Nix, James E.

"World Outlook for Livestock and Poultry", 1004–16.1

Nixon, Scott W.

"Ecology of New England High Salt Marshes: A Community Profile", 5506–9.6

Nnadi, Eucharia E.

"Nigerians' Use of Native and Western Medicine for the Same Illness", 4102–1.417

NOAA

see National Oceanic and Atmospheric Administration

Nober, E. H.

"Waking Effectiveness of Household Smoke and Fire Detection Devices", 2218–70

Noise

Coal transport environmental impacts by type and mode of transport, methodology for assessing alternative systems, 1983 rpt, 3408–28

Environmental quality and protection programs, costs, and Fed Govt enforcement, 1983, detailed annual rpt, 484–1

Fed Govt programs and mgmt cost control proposals, 3-year savings by function and agency, and financial and operating data, 1960s-81, 16908–1.22

Foreign market and trade for pollution control instruments and equipment, and user industry operations and demand, country market research rpts, 2045–17

Neighborhood and housing quality indicators and attitudes, and occupant characteristics, by urban-rural location and region, 1981, annual survey, 2485–7

Nonmetallic minerals and mines

Neighborhood and housing quality indicators and attitudes, by occupant and unit characteristics, region, and metro-nonmetro location, 1981, annual survey, 2485–2

Neighborhood quality, indicators and attitudes by inside-outside central cities, 1979-82 surveys, SMSA rpt series, 2485–6

Smoke alarm sound levels by brand, and response time by circumstances and for older and mentally retarded persons, 1983 rpt, 2218–70

Nolting, Louvan E.

"Integration of Science and Technology in CEMA", 2326–9.7

Non-ferrous metals industry

see Aluminum and aluminum industry

see Copper and copper industry

see Lead and lead industry

see Metals and metal industries

see Tin and tin industry

see Zinc and zinc industry

Nonappropriated funds

Budget of US, CBO analysis of revenue and spending alternatives and projections of economic indicators, FY85-89, annual rpt, 26304–3

Fish and wildlife restoration program of Fed Govt, finances, funding by State, and hunting and fishing equipment excise tax revenue, FY84, annual rpt, 5504–13

Loans and loan guarantees of Fed Govt issued and outstanding, by agency, off-budget entity, or program, FY82, article, 9391–1.403

Postal Service pension and health benefits subsidized by Fed Govt trust funds, and subsidy reduction plans deficit impact, FY79-84 and projected to FY89, 26306–6.82

Statistical Abstract of US, social, political, and economic data, 1950s-83 and trends, annual rpt, 2324–1.2

Nonmetallic minerals and mines

Air pollutant and radiation indoor levels by emissions source, and household exposure and health effects by pollutant type, various periods 1966-83, hearings, 21708–102

Air pollutant emission factors, by detailed source, 3rd edition, 1983-84 supplements, 9198–13

Alaska minerals resources, production, claims on wildlife refuges, oil and gas leases, and exploratory wells, with maps and bibl, 1983, annual rpt, 5664–11

Central America mineral, energy, and water resources, and natural hazards to resource dev, by country, 1981 with trends from 1977, 5668–71

China economic conditions, agricultural and industrial production, trade, and domestic and foreign investment, 1980-85, 2048–106

Coastal environmental characteristics, fish, wildlife, and use, and population socioeconomic data, for individual areas, series, 5506–4

Collective bargaining agreements expiring during year, covered workers by SIC 2-digit industry, firm, and union, with summary of key provisions, 1984, annual rpt, 6784–9

Nonmetallic minerals and mines

County Business Patterns: establishments, employees, and payrolls, by SIC 4-digit industry and county, 1981, annual State rpt series, 2326–8

County Business Patterns: establishments, employees, and payrolls, by SIC 4-digit industry and county, 1982, annual State rpt series, 2326–6

DOE R&D projects and funding at natl labs, universities, and other instns, FY84, annual summary rpt, 3004–18.3

Earnings by major industry group, and personal income per capita and by source, by region and State, 1929-82, 2708–40

Employment by detailed occupation, for 29 SIC 2-digit nonmanufacturing industries, 1981 BLS survey, 6748–60

Employment, earnings, and hours, by selected SIC 1- to 4-digit industry, State, and for 278 major labor areas, 1939-83, annual rpt, 6744–5

Employment, earnings, and hours, by SIC 4-digit nonfarm industry, monthly 1974-Feb 1984, annual update, 6744–4

Energy use and cost for building materials manufacture, by energy source and industry, 1970s-82, article, 2012–1.401

Exports and imports of US, by commodity group, world area, selected country, US coastal area and port, and mode of transport, with seasonal adjustments, monthly rpt, 2422–9

Exports and imports of US, detailed SIC-based commodities by world area, 1983, annual rpts, 2424–6

Exports and imports of US, totals and as percent of domestic production, by SIC 2- to 5-digit commodity, 1981, annual rpt, 2424–3

Exports, imports, tariffs, and industry operating data for nonmetallic minerals and products, TSUSA commodity rpt series, 9885–5

Exports of US, detailed commodities by country of destination, monthly rpt, 2422–3

Exports of US, detailed Schedule B commodities by country of destination, 1983, annual rpt, 2424–9

Foreign minerals production, reserves, and industry role in domestic economy and world supply, country and world region rpt series, 5606–1

Geological Survey and other publications, 1983, annual listing, 5664–4

Great Lakes trade, by SITC 3-digit commodity, port, vessel type, world area, and country, 1982, annual rpt, 7744–3

Imports of US, detailed Schedule A commodities by country and world area of origin, and mode of transport, 1983, annual rpts, 2424–2

Imports of US, detailed Schedule A commodities by country, monthly rpt, 2422–2

Income tax returns of corporations, detailed income and tax items by industry, 1981, annual rpt, 8304–4

Income tax returns of corporations with foreign tax credit, income and deductions by type, asset size, and selected industry group, 1980, article, 8302–2.415

Income tax returns of partnerships, detailed data by industry, 1981 estimates, annual article, 8302–2.404

Income tax returns of sole proprietorships, detailed data by industry div and selected industry group, 1981, annual rpt, 8304–7

Income tax returns of sole proprietorships, receipts, deductions by type, payroll, and net income, by major industry, 1982, annual article, 8302–2.413

Input-output structure of US economy, detailed interindustry transactions for 537 industries, and components of final demand, 1977 benchmark data, 2708–17

Manufacturing census, 1982: financial and operating data, by SIC 2- to 4-digit industry, State, SMSA, and county, preliminary census div rpt series, 2491–3

Manufacturing census, 1982: financial and operating data, for SIC 4-digit industries by product, preliminary rpt series, 2491–1

Mergers of nonfuel minerals companies by SIC 1- to 4-digit industry of acquired and acquiring firm, and asset and earnings measures, various periods 1960-79, 5608–145

Mineral industries census, 1982: financial and operating data, by SIC 2- to 4-digit industry, preliminary summary rpt, 2511–2.1

Mineral industries census, 1982: financial and operating data, including materials consumed, by SIC 4-digit industry and State, preliminary rpt series, 2511–1

Mineral Industry Surveys, commodity reviews of production, trade, and consumption, advance annual rpt series, 5614–5

Mineral Industry Surveys, commodity reviews of production, trade, stocks, and consumption, monthly rpt series, 5612–1

Mineral Industry Surveys, commodity reviews of production, trade, stocks, and consumption, quarterly rpt series, 5612–2

Mineral Industry Surveys, explosives and blasting agents consumption by type, industry, and State, 1983, annual rpt, 5614–22

Mineral Industry Surveys, State reviews of production, 1983, advance annual rpt series, 5614–6

Minerals Yearbook, 1982, Vol 1: commodity reviews of production, reserves, supply, use, and trade, annual rpt, 5604–33

Minerals Yearbook, 1982, Vol 2 preprints: State reviews of production and sales by commodity, and business activity, annual rpt series, 5604–16

Minerals Yearbook, 1982, Vol 2: State reviews of production, sales, and firms, by commodity, and business activity, annual rpt, 5604–34

Minerals Yearbook, 1982, Vol 3: foreign country reviews of production, trade, and policies, by commodity, annual rpt, 5604–35

Minerals Yearbook, 1982, Vol 3 preprints: foreign country reviews of production, trade, and policies, by commodity, annual rpt series, 5604–17

Minerals Yearbook, 1983, Vol 1 preprints: commodity reviews of production, reserves, supply, use, and trade, annual rpt series, 5604–15

Minerals Yearbook, 1983, Vol 3 preprints: foreign country reviews of production, trade, and policies, by commodity, annual rpt series, 5604–23

Index by Subjects and Names

Minority group and women employment, by occupational group and SIC 2- to 3-digit industry, 1981, annual rpt, 9244–1.1

Occupational injury and illness rates, by SIC 2- to 4-digit industry, 1982, annual rpt, 6844–1

Phosphate rock industry environmental protection costs, by control type and selected State, with background operating data, 1977-81 with cost projections to 1990, 5608–143

Phosphate rock reserves in southeastern and northwestern US, by location, 1984 rpt, 5668–74

Potassium chloride from 4 countries, imports injury to US industry from foreign subsidized products, investigation with background financial and operating data, 1984 rpt, 9886–15.52

Producer prices and indexes, by stage of processing and detailed commodity, monthly rpt, 6762–6

Producer prices and indexes, by stage of processing and detailed commodity, monthly 1983, annual supplement, 6764–2

Production, prices, trade, use, employment, tariffs, and stockpiling, by mineral commodity, with foreign comparisons, 1979-83, annual rpt, 5604–18

Productivity, hours, and employment indexes for selected SIC 3- and 4-digit industries, 1954-82, annual rpt, 6824–1.2

Publications and other material of Mines Bur, 1982, annual listing, 5604–40

Publications and patents of Mines Bur, monthly listing, 5602–2

R&D expenditures of US firms foreign affiliates, by selected industry, 1974-82, 9626–2.131

Salt and sulfur from Fed Govt OCS leases, revenue by type, 1953-82, annual rpt, 5734–3

Tariff Schedules of US, Annotated, classifications and rates of duty for detailed imported commodities, 1985 edition, 9886–13

Waterborne commerce of US (domestic and foreign), freight by commodity, traffic, and passengers, by port and waterway, 1982, annual rpt, 3754–3

see also Cement and concrete

see also Clay industry and products

see also Coal and coal mining

see also Fertilizers

see also Gases

see also Gemstones

see also Mine accidents and safety

see also Natural gas and gas industry

see also Offshore mineral resources

see also Offshore oil and gas

see also Oil shale

see also Petroleum and petroleum industry

see also Quarries and stone products

see also Stockpiling

see also Strategic materials

see also Tar sands

see also under By Industry in the "Index by Categories"

Nonmetropolitan areas

see Rural areas

see under By Urban-Rural and Metro-Nonmetro in the "Index by Categories"

Index by Subjects and Names

Nonprofit organizations and foundations

Agricultural exports shipped by voluntary relief agencies under Fed Govt-financed programs, by commodity and country, bimonthly rpt, periodic tables, 1522–1.4

AID activities and funding by project and function, FY85, and developing countries summary socioeconomic data, 1970s-83, by country, annual rpt, 9914–3

AID loan repayment status and terms by program and country, and status of predecessor agency loans, quarterly rpt, 9912–3

Alcohol, Drug Abuse, and Mental Health Admin research grants, awards, and fellowships by recipient, FY83, annual listing, 4044–13

Allergy and Infectious Diseases Natl Inst activities, grants by instn, State, and country, and disease incidence and costs, FY60s-84, annual rpt, 4474–30

Census of Service Industries, 1982: employment, establishments, receipts, and payroll, by SIC 2- to 4-digit kind of business, SMSA, county, and city, State rpt series, 2391–1

Computer specialists sociodemographic, educational, and employment characteristics, and Fed Govt support by agency, 1978, biennial Current Population Rpt, 2546–2.124

County Business Patterns: establishments, employees, and payrolls, by SIC 4-digit industry and county, 1981, annual State rpt series, 2326–8

County Business Patterns: establishments, employees, and payrolls, by SIC 4-digit industry and county, 1982, annual State rpt series, 2326–6

Dental Research Natl Inst research and training funds awarded, by recipient instn, FY83, annual listing, 4474–19

Developing countries disaster preparedness and summary sociodemographic, political, and economic data, country rpt series, 9916–2

Disabled American Veterans financial statements, 1982, GAO rpt, 26111–16

DOD prime contract awards for R&D to educational and nonprofit instns and Federal agencies, by instn and location, FY83, annual listing, 3544–17

DOD procurement, prime contract awards by category, contract and contractor type, and service branch, FY74-1st half FY84, semiannual rpt, 3542–1

DOD procurement, prime contract awards for 25 commodity categories and R&D, by State and census div, FY81-83, annual rpt, 3544–11

DOD procurement, prime contractors for R&D, top 500 and value of contracts, FY83, annual listing, 3544–4

DOE procurement and assistance contracts, by State, contractor type, and top 100 instns, FY83, annual rpt, 3004–21

Engineers sociodemographic, educational, and employment characteristics, and Federal support by agency, 1978, Current Population Rpt, 2546–2.121

Fed Govt employees charity contributions to Combined Federal Campaign, funds by type of recipient, 1982 and trends from 1973, GAO rpt, 26119–66

Fed Govt financial and nonfinancial domestic aid, 1984 annual comprehensive catalog, 104–5

Fed Govt surplus personal property donations to State and local agencies and nonprofit instns, by region and State, FY83, annual rpt, 9454–22

Fed Govt tax litigation, prosecutions, interpretive law decisions, and operating expenses of IRS, with collections, refunds, and taxes due, by region and State, FY83, annual rpt, 8304–3

Foreign aid programs of private voluntary agencies, funding and expenditures, by agency, 1982/83, annual rpt, 9914–9

Foreign countries disasters, persons affected, deaths, damage, and aid by US and others, FY83 and trends from FY64, annual rpt, 9914–12

Homeless population and characteristics, and temporary shelter operations, use, and user characteristics, for selected cities, various periods 1979-84, hearing, 21248–85

Housing (low-income) energy aid of Fed Govt, allocations and average benefits in 13 States, and public interest group assessment, FY81-83, GAO rpt, 26121–75

Input-output structure of US economy, detailed interindustry transactions for 85 industries, and components of final demand, 1977, article, 2702–1.421

Legal fees awarded private parties in cases against Federal, State, and local govts, by case, selected years 1977-83, 6008–19

Mail subsidy for USPS revenue forgone, by class of mail, FY83, annual rpt, 9864–5.3

Mentally retarded and developmentally disabled treatment and services, university-affiliated facility funding, activities, and clients, 1980-FY83, 4608–19

NASA procurement contract awards, by type, contractor, State, and country, FY84, semiannual rpt, 9502–6

Natl Endowment for Arts activities and grants, FY83, annual rpt, 9564–3

Natl Endowment for Humanities activities and grants, FY83, annual rpt, 9564–2

Navy procurement, by contractor and location of work, FY83, annual rpt, 3804–13

NIH extramural grant and contract awards for research, R&D, and construction, FY72-83, annual rpt, 4434–9

Occupational injury and illness rates, by SIC 2- to 4-digit industry, 1982, annual rpt, 6844–1

Philanthropic foundations assets and grants for 50 largest foundations, and for selected foundations by recipient, selected years 1975-82, hearings, 21788–137

Philanthropic foundations detailed financial and operating data, and stock holdings by instn, 1979 with selected trends from 1920, GAO rpt, 26119–53

Philanthropic foundations employment and earnings by organization type, and compared to other nonprofit organizations, selected years 1972-82, article, 6722–1.455

PL 480 exports by commodity, and recipients, by program, sponsor, and country, FY82 and aggregate from FY55, annual rpt, 1924–7

Norfolk, Va.

Political action committee funding to reelect and defeat House and Senate members by candidate, and FEC activities and funding, 1983, annual rpt, 9274–1

Population and health research funded by 4 private organizations, project listing by topic, with funding data, 1981, annual rpt, 4474–16

R&D and science-related Fed Govt funding to higher education and nonprofit instns, by field, instn, agency, and State, FY82, annual rpt, 9627–17

R&D Fed Govt funding, by agency and performer, FY83-84, 9626–2.132

R&D Fed Govt funding by type of performer, and funding for industrial dev by type, program, and agency, selected years FY75-85, 26306–6.81

R&D Fed Govt funding for all performers, by field and supporting agency, selected years FY60-84, annual rpt, 9627–20

Refugee and alien arrivals and resettlements in US, by State, outlying area, country of birth and citizenship, age, sex, and sponsoring agency, monthly rpt, 4702–3

Refugee resettlement program activities and funding, arrivals and population by country of origin and State, and employment and other characteristics, FY83, annual rpt, 4704–8

Runaway and other homeless youth programs, funding by source, activities, and participant characteristics, FY82, annual rpt, 4604–3

Science and engineering doctoral degree recipients, by field, sex, race, age, citizenship, postgrad employment and study status, State, and instn, 1960-82, 9626–6.16

Science and engineering grads of 1980-81, employment characteristics or grad enrollment, by degree level, field, sex, and race, 1982, 9627–25

Scientists and engineers in R&D, salaries by degree, type of establishment, age, experience, and field, 1984, annual rpt, 3004–1

Scientists and engineers in R&D, salary comparisons for DOE labs and non-DOE facilities, Aug 1982-Feb 1984, annual rpt, 3004–9

Statistical Abstract of US, social, political, and economic data, 1950s-83 and trends, annual rpt, 2324–1.1, 2324–1.2

Vietnam Veterans Memorial Fund receipts by source, and disbursements by item and payee, Apr 1979-Mar 1984, GAO rpt, 26111–21

Norfolk, Va.

Census of Housing, 1980: occupancy and unit characteristics, by race, Hispanic origin, and city, SMSA rpt, 2473–1.265

Census of Population and Housing, 1980: detailed population and housing characteristics, by county, city, and census tract, SMSA rpt, 2551–2.265

Port impact on local employment through transport of 5 commodities, by industry for 3 eastern ports, and demand for US coal by country, 1981, 7308–182

Wages of office and plant workers, by occupation, 1984 SMSA survey rpt, 6785–11.5

Waterborne commerce of US (domestic and foreign), freight by commodity, traffic, and passengers, by port and waterway, 1982, annual rpt, 3754–3.1

Norfolk, Va.

see also under By City and By SMSA or MSA in the "Index by Categories"

Normal, Ill.

Census of Housing, 1980: occupancy and unit characteristics, by race, Hispanic origin, and city, SMSA rpt, 2473–1.96

Census of Population and Housing, 1980: detailed population and housing characteristics, by county, city, and census tract, SMSA rpt, 2551–2.96

Housing vacancy rates for single and multifamily units and mobile homes, by county, city, and ZIP code, 1983, annual metro area rpt, 9304–18.2

see also under By SMSA or MSA in the "Index by Categories"

Norman, H. D.

"National Cooperative Dairy Herd Improvement Program Participation Report: State Activities as of Jan. 1, 1984", 1702–2.402

Normile, Mary A.

"Canada's Grain Handling and Transportation System", 1528–176

North America

- Agricultural exports and imports of US, by detailed commodity and country, FY83 and CY83, semiannual rpts, 1522–4
- Agricultural situation in North America and Oceania, by country and commodity, 1983 and outlook for 1984, annual rpt, 1524–4.1
- Agricultural trade of US, by commodity and country, bimonthly rpt with articles, 1522–1
- Carbon dioxide emissions from fossil fuel combustion, and growth rates, by country and country group, 1950-80, 3006–7.6
- China economic conditions, agricultural and industrial production, trade, and domestic and foreign investment, 1980-85, 2048–106
- Electric power transactions of US with Canada and Mexico, by utility and US region, 1983, annual rpt, 3104–10
- Export sales and shipments of US grains, oilseed products, hides, skins, and cotton, by country, weekly rpt, 1922–3
- Exports and imports of US (airborne), by world area and US customs district and city, monthly rpt, 2422–8
- Exports and imports of US (waterborne), by type of service, customs district, port, and world area, monthly rpt, 2422–7
- Exports and imports of US, by commodity group, world area, selected country, US coastal area and port, and mode of transport, with seasonal adjustments, monthly rpt, 2422–9
- Exports and imports of US, detailed SIC-based commodities by world area, 1983, annual rpts, 2424–6
- Exports of US, detailed Schedule E commodities by mode of transport and world area and country of destination, 1983, annual rpts, 2424–5
- Great Lakes trade, by SITC 3-digit commodity, port, vessel type, world area, and country, 1982, annual rpt, 7744–3
- Immigrant and nonimmigrant visas of US issued and refused, and status adjustments, by class and nationality, FY77, annual rpt, 7184–1
- Imports of US, detailed Schedule A commodities by country and world area of origin, and mode of transport, 1983, annual rpts, 2424–2

Military, social, and economic summary data, by world area and country, 1960s-80s, hearing, 25388–47.1

- Military spending, arms trade, and armed forces size, with total govt spending and population, by country, 1972-82, annual rpt, 9824–1
- Population size and growth rates, and latest available benchmark demographic data, by country, 1950-83, biennial rpt, 2324–4
- Precipitation and temperature outlook for US and Northern Hemisphere, and by US and selected foreign weather stations, semimonthly rpt, 2182–1
- Terrorist (intl) incidents, casualties, and attacks on US targets, by attack type and world area, with chronology of events, 1983, annual rpt, 7004–13
- Tidal current tables, daily time and velocity by station for North America and Asia coasts, 1985, annual rpt, 2174–1
- Tide height and time daily at worldwide coastal points, 1985 predictions, annual rpt, 2174–2.1, 2174–2.2
- Travel to and from US on US and foreign flag air carriers, by country, world area, and US port, monthly rpt, 7302–2
- Travel to US and receipts by world area and selected country, 1960-83, and US Travel and Tourism Admin activities, 1983, annual rpt, 2904–6
- USIA info center and reading room operations, by world region, country, and city, FY83, annual rpt, 9854–4

see also Canada

see also Caribbean area

see also Greenland

see also Gulf of Mexico

see also Mexico

see also under By Foreign Country in the "Index by Categories"

North Atlantic Treaty Organization

- DOD budget, organization, personnel, weapons, and property, by service branch, State, and country, 1984 annual summary rpt, 3504–13
- DOD military personnel of US on active duty, by service branch, outlying area, and country, monthly rpt, 3542–14.5
- DOD supply inventory mgmt of for agencies, NATO, and foreign govts, 1970s-83, annual rpt, 21204–1
- Economic conditions in Communist and OECD countries, 1982, annual rpt, 7144–11
- Exports and imports of NATO countries with Council for Mutual Economic Assistance Europe members, by country, 1980-83, annual rpt, 7144–5
- Exports and imports of NATO countries with PRC, by country, 1980-83, annual rpt, 7144–14
- Exports and imports of OECD countries, by country, 1983, annual rpt, 7144–10
- GNP and GNP growth of each OECD member country, 1973-83, annual rpt, 7144–8
- Helsinki Final Act implementation by NATO, Warsaw Pact, and other signatory nations, Dec 1983-Mar 1984, semiannual rpt, 7002–1
- Military commitment of US to NATO, Europe force strengths by service branch and costs by component, FY82 with trends from FY75, GAO rpt, 26123–71

Index by Subjects and Names

- Military expenditures of NATO, by country, selected years 1971-82, hearing, 21388–42
- Military personnel of US abroad, by service branch, world area, and country, quarterly news release, 3542–9
- Military personnel of US on duty overseas, by country, FY83, annual rpt, 3544–1.2
- Military, social, and economic summary data, by world area and country, 1960s-80s, hearing, 25388–47.1
- Military spending, arms trade, and armed forces size, with total govt spending and population, by country, 1972-82, annual rpt, 9824–1
- Military weapons and troop strength of US and NATO compared to USSR and Warsaw Pact, as of Jan 1984, annual rpt, 3564–1
- Military weapons of USSR, Warsaw Pact, and NATO/Japan, with US funding of NATO, selected years 1974-83, annual rpt, 3544–2
- Military weapons systems of USSR and Warsaw Pact, assistance and presence worldwide, and force strengths, with selected US and NATO comparisons, as of 1984, 3508–14
- Nuclear missile deployment and arms control effort of NATO, USSR propaganda response and USSR and NATO nuclear arms in place, 1977-83, narrative rpt, 9828–25
- Space satellites and other objects launched since 1957, quarterly listing, 9502–2

North Carolina

- Agriculture census, 1982: farms, farmland, production and costs, and operator characteristics, preliminary State summary and county rpts, 2330–1.37
- Agriculture census, 1982: farms, farmland, production, finances, and operator characteristics, by county, final State rpt, 2331–1.33
- Albemarle Sound environmental characteristics and mgmt, with related socioeconomic data, 1960s-82 with trends from 1913, 5506–7.1
- Alcohol fuel (ethanol) production in Tennessee Valley, feedstocks, facilities, tax incentives, and related farming data, by State, 1970s-83 and projected to 1992, 9808–69
- Bank deposits in commercial and mutual savings banks and in US branches of foreign banks, by account type, instn, State, SMSA, and county, June 1983, annual rpt, 9295–3.7
- Bank income and expenses, Fed Reserve 5th District member banks, by State, 1983, annual rpt, 9389–10
- Biomass Fuels Program of TVA, technologies and processes dev, costs, and resource requirements, 1970s-90s, series, 9806–9
- Census of Housing, 1980: occupancy and unit characteristics of SMSAs and central cities, by race, Hispanic origin, and city, State rpt, 2473–1.35
- Census of Population and Housing, 1980: detailed population and housing characteristics, by county, city, and census tract, State rpt, 2551–2.35
- Census of Population, 1980: detailed socioeconomic and demographic characteristics, by age, sex, race, Hispanic origin, and industry, State rpt, 2531–4.35

Index by Subjects and Names

North Central States

Cherokee Indians Eastern Band of North Carolina, financial and operating data for Bur of Indian Affairs assistance programs, FY83, annual rpt, 5704–4

Coastal environmental and wildlife characteristics, use, and mgmt, for individual ecosystems, 1970s-83, 5506–9.1

Collective bargaining calendar for Southeast US, 1984, annual rpt, 6946–1.68

County Business Patterns: establishments, employees, and payrolls, by SIC 4-digit industry and county, 1982, annual State rpt, 2326–6.35

Crop insurance participation and operations in 2 States by crop, and Fed Crop Insurance Corp finances, 1980-84, GAO rpt, 26113–132

Dress industry production and related workers, wages, and benefits, by occupation, size of establishment, and union status, for 11 labor market areas, Aug 1982 survey, 6787–6.200

Economic indicators by State, Fed Reserve 5th District, quarterly rpt, 9389–16

Employment (nonagricultural) by industry div and SMSA, earnings, and hours, for 8 southeastern States, monthly press release, 6942–7

Employment and unemployment by SMSA and major industry group, and export-related employment share, for North Carolina, various periods 1967-83, article, 9371–1.410

Employment, earnings, and hours, by selected SIC 1- to 4-digit industry, State, and for 278 major labor areas, 1939-83, annual rpt, 6744–5.2, 6744–5.3

Employment, prices, earnings, and union membership in 8 southeastern States, Oct 1982-83, annual rpt, 6944–2

Environmental quality, pollutant discharge by type and source, and EPA protection activities and funding, 1970s-83, biennial regional rpt, 9184–15.4

Exports of manufactured and agricultural commodities, manufacturing production, and export-related employment, 1960s-82, State rpt, 2046–3.33

Fish and shellfish landings, prices, and cannery production, for Gulf States and North Carolina, by area, weekly rpt, 2162–6.3

HHS aid to each State and local govt or private instn, amount obligated, funding agency, and program, FY83, annual listing, 4004–3.4

Income (personal) per capita and by source, and earnings by industry div, by State, MSA, and county, 1977-82, annual regional rpt, 2704–2.6

Manufacturing census, 1982: financial and operating data, by SIC 2- to 4-digit industry, State, SMSA, and county, preliminary census div rpt, 2491–3.5

Mineral Industry Surveys, phosphate rock production, sales, exports, and use, 1984 crop year, annual rpt, 5614–20

Mineral Industry Surveys, State review of production, 1983, advance annual rpt, 5614–6.33

Minerals Yearbook, 1982, Vol 2 preprints: State review of production and sales by commodity, and business activity, annual rpt, 5604 16.34

Minerals Yearbook, 1982, Vol 2: State reviews of production, sales, and firms, by commodity, and business activity, annual rpt, 5604–34

Peach production, marketing, and prices in 4 Southeastern States and Appalachia, 1983, annual rpt, 1311–12

Phosphate rock reserves in southeastern and northwestern US, by location, 1984 rpt, 5668–74

Population, births, deaths, and net migration, by MSA and county, 1980-82, annual State Current Population Rpt, 2546–4.33

Population size, Apr 1980 and July 1982, and per capita income, 1979 and 1981, by county and city, State Current Population Rpt, 2546–11.33

Retail trade census, 1982: employment, establishments, sales, and payroll, by SIC 2- to 4-digit kind of business, SMSA, county, and city, State rpt, 2397–1.34

Savings and loan assns, FHLB 4th District insured members financial condition and operations, by SMSA, monthly rpt, 9302–1

Seat belt use by race and sex, results of North Carolina projects to increase use, 1981-84, article, 7762–9.408

Textile mill employment and average hours and earnings, for 8 Southeastern States, monthly press release, 6942–1

Timber acreage and resources in North Carolina, by species, ownership class, and county, 1982-83, series, 1206–4

Water supply and quality in streams and lakes, and groundwater levels in wells, by drainage basin, 1983, annual State rpt, 5666–10.32

Water supply and quality in 8 southeastern States, with background socioeconomic data, 1960s-2020 with trends from 1930, 9208–119

Water supply and use in 3 areas with supply problems and total US, and methods to increase supply, selected years 1974-80 and projected to 2010, 9208–125

Wholesale trade census, 1982: employment, establishments, finances, and operations, by SIC 2- to 4-digit kind of business, SMSA, county, and city, State rpt, 2405–1.34

see also Asheville, N.C.
see also Burlington, N.C.
see also Charlotte, N.C.
see also Concord, N.C.
see also Durham, N.C.
see also Fayetteville, N.C.
see also Gastonia, N.C.
see also Greensboro, N.C.
see also Hickory, N.C.
see also High Point, N.C.
see also Jacksonville, N.C.
see also Raleigh, N.C.
see also Salisbury, N.C.
see also Wilmington, N.C.
see also Winston-Salem, N.C.
see also under By State in the "Index by Categories"

North Central States

Air pollutant sulfur dioxide emissions of coal-fired power plants in eastern US, effect of alternative geographic area limits on power and coal industries, 1983 rpt, 3408–32

Army Corps of Engineers activities and projects, FY83 and trends from 1800s, annual rpt, 3754–1

Bridges over navigable waters, with type of bridge and use, owner, dimensions, and location, 1984 regional listing, 7406–5.2, 7406–5.3

Census of Population, 1980: detailed socioeconomic and demographic characteristics, by age, sex, race, Hispanic origin, occupation, and industry, US summary rpt, 2531–4.1

Economic indicators, Fed Reserve 7th District monthly rpt, 9375–9

Economic issues affecting North Central States, Fed Reserve 7th District, working paper series, 9375–13

Electric and gas privately owned utilities, wages and employment by occupation, and benefits, by region, Oct 1982 survey, 6787–6.205

Environmental quality, pollutant discharge by type and source, and EPA protection activities and funding, 1970s-83, biennial regional rpt, 9184–15.5, 9184–15.7, 9184–15.8

Farm credit conditions and economic devs, Fed Reserve 7th District, biweekly rpt, 9375–10

Farm credit conditions, earnings, and expenditures, Fed Reserve 9th District, quarterly rpt, 9383–11

Farm investments, effective rates of Federal/State income and State/local property taxes, by category of structure and equipment, for 7 North Central States, 1981-82, 1548–237

Farm production inputs, outputs, and productivity, by region, 1939-82, annual rpt, 1544–17

Financial and economic devs, Fed Reserve Bank of Chicago bimonthly rpt articles, 9375–1

Financial and economic devs, Fed Reserve Bank of Cleveland quarterly rpt articles, 9377–1

Financial and economic devs, Fed Reserve Bank of Minneapolis quarterly rpt articles, 9383–6

Forest biomass in Northeast and North Central regions, green weight by biomass component and State, 1981, 1208–207

Fruit and vegetable shipments, and arrivals in 23 US and 5 Canada cities, by mode of transport and State or country of origin, 1983, annual rpt, 1311–4.1, 1311–4.2

Govt census, 1982: city govt revenues by source, expenditures by function, debt, and assets, by State and city, 2457–4

Govt revenue and expenditures, surplus/deficit, and tax capacity and effort indexes, for US and 7 western States, selected years 1967-82, article, 9381–1.403

Grain mill production workers, wages, hours, and benefits, by occupation, mill product, and region, June 1982 survey, 6787–6.204

HHS aid to each State and local govt or private instn, amount obligated, funding agency, and program, FY83, annual listing, 4004–3

Hog and pig inventory, value, farrowings, and farms, by State, quarterly release, 1623–3

North Central States

Hog production, producer characteristics, facilities, and marketing, by type and size of enterprise and region, 1975 and 1980, 1568–248

Housing and neighborhood quality indicators and attitudes, and occupant characteristics, by urban-rural location and region, 1981, annual survey, 2485–7.2

Housing and neighborhood quality indicators and attitudes, by occupant and unit characteristics, region, and metro-nonmetro location, 1981, annual survey, 2485–2

Housing census, 1980: inventory, occupancy, and unit characteristics, changes from 1973 by region and inside-outside SMSAs and central cities, series, 2473–3

Housing occupancy and unit and household characteristics, by region and metro-nonmetro residence, 1983, biennial survey, 2485–1

Housing vacancy rates for single and multifamily units and mobile homes in FHLB 10th District, by ZIP code, annual metro area rpt series, 9304–22

Income (personal) by industry group and region, percent change 1959-79 and 1979-83, article, 2702–1.443

Income (personal) per capita and by source, and earnings by industry div, by State, MSA, and county, 1977-82, annual regional rpt, 2704–2.4, 2704–2.5

Income (personal) per capita and by source, earnings by major industry group, and social insurance contributions, by region and State, 1929-82, 2708–40

Iron and steel production workers and wages by occupation, and benefits, by region, Aug 1983 survey, 6787–6.206

IRS tax collections by type of tax, procedures, and interest forgone through processing delay, for selected locations, FY81-82, GAO rpt, 26119–55

Manufacturing activity diffusion indexes, Fed Reserve 4th District 10-year summary charts, monthly rpt, 9377–4

Manufacturing census, 1982: financial and operating data, by SIC 2- to 4-digit industry, State, SMSA, and county, preliminary census div rpt, 2491–3.3, 2491–3.4

Natural gas residential use related to weather, fuels consumed by purpose, and energy share from wood, by North Central State, various periods 1979-83, article, 3162–4.402

Oil and gas extraction production workers, wages, hours, and benefits, by occupation, region, and for 5 States, June 1982 survey, 6787–6.203

Pulpwood production by county, imports, and individual mill capacity, by species for 7 North Central States, 1982, annual rpt, 1204–19

Savings and loan assns, FHLB 6th District insured members financial condition and operations by State, monthly rpt, 9302–11

Savings and loan assns, FHLB 6th District insured members financial condition and operations by State, quarterly rpt, 9302–23

Savings and loan assns, FHLB 7th District insured members cost of funds, and savings flows and mortgage loans closed by SMSA, monthly rpt, 9302–5

Savings and loan assns, FHLB 8th District members financial operations by State and SMSA, monthly rpt, 9302–9

Savings and loan assns, FHLB 8th District members, locations, assets, and savings, 1984, annual listing, 9304–9

Savings and loan assns, FHLB 10th District insured members finances and operations by SMSA, monthly rpt, 9302–22

Timber removals and mill receipts and production, by species, product type, and county, series, 1206–10

Water supply and quality, and effect of coal mining operations, for selected river basins in Eastern and Interior coal provinces, series, 5666–15

Water supply and quality, and effect of coal mining operations, for selected river basins in Western coal provinces, series, 5666–19

Waterborne commerce of US (domestic and foreign), freight by commodity, traffic, and passengers, by port and waterway, 1982, annual rpt, 3754–3.2, 3754–3.3 *see also* under By Region in the "Index by Categories"

see also under names of individual States

North Charleston, S.C.

Census of Housing, 1980: occupancy and unit characteristics, by race, Hispanic origin, and city, SMSA rpt, 2473–1.114

Census of Population and Housing, 1980: detailed population and housing characteristics, by county, city, and census tract, SMSA rpt, 2551–2.114

Wages of office and plant workers, by occupation, 1984 labor market area survey rpt, 6785–3.7

North Dakota

Agricultural cooperatives, membership, activities, and finances, by commodity and selected State, 1900-80 with trends from 1863, 1128–30

Agriculture census, 1982: farms, farmland, production and costs, and operator characteristics, preliminary State summary and county rpts, 2330–1.38

Agriculture census, 1982: farms, farmland, production, finances, and operator characteristics, by county, final State rpt, 2331–1.34

Bank deposits in commercial and mutual savings banks and in US branches of foreign banks, by account type, instn, State, SMSA, and county, June 1983, annual rpt, 9295–3.15

Census of Housing, 1980: occupancy and unit characteristics of SMSAs and central cities, by race, Hispanic origin, and city, State rpt, 2473–1.36

Census of Population, 1980: detailed socioeconomic and demographic characteristics, by age, sex, race, Hispanic origin, and industry, State rpt, 2531–4.36

Coal Fed Govt leases, acreage, production, and prices, by State, and legal and mgmt issues, 1970s-83 with production projections to 2000, 11128–1

Coal production in Montana and North Dakota impact of mining on agricultural land availability and on farm income and production costs, by mining tract, 1982 rpt, 1588–79

County Business Patterns: establishments, employees, and payrolls, by SIC 4-digit industry and county, 1982, annual State rpt, 2326–6.36

Index by Subjects and Names

Employment, earnings, and hours, by selected SIC 1- to 4-digit industry, State, and for 278 major labor areas, 1939-83, annual rpt, 6744–5.2, 6744–5.3

Environmental quality, pollutant discharge by type and source, and EPA protection activities and funding, 1970s-83, biennial regional rpt, 9184–15.8

Exports of manufactured and agricultural commodities, manufacturing production, and export-related employment, 1960s-82, State rpt, 2046–3.34

Farm investments, effective rates of Federal/State income and State/local property taxes, by category of structure and equipment, for 7 North Central States, 1981-82, 1548–237

HHS aid to each State and local govt or private instn, amount obligated, funding agency, and program, FY83, annual listing, 4004–3.8

Income (personal) per capita and by source, and earnings by industry div, by State, MSA, and county, 1977-82, annual regional rpt, 2704–2.5

Manufacturing census, 1982: financial and operating data, by SIC 2- to 4-digit industry, State, SMSA, and county, preliminary census div rpt, 2491–3.4

Mineral Industry Surveys, State review of production, 1983, advance annual rpt, 5614–6.34

Minerals Yearbook, 1982, Vol 2 preprints: State review of production and sales by commodity, and business activity, annual rpt, 5604–16.35

Minerals Yearbook, 1982, Vol 2: State reviews of production, sales, and firms, by commodity, and business activity, annual rpt, 5604–34

Population size and components of change, by MSA and county, 1980-82, annual State Current Population Rpt, 2546–4.34

Population size, Apr 1980 and July 1982, and per capita income, 1979 and 1981, by county and city, State Current Population Rpt, 2546–11.34

Retail trade census, 1982: employment, establishments, sales, and payroll, by SIC 2- to 4-digit kind of business, SMSA, county, and city, State rpt, 2397–1.35

Savings and loan assns, FHLB 8th District members financial operations by State and SMSA, monthly rpt, 9302–9

Service industry census, 1982: employment, establishments, receipts, and payroll, by SIC 2- to 4-digit kind of business, SMSA, county, and city, State rpt, 2391–1.35

Wages for 3 occupational groups, relative average levels in 78 labor market areas, 1983, annual press release, 6785–13

Wages of office and plant workers, by occupation, 1984 labor market area survey rpt, 6785–3.9

Wholesale trade census, 1982: employment, establishments, finances, and operations, by SIC 2- to 4-digit kind of business, SMSA, county, and city, State rpt, 2405–1.35

see also Bismarck, N.Dak.

see also Fargo, N.Dak.

see also Grand Forks, N.Dak.

see also under By State in the "Index by Categories"

Index by Subjects and Names

North Little Rock, Ark.

Census of Housing, 1980: occupancy and unit characteristics, by race, Hispanic origin, and city, SMSA rpt, 2473–1.222

Census of Population and Housing, 1980: detailed population and housing characteristics, by county, city, and census tract, SMSA rpt, 2551–2.222

Wages by occupation, and benefits for office and plant workers, 1984 labor market area survey rpt, 6785–3.8

Northeast States

- Air pollutant sulfur dioxide emissions of coal-fired power plants in eastern US, effect of alternative geographic area limits on power and coal industries, 1983 rpt, 3408–32
- Air pollutant sulfur dioxide emissions reduction proposal, effects on polluting industries and coal production by region and State, projected to 2010, 9188–97 Army Corps of Engineers activities and projects, FY83 and trends from 1800s, annual rpt, 3754–1
- Banks and thrift instns in New England, financial statements by type of instn and State, 1972 and 1982, annual rpt, 9304–3
- Bridges over navigable waters, with type of bridge and use, owner, dimensions, and location, 1984 regional listing, 7406–5.1
- Budget of US, Northeast Corridor rail passenger service funding, effects of Reagan Admin policy changes, FY85, annual rpt, 104–21
- Census of Population, 1980: detailed socioeconomic and demographic characteristics, by age, sex, race, Hispanic origin, occupation, and industry, US summary rpt, 2531–4.1
- Coastal environmental and wildlife characteristics, use, and mgmt, for individual ecosystems, series, 5506–9
- College grads in New England States, employment prospects, 1984, annual narrative rpt, 6916–7.3
- Economic indicators for New England States, Fed Reserve 1st District, monthly rpt with articles, 9373–2
- Electric and gas privately owned utilities, wages and employment by occupation, and benefits, by region, Oct 1982 survey, 6787–6.205
- Employment and price conditions for New England States, series, 6916–7
- Environmental quality, pollutant discharge by type and source, and EPA protection activities and funding, 1970s-83, biennial regional rpt, 9184–15.1
- Environmental quality, pollutant levels, and EPA control activities summary, for New England States, annual rpt, discontinued, 9184–6
- Farm production inputs, outputs, and productivity, by region, 1939-82, annual rpt, 1544–17
- Financial and economic devs, Fed Reserve Bank of Boston bimonthly rpt articles, 9373–1
- Fish and shellfish landings and prices at Boston and other New England ports, and total New England cold storage holdings, weekly rpt, 2162–6.2
- Fish and shellfish landings, life cycles, and environmental needs, for selected species by region, with glossary and bibl, series, 5506–8

Fish landings, employment, gear used, and seafood production, for detailed species by State, 1977, annual rpt, 2164–2.2

- Fishing (ocean sport and commercial) landings and allowable and potential catch of US and Canada, for 34 species in North Atlantic, 1983, annual rpt, 2164–14
- Forest biomass in Northeast and North Central regions, green weight by biomass component and State, 1981, 1208–207
- Forest land owner characteristics in Northeast States, owners and acreage, series, 1206–7
- Fruit and vegetable shipments, and arrivals in 23 US and 5 Canada cities, by mode of transport and State or country of origin, 1983, annual rpt, 1311–4.1
- Govt census, 1982: city govt revenues by source, expenditures by function, debt, and assets, by State and city, 2457–4
- Grain mill production workers, wages, hours, and benefits, by occupation, mill product, and region, June 1982 survey, 6787–6.204
- HHS aid to each State and local govt or private instn, amount obligated, funding agency, and program, FY83, annual listing, 4004–3
- Housing and neighborhood quality indicators and attitudes, and occupant characteristics, by urban-rural location and region, 1981, annual survey, 2485–7.2
- Housing and neighborhood quality indicators and attitudes, by occupant and unit characteristics, region, and metro-nonmetro location, 1981, annual survey, 2485–2
- Housing census, 1980: inventory, occupancy, and unit characteristics, changes from 1973 by region and inside-outside SMSAs and central cities, series, 2473–3
- Housing occupancy and unit and household characteristics, by region and metro-nonmetro residence, 1983, biennial survey, 2485–1
- Income (personal) by industry group and region, percent change 1959-79 and 1979-83, article, 2702–1.443
- Income (personal) per capita and by source, and earnings by industry div, by State, MSA, and county, 1977-82, annual regional rpt, 2704–2.2
- Income (personal) per capita and by source, earnings by major industry group, and social insurance contributions, by region and State, 1929-82, 2708–40
- Iron and steel production workers and wages by occupation, and benefits, by region, Aug 1983 survey, 6787–6.206
- IRS tax collections by type of tax, procedures, and interest forgone through processing delay, for selected locations, FY81-82, GAO rpt, 26119–55
- Mail (1st class), performance ratings for stamped and metered overnight mail in NYC and Northeast US, FY82-83, annual rpt, 9864–5.2
- Pulpwood production and yield per acre, for 14 northeastern States, by county, 1981, TVA technical paper, 9806–2.38
- Radioactive waste generation, by northeast State and reactor and nonreactor source, 1979-81 and projected to 2000, hearing, 25528–93

Northern Mariana Islands

- Railroad improvement project for Northeast Corridor, goals, funding, and progress, and Amtrak finances and operations, FY83, annual rpt, 7604–9
- Savings and loan assns, FHLB 1st District member instns financial operations and related economic and housing indicators, monthly rpt, 9302–4
- Savings bank deposits by type, and commercial banks share of savings in depository instns, by New England State, various dates 1970-83, hearing, 21248–83
- Savings instns, FHLB 1st District members, locations, and financial condition, 1984, annual listing, 9304–26
- Shipbuilding costs and related employment, by coastal district, 1982, annual rpt, 7704–12
- Small business perceived burden of Fed Govt paperwork requirements, and burden for 4 Fed Govt agencies, FY83, 9768–14
- Tide height and time daily at worldwide coastal points, 1985 predictions, annual rpt, 2174–2.2
- Timber growth, removals, products output, and forest ownership and industries in Northeast States, State rpt series, 1206–16
- Timber resources and removals in Northeast States, by species, ownership class, and county, State rpt series, 1206–12
- Water quality and pH of northeast lakes, monitoring results and forecast models, as of 1983, 5506–5.15
- Water supply in Northeastern US, precipitation and stream runoff by station, monthly rpt, 2182–3
- Waterborne commerce of US (domestic and foreign), freight by commodity, traffic, and passengers, by port and waterway, 1982, annual rpt, 3754–3.1
- *see also* Appalachia
- *see also* under By Region in the "Index by Categories"
- *see also* under names of individual States

Northern Mariana Islands

- Govt financial data, audits of Interior Dept Inspector General, FY83, annual rpt, 5304–15.1
- Medical referrals (off-island) of TTPI and American Samoa, costs, and potential savings, by govt, FY83 with comparisons from FY78, GAO rpt, 26123–72
- Population size and components of change, by outlying area, 1970-82, Current Population Rpt, 2546–3.127
- Population size and components of change, by outlying area, 1980-83, Current Population Rpt, 2546–3.134
- Population size and growth rates, and latest available benchmark demographic data, by country, 1950-83, biennial rpt, 2324–4
- Population socioeconomic, health, and govtl data, by TTPI govt, FY82 and selected trends, detailed annual rpt, 7004–6
- Port dev costs and financing through user fees, and shipping industry impact on local economy, by State, other area, industry, commodity, and port, 1970s-82, hearings, 21568–34.1
- Supplemental Security Income and other income maintenance program benefits and beneficiaries, by State, monthly rpt, 4742 2

Northern Mariana Islands

Supplemental Security Income benefits and beneficiaries, by type of eligibility, State, and county, Dec 1983, annual rpt, 4744–27

Supplemental Security Income payments and beneficiaries by State and for Northern Mariana Islands, monthly rpt, 4742–1.4

Supplemental Security Income payments, and recipients by other income source, eligibility type, and other characteristics, by State, 1982, annual rpt, 4744–16

Water supply and quality in streams and lakes, and groundwater levels in wells, by drainage basin, 1983, annual State rpt, 5666–10.10

see also under By Foreign Country in the "Index by Categories"

Norton Shores, Mich.

Census of Housing, 1980: occupancy and unit characteristics, by race, Hispanic origin, and city, SMSA rpt, 2473–1.250

Census of Population and Housing, 1980: detailed population and housing characteristics, by county, city, and census tract, SMSA rpt, 2551–2.250

Norwalk, Conn.

Census of Housing, 1980: occupancy and unit characteristics, by race, Hispanic origin, and city, SMSA rpt, 2473–1.267

Census of Population and Housing, 1980: detailed population and housing characteristics, by county, city, and census tract, SMSA rpt, 2551–2.267

see also under By SMSA or MSA in the "Index by Categories"

Norway

Agricultural and food production indexes, and production of selected commodities, by world region and country, 1974-83, annual rpt, 1524–5

Agricultural imports of 3 countries, by commodity and country of origin, 1981-FY84, article, 1925–34.431

Agricultural situation in Western Europe, by country and commodity, 1983 and outlook for 1984, annual rpt, 1524–4.6

Agricultural supply/demand, trade, and production, and socioeconomic data, by country, 1950s-77, 1528–179

AID loan repayment status and terms by program and country, and status of predecessor agency loans, quarterly rpt, 9912–3

Background Notes, summary social, political, and economic data, 1984 rpt, 7006–2.25

Economic, social, and political summary data, by country, 1984, annual factbook, 244–11

Economic trends in income, production, prices, employment, finances, and trade, 1984 semiannual rpt, 2046–4.90

Exports and imports of NATO countries with Council for Mutual Economic Assistance Europe members, by country, 1980-83, annual rpt, 7144–5

Exports and imports of NATO countries with PRC, by country, 1980-83, annual rpt, 7144–14

Exports and imports of OECD countries, by country, 1983, annual rpt, 7144–10

Exports and imports of US with Western Europe, and US market share and export opportunities for selected commodities, by country, 1982-84, 2048–105

Exports of US, detailed Schedule B commodities by country of destination, 1983, annual rpt, 2424–9

Exports of US, detailed Schedule E commodities by mode of transport and world area and country of destination, 1983, annual rpts, 2424–5

Imports of US, detailed Schedule A commodities by country and world area of origin, and mode of transport, 1983, annual rpts, 2424–2

Imports of US, detailed TSUSA commodities by country of origin, 1983, annual rpt, 2424–4

Lab instruments market and trade, and user industry operations and demand, 1983 country market research rpt, 2045–10.16

Loans and grants for economic and military assistance from US and intl agencies, by program and country, FY46-83, annual rpt, 9914–5

Manufacturing labor productivity and cost indexes for US and 11 OECD countries, 1960-82, annual article, 6722–1.405

Manufacturing productivity and unit labor cost indexes for US and 11 countries, 1950-82 and preliminary 1983, annual rpt, 6864–1

Military aid of US, arms sales, and training programs costs and budget requests by program, world region, and country, FY83-85, annual rpt, 7144–13

Military spending, arms trade, and armed forces size, with total govt spending and population, by country, 1972-82, annual rpt, 9824–1

Minerals Yearbook, 1982, Vol 3: foreign country reviews of production, trade, and policies, by commodity, annual rpt, 5604–35

Minerals Yearbook, 1983, Vol 3 preprints: foreign country review of production, trade, and policies, by commodity, annual rpt, 5604–23.55

Oil and gas undiscovered recoverable resources, cumulative production, and identified reserves, as of 1982, preliminary oil basin rpt, 5666–17.15

Population size and growth rates, and latest available benchmark demographic data, by country, 1950-83, biennial rpt, 2324–4

Ships in world merchant fleet, and tonnage, by country of registry, 1982, annual rpt, 7704–3.1

see also under By Foreign Country in the "Index by Categories"

Norwich, Conn.

Census of Housing, 1980: occupancy and unit characteristics, by race, Hispanic origin, and city, SMSA rpt, 2473–1.258

Census of Population and Housing, 1980: detailed population and housing characteristics, by county, city, and census tract, SMSA rpt, 2551–2.258

see also under By SMSA or MSA in the "Index by Categories"

Norwood, Janet L.

"Jobs and Prices in a Recovering Economy", 6728–28

Nose and throat disorders

see also under By Disease in the "Index by Categories"

Index by Subjects and Names

Notifiable diseases

see Infective and parasitic diseases

Notions

see Clothing and clothing industry

NOW accounts

see Negotiable orders of withdrawal accounts

NSA

see National Security Agency

NSF

see National Science Foundation

Nuclear explosives and explosions

Housing (earth-sheltered) design, energy efficiency, natural and nuclear hazard reduction, and costs, by selected SMSA, 1983 rpt, 3308–71

Radiation from 1940s-70s nuclear weapons tests, levels in air and water, and personnel exposure by military unit and job category, series, 3906–1

Strontium-90 fallout, monitoring results for 67 sites worldwide, quarterly 1976-82 with trends from 1958, annual rpt, 3404–12

Strontium-90 in NYC and San Francisco diet by food item, and in NYC tap water and milk, quarterly 1982 with trends from 1954, annual rpt, 3404–13

see also Nuclear weapons

Nuclear fallout

see Fallout shelters

see Nuclear explosives and explosions

see Nuclear radiation

Nuclear industries

see Nuclear power

Nuclear power

Budget of US, effects of Reagan Admin policy changes, by detailed program, FY85, annual rpt, 104–21

Census of Population, 1980: detailed socioeconomic and demographic characteristics, by age, sex, race, Hispanic origin, occupation, and industry, State rpt series, 2531–4

Communist, OECD, and selected other countries energy reserves, production, and consumption, and oil trade and revenue, 1960s-83, annual rpt, 244–5.5

Consumption, by fuel type, economic sector, and end use, 1983 and 2000, 2006–2.5

Consumption, by fuel type, economic sector, census div, and State, 1960-82, State Energy Data System annual rpt, 3164–39

Consumption per capita, and by economic sector, State, and major energy resource, 1960-82, State Energy Data System annual supplement, 3164–55

Electric power peak demand, generating and interregional transfer capability, and reserve margins, detailed data by region, 1984-93, annual rpt, 3404–6

Electric utilities privately owned, common stock performance measures for companies with and without nuclear facilities, 1963-82, 3168–88

Electric utilities privately owned, detailed financial and operating data by company, with summary data for other distributors by type, 1982, annual rpt, 3164–23

Electric utilities production, plant capacity, and fuel use, by prime mover, census div, and State, 1979-83, annual rpt, 3164–11.1

Electric utility fuel cost, quality, use, receipts, and stocks, and power plant production, by energy source, State and utility, quarterly rpt, 3162–39

Index by Subjects and Names

Electric utility production, fuel consumption, stocks, and costs by fuel type, and sales, by State, monthly rpt, 3162–35

Electrical systems of nuclear power plants, errors in operation and maintenance by circumstance, plant type, and system, 1977-81, 9638–51

Employment in nongovt nuclear industries by industry segment, occupation, and census div, with DOE and NRC nuclear employment, 1968-83, biennial rpt, 3004–11

Energy producers finances and operations, by energy type for US firms domestic and foreign operations, 1974-82, annual rpt, 3164–44

Engineering student enrollments and degrees granted, by State, instn, and subfield, 1983, annual rpt, 3004–5

Environmental quality and protection programs, costs, and Fed Govt enforcement, 1983, detailed annual rpt, 484–1

Exports of equipment with nuclear weapons applications, approvals for shipment to PRC by item and to other foreign markets, July 1981-June 1982, GAO rpt, 26123–76

Fed Govt energy programs proposed budget appropriations, by office or dept and function, FY84-85, annual rpt, 3004–14

Foreign and US energy production, by energy type and country, 1973-83, annual rpt, 3164–50.1, 3164–50.2

Foreign and US nuclear power generation, by non-Communist country, monthly rpt, 242–5

Foreign and US nuclear power plant construction and operation status, and capacity, by plant, region, State, and selected country, 1983 and projected to 2020, annual rpt, 3164–57

Foreign military, social, and economic summary data by world area and country, 1960s-80s, hearing, 25388–47.1

Insurance against nuclear power accidents under Price-Anderson Act, effects on industry finances and operations, with insurance coverage, claims, and costs, various periods 1957-82, 9638–49

Natl Energy Policy Plan, DOE implementation and effect on energy supply/demand, 1983-84, annual rpt, 3024–4

Natl Energy Policy Plan, energy supply, demand, and prices, by fuel and consuming sector, projected 1985-2010, biennial rpt, 3004–13

Nuclear power and weapons policy, fuel supply/demand, waste disposal and siting, environmental effects of radiation, and public attitudes, 1970s-82 with projections to 2000, 3008–88

Nuclear power industry status and outlook, with reactor construction, utility financial and operating data, and foreign comparisons, 1970s-83 with projections to 2010, 26358–99

Prices and expenditures for fuels, by consuming sector, State, and fuel type, 1970-81, annual rpt, 3164–64

Production, reserves, and prices, by fuel type, and selected indicators of energy use, by State, 1982-83 with selected comparisons from 1971, annual rpt, 3164–60

Production, trade, supply, use, conservation, and DOE activities, by energy type, FY83, annual rpt, 3024–2

R&D industry funding and employment of scientists and engineers, by industry group, firm size, and funding source, 1956-82, annual rpt, 9627–21

Regulatory activities, employment, and finances of NRC, and operations of individual power plants by State, FY83, annual rpt, 9634–2

Research publications on energy of DOE and other sources, monthly listing, 3002–2

Safety and emergency technical advisors effectiveness in nuclear power plants, 1983 survey, 9638–55

Safety standards and research, design, licensing, construction, operation, and finances, for nuclear power plants with data by reactor, bimonthly rpt, 3352–4

Science and engineering doctoral degree recipients, by field, sex, race, age, citizenship, postgrad employment and study status, State, and instn, 1960-82, 9626–6.16

Scientists and engineers employed in energy-related fields, supply/demand and effects of R&D funding, by energy type, employer type, field, and age, 1962-91, annual rpt, 3004–19

Scientists and engineers in nuclear-related industry, by field and sector, 1981 and 1983, 3006–8.2

Supply/demand and price forecasts, by fuel type, quarterly rpt, 3162–34

Supply/demand and prices, by energy resource and major producing and consuming country and sector, detailed data, monthly rpt, 3162–24

Supply/demand and prices, by energy source and end-use sector and for 7 electric utilities, 1981-2000 with trends from 1960s, 3008–93

Supply/demand and prices, by fuel type and consuming sector with foreign comparisons, 1949-83, annual rpt, 3164–74

Supply/demand and prices, by fuel type, sector, and end use, detailed trends and projections 1973-95, annual rpt, 3164–75

Supply/demand and prices, by fuel type, sector, and end use, with foreign comparisons, 1960-83 and projected to 1995, annual summary rpt, 3164–76

Transportation and related energy use, for urban areas, late 1970s-82 and projected under lower auto emission standards to 1995, 3408–31

TVA activities, financial and operating data by program and facility, and power sales by customer, FY83, annual rpt, 9804–1

Washington Public Power Supply System nuclear reactors construction financing, with regional economic impacts and power supply/demand, 1980s-2035, hearing, 21448–29

see also Nuclear explosives and explosions
see also Nuclear-powered ships
see also Nuclear radiation
see also Nuclear weapons
see also Power-generating plants and equipment
see also Radioactive waste

Nuclear radiation

see also Uranium

Nuclear-powered ships

Budget of DOD for weapons systems, FY85 requests consistency with US policy and specified treaties, with funding FY83-87, annual rpt, 21384–4

Budget of DOD, itemized account of legislative history, FY84, annual rpt, 3504–7

Budget of DOD, justification, programs, and policies, FY85, annual rpt, 3544–2

Procurement cost estimates for weapons and communications systems, by service branch, quarterly summary rpt, 3502–1

Reactors for domestic use and export by function, with owner, operating characteristics, and location, Apr 1984, semiannual listing, 3002–5

Soviet Union and Warsaw Pact military weapons systems, assistance and presence worldwide, and force strengths, with selected US and NATO comparisons, as of 1984, 3508–14

Nuclear radiation

Atomic Energy Commission and Manhattan Project former research and storage sites, radioactive concentrations, test results series, 3406–1

Clinch River Breeder Reactor proposed site and nearby area, radiation levels in river water and sediment and ground water, 1983, annual rpt, 9804–24

Control program activities, State and local expenditures, personnel, and NRC licenses, by State, FY80- 82, annual rpt, 4064–3

DOE and contractor facility accidents, deaths, illnesses, radiation exposure, and property damage, by facility, 1982, annual rpt, 3004–24

Environmental quality and protection programs, costs, and Fed Govt enforcement, 1983, detailed annual rpt, 484–1

Environmental quality, pollutant discharge by type and source, and EPA protection activities and funding, 1970s-83, biennial regional rpt series, 9184–15

Exposure at DOE-contractor nuclear facilities and for surrounding population, and pollutant releases by type, by site, 1982, annual rpt, 3004–23

Exposure to radiation at DOE and DOE-contractor sites, by facility type and contractor, 1982, annual rpt, 3404–1

Exposure to radiation from 1940s-70s nuclear weapons test by military unit and job category, and levels in air and water, series, 3906–1

FDA investigation and regulatory activities, quarterly rpt, 4062–3

Fed Emergency Mgmt Agency nuclear attack civil defense plans, funding and operations by component, FY81-84 and projected FY85-89, GAO rpt, 26123–61

Great Lakes radioactivity discharges by source, and concentrations in environment, various periods 1963-82, annual rpt, 14644–1.2

Health physics and radiation protection enrollments and degrees granted by State and instn, and grads employment, 1983, annual rpt, 3004–7

Idaho Natl Engineering Lab radiation monitoring results, for 4 onsite facilities and nearby areas, 1983, annual rpt, 3354–10

Nuclear radiation

Indoor air pollutant and radiation levels by emissions source, and household exposure and health effects by pollutant type, various periods 1966-83, hearings, 21708–102

Insurance against nuclear power accidents under Price-Anderson Act, effects on industry finances and operations, with insurance coverage, claims, and costs, various periods 1957-82, 9638–49

Monitoring of radiation and radionuclide concentrations in air, water, and milk, results of EPA and other programs, by State and site, quarterly rpt, 9232–2

Nevada and other nuclear test sites, radionuclide concentrations in nearby air, water, and biota and in milk from western States, by location, 1983, annual rpt, 9234–4

Nevada nuclear test site, radionuclide concentrations in nearby cattle and wildlife, 1957-81, last issue of annual rpt, 9234–5

Nuclear power and weapons policy, fuel supply/demand, waste disposal and siting, environmental effects of radiation, and public attitudes, 1970s-82 with projections to 2000, 3008–88

Nuclear power plant fuel assembly performance and failures, by fuel vendor for US and some foreign reactors, 1982, annual rpt, 9634–8

Nuclear power plant operating and safety data, by plant, 1981, annual rpt, 9634–6

Nuclear power plant radioactive waste, releases and waste composition by plant, 1981, annual rpt, 9634–1

Nuclear power plant safety standards and research, design, licensing, construction, operation, and finances, with data by reactor, bimonthly rpt, 3352–4

Nuclear power plant siting population criteria and estimated compliance of selected regions and sites, 1983 rpt, 9638–54

Nuclear power plants waste and spent fuel generation, inventory, disposal by site, reprocessing, and characteristics, by source, as of 1983 and projected to 2020, annual rpt, 3364–2

Occupational exposure to radiation at individual commercial nuclear power plants, 1969-82, annual rpt, 9634–3

Occupational health risks from hazardous substances and radiation, by industry, occupation, age, and sex, with bibl and glossary, 1920s-82, 9638–50

R&D Fed Govt facilities and services available for private sector use, by field of science, 1984 biennial listing, 2224–4

Radiation from electronic devices, incidents and persons involved by type of device and FDA control program activities, 1983, annual rpt, 4064–13

Regulatory activities, employment, and finances of NRC, and operations of individual power plants by State, FY83, annual rpt, 9634–2

Strontium-90 fallout, monitoring results for 67 sites worldwide, quarterly 1976-82 with trends from 1958, annual rpt, 3404–12

Strontium-90 in NYC and San Francisco diet by food item, and in NYC tap water and milk, quarterly 1982 with trends from 1954, annual rpt, 3404–13

Transport of radioactive materials, surveillance program activities and results, State survey rpt series, 9636–1

Water supply and quality in streams and lakes, and groundwater levels in wells, by drainage basin, 1980, annual State rpt series, 5666–12

Water supply and quality in streams and lakes, and groundwater levels in wells, by drainage basin, 1981, annual State rpt series, 5666–16

Water supply and quality in streams and lakes, and groundwater levels in wells, by drainage basin, 1982, annual State rpt series, 5666–20

Water supply and quality in streams and lakes, and groundwater levels in wells, by drainage basin, 1983, annual State rpt series, 5666–10

see also Electromagnetic radiation

see also Nuclear explosives and explosions

see also Radioactive materials

see also Radioactive waste

see also Radiology

see also Uranium

Nuclear Regulatory Commission

Activities, employment, and finances of NRC, and operations of individual power plants by State, FY83, annual rpt, 9634–2

Budget appropriations, personnel, and workloads, by program, FY83-85, annual rpt, 9634–9

Budget of US Appendix, detailed budgets and personnel summaries, by agency, FY85, annual rpt, 104–3

Budget of US, appropriations, outlays, balances, and budget receipts, by govtl branch and agency, FY83, annual rpt, 8104–2

Cost control proposals for Fed Govt programs and mgmt, 3-year savings by function and agency, and financial and operating data, 1960s-81, 16908–1.4

Electric power plant (nuclear and coal-fired) construction itemized cost estimates, and investment per kilowatt for 20 cities, 1980s-95, 9638–52

Electric power plants (nuclear) fuel assembly performance and failures, by fuel vendor for US and some foreign reactors, 1982, annual rpt, 9634–8

Electric power plants (nuclear), operating and safety data, by plant, 1981, annual rpt, 9634–6

Employment in nuclear energy, 1981-83, biennial rpt, 3004–11.2

Insurance against nuclear power accidents under Price-Anderson Act, effects on industry finances and operations, with insurance coverage, claims, and costs, various periods 1957-82, 9638–49

Nuclear fuel facilities inventory discrepancies, 2nd half 1983, semiannual rpt, 9632–3

Nuclear industry nongovt employment by industry segment, occupation, and census div, and DOE and NRC nuclear employment, 1968-83, biennial rpt, 3004–11

Nuclear power plant electrical systems, errors in operation and maintenance by circumstance, plant type, and system, 1977-81, 9638–51

Index by Subjects and Names

Nuclear power plant licensing actions and status, by action type and plant, monthly rpt, 9632–5

Nuclear power plant licensing 24-month delay, effect on utility financial performance and electric power prices, for plant completed May 1979, 9638–53

Nuclear power plant safety and emergencies, effectiveness of technical advisors, 1983 survey, 9638–55

Nuclear power plant siting population criteria and estimated compliance of selected regions and sites, 1983 rpt, 9638–54

Nuclear reactor operating and inspection data for individual commercial facilities, monthly rpt, 9632–1

Occupational health risks from hazardous substances and radiation, by industry, occupation, age, and sex, with bibl and glossary, 1920s-82, 9638–50

R&D Fed Govt funding for all performers, by field and supporting agency, selected years FY60-84, annual rpt, 9627–20

Radiation control program activities, State and local expenditures, personnel, and NRC licenses, by State, FY80-82, annual rpt, 4064–3

Radiation occupational exposure at individual commercial nuclear power plants, 1969-82, annual rpt, 9634–3

Radioactive waste from nuclear power plants, releases and waste composition by plant, 1981, annual rpt, 9634–1

Transport of radioactive materials, surveillance program activities and results, State survey rpt series, 9636–1

Nuclear weapons

Budget of US, effects of Reagan Admin policy changes, by detailed program, FY85, annual rpt, 104–21

DOD budget, costs of individual weapons or weapons systems, FY83-85, annual rpt, 3504–2

DOD budget, itemized account of legislative history, FY84, annual rpt, 3504–7

DOD budget justification for R&D programs, and acquisition mgmt, FY83-85, annual rpt, 3504–6

DOD budget justification, programs, and policies, FY85, annual rpt, 3544–2

DOD procurement cost estimates for weapons and communications systems, by service branch, quarterly summary rpt, 3502–1

Employment in nuclear industry by industry segment, occupation, and census div, and DOE and NRC nuclear employment, 1968-83, biennial rpt, 3004–11.1

Energy production, trade, supply, use, conservation, and DOE activities, by energy type, FY83, annual rpt, 3024–2

Exports of equipment with nuclear weapons applications, approvals for shipment to PRC by item and to other foreign markets, July 1981-June 1982, GAO rpt, 26123–76

Foreign military, social, and economic summary data by world area and country, 1960s-80s, hearing, 25388–47.1

NATO and US weapons and troop strength compared to Warsaw Pact and USSR, as of Jan 1984, annual rpt, 3564–1

Nuclear power and weapons policy, fuel supply/demand, waste disposal and siting,

Index by Subjects and Names

Nursing homes

environmental effects of radiation, and public attitudes, 1970s-82 with projections to 2000, 3008–88

Nuclear reactors for domestic use and export by function, with owner, operating characteristics, and location, Apr 1984, semiannual listing, 3002–5

Radioactive wastes from DOE defense facilities, interim storage inventories by site and permanent disposal plan costs, 1982 with projections to 2015, 3358–32

Soviet Union and US nuclear weapon under Strategic Arms Reduction Talks and alternative proposals and counting methods, by weapon and system, FY84-96, 26306–6.73

Soviet Union and Warsaw Pact military weapons systems, assistance and presence worldwide, and force strengths, with selected US and NATO comparisons, as of 1984, 3508–14

Soviet Union propaganda campaign against NATO nuclear missile deployment, and USSR and NATO nuclear arms and aircraft in place, 1977-83, narrative rpt, 9828–25

Spent fuel and radioactive waste generation, inventory, disposal by site, reprocessing, and characteristics, by source, as of 1983 and projected to 2020, annual rpt, 3364–2

Statistical Abstract of US, social, political, and economic data, 1950s-83 and trends, annual rpt, 2324–1.2

Tests in 1940s-70s, radiation levels in air and water, and personnel exposure by military unit and job category, series, 3906–1

Treaties on arms control status, and Arms Control and Disarmament Agency activities, 1983, annual rpt, 9824–2

see also Missiles and rockets

see also Nuclear explosives and explosions

see also Strategic Arms Limitation Treaties

see also Strategic Arms Reduction Talks

Numismatics

see Coins and coinage

Nursery products

see Flowers and nursery products

Nurses and nursing

Census of Population, 1980: detailed socioeconomic and demographic characteristics, by age, sex, race, Hispanic origin, occupation, and industry, State rpt series, 2531–4

Census of Population, 1980: labor force, by sex, detailed occupation, and region, with comparison to 1970 census, supplementary rpt, 2535–1.12

Connecticut nurses smoking habits and attitudes on quitting and setting example for others, 1981 with comparisons to nurses nationwide in 1975, article, 4102–1.403

County and City Data Book, detailed socioeconomic and demographic data for States, counties, and cities, selected years 1976-82, 2328–1

DOD medical personnel, trainees, and accessions by source, by occupation, specialty, and service branch, FY83, annual rpt, 3544–24

Employment and population of registered nurses by age and education, and nursing program admissions and grads, projected 1981-90, article, 4102–1.439

Employment in hospitals and nursing homes, total and in selected occupations, by facility bed size, ownership, region, and State, selected years 1969-80, 4147–14.30

Employment of full- and part-time registered and licensed practical nurses in nursing homes, by region, State, and facility characteristics, 1980, 4147–14.29

Foreign and US health care resources, use, and per capita public expenditures, and selected population characteristics, for 7 countries, selected years 1975-81, 21148–33

Health care services of selected medical practitioners, use by patient characteristics, 1980 survey with trends from 1963, 4146–12.4

Health condition and health care resources, use, and expenditures, 1970s-82 with trends and projections 1900-2000, annual compilation, 4144–11

HHS aid to each State and local govt or private instn, amount obligated, funding agency, and program, FY83, annual listing, 4004–3

Hospital employment, vacancies, and vacancy rates, by occupation and by hospital specialty, region, census div, and State, 1980, annual rpt, 4114–12

Hospital nursing cost measurement, by nursing task and patient diagnosis classification, 1973-82, article, 4652–1.427

Income tax returns of sole proprietorships, detailed data by industry div and selected industry group, 1981, annual rpt, 8304–7

Income tax returns of sole proprietorships, receipts, deductions by type, payroll, and net income, by major industry, 1982, annual article, 8302–2.413

Manpower supply and education of health professionals, by occupation, demographic and professional characteristics, and location, 1950s-83 and projected to 2000, biennial rpt, 4114–8

Maternal and child health nursing continuing education at University of Kentucky, course enrollment and student assessment of career value, 1983 article, 4102–1.405

Mental health clinical training funding by NIMH, by program and field, FY80-83, GAO rpt, 26121–86

Mental health facilities, services, staff, and patient characteristics, *Statistical Notes* series, 4506–3

Mental health facilities staffing, by discipline and selected characteristics of health services personnel, selected years 1954-81, annual rpt, 4504–9.4

Military reserve forces medical personnel and wartime requirements by occupation, and medical equipment costs, by reserve component, as of 1983, annual rpt, 3544–27.2

Minority group and women employment and training in health professions, by field, selected years 1962/63-1983/84, 4118–18

Navy and Marine Corps disease incidence, medical care, and deaths, by detailed diagnosis, and medical personnel and workloads, 1978-79, annual rpt, 3804–1

Navy personnel, detailed statistics, quarterly rpt, 3802–4

New Jersey nursing care by nursing unit type, level of care related to length of stay, and costs by diagnosis under 2 allocation methods, as of 1981, article, 4652–1.424

Occupational manpower needs and supply by detailed occupation, and educational and training program enrollees and grads by detailed field, 1982 and 1995, biennial rpt, 6744–3

Occupational Outlook Handbook, 1984-85 biennial rpt, 6744–1

San Diego, Calif, nursing homes receiving Medicaid bonuses for care of severely ill, nursing time and costs by procedure, and bonus amount, 1980-81, article, 4652–1.405

Science and engineering grad enrollment, fields of study, financial support, and other student and instn characteristics, 1975-82, annual survey, 9627–7

Senegal rural health care projects of AID, mgmt and effectiveness, 1978-83, 9916–3.20

South Carolina manufacturing plants with selected employee health care services, by SIC 2-digit industry, 1982, article, 4102–1.408

Southeastern States health care resource availability, and employment by occupation, by facility type, by State and SMSA in Fed Reserve 6th District, 1970s-81, article, 9371–1.425

Statistical Abstract of US, social, political, and economic data, 1950s-83 and trends, annual rpt, 2324–1.1

Temporary health care employees, reasons for desiring temporary and part-time work, and preferences for work time, by skill level, survey, 1984 article, 6722–1.452

VA employment of general and medical personnel, FY59-83, annual rpt, 9924–13.1

VA facilities patients with speech disorders, by severity, patient characteristics, diagnostician occupation, and facility type, FY81, 9926–1.17

VA Medicine and Surgery Dept employment, by medical district and facility, monthly rpt, quarterly data, 9922–5.3

VA Medicine and Surgery Dept trainees, by detailed program and city, FY83, annual rpt, 9924–21

VA physicians, dentists, and nurses, by age, selected employment characteristics, and VA district, quarterly rpt, 9922–11

VA physicians, dentists, and nurses rates by grade, Jan 1984, 21628–54

Wages of hospital workers by sex and occupation, and benefits, for 22 MSAs, Oct 1981 survey, 6787–6.201

see also Midwives

Nursing homes

Arizona hospitals and nursing homes, finances and operations for specified facilities, and itemized expenses for selected cases, 1978-83, hearing, 21148–29

Arizona nursing home patients aged 55 and older in urban and rural areas, impairment levels for specified functions, 1980, article, 4102–1.413

Nursing homes

Census of Population, 1980: detailed socioeconomic and demographic characteristics, by age, sex, race, Hispanic origin, occupation, and industry, State rpt series, 2531–4

Census of Population, 1980: detailed socioeconomic characteristics, by county, city, and inside-outside SMSAs and central cities, State rpt series, 2531–3

Construction put in place, private and public nonresidential, by type, region, and census div, 1979-83, monthly rpt, annual tables, 2382–4.3

County and City Data Book, detailed socioeconomic and demographic data for States, counties, and cities, selected years 1976-82, 2328–1

County Business Patterns: establishments, employees, and payrolls, by SIC 4-digit industry and county, 1981, annual State rpt series, 2326–8

County Business Patterns: establishments, employees, and payrolls, by SIC 4-digit industry and county, 1982, annual State rpt series, 2326–6

Discharges from hospitals and nursing homes, by age, sex, marital status, and selected diagnosis, 1976 and 1979, article, 4102–1.443

Employment, earnings, and hours, by selected SIC 1- to 4-digit industry, State, and for 278 major labor areas, 1939-83, annual rpt, 6744–5

Employment, earnings, and hours, by SIC 4-digit nonfarm industry, monthly 1974-Feb 1984, annual update, 6744–4

Facilities, employees, and use of general and specialty hospitals and nursing homes, by ownership, bed size, region, and State, selected years 1969-80, 4147–14.30

Facilities, use, and characteristics of nursing homes, and nurses employed, by region and State, 1980, 4147–14.29

Florida and California elderly migration by selected State of origin or destination, and Florida elderly, by sociodemographic and housing characteristics, 1970 and 1980, 4478–150

Govt census, 1982: State govt payments to local govts, by program, source of funds, level of govt, and State, with trends from 1902, 2460–3

Govt finances, by level of govt, State, and for large cities and counties, 1981-83, annual rpt series, 2466–2

Health Care Financing Review, Medicare and Medicaid program activity, health care expenditures, and research, quarterly rpt with articles, 4652–1

Health condition and health care resources, use, and expenditures, 1970s-82 with trends and projections 1900-2000, annual compilation, 4144–11

Income tax returns of corporations, detailed income and tax items by industry, 1981, annual rpt, 8304–4

Income tax returns of sole proprietorships, detailed data by industry div and selected industry group, 1981, annual rpt, 8304–7

Income tax returns of sole proprietorships, receipts, deductions by type, payroll, and net income, by major industry, 1982, annual article, 8302–2.413

Input-output structure of US economy, detailed interindustry transactions for 537 industries, and components of final demand, 1977 benchmark data, 2708–17

Medicaid nursing home reimbursement based on level of care, alternative methods of determination, 1983 article, 4652–1.431

Medicare admissions to hospitals and other facilities, and enrollee reimbursement claims, by beneficiary type, 1966-83, annual rpt, 4744–3.7

Medicare and Medicaid eligibility, participation, covered services and use, and reimbursements and payments, various periods 1966-82, annual rpt, 4654–1

Medicare claims approved, total charges, and reimbursements by type of service, from 1974, monthly rpt, quarterly data, 4742–1.11

Medicare coverage of new medical technologies and reimbursements, and health services use and costs, selected years 1966-82, 26358–106

Medicare enrollee nursing home use and coverage, and reimbursements, for aged by region and State, and for disabled, 1969-80, 4656–1.20

Medicare enrollment, reimbursement, and use and covered charges by type of service, by State and census div, 1978-82, 4658–8

Medicare-participating facilities by control, beds, and terminated facilities, by facility type, region, and State, 1975-81, 4656–1.19

Minority group and women employment, by occupational group and SIC 2- to 3-digit industry, 1981, annual rpt, 9244–1.1

NIH grants and awards for R&D, training, construction, and medical libraries, by location and recipient, FY83, annual listings, 4434–7

Nurses in hospitals and nursing homes, earnings by position and selected metro area, 1978 and 1981, biennial rpt, 4114–8

Occupational injury and illness rates, by SIC 2- to 4-digit industry, 1982, annual rpt, 6844–1

Older persons by demographic, socioeconomic, and health characteristics, selected years 1900-81 and projected to 2050, Current Population Rpt, 2546–2.125

Older persons long-term health care and financing alternatives, including nursing home insurance and use of home equity, 1984 conf papers, 4658–7

Older persons nutrition services program operations and assessment, and participant sociodemographic, health, and diet characteristics, 1976 and 1982, 4608–16

Older persons population characteristics, and needs and costs of social services by type, by metro-nonmetro status, 1970s-82 with trends from 1900, 21148–28

Older persons receiving selected services from family and agencies, living arrangements, and need for home mgmt help, selected years 1977-82, article, 1702–1.409

Older persons sociodemographic characteristics, and Fed Govt program participation and funding, 1983 with trends and projections 1900-2060, annual rpt, 25144–3.1

Index by Subjects and Names

Pharmacists employment and sociodemographic characteristics, and reasons for not working in field, by State and overseas, as of 1979, 4147–14.28

Receipts for selected services, by SIC 2- to 4-digit kind of business, 1983, annual rpt, 2413–8

Service industry census, 1982: employment, establishments, receipts, and payroll, by SIC 2- to 4-digit kind of business, SMSA, county, and city, State rpt series, 2391–1

Southeastern States health care resource availability, and employment by occupation, by facility type, by State and SMSA in Fed Reserve 6th District, 1970s-81, article, 9371–1.425

Use of health facilities and manpower, by patient and facility characteristics, Vital and Health Statistics series, 4147–13

Veterans aged 55 and over, socioeconomic characteristics, economic resources, health care and status, and actual and expected use of VA benefits, 1983 survey, 9928–29

Veterans medical care costs, patients, and capacity of VA and non-VA facilties, by service type and patient age, 1970s-83 and projected to 2030, 26306–6.78

see also Veterans health facilities and services

Nutrition and malnutrition

Agricultural production, marketing, trade, supply, food consumption, and food and nutrition programs, 1960s-83, annual chartbook, 1504–3

AID activities and funding by project and function, FY85, and developing countries summary socioeconomic data, 1970s-83, by country, annual rpt, 9914–3

Blood lead levels by sociodemographic and behavioral characteristics, and potential workplace exposure, 1976-80, 4147–11.201

Consumer research and marketing devs, and consumption and price trends, quarterly rpt with articles, 1541–7

Deaths and death rates, by cause and age, provisional 1982-83, US Vital Statistics annual rpt, 4144–7

Deaths and death rates by detailed cause and demographic characteristics, 1979 and selected trends, US Vital Statistics annual rpt, 4144–2.1

Deaths and death rates, by detailed geographic area, cause, and demographic characteristics, 1979, US Vital Statistics annual rpt, 4144–3

Deaths and death rates, by selected cause and demographic characteristics, 1981, US Vital Statistics advance rpt, 4146–5.78

Deaths and death rates, by selected cause and demographic characteristics, 1982, US Vital Statistics advance rpt, 4146–5.81

Developing countries agricultural supply/demand and market for US exports, with socioeconomic indicators, country rpt series, 1526–6

Developing countries disaster preparedness and summary sociodemographic, political, and economic data, country rpt series, 9916–2

Developing countries food production and needs, and related economic trends and outlook, for 67 countries, 1980-86, annual rpt, 1524–6

Index by Subjects and Names

Nuts

Developing countries govt policy, and AID and other foreign assistance, effects on private sector dev and socioeconomic conditions, with case studies for 6 countries, 1960s-80, 9918–12

Developing countries PL 480 Title I funding and socioeconomic impacts, with case studies for 5 countries, 1950s- 81, 9918–13

Education of consumers about cardiovascular disease and nutrition, effectiveness of Natl Heart, Lung, and Blood Inst and Giant Food, Inc, program in DC metro area, 1978-79, 4478–144

Farm finance and credit conditions, forecast 1984, conf papers, annual rpt, 1004–16

Fish nutritional composition, for weakfish and other species in fresh or frozen forms, 1983 articles, 2162–1.401

Foreign human rights conditions in 162 countries, economic and military aid of US, and economic aid of intl organizations, 1981-83, annual rpt, 21384–3

Foreign military, social, and economic summary data by world area and country, 1960s-80s, hearing, 25388–47.1

GAO publications on food, agriculture, and nutrition, 1981-83, annual listing, 26104–11.2

Heart attack and cancer incidence and deaths in men aged 35-59, effects of lowering blood cholesterol levels, with background data on other risk factors, 1973-83, 4478–145

HHS aid to each State and local govt or private instn, amount obligated, funding agency, and program, FY83, annual listing, 4004–3

HHS nutrition research and monitoring activities, 1984 narrative article, 4102–1.454

Jamaica PL 480 Title I assistance effects on economic dev, with data on govt finance, economic indicators, demography, and dev programs, 1970s-81, 9916–1.51

Nutrient intake and food consumption by households, adjustments for meals eaten at home and nutritional requirements of household members, 1977/78, article, 1502–3.401

Nutrient intake and food consumption by individuals, by food group, source, and socioeconomic characteristics, 1977-78 natl survey, final rpt series, 1356–4

Nutrient intake, by age and sex, various periods 1971-80, 028–20

Nutrients available for daily per capita consumption, 1963-83, annual rpt, 1544–4.3

Nutrition status of infants and children, blood and height-weight indicators, and low birth weight risk factors, by age, race, and Hispanic origin, 1981, annual rpt, 4205–24

Nutrition surveillance, blood values and other nutrition indicators by age, race, and Hispanic origin, 1982, annual rpt, 4204–1.3

Older persons by demographic, socioeconomic, and health characteristics, selected years 1900-81 and projected to 2050, Current Population Rpt, 2546–2.125

Older persons nutrition services program operations and assessment, and participant sociodemographic, health, and diet characteristics, 1976 and 1982, 4608–16

Older persons population characteristics, and needs and costs of social services by type, by metro-nonmetro status, 1970s-82 with trends from 1900, 21148–28

Pregnancy health counseling effect on smoking, diet, delivery costs, and birth weight, by sociodemographic characteristics and pregnancy history, 1983 article, 4102–1.401

Research (agricultural) expenditures and scientist years, by topic, commodity, and performing organization, FY82, annual rpt, 1744–2

Research grants awarded competitively by USDA for agricultural science, food and nutrition, and energy dev, FY83, annual listing, 1744–1

Statistical Abstract of US, social, political, and economic data, 1950s-83 and trends, annual rpt, 2324–1.1

Vital and Health Statistics series and other NCHS publications, 1979-83, annual listing,, 4124–1

Youth office visits to physicians by patient and visit characteristics and physician specialty, and drug mentions by brand, 1980-81, 4146–8.100

see also Dietitians and nutritionists
see also Food additives
see also Food assistance
see also Food consumption
see also Food supply
see also Obesity
see also School lunch and breakfast programs

Nuts

Acreage planted and harvested, by crop and State, 1982-83 and planned as of June 1984, annual rpt, 1621–23

Acreage planting intended for 19 crops, by State, as of Feb 1984, annual rpt, 1621–22

Acreage, yield, and production of field crops, by State, 1978-82 and preliminary 1983, 1641–7

Agricultural Stabilization and Conservation Service peanut programs, 1972-84, annual fact sheet, 1806–4.2

Agricultural Statistics, 1983, annual rpt, 1004–1

Agriculture census, 1982: farms, farmland, production, finances, and operator characteristics, by county, final State rpt series, 2331–1

Almond prices, and exports by country of destination, for Spain, 1981/82-1982/83, article, 1925–34.403

Almond production and trade of US and selected countries, 1982/83-1983/84 and forecast 1985, article, 1925–34.425

Candy and confectionery industry sales, shipments, trade, and consumption of selected ingredients, 1983, annual Current Industrial Rpt, 2506–4.5

Cold storage food stocks by commodity and census div, and warehouse cold storage space in use, by State, monthly rpt, 1631–5

Cold storage food stocks of 77 commodities, by region, 1983, annual rpt, 1631–11

Consumption of food and nutrient intake by individuals, by food group, source, and socioeconomic characteristics, 1977-78 natl survey, final rpt series, 1356–4

Consumption, supply, trade, prices, expenditures, and indexes, by food commodity, 1963-83, annual rpt, 1544–4

Cooperatives finances and operations, aggregate for top 100 assns by principal product and revenue source, FY82, annual rpt, 1124–3

Cooperatives, membership, activities, and finances, by commodity and selected State, 1900-80 with trends from 1863, 1128–30

Exports and imports of US, by agricultural commodity and country, bimonthly rpt with articles, 1522–1

Exports and imports of US, by detailed agricultural commodity and country, FY83 and CY83, semiannual rpts, 1522–4

Exports and imports of US, by detailed agricultural commodity for 8 major commodity groups, monthly rpt, 1922–8

Exports and imports of US, detailed SIC-based commodities by world area, 1983, annual rpts, 2424–6

Exports and imports of US, totals and as percent of domestic production, by SIC 2- to 5-digit commodity, 1981, annual rpt, 2424–3

Exports of manufactured and agricultural commodities, manufacturing production, and export-related employment, 1960s-82, State rpt series, 2046–3

Exports of US, detailed commodities by country of destination, monthly rpt, 2422–3

Exports of US, detailed Schedule B commodities by country of destination, 1983, annual rpt, 2424–9

Exports of US, detailed Schedule E commodities by mode of transport and world area and country of destination, 1983, annual rpts, 2424–5

Farm finances, assets, liabilities, income, receipts by commodity and State, and expenses, 1980-83 and trends from 1910, annual rpt, 1544–16

Farm production inputs, outputs, and productivity, by region, 1939-82, annual rpt, 1544–17

Filbert production and trade of US and selected countries, 1981/82-1984/85, article, 1925–34.426

Foreign and US agricultural production, trade, and climatic devs, weekly press release, 1922–4

Foreign and US fresh and processed fruit, vegetable, and nut production and trade, FAS monthly rpt with articles, 1925–34

Great Lakes trade, by SITC 3-digit commodity, port, vessel type, world area, and country, 1982, annual rpt, 7744–3

Imports of US, detailed Schedule A commodities by country and world area of origin, and mode of transport, 1983, annual rpts, 2424–2

Imports of US, detailed Schedule A commodities by country, monthly rpt, 2422–2

Imports of US, detailed TSUSA commodities by country of origin, 1983, annual rpt, 2424–4

Nuts

Income tax returns of partnerships, detailed data by industry, 1981 estimates, annual article, 8302–2.404

Income tax returns of partnerships, receipts by source, deductions by type, and establishments, by selected industry, 1982, annual article, 8302–2.416

Income tax returns of sole proprietorships, receipts, deductions by type, payroll, and net income, by major industry, 1982, annual article, 8302–2.413

Input-output structure of US economy, detailed interindustry transactions for 537 industries, and components of final demand, 1977 benchmark data, 2708–17

Marketing cash receipts of farms, by detailed commodity and State, 1979-82, annual rpt, 1544–18

Peanut itemized production costs, receipts, and net returns, by region, 1981-83, annual rpt, 1544–20

Peanut production, prices, stocks, exports, use, inspection, and quality, by region and State, selected crop years 1974-83, annual rpt, 1311–5

Peanut production, prices, trade by country, and stocks, weekly rpt, 1311–1

Peanut stocks, millings, and processing, Feb-July 1984, semiannual rpt, 1621–6

Pecan wholesale prices, by selected shipping point, 1983, annual rpt, 1311–8

Pistachio imports of EC by country, and US exports by world area, 1981-83, article, 1925–34.424

Prices received by farmers and production value for detailed crops by State, 1981-83, annual rpt, 1621–2

Prices received by farmers for major products, and paid for farm inputs and living items, by commodity and State, monthly rpt, 1629–1

Producer prices and indexes, by stage of processing and detailed commodity, monthly rpt, 6762–6

Producer prices and indexes, by stage of processing and detailed commodity, monthly 1983, annual supplement, 6764–2

Production and farm finances, expenses by type, and domestic economic impact, selected years 1972-82 and preliminary 1983-84, annual rpt, 1544–19

Production, farms, acreage, and related data, by selected crop and State, monthly rpt, 1621–1

Production, prices, and use of noncitrus fruit and nuts, by crop and State, 1981-83, annual rpt, 1621–18.1, 1621–18.3

Production, prices, trade, stocks, and use, by selected crop, periodic situation rpt with articles, 1561–6

USDA agricultural surplus direct purchase program finances, and purchases and food received by schools by commodity, various periods 1936-83, 1548–243

Walnut production, stocks, use, and exports of US and 4 countries, and EC export subsidy, selected years 1977-1984/85, article, 1925–34.429

see also Oils, oilseeds, and fats

see also under By Commodity in the "Index by Categories"

Nuts, metal

see Hardware

Oak Ridge Associated Universities

"Carbon Dioxide Emissions from Fossil Fuels: A Procedure for Estimation and Results for 1950-81", 3008–94

"Occupational Employment in Nuclear-Related Activities, 1983", 3004–11

Oak Ridge National Laboratory

"Age and Capacity Profile of Electric Generation Plants in the U.S.", 3008–98

"Comparison of Actual and Predicted Energy Savings in Minnesota Gas-Heated Single-Family Homes", 3308–74

"Effects of Delaying the Operation of a Nuclear Power Plant", 9638–53

"Evaluation of Utility Home Energy Audit (RCS) Programs", 3308–69

"Hazard Mitigation Potential of Earth-Sheltered Residences", 3308–71

"Impacts of Oil Disturbances: Lessons from Experience", 3108–28

"Loan Impacts in Home Energy Audit Programs: A Minnesota Example", 3308–72

"Population Distribution Analyses for Nuclear Power Plant Siting", 9638–54

"Residential Conservation Service in Connecticut: Evaluation of the CONN SAVE Program", 3308–77

"Transportation Energy Data Book: Edition 7", 3304–5

"Trends in Heavy Truck Energy Use and Efficiency", 3308–70

"Trends in Nuclear Power Plant Capital Investment Cost Estimates, 1976-82", 9638–52

"Use of Electricity Billing Data To Determine Household Energy Use 'Fingerprints'", 3308–76

"Wilderness Designation of Bureau of Land Management Lands and Impacts on the Availability of Energy Resources", 3308–68

see also Department of Energy National Laboratories

Oak Ridge, Tenn.

Clinch River Breeder Reactor proposed site and nearby area, radiation levels in river water and sediment and ground water, 1983, annual rpt, 9804–24

Uranium enrichment facilities operations, finances, uranium stocks, and energy use and capital investment by facility, FY83, annual rpt, 3354–7

Oakes, E. H.

"Wilderness Designation of Bureau of Land Management Lands and Impacts on the Availability of Energy Resources", 3308–68

Oakland, Calif.

Auto dealer repair workers, wages, and benefits, by occupation, size of establishment, and for 24 labor market areas, Nov 1982 survey, 6787–6.202

Cancer cases, incidence, deaths, and death rates, by body site, age, race, Hispanic origin, and sex, for 10 geographic areas, 1973-81, 4478–130

Census of Housing, 1980: occupancy and unit characteristics, by race, Hispanic origin, and city, SMSA rpt, 2473–1.321

Index by Subjects and Names

Census of Population and Housing, 1980: detailed population and housing characteristics, by county, city, and census tract, SMSA rpt, 2551–2.321

CPI by component for US city average, and by region, population size, and for 28 SMSAs, monthly press release, 6762–1

CPI by detailed component, for US city average, 28 SMSAs, and 4 regions by population size, monthly rpt, 6762–2

Dress industry production and related workers, wages, and benefits, by occupation, size of establishment, and union status, for 11 labor market areas, Aug 1982 survey, 6787–6.200

Fruit and vegetable shipments, and arrivals in 23 US and 5 Canada cities, by mode of transport and State or country of origin, 1983, annual rpt, 1311–4.2

Hospital worker wages by sex and occupation, and benefits, for 22 MSAs, Oct 1981 survey, 6787–6.201

Housing and financial characteristics, and unit and neighborhood quality, for 15 SMSAs, 1978, annual survey special supplement, 2485–8

Housing and households detailed characteristics, and unit and neighborhood quality, by inside-outside central cities, 1982 survey, SMSA rpt, 2485–6.34

Repair technicians and apprentices wages and benefits, for 5 types of electrical repair shops in 19 SMSAs, Nov 1981 survey, 6787–6.197

Wages by occupation, and benefits for office and plant workers, 1984 SMSA survey rpt, 6785–11.5

see also under By City and By SMSA or MSA in the "Index by Categories"

OASDHI

see Old-Age, Survivors, Disability, and Health Insurance

Oats

see Grains and grain products

Obesity

Child obesity and low height-for-age, for public food program participants aged 1-4, by race and Hispanic origin, 1982, article, 4202–7.403

Health habits associated with 10 major death causes, prevalence of 8 risk factors in selected States, 1981-83 surveys, article, 4202–7.405

Health habits of adults, including physical activity, smoking, alcohol use, hypertension, and seat belt use, by age and sex, 1982, annual rpt, 4204–1.3

Older persons by demographic, socioeconomic, and health characteristics, selected years 1900-81 and projected to 2050, Current Population Rpt, 2546–2.125

Obstetrics and gynecology

Births, proportion inside-outside hospital and with physician or midwife attending, and prenatal care, 1940-79, US Vital Statistics annual rpt, 4144–1

Black medical residents by specialty, and minority medical faculty by race and Hispanic origin, selected years 1980-83, article, 4102–1.412

Breast-fed infants, by characteristics of mother and source of prenatal care, various periods 1970-75, article, 4102–1.442

Index by Subjects and Names

Cesarean and total births in hospitals affiliated and not affiliated with medical schools, by characteristics of mother, birth, and hospital, 1977, 4186–6.4

DOD medical personnel, trainees, and accessions by source, by occupation, specialty, and service branch, FY83, annual rpt, 3544–24

Drugs (analgesic) provided during visits to office-based physicians, by patient characteristics, drug brand and type, and physician specialty, 1980-81, 4146–8.99

Drugs prescribed, by physician specialty, 1982, annual rpt, 4064–12

Health condition and health care resources, use, and expenditures, 1970s-82 with trends and projections 1900-2000, annual compilation, 4144–11

Hispanic Americans births and birth and fertility rates, by detailed Hispanic origin, characteristics of mother, birth, and prenatal care, and for 22 States, 1981, 4146–5.80

Hospital discharges and length of stay, by patient age and sex, facility size and ownership, procedure performed, and region, 1983, 4146–8.101

Hospital discharges and length of stay, by patient characteristics, facility size, procedure performed, diagnosis, and region, 1982, annual rpt, 4147–13.78

Infections (hospital-related), drug resistance, and associated deaths, for teaching and non-teaching hospitals, 1980-82, article, 4202–7.401

Manpower supply and education of health professionals, by occupation, demographic and professional characteristics, and location, 1950s-83 and projected to 2000, biennial rpt, 4114–8

Menopause symptoms treatment, estrogen prescribed by physicians by dosage and physician specialty, 1974 and 1981, article, 4102–1.444

Mental health facilities, services, staff, and patient characteristics, 1970s-82 with trends from 1954, annual rpt, 4504–9

New Jersey nursing care by nursing unit type, level of care related to length of stay, and costs by diagnosis under 2 allocation methods, as of 1981, article, 4652–1.424

Pelvic inflammatory disease private physician diagnoses by age, race, and reason for visit, 1979-81, article, 4202–7.404

Physician visits for new pain symptoms, by diagnosis, physician specialty, and patient characteristics, and drugs prescribed or used, 1980-81, 4146–8.97

Physicians (not office-based) visits by reason, diagnosis, treatment, patient and physician characteristics, and physician primary activity, 1980, 4147–13.77

Science and engineering grad enrollment, fields of study, financial support, and other student and instn characteristics, 1975-82, annual survey, 9627–7

VA physicians, dentists, and nurses, by age, selected employment characteristics, and VA district, quarterly rpt, 9922–11

Visits to obstetrician-gynecologists and drugs used, by visit reason, diagnosis, treatment, and patient and physician characteristics, 1980-81, 4147–13.76

Youth office visits to physicians by patient and visit characteristics and physician specialty, and drug mentions by brand, 1980-81, 4146–8.100

see also Maternity

Ocala, Fla.

Census of Housing, 1980: occupancy and unit characteristics, by race, Hispanic origin, and city, SMSA rpt, 2473–1.268

Census of Population and Housing, 1980: detailed population and housing characteristics, by county, city, and census tract, SMSA rpt, 2551–2.268

see also under By SMSA or MSA in the "Index by Categories"

Occupational health and safety

Aircraft accident circumstances and severity, by type of flying and aircraft, 1981, annual rpt, 9614–3

Airline and general aviation accident circumstances, severity, and causes, for US operations of domestic and foreign aircraft, periodic rpt, 9612–1

Airline pilots terminated for medical reasons and reinstated by carrier, and aircraft accidents by age of flight crew, selected years 1960-81, hearing, 21148–34

Asbestos workers, exposure levels, cancer incidence, and deaths, by industry and occupation, and asbestos regulation enforcement and costs/benefits, various periods 1940-2027, hearing, 21408–72

Biotechnology commercial uses, R&D funding and output, controls, and industry financial and operating data, for US and 5 countries, 1970s-83 and estimated 1984-85, 26358–98

Budget of US, receipts by source and outlays by function, FY40-89 estimates revised for consistency with FY85 budget definitions, annual rpt, 104–12

Colorado worksite health promotion and disease prevention programs by type, and employers interested in programs, 1984 article, 4102–1.453

Deaths and death rates from accidents, by place, detailed cause, and demographic characteristics, 1979, US Vital Statistics annual rpt, 4144–2.5

Deaths, circumstances and OSHA safety standards violated by type of incident and equipment used, series, 6606–2

Deaths related to work, by industry div and cause, 1981-82, article, 6722–1.422

Disability (work-related), incidence among men aged 22-64 related to sociodemographic and employment characteristics and to self-evaluated mental stress, 1972-74, 4746–5.43

DOE and contractor facility accidents, deaths, illnesses, radiation exposure, and property damage, by facility, 1982, annual rpt, 3004–24

Economic indicators and labor force characteristics, selected years 1880-1995, chartbook, 6728–30

Fed Govt aid to State and local govts, expenditures, and direct payments, by program, agency, and State, FY83, annual rpt, 2464–2

Fed Govt civilian employee occupational injuries, deaths, and illnesses, by agency, 1982, annual rpt, 6604–1

Fed Govt programs and mgmt cost control proposals, 3-year savings by function and agency, and financial and operating data, 1960s-81, 16908–1.15

Occupational health and safety

Hazardous substances and radiation effects on workers health, by industry, occupation, age, and sex, with bibl and glossary, 1920s-82, 9638–50

Health and vital statistics collection, and use in program planning and evaluation, Public Health Conf papers, 1983, biennial rpt, 4164–2

HHS aid to each State and local govt or private instn, amount obligated, funding agency, and program, FY83, annual listing, 4004–3

Injuries, detailed accident circumstances and safety data, by body part injured, type of equipment used, or industry, series, 6846–1

Injuries, illnesses, and workdays lost, by SIC 2-digit industry, 1982-83, annual press release, 6844–3

Injury and illness rates and causes, by SIC 2- to 4-digit industry, 1982, annual rpt, 6844–1

Injury and illness rates, by industry, 1972-81, annual rpt, 6724–1.9

Injury rates, total and by place of accident, by age, region, metro-nonmetro location, and selected SMSA, 1980-81, 4147–10.146

Labor legislation enacted by 48 States, DC, and Guam, 1983, annual summary article, 6722–1.406

Law enforcement officer assaults, murders, and other deaths by circumstances, level of govt, agency, victim and offender characteristics, and location, 1983, annual rpt, 6224–3

Lead levels in blood by sociodemographic and behavioral characteristics, and potential workplace exposure, 1976-80, 4147–11.201

Motor carrier safety inspections by Fed Hwy Admin, audits of driver qualification and vehicle operation records, and violations cited, 1982, annual rpt, 7554–38

NTIS occupational injury and illness data availability, by State, 1981, annual rpt, 6704–2

Nuclear power plant safety and emergencies, effectiveness of technical advisors, 1983 survey, 9638–55

Occupational Outlook Handbook, 1984-85 biennial rpt, 6744–1

Occupational Safety and Health Admin enforcement activities and funding, State programs and staff, and illnesses and injuries by industry div, 1980-82 with FY83-84 estimates, annual rpt, 6604–2

Oil and gas OCS drilling rigs by country, rig losses, and worker injury and death rates, various periods 1966-83, hearing, 21568–35

Pipeline safety regulations enforcement of DOT and States by pipeline type and State, and accidents and commodity losses, selected years 1973-FY84, GAO rpt, 26113–130

Pipelines for natural gas and hazardous liquids, accidents, deaths, and injuries, by cause, 1982, annual rpt, 7304–5

Price indexes and prices for producers of industrial safety equipment by detailed type, monthly rpt, 6762–6

Price indexes and prices for producers of industrial safety equipment by detailed type, monthly 1983, annual supplement, 6764–2

Occupational health and safety

Radioactive materials transport surveillance program activities and results, State survey rpt series, 9636–1

Railroad accidents, casualties, and property damage, Fed Railroad Admin activities, and safety inspectors by State, 1982, annual rpt, 7604–12

Railroad accidents, circumstances, severity, and railroad involved, quarterly rpt, 9612–3

Railroad safety law violations, claims settled FY83, annual rpt, 7604–10

Research and demonstration projects supported by NIOSH, by region and State, annual listing, suspended, 4244–2

South Carolina manufacturing plants with selected employee health care services, by SIC 2-digit industry, 1982, article, 4102–1.408

State govt occupational health and safety program staffing requirements, and occupational injury data, for selected States, selected years 1973-81, hearings, 21348–88

State govt public health labs personnel, finances, workloads, and other activities, by State, FY82, annual rpt, 4204–8

Subway accidents, deaths, injuries, and property damage, by type of accident and victim and cause, for 11 systems, 1983, annual rpt, 7884–5

Terrorist (intl) incidents, casualties, and attacks on US targets, by attack type and world area, with chronology of events, 1983, annual rpt, 7004–13

Truck accidents, injuries, deaths, and property damage, by circumstances, carrier type, and driver age and condition, 1983, annual rpt, 7554–9

Washington State deaths by sex, cause, and detailed occupation, summary data from occupational mortality study, 1950-79, 4248–47

Youth Conservation Corps activities, costs, and participant characteristics, by sponsoring agency, 1982, annual rpt, 5304–12

see also Agricultural accidents and safety

see also Black lung

see also Electromagnetic radiation

see also Mine accidents and safety

see also Nuclear radiation

see also Workers compensation

Occupational Safety and Health Administration

Activities and funding of OSHA, State programs and staff, and illnesses and injuries by industry div, 1980-82 with FY83-84 estimates, annual rpt, 6604–2

Asbestos workers, exposure levels, cancer incidence, and deaths, by industry and occupation, and asbestos regulation enforcement and costs/benefits, various periods 1940-2027, hearing, 21408–72

Cost control proposals for Fed Govt programs and mgmt, 3-year savings by function and agency, and financial and operating data, 1960s-81, 16908–1.3

Deaths, circumstances and OSHA safety standards violated by type of incident and equipment used, series, 6606–2

Fed Govt civilian employee occupational injuries, deaths, and illnesses, by agency, 1982, annual rpt, 6604–1

State govt occupational health and safety program staffing requirements, and occupational injury data, for selected States, selected years 1973-81, hearings, 21348–88

Occupational Safety and Health Review Commission

Budget of US Appendix, detailed budgets and personnel summaries, by agency, FY85, annual rpt, 104–3

Budget of US, appropriations, outlays, balances, and budget receipts, by govtl branch and agency, FY83, annual rpt, 8104–2

Cost control proposals for Fed Govt programs and mgmt, 3-year savings by function and agency, and financial and operating data, 1960s-81, 16908–1.15

Occupational therapy

Census of Population, 1980: detailed socioeconomic and demographic characteristics, by age, sex, race, Hispanic origin, occupation, and industry, State rpt series, 2531–4

Census of Population, 1980: labor force, by sex, detailed occupation, and region, with comparison to 1970 census, supplementary rpt, 2535–1.12

DOD medical personnel, trainees, and accessions by source, by occupation, specialty, and service branch, FY83, annual rpt, 3544–24

Handicapped children public education program enrollment, staff, and funding, by handicap, age, and State, 1981/82-1982/83, annual rpt, 4944–4

Hospital employment, vacancies, and vacancy rates, by occupation and by hospital specialty, region, census div, and State, 1980, annual rpt, 4114–12

Hospital worker wages by sex and occupation, and benefits, for 22 MSAs, Oct 1981 survey, 6787–6.201

Manpower supply of occupational therapists, by sex, 1979-82 and projected 1983-2000, biennial rpt, 4114–8

Occupational manpower needs and supply by detailed occupation, and educational and training program enrollees and grads by detailed field, 1982 and 1995, biennial rpt, 6744–3

Occupational Outlook Handbook, 1984-85 biennial rpt, 6744–1

see also Vocational rehabilitation

Occupational training

see Employee development

see Vocational education and training

Occupational wage surveys

see Area wage surveys

see Industry wage surveys

Occupations

Employment and economic conditions, alternative BLS projections to 1995 with selected trends for 1959-82, 6728–29

License tax revenue from businesses and occupations, by States, FY83, annual rpt, 2466–2.3

Occupational manpower needs and supply by detailed occupation, and educational and training program enrollees and grads by detailed field, 1982 and 1995, biennial rpt, 6744–3

Occupational Outlook Handbook, 1984-85 biennial rpt, 6744–1

Index by Subjects and Names

Occupational trends and outlook, quarterly rpt, 6742–1

see also Agricultural labor

see also Apprenticeship

see also Blue collar workers

see also Clerical workers

see also Employee development

see also Employment and unemployment, specific industries

see also Engineers and engineering

see also Executives

see also Health occupations

see also Household workers

see also Industrial management

see also Judges

see also Lawyers

see also Librarians

see also Pilots

see also Postal employees

see also Professional and technical workers

see also Sales workers

see also Scientists and technicians

see also Teachers

see also Vocational education and training

see also Vocational guidance

see also Vocational rehabilitation

see also under By Occupation in the "Index by Categories"

Ocean County, N.J.

Wages of office and plant workers, by occupation, 1983 labor market area survey rpt, 6785–3.3

see also under By SMSA or MSA in the "Index by Categories"

Ocean floor

see also Continental shelf

see also Offshore mineral resources

Ocean liners

see Passenger ships

Ocean pollution

see Marine pollution

Ocean resources

see Marine resources

Oceania

Agricultural and food production indexes, and production of selected commodities, by world region and country, 1974-83, annual rpt, 1524–5

Agricultural exports and imports of US, by detailed commodity and country, FY83 and CY83, semiannual rpts, 1522–4

Agricultural situation in North America and Oceania, by country and commodity, 1983 and outlook for 1984, annual rpt, 1524–4.1

Agricultural supply/demand, trade, and production, and socioeconomic data, by country, 1950s-77, 1528–179

Agricultural trade of US, by commodity and country, bimonthly rpt with articles, 1522–1

Carbon dioxide emissions from fossil fuel combustion, and growth rates, by country and country group, 1950-80, 3006–7.6

Economic, social, and political summary data, by country, 1984, annual factbook, 244–11

Export sales and shipments of US grains, oilseed products, hides, skins, and cotton, by country, weekly rpt, 1922–3

Exports and imports of US (airborne), by world area and US customs district and city, monthly rpt, 2422–8

Exports and imports of US (waterborne), by type of service, commodity, country, route, and US port, 1982, annual rpt, 7704–2

Index by Subjects and Names

Exports and imports of US (waterborne), by type of service, customs district, port, and world area, monthly rpt, 2422–7

Exports and imports of US, by commodity group, world area, selected country, US coastal area and port, and mode of transport, with seasonal adjustments, monthly rpt, 2422–9

Exports and imports of US, detailed SIC-based commodities by world area, 1983, annual rpts, 2424–6

Exports of US, detailed Schedule B commodities by country of destination, 1983, annual rpt, 2424–9

Exports of US, detailed Schedule E commodities by mode of transport and world area and country of destination, 1983, annual rpts, 2424–5

Great Lakes trade, by SITC 3-digit commodity, port, vessel type, world area, and country, 1982, annual rpt, 7744–3

Immigration, and alien residents, workers, visitors, deportations, and naturalizations, by country of birth, FY81, annual rpt, 6264–2

Imports of US, detailed Schedule A commodities by country and world area of origin, and mode of transport, 1983, annual rpts, 2424–2

Imports of US, detailed TSUSA commodities by country of origin, 1983, annual rpt, 2424–4

Investment (foreign direct) of US, by world area and country, 1977-83, article, 2702–1.442

Loans and grants for economic and military assistance from US and intl agencies, by program and country, FY46-83, annual rpt, 9914–5

Military, social, and economic summary data, by world area and country, 1960s-80s, hearing, 25388–47.1

Military spending, arms trade, and armed forces size, with total govt spending and population, by country, 1972-82, annual rpt, 9824–1

Minerals Yearbook, 1982, Vol 3: foreign country reviews of production, trade, and policies, by commodity, annual rpt, 5604–35

Minerals Yearbook, 1982, Vol 3 preprints: foreign country review of production, trade, and policies, by commodity, annual rpt, 5604–17.90

Minerals Yearbook, 1983, Vol 3 preprints: foreign country review of production, trade, and policies, by commodity, annual rpt, 5604–23.90

Population size and growth rates, and latest available benchmark demographic data, by country, 1950-83, biennial rpt, 2324–4

Travel to and from US on US and foreign flag air carriers, by country, world area, and US port, monthly rpt, 7302–2

Weather conditions and impact assessment, by world area and country, monthly rpt, 2152–9

Weather stations of Natl Weather Service, locations and regular observations made, 1984 annual listing, 2184–5

see also Australia
see also Fiji
see also Nauru
see also New Zealand

see also Papua New Guinea
see also Solomon Islands
see also Tonga
see also Trust Territory of the Pacific Islands
see also Tuvalu
see also Vanuatu
see also Western Samoa
see also under By Foreign Country in the "Index by Categories"

Oceanography

Carbon dioxide atmospheric levels, climatic effects and impacts of fossil and synthetic fuels use, deforestation, and land use patterns, research rpt series, 3406–3

DOE R&D projects and funding at natl labs, universities, and other instns, FY83, annual summary rpt, 3004–18.1

DOE R&D projects and funding at natl labs, universities, and other instns, FY84, annual summary rpt, 3004–18.4

Fish and shellfish of economic importance, biological, fishery, and mgmt data, literature review series, 2166–16

Meteorological services and research of Fed Govt, programs and funding by agency, FY84-85, annual rpt, 2144–2

NOAA scientific and technical publications, monthly listing, 2142–1

NSF grant and award recipients, by State, FY83, annual listing, 9624–11

NSF research programs, activities, and funding, FY82-83, annual rpt, 9624–6

Oceanographic data, stations and cruises recording data for World Data Center A by country, ship, and type of data, 1983, annual rpt, 2144–15

R&D expenditures by higher education instns and federally funded centers, by field, source of funds, instn, and State, FY82, annual rpt, 9627–13

R&D expenditures by source, and scientists education and employment, detailed data by field, selected years 1953-84, annual rpt, 9624–18

R&D expenditures of higher education instns, and science and engineering employment and grad students, by field, 1972-83, biennial rpt, 9627–24

R&D Fed Govt facilities and services available for private sector use, by field of science, 1984 biennial listing, 2224–4

R&D Fed Govt funding for all performers, by field and supporting agency, selected years FY60-84, annual rpt, 9627–20

Research cruises scheduled and ship characteristics, by academic instn or Federal agency, 1984, annual rpt, 3804–6

Science and engineering doctoral degree recipients, by field, sex, race, age, citizenship, postgrad employment and study status, State, and instn, 1960-82, 9626–6.16

Science and engineering grad enrollment, fields of study, financial support, and other student and instn characteristics, 1975-82, annual survey, 9627–7

Scientists and engineers employed at universities and colleges, by field, sex, State, and instn, Jan 1983 and selected trends from 1967, annual survey, 9627–11

Scientists, engineers, and technicians employed in private industry, by occupation and industry group, 1980-81, biennial rpt, 9627–23

Office furniture and equipment

Soviet Union-US science and technology exchange projects, man-hours, and funding, by Fed Govt agency and activity type, FY81-82, 7008–41

Temperature of sea surface by ocean and for US coastal areas, and Bering Sea ice conditions, monthly rpt, 2182–5

Tidal current tables, daily time and velocity by station for North America and Asia coasts, 1985, annual rpt, 2174–1

Tide height and time daily at worldwide coastal points, 1985 predictions, annual rpt series, 2174–2

see also Ice conditions
see also Marine pollution
see also Marine resources
see also Marine resources conservation
see also Navigation

O'Connell, Martin

"Childspacing Among Birth Cohorts of American Women: 1905-59", 2546–1.387

"Fertility of American Women: June 1982", 2546–1.386

O'Connor, Roderick

"New Directions in Youth Services: Experiences with State-Level Coordination", 6068–182

Odessa, Tex.

Census of Housing, 1980: occupancy and unit characteristics, by race, Hispanic origin, and city, SMSA rpt, 2473–1.269

Census of Population and Housing, 1980: detailed population and housing characteristics, by county, city, and census tract, SMSA rpt, 2551–2.269

see also under By SMSA or MSA in the "Index by Categories"

Odum, William E.

"Ecology of the Mangroves of South Florida: A Community Profile", 5506–9.3

"Ecology of Tidal Freshwater Marshes of the U.S. East Coast: A Community Profile", 5506–9.13

OECD

see Organization for Economic Cooperation and Development

Offenbacher, Edward K.

"Empirical Comparisons of Credit and Monetary Aggregates Using Vector Autoregressive Methods", 9389–1.402

Office buildings

see Commercial buildings
see Public buildings

Office for Handicapped Individuals

see Office of Human Development Services

Office furniture and equipment

Air pollutant emission factors, by detailed source, 3rd edition, 1983-84 supplements, 9198–13

Bank financial and operating statements, functional cost analysis for Fed Reserve member banks with average and high earnings, by deposit size, 1982, annual rpt, 9364–6

Census of Population, 1980: detailed socioeconomic and demographic characteristics, by age, sex, race, Hispanic origin, occupation, and industry, State rpt series, 2531–4

Census of Population, 1980: detailed socioeconomic characteristics, by county, city, and inside-outside SMSAs and central cities, State rpt series, 2531–3

Office furniture and equipment

China economic conditions, agricultural and industrial production, trade, and domestic and foreign investment, 1980-85, 2048–106

Collective bargaining agreements expiring during year, covered workers by SIC 2-digit industry, firm, and union, with summary of key provisions, 1984, annual rpt, 6784–9

Computing, accounting, and related office machines shipments, trade, and consumption, by product, 1982-83, annual Current Industrial Rpt, 2506–12.2

County Business Patterns: establishments, employees, and payrolls, by SIC 4-digit industry and county, 1981, annual State rpt series, 2326–8

County Business Patterns: establishments, employees, and payrolls, by SIC 4-digit industry and county, 1982, annual State rpt series, 2326–6

Employment, earnings, and hours, by selected SIC 1- to 4-digit industry, State, and for 278 major labor areas, 1939-83, annual rpt, 6744–5

Employment, earnings, and hours, by SIC 4-digit nonfarm industry, monthly 1974-Feb 1984, annual update, 6744–4

Exports and imports of US, detailed SIC-based commodities by world area, 1983, annual rpts, 2424–6

Exports and imports of US, totals and as percent of domestic production, by SIC 2- to 5-digit commodity, 1981, annual rpt, 2424–3

Exports of US, detailed commodities by country of destination, monthly rpt, 2422–3

Exports of US, detailed Schedule B commodities by country of destination, 1983, annual rpt, 2424–9

Exports of US, detailed Schedule E commodities by mode of transport and world area and country of destination, 1983, annual rpts, 2424–5

Fed Govt programs and mgmt cost control proposals, 3-year savings by function and agency, and financial and operating data, 1960s-81, 16908–1

Great Lakes trade, by SITC 3-digit commodity, port, vessel type, world area, and country, 1982, annual rpt, 7744–3

House of Representatives salaries, expenses, and contingent fund disbursement, detailed listings, quarterly rpt, 21942–1

Imports of US, detailed Schedule A commodities by country and world area of origin, and mode of transport, 1983, annual rpts, 2424–2

Imports of US, detailed Schedule A commodities by country, monthly rpt, 2422–2

Imports of US, detailed TSUSA commodities by country of origin, 1983, annual rpt, 2424–4

Income tax returns of corporations, detailed income and tax items by industry, 1981, annual rpt, 8304–4

Injuries and deaths from use of selected consumer products and related activity, by victim age and sex, 1982, annual rpt, 9164–7

Input-output structure of US economy, detailed interindustry transactions for 85 industries, and components of final demand, 1977, article, 2702–1.421

Input-output structure of US economy, detailed interindustry transactions for 537 industries, and components of final demand, 1977 benchmark data, 2708–17

Manufacturing census, 1982: financial and operating data, by SIC 2- to 4-digit industry, State, SMSA, and county, preliminary census div rpt series, 2491–3

Manufacturing census, 1982: financial and operating data, for SIC 4-digit industries by product, preliminary rpt series, 2491–1

Minority group and women employment, by occupational group and SIC 2- to 3-digit industry, 1981, annual rpt, 9244–1.1

Natural gas interstate pipeline company detailed financial and operating data, by firm, 1983, annual rpt, 3164–38

Occupational injury and illness rates, by SIC 2- to 4-digit industry, 1982, annual rpt, 6844–1

Occupational manpower needs and supply by detailed occupation, and educational and training program enrollees and grads by detailed field, 1982 and 1995, biennial rpt, 6744–3

Occupational Outlook Handbook, 1984-85 biennial rpt, 6744–1

OECD trade, total and for 4 major countries, and US trade by country, by commodity, 1972-82, annual world region rpt series, 244–13

Pens, pencils, and marking devices shipments, trade, and consumption, by product, 1983, annual Current Industrial Rpt, 2506–7.12

Pollution abatement capital and operating costs, by SIC 2- to 4-digit industry, State, and SMSA, 1982, annual Current Industrial Rpt, 2506–3.6

Producer prices and indexes, by stage of processing and detailed commodity, monthly rpt, 6762–6

Producer prices and indexes, by stage of processing and detailed commodity, monthly 1983, annual supplement, 6764–2

R&D industry funding and employment of scientists and engineers, by industry group, firm size, and funding source, 1956-82, annual rpt, 9627–21

Scientists, engineers, and technicians employed in private industry, by occupation and industry group, 1980-81, biennial rpt, 9627–23

Senate salaries, expenses, and contingent fund disbursements, by payee, detailed listings, 1st half FY84, semiannual rpt, 25922–1

Shipments, trade, and consumption of electronic equipment and associated products, by product, 1983, annual Current Industrial Rpt, 2506–12.21

Shipments, trade, and consumption of office supplies and stationery, by product, 1983, annual Current Industrial Rpt, 2506–7.13

Shipments, trade, and consumption of stationery and office supplies, by product, 1983, annual Current Industrial Rpt, 2506–7.11

Thefts, and total value of property stolen and recovered, by property type, 1983, annual rpt, 6224–2.1

Wholesale trade census, 1982: employment, establishments, sales by commodity, and

Index by Subjects and Names

payroll, by SIC 4-digit kind of business and State, preliminary rpt, 2403–1.3, 2403–1.12

Wood and metal office furniture industry productivity, hours, and employment indexes, 1958-81, annual rpt, 6824–1.3

see also Computers

see also under By Commodity in the "Index by Categories"

see also under By Industry in the "Index by Categories"

Office of Child Development

see Office of Human Development Services

Office of Education

see Department of Education

Office of Family Assistance

see Social Security Administration

Office of Federal Statistical Policy and Standards

see Office of Management and Budget

Office of Health Maintenance Organizations

Employer attitudes toward HMOs for employee health insurance, enrollment, premiums, and coverage, by region and industry div, 1982, 4108–32

Enrollment, use, and Fed Govt aid for HMOs and prepaid health plans, FY83, annual rpt, 4104–8

Office of Human Development Services

Adolescent abuse, characteristics of victims and abuse, local agencies contacted, drug and alcohol involvement, and reciprocal violence, 1980-81 survey, 4608–18

Cost control proposals for Fed Govt programs and mgmt, 3-year savings by function and agency, and financial and operating data, 1960s-81, 16908–1.5

Data projects and systems of HHS, by subagency, FY83-84, annual inventory, 4044–3

Fraud and abuse in HHS programs, audits and investigations, 2nd half FY84, semiannual rpt, 4002–6

Head Start Project enrollment, appropriations, and staff, FY65-84, annual rpt, 4604–8

Head Start Project enrollment of handicapped children, by handicap, State, and for Indian and migrant programs, 1982, annual rpt, 4604–1

Head Start Project programs and effect on child dev, literature review with bibl, selected years 1970-83, 4608–17

Head Start Project programs effect on child dev, by characteristics of program, child, and family, literature review, selected years 1965-81, 4608–20

Mentally retarded and developmentally disabled treatment and services, university-affiliated facility funding, activities, and clients, 1980-FY83, 4608–19

Older persons nutrition services program operations and assessment, and participant sociodemographic, health, and diet characteristics, 1976 and 1982, 4608–16

Runaway and other homeless youth programs, funding by source, activities, and participant characteristics, FY82, annual rpt, 4604–3

Office of Justice Assistance, Research and Statistics

Activities of Justice Dept, by subagency, FY82, annual rpt, 6004–1

Index by Subjects and Names

Arson investigation and prosecution, by incident characteristics and outcome, motive, and type of evidence, for 4 jurisdictions, 1981, 6068–184

Coal surface mining reclamation costs and Interior Dept regulatory enforcement activities, impacts on industry in 5 States and 3 regions, various periods 1978-82, 6068–177

Crime and criminal justice data, including justice expenditures and employment by level of govt, 1970s-82 with some trends from 1875, 6068–174

Crime and criminal justice research sponsored by Natl Inst of Justice, summary rpt series, 6066–20

Crime and criminal justice statistics analysis, methodology, and use in courts, 1983 biennial conf proceedings, 6064–20

Crime prevention media campaign, effects on public attitudes and activities, as of Nov 1981, 6068–183

Crime, victimization, offender characteristics, prison population, and other topics, periodic rpt, 6062–2

Crime victimization rates by type of offense, and victim and offense characteristics, Natl Crime Survey series, 6066–3

Criminal case disposition, effect of victim injury and other factors, and law enforcement official and victim attitudes, 1983 survey, 6068–185

Criminal case processing from arrest to sentencing, series, 6066–22

Criminal justice issues, special rpt series, 6066–19

Criminal justice system local operations and costs, series, 6066–21

Data collection programs, missions, and appropriations of Fed Govt statistical agencies, and effect of budget cuts, FY80-84, GAO rpt, 26125–28

Employee theft and misconduct in retail, hospital, and manufacturing establishments, by type and frequency of violation, 1978-80, 6068–178

Juvenile delinquency prevention, Fed Govt programs funding by Federal agency and block grant, FY82, annual rpt, 6064–11

Juvenile delinquency, program activities of Fed Govt for correction of serious, violent, and chronic offenders, 1975-80, narrative rpt, 6068–179

Juvenile Justice and Delinquency Prevention Natl Inst programs and research project funding, FY81-82, annual rpt, 6064–19

Maryland corrections policies, assessments of private citizens and corrections and criminal justice personnel, 1980/81 with prison population trends from 1930, 6068–176

Natl Inst of Justice publications, annual listing, suspended, 6064–8

Parole and prison populations, and Federal and State parole system characteristics and staff, by State, annual rpt, suspended, 6064–14

Police dept performance, analyses of police activities effects on neighborhoods and citizens, 1977, compilation of papers, 6068–181

Pretrial citation release use, cost savings for law enforcement agencies, and failures to appear in court, by offense and selected jurisdiction, 1970s-82, 6068–187

Prisoners in Federal and State correctional instns, by sex, region, and State, quarterly release, 6062–3

Prisoners under death sentence, and executions since 1930, by prisoner characteristics, region, and State, 1982, annual rpt, 6065–1

Robbery rates and circumstances, medical costs and property losses of victims, and offender and victim characteristics, 1960s-81, 6068–180

Telephone conference use in civil and criminal hearings, assessment of lawyers and judges in 2 States and Denver, Colo, 1981, 6068–186

Youth gang criminal activity control, police assessments, staff, and programs in 27 cities, with juvenile arrests nationwide for Crime Index offenses, 1980-81, 6068–175

Youth social services of State govts, coordinating agencies activities, admin, membership, and funding sources, survey, 1984 rpt, 6068–182

Office of Management and Budget

Budget authority rescissions and deferrals, monthly rpt, 102–2

Budget of US Appendix, detailed budgets and personnel summaries, by agency, FY85, annual rpt, 104–3

Budget of US, authority balances in FY85 budget, by agency, FY83-85, annual rpt, 104–8

Budget of US, brief overview, FY85, annual rpt, 104–6

Budget of US, compact budgets by function, agency, and account, FY85 with projections to FY89, annual rpt, 104–2

Budget of US, effects of Reagan Admin policy changes, by detailed program, FY85, annual rpt, 104–21

Budget of US, object class analysis of obligations, by branch of Fed Govt and selected depts and agencies, FY85 estimates, annual rpt, 104–9

Budget of US, receipts by source and outlays by function, FY40-89 estimates revised for consistency with FY85 budget definitions, annual rpt, 104–12

Budget of US, receipts, outlays, and budget authority, by function and agency, FY84-89 revised estimates, midsession review of FY85 budget, annual rpt, 104–7

Budget of US, receipts, outlays, and budget authority, by function and agency, 1st revision of FY85 budget, annual rpt, 104–17

Budget of US, special analyses of economic and social impact, FY85, annual rpt, 104–1

Commercial activities of Fed Govt, savings from performance under contract over in-house, with DOD costs, employees displaced, and small business awards, by service branch, FY81-82, 108–39

Computers and telecommunications systems major acquisition plans and obligations of Fed Govt, by agency, FY84-89, annual listing, 104–20

Cost control proposals for Fed Govt programs and mgmt, 3-year savings by function and agency, and financial and operating data, 1960s-81, 16908–1

Office of Personnel Management

DOD procurement, prime contract awards by type, service branch and command, and for Defense Logistics Agency, last week compared to total year FY83, 108–38

Fed Govt agencies fraud and abuse, Inspectors General investigations and audits by agency, 1st half FY84, semiannual rpt, 102–5

Fed Govt financial and nonfinancial domestic aid, 1984 annual comprehensive catalog, 104–5

Paperwork Reduction Act effects on Fed Govt info collection requirements and respondent burden, by agency, FY80-84, annual rpt, 104–19

Pay comparability of Fed Govt with private industry, and recommended pay rate adjustments, 1983, annual rpt, 104–16

Procurement contract awards of Fed Govt, by State, agency, procurement and contractor type, and for top 100 contractors, quarterly rpt, 102–6

Statistical policies of Fed Govt relating to technical operation of programs, methodology, and use of Federal data, working paper series, 106–4

Statistical programs of Fed Govt, funding by subject and agency, FY74-85, annual rpt, 104–10

Office of Mental Retardation Coordination *see* Office of Human Development Services

Office of Minority Business Enterprise *see* Minority Business Development Agency

Office of Personnel Management

Benefits for Federal civilian employees, retirement, health, and life insurance programs operations and finances, FY81-82, annual rpt, 9844–1

Budget of US Appendix, detailed budgets and personnel summaries, by agency, FY85, annual rpt, 104–3

Budget of US, appropriations, outlays, balances, and budget receipts, by govtl branch and agency, FY83, annual rpt, 8104–2

Budget of US, object class analysis of obligations, by branch of Fed Govt and selected depts and agencies, FY85 estimates, annual rpt, 104–9

Charity contributions of Fed Govt employees to Combined Federal Campaign, funds by type of recipient, 1982 and trends from 1973, GAO rpt, 26119–66

Civil service retirement system actuarial valuation, FY79-83 with projections to FY2060, annual rpt, 9844–34

Collective bargaining agreements of Federal employees, unions involved, and employees covered, by agency for agreements expiring July 1984-June 1985, annual listing, 9847–1

Collective bargaining multi-unit agreements of Federal employees, by labor union and agency, as of July 1983, annual listing, 9847–4

Employment (civilian) of Fed Govt, by location, agency, and pay system, 1982, biennial rpt, 9844–8

Employment and payroll (civilian) of Fed Govt, by agency in DC metro area, total US, and abroad, monthly rpt, 9842–1

Equal Opportunity Recruitment Program implementation, and summary employment data, FY83, annual rpt, 9844–33

Office of Personnel Management

Executive employee dev programs of Fed Govt, employee and candidate attitudes in 5 agencies, 1983 survey, GAO rpt, 26119–69

Handicapped persons employed by Fed Govt, annual rpt, suspended, 9844–23

Labor unions recognized in Fed Govt, agreements and membership by agency and office or installation, Jan 1983, annual listing, 9844–14

Labor unions recognized in Fed Govt, membership by agency and union, as of Jan 1983, annual rpt, 9844–17

Merit system of Office of Personnel Mgmt, implementation and effectiveness, 1982, annual survey, 9494–1

Minority group and handicapped employment of Fed Govt, by race, Hispanic origin, disability, sex, and employment characteristics, as of Sept 1982, biennial rpt, 9844–27

Minority group and women civilian employment of Fed Govt, by pay system and grade level, preliminary annual rpt, discontinued, 9844–13

Minority group and women civilian employment of Fed Govt, by pay system and occupation, annual press release, discontinued, 9844–29

Veterans (disabled and nondisabled) Fed Govt appointments and separations, agency, 2nd half FY82, semiannual rpt, 9842–3

Veterans with disability hired by Fed Govt under noncompetitive temporary hiring authority, by pay system, grade, and agency, 2nd half FY82, semiannual rpt, 9842–4

Office of Research and Statistics, SSA *see* Office of Research, Statistics, and International Policy, SSA

Office of Research, Statistics, and International Policy, SSA

- AFDC recipients and payments, applications by disposition, payment discontinuances by reason, and hearings by outcome, by State, quarterly rpt, 4742–6
- Child Support Enforcement Program cost savings to AFDC, Federal and State govts, and public assistance programs, by State and selected city or county, FY76-85, 4748–37
- Disability Insurance beneficiaries sociodemographic and medical characteristics, 1977-79, annual rpt, 4744–20
- OASDHI, Medicaid, SSI, and other social insurance and public welfare programs benefits, beneficiary characteristics, and trust funds, selected years 1937-83, annual rpt, 4744–3
- OASDI benefits and beneficiaries by demographic characteristics, and use of direct deposit, by SMSA and for rest of US and foreign countries, annual rpt, suspended, 4744–10
- OASDI benefits and beneficiaries, by type of benefit, State, outlying area, and county, Dec 1982, 4748–38
- Older persons income and income sources, by OASDI beneficiary and poverty status, labor force participation, and demographic characteristics, 1982, biennial rpt, 4744–26

Public welfare programs research and evaluations, effects of Fed Govt budget cuts, and statistical projects and techniques, conf papers, 4744–21

Research and Statistics Notes on social security programs and recipient characteristics, series, 4746–16

Research projects of SSA, narrative summary, FY84-86, annual rpt, 4744–11

Social Security Bulletin, OASDHI and other program operations and beneficiary characteristics, from 1940, monthly rpt with articles, 4742–1

Social security programs, research rpt series, 4746–4

Social security programs, staff paper series, 4746–5

- State govt public assistance expenditures, Fed Govt share, local funds, and recipient count, by program, annual rpt, discontinued, 4744–22
- Supplemental Security Income and other income maintenance program benefits and beneficiaries, by State, monthly rpt, 4742–2
- Supplemental Security Income benefits and beneficiaries, by type of eligibility, State, and county, Dec 1983, annual rpt, 4744–27
- Supplemental Security Income payments, and recipients by other income source, eligibility type, and other characteristics, by State, 1982, annual rpt, 4744–16

Office of Revenue Sharing

- Cost control proposals for Fed Govt programs and mgmt, 3-year savings by function and agency, and financial and operating data, 1960s-81, 16908–1.12
- Payments of revenue sharing funds to States, local govts, Indian tribes, and Alaska Native villages, and entitlement computation data, FY84, series, 8066–1
- Revenue sharing and antirecession fiscal assistance program admin and trust funds status, FY83, annual rpt, 8064–1

Office of Saline Water *see* Office of Water Research and Technology

Office of Special Education and Rehabilitative Services

- Handicapped children public education program enrollment, staff, and funding, by handicap, age, and State, 1981/82-1982/83, annual rpt, 4944–4
- Vending stand concessions operated by blind on Federal and non-Federal property, and income, FY82-83, annual rpt, 4944–2
- Vocational rehabilitation, State agency caseloads by status and processing stage, region, and State, FY83 with trends from FY21, annual rpt, 4944–5
- Vocational rehabilitation State agency clients following rehabilitation and employment, annual rpt, suspended, 4944–8
- Vocational rehabilitation State agency expenditures, caseloads, rehabilitations, and staff, under Section 110 of the Rehabilitation Act, by State, FY82, annual rpt, 4944–9
- Vocationally rehabilitated persons under State agency programs, by sociodemographic characteristics and disabling condition, FY79-81, annual rpt, 4944–6

Index by Subjects and Names

Office of Surface Mining Reclamation and Enforcement

- Coal surface mining reclamation costs and Interior Dept regulatory enforcement activities, impacts on industry in 5 States and 3 regions, various periods 1978-82, 6068–177
- Cost control proposals for Fed Govt programs and mgmt, 3-year savings by function and agency, and financial and operating data, 1960s-81, 16908–1.9

Office of Technology Assessment

- Acid rain causes and effects, air pollutant emissions by source, and control costs, by region and State, selected years 1977-83 and projected to 2000, 26358–104
- Biotechnology commercial uses, R&D funding and output, controls, and industry financial and operating data, for US and 5 countries, 1970s-83 and estimated 1984-85, 26358–98
- Budget of US Appendix, detailed budgets and personnel summaries, by agency, FY85, annual rpt, 104–3
- Coal dev on Fed Govt lease land in Western US, surface and mineral rights by State, and environmental protection adequacy, various periods 1978-85, 26358–103
- Foreign and US rail high-speed systems and railcar production, and proposed US projects costs and funding, with population and land area for selected foreign cities, 1940s-82, 26358–97
- Forests (tropical) status by country and world region, conservation methods, and mgmt role of US, foreign, and intl groups, 1977-81 and projected to 2000, 26358–101
- Medicare coverage of new medical technologies and reimbursements, and health services use and costs, selected years 1966-82, 26358–106
- Nuclear power industry status and outlook, with reactor construction, utility financial and operating data, and foreign comparisons, 1970s-83 with projections to 2010, 26358–99
- Polygraph lie detection test accuracy, and Fed Govt use by agency, selected years 1947-83, 26358–96
- Programs, activities, and publications list, 1983, annual rpt, 26354–3
- Robots for industrial use, R&D, training, and employment impacts, US with comparisons to foreign countries, 1980s with projections to 1992, 26358–105
- Satellite Landsat system proposed transfer to private sector, uses and product sales by user type, and university programs and personnel by instn, 1973-85, 26358–100
- Technology-intensive industry employment and establishments by industry and selected location, and venture capital investments by source, 1970s-82, 26358–107
- Wetlands environmental characteristics, acreage, uses, and mgmt, by wetland type and region, 1950s-80, 26358–102

Office of Telecommunications Policy *see also* National Telecommunications and Information Administration

Office of Territorial Affairs

Cost control proposals for Fed Govt programs and mgmt, 3-year savings by function and agency, and financial and operating data, 1960s-81, 16908–1.9

Index by Subjects and Names

Office of the Comptroller of Currency

Activities of Comptroller, and natl banks operations, charters, and mergers, by State, quarterly rpt, 8402–3

Cost control proposals for Fed Govt programs and mgmt, 3-year savings by function and agency, and financial and operating data, 1960s-81, 16908–1.14

Office of the Secretary of Defense

Budget of DOD, expenditures for each service branch and total defense agencies, by function and State, FY85, annual rpt, 3544–23

Budget of DOD, itemized account of legislative history, FY84, annual rpt, 3504–7

Budget of DOD, justification, programs, and policies, FY85, annual rpt, 3544–2

Commercial activities of DOD under contract and performed in-house, costs and work-years, by service branch, defense agency, State, and installation, FY83, annual rpt, 3544–25

Construction and renovation of military bases, DOD budget authorization requests, by DOD component, State, country, and project, FY85, annual rpt, 3544–15

Cost control proposals for Fed Govt programs and mgmt, 3-year savings by function and agency, and financial and operating data, 1960s-81, 16908–1.17

Employment (civilian) of DOD, by service branch and defense agency, with summary military employment data, monthly rpt, 3542–16

Employment (civilian and military) of DOD, by State, service branch, and major installation, as of Sept 1983, annual rpt, 3544–7

Fraud and abuse in DOD programs, audits and investigations, 1st half FY84, semiannual rpt, 3542–18

Manpower active duty strength, recruits, and reenlistment, by race, Hispanic origin, sex, and service branch, quarterly press release, 3542–7

Manpower requirements and cost estimates, DOD budget detailed analysis, FY85, annual rpt, 3504–1

Manpower statistics on active duty, civilian, and reserve personnel, by service branch, monthly rpt, 3542–14

Manpower statistics on active duty, civilian, and retired personnel and dependents, FY83 and historical, annual rpt, 3544–1

Manpower strengths in US and abroad, by service branch, world area, and country, quarterly news release, 3542–9

Manpower strengths, summary by service branch, monthly press release, 3542–2

Medical facilities of DOD in US and abroad, beds, admissions, outpatient visits, and live births by service branch, quarterly rpt, 3542–15

Medical personnel, trainees, and accessions by source, by occupation, specialty, and service branch, FY83, annual rpt, 3544–24

Military women personnel on active duty, by demographic and service characteristics and service branch, with comparisons to men, FY83, annual chartbook, 3544–26

Outlays and obligations of DOD, by function and service branch, quarterly rpt, 3542–3

Procurement, DOD prime contract awards by category, contract and contractor type, and service branch, FY74-1st half FY84, semiannual rpt, 3542–1

Procurement, DOD prime contract awards by detailed procurement category, FY80-83, annual rpt, 3544–18

Procurement, DOD prime contract awards by individual contractor, service branch, State and city, and country, FY83, annual listing, 3544–22

Procurement, DOD prime contract awards by size, dept, and type of contract, FY83, annual rpt, 3544–19

Procurement, DOD prime contract awards, dollar volume for 100 leading contractors and subsidiaries, FY83, annual rpt, 3544–5

Procurement, DOD prime contract awards for military and civil functions, by State, 1st half FY84, semiannual rpt, 3542–5

Procurement, DOD prime contract awards for 25 commodity categories and R&D, by State and census div, FY81-83, annual rpt, 3544–11

Procurement, DOD prime contract awards in labor surplus areas, by service branch, State, and area, 1st half FY84, semiannual rpt, 3542–19

Procurement, DOD prime contract awards to small and total business, for 10 categories and R&D, monthly rpt, 3542–10

Procurement, subcontract awards by DOD contractors to small and disadvantaged business, by firm and service branch, quarterly listing, 3542–17

Property, supplies, and equipment inventory of DOD, by service branch, 1983, annual rpt, 3544–6

Publications of DOD Directorate for Info Operations and Rpts, FY84, annual listing, 3544–16

R&D prime contract awards of DOD to educational and nonprofit instns and Federal agencies, by instn and location, FY83, annual listing, 3544–17

R&D prime contractors for DOD, top 500 and value of contracts, FY83, annual listing, 3544–4

Reserve forces manpower and equipment strengths, readiness, and funding, by reserve component, FY83, annual rpt, 3544–27

Reserve forces manpower strengths and characteristics, by component, quarterly rpt, 3542–4

Office of the Secretary of Energy

DOE in-house energy use, conservation investments, and savings, by type of use and fuel and field office, FY83, annual rpt, 3024–3

Energy production, trade, supply, use, conservation, and DOE activities, by energy type, FY83, annual rpt, 3024–2

Fed Govt energy use, by agency and fuel type, annual rpt, 3024–1

Natl Energy Policy Plan, DOE implementation and effect on energy supply/demand, 1983-84, annual rpt, 3024–4

Office of the Special Representative for Trade Negotiations

see Office of the U.S. Trade Representative

Office of the U.S. Trade Representative

Exports, imports, and economic indicators by country and country group, and US trade policy actions, 1960s-83, annual rpt, 444–1

Services trade regulation proposals of US, with agreements, goods and services trade, intl investment, and GDP, by country, various periods 1970-82, 448–1

Office of Trade Adjustment Assistance

see Employment and Training Administration

Office of Transportation, USDA

Activities and programs of USDA, by subagency, FY83, annual rpt, 1004–3

Grain rail and barge loadings, ship and container car availability, ocean freight rates, and export inspections, prices, and sales, weekly rpt, 1272–2

Truck transport of fruit and vegetables, costs per vehicle-mile by component for fleets and owner-operator trucks, monthly rpt, 1272–1

Office of Water Research and Technology

Cost control proposals for Fed Govt programs and mgmt, 3-year savings by function and agency, and financial and operating data, 1960s-81, 16908–1.9

Office of Water Resources Research

see Office of Water Research and Technology

Office of Youth Development

see Office of Human Development Services

Office on Smoking and Health

Research publications on smoking and health, bimonthly listing, 4042–1

Smoking and health research, article abstracts and indexes, 1983, annual rpt, 4044–8

Smoking related to chronic obstructive lung disease and deaths, by sociodemographic and smoking characteristics, literature review, 1984 annual Surgeon General rpt, 4044–6

Office workers

see Clerical workers

Official publications

see Government documents

Officials

Census of Population, 1980: detailed socioeconomic and demographic characteristics, by age, sex, race, Hispanic origin, occupation, and industry, State rpt series, 2531–4

Census of Population, 1980: detailed socioeconomic characteristics, by county, city, and inside-outside SMSAs and central cities, State rpt series, 2531–3

Commerce Dept Secretaries, 1913-81, and other dept officials as of Sept 1983, annual rpt, 2004–1

Corrupt govt officials prosecutions and convictions, by judicial district and level of govt, 1976-83, annual rpt, 6004–13

Developing countries disaster preparedness and summary sociodemographic, political, and economic data, country rpt series, 9916–2

FDIC officials and operations, 1983, annual rpt, 9294–1.2

Fed Govt civilian pay rates, by branch of govt, employee category, and pay level, as of 1984 with trends from 1789, 21628–54

Officials

Fed Govt officials use of Govt chauffeur services for commuting, driver overtime hours and pay by agency, 4th qtr 1982, GAO rpt, 26123–63

Fed Govt personnel merit system of Office of Personnel Mgmt, implementation and effectiveness, 1982, annual survey, 9494–1

Fed Govt Senior Executive Service employee admin, and program status and effectiveness, by agency and by executive and job characteristics, July 1979-Sept 1983, GAO rpt, 26119–51

Fed Reserve banks and branch officers and employees, and salaries, 1983, annual rpt, 9364–1.1

Foreign economic, social, and political summary data, by country, 1984, annual factbook, 244–11

Foreign govt Chiefs of State and Cabinet members, by country, monthly listing, 242–7

IRS commissioners and other officers, 1862-1983, annual rpt, 8304–3

Public housing under private mgmt, assessment by housing officials and managers, and tenants, with operating costs, crime, and rent delinquency by project type and location, 1982, 5188–103

Soviet Union officials public appearances in and outside of USSR, 1983, annual rpt, 244–8

Statistical Abstract of US, social, political, and economic data, 1950s-83 and trends, annual rpt, 2324–1.3

Terrorist (intl) incidents, casualties, and attacks on US targets, by attack type and world area, with chronology of events, 1983, annual rpt, 7004–13

Witness Security Program costs, participants by arrest record, and prosecutions by offense, offender type, and disposition, various periods FY70-83, GAO rpt, 26119–70

see also Congressional employees
see also Executives
see also Federal employees
see also International employees
see also State and local employees

Offshore mineral resources

Coastal environmental characteristics, fish, wildlife, and use, and population socioeconomic data, for individual areas, series, 5506–4

Fed Govt programs and mgmt cost control proposals, 3-year savings by function and agency, and financial and operating data, 1960s-81, 16908–1.29

Foreign minerals production, reserves, and industry role in domestic economy and world supply, country and world region rpt series, 5606–1

Mineral industries census, 1982: financial and operating data, by State and for 4 offshore regions, preliminary summary rpt, 2511–2.2

Minerals Yearbook, 1982, Vol 2: State reviews of production, sales, and firms, by commodity, and business activity, annual rpt, 5604–34

Nonfuel minerals from marine sources, demand by mineral type, selected years 1978-83 with projections to 2000, 15048–4

Phosphate rock reserves in southeastern and northwestern US, by location, 1984 rpt, 5668–74

Production, revenues, and reserves of oil, gas, and minerals from Fed Govt OCS leases, by State and ocean region, 1950s-82, annual rpt, 5734–3

see also Offshore oil and gas

Offshore oil and gas

Atlantic Ocean Georges Bank oil and gas drilling on Fed Govt leases, marine pollution problems, 1983 hearings, 21568–36

Coastal environmental and wildlife characteristics, use, and mgmt, for individual ecosystems, series, 5506–9

Coastal environmental characteristics, fish, wildlife, and use, and population socioeconomic data, for individual areas, series, 5506–4

Drilling rig construction financing guarantees of MarAd, FY83, annual rpt, 7704–14.1

Environmental and socioeconomic conditions, and potential impacts of oil and gas OCS leases, final statement series, 5736–1

Foreign oil and gas undiscovered recoverable resources, cumulative production, and identified reserves, final oil basin rpt series, 5666–18

Foreign oil and gas undiscovered recoverable resources, cumulative production, and identified reserves, preliminary oil basin rpt series, 5666–17

Gulf of Mexico operating costs and cost indexes for 12- and 18-slot platforms, by depth, 1981-83, annual rpt, 3164–45

Interior Dept programs, activities, and funding, various periods 1967-84, last issue of annual rpt, 5304–13

Leasing OCS oil and gas, 5-year plan and proposed sale off California, acreage, costs, and benefits, various periods 1953-2006, hearing, 21448–30

Natural and supplemental gas production, prices, trade, use, reserves, and pipeline company finances, by firm and State, monthly rpt with articles, 3162–4

Natural gas pipeline and compressor station construction costs, 1979-82, annual rpt, 3084–3

Natural gas production, wells drilled, and contract prices, by Natural Gas Policy Act section, producer and well characteristics, State, and field, selected years 1968-83, 3168–90

Oil and gas OCS drilling rigs by country, rig losses, and worker injury and death rates, various periods 1966-83, hearing, 21568–35

Oil production, total and for surveillance fields, by State and inland and Federal offshore area, 1980-82, biennial rpt, 3164–58

Producers finances and operations, by energy type for US firms domestic and foreign operations, 1974-82, annual rpt, 3164–44.2

Production and exploration expenditures and revenues, and sales volume, 1982, annual Current Industrial Rpt, 2506–8.11

Production and revenues from oil, gas, coal, and other minerals on Fed Govt and Indian lands, by State, 1983 with trends from 1920, annual rpt, 5734–2

Production, leasing and exploration activities, revenues, and costs, for Fed Govt OCS oil and gas reserves, by ocean region, FY83, annual rpt, 5734–4

Production, revenues, and reserves of oil, gas, and minerals from Fed Govt OCS leases, by State and ocean region, 1950s-82, annual rpt, 5734–3

Reserves and production of oil, gas, and gas liquids, by State and selected substate area, 1983, annual rpt, 3164–46

Seismic exploration crews and activity, monthly rpt, 3162–24.5

Supply/demand and prices, by fuel type and consuming sector with foreign comparisons, 1949-83, annual rpt, 3164–74

Supply/demand and prices, by fuel type, sector, and end use, with foreign comparisons, 1960-83 and projected to 1995, annual summary rpt, 3164–76

see also Oil spills

Ogden, E. A.

"Recent Shifts in the Location of U.S. Egg Production", 1561–7.403

Ogden, Utah

Census of Housing, 1980: occupancy and unit characteristics, by race, Hispanic origin, and city, SMSA rpt, 2473–1.317

Census of Population and Housing, 1980: detailed population and housing characteristics, by county, city, and census tract, SMSA rpt, 2551–2.317

Housing unit starts and completions authorized by building permits in 20 MSAs, quarterly rpt, 2382–9

Housing vacancy rates for single and multifamily units and mobile homes, by city and ZIP code, 1983, annual metro area rpt, 9304–21.8

Wages of office and plant workers, by occupation, 1983 SMSA survey rpt, 6785–12.3

see also under By SMSA or MSA in the "Index by Categories"

Ohio

Agriculture census, 1982: farms, farmland, production and costs, and operator characteristics, preliminary State summary and county rpts, 2330–1.39

Bank deposits in commercial and mutual savings banks and in US branches of foreign banks, by account type, instn, State, SMSA, and county, June 1983, annual rpt, 9295–3.10

Census of Population and Housing, 1980: detailed population and housing characteristics, by county, city, and census tract, State rpt, 2551–2.37

Census of Population, 1980: detailed socioeconomic and demographic characteristics, by age, sex, race, Hispanic origin, and industry, State rpt, 2531–4.37

Coal employment and economic losses from utility fuel switching to meet emissions standards, with detail for counties in 5 States, 1970s-83 and projected to 1990, 21368–52

County Business Patterns: establishments, employees, and payrolls, by SIC 4-digit industry and county, 1982, annual State rpt, 2326–6.37

Employment, earnings, and hours, by selected SIC 1- to 4-digit industry, State, and for 278 major labor areas, 1939-83, annual rpt, 6744–5.2, 6744–5.3

Index by Subjects and Names

Oil and gas leases

Environmental quality, pollutant discharge by type and source, and EPA protection activities and funding, 1970s-83, biennial regional rpt, 9184–15.5

Exports of manufactured and agricultural commodities, manufacturing production, and export-related employment, 1960s-82, State rpt, 2046–3.35

Farm investments, effective rates of Federal/State income and State/local property taxes, by category of structure and equipment, for 7 North Central States, 1981-82, 1548–237

Health professionals license sanctions in 3 States, and subsequent Medicare and Medicaid program participation, by specialty, 1977-82, GAO rpt, 26121–80

HHS aid to each State and local govt or private instn, amount obligated, funding agency, and program, FY83, annual listing, 4004–3.5

Income (personal) per capita and by source, and earnings by industry div, by State, MSA, and county, 1977-82, annual regional rpt, 2704–2.4

Manufacturing census, 1982: financial and operating data, by SIC 2- to 4-digit industry, State, SMSA, and county, preliminary census div rpt, 2491–3.3

Mineral Industry Surveys, State review of production, 1983, advance annual rpt, 5614–6.35

Minerals Yearbook, 1982, Vol 2 preprints: State review of production and sales by commodity, and business activity, annual rpt, 5604–16.36

Minerals Yearbook, 1982, Vol 2: State reviews of production, sales, and firms, by commodity, and business activity, annual rpt, 5604–34

Population, births, deaths, and net migration, by MSA and county, 1980-82, annual State Current Population Rpt, 2546–4.35

Population size, Apr 1980 and July 1982, and per capita income, 1979 and 1981, by county and city, State Current Population Rpt, 2546–11.35

Public works capital needs and financing, by project type, level of govt, and selected jurisdiction, 1970s-83 and projected to 2000, hearing, 23848–181

Retail trade census, 1982: employment, establishments, sales, and payroll, by SIC 2- to 4-digit kind of business, SMSA, county, and city, State rpt, 2397–1.36

Savings and loan assns, FHLB 5th District members financial condition and operations by SMSA, monthly rpt, 9302–8

Water supply and quality in streams and lakes, and groundwater levels in wells, by drainage basin, 1980, annual State rpt, 5666–12.34

Water supply and quality in streams and lakes, and groundwater levels in wells, by drainage basin, 1983, annual State rpt, 5666–10.34

see also Akron, Ohio
see also Athens County, Ohio
see also Canton, Ohio
see also Chillicothe, Ohio
see also Cincinnati, Ohio
see also Cleveland, Ohio

see also Columbus, Ohio
see also Cuyahoga County, Ohio
see also Dayton, Ohio
see also Elyria, Ohio
see also Gallipolis, Ohio
see also Hamilton, Ohio
see also Lima, Ohio
see also Logan County, Ohio
see also Lorain, Ohio
see also Mansfield, Ohio
see also Marietta, Ohio
see also Marion County, Ohio
see also Middletown, Ohio
see also Muskingum County, Ohio
see also Newark, Ohio
see also Portsmouth, Ohio
see also Ross County, Ohio
see also Sandusky, Ohio
see also Springfield, Ohio
see also Steubenville, Ohio
see also Toledo, Ohio
see also Warren, Ohio
see also Youngstown, Ohio
see also under By State in the "Index by Categories"

Ohio River

Bridges over navigable waters, with type of bridge and use, owner, dimensions, and location, 1984 regional listing, 7406–5.2

Freight (waterborne domestic and foreign) by commodity, traffic, and passengers, by port and waterway, 1982, annual rpt, 3754–3.2

Water supply and quality in streams and lakes, and groundwater levels in wells, by drainage basin, 1980, annual State rpt series, 5666–12

Water supply and quality in streams and lakes, and groundwater levels in wells, by drainage basin, 1981, annual State rpt series, 5666–16

Water supply and quality in streams and lakes, and groundwater levels in wells, by drainage basin, 1982, annual State rpt series, 5666–20

Water supply and quality in streams and lakes, and groundwater levels in wells, by drainage basin, 1983, annual State rpt series, 5666–10

Water supply in US and Canada, streamflow, well and reservoir levels, and dissolved solids and temperature in 6 US rivers, by station, monthly rpt, 5662–3

Oil

see Aviation fuels
see Diesel fuel
see Gasoline
see Heating oil
see Offshore oil and gas
see Oil and gas leases
see Oil depletion allowances
see Oil shale
see Oil spills
see Oils, oilseeds, and fats
see Petroleum and petroleum industry
see Petroleum exports and imports
see Petroleum prices
see Petroleum reserves
see Tar sands

Oil and gas leases

Alaska minerals resources, production, claims on wildlife refuges, oil and gas leases, and exploratory wells, with maps and bibl, 1983, annual rpt, 5664–11

Atlantic Ocean Georges Bank oil and gas drilling on Fed Govt leases, marine pollution problems, 1983 hearings, 21568–36

Coastal environmental and wildlife characteristics, use, and mgmt, for individual ecosystems, series, 5506–9

Coastal environmental characteristics, fish, wildlife, and use, and population socioeconomic data, for individual areas, series, 5506–4

Environmental and socioeconomic conditions, and potential impacts of oil and gas OCS leases, final statement series, 5736–1

Fed Govt programs and mgmt cost control proposals, 3-year savings by function and agency, and financial and operating data, 1960s-81, 16908–1.9

Fed Govt receipts, tax and other, FY83, annual rpt, 8104–2.2

Govt census, 1982: State govt payments to local govts, by program, source of funds, level of govt, and State, with trends from 1902, 2460–3

Interior Dept programs, activities, and funding, various periods 1967-84, last issue of annual rpt, 5304–13

Land Mgmt Bur activities and finances, and public land acreage and use, annual State rpt series, 5724–11

Land Mgmt Bur public lands admin and program activities in western States, FY82-84, annual rpt, 5724–13

Naval Petroleum and Oil Shale Reserves production, dev, ownership, leasing, sales by purchaser, and Fed Govt revenues, by site, FY83, annual rpt, 3004–22

Offshore OCS oil and gas reserves of Fed Govt, production, leasing and exploration activities, revenues, and costs, by ocean region, FY83, annual rpt, 5734–4

Offshore OCS proposed lease sale areas, oil spill risk analyses, series, 5736–2

Offshore oil and gas 5-year leasing plan and proposed sale off California, acreage, costs, and benefits, various periods 1953-2006, hearing, 21448–30

Offshore oil spills from US OCS platforms and pipelines, and from tankers at sea and in port worldwide, various periods 1964-80, 5738–1

Production and revenues from oil, gas, coal, and other minerals on Fed Govt and Indian lands, by State, 1983 with trends from 1920, annual rpt, 5734–2

Production and royalties from oil, gas, coal, and other minerals on Fed Govt and Indian lands, by State and commodity, annual rpt, discontinued, 5664–3

Production, leases, licenses, patents, and Fed Govt receipts for minerals from public lands, FY83, annual rpt, 5724–1.2

Production of oil and gas, royalties and other revenues, and inspections of leased Fed Govt and Indian lands, annual rpt, discontinued, 5734–1

Production, revenues, and reserves of oil, gas, and minerals from Fed Govt OCS leases, by State and ocean region, 1950s-82, annual rpt, 5734–3

Revenues for on and offshore oil and gas leases, total US and Alaska, 1982, annual Current Industrial Rpt, 2506–8.11

Oil and gas leases

Southeastern US OCS, marine vertebrate abundance and seasonal distribution, with oil and gas dev effects and lease status, early 1980s, 5508–85

Wildlife refuge revenues from economic and recreational uses, and refuge managers attitudes toward expanded use, FY81-83, GAO rpt, 26113–128

Oil depletion allowances

Budget of US, CBO analysis of revenue and spending alternatives and projections of economic indicators, FY85-89, annual rpt, 26304–3.3

Oil and gas finances by firm, and effect of income and excise tax provisions on firms, Fed Govt revenues, and investor tax returns, 1980 and projected to 1992, hearing, 21788–132

Oil shale

- Carbon dioxide emissions, climatic effects, and control costs, projected under alternative emissions controls and energy use restrictions to 2100 with trends 1970s-80, reprint, 9188–88
- Natl Energy Policy Plan, energy supply, demand, and prices, by fuel and consuming sector, projected 1985-2010, biennial rpt, 3004–13
- Naval Petroleum and Oil Shale Reserves production, dev, ownership, leasing, sales by purchaser, and Fed Govt revenues, by site, FY83, annual rpt, 3004–22
- Occupational injuries and incidence, nonmetallic mineral mining and related operations, detailed analysis, 1982, annual rpt, 6664–1
- Producers finances and operations, by energy type for US firms domestic and foreign operations, 1974-82, annual rpt, 3164–44.2
- Production, trade, supply, use, conservation, and DOE activities, by energy type, FY83, annual rpt, 3024–2
- R&D industry funding and employment of scientists and engineers, by industry group, firm size, and funding source, 1956-82, annual rpt, 9627–21
- Transportation and related energy use, for urban areas, late 1970s-82 and projected under lower auto emission standards to 1995, 3408–31
- Western States oil shale dev projects in Green River area, production goals and cost estimates, as of 1983, article, 9381–1.409

Oil spills

- Birds (marine) on southeastern US coast, distribution, abundance, and oil spill effects, by species and State, 1820s-1982, 5508–72
- Birds (shore) on Padre and Mustang Islands, Texas, distribution, abundance, and oil spill effects, by species, 1979-81, 5508–86
- California marine resources and environmental effects of proposed oil and gas dev, for 2 sanctuaries off central and northern coasts, 1980s and projected to 2006, hearing, 21448–30.1
- Coastal and aquatic wildlife habitats oil spills, methodology for cleanup priority rating and listing of wildlife species of concern, 1984 rpt, 5508–87
- Coastal environmental and wildlife characteristics, use, and mgmt, for individual ecosystems, series, 5506–9

Coastal environmental characteristics, fish, wildlife, and use, and population socioeconomic data, for individual areas, series, 5506–4

- Environmental quality and protection programs, costs, and Fed Govt enforcement, 1983, detailed annual rpt, 484–1
- France Brittany coast oil spill cleanup and research costs, marine and tourism industry losses, and recreation losses of tourists and residents, 1971-79, 2178–13
- Offshore OCS oil and gas leases environmental and socioeconomic impacts, and coastal area description, final statement series, 5736–1
- Offshore OCS proposed lease sale areas, oil spill risk analyses, series, 5736–2
- Offshore oil spills and well blowouts in waters under Fed Govt leases, and worldwide tanker oil spills, selected years 1969-FY83, annual rpt, 5734–3.5
- Offshore oil spills from US OCS platforms and pipelines, and from tankers at sea and in port worldwide, various periods 1964-80, 5738–1
- Southeastern US OCS, marine vertebrate abundance and seasonal distribution, with oil and gas dev effects and lease status, early 1980s, 5508–85

Oil wells

see Energy exploration and drilling

Oils, essential

see Spices and herbs

Oils, oilseeds, and fats

- Acreage planted and harvested, by crop and State, 1982-83 and planned as of June 1984, annual rpt, 1621–23
- Acreage planting intended for 19 crops, by State, as of Feb 1984, annual rpt, 1621–22
- Acreage, yield, and production of field crops, by State, 1978-82 and preliminary 1983, 1641–7
- *Agricultural Statistics, 1983,* annual rpt, 1004–1
- Agriculture census, 1982: farms, farmland, production, finances, and operator characteristics, by county, final State rpt series, 2331–1
- Alcohol fuel (ethanol) production in Tennessee Valley, feedstocks, facilities, tax incentives, and related farming data, by State, 1970s-83 and projected to 1992, 9808–69
- Animal and fish oils trade, tariffs, and industry operating data, foreign and US, 1978-82, TSUSA commodity rpt, 9885–1.62
- Argentina grain and oilseed production, effect of agricultural price regulation, 1947-80, 1528–170
- Canada grain handling and rail transport system financial and operating data, and effects of limited capacity on grain and oilseed exports, selected years 1950-82, 1528–176
- Castor oil hydrogenated products from Brazil, imports injury to US industry from removal of duties, investigation with background financial and operating data, 1984 rpt, 9886–18.13
- China economic conditions, agricultural and industrial production, trade, and domestic and foreign investment, 1980-85, 2048–106

Index by Subjects and Names

- China exports and imports by SITC 1- to 5-digit commodity, 1970s-82, annual rpt, 244–12
- Consumption of food and nutrient intake by individuals, by food group, source, and socioeconomic characteristics, 1977-78 natl survey, final rpt series, 1356–4
- Consumption, supply, trade, prices, expenditures, and indexes, by food commodity, 1963-83, annual rpt, 1544–4
- Cooperatives grain marketing, storage, and shipments by mode of transport, by grain type and region, FY80, 1128–28
- Cotton linters production, prices, stocks, use, and trade, monthly rpt, 1309–10
- Cottonseed quality factors, by State, 1983 crop, annual rpt, 1309–5
- County Business Patterns: establishments, employees, and payrolls, by SIC 4-digit industry and county, 1981, annual State rpt series, 2326–8
- County Business Patterns: establishments, employees, and payrolls, by SIC 4-digit industry and county, 1982, annual State rpt series, 2326–6
- Cuba economic conditions, agricultural and industrial production and distribution, trade, and intl economic relations, 1970-82 and trends from 1957, 248–40
- Developing countries food production and needs, and related economic trends and outlook, for 67 countries, 1980-86, annual rpt, 1524–6
- Eastern Europe agricultural production and trade by commodity, food consumption, and farm inputs, for 6 countries, 1960-80 with projections to 1991, 1528–178
- Eastern Europe grain production, consumption, and trade, and US farm cooperatives grain and oilseed export potential, for 4 countries, selected years 1960-90, 1128–27
- EC food supply/demand and market and support prices, with exchange rates, fertilizer price index, GDP, and population, by country, 1960-83, 1528–173
- Employment, earnings, and hours, by selected SIC 1- to 4-digit industry, State, and for 278 major labor areas, 1939-83, annual rpt, 6744–5
- Employment, earnings, and hours, by SIC 4-digit nonfarm industry, monthly 1974-Feb 1984, annual update, 6744–4
- Export sales and shipments of US grains, oilseed products, hides, skins, and cotton, by country, weekly rpt, 1922–3
- Exports and imports of dairy, livestock, and poultry live animals, meat, and products, by commodity and country of destination, FAS quarterly rpt, 1925–32
- Exports and imports of US, and trade balance, by major commodity group, selected country, and world area, with seasonal adjustments, monthly rpt, 2422–6
- Exports and imports of US, by agricultural commodity and country, bimonthly rpt with articles, 1522–1
- Exports and imports of US, by detailed agricultural commodity and country, FY83 and CY83, semiannual rpts, 1522–4
- Exports and imports of US, by detailed agricultural commodity for 8 major commodity groups, monthly rpt, 1922–8

Index by Subjects and Names

Oils, oilseeds, and fats

Exports and imports of US, detailed SIC-based commodities by world area, 1983, annual rpts, 2424–6

Exports and imports of US, totals and as percent of domestic production, by SIC 2- to 5-digit commodity, 1981, annual rpt, 2424–3

Exports and personal expenditures of US and world for selected agricultural commodities, by country, and export share of US farm income, various periods 1926-82, 1528–172

Exports, imports, tariffs, and industry operating data for fatty substances, natural chemicals, and radioactive materials, foreign and US, 1979-83, TSUSA commodity rpt, 9885–4.38

Exports, imports, tariffs, and industry operating data for flavorings, fragrances, perfumes, cosmetics, and toiletries, 1979-83, TSUSA commodity rpt, 9885–4.40

Exports of manufactured and agricultural commodities, manufacturing production, and export-related employment, 1960s-82, State rpt series, 2046–3

Exports of US, detailed commodities by country of destination, monthly rpt, 2422–3

Exports of US, detailed Schedule B commodities by country of destination, 1983, annual rpt, 2424–9

Exports of US, detailed Schedule E commodities by mode of transport and world area and country of destination, 1983, annual rpts, 2424–5

Exports under PL 480 concessional sales program, by commodity and country, 1955-83, semiannual rpt, 1922–6

Exports under PL 480 concessional sales program, by commodity and country, 1978-83, semiannual rpt, 1922–10

Farm finances, assets, liabilities, income, receipts by commodity and State, and expenses, 1980-83 and trends from 1910, annual rpt, 1544–16

Farm production inputs, outputs, and productivity, by region, 1939-82, annual rpt, 1544–17

Fish and fish products production by region and State, and trade, by species and product, 1982-83, annual rpt series, 2166–6

Fish meal and oil, production and trade, monthly rpt, 2162–3

Fish products production, 1977, annual rpt, 2164–2

Fish products, US production and trade, 1982-83, annual rpt, 2164–1

Foreign agricultural production, prices, and trade, by country, 1983 and outlook for 1984/85, annual world region rpt series, 1524–4

Foreign and US agricultural production, trade, and climatic devs, weekly press release, 1922–4

Foreign and US agricultural supply/demand, consumption per capita, and trade, by world area and country group, 1960s-82, 1528–181

Foreign and US production, acreage, and yield for selected crops, forecasts by selected world region and country, FAS monthly rpt, 1925–28

Foreign and US production and trade of fats, oils, and related products, FAS monthly and annual circular series, 1925–1

Futures trading by commodity and exchange, and Commodity Futures Trading Commission activities, funding, and employment, FY83, annual rpt, 11924–2

Futures trading in selected commodities, foreign currencies, and stock indexes, Chicago and other markets activity, monthly rpt, 11922–1

Futures trading in selected commodities, foreign currencies, Treasury securities, and stock indexes, NYC, Chicago, and other markets activity, monthly rpt, 11922–5

Genetic resource (plant and animal) conservation, commercial uses, causes of depletion, and geographic sources, 1984 rpt, 5548–13

Glue, gelatin, and related products trade, tariffs, and industry operating data, 1979-83, TSUSA commodity rpt supplement, 9885–4.48

Great Lakes trade, by SITC 3-digit commodity, port, vessel type, world area, and country, 1982, annual rpt, 7744–3

Imports of US, detailed Schedule A commodities by country and world area of origin, and mode of transport, 1983, annual rpts, 2424–2

Imports of US, detailed Schedule A commodities by country, monthly rpt, 2422–2

Imports of US, detailed TSUSA commodities by country of origin, 1983, annual rpt, 2424–4

Input-output structure of US economy, detailed interindustry transactions for 537 industries, and components of final demand, 1977 benchmark data, 2708–17

Lard production, by State, 1983, annual rpt, 1623–10

Lard production, monthly rpt, 1623–9

Manufacturing census, 1982: financial and operating data, by SIC 2- to 4-digit industry, State, SMSA, and county, preliminary census div rpt series, 2491–3

Manufacturing census, 1982: financial and operating data, for SIC 4-digit industries by product, preliminary rpt series, 2491–1

Marketing cash receipts of farms, by detailed commodity and State, 1979-82, annual rpt, 1544–18

Marshall Islands and Federated States of Micronesia copra production and exports, 1970s-83, annual rpt, 7004–6.2

Mill production, crushings, and stocks of fats and oils by product and State, monthly Current Industrial Rpt, 2506–4.3

Occupational injury and illness rates, by SIC 2- to 4-digit industry, 1982, annual rpt, 6844–1

OECD trade, total and for 4 major countries, and US trade by country, by commodity, 1972-82, annual world region rpt series, 244–13

Peanut production, prices, stocks, exports, use, inspection, and quality, by region and State, selected crop years 1974-83, annual rpt, 1311–5

Peanut production, prices, trade by country, and stocks, weekly rpt, 1311–1

Peanut stocks, millings, and processing, Feb-July 1984, semiannual rpt, 1621–6

PL 480 commodity allocations for long-term credit sales, by country, quarterly press release, 1922–7

Portugal agricultural subsidies, profits, marketing margins, and consumer prices, by commodity or product, and effects of prospective EC membership, 1981, 1528–171

Prices (farm-retail) for foods, marketing cost components, and industry finances and productivity, selected years 1967-83, annual rpt, 1544–9

Prices received by farmers and production value for detailed crops by State, 1981-83, annual rpt, 1621–2

Prices received by farmers for major products, and paid for farm inputs and living items, by commodity and State, monthly rpt, 1629–1

Prices received by farmers for major products, and paid for farm inputs, by commodity and State, 1983, annual rpt, 1629–5

Producer prices and indexes, by stage of processing and detailed commodity, monthly rpt, 6762–6

Producer prices and indexes, by stage of processing and detailed commodity, monthly 1983, annual supplement, 6764–2

Production and farm finances, expenses by type, and domestic economic impact, selected years 1972-82 and preliminary 1983-84, annual rpt, 1544–19

Production, consumption by end use, and stocks, by type of oil and fat, monthly Current Industrial Rpt, 2506–4.4

Production, farms, acreage, and related data, by selected crop and State, monthly rpt, 1621–1

Production itemized costs, receipts, and net returns for sunflower and flaxseed, and peanuts by region, 1981-83, annual rpt, 1544–20

Production, prices, trade, and consumption, periodic situation rpt with articles, 1561–3

Production, prices, trade, and export inspections by US port and country of destination, by grain type, weekly rpt, 1313–2

Production, prices, trade, and marketing, by commodity, current situation and forecast, monthly rpt, 1502–4

Production, prices, trade, stocks, and consumption of fats, oils, and oilseeds and products, annual rpt, suspended, 1564–12

Stocks of grains, oilseeds, and hay on and off farms, by State, 1978-83, 1641–17

Sunflower seed stocks by region and market city, and seed inspected for export, weekly rpt, 1313–4

Tallow and grease foreign and US production, trade, and consumption, FAS semiannual circular, 1925–33

Waterborne commerce of US (domestic and foreign), freight by commodity, traffic, and passengers, by port and waterway, 1982, annual rpt, 3754–3

Waterborne trade of grain and selected other commodities worldwide, and grain ocean freight rates by route, 1966-82, 1548–235

Oils, oilseeds, and fats

see also Animal feed
see also Corn
see also Soybeans
see also under By Commodity in the "Index by Categories"

O'Keefe, Garrett J.

"'Taking a Bite Out of Crime': The Impact of a Mass Media Crime Prevention Campaign", 6068–183

Oklahoma

- Agriculture census, 1982: farms, farmland, production and costs, and operator characteristics, preliminary State summary and county rpts, 2330–1.40
- Agriculture census, 1982: farms, farmland, production, finances, and operator characteristics, by county, final State rpt, 2331–1.36
- Bank deposits in commercial and mutual savings banks and in US branches of foreign banks, by account type, instn, State, SMSA, and county, June 1983, annual rpt, 9295–3.14
- Census of Housing, 1980: occupancy and unit characteristics of SMSAs and central cities, by race, Hispanic origin, and city, State rpt, 2473–1.38
- Census of Population and Housing, 1980: detailed population and housing characteristics, by county, city, and census tract, State rpt, 2551–2.38
- Census of Population, 1980: detailed socioeconomic and demographic characteristics, by age, sex, race, Hispanic origin, and industry, State rpt, 2531–4.38
- County Business Patterns: establishments, employees, and payrolls, by SIC 4-digit industry and county, 1982, annual State rpt, 2326–6.38
- Employment by major nonagricultural industry, and average hours and earnings of manufacturing production workers, for 5 southwestern States, monthly rpt, 6962–2
- Employment, earnings, and hours, by selected SIC 1- to 4-digit industry, State, and for 278 major labor areas, 1939-83, annual rpt, 6744–5.2, 6744–5.3
- Employment, industrial relations, prices, and economic conditions in 5 Southwestern States, regional rpts series, 6966–1
- Environmental quality, pollutant discharge by type and source, and EPA protection activities and funding, 1970s-83, biennial regional rpt, 9184–15.6
- Exports of manufactured and agricultural commodities, manufacturing production, and export-related employment, 1960s-82, State rpt, 2046–3.36
- Hay prices in 10 market areas, for baled alfalfa and prairie hay, weekly rpt, 1313–5
- HHS aid to each State and local govt or private instn, amount obligated, funding agency, and program, FY83, annual listing, 4004–3.6
- Income (personal) per capita and by source, and earnings by industry div, by State, MSA, and county, 1977-82, annual regional rpt, 2704–2.7
- Manufacturing census, 1982: financial and operating data, by SIC 2- to 4-digit industry, State, SMSA, and county, preliminary census div rpt, 2491–3.7

Mineral Industry Surveys, State review of production, 1983, advance annual rpt, 5614–6.36

- *Minerals Yearbook, 1982,* Vol 2 preprints: State review of production and sales by commodity, and business activity, annual rpt, 5604–16.37
- *Minerals Yearbook, 1982,* Vol 2: State reviews of production, sales, and firms, by commodity, and business activity, annual rpt, 5604–34
- Oil and gas extraction production workers, wages, hours, and benefits, by occupation, region, and for 5 States, June 1982 survey, 6787–6.203
- Oil and gas field itemized equipment and operating costs and cost indexes, for 10 producing areas, 1981-83, annual rpt, 3164–45
- Population size and components of change, by MSA and county, 1980-82, annual State Current Population Rpt, 2546–4.36
- Population size, Apr 1980 and July 1982, and per capita income, 1979 and 1981, by county and city, State Current Population Rpt, 2546–11.36
- Retail trade census, 1982: employment, establishments, sales, and payroll, by SIC 2- to 4-digit kind of business, SMSA, county, and city, State rpt, 2397–1.37
- Savings and loan assns, FHLB 10th District insured members finances and operations by SMSA, monthly rpt, 9302–22
- Service industry census, 1982: employment, establishments, receipts, and payroll, by SIC 2- to 4-digit kind of business, SMSA, county, and city, State rpt, 2391–1.37
- Wholesale trade census, 1982: employment, establishments, finances, and operations, by SIC 2- to 4-digit kind of business, SMSA, county, and city, State rpt, 2405–1.37

see also Elk City, Okla.
see also Enid, Okla.
see also Lawton, Okla.
see also Oklahoma City, Okla.
see also Payne County, Okla.
see also Tulsa, Okla.
see also under By State in the "Index by Categories"

Oklahoma City, Okla.

- Census of Housing, 1980: occupancy and unit characteristics, by race, Hispanic origin, and city, SMSA rpt, 2473–1.270
- Census of Population and Housing, 1980: detailed population and housing characteristics, by county, city, and census tract, SMSA rpt, 2551–2.270
- Homeless population and characteristics, and temporary shelter operations, use, and user characteristics, for selected cities, various periods 1979-84, hearing, 21248–85
- Housing and households detailed characteristics, and unit and neighborhood quality, by inside-outside central cities, 1980 survey, SMSA rpt, 2485–6.13
- Wages of office and plant workers, by occupation, 1984 SMSA survey rpt, 6785–11.8

see also under By City and By SMSA or MSA in the "Index by Categories"

Index by Subjects and Names

Old age

see Aged and aging

Old-Age and Survivors Insurance Trust Fund

see Federal trust funds

Old Age Assistance

- Beneficiary families and children, and total and average payments, by public assistance program and State, since 1940, monthly rpt, 4742–1.5
- Benefits and beneficiary characteristics of OASDHI, Medicaid, SSI, and other social insurance and public welfare programs, selected years 1937-82, annual rpt, 4744–3.13
- Benefits, beneficiaries below poverty level, and State expenditures for SSI and 3 earlier programs, selected years 1972-83, article, 4742–1.402
- Outlying areas programs and provisions under Social Security Act, FY82, annual rpt, 4704–9
- Outlying areas public assistance adult recipients and payments, by program, quarterly rpt, 4742–6.1

see also Supplemental Security Income

Old-Age, Survivors, Disability, and Health Insurance

- Actuarial notes on social security, series, 4706–2
- Actuarial studies, Medicare and OASDI future cost estimates and past experience analyses, series, 4706–1
- Beneficiaries of noncash public and employer-based transfer programs, by income source and socioeconomic characteristics, 1982, final Current Population Rpt, 2546–6.37
- Benefit overpayments and OASDI beneficiary status changes reported late, for death, marriage, and leaving school, 1981, GAO rpt, 26121–68
- Benefits and after-tax salary replacement rates by pension type, and older persons income and income sources, by age and marital status, 1950s-82, conf proceedings, 25408–87
- Benefits and beneficiaries by demographic characteristics, and use of direct deposit, by SMSA and for rest of US and foreign countries, annual rpt, suspended, 4744–10
- Benefits and beneficiaries of OASDI, by type of benefit, State, outlying area, and county, Dec 1982, 4748–38
- Benefits and beneficiaries of SSI and other income maintenance programs, by State, monthly rpt, 4742–2
- Benefits and beneficiaries with representative payees by Fed Govt cash benefit program, and OASDI and SSI fraud and misuse, various periods FY74-81, GAO rpt, 26121–85
- Benefits, beneficiary characteristics, and trust funds of OASDHI, Medicaid, SSI, and other social insurance and public welfare programs, selected years 1937-83, annual rpt, 4744–3
- Benefits by county, FY83, annual rpt, 4004–3
- Budget of US, CBO analysis of revenue and spending alternatives and projections of economic indicators, FY85-89, annual rpt, 26304–3.3
- Budget of US, effects of Reagan Admin policy changes, by detailed program, FY85, annual rpt, 104–21

Index by Subjects and Names

Budget of US, receipts, outlays, and budget authority, by function and agency, FY84-89 revised estimates, midsession review of FY85 budget, annual rpt, 104–7

Census of Population and Housing, 1980: detailed population and housing characteristics, by county, city, and census tract, State and SMSA rpt series, 2551–2

Census of Population, 1980: detailed socioeconomic and demographic characteristics, by age, sex, race, Hispanic origin, occupation, and industry, State rpt series, 2531–4

Census of Population, 1980: detailed socioeconomic characteristics, by county, city, and inside-outside SMSAs and central cities, State rpt series, 2531–3

Children and youth benefitting from Fed Govt public welfare programs and tax expenditures, participation and funding for 71 programs, FY81-83, 21968–30

Civil case processing of US Attorneys and amounts involved, by cause of action, FY83, annual rpt, 6004–2.5

Cost control proposals for Fed Govt programs and mgmt, 3-year savings by function and agency, and financial and operating data, 1960s-81, 16908–1.6, 16908–1.23, 16908–1.27

County and City Data Book, detailed socioeconomic and demographic data for States, counties, and cities, selected years 1976-82, 2328–1

Disability (work-related), incidence among men aged 22-64 related to sociodemographic and employment characteristics and to self-evaluated mental stress, 1972-74, 4746–5.43

Disability Insurance beneficiaries sociodemographic and medical characteristics, 1977-79, annual rpt, 4744–20

Disabled workers receiving Social Security allowances, total and for persons with cardiovascular diseases by type, 1975, annual rpt, 4474–22.3

Farm households receiving social security income, farms and amount by characteristics of farm and operator, 1978-82, article, 1702–1.410

Fed Govt aid to State and local govts, expenditures, and direct payments, by program, agency, and State, FY83, annual rpt, 2464–2

Fed Govt consolidated financial statements based on business accounting methods, FY82-83, annual rpt, 8104–5

Fed Govt programs under Ways and Means Committee jurisdiction, program operations and financing data for assessing budgetary requirements, by State, FY70s-83, 21788–117

Fed Govt spending by function, with comparisons to State and local govt spending, selected years 1929-83, annual rpt, 10044–1.1

Finances of OASDHI, trust funds receipts, expenditures, assets, and liabilities, monthly rpt, 8102–9.2

Financial statements of OASDI trust funds, FY83 and selected years 1940s-2060, annual rpt, 4704–4

Financial status of OASDHI trust funds, assets, total and tax income, and outlays, alternative projections to 2060, 4706–2.120

Financial status of OASDI trust funds, and Fed Govt budget balance adjusted for OASDI, various periods 1946-83, article, 9373–1.414

Financing and beneficiaries of OASDI programs, FY83, annual rpt, 4704–6

Food stamp recipient households size and composition, income, and income deductions allowed, Aug 1981, annual rpt, 1364–8

Govt revenues by source, expenditures by function, debt, and assets, by level of govt, 1982-83, annual rpt, 2466–2.6

Income (personal) by source including transfer payments, and social insurance contributions by type, by region, 1982, 2708–40

Income from transfer payments, natl income and product account, *Survey of Current Business,* monthly rpt, monthly and annual tables, 2702–1.23

Income of households, families, and persons, by detailed socioeconomic characteristics and region, 1982, annual Current Population Rpt, 2546–6.39

Life expectancy increase impacts on OASDI and pension policy, with alternative sociodemographic projections to 2100, hearing, 25368–130

Older persons by demographic, socioeconomic, and health characteristics, selected years 1900-81 and projected to 2050, Current Population Rpt, 2546–2.125

Older persons Fed Govt pension and health spending, by program and as percents of budget and GNP, 1965-85 with projections to 2040, 25148–28

Older persons income and income sources, by OASDI beneficiary and poverty status, labor force participation, and demographic characteristics, 1982, biennial rpt, 4744–26

Older persons retirement income by type, and preretirement income replacement, under alternative inflation rates, various periods 1979-84, article, 9373–1.419

Older persons sociodemographic characteristics, and Fed Govt program participation and funding, 1983 with trends and projections 1900-2060, annual rpt, 25144–3.1

Oregon and Montana earnings by SIC 1- to 3-digit industry and payments to retirees by type, for 4 timber dependent communities, 1970, 1208–196

Poverty-level persons and families, by income source, hours of work, earnings, taxes, and family characteristics, various periods 1959-84, 21788–131

Poverty status of families and persons, by detailed socioeconomic characteristics, 1982, annual Current Population Rpt, 2546–6.40

Private pension plans integrated with OASI benefits, and salary replacement rates, by formula type, salary level, and firm collective bargaining status, 1981, article, 6722–1.431

Railroad retirement and unemployment insurance accounts status, and interchange with OASDHI fund, FY82, annual rpt, 9704–2.1

Research and Statistics Notes on social security programs and recipient characteristics, series, 4746–16

Research projects of SSA, narrative summary, FY84-86, annual rpt, 4744–11

Social Security Bulletin, OASDHI and other program operations and beneficiary characteristics, from 1940, monthly rpt with articles, 4742–1

State and local govt employee retirement system members covered by OASDHI, by system, 1982-83, annual rpt, 2466–2.4

Supplementary Security Income beneficiary socioeconomic characteristics and health service use, 1970s-83 and SSI program projections to 1995, 25148–29

Texas farm household income, by income source and substate region, 1979, article, 9379–1.406

Traffic accidents and casualties detailed direct and indirect costs, by characteristics of persons and vehicles involved, 1979-80, 7768–80

Vocationally rehabilitated persons under State agency programs, by sociodemographic characteristics and disabling condition, FY79-81, annual rpt, 4944–6

Women's labor force and OASDHI participation by age, and pension coverage by sex, selected years 1939-82, hearing, 25368–131.1

see also Medicare

see also Social security tax

Old West Regional Commission

Agricultural Stabilization and Conservation Service producer payments under 26 programs, monthly rpt, 1802–10

Older Americans Act

Social services for aged, participation and funding under Act, by program or State, FY70-84, annual rpt, 25144–3.1

Oldfield, Margery L.

"Value of Conserving Genetic Resources", 5548–13

Oleomargarine

see Oils, oilseeds, and fats

Olive oil

see Oils, oilseeds, and fats

Oliver, Julia

"Survey of U.S. Uranium Marketing Activity, 1983", 3164–66

Olives

see Fruit and fruit products

Olsen, David A.

"Ciguatera in the Eastern Caribbean", 2162–1.403

Olsen, Kathryn

"Occupational Employment in Nuclear-Related Activities, 1983", 3004–11

Olympia, Wash.

Census of Housing, 1980: occupancy and unit characteristics, by race, Hispanic origin, and city, SMSA rpt, 2473–1.271

Census of Population and Housing, 1980: detailed population and housing characteristics, by county, city, and census tract, SMSA rpt, 2551–2.271

see also under By SMSA or MSA in the "Index by Categories"

Omaha, Nebr.

Census of Housing, 1980: occupancy and unit characteristics, by race, Hispanic origin, and city, SMSA rpt, 2473–1.272

Census of Population and Housing, 1980: detailed population and housing characteristics, by county, city, and census tract, SMSA rpt, 2551–2.272

Omaha, Nebr.

Housing vacancy rates for single and multifamily units and mobile homes, by county, city, and ZIP code, 1983, annual MSA rpt, 9304–22.6

Wages by occupation, and benefits for office and plant workers, 1983 SMSA survey rpt, 6785–12.2

Wages of office and plant workers, by occupation, 1984 SMSA survey rpt, 6785–11.10

see also under By City and By SMSA or MSA in the "Index by Categories"

Oman

Agricultural situation in Middle East and North Africa, by country and commodity, 1983 and outlook for 1984, annual rpt, 1524–4.3

AID activities and funding by project and function, FY85, and developing countries summary socioeconomic data, 1970s-83, by country, annual rpt, 9914–3

AID economic assistance to developing countries, obligations and disbursements by country, quarterly rpt, 9912–4

AID loan repayment status and terms by program and country, and status of predecessor agency loans, quarterly rpt, 9912–3

Background Notes, summary social, political, and economic data, 1983 rpt, 7006–2.14

Economic, social, and political summary data, by country, 1984, annual factbook, 244–11

Economic trends in income, production, prices, employment, finances, and trade, 1984 annual rpt, 2046–4.35

Exports of US, detailed Schedule B commodities by country of destination, 1983, annual rpt, 2424–9

Exports of US, detailed Schedule E commodities by mode of transport and world area and country of destination, 1983, annual rpts, 2424–5

Imports of US, detailed Schedule A commodities by country and world area of origin, and mode of transport, 1983, annual rpts, 2424–2

Imports of US, detailed TSUSA commodities by country of origin, 1983, annual rpt, 2424–4

Loans and grants for economic and military assistance from US and intl agencies, by program and country, FY46-83, annual rpt, 9914–5

Military aid of US, arms sales, and training programs costs and budget requests by program, world region, and country, FY83-85, annual rpt, 7144–13

Military spending, arms trade, and armed forces size, with total govt spending and population, by country, 1972-82, annual rpt, 9824–1

Minerals Yearbook, 1982, Vol 3: foreign country reviews of production, trade, and policies, by commodity, annual rpt, 5604–35

Minerals Yearbook, 1982, Vol 3 preprints: foreign country review of production, trade, and policies, by commodity, annual rpt, 5604–17.88

Population size and growth rates, and latest available benchmark demographic data, by country, 1950-83, biennial rpt, 2324–4

Telecommunication equipment market and trade, and user industry operations and demand, 1982 country market research rpt, 2045–12.32

see also under By Foreign Country in the "Index by Categories"

Omnibus Budget Reconciliation Act

AFDC eligibility under Omnibus Budget Reconciliation Act, effect on caseloads and recipient benefits and living costs, 1981-83, GAO rpt, 26131–11

O'Neill, David M.

"Growth of the Underground Economy, 1950-81: Some Evidence from the Current Population Survey", 23848–178

O'Neill, Richard P.

"Competition and Other Current Issues in the Natural Gas Market", 3168–89

"Contracts Between Interstate Pipelines and Their Customers", 3162–4.408

"Natural Gas Wellhead Markets: Structures and Trends", 3162–4.403

Onions

see Vegetables and vegetable products

Ontario, Calif.

Census of Housing, 1980: occupancy and unit characteristics, by race, Hispanic origin, and city, SMSA rpt, 2473–1.303

Census of Population and Housing, 1980: detailed population and housing characteristics, by county, city, and census tract, SMSA rpt, 2551–2.303

Housing and financial characteristics, and unit and neighborhood quality, for 15 SMSAs, 1978, annual survey special supplement, 2485–8

Housing and households detailed characteristics, and unit and neighborhood quality, by inside-outside central cities, 1982 survey, SMSA rpt, 2485–6.41

Housing unit starts and completions authorized by building permits in 20 MSAs, quarterly rpt, 2382–9

Housing vacancy rates for single and multifamily units and mobile homes, by city and ZIP code, 1983, annual metro area rpt, 9304–20.9

Ontario, Canada

Great Lakes basin pollutant discharges by source, and control program activities, 1983 annual rpt, 14644–1

OPEC

see Organization of Petroleum Exporting Countries

Open housing

see Discrimination in housing

Open space land programs

Fed Govt aid to State and local govts, expenditures, and direct payments, by program, agency, and State, FY83, annual rpt, 2464–2

Govt census, 1982: State govt payments to local govts, by program, source of funds, level of govt, and State, with trends from 1902, 2460–3

New Communities program of HUD, activities, costs, land sales, and community and population characteristics, for 13 communities, 1970s-83, 5188–107

see also Community Development Block Grants

Operating costs

see Business income and expenses, general

see Business income and expenses, specific industries

Operating ratios

see Operating ratios

see Production costs

Operating ratios

Agricultural cooperative finances and operations, aggregate for top 100 assns by principal product and revenue source, FY82, annual rpt, 1124–3

Agricultural cooperative operating ratios by commodity, and debt financing by source, for 100 largest cooperatives, selected years FY62-83, article, 1122–1.411

Agricultural products trade, tariffs, and industry operating data, 1979-83, TSUSA commodity rpt series, 9885–1

Airline deregulation in 1978, effect on industry operations and finances, air traffic patterns, and CAB programs, various periods FY76-84, 9148–56

Airline financial and operating data for certificated, charter, and cargo carriers, quarterly rpt, 9142–30

Airline financial data, by carrier, carrier group, and for total certificated system, quarterly rpt, 9142–12

Airline income and profitability, by major carrier, 1972-83, annual rpt, 9144–37

Airline intl operations, traffic and financial data for US combination carriers in Atlantic, Pacific, and Latin America regions, quarterly rpt, 9142–41

Airline operations and passenger, cargo, and mail traffic, by type of service, air carrier, State, and country, 1974-83, annual rpt, 7504–1.6

Airline passenger traffic and capacity for US and intl operations of major trunk carriers, and seasonal adjustment factors, monthly rpt, 9142–19

Airline passenger traffic, capacity, yields, and load factors, changes for each system major and short-haul natl carrier, periodic rpt, 9142–45

Airline passenger traffic since 1978 deregulation, by major carrier, quarterly rpt, 9142–49

Airline profit margins, for major operators of large aircraft by carrier group and carrier, quarterly rpt, 9142–43

Airline traffic and financial data, by carrier, FY83 with trends from FY73, annual rpt, 9144–1

Airline traffic, capacity, and performance for medium regionals, by carrier and certification status, quarterly rpt, 9142–44

Airport financing by source, bond issues by region, and airport operations, by airport and operator type, FY75-83 and projected to FY93, 26306–6.75

Auto industry finances and operations by manufacturer, foreign competition, and consumer auto expenditures and attitudes toward car buying, selected years 1968-85, annual rpt, 2004–8

Auto industry finances, employment, production, and cost increases to comply with Fed Govt pollution and safety standards, 1970s-83, annual rpt, 3304–5.4

Bank deposit interest rate deregulation, effect on bank deposits and bank financial performance, 1978-83, hearing, 21248–83

Bank financial ratios and asset and liability composition, for medium-sized commercial instns by profitability and region, 1972-81, research paper, 9371–10.20

Index by Subjects and Names

Operating ratios

Bank holding company ratios of financial involvement in nonbank subsidiaries and subsidiary performance, by holding company size, various periods 1978-82, article, 9377–1.406

Bank profitability, finances, loans and terms, intl earnings, and operating ratios for insured commercial instns, 1980-83, annual article, 9362–1.409

Banks (insured commercial) in Southeastern States, financial ratios by asset size and State, 1979-83, article, 9371–1.419

Banks and thrift instns in New England, financial statements by type of instn and State, 1972 and 1982, annual rpt, 9304–3

Banks in Fed Reserve 5th District, by asset size, finances, and loans and deposits by type, various dates 1979-83, annual article, 9389–1.408

Bus industry collective ratemaking and regulatory reform impacts on operations, finances, and services to older persons and rural areas by State, 1970s-83, 14828–2

Business and financial statistics, historic trends, 1984 annual chartbook, 9364–2

Business and financial statistics, quarterly chartbook, 9362–2.2

Business Conditions Digest, historical supplement on economic, business, and financial conditions and cyclical fluctuations, with methodology, 1947-82, 2708–31

Campground facilities privately owned, and financial and operating data, by region, 1982, annual rpt, 5544–14.5

Chemicals and related products trade, tariffs, and industry operating data, TSUSA commodity rpt series, 9885–4

Coal production, mining employment, exports, and finances, by coal district, 1982, 3008–97

Conrail operations and US Railway Assn finances and activities, FY81-83, annual rpt, 29604–1

Construction industries census, 1982: financial and operating data, by SIC 4-digit industry and State, final rpt series, 2373–1

Corporations financial statements for manufacturing, mining, and trade, by selected SIC 2- to 3-digit industry, quarterly rpt, 2502–1

Corporations profits after taxes, natl compounded annual rates of change, 1964-83, 9391–9.2

Corporations profits by industry div, profit tax liability, and dividends, monthly rpt, quarterly data, 23842–1.1

Credit union financial ratios related to Federal deposit insurance status, various periods 1948-82, article, 9379–1.404

Credit union financial statements by region, State, and type of membership, for Federal and federally insured State unions, 1983, annual rpt, 9534–1

Credit Union Natl Admin Central Liquidity Facility, financial performance, quarterly rpt, 9532–4

Credit unions in Georgia, operating and financial ratios and other performance indicators for 53 large instns, as of Dec 1983, article, 9371–1.427

Electric utilities privately owned, capital investment, finances, equity performance, and operating characteristics, 1950-82 with supply estimates to 2010, 3168–87

Electric utilities privately owned, common stock performance measures, with comparisons to selected industry groups, selected years 1970-82, GAO rpt, 26113–129

Electric utilities privately owned, detailed financial and operating data by company, with summary data for other distributors by type, 1982, annual rpt, 3164–23

Energy producers finances and operations, by energy type for US firms domestic and foreign operations, 1974-82, annual rpt, 3164–44

Farm debt to asset ratio, by southeastern State, 1979-83, article, 9371–1.424

Farm finances, assets, expenses, cash flow, receipts, and loans, selected years 1971-85, annual rpt, 1544–13

Farm finances, liabilities, income, receipts by commodity and State, and expenses, 1980-83 and trends from 1910, annual rpt, 1544–16

Farm finances, expenses by type, loans by purpose and source, and credit detail by Fed Reserve District, quarterly rpt, 9365–3.10

Fed Crop Insurance Corp finances, and insurance participation and operations in 2 States by crop, 1980-84, GAO rpt, 26113–132

Fed Crop Insurance Corp program operations and finances, for FCIC policies and private policies reinsured by FCIC, 1970s-84 with trends from 1948, hearing, 21168–28

Feed grain production, acreage, stocks, use, trade, prices, and price supports, periodic situation rpt with articles, 1561–4

Financial instns income taxes, effective rates, and selected financial data, by instn type and firm, with comparisons to other industries, selected years 1960-82, hearing, 25368–129

Food industry advertising expenditures by media type, and advertising to sales ratio by selected food item, 1970-79 with some trends from 1955, 1548–234

Freight ton-miles and energy consumption rates, by mode of transport, 1970-82, annual rpt, 3164–73

Fresno, Calif, economic, population, labor, and housing indicators, various periods 1974-85, hearing, 21248–84

Fruit and nut production, prices, trade, stocks, and use, by selected crop, periodic situation rpt with articles, 1561–6

Grain cooperatives storage and handling facilities, sales, exports, and financial condition, selected years 1974-82, 1128–31

Import and tariff provisions effect on US industries and products, investigations with background financial and operating data, series, 9886–4

Imports injury to US industries from foreign subsidized products, investigations with background financial and operating data for selected industries and products, series, 9886–15

Imports injury to US industries from import sales at less than fair value, investigations with background financial and operating data, series, 9886–14

Imports injury to US industries from increased import sales, investigations with background financial and operating data, series, 9886–5

Income tax returns of individuals, detailed data, 1982, annual rpt, 8304–2

Income tax returns of sole proprietorships, receipts, deductions by type, payroll, and net income, by major industry, 1982, annual article, 8302–2.413

Insurance industry (property and casualty) financial and operating data, investments, and tax liability, various periods 1951-82, hearing, 25368–128

Manufactured products (miscellaneous) trade, tariffs, and industry operating data, TSUSA commodity rpt series, 9885–7

Manufacturing and trade inventories, sales, and inventory/sales ratios, quarterly article, 2702–1.34

Manufacturing census, 1982: financial and operating data, for SIC 4-digit industries by product, preliminary rpt series, 2491–1

Metals and metal products trade, tariffs, and industry operating data, TSUSA commodity rpt series, 9885–6

Minerals (nonfuel) foreign and US supply under alternative market conditions, reserves, and background industry data, series, 5606–4

Minerals (nonmetallic) and mineral products trade, tariffs, and industry operating data, TSUSA commodity rpt series, 9885–5

Motor and rail carriers regulated by ICC, employment and finances by mode of transport, and ICC activities, FY80-83 and trends, annual rpt, 9484–1

Motor carrier passengers and selected revenue data, for individual large Class I motor carriers, quarterly rpt, 9482–13

Motor carriers (Class I) of household goods operating revenues, net income, and revenue tons, by firm, quarterly rpt, 9482–14

Motor carriers (Class I) of property financial and operating data, by region and firm, quarterly rpt, 9482–5

Motor carriers (Class I interstate) finances, operations, equipment, employment, and payroll, by district, 1982, annual rpt, 9486–5.3

Natural gas interstate pipeline company detailed financial and operating data, by firm, 1983, annual rpt, 3164–38

Nuclear power accident liability insurance under Price-Anderson Act, effects on industry finances and operations, with insurance coverage, claims, and costs, various periods 1957-82, 9638–49

Oil and gas companies production and exploration detailed expenditures, revenues, operating ratios, and sales volume, 1982, annual Current Industrial Rpt, 2506–8.11

Oil and gas finances by firm, and effect of income and excise tax provisions on firms, Fed Govt revenues, and investor tax returns, 1980 and projected to 1992, hearing, 21788–132

Oil companies energy production and imports by type, and financial data, 1975-81, annual rpt, 3164–74

Oil industry foreign-affiliated US firms, selected financial data, 1981-82, annual rpt, 3024–2

Oil pipeline in Alaska, owner companies financial data, and retail gasoline competitive position in 2 States, by company, 1980-83, hearing, 21728–51

Operating ratios

Oil refineries financial and operating impacts from auto use of alcohol fuels, projected to 2000 with trends 1964-80, 3308–75

Pension multiemployer plans in construction, trucking, and entertainment industries, and effect of exemption from withdrawal liability, 1977-81, GAO rpt, 26121–73

Philanthropic foundations detailed financial and operating data, and stock holdings by instn, 1979 with selected trends from 1920, GAO rpt, 26119–53

Pollution abatement expenditures, and effect on economic indicators and industry operations, by major industry, projected under 3 pollution regulation alternatives 1983-95, 9188–84

Postal Service electronic mail system message volume and profitability under proposed rate and service increases, FY82 and projected to FY87, 21408–70

Productivity and costs of labor for private, nonfarm business, and manufacturing sectors, preliminary data, quarterly rpt, 6822–1

Productivity and costs of labor for private, nonfarm business, and manufacturing sectors, revised data, quarterly rpt, 6822–2

Rail high-speed system planned from Chicago, capital and operating costs and profitability by speed class, frequency, and route, 1984 article, 9375–1.406

Railroad finances, operations, and freight rates and shares, by commodity and railroad, 1970s-82, hearings, 25268–80

Railroad freight volume and revenues, by commodity and region of origin and destination, 1982, annual rpt, 7604–6

Railroad revenue, income, freight, and rate of return, by Class I freight railroad and district, quarterly rpt, 9482–2

Retail trade census, 1982: employment, establishments, sales, and payroll, by SIC 2- to 4-digit kind of business, SMSA, county, and city, State rpt series, 2397–1

Retail trade census, 1982: employment, establishments, sales, and payroll, by SIC 4-digit kind of business and State, preliminary rpt series, 2395–1

Retail trade sales, inventories, purchases, gross margin, and accounts receivable, by SIC 2- to 4-digit kind of business and type of ownership, 1983, annual rpt, 2413–5

Rice price variability effect on price margins and profits, various periods 1960-82, article, 1502–3.404

Rural Electrification Admin loans to power supply and distribution firms, and borrower operating and financial data, by firm and State, 1983, annual rpt, 1244–1

Savings and loan assn deregulation impact, financial ratios of S&Ls in 3 States and US, 1980-83, article, 9371–1.426

Savings and loan assns (FSLIC-insured), financial ratios of profitable and unprofitable S&Ls, selected years 1965-82, technical paper, 9316–2.47

Savings and loan assns (FSLIC-insured) income, expenses, and financial and operating ratios, semiannual article, 9312–1

Savings and loan assns, FHLB 1st District member instns financial operations and related economic and housing indicators, monthly rpt, 9302–4

Savings and loan assns, FHLB 4th District members financial ratios and mortgage portfolios by State, 2nd half 1983, semiannual rpt, 9302–3

Savings and loan assns, FHLB 4th District members financial results related to market competition, regression results, 1973-82, article, 9302–2.402

Savings and loan assns, FHLB 5th District members financial condition and operations by SMSA, monthly rpt, 9302–8

Savings and loan assns, FHLB 6th District insured members financial condition and operations by State, monthly rpt, 9302–11

Savings and loan assns, FHLB 6th District insured members financial condition and operations by State, quarterly rpt, 9302–23

Savings and loan assns, FHLB 9th District insured members financial condition and operations by SMSA, monthly rpt, 9302–13

Savings and loan assns, FHLB 10th District insured members finances and operations by SMSA, monthly rpt, 9302–22

Savings and loan assns, FHLB 12th District members financial operations and housing industry indicators by State, monthly rpt, 9302–21

Savings instns, FHLB 2nd District members financial operations, by State, monthly rpt, 9302–14

Savings instns FSLIC-insured, income, expenses, and financial ratios, 2nd half 1983, semiannual rpt, 9312–6

Securities industry finances, for stockbrokers, investment firms, and individual stock exchanges, 1978-82, annual rpt, 9734–2.1

Semiconductor industry subsidies of Japan govt by program, with financial and operating data by firm, R&D, and comparisons to US industry, 1970s-83, hearings, 21368–46.1

Service industry census, 1982: employment, establishments, receipts, and payroll, by SIC 2- to 4-digit kind of business, SMSA, county, and city, State rpt series, 2391–1

Service industry census, 1982: employment, establishments, receipts, and payroll, by SIC 4-digit kind of business and State, preliminary rpt series, 2390–2

Small business economic conditions, with comparisons to larger businesses, selected years 1979-83, annual rpt, 9764–1.1

Southeastern States, financial and operating characteristics of 22 high performance firms and 10 largest banks, 1982-83, article, 9371–1.414

Steel industry finances and operations under proposed import quota, projected 1985-89 with selected foreign comparisons and trends from 1950, 26306–6.80

Steel industry financial and operating data, steel imports by source, and employment situation at Fairless Hills, Pa, plant, 1970s-90, hearing, 25528–94

Student Loan Marketing Assn activities, and financial ratios and stock dividends compared to banks and 4 Fed Govt-sponsored credit assns, 1980-82, GAO rpt, 26121–71

Index by Subjects and Names

Telephone and telegraph firms detailed financial, operating, and employment statistics, 1982, annual rpt, 9284–6

Telephone companies borrowing under rural telephone loan program, and financial and operating data, 1983, annual rpt, 1244–2

Textile fiber and products trade, tariffs, and industry operating data, TSUSA commodity rpt series, 9885–3

Transit system (automated guideway) characteristics and itemized costs, for 16 systems in operation or under construction, 1982, annual rpt, 7884–6

Transit system deficits, effect of cost and service increases and ridership and fare decreases, and govt aid and system operating ratios, 1970-80, 7308–184

Transit system financial and operating data, by mode, function, fleet size, and individual system, FY82, annual rpt, 7884–4

Transportation finances, operations, vehicles, equipment, accidents, and energy use, by mode of transport, 1955-84, annual rpt, 7304–2

Truck transport of fruit and vegetables, costs per vehicle-mile by component for fleets and owner-operator trucks, monthly rpt, 1272–1

Truck transport of fruit and vegetables to 6 major markets, weekly rates by commodity and region, and monthly truck-mile costs, 1983 annual rpt, 1311–15

TVA power distributors detailed operating and financial ratios, for individual municipal and cooperative distributors, FY79-83, annual rpt, 9804–19

Vegetable production, prices, stocks, and consumption, for selected fresh and processed crops, periodic situation rpt with articles, 1561–11

Wheat and rye foreign and US production, prices, trade, stocks, and use, periodic situation rpt with articles, 1561–12

Wholesale trade census, 1982: employment, establishments, finances, and operations, by SIC 2- to 4-digit kind of business, SMSA, county, and city, State rpt series, 2405–1

Wholesale trade census, 1982: employment, establishments, sales by commodity, and payroll, by SIC 4-digit kind of business and State, preliminary rpt series, 2403–1

Wholesale trade sales, inventories, purchases, and gross margins, by SIC 2- to 3-digit kind of business and type of ownership, 1983, annual rpt, 2413–13

Wood, paper, and printed matter trade, tariffs, and industry operating data, TSUSA commodity rpt series, 9885–2

Youth Conservation Corps activities, costs, and participant characteristics, by sponsoring agency, 1982, annual rpt, 5304–12

see also Industrial capacity and utilization

OPIC

see Overseas Private Investment Corp.

Opinion and attitude surveys

Alaska and Alaska Native corporation claims for Fed Govt land, status and Land Mgmt Bur conveyance problems, various dates 1978-FY84, GAO rpt, 26113–125

Banking in-home services, consumer expected use and acceptable costs, 1983 survey, article, 9371–1.422

Index by Subjects and Names

Opinion and attitude surveys

Cancer prevention and risk, public knowledge, attitudes, and behavior, 1983 survey, 4478–149

Coal surface mining Federal inspectors assessments of enforcement methods, 1981 survey, 6068–177

Commerce Dept regional center mgmt assistance operations, assessment, and procurement authority, by subagency, regional rpt series, 2006–4

Community Dev Block Grants to small cities, State admin, project characteristics, and assessments of local officials, 1982, 5188–106

Community services block grants by type of service provider, State mgmt, and opinions of officials and groups involved, for 13 States, FY81-83, GAO rpt, 26121–84

Connecticut nurses smoking habits and attitudes on quitting and setting example for others, 1981 with comparisons to nurses nationwide in 1975, article, 4102–1.403

Court use of telephone conferencing in civil and criminal hearings, assessment of lawyers and judges in 2 States and Denver, Colo, 1981, 6068–186

Crime prevention media campaign, effects on public attitudes and activities, as of Nov 1981, 6068–183

Criminal case disposition, effect of victim injury and other factors, and law enforcement official and victim attitudes, 1983 survey, 6068–185

Criminal justice system problems, assessments of State and local officials, 1983, 6066–20.4

Criminal offenses, public-perceived severity of hypothetical incidents, 1977, 6062–2.402

DOD Dependents Schools students higher education admissions tests scores by sex and subject, and educational goals and attitudes, 1983, annual rpt, 3504–17

Drug (over-the-counter) use related to sociodemographic characteristics and perceived need, by drug type, 1975 survey, article, 4102–1.435

Drug abuse situation, prevention and treatment programs, law enforcement, funding needs, and Fed Govt role, attitudes of State and local officials, 1983 survey, 21968–27

Drug Enforcement Admin cases against major drug traffickers by case characteristics, and agents assessment of activities, in 3 cities, 1979-82, GAO rpt, 26119–57

Election campaign Fed Govt funding, reform and tax deduction proposals, and party assessment, opinion surveys, 1977-82, hearings, 25688–6

Election campaign Fed Govt funding, reform and tax deduction proposals, and TV and political action committee influence, opinion surveys, various dates 1977-83, hearings, 21428–7.1

Elementary and secondary schools use of tests, teacher and student attitudes, with detail for standardized achievement tests, 1980 conf papers, 4918–15

Energy conservation (housing) program of Connecticut utility group, cost effectiveness and characteristics of participants and nonparticipants, 1980-82, 3308–77

Energy conservation devices installation, utility loan program cost effectiveness, and household participation characteristics, Minnesota study, 1980-83, 3308–72

FAA airport maintenance employees attitudes toward reorganization of field offices and automation of facilities, 1980 survey, 7506–10.25

Fed Crop Insurance Corp finances, and insurance participation and operations in 2 States by crop, 1980-84, GAO rpt, 26113–132

Fed Govt employees labor contract negotiations, costs, time spent, and negotiator attitudes, 1983 survey, GAO rpt, 26119–62

Fed Govt executive employee dev programs, employee and candidate attitudes in 5 agencies, 1983 survey, GAO rpt, 26119–69

Fed Govt executive employee performance appraisal system operations, and employee attitudes, 1982 survey, GAO rpt, 26119–61

Fed Govt expenditures in States and local areas, Census Bur data collection, limitation, contributing agency costs, and opinions of congressional users, 1984 GAO rpt, 26111–20

Fed Govt regulatory growth effect on local compliance costs and funding, local officials assessment, and comparisons to State govt regulations, 1970s-82 with trends from 1900, 10048–58

Fed Govt survey questionnaire dev, respondent selection, and other survey procedures, narrative rpt, 106–4.4

Financial services household use and preferred provider, by respondent age and income, 1982-84 surveys, article, 9371–1.417

Forest land owner characteristics in Northeast States, owners and acreage, series, 1206–7

Health behavior survey response correlations with socially desirable answers, 1984 article, 4102–1.438

Health care services for elderly, knowledge, use, and factors affecting service quality, by race and Hispanic origin, 1984 article, 4652–1.406

Health care temporary employees, reasons for desiring temporary and part-time work, and preferences for work time, by skill level, survey, 1984 article, 6722–1.452

Health maintenance organizations for employee health insurance, enrollment, premiums, coverage, and employer attitudes, by region and industry div, 1982, 4108–32

High school classes of 1980 and 1982: educational and sociodemographic characteristics and expectations, natl longitudinal study, series, 4826–2

High school dropout rate and reasons, educational goals and achievement, and required and recommended curricula, by school control, selected years 1972-83, annual rpt, 4824–1.5

High school seniors use and assessment of drugs by type, alcohol, and cigarettes, by sex and region, 1975-83 surveys, annual rpt, 4494–4

Housing (low-income) energy aid of Fed Govt, allocations and average benefits in 13 States, and public interest group assessment, FY81-83, GAO rpt, 26121–75

Housing (rental) unit choice of Pittsburgh, Pa, recent movers related to unit, neighborhood, and town characteristics, 1967 survey, 9306–1.7

Housing and neighborhood quality indicators and attitudes, and occupant characteristics, by urban-rural location and region, 1981, annual survey, 2485–7

Housing and neighborhood quality, indicators and attitudes by inside-outside central cities, 1979-82 surveys, SMSA rpt series, 2485–6

Housing and neighborhood quality indicators and attitudes, by occupant and unit characteristics, region, and metro-nonmetro location, 1981, annual survey, 2485–2

Housing and neighborhood quality, indicators and attitudes for 15 SMSAs, 1978, annual survey special supplement, 2485–8

Hurricane forecasts effect on public evacuation rates, 1983 survey, 2186–4.11

Indian education program operations, funding, student progress measures, and opinions of school staff, parents, and students, selected years 1973-83, 4808–13

IRS taxpayer assistance program operations and use, and users evaluation, selected years 1979-82, GAO rpt, 26119–58

Israel health care in rural clinics under prepaid plan, services use and user satisfaction, 1981 survey, article, 4102–1.456

Labor union leaders attitudes toward labor movement, 1963 and 1983, article, 6722–1.451

Librarians opinions on GPO depository library program quality and mgmt, 1983 survey, GAO rpt, 26111–19

Lumber and wood product production, consumption by end use, shipments, exports, and market channels, for Rocky Mountain States, 1974-76, 1208–208

Mail postage ratemaking and classification cases, processing, and participant costs and attitudes, 1970s-84, GAO rpt, 26119–63

Marijuana cultivation control activity of State law enforcement agencies, and aid from Fed Govt and Natl Guard, 1983 survey, GAO rpt, 26119–64

Maryland corrections policies, assessments of private citizens and corrections and criminal justice personnel, 1980/81 with prison population trends from 1930, 6068–176

Maternal and child health, State govt spending and admin of Fed Govt block grants, by program for 13 States, 1981-83, GAO rpt, 26121–70

Mental health and drug and alcohol abuse treatment funding of State govts, and admin of Fed Govt block grants, for 13 States, FY80-84, GAO rpt, 26121–87

Merit system of Office of Personnel Mgmt, implementation and effectiveness, 1982, annual survey, 9494–1

Opinion and attitude surveys

Monetary policy of Fed Reserve, intermediate target preference among economists and financial analysts, 1983 surveys, article, 9375–1.405

Natural gas utility participation in housing energy conservation programs, and attitudes of mgmt, 1981-83, hearing, 21368–54

Nuclear power and weapons policy, fuel supply/demand, waste disposal and siting, environmental effects of radiation, and public attitudes, 1970s-82 with projections to 2000, 3008–88

Nuclear power plant safety and emergencies, effectiveness of technical advisors, 1983 survey, 9638–55

Nursing continuing education in maternal and child health at University of Kentucky, course enrollment and student assessment of career value, 1983 article, 4102–1.405

Nutrition services for elderly, program operations and assessment, and participant sociodemographic, health, and diet characteristics, 1976 and 1982, 4608–16

NYC families caring for aged relatives, preference for social service and financial programs to provide assistance, 1980, article, 4652–1.403

Physician (family) attitudes toward use of guaiac slide test for colorectal cancer screening, 1982 New York State survey, article, 4102–1.433

Police dept performance, analyses of police activities effects on neighborhoods and citizens, 1977, compilation of papers, 6068–181

Poverty status of young adults related to motivation, psychological factors, and family characteristics, by race and sex, 1970s-82, longitudinal studies, 4008–65

Preventive health services block grants of Fed Govt, State funding by program, and opinions on State program admin, for 13 States, FY81-84, GAO rpt, 26121–88

Public housing under private mgmt, assessment by housing officials and managers, and tenants, with operating costs, crime, and rent delinquency by project type and location, 1982, 5188–103

Real estate broker industry structure and practices, sales commissions, and broker and consumer attitudes, selected years 1975-81, 9408–48

Science Indicators, public attitudes toward science, research, and technological innovations, 1973-82, annual rpt, 9624–10.6

Scientists opinions of acid rain damage and control proposals, 1983 survey, hearings, 25328–25

Seat belt use, effects of driving circumstances and driver characteristics and attitudes, 1981 survey, 7768–82

Small business loans and credit, operational expectations, and NYC metro area owners economic and professional attitudes, by industry div, 1980-83 surveys, hearings, 21728–52

Small business perceived burden of Fed Govt paperwork requirements, and burden for 4 Fed Govt agencies, FY83, 9768–14

Social service spending of State govts by service type and funding source, and

admin of Fed Govt block grants, for 13 States, selected years FY80-84, GAO rpt, 26121–76

Soil conservation program policies of Fed Govt, attitudes of farmers and ranchers in 6 central US counties, 1982/83 survey, hearing, 25168–61

Taxes, tax policy, and intergovtl relations, public opinion survey results, 1972-84, annual rpt, 10044–2

Teaching degrees conferred by specialty and State, required credit hours, and instn officials attitudes, by instn type, 1970s-83, hearings, 21348–89

Transit system mgmt training funded by Urban Mass Transportation Admin, participant characteristics and career impact, 1970-79, 7888–60

Urban revitalization project in Boston, Mass, effect on business conditions by business type, size, and location, 1978 and 1980 surveys, hearings, 21788–140.2

Wildlife refuge revenues from economic and recreational uses, and refuge managers attitudes toward expanded use, FY81-83, GAO rpt, 26113–128

Women's travel patterns, by employment and sociodemographic characteristics and type of child care used, 1980 survey, 7888–62

Youth gang criminal activity control, police assessments, staff, and programs in 27 cities, with juvenile arrests nationwide for Crime Index offenses, 1980-81, 6068–175

see also Consumer surveys

see also Market research

Opinion Research Corp.

"Evaluation of the Nutrition Services for the Elderly", 4608–16

Opium

see Drug abuse and treatment

see Drug and narcotics traffic

see Drugs

Options

see Futures trading

Optometric instruments

see Medical supplies and equipment

Optometry

Air traffic controller color blindness exams, comparison of alternative testing methods, 1983 technical rpt, 7506–10.26

Census of Population, 1980: detailed socioeconomic and demographic characteristics, by age, sex, race, Hispanic origin, occupation, and industry, State rpt series, 2531–4

Census of Population, 1980: labor force, by sex, detailed occupation, and region, with comparison to 1970 census, supplementary rpt, 2535–1.12

Contact lens price and adverse lens-associated eye conditions related to fitting by ophthalomologists, opticians, and optometrists, 1977-80, 9408–49

County Business Patterns: establishments, employees, and payrolls, by SIC 4-digit industry and county, 1981, annual State rpt series, 2326–8

County Business Patterns: establishments, employees, and payrolls, by SIC 4-digit industry and county, 1982, annual State rpt series, 2326–6

Degrees conferred in higher education, by race, Hispanic origin, sex, level, and field, selected years 1949/50-1979/80, annual rpt, 4824–2.16

Index by Subjects and Names

DOD medical personnel, trainees, and accessions by source, by occupation, specialty, and service branch, FY83, annual rpt, 3544–24

Eye care visits and use of corrective lenses by type, by patient and family characteristics, visit location, and specialist type, 1979-80 with selected trends from 1965, 4147–10.145

Health care services of selected medical practitioners, use by patient characteristics, 1980 survey with trends from 1963, 4146–12.4

Health condition and health care resources, use, and expenditures, 1970s-82 with trends and projections 1900-2000, annual compilation, 4144–11

Income tax returns of sole proprietorships, detailed data by industry div and selected industry group, 1981, annual rpt, 8304–7

Income tax returns of sole proprietorships, receipts, deductions by type, payroll, and net income, by major industry, 1982, annual article, 8302–2.413

Manpower supply and education of health professionals, by occupation, demographic and professional characteristics, and location, 1950s-83 and projected to 2000, biennial rpt, 4114–8

Minority group and women employment and training in health professions, by field, selected years 1962/63-1983/84, 4118–18

Occupational manpower needs and supply by detailed occupation, and educational and training program enrollees and grads by detailed field, 1982 and 1995, biennial rpt, 6744–3

Occupational Outlook Handbook, 1984-85 biennial rpt, 6744–1

Older persons health status, health services use and expenditures by type, Medicare enrollment and reimbursement, and private insurance coverage, 1977-84, article, 4652–1.420

Service industry census, 1982: employment, establishments, receipts, and payroll, by SIC 2- to 4-digit kind of business, SMSA, county, and city, State rpt series, 2391–1

Service industry census, 1982: employment, establishments, receipts, and payroll, by SIC 4-digit kind of business and State, preliminary rpt, 2390–2.16

VA Medicine and Surgery Dept trainees, by detailed program and city, FY83, annual rpt, 9924–21

Visual impairment survey methodology and results by age, in 3 SMSAs, Aug 1981-Dec 1982, 4478–147

Youth office visits to physicians by patient and visit characteristics and physician specialty, and drug mentions by brand, 1980-81, 4146–8.100

see also Vision

Orange County, N.Y.

see also under By SMSA or MSA in the "Index by Categories"

Orange, Tex.

Census of Housing, 1980: occupancy and unit characteristics, by race, Hispanic origin, and city, SMSA rpt, 2473–1.87

Census of Population and Housing, 1980: detailed population and housing characteristics, by county, city, and census tract, SMSA rpt, 2551–2.87

Index by Subjects and Names

Wages of office and plant workers, by occupation, 1984 labor market area survey rpt, 6785 3.6

Oranges

see Citrus fruits

Orchardgrass

see Seeds

Orders

see Business orders

Ordnance

see Ammunition

see Military supplies and property

see Military weapons

Oregon

- Agriculture census, 1982: farms, farmland, production and costs, and operator characteristics, preliminary State summary and county rpts, 2330–1.41
- Agriculture census, 1982: farms, farmland, production, finances, and operator characteristics, by county, final State rpt, 2331–1.37
- Bank deposits in commercial and mutual savings banks and in US branches of foreign banks, by account type, instn, State, SMSA, and county, June 1983, annual rpt, 9295–3.19
- Census of Housing, 1980: occupancy and unit characteristics of SMSAs and central cities, by race, Hispanic origin, and city, State rpt, 2473–1.39
- Census of Population and Housing, 1980: detailed population and housing characteristics, by county, city, and census tract, State rpt, 2551–2.39
- Census of Population, 1980: detailed socioeconomic and demographic characteristics, by age, sex, race, Hispanic origin, and industry, State rpt, 2531–4.39
- Coastal environmental and wildlife characteristics, use, and mgmt, for individual ecosystems, series, 5506–9
- County Business Patterns: establishments, employees, and payrolls, by SIC 4-digit industry and county, 1982, annual State rpt, 2326–6.39
- Cranberry production, prices, area, and yield, for 5 States, 1982-83 and forecast 1984, annual rpt, 1621–18.4
- Earnings by SIC 1- to 3-digit industry and payments to retirees by type, for 4 timber dependent communities in Oregon and Montana, 1970 and 1978, 1208–196
- Employment, earnings, and hours, by selected SIC 1- to 4-digit industry, State, and for 278 major labor areas, 1939-83, annual rpt, 6744–5.2, 6744–5.3
- Environmental quality, pollutant discharge by type and source, and EPA protection activities and funding, 1970s-83, biennial regional rpt, 9184–15.10
- Exports of manufactured and agricultural commodities, manufacturing production, and export-related employment, 1960s-82, State rpt, 2046–3.37
- Farms with sales under $2,500, acreage, finances, operations, and operator characteristics, by region and for 6 States, 1978, 1548–241
- Fish and shellfish canned and frozen production, imports, landings, and prices, for Alaska and Northwest States, weekly rpt, 2162–6.5
- Fishermen (ocean sport), fishing activities, and catch by species, by fisherman characteristics and State, for Pacific coast, 1979-80, 2166–17.1, 2166–17.3

Organization for Economic Cooperation and Development

- Forests (natl) timber sales contract operations in Northwest US by forest and firm, and lumber supply/demand, FY76-1983 with trends from 1913, hearings, 25318–57
- HHS aid to each State and local govt or private instn, amount obligated, funding agency, and program, FY83, annual listing, 4004–3.10
- Income (personal) per capita and by source, and earnings by industry div, by State, MSA, and county, 1977-82, annual regional rpt, 2704–2.9
- Lumber production, prices, trade, and employment in Northwest US and British Columbia, quarterly rpt, 1202–3
- Manufacturing census, 1982: financial and operating data, by SIC 2- to 4-digit industry, State, SMSA, and county, preliminary census div rpt, 2491–3.9
- Mineral Industry Surveys, State review of production, 1983, advance annual rpt, 5614–6.37
- *Minerals Yearbook, 1982,* Vol 2 preprints: State review of production and sales by commodity, and business activity, annual rpt, 5604–16.38
- *Minerals Yearbook, 1982,* Vol 2: State reviews of production, sales, and firms, by commodity, and business activity, annual rpt, 5604–34
- Mount St Helens, Wash, volcanic eruptions, effects on water quality and other environmental characteristics of Washington and Oregon watersheds, series, 5666–14
- Population size and components of change, by MSA and county, 1980-82, annual State Current Population Rpt, 2546–4.37
- Population size, Apr 1980 and July 1982, and per capita income, 1979 and 1981, by county and city, State Current Population Rpt, 2546–11.37
- Retail trade census, 1982: employment, establishments, sales, and payroll, by SIC 2- to 4-digit kind of business, SMSA, county, and city, State rpt, 2397–1.38
- Savings and loan assns, FHLB 12th District members financial operations and housing industry indicators by State, monthly rpt, 9302–21
- Service industry census, 1982: employment, establishments, receipts, and payroll, by SIC 2- to 4-digit kind of business, SMSA, county, and city, State rpt, 2391–1.38
- Shipping industry impact on local economy, and port dev financing through user fees, by State, other area, industry, and port, 1970s-2020, hearings, 21568–34
- Water supply and quality in streams and lakes, and groundwater levels in wells, by drainage basin, 1981, annual State rpt, 5666–16.36
- Water supply and quality in streams and lakes, and groundwater levels in wells, by drainage basin, 1982, annual State rpt, 5666–20.36
- Water supply, and snow survey results, monthly State rpt, 1266–2.7
- Water supply in Oregon, streamflow by station and reservoir storage, 1984 water year, annual rpt, 1264–9
- Wholesale trade census, 1982: employment, establishments, finances, and operations, by SIC 2- to 4-digit kind of business, SMSA, county, and city, State rpt, 2405–1.38

see also Albany, Oreg.

see also Bend, Oreg.

see also Eugene, Oreg.

see also Medford, Oreg.

see also Multnomah County, Oreg.

see also Pendleton, Oreg.

see also Portland, Oreg.

see also Redmond, Oreg.

see also Salem, Oreg.

see also Springfield, Oreg.

see also under By State in the "Index by Categories"

Orem, Utah

- Census of Housing, 1980: occupancy and unit characteristics, by race, Hispanic origin, and city, SMSA rpt, 2473–1.294
- Census of Population and Housing, 1980: detailed population and housing characteristics, by county, city, and census tract, SMSA rpt, 2551–2.294
- Housing vacancy rates for single and multifamily units and mobile homes, by city and ZIP code, 1983, annual metro area rpt, 9304–21.7

see also under By SMSA or MSA in the "Index by Categories"

Organ transplants

see Medical transplants

Organization for Economic Cooperation and Development

- Capital formation and steel industry employment costs in US and OECD countries, 1960s-82, 26306–6.69
- Current account balance related to Fed Govt budget deficit, with balance for 14 OECD countries, various periods 1952-83, article, 9373–1.408
- Economic conditions in Communist and OECD countries, 1982, annual rpt, 7144–11
- Economic conditions in Communist, OECD, and selected other countries, 1960s-83, annual rpt, 244–5
- Economic indicators and oil use and imports for US and 6 OECD countries, and oil production by country, biweekly rpt, 242–4
- Economic indicators for 7 OECD countries and US, quarterly rpt, 2042–10
- Energy production by type, and oil prices, trade, and consumption, by country group and selected country, monthly rpt, 242–5
- Energy supply, demand, and prices, by fuel and sector, projected 1985-2010, biennial rpt, 3004–13
- Energy supply/demand and prices, by fuel type and consuming sector with foreign comparisons, 1949-83, annual rpt, 3164–74
- Energy supply/demand and prices, by fuel type, sector, and end use, with foreign comparisons, 1960-83 and projected to 1995, annual summary rpt, 3164–76
- Energy use, oil supply and price, and nuclear generating capacity, for non-Communist markets, by country and country group, various periods 1960-95, annual rpt, 3164–75
- Exports and imports of OECD countries, by country, 1983, annual rpt, 7144–10
- Exports and imports of OECD, total and for 4 major countries, and US trade by country, by commodity, 1972-82, annual world region rpt series, 244–13

Organization for Economic Cooperation and Development

Exports and imports of US, by commodity group, world area, selected country, US coastal area and port, and mode of transport, with seasonal adjustments, monthly rpt, 2422–9

Exports and imports of US, detailed SIC-based commodities by world area, 1983, annual rpts, 2424–6

Exports, imports, and economic indicators by country and country group, and US trade policy actions, 1960s-83, annual rpt, 444–1

Exports of US, detailed Schedule E commodities by mode of transport and world area and country of destination, 1983, annual rpts, 2424–5

GNP and GNP growth of each OECD member country, 1973-83, annual rpt, 7144–8

Imports of US, detailed Schedule A commodities by country and world area of origin, and mode of transport, 1983, annual rpts, 2424–2

Industrial production, consumer price, and stock price indexes for 6 OECD countries and US, *Business Conditions Digest,* monthly rpt, 2702–3.10

Industrial production indexes and CPI, for US and 6 OECD countries, current data and annual trends, monthly rpt, 23842–1.7

Industrial production indexes, 6 OECD countries and US, *Business Conditions Digest,* historical supplement and methodology, 1947-82, 2708–31

Military spending, arms trade, and armed forces size, with total govt spending and population, by country, 1972-82, annual rpt, 9824–1

Nuclear power plant construction and operation status, and capacity, by plant, region, State, and selected country, 1983 and projected to 2020, annual rpt, 3164–57

Oil and refined products stocks of 7 OECD countries, quarterly 1980-83, annual rpt, 3164–50.3

Oil prices impact on US oil trade and energy-intensive industries, with US and foreign reserves and industry operations, 1950-82 and projected to 2020, 9886–4.69

Oil refinery itemized annual costs of OPEC and OECD, under 3 financing assumptions, 1983 hearings, 25368–133.1

Oil stocks in selected OECD countries, monthly rpt, 3162–24.10

Savings (natl) and current account balance ratios to GDP, by OECD country, various periods 1963-81, technical paper, 9366–7.100

Ships in US and OECD merchant fleets, sailors earnings by position, 1983 hearings, 25388–45

see also International Energy Agency

Organization of Petroleum Exporting Countries

Agricultural exports and imports of US, by detailed commodity and country, FY83 and CY83, semiannual rpts, 1522–4

Economic conditions in Communist, OECD, and selected other countries, 1960s-83, annual rpt, 244–5

Energy Energy supply, demand, and prices, by fuel and sector, projected 1985-2010, biennial rpt, 3004–13

Energy Natl Policy Plan, DOE implementation and effect on energy supply/demand, 1983-84, annual rpt, 3024–4

Energy supply/demand and prices, by fuel type and consuming sector with foreign comparisons, 1949-83, annual rpt, 3164–74

Energy supply/demand and prices, by fuel type, sector, and end use, with foreign comparisons, 1960-83 and projected to 1995, annual summary rpt, 3164–76

Energy use, oil supply and price, and nuclear generating capacity, for non-Communist markets, by country or country group, various periods 1960-95, annual rpt, 3164–75

Exports and imports of OECD countries, by country, 1983, annual rpt, 7144–10

Exports and imports of US with OPEC and other oil exporting nations, monthly rpt, 2422–9.1

Exports, imports, and economic indicators by country and country group, and US trade policy actions, 1960s-83, annual rpt, 444–1

Exports of US by selected commodity, and foreign and US economic and employment indicators and balance of payments, by world area and country, 1970s-83, annual rpt, 2044–26

Imports of OPEC from US and 7 OECD countries, quarterly rpt, 2042–10.2

Investment (direct) in US oil and other industries, by OPEC and other countries, 1974-82, annual rpt, 3024–2

Investment (direct) of US, by world area and country, 1977-83, article, 2702–1.442

Investment (direct) worldwide, and US investment flows by major industry, by world region and country, 1982 and trends from 1950, annual rpt, 2044–25

Loans of large US banks to foreigners at all US and foreign offices, by country group and country, quarterly rpt, 13002–1

Military spending, arms trade, and armed forces size, with total govt spending and population, by country, 1972-82, annual rpt, 9824–1

Oil and refined products and natural gas liquids supply/demand, trade, stocks, and refining, by detailed product, State, and PAD district, monthly rpt with articles, 3162–6

Oil and refined products and natural gas liquids supply/demand, trade, stocks, and refining, by detailed product, State, and PAD district, 1983 annual rpt, 3164–2

Oil price and demand relationship and real income effects among developed countries and OPEC and non-OPEC developing countries, 1984 technical paper, 9366–7.96

Oil price changes effects on developed countries and on OPEC and non-OPEC developing countries, model description, 1984 technical paper, 9366–7.93

Oil prices impact on US oil trade and energy-intensive industries, with US and foreign reserves and industry operations, 1950-82 and projected to 2020, 9886–4.69

Oil prices of OPEC and non-OPEC countries, by crude type, weekly rpt, 3162–32

Index by Subjects and Names

Oil prices production by country, and OPEC prices by member, biweekly rpt, 242–4

Oil production, and exports and prices to US, by major exporting country, detailed data, monthly rpt, 3162–24

Oil production, capacity, consumption, exports by country, and sales prices, by OPEC member, monthly rpt, 242–5

Oil refining capacity and production by city, and oil use and exports, by OPEC member, with comparisons to other countries, projected 1985-90, hearings, 25368–133.1

Oil reserves, production, and resource lifespan under alternative production rates, historic and projected, country rpt series, 3166–9

Organized crime

- Drug Enforcement Admin cases against major drug traffickers by case characteristics, and agents assessment of activities, in 3 cities, 1979-82, GAO rpt, 26119–57
- Drug Enforcement Organized Crime Task Forces, funding and staff by agency, region, and city, as of FY83, GAO rpt, 26119–52
- Drug enforcement regional task force program investigation activities, funding, and personnel, with nationwide drug abuse data, 1983 annual rpt, 6004–17
- Labor Dept programs fraud and abuse, audits and investigations, 1st half FY84, semiannual rpt, 6302–2
- Marijuana cultivation control activity of State law enforcement agencies, and aid from Fed Govt and Natl Guard, 1983 survey, GAO rpt, 26119–64
- Wiretapping authorizations by offense, costs, persons involved, arrests, trials, and convictions, 1983, annual rpt, 18204–7
- Witness Security Program costs, participants by arrest record, and prosecutions by offense, offender type, and disposition, various periods FY70-83, GAO rpt, 26119–70

Organized Crime Drug Enforcement Task Forces

Funding and staff of Task Forces, by agency, region, and city, FY83, GAO rpt, 26119–52

Investigation activities, funding, and personnel, with nationwide drug abuse data, 1983 annual rpt, 6004–17

Organized labor

see Labor unions

Organochlorine

see Chemicals and chemical industry

see Pesticides

Oriental Americans

see Asian Americans

Orlando, Fla.

Census of Housing, 1980: occupancy and unit characteristics, by race, Hispanic origin, and city, SMSA rpt, 2473–1.273

Census of Population and Housing, 1980: detailed population and housing characteristics, by county, city, and census tract, SMSA rpt, 2551–2.273

Housing and households detailed characteristics, and unit and neighborhood quality, by inside-outside central cities, 1981 survey, SMSA rpt, 2485–6.23

Wages of office and plant workers, by occupation, 1984 labor market area survey rpt, 6785 3.9

see also under By City and By SMSA or MSA in the "Index by Categories"

Orr, Ann C.

"Job Cuts Are Only One Means Firms Use To Counter Imports", 6722–1.439

Orr, James A.

"Job Cuts Are Only One Means Firms Use To Counter Imports", 6722–1.439

Orthopedic impairments

see Mobility limitations

Orthopedics

- Black medical residents by specialty, and minority medical faculty by race and Hispanic origin, selected years 1980-83, article, 4102–1.412
- Bone injury diagnoses from physical indicators and X-rays, by body site, 1977-79, 4186–2.6
- DOD medical personnel, trainees, and accessions by source, by occupation, specialty, and service branch, FY83, annual rpt, 3544–24
- Drugs (analgesic) provided during visits to office-based physicians, by patient characteristics, drug brand and type, and physician specialty, 1980-81, 4146–8.99
- Hospital discharges and length of stay, by patient characteristics, facility size, procedure performed, diagnosis, and region, 1982, annual rpt, 4147–13.78
- Israel, Tel Aviv Medical Center services and use, by patient age and condition, selected years 1976-83, article, 4102–1.445
- Manpower supply and education of health professionals, by occupation, demographic and professional characteristics, and location, 1950s-83 and projected to 2000, biennial rpt, 4114–8
- Medicare physician charges and reimbursement by enrollee characteristics and carrier, payment limits effects on charges in California, and physician earnings, by specialty, 1950s-84, 25368–127
- VA physicians, dentists, and nurses, by age, selected employment characteristics, and VA district, quarterly rpt, 9922–11

see also Mobility limitations

see also Podiatry

see also Prosthetics and orthotics

Orthotics

see Prosthetics and orthotics

Oshkosh, Wis.

- Census of Housing, 1980: occupancy and unit characteristics, by race, Hispanic origin, and city, SMSA rpt, 2473–1.73
- Census of Population and Housing, 1980: detailed population and housing characteristics, by county, city, and census tract, SMSA rpt, 2551–2.73

see also under By SMSA or MSA in the "Index by Categories"

Osorio, Sandalio R.

"Current Status of the Mule Deer on Tiburon Island, Sonora", 1208–197

Osteen, Craig

"Corn and Soybean Production Losses from Potential Pesticide Regulatory Actions", 1561–16.407

Osteopathy

- County Business Patterns: establishments, employees, and payrolls, by SIC 4-digit industry and county, 1982, annual State rpt series, 2326–6
- Degrees conferred in higher education, by race, Hispanic origin, sex, level, and field, selected years 1949/50-1979/80, annual rpt, 4824–2.16
- Drugs (analgesic) provided during visits to office-based physicians, by patient characteristics, drug brand and type, and physician specialty, 1980-81, 4146–8.99
- Drugs prescribed, by physician specialty, 1982, annual rpt, 4064–12
- Health condition and health care resources, use, and expenditures, 1970s-82 with trends and projections 1900-2000, annual compilation, 4144–11
- Income tax returns of sole proprietorships, detailed data by industry div and selected industry group, 1981, annual rpt, 8304–7
- Income tax returns of sole proprietorships, receipts, deductions by type, payroll, and net income, by major industry, 1982, annual article, 8302–2.413
- License sanctions of health professionals in 3 States, and subsequent Medicare and Medicaid program participation, by specialty, 1977-82, GAO rpt, 26121–80
- Manpower supply and education of health professionals, by occupation, demographic and professional characteristics, and location, 1950s-83 and projected to 2000, biennial rpt, 4114–8
- Minority group and women employment and training in health professions, by field, selected years 1962/63-1983/84, 4118–18
- Physicians (not office-based) visits by reason, diagnosis, treatment, patient and physician characteristics, and physician primary activity, 1980, 4147–13.77
- Service industry census, 1982: employment, establishments, receipts, and payroll, by SIC 2- to 4-digit kind of business, SMSA, county, and city, State rpt series, 2391–1
- Supply of physicians and ratio to population by State and county population size, and counties with shortages and needs, 1960-79 and projected 1982-94, 4118–52
- VA physicians, dentists, and nurses, by age, selected employment characteristics, and VA district, quarterly rpt, 9922–11

Ostrander, David R.

"Counts of 305-Day Lactation Records Excluded from Genetic Evaluations for 1983", 1702–2.403

Oswald, Daniel D.

"Timber Resource Statistics for Eastern Washington", 1206–28.3

Otitis

see Ear diseases and infections

Ott, Mack

"What Can Central Banks Do About the Value of the Dollar?", 9391–1.413

Ott, Robert A., Jr.

- "Changes in the Use of Adjustable-Rate Mortgages in the Fourth FHLB District", 9302–2.403
- "Uses of Adjustable-Rate and Other Mortgages in the Fourth FHLB District", 9302–2.401

Ottawa, Canada

Fruit and vegetable shipments, and arrivals in 23 US and 5 Canada cities, by mode of transport and State or country of origin, 1983, annual rpt, 1311–4.1

Otto, Phyllis F.

"Productivity Growth in the Switchgear Industry Slows After 1973", 6722–1.420

Outdoor recreation

see Recreation

Outer continental shelf

see Continental shelf

Outlying areas

see American Samoa

see Census of Outlying Areas

see Guam

see Northern Mariana Islands

see Puerto Rico

see Territories of the U.S.

see Trust Territory of the Pacific Islands

see Virgin Islands

see under By Outlying Area in the "Index by Categories"

Output of labor

see Labor productivity

Overseas Private Investment Corp.

- Activities of OPIC, foreign and US project impacts, and list of insured projects and companies, FY83, annual rpt, 9904–3
- Budget of US Appendix, detailed budgets and personnel summaries, by agency, FY85, annual rpt, 104–3
- Cost control proposals for Fed Govt programs and mgmt, 3-year savings by function and agency, and financial and operating data, 1960s-81, 16908–1.15
- Credit assistance costs, policies to improve measurement, with loan and loan guarantee data by program, and Federal and private credit instns operations, 1970-84, 26306–6.72
- Currency (foreign) holdings of US, detailed transactions and balances by program and country, 1st half FY84, semiannual rpt, 8102–7
- Debt to US of foreign govts and private obligors, by country and program, periodic rpt, 8002–6
- Investment insurance issued, by type of coverage and world area, FY83, annual rpt, 15344–1.13
- Liabilities (contigent) and claims paid by Fed Govt on federally insured and guaranteed contracts with foreign obligors, by country and program, periodic rpt, 8002–12
- Programs and finances of OPIC, including list of insured projects and companies, FY83, annual rpt, 9904–2

Overstreet, Thomas R., Jr.

"Resale Price Maintenance: Economic Theories and Empirical Evidence", 9406–1.38

Overtime

- *Business Conditions Digest,* cyclical indicators, by economic process, monthly rpt, 2702–3.3
- *Business Conditions Digest,* historical supplement on economic, business, and financial conditions and cyclical fluctuations, with methodology, 1947-82, 2708–31
- Fed Govt officials use of Govt chauffeur services for commuting, driver overtime hours and pay by agency, 4th qtr 1982, GAO rpt, 26123–63

Overtime

Fed Govt programs and mgmt cost control proposals, 3-year savings by function and agency, and financial and operating data, 1960s-81, 16908–1.3, 16908–1.27, 16908–1.33

Manufacturing production and nonsupervisory workers average weekly hours, 1977-Feb 1984, update, 6744–4

Production workers on manufacturing payrolls, average weekly overtime, selected years 1956-82, annual rpt, 6724–1.3

Railroad employee earnings, benefits, and hours, by occupation for Class I railroads, 1983, annual rpt, 9484–5

see also Area wage surveys

Overweight

see Obesity

Owensboro, Ky.

Census of Housing, 1980: occupancy and unit characteristics, by race, Hispanic origin, and city, SMSA rpt, 2473–1.274

Census of Population and Housing, 1980: detailed population and housing characteristics, by county, city, and census tract, SMSA rpt, 2551–2.274

Housing vacancy rates for single and multifamily units and mobile homes, by city and ZIP code, 1984, annual metro area rpt, 9304–27.4

see also under By SMSA or MSA in the "Index by Categories"

Owings, Jeffrey A.

"High School and Beyond Tabulation: Foreign Language Course Taking by 1980 High School Sophomores Who Graduated in 1982", 4828–17

"Patterns of Participation in Secondary Vocational Education, 1978-82", 4826–2.18

Owings, Maria

"Participants in Postsecondary Education: Oct. 1982", 4848–16

Ownership of enterprise

Agriculture census, 1982: farms, farmland, production and costs, and operator characteristics, preliminary State and county rpt series, 2330–1

Agriculture census, 1982: farms, farmland, production, finances, and operator characteristics, by county, final State rpt series, 2331–1

Alaska electric power capacity and generation by fuel type, and marketing, by utility, type of ownership, and location, 1983, annual rpt, 3214–2

Aluminum primary production plant ownership, capacity, and type and source of raw material and energy used, by plant, State, and country, June 1984, semiannual listing, 5602–5

Automated teller machines shared networks by State, and membership and characteristics of top 16 regional and natl networks, Nov 1983, article, 9373–1.403

Business Conditions Digest, historical supplement on economic, business, and financial conditions and cyclical fluctuations, with methodology, 1947-82, 2708–31

Capital (fixed), govt and private nonresidential structures and equipment, residential capital, and consumer-owned durable goods by item, 1980-83, annual article, 2702–1.433

DOE procurement and assistance contracts, by State, contractor type, and top 100 instns, FY83, annual rpt, 3004–21

Enterprise zone and urban revitalization projects of State and local govts, effect on business and employment in selected areas, various dates 1972-83, hearing, 21788–140

Farm business legal organization, finances, operations, tax rates, and State laws restricting farm corporations, 1960s-82, 1548–233

Farm households receiving social security income, farms and amount by characteristics of farm and operator, 1978-82, article, 1702–1.410

Farm houseolds social security tax liability, alternative tax rates by type of legal organization, 1955-90, article, 1702–1.408

Farm population, by farm type and sales size and selected other characteristics, 1975-80, 1598–144

Farmland eroded by rainfall, acreage by crop, and farm operators by selected characteristics, by soil erosion class, 1977-78, 1588–83

Farms with sales under $2,500, acreage, finances, operations, and operator characteristics, by region and for 6 States, 1978, 1548–241

Foreign minerals production, reserves, and industry role in domestic economy and world supply, country and world region rpt series, 5606–1

Foreign-owned US multiestablishment firms, employment, and payroll, by country, State, industry group, and foreign ownership share, 1981-82, annual rpt, 2324–6

Income tax returns filed by type, for US, IRS regions, and service center cities, 1972-82 and projected 1983-90, annual rpt, 8304–9.1

Income tax returns filed by type of filer, selected income items, summary data, quarterly rpt, 8302–2.1

Income tax returns of elderly, by income statement and tax item and income level, 1981 with trends from 1977, article, 8302–2.412

Income tax returns of individuals, detailed data, 1982, annual rpt, 8304–2

Income tax returns of partnerships, receipts by source, deductions by type, and establishments, by selected industry, 1982, annual article, 8302–2.416

Income tax returns of sole proprietorships, detailed data by industry div and selected industry group, 1981, annual rpt, 8304–7

Income tax returns of sole proprietorships, receipts, deductions by type, payroll, and net income, by major industry, 1982, annual article, 8302–2.413

Income tax returns with investment credits, for individuals by income, and for sole proprietorships by industry, 1981, article, 8302–2.409

Partnership finances, tax deductions, and employment, by industry div and size, 1979, article, 8302–2.411

Pharmacists employment and sociodemographic characteristics, and reasons for not working in field, by State and overseas, as of 1979, 4147–14.28

Index by Subjects and Names

Retail trade census, 1982: employment, establishments, sales, and payroll, by SIC 2- to 4-digit kind of business, SMSA, county, and city, State rpt series, 2397–1

Retail trade sales, inventories, purchases, gross margin, and accounts receivable, by SIC 2- to 4-digit kind of business and type of ownership, 1983, annual rpt, 2413–5

Securities purchases, sales, and holdings, by issuer and type and ownership of security, monthly listing, 9732–2

Service industries receipts, by SIC 2- to 4-digit kind of business, 1983, annual rpt, 2413–8

Service industry census, 1982: employment, establishments, receipts, and payroll, by SIC 2- to 4-digit kind of business, SMSA, county, and city, State rpt series, 2391–1

Small business capital formation under securities law exemptions, effects on stocks offered, issuers, and purchasers, series, 9736–2

Small Business Investment Companies finances, funding, licensing, and loan activity, 2nd half FY84, semiannual rpt, 9762–3

Statistical programs of 6 Federal agencies, industry coding system comparability, workload, and updating cycles, 1984 rpt, 106–4.5

Stockbroker firms by type of organization and State, finances, and SEC applications and registrations, 1978-FY83, annual rpt, 9734–2.1

Virgin Islands economic censuses, 1982: employment, establishments, payroll, and receipts, by SIC 1- to 4-digit industry, island, and city, 2593–1

Wholesale trade sales, inventories, purchases, and gross margins, by SIC 2- to 3-digit kind of business and type of ownership, 1983, annual rpt, 2413–13

see also Agricultural cooperatives

see also Bank holding companies

see also Business acquisitions and mergers

see also Cooperatives

see also Corporations

see also Foreign corporations

see also Franchises

see also Government corporations

see also Government ownership

see also Holding companies

see also Minority businesses

see also Multinational corporations

see also Securities

see also Self-employment

Oxnard, Calif.

Census of Housing, 1980: occupancy and unit characteristics, by race, Hispanic origin, and city, SMSA rpt, 2473–1.275

Census of Population and Housing, 1980: detailed population and housing characteristics, by county, city, and census tract, SMSA rpt, 2551–2.275

Housing vacancy rates for single and multifamily units and mobile homes, by city and ZIP code, 1983, annual metro area rpt, 9304–20.12

Wages of office and plant workers, by occupation, 1984 labor market area survey rpt, 6785–3.7

see also under By City and By SMSA or MSA in the "Index by Categories"

Index by Subjects and Names

Oxygen
see Gases

Ozone
see Air pollution

Paarlberg, Philip L.
"When Are Export Subsidies Rational?", 1502–3.401

Pacific Islands Americans
Agriculture census, 1982: farms, farmland, production, finances, and operator characteristics, by county, final State rpt series, 2331–1

Births among Asian and Pacific Islands Americans by ethnic origin and sociodemographic and birth characteristics, with comparisons to blacks and whites, 1978-80, 4146–5.75

Cancer cases, incidence, deaths, and death rates, by body site, age, race, Hispanic origin, and sex, for 10 geographic areas, 1973-81, 4478–130

Census of Housing, 1980: occupancy and unit characteristics of SMSAs and central cities, by race, Hispanic origin, and city, State and SMSA rpt series, 2473–1

Census of Population and Housing, 1980: detailed population and housing characteristics, by county, city, and census tract, State and SMSA rpt series, 2551–2

Census of Population, 1980: Asian and Pacific Islander population, by detailed race and State, supplementary rpt, 2535–1.15

Census of Population, 1980: detailed socioeconomic and demographic characteristics, by age, sex, race, Hispanic origin, occupation, and industry, State rpt series, 2531–4

Census of Population, 1980: detailed socioeconomic characteristics, by county, city, and inside-outside SMSAs and central cities, State rpt series, 2531–3

Census of Population, 1980: migration since 1975, by State and selected demographic characteristics, supplementary rpt, 2535–1.13

County and City Data Book, detailed socioeconomic and demographic data for States, counties, and cities, selected years 1976-82, 2328–1

Statistical Abstract of US, social, political, and economic data, 1950s-83 and trends, annual rpt, 2324–1.1

Pacific Northwest
see Western States

Pacific Northwest Laboratory
"Nuclear Fact Book", 3008–88
"Summary of Environmental Reports, Department of Energy Sites", 3004–23
"U.S. Uranium Mining Industry: Background Information on Economics and Emissions", 9188–96
see also Department of Energy National Laboratories

Pacific Ocean
Coastal environmental and socioeconomic conditions, and potential impacts of oil and gas OCS leases, final statement series, 5736–1

Coastal environmental and wildlife characteristics, use, and mgmt, for individual ecosystems, series, 5506–9

Dumping of low-level radioactive wastes at 4 largest and all disposal sites, 1983 hearings, 21568–36

Dumping of waste materials, EPA permit program and intl London Dumping Convention activities, 1981-83, annual rpt, 9204–8

Exports and imports of US (waterborne), by type of service, commodity, country, route, and US port, 1982, annual rpt, 7704–2

Fish and eggs for stocking distributed from natl hatcheries, by species, hatchery, and jurisdiction, FY83, annual rpt, 5504–10

Fish and shellfish landings, life cycles, and environmental needs, for selected species by region, with glossary and bibl, series, 5506–8

Fish and shellfish landings, prices, trade, consumption, and industry operating data, for US with foreign comparisons, 1982-83, annual rpt, 2164–1

Fish landings, employment, gear used, and seafood production, for detailed species by State, 1977, annual rpt, 2164–2

Fishermen (ocean sport), fishing activities, and catch by species, by fisherman characteristics and State, for Pacific coast, 1979-80, 2166–17.1, 2166–17.3

Hurricanes and tropical storms in northeastern Pacific, paths, surveillance, deaths, and property damage, 1983, annual rpt, 2184–8

Japan fish landings, prices, trade by country, cold storage, and market devs, periodic press release, 2162–7

Marine Mammal Protection Act admin and populations, strandings, and catch permits by type and applicant, by species and location, Apr 1983-Mar 1984, annual rpt, 2164–11

Mineral industries census, 1982: financial and operating data, by State and for 4 offshore regions, preliminary summary rpt, 2511–2.2

Oil and gas OCS reserves of Fed Govt, leasing and exploration activities, production, revenues, and costs, by ocean region, FY83, annual rpt, 5734–4

Oil, gas, and minerals dev, under Fed Govt OCS leases, with production, revenues, reserves, and oil spills, by State and ocean region, 1950s-82, annual rpt, 5734–3

Oil spill risk analyses for OCS proposed lease sale areas, series, 5736–2

Temperature of sea surface by ocean and for US coastal areas, and Bering Sea ice conditions, monthly rpt, 2182–5

Tidal current tables, daily time and velocity by station for North America and Asia coasts, 1985, annual rpt, 2174–1.2

Tide height and time daily at worldwide coastal points, 1985 predictions, annual rpt, 2174–2.1, 2174–2.4

Typhoons in western North Pacific and North Indian Oceans, paths and other characteristics, by mode of surveillance, 1983, annual rpt, 3804–8

Weather and tropical cyclones, quarterly journal with articles, 2152–8

Weather broadcasts for US ships, by major ocean area, as of Jan 1984, biennial rpt, 2184–3

see also Bering Sea

Packaging and containers

see also Gulf of Alaska
see also Oceania

Pacific States
see Western States

Packaging and containers
Agricultural cooperatives, membership, activities, and finances, by commodity and selected State, 1900-80 with trends from 1863, 1128–30

Air pollutant emission factors, by detailed source, 3rd edition, 1983-84 supplements, 9198–13

Bottles (plastic) production by end use, and shipments, 1983, annual rpt, 2506–8.10

Census of Population, 1980: detailed socioeconomic and demographic characteristics, by age, sex, race, Hispanic origin, occupation, and industry, State rpt series, 2531–4

Closures for containers, shipments, trade, consumption, and firms, monthly Current Industrial Rpt, 2506–11.4

County Business Patterns: establishments, employees, and payrolls, by SIC 4-digit industry and county, 1981, annual State rpt series, 2326–8

County Business Patterns: establishments, employees, and payrolls, by SIC 4-digit industry and county, 1982, annual State rpt series, 2326–6

Drums and pails (steel shipping) shipments, trade, consumption, and firms, quarterly Current Industrial Rpt, 2506–11.5

Egg filler flats from Canada at less than fair value, imports injury to US industry, investigation with background financial and operating data, 1984 rpt, 9886–14.119

Employment, earnings, and hours, by selected SIC 1- to 4-digit industry, State, and for 278 major labor areas, 1939-83, annual rpt, 6744–5

Employment, earnings, and hours, by SIC 4-digit nonfarm industry, monthly 1974-Feb 1984, annual update, 6744–4

Exports and imports of US, detailed SIC-based commodities by world area, 1983, annual rpts, 2424–6

Exports and imports of US, totals and as percent of domestic production, by SIC 2- to 5-digit commodity, 1981, annual rpt, 2424–3

Exports of US, detailed commodities by country of destination, monthly rpt, 2422–3

Exports of US, detailed Schedule B commodities by country of destination, 1983, annual rpt, 2424–9

Exports of US, detailed Schedule E commodities by mode of transport and world area and country of destination, 1983, annual rpts, 2424–5

Farm production expenditures, detailed items by farm sales size and region, 1983, annual rpt, 1614–3

Flexible packaging material shipments, by type, 1983, annual Current Industrial Rpt, 2506–7.7

Food prices (farm-retail), marketing cost components, and industry finances and productivity, selected years 1967-83, annual rpt, 1544–9

Food processing and packaging equipment, foreign market and trade, and user industry operations and demand, country market research rpts, 2045–11

Packaging and containers

Glass container production, shipments, stocks, trade, and consumption, by type, monthly Current Industrial Rpt, 2506–9.4

Glass containers trade, tariffs, and industry operating data, foreign and US, 1978-82, TSUSA commodity rpt supplement, 9885–5.14

- Great Lakes trade, by SITC 3-digit commodity, port, vessel type, world area, and country, 1982, annual rpt, 7744–3
- Imports of US, detailed Schedule A commodities by country and world area of origin, and mode of transport, 1983, annual rpts, 2424–2
- Imports of US, detailed Schedule A commodities by country, monthly rpt, 2422–2
- Imports of US, detailed TSUSA commodities by country of origin, 1983, annual rpt, 2424–4
- Income tax returns of corporations, detailed income and tax items by industry, 1981, annual rpt, 8304–4
- Industry finances and operations, by SIC 2- to 4-digit industry, 1970s-83 and projected to 1988, annual rpt, 2014–4
- Injuries and deaths from use of selected consumer products and related activity, by victim age and sex, 1982, annual rpt, 9164–7
- Injuries and deaths from use of selected consumer products, by victim age and medical treatment status, 1982, annual rpt, 9164–6
- Injuries, deaths, and medical costs from consumer products use, and Consumer Product Safety Commission activities and recalls, by product type and brand, FY83, annual rpt, 9164–2
- Input-output structure of US economy, detailed interindustry transactions for 85 industries, and components of final demand, 1977, article, 2702–1.421
- Input-output structure of US economy, detailed interindustry transactions for 537 industries, and components of final demand, 1977 benchmark data, 2708–17
- Manufacturing census, 1982: financial and operating data, by SIC 2- to 4-digit industry, State, SMSA, and county, preliminary census div rpt series, 2491–3
- Manufacturing census, 1982: financial and operating data, for SIC 4-digit industries by product, preliminary rpt series, 2491–1
- Minority group and women employment, by occupational group and SIC 2- to 3-digit industry, 1981, annual rpt, 9244–1.1
- Nuclear power and weapons policy, fuel supply/demand, waste disposal and siting, environmental effects of radiation, and public attitudes, 1970s-82 with projections to 2000, 3008–88
- Occupational injury and illness rates, by SIC 2- to 4-digit industry, 1982, annual rpt, 6844–1
- Producer prices and indexes, by stage of processing and detailed commodity, monthly rpt, 6762–6
- Producer prices and indexes, by stage of processing and detailed commodity, monthly 1983, annual supplement, 6764–2

Productivity, hours, and employment indexes for selected SIC 3- and 4-digit industries, 1954-82, annual rpt, 6824–1.3

- Radioactive materials transport surveillance program activities and results, State survey rpt series, 9636–1
- Technological change, impact on productivity and employment in 4 industries, 1960-90, 6828–23
- Wood used in manufacturing, by type of wood, end use, and SIC 4-digit industry, 1977 with summary trends from 1928, 1208–3

see also Containerization

see also Labeling

Packers and Stockyards Administration

- Activities and programs of USDA, by subagency, FY83, annual rpt, 1004–3
- Livestock packers purchases and feeding, and livestock markets, dealers, and sales, by region and State, 1981-82, annual rpt, 1384–1

Paddock, William C.

"Dairy Outlook", 1004-16.1

Paducah, Ky.

Uranium enrichment facilities operations, finances, uranium stocks, and energy use and capital investment by facility, FY83, annual rpt, 3354–7

Page, William F.

"Health Characteristics of Male Veterans and Nonveterans, Health Interview Surveys, 1971-81", 9926–1.18

Paints and varnishes

- Air pollutant emission factors, by detailed source, 3rd edition, 1983-84 supplements, 9198–13
- Art inks, paints, and related items trade, tariffs, and industry operating data, 1979-83, TSUSA commodity rpt supplement, 9885–4.46
- Business statistics, detailed data for major industries and economic indicators, *Survey of Current Business,* monthly rpt, 2702–1.9
- Census of Population, 1980: detailed socioeconomic and demographic characteristics, by age, sex, race, Hispanic origin, occupation, and industry, State rpt series, 2531–4
- China economic conditions, agricultural and industrial production, trade, and domestic and foreign investment, 1980-85, 2048–106
- County Business Patterns: establishments, employees, and payrolls, by SIC 4-digit industry and county, 1981, annual State rpt series, 2326–8
- County Business Patterns: establishments, employees, and payrolls, by SIC 4-digit industry and county, 1982, annual State rpt series, 2326–6
- Employment, earnings, and hours, by selected SIC 1- to 4-digit industry, State, and for 278 major labor areas, 1939-83, annual rpt, 6744–5
- Employment, earnings, and hours, by SIC 4-digit nonfarm industry, monthly 1974-Feb 1984, annual update, 6744–4
- Energy use and cost for building materials manufacture, by energy source and industry, 1970s-82, article, 2012–1.401
- Exports and imports of US, detailed SIC-based commodities by world area, 1983, annual rpts, 2424–6

Index by Subjects and Names

- Exports and imports of US, totals and as percent of domestic production, by SIC 2- to 5-digit commodity, 1981, annual rpt, 2424–3
- Exports of US, detailed commodities by country of destination, monthly rpt, 2422–3
- Exports of US, detailed Schedule B commodities by country of destination, 1983, annual rpt, 2424–9
- Exports of US, detailed Schedule E commodities by mode of transport and world area and country of destination, 1983, annual rpts, 2424–5
- Franchise business opportunities, by firm and kind of business, 1984 annual listing, 2044–27
- Great Lakes trade, by SITC 3-digit commodity, port, vessel type, world area, and country, 1982, annual rpt, 7744–3
- Imports of US, detailed Schedule A commodities by country and world area of origin, and mode of transport, 1983, annual rpts, 2424–2
- Imports of US, detailed Schedule A commodities by country, monthly rpt, 2422–2
- Imports of US, detailed TSUSA commodities by country of origin, 1983, annual rpt, 2424–4
- Income tax returns of corporations, detailed income and tax items by industry, 1981, annual rpt, 8304–4
- Industry finances and operations, by SIC 2- to 4-digit industry, 1970s-83 and projected to 1988, annual rpt, 2014–4
- Injuries and deaths from use of selected consumer products and related activity, by victim age and sex, 1982, annual rpt, 9164–7
- Input-output structure of US economy, detailed interindustry transactions for 85 industries, and components of final demand, 1977, article, 2702–1.421
- Input-output structure of US economy, detailed interindustry transactions for 537 industries, and components of final demand, 1977 benchmark data, 2708–17
- Manufacturing census, 1982: financial and operating data, by SIC 2- to 4-digit industry, State, SMSA, and county, preliminary census div rpt series, 2491–3
- Manufacturing census, 1982: financial and operating data, for SIC 4-digit industries by product, preliminary rpt, 2491–1.176, 2491–1.189
- *Minerals Yearbook, 1982,* Vol 1: commodity reviews of production, reserves, supply, use, and trade, annual rpt, 5604–33
- *Minerals Yearbook, 1983,* Vol 1 preprints: commodity review of production, reserves, supply, use, and trade, annual rpt, 5604–15.32
- Occupational injury and illness rates, by SIC 2- to 4-digit industry, 1982, annual rpt, 6844–1
- OECD trade, total and for 4 major countries, and US trade by country, by commodity, 1972-82, annual world region rpt series, 244–13
- Oils and fats production, consumption by end use, and stocks, by type, monthly Current Industrial Rpt, 2506–4.4

Index by Subjects and Names

Panama

Pigments (synthetic organic), trade, tariffs, and industry operating data, 1979-83, TSUSA commodity rpt supplement, 9885–4.41

Pigments and other benzenoid chemicals imports by country of origin and product, 1983, annual rpt, 9884–2

Producer prices and indexes, by stage of processing and detailed commodity, monthly rpt, 6762–6

Producer prices and indexes, by stage of processing and detailed commodity, monthly 1983, annual supplement, 6764–2

Production and sales of synthetic organic chemicals by product, and listing of manufacturers, 1983, annual rpt, 9884–3

Production of synthetic organic chemicals, by detailed product, monthly rpt, 9882–1

Production, shipments, PPI, and stocks of building materials, by type, bimonthly rpt, 2012–1.5, 2012–1.6

Productivity, hours, and employment indexes for selected SIC 3- and 4-digit industries, 1954-82, annual rpt, 6824–1.3

Shipments, trade, and consumption of paints and related products, by product, 1983, annual Current Industrial Rpt, 2506–8.16

Shipments, trade, and consumption of paints and related products, monthly Current Industrial Rpt, 2506–8.4

Waterborne commerce of US (domestic and foreign), freight by commodity, traffic, and passengers, by port and waterway, 1982, annual rpt, 3754–3

see also under By Commodity in the "Index by Categories"

Pakistan

Agricultural and food production indexes, and production of selected commodities, by world region and country, 1974-83, annual rpt, 1524–5

Agricultural situation in 5 South Asia countries, by commodity, 1970s-1983/84 and outlook for 1984/85, annual rpt, 1524–4.11

Agricultural supply/demand, trade, and production, and socioeconomic data, by country, 1950s-77, 1528–179

AID activities and funding by project and function, FY85, and developing countries summary socioeconomic data, 1970s-83, by country, annual rpt, 9914–3

AID economic assistance to developing countries, obligations and disbursements by country, quarterly rpt, 9912–4

AID loan repayment status and terms by program and country, and status of predecessor agency loans, quarterly rpt, 9912–3

Background Notes, summary social, political, and economic data, 1984 rpt, 7006–2.26

Cotton towels from Pakistan, imports injury to US industry from sales covered by foreign govt grants, investigation with background financial and operating data, 1980-83, 9886–15.48

Economic conditions in Communist, OECD, and selected other countries, 1960s-83, annual rpt, 244–5

Economic, social, and political summary data, by country, 1984, annual factbook, 244–11

Economic trends in income, production, prices, employment, finances, and trade, 1984 semiannual rpt, 2046–4.52

Exports and imports of US, by commodity and country, 1972-82, annual world region rpt, 244–13.5

Exports of US, detailed Schedule B commodities by country of destination, 1983, annual rpt, 2424–9

Exports of US, detailed Schedule E commodities by mode of transport and world area and country of destination, 1983, annual rpts, 2424–5

Imports of US, detailed Schedule A commodities by country and world area of origin, and mode of transport, 1983, annual rpts, 2424–2

Imports of US, detailed TSUSA commodities by country of origin, 1983, annual rpt, 2424–4

Loans and grants for economic and military assistance from US and intl agencies, by program and country, FY46-83, annual rpt, 9914–5

Military aid of US, arms sales, and training programs costs and budget requests by program, world region, and country, FY83-85, annual rpt, 7144–13

Military spending, arms trade, and armed forces size, with total govt spending and population, by country, 1972-82, annual rpt, 9824–1

Minerals Yearbook, 1982, Vol 3: foreign country reviews of production, trade, and policies, by commodity, annual rpt, 5604–35

Mining industry equipment market and trade, and user industry operations and demand, 1984 country market research rpt, 2045–16.5

Nuclear power generation in US and 18 non-Communist countries, monthly rpt, 3162–24.10

Nuclear power plant construction and operation status, and capacity, by plant, region, State, and selected country, 1983 and projected to 2020, annual rpt, 3164–57

Population size and growth rates, and latest available benchmark demographic data, by country, 1950-83, biennial rpt, 2324–4

see also under By Foreign Country in the "Index by Categories"

Palash, Carl J.

"Did Financial Markets in 1983 Point to Recession?", 9385–1.410

Palm Bay, Fla.

see also under By SMSA or MSA in the "Index by Categories"

Palm oil

see Oils, oilseeds, and fats

Palumbo, George

"Fiscal Disparities: Central Cities and Suburbs, 1981. An Information Report", 10048–61

Palumbo, Thomas J.

"Selected Characteristics of Persons in Computer Specialties: 1978", 2546–2.124

"Selected Characteristics of Persons in Engineering: 1978", 2546–2.121

Panama

Agricultural and food production indexes, and production of selected commodities, by world region and country, 1974-83, annual rpt, 1524–5

Agricultural situation in Latin America, by country, 1981-83 and outlook for 1984, annual rpt, 1524–4.9

Agricultural supply/demand, trade, and production, and socioeconomic data, by country, 1950s-77, 1528–179

AID activities and funding by project and function, FY85, and developing countries summary socioeconomic data, 1970s-83, by country, annual rpt, 9914–3

AID economic assistance to developing countries, obligations and disbursements by country, quarterly rpt, 9912–4

AID economic assistance to 7 Central American countries, by type of aid, FY80-83, GAO rpt, 26123–55

AID loan repayment status and terms by program and country, and status of predecessor agency loans, quarterly rpt, 9912–3

Economic conditions, investment and export opportunities, and trade practices, 1984 country market research rpt, 2046–6.6

Economic, social, and political conditions in 6 Central America countries, 1960s-83 with trends and projections 1930-2010, 028–19

Economic, social, and political summary data, by country, 1984, annual factbook, 244–11

Economic trends in income, production, prices, employment, finances, and trade, 1984 annual rpt, 2046–4.91

Exports and imports of US, by commodity and country, 1972-82, annual world region rpt, 244–13.3

Exports of US, detailed Schedule B commodities by country of destination, 1983, annual rpt, 2424–9

Exports of US, detailed Schedule E commodities by mode of transport and world area and country of destination, 1983, annual rpts, 2424–5

Free zones in developing countries, industry financial and operating data by country, with case studies for 5 countries, 1970s-82, 9918–10

Imports of US, detailed Schedule A commodities by country and world area of origin, and mode of transport, 1983, annual rpts, 2424–2

Imports of US, detailed TSUSA commodities by country of origin, 1983, annual rpt, 2424–4

Loans and grants for economic and military assistance from US and intl agencies, by program and country, FY46-83, annual rpt, 9914–5

Military aid of US, arms sales, and training programs costs and budget requests by program, world region, and country, FY83-85, annual rpt, 7144–13

Military spending, arms trade, and armed forces size, with total govt spending and population, by country, 1972-82, annual rpt, 9824–1

Minerals Yearbook, 1982, Vol 3: foreign country reviews of production, trade, and policies, by commodity, annual rpt, 5604–35

Minerals Yearbook, 1982, Vol 3 preprints: foreign country review of production, trade, and policies, by commodity, annual rpt, 5604–17.86

Panama

Natural resources and hazards to resource dev, with data on mineral, energy, and water resources, by Central American country, 1981 with trends from 1977, 5668–71

Population size and growth rates, and latest available benchmark demographic data, by country, 1950-83, biennial rpt, 2324–4

Refugees from Central America by country of origin and asylum, and aid from US and Mexico, FY82-1984, GAO rpt, 26123–70

Ships in Panama OCS and total merchant fleet, and new registrations, selected years 1978-82, hearing, 21568–35

Ships in world merchant fleet, and tonnage, by country of registry, 1982, annual rpt, 7704–3.1

Tax evasion through nonresidents bank claims and deposits, direct investments, income payments, and other transactions in 5 Caribbean countries, 1978-82, 8008–106

see also Panama Canal

see also under By Foreign Country in the "Index by Categories"

Panama Canal

Commerce on Panama Canal by commodity, and local public utilities and services, FY82, annual rpt, 9664–3

Credit union membership, shares and loans, and asset size, for Federal and federally insured State unions by State, 1984 annual listing, 9534–6

Immigrants admitted under Immigration and Nationality Act, by class of admission, FY78-81, annual rpt, 6264–2

Panama Canal Commission

Budget of US Appendix, detailed budgets and personnel summaries, by agency, FY85, annual rpt, 104–3

Budget of US, appropriations, outlays, balances, and budget receipts, by govtl branch and agency, FY83, annual rpt, 8104–2

Operations, finances, and other activities of Panama Canal Commission, FY82, annual rpt, 9664–3

Panama City, Fla.

Census of Housing, 1980: occupancy and unit characteristics, by race, Hispanic origin, and city, SMSA rpt, 2473–1.276

Census of Population and Housing, 1980: detailed population and housing characteristics, by county, city, and census tract, SMSA rpt, 2551–2.276

Wages by occupation, and benefits for office and plant workers, 1984 labor market area survey rpt, 6785–3.9

see also under By SMSA or MSA in the "Index by Categories"

Panulas, John

"Minerals in the World Economy", 5604–35.1

Papademos, Lucas

"Monetary and Credit Targets in an Open Economy", 9373–3.26

Paper and paper products

Air pollutant emission factors, by detailed source, 3rd edition, 1983-84 supplements, 9198–13

Air pollution abatement equipment shipments by industry, exports, and new and backlog orders, by product, 1983, annual Current Industrial Rpt, 2506–12.5

Business statistics, detailed data for major industries and economic indicators, *Survey of Current Business*, monthly rpt, 2702–1.16

Census of Population, 1980: detailed socioeconomic and demographic characteristics, by age, sex, race, Hispanic origin, occupation, and industry, State rpt series, 2531–4

China economic conditions, agricultural and industrial production, trade, and domestic and foreign investment, 1980-85, 2048–106

China exports and imports by SITC 1- to 5-digit commodity, 1970s-82, annual rpt, 244–12

Collective bargaining agreements expiring during year, covered workers by SIC 2-digit industry, firm, and union, with summary of key provisions, 1984, annual rpt, 6784–9

Communist, OECD, and selected other countries consumer and producer goods production, 1960s-83, annual rpt, 244–5.8

County Business Patterns: establishments, employees, and payrolls, by SIC 4-digit industry and county, 1981, annual State rpt series, 2326–8

County Business Patterns: establishments, employees, and payrolls, by SIC 4-digit industry and county, 1982, annual State rpt series, 2326–6

Cuba economic conditions, agricultural and industrial production and distribution, trade, and intl economic relations, 1970-82 and trends from 1957, 248–40

Earnings by major industry group, and personal income per capita and by source, by region and State, 1929-82, 2708–40

Electric power cogeneration in 5 industries, and fuel use and utility supply/demand effects, by region, 1983-93, 3008–92

Electric power industrial demand model estimates, economic indicators, and supporting data for 5 industries, 1960s-80 with projections to 2000, 3008–87

Employment, earnings, and hours, by selected SIC 1- to 4-digit industry, State, and for 278 major labor areas, 1939-83, annual rpt, 6744–5

Employment, earnings, and hours, by SIC 4-digit nonfarm industry, monthly 1974-Feb 1984, annual update, 6744–4

Energy demand in industry, forecasting model description, detailed technology specifications, and energy use, for 27 SIC 2- to 4-digit industries, 1970s-80 and projected to 2000, 3308–66

Energy use and cost for building materials manufacture, by energy source and industry, 1970s-82, article, 2012–1.401

Energy use, prices, and conservation and efficiency measures, by fuel type, end-use sector, selected industry, and region, 1960-83, annual rpt, 3164–73

Exports and imports of US, by commodity group, world area, selected country, US coastal area and port, and mode of transport, with seasonal adjustments, monthly rpt, 2422–9

Exports and imports of US, detailed SIC-based commodities by world area, 1983, annual rpts, 2424–6

Index by Subjects and Names

Exports and imports of US, totals and as percent of domestic production, by SIC 2- to 5-digit commodity, 1981, annual rpt, 2424–3

Exports, imports, tariffs, and industry operating data for wood, paper, and printed matter, TSUSA commodity rpt series, 9885–2

Exports of manufactured and agricultural commodities, manufacturing production, and export-related employment, 1960s-82, State rpt series, 2046–3

Exports of US, detailed commodities by country of destination, monthly rpt, 2422–3

Exports of US, detailed Schedule B commodities by country of destination, 1983, annual rpt, 2424–9

Exports of US, detailed Schedule E commodities by mode of transport and world area and country of destination, 1983, annual rpts, 2424–5

Financial statements for manufacturing, mining, and trade corporations, by selected SIC 2- to 3-digit industry, quarterly rpt, 2502–1

Great Lakes trade, by SITC 3-digit commodity, port, vessel type, world area, and country, 1982, annual rpt, 7744–3

Imports of US, detailed Schedule A commodities by country and world area of origin, and mode of transport, 1983, annual rpts, 2424–2

Imports of US, detailed Schedule A commodities by country, monthly rpt, 2422–2

Imports of US, detailed TSUSA commodities by country of origin, 1983, annual rpt, 2424–4

Income tax returns of corporations, detailed income and tax items by industry, 1981, annual rpt, 8304–4

Income tax returns of corporations with foreign tax credit, income and deductions by type, asset size, and selected industry group, 1980, article, 8302–2.415

Income tax returns of sole proprietorships, detailed data by industry div and selected industry group, 1981, annual rpt, 8304–7

Industry finances and operations, by SIC 2- to 4-digit industry, 1970s-83 and projected to 1988, annual rpt, 2014–4

Input-output structure of US economy, detailed interindustry transactions for 85 industries, and components of final demand, 1977, article, 2702–1.421

Input-output structure of US economy, detailed interindustry transactions for 537 industries, and components of final demand, 1977 benchmark data, 2708–17

Manufacturing census, 1982: financial and operating data, by SIC 2- to 4-digit industry, State, SMSA, and county, preliminary census div rpt series, 2491–3

Manufacturing census, 1982: financial and operating data, for SIC 4-digit industries by product, preliminary rpt series, 2491–1

Minority group and women employment, by occupational group and SIC 2- to 3-digit industry, 1981, annual rpt, 9244–1.1

North Central States pulpwood production by county, imports, and individual mill capacity, by species, 1982, annual rpt, 1204–19

Index by Subjects and Names

Paraprofessionals

Occupational injury and illness rates, by SIC 2- to 4-digit industry, 1982, annual rpt, 6844–1

OECD trade, total and for 4 major countries, and US trade by country, by commodity, 1972-82, annual world region rpt series, 244–13

Office supplies and stationery shipments, trade, and consumption, by product, 1983, annual Current Industrial Rpt, 2506–7.11, 2506–7.13

Pacific Northwest electricity consumption and prices by end-use sector, and economic and demographic data, 1960s-83 and projected to 2005, annual rpt, 3224–2

Pollution abatement capital and operating costs, by SIC 2- to 4-digit industry, State, and SMSA, 1982, annual Current Industrial Rpt, 2506–3.6

Pollution abatement expenditures, and effect on economic indicators and industry operations, by major industry, projected under 3 pollution regulation alternatives 1983-95, 9188–84

Producer prices and indexes, by stage of processing and detailed commodity, monthly rpt, 6762–6

Producer prices and indexes, by stage of processing and detailed commodity, monthly 1983, annual supplement, 6764–2

Production, prices by region and State, trade by country, and consumption, for timber by species and product, with industry earnings, 1950-83, annual rpt, 1204–29

Productivity, hours, and employment indexes for selected SIC 3- and 4-digit industries, 1954-82, annual rpt, 6824–1.3

R&D industry funding and employment of scientists and engineers, by industry group, firm size, and funding source, 1956-82, annual rpt, 9627–21

Scientists, engineers, and technicians employed in private industry, by occupation and industry group, 1980-81, biennial rpt, 9627–23

Scientists, engineers and technicians employment in transportation, utilities, and retail and wholesale trade, by field of science and industry, 1982, 9628–72

Technological change, impact on productivity and employment in 4 industries, 1960-90, 6828–23

Transportation census, 1982: trucks, by detailed characteristics, miles traveled, and type of product carried, State rpt series, 2573–1

Water pollution fish kills, by State, location, and pollution source, monthly 1978-80, annual rpt, 9204–3

Waterborne commerce of US (domestic and foreign), freight by commodity, traffic, and passengers, by port and waterway, 1982, annual rpt, 3754–3

Wholesale trade census, 1982: employment, establishments, finances, and operations, by SIC 2- to 4-digit kind of business, SMSA, county, and city, State rpt series, 2405–1

Wholesale trade census, 1982: employment, establishments, sales by commodity, and payroll, by SIC 4-digit kind of business and State, preliminary rpt, 2403–1.20, 2403–1.21

Wholesale trade sales and inventories, by SIC 2- to 3-digit kind of business, monthly rpt, 2413–7

Wholesale trade sales, inventories, purchases, and gross margins, by SIC 2- to 3-digit kind of business and type of ownership, 1983, annual rpt, 2413–13

see also under By Commodity in the "Index by Categories"

see also under By Industry in the "Index by Categories"

Paper gold

see Special Drawing Rights

Paperwork Reduction Act

Fed Govt info collection requirements and respondent burden, effects of Act, by agency, FY80-84, annual rpt, 104–19

Papua New Guinea

Background Notes, summary social, political, and economic data, 1984 rpt, 7006–2.50

Economic, social, and political summary data, by country, 1984, annual factbook, 244–11

Exports of US, detailed Schedule B commodities by country of destination, 1983, annual rpt, 2424–9

Exports of US, detailed Schedule E commodities by mode of transport and world area and country of destination, 1983, annual rpts, 2424–5

Imports of US, detailed Schedule A commodities by country and world area of origin, and mode of transport, 1983, annual rpts, 2424–2

Imports of US, detailed TSUSA commodities by country of origin, 1983, annual rpt, 2424–4

Loans and grants for economic and military assistance from US and intl agencies, by program and country, FY46-83, annual rpt, 9914–5

Military aid of US, arms sales, and training programs costs and budget requests by program, world region, and country, FY83-85, annual rpt, 7144–13

Military spending, arms trade, and armed forces size, with total govt spending and population, by country, 1972-82, annual rpt, 9824–1

Minerals Yearbook, 1982, Vol 3: foreign country reviews of production, trade, and policies, by commodity, annual rpt, 5604–35

Minerals Yearbook, 1982, Vol 3 preprints: foreign country review of production, trade, and policies, by commodity, annual rpt, 5604–17.90

Minerals Yearbook, 1983, Vol 3 preprints: foreign country review of production, trade, and policies, by commodity, annual rpt, 5604–23.90

Population size and growth rates, and latest available benchmark demographic data, by country, 1950-83, biennial rpt, 2324–4

Tuna landings by species, and fishery operating data and govt revenues generated, for Papua New Guinea, 1979-81, article, 2162–1.402

see also under By Foreign Country in the "Index by Categories"

Paraguay

Agricultural and food production indexes, and production of selected commodities, by world region and country, 1974-83, annual rpt, 1524–5

Agricultural situation in Latin America, by country, 1981-83 and outlook for 1984, annual rpt, 1524–4.9

Agricultural supply/demand, trade, and production, and socioeconomic data, by country, 1950s-77, 1528–179

AID economic assistance to developing countries, obligations and disbursements by country, quarterly rpt, 9912–4

AID educational program activities and project impacts in 12 developing countries, 1950s-82, 9916–11.8

AID loan repayment status and terms by program and country, and status of predecessor agency loans, quarterly rpt, 9912–3

Economic conditions, income, production, prices, employment, and trade, 1984 annual country rpt, 2046–4.115

Economic, social, and political summary data, by country, 1984, annual factbook, 244–11

Exports of US, detailed Schedule B commodities by country of destination, 1983, annual rpt, 2424–9

Exports of US, detailed Schedule E commodities by mode of transport and world area and country of destination, 1983, annual rpts, 2424–5

Food supply policies of 21 developing countries, with farm sector data, tariff income, and prices and imports of 5 grains, 1960s-81, 1528–168

Imports of US, detailed Schedule A commodities by country and world area of origin, and mode of transport, 1983, annual rpts, 2424–2

Imports of US, detailed TSUSA commodities by country of origin, 1983, annual rpt, 2424–4

Loans and grants for economic and military assistance from US and intl agencies, by program and country, FY46-83, annual rpt, 9914–5

Military aid of US, arms sales, and training programs costs and budget requests by program, world region, and country, FY83-85, annual rpt, 7144–13

Military spending, arms trade, and armed forces size, with total govt spending and population, by country, 1972-82, annual rpt, 9824–1

Minerals Yearbook, 1982, Vol 3: foreign country reviews of production, trade, and policies, by commodity, annual rpt, 5604–35

Minerals Yearbook, 1983, Vol 3 preprints: foreign country review of production, trade, and policies, by commodity, annual rpt, 5604–23.89

Population size and growth rates, and latest available benchmark demographic data, by country, 1950-83, biennial rpt, 2324–4

see also under By Foreign Country in the "Index by Categories"

Paraprofessionals

Census of Population and Housing, 1980: detailed population and housing characteristics, by county, city, and census tract, State and SMSA rpt series, 2551–2

Census of Population, 1980: labor force, by sex, detailed occupation, and region, with comparison to 1970 census, supplementary rpt, 2535–1.12

Paraprofessionals

see also Allied health personnel

Pardons

see also Parole and probation

Paris, David

"Investment Tax Credit for Individual Taxpayers, 1981", 8302–2.409

"70th Year of Individual Income and Tax Statistics, 1913-82", 8302–2.401

Park, Choon B.

"Housing and Housing Finance in the Republic of Korea: Part 1", 9312–1.404

"Housing and Housing Finance in the Republic of Korea: Part 2", 9312–1.406

Park, Thae S.

"Federal Personal Income Taxes: Liabilities and Payments, 1980-82", 2702–1.415

"Personal Income and Adjusted Gross Income, 1980-82", 2702–1.414

Parker, Larry B.

"Distributing Acid Rain Mitigation Costs: Analysis of a Three-Mill User Fee on Fossil Fuel Electricity Generation", 21368–52

"Mitigating Acid Rain: Implications for High-Sulfur Coal Regions", 21368–52

Parker, Robert P.

"Improved Adjustments for Misreporting of Tax Return Information Used To Estimate the National Income and Product Accounts, 1977", 2702–1.422

Parkersburg, W.Va.

Census of Housing, 1980: occupancy and unit characteristics, by race, Hispanic origin, and city, SMSA rpt, 2473–1.277

Census of Population and Housing, 1980: detailed population and housing characteristics, by county, city, and census tract, SMSA rpt, 2551–2.277

see also under By SMSA or MSA in the "Index by Categories"

Parking facilities

Auto and van operating and owning costs by component and vehicle size, for 12 years of operation, 1984 model year, annual rpt, 7304–2, 7304–2.3, 7554–21

Census of Housing, 1980: inventory, occupancy, and unit characteristics, changes from 1973 by region and inside-outside SMSAs and central cities, series, 2473–3

Census of Service Industries, 1982: employment, establishments, receipts, and payroll, by SIC 2- to 4-digit kind of business, SMSA, county, and city, State rpt series, 2391–1

Construction industries census, 1982: financial and operating data, by SIC 4-digit industry and State, final rpt series, 2373–1

Construction industries census, 1982: financial and operating data, by SIC 4-digit industry and State, preliminary rpt series, 2371–1

County Business Patterns: establishments, employees, and payrolls, by SIC 4-digit industry and county, 1981, annual State rpt series, 2326–8

County Business Patterns: establishments, employees, and payrolls, by SIC 4-digit industry and county, 1982, annual State rpt series, 2326–6

Govt revenues by source, expenditures by function, debt, and assets, by level of govt, 1982-83, annual rpt, 2466–2.6

Govt transportation revenues by source and expenditures, by level of govt and mode of transport, and Fed Govt aid by type, FY77-82, 7308–185

Housing characteristics of recent movers for new and previous unit, and household characteristics, by inside-outside central cities, 1979-82 surveys, SMSA rpt series, 2485–6

Housing, new single and multifamily unit physical and financial characteristics, by region and metro-nonmetro location, 1979-83, annual rpt, 2384–1

Income tax returns of sole proprietorships, detailed data by industry div and selected industry group, 1981, annual rpt, 8304–7

Income tax returns of sole proprietorships, receipts, deductions by type, payroll, and net income, by major industry, 1982, annual article, 8302–2.413

Receipts for selected services, by SIC 2- to 4-digit kind of business, 1983, annual rpt, 2413–8

Parkinson, Patrick M.

"Some Implications of Financial Innovations in the U.S.", 9366–1.137

Parks

Acreage of natl park system and other areas under Natl Park Service mgmt, by type of area, ownership, and site, as of Sept 1984, semiannual rpt, 5542–1

Budget of US, effects of Reagan Admin policy changes, by detailed program, FY85, annual rpt, 104–21

Coastal environmental characteristics, fish, wildlife, and use, and population socioeconomic data, for individual areas, series, 5506–4

Foreign and US tropical forests status by country and world region, conservation methods, and mgmt role of US, foreign, and intl groups, 1977-81 and projected to 2000, 26358–101.1

Govt census, 1982: city govt revenues by source, expenditures by function, debt, and assets, by State and city, 2457–4

Govt census, 1982: county govt revenues by source, expenditures by function, debt, and assets, by State and county, 2457–3

Govt census, 1982: State govt payments to local govts, by program, source of funds, level of govt, and State, with trends from 1902, 2460–3

Govt employment and payroll, by function, level of govt, and jurisdiction, 1983, annual rpt series, 2466–1

Govt finances, by level of govt, State, and for large cities and counties, 1981-83, annual rpt series, 2466–2

New Communities program of HUD, activities, costs, land sales, and community and population characteristics, for 13 communities, 1970s-83, 5188–107

Statistical Abstract of US, social, political, and economic data, 1950s-83 and trends, annual rpt, 2324–1.1

see also National park system

see also State parks

Parlett, Ralph L.

"1984 Outlook for Food Prices and Consumption", 1004–16.1

Parochial schools

see Private schools

Index by Subjects and Names

Parole and probation

Arson investigation and prosecution, by incident characteristics and outcome, motive, and type of evidence, for 4 jurisdictions, 1981, 6068–184

Court cases, dispositions, convictions, and sentences of Federal criminal defendants, by offense and district, as of June 1983 with trends from 1945, annual rpt, 18204–1

Court civil and criminal casloads and activity summary, for Federal district, appeals, and bankruptcy courts, 1975-June 1984, annual chartbook, 18204–9

Court criminal case disposition, effect of victim injury and other factors, and law enforcement official and victim attitudes, 1983 survey, 6068–185

Crime and criminal justice data, including justice expenditures and employment by level of govt, 1970s-82 with some trends from 1875, 6068–174

Decisions for parole, guidelines validation and hearing examiner workloads, Parole Commission research rpt series, 6006–2

Drug Enforcement Admin cases against major drug traffickers by case characteristics, and agents assessment of activities, in 3 cities, 1979-82, GAO rpt, 26119–57

Fed Govt correctional instns, discharges for parole and mandatory releases, and recommitments for violation of terms, by facility type and region, monthly rpts, 6242–1

Fed Probation System, persons under supervision by circuit and district, quarterly rpt, annual tables, 18202–1

Govt census, 1982: State govt payments to local govts, by program, source of funds, level of govt, and State, with trends from 1902, 2460–3

Jail capacities, conditions, expenditures, and services, and socioeconomic and other characteristics of inmates, various dates 1976-82, 10048–59

Judicial Conf semiannual proceedings and findings, 1984 annual rpt, 18204–5

Parole and probation population, and entries and exits by reason, by State, 1983, periodic rpt, 6062–2.408

Parolee population, characteristics, and staff of Federal and State parole systems, by State, annual rpt, suspended, 6064–14

Witness Security Program costs, participants by arrest record, and prosecutions by offense, offender type, and disposition, various periods FY70-83, GAO rpt, 26119–70

Parrish, W. A.

"Production and Use of Industrial Wood and Bark Residues for 44 Counties in Alabama, Georgia, Kentucky, and Mississippi", 9806–2.36

Part-time employment

Business Conditions Digest, historical supplement on economic, business, and financial conditions and cyclical fluctuations, with methodology, 1947-82, 2708–31

Computer specialists sociodemographic, educational, and employment characteristics, and Fed Govt support by agency, 1978, biennial Current Population Rpt, 2546–2.124

Index by Subjects and Names

Credit union financial statements by region, State, and type of membership, for Federal and federally insured State unions, 1983, annual rpt, 9534–1

DOD civilian employment, by service branch and defense agency, with summary military employment data, monthly rpt, 3542–16

DOD medical personnel, by full- and part-time status, occupation, and service branch, FY83, annual rpt, 3544–24.2

DOT employment by subagency, State, and selected personnel characteristics, FY83, annual rpt, 7304–18.1

Earnings of couples with both spouses working, by sociodemographic and employment characteristics and age of children, 1981, Current Population Rpt, 2546–2.120

Earnings of full- and part-time workers, quarterly rpt, 6742–19

Educational attainment of labor force, by demographic and employment characteristics, 1982-83 with summary trends from 1940, 6746–1.251

Employment and earnings, detailed data, monthly rpt, 6742–2

Employment and price changes during recession and recovery, by selected employee characteristics, 1979-Jan 1984, 6728–28

Employment and unemployment by selected worker characteristics, annual averages, 1983, article, 6742–2.403

Employment, earnings, and hours, monthly press release, 6742–5

Employment, unemployment, and labor force, by demographic and employment characteristics, State, and for 30 metro areas and 11 large cities, 1983, annual rpt, 6744–7

Employment, unemployment, and labor force, detailed data by sociodemographic and employment characteristics, and industry, 1940s-83, 6748–72

Engineers sociodemographic, educational, and employment characteristics, and Federal support by agency, 1978, Current Population Rpt, 2546–2.121

Fed Govt employee work-years by work schedule and for overtime and holidays, various periods 1980-82, article, 9842–1.401

Florida and California elderly migration by selected State of origin or destination, and Florida elderly, by sociodemographic and housing characteristics, 1970 and 1980, 4478–150

Govt employment and payroll, by function, level of govt, and jurisdiction, 1983, annual rpt series, 2466–1

Handbook of Labor Statistics, employment, earnings, hours, and labor force characteristics, 1982 and trends, detailed annual rpt, 6724–1

Health care temporary employees, reasons for desiring temporary and part-time work, and preferences for work time, by skill level, survey, 1984 article, 6722–1.452

High school classes of 1980 and 1982: educational and sociodemographic characteristics and expectations, natl longitudinal study, series, 4826–2

Higher education enrollment of non-resident aliens, full- and part-time teaching staff, and average undergrad tuition, by instn type, selected years 1970/71-1992/93, annual rpt, 4824–1.2

Income (household) and cash and noncash transfer program participation, by sociodemographic characteristics, quarterly rpt, 2542–2

Income assistance, effects of experimental negative income tax program on employment, earnings, marital status, and other family characteristics in 2 cities, 1970-75, 4008–64

Jail capacities, conditions, expenditures, and services, and socioeconomic and other characteristics of inmates, various dates 1976-82, 10048–59

Kentucky employment growth in 9-county rural area, labor force and establishment characteristics, 1979-80, 1598–194

Labor force status monthly changes, by selected worker characteristics, 1981-82, biennial rpt, 6744–17

Monthly Labor Review, current statistics and articles, 6722–1

Natl income and product, comprehensive accounts and components, *Survey of Current Business,* monthly rpt, monthly and annual tables, 2702–1.27

Nurses employed full- and part-time in nursing homes, by region and State, 1980, 4147–14.29

Occupational employment and percent black, women, and part-time workers, by detailed occupation, 1982, biennial rpt, 6744–3

Occupational Outlook Handbook, 1984-85 biennial rpt, 6744–1

Older persons community service part-time employment and program funding, by State and outlying area, FY84, press release, 6408–60

Older persons income and income sources, by OASDI beneficiary and poverty status, labor force participation, and demographic characteristics, 1982, biennial rpt, 4744–26

Older persons sociodemographic characteristics, and Fed Govt program participation and funding, 1983 with trends and projections 1900-2060, annual rpt, 25144–3.1

Physicians employed in prisons by sociodemographic, employment, and professional characteristics, and compared to all physicians, 1979, article, 4102–1.407

Scientists and engineers employed at universities and colleges, by field, sex, State, and instn, Jan 1983 and selected trends from 1967, annual survey, 9627–11

Small business and all employees sociodemographic characteristics, by industry div and firm size, 1978-1979, annual rpt, 9764–6.3

Statistical Abstract of US, social, political, and economic data, 1950s-83 and trends, annual rpt, 2324–1.3

Steel imports of US from EC and other countries, and US industry operating data, for 15 products limited under arrangement with EC, monthly rpt, 9882–10

Pascagoula, Miss.

TV and radio station employment, total and for minorities and women, by full- and part-time status and individual station, 1983, annual rpt, 9284–7

Unemployment and part-time employment, by race, Hispanic origin, sex, family composition, income, and poverty status, 1980-82, annual report, 6744–15

Unemployment and part-time employment effects on family income, by socioeconomic and labor force characteristics, 1981-82, annual rpt, 6746–1.252

Unemployment, by duration, work experience during year, sex, race, and Hispanic origin, 1982-83, 6748–77

VA employment characteristics and activities, FY83, annual rpt, 9924–1.8

VA physicians, dentists, and nurses, by age, selected employment characteristics, and VA district, quarterly rpt, 9922–11

Veterans income and employment status, by age and war or peacetime service, with comparisons to nonveterans, 1981, annual rpt, 9924–23

Widows with minor children receiving OASI survivor benefits, health insurance coverage and health care services and expenses, 1976-78, article, 4742–1.404

Women in couples with wife as primary earner, socioeconomic and family characteristics, with comparative data for husbands, Mar 1982, 2326–11.9

Women's employment and earnings, by labor force and socioeconomic characteristics, and compared to men, 1978-81 and trends from 1940s, 6568–29

Women's travel patterns, by employment and sociodemographic characteristics and type of child care used, 1980 survey, 7888–62

Youth employment, by high school and college enrollment status, industry div, occupation, and selected demographic characteristics, 1980-82, 6746–1.250

see also Moonlighting

see also Seasonal and summer employment

Particleboard

see Lumber industry and products

Particulates

see Air pollution

Partnerships

see Ownership of enterprise

Pasadena, Calif.

see also under By City in the "Index by Categories"

Pasadena, Tex.

see also under By City in the "Index by Categories"

Pascagoula, Miss.

Census of Housing, 1980: occupancy and unit characteristics, by race, Hispanic origin, and city, SMSA rpt, 2473–1.278

Census of Population and Housing, 1980: detailed population and housing characteristics, by county, city, and census tract, SMSA rpt, 2551–2.278

Wages of office and plant workers, by occupation, 1984 labor market area survey rpt, 6785–3.9

see also under By SMSA or MSA in the "Index by Categories"

Pasco, Wash.

Pasco, Wash.

Census of Housing, 1980: occupancy and unit characteristics, by race, Hispanic origin, and city, SMSA rpt, 2473–1.301

Census of Population and Housing, 1980: detailed population and housing characteristics, by county, city, and census tract, SMSA rpt, 2551–2.301

see also under By SMSA or MSA in the "Index by Categories"

Pasley, Beverly H.

"Prescribing Estrogen During Menopause: Physician Survey of Practices in 1974 and 1981", 4102–1.444

Passaic, N.J.

Census of Housing, 1980: occupancy and unit characteristics, by race, Hispanic origin, and city, SMSA rpt, 2473–1.279

Census of Population and Housing, 1980: detailed population and housing characteristics, by county, city, and census tract, SMSA rpt, 2551–2.279

Housing and financial characteristics, and unit and neighborhood quality, for 15 SMSAs, 1978, annual survey special supplement, 2485–8

Housing and households detailed characteristics, and unit and neighborhood quality, by inside-outside central cities, 1982 survey, SMSA rpt, 2485–6.38

Wages by occupation, and benefits for office and plant workers, 1984 SMSA survey rpt, 6785–11.8

see also under By SMSA or MSA in the "Index by Categories"

Passenger ships

Construction and operating subsidies of MarAd by firm, and ship deliveries and fleet by country, by vessel type, FY83, annual rpt, 7704–14.1, 7704–14.2

Cuba economic conditions, agricultural and industrial production and distribution, trade, and intl economic relations, 1970-82 and trends from 1957, 248–40

Finances, operations, vehicles, equipment, accidents, and energy use, by mode of transport, 1955-84, annual rpt, 7304–2

Foreign travel to US, by characteristics of visit and traveller, country, and State of destination, quarterly rpt, 2902–1

Merchant ships in US fleet, shipping costs, construction, employment, military availability, and Fed Govt subsidies, 1970s-1984 and projected to 2000, 26306–6.83

Merchant ships in world fleet, by selected characteristics and country of registry, as of Jan 1983, annual rpt, 7704–1

Occupational injury and illness rates, by SIC 2- to 4-digit industry, 1982, annual rpt, 6844–1

St Lawrence Seaway ships, cargo and passenger volumes, and toll revenues, 1981-82 and trends from 1959, annual rpt, 7744–2

Passport Office

see Bureau of Consular Affairs

Passports and visas

Developing countries disaster preparedness and summary sociodemographic, political, and economic data, country rpt series, 9916–2

Foreign travel to US, by characteristics of visit and traveller, country, and State of destination, quarterly rpt, 2902–1

Passport applications and estimated travel to Europe, monthly rpt, 7182–2

Passports issued, by holder characteristics, travel purpose, and country of destination, quarterly rpt, 7182–1

Visas issued and refused to immigrants and nonimmigrants, and status adjustments, by class and nationality, FY77, annual rpt, 7184–1

Pasture and rangeland

Acreage harvested and cropland area by crop and region, and potential for expansion, 1982-84 with trends from 1949, annual rpt, 1584–4

Agricultural production, marketing, trade, supply, food consumption, and food and nutrition programs, 1960s-83, annual chartbook, 1504–3

Agricultural Statistics, 1983, annual rpt, 1004–1

Agriculture census, 1982: farms, farmland, production and costs, and operator characteristics, preliminary State and county rpt series, 2330–1

Agriculture census, 1982: farms, farmland, production, finances, and operator characteristics, by county, final State rpt series, 2331–1

Agriculture Fact Book of US, compilation of data for 1983 with trends from 1940, annual rpt, 1004–14

Environmental quality and protection programs, costs, and Fed Govt enforcement, 1983, detailed annual rpt, 484–1

Farm finances, assets, liabilities, income, receipts by commodity and State, and expenses, 1980-83 and trends from 1910, annual rpt, 1544–16

Farm finances, expenses by type, loans by purpose and source, and credit detail by Fed Reserve District, quarterly rpt, 9365–3.10

Farm improvement, acreage and owners by improvement type, funding source, land use, and region, 1978 survey, 1506–5.20

Farm production expenditures, detailed items by farm sales size and region, 1983, annual rpt, 1614–3

Farm production inputs, land mgmt, and environmental effects, for 4 crops, 1940s-80 and projected to 2010, 9188–94

Farm production itemized costs, receipts, and net returns, for 13 crops, 4 livestock types, and milk, by region, 1981-83, annual rpt, 1544–20

Farm real estate value, sales, financing, taxes, and proposed use after purchase, by State, 1970s-84, annual rpt, 1541–8

Farmers prices received for major products and paid for farm inputs and living items, by commodity and State, monthly rpt, 1629–1

Fed Govt-owned real property inventory and costs, worldwide summary by location, agency, and use, 1983, annual rpt, 9454–5

Fed Govt programs and mgmt cost control proposals, 3-year savings by function and agency, and financial and operating data, 1960s-81, 16908–1.9, 16908–1.31

Feed condition of pasture and range, monthly 1970-81, annual rpt, 1564–6.1

Foreign acquisitions of US farmland, by State and county, before 1980 and during 1980-82, 1588–77

Index by Subjects and Names

Foreign and US agricultural supply/demand, consumption per capita, and trade, by world area and country group, 1960s-82, 1528–181

Foreign and US cropland per capita, and total arable land area by use, by selected country and world region, selected years 1955-80, 1528–180

Foreign and US cropland per capita by world region and selected country, and world arable land area by use, selected years 1955-80, summary article, 1522–3.401

Foreign ownership of US agricultural land, acquisitions, dispositions, holdings, and use, by State and type and country of owner, 1983, annual rpt, 1584–2

Foreign ownership of US agricultural land, acreage, value, and use, by State and county, and for 5 leading investor countries, 1983, annual rpt, 1584–3

Genetic resource (plant and animal) conservation, commercial uses, causes of depletion, and geographic sources, 1984 rpt, 5548–13

Grazing on non-irrigated pasture and rangeland, current supply of pasture feed, monthly rpt, 1621–1

Mexico and US range and wildlife characteristics, problems, and research strategies and needs, 1981 conf papers, 1208–197

Montana and North Dakota coal production, impact of mining on agricultural land availability and on farm income and production costs, by mining tract, 1982 rpt, 1588–79

Natl Forest System lands livestock grazing, and losses from predators, poisonous plants, and other causes, by region and State, FY83, annual rpt, 1204–5

Natl Forest System wildlife habitat and fishery improvements, use, and game population and harvest by species and forest, by region, FY83, annual rpt, 1204–31

Public lands grazing and range improvement programs of Land Mgmt Bur, 1982-83, annual rpt, 5724–1.2

Public lands grazing, by animal type and State, FY83, annual rpt, 1204–1.1

Public lands mgmt activities of Land Mgmt Bur in western States, FY82-84, annual rpt, 5724–13

Research project descriptions and bibl for forestry, 1982, annual rpt, 1204–14

Resources use and mgmt assessment and environmental impacts of Forest Service program options, 1977-2030 and trends from 1920, 1208–24

Rocky Mountain forest and rangeland area, and timber resources and removals, by ownership, forest and tree characteristics, and State, 1977, 1208–201

Southwestern States farm credit conditions and real estate values, Fed Reserve 11th District, quarterly rpt, 9379–11

Tennessee Valley ethanol production, feedstocks, facilities, tax incentives, and related farming data, by State, 1970s-83 and projected to 1992, 9808–69

Wildlife refuge revenues from economic and recreational uses, and refuge managers attitudes toward expanded use, FY81-83, GAO rpt, 26113–128

626 ASI Annual Supplement

January-December 1984

Index by Subjects and Names

Payroll

Patent and Trademark Office

Applications, actions taken, litigation, and Patent and Trademark Office services and employment, selected years FY64-83, annual rpt, 2244–1

Budgets and permanent staff positions appropriated for Commerce Dept agencies, FY84-85, annual rpt, 2004–6

Cost control proposals for Fed Govt programs and mgmt, 3-year savings by function and agency, and financial and operating data, 1960s-81, 16908–1.3

DOD prime contract awards for R&D to educational and nonprofit instns and Federal agencies, by instn and location, FY83, annual listing, 3544–17

Patents (US) granted to US and foreign applicants, by applicant type, firm, State, and country, subject rpt series, 2246–2

Patents (US) granted to US and foreign applicants, by patent type, State, and country, 1983, annual press release, 2244–2

Patents (US) granted to US and foreign applicants, by year of grant and application, country, and type of applicant, 1960s-83, annual rpt, 2244–3

Programs, funding, and employment of Commerce Dept agencies, FY83, annual rpt, 2004–1

Publications of Commerce Dept, biweekly listing, 2002–1

Patents

Applications, actions taken, litigation, and Patent and Trademark Office services and employment, selected years FY64-83, annual rpt, 2244–1

Biotechnology commercial uses, R&D funding and output, controls, and industry financial and operating data, for US and 5 countries, 1970s-83 and estimated 1984-85, 26358–98

Biotechnology firms, patents, and trade by country, and effect of industry growth on US drug and chemical trade, selected years 1979-2000, 9886–4.78

County Business Patterns: establishments, employees, and payrolls, by SIC 4-digit industry and county, 1981, annual State rpt series, 2326–8

County Business Patterns: establishments, employees, and payrolls, by SIC 4-digit industry and county, 1982, annual State rpt series, 2326–6

Drug prices by brand and generic category, patent life, FDA approval time, and industry R&D costs and finances, selected years 1962-83, hearing, 25528–98

Fed Govt programs and mgmt cost control proposals, 3-year savings by function and agency, and financial and operating data, 1960s-81, 16908–1.3

Grants of patents to US and foreign inventors, and foreign grants to US citizens, by country and major product group, 1960s-82, annual rpt, 9624–10

Minerals patent applications and patents issued, FY83, annual rpt, 5724–1.2

Mines Bur publications and patents, monthly listing, 5602–2

Multinatl corporation income reallocation through regulation of intercorporate transactions, by tax item, treaty status, asset size, industry, and tax haven country, 1982, 8008–110

NSF-supported activities, number of resulting patents and inventions, FY83, annual rpt, 9624–6

Patents (US) granted to US and foreign applicants, by applicant type, firm, State, and country, subject rpt series, 2246–2

Patents (US) granted to US and foreign applicants, by patent type, State, and country, 1983, annual press release, 2244–2

Patents (US) granted to US and foreign applicants, by year of grant and application, country, and type of applicant, 1960s-83, annual rpt, 2244–3

Soviet Union share of all Council for Mutual Economic Assistance R&D employment, funding, and patents, with enrollment in USSR of science students from member countries, 1970s, 2326–9.7

Statistical Abstract of US, social, political, and economic data, 1950s-83 and trends, annual rpt, 2324–1.3

see also Trademarks

Paterson, N.J.

Census of Housing, 1980: occupancy and unit characteristics, by race, Hispanic origin, and city, SMSA rpt, 2473–1.279

Census of Population and Housing, 1980: detailed population and housing characteristics, by county, city, and census tract, SMSA rpt, 2551–2.279

Housing and financial characteristics, and unit and neighborhood quality, for 15 SMSAs, 1978, annual survey special supplement, 2485–8

Housing and households detailed characteristics, and unit and neighborhood quality, by inside-outside central cities, 1982 survey, SMSA rpt, 2485–6.38

Wages by occupation, and benefits for office and plant workers, 1984 SMSA survey rpt, 6785–11.8

see also under By City in the "Index by Categories"

Pathology

Black medical residents by specialty, and minority medical faculty by race and Hispanic origin, selected years 1980-83, article, 4102–1.412

DOD medical personnel, trainees, and accessions by source, by occupation, specialty, and service branch, FY83, annual rpt, 3544–24

FAA aviation medicine research and studies, technical rpt series, 7506–10

Manpower supply and education of health professionals, by occupation, demographic and professional characteristics, and location, 1950s-83 and projected to 2000, biennial rpt, 4114–8

Medicare physician charges and reimbursement by enrollee characteristics and carrier, payment limits effects on charges in California, and physician earnings, by specialty, 1950s-84, 25368–127

Science and engineering doctoral degree recipients, by field, sex, race, age, citizenship, postgrad employment and study status, State, and instn, 1960-82, 9626–6.16

Science and engineering grad enrollment, fields of study, financial support, and other student and instn characteristics, 1975-82, annual survey, 9627–7

VA physicians, dentists, and nurses, by age, selected employment characteristics, and VA district, quarterly rpt, 9922–11

see also Diseases and disorders

see also Medical examinations and tests

Patinkin, Lynn

"Nonresidential Buildings Energy Consumption Survey: 1979 Consumption and Expenditures. Part 2: Steam, Fuel Oil, LPG, and All Fuels", 3166–8.4

Patzer, R. G.

"Offsite Environmental Monitoring Report, Radiation Monitoring Around U.S. Nuclear Test Areas, 1983", 9234–4

Paull, Mary K.

"Annual Outlook for U.S. Coal, 1984 With Projections to 1995", 3164–68

Paulozzi, Leonard J.

"Outcomes of a Diabetes Education Program", 4102–1.457

Pauly, Peter

"Oil Prices, Welfare Tradeoffs, and International Policy Coordination in a Three Region World Model: An Optimizing Approach", 9366–7.96

Pautler, Paul A.

"Economic Analysis of Taxicab Regulation", 9406–1.37

Pavel, Christine

"Financial Services in Transition: The Effects of Nonbank Competitors", 9375–11.3

Pawtucket, R.I.

Census of Housing, 1980: occupancy and unit characteristics, by race, Hispanic origin, and city, SMSA rpt, 2473–1.293

Census of Population and Housing, 1980: detailed population and housing characteristics, by county, city, and census tract, SMSA rpt, 2551–2.293

Housing and households detailed characteristics, and unit and neighborhood quality, by inside-outside central cities, 1980 survey, SMSA rpt, 2485–6.14

Wages of office and plant workers, by occupation, 1984 SMSA survey rpt, 6785–11.6

see also under By SMSA or MSA in the "Index by Categories"

Payment-in-kind program, USDA

see Agricultural quotas and price supports

Payne County, Okla.

Housing vacancy rates for single and multifamily units and mobile homes, by county, city, and ZIP code, 1983, annual SMSA rpt, 9304–22.2

Housing vacancy rates for single and multifamily units and mobile homes, by county, city, and ZIP code, 1984, annual metro area rpt, 9304–22.14

Payroll

AID Housing Guaranty Program financial statements, and projects by country, FY83, annual rpt, 9914–4

Airline operating and other costs, itemized for domestic and intl trunk and local service carriers, 1st half 1983, semiannual rpt, 9142–47

Bank financial and operating statements, functional cost analysis for Fed Reserve member banks with average and high earnings, by deposit size, 1982, annual rpt, 9364–6

Bus industry collective ratemaking and regulatory reform impacts on operations,

Payroll

finances, and services to older persons and rural areas by State, 1970s-83, 14828–2

- *Business Conditions Digest,* historical supplement on economic, business, and financial conditions and cyclical fluctuations, with methodology, 1947-82, 2708–31
- Construction industries census, 1982: financial and operating data, by SIC 4-digit industry and State, final rpt series, 2373–1
- Construction industries census, 1982: financial and operating data, by SIC 4-digit industry and State, preliminary rpt series, 2371–1
- *County and City Data Book,* detailed socioeconomic and demographic data for States, counties, and cities, selected years 1976-82, 2328–1
- County Business Patterns: establishments, employees, and payrolls, by SIC 4-digit industry and county, 1981, annual State rpt series, 2326–8
- County Business Patterns: establishments, employees, and payrolls, by SIC 4-digit industry and county, 1982, annual State rpt series, 2326–6
- Economic and demographic factors used in OASDI program cost estimates, selected years 1913-82 with alternative projections to 2060, 4706–1.90
- Economic growth, with data on labor force, inflation, and productivity, 1953-83 with inflation and unemployment projections to 1988, article, 9373–1.402
- Economic recovery effect on nonfarm payroll, by industry div and region, 4th qtr 1982-4th qtr 1983, article, 2702–1.412
- Electric utilities privately owned, detailed financial and operating data by company, with summary data for other distributors by type, 1982, annual rpt, 3164–23
- Fish hatchery production, deliveries, and operating costs, and fishery assistance, by region, hatchery, and Fed Govt assistance station, FY82, annual rpt, 5504–9
- Fishing diesel and sail-assisted boats in Hawaiian waters, fuel use, earnings, and operating costs, with fuel and fish price indexes, various periods 1967-81, article, 2162–1.401
- Foreign firms US affiliates financial and operating data, by country of parent firm and industry div, 1980-81, article, 2702–1.402
- Foreign-owned US multiestablishment firms, employment, and payroll, by country, State, industry group, and foreign ownership share, 1981-82, annual rpt, 2324–6
- Forest industry establishments, employment, and payroll in Northeast, by SIC 2- to 4-digit industry, State rpt series, 1206–16
- Hours at work and hours paid ratios and impacts on productivity measures, by firm size and major industry group, with survey methodology, 1981-82, article, 6722–1.434
- Income tax returns filed by type of filer, selected income items, summary data, quarterly rpt, 8302–2.1
- Income tax returns of partnerships, receipts by source, deductions by type, and establishments, by selected industry, 1982, annual article, 8302–2.416

Income tax returns of sole proprietorships, detailed data by industry div and selected industry group, 1981, annual rpt, 8304–7

- Income tax returns of sole proprietorships, receipts, deductions by type, payroll, and net income, by major industry, 1982, annual article, 8302–2.413
- Labor union wage differentials, effect on production and prices by industry div, 1971, technical paper, 9387–8.81
- Manufacturing census, 1982: financial and operating data, by SIC 2- to 4-digit industry, State, SMSA, and county, preliminary census div rpt series, 2491–3
- Manufacturing census, 1982: financial and operating data, for SIC 4-digit industries by product, preliminary rpt series, 2491–1
- Mental health facilities, services, and costs in DC, and effect of St Elizabeths Hospital operations and finances transfer to DC govt, FY83, GAO rpt, 26121–72
- Michigan bankruptcy filings, by filer type, moving history, income, creditor action, debt and asset type, credit status, exemptions claimed, and county, 1979-81, hearings, 21528–57.3
- Mineral industries census, 1982: financial and operating data, by SIC 2- to 4-digit industry and State, preliminary summary rpts, 2511–2
- Mineral industries census, 1982: financial and operating data, including materials consumed, by SIC 4-digit industry and State, preliminary rpt series, 2511–1
- Motor and rail carriers regulated by ICC, employment and finances by mode of transport, and ICC activities, FY80-83 and trends, annual rpt, 9484–1
- Motor carriers (Class I interstate) finances, operations, equipment, employment, and payroll, by district, 1982, annual rpt, 9486–5.3
- Multinatl corporation income reallocation through regulation of intercorporate transactions, by tax item, treaty status, asset size, industry, and tax haven country, 1982, 8008–110
- Natural gas interstate pipeline company detailed financial and operating data, by firm, 1983, annual rpt, 3164–38
- Partnership finances, tax deductions, and employment, by industry div and size, 1979, article, 8302–2.411
- Railroad employee benefits and beneficiaries by type, benefit program finances, and railroad employees and payroll, FY83, annual rpt, 9704–1
- Railroad finances and operations, detailed data by firm, class of service, and district, 1983, annual rpt, 9486–6.1
- Retail trade census, 1982: employment, establishments, sales, and payroll, by SIC 2- to 4-digit kind of business, SMSA, and retail district, State rpt series, 2401–1
- Retail trade census, 1982: employment, establishments, sales, and payroll, by SIC 2- to 4-digit kind of business, SMSA, county, and city, State rpt series, 2397–1
- Retail trade census, 1982: employment, establishments, sales, and payroll, by SIC 4-digit kind of business and State, preliminary rpt series, 2395–1
- Service industry census, 1982: employment, establishments, receipts, and payroll, by SIC 2- to 4-digit kind of business, SMSA, county, and city, State rpt series, 2391–1

Index by Subjects and Names

- Service industry census, 1982: employment, establishments, receipts, and payroll, by SIC 4-digit kind of business and State, preliminary rpt series, 2390–2
- Steel industry hourly employment costs in selected OECD countries, selected years 1969-82, 26306–6.69
- Telephone and telegraph firms, employment by sex, and employee compensation, 1982, annual rpt, 9284–6
- Transit system (automated guideway) characteristics and itemized costs, for 16 systems in operation or under construction, 1982, annual rpt, 7884–6
- Transportation employment, wages, and average annual earnings, by mode of transport, 1972-82, annual rpt, 7304–2.2
- Virgin Islands economic censuses, 1982: employment, establishments, payroll, and receipts, by SIC 1- to 4-digit industry, island, and city, 2593–1
- Wholesale trade census, 1982: employment, establishments, finances, and operations, by SIC 2- to 4-digit kind of business, SMSA, county, and city, State rpt series, 2405–1
- Wholesale trade census, 1982: employment, establishments, sales by commodity, and payroll, by SIC 4-digit kind of business and State, preliminary rpt series, 2403–1

see also Agricultural wages

see also Earnings, general

see also Earnings, specific industries

see also Federal pay

see also Military pay

see also Social security tax

see also State and local employees pay

see also Unemployment insurance tax

Payroll tax

see Social security tax

see Unemployment insurance tax

PCBs

see Hazardous substances

Peace Corps

- Budget of US Appendix, detailed budgets and personnel summaries, by agency, FY85, annual rpt, 104–3
- Budget of US, appropriations, outlays, balances, and budget receipts, by govtl branch and agency, FY83, annual rpt, 8104–2
- Currency (foreign) holdings of US, detailed transactions and balances by program and country, 1st half FY84, semiannual rpt, 8102–7
- Foreign Service positions and union membership by agency, grievances, and pay rates, FY81-83 with ambassador appointments from 1961, GAO rpt, 26123–64
- Intl exchange and training programs of Fed Govt, participants by world region, and funding, by agency, FY83, annual rpt, 9854–8
- Overseas assistance programs, by country, FY46-82, annual rpt, 9914–5
- TTPI Peace Corps volunteers and projects, as of Sept 1983, annual rpt, 7004–6

Peacekeeping forces

see International military forces

Peanuts

see Nuts

see Oils, oilseeds, and fats

Index by Subjects and Names

Pearce, Douglas K.

"Recent Developments in the Credit Union Industry", 9381–1.410

"Stock Prices and Economic News", 9381–10.37

Pearl, Robert B.

"Estimates of Tip Income in Eating Places, 1982", 8302–2.406

Peas

see Vegetables and vegetable products

Peat

see Fertilizers

see Nonmetallic minerals and mines

Peat, Marwick, Mitchell & Co.

"Analysis of Commuter Rail Costs and Cost Allocation Methods", 7888–61

Peck, Raymond C.

"Traffic Safety Impact of Two Experimental Motorcycle Licensing Programs", 7762–9.402

Pedestrians

Census of Housing, 1980: structural, financial, and householder characteristics, by region and State, 2475–4

Census of Population and Housing, 1980: detailed population and housing characteristics, by county, city, and census tract, State and SMSA rpt series, 2551–2

Census of Population, 1980: detailed socioeconomic characteristics, by county, city, and inside-outside SMSAs and central cities, State rpt series, 2531–3

Commuting to work, householder principal mode of transport, distance, and travel time, by race, Hispanic origin, tenure, urban-rural location, and region, 1981, annual survey, 2485–7

Deaths and death rates from traffic accidents, by victim and demographic characteristics, 1979, US Vital Statistics annual rpt, 4144–2.1, 4144–2.5

Deaths in transportation accidents, by mode, 1982-83, annual summary rpt, 9614–6

Hwy safety, accident, and traffic data from Natl Statistics and Analysis Center, series, 7766–10

Safety programs, and accidents, injuries, deaths, hazards, and property damage, by mode of transport, 1983, annual rpt, 7304–19

Traffic accidents and deaths by characteristics of persons and vehicles involved and State, and Natl Hwy Traffic Safety Admin activities, 1961-81, annual rpt, 7764–1

Traffic accidents and occupant and non-occupant deaths, 1972-82, annual rpt, 7304–2

Traffic accidents, circumstances, injuries, deaths, and characteristics of persons and vehicles involved, 1982, annual rpt, 7764–13

Traffic deaths, accident circumstances, and characteristics of persons and vehicles involved, series, 7766–13

Traffic fatal accidents, alcohol levels of drivers and pedestrians by driver age and sex and time of accident, 1980, 7768–81

Traffic fatal accidents, circumstances, and characteristics of persons and vehicles involved, 1983, annual rpt, 7764–14

Traffic fatal accidents detailed circumstances, and characteristics of persons and vehicles involved, 1982, annual rpt, 7764–10

Women's travel patterns, by employment and sociodemographic characteristics and type of child care used, 1980 survey, 7888–62

Pediatrics

Black medical residents by specialty, and minority medical faculty by race and Hispanic origin, selected years 1980-83, article, 4102–1.412

Canada and US hospital use by children by Canada Province and US region, and death rates, by diagnosis and sex, selected years 1977-79, 4147–5.1

DOD medical personnel, trainees, and accessions by source, by occupation, specialty, and service branch, FY83, annual rpt, 3544–24

Drugs (analgesic) provided during visits to office-based physicians, by patient characteristics, drug brand and type, and physician specialty, 1980-81, 4146–8.99

Health condition and health care resources, use, and expenditures, 1970s-82 with trends and projections 1900-2000, annual compilation, 4144–11

Infections (hospital-related), drug resistance, and associated deaths, for teaching and non-teaching hospitals, 1980-82, article, 4202–7.401

Manpower supply and education of health professionals, by occupation, demographic and professional characteristics, and location, 1950s-83 and projected to 2000, biennial rpt, 4114–8

Mental health facilities, services, staff, and patient characteristics, 1970s-82 with trends from 1954, annual rpt, 4504–9

Physician visits for new pain symptoms, by diagnosis, physician specialty, and patient characteristics, and drugs prescribed or used, 1980-81, 4146–8.97

Physicians (not office-based) visits by reason, diagnosis, treatment, patient and physician characteristics, and physician primary activity, 1980, 4147–13.77

Science and engineering grad enrollment, fields of study, financial support, and other student and instn characteristics, 1975-82, annual survey, 9627–7

VA physicians, dentists, and nurses, by age, selected employment characteristics, and VA district, quarterly rpt, 9922–11

Youth office visits to physicians by patient and visit characteristics and physician specialty, and drug mentions by brand, 1980-81, 4146–8.100

Pell Grants

see Student aid

Penalties

see Judgments, civil procedure

see Sentences, criminal procedure

Pendleton, Oreg.

Wages of office and plant workers, by occupation, 1984 labor market area survey rpt, 6785–3.9

Pennsylvania

Agriculture census, 1982: farms, farmland, production, finances, and operator characteristics, by county, final State rpt, 2331–1.38

Apple production, marketing, and prices in 4 Appalachian States, 1983/84 crop year, annual rpt, 1311–13

Bank deposits in commercial and mutual savings banks and in US branches of foreign banks, by account type, instn, State, SMSA, and county, June 1983, annual rpt, 9295–3.3

Bank, S&L, and savings bank deposit and commercial and industrial loan market shares, and loan activity, for Pennsylvania, 1980-83, article, 9387–1.404

Census of Housing, 1980: occupancy and unit characteristics of SMSAs and central cities, by race, Hispanic origin, and city, State rpt, 2473–1.40

Census of Population and Housing, 1980: detailed population and housing characteristics, by county, city, and census tract, State rpt, 2551–2.40

Census of Population, 1980: detailed socioeconomic and demographic characteristics, by age, sex, race, Hispanic origin, and industry, State rpt, 2531–4.40

Coal (anthracite) production and mines by county, prices, productivity, miners, reserves, and stocks, by mining method, 1982-83, annual rpt, 3164–25

Coal (bituminous) mining production and related workers, wages by occupation, and benefits, by size of mine and union status, in 6 States and aggregate for Rocky Mountain States, July 1982 survey, 6787–6.198

Coal (Pennsylvania anthracite) production, consumption, and stocks, weekly rpt, 3162–1

Coal employment and economic losses from utility fuel switching to meet emissions standards, with detail for counties in 5 States, 1970s-83 and projected to 1990, 21368–52

County Business Patterns: establishments, employees, and payrolls, by SIC 4-digit industry and county, 1982, annual State rpt, 2326–6.40

Employment, earnings, and hours, by selected SIC 1- to 4-digit industry, State, and for 278 major labor areas, 1939-83, annual rpt, 6744–5.2, 6744–5.3

Environmental quality, pollutant discharge by type and source, and EPA protection activities and funding, 1970s-83, biennial regional rpt, 9184–15.3

Exports of manufactured and agricultural commodities, manufacturing production, and export-related employment, 1960s-82, State rpt, 2046–3.38

Farms with sales under $2,500, acreage, finances, operations, and operator characteristics, by region and for 6 States, 1978, 1548–241

Health professionals license sanctions in 3 States, and subsequent Medicare and Medicaid program participation, by specialty, 1977-82, GAO rpt, 26121–80

HHS aid to each State and local govt or private instn, amount obligated, funding agency, and program, FY83, annual listing, 4004–3.3

Income (personal) per capita and by source, and earnings by industry div, by State, MSA, and county, 1977-82, annual regional rpt, 2704–2.3

Manufacturing census, 1982: financial and operating data, by SIC 2- to 4-digit industry, State, SMSA, and county, preliminary census div rpt, 2491–3.2

Mineral Industry Surveys, State review of production, 1983, advance annual rpt, 5614–6.38

Pennsylvania

Minerals Yearbook, 1982, Vol 2 preprints: State review of production and sales by commodity, and business activity, annual rpt, 5604–16.39

Minerals Yearbook, 1982, Vol 2: State reviews of production, sales, and firms, by commodity, and business activity, annual rpt, 5604–34

Northeast Pennsylvania wages of office and plant workers, by occupation, 1984 SMSA survey rpt, 6785–11.8

Oil and gas extraction production workers, wages, hours, and benefits, by occupation, region, and for 5 States, June 1982 survey, 6787–6.203

Population, births, deaths, and net migration, by MSA and county, 1980-82, annual State Current Population Rpt, 2546–4.38

Population size, Apr 1980 and July 1982, and per capita income, 1979 and 1981, by county and city, State Current Population Rpt, 2546–11.38

Retail trade census, 1982: employment, establishments, sales, and payroll, by SIC 2- to 4-digit kind of business, SMSA, county, and city, State rpt, 2397–1.39

Steel industry financial and operating data, steel imports by source, and employment situation at Fairless Hills, Pa, plant, 1970s-90, hearing, 25528–94

Uranium ore tailings at inactive mills and DOE remedial action program activities by site, and program funding, FY84, annual rpt, 3354–9

Water supply and quality, and effect of coal mining operations, for selected river basins in Eastern and Interior coal provinces, 1983 rpt, 5666–15.24, 5666–15.25

Water supply and quality in streams and lakes, and groundwater levels in wells, by drainage basin, 1982, annual State rpt, 5666–20.37

Water supply and quality in streams and lakes, and groundwater levels in wells, by drainage basin, 1983, annual State rpt, 5666–10.37

Wholesale trade census, 1982: employment, establishments, finances, and operations, by SIC 2- to 4-digit kind of business, SMSA, county, and city, State rpt, 2405–1.39

see also Allegheny County, Pa.
see also Allentown, Pa.
see also Altoona, Pa.
see also Bethlehem, Pa.
see also Easton, Pa.
see also Erie, Pa.
see also Harrisburg, Pa.
see also Hazelton, Pa.
see also Johnstown, Pa.
see also Lancaster, Pa.
see also Lebanon, Pa.
see also Philadelphia, Pa.
see also Pittsburgh, Pa.
see also Reading, Pa.
see also Scranton, Pa.
see also Sharon, Pa.
see also State College, Pa.
see also Wilkes-Barre, Pa.
see also Williamsport, Pa.
see also York, Pa.
see also under By State in the "Index by Categories"

Pennsylvania Avenue Development Corp.

Budget of US Appendix, detailed budgets and personnel summaries, by agency, FY85, annual rpt, 104–3

Budget of US, appropriations, outlays, balances, and budget receipts, by govtl branch and agency, FY83, annual rpt, 8104–2

Pensacola, Fla.

Census of Housing, 1980: occupancy and unit characteristics, by race, Hispanic origin, and city, SMSA rpt, 2473–1.280

Census of Population and Housing, 1980: detailed population and housing characteristics, by county, city, and census tract, SMSA rpt, 2551–2.280

Wages by occupation, and benefits for office and plant workers, 1984 labor market area survey rpt, 6785–3.9

see also under By SMSA or MSA in the "Index by Categories"

Pension Benefit Guaranty Corp.

Cost control proposals for Fed Govt programs and mgmt, 3-year savings by function and agency, and financial and operating data, 1960s-81, 16908–1.14

Fed Govt programs under Ways and Means Committee jurisdiction, program operations and financing data for assessing budgetary requirements, by State, FY70s-83, 21788–117

Pensions

Beneficiaries of noncash public and employer-based transfer programs, by income source and socioeconomic characteristics, 1982, advance Current Population Rpt, 2546–6.38

Beneficiaries of noncash public and employer-based transfer programs, by income source and socioeconomic characteristics, 1982, final Current Population Rpt, 2546–6.37

Benefits and after-tax salary replacement rates by pension type, and older persons income and income sources, by age and marital status, 1950s-82, conf proceedings, 25408–87

Budget of US, effects of Reagan Admin policy changes, by detailed program, FY85, annual rpt, 104–21

Cost of living postretirement adjustment of pension plans related to employee and employer characteristics, and effect of inflation on benefit purchasing power, 1973-79, 6468–18

Cost of living postretirement benefit increases of pension plans, for banks and manufacturers by size, 1978-83, hearing, 25368–132

Cost of living postretirement benefit increases of pension plans, participants and average increase by occupational group and plan characteristics, 1978-81, article, 6722–1.453

Employee Retirement Income Security Act admin and enforcement, 1982, annual rpt, 6464–4

Fed Govt consolidated financial statements based on business accounting methods, FY82-83, annual rpt, 8104–5

Fed Govt pension and health spending for older persons, by program and as percents of budget and GNP, 1965-85 with projections to 2040, 25148–28

Index by Subjects and Names

Florida and California elderly migration by selected State of origin or destination, and Florida elderly, by sociodemographic and housing characteristics, 1970 and 1980, 4478–150

Flow-of-funds accounts, assets and liabilities by type and economic sector, year-end outstandings, 1960-83, annual rpt, 9364–3

Flow-of-funds accounts savings, investments, and credit statements, quarterly rpt, 9365–3.3

Food stamp recipient households size and composition, income, and income deductions allowed, Aug 1981, annual rpt, 1364–8

Govt finances, by level of govt, State, and for large cities and counties, 1981-83, annual rpt series, 2466–2

Income (household) and cash and noncash transfer program participation, by sociodemographic characteristics, quarterly rpt, 2542–2

Income (legal) not reported on Federal income tax returns by source, and legal and illegal underground income, with bibl, 1974-81, article, 2702–1.419

Income (personal), and BEA and IRS calculations of adjusted gross income, by source, 1981-82, article, 2702–1.414

Income (personal) by source including transfer payments, and social insurance contributions by type, by region, 1929 and 1982, 2708–40

Income (taxable) not reported on individual and corporate returns, and associated Federal revenue losses, by detailed legal and illegal source, 1973-81, 8308–26

Income and income sources of older persons, by OASDI beneficiary and poverty status, labor force participation, and demographic characteristics, 1982, biennial rpt, 4744–26

Income averages of OASI beneficiaries, and beneficiaries by income level, by beneficiary characteristics and income source, before and after receipt of 1st benefit, 1969-77, article, 4742–1.418

Income of households, families, and persons, by detailed socioeconomic characteristics and region, 1982, annual Current Population Rpt, 2546–6.39

Income of retired persons by type, and preretirement income replacement, under alternative inflation rates, various periods 1979-84, article, 9373–1.419

Income tax returns filed by type of filer, selected income items, summary data, quarterly rpt, 8302–2.1

Income tax returns of elderly, by income statement and tax item and income level, 1981 with trends from 1977, article, 8302–2.412

Income tax returns of individuals by tax return item, State, and occupation, and income by source and tax owed, by income level, selected years 1916-80, conf papers, 8308–28.1

Income tax returns of individuals, detailed data, 1982, annual rpt, 8304–2

Income tax returns of partnerships, receipts by source, deductions by type, and establishments, by selected industry, 1982, annual article, 8302–2.416

Index by Subjects and Names

Periodicals

Income tax returns of sole proprietorships, detailed data by industry div and selected industry group, 1981, annual rpt, 8304–7

Income tax returns of sole proprietorships, receipts, deductions by type, payroll, and net income, by major industry, 1982, annual article, 8302–2.413

Life expectancy increase impacts on OASDI and pension policy, with alternative sociodemographic projections to 2100, hearing, 25368–130

Mortgage and mortgage-related investment of financial instns, by instn type and Fed Govt issuing agency, various dates 1981-84, 5008–33

Mortgage-backed securities of Fed Govt, investment by pension plans, yields by issuer, and fund assets by fund type, 1970s-82, conf papers, 5008–32

Mortgage loan activity, by type of lender, loan, and mortgaged property, monthly rpt, 5142–18

Mortgage loan originations, purchases, and acquisitions, for 11 lender types, selected years 1960-82, article, 9312–1.407

Mortgage transactions and holdings, by lender group and type of property and loan, quarterly rpt, 5142–30

Mortgages and mortgage-backed securities of FHLB and 3 Fed Govt mortgage assns, investments by corporate and union pension funds, quarterly rpt, 5002–10

Older persons by demographic, socioeconomic, and health characteristics, selected years 1900-81 and projected to 2050, Current Population Rpt, 2546–2.125

Older persons sociodemographic characteristics, and Fed Govt program participation and funding, 1983 with trends and projections 1900-2060, annual rpt, 25144–3.1

Oregon and Montana earnings by SIC 1- to 3-digit industry and payments to retirees by type, for 4 timber dependent communities, 1970, 1208–196

Poverty-level persons and families, by income source, hours of work, earnings, taxes, and family characteristics, various periods 1959-84, 21788–131

Poverty status of families and persons, by detailed socioeconomic characteristics, 1982, annual Current Population Rpt, 2546–6.40

Private and public pension funds, assets, 1971-82, annual rpt, 9364–5.12

Private and public pension plans funding, assets, benefits, and participants, and State and local plans disclosing finances, selected years 1974-82, hearing, 21788–142

Private industry employee benefits, coverage by benefit type and provisions and occupational group, 1983, annual rpt, 6784–19

Private industry pension and other benefits, pension plans created and terminated since 1939, and NYC retirement systems assets, 1978-83, conf proceedings, 25408–89

Private pension multiemployer plans in construction, trucking, and entertainment industries, and effect of exemption from withdrawal liability, 1977-81, GAO rpt, 26121–73

Private pension multiemployer plans lacking complete participant data for actuarial valuations, 1982-83 survey, GAO rpt, 26121–83

Private pension plan benefits for surviving spouses of workers, by benefit type and collective bargaining status, 1981, article, 6722–1.426

Private pension plans integrated with OASI benefits, and salary replacement rates, by formula type, salary level, and firm collective bargaining status, 1981, article, 6722–1.431

Private plan fund terminations and value of reversion to sponsor, for 12 largest terminations, 1980-83, article, 9385–1.406

Railroad employee benefits and beneficiaries by type, and railroad employees and payrolls, FY82, annual rpt, 9704–2

Railroad employee benefits and beneficiaries by type, benefit program finances, and railroad employees and payroll, FY83, annual rpt, 9704–1

Railroad employee retirement, survivors, unemployment, and sickness insurance programs, monthly rpt, 9702–2

Southeastern States public pension payments and disposable income, and family income by age of household head, by State, selected years 1959-80, article, 9371–1.420

Statistical Abstract of US, social, political, and economic data, 1950s-83 and trends, annual rpt, 2324–1.3

Tax (excise) collections of IRS, by source, quarterly press release, 8302–1

Tax expenditures, Fed Govt revenues foregone through pension and other tax benefit policy changes, FY84-88, and women's labor force and pension participation, 1939-82, hearing, 25368–131

Tax expenditures from employee benefit plans, for income and payroll tax by benefit type and income, with benefits by industry, 1950-83 and projected to 1988, article, 9373–1.404

Telephone and telegraph company benefit and pension cases and amounts paid, for 61 firms, 1982, annual rpt, 9284–6.4

Veterans aged 55 and over, socioeconomic characteristics, economic resources, health care and status, and actual and expected use of VA benefits, 1983 survey, 9928–29

see also Area wage surveys

see also Civil service pensions

see also Employee benefit plans

see also Military pensions

see also Old-Age, Survivors, Disability, and Health Insurance

see also Pension Benefit Guaranty Corp.

see also Social security

see also Veterans benefits and pensions

People's Democratic Republic of Yemen

see Yemen, South

People's Republic of China

see China, Peoples Republic

Peoria, Ill.

Census of Housing, 1980: occupancy and unit characteristics, by race, Hispanic origin, and city, SMSA rpt, 2473–1.281

Census of Population and Housing, 1980: detailed population and housing characteristics, by county, city, and census tract, SMSA rpt, 2551–2.281

see also under By City and By SMSA or MSA in the "Index by Categories"

Per capita income

see Personal and family income

Performing arts

Census of Population, 1980: detailed socioeconomic and demographic characteristics, by age, sex, race, Hispanic origin, occupation, and industry, State rpt series, 2531–4

Census of Population, 1980: detailed socioeconomic characteristics, by county, city, and inside-outside SMSAs and central cities, State rpt series, 2531–3

Census of Population, 1980: labor force, by sex, detailed occupation, and region, with comparison to 1970 census, supplementary rpt, 2535–1.12

County Business Patterns: establishments, employees, and payrolls, by SIC 4-digit industry and county, 1981, annual State rpt series, 2326–8

County Business Patterns: establishments, employees, and payrolls, by SIC 4-digit industry and county, 1982, annual State rpt series, 2326–6

Income tax returns of sole proprietorships, detailed data by industry div and selected industry group, 1981, annual rpt, 8304–7

Kennedy Performing Arts Center income and expenses by type, and Fed Govt share of expenses, FY79-83, GAO rpt, 26119–60

Natl Endowment for Arts activities and grants, FY83, annual rpt, 9564–3

Occupational manpower needs and supply by detailed occupation, and educational and training program enrollees and grads by detailed field, 1982 and 1995, biennial rpt, 6744–3

Occupational Outlook Handbook, 1984-85 biennial rpt, 6744–1

Pension multiemployer plans in construction, trucking, and entertainment industries, and effect of exemption from withdrawal liability, 1977-81, GAO rpt, 26121–73

Service industry census, 1982: employment, establishments, receipts, and payroll, by SIC 2- to 4-digit kind of business, SMSA, county, and city, State rpt series, 2391–1

Statistical Abstract of US, social, political, and economic data, 1950s-83 and trends, annual rpt, 2324–1.1

see also Arts and the humanities

see also Dance

see also Motion pictures

see also Theater

Periodicals

Army morale, welfare, and recreation programs, revenue and expenses worldwide by activity and major command, FY82-83, annual rpt, 3704–12

County Business Patterns: establishments, employees, and payrolls, by SIC 4-digit industry and county, 1981, annual State rpt series, 2326–8

County Business Patterns: establishments, employees, and payrolls, by SIC 4-digit industry and county, 1982, annual State rpt series, 2326–6

Employment, earnings, and hours, by selected SIC 1- to 4-digit industry, State, and for 278 major labor areas, 1939-83, annual rpt, 6744–5

Periodicals

Employment, earnings, and hours, by SIC 4-digit nonfarm industry, monthly 1974-Feb 1984, annual update, 6744–4

- Exports and imports of US, detailed SIC-based commodities by world area, 1983, annual rpts, 2424–6
- Exports and imports of US, totals and as percent of domestic production, by SIC 2- to 5-digit commodity, 1981, annual rpt, 2424–3
- Exports, imports, tariffs, and industry operating data for books, magazines, newspapers, and other printed matter, foreign and US, 1978-82, TSUSA commodity rpt, 9885–2.28
- Exports of US, detailed commodities by country of destination, monthly rpt, 2422–3
- Exports of US, detailed Schedule B commodities by country of destination, 1983, annual rpt, 2424–9
- Exports of US, detailed Schedule E commodities by mode of transport and world area and country of destination, 1983, annual rpts, 2424–5
- Food industry advertising expenditures by media type, and advertising to sales ratio by selected food item, 1970-79 with some trends from 1955, 1548–234
- Imports of US, detailed Schedule A commodities by country, monthly rpt, 2422–2
- Imports of US, detailed TSUSA commodities by country of origin, 1983, annual rpt, 2424–4
- Income tax returns of corporations, detailed income and tax items by industry, 1981, annual rpt, 8304–4
- Input-output structure of US economy, detailed interindustry transactions for 537 industries, and components of final demand, 1977 benchmark data, 2708–17
- Libraries of colleges and universities, expenditures, holdings by type, use, staff by sex, and Federal grants received, 1979-82, biennial rpt, 4854–1
- Manufacturing census, 1982: financial and operating data, by SIC 2- to 4-digit industry, State, SMSA, and county, preliminary census div rpt series, 2491–3
- Manufacturing census, 1982: financial and operating data, for SIC 4-digit industries by product, preliminary rpt, 2491–1.159
- Medicine Natl Library activities, collections, and grants, FY81-83, annual rpt, 4464–1
- Occupational injury and illness rates, by SIC 2- to 4-digit industry, 1982, annual rpt, 6844–1
- Producer prices and indexes, by stage of processing and detailed commodity, monthly rpt, 6762–6
- Producer prices and indexes, by stage of processing and detailed commodity, monthly 1983, annual supplement, 6764–2
- Retail trade census, 1982: employment, establishments, sales, and payroll, for direct selling establishments, by State, preliminary rpt, 2395–1.35
- Senate salaries, expenses, and contingent fund disbursements, by payee, detailed listings, 1st half FY84, semiannual rpt, 25922–1
- USIA info center and reading room operations, by world region, country, and city, FY83, annual rpt, 9854–4

see also Newspapers

Perlite

see Nonmetallic minerals and mines

Permits

see Building permits

see Licenses and permits

see Severance taxes

Perry, Harry

"Evaluation of Selected Provisions of the Federal Coal Leasing Amendments Act of 1976", 25318–58.1

Perry, Samuel W.

"Psychiatric Problems of AIDS Inpatients at the New York Hospital: Preliminary Report", 4102–1.426

Personal and family income

- AFDC eligibility under Omnibus Budget Reconciliation Act, effect on caseloads and recipient benefits and living costs, 1981-83, GAO rpt, 26131–11
- Agricultural production, marketing, trade, supply, food consumption, and food and nutrition programs, 1960s-83, annual chartbook, 1504–3
- Alabama rural black population, education, employment, health services, and economic status, for 16 counties, selected years 1970-81, 11048–180
- Bankruptcy (personal), filers by debt type and other characteristics, selected years 1978-81, hearing, 25528–97.1
- Business activity indicators (nonfinancial), 1982, annual rpt, 9364–5.9
- Business and financial statistics, historic trends, 1984 annual chartbook, 9364–2.4
- Business and financial statistics, quarterly chartbook, 9362–2.2
- *Business Conditions Digest,* current data on economic, business, and financial conditions and cyclical fluctuations, monthly rpt, 2702–3
- *Business Conditions Digest,* historical supplement on economic, business, and financial conditions and cyclical fluctuations, with methodology, 1947-82, 2708–31
- Business statistics, detailed data for major industries and economic indicators, *Survey of Current Business,* monthly rpt, 2702–1
- California housing market, and Los Angeles average home price and mortgage rate, 1969-82 with economic indicators projected to 1989, 9306–1.1
- Census of Housing, 1980: inventory, occupancy, and unit characteristics, changes from 1973 by region and inside-outside SMSAs and central cities, series, 2473–3
- Census of Housing, 1980: occupancy and unit characteristics of SMSAs and central cities, by race, Hispanic origin, and city, State and SMSA rpt series, 2473–1
- Census of Housing, 1980: structural, financial, and householder characteristics, by region and State, 2475–4
- Census of Population and Housing, 1980: detailed population and housing characteristics, by county, city, and census tract, State and SMSA rpt series, 2551–2
- Census of Population, 1980: detailed socioeconomic and demographic characteristics, by age, sex, race, Hispanic origin, occupation, and industry, State rpt series, 2531–4

Index by Subjects and Names

- Census of Population, 1980: detailed socioeconomic characteristics, by county, city, and inside-outside SMSAs and central cities, State rpt series, 2531–3
- City and suburb population characteristics and local govt finances, by region and selected SMSA, 1950s-FY83, 10048–61
- Coal dev plans on Fed Govt lease lands in 12 regions under Fed Coal Mgmt Program, environmental and socioeconomic impacts to 2000, final statement series, 5726–4
- Coastal environmental and socioeconomic conditions, and potential impacts of oil and gas OCS leases, final statement series, 5736–1
- Coastal environmental characteristics, fish, wildlife, and use, and population socioeconomic data, for individual areas, series, 5506–4
- Coastal States per capita personal income, 15 States, 1982, annual rpt, 7704–12.2
- *Consumer Income,* socioeconomic characteristics of persons, families, and households, detailed cross-tabulations, Current Population Rpt series, 2546–6
- *County and City Data Book,* detailed socioeconomic and demographic data for States, counties, and cities, selected years 1976-82, 2328–1
- Developing countries govt policy, and AID and other foreign assistance, effects on private sector dev and socioeconomic conditions, with case studies for 6 countries, 1960s-80, 9918–12
- Developing countries PL 480 Title I funding and socioeconomic impacts, with case studies for 5 countries, 1950s- 81, 9918–13
- Economic and demographic trends for IRS regions, districts, and service centers, 1972-82 and projected to 1990, annual rpt, 8304–8
- Economic and financial trends, natl compounded annual rates of change, 1964-83, annual rpt, 9391–9.2
- Economic and population time series data frequently used in statistical demand analyses, 1941-1982, annual rpt, 1544–21
- Economic growth rates and component economic indicators, selected years 1922-83 and projected under full employment to 1988, hearing, 21348–90
- Economic indicator forecasts, and model estimates of industrial electric power demand, 1960s-80 with projections to 2000, 3008–87
- Economic indicators and components, and Fed Reserve 4th District business and financial conditions, monthly chartbook, 9377–10
- Economic indicators, nonfinancial, monthly rpt, 9362–1.2
- Electric power demand of households in 136 SMSAs and other utility service areas, with fuel prices, family income, and heating degree days, 1975 and projected to 1985, 1588–78
- Employment status of family members, by occupation, family composition, age of children, and other characteristics, 1983 and trends from 1940, 6746–1.253
- Energy conservation programs of utilities under natl conservation act, cost effectiveness and participating household characteristics, 1980s, 3308–69

Index by Subjects and Names

Energy production, reserves, and prices, by energy type, and selected indicators of energy use, by State, 1982-83 with selected comparisons from 1971, annual rpt, 3164–60

Farm finances, assets, liabilities, income, receipts by commodity and State, and expenses, 1980-83 and trends from 1910, annual rpt, 1544–16

Farm income, and income of farm people, 1929-83, annual rpt, 204–1.8

Fed Govt civilian and military employee pay, withholdings by type, and income, special military compensation by type and service branch, 1982-83, GAO rpt, 26123–65

Florida and California elderly migration by selected State of origin or destination, and Florida elderly, by sociodemographic and housing characteristics, 1970 and 1980, 4478–150

Food expenditures for fruit, vegetable, and potato products related to changes in income and other household characteristics, 1977-78, 1548–236

Food stamp recipient households size and composition, income, and income deductions allowed, Aug 1981, annual rpt, 1364–8

Forecasts for selected business activities and natl economic indicators, compilation of representative opinions, 1984, annual rpt, 9389–3

Foreign economic indicators for 7 OECD countries and US, quarterly rpt, 2042–10

High school classes of 1980 and 1982: educational and sociodemographic characteristics and expectations, natl longitudinal study, series, 4826–2

Hispanic Americans socioeconomic and demographic characteristics, and compared to non-Hispanics, selected years 1970-83, chartbook, 2328–48

Home equity mortgaged under 4 hypothetical instruments, effects on current income of elderly Baltimore, Md, residents, 1976, article, 9312–7.402

Home mortgages (graduated payment) FHA-insured, financial, property, and mortgagor characteristics, for US and selected localities, quarterly rpt, 5142–42

Home mortgages (graduated payment) FHA-insured, financial, property, and mortgagor characteristics, for US and selected States, quarterly rpt, 5142–41

Home mortgages (graduated payment) FHA-insured, financial, property, and mortgagor characteristics, US summary, quarterly rpt, 5142–40

Home mortgages FHA-insured, financial, property, and mortgagor characteristics, for US and selected localities, quarterly rpt, 5142–2

Home mortgages FHA-insured, financial, property, and mortgagor characteristics, for US, selected States, and Puerto Rico, quarterly rpt, 5142–3

Home mortgages FHA-insured, financial, property, and mortgagor characteristics, quarterly rpt, 5142–1

Home mortgages FHA-insured for low-cost homes, financial, construction, property, and mortgagor characteristics, quarterly rpt, 5142–4

Homeless population and characteristics, and temporary shelter operations, use, and user characteristics, for selected cities, various periods 1979-84, hearing, 21248–85

Household income and cash and noncash transfer program participation, by sociodemographic characteristics, quarterly rpt, 2542–2

Household income, assets, and debt characteristics, sources of credit, and use of financial services, 1983 survey, article, 9362–1.411

Household income before and after taxes, by socioeconomic characteristics, type of tax paid, and region, 1981, Current Population Rpt, 2546–2.118

Household income before and after taxes, by socioeconomic characteristics, type of tax paid, and region, 1982, annual Current Population Rpt, 2546–2.122

Household income by family type and race, and households receiving noncash benefits by poverty status, 1982 annual Current Population Rpt, 2546–2.119

Household income, home value and equity, and financial assets by type, by household characteristics, 1983 survey with trends from 1970, article, 9362–1.406

Household median income, by household type, race and Hispanic origin, farm-nonfarm residence, region, and number of earners, and change in real income, 1981-82, article, 1702–1.404

Households and housing detailed characteristics, and unit and neighborhood quality, by inside-outside central cities, 1979-82 surveys, SMSA rpt series, 2485–6

Households and housing unit characteristics, and employment, housing finance, and social programs data, selected years 1948-83, hearing, 21968–28

Households and housing unit characteristics, by region and metro-nonmetro residence, 1983, biennial survey, 2485–1

Housing and financial characteristics, and unit and neighborhood quality, for 15 SMSAs, 1978, annual survey special supplement, 2485–8

Housing and neighborhood quality indicators and attitudes, and occupant characteristics, by urban-rural location and region, 1981, annual survey, 2485–7

Housing and neighborhood quality indicators and attitudes, by occupant and unit characteristics, region, and metro-nonmetro location, 1981, annual survey, 2485–2.2

Illegal taxable income not reported, by source, with characteristics of persons involved, methodology, and bibl, 1970s-82, 8008–112

Income (personal) and total and per capita disposable income, 1929-83, annual rpt, 204–1.1

Income of families by selected characteristics, 1980-81, annual rpt, 6724–1.7

Income tax and social security tax burden of households and effect of indexing by income level, 1982, and Fed Govt revenues by source, FY60-89, press release, 8008–109

Personal and family income

Income tax returns filed by type of filer, selected income items, summary data, quarterly rpt, 8302–2.1

Income tax returns of individuals, detailed data, 1982, annual rpt, 8304–2

Income tax returns of individuals, income, and tax, 1913-82, article, 8302–2.401

Income tax returns of individuals, selected income, deduction, and tax credit data by income, preliminary 1982, annual article, 8302–2.402

Income taxes on corporate and personal capital related to capital formation and intl flows, 1984 technical paper, 8006–3.51

IRS and other Fed Govt admin record research methods, data collection and use, 1984 compilation of papers, 8308–28

Jamaica PL 480 Title I assistance effects on economic dev, with data on govt finance, economic indicators, demography, and dev programs, 1970s-81, 9916–1.51

Natl income and product, comprehensive accounts and components, *Survey of Current Business,* monthly rpt, 2702–1.21

New Communities program of HUD, activities, costs, land sales, and community and population characteristics, for 13 communities, 1970s-83, 5188–107

New England States economic indicators, Fed Reserve 1st District, monthly rpt, 9373–2.4

New England States, FHLB 1st District member instns financial operations and housing industry indicators, monthly rpt, 9302–4

OASI beneficiaries by income level, and average income, by beneficiary characteristics and income source, before and after receipt of 1st benefit, 1969-77, article, 4742–1.418

Older persons by demographic, socioeconomic, and health characteristics, selected years 1900-81 and projected to 2050, Current Population Rpt, 2546–2.125

Older persons income and income sources, by OASDI beneficiary and poverty status, labor force participation, and demographic characteristics, 1982, biennial rpt, 4744–26

Older persons income and income sources, including retirement benefits by plan type, by age and marital status, 1950s-82, conf proceedings, 25408–87

Older persons income and percent in poverty, by household composition and sex, with comparisons to nonaged, selected years 1950-82, article, 4742–1.413

Older persons population characteristics, and needs and costs of social services by type, by metro-nonmetro status, 1970s-82 with trends from 1900, 21148–28

Older persons retirement income by type, and preretirement income replacement, under alternative inflation rates, various periods 1979-84, article, 9373–1.419

Older persons sociodemographic characteristics, and Fed Govt program participation and funding, 1983 with trends and projections 1900-2060, annual rpt, 25144–3.1

Personal and family income

Oregon and Montana earnings by SIC 1- to 3-digit industry and payments to retirees by type, for 4 timber dependent communities, 1970, 1208–196

Overseas Business Reports: economic conditions, investment and export opportunities, and trade practices, annual country market research rpt series, 2046–6

Overseas Business Reports: economic conditions, investment and export opportunities, and trade practices, world region rpt series, 2046–5

Pacific Basin economic indicators, US and 12 countries, quarterly rpt, 9393–9

Pacific Northwest electricity consumption and prices by end-use sector, and economic and demographic data, 1960s-83 and projected to 2005, annual rpt, 3224–2

Pension plans with postretirement adjustments related to employee and employer characteristics, and effect of inflation on benefit purchasing power, 1973-79, 6468–18

Per capita income, 1979 and 1981, and population size, Apr 1980 and July 1982, by county and city, State Current Population Rpt series, 2546–11

Personal and per capita income, 1982, and population, July 1983, by State, annual rpt, 2466–2.3

Personal, family, and household income, by detailed socioeconomic characteristics and region, 1982, annual Current Population Rpt, 2546–6.39

Personal income and BEA and IRS calculations of adjusted gross income, by source, 1981-82, article, 2702–1.414

Personal income by industry group and region, percent change 1959-79 and 1979-83, article, 2702–1.443

Personal income, by source, monthly rpt, 23842–1.1

Personal income, natl compounded annual rates of change, monthly rpt, 9391–3

Personal income per capita and by source, and earnings by industry div, by State, MSA, and county, 1977-82, annual regional rpts, 2704–2

Personal income per capita and by source, earnings by major industry group, and social insurance contributions, by region and State, 1929-82, 2708–40

Personal income, per capita and relation to govt revenues and spending by level of govt, by State, selected years 1929-83, annual rpt, 10044–1

Personal income, total and per capita, and earnings by major industry group, by region and State, 1981-83, annual article, 2702–1.432

Personal income totals, by region, census div, and State, quarterly article, 2702–1.32

Personal total and per capita income, by MSA, State, and county, with metro-nonmetro totals, 1980-82, annual article, 2702–1.413

Personal total and taxable income, and Federal income tax liabilities and payments, quarterly 1980-82, annual article, 2702–1.415

Poverty income guidelines of Fed Govt for determining public assistance eligibility, by family size, 1965-84, article, 4742–1.415

Poverty-level persons and families, by income source, hours of work, earnings, taxes, and family characteristics, various periods 1959-84, 21788–131

Poverty population size, effect of counting public noncash transfers as income by recipient characteristics, 1979-83, 2626–2.52

Poverty population size, effects of counting public noncash transfers as income by recipient characteristics, 1979-82, 2626–2.50

Poverty rate by family composition, and effect of noncash transfers, taxes, unemployment benefits, and business cycles, selected years 1959-82, hearings, 21788–141

Poverty status of families and persons, by detailed socioeconomic characteristics, 1982, annual Current Population Rpt, 2546–6.40

Poverty status of young adults related to motivation, psychological factors, and family characteristics, by race and sex, 1970s-82, longitudinal studies, 4008–65

Puerto Rico educational enrollment, finance, completions, curricula, and personnel by instn, and health and vital statistics, selected years 1970-83, hearings, 21348–93

Revenue sharing payments to States, local govts, Indian tribes, and Alaska Native villages, and entitlement computation data, FY84, series, 8066–1

Small business and total employment, income, and number of firms, by State, industry, and size class, selected years 1967-83, annual rpt, 9764–6.1

Social pathology measures including crime and death rates, relation to selected economic indicators, various periods 1950-80, 23848–76

Social security payments as percent of personal income, 1950-82, annual rpt, 4744–3.1

Southeastern States and 5 SMSAs economic indicators, Fed Reserve 8th District, quarterly rpt, 9391–15

Southeastern States economic indicators, by State, Fed Reserve 5th District, quarterly rpt, 9389–16

Southeastern States financial and economic devs, Fed Reserve 6th District, monthly rpt with articles, 9371–1

Southeastern States personal income and employment growth rates, by State, various periods 1958-82 and forecast to 1984, article, 9389–1.403

Statistical Abstract of US, social, political, and economic data, 1950s-83 and trends, annual rpt, 2324–1.3

Student aid need-based program funding, and State Student Incentive Grant funding, recipients, and average income and award, by State, FY67-82, GAO rpt, 26121–69

Student aid Pell grants and recipients, by educational costs, family income, instnl type and control, and State, 1981/82, annual rpt, 4804–1

Supplemental Security Income payments, and recipients by other income source, eligibility type, and other characteristics, by State, 1982, annual rpt, 4744–16

Index by Subjects and Names

Supplementary Security Income beneficiary socioeconomic characteristics and health service use, 1970s-83 and SSI program projections to 1995, 25148–29

Texas farm household income, by income source and substate region, 1979, article, 9379–1.406

Transportation energy use by mode, fuel supplies, and demographic and economic determinants of vehicle use, 1970s-83, annual rpt, 3304–5.1

Underground legal and illegal income, and legal income not reported on Federal income tax returns by source, with bibl, 1974-81, article, 2702–1.419

Unemployment and part-time employment, by race, Hispanic origin, sex, family composition, income, and poverty status, 1980-82, annual report, 6744–15

Unemployment and part-time employment effects on family income, by socioeconomic and labor force characteristics, 1981-82, annual rpt, 6746–1.252

Unemployment effect on family income and poverty status, by demographic, employment, and unemployment characteristics, 1981-82, annual article, 6722–1.412

Urban area socioeconomic and fiscal trends and problems, 1950-83 and Fed Govt funding estimates for FY84-87, biennial rpt, 5124–4

Veterans aged 55 and over, socioeconomic characteristics, economic resources, health care and status, and actual and expected use of VA benefits, 1983 survey, 9928–29

Veterans income and educational attainment compared to nonveterans, by age, 1982-83, annual rpt, 9924–19

Veterans income and employment status, by age and war or peacetime service, with comparisons to nonveterans, 1981, annual rpt, 9924–23

Veterans of Vietnam era, educational attainment and personal and family income, 1980-83, annual rpt, 9924–8.3

Vocationally rehabilitated persons under State agency programs, by sociodemographic characteristics and disabling condition, FY79-81, annual rpt, 4944–6

Western States economic indicators, Fed Reserve 12th District, quarterly rpt, 9393–1.1

Western States housing outlook and economic and demographic trends, FHLB 11th District, urban area rpt series, 9306–2

Women in couples with wife as primary earner, socioeconomic and family characteristics, with comparative data for husbands, Mar 1982, 2326–11.9

Women's employment and earnings, by labor force and socioeconomic characteristics, and compared to men, 1978-81 and trends from 1940s, 6568–29

Women's labor force participation, earnings, and socioeconomic characteristics, 1983, annual fact sheet, 6564–1

see also Child support and alimony

see also under By Income in the "Index by Categories"

Index by Subjects and Names

Personal consumption

Auto industry finances and operations by manufacturer, foreign competition, and consumer auto expenditures and attitudes toward car buying, selected years 1968-85, annual rpt, 2004–8

Business and financial statistics, historic trends, 1984 annual chartbook, 9364–2.2

Business and financial statistics, quarterly chartbook, 9362–2.2

Business Conditions Digest, cyclical indicators, by economic process, monthly rpt, 2702–3.3

Business Conditions Digest, historical supplement on economic, business, and financial conditions and cyclical fluctuations, with methodology, 1947-82, 2708–31

Cigarettes and other tobacco products per capita consumption and total expenditures, 1978-83, annual rpt, 1319–1.4

Consumer expenditures and savings, 1960s-83, annual chartbook, 1504–3

Consumer goods prices and supplies, family finance, and home economics, quarterly rpt with articles, 1702–1

Economic and financial trends, natl compounded annual rates of change, 1964-83, annual rpt, 9391–9.2

Economic and population time series data frequently used in statistical demand analyses, 1941-1982, annual rpt, 1544–21

Economic conditions and employment, alternative BLS projections to 1995 with selected trends for 1959-82, 6728–29

Economic growth rates and component economic indicators, selected years 1922-83 and projected under full employment to 1988, hearing, 21348–90

Economic indicator forecasts, and model estimates of industrial electric power demand, 1960s-80 with projections to 2000, 3008–87

Economic indicators and components, and Fed Reserve 4th District business and financial conditions, monthly chartbook, 9377–10

Economic indicators and components, current data and annual trends, monthly rpt, 23842–1.1

Economic trends, natl compounded annual rates of change, monthly rpt, 9391–3.2

Expenditures for food, beverages, and tobacco as share of per capita income, for US and 54 countries, 1979, 1528–172

Expenditures for personal consumption, 1929-83, annual rpt, 204–1.1

Forecasts for selected business activities and natl economic indicators, compilation of representative opinions, 1984, annual rpt, 9389–3

Inflation measures of CPI and Personal Consumption Expenditures Index, effects of differences in weights and housing treatment, 1977-2nd quarter 1984 article, 6762–2.401

Input-output structure of US economy, detailed interindustry transactions for 85 industries, and components of final demand, 1977, article, 2702–1.421

Input-output structure of US economy, detailed interindustry transactions for 537 industries, and components of final demand, 1977 benchmark data, 2708–17

Natl income and product, comprehensive accounts and components, *Survey of Current Business,* monthly rpt, 2702–1.21

Natl income and product, comprehensive accounts and components, *Survey of Current Business,* monthly rpt, monthly and annual tables, 2702–1.23

Older persons by demographic, socioeconomic, and health characteristics, selected years 1900-81 and projected to 2050, Current Population Rpt, 2546–2.125

Pollution abatement expenditures of govt, business, and consumers, 1972-82, annual article, 2702–1.407

Retail trade per capita, by SIC 2- to 4-digit kind of business, 1983, annual rpt, 2413–5

Textile imports, total and as percents of US domestic production and use, by commodity, 1972- 82, annual rpt, 2044–14

Transportation expenditures by mode of transport, and compared to other personal consumption expenditures, 1972-82, annual rpt, 7304–2.2

Underground economy, household expenditures and participation by type of goods or service and sociodemographic characteristics, with methodology and bibl, 1981 survey, 8308–27

see also Cost of living

see also Food consumption

see also Housing energy use

Personal debt

Bankruptcy (personal), filers by debt type and other characteristics, and impacts in Connecticut and Michigan, various dates 1946-82, hearings, 21528–57

Bankruptcy (personal), filers by debt type and other characteristics, selected years 1978-81, hearing, 25528–97.1

Bankruptcy court cases and admin in districts with and without case trustees, and staff and potential costs of nationwide trustee program, various periods 1979-83, annual rpt, 6004–15

Economic indicators and components, and Fed Reserve 4th District business and financial conditions, monthly chartbook, 9377–10

Financial and business statistics, historic trends, 1984 annual chartbook, 9364–2.7, 9364–2.11

Financial and business statistics, quarterly chartbook, 9362–2.5

Flow-of-funds accounts, assets and liabilities by type and economic sector, year-end outstandings, 1960-83, annual rpt, 9364–3

Flow-of-funds accounts savings, investments, and credit statements, quarterly rpt, 9365–3.3

Income tax proposals to encourage savings, and personal assets and liabilities by type, 1981, article, 8302–2.407

Veterans aged 55 and over, socioeconomic characteristics, economic resources, health care and status, and actual and expected use of VA benefits, 1983 survey, 9928–29

see also Consumer credit

see also Loans

Peru

see also Mortgages

Personal income

see Personal and family income

Personal property

see Housing tenure

see Land ownership

see Ownership of enterprise

see Personal debt

see Property

see Savings

see Wealth

Personick, Martin E.

"White-Collar Pay Determination Under Range-of-Rate Systems", 6722–1.473

Personick, Valerie A.

"Job Outlook Through 1995: Industry Output and Employment Projections", 6728–29

Perth Amboy, N.J.

Census of Housing, 1980: occupancy and unit characteristics, by race, Hispanic origin, and city, SMSA rpt, 2473–1.256

Census of Population and Housing, 1980: detailed population and housing characteristics, by county, city, and census tract, SMSA rpt, 2551–2.256

Peru

Agricultural and food production indexes, and production of selected commodities, by world region and country, 1974-83, annual rpt, 1524–5

Agricultural exports of US to Latin America, by commodity, country group, and selected country, FY81-84 and forecast FY85, article, 1522–1.407

Agricultural situation in Latin America, by country, 1981-83 and outlook for 1984, annual rpt, 1524–4.9

Agricultural supply/demand, trade, and production, and socioeconomic data, by country, 1950s-77, 1528–179

AID activities and funding by project and function, FY85, and developing countries summary socioeconomic data, 1970s-83, by country, annual rpt, 9914–3

AID economic assistance to developing countries, obligations and disbursements by country, quarterly rpt, 9912–4

AID loan repayment status and terms by program and country, and status of predecessor agency loans, quarterly rpt, 9912–3

Cocaine use, user characteristics, medical and botanical research, and South American production and legal policy and enforcement, 1979 intl conf papers, 7008–40

Copper production, production costs, prices, wages, and productivity, for US and 3 countries, 1970s-83 and projected to 1989, 21368–55

Economic conditions, investment and export opportunities, and trade practices, 1983 country market research rpt, 2046–6.7

Economic, social, and political summary data, by country, 1984, annual factbook, 244–11

Economic trends in income, production, prices, employment, finances, and trade, 1984 semiannual rpt, 2046–4.15, 2046–4.92

Exports and imports of US, by commodity and country, 1972-82, annual world region rpt, 244–13.2

Peru

Exports of US, detailed Schedule B commodities by country of destination, 1983, annual rpt, 2424–9

Exports of US, detailed Schedule E commodities by mode of transport and world area and country of destination, 1983, annual rpts, 2424–5

Food supply policies of 21 developing countries, with farm sector data, tariff income, and prices and imports of 5 grains, 1960s-81, 1528–168

Imports of US, detailed Schedule A commodities by country and world area of origin, and mode of transport, 1983, annual rpts, 2424–2

Imports of US, detailed TSUSA commodities by country of origin, 1983, annual rpt, 2424–4

Loans and grants for economic and military assistance from US and intl agencies, by program and country, FY46-83, annual rpt, 9914–5

Military aid of US, arms sales, and training programs costs and budget requests by program, world region, and country, FY83-85, annual rpt, 7144–13

Military spending, arms trade, and armed forces size, with total govt spending and population, by country, 1972-82, annual rpt, 9824–1

Minerals Yearbook, 1982, Vol 3: foreign country reviews of production, trade, and policies, by commodity, annual rpt, 5604–35

Minerals Yearbook, 1982, Vol 3 preprints: foreign country review of production, trade, and policies, by commodity, annual rpt, 5604–17.57

PL 480 Title I funding and socioeconomic impacts in developing countries, with case studies for 5 countries, 1950s-81, 9918–13

Population size and growth rates, and latest available benchmark demographic data, by country, 1950-83, biennial rpt, 2324–4

Weather, effects of El Nino ocean warming off Peru and Ecuador, 1982-83, article, 2152–8.402

see also under By Foreign Country in the "Index by Categories"

Peru, Ind.

Wages of office and plant workers, by occupation, 1984 labor market area survey rpt, 6785–3.5

Pesticides

Agent Orange exposed Air Force personnel diseases and disorders, by disease type, age, and officer status, 1984 rpt, 3604–3

Agent Orange exposure and Vietnam military service effects on veteran health condition, methodology for 3 CDC studies, Nov 1983 rpt, 4208–22

Agricultural Statistics, 1983, annual rpt, 1004–1.2

Agriculture census, 1982: farms, farmland, production, finances, and operator characteristics, by county, final State rpt series, 2331–1

Air pollutant and radiation indoor levels by emissions source, and household exposure and health effects by pollutant type, various periods 1966-83, hearings, 21708–102

Biotechnology firms, patents, and trade by country, and effect of industry growth on US drug and chemical trade, selected years 1979-2000, 9886–4.78

Census of Population, 1980: detailed socioeconomic and demographic characteristics, by age, sex, race, Hispanic origin, occupation, and industry, State rpt series, 2531–4

China economic conditions, agricultural and industrial production, trade, and domestic and foreign investment, 1980-85, 2048–106

Cooperatives farm supply sales programs, services offered, inventory mgmt and marketing methods, and sales force and compensation system, for 4 products, 1982, 1128–24

Cooperatives, membership, activities, and finances, by commodity and selected State, 1900-80 with trends from 1863, 1128–30

County Business Patterns: establishments, employees, and payrolls, by SIC 4-digit industry and county, 1981, annual State rpt series, 2326–8

Eastern Europe agricultural production and trade by commodity, food consumption, and farm inputs, for 6 countries, 1960-80 with projections to 1991, 1528–178

Employment, earnings, and hours, by selected SIC 1- to 4-digit industry, State, and for 278 major labor areas, 1939-83, annual rpt, 6744–5

Employment, earnings, and hours, by SIC 4-digit nonfarm industry, monthly 1974-Feb 1984, annual update, 6744–4

Environmental quality and protection programs, costs, and Fed Govt enforcement, 1983, detailed annual rpt, 484–1

Environmental quality, pollutant discharge by type, and EPA protection activities, 1970s-83, biennial summary rpt, 9184–16

Environmental quality, pollutant discharge by type and source, and EPA protection activities and funding, 1970s-83, biennial regional rpt series, 9184–15

EPA pollution control research and grant assistance program activities, monthly rpt, 9182–8

Ethylene dibromide fumigation of tropical fruit imports, FY82, and cost of EDB and alternative fruit fly treatments for Florida grapefruit and Hawaii papaya, 1984 rpt, 21168–29

Ethylene dibromide residue in grain and grain foods, and effect of processing and cooking, by selected product, 1984 hearing, 25168–62

Exports and imports of US, by agricultural commodity and country, bimonthly rpt with articles, 1522–1

Exports and imports of US, detailed SIC-based commodities by world area, 1983, annual rpts, 2424–6

Exports of US, detailed commodities by country of destination, monthly rpt, 2422–3

Exports of US, detailed Schedule B commodities by country of destination, 1983, annual rpt, 2424–9

Exports of US, detailed Schedule E commodities by mode of transport and world area and country of destination, 1983, annual rpts, 2424–5

Farm finances, assets, liabilities, income, receipts by commodity and State, and expenses, 1980-83 and trends from 1910, annual rpt, 1544–16

Index by Subjects and Names

Farm finances, expenses by type, loans by purpose and source, and credit detail by Fed Reserve District, quarterly rpt, 9365–3.10

Farm finances, production, expenses by type, and domestic economic impact, selected years 1972-82 and preliminary 1983-84, annual rpt, 1544–19

Farm production expenditures, detailed items by farm sales size and region, 1983, annual rpt, 1614–3

Farm production inputs, land mgmt, and environmental effects, for 4 crops, 1940s-80 and projected to 2010, 9188–94

Farm production inputs supply, use, and prices, periodic situation rpt with articles, 1561–16

Farm production itemized costs, receipts, and net returns, for 13 crops, 4 livestock types, and milk, by region, 1981-83, annual rpt, 1544–20

Farm production, prices, marketing, and trade, by commodity, forecast and current situation, monthly rpt, 1502–4

Farm use of pesticides for crops and livestock, acreage treated, application methods, and use of safety equipment and professional services, 1982 survey, 1588–76

Farmers prices received for major products and paid for farm inputs and living items, by commodity and State, monthly rpt, 1629–1

Farmers prices received for major products and paid for farm inputs, by commodity and State, 1983, annual rpt, 1629–5

Forest Service use of pesticides, by type and purpose, FY83, annual rpt, 1204–1.2

Great Lakes basin pollutant discharges by source, and control program activities, 1983 annual rpt, 14644–1

Great Lakes trade, by SITC 3-digit commodity, port, vessel type, world area, and country, 1982, annual rpt, 7744–3

Imports of US, detailed Schedule A commodities by country and world area of origin, and mode of transport, 1983, annual rpts, 2424–2

Imports of US, detailed Schedule A commodities by country, monthly rpt, 2422–2

Income tax returns of corporations, detailed income and tax items by industry, 1981, annual rpt, 8304–4

Industry finances and operations, by SIC 2- to 4-digit industry, 1970s-83 and projected to 1988, annual rpt, 2014–4

Input-output structure of US economy, detailed interindustry transactions for 537 industries, and components of final demand, 1977 benchmark data, 2708–17

Manufacturing census, 1982: financial and operating data, by SIC 2- to 4-digit industry, State, SMSA, and county, preliminary census div rpt series, 2491–3

Manufacturing census, 1982: financial and operating data, for SIC 4-digit industries by product, preliminary rpt, 2491–1.196

Occupational health risks from hazardous substances and radiation, by industry, occupation, age, and sex, with bibl and glossary, 1920s-82, 9638–50

Occupational injury and illness rates, by SIC 2- to 4-digit industry, 1982, annual rpt, 6844–1

Index by Subjects and Names

Petrochemicals

Producer prices and indexes, by stage of processing and detailed commodity, monthly rpt, 6762–6

Producer prices and indexes, by stage of processing and detailed commodity, monthly 1983, annual supplement, 6764–2

Production and sales of synthetic organic chemicals by product, and listing of manufacturers, 1983, annual rpt, 9884–3

Production, trade, and sales, by type of pesticide, 1980-82, annual rpt, 1804–5

Vegetable and melon acreage treated with pesticides, for 12 crops, by type of pesticide, method of application, and region, 1979, 1588–82

Water from urban runoff, quality, pollutant concentrations, and control cost-effectiveness, with monitoring sites rainfall and other characteristics, by city and region, 1978-83, 9208–122

Water pollution fish kills, by State, location, and pollution source, monthly 1978-80, annual rpt, 9204–3

Water supply and quality in streams and lakes, and groundwater levels in wells, by drainage basin, 1980, annual State rpt series, 5666–12

Water supply and quality in streams and lakes, and groundwater levels in wells, by drainage basin, 1981, annual State rpt series, 5666–16

Water supply and quality in streams and lakes, and groundwater levels in wells, by drainage basin, 1982, annual State rpt series, 5666–20

Water supply and quality in streams and lakes, and groundwater levels in wells, by drainage basin, 1983, annual State rpt series, 5666–10

Waterborne commerce of US (domestic and foreign), freight by commodity, traffic, and passengers, by port and waterway, 1982, annual rpt, 3754–3

see also under By Commodity in the "Index by Categories"

Pests and pest control

Agricultural research expenditures and scientist years, by topic, commodity, and performing organization, FY82, annual rpt, 1744–2

Animal damage control research projects of Fish and Wildlife Service, descriptions and results by program, FY83, annual rpt, 5504–20

Census of Service Industries, 1982: employment, establishments, receipts, and payroll, by SIC 2- to 4-digit kind of business, SMSA, county, and city, State rpt series, 2391–1

Census of Service Industries, 1982: employment, establishments, receipts, and payroll, by SIC 4-digit kind of business and State, preliminary rpt, 2390–2.6

County Business Patterns: establishments, employees, and payrolls, by SIC 4-digit industry and county, 1982, annual State rpt series, 2326–6

Forest insect and disease incidence and damage, 1983, annual regional rpt series, 1206–11

Forest insect and disease incidence, by region or State, 1983, annual rpt, 1204–8

Forest research project descriptions and bibl, 1982, annual rpt, 1204–14

Forest Service programs and activities, by State and region, FY83, annual rpt, 1204–1

Forestry activities on State and private lands, Fed Govt and State funding by project and State, FY83, annual tables, 1204–32

Fruit fly control, ethylene dibromide fumigation of tropical fruit imports, FY82, and cost of EDB and alternatives for Florida grapefruit and Hawaii papaya, 1984 rpt, 21168–29

Govt census, 1982: State govt payments to local govts, by program, source of funds, level of govt, and State, with trends from 1902, 2460–3

HHS aid to each State and local govt or private instn, amount obligated, funding agency, and program, FY83, annual listing, 4004–3

Housing and neighborhood quality indicators and attitudes, and occupant characteristics, by urban-rural location and region, 1981, annual survey, 2485–7

Housing and neighborhood quality, indicators and attitudes by inside-outside central cities, 1979-82 surveys, SMSA rpt series, 2485–6

Housing and neighborhood quality indicators and attitudes, by occupant and unit characteristics, region, and metro-nonmetro location, 1981, annual survey, 2485–2

Plant pests and pathogens found entering US, by country of origin, State, and method of interception, FY82, annual rpt, 1394–16

State govt preventive health services funding by program, Fed Govt block grants, and opinions on State program admin, for 13 States, FY81-84, GAO rpt, 26121–88

Timber growth, removals, products output, and forest ownership and industries in Northeast States, State rpt series, 1206–16

Urban area pest control firms, pesticide use by type, employment, and sales, by type of service, 1981 survey, article, 1561–16.408

see also Animal diseases and zoonoses

see also Pesticides

Petaluma, Calif.

Housing vacancy rates for single and multifamily units and mobile homes, by city and ZIP code, 1983, annual metro area rpt, 9304–20.3

Housing vacancy rates for single and multifamily units and mobile homes, by city and ZIP code, 1984, annual metro area rpt, 9304–20.19

see also under By SMSA or MSA in the "Index by Categories"

Petersburg, Va.

Census of Housing, 1980: occupancy and unit characteristics, by race, Hispanic origin, and city, SMSA rpt, 2473–1.282

Census of Population and Housing, 1980: detailed population and housing characteristics, by county, city, and census tract, SMSA rpt, 2551–2.282

see also under By SMSA or MSA in the "Index by Categories"

Peterson, Charles H.

"Ecology of Intertidal Flats of North Carolina: A Community Profile", 5506–9.1

Peterson, James A.

"Assessment of Undiscovered Conventionally Recoverable Petroleum Resources of Northwestern, Central, and Northeastern Africa", 5666–17.13

"Assessment of Undiscovered Conventionally Recoverable Petroleum Resources of Onshore China", 5666–17.14

"Petroleum Geology and Resources of Southeastern Mexico, Northern Guatemala, and Belize", 5666–18.4

Peterson, Milo O.

"Gross Product by Industry, 1983", 2702–1.416

Peterson, Nancy M.

"Ecology of Intertidal Flats of North Carolina: A Community Profile", 5506–9.1

Peterson, R. Neal

"Classification Criteria for Size and Type of Farm", 1544–19.402

Petrochemicals

Air pollutant emission factors, by detailed source, 3rd edition, 1983-84 supplements, 9198–13

Census of Population, 1980: detailed socioeconomic and demographic characteristics, by age, sex, race, Hispanic origin, occupation, and industry, State rpt series, 2531–4

Consumption, by fuel type, economic sector, and end use, 1983 and 2000, 2006–2.5

Employment, earnings, and hours, by SIC 4-digit nonfarm industry, monthly 1974-Feb 1984, annual update, 6744–4

Exports, imports, tariffs, and industry operating data for benzene and other organic chemical crudes, foreign and US, 1979-83, TSUSA commodity rpt, 9885–4.39

Imports of US, detailed Schedule A commodities by country, monthly rpt, 2422–2

Imports of US, detailed TSUSA commodities by country of origin, 1983, annual rpt, 2424–4

Manufacturing census, 1982: financial and operating data, by SIC 2- to 4-digit industry, State, SMSA, and county, preliminary census div rpt series, 2491–3

Manufacturing census, 1982: financial and operating data, for SIC 4-digit industries by product, preliminary rpt, 2491–1.204

Producer prices and indexes, by stage of processing and detailed commodity, monthly rpt, 6762–6

Producer prices and indexes, by stage of processing and detailed commodity, monthly 1983, annual supplement, 6764–2

Producers finances and operations, by energy type for US firms domestic and foreign operations, 1974- 82, annual rpt, 3164–44

Production and sales of synthetic organic chemicals by product, and listing of manufacturers, 1983, annual rpt, 9884–3

Production, dev, and distribution firms revenues and income, quarterly rpt, 3162–38

Petrochemicals

Production of synthetic organic chemicals, by detailed product, monthly rpt, 9882–1

Refinery financial and operating impacts from auto use of alcohol fuels, projected to 2000 with trends 1964-80, 3308–75

Supply/demand and prices, by fuel type, sector, and end use, detailed trends and projections 1973-95, annual rpt, 3164–75

Supply/demand and prices, by fuel type, sector, and end use, with foreign comparisons, 1960-83 and projected to 1995, annual summary rpt, 3164–76

Supply/demand, trade, stocks, and refining of oil and natural gas liquids, by detailed product, State, and PAD district, with fuel oil sulfur content, monthly rpt with articles, 3162–6

Supply/demand, trade, stocks, and refining of oil and natural gas liquids, by detailed product, State, and PAD district, and refineries in US and territories, 1983 annual rpt, 3164–2

Waterborne commerce of US (domestic and foreign), freight by commodity, traffic, and passengers, by port and waterway, 1982, annual rpt, 3754–3

Petroleum and petroleum industry

Agricultural cooperatives, membership, activities, and finances, by commodity and selected State, 1900-80 with trends from 1863, 1128–30

Agricultural cooperatives oil and gas production, supply, and reserves, 1979 and 1982, article, 1122–1.407 1561–16.403

Agriculture census, 1982: farms, farmland, production and costs, and operator characteristics, preliminary State and county rpt series, 2330–1

Agriculture census, 1982: farms, farmland, production, finances, and operator characteristics, by county, final State rpt series, 2331–1

Air pollutant emission factors, by detailed source, 3rd edition, 1983-84 supplements, 9198–13

Air pollutant sulfur dioxide emissions reduction proposal, effects on polluting industries and coal production by region and State, projected to 2010, 9188–97

Air pollution abatement equipment shipments by industry, exports, and new and backlog orders, by product, 1983, annual Current Industrial Rpt, 2506–12.5

Air pollution levels for 5 pollutants, by detailed source, State, and Air Quality Control Region, 1981, annual rpt, 9194–7

Alaska electric power capacity and generation by fuel type, and marketing, by utility, type of ownership, and location, 1983, annual rpt, 3214–2

Alaska minerals resources, production, claims on wildlife refuges, oil and gas leases, and exploratory wells, with maps and bibl, 1983, annual rpt, 5664–11

Alaska potential oil exports to Japan, costs and benefits, with background data on oil prices, Pacific Basin supply/demand, and tankers, various periods 1918-99, hearings, 25388–45

Index by Subjects and Names

American Samoa minimum wage rates, employment, earnings, and benefits, by establishment and industry, Nov 1983, biennial rpt, 6504–6

Asphalt and tar roofing and siding shipments, by product and region, 1983, annual Current Industrial Rpt, 2506–8.6

Budget of US, effects of Reagan Admin policy changes, by detailed program, FY85, annual rpt, 104–21

Building materials manufacture, energy use and cost by source and industry, 1970s-82, article, 2012–1.401

Business statistics, detailed data for major industries and economic indicators, *Survey of Current Business,* monthly rpt, 2702–1.15

Carbon dioxide atmospheric levels, climatic effects and impacts of fossil and synthetic fuels use, deforestation, and land use patterns, research rpt series, 3406–3

Carbon dioxide emissions, climatic effects, and control costs, projected under alternative emissions controls and energy use restrictions to 2100 with trends 1970s-80, reprint, 9188–88

Carbon dioxide emissions from fossil fuel combustion by fuel type, worldwide estimates based on total and non-oxidized fossil fuel production, 1950-81, 3008–94

Census of Population, 1980: detailed socioeconomic and demographic characteristics, by age, sex, race, Hispanic origin, occupation, and industry, State rpt series, 2531–4

China economic conditions, agricultural and industrial production, trade, and domestic and foreign investment, 1980-85, 2048–106

Coal supply and Fed Govt coal leases, by owner, owner industry, and western State, various periods 1950-82 and projected to 2000, hearing, 25318–58

Coastal environmental characteristics, fish, wildlife, and use, and population socioeconomic data, for individual areas, series, 5506–4

Collective bargaining agreements expiring during year, covered workers by SIC 2-digit industry, firm, and union, with summary of key provisions, 1984, annual rpt, 6784–9

Communist, OECD, and selected other countries energy reserves, production, and consumption, and oil trade and revenue, 1960s-83, annual rpt, 244–5.4, 244–5.5

Consumption, by fuel type, economic sector, and end use, 1983 and 2000, 2006–2.5

Consumption, by fuel type, economic sector, census div, and State, 1960-82, State Energy Data System annual rpt, 3164–39

Consumption of energy, by type of air pollutant source and fuel, and State, 1981, annual rpt, 9194–14

Consumption per capita, and by economic sector, State, and major energy resource, 1960-82, State Energy Data System annual supplement, 3164–55

Consumption, prices, and conservation and efficiency measures, by fuel type, end-use sector, selected industry, and region, 1960-83, annual rpt, 3164–73

County Business Patterns: establishments, employees, and payrolls, by SIC 4-digit industry and county, 1981, annual State rpt series, 2326–8

County Business Patterns: establishments, employees, and payrolls, by SIC 4-digit industry and county, 1982, annual State rpt series, 2326–6

Cuba economic conditions, agricultural and industrial production and distribution, trade, and intl economic relations, 1970-82 and trends from 1957, 248–40

Defense Fuel Supply Center procurement, prices, stocks, transport, and other activities and finances, FY83, annual rpt, 3904–8

DOD electric power plants and major fuel-burning facilities conversion from oil and gas, fuel use data, 1983, annual rpt, 3104–9

DOD engineering contract awards by function, contract type, and service branch, and oil and port dredging awards by company, 1970s-83, hearings, 21728–53

DOD expenditures for goods and services, by function, 1972-84, article, 2702–1.440

DOD prime contract awards to small and total business, for 10 categories and R&D, monthly rpt, 3542–10

DOD shipments of military and personal property, loss claims, passenger traffic, and costs, by mode of transport, quarterly rpt, 3702–1

DOE enforcement of oil price and allocation regulations, and overcharge allegations, settlements, and refunds to States, by company, as of June 1983, hearing, 21368–50

Earnings by major industry group, and personal income per capita and by source, by region and State, 1929-82, 2708–40

Electric power plant (steam) fuel deliveries, costs, and quality, by fuel type, State, and utility, 1983, annual rpt, 3164–42

Electric power plant capacity, production, retail sales, and fuel stocks, use, and costs, by State, 1979-83, annual rpt, 3164–11

Electric power plant capital and operating detailed costs, capacity, and fuel use, by plant, plant type, utility, and State, 1982, annual rpt, 3164–9

Electric power plants and industrial facilities prohibited from oil and gas primary use, and exemption petitions, by facility, with summary fuel use, 1983, annual rpt, 3104–8

Electric power plants, by capacity, fuel used, unit type, region, State, and county, for plants added and retired, 1983 and planned through 1993, annual rpt, 3164–36

Electric utility fuel cost, quality, use, receipts, and stocks, and power plant production, by energy source, State and utility, quarterly rpt, 3162–39

Electric utility production, fuel consumption, stocks, and costs by fuel type, and sales, by State, monthly rpt, 3162–35

Employment by detailed occupation, for 29 SIC 2-digit nonmanufacturing industries, 1981 BLS survey, 6748–60

Employment, earnings, and hours, by selected SIC 1- to 4-digit industry, State, and for 278 major labor areas, 1939-83, annual rpt, 6744–5

Employment, earnings, and hours, by SIC 4-digit nonfarm industry, monthly 1974-Feb 1984, annual update, 6744–4

Index by Subjects and Names

Petroleum and petroleum industry

Employment, wages, benefits, and hours of oil and gas extraction production workers, by occupation, region, and for 5 States, June 1982 survey, 6787–6.203

Energy demand in industry, forecasting model description, detailed technology specifications, and energy use, for 27 SIC 2- to 4-digit industries, 1970s-80 and projected to 2000, 3308–66

Enhanced recovery technologies use and environmental impacts, by oil field, county, and State, 1970s-80 and projected to 2000, 3408–29

Environmental quality and protection programs, costs, and Fed Govt enforcement, 1983, detailed annual rpt, 484–1

Farm production expenditures, detailed items by farm sales size and region, 1983, annual rpt, 1614–3

Farm production inputs supply, use, and prices, periodic situation rpt with articles, 1561–16

Fed Govt energy programs proposed budget appropriations, by office or dept and function, FY84-85, annual rpt, 3004–14

Fed Govt programs and mgmt cost control proposals, 3-year savings by function and agency, and financial and operating data, 1960s-81, 16908–1.17

Finances and operations, by SIC 2- to 4-digit industry, 1970s-83 and projected to 1988, annual rpt, 2014–4

Finances by firm, and effect of income and excise tax provisions on firms, Fed Govt revenues, and investor tax returns, 1980 and projected to 1992, hearing, 21788–132

Financial statements for manufacturing, mining, and trade corporations, by selected SIC 2- to 3-digit industry, quarterly rpt, 2502–1

Foreign and US energy production, trade, and reserves, and oil and refined products supply and prices, by country, 1973-83, annual rpt, 3164–50

Foreign and US oil identified and undiscovered reserves, by country and oil type, and cumulative production, as of 1981 and 1983, 5668–72

Foreign and US oil production by country, consumption and imports for US and 6 OECD countries, and OPEC member prices, biweekly rpt, 242–4

Foreign and US oil production, prices, trade, and consumption, by country group and selected country, monthly rpt, 242–5

Foreign direct investment of US, by selected major industry group and world area, 1980-82, annual article, 2702–1.430

Foreign minerals production, reserves, and industry role in domestic economy and world supply, country and world region rpt series, 5606–1

Foreign oil and gas undiscovered recoverable resources, cumulative production, and identified reserves, final oil basin rpt series, 5666–18

Foreign oil and gas undiscovered recoverable resources, cumulative production, and identified reserves, preliminary oil basin rpt series, 5666–17

Foreign oil production and consumption, and economic indicators by country and country group, and US trade policy actions, 1960s-83, annual rpt, 444–1.4

Foreign oil reserves, production, and resource lifespan under alternative production rates, historical and projected, country rpt series, 3166–9

Futures trading by commodity and exchange, and Commodity Futures Trading Commission activities, funding, and employment, FY83, annual rpt, 11924–2

Futures trading in selected commodities, foreign currencies, and stock indexes, Chicago and other markets activity, monthly rpt, 11922–1

Futures trading in selected commodities, foreign currencies, Treasury securities, and stock indexes, NYC, Chicago, and other markets activity, monthly rpt, 11922–5

Housing census, 1980: inventory, occupancy, and unit characteristics, changes from 1973 by region and inside-outside SMSAs and central cities, series, 2473–3

Housing energy use, by fuel type, county, city, and census tract, 1980 Census of Population and Housing, State and SMSA rpt series, 2551–2

Housing energy use in SMSAs and central cities, by fuel type, householder race and Hispanic origin, and city, 1980 Census of Housing, State and SMSA rpt series, 2473–1

Housing occupancy and unit and household characteristics, by region and metro-nonmetro residence, 1983, biennial survey, 2485–1

Housing unit heating fuel, by type, occupant race, Hispanic origin, urban-rural location, and region, 1981, annual survey, 2485–7

Hwy construction expenditures and contracts awarded for Federal-aid system, by type of material used and State, various periods 1944-83, annual rpt, 7554–29.7

Hwy construction materials used per $1 million of total expenditures on Federal-aid system, by State, 1980-82, annual rpt, 7554–29.3

Income tax returns of corporations, detailed income and tax items by industry, 1981, annual rpt, 8304–4

Income tax returns of corporations with foreign tax credit, income and deductions by type, asset size, and selected industry group, 1980, article, 8302–2.415

Income tax returns of foreign subsidiaries of US corporations, income and tax data, by industry and asset size, 1980, article, 8302–2.410

Income tax returns of partnerships, receipts by source, deductions by type, and establishments, by selected industry, 1982, annual article, 8302–2.416

Income tax returns of sole proprietorships, receipts, deductions by type, payroll, and net income, by major industry, 1982, annual article, 8302–2.413

Industrial electric power cogeneration in 5 industries, and fuel use and utility supply/demand effects, by region, 1983-93, 3008–92

Input-output structure of US economy, detailed interindustry transactions for 85 industries, and components of final demand, 1977, article, 2702–1.421

Input-output structure of US economy, detailed interindustry transactions for 537 industries, and components of final demand, 1977 benchmark data, 2708–17

Installment credit held by gasoline companies, monthly rpt, 9365–2.6

Manufacturing census, 1982: financial and operating data, by SIC 2- to 4-digit industry, State, SMSA, and county, preliminary census div rpt series, 2491–3

Manufacturing census, 1982: financial and operating data, for SIC 4-digit industries by product, preliminary rpt series, 2491–1

Manufacturing energy efficiency progress, and energy use by type, by SIC 2-digit industry, 1982, annual rpt, 3304–8

Mexico economic indicators, trade, external accounts and debt, oil industry, and relations with US, 1978-83 with trends from 1959, conf proceedings, 21248–82

Mineral industries census, 1982: financial and operating data, by SIC 2- to 4-digit industry, preliminary summary rpt, 2511–2.1

Mineral industries census, 1982: financial and operating data, including materials consumed, by SIC 4-digit industry and State, preliminary rpt series, 2511–1

Minerals Yearbook, 1982, Vol 3 preprints: foreign country reviews of production, trade, and policies, by commodity, annual rpt series, 5604–17

Minerals Yearbook, 1983, Vol 3 preprints: foreign country reviews of production, trade, and policies, by commodity, annual rpt series, 5604–23

Minority group and women employment, by occupational group and SIC 2- to 3-digit industry, 1981, annual rpt, 9244–1.1

Natl Energy Policy Plan, DOE implementation and effect on energy supply/demand, 1983-84, annual rpt, 3024–4

Natl Energy Policy Plan, energy supply, demand, and prices, by fuel and consuming sector, projected 1985-2010, biennial rpt, 3004–13

Occupational injury and illness rates, by SIC 2- to 4-digit industry, 1982, annual rpt, 6844–1

OECD crude oil consumption related to prices, conservation, and real dollar exchange rates, for 7 countries, various periods 1975-83, article, 9379–1.405

Oil import and refining fees to recover cost of Strategic Petroleum Reserve, with purchases and construction costs, FY84-FY88, 26306–6.68

Pollution abatement capital and operating costs, by SIC 2- to 4-digit industry, State, and SMSA, 1982, annual Current Industrial Rpt, 2506–3.6

Pollution abatement capital and operating costs under Clean Air and Water Acts, for govts and selected industries, various periods 1970-2000, annual rpt, 9184–11

Pollution abatement expenditures, and effect on economic indicators and industry operations, by major industry, projected under 3 pollution regulation alternatives 1983-95, 9188–84

Producers finances and operations, by energy type for US firms domestic and foreign operations, 1974-82, annual rpt, 3164–44

Production and exploration expenditures and revenues, and sales volume, 1982, annual Current Industrial Rpt, 2506–8.11

Petroleum and petroleum industry

Production and reserves of oil, gas, and gas liquids, by State and selected substate area, 1983, annual rpt, 3164–46

Production, dev, and distribution firms revenues and income, quarterly rpt, 3162–38

Production equipment and operating costs and cost indexes, itemized, for oil and gas fields in 10 producing areas, 1981-83, annual rpt, 3164–45

Production, reserves, and prices, by fuel type, and selected indicators of energy use, by State, 1982-83 with selected comparisons from 1971, annual rpt, 3164–60

Production, total and for surveillance fields, by State and inland and Federal offshore area, 1980-82, biennial rpt, 3164–58

Production, trade, use, DOE activities, and foreign direct investment in US oil sources, FY83, annual rpt, 3024–2

R&D expenditures of US firms foreign affiliates, by selected industry, 1974-82, 9626–2.131

R&D industry funding and employment of scientists and engineers, by industry group, firm size, and funding source, 1956-82, annual rpt, 9627–21

Refined products sales of gas plant operators and refiners, price and volume for 13 products, by end-use sector, PAD district, and State, monthly rpt, 3162–11

Refined products surveys, lab analyses of aviation, heating, diesel, and gasoline fuel properties, last issues of annual and semiannual rpt series, 3006–2

Refinery and oilfield construction receipts, 1982 Census of Construction Industries, final rpt series, 2373–1

Refinery construction receipts, 1982 Census of Construction Industries, preliminary rpt series, 2371–1

Refinery financial and operating impacts from auto use of alcohol fuels, projected to 2000 with trends 1964-80, 3308–75

Refinery productivity, hours, and employment indexes, 1954-82, annual rpt, 6824–1.3

Refining capacity and production, and oil use and exports, by OPEC member, with comparisons to other countries, projected 1985-90, hearings, 25368–133.1

Research publications on energy of DOE and other sources, monthly listing, 3002–2

Scientists and engineers employed in energy-related fields, supply/demand and effects of R&D funding, by energy type, employer type, field, and age, 1962-91, annual rpt, 3004–19

Scientists, engineers, and technicians employed in private industry, by occupation and industry group, 1980-81, biennial rpt, 9627–23

Scientists, engineers, and technicians employment in transportation, utilities, and retail and wholesale trade, by field of science and industry, 1982, 9628–72

Sealift Military Command operations for naval fleet support, and transport of DOD and AID cargo by route, quarterly rpt, 3802–2

Ships bunker fuels, oil and coal laden in US on vessels engaged in foreign trade, by port, monthly rpt, 2422–5

Southeastern States financial and economic devs, Fed Reserve 6th District, monthly rpt with articles, 9371–1

Statistical Abstract of US, social, political, and economic data, 1950s-83 and trends, annual rpt, 2324–1.3

Supply and prices of crude oil and refined products, effects of 3 import disruptions, selected years 1972-82, 3108–28

Supply/demand and price forecasts, by fuel type, quarterly rpt, 3162–34

Supply/demand and prices, by energy resource and major producing and consuming country and sector, detailed data, monthly rpt, 3162–24

Supply/demand and prices, by energy source and end-use sector and for 7 electric utilities, 1981-2000 with trends from 1960s, 3008–93

Supply/demand and prices, by fuel type and consuming sector with foreign comparisons, 1949-83, annual rpt, 3164–74

Supply/demand and prices, by fuel type, sector, and end use, with foreign comparisons, 1960-83 and projected to 1995, annual summary rpt, 3164–76

Supply/demand of oil and refined products, refinery capacity and use, and OPEC, non-OPEC, and spot market prices, weekly rpt, 3162–32

Supply/demand, prices, end use, and related technical and socioeconomic data, including impacts of US policy and intl devs, series, 3006–7

Supply/demand, trade, stocks, and refining of oil and natural gas liquids, by detailed product, State, and PAD district, with fuel oil sulfur content, monthly rpt with articles, 3162–6

Supply/demand, trade, stocks, and refining of oil and natural gas liquids, by detailed product, State, and PAD district, and refineries in US and territories, 1983 annual rpt, 3164–2

Transportation and related energy use, for urban areas, late 1970s-82 and projected under lower auto emission standards to 1995, 3408–31

Transportation census, 1982: trucks, by detailed characteristics, miles traveled, and type of product carried, State rpt series, 2573–1

Transportation energy use by mode, fuel supplies, and demographic and economic determinants of vehicle use, 1970s-83, annual rpt, 3304–5

Transportation finances, operations, vehicles, equipment, accidents, and energy use and transport, by mode of transport, 1955-84, annual rpt, 7304–2

Water pollution fish kills, by State, location, and pollution source, monthly 1978-80, annual rpt, 9204–3

Waterborne commerce of US (domestic and foreign), freight by commodity, traffic, and passengers, by port and waterway, 1982, annual rpt, 3754–3

Western US Fed Govt lands by agency and mining restriction status, and energy resources on potential wilderness areas and other lands, 1970s-81 and projected to 1990, 3308–68

Wholesale trade census, 1982: employment, establishments, finances, and operations,

Index by Subjects and Names

by SIC 2- to 4-digit kind of business, SMSA, county, and city, State rpt series, 2405–1

Wholesale trade census, 1982: employment, establishments, sales by commodity, and payroll, by SIC 4-digit kind of business and State, preliminary rpt, 2403–1.36

Windfall profits tax admin of IRS and revenues, tax rates, and nonfilers, 1980-86, GAO rpt, 26119–65

Windfall profits tax collections of IRS, quarterly press release, 8302–1

Windfall profits tax collections, refunds, and taxes due IRS, by State and region, FY83, annual rpt, 8304–3.3

Windfall profits tax credit or refund and deduction for income tax returns of sole proprietorships, 1982, annual article, 8302–2.413

Windfall profits tax liability by tax rate, and exempt oil volume, by oil price control category, quarterly article, 8302–2.2

World oil prices effects on US oil trade and energy-intensive industries, with US and foreign reserves and industry operations, 1950-82 and projected to 2020, 9886–4.69

see also Aviation fuels

see also Diesel fuel

see also Energy exploration and drilling

see also Gasoline

see also Gasoline service stations

see also Heating oil

see also Liquefied petroleum gas

see also Natural gas and gas industry

see also Naval Petroleum Reserves

see also Offshore oil and gas

see also Oil and gas leases

see also Oil depletion allowances

see also Oil shale

see also Oil spills

see also Organization of Petroleum Exporting Countries

see also Petrochemicals

see also Petroleum exports and imports

see also Petroleum prices

see also Petroleum reserves

see also Petroleum stocks

see also Pipelines

see also Strategic Petroleum Reserve

see also Synthetic fuels

see also Tar sands

see also Trans-Alaska Pipeline System

see also under By Commodity in the "Index by Categories"

see also under By Industry in the "Index by Categories"

Petroleum conservation

see Energy conservation

Petroleum consumption

see Petroleum and petroleum industry

Petroleum exports and imports

Alaska potential oil exports to Japan, costs and benefits, with background data on oil prices, Pacific Basin supply/demand, and tankers, various periods 1918-99, hearings, 25388–45

Business statistics, detailed data for major industries and economic indicators, *Survey of Current Business,* monthly rpt, 2702–1.15

China economic conditions, agricultural and industrial production, trade, and domestic and foreign investment, 1980-85, 2048–106

Index by Subjects and Names

China exports and imports, by commodity, world area, and country, quarterly rpt, 242 6

China exports and imports by SITC 1- to 5-digit commodity, 1970s-82, annual rpt, 244–12

China hard currency balance of payments, and intl lines of credit, quarterly rpt, 242–6.1

Communist, OECD, and selected other countries energy reserves, production, and consumption, and oil trade and revenue, 1960s-83, annual rpt, 244–5.5

Cuba economic conditions, agricultural and industrial production and distribution, trade, and intl economic relations, 1970-82 and trends from 1957, 248–40

Export licensing and monitoring activities under Export Admin Act, for selected commodities, and for Communist and other countries, FY83, annual rpt, 2044–22

Exports and imports between US and outlying areas, by detailed commodity and mode of transport, monthly rpt, 2422–4

Exports and imports of oil and refined products, by world region, 1982, annual rpt, 7304–2.5

Exports and imports of US, by principal end-use category, 1965-83, annual rpt, 204–1.9

Exports and imports of US, detailed SIC-based commodities by world area, 1983, annual rpts, 2424–6

Exports and imports of US, totals and as percent of domestic production, by SIC 2- to 5-digit commodity, 1981, annual rpt, 2424–3

Exports, imports, and economic indicators by country and country group, and US trade policy actions, 1960s-83, annual rpt, 444–1.3

Exports, imports, production, prices, and consumption, by country group and selected country, monthly rpt, 242–5

Exports, imports, production, use, DOE activities, and foreign direct investment in US oil sources, FY83, annual rpt, 3024–2

Exports of manufactured and agricultural commodities, manufacturing production, and export-related employment, 1960s-82, State rpt series, 2046–3

Exports of US, detailed commodities by country of destination, monthly rpt, 2422–3

Exports of US, detailed Schedule B commodities by country of destination, 1983, annual rpt, 2424–9

Exports of US, detailed Schedule E commodities by mode of transport and world area and country of destination, 1983, annual rpts, 2424–5

Foreign and US oil production, trade, and stocks, by product and country, 1982, annual rpt, 3164–50.3

Foreign oil price and demand relationships and real income effects among developed countries and OPEC and non-OPEC developing countries, 1984 technical paper, 9366–7.96

Great Lakes trade, by SITC 3-digit commodity, port, vessel type, world area, and country, 1982, annual rpt, 7744–3

Import oil bill of major non-Communist countries, selected years 1965-83, annual rpt, 244–5.4

Imports of oil and refined products, *Business Conditions Digest,* historical supplement and methodology, 1947-82, 2708–31

Imports of oil and refined products, *Business Conditions Digest,* monthly rpt, 2702–3.9

Imports of oil and refined products, by product, monthly rpt, 2422–6

Imports of oil and refined products into US and Virgin Islands, monthly rpt, 2422–6.2

Imports of US and 7 OECD countries, quarterly rpt, 2042–10.2

Imports of US, detailed Schedule A commodities by country and world area of origin, and mode of transport, 1983, annual rpts, 2424–2

Imports of US, detailed Schedule A commodities by country, monthly rpt, 2422–2

Imports of US, detailed TSUSA commodities by country of origin, 1983, annual rpt, 2424–4

Input-output structure of US economy, detailed interindustry transactions for 537 industries, and components of final demand, 1977 benchmark data, 2708–17

Intl trade position of US and 4 OECD countries, and factors affecting US competition, quarterly pamphlet, 2042–25

Intl transactions summary, including impact of oil imports and agricultural exports, 4th qtr 1982-4th qtr 1983, article, 9362–1.403

Mexico economic indicators, trade, external accounts and debt, oil industry, and relations with US, 1978-83 with trends from 1959, conf proceedings, 21248–82

Minerals Yearbook, 1982, Vol 3 preprints: foreign country reviews of production, trade, and policies, by commodity, annual rpt series, 5604–17

Minerals Yearbook, 1983, Vol 3 preprints: foreign country reviews of production, trade, and policies, by commodity, annual rpt series, 5604–23

Natl Energy Policy Plan, DOE implementation and effect on energy supply/demand, 1983-84, annual rpt, 3024–4

Natl Energy Policy Plan, energy supply, demand, and prices, by fuel and consuming sector, projected 1985-2010, biennial rpt, 3004–13

OECD oil consumption and imports, for US and 6 countries, biweekly rpt, 242–4

OECD trade, total and for 4 major countries, and US trade by country, by commodity, 1972-82, annual world region rpt series, 244–13

Oil import and refining fees to recover cost of Strategic Petroleum Reserve, with purchases and construction costs, FY84-FY88, 26306–6.68

OPEC oil refining capacity and production by city, and oil use and exports, by member, with comparisons to other countries, projected 1985-90, hearings, 25368–133.1

Port impact on local employment through transport of 5 commodities, by industry for 3 eastern ports, and demand for US coal by country, 1981, 7308–182

Petroleum prices

Supply and prices of crude oil and refined products, effects of 3 import disruptions, selected years 1972-82, 3108–28

Supply/demand and price forecasts, by fuel type, quarterly rpt, 3162–34

Supply/demand and prices, by energy resource and major producing and consuming country and sector, detailed data, monthly rpt, 3162–24

Supply/demand and prices, by fuel type and consuming sector with foreign comparisons, 1949-83, annual rpt, 3164–74

Supply/demand and prices, by fuel type, sector, and end use, detailed trends and projections 1973-95, annual rpt, 3164–75

Supply/demand and prices, by fuel type, sector, and end use, with foreign comparisons, 1960-83 and projected to 1995, annual summary rpt, 3164–76

Supply/demand of oil and refined products, refinery capacity and use, and OPEC, non-OPEC, and spot market prices, weekly rpt, 3162–32

Supply/demand, trade, stocks, and refining of oil and natural gas liquids, by detailed product, State, and PAD district, with fuel oil sulfur content, monthly rpt with articles, 3162–6

Supply/demand, trade, stocks, and refining of oil and natural gas liquids, by detailed product, State, and PAD district, and refineries in US and territories, 1983 annual rpt, 3164–2

Transportation energy use by mode, fuel supplies, and demographic and economic determinants of vehicle use, 1970s-83, annual rpt, 3304–5.1

Waterborne commerce of US (domestic and foreign), freight by commodity, traffic, and passengers, by port and waterway, 1982, annual rpt, 3754–3

World oil prices effects on US oil trade and energy-intensive industries, with US and foreign reserves and industry operations, 1950-82 and projected to 2020, 9886–4.69

Petroleum prices

Airline fuel use and costs for domestic and intl operations, by US carrier group, monthly rpt, 9142–21

Alaska potential oil exports to Japan, costs and benefits, with background data on oil prices, Pacific Basin supply/demand, and tankers, various periods 1918-99, hearings, 25388–45

Business statistics, detailed data for major industries and economic indicators, *Survey of Current Business,* monthly rpt, 2702–1.15

CPI by detailed component, for US city average, 28 SMSAs, and 4 regions by population size, monthly rpt, 6762–2

Defense Fuel Supply Center procurement, prices, stocks, and other activities, FY83, annual rpt, 3904–6

Defense Fuel Supply Center procurement, prices, stocks, transport, and other activities and finances, FY83, annual rpt, 3904–8

Electric power plant (steam) fuel deliveries, costs, and quality, by fuel type, State, and utility, 1983, annual rpt, 3164–42

Electric power plant capacity, production, retail sales, and fuel stocks, use, and costs, by State, 1979-83, annual rpt, 3164–11

Petroleum prices

Electric power plants (steam), prices paid for fossil fuels, July 1972 and 1982-83, annual rpt, 3084–9

Electric utility fuel cost, quality, use, receipts, and stocks, and power plant production, by energy source, State and utility, quarterly rpt, 3162–39

Electric utility production, fuel consumption, stocks, and costs by fuel type, and sales, by State, monthly rpt, 3162–35

Farm production inputs supply, use, and prices, periodic situation rpt with articles, 1561–16

Farmers prices received for major products and paid for farm inputs and living items, by commodity and State, monthly rpt, 1629–1

Farmers prices received for major products and paid for farm inputs, by commodity and State, 1983, annual rpt, 1629–5

Foreign and US oil prices, tax, and customs duty, by refined product and major city, July 1983 and Jan 1984, annual rpt, 3164–50.4

Foreign and US retail oil prices and tax rates for 5 countries, and OPEC sales prices by member, monthly rpt, 242–5

Foreign economic effects of oil price changes on developed countries and on OPEC and non-OPEC developing countries, model description, 1984 technical paper, 9366–7.93

Foreign oil price and demand relationships and real income effects among developed countries and OPEC and non-OPEC developing countries, 1984 technical paper, 9366–7.96

Gasoline prices, 1970s-82 and projected 1983-92, hearing, 21368–49

Housing energy use, and savings under alternative conservation strategies, by State, with model methodology and energy prices, selected years 1970-81, 21368–48

Natl Energy Policy Plan, energy supply, demand, and prices, by fuel and consuming sector, projected 1985-2010, biennial rpt, 3004–13

OECD crude oil consumption related to prices, conservation, and real dollar exchange rates, for 7 countries, various periods 1975-83, article, 9379–1.405

OPEC countries crude oil prices, 1973-83, annual rpt, 244–5.2

OPEC oil prices, by member, biweekly rpt, 242–4

Pacific Northwest electricity consumption and prices by end-use sector, and economic and demographic data, 1960s-83 and projected to 2005, annual rpt, 3224–2

Prices and expenditures for fuels, by consuming sector, State, and fuel type, 1970-81, annual rpt, 3164–64

Prices and supply/demand, by energy source and end-use sector and for 7 electric utilities, 1981-2000 with trends from 1960s, 3008–93

Prices and supply/demand, by fuel and consuming sector with foreign comparisons, 1949-83, annual rpt, 3164–74

Prices and supply/demand, by fuel, sector, and end use, detailed trends and projections 1973-95, annual rpt, 3164–75

Prices and supply/demand, by fuel, sector, and end use, with foreign comparisons, 1960-83 and projected to 1995, annual summary rpt, 3164–76

Prices and supply/demand forecasts, by fuel, quarterly rpt, 3162–34

Prices of imported and domestic oil and wholesale and retail fuels, and dealer margins, monthly rpt, 3162–24.9

Prices, production, use, and reserves, by energy type, and selected indicators of energy use, by State, 1982-83 with selected comparisons from 1971, annual rpt, 3164–60

Prices, supply/demand, end use, and related technical and socioeconomic data, including impacts of US policy and intl devs, series, 3006–7

Prices, use, and conservation and efficiency measures, by fuel type, end-use sector, selected industry, and region, 1960-83, annual rpt, 3164–73

Producer prices and indexes, by stage of processing and detailed commodity, monthly rpt, 6762–6

Producer prices and indexes, by stage of processing and detailed commodity, monthly 1983, annual supplement, 6764–2

Refined product prices and sales volume, 1981-82, annual rpt, 3164–44.3

Refined products sales of gas plant operators, refiners, and resellers, price and volume for 13 products by end-use sector, PAD district, and State, monthly rpt, 3162–11

Refinery financial and operating impacts from auto use of alcohol fuels, projected to 2000 with trends 1964-80, 3308–75

Regulation of oil prices and allocation, DOE enforcement, and overcharge allegations, settlements, and refunds to States, by company, as of June 1983, hearing, 21368–50

Supply and prices of crude oil and refined products, effects of 3 import disruptions, selected years 1972-82, 3108–28

Supply/demand of oil and refined products, refinery capacity and use, and OPEC, non-OPEC, and spot market prices, weekly rpt, 3162–32

Trans-Alaska Pipeline System owner companies financial data, and retail gasoline competitive position in 2 States, by company, 1980-83, hearing, 21728–51

Transportation energy use by mode, fuel supplies, and demographic and economic determinants of vehicle use, 1970s-83, annual rpt, 3304–5.1

Wholesale prices of oil products by fuel type, 1962-83, hearings, 21728–53

World oil prices effects on US oil trade and energy-intensive industries, with US and foreign reserves and industry operations, 1950-82 and projected to 2020, 9886–4.69

Petroleum reserves

Agricultural cooperatives oil and gas production, supply, and reserves, 1979 and 1982, article, 1561–16.403

Agricultural cooperatives oil and gas production, supply, and reserves, 1982 with comparisons to 1979, article, 1122–1.407

Budget of US Appendix, detailed budgets and personnel summaries, by agency, FY85, annual rpt, 104–3

Coastal environmental characteristics, fish, wildlife, and use, and population socioeconomic data, for individual areas, series, 5506–4

Communist, OECD, and selected other countries energy reserves, production, and consumption, and oil trade and revenue, 1960s-83, annual rpt, 244–5.5

Fed Govt OCS oil and gas reserves, leasing and exploration activities, production, revenues, and costs, by ocean region, FY83, annual rpt, 5734–4

Fed Govt OCS oil, gas, and mineral production, revenues, and reserves, by State and ocean region, 1950s-82, annual rpt, 5734–3

Foreign and US energy reserves, by type of fuel and country, as of Jan 1984, annual rpt, 3164–50.7

Foreign and US oil identified and undiscovered reserves, by country and oil type, and cumulative production, as of 1981 and 1983, 5668–72

Foreign minerals production, reserves, and industry role in domestic economy and world supply, country and world region rpt series, 5606–1

Foreign oil and gas undiscovered recoverable resources, cumulative production, and identified reserves, final oil basin rpt series, 5666–18

Foreign oil and gas undiscovered recoverable resources, cumulative production, and identified reserves, preliminary oil basin rpt series, 5666–17

Foreign oil reserves, production, and resource lifespan under alternative production rates, historical and projected, country rpt series, 3166–9

Mexico economic indicators, trade, external accounts and debt, oil industry, and relations with US, 1978-83 with trends from 1959, conf proceedings, 21248–82

Minerals Yearbook, 1982, Vol 3 preprints: foreign country reviews of production, trade, and policies, by commodity, annual rpt series, 5604–17

Minerals Yearbook, 1983, Vol 3 preprints: foreign country reviews of production, trade, and policies, by commodity, annual rpt series, 5604–23

OCS oil and gas leases environmental and socioeconomic impacts, and coastal area description, final statement series, 5736–1

Pacific Basin and US oil supply/demand, by country or region, various periods 1973-83, hearings, 25388–45

Producers finances and operations, by energy type for US firms domestic and foreign operations, 1974- 82, annual rpt, 3164–44.2

Reserve fields by State and EIA field code, 1983, annual listing, 3164–70

Reserves and production of oil, gas, and gas liquids, by State and selected substate area, 1983, annual rpt, 3164–46

Reserves, production, prices, and use, by energy type, and selected indicators of energy use, by State, 1982-83 with selected comparisons from 1971, annual rpt, 3164–60

Index by Subjects and Names

Supply/demand and prices, by fuel type and consuming sector with foreign comparisons, 1949-83, annual rpt, 3164–74

Supply/demand and prices, by fuel type, sector, and end use, with foreign comparisons, 1960-83 and projected to 1995, annual summary rpt, 3164–76

Western States wilderness areas potential oil and natural gas reserves, for 11 States, 1982-83, compilation of papers, 5668–69

Western US Fed Govt lands by agency and mining restriction status, and energy resources on potential wilderness areas and other lands, 1970s-81 and projected to 1990, 3308–68

World oil prices effects on US oil trade and energy-intensive industries, with US and foreign reserves and industry operations, 1950-82 and projected to 2020, 9886–4.69

see also Naval Petroleum Reserves

see also Strategic Petroleum Reserve

Petroleum stocks

Business statistics, detailed data for major industries and economic indicators, *Survey of Current Business,* monthly rpt, 2702–1.15

Electric power plant capacity, production, retail sales, and fuel stocks, use, and costs, by State, 1979-83, annual rpt, 3164–11

Electric utility fuel cost, quality, use, receipts, and stocks, and power plant production, by energy source, State and utility, quarterly rpt, 3162–39

Electric utility production, fuel consumption, stocks, and costs by fuel type, and sales, by State, monthly rpt, 3162–35

Natl Energy Policy Plan, energy supply, demand, and prices, by fuel and consuming sector, projected 1985-2010, biennial rpt, 3004–13

OECD oil stocks, for US and 16 countries, monthly rpt, 242–5

OECD stocks of crude oil and refined products, for 7 countries, quarterly 1980-83, annual rpt, 3164–50.3

Pacific Basin and US oil supply/demand, by country or region, various periods 1973-83, hearings, 25388–45

Supply and prices of crude oil and refined products, effects of 3 import disruptions, selected years 1972-82, 3108–28

Supply/demand and price forecasts, by fuel type, quarterly rpt, 3162–34

Supply/demand and prices, by energy resource and major producing and consuming country and sector, detailed data, monthly rpt, 3162–24

Supply/demand and prices, by fuel type and consuming sector with foreign comparisons, 1949-83, annual rpt, 3164–74

Supply/demand and prices, by fuel type, sector, and end use, detailed trends and projections 1973-95, annual rpt, 3164–75

Supply/demand and prices, by fuel type, sector, and end use, with foreign comparisons, 1960-83 and projected to 1995, annual summary rpt, 3164–76

Supply/demand of oil and refined products, refinery capacity and use, and OPEC, non-OPEC, and spot market prices, weekly rpt, 3162–32

Supply/demand, trade, stocks, and refining of oil and natural gas liquids, by detailed product, State, and PAD district, with fuel oil sulfur content, monthly rpt with articles, 3162–6

Supply/demand, trade, stocks, and refining of oil and natural gas liquids, by detailed product, State, and PAD district, and refineries in US and territories, 1983 annual rpt, 3164–2

see also Naval Petroleum Reserves

see also Strategic Petroleum Reserve

Pets

see Animals

Pharmaceutical industry

Air pollutant emission factors, by detailed source, 3rd edition, 1983-84 supplements, 9198–13

Biotechnology commercial uses, R&D funding and output, controls, and industry financial and operating data, for US and 5 countries, 1970s-83 and estimated 1984-85, 26358–98

Biotechnology firms, patents, and trade by country, and effect of industry growth on US drug and chemical trade, selected years 1979-2000, 9886–4.78

Census of Population, 1980: detailed socioeconomic and demographic characteristics, by age, sex, race, Hispanic origin, occupation, and industry, State rpt series, 2531–4

China exports and imports by SITC 1- to 5-digit commodity, 1970s-82, annual rpt, 244–12

County Business Patterns: establishments, employees, and payrolls, by SIC 4-digit industry and county, 1981, annual State rpt series, 2326–8

County Business Patterns: establishments, employees, and payrolls, by SIC 4-digit industry and county, 1982, annual State rpt series, 2326–6

Employment, earnings, and hours, by selected SIC 1- to 4-digit industry, State, and for 278 major labor areas, 1939-83, annual rpt, 6744–5

Employment, earnings, and hours, by SIC 4-digit nonfarm industry, monthly 1974-Feb 1984, annual update, 6744–4

Finances and operations, by SIC 2- to 4-digit industry, 1970s-83 and projected to 1988, annual rpt, 2014–4

Financial statements for manufacturing, mining, and trade corporations, by selected SIC 2- to 3-digit industry, quarterly rpt, 2502–1

Income tax returns of corporations, detailed income and tax items by industry, 1981, annual rpt, 8304–4

Income tax returns of corporations with foreign tax credit, income and deductions by type, asset size, and selected industry group, 1980, article, 8302–2.415

Income tax returns of sole proprietorships, detailed data by industry div and selected industry group, 1981, annual rpt, 8304–7

Income tax returns of sole proprietorships, receipts, deductions by type, payroll, and net income, by major industry, 1982, annual article, 8302–2.413

Input-output structure of US economy, detailed interindustry transactions for 85 industries, and components of final demand, 1977, article, 2702–1.421

Pharmacists and pharmacy

Input-output structure of US economy, detailed interindustry transactions for 537 industries, and components of final demand, 1977 benchmark data, 2708–17

Manufacturing census, 1982: financial and operating data, by SIC 2- to 4-digit industry, State, SMSA, and county, preliminary census div rpt series, 2491–3

Manufacturing census, 1982: financial and operating data, for SIC 4-digit industries by product, preliminary rpt, 2491–1.182, 2491–1.183, 2491–1.184

Minority group and women employment, by occupational group and SIC 2- to 3-digit industry, 1981, annual rpt, 9244–1.1

Occupational injury and illness rates, by SIC 2- to 4-digit industry, 1982, annual rpt, 6844–1

Pharmacists employment and sociodemographic characteristics, and reasons for not working in field, by State and overseas, as of 1979, 4147–14.28

Production and sales of synthetic organic chemicals by product, and listing of manufacturers, 1983, annual rpt, 9884–3

Productivity, hours, and employment indexes for selected SIC 3- and 4-digit industries, 1954-82, annual rpt, 6824–1.3

R&D costs and finances of drug industry, drug prices by brand and generic category, patent life, and FDA approval time, selected years 1962-83, hearing, 25528–98

R&D expenditures of US firms foreign affiliates, by selected industry, 1974-82, 9626–2.131

R&D industry funding and employment of scientists and engineers, by industry group, firm size, and funding source, 1956-82, annual rpt, 9627–21

Scientists, engineers, and technicians employment in transportation, utilities, and retail and wholesale trade, by field of science and industry, 1982, 9628–72

Southeastern States health care resource availability, and employment by occupation, by facility type, by State and SMSA in Fed Reserve 6th District, 1970s-81, article, 9371–1.425

Wholesale trade census, 1982: employment, establishments, finances, and operations, by SIC 2- to 4-digit kind of business, SMSA, county, and city, State rpt series, 2405–1

Wholesale trade census, 1982: employment, establishments, sales by commodity, and payroll, by SIC 4-digit kind of business and State, preliminary rpt, 2403–1.22

Wholesale trade sales, inventories, purchases, and gross margins, by SIC 2- to 3-digit kind of business and type of ownership, 1983, annual rpt, 2413–13

see also Drugs

see also Drugstores

see also Pharmacists and pharmacy

see also under By Industry in the "Index by Categories"

Pharmacists and pharmacy

Census of Population, 1980: detailed socioeconomic and demographic characteristics, by age, sex, race, Hispanic origin, occupation, and industry, State rpt series, 2531–4

Costs to pharmacists of brand name prescription drugs, and Medicare maximum allowable costs, by class and manufacturer, July/Aug 1983, 4658–6

Pharmacists and pharmacy

Degrees conferred in higher education, by race, Hispanic origin, sex, level, and field, selected years 1949/50-1979/80, annual rpt, 4824–2.16

DOD medical personnel, trainees, and accessions by source, by occupation, specialty, and service branch, FY83, annual rpt, 3544–24

Employment and sociodemographic characteristics of licensed pharmacists, and reasons for not working in field, by State and overseas, as of 1979, 4147–14.28

General Medical Sciences Natl Inst research programs and funding, FY83, annual rpt, 4474–12

Health condition and health care resources, use, and expenditures, 1970s-82 with trends and projections 1900-2000, annual compilation, 4144–11

Hospital employment, vacancies, and vacancy rates, by occupation and by hospital specialty, region, census div, and State, 1980, annual rpt, 4114–12

Hospital worker wages by sex and occupation, and benefits, for 22 MSAs, Oct 1981 survey, 6787–6.201

License sanctions of health professionals in 3 States, and subsequent Medicare and Medicaid program participation, by specialty, 1977-82, GAO rpt, 26121–80

Manpower supply and education of health professionals, by occupation, demographic and professional characteristics, and location, 1950s-83 and projected to 2000, biennial rpt, 4114–8

Medicaid advisory committees members by type, and operating characteristics, 1979, article, 4652–1.409

Medicare kidney end-stage program, reimbursement by treatment, diagnosis, outcome, and patient characteristics, with covered charges for transplants, 1974-79, article, 4652–1.421

Minority group and women employment and training in health professions, by field, selected years 1962/63-1983/84, 4118–18

Occupational manpower needs and supply by detailed occupation, and educational and training program enrollees and grads by detailed field, 1982 and 1995, biennial rpt, 6744–3

Occupational Outlook Handbook, 1984-85 biennial rpt, 6744–1

Science and engineering doctoral degree recipients, by field, sex, race, age, citizenship, postgrad employment and study status, State, and instn, 1960-82, 9626–6.16

Science and engineering grad enrollment, fields of study, financial support, and other student and instn characteristics, 1975-82, annual survey, 9627–7

Southeastern States health care resource availability, and employment by occupation, by facility type, by State and SMSA in Fed Reserve 6th District, 1970s-81, article, 9371–1.425

VA Medicine and Surgery Dept trainees, by detailed program and city, FY83, annual rpt, 9924–21

VA pharmacies prescriptions and doses dispensed, and other VA activities, FY82-83, annual rpt, 9924–1.4

see also Drugs

see also Drugstores

Pharr, Tex.

Census of Housing, 1980: occupancy and unit characteristics, by race, Hispanic origin, and city, SMSA rpt, 2473–1.236

Census of Population and Housing, 1980: detailed population and housing characteristics, by county, city, and census tract, SMSA rpt, 2551–2.236

Employment and economic impacts on Texas border of Mexican peso devaluation, for 6 counties and 2 SMSAs, 1970s-May 1983, hearing, 21788–133

Wages of office and plant workers, by occupation, 1984 labor market area survey rpt, 6785–3.10

Phaup, Marvin

"New Approaches to the Budgetary Treatment of Federal Credit Assistance", 26306–6.72

Phelps, Robert B.

"Outlook for Timber Products", 1004–16.1

Philadelphia, Pa.

Auto dealer repair workers, wages, and benefits, by occupation, size of establishment, and for 24 labor market areas, Nov 1982 survey, 6787–6.202

Census of Housing, 1980: occupancy and unit characteristics, by race, Hispanic origin, and city, SMSA rpt, 2473–1.283

Census of Population and Housing, 1980: detailed population and housing characteristics, by county, city, and census tract, SMSA rpt, 2551–2.283

CPI by component for US city average, and by region, population size, and for 28 SMSAs, monthly press release, 6762–1

CPI by detailed component, for US city average, 28 SMSAs, and 4 regions by population size, monthly rpt, 6762–2

Dress industry production and related workers, wages, and benefits, by occupation, size of establishment, and union status, for 11 labor market areas, Aug 1982 survey, 6787–6.200

Fruit and vegetable shipments, and arrivals in 23 US and 5 Canada cities, by mode of transport and State or country of origin, 1983, annual rpt, 1311–4.1

Hospital worker wages by sex and occupation, and benefits, for 22 MSAs, Oct 1981 survey, 6787–6.201

Housing and financial characteristics, and unit and neighborhood quality, for 15 SMSAs, 1978, annual survey special supplement, 2485–8

Housing and households detailed characteristics, and unit and neighborhood quality, by inside-outside central cities, 1982 survey, SMSA rpt, 2485–6.33

Population size of top 25 cities, 1980 and 1982, press release, 2328–46

Port impact on local employment through transport of 5 commodities, by industry for 3 eastern ports, and demand for US coal by country, 1981, 7308–182

Repair technicians and apprentices wages and benefits, for 5 types of electrical repair shops in 19 SMSAs, Nov 1981 survey, 6787–6.197

Technology-intensive industry plant location factors and assessment for Philadelphia SMSA, 1984 narrative article, 9387–1.401

Index by Subjects and Names

Wages of office and plant workers, by occupation, 1983 SMSA survey rpt, 6785–12.2

Waterborne commerce of US (domestic and foreign), freight by commodity, traffic, and passengers, by port and waterway, 1982, annual rpt, 3754–3.1

see also under By City and By SMSA or MSA in the "Index by Categories"

Philanthropy

see Gifts and contributions

see Nonprofit organizations and foundations

Philippine Americans

see Asian Americans

Philippines

Agricultural and food production indexes, and production of selected commodities, by world region and country, 1974-83, annual rpt, 1524–5

Agricultural situation in Southeast Asia, by country and commodity, 1983 and outlook for 1984, annual rpt, 1524–4.5

Agricultural supply/demand, trade, and production, and socioeconomic data, by country, 1950s-77, 1528–179

AID activities and funding by project and function, FY85, and developing countries summary socioeconomic data, 1970s-83, by country, annual rpt, 9914–3

AID dev and US military assistance to Philippines, funding data, FY78-84 and proposed FY85-89, GAO rpt, 26123–54

AID economic assistance to developing countries, obligations and disbursements by country, quarterly rpt, 9912–4

AID educational program activities and project impacts in 12 developing countries, 1950s-82, 9916–11.8

AID loan repayment status and terms by program and country, and status of predecessor agency loans, quarterly rpt, 9912–3

Economic indicators of 12 Pacific Basin countries or areas and US, quarterly rpt, 9393–9

Economic, social, and political summary data, by country, 1984, annual factbook, 244–11

Economic trends in income, production, prices, employment, finances, and trade, 1984 semiannual rpt, 2046–4.16, 2046–4.93

Electric power systems equipment market and trade, and user industry operations and demand, 1984 country market research rpt, 2045–15.7

Exports and imports of US, by commodity and country, 1972-82, annual world region rpt, 244–13.5

Exports of US, detailed Schedule B commodities by country of destination, 1983, annual rpt, 2424–9

Exports of US, detailed Schedule E commodities by mode of transport and world area and country of destination, 1983, annual rpts, 2424–5

Food processing and packaging equipment market and trade, and user industry operations and demand, 1984 market research rpt, 2045–11.22

Food supply policies of 21 developing countries, with farm sector data, tariff income, and prices and imports of 5 grains, 1960s-81, 1528–168

Index by Subjects and Names

Photography

Imports of US, detailed Schedule A commodities by country and world area of origin, and mode of transport, 1983, annual rpts, 2424–2

Imports of US, detailed TSUSA commodities by country of origin, 1983, annual rpt, 2424–4

Loans and grants for economic and military assistance from US and intl agencies, by program and country, FY46-83, annual rpt, 9914–5

Military aid of US, arms sales, and training programs costs and budget requests by program, world region, and country, FY83-85, annual rpt, 7144–13

Military spending, arms trade, and armed forces size, with total govt spending and population, by country, 1972-82, annual rpt, 9824–1

Minerals Yearbook, 1982, Vol 3: foreign country reviews of production, trade, and policies, by commodity, annual rpt, 5604–35

Nuclear power plant construction and operation status, and capacity, by plant, region, State, and selected country, 1983 and projected to 2020, annual rpt, 3164–57

Pollution control instruments and equipment market and trade, and user industry operations and demand, 1984 country market research rpt, 2045–17.1

Population size and growth rates, and latest available benchmark demographic data, by country, 1950-83, biennial rpt, 2324–4

Tidal current tables, daily time and velocity by station for North America and Asia coasts, 1985, annual rpt, 2174–1.2

VA selected expenditures, by type, State, and for Puerto Rico, Philippines, and other foreign areas, FY83, annual rpt, 9924–1.9

see also under By Foreign Country in the "Index by Categories"

Phillip, P. Joseph

"Toward a Better Understanding of Hospital Occupancy Rates", 4652–1.418

Phillips, Keith R.

"Effects of Oil Prices and Exchange Rates on World Oil Consumption", 9379–1.405

Phillips, Richard A.

"Mortgage Rate Buydowns: Further Evidence", 9412–2.408

Philosophy

see Arts and the humanities

Phoenix, Ariz.

Auto dealer repair workers, wages, and benefits, by occupation, size of establishment, and for 24 labor market areas, Nov 1982 survey, 6787–6.202

Auto emissions control device tampering and fuel-switching incidence in 6 urban areas, 1983, annual rpt, 9194–15

Carbon monoxide atmospheric concentrations and levels within buildings and along commuting and residential driving routes, for 4 cities, Jan-Mar 1981, 9198–110

Census of Housing, 1980: occupancy and unit characteristics, by race, Hispanic origin, and city, SMSA rpt, 2473–1.284

Census of Population and Housing, 1980: detailed population and housing characteristics, by county, city, and census tract, SMSA rpt, 2551–2.284

Homeless population and characteristics, and temporary shelter operations, use, and user characteristics, for selected cities, various periods 1979-84, hearing, 21248–85

Housing and households detailed characteristics, and unit and neighborhood quality, by inside-outside central cities, 1981 survey, SMSA rpt, 2485–6.24

Housing unit starts and completions authorized by building permits in 20 MSAs, quarterly rpt, 2382–9

Population size of top 25 cities, 1980 and 1982, press release, 2328–46

Wages by occupation, and benefits for office and plant workers, 1984 labor market area survey rpt, 6785–3.9

see also under By City and By SMSA or MSA in the "Index by Categories"

Phonograph

County Business Patterns: establishments, employees, and payrolls, by SIC 4-digit industry and county, 1981, annual State rpt series, 2326–8

Exports and imports of US, detailed SIC-based commodities by world area, 1983, annual rpts, 2424–6

Exports and imports of US, totals and as percent of domestic production, by SIC 2- to 5-digit commodity, 1981, annual rpt, 2424–3

Exports of US, detailed commodities by country of destination, monthly rpt, 2422–3

Exports of US, detailed Schedule B commodities by country of destination, 1983, annual rpt, 2424–9

Exports of US, detailed Schedule E commodities by mode of transport and world area and country of destination, 1983, annual rpts, 2424–5

Great Lakes trade, by SITC 3-digit commodity, port, vessel type, world area, and country, 1982, annual rpt, 7744–3

Imports of US, detailed Schedule A commodities by country and world area of origin, and mode of transport, 1983, annual rpts, 2424–2

Imports of US, detailed Schedule A commodities by country, monthly rpt, 2422–2

Imports of US, detailed TSUSA commodities by country of origin, 1983, annual rpt, 2424–4

Occupational injury and illness rates, by SIC 2- to 4-digit industry, 1982, annual rpt, 6844–1

OECD trade, total and for 4 major countries, and US trade by country, by commodity, 1972-82, annual world region rpt series, 244–13

Producer prices and indexes, by stage of processing and detailed commodity, monthly rpt, 6762–6

Producer prices and indexes, by stage of processing and detailed commodity, monthly 1983, annual supplement, 6764–2

Shipments, trade, and consumption of phonograph and related equipment, by product, 1982-83, annual Current Industrial Rpt, 2506–12.20

see also Recording industry

Phonograph records

see Recording industry

Phosphate rock

see Fertilizers

see Nonmetallic minerals and mines

see Quarries and stone products

Phosphorus

see Chemicals and chemical industry

Photography

Census of Population, 1980: detailed socioeconomic and demographic characteristics, by age, sex, race, Hispanic origin, occupation, and industry, State rpt series, 2531–4

Census of Population, 1980: labor force, by sex, detailed occupation, and region, with comparison to 1970 census, supplementary rpt, 2535–1.12

China economic conditions, agricultural and industrial production, trade, and domestic and foreign investment, 1980-85, 2048–106

County Business Patterns: establishments, employees, and payrolls, by SIC 4-digit industry and county, 1981, annual State rpt series, 2326–8

County Business Patterns: establishments, employees, and payrolls, by SIC 4-digit industry and county, 1982, annual State rpt series, 2326–6

DOD procurement, prime contract awards by category, contract and contractor type, and service branch, FY74-1st half FY84, semiannual rpt, 3542–1

Employment, earnings, and hours, by selected SIC 1- to 4-digit industry, State, and for 278 major labor areas, 1939-83, annual rpt, 6744–5

Employment, earnings, and hours, by SIC 4-digit nonfarm industry, monthly 1974-Feb 1984, annual update, 6744–4

Exports and imports of photographic supplies, by world area, 1983, annual rpt, 2424–6

Exports and imports of US, totals and as percent of domestic production, by SIC 2- to 5-digit commodity, 1981, annual rpt, 2424–3

Exports of equipment, detailed Schedule B commodities by country of destination, 1983, annual rpt, 2424–9

Exports of photographic supplies, by mode of transport and world area and country of destination, 1983, annual rpts, 2424–5

Exports of US, detailed commodities by country of destination, monthly rpt, 2422–3

Foreign market and trade for graphic industries equipment, and user industry operations and demand, country market research rpts, 2045–3

Great Lakes exports and imports of photographic supplies, by port, vessel type, and country and world area, 1982, annual rpt, 7744–3

Imports of equipment, detailed TSUSA commodities by country of origin, 1983, annual rpt, 2424–4

Imports of photographic supplies, by country and world area, and method of transport, 1983, annual rpts, 2424–2

Imports of US, detailed Schedule A commodities by country, monthly rpt, 2422–2

Photography

Income tax returns of corporations, detailed income and tax items by industry, 1981, annual rpt, 8304–4

Income tax returns of sole proprietorships, detailed data by industry div and selected industry group, 1981, annual rpt, 8304–7

Income tax returns of sole proprietorships, receipts, deductions by type, payroll, and net income, by major industry, 1982, annual article, 8302–2.413

Industry finances and operations, by SIC 2- to 4-digit industry, 1970s-83 and projected to 1988, annual rpt, 2014–4

Input-output structure of US economy, detailed interindustry transactions for 537 industries, and components of final demand, 1977 benchmark data, 2708–17

Manufacturing census, 1982: financial and operating data, by SIC 2- to 4-digit industry, State, SMSA, and county, preliminary census div rpt series, 2491–3

Manufacturing census, 1982: financial and operating data, for SIC 4-digit industries by product, preliminary rpt, 2491–1.422

Natl Endowment for Arts activities and grants, FY83, annual rpt, 9564–3

Occupational injury and illness rates, by SIC 2- to 4-digit industry, 1982, annual rpt, 6844–1

Occupational manpower needs and supply by detailed occupation, and educational and training program enrollees and grads by detailed field, 1982 and 1995, biennial rpt, 6744–3

Occupational Outlook Handbook, 1984-85 biennial rpt, 6744–1

OECD trade, total and for 4 major countries, and US trade by country, by commodity, 1972-82, annual world region rpt series, 244–13

Price indexes and prices for producers of photographic equipment by detailed type, monthly 1983, annual supplement, 6762–6, 6764–2

Receipts for selected services, by SIC 2- to 4-digit kind of business, 1983, annual rpt, 2413–8

Retail trade census, 1982: employment, establishments, sales, and payroll, for camera and photographic supply stores, by State, preliminary rpt, 2395–1.32

Service industry census, 1982: employment, establishments, receipts, and payroll, by SIC 2- to 4-digit kind of business, SMSA, county, and city, State rpt series, 2391–1

Service industry census, 1982: employment, establishments, receipts, and payroll, by SIC 4-digit kind of business and State, preliminary rpt, 2390–2.3

Virgin Islands economic censuses, 1982: employment, establishments, payroll, and receipts, by SIC 1- to 4-digit industry, island, and city, 2593–1

Wages of white-collar workers, by occupation, work level, and industry div, Mar 1984, annual rpt, 6784–2

Wholesale trade sales, inventories, purchases, and gross margins, by SIC 2- to 3-digit kind of business and type of ownership, 1983, annual rpt, 2413–13

see also Instruments and measuring devices

PHS

see Public Health Service

Phung, Doan L.

"Economics of Nuclear Power: Past Record, Present Trends, and Future Prospects", 3006–7.5

Physical characteristics

see Body measurements

Physical education and training

Census of Population, 1980: labor force, by sex, detailed occupation, and region, with comparison to 1970 census, supplementary rpt, 2535–1.12

Foreign market and trade for sporting goods and recreational equipment and vehicles, country market research rpts, 2045–14

Handicapped children public education program enrollment, staff, and funding, by handicap, age, and State, 1981/82-1982/83, annual rpt, 4944–4

Health habits of adults, including physical activity, smoking, alcohol use, hypertension, and seat belt use, by age and sex, 1982, annual rpt, 4204–1.3

Teaching degrees conferred by specialty and State, required credit hours, and instn officials attitudes, by instn type, 1970s-83, hearings, 21348–89

see also Health education

see also Sports and athletics

Physical sciences

Degrees conferred in higher education, by race, Hispanic origin, sex, level, and field, selected years 1949/50-1979/80, annual rpt, 4824–2.16

DOE R&D projects and funding at natl labs, universities, and other instns, annual summary rpts, 3004–18

High school classes of 1980 and 1982: educational and sociodemographic characteristics and expectations, natl longitudinal study, series, 4826–2

NASA R&D funding to colleges and universities, by State, field of science, and instn, FY83, annual listing, 9504–7

NOAA scientific and technical publications, monthly listing, 2142–1

NSF grant and award recipients, by State, FY83, annual listing, 9624–11

NSF research programs, activities, and funding, FY82-83, annual rpt, 9624–6

Occupational Outlook Handbook, 1984-85 biennial rpt, 6744–1

R&D and science-related Fed Govt funding and total and federally funded expenditures of universities and colleges, by instn and field of science, FY82, 9626–2.136

R&D and science-related Fed Govt funding to higher education and nonprofit instns, by field, instn, agency, and State, FY82, annual rpt, 9627–17

R&D-employed scientists and engineers salaries by degree, type of establishment, age, experience, and field, 1984, annual rpt, 3004–1

R&D equipment at higher education instns, age, cost, funding sources, and users, for computer and physical sciences and engineering, 1982, 9626–2.138

R&D expenditures by higher education instns and federally funded centers, by field, source of funds, instn, and State, FY82, annual rpt, 9627–13

R&D expenditures by source, and scientists education and employment, detailed data by field, selected years 1953-84, annual rpt, 9624–18

Index by Subjects and Names

R&D expenditures of higher education instns, and science and engineering employment and grad students, by field, 1972-83, biennial rpt, 9627–24

R&D Fed Govt facilities and services available for private sector use, by field of science, 1984 biennial listing, 2224–4

R&D Fed Govt funding, by function, agency, and program, selected years FY80-84 and proposed FY85, 26308–46

R&D Fed Govt funding for all performers, by field and supporting agency, selected years FY60-84, annual rpt, 9627–20

R&D funding by industry, program, and Federal agency, and high-technology trade performance, selected years 1960-FY84, 26306–6.77

Science and engineering doctoral degree recipients, by field, sex, race, age, citizenship, postgrad employment and study status, State, and instn, 1960-82, 9626–6.16

Science and engineering grad enrollment, fields of study, financial support, and other student and instn characteristics, 1975-82, annual survey, 9627–7

Science and engineering grad program enrollment, by field, degree level, source of financial support, race, and Hispanic origin, 1975-81, 9626–2.134

Science and engineering grad program enrollment by field, sources of financial support, and foreign students, 1975-82, 9626–2.141

Science and engineering grads of 1980-81, employment and median salaries by level and field of degree, 1982, 9626–2.137

Science and engineering grads of 1980-81, employment characteristics or grad enrollment, by degree level, field, sex, and race, 1982, 9627–25

Scientists and engineers employed at universities and colleges, by field, sex, and instn, 1973-82, 9626–2.140

Scientists and engineers employed at universities and colleges, by field, sex, State, and instn, Jan 1983 and selected trends from 1967, annual survey, 9627–11

Scientists and engineers employed in energy-related fields, supply/demand and effects of R&D funding, by energy type, employer type, field, and age, 1962-91, annual rpt, 3004–19

Scientists and engineers employment by sector and activity, and share female, black, and Asian descent, by field, 1982, 9626–2.142

Scientists and engineers supply, employment, and education, by sex, race, Hispanic origin, and field, selected years 1965-83, biennial rpt, 9624–20

Scientists, engineers, and technicians employed in private industry, by occupation and industry group, 1980-81, biennial rpt, 9627–23

Scientists, engineers, and technicians needed in defense and nondefense industries, and supply/demand, by field, 1981-87, 9628–71

see also Astronomy

see also Chemistry

see also Earth sciences

see also Environmental sciences

Index by Subjects and Names

Physicians

see also Geography
see also Mathematics
see also Oceanography
see also Physics

Physical therapy

Census of Population, 1980: detailed socioeconomic and demographic characteristics, by age, sex, race, Hispanic origin, occupation, and industry, State rpt series, 2531–4

Census of Population, 1980: labor force, by sex, detailed occupation, and region, with comparison to 1970 census, supplementary rpt, 2535–1.12

DOD medical personnel, trainees, and accessions by source, by occupation, specialty, and service branch, FY83, annual rpt, 3544–24

Handicapped children public education program enrollment, staff, and funding, by handicap, age, and State, 1981/82-1982/83, annual rpt, 4944–4

Health care services of selected medical practitioners, use by patient characteristics, 1980 survey with trends from 1963, 4146–12.4

Hospital employment, vacancies, and vacancy rates, by occupation and by hospital specialty, region, census div, and State, 1980, annual rpt, 4114–12

Hospital worker wages by sex and occupation, and benefits, for 22 MSAs, Oct 1981 survey, 6787–6.201

Manpower supply of physical therapists, by sex, 1978-82 and projected 1983-90, biennial rpt, 4114–8

Medicare-participating facilities by control, beds, and terminated facilities, by facility type, region, and State, 1975-81, 4656–1.19

Occupational manpower needs and supply by detailed occupation, and educational and training program enrollees and grads by detailed field, 1982 and 1995, biennial rpt, 6744–3

Occupational Outlook Handbook, 1984-85 biennial rpt, 6744–1

Youth office visits to physicians by patient and visit characteristics and physician specialty, and drug mentions by brand, 1980-81, 4146–8.100

Physically handicapped

see Blind
see Deaf
see Disabled and handicapped persons

Physicians

Allergy and Infectious Diseases Natl Inst activities, grants by instn, State, and country, and disease incidence and costs, FY60s-84, annual rpt, 4474–30

Births attended by midwives and in nonhospital settings, by mother's sociodemographic and prenatal care characteristics and infant race and birthweight, 1978-79 with trends from 1935, 4147–21.40

Births, by birth weight, Apgar score, infant and mother characteristics, birthplace, and attendant, 1978, article, 4102–1.414

Black medical residents by specialty, and minority medical faculty by race and Hispanic origin, selected years 1980-83, article, 4102–1.412

Breast-fed infants, by characteristics of mother and source of prenatal care, various periods 1970-75, article, 4102–1.442

Canada and US hospital use by children by Canada Province and US region, and death rates, by diagnosis and sex, selected years 1977-79, 4147–5.1

Census of Population, 1980: detailed socioeconomic and demographic characteristics, by age, sex, race, Hispanic origin, occupation, and industry, State rpt series, 2531–4

Census of Population, 1980: labor force, by sex, detailed occupation, and region, with comparison to 1970 census, supplementary rpt, 2535–1.12

Colorectal cancer screening, family physicians attitudes toward use of guaiac slide test, 1982 New York State survey, article, 4102–1.433

Contact lens price and adverse lens-associated eye conditions related to fitting by ophthalomologists, opticians, and optometrists, 1977-80, 9408–49

Contacts with physicians, for 9 diagnoses, weekly rpt, monthly data, 4202–1

County and City Data Book, detailed socioeconomic and demographic data for States, counties, and cities, selected years 1976-82, 2328–1

County Business Patterns: establishments, employees, and payrolls, by SIC 4-digit industry and county, 1981, annual State rpt series, 2326–8

County Business Patterns: establishments, employees, and payrolls, by SIC 4-digit industry and county, 1982, annual State rpt series, 2326–6

DOD medical personnel, trainees, and accessions by source, by occupation, specialty, and service branch, FY83, annual rpt, 3544–24

Drugs prescribed or provided by office-based physicians most often, by patient, physician, and drug characteristics, 1981, series, 4146–8

Employment, earnings, and hours, by SIC 4-digit nonfarm industry, monthly 1974-Feb 1984, annual update, 6744–4

Employment in hospitals and nursing homes, total and in selected occupations, by facility bed size, ownership, region, and State, selected years 1969-80, 4147–14.30

Eye care visits and use of corrective lenses by type, by patient and family characteristics, visit location, and specialist type, 1979-80 with selected trends from 1965, 4147–10.145

Foreign and US health care resources, use, and per capita public expenditures, and selected population characteristics, for 7 countries, selected years 1975-81, 21148–33

Health care expenditures, methodology of natl survey of households, physicians, health insurance firms, and employers, 1977-79, series, 4186–4

Health care expenditures, natl survey on services use, costs, and sources of payment, by patient and physician characteristics, 1977-78, series, 4186–3

Health Care Financing Review, Medicare and Medicaid program activity, health care expenditures, and research, quarterly rpt with articles, 4652–1

Health condition and health care resources, use, and expenditures, 1970s-82 with trends and projections 1900-2000, annual compilation, 4144–11

Health maintenance organizations and prepaid health plans enrollment, use, and Fed Govt aid, FY83, annual rpt, 4104–8

Health maintenance organizations enrollment (total, Medicare, and Medicaid), finances, Fed Govt qualification status, and PHS loan activity, by HMO, FY83, annual rpt, 4044–2

Heart, Lung, and Blood Natl Inst activities and funding, with morbidity and mortality data, various periods 1940-88, annual rpt, 4474–22

Hispanic Americans health services use, illness rates, and disability days, by socioeconomic characteristics, and compared to blacks and whites, 1978-80, 4147–10.147

Hospital employment, vacancies, and vacancy rates, by occupation and by hospital specialty, region, census div, and State, 1980, annual rpt, 4114–12

Income tax returns of corporations, detailed income and tax items by industry, 1981, annual rpt, 8304–4

Income tax returns of partnerships, detailed data by industry, 1981 estimates, annual article, 8302–2.404

Income tax returns of partnerships, receipts by source, deductions by type, and establishments, by selected industry, 1982, annual article, 8302–2.416

Income tax returns of sole proprietorships, detailed data by industry div and selected industry group, 1981, annual rpt, 8304–7

Income tax returns of sole proprietorships, receipts, deductions by type, payroll, and net income, by major industry, 1982, annual article, 8302–2.413

Income tax returns with investment credits, for individuals by income, and for sole proprietorships by industry, 1981, article, 8302–2.409

Input-output structure of US economy, detailed interindustry transactions for 537 industries, and components of final demand, 1977 benchmark data, 2708–17

License sanctions of health professionals in 3 States, and subsequent Medicare and Medicaid program participation, by specialty, 1977-82, GAO rpt, 26121–80

Manpower supply and education of health professionals, by occupation, demographic and professional characteristics, and location, 1950s-83 and projected to 2000, biennial rpt, 4114–8

Medicare aged beneficiaries medical care by usual source, and untreated health conditions, by sociodemographic characteristics, 1980, 4146–12.3

Medicare and Medicaid eligibility, participation, covered services and use, and reimbursements and payments, various periods 1966-82, annual rpt, 4654–1

Medicare claims approved, total charges, and reimbursements by type of service, from 1974, monthly rpt, quarterly data, 4742–1.11

Medicare physician charges and reimbursement by enrollee characteristics and carrier, payment limits effects on charges in California, and physician earnings, by specialty, 1950s-84, 25368–127

Physicians

Medicare reimbursement rates in Massachusetts, and rates used and physicians not certified in designated specialty by selected carrier, various periods 1981-82, GAO rpt, 26121–82

Medicare Supplementary Medical Insurance maximum charges reimbursable for specific services, by State and outlying area, 1983, annual rpt, 4654–4

Mental health facilities, services, staff, and patient characteristics, 1970s-82 with trends from 1954, annual rpt, 4504–9

Military reserve forces medical personnel and wartime requirements by occupation, and medical equipment costs, by reserve component, as of 1983, annual rpt, 3544–27.2

Minority group and women employment and training in health professions, by field, selected years 1962/63-1983/84, 4118–18

Navy and Marine Corps disease incidence, medical care, and deaths, by detailed diagnosis, and medical personnel and workloads, 1978-79, annual rpt, 3804–1

Navy personnel, detailed statistics, quarterly rpt, 3802–4

Occupational manpower needs and supply by detailed occupation, and educational and training program enrollees and grads by detailed field, 1982 and 1995, biennial rpt, 6744–3

Occupational Outlook Handbook, 1984-85 biennial rpt, 6744–1

Older persons by demographic, socioeconomic, and health characteristics, selected years 1900-81 and projected to 2050, Current Population Rpt, 2546–2.125

Older persons nutrition services program operations and assessment, and participant sociodemographic, health, and diet characteristics, 1976 and 1982, 4608–16

Older persons physician visits by age group, projected 1980-2050, and health care expenditures by type, 1981, annual rpt, 25144–3.1

Prison physicians by sociodemographic, employment, and professional characteristics, and compared to all physicians, 1979, article, 4102–1.407

Puerto Rico educational enrollment, finance, completions, curricula, and personnel by instn, and health and vital statistics, selected years 1970-83, hearings, 21348–93

R&D-employed scientists and engineers salaries by degree, type of establishment, age, experience, and field, 1984, annual rpt, 3004–1

Receipts for selected services, by SIC 2- to 4-digit kind of business, 1983, annual rpt, 2413–8

Reporting of communicable diseases to public health depts, physician reasons for underreporting, 1982 survey, article, 4102–1.411

Research activities and grants of HCFA by research area, as of June 1984, semiannual listing, 4652–8

Senegal rural health care projects of AID, mgmt and effectiveness, 1978-83, 9916–3.20

Service industry census, 1982: employment, establishments, receipts, and payroll, by SIC 2- to 4-digit kind of business, SMSA, county, and city, State rpt series, 2391–1

Service industry census, 1982: employment, establishments, receipts, and payroll, by SIC 4-digit kind of business and State, preliminary rpt, 2390–2.14

South Carolina manufacturing plants with selected employee health care services, by SIC 2-digit industry, 1982, article, 4102–1.408

Southeastern States health care resource availability, and employment by occupation, by facility type, by State and SMSA in Fed Reserve 6th District, 1970s-81, article, 9371–1.425

Statistical Abstract of US, social, political, and economic data, 1950s-83 and trends, annual rpt, 2324–1.1

Supplementary Security Income beneficiary socioeconomic characteristics and health service use, 1970s-83 and SSI program projections to 1995, 25148–29

Supply of physicians and ratio to population by State and county population size, and counties with shortages and needs, 1960-79 and projected 1982-94, 4118–52

Traffic accidents and casualties detailed direct and indirect costs, by characteristics of persons and vehicles involved, 1979-80, 7768–80

VA employment of general and medical personnel, FY59-83, annual rpt, 9924–13.1

VA facilities patients with speech disorders, by severity, patient characteristics, diagnostician occupation, and facility type, FY81, 9926–1.17

VA facilities psychological services, staffing, research, and training programs, 1984 annual listing, 9924–10

VA Medicine and Surgery Dept employment, by medical district and facility, monthly rpt, quarterly data, 9922–5.3

VA Medicine and Surgery Dept trainees, by detailed program and city, FY83, annual rpt, 9924–21

VA physicians, dentists, and nurses, by age, selected employment characteristics, and VA district, quarterly rpt, 9922–11

VA physicians, dentists, and nurses pay rates by grade, as of Jan 1984, 21628–54

Veterans and nonveterans health condition, and veteran use of VA and non-VA hospitals by disease, by age, race, income, and metro-nonmetro location, various periods 1971-81, 9926–1.18

Visits to physicians and dentists, by age, metro-nonmetro location, region, and selected SMSA, 1980-81, 4147–10.146

Visits to physicians, by reason, diagnosis, treatment, and characteristics of patient and physician, Vital and Health Statistics series, 4147–13

Visits to physicians for new pain symptoms, by diagnosis, physician specialty, and patient characteristics, and drugs prescribed or used, 1980-81, 4146–8.97

Widows with minor children receiving OASI survivor benefits, health insurance coverage and health care services and expenses, 1976-78, article, 4742–1.404

Workers compensation law provisions of States and Fed Govt, by jurisdiction, as of July 1984, semiannual rpt, 6502–1

see also Coroners

Index by Subjects and Names

see also Foreign medical graduates
see also Medical education
see also Medical ethics
see also Obstetrics and gynecology
see also Orthopedics
see also Osteopathy
see also Pathology
see also Pediatrics
see also Podiatry
see also Psychiatry
see also Radiology
see also Surgeons and surgery

Physicians assistants

see Allied health personnel

Physics

Census of Population, 1980: detailed socioeconomic and demographic characteristics, by age, sex, race, Hispanic origin, occupation, and industry, State rpt series, 2531–4

High school class of 1982: science and math coursework and assessment, by sociodemographic and school characteristics and educational goal, 4826–2.14

NSF grant and award recipients, by State, FY83, annual listing, 9624–11

Nuclear industry nongovt employment by industry segment, occupation, and census div, and DOE and NRC nuclear employment, 1968-83, biennial rpt, 3004–11

Occupational Outlook Handbook, 1984-85 biennial rpt, 6744–1

R&D-employed scientists and engineers salaries by degree, type of establishment, age, experience, and field, 1984, annual rpt, 3004–1

R&D expenditures by higher education instns and federally funded centers, by field, source of funds, instn, and State, FY82, annual rpt, 9627–13

R&D expenditures by source, and scientists education and employment, detailed data by field, selected years 1953-84, annual rpt, 9624–18

R&D expenditures of higher education instns, and science and engineering employment and grad students, by field, 1972-83, biennial rpt, 9627–24

R&D Fed Govt funding for all performers, by field and supporting agency, selected years FY60-84, annual rpt, 9627–20

Science and engineering doctoral degree recipients, by field, sex, race, age, citizenship, postgrad employment and study status, State, and instn, 1960-82, 9626–6.16

Science and engineering grad enrollment, fields of study, financial support, and other student and instn characteristics, 1975-82, annual survey, 9627–7

Science and engineering grads of 1980-81, employment characteristics or grad enrollment, by degree level, field, sex, and race, 1982, 9627–25

Scientists and engineers employed at universities and colleges, by field, sex, State, and instn, Jan 1983 and selected trends from 1967, annual survey, 9627–11

Scientists and engineers employed in energy-related fields, supply/demand and effects of R&D funding, by energy type, employer type, field, and age, 1962-91, annual rpt, 3004–19

Index by Subjects and Names

Scientists, engineers, and technicians employed in private industry, by occupation and industry group, 1980-81, biennial rpt, 9627–23

Scientists, engineers, and technicians needed in defense and nondefense industries, and supply/demand, by field, 1981-87, 9628–71

see also Electromagnetic radiation
see also Nuclear radiation
see also Weights and measures

Physiology

Cocaine use, user characteristics, medical and botanical research, and South American production and legal policy and enforcement, 1979 intl conf papers, 7008–40

FAA aviation medicine research and studies, technical rpt series, 7506–10

General Medical Sciences Natl Inst research programs and funding, FY83, annual rpt, 4474–12

NSF research programs, activities, and funding, FY82-83, annual rpt, 9624–6

Science and engineering doctoral degree recipients, by field, sex, race, age, citizenship, postgrad employment and study status, State, and instn, 1960-82, 9626–6.16

Science and engineering grad enrollment, fields of study, financial support, and other student and instn characteristics, 1975-82, annual survey, 9627–7

Pickrel, Evan W.

"Color Perception and ATC Job Performance", 7506–10.26

Pickrell, Don H.

"Causes of Rising Transit Operating Deficits", 7308–184

Pierce, David A.

"Four Discussions", 9366–6.75

"Transmission of Data Noise into Policy Noise in Monetary Control", 9366–6.74

Piet, Patrick

"Partnership Returns for 1981 Reflect Tax Shelter Activity", 8302–2.404

"Partnership Returns, 1982", 8302–2.416

Pigments

see Chemicals and chemical industry
see Paints and varnishes

Pigott, Charles

"Indicators of Long-Term Real Interest Rates", 9393–8.406

Pigs

see Livestock and livestock industry

Pilots

Active pilot and nonpilot certificates held and issued, by type of certificate, region, State, and for women, 1983, annual rpt, 7504–1.7

Active pilots and nonpilots, by type of certificate, age, sex, region, and State, 1983, annual rpt, 7504–2

Active pilots, total and per registered aircraft, by State, 1983, annual rpt, 7504–3

Aircraft accident circumstances and severity, by type of flying and aircraft, 1981, annual rpt, 9614–3

Aircraft collisions, and near collisions by circumstances and State, by type of aircraft, various periods 1980-84, 7508–61

Airline and general aviation accident circumstances, severity, and causes, for US operations of domestic and foreign aircraft, periodic rpt, 9612–1

Airline pilots terminated for medical reasons and reinstated by carrier, and aircraft accidents by age of flight crew, selected years 1960-81, hearing, 21148–34

Alcohol-related fatal accidents of comuter airlines, air taxis, and general aviation, by pilot characteristics and circumstances, 1975-81, 9618–11

Aviation traffic, aircraft, pilots, airport activity, and fuel use, forecast FY84-95 with FY79-83 trends, annual rpt, 7504–6

Census of Population, 1980: labor force, by sex, detailed occupation, and region, with comparison to 1970 census, supplementary rpt, 2535–1.12

Commuter air carriers and air taxi accidents by seating capacity and cause, and deaths, 1975-82, GAO rpt, 26113–116

FAA aviation medicine research and studies, technical rpt series, 7506–10

Instrument-rated and total pilots under FAA Natl Airspace System Plan, 1982-2000, annual rpt, 7504–12

Natl Guard (Army and Air) activities, manpower, and facilities, FY83, annual rpt, 3704–3

Occupational Outlook Handbook, 1984-85 biennial rpt, 6744–1

Veterans education assistance program participation and costs under GI Bill and other programs, WW II through Sept 1983, annual rpt, 9924–22

Pine Bluff, Ark.

Census of Housing, 1980: occupancy and unit characteristics, by race, Hispanic origin, and city, SMSA rpt, 2473–1.285

Census of Population and Housing, 1980: detailed population and housing characteristics, by county, city, and census tract, SMSA rpt, 2551–2.285

Housing vacancy rates for single and multifamily units and mobile homes, by city and ZIP code, 1984, annual metro area rpt, 9304–19.26

Wages of office and plant workers, by occupation, 1984 labor market area survey rpt, 6785–3.2

see also under By SMSA or MSA in the "Index by Categories"

Pinellas County, Fla.

Home mortgage creative financing, effect on home sales price, model results for Pinellas County, Fla, 1981/82, article, 9412–2.406

Pinn, Vivian W.

"Underrepresented in Graduate Medical Education and Medical Research", 4102–1.412

Pipelines

Accident deaths in transportation, by mode, 1982-83, annual summary rpt, 9614–6

Accident investigations and recommendations by Natl Transportation Safety Board, 1983, annual rpt, 9614–1

Bridges over navigable waters, with type of bridge and use, owner, dimensions, and location, 1984 regional listing series, 7406–5

Census of Population, 1980: detailed socioeconomic and demographic characteristics, by age, sex, race, Hispanic origin, occupation, and industry, State rpt series, 2531–4

China economic conditions, agricultural and industrial production, trade, and domestic and foreign investment, 1980-85, 2048–106

Coal production and stocks by district, and shipments by district of origin, State of destination, consuming sector, and mode of transport, quarterly rpt, 3162–8

Coal supply and Fed Govt coal leases, by owner, industry, and western State, various periods 1950-82 and projected to 2000, hearing, 25318–58

Coal transport environmental impacts by type and mode of transport, methodology for assessing alternative systems, 1983 rpt, 3408–28

Coastal environmental characteristics, fish, wildlife, and use, and population socioeconomic data, for individual areas, series, 5506–4

Communist, OECD, and selected other countries freight and carrier inventories, by mode of transport, 1960s-83, annual rpt, 244–5.10

Construction industries census, 1982: financial and operating data, by SIC 4-digit industry and State, preliminary rpt series, 2371–1

Construction put in place, permits authorized by region, State, and MSA, and Federal contract awards, by construction type, bimonthly rpt with articles, 2012–1

Construction put in place, value of new public and private structures, by type, monthly rpt, 2382–4

County Business Patterns: establishments, employees, and payrolls, by SIC 4-digit industry and county, 1981, annual State rpt series, 2326–8

County Business Patterns: establishments, employees, and payrolls, by SIC 4-digit industry and county, 1982, annual State rpt series, 2326–6

Defense Fuel Supply Center procurement, prices, stocks, transport, and other activities and finances, FY83, annual rpt, 3904–8

DOD shipments of military and personal property, loss claims, passenger traffic, and costs, by mode of transport, quarterly rpt, 3702–1

DOT grant awards for transportation planning and safety programs, by region, State, and for 35 largest SMSAs, FY83, annual rpt, 7304–7

Employment, earnings, and hours, by SIC 4-digit nonfarm industry, monthly 1974-Feb 1984, annual update, 6744–4

Energy producers finances and operations, by energy type for US firms domestic and foreign operations, 1974-82, annual rpt, 3164–44.1

Energy production, dev, and distribution firms revenues and income, quarterly rpt, 3162–38

Energy use in transportation sector by mode, fuel supplies, and demographic and economic determinants of vehicle use, 1970s-83, annual rpt, 3304–5

Fed Govt aid to State and local govts, expenditures, and direct payments, by program, agency, and State, FY83, annual rpt, 2464–2

Fed Govt reclamation projects in western US, electric power capacities and transmission miles, and water storage and carriage facilities, by State, FY81, annual rpt, 5824–1.1

Pipelines

Finances, operations, vehicles, equipment, accidents, and energy use, by mode of transport, 1955-84, annual rpt, 7304-2

Foreign economic, social, and political summary data, by country, 1984, annual factbook, 244-11

Govt transportation revenues by source and expenditures, by level of govt and mode of transport, and Fed Govt aid by type, FY77-82, 7308-185

Industry finances and operations, by SIC 2- to 4-digit industry, 1970s-83 and projected to 1988, annual rpt, 2014-4

Input-output structure of US economy, detailed interindustry transactions for 537 industries, and components of final demand, 1977 benchmark data, 2708-17

Minority group and women employment, by occupational group and SIC 2- to 3-digit industry, 1981, annual rpt, 9244-1.1

Natural and supplemental gas production, prices, trade, use, reserves, and pipeline company finances, by firm and State, monthly rpt with articles, 3162-4

Natural gas and hazardous liquid pipelines accidents and casualties, and DOT and State govt safety activities, 1982, annual rpt, 7304-5

Natural gas and liquid pipeline failures, deaths, and injuries, 1970-80, annual rpt, 7304-1

Natural gas composition and occurrence of helium, analyses of samples from individual wells and pipelines in 26 States and 2 countries, 1983, annual survey, 5604-2

Natural gas interstate pipeline company detailed financial and operating data, by firm, 1983, annual rpt, 3164-38

Natural gas interstate pipeline company sales and price trends, monthly rpt, 3162-24.4, 3162-24.9

Natural gas interstate pipeline company supplies, reserves, production, purchases, and contracts, by firm, 1983 with projected deliverability to 2003, annual rpt, 3164-33

Natural gas interstate pipeline sales, total and under minimum fee contract provision, by service type, contract date, and region, 1981, 3168-91

Natural gas pipeline and compressor station construction costs, 1979-82, annual rpt, 3084-3

Natural gas pipeline rate increases and rate applications, and FERC activities and funding by program, FY83 annual rpt, 3084-9

Natural gas prices, reserves, consumption, and production, projected under alternative price controls 1983-95 with market data for various periods 1970-Mar 1984, 3008-96

Natural gas privately owned utilities, wages and employment by occupation, and benefits, by region, Oct 1982 survey, 6787-6.205

Natural gas supply, contract prices, pipeline operations and finances, and residential use, various periods 1966-1983/84, 3168-89

Natural gas utilities and pipelines in Iowa, financial and operating data, selected years 1969-81, hearings, 23848-177

Natural gas volume and prices for interstate pipeline market activities, and price decontrol effects, 1978-80s, 3168-50

Oil and gas OCS reserves of Fed Govt, leasing and exploration activities, production, revenues, and costs, by ocean region, FY83, annual rpt, 5734-4

Oil and refined products stocks, and interdistrict shipments by mode of transport, monthly rpt, 3162-6.2

Oil and refined products stocks, and interdistrict shipments by mode of transport, 1983, annual rpt, 3164-2

Oil pipeline industry competition, market shares and throughput capacity by firm and market area, as of 1983, 6008-18

Oil spills from US OCS platforms and pipelines, and from tankers at sea and in port worldwide, various periods 1964-80, 5738-1

Productivity, hours, and employment indexes for selected SIC 3- and 4-digit industries, 1954-82, annual rpt, 6824-1.4

Safety programs, and accidents, injuries, deaths, hazards, and property damage, by mode of transport, 1983, annual rpt, 7304-19

Safety regulations enforcement of DOT and States by pipeline type and State, and accidents and commodity losses, selected years 1973-FY84, GAO rpt, 26113-130

Scientists, engineers, and technicians employment in transportation, utilities, and retail and wholesale trade, by field of science and industry, 1982, 9628-72

Water pollution fish kills, by State, location, and pollution source, monthly 1978-80, annual rpt, 9204-3

Water storage and carriage facilities of Reclamation Bur, by type, as of Sept 1983, annual listing, 5824-7

see also Trans-Alaska Pipeline System

Pistols

see Firearms

Pitcher, C. B.

"Directory of National Trade Associations, Professional Societies, and Labor Unions of the Construction and Building Materials Industries", 2012-1.405

"Energy Use and Conservation in the Construction Materials Industries", 2012-1.401

Pittsburgh and Lake Erie Railroad

Finances and operations of 7 commuter rail systems, and public agency cost reimbursement, 1980, 7888-61

Pittsburgh, Pa.

Auto dealer repair workers, wages, and benefits, by occupation, size of establishment, and for 24 labor market areas, Nov 1982 survey, 6787-6.202

Census of Housing, 1980: occupancy and unit characteristics, by race, Hispanic origin, and city, SMSA rpt, 2473-1.286

Census of Population and Housing, 1980: detailed population and housing characteristics, by county, city, and census tract, SMSA rpt, 2551-2.287

CPI by component for US city average, and by region, population size, and for 28 SMSAs, monthly press release, 6762-1

CPI by detailed component, for US city average, 28 SMSAs, and 4 regions by population size, monthly rpt, 6762-2

Index by Subjects and Names

Employment in traditional and high technology industry by occupation, and wages by industry, for Massachusetts and compared to US and 3 SMSAs, various periods 1976-82, article, 9373-1.416

Fruit and vegetable shipments, and arrivals in 23 US and 5 Canada cities, by mode of transport and State or country of origin, 1983, annual rpt, 1311-4.1

Homeless population and characteristics, and temporary shelter operations, use, and user characteristics, for selected cities, various periods 1979-84, hearing, 21248-85

Housing (rental) unit choice of Pittsburgh, Pa, recent movers related to unit, neighborhood, and town characteristics, 1967 survey, 9306-1.7

Housing and households detailed characteristics, and unit and neighborhood quality, by inside-outside central cities, 1981 survey, SMSA rpt, 2485-6.25

Wages of office and plant workers, by occupation, 1984 SMSA survey rpt, 6785-11.1

Waterborne commerce of US (domestic and foreign), freight by commodity, traffic, and passengers, by port and waterway, 1982, annual rpt, 3754-3.2

see also under By City and By SMSA or MSA in the "Index by Categories"

Pittsfield, Mass.

Census of Housing, 1980: occupancy and unit characteristics, by race, Hispanic origin, and city, SMSA rpt, 2473-1.287

Census of Population and Housing, 1980: detailed population and housing characteristics, by county, city, and census tract, SMSA rpt, 2551-2.287

see also under By SMSA or MSA in the "Index by Categories"

Place of birth

see Birthplace

Placek, Paul J.

"Electronic Fetal Monitoring in Relation to Cesarean Section Delivery, for Live Births and Stillbirths in the U.S., 1980", 4102-1.424

"Maternal and Infant Characteristics Associated with Cesarean Section Delivery", 4144-11.1

Planned parenthood

see Family planning

Planning

see City and town planning

see Economic policy

see Health planning and evaluation

see Military strategy

see Regional planning

Plants and equipment

see Business firms and establishments, number

see Capital investments, general

see Capital investments, specific industries

see Industrial plants and equipment

see Power-generating plants and equipment

Plants and vegetation

Acid rain causes and effects, air pollutant emissions by source in US and selected countries, control costs, and Fed Govt research funding, 1960s-82, 3408-27

Air pollution and acid rain environmental effects, and methods of neutralizing acidified water bodies, summary research rpt series, 5506-5

Index by Subjects and Names

Plastics and plastics industry

Alaska Arctic Natl Wildlife Refuge resources, resident and visitor activities, and environmental impacts of energy exploration, 1983, annual update rpt, 5504–26

Biotechnology commercial uses, R&D funding and output, controls, and industry financial and operating data, for US and 5 countries, 1970s-83 and estimated 1984-85, 26358–98

Carbon dioxide atmospheric levels, climatic effects and impacts of fossil and synthetic fuels use, deforestation, and land use patterns, research rpt series, 3406–3

Coastal environmental and wildlife characteristics, use, and mgmt, for individual ecosystems, series, 5506–9

Coastal environmental characteristics, fish, wildlife, and use, and population socioeconomic data, for individual areas, series, 5506–4

Cocaine use, user characteristics, medical and botanical research, and South American production and legal policy and enforcement, 1979 intl conf papers, 7008–40

DOE R&D projects and funding at natl labs, universities, and other instns, FY83, annual summary rpt, 3004–18.1

Endangered animals and plants foreign trade including reexports of live specimens and products, by purpose, country, and species, 1982, annual rpt, 5504–19

Exports of US, detailed commodities by country of destination, monthly rpt, 2422–3

Genetic resource (plant and animal) conservation, commercial uses, causes of depletion, and geographic sources, 1984 rpt, 5548–13

Imports of US, detailed Schedule A commodities by country, monthly rpt, 2422–2

Natl Forest System wildlife habitat and fishery improvements, use, and game population and harvest by species and forest, by region, FY83, annual rpt, 1204–31

R&D in botany and other plant sciences at higher education instns, funding by source, grad students, and staff, 1983, 9626–2.143

Radionuclide concentrations in air, water, and biota near Nevada and other nuclear test sites, and in milk from western States, by location, 1983, annual rpt, 9234–4

see also Botany

see also Farms and farmland

see also Flowers and nursery products

see also Forests and forestry

see also Horticulture

see also Pasture and rangeland

see also Wetlands

Plastics and plastics industry

Acrylic sheet from Taiwan at less than fair value, imports injury to US industry, investigation with background financial and operating data, 1984 rpt, 9886–14.105

Bottles (plastic) production by end use, and shipments, 1983, annual rpt, 2506–8.10

Business statistics, detailed data for major industries and economic indicators, *Survey of Current Business,* monthly rpt, 2702–1.9

Census of Population, 1980: detailed socioeconomic and demographic characteristics, by age, sex, race, Hispanic origin, occupation, and industry, State rpt series, 2531–4

China economic conditions, agricultural and industrial production, trade, and domestic and foreign investment, 1980-85, 2048–106

China exports and imports by SITC 1- to 5-digit commodity, 1970s-82, annual rpt, 244–12

Collective bargaining agreements expiring during year, covered workers by SIC 2-digit industry, firm, and union, with summary of key provisions, 1984, annual rpt, 6784–9

Communist, OECD, and selected other countries consumer and producer goods production, 1960s-83, annual rpt, 244–5.7

County Business Patterns: establishments, employees, and payrolls, by SIC 4-digit industry and county, 1981, annual State rpt series, 2326–8

County Business Patterns: establishments, employees, and payrolls, by SIC 4-digit industry and county, 1982, annual State rpt series, 2326–6

Earnings by major industry group, and personal income per capita and by source, by region and State, 1929-82, 2708–40

Employment, earnings, and hours, by selected SIC 1- to 4-digit industry, State, and for 278 major labor areas, 1939-83, annual rpt, 6744–5

Employment, earnings, and hours, by SIC 4-digit nonfarm industry, monthly 1974-Feb 1984, annual update, 6744–4

Exports and imports of US, by commodity group, world area, selected country, US coastal area and port, and mode of transport, with seasonal adjustments, monthly rpt, 2422–9

Exports and imports of US, detailed SIC-based commodities by world area, 1983, annual rpts, 2424–6

Exports and imports of US, totals and as percent of domestic production, by SIC 2- to 5-digit commodity, 1981, annual rpt, 2424–3

Exports of manufactured and agricultural commodities, manufacturing production, and export-related employment, 1960s-82, State rpt series, 2046–3

Exports of US, detailed commodities by country of destination, monthly rpt, 2422–3

Exports of US, detailed Schedule B commodities by country of destination, 1983, annual rpt, 2424–9

Exports of US, detailed Schedule E commodities by mode of transport and world area and country of destination, 1983, annual rpts, 2424–5

Finances and operations, by SIC 2- to 4-digit industry, 1970s-83 and projected to 1988, annual rpt, 2014–4

Financial statements for manufacturing, mining, and trade corporations, by selected SIC 2- to 3-digit industry, quarterly rpt, 2502–1

Footwear imports of US, by category, value class, and selected country, monthly rpt, 2042–29

Footwear production, shipments, trade, and consumption, by product, 1983, annual Current Industrial Rpt, 2506–6.8

Great Lakes trade, by SITC 3-digit commodity, port, vessel type, world area, and country, 1982, annual rpt, 7744–3

Hose and belting shipments, by detailed product class, 1983, annual Current Industrial Rpt, 2506–8.12

Imports of US, detailed Schedule A commodities by country and world area of origin, and mode of transport, 1983, annual rpts, 2424–2

Imports of US, detailed Schedule A commodities by country, monthly rpt, 2422–2

Imports of US, detailed TSUSA commodities by country of origin, 1983, annual rpt, 2424–4

Income tax returns of corporations, detailed income and tax items by industry, 1981, annual rpt, 8304–4

Income tax returns of corporations with foreign tax credit, income and deductions by type, asset size, and selected industry group, 1980, article, 8302–2.415

Input-output structure of US economy, detailed interindustry transactions for 85 industries, and components of final demand, 1977, article, 2702–1.421

Input-output structure of US economy, detailed interindustry transactions for 537 industries, and components of final demand, 1977 benchmark data, 2708–17

Machines for plastic and rubber molding trade, tariffs, and industry operating data, foreign and US, 1979-83, TSUSA commodity rpt, 9885–6.61

Manufacturing census, 1982: financial and operating data, by SIC 2- to 4-digit industry, State, SMSA, and county, preliminary census div rpt series, 2491–3

Manufacturing census, 1982: financial and operating data, for SIC 4-digit industries by product, preliminary rpt series, 2491–1

Minority group and women employment, by occupational group and SIC 2- to 3-digit industry, 1981, annual rpt, 9244–1.1

Occupational health risks from hazardous substances and radiation, by industry, occupation, age, and sex, with bibl and glossary, 1920s-82, 9638–50

Occupational injury and illness rates, by SIC 2- to 4-digit industry, 1982, annual rpt, 6844–1

OECD trade, total and for 4 major countries, and US trade by country, by commodity, 1972-82, annual world region rpt series, 244–13

Oils and fats production, consumption by end use, and stocks, by type, monthly Current Industrial Rpt, 2506–4.4

Pollution abatement capital and operating costs, by SIC 2- to 4-digit industry, State, and SMSA, 1982, annual Current Industrial Rpt, 2506–3.6

Producer prices and indexes, by stage of processing and detailed commodity, monthly rpt, 6762–6

Producer prices and indexes, by stage of processing and detailed commodity, monthly 1983, annual supplement, 6764–2

Plastics and plastics industry

Production and sales of synthetic organic chemicals by product, and listing of manufacturers, 1983, annual rpt, 9884–3

Production of synthetic organic chemicals, by detailed product, monthly rpt, 9882–1

Productivity, hours, and employment indexes for selected SIC 3- and 4-digit industries, 1954-82, annual rpt, 6824–1.3

R&D industry funding and employment of scientists and engineers, by industry group, firm size, and funding source, 1956-82, annual rpt, 9627–21

Scientists, engineers, and technicians employed in private industry, by occupation and industry group, 1980-81, biennial rpt, 9627–23

Shipments of plastics, by product, 1982-83, annual Current Industrial Rpt, 2506–8.9

Transportation census, 1982: trucks, by detailed characteristics, miles traveled, and type of product carried, State rpt series, 2573–1

Vinyl sheet flooring, tariff and nontariff trade barriers impact on US industry, 1984 rpt, 9886–4.76

Waterborne commerce of US (domestic and foreign), freight by commodity, traffic, and passengers, by port and waterway, 1982, annual rpt, 3754–3

see also Petrochemicals

see also under By Commodity in the "Index by Categories"

see also under By Industry in the "Index by Categories"

Platinum

see Metals and metal industries

Plato, Gerald

"Stockpiling U.S. Agricultural Commodities with Volatile World Markets: The Case of Soybeans", 1502–3.402

Platonium

see Radioactive materials

Plowden, Ray

"Statistics of Income for Individuals: A Historical Perspective", 8308–28.1

Plumbing and heating

Air pollutant and radiation indoor levels by emissions source, and household exposure and health effects by pollutant type, various periods 1966-83, hearings, 21708–102

Buildings heating and air conditioning fuel by type, for new private nonresidential and public buildings, by region, 1979-83, monthly rpt, annual tables, 2382–4.4

Business statistics, detailed data for major industries and economic indicators, *Survey of Current Business,* monthly rpt, 2702–1.14

Census of Agriculture, 1982: farms, farmland, production, finances, and operator characteristics, by county, final State rpt series, 2331–1

Census of Housing, 1980: inventory, occupancy, and unit characteristics, changes from 1973 by region and inside-outside SMSAs and central cities, series, 2473–3

Census of Housing, 1980: occupancy and unit characteristics of SMSAs and central cities, by race, Hispanic origin, and city, State and SMSA rpt series, 2473–1

Census of Housing, 1980: structural, financial, and householder characteristics, by region and State, 2475–4

Census of Population and Housing, 1980: detailed population and housing characteristics, by county, city, and census tract, State and SMSA rpt series, 2551–2

Census of Population, 1980: detailed socioeconomic and demographic characteristics, by age, sex, race, Hispanic origin, occupation, and industry, State rpt series, 2531–4

Census of Population, 1980: labor force, by sex, detailed occupation, and region, with comparison to 1970 census, supplementary rpt, 2535–1.12

China economic conditions, agricultural and industrial production, trade, and domestic and foreign investment, 1980-85, 2048–106

China exports and imports by SITC 1- to 5-digit commodity, 1970s-82, annual rpt, 244–12

Connecticut utility group housing energy conservation program, cost effectiveness and characteristics of participants and nonparticipants, 1980-82, 3308–77

Construction industries census, 1982: financial and operating data, by SIC 4-digit industry and State, final rpt series, 2373–1

Construction industries census, 1982: financial and operating data, by SIC 4-digit industry and State, preliminary rpt, 2371–1.10

County Business Patterns: establishments, employees, and payrolls, by SIC 4-digit industry and county, 1981, annual State rpt series, 2326–8

County Business Patterns: establishments, employees, and payrolls, by SIC 4-digit industry and county, 1982, annual State rpt series, 2326–6

Electric power rate schedules, by user type, utility, and city, Jan 1984, annual rpt, 3164–40

Employment, earnings, and hours, by selected SIC 1- to 4-digit industry, State, and for 278 major labor areas, 1939-83, annual rpt, 6744–5

Employment, earnings, and hours, by SIC 4-digit nonfarm industry, monthly 1974-Feb 1984, annual update, 6744–4

Energy aid of Fed Govt for low-income households, allocations and average benefits in 13 States, and public interest group assessment, FY81-83, GAO rpt, 26121–75

Energy aid of Fed Govt for low-income households, by income, aid type, and State, FY83, annual rpt, 4744–3.13

Energy conservation devices installation, utility loan program cost effectiveness, and household participation characteristics, Minnesota study, 1980-83, 3308–72

Energy conservation programs of utilities, actual and predicted gas savings by conservation measure, Minnesota study, 1980-83, 3308–74

Energy conservation programs of utilities under natl conservation act, cost effectiveness and participating household characteristics, 1980s, 3308–69

Energy supply/demand and prices, by fuel type and consuming sector with foreign comparisons, 1949-83, annual rpt, 3164–74

Index by Subjects and Names

Energy supply/demand and prices, by fuel type, sector, and end use, detailed trends and projections 1973-95, annual rpt, 3164–75

Energy supply/demand and prices, by fuel type, sector, and end use, with foreign comparisons, 1960-83 and projected to 1995, annual summary rpt, 3164–76

Energy use and costs in multifamily rental housing, conservation effect on rental marketing, and effect of utility bill payment methods on conservation efforts, 1970s-80s, 3308–73

Energy use, by economic sector, end use, and energy source, 1983 and 2000, 2006–2.5

Energy use, costs, expenditures, and conservation, and household and housing characteristics, EIA survey series, 3166–7

Energy use in housing, and savings under alternative conservation strategies, by State, with model methodology and energy prices, selected years 1970-81, 21368–48

Energy use in nonresidential buildings, expenditures, and conservation, by building characteristics, EIA survey series, 3166–8

Environmental quality and protection programs, costs, and Fed Govt enforcement, 1983, detailed annual rpt, 484–1

Exports and imports of equipment, detailed SIC-based commodities by world area, 1983, annual rpt, 2424–6

Exports and imports of US, totals and as percent of domestic production, by SIC 2- to 5-digit commodity, 1981, annual rpt, 2424–3

Exports, imports, tariffs, and industry operating data for miscellaneous machines and equipment, 1979-83, TSUSA commodity rpt, 9885–6.84

Exports of equipment, detailed Schedule B commodities by country of destination, 1983, annual rpt, 2424–9

Exports of equipment, detailed Schedule E commodities by mode of transport and world area and country of destination, 1983, annual rpts, 2424–5

Exports of US, detailed commodities by country of destination, monthly rpt, 2422–3

Florida and California elderly migration by selected State of origin or destination, and Florida elderly, by sociodemographic and housing characteristics, 1970 and 1980, 4478–150

Furnace shipments, trade, and consumption, 1983, annual Current Industrial Rpt, 2506–12.7

Furnace and cooling equipment industry productivity trends and technological innovations, 1967-82, article, 6722–1.471

Great Lakes trade, by SITC 3-digit commodity, port, vessel type, world area, and country, 1982, annual rpt, 7744–3

Heating and cooling degree days by State, and housing energy bills and departures from normal, by census div, monthly rpt, 2152–12

Heating and cooling degree days by State, and housing energy bills and departures from normal by fuel type, by census div, monthly rpt, 2152–11

Index by Subjects and Names

Heating equipment shipments, inventories, and exports, by product, 1983, annual Current Industrial Rpt, 2506–11.6

Home heating costs of low-income households, natural gas price decontrol effects, aid programs, and gas supply/demand data, by income level and State, 1970s-95, hearing, 25148–26

Home mortgages (graduated payment) FHA-insured, financial, property, and mortgagor characteristics, for US and selected localities, quarterly rpt, 5142–42

Home mortgages (graduated payment) FHA-insured, financial, property, and mortgagor characteristics, for US and selected States, quarterly rpt, 5142–41

Home mortgages (graduated payment) FHA-insured, financial, property, and mortgagor characteristics, US summary, quarterly rpt, 5142–40

Home mortgages FHA-insured, financial, property, and mortgagor characteristics, for US and selected localities, quarterly rpt, 5142–2

Home mortgages FHA-insured, financial, property, and mortgagor characteristics, for US, selected States, and Puerto Rico, quarterly rpt, 5142–3

Home mortgages FHA-insured, financial, property, and mortgagor characteristics, quarterly rpt, 5142–1

Home mortgages FHA-insured, financial, property, and mortgagor characteristics, 1983, annual rpt, 5144–17

Home mortgages FHA-insured for low-cost homes, financial, construction, property, and mortgagor characteristics, quarterly rpt, 5142–4

Housing alteration and repair expenditures by characteristics of property and region, 1983, annual rpt, 2384–4

Housing alteration and repair expenditures, by type and property size, various periods 1963-83, article, 2012–1.406

Housing and financial characteristics, and unit and neighborhood quality, for 15 SMSAs, 1978, annual survey special supplement, 2485–8

Housing and households detailed characteristics, and unit and neighborhood quality, by inside-outside central cities, 1979-82 surveys, SMSA rpt series, 2485–6

Housing and neighborhood quality indicators and attitudes, and occupant characteristics, by urban-rural location and region, 1981, annual survey, 2485–7

Housing and neighborhood quality indicators and attitudes, by occupant and unit characteristics, region, and metro-nonmetro location, 1981, annual survey, 2485–2

Housing completions, and new unit sales price, cost per square foot, and heating fuel use, by metro-nonmetro area, 1976-82, 1598–190

Housing energy conservation programs of utilities, financing, costs, participation, and energy savings, various periods 1981-84, hearing, 21368–54

Housing, new single and multifamily unit physical and financial characteristics, by region and metro-nonmetro location, 1979-83, annual rpt, 2384–1

Housing occupancy and unit and household characteristics, by region and metro-nonmetro residence, 1983, biennial survey, 2485–1

Housing units heating fuel mix, for new 1-family and multifamily units, selected years 1966-83, annual rpt, 3164–73

Housing vacancy and occupancy rates, and vacant unit characteristics, by metro-nonmetro location and region, selected years 1960-83, annual rpt, 2484–1

Housing vacant unit characteristics and costs, and occupancy and vacancy rates, by region and metro-nonmetro location, quarterly rpt, 2482–1

Housing water conservation programs and savings of water and energy, for selected cities and suburbs, 1980-83, 5188–109

Imports of equipment, detailed Schedule A commodities by country and world area, and method of transport, 1983, annual rpts, 2424–2

Imports of equipment, detailed TSUSA commodities by country of origin, 1983, annual rpt, 2424–4

Imports of US, detailed Schedule A commodities by country, monthly rpt, 2422–2

Income tax returns of corporations, detailed income and tax items by industry, 1981, annual rpt, 8304–4

Income tax returns of partnerships, detailed data by industry, 1981 estimates, annual article, 8302–2.404

Income tax returns of sole proprietorships, detailed data by industry div and selected industry group, 1981, annual rpt, 8304–7

Industry finances and operations, by SIC 2- to 4-digit industry, 1970s-83 and projected to 1988, annual rpt, 2014–4

Injuries and deaths from use of selected consumer products and related activity, by victim age and sex, 1982, annual rpt, 9164–7

Injuries and deaths from use of selected consumer products, by victim age and medical treatment status, 1982, annual rpt, 9164–6

Injuries, deaths, and medical costs from consumer products use, and Consumer Product Safety Commission activities and recalls, by product type and brand, FY83, annual rpt, 9164–2

Input-output structure of US economy, detailed interindustry transactions for 85 industries, and components of final demand, 1977, article, 2702–1.421

Input-output structure of US economy, detailed interindustry transactions for 537 industries, and components of final demand, 1977 benchmark data, 2708–17

Liquefied petroleum gas ethane sales, by principal use, PAD district, and State, 1981-83, annual rpt, 3164–2

Manufacturing census, 1982: financial and operating data, by SIC 2- to 4-digit industry, State, SMSA, and county, preliminary census div rpt series, 2491–3

Manufacturing census, 1982: financial and operating data, for SIC 4-digit industries by product, preliminary rpt, 2491–1.283

Manufacturing census, 1982: financial and operating data, for SIC 4-digit industries by product, preliminary rpt series, 2491–1

Pneumonia and influenza

Occupational injury and illness rates, by SIC 2- to 4-digit industry, 1982, annual rpt, 6844–1

Occupational Outlook Handbook, 1984-85 biennial rpt, 6744–1

OECD trade, total and for 4 major countries, and US trade by country, by commodity, 1972-82, annual world region rpt series, 244–13

Pacific Northwest electricity consumption and prices by end-use sector, and economic and demographic data, 1960s-83 and projected to 2005, annual rpt, 3224–2

Plumbing fixtures shipments, stocks, trade, and consumption, quarterly Current Industrial Rpt, 2506–11.2

Producer prices and indexes, by stage of processing and detailed commodity, monthly rpt, 6762–6

Producer prices and indexes, by stage of processing and detailed commodity, monthly 1983, annual supplement, 6764–2

Production, shipments, PPI, and stocks of building materials, by type, bimonthly rpt, 2012–1.5, 2012–1.6

Retail trade census, 1982: employment, establishments, sales, and payroll, for hardware stores by State, preliminary rpt, 2395–1.3

Scientists, engineers, and technicians employment in transportation, utilities, and retail and wholesale trade, by field of science and industry, 1982, 9628–72

Solar collector and photovoltaic module production, sales, and use, with listing of manufacturers, 1983, annual rpt, 3164–62

Underground economy, household expenditures and participation by type of goods or service and sociodemographic characteristics, with methodology and bibl, 1981 survey, 8308–27

Virgin Islands economic censuses, 1982: employment, establishments, payroll, and receipts, by SIC 1- to 4-digit industry, island, and city, 2593–1

Wholesale trade census, 1982: employment, establishments, sales by commodity, and payroll, by SIC 4-digit kind of business and State, preliminary rpt, 2403–1.11

Wholesale trade sales and inventories, by SIC 2- to 3-digit kind of business, monthly rpt, 2413–7

Wholesale trade sales, inventories, purchases, and gross margins, by SIC 2- to 3-digit kind of business and type of ownership, 1983, annual rpt, 2413–13

Wood acquired and used for home heating, by household characteristics and wood sources, 1980/81, 1208–204

see also Air conditioning

see also Heating oil

see also Household appliances and equipment

Plums and prunes

see Fruit and fruit products

Pneumonia and influenza

Cases of notifiable infectious diseases and current outbreaks, by region and State, weekly rpt, 4202–1

Deaths and death rates, by cause and age, provisional 1982-83, US Vital Statistics annual rpt, 4144–7

Pneumonia and influenza

Deaths and death rates by detailed cause and demographic characteristics, 1979 and selected trends, US Vital Statistics annual rpt, 4144–2.1

Deaths and death rates, by detailed geographic area, cause, and demographic characteristics, 1979, US Vital Statistics annual rpt, 4144–3

Deaths and death rates, by selected cause and demographic characteristics, 1981, US Vital Statistics advance rpt, 4146–5.78

Deaths and death rates, by selected cause and demographic characteristics, 1982, US Vital Statistics advance rpt, 4146–5.81

Deaths due to cold weather and related causes, by age, race, State, and city, selected periods 1962-83, 21148–30

Deaths recorded in 121 cities, weekly rpt, 4202–1

Health condition and health care resources, use, and expenditures, 1970s-82 with trends and projections 1900-2000, annual compilation, 4114–11

Hospital discharges and length of stay, by patient characteristics, facility size, procedure performed, diagnosis, and region, 1982, annual rpt, 4147–13.78

Infant deaths by detailed cause, geographic location, age, race, and sex, 1979, US Vital Statistics annual rpt, 4144–2.2

Influenza deaths, viruses identified by State and country, epidemiology, and vaccine effects and recommended dosages by age, 1979/80-1980/81, annual rpt, 4205–3

Older persons by demographic, socioeconomic, and health characteristics, selected years 1900-81 and projected to 2050, Current Population Rpt, 2546–2.125

Plague (bubonic and pneumonia-inducing) deaths, and cases by onset date, patient characteristics, and source, 1983 and trends from 1950, article, 4202–7.408

Reye syndrome cases by State, and mortality rate by influenza strain, with patient characteristics, various years 1974-82, article, 4202–7.402

see also under By Disease in the "Index by Categories"

Podgursky, Michael

"Sources of Secular Increases in the Unemployment Rate, 1969-82", 6722–1.444

Podiatry

Census of Population, 1980: detailed socioeconomic and demographic characteristics, by age, sex, race, Hispanic origin, occupation, and industry, State rpt series, 2531–4

Census of Population, 1980: labor force, by sex, detailed occupation, and region, with comparison to 1970 census, supplementary rpt, 2535–1.12

Degrees conferred in higher education, by race, Hispanic origin, sex, level, and field, selected years 1949/50-1979/80, annual rpt, 4824–2.16

DOD medical personnel, trainees, and accessions by source, by occupation, specialty, and service branch, FY83, annual rpt, 3544–24

Health care services of selected medical practitioners, use by patient characteristics, 1980 survey with trends from 1963, 4146–12.4

Health condition and health care resources, use, and expenditures, 1970s-82 with trends and projections 1900-2000, annual compilation, 4144–11

License sanctions of health professionals in 3 States, and subsequent Medicare and Medicaid program participation, by specialty, 1977-82, GAO rpt, 26121–80

Manpower supply and education of health professionals, by occupation, demographic and professional characteristics, and location, 1950s-83 and projected to 2000, biennial rpt, 4114–8

Minority group and women employment and training in health professions, by field, selected years 1962/63-1983/84, 4118–18

Occupational manpower needs and supply by detailed occupation, and educational and training program enrollees and grads by detailed field, 1982 and 1995, biennial rpt, 6744–3

Occupational Outlook Handbook, 1984-85 biennial rpt, 6744–1

VA Medicine and Surgery Dept trainees, by detailed program and city, FY83, annual rpt, 9924–21

Poe, Gail S.

"Eye Care Visits and Use of Eyeglasses or Contact Lenses: U.S., 1979 and 1980", 4147–10.145

Poisoning and drug reaction

Death rates by sex, race, and age for 40 causes, projected for 10-year period, 1982 rpt, 4208–21

Deaths and death rates from accidents, by place, detailed cause, and demographic characteristics, 1979, US Vital Statistics annual rpt, 4144–2.1, 4144–2.5

Deaths by principal or contributing cause, with type of injury reported in accidental, poisoning, and violent deaths, by age, sex, and race, 1978, 4146–5.76

Homicides, by circumstance and type of weapon, 1983, annual rpt, 6224–2.1

Immunization and preventive medicine programs for children in US and Mexico, and disease cases, vaccine reactions, and deaths, 1984 conf papers, 4204–15

Injuries and deaths from use of selected consumer products and related activity, by victim age and sex, 1982, annual rpt, 9164–7

Injuries and deaths from use of selected consumer products, by victim age and medical treatment status, 1982, annual rpt, 9164–6

Injuries, deaths, and medical costs from consumer products use, and Consumer Product Safety Commission activities and recalls, by product type and brand, FY83, annual rpt, 9164–2

Suicide and homicide rates for youth, by sex, race, and circumstances, selected years 1970-79, and stress and violent behavior reduction goals for 1990, 4102–1.437

see also Drug abuse and treatment

see also Food and waterborne diseases

see also Lead poisoning and pollution

see also Pesticides

see also under By Disease in the "Index by Categories"

Index by Subjects and Names

Pojar, Michael G.

"Gold and Silver Leaching Practices in the U.S.", 5606–6.1

Pokras, Robert

"Diagnosis-Related Groups Using Data from the National Hospital Discharge Survey: U.S., 1981", 4146–8.98

Polak, Jacques J.

"Role of the Fund", 9373–3.28

Poland

Agricultural and food production indexes, and production of selected commodities, by world region and country, 1974-83, annual rpt, 1524–5

Agricultural production and trade by commodity, food consumption, and farm inputs, for 6 countries, 1960-80 with projections to 1991, 1528–178

Agricultural situation in Eastern Europe, by country, 1983 and outlook for 1984, annual report, 1524–4.7

AID economic assistance to developing countries, obligations and disbursements by country, quarterly rpt, 9912–4

AID loan repayment status and terms by program and country, and status of predecessor agency loans, quarterly rpt, 9912–3

Cuba economic conditions, agricultural and industrial production and distribution, trade, and intl economic relations, 1970-82 and trends from 1957, 248–40

Economic conditions in Communist, OECD, and selected other countries, 1960s-83, annual rpt, 244–5

Economic conditions, income, production, prices, employment, and trade, 1984 annual country rpt, 2046–4.116

Economic, social, and political summary data, by country, 1984, annual factbook, 244–11

Export licensing and monitoring activities under Export Admin Act, for selected commodities, and for Communist and other countries, FY83, annual rpt, 2044–22

Exports and imports of NATO countries with Council for Mutual Economic Assistance Europe members, by country, 1980-83, annual rpt, 7144–5

Exports and imports of US with Communist countries, by detailed commodity and country, quarterly rpt with articles, 9882–2

Exports of US, detailed Schedule B commodities by country of destination, 1983, annual rpt, 2424–9

Exports of US, detailed Schedule E commodities by mode of transport and world area and country of destination, 1983, annual rpts, 2424–5

Grain production, consumption, and trade, and US farm cooperatives grain and oilseed export potential, for 4 countries, selected years 1960-90, 1128–27

Imports of US, detailed Schedule A commodities by country and world area of origin, and mode of transport, 1983, annual rpts, 2424–2

Imports of US, detailed TSUSA commodities by country of origin, 1983, annual rpt, 2424–4

Loans and grants for economic and military assistance from US and intl agencies, by program and country, FY46-83, annual rpt, 9914–5

Index by Subjects and Names

Military spending, arms trade, and armed forces size, with total govt spending and population, by country, 1972-82, annual rpt, 9824–1

Minerals Yearbook, 1982, Vol 3: foreign country reviews of production, trade, and policies, by commodity, annual rpt, 5604–35

Minerals Yearbook, 1982, Vol 3 preprints: foreign country review of production, trade, and policies, by commodity, annual rpt, 5604–17.59

Population size and growth rates, and latest available benchmark demographic data, by country, 1950-83, biennial rpt, 2324–4

Refugee arrivals in US, by world area of origin and processing and nationality, monthly rpt, 7002–4, 7002–5

Refugee resettlement program activities and funding, arrivals and population by country of origin and State, and employment and other characteristics, FY83, annual rpt, 4704–8

Science and technology dev and transfer between USSR and other members of Council for Mutual Economic Assistance, 1940s-81, 2326–9.7

Steel wire rod from Poland at less than fair value, imports injury to US industry, investigation with background financial and operating data, 1984 rpt, 9886–14.116

Steel wire rod from 4 countries, imports injury to US industry from sales covered by foreign govt grants, investigation with background financial and operating data, 1980-83, 9886–15.47

see also under By Foreign Country in the "Index by Categories"

Poland, Jack D.

"Plague in the U.S., 1983", 4202–7.408

Police

Assaults, murders, and other deaths of law enforcement officers, by circumstances, level of govt, agency, victim and offender characteristics, and location, 1983, annual rpt, 6224–3

Auto fleet size, trip characteristics, and energy use, by fleet type, 1970s-83, annual rpt, 3304–5.2

Bombing (explosive and incendiary) and arson incidents by target, State, and circumstances, and explosives theft and recovery, 1982-83, annual rpt, 8484–4

Bombing (explosive and incendiary) incidents, damage, injuries, and deaths, by target, State, and circumstances, 1983, annual rpt, 6224–5

Census of Population, 1980: detailed socioeconomic and demographic characteristics, by age, sex, race, Hispanic origin, occupation, and industry, State rpt series, 2531–4

Census of Population, 1980: detailed socioeconomic characteristics, by county, city, and inside-outside SMSAs and central cities, State rpt series, 2531–3

Census of Population, 1980: labor force, by sex, detailed occupation, and region, with comparison to 1970 census, supplementary rpt, 2535–1.12

Crime victimization rates and reports to police, by offense, 1973-83, 6062–2.405

Crime victimization rates by type of offense, and victim and offense characteristics, Natl Crime Survey series, 6066–3

Crimes of violence involving relatives, by victim-offender relationship, circumstances, and victim characteristics, aggregate 1973-81, 6066–19.5

Criminal case disposition, effect of victim injury and other factors, and law enforcement official and victim attitudes, 1983 survey, 6068–185

Drug abuse situation, prevention and treatment programs, law enforcement, funding needs, and Fed Govt role, attitudes of State and local officials, 1983 survey, 21968–27

Employment and payroll, by function and level of govt, 1983, annual rpt series, 2466–1

Employment of State and local law enforcement personnel and officers, by sex, population size, census div, and jurisdiction, 1983, annual rpt, 6224–2.3

Govt census, 1982: city govt revenues by source, expenditures by function, debt, and assets, by State and city, 2457–4

Govt census, 1982: county govt revenues by source, expenditures by function, debt, and assets, by State and county, 2457–3

Govt census, 1982: employment, payrolls, and average earnings, by function, level of govt, State, county, population size, and inside-outside SMSAs, 2455–2

Govt census, 1982: local govt employment by function, payroll, and average earnings, for individual counties, cities, and school and special districts, 2455–1

Govt census, 1982: State govt payments to local govts, by program, source of funds, level of govt, and State, with trends from 1902, 2460–3

Govt expenditures for police services, by level of govt, 1981, 6066–20.8

Govt finances, by level of govt, State, and for large cities and counties, 1981-83, annual rpt series, 2466–2

Govt revenues by source and expenditures by function, natl income and product account, *Survey of Current Business,* monthly rpt, monthly and annual tables, 2702–1.24

Local govt per capita expenditures, by function and State, 1981-82, annual rpt, 10044–1.7

Neighborhood and housing quality indicators and attitudes, and occupant characteristics, by urban-rural location and region, 1981, annual survey, 2485–7

Neighborhood and housing quality indicators and attitudes, by occupant and unit characteristics, region, and metro-nonmetro location, 1981, annual survey, 2485–2

Neighborhood quality, indicators and attitudes by inside-outside central cities, 1979-82 surveys, SMSA rpt series, 2485–6

Occupational manpower needs and supply by detailed occupation, and educational and training program enrollees and grads by detailed field, 1982 and 1995, biennial rpt, 6744–3

Occupational Outlook Handbook, 1984-85 biennial rpt, 6744–1

Police dept costs and operations, patrol car use, investigations, arrests, and recruit training, by city population size, 1982, 6066–21.1

Political campaign funds

Police dept performance, analyses of police activities effects on neighborhoods and citizens, 1977, compilation of papers, 6068–181

Traffic accidents and casualties detailed direct and indirect costs, by characteristics of persons and vehicles involved, 1979-80, 7768–80

Youth gang criminal activity control, police assessments, staff, and programs in 27 cities, with juvenile arrests nationwide for Crime Index offenses, 1980-81, 6068–175

see also Detective and protective services

see also Federal aid to law enforcement

see also Law enforcement

see also State police

Policy Development and Research, HUD

Community Dev Block Grants admin, allocation, and family social benefits, effect of policy changes to increase local admin responsibility, for 10 cities, as of 1982, 5188–105

Community Dev Block Grants to small cities, State admin, project characteristics, and assessments of local officials, 1982, 5188–106

Discrimination in housing, complaints collected through HUD-sponsored fair housing study in 9 cities, with nationwide comparisons, 1978/79-1980/81, 5188–102

Homeless population and characteristics, and temporary shelter operations, use, and user characteristics, by region and selected city, 1983, 5188–108

Housing water conservation programs and savings of water and energy, for selected cities and suburbs, 1980-83, 5188–109

New Communities program of HUD, activities, costs, land sales, and community and population characteristics, for 13 communities, 1970s-83, 5188–107

Public housing under private mgmt, assessment by housing officials and managers, and tenants, with operating costs, crime, and rent delinquency by project type and location, 1982, 5188–103

Rental housing, effects of Fed Govt tax policies on real estate investment, 1969-81, 5188–104

Polio

see Infective and parasitic diseases

Politano, Arturo

"Financing Urban Transportation Improvements, Report 1: Cost-Effectiveness Considerations in Corridor Planning and Project Programming", 7556–7.1

Political broadcasting

Radio Free Europe and Radio Liberty broadcast and financial data, with comparisons to other intl broadcasters, FY83, annual rpt, 10314–1

USIA activities, employment, and funding, FY83-84, annual rpt, 17594–1

see also Propaganda

see also Radio Free Europe

see also Radio Liberty

see also Voice of America

Political campaign funds

see Campaign funds

Political conventions

Political conventions

Campaign finances and Fed Election Commission monitoring activities, 1984 Federal elections, biennial rpt series, 9276–2

Campaign finances, election procedures, and Fed Election Commission monitoring activities, press release series, 9276–1

Political ethics

Campaign funding by political action committees, and voting on FTC rules, for individual congressmen, 1978-82, hearings, 25688–6.2

Campaign funding by political action committees to individual congressmen, and public opinion on reform proposals and assn influence, 1970s-83, hearings, 21428–7

Corrupt govt officials prosecutions and convictions, by judicial district and level of govt, 1976-83, annual rpt, 6004–13

see also Corruption and bribery

see also Lobbying

Political parties

Campaign finances and Fed Election Commission monitoring activities, 1984 Federal elections, biennial rpt series, 9276–2

Campaign finances, election procedures, and Fed Election Commission monitoring activities, press release series, 9276–1

Campaign funding and activities of Fed Election Commission, and political action committees funding, 1983, annual rpt, 9274–1

County Business Patterns: establishments, employees, and payrolls, by SIC 4-digit industry and county, 1981, annual State rpt series, 2326–8

County Business Patterns: establishments, employees, and payrolls, by SIC 4-digit industry and county, 1982, annual State rpt series, 2326–6

Developing countries disaster preparedness and summary sociodemographic, political, and economic data, country rpt series, 9916–2

Foreign countries *Background Notes,* summary social, political, and economic data, series, 7006–2

Foreign economic, social, and political summary data, by country, 1984, annual factbook, 244–11

Foreign human rights conditions in 162 countries, economic and military aid of US, and economic aid of intl organizations, 1981-83, annual rpt, 21384–3

Public opinion on taxes, tax policy, and intergovtl relations, 1972-84 surveys, annual rpt, 10044–2

Statistical Abstract of US, social, political, and economic data, 1950s-83 and trends, annual rpt, 2324–1.2

see also Communist parties

see also Democratic Party

see also Political conventions

see also Republican Party

Political rights

see Civil rights

Pollack, Earl S.

"Epidemiology of Cancer and the Delivery of Medical Care Services", 4102–1.448

Polls

see Elections

see Opinion and attitude surveys

Pollution

see Air pollution

see Electromagnetic radiation

see Environmental pollution and control

see Marine pollution

see Mercury pollution

see Noise

see Nuclear radiation

see Soil pollution

see Water pollution

Polychlorinated biphenyls

see Hazardous substances

Polyester

see Synthetic fibers and fabrics

Polzin, Paul E.

"Considering Departures from Current Timber Harvesting Policies: Case Studies of Four Communities in the Pacific Northwest", 1208–196

Pompano Beach, Fla.

see also under By SMSA or MSA in the "Index by Categories"

Ponce, P.R.

see also under By SMSA or MSA in the "Index by Categories"

Poor

see Poverty

Popcorn

see Corn

Population census

see Census of Population

see Census of Population and Housing

Population characteristics

Census of Population and Housing, 1980: data coverage, availability, and uses for urban and transportation planning, 1984 guide, 7558–101

Census of Population and Housing, 1980: detailed population and housing characteristics, by county, city, and census tract, State and SMSA rpt series, 2551–2

Census of Population, 1980: detailed socioeconomic and demographic characteristics, by age, sex, race, Hispanic origin, occupation, and industry, State rpt series, 2531–4

Census of Population, 1980: detailed socioeconomic characteristics, by county, city, and inside-outside SMSAs and central cities, State rpt series, 2531–3

Census of Population, 1980: population characteristics, selected and advance data, supplementary rpt series, 2535–1

Census of Population, 1980: selected socioeconomic data, with trends and projections 1960-2050, young readers pamphlet series, 2326–1

Central America socioeconomic and political conditions in 6 countries, 1960s-83 with trends and projections 1930-2010, Commission rpt, 028–19.2

Coal dev plans on Fed Govt lease lands in 12 regions under Fed Coal Mgmt Program, environmental and socioeconomic impacts to 2000, final statement series, 5726–4

Coastal environmental and socioeconomic conditions, and potential impacts of oil and gas OCS leases, final statement series, 5736–1

Coastal environmental characteristics, fish, wildlife, and use, and population socioeconomic data, for individual areas, series, 5506–4

Index by Subjects and Names

County and City Data Book, detailed socioeconomic and demographic data for States, counties, and cities, selected years 1976-82, 2328–1

Current Population Reports, demographic, social, and economic characteristics, series, 2546–1

Current Population Reports, demographic subjects, special study series, 2546–2

Current Population Reports, income and socioeconomic characteristics of persons, families, and households, detailed cross-tabulations, series, 2546–6

Developing countries disaster preparedness and summary sociodemographic, political, and economic data, country rpt series, 9916–2

Developing countries govt policy, and AID and other foreign assistance, effects on private sector dev and socioeconomic conditions, with case studies for 6 countries, 1960s-80, 9918–12

Developing countries sociodemographic data, and AID dev assistance project activities, special study series, 9916–3

Developing countries summary socioeconomic data, 1970s-83, and AID activities and funding by project and function, FY82-85, by country, annual rpt, 9914–3

Economic indicator forecasts, and model estimates of industrial electric power demand, 1960s-80 with projections to 2000, 3008–87

Foreign aged population characteristics, with related health care data and vital statistics, by world area and selected country, 1950-80 and projected to 2020, 2546–10.12

Foreign countries *Background Notes,* summary social, political, and economic data, series, 7006–2

Foreign economic, social, and political summary data, by country, 1984, annual factbook, 244–11

Foreign population size and growth rates, and latest available benchmark demographic data, by country, 1950-83, biennial rpt, 2324–4

Foreign women sociodemographic, economic, and fertility characteristics, with comparisons to men, by country, 1960s-85, world region rpt series, 2326–15

Hispanic Americans socioeconomic and demographic characteristics, and compared to non-Hispanics, selected years 1970-83, chartbook, 2328–48

Mental health facilities needs assessment and program evaluation for small areas, methodology, use of census data, analysis, and sample data, series, 4506–8

Overseas Business Reports: economic conditions, investment and export opportunities, and trade practices, world region rpt series, 2046–5

Population and health research funded by 4 private organizations, project listing by topic, with funding data, 1981, annual rpt, 4474–16

Population demographic and socioeconomic trends, special analyses series, 2326–11

Statistical Abstract of US, social, political, and economic data, 1950s-83 and trends, annual rpt, 2324–1.1

Index by Subjects and Names

Population size

TTPI socioeconomic, health, and govtl data, by TTPI govt, FY83 and selected trends, detailed annual rpt, 7004–6

Virgin Islands socioeconomic and govtl data, FY81, annual rpt, 5304–4

see also Aged and aging
see also Birthplace
see also Body measurements
see also Children
see also Disabled and handicapped persons
see also Earnings, general
see also Educational attainment
see also Educational enrollment
see also Employment and unemployment, general
see also Families and households
see also Farm population
see also Fertility
see also Health condition
see also Housing condition and occupancy
see also Manpower
see also Marriage and divorce
see also Men
see also Migration
see also Nutrition and malnutrition
see also Occupations
see also Personal and family income
see also Personal consumption
see also Population size
see also Poverty
see also Vital statistics
see also Wealth
see also Women
see also Youth

Population Council

Population and health research funded by 4 private organizations, project listing by topic, with funding data, 1981, annual rpt, 4474–16

Population size

- Alabama rural black population, education, employment, health services, and economic status, for 16 counties, selected years 1970-81, 11048–180
- Appalachia population by age and urban-rural location, and employment and net employment change by industry, selected years 1960-90, article, 9088–33
- Appalachian States population, by county, 1980-81, annual rpt, 9084–1
- Assaults, murders, and other deaths of law enforcement officers, by circumstances, level of govt, agency, victim and offender characteristics, and location, 1983, annual rpt, 6224–3
- Business and financial statistics, historic trends, 1984 annual chartbook, 9364–2.4
- Census of Govts, 1982: employment, payrolls, and average earnings, by function, level of govt, State, county, population size, and inside-outside SMSAs, 2455–2
- Census of Population and Housing, 1980: detailed population and housing characteristics, by county, city, and census tract, State and SMSA rpt series, 2551–2
- Census of Population, 1980: detailed socioeconomic and demographic characteristics, by age, sex, race, Hispanic origin, occupation, and industry, State rpt series, 2531–4
- Census of Population, 1980: detailed socioeconomic characteristics, by county, city, and inside-outside SMSAs and central cities, State rpt series, 2531–3

Census of Population, 1980: population characteristics, selected and advance data, supplementary rpt series, 2535–1

Census of Population, 1980: selected socioeconomic data, with trends and projections 1960-2050, young readers pamphlet series, 2326–1

- Central America socioeconomic and political conditions in 6 countries, 1960s-83 with trends and projections 1930-2010, Commission rpt, 028–19.2
- Central cities and suburbs population and employment, effect of region, neighborhood, population, and labor characteristics, 1970-80, technical paper, 9387–8.89
- City and suburb population characteristics and local govt finances, by region and selected SMSA, 1950s-FY83, 10048–61
- City govt employment and payroll, by function and population size, for 447 largest cities, Oct 1983, annual rpt, 2466–1.1
- City govt revenue sharing program allocations and use by function, and response to program cuts, by city size and region, 1982 survey, hearings, 25408–86.2
- City population size for 25 top cities, 1980 and 1982, press release, 2328–46
- Coastal environmental characteristics, fish, wildlife, and use, and population socioeconomic data, for individual areas, series, 5506–4
- Communist and and OECD countries economic conditions, 1982, annual rpt, 7144–11
- Communist, OECD, and selected other countries economic statistics, 1960s-83, annual rpt, 244–5.2
- *County and City Data Book,* detailed socioeconomic and demographic data for States, counties, and cities, selected years 1976-82, 2328–1
- County govt employment and payroll, by function and population size, for 375 largest counties, Oct 1983, annual rpt, 2466–1.2
- Crimes, arrests by offender characteristics, and rates, by offense, and law enforcement employees, by population size and jurisdiction, 1970s-83, annual rpt, 6224–2
- Cuba economic conditions, agricultural and industrial production and distribution, trade, and intl economic relations, 1970-82 and trends from 1957, 248–40
- *Current Population Reports,* demographic, social, and economic characteristics, series, 2546–1
- *Current Population Reports,* population estimates and projections, by region and State, series, 2546–3
- *Current Population Reports,* population estimates for civilian, resident, and total population, monthly rpt, 2542–1
- *Current Population Reports,* population size and components of change, by MSA and county, annual State rpt series, 2546–4
- *Current Population Reports,* population size, Apr 1980 and July 1982, and per capita income, 1979 and 1981, by county and city, State rpt series, 2546–11
- Developing countries agricultural supply/demand and market for US exports, with socioeconomic indicators, country rpt series, 1526–6

Developing countries disaster preparedness and summary sociodemographic, political, and economic data, country rpt series, 9916–2

- Developing countries govt policy, and AID and other foreign assistance, effects on private sector dev and socioeconomic conditions, with case studies for 6 countries, 1960s-80, 9918–12
- Developing countries PL 480 Title I funding and socioeconomic impacts, with case studies for 5 countries, 1950s- 81, 9918–13
- Developing countries sociodemographic data, and AID dev assistance project activities, special study series, 9916–3
- Developing countries summary socioeconomic data, 1970s-83, and AID activities and funding by project and function, FY82-85, by country, annual rpt, 9914–3
- EC food supply/demand and market and support prices, with exchange rates, fertilizer price index, GDP, and population, by country, 1960-83, 1528–173
- Economic and demographic factors used in OASDI program cost estimates, selected years 1913-82 with alternative projections to 2060, 4706–1.90
- Economic and demographic trends for IRS regions, districts, and service centers, 1972-82 and projected to 1990, annual rpt, 8304–8
- Economic and population time series data frequently used in statistical demand analyses, 1941-1982, annual rpt, 1544–21
- El Salvador socioeconomic and political conditions, and US economic and military assistance, 1977-FY84, 7008–39
- Energy production, reserves, and prices, by energy type, and selected indicators of energy use, by State, 1982-83 with selected comparisons from 1971, annual rpt, 3164–60
- Environmental quality and protection programs, costs, and Fed Govt enforcement, 1983, detailed annual rpt, 484–1
- Foreign aged population characteristics, with related health care data and vital statistics, by world area and selected country, 1950-80 and projected to 2020, 2546–10.12
- Foreign and US agricultural supply/demand indicators by commodity and world area, and related research and extension program needs, 1950s-2020, 1008–47
- Foreign and US agricultural supply/demand, trade, and production, and socioeconomic data, by country, 1950s-77, 1528–179
- Foreign and US population by age and percent urban, for 7 countries, selected years 1975-81, 21148–33
- Foreign and US rail high-speed systems and railcar production, and proposed US projects costs and funding, with population and land area for selected foreign cities, 1940s-82, 26358–97
- Foreign countries *Background Notes,* summary social, political, and economic data, series, 7006–2
- Foreign economic indicators and trade by country and country group, and US trade policy actions, 1960s-83, annual rpt, 444–1.4

Population size

Foreign economic, social, and political summary data, by country, 1984, annual factbook, 244–11

Foreign military, social, and economic summary data by world area and country, 1960s-80s, hearing, 25388–47.1

Foreign military spending, arms trade, and armed forces size, with total govt spending and population, by country, 1972-82, annual rpt, 9824–1

Foreign population, and agriculture and food production indexes, by country and world region, 1974-83, annual rpt, 1524–5

Foreign population size and growth rates, and latest available benchmark demographic data, by country, 1950-83, biennial rpt, 2324–4

Foreign women sociodemographic, economic, and fertility characteristics, with comparisons to men, by country, 1960s-85, world region rpt series, 2326–15

Fresno, Calif, economic, population, labor, and housing indicators, various periods 1974-85, hearing, 21248–84

Health care expenditures, growth factors, medical equipment and drugs trade, and physician income, 1950-90, article, 4652–1.407

Health condition and health care resources, use, and expenditures, 1970s-82 with trends and projections 1900-2000, annual compilation, 4144–11

Hispanic Americans socioeconomic and demographic characteristics, and compared to non-Hispanics, selected years 1970-83, chartbook, 2328–48

Homeless population and characteristics, and temporary shelter operations, use, and user characteristics, by region and selected city, 1983, 5188–108

Jamaica PL 480 Title I assistance effects on economic dev, with data on govt finance, economic indicators, demography, and dev programs, 1970s-81, 9916–1.51

Metro and nonmetro areas and central cities population size and change by census div, and growth of areas with large black and aged populations, 1970-82, 2328–47

New Communities program of HUD, activities, costs, land sales, and community and population characteristics, for 13 communities, 1970s-83, 5188–107

Nuclear power plant siting population criteria and estimated compliance of selected regions and sites, 1983 rpt, 9638–54

NYC population size, demographic characteristics, and rental housing, in 5 neighborhoods by census tract, 1980 with percent change from 1970, article, 9385–1.403

OASDI and pension policy, impacts of increased life expectancy, with alternative sociodemographic projections to 2100, hearing, 25368–130

Older persons by demographic, socioeconomic, and health characteristics, selected years 1900-81 and projected to 2050, Current Population Rpt, 2546–2.125

Older persons sociodemographic characteristics, and Fed Govt program participation and funding by agency, 1983 with trends and projections 1900-2080, annual rpt, 25144–3

Older persons sociodemographic characteristics and transportation needs, selected years 1900-2040, 7308–183

Outlying area population size and components of change, by area, 1970-82, Current Population Rpt, 2546–3.127

Overseas Business Reports: economic conditions, investment and export opportunities, and trade practices, world region rpt series, 2046–5

Pacific Northwest electricity consumption and prices by end-use sector, and economic and demographic data, 1960s-83 and projected to 2005, annual rpt, 3224–2

Population and health research funded by 4 private organizations, project listing by topic, with funding data, 1981, annual rpt, 4474–16

Population demographic and socioeconomic trends, special analyses series, 2326–11

Population size and components of change, by region and State, 1970s-83 with projections to 2050, annual Current Population Rpt, 2546–2.119

Population size, by State, July 1983, annual rpt, 2466–2.3

Projections of population size and components of change, under 3 fertility assumptions, 1982-2080, SSA actuarial rpt, 4706–1.92

Regional councils involved in service activities, by type of service and region population size, 1982 survey, hearing, 25408–88

Revenue sharing payments to States, local govts, Indian tribes, and Alaska Native villages, and entitlement computation data, FY84, series, 8066–1

Rural communities losing bus service, with total and older persons population size, 1984 rpt, 14828–2

Southeastern US water supply and quality, with background socioeconomic data, for 8 States, 1960s-2020 with trends from 1930, 9208–119

Soviet Union industrial and agricultural production by selected commodity, and demographic trends and projections by Republic, 1950s-2000, hearings, 23848–180

State population size, and relation to govt revenues and spending by level of govt, by State, selected years 1929-83, annual rpt, 10044–1

Statistical Abstract of US, social, political, and economic data, 1950s-83 and trends, annual rpt, 2324–1.1

Transportation energy use by mode, fuel supplies, and demographic and economic determinants of vehicle use, 1970s-83, annual rpt, 3304–5.1

TTPI socioeconomic, health, and govtl data, by TTPI govt, FY83 and selected trends, detailed annual rpt, 7004–6

Urban runoff water quality, pollutant concentrations, and control cost-effectiveness, with monitoring sites rainfall and other characteristics, by city and region, 1978-83, 9208–122

Vital statistics, births, marriages, divorces, and deaths, provisional data, monthly rpt, 4142–1

Voting age population, by congressional district, biennial rpt, discontinued, 2544–2

Index by Subjects and Names

Voting age population, by State, 1984 Federal elections, press release, 9276–1.19

Voting age population selected characteristics and participation in presidential elections, 1964-80 with projections to 2000, Current Population Rpt, 2546–2.117

Washington Public Power Supply System nuclear reactors construction financing, with regional economic impacts and power supply/demand, 1980s-2035, hearing, 21448–29

Western States, FHLB 11th District housing, employment, and economic indicators, by SMSA, quarterly rpt, 9302–18

Western States, FHLB 11th District member S&L offices, locations, savings balances, and accounts, quarterly listing, 9302–20

Western States housing outlook and economic and demographic trends, FHLB 11th District, urban area rpt series, 9306–2

see also Family planning

see also Farm population

see also Fertility

see also Vital statistics

Porcelain electrical supplies

see Electrical machinery and equipment

Port Arthur, Tex.

Census of Housing, 1980: occupancy and unit characteristics, by race, Hispanic origin, and city, SMSA rpt, 2473–1.87

Census of Population and Housing, 1980: detailed population and housing characteristics, by county, city, and census tract, SMSA rpt, 2551–2.87

Wages of office and plant workers, by occupation, 1984 labor market area survey rpt, 6785–3.6

see also under By SMSA or MSA in the "Index by Categories"

Portage, Mich.

Census of Housing, 1980: occupancy and unit characteristics, by race, Hispanic origin, and city, SMSA rpt, 2473–1.198

Census of Population and Housing, 1980: detailed population and housing characteristics, by county, city, and census tract, SMSA rpt, 2551–2.198

Porter, Richard D.

"Empirical Comparisons of Credit and Monetary Aggregates Using Vector Autoregressive Methods", 9389–1.402

"Monetary Perspective on Underground Economic Activity in the U.S.", 9362–1.402

Porterville, Calif.

Census of Housing, 1980: occupancy and unit characteristics, by race, Hispanic origin, and city, SMSA rpt, 2473–1.363

Census of Population and Housing, 1980: detailed population and housing characteristics, by county, city, and census tract, SMSA rpt, 2551–2.363

Housing vacancy rates for single and multifamily units and mobile homes, by city and ZIP code, 1983, annual metro area rpt, 9304–20.10

Housing vacancy rates for single and multifamily units and mobile homes, by city and ZIP code, 1984, annual metro area rpt, 9304–20.18

Index by Subjects and Names

Postal employees

see also under By SMSA or MSA in the "Index by Categories"

Portland, Maine

Census of Housing, 1980: occupancy and unit characteristics, by race, Hispanic origin, and city, SMSA rpt, 2473–1.289

Census of Population and Housing, 1980: detailed population and housing characteristics, by county, city, and census tract, SMSA rpt, 2551–2.289

Fish and shellfish landings and prices at Boston and other New England ports, and total New England cold storage holdings, weekly rpt, 2162–6.2

Wages of office and plant workers, by occupation, 1983 SMSA survey rpt, 6785–12.3

see also under By SMSA or MSA in the "Index by Categories"

Portland, Oreg.

Auto dealer repair workers, wages, and benefits, by occupation, size of establishment, and for 24 labor market areas, Nov 1982 survey, 6787–6.202

Census of Population and Housing, 1980: detailed population and housing characteristics, by county, city, and census tract, SMSA rpt, 2551–2.290

CPI by component for US city average, and by region, population size, and for 28 SMSAs, monthly press release, 6762–1

CPI by detailed component, for US city average, 28 SMSAs, and 4 regions by population size, monthly rpt, 6762–2

Home mortgage creative financing, effect on home sales price, model results for sales near Portland, Ore, July 1981-June 1982, article, 9412–2.405

Housing unit starts and completions authorized by building permits in 20 MSAs, quarterly rpt, 2382–9

Housing vacancy rates for single and multifamily units and mobile homes, by city and ZIP code, 1983, annual metro area rpt, 9304–21.4

Shipping industry impact on local economy, and port dev financing through user fees, by State, other area, industry, and port, 1970s-2020, hearings, 21568–34

Wages of office and plant workers, by occupation, 1984 SMSA survey rpt, 6785–11.8

Waterborne commerce of US (domestic and foreign), freight by commodity, traffic, and passengers, by port and waterway, 1982, annual rpt, 3754–3.4

see also under By City and By SMSA or MSA in the "Index by Categories"

Ports

see Harbors and ports

Portsmouth, N.H.

Census of Housing, 1980: occupancy and unit characteristics, by race, Hispanic origin, and city, SMSA rpt, 2473–1.291

Census of Population and Housing, 1980: detailed population and housing characteristics, by county, city, and census tract, SMSA rpt, 2551–2.291

see also under By SMSA or MSA in the "Index by Categories"

Portsmouth, Ohio

Uranium enrichment facilities operations, finances, uranium stocks, and energy use and capital investment by facility, FY83, annual rpt, 3354–7

Wages by occupation, and benefits for office and plant workers, 1984 labor market area survey rpt, 6785–3.7

Portsmouth, Va.

Census of Housing, 1980: occupancy and unit characteristics, by race, Hispanic origin, and city, SMSA rpt, 2473–1.265

Census of Population and Housing, 1980: detailed population and housing characteristics, by county, city, and census tract, SMSA rpt, 2551–2.265

Wages of office and plant workers, by occupation, 1984 SMSA survey rpt, 6785–11.5

see also under By City in the "Index by Categories"

Portugal

Agricultural and food production indexes, and production of selected commodities, by world region and country, 1974-83, annual rpt, 1524–5

Agricultural situation in Western Europe, by country and commodity, 1983 and outlook for 1984, annual rpt, 1524–4.6

Agricultural subsidies, profits, marketing margins, and consumer prices in Portugal, by commodity or product, and effects of prospective EC membership, 1981, 1528–171

Agricultural supply/demand, trade, and production, and socioeconomic data, by country, 1950s-77, 1528–179

AID activities and funding by project and function, FY85, and developing countries summary socioeconomic data, 1970s-83, by country, annual rpt, 9914–3

AID economic assistance to developing countries, obligations and disbursements by country, quarterly rpt, 9912–4

AID loan repayment status and terms by program and country, and status of predecessor agency loans, quarterly rpt, 9912–3

Almond production and trade of US and selected countries, 1982/83-1983/84 and forecast 1985, article, 1925–34.425

Economic, social, and political summary data, by country, 1984, annual factbook, 244–11

Economic trends in income, production, prices, employment, finances, and trade, 1984 annual rpt, 2046–4.53

Export and import statistics country classifications, Census Bur codes and designations, 1984 revisions, 2428–3.1, 2428–3.2

Exports and imports of NATO countries with Council for Mutual Economic Assistance Europe members, by country, 1980-83, annual rpt, 7144–5

Exports and imports of NATO countries with PRC, by country, 1980-83, annual rpt, 7144–14

Exports and imports of OECD countries, by country, 1983, annual rpt, 7144–10

Exports and imports of US with Western Europe, and US market share and export opportunities for selected commodities, by country, 1982-84, 2048–105

Exports of US, detailed Schedule B commodities by country of destination, 1983, annual rpt, 2424–9

Exports of US, detailed Schedule E commodities by mode of transport and world area and country of destination, 1983, annual rpts, 2424–5

Fish and shellfish wholesale prices and market activity in 8 West Europe countries, weekly rpt, 2162–8

Fruit and vegetable product trade and tariffs of EC, 1966-78, and effect of Greece, Spain, and Portugal entry into EC, projected to 1986, 1528–182

Imports of US, detailed Schedule A commodities by country and world area of origin, and mode of transport, 1983, annual rpts, 2424–2

Imports of US, detailed TSUSA commodities by country of origin, 1983, annual rpt, 2424–4

Loans and grants for economic and military assistance from US and intl agencies, by program and country, FY46-83, annual rpt, 9914–5

Machine tool and equipment market and trade, and user industry operations and demand, 1984 country market research rpt, 2045–9.3

Military aid of US, arms sales, and training programs costs and budget requests by program, world region, and country, FY83-85, annual rpt, 7144–13

Military spending, arms trade, and armed forces size, with total govt spending and population, by country, 1972-82, annual rpt, 9824–1

Minerals Yearbook, 1982, Vol 3: foreign country reviews of production, trade, and policies, by commodity, annual rpt, 5604–35

Minerals Yearbook, 1983, Vol 3 preprints: foreign country review of production, trade, and policies, by commodity, annual rpt, 5604–23.60

Nuclear power plant construction and operation status, and capacity, by plant, region, State, and selected country, 1983 and projected to 2020, annual rpt, 3164–57

Population size and growth rates, and latest available benchmark demographic data, by country, 1950-83, biennial rpt, 2324–4

see also Macao

see also under By Foreign Country in the "Index by Categories"

Post exchanges

Army morale, welfare, and recreation programs, revenue and expenses worldwide by activity and major command, FY82-83, annual rpt, 3704–12

Budget of DOD, itemized account of legislative history, FY84, annual rpt, 3504–7

Cost control proposals for Fed Govt programs and mgmt, 3-year savings by function and agency, and financial and operating data, 1960s-81, 16908–1.17, 16908–1.23, 16908–1.28

Fraud and abuse in DOD programs, audits and investigations, 1st half FY84, semiannual rpt, 3542–18

Operations of post exchanges, locations worldwide, sales by type of commodity or service and facility, and employment, FY83, annual rpt, 3504–10

Postal employees

Assaults, murders, and other deaths of law enforcement officers, by circumstances, level of govt, agency, victim and offender characteristics, and location, 1983, annual rpt, 6224–3

Postal employees

Census of Govts, 1982: employment, payrolls, and average earnings, by function, level of govt, State, county, population size, and inside-outside SMSAs, 2455–2

Census of Population, 1980: detailed socioeconomic and demographic characteristics, by age, sex, race, Hispanic origin, occupation, and industry, State rpt series, 2531–4

Census of Population, 1980: detailed socioeconomic characteristics, by county, city, and inside-outside SMSAs and central cities, State rpt series, 2531–3

Census of Population, 1980: labor force, by sex, detailed occupation, and region, with comparison to 1970 census, supplementary rpt, 2535–1.12

Cost control proposals for Fed Govt programs and mgmt, 3-year savings by function and agency, and financial and operating data, 1960s-81, 16908–1.16

Employment (civilian) of Fed Govt, by location, agency, and pay system, 1982, biennial rpt, 9844–8

Employment and economic conditions, alternative BLS projections to 1995 with selected trends for 1959-82, 6728–29

Employment, earnings, and hours, by level and branch of govt, and function, monthly 1977-Feb 1984, annual update, 6744–4

Employment, earnings, and hours, by selected SIC 1- to 4-digit industry, State, and for 278 major labor areas, 1939-83, annual rpt, 6744–5

Health benefit plans enrollment and premiums, for individual private and employee organization plans, FY81-82, annual rpt, 9844–1.2

Labor unions recognized in Fed Govt, agreements and membership by agency and office or installation, Jan 1983, annual listing, 9844–14

Minority group and women employment of USPS, by race, Hispanic origin, and pay grade, 1977-83, hearings, 21628–55

Occupational manpower needs and supply by detailed occupation, and educational and training program enrollees and grads by detailed field, 1982 and 1995, biennial rpt, 6744–3

Occupational Outlook Handbook, 1984-85 biennial rpt, 6744–1

Pay comparability of Fed Govt with private industry, and recommended and actual pay increase, various dates 1971-84, annual rpt, 10104–1

Pay for USPS employees, value of premium pay and all wages and benefits, FY81-82, article, 9842–1.401

Pay rates of Fed Govt civilian employees, by branch of govt, employee category, and pay level, as of 1984 with trends from 1789, 21628–54

Payroll of USPS, total payments by State, FY83, annual rpt, 2464–2

Pension and health benefits of USPS subsidized through Fed Govt trust funds, and subsidy reduction plans deficit impact, FY79-84 and projected to FY89, 26306–6.82

Postal Service finances, organization, and services since 1775, and current operations, FY81-82, annual rpt, 9864–6

Postal Service operating costs, itemized by class of mail, FY83, annual rpt, 9864–4

Postal Service operations, employment, productivity, and financial statements, FY79-83, annual rpt, 9864–1

Productivity and performance, earnings compared to private industry, and workers compensation costs and 3rd-party recovery program data, FY83, annual rpt, 9864–5

Postal Rate Commission

Mail postage ratemaking and classification cases, processing, and participant costs and attitudes, 1970s-84, GAO rpt, 26119–63

Postal service

Air mail (foreign and US) carried by US certificated carriers, by airport and airline, 1982, annual rpt, 7504–35

Air mail (foreign and US) carried by US scheduled service carriers, by carrier, monthly rpt, 9142–13

Air mail, passenger, and cargo traffic, and airline operations, by type of service, air carrier, State, and country, 1974-83, annual rpt, 7504–1.4, 7504–1.6

Airline financial data, by carrier, carrier group, and for total certificated system, quarterly rpt, 9142–12

Bombing (explosive and incendiary) and arson incidents by target, State, and circumstances, and explosives theft and recovery, 1982-83, annual rpt, 8484–4

Bombing (explosive and incendiary) incidents, damage, injuries, and deaths, by target, State, and circumstances, 1983, annual rpt, 6224–5

China economic conditions, agricultural and industrial production, trade, and domestic and foreign investment, 1980-85, 2048–106

Cost control proposals for Fed Govt programs and mgmt, 3-year savings by function and agency, and financial and operating data, 1960s-81, 16908–1

Electronic mail system message volume and profitability under proposed rate and service increases, FY82 and projected to FY87, 21408–70

Fed Govt revenues by source, expenditures by function, debt, and assets, 1982-83, annual rpt, 2466–2.6

Finances, organization, and services of USPS since 1775, and current operations, FY81-82, annual rpt, 9864–6

Foreign govts and private obligors debt to US, by country and program, periodic rpt, 8002–6

Foreign postal rates for domestic letters in US and 14 countries, 1983, annual rpt, 9864–1

Govt revenues by source and expenditures by function, natl income and product account, *Survey of Current Business,* monthly rpt, monthly and annual tables, 2702–1.24

House of Representatives salaries, expenses, and contingent fund disbursement, detailed listings, quarterly rpt, 21942–1

Mail postage ratemaking and classification cases, processing, and participant costs and attitudes, 1970s-84, GAO rpt, 26119–63

Mail postage rates and productivity, FY83, annual rpt, 9864–1

Index by Subjects and Names

Mail postage rates, volume by class of mail, service performance, and productivity, FY83, annual rpt, 9864–5

Mail revenue and volume by class of mail, and special service transactions, quarterly rpt, 9862–1

Mail revenues and volume by class, and postal money orders sent to Latin America by area, FY83 with estimated USPS electronic mail promotion costs, FY82-87, hearings, 21628–55

Postage stamp new issues delivered by Bur of Engraving and Printing, annual rpt, discontinued, 8164–1

Producer prices and indexes, by stage of processing and detailed commodity, monthly rpt, 6762–6

Producer prices and indexes, by stage of processing and detailed commodity, monthly 1983, annual supplement, 6764–2

Senate salaries, expenses, and contingent fund disbursements, by payee, detailed listings, 1st half FY84, semiannual rpt, 25922–1

User fees to recover costs of 7 federally subsidized public service programs, by type of fee, user, and service, FY84-88, 26306–6.68

see also Postal employees

see also U.S. Postal Service

see also ZIP codes

Potash

see Fertilizers

see Nonmetallic minerals and mines

Potatoes

see Vegetables and vegetable products

Poterba, James M.

"Response Variation in the CPS: Caveats for the Unemployment Analyst", 6722–1.421

Potomac River

Bridges over navigable waters, with type of bridge and use, owner, dimensions, and location, 1984 regional listing, 7406–5.1

Freight (waterborne domestic and foreign) by commodity, traffic, and passengers, by port and waterway, 1982, annual rpt, 3754–3.1

Water supply and quality in streams and lakes, and groundwater levels in wells, by drainage basin, 1981, annual State rpt series, 5666–16

Water supply and quality in streams and lakes, and groundwater levels in wells, by drainage basin, 1982, annual State rpt series, 5666–20

Water supply and quality in streams and lakes, and groundwater levels in wells, by drainage basin, 1983, annual State rpt series, 5666–10

Water supply in US and Canada, streamflow, well and reservoir levels, and dissolved solids and temperature in 6 US rivers, by station, monthly rpt, 5662–3

Poughkeepsie, N.Y.

Census of Housing, 1980: occupancy and unit characteristics, by race, Hispanic origin, and city, SMSA rpt, 2473–1.292

Census of Population and Housing, 1980: detailed population and housing characteristics, by county, city, and census tract, SMSA rpt, 2551–2.292

Wages by occupation, and benefits for office and plant workers, 1983 SMSA survey rpt, 6785–12.1, 6785–12.2

Index by Subjects and Names

Wages of office and plant workers, by occupation, 1984 SMSA survey rpt, 6785–11.10

see also under By SMSA or MSA in the "Index by Categories"

Poultry industry and products

Agricultural Statistics, 1983, annual rpt, 1004–1

- Agriculture census, 1982: farms, farmland, production and costs, and operator characteristics, preliminary State and county rpt series, 2330–1
- Agriculture census, 1982: farms, farmland, production, finances, and operator characteristics, by county, final State rpt series, 2331–1
- Business statistics, detailed data for major industries and economic indicators, *Survey of Current Business,* monthly rpt, 2702–1.11
- Chicken and turkey hatchery production, by State, 1983, annual rpt, 1625–8
- Cold storage food stocks by commodity and census div, and warehouse cold storage space in use, by State, monthly rpt, 1631–5
- Cold storage food stocks of 77 commodities, by region, 1983, annual rpt, 1631–11
- Consumption of food and nutrient intake by individuals, by food group, source, and socioeconomic characteristics, 1977-78 natl survey, final rpt series, 1356–4
- Consumption of meat and poultry, impact of hypothetical consumer demand changes in price structure and industry performance, model, 1982-91, article, 1502–3.402
- Consumption, supply, trade, prices, expenditures, and indexes, by food commodity, 1963-83, annual rpt, 1544–4
- Cooperatives finances and operations, aggregate for top 100 assns by principal product and revenue source, FY82, annual rpt, 1124–3
- Cooperatives, membership, activities, and finances, by commodity and leading State, 1900-80 with trends from 1863, 1128–30
- County Business Patterns: establishments, employees, and payrolls, by SIC 4-digit industry and county, 1981, annual State rpt series, 2326–8
- County Business Patterns: establishments, employees, and payrolls, by SIC 4-digit industry and county, 1982, annual State rpt series, 2326–6
- CPI by detailed component, for US city average, 28 SMSAs, and 4 regions by population size, monthly rpt, 6762–2
- Cuba economic conditions, agricultural and industrial production and distribution, trade, and intl economic relations, 1970-82 and trends from 1957, 248–40
- Eastern Europe agricultural production and trade by commodity, food consumption, and farm inputs, for 6 countries, 1960-80 with projections to 1991, 1528–178
- EC food supply/demand and market and support prices, with exchange rates, fertilizer price index, GDP, and population, by country, 1960-83, 1528–173
- Egg, chicken, and turkey production and inventories, monthly rpt, 1625–1
- Egg production and layer inventory, by State, 1982-83, annual rpt, 1625–7

Egg production by type of product, and shell eggs broken under Fed Govt inspection by region, monthly rpt, 1625–2

- Employment, earnings, and hours, by selected SIC 1- to 4-digit industry, State, and for 278 major labor areas, 1939-83, annual rpt, 6744–5
- Employment, earnings, and hours, by SIC 4-digit nonfarm industry, monthly 1974-Feb 1984, annual update, 6744–4
- Exports and imports of dairy, livestock, and poultry live animals, meat, and products, by commodity and country of destination, FAS quarterly rpt, 1925 32
- Exports and imports of US, by agricultural commodity and country, bimonthly rpt with articles, 1522–1
- Exports and imports of US, by detailed agricultural commodity and country, FY83 and CY83, semiannual rpts, 1522–4
- Exports and imports of US, by detailed agricultural commodity for 8 major commodity groups, monthly rpt, 1922–8
- Exports and imports of US, detailed SIC-based commodities by world area, 1983, annual rpts, 2424–6
- Exports and imports of US, totals and as percent of domestic production, by SIC 2- to 5-digit commodity, 1981, annual rpt, 2424–3
- Exports of manufactured and agricultural commodities, manufacturing production, and export-related employment, 1960s-82, State rpt series, 2046–3
- Exports of US, detailed commodities by country of destination, monthly rpt, 2422–3
- Exports of US, detailed Schedule B commodities by country of destination, 1983, annual rpt, 2424–9
- Exports of US, detailed Schedule E commodities by mode of transport and world area and country of destination, 1983, annual rpts, 2424–5
- Farm finances, assets, liabilities, income, receipts by commodity and State, and expenses, 1980-83 and trends from 1910, annual rpt, 1544–16
- Farm production inputs, outputs, and productivity, by region, 1939-82, annual rpt, 1544–17
- Foreign agricultural production, prices, and trade, by country, 1983 and outlook for 1984/85, annual world region rpt series, 1524–4
- Foreign and US agricultural production, prices, trade, and consumption, quarterly rpt with articles, 1522–3
- Foreign and US agricultural production, trade, and climatic devs, with EC price supports, weekly press release, 1922–4
- Foreign and US agricultural supply/demand, consumption per capita, and trade, by world area and country group, 1960s-82, 1528–181
- Foreign and US feed and livestock trade by product and world region, and ocean freight rates between selected countries of origin and destination, selected years 1960-82, 1528–177
- Foreign and US livestock, poultry, and products production, consumption, and trade, FAS semiannual circular, 1925–33

Poultry industry and products

- Futures trading by commodity and exchange, and Commodity Futures Trading Commission activities, funding, and employment, FY83, annual rpt, 11924–2
- Genetic resource (plant and animal) conservation, commercial uses, causes of depletion, and geographic sources, 1984 rpt, 5548–13
- Hatchery participation and flocks included in Natl Poultry Improvement Plan, by disease program, region, and State, 1981-83, annual rpt, 1394–15
- Imports of US, detailed Schedule A commodities by country and world area of origin, and mode of transport, 1983, annual rpts, 2424–2
- Imports of US, detailed TSUSA commodities by country of origin, 1983, annual rpt, 2424–4
- Income tax returns of partnerships, detailed data by industry, 1981 estimates, annual article, 8302–2.404
- Income tax returns of partnerships, receipts by source, deductions by type, and establishments, by selected industry, 1982, annual article, 8302–2.416
- Input-output structure of US economy, detailed interindustry transactions for 537 industries, and components of final demand, 1977 benchmark data, 2708–17
- Inspection of meat and poultry by Food Safety and Inspection Service, FY83, annual rpt, 1374–3
- Inspection of meat and poultry, Federal aid to State and local programs by agency and State, FY83, annual rpt, 2464–2
- Inspection of meat and poultry, Federal, State, and foreign govts activities and personnel, FY83, annual rpt, 1374–1
- Manufacturing census, 1982: financial and operating data, by SIC 2- to 4-digit industry, State, SMSA, and county, preliminary census div rpt series, 2491–3
- Manufacturing census, 1982: financial and operating data, for SIC 4-digit industries by product, preliminary rpt, 2491–1.2
- Marketing and price data for poultry and eggs, for selected regions, States, and SMSAs, monthly 1983, annual rpt, 1317–2
- Marketing cash receipts of farms, by detailed commodity and State, 1979-82, annual rpt, 1544–18
- Occupational injury and illness rates, by SIC 2- to 4-digit industry, 1982, annual rpt, 6844–1
- Portugal agricultural subsidies, profits, marketing margins, and consumer prices, by commodity or product, and effects of prospective EC membership, 1981, 1528–171
- Prices (farm-retail) for foods, marketing cost components, and industry finances and productivity, selected years 1967-83, annual rpt, 1544–9
- Prices received by farmers for chickens, turkeys, and eggs, by State, monthly and annual average, 1959-78, 1651–3
- Prices received by farmers for major products, and paid for farm inputs and living items, by commodity and State, monthly rpt, 1629–1
- Prices received by farmers for major products, and paid for farm inputs, by commodity and State, 1983, annual rpt, 1629–5

Poultry industry and products

Producer prices and indexes, by stage of processing and detailed commodity, monthly rpt, 6762–6

Producer prices and indexes, by stage of processing and detailed commodity, monthly 1983, annual supplement, 6764–2

Production and farm finances, expenses by type, and domestic economic impact, selected years 1972-82 and preliminary 1983-84, annual rpt, 1544–19

Production and supply/demand data, for US livestock and dairy products, and for selected US and world crops, periodic rpt, 1522–5

Production expenditures, detailed items by farm sales size and region, 1983, annual rpt, 1614–3

Production, prices, and producers gross income, by State, 1982-83, annual rpt, 1625–5

Production, prices, trade, and marketing, by commodity, current situation and forecast, monthly rpt, 1502–4

Production, prices, trade, stocks, and consumption, periodic situation rpt, 1561–7

Slaughter of poultry under Fed Govt inspection, pounds certified, and condemnations by cause, by State, monthly rpt, 1625–3

Small farms with sales under $2,500, acreage, finances, operations, and operator characteristics, by region and for 6 States, 1978, 1548–241

Turkey hatcheries incubator egg inventory and poult placements, by region, monthly rpt, 1625–10

Turkey inventories and production, by State, 1981-83 with 1984 breeding intentions, annual release, 1625–6

Underground economy, household expenditures and participation by type of goods or service and sociodemographic characteristics, with methodology and bibl, 1981 survey, 8308–27

USDA agricultural surplus direct purchase program finances, and purchases and food received by schools by commodity, various periods 1936-83, 1548–243

Wholesale trade census, 1982: employment, establishments, sales by commodity, and payroll, by SIC 4-digit kind of business and State, preliminary rpt, 2403–1.30

see also Animal diseases and zoonoses

see also Animal feed

see also under By Commodity in the "Index by Categories"

Poverty

Agricultural Conservation Program participation by low-income farmers, by State, FY83, annual rpt, 1804–7

Alabama rural black population, education, employment, health services, and economic status, for 16 counties, selected years 1970-81, 11048–180

Bankruptcy (personal), filers by debt type and other characteristics, selected years 1978-81, hearing, 25528–97.1

Births, fertility rates, expected births, and childless women, by socioeconomic characteristics, June 1982, annual Current Population Rpt, 2546–1.386

Births, fertility rates, expected births, and childless women, by socioeconomic characteristics, June 1983, annual Current Population Rpt, 2546–1.393

CCC dairy price support program foreign donations and domestic donations to poor, schools, Prisons Bur, DOD, and VA, monthly rpt, 1802–2

Census of Housing, 1980: occupancy and unit characteristics of SMSAs and central cities, by race, Hispanic origin, and city, State and SMSA rpt series, 2473–1

Census of Housing, 1980: structural, financial, and householder characteristics, by region and State, 2475–4

Census of Population and Housing, 1980: detailed population and housing characteristics, by county, city, and census tract, State and SMSA rpt series, 2551–2

Census of Population, 1980: detailed socioeconomic and demographic characteristics, by age, sex, race, Hispanic origin, occupation, and industry, State rpt series, 2531–4

Census of Population, 1980: detailed socioeconomic characteristics, by county, city, and inside-outside SMSAs and central cities, State rpt series, 2531–3

Central America socioeconomic and political conditions in 6 countries, 1960s-83 with trends and projections 1930-2010, Commission rpt, 028–19.2

County and City Data Book, detailed socioeconomic and demographic data for States, counties, and cities, selected years 1976-82, 2328–1

Educational attainment of population over age 22 and below poverty level, by sex, race, and age, 1981, annual rpt, 4824–1.4

Employment and unemployment in metro and nonmetro poverty and nonpoverty areas, annual averages, 1983, article, 6742–2.403

Employment and unemployment in metro and nonmetro poverty and nonpoverty areas, monthly rpt, quarterly data, 6742–2.8

Employment status of family members, by occupation, family composition, age of children, and other characteristics, 1983 and trends from 1940, 6746–1.253

Energy price increases related to economic indicators, and to household energy use by socioeconomic characteristics, selected years 1978-95, 3004–13.3

Families and persons in poverty, by detailed socioeconomic characteristics, 1982, annual Current Population Rpt, 2546–6.40

Families and persons in poverty, by income source, hours of work, earnings, and taxes paid, and family characteristics, various periods 1959-84, 21788–131

Families and persons in poverty by labor force status, and effect of public welfare changes and recession, by family status, FY82, 21788–139

Families and persons in poverty by selected characteristics, public welfare funding, and effect of counting transfer payments as income, selected years 1950-83, 25928–4

Family poverty rate by family composition, and effect of noncash transfers, taxes, unemployment benefits, and business cycles, selected years 1959-82, hearings, 21788–141

Family poverty status, by sex, age, and work experience of householder, 1959-83, annual rpt, 4744–3.1

Index by Subjects and Names

Farm population, by employment and socioeconomic characteristics, 1983, annual rpt, 2544–1

Farmers, farm population, and managers health insurance coverage by insurance type and selected sociodemographic characteristics, 1976, 1598–191

Fed Govt poverty income guidelines for determining public assistance eligibility, by family size, 1965-84, article, 4742–1.415

Florida and California elderly migration by selected State of origin or destination, and Florida elderly, by sociodemographic and housing characteristics, 1970 and 1980, 4478–150

Food aid programs of Fed Govt and others, funding, participant characteristics, and nutrition and poverty data, 1970s-83, 028–20

Food stamp recipient households size and composition, income, and income deductions allowed, Aug 1981, annual rpt, 1364–8

Foreign military, social, and economic summary data by world area and country, 1960s-80s, hearing, 25388–47.1

Health care expenditures, natl survey on services use, costs, and sources of payment, by patient and physician characteristics, 1977-78, series, 4186–3

Health facilities and manpower use, by patient and facility characteristics, Vital and Health Statistics series, 4147–13

Health Services Research Natl Center grants and contracts, by program area, FY83, annual listing, 4184–2

HHS aid to each State and local govt or private instn, amount obligated, funding agency, and program, FY83, annual listing, 4004–3

Hispanic Americans socioeconomic and demographic characteristics, and compared to non-Hispanics, selected years 1970-83, chartbook, 2328–48

Home heating costs of low-income households, natural gas price decontrol effects, aid programs, and gas supply/demand data, by income level and State, 1970s-95, hearing, 25148–26

Homeless population and characteristics, and temporary shelter operations, use, and user characteristics, for selected cities, various periods 1979-84, hearing, 21248–85

Households and housing unit characteristics, and employment, housing finance, and social programs data, selected years 1948-83, hearing, 21968–28

Income (household) before and after taxes, by socioeconomic characteristics, type of tax paid, and region, 1981, Current Population Rpt, 2546–2.118

Income (household) before and after taxes, by socioeconomic characteristics, type of tax paid, and region, 1982, annual Current Population Rpt, 2546–2.122

Income of families and persons, by sociodemographic characteristics, 1983, advance annual Current Population Rpt, 2546–6.41

Income of families, by household type, race and Hispanic origin, farm-nonfarm residence, region, and number of earners, and change in real income, 1981-82, article, 1702–1.404

Index by Subjects and Names

Income tax and social security tax burden of households and effect of indexing by income level, 1982, and Fed Govt revenues by source, FY60-89, press release, 8008–109

Job Training Partnership Act dislocated workers program performance standards guide for States, with data on previous programs, by State and client characteristics, FY81-82, 6408–59.2

Job Training Partnership Act participants, by program and socioeconomic characteristics, Oct 1983-June 1984 with funding to 1985/86, 6408–63

Mobility of population, detailed data by demographic and socioeconomic characteristics of movers and nonmovers, Mar 1981-82, annual Current Population Rpt, 2546–1.384

Motivation, psychological factors, and family characteristics of young adults, relationship to poverty status by race and sex, 1970s-82, longitudinal studies, 4008–65

Older persons by demographic, socioeconomic, and health characteristics, selected years 1900-81 and projected to 2050, Current Population Rpt, 2546–2.125

Older persons entitled to both Medicare and Medicaid, demographic characteristics, and health condition and services use, 1980, article, 4652–1.433

Older persons health care total and out-of-pocket expenditures, by sociodemographic characteristics, poverty and health status, and degree of functional limitation, 1980, 4146–11.4

Older persons income and income sources, by OASDI beneficiary and poverty status, labor force participation, and demographic characteristics, 1982, biennial rpt, 4744–26

Older persons income and percent in poverty, by household composition and sex, with comparisons to nonaged, selected years 1950-82, article, 4742–1.413

Older persons population characteristics, and needs and costs of social services by type, by metro-nonmetro status, 1970s-82 with trends from 1900, 21148–28

Older persons sociodemographic characteristics, and Fed Govt program participation and funding, 1983 with trends and projections 1900-2060, annual rpt, 25144–3.1

Older persons sociodemographic characteristics and transportation needs, selected years 1900-2040, 7308–183

Population demographic and economic characteristics, 1982 with projections of population size to 2050, annual Current Population Rpt, 2546–2.119

Public and employer-based noncash transfer program recipients, by income source and socioeconomic characteristics, 1982, advance Current Population Rpt, 2546–6.38

Public and employer-based noncash transfer program recipients, by income source and socioeconomic characteristics, 1982, final Current Population Rpt, 2546–6.37

Public noncash transfers counted as income, effect on poverty population size by selected recipient characteristics, 1979-83, 2626–2.52

Power-generating plants and equipment

Public noncash transfers counted as income, effects on poverty population size by recipient characteristics, 1979-82, 2626–2.50

School lunch program school and student participation, families eligible, and Federal reimbursement rates, FY79-83, GAO rpt, 26113–123

Statistical Abstract of US, social, political, and economic data, 1950s-83 and trends, annual rpt, 2324–1.3

Supplemental Security Income and 3 earlier programs benefits, beneficiaries below poverty level, and State program expenditures, various periods 1972-83, article, 4742–1.402

Supplementary Security Income beneficiary socioeconomic characteristics and health service use, 1970s-83 and SSI program projections to 1995, 25148–29

Unemployment and part-time employment, by race, Hispanic origin, sex, family composition, income, and poverty status, 1980-82, annual report, 6744–15

Unemployment and part-time employment effects on family income, by socioeconomic and labor force characteristics, 1981-82, annual rpt, 6746–1.252

Unemployment effect on family income and poverty status, by demographic, employment, and unemployment characteristics, 1981-82, annual article, 6722–1.412

Urban area economic distress index and components, for 153 cities, 1975 and 1980, article, 9373–1.413

Urban area socioeconomic and fiscal trends and problems, 1950-83 and Fed Govt funding estimates for FY84-87, biennial rpt, 5124–4

Women in couples with wife as primary earner, socioeconomic and family characteristics, with comparative data for husbands, Mar 1982, 2326–11.9

Women's employment and earnings, by labor force and socioeconomic characteristics, and compared to men, 1978-81 and trends from 1940s, 6568–29

Women's labor force participation, earnings, and socioeconomic characteristics, 1983, annual fact sheet, 6564–1

see also under By Income in the "Index by Categories"

Powell, Douglas S.

"Forest Statistics for Maine, 1971 and 1982", 1206–12.7

Powell, Rex L.

"State and National Standardized Lactation Averages by Breed for Cows on Official Test, Calving in 1982", 1702–2.403

Power-generating plants and equipment

Acid rain causes and effects, air pollutant emissions by source in US and selected countries, control costs, and Fed Govt research funding, 1960s-82, 3408–27

Air pollutant emissions, control costs, and acid rain causes and effects, selected years 1977-83 and projected to 2000, 26358–104

Air pollutant emissions in US and selected countries, control costs, and acid rain causes and effects, 1970s-83 and projected to 2000, 21368–52

Air pollutant sulfur dioxide emissions of coal-fired power plants in eastern US, effect of alternative geographic area limits on power and coal industries, 1983 rpt, 3408–32

Air pollutant sulfur dioxide emissions reduction proposal, effects on polluting industries and coal production by region and State, projected to 2010, 9188–97

Air pollution abatement equipment shipments by industry, exports, and new and backlog orders, by product, 1983, annual Current Industrial Rpt, 2506–12.5

Air pollution abatement under Clean Air Act, emissions by source, standards, and effects on auto industry and health, 1970s-83, hearings, 25328–25

Air pollution levels for 5 pollutants, by detailed source, State, and Air Quality Control Region, 1981, annual rpt, 9194–7

Air pollution levels for 5 pollutants, by source, 1970- 82 with trends from 1940, annual rpt, 9194–13

Alaska electric power capacity and generation by fuel type, and marketing, by utility, type of ownership, and location, 1983, annual rpt, 3214–2

Army Corps of Engineers activities and projects, FY83 and trends from 1800s, annual rpt, 3754–1

Bond tax-exempt issues for private activity, by purpose, face value, major industry, and State, 1983, article, 8302–2.417

Bonneville Power Admin operations, and Columbia River power system sales and financial statements, FY83, annual rpt, 3224–1

Budget of US, effects of Reagan Admin policy changes, by detailed program, FY85, annual rpt, 104–21

Capacity utilization in 15 manufacturing industries, mining, electric and all utilities, and industrial materials including energy, monthly rpt, 9365–2.19

Carbon dioxide emissions, climatic effects, and control costs, projected under alternative emissions controls and energy use restrictions to 2100 with trends 1970s-80, reprint, 9188–88

Census of Population, 1980: detailed socioeconomic and demographic characteristics, by age, sex, race, Hispanic origin, occupation, and industry, State rpt series, 2531–4

China economic conditions, agricultural and industrial production, trade, and domestic and foreign investment, 1980-85, 2048–106

Coal, coke, and breeze supply/demand, prices, trade, and stocks, by end-use sector and State, quarterly rpt with articles, 3162–37

Coal production and stocks, and electric utility generation, capacity, and coal use, alternative estimates 1977-82, annual rpt, 3164–63

Coal production and stocks by district, and shipments by district of origin, State of destination, consuming sector, and mode of transport, quarterly rpt, 3162–8

Coal receipts, consumption, stocks, and delivered price to electric utilities, by State, weekly rpt, monthly data, 3162–1.2

Power-generating plants and equipment

Colorado River Storage Project finances, water resource dev, power production, and other activities in western States, FY83, annual rpt, 5824–3

Communist, OECD, and selected other countries consumer and producer goods production, 1960s-83, annual rpt, 244–5.8

Construction industries census, 1982: financial and operating data, by SIC 4-digit industry and State, final rpt series, 2373–1

Construction industries census, 1982: financial and operating data, by SIC 4-digit industry and State, preliminary rpt series, 2371–1

Construction put in place, permits authorized by region, State, and MSA, and Federal contract awards, by construction type, bimonthly rpt with articles, 2012–1

County Business Patterns: establishments, employees, and payrolls, by SIC 4-digit industry and county, 1982, annual State rpt series, 2326–6

Electric power cogeneration in 5 industries, and fuel use and utility supply/demand effects, by region, 1983-93, 3008–92

Electric power generating capacity, demand, and cost, by energy source and end-use sector and for 7 electric utilities, 1981-2000 with trends from 1960s, 3008–93

Electric power peak demand, generating and interregional transfer capability, and reserve margins, detailed data by region, 1984-93, annual rpt, 3404–6

Electric power plant (coal-fired) capacity addition estimation to forecast coal demand, methodology and input data, series, 3166–11

Electric power plant (coal-fired) capacity, coal demand, and coal supply by mode of transport and region of origin, by State, for units planned 1983-92, 3088–18

Electric power plant (nuclear and coal-fired) construction itemized cost estimates, and investment per kilowatt for 20 cities, 1980s-95, 9638–52

Electric power plant (steam) fuel deliveries, costs, and quality, by fuel type, State, and utility, 1983, annual rpt, 3164–42

Electric power plant capacity, by plant type, age, and DOE region, 1982, and new and replacement capacity trends and projections, 1900-2020, 3008–98

Electric power plant capacity, production, retail sales, and fuel stocks, use, and costs, by State, 1979-83, annual rpt, 3164–11

Electric power plant capital and operating detailed costs, capacity, and fuel use, by plant, plant type, utility, and State, 1982, annual rpt, 3164–9

Electric power plants and industrial facilities prohibited from oil and gas primary use, and exemption petitions, by facility, with summary fuel use, 1983, annual rpt, 3104–8

Electric power plants, by capacity, fuel used, unit type, region, State, and county, for plants added and retired, 1983 and planned through 1993, annual rpt, 3164–36

Electric utilities privately owned, capital investment, finances, equity performance, and operating characteristics, 1950-82 with supply estimates to 2010, 3168–87

Electric utilities privately owned, detailed financial and operating data by company, with summary data for other distributors by type, 1982, annual rpt, 3164–23

Electric utilities publicly owned, detailed financial and operating data by company, annual rpt, discontinued, 3164–24

Electric utility fuel cost, quality, use, receipts, and stocks, and power plant production, by energy source, State and utility, quarterly rpt, 3162–39

Electric utility production, fuel consumption, stocks, and costs by fuel type, and sales, by State, monthly rpt, 3162–35

Employment, earnings, and hours, by selected SIC 1- to 4-digit industry, State, and for 278 major labor areas, 1939-83, annual rpt, 6744–5

Employment, earnings, and hours, by SIC 4-digit nonfarm industry, monthly 1974-Feb 1984, annual update, 6744–4

Energy consumption of electric utilities and total US, by fuel, projected 1983-95, annual rpt, 3164–68

Energy demand in industry, forecasting model description, detailed technology specifications, and energy use, for 27 SIC 2- to 4-digit industries, 1970s-80 and projected to 2000, 3308–66

Energy prices and expenditures for fuels and electricity, by consuming sector, State, and fuel type, 1970-81, annual rpt, 3164–64

Energy production, reserves, and prices, by energy type, and selected indicators of energy use, by State, 1982-83 with selected comparisons from 1971, annual rpt, 3164–60

Energy supply/demand and price forecasts, by fuel type, quarterly rpt, 3162–34

Energy supply/demand and prices, by energy resource and major producing and consuming country and sector, detailed data, monthly rpt, 3162–24

Energy supply/demand and prices, by fuel type, sector, and end use, detailed trends and projections 1973-95, annual rpt, 3164–75

Energy supply/demand and prices, by fuel type, sector, and end use, with foreign comparisons, 1960-83 and projected to 1995, annual summary rpt, 3164–76

Energy use, by economic sector, State, census div, and detailed energy resource, 1960-82, State Energy Data System annual rpt, 3164–39

Energy use, by type of air pollutant source and fuel, and State, 1981, annual rpt, 9194–14

Energy use in transportation and other sectors, by fuel, selected years 1970-83, annual rpt, 3304–5

Environmental quality and protection programs, costs, and Fed Govt enforcement, 1983, detailed annual rpt, 484–1

Exports of US, detailed commodities by country of destination, monthly rpt, 2422–3

Exports of US, detailed Schedule E commodities by mode of transport and world area and country of destination, 1983, annual rpts, 2424–5

Fed Govt reclamation projects in western US, electric power capacities and

Index by Subjects and Names

transmission miles, and water storage and carriage facilities, by State, FY81, annual rpt, 5824–1.1

Finances and operations, by SIC 2- to 4-digit industry, 1970s-83 and projected to 1988, annual rpt, 2014–4

Foreign market and trade for electric power systems equipment, and user industry operations and demand, country market research rpts, 2045–15

Generator shipments, interplant transfers, and trade, by product, 1983, annual Current Industrial Rpt, 2506–12.17

Great Lakes radioactivity discharges by source, and concentrations in environment, various periods 1963-82, annual rpt, 14644–1.2

Great Lakes trade, by SITC 3-digit commodity, port, vessel type, world area, and country, 1982, annual rpt, 7744–3

Hydroelectric power plants construction and production costs, capacities, and hydraulic characteristics, by plant, annual rpt, discontinued, 3164–37

Hydroelectric power plants, listing of major foreign and US plants with location and characteristics, as of June 1983, 5828–13

Imports of US, detailed Schedule A commodities by country, monthly rpt, 2422–2

Input-output structure of US economy, detailed interindustry transactions for 537 industries, and components of final demand, 1977 benchmark data, 2708–17

Mechanical power transmission equipment trade, tariffs, and industry operating data, foreign and US, 1979-83, TSUSA commodity rpt, 9885–6.64

Minority group and women employment, by occupational group and SIC 2- to 3-digit industry, 1981, annual rpt, 9244–1.1

Natural and supplemental gas production, prices, trade, use, reserves, and pipeline company finances, by firm and State, monthly rpt with articles, 3162–4

Nuclear power accident liability insurance under Price-Anderson Act, effects on industry finances and operations, with insurance coverage, claims, and costs, various periods 1957-82, 9638–49

Nuclear power and weapons policy, fuel supply/demand, waste disposal and siting, environmental effects of radiation, and public attitudes, 1970s-82 with projections to 2000, 3008–88

Nuclear power industry status and outlook, with reactor construction, utility financial and operating data, and foreign comparisons, 1970s-83 with projections to 2010, 26358–99

Nuclear power plant and reactor construction costs, by plant and reactor, for start-up dates 1960-82 and projected to 1995, 3006–7.5

Nuclear power plant capacity, generation, shutdowns, operation status and costs, and fuel, quarterly rpt, 3352–3

Nuclear power plant construction and operation status, and capacity, by plant, region, State, and selected country, 1983 and projected to 2020, annual rpt, 3164–57

Nuclear power plant construction costs and status, and capacity, by plant and State, as of Mar 1984, annual rpt, 3164–69

Index by Subjects and Names

Prefabricated buildings

Nuclear power plant construction costs and status, capacity, and revenue requirements, by plant and utility, various dates Dec 1983-Mar 1984, article, 9385–1.412

Nuclear power plant electrical systems, errors in operation and maintenance by circumstance, plant type, and system, 1977-81, 9638–51

Nuclear power plant fuel assembly performance and failures, by fuel vendor for US and some foreign reactors, 1982, annual rpt, 9634–8

Nuclear power plant licensing actions and status, by action type and plant, monthly rpt, 9632–5

Nuclear power plant licensing 24-month delay, effect on utility financial performance and electric power prices, for plant completed May 1979, 9638–53

Nuclear power plant occupational exposure to radiation at individual commercial facilities, 1969-82, annual rpt, 9634–3

Nuclear power plant operating and safety data, by plant, 1981, annual rpt, 9634–6

Nuclear power plant radioactive waste, releases and waste composition by plant, 1981, annual rpt, 9634–1

Nuclear power plant safety and emergencies, effectiveness of technical advisors, 1983 survey, 9638–55

Nuclear power plant safety standards and research, design, licensing, construction, operation, and finances, with data by reactor, bimonthly rpt, 3352–4

Nuclear power plant siting population criteria and estimated compliance of selected regions and sites, 1983 rpt, 9638–54

Nuclear power plant spent fuel and demand for uranium and enrichment services, for US and non-Communist country groups, 1983 and projected to 2020, annual rpt, 3164–72

Nuclear power plant spent fuel discharges and additional storage capacity required, by reactor, projected 1984-93, annual rpt, 3354–2

Nuclear power plant spent fuel generation, inventory, disposal by site, reprocessing, and characteristics, by source, as of 1983 and projected to 2020, annual rpt, 3364–2

Nuclear reactor components and other atomic energy products and services, orders, total and Fed Govt shipments, and exports, 1983, annual Current Industrial Rpt, 2506–12.27

Nuclear reactor operating and inspection data for individual commercial facilities, monthly rpt, 9632–1

Nuclear reactors at central station power plants, operating status and other characteristics by plant, utility, and State, as of Jan 1984, annual rpt, 3354–11

Nuclear reactors for domestic use and export by function, with owner, operating characteristics, and location, Apr 1984, semiannual listing, 3002–5

Nuclear Regulatory Commission activities, employment, and finances, and operations of individual power plants by State, FY83, annual rpt, 9634–2

OECD energy prices and taxes by energy source and end-use sector, for US and 9 countries, quarterly 1979-83, annual rpt, 3164–71

OECD trade, total and for 4 major countries, and US trade by country, by commodity, 1972-82, annual world region rpt series, 244–13

Oil enhanced recovery technologies use and environmental impacts, by oil field, county, and State, 1970s-80 and projected to 2000, 3408–29

Pollution abatement capital and operating costs under Clean Air and Water Acts, for govts and selected industries, various periods 1970-2000, annual rpt, 9184–11

Pollution abatement expenditures, and effect on economic indicators and industry operations, by major industry, projected under 3 pollution regulation alternatives 1983-95, 9188–84

Producer prices and indexes, by stage of processing and detailed commodity, monthly rpt, 6762–6

Producer prices and indexes, by stage of processing and detailed commodity, monthly 1983, annual supplement, 6764–2

Productivity, hours, and employment indexes for selected SIC 3- and 4-digit industries, 1954-82, annual rpt, 6824–1.4

Rural Electrification Admin financed electric power plants, with location, capacity, and owner, as of Jan 1984, annual listing, 1244–6

Rural Electrification Admin loans to power supply and distribution firms, and borrower operating and financial data, by firm and State, 1983, annual rpt, 1244–1

Southeastern Power Admin sales by customer, plants, and capacity, and financial statements of Southeastern Fed Power Program, FY83, annual rpt, 3234–1

Switchgear and switchboard apparatus, productivity, hours, and employment indexes, 1963-82, annual rpt, 6824–1.3

Switchgear industry labor productivity trends and technological innovations, 1963-82, article, 6722–1.420

Tennessee Valley river control and reservoir elevations, storage, flows, and hydroelectric generating capacity use, 1981, annual rpt, 9804–7

TVA activities, financial and operating data by program and facility, and power sales by customer, FY83, annual rpt, 9804–1

TVA construction projects employment, and impacts on nearby areas, survey rpt series, 9806–7

TVA power program finances and operations, by plant and distributor, FY83, annual rpt, 9804–23

Uranium reserves and mining and milling industries operations and finances, with selected foreign comparisons, various periods 1964-83 and projected to 2000, 3008–95

Washington Public Power Supply System nuclear reactors construction financing, with regional economic impacts and power supply/demand, 1980s-2035, hearing, 21448–29

Western Area Power Admin electric power plant generating capacities, by plant and operating agency, FY83, annual rpt, 3254–1

Western Area Power Admin small-scale potential hydroelectric generation, site inventory, characteristics, and costs, by State and county, 1984 rpt, 3258–1

Wholesale trade census, 1982: employment, establishments, sales by commodity, and payroll, by SIC 4-digit kind of business and State, preliminary rpt, 2403–1.15

Wood fuel consumption, by end-use sector, SIC 2-digit industry, region, State, and selected industrial and power plant, 1980-83, biennial rpt, 3164–78

see also Electrical machinery and equipment

Power resources

see terms listed under Energy resources

Prager, Kate

"Maternal Smoking and Drinking Behavior Before and During Pregnancy", 4144–11.1

"Smoking and Drinking Behavior Before and During Pregnancy of Married Mothers of Live-Born Infants and Stillborn Infants", 4102–1.418

Precious metals

see Gold

see Silver

Precious stones

see Gemstones

Precipitation

see Weather

Predictions

see Projections

Prefabricated buildings

County Business Patterns: establishments, employees, and payrolls, by SIC 4-digit industry and county, 1981, annual State rpt series, 2326–8

County Business Patterns: establishments, employees, and payrolls, by SIC 4-digit industry and county, 1982, annual State rpt series, 2326–6

Employment, earnings, and hours, by selected SIC 1- to 4-digit industry, State, and for 278 major labor areas, 1939-83, annual rpt, 6744–5

Exports, imports, tariffs, and industry operating data for miscellaneous wood products, foreign and US, 1979-83, TSUSA commodity rpt, 9885–2.30

Exports of US, detailed commodities by country of destination, monthly rpt, 2422–3

Finances and operations, by SIC 2- to 4-digit industry, 1970s-83 and projected to 1988, annual rpt, 2014–4

Home mortgages (graduated payment) FHA-insured, financial, property, and mortgagor characteristics, for US and selected localities, quarterly rpt, 5142–42

Home mortgages (graduated payment) FHA-insured, financial, property, and mortgagor characteristics, for US and selected States, quarterly rpt, 5142–41

Home mortgages (graduated payment) FHA-insured, financial, property, and mortgagor characteristics, US summary, quarterly rpt, 5142–40

Home mortgages FHA-insured, financial, property, and mortgagor characteristics, for US and selected localities, quarterly rpt, 5142–2

Home mortgages FHA-insured, financial, property, and mortgagor characteristics, for US, selected States, and Puerto Rico, quarterly rpt, 5142–3

Home mortgages FHA-insured, financial, property, and mortgagor characteristics, quarterly rpt, 5142–1

Prefabricated buildings

Home mortgages FHA-insured, financial, property, and mortgagor characteristics, 1983, annual rpt, 5144–17

Home mortgages FHA-insured for low-cost homes, financial, construction, property, and mortgagor characteristics, quarterly rpt, 5142–4

Imports of US, detailed Schedule A commodities by country, monthly rpt, 2422–2

Input-output structure of US economy, detailed interindustry transactions for 537 industries, and components of final demand, 1977 benchmark data, 2708–17

Manufacturing census, 1982: financial and operating data, by SIC 2- to 4-digit industry, State, SMSA, and county, preliminary census div rpt series, 2491–3

Manufacturing census, 1982: financial and operating data, for SIC 4-digit industries by product, preliminary rpt, 2491–1.127, 2491–1.290

New Jersey and Maryland prison capacity and population, and New Jersey construction costs by type and funding source, by facility, 1977-82 and projected to 1988, 25528–99

Producer prices and indexes, by stage of processing and detailed commodity, monthly rpt, 6762–6

Producer prices and indexes, by stage of processing and detailed commodity, monthly 1983, annual supplement, 6764–2

Puerto Rico wood and wood product shipments from US by type, and from selected foreign sources, 1971-81, 1208–205

Safety standards, program inspections, enforcement actions, and accidents and casualties in manufactured homes by victim characteristics, 1982-83 biennial rpt, 5004–4

Pregnancy

see Maternity

Prentice, Barry E.

"Barriers to Trade in Agricultural Products Between Canada and the U.S.", 1528–175

Preschool education

- Census of Population and Housing, 1980: detailed population and housing characteristics, by county, city, and census tract, State and SMSA rpt series, 2551–2
- Census of Population, 1980: detailed socioeconomic and demographic characteristics, by age, sex, race, Hispanic origin, occupation, and industry, State rpt series, 2531–4
- Census of Population, 1980: detailed socioeconomic characteristics, by county, city, and inside-outside SMSAs and central cities, State rpt series, 2531–3
- *Condition of Education,* detailed data on enrollment, staff, achievement, finances, curricula, and education effects on employment, 1982-83, annual rpt, 4824–1.1
- Enrollment in preprimary programs, by sociodemographic characteristics of child and mother or household head, annual rpt, suspended, 4834–7
- Enrollment in preprimary school and child day care services, by age of child and labor force participation of mother, 1980, 6746–1.253

Enrollment in public elementary and secondary schools, by grade level and State, fall 1982, annual rpt, 4834–10

Enrollment of persons aged 3-34, by grade level and student characteristics, Oct 1982, advance annual Current Population Rpt, 2546–1.391

Enrollment of persons aged 3-34, by grade level, instn control, and student characteristics, Oct 1983, advance annual Current Population Rpt, 2546–1.392

Enrollment of 3-5 year olds, by type of program, Oct 1979-80, annual rpt, 4824–2.7

Fed Govt educational grants, State allocations by program, type of recipient agency, and State, FY83, annual rpt, 4804–8

Teaching degrees conferred by specialty and State, required credit hours, and instn officials attitudes, by instn type, 1970s-83, hearings, 21348–89

see also Head Start Project

Prescott, Richard

"Size Characteristics and Spending Patterns for Corn Belt Grain Farms in 1982, from the Farm Production Expenditure Survey", 1544–19.404

Prescription drugs

see Drugs

Presidency of the U.S.

- Election voting decisions, and assessment of political parties and Reagan Admin performance, by party affiliation, Nov 1981-82, hearings, 25688–6.1
- Pay rates of Fed Govt civilian employees, by branch of govt, employee category, and pay level, as of 1984 with trends from 1789, 21628–54
- *see also* Executive Office of the President
- *see also* Presidential appointments
- *see also* Presidential powers

Presidential advisory bodies

see Federal boards, committees, and commissions

Presidential appointments

- Ambassador career and noncareer appointments, 1961-83, and Foreign Service positions and union membership by agency, grievances, and pay rates, FY81-83, GAO rpt, 26123–64
- Cost control proposals for Fed Govt programs and mgmt, 3-year savings by function and agency, and financial and operating data, 1960s-81, 16908–1.25
- Pay rates of Fed Govt civilian employees, by branch of govt, employee category, and pay level, as of 1984 with trends from 1789, 21628–54

Presidential commissions

see Federal boards, committees, and commissions

Presidential communications and messages

see Presidency of the U.S.

Presidential-congressional relations

see Congressional-executive relations

Presidential elections

see Elections

Presidential powers

- Cost control proposals for Fed Govt programs and mgmt, 3-year savings by function and agency, and financial and operating data, 1960s-81, 16908–1
- *see also* Congressional-executive relations

Index by Subjects and Names

see also Executive agreements

see also Executive impoundment of appropriated funds

see also Presidential appointments

President's Commission for the Study of Ethical Problems in Medicine and Biomedical and Behavioral Research

Budget of US, appropriations, outlays, balances, and budget receipts, by govtl branch and agency, FY83, annual rpt, 8104–2

President's Commission on Pension Policy

Budget of US, appropriations, outlays, balances, and budget receipts, by govtl branch and agency, FY83, annual rpt, 8104–2

President's Commission on Strategic Forces

Missile experimental (MX) basing proposals of Reagan Admin, 1984 narrative rpt update, 3508–17

President's Committee on Employment of the Handicapped

- Disabled women, by socioeconomic and demographic characteristics, and compared to nondisabled women and disabled men, 1981, chartbook, 16598–4
- Hispanic Americans with disabilities, by disability type and severity and for 5 States, selected years 1970-78, conf proceedings, 16598–5

President's Private Sector Survey on Cost Control

- Cost control proposals for Fed Govt programs and mgmt, CBO and GAO estimates of savings by function and agency, FY85-89, 26308–45
- Cost control proposals for Fed Govt programs and mgmt, 3-year savings by function and agency, and financial and operating data, 1960s-81, 16908–1

Presler, Elizabeth P.

"Continuing Education for Maternal Child Health Nurses: A Means To Improve the Health Care of Mothers and Children", 4102–1.405

Press

see Freedom of the press

see Journalism

see Newspapers

Pressure groups

see Lobbying

Pretrial detention and release

- Alcohol-related and total traffic deaths, and drunk driver license revocations and other deterrence measures in selected States, 1980-82, 9618–10
- Bank robbery court cases by case processing, sentencing, and offender characteristics, and compared to other Fed Govt felony cases, 1979-80, periodic rpt, 6062–2.407
- Citation release use, cost savings for law enforcement agencies, and failures to appear in court, by offense and selected jurisdiction, 1970s-82, 6068–187
- Crime and criminal justice data, including justice expenditures and employment by level of govt, 1970s-82 with some trends from 1875, 6068–174
- DC criminal cases involving drug users, and user and nonuser rates of detention, pretrial rearrest, and failure to appear in court, 1979-81, 6066–20.7
- Drug defendants, by sociodemographic and case processing characteristics, with comparisons to Federal fraud and bank robbery defendants, 1979, 6062–2.403

Index by Subjects and Names

Prices

Illinois pretrial detention time credited to prison terms, by offense, for prisoners released 1978-82, 6066–19.7

Jail capacities, conditions, expenditures, and services, and socioeconomic and other characteristics of inmates, various dates 1976-82, 10048–59

see also Arrest

see also Habeas corpus

Preventive medicine

Blood pressure screening and hypertension treatment itemized costs at 9 worksites, 1978-80, 4478–148

Child immunization and preventive medicine programs in US and Mexico, disease cases, vaccine reactions, and deaths, 1984 conf papers, 4204–15

Children and youth benefitting from Fed Govt public welfare programs and tax expenditures, participation and funding for 71 programs, FY81-83, 21968–30

Fed Govt aid to State and local govts, expenditures, and direct payments, by program, agency, and State, FY83, annual rpt, 2464–2

Govt census, 1982: State govt payments to local govts, by program, source of funds, level of govt, and State, with trends from 1902, 2460–3

Health Care Financing Admin research activities and grants by research area, as of June 1984, semiannual listing, 4652–8

Health Services Research Natl Center grants and contracts, by program area, FY83, annual listing, 4184–2

HHS aid to each State and local govt or private instn, amount obligated, funding agency, and program, FY83, annual listing, 4004–3

Public Health Reports, articles and special studies rpts, bimonthly journal, 4102–1

Public Health Service activities, and funding by function and subagency, FY83, annual rpt, 4044–2

Refugee resettlement program activities and funding, arrivals and population by country of origin and State, and employment and other characteristics, FY83, annual rpt, 4704–8

State govt maternal and child health funding, and admin of Fed Govt block grants, by program for 13 States, 1981-83, GAO rpt, 26121–70

State govt preventive health services funding by program, Fed Govt block grants, and opinions on State program admin, for 13 States, FY81-84, GAO rpt, 26121–88

Vital and Health Statistics series and other NCHS publications, 1979-83, annual listing,, 4124–1

see also Health maintenance organizations

see also Medical examinations and tests

see also Occupational health and safety

see also Vaccination and vaccines

Pribilof Islands, Alaska

Seal harvest, mgmt, and skins taken and rejected for northern fur seals of Pribolof Islands, Alaska, various dates 1786-1981, 2168–79

Price-Anderson Act

Nuclear power accident liability insurance under Price-Anderson Act, effects on industry finances and operations, with insurance coverage, claims, and costs, various periods 1957-82, 9638–49

Price, Bob

"Cattle Outlook Discussion", 1004–16.1

Price, Daniel N.

"Cash Benefits for Short-Term Sickness, 1948-81", 4742–1.417

"Workers' Compensation: Coverage, Benefits, and Costs, 1982", 4742–1.424

"Workers' Compensation Program Experience, 1981", 4742–1.409

"Workers' Compensation: 1976-80 Benchmark Revisions", 4742–1.414

Price, Deborah S.

"Urban Travel Trends: Historical Observations and Future Forecasts, Final Report, May 1984", 7888–63

Price indexes

see Consumer Price Index

see Producer Price Index

Price regulation

Airline deregulation in 1978, effect on industry operations and finances, air traffic patterns, and CAB programs, various periods FY76-84, 9148–56

Airline deregulation in 1978, traffic and service changes by city, with market shares, fares, and load factors, quarterly rpt, 9142–42

Bus industry collective ratemaking and regulatory reform impacts on operations, finances, and services to older persons and rural areas by State, 1970s-83, 14828–2

Developing countries food supply policies, with farm sector data, tariff income, and prices and imports of 5 grains, for 21 countries, 1960s-81, 1528–168

Electric and gas utility ratemaking and regulatory policy standards, and consumers and sales covered, by type of consumer and utility, 1983, annual rpt, 3104–7

Electric utility rate minimization from improved efficiency, proposed FERC incentive program operations and costs, with comparisons to 3 State programs, 1950s-82, 3088–17

FERC activities and funding by program, with some natural gas and electric power industry data, FY83, annual rpt, 3084–9

Jamaica PL 480 Title I assistance effects on economic dev, with data on govt finance, economic indicators, demography, and dev programs, 1970s-81, 9916–1.51

Natural gas price decontrol alternatives effect on farm production by crop, prices, and fertilizer use and costs, 1982-90, model results, 1548–239

Natural gas price decontrol alternatives effect on supply/demand, prices, and home heating costs of households, 1970s-95, hearing, 25148–26

Natural gas price decontrol effect on supply/demand and prices, 1970s-83, 3168–50

Natural gas prices, reserves, consumption, and production, projected under alternative price controls 1983-95 with market data for various periods 1970-Mar 1984, 3008–96

Natural gas supply, contract prices, pipeline operations and finances, and residential use, various periods 1966-1983/84, 3168–89

Oil price and allocation regulations enforcement by DOE, and overcharge

allegations, settlements, and refunds to States, by company, as of June 1983, hearing, 21368–50

Oil windfall profits tax liability by tax rate, and exempt oil volume, by price control category, quarterly article, 8302–2.2

Retail prices set by manufacturers under fair-trade law by brand and product, with manufacturers, market concentration, and sales, by industry, selected years 1952-82, 9406–1.38

see also Agricultural quotas and price supports

Prices

Airline deregulation in 1978, effect on industry operations and finances, air traffic patterns, and CAB programs, various periods FY76-84, 9148–56

Airline deregulation in 1978, traffic and service changes by city, with market shares, fares, and load factors, quarterly rpt, 9142–42

Business activity indicators (nonfinancial), 1982, annual rpt, 9364–5.9

Business and financial statistics, historic trends, 1984 annual chartbook, 9364–2.6

Business Conditions Digest, current data on economic, business, and financial conditions and cyclical fluctuations, monthly rpt, 2702–3

Business Conditions Digest, historical supplement on economic, business, and financial conditions and cyclical fluctuations, with methodology, 1947-82, 2708–31

Business statistics, detailed data for major industries and economic indicators, *Survey of Current Business,* monthly rpt, 2702–1

Communications satellite intl systems charges, operations, investment shares by country, and competition impacts, 1964-83 with projections to 2003, hearings, 25388–46

Communist, OECD, and selected other countries economic statistics, 1960s-83, annual rpt, 244–5.2

Department store inventory price indexes, July 1984, semiannual rpt, 6762–7

Economic indicators, nonfinancial, monthly rpt, 9362–1.2

Export and import price indexes for food and manufactured products, quarterly press release, 6762–13

Export and import price indexes for selected commodities, 1st half 1984, semiannual article, 6722–1.459

Export and import price indexes for selected commodities, 1983, semiannual article, 6722–1.424

Foreign and US indexes of consumer, producer, and major commodity prices, nonfarm wages, and currency value, US and 4 countries, bimonthly rpt, 2042–11

Foreign economic indicators and currency exchange rates, by world area and selected country, mid-1960s-83, annual rpt, 204–1.9

Foreign economic indicators for 7 OECD countries and US, quarterly rpt, 2042–10

Foreign exchange rates correlation with price and trade indicators, for 14 countries, 1977-83, article, 9373–1.418

Foreign exchange rates for currencies of US and 2 countries with yen, and measures of

Prices

manufacturing competitiveness, 1983 with 1974-80 and 1979-80 averages, article, 9385–1.404

Foreign investment, US intl position net change by component, investment type, and world region, and for 2 countries, 1982-83, annual article, 2702–1.424

Fresno, Calif, economic, population, labor, and housing indicators, various periods 1974-85, hearing, 21248–84

Import and tariff provisions effect on US industries and products, investigations with background financial and operating data, series, 9886–4

Imports from Communist countries, injury to US industries, investigations with background financial and operating data, selected industries and products, series, 9886–12

Imports injury to US industries from foreign subsidized products, investigations with background financial and operating data for selected industries and products, series, 9886–15

Imports injury to US industries from import sales at less than fair value, investigations with background financial and operating data, series, 9886–14

Imports injury to US industries from increased import sales, investigations with background financial and operating data, series, 9886–5

Imports injury to US industries from removal of duties on foreign subsidized products, investigations with background financial and operating data, series, 9886–18

Jamaica PL 480 Title I assistance effects on economic dev, with data on govt finance, economic indicators, demography, and dev programs, 1970s-81, 9916–1.51

OECD economic indicators, for US and 6 countries, biweekly rpt, 242–4

Pacific Basin economic indicators, US and 12 countries, quarterly rpt, 9393–9

Prices, costs, and productivity of labor and capital, by selected industry, and compared to 6 OECD countries, selected years 1947-82, 17898–1

Railroad finances, operations, and freight rates and shares, by commodity and railroad, 1970s-82, hearings, 25268–80

Recording industry operations and sales lost from home taping, home taping costs, and material taped by source, 1969-83, hearings with chartbook, 25528–100

Retail prices set by manufacturers under fair-trade law by brand and product, with manufacturers, market concentration, and sales, by industry, selected years 1952-82, 9406–1.38

Small business owners expectations of operations, expansion opportunity, and loan availability during coming quarter, July 1983 survey, hearings, 21728–52.2

Statistical Abstract of US, social, political, and economic data, 1950s-83 and trends, annual rpt, 2324–1.3

Taxicab licenses, density, fares, license prices, and deregulation effects, by selected city, various dates 1970-84, 9406–1.37

Telecommunications service rates for messages sent within US and to selected countries, by type and country, as of May 1982-Oct 1983, annual rpt, 9284–6.6

Transportation average passenger fares, by mode of transport, 1972-82, annual rpt, 7304–2.1

see also Agricultural prices

see also Agricultural quotas and price supports

see also Coal prices

see also Consumer Price Index

see also Electric power prices

see also Energy prices

see also Food prices

see also Housing costs and financing

see also Inflation

see also Medical costs

see also Natural gas prices

see also Petroleum prices

see also Price regulation

see also Producer Price Index

see also under names of specific commodities or commodity groups

Pridgen, Vermelle

"Domestic Natural Gas Reserves and Production Dedicated to Interstate Pipeline Companies, 1983", 3162–4.405

"Domestic Natural Gas Reserves and Production Dedicated to Interstate Pipeline Companies, 1983 (Preliminary Data Report)", 3164–33

"Gas Supplies of Interstate Natural Gas Pipeline Companies, 1983", 3164–33

Prihoda, Ronald

"Use and Costs of Medicare Services in the Last Years of Life", 4144–11.1

"Use and Costs of Medicare Services in the Last 2 Years of Life", 4652–1.412

Primary Metropolitan Statistical Areas

see Metropolitan Statistical Areas

see under By SMSA or MSA in the "Index by Categories"

Printing and publishing industry

Air pollutant emission factors, by detailed source, 3rd edition, 1983-84 supplements, 9198–13

American Samoa minimum wage rates, employment, earnings, and benefits, by establishment and industry, Nov 1983, biennial rpt, 6504–6

Census of Population, 1980: detailed socioeconomic and demographic characteristics, by age, sex, race, Hispanic origin, occupation, and industry, State rpt series, 2531–4

Census of Population, 1980: detailed socioeconomic characteristics, by county, city, and inside-outside SMSAs and central cities, State rpt series, 2531–3

Collective bargaining agreements expiring during year, covered workers by SIC 2-digit industry, firm, and union, with summary of key provisions, 1984, annual rpt, 6784–9

County Business Patterns: establishments, employees, and payrolls, by SIC 4-digit industry and county, 1981, annual State rpt series, 2326–8

County Business Patterns: establishments, employees, and payrolls, by SIC 4-digit industry and county, 1982, annual State rpt series, 2326–6

Earnings by major industry group, and personal income per capita and by source, by region and State, 1929-82, 2708–40

Employment, earnings, and hours, by selected SIC 1- to 4-digit industry, State, and for 278 major labor areas, 1939-83, annual rpt, 6744–5

Index by Subjects and Names

Employment, earnings, and hours, by SIC 4-digit nonfarm industry, monthly 1974-Feb 1984, annual update, 6744–4

Exports and imports of US, by commodity group, world area, selected country, US coastal area and port, and mode of transport, with seasonal adjustments, monthly rpt, 2422–9

Exports and imports of US, detailed SIC-based commodities by world area, 1983, annual rpts, 2424–6

Exports and imports of US, totals and as percent of domestic production, by SIC 2- to 5-digit commodity, 1981, annual rpt, 2424–3

Exports, imports, tariffs, and industry operating data for wood, paper, and printed matter, TSUSA commodity rpt series, 9885–2

Exports of manufactured and agricultural commodities, manufacturing production, and export-related employment, 1960s-82, State rpt series, 2046–3

Exports of US, detailed commodities by country of destination, monthly rpt, 2422–3

Exports of US, detailed Schedule B commodities by country of destination, 1983, annual rpt, 2424–9

Exports of US, detailed Schedule E commodities by mode of transport and world area and country of destination, 1983, annual rpts, 2424–5

Fed Govt classified info security clearances of Govt and contractor employees, polygraph use, and prepublication reviews, by agency, 1979-83, GAO rpt, 26123–66

Fed Govt procurement contract awards, by State, agency, procurement and contractor type, and for top 100 contractors, quarterly rpt, 102–6

Fed Govt programs and mgmt cost control proposals, 3-year savings by function and agency, and financial and operating data, 1960s-81, 16908–1.32

Finances and operations, by SIC 2- to 4-digit industry, 1970s-83 and projected to 1988, annual rpt, 2014–4

Financial statements for manufacturing, mining, and trade corporations, by selected SIC 2- to 3-digit industry, quarterly rpt, 2502–1

Foreign market and trade for graphic industries equipment, and user industry operations and demand, country market research rpts, 2045–3

Franchise business opportunities, by firm and kind of business, 1984 annual listing, 2044–27

Franchises of firms engaged in distribution of goods and services by kind of business, establishments by State, and sales, 1982-84, annual rpt, 2014–5

GPO activities, finances, and production, FY83, annual rpt, 26204–1

Great Lakes trade, by SITC 3-digit commodity, port, vessel type, world area, and country, 1982, annual rpt, 7744–3

Imports of US, detailed Schedule A commodities by country and world area of origin, and mode of transport, 1983, annual rpts, 2424–2

Imports of US, detailed Schedule A commodities by country, monthly rpt, 2422–2

Index by Subjects and Names

Imports of US, detailed TSUSA commodities by country of origin, 1983, annual rpt, 2424–4

Income tax returns of corporations, detailed income and tax items by industry, 1981, annual rpt, 8304–4

Income tax returns of corporations with foreign tax credit, income and deductions by type, asset size, and selected industry group, 1980, article, 8302–2.415

Income tax returns of sole proprietorships, detailed data by industry div and selected industry group, 1981, annual rpt, 8304–7

Income tax returns of sole proprietorships, receipts, deductions by type, payroll, and net income, by major industry, 1982, annual article, 8302–2.413

Input-output structure of US economy, detailed interindustry transactions for 85 industries, and components of final demand, 1977, article, 2702–1.421

Input-output structure of US economy, detailed interindustry transactions for 537 industries, and components of final demand, 1977 benchmark data, 2708–17

Manufacturing census, 1982: financial and operating data, by SIC 2- to 4-digit industry, State, SMSA, and county, preliminary census div rpt series, 2491–3

Manufacturing census, 1982: financial and operating data, for SIC 4-digit industries by product, preliminary rpt series, 2491–1

Minority group and women employment, by occupational group and SIC 2- to 3-digit industry, 1981, annual rpt, 9244–1.1

Occupational injury and illness rates, by SIC 2- to 4-digit industry, 1982, annual rpt, 6844–1

Occupational manpower needs and supply by detailed occupation, and educational and training program enrollees and grads by detailed field, 1982 and 1995, biennial rpt, 6744–3

Occupational Outlook Handbook, 1984-85 biennial rpt, 6744–1

Pollution abatement capital and operating costs, by SIC 2- to 4-digit industry, State, and SMSA, 1982, annual Current Industrial Rpt, 2506–3.6

Producer prices and indexes, by stage of processing and detailed commodity, monthly rpt, 6762–6

Producer prices and indexes, by stage of processing and detailed commodity, monthly, 1983, annual supplement, 6764–2

Scientific publications and research articles, by field of author and journal, 1970s-80, annual rpt, 9624–10

Scientists, engineers, and technicians employed in private industry, by occupation and industry group, 1980-81, biennial rpt, 9627–23

Tariff Schedules of US, Annotated, classifications and rates of duty for detailed imported commodities, 1985 edition, 9886–13

Virgin Islands economic censuses, 1982: employment, establishments, payroll, and receipts, by SIC 1- to 4-digit industry, island, and city, 2593–1

Waterborne commerce of US (domestic and foreign), freight by commodity, traffic, and passengers, by port and waterway, 1982, annual rpt, 3754–3

see also Books and bookselling
see also Copyright
see also Microforms
see also Newspapers
see also Periodicals
see also under By Commodity in the "Index by Categories"
see also under By Industry in the "Index by Categories"

Prison sentences
see Sentences, criminal procedure

Prisoners of war

Claims against foreign govts by US natls, by country and type of claim, 1983, annual rpt, 6004–16

Disabled prisoners of war filing disability claims by period of service, and disability ratings by type and degree, various dates Oct 1981-May 1984, chartbook, 9928–30

Veterans aged 55 and over, socioeconomic characteristics, economic resources, health care and status, and actual and expected use of VA benefits, 1983 survey, 9928–29

Prisons and prisoners
see Correctional institutions
see Prisoners of war
see Sentences, criminal procedure

Privacy
see Right of privacy

Private schools

Alabama rural black population, education, employment, health services, and economic status, for 16 counties, selected years 1970-81, 11048–180

Census of Population and Housing, 1980: detailed population and housing characteristics, by county, city, and census tract, State and SMSA rpt series, 2551–2

Census of Population, 1980: detailed socioeconomic and demographic characteristics, by age, sex, race, Hispanic origin, occupation, and industry, State rpt series, 2531–4

Census of Population, 1980: detailed socioeconomic characteristics, by county, city, and inside-outside SMSAs and central cities, State rpt series, 2531–3

Condition of Education, detailed data on enrollment, staff, achievement, finances, curricula, and education effects on employment, 1982-83, annual rpt, 4824–1

Digest of Education Statistics, detailed data on students, staff, finances, and facilities, 1982 and selected trends, annual rpt, 4824–2

Elementary and secondary enrollment, households with children enrolled by school control, householder characteristics, and region, Oct 1982, 4838–13

Enrollment and teacher employment in all schools, by grade level and instn control, fall 1983-84, annual press release, 4804–19

Enrollment of persons aged 3-34, by grade level, instn control, and student characteristics, Oct 1983, advance annual Current Population Rpt, 2546–1.392

Fed Govt funding for elementary and secondary education by agency, and Education Dept funding for special education by program, selected years FY60-84, 4808–9.3

Private schools

Health professionals supply and education, by occupation, demographic and professional characteristics, and location, 1950s-83 and projected to 2000, biennial rpt, 4114–8

High school class of 1982: coursework compared to graduation criteria of natl commission, by student and school characteristics, 4828–16

High school class of 1982: foreign language course enrollment, by language, student and school characteristics, and location, 1984 rpt, 4838–11

High school class of 1982: foreign language coursework, by language, course level, student and school characteristics, and location, 1984 rpt, 4828–17

High school classes of 1980 and 1982: educational and sociodemographic characteristics and expectations, natl longitudinal study, series, 4826–2

Higher education enrollment, by student characteristics, instn type, State, and for 150 instns, fall 1982, annual rpt, 4844–2

Higher education instns, by type, location, and other characteristics, 1983/84 annual listing, 4844–3

Higher education instns, type, location, enrollment, and student charges, by State and congressional district, 1983/84, biennial listing, 4844–11

Higher education tuition and other student charges, for each public and private 2- and 4-year instn, by State, 1983/84, annual listing, 4844–10

Kentucky Higher Education Student Loan Corp student loans, loan purchases and defaults by instn, and revenue bonds status, various dates 1979-84, hearing, 21348–92

Neighborhood and housing quality indicators and attitudes, and occupant characteristics, by urban-rural location and region, 1981, annual survey, 2485–7

Neighborhood and housing quality indicators and attitudes, by occupant and unit characteristics, region, and metro-nonmetro location, 1981, annual survey, 2485–2

Science and engineering employment and grad students in higher education instns, and R&D expenditures, by field, 1972-83, biennial rpt, 9627–24

Southeastern States economic dev effect on education, for Fed Reserve 6th District States, selected years 1900-82, article, 9371–1.428

Statistical Abstract of US, social, political, and economic data, 1950s-83 and trends, annual rpt, 2324–1.1

Student aid Federal programs funding and participation, by instn type and control, State, and outlying area, with student loan defaults and collections, FY82, annual rpt, 4804–28

Student aid Pell grants and recipients, by educational costs, family income, instnl type and control, and State, 1981/82, annual rpt, 4804–1

Teaching degrees conferred by specialty and State, required credit hours, and instn officials attitudes, by instn type, 1970s-83, hearings, 21348–89

Truman, Harry S, Scholarship Foundation, program operation, financial status, and

Private schools

awards by student characteristics, 1983 with trends from 1977, annual rpt, 14314–1

Prizes

see Awards, medals, and prizes

Probation

see Parole and probation

Processed foods

see Food and food industry

Proctor, Allen J.

"Commercial Bank Investment in Municipal Securities", 9385–1.402

Procurement

see Defense contracts and procurement

see Government contracts and procurement

Producer Price Index

- Agricultural and food products prices, monthly rpt, 1502–4
- Building materials, by selected group and commodity, bimonthly rpt, 2012–1.5
- Business and financial statistics, historic trends, 1984 annual chartbook, 9364–2.6
- Business and financial statistics, quarterly chartbook, 9362–2.3
- Business statistics, detailed data for major industries and economic indicators, *Survey of Current Business,* monthly rpt, 2702–1.2
- Dairy products PPI, monthly rpt, 1317–4.2
- Economic and financial trends, natl compounded annual rates of change, 1964-83, annual rpt, 9391–9.2
- Economic and population time series data frequently used in statistical demand analyses, 1941-1982, annual rpt, 1544–21
- Economic indicators and components, and Fed Reserve 4th District business and financial conditions, monthly chartbook, 9377–10
- Economic indicators and components, current data and annual trends, monthly rpt, 23842–1.4
- Economic indicators and labor force characteristics, selected years 1880-1995, chartbook, 6728–30
- Economic indicators, nonfinancial, monthly rpt, 9362–1.2
- Economic performance of US, and Reagan Admin 1984 spending, tax, and monetary policy proposals, with data for 1950s-83 and projected to 1988, press release, 8008–107
- Economic trends, natl compounded annual rates of change, monthly rpt, 9391–3.1
- Fish prices, exvessel 1978-83, and wholesale and retail 1983, annual rpt, 2164–1.8
- Food price indexes (consumer and producer) and retail prices for selected items, and CPI for 25 cities, 1963-83, annual rpt, 1544–4.5
- Footwear production, employment, consumption, prices, and US trade by country, quarterly rpt, 9882–6
- Forecasts for selected business activities and natl economic indicators, compilation of representative opinions, 1984, annual rpt, 9389–3
- Foreign and US indexes of consumer, producer, and major commodity prices, nonfarm wages, and currency value, US and 4 countries, bimonthly rpt, 2042–11
- Foreign economic and monetary trends, compounded annual rates of change for US and 10 major trading partners, quarterly rpt, 9391–7

Foreign economic indicators for 7 OECD countries and US, quarterly rpt, 2042–10

- Foreign economic trends and implications for US, annual and semiannual country rpt series, 2046–4
- Foreign price indexes, by selected country, 1950-82, annual rpt, 6724–1.10
- Industry finances and operations, by SIC 2- to 4-digit industry, 1970s-83 and projected to 1988, annual rpt, 2014–4
- Inflationary impact of PPI changes, by processing stage, quarterly 1982-83, article, 6722–1.407
- Intl trade position of US and 4 OECD countries, and factors affecting US competition, quarterly pamphlet, 2042–25
- *Monthly Labor Review,* CPI and PPI current statistics, 6722–1.5
- North Central States farm credit conditions and economic devs, Fed Reserve 7th District, biweekly rpt, 9375–10
- OECD countries wholesale price indexes, 1960s-83, annual rpt, 244–5.2
- Price indexes (consumer and producer) by commodity and service group, and expenditure class, selected years 1929-83, annual rpt, 204–1.4
- Price indexes (consumer and producer) changes for selected items, and changes in CPI for selected services, 1982-83, article, 6722–1.429
- Price indexes (producer), by major commodity group and subgroup, and processing stage, monthly press release, 6762–5
- Price indexes, *Business Conditions Digest,* historical supplement and methodology, 1947-82, 2708–31
- Price indexes, *Business Conditions Digest,* monthly rpt, 2702–3.6
- Prices and living costs, selected years 1913-82, annual rpt, 6724–1.7
- Prices and price indexes, by stage of processing and detailed commodity, monthly rpt, 6762–6
- Prices and price indexes, by stage of processing and detailed commodity, monthly 1983, annual supplement, 6764–2
- Recession and recovery effect on labor cost and price indexes, changes by index component, various periods 1949-82, article, 6722–1.464
- Timber production, prices by region and State, trade by country, and consumption, by species and product, with industry earnings, 1950-83, annual rpt, 1204–29

Product safety

- Consumer Product Safety Commission activities, recalls, and product-related injuries, deaths, and medical costs, by product type and brand, FY83, annual rpt, 9164–2
- FDA investigation and regulatory activities, quarterly rpt, 4062–3
- Imports detained by FDA, by product, shipper or manufacturer, country, and detention reasons, monthly listing, 4062–2
- Injuries and deaths from use of selected consumer products and related activity, by victim age and sex, 1982, annual rpt, 9164–7

Index by Subjects and Names

- Injuries and deaths from use of selected consumer products, by victim age and medical treatment status, 1982, annual rpt, 9164–6
- Mobile and manufactured home safety standards, program inspections, enforcement actions, and accidents and casualties by victim characteristics, 1982-83, biennial rpt, 5004–4
- Radiation from electronic devices, incidents and persons involved by type of device and FDA control program activities, 1983, annual rpt, 4064–13
- Standards Natl Bur publications, 1983 annual listing, 2214–1
- *see also* Defective products
- *see also* Food additives
- *see also* Food inspection
- *see also* Hazardous substances
- *see also* Motor vehicle safety devices
- *see also* Poisoning and drug reaction
- *see also* Quality control and testing

Production

- *see* Agricultural production
- *see* Industrial production
- *see* Industrial production indexes
- *see* Production costs
- *see* Productivity

Production capacity

see Industrial capacity and utilization

Production costs

- Auto industry finances, employment, production, and cost increases to comply with Fed Govt pollution and safety standards, 1970s-83, annual rpt, 3304–5.4
- *Business Conditions Digest,* current data on economic, business, and financial conditions and cyclical fluctuations, monthly rpt, 2702–3
- *Business Conditions Digest,* historical supplement on economic, business, and financial conditions and cyclical fluctuations, with methodology, 1947-82, 2708–31
- Copper mine expansion in Cananea, Mexico, effects on US air pollution and copper industry, with US and foreign industry data, 1960s-95, hearing, 21448–31
- Copper production, production costs, prices, wages, and productivity, for US and 3 countries, 1970s-83 and projected to 1989, 21368–55
- Costs, prices, and productivity of labor and capital, by selected industry, and compared to 6 OECD countries, selected years 1947-82, 17898–1
- DOD-owned manufacturing and R&D facilities, operating data by selected SIC 2- to 3-digit industry, State, and SMSA, 1982, annual Current Industrial Rpt, 2506–3.4
- Fish hatchery production, deliveries, and operating costs, and fishery assistance, by region, hatchery, and Fed Govt assistance station, FY82, annual rpt, 5504–9
- Food prices (farm-retail), marketing cost components, and industry finances and productivity, selected years 1967-83, annual rpt, 1544–9
- Foreign manufacturing productivity and unit labor cost indexes for US and 11 countries, 1950-82 and preliminary 1983, annual rpt, 6864–1

Index by Subjects and Names

Income tax returns of corporations, detailed income and tax items by industry, 1981, annual rpt, 8304–4

Income tax returns of partnerships, receipts by source, deductions by type, and establishments, by selected industry, 1982, annual article, 8302–2.416

Manufacturing census, 1982: financial and operating data, by SIC 2- to 4-digit industry, State, SMSA, and county, preliminary census div rpt series, 2491–3

Manufacturing census, 1982: financial and operating data, for SIC 4-digit industries by product, preliminary rpt series, 2491–1

Mineral industries census, 1982: financial and operating data, including materials consumed, by SIC 4-digit industry and State, preliminary rpt series, 2511–1

Minerals (nonfuel) foreign and US supply under alternative market conditions, reserves, and background industry data, series, 5606–4

Partnership finances, tax deductions, and employment, by industry div and size, 1979, article, 8302–2.411

Pollution abatement capital and operating costs, by SIC 2- to 4-digit industry, State, and SMSA, 1982, annual Current Industrial Rpt, 2506–3.6

Private, nonfarm business, and manufacturing sectors, labor productivity and costs, preliminary data, quarterly rpt, 6822–1

Sausage potential use of fish, with fish supply, cost effectiveness, and nutritional value, various periods 1977-82, article, 2162–1.401

Shipbuilding costs and related employment, by coastal district, 1982, annual rpt, 7704–12

Steel industry finances and operations under proposed import quota, projected 1985-89 with selected foreign comparisons and trends from 1950, 26306–6.80

Steel industry financial and operating data, steel imports by source, and employment situation at Fairless Hills, Pa, plant, 1970s-90, hearing, 25528–94

Timber harvest residue recovery for energy, cost-effectiveness of 3 logging systems, 1983 technical paper, 9806–2.37

see also Agricultural production costs

see also Business income and expenses, general

see also Business income and expenses, specific industries

see also Capital investments, general

see also Capital investments, specific industries

see also Energy production costs

see also Labor cost indexes

see also Payroll

Production Credit Associations

see Farm Credit System

Production workers

see Blue collar workers

Productivity

Agricultural Statistics, 1983, annual rpt, 1004–1.2

Copper mine expansion in Cananea, Mexico, effects on US air pollution and copper industry, with US and foreign industry data, 1960s-95, hearing, 21448–31

Electric utility rate minimization from improved efficiency, proposed FERC incentive program operations and costs, with comparisons to 3 State programs, 1950s-82, 3088–17

Intl trade position of US and 4 OECD countries, and factors affecting US competition, quarterly pamphlet, 2042–25

Monthly labor Review, output, compensation, labor and nonlabor unit costs, and indexes, 6722–1.6

Oil (Alaskan) potential exports to Japan, costs and benefits, with background data on oil prices, Pacific Basin supply/demand, and tankers, various periods 1918-99, hearings, 25388–45

Pacific Northwest electricity consumption and prices by end-use sector, and economic and demographic data, 1960s-83 and projected to 2005, annual rpt, 3224–2

Productivity of labor and capital, costs, and prices, by selected industry, and compared to 6 OECD countries, selected years 1947-82, 17898–1

Productivity of labor and capital, growth by SIC 1- to 2-digit industry, and measurement methods and bibl, various periods 1948-78 with trends from 1800, 2218–69

Productivity of labor and capital in manufacturing, all nonfarm business, and all private business, indexes and percent change, 1948-83, annual rpt, 6824–2

Soviet Union aggregate and industrial factor productivity, annual growth rate 1961-83, annual rpt, 244–5.3

see also Agricultural productivity

see also Government efficiency

see also Industrial capacity and utilization

see also Industrial production indexes

see also Labor productivity

Professional and technical workers

Aircraft mechanics certified by FAA, by age, sex, region, and State, 1983, annual rpt, 7504–2

Census of Housing, 1980: structural, financial, and householder characteristics, by region and State, 2475–4

Census of Population and Housing, 1980: detailed population and housing characteristics, by county, city, and census tract, State and SMSA rpt series, 2551–2

Census of Population, 1980: detailed socioeconomic and demographic characteristics, by age, sex, race, Hispanic origin, occupation, and industry, State rpt series, 2531–4

Census of Population, 1980: detailed socioeconomic characteristics, by county, city, and inside-outside SMSAs and central cities, State rpt series, 2531–3

Census of Population, 1980: labor force, by sex, detailed occupation, and region, with comparison to 1970 census, supplementary rpt, 2535–1.12

Employee benefits in private industry, coverage by benefit type and provisions and occupational group, 1983, annual rpt, 6784–19

Employment and economic conditions, alternative BLS projections to 1995 with selected trends for 1959-82, 6728–29

Professional and technical workers

Employment by detailed occupation, for 29 SIC 2-digit nonmanufacturing industries, 1981 BLS survey, 6748–60

Employment, earnings, and hours, monthly press release, 6742–5

Employment situation, earnings, hours, and other BLS economic indicators, transcripts of BLS Commissioner's monthly testimony, periodic rpt, 23846–4

Employment, unemployment, and labor force, by demographic and employment characteristics, State, and for 30 metro areas and 11 large cities, 1983, annual rpt, 6744–7

Fed Govt civilian employment by occupation, total and for 25 agencies, as of Oct 1983, annual article, 9842–1.405

Fed Govt middle mgmt positions, labor cost savings under alternative grade reduction proposals, FY85-89, 26306–6.84

Fed Govt minority group and handicapped employment, by race, Hispanic origin, disability, sex, and employment characteristics, as of Sept 1982, biennial rpt, 9844–27

Fed Govt pay comparability with private industry, and recommended and actual pay increase, various dates 1971-84, annual rpt, 10104–1

Fed Govt pay comparability with private industry, and recommended pay rate adjustments, 1983, annual rpt, 104–16

Foreign women sociodemographic, economic, and fertility characteristics, with comparisons to men, by country, 1960s-85, world region rpt series, 2326–15

Handbook of Labor Statistics, employment, earnings, hours, and labor force characteristics, 1982 and trends, detailed annual rpt, 6724–1

Income of households, families, and persons, by detailed socioeconomic characteristics and region, 1982, annual Current Population Rpt, 2546–6.39

Labor unions recognized in Fed Govt, agreements and membership by agency and office or installation, Jan 1983, annual listing, 9844–14

Minority group and women's employment, by occupational group, SIC 2- to 3-digit industry, State, and SMSA, 1981, annual rpt, 9244–1

New England States college grads employment prospects in 1984, annual narrative rpt, 6916–7.3

Occupational manpower needs and supply by detailed occupation, and educational and training program enrollees and grads by detailed field, 1982 and 1995, biennial rpt, 6744–3

Occupational Outlook Handbook, 1984-85 biennial rpt, 6744–1

Pay ranges for white collar employees, and employees by characteristics of salary policy, by occupation, Mar 1983-84, article, 6722–1.473

Pension plans with postretirement benefit increases, participants and average increase by occupational group and plan characteristics, 1978-81, article, 6722–1.453

Poverty status of families and persons, by detailed socioeconomic characteristics, 1982, annual Current Population Rpt, 2546–6.40

Professional and technical workers

Seat belt use by blue and white collar workers, results of Virginia projects to increase use, 1983, article, 7762–9.409
TV and radio industry minority and women employment by occupation, and business owners, by race and State, with revenues and stations, 1971-81, hearing, 21368–45
Wages of white-collar workers, by occupation, work level, and industry div, Mar 1984, annual rpt, 6784–2
Washington State deaths by sex, cause, and detailed occupation, summary data from occupational mortality study, 1950-79, 4248–47
Women's employment and earnings, by labor force and socioeconomic characteristics, and compared to men, 1978-81 and trends from 1940s, 6568–29
see also Area wage surveys
see also Engineers and engineering
see also Executives
see also Health occupations
see also Industry wage surveys
see also Paraprofessionals
see also Scientists and technicians
see also under By Occupation in the "Index by Categories"
see also under names of specific professions

Professional associations
see Associations

Profits
see Business income and expenses, general
see Business income and expenses, specific industries
see Farm income
see Operating ratios

Project listings
see Directories

Projections

- Agricultural economics technical research, quarterly journal, 1502–3
- Agricultural exports and imports, outlook and current situation, quarterly rpt, 1542–4
- Air passenger traffic, and aircraft operations by type, by airport, region, and State, projected FY82-95 and trends from FY76, annual rpt, 7504–7
- Air pollutant emission effects of solar and biomass energy use, by region, and projected to 2000, 3408–30
- Air pollutant sulfur dioxide emissions reduction proposal, effects on polluting industries and coal production by region and State, projected to 2010, 9188–97
- Air quality and transportation and related energy use, for urban areas and Chicago area, late 1970s-82 and projected under lower auto emission standards to 1995, 3408–31
- Air traffic control and airway facilities and equipment, FAA improvement activities and R&D under Natl Airspace System Plan, 1982-2000, annual rpt, 7504–12
- Aircraft handled by instrument flight rule, by user type, FAA traffic control center, and region, FY69-83 and forecast to FY95, annual rpt, 7504–15
- Aviation activity forecasts, methodology, data sources, and coverage, Feb 1983 conf papers, annual rpt, 7504–28
- Aviation traffic, aircraft, pilots, airport activity, and fuel use, forecast FY84-95 with FY79-83 trends, annual rpt, 7504–6

BLS projections of employment by industry and GNP by component, analysis of projections to 1980 made selected years 1970-76, article, 6722–1.450
Budget of US, CBO analysis of revenue and spending alternatives and projections of economic indicators, FY85-89, annual rpt, 26304–3
Budget of US, compact budgets by function, agency, and account, FY85 with projections to FY89, annual rpt, 104–2
Budget of US, receipts, outlays, and budget authority, by function and agency, FY84-89 revised estimates, midsession review of FY85 budget, annual rpt, 104–7
Carbon dioxide emissions, climatic effects, and control costs, projected under alternative emissions controls and energy use restrictions to 2100 with trends 1970s-80, reprint, 9188–88
Civil Service Retirement Fund income by source, projected 1983-92, conf proceedings, 25408–87
Civil service retirement system actuarial valuation, FY79-83 with projections to FY2060, annual rpt, 9844–34
Coal dev plans on Fed Govt lease lands in 12 regions under Fed Coal Mgmt Program, environmental and socioeconomic impacts to 2000, final statement series, 5726–4
Coal Fed Govt leases, acreage, production, and prices, by State, and legal and mgmt issues, 1970s-83 with production projections to 2000, 11128–1
Coal miners working daily, mines, and labor productivity, trends and projections, quarterly rpt, 3162–37.4
Coal supply/demand, projected 1983-95 with summary trends from 1865, annual rpt, 3164–68
Coastal environmental and socioeconomic conditions, and potential impacts of oil and gas OCS leases, final statement series, 5736–1
Coastal environmental characteristics, fish, wildlife, and use, and population socioeconomic data, for individual areas, series, 5506–4
Computers and computer equipment foreign market and trade, and user industry operations and demand, country market research rpts, 2045–1
Construction industry activity, employment and earnings, prices, Federal aid, and foreign contracts, 1970s-83 with projections to 1988, annual article, 2012–1.402
Death rates by sex, race, and age for 40 causes, projected for 10-year period, 1982 rpt, 4208–21
Eastern Europe agricultural production and trade by commodity, food consumption, and farm inputs, for 6 countries, 1960-80 with projections to 1991, 1528–178
Economic conditions and employment, alternative BLS projections to 1995 with selected trends for 1959-82, 6728–29
Economic conditions of US, with some foreign comparisons, 1960s-82 and alternative projections to 1992, hearing, 21248–79
Economic growth, with data on labor force, inflation, and productivity, 1953-83 with inflation and unemployment projections to 1988, article, 9373–1.402

Index by Subjects and Names

Economic indicators and labor force characteristics, selected years 1880-1995, chartbook, 6728–30
Economic Report of the President for 1984, economic effects of budget proposals, and trends and projections 1950s-89, annual hearings, 23844–4
Electric power cogeneration in 5 industries, and fuel use and utility supply/demand effects, by region, 1983-93, 3008–92
Electric power demand of households in 136 SMSAs and other utility service areas, with fuel prices, family income, and heating degree days, 1975 and projected to 1985, 1588–78
Electric power industrial demand model estimates, economic indicators, and supporting data for 5 industries, 1960s-80 with projections to 2000, 3008–87
Electric power peak demand, generating and interregional transfer capability, and reserve margins, detailed data by region, 1984-93, annual rpt, 3404–6
Electric power plant (coal-fired) capacity addition estimation to forecast coal demand, methodology and input data, series, 3166–11
Electric power plant (coal-fired) capacity, coal demand, and coal supply by mode of transport and region of origin, by State, for units planned 1983-92, 3088–18
Electric power plant capacity, by plant type, age, and DOE region, 1982, and new and replacement capacity trends and projections, 1900-2020, 3008–98
Electric power systems equipment foreign market and trade, and user industry operations and demand, country market research rpts, 2045–15
Electronic component equipment foreign market and trade, and user industry operations and demand, country market research rpts, 2045–4
Electronic component manufacturing equipment foreign market and trade, and user industry operations and demand, country market research rpts, 2045–5
Energy demand in industry, forecasting model description, detailed technology specifications, and energy use, for 27 SIC 2- to 4-digit industries, 1970s-80 and projected to 2000, 3308–66
Energy Natl Policy Plan, energy supply, demand, and prices, by fuel and sector, projected 1985-2010, biennial rpt, 3004–13
Energy supply/demand and price forecasts, by fuel type, quarterly rpt, 3162–34
Energy supply/demand and prices, by energy source and end-use sector and for 7 electric utilities, 1981-2000 with trends from 1960s, 3008–93
Energy supply/demand and prices, by fuel type, sector, and end use, detailed trends and projections 1973-95, annual rpt, 3164–75
Energy supply/demand and prices, by fuel type, sector, and end use, with foreign comparisons, 1960-83 and projected to 1995, annual summary rpt, 3164–76
Energy supply/demand projections, by energy source and end use, series, 2006–2
Farm machinery and equipment foreign market and trade, and user industry operations and demand, country market research rpts, 2045–13

Index by Subjects and Names

Projections

Farm production inputs, land mgmt, and environmental effects, for 4 crops, 1940s-80 and projected to 2010, 9188–94

Fed Govt programs and mgmt cost control proposals, 3-year savings by function and agency, and financial and operating data, 1960s-81, 16908–1

Fed Govt programs of congressional legislative interest, objectives, feasibility, benefits, and costs, CBO study series, 26306–6

Food processing and packaging equipment, foreign market and trade, and user industry operations and demand, country market research rpts, 2045–11

Foreign aged population characteristics, with related health care data and vital statistics, by world area and selected country, 1950-80 and projected to 2020, 2546–10.12

Foreign and US coal reserves, production, demand indicators, and trade, by country, selected years 1973-82 and alternative trade projections to 1995, annual rpt, 3164–77

Foreign and US production, acreage, and yield for selected crops, forecasts by selected world region and country, FAS monthly rpt, 1925–28

Forest, range, and associated waters use and mgmt assessment, and environmental impacts of Forest Service program options, 1977-2030 and trends from 1920, 1208–24

Forests (tropical) status by country and world region, conservation methods, and mgmt role of US, foreign, and intl groups, 1977-80s and projected to 2000, 26358–101.1

Graphic industries equipment foreign market and trade, and user industry operations and demand, country market research rpts, 2045–3

Health care expenditures, growth factors, medical equipment and drugs trade, and physician income, 1950-90, article, 4652–1.407

Health professionals supply and education, by occupation, demographic and professional characteristics, and location, 1950s-83 and projected to 2000, biennial rpt, 4114–8

Income tax returns and collections and economic and demographic trends for IRS regions, districts, and service centers, 1972-82 and projected to 1990, annual rpt, 8304–8

Income tax returns filed, by type of return, 1972-82 and projected 1983-90, annual rpt, 8304–9

Industrial process control equipment foreign market and trade, and user industry operations and demand, country market research rpts, 2045–6

Industry finances and operations, by SIC 2- to 4-digit industry, 1970s-83 and projected to 1988, annual rpt, 2014–4

Industry R&D expenditures by funding source, and projected impact on output, employment, and hours of labor, by selected industry, various periods 1953-90, hearings, 25368–133

Inflation, real GNP, and Treasury bill rate forecasts, and forecasting errors, 1971-84, summary article, 9389–1.404

Lab instruments foreign market and trade, and user industry operations and demand, country market research rpts, 2045–10

Life expectancy increase impacts on OASDI and pension policy, with alternative sociodemographic projections to 2100, hearing, 25368–130

Machine tools and equipment foreign market and trade, and user industry operations and demand, country market research rpts, 2045–9

Mail electronic system message volume and profitability under USPS proposed rate and service increases, FY82 and projected to FY87, 21408–70

Medical and health care equipment foreign market and trade, and user industry operations and demand, country market research rpts, 2045–2

Medicare Hospital Insurance Trust Fund financial operations and payroll taxes, FY83 and selected years 1966-2005, annual rpt, 4704–5

Medicare Supplementary Medical Insurance Trust Fund financial operations, FY83 and selected years 1966-87, annual rpt, 4704–3

Medicare trust funds financial operations and payroll taxes, annual summary of 1984 trustees rpts, 4654–8

Methanol fuel for autos, regulatory barriers to market dev, with supply/demand and auto fleet use and fuel economy, mid-1970s-82 and projected to 2000, GAO rpt, 26113–112

Milk price support alternatives, effects on production, use, prices, and farm receipts, projected 1983/84-1988/89 and actual 1982/83, 1568–246

Milk price supports effect on production, use, prices, and farm receipts, by region and State, 1940s-83 and alternative projections to 1988/89, 1568–245

Minerals (nonfuel) foreign and US supply under alternative market conditions, reserves, and background industry data, series, 5606–4

Minerals (nonfuel) from marine sources, demand by mineral type, selected years 1978-83 with projections to 2000, 15048–4

Mining industry equipment foreign market and trade, and user industry operations and demand, country market research rpts, 2045–16

Montana and North Dakota coal production, impact of mining on agricultural land availability and on farm income and production costs, by mining tract, 1982 rpt, 1588–79

Natural gas interstate pipeline company supplies, reserves, production, purchases, and contracts, by firm, 1983 with projected deliverability to 2003, annual rpt, 3164–33

Natural gas price changes effect on farm income and fertilizer use, 1980 and projected to 1990, 1548–240

Natural gas price decontrol alternatives effect on farm production by crop, prices, and fertilizer use and costs, 1982-90, model results, 1548–239

Natural gas price decontrol alternatives effect on supply/demand, prices, and home heating costs of low-income households, 1970s-95, hearing, 25148–26

Natural gas price decontrol effect on prices, Iowa supply/demand, and economic indicators, with US imports from Canada, various periods 1969-95, hearings, 23848–177

Natural gas prices, reserves, consumption, and production, projected under alternative price controls 1983-95 with market data for various periods 1970-Mar 1984, 3008–96

Northern Mariana Islands economic, govtl, and population data, 1970s-FY83 and population projections to 1990, annual rpt, 7004–6.2

Nuclear power industry status and outlook, with reactor construction, utility financial and operating data, and foreign comparisons, 1970s-83 with projections to 2010, 26358–99

Nuclear power plant construction and operation status, and capacity, by plant, region, State, and selected country, 1983 and projected to 2020, annual rpt, 3164–57

Nuclear power plant spent fuel and demand for uranium and enrichment services, US and non-Communist country groups, 1983 and projected to 2020, annual rpt, 3164–72

Nuclear power plant spent fuel discharges and additional storage capacity required, by reactor, projected 1984-93, annual rpt, 3354–2

Nuclear power plant spent fuel permanent disposal site and transport costs, and Nuclear Waste Fund financing, alternative projections FY83-2037, 26308–49

Nuclear power plants construction financing of Washington Public Power Supply System, with regional economic impacts and power supply/demand, 1980s-2035, hearing, 21448–29

Nuclear weapon forces of US and USSR under Strategic Arms Reduction Talks and alternative proposals and counting methods, by weapon and system, FY84-96, 26306–6.73

Nurses (registered) population and employment by age and education, and nursing program admissions and grads, projected 1981-90, article, 4102–1.439

OASDHI and Supplementary Medical Insurance trust fund financial status summary, as of 1983 with projections to 2000, articles, 4742–1.410, 4742–1.411

OASDHI benefits wage replacement rate and delayed retirement credits, by retirement age, selected years 1986-2050, article, 4742–1.420

OASDHI future cost estimates, actuarial studies series, 4706–1

OASDHI trust fund assets, total and tax income, and outlays, alternative projections to 2060, 4706–2.120

OASDI trust funds financial operations, FY83 and selected years 1940s-2060, annual rpt, 4704–4

Occupational manpower needs and supply by detailed occupation, and educational and training program enrollees and grads by detailed field, 1982 and 1995, biennial rpt, 6744–3

Occupational Outlook Handbook, 1984-85 biennial rpt, 6744–1

Projections

Oil (Alaskan) potential exports to Japan, costs and benefits, with background data on oil prices, Pacific Basin supply/demand, and tankers, various periods 1918-99, hearings, 25388–45

Oil and gas 5-year OCS leasing plan and proposed sale off California coast, acreage, costs, and benefits, various periods 1953-2006, hearing, 21448–30

Oil enhanced recovery technologies use and environmental impacts, by oil field, county, and State, 1970s-80 and projected to 2000, 3408–29

Oil prices impact on US oil trade and energy-intensive industries, with US and foreign reserves and industry operations, 1950-82 and projected to 2020, 9886–4.69

Oil refineries financial and operating impacts from auto use of alcohol fuels, projected to 2000 with trends 1964-80, 3308–75

Oil reserves, production, and resource lifespan under alternative production rates, historic and projected, country rpt series, 3166–9

Older persons by demographic, socioeconomic, and health characteristics, selected years 1900-81 and projected to 2050, Current Population Rpt, 2546–2.125

Older persons Fed Govt pension and health spending, by program and as percents of budget and GNP, 1965-85 with projections to 2040, 25148–28

OPEC oil refining capacity and production by city, and oil use and exports, by member, with comparisons to other countries, projected 1985-90, hearings, 25368–133.1

Pacific Northwest electricity consumption and prices by end-use sector, and economic and demographic data, 1960s-83 and projected to 2005, annual rpt, 3224–2

Phosphate rock industry environmental protection costs, by control type and selected State, with background operating data, 1977-81 with cost projections to 1990, 5608–143

Physician supply and ratio to population by State and county population size, and counties with shortages and needs, 1960-79 and projected 1982-94, 4118–52

Pollution abatement capital and operating costs under Clean Air and Water Acts, for govts and selected industries, various periods 1970-2000, annual rpt, 9184–11

Pollution abatement expenditures, and effect on economic indicators and industry operations, by major industry, projected under 3 pollution regulation alternatives 1983-95, 9188–84

Pollution control instruments and equipment foreign market and trade, and user industry operations and demand, country market research rpts, 2045–17

Population census, 1980: selected socioeconomic data, with trends and projections 1960-2050, young readers pamphlet series, 2326–1

Population estimates and projections, by region and State, Current Population Rpt series, 2546–3

Population size and components of change, by region and State, 1970s-83 with projections to 2050, annual Current Population Rpt, 2546–2.119

Prison population and capacity by State and individual DC and Federal instn, construction costs, and Fed Govt operating costs, 1983 and projected to 1990, GAO rpt, 26119–59

Radioactive waste and spent fuel generation, inventory, disposal by site, reprocessing, and characteristics, by source, as of 1983 and projected to 2020, annual rpt, 3364–2

Radioactive waste generation, by northeast State and reactor and nonreactor source, 1979-81 and projected to 2000, hearing, 25528–93

Recreation (outdoor) participation, by type of activity, projected 1985-2030, 1208–195

Scientists and engineers employed in energy-related fields, supply/demand and effects of R&D funding, by energy type, employer type, field, and age, 1962-91, annual rpt, 3004–19

Scientists, engineers, and technicians needed in defense and nondefense industries, and supply/demand, by field, 1981-87, 9628–71

Seasonal adjustment methodology for economic time series, dev and design of Census Bur and other systems, with illustrative data, 1981 conf papers, 2626–7.5

Southeastern States employment measures by occupation, for Fed Reserve 6th District States, 1982 and projected to 1995, article, 9371–1.430

Southeastern US water supply and quality, with background socioeconomic data, for 8 States, 1960s-2020 with trends from 1930, 9208–119

Sporting goods and recreational equipment and vehicles foreign market and trade, country market research rpts, 2045–14

Statistical Abstract of US, social, political, and economic data, 1950s-83 and trends, annual rpt, 2324–1

Tax expenditures, Fed Govt revenues foregone through income tax deductions and exclusions by type, and effect of Deficit Reduction Act, FY84-89, annual rpt, 21784–10

Tax expenditures from employee benefit plans, for income and payroll tax by benefit type and income, with benefits by industry, 1950-83 and projected to 1988, article, 9373–1.404

Telecommunication equipment foreign market and trade, and user industry operations and demand, country market research rpts, 2045–12

Trucks (heavy) energy use, efficiency, and conservation technologies, selected years 1958-82 and projected to 2000, 3308–70

Uranium enrichment plants of DOE, production and other costs and selling prices, FY71-83 and projected to FY94, GAO rpt, 26113–137

Uranium enrichment prices of DOE under alternative TVA power rates, and effects of TVA charges for power not taken, FY84-95, GAO rpt, 26113–114

Uranium mining operations, finances, and costs of alternative methods to meet emissions standards, for industry and selected mines, selected years 1948-90, 9188–96

Index by Subjects and Names

Uranium reserves and mining and milling industries operations and finances, with selected foreign comparisons, various periods 1964-83 and projected to 2000, 3008–95

Urban travel by purpose, effect of telecommunication advances, land use changes, and alternative work schedules, projected to 2000 with some trends 1950-80, 7888–63

Veteran women, by period of service, age, and State, Mar 1983 and projected to 2030, 9928–28

Voting age population selected characteristics and participation in presidential elections, 1964-80 with projections to 2000, Current Population Rpt, 2546–2.117

Washington State telephone rates including govt long-distance access charges, by company, 1983-89, hearing, 21148–32

Water supply and use in 3 areas with supply problems and total US, and methods to increase supply, selected years 1974-80 and projected to 2010, 9208–125

Water supply in Western US, streamflow and reservoir storage forecasts by stream and station, Jan-May monthly rpt, 1262–1

Western Area Power Admin small-scale potential hydroelectric generation, site inventory, characteristics, and costs, by State and county, 1984 rpt, 3258–1

Propaganda

Fed Govt programs and mgmt cost control proposals, 3-year savings by function and agency, and financial and operating data, 1960s-81, 16908–1.32

Soviet Union propaganda campaign against NATO nuclear missile deployment, and USSR and NATO nuclear arms and aircraft in place, 1977-83, narrative rpt, 9828–25

see also Political broadcasting

Property

AFDC eligibility under Omnibus Budget Reconciliation Act, effect on caseloads and recipient benefits and living costs, 1981-83, GAO rpt, 26131–11

Arson investigation and prosecution, by incident characteristics and outcome, motive, and type of evidence, for 4 jurisdictions, 1981, 6068–184

Bombing (explosive and incendiary) and arson incidents by target, State, and circumstances, and explosives theft and recovery, 1982-83, annual rpt, 8484–4

Bombing (explosive and incendiary) incidents, damage, injuries, and deaths, by target, State, and circumstances, 1983, annual rpt, 6224–5

Census of Govts, 1982: properties, govt-assessed value, sales, and tax rates, by property type, State, SMSA, county, and city, 2453–1

Court caseloads for Federal district, appeals, and bankruptcy courts, by type of suit and offense, circuit, and district, quarterly rpt, 18202–1

Crime victim medical expenses and property loss, and median loss by victim characteristics, by offense type, 1975-81, 6066–19.6

Index by Subjects and Names

Property tax

Crimes, arrests by offender characteristics, and rates, by offense, and law enforcement employees, by population size and jurisdiction, 1970s-83, annual rpt, 6224–2

Earthquake intensity, damage, and deaths, by location for major earthquakes since 1755, and hazard areas and natl reduction program activities, as of 1984, 5668–73

Earthquake intensity, damage, time of origin, and seismic characteristics of all US and major foreign earthquakes, 1981, annual rpt, 5664–13

FBI undercover operations convictions, fines, recoveries, victim compensation, and status of lawsuits against FBI by operation, FY82, GAO rpt, 26119–67

Foreign countries disasters, persons affected, deaths, damage, and aid by US and others, FY83 and trends from FY64, annual rpt, 9914–12

Hazardous material transport accidents, casualties, and property damage, by mode of transport, with DOT control activities, 1983, annual rpt, 7304–4

Hurricanes and tropical storms in North Atlantic and Caribbean area, paths, surveillance, deaths, property damage, and landfall probabilities by city, 1983, annual rpt, 2184–7

Hurricanes and tropical storms in northeastern Pacific, paths, surveillance, deaths, and property damage, 1983, annual rpt, 2184–8

Income tax proposals to encourage savings, and personal assets and liabilities by type, 1981, article, 8302–2.407

Income tax returns of individuals, detailed data, 1982, annual rpt, 8304–2

Marijuana cultivation control activity of State law enforcement agencies, and aid from Fed Govt and Natl Guard, 1983 survey, GAO rpt, 26119–64

Marine property loss, and losses prevented by Coast Guard search and rescue missions, by district, station, and rescue vessel, FY83, annual rpt, 7404–2

Michigan bankruptcy filings, by filer type, moving history, income, creditor action, debt and asset type, credit status, exemptions claimed, and county, 1979-81, hearings, 21528–57.3

Military personnel personal property shipped worldwide, and loss and damage claims, quarterly rpt, 3702–1

Natural gas interstate pipeline company detailed financial and operating data, by firm, 1983, annual rpt, 3164–38

Robbery rates and circumstances, medical costs and property losses of victims, and offender and victim characteristics, 1960s-81, 6068–180

Storms and unusual weather phenomena characteristics, casualties, and property damage, by State and outlying area, monthly listing, 2152–3

Tax expenditures, Fed Govt revenues foregone through income tax deductions and exclusions by type, and effect of Deficit Reduction Act, FY84-89, annual rpt, 21784–10

Truck accidents, injuries, deaths, and property damage, by circumstances, carrier type, and driver age and condition, 1983, annual rpt, 7554–9

Trust assets of banks and trust companies, by type of asset and fund and State, 1983, annual rpt, 13004–1

Weather events socioeconomic impacts and costs, heating and cooling degree days, and housing energy bills, by census div and State, monthly rpt, 2152–12

see also Business assets and liabilities, general

see also Business assets and liabilities, specific industries

see also Educational facilities

see also Farms and farmland

see also Government property

see also Housing tenure

see also Land ownership

see also Land use

see also Military bases, posts, and reservations

see also Military supplies and property

see also Mortgages

see also Property tax

see also Property value

see also Public buildings

see also Public lands

see also Real estate business

see also Rent

see also Surplus government property

see also Wealth

Property insurance

see Insurance

Property tax

Boston, Mass, govt budget and impact of reduced local revenue and Fed Govt aid, and other devs, FY80-86, article, 9373–1.406

Census of Govts, 1982: city govt revenues by source, expenditures by function, debt, and assets, by State and city, 2457–4

Census of Govts, 1982: county govt revenues by source, expenditures by function, debt, and assets, by State and county, 2457–3

Census of Govts, 1982: properties, govt-assessed value, sales, and tax rates, by property type, State, SMSA, county, and city, 2453–1

Census of Govts, 1982: school districts revenues, expenditures, debt, and assets, by district and State, 2457–1

Census of Govts, 1982: State govt payments to local govts, by program, source of funds, level of govt, and State, with trends from 1902, 2460–3

City govt fiscal condition, plans to raise or lower taxes and city employment, and use of municipal bonds, FY81-83, survey, hearings, 25408–86.1

Coal taxes for surface and underground mines, by type of tax and State, 1984 rpt, 11128–1

Farm investments, effective rates of Federal/State income and State/local property taxes, by category of structure and equipment, for 7 North Central States, 1981-82, 1548–237

Farm production expenditures, detailed items by farm sales size and region, 1983, annual rpt, 1614–3

Farm real estate taxes, by State, selected years 1940-82 and trends from 1890, annual rpt, 1541–8.6

Farm real estate taxes, by State, 1979-82, annual rpt, 1544–18

Farmers prices received for major products and paid for farm inputs and living items, by commodity and State, monthly rpt, 1629–1

Govt finances, by level of govt and State, selected years 1929-83, annual rpt, 10044–1

Govt finances, by level of govt, State, and for large cities and counties, 1981-83, annual rpt series, 2466–2

Govt revenues by source and expenditures by function, natl income and product account, *Survey of Current Business,* monthly rpt, monthly and annual tables, 2702–1.24

Govt tax revenues, by level of govt, type of tax, State, and selected counties, quarterly rpt, 2462–3

Home mortgages (graduated payment) FHA-insured, financial, property, and mortgagor characteristics, for US and selected localities, quarterly rpt, 5142–42

Home mortgages (graduated payment) FHA-insured, financial, property, and mortgagor characteristics, for US and selected States, quarterly rpt, 5142–41

Home mortgages (graduated payment) FHA-insured, financial, property, and mortgagor characteristics, US summary, quarterly rpt, 5142–40

Home mortgages FHA-insured, financial, property, and mortgagor characteristics, for US and selected localities, quarterly rpt, 5142–2

Home mortgages FHA-insured, financial, property, and mortgagor characteristics, for US, selected States, and Puerto Rico, quarterly rpt, 5142–3

Home mortgages FHA-insured, financial, property, and mortgagor characteristics, quarterly rpt, 5142–1

Home mortgages FHA-insured, financial, property, and mortgagor characteristics, 1983, annual rpt, 5144–17

Home mortgages FHA-insured for low-cost homes, financial, construction, property, and mortgagor characteristics, quarterly rpt, 5142–4

Housing and financial characteristics, and unit and neighborhood quality, for 15 SMSAs, 1978, annual survey special supplement, 2485–8

Housing and neighborhood quality indicators and attitudes, and occupant characteristics, by urban-rural location and region, 1981, annual survey, 2485–7

Housing occupancy and unit and household characteristics, by region and metro-nonmetro residence, 1983, biennial survey, 2485–1

Housing value or rent, and household income groups, by housing and household characteristics, and inside-outside central cities, 1979-82 surveys, SMSA rpt series, 2485–6

Hwy receipts by source, and expenditures by function, by level of govt and State, 1983, annual rpt, 7554–1.3

Income (household) before and after taxes, by socioeconomic characteristics, type of tax paid, and region, 1981, Current Population Rpt, 2546–2.118

Income (household) before and after taxes, by socioeconomic characteristics, type of tax paid, and region, 1982, annual Current Population Rpt, 2546–2.122

Property tax

Income tax returns of elderly, by income statement and tax item and income level, 1981 with trends from 1977, article, 8302–2.412

Income tax returns of individuals, detailed data, 1982, annual rpt, 8304–2

Local govt finances and population characteristics for cities and suburbs, by region and selected SMSA, selected years 1957-FY83, 10048–61

Louisiana property tax on forest, agricultural, and marsh lands, impact of change from market to use valuation by parish, 1977-78, 1208–206

Public lands, Fed Govt payments to local govts in lieu of property taxes by State, FY84, annual press release, 5724–9

Public opinion on taxes, tax policy, and intergovtl relations, 1972-84 surveys, annual rpt, 10044–2

State and local tax rates by selected jurisdiction, and average family tax burden by income level and selected city, by type of tax, 1982, 10046–8.2

Tax assessment, local jurisdictions reporting data on property size, use, location, ownership, and value, 1972-82, 1588–81

Tax expenditures, Fed Govt revenues foregone through income tax deductions and exclusions by type, and effect of Deficit Reduction Act, FY84-89, annual rpt, 21784–10

Urban Dev Action Grant awards to local areas, preliminary approvals, with project descriptions, private investment, and jobs and taxes to be created, by city, quarterly press release series, 5002–7

Property value

Agriculture census, 1982: farms, farmland, production and costs, and operator characteristics, preliminary State and county rpt series, 2330–1

California (southern) housing demand by county, prices and sales, and costs after homeowner tax deductions, 1970s-80, hearing, 21148–31

Capital (fixed), govt and private nonresidential structures and equipment, residential capital, and consumer-owned durable goods by item, 1980-83, annual article, 2702–1.433

Census of Govts, 1982: properties, govt-assessed value, sales, and tax rates, by property type, State, SMSA, county, and city, 2453–1

Census of Housing, 1980: inventory, occupancy, and unit characteristics, changes from 1973 by region and inside-outside SMSAs and central cities, series, 2473–3

Census of Housing, 1980: occupancy and unit characteristics of SMSAs and central cities, by race, Hispanic origin, and city, State and SMSA rpt series, 2473–1

Census of Population and Housing, 1980: detailed population and housing characteristics, by county, city, and census tract, State and SMSA rpt series, 2551–2

Construction put in place, value of new public and private structures, by type, monthly rpt, 2382–4

County and City Data Book, detailed socioeconomic and demographic data for States, counties, and cities, selected years 1976-82, 2328–1

Farm finances, assets, expenses, cash flow, receipts, and loans, selected years 1971-85, annual rpt, 1544–13

Farm finances, expenses by type, loans by purpose and source, and credit detail by Fed Reserve District, quarterly rpt, 9365–3.10

Farm real estate value, for land, service structures, and operator dwellings, 1940-84, annual rpt, 1544–16.2

Farm real estate value, sales, financing, taxes, and proposed use after purchase, by State, 1970s-84, annual rpt, 1541–8

Fed Govt programs and mgmt cost control proposals, 3-year savings by function and agency, and financial and operating data, 1960s-81, 16908–1

Foreign direct investment in US, major investors and investments by SIC 4-digit industry, transaction type and value, and location, 1983, annual rpt, 2044–20

Home mortgages (graduated payment) FHA-insured, financial, property, and mortgagor characteristics, for US and selected localities, quarterly rpt, 5142–42

Home mortgages (graduated payment) FHA-insured, financial, property, and mortgagor characteristics, for US and selected States, quarterly rpt, 5142–41

Home mortgages (graduated payment) FHA-insured, financial, property, and mortgagor characteristics, US summary, quarterly rpt, 5142–40

Home mortgages FHA-insured, financial, property, and mortgagor characteristics, for US and selected localities, quarterly rpt, 5142–2

Home mortgages FHA-insured, financial, property, and mortgagor characteristics, for US, selected States, and Puerto Rico, quarterly rpt, 5142–3

Home mortgages FHA-insured, financial, property, and mortgagor characteristics, quarterly rpt, 5142–1

Home mortgages FHA-insured, financial, property, and mortgagor characteristics, 1983, annual rpt, 5144–17

Home mortgages FHA-insured for low-cost homes, financial, construction, property, and mortgagor characteristics, quarterly rpt, 5142–4

Household income, assets, and debt characteristics, sources of credit, and use of financial services, 1983 survey, article, 9362–1.411

Household income, home value and equity, and financial assets by type, by household characteristics, 1983 survey with trends from 1970, article, 9362–1.406

Housing and financial characteristics, and unit and neighborhood quality, for 15 SMSAs, 1978, annual survey special supplement, 2485–8

Housing and households detailed characteristics, and unit and neighborhood quality, by inside-outside central cities, 1979-82 surveys, SMSA rpt series, 2485–6

Housing and neighborhood quality indicators and attitudes, and occupant characteristics, by urban-rural location and region, 1981, annual survey, 2485–7

Housing and neighborhood quality indicators and attitudes, by occupant and unit characteristics, region, and metro-nonmetro location, 1981, annual survey, 2485–2.2

Index by Subjects and Names

Housing, new single and multifamily unit physical and financial characteristics, by region and metro-nonmetro location, 1979-83, annual rpt, 2384–1

Housing, new single-family units sold and for sale by price, stage of construction, months on market, and region, and seasonal adjustments, monthly rpt, 2382–3

Housing occupancy and unit and household characteristics, by region and metro-nonmetro residence, 1983, biennial survey, 2485–1

Income tax returns of corporations, detailed income and tax items by industry, 1981, annual rpt, 8304–4

Louisiana property tax on forest, agricultural, and marsh lands, impact of change from market to use valuation by parish, 1977-78, 1208–206

NASA building size, value, employees, costs of GSA rental and services, and construction budget, by facility, FY82-88, hearings, 25328–23

Natural gas interstate pipeline company detailed financial and operating data, by firm, 1983, annual rpt, 3164–38

New Communities program of HUD, activities, costs, land sales, and community and population characteristics, for 13 communities, 1970s-83, 5188–107

Public lands sales of Land Mgmt Bur, prices of Nevada and California acreage, and effect on Forest Service land acquisition program, 1983, GAO rpt, 26113–122

Southeastern States economic indicators, by State, Fed Reserve 5th District, quarterly rpt, 9389–16

Southeastern States farm credit conditions and real estate values, Fed Reserve 5th District, quarterly rpt, 9389–17

Southeastern States financial and economic devs, Fed Reserve 6th District, monthly rpt with articles, 9371–1

Southwestern States farm credit conditions and real estate values, Fed Reserve 11th District, quarterly rpt, 9379–11

Tax assessment, local jurisdictions reporting data on property size, use, location, ownership, and value, 1972-82, 1588–81

Tax evasion through tax haven countries, with income, investments, and taxes withheld by country, various periods 1975- 83, hearings, 21408–71

Traffic accidents and casualties detailed direct and indirect costs, by characteristics of persons and vehicles involved, 1979-80, 7768–80

Transportation safety programs, and accidents, injuries, deaths, hazards, and property damage, by mode of transport, 1983, annual rpt, 7304–19

Uranium mining operations, finances, and costs of alternative methods to meet emissions standards, for industry and selected mines, selected years 1948-90, 9188–96

Vacancy and occupancy rates, and vacant housing characteristics, by region and metro-nonmetro location, selected years 1960-83, annual rpt, 2484–1

Vacant housing characteristics and costs, and occupancy and vacancy rates, by region and metro-nonmetro location, quarterly rpt, 2482–1

Index by Subjects and Names

Western States farm real estate values, and nonreal estate farm loan trends, monthly rpt, quarterly data, 9381–2

Western States, FHLB 11th District housing, employment, and economic indicators, by SMSA, quarterly rpt, 9302–18

Proprietorships

see Business firms and establishments, number

see Ownership of enterprise

Prosthetics and orthotics

Exports and imports of US, detailed SIC-based commodities by world area, 1983, annual rpts, 2424–6

Exports and imports of US, totals and as percent of domestic production, by SIC 2- to 5-digit commodity, 1981, annual rpt, 2424–3

Exports of US, detailed Schedule B commodities by country of destination, 1983, annual rpt, 2424–9

Exports of US, detailed Schedule E commodities by mode of transport and world area and country of destination, 1983, annual rpts, 2424–5

Imports of US, detailed Schedule A commodities by country and world area of origin, and mode of transport, 1983, annual rpts, 2424–2

Imports of US, detailed TSUSA commodities by country of origin, 1983, annual rpt, 2424–4

Medicare Supplementary Medical Insurance maximum charges reimbursable for specific services, by State and outlying area, 1983, annual rpt, 4654–4

Veterans aged 55 and over, socioeconomic characteristics, economic resources, health care and status, and actual and expected use of VA benefits, 1983 survey, 9928–29

Vital and Health Statistics series and other NCHS publications, 1979-83, annual listing,, 4124–1

Prostitution

Arrests and arrest rates, by offense, offender characteristics, population size, and State, 1970s-83, annual rpt, 6224–2.2

Income (taxable) not reported, by illegal source, with characteristics of persons involved, methodology, and bibl, 1970s-82, 8008–112

Income (taxable) not reported on individual and corporate returns, and associated Federal revenue losses, by detailed legal and illegal source, 1973-81, 8308–26

Pretrial citation release use, cost savings for law enforcement agencies, and failures to appear in court, by offense and selected jurisdiction, 1970s-82, 6068–187

Protection of animals

see Birds and bird conservation

see Marine resources conservation

see Wildlife and wildlife conservation

Protection of nature

see Conservation of natural resources

Protective services

see Detective and protective services

Protopapadakis, Aris

"General Equilibrium Properties of the Term Structure of Interest Rates", 9387–8.91

Providence, R.I.

Census of Housing, 1980: occupancy and unit characteristics, by race, Hispanic origin, and city, SMSA rpt, 2473–1.293

Census of Population and Housing, 1980: detailed population and housing characteristics, by county, city, and census tract, SMSA rpt, 2551–2.293

Housing and households detailed characteristics, and unit and neighborhood quality, by inside-outside central cities, 1980 survey, SMSA rpt, 2485–6.14

Wages of office and plant workers, by occupation, 1984 SMSA survey rpt, 6785–11.6

see also under By City and By SMSA or MSA in the "Index by Categories"

Provo, Utah

Census of Population and Housing, 1980: detailed population and housing characteristics, by county, city, and census tract, SMSA rpt, 2551–2.294

Housing vacancy rates for single and multifamily units and mobile homes, by city and ZIP code, 1983, annual metro area rpt, 9304–21.7

see also under By SMSA or MSA in the "Index by Categories"

Pryor, Frederic L.

"Incentives in Manufacturing: The Carrot and the Stick", 6722–1.447

Psittacosis

see Animal diseases and zoonoses

Psychiatry

Alcoholism research, treatment programs, and patient characteristics, quarterly journal, 4482–1

Black medical residents by specialty, and minority medical faculty by race and Hispanic origin, selected years 1980-83, article, 4102–1.412

DOD medical personnel, trainees, and accessions by source, by occupation, specialty, and service branch, FY83, annual rpt, 3544–24

Drugs (analgesic) provided during visits to office-based physicians, by patient characteristics, drug brand and type, and physician specialty, 1980-81, 4146–8.99

Handicapped children public education program enrollment, staff, and funding, by handicap, age, and State, 1981/82-1982/83, annual rpt, 4944–4

Health care services of selected medical practitioners, use by patient characteristics, 1980 survey with trends from 1963, 4146–12.4

Homeless population and characteristics, and temporary shelter operations, use, and user characteristics, by region and selected city, 1983, 5188–108

Mental health clinical training funding by NIMH, by program and field, FY80-83, GAO rpt, 26121–86

Mental health facilities, services, staff, and patient characteristics, *Statistical Notes* series, 4506–3

Mental health facilities, services, staff, and patient characteristics, 1970s-82 with trends from 1954, annual rpt, 4504–9

Mental health office and clinic visits, average charges, and total expenditures for services, by type of provider and patient characteristics, 1980, 4146–11.5

Psychology

New Jersey nursing care by nursing unit type, level of care related to length of stay, and costs by diagnosis under 2 allocation methods, as of 1981, article, 4652–1.424

Physicians (not office-based) visits by reason, diagnosis, treatment, patient and physician characteristics, and physician primary activity, 1980, 4147–13.77

Science and engineering grad enrollment, fields of study, financial support, and other student and instn characteristics, 1975-82, annual survey, 9627–7

VA facilities psychological services, staffing, research, and training programs, 1984 annual listing, 9924–10

VA physicians, dentists, and nurses, by age, selected employment characteristics, and VA district, quarterly rpt, 9922–11

Youth office visits to physicians by patient and visit characteristics and physician specialty, and drug mentions by brand, 1980-81, 4146–8.100

Psychological disorders

see Mental health and illness

Psychology

Census of Population, 1980: detailed socioeconomic and demographic characteristics, by age, sex, race, Hispanic origin, occupation, and industry, State rpt series, 2531–4

Degrees conferred in higher education, by race, Hispanic origin, sex, level, and field, selected years 1949/50-1979/80, annual rpt, 4824–2.16

NASA R&D funding to colleges and universities, by State, field of science, and instn, FY83, annual listing, 9504–7

Occupational manpower needs and supply by detailed occupation, and educational and training program enrollees and grads by detailed field, 1982 and 1995, biennial rpt, 6744–3

Occupational Outlook Handbook, 1984-85 biennial rpt, 6744–1

R&D and science-related Fed Govt funding and total and federally funded expenditures of universities and colleges, by instn and field of science, FY82, 9626–2.136

R&D and science-related Fed Govt funding to higher education and nonprofit instns, by field, instn, agency, and State, FY82, annual rpt, 9627–17

R&D-employed scientists and engineers salaries by degree, type of establishment, age, experience, and field, 1984, annual rpt, 3004–1

R&D expenditures by higher education instns and federally funded centers, by field, source of funds, instn, and State, FY82, annual rpt, 9627–13

R&D expenditures by source, and scientists education and employment, detailed data by field, selected years 1953-84, annual rpt, 9624–18

R&D expenditures of higher education instns, and science and engineering employment and grad students, by field, 1972-83, biennial rpt, 9627–24

R&D Fed Govt funding for all performers, by field and supporting agency, selected years FY60-84, annual rpt, 9627–20

Science and engineering doctoral degree recipients, by field, sex, race, age,

Psychology

citizenship, postgrad employment and study status, State, and instn, 1960-82, 9626–6.16

Science and engineering grad enrollment, fields of study, financial support, and other student and instn characteristics, 1975-82, annual survey, 9627–7

Science and engineering grad program enrollment, by field, degree level, source of financial support, race, and Hispanic origin, 1975-81, 9626–2.134

Science and engineering grad program enrollment by field, sources of financial support, and foreign students, 1975-82, 9626–2.141

Science and engineering grads of 1980-81, employment and median salaries by level and field of degree, 1982, 9626–2.137

Science and engineering grads of 1980-81, employment characteristics or grad enrollment, by degree level, field, sex, and race, 1982, 9627–25

Scientists and engineers employed at universities and colleges, by field, sex, and instn, 1973-82, 9626–2.140

Scientists and engineers employed at universities and colleges, by field, sex, State, and instn, Jan 1983 and selected trends from 1967, annual survey, 9627–11

Scientists and engineers employment by sector and activity, and share female, black, and Asian descent, by field, 1982, 9626–2.142

Scientists and engineers supply, employment, and education, by sex, race, Hispanic origin, and field, selected years 1965-83, biennial rpt, 9624–20

Scientists, engineers, and technicians employed in private industry, by occupation and industry group, 1980-81, biennial rpt, 9627–23

Scientists, engineers, and technicians needed in defense and nondefense industries, and supply/demand, by field, 1981-87, 9628–71

VA Medicine and Surgery Dept trainees, by detailed program and city, FY83, annual rpt, 9924–21

Public administration

Budget of US Appendix, detailed budgets and personnel summaries, by agency, FY85, annual rpt, 104–3

Budget of US, CBO analysis and review of FY85 budget by function, annual rpt, 26304–2

Budget of US, compact budgets by function, agency, and account, FY85 with projections to FY89, annual rpt, 104–2

Budget of US, loans and loan guarantees, and Admin proposed limits on credit assistance, by program, FY83-89, annual rpt, 26306–3.65

Budget of US, receipts by source and outlays by agency and program, monthly rpt, 8102–3

Budget of US, receipts by source and outlays by function, FY40-89 estimates revised for consistency with FY85 budget definitions, annual rpt, 104–12

Budget of US, receipts, outlays, and budget authority, by function and agency, FY84-89 revised estimates, midsession review of FY85 budget, annual rpt, 104–7

Budget of US, receipts, outlays, and budget authority, by function and agency, 1st revision of FY85 budget, annual rpt, 104–17

Census of Govts, 1982: city govt revenues by source, expenditures by function, debt, and assets, by State and city, 2457–4

Census of Govts, 1982: county govt revenues by source, expenditures by function, debt, and assets, by State and county, 2457–3

Census of Govts, 1982: employment, payrolls, and average earnings, by function, level of govt, State, county, population size, and inside-outside SMSAs, 2455–2

Census of Govts, 1982: State govt payments to local govts, by program, source of funds, level of govt, and State, with trends from 1902, 2460–3

Census of Population, 1980: detailed socioeconomic and demographic characteristics, by age, sex, race, Hispanic origin, occupation, and industry, State rpt series, 2531–4

Census of Population, 1980: detailed socioeconomic characteristics, by county, city, and inside-outside SMSAs and central cities, State rpt series, 2531–3

Degrees conferred in higher education, by race, Hispanic origin, sex, level, and field, selected years 1949/50-1979/80, annual rpt, 4824–2.16

Fed Govt programs and mgmt cost control proposals, 3-year savings by function and agency, and financial and operating data, 1960s-81, 16908–1

Foreign direct investment in US, major investors and investments by SIC 4-digit industry, transaction type and value, and location, 1983, annual rpt, 2044–20

Govt census, 1982: city govt revenues by source, expenditures by function, debt, and assets, by State and city, 2457–4

Govt census, 1982: local govt employment by function, payroll, and average earnings, for individual counties, cities, and school and special districts, 2455–1

Govt employment and payroll, by function, level of govt, and jurisdiction, 1983, annual rpt series, 2466–1

Govt finances, by level of govt, State, and for large cities and counties, 1981-83, annual rpt series, 2466–2

Govt revenues by source and expenditures by function, natl income and product account, *Survey of Current Business*, monthly rpt, monthly and annual tables, 2702–1.24

Regional councils involved in service activities, by type of service and region population size, 1982 survey, hearing, 25408–88

Truman, Harry S, Scholarship Foundation, program operation, financial status, and awards by student characteristics, 1983 with trends from 1977, annual rpt, 14314–1

see also Administrative law and procedure

see also Civil service system

see also Federal boards, committees, and commissions

see also Federal employees

see also Federal executive departments

Index by Subjects and Names

see also Federal independent agencies

see also Government and business

see also Government efficiency

see also Government property

see also Government revenues

see also Government spending

see also Labor-management relations in government

see also Local government

see also Officials

see also School administration and staff

see also State and local employees

see also State government

Public assistance

see Public welfare programs

Public broadcasting

Budget of US, effects of Reagan Admin policy changes, by detailed program, FY85, annual rpt, 104–21

Minority group and women employment by occupation, and business owners, by race and State, with TV and radio revenues and stations, 1971-81, hearing, 21368–45

TV and radio industry employment, total and for minorities, women, and youth, by job category and State, 1979-83, annual rpt, 9284–16

TV and radio station employment, total and for minorities and women, by full- and part-time status and individual station, 1983, annual rpt, 9284–7

TV channels allocation and licensing status, for commercial and noncommercial UHF and VHF TV by market and community, as of Dec 1983, semiannual rpt, 9282–6

see also Educational broadcasting

Public buildings

Bombing (explosive and incendiary) and arson incidents by target, State, and circumstances, and explosives theft and recovery, 1982-83, annual rpt, 8484–4

Bombing (explosive and incendiary) incidents, damage, injuries, and deaths, by target, State, and circumstances, 1983, annual rpt, 6224–5

Bonneville Power Admin energy conservation program activities and funding data, FY82 and estimated FY83-87, 3228–2

Capital (fixed), govt and private nonresidential structures and equipment, residential capital, and consumer-owned durable goods by item, 1980-83, annual article, 2702–1.433

Capitol Architect detailed expenditures for buildings and grounds, salaries, supplies, and services, 1st half FY84, semiannual rpt, 25922–2

Carbon monoxide atmospheric concentrations and levels within buildings and along commuting and residential driving routes, for 4 cities, Jan-Mar 1981, 9198–110

Construction, alteration, and leasing projects, description and cost by location, Dec 1983, annual listing, 9454–12

Construction industries census, 1982: financial and operating data, by SIC 4-digit industry and State, final rpt series, 2373–1

Construction industries census, 1982: financial and operating data, by SIC 4-digit industry and State, preliminary rpt series, 2371–1

Index by Subjects and Names

Construction put in place, permits authorized by region, State, and MSA, and Federal contract awards, by construction type, bimonthly rpt with articles, 2012–1

Construction put in place, value of new public and private structures, by type, monthly rpt, 2382–4

DOE in-house energy use, conservation investments, and savings, by type of use and fuel and field office, FY83, annual rpt, 3024–3

Energy conservation grants of Fed Govt to public and nonprofit private instns, by building type and State, 1983, annual rpt, 3304–15

Energy use and efficiency of Fed Govt, by agency and fuel type, FY83, annual rpt, 3304–22

Energy use by Fed Govt, by agency and fuel type, FY75-83, annual rpt, 3164–74.1

Fed Govt consolidated financial statements based on business accounting methods, FY82-83, annual rpt, 8104–5

Fed Govt construction, acquisition, and alteration proposals for historic and other building projects, costs and tenure by city and project, as of 1983, hearings, 25328–23

Fed Govt programs and mgmt cost control proposals, 3-year savings by function and agency, and financial and operating data, 1960s-81, 16908–1

Fed Reserve banks financial statements and employees, 1983, annual rpt, 9364–1.1

Govt census, 1982: city govt revenues by source, expenditures by function, debt, and assets, by State and city, 2457–4

Govt census, 1982: county govt revenues by source, expenditures by function, debt, and assets, by State and county, 2457–3

Govt finances, by level of govt, State, and for large cities and counties, 1981-83, annual rpt series, 2466–2

GPO document sales program mgmt and finances, and bookstore operations by location, FY78-82, GAO rpt, 26111–17

GSA mgmt activities and finances, FY78-83, annual rpt, 9454–23

GSA programs fraud and abuse, audits and investigations, 2nd half FY84, semiannual rpt, 9452–8

Handicapped persons access to Fed Govt or federally funded buildings, compliance activities and complaints by agency, FY83, annual rpt, 17614–1

Inventory and costs of Fed Govt-owned real property, worldwide summary by location, agency, and use, 1983, annual rpt, 9454–5

NIH activities, staff, funding, and facilities, historical data, 1984 annual rpt, 4434–1

Postal Service finances, organization, and services since 1775, and current operations, FY81-82, annual rpt, 9864–6

see also Educational facilities

see also Military bases, posts, and reservations

Public contracts

see Defense contracts and procurement

see Government contracts and procurement

Public debt

Bond tax-exempt issues for public and private purposes, by use of proceeds, 1975-83, article, 9362–1.408

Boston, Mass, govt budget and impact of reduced local revenue and Fed Govt aid, and other devs, FY80-86, article, 9373–1.406

Budget deficit, actual and assuming efficient tax system, FY75-83 and projected FY85-95, article, 9387–1.402

Budget deficit impacts on economy, projected FY84-88 with trends and foreign comparisons from 1946, conf papers, 9373–3.27

Budget deficit-interest rate relationship, and deficit cyclical and structural components, various periods 1955-83 and projected FY84-89, article, 9391–1.415

Budget of US Appendix, detailed budgets and personnel summaries, by agency, FY85, annual rpt, 104–3

Budget of US, CBO analysis and review of FY85 budget by function, annual rpt, 26304–2

Budget of US, CBO analysis of revenue and spending alternatives and projections of economic indicators, FY85-89, annual rpt, 26304–3

Budget of US, compact budgets by function, agency, and account, FY85 with projections to FY89, annual rpt, 104–2

Budget of US, deficit effect on inflation, and debt outstanding by holder, Reagan Admin mid-1983 outlook for FY83-84 with supporting data from 1949, article, 9371–1.402

Budget of US, receipts by source and outlays by function, FY40-89 estimates revised for consistency with FY85 budget definitions, annual rpt, 104–12

Budget of US, receipts, outlays, and budget authority, by function and agency, FY84-89 revised estimates, midsession review of FY85 budget, annual rpt, 104–7

Budget of US, receipts, outlays, and budget authority, by function and agency, 1st revision of FY85 budget, annual rpt, 104–17

Budget of US, special analysis of debt outstanding and interest cost, FY83-85, annual rpt, 104–1.5

Business statistics, detailed data for major industries and economic indicators, *Survey of Current Business,* monthly rpt, 2702–1.6

Census of Govts, 1982: school districts revenues, expenditures, debt, and assets, by district and State, 2457–1

City govt revenue sharing program allocations and use by function, and response to program cuts, by city size and region, 1982 survey, hearings, 25408–86.2

Economic conditions of US, with some foreign comparisons, 1960s-82 and alternative projections to 1992, hearing, 21248–79

Fed Govt budget and debt, cyclically adjusted estimates assuming mid-level unemployment and GNP, and methodology, quarterly 1955-83, 2706–5.31

Fed Govt consolidated financial statements based on business accounting methods, FY82-83, annual rpt, 8104–5

Fed Govt debt by holder, interest rates and costs, and financing mechanisms, projected FY84-89 with data for FY80-83, 26308–50

Fed Govt debt, by type and holder, monthly rpt, 9362–1.1

Fed Govt debt, by type and holder, 1982, annual rpt, 9364–5.5

Fed Govt debt issued, redeemed, and outstanding, by individual issue and source, monthly rpt, 8242–2

Fed Govt debt outstanding, FY82-83, annual rpt, 8104–2.1

Fed Govt financial operations, detailed data, *Treasury Bulletin,* quarterly rpt, 8002–4

Fed Govt interest payments and budget deficit, various periods FY50-81, article, 9379–1.407

Fed Govt liabilities and other financial commitments, by agency, as of Sept 1983, annual rpt, 8104–3

Fed Govt programs and mgmt cost control proposals, 3-year savings by function and agency, and financial and operating data, 1960s-81, 16908–1

Fed Govt programs under Ways and Means Committee jurisdiction, program operations and financing data for assessing budgetary requirements, by State, FY70s-83, 21788–117

Fed Govt receipts and outlays, FY29-85, and financing and debt, FY74-85, Council of Economic Advisers annual rpt, 204–1.6

Fed Govt receipts, expenditures, and debt, Fed Reserve Bank of St Louis monthly rpt, 9391–2

Fed Govt receipts, outlays, and debt account transactions, daily statement, 8102–4

Fed Govt receipts, outlays, and debt shares of GNP, and tax expenditures as percentage of outlays and revenue, FY66-83 and projected FY84-87, article, 9383–2

Fed Govt revenues, deficits, and debt, and GNP and unemployment, cyclically adjusted estimates assuming middle-range unemployment, 1955-3rd qtr 1983, article, 2702–1.403

Financial and business statistics, historic trends, 1984 annual chartbook, 9364–2.7, 9364–2.8, 9364–2.9

Flow-of-funds accounts, assets and liabilities by type and economic sector, year-end outstandings, 1960-83, annual rpt, 9364–3

Foreign and US budget deficits effect on interest rates and economic indicators, with govt borrowing and saving, for US and 6 OECD countries, 1975-83, technical paper, 9366–7.89

Foreign economic trends and implications for US, annual and semiannual country rpt series, 2046–4

Govt census, 1982: city govt revenues by source, expenditures by function, debt, and assets, by State and city, 2457–4

Govt census, 1982: county govt revenues by source, expenditures by function, debt, and assets, by State and county, 2457–3

Public debt

Govt finances, by level of govt and State, selected years 1929-83, annual rpt, 10044–1

Govt finances, by level of govt, State, and for large cities and counties, 1981-83, annual rpt series, 2466–2

Govt finances, quarterly chartbook, 9362–2.4

Interest paid on Fed Govt debt, cumulative for fiscal year, annual trends, and quarterly data, monthly rpt, 23842–1.6

Jamaica PL 480 Title I assistance effects on economic dev, with data on govt finance, economic indicators, demography, and dev programs, 1970s-81, 9916–1.51

Japan yen/dollar exchange rate, 2-country model of sterilized intervention and effect of fiscal balance and private savings, 1973-82, article, 9393–8.405

Monetary and fiscal policy analysis using inflation-adjusted public debt, 1983 technical paper, 9387–8.86

Statistical Abstract of US, social, political, and economic data, 1950s-83 and trends, annual rpt, 2324–1.2

see also Government securities

see also Municipal bonds

see also U.S. savings bonds

Public defenders

see Legal aid

see Right to counsel

Public demonstrations

see also Right of assembly

see also Riots and disorders

Public documents

see Government documents

Public finance

see Budget of the U.S.

see Fiscal policy

see Government revenues

see Government securities

see Government spending

see Monetary policy

see Public debt

see Taxation

Public health

Alcohol auto fuels health effects and safety review, as of 1983, 3308–75

Budget of US, effects of Reagan Admin policy changes, by detailed program, FY85, annual rpt, 104–21

Census of Govts, 1982: city govt revenues by source, expenditures by function, debt, and assets, by State and city, 2457–4

Census of Govts, 1982: county govt revenues by source, expenditures by function, debt, and assets, by State and county, 2457–3

Census of Govts, 1982: State govt payments to local govts, by program, source of funds, level of govt, and State, with trends from 1902, 2460–3

Central America socioeconomic and political conditions in 6 countries, 1960s-83 with trends and projections 1930-2010, Commission rpt, 028–19.2

City govt revenue sharing program allocations and use by function, and response to program cuts, by city size and region, 1982 survey, hearings, 25408–86.2

Cost control proposals for Fed Govt programs and mgmt, 3-year savings by function and agency, and financial and operating data, 1960s-81, 16908–1.7

Fed Govt financial and nonfinancial domestic aid, 1984 annual comprehensive catalog, 104–5

Fed Govt procurement contract awards, by State, agency, procurement and contractor type, and for top 100 contractors, quarterly rpt, 102–6

Fed Govt programs and mgmt cost control proposals, CBO and GAO estimates of savings by function and agency, FY85-89, 26308–45

Foreign and US health care resources, use, and per capita public expenditures, and selected population characteristics, for 7 countries, selected years 1975-81, 21148–33

Foreign military, social, and economic summary data by world area and country, 1960s-80s, hearing, 25388–47.1

Govt expenditures for social welfare by program and level of govt, and private expenditures for health care, selected years FY50-82, annual article, 4742–1.425

Govt finances, by level of govt, State, and for large cities and counties, 1981-83, annual rpt series, 2466–2

Govt revenues by source and expenditures by function, natl income and product account, *Survey of Current Business,* monthly rpt, monthly and annual tables, 2702–1.24

Health care expenditures, growth factors, medical equipment and drugs trade, and physician income, 1950-90, article, 4652–1.407

Health care expenditures, natl and personal total and per capita amounts, by type of service and source of funds, 1983 and trends from 1929, annual article, 4652–1.429

HHS aid to each State and local govt or private instn, amount obligated, funding agency, and program, FY83, annual listing, 4004–3

Infectious notifiable diseases and other public health concerns, cases and mortality trends, quarterly rpt articles, 4202–7

Infectious notifiable diseases, cases and incidence, by census div and State, 1982, annual rpt, 4204–1

Input-output structure of US economy, detailed interindustry transactions for 85 industries, and components of final demand, 1977, article, 2702–1.421

Labs (public health) of States, pay scales and job requirements by occupation and State, FY81-83, annual rpt, 4204–7

Local govt finances and population characteristics for cities and suburbs, by region and selected SMSA, selected years 1957-FY83, 10048–61

Manpower supply and education of health professionals, by occupation, demographic and professional characteristics, and location, 1950s-83 and projected to 2000, biennial rpt, 4114–8

Michigan health funding, Blue Cross-Blue Shield and welfare participation, and unemployment, poverty, and food assistance by county, 1979-83, hearing, 21348–86

Minority group and women employment and training in health professions, by field, selected years 1962/63-1983/84, 4118–18

Index by Subjects and Names

Neighborhood and housing quality indicators and attitudes, and occupant characteristics, by urban-rural location and region, 1981, annual survey, 2485–7

Neighborhood and housing quality indicators and attitudes, by occupant and unit characteristics, region, and metro-nonmetro location, 1981, annual survey, 2485–2

New Mexico health clinics staffed by Natl Health Service Corps, income by source and service, and effect of revised system for Federal payback, 1980-83, hearings, 21368–47

Public Health Reports, articles and special studies rpts, bimonthly journal, 4102–1

Reporting of communicable diseases to public health depts, physician reasons for underreporting, 1982 survey, article, 4102–1.411

State govt food, drugs, and cosmetics control programs, expenditures, personnel, and labs, biennial rpt, suspended, 4064–11

State govt public health labs personnel, finances, workloads, and other activities, by State, FY82, annual rpt, 4204–8

Statistical Abstract of US, social, political, and economic data, 1950s-83 and trends, annual rpt, 2324–1.1

see also Accidents and accident prevention

see also Air pollution

see also Birth defects

see also Carcinogens

see also Child abuse and neglect

see also Child welfare

see also Community health services

see also Diseases and disorders

see also Domestic violence

see also Electromagnetic radiation

see also Environmental pollution and control

see also Food inspection

see also Hazardous substances

see also Health condition

see also Health education

see also Health facilities administration

see also Health facilities and services

see also Health insurance

see also Health maintenance organizations

see also Health occupations

see also Infant mortality

see also Lead poisoning and pollution

see also Medicaid

see also Medical assistance

see also Medical costs

see also Medical education

see also Medical research

see also Medical supplies and equipment

see also Medical transplants

see also Medicine

see also Mental health facilities and services

see also Noise

see also Nuclear radiation

see also Occupational health and safety

see also Pesticides

see also Pests and pest control

see also Poisoning and drug reaction

see also Preventive medicine

see also Refuse and refuse disposal

see also Regional medical programs

see also Sewage and wastewater treatment systems

see also Smoking

see also Soil pollution

Index by Subjects and Names

see also Vaccination and vaccines
see also Vital statistics
see also Water supply and use

Public Health Service

- Acquired immune deficiency syndrome (AIDS) cases, and research funding and activities, monthly rpt, 4042–2
- Activities of PHS, funding by function and subagency, and HMO financing and enrollment, FY83, annual rpt, 4044–2
- Cost control proposals for Fed Govt programs and mgmt, 3-year savings by function and agency, and financial and operating data, 1960s-81, 16908–1.7
- Data projects and systems of HHS, by subagency, FY83-84, annual inventory, 4044–3
- Family planning program activities and funding of HHS, annual rpt, suspended, 4044–4
- Fraud and abuse in HHS programs, audits and investigations, 2nd half FY84, semiannual rpt, 4002–6
- Health info offices and services of HHS and other Fed Govt agencies, by subject, 1984 listing, 4048–18
- Health professionals supply and education, by occupation, demographic and professional characteristics, and location, 1950s-83 and projected to 2000, biennial rpt, 4114–8
- Medical facilities of Navy, use by active and retired military personnel, dependents, and others by facility and type, quarterly rpt, 3802–1
- *Public Health Reports,* articles and special studies rpts, bimonthly journal, 4102–1
- Refugee resettlement program activities and funding, arrivals and population by country of origin and State, and employment and other characteristics, FY83, annual rpt, 4704–8

see also Alcohol, Drug Abuse and Mental Health Administration
see also Bureau of Health Professions
see also Centers for Disease Control
see also Food and Drug Administration
see also Health Resources and Services Administration
see also Indian Health Service
see also National Center for Health Services Research
see also National Center for Health Statistics
see also National Institute for Occupational Safety and Health
see also National Institute of Mental Health
see also National Institute on Alcohol Abuse and Alcoholism
see also National Institute on Drug Abuse
see also National Institutes of Health
see also National Library of Medicine
see also Office on Smoking and Health

Public housing

- AFDC eligibility under Omnibus Budget Reconciliation Act, effect on caseloads and recipient benefits and living costs, 1981-83, GAO rpt, 26131–11
- Beneficiaries of noncash public and employer-based transfer programs, by income source and socioeconomic characteristics, 1982, advance Current Population Rpt, 2546–6.38
- Beneficiaries of noncash public and employer-based transfer programs, by income source and socioeconomic characteristics, 1982, final Current Population Rpt, 2546–6.37
- Budget of US, effects of Reagan Admin policy changes, by detailed program, FY85, annual rpt, 104–21
- Capital (fixed), govt and private nonresidential structures and equipment, residential capital, and consumer-owned durable goods by item, 1980-83, annual article, 2702–1.433
- Census of Housing, 1980: inventory, occupancy, and unit characteristics, changes from 1973 by region and inside-outside SMSAs and central cities, series, 2473–3
- Children and youth benefitting from Fed Govt public welfare programs and tax expenditures, participation and funding for 71 programs, FY81-83, 21968–30
- Construction put in place, permits authorized by region, State, and MSA, and Federal contract awards, by construction type, bimonthly rpt with articles, 2012–1
- Construction put in place, value of new public and private structures, by type, monthly rpt, 2382–4
- Construction starts and completions of public and subsidized rental housing, 1975-84, hearing, 21968–28
- Fed Govt aid to State and local govts, expenditures, and direct payments, by program, agency, and State, FY83, annual rpt, 2464–2
- Fed Govt-owned real property inventory and costs, worldwide summary by location, agency, and use, 1983, annual rpt, 9454–5
- Fed Govt programs and mgmt cost control proposals, 3-year savings by function and agency, and financial and operating data, 1960s-81, 16908–1.22, 16908–1.23
- Govt census, 1982: city govt revenues by source, expenditures by function, debt, and assets, by State and city, 2457–4
- Govt census, 1982: county govt revenues by source, expenditures by function, debt, and assets, by State and county, 2457–3
- Govt census, 1982: State govt payments to local govts, by program, source of funds, level of govt, and State, with trends from 1902, 2460–3
- Govt employment and payroll, by function, level of govt, and jurisdiction, 1983, annual rpt series, 2466–1
- Govt expenditures for social welfare by program and level of govt, and private expenditures for health care, selected years FY50-82, annual article, 4742–1.425
- Govt finances, by level of govt, State, and for large cities and counties, 1981-83, annual rpt series, 2466–2
- Housing and households detailed characteristics, and unit and neighborhood quality, by inside-outside central cities, 1979-82 surveys, SMSA rpt series, 2485–6
- Housing and neighborhood quality indicators and attitudes, and occupant characteristics, by urban-rural location and region, 1981, annual survey, 2485–7
- Housing occupancy and unit and household characteristics, by region and metro-nonmetro residence, 1983, biennial survey, 2485–1

Income (household) and cash and noncash transfer program participation, by sociodemographic characteristics, quarterly rpt, 2542–2

- Indian and Alaska Native housing and community dev program operations, FY82 with Community Dev Block Grant funding by tribe and State for FY81, annual rpt, 5004–5
- New Communities program of HUD, activities, costs, land sales, and community and population characteristics, for 13 communities, 1970s-83, 5188–107
- New housing units authorized, by public and private ownership, by region, div, State, selected MSA, and 4,700 permit-issuing places, monthly rpt, 2382–5
- New housing units authorized, by public and private ownership, State, and permit-issuing place, 1983, annual rpt, 2384–2
- New housing units completed and under construction, by units per structure, region, and inside-outside SMSAs, monthly rpt, 2382–2
- Older persons receiving selected services from family and agencies, living arrangements, and need for home mgmt help, selected years 1977-82, article, 1702–1.409
- Private mgmt of public housing, assessment by housing officials and managers, and tenants, with operating costs, crime, and rent delinquency by project type and location, 1982, 5188–103
- Regional councils involved in service activities, by type of service and region population size, 1982 survey, hearing, 25408–88
- *Statistical Abstract of US,* social, political, and economic data, 1950s-83 and trends, annual rpt, 2324–1.3
- Tenure and units in structure, and detailed socioeconomic characteristics of families and households, Mar 1982, annual Current Population Rpt, 2546–1.383

see also Low-income housing

Public lands

- Acreage of natl park system and other areas under Natl Park Service mgmt, by type of area, ownership, and site, as of Sept 1984, semiannual rpt, 5542–1
- Alaska and Alaska Native corporation claims for Fed Govt land, status and Land Mgmt Bur conveyance problems, various dates 1978-FY84, GAO rpt, 26113–125
- Army Corps of Engineers water resources dev projects, recreation activities by district and project, 1982, annual rpt, 3754–5
- Budget of US, effects of Reagan Admin policy changes, by detailed program, FY85, annual rpt, 104–21
- Budget of US, receipts by source and outlays by agency and program, monthly rpt, 8102–3
- Coal dev plans on Fed Govt lease lands in 12 regions under Fed Coal Mgmt Program, environmental and socioeconomic impacts to 2000, final statement series, 5726–4
- Cost control proposals for Fed Govt programs and mgmt, 3-year savings by function and agency, and financial and operating data, 1960s-81, 16908–1.9, 16908–1.31

Public lands

Environmental quality and protection programs, costs, and Fed Govt enforcement, 1983, detailed annual rpt, 484–1

Fed Govt consolidated financial statements based on business accounting methods, FY82-83, annual rpt, 8104–5

Fish and Wildlife Service restoration programs, including new sites, funding, and research, by State, FY81, annual rpt, 5504–1

Fish hatchery production, deliveries, and operating costs, and fishery assistance, by region, hatchery, and Fed Govt assistance station, FY82, annual rpt, 5504–9

Forest and windbarrier planting and seeding, by State, FY83, annual rpt, 1204–7

Forest, range, and associated waters use and mgmt assessment, and environmental impacts of Forest Service program options, 1977-2030 and trends from 1920, 1208–24

GAO publications on land use, ownership, mgmt, and planning, 1979-83, annual listing, 26104–11.3

Hazardous waste sites and activities of Fed Govt civil agencies, and EPA data mgmt, by waste location, 1984, GAO rpt, 26113–139

Horse and burro wild herd areas in western States, population, adoption, and protection and mgmt costs, as of 1984, biennial rpt, 5724–8

Hwy and bridge Fed Hwy Admin allocations, by project and State, FY85, 7556–3.2

Inventory and costs of Fed Govt-owned real property, worldwide summary by location, agency, and use, 1983, annual rpt, 9454–5

Land Mgmt Bur activities and finances, and public land acreage and use, annual State rpt series, 5724–11

Land Mgmt Bur activities, and grants, sales, and use of public lands, by State, FY83 and historical, annual rpt, 5724–1

Land Mgmt Bur public lands admin and program activities in western States, FY82-84, annual rpt, 5724–13

Land Mgmt Bur public lands sales, prices of Nevada and California acreage, and effect on Forest Service land acquisition program, 1983, GAO rpt, 26113–122

Local govt receipts from Fed Govt in lieu of property taxes on public lands, by State, FY84, annual press release, 5724–9

Marijuana cultivation control activity of State law enforcement agencies, and aid from Fed Govt and Natl Guard, 1983 survey, GAO rpt, 26119–64

NIH activities, staff, funding, and facilities, historical data, 1984 annual rpt, 4434–1

Northwest US and British Columbia forest industry production, prices, trade, and employment, quarterly rpt, 1202–3

Rocky Mountain forest and rangeland area, and timber resources and removals, by ownership, forest and tree characteristics, and State, 1977, 1208–201

Schools in federally impacted areas, Fed Govt funding by county and school and congressional district, and eligible pupils, by State, FY83, annual rpt, 4804–10

Statistical Abstract of US, social, political, and economic data, 1950s-83 and trends, annual rpt, 2324–1.1

Index by Subjects and Names

Timber growth, removals, products output, and forest ownership and industries in Northeast States, State rpt series, 1206–16

Timber resources and removals in Northeast States, by species, ownership class, and county, State rpt series, 1206–12

US Attorneys civil case processing and amounts involved, by cause of action, FY83, annual rpt, 6004–2.5

Western US Fed Govt lands by agency and mining restriction status, and energy resources on potential wilderness areas and other lands, 1970s-81 and projected to 1990, 3308–68

see also Homesteads

see also Mineral leases

see also National forests

see also National grasslands

see also National park system

see also Oil and gas leases

see also Public buildings

see also Wilderness areas

see also Wildlife refuges

Public Law 480

AID activities and funding by project and function, FY85, and developing countries summary socioeconomic data, 1970s-83, by country, annual rpt, 9914–3

Budget of US, effects of Reagan Admin policy changes, by detailed program, FY85, annual rpt, 104–21

Budget of US, Reagan Admin funding requests for foreign economic and military aid by program and country, FY82-85, annual rpt, 7004–14

CCC dairy price support program foreign donations and domestic donations to poor, schools, Prisons Bur, DOD, and VA, monthly rpt, 1802–2

CCC finances and program operations, FY83, annual rpt, 1824–1

Central America economic assistance from AID by type of aid, for 7 countries, FY80-83, GAO rpt, 26123–55

Commodity allocations for long-term credit sales, by country, quarterly press release, 1922–7

Cost control proposals for Fed Govt programs and mgmt, 3-year savings by function and agency, and financial and operating data, 1960s-81, 16908–1.10

Credit sales agreement terms, by commodity and country, FY83, annual rpt, 15344–1.11

Currency (foreign) accounts owned by US under AID admin and by foreign govts with joint AID control, status by program and country, quarterly rpt, 9912–1

Currency (foreign) holdings of US, detailed transactions and balances by program and country, 1st half FY84, semiannual rpt, 8102–7

Developing countries agricultural supply/demand and market for US exports, with socioeconomic indicators, country rpt series, 1526–6

Disasters, persons affected, deaths, damage, and aid by US and others, by country, FY83 and trends from FY64, annual rpt, 9914–12

Exports under Fed Govt-financed programs, by commodity and country, bimonthly rpt, periodic tables, 1522–1.4

Exports under PL 480 by commodity, and recipients, by program, sponsor, and country, FY82 and aggregate from FY55, annual rpt, 1924–7

Exports under PL 480 concessional sales program, by commodity and country, 1955-83, semiannual rpt, 1922–6

Exports under PL 480 concessional sales program, by commodity and country, 1978-83, semiannual rpt, 1922–10

Food production and needs, and related economic trends and outlook, for 67 developing countries, 1980-86, annual rpt, 1524–6

Grain and feed export agreements with selected countries under PL 480, FAS monthly rpt, 1925–2.4

Jamaica PL 480 Title I assistance effects on economic dev, with data on govt finance, economic indicators, demography, and dev programs, 1970s-81, 9916–1.51

Loan repayment status and terms by program and country, AID and predecessor agencies, quarterly rpt, 9912–3

Refugee arrivals in US by world area of origin and State of settlement, and Fed Govt intl and domestic assistance costs, FY85, annual rpt, 7004–16

Shipping costs and foreign cargo shipments of Fed Govt by agency or program and route, and employment and economic impacts of US vessel preference, 1980, GAO rpt, 26117–30

Strategic materials stockpiles, and imports in exchange for CCC commodity exports by world region and country, various periods 1950-83, hearings, 21208–20

Title I and II aid, by country, FY46-83, annual rpt, 9914–5

Title I and III allocations, by commodity and country, FY85, semiannual rpt, 1542–6

Title I assistance funding and socioeconomic impacts, with case studies for 5 countries, 1950s-81, 9918–13

Title I, IV, and I/III concessional sales agreements, value and date signed, by country, 1954-83, annual rpt, 1924–6

Voluntary agencies overseas foreign aid programs funding and expenditures, by agency, 1982/83, annual rpt, 9914–9

Public libraries

see Libraries

Public opinion

see Consumer surveys

see Opinion and attitude surveys

Public ownership

see Government ownership

Public schools

see Elementary and secondary education

see Higher education

see terms listed under Education and beginning with School

Public service employment

AFDC workfare program participation and requirements in 16 States, Feb 1983, GAO rpt, 26131–9

Budget of US Appendix, detailed budgets and personnel summaries, by agency, FY85, annual rpt, 104–3

CETA participants by sociodemographic characteristics, and Labor Dept activities and staff, FY83, annual rpt, 6304–1

Index by Subjects and Names

Public utilities

Fed Govt aid to State and local govts, expenditures, and direct payments, by program, agency, and State, FY83, annual rpt, 2464–2

Fed Govt public service job creation program for unemployed, funding by agency, as of June 1983, GAO rpt, 26115–51

HHS aid to each State and local govt or private instn, amount obligated, funding agency, and program, FY83, annual listing, 4004–3

Older persons community service part-time employment and program funding, by State and outlying area, FY84, press release, 6408–60

Youth summer job program of Fed Govt, funding and jobs by State and for Indians, summer 1984, press release, 6408–62

Public Services Administration

see Office of Human Development Services

Public transportation

see Subways

see Urban transportation

Public utilities

- AFDC eligibility under Omnibus Budget Reconciliation Act, effect on caseloads and recipient benefits and living costs, 1981-83, GAO rpt, 26131–11
- Alaska electric power capacity and generation by fuel type, and marketing, by utility, type of ownership, and location, 1983, annual rpt, 3214–2
- American Samoa minimum wage rates, employment, earnings, and benefits, by establishment and industry, Nov 1983, biennial rpt, 6504–6
- Bankruptcy (personal), filers by debt type and other characteristics, selected years 1978-81, hearing, 25528–97.1
- Bombing (explosive and incendiary) and arson incidents by target, State, and circumstances, and explosives theft and recovery, 1982-83, annual rpt, 8484–4
- Bombing (explosive and incendiary) incidents, damage, injuries, and deaths, by target, State, and circumstances, 1983, annual rpt, 6224–5
- Capacity utilization in 15 manufacturing industries, mining, electric and all utilities, and industrial materials including energy, monthly rpt, 9365–2.19
- Capital expenditures for new plants and equipment, by industry div, monthly rpt, quarterly data, 23842–1.1
- Census of Housing, 1980: inventory, occupancy, and unit characteristics, changes from 1973 by region and inside-outside SMSAs and central cities, series, 2473–3
- Census of Population, 1980: detailed socioeconomic and demographic characteristics, by age, sex, race, Hispanic origin, occupation, and industry, State rpt series, 2531–4
- Census of Population, 1980: detailed socioeconomic characteristics, by county, city, and inside-outside SMSAs and central cities, State rpt series, 2531–3
- China economic conditions, agricultural and industrial production, trade, and domestic and foreign investment, 1980-85, 2048–106
- Coal supply and Fed Govt coal leases, by owner, owner industry, and western State, various periods 1950-82 and projected to 2000, hearing, 25318–58

Coastal environmental characteristics, fish, wildlife, and use, and population socioeconomic data, for individual areas, series, 5506–4

- Collective bargaining agreements expiring during year, covered workers by SIC 2-digit industry, firm, and union, with summary of key provisions, 1984, annual rpt, 6784–9
- Construction put in place, permits authorized by region, State, and MSA, and Federal contract awards, by construction type, bimonthly rpt with articles, 2012–1
- Construction put in place, value of new public and private structures, by type, monthly rpt, 2382–4
- County Business Patterns: establishments, employees, and payrolls, by SIC 4-digit industry and county, 1981, annual State rpt series, 2326–8
- County Business Patterns: establishments, employees, and payrolls, by SIC 4-digit industry and county, 1982, annual State rpt series, 2326–6
- Developing countries govt policy, and AID and other foreign assistance, effects on private sector dev and socioeconomic conditions, with case studies for 6 countries, 1960s-80, 9918–12
- Earnings by industry div, and personal income per capita and by source, by State, MSA, and county, 1977-82, annual regional rpts, 2704–2
- Earnings by major industry group, and personal income per capita and by source, by region and State, 1929-82, 2708–40
- Employment and earnings, detailed data, monthly rpt, 6742–2.5
- Employment, earnings, and hours, by selected SIC 1- to 4-digit industry, State, and for 278 major labor areas, 1939-83, annual rpt, 6744–5
- Employment, earnings, and hours, by SIC 4-digit nonfarm industry, monthly 1974-Feb 1984, annual update, 6744–4
- Employment, unemployment, and labor force, by demographic and employment characteristics, State, and for 30 metro areas and 11 large cities, 1983, annual rpt, 6744–7
- Energy conservation programs of State govts, Fed Govt financial and technical aid, and reported energy savings, by State, 1983, annual rpt, 3304–1
- Energy supply/demand and prices, by energy source and end-use sector and for 7 electric utilities, 1981-2000 with trends from 1960s, 3008–93
- Fed Govt loans, grants, and tax benefits to business, by program and economic sector, projected FY84-88 with effective tax rates for FY80-82, 26306–6.70
- Fed Govt programs and mgmt cost control proposals, 3-year savings by function and agency, and financial and operating data, 1960s-81, 16908–1.22
- Foreign market and trade for electric power systems equipment, and user industry operations and demand, country market research rpts, 2045–15
- Govt census, 1982: city govt revenues by source, expenditures by function, debt, and assets, by State and city, 2457–4

Govt census, 1982: county govt revenues by source, expenditures by function, debt, and assets, by State and county, 2457–3

- Govt census, 1982: employment, payrolls, and average earnings, by function, level of govt, State, county, population size, and inside-outside SMSAs, 2455–2
- Govt census, 1982: local govt employment by function, payroll, and average earnings, for individual counties, cities, and school and special districts, 2455–1
- Govt census, 1982: properties, govt-assessed value, sales, and tax rates, by property type, State, SMSA, county, and city, 2453–1
- Govt census, 1982: State govt payments to local govts, by program, source of funds, level of govt, and State, with trends from 1902, 2460–3
- Govt employment and payroll, by function, level of govt, and jurisdiction, 1983, annual rpt series, 2466–1
- Govt finances, by level of govt, State, and for large cities and counties, 1981-83, annual rpt series, 2466–2
- Govt revenues by source and expenditures by function, natl income and product account, *Survey of Current Business,* monthly rpt, monthly and annual tables, 2702–1.24
- *Handbook of Labor Statistics,* employment, earnings, hours, and labor force characteristics, 1982 and trends, detailed annual rpt, 6724–1
- Holding companies of public utilities finances, securities issued, and subsidiaries by type, by firm, FY83, annual rpt, 9734–2.6
- Home mortgages (graduated payment) FHA-insured, financial, property, and mortgagor characteristics, for US and selected localities, quarterly rpt, 5142–42
- Home mortgages (graduated payment) FHA-insured, financial, property, and mortgagor characteristics, for US and selected States, quarterly rpt, 5142–41
- Home mortgages (graduated payment) FHA-insured, financial, property, and mortgagor characteristics, US summary, quarterly rpt, 5142–40
- Home mortgages FHA-insured, financial, property, and mortgagor characteristics, for US and selected localities, quarterly rpt, 5142–2
- Home mortgages FHA-insured, financial, property, and mortgagor characteristics, for US, selected States, and Puerto Rico, quarterly rpt, 5142–3
- Home mortgages FHA-insured, financial, property, and mortgagor characteristics, quarterly rpt, 5142–1
- Home mortgages FHA-insured, financial, property, and mortgagor characteristics, 1983, annual rpt, 5144–17
- Home mortgages FHA-insured for low-cost homes, financial, construction, property, and mortgagor characteristics, quarterly rpt, 5142–4
- Housing and households detailed characteristics, and unit and neighborhood quality, by inside-outside central cities, 1979-82 surveys, SMSA rpt series, 2485–6
- Housing and neighborhood quality indicators and attitudes, and occupant characteristics, by urban-rural location and region, 1981, annual survey, 2485–7

Public utilities

Housing electricity and gas costs for 306 cities, by utility, with climatological data, fall 1982, 3308–67

Housing energy conservation devices installation, utility loan program cost effectiveness, and household participation characteristics, Minnesota study, 1980-83, 3308–72

Income tax returns of corporations, detailed income and tax items by industry, 1981, annual rpt, 8304–4

Income tax returns of corporations, summary data by industry div, 1981 estimates, annual article, 8302–2.403

Income tax returns of corporations with foreign tax credit, income and deductions by type, asset size, and selected industry group, 1980, article, 8302–2.415

Income tax returns of foreign subsidiaries of US corporations, income and tax data, by industry and asset size, 1980, article, 8302–2.410

Income tax returns of partnerships, detailed data by industry, 1981 estimates, annual article, 8302–2.404

Income tax returns of partnerships, receipts by source, deductions by type, and establishments, by selected industry, 1982, annual article, 8302–2.416

Income tax returns of sole proprietorships, detailed data by industry div and selected industry group, 1981, annual rpt, 8304–7

Income tax returns of sole proprietorships, receipts, deductions by type, payroll, and net income, by major industry, 1982, annual article, 8302–2.413

Input-output structure of US economy, detailed interindustry transactions for 85 industries, and components of final demand, 1977, article, 2702–1.421

Input-output structure of US economy, detailed interindustry transactions for 537 industries, and components of final demand, 1977 benchmark data, 2708–17

Michigan bankruptcy filings, by filer type, moving history, income, creditor action, debt and asset type, credit status, exemptions claimed, and county, 1979-81, hearings, 21528–57.3

Minority group and women employment, by occupational group and SIC 2- to 3-digit industry, 1981, annual rpt, 9244–1.1

Natl income and product, comprehensive accounts and components, *Survey of Current Business,* monthly rpt, monthly and annual tables, 2702–1.27

Occupational injuries, illnesses, and workdays lost, by SIC 2-digit industry, 1982-83, annual press release, 6844–3

Occupational injury and illness rates, by SIC 2- to 4-digit industry, 1982, annual rpt, 6844–1

Occupational manpower needs and supply by detailed occupation, and educational and training program enrollees and grads by detailed field, 1982 and 1995, biennial rpt, 6744–3

Pacific Northwest electricity consumption and prices by end-use sector, and economic and demographic data, 1960s-83 and projected to 2005, annual rpt, 3224–2

Pollution abatement capital and operating costs under Clean Air and Water Acts, for govts and selected industries, various periods 1970-2000, annual rpt, 9184–11

Index by Subjects and Names

Scientists, engineers, and technicians employment in transportation, utilities, and retail and wholesale trade, by field of science and industry, 1982, 9628–72

Seasonal adjustment methodology for economic time series, dev and design of Census Bur and other systems, with illustrative data, 1981 conf papers, 2626–7.5

Small and minority-owned businesses finances and operations, Federal contracts by agency, and worker characteristics, by industry, race, sex, and State, 1950s-83, annual rpt, 9764–6

State and local govt productivity measurement, with background data and output indexes for 7 govt services, various periods 1955-82, 6728–27

Statistical Abstract of US, social, political, and economic data, 1950s-83 and trends, annual rpt, 2324–1.3

Stock (common) prices and yields, current data and annual trends, monthly rpt, 23842–1.5

Tax (excise) revenue of local govts, by excise type and State, average annual growth FY72-82, article, 10042–1.403

Tax revenues, by level of govt, type of tax, State, and selected large counties, quarterly rpt, 2462–3

Transportation census, 1982: trucks, by detailed characteristics, miles traveled, and type of product carried, State rpt series, 2573–1

Virgin Islands socioeconomic and govtl data, FY81, annual rpt, 5304–4

Wages by occupation, and benefits for office and plant workers in 70 SMSAs, 1983, annual rpt, 6785–1

Wages by occupation, and benefits for office and plant workers, 1983, annual SMSA survey rpt series, 6785–12

Wages by occupation, and benefits for office and plant workers, 1984, annual SMSA survey rpt series, 6785–11

Water pollution fish kills, by State, location, and pollution source, monthly 1978-80, annual rpt, 9204–3

see also Buses

see also Electric power

see also Electric power prices

see also Natural gas and gas industry

see also Natural gas prices

see also Power-generating plants and equipment

see also Railroads

see also Refuse and refuse disposal

see also Rural electrification

see also Sewage and wastewater treatment systems

see also Subways

see also Telephone and telephone industry

see also Water supply and use

see also under By Industry in the "Index by Categories"

Public welfare programs

Bankruptcy (personal), filers by debt type and other characteristics, selected years 1978-81, hearing, 25528–97.1

Beneficiaries of noncash public and employer-based transfer programs, by income source and socioeconomic characteristics, 1982, advance Current Population Rpt, 2546–6.38

Beneficiaries of noncash public and employer-based transfer programs, by income source and socioeconomic characteristics, 1982, final Current Population Rpt, 2546–6.37

Beneficiary families and children, and total and average payments, by public assistance program and State, since 1940, monthly rpt, 4742–1.5

Budget of US Appendix, detailed budgets and personnel summaries, by agency, FY85, annual rpt, 104–3

Budget of US, CBO analysis and review of FY85 budget by function, annual rpt, 26304–2

Budget of US, CBO analysis of revenue and spending alternatives and projections of economic indicators, FY85-89, annual rpt, 26304–3.3

Budget of US, compact budgets by function, agency, and account, FY85 with projections to FY89, annual rpt, 104–2

Budget of US, effects of Reagan Admin policy changes, by detailed program, FY85, annual rpt, 104–21

Budget of US, receipts by source and outlays by agency and program, monthly rpt, 8102–3

Budget of US, receipts by source and outlays by function, FY40-89 estimates revised for consistency with FY85 budget definitions, annual rpt, 104–12

Budget of US, receipts, outlays, and budget authority, by function and agency, FY84-89 revised estimates, midsession review of FY85 budget, annual rpt, 104–7

Census of Population and Housing, 1980: detailed population and housing characteristics, by county, city, and census tract, State and SMSA rpt series, 2551–2

Census of Population, 1980: detailed socioeconomic and demographic characteristics, by age, sex, race, Hispanic origin, occupation, and industry, State rpt series, 2531–4

Census of Population, 1980: detailed socioeconomic characteristics, by county, city, and inside-outside SMSAs and central cities, State rpt series, 2531–3

Child Support Enforcement Program cost savings to AFDC, Federal and State govts, and public assistance programs, by State and selected city or county, FY76-85, 4748–37

Children and youth benefitting from Fed Govt public welfare programs and tax expenditures, participation and funding for 71 programs, FY81-83, 21968–30

Coastal environmental characteristics, fish, wildlife, and use, and population socioeconomic data, for individual areas, series, 5506–4

Fed Govt aid to State and local govts, expenditures, and direct payments, by program, agency, and State, FY83, annual rpt, 2464–2

Fed Govt financial and nonfinancial domestic aid, 1984 annual comprehensive catalog, 104–5

Fed Govt programs and mgmt cost control proposals, CBO and GAO estimates of savings by function and agency, FY85-89, 26308–45

Index by Subjects and Names

Public welfare programs

Fed Govt programs and mgmt cost control proposals, 3-year savings by function and agency, and financial and operating data, 1960s-81, 16908–1

Fed Govt programs under Ways and Means Committee jurisdiction, program operations and financing data for assessing budgetary requirements, by State, FY70s-83, 21788–117

Govt census, 1982: city govt revenues by source, expenditures by function, debt, and assets, by State and city, 2457–4

Govt census, 1982: county govt revenues by source, expenditures by function, debt, and assets, by State and county, 2457–3

Govt census, 1982: employment, payrolls, and average earnings, by function, level of govt, State, county, population size, and inside-outside SMSAs, 2455–2

Govt census, 1982: local govt employment by function, payroll, and average earnings, for individual counties, cities, and school and special districts, 2455–1

Govt census, 1982: State govt payments to local govts, by program, source of funds, level of govt, and State, with trends from 1902, 2460–3

Govt employment and payroll, by function, level of govt, and jurisdiction, 1983, annual rpt series, 2466–1

Govt expenditures for public welfare, by level of govt and type of program, selected years FY50-82, 4746–16.1

Govt expenditures for social welfare by program and level of govt, and private expenditures for health care, selected years FY50-82, annual article, 4742–1.425

Govt finances, by level of govt and State, selected years 1929-83, annual rpt, 10044–1

Govt finances, by level of govt, State, and for large cities and counties, 1981-83, annual rpt series, 2466–2

Govt revenues by source and expenditures by function, natl income and product account, *Survey of Current Business,* monthly rpt, monthly and annual tables, 2702–1.24

HHS aid to each State and local govt or private instn, amount obligated, funding agency, and program, FY83, annual listing, 4004–3

HHS programs fraud and abuse, audits and investigations, 2nd half FY84, semiannual rpt, 4002–6

Homeless population and characteristics, and temporary shelter operations, use, and user characteristics, by region and selected city, 1983, 5188–108

Homeless population and characteristics, and temporary shelter operations, use, and user characteristics, for selected cities, various periods 1979-84, hearing, 21248–85

Household income by family type and race, and households receiving noncash benefits by poverty status, 1982 annual Current Population Rpt, 2546–2.119

Household,family, and personal income, by detailed socioeconomic characteristics and region, 1982, annual Current Population Rpt, 2546–6.39

Households and housing unit characteristics, and employment, housing finance, and social programs data, selected years 1948-83, hearing, 21968–28

Income (household) and cash and noncash transfer program participation, by sociodemographic characteristics, quarterly rpt, 2542–2

Income averages of OASI beneficiaries, and beneficiaries by income level, by beneficiary characteristics and income source, before and after receipt of 1st benefit, 1969-77, article, 4742–1.418

Job Training Partnership Act performance standards guide for States, with data on previous job training programs by State or local area, FY81-82, 6408–59

Local govt finances and population characteristics for cities and suburbs, by region and selected SMSA, selected years 1957-FY83, 10048–61

Mobility of population, detailed data by demographic and socioeconomic characteristics of movers and nonmovers, Mar 1981-82, annual Current Population Rpt, 2546–1.384

New York State home health care program info system on public assistance benefits and services received by program participants, 1984 article, 4652–1.402

OASDHI, Medicaid, SSI, and other social insurance and public welfare programs benefits, beneficiary characteristics, and trust funds, selected years 1937-83, annual rpt, 4744–3

Older persons by demographic, socioeconomic, and health characteristics, selected years 1900-81 and projected to 2050, Current Population Rpt, 2546–2.125

Older persons discrimination in Fed Govt aid programs, Age Discrimination Act enforcement by 28 agencies, FY83, annual rpt, 4004–27

Older persons income and income sources, by OASDI beneficiary and poverty status, labor force participation, and demographic characteristics, 1982, biennial rpt, 4744–26

Older persons sociodemographic characteristics, and Fed Govt program participation and funding by agency, 1983 with trends and projections 1900-2080, annual rpt, 25144–3

Poverty income guidelines of Fed Govt for determining public assistance eligibility, by family size, 1965-84, article, 4742–1.415

Poverty-level persons and families, by income source, hours of work, earnings, taxes, and family characteristics, various periods 1959-84, 21788–131

Poverty population by labor force status, and effect of public welfare changes and recession, by family status, FY82, 21788–139

Poverty rate by family composition, and effect of noncash transfers, taxes, unemployment benefits, and business cycles, selected years 1959-82, hearings, 21788–141

Poverty status of families and persons, by detailed socioeconomic characteristics, 1982, annual Current Population Rpt, 2546–6.40

Poverty status of families and persons by selected characteristics, public welfare funding, and effect of counting transfer payments as income, selected years 1950-83, 25928–4

Poverty status of young adults related to motivation, psychological factors, and family characteristics, by race and sex, 1970s-82, longitudinal study, 4008–65.1

Public opinion on taxes, tax policy, and intergovtl relations, 1972-84 surveys, annual rpt, 10044–2

Refugee arrivals in US by world area of origin and State of settlement, and Fed Govt intl and domestic assistance costs, FY85, annual rpt, 7004–16

Refugee resettlement program activities and funding, arrivals and population by country of origin and State, and employment and other characteristics, FY83, annual rpt, 4704–8

Research and statistical projects and techniques, and evaluation of public welfare programs, 1983 conf papers, 4704–11

State govt public assistance expenditures, Fed Govt share, local funds, and recipient count, by program, annual rpt, discontinued, 4744–22

Statistical Abstract of US, social, political, and economic data, 1950s-83 and trends, annual rpt, 2324–1.2

Tax expenditures, Fed Govt revenues foregone through income tax deductions and exclusions by type, and effect of Deficit Reduction Act, FY84-89, annual rpt, 21784–10

Traffic accidents and casualties detailed direct and indirect costs, by characteristics of persons and vehicles involved, 1979-80, 7768–80

Virgin Islands socioeconomic and govtl data, FY81, annual rpt, 5304–4

Vocationally rehabilitated persons under State agency programs, by sociodemographic characteristics and disabling condition, FY79-81, annual rpt, 4944–6

see also Aid to Blind

see also Aid to Families with Dependent Children

see also Aid to Permanently and Totally Disabled

see also Child day care

see also Child welfare

see also Disability insurance

see also Disaster relief

see also Food assistance

see also Food stamp programs

see also Foster home care

see also Homemaker services

see also Income maintenance

see also Legal aid

see also Medicaid

see also Medical assistance

see also Medicare

see also Old Age Assistance

see also Public service employment

see also Rent supplements

see also School lunch and breakfast programs

see also Social security

see also Social services

see also Social work

see also Supplemental Security Income

see also Vocational rehabilitation

see also Work Incentive Program

Public works

Public works

Army Corps of Engineers activities and projects, FY83 and trends from 1800s, annual rpt, 3754–1

Bond tax-exempt issues by purpose, and Fed Govt mortgage bond revenue losses and borrower characteristics, selected years 1971-85, hearings, 21788–135

Budget of US Appendix, detailed budgets and personnel summaries, by agency, FY85, annual rpt, 104–3

Capital needs and financing for public works, by project type, level of govt, and selected jurisdiction, 1970s-83 and projected to 2000, hearing, 23848–181

Capital needs and intergovtl financing for public works, by type of project and selected city, various periods 1950-83, 10048–60

Community Dev Block Grants to small cities, State admin, project characteristics, and assessments of local officials, 1982, 5188–106

Community dev programs funding and activities, for 5 HUD programs, FY83, annual rpt, 5124–5

Construction industry activity, employment and earnings, prices, Federal aid, and foreign contracts, 1970s-83 with projections to 1988, annual article, 2012–1.402

Economic Dev Admin loans and grants, by program, State, county, and project or recipient, FY83 and cumulative FY66-83, annual rpt, 2064–2

Fed Govt aid to State and local govts, expenditures, and direct payments, by program, agency, and State, FY83, annual rpt, 2464–2

Fed Govt programs and mgmt cost control proposals, 3-year savings by function and agency, and financial and operating data, 1960s-81, 16908–1.22

Govt census, 1982: State govt payments to local govts, by program, source of funds, level of govt, and State, with trends from 1902, 2460–3

Public opinion on taxes, tax policy, and intergovtl relations, 1972-84 surveys, annual rpt, 10044–2

see also Public buildings

see also Public service employment

Publications catalogs

see Bibliographies

see Government publications lists

Publishing industry

see Printing and publishing industry

Pueblo, Colo.

Census of Housing, 1980: occupancy and unit characteristics, by race, Hispanic origin, and city, SMSA rpt, 2473–1.295

Census of Population and Housing, 1980: detailed population and housing characteristics, by county, city, and census tract, SMSA rpt, 2551–2.295

Housing vacancy rates for single and multifamily units and mobile homes, by county, city, and ZIP code, 1984, annual metro area rpt, 9304–22.7

see also under By City and By SMSA or MSA in the "Index by Categories"

Puerto Ricans

see Hispanic Americans

see Puerto Rico

Puerto Rico

Agriculture census, 1982: farms, farmland, production, finances, and operator characteristics, by municipio, final outlying area rpt, 2331–1.52

AID contracts and grants for technical and support services, by instn, country, and State, FY83, annual listing, 9914–7

Aircraft (general aviation), hours flown, and equipment, by type, use, and model of aircraft, region, and State, 1982, annual rpt, 7504–29

Airlines (commuter and intrastate) operating in 1978 by region and State, and listing by city, by operation status in 1984, article, 9142–42.404

Animal protection, licensing, and inspection activities of USDA, and animals used in research, by State, FY83, annual rpt, 1394–10

Bank deposits in commercial and mutual savings banks and in US branches of foreign banks, by account type, instn, State, SMSA, and county, June 1983, annual rpt, 9295–3.2

Births (live) by selected demographic characteristics, for 3 outlying areas, 1979, US Vital Statistics annual rpt, 4144–1.3

Bombing (explosive and incendiary) incidents, damage, injuries, and deaths, by target, State, and circumstances, 1983, annual rpt, 6224–5

Budget of US, food stamp and nutrition assistance funding, effects of Reagan Admin policy changes, FY85, annual rpt, 104–21

Cancer cases, incidence, deaths, and death rates, by body site, age, race, Hispanic origin, and sex, for 10 geographic areas, 1973-81, 4478–130

Cattle brucellosis eradication, and testing of goats and swine, cooperative Federal-State program activities, by State, FY83, annual rpt, 1394–6

Cattle tuberculosis eradication and surveillance, cooperative Federal-State program activities, by State, FY83, annual rpt, 1394–13

Cement (portland) shipments from plants in US and Puerto Rico, by destination, bimonthly rpt, 2012–1.6

Census of Population, 1980: detailed socioeconomic and demographic characteristics, by age, sex, occupation, and industry, outlying area rpt, 2531–4.53

Census of Population, 1980: detailed socioeconomic and demographic characteristics, by age, sex, race, Hispanic origin, occupation, and industry, State rpt series, 2531–4

Census of Population, 1980: detailed socioeconomic characteristics, by municipio, city, and inside-outside SMSAs and central cities, outlying area rpt, 2531–3.53

County Business Patterns: establishments, employees, and payrolls, by SIC 4-digit industry and county, 1981, annual State rpt, 2326–8.53

County Business Patterns: establishments, employees, and payrolls, by SIC 4-digit industry and county, 1982, annual State rpt, 2326–6.53

Index by Subjects and Names

Crime and crime rates, by offense, MSA, and central city, 1983, annual rpt, 6224–2.5

Dengue and dengue-like illness cases reported and confirmed in Puerto Rico by month or week of onset, and cases by State, 1982, article, 4202–7.407

Disability Insurance beneficiaries sociodemographic and medical characteristics, 1977-79, annual rpt, 4744–20

DOD budget, expenditures for each service branch and total defense agencies, by function and State, FY85, annual rpt, 3544–23

DOD prime contract awards in labor surplus areas, by service branch, State, and area, 1st half FY84, semiannual rpt, 3542–19

Earthquake intensity, damage, and deaths, by location for major earthquakes since 1755, and hazard areas and natl reduction program activities, as of 1984, 5668–73

Educational enrollment, finance, completions, curricula, and personnel by instn, and health and vital statistics, selected years 1970-83, hearings, 21348–93

Employment and wages of workers covered by State unemployment insurance laws and Fed Govt unemployment compensation, by SIC 4-digit industry and State, 1982, annual rpt, 6744–16

Employment, earnings, and hours, by selected SIC 1- to 4-digit industry, State, and for 278 major labor areas, 1939-83, annual rpt, 6744–5.2, 6744–5.3

Environmental quality, pollutant discharge by type and source, and EPA protection activities and funding, 1970s-83, biennial regional rpt, 9184–15.2

Exports and imports between US and outlying areas, by detailed commodity and mode of transport, monthly rpt, 2422–4

Fed Govt Equal Opportunity Recruitment Program implementation, and summary employment data, FY83, annual rpt, 9844–33

Fed Home Loan Bank System members, with assets of S&Ls, by instn, city, and State, 1983, annual listing, 9314–5

Fertilizer consumption, by fertilizer type and State, years ended June 1983-84, annual rpt, 1631–13

Fish landings, by species, 1957-77, annual rpt, 2164–2.11

Fishery cooperatives in US, Puerto Rico, and Guam, 1983, annual rpt, 2164–1.10

Fishing (ocean sport) effort and catch, and Natl Marine Fisheries Service tagging and research activity, by species and location, 1983, annual rpt, 2164–7

Foreign firms US affiliates financial and operating data, by country of parent firm and industry div, 1980-81, article, 2702–1.402

Govt census, 1982: properties, govt-assessed value, sales, and tax rates, by property type, State, SMSA, county, and city, 2453–1

HHS aid to each State and local govt or private instn, amount obligated, funding agency, and program, FY83, annual listing, 4004–3.2

Home mortgage loan originations, by State and for Puerto Rico, 1978-83, press release, 5148–6

Index by Subjects and Names

Puerto Rico

Home mortgages FHA-insured, financial, property, and mortgagor characteristics, for US, selected States, and Puerto Rico, quarterly rpt, 5142–3

Housing units authorized, by public and private ownership, by region, div, State, selected MSA, and 4,700 permit-issuing places, monthly rpt, 2382–5

Housing units authorized, by public and private ownership, State, and permit-issuing place, 1983, annual rpt, 2384–2

HUD rental rehabilitation grants for low- and moderate-income housing, by community, 1984 press release, 5006–3.33

HUD rental rehabilitation program allocations, by State, county, and city, FY85, press release, 5006–3.39

HUD rental rehabilitation projects, local funding and Section 8 rent supplements for 22 States and 275 communities, 1984 press release, 5006–3.30

Hwy construction expenditures and contracts awarded for Federal-aid system, by type of material used and State, various periods 1944-83, annual rpts, 7554–29

Hwy interstate system mileage, costs, and Fed Govt funding, by hwy completion status and State, as of June 1984, 7556–3.4

Hwy speed averages and vehicles exceeding 55 mph, by State, quarterly rpt, 7552–14

Hwy Statistics, detailed data on traffic, govt finances, fuel use, vehicles, driver licenses, and hwy characteristics, 1983, annual rpt, 7554–1.6

Income tax returns of individuals, selected income, deduction, and tax credit data by income, preliminary 1982, annual article, 8302–2.402

Marriages, divorces, and rates, by detailed demographic characteristics, 1979 and trends, US Vital Statistics annual rpt, 4144–4.3

Medicare enrollment, reimbursement, and use and covered charges by type of service, by State and census div, 1978-82, 4658–8

Medicare program operations and admin efficiency, Blue Shield participants, and end-stage renal disease program activity, FY81, annual rpt, 4654–5

Medicare Supplementary Medical Insurance maximum charges reimbursable for specific services, by State and outlying area, 1983, annual rpt, 4654–4

Mineral Industry Surveys, State review of production, 1983, advance annual rpt, 5614–6.51

Minerals Yearbook, 1982, Vol 2 preprints: State review of production and sales by commodity, and business activity, annual rpt, 5604–16.40

Minerals Yearbook, 1982, Vol 2: State reviews of production, sales, and firms, by commodity, and business activity, annual rpt, 5604–34

Mines, mills, and quarries occupational injuries, and employees and hours, by State, quarterly rpt, 6662–1

Motor fuel State tax provisions, motor vehicle registration fees, and disposition of receipts, by State, as of Jan 1984, biennial rpt, 7554–37

Natural gas pipeline safety, Fed Govt expenditures, FY81, and State inspection personnel, enforcement actions, and accidents investigated, by State, 1982, annual rpt, 7304–5

NIH grants, awards, and obligations by State and type of recipient, and full-time personnel, by inst, FY83, annual rpt, 4434–3

NSF grant and award recipients, by State, FY83, annual listing, 9624–11

Oil exports to US by OPEC and non-OPEC countries, monthly rpt, 3162–24.3

Philanthropic grants to Puerto Rican organizations in US and Puerto Rico, by foundation, purpose, and recipient, 1979-81, hearings, 21788–137.1

Population size and components of change, by outlying area, 1970-82, Current Population Rpt, 2546–3.127

Population size and components of change, by outlying area, 1980-83, Current Population Rpt, 2546–3.134

Population size and growth rates, and latest available benchmark demographic data, by country, 1950-83, biennial rpt, 2324–4

Radiation control program activities, State and local expenditures, personnel, and NRC licenses, by State, FY80-82, annual rpt, 4064–3

Rum production, trade by selected country, consumption, and shipments from Puerto Rico and Virgin Islands, Jan-June 1983-84, annual rpt, 9884–15

Rural Electrification Admin loans to power supply and distribution firms, and borrower operating and financial data, by firm and State, 1983, annual rpt, 1244–1

Rural Electrification Program loan activities summary, by State, FY83 and cumulative from 1935, annual rpt, 1244–7

Savings and loan assns assets and liabilities, by FHLB district and State, selected years 1955-82, annual rpt, 9314–1

Savings instns, FHLB 2nd District members financial operations, by State, monthly rpt, 9302–14

Science and engineering doctoral degree recipients, by field, sex, race, age, citizenship, postgrad employment and study status, State, and instn, 1960-82, 9626–6.16

Storms and unusual weather phenomena characteristics, casualties, and property damage, by State and outlying area, monthly listing, 2152–3

Sugar cane growers, acreage, yield, and cane sugar production, quarterly rpt, 1561–14

Sugar production, consumption, supply, and trade, quarterly rpt, 1621–28

Telephone companies borrowing under rural telephone loan program, and financial and operating data, 1983, annual rpt, 1244–2.3

Tobacco production, prices, stocks, taxes by State, and trade and foreign production by country, 1983, annual rpt, 1319–1

Traffic fatal accidents detailed circumstances, and characteristics of persons and vehicles involved, 1982, annual rpt, 7764–10

Trust assets of banks and trust companies, by type of asset and fund and State, 1983, annual rpt, 13004–1

TVA fertilizer distribution in farmer education programs by State, dev costs, and shipments by type and purpose, FY83, annual rpt, 9804–1.2

Unemployment insurance State govt program admin, quality appraisal results, FY84, annual rpt, 6404–16

Unemployment insurance State govt program benefits, coverage, and tax provisions, July 1984, semiannual listing, 6402–7

Unemployment insurance system finances, claims, payments, and covered employment and wages, by State, 1938-82, 6408–5

Unemployment, labor surplus areas eligible for preferential Fed Govt contracts, and labor force data for 150 major labor markets, monthly listing, 6402–1

VA selected expenditures, by type, State, and for Puerto Rico, Philippines, and other foreign areas, FY83, annual rpt, 9924–1.9

Veteran population, by period of service, age, and State, Sept 1984, semiannual rpt, 9922–3

Veteran women, by period of service, age, and State, Mar 1983 and projected to 2030, 9928–28

Veterans education assistance program participation and costs under GI Bill and other programs, WW II through Sept 1983, annual rpt, 9924–22

Veterans of Vietnam era, by age, sex, State, and for Puerto Rico, FY83, annual rpt, 9924–8.1

Vital statistics, births, marriages, divorces, and deaths, provisional data, monthly rpt, 4142–1

Wages for 3 occupational groups, relative average levels in 78 labor market areas, 1983, annual press release, 6785–13

Water supply and quality, floods, drought, mudslides, and other hydrologic events, by State, 1983, annual rpt, 5664–12

Water supply and quality in streams and lakes, and groundwater levels in wells, by drainage basin, 1982, annual State rpt, 5666–20.48

Water supply contamination by volatile organic chemicals, monitoring results for each State and Puerto Rico, 1981, 9208–120

Water supply in US and Canada, streamflow, well and reservoir levels, and dissolved solids and temperature in 6 US rivers, by station, monthly rpt, 5662–3

Waterborne commerce of US (domestic and foreign), freight by commodity, traffic, and passengers, by port and waterway, 1982, annual rpt, 3754–3.2

Weather conditions and effect on agriculture, by US region, State, and city, and world area, weekly rpt, 2152–2

Wood and wood product shipments from US by type, and from selected foreign sources, 1971-81, 1208–205

Workers compensation law provisions of States and Fed Govt, by jurisdiction, as of July 1984, semiannual rpt, 6502–1

see also under By Outlying Area in the "Index by Categories"

Pulp

Pulp
see Lumber industry and products
see Paper and paper products

Pulses
see Vegetables and vegetable products

Pumice
see Abrasive materials

Pumps and compressors
see Machines and machinery industry

Purchasing power
see Personal and family income

Putnam, Hayes & Bartlett, Inc.
"Alternative Energy Futures: A Review of Low-Energy-Growth Forecasts and Least-Cost Planning Studies", 3008–93

Pyrites
see Nonmetallic minerals and mines

Pyrophyllite
see Nonmetallic minerals and mines

Qatar

- Agricultural situation in Middle East and North Africa, by country and commodity, 1983 and outlook for 1984, annual rpt, 1524–4.3
- Economic, social, and political summary data, by country, 1984, annual factbook, 244–11
- Exports and imports of US, by commodity and country, 1972-82, annual world region rpt, 244–13.1
- Exports of US, detailed Schedule B commodities by country of destination, 1983, annual rpt, 2424–9
- Exports of US, detailed Schedule E commodities by mode of transport and world area and country of destination, 1983, annual rpts, 2424–5
- Imports of US, detailed Schedule A commodities by country and world area of origin, and mode of transport, 1983, annual rpts, 2424–2
- Imports of US, detailed TSUSA commodities by country of origin, 1983, annual rpt, 2424–4
- Military aid of US, arms sales, and training programs costs and budget requests by program, world region, and country, FY83-85, annual rpt, 7144–13
- Military spending, arms trade, and armed forces size, with total govt spending and population, by country, 1972-82, annual rpt, 9824–1
- *Minerals Yearbook, 1982,* Vol 3: foreign country reviews of production, trade, and policies, by commodity, annual rpt, 5604–35
- *Minerals Yearbook, 1982,* Vol 3 preprints: foreign country review of production, trade, and policies, by commodity, annual rpt, 5604–17.88
- Oil production by major exporting countries, monthly rpt, 3162–24.10
- Population size and growth rates, and latest available benchmark demographic data, by country, 1950-83, biennial rpt, 2324–4
- Telecommunication equipment market and trade, and user industry operations and demand, 1982 country market research rpt, 2045–12.32
- *see also* under By Foreign Country in the "Index by Categories"

Index by Subjects and Names

Quality control and testing

- Census of Population, 1980: detailed socioeconomic and demographic characteristics, by age, sex, race, Hispanic origin, occupation, and industry, State rpt series, 2531–4
- Census of Population, 1980: labor force, by sex, detailed occupation, and region, with comparison to 1970 census, supplementary rpt, 2535–1.12
- Coal purchases of Fed Govt, quality control analyses by mine and location, FY82-83, annual rpt, 3004–15
- Cobalt consumption by end use, and stockpile inventories and quality, selected years 1950-82, hearings, 25208–27
- Computer specialists sociodemographic, educational, and employment characteristics, and Fed Govt support by agency, 1978, biennial Current Population Rpt, 2546–2.124
- Cotton acreage planted, by State and county, and fiber quality, by variety, 1980-84, annual rpt, 1309–6
- Cotton fiber and processing test results, by staple, region, State, and production area, seasonal biweekly rpt, 1309–3
- Cotton fiber and processing test results, by State, 1983, annual rpt, 1309–4
- Cotton fiber grade, staple, and mike, for upland and American Pima cotton by State, monthly rpt, 1309–11
- Cotton quality specifications, by State, 1983/84, annual rpt, 1309–7
- Cottonseed quality factors, by State, 1983 crop, annual rpt, 1309–5
- Electric power plant (steam) fuel deliveries, costs, and quality, by fuel type, State, and utility, 1983, annual rpt, 3164–42
- Employment, earnings, and hours, by SIC 4-digit nonfarm industry, monthly 1974-Feb 1984, annual update, 6744–4
- Fed Govt procurement contract awards, by State, agency, procurement and contractor type, and for top 100 contractors, quarterly rpt, 102–6
- Foreign trade zones, activities, and value of goods entering and leaving zones, 1973-82, GAO rpt, 26119–56
- Hearing aid performance evaluation, by model and manufacturer, 1984, annual rpt, 9924–5
- Mobile and manufactured home safety standards, program inspections, enforcement actions, and accidents and casualties by victim characteristics, 1982-83, biennial rpt, 5004–4
- Nuclear reactors for domestic use and export by function, with owner, operating characteristics, and location, Apr 1984, semiannual listing, 3002–5
- Nuclear Regulatory Commission activities, employment, and finances, and operations of individual power plants by State, FY83, annual rpt, 9634–2
- Oil product surveys, lab analyses of aviation, heating, diesel, and gasoline fuel properties, last issues of annual and semiannual rpt series, 3006–2
- Scientists and engineers employed in energy-related fields, supply/demand and effects of R&D funding, by energy type, employer type, field, and age, 1962-91, annual rpt, 3004–19

Shipments, trade, and consumption of industrial control and other equipment, by product, 1983, annual Current Industrial Rpt, 2506–12.11

- Water supply and quality in 8 southeastern States, with background socioeconomic data, 1960s-2020 with trends from 1930, 9208–119
- *see also* Food inspection

Quality of life

- Black young adults economic status and educational attainment related to motivation, goals, family characteristics, and social factors, 1982, longitudinal study, 4008–65.2
- Communist, OECD, and selected other countries living standards and commodity production, 1960s-83, annual rpt, 244–5.1
- Developing countries govt policy, and AID and other foreign assistance, effects on private sector dev and socioeconomic conditions, with case studies for 6 countries, 1960s-80, 9918–12
- Florida and California elderly migration by selected State of origin or destination, and Florida elderly, by sociodemographic and housing characteristics, 1970 and 1980, 4478–150
- Housing (rental) unit choice of Pittsburgh, Pa, recent movers related to unit, neighborhood, and town characteristics, 1967 survey, 9306–1.7
- Housing and neighborhood quality indicators and attitudes, and occupant characteristics, by urban-rural location and region, 1981, annual survey, 2485–7
- Housing and neighborhood quality, indicators and attitudes by inside-outside central cities, 1979-82 surveys, SMSA rpt series, 2485–6
- Housing and neighborhood quality indicators and attitudes, by occupant and unit characteristics, region, and metro-nonmetro location, 1981, annual survey, 2485–2
- NYC metro area small business owners and accountants, assessment of economy, professional activities, and community problems, by county and industry div, 1983 survey, hearings, 21728–52.3
- Older persons nutrition services program operations and assessment, and participant sociodemographic, health, and diet characteristics, 1976 and 1982, 4608–16

Quarries and stone products

- Air pollutant emission factors, by detailed source, 3rd edition, 1983-84 supplements, 9198–13
- Alaska minerals resources, production, claims on wildlife refuges, oil and gas leases, and exploratory wells, with maps and bibl, 1983, annual rpt, 5664–11
- Census of Population, 1980: detailed socioeconomic and demographic characteristics, by age, sex, race, Hispanic origin, occupation, and industry, State rpt series, 2531–4
- Collective bargaining agreements expiring during year, covered workers by SIC 2-digit industry, firm, and union, with summary of key provisions, 1984, annual rpt, 6784–9
- County Business Patterns: establishments, employees, and payrolls, by SIC 4-digit industry and county, 1981, annual State rpt series, 2326–8

Index by Subjects and Names

County Business Patterns: establishments, employees, and payrolls, by SIC 4-digit industry and county, 1982, annual State rpt series, 2326–6

Cuba economic conditions, agricultural and industrial production and distribution, trade, and intl economic relations, 1970-82 and trends from 1957, 248–40

Earnings by major industry group, and personal income per capita and by source, by region and State, 1929-82, 2708–40

Employment, earnings, and hours, by selected SIC 1- to 4-digit industry, State, and for 278 major labor areas, 1939-83, annual rpt, 6744–5

Employment, earnings, and hours, by SIC 4-digit nonfarm industry, monthly 1974-Feb 1984, annual update, 6744–4

Exports and imports of US, detailed SIC-based commodities by world area, 1983, annual rpts, 2424–6

Exports and imports of US, totals and as percent of domestic production, by SIC 2- to 5-digit commodity, 1981, annual rpt, 2424–3

Exports of US, detailed commodities by country of destination, monthly rpt, 2422–3

Exports of US, detailed Schedule B commodities by country of destination, 1983, annual rpt, 2424–9

Exports of US, detailed Schedule E commodities by mode of transport and world area and country of destination, 1983, annual rpts, 2424–5

Foreign minerals production, reserves, and industry role in domestic economy and world supply, country and world region rpt series, 5606–1

Great Lakes trade, by SITC 3-digit commodity, port, vessel type, world area, and country, 1982, annual rpt, 7744–3

Hwy construction expenditures and contracts awarded for Federal-aid system, by type of material used and State, various periods 1944-83, annual rpt, 7554-29.1, 7554–29.5

Imports of US, detailed Schedule A commodities by country and world area of origin, and mode of transport, 1983, annual rpts, 2424–2

Imports of US, detailed Schedule A commodities by country, monthly rpt, 2422–2

Imports of US, detailed TSUSA commodities by country of origin, 1983, annual rpt, 2424–4

Income tax returns of corporations, detailed income and tax items by industry, 1981, annual rpt, 8304–4

Income tax returns of sole proprietorships, detailed data by industry div and selected industry group, 1981, annual rpt, 8304–7

Income tax returns of sole proprietorships, receipts, deductions by type, payroll, and net income, by major industry, 1982, annual article, 8302-2.413

Input-output structure of US economy, detailed interindustry transactions for 85 industries, and components of final demand, 1977, article, 2702–1.421

Input-output structure of US economy, detailed interindustry transactions for 537 industries, and components of final demand, 1977 benchmark data, 2708–17

Manufacturing census, 1982: financial and operating data, by SIC 2- to 4-digit industry, State, SMSA, and county, preliminary census div rpt series, 2491–3

Manufacturing census, 1982: financial and operating data, for SIC 4-digit industries by product, preliminary rpt series, 2491–1

Mineral industries census, 1982: financial and operating data, by SIC 2- to 4-digit industry, preliminary summary rpt, 2511–2.1

Mineral industries census, 1982: financial and operating data, including materials consumed, by SIC 4-digit industry and State, preliminary rpt, 2511–1.8, 2511–1.9

Mineral Industry Surveys, commodity reviews of production, trade, and consumption, advance annual rpt series, 5614–5

Mineral Industry Surveys, explosives and blasting agents consumption by type, industry, and State, 1983, annual rpt, 5614–22

Mineral Industry Surveys, phosphate rock production, sales, exports, and use, 1984 crop year, annual rpt, 5614–20

Minerals Yearbook, 1982, Vol 1: commodity reviews of production, reserves, supply, use, and trade, annual rpt, 5604–33

Minerals Yearbook, 1982, Vol 2 preprints: State reviews of production and sales by commodity, and business activity, annual rpt series, 5604–16

Minerals Yearbook, 1982, Vol 2: State reviews of production, sales, and firms, by commodity, and business activity, annual rpt, 5604–34

Minerals Yearbook, 1982, Vol 3: foreign country reviews of production, trade, and policies, by commodity, annual rpt, 5604–35

Minerals Yearbook, 1982, Vol 3 preprints: foreign country reviews of production, trade, and policies, by commodity, annual rpt series, 5604–17

Minerals Yearbook, 1983, Vol 1 preprints: commodity review of production, reserves, supply, use, and trade, annual rpt, 5604–15.57, 5604–15.61

Minerals Yearbook, 1983, Vol 3 preprints: foreign country reviews of production, trade, and policies, by commodity, annual rpt series, 5604–23

Minority group and women employment, by occupational group and SIC 2- to 3-digit industry, 1981, annual rpt, 9244–1.1

Occupational injuries, and employees and hours, of mines, mills, and quarries, by State, quarterly rpt, 6662–1

Occupational injuries and incidence rates at sand and gravel mines and related operations, 1982, annual rpt, 6664–2

Occupational injuries and incidence rates at stone mines and related operations, detailed analysis, 1982, annual rpt, 6664–5

Occupational injury and illness rates, by SIC 2- to 4-digit industry, 1982, annual rpt, 6844–1

Pollution abatement capital and operating costs, by SIC 2- to 4-digit industry, State, and SMSA, 1982, annual Current Industrial Rpt, 2506–3.6

Producer prices and indexes, by stage of processing and detailed commodity, monthly rpt, 6762–6

Producer prices and indexes, by stage of processing and detailed commodity, monthly 1983, annual supplement, 6764–2

Production, prices, trade, use, employment, tariffs, and stockpiling, by mineral commodity, with foreign comparisons, 1979-83, annual rpt, 5604–18

Production, shipments, PPI, and stocks of building materials, by type, bimonthly rpt, 2012–1.5

Productivity, hours, and employment indexes for selected SIC 3- and 4-digit industries, 1954-82, annual rpt, 6824–1.2

Scientists, engineers, and technicians employed in private industry, by occupation and industry group, 1980-81, biennial rpt, 9627–23

Water pollution from nonpoint sources, source land uses and acreage, and control program funding, by State or region, various periods 1974-FY84, 9208–123

Waterborne commerce of US (domestic and foreign), freight by commodity, traffic, and passengers, by port and waterway, 1982, annual rpt, 3754–3

see also Abrasive materials

see also Cement and concrete

see also Oil shale

see also under By Commodity in the "Index by Categories"

see also under By Industry in the "Index by Categories"

Quartz

see Nonmetallic minerals and mines

Quasebarth, Mollie V.

"Nuclear Waste Disposal: Achieving Adequate Financing, Special Study", 26308–49

Quasi-official agencies

see also American National Red Cross

see also National Railroad Passenger Corp.

see also U.S. Railway Association

see also U.S. Synthetic Fuels Corp.

see also Washington Metropolitan Area Transit Authority

Quayle, Robert G.

"Comparisons Between Ship and Buoy Climatologies", 2152–8.403

Questionnaires

see Consumer surveys

see Opinion and attitude surveys

see Statistical programs and activities

Quigley, John M.

"Consumer Choice of Dwelling, Neighborhood, and Public Services", 9306–1.7

"Production of Housing Services and the Derived Demand for Residential Energy", 9306–1.2

Quits

see Labor turnover

Rabaj, Serafin

"Profiles of the Problems of Coca in Bolivia", 7008–40

Rabies

Cases and incidence of infectious notifiable diseases and other public health concerns, by census div and State, 1982, annual rpt, 4204–1

Rabies

Cases in animals and humans, for US and Mexico by State and for Canada by Province, 1980-82, annual rpt, 4205-28

Cases of notifiable infectious diseases and current outbreaks, by region and State, weekly rpt, 4202-1

Deaths and death rates by detailed cause and demographic characteristics, 1979 and selected trends, US Vital Statistics annual rpt, 4144-2.1

Foreign countries free of rabies, and disease prevention recommendations, 1984 annual rpt, 4204-11

Race/ethnic groups

see Alaska Natives

see Asian Americans

see Black Americans

see Hispanic Americans

see Indians

see Minority groups

see Pacific Islands Americans

see Racial discrimination

see under By Race in the "Index by Categories"

Racial discrimination

Black young adults economic status and educational attainment related to motivation, goals, family characteristics, and social factors, 1982, longitudinal study, 4008-65.2

Civil rights progress of minorities and women, Supreme Court decisions, and legislative action, 1957-83, last issue of narrative annual rpt, 11044-3

Community Relations Service investigation and mediation of minority discrimination disputes, FY83, annual rpt, 6004-9

Fed Govt Equal Opportunity Recruitment Program implementation, and summary employment data, FY83, annual rpt, 9844-33

Foreign human rights conditions in 162 countries, economic and military aid of US, and economic aid of intl organizations, 1981-83, annual rpt, 21384-3

TVA employment of minorities and women, by detailed occupation, pay level, and grade, FY83 and goals for FY84, annual rpt, 9804-17

Racine, Wis.

Census of Housing, 1980: occupancy and unit characteristics, by race, Hispanic origin, and city, SMSA rpt, 2473-1.296

Census of Population and Housing, 1980: detailed population and housing characteristics, by county, city, and census tract, SMSA rpt, 2551-2.296

see also under By SMSA or MSA in the "Index by Categories"

Racketeering

see Organized crime

Radar

Air traffic control and airway facilities and equipment, FAA improvement activities and R&D under Natl Airspace System Plan, 1982-2000, annual rpt, 7504-12

Air traffic control and airway facilities and services, operations, and finances, FY83, annual rpt, 7504-37

Air traffic control facilities of FAA, operations and services by service type, aviation category, and facility, 1974-83, annual rpt, 7504-1.2

Air traffic levels at FAA-operated control facilities, including instrument operations, by airport and State, FY83, annual rpt, 7504-27

Aircraft (general aviation), hours flown, and equipment, by type, use, and model of aircraft, region, and State, 1982, annual rpt, 7504-29

DOD budget, FY85 weapons system requests consistency with US policy and specified treaties, with funding FY83-87, annual rpt, 21384-4

DOD budget justification, programs, and policies, FY85, annual rpt, 3544-2

DOD procurement cost estimates for weapons and communications systems, by service branch, quarterly summary rpt, 3502-1

Exports of US, detailed commodities by country of destination, monthly rpt, 2422-3

Exports of US, detailed Schedule B commodities by country of destination, 1983, annual rpt, 2424-9

FAA aviation medicine research and studies, technical rpt series, 7506-10

Hurricanes and tropical storms in North Atlantic and Caribbean area, paths, surveillance, deaths, property damage, and landfall probabilities by city, 1983, annual rpt, 2184-7

Hurricanes and tropical storms in northeastern Pacific, paths, surveillance, deaths, and property damage, 1983, annual rpt, 2184-8

Imports of US, detailed Schedule A commodities by country, monthly rpt, 2422-2

Natl Weather Service, effects of proposed reorganization and technological improvement on staff and expenditures, FY82 and projected to 2000, 2188-16

Shipments, trade, and consumption of electronic equipment and associated products, by product, 1983, annual Current Industrial Rpt, 2506-12.21

Soviet Union and US satellites by mission and vulnerability to attack, and USSR anti-satellite missiles, 1983 and projected to 1989, hearing, 21208-18

Typhoons in western North Pacific and North Indian Oceans, paths and other characteristics, by mode of surveillance, 1983, annual rpt, 3804-8

Radecki, Lawrence J.

"Did Financial Markets in 1983 Point to Recession?", 9385-1.410

Radiation

see Electromagnetic radiation

see Nuclear radiation

see Radioactive materials

see Radioactive waste

see Radiology

see Uranium

see X-rays

Radiation Control for Health and Safety Act

FDA admin of Act, and radiation incidents involving electronic devices, 1983, annual rpt, 4064-13

Radio

Business statistics, detailed data for major industries and economic indicators, *Survey of Current Business,* monthly rpt, 2702-1.14

Index by Subjects and Names

Cellular telephones and parts from Japan at less than fair value, imports injury to US industry, investigation with background financial and operating data, 1984 rpt, 9886-14.130

Census of Population, 1980: detailed socioeconomic and demographic characteristics, by age, sex, race, Hispanic origin, occupation, and industry, State rpt series, 2531-4

China economic conditions, agricultural and industrial production, trade, and domestic and foreign investment, 1980-85, 2048-106

County Business Patterns: establishments, employees, and payrolls, by SIC 4-digit industry and county, 1981, annual State rpt series, 2326-8

County Business Patterns: establishments, employees, and payrolls, by SIC 4-digit industry and county, 1982, annual State rpt series, 2326-6

Developing countries disaster preparedness and summary sociodemographic, political, and economic data, country rpt series, 9916-2

Employment, earnings, and hours, by selected SIC 1- to 4-digit industry, State, and for 278 major labor areas, 1939-83, annual rpt, 6744-5

Employment, earnings, and hours, by SIC 4-digit nonfarm industry, monthly 1974-Feb 1984, annual update, 6744-4

Employment in TV and radio industry, total and for minorities, women, and youth, by job category and State, 1979-83, annual rpt, 9284-16

Employment in TV and radio stations, total and for minorities and women, by full- and part-time status and individual station, 1983, annual rpt, 9284-7

Exports and imports of US, detailed SIC-based commodities by world area, 1983, annual rpts, 2424-6

Exports and imports of US, totals and as percent of domestic production, by SIC 2- to 5-digit commodity, 1981, annual rpt, 2424-3

Exports of US, detailed commodities by country of destination, monthly rpt, 2422-3

Exports of US, detailed Schedule B commodities by country of destination, 1983, annual rpt, 2424-9

Exports of US, detailed Schedule E commodities by mode of transport and world area and country of destination, 1983, annual rpts, 2424-5

Fed Govt programs and mgmt cost control proposals, 3-year savings by function and agency, and financial and operating data, 1960s-81, 16908-1.3

Fed Govt radio frequency assignments, by agency, 2nd half 1983, semiannual rpt, 2802-1

Food industry advertising expenditures by media type, and advertising to sales ratio by selected food item, 1970-79 with some trends from 1955, 1548-234

Foreign economic, social, and political summary data, by country, 1984, annual factbook, 244-11

Foreign market and trade for telecommunications equipment, and user industry operations and demand, country market research rpts, 2045-12

Index by Subjects and Names

Radioactive materials

Great Lakes trade, by SITC 3-digit commodity, port, vessel type, world area, and country, 1982, annual rpt, 7744–3

Home taping costs, material taped by source, and recording industry operations and sales lost from home taping, 1969-83, hearings with chartbook, 25528–100

Import quotas and tariffs, jobs protected and cost per job for selected products, and foreign trade balance by industry div, various periods 1958-81, article, 9381–1.412

Imports of mobile cellular radio transceivers and parts from Japan at less than fair value, injury to US industry, investigation with background financial and operating data, 1984 rpt, 9886–14.95

Imports of US, detailed Schedule A commodities by country and world area of origin, and mode of transport, 1983, annual rpts, 2424–2

Imports of US, detailed Schedule A commodities by country, monthly rpt, 2422–2

Imports of US, detailed TSUSA commodities by country of origin, 1983, annual rpt, 2424–4

Income tax returns of corporations, detailed income and tax items by industry, 1981, annual rpt, 8304–4

Income tax returns of sole proprietorships, detailed data by industry div and selected industry group, 1981, annual rpt, 8304–7

Income tax returns of sole proprietorships, receipts, deductions by type, payroll, and net income, by major industry, 1982, annual article, 8302–2.413

Industry finances and operations, by SIC 2- to 4- digit industry, 1970s-83 and projected to 1988, annual rpt, 2014–4

Input-output structure of US economy, detailed interindustry transactions for 85 industries, and components of final demand, 1977, article, 2702–1.421

Input-output structure of US economy, detailed interindustry transactions for 537 industries, and components of final demand, 1977 benchmark data, 2708–17

Manufacturing census, 1982: financial and operating data, by SIC 2- to 4-digit industry, State, SMSA, and county, preliminary census div rpt series, 2491–3

Manufacturing census, 1982: financial and operating data, for SIC 4-digit industries by product, preliminary rpt, 2491–1.377, 2491–1.380

Marine weather broadcasts for US ships, by major ocean area, as of Jan 1984, biennial rpt, 2184–3

Minority group and women employment by occupation, and business owners, by race and State, with TV and radio revenues and stations, 1971-81, hearing, 21368–45

Natl Endowment for Arts activities and grants, FY83, annual rpt, 9564–3

Natl Endowment for Humanities activities and grants, FY83, annual rpt, 9564–2

Nuclear attack civil defense plans of Fed Emergency Mgmt Agency, funding and operations by component, FY81-84 and projected FY85-89, GAO rpt, 26123–61

Occupational injury and illness rates, by SIC 2- to 4-digit industry, 1982, annual rpt, 6844–1

Occupational Outlook Handbook, 1984-85 biennial rpt, 6744–1

OECD trade, total and for 4 major countries, and US trade by country, by commodity, 1972-82, annual world region rpt series, 244–13

Patents (US) for telecommunication equipment granted to US and foreign applicants, by applicant type, firm, State, and country, various periods 1963-83, 2246–2.7

Producer prices and indexes, by stage of processing and detailed commodity, monthly rpt, 6762–6

Producer prices and indexes, by stage of processing and detailed commodity, monthly 1983, annual supplement, 6764–2

Receiving set industries productivity, hours, and employment indexes, for radio and TV, 1958-81, annual rpt, 6824–1.3

Repair of TV and radio, industry receipts, 1983, annual rpt, 2413–8

Repair technicians and apprentices wages and benefits, for 5 types of electrical repair shops in 19 SMSAs, Nov 1981 survey, 6787–6.197

Scientists, engineers, and technicians employment in transportation, utilities, and retail and wholesale trade, by field of science and industry, 1982, 9628–72

Service industry census, 1982: employment, establishments, receipts, and payroll, by SIC 2- to 4-digit kind of business, SMSA, county, and city, State rpt series, 2391–1

Service industry census, 1982: employment, establishments, receipts, and payroll, by SIC 4-digit kind of business and State, preliminary rpt, 2390–2.11

Shipments, trade, and consumption of radio and related equipment, by product, 1982-83, annual Current Industrial Rpt, 2506–12.20

Stations on the air, by class of operation, monthly press release, 9282–4

Virgin Islands economic censuses, 1982: employment, establishments, payroll, and receipts, by SIC 1- to 4-digit industry, island, and city, 2593–1

Wholesale trade census, 1982: employment, establishments, sales by commodity, and payroll, by SIC 4-digit kind of business and State, preliminary rpt, 2403–1.9

see also Educational broadcasting

see also Political broadcasting

see also Public broadcasting

see also Recording industry

Radio Free Europe

Broadcast and financial data for Radio Free Europe and Radio Liberty, with comparisons to other intl broadcasters, FY83, annual rpt, 10314–1

Radio Liberty

Broadcast and financial data for Radio Free Europe and Radio Liberty, with comparisons to other intl broadcasters, FY83, annual rpt, 10314–1

Radioactive materials

Exports, imports, tariffs, and industry operating data for fatty substances, natural chemicals, and radioactive materials, foreign and US, 1979-83, TSUSA commodity rpt, 9885–4.38

Exports of US, detailed commodities by country of destination, monthly rpt, 2422–3

Exports of US, detailed Schedule B commodities by country of destination, 1983, annual rpt, 2424–9

Exports of US, detailed Schedule E commodities by mode of transport and world area and country of destination, 1983, annual rpts, 2424–5

FDA investigation and regulatory activities, quarterly rpt, 4062–3

Great Lakes trade, by SITC 3-digit commodity, port, vessel type, world area, and country, 1982, annual rpt, 7744–3

Imports of US, detailed Schedule A commodities by country and world area of origin, and mode of transport, 1983, annual rpts, 2424–2

Imports of US, detailed Schedule A commodities by country, monthly rpt, 2422–2

Imports of US, detailed TSUSA commodities by country of origin, 1983, annual rpt, 2424–4

Inventory discrepancies for strategic nuclear materials at DOE facilities, 1st half FY83, semiannual rpt, 3002–4

Mineral industries census, 1982: financial and operating data, by SIC 2- to 4-digit industry, preliminary summary rpt, 2511–2.1

Mineral industries census, 1982: financial and operating data, including materials consumed, by SIC 4-digit industry and State, preliminary rpt, 2511–1.3

Minerals Yearbook, 1982, Vol 1: commodity reviews of production, reserves, supply, use, and trade, annual rpt, 5604–33

Minerals Yearbook, 1982, Vol 3: foreign country reviews of production, trade, and policies, by commodity, annual rpt, 5604–35

Nuclear fuel facilities inventory discrepancies, 2nd half 1983, semiannual rpt, 9632–3

Nuclear power and weapons policy, fuel supply/demand, waste disposal and siting, environmental effects of radiation, and public attitudes, 1970s-82 with projections to 2000, 3008–88

Nuclear power plant safety standards and research, design, licensing, construction, operation, and finances, with data by reactor, bimonthly rpt, 3352–4

Nuclear Regulatory Commission activities, employment, and finances, and operations of individual power plants by State, FY83, annual rpt, 9634–2

Sealift Military Command operations for naval fleet support, and transport of DOD and AID cargo by route, quarterly rpt, 3802–2

Transport of radioactive materials, surveillance program activities and results, State survey rpt series, 9636–1

Transportation census, 1982: trucks, by detailed characteristics, miles traveled, and type of product carried, State rpt series, 2573–1

see also Nuclear explosives and explosions

see also Nuclear radiation

see also Radioactive waste

see also Uranium

Radioactive waste

Radioactive waste

- Budget of US, effects of Reagan Admin policy changes, by detailed program, FY85, annual rpt, 104–21
- Defense wastes from DOE facilities, interim storage inventories by site and permanent disposal plan costs, 1982 with projections to 2015, 3358–32
- Disposal of low-level wastes, status of interstate compacts, waste generation and shipments, 1979-82, hearing, 25528–93
- DOE Office of Civilian Radioactive Waste Mgmt activities and financing, FY83-85, annual rpt, 3364–1
- Energy production, trade, supply, use, conservation, and DOE activities, by energy type, FY83, annual rpt, 3024–2
- Environmental quality and protection programs, costs, and Fed Govt enforcement, 1983, detailed annual rpt, 484–1
- Environmental quality, pollutant discharge by type, and EPA protection activities, 1970s-83, biennial summary rpt, 9184–16
- Environmental quality, pollutant discharge by type and source, and EPA protection activities and funding, 1970s-83, biennial regional rpt series, 9184–15
- Fed Govt energy programs proposed budget appropriations, by office or dept and function, FY84-85, annual rpt, 3004–14
- Fed Govt programs and mgmt cost control proposals, 3-year savings by function and agency, and financial and operating data, 1960s-81, 16908–1.4
- Great Lakes radioactivity discharges by source, and concentrations in environment, various periods 1963-82, annual rpt, 14644–1.2
- Idaho Natl Engineering Lab radiation monitoring results, for 4 onsite facilities and nearby areas, 1983, annual rpt, 3354–10
- Nuclear industry nongovt employment by industry segment, occupation, and census div, and DOE and NRC nuclear employment, 1968-83, biennial rpt, 3004–11.1
- Nuclear power and weapons policy, fuel supply/demand, waste disposal and siting, environmental effects of radiation, and public attitudes, 1970s-82 with projections to 2000, 3008–88
- Nuclear power plant radioactive waste, releases and waste composition by plant, 1981, annual rpt, 9634–1
- Nuclear power plant safety standards and research, design, licensing, construction, operation, and finances, with data by reactor, bimonthly rpt, 3352–4
- Nuclear Regulatory Commission activities, employment, and finances, and operations of individual power plants by State, FY83, annual rpt, 9634–2
- Nuclear Waste Fund obligations by function and receipts, and DOE Civilian Radioactive Mgmt Office activities and staff, quarterly GAO rpt, 26102–4
- Ocean dumping of low-level radioactive wastes at 4 largest and all disposal sites, 1983 hearings, 21568–36
- Spent fuel and demand for uranium and enrichment services of nuclear power plants, for US and non-Communist country groups, 1983 and projected to 2020, annual rpt, 3164–72

Spent fuel and radioactive waste generation, inventory, disposal by site, reprocessing, and characteristics, by source, as of 1983 and projected to 2020, annual rpt, 3364–2

- Spent fuel from nuclear power plants and additional storage capacity required, by reactor, projected 1984-93, annual rpt, 3354–2
- Spent fuel from nuclear power plants, permanent disposal site and transport costs and Nuclear Waste Fund financing, alternative projections FY83-2037, 26308–49
- Spent fuel storage capability, by nuclear power unit, monthly rpt, 9632–1.4
- Uranium ore tailings at active mills, EPA radon and radionuclide emmission standards and US and foreign exposure and health effects, various periods 1957-83, hearings, 21208–17
- Uranium ore tailings at inactive mills and DOE remedial action program activities by site, and program funding, FY84, annual rpt, 3354–9

Radiology

- Black medical residents by specialty, and minority medical faculty by race and Hispanic origin, selected years 1980-83, article, 4102–1.412
- Census of Population, 1980: labor force, by sex, detailed occupation, and region, with comparison to 1970 census, supplementary rpt, 2535–1.12
- DOD medical personnel, trainees, and accessions by source, by occupation, specialty, and service branch, FY83, annual rpt, 3544–24
- FDA investigation and regulatory activities, quarterly rpt, 4062–3
- Hospital employment, vacancies, and vacancy rates, by occupation and by hospital specialty, region, census div, and State, 1980, annual rpt, 4114–12
- Hospital worker wages by sex and occupation, and benefits, for 22 MSAs, Oct 1981 survey, 6787–6.201
- Manpower supply and education of health professionals, by occupation, demographic and professional characteristics, and location, 1950s-83 and projected to 2000, biennial rpt, 4114–8
- Medicare fee assignments, physician acceptance rates for selected services related to professional characteristics, FY76-78, article, 4652–1.416
- Medicare kidney end-stage program, reimbursement by treatment, diagnosis, outcome, and patient characteristics, with covered charges for transplants, 1974-79, article, 4652–1.421
- Medicare physician charges and reimbursement by enrollee characteristics and carrier, payment limits effects on charges in California, and physician earnings, by specialty, 1950s-84, 25368–127
- Medicare Supplementary Medical Insurance maximum charges reimbursable for specific services, by State and outlying area, 1983, annual rpt, 4654–4
- Occupational manpower needs and supply by detailed occupation, and educational and training program enrollees and grads by detailed field, 1982 and 1995, biennial rpt, 6744–3

Index by Subjects and Names

Occupational Outlook Handbook, 1984-85 biennial rpt, 6744–1

- Physicians (not office-based) visits by reason, diagnosis, treatment, patient and physician characteristics, and physician primary activity, 1980, 4147–13.77
- Radiation control program activities, State and local expenditures, personnel, and NRC licenses, by State, FY80-82, annual rpt, 4064–3
- Radiation from electronic devices, incidents and persons involved by type of device and FDA control program activities, 1983, annual rpt, 4064–13
- Science and engineering grad enrollment, fields of study, financial support, and other student and instn characteristics, 1975-82, annual survey, 9627–7
- VA Medicine and Surgery Dept trainees, by detailed program and city, FY83, annual rpt, 9924–21
- VA physicians, dentists, and nurses, by age, selected employment characteristics, and VA district, quarterly rpt, 9922–11

see also X-rays

Radium

see Radioactive materials

Rae, Douglas A.

"Value to Visitors of Improving Visibility at Mesa Verde and Great Smoky National Parks", 21368–52

Raile, Gerhard K.

"Biomass Statistics for the Northern U.S.", 1208–207

"Michigan Forest Statistics, 1980", 1206–31.5

Railpax

see National Railroad Passenger Corp.

Railroad accidents and safety

- Accident investigations and recommendations by Natl Transportation Safety Board, 1983, annual rpt, 9614–1
- Accidents and deaths in transportation, by mode of transport, 1972-82, annual rpt, 7304–2
- Accidents, casualties, and property damage involving railroads, Fed Railroad Admin activities, and safety inspectors by State, 1982, annual rpt, 7604–12
- Accidents, circumstances, severity, and railroad involved, quarterly rpt, 9612–3
- Accidents investigated by Fed Railroad Admin, casualties, damage, and circumstances, 1982, annual rpt, 7604–3
- Deaths and death rates by detailed cause and demographic characteristics, 1979 and selected trends, US Vital Statistics annual rpt, 4144–2.1
- Deaths in transportation accidents, by mode, 1982-83, annual summary rpt, 9614–6
- DOT grant awards for transportation planning and safety programs, by region, State, and for 35 largest SMSAs, FY83, annual rpt, 7304–7
- Hazardous material transport accidents, casualties, and property damage, by mode of transport, with DOT control activities, 1983, annual rpt, 7304–4
- Hwy-railroad grade-crossing accidents, deaths, and injuries, 1972-80, annual rpt, 7304 1
- Hwy-railroad grade-crossing accidents, detailed data by State and railroad, 1982, annual rpt, 7604–2

Index by Subjects and Names

Railroads

Hwy safety improvement, federally funded programs implementation by State, FY83, annual rpt, 7554–26

Safety law violations, claims settled FY83, annual rpt, 7604–10

Safety programs, and accidents, injuries, deaths, hazards, and property damage, by mode of transport, 1983, annual rpt, 7304–19

Railroad equipment and vehicles

Air pollutant emission factors, by detailed source, 3rd edition, 1983-84 supplements, 9198–13

Bearings (roller) for rail vehicles from Italy and Japan at less than fair value, imports injury to US industry, investigation with background financial and operating data, 1984 rpt, 9886–14.96

Business statistics, detailed data for major industries and economic indicators, *Survey of Current Business,* monthly rpt, 2702–1.20

Canada grain handling and rail transport system financial and operating data, and effects of limited capacity on grain and oilseed exports, selected years 1950-82, 1528–176

Cars, ownership, supply, and turnaround time, by type, selected years FY68-83, annual rpt, 9484–1

Census of Population, 1980: detailed socioeconomic and demographic characteristics, by age, sex, race, Hispanic origin, occupation, and industry, State rpt series, 2531–4

China economic conditions, agricultural and industrial production, trade, and domestic and foreign investment, 1980-85, 2048–106

Communist, OECD, and selected other countries production, inventories, and freight, by mode of transport, 1960s-83, annual rpt, 244–5.8

Conrail operations and US Railway Assn finances and activities, FY81-83, annual rpt, 29604–1

County Business Patterns: establishments, employees, and payrolls, by SIC 4-digit industry and county, 1981, annual State rpt series, 2326–8

County Business Patterns: establishments, employees, and payrolls, by SIC 4-digit industry and county, 1982, annual State rpt series, 2326–6

Cuba economic conditions, agricultural and industrial production and distribution, trade, and intl economic relations, 1970-82 and trends from 1957, 248–40

Employment, earnings, and hours, by SIC 4-digit nonfarm industry, monthly 1974-Feb 1984, annual update, 6744–4

Exports and imports of US, detailed SIC-based commodities by world area, 1983, annual rpts, 2424–6

Exports and imports of US, totals and as percent of domestic production, by SIC 2- to 5-digit commodity, 1981, annual rpt, 2424–3

Exports of US, detailed commodities by country of destination, monthly rpt, 2422–3

Exports of US, detailed Schedule B commodities by country of destination, 1983, annual rpt, 2424–9

Exports of US, detailed Schedule E commodities by mode of transport and world area and country of destination, 1983, annual rpts, 2424–5

Finances and operations, by SIC 2- to 4-digit industry, 1970s-83 and projected to 1988, annual rpt, 2014–4

Foreign and US rail high-speed systems and railcar production, and proposed US projects costs and funding, with population and land area for selected foreign cities, 1940s-82, 26358–97

Grain rail and barge loadings, ship and container car availability, ocean freight rates, and export inspections, prices, and sales, weekly rpt, 1272–2

Great Lakes trade, by SITC 3-digit commodity, port, vessel type, world area, and country, 1982, annual rpt, 7744–3

Imports of US, detailed Schedule A commodities by country and world area of origin, and mode of transport, 1983, annual rpts, 2424–2

Imports of US, detailed Schedule A commodities by country, monthly rpt, 2422–2

Imports of US, detailed TSUSA commodities by country of origin, 1983, annual rpt, 2424–4

Income tax returns of corporations, detailed income and tax items by industry, 1981, annual rpt, 8304–4

Input-output structure of US economy, detailed interindustry transactions for 537 industries, and components of final demand, 1977 benchmark data, 2708–17

Manufacturing census, 1982: financial and operating data, by SIC 2- to 4-digit industry, State, SMSA, and county, preliminary census div rpt series, 2491–3

Manufacturing census, 1982: financial and operating data, for SIC 4-digit industries by product, preliminary rpt, 2491–1.406

Northeast Corridor rail improvement project goals, funding, and progress, and Amtrak finances and operations, FY83, annual rpt, 7604–9

Occupational injury and illness rates, by SIC 2- to 4-digit industry, 1982, annual rpt, 6844–1

OECD trade, total and for 4 major countries, and US trade by country, by commodity, 1972-82, annual world region rpt series, 244–13

Operations and finances, detailed data by firm, class of service, and district, 1983, annual rpt, 9486–6.1

Producer prices and indexes, by stage of processing and detailed commodity, monthly rpt, 6762–6

Producer prices and indexes, by stage of processing and detailed commodity, monthly 1983, annual supplement, 6764–2

Transportation finances, operations, vehicles, equipment, accidents, and energy use, by mode of transport, 1955-84, annual rpt, 7304–2

Wood railroad ties trade, tariffs, and industry operating data, foreign and US, 1979-83, TSUSA commidty rpt, 9885–2.31

see also Railroad accidents and safety

Railroad Retirement Accounts

see Federal trust funds

Railroad Retirement Board

Budget of US Appendix, detailed budgets and personnel summaries, by agency, FY85, annual rpt, 104–3

Budget of US, appropriations, outlays, balances, and budget receipts, by govtl branch and agency, FY83, annual rpt, 8104–2

Budget of US, object class analysis of obligations, by branch of Fed Govt and selected depts and agencies, FY85 estimates, annual rpt, 104–9

Cost control proposals for Fed Govt programs and mgmt, 3-year savings by function and agency, and financial and operating data, 1960s-81, 16908–1.14

Railroad employee benefits and beneficiaries by type, and railroad employees and payrolls, FY82, annual rpt, 9704–2

Railroad employee benefits and beneficiaries by type, benefit program finances, and railroad employees and payroll, FY83, annual rpt, 9704–1

Railroad employee retirement, survivors, unemployment, and sickness insurance programs, monthly rpt, 9702–2

Unemployment insurance claims, insured unemployment, and exhaustions, by program, weekly rpt, 6402–14

Railroads

Air pollution levels for 5 pollutants, by detailed source, State, and Air Quality Control Region, 1981, annual rpt, 9194–7

Bridges over navigable waters, with type of bridge and use, owner, dimensions, and location, 1984 regional listing series, 7406–5

Business statistics, detailed data for major industries and economic indicators, *Survey of Current Business,* monthly rpt, 2702–1.8

Canada grain handling and rail transport system financial and operating data, and effects of limited capacity on grain and oilseed exports, selected years 1950-82, 1528–176

Census of Govts, 1982: properties, govt-assessed value, sales, and tax rates, by property type, State, SMSA, county, and city, 2453–1

Census of Housing, 1980: structural, financial, and householder characteristics, by region and State, 2475–4

Census of Population and Housing, 1980: detailed population and housing characteristics, by county, city, and census tract, State and SMSA rpt series, 2551–2

Census of Population, 1980: detailed socioeconomic and demographic characteristics, by age, sex, race, Hispanic origin, occupation, and industry, State rpt series, 2531–4

Census of Population, 1980: detailed socioeconomic characteristics, by county, city, and inside-outside SMSAs and central cities, State rpt series, 2531–3

China economic conditions, agricultural and industrial production, trade, and domestic and foreign investment, 1980-85, 2048–106

Coal dev plans on Fed Govt lease lands in 12 regions under Fed Coal Mgmt

Railroads

Program, environmental and socioeconomic impacts to 2000, final statement series, 5726–4

- Coal transport environmental impacts by type and mode of transport, methodology for assessing alternative systems, 1983 rpt, 3408–28
- Coastal environmental characteristics, fish, wildlife, and use, and population socioeconomic data, for individual areas, series, 5506–4
- Collective bargaining agreements expiring during year, covered workers by SIC 2-digit industry, firm, and union, with summary of key provisions, 1984, annual rpt, 6784–9
- Construction put in place, permits authorized by region, State, and MSA, and Federal contract awards, by construction type, bimonthly rpt with articles, 2012–1
- Construction put in place, value of new public and private structures, by type, monthly rpt, 2382–4
- Cuba economic conditions, agricultural and industrial production and distribution, trade, and intl economic relations, 1970-82 and trends from 1957, 248–40
- Developing countries disaster preparedness and summary sociodemographic, political, and economic data, country rpt series, 9916–2
- DOD shipments of military and personal property, loss claims, passenger traffic, and costs, by mode of transport, quarterly rpt, 3702–1
- Earnings by major industry group, and personal income per capita and by source, by region and State, 1929-82, 2708–40
- Electric railroad mileage by country, subway system mileage by US city, and trolley and motor bus capital and operating costs, selected years 1960-80, 3006–7.7
- Employee benefits and beneficiaries by type, and railroad employees and payrolls, FY82, annual rpt, 9704–2
- Employee benefits and beneficiaries by type, benefit program finances, and railroad employees and payroll, FY83, annual rpt, 9704–1
- Employee earnings, benefits, and hours, by occupation, Class I railroads, 1983, annual rpt, 9484–5
- Employee retirement average monthly benefit, and beneficiaries with representative payees by relation to payee, as of June 1983, GAO rpt, 26121–85
- Employee retirement, disability, and unemployment insurance programs, beneficiaries and collections, monthly rpt, 4742–1.1
- Employee retirement, survivors, unemployment, and sickness insurance programs, monthly rpt, 9702–2
- Employee unemployment insurance benefits and claims, Monthly Labor Review, 6722–1.4
- Employment and finances of ICC-regulated carriers by mode of transport, and ICC activities, FY80-83 and trends, annual rpt, 9484–1
- Employment by functional group, for Class I line-haul railroads, monthly rpt, 9482–3
- Employment, earnings, and hours, by selected SIC 1- to 4-digit industry, State, and for 278 major labor areas, 1939-83, annual rpt, 6744–5

Employment, earnings, and hours, by SIC 4-digit nonfarm industry, monthly 1974-Feb 1984, annual update, 6744–4

- Energy use in transportation sector by mode, fuel supplies, and demographic and economic determinants of vehicle use, 1970s-83, annual rpt, 3304–5
- Finances and operations, detailed data by firm, class of service, and district, 1983, annual rpt, 9486–6.1
- Finances and operations of 7 commuter rail systems, and public agency cost reimbursement, 1980, 7888–61
- Finances, operations, and freight rates and shares, by commodity and railroad, 1970s-82, hearings, 25268–80
- Finances, operations, vehicles, equipment, accidents, and energy use, by mode of transport, 1955-84, annual rpt, 7304–2
- Foreign and US rail high-speed systems and railcar production, and proposed US projects costs and funding, with population and land area for selected foreign cities, 1940s-82, 26358–97
- Foreign economic, social, and political summary data, by country, 1984, annual factbook, 244–11
- Govt transportation revenues by source and expenditures, by level of govt and mode of transport, and Fed Govt aid by type, FY77-82, 7308–185
- Grain cooperatives storage capacity, by rail line abandonment status, railroad, and region, FY80, 1128–28
- Income tax returns of corporations, detailed income and tax items by industry, 1981, annual rpt, 8304–4
- Input-output structure of US economy, detailed interindustry transactions for 537 industries, and components of final demand, 1977 benchmark data, 2708–17
- Minority group and women employment, by occupational group and SIC 2- to 3-digit industry, 1981, annual rpt, 9244–1.1
- Northeast Corridor rail improvement project goals, funding, and progress, and Amtrak finances and operations, FY83, annual rpt, 7604–9
- Occupational manpower needs and supply by detailed occupation, and educational and training program enrollees and grads by detailed field, 1982 and 1995, biennial rpt, 6744–3
- Productivity, hours, and employment indexes for selected SIC 3- and 4-digit industries, 1954-82, annual rpt, 6824–1.4
- Research publications on public transit, 2nd half FY83, semiannual listing, 7882–1
- Revenue, income, freight, and rate of return, by Class I freight railroad and district, quarterly rpt, 9482–2
- *Statistical Abstract of US,* social, political, and economic data, 1950s-83 and trends, annual rpt, 2324–1.3
- Water pollution fish kills, by State, location, and pollution source, monthly 1978-80, annual rpt, 9204–3
- *see also* Consolidated Rail Corp.
- *see also* Federal aid to railroads
- *see also* Freight
- *see also* High-speed ground transportation
- *see also* National Railroad Passenger Corp.
- *see also* Railroad accidents and safety
- *see also* Railroad equipment and vehicles

Index by Subjects and Names

see also Subways

see also U.S. Railway Association

see also under By Individual Company or Institution in the "Index by Categories"

see also under By Industry in the "Index by Categories"

Raines, Fredric

"Output and Employment Trends in Basic Manufacturing Industries: The Role of R&D", 25368–133

Rainfall

see Weather

Rainy River

see Souris-Red-Rainy Rivers

Raisins

see Fruit and fruit products

Raleigh, N.C.

- Census of Population and Housing, 1980: detailed population and housing characteristics, by county, city, and census tract, SMSA rpt, 2551–2.297
- Wages of office and plant workers, by occupation, 1984 labor market area survey rpt, 6785–3.6
- *see also* under By City and By SMSA or MSA in the "Index by Categories"

Ramirez, Ruben H.

"Coca Production in Peru", 7008–40

Ramirez, Yonel

"Illicit Traffic and Undue Use of Coca and Cocaine in Peru in 1978", 7008–40

Rand, Michael R.

"Family Violence", 6066–19.5

Rand, William M.

"International Network of Food Data Systems (INFOODS)", 1004–16.1

Rantoul, Ill.

- Census of Housing, 1980: occupancy and unit characteristics, by race, Hispanic origin, and city, SMSA rpt, 2473–1.113
- Census of Population and Housing, 1980: detailed population and housing characteristics, by county, city, and census tract, SMSA rpt, 2551–2.113
- Housing vacancy rates for single and multifamily units and mobile homes, by county, city, and ZIP code, 1983, annual metro area rpt, 9304–18.1
- Wages by occupation, and benefits for office and plant workers, 1984 labor market area survey rpt, 6785–3.7
- *see also* under By SMSA or MSA in the "Index by Categories"

Rape

- Abortions funded by Medicaid by justification, and expenditures, by State, FY78-83, annual rpt, 4654–9
- Convictions, prison sentences, and average sentence lengths, by offense, offender class, and selected State, various periods 1971-84, 6066–19.10
- Court cases, dispositions, convictions, and sentences of Federal criminal defendants, by offense and district, as of June 1983 with trends from 1945, annual rpt, 18204–1
- Court criminal case disposition, effect of victim injury and other factors, and law enforcement official and victim attitudes, 1983 survey, 6068–185
- Crime and criminal justice data, including justice expenditures and employment by level of govt, 1970s-82 with some trends from 1875, 6068–174

Index by Subjects and Names

Crime Index by population size and region, and offenses known to police by large city, Jan-June 1984, semiannual rpt, 6222–1

Crimes, arrests by offender characteristics, and rates, by offense, and law enforcement employees, by population size and jurisdiction, 1970s-83, annual rpt, 6224–2

Criminal case processing from arrest to sentencing, cases and processing time by disposition, dismissal reason, and offense, for 14 cities, 1979, 6066–22.1

Executions since 1930, and prisoners under death sentence, by prisoner characteristics, region, and State, 1982, annual rpt, 6065–1

Prison terms actually served by selected State, and Illinois pretrial detention time credited to sentence, by offense, various periods 1977-83, 6066–19.7

Prisoners in State prisons median sentence, and admissions and releases by prisoner and sentencing characteristics, by offense and State, 1981 and trends from 1926, 6066–19.9

School crime against students, teachers, and others, by offense, circumstances, and offender sex and race, 1974-76, 6066–20.2

Victimization of households, by offense type, race of household head, and family income and urban-rural residence, 1975-83, periodic rpt, 6062–2.404

Victimization rates and reports to police, by offense, 1973-83, 6062–2.405

Victimization rates by type of offense, and victim and offense characteristics, Natl Crime Survey series, 6066–3

Victims of crime, medical expenses and property loss, and median loss by victim characteristics, by offense type, 1975-81, 6066–19.6

Rapid transit

see High-speed ground transportation

see Metroliner

see Subways

see Urban transportation

Rare earths

see Nonmetallic minerals and mines

Ras al-Khaimah

see United Arab Emirates

Rasberry, Theodosia P.

"Program and Demographic Characteristics of Supplemental Security Income Beneficiaries, Dec. 1982", 4744–16

"Supplemental Security Income: State and County Data, Dec. 1983.", 4744–27

Raw materials

see Stockpiling

see Strategic materials

see terms listed under Agricultural commodities

see terms listed under Commodities

see terms listed under Natural resources

Rawlings, Steve W.

"Household and Family Characteristics: Mar. 1982", 2546–1.383

Rayon

see Synthetic fibers and fabrics

RCA Global Communications

Financial and operating data for 7 major telegraph carriers, quarterly rpt, 9282–1

REA

see Rural Electrification Administration

Reactors

see Nuclear power

see Power-generating plants and equipment

Reading ability and habits

Blood pressure and heart rate effects of reading aloud, results of study of Baltimore, Md, 5th graders, 1984 article, 4102–1.415

DOD Dependents Schools students higher education admissions tests scores by sex and subject, and educational goals and attitudes, 1983, annual rpt, 3504–17

DOD Dependents Schools 1st grader basic skills test scores, by world area and English fluency, fall 1983, annual rpt, 3504–18

Education Dept programs funding, operations, and effectiveness, FY83, annual rpt, 4804–5

Educational progress, natl assessment summary data for 7 learning areas, by characteristics of participants, selected years 1971-82, annual rpt, 4824–2.6

High school classes of 1972 and 1980: achievement test scores by sex and whether planning education major, hearings, 21348–89

High school classes of 1980 and 1982: educational and sociodemographic characteristics and expectations, natl longitudinal study, series, 4826–2

Indian education program operations, funding, student progress measures, and opinions of school staff, parents, and students, selected years 1973-83, 4808–13

see also Illiteracy

Reading, Pa.

Census of Housing, 1980: occupancy and unit characteristics, by race, Hispanic origin, and city, SMSA rpt, 2473–1.298

Census of Population and Housing, 1980: detailed population and housing characteristics, by county, city, and census tract, SMSA rpt, 2551–2.298

see also under By SMSA or MSA in the "Index by Categories"

Readling, Charles L.

"Natural Gas Production and Wellhead Price, 1983 (Preliminary)", 3162–4.410

Real estate

see Apartment houses

see Commercial buildings

see Condominiums and cooperatives

see Farms and farmland

see Government property

see Homesteads

see Housing condition and occupancy

see Housing construction

see Housing costs and financing

see Housing tenure

see Industrial plants and equipment

see Land area

see Land ownership

see Land reform

see Land use

see Landlord-tenant relations

see Military bases, posts, and reservations

see Mortgages

see Open space land programs

see Property

see Property value

Real estate business

see Public buildings

see Public lands

see Real estate business

see Reclamation of land

Real estate business

Apartment market absorption rates and characteristics for nonsubsidized privately financed furnished and unfurnished units completed in 1982, annual Current Housing Rpt, 2484–2

Apartment market absorption rates and characteristics for nonsubsidized privately financed units completed in 1983, preliminary annual Current Housing Rpt, 2484–3

Brokerage (real estate) industry structure and practices, sales commissions, and broker and consumer attitudes, selected years 1975-81, 9408–48

Business statistics, detailed data for major industries and economic indicators, *Survey of Current Business,* monthly rpt, 2702–1.3

Census of Construction Industries, 1982: financial and operating data, by SIC 4-digit industry and State, final rpt series, 2373–1

Census of Population, 1980: detailed socioeconomic and demographic characteristics, by age, sex, race, Hispanic origin, occupation, and industry, State rpt series, 2531–4

Census of Population, 1980: detailed socioeconomic characteristics, by county, city, and inside-outside SMSAs and central cities, State rpt series, 2531–3

Census of Population, 1980: labor force, by sex, detailed occupation, and region, with comparison to 1970 census, supplementary rpt, 2535–1.12

Coal supply and Fed Govt coal leases, by owner, owner industry, and western State, various periods 1950-82 and projected to 2000, hearing, 25318–58

Collective bargaining agreements expiring during year, covered workers by SIC 2-digit industry, firm, and union, with summary of key provisions, 1984, annual rpt, 6784–9

County Business Patterns: establishments, employees, and payrolls, by SIC 4-digit industry and county, 1981, annual State rpt series, 2326–8

County Business Patterns: establishments, employees, and payrolls, by SIC 4-digit industry and county, 1982, annual State rpt series, 2326–6

Employment and earnings, detailed data, monthly rpt, 6742–2.5

Employment by detailed occupation, for 29 SIC 2-digit nonmanufacturing industries, 1981 BLS survey, 6748–60

Employment, earnings, and hours, by selected SIC 1- to 4-digit industry, State, and for 278 major labor areas, 1939-83, annual rpt, 6744–5

Employment, earnings, and hours, by SIC 4-digit nonfarm industry, monthly 1974-Feb 1984, annual update, 6744–4

Farm real estate value, sales, financing, taxes, and proposed use after purchase, by State, 1970s-84, annual rpt, 1541–8

Fed Govt loans, grants, and tax benefits to business, by program and economic sector, projected FY84-88 with effective tax rates for FY80-82, 26306–6.70

Real estate business

Flow-of-funds accounts, assets and liabilities by type and economic sector, year-end outstandings, 1960-83, annual rpt, 9364–3

Flow-of-funds accounts savings, investments, and credit statements, quarterly rpt, 9365–3.3

Foreign direct investment in US, major investors and investments by SIC 4-digit industry, transaction type and value, and location, 1983, annual rpt, 2044–20

Franchise business opportunities, by firm and kind of business, 1984 annual listing, 2044–27

Franchises of firms engaged in distribution of goods and services by kind of business, establishments by State, and sales, 1982-84, annual rpt, 2014–5

Income tax returns of corporations, detailed income and tax items by industry, 1981, annual rpt, 8304–4

Income tax returns of corporations, summary data by industry div, 1981 estimates, annual article, 8302–2.403

Income tax returns of corporations with foreign tax credit, income and deductions by type, asset size, and selected industry group, 1980, article, 8302–2.415

Income tax returns of partnerships, detailed data by industry, 1981 estimates, annual article, 8302–2.404

Income tax returns of partnerships, receipts by source, deductions by type, and establishments, by selected industry, 1982, annual article, 8302–2.416

Income tax returns of sole proprietorships, detailed data by industry div and selected industry group, 1981, annual rpt, 8304–7

Income tax returns of sole proprietorships, receipts, deductions by type, payroll, and net income, by major industry, 1982, annual article, 8302–2.413

Income tax returns with investment credits, for individuals by income, and for sole proprietorships by industry, 1981, article, 8302–2.409

Input-output structure of US economy, detailed interindustry transactions for 85 industries, and components of final demand, 1977, article, 2702–1.421

Input-output structure of US economy, detailed interindustry transactions for 537 industries, and components of final demand, 1977 benchmark data, 2708–17

Land privately held, acreage and owners by owner characteristics, land use, and region, and purchase and improvement funding, 1978 survey, series, 1506–5

Minority group and women employment, by occupational group and SIC 2- to 3-digit industry, 1981, annual rpt, 9244–1.1

North Central States agricultural credit conditions, earnings, and expenditures, Fed Reserve 9th District, quarterly rpt, 9383–11

Occupational injury and illness rates, by SIC 2- to 4-digit industry, 1982, annual rpt, 6844–1

Occupational manpower needs and supply by detailed occupation, and educational and training program enrollees and grads by detailed field, 1982 and 1995, biennial rpt, 6744–3

Occupational Outlook Handbook, 1984-85 biennial rpt, 6744–1

Public lands sales of Land Mgmt Bur, prices of Nevada and California acreage, and effect on Forest Service land acquisition program, 1983, GAO rpt, 26113–122

Scientists, engineers, and technicians employed in private industry, by occupation and industry group, 1980-81, biennial rpt, 9627–23

Small and minority-owned businesses finances and operations, Federal contracts by agency, and worker characteristics, by industry, race, sex, and State, 1950s-83, annual rpt, 9764–6

Uranium exploration, land acquisition expenditures, and employment, various periods 1966-83 and planned 1984-85, annual rpt, 3164–65

see also Housing costs and financing

see also Housing sales

see also Property value

see also Rent

see also under By Industry in the "Index by Categories"

Real property

see Property

Recession

see Business cycles

Recksiek, Conrad W.

"Microcomputer Program for the Calculation of a Trawlnet Section Taper", 2162–1.402

"Shaping and Assembling Webbing", 2162–1.402

Reclamation of land

Coal dev plans on Fed Govt lease lands in 12 regions under Fed Coal Mgmt Program, environmental and socioeconomic impacts to 2000, final statement series, 5726–4

Coal surface mining reclamation costs and Interior Dept regulatory enforcement activities, impacts on industry in 5 States and 3 regions, various periods 1978-82, 6068–177

Coal taxes for surface and underground mines, by type of tax and State, 1984 rpt, 11128–1

Environmental quality and protection programs, costs, and Fed Govt enforcement, 1983, detailed annual rpt, 484–1

Fed Govt-owned real property inventory and costs, worldwide summary by location, agency, and use, 1983, annual rpt, 9454–5

Fed Govt reclamation programs in western US, finances and operations by project and State, 1981-82, annual rpts, 5824–1

Foreign and US tropical forests status by country and world region, conservation methods, and mgmt role of US, foreign, and intl groups, 1977-81 and projected to 2000, 26358–101

Liberia socioeconomic impacts of AID rural dev assistance program, 1976-77, 9916–1.53

Mining (surface) acreage by type and whether reclamation required, and effects on water quality, as of July 1977, 9208–123

Montana and North Dakota coal production, impact of mining on agricultural land availability and on farm income and production costs, by mining tract, 1982 rpt, 1588–79

Index by Subjects and Names

Phosphate rock industry environmental protection costs, by control type and selected State, with background operating data, 1977-81 with cost projections to 1990, 5608–143

Reclamation Bur water storage and carriage facilities, by type, as of Sept 1983, annual listing, 5824–7

Reclamation fund, amounts credited from public land and timber sales, 1901-FY83, annual rpt, 5724–1.4

TVA activities, financial and operating data by program and facility, and power sales by customer, FY83, annual rpt, 9804–1

see also Irrigation

Recording industry

Copyright royalty fees collected for secondary cable TV transmissions and jukeboxes, FY82, annual rpt, 26404–2

Counterfeiting of brand-name products by foreign manufacturers, effects on 6 US industries, investigation with financial and operating data, 1984 rpt, 9886–4.67

County Business Patterns: establishments, employees, and payrolls, by SIC 4-digit industry and county, 1981, annual State rpt series, 2326–8

Equipment (electronic) and associated product shipments, trade, and consumption, by product, 1983, annual Current Industrial Rpt, 2506–12.21

Exports and imports of US, detailed SIC-based commodities by world area, 1983, annual rpts, 2424–6

Exports of US, detailed commodities by country of destination, monthly rpt, 2422–3

Exports of US, detailed Schedule B commodities by country of destination, 1983, annual rpt, 2424–9

Exports of US, detailed Schedule E commodities by mode of transport and world area and country of destination, 1983, annual rpts, 2424–5

Great Lakes trade, by SITC 3-digit commodity, port, vessel type, world area, and country, 1982, annual rpt, 7744–3

Home taping costs, material taped by source, and recording industry operations and sales lost from home taping, 1969-83, hearings with chartbook, 25528–100

Imports of US, detailed Schedule A commodities by country and world area of origin, and mode of transport, 1983, annual rpts, 2424–2

Imports of US, detailed Schedule A commodities by country, monthly rpt, 2422–2

Imports of US, detailed TSUSA commodities by country of origin, 1983, annual rpt, 2424–4

Input-output structure of US economy, detailed interindustry transactions for 537 industries, and components of final demand, 1977 benchmark data, 2708–17

Manufacturing census, 1982: financial and operating data, by SIC 2- to 4-digit industry, State, SMSA, and county, preliminary census div rpt series, 2491–3

Manufacturing census, 1982: financial and operating data, for SIC 4-digit industries by product, preliminary rpt, 2491–1.378

Occupational injury and illness rates, by SIC 2- to 4-digit industry, 1982, annual rpt, 6844–1

Index by Subjects and Names

Recreation

Aircraft accident circumstances and severity, by type of flying and aircraft, 1981, annual rpt, 9614–3

Airline and general aviation accident circumstances, severity, and causes, for US operations of domestic and foreign aircraft, periodic rpt, 9612–1

Amusement and recreational services receipts, 1983, annual rpt, 2413–8

Amusement park automated guideway transit systems itemized costs, and design and operating characteristics, 1982, annual rpt, 7884–6

Army Corps of Engineers water resources dev projects, recreation activities by district and project, 1982, annual rpt, 3754–5

Army morale, welfare, and recreation programs, revenue and expenses worldwide by activity and major command, FY82-83, annual rpt, 3704–12

Bombing (explosive and incendiary) incidents, damage, injuries, and deaths, by target, State, and circumstances, 1983, annual rpt, 6224–5

Bond tax-exempt issues for private activity, by purpose, face value, major industry, and State, 1983, article, 8302–2.417

Budget of US, receipts by source and outlays by function, FY40-89 estimates revised for consistency with FY85 budget definitions, annual rpt, 104–12

Census of Population, 1980: detailed socioeconomic and demographic characteristics, by age, sex, race, Hispanic origin, occupation, and industry, State rpt series, 2531–4

Census of Population, 1980: detailed socioeconomic characteristics, by county, city, and inside-outside SMSAs and central cities, State rpt series, 2531–3

City govt revenue sharing program allocations and use by function, and response to program cuts, by city size and region, 1982 survey, hearings, 25408–86.2

Coal dev plans on Fed Govt lease lands in 12 regions under Fed Coal Mgmt Program, environmental and socioeconomic impacts to 2000, final statement series, 5726–4

Coastal environmental and socioeconomic conditions, and potential impacts of oil and gas OCS leases, final statement series, 5736–1

Coastal environmental characteristics, fish, wildlife, and use, and population socioeconomic data, for individual areas, series, 5506–4

Collective bargaining agreements expiring during year, covered workers by SIC 2-digit industry, firm, and union, with summary of key provisions, 1984, annual rpt, 6784–9

Colorado River Storage Project finances, water resource dev, power production, and other activities in western States, FY83, annual rpt, 5824–3

Construction industries census, 1982: financial and operating data, by SIC 4-digit industry and State, final rpt series, 2373–1

Construction industries census, 1982: financial and operating data, by SIC 4-digit industry and State, preliminary rpt series, 2371–1

Construction put in place, permits authorized by region, State, and MSA, and Federal contract awards, by construction type, bimonthly rpt with articles, 2012–1

County Business Patterns: establishments, employees, and payrolls, by SIC 4-digit industry and county, 1981, annual State rpt series, 2326–8

County Business Patterns: establishments, employees, and payrolls, by SIC 4-digit industry and county, 1982, annual State rpt series, 2326–6

CPI by detailed component, for US city average, 28 SMSAs, and 4 regions by population size, monthly rpt, 6762–2

CPI components relative importance, for selected SMSAs, and US city average by region and population size, 1983, annual rpt, 6884–1

Deaths and death rates from accidents, by place, detailed cause, and demographic characteristics, 1979, US Vital Statistics annual rpt, 4144–2.1, 4144–2.5

Earnings by major industry group, and personal income per capita and by source, by region and State, 1929-82, 2708–40

Employment by detailed occupation, for 29 SIC 2-digit nonmanufacturing industries, 1981 BLS survey, 6748–60

Employment, earnings, and hours, by selected SIC 1- to 4-digit industry, State, and for 278 major labor areas, 1939-83, annual rpt, 6744–5

Employment, earnings, and hours, by SIC 4-digit nonfarm industry, monthly 1974-Feb 1984, annual update, 6744–4

Environmental quality and protection programs, costs, and Fed Govt enforcement, 1983, detailed annual rpt, 484–1

Exports and imports of recreation equipment, detailed SIC-based commodities by world area, 1983, annual rpt, 2424–6

Exports of recreation equipment, detailed Schedule E commodities by mode of transport and world area and country of destination, 1983, annual rpts, 2424–5

Farm real estate transfers, by proposed use of property, region, and State, 1982-83, annual rpt, 1541–8.4

Fed Govt programs and mgmt cost control proposals, 3-year savings by function and agency, and financial and operating data, 1960s-81, 16908–1.31

FmHA loans and grants by program and State, and summary of services, FY83 with trends from FY63, annual rpt, 1184–17

FmHA loans, by type, race, Hispanic origin, and State, quarterly rpt, 1182–5

Forest land owner characteristics in Northeast States, owners and acreage, series, 1206–7

Forest, range, and associated waters use and mgmt assessment, and environmental impacts of Forest Service program options, 1977-2030 and trends from 1920, 1208–24

France Brittany coast oil spill cleanup and research costs, marine and tourism industry losses, and recreation losses of tourists and residents, 1971-79, 2178–13

Franchise business opportunities, by firm and kind of business, 1984 annual listing, 2044–27

Franchises of firms engaged in distribution of goods and services by kind of business, establishments by State, and sales, 1982-84, annual rpt, 2014–5

Govt census, 1982: city govt revenues by source, expenditures by function, debt, and assets, by State and city, 2457–4

Govt census, 1982: county govt revenues by source, expenditures by function, debt, and assets, by State and county, 2457–3

Govt census, 1982: employment, payrolls, and average earnings, by function, level of govt, State, county, population size, and inside-outside SMSAs, 2455–2

Govt census, 1982: local govt employment by function, payroll, and average earnings, for individual counties, cities, and school and special districts, 2455–1

Govt census, 1982: State govt payments to local govts, by program, source of funds, level of govt, and State, with trends from 1902, 2460–3

Govt employment and payroll, by function, level of govt, and jurisdiction, 1983, annual rpt series, 2466–1

Govt finances, by level of govt, State, and for large cities and counties, 1981-83, annual rpt series, 2466–2

Idaho and Montana recreation sites of Forest Service, itemized operating and maintenance costs by type of site, 1980, 1208–202

Imports of recreation equipment, detailed Schedule A commodities by country and world area of origin, and method of transport, 1983, annual rpts, 2424–2

Income tax returns of corporations, detailed income and tax items by industry, 1981, annual rpt, 8304–4

Income tax returns of corporations with foreign tax credit, income and deductions by type, asset size, and selected industry group, 1980, article, 8302–2.415

Income tax returns of partnerships, detailed data by industry, 1981 estimates, annual article, 8302–2.404

Income tax returns of partnerships, receipts by source, deductions by type, and establishments, by selected industry, 1982, annual article, 8302–2.416

Income tax returns of sole proprietorships, detailed data by industry div and selected industry group, 1981, annual rpt, 8304–7

Income tax returns of sole proprietorships, receipts, deductions by type, payroll, and net income, by major industry, 1982, annual article, 8302–2.413

Income tax returns with investment credits, for individuals by income, and for sole proprietorships by industry, 1981, article, 8302–2.409

Injuries and deaths from use of selected consumer products and related activity, by victim age and sex, 1982, annual rpt, 9164–7

Input-output structure of US economy, detailed interindustry transactions for 85 industries, and components of final demand, 1977, article, 2702–1.421

Input-output structure of US economy, detailed interindustry transactions for 537 industries, and components of final demand, 1977 benchmark data, 2708–17

Recreation

Jail capacities, conditions, expenditures, and services, and socioeconomic and other characteristics of inmates, various dates 1976-82, 10048–59

Land Mgmt Bur activities and finances, and public land acreage and use, annual State rpt series, 5724–11

Land Mgmt Bur public lands admin and program activities in western States, FY82-84, annual rpt, 5724–13

Minority group and women employment, by occupational group and SIC 2- to 3-digit industry, 1981, annual rpt, 9244–1.1

Natl Forest System wildlife habitat and fishery improvements, use, and game population and harvest by species and forest, by region, FY83, annual rpt, 1204–31

Neighborhood and housing quality indicators and attitudes, and occupant characteristics, by urban-rural location and region, 1981, annual survey, 2485–7

Neighborhood and housing quality indicators and attitudes, by occupant and unit characteristics, region, and metro-nonmetro location, 1981, annual survey, 2485–2

Occupational injury and illness rates, by SIC 2- to 4-digit industry, 1982, annual rpt, 6844–1

Occupational manpower needs and supply by detailed occupation, and educational and training program enrollees and grads by detailed field, 1982 and 1995, biennial rpt, 6744–3

Occupational Outlook Handbook, 1984-85 biennial rpt, 6744–1

Oil spill risk analyses for OCS proposed lease sale areas, series, 5736–2

Older persons nutrition services program operations and assessment, and participant sociodemographic, health, and diet characteristics, 1976 and 1982, 4608–16

Outdoor recreation area dev, Interior Dept Land and Water Conservation Fund grants by State, FY85, annual press release, 5544–15

Outdoor recreation fees and collection costs, visitors, and capacity of Fed Govt, State, and private facilities, by managing agency and State, 1983, annual rpt, 5544–14

Outdoor recreation participation, by type of activity, projected 1985-2030, 1208–195

Outdoor recreation use of public lands, area and visits, FY83, annual rpt, 5724–1.2

Personal consumption expenditures, natl income and product account, *Survey of Current Business,* monthly rpt, monthly and annual tables, 2702–1.23

Public opinion on taxes, tax policy, and intergovtl relations, 1972-84 surveys, annual rpt, 10044–2

Service industry census, 1982: employment, establishments, receipts, and payroll, by SIC 2- to 4-digit kind of business, SMSA, county, and city, State rpt series, 2391–1

Service industry census, 1982: employment, establishments, receipts, and payroll, by SIC 4-digit kind of business and State, preliminary rpt, 2390–2.13

Statistical Abstract of US, social, political, and economic data, 1950s-83 and trends, annual rpt, 2324–1.1

Tax collections, refunds, and taxes due IRS, by State and region, and IRS court activity and operating expenses, FY83, annual rpt, 8304–3.3

TVA activities, financial and operating data by program and facility, and power sales by customer, FY83, annual rpt, 9804–1

Utah timber acreage and resources, and forest recreational use and big game population by species, 1977-78, 1206–22.6

Virgin Islands economic censuses, 1982: employment, establishments, payroll, and receipts, by SIC 1- to 4-digit industry, island, and city, 2593–1

Water resources dev projects recreation construction, for Army Corps of Engineers and Reclamation Bur, unfunded costs by project, FY82, GAO rpt, 26113–115

Waterborne disease outbreaks and cases, by type, source, and location, 1983, annual rpt, 4205–35

Women's travel patterns, by employment and sociodemographic characteristics and type of child care used, 1980 survey, 7888–62

see also Boats and boating
see also Camping
see also Fishing, sport
see also Horse racing
see also Hunting and trapping
see also Motion pictures
see also National forests
see also National park system
see also Parks
see also Recreational vehicles
see also Sporting goods
see also Sports and athletics
see also Swimming
see also Travel
see also Wilderness areas
see also Winter sports

Recreational vehicles

Air pollutant emission factors, by detailed source, 3rd edition, 1983-84 supplements, 9198–13

County Business Patterns: establishments, employees, and payrolls, by SIC 4-digit industry and county, 1981, annual State rpt series, 2326–8

County Business Patterns: establishments, employees, and payrolls, by SIC 4-digit industry and county, 1982, annual State rpt series, 2326–6

Employment, earnings, and hours, by SIC 4-digit nonfarm industry, monthly 1974-Feb 1984, annual update, 6744–4

Energy use in transportation sector by mode, fuel supplies, and demographic and economic determinants of vehicle use, 1970s-83, annual rpt, 3304–5

Exports and imports of US, detailed SIC-based commodities by world area, 1983, annual rpts, 2424–6

Exports and imports of US, totals and as percent of domestic production, by SIC 2- to 5-digit commodity, 1981, annual rpt, 2424–3

Exports, imports, tariffs, and industry operating data for military and special-purpose vehicles, 1979-83, TSUSA commodity rpt, 9885–6.78

Exports of US, detailed commodities by country of destination, monthly rpt, 2422–3

Exports of US, detailed Schedule B commodities by country of destination, 1983, annual rpt, 2424–9

Index by Subjects and Names

Exports of US, detailed Schedule E commodities by mode of transport and world area and country of destination, 1983, annual rpts, 2424–5

Foreign market and trade for sporting goods and recreational equipment and vehicles, country market research rpts, 2045–14

Imports of US, detailed Schedule A commodities by country and world area of origin, and mode of transport, 1983, annual rpts, 2424–2

Imports of US, detailed Schedule A commodities by country, monthly rpt, 2422–2

Imports of US, detailed TSUSA commodities by country of origin, 1983, annual rpt, 2424–4

Income tax returns of sole proprietorships, detailed data by industry div and selected industry group, 1981, annual rpt, 8304–7

Income tax returns of sole proprietorships, receipts, deductions by type, payroll, and net income, by major industry, 1982, annual article, 8302–2.413

Input-output structure of US economy, detailed interindustry transactions for 537 industries, and components of final demand, 1977 benchmark data, 2708–17

Manufacturing census, 1982: financial and operating data, for SIC 4-digit industries by product, preliminary rpt, 2491–1.397, 2491–1.408

Natl forests recreational use, visitor-days by type of activity, forest, and State, FY83 with trends from 1924, annual rpt series, 1204–17

Natl park area visits and overnight stays, visitors, and vehicles, by State and park, 1983, annual rpt, 5544–12

OECD trade, total and for 4 major countries, and US trade by country, by commodity, 1972-82, annual world region rpt series, 244–13

Recreation (outdoor) participation, by type of activity, projected 1985-2030, 1208–195

Retail trade census, 1982: employment, establishments, sales, and payroll, for recreational and utility trailer dealers, by State, preliminary rpt, 2395–1.14

Sales, prices, and registrations of autos and auto products in US, and trade of 8 countries with US, by make and model, 1964-83, annual rpt, 9884–7

Recruiting

see Voluntary military service

Recycling of waste materials

Census of Population, 1980: detailed socioeconomic and demographic characteristics, by age, sex, race, Hispanic origin, occupation, and industry, State rpt series, 2531–4

Electric power plants, by capacity, fuel used, unit type, region, State, and county, for plants added and retired, 1983 and planned through 1993, annual rpt, 3164–36

Employment, earnings, and hours, by SIC 4-digit nonfarm industry, monthly 1974-Feb 1984, annual update, 6744–4

Energy demand in industry, forecasting model description, detailed technology specifications, and energy use, for 27 SIC 2- to 4-digit industries, 1970s-80 and projected to 2000, 3308–66

Index by Subjects and Names

Energy production, trade, supply, use, conservation, and DOE activities, by energy type, FY83, annual rpt, 3024–2

Environmental quality and protection programs, costs, and Fed Govt enforcement, 1983, detailed annual rpt, 484–1

Exports, imports, tariffs, and industry operating data for waste and scrap material, 1979-83, TSUSA commodity rpt, 9885–7.58

Manufacturing energy efficiency progress, and energy use by type, by SIC 2-digit industry, 1982, annual rpt, 3304–8

Manufacturing pollution abatement costs recovered, by SIC 2- to 4-digit industry, State, and SMSA, 1982, annual Current Industrial Rpt, 2506–3.6

Minerals and metal recycling and scrap, by commodity, 1983, annual rpt, 5604–18

North Central States timber mill residue, by county and type of use, series, 1206–10

Producer prices and indexes, by stage of processing and detailed commodity, monthly rpt, 6762–6

Producer prices and indexes, by stage of processing and detailed commodity, monthly 1983, annual supplement, 6764–2

Radioactive waste and spent fuel generation, inventory, disposal by site, reprocessing, and characteristics, by source, as of 1983 and projected to 2020, annual rpt, 3364–2

Wholesale trade census, 1982: employment, establishments, sales by commodity, and payroll, by SIC 4-digit kind of business and State, revised preliminary rpt, 2403–1.18

see also Scrap metals

Red River

Bridges over navigable waters, with type of bridge and use, owner, dimensions, and location, 1984 regional listing, 7406–5.2

Freight (waterborne domestic and foreign) by commodity, traffic, and passengers, by port and waterway, 1982, annual rpt, 3754–3.2

Water supply and quality in streams and lakes, and groundwater levels in wells, by drainage basin, 1981, annual State rpt series, 5666–16

Water supply and quality in streams and lakes, and groundwater levels in wells, by drainage basin, 1982, annual State rpt series, 5666–20

Water supply in US and Canada, streamflow, well and reservoir levels, and dissolved solids and temperature in 6 US rivers, by station, monthly rpt, 5662–3

Red River of the North

see Souris-Red-Rainy Rivers

Redding, Calif.

Census of Housing, 1980: occupancy and unit characteristics, by race, Hispanic origin, and city, SMSA rpt, 2473–1.299

Census of Population and Housing, 1980: detailed population and housing characteristics, by county, city, and census tract, SMSA rpt, 2551–2.299

Housing vacancy rates for single and multifamily units and mobile homes, by city and ZIP code, 1983, annual metro area rpt, 9304–20.5

Housing vacancy rates for single and multifamily units and mobile homes, by city and ZIP code, 1984, annual metro area rpt, 9304–20.17

see also under By SMSA or MSA in the "Index by Categories"

Redick, Richard W.

"Distribution of Psychiatric Beds, U.S. and Each State, 1982", 4506–3.14

"History of the U.S. National Reporting Program for Mental Health Statistics, 1840-1983. Mental Health Service System Reports, Series HN", 4508–5

"State and County Mental Hospitals, U.S., 1980-81 and 1981-82", 4506–3.13

Redmond, Oreg.

Housing vacancy rates for single and multifamily units and mobile homes, by city and ZIP code, 1984, annual metro area rpt, 9304–21.10

Reed, R. K.

"Oceanographic Observations Off the Pacific Northwest Following the 1982 El Nino Event", 2162–1.403

Rees, John

"New Technology in the American Machinery Industry: Trends and Implications", 23848–179

Refractories

see Clay industry and products

Refrigeration

see Air conditioning

see Cold storage and refrigeration

see Household appliances and equipment

Refugees

AID economic assistance to developing countries, obligations and disbursements by country, quarterly rpt, 9912–4

Arrivals in US, by world area of origin and processing and nationality, monthly rpt, 7002–4, 7002–5

Arrivals in US by world area of origin and State of settlement, and intl and Fed Govt assistance program costs and funding, FY85, annual rpt, 7004–16

Bilingual education programs, teachers, enrollment, and funding, selected years 1976-FY83, biennial rpt, 4804–14

Budget of US, effects of Reagan Admin policy changes, by detailed program, FY85, annual rpt, 104–21

Central America economic assistance from AID by type of aid, for 7 countries, FY80-83, GAO rpt, 26123–55

Central America socioeconomic and political conditions in 6 countries, 1960s-83 with trends and projections 1930-2010, Commission rpt, 028–19.2

Central American refugees by country of origin and asylum, and aid from US and Mexico, FY82-1984, GAO rpt, 26123–70

Children and youth benefitting from Fed Govt public welfare programs and tax expenditures, participation and funding for 71 programs, FY81-83, 21968–30

Education Dept programs funding, operations, and effectiveness, FY83, annual rpt, 4804–5

Fed Govt programs and mgmt cost control proposals, 3-year savings by function and agency, and financial and operating data, 1960s-81, 16908–1.10

Foreign countries disasters, persons affected, deaths, damage, and aid by US and others, FY83 and trends from FY64, annual rpt, 9914–12

Refuse and refuse disposal

Foreign military, social, and economic summary data by world area and country, 1960s-80s, hearing, 25388–47.1

Govt census, 1982: State govt payments to local govts, by program, source of funds, level of govt, and State, with trends from 1902, 2460–3

HHS aid to each State and local govt or private instn, amount obligated, funding agency, and program, FY83, annual listing, 4004–3

Immigration, and alien residents, workers, visitors, deportations, and naturalizations, by country of birth, FY81, annual rpt, 6264–2

Indochina refugee arrivals in US, by country of origin and State of destination, tuberculosis cases, and unexplained sudden deaths, 1982, annual rpt, 4204–1.3

Indochina refugee population, arrivals, and departures, by country of origin and resettlement, camp, and ethnicity, monthly rpt, 7002–4

Malaria cases reported in US, including military personnel and foreign civilians, 1966-82, annual rpt, 4205–4

Migration, settlement status, and assistance of refugees, by world area and country of origin and asylum, as of May 1984, annual rpt, 7004–15

PL 480 exports by commodity, and recipients, by program, sponsor, and country, FY82 and aggregate from FY55, annual rpt, 1924–7

Red Cross program operations and financial statements, 1982/83, annual rpt, 29254–1

Resettlement program activities and funding, refugee arrivals and population by country of origin and State, and employment and other characteristics, FY83, annual rpt, 4704–8

Resettlements and arrivals of refugees and aliens in US, by State, outlying area, country of birth and citizenship, age, sex, and sponsoring agency, monthly rpt, 4702–3

Southeast Asia refugee children nutrition status, blood and height-weight indicators, by age, 1981, annual rpt, 4205–24

Statistical Abstract of US, social, political, and economic data, 1950s-83 and trends, annual rpt, 2324–1.1

Visas issued and refused to immigrants and nonimmigrants, and status adjustments, by class and nationality, FY77, annual rpt, 7184–1

Refuse and refuse disposal

Air pollution levels for 5 pollutants, by detailed source, State, and Air Quality Control Region, 1981, annual rpt, 9194–7

Army Corps of Engineers activities and projects, FY83 and trends from 1800s, annual rpt, 3754–1

Bond tax-exempt issues for private activity, by purpose, face value, major industry, and State, 1983, article, 8302–2.417

Census of Population, 1980: detailed socioeconomic and demographic characteristics, by age, sex, race, Hispanic origin, occupation, and industry, State rpt series, 2531–4

Refuse and refuse disposal

Census of Population, 1980: detailed socioeconomic characteristics, by county, city, and inside-outside SMSAs and central cities, State rpt series, 2531–3

Coal transport environmental impacts by type and mode of transport, methodology for assessing alternative systems, 1983 rpt, 3408–28

Coastal environmental characteristics, fish, wildlife, and use, and population socioeconomic data, for individual areas, series, 5506–4

County Business Patterns: establishments, employees, and payrolls, by SIC 4-digit industry and county, 1981, annual State rpt series, 2326–8

County Business Patterns: establishments, employees, and payrolls, by SIC 4-digit industry and county, 1982, annual State rpt series, 2326–6

Employment, earnings, and hours, by SIC 4-digit nonfarm industry, monthly 1974-Feb 1984, annual update, 6744–4

Environmental quality and protection programs, costs, and Fed Govt enforcement, 1983, detailed annual rpt, 484–1

EPA budget and full-time staff positions by type of activity, and grants to States, by program, FY75-84 and proposed FY85, 26308–47

EPA Office of R&D environmental research plans, and outlays by program, FY84-88, annual rpt, 9184–10

EPA pollution control research and grant assistance program activities, monthly rpt, 9182–8

EPA publications in NTIS collection, quarterly listing, 9182–5

Fed Govt programs and mgmt cost control proposals, 3-year savings by function and agency, and financial and operating data, 1960s-81, 16908–1.22

FmHA loans and grants by program and State, and summary of services, FY83 with trends from FY63, annual rpt, 1184–17

Foreign market and trade for pollution control instruments and equipment, and user industry operations and demand, country market research rpts, 2045–17

Govt census, 1982: city govt revenues by source, expenditures by function, debt, and assets, by State and city, 2457–4

Govt census, 1982: county govt revenues by source, expenditures by function, debt, and assets, by State and county, 2457–3

Govt census, 1982: employment, payrolls, and average earnings, by function, level of govt, State, county, population size, and inside-outside SMSAs, 2455–2

Govt census, 1982: local govt employment by function, payroll, and average earnings, for individual counties, cities, and school and special districts, 2455–1

Govt census, 1982: State govt payments to local govts, by program, source of funds, level of govt, and State, with trends from 1902, 2460–3

Govt employment and payroll, by function, level of govt, and jurisdiction, 1983, annual rpt series, 2466–1

Govt finances, by level of govt, State, and for large cities and counties, 1981-83, annual rpt series, 2466–2

Hazardous waste generation and disposal taxes in 3 States, and effects on waste mgmt, 1981-83, with assessment of 3 Fed Govt tax proposals, GAO rpt, 26113–124

Hazardous waste sites and activities of Fed Govt civil agencies, and EPA data mgmt, by waste location, 1984, GAO rpt, 26113–139

Home mortgages FHA-insured, financial, property, and mortgagor characteristics, for US, selected States, and Puerto Rico, quarterly rpt, 5142–3

Housing and financial characteristics, and unit and neighborhood quality, for 15 SMSAs, 1978, annual survey special supplement, 2485–8

Income tax returns of corporations, detailed income and tax items by industry, 1981, annual rpt, 8304–4

Income tax returns of sole proprietorships, detailed data by industry div and selected industry group, 1981, annual rpt, 8304–7

Income tax returns of sole proprietorships, receipts, deductions by type, payroll, and net income, by major industry, 1982, annual article, 8302–2.413

Indian and Alaska Native health program activities, and funding for scholarships, care services, and facilities construction, by city, FY82, annual rpt, 4104–11

Local govt per capita expenditures, by function and State, 1981-82, annual rpt, 10044–1.7

Manufacturing pollution abatement costs recovered, by SIC 2- to 4-digit industry, State, and SMSA, 1982, annual Current Industrial Rpt, 2506–3.6

Neighborhood and housing quality indicators and attitudes, and occupant characteristics, by urban-rural location and region, 1981, annual survey, 2485–7

Neighborhood and housing quality indicators and attitudes, by occupant and unit characteristics, region, and metro-nonmetro location, 1981, annual survey, 2485–2

Occupational injury and illness rates, by SIC 2- to 4-digit industry, 1982, annual rpt, 6844–1

Oil enhanced recovery technologies use and environmental impacts, by oil field, county, and State, 1970s-80 and projected to 2000, 3408–29

Pollution abatement capital expenditures, by pollution type and selected industry, 1973-84, annual article, 2702–1.423

Pollution abatement expenditures, and effect on economic indicators and industry operations, by major industry, projected under 3 pollution-regulation alternatives 1983-95, 9188–84

Pollution abatement expenditures of govt, business, and consumers, 1972-82, annual article, 2702–1.407

Scientists, engineers, and technicians employment in transportation, utilities, and retail and wholesale trade, by field of science and industry, 1982, 9628–72

State and local govt productivity measurement, with background data and output indexes for 7 govt services, various periods 1955-82, 6728–27

Tennessee Valley ethanol production, feedstocks, facilities, tax incentives, and related farming data, by State, 1970s-83 and projected to 1992, 9808–69

Index by Subjects and Names

Transportation census, 1982: trucks, by detailed characteristics, miles traveled, and type of product carried, State rpt series, 2573–1

see also Air pollution

see also Marine pollution

see also Radioactive waste

see also Recycling of waste materials

see also Sewage and wastewater treatment systems

see also Water pollution

Regier, Darrel A.

"Epidemiology and Health Service Resource Allocation Policy for Alcohol, Drug Abuse, and Mental Disorders", 4102–1.449

Regional medical programs

Appalachia regional dev spending, by program area and source of funds, FY82, annual rpt, 9084–1

HHS aid to each State and local govt or private instn, amount obligated, funding agency, and program, FY83, annual listing, 4004–3

Regional planning

Appalachia regional dev spending, by program area and source of funds, FY82, annual rpt, 9084–1

Coal dev plans on Fed Govt lease lands in 12 regions under Fed Coal Mgmt Program, environmental and socioeconomic impacts to 2000, final statement series, 5726–4

DC metro area Metrorail transit system, land use planning dev and impacts, 1984 narrative rpt, 7306–8.3

Fed Govt aid to State and local govts, expenditures, and direct payments, by program, agency, and State, FY83, annual rpt, 2464–2

Fed Govt financial and nonfinancial domestic aid, 1984 annual comprehensive catalog, 104–5

GAO publications on land use, ownership, mgmt, and planning, 1979-83, annual listing, 26104–11.3

Occupational manpower needs and supply by detailed occupation, and educational and training program enrollees and grads by detailed field, 1982 and 1995, biennial rpt, 6744–3

Occupational Outlook Handbook, 1984-85 biennial rpt, 6744–1

Regional councils involved in service activities, by type of service and region population size, 1982 survey, hearing, 25408–88

Transit system mgmt training funded by Urban Mass Transportation Admin, participant characteristics and career impact, 1970-79, 7888–60

TVA activities, financial and operating data by program and facility, and power sales by customer, FY83, annual rpt, 9804–1

TVA construction projects employment, and impacts on nearby areas, survey rpt series, 9806–7

see also Open space land programs

Regions of the U.S.

see Middle Atlantic States

see North Central States

see Northeast States

see Southeastern States

see Southwestern States

Index by Subjects and Names

see Western States
see under By Region, By Census Division, and By State in the "Index by Categories"
see under names of individual States

Regions of the world

see Africa
see Antarctic
see Arctic
see Asia
see Atlantic Ocean
see Caribbean area
see Central America
see Central Europe
see Eastern Europe
see Europe
see Gulf of Mexico
see Indian Ocean
see Mediterranean Sea
see Micronesia
see Middle East
see North America
see Oceania
see Pacific Ocean
see South America
see Southeast Asia

Regulatory commissions

see Administrative law and procedure
see under names of individual agencies (listed under Federal independent agencies)

Rehabilitation

see Drug abuse and treatment
see Housing maintenance and repair
see Methadone treatment
see Rehabilitation of criminals
see Rehabilitation of the disabled
see Veterans rehabilitation
see Vocational rehabilitation

Rehabilitation of criminals

Jail capacities, conditions, expenditures, and services, and socioeconomic and other characteristics of inmates, various dates 1976-82, 10048–59
see also Drug abuse and treatment
see also Halfway houses
see also Parole and probation

Rehabilitation of the disabled

Budget of US, effects of Reagan Admin policy changes, by detailed program, FY85, annual rpt, 104–21
Census of Population, 1980: detailed socioeconomic and demographic characteristics, by age, sex, race, Hispanic origin, occupation, and industry, State rpt series, 2531–4
Fed Govt aid to State and local govts, expenditures, and direct payments, by program, agency, and State, FY83, annual rpt, 2464–2
HHS aid to each State and local govt or private instn, amount obligated, funding agency, and program, FY83, annual listing, 4004–3
Supplementary Security Income beneficiary socioeconomic characteristics and health service use, 1970s-83 and SSI program projections to 1995, 25148–29
Workers compensation law provisions of States and Fed Govt, by jurisdiction, as of July 1984, semiannual rpt, 6502–1
see also Veterans rehabilitation
see also Vocational rehabilitation

Reid, J. Norman

"Counting Community Capital: The Status of Rural Infrastructure", 1004–16.1

Reister, David B.

"Aggregate Energy Demand Patterns in the Manufacturing Sector", 3006–7.4

Relief

see Disaster relief
see International relief
see Public welfare programs
see Refugees
see War relief

Religion

Army morale, welfare, and recreation programs, revenue and expenses worldwide by activity and major command, FY82-83, annual rpt, 3704–12
Black young adults economic status and educational attainment related to motivation, goals, family characteristics, and social factors, 1982, longitudinal study, 4008–65.2
Degrees conferred in higher education, by race, Hispanic origin, sex, level, and field, selected years 1949/50-1979/80, annual rpt, 4824–2.16
Developing countries disaster preparedness and summary sociodemographic, political, and economic data, country rpt series, 9916–2
Education statistics, detailed data on students, staff, finances, and facilities, 1982 and selected trends, annual rpt, 4824–2
Foreign economic, social, and political summary data, by country, 1984, annual factbook, 244–11
High school classes of 1980 and 1982: educational and sociodemographic characteristics and expectations, natl longitudinal study, series, 4826–2
High school dropout rate and reasons, educational goals and achievement, and required and recommended curricula, by school control, selected years 1972-83, annual rpt, 4824–1.5
Higher education instns, by type, location, and other characteristics, 1983/84 annual listing, 4844–3
Jail capacities, conditions, expenditures, and services, and socioeconomic and other characteristics of inmates, various dates 1976-82, 10048–59
Marriages in civil and religious ceremonies, by detailed demographic and geographic characteristics, 1979 and trends, US Vital Statistics annual rpt, 4144–4.1
Nigeria native and Western health care use, by sociodemographic characteristics, 1984 article, 4102–1.417
Personal consumption expenditures, natl income and product account, *Survey of Current Business,* monthly rpt, monthly and annual tables, 2702–1.23
VA Medicine and Surgery Dept chaplaincy trainees, by city, FY83, annual rpt, 9924–21
see also Religious liberty
see also Religious organizations

Religious liberty

Foreign human rights conditions in 162 countries, economic and military aid of US, and economic aid of intl organizations, 1981-83, annual rpt, 21384–3

Religious organizations

Bombing (explosive and incendiary) incidents, damage, injuries, and deaths, by target, State, and circumstances, 1983, annual rpt, 6224–5
Census of Population, 1980: detailed socioeconomic and demographic characteristics, by age, sex, race, Hispanic origin, occupation, and industry, State rpt series, 2531–4
Census of Population, 1980: detailed socioeconomic characteristics, by county, city, and inside-outside SMSAs and central cities, State rpt series, 2531–3
Census of Population, 1980: labor force, by sex, detailed occupation, and region, with comparison to 1970 census, supplementary rpt, 2535–1.12
Construction industries census, 1982: financial and operating data, by SIC 4-digit industry and State, final rpt series, 2373–1
Construction industries census, 1982: financial and operating data, by SIC 4-digit industry and State, preliminary rpt series, 2371–1
Construction put in place, permits authorized by region, State, and MSA, and Federal contract awards, by construction type, bimonthly rpt with articles, 2012–1
Construction put in place, value of new public and private structures, by type, monthly rpt, 2382–4
County Business Patterns: establishments, employees, and payrolls, by SIC 4-digit industry and county, 1981, annual State rpt series, 2326–8
County Business Patterns: establishments, employees, and payrolls, by SIC 4-digit industry and county, 1982, annual State rpt series, 2326–6
Employment and earnings in philanthropic organizations by organization type, and compared to other nonprofit organizations, selected years 1972-82, article, 6722–1.455
Higher education instns, type, location, enrollment, and student charges, by State and congressional district, 1983/84, biennial listing, 4844–11
Homeless population and characteristics, and temporary shelter operations, use, and user characteristics, for selected cities, various periods 1979-84, hearing, 21248–85
Immigrants admitted under Immigration and Nationality Act, by class of admission, FY78-81, annual rpt, 6264–2
Input-output structure of US economy, detailed interindustry transactions for 537 industries, and components of final demand, 1977 benchmark data, 2708–17
Occupational manpower needs and supply by detailed occupation, and educational and training program enrollees and grads by detailed field, 1982 and 1995, biennial rpt, 6744–3
Occupational Outlook Handbook, 1984-85 biennial rpt, 6744–1
Statistical Abstract of US, social, political, and economic data, 1950s-83 and trends, annual rpt, 2324–1.1

Relocation

Relocation

Community dev programs funding and activities, for 5 HUD programs, FY83, annual rpt, 5124–5

Fed Govt Senior Executive Service employee admin, and program status and effectiveness, by agency and by executive and job characteristics, July 1979-Sept 1983, GAO rpt, 26119–51

Uranium mining operations, finances, and costs of alternative methods to meet emissions standards, for industry and selected mines, selected years 1948-90, 9188–96

see also Urban renewal

Reno, Nev.

Census of Housing, 1980: occupancy and unit characteristics, by race, Hispanic origin, and city, SMSA rpt, 2473–1.300

Census of Population and Housing, 1980: detailed population and housing characteristics, by county, city, and census tract, SMSA rpt, 2551–2.300

Wages of office and plant workers, by occupation, 1983 labor market area survey rpt, 6785–3.2

Wages of office and plant workers, by occupation, 1984 labor market area survey rpt, 6785–3.10

see also under By City and By SMSA or MSA in the "Index by Categories"

Renshaw, Derwent

"Effect of Changes in the Cap on U.S. Agricultural Trade", 1004–16.1

Rent

- AFDC eligibility under Omnibus Budget Reconciliation Act, effect on caseloads and recipient benefits and living costs, 1981-83, GAO rpt, 26131–11
- Airline financial data, by carrier, carrier group, and for total certificated system, quarterly rpt, 9142–12
- Airline operating and other costs, itemized for domestic and intl trunk and local service carriers, 1st half 1983, semiannual rpt, 9142–47
- Apartment and condominium completions by rent class and sales price, and market absorption rates, quarterly rpt, 2482–2
- Apartment market absorption rates and characteristics for nonsubsidized privately financed furnished and unfurnished units completed in 1982, annual Current Housing Rpt, 2484–2
- Apartment market absorption rates and characteristics for nonsubsidized privately financed units completed in 1983, preliminary annual Current Housing Rpt, 2484–3
- Bank financial and operating statements, functional cost analysis for Fed Reserve member banks with average and high earnings, by deposit size, 1982, annual rpt, 9364–6
- Bankruptcy (personal), filers by debt type and other characteristics, selected years 1978-81, hearing, 25528–97.1
- Business and financial statistics, historic trends, 1984 annual chartbook, 9364–2.6
- Census of Housing, 1980: inventory, occupancy, and unit characteristics, changes from 1973 by region and inside-outside SMSAs and central cities, series, 2473–3

Census of Housing, 1980: occupancy and unit characteristics of SMSAs and central cities, by race, Hispanic origin, and city, State and SMSA rpt series, 2473–1

Census of Housing, 1980: structural, financial, and householder characteristics, by region and State, 2475–4

Census of Population and Housing, 1980: detailed population and housing characteristics, by county, city, and census tract, State and SMSA rpt series, 2551–2

Community dev programs funding and activities, for 5 HUD programs, FY83, annual rpt, 5124–5

Construction industries census, 1982: financial and operating data, by SIC 4-digit industry and State, final rpt series, 2373–1

County and City Data Book, detailed socioeconomic and demographic data for States, counties, and cities, selected years 1976-82, 2328–1

CPI by detailed component, for US city average, 28 SMSAs, and 4 regions by population size, monthly rpt, 6762–2

CPI for rent, bimonthly rpt, 2012–1.5

Electric utilities privately owned, detailed financial and operating data by company, with summary data for other distributors by type, 1982, annual rpt, 3164–23

Farm, cropland, and pasture rent rates, for selected States, 1980-84, annual rpt, 1541–8.2

Farm finances, assets, liabilities, income, receipts by commodity and State, and expenses, 1980-83 and trends from 1910, annual rpt, 1544–16

Farm finances, production, expenses by type, and domestic economic impact, selected years 1972-82 and preliminary 1983-84, annual rpt, 1544–19

Farm production expenditures, detailed items by farm sales size and region, 1983, annual rpt, 1614–3

Farm production expenses, by type and State, 1979-82, annual rpt, 1544–18

Fed Govt-leased real property inventory and rental costs, worldwide summary by location and agency, 1983, annual rpt, 9454–10

Fed Govt receipts, tax and other, FY83, annual rpt, 8104–2.2

Govt census, 1982: State govt payments to local govts, by program, source of funds, level of govt, and State, with trends from 1902, 2460–3

House of Representatives salaries, expenses, and contingent fund disbursement, detailed listings, quarterly rpt, 21942–1

Housing (multifamily rental) energy use and costs, conservation effect on rental marketing, and effect of utility bill payment methods on conservation efforts, 1970s-80s, 3308–73

Housing (rental) unit choice of Pittsburgh, Pa, recent movers related to unit, neighborhood, and town characteristics, 1967 survey, 9306–1.7

Housing adequacy, quality, and affordability by condition and age of unit, rent paid or owner expense and share of income, and metro-nonmetro location, 1980, article, 1702–1.406

Housing and financial characteristics, and unit and neighborhood quality, for 15 SMSAs, 1978, annual survey special supplement, 2485–8

Index by Subjects and Names

Housing and households detailed characteristics, and unit and neighborhood quality, by inside-outside central cities, 1979-82 surveys, SMSA rpt series, 2485–6

Housing and neighborhood quality indicators and attitudes, and occupant characteristics, by urban-rural location and region, 1981, annual survey, 2485–7

Housing and neighborhood quality indicators and attitudes, by occupant and unit characteristics, region, and metro-nonmetro location, 1981, annual survey, 2485–2.2

Housing energy use, costs, expenditures, and conservation, and household and housing characteristics, survey series, 3166–7

Housing occupancy and unit and household characteristics, by region and metro-nonmetro residence, 1983, biennial survey, 2485–1

Housing vacancy and occupancy rates, and vacant unit characteristics, by metro-nonmetro location and region, selected years 1960-83, annual rpt, 2484–1

Income (household) and cash and noncash transfer program participation, by sociodemographic characteristics, quarterly rpt, 2542–2

Income (legal) not reported on Federal income tax returns by source, and legal and illegal underground income, with bibl, 1974-81, article, 2702–1.419

Income (natl) by type, 1929-83, annual rpt, 204–1.1

Income (personal), and BEA and IRS calculations of adjusted gross income, by source, 1981-82, article, 2702–1.414

Income (personal) per capita and by source, and earnings by industry div, by State, MSA, and county, 1977-82, annual regional rpts, 2704–2

Income (personal) per capita and by source, earnings by major industry group, and social insurance contributions, by region and State, 1929-82, 2708–40

Income (taxable) not reported on individual and corporate returns, and associated Federal revenue losses, by detailed legal and illegal source, 1973-81, 8308–26

Income averages of OASI beneficiaries, and beneficiaries by income level, by beneficiary characteristics and income source, before and after receipt of 1st benefit, 1969-77, article, 4742–1.418

Income from rent, *Business Conditions Digest,* historical supplement and methodology, 2708–31

Income from rent, *Business Conditions Digest,* monthly rpt, 2702–3.5

Income tax returns of corporations, detailed income and tax items by industry, 1981, annual rpt, 8304–4

Income tax returns of corporations with foreign tax credit, income and deductions by type, asset size, and selected industry group, 1980, article, 8302–2.415

Income tax returns of elderly, by income statement and tax item and income level, 1981 with trends from 1977, article, 8302–2.412

Income tax returns of individuals by tax return item, State, and occupation, and income by source and tax owed, by income level, selected years 1916-80, conf papers, 8308–28.1

Index by Subjects and Names

Rental industries

Income tax returns of individuals, detailed data, 1982, annual rpt, 8304–2

Income tax returns of partnerships, receipts by source, deductions by type, and establishments, by selected industry, 1982, annual article, 8302–2.416

Income tax returns of sole proprietorships, receipts, deductions by type, payroll, and net income, by major industry, 1982, annual article, 8302–2.413

Michigan bankruptcy filings, by filer type, moving history, income, creditor action, debt and asset type, credit status, exemptions claimed, and county, 1979-81, hearings, 21528–57.3

Multinatl corporation income reallocation through regulation of intercorporate transactions, by tax item, treaty status, asset size, industry, and tax haven country, 1982, 8008–110

Natural gas interstate pipeline company detailed financial and operating data, by firm, 1983, annual rpt, 3164–38

New Communities program of HUD, activities, costs, land sales, and community and population characteristics, for 13 communities, 1970s-83, 5188–107

NYC population size, demographic characteristics, and rental housing, in 5 neighborhoods by census tract, 1980 with percent change from 1970, article, 9385–1.403

Partnership finances, tax deductions, and employment, by industry div and size, 1979, article, 8302–2.411

Personal consumption expenditures, natl income and product account, *Survey of Current Business,* monthly rpt, monthly and annual tables, 2702–1.23

Public building construction, alteration, and leasing projects, description and cost by location, Dec 1983, annual listing, 9454–12

Public housing under private mgmt, assessment by housing officials and managers, and tenants, with operating costs, crime, and rent delinquency by project type and location, 1982, 5188–103

Railroad finances and operations, detailed data by firm, class of service, and district, 1983, annual rpt, 9486–6.1

Royalty receipts and payments, for US and selected foreign countries, selected years 1967-81, annual rpt, 9624–10.1

Senate salaries, expenses, and contingent fund disbursements, by payee, detailed listings, 1st half FY84, semiannual rpt, 25922–1

Small Business Admin loan and contract activity by program, and balance sheets, FY83, annual rpt, 9764–1.1

Vacant housing characteristics and costs, and occupancy and vacancy rates, by region and metro-nonmetro location, quarterly rpt, 2482–1

1 Western States rent and homeownership costs, Fed Reserve 12th District, quarterly rpt, 9393–1.4

see also Housing tenure

see also Landlord-tenant relations

see also Rent supplements

see also Rental industries

Rent supplements

AFDC eligibility under Omnibus Budget Reconciliation Act, effect on caseloads and recipient benefits and living costs, 1981-83, GAO rpt, 26131–11

Budget of US, effects of Reagan Admin policy changes, by detailed program, FY85, annual rpt, 104–21

Census of Housing, 1980: inventory, occupancy, and unit characteristics, changes from 1973 by region and inside-outside SMSAs and central cities, series, 2473–3

Children and youth benefitting from Fed Govt public welfare programs and tax expenditures, participation and funding for 71 programs, FY81-83, 21968–30

Community dev programs funding and activities, for 5 HUD programs, FY83, annual rpt, 5124–5

Fed Govt programs and mgmt cost control proposals, 3-year savings by function and agency, and financial and operating data, 1960s-81, 16908–1.23

Fresno, Calif, economic, population, labor, and housing indicators, various periods 1974-85, hearing, 21248–84

Hispanic Americans socioeconomic and demographic characteristics, and compared to non-Hispanics, selected years 1970-83, chartbook, 2328–48

Housing and households characteristics, and low-income housing construction and availability, 1970s-83, hearing, 21968–28.1

Housing and neighborhood quality indicators and attitudes, and occupant characteristics, by urban-rural location and region, 1981, annual survey, 2485–7

HUD rental assistance certificates for low-income single parents, by community, 1984 press release, 5006–3.35

HUD rental rehabilitation projects, local funding and Section 8 rent supplements for 22 States and 275 communities, 1984 press release, 5006–3.30

Older persons nutrition services program operations and assessment, and participant sociodemographic, health, and diet characteristics, 1976 and 1982, 4608–16

Public noncash transfers counted as income, effect on poverty population size by selected recipient characteristics, 1979-83, 2626–2.52

Public noncash transfers counted as income, effects on poverty population size by recipient characteristics, 1979-82, 2626–2.50

Rental industries

Agriculture census, 1982: farms, farmland, production, finances, and operator characteristics, by county, final State rpt series, 2331–1

Auto and truck rental receipts, 1983, annual rpt, 2413–8

Auto fleet size, trip characteristics, and energy use, by fleet type, 1970s-83, annual rpt, 3304–5.2

Census of Construction Industries, 1982: financial and operating data, by SIC 4-digit industry and State, final rpt series, 2373–1

Census of Service Industries, 1982: employment, establishments, receipts, and payroll, by SIC 2- to 4-digit kind of business, SMSA, county, and city, State rpt series, 2391–1

Census of Service Industries, 1982: employment, establishments, receipts, and payroll, by SIC 4-digit kind of business and State, preliminary rpt, 2390–2.8

Computer systems and equipment of Fed Govt, inventory by manufacturer, type, agency, and location, FY83, last issue of annual rpt, 9454–4

Construction industries census, 1982: financial and operating data, by SIC 4-digit industry and State, preliminary rpt series, 2371–1

County Business Patterns: establishments, employees, and payrolls, by SIC 4-digit industry and county, 1981, annual State rpt series, 2326–8

County Business Patterns: establishments, employees, and payrolls, by SIC 4-digit industry and county, 1982, annual State rpt series, 2326–6

DOD procurement, prime contract awards by detailed procurement category, FY80-83, annual rpt, 3544–18

Employment, earnings, and hours, by SIC 4-digit nonfarm industry, monthly 1974-Feb 1984, annual update, 6744–4

Farm finances, production, expenses by type, and domestic economic impact, selected years 1972-82 and preliminary 1983-84, annual rpt, 1544–19

Fed Govt motor vehicle fleet costs and operating data, by agency, FY83, annual rpt, 9454–9

Fed Govt procurement contract awards, by State, agency, procurement and contractor type, and for top 100 contractors, quarterly rpt, 102–6

Fed Govt programs and mgmt cost control proposals, 3-year savings by function and agency, and financial and operating data, 1960s-81, 16908–1.29

Finances and operations, by SIC 2- to 4-digit industry, 1970s-83 and projected to 1988, annual rpt, 2014–4

Franchise business opportunities, by firm and kind of business, 1984 annual listing, 2044–27

Franchises of firms engaged in distribution of goods and services by kind of business, establishments by State, and sales, 1982-84, annual rpt, 2014–5

Income tax returns of sole proprietorships, detailed data by industry div and selected industry group, 1981, annual rpt, 8304–7

Input-output structure of US economy, detailed interindustry transactions for 537 industries, and components of final demand, 1977 benchmark data, 2708–17

Intermodal containers and equipment owned by US shipping and leasing companies, inventory by type and size, 1983, annual rpt, 7704–10

Lease financing receivables of 34 nonbank firms and their subsidiaries, 1982, technical paper, 9375–11.3

Leasing and other financial services of interstate bank service offices, by instn and State, 1981-83, 9371–13

Motor carriers (Class I interstate) finances, operations, equipment, employment, and payroll, by district, 1982, annual rpt, 9486–5.3

Pollution abatement equipment leasing costs, by SIC 2- to 4-digit industry, State, and SMSA, 1982, annual Current Industrial Rpt, 2506–3.6

Rental industries

Retail trade census, 1982: employment, establishments, sales, and payroll, by SIC 4-digit kind of business and State, preliminary rpt series, 2395–1

Transportation census, 1982: trucks, by detailed characteristics, miles traveled, and type of product carried, State rpt series, 2573–1

Virgin Islands economic censuses, 1982: employment, establishments, payroll, and receipts, by SIC 1- to 4-digit industry, island, and city, 2593–1

see also under By Industry in the "Index by Categories"

Renter households

see Housing tenure

Reorganization of government

see Government reorganization

Repair industries

- Aircraft operating costs by component for privately owned small planes, and Fed Govt mileage reimbursement rates, 1983, annual rpt, 9454–13.2
- Census of Population and Housing, 1980: detailed population and housing characteristics, by county, city, and census tract, State and SMSA rpt series, 2551–2
- Census of Population, 1980: detailed socioeconomic and demographic characteristics, by age, sex, race, Hispanic origin, occupation, and industry, State rpt series, 2531–4
- Census of Population, 1980: detailed socioeconomic characteristics, by county, city, and inside-outside SMSAs and central cities, State rpt series, 2531–3
- Census of Population, 1980: labor force, by sex, detailed occupation, and region, with comparison to 1970 census, supplementary rpt, 2535–1.12
- Census of Service Industries, 1982: employment, establishments, receipts, and payroll, by SIC 2- to 4-digit kind of business, SMSA, county, and city, State rpt series, 2391–1
- Census of Service Industries, 1982: employment, establishments, receipts, and payroll, by SIC 4-digit kind of business and State, preliminary rpt, 2390–2.11
- Collective bargaining agreements expiring during year, covered workers by SIC 2-digit industry, firm, and union, with summary of key provisions, 1984, annual rpt, 6784–9
- Construction industries census, 1982: financial and operating data, by SIC 4-digit industry and State, final rpt series, 2373–1
- County Business Patterns: establishments, employees, and payrolls, by SIC 4-digit industry and county, 1981, annual State rpt series, 2326–8
- County Business Patterns: establishments, employees, and payrolls, by SIC 4-digit industry and county, 1982, annual State rpt series, 2326–6
- Employment by detailed occupation, for 29 SIC 2-digit nonmanufacturing industries, 1981 BLS survey, 6748–60
- Employment, earnings, and hours, by selected SIC 1- to 4-digit industry, State, and for 278 major labor areas, 1939-83, annual rpt, 6744–5
- Employment, earnings, and hours, by SIC 4-digit nonfarm industry, monthly 1974-Feb 1984, annual update, 6744–4

Finances and operations, by SIC 2- to 4-digit industry, 1970s-83 and projected to 1988, annual rpt, 2014–4

- Foreign trade zones, activities, and value of goods entering and leaving zones, 1973-82, GAO rpt, 26119–56
- Franchise business opportunities, by firm and kind of business, 1984 annual listing, 2044–27
- Income tax returns of corporations, detailed income and tax items by industry, 1981, annual rpt, 8304–4
- Income tax returns of partnerships, detailed data by industry, 1981 estimates, annual article, 8302–2.404
- Income tax returns of partnerships, receipts by source, deductions by type, and establishments, by selected industry, 1982, annual article, 8302–2.416
- Income tax returns of sole proprietorships, detailed data by industry div and selected industry group, 1981, annual rpt, 8304–7
- Income tax returns of sole proprietorships, receipts, deductions by type, payroll, and net income, by major industry, 1982, annual article, 8302–2.413
- Input-output structure of US economy, detailed interindustry transactions for 537 industries, and components of final demand, 1977 benchmark data, 2708–17
- Minority group and women employment, by occupational group and SIC 2- to 3-digit industry, 1981, annual rpt, 9244–1.1
- Occupational injury and illness rates, by SIC 2- to 4-digit industry, 1982, annual rpt, 6844–1
- Occupational manpower needs and supply by detailed occupation, and educational and training program enrollees and grads by detailed field, 1982 and 1995, biennial rpt, 6744–3
- *Occupational Outlook Handbook,* 1984-85 biennial rpt, 6744–1
- Receipts for selected services, by SIC 2- to 4-digit kind of business, 1983, annual rpt, 2413–8
- Retail trade census, 1982: employment, establishments, sales, and payroll, by SIC 4-digit kind of business and State, preliminary rpt series, 2395–1
- Underground economy, household expenditures and participation by type of goods or service and sociodemographic characteristics, with methodology and bibl, 1981 survey, 8308–27
- Virgin Islands economic censuses, 1982: employment, establishments, payroll, and receipts, by SIC 1- to 4-digit industry, island, and city, 2593–1
- Wages and benefits of technicians and apprentices, for 5 types of electrical repair shops in 19 SMSAs, Nov 1981 survey, 6787–6.197

see also Automobile repair

see also Housing maintenance and repair

see also under By Industry in the "Index by Categories"

Republic of China

see Taiwan

Republic of Korea

see Korea, South

Republican Party

Campaign finances and Fed Election Commission monitoring activities, 1984 Federal elections, biennial rpt series, 9276–2

Index by Subjects and Names

- Campaign finances, election procedures, and Fed Election Commission monitoring activities, press release series, 9276–1
- Campaign funding and activities of Fed Election Commission, and political action committees funding, 1983, annual rpt, 9274–1
- Campaign funding by political action committee and candidate, proposed candidate spending limits, voting rates by party, and political opinions, by State, 1960-82, hearings, 25688–6
- Campaign funding by political action committees to individual congressmen, and public opinion on reform proposals and assn influence, 1970s-83, hearings, 21428–7

Research

- Animal protection, licensing, and inspection activities of USDA, and animals used in research, by State, FY83, annual rpt, 1394–10
- Corporate income tax returns, detailed income and tax items by industry, 1981, annual rpt, 8304–4
- Council for Mutual Economic Assistance science and technology dev and transfer between USSR and other member countries, 1940s-81, 2326–9.7
- County Business Patterns: establishments, employees, and payrolls, by SIC 4-digit industry and county, 1982, annual State rpt series, 2326–6
- Crime and criminal justice research sponsored by Natl Inst of Justice, summary rpt series, 6066–20
- Economic Analysis Bur specialized and preliminary economic research, staff paper series, 2706–5
- Employment, earnings, and hours, by SIC 4-digit nonfarm industry, monthly 1974-Feb 1984, annual update, 6744–4
- Endangered animals and plants foreign trade including reexports of live specimens and products, by purpose, country, and species, 1982, annual rpt, 5504–19
- Fed Govt statistical policies relating to technical operation of programs, methodology, and use of Federal data, working paper series, 106–4
- Forest research project descriptions and bibl, 1982, annual rpt, 1204–14
- Forest Service research funding and number of publications issued, FY80-83, annual rpt, 1204–1.3
- France Brittany coast oil spill cleanup and research costs, marine and tourism industry losses, and recreation losses of tourists and residents, 1971-79, 2178–13
- Natl Bur of Standards standard reference and research materials available, 1984-85, biennial catalog, 2214–2
- NOAA scientific and technical publications, monthly listing, 2142–1
- NSF research programs, activities, and funding, FY82-83, annual rpt, 9624–6
- OASDHI economic effects, use of models in research, 1984 narrative article, 4742–1.419
- Puerto Rico organizations in US and Puerto Rico, philanthropic grants received, by foundation, purpose, and recipient, 1979-81, hearings, 21788–137.1
- Radioactive waste and spent fuel generation, inventory, disposal by site, reprocessing,

and characteristics, by source, as of 1983 and projected to 2020, annual rpt, 3364–2

Science Indicators, R&D expenditures, innovations, research, and higher education, with foreign comparisons, 1960s- 83, annual rpt, 9624–10

Social security research projects of SSA, narrative summary, FY84-86, annual rpt, 4744–11

see also Consumer surveys
see also Defense research
see also Educational research
see also Energy research and development
see also Federal funding for research and development
see also Market research
see also Medical research
see also Opinion and attitude surveys
see also Research and development
see also under specific academic and scientific disciplines

Research & Forecasts, Inc.

"Small Business Speaks: The Chemical Bank Report", 21728–52.3

Research and development

- Aerial survey R&D publications, and sources of natural resource and environmental data gathered by air- and spacecraft, quarterly listing, 9502–7
- Air pollution control programs, emissions standards dev, monitoring, and enforcement, 1982, annual rpt, 9194–4
- Auto safety and experimental vehicle designs, 1982, conf proceedings, annual rpt, 7764–3
- Census of Population, 1980: detailed socioeconomic and demographic characteristics, by age, sex, race, Hispanic origin, occupation, and industry, State rpt series, 2531–4
- Computer specialists sociodemographic, educational, and employment characteristics, and Fed Govt support by agency, 1978, biennial Current Population Rpt, 2546–2.124
- Council for Mutual Economic Assistance science and technology dev and transfer between USSR and other member countries, 1940s-81, 2326–9.7
- County Business Patterns: establishments, employees, and payrolls, by SIC 4-digit industry and county, 1981, annual State rpt series, 2326–8
- County Business Patterns: establishments, employees, and payrolls, by SIC 4-digit industry and county, 1982, annual State rpt series, 2326–6
- EC trade promotion policies and financing by industry, and effect on competing US industries, 1970s-82, 9886–4.73
- Engineers sociodemographic, educational, and employment characteristics, and Federal support by agency, 1978, Current Population Rpt, 2546–2.121
- Expenditures for R&D, by industry, program, and Federal agency, and high-technology trade performance, selected years 1960-FY84, 26306–6.77
- Expenditures for R&D by source, and scientists education and employment, detailed data by field, selected years 1953-84, annual rpt, 9624–18
- Foreign and US economic and employment indicators and balance of payments, and

US exports by selected commodity, by world area and country, 1970s-83, annual rpt, 2044–26

- Foreign and US R&D expenditures, ratio to GNP, 1961-80, annual rpt, 444–1.4
- Forests (tropical) status by country and world region, conservation methods, and mgmt role of US, foreign, and intl groups, 1977-80s and projected to 2000, 26358–101.1
- Higher education instn and federally funded center expenditures for R&D, by field, source of funds, instn, and State, FY82, annual rpt, 9627–13
- Higher education instns R&D equipment age, cost, funding sources, and users, for computer and physical sciences and engineering, 1982, 9626–2.138
- Higher education instns R&D expenditures, and science and engineering employment and grad students, by field, 1972-83, biennial rpt, 9627–24
- Higher education R&D and science-related Fed Govt funding, and total and federally funded expenditures, by instn, FY82, 9626–2.136
- Hwy design and construction R&D, quarterly journal, 7552–3
- Income tax returns of corporations with foreign tax credit, income and deductions by type, asset size, and selected industry group, 1980, article, 8302–2.415
- Industry R&D expenditures by funding source, and projected impact on output, employment, and hours of labor, by selected industry, various periods 1953-90, hearings, 25368–133
- Industry R&D expenditures by funding source, and scientists and engineers employed, by SIC 2- and 3-digit industry, 1982 with trends from 1962, annual rpt, 9626–2.139
- Industry R&D funding and employment of scientists and engineers, by industry group, firm size, and funding source, 1956-82, annual rpt, 9627–21
- Input-output structure of US economy, detailed interindustry transactions for 537 industries, and components of final demand, 1977 benchmark data, 2708–17
- Metals resource recovery through leaching technologies, characteristics of methods and operations, regulation, and research, series, 5606–6
- Multinatl corporation income reallocation through regulation of intercorporate transactions, by tax item, treaty status, asset size, industry, and tax haven country, 1982, 8008–110
- NSF Science Resources Studies Div activities, project descriptions, and 1973-83 publications, 1983 annual listing, 9624–21
- Nuclear industry nongovt employment by industry segment, occupation, and census div, and DOE and NRC nuclear employment, 1968-83, biennial rpt, 3004–11
- Office of Technology Assessment activities, programs, and publications list, 1983, annual rpt, 26354–3
- Pharmaceutical industry R&D costs and finances, selected years 1962-83, hearing, 25528–98

Robots for industrial use, R&D, training, and employment impacts, US with comparisons to foreign countries, 1980s with projections to 1992, 26358–105

- Science and engineering enrollment, degrees, and employment, R&D funding, and related topics, highlights series, 9626–2
- Science and engineering grads of 1980-81, employment characteristics or grad enrollment, by degree level, field, sex, and race, 1982, 9627–25
- *Science Indicators,* R&D expenditures, innovations, research, and higher education, with foreign comparisons, 1960s- 83, annual rpt, 9624–10
- Scientists and engineers employed at universities and colleges, by field, sex, State, and instn, Jan 1983 and selected trends from 1967, annual survey, 9627–11
- Scientists and engineers in R&D, salaries by degree, type of establishment, age, experience, and field, 1984, annual rpt, 3004–1
- Semiconductor industry subsidies of Japan govt by program, with financial and operating data by firm, R&D, and comparisons to US industry, 1970s-83, hearings, 21368–46.1
- Service industry census, 1982: employment, establishments, receipts, and payroll, by SIC 2- to 4-digit kind of business, SMSA, county, and city, State rpt series, 2391–1
- *Statistical Abstract of US,* social, political, and economic data, 1950s-83 and trends, annual rpt, 2324–1.3
- Transit systems research publications, 2nd half FY83, semiannual listing, 7882–1
- *see also* Defense research
- *see also* Energy research and development
- *see also* Federal funding for research and development
- *see also* Federally Funded R&D Centers
- *see also* Inventions
- *see also* Technological innovations

Resek, Robert W.

- "Comparative Performance of Multiple Reaction Function Equations Estimated by Canonical Methods", 9373–3.26
- "Determinants of Monetary Policy in France, The Federal Republic of Germany, Italy and the UK: A Comparative Analysis", 9373–3.26

Reserve components

see Armed services reserves
see Coast Guard Reserve
see National guard

Reserve Officers Training Corps

- Budget of DOD, itemized account of legislative history, FY84, annual rpt, 3504–7
- Enrollment in college ROTC, by service branch, monthly rpt, 3542–14.1
- Medical personnel, trainees, and accessions by source, by occupation, specialty, and service branch, FY83, annual rpt, 3544–24
- Training and education programs of DOD, funding, staff, students, and facilities, by service branch and reserve component, FY85, annual rpt, 3504–5

Reservoirs

Army Corps of Engineers activities and projects, FY83 and trends from 1800s, annual rpt, 3754–1

Reservoirs

Colorado River Storage Project finances, water resource dev, power production, and other activities in western States, FY83, annual rpt, 5824–3

Construction industries census, 1982: financial and operating data, by SIC 4-digit industry and State, preliminary rpt series, 2371–1

Fed Govt reclamation projects in western US, electric power capacities and transmission miles, and water storage and carriage facilities, by State, FY81, annual rpt, 5824–1.1

Fish and eggs for stocking distributed from natl hatcheries, by species, hatchery, and jurisdiction, FY83, annual rpt, 5504–10

Fish and Wildlife Service conservation and research project descriptions and results, by program, FY83, annual rpt, 5504–20

Foreign and US major dams, reservoirs, and hydroelectric plants, listing with location and characteristics, as of June 1983, 5828–13

Nevada water supply, streamflow, reservoir storage, and precipitation, 1984 water year, annual rpt, 1264–8

Oregon water supply, streamflow by station and reservoir storage, 1984 water year, annual rpt, 1264–9

Pollution-caused fish kills, by State, location, and pollution source, monthly 1978-80, annual rpt, 9204–3

Reclamation Bur water storage and carriage facilities, by type, as of Sept 1983, annual listing, 5824–7

Sedimentation control, surveillance, and research activity of Fed Govt, by project, agency, region, and State, 1982, annual rpt, 5664–9

Tennessee Valley river control and reservoir elevations, storage, flows, and hydroelectric generating capacity use, 1981, annual rpt, 9804–7

TVA activities, financial and operating data by program and facility, and power sales by customer, FY83, annual rpt, 9804–1

Utah water supply, streamflow, reservoir storage, and precipitation, 1984 water year, annual rpt, 1264–6

Water supply and quality, and effect of coal mining operations, for selected river basins in Eastern and Interior coal provinces, series, 5666–15

Water supply and quality, and effect of coal mining operations, for selected river basins in Western coal provinces, series, 5666–19

Water supply and quality, floods, drought, mudslides, and other hydrologic events, by State, 1983, annual rpt, 5664–12

Water supply and quality in streams and lakes, and groundwater levels in wells, by drainage basin, 1980, annual State rpt series, 5666–12

Water supply and quality in streams and lakes, and groundwater levels in wells, by drainage basin, 1981, annual State rpt series, 5666–16

Water supply and quality in streams and lakes, and groundwater levels in wells, by drainage basin, 1982, annual State rpt series, 5666–20

Water supply and quality in streams and lakes, and groundwater levels in wells, by drainage basin, 1983, annual State rpt series, 5666–10

Water supply in US and Canada, streamflow, well and reservoir levels, and dissolved solids and temperature in 6 US rivers, by station, monthly rpt, 5662–3

Waterborne disease outbreaks and cases, by type, source, and location, 1983, annual rpt, 4205–35

Western US water supply, and snow survey results, monthly State rpt series, 1266–2

Western US water supply, reservoir storage by large reservoir and State, and streamflow conditions, as of Oct 1984, annual rpt, 1264–4

Western US water supply, streamflow and reservoir storage forecasts by stream and station, Jan-May monthly rpt, 1262–1

Residential energy use see Housing energy use

Resins see Chemicals and chemical industry see Gum and wood chemicals see Plastics and plastics industry

Resorts see Hotels and motels

Resource Planning Associates, Inc. "Potential for Industrial Cogeneration Development To Defer New-Utility Electric-Power Capacity over the Next Decade", 3008–92

Resources Consulting Group, Inc. "Incentive Regulation in the Electric Utility Industry, Final Report", 3088–17

Resources for the Future, Inc. "Meeting Future Needs for U.S. Food, Fiber, and Forest Products", 1008–47.2 "Resource and Environmental Impacts of Trends in U.S. Agriculture", 9188–94

Respiratory diseases Agent Orange exposed Air Force personnel diseases and disorders, by disease type, age, and officer status, 1984 rpt, 3604–3

Air pollutant and radiation indoor levels by emissions source, and household exposure and health effects by pollutant type, various periods 1966-83, hearings, 21708–102

Air pollutant sulfur dioxide health effects studies, and cases of selected respiratory diseases by sex and age, 1970s-80, hearings, 25328–25

Deaths and death rates, by cause and age, provisional 1982-83, US Vital Statistics annual rpt, 4144–7

Deaths and death rates by detailed cause and demographic characteristics, 1979 and selected trends, US Vital Statistics annual rpt, 4144–2.1

Deaths and death rates, by detailed geographic area, cause, and demographic characteristics, 1979, US Vital Statistics annual rpt, 4144–3

Deaths and death rates, by selected cause and demographic characteristics, 1981, US Vital Statistics advance rpt, 4146–5.78

Deaths and death rates, by selected cause and demographic characteristics, 1982, US Vital Statistics advance rpt, 4146–5.81

Disability Insurance beneficiaries sociodemographic and medical characteristics, 1977-79, annual rpt, 4744–20

Environmental pollution-related disease research activities and publications, Sept 1982-Aug 1983, annual rpt, 9184–9

Index by Subjects and Names

Hospital discharges and length of stay, by patient characteristics, facility size, procedure performed, diagnosis, and region, 1982, annual rpt, 4147–13.78

Infant deaths by detailed cause, geographic location, age, race, and sex, 1979, US Vital Statistics annual rpt, 4144–2.2

Natl Heart, Lung, and Blood Inst activities and funding, with morbidity and mortality data, various periods 1940-88, annual rpt, 4474–22

Natl Heart, Lung, and Blood Inst organization, disease and mortality data, and funds and recipients, FY83 with trends from 1900, annual fact book, 4474–15

Older persons by demographic, socioeconomic, and health characteristics, selected years 1900-81 and projected to 2050, Current Population Rpt, 2546–2.125

Smoking and health research, article abstracts and indexes, 1983, annual rpt, 4044–8

Smoking related to chronic obstructive lung disease and deaths, by sociodemographic and smoking characteristics, literature review, 1984 annual Surgeon General rpt, 4044–6

Uranium ore tailings at active mills, EPA radon and radionuclide emmission standards and US and foreign exposure and health effects, various periods 1957-83, hearings, 21208–17

see also Allergies *see also* Black lung *see also* Pneumonia and influenza *see also* Tuberculosis *see also* under By Disease in the "Index by Categories"

Rest homes see Nursing homes

Restaurants and restaurant industry Advertising expenditures by media type, and advertising to sales ratio, by selected food item, 1970-79 with some trends from 1955, 1548–234

Carbon monoxide atmospheric concentrations and levels within buildings and along commuting and residential driving routes, for 4 cities, Jan-Mar 1981, 9198–110

Census of Population, 1980: detailed socioeconomic and demographic characteristics, by age, sex, race, Hispanic origin, occupation, and industry, State rpt series, 2531–4

Census of Population, 1980: detailed socioeconomic characteristics, by county, city, and inside-outside SMSAs and central cities, State rpt series, 2531–3

Census of Population, 1980: labor force, by sex, detailed occupation, and region, with comparison to 1970 census, supplementary rpt, 2535–1.12

Census of Retail Trade, 1982: employment, establishments, sales, and payroll, by SIC 2- to 4-digit kind of business, SMSA, and retail district, State rpt series, 2401–1

Census of Retail Trade, 1982: employment, establishments, sales, and payroll, by SIC 2- to 4-digit kind of business, SMSA, county, and city, State rpt series, 2397–1

Census of Retail Trade, 1982: employment, establishments, sales, and payroll, by State, preliminary rpt, 2395–1.23, 2395–1.24, 2395–1.25

Index by Subjects and Names

Retail trade

Collective bargaining agreements expiring during year, covered workers by SIC 2-digit industry, firm, and union, with summary of key provisions, 1984, annual rpt, 6784–9

Construction industries census, 1982: financial and operating data, by SIC 4-digit industry and State, final rpt series, 2373–1

Construction industries census, 1982: financial and operating data, by SIC 4-digit industry and State, preliminary rpt series, 2371–1

Consumer research and marketing devs, and consumption and price trends, quarterly rpt with articles, 1541–7

County Business Patterns: establishments, employees, and payrolls, by SIC 4-digit industry and county, 1981, annual State rpt series, 2326–8

County Business Patterns: establishments, employees, and payrolls, by SIC 4-digit industry and county, 1982, annual State rpt series, 2326–6

CPI by detailed component, for US city average, 28 SMSAs, and 4 regions by population size, monthly rpt, 6762–2

Employment, earnings, and hours, by selected SIC 1- to 4-digit industry, State, and for 278 major labor areas, 1939-83, annual rpt, 6744–5

Employment, earnings, and hours, by SIC 4-digit nonfarm industry, monthly 1974-Feb 1984, annual update, 6744–4

Energy use in nonresidential buildings, expenditures, and conservation, by building characteristics, EIA survey series, 3166–8

Fed Govt employee travel expenses for official business trips, and reimbursement rates, for high rate cities, 1983, annual rpt, 9454–16

Fed Govt programs and mgmt cost control proposals, 3-year savings by function and agency, and financial and operating data, 1960s-81, 16908–1.23

Food consumption and nutrient intake by individuals, by food group, source, and socioeconomic characteristics, 1977-78 natl survey, final rpt series, 1356–4

Food prices (farm-retail), marketing cost components, and industry finances and productivity, selected years 1967-83, annual rpt, 1544–9

France Brittany coast oil spill cleanup and research costs, marine and tourism industry losses, and recreation losses of tourists and residents, 1971-79, 2178–13

Franchise business opportunities, by firm and kind of business, 1984 annual listing, 2044–27

Franchises of firms engaged in distribution of goods and services by kind of business, establishments by State, and sales, 1982-84, annual rpt, 2014–5

Income tax returns of corporations, detailed income and tax items by industry, 1981, annual rpt, 8304–4

Income tax returns of corporations with foreign tax credit, income and deductions by type, asset size, and selected industry group, 1980, article, 8302–2.415

Income tax returns of partnerships, detailed data by industry, 1981 estimates, annual article, 8302–2.404

Income tax returns of partnerships, receipts by source, deductions by type, and establishments, by selected industry, 1982, annual article, 8302–2.416

Income tax returns of sole proprietorships, detailed data by industry div and selected industry group, 1981, annual rpt, 8304–7

Income tax returns of sole proprietorships, receipts, deductions by type, payroll, and net income, by major industry, 1982, annual article, 8302–2.413

Income tax returns with investment credits, for individuals by income, and for sole proprietorships by industry, 1981, article, 8302–2.409

Input-output structure of US economy, detailed interindustry transactions for 85 industries, and components of final demand, 1977, article, 2702–1.421

Input-output structure of US economy, detailed interindustry transactions for 537 industries, and components of final demand, 1977 benchmark data, 2708–17

Meat marketing and distribution establishments, sales, and per capita consumption, 1950s-82 with trends from 1929, 1548–232

Minority group and women employment, by occupational group and SIC 2- to 3-digit industry, 1981, annual rpt, 9244–1.1

Occupational injury and illness rates, by SIC 2- to 4-digit industry, 1982, annual rpt, 6844–1

Occupational manpower needs and supply by detailed occupation, and educational and training program enrollees and grads by detailed field, 1982 and 1995, biennial rpt, 6744–3

Occupational Outlook Handbook, 1984-85 biennial rpt, 6744–1

Productivity, hours, and employment indexes for eating and drinking places, 1958-82, annual rpt, 6824–1.4

Sales and inventories, by kind of business, region, census div, and selected State, SMSA, and city, and seasonal adjustments, monthly rpt, 2413–3

Sales, inventories, purchases, gross margin, and accounts receivable, by SIC 2- to 4-digit kind of business and type of ownership, 1983, annual rpt, 2413–5

Scientists, engineers, and technicians employment in transportation, utilities, and retail and wholesale trade, by field of science and industry, 1982, 9628–72

Tips and meal expenditures at eating places, visits to eating places, 1982, article, 8302–2.406

Virgin Islands economic censuses, 1982: employment, establishments, payroll, and receipts, by SIC 1- to 4-digit industry, island, and city, 2593–1

see also under By Industry in the "Index by Categories"

Retail centers

see Shopping centers

Retail trade

American Samoa minimum wage rates, employment, earnings, and benefits, by establishment and industry, Nov 1983, biennial rpt, 6504–6

Business activity indicators (nonfinancial), 1982, annual rpt, 9364–5.9

Business and financial statistics, quarterly chartbook, 9362–2.2

Business Conditions Digest, current data on economic, business, and financial conditions and cyclical fluctuations, monthly rpt, 2702–3

Business Conditions Digest, historical supplement on economic, business, and financial conditions and cyclical fluctuations, with methodology, 1947-82, 2708–31

Business statistics, detailed data for major industries and economic indicators, *Survey of Current Business,* monthly rpt, 2702–1.4

Census of Construction Industries, 1982: financial and operating data, by SIC 4-digit industry and State, final rpt series, 2373–1

Census of Population and Housing, 1980: detailed population and housing characteristics, by county, city, and census tract, State and SMSA rpt series, 2551–2

Census of Population, 1980: detailed socioeconomic and demographic characteristics, by age, sex, race, Hispanic origin, occupation, and industry, State rpt series, 2531–4

Census of Population, 1980: detailed socioeconomic characteristics, by county, city, and inside-outside SMSAs and central cities, State rpt series, 2531–3

Census of Population, 1980: labor force, by sex, detailed occupation, and region, with comparison to 1970 census, supplementary rpt, 2535–1.12

Census of Transportation, 1982: trucks, by detailed characteristics, miles traveled, and type of product carried, State rpt series, 2573–1

China economic conditions, agricultural and industrial production, trade, and domestic and foreign investment, 1980-85, 2048–106

Clothing (retail) business labor productivity, by kind of business, 1967-83, article, 6722–1.463

Coastal environmental characteristics, fish, wildlife, and use, and population socioeconomic data, for individual areas, series, 5506–4

Collective bargaining agreements expiring during year, covered workers by SIC 2-digit industry, firm, and union, with summary of key provisions, 1984, annual rpt, 6784–9

Construction industries census, 1982: financial and operating data, by SIC 4-digit industry and State, preliminary rpt series, 2371–1

County and City Data Book, detailed socioeconomic and demographic data for States, counties, and cities, selected years 1976-82, 2328–1

County Business Patterns: establishments, employees, and payrolls, by SIC 4-digit industry and county, 1981, annual State rpt series, 2326–8

County Business Patterns: establishments, employees, and payrolls, by SIC 4-digit industry and county, 1982, annual State rpt series, 2326–6

Earnings by industry div, and personal income per capita and by source, by State, MSA, and county, 1977-82, annual regional rpts, 2704–2

Retail trade

Earnings by major industry group, and personal income per capita and by source, by region and State, 1929-82, 2708-40

Earnings, weekly averages, monthly rpt, 23842-1.2

Economic and demographic trends for IRS regions, districts, and service centers, 1972-82 and projected to 1990, annual rpt, 8304-8

Economic and financial trends, natl compounded annual rates of change, 1964-83, annual rpt, 9391-9.2

Economic indicators and components, and Fed Reserve 4th District business and financial conditions, monthly chartbook, 9377-10

Economic indicators, nonfinancial, monthly rpt, 9362-1.2

Economic trends, natl compounded annual rates of change, monthly rpt, 9391-3

Employee theft and misconduct in retail, hospital, and manufacturing establishments, by type and frequency of violation, 1978-80, 6068-178

Employment and earnings, detailed data, monthly rpt, 6742-2.5

Employment, earnings, and hours, by selected SIC 1- to 4-digit industry, State, and for 278 major labor areas, 1939-83, annual rpt, 6744-5

Employment, earnings, and hours, by SIC 4-digit nonfarm industry, monthly 1974-Feb 1984, annual update, 6744-4

Employment, earnings and hours, monthly press release, 6742-5

Employment situation, earnings, hours, and other BLS economic indicators, transcripts of BLS Commissioner's monthly testimony, periodic rpt, 23846-4

Employment, unemployment, and labor force, by demographic and employment characteristics, State, and for 30 metro areas and 11 large cities, 1983, annual rpt, 6744-7

Finances and operations, by SIC 2- to 4-digit industry, 1970s-83 and projected to 1988, annual rpt, 2014-4

Financial statements for manufacturing, mining, and trade corporations, by selected SIC 2- to 3-digit industry, quarterly rpt, 2502-1

Food consumer research and marketing devs, and consumption and price trends, quarterly rpt with articles, 1541-7

Foreign direct investment in US, major investors and investments by SIC 4-digit industry, transaction type and value, and location, 1983, annual rpt, 2044-20

Handbook of Labor Statistics, employment, earnings, hours, and labor force characteristics, 1982 and trends, detailed annual rpt, 6724-1

Income tax returns of corporations, detailed income and tax items by industry, 1981, annual rpt, 8304-4

Income tax returns of corporations, summary data by industry div, 1981 estimates, annual article, 8302-2.403

Income tax returns of corporations with foreign tax credit, income and deductions by type, asset size, and selected industry group, 1980, article, 8302-2.415

Income tax returns of foreign subsidiaries of US corporations, income and tax data, by industry and asset size, 1980, article, 8302-2.410

Income tax returns of partnerships, detailed data by industry, 1981 estimates, annual article, 8302-2.404

Income tax returns of partnerships, receipts by source, deductions by type, and establishments, by selected industry, 1982, annual article, 8302-2.416

Income tax returns of sole proprietorships, detailed data by industry div and selected industry group, 1981, annual rpt, 8304-7

Income tax returns of sole proprietorships, receipts, deductions by type, payroll, and net income, by major industry, 1982, annual article, 8302-2.413

Income tax returns with investment credits, for individuals by income, and for sole proprietorships by industry, 1981, article, 8302-2.409

Input-output structure of US economy, detailed interindustry transactions for 85 industries, and components of final demand, 1977, article, 2702-1.421

Input-output structure of US economy, detailed interindustry transactions for 537 industries, and components of final demand, 1977 benchmark data, 2708-17

Manufacturer-set retail prices under fair-trade law by brand and product, with manufacturers, market concentration, and sales, by industry, selected years 1952-82, 9406-1.38

Military post exchange operations, locations worldwide, sales by type of commodity or service and facility, and employment, FY83, annual rpt, 3504-10

Minority group and women's employment, by occupational group, SIC 2- to 3-digit industry, State, and SMSA, 1981, annual rpt, 9244-1

Natl income and product, comprehensive accounts and components, *Survey of Current Business,* monthly rpt, monthly and annual tables, 2702-1.27

New England States economic indicators, Fed Reserve 1st District, monthly rpt, 9373-2.4

New England States, FHLB 1st District member instns financial operations and housing industry indicators, monthly rpt, 9302-4

North Central States economic indicators, Fed Reserve 7th District monthly rpt, 9375-9

Occupational injuries, illnesses, and workdays lost, by SIC 2-digit industry, 1982-83, annual press release, 6844-3

Occupational injury and illness rates, by SIC 2- to 4-digit industry, 1982, annual rpt, 6844-1

Occupational manpower needs and supply by detailed occupation, and educational and training program enrollees and grads by detailed field, 1982 and 1995, biennial rpt, 6744-3

Occupational Outlook Handbook, 1984-85 biennial rpt, 6744-1

Sales and inventories, by kind of business, region, census div, and selected State, SMSA, and city, and seasonal adjustments, monthly rpt, 2413-3

Sales and inventories, monthly rpt, 23842-1.3

Sales, inventories, and inventory/sales ratios for manufacturing and trade, quarterly article, 2702-1.34

Index by Subjects and Names

Sales, inventories, purchases, gross margin, and accounts receivable, by SIC 2- to 4-digit kind of business and type of ownership, 1983, annual rpt, 2413-5

Sales of retailers, by kind of business, advance monthly rpt, 2413-2

Scientists, engineers, and technicians employment in transportation, utilities, and retail and wholesale trade, by field of science and industry, 1982, 9628-72

Seasonal adjustment methodology for economic time series, dev and design of Census Bur and other systems, with illustrative data, 1981 conf papers, 2626-7.5

Small and minority-owned businesses finances and operations, Federal contracts by agency, and worker characteristics, by industry, race, sex, and State, 1950s-83, annual rpt, 9764-6

Southeastern States financial and economic devs, Fed Reserve 6th District, monthly rpt with articles, 9371-1

Statistical Abstract of US, social, political, and economic data, 1950s-83 and trends, annual rpt, 2324-1.3

Texas border employment and economic impacts of Mexican peso devaluation, for 6 counties and 2 SMSAs, 1970s-May 1983, hearing, 21788-133

Underground economy, household expenditures and participation by type of goods or service and sociodemographic characteristics, with methodology and bibl, 1981 survey, 8308-27

Utah power plant construction effect on consumer demand for small retail and service businesses, for 2 rural counties, 1982-90, hearing, 25728-36

Virgin Islands economic censuses, 1982: employment, establishments, payroll, and receipts, by SIC 1- to 4-digit industry, island, and city, 2593-1

Western States economic indicators, Fed Reserve 12th District, quarterly rpt, 9393-1.1

see also Advertising

see also Agricultural marketing

see also Census of Retail Trade

see also Consumer credit

see also Consumer protection

see also Credit cards

see also Department stores

see also Drugstores

see also Food stores

see also Franchises

see also Gasoline service stations

see also Labeling

see also Packaging and containers

see also Post exchanges

see also Restaurants and restaurant industry

see also Sales promotion

see also Sales workers

see also Shopping centers

see also Vending machines and stands

see also Warehouses

see also Wholesale trade

see also under By Industry in the "Index by Categories"

see also under names of specific commodities or commodity groups

Retired military personnel

Annuitants, DOD retired military personnel, FY50-83, annual rpt, 3544-1.4

Index by Subjects and Names

Rhode Island

Army personnel health status, and use of Army medical services in US and abroad by personnel, retirees, and dependents, monthly rpt, 3702–4.1

Budget of DOD, itemized account of legislative history, FY84, annual rpt, 3504–7

Civilian Health and Medical Program of the Uniformed Services costs and operations, FY83-84 with trends from FY79, semiannual rpt, 3502–2

Cost control proposals for Fed Govt programs and mgmt, 3-year savings by function and agency, and financial and operating data, 1960s-81, 16908–1

Health care expenditures, natl and personal total and per capita amounts, by type of service and source of funds, 1983 and trends from 1929, annual article, 4652–1.429

Manpower of DOD, and organization, budget, weapons, and property, by service branch, State, and country, 1984 annual summary rpt, 3504–13

Medical facilities of DOD in US and abroad, beds, admissions, outpatient visits, and live births by service branch, quarterly rpt, 3542–15

Medical services for military, potential effects of alternative financing proposals on DOD costs, with service use and out-of-pocket medical costs by type of recipient, FY84-89, 26306–6.74

Navy medical facility use by active and retired military personnel, dependents, and others, by facility and type, quarterly rpt, 3802–1

Navy personnel, detailed statistics, quarterly rpt, 3802–4

Reserve forces manpower and equipment strengths, readiness, and funding, by reserve component, FY83, annual rpt, 3544–27

Reserve forces manpower strengths and characteristics, by component, quarterly rpt, 3542–4

see also Civilian Health and Medical Program of the Uniformed Services

see also Military pensions

see also Veterans

Retired Senior Volunteer Program

Activities, volunteer characteristics, and budget of ACTION, by program, FY82, annual rpt, 9024–2

Retirement

Employment status of family members, by occupation, family composition, age of children, and other characteristics, 1983 and trends from 1940, 6746–1.253

Fed Govt programs and mgmt cost control proposals, 3-year savings by function and agency, and financial and operating data, 1960s-81, 16908–1.27, 16908–1.34

Fed Govt Senior Executive Service employee admin, and program status and effectiveness, by agency and by executive and job characteristics, July 1979-Sept 1983, GAO rpt, 26119–51

NYC metro area small business owners and accountants, assessment of economy, professional activities, and community problems, by county and industry div, 1983 survey, hearings, 21728–52.3

OASDI retirement age proposed revisions based on increased life expectancy, by sex under 4 measurement methods, selected years 1940-2050, article, 4742–1.406

Older persons sociodemographic characteristics, and Fed Govt program participation and funding by agency, 1983 with trends and projections 1900-2080, annual rpt, 25144–3

Older white men retirement status, and 2-year transition and continuation rates, by age, selected years 1969-75, article, 6722–1.445

Railroad employee benefits and beneficiaries by type, and railroad employees and payrolls, FY82, annual rpt, 9704–2

see also Civil service pensions

see also Employee benefit plans

see also Individual retirement arrangements

see also Military pensions

see also Old-Age, Survivors, Disability, and Health Insurance

see also Pensions

see also Retired military personnel

see also Retired Senior Volunteer Program

Reunion

see Africa

Revenue sharing

Budget of US Appendix, detailed budgets and personnel summaries, by agency, FY85, annual rpt, 104–3

Budget of US, CBO analysis and review of FY85 budget by function, annual rpt, 26304–2

Budget of US, compact budgets by function, agency, and account, FY85 with projections to FY89, annual rpt, 104–2

Budget of US, effects of Reagan Admin policy changes, by detailed program, FY85, annual rpt, 104–21

Budget of US, receipts by source and outlays by function, FY40-89 estimates revised for consistency with FY85 budget definitions, annual rpt, 104–12

Budget of US, receipts, outlays, and budget authority, by function and agency, FY84-89 revised estimates, midsession review of FY85 budget, annual rpt, 104–7

Budget of US, receipts, outlays, and budget authority, by function and agency, 1st revision of FY85 budget, annual rpt, 104–17

Census of Govts, 1982: city govt revenues by source, expenditures by function, debt, and assets, by State and city, 2457–4

Census of Govts, 1982: county govt revenues by source, expenditures by function, debt, and assets, by State and county, 2457–3

Census of Govts, 1982: school districts revenues, expenditures, debt, and assets, by district and State, 2457–1

Census of Govts, 1982: State govt payments to local govts, by program, source of funds, level of govt, and State, with trends from 1902, 2460–3

Cost control proposals for Fed Govt programs and mgmt, 3-year savings by function and agency, and financial and operating data, 1960s-81, 16908–1.12

Fed Govt aid to State and local areas, by type of payment, State, county, and city, FY83, annual rpt, 2464–3.2

Fed Govt aid to State and local govts, expenditures, and direct payments, by program, agency, and State, FY83, annual rpt, 2464–2

Fed Govt revenue sharing and antirecession fiscal assistance program admin and trust funds status, FY83, annual rpt, 8064–1

Fed Govt revenue sharing and other grant program alternative allocations, with city govt finances and responses to program cuts, FY79-83, hearings, 25408–86

Govt finances, by level of govt and State, selected years 1929-83, annual rpt, 10044–1

Govt finances, by level of govt, State, and for large cities and counties, 1981-83, annual rpt series, 2466–2

Hwy Trust Fund receipts by source, and apportionments, by State, 1983, annual rpt, 7554–1.3

Local govt finances and population characteristics for cities and suburbs, by region and selected SMSA, selected years 1957-FY83, 10048–61

Payments of revenue sharing funds to States, local govts, Indian tribes, and Alaska Native villages, and entitlement computation data, FY84, series, 8066–1

Public land acreage and use, and Land Mgmt Bur activities and finances, annual State rpt series, 5724–11

Public opinion on taxes, tax policy, and intergovtl relations, 1972-84 surveys, annual rpt, 10044–2

Revis, Joseph S.

"Transportation for Older Americans: Issues and Options for the Decade of the 1980's", 7308–183

Revolutionary War

see War

Revolvers

see Firearms

Reyes, J. A., Associates, Inc.

"Solar Collector Manufacturing Activity, 1983", 3164–62

Reynolds, William E.

"Dental Record Documentation in Selected Ambulatory Care Facilities", 4102–1.458

Rhenium

see Metals and metal industries

Rheumatism

see Musculoskeletal diseases

Rhoades, Stephen A.

"Implications for Bank Merger Policy of Financial Deregulation, Interstate Banking, and Financial Supermarkets", 9366–1.135

Rhode Island

Bank deposits in commercial and mutual savings banks and in US branches of foreign banks, by account type, instn, State, SMSA, and county, June 1983, annual rpt, 9295–3.1

Census of Housing, 1980: occupancy and unit characteristics of SMSAs and central cities, by race, Hispanic origin, and city, State rpt, 2473–1.41

Census of Population and Housing, 1980: detailed population and housing characteristics, by county, city, and census tract, State rpt, 2551–2.41

County Business Patterns: establishments, employees, and payrolls, by SIC 4-digit industry and county, 1982, annual State rpt, 2326–6.41

Economic indicators for New England States, Fed Reserve 1st District, monthly rpt with articles, 9373–2

Rhode Island

Employment, earnings, and hours, by selected SIC 1- to 4-digit industry, State, and for 278 major labor areas, 1939-83, annual rpt, 6744-5.2, 6744-5.3

Environmental quality, pollutant discharge by type and source, and EPA protection activities and funding, 1970s-83, biennial regional rpt, 9184-15.1

Exports of manufactured and agricultural commodities, manufacturing production, and export-related employment, 1960s-82, State rpt, 2046-3.39

Fish and shellfish landings and prices at Boston and other New England ports, and total New England cold storage holdings, weekly rpt, 2162-6.2

Health insurance claims and benefit-cost ratio, by income and Medicare eligibility status, for Rhode Island State program, various periods 1975-79, article, 4652-1.423

HHS aid to each State and local govt or private instn, amount obligated, funding agency, and program, FY83, annual listing, 4004-3.1

Income (personal) per capita and by source, and earnings by industry div, by State, MSA, and county, 1977-82, annual regional rpt, 2704-2.2

Mineral Industry Surveys, State review of production, 1983, advance annual rpt, 5614-6.39

Minerals Yearbook, 1982, Vol 2 preprints: State review of production and sales by commodity, and business activity, annual rpt, 5604-16.41

Minerals Yearbook, 1982, Vol 2: State reviews of production, sales, and firms, by commodity, and business activity, annual rpt, 5604-34

Population size and components of change, by MSA and county, 1980-82, annual State Current Population Rpt, 2546-4.39

Population size, Apr 1980 and July 1982, and per capita income, 1979 and 1981, by county and city, State Current Population Rpt, 2546-11.39

Retail trade census, 1982: employment, establishments, sales, and payroll, by SIC 2- to 4-digit kind of business, SMSA, county, and city, State rpt, 2397-1.40

Savings and loan assns, FHLB 1st District member instns financial operations and related economic and housing indicators, monthly rpt, 9302-4

Service industry census, 1982: employment, establishments, receipts, and payroll, by SIC 2- to 4-digit kind of business, SMSA, county, and city, State rpt, 2391-1.40

Transportation census, 1982: trucks, by detailed characteristics, miles traveled, and type of product carried, State rpt, 2573-1.40

Water supply and quality in streams and lakes, and groundwater levels in wells, by drainage basin, 1982, annual State rpt, 5666-20.20

Wholesale trade census, 1982: employment, establishments, finances, and operations, by SIC 2- to 4-digit kind of business, SMSA, county, and city, State rpt, 2405-1.40

see also Pawtucket, R.I. *see also* Providence, R.I.

see also Warwick, R.I. *see also* under By State in the "Index by Categories"

Rhodesia *see* Zimbabwe

Rhorer, Thomas L.

"Personal Bankruptcy Data for Opt-Out Hearings and Other Purposes", 21528-57.1

Rice

- Acreage planted and harvested, by crop and State, 1982-83 and planned as of June 1984, annual rpt, 1621-23
- Acreage planting intended for 19 crops, by State, as of Feb 1984, annual rpt, 1621-22
- Acreage reduction payment-in-kind program costs, requirements, producer and diversion payments, and loan interest forgiven, by crop, as of 1983, hearing, 21788-138
- Acreage, yield, and production of field crops, by State, 1978-82 and preliminary 1983, 1641-7
- Agricultural Stabilization and Conservation Service producer payments under 26 programs, monthly rpt, 1802-10
- Agricultural Stabilization and Conservation Service rice programs, 1955-84, annual fact sheet, 1806-4.6
- *Agricultural Statistics, 1983,* annual rpt, 1004-1
- Agriculture census, 1982: farms, farmland, production, finances, and operator characteristics, by county, final State rpt series, 2331-1
- Beer production, stocks, materials used, tax-free removals, and taxable removals by State, monthly rpt, 8486-1.1
- China economic conditions, agricultural and industrial production, trade, and domestic and foreign investment, 1980-85, 2048-106
- Communist, OECD, and selected other countries agricultural production, by commodity, 1960s-83, annual rpt, 244-5.9
- Consumption, supply, trade, prices, expenditures, and indexes, by food commodity, 1963-83, annual rpt, 1544-4
- Cooperatives finances and operations, aggregate for top 100 assns by principal product and revenue source, FY82, annual rpt, 1124-3
- Cooperatives grain marketing, storage, and shipments by mode of transport, by grain type and region, FY80, 1128-28
- Cooperatives, membership, activities, and finances, by commodity and selected State, 1900-80 with trends from 1863, 1128-30
- County Business Patterns: establishments, employees, and payrolls, by SIC 4-digit industry and county, 1982, annual State rpt series, 2326-6
- Cuba economic conditions, agricultural and industrial production and distribution, trade, and intl economic relations, 1970-82 and trends from 1957, 248-40
- Developing countries food supply policies, with farm sector data, tariff income, and prices and imports of 5 grains, for 21 countries, 1960s-81, 1528-168
- Eastern Europe agricultural production and trade by commodity, food consumption, and farm inputs, for 6 countries, 1960-80 with projections to 1991, 1528-178

Index by Subjects and Names

- EC food supply/demand and market and support prices, with exchange rates, fertilizer price index, GDP, and population, by country, 1960-83, 1528-173
- Export licensing and monitoring activities under Export Admin Act, for selected commodities, and for Communist and other countries, FY83, annual rpt, 2044-22
- Export sales and shipments of US grains, oilseed products, hides, skins, and cotton, by country, weekly rpt, 1922-3
- Exports and imports of US, by agricultural commodity and country, bimonthly rpt with articles, 1522-1
- Exports and imports of US, detailed SIC-based commodities by world area, 1983, annual rpts, 2424-6
- Exports and imports of US, totals and as percent of domestic production, by SIC 2- to 5-digit commodity, 1981, annual rpt, 2424-3
- Exports, imports, tariffs, and industry operating data for rice and rice products, foreign and US, 1979-83, TSUSA commodity rpt, 9885-1.63
- Exports of manufactured and agricultural commodities, manufacturing production, and export-related employment, 1960s-82, State rpt series, 2046-3
- Exports of US, detailed commodities by country of destination, monthly rpt, 2422-3
- Exports of US, detailed Schedule B commodities by country of destination, 1983, annual rpt, 2424-9
- Exports of US, detailed Schedule E commodities by mode of transport and world area and country of destination, 1983, annual rpts, 2424-5
- Exports under PL 480 concessional sales program, by commodity and country, 1955-83, semiannual rpt, 1922-6
- Exports under PL 480 concessional sales program, by commodity and country, 1978-83, semiannual rpt, 1922-10
- Farm finances, assets, liabilities, income, receipts by commodity and State, and expenses, 1980-83 and trends from 1910, annual rpt, 1544-16
- Foreign agricultural production, prices, and trade, by country, 1983 and outlook for 1984/85, annual world region rpt series, 1524-4
- Foreign and US agricultural production, prices, trade, and consumption, quarterly rpt with articles, 1522-3
- Foreign and US agricultural supply/demand and production data, for selected US and world crops, and for US livestock and dairy products, periodic rpt, 1522-5
- Foreign and US grain production, trade, stocks, consumption, and prices, FAS monthly and annual rpt series, 1925-2
- Foreign and US production, acreage, and yield for selected crops, forecasts by selected world region and country, FAS monthly rpt, 1925-28
- Futures trading by commodity and exchange, and Commodity Futures Trading Commission activities, funding, and employment, FY83, annual rpt, 11924-2

710 ASI Annual Supplement January-December 1984

Index by Subjects and Names

Rivers and waterways

Futures trading in selected commodities, foreign currencies, and stock indexes, Chicago and other markets activity, monthly rpt, 11922–1

Futures trading in selected commodities, foreign currencies, Treasury securities, and stock indexes, NYC, Chicago, and other markets activity, monthly rpt, 11922–5

Great Lakes trade, by SITC 3-digit commodity, port, vessel type, world area, and country, 1982, annual rpt, 7744–3

Imports of US, detailed Schedule A commodities by country and world area of origin, and mode of transport, 1983, annual rpts, 2424–2

Imports of US, detailed Schedule A commodities by country, monthly rpt, 2422–2

Input-output structure of US economy, detailed interindustry transactions for 537 industries, and components of final demand, 1977 benchmark data, 2708–17

Loan support programs of USDA for grains, activity and status by type of grain and State, monthly rpt, 1802–3

Manufacturing census, 1982: financial and operating data, for SIC 4-digit industries by product, preliminary rpt, 2491–1.16

Marketing cash receipts of farms, by detailed commodity and State, 1979-82, annual rpt, 1544–18

Mill production workers, wages, hours, and benefits, by occupation, mill product, and region, June 1982 survey, 6787–6.204

OECD trade, total and for 4 major countries, and US trade by country, by commodity, 1972-82, annual world region rpt series, 244–13

PL 480 commodity allocations for long-term credit sales, by country, quarterly press release, 1922–7

Price variability effect on price margins and profits, and futures market hedging and price forecasting efficiency, various periods, 1960-83, article, 1502–3.404

Prices, market activities, inspections, sales, trade, supply, and use of rice, for US and selected foreign markets, weekly rpt, 1313–8

Prices received by farmers and production value for detailed crops by State, 1981-83, annual rpt, 1621–2

Prices received by farmers for major products, and paid for farm inputs and living items, by commodity and State, monthly rpt, 1629–1

Production, acreage, and yield, for selected grains by State, 1982-84 with wheat and rye seedings for 1985, annual rpt, 1621–24

Production and farm finances, expenses by type, and domestic economic impact, selected years 1972-82 and preliminary 1983-84, annual rpt, 1544–19

Production, farms, acreage, and related data, by selected crop and State, monthly rpt, 1621–1

Production itemized costs, receipts, and net returns, for 13 crops, 4 livestock types, and milk, by region, 1981-83, annual rpt, 1544–20

Production, prices, trade, and marketing, by commodity, current situation and forecast, monthly rpt, 1502–4

Production, prices, trade, stocks, and use, 1978-July 1984 and 1984/85 outlook, semiannual situation rpt, 1561–8

Productivity, hours, and employment indexes for selected SIC 3- and 4-digit industries, 1954-82, annual rpt, 6824–1.3

Stocks of grain on and off farms and total in all positions, by crop, periodic rpt, 1621–4

Stocks of rice on and off farms and total, periodic rpt, 1621–7

Waterborne commerce of US (domestic and foreign), freight by commodity, traffic, and passengers, by port and waterway, 1982, annual rpt, 3754–3

see also under By Commodity in the "Index by Categories"

Rice, Thomas

"Determinants of Physician Assignment Rates by Type of Service", 4652–1.416

Richa, Hugo T.

"Regulation of Safety on Panamian Flag Vessels: The Panama Offshore Industry Advisory Committee as a Model for Successful Government Industry Interface", 21568–35

Richards, William J.

"Kinds and Abundances of Fish Larvae in the Caribbean Sea and Adjacent Areas", 2168–80

Richardson, Charles J.

"Federal Debt and Interest Costs, Special Study", 26308–50

Richland, Wash.

Census of Housing, 1980: occupancy and unit characteristics, by race, Hispanic origin, and city, SMSA rpt, 2473–1.301

Census of Population and Housing, 1980: detailed population and housing characteristics, by county, city, and census tract, SMSA rpt, 2551–2.301

Wages of office and plant workers, by occupation, 1984 labor market area survey rpt, 6785–3.9

see also under By SMSA or MSA in the "Index by Categories"

Richmond, Barry

"Generation of Behavioral Lags for ISTUM2", 3308–66.8

Richmond, Va.

Census of Housing, 1980: occupancy and unit characteristics, by race, Hispanic origin, and city, SMSA rpt, 2473–1.302

Census of Population and Housing, 1980: detailed population and housing characteristics, by county, city, and census tract, SMSA rpt, 2551–2.302

Wages of office and plant workers, by occupation, 1984 SMSA survey rpt, 6785–11.6

see also under By City and By SMSA or MSA in the "Index by Categories"

Ries, John C.

"Unemployment in 1982: Beyond the Official Labor Force Statistics", 9373–1.410

Rifles

see Firearms

Riggan, Wilson B.

"U.S. Cancer Mortality Rates and Trends, 1950-79", 4478–146

Right of assembly

Foreign human rights conditions in 162 countries, economic and military aid of US, and economic aid of intl organizations, 1981-83, annual rpt, 21384–3

Right of privacy

Foreign human rights conditions in 162 countries, economic and military aid of US, and economic aid of intl organizations, 1981-83, annual rpt, 21384–3

IRS prosecutions, litigations, and interpretive law decisions, FY83 with comparisons to FY82, annual rpt, 8304–3.2

Labor legislation enacted by 48 States, DC, and Guam, 1983, annual summary article, 6722–1.406

see also Electronic surveillance

Right to counsel

Foreign human rights conditions in 162 countries, economic and military aid of US, and economic aid of intl organizations, 1981-83, annual rpt, 21384–3

see also Legal aid

Riley, Dorothea

"Individual Income Tax Returns: Selected Characteristics from the 1983 Taxpayer Usage Study", 8302–2.414

Rio Grande River

Bridges over navigable waters, with type of bridge and use, owner, dimensions, and location, 1984 regional listing, 7406–5.2

Reclamation programs of Fed Govt in western US, finances and operations by project and State, 1981-82, annual rpts, 5824–1

Water supply and quality in streams and lakes, and groundwater levels in wells, by drainage basin, 1981, annual State rpt series, 5666–16

Water supply and quality in streams and lakes, and groundwater levels in wells, by drainage basin, 1982, annual State rpt series, 5666–20

Water supply in US and Canada, streamflow, well and reservoir levels, and dissolved solids and temperature in 6 US rivers, by station, monthly rpt, 5662–3

Riots and disorders

Natl Guard (Army and Air) activities, manpower, and facilities, FY83, annual rpt, 3704–3

Ritchie, Eleanor H.

"Astronautics and Aeronautics, 1976", 9504–2

Ritter, Clay J.

"Computerization of Market News Reports", 1004–16.1

Rivers and waterways

Acid rain causes and effects, air pollutant emissions by source, and control costs, by region and State, selected years 1977-83 and projected to 2000, 26358–104

Acid rain causes and effects, air pollutant emissions by source in US and selected countries, and control costs, 1970s-83 and projected to 2000, 21368–52

Appalachia regional dev spending, by program area and source of funds, FY82, annual rpt, 9084–1

Army Corps of Engineers activities and projects, FY83 and trends from 1800s, annual rpt, 3754–1

Coast Guard search and rescue activities, by district, station, and rescue vessel, FY83 and projected FY88, annual rpt, 7404–2

Coastal environmental characteristics, fish, wildlife, and use, and population socioeconomic data, for individual areas, series, 5506–4

Rivers and waterways

County Business Patterns: establishments, employees, and payrolls, by SIC 4-digit industry and county, 1982, annual State rpt series, 2326–6

Developing countries disaster preparedness and summary sociodemographic, political, and economic data, country rpt series, 9916–2

Environmental quality and protection programs, costs, and Fed Govt enforcement, 1983, detailed annual rpt, 484–1

Fed Govt programs and mgmt cost control proposals, 3-year savings by function and agency, and financial and operating data, 1960s-81, 16908–1.22

Fed Govt reclamation programs in western US, finances and operations by project and State, 1981-82, annual rpts, 5824–1

Fish and eggs for stocking distributed from natl hatcheries, by species, hatchery, and jurisdiction, FY83, annual rpt, 5504–10

Foreign and US major dams, reservoirs, and hydroelectric plants, listing with location and characteristics, as of June 1983, 5828–13

Freight (waterborne domestic and foreign) by commodity, traffic, and passengers, by port and waterway, 1982, annual rpt, 3754–3

Mount St Helens, Wash, volcanic eruptions, effects on water quality and other environmental characteristics of Washington and Oregon watersheds, series, 5666–14

Natl Forest System wildlife habitat and fishery improvements, use, and game population and harvest by species and forest, by region, FY83, annual rpt, 1204–31

Natl park system and other areas under Natl Park Service mgmt, acreage by type of area, ownership, and site, as of Sept 1984, semiannual rpt, 5542–1

Nevada water supply, streamflow, reservoir storage, and precipitation, 1984 water year, annual rpt, 1264–8

Northeastern US water supply, precipitation and stream runoff by station, monthly rpt, 2182–3

Oregon water supply, streamflow by station and reservoir storage, 1984 water year, annual rpt, 1264–9

Pollution-caused fish kills, by State, location, and pollution source, monthly 1978-80, annual rpt, 9204–3

Sedimentation control, surveillance, and research activity of Fed Govt, by project, agency, region, and State, 1982, annual rpt, 5664–9

Urban runoff water quality, pollutant concentrations, and control cost-effectiveness, with monitoring sites rainfall and other characteristics, by city and region, 1978-83, 9208–122

Utah water supply, streamflow, reservoir storage, and precipitation, 1984 water year, annual rpt, 1264–6

Water supply and quality, and effect of coal mining operations, for selected river basins in Eastern and Interior coal provinces, series, 5666–15

Water supply and quality, and effect of coal mining operations, for selected river basins in Western coal provinces, series, 5666–19

Water supply and quality in streams and lakes, and groundwater levels in wells, by drainage basin, 1980, annual State rpt series, 5666–12

Water supply and quality in streams and lakes, and groundwater levels in wells, by drainage basin, 1981, annual State rpt series, 5666–16

Water supply and quality in streams and lakes, and groundwater levels in wells, by drainage basin, 1982, annual State rpt series, 5666–20

Water supply and quality in streams and lakes, and groundwater levels in wells, by drainage basin, 1983, annual State rpt series, 5666–10

Water supply in US and Canada, streamflow, well and reservoir levels, and dissolved solids and temperature in 6 US rivers, by station, monthly rpt, 5662–3

Waterborne disease outbreaks and cases, by type, source, and location, 1983, annual rpt, 4205–35

Western Area Power Admin small-scale potential hydroelectric generation, site inventory, characteristics, and costs, by State and county, 1984 rpt, 3258–1

Western US water supply, and snow survey results, monthly State rpt series, 1266–2

Western US water supply, snow depth measurements by station, State rpt series, 1266–3

Western US water supply, streamflow and reservoir storage forecasts by stream and station, Jan-May monthly rpt, 1262–1

Wild and scenic rivers in natl forests, Sept 1983, annual rpt, 1204–2

see also Arkansas River
see also Bridges
see also Canals
see also Chesapeake Bay
see also Colorado River
see also Columbia River
see also Dams
see also Delaware River
see also Dredging
see also Estuaries
see also Floods
see also Great Lakes
see also Harbors and ports
see also Hudson River
see also Illinois River
see also Lakes and lakeshores
see also Mississippi River
see also Missouri River
see also New York Bight
see also Ohio River
see also Potomac River
see also Red River
see also Rio Grande River
see also Snake River
see also Souris-Red-Rainy Rivers
see also St. Lawrence River
see also Susquehanna River
see also Tennessee River
see also Water resources development
see also Water supply and use
see also Willamette River

Riverside, Calif.

Census of Housing, 1980: occupancy and unit characteristics, by race, Hispanic origin, and city, SMSA rpt, 2473–1.303

Census of Population and Housing, 1980: detailed population and housing characteristics, by county, city, and census tract, SMSA rpt, 2551–2.303

Index by Subjects and Names

Housing and financial characteristics, and unit and neighborhood quality, for 15 SMSAs, 1978, annual survey special supplement, 2485–8

Housing and households detailed characteristics, and unit and neighborhood quality, by inside-outside central cities, 1982 survey, SMSA rpt, 2485–6.41

Housing unit starts and completions authorized by building permits in 20 MSAs, quarterly rpt, 2382–9

Housing vacancy rates for single and multifamily units and mobile homes, by city and ZIP code, 1983, annual metro area rpt, 9304–20.9

see also under By City and By SMSA or MSA in the "Index by Categories"

Rivets

see Machines and machinery industry

Rizek, Robert L.

"USDA's Nutrient Data Bases", 1004–16.1

Roads

see Highways

Roanoke, Va.

Census of Housing, 1980: occupancy and unit characteristics, by race, Hispanic origin, and city, SMSA rpt, 2473–1.304

Census of Population and Housing, 1980: detailed population and housing characteristics, by county, city, and census tract, SMSA rpt, 2551–2.304

see also under By City and By SMSA or MSA in the "Index by Categories"

Robbery and theft

Bank robbery court cases by case processing, sentencing, and offender characteristics, and compared to other Fed Govt felony cases, 1979-80, periodic rpt, 6062–2.407

Convictions, prison sentences, and average sentence lengths, by offense, offender class, and selected State, various periods 1971-84, 6066–19.10

Court cases, dispositions, convictions, and sentences of Federal criminal defendants, by offense and district, as of June 1983 with trends from 1945, annual rpt, 18204–1

Court criminal case disposition, effect of victim injury and other factors, and law enforcement official and victim attitudes, 1983 survey, 6068–185

Crime and criminal justice data, including justice expenditures and employment by level of govt, 1970s-82 with some trends from 1875, 6068–174

Crime Index by population size and region, and offenses known to police by large city, Jan-June 1984, semiannual rpt, 6222–1

Crimes, arrests by offender characteristics, and rates, by offense, and law enforcement employees, by population size and jurisdiction, 1970s-83, annual rpt, 6224–2

Criminal case processing from arrest to sentencing, cases and processing time by disposition, dismissal reason, and offense, for 14 cities, 1979, 6066–22.1

Criminal drug, fraud, and bank robbery Federal defendants, by sociodemographic and case processing characteristics, 1979, 6062–2.403

Employee theft and misconduct in retail, hospital, and manufacturing establishments, by type and frequency of violation, 1978-80, 6068–178

Index by Subjects and Names — Romania

Explosives stolen and recovered, by State, 1982-83, annual rpt, 8484–4.2

Financial instns, crimes committed against, by State, semiannual article, 9312–1

Income (taxable) not reported, by illegal source, with characteristics of persons involved, methodology, and bibl, 1970s-82, 8008–112

Minnesota crime sentencing guidelines by type and severity of offense, 1982, 10048–59

Pretrial citation release use, cost savings for law enforcement agencies, and failures to appear in court, by offense and selected jurisdiction, 1970s-82, 6068–187

Prison terms actually served by selected State, and Illinois pretrial detention time credited to sentence, by offense, various periods 1977-83, 6066–19.7

Prisoners in State prisons median sentence, and admissions and releases by prisoner and sentencing characteristics, by offense and State, 1981 and trends from 1926, 6066–19.9

Public housing under private mgmt, assessment by housing officials and managers, and tenants, with operating costs, crime, and rent delinquency by project type and location, 1982, 5188–103

Robbery rates and circumstances, medical costs and property losses of victims, and offender and victim characteristics, 1960s-81, 6068–180

School crime against students, teachers, and others, by offense, circumstances, and offender sex and race, 1974-76, 6066–20.2

School crime, assaults and robberies of secondary students and teachers, 1972-83, 4918–13

School crime, assaults and robberies of teachers and minority and all students, and vandalism incidents, 1976/77, 4808–12

Victimization of households, by offense type, race of household head, and family income and urban-rural residence, 1975-83, periodic rpt, 6062–2.404

Victimization rates and reports to police, by offense, 1973-83, 6062–2.405

Victimization rates by type of offense, and victim and offense characteristics, Natl Crime Survey series, 6066–3

Victims of crime, medical expenses and property loss, and median loss by victim characteristics, by offense type, 1975-81, 6066–19.6

Wiretapping authorizations by offense, costs, persons involved, arrests, trials, and convictions, 1983, annual rpt, 18204–7

see also Federal Inspectors General reports

Roberts, Glenn F.

"Trends in Heavy Truck Energy Use and Efficiency", 3308–70

Robinette, H. Randall

"Species Profiles: Life Histories and Environmental Requirements of Coastal Fishes and Invertebrates (Gulf of Mexico), Bay Anchovy and Striped Anchovy", 5506–8.17

Robinson, Elmer

"Atmospheric Turbidity over the U.S. from 1967-76", 9198–106

Robotics

see Automation

Rochester, Minn.

Census of Housing, 1980: occupancy and unit characteristics, by race, Hispanic origin, and city, SMSA rpt, 2473–1.305

Census of Population and Housing, 1980: detailed population and housing characteristics, by county, city, and census tract, SMSA rpt, 2551–2.305

see also under By SMSA or MSA in the "Index by Categories"

Rochester, N.H.

Census of Housing, 1980: occupancy and unit characteristics, by race, Hispanic origin, and city, SMSA rpt, 2473–1.291

Census of Population and Housing, 1980: detailed population and housing characteristics, by county, city, and census tract, SMSA rpt, 2551–2.291

see also under By SMSA or MSA in the "Index by Categories"

Rochester, N.Y.

Census of Housing, 1980: occupancy and unit characteristics, by race, Hispanic origin, and city, SMSA rpt, 2473–1.306

Census of Population and Housing, 1980: detailed population and housing characteristics, by county, city, and census tract, SMSA rpt, 2551–2.306

Housing and financial characteristics, and unit and neighborhood quality, for 15 SMSAs, 1978, annual survey special supplement, 2485–8

Housing and households detailed characteristics, and unit and neighborhood quality, by inside-outside central cities, 1982 survey, SMSA rpt, 2485–6.39

see also under By City and By SMSA or MSA in the "Index by Categories"

Rock Hill, S.C.

Census of Housing, 1980: occupancy and unit characteristics, by race, Hispanic origin, and city, SMSA rpt, 2473–1.308

Census of Population and Housing, 1980: detailed population and housing characteristics, by county, city, and census tract, SMSA rpt, 2551–2.308

see also under By SMSA or MSA in the "Index by Categories"

Rock Island, Ill.

Census of Housing, 1980: occupancy and unit characteristics, by race, Hispanic origin, and city, SMSA rpt, 2473–1.134

Census of Population and Housing, 1980: detailed population and housing characteristics, by county, city, and census tract, SMSA rpt, 2551–2.134

Housing vacancy rates for single and multifamily units and mobile homes, by county, city, and ZIP code, 1983, annual metro area rpt, 9304–18.3

Wages of office and plant workers, by occupation, 1984 SMSA survey rpt, 6785–11.4

Waterborne commerce of US (domestic and foreign), freight by commodity, traffic, and passengers, by port and waterway, 1982, annual rpt, 3754–3.2, 3754–3.3

see also under By SMSA or MSA in the "Index by Categories"

Rockefeller Foundation

Population and health research funded by 4 private organizations, project listing by topic, with funding data, 1981, annual rpt, 4474–16

Rockel, Mark

"Future Consumption of Timber Growth in Northern Minnesota: 1980-2030", 1206–24.9

Rockets

see Missiles and rockets

Rockford, Ill.

Census of Housing, 1980: occupancy and unit characteristics, by race, Hispanic origin, and city, SMSA rpt, 2473–1.307

Census of Population and Housing, 1980: detailed population and housing characteristics, by county, city, and census tract, SMSA rpt, 2551–2.307

Housing vacancy rates for single and multifamily units and mobile homes, by county, city, and ZIP code, 1984, annual metro area rpt, 9304–18.6

see also under By City and By SMSA or MSA in the "Index by Categories"

Rogers, Carolyn C.

"Childspacing Among Birth Cohorts of American Women: 1905-59", 2546–1.387

"Fertility of American Women: June 1982", 2546–1.386

"Fertility of American Women: June 1983", 2546–1.393

Rogers, Martha F.

"Reye Syndrome Surveillance, 1981-82", 4202–7.402

Rogers, S. Gordon

"Species Profiles: Life Histories and Environmental Requirements of Coastal Fishes and Invertebrates (South Atlantic), Atlantic Menhaden", 5506–8.15, 5506–8.25

Rogoff, Kenneth

"Can Exchange Rate Predictability Be Achieved Without Monetary Convergence? Evidence from the EMS", 9366–7.101

"Time-Series of the Relationship Between Exchange Rates and Intervention: A Review of the Techniques and Literature", 9366–1.131

Roley, V. Vance

"Impact of Discount Rate Changes on Market Interest Rates", 9381–1.404

"Stock Prices and Economic News", 9381–10.37

Romania

Agricultural and food production indexes, and production of selected commodities, by world region and country, 1974-83, annual rpt, 1524–5

Agricultural production and trade by commodity, food consumption, and farm inputs, for 6 countries, 1960-80 with projections to 1991, 1528–178

Agricultural situation in Eastern Europe, by country, 1983 and outlook for 1984, annual report, 1524–4.7

Cuba economic conditions, agricultural and industrial production and distribution, trade, and intl economic relations, 1970-82 and trends from 1957, 248–40

Economic conditions in Communist, OECD, and selected other countries, 1960s-83, annual rpt, 244–5

Economic, social, and political summary data, by country, 1984, annual factbook, 244–11

Economic trends in income, production, prices, employment, finances, and trade, 1984 annual rpt, 2046–4.71

Romania

Export licensing and monitoring activities under Export Admin Act, for selected commodities, and for Communist and other countries, FY83, annual rpt, 2044–22

Exports and imports of NATO countries with Council for Mutual Economic Assistance Europe members, by country, 1980-83, annual rpt, 7144–5

Exports and imports of US with Communist countries, by detailed commodity and country, quarterly rpt with articles, 9882–2

Exports of US, detailed Schedule B commodities by country of destination, 1983, annual rpt, 2424–9

Exports of US, detailed Schedule E commodities by mode of transport and world area and country of destination, 1983, annual rpts, 2424–5

Imports of US, detailed Schedule A commodities by country and world area of origin, and mode of transport, 1983, annual rpts, 2424–2

Imports of US, detailed TSUSA commodities by country of origin, 1983, annual rpt, 2424–4

Loans and grants for economic and military assistance from US and intl agencies, by program and country, FY46-83, annual rpt, 9914–5

Military spending, arms trade, and armed forces size, with total govt spending and population, by country, 1972-82, annual rpt, 9824–1

Minerals Yearbook, 1982, Vol 3: foreign country reviews of production, trade, and policies, by commodity, annual rpt, 5604–35

Minerals Yearbook, 1982, Vol 3 preprints: foreign country review of production, trade, and policies, by commodity, annual rpt, 5604–17.61

Population size and growth rates, and latest available benchmark demographic data, by country, 1950-83, biennial rpt, 2324–4

Refugee arrivals in US, by world area of origin and processing and nationality, monthly rpt, 7002–4, 7002–5

Refugee resettlement program activities and funding, arrivals and population by country of origin and State, and employment and other characteristics, FY83, annual rpt, 4704–8

Science and technology dev and transfer between USSR and other members of Council for Mutual Economic Assistance, 1940s-81, 2326–9.7

see also under By Foreign Country in the "Index by Categories"

Rome, N.Y.

Census of Housing, 1980: occupancy and unit characteristics, by race, Hispanic origin, and city, SMSA rpt, 2473–1.359

Census of Population and Housing, 1980: detailed population and housing characteristics, by county, city, and census tract, SMSA rpt, 2551–2.359

see also under By SMSA or MSA in the "Index by Categories"

Rones, Philip L.

"Recent Recessions Swell Ranks of the Long-Term Unemployed", 6722–1.411

Roof, James B.

"Farmer Owned Share of Market Up Despite Fewer Dairy Co-ops", 1122–1.404

"Marketing Operations of Dairy Cooperatives", 1128–29

Rooming and boarding houses

Census of Population and Housing, 1980: detailed population and housing characteristics, by county, city, and census tract, State and SMSA rpt series, 2551–2

Census of Population, 1980: detailed socioeconomic and demographic characteristics, by age, sex, race, Hispanic origin, occupation, and industry, State rpt series, 2531–4

County Business Patterns: establishments, employees, and payrolls, by SIC 4-digit industry and county, 1982, annual State rpt series, 2326–6

Income tax returns of sole proprietorships, receipts, deductions by type, payroll, and net income, by major industry, 1982, annual article, 8302–2.413

Service industry census, 1982: employment, establishments, receipts, and payroll, by SIC 2- to 4-digit kind of business, SMSA, county, and city, State rpt series, 2391–1

Roosa, Robert V.

"Exchange Rate Arrangements in the Eighties", 9373–3.28

Roosevelt, Franklin Delano, Memorial Commission

Budget of US, appropriations, outlays, balances, and budget receipts, by govtl branch and agency, FY83, annual rpt, 8104–2

Roppel, Alton Y.

"Management of Northern Fur Seals on the Pribilof Islands, Alaska, 1786-1981", 2168–79

Rosen, Harvey S.

"Housing Tenure, Uncertainty, and Taxation", 8006–3.50

Rosen, Kenneth T.

"Creative Financing and House Prices: A Study of Capitalization Effects", 9412–2.402

Rosen, Richard J.

"Regional Variations in Employment and Unemployment During 1970-82", 6722–1.413

Rosenblum, Harvey

"Financial Services in Transition: The Effects of Nonbank Competitors", 9375–11.3

Rosenkranz, R. D.

"Copper Availability, Market Economy Countries. A Minerals Availability Program Appraisal", 5606–4.11

Ross County, Ohio

Housing vacancy rates for single and multifamily units and mobile homes, by city and ZIP code, 1984, annual metro area rpt, 9304–27.2

Ross, Leslie E.

"Thailand's Rice Export Potential", 1561–8.402

Rossana, Robert J.

"Empirical Estimates of Investment in Employment, Inventories of Finished Goods and Unfilled Orders", 9387–8.80

"Joint Production, Quasi-Fixed Factors of Production and Investment in Finished Goods Inventories", 9387–8.79

Index by Subjects and Names

ROTC

see Reserve Officers Training Corps

Roth, Howard L.

"Recent Experience with M1 as a Policy Guide", 9381–1.406

Roth, Melanie

"Nonmetro Areas Gain in New Housing Market", 1598–190

Rotty, Ralph M.

"Carbon Dioxide Emissions from Fossil Fuels: A Procedure for Estimation and Results for 1950-81", 3008–94

"Changing Pattern of CO_2 Emissions", 3006–7.6

Rourke, John P.

"Adjusting In-Area Fluid Milk Sales for Calendar Composition", 1317–4.401

"Cooperatives in Federal Milk Order Markets", 1317–4.403

"Minnesota-Wisconsin Manufacturing Grade Milk Price Series", 1317–4.404

"Producer Milk Marketed Under Federal Milk Orders by State of Origin", 1317–4.405

Rovner, Bruce A.

"General Aviation Activity and Avionics Survey", 7504–29

Rowland, Michael

"Changes in Heart Disease Risk Factors", 4144–11.1

Rozwadowski, Franek

"Monetary and Credit Targets in an Open Economy", 9373–3.26

Rubber and rubber industry

Air pollutant emission factors, by detailed source, 3rd edition, 1983-84 supplements, 9198–13

Business statistics, detailed data for major industries and economic indicators, *Survey of Current Business,* monthly rpt, 2702–1.17

Census of Population, 1980: detailed socioeconomic and demographic characteristics, by age, sex, race, Hispanic origin, occupation, and industry, State rpt series, 2531–4

China economic conditions, agricultural and industrial production, trade, and domestic and foreign investment, 1980-85, 2048–106

China exports and imports by SITC 1- to 5-digit commodity, 1970s-82, annual rpt, 244–12

Collective bargaining agreements expiring during year, covered workers by SIC 2-digit industry, firm, and union, with summary of key provisions, 1984, annual rpt, 6784–9

Communist, OECD, and selected other countries consumer and producer goods production, 1960s-83, annual rpt, 244–5.7, 244–5.8

County Business Patterns: establishments, employees, and payrolls, by SIC 4-digit industry and county, 1981, annual State rpt series, 2326–8

County Business Patterns: establishments, employees, and payrolls, by SIC 4-digit industry and county, 1982, annual State rpt series, 2326–6

Earnings by major industry group, and personal income per capita and by source, by region and State, 1929-82, 2708–40

Employment, earnings, and hours, by selected SIC 1- to 4-digit industry, State, and for 278 major labor areas, 1939-83, annual rpt, 6744–5

Index by Subjects and Names

Rural areas

Employment, earnings, and hours, by SIC 4-digit nonfarm industry, monthly 1974-Feb 1984, annual update, 6744–4

Exports and imports of US, by agricultural commodity and country, bimonthly rpt with articles, 1522–1

Exports and imports of US, by commodity group, world area, selected country, US coastal area and port, and mode of transport, with seasonal adjustments, monthly rpt, 2422–9

Exports and imports of US, by detailed agricultural commodity and country, FY83 and CY83, semiannual rpts, 1522–4

Exports and imports of US, by detailed agricultural commodity for 8 major commodity groups, monthly rpt, 1922–8

Exports and imports of US, detailed SIC-based commodities by world area, 1983, annual rpts, 2424–6

Exports and imports of US, totals and as percent of domestic production, by SIC 2- to 5-digit commodity, 1981, annual rpt, 2424–3

Exports of manufactured and agricultural commodities, manufacturing production, and export-related employment, 1960s-82, State rpt series, 2046–3

Exports of US, detailed commodities by country of destination, monthly rpt, 2422–3

Exports of US, detailed Schedule B commodities by country of destination, 1983, annual rpt, 2424–9

Exports of US, detailed Schedule E commodities by mode of transport and world area and country of destination, 1983, annual rpts, 2424–5

Finances and operations, by SIC 2- to 4-digit industry, 1970s-83 and projected to 1988, annual rpt, 2014–4

Financial statements for manufacturing, mining, and trade corporations, by selected SIC 2- to 3-digit industry, quarterly rpt, 2502–1

Footwear (rubber) trade, tariffs, and industry operating data, 1979-83, TSUSA commodity rpt supplement, 9885–7.59

Footwear imports of US, by category, value class, and selected country, monthly rpt, 2042–29

Footwear production, shipments, trade, and consumption, by product, 1983, annual Current Industrial Rpt, 2506–6.8

Foreign agricultural production, prices, and trade, by country, 1983 and outlook for 1984/85, annual world region rpt series, 1524–4

Great Lakes trade, by SITC 3-digit commodity, port, vessel type, world area, and country, 1982, annual rpt, 7744–3

Hose and belting shipments, by detailed product class, 1983, annual Current Industrial Rpt, 2506–8.12

Imports of fabric and neoprene laminate from Japan at less than fair value, injury to US industry, investigation with background financial and operating data, 1984 rpt, 9886–14.128

Imports of US, detailed Schedule A commodities by country and world area of origin, and mode of transport, 1983, annual rpts, 2424–2

Imports of US, detailed Schedule A commodities by country, monthly rpt, 2422–2

Imports of US, detailed TSUSA commodities by country of origin, 1983, annual rpt, 2424–4

Income tax returns of corporations, detailed income and tax items by industry, 1981, annual rpt, 8304–4

Income tax returns of corporations with foreign tax credit, income and deductions by type, asset size, and selected industry group, 1980, article, 8302–2.415

Input-output structure of US economy, detailed interindustry transactions for 85 industries, and components of final demand, 1977, article, 2702–1.421

Input-output structure of US economy, detailed interindustry transactions for 537 industries, and components of final demand, 1977 benchmark data, 2708–17

Machines for plastic and rubber molding trade, tariffs, and industry operating data, foreign and US, 1979-83, TSUSA commodity rpt, 9885–6.61

Manufacturing census, 1982: financial and operating data, by SIC 2- to 4-digit industry, State, SMSA, and county, preliminary census div rpt series, 2491–3

Manufacturing census, 1982: financial and operating data, for SIC 4-digit industries by product, preliminary rpt series, 2491–1

Minority group and women employment, by occupational group and SIC 2- to 3-digit industry, 1981, annual rpt, 9244–1.1

Occupational injury and illness rates, by SIC 2- to 4-digit industry, 1982, annual rpt, 6844–1

OECD trade, total and for 4 major countries, and US trade by country, by commodity, 1972-82, annual world region rpt series, 244–13

Plant and animal genetic resource conservation, commercial uses, causes of depletion, and geographic sources, 1984 rpt, 5548–13

Pollution abatement capital and operating costs, by SIC 2- to 4-digit industry, State, and SMSA, 1982, annual Current Industrial Rpt, 2506–3.6

Producer prices and indexes, by stage of processing and detailed commodity, monthly rpt, 6762–6

Producer prices and indexes, by stage of processing and detailed commodity, monthly 1983, annual supplement, 6764–2

Production and sales of synthetic organic chemicals by product, and listing of manufacturers, 1983, annual rpt, 9884–3

Production, shipments, trade, and stocks, by product, 1983, annual Current Industrial Rpt, 2506–8.7

R&D industry funding and employment of scientists and engineers, by industry group, firm size, and funding source, 1956-82, annual rpt, 9627–21

Scientists, engineers, and technicians employed in private industry, by occupation and industry group, 1980-81, biennial rpt, 9627–23

Stockpiling of strategic and critical materials, Fed Govt activities and inventories by commodity, Oct 1983-Mar 1984, semiannual rpt, 9432–1

Stockpiling of strategic materials, inventories, costs, and goals, by commodity, as of June 1984, semiannual rpt, 9452–7

Transportation census, 1982: trucks, by detailed characteristics, miles traveled, and type of product carried, State rpt series, 2573–1

Waterborne commerce of US (domestic and foreign), freight by commodity, traffic, and passengers, by port and waterway, 1982, annual rpt, 3754–3

see also Tires and tire industry

see also under By Commodity in the "Index by Categories"

see also under By Industry in the "Index by Categories"

Rubella

see Infective and parasitic diseases

Ruben, George

"Economy Improves; Bargaining Problems Persist in 1983", 6722–1.403

Rubidium

see Metals and metal industries

Rubin, Laura S.

"Recent Developments in the State and Local Government Sector", 9362–1.408

Rubin, Robert J.

"Epidemiology of End Stage Renal Disease and Implications for Public Policy", 4102–1.450

Rubinstein, Nathan

"Residential Alterations and Repairs", 2012–1.406

Rudney, Gabriel

"Trends in Employment and Earnings in the Philanthropic Sector", 6722–1.455

Rudy, Dennis

"U.S. Production, Imports & Import/Production Ratios for Cotton, Wool & Man-Made Fiber Textiles & Apparel", 2044–14

Ruff, Samuel R.

"Brazil: An Export Market Profile", 1526–6.4

Ruffin, Marilyn D.

"Contribution of the Family to the Economic Support of the Elderly", 1702–1.409

Ruffing, Kathy A.

"Federal Debt and Interest Costs, Special Study", 26308–50

Rugs

see Textile industry and fabrics

Ruiz, Pedro

"Illicit Traffic and Undue Use of Coca and Cocaine in Peru in 1978", 7008–40

Runner, Diana

"Changes in Unemployment Insurance Legislation During 1983", 6722–1.414

Rural areas

Agricultural and rural area dev research, scientist years and funds expended, FY82, annual rpt, 1744–2

Agricultural production, marketing, trade, supply, food consumption, and food and nutrition programs, 1960s-83, annual chartbook, 1504–3

Agricultural Statistics, 1983, annual rpt, 1004–1

Agriculture Fact Book of US, compilation of data for 1983 with trends from 1940, annual rpt, 1004–14

AID dev assistance activities, special study series, 9916–3

Rural areas

Airline subsidies of Fed Govt paid since 1979 to air carriers serving small communities, by carrier, monthly rpt, 9142–48

Alabama rural black population, education, employment, health services, and economic status, for 16 counties, selected years 1970-81, 11048–180

Assaults, murders, and other deaths of law enforcement officers, by circumstances, level of govt, agency, victim and offender characteristics, and location, 1983, annual rpt, 6224–3

Bus industry collective ratemaking and regulatory reform impacts on operations, finances, and services to older persons and rural areas by State, 1970s-83, 14828–2

Census of Govts, 1982: properties, govt-assessed value, sales, and tax rates, by property type, State, SMSA, county, and city, 2453–1

Census of Population, 1980: detailed socioeconomic and demographic characteristics, by age, sex, race, Hispanic origin, occupation, and industry, State rpt series, 2531–4

Census of Population, 1980: detailed socioeconomic characteristics, by county, city, and inside-outside SMSAs and central cities, State rpt series, 2531–3

Conservation practices in rural areas, Agricultural Conservation Program participation and payments, by State, FY83, annual rpt, 1804–7

Crime Index by population size and region, and offenses known to police by large city, Jan-June 1984, semiannual rpt, 6222–1

Crimes, arrests by offender characteristics, and rates, by offense, and law enforcement employees, by population size and jurisdiction, 1970s-83, annual rpt, 6224–2

Disability days, injury and illness rates by type, and use of health services and Medicaid, by age, region, metro-nonmetro location, and selected SMSA, 1980-81, 4147–10.146

Emergency Conservation Program participation and payments for farmland restoration from natural disaster, by practice and State, FY83, annual rpt, 1804–22

Employment and unemployment in metro and nonmetro areas, annual averages, 1983, article, 6742–2.403

Food consumption and nutrient intake by individuals, by food group, source, and socioeconomic characteristics, 1977-78 natl survey, final rpt series, 1356–4

Foreign women sociodemographic, economic, and fertility characteristics, with comparisons to men, by country, 1960s-85, world region rpt series, 2326–15

Housing and neighborhood quality indicators and attitudes, and occupant characteristics, by urban-rural location and region, 1981, annual survey, 2485–7

Housing completions, and new unit sales price, cost per square foot, and heating fuel use, by metro-nonmetro area, 1976-82, 1598–190

Housing vacant unit characteristics and costs, and occupancy and vacancy rates, by region and metro-nonmetro location, quarterly rpt, 2482–1

Hwy Statistics, detailed data on traffic, govt finances, fuel use, vehicles, driver licenses, and hwy characteristics, by State, 1983, annual rpt, 7554–1

Hwy traffic volume on rural roads and city streets, by region, monthly rpt, 7552–8

Income of families and persons, by sociodemographic characteristics, 1983, advance annual Current Population Rpt, 2546–6.41

Israel health care in rural clinics under prepaid plan, services use and user satisfaction, 1981 survey, article, 4102–1.456

Kentucky employment growth in 9-county rural area, labor force and establishment characteristics, 1979-80, 1598–194

Older persons by demographic, socioeconomic, and health characteristics, selected years 1900-81 and projected to 2050, Current Population Rpt, 2546–2.125

Older persons population characteristics, and needs and costs of social services by type, by metro-nonmetro status, 1970s-82 with trends from 1900, 21148–28

Older persons rural housing condition, selected householder and housing characteristics with comparisons to urban and nonaged population, 1979, 1598–193

Population size and change for metro and nonmetro areas and central cities by census div, and growth of areas with large black and aged populations, 1970-82, 2328–47

Rural area situation and dev, periodic rpt articles, 1502–7

Statistical Abstract of US, social, political, and economic data, 1950s-83 and trends, annual rpt, 2324–1.1

Transit systems research publications, 2nd half FY83, semiannual listing, 7882–1

see also Agricultural cooperatives

see also Farm income

see also Farm population

see also Farms and farmland

see also Federal aid to rural areas

see also Migrant workers

see also Rural electrification

see also under Agriculture and terms beginning with Agricultural

see also under By Urban-Rural and Metro-Nonmetro in the "Index by Categories"

Rural cooperatives

see Agricultural cooperatives

Rural Development Service

see Farmers Home Administration

Rural electrification

Agricultural Statistics, 1983, annual rpt, 1004–1.2

Electric power average bills, by supplier type, consumption level, and State, Jan 1984, annual rpt, 3164–40.3

Electric utilities privately owned, detailed financial and operating data by company, with summary data for other distributors by type, 1982, annual rpt, 3164–23

Fed Govt aid to State and local govts, expenditures, and direct payments, by program, agency, and State, FY83, annual rpt, 2464–2

Index by Subjects and Names

Loan activities of Rural Electrification Program, by State, FY83 and cumulative from 1935, annual rpt, 1244–7

Loans by REA to electric power supply and distribution companies, and borrower operating and financial data, by firm and State, 1983, annual rpt, 1244–1

Plants financed by REA, with location, capacity, and owner, as of Jan 1984, annual listing, 1244–6

Purchases (wholesale) and costs for individual REA borrowers, by supplier and State, 1940-83, annual rpt, 1244–5

Southwestern Fed Power System financial statements, electric power sales by customer, and project capacity, production, and costs, FY83, annual rpt, 3244–1

Western Area Power Admin operations by plant, financial statements, and electric power sales by customer, FY83, annual rpt, 3254–1

Rural Electrification Administration

Activities and programs of USDA, by subagency, FY83, annual rpt, 1004–3

Agricultural Statistics, 1983, annual rpt, 1004–1.2

Budget of US, appropriations, outlays, balances, and budget receipts, by govtl branch and agency, FY83, annual rpt, 8104–2

Budget of US, CBO analysis of revenue and spending alternatives and projections of economic indicators, FY85-89, annual rpt, 26304–3.3

Budget of US, loans and loan guarantees, and Admin proposed limits on credit assistance, by program, FY83-89, annual rpt, 26306–3.65

Cost control proposals for Fed Govt programs and mgmt, 3-year savings by function and agency, and financial and operating data, 1960s-81, 16908–1.2

Credit assistance costs, policies to improve measurement, with loan and loan guarantee data by program, and Federal and private credit instns operations, 1970-84, 26306–6.72

Electric utilities privately owned, detailed financial and operating data by company, with summary data for other distributors by type, 1982, annual rpt, 3164–23

Fed Govt off-budget outlays, by function FY62-89, and by entity FY73-89, annual rpt, 104–12

Finances of Federal off-budget entities, US Budget Appendix, FY85, detailed annual rpt, 104–3.3

Fraud and abuse in USDA programs, audits and investigations, 2nd half FY84, semiannual rpt, 1002–4

Loan activities of Rural Electrification Program, by State, FY83 and cumulative from 1935, annual rpt, 1244–7

Loan activities of Rural Telephone Program, by State, FY83, annual rpt, 1244–8

Loans to electric power supply and distribution companies, and borrower operating and financial data, by firm and State, 1983, annual rpt, 1244–1

Loans to telephone companies under rural telephone program, and borrower operations and finances, 1983, annual rpt, 1244–2

Index by Subjects and Names

Plants financed by REA, with location, capacity, and owner, as of Jan 1984, annual listing, 1244–6

Purchases (wholesale) and costs for individual REA borrowers, by supplier and State, 1940-83, annual rpt, 1244–5

see also Rural Telephone Bank

Rural Electrification and Telephone Revolving Fund

see Federal trust funds

Rural Telephone Bank

Agricultural Statistics, 1983, annual rpt, 1004–1.2

Fed Govt off-budget outlays, by function FY62-89, and by entity FY73-89, annual rpt, 104–12

Finances of Federal off-budget entities, US Budget Appendix, FY85, detailed annual rpt, 104–3.3

Loan activities of Rural Telephone Program, by State, FY83, annual rpt, 1244–8

Loans to telephone companies under rural telephone program, and borrower operations and finances, 1983, annual rpt, 1244–2

Russell, Jesse R.

"Use and Cost of Soil Conservation and Water Quality Practices in the Southeast", 1588–84

Russell, Mark S.

"Female Veteran Population", 9928–28

Russia

see Soviet Union

Russo, William J., Jr.

"Plant and Equipment Expenditures by Business for Pollution Abatement, 1983 and Planned 1984", 2702–1.423

Rutledge, Gary L.

"Plant and Equipment Expenditures by Business for Pollution Abatement, 1983 and Planned 1984", 2702–1.423

Rwanda

Agricultural and food production indexes, and production of selected commodities, by world region and country, 1974-83, annual rpt, 1524–5

Agricultural situation in sub-Saharan Africa, by country, 1982-83 and outlook for 1984, annual rpt, 1524–4.10

AID activities and funding by project and function, FY85, and developing countries summary socioeconomic data, 1970s-83, by country, annual rpt, 9914–3

AID economic assistance to developing countries, obligations and disbursements by country, quarterly rpt, 9912–4

Economic conditions and foreign marketing prospects in 46 Sub-Saharan countries, 1983 world region rpt, 2046–5.1

Economic, social, and political summary data, by country, 1984, annual factbook, 244–11

Economic trends in income, production, prices, employment, finances, and trade, 1984 annual rpt, 2046–4.72

Exports of US, detailed Schedule B commodities by country of destination, 1983, annual rpt, 2424–9

Exports of US, detailed Schedule E commodities by mode of transport and world area and country of destination, 1983, annual rpts, 2424–5

Imports of US, detailed Schedule A commodities by country and world area of origin, and mode of transport, 1983, annual rpts, 2424–2

Imports of US, detailed TSUSA commodities by country of origin, 1983, annual rpt, 2424–4

Loans and grants for economic and military assistance from US and intl agencies, by program and country, FY46-83, annual rpt, 9914–5

Military aid of US, arms sales, and training programs costs and budget requests by program, world region, and country, FY83-85, annual rpt, 7144–13

Military spending, arms trade, and armed forces size, with total govt spending and population, by country, 1972-82, annual rpt, 9824–1

Minerals Yearbook, 1982, Vol 3: foreign country reviews of production, trade, and policies, by commodity, annual rpt, 5604–35

Minerals Yearbook, 1982, Vol 3 preprints: foreign country review of production, trade, and policies, by commodity, annual rpt, 5604–17.83

Population size and growth rates, and latest available benchmark demographic data, by country, 1950-83, biennial rpt, 2324–4

see also under By Foreign Country in the "Index by Categories"

Rye

see Grains and grain products

Rykwalder, Annette

"Licensed Physicians Who Work in Prisons: A Profile", 4102–1.407

Rytina, Nancy F.

"Occupational Reclassification and Changes in Distribution by Gender", 6722–1.417

Sabre Foundation

"Enterprise Zone Activity in the States: Summary of Survey Findings", 21788–140.1

"Free Zones in Developing Countries: Expanding Opportunities for the Private Sector", 9918–10

Saccoccio, Marjorie

"Transportation Safety Information Report, 1983 Annual Summary", 7304–19

Sachs, Abner

"Implicit Price Deflators for Military Construction", 2702–1.401

Sacks, Seymour

"Fiscal Disparities: Central Cities and Suburbs, 1981. An Information Report", 10048–61

Sacramento, Calif.

Census of Housing, 1980: occupancy and unit characteristics, by race, Hispanic origin, and city, SMSA rpt, 2473–1.309

Census of Population and Housing, 1980: detailed population and housing characteristics, by county, city, and census tract, SMSA rpt, 2551–2.309

Housing and households detailed characteristics, and unit and neighborhood quality, by inside-outside central cities, 1980 survey, SMSA rpt, 2485–6.15

Housing unit starts and completions authorized by building permits in 20 MSAs, quarterly rpt, 2382–9

Wages by occupation, and benefits for office and plant workers, 1983 SMSA survey rpt, 6785–12.4

Waterborne commerce of US (domestic and foreign), freight by commodity, traffic, and passengers, by port and waterway, 1982, annual rpt, 3754–3.4

Sales, business

see also under By City and By SMSA or MSA in the "Index by Categories"

Safety

see Accidents and accident prevention

see Aviation accidents and safety

see Marine accidents and safety

see Mine accidents and safety

see Motor vehicle safety devices

see Occupational health and safety

see Product safety

see Railroad accidents and safety

see Traffic accidents and safety

Saginaw, Mich.

Census of Housing, 1980: occupancy and unit characteristics, by race, Hispanic origin, and city, SMSA rpt, 2473–1.310

Census of Population and Housing, 1980: detailed population and housing characteristics, by county, city, and census tract, SMSA rpt, 2551–2.310

Housing and households detailed characteristics, and unit and neighborhood quality, by inside-outside central cities, 1980 survey, SMSA rpt, 2485–6.5

Wages of office and plant workers, by occupation, 1983 SMSA survey rpt, 6785–12.2

Wages of office and plant workers, by occupation, 1984 SMSA survey rpt, 6785–11.10

see also under By SMSA or MSA in the "Index by Categories"

Sailer, Peter

"Coming Soon: Taxpayer Data Classified by Occupation", 8308–28.1

"Results of Coverage and Processing Changes to the 1980 Individual Statistics of Income Program", 8308–28.1

Sailors

see Merchant seamen

see Military personnel

Saint

see under terms beginning St.

Salaries

see Agricultural wages

see Earnings, general

see Earnings, local and regional

see Earnings, specific industries

see Federal pay

see Minimum wage

see Payroll

see State and local employees pay

Salathe, Larry E.

"Dairy Program Alternatives for the 1980's", 1568–246

Salem, Mass.

see also under By SMSA or MSA in the "Index by Categories"

Salem, Oreg.

Census of Population and Housing, 1980: detailed population and housing characteristics, by county, city, and census tract, SMSA rpt, 2551–2.314

Housing vacancy rates for single and multifamily units and mobile homes, by city and ZIP code, 1983, annual metro area rpt, 9304–21.1

see also under By SMSA or MSA in the "Index by Categories"

Sales, business

see Business income and expenses, general

see Business income and expenses, specific industries

see Farm income

Sales promotion

Sales promotion

Agricultural commodities generic advertising, activities and funding by source, selected years 1972-82, 1548–242

Agricultural cooperatives farm supply sales programs, services offered, inventory mgmt and marketing methods, and sales force and compensation system, for 4 products, 1982, 1128–24

Census of Population, 1980: detailed socioeconomic and demographic characteristics, by age, sex, race, Hispanic origin, occupation, and industry, State rpt series, 2531–4

Census of Population, 1980: labor force, by sex, detailed occupation, and region, with comparison to 1970 census, supplementary rpt, 2535–1.12

Cigarette sales, market shares, advertising expenditures and methods, and tar and nicotine content, by cigarette type, selected years 1963-81, annual rpt, 9404–4

Electric utilities privately owned, advertising and sales expenses, by company, 1982, annual rpt, 3164–23.2

Food industry advertising expenditures by media type, and advertising to sales ratio by selected food item, 1970-79 with some trends from 1955, 1548–234

Milk order advertising and promotion programs finances, fees, and producer participation, by region, 1983, article, 1317–4.406

Multinatl corporation income reallocation through regulation of intercorporate transactions, by tax item, treaty status, asset size, industry, and tax haven country, 1982, 8008–110

Natural gas interstate pipeline company detailed financial and operating data, by firm, 1983, annual rpt, 3164–38

see also Market research

see also Sales workers

Sales tax

Auto and van operating and owning costs by component and vehicle size, for 12 years of operation, 1984 model year, biennial rpt, 7554–21

Auto operating costs by component and vehicle size, and Fed Govt mileage reimbursement rates, 1983, annual rpt, 9454–13.1

Census of Govts, 1982: city govt revenues by source, expenditures by function, debt, and assets, by State and city, 2457–4

Census of Govts, 1982: county govt revenues by source, expenditures by function, debt, and assets, by State and county, 2457–3

Census of Govts, 1982: State govt payments to local govts, by program, source of funds, level of govt, and State, with trends from 1902, 2460–3

Coal taxes for surface and underground mines, by type of tax and State, 1984 rpt, 11128–1

Govt finances, by level of govt and State, selected years 1929-83, annual rpt, 10044–1

Govt finances, by level of govt, State, and for large cities and counties, 1981-83, annual rpt series, 2466–2

Govt revenues by source and expenditures by function, natl income and product

account, *Survey of Current Business,* monthly rpt, monthly and annual tables, 2702–1.24

Govt tax revenues, by level of govt, type of tax, State, and selected counties, quarterly rpt, 2462–3

Income tax returns of elderly, by income statement and tax item and income level, 1981 with trends from 1977, article, 8302–2.412

Income tax returns of individuals, detailed data, 1982, annual rpt, 8304–2

Local govt spending, reliance on State aid and local taxes by type, and excise tax growth by State, selected years FY57-83, article, 10042–1.403

Motor fuel State tax provisions, motor vehicle registration fees, and disposition of receipts, by State, as of Jan 1984, biennial rpt, 7554–37

Motor fuel tax rates, by fuel type and State, monthly rpt, 7552–1

Public opinion on taxes, tax policy, and intergovtl relations, 1972-84 surveys, annual rpt, 10044–2

Retail store sales tax as percent of sales, by SIC 2- to 4-digit kind of business, 1983, annual rpt, 2413–5

State and local tax rates by selected jurisdiction, and average family tax burden by income level and selected city, by type of tax, 1982, 10046–8.2

Tax expenditures, Fed Govt revenues foregone through income tax deductions and exclusions by type, and effect of Deficit Reduction Act, FY84-89, annual rpt, 21784–10

Texas border employment and economic impacts of Mexican peso devaluation, for 6 counties and 2 SMSAs, 1970s-May 1983, hearing, 21788–133

Transportation finances, operations, vehicles, equipment, accidents, and energy use, by mode of transport, 1955-84, annual rpt, 7304–2

Wholesale trade sales tax as a percent of sales, by SIC 2- to 3-digit kind of business, 1983, annual rpt, 2413–13

see also Excise tax

Sales workers

Agricultural cooperatives farm supply sales programs, services offered, inventory mgmt and marketing methods, and sales force and compensation system, for 4 products, 1982, 1128–24

Census of Housing, 1980: structural, financial, and householder characteristics, by region and State, 2475–4

Census of Population and Housing, 1980: detailed population and housing characteristics, by county, city, and census tract, State and SMSA rpt series, 2551–2

Census of Population, 1980: detailed socioeconomic and demographic characteristics, by age, sex, race, Hispanic origin, occupation, and industry, State rpt series, 2531–4

Census of Population, 1980: detailed socioeconomic characteristics, by county, city, and inside-outside SMSAs and central cities, State rpt series, 2531–3

Census of Population, 1980: labor force, by sex, detailed occupation, and region, with comparison to 1970 census, supplementary rpt, 2535–1.12

Index by Subjects and Names

Employment and economic conditions, alternative BLS projections to 1995 with selected trends for 1959-82, 6728–29

Employment by detailed occupation, for 29 SIC 2-digit nonmanufacturing industries, 1981 BLS survey, 6748–60

Employment, unemployment, and labor force, by demographic and employment characteristics, State, and for 30 metro areas and 11 large cities, 1983, annual rpt, 6744–7

Handbook of Labor Statistics, employment, earnings, hours, and labor force characteristics, 1982 and trends, detailed annual rpt, 6724–1

Income of households, families, and persons, by detailed socioeconomic characteristics and region, 1982, annual Current Population Rpt, 2546–6.39

Minority group and women's employment, by occupational group, SIC 2- to 3-digit industry, State, and SMSA, 1981, annual rpt, 9244–1

Occupational manpower needs and supply by detailed occupation, and educational and training program enrollees and grads by detailed field, 1982 and 1995, biennial rpt, 6744–3

Occupational Outlook Handbook, 1984-85 biennial rpt, 6744–1

Poverty status of families and persons, by detailed socioeconomic characteristics, 1982, annual Current Population Rpt, 2546–6.40

TV and radio industry minority and women employment by occupation, and business owners, by race and State, with revenues and stations, 1971-81, hearing, 21368–45

Washington State deaths by sex, cause, and detailed occupation, summary data from occupational mortality study, 1950-79, 4248–47

Women's employment and earnings, by labor force and socioeconomic characteristics, and compared to men, 1978-81 and trends from 1940s, 6568–29

see also under By Occupation in the "Index by Categories"

Sali, Gregory J.

"Evaluation of Boise Selective Traffic Enforcement Project", 7762–9.406

Salina, Kans.

Wages of office and plant workers, by occupation, 1983 labor market area survey rpt, 6785–3.3

Salinas, Calif.

Census of Housing, 1980: occupancy and unit characteristics, by race, Hispanic origin, and city, SMSA rpt, 2473–1.315

Census of Population and Housing, 1980: detailed population and housing characteristics, by county, city, and census tract, SMSA rpt, 2551–2.315

Housing vacancy rates for single and multifamily units and mobile homes, by city and ZIP code, 1983, annual metro area rpt, 9304–20.6

see also under By SMSA or MSA in the "Index by Categories"

Saline water conversion

Water supply and use in 3 areas with supply problems and total US, and methods to increase supply, selected years 1974-80 and projected to 2010, 9208–125

Index by Subjects and Names

Salisbury, Dallas L.
"Development and Design of Private Employer Pensions", 25408–89

Salisbury, N.C.
Census of Housing, 1980: occupancy and unit characteristics, by race, Hispanic origin, and city, SMSA rpt, 2473–1.316
Census of Population and Housing, 1980: detailed population and housing characteristics, by county, city, and census tract, SMSA rpt, 2551–2.316

Salmonella
see Food and waterborne diseases

Solomon, S. N.
"State Surveillance of Radioactive Material Transportation, Final Report", 9636–1.23

Salt
see Nonmetallic minerals and mines

SALT
see Strategic Arms Limitation Treaties

Salt Lake City, Utah
Census of Housing, 1980: occupancy and unit characteristics, by race, Hispanic origin, and city, SMSA rpt, 2473–1.317
Census of Population and Housing, 1980: detailed population and housing characteristics, by county, city, and census tract, SMSA rpt, 2551–2.317
Housing and households detailed characteristics, and unit and neighborhood quality, by inside-outside central cities, 1980 survey, SMSA rpt, 2485–6.6
Housing unit starts and completions authorized by building permits in 20 MSAs, quarterly rpt, 2382–9
Housing vacancy rates for single and multifamily units and mobile homes, by city and ZIP code, 1983, annual metro area rpt, 9304–21.8
Wages of office and plant workers, by occupation, 1983 SMSA survey rpt, 6785–12.3
see also under By City and By SMSA or MSA in the "Index by Categories"

Salt water conversion
see Saline water conversion

Saluter, Arlene F.
"Marital Status and Living Arrangements: Mar. 1983", 2546–1.388

Salvage
see also Recycling of waste materials
see also Scrap metals

Salvo, Joseph J.
"Lifetime Work Experience and Its Effect on Earnings: Retrospective Data from the 1979 Income Survey Development Program", 2546–2.123

Samoa
see American Samoa
see Western Samoa

Samples, Karl C.
"Economic appraisal of Sail-Assisted Commercial Fishing Vessels in Hawaiian Waters", 2162–1.401

Samuels, William B.
"Oilspill Risk Analysis for the St. George Basin (Dec. 1984) and North Aleutian Basin (Apr. 1985) Outer Continental Shelf Lease Offerings", 5736–2.8

Samuelson, Ray
"Corporation Income Tax Returns, 1981", 8302–2.403

San Angelo, Tex.
Census of Housing, 1980: occupancy and unit characteristics, by race, Hispanic origin, and city, SMSA rpt, 2473–1.318
Census of Population and Housing, 1980: detailed population and housing characteristics, by county, city, and census tract, SMSA rpt, 2551–2.318
see also under By SMSA or MSA in the "Index by Categories"

San Antonio, Tex.
Census of Housing, 1980: occupancy and unit characteristics, by race, Hispanic origin, and city, SMSA rpt, 2473–1.319
Census of Population and Housing, 1980: detailed population and housing characteristics, by county, city, and census tract, SMSA rpt, 2551–2.319
Fruit and vegetable shipments, and arrivals in 23 US and 5 Canada cities, by mode of transport and State or country of origin, 1983, annual rpt, 1311–4.2
Housing and financial characteristics, and unit and neighborhood quality, for 15 SMSAs, 1978, annual survey special supplement, 2485–8
Housing and households detailed characteristics, and unit and neighborhood quality, by inside-outside central cities, 1982 survey, SMSA rpt, 2485–6.40
Housing vacancy rates for single and multifamily units and mobile homes, by city and ZIP code, 1983, annual metro area rpt, 9304–19.3
Population size of top 25 cities, 1980 and 1982, press release, 2328–46
Wages of office and plant workers, by occupation, 1984 SMSA survey rpt, 6785–11.5
Water supply and use in 3 areas with supply problems and total US, and methods to increase supply, selected years 1974-80 and projected to 2010, 9208–125
see also under By City and By SMSA or MSA in the "Index by Categories"

San Benito, Tex.
Census of Housing, 1980: occupancy and unit characteristics, by race, Hispanic origin, and city, SMSA rpt, 2473–1.104
Census of Population and Housing, 1980: detailed population and housing characteristics, by county, city, and census tract, SMSA rpt, 2551–2.104
Employment and economic impacts on Texas border of Mexican peso devaluation, for 6 counties and 2 SMSAs, 1970s-May 1983, hearing, 21788–133
Wages of office and plant workers, by occupation, 1984 labor market area survey rpt, 6785–3.10

San Bernardino, Calif.
Census of Housing, 1980: occupancy and unit characteristics, by race, Hispanic origin, and city, SMSA rpt, 2473–1.303
Census of Population and Housing, 1980: detailed population and housing characteristics, by county, city, and census tract, SMSA rpt, 2551–2.303
Housing and financial characteristics, and unit and neighborhood quality, for 15 SMSAs, 1978, annual survey special supplement, 2485–8
Housing and households detailed characteristics, and unit and neighborhood quality, by inside-outside central cities, 1982 survey, SMSA rpt, 2485–6.41

San Francisco, Calif.

Housing unit starts and completions authorized by building permits in 20 MSAs, quarterly rpt, 2382–9
Housing vacancy rates for single and multifamily units and mobile homes, by city and ZIP code, 1983, annual metro area rpt, 9304–20.9
see also under By City and By SMSA or MSA in the "Index by Categories"

San Diego, Calif.
Census of Housing, 1980: occupancy and unit characteristics, by race, Hispanic origin, and city, SMSA rpt, 2473–1.320
Census of Population and Housing, 1980: detailed population and housing characteristics, by county, city, and census tract, SMSA rpt, 2551–2.320
CPI by component for US city average, and by region, population size, and for 28 SMSAs, monthly press release, 6762–1
CPI by detailed component, for US city average, 28 SMSAs, and 4 regions by population size, monthly rpt, 6762–2
Housing and financial characteristics, and unit and neighborhood quality, for 15 SMSAs, 1978, annual survey special supplement, 2485–8
Housing and households detailed characteristics, and unit and neighborhood quality, by inside-outside central cities, 1982 survey, SMSA rpt, 2485–6.42
Housing unit starts and completions authorized by building permits in 20 MSAs, quarterly rpt, 2382–9
Nursing homes in San Diego, Calif, receiving Medicaid bonuses for care of severely ill, nursing time and costs by procedure, and bonus amount, 1980-81, article, 4652–1.405
Population size of top 25 cities, 1980 and 1982, press release, 2328–46
Wages by occupation, and benefits for office and plant workers, 1983 SMSA survey rpt, 6785–12.3
see also under By City and By SMSA or MSA in the "Index by Categories"

San Diego County, Calif.
Arson investigation and prosecution, by incident characteristics and outcome, motive, and type of evidence, for 4 jurisdictions, 1981, 6068–184

San Francisco, Calif.
Auto dealer repair workers, wages, and benefits, by occupation, size of establishment, and for 24 labor market areas, Nov 1982 survey, 6787–6.202
Cancer cases, incidence, deaths, and death rates, by body site, age, race, Hispanic origin, and sex, for 10 geographic areas, 1973-81, 4478–130
Census of Housing, 1980: occupancy and unit characteristics, by race, Hispanic origin, and city, SMSA rpt, 2473–1.321
Census of Population and Housing, 1980: detailed population and housing characteristics, by county, city, and census tract, SMSA rpt, 2551–2.321
CPI by component for US city average, and by region, population size, and for 28 SMSAs, monthly press release, 6762–1
CPI by detailed component, for US city average, 28 SMSAs, and 4 regions by population size, monthly rpt, 6762–2
Dress industry production and related workers, wages, and benefits, by

San Francisco, Calif.

occupation, size of establishment, and union status, for 11 labor market areas, Aug 1982 survey, 6787–6.200

Fruit and vegetable shipments, and arrivals in 23 US and 5 Canada cities, by mode of transport and State or country of origin, 1983, annual rpt, 1311–4.2

Hospital worker wages by sex and occupation, and benefits, for 22 MSAs, Oct 1981 survey, 6787–6.201

Housing and financial characteristics, and unit and neighborhood quality, for 15 SMSAs, 1978, annual survey special supplement, 2485–8

Housing and households detailed characteristics, and unit and neighborhood quality, by inside-outside central cities, 1982 survey, SMSA rpt, 2485–6.34

Population size of top 25 cities, 1980 and 1982, press release, 2328–46

Port dev costs and financing through user fees, and shipping industry impact on local economy, by State, other area, industry, commodity, and port, 1970s-2020, hearings, 21568–34

Radioactive strontium in NYC and San Francisco diet by food item, and in NYC tap water and milk, quarterly 1982 with trends from 1954, annual rpt, 3404–13

Repair technicians and apprentices wages and benefits, for 5 types of electrical repair shops in 19 SMSAs, Nov 1981 survey, 6787–6.197

Ships in Natl Defense Reserve Fleet at Suisun Bay, Jan 1984, semiannual inventory, 7702–2

Wages by occupation, and benefits for office and plant workers, 1984 SMSA survey rpt, 6785–11.5

Waterborne commerce of US (domestic and foreign), freight by commodity, traffic, and passengers, by port and waterway, 1982, annual rpt, 3754–3.4

see also under By City and By SMSA or MSA in the "Index by Categories"

San Jose, Calif.

Census of Housing, 1980: occupancy and unit characteristics, by race, Hispanic origin, and city, SMSA rpt, 2473–1.322

Census of Population and Housing, 1980: detailed population and housing characteristics, by county, city, and census tract, SMSA rpt, 2551–2.322

Housing unit starts and completions authorized by building permits in 20 MSAs, quarterly rpt, 2382–9

Housing vacancy rates for single and multifamily units and mobile homes, by city and ZIP code, 1983, annual metro area rpt, 9304–20.15

Population size of top 25 cities, 1980 and 1982, press release, 2328–46

Wages by occupation, and benefits for office and plant workers, 1984 SMSA survey rpt, 6785–11.5

see also under By City and By SMSA or MSA in the "Index by Categories"

San Juan, P.R.

see also under By SMSA or MSA in the "Index by Categories"

San Marino

Economic, social, and political summary data, by country, 1984, annual factbook, 244–11

Imports of US, detailed TSUSA commodities by country of origin, 1983, annual rpt, 2424–4

Population size and growth rates, and latest available benchmark demographic data, by country, 1950-83, biennial rpt, 2324–4

see also under By Foreign Country in the "Index by Categories"

San Mateo County, Calif.

Housing vacancy rates for single and multifamily units and mobile homes, by city and ZIP code, 1983, annual metro area rpt, 9304–20.14

Sana

see Yemen, North

Sanctions

see International sanctions

Sand and gravel

see Quarries and stone products

Sandia Laboratories

see also Department of Energy National Laboratories

Sandusky, Ohio

Wages by occupation, and benefits for office and plant workers, 1984 labor market area survey rpt, 6785–3.7

Sanik, Margaret M.

"Technology and Household Production", 1004–16.1

Sanitary districts

see Special districts

Sanitary engineering

see Plumbing and heating

see Refuse and refuse disposal

see Sewage and wastewater treatment systems

Santa Ana, Calif.

Census of Housing, 1980: occupancy and unit characteristics, by race, Hispanic origin, and city, SMSA rpt, 2473–1.67

Census of Population and Housing, 1980: detailed population and housing characteristics, by county, city, and census tract, SMSA rpt, 2551–2.67

Housing and households detailed characteristics, and unit and neighborhood quality, by inside-outside central cities, 1981 survey, SMSA rpt, 2485–6.19

Housing unit starts and completions authorized by building permits in 20 MSAs, quarterly rpt, 2382–9

Housing vacancy rates for single and multifamily units and mobile homes, by city and ZIP code, 1983, annual metro area rpt, 9304–20.7

Wages of office and plant workers, by occupation, 1983 SMSA survey rpt, 6785–12.2

see also under By City and By SMSA or MSA in the "Index by Categories"

Santa Barbara, Calif.

Census of Housing, 1980: occupancy and unit characteristics, by race, Hispanic origin, and city, SMSA rpt, 2473–1.324

Census of Population and Housing, 1980: detailed population and housing characteristics, by county, city, and census tract, SMSA rpt, 2551–2.324

Wages of office and plant workers, by occupation, 1984 labor market area survey rpt, 6785–3.7

see also under By SMSA or MSA in the "Index by Categories"

Index by Subjects and Names

Santa Cruz, Calif.

Census of Housing, 1980: occupancy and unit characteristics, by race, Hispanic origin, and city, SMSA rpt, 2473–1.325

Census of Population and Housing, 1980: detailed population and housing characteristics, by county, city, and census tract, SMSA rpt, 2551–2.325

Housing vacancy rates for single and multifamily units and mobile homes, by city and ZIP code, 1983, annual metro area rpt, 9304–20.13

see also under By SMSA or MSA in the "Index by Categories"

Santa Maria, Calif.

Census of Housing, 1980: occupancy and unit characteristics, by race, Hispanic origin, and city, SMSA rpt, 2473–1.324

Census of Population and Housing, 1980: detailed population and housing characteristics, by county, city, and census tract, SMSA rpt, 2551–2.324

Wages of office and plant workers, by occupation, 1984 labor market area survey rpt, 6785–3.7

see also under By SMSA or MSA in the "Index by Categories"

Santa Rosa, Calif.

Census of Housing, 1980: occupancy and unit characteristics, by race, Hispanic origin, and city, SMSA rpt, 2473–1.326

Census of Population and Housing, 1980: detailed population and housing characteristics, by county, city, and census tract, SMSA rpt, 2551–2.326

Housing vacancy rates for single and multifamily units and mobile homes, by city and ZIP code, 1983, annual metro area rpt, 9304–20.3

Housing vacancy rates for single and multifamily units and mobile homes, by city and ZIP code, 1984, annual metro area rpt, 9304–20.19

see also under By SMSA or MSA in the "Index by Categories"

Santoni, G. J.

"Business Cycles and the Eighth District", 9391–1.402

"Employment Trends in St. Louis: 1954-82", 9391–1.405

"Interest Rate Risk and the Stock Prices of Financial Institutions", 9391–1.419

"Private Central Bank: Some Olde English Lessons", 9391–1.410

Sao Tome and Principe

AID economic assistance to developing countries, obligations and disbursements by country, quarterly rpt, 9912–4

Economic conditions and foreign marketing prospects in 46 Sub-Saharan countries, 1983 world region rpt, 2046–5.1

Economic, social, and political summary data, by country, 1984, annual factbook, 244–11

Imports of US, detailed TSUSA commodities by country of origin, 1983, annual rpt, 2424–4

Loans and grants for economic and military assistance from US and intl agencies, by program and country, FY46-83, annual rpt, 9914–5

Military spending, arms trade, and armed forces size, with total govt spending and population, by country, 1972-82, annual rpt, 9824–1

Index by Subjects and Names

Savings

Minerals Yearbook, 1982, Vol 3: foreign country reviews of production, trade, and policies, by commodity, annual rpt, 5604–35

Minerals Yearbook, 1982, Vol 3 preprints: foreign country review of production, trade, and policies, by commodity, annual rpt, 5604–17.82

Population size and growth rates, and latest available benchmark demographic data, by country, 1950-83, biennial rpt, 2324–4

see also under By Foreign Country in the "Index by Categories"

Sarasota, Fla.

Census of Housing, 1980: occupancy and unit characteristics, by race, Hispanic origin, and city, SMSA rpt, 2473–1.327

Census of Population and Housing, 1980: detailed population and housing characteristics, by county, city, and census tract, SMSA rpt, 2551–2.327

see also under By SMSA or MSA in the "Index by Categories"

Saricks, C. L.

"Effects of Relaxing Automobile Emission Standards: A Generic Analysis and an Urban Case Study", 3408–31

Sarris, Alexander H.

"World Trade in Fruits and Vegetables: Projections for an Enlarged European Community", 1528–182

Satellites

- Aerial survey R&D publications, and sources of natural resource and environmental data gathered by air- and spacecraft, quarterly listing, 9502–7
- DOD budget, costs of individual weapons or weapons systems, FY83-85, annual rpt, 3504–2
- DOD budget, FY85 weapons system requests consistency with US policy and specified treaties, with funding FY83-87, annual rpt, 21384–4
- DOD budget, itemized account of legislative history, FY84, annual rpt, 3504–7
- DOD space and related R&D program activities and funding, FY84-85, annual rpt, 3504–9
- Fed Govt programs and mgmt cost control proposals, 3-year savings by function and agency, and financial and operating data, 1960s-81, 16908–1.3
- Foreign and US astronautic and aeronautic events, comprehensive chronology, 1976, annual rpt, 9504–2
- Foreign and US satellite systems for civil observation, data product revenue, and proposed transfer of Fed Govt system to private sector, selected years 1978-FY84, 2148–47
- Landsat satellite system proposed transfer to private sector, uses and product sales by user, and university programs and personnel by instn, 1973-85, 26358–100
- Launchings of satellites and other space objects since 1957, quarterly listing, 9502–2
- NASA-launched communications and other satellites, and USSR launches by type, 1957-83, annual rpt, 9504–6.1
- NASA project launch schedules and technical descriptions, press release series, 9506–2
- Soviet Union and US satellites by mission and vulnerability to attack, and USSR anti-satellite missiles, 1983 and projected to 1989, hearing, 21208–18

Space and aeronautics programs and budgets of Fed Govt by agency, and foreign programs, 1957-FY85, annual rpt, 9504–9

see also Communications satellites

see also Meteorological satellites

Sattin, Richard W.

"Epidemic of Gynecomastia Among Illegal Haitian Entrants", 4102–1.451

Saudi Arabia

- Agricultural and food production indexes, and production of selected commodities, by world region and country, 1974-83, annual rpt, 1524–5
- Agricultural situation in Middle East and North Africa, by country and commodity, 1983 and outlook for 1984, annual rpt, 1524–4.3
- Computers and computer technology market and trade, and user industry operations and demand, 1984 country market research rpt, 2045–1.45
- Economic conditions in Communist, OECD, and selected other countries, 1960s-83, annual rpt, 244–5
- Economic, social, and political summary data, by country, 1984, annual factbook, 244–11
- Economic trends in income, production, prices, employment, finances, and trade, 1984 annual rpt, 2046–4.94
- Exports and imports of US, by commodity and country, 1972-82, annual world region rpt, 244–13.1
- Exports of US, detailed Schedule B commodities by country of destination, 1983, annual rpt, 2424–9
- Exports of US, detailed Schedule E commodities by mode of transport and world area and country of destination, 1983, annual rpts, 2424–5
- Food processing and packaging equipment market and trade, and user industry operations and demand, 1983 market research rpt, 2045–11.19
- Imports of US, detailed Schedule A commodities by country and world area of origin, and mode of transport, 1983, annual rpts, 2424–2
- Imports of US, detailed TSUSA commodities by country of origin, 1983, annual rpt, 2424–4
- Loans and grants for economic and military assistance from US and intl agencies, by program and country, FY46-83, annual rpt, 9914–5
- Military aid of US, arms sales, and training programs costs and budget requests by program, world region, and country, FY83-85, annual rpt, 7144–13
- Military spending, arms trade, and armed forces size, with total govt spending and population, by country, 1972-82, annual rpt, 9824–1
- *Minerals Yearbook, 1982,* Vol 3: foreign country reviews of production, trade, and policies, by commodity, annual rpt, 5604–35
- *Minerals Yearbook, 1982,* Vol 3 preprints: foreign country review of production, trade, and policies, by commodity, annual rpt, 5604–17.62
- Oil production, and exports and prices to US, by major exporting country, detailed data, monthly rpt, 3162–24

Population size and growth rates, and latest available benchmark demographic data, by country, 1950-83, biennial rpt, 2324–4

- Sporting goods and recreational equipment and vehicles market and trade, 1984 country market research rpt, 2045–14.5
- Telecommunication equipment market and trade, and user industry operations and demand, 1982 country market research rpt, 2045–12.32
- US-Saudi Arabian Joint Commission on Economic Cooperation project activities and costs, and related contract awards by Fed Govt agency, as of 1983, GAO rpt, 26123–80

see also under By Foreign Country in the "Index by Categories"

Saul, Richard

"Out in the Cold: The Expected Impact of Rising Natural Gas Prices on the Poor, the Elderly, and the Unemployed", 25148–26.401

Savannah, Ga.

- Census of Housing, 1980: occupancy and unit characteristics, by race, Hispanic origin, and city, SMSA rpt, 2473–1.328
- Census of Population and Housing, 1980: detailed population and housing characteristics, by county, city, and census tract, SMSA rpt, 2551–2.328
- Wages by occupation, and benefits for office and plant workers, 1984 labor market area survey rpt, 6785–3.5
- Waterborne commerce of US (domestic and foreign), freight by commodity, traffic, and passengers, by port and waterway, 1982, annual rpt, 3754–3.1

see also under By City and By SMSA or MSA in the "Index by Categories"

Savings

- AFDC eligibility under Omnibus Budget Reconciliation Act, effect on caseloads and recipient benefits and living costs, 1981-83, GAO rpt, 26131–11
- Bank financial and operating statements, functional cost analysis for Fed Reserve member banks with average and high earnings, by deposit size, 1982, annual rpt, 9364–6
- Consumer expenditures and savings, 1960s-83, annual chartbook, 1504–3
- *County and City Data Book,* detailed socioeconomic and demographic data for States, counties, and cities, selected years 1976-82, 2328–1
- Deposits, debits, and deposit turnover at financial instns, 1982, annual rpt, 9364–5.1
- Economic and population time series data frequently used in statistical demand analyses, 1941-1982, annual rpt, 1544–21
- Economic indicators and components, and Fed Reserve 4th District business and financial conditions, monthly chartbook, 9377–10
- Economic indicators, nonfinancial, monthly rpt, 9362–1.2
- Economic trends and projections, 1970s-83, and Budget of US under current fiscal policy and alternatives, FY85-89, annual rpt, 26304–3.1
- Farm finances, production, expenses by type, and domestic economic impact, selected years 1972-82 and preliminary 1983-84, annual rpt, 1544–19

Savings

Fed Govt budget deficit related to current account balance, with balance for 14 OECD countries, various periods 1952-83, article, 9373–1.408

Financial and business statistics, historic trends, 1984 annual chartbook, 9364–2.4, 9364–2.11

Financial and business statistics, quarterly chartbook, 9362–2.2

Financial and economic trends, compounded annual rates of change, 1964-83, annual rpt, 9391–9.1

Financial and monetary conditions, selected US summary data, weekly rpt, 9391–4

Financial instns income taxes, effective rates, and selected financial data, by instn type and firm, with comparisons to other industries, selected years 1960-82, hearing, 25368–129

Flow-of-funds accounts, assets and liabilities by type and economic sector, year-end outstandings, 1960-83, annual rpt, 9364–3

Flow-of-funds accounts savings, investments, and credit statements, quarterly rpt, 9365–3.3

Forecasts for selected business activities and natl economic indicators, compilation of representative opinions, 1984, annual rpt, 9389–3

Foreign and US budget deficits effect on interest rates and economic indicators, with govt borrowing and saving, for US and 6 OECD countries, 1975-83, technical paper, 9366–7.89

Foreign and US economic and employment indicators and balance of payments, and US exports by selected commodity, by world area and country, 1970s-83, annual rpt, 2044–26

Foreign economic indicators for 7 OECD countries and US, quarterly rpt, 2042–10

Foreign economic trends and implications for US, annual and semiannual country rpt series, 2046–4

Gross saving and saving by individuals, 1929-83, annual rpt, 204–1.1

Household income, assets, and debt characteristics, sources of credit, and use of financial services, 1983 survey, article, 9362–1.411

Household income, home value and equity, and financial assets by type, by household characteristics, 1983 survey with trends from 1970, article, 9362–1.406

Income tax proposals to encourage savings, and personal assets and liabilities by type, 1981, article, 8302–2.407

Interest rates on time and savings deposits, maximum payable at federally insured instns, Dec 1983, annual rpt, 9364–1.2

Japan yen/dollar exchange rate, 2-country model of sterilized intervention and effect of fiscal balance and private savings, 1973-82, article, 9393–8.405

Monetary and Fed Govt budget trends, Fed Reserve Bank of St Louis monthly rpt, 9391–2

Natl income and product, comprehensive accounts and components, *Survey of Current Business,* monthly rpt, 2702–1.21

Natl income and product, comprehensive accounts and components, *Survey of Current Business,* monthly rpt, monthly and annual tables, 2702–1.26

North Central States, FHLB 6th District insured S&Ls financial condition and operations by State, quarterly rpt, 9302–23

OECD countries natl savings and current account balance ratios to GDP, by country, various periods 1963-81, technical paper, 9366–7.100

OECD countries personal savings rates, 1960s-83, annual rpt, 244–5.2

Older persons income and income sources, by OASDI beneficiary and poverty status, labor force participation, and demographic characteristics, 1982, biennial rpt, 4744–26

Older persons income and income sources, including retirement benefits by plan type, by age and marital status, 1950s-82, conf proceedings, 25408–87

Older persons sociodemographic characteristics, and Fed Govt program participation and funding, 1983 with trends and projections 1900-2060, annual rpt, 25144–3.1

Personal and govt savings, *Business Conditions Digest,* historical supplement and methodology, 1947-82, 2708–31

Personal, corporate, and govt savings, *Business Conditions Digest,* monthly rpt, 2702–3.5

Personal savings measures from natl income and product and flow-of-funds accounts, 1977 and 1982, article, 2702–1.441

Southeastern States financial and economic devs, Fed Reserve 6th District, monthly rpt with articles, 9371–1

Veterans aged 55 and over, socioeconomic characteristics, economic resources, health care and status, and actual and expected use of VA benefits, 1983 survey, 9928–29

Western States, FHLB 11th District member S&L offices, locations, savings balances, and accounts, quarterly listing, 9302–20

Western States, FHLB 11th District member S&Ls financial condition and operations by State, quarterly rpt, 9302–19

Western States, FHLB 12th District member S&Ls financial operations and housing industry indicators by State, monthly rpt, 9302–21

see also Bank deposits

see also Certificates of deposit

see also Credit unions

see also Individual retirement arrangements

see also Investments

see also Negotiable orders of withdrawal accounts

see also Savings and loan associations

see also Savings banks

Savings and loan associations

Appalachian States, FHLB 5th District member S&Ls financial condition and operations by SMSA, monthly rpt, 9302–8

Assets and liabilities, by FHLB district and State, selected years 1955-82, annual rpt, 9314–1

Assets and liabilities of depository instns, monthly rpt, 9362–1.1

Assets and liabilities of savings instns, by type of instn, 1980-82, annual rpt, 9364–5.4

Assets, liabilities, and deposit and loan activity, for all S&Ls and FSLIC-insured savings banks and S&Ls, monthly rpt, 9312–4

Index by Subjects and Names

Automated teller machines shared networks by State, and membership and characteristics of top 16 regional and natl networks, Nov 1983, article, 9373–1.403

Brokered certificates of deposit in acquired and closed individual banks and S&Ls, and disposition of instns, 1982-Oct 1983, hearing, 21248–83

Census of Population, 1980: detailed socioeconomic and demographic characteristics, by age, sex, race, Hispanic origin, occupation, and industry, State rpt series, 2531–4

County Business Patterns: establishments, employees, and payrolls, by SIC 4-digit industry and county, 1981, annual State rpt series, 2326–8

County Business Patterns: establishments, employees, and payrolls, by SIC 4-digit industry and county, 1982, annual State rpt series, 2326–6

Deposits in FSLIC-insured savings instns, and offices, by State, SMSA, and county, 1983, annual rpt, 9314–4

Deregulation of S&Ls, effect on lending activity and noninterest-earning negotiable orders of withdrawal accounts, for US and 3 States, as of June 1980-83, article, 9371–1.432

Employment by detailed occupation, for 29 SIC 2-digit nonmanufacturing industries, 1981 BLS survey, 6748–60

Employment, earnings, and hours, by SIC 4-digit nonfarm industry, monthly 1974-Feb 1984, annual update, 6744–4

Fed Home Loan Bank of New York financial statements, 1982-83, annual rpt, 9304–12

Fed Home Loan Bank System members, with assets of S&Ls, by instn, city, and State, 1983, annual listing, 9314–5

Finances and operations, by SIC 2- to 4-digit industry, 1970s-83 and projected to 1988, annual rpt, 2014–4

Financial and business statistics, historic trends, 1984 annual chartbook, 9364–2.14

Financial and business statistics, quarterly chartbook, 9362–2.7

Financial condition and mortgage loan activity, monthly rpt with articles, 9312–1

Financial ratios, income, and expenses of FSLIC-insured savings instns, 2nd half 1983, semiannual rpt, 9312–6

Financial ratios of profitable and unprofitable FSLIC-insured S&Ls, selected years 1965-82, technical paper, 9316–2.47

Financial ratios of S&Ls in 3 States and US, deregulation impact, 1980-83, article, 9371–1.426

Flow-of-funds accounts, assets and liabilities by type and economic sector, year-end outstandings, 1960-83, annual rpt, 9364–3

Flow-of-funds accounts savings, investments, and credit statements, quarterly rpt, 9365–3.3

Futures trading in Treasury security put options, hypothetical thrift instn losses, 1983 technical paper, 9316–1.102

Home mortgage (conventional) terms on loans closed, and commitment rates, by type of loan and lender and for 32 SMSAs, monthly rpt, 9312–2

Index by Subjects and Names

Savings banks

Housing finance studies, technical paper series, 9306–1

Housing financing of S&Ls and others, mortgage terms and debt outstanding, and balance sheets of S&Ls and FHLBs, 1983, annual rpt, 9314–3

Income tax returns of corporations, detailed income and tax items by industry, 1981, annual rpt, 8304–4

Income taxes, effective rates, and selected financial data, for financial instns by type and individual firm, with comparisons to other industries, selected 1960-82, hearing, 25368–129

Installment credit outstanding, by type of financial instn and credit, monthly rpt, 9365–2.6

Interstate bank offices by type, and electronic funds transfer networks, for Fed Reserve 7th District by State of origin and coverage, 1981-83, article, 9375–1.403

Interstate bank service offices, including S&Ls, bank branches, and nonbank subsidiaries offering financial services, by instn and State, 1981-83, 9371–13

Middle Atlantic States, FHLB 2nd District member savings instns financial operations, by State, monthly rpt, 9302–14

Middle Atlantic States, FHLB 3rd District member S&Ls financial operations and housing industry indicators, by SMSA, monthly rpt, suspended, 9302–16

New England States, FHLB 1st District member instns financial operations and housing industry indicators, monthly rpt, 9302–4

New England States, FHLB 1st District member savings instns, locations, and financial condition, 1984, annual listing, 9304–26

New England States financial instn assets and liabilities, Fed Reserve 1st District, monthly rpt, 9373–2.5

New England States thrift and commercial banking instns financial statements, by type of instn and State, 1972 and 1982, annual rpt, 9304–3

North Central States, FHLB 6th District insured S&Ls financial condition and operations by State, monthly rpt, 9302–11

North Central States, FHLB 6th District insured S&Ls financial condition and operations by State, quarterly rpt, 9302–23

North Central States, FHLB 7th District insured S&Ls cost of funds, and savings flows and mortgage loans closed by SMSA, monthly rpt, 9302–5

North Central States, FHLB 8th District member S&Ls financial operations by State and SMSA, monthly rpt, 9302–9

North Central States, FHLB 8th District member S&Ls, locations, assets, and savings, 1984, annual listing, 9304–9

Pennsylvania bank, S&L, and savings bank deposit and commercial and industrial loan market shares, and loan activity, 1980-83, article, 9387–1.404

South Central States, FHLB 9th District insured S&Ls financial condition and operations by SMSA, monthly rpt, 9302–13

Southeastern States economic indicators, by State, Fed Reserve 5th District, quarterly rpt, 9389–16

Southeastern States, FHLB 4th District insured S&Ls financial condition and operations, by SMSA, monthly rpt, 9302–1

Southeastern States, FHLB 4th District member S&Ls financial ratios and mortgage portfolios by State, 2nd half 1983, semiannual rpt, 9302–3

Southeastern States financial and economic devs, Fed Reserve 6th District, monthly rpt with articles, 9371–1

Southeastern States S&L industry review, periodic rpt articles, 9302–2

Stock S&Ls, market value related to risk and return for midwestern S&Ls, 1974-78, regression results, technical paper, 9316–2.46

West Central States, FHLB 10th District insured S&Ls finances and operations by SMSA, monthly rpt, 9302–22

Western States economic indicators, Fed Reserve 12th District, quarterly rpt, 9393–1.5

Western States, FHLB 10th District member S&Ls, locations, assets, and savings, 1984, annual listing, 9304–17

Western States, FHLB 11th District member S&L offices, locations, savings balances, and accounts, quarterly listing, 9302–20

Western States, FHLB 11th District member S&Ls financial condition and operations by State, quarterly rpt, 9302–19

Western States, FHLB 11th District member S&Ls financial operations and housing industry indicators by State, monthly rpt, 9302–17

Western States, FHLB 12th District member S&Ls financial operations and housing industry indicators by State, monthly rpt, 9302–21

see also Mortgages

see also Negotiable orders of withdrawal accounts

Savings banks

Assets and liabilities of depository instns, monthly rpt, 9362–1.1

Assets and liabilities of Fed Reserve member and nonmember banks, 1982-83, annual rpt, 9364–1.2

Assets and liabilities of savings instns, by type of instn, 1980-82, annual rpt, 9364–5.4

Assets, liabilities, and deposit and loan activity, for all S&Ls and FSLIC-insured savings banks and S&Ls, monthly rpt, 9312–4

County Business Patterns: establishments, employees, and payrolls, by SIC 4-digit industry and county, 1982, annual State rpt series, 2326–6

Deposits in commercial and mutual savings banks and in US branches of foreign banks, by account type, instn, State, SMSA, and county, June 1983, annual rpt, 9295–3

Deposits in FSLIC-insured savings instns, and offices, by State, SMSA, and county, 1983, annual rpt, 9314–4

Employment, earnings, and hours, by SIC 4-digit nonfarm industry, monthly 1974-Feb 1984, annual update, 6744–4

FDIC bank examination activities and supervisory actions, 1983, annual rpt, 9294–1

Fed Home Loan Bank System members, with assets of S&Ls, by instn, city, and State, 1983, annual listing, 9314–5

Financial and business statistics, historic trends, 1984 annual chartbook, 9364–2.14

Financial and business statistics, quarterly chartbook, 9362–2.7

Financial ratios, income, and expenses of FSLIC-insured savings instns, 2nd half 1983, semiannual rpt, 9312–6

Flow-of-funds accounts, assets and liabilities by type and economic sector, year-end outstandings, 1960-83, annual rpt, 9364–3

Flow-of-funds accounts savings, investments, and credit statements, quarterly rpt, 9365–3.3

Futures trading in Treasury security put options, hypothetical thrift instn losses, 1983 technical paper, 9316–1.102

Home mortgage (conventional) terms on loans closed, and commitment rates, by type of loan and lender and for 32 SMSAs, monthly rpt, 9312–2

Income tax returns of corporations, detailed income and tax items by industry, 1981, annual rpt, 8304–4

Income taxes, effective rates, and selected financial data, for financial instns by type and individual firm, with comparisons to other industries, selected years 1960-82, hearing, 25368–129

Installment credit outstanding, by type of financial instn and credit, monthly rpt, 9365–2.6

Middle Atlantic States, FHLB 2nd District member savings instns financial operations, by State, monthly rpt, 9302–14

Minority group and women employment, by occupational group and SIC 2- to 3-digit industry, 1981, annual rpt, 9244–1.1

Mortgage loan activity, by type of lender, loan, and mortgaged property, monthly rpt, 5142–18

Mortgage loan originations, purchases, and acquisitions, for 11 lender types, selected years 1960-82, article, 9312–1.407

Mortgage transactions and holdings, by lender group and type of property and loan, quarterly rpt, 5142–30

Mortgages (home) and mortgage pool participation by lender type, and FHA mortgage yields, various periods 1950-84 with trends from 1900, technical paper, 9375–11.4

Negotiable orders of withdrawal accounts authorized and offered at industrial banks, S&Ls, and savings banks, and instns and deposits, by State, as of Dec 1983, press release, 9368–75

New England States, FHLB 1st District member instns financial operations and housing industry indicators, monthly rpt, 9302–4

New England States, FHLB 1st District member savings instns, locations, and financial condition, 1984, annual listing, 9304–26

New England States financial instn assets and liabilities, Fed Reserve 1st District, monthly rpt, 9373–2.5

Savings banks

New England States thrift and commercial banking instns financial statements, by type of instn and State, 1972 and 1982, annual rpt, 9304–3

Northeast States savings bank deposits by type, and commercial banks share of savings in depository instns, by State, various dates 1970-83, hearing, 21248–83

Pennsylvania bank, S&L, and savings bank deposit and commercial and industrial loan market shares, and loan activity, 1980-83, article, 9387–1.404

Savings bonds *see* U.S. savings bonds

Sawhill, Isabel V. "Human Resources", 21968–28

Sawyer, Darwin "Medicare and Medicaid Data Book, 1983", 4654–1

Sayreville, N.J.

Census of Housing, 1980: occupancy and unit characteristics, by race, Hispanic origin, and city, SMSA rpt, 2473–1.256 Census of Population and Housing, 1980: detailed population and housing characteristics, by county, city, and census tract, SMSA rpt, 2551–2.256

SBA *see* Small Business Administration

Scabies *see* Animal diseases and zoonoses

Scales and balances *see* Instruments and measuring devices

Scandium *see* Metals and metal industries

Schallau, Con H. "Considering Departures from Current Timber Harvesting Policies: Case Studies of Four Communities in the Pacific Northwest", 1208–196

Schaub, James D. "New and Expanding Firms Provide New Jobs in Rural Georgia", 1502–7.401

Schendler, Carol E. "Health Spending in the 1980s: Integration of Clinical Practice Patterns with Management", 4652–1.407

Schenectady, N.Y.

Census of Housing, 1980: occupancy and unit characteristics, by race, Hispanic origin, and city, SMSA rpt, 2473–1.61

Census of Population and Housing, 1980: detailed population and housing characteristics, by county, city, and census tract, SMSA rpt, 2551–2.61

Housing and households detailed characteristics, and unit and neighborhood quality, by inside-outside central cities, 1980 survey, SMSA rpt, 2485–6.2

Public works capital needs and financing, by project type, level of govt, and selected jurisdiction, 1970s-83 and projected to 2000, hearing, 23848–181

Wages of office and plant workers, by occupation, 1984 SMSA survey rpt, 6785–11.9

see also under By SMSA or MSA in the "Index by Categories"

Schlenger, William E. "Access to Health Care Among Aged Medicare Beneficiaries", 4146–12.3 "Health Status of Aged Medicare Beneficiaries", 4146–12.2

Schlenker, Robert E. "Case Mix, Quality, and Cost Relationships in Colorado Nursing Homes", 4652–1.432

Schloss, Nathan "Use of Employment Data To Estimate Office Space Demand", 6722–1.474

Schmidt, S. C. "Cooperative Grain Trade Opportunities in Eastern Europe", 1128–27

Schmitt, Donald G. "Postretirement Increases Under Private Pension Plans", 6722–1.453

Schneider, Suzanne "Financing U.S. Airports in the 1980s", 26306–6.75

Scholarships *see* Student aid

Scholastic Apptitude Test *see* Educational tests

Scholl, Kathleen K. "Farm Operator Households Receiving Social Security Income, 1979", 1702–1.410 "Social Security Program of Self-Employed Farm Operator Families", 1702–1.408

Scholl, Russell B. "International Investment Position of the U.S. in 1983", 2702–1.424

School administration and staff

Alabama rural black population, education, employment, health services, and economic status, for 16 counties, selected years 1970-81, 11048–180

Botany and other plant science R&D at higher education instns, funding by source, grad students, and staff, 1983, 9626–2.143

Census of Population, 1980: detailed socioeconomic and demographic characteristics, by age, sex, race, Hispanic origin, occupation, and industry, State rpt series, 2531–4

Census of Population, 1980: detailed socioeconomic characteristics, by county, city, and inside-outside SMSAs and central cities, State rpt series, 2531–3

Census of Population, 1980: labor force, by sex, detailed occupation, and region, with comparison to 1970 census, supplementary rpt, 2535–1.12

Condition of Education, detailed data on enrollment, staff, achievement, finances, curricula, and education effects on employment, 1982-83, annual rpt, 4824–1

County Business Patterns: establishments, employees, and payrolls, by SIC 4-digit industry and county, 1981, annual State rpt series, 2326–8

County Business Patterns: establishments, employees, and payrolls, by SIC 4-digit industry and county, 1982, annual State rpt series, 2326–6

Crime against students, teachers, and others, by offense, circumstances, and offender sex and race, 1974-76, 6066–20.2

Digest of Education Statistics, detailed data on students, staff, finances, and facilities, 1982 and selected trends, annual rpt, 4824–2

DOD Dependents Schools and Uniformed Services University of Health Sciences civilian and military personnel, monthly rpt, 3542–14.1

Index by Subjects and Names

Earnings by major industry group, and personal income per capita and by source, by region and State, 1929-82, 2708–40

Education statistics summary compilation, 1980/81-1982/83 with selected trends from 1869, biennial rpt, 4804–27

Elementary and secondary public school districts, schools, enrollment, staff, and finances, by State, 1981/82, annual rpt, 4834–13

Employment and earnings in philanthropic organizations by organization type, and compared to other nonprofit organizations, selected years 1972-82, article, 6722–1.455

Employment, earnings, and hours, by level and branch of govt, and function, monthly 1977-Feb 1984, annual update, 6744–4

Employment, earnings, and hours, by selected SIC 1- to 4-digit industry, State, and for 278 major labor areas, 1939-83, annual rpt, 6744–5

Employment, earnings, and hours, by SIC 4-digit nonfarm industry, monthly 1974-Feb 1984, annual update, 6744–4

Finances and operations, by SIC 2- to 4-digit industry, 1970s-83 and projected to 1988, annual rpt, 2014–4

Govt census, 1982: employment, payrolls, and average earnings, by function, level of govt, State, county, population size, and inside-outside SMSAs, 2455–2

Govt census, 1982: local govt employment by function, payroll, and average earnings, for individual counties, cities, and school and special districts, 2455–1

Govt census, 1982: State govt payments to local govts, by program, source of funds, level of govt, and State, with trends from 1902, 2460–3

Govt employment and payroll, by function, level of govt, and jurisdiction, 1983, annual rpt series, 2466–1

Govt employment and payrolls, for State and local govts, monthly rpt, 6742–4

Head Start Project programs and effect on child dev, literature review with bibl, selected years 1970-83, 4608–17

Health insurance plans for school employees in 7 cities, as of 1980, hearing, 21788–136

Howard University salaries, academic standing, medical research, and library operations, and finances of Howard Inn, selected years 1976-83, GAO rpt, 26121–74

Indian education program operations, funding, student progress measures, and opinions of school staff, parents, and students, selected years 1973-83, 4808–13

Law enforcement personnel and officers at higher education instns, by instn, 1983, annual rpt, 6224–2.3

Minority group and women employment, by occupational group and SIC 2- to 3-digit industry, 1981, annual rpt, 9244–1.1

Occupational injury and illness rates, by SIC 2- to 4-digit industry, 1982, annual rpt, 6844–1

Occupational manpower needs and supply by detailed occupation, and educational and training program enrollees and grads by detailed field, 1982 and 1995, biennial rpt, 6744–3

Index by Subjects and Names

Occupational Outlook Handbook, 1984-85 biennial rpt, 6744–1

Pension systems of State and local govts finances, membership, beneficiaries, and benefits, by system, 1982-83, annual rpt, 2466–2.4

Puerto Rico University enrollment, tuition, construction costs, degrees granted, personnel by sex, and Fed Govt funding of medical research, 1970s-87, hearings, 21348–93

Science and engineering employment in higher education instns, by sex, field of science, and instn type, 1972-83, biennial rpt, 9627–24.2

Scientists and engineers employment by sector and activity, and share female, black, and Asian descent, by field, 1982, 9626–2.142

Service industry census, 1982: employment, establishments, receipts, and payroll, by SIC 2- to 4-digit kind of business, SMSA, county, and city, State rpt series, 2391–1

Special education programs for handicapped children, enrollment, staff, and funding, by handicap, age, and State, 1981/82-1982/83, annual rpt, 4944–4

Statistical Abstract of US, social, political, and economic data, 1950s-83 and trends, annual rpt, 2324–1.1

Teaching degrees conferred by specialty and State, required credit hours, and instn officials attitudes, by instn type, 1970s-83, hearings, 21348–89

see also Educational finance

see also School districts

see also Teachers

School buildings

see Educational facilities

School busing

Accidents (fatal), circumstances, and characteristics of persons and vehicles involved, detailed data, 1982, annual rpt, 7764–10

Education highlights, trends in enrollment, expenditures, curricula, and other topics of current interest, periodic press release, 4822–1

Energy use in transportation sector by mode, fuel supplies, and demographic and economic determinants of vehicle use, 1970s-83, annual rpt, 3304–5

Govt census, 1982: school districts revenues, expenditures, debt, and assets, by district and State, 2457–1

Govt census, 1982: State govt payments to local govts, by program, source of funds, level of govt, and State, with trends from 1902, 2460–3

Statistical Abstract of US, social, political, and economic data, 1950s-83 and trends, annual rpt, 2324–1.1

Students of public schools transported at public expense, number and expenditures, 1979/80, annual rpt, 4824–2.7

Transportation finances, operations, vehicles, equipment, accidents, and energy use, by mode of transport, 1955-84, annual rpt, 7304–2

School desegregation

see Discrimination in education

School districts

Census of Govts, 1982: local govt employment by function, payroll, and average earnings, for individual counties, cities, and school and special districts, 2455–1

Census of Govts, 1982: properties, govt-assessed value, sales, and tax rates, by property type, State, SMSA, county, and city, 2453–1

Census of Govts, 1982: school districts revenues, expenditures, debt, and assets, by district and State, 2457–1

Census of Govts, 1982: school system total and instructional employment, payroll, and average earnings, by enrollment size and State, 2455–2

Census of Govts, 1982: State govt payments to local govts, by program, source of funds, level of govt, and State, with trends from 1902, 2460–3

Central city jurisdictional areas, by govt type and selected SMSA, 1981, 10048–61

Districts and schools, total units, selected years 1929/30-80/81, and pupils enrolled 1981, annual rpt, 4824–2.9

Educational trends, 1972/73-1992/93, biennial pocket-size card, 4824–3

Elementary and secondary public school districts, schools, enrollment, staff, and finances, by State, 1981/82, annual rpt, 4834–13

Elementary and secondary public school systems, annual listing, discontinued, 4834–1

Employment and payroll, by function and level of govt in 75 SMSAs and 69 large counties, Oct 1983, annual rpt, 2466–1.3

Fed Govt education block grants, State allocations by program and selected school district, FY82-84 and trends from FY60, hearing, 21408–75

Govt finances, by level of govt and State, selected years 1929-83, annual rpt, 10044–1

Govt finances, by level of govt, State, and for large cities and counties, 1981-83, annual rpt series, 2466–2

Impacted area schools, Fed Govt funding by county and school and congressional district, and eligible pupils, by State, FY83, annual rpt, 4804–10

Indian education program operations, funding, student progress measures, and opinions of school staff, parents, and students, selected years 1973-83, 4808–13

Neighborhood quality, indicators and attitudes by inside-outside central cities, 1979-82 surveys, SMSA rpt series, 2485–6

Tax burden for average family by income level and selected city, and tax rates by selected jurisdiction, by type of tax, 1982, 10046–8.2

Texas school districts and higher education instns scholarship awards from Houston Endowment Inc, 1981, hearings, 21788–137

School dropouts

Census of Population and Housing, 1980: detailed population and housing characteristics, by county, city, and census tract, State and SMSA rpt series, 2551–2

Employment of youth and hours worked, by high school and college enrollment status, sex, race, and Hispanic origin, 1982-83, annual article, 6722–1.446

Employment status and occupation groups, school dropouts and high school grads not attending college, 1981, annual rpt, 4824–2.23

School lunch and breakfast programs

High school classes of 1980 and 1982: educational and sociodemographic characteristics and expectations, natl longitudinal study, series, 4826–2

High school dropout rate and reasons, educational goals and achievement, and required and recommended curricula, by school control, selected years 1972-83, annual rpt, 4824–1.5

High school dropouts, percent aged 14-34, by race, age, and sex, 1971 and 1981, annual rpt, 4824–2.10

Indian education program operations, funding, student progress measures, and opinions of school staff, parents, and students, selected years 1973-83, 4808–13

Job Training Partnership Act participants, by program and socieconomic characteristics, Oct 1983-June 1984 with funding to 1985/86, 6408–63

Puerto Rico educational enrollment, finance, completions, curricula, and personnel by instn, and health and vital statistics, selected years 1970-83, hearings, 21348–93

Women's employment and earnings, by labor force and socioeconomic characteristics, and compared to men, 1978-81 and trends from 1940s, 6568–29

Youth employment, by high school and college enrollment status, industry div, occupation, and selected demographic characteristics, 1980-82, 6746–1.250

see also Educational retention rates

School enrollment

see Educational enrollment

School finance

see Educational finance

School lunch and breakfast programs

Activities and finances of USDA child nutrition programs, FY79-83, annual rpt, 1364–14

Agricultural production, marketing, trade, supply, food consumption, and food and nutrition programs, 1960s-83, annual chartbook, 1504–3

Alabama rural black population, education, employment, health services, and economic status, for 16 counties, selected years 1970-81, 11048–180

Beneficiaries of noncash public and employer-based transfer programs, by income source and socioeconomic characteristics, 1982, advance Current Population Rpt, 2546–6.38

Beneficiaries of noncash public and employer-based transfer programs, by income source and socioeconomic characteristics, 1982, final Current Population Rpt, 2546–6.37

CCC dairy price support program foreign donations and domestic donations to poor, schools, Prisons Bur, DOD, and VA, monthly rpt, 1802–2

Children and youth benefitting from Fed Govt public welfare programs and tax expenditures, participation and funding for 71 programs, FY81-83, 21968–30

Consumer research and marketing devs, and consumption and price trends, quarterly rpt with articles, 1541–7

Cost control proposals for Fed Govt programs and mgmt, 3-year savings by function and agency, and financial and operating data, 1960s-81, 16908–1.2, 16908–1.23

School lunch and breakfast programs

Fed Govt aid to State and local govts, expenditures, and direct payments, by program, agency, and State, FY83, annual rpt, 2464–2

Fed Govt and other food aid programs, funding, participant characteristics, and nutrition and poverty data, 1970s-83, 028–20

Govt census, 1982: school districts revenues, expenditures, debt, and assets, by district and State, 2457–1

Govt census, 1982: State govt payments to local govts, by program, source of funds, level of govt, and State, with trends from 1902, 2460–3

Hispanic Americans socioeconomic and demographic characteristics, and compared to non-Hispanics, selected years 1970-83, chartbook, 2328–48

Income (household) and cash and noncash transfer program participation, by sociodemographic characteristics, quarterly rpt, 2542–2

Participation and costs of USDA food aid programs, by program, region, and State, monthly rpt, 1362–14

Participation and finances of USDA child nutrition programs, by region and State, annual rpt series, 1364–13

Participation of schools and students, families eligible, and Federal reimbursement rates, FY79-83, GAO rpt, 26113–123

Participation of USDA food aid programs, monthly rpt, 1362–13

Public noncash transfers counted as income, effects on poverty population size by recipient characteristics, 1979-82, 2626–2.50

TTPI socioeconomic, health, and govtl data, by TTPI govt, FY83 and selected trends, detailed annual rpt, 7004–6

USDA agricultural surplus direct purchase program finances, and purchases and food received by schools by commodity, various periods 1936-83, 1548–243

USDA funding for school lunch, milk, other food assistance, and nutrition education programs, by State and outlying area, FY82, annual rpt, 4824–2.22

Schools

see Educational facilities

see Private schools

see terms listed under Education and beginning with School

Schorsch, Louis L.

"Effects of Import Quotas on the Steel Industry", 26306–6.80

"Federal Support for R&D and Innovation", 26306–6.77

"Research and Development Funding in the Proposed FY85 Budget, Special Study", 26308–46

Schroeder, David J.

"Bibliography on Shift Work Research: 1950-82", 7506–10.29

"Job Attitudes Toward the New Maintenance Concept of the Airway Facilities Service", 7506–10.25

Schumann, Richard

"Workers' Purchasing Power Rises Despite Slowdown in Wage and Salary Gains", 6722–1.430

Schussheim, Morton J.

"Housing: An Overview", 21968–28

Schuster, Ervin G.

"Costs of Developed Recreation Sites in the Northern Region, USDA Forest Service", 1208–202

Schwartz, Arthur L., Jr.

"Economic Implications of Alternative Home Financing", 9412–2.406

Schwartz, Elliot

"Federal Role in State Industrial Development Programs", 26306–6.81

"Industrial Policy Debate", 26306–6.69

Schwenk, Judith C.

"General Aviation Activity and Avionics Survey", 7504–29

Science and Education Administration, USDA

see Agricultural Research Service

see Cooperative State Research Service

see Human Nutrition Information Service

Science and technology

NSF research programs, activities, and funding, FY82-83, annual rpt, 9624–6

NSF Science Resources Studies Div activities, project descriptions, and 1973-83 publications, 1983 annual listing, 9624–21

Science Indicators, R&D expenditures, innovations, research, and higher education, with foreign comparisons, 1960s- 83, annual rpt, 9624–10

Science resources, special rpts series, 9626–6

Standards Natl Bur publications, 1983 annual listing, 2214–1

Statistical Abstract of US, social, political, and economic data, 1950s-83 and trends, annual rpt, 2324–1.3

see also Agricultural sciences

see also Astronomy

see also Atmospheric sciences

see also Aviation sciences

see also Biological sciences

see also Biomedical engineering

see also Botany

see also Chemistry

see also Computer sciences

see also Defense research

see also Earth sciences

see also Educational research

see also Educational technology

see also Energy research and development

see also Engineers and engineering

see also Environmental sciences

see also Federal aid to medicine

see also Federal funding for energy programs

see also Federal funding for research and development

see also Federally Funded R&D Centers

see also Genetics

see also International cooperation in science and technology

see also Inventions

see also Mathematics

see also Medical research

see also Medicine

see also Meteorology

see also Oceanography

see also Physical sciences

see also Physics

see also Physiology

see also Psychology

see also Research

see also Research and development

Index by Subjects and Names

see also Scientific education

see also Scientists and technicians

see also Social sciences

see also Space programs

see also Space sciences

see also Technological innovations

see also Technology transfer

see also Zoology

Science Applications, Inc.

"Wilderness Designation of Bureau of Land Management Lands and Impacts on the Availability of Energy Resources", 3308–68

Scientific education

Census of Population, 1980: labor force, by sex, detailed occupation, and region, with comparison to 1970 census, supplementary rpt, 2535–1.12

Condition of Education, detailed data on enrollment, staff, achievement, finances, curricula, and education effects on employment, 1982-83, annual rpt, 4824–1

Degree (doctoral) recipients in science and engineering, by field, sex, race, age, citizenship, postgrad employment and study status, State, and instn, 1960-82, 9626–6.16

Degrees conferred in higher education, by race, Hispanic origin, sex, level, and field, selected years 1949/50-1979/80, annual rpt, 4824–2.16

Degrees, employment, and salaries of scientists and engineers, by field, type of employer, race, and sex, selected years 1960-81, annual rpt, 9624–18.4, 9624–18.5

Education Dept programs funding, operations, and effectiveness, FY83, annual rpt, 4804–5

Elementary and secondary educational progress, natl assessment summary data for 7 learning areas, by selected characteristics of participants, selected years 1971-82, annual rpt, 4824–2.6

Employment of scientists and engineers at universities and colleges, by field, sex, and instn, 1973-82, 9626–2.140

Employment of scientists and engineers at universities and colleges, by field, sex, State, and instn, Jan 1983 and selected trends from 1967, annual survey, 9627–11

Energy R&D and science and engineering education, DOE and DOE natl labs aid to selected higher education instns, 1960s-84, 3008–89

Enrollment in grad program or employment characteristics of science and engineering grads of 1980-81, by degree level, field, sex, and race, 1982, 9627–25

Enrollment in grad science and engineering, fields of study, financial support, and other student and instn characteristics, 1975-82, annual survey, 9627–7

Enrollment in science and engineering grad programs, by field, degree level, source of financial support, race, and Hispanic origin, 1975-81, 9626–2.134

Enrollment in science and engineering grad programs, by field, sex, and instn, 1973-82, 9626–2.141

Fed Govt science-related and R&D funding for higher education instns, by field, instn, agency, and State, FY82, annual rpt, 9627–17

Index by Subjects and Names

Scranton, Pa.

High school class of 1982: science and math coursework and assessment, by sociodemographic and school characteristics and educational goal, 4826–2.14

NSF grant and award recipients, by State, FY83, annual listing, 9624–11

NSF research programs, activities, and funding, FY82-83, annual rpt, 9624–6

Nuclear engineering student enrollments and degrees granted, by State, instn, and subfield, and placements by sector, 1983, annual rpt, 3004–5

R&D-employed scientists and engineers salaries by degree, type of establishment, age, experience, and field, 1984, annual rpt, 3004–1

Radiation protection and health physics enrollments and degrees granted by State and instn, and grads employment, 1983, annual rpt, 3004–7

Satellite Landsat system proposed transfer to private sector, uses and product sales by user type, and university programs and personnel by instn, 1973-85, 26358–100

Science and engineering enrollment, degrees, and employment, R&D funding, and related topics, highlights series, 9626–2

Science and engineering grad students, by field, type of financial aid, sex, race, Hispanic origin, and citizenship, 1972-83, biennial rpt, 9627–24.3

Science Indicators, R&D expenditures, innovations, research, and higher education, with foreign comparisons, 1960s- 83, annual rpt, 9624–10

Scientists and engineers supply, employment, and education, by sex, race, Hispanic origin, and field, selected years 1965-83, biennial rpt, 9624–20

Soviet Union share of all Council for Mutual Economic Assistance R&D employment, funding, and patents, with enrollment in USSR of science students from member countries, 1970s, 2326–9.7

Teaching degrees conferred by specialty and State, required credit hours, and instn officials attitudes, by instn type, 1970s-83, hearings, 21348–89

Scientific research

see Research

Scientists and technicians

Agricultural research expenditures and scientist years, by topic, commodity, and performing organization, FY82, annual rpt, 1744–2

Biotechnology commercial uses, R&D funding and output, controls, and industry financial and operating data, for US and 5 countries, 1970s-83 and estimated 1984-85, 26358–98

Census of Housing, 1980: structural, financial, and householder characteristics, by region and State, 2475–4

Census of Population and Housing, 1980: detailed population and housing characteristics, by county, city, and census tract, State and SMSA rpt series, 2551–2

Census of Population, 1980: detailed socioeconomic and demographic characteristics, by age, sex, race, Hispanic origin, occupation, and industry, State rpt series, 2531–4

Census of Population, 1980: detailed socioeconomic characteristics, by county, city, and inside-outside SMSAs and central cities, State rpt series, 2531–3

Census of Population, 1980: labor force, by sex, detailed occupation, and region, with comparison to 1970 census, supplementary rpt, 2535–1.12

Council for Mutual Economic Assistance science and technology dev and transfer between USSR and other member countries, 1940s-81, 2326–9.7

DOT employment by subagency, State, and selected personnel characteristics, FY83, annual rpt, 7304–18

Employment and economic conditions, alternative BLS projections to 1995 with data for selected years 1959-82, 6728–29

Employment characteristics or grad enrollment of science and engineering grads of 1980-81, by degree level, field, sex, and race, 1982, 9627–25

Employment, enrollment, and degrees of scientists and engineers, R&D funding, and related topics, highlights series, 9626–2

Employment of scientists and engineers at universities and colleges and federally funded R&D centers, by field, sex, State, and instn, Jan 1983 and selected trends from 1967, annual survey, 9627–11

Employment of scientists, engineers, and technicians in defense and nondefense industries, and supply/demand, by field, 1981-87, 9628–71

Employment of scientists, engineers, and technicians in private industry, by occupation and industry group, 1980-81, biennial rpt, 9627–23

Employment of scientists, engineers, and technicians in transportation, utilities, and retail and wholesale trade, by field of science and industry, 1982, 9628–72

Employment, supply, and education of scientists and engineers, by sex, race, Hispanic origin, and field, selected years 1965-83, biennial rpt, 9624–20

Employment, unemployment, and labor force, by demographic and employment characteristics, State, and for 30 metro areas and 11 large cities, 1983, annual rpt, 6744–7

Energy R&D and science and engineering education, DOE and DOE natl labs aid to selected higher education instns, 1960s-84, 3008–89.2

Energy-related employment of scientists and engineers, supply/demand and effects of R&D funding, by sector, energy type, field, and age, 1962-91, annual rpt, 3004–19

Exports and imports of US, relative contributions of labor by type and capital to trade balance, selected years 1958-80, technical paper, 9381–10.30

Handbook of Labor Statistics, employment, earnings, hours, and labor force characteristics, 1982 and trends, detailed annual rpt, 6724–1

Heart, Lung, and Blood Natl Inst activities and funding, with morbidity and mortality data, various periods 1940-88, annual rpt, 4474–22

Industry R&D funding and employment of scientists and engineers, by industry group, firm size, and funding source, 1956-82, annual rpt, 9627–21

NSF Science Resources Studies Div activities, project descriptions, and 1973-83 publications, 1983 annual listing, 9624–21

Nuclear industry nongovt employment by industry segment, occupation, and census div, and DOE and NRC nuclear employment, 1968-83, biennial rpt, 3004–11

Nuclear-related employment of scientists and engineers, by field and sector, 1981 and 1983, 3006–8.2

Occupational manpower needs and supply by detailed occupation, and educational and training program enrollees and grads by detailed field, 1982 and 1995, biennial rpt, 6744–3

Occupational Outlook Handbook, 1984-85 biennial rpt, 6744–1

Oceanographic research cruise schedules and ship characteristics, by academic instn or Federal agency, 1984, annual rpt, 3804–6

R&D equipment at higher education instns, age, cost, funding sources, and users, for computer and physical sciences and engineering, 1982, 9626–2.138

R&D expenditures by source, and scientists education and employment, detailed data by field, selected years 1953-84, annual rpt, 9624–18

Radiation protection and health physics enrollments and degrees granted by State and instn, and grads employment, 1983, annual rpt, 3004–7

Salaries of scientists and engineers in R&D at DOE labs and non-DOE facilities, Aug 1982-Feb 1984, annual rpt, 3004–9

Salaries of scientists and engineers in R&D, by degree, type of establishment, age, experience, and field, 1984, annual rpt, 3004–1

Science Indicators, R&D expenditures, innovations, research, and higher education, with foreign comparisons, 1960s- 83, annual rpt, 9624–10

Statistical Abstract of US, social, political, and economic data, 1950s-83 and trends, annual rpt, 2324–1.3

Wages of white-collar workers, by occupation, work level, and industry div, Mar 1984, annual rpt, 6784–2

see also Scientific education

see also Statisticians

see also under specific scientific disciplines (listed under Science and technology)

Scioto, Colo.

Housing vacancy rates for single and multifamily units and mobile homes, by county, city, and ZIP code, 1984, annual metro area rpt, 9304–22.9

Scotland

see United Kingdom

Scott, Jonathan A.

"Credit, Banks and Small Business", 21728–52.1

Scranton, Pa.

Census of Housing, 1980: occupancy and unit characteristics, by race, Hispanic origin, and city, SMSA rpt, 2473–1.266

Census of Population and Housing, 1980: detailed population and housing characteristics, by county, city, and census tract, SMSA rpt, 2551–2.266

CPI by detailed component, for US city average, 28 SMSAs, and 4 regions by population size, monthly rpt, 6762–2

Wages of office and plant workers, by occupation, 1984 SMSA survey rpt, 6785–11.8

Scranton, Pa.

see also under By SMSA or MSA in the "Index by Categories"

Scrap metals

Business statistics, detailed data for major industries and economic indicators, *Survey of Current Business,* monthly rpt, 2702–1.14

Census of Population, 1980: detailed socioeconomic and demographic characteristics, by age, sex, race, Hispanic origin, occupation, and industry, State rpt series, 2531–4

County Business Patterns: establishments, employees, and payrolls, by SIC 4-digit industry and county, 1981, annual State rpt series, 2326–8

County Business Patterns: establishments, employees, and payrolls, by SIC 4-digit industry and county, 1982, annual State rpt series, 2326–6

Exports and imports of US, detailed SIC-based commodities by world area, 1983, annual rpts, 2424–6

Exports of US, detailed commodities by country of destination, monthly rpt, 2422–3

Exports of US, detailed Schedule B commodities by country of destination, 1983, annual rpt, 2424–9

Exports of US, detailed Schedule E commodities by mode of transport and world area and country of destination, 1983, annual rpts, 2424–5

Great Lakes trade, by SITC 3-digit commodity, port, vessel type, world area, and country, 1982, annual rpt, 7744–3

Imports of US, detailed Schedule A commodities by country and world area of origin, and mode of transport, 1983, annual rpts, 2424–2

Imports of US, detailed Schedule A commodities by country, monthly rpt, 2422–2

Imports of US, detailed TSUSA commodities by country of origin, 1983, annual rpt, 2424–4

Iron and steel castings and scrap production, shipments, unfilled orders, stocks, receipts, and trade, by census div and State, monthly Current Industrial Rpt, 2506–10.1

Mineral Industry Surveys, commodity review of production, trade, stocks, and consumption, monthly rpt, 5612–1.11

Minerals (strategic) supply/demand, trade, and foreign and US industry devs by firm and country, by commodity, bimonthly rpt, 5602–4

Minerals and metals recycling and scrap, by commodity, 1983, annual rpt, 5604–18

Minerals Yearbook, 1982, Vol 1: commodity reviews of production, reserves, supply, use, and trade, annual rpt, 5604–33

Minerals Yearbook, 1982, Vol 3: foreign country reviews of production, trade, and policies, by commodity, annual rpt, 5604–35

Minerals Yearbook, 1983, Vol 1 preprints: commodity review of production, reserves, supply, use, and trade, annual rpt, 5604–15.34

Waterborne commerce of US (domestic and foreign), freight by commodity, traffic, and passengers, by port and waterway, 1982, annual rpt, 3754–3

Wholesale trade census, 1982: employment, establishments, sales by commodity, and payroll, by SIC 4-digit kind of business and State, revised preliminary rpt, 2403–1.18

Screws

see Hardware

Screwworms

see Animal diseases and zoonoses

Sea pollution

see Marine pollution

Seaboard System Railroad

Employee earnings, benefits, and hours, by occupation, Class I railroads, 1983, annual rpt, 9484–5

Seafood

see Fish and fishing industry

see Shellfish

Seals

see Marine mammals

Seaman, William, Jr.

"Species Profiles: Life Histories and Environmental Requirements of Coastal Fishes and Invertebrates (South Florida), Snook", 5506–8.27

Seamen

see Merchant seamen

Searches and seizures

Airport security operations to prevent hijacking, screening results, enforcement actions, and hijacking attempts, 1st half 1984, semiannual rpt, 7502–5

Alcohol, tobacco, firearms, and explosives arrests and seizures, by State, FY82, last issue of annual rpt, 8484–1.6

Drug (illegal) supply, use, casualties, treatment program and emergency room admissions in major cities, arrests, and seizures, by drug type, 1982, annual rpt, 15894–1

Drug and narcotics foreign production, acreage, eradication, and seizures, by substance, with labs destroyed and US aid, by country, 1981-85, annual rpt, 7004–17

Drug Enforcement Admin cases against major drug traffickers by case characteristics, and agents assessment of activities, in 3 cities, 1979-82, GAO rpt, 26119–57

Drug enforcement regional task force program investigation activities, funding, and personnel, with nationwide drug abuse data, 1983 annual rpt, 6004–17

Fed Govt programs and mgmt cost control proposals, 3-year savings by function and agency, and financial and operating data, 1960s-81, 16908–1.9

Foreign human rights conditions in 162 countries, economic and military aid of US, and economic aid of intl organizations, 1981-83, annual rpt, 21384–3

Immigration and Naturalization Service illegal alien and narcotics activities, FY72-81, annual rpt, 6264–2

Marijuana cultivation control activity of State law enforcement agencies, and aid from Fed Govt and Natl Guard, 1983 survey, GAO rpt, 26119–64

Motor carrier safety inspections on interstate hwys, violations cited, and vehicles and drivers ordered out of service, 1982, annual rpt, 7554–35

Index by Subjects and Names

Motor carrier safety inspections on interstate hwys, violations cited, and vehicles and drivers ordered out of service, May 1983, semiannual rpt, 7552–15

Peru cocaine addicts and arrested traffickers and users socioeconomic characteristics, and cocaine confiscated, 1974-78, intl conf papers, 7008–40

Seashores

Army Corps of Engineers activities and projects, FY83 and trends from 1800s, annual rpt, 3754–1

Birds (shore) on Padre and Mustang Islands, Texas, distribution, abundance, and oil spill effects, by species, 1979-81, 5508–86

California marine resources and environmental effects of proposed oil and gas dev, for 2 sanctuaries off central and northern coasts, 1980s and projected to 2006, hearing, 21448–30.1

Environmental characteristics, fish, wildlife, and use, and population socioeconomic data, for individual coastal areas, series, 5506–4

Environmental characteristics, fish, wildlife, uses, and mgmt, for individual estuaries, series, 5506–7

Environmental characteristics, fish, wildlife, uses, and mgmt of individual coastal ecosystems, series, 5506–9

France Brittany coast oil spill cleanup and research costs, marine and tourism industry losses, and recreation losses of tourists and residents, 1971-79, 2178–13

Natl park system and other areas under Natl Park Service mgmt, acreage by type of area, ownership, and site, as of Sept 1984, semiannual rpt, 5542–1

Oil spill risk analyses for OCS proposed lease sale areas, series, 5736–2

Oil spills in coastal and aquatic wildlife habitats, methodology for cleanup priority rating and listing of wildlife species of concern, 1984 rpt, 5508–87

Sedimentation control, surveillance, and research activity of Fed Govt, by project, agency, region, and State, 1982, annual rpt, 5664–9

Seaside, Calif.

Census of Housing, 1980: occupancy and unit characteristics, by race, Hispanic origin, and city, SMSA rpt, 2473–1.315

Census of Population and Housing, 1980: detailed population and housing characteristics, by county, city, and census tract, SMSA rpt, 2551–2.315

Housing vacancy rates for single and multifamily units and mobile homes, by city and ZIP code, 1983, annual metro area rpt, 9304–20.6

see also under By SMSA or MSA in the "Index by Categories"

Seasonal adjustment factors

Airline passenger traffic and capacity for US and intl operations of major trunk carriers, and seasonal adjustment factors, monthly rpt, 9142–19

BLS data collection, analysis, and presentation methods, by program, 1984 handbook, 6888–1

Construction put in place, cost indexes and seasonal adjustment factors for estimating value, by type of construction, monthly rpt, 2382–4.1

Index by Subjects and Names

Securities

Earnings, revised seasonally adjusted estimates of real average hourly and weekly rates based on 1983 CPI changes, monthly 1964-83, article, 6742–2.405

Economic time series seasonal adjustment methodology, dev and design of Census Bur and other systems, with illustrative data, 1981 conf papers, 2626–7.5

Employment, earnings, and hours, benchmarks for establishment-based time series, by SIC 2- to 4-digit industry, 1976-83, and seasonal adjustment factors, 1984-85, article, 6742–2.409

Employment situation, earnings, hours, and other BLS economic indicators, transcripts of BLS Commissioner's monthly testimony, periodic rpt, 23846–4

Housing, new single-family units sold and for sale by price, stage of construction, months on market, and region, and seasonal adjustments, monthly rpt, 2382–3

Housing starts, by region, number of units per structure, and metro-nonmetro location, monthly rpt, supplemental tables, 2382–1

Housing units authorized, by public and private ownership, by region, div, State, selected MSA, and 4,700 permit-issuing places, monthly rpt, 2382–5

Labor force data series of BLS, revised seasonal adjustment factors and estimating formulas, Jan 1983-June 1984, annual article, 6742–2.401

Labor force data series of BLS, revised seasonal adjustment factors for 12 series, July-Dec 1984, article, 6742–2.411

Labor force, revised seasonally adjusted estimates based on 1983 seasonal adjustment factors, monthly 1979-83, article, 6742–2.404

Monetary growth rate, seasonal adjustments to M1, accuracy assessment and behavior of various components, Aug 1973-Feb 1984, article, 9389–1.405

Monetary growth rates, revisions to M1, M2, and M3, and effects of seasonal and benchmark adjustments, various periods 1978-84, article, 9362–1.404

Retail trade sales and inventories, by kind of business, region, census div, and selected State, SMSA, and city, and seasonal adjustments, monthly rpt, 2413–3

Traffic deaths, accident circumstances, and characteristics of persons and vehicles involved, series, 7766–13

Wholesale trade sales and inventories, by SIC 2- to 3-digit kind of business, monthly rpt, 2413–7

Seasonal and summer employment

Farm labor, farms, and labor costs, by labor and farm type and State, with immigrant labor law effect on farm work force, 1978, 1598–192

Fed Govt employment and training program funding under Job Training Partnership Act, and required matching funds, for 3 programs by State, 1984/85, press release, 6408–58

Recreation fees at State outdoor facilities, visits, revenue, costs, and employee salaries, by State, 1982/83, annual rpt, 5544–14.4

Unemployment and part-time employment effects on family income, by

socioeconomic and labor force characteristics, 1981-82, annual rpt, 6746–1.252

Youth Conservation Corps activities, costs, and participant characteristics, by sponsoring agency, 1982, annual rpt, 5304–12

Youth labor force participation, by age group, Apr and July 1984 and change from 1983, annual press release, 6744–13

Youth summer employment, by sex, race, and class of worker, 1979-84, annual press release, 6744–14

Youth summer job program of Fed Govt, funding and jobs by State and for Indians, summer 1984, press release, 6408–62

see also Migrant workers

Seat belts

see Motor vehicle safety devices

Seattle, Wash.

Cancer cases, incidence, deaths, and death rates, by body site, age, race, Hispanic origin, and sex, for 10 geographic areas, 1973-81, 4478–130

Census of Housing, 1980: occupancy and unit characteristics, by race, Hispanic origin, and city, SMSA rpt, 2473–1.329

Census of Population and Housing, 1980: detailed population and housing characteristics, by county, city, and census tract, SMSA rpt, 2551–2.329

CPI by component for US city average, and by region, population size, and for 28 SMSAs, monthly press release, 6762–1

CPI by detailed component, for US city average, 28 SMSAs, and 4 regions by population size, monthly rpt, 6762–2

Fish and shellfish canned and frozen production, imports, landings, and prices, for Alaska and Northwest States, weekly rpt, 2162–6.5

Fruit and vegetable shipments, and arrivals in 23 US and 5 Canada cities, by mode of transport and State or country of origin, 1983, annual rpt, 1311–4.2

Hospital worker wages by sex and occupation, and benefits, for 22 MSAs, Oct 1981 survey, 6787–6.201

Housing unit starts and completions authorized by building permits in 20 MSAs, quarterly rpt, 2382–9

Income assistance, effects of experimental negative income tax program on employment, earnings, marital status, and other family characteristics in 2 cities, 1970-75, 4008–64

Population size of top 25 cities, 1980 and 1982, press release, 2328–46

Wages of office and plant workers, by occupation, 1983 SMSA survey rpt, 6785–12.4

Waterborne commerce of US (domestic and foreign), freight by commodity, traffic, and passengers, by port and waterway, 1982, annual rpt, 3754–3.4

see also under By City and By SMSA or MSA in the "Index by Categories"

Sebranek, Lyle J.

"Outlook for Feed Grains", 1004–16.1

SEC

see Securities and Exchange Commission

Secondary education

see Elementary and secondary education

Secret Service

see U.S. Secret Service

Securities

Agricultural cooperative operating ratios by commodity, and debt financing by source, for 100 largest cooperatives, selected years FY62-83, article, 1122–1.411

Airline common stock average price for major carriers, and compared to New York Stock Exchange indexes, quarterly Dec 1977-June 1984, semiannual rpt, 9142–36

Bank stock ownership changes, monthly rpt, 9365–2.15

Banking and financial data, 1982, annual rpt, 9364–5

Banks (natl) domestic and intl operations, charters, mergers, and liquidations, by State and instn, and Comptroller of Currency activities, quarterly rpt, 8402–3

Biotechnology commercial uses, R&D funding and output, controls, and industry financial and operating data, for US and 5 countries, 1970s-83 and estimated 1984-85, 26358–98

Business Conditions Digest, current data on economic, business, and financial conditions and cyclical fluctuations, monthly rpt, 2702–3

Business Conditions Digest, historical supplement on economic, business, and financial conditions and cyclical fluctuations, with methodology, 1947-82, 2708–31

Business statistics, detailed data for major industries and economic indicators, *Survey of Current Business,* monthly rpt, 2702–1.6

Census of Govts, 1982: school districts revenues, expenditures, debt, and assets, by district and State, 2457–1

Common stock and bonds prices and yields, current data and annual trends, monthly rpt, 23842–1.5

Corporate bond rate related to stock price index changes, regression results, 1961-83, article, 9391–1.419

Corporate bonds performance, comparison with municipal bonds, 1980-3rd quarter 1982, hearings, 25408–86.1

Corporate Eurobonds issued by US firms and their finance subsidiaries, value, and average yields and interest rates, by firm, various periods 1975-82, hearings, 21408–71

Corporations debt and equity funds raised by type, bonds placed, and stock market performance, various periods 1977-1st qtr 1984, article, 9362–1.405

Corporations historic financial and business statistics, 1984 annual chartbook, 9364–2.10

Economic trends and projections, 1970s-83, and Budget of US under current fiscal policy and alternatives, FY85-89, annual rpt, 26304–3.1

Electric utilities privately owned, capital investment, finances, equity performance, and operating characteristics, 1950-82 with supply estimates to 2010, 3168–87

Electric utilities privately owned, common stock performance measures for companies with and without nuclear facilities, 1963-82, 3168–88

Securities

Electric utilities privately owned, common stock performance measures, with comparisons to selected industry groups, selected years 1970-82, GAO rpt, 26113–129

Electric utilities privately owned, detailed financial and operating data by company, with summary data for other distributors by type, 1982, annual rpt, 3164–23

Electric utility bond rating, by utility, Dec 1970 and Oct 1983, hearing, 21368–53

Employee stock ownership plans in developing countries, and firms finances and operations, with case studies of US and 3 countries, 1970s-82, 9916–3.19

Employment, earnings, and hours, by selected SIC 1- to 4-digit industry, State, and for 278 major labor areas, 1939-83, annual rpt, 6744–5

Farm Credit System mortgage and other loans, and financial statements, 1982 and selected trends from 1961, annual rpt, 9264–2

Fed Home Loan Bank of Des Moines financial statements, 1982-83, annual rpt, 9304–7

Fed Reserve Bank of Chicago financial statements, 1983, annual rpt, 9375–5

Fed Reserve Bank of Kansas City financial statements, 1982-83, annual rpt, 9381–3

Fed Reserve Bank of Minneapolis financial statements, 1981-82, annual rpt, 9383–2

Fed Reserve payments services provided depository instns, financial statements, and costs and revenues by service and district bank, 1983, annual press release, 9364–9

Financial and business statistics, historic trends, 1984 annual chartbook, 9364–2.11, 9364–2.15

Financial and business statistics, quarterly chartbook, 9362–2.5, 9362–2.8

Flow-of-funds accounts, assets and liabilities by type and economic sector, year-end outstandings, 1960-83, annual rpt, 9364–3

Forecasts for selected business activities and natl economic indicators, compilation of representative opinions, 1984, annual rpt, 9389–3

Foreign industrial stock indices and long-term government bond yields, US and 7 foreign countries, weekly chartbook, 9365–1.5

Foreign official assets and liabilities, and transactions in securities, monthly rpt, 9362–1.3

Foreign stock price indexes, 6 OECD countries and US, *Business Conditions Digest,* historical supplement and methodology, 1947-82, 2708–31

Foreign stock price indexes, 6 OECD countries and US, *Business Conditions Digest,* monthly rpt, 2702–3.10

Foreign transactions in long-term domestic and foreign securities, purchases and sales, by country, *Treasury Bulletin,* quarterly rpt, 8002–4.12

Futures trading in selected commodities, foreign currencies, and stock indexes, Chicago and other markets activity, monthly rpt, 11922–1

Futures trading in selected commodities, foreign currencies, Treasury securities, and stock indexes, NYC, Chicago, and other markets activity, monthly rpt, 11922–5

Futures trading in selected commodities, Treasury securities, and stock indexes, NYC market activity, monthly rpt, 11922–2

Futures trading summary data by type of investment, and Commodity Futures Trading Commission activities, funding, and employment, FY83, annual rpt, 11924–2

Govt census, 1982: city govt revenues by source, expenditures by function, debt, and assets, by State and city, 2457–4

Govt census, 1982: county govt revenues by source, expenditures by function, debt, and assets, by State and county, 2457–3

Household income, assets, and debt characteristics, sources of credit, and use of financial services, 1983 survey, article, 9362–1.411

Household income, home value and equity, and financial assets by type, by household characteristics, 1983 survey with trends from 1970, article, 9362–1.406

Income tax proposals to encourage savings, and personal assets and liabilities by type, 1981, article, 8302–2.407

Income tax returns of corporations, detailed income and tax items by industry, 1981, annual rpt, 8304–4

Income tax returns of foreign subsidiaries of US corporations, income and tax data, by industry and asset size, 1980, article, 8302–2.410

Industry financial statements and profitability, by size and type of firm, and market operations, annual rpt, discontinued, 9734–3

Intl investment position of US, net change by component, investment type, and world region, and for 2 countries, 1982-83, annual article, 2702–1.424

Intl investment position of US, net position and components, selected years 1897-1982, annual rpt, 2044–25

Intl transactions, *Survey of Current Business,* monthly rpt, quarterly tables, 2702–1.31

Margin requirements, Fed Reserve member and nonmember banks, 1934-83, annual rpt, 9364–1.2

Natural gas interstate pipeline company detailed financial and operating data, by firm, 1983, annual rpt, 3164–38

Nuclear power accident liability insurance under Price-Anderson Act, effects on industry finances and operations, with insurance coverage, claims, and costs, various periods 1957-82, 9638–49

Nuclear power industry status and outlook, with reactor construction, utility financial and operating data, and foreign comparisons, 1970s-83 with projections to 2010, 26358–99

NYC retirement systems assets, by type for 6 systems, selected years 1978-83, conf proceedings, 25408–89

Offerings of State, municipal, and corporate securities, 1934-83, and common stock prices and earnings, 1949-83, annual rpt, 204–1.7

Pension systems of State and local govts finances, membership, beneficiaries, and benefits, by system, 1982-83, annual rpt, 2466–2.4

Philanthropic foundations detailed financial and operating data, and stock holdings by instn, 1979 with selected trends from 1920, GAO rpt, 26119–53

Index by Subjects and Names

Prices of stocks and margin credit, and new govt and corporate issues, monthly rpt, 9362–1.1

Prices of stocks, impact of announced changes in money supply, CPI, economic activity, and Fed Reserve discount rates, 1977-82, technical paper, 9381–10.37

Purchases, sales, and holdings, by issuer and type and ownership of security, monthly listing, 9732–2

Savings and loan assn balance sheet items by State and SMSA, and finances of FHLBs, 1983, annual rpt, 9314–3

Savings and loan assns assets and liabilities, by FHLB district and State, selected years 1955-82, annual rpt, 9314–1

SEC regulatory activities and operations, securities industry finances, and securities exchange activity, selected years 1935-FY83, annual rpt, 9734–2

Small business capital formation under securities law exemptions, effects on stocks offered, issuers, and purchasers, series, 9736–2

Southeastern States banks by asset size, finances, and loans and deposits by type, Fed Reserve 5th District, various dates 1979-83, annual article, 9389–1.408

State and local govt retirement systems, cash and security holdings and finances, quarterly rpt, 2462–2

Statistical Abstract of US, social, political, and economic data, 1950s-83 and trends, annual rpt, 2324–1.3

Stockbroker earnings concentrations, for debt and equity issues, 1970-77 and 1980-82, article, 9371–1.418

Stockholder distributions by US corporations, quarterly rpt, 8302–2.1

Stockholder distributions of US corporations, 1981 estimates, annual article, 8302–2.403

Technology-intensive industry firms stock offerings, 1972-81, annual rpt, 9624–10.4

Trust assets of banks and trust companies, by type of asset and fund and State, 1983, annual rpt, 13004–1

Western States depository instns financial activity by State, and large commercial banks by city, Fed Reserve 10th District, monthly rpt, 9381–11

Western States, Fed Reserve 10th District depository instns deposits, loans, investments, and borrowings, monthly rpt, 9381–2

Yields and interest rates, govt and private issues, weekly rpt, 9391–4

Yields and interest rates on public and private securities, 1929-83, annual rpt, 204–1.5

Yields, interest rates, and bond prices, for commercial paper and govt securities, monthly rpt, 9365–2.14

Yields of Treasury, corporate, and municipal long-term bonds, *Treasury Bulletin,* quarterly rpt, 8002–4.9

see also American Stock Exchange

see also Foreign investments

see also Government securities

see also Mortgages

see also Municipal bonds

see also Mutual funds

see also New York Stock Exchange

see also Public debt

Index by Subjects and Names

see also Stockbrokers
see also Tax exempt securities
see also U.S. savings bonds

Securities Act

Small business capital formation under securities law exemptions, effects on stocks offered, issuers, and purchasers, series, 9736–2

Securities and Exchange Commission

Budget of US Appendix, detailed budgets and personnel summaries, by agency, FY85, annual rpt, 104–3

Budget of US, appropriations, outlays, balances, and budget receipts, by govtl branch and agency, FY83, annual rpt, 8104–2

Investment companies classification, assets, and location, Sept 1982, annual directory, 9734–1

Regulatory activities and operations, securities industry finances, and securities exchange activity, selected years 1935-FY83, annual rpt, 9734–2

Securities market operations and industry financial statements and profitability, by size and type of firm, annual rpt, discontinued, 9734–3

Securities purchases, sales, and holdings, by issuer and type and ownership of security, monthly listing, 9732–2

Small business capital formation, sources, needs, and tax and other investment incentives and barriers, 1983 annual conf rpt, 9734–4

Small business capital formation under securities law exemptions, effects on stocks offered, issuers, and purchasers, series, 9736–2

Stock market transactions volume and proceeds and new issue registrations, for US registered exchanges, SEC monthly rpt, 9732–1

Securities exchange

see American Stock Exchange
see New York Stock Exchange
see Stock exchanges

Security clearance

see Internal security

Sedatives

see Drug abuse and treatment
see Drugs

Sedberry, George R.

"Food Habits and Trophic Relationships of a Community of Fishes on the Outer Continental Shelf", 2168–78

Seeborg, Michael

"Female-Male Unemployment Differential: Effects of Changes in Industry Employment", 6722–1.465

Seeds

Acreage planted and harvested, by crop and State, 1982-83 and planned as of June 1984, annual rpt, 1621–23

Agricultural Statistics, 1983, annual rpt, 1004–1

Agriculture census, 1982: farms, farmland, production and costs, and operator characteristics, preliminary State and county rpt series, 2330–1

Agriculture census, 1982: farms, farmland, production, finances, and operator characteristics, by county, final State rpt series, 2331–1

Cooperatives farm supply sales programs, services offered, inventory mgmt and

marketing methods, and sales force and compensation system, for 4 products, 1982, 1128–24

Cooperatives, membership, activities, and finances, by commodity and selected State, 1900-80 with trends from 1863, 1128–30

Exports and imports of US, by agricultural commodity and country, bimonthly rpt with articles, 1522–1

Exports and imports of US, by detailed agricultural commodity and country, FY83 and CY83, semiannual rpts, 1522–4

Exports and imports of US, detailed SIC-based commodities by world area, 1983, annual rpts, 2424–6

Exports and imports of US, totals and as percent of domestic production, by SIC 2- to 5-digit commodity, 1981, annual rpt, 2424–3

Exports and personal expenditures of US and world for selected agricultural commodities, by country, and export share of US farm income, various periods 1926-82, 1528–172

Exports of manufactured and agricultural commodities, manufacturing production, and export-related employment, 1960s-82, State rpt series, 2046–3

Exports of US, detailed commodities by country of destination, monthly rpt, 2422–3

Exports of US, detailed Schedule B commodities by country of destination, 1983, annual rpt, 2424–9

Exports of US, detailed Schedule E commodities by mode of transport and world area and country of destination, 1983, annual rpts, 2424–5

Exports of US seeds, by type of seed, world region, and country, FAS quarterly rpt, 1925–13

Farm finances, assets, liabilities, income, receipts by commodity and State, and expenses, 1980-83 and trends from 1910, annual rpt, 1544–16

Farm finances, expenses by type, loans by purpose and source, and credit detail by Fed Reserve District, quarterly rpt, 9365–3.10

Farm finances, production, expenses by type, and domestic economic impact, selected years 1972-82 and preliminary 1983-84, annual rpt, 1544–19

Farm production expenditures, detailed items by farm sales size and region, 1983, annual rpt, 1614–3

Farm production inputs, outputs, and productivity, by region, 1939-82, annual rpt, 1544–17

Farm production itemized costs, receipts, and net returns, for 13 crops, 4 livestock types, and milk, by region, 1981-83, annual rpt, 1544–20

Farmers prices received for major products and paid for farm inputs and living items, by commodity and State, monthly rpt, 1629–1

Farmers prices received for major products and paid for farm inputs, by commodity and State, 1983, annual rpt, 1629–5

Feed grain production, acreage, stocks, use, trade, prices, and price supports, periodic situation rpt with articles, 1561–4

Selective Service System

Futures market hedging and price forecasting efficiency, for rice, sunflower seeds, and soybeans, 1980-83, article, 1502–3.404

Imports of US, detailed Schedule A commodities by country and world area of origin, and mode of transport, 1983, annual rpts, 2424–2

Imports of US, detailed Schedule A commodities by country, monthly rpt, 2422–2

Imports of US, detailed TSUSA commodities by country of origin, 1983, annual rpt, 2424–4

Input-output structure of US economy, detailed interindustry transactions for 537 industries, and components of final demand, 1977 benchmark data, 2708–17

Marketing cash receipts of farms, by detailed commodity and State, 1979-82, annual rpt, 1544–18

Prices received by farmers and production value for detailed crops by State, 1981-83, annual rpt, 1621–2

Production, farms, acreage, and related data, by selected crop and State, monthly rpt, 1621–1

Wheat (durum) acreage, production, prices, stocks, use, and US and Canada exports by country, quarterly rpt, 1313–6

see also Oils, oilseeds, and fats
see also under By Commodity in the "Index by Categories"

Segregation

see Discrimination in education
see Discrimination in housing
see School busing

Sehgal, Ellen

"Occupational Mobility and Job Tenure in 1983", 6722–1.460

"Work Experience in 1983 Reflects the Effects of the Recovery", 6722–1.472

Seidel, Stephen

"Can We Delay a Greenhouse Warming? The Effectiveness and Feasibility of Options To Slow a Build-Up of Carbon Dioxide in the Atmosphere", 9188–88

Seizures

see Searches and seizures

Select Commission on Immigration and Refugee Policy

Budget of US, appropriations, outlays, balances, and budget receipts, by govtl branch and agency, FY83, annual rpt, 8104–2

Selective service

Criminal cases of Federal defendants, disposition, convictions, and sentences, by offense and district, as of June 1983, annual rpt, 18204–1

Registrants by State, and nonregistrant prosecution status, 2nd half FY84, semiannual rpt, 9742–1

see also Voluntary military service

Selective Service System

Activities and staff of SSS, nonregistrant prosecution status, and registrants by State, 2nd half FY84, semiannual rpt, 9742–1

Budget of US Appendix, detailed budgets and personnel summaries, by agency, FY85, annual rpt, 104–3

Budget of US, appropriations, outlays, balances, and budget receipts, by govtl branch and agency, FY83, annual rpt, 8104–2

Selenium

Selenium

see Nonmetallic minerals and mines

Self-employment

Agriculture census, 1982: farms, farmland, production and costs, and operator characteristics, preliminary State and county rpt series, 2330–1

Census of Population and Housing, 1980: detailed population and housing characteristics, by county, city, and census tract, State and SMSA rpt series, 2551–2

Census of Population, 1980: detailed socioeconomic and demographic characteristics, by age, sex, race, Hispanic origin, occupation, and industry, State rpt series, 2531–4

Census of Population, 1980: detailed socioeconomic characteristics, by county, city, and inside-outside SMSAs and central cities, State rpt series, 2531–3

China economic conditions, agricultural and industrial production, trade, and domestic and foreign investment, 1980-85, 2048–106

Disability (short-term) earnings lost, insurance benefits, sick leave, and work days lost by sex, by type of worker, 1948-81, article, 4742–1.417

Economic and demographic factors used in OASDI program cost estimates, selected years 1913-82 with alternative projections to 2060, 4706–1.90

Employment and earnings, detailed data, monthly rpt, 6742–2

Employment and unemployment by selected worker characteristics, annual averages, 1983, article, 6742–2.403

Employment, earnings, and hours, monthly press release, 6742–5

Employment, earnings, and hours of self-employed, wage and salary, and unpaid family workers, by industry div and occupation, 1970-83, article, 6722–1.443

Employment situation, earnings, hours, and other BLS economic indicators, transcripts of BLS Commissioner's monthly testimony, periodic rpt, 23846–4

Employment, unemployment, and labor force, detailed data by sociodemographic and employment characteristics, and industry, 1940s-83, 6748–72

Farm houseolds social security tax liability, alternative tax rates by type of legal organization, 1955-90, article, 1702–1.408

Farm labor, wages, hours, and perquisites, by State, quarterly rpt, 1631–1

Farm population, by employment and socioeconomic characteristics, 1983, annual rpt, 2544–1

Govt taxation and revenue systems, by type of tax and system, level of govt, and State, selected years 1958-83, annual rpt, 10044–1.3

Income (legal) not reported on Federal income tax returns by source, and legal and illegal underground income, with bibl, 1974-81, article, 2702–1.419

Income (personal) per capita and by source, earnings by major industry group, and social insurance contributions, by region and State, 1929-82, 2708–40

Income (taxable) not reported on individual and corporate returns, and associated Federal revenue losses, by detailed legal and illegal source, 1973-81, 8308–26

Income of households, families, and persons, by detailed socioeconomic characteristics and region, 1982, annual Current Population Rpt, 2546–6.39

Income tax returns of elderly, by income statement and tax item and income level, 1981 with trends from 1977, article, 8302–2.412

Income tax returns of individuals, by filing and deduction characteristics and income level, 1983, annual article, 8302–2.414

Income tax returns of individuals by tax return item, State, and occupation, and income by source and tax owed, by income level, selected years 1916-80, conf papers, 8308–28.1

Income tax returns of individuals, detailed data, 1982, annual rpt, 8304–2

Kentucky employment growth in 9-county rural area, labor force and establishment characteristics, 1979-80, 1598–194

Natl income and product, comprehensive accounts and components, *Survey of Current Business,* monthly rpt, monthly and annual tables, 2702–1.27

OASDHI and selected social insurance programs, covered workers earnings and characteristics, selected years 1937-82, annual rpt, 4744–3.3

OASI beneficiaries by income level, and average income, by beneficiary characteristics and income source, before and after receipt of 1st benefit, 1969-77, article, 4742–1.418

Older persons by demographic, socioeconomic, and health characteristics, selected years 1900-81 and projected to 2050, Current Population Rpt, 2546–2.125

Older persons income and income sources, by OASDI beneficiary and poverty status, labor force participation, and demographic characteristics, 1982, biennial rpt, 4744–26

Poverty status of families and persons, by detailed socioeconomic characteristics, 1982, annual Current Population Rpt, 2546–6.40

Science and engineering doctoral degree recipients, by field, sex, race, age, citizenship, postgrad employment and study status, State, and instn, 1960-82, 9626–6.16

Small and minority-owned businesses finances and operations, Federal contracts by agency, and worker characteristics, by industry, race, sex, and State, 1950s-83, annual rpt, 9764–6

Small business loans and credit, operational expectations, and NYC metro area owners economic and professional attitudes, by industry div, 1980-83 surveys, hearings, 21728–52

Texas farm household income, by income source and substate region, 1979, article, 9379–1.406

Virgin Islands economic censuses, 1982: employment, establishments, payroll, and receipts, by SIC 1- to 4-digit industry, island, and city, 2593–1

Wage growth and turnover rates related to marital status, sex, age, establishment type, and employer size, 1979/80, article, 9393–8.403

Index by Subjects and Names

Youth employment, by high school and college enrollment status, industry div, occupation, and selected demographic characteristics, 1980-82, 6746–1.250

Seliskar, Denise M.

"Ecology of Tidal Marshes of the Pacific Northwest Coast: A Community Profile", 5506–9.11

Sellon, Gordon H., Jr.

"Instruments of Monetary Policy", 9381–1.408

"Monetary Control: A Comparison of the U.S. and Canadian Experiences, 1975-79", 9381–10.38

Semiconductor Industry Association

"Effect of Government Targeting on World Semiconductor Competition: A Case History of Japanese Industrial Strategy and Its Costs for America", 21368–46.1

Senate

Budget of US Appendix, detailed budgets and personnel summaries, by agency, FY85, annual rpt, 104–3

Budget of US, appropriations, outlays, balances, and budget receipts, by govtl branch and agency, FY83, annual rpt, 8104–2

Budget of US, compact budgets by function, agency, and account, FY85 with projections to FY89, annual rpt, 104–2

Campaign finances and Fed Election Commission monitoring activities, 1984 Federal elections, biennial rpt series, 9276–2

Campaign finances, election procedures, and Fed Election Commission monitoring activities, press release series, 9276–1

Campaign funding by political action committee and candidate, proposed candidate spending limits, voting rates by party, and political opinions, by State, 1960-82, hearings, 25688–6

Campaign funding by political action committees to individual congressmen, and public opinion on reform proposals and assn influence, 1970s-83, hearings, 21428–7

Campaign funding by political action committees to reelect and defeat House and Senate members by candidate, and FEC activities and funding, 1983, annual rpt, 9274–1

Election campaign political action committee funding, by House and Senate candidate, 1978-82 Federal elections, biennial rpt, 9274–4

Salaries, expenses, and contingent fund disbursements, by payee, detailed listings, 1st half FY84, semiannual rpt, 25922–1

see also Senate Documents

see also Senate Special Publications

see also under names of individual committees (starting with Senate or Joint)

see also under names of individual subcommittees (starting with Subcommittee)

Senate Aging Committee, Special

Home heating costs of low-income households, natural gas price decontrol effects, aid programs, and gas supply/demand data, by income level and State, 1970s-95, hearing, 25148–26

Older persons Fed Govt pension and health spending, by program and as percents of budget and GNP, 1965-85 with projections to 2040, 25148–28

Index by Subjects and Names

Older persons health care expenditures, costs, and insurance, and effects of proposed Medicare cost share increase, selected years 1965-81, 25148–27

Older persons sociodemographic characteristics, and Fed Govt program participation and funding by agency, 1983 with trends and projections 1900-2080, annual rpt, 25144–3

Supplementary Security Income beneficiary socioeconomic characteristics and health service use, 1970s-83 and SSI program projections to 1995, 25148–29

Senate Agriculture and Forestry Committee *see* Senate Agriculture, Nutrition, and Forestry Committee

Senate Agriculture, Nutrition, and Forestry Committee

Pesticide (ethylene dibromide) residue in grain and grain foods, and effect of processing and cooking, by selected product, 1984 hearing, 25168–62

Soil conservation program policies of Fed Govt, attitudes of farmers and ranchers in 6 central US counties, 1982/83 survey, hearing, 25168–61

Senate Armed Services Committee

Strategic material stockpile mgmt, with cobalt use and stockpiles, and CCC appropriations and inventories, selected years 1950-83, hearings, 25208–27

Senate Banking, Housing, and Urban Affairs Committee

Eximbank loan guarantees and insurance currently provided and needed by Mexico and Brazil, and value of worldwide and US trade, 1981-84, hearings, 25248–97

Senate Commerce, Science and Transportation Committee

Railroad finances, operations, and freight rates and shares, by commodity and railroad, 1970s-82, hearings, 25268–80

Travel agency financial and operating data, and airline ticket sales by type of distributor, 1970s-82, hearing, 25268–81

Senate Documents

Capitol Architect detailed expenditures for buildings and grounds, salaries, supplies, and services, 1st half FY84, semiannual rpt, 25922–2

Poverty status of families and persons by selected characteristics, public welfare funding, and effect of counting transfer payments as income, selected years 1950-83, 25928–4

Senate salaries, expenses, and contingent fund disbursements, by payee, detailed listings, 1st half FY84, semiannual rpt, 25922–1

Senate Energy and Natural Resources Committee

Coal supply and Fed Govt coal leases, by owner, owner industry, and western State, various periods 1950-82 and projected to 2000, hearing, 25318–58

Forests (natl) timber sales contract operations in Northwest US by forest and firm, and lumber supply/demand, FY76-1983 with trends from 1913, hearings, 25318–57

Senate Environment and Public Works Committee

Air pollution abatement under Clean Air Act, emissions by source, standards, and effects on auto industry and health, 1970s-83, hearings, 25328–25

Building construction, acquisition, and alteration proposals for historic and other Fed Govt projects, costs and tenure by city and project, as of 1983, hearings, 25328–23

Trucking industry economic effects of size and weight limits, and hwy use taxes by tax type, 1982-83 and projected 1984-87, hearings, 25328–24

Senate Finance Committee

EC agricultural self-sufficiency and trade by selected product, with comparisons to other countries, selected years 1959/60-1983/84, hearing, 25368–135

Eurodollar bond market issues of US corporations, and amount raised and savings relative to domestic market, by company, 1975-82, hearing, 25368–132

Income taxes, effective rates, and selected financial data, for financial instns by type and individual firm, with comparisons to other industries, selected years 1960-82, hearing, 25368–129

Insurance industry (property and casualty) financial and operating data, investments, and tax liability, various periods 1951-82, hearing, 25368–128

Life expectancy increase impacts on OASDI and pension policy, with alternative sociodemographic projections to 2100, hearing, 25368–130

Medicare physician charges and reimbursement by enrollee characteristics and carrier, payment limits effects on charges in California, and physician earnings, by specialty, 1950s-84, 25368–127

R&D spending and industry growth, and OPEC oil refining operations, various periods 1953-90, hearings, 25368–133

Steel pipe and tube shipments, imports from EC by country, and exports, by product type, various periods 1978-83 with import duties to 1987, hearing, 25368–134

Tax expenditures, Fed Govt revenues foregone through income tax deductions and exclusions by type, and effect of Deficit Reduction Act, FY84-89, annual rpt, 21784–10

Tax expenditures, Fed Govt revenues foregone through pension and other tax benefit policy changes, FY84-88, and women's labor force and pension participation, 1939-82, hearing, 25368–131

Senate Foreign Relations Committee

Communications satellite intl systems charges, operations, investment shares by country, and competition impacts, 1964-83 with projections to 2003, hearings, 25388–46

DOD budget, FY85 weapons system requests consistency with US policy and specified treaties, with funding FY83-87, annual rpt, 21384–4

Foreign military, social, and economic summary data by world area and country, and US-USSR relations, 1960s-80s, hearing, 25388–47

Human rights conditions in 162 countries, economic and military aid of US, and economic aid of intl organizations, 1981-83, annual rpt, 21384–3

Machine tool orders by selected industry, trade, and shipments and Japan share of US market by type of tool, various dates 1972-84, hearing, 25388–48

Senate Small Business Committee, Select

Oil (Alaskan) potential exports to Japan, costs and benefits, with background data on oil prices, Pacific Basin supply/demand, and tankers, various periods 1918-99, hearings, 25388–45

Senate Governmental Affairs Committee

Machine tool orders by selected industry, trade, and shipments and Japan share of US market by type of tool, various dates 1972-84, hearing, 25388–48

Pension and other benefits of private industry, pension plans created and terminated since 1939, and NYC retirement systems assets, 1978-83, conf proceedings, 25408–89

Pension benefits and after-tax salary replacement rates by plan type, and older persons income and income sources, by age and marital status, 1950s-82, conf proceedings, 25408–87

Regional councils involved in service activities, by type of service and region population size, 1982 survey, hearing, 25408–88

Revenue sharing and other Fed Govt grant program alternative allocations, with city govt finances and responses to program cuts, FY79-83, hearings, 25408–86

Senate Judiciary Committee

Bankruptcy caseloads in Federal district courts and new judges needed, by circuit and district, and characteristics of bankruptcy filers, 1978-83, hearing, 25528–97

Drug prices by brand and generic category, patent life, FDA approval time, and industry R&D costs and finances, selected years 1962-83, hearing, 25528–98

Fed Govt administrative law judges by agency and grade, various dates 1947-82, and New Jersey administrative law cases, FY80-84, hearings, 25528–96

Kidnapping by parents over intl and interstate boundaries, characteristics of cases referred to State Dept and FBI by State and country, 1979-83, hearing, 25528–95

New Jersey and Maryland prison capacity and population, and New Jersey construction costs by type and funding source, by facility, 1977-82 and projected to 1988, 25528–99

Radioactive low-level waste disposal, status of interstate compacts, and waste generation and shipments, 1979-82, hearing, 25528–93

Recording industry operations and sales lost from home taping, home taping costs, and material taped by source, 1969-83, hearings with chartbook, 25528–100

Steel industry financial and operating data, steel imports by source, and employment situation at Fairless Hills, Pa, plant, 1970s-90, hearing, 25528–94

Senate Rules and Administration Committee

Election campaign funding by political action committee and candidate, proposed candidate spending limits, voting rates by party, and political opinions, by State, 1960-82, hearings, 25688–6

Senate Small Business Committee, Select

Small business mgmt counseling by university centers, costs, funding, and businesses served by industry, with detail for 2 States, 1980-83, hearing, 25728–36

Senate Special Publications

Senate Special Publications
Military weapons transfers to developing countries from US, USSR, and Europe, by weapon type and world region, 1974-82, 25948–3

Senegal

- Agricultural and food production indexes, and production of selected commodities, by world region and country, 1974-83, annual rpt, 1524–5
- Agricultural situation in sub-Saharan Africa, by country, 1982-83 and outlook for 1984, annual rpt, 1524–4.10
- Agricultural supply/demand, trade, and production, and socioeconomic data, by country, 1950s-77, 1528–179
- AID activities and funding by project and function, FY85, and developing countries summary socioeconomic data, 1970s-83, by country, annual rpt, 9914–3
- AID economic assistance to developing countries, obligations and disbursements by country, quarterly rpt, 9912–4
- AID loan repayment status and terms by program and country, and status of predecessor agency loans, quarterly rpt, 9912–3
- AID rural health care projects in Sengal, mgmt and effectiveness, and population sociodemographic characteristics, 1978-83, 9916–3.20

Background Notes, summary social, political, and economic data, 1984 rpt, 7006–2.51

- Economic conditions and foreign marketing prospects in 46 Sub-Saharan countries, 1983 world region rpt, 2046–5.1
- Economic, social, and political summary data, by country, 1984, annual factbook, 244–11
- Exports of US, detailed Schedule B commodities by country of destination, 1983, annual rpt, 2424–9
- Exports of US, detailed Schedule E commodities by mode of transport and world area and country of destination, 1983, annual rpts, 2424–5
- Food supply policies of 21 developing countries, with farm sector data, tariff income, and prices and imports of 5 grains, 1960s-81, 1528–168
- Free zones in developing countries, industry financial and operating data by country, with case studies for 5 countries, 1970s-82, 9918–10
- Imports of US, detailed Schedule A commodities by country and world area of origin, and mode of transport, 1983, annual rpts, 2424–2
- Imports of US, detailed TSUSA commodities by country of origin, 1983, annual rpt, 2424–4
- Loans and grants for economic and military assistance from US and intl agencies, by program and country, FY46-83, annual rpt, 9914–5
- Military aid of US, arms sales, and training programs costs and budget requests by program, world region, and country, FY83-85, annual rpt, 7144–13
- Military spending, arms trade, and armed forces size, with total govt spending and population, by country, 1972-82, annual rpt, 9824–1

Minerals Yearbook, 1982, Vol 3: foreign country reviews of production, trade, and policies, by commodity, annual rpt, 5604–35

Minerals Yearbook, 1982, Vol 3 preprints: foreign country review of production, trade, and policies, by commodity, annual rpt, 5604–17.84

- Population size and growth rates, and latest available benchmark demographic data, by country, 1950-83, biennial rpt, 2324–4

see also under By Foreign Country in the "Index by Categories"

Senior citizens

see Aged and aging

Sentences, criminal procedure

- Aircraft hijackings, on-board explosions, other crimes against civil aviation, and circumstances, US and worldwide, 1931-83, annual rpt, 7504–31
- Arson investigation and prosecution, by incident characteristics and outcome, motive, and type of evidence, for 4 jurisdictions, 1981, 6068–184
- Assaults, murders, and other deaths of law enforcement officers, by circumstances, level of govt, agency, victim and offender characteristics, and location, 1983, annual rpt, 6224–3
- Bank robbery court cases by case processing, sentencing, and offender characteristics, and compared to other Fed Govt felony cases, 1979-80, periodic rpt, 6062–2.407
- Court criminal case disposition, effect of victim injury and other factors, and law enforcement official and victim attitudes, 1983 survey, 6068–185
- Crime and criminal justice data, including justice expenditures and employment by level of govt, 1970s-82 with some trends from 1875, 6068–174
- Criminal case processing from arrest to sentencing, series, 6066–22
- DOE programs fraud and abuse, audits and investigations, 2nd half FY84, semiannual rpt, 3002–12
- DOT programs fraud and abuse, audits and investigations, 1st half FY84, semiannual rpt, 7302–4
- Drug defendants, by sociodemographic and case processing characteristics, with comparisons to Federal fraud and bank robbery defendants, 1979, 6062–2.403
- Drug Enforcement Admin cases against major drug traffickers by case characteristics, and agents assessment of activities, in 3 cities, 1979-82, GAO rpt, 26119–57
- Education Dept programs fraud and abuse, audits and investigations, 2nd half FY84, semiannual rpt, 4802–1
- EPA programs fraud and abuse, audits and investigations, 2nd half FY84, semiannual rpt, 9182–10
- FBI undercover operations convictions, fines, recoveries, victim compensation, and status of lawsuits against FBI by operation, FY82, GAO rpt, 26119–67
- Fed Govt agencies fraud and abuse, Inspectors General investigations and audits by agency, 1st half FY84, semiannual rpt, 102–5
- Fed Govt criminal cases, disposition, convictions, and sentences, by offense and district, as of June 1983 and trends from 1945, annual rpt, 18204–1

Index by Subjects and Names

- HUD programs fraud and abuse, audits and investigations, 2nd half FY84, semiannual rpt, 5002–8
- Marijuana cultivation control activity of State law enforcement agencies, and aid from Fed Govt and Natl Guard, 1983 survey, GAO rpt, 26119–64
- Minnesota crime sentencing guidelines by type and severity of offense, 1982, 10048–59
- NASA programs fraud and abuse, audits and investigations, 2nd half FY84, semiannual rpt, 9502–9
- Prison mandatory sentencing effects on Crime Index offense rates and prison population, selected years 1960-76, 6066–20.3
- Prison sentences, convictions, and average sentence lengths, by offense, offender class, and selected State, various periods 1971-84, 6066–19.10
- Prison terms actually served by selected State, and Illinois pretrial detention time credited to sentence, by offense, various periods 1977-83, 6066–19.7
- Prisoners in State prisons median sentence, and admissions and releases by prisoner and sentencing characteristics, by offense and State, 1981 and trends from 1926, 6066–19.9
- Supplemental Security Income representative payee fraud cases and convictions, various periods FY74-81, GAO rpt, 26121–85
- Tax prosecutions and litigations of IRS, and cases received, amounts in dispute, and disposition, FY83, annual rpt, 8304–3
- US Attorneys civil and criminal case processing in district, appellate, and State courts, by district, FY83, annual rpt, 6004–2
- USDA programs fraud and abuse, audits and investigations, 2nd half FY84, semiannual rpt, 1002–4
- VA programs fraud and abuse, audits and investigations, 2nd half FY84, semiannual rpt, 9922–13
- Witness Security Program costs, participants by arrest record, and prosecutions by offense, offender type, and disposition, various periods FY70-83, GAO rpt, 26119–70

see also Capital punishment

see also Parole and probation

Separation of powers

see also Congressional-executive relations

Seron, Carroll

"Roles of Magistrates in Federal District Courts", 18408–24

Servants

see Household workers

Service academies

- Budget of US, effects of Reagan Admin policy changes, by detailed program, FY85, annual rpt, 104–21
- Cost control proposals for Fed Govt programs and mgmt, 3-year savings by function and agency, and financial and operating data, 1960s-81, 16908–1.11
- Enrollment in higher education, by student characteristics, instn type, State, and for 150 instns, fall 1982, annual rpt, 4844–2
- Higher education instns, by type, location, and other characteristics, 1983/84 annual listing, 4844–3

Index by Subjects and Names

Service industries

Higher education instns, type, location, enrollment, and student charges, by State and congressional district, 1983/84, biennial listing, 4844–11

Manpower of DOD, and organization, budget, weapons, and property, by service branch, State, and country, 1984 annual summary rpt, 3504–13

Officer candidates, by service branch, monthly rpt, 3542–14

Officer candidates, FY46-83, annual rpt, 3544–1.2

Training and education programs of DOD, funding, staff, students, and facilities, by service branch and reserve component, FY85, annual rpt, 3504–5

Service industries

Business Conditions Digest, historical supplement on economic, business, and financial conditions and cyclical fluctuations, with methodology, 1947-82, 2708–31

Census of Population and Housing, 1980: detailed population and housing characteristics, by county, city, and census tract, State and SMSA rpt series, 2551–2

Census of Population, 1980: detailed socioeconomic and demographic characteristics, by age, sex, race, Hispanic origin, occupation, and industry, State rpt series, 2531–4

Census of Population, 1980: detailed socioeconomic characteristics, by county, city, and inside-outside SMSAs and central cities, State rpt series, 2531–3

Census of Population, 1980: labor force, by sex, detailed occupation, and region, with comparison to 1970 census, supplementary rpt, 2535–1.12

Collective bargaining agreements expiring during year, covered workers by SIC 2-digit industry, firm, and union, with summary of key provisions, 1984, annual rpt, 6784–9

Consumer expenditures, monthly rpt, quarterly data, 23842–1.1

County and City Data Book, detailed socioeconomic and demographic data for States, counties, and cities, selected years 1976-82, 2328–1

County Business Patterns: establishments, employees, and payrolls, by SIC 4-digit industry and county, 1981, annual State rpt series, 2326–8

County Business Patterns: establishments, employees, and payrolls, by SIC 4-digit industry and county, 1982, annual State rpt series, 2326–6

Developing countries govt policy, and AID and other foreign assistance, effects on private sector dev and socioeconomic conditions, with case studies for 6 countries, 1960s-80, 9918–12

Developing countries PL 480 Title I funding and socioeconomic impacts, with case studies for 5 countries, 1950s- 81, 9918–13

DOD procurement, prime contract awards by category, contract and contractor type, and service branch, FY74-1st half FY84, semiannual rpt, 3542–1

DOD procurement, prime contract awards by detailed procurement category, FY80-83, annual rpt, 3544–18

Earnings by industry div, and personal income per capita and by source, by State, MSA, and county, 1977-82, annual regional rpts, 2704–2

Earnings by major industry group, and personal income per capita and by source, by region and State, 1929-82, 2708–40

Employment and earnings, detailed data, monthly rpt, 6742–2.5

Employment by detailed occupation, for 29 SIC 2-digit nonmanufacturing industries, 1981 BLS survey, 6748–60

Employment, by sector, major industry group, and sex, selected years 1850-1982, article, 6722–1.425

Employment, earnings, and hours, by selected SIC 1- to 4-digit industry, State, and for 278 major labor areas, 1939-83, annual rpt, 6744–5

Employment, earnings, and hours, by SIC 4-digit nonfarm industry, monthly 1974-Feb 1984, annual update, 6744–4

Employment, earnings, and hours, monthly press release, 6742–5

Employment situation, earnings, hours, and other BLS economic indicators, transcripts of BLS Commissioner's monthly testimony, periodic rpt, 23846–4

Employment, unemployment, and labor force, by demographic and employment characteristics, State, and for 30 metro areas and 11 large cities, 1983, annual rpt, 6744–7

Exports, imports, and economic indicators by country and country group, and US trade policy actions, 1960s-83, annual rpt, 444–1

Fed Govt loans, grants, and tax benefits to business, by program and economic sector, projected FY84-88 with effective tax rates for FY80-82, 26306–6.70

Fed Govt procurement contract awards, by State, agency, procurement and contractor type, and for top 100 contractors, quarterly rpt, 102–6

Finances and operations, by SIC 2- to 4-digit industry, 1970s-83 and projected to 1988, annual rpt, 2014–4

Foreign direct investment in US, major investors and investments by SIC 4-digit industry, transaction type and value, and location, 1983, annual rpt, 2044–20

Handbook of Labor Statistics, employment, earnings, hours, and labor force characteristics, 1982 and trends, detailed annual rpt, 6724–1

Income tax returns of corporations, detailed income and tax items by industry, 1981, annual rpt, 8304–4

Income tax returns of corporations, summary data by industry div, 1981 . estimates, annual article, 8302–2.403

Income tax returns of corporations with foreign tax credit, income and deductions by type, asset size, and selected industry group, 1980, article, 8302–2.415

Income tax returns of foreign subsidiaries of US corporations, income and tax data, by industry and asset size, 1980, article, 8302–2.410

Income tax returns of partnerships, detailed data by industry, 1981 estimates, annual article, 8302–2.404

Income tax returns of partnerships, receipts by source, deductions by type, and establishments, by selected industry, 1982, annual article, 8302–2.416

Income tax returns of sole proprietorships, detailed data by industry div and selected industry group, 1981, annual rpt, 8304–7

Income tax returns of sole proprietorships, receipts, deductions by type, payroll, and net income, by major industry, 1982, annual article, 8302–2.413

Income tax returns with investment credits, for individuals by income, and for sole proprietorships by industry, 1981, article, 8302–2.409

Input-output structure of US economy, detailed interindustry transactions for 537 industries, and components of final demand, 1977 benchmark data, 2708–17

Intl services trade agreements, goods and services trade, intl investment, and GDP, by country, and US regulatory proposals, various periods 1970-82, 448–1

Intl services transactions by type, and sales, assets, and employment of US multinatl service firms by industry and world region, 1977-82, 2706–5.30

Mineral industries census, 1982: financial and operating data, by SIC 2- to 4-digit industry, preliminary summary rpt, 2511–2.1

Mineral industries census, 1982: financial and operating data, including materials consumed, by SIC 4-digit industry and State, preliminary rpt series, 2511–1

Minority group and women's employment, by occupational group, SIC 2- to 3-digit industry, State, and SMSA, 1981, annual rpt, 9244–1

Natl income and product, comprehensive accounts and components, *Survey of Current Business,* monthly rpt, monthly and annual tables, 2702–1.27

Occupational injuries, illnesses, and workdays lost, by SIC 2-digit industry, 1982-83, annual press release, 6844–3

Occupational injury and illness rates, by SIC 2- to 4-digit industry, 1982, annual rpt, 6844–1

Occupational manpower needs and supply by detailed occupation, and educational and training program enrollees and grads by detailed field, 1982 and 1995, biennial rpt, 6744–3

Occupational Outlook Handbook, 1984-85 biennial rpt, 6744–1

Pollution abatement capital and operating costs under Clean Air and Water Acts, for govts and selected industries, various periods 1970-2000, annual rpt, 9184–11

Price indexes (consumer and producer) by commodity and service group, and expenditure class, selected years 1929-83, annual rpt, 204–1.4

Price indexes and prices for producers of service industry equipment by detailed type, monthly 1983, annual supplement, 6762–6, 6764–2

Productivity growth adjusted for wage and price controls of early 1970s, and regression results, by industry, 1948-81, article, 9381–1.407

Receipts for selected services, by SIC 2- to 4-digit kind of business, 1983, annual rpt, 2413–8

Retail trade census, 1982: employment, establishments, sales, and payroll, by SIC 4-digit kind of business and State, preliminary rpt series, 2395–1

Service industries

Scientists, engineers, and technicians employed in private industry, by occupation and industry group, 1980-81, biennial rpt, 9627–23

- Small and minority-owned businesses finances and operations, Federal contracts by agency, and worker characteristics, by industry, race, sex, and State, 1950s-83, annual rpt, 9764–6
- *Statistical Abstract of US,* social, political, and economic data, 1950s-83 and trends, annual rpt, 2324–1.3
- Trade policy of Fed Govt, with data on US industry foreign trade and revenues, and Japan semiconductor industry subsidies, 1970s-83, hearings, 21368–46
- Transportation census, 1982: trucks, by detailed characteristics, miles traveled, and type of product carried, State rpt series, 2573–1
- Underground economy, household expenditures and participation by type of goods or service and sociodemographic characteristics, with methodology and bibl, 1981 survey, 8308–27
- Utah power plant construction effect on consumer demand for small retail and service businesses, for 2 rural counties, 1982-90, hearing, 25728–36
- Virgin Islands economic censuses, 1982: employment, establishments, payroll, and receipts, by SIC 1- to 4-digit industry, island, and city, 2593–1
- Wholesale trade census, 1982: employment, establishments, sales by commodity, and payroll for service industry suppliers, by State, preliminary rpt, 2403–1.17
- Women's employment and earnings, by labor force and socioeconomic characteristics, and compared to men, 1978-81 and trends from 1940s, 6568–29

see also Accounting and auditing

see also Advertising

see also Agricultural services

see also Automobile repair

see also Barber and beauty shops

see also Census of Service Industries

see also Child day care

see also Detective and protective services

see also Elementary and secondary education

see also Franchises

see also Gasoline service stations

see also Health facilities and services

see also Hotels and motels

see also Household workers

see also Information services

see also Labor unions

see also Laundry and cleaning services

see also Lawyers

see also Legal aid

see also Motion pictures

see also Museums

see also Nonprofit organizations and foundations

see also Rental industries

see also Repair industries

see also under By Industry in the "Index by Categories"

Service stations

see Gasoline service stations

Servicemen's life insurance programs

Actuarial analysis of 5 life insurance programs for veterans and servicemen, 1982, annual rpt, 9924–16

Army Medical/Life, Central Insurance, and Central Retirement Fund financial statements, FY83, annual rpt, 3704–12

- Budget of US, effects of Reagan Admin policy changes, by detailed program, FY85, annual rpt, 104–21
- Cost control proposals for Fed Govt programs and mgmt, 3-year savings by function and agency, and financial and operating data, 1960s-81, 16908–1.10
- Income (personal) by source including transfer payments, and social insurance contributions by type, by region, 1929 and 1982, 2708–40
- Income, expenses, and death rates for servicemen's and veterans group programs, as of June 1983, annual rpt, 9924–3
- VA insurance programs operations and other activities, FY83 and cumulative from Sept 1965, annual rpt, 9924–1.7
- VA life insurance for veterans and servicemen, finances and coverage of 8 programs, 1983, annual rpt, 9924–2
- VA mortgage loan guarantee and life insurance programs, activities and enrollees, FY59-83, annual rpt, 9924–13.3
- VA programs and activities, monthly rpt, 9922–2

see also Veterans benefits and pensions

Sesame seed

see Oils, oilseeds, and fats

Seskin, Eugene P.

"Plant and Equipment Expenditures, 1984", 2702–1.404

Set-aside programs

see Agricultural quotas and price supports

see Defense contracts and procurement

see Small business

Settle, Russell F.

"Benefits and Costs of the Federal Asbestos Standard", 21408–72

Severance taxes

- Coal taxes for surface and underground mines, by type of tax and State, 1984 rpt, 11128–1
- Govt revenues by source and expenditures by function, natl income and product account, *Survey of Current Business,* monthly rpt, monthly and annual tables, 2702–1.24
- Govt taxation and revenue systems, by type of tax and system, level of govt, and State, selected years 1958-83, annual rpt, 10044–1.3
- Minerals production, State severance tax and royalty revenue by selected State, selected years FY73-83, article, 9375–1.407
- State govt revenues by source, expenditures by function, debt, and holdings by type, FY83, annual rpt, 2466–2.5
- State govt tax collections, by detailed type of tax and tax rates, by State, FY83, annual rpt, 2466–2.3

Sewage and wastewater treatment systems

- Army Corps of Engineers activities and projects, FY83 and trends from 1800s, annual rpt, 3754–1
- Bond tax-exempt issues for private activity, by purpose, face value, major industry, and State, 1983, article, 8302–2.417
- Budget of US, effects of Reagan Admin policy changes, by detailed program, FY85, annual rpt, 104–21

Index by Subjects and Names

- Capital (fixed), govt and private nonresidential structures and equipment, residential capital, and consumer-owned durable goods by item, 1980-83, annual article, 2702–1.433
- Capital needs and financing for public works, by project type, level of govt, and selected jurisdiction, 1970s-83 and projected to 2000, hearing, 23848–181
- Capital needs and intergovtl financing for public works, by type of project and selected city, various periods 1950-83, 10048–60
- Census of Housing, 1980: inventory, occupancy, and unit characteristics, changes from 1973 by region and inside-outside SMSAs and central cities, series, 2473–3
- Census of Housing, 1980: structural, financial, and householder characteristics, by region and State, 2475–4
- Census of Population and Housing, 1980: detailed population and housing characteristics, by county, city, and census tract, State and SMSA rpt series, 2551–2
- Coal dev plans on Fed Govt lease lands in 12 regions under Fed Coal Mgmt Program, environmental and socioeconomic impacts to 2000, final statement series, 5726–4
- Coastal environmental characteristics, fish, wildlife, and use, and population socioeconomic data, for individual areas, series, 5506–4
- Community Dev Block Grants to small cities, State admin, project characteristics, and assessments of local officials, 1982, 5188–106
- Construction grants, loans, and loan guarantees of Fed Govt, by program and type of structure, FY80-83 and estimated FY84-85, annual article, 2012–1.404
- Construction industries census, 1982: financial and operating data, by SIC 4-digit industry and State, final rpt series, 2373–1
- Construction industries census, 1982: financial and operating data, by SIC 4-digit industry and State, preliminary rpt series, 2371–1
- Construction put in place, permits authorized by region, State, and MSA, and Federal contract awards, by construction type, bimonthly rpt with articles, 2012–1
- Construction put in place, value of new public and private structures, by type, monthly rpt, 2382–4
- Environmental quality and protection programs, costs, and Fed Govt enforcement, 1983, detailed annual rpt, 484–1
- Environmental quality, pollutant discharge by type, and EPA protection activities, 1970s-83, biennial summary rpt, 9184–16
- Environmental quality, pollutant discharge by type and source, and EPA protection activities and funding, 1970s-83, biennial regional rpt series, 9184–15
- EPA pollution control research and grant assistance program activities, monthly rpt, 9182–8
- Estuary environmental characteristics, fish, wildlife, uses, and mgmt, for individual estuaries, series, 5506–7

Index by Subjects and Names

Sexual sterilization

Fed Govt aid to State and local govts, expenditures, and direct payments, by program, agency, and State, FY83, annual rpt, 2464–2

Fed Govt industrial dev funding by type, program, and agency, and State govt policies and support, selected years FY75-85, 26306–6.81

Fed Govt programs and mgmt cost control proposals, 3-year savings by function and agency, and financial and operating data, 1960s-81, 16908–1.22, 16908–1.31

Fish kills from water pollution, by State, location, and pollution source, monthly 1978-80, annual rpt, 9204–3

FmHA loans and grants by program and State, and summary of services, FY83 with trends from FY63, annual rpt, 1184–17

Foreign market and trade for pollution control instruments and equipment, and user industry operations and demand, country market research rpts, 2045–17

Govt census, 1982: city govt revenues by source, expenditures by function, debt, and assets, by State and city, 2457–4

Govt census, 1982: county govt revenues by source, expenditures by function, debt, and assets, by State and county, 2457–3

Govt census, 1982: employment, payrolls, and average earnings, by function, level of govt, State, county, population size, and inside-outside SMSAs, 2455–2

Govt census, 1982: State govt payments to local govts, by program, source of funds, level of govt, and State, with trends from 1902, 2460–3

Govt employment and payroll, by function, level of govt, and jurisdiction, 1983, annual rpt series, 2466–1

Govt finances, by level of govt, State, and for large cities and counties, 1981-83, annual rpt series, 2466–2

Great Lakes basin pollutant discharges by source, and control program activities, 1983 annual rpt, 14644–1

Home mortgages (graduated payment) FHA-insured, financial, property, and mortgagor characteristics, for US and selected localities, quarterly rpt, 5142–42

Home mortgages (graduated payment) FHA-insured, financial, property, and mortgagor characteristics, for US and selected States, quarterly rpt, 5142–41

Home mortgages (graduated payment) FHA-insured, financial, property, and mortgagor characteristics, US summary, quarterly rpt, 5142–40

Home mortgages FHA-insured, financial, property, and mortgagor characteristics, for US and selected localities, quarterly rpt, 5142–2

Home mortgages FHA-insured, financial, property, and mortgagor characteristics, for US, selected States, and Puerto Rico, quarterly rpt, 5142–3

Home mortgages FHA-insured, financial, property, and mortgagor characteristics, quarterly rpt, 5142–1

Home mortgages FHA-insured, financial, property, and mortgagor characteristics, 1983, annual rpt, 5144–17

Housing and households detailed characteristics, and unit and neighborhood quality, by inside-outside central cities, 1979-82 surveys, SMSA rpt series, 2485–6

Housing and neighborhood quality indicators and attitudes, and occupant characteristics, by urban-rural location and region, 1981, annual survey, 2485–7

Housing and neighborhood quality indicators and attitudes, by occupant and unit characteristics, region, and metro-nonmetro location, 1981, annual survey, 2485–2

Housing occupancy and unit and household characteristics, by region and metro-nonmetro residence, 1983, biennial survey, 2485–1

Indian and Alaska Native health program activities, and funding for scholarships, care services, and facilities construction, by city, FY82, annual rpt, 4104–11

Input-output structure of US economy, detailed interindustry transactions for 537 industries, and components of final demand, 1977 benchmark data, 2708–17

Local govt per capita expenditures, by function and State, 1981-82, annual rpt, 10044–1.7

Manufacturing pollution abatement costs recovered, by SIC 2- to 4-digit industry, State, and SMSA, 1982, annual Current Industrial Rpt, 2506–3.6

New York Bight pollutant loadings from ocean dumping of municipal wastes by type and source, and concentrations in fish and sediments, 1970s-82, hearings, 21568–36

Occupational Outlook Handbook, 1984-85 biennial rpt, 6744–1

Ocean dumping of waste materials, EPA permit program and intl London Dumping Convention activities, 1981-83, annual rpt, 9204–8

Pollution abatement expenditures of govt, business, and consumers, 1972-82, annual article, 2702–1.407

Rural housing conditions of aged, selected householder and housing characteristics with comparisons to urban and nonaged population, 1979, 1598–193

Southeastern US water supply and quality, with background socioeconomic data, for 8 States, 1960s-2020 with trends from 1930, 9208–119

TTPI budget, vital statistics, and health services data, often by TTPI govt, FY83 and selected trends, annual rpt, 7004–6.1

Water pollution regulation under EPA wastewater discharge system, operations and funding, various periods FY79-83, GAO rpt, 26113–113

Water supply and use in 3 areas with supply problems and total US, and methods to increase supply, selected years 1974-80 and projected to 2010, 9208–125

Waterborne disease outbreaks and cases, by type, source, and location, 1983, annual rpt, 4205–35

Sex

see Men

see Sex discrimination

see Sexual behavior

see Sexual sterilization

see Women

see under By Sex in the "Index by Categories"

Sex discrimination

Black young adults economic status and educational attainment related to motivation, goals, family characteristics, and social factors, 1982, longitudinal study, 4008–65.2

Civil rights progress of minorities and women, Supreme Court decisions, and legislative action, 1957-83, last issue of narrative annual rpt, 11044–3

Fed Govt Equal Opportunity Recruitment Program implementation, and summary employment data, FY83, annual rpt, 9844–33

Foreign human rights conditions in 162 countries, economic and military aid of US, and economic aid of intl organizations, 1981-83, annual rpt, 21384–3

TVA employment of minorities and women, by detailed occupation, pay level, and grade, FY83 and goals for FY84, annual rpt, 9804–17

Sexual behavior

Acquired immune deficiency syndrome (AIDS) cases by patient sexual prefernce, 1979-83, article, 4102–1.431

Acquired immune deficiency syndrome (AIDS) cases by sexual preference and intravenous drug use, and drug abusers characteristics, 1979-81, article, 4102–1.427

Aliens excluded and deported by cause, 1892-FY81, annual rpt, 6264–2

Arrests and arrest rates, by offense, offender characteristics, population size, and State, 1970s-83, annual rpt, 6224–2.2

Criminal cases of Federal defendants, disposition, convictions, and sentences, by offense and district, as of June 1983, annual rpt, 18204–1

Teenage girls births and sexual experience by race, abortions, and birth control use, by age, 1970s-80 with birth trends from 1920, hearings, 21968–29

see also Family planning

see also Rape

Sexual sterilization

Hospital discharges and length of stay, by patient age and sex, facility size and ownership, procedure performed, and region, 1983, 4146–8.101

Hospital discharges and length of stay, by patient characteristics, facility size, procedure performed, diagnosis, and region, 1982, annual rpt, 4147–13.78

Hysterectomy and tubal sterilization rates for women aged 15-44, 1979-80, annual rpt, 4204–1.3

Medicare and Medicaid eligibility, participation, covered services and use, and reimbursements and payments, various periods 1966-82, annual rpt, 4654–1

Women sterilized following hospital delivery of live or stillborn infants, by sociodemographic and maternity characteristics, 1972 and 1980, article, 4102–1.419

Women's contraceptives use, by method, marital status, age, and race, 1982, 4146–8.103

Women's family planning and infertility services use, by source of service, marital status, age, race, and Hispanic origin, 1982, 4146–8.104

Seychelles Islands

Seychelles Islands

AID activities and funding by project and function, FY85, and developing countries summary socioeconomic data, 1970s-83, by country, annual rpt, 9914–3

AID economic assistance to developing countries, obligations and disbursements by country, quarterly rpt, 9912–4

Economic conditions and foreign marketing prospects in 46 Sub-Saharan countries, 1983 world region rpt, 2046–5.1

Economic, social, and political summary data, by country, 1984, annual factbook, 244–11

Exports of US, detailed Schedule B commodities by country of destination, 1983, annual rpt, 2424–9

Exports of US, detailed Schedule E commodities by mode of transport and world area and country of destination, 1983, annual rpts, 2424–5

Imports of US, detailed Schedule A commodities by country and world area of origin, and mode of transport, 1983, annual rpts, 2424–2

Imports of US, detailed TSUSA commodities by country of origin, 1983, annual rpt, 2424–4

Loans and grants for economic and military assistance from US and intl agencies, by program and country, FY46-83, annual rpt, 9914–5

Military aid of US, arms sales, and training programs costs and budget requests by program, world region, and country, FY83-85, annual rpt, 7144–13

Minerals Yearbook, 1982, Vol 3: foreign country reviews of production, trade, and policies, by commodity, annual rpt, 5604–35

Minerals Yearbook, 1982, Vol 3 preprints: foreign country review of production, trade, and policies, by commodity, annual rpt, 5604–17.83

Population size and growth rates, and latest available benchmark demographic data, by country, 1950-83, biennial rpt, 2324–4

see also under By Foreign Country in the "Index by Categories"

Shaber, Sandra

"Consumer Spending: Recovery and Beyond", 1702–1.405

Shack-Marquez, Janice

"Earnings Differences Between Men and Women: An Introductory Note", 6722–1.436

Shale oil

see Oil shale

Shannon, John

"Dealing with Deficits—Striking a New Fiscal Balance?", 10042–1.401

Shapira, Philip

"Shutdowns and Job Loss in California: The Need for New National Priorities", 21348–84.1

Sharitz, Rebecca R.

"Ecology of Southeastern Shrub Bogs (Pocosins) and Carolina Bays: A Community Profile", 5506–9.9

Sharjah

see United Arab Emirates

Sharon, Pa.

Census of Housing, 1980: occupancy and unit characteristics, by race, Hispanic origin, and city, SMSA rpt, 2473–1.330

Census of Population and Housing, 1980: detailed population and housing characteristics, by county, city, and census tract, SMSA rpt, 2551–2.330

see also under By SMSA or MSA in the "Index by Categories"

Sharples, Jerry A.

"Global Stocks of Grain: Implications for U.S. Policy", 1528–184

"World Trade and U.S. Farm Policy", 1528–183

Shaughnessy, Peter W.

"Case Mix, Quality, and Cost Relationships in Colorado Nursing Homes", 4652–1.432

Sheboygan, Wis.

Census of Housing, 1980: occupancy and unit characteristics, by race, Hispanic origin, and city, SMSA rpt, 2473–1.331

Census of Population and Housing, 1980: detailed population and housing characteristics, by county, city, and census tract, SMSA rpt, 2551–2.331

see also under By SMSA or MSA in the "Index by Categories"

Sheep

see Livestock and livestock industry

Sheffield, Raymond M.

"Georgia's Forests", 1206–26.7

Sheldrick, William F.

"Current World Fertilizer Situation and Outlook, 1982/83-1992/93", 1004–16.1

Shellfish

Atlantic Ocean sport and commercial landings and allowable and potential catch of US and Canada, for 34 species, 1983, annual rpt, 2164–14

California marine resources and environmental effects of proposed oil and gas dev, for 2 sanctuaries off central and northern coasts, 1980s and projected to 2006, hearing, 21448–30.1

Coastal environmental and wildlife characteristics, use, and mgmt, for individual ecosystems, series, 5506–9

Coastal environmental characteristics, fish, wildlife, and use, and population socioeconomic data, for individual areas, series, 5506–4

Coastal fish and shellfish landings, life cycles, and environmental needs, for selected species by region, with glossary and bibl, series, 5506–8

Cold storage holdings of fish and shellfish products, weight by species and form, preliminary data, monthly rpt, 2162–2

Consumption of food and nutrient intake by individuals, by food group, source, and socioeconomic characteristics, 1977-78 natl survey, final rpt series, 1356–4

Consumption, supply, trade, prices, expenditures, and indexes, by food commodity, 1963-83, annual rpt, 1544–4

Environmental quality, pollutant discharge by type and source, and EPA protection activities and funding, 1970s-83, biennial regional rpt series, 9184–15

Estuary environmental characteristics, fish, wildlife, uses, and mgmt, for individual estuaries, series, 5506–7

Europe (Western) fish and shellfish wholesale prices and market activity in 8 countries, weekly rpt, 2162–8

Exports and imports of US, detailed SIC-based commodities by world area, 1983, annual rpts, 2424–6

Index by Subjects and Names

Exports and imports of US, totals and as percent of domestic production, by SIC 2- to 5-digit commodity, 1981, annual rpt, 2424–3

Exports of US, detailed commodities by country of destination, monthly rpt, 2422–3

Exports of US, detailed Schedule B commodities by country of destination, 1983, annual rpt, 2424–9

Exports of US, detailed Schedule E commodities by mode of transport and world area and country of destination, 1983, annual rpts, 2424–5

Fish and fish products production by region and State, and trade, by species and product, 1982-83, annual rpt series, 2166–6

Fish and shellfish of economic importance, biological, fishery, and mgmt data, literature review series, 2166–16

France Brittany coast oil spill cleanup and research costs, marine and tourism industry losses, and recreation losses of tourists and residents, 1971-79, 2178–13

Great Lakes trade, by SITC 3-digit commodity, port, vessel type, world area, and country, 1982, annual rpt, 7744–3

Imports of US, detailed Schedule A commodities by country and world area of origin, and mode of transport, 1983, annual rpts, 2424–2

Imports of US, detailed Schedule A commodities by country, monthly rpt, 2422–2

Imports of US, detailed TSUSA commodities by country of origin, 1983, annual rpt, 2424–4

Landings, employment, gear used, and seafood production, for detailed species by State, 1977, annual rpt, 2164–2

Landings, prices, trade, consumption, and industry operating data, for US with foreign comparisons, 1982-83, annual rpt, 2164–1

Landings, prices, trade, wholesaler receipts, and market activities at 5 major US ports, weekly rpts, 2162–6

Manufacturing census, 1982: financial and operating data, for SIC 4-digit industries by product, preliminary rpt, 2491–1.38, 2491–1.39

Marine Fisheries Review, US and foreign fisheries resources, conservation, operations, and research, quarterly rpt articles, 2162–1

New York Bight pollutant loadings from ocean dumping of municipal wastes by type and source, and concentrations in fish and sediments, 1970s-82, hearings, 21568–36

Producer prices and indexes, by stage of processing and detailed commodity, monthly rpt, 6762–6

Producer prices and indexes, by stage of processing and detailed commodity, monthly 1983, annual supplement, 6764–2

Shrimp landings in South Atlantic and Gulf of Mexico, by species, size, type of gear, depth, and area, 1977, annual rpt, 2164–2.5, 2164–2.6

Waterborne commerce of US (domestic and foreign), freight by commodity, traffic, and passengers, by port and waterway, 1982, annual rpt, 3754–3

Index by Subjects and Names

Wetlands environmental characteristics, acreage, uses, and mgmt, by wetland type and region, 1950s-80, 26358–102
see also Fish and fishing industry
see also under By Commodity in the "Index by Categories"

Shelton, Ella M.
"Aviation Fuels, 1983", 3006–2.2
"Heating Oils, 1984", 3006–2.4
"Motor Gasolines, Summer 1983", 3006–2.1
"Motor Gasolines, Winter 1983-84", 3006–2.3

Shelton, Wash.
Wages by occupation, and benefits for office and plant workers, 1984 labor market area survey rpt, 6785–3.4

Shen, Susan
"Sustaining Tropical Forest Resources: Reforestation of Degraded Lands", 26358–101.2

Shenk, J. Frederick
"Economic Cost of Crime to Victims", 6066–19.6

Sherman, Kenneth
"Ichyoplankton and Fish Recruitment Studies in Large Marine Ecosystems", 2162–1.402

Sherman, Tex.
Census of Housing, 1980: occupancy and unit characteristics, by race, Hispanic origin, and city, SMSA rpt, 2473–1.332
Census of Population and Housing, 1980: detailed population and housing characteristics, by county, city, and census tract, SMSA rpt, 2551–2.332
Wages of office and plant workers, by occupation, 1984 labor market area survey rpt, 6785–3.10
see also under By SMSA or MSA in the "Index by Categories"

Shigella
see Food and waterborne diseases

Shilling, Sharon
"Maternal Occupation and Industry and the Pregnancy Outcome of U.S. Married Women, 1980", 4102–1.422

Shindelman, Lois W.
"Social and Economic Incentives for Family Caregivers", 4652–1.403

Shipbuilding and operating subsidies
Budget of US, effects of Reagan Admin policy changes, by detailed program, FY85, annual rpt, 104–21
Construction and repair facilities, construction capability, number and value of ships under construction, and employment, by shipyard, 1983, annual rpt, 7704–9
Construction, govt-subsidized contracts awarded 1971-81, annual rpt, 7704–12.1
Cost control proposals for Fed Govt programs and mgmt, 3-year savings by function and agency, and financial and operating data, 1960s-81, 16908–1.11
Fed Govt financial and nonfinancial domestic aid, 1984 annual comprehensive catalog, 104–5
Fed Govt foreign cargo shipments and costs by agency or program and route, and employment and economic impacts of US vessel preference, 1980, GAO rpt, 26117–30
Foreign and US shipping and shipbuilding subsidies and aid, with summary fleet, trade, and GNP data, for 48 countries, 1979-80, biennial rpt, 7704–18

Ships and shipping

MarAd shipbuilding and operating subsidies and other activities, and world merchant fleets operations, FY83, annual rpt, 7704–14
Merchant ships and percent of construction costs under government subsidy, monthly rpt, 7702–1
Merchant ships in US fleet, shipping costs, construction, employment, military availability, and Fed Govt subsidies, 1970s-1984 and projected to 2000, 26306–6.83
Military Sealift Command operations for naval fleet support, and transport of DOD and AID cargo by route, quarterly rpt, 3802–2

Shipments, industrial
see Industrial production

Shipp, P. Royal
"Current Federal Retirement System", 25408–87

Ships and shipping
Air pollutant emission factors, by detailed source, 3rd edition, 1983-84 supplements, 9198–13
Air pollution levels for 5 pollutants, by detailed source, State, and Air Quality Control Region, 1981, annual rpt, 9194–7
American Samoa minimum wage rates, employment, earnings, and benefits, by establishment and industry, Nov 1983, biennial rpt, 6504–6
Asbestos workers, exposure levels, cancer incidence, and deaths, by industry and occupation, and asbestos regulation enforcement and costs/benefits, various periods 1940-2027, hearing, 21408–72
Bulk carrier ships in world fleet, characteristics by country of registry, 1982, annual rpt, 7704–13
Bunker fuels, oil, and coal laden in US on vessels engaged in foreign trade, by port, monthly rpt, 2422–5
Census of Population, 1980: detailed socioeconomic and demographic characteristics, by age, sex, race, Hispanic origin, occupation, and industry, State rpt series, 2531–4
China economic conditions, agricultural and industrial production, trade, and domestic and foreign investment, 1980-85, 2048–106
Coastal environmental characteristics, fish, wildlife, and use, and population socioeconomic data, for individual areas, series, 5506–4
Collective bargaining agreements expiring during year, covered workers by SIC 2-digit industry, firm, and union, with summary of key provisions, 1984, annual rpt, 6784–9
Communist, OECD, and selected other countries freight and carrier inventories, by mode of transport, 1960s-83, annual rpt, 244–5.10
Construction and conversion costs for merchant ships by owner and builder, fleet size, and employment, monthly rpt, 7702–1
Construction and repair facilities, construction capability, number and value of ships under construction, and employment, by shipyard, 1983, annual rpt, 7704–9

Construction costs and shipbuilding employment, by coastal district, 1982, annual rpt, 7704–12
Construction of new ships, by type and by country of construction and registry, 1982, annual rpt, 7704–4
Containerized cargo carried over principal trade routes, by flag of vessel, port, and US coastal district, 1982, annual rpt, 7704–8
County Business Patterns: establishments, employees, and payrolls, by SIC 4-digit industry and county, 1981, annual State rpt series, 2326–8
County Business Patterns: establishments, employees, and payrolls, by SIC 4-digit industry and county, 1982, annual State rpt series, 2326–6
Developing countries disaster preparedness and summary sociodemographic, political, and economic data, country rpt series, 9916–2
Earnings by major industry group, and personal income per capita and by source, by region and State, 1929-82, 2708–40
Employment, earnings, and hours, by selected SIC 1- to 4-digit industry, State, and for 278 major labor areas, 1939-83, annual rpt, 6744–5
Employment, earnings, and hours, by SIC 4-digit nonfarm industry, monthly 1974-Feb 1984, annual update, 6744–4
Energy use, by type of air pollutant source and fuel, and State, 1981, annual rpt, 9194–14
Energy use in transportation sector by mode, fuel supplies, and demographic and economic determinants of vehicle use, 1970s-83, annual rpt, 3304–5
Exports and imports between US and outlying areas, by detailed commodity and mode of transport, monthly rpt, 2422–4
Exports and imports of US (waterborne), by type of service, customs district, port, and world area, monthly rpt, 2422–7
Exports and imports of US, by commodity group, world area, selected country, US coastal area and port, and mode of transport, with seasonal adjustments, monthly rpt, 2422–9
Exports and imports of US, detailed SIC-based commodities by world area, 1983, annual rpts, 2424–6
Exports and imports of US, totals and as percent of domestic production, by SIC 2- to 5-digit commodity, 1981, annual rpt, 2424–3
Exports of US, detailed commodities by country of destination, monthly rpt, 2422–3
Exports of US, detailed Schedule B commodities by country of destination, 1983, annual rpt, 2424–9
Exports of US, detailed Schedule E commodities by mode of transport and world area and country of destination, 1983, annual rpts, 2424–5
Fed Govt foreign cargo shipments and costs by agency or program and route, and employment and economic impacts of US vessel preference, 1980, GAO rpt, 26117–30
Finances and operations, by SIC 2- to 4-digit industry, 1970s-83 and projected to 1988, annual rpt, 2014–4

Ships and shipping

Finances, operations, vehicles, equipment, accidents, and energy use, by mode of transport, 1955-84, annual rpt, 7304–2

Fishery and fish processing employment, firms, and vessels, 1950s-83, annual rpt, 2164–1.10

Fishing craft, by size and type, and catch, 1977, annual rpt, 2164–2

Foreign and US shipping and shipbuilding subsidies and aid, with summary fleet, trade, and GNP data, for 48 countries, 1979-80, biennial rpt, 7704–18

Fuel oil (distillate and residual) and kerosene deliveries, by end use, PAD district, and State, selected years 1978-83, annual rpt, 3164–2

Grain rail and barge loadings, ship and container car availability, ocean freight rates, and export inspections, prices, and sales, weekly rpt, 1272–2

Great Lakes trade, by SITC 3-digit commodity, port, vessel type, world area, and country, 1982, annual rpt, 7744–3

Imports of US, detailed Schedule A commodities by country and world area of origin, and mode of transport, 1983, annual rpts, 2424–2

Imports of US, detailed TSUSA commodities by country of origin, 1983, annual rpt, 2424–4

Income tax returns of corporations, detailed income and tax items by industry, 1981, annual rpt, 8304–4

Income tax returns of corporations with foreign tax credit, income and deductions by type, asset size, and selected industry group, 1980, article, 8302–2.415

Income tax returns of sole proprietorships, detailed data by industry div and selected industry group, 1981, annual rpt, 8304–7

Income tax returns of sole proprietorships, receipts, deductions by type, payroll, and net income, by major industry, 1982, annual article, 8302–2.413

Input-output structure of US economy, detailed interindustry transactions for 537 industries, and components of final demand, 1977 benchmark data, 2708–17

Intermodal containers and equipment owned by US shipping and leasing companies, inventory by type and size, 1983, annual rpt, 7704–10

Manufacturing census, 1982: financial and operating data, by SIC 2- to 4-digit industry, State, SMSA, and county, preliminary census div rpt series, 2491–3

Manufacturing census, 1982: financial and operating data, for SIC 4-digit industries by product, preliminary rpt, 2491–1.404

Maritime Commission mgmt and enforcement activities, filings by type and disposition, and civil penalties by shipper, FY83, annual rpt, 9334–1

Merchant fleets operations, and MarAd shipbuilding and operating subsidies and other activities, and FY83, annual rpt, 7704–14

Merchant ships in active US fleet and Natl Defense Reserve Fleet, number and tonnage by owner/operator, Jan 1984, semiannual inventory, 7702–2

Merchant ships in US fleet, shipping costs, construction, employment, military availability, and Fed Govt subsidies, 1970s-1984 and projected to 2000, 26306–6.83

Merchant ships in world fleet, and tonnage, by country of registry, 1982, annual rpt, 7704–3

Merchant ships in world fleet, and tonnage, by vessel type, 1961-81, 1548–235

Merchant ships in world fleet, and tonnage, by vessel type, 1977-81, annual rpt, 5604–35.1

Merchant ships in world fleet, by selected characteristics and country of registry, as of Jan 1983, annual rpt, 7704–1

Military Sealift Command operations for naval fleet support, and transport of DOD and AID cargo by route, quarterly rpt, 3802–2

Minority group and women employment, by occupational group and SIC 2- to 3-digit industry, 1981, annual rpt, 9244–1.1

Occupational injury and illness rates, by SIC 2- to 4-digit industry, 1982, annual rpt, 6844–1

Oceanographic data, stations and cruises recording data for World Data Center A by country, ship, and type of data, 1983, annual rpt, 2144–15

Oceanographic research cruise schedules and ship characteristics, by academic instn or Federal agency, 1984, annual rpt, 3804–6

OECD trade, total and for 4 major countries, and US trade by country, by commodity, 1972-82, annual world region rpt series, 244–13

Overseas Business Reports: economic conditions, investment and export opportunities, and trade practices, annual country market research rpt series, 2046–6

Pacific coast States and selected areas, impact of shipping industry activities, 1970s-83, hearings, 21568–34

Panama Canal commerce, by commodity, flag of vessel, and trade routes, FY82, annual rpt, 9664–3.2

Panama merchant fleet, OCS and total vessels, and new registrations, selected years 1978-82, hearing, 21568–35

PL 480 concessional sales agreements, market value and date signed, and shipping costs, by country, 1954-83, annual rpt, 1924–6

Producer prices and indexes, by stage of processing and detailed commodity, monthly rpt, 6762–6

Producer prices and indexes, by stage of processing and detailed commodity, monthly 1983, annual supplement, 6764–2

Scientists, engineers, and technicians employment in transportation, utilities, and retail and wholesale trade, by field of science and industry, 1982, 9628–72

Ships and tonnage entering and clearing US Customs, by district and port of entry, 1983, annual rpt, 2424–7

St Lawrence Seaway Dev Corp finances and activities, and seaway toll charges and cargo tonnage by type of cargo, 1983, annual rpt, 7744–1

St Lawrence Seaway ships, cargo and passenger volumes, and toll revenues, 1981-82 and trends from 1959, annual rpt, 7744–2

Statistical Abstract of US, social, political, and economic data, 1950s-83 and trends, annual rpt, 2324–1.3

Index by Subjects and Names

Traffic, freight by commodity, and passengers, domestic and foreign waterborne commerce by port and waterway, 1982, annual rpt, 3754–3

User fees to recover costs of 7 federally subsidized public service programs, by type of fee, user, and service, FY84-88, 26306–6.68

Weather reports received from US ships and gale and wave observations by US and foreign ships, quarterly journal, 2152–8

see also Barges

see also Boats and boating

see also Freight

see also Harbors and ports

see also Inland water transportation

see also Longshoremen

see also Marine accidents and safety

see also Merchant seamen

see also Naval vessels

see also Navigation

see also Nuclear-powered ships

see also Oil spills

see also Passenger ships

see also Service academies

see also Shipbuilding and operating subsidies

see also Tanker ships

see also under By Industry in the "Index by Categories"

Shirley, Duveen L.

"Nuclear Engineering Enrollments and Degrees, 1983", 3004–5

Shoe industry

Business statistics, detailed data for major industries and economic indicators, *Survey of Current Business*, monthly rpt, 2702–1.12

Census of Population, 1980: detailed socioeconomic and demographic characteristics, by age, sex, race, Hispanic origin, occupation, and industry, State rpt series, 2531–4

China economic conditions, agricultural and industrial production, trade, and domestic and foreign investment, 1980-85, 2048–106

China exports and imports by SITC 1- to 5-digit commodity, 1970s-82, annual rpt, 244–12

Counterfeiting of brand-name products by foreign manufacturers, effects on 6 US industries, investigation with financial and operating data, 1984 rpt, 9886–4.67

County Business Patterns: establishments, employees, and payrolls, by SIC 4-digit industry and county, 1981, annual State rpt series, 2326–8

County Business Patterns: establishments, employees, and payrolls, by SIC 4-digit industry and county, 1982, annual State rpt series, 2326–6

Cuba economic conditions, agricultural and industrial production and distribution, trade, and intl economic relations, 1970-82 and trends from 1957, 248–40

Employment, earnings, and hours, by selected SIC 1- to 4-digit industry, State, and for 278 major labor areas, 1939-83, annual rpt, 6744–5

Employment, earnings, and hours, by SIC 4-digit nonfarm industry, monthly 1974-Feb 1984, annual update, 6744–4

Endangered animals and plants foreign trade including reexports of live specimens and products, by purpose, country, and species, 1982, annual rpt, 5504–19

Index by Subjects and Names

Exports and imports of US by country, and trade shifts by commodity, USITC quarterly monitoring rpt, 9882–9

Exports and imports of US, detailed SIC-based commodities by world area, 1983, annual rpts, 2424–6

Exports and imports of US, totals and as percent of domestic production, by SIC 2- to 5-digit commodity, 1981, annual rpt, 2424–3

Exports, imports, tariffs, and industry operating data for rubber footwear, 1979-83, TSUSA commodity rpt supplement, 9885–7.59

Exports of US, detailed commodities by country of destination, monthly rpt, 2422–3

Exports of US, detailed Schedule B commodities by country of destination, 1983, annual rpt, 2424–9

Exports of US, detailed Schedule E commodities by mode of transport and world area and country of destination, 1983, annual rpts, 2424–5

Finances and operations, by SIC 2- to 4-digit industry, 1970s-83 and projected to 1988, annual rpt, 2014–4

Franchise business opportunities, by firm and kind of business, 1984 annual listing, 2044–27

Great Lakes trade, by SITC 3-digit commodity, port, vessel type, world area, and country, 1982, annual rpt, 7744–3

Import quotas and tariffs, jobs protected and cost per job for selected products, and foreign trade balance by industry div, various periods 1958-81, article, 9381–1.412

Imports of footwear by US, by category, value class, and selected country, monthly rpt, 2042–29

Imports of nonrubber footwear, injury to US industry from increased import sales, investigation with background financial and operating data, 1984 rpt, 9886–5.49

Imports of US, detailed Schedule A commodities by country and world area of origin, and mode of transport, 1983, annual rpts, 2424–2

Imports of US, detailed Schedule A commodities by country, monthly rpt, 2422–2

Imports of US, detailed TSUSA commodities by country of origin, 1983, annual rpt, 2424–4

Income tax returns of corporations, detailed income and tax items by industry, 1981, annual rpt, 8304–4

Income tax returns of sole proprietorships, detailed data by industry div and selected industry group, 1981, annual rpt, 8304–7

Income tax returns of sole proprietorships, receipts, deductions by type, payroll, and net income, by major industry, 1982, annual article, 8302–2.413

Input-output structure of US economy, detailed interindustry transactions for 85 industries, and components of final demand, 1977, article, 2702–1.421

Input-output structure of US economy, detailed interindustry transactions for 537 industries, and components of final demand, 1977 benchmark data, 2708–17

Manufacturing census, 1982: financial and operating data, by SIC 2- to 4-digit industry, State, SMSA, and county, preliminary census div rpt series, 2491–3

Manufacturing census, 1982: financial and operating data, for SIC 4-digit industries by product, preliminary rpt series, 2491–1

Minority group and women employment, by occupational group and SIC 2- to 3-digit industry, 1981, annual rpt, 9244–1.1

Occupational injury and illness rates, by SIC 2- to 4-digit industry, 1982, annual rpt, 6844–1

Occupational Outlook Handbook, 1984-85 biennial rpt, 6744–1

OECD trade, total and for 4 major countries, and US trade by country, by commodity, 1972-82, annual world region rpt series, 244–13

Personal consumption expenditures for clothing and shoes, 1960-83, and percent price change, Dec 1982-Aug 1983, article, 1702–1.403

Producer prices and indexes, by stage of processing and detailed commodity, monthly rpt, 6762–6

Producer prices and indexes, by stage of processing and detailed commodity, monthly 1983, annual supplement, 6764–2

Production, employment, consumption, prices, and US trade by country, quarterly rpt, 9882–6

Production, shipments, trade, and consumption, by product, 1983, annual Current Industrial Rpt, 2506–6.8

Production, shipments, trade, and consumption of footwear, monthly Current Industrial Rpt, 2506–6.7

Productivity, hours, and employment indexes for selected SIC 3- and 4-digit industries, 1954-82, annual rpt, 6824–1.3

Retail clothing business labor productivity, by kind of business, 1967-83, article, 6722–1.463

Retail trade census, 1982: employment, establishments, sales, and payroll, by SIC 2- to 4-digit kind of business, SMSA, and retail district, State rpt series, 2401–1

Retail trade census, 1982: employment, establishments, sales, and payroll, for shoe stores by State, preliminary rpt, 2395–1.18

Retail trade sales and inventories, by kind of business, region, census div, and selected State, SMSA, and city, and seasonal adjustments, monthly rpt, 2413–3

Retail trade sales, inventories, purchases, gross margin, and accounts receivable, by SIC 2- to 4-digit kind of business and type of ownership, 1983, annual rpt, 2413–5

Virgin Islands economic censuses, 1982: employment, establishments, payroll, and receipts, by SIC 1- to 4-digit industry, island, and city, 2593–1

Wholesale trade census, 1982: employment, establishments, sales by commodity, and payroll, by SIC 4-digit kind of business and State, preliminary rpt, 2403–1.26

see also under By Industry in the "Index by Categories"

Shopping centers

Census of Retail Trade, 1982: employment, establishments, sales, and payroll, by SIC 2- to 4-digit kind of business, SMSA, and retail district, State rpt series, 2401–1

Siegel, Jacob S.

Enterprise zone and urban revitalization projects of State and local govts, effect on business and employment in selected areas, various dates 1972-83, hearing, 21788–140

Neighborhood and housing quality indicators and attitudes, and occupant characteristics, by urban-rural location and region, 1981, annual survey, 2485–7

Neighborhood and housing quality indicators and attitudes, by occupant and unit characteristics, region, and metro-nonmetro location, 1981, annual survey, 2485–2

Neighborhood quality, indicators and attitudes by inside-outside central cities, 1979-82 surveys, SMSA rpt series, 2485–6

Transit system (automated guideway) characteristics and itemized costs, for 16 systems in operation or under construction, 1982, annual rpt, 7884–6

Shortle, James S.

"Investments in Soil Conservation Structures: The Role of Operator and Operation Characteristics", 1502–3.402

Shoven, John B.

"Effect of Interest Rates on Mortgage Prepayments", 9306–1.6

Shover, Neal

"Developing a Regulatory Bureaucracy: The Office of Surface Mining Reclamation and Enforcement", 6068–177

Shreveport, La.

Census of Housing, 1980: occupancy and unit characteristics, by race, Hispanic origin, and city, SMSA rpt, 2473–1.333

Census of Population and Housing, 1980: detailed population and housing characteristics, by county, city, and census tract, SMSA rpt, 2551–2.333

see also under By City and By SMSA or MSA in the "Index by Categories"

Shrimp

see Shellfish

Shuchman, Philip

"Average Bankrupt: A Description and Analysis of 753 Personal Bankruptcy Filings in Nine States", 25528–97.1

"Personal Bankruptcy Data for Opt-Out Hearings and Other Purposes", 21528–57.1

Sibert, Anne C.

"Macroeconomic Implications of Labor Contracting with Asymmetric Information", 9366–7.104

Sickness

see Disabled and handicapped persons

see Diseases and disorders

see Hospitalization

Sider, Hal

"Changing Composition of the Military and the Effect on Labor Force Data", 6722–1.442

Sidman, Barry

"Jamaica: The Impact and Effectiveness of the PL 480 Title I Program", 9916–1.51

Siegel, Jacob S.

"Demographic and Socioeconomic Aspects of Aging in the U.S.", 2546–2.125

"International Trends and Perspectives: Aging", 2546–10.12

Siek, Robert F.

Siek, Robert F.

"New York State Police Controlled Access Highway Task Force", 7762–9.403

Sieling, Mark S.

"Staffing Patterns Prominent in Female-Male Earnings Gap", 6722–1.438

Sierra Leone

- Agricultural and food production indexes, and production of selected commodities, by world region and country, 1974-83, annual rpt, 1524–5
- Agricultural situation in sub-Saharan Africa, by country, 1982-83 and outlook for 1984, annual rpt, 1524–4.10
- Agricultural supply/demand, trade, and production, and socioeconomic data, by country, 1950s-77, 1528–179
- AID activities and funding by project and function, FY85, and developing countries summary socioeconomic data, 1970s-83, by country, annual rpt, 9914–3
- AID economic assistance to developing countries, obligations and disbursements by country, quarterly rpt, 9912–4
- *Background Notes,* summary social, political, and economic data, 1984 rpt, 7006–2.20
- Economic conditions and foreign marketing prospects in 46 Sub-Saharan countries, 1983 world region rpt, 2046–5.1
- Economic, social, and political summary data, by country, 1984, annual factbook, 244–11
- Economic trends in income, production, prices, employment, finances, and trade, 1984 annual rpt, 2046–4.36
- Exports of US, detailed Schedule B commodities by country of destination, 1983, annual rpt, 2424–9
- Exports of US, detailed Schedule E commodities by mode of transport and world area and country of destination, 1983, annual rpts, 2424–5
- Imports of US, detailed Schedule A commodities by country and world area of origin, and mode of transport, 1983, annual rpts, 2424–2
- Imports of US, detailed TSUSA commodities by country of origin, 1983, annual rpt, 2424–4
- Loans and grants for economic and military assistance from US and intl agencies, by program and country, FY46-83, annual rpt, 9914–5
- Military aid of US, arms sales, and training programs costs and budget requests by program, world region, and country, FY83-85, annual rpt, 7144–13
- Military spending, arms trade, and armed forces size, with total govt spending and population, by country, 1972-82, annual rpt, 9824–1
- *Minerals Yearbook, 1982,* Vol 3: foreign country reviews of production, trade, and policies, by commodity, annual rpt, 5604–35
- Population size and growth rates, and latest available benchmark demographic data, by country, 1950-83, biennial rpt, 2324–4
- *see also* under By Foreign Country in the "Index by Categories"

Sigmon, E. Brent

"Tests of Consistency Among Five EIA Natural Gas Data Collections", 3008–90

Silk

- *Agricultural Statistics, 1983,* annual rpt, 1004–1
- Broadwoven gray goods production, by fabric type, quarterly Current Industrial Rpt, 2506–5.11
- China economic conditions, agricultural and industrial production, trade, and domestic and foreign investment, 1980-85, 2048–106
- Exports and imports of US, by detailed agricultural commodity and country, FY83 and CY83, semiannual rpts, 1522–4
- Exports and imports of US, detailed SIC-based commodities by world area, 1983, annual rpts, 2424–6
- Exports and imports of US, totals and as percent of domestic production, by SIC 2- to 5-digit commodity, 1981, annual rpt, 2424–3
- Exports, imports, tariffs, and industry operating data for textile fiber and products, TSUSA commodity rpt series, 9885–3
- Exports of US, detailed commodities by country of destination, monthly rpt, 2422–3
- Exports of US, detailed Schedule B commodities by country of destination, 1983, annual rpt, 2424–9
- Exports of US, detailed Schedule E commodities by mode of transport and world area and country of destination, 1983, annual rpts, 2424–5
- Great Lakes trade, by SITC 3-digit commodity, port, vessel type, world area, and country, 1982, annual rpt, 7744–3
- Imports of textile manufactures other than cotton, wool, or man-made fibers, by product and country of origin, June 1984, semiannual rpt, 2046–8.5
- Imports of US, detailed Schedule A commodities by country and world area of origin, and mode of transport, 1983, annual rpts, 2424–2
- Imports of US, detailed Schedule A commodities by country, monthly rpt, 2422–2
- Imports of US, detailed TSUSA commodities by country of origin, 1983, annual rpt, 2424–4
- Manufacturing census, 1982: financial and operating data, by SIC 2- to 4-digit industry, State, SMSA, and county, preliminary census div rpt series, 2491–3
- *see also* under By Commodity in the "Index by Categories"

Silver

- Alaska minerals resources, production, claims on wildlife refuges, oil and gas leases, and exploratory wells, with maps and bibl, 1983, annual rpt, 5664–11
- Business statistics, detailed data for major industries and economic indicators, *Survey of Current Business,* monthly rpt, 2702–1.6
- County Business Patterns: establishments, employees, and payrolls, by SIC 4-digit industry and county, 1982, annual State rpt series, 2326–6
- Exports and imports of US, detailed SIC-based commodities by world area, 1983, annual rpts, 2424–6

Index by Subjects and Names

- Exports and imports of US, totals and as percent of domestic production, by SIC 2- to 5-digit commodity, 1981, annual rpt, 2424–3
- Exports of US, detailed commodities by country of destination, monthly rpt, 2422–3
- Exports of US, detailed Schedule B commodities by country of destination, 1983, annual rpt, 2424–9
- Exports of US, detailed Schedule E commodities by mode of transport and world area and country of destination, 1983, annual rpts, 2424–5
- Foreign minerals production, reserves, and industry role in domestic economy and world supply, country and world region rpt series, 5606–1
- Futures trading by commodity and exchange, and Commodity Futures Trading Commission activities, funding, and employment, FY83, annual rpt, 11924–2
- Futures trading in selected commodities, foreign currencies, and stock indexes, Chicago and other markets activity, monthly rpt, 11922–1
- Futures trading in selected commodities, foreign currencies, Treasury securities, and stock indexes, NYC, Chicago, and other markets activity, monthly rpt, 11922–5
- Futures trading in selected commodities, Treasury securities, and stock indexes, NYC market activity, monthly rpt, 11922–2
- Imports of US, detailed Schedule A commodities by country and world area of origin, and mode of transport, 1983, annual rpts, 2424–2
- Imports of US, detailed Schedule A commodities by country, monthly rpt, 2422–2
- Imports of US, detailed TSUSA commodities by country of origin, 1983, annual rpt, 2424–4
- Mineral industries census, 1982: financial and operating data, by SIC 2- to 4-digit industry, preliminary summary rpt, 2511–2.1
- Mineral industries census, 1982: financial and operating data, including materials consumed, by SIC 4-digit industry and State, preliminary rpt, 2511–1.2
- Mineral Industry Surveys, commodity review of production, trade, stocks, and consumption, monthly rpt, 5612–1.10
- *Minerals Yearbook, 1982,* Vol 1: commodity reviews of production, reserves, supply, use, and trade, annual rpt, 5604–33
- *Minerals Yearbook, 1982,* Vol 2 preprints: State reviews of production and sales by commodity, and business activity, annual rpt series, 5604–16
- *Minerals Yearbook, 1982,* Vol 2: State reviews of production, sales, and firms, by commodity, and business activity, annual rpt, 5604–34
- *Minerals Yearbook, 1982,* Vol 3: foreign country reviews of production, trade, and policies, by commodity, annual rpt, 5604–35
- *Minerals Yearbook, 1982,* Vol 3 preprints: foreign country reviews of production, trade, and policies, by commodity, annual rpt series, 5604–17

Index by Subjects and Names

Minerals Yearbook, 1983, Vol 1 preprints: commodity review of production, reserves, supply, use, and trade, annual rpt, 5604–15.59

Minerals Yearbook, 1983, Vol 3 preprints: foreign country reviews of production, trade, and policies, by commodity, annual rpt series, 5604–23

Mint Bur activities and finances, production of medals and US and foreign coins, and gold and silver stocks and transactions, by office, FY83, annual rpt, 8204–1

Occupational injuries and incidence rates at metal mines and related operations, detailed analysis, 1982, annual rpt, 6664–3

Occupational injury and illness rates, by SIC 2- to 4-digit industry, 1982, annual rpt, 6844–1

Producer prices and indexes, by stage of processing and detailed commodity, monthly rpt, 6762–6

Producer prices and indexes, by stage of processing and detailed commodity, monthly 1983, annual supplement, 6764–2

Production, prices, trade, use, employment, tariffs, and stockpiling, by mineral commodity, with foreign comparisons, 1979-83, annual rpt, 5604–18

Recovery of metal resources through leaching technologies, characteristics of methods and operations, as of 1984, 5606–6.1

Stockpiling of strategic and critical materials, Fed Govt activities and inventories by commodity, Oct 1983-Mar 1984, semiannual rpt, 9432–1

Stockpiling of strategic materials, inventories, costs, and goals, by commodity, as of June 1984, semiannual rpt, 9452–7

see also Coins and coinage

see also under By Commodity in the "Index by Categories"

Silver, Barbara J.

"1990 Objectives for the Nation for Control of Stress and Violent Behavior: Progress Report", 4102–1.437

Silver, E. G.

"Nuclear Power Plant Operating Experience, 1981", 9634–6

Silverman, Jerry M.

"AID Assistance to Local Government: Experience and Issues", 9918–11

Silvestri, George T.

"Occupational Employment Projections Through 1995", 6728–29

Simenstad, Charles A.

"Ecology of Estuarine Channels of the Pacific Northwest Coast: A Community Profile", 5506–9.12

Simi Valley, Calif.

Census of Housing, 1980: occupancy and unit characteristics, by race, Hispanic origin, and city, SMSA rpt, 2473–1.275

Census of Population and Housing, 1980: detailed population and housing characteristics, by county, city, and census tract, SMSA rpt, 2551–2.275

Wages of office and plant workers, by occupation, 1984 labor market area survey rpt, 6785–3.7

Simon, Jennifer

"Acid Rain: A Survey of Data and Current Analyses", 21368–52

Simpson, Thomas D.

"Annual Revisions to the Money Stock", 9362–1.404

"Some Implications of Financial Innovations in the U.S.", 9366–1.137

Singapore

Agricultural situation in Southeast Asia, by country and commodity, 1983 and outlook for 1984, annual rpt, 1524–4.5

Background Notes, summary social, political, and economic data, 1984 rpt, 7006–2.52

Economic indicators of 12 Pacific Basin countries or areas and US, quarterly rpt, 9393–9

Economic, social, and political summary data, by country, 1984, annual factbook, 244–11

Economic trends in income, production, prices, employment, finances, and trade, 1984 annual rpt, 2046–4.73

Exports and imports of US, by commodity and country, 1972-82, annual world region rpt, 244–13.5

Exports of US, detailed Schedule B commodities by country of destination, 1983, annual rpt, 2424–9

Exports of US, detailed Schedule E commodities by mode of transport and world area and country of destination, 1983, annual rpts, 2424–5

Foreign exchange bank and nonbank activity, and currency futures turnover in US and 3 foreign markets, Mar 1980 and Apr 1983, article, 9385–1.411

Imports of US, detailed Schedule A commodities by country and world area of origin, and mode of transport, 1983, annual rpts, 2424–2

Imports of US, detailed TSUSA commodities by country of origin, 1983, annual rpt, 2424–4

Industrial process control equipment market and trade, and user industry operations and demand, 1984 country market research rpt, 2045–6.41

Loans and grants for economic and military assistance from US and intl agencies, by program and country, FY46-83, annual rpt, 9914–5

Military aid of US, arms sales, and training programs costs and budget requests by program, world region, and country, FY83-85, annual rpt, 7144–13

Military spending, arms trade, and armed forces size, with total govt spending and population, by country, 1972-82, annual rpt, 9824–1

Minerals Yearbook, 1982, Vol 3: foreign country reviews of production, trade, and policies, by commodity, annual rpt, 5604–35

Minerals Yearbook, 1982, Vol 3 preprints: foreign country review of production, trade, and policies, by commodity, annual rpt, 5604–17.87

Population size and growth rates, and latest available benchmark demographic data, by country, 1950-83, biennial rpt, 2324–4

Ships in world merchant fleet, and tonnage, by country of registry, 1982, annual rpt, 7704–3.1

Vegetable (fresh) imports from US, 1982-84, and onion and potato imports by selected country, 1979-82, article, 1925–34.422

see also under By Foreign Country in the "Index by Categories"

Singer, Neil M.

"Modifying Military Retirement: Alternative Approaches", 26306–6.76

Singh, Hanwant B.

"Volatile Organic Chemicals in the Atmosphere: An Assessment of Available Data", 9198–109

Sioux City, Iowa

Census of Housing, 1980: occupancy and unit characteristics, by race, Hispanic origin, and city, SMSA rpt, 2473–1.334

Census of Population and Housing, 1980: detailed population and housing characteristics, by county, city, and census tract, SMSA rpt, 2551–2.334

see also under By SMSA or MSA in the "Index by Categories"

Sioux Falls, S.Dak.

Census of Population and Housing, 1980: detailed population and housing characteristics, by county, city, and census tract, SMSA rpt, 2551–2.335

see also under By SMSA or MSA in the "Index by Categories"

Sirmans, G. Stacy

"Assumable Loan Value in Creative Financing", 9412–2.404

Sirrocco, Al

"Nursing and Related Care Homes as Reported from the 1980 NMFI Survey", 4147–14.29

Sivard, Ruth L.

"World Military and Social Expenditures, 1983: An Annual Report on World Priorities", 25388–47.1

Skaperdas, Peter D.

"State and Local Governments: An Assessment of Their Financial Position and Fiscal Policies", 9385–1.401

Skelly, Carol

"Review of the Upland Cotton Acreage Base", 1561–1.403

Skin diseases

Agent Orange exposed Air Force personnel diseases and disorders, by disease type, age, and officer status, 1984 rpt, 3604–3

Deaths and death rates by detailed cause and demographic characteristics, 1979 and selected trends, US Vital Statistics annual rpt, 4144–2.1

Disability Insurance beneficiaries sociodemographic and medical characteristics, 1977-79, annual rpt, 4744–20

Hospital discharges and length of stay, by patient characteristics, facility size, procedure performed, diagnosis, and region, 1982, annual rpt, 4147–13.78

see also Allergies

see also under By Disease in the "Index by Categories"

Skinner, Robert A.

"Bargaining Co-ops Remain Stable, Strongest in West Coast States", 1122–1.403

Skog, Kenneth E.

"Residential Fuelwood Use in the U.S.: 1980-81", 1208–204

Skyjacking

Index by Subjects and Names

Skyjacking
see Air piracy

Slackman, Joel
"Options for Change in Military Medical Care", 26306–6.74

Slag
see Iron and steel industry

Sloggett, Gordon
"Energy and Irrigation", 1561–16.406

Sludge
see Sewage and wastewater treatment systems

Slum clearance
see Urban renewal

Small business

- AID activities and funding by project and function, FY85, and developing countries summary socioeconomic data, 1970s-83, by country, annual rpt, 9914–3
- Capital formation for small business, sources, needs, and tax and other investment incentives and barriers, 1983 annual conf rpt, 9734–4
- Defense Fuel Supply Center procurement, prices, stocks, and other activities, FY83, annual rpt, 3904–6
- Defense Fuel Supply Center procurement, prices, stocks, transport, and other activities and finances, FY83, annual rpt, 3904–8
- DOD awards by service branch, and Fed Govt savings from performance of commercial activities under contract over in-house, FY81-82, 108–39
- DOD contractor subcontract awards to small and disadvantaged business, by firm and service branch, quarterly listing, 3542–17
- DOD prime contract awards to small and total business, for 10 categories and R&D, monthly rpt, 3542–10
- DOD procurement, prime contract awards by category, contract and contractor type, and service branch, FY74-1st half FY84, semiannual rpt, 3542–1
- DOD procurement, prime contractors for R&D, top 500 and value of contracts, FY83, annual listing, 3544–4
- DOE procurement and assistance contracts, by State, contractor type, and top 100 instns, FY83, annual rpt, 3004–21
- DOE R&D projects and funding at natl labs, universities, and other instns, annual summary rpts, 3004–18
- Enterprise zone and urban revitalization projects of State and local govts, effect on business and employment in selected areas, various dates 1972-83, hearing, 21788–140
- Fed Govt aid to State and local govts, expenditures, and direct payments, by program, agency, and State, FY83, annual rpt, 2464–2
- Fed Govt contract award employment and receipt size standards for small business by industry, and DOD contract awards data, 1970s-83, hearings, 21728–53
- Fed Govt industrial dev funding by type, program, and agency, and State govt policies and support, selected years FY75-85, 26306–6.81
- Fed Govt paperwork requirements, small business perceived burden, and burden for 4 Fed Govt agencies, FY83, 9768–14
- Fed Govt procurement contract awards, by State, agency, procurement and contractor type, and for top 100 contractors, quarterly rpt, 102–6
- Fed Govt programs and mgmt cost control proposals, 3-year savings by function and agency, and financial and operating data, 1960s-81, 16908–1
- Finances and operations for small and minority-owned businesses, Federal contracts by agency, and worker characteristics, by industry, race, sex, and State, 1950s- 83, annual rpt, 9764–6
- Forests (natl) set-aside sales in Pacific Northwest region, quarterly rpt, 1202–3
- Income (legal) not reported on Federal income tax returns by source, and legal and illegal underground income, with bibl, 1974-81, article, 2702–1.419
- Income tax returns filed by type of filer, selected income items, summary data, quarterly rpt, 8302–2.1
- Income tax returns of corporations, detailed income and tax items by industry, 1981, annual rpt, 8304–4
- Income tax returns of elderly, by income statement and tax item and income level, 1981 with trends from 1977, article, 8302–2.412
- Income tax returns of individuals, detailed data, 1982, annual rpt, 8304–2
- Income tax returns of sole proprietorships, detailed data by industry div and selected industry group, 1981, annual rpt, 8304–7
- Loans and credit of small business, operational expectations, and NYC metro area owners economic and professional attitudes, by industry div, 1980-83 surveys, hearings, 21728–52
- Mgmt counseling of small business by university centers, costs, funding, and businesses served by industry, with detail for 2 States, 1980-83, hearing, 25728–36
- Minority business Fed Govt funding, procurement, and subsidies, and deposits in minority-owned banks, by agency, FY69-83, annual rpt, 2104–5
- NASA procurement contract awards, by type, contractor, State, and country, FY84, semiannual rpt, 9502–6
- Navy procurement, by contractor and location of work, FY83, annual rpt, 3804–13
- Securities law exemptions and small business capital formation, effect on stocks offered, issuers, and purchasers, series, 9736–2
- Small Business Admin activities, balance sheets, and loans and contracts by firm, with small business economic conditions, FY83, annual rpt, 9764–1
- *see also* Franchises
- *see also* Small Business Investment Companies

Small Business Administration

- Budget of US Appendix, detailed budgets and personnel summaries, by agency, FY85, annual rpt, 104–3
- Budget of US, appropriations, outlays, balances, and budget receipts, by govtl branch and agency, FY83, annual rpt, 8104–2
- Budget of US, CBO analysis of revenue and spending alternatives and projections of economic indicators, FY85-89, annual rpt, 26304–3.3

- Budget of US, loans and loan guarantees, and Admin proposed limits on credit assistance, by program, FY83-89, annual rpt, 26306–3.65
- Budget of US, object class analysis of obligations, by branch of Fed Govt and selected depts and agencies, FY85 estimates, annual rpt, 104–9
- Cost control proposals for Fed Govt programs and mgmt, 3-year savings by function and agency, and financial and operating data, 1960s-81, 16908–1.13
- Credit assistance costs, policies to improve measurement, with loan and loan guarantee data by program, and Federal and private credit instns operations, 1970-84, 26306–6.72
- Data collection and use, IRS and other Fed Govt admin record research methods, 1984 compilation of papers, 8308–28
- Fraud and abuse in SBA programs, audits and investigations, 1st half FY84, semiannual rpt, 9762–5
- Land privately held, acreage and owners by owner characteristics, land use, and region, and purchase and improvement funding, 1978 survey, series, 1506–5
- Mgmt counseling of small business by university centers, costs, funding, and businesses served by industry, with detail for 2 States, 1980-83, hearing, 25728–36
- Paperwork requirements of Fed Govt, small business perceived burden, and burden for 4 Fed Govt agencies, FY83, 9768–14
- Securities law exemptions and small business capital formation, effect on stocks offered, issuers, and purchasers, series, 9736–2
- Small and minority-owned businesses finances and operations, Federal contracts by agency, and worker characteristics, by industry, race, sex, and State, 1950s-83, annual rpt, 9764–6
- Small business economic conditions, and SBA activities, balance sheets, and loans and contracts by firm, FY83, annual rpt, 9764–1
- Small Business Investment Companies finances, funding, licensing, and loan activity, 2nd half FY84, semiannual rpt, 9762–3

Small Business Investment Companies

- Cost control proposals for Fed Govt programs and mgmt, 3-year savings by function and agency, and financial and operating data, 1960s-81, 16908–1.26
- Finances, firms, and SEC registrations and terminations, by type of investment firm, as of FY83, annual rpt, 9734–2.2
- Finances, funding, licensing, and loan activity of SBICs, 2nd half FY84, semiannual rpt, 9762–3
- Financing disbursements, SBA loans, and companies operating, by type of SBIC, various dates FY80-83, annual rpt, 9764–1.1
- Fraud and abuse in SBA programs, audits and investigations, 1st half FY84, semiannual rpt, 9762–5

Smallwood, David M.

- "Household Characteristics and the Demand for Vegetables and Potatoes", 1561–11.401
- "Household Characteristics, Frequency of Use, and the Demand for Dairy Products", 1561–2.404

Index by Subjects and Names

"Household Expenditures for Fruits, Vegetables, and Potatoes", 1548–236
"Scaling Household Nutrient Data", 1502–3.401

Smith, Bruce D.
"Money and Inflation in Colonial Massachusetts", 9383–6.402

Smith, Donald D.
"Animal Investigation Program for the Nevada Test Site: 1957-81", 9234–5

Smith, Hilary H.
"Farmers and Economic Shocks: Ranking Texas Agricultural Production Regions", 9379–1.406

Smith, James D.
"Measurement of Selected Income Flows in Informal Markets", 8308–27

Smith, Joyce A.
"Sewing for Profit Utilizes Home Economics Skills", 1004–16.1

Smith, Sandra R.
"Coal-Fired Capacity Additions System: Evaluation and Testing", 3166–11.1

Smith, Stanley D.
"Valuation of Creative Financing in Housing", 9412–2.403

Smith, W. Brad
"Michigan Forest Statistics, 1980", 1206–31.5
"Michigan's Predicted Timber Yields, 1981-2010", 1208–193
"Pulpwood Production in the North-Central Region, By County, 1982", 1204–19

Smithsonian Institution
Budget of US Appendix, detailed budgets and personnel summaries, by agency, FY85, annual rpt, 104–3
Budget of US, appropriations, outlays, balances, and budget receipts, by govtl branch and agency, FY83, annual rpt, 8104–2
DOD prime contract awards for R&D to educational and nonprofit instns and Federal agencies, by instn and location, FY83, annual listing, 3544–17
Finances, activities, and visitors, FY83, annual rpt, 9774–3
R&D Fed Govt funding for all performers, by field and supporting agency, selected years FY60-84, annual rpt, 9627–20
Zoological Natl Park in DC, species in collections and other activities, annual rpt, suspended, 9774–2

Smog
see Air pollution

Smoking
Air passenger and shipper complaints to CAB, by US and foreign air carrier and type of complaint, monthly rpt, 9142–20
Births by outcome, and mother's sociodemographic, life style, and maternity characteristics, 1980, article, 4102–1.418, 4102–1.420, 4102–1.422
Births of low birth weight by maternal risk including smoking, blood pressure, and blood value factors, by mothers age, race, and Hispanic origin, 1981, annual rpt, 4205–24
Blood lead levels by sociodemographic and behavioral characteristics, and potential workplace exposure, 1976-80, 4147–11.201
Cigarette sales, market shares, advertising expenditures and methods, and tar and nicotine content, by cigarette type, selected years 1963-81, annual rpt, 9404–4

Cigarette tar, nicotine, and carbon monoxide content in 207 varieties, 1982, periodic rpt, 9402–2
Cigarettes and other tobacco products per capita consumption and total expenditures, quarterly situation rpt with articles, 1561–10
Cigarettes and other tobacco products per capita consumption and total expenditures, 1978-83, annual rpt, 1319–1.4
Fed Govt plan to reduce drug abuse and trafficking, funding by agency and background data on drug use by substance, selected years FY81-85, biennial rpt, 024–1
Fire (forest) damage and causes, by State and region, 1981, annual rpt, 1204–4
Fires on Forest Service land and acres burned, by cause, forest, and State, 1983, annual rpt, 1204–6
Health condition and health care resources, use, and expenditures, 1970s-82 with trends and projections 1900-2000, annual compilation, 4144–11
Health effects of indoor air pollutants and radiation, by pollutant type, various periods 1966-83, hearings, 21708–102
Health habits associated with 10 major death causes, prevalence of 8 risk factors in selected States, 1981-83 surveys, article, 4202–7.405
Health habits of adults, including physical activity, smoking, alcohol use, hypertension, and seat belt use, by age and sex, 1982, annual rpt, 4204–1.3
Heart attack and cancer incidence and deaths in men aged 35-59, effects of lowering blood cholesterol levels, with background data on other risk factors, 1973-83, 4478–145
High school classes of 1980 and 1982: educational and sociodemographic characteristics and expectations, natl longitudinal study, series, 4826–2
High school seniors use and assessment of drugs by type, alcohol, and cigarettes, by sex and region, 1975-83 surveys, annual rpt, 4494–4
High school seniors use of drugs, alcohol, and cigarettes, 1975-82, article, 4102–1.410
Israel and France urban youths use of selected drugs, alcohol, and cigarettes, by age and sex, 1977 and 1979, article, 4102–1.430
Legislation on smoking and tobacco marketing introduced and enacted in State legislatures, by State, 1982, annual rpt, 4204–13
Lung obstructive diseases (chronic) related to smoking, by sociodemographic and smoking characteristics, literature review, 1984 annual Surgeon General rpt, 4044–6
Nurses in Connecticut, smoking habits and attitudes on quitting and setting example for others, 1981 with comparisons to nurses nationwide in 1975, article, 4102–1.403
Older persons by demographic, socioeconomic, and health characteristics, selected years 1900-81 and projected to 2050, Current Population Rpt, 2546–2.125

Pipes, lighters, and other smoking articles trade, tariffs, and industry operating data, foreign and US, 1979-83, TSUSA commodity rpt, 9885–7.54
Pregnancy health counseling effect on smoking, diet, delivery costs, and birth weight, by sociodemographic characteristics and pregnancy history, 1983 article, 4102–1.401
Research on smoking and health, article abstracts and indexes, 1983, annual rpt, 4044–8
Research publications on smoking and health, bimonthly listing, 4042–1
South Carolina manufacturing plants with selected employee health care services, by SIC 2-digit industry, 1982, article, 4102–1.408
Statistical Abstract of US, social, political, and economic data, 1950s-83 and trends, annual rpt, 2324–1.1
Use of drugs and health consequences of drug abuse, and Natl Inst on Drug Abuse and other HHS prevention activities, FY82, annual rpt, 4004–26
Vital and Health Statistics series and other NCHS publications, 1979-83, annual listing,, 4124–1
see also Tobacco industry and products

SMSA
see Metropolitan Statistical Areas
see under By SMSA or MSA in the "Index by Categories"

Smuggling
Aliens smuggled into US, and smugglers located, FY72-81, annual rpt, 6264–2
Customs Service activities, operations, and staff, FY79-83, annual rpt, 8144–1
Drug Enforcement Admin cases against major drug traffickers by case characteristics, and agents assessment of activities, in 3 cities, 1979-82, GAO rpt, 26119–57
Drug enforcement regional task force program investigation activities, funding, and personnel, with nationwide drug abuse data, 1983 annual rpt, 6004–17

Snake River
Bridges over navigable waters, with type of bridge and use, owner, dimensions, and location, 1984 regional listing, 7406–5.4
Freight (waterborne domestic and foreign) by commodity, traffic, and passengers, by port and waterway, 1982, annual rpt, 3754–3.4
Ports, port facilities by type, and inland waterways by size, by location, 1982-83, annual rpt, 7704–16
Reclamation programs of Fed Govt in western US, finances and operations by project and State, 1981-82, annual rpts, 5824–1
Water supply and quality in streams and lakes, and groundwater levels in wells, by drainage basin, 1981, annual State rpt series, 5666–16
Water supply in US and Canada, streamflow, well and reservoir levels, and dissolved solids and temperature in 6 US rivers, by station, monthly rpt, 5662–3

Sniderman, Mark S.
"Prevailing Wage Laws, the Federal Reserve, and the Service Contract Act", 9377–1.402

Snyder, Thomas D.

Snyder, Thomas D.
"Digest of Education Statistics, 1983-84", 4824–2

Soap and detergent industry
Air pollutant emission factors, by detailed source, 3rd edition, 1983-84 supplements, 9198–13
Census of Population, 1980: detailed socioeconomic and demographic characteristics, by age, sex, race, Hispanic origin, occupation, and industry, State rpt series, 2531–4
China economic conditions, agricultural and industrial production, trade, and domestic and foreign investment, 1980-85, 2048–106
County Business Patterns: establishments, employees, and payrolls, by SIC 4-digit industry and county, 1981, annual State rpt series, 2326–8
County Business Patterns: establishments, employees, and payrolls, by SIC 4-digit industry and county, 1982, annual State rpt series, 2326–6
Cuba economic conditions, agricultural and industrial production and distribution, trade, and intl economic relations, 1970-82 and trends from 1957, 248–40
Employment, earnings, and hours, by selected SIC 1- to 4-digit industry, State, and for 278 major labor areas, 1939-83, annual rpt, 6744–5
Employment, earnings, and hours, by SIC 4-digit nonfarm industry, monthly 1974-Feb 1984, annual update, 6744–4
Exports and imports of US, detailed SIC-based commodities by world area, 1983, annual rpts, 2424–6
Exports and imports of US, totals and as percent of domestic production, by SIC 2- to 5-digit commodity, 1981, annual rpt, 2424–3
Exports, imports, tariffs, and industry operating data for fatty substances, natural chemicals, and radioactive materials, foreign and US, 1979-83, TSUSA commodity rpt, 9885–4.38
Exports of US, detailed commodities by country of destination, monthly rpt, 2422–3
Exports of US, detailed Schedule B commodities by country of destination, 1983, annual rpt, 2424–9
Exports of US, detailed Schedule E commodities by mode of transport and world area and country of destination, 1983, annual rpts, 2424–5
Finances and operations, by SIC 2- to 4-digit industry, 1970s-83 and projected to 1988, annual rpt, 2014–4
Great Lakes trade, by SITC 3-digit commodity, port, vessel type, world area, and country, 1982, annual rpt, 7744–3
Imports of US, detailed Schedule A commodities by country and world area of origin, and mode of transport, 1983, annual rpts, 2424–2
Imports of US, detailed Schedule A commodities by country, monthly rpt, 2422–2
Imports of US, detailed TSUSA commodities by country of origin, 1983, annual rpt, 2424–4
Income tax returns of corporations, detailed income and tax items by industry, 1981, annual rpt, 8304–4

Injuries and deaths from use of selected consumer products and related activity, by victim age and sex, 1982, annual rpt, 9164–7
Input-output structure of US economy, detailed interindustry transactions for 537 industries, and components of final demand, 1977 benchmark data, 2708–17
Manufacturing census, 1982: financial and operating data, by SIC 2- to 4-digit industry, State, SMSA, and county, preliminary census div rpt series, 2491–3
Manufacturing census, 1982: financial and operating data, for SIC 4-digit industries by product, preliminary rpt, 2491–1.185, 2491–1.186
Minority group and women employment, by occupational group and SIC 2- to 3-digit industry, 1981, annual rpt, 9244–1.1
Occupational injury and illness rates, by SIC 2- to 4-digit industry, 1982, annual rpt, 6844–1
Oils and fats production, consumption by end use, and stocks, by type, monthly Current Industrial Rpt, 2506–4.4
Producer prices and indexes, by stage of processing and detailed commodity, monthly rpt, 6762–6
Producer prices and indexes, by stage of processing and detailed commodity, monthly 1983, annual supplement, 6764–2
Production and sales of synthetic organic chemicals by product, and listing of manufacturers, 1983, annual rpt, 9884–3
Productivity, hours, and employment indexes for selected SIC 3- and 4-digit industries, 1954-82, annual rpt, 6824–1.3
Waterborne commerce of US (domestic and foreign), freight by commodity, traffic, and passengers, by port and waterway, 1982, annual rpt, 3754–3

Soapstone
see Nonmetallic minerals and mines

Sobel, Solomon
"Role of Epidemiology in the Regulation of Oral Contraceptives", 4102–1.436

Social and Economic Statistics Administration
see Bureau of Census
see Bureau of Economic Analysis

Social and Rehabilitation Service
see Health Care Financing Administration
see Office of Human Development Services
see Office of Research, Statistics, and International Policy, SSA

Social indicators
see Quality of life
see under names of specific indicators

Social sciences
Census of Population, 1980: detailed socioeconomic and demographic characteristics, by age, sex, race, Hispanic origin, occupation, and industry, State rpt series, 2531–4
Census of Population, 1980: labor force, by sex, detailed occupation, and region, with comparison to 1970 census, supplementary rpt, 2535–1.12
Degrees conferred in higher education, by race, Hispanic origin, sex, level, and field, selected years 1949/50-1979/80, annual rpt, 4824–2.16
Educational progress, natl assessment summary data for 7 learning areas, by characteristics of participants, selected years 1971-82, annual rpt, 4824–2.6

Index by Subjects and Names

High school classes of 1980 and 1982: educational and sociodemographic characteristics and expectations, natl longitudinal study, series, 4826–2
NASA R&D funding to colleges and universities, by State, field of science, and instn, FY83, annual listing, 9504–7
NSF grant and award recipients, by State, FY83, annual listing, 9624–11
NSF research programs, activities, and funding, FY82-83, annual rpt, 9624–6
Occupational manpower needs and supply by detailed occupation, and educational and training program enrollees and grads by detailed field, 1982 and 1995, biennial rpt, 6744–3
Occupational Outlook Handbook, 1984-85 biennial rpt, 6744–1
Population and health research funded by 4 private organizations, project listing by topic, with funding data, 1981, annual rpt, 4474–16
R&D and science-related Fed Govt funding and total and federally funded expenditures of universities and colleges, by instn and field of science, FY82, 9626–2.136
R&D and science-related Fed Govt funding to higher education and nonprofit instns, by field, instn, agency, and State, FY82, annual rpt, 9627–17
R&D-employed scientists and engineers salaries by degree, type of establishment, age, experience, and field, 1984, annual rpt, 3004–1
R&D expenditures by higher education instns and federally funded centers, by field, source of funds, instn, and State, FY82, annual rpt, 9627–13
R&D expenditures by source, and scientists education and employment, detailed data by field, selected years 1953-84, annual rpt, 9624–18
R&D expenditures of higher education instns, and science and engineering employment and grad students, by field, 1972-83, biennial rpt, 9627–24
R&D Fed Govt funding, by function, agency, and program, selected years FY80-84 and proposed FY85, 26308–46
R&D Fed Govt funding for all performers, by field and supporting agency, selected years FY60-84, annual rpt, 9627–20
R&D funding by industry, program, and Federal agency, and high-technology trade performance, selected years 1960-FY84, 26306–6.77
Science and engineering doctoral degree recipients, by field, sex, race, age, citizenship, postgrad employment and study status, State, and instn, 1960-82, 9626–6.16
Science and engineering grad enrollment, fields of study, financial support, and other student and instn characteristics, 1975-82, annual survey, 9627–7
Science and engineering grad program enrollment, by field, degree level, source of financial support, race, and Hispanic origin, 1975-81, 9626–2.134
Science and engineering grad program enrollment by field, sources of financial support, and foreign students, 1975-82, 9626–2.141

Index by Subjects and Names

Science and engineering grads of 1980-81, employment and median salaries by level and field of degree, 1982, 9626–2.137

Science and engineering grads of 1980-81, employment characteristics or grad enrollment, by degree level, field, sex, and race, 1982, 9627–25

Scientists and engineers employed at universities and colleges, by field, sex, and instn, 1973-82, 9626–2.140

Scientists and engineers employed at universities and colleges, by field, sex, State, and instn, Jan 1983 and selected trends from 1967, annual survey, 9627–11

Scientists and engineers employed in energy-related fields, supply/demand and effects of R&D funding, by energy type, employer type, field, and age, 1962-91, annual rpt, 3004–19

Scientists and engineers employment by sector and activity, and share female, black, and Asian descent, by field, 1982, 9626–2.142

Scientists and engineers supply, employment, and education, by sex, race, Hispanic origin, and field, selected years 1965-83, biennial rpt, 9624–20

Scientists, engineers, and technicians employed in private industry, by occupation and industry group, 1980-81, biennial rpt, 9627–23

Scientists, engineers, and technicians needed in defense and nondefense industries, and supply/demand, by field, 1981-87, 9628–71

see also Anthropology
see also Economics
see also Geography
see also History
see also Psychology
see also Sociology

Social security

EC social security programs benefits and expenditures, and unemployment rate, and economic indicators growth, 1960-82, article, 4742–1.405

Foreign social security programs coverage, funding, eligibility, and benefits, by country, 1983, biennial rpt, 4746–4.58

Research on social security programs, series, 4746–4

Research projects of SSA, narrative summary, FY84-86, annual rpt, 4744–11

see also Aid to Families with Dependent Children

see also Health insurance

see also Health maintenance organizations

see also Income maintenance

see also Medicaid

see also Medicare

see also Old-Age, Survivors, Disability, and Health Insurance

see also Public welfare programs

see also Social security tax

see also Supplemental Security Income

see also Unemployment insurance

see also Workers compensation

Social Security Act

AFDC programs and provisions of States under Social Security Act, FY82, annual rpt, 4704–9

Unemployment insurance laws, comparisons of State provisions, as of Sept 1984, semiannual revision, 6402–2

Social Security Administration

Activities, programs, finances, and staff of SSA, FY83, annual rpt, 4704–6

ctuarial notes on social security, series, 4706–2

Actuarial studies, Medicare and OASDI future cost estimates and past experience analyses, series, 4706–1

AFDC programs and provisions of States under Social S urity Act, FY82, annual rpt, 4704–9

AFDC State admin agencies performance measures, caseloads, payments, and costs, by State, FY81, annual rpt, 4704–10

Benefits and beneficiaries with representative payees by Fed Govt cash benefit program, and OASDI and SSI fraud and misuse, various periods FY74-81, GAO rpt, 26121–85

Cost control proposals for Fed Govt programs and mgmt, 3-year savings by function and agency, and financial and operating data, 1960s-81, 16908–1.6, 16908–1.28

Data collection and use, IRS and other Fed Govt admin record research methods, 1984 annual conf papers, 8304–17

Data collection and use, IRS and other Fed Govt admin record research methods, 1984 compilation of papers, 8308–28

Data collection programs, missions, and appropriations of Fed Govt statistical agencies, and effect of budget cuts, FY80-84, GAO rpt, 26125–28

Fraud and abuse in HHS programs, audits and investigations, 2nd half FY84, semiannual rpt, 4002–6

Industry coding systems for statistical programs of 6 Federal agencies, comparability, workload, and updating cycles, 1984 rpt, 106–4.5

Medicare Hospital Insurance Trust Fund financial operations and payroll taxes, FY83 and selected years 1966-2005, annual rpt, 4704–5

Medicare Supplementary Medical Insurance Trust Fund financial operations, FY83 and selected years 1966-87, annual rpt, 4704–3

OASDI beneficiary status changes reported late and benefit overpayments, for death, marriage, and leaving school, 1981, GAO rpt, 26121–68

OASDI trust funds financial operations, FY83 and selected years 1940s-2060, annual rpt, 4704–4

Public welfare programs evaluation, and research and statistical projects and techniques, 1983 conf papers, 4704–11

Refugee and alien arrivals and resettlements in US, by State, outlying area, country of birth and citizenship, age, sex, and sponsoring agency, monthly rpt, 4702–3

Refugee resettlement program activities and funding, arrivals and population by country of origin and State, and employment and other characteristics, FY83, annual rpt, 4704–8

see also Office of Research, Statistics, and International Policy, SSA

Social security tax

Budget of US, CBO analysis of revenue and spending alternatives and projections of economic indicators, FY85-89, annual rpt, 26304–3

Social security tax

Budget of US, receipts by source and outlays by agency and program, monthly rpt, 8102–3

Budget of US, receipts by source and outlays by function, FY40-89 estimates revised for consistency with FY85 budget definitions, annual rpt, 104–12

Budget of US, receipts, outlays, and budget authority, by function and agency, FY84-89 revised estimates, midsession review of FY85 budget, annual rpt, 104–7

Cost control proposals for Fed Govt programs and mgmt, 3-year savings by function and agency, and financial and operating data, 1960s-81, 16908–1.26, 16908–1.27

EC social security programs benefits and expenditures, and unemployment rate, and economic indicators growth, 1960-82, article, 4742–1.405

Employee benefit plans effects on income and payroll tax revenue by benefit type and income, with benefits by industry, 1950-83 and projected to 1988, article, 9373–1.404

Family tax burden by income level and selected city, and tax rates by selected jurisdiction, by type of tax, 1982, 10046–8.2

Farm households social security tax liability, alternative tax rates by type of legal organization, 1955-90, article, 1702–1.408

Fed Govt civilian and military employee pay, withholdings by type, and income, and special military compensation by type and service branch, 1982-83, GAO rpt, 26123–65

Fed Govt consolidated financial statements based on business accounting methods, FY82-83, annual rpt, 8104–5

Fed Govt internal revenue, by type of tax, quarterly rpt, 8302–2.1

Fed Govt programs under Ways and Means Committee jurisdiction, program operations and financing data for assessing budgetary requirements, by State, FY70s-83, 21788–117

Fed Govt receipts by source and outlays by agency, *Treasury Bulletin,* quarterly rpt, 8002–4.1

Foreign social security programs coverage, funding, eligibility, and benefits, by country, 1983, biennial rpt, 4746–4.58

Govt taxation and revenue systems, by type of tax and system, level of govt, and State, selected years 1958-83, annual rpt, 10044–1.3

Household income and social security tax burden and effect of indexing by income level, 1982, and Fed Govt revenues by source, FY60-89, press release, 8008–109

Household income before and after taxes, by socioeconomic characteristics, type of tax paid, and region, 1981, Current Population Rpt, 2546–2.118

Household income before and after taxes, by socioeconomic characteristics, type of tax paid, and region, 1982, annual Current Population Rpt, 2546–2.122

IRS collections, by type of tax, region, and State, FY83, annual rpt, 8304–3.3

IRS collections, FY83, annual rpt, 8104–2.2

Social security tax

IRS tax collections by type of tax, procedures, and interest forgone through processing delay, for selected locations, FY81-82, GAO rpt, 26119-55

Medicare Hospital Insurance Trust Fund financial operations and payroll taxes, FY83 and selected years 1966-2005, annual rpt, 4704-5

Medicare recommendations of Advisory Council on Social Security, and trust fund and program operations, 1982 quadrennial rpt, 10178-1

Medicare trust funds financial operations and payroll taxes, annual summary of 1984 trustees rpts, 4654-8

Natl income and product, comprehensive accounts and components, *Survey of Current Business,* monthly rpt, 2702-1.21

OASDHI taxable wages, number of employers reporting, selected years 1937-82, annual rpt, 4744-3.3

OASDHI trust fund assets, total and tax income, and outlays, alternative projections to 2060, 4706-2.120

OASDI trust funds financial operations, FY83 and selected years 1940s-2060, annual rpt, 4704-4

Older persons sociodemographic characteristics, and Fed Govt program participation and funding, 1983 with trends and projections 1900-2060, annual rpt, 25144-3.1

Personal income per capita and by source, earnings by major industry group, and social insurance contributions, by region and State, 1929-82, 2708-40

Poverty-level persons and families, by income source, hours of work, earnings, taxes, and family characteristics, various periods 1959-84, 21788-131

Taxes collected and beneficiaries for social insurance programs, monthly rpt, 4742-1.1

Wage deductions for social insurance, by State, MSA, and county, 1977-82, annual regional rpts, 2704-2

see also Labor cost indexes

Social services

Budget of US, effects of Reagan Admin policy changes, by detailed program, FY85, annual rpt, 104-21

Budget of US, receipts by source and outlays by agency and program, monthly rpt, 8102-3

Census of Population, 1980: detailed socioeconomic and demographic characteristics, by age, sex, race, Hispanic origin, occupation, and industry, State rpt series, 2531-4

Census of Population, 1980: detailed socioeconomic characteristics, by county, city, and inside-outside SMSAs and central cities, State rpt series, 2531-3

Children and youth benefitting from Fed Govt public welfare programs and tax expenditures, participation and funding for 71 programs, FY81-83, 21968-30

City govt revenue sharing program allocations and use by function, and response to program cuts, by city size and region, 1982 survey, hearings, 25408-86.2

Community Dev Block Grants to small cities, State admin, project characteristics, and assessments of local officials, 1982, 5188-106

Community services block grants by type of service provider, State mgmt, and opinions of officials and groups involved, for 13 States, FY81-83, GAO rpt, 26121-84

County Business Patterns: establishments, employees, and payrolls, by SIC 4-digit industry and county, 1981, annual State rpt series, 2326-8

County Business Patterns: establishments, employees, and payrolls, by SIC 4-digit industry and county, 1982, annual State rpt series, 2326-6

DOD contract and in-house commercial activities costs and work-years, by service branch, defense agency, State, and installation, FY83, annual rpt, 3544-25

Earnings by major industry group, and personal income per capita and by source, by region and State, 1929-82, 2708-40

Employment and earnings in philanthropic organizations by organization type, and compared to other nonprofit organizations, selected years 1972-82, article, 6722-1.455

Employment by detailed occupation, for 29 SIC 2-digit nonmanufacturing industries, 1981 BLS survey, 6748-60

Employment, earnings, and hours, by selected SIC 1- to 4-digit industry, State, and for 278 major labor areas, 1939-83, annual rpt, 6744-5

Employment, earnings, and hours, by SIC 4-digit nonfarm industry, monthly 1974-Feb 1984, annual update, 6744-4

Fed Govt aid to State and local govts, expenditures, and direct payments, by program, agency, and State, FY83, annual rpt, 2464-2

Fed Govt financial and nonfinancial domestic aid, 1984 annual comprehensive catalog, 104-5

Fed Govt grants-in-aid for 13 program areas, FY82-84, annual article, 10042-1.402

Fed Govt health info offices and services of HHS and other agencies, by subject, 1984 listing, 4048-18

Fed Govt procurement contract awards, by State, agency, procurement and contractor type, and for top 100 contractors, quarterly rpt, 102-6

Fed Govt programs under Ways and Means Committee jurisdiction, program operations and financing data for assessing budgetary requirements, by State, FY70s-83, 21788-117

Govt employment and payroll, by function, level of govt, and jurisdiction, 1983, annual rpt series, 2466-1

HHS aid to each State and local govt or private instn, amount obligated, funding agency, and program, FY83, annual listing, 4004-3

Income tax returns of corporations, detailed income and tax items by industry, 1981, annual rpt, 8304-4

Input-output structure of US economy, detailed interindustry transactions for 85 industries, and components of final demand, 1977, article, 2702-1.421

Input-output structure of US economy, detailed interindustry transactions for 537 industries, and components of final demand, 1977 benchmark data, 2708-17

Index by Subjects and Names

Maternal and child health, State govt spending and admin of Fed Govt block grants, by program for 13 States, 1981-83, GAO rpt, 26121-70

Minority group and women employment, by occupational group and SIC 2- to 3-digit industry, 1981, annual rpt, 9244-1.1

NYC families caring for aged relatives, preference for social service and financial programs to provide assistance, 1980, article, 4652-1.403

Older persons Fed Govt pension and health spending, by program and as percents of budget and GNP, 1965-85 with projections to 2040, 25148-28

Older persons nutrition services program operations and assessment, and participant sociodemographic, health, and diet characteristics, 1976 and 1982, 4608-16

Older persons population characteristics, and needs and costs of social services by type, by metro-nonmetro status, 1970s-82 with trends from 1900, 21148-28

Older persons receiving selected services from family and agencies, living arrangements, and need for home mgmt help, selected years 1977-82, article, 1702-1.409

Older persons sociodemographic characteristics, and Fed Govt program participation and funding by agency, 1983 with trends and projections 1900-2080, annual rpt, 25144-3

Public opinion on taxes, tax policy, and intergovtl relations, 1972-84 surveys, annual rpt, 10044-2

Puerto Rico organizations in US and Puerto Rico, philanthropic grants received, by foundation, purpose, and recipient, 1979-81, hearings, 21788-137.1

Refugee resettlement program activities and funding, arrivals and population by country of origin and State, and employment and other characteristics, FY83, annual rpt, 4704-8

Regional councils involved in service activities, by type of service and region population size, 1982 survey, hearing, 25408-88

Research and statistical projects and techniques, and evaluation of public welfare programs, 1983 conf papers, 4704-11

Service industry census, 1982: employment, establishments, receipts, and payroll, by SIC 2- to 4-digit kind of business, SMSA, county, and city, State rpt series, 2391-1

State govt alcohol, drug abuse, and mental health treatment funding, and admin of Fed Govt block grants, for 13 States, FY80-84, GAO rpt, 26121-87

State govt public assistance expenditures, Fed Govt share, local funds, and recipient count, by program, annual rpt, discontinued, 4744-22

State govt social services spending by type and funding source, and admin of Fed Govt block grants, for 13 States, selected years FY80-84, GAO rpt, 26121-76

Youth social services of State govts, coordinating agencies activities, admin, membership, and funding sources, survey, 1984 rpt, 6068-182

see also Adult day care

Index by Subjects and Names

Soil Conservation Service

see also Child day care
see also Child welfare
see also Community health services
see also Disaster relief
see also Foster home care
see also Homemaker services
see also Legal aid
see also School lunch and breakfast programs
see also Social work
see also Vocational rehabilitation
see also Work Incentive Program

Social work

- Census of Population, 1980: detailed socioeconomic and demographic characteristics, by age, sex, race, Hispanic origin, occupation, and industry, State rpt series, 2531–4
- Census of Population, 1980: labor force, by sex, detailed occupation, and region, with comparison to 1970 census, supplementary rpt, 2535–1.12
- DOD medical personnel, trainees, and accessions by source, by occupation, specialty, and service branch, FY83, annual rpt, 3544–24
- Fed Govt aid to State and local govts, expenditures, and direct payments, by program, agency, and State, FY83, annual rpt, 2464–2
- Handicapped children public education program enrollment, staff, and funding, by handicap, age, and State, 1981/82-1982/83, annual rpt, 4944–4
- Health care services of selected medical practitioners, use by patient characteristics, 1980 survey with trends from 1963, 4146–12.4
- HHS aid to each State and local govt or private instn, amount obligated, funding agency, and program, FY83, annual listing, 4004–3
- Hospital employment, vacancies, and vacancy rates, by occupation and by hospital specialty, region, census div, and State, 1980, annual rpt, 4114–12
- Hospital worker wages by sex and occupation, and benefits, for 22 MSAs, Oct 1981 survey, 6787–6.201
- Mental health clinical training funding by NIMH, by program and field, FY80-83, GAO rpt, 26121–86
- Mental health facilities, services, staff, and patient characteristics, *Statistical Notes* series, 4506–3
- Mental health facilities staffing, by discipline and selected characteristics of health services personnel, selected years 1954-81, annual rpt, 4504–9.4
- Occupational manpower needs and supply by detailed occupation, and educational and training program enrollees and grads by detailed field, 1982 and 1995, biennial rpt, 6744–3
- *Occupational Outlook Handbook,* 1984-85 biennial rpt, 6744–1
- VA Medicine and Surgery Dept trainees, by detailed program and city, FY83, annual rpt, 9924–21
- *see also* Homemaker services
- *see also* Social services

Socialism

Cuba economic conditions, agricultural and industrial production and distribution, trade, and intl economic relations, 1970-82 and trends from 1957, 248–40

see also Government ownership

Sociology

- Occupational manpower needs and supply by detailed occupation, and educational and training program enrollees and grads by detailed field, 1982 and 1995, biennial rpt, 6744–3
- *Occupational Outlook Handbook,* 1984-85 biennial rpt, 6744–1
- R&D expenditures by higher education instns and federally funded centers, by field, source of funds, instn, and State, FY82, annual rpt, 9627–13
- R&D expenditures by source, and scientists education and employment, detailed data by field, selected years 1953-84, annual rpt, 9624–18
- R&D expenditures of higher education instns, and science and engineering employment and grad students, by field, 1972-83, biennial rpt, 9627–24
- R&D Fed Govt funding for all performers, by field and supporting agency, selected years FY60-84, annual rpt, 9627–20
- Science and engineering doctoral degree recipients, by field, sex, race, age, citizenship, postgrad employment and study status, State, and instn, 1960-82, 9626–6.16
- Science and engineering grad enrollment, fields of study, financial support, and other student and instn characteristics, 1975-82, annual survey, 9627–7
- Science and engineering grads of 1980-81, employment characteristics or grad enrollment, by degree level, field, sex, and race, 1982, 9627–25
- Scientists and engineers employed at universities and colleges, by field, sex, State, and instn, Jan 1983 and selected trends from 1967, annual survey, 9627–11
- Scientists, engineers, and technicians needed in defense and nondefense industries, and supply/demand, by field, 1981-87, 9628–71

Sodium

see Metals and metal industries

Soft drink industry

- Consumption of food and nutrient intake by individuals, by food group, source, and socioeconomic characteristics, 1977-78 natl survey, final rpt series, 1356–4
- Consumption, supply, trade, prices, expenditures, and indexes, by food commodity, 1963-83, annual rpt, 1544–4
- County Business Patterns: establishments, employees, and payrolls, by SIC 4-digit industry and county, 1981, annual State rpt series, 2326–8
- County Business Patterns: establishments, employees, and payrolls, by SIC 4-digit industry and county, 1982, annual State rpt series, 2326–6
- CPI by detailed component, for US city average, 28 SMSAs, and 4 regions by population size, monthly rpt, 6762–2
- Employment, earnings, and hours, by SIC 4-digit nonfarm industry, monthly 1974-Feb 1984, annual update, 6744–4
- Exports and imports of US, detailed SIC-based commodities by world area, 1983, annual rpts, 2424–6
- Exports and imports of US, totals and as percent of domestic production, by SIC 2- to 5-digit commodity, 1981, annual rpt, 2424–3

Exports of US, detailed commodities by country of destination, monthly rpt, 2422–3

- Exports of US, detailed Schedule B commodities by country of destination, 1983, annual rpt, 2424–9
- Exports of US, detailed Schedule E commodities by mode of transport and world area and country of destination, 1983, annual rpts, 2424–5
- Finances and operations, by SIC 2- to 4-digit industry, 1970s-83 and projected to 1988, annual rpt, 2014–4
- Franchises of soft drink bottling firms, establishments by State, and sales, 1982-84, annual rpt, 2014–5
- Imports of products containing sugar, injury to price-supported US sugar industries, investigation with background financial and operating data, 1983 rpt, 9886–10.7
- Imports of US, detailed Schedule A commodities by country and world area of origin, and mode of transport, 1983, annual rpts, 2424–2
- Imports of US, detailed TSUSA commodities by country of origin, 1983, annual rpt, 2424–4
- Income tax returns of corporations, detailed income and tax items by industry, 1981, annual rpt, 8304–4
- Input-output structure of US economy, detailed interindustry transactions for 537 industries, and components of final demand, 1977 benchmark data, 2708–17
- Manufacturing census, 1982: financial and operating data, by SIC 2- to 4-digit industry, State, SMSA, and county, preliminary census div rpt series, 2491–3
- Manufacturing census, 1982: financial and operating data, for SIC 4-digit industries by product, preliminary rpt, 2491–1.36
- Occupational injury and illness rates, by SIC 2- to 4-digit industry, 1982, annual rpt, 6844–1
- Producer prices and indexes, by stage of processing and detailed commodity, monthly rpt, 6762–6
- Producer prices and indexes, by stage of processing and detailed commodity, monthly 1983, annual supplement, 6764–2
- Productivity, hours, and employment indexes for selected SIC 3- and 4-digit industries, 1954-82, annual rpt, 6824–1.3
- *see also* under By Commodity in the "Index by Categories"

Software

see Computers

Soil Conservation Service

- Activities and programs of USDA, by subagency, FY83, annual rpt, 1004–3
- Activities, services, and acreage covered under programs of Service, by program, FY83, annual rpt, 1264–2
- Cost control proposals for Fed Govt programs and mgmt, 3-year savings by function and agency, and financial and operating data, 1960s-81, 16908–1.2, 16908–1.31
- Fraud and abuse in USDA programs, audits and investigations, 2nd half FY84, semiannual rpt, 1002–4
- Montana water supply, snow water accumulations and reservoir storage, annual rpt, suspended, 1264–7

Soil Conservation Service

Nevada water supply, streamflow, reservoir storage, and precipitation, 1984 water year, annual rpt, 1264–8

Oregon water supply, streamflow by station and reservoir storage, 1984 water year, annual rpt, 1264–9

Publications of USDA, soil survey county descriptions and maps, 1899-1983, annual listing, 1264–11

Sedimentation control, surveillance, and research activity of Fed Govt, by project, agency, region, and State, 1982, annual rpt, 5664–9

Soil and water conservation districts, farms, and area covered, by State, annual rpt, suspended, 1264–1

Utah water supply, streamflow, reservoir storage, and precipitation, 1984 water year, annual rpt, 1264–6

Western US water supply, and snow survey results, monthly State rpt series, 1266–2

Western US water supply, reservoir storage by large reservoir and State, and streamflow conditions, as of Oct 1984, annual rpt, 1264–4

Western US water supply, snow depth measurements by station, State rpt series, 1266–3

Western US water supply, streamflow and reservoir storage forecasts by stream and station, Jan-May monthly rpt, 1262–1

Soil pollution

- Acid Precipitation Natl Assessment Program activities, and funding by Federal agency, 1983, annual rpt, 14354–1
- Acid rain and air pollution environmental effects, and methods for neutralizing acidified water bodies, summary research rpt series, 5506–5
- Acid rain causes and effects, air pollutant emissions by source, and control costs, by region and State, selected years 1977-83 and projected to 2000, 26358–104
- Acid rain causes and effects, air pollutant emissions by source in US and selected countries, and control costs, 1970s-83 and projected to 2000, 21368–52
- Acid rain causes and effects, air pollutant emissions by source in US and selected countries, control costs, and Fed Govt research funding, 1960s-82, 3408–27
- Clinch River Breeder Reactor proposed site and nearby area, radiation levels in river water and sediment and ground water, 1983, annual rpt, 9804–24
- Coal dev plans on Fed Govt lease lands in 12 regions under Fed Coal Mgmt Program, environmental and socioeconomic impacts to 2000, final statement series, 5726–4
- Coastal environmental and wildlife characteristics, use, and mgmt, for individual ecosystems, series, 5506–9
- Environmental quality and protection programs, costs, and Fed Govt enforcement, 1983, detailed annual rpt, 484–1
- Environmental quality, pollutant discharge by type, and EPA protection activities, 1970s-83, biennial summary rpt, 9184–16
- Environmental quality, pollutant discharge by type and source, and EPA protection activities and funding, 1970s-83, biennial regional rpt series, 9184–15

Great Lakes radioactivity discharges by source, and concentrations in environment, various periods 1963-82, annual rpt, 14644–1.2

Idaho Natl Engineering Lab radiation monitoring results, for 4 onsite facilities and nearby areas, 1983, annual rpt, 3354–10

Radioactive waste and spent fuel generation, inventory, disposal by site, reprocessing, and characteristics, by source, as of 1983 and projected to 2020, annual rpt, 3364–2

Uranium ore tailings at active mills, EPA radon and radionuclide emmission standards and US and foreign exposure and health effects, various periods 1957-83, hearings, 21208–17

Soils and soil conservation

- Agricultural Conservation Program participation and payments, by State, FY83, annual rpt, 1804–7
- Agricultural Stabilization and Conservation Service producer payments under 26 programs, monthly rpt, 1802–10
- *Agricultural Statistics, 1983,* annual rpt, 1004–1.2
- Alaska Arctic Natl Wildlife Refuge resources, resident and visitor activities, and environmental impacts of energy exploration, 1983, annual update rpt, 5504–26
- Army Corps of Engineers activities and projects, FY83 and trends from 1800s, annual rpt, 3754–1
- Budget of US, effects of Reagan Admin policy changes, by detailed program, FY85, annual rpt, 104–21
- Carbon dioxide atmospheric levels, climatic effects and impacts of fossil and synthetic fuels use, deforestation, and land use patterns, research rpt series, 3406–3
- Coastal environmental and wildlife characteristics, use, and mgmt, for individual ecosystems, series, 5506–9
- Coastal environmental characteristics, fish, wildlife, and use, and population socioeconomic data, for individual areas, series, 5506–4
- Corn and soybean yields, itemized production costs, and input use, effects of alternative tillage systems, by region and for 10 States, 1980, 1588–80
- County Business Patterns: establishments, employees, and payrolls, by SIC 4-digit industry and county, 1981, annual State rpt series, 2326–8
- County Business Patterns: establishments, employees, and payrolls, by SIC 4-digit industry and county, 1982, annual State rpt series, 2326–6
- Developing countries disaster preparedness and summary sociodemographic, political, and economic data, country rpt series, 9916–2
- Emergency Conservation Program participation and payments for farmland restoration from natural disaster, by practice and State, FY83, annual rpt, 1804–22
- Environmental quality and protection programs, costs, and Fed Govt enforcement, 1983, detailed annual rpt, 484–1

Index by Subjects and Names

Erosion rates for cropland and construction sites, with water quality effects, 1984 rpt, 9208–123

Farm improvement, acreage and owners by improvement type, funding source, land use, and region, 1978 survey, 1506–5.20

Farm production inputs, land mgmt, and environmental effects, for 4 crops, 1940s-80 and projected to 2010, 9188–94

Farmland eroded by rainfall, acreage by crop, and farm operators by selected characteristics, by soil erosion class, 1977-78, 1588–83

Fed Govt programs and mgmt cost control proposals, 3-year savings by function and agency, and financial and operating data, 1960s-81, 16908–1.2, 16908–1.31

Fed Govt soil conservation program policies, attitudes of farmers and ranchers in 6 central US counties, 1982/82 survey, hearing, 25168–61

FmHA loans and grants by program and State, and summary of services, FY83 with trends from FY63, annual rpt, 1184–17

FmHA soil and water loans, by race, Hispanic origin, and State, quarterly rpt, 1182–5

Foreign and US tropical forests status by country and world region, conservation methods, and mgmt role of US, foreign, and intl groups, 1977-81 and projected to 2000, 26358–101

Forest, range, and associated waters use and mgmt assessment, and environmental impacts of Forest Service program options, 1977-2030 and trends from 1920, 1208–24

Govt census, 1982: State govt payments to local govts, by program, source of funds, level of govt, and State, with trends from 1902, 2460–3

Natl Forest System wildlife habitat and fishery improvements, use, and game population and harvest by species and forest, by region, FY83, annual rpt, 1204–31

Public lands programs of Land Mgmt Bur, FY83, annual rpt, 5724–1.2

Research (agricultural) expenditures and scientist years, by topic, commodity, and performing organization, FY82, annual rpt, 1744–2

Science and engineering doctoral degree recipients, by field, sex, race, age, citizenship, postgrad employment and study status, State, and instn, 1960-82, 9626–6.16

Sedimentation control, surveillance, and research activity of Fed Govt, by project, agency, region, and State, 1982, annual rpt, 5664–9

Soil and water conservation districts, farms, and area covered, by State, annual rpt, suspended, 1264–1

Soil Conservation Service activities, services, and acreage covered, by program, FY83, annual rpt, 1264–2

Southeastern States soil conservation and water pollution reduction participants, costs, and acreage, by conservation method and State, selected years 1973-82, 1588–84

Tennessee Valley ethanol production, feedstocks, facilities, tax incentives, and related farming data, by State, 1970s-83 and projected to 1992, 9808–69

Index by Subjects and Names

Sorensen, James E.

USDA soil survey county descriptions and map publications, 1899-1983, annual listing, 1264–11

Water supply and quality, and effect of coal mining operations, for selected river basins in Eastern and Interior coal provinces, series, 5666–15

Water supply and quality, and effect of coal mining operations, for selected river basins in Western coal provinces, series, 5666–19

Water supply and quality, floods, drought, mudslides, and other hydrologic events, by State, 1983, annual rpt, 5664–12

Windbarrier planting, by State, FY83, annual rpt, 1204–7

see also Flood control

see also Irrigation

see also Reclamation of land

see also Soil pollution

Solar energy

Air pollutant emission effects of solar and biomass energy use, by region, and projected to 2000, 3408–30

Budget of US, effects of Reagan Admin policy changes, by detailed program, FY85, annual rpt, 104–21

Consumption by fuel type, and estimated supply from renewable resources, 1977 and projected 2000, hearing, 21448–30

Consumption, by fuel type, economic sector, and end use, 1983 and 2000, 2006–2.5

Electric power plants, by capacity, fuel used, unit type, region, State, and county, for plants added and retired, 1983 and planned through 1993, annual rpt, 3164–36

Energy R&D and technology publications, quarterly listing, 9502–4

Environmental quality and protection programs, costs, and Fed Govt enforcement, 1983, detailed annual rpt, 484–1

Exports of US, detailed commodities by country of destination, monthly rpt, 2422–3

Exports of US, detailed Schedule B commodities by country of destination, 1983, annual rpt, 2424–9

Fed Govt energy programs proposed budget appropriations, by office or dept and function, FY84-85, annual rpt, 3004–14

Housing census, 1980: inventory, occupancy, and unit characteristics, changes from 1973 by region and inside-outside SMSAs and central cities, series, 2473–3

Housing energy use, costs, expenditures, and conservation, and household and housing characteristics, survey series, 3166–7

Housing solar energy and energy conservation projects, HUD grants by State and outlying area, 1984 press release, 5006–3.36

Natl Energy Policy Plan, energy supply, demand, and prices, by fuel and consuming sector, projected 1985-2010, biennial rpt, 3004–13

Photovoltaic system R&D sponsored by DOE, project descriptions and publications, FY83, annual listing, 3304–20

Production, sales, and use of solar collectors and photovoltaic modules, with listing of manufacturers, 1983, annual rpt, 3164–62

Production, trade, supply, use, conservation, and DOE activities, by energy type, FY83, annual rpt, 3024–2

R&D industry funding and employment of scientists and engineers, by industry group, firm size, and funding source, 1956-82, annual rpt, 9627–21

Radiation (solar) mean daily levels and related data for solar heating and cooling system design, for 306 cities, fall 1982, 3308–67

Research publications on energy of DOE and other sources, monthly listing, 3002–2

Scientists and engineers employed in energy-related fields, supply/demand and effects of R&D funding, by energy type, employer type, field, and age, 1962-91, annual rpt, 3004–19

Supply/demand and prices, by energy source and end-use sector and for 7 electric utilities, 1981-2000 with trends from 1960s, 3008–93

Supply/demand and prices, by fuel type and consuming sector with foreign comparisons, 1949-83, annual rpt, 3164–74

Supply/demand and prices, by fuel type, sector, and end use, with foreign comparisons, 1960-83 and projected to 1995, annual summary rpt, 3164–76

see also Biomass energy

see also Wind energy

Solar Energy Research Laboratory

"Photovoltaic Energy Systems: Program Summary, FY83", 3304–20

see also Department of Energy National Laboratories

Soldiers

see Military personnel

Soldiers pay and allowances

see Military pay

Solid waste

see Recycling of waste materials

see Refuse and refuse disposal

see Sewage and wastewater treatment systems

Solomon Islands

Economic, social, and political summary data, by country, 1984, annual factbook, 244–11

Military aid of US, arms sales, and training programs costs and budget requests by program, world region, and country, FY83-85, annual rpt, 7144–13

Minerals Yearbook, 1982, Vol 3: foreign country reviews of production, trade, and policies, by commodity, annual rpt, 5604–35

Minerals Yearbook, 1982, Vol 3 preprints: foreign country review of production, trade, and policies, by commodity, annual rpt, 5604–17.90

Minerals Yearbook, 1983, Vol 3 preprints: foreign country review of production, trade, and policies, by commodity, annual rpt, 5604–23.90

Population size and growth rates, and latest available benchmark demographic data, by country, 1950-83, biennial rpt, 2324–4

Somalia

Agricultural situation in sub-Saharan Africa, by country, 1982-83 and outlook for 1984, annual rpt, 1524–4.10

AID activities and funding by project and function, FY85, and developing countries summary socioeconomic data, 1970s-83, by country, annual rpt, 9914–3

AID economic assistance to developing countries, obligations and disbursements by country, quarterly rpt, 9912–4

AID loan repayment status and terms by program and country, and status of predecessor agency loans, quarterly rpt, 9912–3

Background Notes, summary social, political, and economic data, 1984 rpt, 7006–2.27

Economic conditions and foreign marketing prospects in 46 Sub-Saharan countries, 1983 world region rpt, 2046–5.1

Economic, social, and political summary data, by country, 1984, annual factbook, 244–11

Economic trends in income, production, prices, employment, finances, and trade, 1983 annual rpt, 2046–4.8

Exports of US, detailed Schedule B commodities by country of destination, 1983, annual rpt, 2424–9

Exports of US, detailed Schedule E commodities by mode of transport and world area and country of destination, 1983, annual rpts, 2424–5

Imports of US, detailed Schedule A commodities by country and world area of origin, and mode of transport, 1983, annual rpts, 2424–2

Imports of US, detailed TSUSA commodities by country of origin, 1983, annual rpt, 2424–4

Loans and grants for economic and military assistance from US and intl agencies, by program and country, FY46-83, annual rpt, 9914–5

Military aid of US, arms sales, and training programs costs and budget requests by program, world region, and country, FY83-85, annual rpt, 7144–13

Military spending, arms trade, and armed forces size, with total govt spending and population, by country, 1972-82, annual rpt, 9824–1

Minerals Yearbook, 1982, Vol 3: foreign country reviews of production, trade, and policies, by commodity, annual rpt, 5604–35

Minerals Yearbook, 1982, Vol 3 preprints: foreign country review of production, trade, and policies, by commodity, annual rpt, 5604–17.83

Oil and gas undiscovered recoverable resources, cumulative production, and identified reserves, as of 1982, preliminary oil basin rpt, 5666–17.13

Population size and growth rates, and latest available benchmark demographic data, by country, 1950-83, biennial rpt, 2324–4

see also under By Foreign Country in the "Index by Categories"

Somerset County, N.J.

see also under By SMSA or MSA in the "Index by Categories"

Sorensen, James E.

"Accounting and Budgeting Systems for Mental Health Organizations", 4506–2.6

Sorghum

Sorghum
see Grains and grain products

Sorrentino, Constance
"Japan's Low Unemployment: An In-Depth Analysis", 6722–1.418

Sosslau, Arthur B.
"Transportation Planners' Guide to Using the 1980 Census", 7558–101

Souris-Red-Rainy Rivers
Water supply and quality in streams and lakes, and groundwater levels in wells, by drainage basin, 1981, annual State rpt series, 5666–16

Water supply and quality in streams and lakes, and groundwater levels in wells, by drainage basin, 1982, annual State rpt series, 5666–20

Water supply in US and Canada, streamflow, well and reservoir levels, and dissolved solids and temperature in 6 US rivers, by station, monthly rpt, 5662–3

South Africa
Agricultural and food production indexes, and production of selected commodities, by world region and country, 1974-83, annual rpt, 1524–5

Agricultural exports of US to South Africa, Nigeria, and total sub-Saharan Africa, 1981-83, and forecast 1984, article, 1522–1.401

Agricultural situation in sub-Saharan Africa, by country, 1982-83 and outlook for 1984, annual rpt, 1524–4.10

Agricultural supply/demand, trade, and production, and socioeconomic data, by country, 1950s-77, 1528–179

AID economic assistance to developing countries, obligations and disbursements by country, quarterly rpt, 9912–4

Economic conditions and foreign marketing prospects in 46 Sub-Saharan countries, 1983 world region rpt, 2046–5.1

Economic conditions, income, production, prices, employment, and trade, 1984 semiannual country rpt, 2046–4.117

Economic conditions, investment and export opportunities, and trade practices, 1984 country market research rpt, 2046–6.10

Economic, social, and political summary data, by country, 1984, annual factbook, 244–11

Economic trends in income, production, prices, employment, finances, and trade, 1984 semiannual rpt, 2046–4.37

Exports of US, detailed Schedule B commodities by country of destination, 1983, annual rpt, 2424–9

Exports of US, detailed Schedule E commodities by mode of transport and world area and country of destination, 1983, annual rpts, 2424–5

Fruit (deciduous) grower prices and processor net cost and subsidies in 4 countries and EC, 1982/83-1983/84, article, 1925–34.414

Graphic industries equipment market and trade, and user industry operations and demand, 1984 country market research rpt, 2045–3.32

Imports of US, detailed Schedule A commodities by country and world area of origin, and mode of transport, 1983, annual rpts, 2424–2

Imports of US, detailed TSUSA commodities by country of origin, 1983, annual rpt, 2424–4

Intl transactions of US with 10 countries, 1981-83, *Survey of Current Business,* monthly rpt, annual table, 2702–1.31

Loans and grants for economic and military assistance from US and intl agencies, by program and country, FY46-83, annual rpt, 9914–5

Military spending, arms trade, and armed forces size, with total govt spending and population, by country, 1972-82, annual rpt, 9824–1

Minerals Yearbook, 1982, Vol 3: foreign country reviews of production, trade, and policies, by commodity, annual rpt, 5604–35

Minerals Yearbook, 1982, Vol 3 preprints: foreign country review of production, trade, and policies, by commodity, annual rpt, 5604–17.64

Nuclear power generation in US and 18 non-Communist countries, monthly rpt, 3162–24.10

Nuclear power plant construction and operation status, and capacity, by plant, region, State, and selected country, 1983 and projected to 2020, annual rpt, 3164–57

Population size and growth rates, and latest available benchmark demographic data, by country, 1950-83, biennial rpt, 2324–4

Raisin and dried prune stocks, production, and exports for 4 countries, 1982-83 and forecast 1984, article, 1925–34.416

Steel from 5 countries, injury to US industry from foreign subsidized products and sales at less than fair value, investigation with background financial and operating data, 1984 rpt, 9886–19.8

see also Namibia

see also under By Foreign Country in the "Index by Categories"

South America
Agricultural and food production indexes, and production of selected commodities, by world region and country, 1974-83, annual rpt, 1524–5

Agricultural exports and imports of US, by detailed commodity and country, FY83 and CY83, semiannual rpts, 1522–4

Agricultural exports of Argentina and total South America, and coffee exports of Colombia and Brazil to US and world, market share analysis, 1960-79, 1528–169

Agricultural situation in Latin America, by country, 1981-83 and outlook for 1984, annual rpt, 1524–4.9

Agricultural supply/demand, trade, and production, and socioeconomic data, by country, 1950s-77, 1528–179

Agricultural trade of US, by commodity and country, bimonthly rpt with articles, 1522–1

AID activities and funding by project and function, FY85, and developing countries summary socioeconomic data, 1970s-83, by country, annual rpt, 9914–3

AID community dev assistance to local govts in developing countries, program activities and funding, 1960s-80s, 9918–11

AID contracts and grants for technical and support services, by instn, country, and State, FY83, annual listing, 9914–7

Index by Subjects and Names

AID economic assistance to developing countries, obligations and disbursements by country, quarterly rpt, 9912–4

AID Housing Guaranty Program financial statements, and projects by country, FY83, annual rpt, 9914–4

AID loan repayment status and terms by program and country, and status of predecessor agency loans, quarterly rpt, 9912–3

AID loans authorized, signed, and canceled, by country and world area, monthly rpt, 9912–2

Carbon dioxide emissions from fossil fuel combustion, and growth rates, by country and country group, 1950-80, 3006–7.6

China economic conditions, agricultural and industrial production, trade, and domestic and foreign investment, 1980-85, 2048–106

Cocaine use, user characteristics, medical and botanical research, and South American production and legal policy and enforcement, 1979 intl conf papers, 7008–40

Defense and total govt expenditures, military imports, GNP, and intl reserves of countries receiving US economic aid, by country, 1976-81, annual rpt, 9914–1

Elections in Latin America, votes and share of population voting by country and election type, selected years 1962-83, 7008–42

Energy production by type, and oil prices, trade, and consumption, by country group and selected country, monthly rpt, 242–5

Eurocurrency syndicated loans, loan fees, and interest rate spread, by country group and selected country, 1981-83, technical paper, 9366–7.105

Export sales and shipments of US grains, oilseed products, hides, skins, and cotton, by country, weekly rpt, 1922–3

Exports and imports of OECD, total and for 4 major countries, and US trade by country, by commodity, 1972-82, annual world region rpt, 244–13.2

Exports and imports of US (airborne), by world area and US customs district and city, monthly rpt, 2422–8

Exports and imports of US (waterborne), by type of service, commodity, country, route, and US port, 1982, annual rpt, 7704–2

Exports and imports of US (waterborne), by type of service, customs district, port, and world area, monthly rpt, 2422–7

Exports and imports of US, by commodity group, world area, selected country, US coastal area and port, and mode of transport, with seasonal adjustments, monthly rpt, 2422–9

Exports and imports of US, detailed SIC-based commodities by world area, 1983, annual rpts, 2424–6

Exports of US, detailed Schedule E commodities by mode of transport and world area and country of destination, 1983, annual rpts, 2424–5

Food production and needs, and related economic trends and outlook, for 67 developing countries, 1980-86, annual rpt, 1524–6

Great Lakes trade, by SITC 3-digit commodity, port, vessel type, world area, and country, 1982, annual rpt, 7744–3

Index by Subjects and Names

South Carolina

Immigrant and nonimmigrant visas of US issued and refused, and status adjustments, by class and nationality, FY77, annual rpt, 7184–1

Immigration, and alien residents, workers, visitors, deportations, and naturalizations, by country of birth, FY81, annual rpt, 6264–2

Imports of US, detailed Schedule A commodities by country and world area of origin, and mode of transport, 1983, annual rpts, 2424–2

Inter-American Foundation activities, grants, and fellowships, by country, FY83, annual rpt, 14424–1

Inter-American Foundation activities, 1984 narrative semiannual rpt, 14422–2

Investment (foreign direct) in US, by major industry group, world area, and selected country, 1980-83, annual article, 2702–1.439

Investment (foreign direct) of US, by selected major industry group and world area, 1982-83, annual article, 2702–1.430

Investment (foreign direct) of US, by world area and country, 1977-83, article, 2702–1.442

Investment (intl direct) worldwide, and US investment flows by major industry, by world region and country, 1982 and trends from 1950, annual rpt, 2044–25

Loans and grants for economic and military assistance from US and intl agencies, by program and country, FY46-83, annual rpt, 9914–5

Loans, debts, exchange rates, and intl reserves, for US and selected countries, various periods 1949-84, conf papers, 9373–3.28

Loans of large US banks to foreigners at all US and foreign offices, by country group and country, quarterly rpt, 13002–1

Military aid of US, arms sales, and training programs costs and budget requests by program, world region, and country, FY83-85, annual rpt, 7144–13

Military, social, and economic summary data, by world area and country, 1960s-80s, hearing, 25388–47.1

Military spending, arms trade, and armed forces size, with total govt spending and population, by country, 1972-82, annual rpt, 9824–1

Minerals Yearbook, 1982, Vol 3: foreign country reviews of production, trade, and policies, by commodity, annual rpt, 5604–35

Money orders of USPS sent to Latin America, volume and amount by area, 1983 hearings, 21628–55

Multilateral dev banks economic dev projects, environmental and cultural impacts in developing countries, 1970s-83, hearings, 21248–80

Population size and growth rates, and latest available benchmark demographic data, by country, 1950-83, biennial rpt, 2324–4

R&D Fed Govt funding for foreign performers, by world region and country, FY82-84, annual rpt, 9627–20.2

Refugee arrivals in US, by world area of origin and processing and nationality, monthly rpt, 7002–4, 7002–5

Refugee arrivals in US by world area of origin and State of settlement, and Fed Govt intl and domestic assistance costs, FY85, annual rpt, 7004–16

Refugee migration, settlement status, and assistance, by world area and country of origin and asylum, as of May 1984, annual rpt, 7004–15

Students in US and Soviet bloc training programs, by program type and Latin American country or world region of student origin, selected years 1972-82, GAO rpt, 26123–77

Terrorist (intl) incidents, casualties, and attacks on US targets, by attack type and world area, with chronology of events, 1983, annual rpt, 7004–13

Tide height and time daily at worldwide coastal points, 1985 predictions, annual rpt, 2174–2.1, 2174–2.2

Travel to and from US and travel receipts and payments by world area, and travel to US by country, 1977-83, annual rpt, 2904–10

Travel to and from US, by world area and selected country, projected 1984-85, annual rpt, 2904–9

Travel to and from US on US and foreign flag air carriers, by country, world area, and US port, monthly rpt, 7302–2

Travel to US and receipts by world area and selected country, 1960-83, and US Travel and Tourism Admin activities, 1983, annual rpt, 2904–6

USIA info center and reading room operations, by world region, country, and city, FY83, annual rpt, 9854–4

Weather conditions and effect on agriculture, by US region, State, and city, and world area, weekly rpt, 2152–2

Weather conditions and impact assessment, by world area and country, monthly rpt, 2152–9

Weather stations of Natl Weather Service, locations and regular observations made, 1984 annual listing, 2184–5

Weather stations of Upper Air Observational Network, by US and foreign location, 1984 annual listing, 2184–6

Women sociodemographic, economic, and fertility characteristics, with comparisons to men, by country, 1960s-85, world region rpt, 2326–15.1

see also Argentina
see also Bolivia
see also Brazil
see also Caribbean area
see also Central America
see also Chile
see also Colombia
see also Ecuador
see also French Guiana
see also Guyana
see also Inter-American Development Bank
see also Latin American Free Trade Association
see also Paraguay
see also Peru
see also Suriname
see also Uruguay
see also Venezuela
see also under By Foreign Country in the "Index by Categories"

South Bend, Ind.

Census of Housing, 1980: occupancy and unit characteristics, by race, Hispanic origin, and city, SMSA rpt, 2473–1.336

Census of Population and Housing, 1980: detailed population and housing characteristics, by county, city, and census tract, SMSA rpt, 2551–2.336

Wages of office and plant workers, by occupation, 1984 SMSA survey rpt, 6785–11.8

see also under By City and By SMSA or MSA in the "Index by Categories"

South Carolina

Agriculture census, 1982: farms, farmland, production and costs, and operator characteristics, preliminary State summary and county rpts, 2330–1.45

Agriculture census, 1982: farms, farmland, production, finances, and operator characteristics, by county, final State rpt, 2331–1.40

Bank deposits in commercial and mutual savings banks and in US branches of foreign banks, by account type, instn, State, SMSA, and county, June 1983, annual rpt, 9295–3.7

Bank income and expenses, Fed Reserve 5th District member banks, by State, 1983, annual rpt, 9389–10

Biomass Fuels Program of TVA, technologies and processes dev, costs, and resource requirements, 1970s-90s, series, 9806–9

Census of Housing, 1980: occupancy and unit characteristics of SMSAs and central cities, by race, Hispanic origin, and city, State rpt, 2473–1.42

Census of Population and Housing, 1980: detailed population and housing characteristics, by county, city, and census tract, State rpt, 2551–2.42

Census of Population, 1980: detailed socioeconomic and demographic characteristics, by age, sex, race, Hispanic origin, and industry, State rpt, 2531–4.42

Collective bargaining calendar for Southeast US, 1984, annual rpt, 6946–1.68

County Business Patterns: establishments, employees, and payrolls, by SIC 4-digit industry and county, 1982, annual State rpt, 2326–6.42

Dress industry production and related workers, wages, and benefits, by occupation, size of establishment, and union status, for 11 labor market areas, Aug 1982 survey, 6787–6.200

Economic indicators by State, Fed Reserve 5th District, quarterly rpt, 9389–16

Economic indicators in South Carolina, including unemployment rate by county, and textile manufacturing employment, quarterly 1970-83 with estimated unemployment for 1984, article, 9371–1.411

Employment (nonagricultural) by industry div and SMSA, earnings, and hours, for 8 southeastern States, monthly press release, 6942–7

Employment, earnings, and hours, by selected SIC 1- to 4-digit industry, State, and for 278 major labor areas, 1939-83, annual rpt, 6744–5.2, 6744–5.3

Employment, prices, earnings, and union membership in 8 southeastern States, Oct 1982-83, annual rpt, 6944–2

Environmental quality, pollutant discharge by type and source, and EPA protection activities and funding, 1970s-83, biennial regional rpt, 9184–15.4

Exports of manufactured and agricultural commodities, manufacturing production, and export-related employment, 1960s-82, State rpt, 2046–3.40

South Carolina

Foster care children permanent placement, Fed Govt incentive program funding and operations in 7 States, FY80-82, GAO rpt, 26121-81

HHS aid to each State and local govt or private instn, amount obligated, funding agency, and program, FY83, annual listing, 4004-3.4

Income (personal) per capita and by source, and earnings by industry div, by State, MSA, and county, 1977-82, annual regional rpt, 2704-2.6

Manufacturing census, 1982: financial and operating data, by SIC 2- to 4-digit industry, State, SMSA, and county, preliminary census div rpt, 2491-3.5

Manufacturing plants in South Carolina with selected employee health care services, by SIC 2-digit industry, 1982, 4102-1.408

Mineral Industry Surveys, State review of production, 1983, advance annual rpt, 5614-6.40

Minerals Yearbook, 1982, Vol 2 preprints: State review of production and sales by commodity, and business activity, annual rpt, 5604-16.42

Minerals Yearbook, 1982, Vol 2: State reviews of production, sales, and firms, by commodity, and business activity, annual rpt, 5604-34

Peach production, marketing, and prices in 4 Southeastern States and Appalachia, 1983, annual rpt, 1311-12

Phosphate rock reserves in southeastern and northwestern US, by location, 1984 rpt, 5668-74

Population, births, deaths, and net migration, by MSA and county, 1980-82, annual State Current Population Rpt, 2546-4.40

Population size, Apr 1980 and July 1982, and per capita income, 1979 and 1981, by county and city, State Current Population Rpt, 2546-11.40

Retail trade census, 1982: employment, establishments, sales, and payroll, by SIC 2- to 4-digit kind of business, SMSA, county, and city, State rpt, 2397-1.41

Savings and loan assns, FHLB 4th District insured members financial condition and operations, by SMSA, monthly rpt, 9302-1

Textile mill employment and average hours and earnings, for 8 Southeastern States, monthly press release, 6942-1

Timber (pine) resources and removals in South Carolina, by ownership, 1978 and 1983, 1206-32.1

Timber (roundwood) production and residue volume in South Carolina, by species, product type, State region, and county, 1977-81, 1208-203

Water supply and quality in streams and lakes, and groundwater levels in wells, by drainage basin, 1982, annual State rpt, 5666-20.38

Water supply and quality in 8 southeastern States, with background socioeconomic data, 1960s-2020 with trends from 1930, 9208-119

Water supply and use in 3 areas with supply problems and total US, and methods to increase supply, selected years 1974-80 and projected to 2010, 9208-125

Wholesale trade census, 1982: employment, establishments, finances, and operations, by SIC 2- to 4-digit kind of business, SMSA, county, and city, State rpt, 2405-1.41

see also Charleston, S.C.
see also Columbia, S.C.
see also Florence, S.C.
see also Greenville, S.C.
see also North Charleston, S.C.
see also Rock Hill, S.C.
see also Spartanburg, S.C.
see also Walterboro, S.C.
see also under By State in the "Index by Categories"

South Dakota

Agriculture census, 1982: farms, farmland, production and costs, and operator characteristics, preliminary State summary and county rpts, 2330-1.46

Agriculture census, 1982: farms, farmland, production, finances, and operator characteristics, by county, final State rpt, 2331-1.41

Bank deposits in commercial and mutual savings banks and in US branches of foreign banks, by account type, instn, State, SMSA, and county, June 1983, annual rpt, 9295-3.15

Census of Population and Housing, 1980: detailed population and housing characteristics, by county, city, and census tract, State rpt, 2551-2.43

Census of Population, 1980: detailed socioeconomic and demographic characteristics, by age, sex, race, Hispanic origin, and industry, State rpt, 2531-4.43

County Business Patterns: establishments, employees, and payrolls, by SIC 4-digit industry and county, 1982, annual State rpt, 2326-6.43

Employment, earnings, and hours, by selected SIC 1- to 4-digit industry, State, and for 278 major labor areas, 1939-83, annual rpt, 6744-5.2, 6744-5.3

Environmental quality, pollutant discharge by type and source, and EPA protection activities and funding, 1970s-83, biennial regional rpt, 9184-15.8

Exports of manufactured and agricultural commodities, manufacturing production, and export-related employment, 1960s-82, State rpt, 2046-3.41

Farm investments, effective rates of Federal/State income and State/local property taxes, by category of structure and equipment, for 7 North Central States, 1981-82, 1548-237

Forest biomass in Rocky Mountain States, conversion from volume to dry weight, for softwood and hardwood species, 1977, 1208-200

HHS aid to each State and local govt or private instn, amount obligated, funding agency, and program, FY83, annual listing, 4004-3.8

Income (personal) per capita and by source, and earnings by industry div, by State, MSA, and county, 1977-82, annual regional rpt, 2704-2.5

Manufacturing census, 1982: financial and operating data, by SIC 2- to 4-digit industry, State, SMSA, and county, preliminary census div rpt, 2491-3.4

Index by Subjects and Names

Mineral Industry Surveys, State review of production, 1983, advance annual rpt, 5614-6.41

Minerals Yearbook, 1982, Vol 2 preprints: State review of production and sales by commodity, and business activity, annual rpt, 5604-16.43

Minerals Yearbook, 1982, Vol 2: State reviews of production, sales, and firms, by commodity, and business activity, annual rpt, 5604-34

Population size and components of change, by MSA and county, 1980-82, annual State Current Population Rpt, 2546-4.41

Population size, Apr 1980 and July 1982, and per capita income, 1979 and 1981, by county and city, State Current Population Rpt, 2546-11.41

Retail trade census, 1982: employment, establishments, sales, and payroll, by SIC 2- to 4-digit kind of business, SMSA, county, and city, State rpt, 2397-1.42

Savings and loan assns, FHLB 8th District members financial operations by State and SMSA, monthly rpt, 9302-9

Service industry census, 1982: employment, establishments, receipts, and payroll, by SIC 2- to 4-digit kind of business, SMSA, county, and city, State rpt, 2391-1.42

Timber resources and removals in 9 Rocky Mountain States, and forest and rangeland area, by ownership, forest and tree characteristics, and State, 1977, 1208-201

Transportation census, 1982: trucks, by detailed characteristics, miles traveled, and type of product carried, State rpt, 2573-1.42

Wages for 3 occupational groups, relative average levels in 78 labor market areas, 1983, annual press release, 6785-13

Wages of office and plant workers, by occupation, 1984 labor market area survey rpt, 6785-3.7

Water supply and quality in streams and lakes, and groundwater levels in wells, by drainage basin, 1983, annual State rpt, 5666-10.39

Wholesale trade census, 1982: employment, establishments, finances, and operations, by SIC 2- to 4-digit kind of business, SMSA, county, and city, State rpt, 2405-1.42

see also Sioux Falls, S.Dak.
see also under By State in the "Index by Categories"

South West Africa

see Namibia

Southard, Leland W.

"Red Meats Outlook", 1004-16.1

Southeast Asia

Agricultural situation in Southeast Asia, by country and commodity, 1983 and outlook for 1984, annual rpt, 1524-4.5

Agricultural supply/demand, trade, and production, and socioeconomic data, by country, 1950s-77, 1528-179

AID activities and funding by project and function, FY85, and developing countries summary socioeconomic data, 1970s-83, by country, annual rpt, 9914-3

AID community dev assistance to local govts in developing countries, program activities and funding, 1960s-80s, 9918-11

Index by Subjects and Names

AID loans authorized, signed, and canceled, by country and world area, monthly rpt, 9912–2

China economic conditions, agricultural and industrial production, trade, and domestic and foreign investment, 1980-85, 2048–106

Exports and imports of US (waterborne), by type of service, commodity, country, route, and US port, 1982, annual rpt, 7704–2

Exports and imports of US, by commodity group, world area, selected country, US coastal area and port, and mode of transport, with seasonal adjustments, monthly rpt, 2422–9

Exports of US, detailed Schedule E commodities by mode of transport and world area and country of destination, 1983, annual rpts, 2424–5

Food production and needs, and related economic trends and outlook, for 67 developing countries, 1980-86, annual rpt, 1524–6

Great Lakes trade, by SITC 3-digit commodity, port, vessel type, world area, and country, 1982, annual rpt, 7744–3

Immigration and alien residents, workers, visitors, deportations, and naturalizations, by country of birth, FY81, annual rpt, 6264–2

Loans and grants for economic and military assistance from US and intl agencies, by program and country, FY46-83, annual rpt, 9914–5

Military, social, and economic summary data, by world area and country, 1960s-80s, hearing, 25388–47.1

Military spending, arms trade, and armed forces size, with total govt spending and population, by country, 1972-82, annual rpt, 9824–1

Multilateral dev banks economic dev projects, environmental and cultural impacts in developing countries, 1970s-83, hearings, 21248–80

Population size and growth rates, and latest available benchmark demographic data, by country, 1950-83, biennial rpt, 2324–4

Refugee arrivals in US, by world area of origin and processing and nationality, monthly rpt, 7002–5

Refugee arrivals in US by world area of origin and State of settlement, and Fed Govt intl and domestic assistance costs, FY85, annual rpt, 7004–16

Refugee Indochinese population, arrivals, and departures, by country of origin and resettlement, camp, and ethnicity, monthly rpt, 7002–4

Refugee migration, settlement status, and assistance, by world area and country of origin and asylum, as of May 1984, annual rpt, 7004–15

Refugee resettlement program activities and funding, arrivals and population by country of origin and State, and employment and other characteristics, FY83, annual rpt, 4704–8

Weather conditions and impact assessment, by world area and country, monthly rpt, 2152–9

see also Association of South East Asian Nations

see also Burma
see also Indonesia
see also Kampuchea
see also Laos
see also Malaysia
see also Papua New Guinea
see also Philippines
see also Singapore
see also Thailand
see also Vietnam
see also under By Foreign Country in the "Index by Categories"

Southeastern Power Administration

Budget appropriations proposed for Fed Govt energy programs, by office or dept and function, FY84-85, annual rpt, 3004–14

Budget of US, effects of Reagan Admin policy changes, by detailed program, FY85, annual rpt, 104–21

Cost control proposals for Fed Govt programs and mgmt, 3-year savings by function and agency, and financial and operating data, 1960s-81, 16908–1

Electric power wholesale purchases and costs for individual REA borrowers, by supplier and State, 1940-83, annual rpt, 1244–5

Electric utilities privately owned, detailed financial and operating data by company, with summary data for other distributors by type, 1982, annual rpt, 3164–23

Sales by customer, plants, and capacity of Southeastern Power Admin, and financial statements of Southeastern Fed Power Program, FY83, annual rpt, 3234–1

Southeastern States

Agricultural conditions in Southeastern States, Fed Reserve 8th District, quarterly rpt, 9391–13

Air pollutant sulfur dioxide emissions of coal-fired power plants in eastern US, effect of alternative geographic area limits on power and coal industries, 1983 rpt, 3408–32

Air pollutant sulfur dioxide emissions reduction proposal, effects on polluting industries and coal production by region and State, projected to 2010, 9188–97

Army Corps of Engineers activities and projects, FY83 and trends from 1800s, annual rpt, 3754–1

Bank income and expenses, Fed Reserve 5th District member banks, by State, 1983, annual rpt, 9389–10

Banking and financial conditions, Fed Reserve 8th District, quarterly rpt, 9391–14

Birds (marine) on southeastern US coast, distribution, abundance, and oil spill effects, by species and State, 1820s-1982, 5508–72

Bridges over navigable waters, with type of bridge and use, owner, dimensions, and location, 1984 regional listing, 7406–5.1, 7406–5.2

Census of Population, 1980: detailed socioeconomic and demographic characteristics, by age, sex, race, Hispanic origin, occupation, and industry, US summary rpt, 2531–4.1

Coastal environmental and wildlife characteristics, use, and mgmt, for individual ecosystems, series, 5506–9

Economic indicators by State, Fed Reserve 5th District, quarterly rpt, 9389–16

Economic indicators for Southeastern States and 5 SMSAs, Fed Reserve 8th District, quarterly rpt, 9391–15

Electric and gas privately owned utilities, wages and employment by occupation, and benefits, by region, Oct 1982 survey, 6787–6.205

Employment (nonagricultural) by industry div and SMSA, earnings, and hours, for 8 southeastern States, monthly press release, 6942–7

Employment conditions for Southeast region, series, 6946–1

Employment, prices, earnings, and union membership in 8 southeastern States, Oct 1982-83, annual rpt, 6944–2

Environmental quality, pollutant discharge by type and source, and EPA protection activities and funding, 1970s-83, biennial regional rpt, 9184–15.3, 9184–15.4

Farm credit conditions and real estate values, Fed Reserve 5th District, quarterly rpt, 9389–17

Farm production inputs, outputs, and productivity, by region, 1939-82, annual rpt, 1544–17

Farm soil conservation and water pollution reduction participants, costs, and acreage, by conservation method and southeastern State, selected years 1973-82, 1588–84

Financial and banking devs in southeastern States, research paper series, 9371–10

Financial and economic devs, Fed Reserve Bank of Atlanta monthly rpt with articles, 9371–1

Financial and economic devs, Fed Reserve Bank of Richmond bimonthly rpt articles, 9389–1

Fish and shellfish landings, life cycles, and environmental needs, for selected species by region, with glossary and bibl, series, 5506–8

Fish landings, employment, gear used, and seafood production, for detailed species by State, 1977, annual rpt, 2164–2.5

Forest biomass in southeast region, trees, volume, and green weight by species, site and diameter class, and stand age, 1982, 1208–199

Fruit and vegetable shipments, and arrivals in 23 US and 5 Canada cities, by mode of transport and State or country of origin, 1983, annual rpt, 1311–4.1

Grain mill production workers, wages, hours, and benefits, by occupation, mill product, and region, June 1982 survey, 6787–6.204

HHS aid to each State and local govt or private instn, amount obligated, funding agency, and program, FY83, annual listing, 4004–3

Hog and pig inventory, value, farrowings, and farms, by State, quarterly release, 1623–3

Hog production, producer characteristics, facilities, and marketing, by type and size of enterprise and region, 1975 and 1980, 1568–248

Housing and neighborhood quality indicators and attitudes, and occupant characteristics, by urban-rural location and region, 1981, annual survey, 2485–7.2

Southeastern States

Housing and neighborhood quality indicators and attitudes, by occupant and unit characteristics, region, and metro-nonmetro location, 1981, annual survey, 2485–2

Housing census, 1980: inventory, occupancy, and unit characteristics, changes from 1973 by region and inside-outside SMSAs and central cities, series, 2473–3

Housing occupancy and unit and household characteristics, by region and metro-nonmetro residence, 1983, biennial survey, 2485–1

Housing vacancy rates for single and multifamily units and mobile homes in FHLB 9th District, by ZIP code, annual metro area rpt series, 9304–19

Income (personal) by industry group and region, percent change 1959-79 and 1979-83, article, 2702–1.443

Income (personal) per capita and by source, and earnings by industry div, by State, MSA, and county, 1977-82, annual regional rpt, 2704–2.3, 2704–2.6

Income (personal) per capita and by source, earnings by major industry group, and social insurance contributions, by region and State, 1929-82, 2708–40

Iron and steel production workers and wages by occupation, and benefits, by region, Aug 1983 survey, 6787–6.206

Manufacturing census, 1982: financial and operating data, by SIC 2- to 4-digit industry, State, SMSA, and county, preliminary census div rpt, 2491–3.5, 2491–3.6

Marine vertebrates off southeastern US coast, abundance and seasonal distribution, with oil and gas dev effects and lease status, early 1980s, 5508–85

Peach production, marketing, and prices in 4 Southeastern States and Appalachia, 1983, annual rpt, 1311–12

Peanut production, prices, stocks, exports, use, inspection, and quality, by region and State, selected crop years 1974-83, annual rpt, 1311–5

Phosphate rock reserves in southeastern and northwestern US, by location, 1984 rpt, 5668–74

Pulpwood prices, expenditures, and transportation modes in Southeast, 1981-82, annual rpt, 1204–22

Savings and loan assn acquisitions in Southeastern States related to market concentration and acquired S&L market share, 1974-81, article, 9312–1.401

Savings and loan assns, FHLB 4th District insured members financial condition and operations, by SMSA, monthly rpt, 9302–1

Savings and loan assns, FHLB 4th District members financial ratios and mortgage portfolios by State, 2nd half 1983, semiannual rpt, 9302–3

Savings and loan assns, FHLB 9th District insured members financial condition and operations by SMSA, monthly rpt, 9302–13

Savings and loan industry review, periodic rpt articles, 9302–2

Shipbuilding costs and related employment, by coastal district, 1982, annual rpt, 7704–12

Southeastern Power Admin sales by customer, plants, and capacity, and financial statements of Southeastern Fed Power Program, FY83, annual rpt, 3234–1

Technology-intensive industry employment and share of total employment in 8 southeastern States, 1982 and percent change 1975-82, press release, 6948–6

Textile mill employment and average hours and earnings, for 8 Southeastern States, monthly press release, 6942–1

Textile mill employment in Southeastern States, monthly 1951-83, annual summary rpt, 6944–1

Tide height and time daily at worldwide coastal points, 1985 predictions, annual rpt, 2174–2.2

Timber resources and removals in 5 States, interim rpt series, 1206–32

Water supply and quality, and effect of coal mining operations, for selected river basins in Eastern and Interior coal provinces, series, 5666–15

Water supply and quality in 8 southeastern States, with background socioeconomic data, 1960s-2020 with trends from 1930, 9208–119

Waterborne commerce of US (domestic and foreign), freight by commodity, traffic, and passengers, by port and waterway, 1982, annual rpt, 3754–3.1, 3754–3.2

see also Appalachia

see also under By Region in the "Index by Categories"

see also under names of individual States

Southern Pacific Railroad

Finances and operations of 7 commuter rail systems, and public agency cost reimbursement, 1980, 7888–61

Southwestern Power Administration

Budget appropriations proposed for Fed Govt energy programs, by office or dept and function, FY84-85, annual rpt, 3004–14

Budget of US, effects of Reagan Admin policy changes, by detailed program, FY85, annual rpt, 104–21

Cost control proposals for Fed Govt programs and mgmt, 3-year savings by function and agency, and financial and operating data, 1960s-81, 16908–1

Electric power sales by customer, financial statements, and project capacity, production, and costs, for Southwestern Fed Power System, FY83, annual rpt, 3244–1

Electric power wholesale purchases and costs for individual REA borrowers, by supplier and State, 1940-83, annual rpt, 1244–5

Electric utilities privately owned, detailed financial and operating data by company, with summary data for other distributors by type, 1982, annual rpt, 3164–23

Southwestern States

Army Corps of Engineers activities and projects, FY83 and trends from 1800s, annual rpt, 3754–1

Bridges over navigable waters, with type of bridge and use, owner, dimensions, and location, 1984 regional listing, 7406–5.2

Census of Population, 1980: detailed socioeconomic and demographic characteristics, by age, sex, race, Hispanic origin, occupation, and industry, US summary rpt, 2531–4.1

Index by Subjects and Names

Electric and gas privately owned utilities, wages and employment by occupation, and benefits, by region, Oct 1982 survey, 6787–6.205

Electric power sales by customer, financial statements, and project capacity, production, and costs, for Southwestern Fed Power System, FY83, annual rpt, 3244–1

Electric power sales by customer, operations by plant, and financial statements of Western Area Power Admin, FY83, annual rpt, 3254–1

Employment by major nonagricultural industry, and average hours and earnings of manufacturing production workers, for 5 southwestern States, monthly rpt, 6962–2

Employment, industrial relations, prices, and economic conditions in 5 Southwestern States, regional rpts series, 6966–1

Environmental quality, pollutant discharge by type and source, and EPA protection activities and funding, 1970s-83, biennial regional rpt, 9184–15.6

Farm credit conditions and real estate values, Fed Reserve 11th District, quarterly rpt, 9379–11

Farm production inputs, outputs, and productivity, by region, 1939-82, annual rpt, 1544–17

Farm real estate value per acre indexes, 15 western States, 1970s-84, annual rpt, 1541–8.1

Financial and economic devs, Fed Reserve Bank of Dallas bimonthly rpt articles, 9379–1

Fish and shellfish landings, life cycles, and environmental needs, for selected species by region, with glossary and bibl, series, 5506–8

Forest insect and disease incidence and damage, 1983, annual regional rpt, 1206–11.2

Fruit and vegetable shipments, and arrivals in 23 US and 5 Canada cities, by mode of transport and State or country of origin, 1983, annual rpt, 1311–4.2

Grain mill production workers, wages, hours, and benefits, by occupation, mill product, and region, June 1982 survey, 6787–6.204

HHS aid to each State and local govt or private instn, amount obligated, funding agency, and program, FY83, annual listing, 4004–3

Housing occupancy and unit and household characteristics, by region and metro-nonmetro residence, 1983, biennial survey, 2485–1

Housing vacancy rates for single and multifamily units and mobile homes in FHLB 9th District, by ZIP code, annual metro area rpt series, 9304–19

Income (personal) by industry group and region, percent change 1959-79 and 1979-83, article, 2702–1.443

Income (personal) per capita and by source, and earnings by industry div, by State, MSA, and county, 1977-82, annual regional rpt, 2704–2.7

Income (personal) per capita and by source, earnings by major industry group, and social insurance contributions, by region and State, 1929-82, 2708–40

Index by Subjects and Names

Soviet Union

Iron and steel production workers and wages by occupation, and benefits, by region, Aug 1983 survey, 6787–6.206

Manufacturing census, 1982: financial and operating data, by SIC 2- to 4-digit industry, State, SMSA, and county, preliminary census div rpt, 2491–3.7

Oil and gas extraction production workers, wages, hours, and benefits, by occupation, region, and for 5 States, June 1982 survey, 6787–6.203

Peanut production, prices, stocks, exports, use, inspection, and quality, by region and State, selected crop years 1974-83, annual rpt, 1311–5

Range and wildlife characteristics, problems, and research strategies and needs, northern Mexico and southwestern US, 1981 conf papers, 1208–197

Reclamation programs of Fed Govt in western US, finances and operations by project and State, 1981-82, annual rpts, 5824–1

Savings and loan assns, FHLB 9th District insured members financial condition and operations by SMSA, monthly rpt, 9302–13

Water supply and quality, and effect of coal mining operations, for selected river basins in Western coal provinces, series, 5666–19

see also under By Region in the "Index by Categories"

see also under names of individual States

Soviet Union

- Acid rain causes and effects, air pollutant emissions by source in US and selected countries, and control costs, 1970s-83 and projected to 2000, 21368–52
- Agricultural and food production indexes, and production of selected commodities, by world region and country, 1974-83, annual rpt, 1524–5
- Agricultural exports and imports of US, by detailed commodity and country, FY83 and CY83, semiannual rpts, 1522–4
- Agricultural situation in USSR, 1983 and outlook for 1984, annual report, 1524–4.4
- Arms control treaties with US, status as of Dec 1983, annual rpt, 9824–2
- Astronautic and aeronautic events, foreign and US, comprehensive chronology, 1976, annual rpt, 9504–2
- Carbon dioxide emissions from fossil fuel combustion, and growth rates, by country and country group, 1950-80, 3006–7.6
- Cotton production, consumption, and trade, selected countries, FAS monthly rpt, 1925–4.2
- Cuba economic conditions, agricultural and industrial production and distribution, trade, and intl economic relations, 1970-82 and trends from 1957, 248–40
- Economic conditions in Communist and OECD countries, 1982, annual rpt, 7144–11
- Economic conditions in Communist, OECD, and selected other countries, 1960s-83, annual rpt, 244–5
- Economic, social, and political summary data, by country, 1984, annual factbook, 244–11
- Economic trends in income, production, prices, employment, finances, and trade, 1984 annual rpt, 2046–4.98

Export and import statistics country classifications, Census Bur codes and designations, 1984 revisions, 2428–3.1, 2428–3.2

Export licensing and monitoring activities under Export Admin Act, for selected commodities, and for Communist and other countries, FY83, annual rpt, 2044–22

Export sales and shipments of US grains, oilseed products, hides, skins, and cotton, by country, weekly rpt, 1922–3

Exports and imports of NATO countries with Council for Mutual Economic Assistance Europe members, by country, 1980-83, annual rpt, 7144–5

Exports and imports of OECD countries, by country, 1983, annual rpt, 7144–10

Exports and imports of US with Communist countries, by detailed commodity and country, quarterly rpt with articles, 9882–2

Exports of US, detailed Schedule B commodities by country of destination, 1983, annual rpt, 2424–9

Exports of US, detailed Schedule E commodities by mode of transport and world area and country of destination, 1983, annual rpts, 2424–5

Ferrosilicon from USSR, injury to US industry, investigation with background financial and operating data, 1965-82, 9886–12.8

Grain area, yield, production, trade, supply, and use forecasts, FAS monthly rpt, 1925–2.3

Grenada arms and equipment commitments of USSR and other Communist countries, 1980-85, and arms discovered and personnel evacuated by US, Oct 1983, hearings, 21388–43

Helsinki Final Act implementation by NATO, Warsaw Pact, and other signatory nations, Dec 1983-Mar 1984, semiannual rpt, 7002–1

Imports of US, detailed Schedule A commodities by country and world area of origin, and mode of transport, 1983, annual rpts, 2424–2

Imports of US, detailed TSUSA commodities by country of origin, 1983, annual rpt, 2424–4

Livestock numbers, and hog and cattle slaughter, FAS monthly rpt, 1925–2.3

Loans and grants for economic and military assistance from US and intl agencies, by program and country, FY46-83, annual rpt, 9914–5

Military pension lifetime earnings in US and 7 countries, as of 1983, 26306–6.76

Military, social, and economic summary data, by world area and country, 1960s-80s, hearing, 25388–47.1

Military spending, arms trade, and armed forces size, with total govt spending and population, by country, 1972-82, annual rpt, 9824–1

Military weapons and troop strength of US and NATO compared to USSR and Warsaw Pact, as of Jan 1984, annual rpt, 3564–1

Military weapons of USSR, Warsaw Pact, and NATO/Japan, selected years 1974-83, annual rpt, 3544–2

Military weapons systems of USSR and Warsaw Pact, assistance and presence worldwide, and force strengths, with selected US and NATO comparisons, as of 1984, 3508–14

Military weapons transfers to developing countries from US, USSR, and Europe, by weapon type and world region, 1974-82, 25948–3

Minerals Yearbook, 1982, Vol 3: foreign country reviews of production, trade, and policies, by commodity, annual rpt, 5604–35

Minerals Yearbook, 1982, Vol 3 preprints: foreign country review of production, trade, and policies, by commodity, annual rpt, 5604–17.74

Nuclear missile deployment of NATO, USSR propaganda response and USSR and NATO nuclear arms and aircraft in place, 1977-83, narrative rpt, 9828–25

Nuclear weapon forces of US and USSR under Strategic Arms Reduction Talks and alternative proposals and counting methods, by weapon and system, FY84-96, 26306–6.73

Officials appearances in and outside of USSR, 1983, annual rpt, 244–8

Oil and gas production, consumption, and trade by country, for Communist countries, monthly rpt, 242–5

Oil production by major exporting countries, monthly rpt, 3162–24.10

Population demographic trends and projections by Republic, and industrial and agricultural production by selected commodity, 1950s-2000, hearings, 23848–180

Population size and growth rates, and latest available benchmark demographic data, by country, 1950-83, biennial rpt, 2324–4

Potassium chloride from 4 countries, imports injury to US industry from foreign subsidized products, investigation with background financial and operating data, 1984 rpt, 9886–15.52

R&D expenditures and employment in science and technology, for US and 4 countries, selected years 1953-84, annual rpt, 9624–18.1

Radio Free Europe and Radio Liberty broadcast and financial data, with comparisons to other intl broadcasters, FY83, annual rpt, 10314–1

Refugee arrivals in US, by world area of origin and processing and nationality, monthly rpt, 7002–4, 7002–5

Refugee arrivals in US by world area of origin and State of settlement, and Fed Govt intl and domestic assistance costs, FY85, annual rpt, 7004–16

Refugee migration, settlement status, and assistance, by world area and country of origin and asylum, as of May 1984, annual rpt, 7004–15

Refugee resettlement program activities and funding, arrivals and population by country of origin and State, and employment and other characteristics, FY83, annual rpt, 4704–8

Science and technology dev and transfer between USSR and other members of Council for Mutual Economic Assistance, 1940s-81, 2326–9.7

Soviet Union

Science and technology exchange with US, projects, man-hours, and funding, by Fed Govt agency and activity type, FY81-82, 7008–41

Science Indicators, R&D expenditures, innovations, research, and higher education, with foreign comparisons, 1960s- 83, annual rpt, 9624–10.1

Ships in world merchant fleet, and tonnage, by country of registry, 1982, annual rpt, 7704–3.1

Space flights of US and USSR, and NASA financial and employment data, 1957-83, annual rpt, 9504–6

Space launchings attaining Earth orbit or beyond, by country, 1957-83, annual rpt, 9504–9.1

Space satellites and other objects launched since 1957, quarterly listing, 9502–2

Space satellites of USSR and US by mission and vulnerability to attack, and USSR anti-satellite missiles, 1983 and projected to 1989, hearing, 21208–18

Students in US and Soviet bloc training programs, by program type and Latin American country or world region of student origin, selected years 1972-82, GAO rpt, 26123–77

Weather conditions and effect on agriculture, by US region, State, and city, and world area, weekly rpt, 2152–2

Weather conditions and impact assessment, by world area and country, monthly rpt, 2152–9

see also under By Foreign Country in the "Index by Categories"

Soybeans

Acreage harvested and cropland area by crop and region, and potential for expansion, 1982-84 with trends from 1949, annual rpt, 1584–4

Acreage planted and harvested, by crop and State, 1982-83 and planned as of June 1984, annual rpt, 1621–23

Acreage planting intended for 19 crops, by State, as of Feb 1984, annual rpt, 1621–22

Acreage, yield, and production of field crops, by State, 1978-82 and preliminary 1983, 1641–7

Agricultural Stabilization and Conservation Service soybean programs, 1955-84, annual fact sheet, 1806–4.4

Agricultural Statistics, 1983, annual rpt, 1004–1

Agriculture census, 1982: farms, farmland, production and costs, and operator characteristics, preliminary State and county rpt series, 2330–1

Agriculture census, 1982: farms, farmland, production, finances, and operator characteristics, by county, final State rpt series, 2331–1

Agriculture Fact Book of US, compilation of data for 1983 with trends from 1940, annual rpt, 1004–14

Alcohol fuel (ethanol) production in Tennessee Valley, feedstocks, facilities, tax incentives, and related farming data, by State, 1970s-83 and projected to 1992, 9808–69

Argentina grain production, exports by firm, storage by facility type and port, and shipments to ports by mode of transport, by grain type, selected years 1954-81, 1528–185

Beer production, stocks, materials used, tax-free removals, and taxable removals by State, monthly rpt, 8486–1.1

China economic conditions, agricultural and industrial production, trade, and domestic and foreign investment, 1980-85, 2048–106

Cooperatives finances and operations, aggregate for top 100 assns by principal product and revenue source, FY82, annual rpt, 1124–3

Cooperatives grain marketing, storage, and shipments by mode of transport, by grain type and region, FY80, 1128–28

County Business Patterns: establishments, employees, and payrolls, by SIC 4-digit industry and county, 1982, annual State rpt series, 2326–6

Eastern Europe agricultural production and trade by commodity, food consumption, and farm inputs, for 6 countries, 1960-80 with projections to 1991, 1528–178

Eastern Europe grain production, consumption, and trade, and US farm cooperatives grain and oilseed export potential, for 4 countries, selected years 1960-90, 1128–27

Export licensing and monitoring activities under Export Admin Act, for selected commodities, and for Communist and other countries, FY83, annual rpt, 2044–22

Export sales and shipments of US grains, oilseed products, hides, skins, and cotton, by country, weekly rpt, 1922–3

Exports and imports of US, by agricultural commodity and country, bimonthly rpt with articles, 1522–1

Exports and imports of US, by detailed agricultural commodity and country, FY83 and CY83, semiannual rpts, 1522–4

Exports and imports of US, detailed SIC-based commodities by world area, 1983, annual rpts, 2424–6

Exports and imports of US, totals and as percent of domestic production, by SIC 2- to 5-digit commodity, 1981, annual rpt, 2424–3

Exports and personal expenditures of US and world for selected agricultural commodities, by country, and export share of US farm income, various periods 1926-82, 1528–172

Exports of grain, prices and sales by type of grain, weekly rpt, 1272–2

Exports of manufactured and agricultural commodities, manufacturing production, and export-related employment, 1960s-82, State rpt series, 2046–3

Exports of US, detailed Schedule B commodities by country of destination, 1983, annual rpt, 2424–9

Exports of US, detailed Schedule E commodities by mode of transport and world area and country of destination, 1983, annual rpts, 2424–5

Exports, stocks, and prices of wheat, corn, and soybeans, effects of appreciated dollar exchange rates, 1980-82 and for hypothetical 20-year period, 1528–174

Farm finances, assets, liabilities, income, receipts by commodity and State, and expenses, 1980-83 and trends from 1910, annual rpt, 1544–16

Index by Subjects and Names

Fed Govt cost control through ground meat soy-extenders in feeding programs, proposed 3-year savings, and background data, FY70s-83, 16908–1.23

Fertilizer use and acreage of corn and soybeans, for alternative tillage systems by region, 1980 and 1982, article, 1561–16.401

Foreign and US agricultural production, prices, trade, and consumption, quarterly rpt with articles, 1522–3

Foreign and US agricultural supply/demand and production data, for selected US and world crops, and for US livestock and dairy products, periodic rpt, 1522–5

Foreign and US production, acreage, and yield for selected crops, forecasts by selected world region and country, FAS monthly rpt, 1925–28

Foreign and US production and trade of fats, oils, and related products, FAS monthly and annual circular series, 1925–1

Futures contracts, stocks in deliverable position by type and grade, weekly table, 11922–4.3

Futures market hedging and price forecasting efficiency, for rice, sunflower seeds, and soybeans, 1980-83, article, 1502–3.404

Futures trading by commodity and exchange, and Commodity Futures Trading Commission activities, funding, and employment, FY83, annual rpt, 11924–2

Imports of US, detailed Schedule A commodities by country, monthly rpt, 2422–2

Input-output structure of US economy, detailed interindustry transactions for 537 industries, and components of final demand, 1977 benchmark data, 2708–17

Loan support programs of USDA for grains, activity and status by type of grain and State, monthly rpt, 1802–3

Manufacturing census, 1982: financial and operating data, for SIC 4-digit industries by product, preliminary rpt, 2491–1.28

Marketing cash receipts of farms, by detailed commodity and State, 1979-82, annual rpt, 1544–18

OECD trade, total and for 4 major countries, and US trade by country, by commodity, 1972-82, annual world region rpt series, 244–13

Oils and fats production, consumption by end use, and stocks, by type, monthly Current Industrial Rpt, 2506–4.4

Oilseed mill production, crushings, and stocks by State, and trade, by oilseed type, monthly Current Industrial Rpt, 2506–4.3

Pesticide use effect on corn and soybean production, losses from hypothetical ban on selected pesticides by pest and region, 1984 article, 1561–16.407

Prices on US farms and for imports at Rotterdam, and EC price supports, by type of grain, weekly press release, 1922–4

Prices received by farmers and production value for detailed crops by State, 1981-83, annual rpt, 1621–2

Prices received by farmers for major products, and paid for farm inputs and living items, by commodity and State, monthly rpt, 1629–1

Index by Subjects and Names

Spain

Producer prices and indexes, by stage of processing and detailed commodity, monthly rpt, 6762–6

Producer prices and indexes, by stage of processing and detailed commodity, monthly 1983, annual supplement, 6764–2

Production and farm finances, expenses by type, and domestic economic impact, selected years 1972-82 and preliminary 1983-84, annual rpt, 1544–19

Production, farms, acreage, and related data, by selected crop and State, monthly rpt, 1621–1

Production inputs, land mgmt, and environmental effects, for 4 crops, 1940s-80 and projected to 2010, 9188–94

Production itemized costs, receipts, and net returns, for 13 crops, 4 livestock types, and milk, by region, 1981-83, annual rpt, 1544–20

Production, prices, trade, and consumption, periodic situation rpt with articles, 1561–3

Production, prices, trade, and export inspections by US port and country of destination, by grain type, weekly rpt, 1313–2

Production, prices, trade, and marketing, by commodity, current situation and forecast, monthly rpt, 1502–4

Southeastern States soil conservation and water pollution reduction participants, costs, and acreage, by conservation method and State, selected years 1973-82, 1588–84

Stocks of grain by region and market city, and grain inspected for export, by type, weekly rpt, 1313–4

Stocks of grain on and off farms and total in all positions, by crop, periodic rpt, 1621–4

Stocks of grains, oilseeds, and hay on and off farms, by State, 1978-83, 1641–17

Stocks on and off farms, by State, various dates 1983-84, annual rpt, 1621–5

Supply/demand, prices, and commodity program operations, for selected crops and livestock, 1983 and outlook for 1984, annual article, 9381–1.402

Tillage system effects on corn and soybean yields, itemized production costs, and input use, by region and for 10 States, 1980, 1588–80

Waterborne commerce of US (domestic and foreign), freight by commodity, traffic, and passengers, by port and waterway, 1982, annual rpt, 3754–3

see also under By Commodity in the "Index by Categories"

Space medicine

Foreign and US astronautic and aeronautic events, comprehensive chronology, 1976, annual rpt, 9504–2

Space programs

Aerial survey R&D publications, and sources of natural resource and environmental data gathered by air- and spacecraft, quarterly listing, 9502–7

Budget of US Appendix, detailed budgets and personnel summaries, by agency, FY85, annual rpt, 104–3

Budget of US, CBO analysis and review of FY85 budget by function, annual rpt, 26304–2

Budget of US, CBO analysis of revenue and spending alternatives and projections of economic indicators, FY85-89, annual rpt, 26304–3.3

Budget of US, compact budgets by function, agency, and account, FY85 with projections to FY89, annual rpt, 104–2

Budget of US, effects of Reagan Admin policy changes, by detailed program, FY85, annual rpt, 104–21

Budget of US, loans and loan guarantees, and Admin proposed limits on credit assistance, by program, FY83-89, annual rpt, 26306–3.65

Budget of US, receipts by source and outlays by function, FY40-89 estimates revised for consistency with FY85 budget definitions, annual rpt, 104–12

Budget of US, receipts, outlays, and budget authority, by function and agency, FY84-89 revised estimates, midsession review of FY85 budget, annual rpt, 104–7

Cost control proposals for Fed Govt programs and mgmt, CBO and GAO estimates of savings by function and agency, FY85-89, 26308–45

Cost control proposals for Fed Govt programs and mgmt, 3-year savings by function and agency, and financial and operating data, 1960s-81, 16908–1.28, 16908–1.30

Credit assistance costs, policies to improve measurement, with loan and loan guarantee data by program, and Federal and private credit instns operations, 1970-84, 26306–6.72

DOD budget, FY85 weapons system requests consistency with US policy and specified treaties, with funding FY83-87, annual rpt, 21384–4

DOD space and related R&D program activities and funding, FY84-85, annual rpt, 3504–9

Fed Govt revenues by source, expenditures by function, debt, and assets, 1982-83, annual rpt, 2466–2.6

Foreign and US astronautic and aeronautic events, comprehensive chronology, 1976, annual rpt, 9504–2

Govt revenues by source and expenditures by function, natl income and product account, *Survey of Current Business,* monthly and annual tables, 2702–1.24

Guests at space shuttle launches by type, and itemized Fed Govt costs by agency, Apr 1981-Nov 1983, GAO rpt, 26123–78

Meteorological services and research of Fed Govt, programs and funding by agency, FY84-85, annual rpt, 2144–2

NASA programs fraud and abuse, audits and investigations, 2nd half FY84, semiannual rpt, 9502–9

NASA project launch schedules and technical descriptions, press release series, 9506–2

Programs and budgets of Fed Govt by agency, and foreign programs, 1957-FY85, annual rpt, 9504–9

R&D expenditures by source, and scientists education and employment, detailed data by field, selected years 1953-84, annual rpt, 9624–18

R&D Fed Govt funding, by function, agency, and program, selected years FY80-84 and proposed FY85, 26308–46

Soviet Union and US space flights, and NASA financial and employment data, 1957-83, annual rpt, 9504–6

Soviet Union and Warsaw Pact military weapons systems, assistance and presence worldwide, and force strengths, with selected US and NATO comparisons, as of 1984, 3508–14

Space vehicle and selected parts production, quarterly Current Industrial Rpt, 2506–12.22

Statistical Abstract of US, social, political, and economic data, 1950s-83 and trends, annual rpt, 2324–1.3

see also Communications satellites

see also Meteorological satellites

see also Satellites

Space sciences

Aerial survey R&D publications, and sources of natural resource and environmental data gathered by air- and spacecraft, quarterly listing, 9502–7

DOD space and related R&D program activities and funding, FY84-85, annual rpt, 3504–9

Foreign and US astronautic and aeronautic events, comprehensive chronology, 1976, annual rpt, 9504–2

NASA project launch schedules and technical descriptions, press release series, 9506–2

NASA R&D funding to colleges and universities, by State, field of science, and instn, FY83, annual listing, 9504–7

R&D-employed scientists and engineers salaries by degree, type of establishment, age, experience, and field, 1984, annual rpt, 3004–1

R&D expenditures by source, and scientists education and employment, detailed data by field, selected years 1953-84, annual rpt, 9624–18

R&D expenditures of higher education instns, and science and engineering employment and grad students, by field, 1972-83, biennial rpt, 9627–24

R&D Fed Govt facilities and services available for private sector use, by field of science, 1984 biennial listing, 2224–4

Science and engineering grad enrollment, fields of study, financial support, and other student and instn characteristics, 1975-82, annual survey, 9627–7

Soviet Union-US science and technology exchange projects, man-hours, and funding, by Fed Govt agency and activity type, FY81-82, 7008–41

see also Communications satellites

see also Meteorological satellites

see also Satellites

see also Space medicine

see also Space programs

Spain

Agricultural and food production indexes, and production of selected commodities, by world region and country, 1974-83, annual rpt, 1524–5

Agricultural situation in Western Europe, by country and commodity, 1983 and outlook for 1984, annual rpt, 1524–4.6

Agricultural supply/demand, trade, and production, and socioeconomic data, by country, 1950s-77, 1528–179

Spain

AID economic assistance to developing countries, obligations and disbursements by country, quarterly rpt, 9912–4

AID loan repayment status and terms by program and country, and status of predecessor agency loans, quarterly rpt, 9912–3

Almond prices, and exports by country of destination, for Spain, 1981/82-1982/83, article, 1925–34.403

Almond production and trade of US and selected countries, 1982/83-1983/84 and forecast 1985, article, 1925–34.425

Economic and monetary trends, compounded annual rates of change for US and 13 trading partners, quarterly rpt annual supplement, 9391–7

Economic conditions in Communist, OECD, and selected other countries, 1960s-83, annual rpt, 244–5

Economic, social, and political summary data, by country, 1984, annual factbook, 244–11

Economic trends in income, production, prices, employment, finances, and trade, 1984 semiannual rpt, 2046–4.54

Electric power systems equipment market and trade, and user industry operations and demand, 1984 country market research rpt, 2045–15.8

Export and import statistics country classifications, Census Bur codes and designations, 1984 revisions, 2428–3.1, 2428–3.2

Exports and imports of NATO countries with Council for Mutual Economic Assistance Europe members, by country, 1980-83, annual rpt, 7144–5

Exports and imports of NATO countries with PRC, by country, 1980-83, annual rpt, 7144–14

Exports and imports of OECD countries, by country, 1983, annual rpt, 7144–10

Exports and imports of US with Western Europe, and US market share and export opportunities for selected commodities, by country, 1982-84, 2048–105

Exports of US, detailed Schedule B commodities by country of destination, 1983, annual rpt, 2424–9

Exports of US, detailed Schedule E commodities by mode of transport and world area and country of destination, 1983, annual rpts, 2424–5

Filbert production and trade of US and selected countries, 1981/82-1984/85, article, 1925–34.426

Fish and shellfish wholesale prices and market activity in 8 West Europe countries, weekly rpt, 2162–8

Fruit and vegetable product trade and tariffs of EC, 1966-78, and effect of Greece, Spain, and Portugal entry into EC, projected to 1986, 1528–182

Imports of US, detailed Schedule A commodities by country and world area of origin, and mode of transport, 1983, annual rpts, 2424–2

Imports of US, detailed TSUSA commodities by country of origin, 1983, annual rpt, 2424–4

Industrial process control equipment market and trade, and user industry operations and demand, 1984 country market research rpt, 2045–6.36

Loans and grants for economic and military assistance from US and intl agencies, by program and country, FY46-83, annual rpt, 9914–5

Military aid of US, arms sales, and training programs costs and budget requests by program, world region, and country, FY83-85, annual rpt, 7144–13

Military spending, arms trade, and armed forces size, with total govt spending and population, by country, 1972-82, annual rpt, 9824–1

Minerals Yearbook, 1982, Vol 3: foreign country reviews of production, trade, and policies, by commodity, annual rpt, 5604–35

Minerals Yearbook, 1982, Vol 3 preprints: foreign country review of production, trade, and policies, by commodity, annual rpt, 5604–17.65

Nuclear power generation in US and 18 non-Communist countries, monthly rpt, 3162–24.10

Nuclear power plant construction and operation status, and capacity, by plant, region, State, and selected country, 1983 and projected to 2020, annual rpt, 3164–57

Oil field equipment from 5 countries, injury to US industry from foreign subsidized imports and less than fair value sales, investigation with background financial and operating data, 1984 rpt, 9886–19.11

Olives (bottled) from Spain, imports injury to US industry from removal of duties on foreign subsidized products, investigation with selected financial and operating data, 1984 rpt, 9886–18.15

Population size and growth rates, and latest available benchmark demographic data, by country, 1950-83, biennial rpt, 2324–4

Potassium chloride from Israel and Spain, imports injury to US industry from foreign subsidized products, investigation with background financial and operating data, 1984 rpt, 9886–15.54

Potassium chloride from 4 countries, imports injury to US industry from foreign subsidized products, investigation with background financial and operating data, 1984 rpt, 9886–15.52

Potassium permanganate from Spain at less than fair value, imports injury to US industry, investigation with background financial and operating data, 1984 rpt supplement, 9886–14.92

Ships in world merchant fleet, and tonnage, by country of registry, 1982, annual rpt, 7704–3.1

Space satellites and other objects launched since 1957, quarterly listing, 9502–2

Stainless steel sheet and strip from Spain at less than fair value, imports injury to US industry, investigation with background financial and operating data, 1984 rpt, 9886–14.97

Steel (carbon) wire rod from Spain and Argentina at less than fair value, imports injury to US industry, investigation with background financial and operating data, 1984 rpt, 9886–14.126

Steel (stainless) products from Spain at less than fair value, imports injury to US industry, investigation with background financial and operating data, 1984 rpt, 9886–14.125

Index by Subjects and Names

Steel from 5 countries, injury to US industry from foreign subsidized products and sales at less than fair value, investigation with background financial and operating data, 1984 rpt, 9886–19.8

Steel imports of US from EC and other countries, and US industry operating data, for 15 products limited under arrangement with EC, monthly rpt, 9882–10

Steel pipes and tubes from Brazil and Spain, injury to US industry from foreign subsidized and less than fair value imports, investigation with background financial and operating data, 1984 rpt, 9886–19.12

Steel wire rod from Spain, imports injury to US industry from foreign subsidized products, investigation with background financial and operating data, 1984 rpt, 9886–15.50

Steel wire rod from 4 countries, imports injury to US industry from sales covered by foreign govt grants, investigation with background financial and operating data, 1980-83, 9886–15.47

see also under By Foreign Country in the "Index by Categories"

Spanish-American War
see War

Spanish heritage Americans
see Hispanic Americans

Spanish Sahara
see Morocco

Spartanburg, S.C.

Census of Housing, 1980: occupancy and unit characteristics, by race, Hispanic origin, and city, SMSA rpt, 2473–1.177

Census of Population and Housing, 1980: detailed population and housing characteristics, by county, city, and census tract, SMSA rpt, 2551–2.177

Wages of office and plant workers, by occupation, 1984 SMSA survey rpt, 6785–11.6

see also under By SMSA or MSA in the "Index by Categories"

Spaulding, Pamela

"National Transportation Statistics", 7304–2

Speaker, D. M.

"Identification and Analysis of Human Errors Underlying Electrical/Electronic Component Related Events Reported by Nuclear Power Plant Licensees", 9638–51

Special districts

Airport financing by source, bond issues by region, and airport operations, by airport and operator type, FY75-83 and projected to FY93, 26306–6.75

Census of Govts, 1982: employment, payrolls, and average earnings, by function, level of govt, State, county, population size, and inside-outside SMSAs, 2455–2

Census of Govts, 1982: local govt employment by function, payroll, and average earnings, for individual counties, cities, and school and special districts, 2455–1

Census of Govts, 1982: properties, govt-assessed value, sales, and tax rates, by property type, State, SMSA, county, and city, 2453–1

Index by Subjects and Names

Census of Govts, 1982: State govt payments to local govts, by program, source of funds, level of govt, and State, with trends from 1902, 2460–3

Central city jurisdictional areas, by govt type and selected SMSA, 1981, 10048–61

Electric power wholesale purchases and costs for individual REA borrowers, by supplier and State, 1940-83, annual rpt, 1244–5

Employment and payroll, by function and level of govt in 75 SMSAs and 69 large counties, Oct 1983, annual rpt, 2466–1.3

Enterprise zone and urban revitalization projects of State and local govts, effect on business and employment in selected areas, various dates 1972-83, hearing, 21788–140

Foreign trade zones operations and economic effects, with data on merchandise shipments, value added, employment, hours, and customs revenue, 1978-83, 9886–4.70

Govt finances, by level of govt and State, selected years 1929-83, annual rpt, 10044–1

Govt finances, by level of govt, State, and for large cities and counties, 1981-83, annual rpt series, 2466–2

Tax burden for average family by income level and selected city, and tax rates by selected jurisdiction, by type of tax, 1982, 10046–8.2

Transit systems, expenditures by level of govt, and revenues by source, with distribution of commuter trips by mode of transport, 1980-82, article, 10042–1.404

Western Area Power Admin operations by plant, financial statements, and electric power sales by customer, FY83, annual rpt, 3254–1

see also Central business districts

see also Common markets and free trade areas

see also Congressional districts

see also School districts

Special Drawing Rights

Economic indicators and components, current data and annual trends, monthly rpt, 23842–1.7

Fed Govt receipts by source and outlays by agency, *Treasury Bulletin,* quarterly rpt, 8002–4.1

Fed Reserve Bank of Atlanta financial statements, 1982-83, annual rpt, 9371–4

Fed Reserve Bank of Chicago financial statements, 1983, annual rpt, 9375–5

Fed Reserve Bank of Cleveland financial statements, 1982-83, annual rpt, 9377–5

Fed Reserve Bank of Kansas City financial statements, 1982-83, annual rpt, 9381–3

Fed Reserve Bank of Minneapolis financial statements, 1981-82, annual rpt, 9383–2

Fed Reserve Bank of New York financial statements, 1982-83, annual rpt, 9385–2

Fed Reserve Bank of Philadelphia financial statements, 1982-83, annual rpt, 9387–3

Fed Reserve Bank of Richmond financial statements, 1983, annual rpt, 9389–2

Fed Reserve Bank of San Francisco financial statements, 1982-83, annual rpt, 9393–2

Fed Reserve banks financial statements and employees, 1983, annual rpt, 9364–1.1

Financial and business statistics, historic trends, 1984 annual chartbook, 9364–2.17

Flow-of-funds accounts, assets and liabilities by type and economic sector, year-end outstandings, 1960-83, annual rpt, 9364–3

Flow-of-funds accounts savings, investments, and credit statements, quarterly rpt, 9365–3.3

IMF currency transactions and Special Drawing Rights positions, by country, FY83, annual rpt, 15344–1.3

Intl finance, loans, debts, exchange rates, and intl reserves, for US and selected countries, various periods 1949-84, conf papers, 9373–3.28

Intl investment position of US, net change by component, investment type, and world region, and for 2 countries, 1982-83, annual article, 2702–1.424

Reserve assets of US by type, *Treasury Bulletin,* quarterly rpt, 8002–4.11

Reserve assets of US, monthly rpt, 9362–1.3

Special education

Census of Population, 1980: detailed socioeconomic and demographic characteristics, by age, sex, race, Hispanic origin, occupation, and industry, State rpt series, 2531–4

Census of Population, 1980: labor force, by sex, detailed occupation, and region, with comparison to 1970 census, supplementary rpt, 2535–1.12

Condition of Education, detailed data on enrollment, staff, achievement, finances, curricula, and education effects on employment, 1982-83, annual rpt, 4824–1.1

Early education for handicapped children, research and service project activities and characteristics, and grants to States for program dev, 1983-84, annual listing, 4804–30

Education Dept financial aid programs for educational instns and individuals, 1984 annual listing, 4804–3

Education Dept programs and activities, FY83, annual rpt, 4804–6

Education Dept programs funding, operations, and effectiveness, FY83, annual rpt, 4804–5

Enrollment of children in special education programs, by amount of participation and type of handicap, fall 1980, annual rpt, 4824–2.7

Enrollment, staffing, and funding for handicapped children public education programs, by handicap, age, and State, 1981/82-1982/83, annual rpt, 4944–4

Fed Govt educational grants, State allocations by program, type of recipient agency, and State, FY83, annual rpt, 4804–8

Fed Govt funding for elementary and secondary education by agency, and Education Dept funding for special education by program, selected years FY60-84, 4808–9.3

Fed Govt public welfare programs and tax expenditures benefitting children and youth, participation and funding for 71 programs, FY81-83, 21968–30

Speech pathology and audiology

Govt census, 1982: State govt payments to local govts, by program, source of funds, level of govt, and State, with trends from 1902, 2460–3

Head Start Project enrollment of handicapped children, by handicap, State, and for Indian and migrant programs, 1982, annual rpt, 4604–1

Statistical Abstract of US, social, political, and economic data, 1950s-83 and trends, annual rpt, 2324–1.1

Teaching degrees conferred by specialty and State, required credit hours, and instn officials attitudes, by instn type, 1970s-83, hearings, 21348–89

Special Food Service Program

see School lunch and breakfast programs

Special foreign currency programs

AID activities and funding by project and function, FY85, and developing countries summary socioeconomic data, 1970s-83, by country, annual rpt, 9914–3

Currency (foreign) accounts owned by US under AID admin and by foreign govts with joint AID control, status by program and country, quarterly rpt, 9912–1

Currency (foreign) holdings of US, detailed transactions and balances by program and country, 1st half FY84, semiannual rpt, 8102–7

DOD budget, itemized account of legislative history, FY84, annual rpt, 3504–7

DOD outlays and obligations, by function and service branch, quarterly rpt, 3542–3

NIH intl program activities and funding, by inst and country, FY83, annual rpt, 4474–6

NSF grant and award recipients, by State, FY83, annual listing, 9624–11

PL 480 commodity sales, status of foreign currencies, by country and specified use, FY82, annual rpt, 1924–7

R&D Fed Govt funding for foreign performers, by world region and country, FY82-84, annual rpt, 9627–20.2

Smithsonian Instn finances, activities, and visitors, FY83, annual rpt, 9774–3

Special Milk Program

see School lunch and breakfast programs

Speech pathology and audiology

Census of Population, 1980: labor force, by sex, detailed occupation, and region, with comparison to 1970 census, supplementary rpt, 2535–1.12

Dental Research Natl Inst research and training funds awarded, by recipient instn, FY83, annual listing, 4474–19

DOD medical personnel, trainees, and accessions by source, by occupation, specialty, and service branch, FY83, annual rpt, 3544–24

Fed Govt minority group and handicapped employment, by race, Hispanic origin, disability, sex, and employment characteristics, as of Sept 1982, biennial rpt, 9844–27

Handicapped children early education research and service project activities and characteristics, and grants to States for program dev, 1983-84, annual listing, 4804–30

Handicapped children public education program enrollment, staff, and funding, by handicap, age, and State, 1981/82-1982/83, annual rpt, 4944–4

Speech pathology and audiology

Head Start Project enrollment of handicapped children, by handicap, State, and for Indian and migrant programs, 1982, annual rpt, 4604–1

HHS aid to each State and local govt or private instn, amount obligated, funding agency, and program, FY83, annual listing, 4004–3

Hospital worker wages by sex and occupation, and benefits, for 22 MSAs, Oct 1981 survey, 6787–6.201

Medicare-participating facilities by control, beds, and terminated facilities, by facility type, region, and State, 1975-81, 4656–1.19

Occupational manpower needs and supply by detailed occupation, and educational and training program enrollees and grads by detailed field, 1982 and 1995, biennial rpt, 6744–3

Occupational Outlook Handbook, 1984-85 biennial rpt, 6744–1

Science and engineering grad enrollment, fields of study, financial support, and other student and instn characteristics, 1975-82, annual survey, 9627–7

VA facilities patients with speech disorders, by severity, patient characteristics, diagnostician occupation, and facility type, FY81, 9926–1.17

VA Medicine and Surgery Dept trainees, by detailed program and city, FY83, annual rpt, 9924–21

VA patients with communicative disorders, by age, disease and treatment characteristics, and facility type, 1981 survey, 9926–4.8, 9926–4.9

see also Ear diseases and infections

Spencer, Gregory

"Projections of the Population of the U.S., by Age, Sex, and Race: 1983-2080", 2546–3.132

Spencer, John S., Jr.

"Michigan's Fourth Forest Inventory: Area", 1208–192

"Michigan's Fourth Forest Inventory: Timber Volumes and Projections of Timber Supply", 1206–31.6

Spices and herbs

Consumption, supply, trade, prices, expenditures, and indexes, by food commodity, 1963-83, annual rpt, 1544–4

Exports and imports of US, by agricultural commodity and country, bimonthly rpt with articles, 1522–1

Exports and imports of US, by detailed agricultural commodity and country, FY83 and CY83, semiannual rpts, 1522–4

Exports and imports of US, by detailed agricultural commodity for 8 major commodity groups, monthly rpt, 1922–8

Exports and imports of US, detailed SIC-based commodities by world area, 1983, annual rpts, 2424–6

Exports and imports of US, totals and as percent of domestic production, by SIC 2- to 5-digit commodity, 1981, annual rpt, 2424–3

Exports, imports, tariffs, and industry operating data for spices and herbs, 1979-83, TSUSA commodity rpt, 9885–1.66

Exports of US, detailed commodities by country of destination, monthly rpt, 2422–3

Exports of US, detailed Schedule B commodities by country of destination, 1983, annual rpt, 2424–9

Exports of US, detailed Schedule E commodities by mode of transport and world area and country of destination, 1983, annual rpts, 2424–5

Foreign agricultural production, prices, and trade, by country, 1983 and outlook for 1984/85, annual world region rpt series, 1524–4

Foreign and US production, prices, and trade of spices, essential oils, and tea, FAS annual rpt series, 1925–15

Great Lakes trade, by SITC 3-digit commodity, port, vessel type, world area, and country, 1982, annual rpt, 7744–3

Imports of US, detailed Schedule A commodities by country and world area of origin, and mode of transport, 1983, annual rpts, 2424–2

Imports of US, detailed Schedule A commodities by country, monthly rpt, 2422–2

Imports of US, detailed TSUSA commodities by country of origin, 1983, annual rpt, 2424–4

Mint oil acreage, yield, and production, by State, 1978-82 and preliminary 1983, 1641–7

Prices received by farmers and production value for detailed crops by State, 1981-83, annual rpt, 1621–2

see also under By Commodity in the "Index by Categories"

Spindt, Paul A.

"Federal Reserve's New Operating Procedures: A Post Mortem", 9366–6.78

Spokane, Wash.

Census of Housing, 1980: occupancy and unit characteristics, by race, Hispanic origin, and city, SMSA rpt, 2473–1.337

Census of Population and Housing, 1980: detailed population and housing characteristics, by county, city, and census tract, SMSA rpt, 2551–2.337

Housing and households detailed characteristics, and unit and neighborhood quality, by inside-outside central cities, 1981 survey, SMSA rpt, 2485–6.26

see also under By City and By SMSA or MSA in the "Index by Categories"

Sporting goods

Census of Population, 1980: detailed socioeconomic and demographic characteristics, by age, sex, race, Hispanic origin, occupation, and industry, State rpt series, 2531–4

Counterfeiting of brand-name products by foreign manufacturers, effects on 6 US industries, investigation with financial and operating data, 1984 rpt, 9886–4.67

County Business Patterns: establishments, employees, and payrolls, by SIC 4-digit industry and county, 1981, annual State rpt series, 2326–8

County Business Patterns: establishments, employees, and payrolls, by SIC 4-digit industry and county, 1982, annual State rpt series, 2326–6

Employment, earnings, and hours, by selected SIC 1- to 4-digit industry, State, and for 278 major labor areas, 1939-83, annual rpt, 6744–5

Employment, earnings, and hours, by SIC 4-digit nonfarm industry, monthly 1974-Feb 1984, annual update, 6744–4

Exports and imports of US, detailed SIC-based commodities by world area, 1983, annual rpts, 2424–6

Exports and imports of US, totals and as percent of domestic production, by SIC 2- to 5-digit commodity, 1981, annual rpt, 2424–3

Exports, imports, tariffs, and industry operating data for sporting goods, foreign and US, 1979-83, TSUSA commodity rpt supplement, 9885–7.56

Exports of US, detailed commodities by country of destination, monthly rpt, 2422–3

Exports of US, detailed Schedule B commodities by country of destination, 1983, annual rpt, 2424–9

Exports of US, detailed Schedule E commodities by mode of transport and world area and country of destination, 1983, annual rpts, 2424–5

Footwear imports of US, by category, value class, and selected country, monthly rpt, 2042–29

Foreign market and trade for sporting goods and recreational equipment and vehicles, country market research rpts, 2045–14

Great Lakes trade, by SITC 3-digit commodity, port, vessel type, world area, and country, 1982, annual rpt, 7744–3

Imports of US, detailed Schedule A commodities by country and world area of origin, and mode of transport, 1983, annual rpts, 2424–2

Imports of US, detailed Schedule A commodities by country, monthly rpt, 2422–2

Imports of US, detailed TSUSA commodities by country of origin, 1983, annual rpt, 2424–4

Income tax returns of corporations, detailed income and tax items by industry, 1981, annual rpt, 8304–4

Income tax returns of sole proprietorships, detailed data by industry div and selected industry group, 1981, annual rpt, 8304–7

Income tax returns of sole proprietorships, receipts, deductions by type, payroll, and net income, by major industry, 1982, annual article, 8302–2.413

Industry finances and operations, by SIC 2- to 4-digit industry, 1970s-83 and projected to 1988, annual rpt, 2014–4

Injuries and deaths from use of selected consumer products and related activity, by victim age and sex, 1982, annual rpt, 9164–7

Injuries and deaths from use of selected consumer products, by victim age and medical treatment status, 1982, annual rpt, 9164–6

Injuries, deaths, and medical costs from consumer products use, and Consumer Product Safety Commission activities and recalls, by product type and brand, FY83, annual rpt, 9164–2

Input-output structure of US economy, detailed interindustry transactions for 537 industries, and components of final demand, 1977 benchmark data, 2708–17

Manufacturing census, 1982: financial and operating data, by SIC 2- to 4-digit industry, State, SMSA, and county, preliminary census div rpt series, 2491–3

Index by Subjects and Names

SRI International

Minority group and women employment, by occupational group and SIC 2- to 3-digit industry, 1981, annual rpt, 9244–1.1

Occupational injury and illness rates, by SIC 2- to 4-digit industry, 1982, annual rpt, 6844–1

Pollution abatement capital and operating costs, by SIC 2- to 4-digit industry, State, and SMSA, 1982, annual Current Industrial Rpt, 2506–3.6

Producer prices and indexes, by stage of processing and detailed commodity, monthly rpt, 6762–6

Producer prices and indexes, by stage of processing and detailed commodity, monthly 1983, annual supplement, 6764–2

Retail trade census, 1982: employment, establishments, sales, and payroll, for sporting goods stores and bicycle shops, by State, preliminary rpt, 2395–1.28

Tax (excise) collections of IRS, by source, quarterly press release, 8302–1

Tax (excise) on hunting and fishing equipment, revenue of Fed Govt fish and wildlife restoration program by type of equipment, FY84, annual rpt, 5504–13

Tax collections, refunds, and taxes due IRS, by State and region, and IRS court activity and operating expenses, FY83, annual rpt, 8304–3.3

Virgin Islands economic censuses, 1982: employment, establishments, payroll, and receipts, by SIC 1- to 4-digit industry, island, and city, 2593–1

Wholesale trade census, 1982: employment, establishments, finances, and operations, by SIC 2- to 4-digit kind of business, SMSA, county, and city, State rpt series, 2405–1

Wholesale trade sales, inventories, purchases, and gross margins, by SIC 2- to 3-digit kind of business and type of ownership, 1983, annual rpt, 2413–13

see also Bicycles

see also Boats and boating

see also Recreational vehicles

see also under By Commodity in the "Index by Categories"

Sports and athletics

Army morale, welfare, and recreation programs, revenue and expenses worldwide by activity and major command, FY82-83, annual rpt, 3704–12

Census of Population, 1980: detailed socioeconomic and demographic characteristics, by age, sex, race, Hispanic origin, occupation, and industry, State rpt series, 2531–4

Census of Population, 1980: labor force, by sex, detailed occupation, and region, with comparison to 1970 census, supplementary rpt, 2535–1.12

County Business Patterns: establishments, employees, and payrolls, by SIC 4-digit industry and county, 1981, annual State rpt series, 2326–8

County Business Patterns: establishments, employees, and payrolls, by SIC 4-digit industry and county, 1982, annual State rpt series, 2326–6

Educational services in underground economy, household expenditures and participation by type of instruction, 1981 survey, 8308–27

Income (taxable) not reported, by illegal source, with characteristics of persons involved, methodology, and bibl, 1970s-82, 8008–112

Income (taxable) not reported on individual and corporate returns, and associated Federal revenue losses, by detailed legal and illegal source, 1973-81, 8308–26

Income tax returns of sole proprietorships, detailed data by industry div and selected industry group, 1981, annual rpt, 8304–7

Industry finances and operations, by SIC 2- to 4-digit industry, 1970s-83 and projected to 1988, annual rpt, 2014–4

Injuries and deaths from use of selected consumer products and related activity, by victim age and sex, 1982, annual rpt, 9164–7

Input-output structure of US economy, detailed interindustry transactions for 537 industries, and components of final demand, 1977 benchmark data, 2708–17

Occupational manpower needs and supply by detailed occupation, and educational and training program enrollees and grads by detailed field, 1982 and 1995, biennial rpt, 6744–3

Outdoor recreation participation, by type of activity, projected 1985-2030, 1208–195

Service industry census, 1982: employment, establishments, receipts, and payroll, by SIC 2- to 4-digit kind of business, SMSA, county, and city, State rpt series, 2391–1

Statistical Abstract of US, social, political, and economic data, 1950s-83 and trends, annual rpt, 2324–1.1

see also Basketball

see also Bicycles

see also Boats and boating

see also Fishing, sport

see also Football

see also Golf

see also Horse racing

see also Sporting goods

see also Swimming

see also Winter sports

Sprafka, J. Michael

"Environmental Levels of PCB in Great Lakes Fish", 9208–126

Sprague, Merritt W.

"Program Outlook for Crop Insurance in 1984", 1004–16.1

Sprague, Willard F.

"California's Prospects for the Rest of the 1980's: Economic Growth and Housing Production", 9306–1.1

"Tucson Area Economy and Housing Market: Outlook to 1992", 9306–2.1

Springdale, Ark.

Census of Housing, 1980: occupancy and unit characteristics, by race, Hispanic origin, and city, SMSA rpt, 2473–1.154

Census of Population and Housing, 1980: detailed population and housing characteristics, by county, city, and census tract, SMSA rpt, 2551–2.154

see also under By SMSA or MSA in the "Index by Categories"

Springer, Philip B.

"Health Care Coverage of Survivor Families with Children: Determinants and Consequences", 4742–1.404

Springfield, Ill.

Census of Housing, 1980: occupancy and unit characteristics, by race, Hispanic origin, and city, SMSA rpt, 2473–1.338

Census of Population and Housing, 1980: detailed population and housing characteristics, by county, city, and census tract, SMSA rpt, 2551–2.338

Wages of office and plant workers, by occupation, 1983 labor market area survey rpt, 6785–3.2

see also under By SMSA or MSA in the "Index by Categories"

Springfield, Mass.

Census of Housing, 1980: occupancy and unit characteristics, by race, Hispanic origin, and city, SMSA rpt, 2473–1.341

Census of Population and Housing, 1980: detailed population and housing characteristics, by county, city, and census tract, SMSA rpt, 2551–2.341

Housing and financial characteristics, and unit and neighborhood quality, for 15 SMSAs, 1978, annual survey special supplement, 2485–8

see also under By City and By SMSA or MSA in the "Index by Categories"

Springfield, Mo.

Census of Housing, 1980: occupancy and unit characteristics, by race, Hispanic origin, and city, SMSA rpt, 2473–1.339

Census of Population and Housing, 1980: detailed population and housing characteristics, by county, city, and census tract, SMSA rpt, 2551–2.339

see also under By City and By SMSA or MSA in the "Index by Categories"

Springfield, Ohio

Census of Housing, 1980: occupancy and unit characteristics, by race, Hispanic origin, and city, SMSA rpt, 2473–1.340

Census of Population and Housing, 1980: detailed population and housing characteristics, by county, city, and census tract, SMSA rpt, 2551–2.340

see also under By SMSA or MSA in the "Index by Categories"

Springfield, Oreg.

Census of Housing, 1980: occupancy and unit characteristics, by race, Hispanic origin, and city, SMSA rpt, 2473–1.149

Census of Population and Housing, 1980: detailed population and housing characteristics, by county, city, and census tract, SMSA rpt, 2551–2.149

Housing vacancy rates for single and multifamily units and mobile homes, by city and ZIP code, 1983, annual metro area rpt, 9304–21.6

see also under By SMSA or MSA in the "Index by Categories"

Sproat, Kezia

"How Do Families Fare when the Breadwinner Retires?", 6746–1.253

Squire, James L., Jr.

"Weight Frequencies for Striped Marlin Caught Off Southern California", 2162–1.401

SRI International

"Final Report of the Seattle-Denver Income Maintenance Experiment. Vol. 1: Design and Results", 4008–64.2

Sri Lanka

Sri Lanka

Agricultural and food production indexes, and production of selected commodities, by world region and country, 1974-83, annual rpt, 1524–5

Agricultural situation in 5 South Asia countries, by commodity, 1970s-1983/84 and outlook for 1984/85, annual rpt, 1524–4.11

Agricultural supply/demand, trade, and production, and socioeconomic data, by country, 1950s-77, 1528–179

AID activities and funding by project and function, FY85, and developing countries summary socioeconomic data, 1970s-83, by country, annual rpt, 9914–3

AID and other foreign assistance, and govt policy, effects on private sector dev and socioeconomic conditions, with case studies for 6 countries, 1960s-80, 9918–12

AID economic assistance to developing countries, obligations and disbursements by country, quarterly rpt, 9912–4

AID loan repayment status and terms by program and country, and status of predecessor agency loans, quarterly rpt, 9912–3

Economic, social, and political summary data, by country, 1984, annual factbook, 244–11

Economic trends in income, production, prices, employment, finances, and trade, 1984 annual rpt, 2046–4.95

Exports of US, detailed Schedule B commodities by country of destination, 1983, annual rpt, 2424–9

Exports of US, detailed Schedule E commodities by mode of transport and world area and country of destination, 1983, annual rpts, 2424–5

Food supply policies of 21 developing countries, with farm sector data, tariff income, and prices and imports of 5 grains, 1960s-81, 1528–168

Free zones in developing countries, industry financial and operating data by country, with case studies for 5 countries, 1970s-82, 9918–10

Housing finance and low-income housing projects in Asian developing countries, and activities of 2 countries, 1970s-82, annual conf proceedings, 9914–11

Imports of US, detailed Schedule A commodities by country and world area of origin, and mode of transport, 1983, annual rpts, 2424–2

Imports of US, detailed TSUSA commodities by country of origin, 1983, annual rpt, 2424–4

Loans and grants for economic and military assistance from US and intl agencies, by program and country, FY46-83, annual rpt, 9914–5

Military aid of US, arms sales, and training programs costs and budget requests by program, world region, and country, FY83-85, annual rpt, 7144–13

Military spending, arms trade, and armed forces size, with total govt spending and population, by country, 1972-82, annual rpt, 9824–1

Minerals Yearbook, 1982, Vol 3: foreign country reviews of production, trade, and policies, by commodity, annual rpt, 5604–35

Minerals Yearbook, 1982, Vol 3 preprints: foreign country review of production, trade, and policies, by commodity, annual rpt, 5604–17.87

PL 480 Title I funding and socioeconomic impacts in developing countries, with case studies for 5 countries, 1950s-81, 9918–13

Population size and growth rates, and latest available benchmark demographic data, by country, 1950-83, biennial rpt, 2324–4

Tea exports of 3 Asian countries, by country of destination, 1982-83, FAS annual rpt, 1925–15.3

see also under By Foreign Country in the "Index by Categories"

St. Christopher and Nevis

Economic, social, and political summary data, by country, 1984, annual factbook, 244–11

St. Cloud, Minn.

Census of Housing, 1980: occupancy and unit characteristics, by race, Hispanic origin, and city, SMSA rpt, 2473–1.311

Census of Population and Housing, 1980: detailed population and housing characteristics, by county, city, and census tract, SMSA rpt, 2551–2.311

see also under By SMSA or MSA in the "Index by Categories"

St. Elizabeths Hospital, D.C.

Budget of US, effects of Reagan Admin policy changes, by detailed program, FY85, annual rpt, 104–21

Mental health facilities, services, and costs in DC, and effect of St Elizabeths Hospital operations and finances transfer to DC govt, FY83, GAO rpt, 26121–72

St. Joseph, Mo.

Census of Housing, 1980: occupancy and unit characteristics, by race, Hispanic origin, and city, SMSA rpt, 2473–1.312

Census of Population and Housing, 1980: detailed population and housing characteristics, by county, city, and census tract, SMSA rpt, 2551–2.312

see also under By SMSA or MSA in the "Index by Categories"

St. Lawrence River

PCB (polychlorinated biphenyl) concentrations in Great Lakes fish, for 29 species monitored at 24 sites, selected dates 1969-77, 9208–126

Pollution control programs and discharges in Great Lakes basin, 1983 annual rpt, 14644–1

Port dev costs and financing through user fees, and shipping industry impact on local economy, by State, other area, industry, commodity, and port, 1970s-2020, hearings, 21568–34

Traffic rpt on ships, cargo and passenger volumes, and toll revenues, St Lawrence Seaway, 1981-82 and trends from 1959, annual rpt, 7744–2

Water levels of Great Lakes and connecting channels, recorded and expected, biweekly rpt, 3752–2

Water supply and quality in streams and lakes, and groundwater levels in wells, by drainage basin, 1980, annual State rpt series, 5666–12

Water supply and quality in streams and lakes, and groundwater levels in wells, by drainage basin, 1981, annual State rpt series, 5666–16

Index by Subjects and Names

Water supply and quality in streams and lakes, and groundwater levels in wells, by drainage basin, 1982, annual State rpt series, 5666–20

Water supply and quality in streams and lakes, and groundwater levels in wells, by drainage basin, 1983, annual State rpt series, 5666–10

Water supply in US and Canada, streamflow, well and reservoir levels, and dissolved solids and temperature in 6 US rivers, by station, monthly rpt, 5662–3

St. Lawrence Seaway Development Corp.

Activities and finances of St Lawrence Seaway Dev Corp, and seaway toll charges and cargo tonnage by type of cargo, 1983, annual rpt, 7744–1

Cost control proposals for Fed Govt programs and mgmt, 3-year savings by function and agency, and financial and operating data, 1960s-81, 16908–1.11

Employment at DOT, by subagency, State, and selected personnel characteristics, FY83, annual rpt, 7304–18

Great Lakes trade, by SITC 3-digit commodity, port, vessel type, world area, and country, 1982, annual rpt, 7744–3

Traffic rpt on ships, cargo and passenger volumes, and toll revenues, St Lawrence Seaway, 1981-82 and trends from 1959, annual rpt, 7744–2

St. Louis, Mo.

Auto dealer repair workers, wages, and benefits, by occupation, size of establishment, and for 24 labor market areas, Nov 1982 survey, 6787–6.202

Census of Housing, 1980: occupancy and unit characteristics, by race, Hispanic origin, and city, SMSA rpt, 2473–1.313

Census of Population and Housing, 1980: detailed population and housing characteristics, by county, city, and census tract, SMSA rpt, 2551–2.313

CPI by component for US city average, and by region, population size, and for 28 SMSAs, monthly press release, 6762–1

CPI by detailed component, for US city average, 28 SMSAs, and 4 regions by population size, monthly rpt, 6762–2

Economic indicators for Southeastern States and 5 SMSAs, Fed Reserve 8th District, quarterly rpt, 9391–15

Employment, earnings, and CPI changes in St Louis, Mo, SMSA, 1983, annual rpt, 6974–3

Employment growth rate in nonagricultural industry, for St Louis SMSA, with comparisons to US and 4 aggregated SMSAs, 1955-82, article, 9391–1.405

Fruit and vegetable shipments, and arrivals in 23 US and 5 Canada cities, by mode of transport and State or country of origin, 1983, annual rpt, 1311–4.2

Homeless population and characteristics, and temporary shelter operations, use, and user characteristics, for selected cities, various periods 1979-84, hearing, 21248–85

Hospital worker wages by sex and occupation, and benefits, for 22 MSAs, Oct 1981 survey, 6787–6.201

Housing and households detailed characteristics, and unit and neighborhood quality, by inside-outside central cities, 1980 survey, SMSA rpt, 2485–6.16

Index by Subjects and Names

State aid to education

Rail high-speed system planned from Chicago, capital and operating costs and profitability by speed class, frequency, and route, 1984 article, 9375–1.406

Repair technicians and apprentices wages and benefits, for 5 types of electrical repair shops in 19 SMSAs, Nov 1981 survey, 6787–6.197

Wages of office and plant workers, by occupation, 1984 SMSA survey rpt, 6785–11.4

Waterborne commerce of US (domestic and foreign), freight by commodity, traffic, and passengers, by port and waterway, 1982, annual rpt, 3754–3.2

see also under By City and By SMSA or MSA in the "Index by Categories"

St. Lucia

Background Notes, summary social, political, and economic data, 1984 rpt, 7006–2.53

Economic, social, and political summary data, by country, 1984, annual factbook, 244–11

Population size and growth rates, and latest available benchmark demographic data, by country, 1950-83, biennial rpt, 2324–4

see also under By Foreign Country in the "Index by Categories"

St. Paul, Minn.

Auto dealer repair workers, wages, and benefits, by occupation, size of establishment, and for 24 labor market areas, Nov 1982 survey, 6787–6.202

Census of Housing, 1980: occupancy and unit characteristics, by race, Hispanic origin, and city, SMSA rpt, 2473–1.244

Census of Population and Housing, 1980: detailed population and housing characteristics, by county, city, and census tract, SMSA rpt, 2551–2.244

CPI by component for US city average, and by region, population size, and for 28 SMSAs, monthly press release, 6762–1

CPI by detailed component, for US city average, 28 SMSAs, and 4 regions by population size, monthly rpt, 6762–2

Energy conservation devices installation, utility loan program cost effectiveness, and household participation characteristics, Minnesota study, 1980-83, 3308–72

Hospital worker wages by sex and occupation, and benefits, for 22 MSAs, Oct 1981 survey, 6787–6.201

Housing and households detailed characteristics, and unit and neighborhood quality, by inside-outside central cities, 1981 survey, SMSA rpt, 2485–6.29

Repair technicians and apprentices wages and benefits, for 5 types of electrical repair shops in 19 SMSAs, Nov 1981 survey, 6787–6.197

Wages by occupation, and benefits for office and plant workers, 1984 SMSA survey rpt, 6785–11.1

Waterborne commerce of US (domestic and foreign), freight by commodity, traffic, and passengers, by port and waterway, 1982, annual rpt, 3754–3.2, 3754–3.3

see also under By City and By SMSA or MSA in the "Index by Categories"

St. Petersburg, Fla.

Census of Housing, 1980: occupancy and unit characteristics, by race, Hispanic origin, and city, SMSA rpt, 2473–1.349

Census of Population and Housing, 1980: detailed population and housing characteristics, by county, city, and census tract, SMSA rpt, 2551–2.349

Wages by occupation, and benefits for office and plant workers, 1984 labor market area survey rpt, 6785–3.9

see also under By City and By SMSA or MSA in the "Index by Categories"

St. Vincent and The Grenadines

Economic, social, and political summary data, by country, 1984, annual factbook, 244–11

Population size and growth rates, and latest available benchmark demographic data, by country, 1950-83, biennial rpt, 2324–4

see also under By Foreign Country in the "Index by Categories"

Stacey, Helen

"In-Store ATMs: Steppingstone to POS", 9371–1.403

Stafford, Thomas H.

"Farmer Owned Share of Market Up Despite Fewer Dairy Co-ops", 1122–1.404

"Marketing Operations of Dairy Cooperatives", 1128–29

Staggers Rail Act

Railroad finances, operations, and freight rates and shares, by commodity and railroad, 1970s-82, hearings, 25268–80

Stamas, George D.

"State and Regional Employment and Unemployment in 1983", 6722–1.454

Stamford, Conn.

Carbon monoxide atmospheric concentrations and levels within buildings and along commuting and residential driving routes, for 4 cities, Jan-Mar 1981, 9198–110

Census of Housing, 1980: occupancy and unit characteristics, by race, Hispanic origin, and city, SMSA rpt, 2473–1.342

Census of Population and Housing, 1980: detailed population and housing characteristics, by county, city, and census tract, SMSA rpt, 2551–2.342

see also under By City and By SMSA or MSA in the "Index by Categories"

Standard Consolidated Areas

see Metropolitan Statistical Areas

Standard Metropolitan Statistical Areas

see Metropolitan Statistical Areas

see under By SMSA or MSA in the "Index by Categories"

see under By Urban-Rural and Metro-Nonmetro in the "Index by Categories"

Standard of living

see Cost of living

see Personal and family income

see Quality of life

Standards

see Industrial standards

see Quality control and testing

see Weights and measures

Standards Bureau

see National Bureau of Standards

Standish, Mich.

Wages of office and plant workers, by occupation, 1984 labor market area survey rpt, 6785–3.7

Stanford Research Institute

see SRI International

Stanley, Jon G.

"Species Profiles: Life Histories and Environmental Requirements of Coastal Fishes and Invertebrates (North Atlantic), White Perch", 5506–8.9, 5506–8.23

Stapleton, William V.

"Police Handling of Youth Gangs", 6068–175

Starsinic, Donald E.

"Projections of the Population of Voting Age for States: Nov. 1984", 2546–3.129

START

see Strategic Arms Reduction Talks

State aid to education

Appalachia regional dev spending, by program area and source of funds, FY82, annual rpt, 9084–1

Bilingual education programs, teachers, enrollment, and funding, selected years 1976-FY83, biennial rpt, 4804–14

Census of Govts, 1982: city govt revenues by source, expenditures by function, debt, and assets, by State and city, 2457–4

Census of Govts, 1982: county govt revenues by source, expenditures by function, debt, and assets, by State and county, 2457–3

Census of Govts, 1982: school districts revenues, expenditures, debt, and assets, by district and State, 2457–1

Census of Govts, 1982: State govt payments to local govts, by program, source of funds, level of govt, and State, with trends from 1902, 2460–3

Condition of Education, detailed data on enrollment, staff, achievement, finances, curricula, and education effects on employment, 1982-83, annual rpt, 4824–1.1

Digest of Education Statistics, detailed data on students, staff, finances, and facilities, 1982 and selected trends, annual rpt, 4824–2

Elementary and secondary education revenue by level of govt, and change in enrollment, teachers, and expenditures, by State, 1973-83, hearings, 21348–89

Elementary and secondary public school districts, schools, enrollment, staff, and finances, by State, 1981/82, annual rpt, 4834–13

Elementary and secondary public school systems revenues, by level of govt, selected years 1919/20-1981/82, press release, 4838–12

Govt expenditures for public welfare, by level of govt and type of program, selected years FY50-82, 4746–16.1

Govt finances, by level of govt and State, selected years 1929-83, annual rpt, 10044–1

Govt finances, by level of govt, State, and for large cities and counties, 1981-83, annual rpt series, 2466–2

Govt revenues by source and expenditures by function, natl income and product account, *Survey of Current Business,* monthly rpt, monthly and annual tables, 2702–1.24

State aid to education

Handicapped children public education program enrollment, staff, and funding, by handicap, age, and State, 1981/82-1982/83, annual rpt, 4944–4

- Input-output structure of US economy, detailed interindustry transactions for 85 industries, and components of final demand, 1977, article, 2702–1.421
- Local govt finances and population characteristics for cities and suburbs, by region and selected SMSA, selected years 1957-FY83, 10048–61
- Local govt spending, reliance on State aid and local taxes by type, and excise tax growth by State, selected years FY57-83, article, 10042–1.403
- Southeastern States educational finances and indicators of cost burden, for Fed Reserve 6th District States, selected years 1970-83, article, 9371–1.429
- *Statistical Abstract of US,* social, political, and economic data, 1950s-83 and trends, annual rpt, 2324–1.1
- Vocational Education Research Natl Center funding, by purpose and source, selected years 1978-84, GAO rpt, 26121–79

see also State aid to higher education

State aid to higher education

- Agricultural research funding from Fed Govt and States, by region, State, and outlying area, FY78-82, GAO rpt, 26113–111
- Botany and other plant science R&D at higher education instns, funding by source, grad students, and staff, 1983, 9626–2.143
- Census of Govts, 1982: school districts revenues, expenditures, debt, and assets, by district and State, 2457–1
- Census of Govts, 1982: State govt payments to local govts, by program, source of funds, level of govt, and State, with trends from 1902, 2460–3
- *Condition of Education,* detailed data on enrollment, staff, achievement, finances, curricula, and education effects on employment, 1982-83, annual rpt, 4824–1.2
- Govt finances, by level of govt, State, and for large cities and counties, 1981-83, annual rpt series, 2466–2
- R&D expenditures by higher education instns and federally funded centers, by field, source of funds, instn, and State, FY82, annual rpt, 9627–13
- Small business mgmt counseling by university centers, costs, funding, and businesses served by industry, with detail for 2 States, 1980-83, hearing, 25728–36
- Student aid Federal programs funding and participation, by instn type and control, State, and outlying area, with student loan defaults and collections, FY82, annual rpt, 4804–28
- Student aid need-based program funding, and State Student Incentive Grant funding, recipients, and average income and award, by State, FY67-82, GAO rpt, 26121–69

State aid to local areas

- Appalachia regional dev spending, by program area and source of funds, FY82, annual rpt, 9084–1
- Boston, Mass, govt budget and impact of reduced local revenue and Fed Govt aid, and other devs, FY80-86, article, 9373–1.406

Bus intercity service funding of State govts, and impacts of regulatory reform on bus industry, by State, 1970s-83, 14828–2.2

- Census of Govts, 1982: city govt revenues by source, expenditures by function, debt, and assets, by State and city, 2457–4
- Census of Govts, 1982: county govt revenues by source, expenditures by function, debt, and assets, by State and county, 2457–3
- Census of Govts, 1982: State govt payments to local govts, by program, source of funds, level of govt, and State, with trends from 1902, 2460–3
- Community Dev Block Grants to small cities, State admin, project characteristics, and assessments of local officials, 1982, 5188–106
- Forestry activities on State and private lands, Fed Govt and State funding by project and State, FY83, annual tables, 1204–32
- Govt finances, by level of govt and State, selected years 1929-83, annual rpt, 10044–1
- Govt finances, by level of govt, State, and for large cities and counties, 1981-83, annual rpt series, 2466–2
- Hwy receipts by source, and expenditures by function, by level of govt and State, 1983, annual rpt, 7554–1.4
- Jail capacities, conditions, expenditures, and services, and socioeconomic and other characteristics of inmates, various dates 1976-82, 10048–59
- Local govt finances and population characteristics for cities and suburbs, by region and selected SMSA, selected years 1957-FY83, 10048–61
- Local govt spending, reliance on State aid and local taxes by type, and excise tax growth by State, selected years FY57-83, article, 10042–1.403
- Public defender systems, costs, cases, and expenditures by level of govt and State, with system characteristics and lawyer fee ranges, 1981, 6066–19.8
- Public opinion on taxes, tax policy, and intergovtl relations, 1972-84 surveys, annual rpt, 10044–2
- Regulatory growth of Fed Govt effect on local compliance costs and funding, local officials assessment, and comparisons to State govt regulations, 1970s-82 with trends from 1900, 10048–58
- Transit system deficits, effect of cost and service increases and ridership and fare decreases, and govt aid and system operating ratios, 1970-80, 7308–184
- Transit systems, expenditures by level of govt, and revenues by source, with distribution of commuter trips by mode of transport, 1980-82, article, 10042–1.404

State and local employees

- Assaults, murders, and other deaths of law enforcement officers, by circumstances, level of govt, agency, victim and offender characteristics, and location, 1983, annual rpt, 6224–3
- Census of Govts, 1982: employment, payrolls, and average earnings, by function, level of govt, State, county, population size, and inside-outside SMSAs, 2455–2

Index by Subjects and Names

- Census of Govts, 1982: local govt employment by function, payroll, and average earnings, for individual counties, cities, and school and special districts, 2455–1
- Census of Population and Housing, 1980: detailed population and housing characteristics, by county, city, and census tract, State and SMSA rpt series, 2551–2
- Census of Population, 1980: detailed socioeconomic and demographic characteristics, by age, sex, race, Hispanic origin, occupation, and industry, State rpt series, 2531–4
- Census of Population, 1980: detailed socioeconomic characteristics, by county, city, and inside-outside SMSAs and central cities, State rpt series, 2531–3
- City govt fiscal condition, revenue sharing program allocations, and responses to program cuts, FY81-83, surveys, hearings, 25408–86
- Computer specialists sociodemographic, educational, and employment characteristics, and Fed Govt support by agency, 1978, biennial Current Population Rpt, 2546–2.124
- *County and City Data Book,* detailed socioeconomic and demographic data for States, counties, and cities, selected years 1976-82, 2328–1
- Crime and criminal justice data, including justice expenditures and employment by level of govt, 1970s-82 with some trends from 1875, 6068–174
- Criminal justice employment by job category and level of govt, and arrests for serious crimes in 5 States by disposition, Dec 1983 rpt, 6062–2.401
- DC employees workers compensation under Fed Govt-administered program, cases and dispositions, FY79-83, annual compilation, 6504–5
- Disability (short-term) earnings lost, insurance benefits, sick leave, and work days lost by sex, by type of worker, 1948-81, article, 4742–1.417
- Drug abuse situation, prevention and treatment programs, law enforcement, funding needs, and Fed Govt role, attitudes of State and local officials, 1983 survey, 21968–27
- Employment and earnings, by level of govt and State, selected years 1929-82, annual rpt, 10044–1.5
- Employment and earnings, detailed data, monthly rpt, 6742–2.5
- Employment and payroll, by function and level of govt, 1983, annual rpt series, 2466–1
- Employment and payrolls of State and local govts, monthly rpt, 6742–4
- Employment and wages of workers covered by State unemployment insurance laws and Fed Govt unemployment compensation, by SIC 4-digit industry and State, 1982, annual rpt, 6744–16
- Employment, earnings, and hours, by level and branch of govt, and function, monthly 1977-Feb 1984, annual update, 6744–4
- Employment, earnings, and hours, by selected SIC 1- to 4-digit industry, State, and for 278 major labor areas, 1939-83, annual rpt, 6744–5

Index by Subjects and Names

State and local employees pay

Employment of Federal and State/local workers, monthly press release, 6742–5

Employment situation, earnings, hours, and other BLS economic indicators, transcripts of BLS Commissioner's monthly testimony, periodic rpt, 23846–4

Engineers sociodemographic, educational, and employment characteristics, and Federal support by agency, 1978, Current Population Rpt, 2546–2.121

Health professionals supply and education, by occupation, demographic and professional characteristics, and location, 1950s-83 and projected to 2000, biennial rpt, 4114–8

Marijuana cultivation control activity of State law enforcement agencies, and aid from Fed Govt and Natl Guard, 1983 survey, GAO rpt, 26119–64

Meat and poultry inspection activities and personnel of Federal, State, and foreign govts, FY83, annual rpt, 1374–1

Natural gas and hazardous liquid pipelines accidents and casualties, and DOT and State govt safety activities, 1982, annual rpt, 7304–5

Occupational health and safety State govt program staffing requirements, and occupational injury data, for selected States, selected years 1973-81, hearings, 21348–88

Occupational Outlook Handbook, 1984-85 biennial rpt, 6744–1

Occupational Safety and Health Admin enforcement activities and funding, and State programs and staff, 1982, annual rpt, 6604–2.1

Pension plans for public employees, benefits and beneficiaries by eligibility reason, level of govt, and Federal plan, selected years 1954-80, article, 4742–1.403

Pension systems of State and local govts finances, membership, beneficiaries, and benefits, by system, 1982-83, annual rpt, 2466–2.4

Productivity measurement of State and local govt, with background data and output indexes for 7 govt services, various periods 1955-82, 6728–27

Public health labs of States, personnel, finances, workloads, and other activities, by State, FY82, annual rpt, 4204–8

Radiation control program activities, State and local expenditures, personnel, and NRC licenses, by State, FY80-82, annual rpt, 4064–3

Radiological health personnel of State and local govts, FY77-82, biennial rpt, 3004–11

Railroad accidents, casualties, and property damage, Fed Railroad Admin activities, and safety inspectors by State, 1982, annual rpt, 7604–12

Recreation fees at State outdoor facilities, visits, revenue, costs, and employee salaries, by State, 1982/83, annual rpt, 5544–14.4

Science and engineering grads of 1980-81, employment characteristics or grad enrollment, by degree level, field, sex, and race, 1982, 9627–25

Scientists and engineers in nuclear-related industry, by field and sector, 1981 and 1983, 3006–8.2

Southwestern States nonagricultural employment, including Federal and State/local govts, monthly rpt, 6962–2

Statistical Abstract of US, social, political, and economic data, 1950s-83 and trends, annual rpt, 2324–1.2

Traffic accidents and casualties detailed direct and indirect costs, by characteristics of persons and vehicles involved, 1979-80, 7768–80

Transit system financial and operating data, by mode, function, fleet size, and individual system, FY82, annual rpt, 7884–4

Transit system mgmt training funded by Urban Mass Transportation Admin, participant characteristics and career impact, 1970-79, 7888–60

Transit system operations, tax burden related to ridership, fares, and govt funding, for selected States and cities, 1950s-82, reprint, 7888–59

Unemployment insurance benefits and claims, by program, Monthly Labor Review, 6722–1.4

Vocational rehabilitation State agency expenditures, caseloads, rehabilitations, and staff, under Section 110 of the Rehabilitation Act, by State, FY82, annual rpt, 4944–9

see also Civil service system
see also Fire departments
see also Labor-management relations in government
see also Officials
see also Police
see also State and local employees pay
see also Teachers

State and local employees pay

AFDC State admin agencies performance measures, caseloads, payments, and costs, by State, FY81, annual rpt, 4704–10

Census of Govts, 1982: city govt revenues by source, expenditures by function, debt, and assets, by State and city, 2457–4

Census of Govts, 1982: county govt revenues by source, expenditures by function, debt, and assets, by State and county, 2457–3

Census of Govts, 1982: employment, payrolls, and average earnings, by function, level of govt, State, county, population size, and inside-outside SMSAs, 2455–2

Census of Govts, 1982: local govt employment by function, payroll, and average earnings, for individual counties, cities, and school and special districts, 2455–1

Census of Govts, 1982: school districts revenues, expenditures, debt, and assets, by district and State, 2457–1

Collective bargaining wage and benefit changes, and workers affected, 1979-84, semiannual press release, 6782–6

Collective bargaining wage and compensation changes, periodic article, 6782–1

County and City Data Book, detailed socioeconomic and demographic data for States, counties, and cities, selected years 1976-82, 2328–1

Crime and criminal justice data, including justice expenditures and employment by level of govt, 1970s-82 with some trends from 1875, 6068–174

Disability (short-term) earnings lost, insurance benefits, sick leave, and work days lost by sex, by type of worker, 1948-81, article, 4742–1.417

Earnings by industry div, and personal income per capita and by source, by State, MSA, and county, 1977-82, annual regional rpts, 2704–2

Earnings by major industry group, and personal income per capita and by source, by region and State, 1929-82, 2708–40

Employment and earnings, by level of govt and State, selected years 1929-82, annual rpt, 10044–1.5

Employment and payroll, by function and level of govt, 1983, annual rpt series, 2466–1

Employment and payrolls of State and local govts, monthly rpt, 6742–4

Employment and wages of workers covered by State unemployment insurance laws and Fed Govt unemployment compensation, by SIC 4-digit industry and State, 1982, annual rpt, 6744–16

Employment Cost Index, by occupation and industry div, quarterly rpt, 6782–5

Employment, earnings, and hours, by level and branch of govt, and function, monthly 1977-Feb 1984, annual update, 6744–4

Employment situation, earnings, hours, and other BLS economic indicators, transcripts of BLS Commissioner's monthly testimony, periodic rpt, 23846–4

Govt finances, by level of govt, State, and for large cities and counties, 1981-83, annual rpt series, 2466–2

Occupational Outlook Handbook, 1984-85 biennial rpt, 6744–1

Police dept costs and operations, patrol car use, investigations, arrests, and recruit training, by city population size, 1982, 6066–21.1

Public health labs of States, pay scales and job requirements by occupation and State, FY81-83, annual rpt, 4204–7

Radiation control program activities, State and local expenditures, personnel, and NRC licenses, by State, FY80-82, annual rpt, 4064–3

Recreation fees at State outdoor facilities, visits, revenue, costs, and employee salaries, by State, 1982/83, annual rpt, 5544–14.4

Science and engineering grads of 1980-81, employment characteristics or grad enrollment, by degree level, field, sex, and race, 1982, 9627–25

Statistical Abstract of US, social, political, and economic data, 1950s-83 and trends, annual rpt, 2324–1.2

Teachers average salary by State, 1983 and percent change from 1973, hearings, 21348–89

Teachers salaries in schools and colleges by State, 1982/83, and school employees health insurance plans in 7 cities, as of 1980, hearing, 21788–136

Transit system financial and operating data, by mode, function, fleet size, and individual system, FY82, annual rpt, 7884–4

Transit system operations, tax burden related to ridership, fares, and govt funding, for selected States and cities, 1950s-82, reprint, 7888–59

State and local employees pay

see also Civil service pensions

State and local taxes

- Boston, Mass, govt budget and impact of reduced local revenue and Fed Govt aid, and other devs, FY80-86, article, 9373–1.406
- Budget of US, CBO analysis of revenue and spending alternatives and projections of economic indicators, FY85-89, annual rpt, 26304–3.3
- Census of Govts, 1982: city govt revenues by source, expenditures by function, debt, and assets, by State and city, 2457–4
- Census of Govts, 1982: county govt revenues by source, expenditures by function, debt, and assets, by State and county, 2457–3
- Census of Govts, 1982: properties, govt-assessed value, sales, and tax rates, by property type, State, SMSA, county, and city, 2453–1
- Census of Govts, 1982: school districts revenues, expenditures, debt, and assets, by district and State, 2457–1
- Census of Govts, 1982: State govt payments to local govts, by program, source of funds, level of govt, and State, with trends from 1902, 2460–3
- Central cities and suburbs population and employment, effect of region, neighborhood, population, and labor characteristics, 1970-80, technical paper, 9387–8.89
- Child support overdue payments deducted from income tax refunds and unemployment benefits, by State, FY83, annual rpt, 4004–16.3
- Coal production, mining employment, exports, and finances, by coal district, 1982, 3008–97
- *County and City Data Book,* detailed socioeconomic and demographic data for States, counties, and cities, selected years 1976-82, 2328–1
- Economic and demographic trends for IRS regions, districts, and service centers, 1972-82 and projected to 1990, annual rpt, 8304–8
- Fed Govt civilian and military employee pay, withholdings by type, and income, and special military compensation by type and service branch, 1982-83, GAO rpt, 26123–65
- Financial and business statistics, historic trends, 1984 annual chartbook, 9364–2.9
- Georgia small businesses, effect of mgmt counseling on sales, employment, profits, and taxes paid, 1980-81, hearing, 25728–36
- Govt finances, by level of govt and State, selected years 1929-83, annual rpt, 10044–1
- Govt finances, by level of govt, State, and for large cities and counties, 1981-83, annual rpt series, 2466–2
- Govt revenue and expenditures, surplus/deficit, and tax capacity and effort indexes, for US and 7 western States, selected years 1967-82, article, 9381–1.403
- Govt revenue by source and expenditures by function, for State and local govts, 1980-83, article, 2702–1.436
- Govt revenues by source and expenditures by type, for State and local govts, 1978-83, annual article, 2702–1.405

Govt tax revenues, by level of govt, type of tax, State, and selected counties, quarterly rpt, 2462–3

- Hazardous waste generation and disposal taxes in 3 States, and effects on waste mgmt, 1981-83, with assessment of 3 Fed Govt tax proposals, GAO rpt, 26113–124
- Hwy and urban transit systems financing methods of govts and private sector, with case studies for selected metro areas, series, 7556–7
- Hwy receipts by source, and expenditures by function, by level of govt and State, 1983, annual rpt, 7554–1.3, 7554–1.4
- Income (household) before and after taxes, by socioeconomic characteristics, type of tax paid, and region, 1981, Current Population Rpt, 2546–2.118
- Income (household) before and after taxes, by socioeconomic characteristics, type of tax paid, and region, 1982, annual Current Population Rpt, 2546–2.122
- Income tax returns of elderly, by income statement and tax item and income level, 1981 with trends from 1977, article, 8302–2.412
- Income tax returns of individuals, detailed data, 1982, annual rpt, 8304–2
- Local govt finances and population characteristics for cities and suburbs, by region and selected SMSA, selected years 1957-FY83, 10048–61
- Local govt spending, reliance on State aid and local taxes by type, and excise tax growth by State, selected years FY57-83, article, 10042–1.403
- Minerals production, State severance tax and royalty revenue by selected State, selected years FY73-83, article, 9375–1.407
- Motor fuel State tax provisions, motor vehicle registration fees, and disposition of receipts, by State, as of Jan 1984, biennial rpt, 7554–37
- Multinatl and multistate corporations income under alternative State income tax treatment methods, by major industry, 1977, article, 9373–1.412
- North Central States farm investments, effective rates of Federal/State income and State/local property taxes, by category of structure and equipment and State, 1981-82, 1548–237
- Public lands, Fed Govt payments to local govts in lieu of property taxes by State, FY84, annual press release, 5724–9
- Public opinion on taxes, tax policy, and intergovtl relations, 1972-84 surveys, annual rpt, 10044–2
- Smoking and tobacco marketing legislation introduced and enacted in State legislatures, by State, 1982, annual rpt, 4204–13
- Tax burden for average family by income level and selected city, and tax rates by selected jurisdiction, by type of tax, 1982, 10046–8.2
- Tax expenditures, Fed Govt revenues foregone through income tax deductions and exclusions by type, and effect of Deficit Reduction Act, FY84-89, annual rpt, 21784–10
- Transit system financial and operating data, by mode, function, fleet size, and individual system, FY82, annual rpt, 7884–4

Index by Subjects and Names

- Transit system operations, tax burden related to ridership, fares, and govt funding, for selected States and cities, 1950s-82, reprint, 7888–59
- Transportation finances, operations, vehicles, equipment, accidents, and energy use, by mode of transport, 1955-84, annual rpt, 7304–2
- Transportation revenues by source and expenditures, by level of govt and mode of transport, and Fed Govt aid by type, FY77-82, 7308–185
- Urban area economic distress index and components, for 153 cities, 1975 and 1980, article, 9373–1.413
- Urban Dev Action Grant awards, private and public investment, and jobs, housing units, and taxes generated, by city and project, FY83, annual rpt, 5124–5
- Urban Dev Action Grant awards to local areas, preliminary approvals, with project descriptions, private investment, and jobs and taxes to be created, by city, quarterly press release series, 5002–7
- Urban Dev Action Grant program effectiveness, and participation of small cities by State, 1978-82, GAO rpt, 26113–118
- Virgin Islands govt fiscal condition, FY81, annual rpt, 5304–10
- *see also* Excise tax
- *see also* Property tax
- *see also* Revenue sharing
- *see also* Sales tax
- *see also* Severance taxes

State College, Pa.

- Census of Housing, 1980: occupancy and unit characteristics, by race, Hispanic origin, and city, SMSA rpt, 2473–1.343
- Census of Population and Housing, 1980: detailed population and housing characteristics, by county, city, and census tract, SMSA rpt, 2551–2.343
- *see also* under By SMSA or MSA in the alternative "Index by Categories"

State courts

- Case filings in State trial courts by case type, and appellate court filings and dispositions by court type, by State, 1978-83, periodic rpt, 6062–2.409
- Marijuana cultivation control activity of State law enforcement agencies, and aid from Fed Govt and Natl Guard, 1983 survey, GAO rpt, 26119–64
- New Jersey administrative law cases, disposition, and processing time, by govt agency, selected years FY80-84, hearings, 25528–96
- US Attorneys civil and criminal case processing in district, appellate, and State courts, by district, FY83, annual rpt, 6004–2
- Wiretapping authorizations by offense, costs, persons involved, arrests, trials, and convictions, 1983, annual rpt, 18204–7

State Department

see Department of State

State government

- AFDC programs and provisions of States under Social Security Act, FY82, annual rpt, 4704–9
- AFDC State admin agencies performance measures, caseloads, payments, and costs, by State, FY81, annual rpt, 4704–10

Index by Subjects and Names

State government

Air pollution control programs, emissions standards dev, monitoring, and enforcement, 1982, annual rpt, 9194–4

Airport financing by source, bond issues by region, and airport operations, by airport and operator type, FY75-83 and projected to FY93, 26306–6.75

Arts and humanities funding, by source and State, FY82-83 with trends from FY66, 21408–69

Community services block grants by type of service provider, State mgmt, and opinions of officials and groups involved, for 13 States, FY81-83, GAO rpt, 26121–84

Construction put in place, value of new public and private structures, by type, monthly rpt, 2382–4

Electric utilities privately owned, sales revenues by company and consuming sector, 1982, annual rpt, 3164–23

Energy conservation programs of State govts, Fed Govt financial and technical aid, and reported energy savings, by State, 1983, annual rpt, 3304–1

Farm business legal organization, finances, operations, tax rates, and State laws restricting farm corporations, 1960s-82, 1548–233

Financial and business statistics, historic trends, 1984 annual chartbook, 9364–2.9

Flow-of-funds accounts, assets and liabilities by type and economic sector, year-end outstandings, 1960-83, annual rpt, 9364–3

Flow-of-funds accounts savings, investments, and credit statements, quarterly rpt, 9365–3.3

Food aid programs of Fed Govt and others, funding, participant characteristics, and nutrition and poverty data, 1970s-83, 028–20

Govt expenditures for social welfare by program and level of govt, and private expenditures for health care, selected years FY50-82, annual article, 4742–1.425

Govt finances, by level of govt and State, selected years 1929-83, annual rpt, 10044–1

Govt finances, by level of govt, State, and for large cities and counties, 1981-83, annual rpt series, 2466–2

Govt finances, policy, and intergovtl relations of Federal, State, and local govts, series, 10046–8

Govt finances, quarterly chartbook, 9362–2.4

Govt revenue and expenditures, surplus/deficit, and tax capacity and effort indexes, for US and 7 western States, selected years 1967-82, article, 9381–1.403

Govt revenue and spending growth rates, and bond offerings by purpose, for State and local govts, various periods 1948-84, article, 9362–1.408

Govt revenue by source and expenditures by function, for State and local govts, 1980-83, article, 2702–1.436

Govt revenues and expenditures, State and local govt, selected years FY27-82, annual rpt, 204–1.6

Govt revenues by source and expenditures by function, natl income and product account, *Survey of Current Business,* monthly rpt, 2702–1.21, 2702–1.24

Govt revenues by source and expenditures by type, for State and local govts, 1978-83, annual article, 2702–1.405

Hwy Statistics, detailed data on traffic, govt finances, fuel use, vehicles, driver licenses, and hwy characteristics, by State, 1983, annual rpt, 7554–1

Input-output structure of US economy, detailed interindustry transactions for 85 industries, and components of final demand, 1977, article, 2702–1.421

Input-output structure of US economy, detailed interindustry transactions for 537 industries, and components of final demand, 1977 benchmark data, 2708–17

Legal fees awarded private parties in cases against Federal, State, and local govts, by case, selected years 1977-83, 6008–19

Marijuana cultivation control activity of State law enforcement agencies, and aid from Fed Govt and Natl Guard, 1983 survey, GAO rpt, 26119–64

Maternal and child health, State govt spending and admin of Fed Govt block grants, by program for 13 States, 1981-83, GAO rpt, 26121–70

Mental health and drug and alcohol abuse treatment funding of State govts, and admin of Fed Govt block grants, for 13 States, FY80-84, GAO rpt, 26121–87

Mortgage loan activity, by type of lender, loan, and mortgaged property, monthly rpt, 5142–18

Mortgage loan transactions and holdings of State and local govt retirement funds and credit agencies, by type of property and loan, quarterly rpt, 5142–30

New England State govts revenues, expenditures, and year-end closing balances, for 6 States, FY83 and projected FY84, article, 9373–2.401

New Jersey and Maryland prison capacity and population, and New Jersey construction costs by type and funding source, by facility, 1977-82 and projected to 1988, 25528–99

Nuclear attack civil defense plans of Fed Emergency Mgmt Agency, funding and operations by component, FY81-84 and projected FY85-89, GAO rpt, 26123–61

Pollution abatement capital and operating costs under Clean Air and Water Acts, for govts and selected industries, various periods 1970-2000, annual rpt, 9184–11

Preventive health services block grants of Fed Govt, State funding by program, and opinions on State program admin, for 13 States, FY81-84, GAO rpt, 26121–88

Procurement of goods and services, and budget surplus and deficit, by level of govt, *Business Conditions Digest,* historical supplement and methodology, 1947-82, 2708–31

Procurement of goods and services by level of govt, *Business Conditions Digest,* monthly rpt, 2702–3.5

Productivity measurement of State and local govt, with background data and output indexes for 7 govt services, various periods 1955-82, 6728–27

Public health labs of States, personnel, finances, workloads, and other activities, by State, FY82, annual rpt, 4204–8

Public welfare expenditures by level of govt and program type, selected years FY50-82, 4746–16.1

Public welfare programs evaluation, and research and statistical projects and techniques, 1983 conf papers, 4704–11

R&D Fed Govt funding, by agency and performer, FY83-84, 9626–2.132

R&D Fed Govt funding for all performers, by field and supporting agency, selected years FY60-84, annual rpt, 9627–20

Radiation control program activities, State and local expenditures, personnel, and NRC licenses, by State, FY80-82, annual rpt, 4064–3

Real estate broker govt certification requirements, licenses, and exam results, by State and Canada Province, 1977-78, 9408–48

Retirement systems of State and local govts, cash and security holdings and finances, quarterly rpt, 2462–2

Revenue sharing payments to States, local govts, Indian tribes, and Alaska Native villages, and entitlement computation data, FY84, series, 8066–1

Runaway and other homeless youth programs, funding by source, activities, and participant characteristics, FY82, annual rpt, 4604–3

Security issues of State and local govts and corporations, 1982, annual rpt, 9364–5.5

Social service spending of State govts by service type and funding source, and admin of Fed Govt block grants, for 13 States, selected years FY80-84, GAO rpt, 26121–76

Statistical Abstract of US, social, political, and economic data, 1950s-83 and trends, annual rpt, 2324–1.2

Transit system operations, tax burden related to ridership, fares, and govt funding, for selected States and cities, 1950s-82, reprint, 7888–59

Transit systems, expenditures by level of govt, and revenues by source, with distribution of commuter trips by mode of transport, 1980-82, article, 10042–1.404

Unemployment compensation payments of State govts, by State, FY83, annual rpt, 2464–2

Unemployment insurance State govt program admin, quality appraisal results, FY84, annual rpt, 6404–16

Veterans medical and nursing home care in State homes, and construction projects, by district and facility, monthly rpt, 9922–5

Workers compensation benefits under State programs, by benefit type, insurance source, and State, and Fed Govt black lung program payments, 1980-82, article, 4742–1.424

Workers compensation coverage by State, benefits, degree of disability, employer costs, and insurance industry finances, 1939-80, article, 4742–1.414

Youth social services of State govts, coordinating agencies activities, admin, membership, and funding sources, survey, 1984 rpt, 6068–182

see also Census of Governments

see also Federal aid to States

see also Federal-State relations

see also State aid to education

see also State aid to higher education

see also State aid to local areas

see also State and local employees

State government

see also State and local employees pay
see also State and local taxes
see also State courts
see also State legislatures
see also State-local relations
see also State parks
see also State police
see also under By State in the "Index by Categories"
see also under names of individual States

State legislatures

Alcohol-related and total traffic deaths, and drunk driver license revocations and other deterrence measures in selected States, 1980-82, 9618–10

Smoking and tobacco marketing legislation introduced and enacted in State legislatures, by State, 1982, annual rpt, 4204–13

State-local relations

Community Dev Block Grants to small cities, State admin, project characteristics, and assessments of local officials, 1982, 5188–106

Medicaid medical vendor payment expenditures of Federal, State, and local govt, with Medicare and Medicaid program data, various periods 1966-82, annual rpt, 4654–1

Regulatory growth of Fed Govt effect on local compliance costs and funding, local officials assessment, and comparisons to State govt regulations, 1970s-82 with trends from 1900, 10048–58

see also State aid to local areas

State parks

Recreation fees at State outdoor facilities, visits, revenue, costs, and employee salaries, by State, 1982/83, annual rpt, 5544–14.4

State police

Employment of State and local law enforcement personnel and officers, by sex, population size, census div, and jurisdiction, 1983, annual rpt, 6224–2.3

Govt census, 1982: employment, payrolls, and average earnings, by function, level of govt, State, county, population size, and inside-outside SMSAs, 2455–2

Govt expenditures for police services, by level of govt, 1981, 6066–20.8

Hwy speeding and accident rates related to use of marked and unmarked New York State patrol cars, 1977-79, article, 7762–9.403

State prisons

see Correctional institutions

State taxation

see State and local taxes

States

see terms beginning with State
see under By State in the "Index by Categories"
see under names of individual States

States' rights

see Federal-State relations

States, William

"Corporate Foreign Tax Credit, 1980: An Industry Focus", 8302–2.415

Statistical programs and activities

BLS activities and terms of commissioners, and related historical and economic events, 1884-1983, article, 6722–1.467

BLS major statistical and analytical programs and publications, annual listing, suspended, 6704–1

BLS measures of unemployment, labor productivity, and CPI, effects of undisclosed economic activity, with illustrative data, 1958-79, article, 6722–1.401

BLS wage statistics programs dev, 1884-1984, narrative article, 6722–1.466

Cancer Natl Inst epidemiology and biometry activities, staff, budget, and contract awards by project and recipient instn, FY83, annual rpt, 4474–29

Census Bur activities, publications, and user services, monthly rpt, 2302–3

Census Bur data collection methodology, programs, and measurement techniques, technical paper series, 2626–2

Census Bur data coverage and availability for 1982 economic censuses and related statistics, 1984 guide, 2308–5

Census Bur data coverage policy for agriculture and economic censuses, and Federal agency data use, 1984 GAO narrative rpt, 26125–26

Census Bur publications data coverage and availability, 1984 annual listing, 2304–2

Census Bur publications, data coverage, and suggested uses, series, 2326–7

Census of Agriculture, 1982: data coverage and availability for agriculture census and related statistics, 1984 guide, 2308–55

Census of Population and Housing, 1980: data coverage, availability, and uses for urban and transportation planning, 1984 guide, 7558–101

Commerce Dept budgets and permanent staff positions appropriated, by activity, FY84-85, annual rpt, 2004–6

CPI planned 1987 revisions to urban areas sampled and index publication schedule, 1984 press release, 6888–29

Crime and criminal justice research sponsored by Natl Inst of Justice, summary rpt series, 6066–20

Crime and criminal justice statistics analysis, methodology, and use in courts, 1983 biennial conf proceedings, 6064–20

Drugs nonmedical use and effects, research compilations and summaries, bibls, and survey instruments, series, 4496–1

Earnings (real spendable) measures, BLS weekly series and proposed hourly series and results, 1948-81, article, 6722–1.468

Economic Analysis Bur specialized and preliminary economic research, staff paper series, 2706–5

Economic and population time series data frequently used in statistical demand analyses, 1941-1982, annual rpt, 1544–21

Economic Research Service activities, funding, and staff in DC and other locations, by detailed branch and section, FY83, annual rpt, 1504–7

Economic Research Service activities, funding, and staff in DC and other locations, by detailed branch and section, FY84, annual rpt, 1504–6

Economic time series of Fed Govt, content, design, and methodology, research rpt and conf proceedings series, 2626–7

Education data, current natl estimates from Fast Response Survey System, series, 4826–1

Employment and sample characteristics of 82 SIC 3- to 4-digit service-producing industries added to BLS survey, as of Mar 1984, article, 6742–2.410

Index by Subjects and Names

Energy Info Admin data collection and analysis activities, Jan 1982-Sept 1983, GAO annual rpt, 26104–14

Energy Info Admin natural gas supply estimates based on alternative data sources, for production and trade by State, and underground storage changes, 1980-81, 3008–90

Energy Info Admin surveys, data analysis models, and publications, 1983, annual rpt, 3164–29

Energy prices and expenditures for fuels and electricity, by consuming sector, State, and fuel type, 1970-81, annual rpt, 3164–64

Energy use, by economic sector, State, census div, and detailed energy resource, 1960-82, State Energy Data System annual rpt, 3164–39

Fed Govt expenditures in States and local areas, Census Bur data collection, limitation, contributing agency costs, and opinions of congressional users, 1984 GAO rpt, 26111–20

Fed Govt principal statistical programs, funding by subject and agency, FY74-85, annual rpt, 104–10

Fed Govt programs and mgmt cost control proposals, 3-year savings by function and agency, and financial and operating data, 1960s-81, 16908–1

Fed Govt statistical agencies appropriations and missions, and effect of budget cuts on principal programs, FY80-84, GAO rpt, 26125–28

Fed Govt statistical policies relating to technical operation of programs, methodology, and use of Federal data, working paper series, 106–4

Fed Reserve, concordance of data in monthly *Federal Reserve Bulletin* and *Annual Statistical Digest,* 1983, annual rpt, 9364–8

Fed Reserve System, statistical series additions and revisions, monthly rpt with articles, 9362–1

Health care expenditures, methodology of natl survey of households, physicians, health insurance firms, and employers, 1977-79, series, 4186–4

Health survey design and research methods, 1982 biennial conf proceedings, 4184–1

HHS health data projects and systems, by subagency, FY83-84, annual inventory, 4044–3

HHS nutrition research and monitoring activities, 1984 narrative article, 4102–1.454

IRS and other Fed Govt admin record research methods, data collection and use, 1984 annual conf papers, 8304–17

IRS and other Fed Govt admin record research methods, data collection and use, 1984 compilation of papers, 8308–28

Mental health facilities needs assessment and program evaluation for small areas, methodology, use of census data, analysis, and sample data, series, 4506–8

Mental health statistics, natl reporting program historical overview, 1840-1983, narrative rpt, 4508–5

Milk of manufacturing grade, Minnesota-Wisconsin price series description and data, 1981-83, article, 1317–4.404

Index by Subjects and Names

Stockbrokers

Public Health Service activities, and funding by function and subagency, FY83, annual rpt, 4044–2

Public welfare programs evaluation, and research and statistical projects and techniques, 1983 conf papers, 4704–11

R&D Fed Govt facilities and services available for private sector use, by field of science, 1984 biennial listing, 2224–4

Revenue sharing and other Fed Govt grant program alternative allocations, with city govt finances and responses to program cuts, FY79-83, hearings, 25408–86

Social security programs and recipient characteristics, *Research and Statistics Notes,* series, 4746–16

SSA research projects, narrative summary, FY84-86, annual rpt, 4744–11

Visual impairment survey methodology and results by age, in 3 SMSAs, Aug 1981-Dec 1982, 4478–147

see also Accounting and auditing

see also Bibliographies

see also Classifications

see also Computer data file guides

see also Consumer surveys

see also Economic and econometric models

see also Information storage and retrieval systems

see also Methodology

see also Opinion and attitude surveys

see also Seasonal adjustment factors

see also Statisticians

see also under names of individual surveys (listed under Surveys)

Statistical Reporting Service

Activities and programs of USDA, by subagency, FY83, annual rpt, 1004–3

Data collection programs, missions, and appropriations of Fed Govt statistical agencies, and effect of budget cuts, FY80-84, GAO rpt, 26125–28

Fraud and abuse in USDA programs, audits and investigations, 2nd half FY84, semiannual rpt, 1002–4

see also Crop Reporting Board

Statisticians

Census of Population, 1980: detailed socioeconomic and demographic characteristics, by age, sex, race, Hispanic origin, occupation, and industry, State rpt series, 2531–4

Census of Population, 1980: labor force, by sex, detailed occupation, and region, with comparison to 1970 census, supplementary rpt, 2535–1.12

Crime and criminal justice statistics analysis, methodology, and use in courts, 1983 biennial conf proceedings, 6064–20

Occupational Outlook Handbook, 1984-85 biennial rpt, 6744–1

R&D-employed scientists and engineers salaries by degree, type of establishment, age, experience, and field, 1984, annual rpt, 3004–1

R&D expenditures by source, and scientists education and employment, detailed data by field, selected years 1953-84, annual rpt, 9624–18

Science and engineering doctoral degree recipients, by field, sex, race, age, citizenship, postgrad employment and study status, State, and instn, 1960-82, 9626–6.16

Science and engineering grad enrollment, fields of study, financial support, and other student and instn characteristics, 1975-82, annual survey, 9627–7

Science and engineering grads of 1980-81, employment characteristics or grad enrollment, by degree level, field, sex, and race, 1982, 9627–25

Scientists, engineers, and technicians employed in private industry, by occupation and industry group, 1980-81, biennial rpt, 9627–23

Status of forces agreements

see Strategic Arms Limitation Treaties

see Strategic Arms Reduction Talks

Steadman, Henry J.

"Crime and Mental Disorder", 6066–20.5

Steel industry

see Iron and steel industry

Steele, Christine E.

"Full-Time Federal Civilian Employment in White- and Blue-Collar Occupations as of Oct. 31, 1983", 9842–1.405

Steinberg, David I.

"Korean Agricultural Services: The Invisible Hand in the Iron Glove. Market and Nonmarket Forces in Korean Rural Development", 9916–1.52

Steinberg, Harold

"World Nuclear Fuel Cycle Requirements, 1984", 3164–72

Steinmeier, Thomas L.

"Modeling the Retirement Process for Policy Evaluation and Research", 6722–1.445

Stellmacher, Michael J.

"1984 Outlook for Vegetables", 1004–16.1

Sterilization

see Sexual sterilization

Sterling Heights, Mich.

see also under By City in the "Index by Categories"

Stern, Gary H.

"Money Market Mutual Funds Are Hardly Money", 9383–6.403

Sterrett, Velma J.

"Forest Area and Timber Resource Statistics for State and Private Lands in New Mexico, 1980", 1206–23.7

"Forest Area and Timber Resource Statistics for State and Private Lands in Southwestern Montana, 1978", 1206–25.6

Steubenville, Ohio

Census of Housing, 1980: occupancy and unit characteristics, by race, Hispanic origin, and city, SMSA rpt, 2473–1.344

Census of Population and Housing, 1980: detailed population and housing characteristics, by county, city, and census tract, SMSA rpt, 2551–2.344

see also under By SMSA or MSA in the "Index by Categories"

Steuerle, Eugene

"Tax Incentives for Saving", 8302–2.407

"Taxation of Income Flowing Through Life Insurance Companies", 8006–3.49

Stevedores

see Longshoremen

Stevens, Guy V.

"U.S. Economy in an Interdependent World: A Multicountry Model", 9368–78

Stewart, Clyde E.

"Economic Impacts of the Fort Union Coal Project on Farms and Ranches, Montana and North Dakota", 1588–79

Stillman, Richard P.

"Hog Operations Becoming Fewer, Larger, and More Efficient", 1561–7.405

Stimulants

see Drug abuse and treatment

see Drugs

Stiner, Frederic M., Jr.

"Examination of Auditor Concentration in the Savings and Loan Industry", 9312–1.403

Stock exchanges

Employment, earnings, and hours, by SIC 4-digit nonfarm industry, monthly 1974-Feb 1984, annual update, 6744–4

Financial and business statistics, historic trends, 1984 annual chartbook, 9364–2.15

Occupational injury and illness rates, by SIC 2- to 4-digit industry, 1982, annual rpt, 6844–1

Prices, trading, and customer financing, 1982, annual rpt, 9364–5.4

Trading volume on New York and American Stock Exchanges, monthly rpt, 9362–1.1

Trading volume, securities listed by type, and exchange finances, by stock exchange, selected years 1935-82, annual rpt, 9734–2.1, 9734–2.3

Transactions volume and proceeds and new issue registrations, for US registered exchanges, SEC monthly rpt, 9732–1

see also American Stock Exchange

see also New York Stock Exchange

see also Securities

see also Stockbrokers

Stock market

see New York Stock Exchange

see Stock exchanges

see Stockbrokers

Stockbrokers

Census of Population, 1980: detailed socioeconomic and demographic characteristics, by age, sex, race, Hispanic origin, occupation, and industry, State rpt series, 2531–4

Concentrations of earnings, for brokers offering debt and equity issues, 1970-77 and 1980-82, article, 9371–1.418

County Business Patterns: establishments, employees, and payrolls, by SIC 4-digit industry and county, 1981, annual State rpt series, 2326–8

County Business Patterns: establishments, employees, and payrolls, by SIC 4-digit industry and county, 1982, annual State rpt series, 2326–6

Employment by detailed occupation, for 29 SIC 2-digit nonmanufacturing industries, 1981 BLS survey, 6748–60

Employment, earnings, and hours, by selected SIC 1- to 4-digit industry, State, and for 278 major labor areas, 1939-83, annual rpt, 6744–5

Employment, earnings, and hours, by SIC 4-digit nonfarm industry, monthly 1974-Feb 1984, annual update, 6744–4

Finances and broker services of brokerage firms and New England banks and thrifts, and brokerage acquisitions by firm, selected years 1977-84, article, 9373–1.417

Stockbrokers

Finances of stockbrokers, firms by type of organization and State, and SEC applications and registrations, 1978-82, annual rpt, 9734–2.1

Financial info, including revenues and expenses, for selected broker-dealers, monthly rpt, annual tables, 9732–1.3

Flow-of-funds accounts, assets and liabilities by type and economic sector, year-end outstandings, 1960-83, annual rpt, 9364–3

Flow-of-funds accounts savings, investments, and credit statements, quarterly rpt, 9365–3.3

Income tax returns of corporations, detailed income and tax items by industry, 1981, annual rpt, 8304–4

Income tax returns of corporations with foreign tax credit, income and deductions by type, asset size, and selected industry group, 1980, article, 8302–2.415

Income tax returns of partnerships, detailed data by industry, 1981 estimates, annual article, 8302–2.404

Income tax returns of partnerships, receipts by source, deductions by type, and establishments, by selected industry, 1982, annual article, 8302–2.416

Income tax returns of sole proprietorships, detailed data by industry div and selected industry group, 1981, annual rpt, 8304–7

Income tax returns of sole proprietorships, receipts, deductions by type, payroll, and net income, by major industry, 1982, annual article, 8302–2.413

Input-output structure of US economy, detailed interindustry transactions for 537 industries, and components of final demand, 1977 benchmark data, 2708–17

Investment companies classification, assets, and location, Sept 1982, annual directory, 9734–1

Minority group and women employment, by occupational group and SIC 2- to 3-digit industry, 1981, annual rpt, 9244–1.1

Occupational injury and illness rates, by SIC 2- to 4-digit industry, 1982, annual rpt, 6844–1

Occupational manpower needs and supply by detailed occupation, and educational and training program enrollees and grads by detailed field, 1982 and 1995, biennial rpt, 6744–3

Occupational Outlook Handbook, 1984-85 biennial rpt, 6744–1

Securities purchases, sales, and holdings, by issuer and type and ownership of security, monthly listing, 9732–2

Stockford, Donald

"Communicative Disorders Among Patients in VA Medical Facilities", 9926–1.17

Stockpiling

Budget of US, effects of Reagan Admin policy changes, by detailed program, FY85, annual rpt, 104–21

DOD budget, itemized account of legislative history, FY84, annual rpt, 3504–7

Fed Govt consolidated financial statements based on business accounting methods, FY82-83, annual rpt, 8104–5

Fed Govt programs and mgmt cost control proposals, 3-year savings by function and agency, and financial and operating data, 1960s-81, 16908–1

GSA mgmt activities and finances, FY78-83, annual rpt, 9454–23

Minerals production, prices, trade, use, employment, tariffs, and stockpiling, by commodity, with foreign comparisons, 1979-83, annual rpt, 5604–18

Strategic and critical materials stockpiling activities and inventories of Fed Govt, by commodity, as of Mar 1984, semiannual rpt, 9432–1

Strategic material stockpile mgmt, with cobalt use and stockpiles, and CCC appropriations and inventories, selected years 1950-83, hearings, 25208–27

Strategic materials stockpile inventories, costs, and goals, by commodity, as of June 1984, semiannual rpt, 9452–7

Strategic materials stockpiles, and imports in exchange for CCC commodity exports by world region and country, various periods 1950-83, hearings, 21208–20

Strategic minerals supply/demand, trade, and foreign and US industry devs by firm and country, by commodity, bimonthly rpt, 5602–4

see also Naval Petroleum Reserves

see also Strategic Petroleum Reserve

Stocks

see Agricultural stocks

see Business inventories

see Coal stocks

see Energy stocks and inventories

see Petroleum stocks

see Securities

see Stock exchanges

see Stockbrokers

see Stockpiling

Stockton, Calif.

Census of Housing, 1980: occupancy and unit characteristics, by race, Hispanic origin, and city, SMSA rpt, 2473–1.345

Census of Population and Housing, 1980: detailed population and housing characteristics, by county, city, and census tract, SMSA rpt, 2551–2.345

Wages of office and plant workers, by occupation, 1984 labor market area survey rpt, 6785–3.9

see also under By City and By SMSA or MSA in the "Index by Categories"

Stoeckel, Andy

"Issues in World Agricultural Trade", 1004–16.1

Stoga, Alan

"Crisis in Central America: Economic Problems, Prospects and Proposals", 028–19.2

Stone products

see Quarries and stone products

Storage

see Agricultural stocks

see Agricultural surpluses

see Cold storage and refrigeration

see Warehouses

Storms

Developing countries disaster preparedness and summary sociodemographic, political, and economic data, country rpt series, 9916–2

Farmland restoration from natural disaster, Emergency Conservation Program participation and payments, by practice and State, FY83, annual rpt, 1804–22

Fed Emergency Mgmt Agency activities and funding for disaster and emergency relief, and major disasters, 1983, annual rpt, 9434–2

Index by Subjects and Names

Forecast methodology, accuracy, and applications, technical rpt series, 2186–4

Foreign countries disasters, persons affected, deaths, damage, and aid by US and others, FY83 and trends from FY64, annual rpt, 9914–12

Foreign weather conditions and impact assessment, by world area and country, monthly rpt, 2152–9

Hurricanes and tropical storms in North Atlantic and Caribbean area, paths, surveillance, deaths, property damage, and landfall probabilities by city, 1983, annual rpt, 2184–7

Hurricanes and tropical storms in northeastern Pacific, paths, surveillance, deaths, and property damage, 1983, annual rpt, 2184–8

Marine weather and tropical cyclones, quarterly journal with articles, 2152–8

Meteorological services and research of Fed Govt, programs and funding by agency, FY84-85, annual rpt, 2144–2

Typhoons in western North Pacific and North Indian Oceans, paths and other characteristics, by mode of surveillance, 1983, annual rpt, 3804–8

Urban runoff water quality, pollutant concentrations, and control cost-effectiveness, with monitoring sites rainfall and other characteristics, by city and region, 1978-83, 9208–122

Water supply and quality, floods, drought, mudslides, and other hydrologic events, by State, 1983, annual rpt, 5664–12

Weather events socioeconomic impacts and costs, heating and cooling degree days, and housing energy bills, by census div and State, monthly rpt, 2152–12

Weather phenomena and storm characteristics, casualties, and property damage, by State, monthly listing, 2152–3

see also Floods

Stover, C. W.

"Earthquakes in the U.S.", 5662–4

Strahan, Genevieve W.

"Trends in Nursing and Related Care Homes and Hospitals: U.S., Selected Years, 1969-80", 4147–14.30

Strategic Arms Limitation Treaties

DOD budget, FY85 weapons system requests consistency with US policy and specified treaties, with funding FY83-87, annual rpt, 21384–4

Nuclear weapon forces of US and USSR under Strategic Arms Reduction Talks and alternative proposals and counting methods, by weapon and system, FY84-96, 26306–6.73

Strategic Arms Reduction Talks

Arms control treaties status, and Arms Control and Disarmament Agency activities, 1983, annual rpt, 9824–2

DOD budget, FY85 weapons system requests consistency with US policy and specified treaties, with funding FY83-87, annual rpt, 21384–4

Nuclear weapon forces of US and USSR under Strategic Arms Reduction Talks and alternative proposals and counting methods, by weapon and system, FY84-96, 26306–6.73

Index by Subjects and Names

Student aid

Strategic materials

Alaska minerals resources, production, claims on wildlife refuges, oil and gas leases, and exploratory wells, with maps and bibl, 1983, annual rpt, 5664–11

Minerals (strategic) supply/demand, trade, and foreign and US industry devs by firm and country, by commodity, bimonthly rpt, 5602–4

Nuclear strategic materials, inventory discrepancies at DOE facilities, 1st half FY83, semiannual rpt, 3002–4

Prices for sensitive materials, and indexes, *Business Conditions Digest,* cyclical indicators, monthly rpt, 2702–3.3

Prices for sensitive materials, and indexes, *Business Conditions Digest,* historical supplement and methodology, 1947-82, 2708–31

see also Naval Petroleum Reserves

see also Stockpiling

see also Strategic Petroleum Reserve

see also Uranium

Strategic Petroleum Reserve

Activities and funding of Strategic Petroleum Reserve, by supplier and site, quarterly GAO rpt, 26102–3

Budget appropriations proposed for Fed Govt energy programs, by office or dept and function, FY84-85, annual rpt, 3004–14

Budget of US, appropriations, outlays, balances, and budget receipts, by govtl branch and agency, FY83, annual rpt, 8104–2

Budget of US, effects of Reagan Admin policy changes, by detailed program, FY85, annual rpt, 104–21

Capacity, inventory, fill rate, and finances of Strategic Petroleum Reserve, quarterly rpt, 3002–13

Cost control proposals for Fed Govt programs and mgmt, 3-year savings by function and agency, and financial and operating data, 1960s-81, 16908–1.4

Defense Fuel Supply Center procurement, prices, stocks, and other activities, FY83, annual rpt, 3904–6

Defense Fuel Supply Center procurement, prices, stocks, transport, and other activities and finances, FY83, annual rpt, 3904–8

Energy supply/demand and price forecasts, by fuel type, quarterly rpt, 3162–34

Energy supply/demand and prices, by fuel type and consuming sector with foreign comparisons, 1949-83, annual rpt, 3164–74

Energy supply/demand and prices, by fuel type, sector, and end use, detailed trends and projections 1973-95, annual rpt, 3164–75

Energy supply/demand and prices, by fuel type, sector, and end use, with foreign comparisons, 1960-83 and projected to 1995, annual summary rpt, 3164–76

Finances of Federal off-budget entities, US Budget Appendix, FY85, detailed annual rpt, 104–3.3

Oil import and refining fees to recover cost of Strategic Petroleum Reserve, with purchases and construction costs, FY84-88, 26306–6.68

Oil imports and withdrawals from stocks, monthly rpt, 3162–24.3

Operational status, funding, and technical evaluation, 1983 rpt, 3008–91

Operational status, storage capacities, funding, and costs, by site, 1983, annual rpt, 3004–20

Sealift Military Command operations for naval fleet support, and transport of DOD and AID cargo by route, quarterly rpt, 3802–2

Shipping costs and foreign cargo shipments of Fed Govt by agency or program and route, and employment and economic impacts of US vessel preference, 1980, GAO rpt, 26117–30

Strathman, James G.

"Creative Financing 'Concessions' in Residential Sales: Effects and Implications", 9412–2.405

Stratosphere

Weather stations of Upper Air Observational Network, by US and foreign location, 1984 annual listing, 2184–6

Straub, Conrad P.

"Environmental Levels of PCB in Great Lakes Fish", 9208–126

Strawberries

see Fruit and fruit products

Streams

see Rivers and waterways

Street, Donald W.

"Ag Decline Prompts Top 100 To Cut Debt, Prune Assets", 1122–1.410

"Cooperative Vessel Still Afloat; Losses Slashed, Net Margins Tripled", 1122–1.412

"Top 100 Boost Margins Despite Lower Volume", 1122–1.408

"Top 100 Cooperatives, 1982 Financial Profile", 1124–3

"Top 100 Raise Cash Refunds, Retains; Reduce Borrowings from Co-op Banks", 1122–1.411

Streetcars

see Urban transportation

Streets, D. G.

"Regional, New-Source Bubble Policy for Sulfur Dioxide Emissions in the Eastern U.S.", 3408–32

Strickland, Roger P.

"Value of Net Change in Farm Inventories, 1974-83", 1544–19.405

Strikes and lockouts

see Work stoppages

Stroke

see Cerebrovascular diseases

see Circulatory diseases

Strontium

see Radioactive materials

Student aid

Alcohol, Drug Abuse, and Mental Health Admin research grants, awards, and fellowships by recipient, FY83, annual listing, 4044–13

Bankruptcy (personal), filers by debt type and other characteristics, selected years 1978-81, hearing, 25528–97.1

Bond tax-exempt issues by purpose, and Fed Govt mortgage bond revenue losses and borrower characteristics, selected years 1971-85, hearings, 21788–135

Bond tax-exempt issues for private activity, by purpose, face value, major industry, and State, 1983, article, 8302–2.417

Bond tax-exempt issues for public and private purposes, by use of proceeds, 1975-83, article, 9362–1.408

Botany and other plant science R&D at higher education instns, funding by source, grad students, and staff, 1983, 9626–2.143

Budget of US, CBO analysis of revenue and spending alternatives and projections of economic indicators, FY85-89, annual rpt, 26304–3.3

Budget of US, effects of Reagan Admin policy changes, by detailed program, FY85, annual rpt, 104–21

Civil case processing of US Attorneys and amounts involved, by cause of action, FY83, annual rpt, 6004–2.5

DOD medical personnel, trainees, and accessions by source, by occupation, specialty, and service branch, FY83, annual rpt, 3544–24

DOD training and education programs funding, staff, students, and facilities, by service branch and reserve component, FY85, annual rpt, 3504–5

Education Dept financial aid programs for educational instns and individuals, 1984 annual listing, 4804–3

Education Dept programs fraud and abuse, audits and investigations, 2nd half FY84, semiannual rpt, 4802–1

Fed Govt aid to State and local govts, expenditures, and direct payments, by program, agency, and State, FY83, annual rpt, 2464–2

Fed Govt credit assistance costs, policies to improve measurement, with loan and loan guarantee data by program, and Federal and private credit instns operations, 1970-84, 26306–6.72

Fed Govt programs and mgmt cost control proposals, 3-year savings by function and agency, and financial and operating data, 1960s-81, 16908–1.5, 16908–1.26, 16908–1.34

Fed Govt share of student aid basic grant, loan, and work-study awards, by instn and State, 1984/85, annual rpt, 4804–17

Flow-of-funds accounts, assets and liabilities by type and economic sector, year-end outstandings, 1960-83, annual rpt, 9364–3

Govt census, 1982: State govt payments to local govts, by program, source of funds, level of govt, and State, with trends from 1902, 2460–3

Health professionals supply and education, by occupation, demographic and professional characteristics, and location, 1950s-83 and projected to 2000, biennial rpt, 4114–8

HHS aid to each State and local govt or private instn, amount obligated, funding agency, and program, FY83, annual listing, 4004–3

High school class of 1980: use of student aid and earnings to pay higher education costs, by instn type and family income, 1980-82, 4848–15

High school classes of 1980 and 1982: educational and sociodemographic characteristics and expectations, natl longitudinal study, series, 4826–2

Higher education student aid, Federal programs funding and participation, by instn type and control, State, and outlying area, with student loan defaults and collections, FY82, annual rpt, 4804–28

Student aid

Higher education student aid sources, by selected school and student characteristics, 1967-83, annual rpt, 4804–5

Income (personal) by source including transfer payments, and social insurance contributions by type, by region, 1929 and 1982, 2708–40

Indian and Alaska Native health program activities, and funding for scholarships, care services, and facilities construction, by city, FY82, annual rpt, 4104–11

Indian Education Act, Fed Govt grants and fellowships awarded by State, FY83, and natl advisory council funding, FY73-84, annual rpt, 14874–1

Inter-American Foundation activities, grants, and fellowships, by country, FY83, annual rpt, 14424–1

Japan-US Friendship Commission educational and cultural exchange activities, grants, and trust fund status, FY83, annual rpt, 14694–1

Kentucky Higher Education Student Loan Corp student loans, loan purchases and defaults by instn, and revenue bonds status, various dates 1979-84, hearing, 21348–92

Latin America students in US and Soviet bloc training programs, by program type and student country, and summary by world region, selected years 1972-82, GAO rpt, 26123–77

Maritime academy students receiving Fed Govt aid, monthly rpt, 7702–1

Mental health clinical training funding by NIMH, by program and field, FY80-83, GAO rpt, 26121–86

Natl Endowment for Humanities activities and grants, FY83, annual rpt, 9564–2

NIH grants and awards for R&D, training, construction, and medical libraries, by location and recipient, FY83, annual listings, 4434–7

Pell student aid grants and recipients, by educational costs, family income, instnl type and control, and State, 1981/82, annual rpt, 4804–1

Puerto Rico educational enrollment, finance, completions, curricula, and personnel by instn, and health and vital statistics, selected years 1970-83, hearings, 21348–93

Scholarship and fellowship awards of higher education instns, selected years 1975/76-1979/80, annual rpt, 4824–2.18

Science and engineering doctoral degree recipients, by race and grad education funding source, 1982, biennial rpt, 9624–20.2

Science and engineering grad enrollment, fields of study, financial support, and other student and instn characteristics, 1975-82, annual survey, 9627–7

Science and engineering grad students, by field, type of financial aid, sex, race, Hispanic origin, and citizenship, 1972-83, biennial rpt, 9627–24.3

Science fellowships and traineeships, Fed Govt funding, by field, instn, agency, and State, FY82, annual rpt, 9627–17

State Student Incentive Grant funding and recipients and average income and award, and other aid need-based program funding, by State, FY67-82, GAO rpt, 26121–69

Student Loan Marketing Assn activities, and financial ratios and stock dividends compared to banks and 4 Fed Govt-sponsored credit assns, 1980-82, GAO rpt, 26121–71

Student Loan Marketing Assn, detailed budget, US Budget Appendix, FY85, annual rpt, 104–3.5

Texas school districts and higher education instns scholarship awards from Houston Endowment Inc, 1981, hearings, 21788–137

Truman, Harry S, Scholarship Foundation, program operation, financial status, and awards by student characteristics, 1983 with trends from 1977, annual rpt, 14314–1

Truman, Harry S, Scholarship Fund receipts by source, transfers, and investment holdings and transactions, monthly rpt, 14312–1

VA education assistance, job training, and other activities, FY79-83, annual rpt, 9924–1.7

VA educational assistance, monthly rpt, 9922–2

Veteran women population, and use of benefits by type, by age, period of service, and State, with comparisons to men, FY83, annual rpt, 9924–24

Veterans education assistance program participation and costs under GI Bill and other programs, WW II through Sept 1983, annual rpt, 9924–22

Veterans participation in training, rehabilitation, and housing loan programs, Vietnam era compared with WW II and Korea veterans, FY83, annual rpt, 9924–8.6

see also School lunch and breakfast programs

see also Work-study programs

Student employment

see Seasonal and summer employment

see Work-study programs

see Youth employment

Student Loan Marketing Association

Financial ratios and stock dividends of Student Loan Marketing Assn compared to banks and 4 Fed Govt-sponsored credit assns, 1980-82, GAO rpt, 26121–71

Student loans

see Student aid

Students

Census of Population, 1980: migration since 1975, by county and selected demographic characteristics, supplementary rpt, 2535–1.14

Census of Population, 1980: migration since 1975, by State and selected demographic characteristics, supplementary rpt, 2535–1.13

CETA participants by sociodemographic characteristics, and Labor Dept activities and staff, FY83, annual rpt, 6304–1

Condition of Education, detailed data on enrollment, staff, achievement, finances, curricula, and education effects on employment, 1982-83, annual rpt, 4824–1

Crime against students, teachers, and others, by offense, circumstances, and offender sex and race, 1974-76, 6066–20.2

Crime in public schools, assaults and robberies of teachers and minority and other students, and vandalism incidents, 1976/77, 4808–12

Index by Subjects and Names

Crime in secondary schools, assaults and robberies of students and teachers, 1972-83, 4918–13

Digest of Education Statistics, detailed data on students, staff, finances, and facilities, 1982 and selected trends, annual rpt, 4824–2

DOD Dependents Schools students higher education admissions tests scores by sex and subject, and educational goals and attitudes, 1983, annual rpt, 3504–17

DOD Dependents Schools 1st grader basic skills test scores, by world area and English fluency, fall 1983, annual rpt, 3504–18

DOD training and education programs funding, staff, students, and facilities, by service branch and reserve component, FY85, annual rpt, 3504–5

Drugs, alcohol, and cigarettes, high school seniors use and assessment by drug type, sex, and region, 1975-83 surveys, annual rpt, 4494–4

Education statistics summary compilation, 1980/81-1982/83 with selected trends from 1869, biennial rpt, 4804–27

Employment of youth and hours worked, by high school and college enrollment status, sex, race, and Hispanic origin, 1982-83, annual article, 6722–1.446

High school class of 1982: foreign language course enrollment, by language, student and school characteristics, and location, 1984 rpt, 4838–11

High school class of 1982: foreign language coursework, by language, course level, student and school characteristics, and location, 1984 rpt, 4828–17

High school classes of 1980 and 1982: educational and sociodemographic characteristics and expectations, natl longitudinal study, series, 4826–2

Indian Education Act grants to local agencies, Education Dept audit results by region, FY82, annual rpt, 4804–29

Indian education program operations, funding, student progress measures, and opinions of school staff, parents, and students, selected years 1973-83, 4808–13

New England States college grads employment prospects in 1984, annual narrative rpt, 6916–7.3

OASDHI, Medicaid, SSI, and other social insurance and public welfare programs benefits, beneficiary characteristics, and trust funds, selected years 1937-82, annual rpt, 4744–3.6

OASDI beneficiary status changes reported late and benefit overpayments, for death, marriage, and leaving school, 1981, GAO rpt, 26121–68

Pilots and nonpilots certified by FAA, by type of certificate, age, sex, region, and State, 1983, annual rpt, 7504–2

Science and engineering grad enrollment, fields of study, financial support, and other student and instn characteristics, 1975-82, annual survey, 9627–7

see also Black students

see also Educational attainment

see also Educational enrollment

see also Foreign students

see also School dropouts

see also Student aid

Stutts, Jane C.

"Three Studies Evaluating the Effectiveness of Incentives for Increasing Safety Belt Use", 7762–9.408

Subcommittee on Administrative Law and Governmental Relations. House

FTC budget authority and expenditures for regulatory analysis, by prospective regulation and contractor, 1983, hearings, 21528–56

Subcommittee on Administrative Practice and Procedure. Senate

Fed Govt administrative law judges by agency and grade, various dates 1947-82, and New Jersey administrative law cases, FY80-84, hearings, 25528–96

Subcommittee on Agriculture and Transportation. Joint

Telephone operating data, costs, and billings for American Telephone and Telegraph Co local and long distance lines, by State, 1980-82 with trends from 1970, 23848–176

Subcommittee on Arms Control, Oceans, International Operations, and Environment. Senate

Communications satellite intl systems charges, operations, investment shares by country, and competition impacts, 1964-83 with projections to 2003, hearings, 25388–46

Subcommittee on Aviation. Senate

Travel agency financial and operating data, and airline ticket sales by type of distributor, 1970s-82, hearing, 25268–81

Subcommittee on Civil and Constitutional Rights. House

Higher education desegregation, Louisiana black instn funding, and Virginia students needed to meet desegregation goals, by instn, late 1970s-85, hearings, 21348–91

Subcommittee on Civil Service, Post Office, and General Services. Senate

Pension and other benefits of private industry, pension plans created and terminated since 1939, and NYC retirement systems assets, 1978-83, conf proceedings, 25408–89

Pension benefits and after-tax salary replacement rates by plan type, and older persons income and income sources, by age and marital status, 1950s-82, conf proceedings, 25408–87

Subcommittee on Commerce, Consumer and Monetary Affairs. House

Foreign and US Commercial Service of ITA, overseas staff by category, and trade promotion costs by activity, by country, 1982-83, hearing, 21408–73

Tax evasion through tax haven countries, with income, investments, and taxes withheld by country, various periods 1975- 83, hearings, 21408–71

Subcommittee on Commerce, Transportation, and Tourism. House

Trade policy of Fed Govt, with data on US industry foreign trade and revenues, and Japan semiconductor industry subsidies, 1970s-83, hearings, 21368–46

Subcommittee on Conservation, Credit, and Rural Development. House

Fed Crop Insurance Corp program operations and finances, for FCIC policies and private policies reinsured by FCIC, 1970s-84 with trends from 1948, hearing, 21168–28

Subcommittee on Crime. House

Alcohol, Tobacco, and Firearms Bur activities nationwide and in 20 cities, funding, and jobs to be transferred to Customs and Secret Service, 1979-82, hearings, 21528–55

Subcommittee on Criminal Law. Senate

New Jersey and Maryland prison capacity and population, and New Jersey construction costs by type and funding source, by facility, 1977-82 and projected to 1988, 25528–99

Subcommittee on Domestic Monetary Policy. House

Fresno, Calif, economic, population, labor, and housing indicators, various periods 1974-85, hearing, 21248–84

Subcommittee on East Asian and Pacific Affairs. Senate

Oil (Alaskan) potential exports to Japan, costs and benefits, with background data on oil prices, Pacific Basin supply/demand, and tankers, various periods 1918-99, hearings, 25388–45

Subcommittee on Economic Goals and Intergovernmental Policy. Joint

Social pathology measures including crime and death rates, relation to selected economic indicators, various periods 1950-80, 23848–76

Soviet Union industrial and agricultural production by selected commodity, and demographic trends and projections by Republic, 1950s-2000, hearings, 23848–180

Subcommittee on Economic Growth, Employment, and Revenue Sharing. Senate

R&D spending and industry growth, and OPEC oil refining operations, various periods 1953-90, hearings, 25368–133

Subcommittee on Economic Stabilization. House

Economic conditions of US, with some foreign comparisons, 1960s-82 and alternative projections to 1992, hearing, 21248–79

Subcommittee on Employment Opportunities. House

Business failures, plant closings, layoffs, and relocations, for California by industry, individual plant, county, and city, 1980-83, hearing, 21348–84

Economic growth rates and component economic indicators, selected years 1922-83 and projected under full employment to 1988, hearing, 21348–90

Fed Govt civilian employment of minority groups and women, by grade and agency, 1980 and 1983, 21348–41

Subcommittee on Energy and Mineral Resources. Senate

Coal supply and Fed Govt coal leases, by owner, owner industry, and western State, various periods 1950-82 and projected to 2000, hearing, 25318–58

Subcommittee on Energy Conservation and Power. House

Auto and light truck fuel use, economy standards and manufacturer compliance, and gas prices and taxes, with selected foreign comparisons, FY80-83 and projected to 2000, hearing, 21368–49

Electric and gas utility diversification activity by type, and finances and bond ratings by selected firm, various periods 1970-83, hearing, 21368–53

Subcommittee on Health and Long-Term Care. House

Housing energy conservation programs of utilities, financing, costs, participation, and energy savings, various periods 1981-84, hearing, 21368–54

Housing energy use, and savings under alternative conservation strategies, by State, with model methodology and energy prices, selected years 1970-81, 21368–48

Subcommittee on Energy Development and Applications. House

Air pollutant and radiation indoor levels by emissions source, and household exposure and health effects by pollutant type, various periods 1966-83, hearings, 21708–102

Subcommittee on Energy, Nuclear Proliferation, and Government Processes. Senate

Machine tool orders by selected industry, trade, and shipments and Japan share of US market by type of tool, various dates 1972-84, hearing, 25388–48

Subcommittee on Europe and the Middle East. House

NATO military expenditures, by country, selected years 1971-82, hearing, 21388–42

Soviet Union industrial and agricultural production by selected commodity, and demographic trends and projections by Republic, 1950s-2000, hearings, 23848–180

Subcommittee on Financial Institutions Supervision, Regulation, and Insurance. House

Bank deposit interest rate deregulation, effect on bank deposits and bank financial performance, 1978-83, hearing, 21248–83

Subcommittee on Fisheries and Wildlife Conservation and the Environment. House

Marine pollution problems from municipal waste dumping in New York Bight, oil and gas drilling on Georges Bank, and radioactive waste disposal in oceans, 1970s-82, hearings, 21568–36

Subcommittee on General Oversight and the Economy. House

Robots installed for manufacturing, and jobs displaced and created by occupation, by type of robot use, 1980s-2000, hearings, 21728–54

Trans-Alaska Pipeline System owner companies financial data, and retail gasoline competitive position in 2 States, by company, 1980-83, hearing, 21728–51

Subcommittee on Government Activities and Transportation. House

Art appraisals accepted and rejected on estate, gift, and income tax returns, and valuation by taxpayers, IRS, and US courts, 1978-82, hearings, 21408–74

Arts and humanities funding, by source and State, FY82-83 with trends from FY66, 21408–69

Subcommittee on Government Information, Justice, and Agriculture. House

Mail electronic system message volume and profitability under USPS proposed rate and service increases, FY82 and projected to FY87, 21408–70

Subcommittee on Health and Long-Term Care. House

Airline pilots terminated for medical reasons and reinstated by carrier, and aircraft accidents by age of flight crew, selected years 1960-81, hearing, 21148–34

Subcommittee on Health and Long-Term Care. House

Deaths due to cold weather and related causes, by age, race, State, and city, selected periods 1962-83, 21148–30

Hospitals and nursing homes in Arizona, finances and operations for specified facilities, and itemized expenses for selected cases, 1978-83, hearing, 21148–29

Subcommittee on Health and Safety. House Occupational health and safety State govt program staffing requirements, and occupational injury data, for selected States, selected years 1973-81, hearings, 21348–88

Subcommittee on Health and the Environment. House

Abortions (legal), and deaths from abortion and childbirth, by medical and sociodemographic characteristics, and New Mexico health clinics financial data, 1972-83, hearings, 21368–47

Acid rain causes and effects, air pollutant emissions by source in US and selected countries, and control costs, 1970s-83 and projected to 2000, 21368–52

Subcommittee on Health. House Teachers salaries in schools and colleges by State, 1982/83, and school employees health insurance plans in 7 cities, as of 1980, hearing, 21788–136

Subcommittee on Housing and Community Development. House

- Flood insurance program of Fed Govt, average premiums, premium income, and program costs, selected years FY68-84, hearing, 21248–81
- Homeless population and characteristics, and temporary shelter operations, use, and user characteristics, for selected cities, various periods 1979-84, hearing, 21248–85

Subcommittee on Housing and Consumer Interests. House

California (southern) housing demand by county, prices and sales, and costs after homeowner tax deductions, 1970s-80, hearing, 21148–31

Washington State telephone rates including govt long-distance access charges, by company, 1983-89, hearing, 21148–32

Subcommittee on Human Resources, Education and Labor. House

Elementary level Follow Through compensatory education programs beneficiaries, costs, funding, and participant test scores, selected years 1968-82, hearing, 21348–87

Subcommittee on Human Rights and International Organizations. House

El Salvador terrorist acts against property, casualties, kidnappings, and hostages, Oct 1979-June 1983, human rights certification hearing, 21388–41

Subcommittee on Intergovernmental Relations and Human Resources. House Education block grants of Fed Govt, State allocations by program and selected school district, FY82-84 and trends from FY60, hearing, 21408–75

Subcommittee on Intergovernmental Relations. Senate

Regional councils involved in service activities, by type of service and region and population size, 1982 survey, hearing, 25408–88

Revenue sharing and other Fed Govt grant program alternative allocations, with city govt finances and responses to program cuts, FY79-83, hearings, 25408–86

Subcommittee on International Development Institutions and Finance. House

Multilateral dev banks economic dev projects, environmental and cultural impacts in developing countries, 1970s-83, hearings, 21248–80

Subcommittee on International Finance and Monetary Policy. Senate

Eximbank loan guarantees and insurance currently provided and needed by Mexico and Brazil, and value of worldwide and US trade, 1981-84, hearings, 25248–97

Subcommittee on International Trade, Investment, and Monetary Policy. House

Mexico economic indicators, trade, external accounts and debt, oil industry, and relations with US, 1978-83 with trends from 1959, conf proceedings, 21248–82

Subcommittee on International Trade. Senate Steel pipe and tube shipments, imports from EC by country, and exports, by product type, various periods 1978-83 with import duties to 1987, hearing, 25368–134

Subcommittee on Investigations, Armed Services. House

Fed Govt supply inventory and automated cataloging system, and DOD mgmt of inventory items for agencies, NATO, and foreign govts, 1970s-83, annual rpt, 21204–1

Soviet Union and US satellites by mission and vulnerability to attack, and USSR anti-satellite missiles, 1983 and projected to 1989, hearing, 21208–18

Subcommittee on Juvenile Justice. Senate Kidnapping by parents over intl and interstate boundaries, characteristics of cases referred to State Dept and FBI by State and country, 1979-83, hearing, 25528–95

Subcommittee on Labor-Management Relations. House

- Business failures, plant closings, layoffs, and relocations, for California by industry, individual plant, county, and city, 1980-83, hearing, 21348–84
- Pension plan funding, assets, benefits, and participants for private and public systems, and State and local plans disclosing finances, selected years 1974-82, hearing, 21788–142

Subcommittee on Labor Standards. House

Asbestos-related occupational disease compensation paid and defendant and plaintiff litigation costs, with comparisons to other tort suits, selected years 1968-82, hearings, 21348–85

Fed Govt and total law enforcement officers and firefighters killed, death benefit claims, and non-Fed Govt firefighters death benefits by State and city, 1972-82, hearing, 21348–94

Michigan health funding, Blue Cross-Blue Shield and welfare participation, and unemployment, poverty, and food assistance by county, 1979-83, hearing, 21348–86

Subcommittee on Legislation and National Security. House

DOD aircraft for noncombat use, costs, Navy and Air Force requirements, and Navy losses, by aircraft type, selected years FY73-86, hearing, 21408–76

Index by Subjects and Names

Subcommittee on Manpower and Housing. House

Asbestos workers, exposure levels, cancer incidence, and deaths, by industry and occupation, and asbestos regulation enforcement and costs/benefits, various periods 1940-2027, hearing, 21408–72

Subcommittee on Merchant Marine. House Port dev costs and financing through user fees, and shipping industry impact on local economy, by State, other area, industry, commodity, and port, 1970s-2020, hearings, 21568–34

Subcommittee on Military Personnel and Compensation. House

Pension benefits for military retirees and compared to US civil and foreign service and foreign countries, and Air Force personnel costs, FY75-84, hearings, 21208–19

Subcommittee on Mining, Forest Management, and Bonneville Power Administration. House

Copper mine expansion in Cananea, Mexico, effects on US air pollution and copper industry, with US and foreign industry data, 1960s-95, hearing, 21448–31

Nuclear power plants construction financing of Washington Public Power Supply System, with regional economic impacts and power supply/demand, 1980s-2035, hearing, 21448–29

Subcommittee on Monopolies and Commercial Law. House

Bankruptcy (personal), filers by debt type and other characteristics, and impacts in Connecticut and Michigan, various dates 1946-82, hearings, 21528–57

Subcommittee on Natural Resources, Agriculture Research, and Environment. House

Air pollutant and radiation indoor levels by emissions source, and household exposure and health effects by pollutant type, various periods 1966-83, hearings, 21708–102

Subcommittee on Oceanography. House

Marine pollution problems from municipal waste dumping in New York Bight, oil and gas drilling on Georges Bank, and radioactive waste disposal in oceans, 1970s-82, hearings, 21568–36

Subcommittee on Oversight and Investigations, Energy and Commerce. House

Copper production, production costs, prices, wages, and productivity, for US and 3 countries, 1970s-83 and projected to 1989, 21368–55

Oil price and allocation regulations enforcement by DOE, and overcharge allegations, settlements, and refunds to States, by company, as of June 1983, hearing, 21368–50

Steel import trigger prices to prevent Japan dumping, and domestic steel prices, employment, and imports, by product and region, various dates 1977-1983, hearings, 21368–51

Subcommittee on Oversight and Investigations, Interior and Insular Affairs. House

Oil and gas finances by firm, and effect of income and excise tax provisions on firms, Fed Govt revenues, and investor tax returns, 1980 and projected to 1992, hearing, 21788–132

Index by Subjects and Names

Submarines

Oil and gas 5-year OCS leasing plan and proposed sale off California coast, acreage, costs, and benefits, various periods 1953-2006, hearing, 21448–30

Pension plan funding, assets, benefits, and participants for private and public systems, and State and local plans disclosing finances, selected years 1974-82, hearing, 21788–142

Philanthropic foundations assets and grants for 50 largest foundations, and for selected foundations by recipient, selected years 1975-82, hearings, 21788–137

Poverty-level persons and families, by income source, hours of work, earnings, taxes, and family characteristics, various periods 1959-84, 21788–131

Poverty population by labor force status, and effect of public welfare changes and recession, by family status, FY82, 21788–139

Poverty rate by family composition, and effect of noncash transfers, taxes, unemployment benefits, and business cycles, selected years 1959-82, hearings, 21788–141

Subcommittee on Panama Canal and Outer Continental Shelf. House

Oil and gas OCS drilling rigs by country, rig losses, and worker injury and death rates, various periods 1966-83, hearing, 21568–35

Subcommittee on Patents, Copyrights, and Trademarks. Senate

Drug prices by brand and generic category, patent life, FDA approval time, and industry R&D costs and finances, selected years 1962-83, hearing, 25528–98

Recording industry operations and sales lost from home taping, home taping costs, and material taped by source, 1969-83, hearings with chartbook, 25528–100

Subcommittee on Postal Operations and Services. House

Postal Service operations, revenues by source, and employee characteristics, 1970s-83, and electronic mail promotion costs, FY82-87, hearings, 21628–55

Subcommittee on Postal Personnel and Modernization. House

Postal Service operations, revenues by source, and employee characteristics, 1970s-83, and electronic mail promotion costs, FY82-87, hearings, 21628–55

Subcommittee on Postsecondary Education. House

Education of teachers, teaching degrees and salaries, high school seniors achievement test scores, and school enrollment and finances, 1970s-83, hearings, 21348–89

Higher education desegregation, Louisiana black instn funding, and Virginia students needed to meet desegregation goals, by instn, late 1970s-85, hearings, 21348–91

Kentucky Higher Education Student Loan Corp student loans, loan purchases and defaults by instn, and revenue bonds status, various dates 1979-84, hearing, 21348–92

Puerto Rico educational enrollment, finance, completions, curricula, and personnel by instn, and health and vital statistics, selected years 1970-83, hearings, 21348–93

Subcommittee on Preparedness. Senate

Strategic material stockpile mgmt, with cobalt use and stockpiles, and CCC appropriations and inventories, selected years 1950-83, hearings, 25208–27

Subcommittee on Procurement and Military Nuclear Systems. House

Uranium ore tailings at active mills, EPA radon and radionuclide emmission standards and US and foreign exposure and health effects, various periods 1957-83, hearings, 21208–17

Subcommittee on Public Assistance and Unemployment Compensation. House

Poverty-level persons and families, by income source, hours of work, earnings, taxes, and family characteristics, various periods 1959-84, 21788–131

Poverty population by labor force status, and effect of public welfare changes and recession, by family status, FY82, 21788–139

Poverty rate by family composition, and effect of noncash transfers, taxes, unemployment benefits, and business cycles, selected years 1959-82, hearings, 21788–141

Texas border employment and economic impacts of Mexican peso devaluation, for 6 counties and 2 SMSAs, 1970s-May 1983, hearing, 21788–133

Subcommittee on Public Lands and Reserved Water. Senate

Forests (natl) timber sales contract operations in Northwest US by forest and firm, and lumber supply/demand, FY76-1983 with trends from 1913, hearings, 25318–57

Subcommittee on Research and Development. House

Soviet Union and US satellites by mission and vulnerability to attack, and USSR anti-satellite missiles, 1983 and projected to 1989, hearing, 21208–18

Subcommittee on Savings, Pensions, and Investment Policy. Senate

Life expectancy increase impacts on OASDI and pension policy, with alternative sociodemographic projections to 2100, hearing, 25368–130

Pension plans with postretirement benefit increases, for banks and manufacturers by size, 1978-83, hearing, 25368–132

Subcommittee on SBA and SBIC Authority, Minority Enterprise, and General Small Business Problems. House

Small business employment and receipts size standards for Fed Govt contract awards by industry, and DOD contract awards data, 1970s-83, hearings, 21728–53

Subcommittee on Seapower and Strategic and Critical Materials. House

Strategic materials stockpiles, and imports in exchange for CCC commodity exports by world region and country, various periods 1950-83, hearings, 21208–20

Subcommittee on Select Revenue Measures. House

Crop acreage reduction payment-in-kind program costs, requirements, producer and diversion payments, and loan interest forgiven, by crop, as of 1983, hearing, 21788–138

Subcommittee on Soil and Water Conservation, Forestry, and Environment. Senate

Soil conservation program policies of Fed Govt, attitudes of farmers and ranchers in 6 central US counties, 1982/83 survey, hearing, 25168–61

Subcommittee on Surface Transportation. Senate

Railroad finances, operations, and freight rates and shares, by commodity and railroad, 1970s-82, hearings, 25268–80

Subcommittee on Tax, Access to Equity Capital, and Business Opportunities. House

Small business loans and credit, operational expectations, and NYC metro area owners economic and professional attitudes, by industry div, 1980-83 surveys, hearings, 21728–52

Subcommittee on Taxation and Debt Management. Senate

Eurodollar bond market issues of US corporations, and amount raised and savings relative to domestic market, by company, 1975-82, hearing, 25368–132

Subcommittee on Telecommunications, Consumer Protection, and Finance. House

Electric and gas utility diversification activity by type, and finances and bond ratings by selected firm, various periods 1970-83, hearing, 21368–53

TV and radio industry minority and women employment by occupation, and business owners, by race and State, with revenues and stations, 1971-81, hearing, 21368–45

Subcommittee on Trade. House

Auto industry operations, trade, and registrations, foreign and US, selected years 1928-82, domestic content requirement hearings, 21788–134

Subcommittee on Transportation. Senate

Trucking industry economic effects of size and weight limits, and hwy use taxes by tax type, 1982-83 and projected 1984-87, hearings, 25328–24

Subcommittee on Western Hemisphere Affairs. House

El Salvador terrorist acts against property, casualties, kidnappings, and hostages, Oct 1979-June 1983, human rights certification hearing, 21388–41

Mexico economic indicators, trade, external accounts and debt, oil industry, and relations with US, 1978-83 with trends from 1959, conf proceedings, 21248–82

Submarines

Developing countries arms transfers from US, USSR, and Europe, by weapon type and world region, 1974-82, 25948–3

DOD budget, costs of individual weapons or weapons systems, FY83-85, annual rpt, 3504–2

DOD budget, FY85 weapons system requests consistency with US policy and specified treaties, with funding FY83-87, annual rpt, 21384–4

DOD budget, itemized account of legislative history, FY84, annual rpt, 3504–7

DOD budget justification, programs, and policies, FY85, annual rpt, 3544–2

DOD procurement cost estimates for weapons and communications systems, by service branch, quarterly summary rpt, 3502–1

Submarines

Foreign military spending, arms trade, and armed forces size, with total govt spending and population, by country, 1972-82, annual rpt, 9824–1

NATO and US weapons and troop strength compared to Warsaw Pact and USSR, as of Jan 1984, annual rpt, 3564–1

Soviet Union and Warsaw Pact military weapons systems, assistance and presence worldwide, and force strengths, with selected US and NATO comparisons, as of 1984, 3508–14

Submerged lands

see also Continental shelf

see also Offshore oil and gas

Subsidies

- Alcohol fuel production costs, related employment, and Fed Govt subsidies and impact on farm income, selected years 1978-90, GAO rpt, 26113–140
- Budget of US, effects of Reagan Admin policy changes, by detailed program, FY85, annual rpt, 104–21
- Chrysler Corp Loan Guarantee Act implementation, with related financial and operating data, FY83, last issue of annual rpt, 8004–14
- Cost control proposals for Fed Govt programs and mgmt, 3-year savings by function and agency, and financial and operating data, 1960s-81, 16908–1
- EC trade promotion policies and financing by industry, and effect on competing US industries, 1970s-82, 9886–4.73
- Fed Govt loans, grants, and tax benefits to business, by program and economic sector, projected FY84-88 with effective tax rates for FY80-82, 26306–6.70
- Govt revenues by source and expenditures by function, natl income and product account, *Survey of Current Business,* monthly rpt, monthly and annual tables, 2702–1.24
- Japan semiconductor industry govt subsidies by program, with financial and operating data by firm, R&D, and comparisons to US industry, 1970s-83, hearings, 21368–46.1
- Minerals depletion allowance of foreign countries and US, and financial assistance for exploration and R&D, for 87 commodities, 1983, annual rpt, 5604–18
- Minority business Fed Govt funding, procurement, and subsidies, and deposits in minority-owned banks, by agency, FY69-83, annual rpt, 2104–5
- Postal Service costs of free mail, FY83, annual rpt, 9864–4
- Postal Service pension and health benefits subsidized by Fed Govt trust funds, and subsidy reduction plans deficit impact, FY79-84 and projected to FY89, 26306–6.82
- Postal Service revenue forgone by class of subsidized mail, FY83, annual rpt, 9864–5.3
- Postal Service revenue forgone subsidy, by class of mail, FY83, annual rpt, 9864–1
- Public services subsidized by Fed Govt, user fees to recover costs of 7 programs, by type of fee, user, and service, FY84-88, 26306–6.68

see also Agricultural quotas and price supports

see also Agricultural subsidies

see also Federal aid programs

see also Federal aid to arts and humanities

see also Federal aid to education

see also Federal aid to higher education

see also Federal aid to highways

see also Federal aid to housing

see also Federal aid to law enforcement

see also Federal aid to libraries

see also Federal aid to local areas

see also Federal aid to medical education

see also Federal aid to medicine

see also Federal aid to railroads

see also Federal aid to rural areas

see also Federal aid to States

see also Federal aid to transportation

see also Federal aid to vocational education

see also Federal funding for research and development

see also Rent supplements

see also Shipbuilding and operating subsidies

see also Tax expenditures

see also Tax incentives and shelters

see also Trade adjustment assistance

Suburbs

- Apartment market absorption rates and characteristics for nonsubsidized privately financed furnished and unfurnished units completed in 1982, annual Current Housing Rpt, 2484–2
- Apartment market absorption rates and characteristics for nonsubsidized privately financed units completed in 1983, preliminary annual Current Housing Rpt, 2484–3
- Assaults, murders, and other deaths of law enforcement officers, by circumstances, level of govt, agency, victim and offender characteristics, and location, 1983, annual rpt, 6224–3
- Births and birth rates, by detailed demographic characteristics and geographic area, 1979 and trends, US Vital Statistics annual rpt, 4144–1
- Census of Housing, 1980: inventory, occupancy, and unit characteristics, changes from 1973 by region and inside-outside SMSAs and central cities, series, 2473–3
- Census of Housing, 1980: occupancy and unit characteristics of SMSAs and central cities, by race, Hispanic origin, and city, State and SMSA rpt series, 2473–1
- Census of Population and Housing, 1980: detailed population and housing characteristics, by county, city, and census tract, State and SMSA rpt series, 2551–2
- Census of Population, 1980: detailed socioeconomic characteristics, by county, city, and inside-outside SMSAs and central cities, State rpt series, 2531–3
- Crime Index by population size and region, and offenses known to police by large city, Jan-June 1984, semiannual rpt, 6222–1
- Crime victimization rates by type of offense, and victim and offense characteristics, Natl Crime Survey series, 6066–3
- Crimes, arrests by offender characteristics, and rates, by offense, and law enforcement employees, by population size and jurisdiction, 1970s-83, annual rpt, 6224–2
- DC metro area Metrorail transit system, effect on commuting patterns, population, business, land use, and environment, series, 7306–8

Index by Subjects and Names

- Disability days, injury and illness rates by type, and use of health services and Medicaid, by age, region, metro-nonmetro location, and selected SMSA, 1980-81, 4147–10.146
- Employment and unemployment in metro and nonmetro areas, annual averages, 1983, article, 6742–2.403
- Employment and unemployment in metro and nonmetro areas, monthly rpt, quarterly data, 6742–2.8
- Families and households detailed socioeconomic characteristics, Mar 1982, annual Current Population Rpt, 2546–1.383
- Food consumption and nutrient intake by individuals, by food group, source, and socioeconomic characteristics, 1977-78 natl survey, final rpt series, 1356–4
- Home mortgages (graduated payment) FHA-insured, financial, property, and mortgagor characteristics, for US and selected localities, quarterly rpt, 5142–42
- Home mortgages (graduated payment) FHA-insured, financial, property, and mortgagor characteristics, for US and selected States, quarterly rpt, 5142–41
- Home mortgages (graduated payment) FHA-insured, financial, property, and mortgagor characteristics, US summary, quarterly rpt, 5142–40
- Home mortgages FHA-insured, financial, property, and mortgagor characteristics, for US and selected localities, quarterly rpt, 5142–2
- Home mortgages FHA-insured, financial, property, and mortgagor characteristics, for US, selected States, and Puerto Rico, quarterly rpt, 5142–3
- Home mortgages FHA-insured, financial, property, and mortgagor characteristics, quarterly rpt, 5142–1
- Home mortgages FHA-insured, financial, property, and mortgagor characteristics, 1983, annual rpt, 5144–17
- Home mortgages FHA-insured for low-cost homes, financial, construction, property, and mortgagor characteristics, quarterly rpt, 5142–4
- Housing and households detailed characteristics, and unit and neighborhood quality, by inside-outside central cities, 1979-82 surveys, SMSA rpt series, 2485–6
- Housing and neighborhood quality indicators and attitudes, by occupant and unit characteristics, region, and metro-nonmetro location, 1981, annual survey, 2485–2
- Housing occupancy and unit and household characteristics, by region and metro-nonmetro residence, 1983, biennial survey, 2485–1
- Housing units authorized, by public and private ownership, State, and permit-issuing place, 1983, annual rpt, 2384–2
- Housing vacancy and occupancy rates, and vacant unit characteristics, by metro-nonmetro location and region, selected years 1960-83, annual rpt, 2484–1.1
- Housing vacant unit characteristics and costs, and occupancy and vacancy rates, by region and metro-nonmetro location, quarterly rpt, 2482–1

Index by Subjects and Names

Income of families and persons, by sociodemographic characteristics, 1983, advance annual Current Population Rpt, 2546–6.41

Local govt finances and population characteristics for cities and suburbs, by region and selected SMSA, selected years 1957-FY83, 10048–61

Mobility of population, detailed data by demographic and socioeconomic characteristics of movers and nonmovers, Mar 1981-82, annual Current Population Rpt, 2546–1.384

Older persons by demographic, socioeconomic, and health characteristics, selected years 1900-81 and projected to 2050, Current Population Rpt, 2546–2.125

Population and employment in central cities and suburbs, effect of region, neighborhood, population, and labor characteristics on change, 1970-80, technical paper, 9387–8.89

Poverty status of families and persons, by detailed socioeconomic characteristics, 1982, annual Current Population Rpt, 2546–6.40

see also Neighborhoods

see also New towns

see also Urban renewal

see also under By Urban-Rural and Metro-Nonmetro in the "Index by Categories"

Subversive activities

see Internal security

see Underground movements

Subways

Accidents, deaths, injuries, and property damage, by type of accident and victim and cause, for 11 subway systems, 1983, annual rpt, 7884–5

Census of Housing, 1980: structural, financial, and householder characteristics, by region and State, 2475–4

Census of Population and Housing, 1980: detailed population and housing characteristics, by county, city, and census tract, State and SMSA rpt series, 2551–2

Census of Population, 1980: detailed socioeconomic characteristics, by county, city, and inside-outside SMSAs and central cities, State rpt series, 2531–3

DC metro area Metrorail transit system, effect on commuting patterns, population, business, land use, and environment, series, 7306–8

Electric railroad mileage by country, subway system mileage by US city, and trolley and motor bus capital and operating costs, selected years 1960-80, 3006–7.7

Finances and operations of transit systems, by mode of transport, function, fleet size, and system, FY82, annual rpt, 7884–4

Finances, operations, vehicles, equipment, accidents, and energy use, by mode of transport, 1955-84, annual rpt, 7304–2

Research publications on public transit, 2nd half FY83, semiannual listing, 7882–1

State and local govt productivity measurement, with background data and output indexes for 7 govt services, various periods 1955-82, 6728–27

Sudan

Agricultural and food production indexes, and production of selected commodities, by world region and country, 1974-83, annual rpt, 1524–5

Agricultural situation in sub-Saharan Africa, by country, 1982-83 and outlook for 1984, annual rpt, 1524–4.10

Agricultural supply/demand, trade, and production, and socioeconomic data, by country, 1950s-77, 1528–179

AID activities and funding by project and function, FY85, and developing countries summary socioeconomic data, 1970s-83, by country, annual rpt, 9914–3

AID economic assistance to developing countries, obligations and disbursements by country, quarterly rpt, 9912–4

AID loan repayment status and terms by program and country, and status of predecessor agency loans, quarterly rpt, 9912–3

Economic conditions and foreign marketing prospects in 46 Sub-Saharan countries, 1983 world region rpt, 2046–5.1

Economic, social, and political summary data, by country, 1984, annual factbook, 244–11

Economic trends in income, production, prices, employment, finances, and trade, 1984 annual rpt, 2046–4.38

Exports of US, detailed Schedule B commodities by country of destination, 1983, annual rpt, 2424–9

Exports of US, detailed Schedule E commodities by mode of transport and world area and country of destination, 1983, annual rpts, 2424–5

Food supply policies of 21 developing countries, with farm sector data, tariff income, and prices and imports of 5 grains, 1960s-81, 1528–168

Imports of US, detailed Schedule A commodities by country and world area of origin, and mode of transport, 1983, annual rpts, 2424–2

Imports of US, detailed TSUSA commodities by country of origin, 1983, annual rpt, 2424–4

Loans and grants for economic and military assistance from US and intl agencies, by program and country, FY46-83, annual rpt, 9914–5

Military aid of US, arms sales, and training programs costs and budget requests by program, world region, and country, FY83-85, annual rpt, 7144–13

Military spending, arms trade, and armed forces size, with total govt spending and population, by country, 1972-82, annual rpt, 9824–1

Minerals Yearbook, 1982, Vol 3: foreign country reviews of production, trade, and policies, by commodity, annual rpt, 5604–35

Minerals Yearbook, 1983, Vol 3 preprints: foreign country review of production, trade, and policies, by commodity, annual rpt, 5604–23.66

Oil and gas undiscovered recoverable resources, cumulative production, and identified reserves, as of 1982, preliminary oil basin rpt, 5666–17.13

Population size and growth rates, and latest available benchmark demographic data, by country, 1950-83, biennial rpt, 2324–4

Sugar industry and products

see also under By Foreign Country in the "Index by Categories"

Suddendorf, Sandra

"Leasing of Agricultural Inputs", 1544–19.406

Suez Canal

Traffic, mineral commodity and other, 1981-82, *Minerals Yearbook,* annual rpt, 5604–35.1

Suffolk County, N.Y.

Auto dealer repair workers, wages, and benefits, by occupation, size of establishment, and for 24 labor market areas, Nov 1982 survey, 6787–6.202

Census of Housing, 1980: occupancy and unit characteristics, by race, Hispanic origin, and city, SMSA rpt, 2473–1.253

Census of Population and Housing, 1980: detailed population and housing characteristics, by county, city, and census tract, SMSA rpt, 2551–2.253

Repair technicians and apprentices wages and benefits, for 5 types of electrical repair shops in 19 SMSAs, Nov 1981 survey, 6787–6.197

Wages by occupation, and benefits for office and plant workers, 1984 SMSA survey rpt, 6785–11.9

see also under By SMSA or MSA in the "Index by Categories"

Sugar industry and products

Acreage planted and harvested, by crop and State, 1982-83 and planned as of June 1984, annual rpt, 1621–23

Acreage planting intended for 19 crops, by State, as of Feb 1984, annual rpt, 1621–22

Acreage, yield, and production of field crops, by State, 1978-82 and preliminary 1983, 1641–7

Agricultural Stabilization and Conservation Service sugar programs, 1955-83, annual fact sheet, 1806–4.3

Agricultural Statistics, 1983, annual rpt, 1004–1

Agriculture census, 1982: farms, farmland, production, finances, and operator characteristics, by county, final State rpt series, 2331–1

Air pollutant emission factors, by detailed source, 3rd edition, 1983-84 supplements, 9198–13

Alcoholic beverage production, stocks, materials used, and taxable and tax-free removals, for beer and distilled spirits by State, monthly rpt, 8486–1.1, 8486–1.3

Business statistics, detailed data for major industries and economic indicators, *Survey of Current Business,* monthly rpt, 2702–1.11

Census of Population, 1980: detailed socioeconomic and demographic characteristics, by age, sex, race, Hispanic origin, occupation, and industry, State rpt series, 2531–4

China economic conditions, agricultural and industrial production, trade, and domestic and foreign investment, 1980-85, 2048–106

China exports and imports by SITC 1- to 5-digit commodity, 1970s-82, annual rpt, 244–12

Communist, OECD, and selected other countries agricultural production, by commodity, 1960s-83, annual rpt, 244–5.9

Sugar industry and products

Consumption of food and nutrient intake by individuals, by food group, source, and socioeconomic characteristics, 1977-78 natl survey, final rpt series, 1356–4

Consumption, supply, trade, prices, expenditures, and indexes, by food commodity, 1963-83, annual rpt, 1544–4

Cooperatives finances and operations, aggregate for top 100 assns by principal product and revenue source, FY82, annual rpt, 1124–3

Cooperatives, membership, activities, and finances, by commodity and selected State, 1900-80 with trends from 1863, 1128–30

County Business Patterns: establishments, employees, and payrolls, by SIC 4-digit industry and county, 1981, annual State rpt series, 2326–8

County Business Patterns: establishments, employees, and payrolls, by SIC 4-digit industry and county, 1982, annual State rpt series, 2326–6

CPI by detailed component, for US city average, 28 SMSAs, and 4 regions by population size, monthly rpt, 6762–2

Cuba economic conditions, agricultural and industrial production and distribution, trade, and intl economic relations, 1970-82 and trends from 1957, 248–40

Eastern Europe agricultural production and trade by commodity, food consumption, and farm inputs, for 6 countries, 1960-80 with projections to 1991, 1528–178

EC food supply/demand and market and support prices, with exchange rates, fertilizer price index, GDP, and population, by country, 1960-83, 1528–173

Employment, earnings, and hours, by selected SIC 1- to 4-digit industry, State, and for 278 major labor areas, 1939-83, annual rpt, 6744–5

Employment, earnings, and hours, by SIC 4-digit nonfarm industry, monthly 1974-Feb 1984, annual update, 6744–4

Exports and imports of US, by agricultural commodity and country, bimonthly rpt with articles, 1522–1

Exports and imports of US, by detailed agricultural commodity and country, FY83 and CY83, semiannual rpts, 1522–4

Exports and imports of US, by detailed agricultural commodity for 8 major commodity groups, monthly rpt, 1922–8

Exports and imports of US, detailed SIC-based commodities by world area, 1983, annual rpts, 2424–6

Exports and imports of US, totals and as percent of domestic production, by SIC 2- to 5-digit commodity, 1981, annual rpt, 2424–3

Exports, imports, tariffs, and industry operating data for sugar, syrups, and honey, 1979-83, TSUSA commodity rpt, 9885–1.71

Exports of US, detailed commodities by country of destination, monthly rpt, 2422–3

Exports of US, detailed Schedule B commodities by country of destination, 1983, annual rpt, 2424–9

Exports of US, detailed Schedule E commodities by mode of transport and world area and country of destination, 1983, annual rpts, 2424–5

Farm finances, assets, liabilities, income, receipts by commodity and State, and expenses, 1980-83 and trends from 1910, annual rpt, 1544–16

Farm production inputs, outputs, and productivity, by region, 1939-82, annual rpt, 1544–17

Foreign agricultural production, prices, and trade, by country, 1983 and outlook for 1984/85, annual world region rpt series, 1524–4

Foreign and US agricultural supply/demand, consumption per capita, and trade, by world area and country group, 1960s-82, 1528–181

Foreign and US production, trade, and consumption, by country, FAS annual rpt series, 1925–14

Futures trading by commodity and exchange, and Commodity Futures Trading Commission activities, funding, and employment, FY83, annual rpt, 11924–2

Futures trading in selected commodities, foreign currencies, Treasury securities, and stock indexes, NYC, Chicago, and other markets activity, monthly rpt, 11922–5

Futures trading in selected commodities, Treasury securities, and stock indexes, NYC market activity, monthly rpt, 11922–2

Gasohol production and costs by feedstock, prices, and market penetration rates and excise tax exemption by State, 1983, article, 1561–16.404

Great Lakes trade, by SITC 3-digit commodity, port, vessel type, world area, and country, 1982, annual rpt, 7744–3

Import quotas for sugars, syrups, and molasses, and charges against quota, by country of origin, monthly rpt, 8146–1.9

Imports of products containing sugar, injury to price-supported US sugar industries, investigation with background financial and operating data, 1983 rpt, 9886–10.7

Imports of sugar and specialty sugar under quota, by country, weekly rpt, 1922–9

Imports of US, detailed Schedule A commodities by country and world area of origin, and mode of transport, 1983, annual rpts, 2424–2

Imports of US, detailed Schedule A commodities by country, monthly rpt, 2422–2

Imports of US, detailed TSUSA commodities by country of origin, 1983, annual rpt, 2424–4

Income tax returns of corporations, detailed income and tax items by industry, 1981, annual rpt, 8304–4

Input-output structure of US economy, detailed interindustry transactions for 537 industries, and components of final demand, 1977 benchmark data, 2708–17

Manufacturing census, 1982: financial and operating data, by SIC 2- to 4-digit industry, State, SMSA, and county, preliminary census div rpt series, 2491–3

Manufacturing census, 1982: financial and operating data, for SIC 4-digit industries by product, preliminary rpt, 2491–1.23, 2491–1.24

Marketing cash receipts of farms, by detailed commodity and State, 1979-82, annual rpt, 1544–18

Index by Subjects and Names

Molasses (feed) production, wholesale prices by market area, and US imports by customs district and country, weekly rpt, 1311–16

Occupational injury and illness rates, by SIC 2- to 4-digit industry, 1982, annual rpt, 6844–1

OECD trade, total and for 4 major countries, and US trade by country, by commodity, 1972-82, annual world region rpt series, 244–13

Prices (farm-retail) for foods, marketing cost components, and industry finances and productivity, selected years 1967-83, annual rpt, 1544–9

Prices received by farmers and production value for detailed crops by State, 1981-83, annual rpt, 1621–2

Producer prices and indexes, by stage of processing and detailed commodity, monthly rpt, 6762–6

Producer prices and indexes, by stage of processing and detailed commodity, monthly 1983, annual supplement, 6764–2

Production, consumption, prices, supply, stocks, and trade, quarterly rpt with articles, 1561–14

Production, consumption, supply, and trade, quarterly rpt, 1621–28

Production, farms, acreage, and related data, by selected crop and State, monthly rpt, 1621–1

Production itemized costs, receipts, and net returns, for sugar beets and sugarcane, by region, 1981-83, annual rpt, 1544–20

Production, prices, trade, and marketing, by commodity, current situation and forecast, monthly rpt, 1502–4

Production, prices, trade, stocks, and marketing of sugar, weekly rpt, 1311–2

Productivity, hours, and employment indexes for selected SIC 3- and 4-digit industries, 1954-82, annual rpt, 6824–1.3

Waterborne commerce of US (domestic and foreign), freight by commodity, traffic, and passengers, by port and waterway, 1982, annual rpt, 3754–3

see also Candy and confectionery products

see also Syrups and sweeteners

see also under By Commodity in the "Index by Categories"

Suicide

Aircraft hijackings, on-board explosions, other crimes against civil aviation, and circumstances, US and worldwide, 1931-83, annual rpt, 7504–31

Bombing (explosive and incendiary) and arson incidents by target, State, and circumstances, and explosives theft and recovery, 1982-83, annual rpt, 8484–4

Death rates by sex, race, and age for 40 causes, projected for 10-year period, 1982 rpt, 4208–21

Deaths and death rates, by cause and age, provisional 1982-83, US Vital Statistics annual rpt, 4144–7

Deaths and death rates by detailed cause and demographic characteristics, 1979 and selected trends, US Vital Statistics annual rpt, 4144–2.1

Deaths and death rates, by detailed geographic area, cause, and demographic characteristics, 1979, US Vital Statistics annual rpt, 4144–3

Index by Subjects and Names

Deaths and death rates, by selected cause and demographic characteristics, 1981, US Vital Statistics advance rpt, 4146–5.78

Deaths and death rates, by selected cause and demographic characteristics, 1982, US Vital Statistics advance rpt, 4146–5.81

Deaths and death rates from homicide, by location, circumstances, and victim characteristics, and years of life lost from homicide and other leading causes of death, 1970-78, 4205–38

Deaths by principal or contributing cause, with type of injury reported in accidental, poisoning, and violent deaths, by age, sex, and race, 1978, 4146–5.76

Economic indicators relation to measures of social pathology including crime and death rates, various periods 1950-80, 23848–76

Health condition and health care resources, use, and expenditures, 1970s-82 with trends and projections 1900-2000, annual compilation, 4144–11

Indian births, morbidity, and deaths and rates, and health services facilities and use, 1954-83, annual compilation, 4104–7

Micronesia Federated States, arrests by type, and traffic and other accidents and deaths, Jan-Aug 1983, annual rpt, 7004–6.2

Statistical Abstract of US, social, political, and economic data, 1950s-83 and trends, annual rpt, 2324–1.1

Youth homicide and suicide rates, by sex, race, and circumstances, selected years 1970-79, and stress and violent behavior reduction goals for 1990, 4102–1.437

Sulfur

see Nonmetallic minerals and mines

Sulfur oxides

see Air pollution

Sulfuric acid

see Chemicals and chemical industry

Sullivan, Gene D.

"Crucial Year for Southeastern Farmers", 9371–1.424

"Educational Inventory: Where Does the Southeast Stand?", 9371–1.428

"Financing Education in the Southeast", 9371–1.429

"Mississippi: A State in Transition", 9371–1.409

Sullivan, Patrick J.

"Counting Community Capital: The Status of Rural Infrastructure", 1004–16.1

Summer employment

see Seasonal and summer employment

Summers, Lawrence H.

"Response Variation in the CPS: Caveats for the Unemployment Analyst", 6722–1.421

Sunflowers and sunflower seeds

see Oils, oilseeds, and fats

Sunnyvale, Calif.

see also under By City in the "Index by Categories"

Superior, Wis.

Census of Housing, 1980: occupancy and unit characteristics, by race, Hispanic origin, and city, SMSA rpt, 2473–1.142

Census of Population and Housing, 1980: detailed population and housing characteristics, by county, city, and census tract, SMSA rpt, 2551–2.142

Wages of office and plant workers, by occupation, 1984 labor market area survey rpt, 6785–3.6

Supplementary Medical Insurance Trust Fund

Supermarkets

see Food stores

Supervisors

see Executives

see Industrial management

Supplemental Educational Opportunity Grants

see Student aid

Supplemental Security Income

Beneficiaries of noncash public and employer-based transfer programs, by income source and socioeconomic characteristics, 1982, final Current Population Rpt, 2546–6.37

Beneficiary socioeconomic characteristics and health service use, 1970s-83 and SSI program projections to 1995, 25148–29

Benefit overpayments, payment error rates, and sanctions imposed, for food stamp, AFDC, and SSI programs, by State, various dates 1980-82, GAO rpt, 26113–136

Benefits, and beneficiaries by other income source, eligibility type, and other characteristics, by State, 1982, annual rpt, 4744–16

Benefits and beneficiaries of SSI and other income maintenance programs, by State, monthly rpt, 4742–2

Benefits and beneficiaries of SSI, by type of eligibility, State, and county, Dec 1983, annual rpt, 4744–27

Benefits and beneficiaries with representative payees by Fed Govt cash benefit program, and OASDI and SSI fraud and misuse, various periods FY74-81, GAO rpt, 26121–85

Benefits and beneficiary characteristics of OASDHI, Medicaid, SSI, and other social insurance and public welfare programs, selected years 1937-82, annual rpt, 4744–3.11, 4744–3.12

Benefits, beneficiaries below poverty level, and State expenditures for SSI and 3 earlier programs, selected years 1972-83, article, 4742–1.402

Benefits by county, FY83, annual rpt, 4004–3

Budget of US, effects of Reagan Admin policy changes, by detailed program, FY85, annual rpt, 104–21

Children and youth benefitting from Fed Govt public welfare programs and tax expenditures, participation and funding for 71 programs, FY81-83, 21968–30

Claims processing, disability awards, and payment error by reason, various dates 1974-83, article, 4742–1.416

Cost control proposals for Fed Govt programs and mgmt, 3-year savings by function and agency, and financial and operating data, 1960s-81, 16908–1.6, 16908–1.23

County and City Data Book, detailed socioeconomic and demographic data for States, counties, and cities, selected years 1976-82, 2328–1

Deficit Reduction Act provisions related to OASDI and SSI, 1984 narrative article, 4742–1.421

Fed Govt aid to State and local govts, expenditures, and direct payments, by program, agency, and State, FY83, annual rpt, 2464–2

Fed Govt programs under Ways and Means Committee jurisdiction, program operations and financing data for assessing budgetary requirements, by State, FY70s-83, 21788–117

Food stamp recipient households size and composition, income, and income deductions allowed, Aug 1981, annual rpt, 1364–8

Fraud in Fed Govt benefit programs and other unreported taxable income from illegal activities, with methodology and bibl, 1970s-82, 8008–112

Income (household) and cash and noncash transfer program participation, by sociodemographic characteristics, quarterly rpt, 2542–2

Income (personal) by source including transfer payments, and social insurance contributions by type, by region, 1982, 2708–40

Income of households, families, and persons, by detailed socioeconomic characteristics and region, 1982, annual Current Population Rpt, 2546–6.39

Maternal and child health, State govt spending and admin of Fed Govt block grants, by program for 13 States, 1981-83, GAO rpt, 26121–70

Older persons income and income sources, by OASDI beneficiary and poverty status, labor force participation, and demographic characteristics, 1982, biennial rpt, 4744–26

Older persons population characteristics, and needs and costs of social services by type, by metro-nonmetro status, 1970s-82 with trends from 1900, 21148–28

Older persons sociodemographic characteristics, and Fed Govt program participation and funding, 1983 with trends and projections 1900-2060, annual rpt, 25144–3.1

Poverty-level persons and families, by income source, hours of work, earnings, taxes, and family characteristics, various periods 1959-84, 21788–131

Poverty status of families and persons, by detailed socioeconomic characteristics, 1982, annual Current Population Rpt, 2546–6.40

Refugee arrivals in US by world area of origin and State of settlement, and Fed Govt intl and domestic assistance costs, FY85, annual rpt, 7004–16

Research and Statistics Notes on social security programs and recipient characteristics, series, 4746–16

Research projects of SSA, narrative summary, FY84-86, annual rpt, 4744–11

Social Security Bulletin, OASDHI and other program operations and beneficiary characteristics, from 1940, monthly rpt with articles, 4742–1

SSA programs, finances, staff, and litigation, FY83, annual rpt, 4704–6

Traffic accidents and casualties detailed direct and indirect costs, by characteristics of persons and vehicles involved, 1979-80, 7768–80

Supplementary Medical Insurance Trust Fund

see Federal trust funds

Supplementary wage benefits

Supplementary wage benefits
see Employee benefit plans

Supreme Court

- Budget of US Appendix, detailed budgets and personnel summaries, by agency, FY85, annual rpt, 104–3
- Budget of US, appropriations, outlays, balances, and budget receipts, by govtl branch and agency, FY83, annual rpt, 8104–2
- Budget of US, compact budgets by function, agency, and account, FY85 with projections to FY89, annual rpt, 104–2
- Capitol Architect detailed expenditures for buildings and grounds, salaries, supplies, and services, 1st half FY84, semiannual rpt, 25922–2
- Cases and case dispositions, by type of Justice Dept participation, 1976-80, annual rpt, 6004–1
- Civil rights progress of minorities and women, Supreme Court decisions, and legislative action, 1957-83, last issue of narrative annual rpt, 11044–3
- Pay rates of Fed Govt civilian employees, by branch of govt, employee category, and pay level, as of 1984 with trends from 1789, 21628–54

Surety bonds

- Companies (surety) authorized to post bonds with Fed Govt, location and bonding limits, as of July 1983, annual listing, 8104–4
- Small Business Admin loans, contract awards, and surety bonds, by firm, State, and city, FY83, annual rpt, 9764–1.2

Surface Mining Control and Reclamation Act

- Coal surface mining reclamation costs and Interior Dept regulatory enforcement activities, impacts on industry in 5 States and 3 regions, various periods 1978-82, 6068–177

Surface Transportation Assistance Act

- Hwys designated for use by large trucks, mileage by State, as of June 1984, press release, 7556–3.1
- Trucking industry economic effects of size and weight limits, and hwy use taxes by tax type, 1982-83 and projected 1984-87, hearings, 25328–24
- Trucking industry economic effects of tax and size and weight rules, and hwy use taxes and Trust Fund revenues by tax type, FY82-84 and projected to 1990, GAO rpt, 26117–31

Surgeons and surgery

- Black medical residents by specialty, and minority medical faculty by race and Hispanic origin, selected years 1980-83, article, 4102–1.412
- Canada and US hospital use by children by Canada Province and US region, and death rates, by diagnosis and sex, selected years 1977-79, 4147–5.1
- Cesarean sections and electronic fetal monitoring, by birth outcome, and mother's sociodemographic and maternity characteristics, 1980, article, 4102–1.424
- Deaths and death rates by detailed cause and demographic characteristics, 1979 and selected trends, US Vital Statistics annual rpt, 4144–2.1
- DOD Civilian Health and Medical Program of the Uniformed Services costs and operations, FY83-84 with trends from FY79, semiannual rpt, 3502–2

DOD medical personnel, trainees, and accessions by source, by occupation, specialty, and service branch, FY83, annual rpt, 3544–24

- Drugs (analgesic) provided during visits to office-based physicians, by patient characteristics, drug brand and type, and physician specialty, 1980-81, 4146–8.99
- Drugs prescribed, by physician specialty, 1982, annual rpt, 4064–12
- *Health Care Financing Review,* Medicare and Medicaid program activity, health care expenditures, and research, quarterly rpt with articles, 4652–1
- Health condition and health care resources, use, and expenditures, 1970s-82 with trends and projections 1900-2000, annual compilation, 4144–11
- Hospital discharges and length of stay, by patient age and sex, facility size and ownership, procedure performed, and region, 1982, 4146–8.96, 4146–8.101
- Infections (hospital-related), drug resistance, and associated deaths, for teaching and non-teaching hospitals, 1980-82, article, 4202–7.401
- Israel, Tel Aviv Medical Center services and use, by patient age and condition, selected years 1976-83, article, 4102–1.445
- Manpower supply and education of health professionals, by occupation, demographic and professional characteristics, and location, 1950s-83 and projected to 2000, biennial rpt, 4114–8
- Medicare fee assignments, physician acceptance rates for selected services related to professional characteristics, FY76-78, article, 4652–1.416
- Medicare physician charges and reimbursement by enrollee characteristics and carrier, payment limits effects on charges in California, and physician earnings, by specialty, 1950s-84, 25368–127
- Medicare Supplementary Medical Insurance maximum charges reimbursable for specific services, by State and outlying area, 1983, annual rpt, 4654–4
- Military reserve forces medical personnel and wartime requirements by occupation, and medical equipment costs, by reserve component, as of 1983, annual rpt, 3544–27.2
- New Jersey nursing care by nursing unit type, level of care related to length of stay, and costs by diagnosis under 2 allocation methods, as of 1981, article, 4652–1.424
- Obstetrician-gynecologist office visits and drugs used, by visit reason, diagnosis, treatment, and patient and physician characteristics, 1980-81, 4147–13.76
- *Occupational Outlook Handbook,* 1984-85 biennial rpt, 6744–1
- Physician visits for new pain symptoms, by diagnosis, physician specialty, and patient characteristics, and drugs prescribed or used, 1980-81, 4146–8.97
- Physicians (not office-based) visits by reason, diagnosis, treatment, patient and physician characteristics, and physician primary activity, 1980, 4147–13.77
- Science and engineering grad enrollment, fields of study, financial support, and other student and instn characteristics, 1975-82, annual survey, 9627–7

Index by Subjects and Names

- Surgery performed at short-stay hospitals, by type and patient age, sex, and race, 1982, annual rpt, 4147–13.78
- VA facilities psychological services, staffing, research, and training programs, 1984 annual listing, 9924–10
- VA Medicine and Surgery Dept trainees, by detailed program and city, FY83, annual rpt, 9924–21
- VA physicians, dentists, and nurses, by age, selected employment characteristics, and VA district, quarterly rpt, 9922–11
- Veterans aged 55 and over, socioeconomic characteristics, economic resources, health care and status, and actual and expected use of VA benefits, 1983 survey, 9928–29
- Veterans inpatient care in VA hospitals by diagnosis, facilities operating costs, and other VA activities, FY83, annual rpt, 9924–1.3
- Visits to office-based surgeons and drugs provided, by characteristics of visit, patient, and physician, and location, 1980-81, 4147–13.79
- Youth office visits to physicians by patient and visit characteristics and physician specialty, and drug mentions by brand, 1980-81, 4146–8.100
- *see also* Medical transplants

Suriname

- Agricultural and food production indexes, and production of selected commodities, by world region and country, 1974-83, annual rpt, 1524–5
- Agricultural situation in Latin America, by country, 1981-83 and outlook for 1984, annual rpt, 1524–4.9
- AID economic assistance to developing countries, obligations and disbursements by country, quarterly rpt, 9912–4
- AID loan repayment status and terms by program and country, and status of predecessor agency loans, quarterly rpt, 9912–3
- Economic conditions, income, production, prices, employment, and trade, 1984 annual country rpt, 2046–4.107
- Economic, social, and political summary data, by country, 1984, annual factbook, 244–11
- Exports of US, detailed Schedule B commodities by country of destination, 1983, annual rpt, 2424–9
- Exports of US, detailed Schedule E commodities by mode of transport and world area and country of destination, 1983, annual rpts, 2424–5
- Imports of US, detailed Schedule A commodities by country and world area of origin, and mode of transport, 1983, annual rpts, 2424–2
- Imports of US, detailed TSUSA commodities by country of origin, 1983, annual rpt, 2424–4
- Loans and grants for economic and military assistance from US and intl agencies, by program and country, FY46-83, annual rpt, 9914–5
- Military aid of US, arms sales, and training programs costs and budget requests by program, world region, and country, FY83-85, annual rpt, 7144–13
- Military spending, arms trade, and armed forces size, with total govt spending and population, by country, 1972-82, annual rpt, 9824–1

Minerals Yearbook, 1982, Vol 3: foreign country reviews of production, trade, and policies, by commodity, annual rpt, 5604–35

Minerals Yearbook, 1983, Vol 3 preprints: foreign country review of production, trade, and policies, by commodity, annual rpt, 5604–23.89

Population size and growth rates, and latest available benchmark demographic data, by country, 1950-83, biennial rpt, 2324–4

see also under By Foreign Country in the "Index by Categories"

Surplus government property

AID activities and funding by project and function, FY85, and developing countries summary socioeconomic data, 1970s-83, by country, annual rpt, 9914–3

Cost control proposals for Fed Govt programs and mgmt, 3-year savings by function and agency, and financial and operating data, 1960s-81, 16908–1

Donations of surplus Fed Govt personal property to State and local agencies and nonprofit instns, by region and State, FY83, annual rpt, 9454–22

Foreign aid programs of private voluntary agencies, funding and expenditures, by agency, 1982/83, annual rpt, 9914–9

Foreign military aid of US and sales of arms, equipment, and training, by item and country, FY50-83, annual rpt, 3904–3

GSA mgmt activities and finances, FY78-83, annual rpt, 9454–23

Navy vessels sold to foreign govts, sales prices, fair market value, and Navy costs, for surplus ships sold 1981-82, GAO rpt, 26123–60

Surveillance

see Electronic surveillance

Survey of Disabled and Nondisabled Adults

Disability (work-related), incidence among men aged 22-64 related to sociodemographic and employment characteristics and to self-evaluated mental stress, 1972-74, 4746–5.43

Survey of Income and Program Participation

Income (household) and cash and noncash transfer program participation, by sociodemographic characteristics, quarterly rpt, 2542–2

Older persons sociodemographic characteristics, and Fed Govt program participation and funding by agency, 1983 with trends and projections 1900-2080, annual rpt, 25144–3

Survey of Minority-Owned Business Enterprises

Data coverage and availability for 1982 economic censuses and related statistics, 1984 guide, 2308–5

Survey of Women-Owned Businesses

Data coverage and availability for 1982 economic censuses and related statistics, 1984 guide, 2308–5

Surveys

see Annual Housing Survey

see Annual Survey of Manufactures

see Area wage surveys

see Consumer Expenditure Survey

see Consumer surveys

see Current Employment Survey

see Current Population Survey

see High School and Beyond Survey

see Industry wage surveys

see Methodology

see Mineral Industry Surveys

see National Ambulatory Medical Care Complement Survey

see National Ambulatory Medical Care Survey

see National Assessment of Educational Progress

see National Crime Survey

see National Health and Nutrition Examination Survey

see National Health Interview Survey

see National Hospital Discharge Survey

see National Master Facility Inventory survey

see National Medical Care Expenditure Survey

see National Medical Care Utilization and Expenditure Survey

see National Nursing Home Survey

see National Reporting System for Family Planning Services

see National Survey of Family Growth

see Nationwide Food Consumption Survey

see Nationwide Personal Transportation Study

see Opinion and attitude surveys

see Statistical programs and activities

see Survey of Disabled and Nondisabled Adults

see Survey of Income and Program Participation

see Survey of Minority-Owned Business Enterprises

see Survey of Women-Owned Businesses

Survivors

see Old-Age, Survivors, Disability, and Health Insurance

see Widows and widowers

Susquehanna River

Bridges over navigable waters, with type of bridge and use, owner, dimensions, and location, 1984 regional listing, 7406–5.1

Freight (waterborne domestic and foreign) by commodity, traffic, and passengers, by port and waterway, 1982, annual rpt, 3754–3.1

Water supply and quality in streams and lakes, and groundwater levels in wells, by drainage basin, 1980, annual State rpt series, 5666–12

Water supply and quality in streams and lakes, and groundwater levels in wells, by drainage basin, 1981, annual State rpt series, 5666 16

Water supply and quality in streams and lakes, and groundwater levels in wells, by drainage basin, 1982, annual State rpt series, 5666–20

Water supply and quality in streams and lakes, and groundwater levels in wells, by drainage basin, 1983, annual State rpt series, 5666–10

Water supply in US and Canada, streamflow, well and reservoir levels, and dissolved solids and temperature in 6 US rivers, by station, monthly rpt, 5662–3

Sutton, William

"Controlled Foreign Corporations, 1980", 8302–2.410

Swamps

see Wetlands

Swamy, P. A.

"Foundations of Econometrics, Are There Any?", 9366–6.76

Swan, James H.

"Medicaid Nursing Home Reimbursement Policies, Rates, and Expenditures", 4652–1.422

Swant, Frank T.

"Washington State Patrol Heavy Truck Inspection Program", 7762–9.407

Swartz, T. A.

"Prevention of Measles in Israel: Implications of a Long-Term Partial Immunization Program", 4102–1.429

Swaziland

AID activities and funding by project and function, FY85, and developing countries summary socioeconomic data, 1970s-83, by country, annual rpt, 9914–3

AID economic assistance to developing countries, obligations and disbursements by country, quarterly rpt, 9912–4

AID loan repayment status and terms by program and country, and status of predecessor agency loans, quarterly rpt, 9912–3

Economic conditions and foreign marketing prospects in 46 Sub-Saharan countries, 1983 world region rpt, 2046–5.1

Economic, social, and political summary data, by country, 1984, annual factbook, 244–11

Exports of US, detailed Schedule B commodities by country of destination, 1983, annual rpt, 2424–9

Exports of US, detailed Schedule E commodities by mode of transport and world area and country of destination, 1983, annual rpts, 2424–5

Imports of US, detailed Schedule A commodities by country and world area of origin, and mode of transport, 1983, annual rpts, 2424–2

Imports of US, detailed TSUSA commodities by country of origin, 1983, annual rpt, 2424–4

Loans and grants for economic and military assistance from US and intl agencies, by program and country, FY46-83, annual rpt, 9914–5

Military aid of US, arms sales, and training programs costs and budget requests by program, world region, and country, FY83-85, annual rpt, 7144–13

Military spending, arms trade, and armed forces size, with total govt spending and population, by country, 1972-82, annual rpt, 9824–1

Minerals Yearbook, 1982, Vol 3: foreign country reviews of production, trade, and policies, by commodity, annual rpt, 5604–35

Minerals Yearbook, 1982, Vol 3 preprints: foreign country review of production, trade, and policies, by commodity, annual rpt, 5604–17.83

Population size and growth rates, and latest available benchmark demographic data, by country, 1950-83, biennial rpt, 2324–4

see also under By Foreign Country in the "Index by Categories"

Sweden

Sweden

Agricultural and food production indexes, and production of selected commodities, by world region and country, 1974-83, annual rpt, 1524–5

Agricultural imports of 3 countries, by commodity and country of origin, 1981-FY84, article, 1925–34.431

Agricultural situation in Western Europe, by country and commodity, 1983 and outlook for 1984, annual rpt, 1524–4.6

Agricultural supply/demand, trade, and production, and socioeconomic data, by country, 1950s-77, 1528–179

AID loan repayment status and terms by program and country, and status of predecessor agency loans, quarterly rpt, 9912–3

Auto and auto products sales, prices, and registrations in US, and trade of 8 countries with US, by make and model, 1964-83, annual rpt, 9884–7

Auto safety and experimental vehicle designs, 1982, conf proceedings, annual rpt, 7764–3

Computers and computer equipment market and trade, and user industry operations and demand, 1984 country market research rpt, 2045–1.49

Economic and monetary trends, compounded annual rates of change for US and 10 major trading partners, quarterly rpt, 9391–7

Economic conditions in Communist, OECD, and selected other countries, 1960s-83, annual rpt, 244–5

Economic conditions, income, production, prices, employment, and trade, 1984 semiannual country rpt, 2046–4.118

Economic, social, and political summary data, by country, 1984, annual factbook, 244–11

Economic trends in income, production, prices, employment, finances, and trade, 1984 semiannual rpt, 2046–4.48

Employment, labor force, and participation and unemployment rates by sex, in US and 9 OECD countries, various periods 1970-3rd qtr 1983, annual article, 6722–1.404

Energy prices and taxes by energy source and end-use sector, for US and 9 OECD countries, quarterly 1979-83, annual rpt, 3164–71

Exports and imports of OECD countries, by country, 1983, annual rpt, 7144–10

Exports and imports of US with Western Europe, and US market share and export opportunities for selected commodities, by country, 1982-84, 2048–105

Exports of US, detailed Schedule B commodities by country of destination, 1983, annual rpt, 2424–9

Exports of US, detailed Schedule E commodities by mode of transport and world area and country of destination, 1983, annual rpts, 2424–5

Health care resources, use, and per capita public expenditures, and selected population characteristics, for US and 6 countries, selected years 1975-81, 21148–33

Imports of US, detailed Schedule A commodities by country and world area of origin, and mode of transport, 1983, annual rpts, 2424–2

Imports of US, detailed TSUSA commodities by country of origin, 1983, annual rpt, 2424–4

Loans and grants for economic and military assistance from US and intl agencies, by program and country, FY46-83, annual rpt, 9914–5

Manufacturing labor productivity and cost indexes for US and 11 OECD countries, 1960-82, annual article, 6722–1.405

Manufacturing productivity and unit labor cost indexes for US and 11 countries, 1950-82 and preliminary 1983, annual rpt, 6864–1

Military aid of US, arms sales, and training programs costs and budget requests by program, world region, and country, FY83-85, annual rpt, 7144–13

Military spending, arms trade, and armed forces size, with total govt spending and population, by country, 1972-82, annual rpt, 9824–1

Minerals Yearbook, 1982, Vol 3: foreign country reviews of production, trade, and policies, by commodity, annual rpt, 5604–35

Minerals Yearbook, 1982, Vol 3 preprints: foreign country review of production, trade, and policies, by commodity, annual rpt, 5604–17.67

Nuclear power generation in US and 18 non-Communist countries, monthly rpt, 3162–24.10

Nuclear power plant construction and operation status, and capacity, by plant, region, State, and selected country, 1983 and projected to 2020, annual rpt, 3164–57

Population size and growth rates, and latest available benchmark demographic data, by country, 1950-83, biennial rpt, 2324–4

Sporting goods and recreational equipment and vehicles market and trade, 1984 country market research rpt, 2045–14.6

Telecommunication equipment market and trade, and user industry operations and demand, 1982 country market research rpt, 2045–12.36

see also under By Foreign Country in the "Index by Categories"

Sweeney, Deborah H.

"Nuclear Engineering Enrollments and Degrees, 1983", 3004–5

Sweeteners

see Honey and beekeeping

see Sugar industry and products

see Syrups and sweeteners

Swimming

Apartment market absorption rates and characteristics for nonsubsidized privately financed furnished and unfurnished units completed in 1982, annual Current Housing Rpt, 2484–2

Army Corps of Engineers water resources dev projects, recreation activities by district and project, 1982, annual rpt, 3754–5

Death rates by sex, race, and age for 40 causes, projected for 10-year period, 1982 rpt, 4208–21

Deaths from accidents by selected cause, 1981 with trends from 1960s and reduction goals for 1990, article, 4102–1.409

Index by Subjects and Names

Injuries and deaths from use of selected consumer products and related activity, by victim age and sex, 1982, annual rpt, 9164–7

Natl forests recreation sites, area, and capacity, by type of activity, as of Nov 1983, annual rpt, 1204–28

Natl forests recreational use, visitor-days by State and activity, FY79-83, annual rpt, 1204–1.1

Natl forests recreational use, visitor-days by type of activity, forest, and State, FY83 with trends from 1924, annual rpt series, 1204–17

Natl park system visitor deaths, by park and type of accident, 1973-83, annual rpt, 5544–6

Pool construction and maintenance franchise business opportunities, 1984 annual listing, 2044–27

Pool construction receipts, by State, 1982 Census of Construction Industries, preliminary rpt series, 2371–1

Pool solar heating system manufacturing, 1983, annual rpt, 3164–62

Recreation (outdoor) participation, by type of activity, projected 1985-2030, 1208–195

Red Cross program operations and financial statements, 1982/83, annual rpt, 29254–1

Waterborne disease outbreaks and cases, by type, source, and location, 1983, annual rpt, 4205–35

Swine

see Livestock and livestock industry

Switzerland

Agricultural and food production indexes, and production of selected commodities, by world region and country, 1974-83, annual rpt, 1524–5

Agricultural situation in Western Europe, by country and commodity, 1983 and outlook for 1984, annual rpt, 1524–4.6

Agricultural supply/demand, trade, and production, and socioeconomic data, by country, 1950s-77, 1528–179

Biotechnology commercial uses, R&D funding and output, controls, and industry financial and operating data, for US and 5 countries, 1970s-83 and estimated 1984-85, 26358–98

Economic and monetary trends, compounded annual rates of change for US and 10 major trading partners, quarterly rpt, 9391–7

Economic conditions in Communist, OECD, and selected other countries, 1960s-83, annual rpt, 244–5

Economic, social, and political summary data, by country, 1984, annual factbook, 244–11

Economic trends in income, production, prices, employment, finances, and trade, 1984 annual rpt, 2046–4.39

Exports and imports of OECD countries, by country, 1983, annual rpt, 7144–10

Exports and imports of US with Western Europe, and US market share and export opportunities for selected commodities, by country, 1982-84, 2048–105

Exports of US, detailed Schedule B commodities by country of destination, 1983, annual rpt, 2424–9

Index by Subjects and Names

Synthetic fuels

Exports of US, detailed Schedule E commodities by mode of transport and world area and country of destination, 1983, annual rpts, 2424–5

Foreign exchange rate intervention in 3 currency markets by Fed Reserve, various periods Sept 1977-Dec 1979, technical paper, 9366–1.140

Imports of US, detailed Schedule A commodities by country and world area of origin, and mode of transport, 1983, annual rpts, 2424–2

Imports of US, detailed TSUSA commodities by country of origin, 1983, annual rpt, 2424–4

Investment (foreign direct) in US, major investors and investments by SIC 4-digit industry, transaction type and value, and location, 1983, annual rpt, 2044–20

Loans and grants for economic and military assistance from US and intl agencies, by program and country, FY46-83, annual rpt, 9914–5

Military aid of US, arms sales, and training programs costs and budget requests by program, world region, and country, FY83-85, annual rpt, 7144–13

Military spending, arms trade, and armed forces size, with total govt spending and population, by country, 1972-82, annual rpt, 9824–1

Minerals Yearbook, 1982, Vol 3: foreign country reviews of production, trade, and policies, by commodity, annual rpt, 5604–35

Minerals Yearbook, 1983, Vol 3 preprints: foreign country review of production, trade, and policies, by commodity, annual rpt, 5604–23.68

Nuclear power generation in US and 18 non-Communist countries, monthly rpt, 3162–24.10

Nuclear power plant construction and operation status, and capacity, by plant, region, State, and selected country, 1983 and projected to 2020, annual rpt, 3164–57

Population size and growth rates, and latest available benchmark demographic data, by country, 1950-83, biennial rpt, 2324–4

Sporting goods and recreational equipment and vehicles market and trade, 1984 country market research rpt, 2045–14.7

see also Liechtenstein

see also under By Foreign Country in the "Index by Categories"

Symansky, Steven A.

"Alternative Financial Strategies: The Results of Some Policy Simulations with the Multi-Country Model", 9366–7.90

Synthetic fibers and fabrics

Air pollutant and radiation indoor levels by emissions source, and household exposure and health effects by pollutant type, various periods 1966-83, hearings, 21708–102

Broadwoven fabric production by region and State, inventory, orders, and exports, by product, 1983, annual Current Industrial Rpt, 2506–5.10

Business statistics, detailed data for major industries and economic indicators, *Survey of Current Business,* monthly rpt, 2702–1.19

Census of Population, 1980: detailed socioeconomic and demographic characteristics, by age, sex, race, Hispanic origin, occupation, and industry, State rpt series, 2531–4

China economic conditions, agricultural and industrial production, trade, and domestic and foreign investment, 1980-85, 2048–106

Communist, OECD, and selected other countries consumer and producer goods production, 1960s-83, annual rpt, 244–5.8

County Business Patterns: establishments, employees, and payrolls, by SIC 4-digit industry and county, 1981, annual State rpt series, 2326–8

County Business Patterns: establishments, employees, and payrolls, by SIC 4-digit industry and county, 1982, annual State rpt series, 2326–6

Cuba economic conditions, agricultural and industrial production and distribution, trade, and intl economic relations, 1970-82 and trends from 1957, 248–40

Employment, earnings, and hours, by selected SIC 1- to 4-digit industry, State, and for 278 major labor areas, 1939-83, annual rpt, 6744–5

Employment, earnings, and hours, by SIC 4-digit nonfarm industry, monthly 1974-Feb 1984, annual update, 6744–4

Exports and imports of US, detailed SIC-based commodities by world area, 1983, annual rpts, 2424–6

Exports, imports, tariffs, and industry operating data for textile fiber and products, TSUSA commodity rpt series, 9885–3

Exports of textiles, by product and country of destination, monthly rpt, 2042–26

Exports of US, detailed commodities by country of destination, monthly rpt, 2422–3

Exports of US, detailed Schedule B commodities by country of destination, 1983, annual rpt, 2424–9

Great Lakes trade, by SITC 3-digit commodity, port, vessel type, world area, and country, 1982, annual rpt, 7744–3

Handbags trade, tariffs, and industry operating data, 1979-83, TSUSA commodity rpt supplement, 9885–7.60

Imports and import limits for textiles under Multifiber Arrangement by product and country, with US exports and use, 1970-83, semiannual rpt, 9882–11

Imports of textiles, by country of origin, monthly rpt, 2042–27

Imports of textiles, by product and country of origin, monthly rpt, 2422–1

Imports of textiles, by product and country of origin, monthly rpt series, 2046–9

Imports of textiles, by product and country of origin, periodic rpt series, 2046–8

Imports of textiles, monthly rpt, 2042–18

Imports of textiles, total and as percents of US production and use, by commodity, 1972-82, annual rpt, 2044–14

Imports of US, detailed Schedule A commodities by country and world area of origin, and mode of transport, 1983, annual rpts, 2424–2

Imports of US, detailed Schedule A commodities by country, monthly rpt, 2422–2

Imports of US, detailed TSUSA commodities by country of origin, 1983, annual rpt, 2424–4

Input-output structure of US economy, detailed interindustry transactions for 537 industries, and components of final demand, 1977 benchmark data, 2708–17

Manufacturing census, 1982: financial and operating data, by SIC 2- to 4-digit industry, State, SMSA, and county, preliminary census div rpt series, 2491–3

Manufacturing census, 1982: financial and operating data, for SIC 4-digit industries by product, preliminary rpt series, 2491–1

Manufacturing census, 1982: textile mill machinery in place, by machine type and textile industry, special preliminary rpts, 2491–2

Occupational injury and illness rates, by SIC 2- to 4-digit industry, 1982, annual rpt, 6844–1

Producer prices and indexes, by stage of processing and detailed commodity, monthly rpt, 6762–6

Producer prices and indexes, by stage of processing and detailed commodity, monthly 1983, annual supplement, 6764–2

Production, consumption, prices, and trade, periodic situation rpt with articles, 1561–1

Production, stocks, materials used, and orders, by product and major State, and trade by country, periodic Current Industrial Rpt series, 2506–5

Productivity, hours, and employment indexes for selected SIC 3- and 4-digit industries, 1954-82, annual rpt, 6824–1.3

Waterborne commerce of US (domestic and foreign), freight by commodity, traffic, and passengers, by port and waterway, 1982, annual rpt, 3754–3

Wholesale trade census, 1982: employment, establishments, sales by commodity, and payroll, by SIC 4-digit kind of business and State, preliminary rpt, 2403–1.23

Yarn (textured) production by end use, trade, and consumption, by product, 1983, annual Current Industrial Rpt, 2506–5.4

see also under By Commodity in the "Index by Categories"

Synthetic fuels

Budget of US, effects of Reagan Admin policy changes, by detailed program, FY85, annual rpt, 104–21

Carbon dioxide atmospheric levels, climatic effects and impacts of fossil and synthetic fuels use, deforestation, and land use patterns, research rpt series, 3406–3

Electric power plants, by capacity, fuel used, unit type, region, State, and county, for plants added and retired, 1983 and planned through 1993, annual rpt, 3164–36

Natl Energy Policy Plan, energy supply, demand, and prices, by fuel and consuming sector, projected 1985-2010, biennial rpt, 3004–13

Oil refineries financial and operating impacts from auto use of alcohol fuels, projected to 2000 with trends 1964-80, 3308–75

Production, trade, supply, use, conservation, and DOE activities, by energy type, FY83, annual rpt, 3024–2

Synthetic fuels

R&D industry funding and employment of scientists and engineers, by industry group, firm size, and funding source, 1956-82, annual rpt, 9627–21

Research publications on energy of DOE and other sources, monthly listing, 3002–2

Supply/demand and prices, by fuel type and consuming sector with foreign comparisons, 1949-83, annual rpt, 3164–74

Western States oil shale dev projects in Green River area, production goals and cost estimates, as of 1983, article, 9381–1.409

see also Alcohol fuels

see also Biomass energy

see also Gasohol

Synthetic Fuels Corp.

see U.S. Synthetic Fuels Corp.

Synthetic products

see Chemicals and chemical industry

see Plastics and plastics industry

see Synthetic fibers and fabrics

see Synthetic fuels

Syphilis

see Venereal diseases

Syracuse, N.Y.

Census of Housing, 1980: occupancy and unit characteristics, by race, Hispanic origin, and city, SMSA rpt, 2473–1.346

Census of Population and Housing, 1980: detailed population and housing characteristics, by county, city, and census tract, SMSA rpt, 2551–2.346

see also under By City and By SMSA or MSA in the "Index by Categories"

Syria

- Agricultural and food production indexes, and production of selected commodities, by world region and country, 1974-83, annual rpt, 1524–5
- Agricultural situation in Middle East and North Africa, by country and commodity, 1983 and outlook for 1984, annual rpt, 1524–4.3
- Agricultural supply/demand, trade, and production, and socioeconomic data, by country, 1950s-77, 1528–179
- AID economic assistance to developing countries, obligations and disbursements by country, quarterly rpt, 9912–4
- AID loan repayment status and terms by program and country, and status of predecessor agency loans, quarterly rpt, 9912–3
- *Background Notes,* summary social, political, and economic data, 1983 rpt, 7006–2.15
- Economic, social, and political summary data, by country, 1984, annual factbook, 244–11
- Economic trends in income, production, prices, employment, finances, and trade, 1984 annual rpt, 2046–4.64
- Exports of US, detailed Schedule B commodities by country of destination, 1983, annual rpt, 2424–9
- Exports of US, detailed Schedule E commodities by mode of transport and world area and country of destination, 1983, annual rpts, 2424–5
- Imports of US, detailed Schedule A commodities by country and world area of origin, and mode of transport, 1983, annual rpts, 2424 2

Imports of US, detailed TSUSA commodities by country of origin, 1983, annual rpt, 2424–4

- Loans and grants for economic and military assistance from US and intl agencies, by program and country, FY46-83, annual rpt, 9914–5
- Military spending, arms trade, and armed forces size, with total govt spending and population, by country, 1972-82, annual rpt, 9824–1
- *Minerals Yearbook, 1982,* Vol 3: foreign country reviews of production, trade, and policies, by commodity, annual rpt, 5604–35
- *Minerals Yearbook, 1982,* Vol 3 preprints: foreign country review of production, trade, and policies, by commodity, annual rpt, 5604–17.88
- Population size and growth rates, and latest available benchmark demographic data, by country, 1950-83, biennial rpt, 2324–4

see also under By Foreign Country in the "Index by Categories"

Syron, Richard F.

"Interstate Banking: The Drive To Consolidate", 9373–1.409

"'New England Experiment' in Interstate Banking", 9373–1.405

Syrups and sweeteners

Agricultural Statistics, 1983, annual rpt, 1004–1

- Consumption per capita and prices of caloric and noncaloric sweeteners, quarterly rpt, 1561–14.2
- Consumption, supply, trade, prices, expenditures, and indexes, by food commodity, 1963-83, annual rpt, 1544–4
- Exports and imports of US, by agricultural commodity and country, bimonthly rpt with articles, 1522–1
- Exports and imports of US, by detailed agricultural commodity and country, FY83 and CY83, semiannual rpts, 1522–4
- Exports and imports of US, detailed SIC-based commodities by world area, 1983, annual rpts, 2424–6
- Exports and imports of US, totals and as percent of domestic production, by SIC 2- to 5-digit commodity, 1981, annual rpt, 2424–3
- Exports, imports, tariffs, and industry operating data for sugar, syrups, and honey, 1979-83, TSUSA commodity rpt, 9885–1.71
- Exports of US, detailed commodities by country of destination, monthly rpt, 2422–3
- Exports of US, detailed Schedule B commodities by country of destination, 1983, annual rpt, 2424–9
- Exports of US, detailed Schedule E commodities by mode of transport and world area and country of destination, 1983, annual rpts, 2424–5
- Farm finances, assets, liabilities, income, receipts by commodity and State, and expenses, 1980-83 and trends from 1910, annual rpt, 1544–16
- Foreign and US production, trade, and consumption, by country, FAS annual rpt series, 1925–14
- Great Lakes trade, by SITC 3-digit commodity, port, vessel type, world area, and country, 1982, annual rpt, 7744–3

Index by Subjects and Names

- Import quotas for sugars, syrups, and molasses, and charges against quota, by country of origin, monthly rpt, 8146–1.9
- Imports of products containing sugar, injury to price-supported US sugar industries, investigation with background financial and operating data, 1983 rpt, 9886–10.7
- Imports of US, detailed Schedule A commodities by country and world area of origin, and mode of transport, 1983, annual rpts, 2424–2
- Imports of US, detailed Schedule A commodities by country, monthly rpt, 2422–2
- Imports of US, detailed TSUSA commodities by country of origin, 1983, annual rpt, 2424–4
- Input-output structure of US economy, detailed interindustry transactions for 537 industries, and components of final demand, 1977 benchmark data, 2708–17
- Manufacturing census, 1982: financial and operating data, by SIC 2- to 4-digit industry, State, SMSA, and county, preliminary census div rpt series, 2491–3
- Manufacturing census, 1982: financial and operating data, for SIC 4-digit industries by product, preliminary rpt, 2491–1.37
- Maple syrup production, by State, 1978-81, 1641–7
- Molasses trade, tariffs, and industry operating data, foreign and US, 1978-82, TSUSA commodity rpt supplemental, 9885–1.60
- Producer prices and indexes, by stage of processing and detailed commodity, monthly rpt, 6762–6
- Producer prices and indexes, by stage of processing and detailed commodity, monthly 1983, annual supplement, 6764–2

see also Honey and beekeeping

see also Sugar industry and products

see also under By Commodity in the "Index by Categories"

Systan, Inc.

"Study of the Careers of Participants in UMTA's Transit Management Programs (Section 10)", 7888–60

Szarek, Patricia

"Effects of Strong Dollar, Economic Recovery Apparent in First-Half Import and Export Prices", 6722–1.459

Szatan, Jerry

"Economic Recovery and Jobs in the Seventh District", 9375–1.408

Tacoma, Wash.

- Census of Housing, 1980: occupancy and unit characteristics, by race, Hispanic origin, and city, SMSA rpt, 2473–1.347
- Census of Population and Housing, 1980: detailed population and housing characteristics, by county, city, and census tract, SMSA rpt, 2551–2.347
- Fruit and vegetable shipments, and arrivals in 23 US and 5 Canada cities, by mode of transport and State or country of origin, 1983, annual rpt, 1311–4.2
- Housing and households detailed characteristics, and unit and neighborhood quality, by inside-outside central cities, 1981 survey, SMSA rpt, 2485–6.27

Index by Subjects and Names

Wages of office and plant workers, by occupation, 1984 labor market area survey rpt, 6785–3.3

see also under By City and By SMSA or MSA in the "Index by Categories"

Taffel, Selma

"Birth and Fertility Rates for States: U.S., 1980", 4147–21.42

"Characteristics of Asian Births: U.S., 1980", 4146–5.75

"Midwife and Out-of-Hospital Deliveries: U.S.", 4147–21.40

Taiwan

- Acrylic sheet from Taiwan at less than fair value, imports injury to US industry, investigation with background financial and operating data, 1984 rpt, 9886–14.105
- Agricultural and food production indexes, and production of selected commodities, by world region and country, 1974-83, annual rpt, 1524–5
- Agricultural situation in 4 East Asian countries, by commodity, 1983 and outlook for 1984, annual rpt, 1524–4.2
- Agricultural supply/demand, trade, and production, and socioeconomic data, by country, 1950s-77, 1528–179
- AID loan repayment status and terms by program and country, and status of predecessor agency loans, quarterly rpt, 9912–3
- Bicycle tires and tubes from Taiwan at less than fair value, imports injury to US industry, investigation with background financial and operating data, 1984 rpt, 9886–14.106
- Chairs (metal stacking) from Italy and Taiwan at less than fair value, imports injury to US industry, investigation with background financial and operating data, 1984 rpt, 9886–14.121
- Economic conditions in Communist, OECD, and selected other countries, 1960s-83, annual rpt, 244–5
- Economic conditions, income, production, prices, employment, and trade, 1984 semiannual country rpt, 2046–4.119
- Economic indicators of 12 Pacific Basin countries or areas and US, quarterly rpt, 9393–9
- Economic, social, and political summary data, by country, 1984, annual factbook, 244–11
- Exports and imports of US, by commodity and country, 1972-82, annual world region rpt, 244–13.5
- Exports of US, detailed Schedule B commodities by country of destination, 1983, annual rpt, 2424–9
- Exports of US, detailed Schedule E commodities by mode of transport and world area and country of destination, 1983, annual rpts, 2424–5
- Imports of US, detailed Schedule A commodities by country and world area of origin, and mode of transport, 1983, annual rpts, 2424–2
- Imports of US, detailed TSUSA commodities by country of origin, 1983, annual rpt, 2424–4
- Industrial process control equipment market and trade, and user industry operations and demand, 1984 country market research rpt, 2045–6.38

Tanker ships

- Loans and grants for economic and military assistance from US and intl agencies, by program and country, FY46-83, annual rpt, 9914–5
- Military aid of US, arms sales, and training programs costs and budget requests by program, world region, and country, FY83-85, annual rpt, 7144–13
- Military spending, arms trade, and armed forces size, with total govt spending and population, by country, 1972-82, annual rpt, 9824–1
- *Minerals Yearbook, 1982,* Vol 3: foreign country reviews of production, trade, and policies, by commodity, annual rpt, 5604–35
- Nuclear power generation in US and 18 non-Communist countries, monthly rpt, 3162–24.10
- Nuclear power plant construction and operation status, and capacity, by plant, region, State, and selected country, 1983 and projected to 2020, annual rpt, 3164–57
- Population size and growth rates, and latest available benchmark demographic data, by country, 1950-83, biennial rpt, 2324–4
- Steel pipes and tubes from South Korea and Taiwan at less than fair value, imports injury to US industry, investigation with background financial and operating data, 1984 rpt, 9886–14.104
- TVs (color) from South Korea and Taiwan at less than fair value, imports injury to US industry, investigation with background financial and operating data, 1984 rpt, 9886–14.101

see also under By Foreign Country in the "Index by Categories"

Talc

see Nonmetallic minerals and mines

Tallahassee, Fla.

- Census of Housing, 1980: occupancy and unit characteristics, by race, Hispanic origin, and city, SMSA rpt, 2473–1.348
- Census of Population and Housing, 1980: detailed population and housing characteristics, by county, city, and census tract, SMSA rpt, 2551–2.348

see also under By SMSA or MSA in the "Index by Categories"

Tallow and greases

see Oils, oilseeds, and fats

Tampa, Fla.

- Census of Housing, 1980: occupancy and unit characteristics, by race, Hispanic origin, and city, SMSA rpt, 2473–1.349
- Census of Population and Housing, 1980: detailed population and housing characteristics, by county, city, and census tract, SMSA rpt, 2551–2.349
- Wages by occupation, and benefits for office and plant workers, 1984 labor market area survey rpt, 6785–3.9

see also under By City and By SMSA or MSA in the "Index by Categories"

Tanker ships

- Bulk carrier ships in world fleet, characteristics by country of registry, 1982, annual rpt, 7704–13
- Communist, OECD, and selected other countries freight and carrier inventories, by mode of transport, 1960s-83, annual rpt, 244–5.10
- Construction and conversion costs for merchant ships by owner and builder, fleet size, and employment, monthly rpt, 7702–1
- Construction and operating subsidies of MarAd by firm, and ship deliveries and fleet by country, by vessel type, FY83, annual rpt, 7704–14.1, 7704–14.2
- Construction of new ships, by type and by country of construction and registry, 1982, annual rpt, 7704–4
- Defense Fuel Supply Center procurement, prices, stocks, transport, and other activities and finances, FY83, annual rpt, 3904–8
- Exports and imports of US (waterborne), by type of service, commodity, country, route, and US port, 1982, annual rpt, 7704–2
- Exports and imports of US (waterborne), by type of service, customs district, port, and world area, monthly rpt, 2422–7
- Finances, operations, vehicles, equipment, accidents, and energy use, by mode of transport, 1955-84, annual rpt, 7304–2
- Foreign and US shipping and shipbuilding subsidies and aid, with summary fleet, trade, and GNP data, for 48 countries, 1979-80, biennial rpt, 7704–18
- Foreign and US tankers, by selected characteristics and country of registry, 1982, annual rpt, 7704–17
- Freight (waterborne domestic and foreign) by commodity, traffic, and passengers, by port and waterway, 1982, annual rpt, 3754–3
- Great Lakes trade, by SITC 3-digit commodity, port, vessel type, world area, and country, 1982, annual rpt, 7744–3
- Merchant ships in active US fleet and Natl Defense Reserve Fleet, number and tonnage by owner/operator, Jan 1984, semiannual inventory, 7702–2
- Merchant ships in US fleet, shipping costs, construction, employment, military availability, and Fed Govt subsidies, 1970s-1984 and projected to 2000, 26306–6.83
- Merchant ships in world fleet, and tonnage, by country of registry, 1982, annual rpt, 7704–3
- Merchant ships in world fleet, and tonnage, by vessel type, 1961-81, 1548–235
- Merchant ships in world fleet, and tonnage, by vessel type, 1977-81, annual rpt, 5604–35.1
- Merchant ships in world fleet, by selected characteristics and country of registry, as of Jan 1983, annual rpt, 7704–1
- Military Sealift Command operations for naval fleet support, and transport of DOD and AID cargo by route, quarterly rpt, 3802–2
- Oil (Alaskan) potential exports to Japan, costs and benefits, with background data on oil prices, Pacific Basin supply/demand, and tankers, various periods 1918-99, hearings, 25388–45
- Oil and refined products stocks, and interdistrict shipments by mode of transport, monthly rpt, 3162–6.2
- Oil and refined products stocks, and interdistrict shipments by mode of transport, 1983, annual rpt, 3164–2

Tanker ships

Oil spills from US OCS platforms and pipelines, and from tankers at sea and in port worldwide, various periods 1964-80, 5738–1

Ports, port facilities by type, and inland waterways by size, by location, 1982-83, annual rpt, 7704–16

St Lawrence Seaway ships, cargo and passenger volumes, and toll revenues, 1981-82 and trends from 1959, annual rpt, 7744–2

see also Oil spills

Tanks

see Military vehicles

Tannenwald, Robert

"Pros and Cons of Worldwide Unitary Taxation", 9373–1.412

"Why Has the Unemployment Rate Declined So Rapidly?", 9373–1.415

Tanning industry

see Hides and skins

see Leather industry and products

Tansey, John B.

"Forest Statistics for the Southern Coastal Plain of North Carolina, 1983", 1206–4.5

"Pine Resource in South Carolina: An Interim Assessment, 1983", 1206–32.1

"South Carolina's Industrial Timber Products Output, 1977-81", 1208–203

Tantalum

see Metals and metal industries

Tanzania

- Agricultural and food production indexes, and production of selected commodities, by world region and country, 1974-83, annual rpt, 1524–5
- Agricultural situation in sub-Saharan Africa, by country, 1982-83 and outlook for 1984, annual rpt, 1524–4.10
- Agricultural supply/demand, trade, and production, and socioeconomic data, by country, 1950s-77, 1528–179
- AID activities and funding by project and function, FY85, and developing countries summary socioeconomic data, 1970s-83, by country, annual rpt, 9914–3
- AID economic assistance to developing countries, obligations and disbursements by country, quarterly rpt, 9912–4
- AID loan repayment status and terms by program and country, and status of predecessor agency loans, quarterly rpt, 9912–3
- *Background Notes,* summary social, political, and economic data, 1984 rpt, 7006–2.21
- Economic conditions and foreign marketing prospects in 46 Sub-Saharan countries, 1983 world region rpt, 2046–5.1
- Economic, social, and political summary data, by country, 1984, annual factbook, 244–11
- Exports of US, detailed Schedule B commodities by country of destination, 1983, annual rpt, 2424–9
- Exports of US, detailed Schedule E commodities by mode of transport and world area and country of destination, 1983, annual rpts, 2424–5
- Food supply policies of 21 developing countries, with farm sector data, tariff income, and prices and imports of 5 grains, 1960s-81, 1528–168
- Imports of US, detailed Schedule A commodities by country and world area of origin, and mode of transport, 1983, annual rpts, 2424–2

Imports of US, detailed TSUSA commodities by country of origin, 1983, annual rpt, 2424–4

- Loans and grants for economic and military assistance from US and intl agencies, by program and country, FY46-83, annual rpt, 9914–5
- Military aid of US, arms sales, and training programs costs and budget requests by program, world region, and country, FY83-85, annual rpt, 7144–13
- Military spending, arms trade, and armed forces size, with total govt spending and population, by country, 1972-82, annual rpt, 9824–1
- *Minerals Yearbook, 1982,* Vol 3: foreign country reviews of production, trade, and policies, by commodity, annual rpt, 5604–35
- *Minerals Yearbook, 1982,* Vol 3 preprints: foreign country review of production, trade, and policies, by commodity, annual rpt, 5604–17.83
- Population size and growth rates, and latest available benchmark demographic data, by country, 1950-83, biennial rpt, 2324–4

see also under By Foreign Country in the "Index by Categories"

Tape recordings

see Recording industry

Tar sands

- Natl Energy Policy Plan, energy supply, demand, and prices, by fuel and consuming sector, projected 1985-2010, biennial rpt, 3004–13
- Producers finances and operations, by energy type for US firms domestic and foreign operations, 1974-82, annual rpt, 3164–44.2

Tarhan, Vefa

"Federal Reserve's New Operating Procedures: A Post Mortem", 9366–6.78

Tariff Commission

see U.S. International Trade Commission

Tariffs and foreign trade controls

- Agricultural production, trade, and climatic devs, weekly press release, 1922–4
- Agricultural products trade, tariffs, and industry operating data, 1979-83, TSUSA commodity rpt series, 9885–1
- Auto and auto products sales, prices, and registrations in US, and trade of 8 countries with US, by make and model, 1964-83, annual rpt, 9884–7
- Auto industry operations, trade, and registrations, foreign and US, selected years 1928-82, domestic content requirement hearings, 21788–134
- Biotechnology commercial uses, R&D funding and output, controls, and industry financial and operating data, for US and 5 countries, 1970s-83 and estimated 1984-85, 26358–98
- Brooms (broomcorn) shipments, trade, and apparent consumption data for USITC import quota determination, 1983, annual rpt, 9884–6
- Budget of US, projected under current fiscal policies, FY85-89, annual rpt, 26304–3.2
- Budget of US, receipts by source and outlays by agency and program, monthly rpt, 8102–3
- Budget of US, receipts, outlays, and budget authority, by function and agency, FY84-89 revised estimates, midsession review of FY85 budget, annual rpt, 104–7

Index by Subjects and Names

- *Business America,* foreign and domestic commerce, and US investment and trade opportunities, biweekly rpt articles, 2042–24
- Canada agricultural trade with US, effects of nontariff trade barriers, selected years 1955-81, 1528–175
- Chemicals (benzenoid), imports by country of origin and product, 1983, annual rpt, 9884–2
- Chemicals and related products trade, tariffs, and industry operating data, TSUSA commodity rpt series, 9885–4
- China economic and business investment conditions, trade practices, and trade with US by detailed commodity, 1978-82, 2048–72
- Classification codes for countries for Census Bur foreign trade statistics, revisions to 1981 base edition, 2428–3
- Coffee production, trade and quotas, and consumption, by country, with US and intl prices, FAS periodic circular, 1925–5
- Computers and other equipment with nuclear weapons applications, approvals for export to PRC by item and to other foreign markets, July 1981-June 1982, GAO rpt, 26123–76
- Customs collections, Budget of US estimates revised for consistency with FY85 budget definitions, FY40-89, annual rpt, 104–12
- Customs collections, by district and port, FY83, annual rpt, 8104–2.2
- Customs collections of 15 largest collection districts, by port, quarterly rpt, 8142–1
- Customs Service activities, operations, and staff, FY79-83, annual rpt, 8144–1
- Dairy imports subject to quota by commodity, and meat imports subject to Meat Import Law, by country of origin, FAS monthly circular, 1925–31
- Developing countries agricultural supply/demand and market for US exports, with socioeconomic indicators, country rpt series, 1526–6
- Developing countries food supply policies, with farm sector data, tariff income, and prices and imports of 5 grains, for 21 countries, 1960s-81, 1528–168
- Developing countries free zones, industry financial and operating data by country, with case studies for 5 countries, 1970s-82, 9918–10
- Developing countries govt policy, and AID and other foreign assistance, effects on private sector dev and socioeconomic conditions, with case studies for 6 countries, 1960s-80, 9918–12
- EC fruit and vegetable product trade and tariffs, 1966-78, and effect of Greece, Spain, and Portugal entry into EC, projected to 1986, 1528–182
- Export licensing and monitoring activities under Export Admin Act, for selected commodities, and for Communist and other countries, FY83, annual rpt, 2044–22
- Exports, imports, and economic indicators by country and country group, and US trade policy actions, 1960s-83, annual rpt, 444–1
- Exports, imports, and tariffs, USITC investigation publications issued, 1960-83, annual listing, 9884–12

Index by Subjects and Names

Tawas City, Mich.

Exports, imports, and tariffs, USITC investigations, publications, and other activities, FY83, annual rpt, 9884–1

Fed Govt consolidated financial statements based on business accounting methods, FY82-83, annual rpt, 8104–5

Fed Govt programs and mgmt cost control proposals, 3-year savings by function and agency, and financial and operating data, 1960s-81, 16908–1

Fed Govt receipts by source and outlays by agency, *Treasury Bulletin,* quarterly rpt, 8002–4.1

Fed Govt tax revenues, including customs duties collections, by State and selected counties, quarterly rpt, 2462–3

Fish imports, duties, and quotas, 1982-83, annual rpt, 2164–1.6

Foreign trade zones operations and economic effects, with data on merchandise shipments, value added, employment, hours, and customs revenue, 1978-83, 9886–4.70

Generalized System of Preferences status of 29 commodities, with US production, consumption, tariffs, and trade by country, selected years 1978-87, 9888–17

Govt revenues by source and expenditures by function, natl income and product account, *Survey of Current Business,* monthly rpt, monthly and annual tables, 2702–1.24

Govt revenues, by type, level of govt, and State, selected years 1902-83, annual rpt, 10044–1.2

Hong Kong wine and champagne import duties, 1984, article, 1925–34.408

Import and tariff provisions effect on US industries and products, investigations with background financial and operating data, series, 9886–4

Import duties, exports, and imports, by SIC 2-digit commodity, 1981, annual rpt, 2424–3

Import quotas and imports for selected commodities, by country of origin, monthly rpt, 8146–1

Import quotas and tariffs, jobs protected and cost per job for selected products, and foreign trade balance by industry div, various periods 1958-81, article, 9381–1.412

Imports from Communist countries, injury to US industries, investigations with background financial and operating data, selected industries and products, series, 9886–12

Imports injury to US industries from foreign subsidized products and sales in US at less than fair value, investigations with background financial and operating data, series, 9886–19

Imports injury to US industries from foreign subsidized products, investigations with background financial and operating data for selected industries and products, series, 9886–15

Imports injury to US industries from import sales at less than fair value, investigations with background financial and operating data, series, 9886–14

Imports injury to US industries from increased import sales, investigations with background financial and operating data, series, 9886–5

Imports injury to US industries from removal of duties on foreign subsidized products, investigations with background financial and operating data, series, 9886–18

Imports of US given duty-free treatment for value of US materials or parts sent abroad for processing or assembly, by country and commodity, 1979-82, biennial rpt, 9884–14

Japan auto export voluntary restraint, effect on US auto industry and import sales and prices, 2nd qtr 1981-1st qtr 1984, article, 9377–1.407

Manufactured products (miscellaneous) trade, tariffs, and industry operating data, TSUSA commodity rpt series, 9885–7

Maritime Commission mgmt and enforcement activities, filings by type and disposition, and civil penalties by shipper, FY83, annual rpt, 9334–1

Metals and metal products trade, tariffs, and industry operating data, TSUSA commodity rpt series, 9885–6

Minerals (nonmetallic) and mineral products trade, tariffs, and industry operating data, TSUSA commodity rpt series, 9885–5

Minerals production, prices, trade, use, employment, tariffs, and stockpiling, by commodity, with foreign comparisons, 1979-83, annual rpt, 5604–18

Oil (Alaskan) potential exports to Japan, costs and benefits, with background data on oil prices, Pacific Basin supply/demand, and tankers, various periods 1918-99, hearings, 25388–45

Oil import and refining fees to recover cost of Strategic Petroleum Reserve, with purchases and construction costs, FY84-FY88, 26306–6.68

Oil prices, tax, and customs duty, by refined product for major foreign and US cities, July 1983 and Jan 1984, annual rpt, 3164–50.4

Overseas Business Reports: economic conditions, investment and export opportunities, and trade practices, annual country market research rpt series, 2046–6

Overseas Business Reports: economic conditions, investment and export opportunities, and trade practices, world region rpt series, 2046–5

Port dev costs and financing through user fees, and shipping industry impact on local economy, by State, other area, industry, commodity, and port, 1970s-2020, hearings, 21568–34

Rum imports (duty-free) of US under Caribbean Basin Initiative, by country, Jan-June 1983-84, annual rpt, 9884–15

Services trade regulation proposals of US, with agreements, goods and services trade, intl investment, and GDP, by country, various periods 1970-82, 448–1

Shipping and shipbuilding subsidies and aid, and summary fleet, trade, and GNP data, for US and 47 countries, 1979-80, biennial rpt, 7704–18

Steel import trigger prices to prevent Japan dumping, and domestic steel prices, employment, and imports, by product and region, various dates 1977-1983, hearings, 21368–51

Steel imports of US from EC and other countries, and US industry operating data, for 15 products limited under arrangement with EC, monthly rpt, 9882–10

Steel industry finances and operations under proposed import quota, projected 1985-89 with selected foreign comparisons and trends from 1950, 26306–6.80

Steel pipe and tube shipments, imports from EC by country, and exports, by product type, various periods 1978-83 with import duties to 1987, hearing, 25368–134

Sugar and specialty sugar imports of US under quota, by country, weekly rpt, 1922–9

Sugar, molasses, and honey foreign and US production, trade, and consumption, FAS annual rpt series, 1925–14

Tariff Schedules of US, Annotated, classifications and rates of duty for detailed imported commodities, and codes for ports and foreign countries, 1985 edition, 9886–13

Tariff Schedules of US, Annotated, commodity classification revisions under proposed internatl system, 1984 rpt, 9886–4.66

Textile fiber and products trade, tariffs, and industry operating data, TSUSA commodity rpt series, 9885–3

Tobacco tariff rates for unmanufactured tobacco and products, as of Jan 1983-84, annual rpt, 1319–1.5

USITC analysts assigned to cover individual commodities, grouped by TSUSA schedule, 1983 listing, 9888–12

Virgin Islands import duty collections, and reimbursement of US Customs Service collections expenses, FY81-83, GAO rpt, 26119–54

Wood, paper, and printed matter trade, tariffs, and industry operating data, TSUSA commodity rpt series, 9885–2

see also Common markets and free trade areas

see also Dumping

see also International sanctions

Tarpgaard, Peter T.

"U.S. Shipping and Shipbuilding: Trends and Policy Choices", 26306–6.83

Task Force on Elections

Election campaign funding by political action committees to individual congressmen, and public opinion on reform proposals and assn influence, 1970s-83, hearings, 21428–7

Tatom, John A.

"Perspective on the Federal Deficit Problem", 9391–1.415

Taube, Carl A.

"Utilization and Expenditures for Ambulatory Mental Health Care During 1980", 4146–11.5

Taube, Sheila

"Science Base Underlying Research on Acquired Immune Deficiency Syndrome", 4102–1.404

Tautin, John

"Status of American Woodcock, 1984", 5504–11

Tawas City, Mich.

Wages of office and plant workers, by occupation, 1984 labor market area survey rpt, 6785–3.7

Tax appeals

Tax appeals
see Tax protests and appeals

Tax Court of the U.S.

Budget of US Appendix, detailed budgets and personnel summaries, by agency, FY85, annual rpt, 104–3

Budget of US, appropriations, outlays, balances, and budget receipts, by govtl branch and agency, FY83, annual rpt, 8104–2

IRS prosecutions and litigations, cases received, amounts in dispute, and disposition, FY83, annual rpt, 8304–3

Tax courts
see Tax Court of the U.S.
see Tax laws and courts

Tax credits
see Tax expenditures
see Tax incentives and shelters

Tax evasion

Art appraisals accepted and rejected on estate, gift, and income tax returns, and valuation by taxpayers, IRS, and US courts, 1978-82, hearings, 21408–74

Court caseloads for Federal district courts, disposition, and convictions, as of June 1961-83, annual rpt, 18204–1

Drug traffickers income tax evasion assessments, FY82, annual rpt, 15894–1

Fed Govt programs and mgmt cost control proposals, 3-year savings by function and agency, and financial and operating data, 1960s-81, 16908–1.12

Foreign residents tax evasion through bank claims and deposits, direct investments, income payments, and other transactions in 5 Caribbean countries, 1978-82, 8008–106

Income (legal) not reported on Federal income tax returns by source, and legal and illegal underground income, with bibl, 1974-81, article, 2702–1.419

Income (taxable) not reported, by illegal source, with characteristics of persons involved, methodology, and bibl, 1970s-82, 8008–112

Income (taxable) not reported, methodology using Current Population Survey labor force data to estimate share of output and nonreporters, 1950s-81, 23848–178

Income (taxable) not reported on individual and corporate returns, and associated Federal revenue losses, by detailed legal and illegal source, 1973-81, 8308–26 Natl income and product revised estimates, adjustment for misreporting of income tax returns info, 1977, article, 2702–1.422

Oil windfall profits tax admin of IRS and revenues, tax rates, and nonfilers, 1980-86, GAO rpt, 26119–65

Prosecutions, litigation, interpretive law decisions, and operating expenses of IRS, with collections, refunds, and taxes due, by region and State, FY83, annual rpt, 8304–3

Tax haven countries use for ta evasion, with income, investments, and taxes withheld by country, various periods 1975-83, hearings, 21408–71

Trans-Alaska Pipeline System owner companies financial data, and retail gasoline competitive position in 2 States, by company, 1980-83, hearing, 21728–51

Tax exempt organizations

Fed Govt tax litigation, prosecutions, interpretive law decisions, and operating expenses of IRS, with collections, refunds, and taxes due, by region and State, FY83, annual rpt, 8304–3

Income (taxable) not reported on individual and corporate returns, and associated Federal revenue losses, by detailed legal and illegal source, 1973-81, 8308–26

Income tax returns filed by type, for US, IRS regions, and service center cities, 1972-82 and projected 1983-90, annual rpt, 8304–9.1

Philanthropic foundations assets and grants for 50 largest foundations, and for selected foundations by recipient, selected years 1975-82, hearings, 21788–137

Philanthropic foundations detailed financial and operating data, and stock holdings by instn, 1979 with selected trends from 1920, GAO rpt, 26119–53

Service industry census, 1982: employment, establishments, receipts, and payroll, by SIC 2- to 4-digit kind of business, SMSA, county, and city, State rpt series, 2391–1

Tax (excise) collections of IRS, by source, quarterly press release, 8302–1

Tax exempt securities

Agricultural cooperative operating ratios by commodity, and debt financing by source, for 100 largest cooperatives, selected years FY62-83, article, 1122–1.411

Airport financing by source, bond issues by region, and airport operations, by airport and operator type, FY75-83 and projected to FY93, 26306–6.75

Bond tax-exempt issues by purpose, and Fed Govt mortgage bond revenue losses and borrower characteristics, selected years 1971-85, hearings, 21788–135

Bond tax-exempt issues for private activity, by purpose, face value, major industry, and State, 1983, article, 8302–2.417

Bond tax-exempt issues for public and private purposes, by use of proceeds, 1975-83, article, 9362–1.408

Budget of US, CBO analysis of revenue and spending alternatives and projections of economic indicators, FY85-89, annual rpt, 26304–3.3

Census of Govts, 1982: school districts revenues, expenditures, debt, and assets, by district and State, 2457–1

Fed Govt programs and mgmt cost control proposals, 3-year savings by function and agency, and financial and operating data, 1960s-81, 16908–1.37

Flow-of-funds accounts, assets and liabilities by type and economic sector, year-end outstandings, 1960-83, annual rpt, 9364–3

Household income, home value and equity, and financial assets by type, by household characteristics, 1983 survey with trends from 1970, article, 9362–1.406

Income tax returns of corporations, detailed income and tax items by industry, 1981, annual rpt, 8304–4

Insurance industry (property and casualty) financial and operating data, investments, and tax liability, various periods 1951-82, hearing, 25368–128

Mortgage (home) subsidy bonds Fed Govt costs, and loans, mortgage value, and

Index by Subjects and Names

borrowers by jurisdiction, by borrower income, Dec 1981-July 1982, GAO rpt, 26113–127

Mortgage (home) subsidy bonds, issuance and purchase price limits for tax-exempt status, by State and MSA, 1984, annual press releases, 8304–16

North Central States tax exempt industrial revenue bonds issued by local govts, by Fed Reserve 7th District State, county, and city, with interest rate spread, 1975-80, 9375–13.2

Tax expenditures, Fed Govt revenues foregone through income tax deductions and exclusions by type, and effect of Deficit Reduction Act, FY84-89, annual rpt, 21784–10

Washington Public Power Supply System nuclear reactors construction financing, with regional economic impacts and power supply/demand, 1980s-2035, hearing, 21448–29

see also Municipal bonds

Tax expenditures

Alcohol fuel production costs, related employment, and Fed Govt subsidies and impact on farm income, selected years 1978-90, GAO rpt, 26113–140

Budget of US, CBO analysis and review of FY85 budget by function, annual rpt, 26304–2

Budget of US, CBO analysis of revenue and spending alternatives and projections of economic indicators, FY85-89, annual rpt, 26304–3.3

Budget of US, receipts, outlays, and budget authority, by function and agency, FY84-89 revised estimates, midsession review of FY85 budget, annual rpt, 104–7

Budget of US, special analysis of tax expenditures, FY85, annual rpt, 104–1.7

Business loans, grants, and tax benefits of Fed Govt, by program and economic sector, projected FY84-88 with effective tax rates for FY80-82, 26306–6.70

Children and youth benefitting from Fed Govt public welfare programs and tax expenditures, participation and funding for 71 programs, FY81-83, 21968–30

EC trade promotion policies and financing by industry, and effect on competing US industries, 1970s-82, 9886–4.73

Employee benefit plans effects on income and payroll tax revenue by benefit type and income, with benefits by industry, 1950-83 and projected to 1988, article, 9373–1.404

Fed Govt consolidated financial statements based on business accounting methods, FY82-83, annual rpt, 8104–5

Fed Govt industrial dev funding by type, program, and agency, and State govt policies and support, selected years FY75-85, 26306–6.81

Fed Govt programs and mgmt cost control proposals, CBO and GAO estimates of savings by function and agency, FY85-89, 26308–45

Fed Govt programs and mgmt cost control proposals, 3-year savings by function and agency, and financial and operating data, 1960s-81, 16908–1

Fed Govt receipts, outlays, and debt shares of GNP, and tax expenditures as

January-December 1984

Index by Subjects and Names

Tax sharing

percentage of outlays and revenue, FY66-83 and projected FY84-87, article, 9383–2

Gasohol and ethanol plant capacity and production, tax exemptions and sales by State, and prices, 1983, annual rpt, 3304–9

Govt taxation and revenue systems, by type of tax and system, level of govt, and State, selected years 1958-83, annual rpt, 10044–1.3

Mortgage (home) subsidy bonds Fed Govt costs, and loans, mortgage value, and borrowers by jurisdiction, by borrower income, Dec 1981-July 1982, GAO rpt, 26113–127

Mortgage (home) subsidy bonds, Fed Govt revenue losses and borrower characteristics, various periods 1972-82, hearings, 21788–135

Oil and gas finances by firm, and effect of income and excise tax provisions on firms, Fed Govt revenues, and investor tax returns, 1980 and projected to 1992, hearing, 21788–132

Pension and other tax benefit policy changes tax expenditures of Fed Govt, FY84-88, hearing, 25368–131

R&D tax credit, Federal revenue foregone, projected FY82-88, 26306–6.77

Rental housing, effects of Fed Govt tax policies on real estate investment, 1969-81, 5188–104

Tax expenditures, Fed Govt revenues foregone through income tax deductions and exclusions by type, and effect of Deficit Reduction Act, FY84-89, annual rpt, 21784–10

Tax incentives and shelters

Alcohol fuel (ethanol) production in Tennessee Valley, feedstocks, facilities, tax incentives, and related farming data, by State, 1970s-83 and projected to 1992, 9808–69

Art appraisals accepted and rejected on estate, gift, and income tax returns, and valuation by taxpayers, IRS, and US courts, 1978-82, hearings, 21408–74

Auto and light truck fuel use, economy standards and manufacturer compliance, and gas prices and taxes, with selected foreign comparisons, FY80-83 and projected to 2000, hearing, 21368–49

Bank investment returns on capital assets for leasing, and municipal bond holdings, for 16 States, 1982, article, 9385–1.402

Biotechnology commercial uses, R&D funding and output, controls, and industry financial and operating data, for US and 5 countries, 1970s-83 and estimated 1984-85, 26358–98

Budget of US, CBO analysis of revenue and spending alternatives and projections of economic indicators, FY85-89, annual rpt, 26304–3.3

Budget of US, effects of Reagan Admin policy changes, by detailed program, FY85, annual rpt, 104–21

Budget of US, receipts, outlays, and budget authority, by function and agency, FY84-89 revised estimates, midsession review of FY85 budget, annual rpt, 104–7

Business loans, grants, and tax benefits of Fed Govt, by program and economic sector, projected FY84-88 with effective tax rates for FY80-82, 26306–6.70

California (southern) housing demand by county, prices and sales, and costs after homeowner tax deductions, 1970s-80, hearing, 21148–31

Corporate income tax returns, detailed income and tax items by industry, 1981, annual rpt, 8304–4

Corporate income tax returns, summary data by industry div, 1981 estimates, annual article, 8302–2.403

EC trade promotion policies and financing by industry, and effect on competing US industries, 1970s-82, 9886–4.73

Election campaign Fed Govt funding, reform and tax deduction proposals, and party assessment, opinion surveys, 1977-82, hearings, 25688–6

Election campaign Fed Govt funding, reform and tax deduction proposals, and TV and political action committee influence, opinion surveys, various dates 1977-83, hearings, 21428–7.1

Electric power cogeneration in 5 industries, and fuel use and utility supply/demand effects, by region, 1983-93, 3008–92

Farm business legal organization, finances, operations, tax rates, and State laws restricting farm corporations, 1960s-82, 1548–233

Farm investments, effect of Fed Govt and State tax rates under alternative depreciation methods and inflation rates, 1950-84, 1548–231

Govt taxation and revenue systems, by type of tax and system, level of govt, and State, selected years 1958-83, annual rpt, 10044–1.3

Housing tenure related to housing price uncertainty and changes in home-owner tax shelters, 1984 technical paper, 8006–3.50

Income tax returns filed by type of filer, detailed preliminary and supplementary data, quarterly rpt with articles, 8302–2

Income tax returns of individuals by tax return item, State, and occupation, and income by source and tax owed, by income level, selected years 1916-80, conf papers, 8308–28.1

Income tax returns of individuals, detailed data, 1982, annual rpt, 8304–2

Income tax returns of individuals, selected income, deduction, and tax credit data by income, preliminary 1982, annual article, 8302–2.402

Litigation, prosecutions, interpretive law decisions, and operating expenses of IRS, with collections, refunds, and taxes due, by region and State, FY83, annual rpt, 8304–3

Natural gas interstate pipeline company detailed financial and operating data, by firm, 1983, annual rpt, 3164–38

NYC families caring for aged relatives, preference for social service and financial programs to provide assistance, 1980, article, 4652–1.403

Oil and gas finances by firm, and effect of income and excise tax provisions on firms, Fed Govt revenues, and investor tax returns, 1980 and projected to 1992, hearing, 21788–132

Poverty-level persons and families, by income source, hours of work, earnings, taxes, and family characteristics, various periods 1959-84, 21788–131

Public opinion on taxes, tax policy, and intergovtl relations, 1972-84 surveys, annual rpt, 10044–2

Rental housing, effects of Fed Govt tax policies on real estate investment, 1969-81, 5188–104

Shipping and shipbuilding subsidies and aid, and summary fleet, trade, and GNP data, for US and 47 countries, 1979-80, biennial rpt, 7704–18

Sole proprietorships income tax returns, detailed data by industry div and selected industry group, 1981, annual rpt, 8304–7

Tax haven countries use for ta evasion, with income, investments, and taxes withheld by country, various periods 1975-83, hearings, 21408–71

see also Individual retirement arrangements

see also Oil depletion allowances

see also Tax exempt organizations

see also Tax exempt securities

see also Tax expenditures

Tax laws and courts

Art appraisals accepted and rejected on estate, gift, and income tax returns, and valuation by taxpayers, IRS, and US courts, 1978-82, hearings, 21408–74

Civil case processing of US Attorneys and amounts involved, by cause of action, FY83, annual rpt, 6004–2.5

Fed Govt programs and mgmt cost control proposals, 3-year savings by function and agency, and financial and operating data, 1960s-81, 16908–1.12

Fraud cases disposition and convictions for Federal district courts, as of June 1961-83, annual rpt, 18204–1

Justice Dept Tax Div caseload, 1977-81, annual rpt, 6004–1

Multinatl corporation income reallocation through regulation of intercorporate transactions, by tax item, treaty status, asset size, industry, and tax haven country, 1982, 8008–110

Penalty abatements of IRS, 1978-83, and estimated error rates by category of taxpayer excuse, FY81, GAO rpt, 26119–68

Prosecutions, litigation, interpretive law decisions, and operating expenses of IRS, with collections, refunds, and taxes due, by region and State, FY83, annual rpt, 8304–3

see also Tax evasion

see also Tax protests and appeals

Tax loopholes

see Tax incentives and shelters

Tax protests and appeals

Alcohol and tobacco tax refund claims, FY81-82, last issue of annual rpt, 8484–1.6

Civil case processing of US Attorneys and amounts involved, by cause of action, FY83, annual rpt, 6004–2.5

Litigations and prosecutions of IRS, cases received, amounts in dispute, and disposition, FY83, annual rpt, 8304–3

Penalty abatements of IRS, 1978-83, and estimated error rates by category of taxpayer excuse, FY81, GAO rpt, 26119–68

Tax sharing

see Revenue sharing

Taxation

Taxation

Agricultural Statistics, 1983, annual rpt, 1004–1.2

Budget deficit, actual and assuming efficient tax system, FY75-83 and projected FY85-95, article, 9387–1.402

Budget of US, CBO analysis of revenue and spending alternatives and projections of economic indicators, FY85-89, annual rpt, 26304–3

Budget of US, compact budgets by function, agency, and account, FY85 with projections to FY89, annual rpt, 104–2

Budget of US, receipts by source and outlays by agency and program, monthly rpt, 8102–3

Budget of US, receipts, outlays, and budget authority, by function and agency, FY84-89 revised estimates, midsession review of FY85 budget, annual rpt, 104–7

Budget of US, revenues and expenditures, and effects of 1981-82 tax legislation, FY81 and projected FY86, article, 9383–6.401

City govt revenue sharing program allocations and use by function, and response to program cuts, by city size and region, 1982 survey, hearings, 25408–86.2

Economic Report of the President for 1984, economic trends from 1929 and Reagan Admin proposals, annual rpt, 204–1

Farm production expenses, by type and State, 1979-82, annual rpt, 1544–18

Farm production inputs, outputs, and productivity, by region, 1939-82, annual rpt, 1544–17

Farm production itemized costs, receipts, and net returns, for 13 crops, 4 livestock types, and milk, by region, 1981-83, annual rpt, 1544–20

Fed Govt consolidated financial statements based on business accounting methods, FY82-83, annual rpt, 8104–5

Fed Govt internal revenue, by type of tax, quarterly rpt, 8302–2.1

Fed Govt internal revenue from personal taxes under current tax law and 3 flat-rate proposals, and consumption tax characteristics, 1984 article, 9381–1.415

Fed Govt programs and mgmt cost control proposals, CBO and GAO estimates of savings by function and agency, FY85-89, 26308–45

Fed Govt programs and mgmt cost control proposals, 3-year savings by function and agency, and financial and operating data, 1960s-81, 16908–1

Fed Govt programs under Ways and Means Committee jurisdiction, program operations and financing data for assessing budgetary requirements, by State, FY70s-83, 21788–117

Fed Govt receipts by source and outlays by agency, *Treasury Bulletin,* quarterly rpt, 8002–4.1

Fed Govt receipts, tax and other, FY83, annual rpt, 8104–2.2

Fed Govt tax litigation, prosecutions, interpretive law decisions, and operating expenses of IRS, with collections, refunds, and taxes due, by region and State, FY83, annual rpt, 8304–3

Fed Govt tax receipts, cumulative for fiscal year, annual trends, and quarterly data, monthly rpt, 23842–1.6

Fed Govt tax returns and collections, for IRS regions, districts, and service centers, 1972-82 and projections to 1990, annual rpt, 8304–8

Fed Govt tax returns filed, by type of return, 1972-82 and projected 1983-90, annual rpt, 8304–9

Fed Tax Deposit System, taxes received by type, daily statement, 8102–4

Flow-of-funds accounts savings, investments, and credit statements, quarterly rpt, 9365–3.3

Govt finances, by level of govt and State, selected years 1929-83, annual rpt, 10044–1

Hazardous waste generation and disposal taxes in 3 States, and effects on waste mgmt, 1981-83, with assessment of 3 Fed Govt tax proposals, GAO rpt, 26113–124

Internal revenue stamp new issues delivered by Bur of Engraving and Printing, annual rpt, discontinued, 8164–1

IRS and other Fed Govt admin record research methods, data collection and use, 1984 compilation of papers, 8308–28

IRS tax collections by type of tax, procedures, and interest forgone through processing delay, for selected locations, FY81-82, GAO rpt, 26119–55

Motor and rail carriers regulated by ICC, employment and finances by mode of transport, and ICC activities, FY80-83 and trends, annual rpt, 9484–1

Natural gas interstate pipeline company detailed financial and operating data, by firm, 1983, annual rpt, 3164–38

Oil and gas finances by firm, and effect of income and excise tax provisions on firms, Fed Govt revenues, and investor tax returns, 1980 and projected to 1992, hearing, 21788–132

Port dev costs and financing through user fees, and shipping industry impact on local economy, by State, other area, industry, commodity, and port, 1970s-2020, hearings, 21568–34

Public opinion on taxes, tax policy, and intergovtl relations, 1972-84 surveys, annual rpt, 10044–2

Statistical Abstract of US, social, political, and economic data, 1950s-83 and trends, annual rpt, 2324–1.2

Tax burden for average family by income level and selected city, and tax rates by selected jurisdiction, by type of tax, 1982, 10046–8.2

Tax-related economic and fiscal topics, technical research paper series, 8006–3

Telephone and telegraph tax accruals and excise taxes collected from users, 1982 annual rpt, 9284–6.1

Virgin Islands socioeconomic and govtl data, FY81, annual rpt, 5304–4

see also Estate tax

see also Excise tax

see also Gift tax

see also Income taxes

see also Licenses and permits

see also Oil depletion allowances

see also Property tax

see also Revenue sharing

see also Sales tax

see also Severance taxes

see also Social security tax

see also State and local taxes

see also Tariffs and foreign trade controls

see also Tax evasion

see also Tax exempt organizations

see also Tax exempt securities

see also Tax expenditures

see also Tax incentives and shelters

see also Tax laws and courts

see also Tax protests and appeals

see also Unemployment insurance tax

Taxicabs

Auto fleet size, trip characteristics, and energy use, by fleet type, 1970s-83, annual rpt, 3304–5.2

Census of Housing, 1980: structural, financial, and householder characteristics, by region and State, 2475–4

Census of Population, 1980: detailed socioeconomic and demographic characteristics, by age, sex, race, Hispanic origin, occupation, and industry, State rpt series, 2531–4

Census of Population, 1980: detailed socioeconomic characteristics, by county, city, and inside-outside SMSAs and central cities, State rpt series, 2531–3

Commuting to work, householder principal mode of transport, distance, and travel time, by race, Hispanic origin, tenure, urban-rural location, and region, 1981, annual survey, 2485–7

County Business Patterns: establishments, employees, and payrolls, by SIC 4-digit industry and county, 1981, annual State rpt series, 2326–8

County Business Patterns: establishments, employees, and payrolls, by SIC 4-digit industry and county, 1982, annual State rpt series, 2326–6

Employment, earnings, and hours, by SIC 4-digit nonfarm industry, monthly 1974-Feb 1984, annual update, 6744–4

Finances, operations, vehicles, equipment, accidents, and energy use, by mode of transport, 1955-84, annual rpt, 7304–2

Income tax returns of sole proprietorships, detailed data by industry div and selected industry group, 1981, annual rpt, 8304–7

Income tax returns of sole proprietorships, receipts, deductions by type, payroll, and net income, by major industry, 1982, annual article, 8302–2.413

Licenses, density, fares, license prices, and deregulation effects for taxis, by selected city, various dates 1970-84, 9406–1.37

Occupational injury and illness rates, by SIC 2- to 4-digit industry, 1982, annual rpt, 6844–1

Research publications on public transit, 2nd half FY83, semiannual listing, 7882–1

Ridership for transit services, by service type, 1983 rpt, 7306–9.6

Scientists, engineers, and technicians employment in transportation, utilities, and retail and wholesale trade, by field of science and industry, 1982, 9628–72

Taylor, Herb

"Return Banks Have Paid on NOW Accounts", 9387–1.403

"Role of the Discount Window in Monetary Policy Under Alternative Operating Procedures and Reserve Requirement Systems", 9387–8.87

Index by Subjects and Names

Teachers

Taylor, Jeffrey R.
"Estimating the Input-Output Tables from Scarce Data: Experiences of the U.S. Census Bureau's Center for International Research", 2546–10.13

Taylor, John B.
"International Capital Mobility and the Coordination of Monetary Rules", 9387–8.85

Taylor, Ralph B.
"Correctional Crisis: Prison Populations and Public Policy", 6068–176

Taylor, Todd H.
"Growing Role of Private Security", 6066–20.8

Tea

Agricultural Statistics, 1983, annual rpt, 1004–1

Births by outcome, and mother's sociodemographic, life style, and maternity characteristics, 1980, article, 4102–1.422

Business statistics, detailed data for major industries and economic indicators, *Survey of Current Business,* monthly rpt, 2702–1.11

China economic conditions, agricultural and industrial production, trade, and domestic and foreign investment, 1980-85, 2048–106

Consumption of food and nutrient intake by individuals, by food group, source, and socioeconomic characteristics, 1977-78 natl survey, final rpt series, 1356–4

Consumption, supply, trade, prices, expenditures, and indexes, by food commodity, 1963-83, annual rpt, 1544–4

Exports and imports of US, by agricultural commodity and country, bimonthly rpt with articles, 1522–1

Exports and imports of US, by detailed agricultural commodity and country, FY83 and CY83, semiannual rpts, 1522–4

Exports and imports of US, by detailed agricultural commodity for 8 major commodity groups, monthly rpt, 1922–8

Exports and imports of US, detailed SIC-based commodities by world area, 1983, annual rpts, 2424–6

Exports and imports of US, totals and as percent of domestic production, by SIC 2- to 5-digit commodity, 1981, annual rpt, 2424–3

Exports of US, detailed commodities by country of destination, monthly rpt, 2422–3

Exports of US, detailed Schedule B commodities by country of destination, 1983, annual rpt, 2424–9

Exports of US, detailed Schedule E commodities by mode of transport and world area and country of destination, 1983, annual rpts, 2424–5

Foreign agricultural production, prices, and trade, by country, 1983 and outlook for 1984/85, annual world region rpt series, 1524–4

Foreign and US agricultural production, trade, and climatic devs, weekly press release, 1922–4

Foreign and US production, prices, and trade of spices, essential oils, and tea, FAS annual rpt series, 1925–15

Great Lakes trade, by SITC 3-digit commodity, port, vessel type, world area, and country, 1982, annual rpt, 7744–3

Imports of US, detailed Schedule A commodities by country and world area of origin, and mode of transport, 1983, annual rpts, 2424–2

Imports of US, detailed Schedule A commodities by country, monthly rpt, 2422–2

Imports of US, detailed TSUSA commodities by country of origin, 1983, annual rpt, 2424–4

see also under By Commodity in the "Index by Categories"

Teacher education

AID educational program activities and project impacts in 12 developing countries, 1950s-82, 9916–11.8

Bilingual education programs, teachers, enrollment, and funding, selected years 1976-FY83, biennial rpt, 4804–14

Bilingual vocational training projects, participants, characteristics, and costs, by program, FY82, annual rpt, 4804–26

Degrees conferred in higher education, by race, Hispanic origin, sex, level, and field, selected years 1949/50-1979/80, annual rpt, 4824–2.16

Degrees conferred in teaching by specialty and State, required credit hours, and instn officials attitudes, by instn type, 1970s-83, hearings, 21348–89

Education Dept programs funding, operations, and effectiveness, FY83, annual rpt, 4804–5

English teaching programs and teacher seminars supported by USIA, by world region and country, FY83, annual rpt, 9854–2

Fed Govt aid to State and local govts, expenditures, and direct payments, by program, agency, and State, FY83, annual rpt, 2464–2

Testing in elementary and secondary schools, teacher and student attitudes, with detail for standardized achievement tests, 1980 conf papers, 4918–15

Teachers

Alabama rural black population, education, employment, health services, and economic status, for 16 counties, selected years 1970-81, 11048–180

Bilingual education programs, teachers, enrollment, and funding, selected years 1976-FY83, biennial rpt, 4804–14

Census of Population, 1980: detailed socioeconomic and demographic characteristics, by age, sex, race, Hispanic origin, occupation, and industry, State rpt series, 2531–4

Census of Population, 1980: detailed socioeconomic characteristics, by county, city, and inside-outside SMSAs and central cities, State rpt series, 2531–3

Census of Population, 1980: labor force, by sex, detailed occupation, and region, with comparison to 1970 census, supplementary rpt, 2535–1.12

Computer access and use in elementary and secondary schools, by region, urban-rural location, and Title I status, spring 1982, 4826–1.10

Condition of Education, detailed data on enrollment, staff, achievement, finances,

curricula, and education effects on employment, 1982-83, annual rpt, 4824–1

Crime against students, teachers, and others, by offense, circumstances, and offender sex and race, 1974-76, 6066–20.2

Crime in public schools, assaults and robberies of teachers and minority and other students, and vandalism incidents, 1976/77, 4808–12

Crime in secondary schools, assaults and robberies of students and teachers, 1972-83, 4918–13

Digest of Education Statistics, detailed data on students, staff, finances, and facilities, 1982 and selected trends, annual rpt, 4824–2

DOD training and education programs funding, staff, students, and facilities, by service branch and reserve component, FY85, annual rpt, 3504–5

Education statistics summary compilation, 1980/81-1982/83 with selected trends from 1869, biennial rpt, 4804–27

Educational trends, 1972/73-1992/93, biennial pocket-size card, 4824–3

Elementary and secondary education revenue by level of govt, and change in enrollment, teachers, and expenditures, by State, 1973-83, hearings, 21348–89

Elementary and secondary public school districts, schools, enrollment, staff, and finances, by State, 1981/82, annual rpt, 4834–13

Employment and economic conditions, alternative BLS projections to 1995 with selected trends for 1959-82, 6728–29

Employment of teachers and enrollment in all schools, by grade level and instn control, fall 1983-84, annual press release, 4804–19

Employment, unemployment, and labor force, by demographic and employment characteristics, State, and for 30 metro areas and 11 large cities, 1983, annual rpt, 6744–7

English teaching programs and teacher seminars supported by USIA, by world region and country, FY83, annual rpt, 9854–2

Flight and ground inspector certificates held and issued, by region, State, and for women, 1983, annual rpt, 7504–1.7

Flight and ground instructors certified by FAA, by age, sex, region, and State, 1983, annual rpt, 7504–2

Foreign military, social, and economic summary data by world area and country, 1960s-80s, hearing, 25388–47.1

Foreign women sociodemographic, economic, and fertility characteristics, with comparisons to men, by country, 1960s-85, world region rpt series, 2326–15

Govt census, 1982: employment, payrolls, and average earnings, by function, level of govt, State, county, population size, and inside-outside SMSAs, 2455–2

Govt employment and payroll, by function, level of govt, and jurisdiction, 1983, annual rpt series, 2466–1

Head Start Project programs and effect on child dev, literature review with bibl, selected years 1970-83, 4608–17

Teachers

Head Start Project programs effect on child dev, by characteristics of program, child, and family, literature review, selected years 1965-81, 4608–20

Health professionals supply and education, by occupation, demographic and professional characteristics, and location, 1950s-83 and projected to 2000, biennial rpt, 4114–8

Hospital worker wages by sex and occupation, and benefits, for 22 MSAs, Oct 1981 survey, 6787–6.201

Indian education program operations, funding, student progress measures, and opinions of school staff, parents, and students, selected years 1973-83, 4808–13

Occupational manpower needs and supply by detailed occupation, and educational and training program enrollees and grads by detailed field, 1982 and 1995, biennial rpt, 6744–3

Occupational Outlook Handbook, 1984-85 biennial rpt, 6744–1

Pension systems of State and local govts finances, membership, beneficiaries, and benefits, by system, 1982-83, annual rpt, 2466–2.4

Physicians (not office-based) visits by reason, diagnosis, treatment, patient and physician characteristics, and physician primary activity, 1980, 4147–13.77

Psychologists in health service provision by degree level, employment and service setting, services provided, and weekly hours worked, 1978, annual rpt, 4504–9.4

Puerto Rico educational enrollment, finance, completions, curricula, and personnel by instn, and health and vital statistics, selected years 1970-83, hearings, 21348–93

Salaries of teachers in schools and colleges by State, 1982/83, and school employees health insurance plans in 7 cities, as of 1980, hearing, 21788–136

Satellite Landsat system proposed transfer to private sector, uses and product sales by user type, and university programs and personnel by instn, 1973-85, 26358–100

Science and engineering doctoral degree recipients, by field, sex, race, age, citizenship, postgrad employment and study status, State, and instn, 1960-82, 9626–6.16

Science and engineering faculty at grad instns, by dept, 1975-82, annual survey, 9627–7

Science and engineering grads of 1980-81, employment characteristics or grad enrollment, by degree level, field, sex, and race, 1982, 9627–25

Scientists and engineers employed at universities and colleges, by field, sex, and instn, 1973-82, 9626–2.140

Scientists and engineers employed at universities and colleges, by field, sex, State, and instn, Jan 1983 and selected trends from 1967, annual survey, 9627–11

Scientists and engineers employed in energy-related fields, supply/demand and effects of R&D funding, by energy type, employer type, field, and age, 1962-91, annual rpt, 3004–19

Scientists and engineers employment by sector and activity, and share female, black, and Asian descent, by field, 1982, 9626–2.142

Southeastern States economic dev effect on education, for Fed Reserve 6th District States, selected years 1900-82, article, 9371–1.428

Special education programs for handicapped children, enrollment, staff, and funding, by handicap, age, and State, 1981/82-1982/83, annual rpt, 4944–4

Testing in elementary and secondary schools, teacher and student attitudes, with detail for standardized achievement tests, 1980 conf papers, 4918–15

TTPI socioeconomic, health, and govtl data, by TTPI govt, FY83 and selected trends, detailed annual rpt, 7004–6

see also Teacher education

Teaching aids and devices

see Audiovisual education

see Educational materials

Technical assistance

see Foreign assistance

see Military assistance

Technical education

see Vocational education and training

Technicians

see Clinical laboratory technicians

see Scientists and technicians

Technological innovations

Biotechnology commercial uses, R&D funding and output, controls, and industry financial and operating data, for US and 5 countries, 1970s-83 and estimated 1984-85, 26358–98

Biotechnology firms, patents, and trade by country, and effect of industry growth on US drug and chemical trade, selected years 1979-2000, 9886–4.78

Cooling and heating equipment industry productivity trends and technological innovations, 1967-82, article, 6722–1.471

Council for Mutual Economic Assistance science and technology dev and transfer between USSR and other member countries, 1940s-81, 2326–9.7

Employment and productivity and effects of technological change in 4 industries, 1960 90, 6828–23

Fiber optics displacement of copper in telecommunications, with Bell System use and copper and fiber optics industry data, 1978-88, 2048–104

Industry finances and operations, by SIC 2- to 4-digit industry, 1970s-83 and projected to 1988, annual rpt, 2014–4

Meatpacking and prepared meats industry productivity trends and technological innovations, 1967-82, article, 6722–1.428

Medical technologies coverage and reimbursements of Medicare, and health services use and costs, selected years 1966-82, 26358–106

Motor vehicles powered by electricity, Fed Govt dev program implementation, with bibl, FY83, annual rpt, 3304–2

Natl Weather Service, effects of proposed reorganization and technological improvement on staff and expenditures, FY82 and projected to 2000, 2188–16

NSF grant and award recipients, by State, FY83, annual listing, 9624–11

Index by Subjects and Names

Rail high-speed systems and railcar production of US and selected countries, and proposed US projects costs and funding, 1940s-82, 26358–97

Science Indicators, R&D expenditures, innovations, research, and higher education, with foreign comparisons, 1960s- 83, annual rpt, 9624–10

Switchgear industry labor productivity trends and technological innovations, 1963-82, article, 6722–1.420

Transit systems research publications, 2nd half FY83, semiannual listing, 7882–1

Trucks (heavy) energy use, efficiency, and conservation technologies, selected years 1958-82 and projected to 2000, 3308–70

see also Automation

see also Energy research and development

see also Inventions

see also Lasers

see also Patents

see also Research

see also Research and development

see also Solar energy

see also Technology transfer

see also Wind energy

Technology

see Inventions

see Research

see Research and development

see Science and technology

see Technological innovations

see Technology transfer

Technology transfer

AID activities and funding by project and function, FY85, and developing countries summary socioeconomic data, 1970s-83, by country, annual rpt, 9914–3

AID contracts and grants to universities for technical assistance to foreign countries and other services, FY83, annual listing, 9914–6

AID economic assistance to developing countries, obligations and disbursements by country, quarterly rpt, 9912–4

Council for Mutual Economic Assistance science and technology dev and transfer between USSR and other member countries, 1940s-81, 2326–9.7

Export licensing and monitoring activities under Export Admin Act, for selected commodities, and for Communist and other countries, FY83, annual rpt, 2044–22

Fed Govt R&D labs required technology transfer to public and private sector, labs complying, funding, and requests, by agency, FY82, GAO rpt, 26113–141

Forests (tropical) status by country and world region, conservation methods, and mgmt role of US, foreign, and intl groups, 1977-80s and projected to 2000, 26358–101.1

R&D-intensive products, transfers from US multinatl corporations to affiliates abroad, 1945-77, annual rpt, 9624–10.1

Science Indicators, R&D expenditures, innovations, research, and higher education, with foreign comparisons, 1960s- 83, annual rpt, 9624–10

Soviet Union-US science and technology exchange projects, man-hours, and funding, by Fed Govt agency and activity type, FY81-82, 7008–41

Index by Subjects and Names

Teenagers

see Children
see Elementary and secondary education
see Juvenile delinquency
see Youth
see Youth employment

Telecommunication

Air traffic control and airway facilities and equipment, FAA improvement activities and R&D under Natl Airspace System Plan, 1982-2000, annual rpt, 7504–12

Air traffic control and airway facilities and services, operations, and finances, FY83, annual rpt, 7504–37

American Telephone and Telegraph Co divestiture effect on telecommunications equipment industry, with background financial and operating data, 1984 rpt, 9886–4.75

China economic conditions, agricultural and industrial production, trade, and domestic and foreign investment, 1980-85, 2048–106

County Business Patterns: establishments, employees, and payrolls, by SIC 4-digit industry and county, 1981, annual State rpt series, 2326–8

Developing countries disaster preparedness and summary sociodemographic, political, and economic data, country rpt series, 9916–2

Employment, earnings, and hours, by SIC 4-digit nonfarm industry, monthly 1974-Feb 1984, annual update, 6744–4

Equipment (electronic) and associated product shipments, trade, and consumption, by product, 1983, annual Current Industrial Rpt, 2506–12.21

Exports and imports of US, detailed SIC-based commodities by world area, 1983, annual rpts, 2424–6

Exports of US, detailed Schedule B commodities by country of destination, 1983, annual rpt, 2424–9

Exports of US, detailed Schedule E commodities by mode of transport and world area and country of destination, 1983, annual rpts, 2424–5

Fed Govt computers and telecommunications systems acquisition plans and obligations, by agency, FY84-89, annual rpt, 104–20

Fed Govt programs and mgmt cost control proposals, 3-year savings by function and agency, and financial and operating data, 1960s-81, 16908–1.21

Fiber optics displacement of copper in telecommunications, with Bell System use and copper and fiber optics industry data, 1978-88, 2048–104

Foreign economic, social, and political summary data, by country, 1984, annual factbook, 244–11

Foreign market and trade for telecommunications equipment, and user industry operations and demand, country market research rpts, 2045–12

GAO publications on computers, computer use, and telecommunication, as of 1983, annual listing, 26104–11.1

Great Lakes trade, by SITC 3-digit commodity, port, vessel type, world area, and country, 1982, annual rpt, 7744–3

GSA mgmt activities and finances, FY78-83, annual rpt, 9454–23

Imports of US, detailed TSUSA commodities by country of origin, 1983, annual rpt, 2424–4

Industry finances and operations, by SIC 2- to 4-digit industry, 1970s-83 and projected to 1988, annual rpt, 2014–4

Minority group and women employment by occupation, and business owners, by race and State, with TV and radio revenues and stations, 1971-81, hearing, 21368–45

Natl Endowment for Arts activities and grants, FY83, annual rpt, 9564–3

Occupational injury and illness rates, by SIC 2- to 4-digit industry, 1982, annual rpt, 6844–1

OECD trade, total and for 4 major countries, and US trade by country, by commodity, 1972-82, annual world region rpt series, 244–13

Patents (US) for telecommunication equipment granted to US and foreign applicants, by applicant type, firm, State, and country, various periods 1963-83, 2246–2.7

Postal Service electronic mail system message volume and profitability under proposed rate and service increases, FY82 and projected to FY87, 21408–70

Research and engineering rpts of Natl Telecommunications and Info Admin, FY83, annual listing, 2804–3

Urban travel by purpose, effect of telecommunication advances, land use changes, and alternative work schedules, projected to 2000 with some trends 1950-80, 7888–63

see also Communications satellites
see also Educational broadcasting
see also Public broadcasting
see also Radio
see also Telegraph
see also Telephone and telephone industry
see also Television

Telegraph

Business statistics, detailed data for major industries and economic indicators, *Survey of Current Business,* monthly rpt, 2702–1.8

Census of Population, 1980: detailed socioeconomic and demographic characteristics, by age, sex, race, Hispanic origin, occupation, and industry, State rpt series, 2531–4

Construction put in place, permits authorized by region, State, and MSA, and Federal contract awards, by construction type, bimonthly rpt with articles, 2012–1

County Business Patterns: establishments, employees, and payrolls, by SIC 4-digit industry and county, 1981, annual State rpt series, 2326–8

County Business Patterns: establishments, employees, and payrolls, by SIC 4-digit industry and county, 1982, annual State rpt series, 2326–6

Employment, earnings, and hours, by selected SIC 1- to 4-digit industry, State, and for 278 major labor areas, 1939-83, annual rpt, 6744–5

Employment, earnings, and hours, by SIC 4-digit nonfarm industry, monthly 1974-Feb 1984, annual update, 6744–4

Equipment (electronic) and associated product shipments, trade, and consumption, by product, 1983, annual Current Industrial Rpt, 2506–12.21

Telephone and telephone industry

Exports of US, detailed commodities by country of destination, monthly rpt, 2422–3

Finances and operations, by SIC 2- to 4-digit industry, 1970s-83 and projected to 1988, annual rpt, 2014–4

Financial and operating data for 7 major telegraph carriers, quarterly rpt, 9282–1

Financial, operating, and employment detailed statistics, 1982, annual rpt, 9284–6

Income tax returns of corporations, detailed income and tax items by industry, 1981, annual rpt, 8304–4

Input-output structure of US economy, detailed interindustry transactions for 537 industries, and components of final demand, 1977 benchmark data, 2708–17

Manufacturing census, 1982: financial and operating data, by SIC 2- to 4-digit industry, State, SMSA, and county, preliminary census div rpt series, 2491–3

Manufacturing census, 1982: financial and operating data, for SIC 4-digit industries by product, preliminary rpt, 2491–1.379

Rates for messages sent within US and to selected countries, by type and country, 1982, annual rpt, 9284–6.6

Scientists, engineers, and technicians employment in transportation, utilities, and retail and wholesale trade, by field of science and industry, 1982, 9628–72

Wages and employment in telephone and telegraph industry by occupation and sex, 1981, annual survey, 6787–6.199

Telephone and telephone industry

American Telephone and Telegraph Co divestiture effect on telecommunications equipment industry, with background financial and operating data, 1984 rpt, 9886–4.75

American Telephone and Telegraph Co operating data, costs, and billings for local and long distance lines, by State, 1980-82 with trends from 1970, 23848–176

Bombing (explosive and incendiary) incidents, damage, injuries, and deaths, by target, State, and circumstances, 1983, annual rpt, 6224–5

Business statistics, detailed data for major industries and economic indicators, *Survey of Current Business,* monthly rpt, 2702–1.8

Cellular telephones and parts from Japan at less than fair value, imports injury to US industry, investigation with background financial and operating data, 1984 rpt, 9886–14.130

Census of Housing, 1980: inventory, occupancy, and unit characteristics, changes from 1973 by region and inside-outside SMSAs and central cities, series, 2473–3

Census of Housing, 1980: structural, financial, and householder characteristics, by region and State, 2475–4

Census of Population and Housing, 1980: detailed population and housing characteristics, by county, city, and census tract, State and SMSA rpt series, 2551–2

Census of Population, 1980: detailed socioeconomic and demographic characteristics, by age, sex, race, Hispanic origin, occupation, and industry, State rpt series, 2531–4

Telephone and telephone industry

Collective bargaining agreements expiring during year, covered workers by SIC 2-digit industry, firm, and union, with summary of key provisions, 1984, annual rpt, 6784–9

Communist, OECD, and selected other countries telephones in use, by country, 1983, annual rpt, 244–5.1

Construction put in place, permits authorized by region, State, and MSA, and Federal contract awards, by construction type, bimonthly rpt with articles, 2012–1

Construction put in place, value of new public and private structures, by type, monthly rpt, 2382–4

County Business Patterns: establishments, employees, and payrolls, by SIC 4-digit industry and county, 1981, annual State rpt series, 2326–8

County Business Patterns: establishments, employees, and payrolls, by SIC 4-digit industry and county, 1982, annual State rpt series, 2326–6

Court use of telephone conferencing in civil and criminal hearings, assessment of lawyers and judges in 2 States and Denver, Colo, 1981, 6068–186

Developing countries disaster preparedness and summary sociodemographic, political, and economic data, country rpt series, 9916–2

Employment, earnings, and hours, by selected SIC 1- to 4-digit industry, State, and for 278 major labor areas, 1939-83, annual rpt, 6744–5

Employment, earnings, and hours, by SIC 4-digit nonfarm industry, monthly 1974-Feb 1984, annual update, 6744–4

Equipment (electronic) and associated product shipments, trade, and consumption, by product, 1983, annual Current Industrial Rpt, 2506–12.21

Exports and imports of US, detailed SIC-based commodities by world area, 1983, annual rpts, 2424–6

Exports and imports of US, totals and as percent of domestic production, by SIC 2- to 5-digit commodity, 1981, annual rpt, 2424–3

Exports of US, detailed commodities by country of destination, monthly rpt, 2422–3

Exports of US, detailed Schedule B commodities by country of destination, 1983, annual rpt, 2424–9

Exports of US, detailed Schedule E commodities by mode of transport and world area and country of destination, 1983, annual rpts, 2424–5

Farm production expenditures, detailed items by farm sales size and region, 1983, annual rpt, 1614–3

Farmers average monthly local and total telephone bill, monthly rpt, annual table, 1629–1

Fed Govt programs and mgmt cost control proposals, 3-year savings by function and agency, and financial and operating data, 1960s-81, 16908–1

Fiber optics displacement of copper in telecommunications, with Bell System use and copper and fiber optics industry data, 1978-88, 2048–104

Index by Subjects and Names

Finances and operations, by SIC 2- to 4-digit industry, 1970s-83 and projected to 1988, annual rpt, 2014–4

Financial and operating data by company type, with fixed cost recovery from interstate revenue by Bell company and State, 1981-82 with trends from 1945, 26306–6.79

Financial and operating data for major and other telephone carriers, quarterly rpt, discontinued, 9282–2

Financial, operating, and employment detailed statistics, 1982, annual rpt, 9284–6

Foreign economic, social, and political summary data, by country, 1984, annual factbook, 244–11

Foreign market and trade for telecommunications equipment, and user industry operations and demand, country market research rpts, 2045–12

House of Representatives salaries, expenses, and contingent fund disbursement, detailed listings, quarterly rpt, 21942–1

Housing occupancy and unit and household characteristics, by region and metro-nonmetro residence, 1983, biennial survey, 2485–1

Housing units with telephone, by inside-outside central cities, 1979-82 surveys, SMSA rpt series, 2485–6

Housing units with telephone, by occupant race, Hispanic origin, urban-rural location, and region, 1981, annual survey, 2485–7

Imports of US, detailed Schedule A commodities by country and world area of origin, and mode of transport, 1983, annual rpts, 2424–2

Imports of US, detailed Schedule A commodities by country, monthly rpt, 2422–2

Imports of US, detailed TSUSA commodities by country of origin, 1983, annual rpt, 2424–4

Income tax returns of corporations, detailed income and tax items by industry, 1981, annual rpt, 8304–4

Input-output structure of US economy, detailed interindustry transactions for 537 industries, and components of final demand, 1977 benchmark data, 2708–17

Manufacturing census, 1982: financial and operating data, by SIC 2- to 4-digit industry, State, SMSA, and county, preliminary census div rpt series, 2491–3

Manufacturing census, 1982: financial and operating data, for SIC 4-digit industries by product, preliminary rpt, 2491–1.379

Minority group and women employment, by occupational group and SIC 2- to 3-digit industry, 1981, annual rpt, 9244–1.1

Occupational injury and illness rates, by SIC 2- to 4-digit industry, 1982, annual rpt, 6844–1

Occupational Outlook Handbook, 1984-85 biennial rpt, 6744–1

Patents (US) for telecommunication equipment granted to US and foreign applicants, by applicant type, firm, State, and country, various periods 1963-83, 2246–2.7

Personal consumption expenditures, natl income and product account, *Survey of Current Business,* monthly rpt, monthly and annual tables, 2702–1.23

Productivity, hours, and employment indexes for selected SIC 3- and 4-digit industries, 1954-82, annual rpt, 6824–1.4

Rates for messages sent within US and to selected countries, by type and country, 1982, annual rpt, 9284–6.6

Rural Telephone Program loan activities summary, by State, FY83, annual rpt, 1244–8

Rural telephone program loans to telephone companies, and borrower operations and finances, 1983, annual rpt, 1244–2

Savings and loan assn and all thrifts offering telephone bill paying services, 1975-2nd qtr 1982, article, 9312–1.409

Scientists, engineers, and technicians employment in transportation, utilities, and retail and wholesale trade, by field of science and industry, 1982, 9628–72

Seasonal adjustment methodology for economic time series, dev and design of Census Bur and other systems, with illustrative data, 1981 conf papers, 2626–7.5

Senate salaries, expenses, and contingent fund disbursements, by payee, detailed listings, 1st half FY84, semiannual rpt, 25922–1

Service industry census, 1982: employment, establishments, receipts, and payroll, by SIC 2- to 4-digit kind of business, SMSA, county, and city, State rpt series, 2391–1

Tax (excise) collections of IRS, by source, quarterly press release, 8302–1

Tax collections, refunds, and taxes due IRS, by State and region, and IRS court activity and operating expenses, FY83, annual rpt, 8304–3.3

Wages and employment in telephone and telegraph industry by occupation and sex, 1981, annual survey, 6787–6.199

Washington State telephone rates including govt long-distance access charges, by company, 1983-89, hearing, 21148–32

Television

Business statistics, detailed data for major industries and economic indicators, *Survey of Current Business,* monthly rpt, 2702–1.14

Census of Population, 1980: detailed socioeconomic and demographic characteristics, by age, sex, race, Hispanic origin, occupation, and industry, State rpt series, 2531–4

China economic conditions, agricultural and industrial production, trade, and domestic and foreign investment, 1980-85, 2048–106

Communist, OECD, and selected other countries consumer and producer goods production, 1960s-83, annual rpt, 244–5.8

County Business Patterns: establishments, employees, and payrolls, by SIC 4-digit industry and county, 1981, annual State rpt series, 2326–8

County Business Patterns: establishments, employees, and payrolls, by SIC 4-digit industry and county, 1982, annual State rpt series, 2326–6

Developing countries disaster preparedness and summary sociodemographic, political, and economic data, country rpt series, 9916–2

Index by Subjects and Names

Tennessee

Election campaign expenditures for network and local TV ads, and public opinion on TV influence, selected years 1972-83, hearings, 21428–7

Employment, earnings, and hours, by selected SIC 1- to 4-digit industry, State, and for 278 major labor areas, 1939-83, annual rpt, 6744–5

Employment, earnings, and hours, by SIC 4-digit nonfarm industry, monthly 1974-Feb 1984, annual update, 6744–4

Employment in TV and radio industry, total and for minorities, women, and youth, by job category and State, 1979-83, annual rpt, 9284–16

Employment in TV and radio stations, total and for minorities and women, by full- and part-time status and individual station, 1983, annual rpt, 9284–7

Exports and imports of US, detailed SIC-based commodities by world area, 1983, annual rpts, 2424–6

Exports and imports of US, totals and as percent of domestic production, by SIC 2- to 5-digit commodity, 1981, annual rpt, 2424–3

Exports, imports, tariffs, and industry operating data for TV receivers and other apparatus, TSUSA commodity rpt supplement, 9885–6.69

Exports of US, detailed commodities by country of destination, monthly rpt, 2422–3

Exports of US, detailed Schedule B commodities by country of destination, 1983, annual rpt, 2424–9

Exports of US, detailed Schedule E commodities by mode of transport and world area and country of destination, 1983, annual rpts, 2424–5

Food industry advertising expenditures by media type, and advertising to sales ratio by selected food item, 1970-79 with some trends from 1955, 1548–234

Foreign economic, social, and political summary data, by country, 1984, annual factbook, 244–11

Great Lakes trade, by SITC 3-digit commodity, port, vessel type, world area, and country, 1982, annual rpt, 7744–3

Household energy use, appliances, motor vehicles, and vehicle fuel economy, by census region and urban-rural location, various periods Oct 1980-Mar 1983, annual rpt, 3164–74

Imports of color TVs from South Korea and Taiwan at less than fair value, injury to US industry, investigation with background financial and operating data, 1984 rpt, 9886–14.101

Imports of US, detailed Schedule A commodities by country and world area of origin, and mode of transport, 1983, annual rpts, 2424–2

Imports of US, detailed Schedule A commodities by country, monthly rpt, 2422–2

Imports of US, detailed TSUSA commodities by country of origin, 1983, annual rpt, 2424–4

Income tax returns of corporations, detailed income and tax items by industry, 1981, annual rpt, 8304–4

Income tax returns of sole proprietorships, detailed data by industry div and selected industry group, 1981, annual rpt, 8304–7

Income tax returns of sole proprietorships, receipts, deductions by type, payroll, and net income, by major industry, 1982, annual article, 8302–2.413

Industry finances and operations, by SIC 2- to 4-digit industry, 1970s-83 and projected to 1988, annual rpt, 2014–4

Injuries and deaths from use of selected consumer products and related activity, by victim age and sex, 1982, annual rpt, 9164–7

Input-output structure of US economy, detailed interindustry transactions for 85 industries, and components of final demand, 1977, article, 2702–1.421

Input-output structure of US economy, detailed interindustry transactions for 537 industries, and components of final demand, 1977 benchmark data, 2708–17

License status and allocations of commercial and noncommercial UHF and VHF TV channels, by market and community, as of Dec 1983, semiannual rpt, 9282–6

Manufacturing census, 1982: financial and operating data, by SIC 2- to 4-digit industry, State, SMSA, and county, preliminary census div rpt series, 2491–3

Manufacturing census, 1982: financial and operating data, for SIC 4-digit industries by product, preliminary rpt, 2491–1.377, 2491–1.380

Minority group and women employment by occupation, and business owners, by race and State, with TV and radio revenues and stations, 1971-81, hearing, 21368–45

Natl Endowment for Arts activities and grants, FY83, annual rpt, 9564–3

Natl Endowment for Humanities activities and grants, FY83, annual rpt, 9564–2

Nuclear attack civil defense plans of Fed Emergency Mgmt Agency, funding and operations by component, FY81-84 and projected FY85-89, GAO rpt, 26123–61

Occupational injury and illness rates, by SIC 2- to 4-digit industry, 1982, annual rpt, 6844–1

Occupational Outlook Handbook, 1984-85 biennial rpt, 6744–1

OECD trade, total and for 4 major countries, and US trade by country, by commodity, 1972-82, annual world region rpt series, 244–13

Patents (US) for telecommunication equipment granted to US and foreign applicants, by applicant type, firm, State, and country, various periods 1963-83, 2246–2.7

Producer prices and indexes, by stage of processing and detailed commodity, monthly rpt, 6762–6

Producer prices and indexes, by stage of processing and detailed commodity, monthly 1983, annual supplement, 6764–2

Receiving set industries productivity, hours, and employment indexes, for radio and TV, 1958-81, annual rpt, 6824–1.3

Repair of TV and radio, industry receipts, 1983, annual rpt, 2413–8

Repair technicians and apprentices wages and benefits, for 5 types of electrical repair shops in 19 SMSAs, Nov 1981 survey, 6787–6.197

Retail trade census, 1982: employment, establishments, sales, and payroll, for household appliance stores, by State, preliminary rpt, 2395–1.21

Scientists, engineers, and technicians employment in transportation, utilities, and retail and wholesale trade, by field of science and industry, 1982, 9628–72

Service industry census, 1982: employment, establishments, receipts, and payroll, by SIC 2- to 4-digit kind of business, SMSA, county, and city, State rpt series, 2391–1

Service industry census, 1982: employment, establishments, receipts, and payroll, by SIC 4-digit kind of business and State, preliminary rpt, 2390–2.11

Shipments, trade, and consumption of TV and related equipment, by product, 1982-83, annual Current Industrial Rpt, 2506–12.20

Stations on the air, by class of operation, monthly press release, 9282–4

Virgin Islands economic censuses, 1982: employment, establishments, payroll, and receipts, by SIC 1- to 4-digit industry, island, and city, 2593–1

Wholesale trade census, 1982: employment, establishments, sales by commodity, and payroll, by SIC 4-digit kind of business and State, preliminary rpt, 2403–1.9

see also Cable television

see also Educational broadcasting

see also Political broadcasting

Tellurium

see Metals and metal industries

Tempe, Ariz.

see also under By City in the "Index by Categories"

Temperature

see Weather

Temple, Tex.

Census of Housing, 1980: occupancy and unit characteristics, by race, Hispanic origin, and city, SMSA rpt, 2473–1.202

Census of Population and Housing, 1980: detailed population and housing characteristics, by county, city, and census tract, SMSA rpt, 2551–2.202

Housing vacancy rates for single and multifamily units and mobile homes, by city and ZIP code, 1984, annual metro area rpt, 9304–19.31

Wages of office and plant workers, by occupation, 1984 labor market area survey rpt, 6785–3.7

see also under By SMSA or MSA in the "Index by Categories"

Tennessee

Agriculture census, 1982: farms, farmland, production and costs, and operator characteristics, preliminary State summary and county rpts, 2330–1.47

Agriculture census, 1982: farms, farmland, production, finances, and operator characteristics, by county, final State rpt, 2331–1.42

Alcohol fuel (ethanol) production in Tennessee Valley, feedstocks, facilities, tax incentives, and related farming data, by State, 1970s-83 and projected to 1992, 9808–69

Bank deposits in commercial and mutual savings banks and in US branches of foreign banks, by account type, instn, State, SMSA, and county, June 1983, annual rpt, 9295–3.6

Biomass Fuels Program of TVA, technologies and processes dev, costs, and resource requirements, 1970s-90s, series, 9806–9

Tennessee

Census of Housing, 1980: occupancy and unit characteristics of SMSAs and central cities, by race, Hispanic origin, and city, State rpt, 2473–1.44

Census of Population and Housing, 1980: detailed population and housing characteristics, by county, city, and census tract, State rpt, 2551–2.44

Census of Population, 1980: detailed socioeconomic and demographic characteristics, by age, sex, race, Hispanic origin, and industry, State rpt, 2531–4.44

Collective bargaining calendar for Southeast US, 1984, annual rpt, 6946–1.68

County Business Patterns: establishments, employees, and payrolls, by SIC 4-digit industry and county, 1982, annual State rpt, 2326–6.44

Economic indicators by Tennessee region, manufacturing employment and farm receipts, and employment concentration ratios by SMSA and industry div, 1980-83, article, 9371–1.406

Employment (nonagricultural) by industry div and SMSA, earnings, and hours, for 8 southeastern States, monthly press release, 6942–7

Employment, earnings, and hours, by selected SIC 1- to 4-digit industry, State, and for 278 major labor areas, 1939-83, annual rpt, 6744–5.2, 6744–5.3

Employment, prices, earnings, and union membership in 8 southeastern States, Oct 1982-83, annual rpt, 6944–2

Environmental quality, pollutant discharge by type and source, and EPA protection activities and funding, 1970s-83, biennial regional rpt, 9184–15.4

Exports of manufactured and agricultural commodities, manufacturing production, and export-related employment, 1960s-82, State rpt, 2046–3.42

Farms in TVA mgmt program in Tennessee, and income at start and end of program, 1971-81, 9808–68

Farms with sales under $2,500, acreage, finances, operations, and operator characteristics, by region and for 6 States, 1978, 1548–241

Financial and economic devs, Fed Reserve Bank of Atlanta monthly rpt with articles, 9371–1

Foster care children permanent placement, Fed Govt incentive program funding and operations in 7 States, FY80-82, GAO rpt, 26121–81

HHS aid to each State and local govt or private instn, amount obligated, funding agency, and program, FY83, annual listing, 4004–3.4

Income (personal) per capita and by source, and earnings by industry div, by State, MSA, and county, 1977-82, annual regional rpt, 2704–2.6

Manufacturing census, 1982: financial and operating data, by SIC 2- to 4-digit industry, State, SMSA, and county, preliminary census div rpt, 2491–3.6

Mineral Industry Surveys, phosphate rock production, sales, exports, and use, 1984 crop year, annual rpt, 5614–20

Mineral Industry Surveys, State review of production, 1983, advance annual rpt, 5614–6.42

Index by Subjects and Names

Minerals Yearbook, 1982, Vol 2 preprints: State review of production and sales by commodity, and business activity, annual rpt, 5604–16.44

Minerals Yearbook, 1982, Vol 2: State reviews of production, sales, and firms, by commodity, and business activity, annual rpt, 5604–34

Population, births, deaths, and net migration, by MSA and county, 1980-82, annual State Current Population Rpt, 2546–4.42

Population size, Apr 1980 and July 1982, and per capita income, 1979 and 1981, by county and city, State Current Population Rpt, 2546–11.42

Retail trade census, 1982: employment, establishments, sales, and payroll, by SIC 2- to 4-digit kind of business, SMSA, county, and city, State rpt, 2397–1.43

Retail trade in Tennessee, firms and sales by city, county, and kind of business, annual rpt, discontinued, 9804–15

Savings and loan assns, FHLB 5th District members financial condition and operations by SMSA, monthly rpt, 9302–8

Textile mill employment and average hours and earnings, for 8 Southeastern States, monthly press release, 6942–1

Water supply and quality, and effect of coal mining operations, for selected river basins in Eastern and Interior coal provinces, 1983 rpt, 5666–15.23

Water supply and quality in streams and lakes, and groundwater levels in wells, by drainage basin, 1983, annual State rpt, 5666–10.40

Water supply and quality in 8 southeastern States, with background socioeconomic data, 1960s-2020 with trends from 1930, 9208–119

see also Bristol, Tenn.
see also Chattanooga, Tenn.
see also Clarksville, Tenn.
see also Johnson City, Tenn.
see also Kingsport, Tenn.
see also Knoxville, Tenn.
see also Memphis, Tenn.
see also Nashville, Tenn.
see also Oak Ridge, Tenn.
see also Tennessee River
see also Tennessee Valley
see also under By State in the "Index by Categories"

Tennessee River

Bridges over navigable waters, with type of bridge and use, owner, dimensions, and location, 1984 regional listing, 7406–5.2

Control operations, and reservoir elevations, storage, flows, and hydroelectric generating capacity use, 1981, annual rpt, 9804–7

Freight (waterborne domestic and foreign) by commodity, traffic, and passengers, by port and waterway, 1982, annual rpt, 3754–3.2

Water supply and quality in streams and lakes, and groundwater levels in wells, by drainage basin, 1980, annual State rpt series, 5666–12

Water supply and quality in streams and lakes, and groundwater levels in wells, by drainage basin, 1981, annual State rpt series, 5666–16

Water supply and quality in streams and lakes, and groundwater levels in wells, by drainage basin, 1982, annual State rpt series, 5666–20

Water supply and quality in streams and lakes, and groundwater levels in wells, by drainage basin, 1983, annual State rpt series, 5666–10

see also Tennessee Valley

Tennessee Valley

Alcohol fuel (ethanol) production in Tennessee Valley, feedstocks, facilities, tax incentives, and related farming data, by State, 1970s-83 and projected to 1992, 9808–69

Biomass Fuels Program of TVA, technologies and processes dev, costs, and resource requirements, 1970s-90s, series, 9806–9

Electric power distributors detailed operating and financial ratios, for individual municipal and cooperative distributors, FY79-83, annual rpt, 9804–19

Electric power distributors purchases and resales of TVA power and rates charged, by consumer class, 1983, annual rpt, 9804–14

Electric power program of TVA, finances and operations by plant and distributor, FY83, annual rpt, 9804–23

Fertilizer shipments of TVA agricultural dev program by fertilizer type, and farms participating, 1935-60, 9808–68

Forest, fish, and wildlife resources, TVA technical papers series, 9806–2

Industrial dev in Tennessee Valley and effects on employment, investment, and TVA power demand, by location and company, 1983, annual rpt, 9804–3

River control and reservoir elevations, storage, flows, and hydroelectric generating capacity use, 1981, annual rpt, 9804–7

TVA activities, financial and operating data by program and facility, and power sales by customer, FY83, annual rpt, 9804–1

Tennessee Valley Authority

Agricultural dev program of TVA, activities, and fertilizer shipments by fertilizer type, selected years 1935-81, 9808–68

Alcohol fuel (ethanol) production in Tennessee Valley, feedstocks, facilities, tax incentives, and related farming data, by State, 1970s-83 and projected to 1992, 9808–69

Biomass Fuels Program of TVA, technologies and processes dev, costs, and resource requirements, 1970s-90s, series, 9806–9

Budget of US Appendix, detailed budgets and personnel summaries, by agency, FY85, annual rpt, 104–3

Budget of US, appropriations, outlays, balances, and budget receipts, by govtl branch and agency, FY83, annual rpt, 8104–2

Clinch River Breeder Reactor proposed site and nearby area, radiation levels in river water and sediment and ground water, 1983, annual rpt, 9804–24

Construction projects of TVA, employment and impacts on nearby areas, survey rpt series, 9806–7

Index by Subjects and Names

Cost control proposals for Fed Govt programs and mgmt, 3-year savings by function and agency, and financial and operating data, 1960s-81, 16908–1.16, 16908–1.28, 16908–1.31

Electric power distributors detailed operating and financial ratios, for individual municipal and cooperative distributors, FY79-83, annual rpt, 9804–19

Electric power distributors purchases and resales of TVA power and rates charged, by consumer class, 1983, annual rpt, 9804–14

Electric power for DOE uranium enrichment, DOE prices under alternative TVA power rates and effects of TVA charges for power not taken, FY84-95, GAO rpt, 26113–114

Electric power program of TVA, finances and operations by plant and distributor, FY83, annual rpt, 9804–23

Electric power purchases of municipal and cooperative distributors, and prices and consumption by distributor and consumer sector, for TVA, monthly rpt, 9802–1

Electric power wholesale purchases and costs for individual REA borrowers, by supplier and State, 1940-83, annual rpt, 1244–5

Electric utilities privately owned, detailed financial and operating data by company, with summary data for other distributors by type, 1982, annual rpt, 3164–23

Employment (civilian) of Fed Govt, by location, agency, and pay system, 1982, biennial rpt, 9844–8

Financial and operating data, by program and facility, and power sales, by customer, FY83, annual rpt, 9804–1

Forest, fish, and wildlife resources, TVA technical papers series, 9806–2

Industrial dev in Tennessee Valley and effects on employment, investment, and TVA power demand, by location and company, 1983, annual rpt, 9804–3

Minority group and women employment of TVA, by detailed occupation, pay level, and grade, FY83 and goals for FY84, annual rpt, 9804–17

R&D Fed Govt funding for all performers, by field and supporting agency, selected years FY60-84, annual rpt, 9627–20

Recreation fees and collection costs, visitors, and capacity of outdoor Fed Govt, State, and private facilities, by managing agency and State, 1983, annual rpt, 5544–14

Retail trade in Tennessee, firms and sales by city, county, and kind of business, annual rpt, discontinued, 9804–15

River control and reservoir elevations, storage, flows, and hydroelectric generating capacity use, 1981, annual rpt, 9804–7

Sedimentation control, surveillance, and research activity of Fed Govt, by project, agency, region, and State, 1982, annual rpt, 5664–9

Terre Haute, Ind.

Census of Housing, 1980: occupancy and unit characteristics, by race, Hispanic origin, and city, SMSA rpt, 2473–1.350

Census of Population and Housing, 1980: detailed population and housing characteristics, by county, city, and census tract, SMSA rpt, 2551–2.350

see also under By SMSA or MSA in the "Index by Categories"

Terrell, Henry S.

"Bank Lending to Developing Countries: Recent Developments and Some Considerations for the Future", 9362–1.407

"Determination of Front-End Fees on Syndicated Eurocurrency Credits", 9366–7.105

Territorial waters

Developing countries disaster preparedness and summary sociodemographic, political, and economic data, country rpt series, 9916–2

Foreign economic, social, and political summary data, by country, 1984, annual factbook, 244–11

see also Continental shelf

Territories of the U.S.

Census of Population, 1980: detailed socioeconomic and demographic characteristics, by age, sex, race, Hispanic origin, occupation, and industry, State rpt series, 2531–4

DOD base support costs by function, and personnel and acreage by installation, by service branch, FY85, annual rpt, 3504–11

DOD budget, organization, personnel, weapons, and property, by service branch, State, and country, 1984 annual summary rpt, 3504–13

Environmental quality, pollutant discharge by type and source, and EPA protection activities and funding, 1970s-83, biennial regional rpt, 9184–15.2, 9184–15.9

Fed Govt civil service retirees and survivors, and monthly benefit, for US territories and foreign countries, and by State, age, and sex, FY81-82, annual rpt, 9844–1.1

Fed Govt civilian employee accessions and separations, by citizenship status and agency for DC metro area and elsewhere, monthly rpt, 9842–1.3

Fed Govt civilian employment, by US citizenship, selected agency, and outlying area, 1982, biennial rpt, 9844–8

Fed Govt financial and nonfinancial domestic aid, 1984 annual comprehensive catalog, 104–5

Food stamp recipient households size and composition, income, and income deductions allowed, Aug 1981, annual rpt, 1364–8

Pharmacists employment and sociodemographic characteristics, and reasons for not working in field, by State and overseas, as of 1979, 4147–14.28

Population size and components of change, by outlying area, 1970-82, Current Population Rpt, 2546–3.127

Population size and components of change, by outlying area, 1980-83, Current Population Rpt, 2546–3.134

R&D expenditures by higher education instns and federally funded centers, by field, source of funds, instn, and State, FY82, annual rpt, 9627–13

R&D expenditures of higher education instns, by source, field of science, census div, and State, 1972-83, biennial rpt, 9627–24.1

Statistical Abstract of US, selected social, political, and economic data, by country, 1945-83 and trends, annual rpt, 2324–1.4

Texarkana, Ark.

TV channels allocation and licensing status, for commercial and noncommercial UHF and VHF TV by market and community, as of Dec 1983, semiannual rpt, 9282–6

see also American Samoa

see also Guam

see also Northern Mariana Islands

see also Puerto Rico

see also Trust Territory of the Pacific Islands

see also Virgin Islands

see also under By Outlying Area in the "Index by Categories"

Terrorism

Bombing (explosive and incendiary) and arson incidents by target, State, and circumstances, and explosives theft and recovery, 1982-83, annual rpt, 8484–4

Bombing (explosive and incendiary) incidents, damage, injuries, and deaths, by target, State, and circumstances, 1983, annual rpt, 6224–5

Central America socioeconomic and political conditions in 6 countries, 1960s-83 with trends and projections 1930-2010, Commission rpt, 028–19.2

El Salvador socioeconomic and political conditions, and US economic and military assistance, 1977-FY84, 7008–39

El Salvador terrorist acts against property, casualties, kidnappings, and hostages, Oct 1979-June 1983, human rights certification hearing, 21388–41

Foreign human rights conditions in 162 countries, economic and military aid of US, and economic aid of intl organizations, 1981-83, annual rpt, 21384–3

Foreign military, social, and economic summary data by world area and country, 1960s-80s, hearing, 25388–47.1

Intl terrorist incidents, casualties, and attacks on US targets, by attack type and world area, with chronology of events, 1983, annual rpt, 7004–13

see also Air piracy

see also Assassination

see also Hostages

see also Kidnapping

see also Riots and disorders

see also Underground movements

Testa, William A.

"Economic Recovery and Jobs in the Seventh District", 9375–1.408

"Natural Gas Policy and the Midwest Region", 9375–13.3

"State Taxation of Energy Production: Regional and National Issues", 9375–1.407

Tests

see Educational tests

see Medical examinations and tests

see Quality control and testing

Tetanus

see Infective and parasitic diseases

Texarkana, Ark.

Census of Housing, 1980: occupancy and unit characteristics, by race, Hispanic origin, and city, SMSA rpt, 2473–1.351

Census of Population and Housing, 1980: detailed population and housing characteristics, by county, city, and census tract, SMSA rpt, 2551–2.351

Housing vacancy rates for single and multifamily units and mobile homes, by city and ZIP code, l983, annual metro area rpt, 9304–19.7

Texarkana, Ark.

Housing vacancy rates for single and multifamily units and mobile homes, by city and ZIP code, 1983, annual metro area rpt, 9304–19.6

see also under By SMSA or MSA in the "Index by Categories"

Texarkana, Tex.

Census of Housing, 1980: occupancy and unit characteristics, by race, Hispanic origin, and city, SMSA rpt, 2473–1.351

Census of Population and Housing, 1980: detailed population and housing characteristics, by county, city, and census tract, SMSA rpt, 2551–2.351

Housing vacancy rates for single and multifamily units and mobile homes, by city and ZIP code, 1983, annual metro area rpt, 9304–19.7

Housing vacancy rates for single and multifamily units and mobile homes, by city and ZIP code, 1983, annual metro area rpt, 9304–19.6

see also under By SMSA or MSA in the "Index by Categories"

Texas

- Agricultural cooperatives, membership, activities, and finances, by commodity and selected State, 1900-80 with trends from 1863, 1128–30
- Agriculture census, 1982: farms, farmland, production, finances, and operator characteristics, by county, final State rpt, 2331–1.43
- Bank deposits in commercial and mutual savings banks and in US branches of foreign banks, by account type, instn, State, SMSA, and county, June 1983, annual rpt, 9295–3.16
- Birds (shore) on Padre and Mustang Islands, Texas, distribution, abundance, and oil spill effects, by species, 1979-81, 5508–86
- Census of Housing, 1980: occupancy and unit characteristics of SMSAs and central cities, by race, Hispanic origin, and city, State rpt, 2473–1.45
- Census of Population and Housing, 1980: detailed population and housing characteristics, by county, city, and census tract, State rpt, 2551–2.45
- Census of Population, 1980: detailed socioeconomic and demographic characteristics, by age, sex, race, Hispanic origin, and industry, State rpt, 2531–4.45
- County Business Patterns: establishments, employees, and payrolls, by SIC 4-digit industry and county, 1982, annual State rpt, 2326–6.45
- Economic forecast for Texas, 1969-80, model description, technical paper, 9377–9.10
- Economic indicators, predictive value of 5 model types for 7 Texas indicators over 1-6 quarters, 1984 article, 9379–1.403
- Employment and economic impacts on Texas border of Mexican peso devaluation, for 6 counties and 2 SMSAs, 1970s-May 1983, hearing, 21788–133
- Employment by major nonagricultural industry, and average hours and earnings of manufacturing production workers, for 5 southwestern States, monthly rpt, 6962–2
- Employment, earnings, and hours, by selected SIC 1- to 4-digit industry, State, and for 278 major labor areas, 1939-83, annual rpt, 6744–5.2, 6744–5.3

Employment, industrial relations, prices, and economic conditions in 5 Southwestern States, regional rpts series, 6966–1

- Environmental quality, pollutant discharge by type and source, and EPA protection activities and funding, 1970s-83, biennial regional rpt, 9184–15.6
- Exports of manufactured and agricultural commodities, manufacturing production, and export-related employment, 1960s-82, State rpt, 2046–3.43
- Farm households income in Texas, by income source and substate region, 1979, article, 9379–1.406
- Fish and shellfish landings, prices, and cannery production, for Gulf States and North Carolina, by area, weekly rpt, 2162–6.3
- Fruit (citrus) production and use, by crop and State, 1977/78-1981/82, 1641–4
- Goat inventory in Texas, 1981-84, annual press release, 1623–4
- HHS aid to each State and local govt or private instn, amount obligated, funding agency, and program, FY83, annual listing, 4004–3.6
- Income (personal) per capita and by source, and earnings by industry div, by State, MSA, and county, 1977-82, annual regional rpt, 2704–2.7
- Manufacturing census, 1982: financial and operating data, by SIC 2- to 4-digit industry, State, SMSA, and county, preliminary census div rpt, 2491–3.7
- Mineral Industry Surveys, State review of production, 1983, advance annual rpt, 5614–6.43
- *Minerals Yearbook,* 1982, Vol 2 preprints: State review of production and sales by commodity, and business activity, annual rpt, 5604–16.45
- *Minerals Yearbook,* 1982, Vol 2: State reviews of production, sales, and firms, by commodity, and business activity, annual rpt, 5604–34
- Northwest Texas wages by occupation, and benefits for office and plant workers, 1984 labor market area survey rpt, 6785–3.10
- Oil and gas extraction production workers, wages, hours, and benefits, by occupation, region, and for 5 States, June 1982 survey, 6787 6.203
- Oil and gas field itemized equipment and operating costs and cost indexes, for 10 producing areas, 1981-83, annual rpt, 3164–45
- Philanthropic foundations assets and grants for 50 largest foundations, and for selected foundations by recipient, selected years 1975-82, hearings, 21788–137
- Population, births, deaths, and net migration, by MSA and county, 1980-82, annual State Current Population Rpt, 2546–4.43
- Population size, Apr 1980 and July 1982, and per capita income, 1979 and 1981, by county and city, State Current Population Rpt, 2546–11.43
- Retail trade census, 1982: employment, establishments, sales, and payroll, by SIC 2- to 4-digit kind of business, SMSA, county, and city, State rpt, 2397–1.44
- Rice market activities, prices, inspections, sales, trade, supply, and use, for US and selected foreign markets, weekly rpt, 1313–8

Index by Subjects and Names

- Rice stocks on and off farms and total, periodic rpt, 1621–7
- Savings and loan assn deregulation effect on lending activity, for US and 3 States, as of June 1980-83, article, 9371–1.432
- Savings and loan assn deregulation impact, financial ratios of S&Ls in 3 States and US, 1980-83, article, 9371–1.426
- Savings and loan assns, FHLB 9th District insured members financial condition and operations by SMSA, monthly rpt, 9302–13
- Service industry census, 1982: employment, establishments, receipts, and payroll, by SIC 2- to 4-digit kind of business, SMSA, county, and city, State rpt, 2391–1.44
- Water supply and use in 3 areas with supply problems and total US, and methods to increase supply, selected years 1974-80 and projected to 2010, 9208–125
- Wool and mohair production and prices, 1981-83, annual release, 1623–6

see also Abilene, Tex.

see also Amarillo, Tex.

see also Austin, Tex.

see also Beaumont, Tex.

see also Brownsville, Tex.

see also Bryan, Tex.

see also College Station, Tex.

see also Corpus Christi, Tex.

see also Dallas, Tex.

see also Denison, Tex.

see also Edinburg, Tex.

see also El Paso, Tex.

see also Fort Worth, Tex.

see also Galveston, Tex.

see also Harlingen, Tex.

see also Houston, Tex.

see also Killeen, Tex.

see also Laredo, Tex.

see also Longview, Tex.

see also Lubbock, Tex.

see also Marshall, Tex.

see also McAllen, Tex.

see also Midland, Tex.

see also Mission, Tex.

see also Odessa, Tex.

see also Orange, Tex.

see also Pharr, Tex.

see also Port Arthur, Tex.

see also San Angelo, Tex.

see also San Antonio, Tex.

see also San Benito, Tex.

see also Sherman, Tex.

see also Temple, Tex.

see also Texarkana, Tex.

see also Texas City, Tex.

see also Tyler, Tex.

see also Val Verde County, Tex.

see also Victoria, Tex.

see also Waco, Tex.

see also Wichita Falls, Tex.

see also under By State in the "Index by Categories"

Texas City, Tex.

Census of Housing, 1980: occupancy and unit characteristics, by race, Hispanic origin, and city, SMSA rpt, 2473–1.168

Census of Population and Housing, 1980: detailed population and housing characteristics, by county, city, and census tract, SMSA rpt, 2551–2.168

see also under By SMSA or MSA in the "Index by Categories"

Index by Subjects and Names

Textile industry and fabrics

Air pollutant emission factors, by detailed source, 3rd edition, 1983-84 supplements, 9198–13

Air pollution levels for 5 pollutants, by detailed source, State, and Air Quality Control Region, 1981, annual rpt, 9194–7

Business statistics, detailed data for major industries and economic indicators, *Survey of Current Business,* monthly rpt, 2702–1.19

Census of Population, 1980: detailed socioeconomic and demographic characteristics, by age, sex, race, Hispanic origin, occupation, and industry, State rpt series, 2531–4

Census of Population, 1980: detailed socioeconomic characteristics, by county, city, and inside-outside SMSAs and central cities, State rpt series, 2531–3

Census of Population, 1980: labor force, by sex, detailed occupation, and region, with comparison to 1970 census, supplementary rpt, 2535–1.12

China economic conditions, agricultural and industrial production, trade, and domestic and foreign investment, 1980-85, 2048–106

China exports and imports by SITC 1- to 5-digit commodity, 1970s-82, annual rpt, 244–12

China exports to US of selected textile and leather goods harmful to competing US industries, and US consumption and producer shipments, 1978-83, 9882–2.401

Collective bargaining agreements expiring during year, covered workers by SIC 2-digit industry, firm, and union, with summary of key provisions, 1984, annual rpt, 6784–9

Communist, OECD, and selected other countries consumer and producer goods production, 1960s-83, annual rpt, 244–5.8

County Business Patterns: establishments, employees, and payrolls, by SIC 4-digit industry and county, 1981, annual State rpt series, 2326–8

County Business Patterns: establishments, employees, and payrolls, by SIC 4-digit industry and county, 1982, annual State rpt series, 2326–6

DOD expenditures for goods and services, by function, 1972-84, article, 2702–1.440

DOD procurement, prime contract awards by category, contract and contractor type, and service branch, FY74-1st half FY84, semiannual rpt, 3542–1

Earnings by major industry group, and personal income per capita and by source, by region and State, 1929-82, 2708–40

Employment, earnings, and hours, by selected SIC 1- to 4-digit industry, State, and for 278 major labor areas, 1939-83, annual rpt, 6744–5

Employment, earnings, and hours, by SIC 4-digit nonfarm industry, monthly 1974-Feb 1984, annual update, 6744–4

Employment in regionally concentrated and all industries, and population size, by State, 1970-82, article, 6722–1.413

Exports and imports between US and outlying areas, by detailed commodity and mode of transport, monthly rpt, 2422–4

Exports and imports of US, by commodity group, world area, selected country, US coastal area and port, and mode of transport, with seasonal adjustments, monthly rpt, 2422–9

Exports and imports of US by country, and trade shifts by commodity, USITC quarterly monitoring rpt, 9882–9

Exports and imports of US, detailed SIC-based commodities by world area, 1983, annual rpts, 2424–6

Exports and imports of US, totals and as percent of domestic production, by SIC 2- to 5-digit commodity, 1981, annual rpt, 2424–3

Exports, imports, tariffs, and industry operating data for textile fiber and products, TSUSA commodity rpt series, 9885–3

Exports of manufactured and agricultural commodities, manufacturing production, and export-related employment, 1960s-82, State rpt series, 2046–3

Exports of textiles, by product and country of destination, monthly rpt, 2042–26

Exports of US, detailed commodities by country of destination, monthly rpt, 2422–3

Exports of US, detailed Schedule B commodities by country of destination, 1983, annual rpt, 2424–9

Exports of US, detailed Schedule E commodities by mode of transport and world area and country of destination, 1983, annual rpts, 2424–5

Finances and operations, by SIC 2- to 4-digit industry, 1970s-83 and projected to 1988, annual rpt, 2014–4

Financial statements for manufacturing, mining, and trade corporations, by selected SIC 2- to 3-digit industry, quarterly rpt, 2502–1

Foreign and US production and trade of textiles, FAS monthly and annual rpt series, 1925–4

Great Lakes trade, by SITC 3-digit commodity, port, vessel type, world area, and country, 1982, annual rpt, 7744–3

Import quotas and imports, by country of origin, monthly rpt, 8146–1.4

Imports and import limits for textiles under Multifiber Arrangement by product and country, with US exports and use, 1970-83, semiannual rpt, 9882–11

Imports of fabric and neoprene laminate from Japan at less than fair value, injury to US industry, investigation with background financial and operating data, 1984 rpt, 9886–14.128

Imports of textiles, by country of origin, monthly rpt, 2042–27

Imports of textiles, by product and country of origin, monthly rpt, 2422–1

Imports of textiles, by product and country of origin, monthly rpt series, 2046–9

Imports of textiles, by product and country of origin, periodic rpt series, 2046–8

Imports of textiles, monthly rpt, 2042–18

Imports of textiles, total and as percents of US production and use, by commodity, 1972-82, annual rpt, 2044–14

Imports of US, detailed Schedule A commodities by country and world area of origin, and mode of transport, 1983, annual rpts, 2424–2

Textile industry and fabrics

Imports of US, detailed Schedule A commodities by country, monthly rpt, 2422–2

Imports of US, detailed TSUSA commodities by country of origin, 1983, annual rpt, 2424–4

Income tax returns of corporations, detailed income and tax items by industry, 1981, annual rpt, 8304–4

Income tax returns of corporations with foreign tax credit, income and deductions by type, asset size, and selected industry group, 1980, article, 8302–2.415

Income tax returns of sole proprietorships, detailed data by industry div and selected industry group, 1981, annual rpt, 8304–7

Income tax returns of sole proprietorships, receipts, deductions by type, payroll, and net income, by major industry, 1982, annual article, 8302–2.413

Input-output structure of US economy, detailed interindustry transactions for 85 industries, and components of final demand, 1977, article, 2702–1.421

Input-output structure of US economy, detailed interindustry transactions for 537 industries, and components of final demand, 1977 benchmark data, 2708–17

Linens production, shipments, trade, inventories, and consumption, quarterly Current Industrial Rpt, 2506–6.6

Manufacturing census, 1982: financial and operating data, by SIC 2- to 4-digit industry, State, SMSA, and county, preliminary census div rpt series, 2491–3

Manufacturing census, 1982: financial and operating data, for SIC 4-digit industries by product, preliminary rpt series, 2491–1

Manufacturing census, 1982: textile mill machinery in place, by machine type and textile industry, special preliminary rpts, 2491–2

Minority group and women employment, by occupational group and SIC 2- to 3-digit industry, 1981, annual rpt, 9244–1.1

Occupational injury and illness rates, by SIC 2- to 4-digit industry, 1982, annual rpt, 6844–1

Occupational manpower needs and supply by detailed occupation, and educational and training program enrollees and grads by detailed field, 1982 and 1995, biennial rpt, 6744–3

OECD trade, total and for 4 major countries, and US trade by country, by commodity, 1972-82, annual world region rpt series, 244–13

Pollution abatement capital and operating costs, by SIC 2- to 4-digit industry, State, and SMSA, 1982, annual Current Industrial Rpt, 2506–3.6

Producer prices and indexes, by stage of processing and detailed commodity, monthly rpt, 6762–6

Producer prices and indexes, by stage of processing and detailed commodity, monthly 1983, annual supplement, 6764–2

Production, consumption, prices, and trade of cotton, wool, and synthetic fibers, periodic situation rpt with articles, 1561–1

Production, stocks, materials used, and orders, by product and major State, and trade by country, periodic Current Industrial Rpt series, 2506–5

Textile industry and fabrics

- R&D industry funding and employment of scientists and engineers, by industry group, firm size, and funding source, 1956-82, annual rpt, 9627–21
- Retail trade census, 1982: employment, establishments, sales, and payroll, for floor covering stores by State, preliminary rpt, 2395–1.20
- Scientists, engineers, and technicians employed in private industry, by occupation and industry group, 1980-81, biennial rpt, 9627–23
- South Carolina economic indicators, including unemployment rate by county, and textile manufacturing employment, quarterly 1970-83 with estimated unemployment for 1984, article, 9371–1.411
- Southeastern States textile mill employment and average hours and earnings, for 8 States, monthly press release, 6942–1
- Southeastern States textile mill employment, monthly 1951-83, annual summary rpt, 6944–1
- Tariff Schedules of US, Annotated, classifications and rates of duty for detailed imported commodities, 1985 edition, 9886–13
- Transportation census, 1982: trucks, by detailed characteristics, miles traveled, and type of product carried, State rpt series, 2573–1
- Waterborne commerce of US (domestic and foreign), freight by commodity, traffic, and passengers, by port and waterway, 1982, annual rpt, 3754–3
- Wholesale trade census, 1982: employment, establishments, finances, and operations, by SIC 2- to 4-digit kind of business, SMSA, county, and city, State rpt series, 2405–1
- Wholesale trade census, 1982: employment, establishments, sales by commodity, and payroll, by SIC 4-digit kind of business and State, preliminary rpt series, 2403–1
- *see also* Clothing and clothing industry
- *see also* Cotton
- *see also* Fibers
- *see also* Silk
- *see also* Synthetic fibers and fabrics
- *see also* Wool and wool trade
- *see also* under By Commodity in the "Index by Categories"
- *see also* under By Industry in the "Index by Categories"

Thailand

- Agricultural and food production indexes, and production of selected commodities, by world region and country, 1974-83, annual rpt, 1524–5
- Agricultural situation in Southeast Asia, by country and commodity, 1983 and outlook for 1984, annual rpt, 1524–4.5
- Agricultural supply/demand, trade, and production, and socioeconomic data, by country, 1950s-77, 1528–179
- AID activities and funding by project and function, FY85, and developing countries summary socioeconomic data, 1970s-83, by country, annual rpt, 9914–3
- AID and other foreign assistance, and govt policy, effects on private sector dev and socioeconomic conditions, with case studies for 6 countries, 1960s-80, 9918–12
- AID economic assistance to developing countries, obligations and disbursements by country, quarterly rpt, 9912–4
- AID educational program activities and project impacts in 12 developing countries, 1950s-82, 9916–11.8
- AID loan repayment status and terms by program and country, and status of predecessor agency loans, quarterly rpt, 9912–3
- Economic conditions, investment and export opportunities, and trade practices, 1984 country market research rpt, 2046–6.3
- Economic indicators of 12 Pacific Basin countries or areas and US, quarterly rpt, 9393–9
- Economic, social, and political summary data, by country, 1984, annual factbook, 244–11
- Economic trends in income, production, prices, employment, finances, and trade, 1984 annual rpt, 2046–4.74
- Electric power systems equipment market and trade, and user industry operations and demand, 1984 country market research rpt, 2045–15.4
- Employee stock ownership plans in developing countries, and firms finances and operations, with case studies of US and 3 countries, 1970s-82, 9916–3.19
- Exports and imports of US, by commodity and country, 1972-82, annual world region rpt, 244–13.5
- Exports of US, detailed Schedule B commodities by country of destination, 1983, annual rpt, 2424–9
- Exports of US, detailed Schedule E commodities by mode of transport and world area and country of destination, 1983, annual rpts, 2424–5
- Food processing and packaging equipment market and trade, and user industry operations and demand, 1984 market research rpt, 2045–11.23
- Food supply policies of 21 developing countries, with farm sector data, tariff income, and prices and imports of 5 grains, 1960s-81, 1528–168
- Imports of US, detailed Schedule A commodities by country and world area of origin, and mode of transport, 1983, annual rpts, 2424–2
- Imports of US, detailed TSUSA commodities by country of origin, 1983, annual rpt, 2424–4
- Loans and grants for economic and military assistance from US and intl agencies, by program and country, FY46-83, annual rpt, 9914–5
- Military aid of US, arms sales, and training programs costs and budget requests by program, world region, and country, FY83-85, annual rpt, 7144–13
- Military spending, arms trade, and armed forces size, with total govt spending and population, by country, 1972-82, annual rpt, 9824–1
- *Minerals Yearbook, 1982,* Vol 3: foreign country reviews of production, trade, and policies, by commodity, annual rpt, 5604–35
- *Minerals Yearbook, 1982,* Vol 3 preprints: foreign country review of production, trade, and policies, by commodity, annual rpt, 5604–17.71

Index by Subjects and Names

- Natural gas composition and occurrence of helium, analyses of samples from individual wells and pipelines in 26 States and 2 countries, 1983, annual survey, 5604–2
- Oil reserves, production, and resource lifespan under alternative production rates, for 4 Asian countries, late 1800s-1982 and projected to 2030, 3166–9.9
- Population size and growth rates, and latest available benchmark demographic data, by country, 1950-83, biennial rpt, 2324–4
- Refugee migration, settlement status, and assistance, by world area and country of origin and asylum, as of May 1984, annual rpt, 7004–15
- Rice market activities, prices, inspections, sales, trade, supply, and use, for US and selected foreign markets, weekly rpt, 1313–8
- Rice production, prices, exports, and stocks, 1970-84 with projections to 1995, article, 1561–8.402
- *see also* under By Foreign Country in the "Index by Categories"

Thallium

see Metals and metal industries

Theater

- Army morale, welfare, and recreation programs, revenue and expenses worldwide by activity and major command, FY82-83, annual rpt, 3704–12
- Census of Population, 1980: detailed socioeconomic and demographic characteristics, by age, sex, race, Hispanic origin, occupation, and industry, State rpt series, 2531–4
- Census of Population, 1980: labor force, by sex, detailed occupation, and region, with comparison to 1970 census, supplementary rpt, 2535–1.12
- County Business Patterns: establishments, employees, and payrolls, by SIC 4-digit industry and county, 1981, annual State rpt series, 2326–8
- County Business Patterns: establishments, employees, and payrolls, by SIC 4-digit industry and county, 1982, annual State rpt series, 2326–6
- Input-output structure of US economy, detailed interindustry transactions for 537 industries, and components of final demand, 1977 benchmark data, 2708–17
- Natl Endowment for Arts activities and grants, FY83, annual rpt, 9564–3
- Service industry census, 1982: employment, establishments, receipts, and payroll, by SIC 2- to 4-digit kind of business, SMSA, county, and city, State rpt series, 2391–1

Theft

see Robbery and theft

Therapy

- *see* Occupational therapy
- *see* Physical therapy
- *see* Rehabilitation of the disabled

Thermal pollution

see Water pollution

Thermal power

- *see* Cogeneration of heat and electricity
- *see* Geothermal resources

Thibodaux, La.

Housing vacancy rates for single and multifamily units and mobile homes, by city and ZIP code, 1984, annual metro area rpt, 9304–19.20

Index by Subjects and Names

see also under By SMSA or MSA in the "Index by Categories"

Third World countries
see Developing countries

Thomas, P. R.
"Chromium Availability, Market Economy Countries. A Minerals Availability Program Appraisal", 5606–4.12

Thomas, Sue A.
"Blood Pressure and Heart Rate Changes in Children when They Read Aloud", 4102–1.415

Thompson, A. Frank, Jr.
"Examination of Auditor Concentration in the Savings and Loan Industry", 9312–1.403

Thompson, Catherine
"Residential Energy Consumption Survey. Consumption and Expenditures, Apr. 1982-Mar. 1983. Part 2: Regional Data", 3166–7.22

Thompson, John D.
"Measurement of Nursing Intensity", 4652–1.427

Thorium
see Radioactive materials

Thornton, Daniel L.
"Early Look at the Volatility of Money and Interest Rates under CRR", 9391–1.422
"How Robust Are the Policy Conclusions of the St. Louis Equation?: Some Further Evidence", 9391–1.417
"Why Does Velocity Matter?", 9391–1.401

Thurman, S. S.
"Examination of Distributed Lag Model Coefficients Estimated with Smoothness Priors", 9366–6.77

Tichler, J.
"Radioactive Materials Released from Nuclear Power Plants, Annual Report, 1981", 9634–1

Ticks
see Animal diseases and zoonoses

Tides and currents
see Oceanography

Tilsley, James M.
"Major Dams, Reservoirs, and Hydroelectric Plants: Worldwide and Bureau of Reclamation", 5828–13

Timber
see Forests and forestry
see Lumber industry and products

Time deposits
see Bank deposits
see Certificates of deposit

Time of day
Aircraft accident circumstances and severity, by type of flying and aircraft, 1981, annual rpt, 9614–3
Assaults, murders, and other deaths of law enforcement officers, by circumstances, level of govt, agency, victim and offender characteristics, and location, 1983, annual rpt, 6224–3
Boat accidents, injuries, and fatalities, by age of operator and circumstances, 1983, annual rpt, 7404–1.2
Bombing (explosive and incendiary) incidents, damage, injuries, and deaths, by target, State, and circumstances, 1983, annual rpt, 6224–5
Crime victimization rates by type of offense, and victim and offense characteristics, Natl Crime Survey series, 6066–3

Earthquake intensity, damage, time of origin, and seismic characteristics of all US and major foreign earthquakes, 1981, annual rpt, 5664–13
Electric and gas utility ratemaking and regulatory policy standards, and consumers and sales covered, by type of consumer and utility, 1983, annual rpt, 3104–7
Fires (housing electrical) in 10 cities, by type of wiring and equipment involved and circumstances, 1980-81, 2218–71
Health care temporary employees, reasons for desiring temporary and part-time work, and preferences for work time, by skill level, survey, 1984 article, 6722–1.452
Hwy-railroad grade-crossing accidents, detailed data by State and railroad, 1982, annual rpt, 7604–2
Hwy safety, accident, and traffic data from Natl Statistics and Analysis Center, series, 7766–10
Railroad accidents, circumstances, severity, and railroad involved, quarterly rpt, 9612–3
Railroad accidents investigated by Fed Railroad Admin, casualties, damage, and circumstances, 1982, annual rpt, 7604–3
Sunrise and sunset local mean times, every 5th day by date and degree of latitude, 1985 predictions, annual rpt series, 2174–2
Traffic accidents alcohol-related in 3 Idaho counties, effect of reduction program, model results, 1970-80, article, 7762–9.404
Traffic accidents, circumstances, injuries, deaths, and characteristics of persons and vehicles involved, 1982, annual rpt, 7764–13
Traffic fatal accidents, alcohol levels of drivers and pedestrians by driver age and sex and time of accident, 1980, 7768–81
Traffic fatal accidents, circumstances, and characteristics of persons and vehicles involved, 1983, annual rpt, 7764–14
Traffic fatal accidents detailed circumstances, and characteristics of persons and vehicles involved, 1982, annual rpt, 7764–10
Travel patterns, personal and household characteristics, auto use, and public transport availability, 1977 survey, series, 7556–6
Truck accidents, injuries, deaths, and property damage, by circumstances, carrier type, and driver age and condition, 1983, annual rpt, 7554–9
Weather broadcasts for US ships, by major ocean area, as of Jan 1984, biennial rpt, 2184–3

Timson, Floyd G.
"Personal-Use Firewood Program on Three National Forests: A Cost Analysis", 1208–191

Tin and tin industry
Alaska minerals resources, production, claims on wildlife refuges, oil and gas leases, and exploratory wells, with maps and bibl, 1983, annual rpt, 5664–11
Business statistics, detailed data for major industries and economic indicators, *Survey of Current Business,* monthly rpt, 2702–1.14

Tin and tin industry

Communist, OECD, and selected other countries minerals and metals production, by commodity, 1960s-83, annual rpt, 244–5.6
County Business Patterns: establishments, employees, and payrolls, by SIC 4-digit industry and county, 1981, annual State rpt series, 2326–8
Cuba economic conditions, agricultural and industrial production and distribution, trade, and intl economic relations, 1970-82 and trends from 1957, 248–40
Exports and imports of US, totals and as percent of domestic production, by SIC 2- to 5-digit commodity, 1981, annual rpt, 2424–3
Exports of US, detailed commodities by country of destination, monthly rpt, 2422–3
Exports of US, detailed Schedule B commodities by country of destination, 1983, annual rpt, 2424–9
Exports of US, detailed Schedule E commodities by mode of transport and world area and country of destination, 1983, annual rpts, 2424–5
Foreign minerals production, reserves, and industry role in domestic economy and world supply, country and world region rpt series, 5606–1
Great Lakes trade, by SITC 3-digit commodity, port, vessel type, world area, and country, 1982, annual rpt, 7744–3
Imports of US, detailed Schedule A commodities by country and world area of origin, and mode of transport, 1983, annual rpts, 2424–2
Imports of US, detailed Schedule A commodities by country, monthly rpt, 2422–2
Imports of US, detailed TSUSA commodities by country of origin, 1983, annual rpt, 2424–4
Mineral Industry Surveys, commodity review of production, trade, stocks, and consumption, monthly rpt, 5612–1.24
Minerals Yearbook, 1982, Vol 1: commodity reviews of production, reserves, supply, use, and trade, annual rpt, 5604–33
Minerals Yearbook, 1982, Vol 2 preprints: State reviews of production and sales by commodity, and business activity, annual rpt series, 5604–16
Minerals Yearbook, 1982, Vol 2: State reviews of production, sales, and firms, by commodity, and business activity, annual rpt, 5604–34
Minerals Yearbook, 1982, Vol 3: foreign country reviews of production, trade, and policies, by commodity, annual rpt, 5604–35
Minerals Yearbook, 1982, Vol 3 preprints: foreign country reviews of production, trade, and policies, by commodity, annual rpt series, 5604–17
Minerals Yearbook, 1983, Vol 1 preprints: commodity review of production, reserves, supply, use, and trade, annual rpt, 5604–15.6S
Minerals Yearbook, 1983, Vol 3 preprints: foreign country reviews of production, trade, and policies, by commodity, annual rpt series, 5604–23

Tin and tin industry

Occupational injuries and incidence rates at metal mines and related operations, detailed analysis, 1982, annual rpt, 6664–3

Production, prices, trade, use, employment, tariffs, and stockpiling, by mineral commodity, with foreign comparisons, 1979-83, annual rpt, 5604–18

Stockpiling of strategic and critical materials, Fed Govt activities and inventories by commodity, Oct 1983-Mar 1984, semiannual rpt, 9432–1

Stockpiling of strategic materials, inventories, costs, and goals, by commodity, as of June 1984, semiannual rpt, 9452–7

Strategic minerals supply/demand, trade, and foreign and US industry devs by firm and country, by commodity, bimonthly rpt, 5602–4

see also under By Commodity in the "Index by Categories"

see also under By Industry in the "Index by Categories"

Tiner, Ralph W., Jr.

"Wetlands of the U.S.: Current Status and Recent Trends", 5508–89

Tinney, Richard

"Offshore Petroleum Exploration: Capabilities and Constraints", 21448–30

"Oil Drilling Prohibitions at the Channel Islands and Pt. Reyes-Farallon Islands National Marine Sanctuaries: Some Costs and Benefits", 21448–30.1

Tinsley, LaVerne C.

"Workers' Compensation: Significant Enactments in 1983", 6722–1.415

Tips and tipping

Expenditures for tips and meals at eating places, and visits to eating places, 1982, article, 8302–2.406

Tires and tire industry

- Auto and van operating and owning costs by component and vehicle size, for 12 years of operation, 1984 model year, annual rpt, 7304–2, 7304–2.3, 7554–21
- Auto, small airplane, and motorcycle operating costs by component and vehicle size or make, and Fed Govt mileage reimbursement rates, 1983, annual rpt, 9454–13
- Bicycle tires and tubes from Taiwan at less than fair value, imports injury to US industry, investigation with background financial and operating data, 1984 rpt, 9886–14.106
- Business statistics, detailed data for major industries and economic indicators, *Survey of Current Business,* monthly rpt, 2702–1.17
- China economic conditions, agricultural and industrial production, trade, and domestic and foreign investment, 1980-85, 2048–106
- Communist, OECD, and selected other countries consumer and producer goods production, 1960s-83, annual rpt, 244–5.8
- County Business Patterns: establishments, employees, and payrolls, by SIC 4-digit industry and county, 1981, annual State rpt series, 2326–8
- County Business Patterns: establishments, employees, and payrolls, by SIC 4-digit industry and county, 1982, annual State rpt series, 2326–6

Cuba economic conditions, agricultural and industrial production and distribution, trade, and intl economic relations, 1970-82 and trends from 1957, 248–40

Employment, earnings, and hours, by selected SIC 1- to 4-digit industry, State, and for 278 major labor areas, 1939-83, annual rpt, 6744–5

Employment, earnings, and hours, by SIC 4-digit nonfarm industry, monthly 1974-Feb 1984, annual update, 6744–4

Exports and imports of US, detailed SIC-based commodities by world area, 1983, annual rpts, 2424–6

Exports and imports of US, totals and as percent of domestic production, by SIC 2- to 5-digit commodity, 1981, annual rpt, 2424–3

Exports of US, detailed commodities by country of destination, monthly rpt, 2422–3

Exports of US, detailed Schedule B commodities by country of destination, 1983, annual rpt, 2424–9

Exports of US, detailed Schedule E commodities by mode of transport and world area and country of destination, 1983, annual rpts, 2424–5

Farm production expenditures, detailed items by farm sales size and region, 1983, annual rpt, 1614–3

Great Lakes trade, by SITC 3-digit commodity, port, vessel type, world area, and country, 1982, annual rpt, 7744–3

Imports of radial passenger car tires from South Korea at less than fair value, injury to US industry, investigation with background financial and operating data, 1984 rpt, 9886–14.117

Imports of US, detailed Schedule A commodities by country and world area of origin, and mode of transport, 1983, annual rpts, 2424–2

Imports of US, detailed Schedule A commodities by country, monthly rpt, 2422–2

Imports of US, detailed TSUSA commodities by country of origin, 1983, annual rpt, 2424–4

Input-output structure of US economy, detailed interindustry transactions for 537 industries, and components of final demand, 1977 benchmark data, 2708–17

Manufacturing census, 1982: financial and operating data, by SIC 2- to 4-digit industry, State, SMSA, and county, preliminary census div rpt series, 2491–3

Manufacturing census, 1982: financial and operating data, for SIC 4-digit industries by product, preliminary rpt, 2491–1.74, 2491–1.206

Mineral industries census, 1982: financial and operating data, including materials consumed, by SIC 4-digit industry and State, preliminary rpt series, 2511–1

Minority group and women employment, by occupational group and SIC 2- to 3-digit industry, 1981, annual rpt, 9244–1.1

Occupational injury and illness rates, by SIC 2- to 4-digit industry, 1982, annual rpt, 6844–1

Producer prices and indexes, by stage of processing and detailed commodity, monthly rpt, 6762–6

Index by Subjects and Names

Producer prices and indexes, by stage of processing and detailed commodity, monthly 1983, annual supplement, 6764–2

Productivity, hours, and employment indexes for selected SIC 3- and 4-digit industries, 1954-82, annual rpt, 6824–1.3

Recalls of motor vehicles and equipment with safety-related defects, by make, quarterly listing, 7762–2

Retail trade census, 1982: employment, establishments, sales, and payroll, for tire, battery, and auto accessory dealers by State, preliminary rpt, 2395–1.11

Tax (excise) collections of IRS, by source, quarterly press release, 8302–1

Tax collections, refunds, and taxes due IRS, by State and region, and IRS court activity and operating expenses, FY83, annual rpt, 8304–3.3

Taxes for hwy use and Trust Fund revenues by tax type, and trucking industry economic effects of tax and size and weight rules, FY82-84 and projected to 1990, GAO rpt, 26117–31

Taxes for hwy use by tax type, and truck size and weight limits, economic effects on trucking industry, 1982-83 and projected 1984-87, hearings, 25328–24

Tire cord fabrics production, quarterly Current Industrial Rpt, 2506–5.11

Truck transport of fruit and vegetables, costs per vehicle-mile by component for fleets and owner-operator trucks, monthly rpt, 1272–1

see also under By Commodity in the "Index by Categories"

Titanium

see Metals and metal industries

Titusville, Fla.

Census of Housing, 1980: occupancy and unit characteristics, by race, Hispanic origin, and city, SMSA rpt, 2473–1.238

Census of Population and Housing, 1980: detailed population and housing characteristics, by county, city, and census tract, SMSA rpt, 2551–2.238

see also under By SMSA or MSA in the "Index by Categories"

Tkacz, Borys M.

"Forest Insect and Disease Conditions, Intermountain Region, 1983", 1206–11.3

Tobacco industry and products

- Acreage planted and harvested, by crop and State, 1982-83 and planned as of June 1984, annual rpt, 1621–23
- Acreage planting intended for 19 crops, by State, as of Feb 1984, annual rpt, 1621–22
- Acreage, yield, and production of field crops, by State, 1978-82 and preliminary 1983, 1641–7
- Agricultural cooperatives, membership, activities, and finances, by commodity and selected State, 1900-80 with trends from 1863, 1128–30
- Agricultural Stabilization and Conservation Service flue-cured, burley, and other tobacco programs, 1960-84, annual fact sheet, 1806–4.14, 1806–4.15, 1806–4.16
- *Agricultural Statistics, 1983,* annual rpt, 1004–1
- Agriculture census, 1982: farms, farmland, production and costs, and operator characteristics, preliminary State and county rpt series, 2330–1

Index by Subjects and Names

Tobacco industry and products

Agriculture census, 1982: farms, farmland, production, finances, and operator characteristics, by county, final State rpt series, 2331–1

Business statistics, detailed data for major industries and economic indicators, *Survey of Current Business,* monthly rpt, 2702–1.11

CCC tobacco support program itemized costs, adequacy of assessed producer payments, and crop loans and accrued interest, for flue-cured and burley tobacco, various periods 1981-84, GAO rpt, 26113–117

Census of Population, 1980: detailed socioeconomic and demographic characteristics, by age, sex, race, Hispanic origin, occupation, and industry, State rpt series, 2531–4

China economic conditions, agricultural and industrial production, trade, and domestic and foreign investment, 1980-85, 2048–106

China exports and imports by SITC 1- to 5-digit commodity, 1970s-82, annual rpt, 244–12

Cigarette and cigar production, stocks, and Fed Govt tax and enforcement activities, by State, FY81-82, last issue of annual rpt, 8484–1

Cigarette and cigar production, stocks, imports, and taxable and tax-free removals, monthly rpt, 8486–1.4

Cigarette sales, market shares, advertising expenditures and methods, and tar and nicotine content, by cigarette type, selected years 1963-81, annual rpt, 9404–4

Cigarette tar, nicotine, and carbon monoxide content in 207 varieties, 1982, periodic rpt, 9402–2

Collective bargaining agreements expiring during year, covered workers by SIC 2-digit industry, firm, and union, with summary of key provisions, 1984, annual rpt, 6784–9

County Business Patterns: establishments, employees, and payrolls, by SIC 4-digit industry and county, 1981, annual State rpt series, 2326–8

County Business Patterns: establishments, employees, and payrolls, by SIC 4-digit industry and county, 1982, annual State rpt series, 2326–6

CPI by detailed component, for US city average, 28 SMSAs, and 4 regions by population size, monthly rpt, 6762–2

Cuba economic conditions, agricultural and industrial production and distribution, trade, and intl economic relations, 1970-82 and trends from 1957, 248–40

Earnings by major industry group, and personal income per capita and by source, by region and State, 1929-82, 2708–40

Eastern Europe agricultural production and trade by commodity, food consumption, and farm inputs, for 6 countries, 1960-80 with projections to 1991, 1528–178

Employment, earnings, and hours, by selected SIC 1- to 4-digit industry, State, and for 278 major labor areas, 1939-83, annual rpt, 6744–5

Employment, earnings, and hours, by SIC 4-digit nonfarm industry, monthly 1974-Feb 1984, annual update, 6744–4

Exports and imports of US, and trade balance, by major commodity group, selected country, and world area, with seasonal adjustments, monthly rpt, 2422–6

Exports and imports of US, by agricultural commodity and country, bimonthly rpt with articles, 1522–1

Exports and imports of US, by commodity group, world area, selected country, US coastal area and port, and mode of transport, with seasonal adjustments, monthly rpt, 2422–9

Exports and imports of US, by detailed agricultural commodity and country, FY83 and CY83, semiannual rpts, 1522–4

Exports and imports of US, by detailed agricultural commodity for 8 major commodity groups, monthly rpt, 1922–8

Exports and imports of US, detailed SIC-based commodities by world area, 1983, annual rpts, 2424–6

Exports and imports of US, totals and as percent of domestic production, by SIC 2- to 5-digit commodity, 1981, annual rpt, 2424–3

Exports and personal expenditures of US and world for selected agricultural commodities, by country, and export share of US farm income, various periods 1926-82, 1528–172

Exports, imports, tariffs, and industry operating data for tobacco and products, foreign and US, 1979-83, TSUSA commodity rpt, 9885–1.65

Exports of cheese and tobacco by country of origin, various periods 1974-82, strategic material stockpile mgmt hearings, 25208–27

Exports of manufactured and agricultural commodities, manufacturing production, and export-related employment, 1960s-82, State rpt series, 2046–3

Exports of US, detailed commodities by country of destination, monthly rpt, 2422–3

Exports of US, detailed Schedule B commodities by country of destination, 1983, annual rpt, 2424–9

Exports of US, detailed Schedule E commodities by mode of transport and world area and country of destination, 1983, annual rpts, 2424–5

Exports under PL 480 concessional sales program, by commodity and country, 1955-83, semiannual rpt, 1922–6

Exports under PL 480 concessional sales program, by commodity and country, 1978-83, semiannual rpt, 1922–10

Farm finances, assets, liabilities, income, receipts by commodity and State, and expenses, 1980-83 and trends from 1910, annual rpt, 1544–16

Farm production inputs, outputs, and productivity, by region, 1939-82, annual rpt, 1544–17

Financial statements for manufacturing, mining, and trade corporations, by selected SIC 2- to 3-digit industry, quarterly rpt, 2502–1

Foreign agricultural production, prices, and trade, by country, 1983 and outlook for 1984/85, annual world region rpt series, 1524–4

Foreign and US agricultural production, trade, and climatic devs, weekly press release, 1922–4

Foreign and US tobacco production, prices, trade, and acreage, FAS monthly rpt with articles, 1925–16

Great Lakes trade, by SITC 3-digit commodity, port, vessel type, world area, and country, 1982, annual rpt, 7744–3

Imports of US, detailed Schedule A commodities by country and world area of origin, and mode of transport, 1983, annual rpts, 2424–2

Imports of US, detailed Schedule A commodities by country, monthly rpt, 2422–2

Imports of US, detailed TSUSA commodities by country of origin, 1983, annual rpt, 2424–4

Income tax returns of corporations, detailed income and tax items by industry, 1981, annual rpt, 8304–4

Income tax returns of corporations with foreign tax credit, income and deductions by type, asset size, and selected industry group, 1980, article, 8302–2.415

Income tax returns of sole proprietorships, detailed data by industry div and selected industry group, 1981, annual rpt, 8304–7

Income tax returns of sole proprietorships, receipts, deductions by type, payroll, and net income, by major industry, 1982, annual article, 8302–2.413

Input-output structure of US economy, detailed interindustry transactions for 85 industries, and components of final demand, 1977, article, 2702–1.421

Input-output structure of US economy, detailed interindustry transactions for 537 industries, and components of final demand, 1977 benchmark data, 2708–17

Law enforcement activities of Alcohol, Tobacco, and Firearms Bur in 20 cities and nationwide, funding, and jobs to be transferred to Customs and Secret Service, 1979-82, hearings, 21528–55

Legislation on smoking and tobacco marketing introduced and enacted in State legislatures, by State, 1982, annual rpt, 4204–13

Manufacturing census, 1982: financial and operating data, for SIC 4-digit industries by product, preliminary rpt series, 2491–1

Marketing cash receipts of farms, by detailed commodity and State, 1979-82, annual rpt, 1544–18

Minority group and women employment, by occupational group and SIC 2- to 3-digit industry, 1981, annual rpt, 9244–1.1

Occupational injury and illness rates, by SIC 2- to 4-digit industry, 1982, annual rpt, 6844–1

OECD trade, total and for 4 major countries, and US trade by country, by commodity, 1972-82, annual world region rpt series, 244–13

Pollution abatement capital and operating costs, by SIC 2- to 4-digit industry, State, and SMSA, 1982, annual Current Industrial Rpt, 2506–3.6

Prices, marketing, grades, and types for 3 classes of tobacco, 1983 crop and 1983/84 season, annual rpt series, 1319–5

Tobacco industry and products

Prices received by farmers and production value for detailed crops by State, 1981-83, annual rpt, 1621–2

Prices received by farmers for major products, and paid for farm inputs and living items, by commodity and State, monthly rpt, 1629–1

Prices received by farmers for major products, and paid for farm inputs, by commodity and State, 1983, annual rpt, 1629–5

Producer prices and indexes, by stage of processing and detailed commodity, monthly rpt, 6762–6

Producer prices and indexes, by stage of processing and detailed commodity, monthly 1983, annual supplement, 6764–2

Production and farm finances, expenses by type, and domestic economic impact, selected years 1972-82 and preliminary 1983-84, annual rpt, 1544–19

Production, farms, acreage, and related data, by selected crop and State, monthly rpt, 1621–1

Production, price, stocks, and taxes by State, and trade and foreign production by country, 1983, annual rpt, 1319–1

Production, prices, trade, and marketing, by commodity, current situation and forecast, monthly rpt, 1502–4

Production, trade, consumption, marketing, taxes, and price supports, quarterly situation rpt with articles, 1561–10

Productivity, hours, and employment indexes for selected SIC 3- and 4-digit industries, 1954-82, annual rpt, 6824–1.3

Research on smoking and health, article abstracts and indexes, 1983, annual rpt, 4044–8

Research publications on smoking and health, bimonthly listing, 4042–1

Scientists, engineers, and technicians employed in private industry, by occupation and industry group, 1980-81, biennial rpt, 9627–23

Stocks of leaf tobacco, and products manufactured and sold, quarterly rpt, 1319–3

Tax (excise) collections of IRS, by source, quarterly press release, 8302–1

Tax (excise) revenue of local govts, by excise type and State, average annual growth FY72-82, article, 10042–1.403

Tax collections of State govts, by detailed type of tax and tax rates, by State, FY83, annual rpt, 2466–2.3

Tax collections, refunds, and taxes due IRS, by State and region, and IRS court activity and operating expenses, FY83, annual rpt, 8304–3.3

Tax revenues, by level of govt, type of tax, State, and selected large counties, quarterly rpt, 2462–3

Taxation and revenue systems, by type of tax and system, level of govt, and State, selected years 1958-83, annual rpt, 10044–1.3

Waterborne commerce of US (domestic and foreign), freight by commodity, traffic, and passengers, by port and waterway, 1982, annual rpt, 3754–3

see also Smoking

see also under By Commodity in the "Index by Categories"

see also under By Industry in the "Index by Categories"

Toborg, Mary A.

"Drug Use and Pretrial Crime in the District of Columbia", 6066–20.7

Toby, Jackson

"Violence in School", 6066–20.2

Togo

Agricultural and food production indexes, and production of selected commodities, by world region and country, 1974-83, annual rpt, 1524–5

Agricultural situation in sub-Saharan Africa, by country, 1982-83 and outlook for 1984, annual rpt, 1524–4.10

AID activities and funding by project and function, FY85, and developing countries summary socioeconomic data, 1970s-83, by country, annual rpt, 9914–3

AID economic assistance to developing countries, obligations and disbursements by country, quarterly rpt, 9912–4

Background Notes, summary social, political, and economic data, 1984 rpt, 7006–2.61

Economic conditions and foreign marketing prospects in 46 Sub-Saharan countries, 1983 world region rpt, 2046–5.1

Economic, social, and political summary data, by country, 1984, annual factbook, 244–11

Exports of US, detailed Schedule B commodities by country of destination, 1983, annual rpt, 2424–9

Exports of US, detailed Schedule E commodities by mode of transport and world area and country of destination, 1983, annual rpts, 2424–5

Imports of US, detailed Schedule A commodities by country and world area of origin, and mode of transport, 1983, annual rpts, 2424–2

Imports of US, detailed TSUSA commodities by country of origin, 1983, annual rpt, 2424–4

Loans and grants for economic and military assistance from US and intl agencies, by program and country, FY46-83, annual rpt, 9914–5

Military aid of US, arms sales, and training programs costs and budget requests by program, world region, and country, FY83-85, annual rpt, 7144–13

Military spending, arms trade, and armed forces size, with total govt spending and population, by country, 1972-82, annual rpt, 9824–1

Minerals Yearbook, 1982, Vol 3: foreign country reviews of production, trade, and policies, by commodity, annual rpt, 5604–35

Minerals Yearbook, 1982, Vol 3 preprints: foreign country review of production, trade, and policies, by commodity, annual rpt, 5604–17.84

Population size and growth rates, and latest available benchmark demographic data, by country, 1950-83, biennial rpt, 2324–4

see also under By Foreign Country in the "Index by Categories"

Toiletries

see Cosmetics

Index by Subjects and Names

Tokar, M.

"Fuel Performance Annual Report for 1982", 9634–8

Toledo, Ohio

- Census of Housing, 1980: occupancy and unit characteristics, by race, Hispanic origin, and city, SMSA rpt, 2473–1.352
- Census of Population and Housing, 1980: detailed population and housing characteristics, by county, city, and census tract, SMSA rpt, 2551–2.352
- Housing vacancy rates for single and multifamily units and mobile homes, by city and ZIP code, 1984, annual metro area rpt, 9304–27.11
- Wages by occupation, and benefits for office and plant workers, 1984 SMSA survey rpt, 6785–11.6

see also under By City and By SMSA or MSA in the "Index by Categories"

Tolls

- Auto and van operating and owning costs by component and vehicle size, for 12 years of operation, 1984 model year, annual rpt, 7304–2, 7304–2.3, 7554–21
- Hwy and urban transit systems financing methods of govts and private sector, with case studies for selected metro areas, series, 7556–7
- Hwy receipts by source, and expenditures by function, by level of govt and State, 1983, annual rpt, 7554–1.3, 7554–1.4
- Public services subsidized by Fed Govt, user fees to recover costs of 7 programs, by type of fee, user, and service, FY84-88, 26306–6.68
- St Lawrence Seaway Dev Corp finances and activities, and seaway toll charges and cargo tonnage by type of cargo, 1983, annual rpt, 7744–1
- St Lawrence Seaway ships, cargo and passenger volumes, and toll revenues, 1981-82 and trends from 1959, annual rpt, 7744–2
- St Lawrence Seaway US and total tolls, and costs to users under proposed natl port user fee, 1983, hearings, 21568–34
- State govt revenues by source, expenditures by function, debt, and holdings by type, FY83, annual rpt, 2466–2.5
- Transportation revenues by source and expenditures, by level of govt and mode of transport, and Fed Govt aid by type, FY77-82, 7308–185

Tomatoes

see Vegetables and vegetable products

Tonga

- Economic, social, and political summary data, by country, 1984, annual factbook, 244–11
- Imports of US, detailed Schedule A commodities by country and world area of origin, and mode of transport, 1983, annual rpts, 2424–2
- Imports of US, detailed TSUSA commodities by country of origin, 1983, annual rpt, 2424–4
- Military aid of US, arms sales, and training programs costs and budget requests by program, world region, and country, FY83-85, annual rpt, 7144–13
- *Minerals Yearbook, 1982,* Vol 3: foreign country reviews of production, trade, and policies, by commodity, annual rpt, 5604–35

Index by Subjects and Names

Minerals Yearbook, 1982, Vol 3 preprints: foreign country review of production, trade, and policies, by commodity, annual rpt, 5604–17.90

Minerals Yearbook, 1983, Vol 3 preprints: foreign country review of production, trade, and policies, by commodity, annual rpt, 5604–23.90

Population size and growth rates, and latest available benchmark demographic data, by country, 1950-83, biennial rpt, 2324–4

see also under By Foreign Country in the "Index by Categories"

Tonn, Bruce

"Loan Impacts in Home Energy Audit Programs: A Minnesota Example", 3308–72

Tool and die industry

see Machines and machinery industry

Tools

see Hand tools

see Machines and machinery industry

Topeka, Kans.

- Census of Housing, 1980: occupancy and unit characteristics, by race, Hispanic origin, and city, SMSA rpt, 2473–1.353
- Census of Population and Housing, 1980: detailed population and housing characteristics, by county, city, and census tract, SMSA rpt, 2551–2.353
- Housing vacancy rates for single and multifamily units and mobile homes, by county, city, and ZIP code, 1984, annual metro area rpt, 9304–22.10
- Wages of office and plant workers, by occupation, 1984 labor market area survey rpt, 6785–3.9

see also under By City and By SMSA or MSA in the "Index by Categories"

Tornadoes

see Storms

Toronto, Canada

Fruit and vegetable shipments, and arrivals in 23 US and 5 Canada cities, by mode of transport and State or country of origin, 1983, annual rpt, 1311–4.1

Torpedoes

- DOD budget, costs of individual weapons or weapons systems, FY83-85, annual rpt, 3504–2
- DOD budget justification, programs, and policies, FY85, annual rpt, 3544–2
- Fed Govt programs and mgmt cost control proposals, 3-year savings by function and agency, and financial and operating data, 1960s-81, 16908–1.19

Torrance, Calif.

Uranium enrichment facilities operations, finances, uranium stocks, and energy use and capital investment by facility, FY83, annual rpt, 3354–7

see also under By City in the "Index by Categories"

Torts

- Asbestos-related occupational disease compensation paid and defendant and plaintiff litigation costs, with comparisons to other tort suits, selected years 1968-82, hearings, 21348–85
- Court caseloads for Federal district, appeals, and bankruptcy courts, by type of suit and offense, circuit, and district, quarterly rpt, 18202–1
- US Attorneys civil case processing and amounts involved, by cause of action, FY83, annual rpt, 6004–2.5

Tourist travel

see Travel

Towels

see Household furnishings

Town planning

see City and town planning

see New towns

Towns

see Central cities

see Cities

see Rural areas

see Suburbs

see Urban areas

Townsend, Terry

"Domestic Cotton Outlook", 1004–16.1

"Outlook for Participation in the 1985 Upland Cotton Program", 1561–1.404

"U.S. Raw Cotton Content of Textile Imports by Country of Origin, 1983", 1561–1.401

Toxic substances

see Hazardous substances

see Pesticides

see Poisoning and drug reaction

Toys and toy industry

- Census of Population, 1980: detailed socioeconomic and demographic characteristics, by age, sex, race, Hispanic origin, occupation, and industry, State rpt series, 2531–4
- County Business Patterns: establishments, employees, and payrolls, by SIC 4-digit industry and county, 1981, annual State rpt series, 2326–8
- County Business Patterns: establishments, employees, and payrolls, by SIC 4-digit industry and county, 1982, annual State rpt series, 2326–6
- Employment, earnings, and hours, by selected SIC 1- to 4-digit industry, State, and for 278 major labor areas, 1939-83, annual rpt, 6744–5
- Employment, earnings, and hours, by SIC 4-digit nonfarm industry, monthly 1974-Feb 1984, annual update, 6744–4
- Exports and imports of US, detailed SIC-based commodities by world area, 1983, annual rpts, 2424–6
- Exports and imports of US, totals and as percent of domestic production, by SIC 2- to 5-digit commodity, 1981, annual rpt, 2424–3
- Exports of US, detailed commodities by country of destination, monthly rpt, 2422–3
- Exports of US, detailed Schedule B commodities by country of destination, 1983, annual rpt, 2424–9
- Exports of US, detailed Schedule E commodities by mode of transport and world area and country of destination, 1983, annual rpts, 2424–5
- Finances and operations, by SIC 2- to 4-digit industry, 1970s-83 and projected to 1988, annual rpt, 2014–4
- Great Lakes trade, by SITC 3-digit commodity, port, vessel type, world area, and country, 1982, annual rpt, 7744–3
- Imports of US, detailed Schedule A commodities by country and world area of origin, and mode of transport, 1983, annual rpts, 2424–2
- Imports of US, detailed Schedule A commodities by country, monthly rpt, 2422–2

Imports of US, detailed TSUSA commodities by country of origin, 1983, annual rpt, 2424–4

- Income tax returns of sole proprietorships, detailed data by industry div and selected industry group, 1981, annual rpt, 8304–7
- Income tax returns of sole proprietorships, receipts, deductions by type, payroll, and net income, by major industry, 1982, annual article, 8302–2.413
- Injuries and deaths from use of selected consumer products and related activity, by victim age and sex, 1982, annual rpt, 9164–7
- Injuries and deaths from use of selected consumer products, by victim age and medical treatment status, 1982, annual rpt, 9164–6
- Injuries, deaths, and medical costs from consumer products use, and Consumer Product Safety Commission activities and recalls, by product type and brand, FY83, annual rpt, 9164–2
- Input-output structure of US economy, detailed interindustry transactions for 537 industries, and components of final demand, 1977 benchmark data, 2708–17
- Manufacturing census, 1982: financial and operating data, by SIC 2- to 4-digit industry, State, SMSA, and county, preliminary census div rpt series, 2491–3
- Manufacturing census, 1982: financial and operating data, for SIC 4-digit industries by product, preliminary rpt, 2491–1.428, 2491–1.429
- Minority group and women employment, by occupational group and SIC 2- to 3-digit industry, 1981, annual rpt, 9244–1.1
- Occupational injury and illness rates, by SIC 2- to 4-digit industry, 1982, annual rpt, 6844–1
- OECD trade, total and for 4 major countries, and US trade by country, by commodity, 1972-82, annual world region rpt series, 244–13
- Pollution abatement capital and operating costs, by SIC 2- to 4-digit industry, State, and SMSA, 1982, annual Current Industrial Rpt, 2506–3.6
- Producer prices and indexes, by stage of processing and detailed commodity, monthly rpt, 6762–6
- Producer prices and indexes, by stage of processing and detailed commodity, monthly 1983, annual supplement, 6764–2
- Video games and game software and components, effects of foreign imports on US industry, investigation with background financial and operating data, 1984 rpt, 9886–4.71
- Wholesale trade census, 1982: employment, establishments, sales by commodity, and payroll, by SIC 4-digit kind of business and State, preliminary rpt, 2403–1.6
- Wholesale trade sales, inventories, purchases, and gross margins, by SIC 2- to 3-digit kind of business and type of ownership, 1983, annual rpt, 2413–13

see also Sporting goods

see also under By Commodity in the "Index by Categories"

see also under By Industry in the "Index by Categories"

Trace metals

Trace metals

Acid rain and air pollution environmental effects, and methods for neutralizing acidified water bodies, summary research rpt series, 5506–5

Air pollutant and radiation indoor levels by emissions source, and household exposure and health effects by pollutant type, various periods 1966-83, hearings, 21708–102

Air pollutant metal levels, by monitoring site, State, and urban-rural location, 1977-79, last issue of annual rpt, 9194–10

Environmental quality, pollutant discharge by type, and EPA protection activities, 1970s-83, biennial summary rpt, 9184–16

Environmental quality, pollutant discharge by type and source, and EPA protection activities and funding, 1970s-83, biennial regional rpt series, 9184–15

Great Lakes basin pollutant discharges by source, and control program activities, 1983 annual rpt, 14644–1

Mount St Helens, Wash, volcanic eruptions, effects on water quality of selected Washington rivers, various dates Mar-June 1980, 5666–14.9

New York Bight pollutant loadings from ocean dumping of municipal wastes by type and source, and concentrations in fish and sediments, 1970s-82, hearings, 21568–36

Occupational health risks from hazardous substances and radiation, by industry, occupation, age, and sex, with bibl and glossary, 1920s-82, 9638–50

Water from urban runoff, quality, pollutant concentrations, and control cost-effectiveness, with monitoring sites rainfall and other characteristics, by city and region, 1978-83, 9208–122

Water pollution from nonpoint sources, source land uses and acreage, and control program funding, by State or region, various periods 1974-FY84, 9208–123

Water supply and quality, floods, drought, mudslides, and other hydrologic events, by State, 1983, annual rpt, 5664–12

Water supply and quality in streams and lakes, and groundwater levels in wells, by drainage basin, 1980, annual State rpt series, 5666–12

Water supply and quality in streams and lakes, and groundwater levels in wells, by drainage basin, 1981, annual State rpt series, 5666–16

Water supply and quality in streams and lakes, and groundwater levels in wells, by drainage basin, 1982, annual State rpt series, 5666–20

Water supply and quality in streams and lakes, and groundwater levels in wells, by drainage basin, 1983, annual State rpt series, 5666–10

see also Lead poisoning and pollution

see also Mercury pollution

Tractors

see Agricultural machinery and equipment

Trade

see Agricultural exports and imports

see Arms sales

see Common markets and free trade areas

see Foreign assistance

see Foreign trade

see Foreign trade promotion

see International transactions

see Interstate commerce

see Marketing

see Military assistance

see Retail trade

see Tariffs and foreign trade controls

see Trade adjustment assistance

see Trade agreements

see Wholesale trade

Trade adjustment assistance

Assistance centers to help firms apply for ITA trade adjustment aid, operations, annual rpt, suspended, 2044–24

Budget of US, effects of Reagan Admin policy changes, by detailed program, FY85, annual rpt, 104–21

EC trade promotion policies and financing by industry, and effect on competing US industries, 1970s-82, 9886–4.73

Eligibility and certification of workers and companies, by industry, and labor union, 1975-83, annual rpt, 444–1.2

Eligibility for assistance, reemployment opportunities, and worker characteristics, investigations of industries injured by import competition, series, 6406–9

Eligibility of workers, petitions, investigations, and determinations, by major industry group, union, and State, monthly rpt, 6402–13

Fed Govt programs under Ways and Means Committee jurisdiction, program operations and financing data for assessing budgetary requirements, by State, FY70s-83, 21788–117

Research contracts of Bur of Intl Labor Affairs, by project and contractor, FY73-84, annual listing, 6364–1

USITC investigations of countervailing duties on foreign subsidized products, with background financial and operating data, series, 9886–18

USITC investigations of foreign subsidized imports, with background financial and operating data for selected industries and products, series, 9886–15

USITC investigations of import sales in US at less than fair value, with background financial and operating data for selected industries and products, series, 9886–14

USITC investigations of imports from Communist countries injury to US industries, with background financial and operating data for selected industries and products, series, 9886–12

USITC investigations of injury to US industries from increased import sales, with background financial and operating data, series, 9886–5

see also Dumping

Trade agreements

Agricultural product rates of duty under Multilateral Trade Negotiations, by commodity, projected for 1980s with pre-MTN comparisons, TSUSA commodity rpt series, 9885–1

Bilateral and multilateral agreements of US in force, by country, Jan 1984, annual listing, 7004–1

Chemicals and related products rates of duty under Multilateral Trade Negotiations, by commodity, projected for 1980s with pre-MTN comparisons, TSUSA commodity rpt series, 9885–4

Index by Subjects and Names

Exports, imports, and economic indicators by country and country group, and US trade policy actions, 1960s-83, annual rpt, 444–1

Exports, imports, and tariffs, USITC investigations, publications, and other activities, FY83, annual rpt, 9884–1

Generalized System of Preferences status of 29 commodities, with US production, consumption, tariffs, and trade by country, selected years 1978-87, 9888–17

Intl trade agreement devs, US trade relations, and USITC investigations, 1983, annual rpt, 9884–5

Manufactured products (miscellaneous) rates of duty under Multilateral Trade Negotiations, by commodity, TSUSA commodity rpt series, 9885–7

Metals and metal products rates of duty under Multilateral Trade Negotiations, by commodity, TSUSA commodity rpt series, 9885–6

Minerals (nonmetallic) and mineral products trade, tariffs, and industry operating data, TSUSA commodity rpt series, 9885–5

Overseas Business Reports: economic conditions, investment and export opportunities, and trade practices, annual country market research rpt series, 2046–6

Services trade regulation proposals of US, with agreements, goods and services trade, intl investment, and GDP, by country, various periods 1970-82, 448–1

Strategic materials stockpiles, and imports in exchange for CCC commodity exports by world region and country, various periods 1950-83, hearings, 21208–20

Textile fiber and products rates of duty under Multilateral Trade Negotiations, by commodity, projected for 1980s with pre-MTN comparisons, TSUSA commodity rpt series, 9885–3

Textile imports and import limits under Multifiber Arrangement by product and country, with US exports and use, 1970-83, semiannual rpt, 9882–11

Wood, paper, and printed matter rates of duty under Multilateral Trade Negotiations, by commodity, projected for 1980s with pre-MTN comparisons, TSUSA commodity rpt series, 9885–2

see also Common markets and free trade areas

see also Tariffs and foreign trade controls

Trade balances

see Foreign trade

see International transactions

Trade fairs

see Exhibitions and trade fairs

Trade investigations

see Government investigations

Trade promotion

see Foreign trade promotion

Trade regulation

see Antitrust law

see Consumer protection

see Copyright

see Fuel allocation

see Interstate commerce

see Licenses and permits

see Patents

see Price regulation

see Tariffs and foreign trade controls

Index by Subjects and Names

see Trade adjustment assistance
see Trademarks

Trade unions
see Labor unions

Trademarks

Applications, actions taken, litigation, and Patent and Trademark Office services and employment, selected years FY64-83, annual rpt, 2244–1

Counterfeiting of brand-name products by foreign manufacturers, effects on 6 US industries, investigation with financial and operating data, 1984 rpt, 9886–4.67

Fed Govt programs and mgmt cost control proposals, 3-year savings by function and agency, and financial and operating data, 1960s-81, 16908–1.3

Multinatl corporation income reallocation through regulation of intercorporate transactions, by tax item, treaty status, asset size, industry, and tax haven country, 1982, 8008–110

Statistical Abstract of US, social, political, and economic data, 1950s-83 and trends, annual rpt, 2324–1.3

Traffic accidents and safety

Accident investigations and recommendations by Natl Transportation Safety Board, 1983, annual rpt, 9614–1

Accidents (fatal), circumstances, and characteristics of persons and vehicles involved, detailed data, 1982, annual rpt, 7764–10

Accidents (fatal), circumstances, and characteristics of persons and vehicles involved, 1983, annual rpt, 7764–14

Accidents and deaths by characteristics of persons and vehicles involved and State, and Natl Hwy Traffic Safety Admin activities, 1961-81, annual rpt, 7764–1.

Accidents, circumstances, injuries, deaths, and characteristics of persons and vehicles involved, 1982, annual rpt, 7764–13

Alcohol levels of drivers and pedestrians involved in fatal traffic accidents, by driver age and sex and time of accident, 1980, 7768–81

Auto and light truck safety, crash test results of selected new domestic and foreign models for model year to date, press release series, 7766–7

Auto safety and experimental vehicle designs, 1982, conf proceedings, annual rpt, 7764–3

Bridge replacement and rehabilitation program of Fed Govt, funding by bridge and bridge status by State, 1983, annual rpt, 7554–27

Budget of US, effects of Reagan Admin policy changes, by detailed program, FY85, annual rpt, 104–21

Coal dev plans on Fed Govt lease lands in 12 regions under Fed Coal Mgmt Program, environmental and socioeconomic impacts to 2000, final statement series, 5726–4

Costs (direct and indirect) of traffic accidents and casualties, by characteristics of persons and vehicles involved, with DOT safety program funding, 1979-80, 7768–80

Death rates by sex, race, and age for 40 causes, projected for 10-year period, 1982 rpt, 4208–21

Deaths and death rates, by cause and age, provisional 1982-83, US Vital Statistics annual rpt, 4144–7

Deaths and death rates, by detailed geographic area, cause, and demographic characteristics, 1979, US Vital Statistics annual rpt, 4144–3

Deaths and death rates, by selected cause and demographic characteristics, 1981, US Vital Statistics advance rpt, 4146–5.78

Deaths and death rates, by selected cause and demographic characteristics, 1982, US Vital Statistics advance rpt, 4146–5.81

Deaths and death rates from traffic accidents, by victim and demographic characteristics, 1979, US Vital Statistics annual rpt, 4144–2.1, 4144–2.5

Deaths and injuries in traffic accidents, and rates, by type of hwy and State, 1982, annual rpt, 7554–2

Deaths by principal or contributing cause, with type of injury reported in accidental, poisoning, and violent deaths, by age, sex, and race, 1978, 4146–5.76

Deaths from accidents by selected cause, 1981 with trends from 1960s and reduction goals for 1990, article, 4102–1.409

Deaths in traffic accidents by region, and death rates for miles traveled, monthly rpt, 7762–7

Deaths in traffic accidents, circumstances, and characteristics of persons and vehicles involved, series, 7766–13

Deaths in traffic accidents, total and alcohol-related, and drunk driver license revocations and other deterrence programs in selected States, 1980-82, 9618–10

Deaths in transportation accidents, by mode, 1982-83, annual summary rpt, 9614–6

DOE and contractor facility accidents, deaths, illnesses, radiation exposure, and property damage, by facility, 1982, annual rpt, 3004–24

DOT grant awards for transportation planning and safety programs, by region, State, and for 35 largest SMSAs, FY83, annual rpt, 7304–7

Fed Govt programs and mgmt cost control proposals, 3-year savings by function and agency, and financial and operating data, 1960s-81, 16908–1.11

Govt census, 1982: State govt payments to local govts, by program, source of funds, level of govt, and State, with trends from 1902, 2460–3

Hazardous material transport accidents, casualties, and property damage, by mode of transport, with DOT control activities, 1983, annual rpt, 7304–4

Health condition and health care resources, use, and expenditures, 1970s-82 with trends and projections 1900-2000, annual compilation, 4144–11

Hwy-railroad grade-crossing accidents, circumstances, severity, and railroad involved, quarterly rpt, 9612–3

Hwy-railroad grade-crossing accidents, deaths, and injuries, and Fed Railroad Admin safety programs, 1982, annual rpt, 7604–12

Hwy-railroad grade-crossing accidents, detailed data by State and railroad, 1982, annual rpt, 7604–2

Traffic accidents and safety

Hwy safety, accident, and traffic data from Natl Statistics and Analysis Center, series, 7766–10

Hwy safety improvement, federally funded programs implementation by State, FY83, annual rpt, 7554–26

Hwy safety program Fed Govt appropriations, by State and program, quarterly rpt, 7552–9

Hwy Statistics, detailed data on traffic, govt finances, fuel use, vehicles, driver licenses, and hwy characteristics, by State, 1983, annual rpt, 7554–1

Indian births, morbidity, and deaths and rates, and health services facilities and use, 1954-83, annual compilation, 4104–7

Injury rates, total and by place of accident, by age, region, metro-nonmetro location, and selected SMSA, 1980-81, 4147–10.146

Law enforcement officer assaults, murders, and other deaths by circumstances, level of govt, agency, victim and offender characteristics, and location, 1983, annual rpt, 6224–3

Micronesia Federated States, arrests by type, and traffic and other accidents and deaths, Jan-Aug 1983, annual rpt, 7004–6.2

Motor carrier safety inspections by Fed Hwy Admin, audits of driver qualification and vehicle operation records, and violations cited, 1982, annual rpt, 7554–38

Motor carrier safety inspections on interstate hwys, violations cited, and vehicles and drivers ordered out of service, 1982, annual rpt, 7554–35

Motor carrier safety inspections on interstate hwys, violations cited, and vehicles and drivers ordered out of service, May 1983, semiannual rpt, 7552–15

Natl park system visitor deaths, by park and type of accident, 1973-83, annual rpt, 5544–6

Occupational deaths, by industry div and cause, 1981-82, article, 6722–1.422

Older persons by demographic, socioeconomic, and health characteristics, selected years 1900-81 and projected to 2050, Current Population Rpt, 2546–2.125

Safety programs, and accidents, injuries, deaths, hazards, and property damage, by mode of transport, 1983, annual rpt, 7304–19

Safety projects research and evaluation, quarterly rpt articles, 7762–9

Speed averages and vehicles exceeding 55 mph, by State, quarterly rpt, 7552–14

Statistical Abstract of US, social, political, and economic data, 1950s-83 and trends, annual rpt, 2324–1.3

Traffic accidents and occupant and non-occupant deaths, 1972-82, annual rpt, 7304–2

Transportation summary data, traffic, accidents, and deaths, FY81, annual rpt, 7304–1

Truck accidents, injuries, deaths, and property damage, by circumstances, carrier type, and driver age and condition, 1983, annual rpt, 7554–9

Traffic accidents and safety

Virgin Islands socioeconomic and govtl data, FY81, annual rpt, 5304–4
see also Driving while intoxicated
see also Motor vehicle safety devices
see also Pedestrians
see also Traffic engineering
see also Traffic laws and courts

Traffic engineering

- Census of Population and Housing, 1980: data coverage, availability, and uses for urban and transportation planning, 1984 guide, 7558–101
- City govt revenue sharing program allocations and use by function, and response to program cuts, by city size and region, 1982 survey, hearings, 25408–86.2
- Construction industries census, 1982: financial and operating data, by SIC 4-digit industry and State, final rpt series, 2373–1
- Construction industries census, 1982: financial and operating data, by SIC 4-digit industry and State, preliminary rpt series, 2371–1
- Hwy and bridge repair projects funded by Fed Govt, and costs, for 7 States, FY81-82, GAO rpt, 26113–121
- Hwy safety improvement, federally funded programs implementation by State, FY83, annual rpt, 7554–26
- Hwy safety program Fed Govt appropriations, by State and program, quarterly rpt, 7552–9
- R&D projects funded by Fed Hwy Admin, FY83, annual summary rpt, 7554–14
- Traffic accidents, circumstances, injuries, deaths, and characteristics of persons and vehicles involved, 1982, annual rpt, 7764–13
- Transit services for commuting and other purposes, dev and effects, series, 7306–9
- Transit system operations, tax burden related to ridership, fares, and govt funding, for selected States and cities, 1950s-82, reprint, 7888–59
- Transit systems research publications, 2nd half FY83, semiannual listing, 7882–1
- Urban transit and hwy systems financing methods of govts and private sector, with case studies for selected metro areas, series, 7556–7

see also Parking facilities

Traffic laws and courts

- Accidents, circumstances, injuries, deaths, and characteristics of persons and vehicles involved, 1982, annual rpt, 7764–13
- Case filings in State trial courts by case type, and appellate court filings and dispositions by court type, by State, 1978-83, periodic rpt, 6062–2.409
- Costs (direct and indirect) of traffic accidents and casualties, by characteristics of persons and vehicles involved, 1979-80, 7768–80
- Criminal cases of Federal defendants, disposition, convictions, and sentences, by offense and district, as of June 1983, annual rpt, 18204–1
- Drivers license revocation and other drunk driving deterrence measures in selected States, and total and alcohol-related traffic deaths, 1980-82, 9618–10
- Hwy safety, accident, and traffic data from Natl Statistics and Analysis Center, series, 7766–10

Hwy Statistics, detailed data on traffic, govt finances, fuel use, vehicles, driver licenses, and hwy characteristics, by State, 1983, annual rpt, 7554–1

- Motor carrier safety inspections by Fed Hwy Admin, audits of driver qualification and vehicle operation records, and violations cited, 1982, annual rpt, 7554–38
- Motor carrier safety inspections on interstate hwys, violations cited, and vehicles and drivers ordered out of service, 1982, annual rpt, 7554–35
- Motor carrier safety inspections on interstate hwys, violations cited, and vehicles and drivers ordered out of service, May 1983, semiannual rpt, 7552–15
- Natl Hwy Traffic Safety Admin activities and funding, and traffic accident data, 1981, annual rpt, 7764–1.1
- Police dept costs and operations, patrol car use, investigations, arrests, and recruit training, by city population size, 1982, 6066–21.1
- Pretrial citation release use, cost savings for law enforcement agencies, and failures to appear in court, by offense and selected jurisdiction, 1970s-82, 6068–187
- Safety projects research and evaluation, quarterly rpt articles, 7762–9
- Speed averages and vehicles exceeding 55 mph, by State, quarterly rpt, 7552–14

see also Driving while intoxicated

Traffic violations

see Traffic accidents and safety
see Traffic laws and courts

Trailways, Inc.

Bus industry collective ratemaking and regulatory reform impacts on operations, finances, and services to older persons and rural areas by State, 1970s-83, 14828–2

Training

see Apprenticeship
see Employee development
see Manpower training programs
see Military training
see Vocational education and training

Tranquilizers

see Drug abuse and treatment
see Drugs

Trans-Alaska Pipeline System

Owner companies financial data, and retail gasoline price competition in 2 States, by company, 1980-83, hearing, 21728–51

Transfer payments

see terms listed under Income maintenance

Transient housing

- Army morale, welfare, and recreation programs, revenue and expenses worldwide by activity and major command, FY82-83, annual rpt, 3704–12
- County Business Patterns: establishments, employees, and payrolls, by SIC 4-digit industry and county, 1982, annual State rpt series, 2326–6
- Homeless population and characteristics, and reasons for homelessness, for selected cities, early 1980s, 028–20
- Homeless population and characteristics, and temporary shelter operations, use, and user characteristics, by region and selected city, 1983, 5188–108

Index by Subjects and Names

Homeless population and characteristics, and temporary shelter operations, use, and user characteristics, for selected cities, various periods 1979-84, hearing, 21248–85

see also Hotels and motels

Transit districts

see Special districts

Transportation and transportation equipment

- Agricultural production, marketing, trade, supply, food consumption, and food and nutrition programs, 1960s-83, annual chartbook, 1504–3
- Air pollutant emission factors, by detailed source, 3rd edition, 1983-84 supplements, 9198–13
- American Samoa minimum wage rates, employment, earnings, and benefits, by establishment and industry, Nov 1983, biennial rpt, 6504–6
- Bombing (explosive and incendiary) and arson incidents by target, State, and circumstances, and explosives theft and recovery, 1982-83, annual rpt, 8484–4
- Bombing (explosive and incendiary) incidents, damage, injuries, and deaths, by target, State, and circumstances, 1983, annual rpt, 6224–5
- Capital expenditures for new plants and equipment, by industry div, monthly rpt, quarterly data, 23842–1.1
- Census Bur data coverage and availability of transportation industry statistics, 1983 pamphlet, 2326–7.61
- Census of Population and Housing, 1980: data coverage, availability, and uses for urban and transportation planning, 1984 guide, 7558–101
- Census of Population, 1980: detailed socioeconomic and demographic characteristics, by age, sex, race, Hispanic origin, occupation, and industry, State rpt series, 2531–4
- Census of Population, 1980: detailed socioeconomic characteristics, by county, city, and inside-outside SMSAs and central cities, State rpt series, 2531–3
- Census of Population, 1980: labor force, by sex, detailed occupation, and region, with comparison to 1970 census, supplementary rpt, 2535–1.12
- China economic conditions, agricultural and industrial production, trade, and domestic and foreign investment, 1980-85, 2048–106
- China exports and imports by SITC 1- to 5-digit commodity, 1970s-82, annual rpt, 244–12
- Coal transport environmental impacts by type and mode of transport, methodology for assessing alternative systems, 1983 rpt, 3408–28
- Collective bargaining agreements expiring during year, covered workers by SIC 2-digit industry, firm, and union, with summary of key provisions, 1984, annual rpt, 6784–9
- Communist, OECD, and selected other countries freight and carrier inventories, by mode of transport, 1960s-83, annual rpt, 244–5.10
- Counterfeiting of brand-name products by foreign manufacturers, effects on 6 US industries, investigation with financial and operating data, 1984 rpt, 9886–4.67

Index by Subjects and Names

Transportation and transportation equipment

County Business Patterns: establishments, employees, and payrolls, by SIC 4-digit industry and county, 1981, annual State rpt series, 2326–8

County Business Patterns: establishments, employees, and payrolls, by SIC 4-digit industry and county, 1982, annual State rpt series, 2326–6

CPI by detailed component, for US city average, 28 SMSAs, and 4 regions by population size, monthly rpt, 6762–2

CPI components relative importance, for selected SMSAs, and US city average by region and population size, 1983, annual rpt, 6884–1

Developing countries disaster preparedness and summary sociodemographic, political, and economic data, country rpt series, 9916–2

Developing countries govt policy, and AID and other foreign assistance, effects on private sector dev and socioeconomic conditions, with case studies for 6 countries, 1960s-80, 9918–12

DOD procurement, prime contract awards by detailed procurement category, FY80-83, annual rpt, 3544–18

DOT admin and funding activities, and transportation traffic and accident data, FY81, annual rpt, 7304–1

Earnings by industry div, and personal income per capita and by source, by State, MSA, and county, 1977-82, annual regional rpts, 2704–2

Earnings by major industry group, and personal income per capita and by source, by region and State, 1929-82, 2708–40

Employment and earnings, detailed data, monthly rpt, 6742–2.5

Employment, earnings, and hours, by selected SIC 1- to 4-digit industry, State, and for 278 major labor areas, 1939-83, annual rpt, 6744–5

Employment, earnings, and hours, by SIC 4-digit nonfarm industry, monthly 1974-Feb 1984, annual update, 6744–4

Employment, unemployment, and labor force, by demographic and employment characteristics, State, and for 30 metro areas and 11 large cities, 1983, annual rpt, 6744–7

Employment, unemployment, hours, and women's employment, for all durables manufacturing and for 5 metals industries, 1979-82, article, 6722–1.410

Environmental quality and protection programs, costs, and Fed Govt enforcement, 1983, detailed annual rpt, 484–1

Exports and imports of US, and trade balance, by major commodity group, selected country, and world area, with seasonal adjustments, monthly rpt, 2422–2

Exports and imports of US, by commodity group, world area, selected country, US coastal area and port, and mode of transport, with seasonal adjustments, monthly rpt, 2422–9

Exports and imports of US, detailed SIC-based commodities by world area, 1983, annual rpts, 2424–6

Exports and imports of US, totals and as percent of domestic production, by SIC 2- to 5-digit commodity, 1981, annual rpt, 2424–3

Exports, imports, tariffs, and industry operating data for military and special-purpose vehicles, 1979-83, TSUSA commodity rpt, 9885–6.78

Exports of manufactured and agricultural commodities, manufacturing production, and export-related employment, 1960s-82, State rpt series, 2046–3

Exports of US, detailed commodities by country of destination, monthly rpt, 2422–3

Exports of US, detailed Schedule B commodities by country of destination, 1983, annual rpt, 2424–9

Exports of US, detailed Schedule E commodities by mode of transport and world area and country of destination, 1983, annual rpts, 2424–5

Fed Govt procurement contract awards, by State, agency, procurement and contractor type, and for top 100 contractors, quarterly rpt, 102–6

Finances and operations, by SIC 2- to 4-digit industry, 1970s-83 and projected to 1988, annual rpt, 2014–4

Finances and operations of rail and motor carriers, detailed statistics, 1982, annual rpt series, 9486–5

Finances and operations of rail and motor carriers, detailed statistics, 1983, annual rpt series, 9486–6

Finances and operations of transit systems, by mode of transport, function, fleet size, and system, FY82, annual rpt, 7884–4

Finances, operations, vehicles, equipment, accidents, and energy use, by mode of transport, 1955-84, annual rpt, 7304–2

Financial statements for manufacturing, mining, and trade corporations, by selected SIC 2- to 3-digit industry, quarterly rpt, 2502–1

Foreign direct investment in US, major investors and investments by SIC 4-digit industry, transaction type and value, and location, 1983, annual rpt, 2044–20

Foreign direct investment of US, by selected major industry group and world area, 1980-82, annual article, 2702–1.430

Foreign economic, social, and political summary data, by country, 1984, annual factbook, 244–11

Govt census, 1982: city govt revenues by source, expenditures by function, debt, and assets, by State and city, 2457–4

Govt census, 1982: county govt revenues by source, expenditures by function, debt, and assets, by State and county, 2457–3

Govt transportation revenues by source and expenditures, by level of govt and mode of transport, and Fed Govt aid by type, FY77-82, 7308–185

Imports of US, detailed Schedule A commodities by country and world area of origin, and mode of transport, 1983, annual rpts, 2424–2

Imports of US, detailed Schedule A commodities by country, monthly rpt, 2422–2

Imports of US, detailed TSUSA commodities by country of origin, 1983, annual rpt, 2424–4

Income tax returns of corporations, detailed income and tax items by industry, 1981, annual rpt, 8304–4

Income tax returns of corporations, summary data by industry div, 1981 estimates, annual article, 8302–2.403

Income tax returns of corporations with foreign tax credit, income and deductions by type, asset size, and selected industry group, 1980, article, 8302–2.415

Income tax returns of foreign subsidiaries of US corporations, income and tax data, by industry and asset size, 1980, article, 8302–2.410

Income tax returns of partnerships, detailed data by industry, 1981 estimates, annual article, 8302–2.404

Income tax returns of partnerships, receipts by source, deductions by type, and establishments, by selected industry, 1982, annual article, 8302–2.416

Income tax returns of sole proprietorships, detailed data by industry div and selected industry group, 1981, annual rpt, 8304–7

Income tax returns of sole proprietorships, receipts, deductions by type, payroll, and net income, by major industry, 1982, annual article, 8302–2.413

Income tax returns with investment credits, for individuals by income, and for sole proprietorships by industry, 1981, article, 8302–2.409

Input-output structure of US economy, detailed interindustry transactions for 85 industries, and components of final demand, 1977, article, 2702–1.421

Input-output structure of US economy, detailed interindustry transactions for 537 industries, and components of final demand, 1977 benchmark data, 2708–17

Manufacturing census, 1982: financial and operating data, by SIC 2- to 4-digit industry, State, SMSA, and county, preliminary census div rpt series, 2491–3

Manufacturing census, 1982: financial and operating data, for SIC 4-digit industries by product, preliminary rpt series, 2491–1

Mineral industries census, 1982: financial and operating data, including materials consumed, by SIC 4-digit industry and State, preliminary rpt series, 2511–1

Minority group and women's employment, by occupational group, SIC 2- to 3-digit industry, State, and SMSA, 1981, annual rpt, 9244–1

Motor and rail carriers regulated by ICC, employment and finances by mode of transport, and ICC activities, FY80-83 and trends, annual rpt, 9484–1

Natl income and product, comprehensive accounts and components, *Survey of Current Business,* monthly rpt, 2702–1.21

Natl income and product, comprehensive accounts and components, *Survey of Current Business,* monthly rpt, monthly and annual tables, 2702–1.27

Nuclear power and weapons policy, fuel supply/demand, waste disposal and siting, environmental effects of radiation, and public attitudes, 1970s-82 with projections to 2000, 3008–88

Occupational injuries, illnesses, and workdays lost, by SIC 2-digit industry, 1982-83, annual press release, 6844–3

Occupational injury and illness rates, by SIC 2- to 4-digit industry, 1982, annual rpt, 6844–1

Transportation and transportation equipment

Occupational manpower needs and supply by detailed occupation, and educational and training program enrollees and grads by detailed field, 1982 and 1995, biennial rpt, 6744–3

Occupational Outlook Handbook, 1984-85 biennial rpt, 6744–1

OECD trade, total and for 4 major countries, and US trade by country, by commodity, 1972-82, annual world region rpt series, 244–13

Older persons population characteristics, and needs and costs of social services by type, by metro-nonmetro status, 1970s-82 with trends from 1900, 21148–28

Pollution abatement capital and operating costs, by SIC 2- to 4-digit industry, State, and SMSA, 1982, annual Current Industrial Rpt, 2506–3.6

Producer prices and indexes, by stage of processing and detailed commodity, monthly rpt, 6762–6

Producer prices and indexes, by stage of processing and detailed commodity, monthly 1983, annual supplement, 6764–2

R&D Fed Govt facilities and services available for private sector use, by field of science, 1984 biennial listing, 2224–4

R&D industry funding and employment of scientists and engineers, by industry group, firm size, and funding source, 1956-82, annual rpt, 9627–21

Radioactive materials transport surveillance program activities and results, State survey rpt series, 9636–1

Regional councils involved in service activities, by type of service and region population size, 1982 survey, hearing, 25408–88

Scientists, engineers, and technicians employed in private industry, by occupation and industry group, 1980-81, biennial rpt, 9627–23

Scientists, engineers, and technicians employment in transportation, utilities, and retail and wholesale trade, by field of science and industry, 1982, 9628–72

Small and minority-owned businesses finances and operations, Federal contracts by agency, and worker characteristics, by industry, race, sex, and State, 1950s-83, annual rpt, 9764–6

Soviet Union-US science and technology exchange projects, man-hours, and funding, by Fed Govt agency and activity type, FY81-82, 7008–41

Statistical Abstract of US, social, political, and economic data, 1950s-83 and trends, annual rpt, 2324–1.3

Stock (common) prices and yields, current data and annual trends, monthly rpt, 23842–1.5

Transit services for commuting and other purposes, dev and effects, series, 7306–9

Transit system (automated guideway) characteristics and itemized costs, for 16 systems in operation or under construction, 1982, annual rpt, 7884–6

Wages by occupation, and benefits for office and plant workers in 70 SMSAs, 1983, annual rpt, 6785–1

Water pollution fish kills, by State, location, and pollution source, monthly 1978-80, annual rpt, 9204–3

Waterborne commerce of US (domestic and foreign), freight by commodity, traffic, and passengers, by port and waterway, 1982, annual rpt, 3754–3

Wholesale trade census, 1982: employment, establishments, sales by commodity, and payroll, by SIC 4-digit kind of business and State, preliminary rpt series, 2403–1

see also Air travel
see also Aircraft
see also Airlines
see also Automobiles
see also Aviation accidents and safety
see also Bicycles
see also Boats and boating
see also Bridges
see also Buses
see also Canals
see also Census of Transportation
see also Commuting
see also Federal aid to transportation
see also Freight
see also Harbors and ports
see also High-speed ground transportation
see also Highways
see also Inland water transportation
see also Marine accidents and safety
see also Metroliner
see also Military vehicles
see also Mopeds
see also Motor vehicle industry
see also Motor vehicle registrations
see also Motorcycles
see also Passenger ships
see also Pipelines
see also Railroad accidents and safety
see also Railroad equipment and vehicles
see also Railroads
see also Recreational vehicles
see also Rivers and waterways
see also Ships and shipping
see also Subways
see also Tanker ships
see also Taxicabs
see also Traffic accidents and safety
see also Transportation energy use
see also Travel
see also Trucks and trucking industry
see also Urban transportation
see also under By Commodity in the "Index by Categories"
see also under By Industry in the "Index by Categories"

Transportation census
see Census of Transportation

Transportation Department
see Department of Transportation

Transportation energy use

Air pollutant emission factors, by detailed source, 3rd edition, 1983-84 supplements, 9198–13

Air pollution levels for 5 pollutants, by detailed source, State, and Air Quality Control Region, 1981, annual rpt, 9194–7

Air pollution levels for 5 pollutants, by source, 1970- 82 with trends from 1940, annual rpt, 9194–13

Air quality and transportation and related energy use, for urban areas and Chicago area, late 1970s-82 and projected under lower auto emission standards to 1995, 3408–31

Auto and light truck fuel economy performance by make, and standards, 1978-85 model years, annual rpt, 7764–9

Index by Subjects and Names

Auto and light truck fuel use, economy standards and manufacturer compliance, and gas prices and taxes, with selected foreign comparisons, FY80-83 and projected to 2000, hearing, 21368–49

Auto and van operating and owning costs by component and vehicle size, for 12 years of operation, 1984 model year, biennial rpt, 7554–21

Auto emissions control device tampering and fuel-switching incidence in 6 urban areas, 1983, annual rpt, 9194–15

Auto fuel economy test results for models complying with California emission standards, 1984 model year, annual rpt, 3304–13

Auto fuel economy test results, 1985 model year, annual rpt, 3304–11

Auto, small airplane, and motorcycle operating costs by component and vehicle size or make, and Fed Govt mileage reimbursement rates, 1983, annual rpt, 9454–13

Electric utilities privately owned, sales revenues by company and consuming sector, 1982, annual rpt, 3164–23

Energy prices and expenditures for fuels and electricity, by consuming sector, State, and fuel type, 1970-81, annual rpt, 3164–64

Energy production, reserves, and prices, by energy type, and selected indicators of energy use, by State, 1982-83 with selected comparisons from 1971, annual rpt, 3164–60

Energy supply/demand and prices, by energy resource and major producing and consuming country and sector, detailed data, monthly rpt, 3162–24

Energy supply/demand and prices, by energy source and end-use sector and for 7 electric utilities, 1981-2000 with trends from 1960s, 3008–93

Energy supply/demand and prices, by fuel type and consuming sector with foreign comparisons, 1949-83, annual rpt, 3164–74

Energy supply/demand and prices, by fuel type, sector, and end use, detailed trends and projections 1973-95, annual rpt, 3164–75

Energy supply/demand and prices, by fuel type, sector, and end use, with foreign comparisons, 1960-83 and projected to 1995, annual summary rpt, 3164–76

Energy supply/demand, prices, end use, and related technical and socioeconomic data, including impacts of US policy and intl devs, series, 3006–7

Energy use, by economic sector, end use, and energy source, 1983 and 2000, 2006–2.5

Energy use, by economic sector, State, census div, and detailed energy resource, 1960-82, State Energy Data System annual rpt, 3164–39

Energy use, by type of air pollutant source and fuel, and State, 1981, annual rpt, 9194–14

Energy use in transportation sector by mode, fuel supplies, and demographic and economic determinants of vehicle use, 1970s-83, annual rpt, 3304–5

Energy use, per capita and by economic sector, State, and major energy resource, 1960-82, State Energy Data System annual supplement, 3164–55

Index by Subjects and Names

Energy use, prices, and conservation and efficiency measures, by fuel type, end-use sector, selected industry, and region, 1960-83, annual rpt, 3164–73

Environmental quality and protection programs, costs, and Fed Govt enforcement, 1983, detailed annual rpt, 484–1

Fed Govt energy use and efficiency, by agency and fuel type, FY83, annual rpt, 3304–22

Fed Govt motor vehicle fleet costs and operating data, by agency, FY83, annual rpt, 9454–9

Fuel oil (distillate and residual) and kerosene deliveries, by end use, PAD district, and State, selected years 1978-83, annual rpt, 3164–2

Input-output structure of US economy, detailed interindustry transactions for 537 industries, and components of final demand, 1977 benchmark data, 2708–17

Methanol fuel for autos, regulatory barriers to market dev, with supply/demand and auto fleet use and fuel economy, mid-1970s-82 and projected to 2000, GAO rpt, 26113–112

Motor fuel consumption by consuming sector, hwy-nonhwy use, and State, 1983, annual rpt, 7554–1.1

Natl Energy Policy Plan, energy supply, demand, and prices, by fuel and consuming sector, projected 1985-2010, biennial rpt, 3004–13

New England States electricity and gasoline sales, Fed Reserve 1st District, monthly rpt, 9373–2.6

OECD energy prices and taxes by energy source and end-use sector, for US and 9 countries, quarterly 1979-83, annual rpt, 3164–71

State govt energy conservation programs, Fed Govt financial and technical aid, and reported energy savings, by State, 1983, annual rpt, 3304–1

Statistical Abstract of US, social, political, and economic data, 1950s-83 and trends, annual rpt, 2324–1.3

Transit services for commuting and other purposes, dev and effects, series, 7306–9

Transit system deficits, effect of cost and service increases and ridership and fare decreases, and govt aid and system operating ratios, 1970-80, 7308–184

Transit system financial and operating data, by mode, function, fleet size, and individual system, FY82, annual rpt, 7884–4

Transit system operations, tax burden related to ridership, fares, and govt funding, for selected States and cities, 1950s-82, reprint, 7888–59

Transit systems research publications, 2nd half FY83, semiannual listing, 7882–1

Transportation census, 1982: trucks, by detailed characteristics, miles traveled, and type of product carried, State rpt series, 2573–1

Transportation finances, operations, vehicles, equipment, accidents, and energy use and transport, by mode of transport, 1955-84, annual rpt, 7304–2

Truck transport of fruit and vegetables, costs per vehicle-mile by component for fleets and owner-operator trucks, monthly rpt, 1272–1

Trucks (heavy) energy use, efficiency, and conservation technologies, selected years 1958-82 and projected to 2000, 3308–70 *see also* Aviation fuels

Transports

see Naval vessels

Trapido, Paul J.

"Venezuela: An Export Market Profile", 1526–6.5

Trapnell, Gordon R.

"Private Health Insurance: New Measures of a Complex and Changing Industry", 4652–1.430

Trapping

see Hunting and trapping

Traub, Larry G.

"Influences on U.S. Direct Food Purchase Program", 1548–243

Travel

- Agencies financial and operating data, and airline ticket sales by type of distributor, 1970s-82, hearing, 25268–81
- American Samoa minimum wage rates, employment, earnings, and benefits, by establishment and industry, Nov 1983, biennial rpt, 6504–6
- Bus industry collective ratemaking and regulatory reform impacts on operations, finances, and services to older persons and rural areas by State, 1970s-83, 14828–2
- Business statistics, detailed data for major industries and economic indicators, *Survey of Current Business,* monthly rpt, 2702–1.8
- County Business Patterns: establishments, employees, and payrolls, by SIC 4-digit industry and county, 1982, annual State rpt series, 2326–6
- Cuba economic conditions, agricultural and industrial production and distribution, trade, and intl economic relations, 1970-82 and trends from 1957, 248–40
- Developing countries disaster preparedness and summary sociodemographic, political, and economic data, country rpt series, 9916–2
- DOD expenditures for goods and services, by function, 1972-84, article, 2702–1.440
- Energy use in transportation sector by mode, fuel supplies, and demographic and economic determinants of vehicle use, 1970s-83, annual rpt, 3304–5
- Europe travel by US citizens, monthly rpt, 7182–2
- Fed Govt employee travel expenses for official business trips, and reimbursement rates, for high rate cities, 1983, annual rpt, 9454–16
- Fed Govt employee travel expenses, operating costs for private autos, airplanes, and motorcycles and reimbursement rates for business use, 1983, annual rpt, 9454–13
- Fed Govt programs and mgmt cost control proposals, 3-year savings by function and agency, and financial and operating data, 1960s-81, 16908–1
- Foreign countries *Background Notes,* summary social, political, and economic data, travel notes, series, 7006–2
- Foreign economic trends and implications for US, annual and semiannual country rpt series, 2046–4

Travel

- Foreign travel balance of US, current and annual trends, monthly rpt, 23842–1.7
- Foreign travel from US, passports issued by holder characteristics, travel purpose, and country of destination, quarterly rpt, 7182–1
- Foreign travel to and from US and travel receipts and payments by world area, and travel to US by country, 1977-83, annual rpt, 2904–10
- Foreign travel to and from US, by world area and selected country, projected 1984-85, annual rpt, 2904–9
- Foreign travel to and from US, receipts and expenditures by world area and country, 1979-83, annual article, 2702–1.417
- Foreign travel to US and receipts by world area and selected country, 1960-83, and US Travel and Tourism Admin activities, 1983, annual rpt, 2904–6
- Foreign travel to US, by characteristics of visit and traveller, country, and State of destination, quarterly rpt, 2902–1
- Foreign visitors and other nonimmigrants admitted to US, by country of last residence, FY81, annual rpt, 6264–2
- France Brittany coast oil spill cleanup and research costs, marine and tourism industry losses, and recreation losses of tourists and residents, 1971-79, 2178–13
- Franchise business opportunities, by firm and kind of business, 1984 annual listing, 2044–27
- Franchises of firms engaged in distribution of goods and services by kind of business, establishments by State, and sales, 1982-84, annual rpt, 2014–5
- Govt census, 1982: State govt payments to local govts, by program, source of funds, level of govt, and State, with trends from 1902, 2460–3
- House of Representatives salaries, expenses, and contingent fund disbursement, detailed listings, quarterly rpt, 21942–1
- Hwy traffic volume on rural roads and city streets, by region, monthly rpt, 7552–8
- Income tax returns of sole proprietorships, detailed data by industry div and selected industry group, 1981, annual rpt, 8304–7
- Industry finances and operations, by SIC 2- to 4- digit industry, 1970s-83 and projected to 1988, annual rpt, 2014–4
- Input-output structure of US economy, detailed interindustry transactions for 537 industries, and components of final demand, 1977 benchmark data, 2708–17
- Intl services transactions by type, and sales, assets, and employment of US multinatl service firms by industry and world region, 1977-82, 2706–5.30
- Jamaica PL 480 Title I assistance effects on economic dev, with data on govt finance, economic indicators, demography, and dev programs, 1970s-81, 9916–1.51
- Motor carrier passengers and selected revenue data, for individual large Class I motor carriers, quarterly rpt, 9482–13
- Multinatl corporation income reallocation through regulation of intercorporate transactions, by tax item, treaty status, asset size, industry, and tax haven country, 1982, 8008–110
- Natl park area visits and overnight stays, visitors, and vehicles, by State and park, 1983, annual rpt, 5544–12

Travel

Occupational manpower needs and supply by detailed occupation, and educational and training program enrollees and grads by detailed field, 1982 and 1995, biennial rpt, 6744–3

Occupational Outlook Handbook, 1984-85 biennial rpt, 6744–1

Overseas Business Reports: economic conditions, investment and export opportunities, and trade practices, annual country market research rpt series, 2046–6

Patterns of travel, personal and household characteristics, auto use, and public transport availability, 1977 survey, series, 7556–6

Personal consumption expenditures, natl income and product account, *Survey of Current Business,* monthly rpt, monthly and annual tables, 2702–1.23

Railroad improvement project for Northeast Corridor, goals, funding, and progress, and Amtrak finances and operations, FY83, annual rpt, 7604–9

Recreation (outdoor) participation, by type of activity, projected 1985-2030, 1208–195

Scientists, engineers, and technicians employment in transportation, utilities, and retail and wholesale trade, by field of science and industry, 1982, 9628–72

Senate salaries, expenses, and contingent fund disbursements, by payee, detailed listings, 1st half FY84, semiannual rpt, 25922–1

Statistical Abstract of US, social, political, and economic data, 1950s-83 and trends, annual rpt, 2324–1.1

Transportation finances, operations, vehicles, equipment, accidents, and energy use, by mode of transport, 1955-84, annual rpt, 7304–2

TTPI tourists, by visitor country of origin, FY80-82, annual rpt, 7004–6

Urban travel by purpose, effect of telecommunication advances, land use changes, and alternative work schedules, projected to 2000 with some trends 1950-80, 7888–63

Vaccination requirements for intl travel by country, and disease prevention recommendations, 1984 annual rpt, 4204–11

Virgin Islands economic censuses, 1982: employment, establishments, payroll, and receipts, by SIC 1- to 4-digit industry, island, and city, 2593–1

Virgin Islands visitor entries, FY81, annual rpt, 5304–4

Waterborne commerce of US (domestic and foreign), freight by commodity, traffic, and passengers, by port and waterway, 1982, annual rpt, 3754–3

Women's travel patterns, by employment and sociodemographic characteristics and type of child care used, 1980 survey, 7888–62

see also Air travel

see also Commuting

see also Passports and visas

Travel and Tourism Administration

see U.S. Travel and Tourism Administration

Treasury Department

see Department of Treasury

Treat, Ned L.

"Electric Railroads and Trolley Systems: Past, Present, and Future", 3006–7.7

Treaties and conventions

Arms control treaties status, and Arms Control and Disarmament Agency activities, 1983, annual rpt, 9824–2

Bilateral and multilateral agreements of US in force, by country, Jan 1984, annual listing, 7004–1

Copyright activities of Register of Copyrights, including intl relations, registrations, fees earned, and royalties collected, FY82, annual rpt, 26404–2

Developing countries disaster preparedness and summary sociodemographic, political, and economic data, country rpt series, 9916–2

DOD budget, FY85 weapons system requests consistency with US policy and specified treaties, with funding FY83-87, annual rpt, 21384–4

DOD budget, organization, personnel, weapons, and property, by service branch, State, and country, 1984 annual summary rpt, 3504–13

Foreign military, social, and economic summary data by world area and country, 1960s-80s, hearing, 25388–47.1

Helsinki Final Act implementation by NATO, Warsaw Pact, and other signatory nations, Dec 1983-Mar 1984, semiannual rpt, 7002–1

Multinatl corporation income reallocation through regulation of intercorporate transactions, by tax item, treaty status, asset size, industry, and tax haven country, 1982, 8008–110

Ocean dumping of waste materials, EPA permit program and intl London Dumping Convention activities, 1981-83, annual rpt, 9204–8

Soviet Union and Warsaw Pact military weapons systems, assistance and presence worldwide, and force strengths, with selected US and NATO comparisons, as of 1984, 3508–14

see also Executive agreements

see also Strategic Arms Limitation Treaties

see also Strategic Arms Reduction Talks

see also Trade agreements

Trees

see Forests and forestry

Trembley, Nancy

"FAA Air Traffic Activity, FY83", 7504–27

Trenton, N.J.

Census of Housing, 1980: occupancy and unit characteristics, by race, Hispanic origin, and city, SMSA rpt, 2473–1.354

Census of Population and Housing, 1980: detailed population and housing characteristics, by county, city, and census tract, SMSA rpt, 2551–2.354

Wages of office and plant workers, by occupation, 1983 SMSA survey rpt, 6785–12.1

see also under By SMSA or MSA in the "Index by Categories"

Trevino, Fernando

"Health Insurance Coverage and Physician Visits Among Hispanic and Non-Hispanic People", 4144–11.1

Index by Subjects and Names

Trevino, Fernando M.

"Health Indicators for Hispanic, Black, and White Americans", 4147–10.147

Trials

- Arson investigation and prosecution, by incident characteristics and outcome, motive, and type of evidence, for 4 jurisdictions, 1981, 6068–184
- Bank robbery court cases by case processing, sentencing, and offender characteristics, and compared to other Fed Govt felony cases, 1979-80, periodic rpt, 6062–2.407
- Court caseloads, actions, procedure duration, judges, and jurors, by Federal district and appeals court, 1979-84, annual rpt, 18204–3
- Court cases, dispositions, convictions, and sentences of Federal criminal defendants, by offense and district, as of June 1983 with trends from 1945, annual rpt, 18204–1
- Crime and criminal justice statistics analysis, methodology, and use in courts, 1983 biennial conf proceedings, 6064–20
- Criminal case processing from arrest to sentencing, series, 6066–22
- Fed Govt district court magistrates case processing duties, by type of case, duty, and district, 1983 rpt, 18408–24
- Federal district court grand and petit juror use and costs, trials, and trial days, by court, years ended June 1980-84, annual rpt, 18204–4
- US Attorneys civil and criminal case processing in district, appellate, and State courts, by district, FY83, annual rpt, 6004–2
- Wiretapping authorizations, costs, persons involved, arrests, trials, and convictions, 1977-83, annual rpt, 18204–7.2
- Witness Security Program costs, participants by arrest record, and prosecutions by offense, offender type, and disposition, various periods FY70-83, GAO rpt, 26119–70

see also Courts-martial and courts of inquiry

see also Juries

Trichinosis

see Food and waterborne diseases

Triffin, Robert

"European Monetary System: Tombstone or Cornerstone?", 9373–3.28

Trinidad and Tobago

- Agricultural and food production indexes, and production of selected commodities, by world region and country, 1974-83, annual rpt, 1524–5
- Agricultural situation in Latin America, by country, 1981-83 and outlook for 1984, annual rpt, 1524–4.9
- *Background Notes,* summary social, political, and economic data, 1984 rpt, 7006–2.62
- Economic, social, and political summary data, by country, 1984, annual factbook, 244–11
- Exports of US, detailed Schedule B commodities by country of destination, 1983, annual rpt, 2424–9
- Exports of US, detailed Schedule E commodities by mode of transport and world area and country of destination, 1983, annual rpts, 2424–5
- Imports of US, detailed Schedule A commodities by country and world area of origin, and mode of transport, 1983, annual rpts, 2424–2

Index by Subjects and Names

Imports of US, detailed TSUSA commodities by country of origin, 1983, annual rpt, 2424–4

Loans and grants for economic and military assistance from US and intl agencies, by program and country, FY46-83, annual rpt, 9914–5

Military aid of US, arms sales, and training programs costs and budget requests by program, world region, and country, FY83-85, annual rpt, 7144–13

Military spending, arms trade, and armed forces size, with total govt spending and population, by country, 1972-82, annual rpt, 9824–1

Minerals Yearbook, 1982, Vol 3: foreign country reviews of production, trade, and policies, by commodity, annual rpt, 5604–35

Minerals Yearbook, 1983, Vol 3 preprints: foreign country review of production, trade, and policies, by commodity, annual rpt, 5604–23.85

Oil exports to US by OPEC and non-OPEC countries, monthly rpt, 3162–24.3

Population size and growth rates, and latest available benchmark demographic data, by country, 1950-83, biennial rpt, 2324–4

see also under By Foreign Country in the "Index by Categories"

Troll, Rick

"Impact of Discount Rate Changes on Market Interest Rates", 9381–1.404

Troop ships

see Naval vessels

Trophies

see Awards, medals, and prizes

Tross, Susan

"Psychiatric Problems of AIDS Inpatients at the New York Hospital: Preliminary Report", 4102–1.426

Trostle, Ron

"Recent CAP Changes: Will They Reduce Subsidized Exports?", 1522–3.402

Trout, John

"10-Year Review of the Supplemental Security Income Program", 4742–1.402

Trowbridge, Frederick L.

"Prevalence of Growth Stunting and Obesity: Pediatric Nutrition Surveillance System, 1982", 4202–7.403

Troy, N.Y.

- Census of Housing, 1980: occupancy and unit characteristics, by race, Hispanic origin, and city, SMSA rpt, 2473–1.61
- Census of Population and Housing, 1980: detailed population and housing characteristics, by county, city, and census tract, SMSA rpt, 2551–2.61
- Housing and households detailed characteristics, and unit and neighborhood quality, by inside-outside central cities, 1980 survey, SMSA rpt, 2485–6.2
- Public works capital needs and financing, by project type, level of govt, and selected jurisdiction, 1970s-83 and projected to 2000, hearing, 23848–181
- Wages of office and plant workers, by occupation, 1984 SMSA survey rpt, 6785–11.9

see also under By SMSA or MSA in the "Index by Categories"

TRT Telecommunications Corp.

Financial and operating data for 7 major telegraph carriers, quarterly rpt, 9282–1

Trucks and trucking industry

- Accident deaths in transportation, by mode, 1982-83, annual summary rpt, 9614–6
- Accidents (fatal), circumstances, and characteristics of persons and vehicles involved, detailed data, 1982, annual rpt, 7764–10
- Accidents (fatal), circumstances, and characteristics of persons and vehicles involved, 1983, annual rpt, 7764–14
- Accidents (traffic), deaths, circumstances, and characteristics of persons and vehicles involved, series, 7766–13
- Accidents and casualties detailed direct and indirect costs, by characteristics of persons and vehicles involved, 1979-80, 7768–80
- Accidents, circumstances, injuries, deaths, and characteristics of persons and vehicles involved, 1982, annual rpt, 7764–13
- Accidents, injuries, deaths, and property damage, by circumstances, carrier type, and driver age and condition, 1983, annual rpt, 7554–9
- Agriculture census, 1982: farms, farmland, production and costs, and operator characteristics, preliminary State and county rpt series, 2330–1
- Agriculture census, 1982: farms, farmland, production, finances, and operator characteristics, by county, final State rpt series, 2331–1
- Business statistics, detailed data for major industries and economic indicators, *Survey of Current Business,* monthly rpt, 2702–1.8, 2702–1.20
- Census of Housing, 1980: inventory, occupancy, and unit characteristics, changes from 1973 by region and inside-outside SMSAs and central cities, series, 2473–3
- Census of Housing, 1980: occupancy and unit characteristics of SMSAs and central cities, by race, Hispanic origin, and city, State and SMSA rpt series, 2473–1
- Census of Population, 1980: detailed socioeconomic and demographic characteristics, by age, sex, race, Hispanic origin, occupation, and industry, State rpt series, 2531–4
- Census of Population, 1980: detailed socioeconomic characteristics, by county, city, and inside-outside SMSAs and central cities, State rpt series, 2531–3
- Census of Transportation, 1982: trucks, by detailed characteristics, miles traveled, and type of product carried, State rpt series, 2573–1
- Coal transport environmental impacts by type and mode of transport, methodology for assessing alternative systems, 1983 rpt, 3408–28
- Collective bargaining agreements expiring during year, covered workers by SIC 2-digit industry, firm, and union, with summary of key provisions, 1984, annual rpt, 6784–9
- Communist, OECD, and selected other countries freight and carrier inventories, by mode of transport, 1960s-83, annual rpt, 244–5.10

Trucks and trucking industry

- County Business Patterns: establishments, employees, and payrolls, by SIC 4-digit industry and county, 1981, annual State rpt series, 2326–8
- County Business Patterns: establishments, employees, and payrolls, by SIC 4-digit industry and county, 1982, annual State rpt series, 2326–6
- Deregulation of trucking, effects on marketing food and agricultural commodities, 1976-82, 1548–238
- DOE in-house energy use, conservation investments, and savings, by type of use and fuel and field office, FY83, annual rpt, 3024–3
- Earnings by major industry group, and personal income per capita and by source, by region and State, 1929-82, 2708–40
- Employment and finances of ICC-regulated carriers by mode of transport, and ICC activities, FY80-83 and trends, annual rpt, 9484–1
- Employment, earnings, and hours, by selected SIC 1- to 4-digit industry, State, and for 278 major labor areas, 1939-83, annual rpt, 6744–5
- Employment, earnings, and hours, by SIC 4-digit nonfarm industry, monthly 1974-Feb 1984, annual update, 6744–4
- Energy economy and registrations, by type of vehicle, 1960-83, annual rpt, 3164–74.3
- Energy economy measures for autos and light trucks, selected years 1960-83, annual rpt, 3164–73
- Energy economy performance of autos and light trucks by make, and standards, 1978-85 model years, annual rpt, 7764–9
- Energy supply/demand and prices, by fuel type, sector, and end use, detailed trends and projections 1973-95, annual rpt, 3164–75
- Energy use, by type of air pollutant source and fuel, and State, 1981, annual rpt, 9194–14
- Energy use, efficiency, and conservation technologies, and vehicle sales, for heavy trucks, selected years 1958-82 and projected to 2000, 3308–70
- Energy use in transportation sector by mode, fuel supplies, and demographic and economic determinants of vehicle use, 1970s-83, annual rpt, 3304–5
- Energy use of autos and light trucks, economy standards and manufacturer compliance, and gas prices and taxes, with selected foreign comparisons, FY80-83 and projected to 2000, hearing, 21368–49
- Exports and imports of autos and trucks by country, retail prices of selected US and Japan models, and industry operating data, monthly rpt, 9882–8
- Exports and imports of US, detailed SIC-based commodities by world area, 1983, annual rpts, 2424–6
- Exports and imports of US, totals and as percent of domestic production, by SIC 2- to 5-digit commodity, 1981, annual rpt, 2424–3
- Exports, imports, tariffs, and industry operating data for motor vehicles and bodies and chassis, foreign and US, 1979-83, TSUSA commodity rpt, 9885–6.63

Trucks and trucking industry

Exports of US, detailed commodities by country of destination, monthly rpt, 2422–3

Exports of US, detailed Schedule B commodities by country of destination, 1983, annual rpt, 2424–9

Exports of US, detailed Schedule E commodities by mode of transport and world area and country of destination, 1983, annual rpts, 2424–5

Farm finances, assets, liabilities, income, receipts by commodity and State, and expenses, 1980-83 and trends from 1910, annual rpt, 1544–16

Farm finances, expenses by type, loans by purpose and source, and credit detail by Fed Reserve District, quarterly rpt, 9365–3.10

Farm finances, production, expenses by type, and domestic economic impact, selected years 1972-82 and preliminary 1983-84, annual rpt, 1544–19

Farm production expenditures, detailed items by farm sales size and region, 1983, annual rpt, 1614–3

Fed Govt motor vehicle fleet and mileage, GSA mgmt activities and finances, FY78-83, annual rpt, 9454–23

Fed Govt motor vehicle fleet costs and operating data, by agency, FY83, annual rpt, 9454–9

Fed Govt programs and mgmt cost control proposals, 3-year savings by function and agency, and financial and operating data, 1960s-81, 16908–1

Fed Reserve System coin and currency transport truck driver and guard wages in 12 cities, effects of locally prevailing wage rate requirements, 1980, article, 9377–1.402

Finances and operations, by SIC 2- to 4-digit industry, 1970s-83 and projected to 1988, annual rpt, 2014–4

Finances and operations for Class I motor carriers of property, by region and firm, quarterly rpt, 9482–5

Finances, operations, equipment, employment, and payroll for Class I interstate motor carriers, by district, 1982, annual rpt, 9486–5.3

Finances, operations, vehicles, equipment, accidents, and energy use, by mode of transport, 1955-84, annual rpt, 7304–2

Financial and operating data for Class II motor carriers of property, by region, 1982, annual rpt, 9484–10

Franchises of firms engaged in distribution of goods and services by kind of business, establishments by State, and sales, 1982-84, annual rpt, 2014–5

Great Lakes trade, by SIC 3-digit commodity, port, vessel type, world area, and country, 1982, annual rpt, 7744–3

Household goods carriers (Class I) operating revenues, net income, and revenue tons, by firm, quarterly rpt, 9482–14

Housing units with cars and trucks available, by inside-outside central cities, 1979-82 surveys, SMSA rpt series, 2485–6

Hwy-railroad grade-crossing accidents, detailed data by State and railroad, 1982, annual rpt, 7604–2

Hwy safety, accident, and traffic data from Natl Statistics and Analysis Center, series, 7766–10

Hwy Statistics, detailed data on traffic, govt finances, fuel use, vehicles, driver licenses, and hwy characteristics, by State, 1983, annual rpt, 7554–1

Hwy use taxes and Trust Fund revenues by tax type, and tax and truck size and weight limits effects on trucking industry, FY82-84 and projected to 1990, GAO rpt, 26117–31

Hwy use taxes by tax type, and truck size and weight limits, economic effects on trucking industry, 1982-83 and projected 1984-87, hearings, 25328–24

Hwys designated for use by large trucks, mileage by State, as of June 1984, press release, 7556–3.1

ICC enforcement of motor carrier regulations, staff by position, and caseload by violation type, by ICC region, selected years FY80-85, GAO rpt, 26113–133

Imports of US, detailed Schedule A commodities by country and world area of origin, and mode of transport, 1983, annual rpts, 2424–2

Imports of US, detailed Schedule A commodities by country, monthly rpt, 2422–2

Imports of US, detailed TSUSA commodities by country of origin, 1983, annual rpt, 2424–4

Income tax returns of corporations, detailed income and tax items by industry, 1981, annual rpt, 8304–4

Income tax returns of sole proprietorships, detailed data by industry div and selected industry group, 1981, annual rpt, 8304–7

Income tax returns of sole proprietorships, receipts, deductions by type, payroll, and net income, by major industry, 1982, annual article, 8302–2.413

Income tax returns with investment credits, for individuals by income, and for sole proprietorships by industry, 1981, article, 8302–2.409

Input-output structure of US economy, detailed interindustry transactions for 537 industries, and components of final demand, 1977 benchmark data, 2708–17

Japan auto, truck, and bus production, by make, 1982, hearings, 21788–134

Light truck sales and consumer attitudes, 1978-82, annual rpt, 2004–8

Manufacturing census, 1982: financial and operating data, for SIC 4-digit industries by product, preliminary rpt, 2491–1.396

Minority group and women employment, by occupational group and SIC 2- to 3-digit industry, 1981, annual rpt, 9244–1.1

Natl income and product, comprehensive accounts and components, *Survey of Current Business,* monthly rpt, 2702–1.22

Occupational injury and illness rates, by SIC 2- to 4-digit industry, 1982, annual rpt, 6844–1

Occupational Outlook Handbook, 1984-85 biennial rpt, 6744–1

OECD trade, total and for 4 major countries, and US trade by country, by commodity, 1972-82, annual world region rpt series, 244–13

Operating costs for transporting fruit and vegetables, per vehicle-mile by component for fleets and owner-operator trucks, monthly rpt, 1272–1

Index by Subjects and Names

Pension multiemployer plans in construction, trucking, and entertainment industries, and effect of exemption from withdrawal liability, 1977-81, GAO rpt, 26121–73

Producer prices and indexes, by stage of processing and detailed commodity, monthly rpt, 6762–6

Producer prices and indexes, by stage of processing and detailed commodity, monthly 1983, annual supplement, 6764–2

Productivity, hours, and employment indexes for intercity truckers, 1954-82, annual rpt, 6824–1.4

Registrations of motor vehicles, by State and type of vehicle, 1982-83, annual summary rpt, 7554–24

Rental of autos and trucks, industry receipts, 1983, annual rpt, 2413–8

Safety inspections of motor carriers by Fed Hwy Admin, audits of driver qualification and vehicle operation records, and violations cited, 1982, annual rpt, 7554–38

Safety inspections of motor carriers on interstate hwys, violations cited, and vehicles and drivers ordered out of service, 1982, annual rpt, 7554–35

Safety inspections of motor carriers on interstate hwys, violations cited, and vehicles and drivers ordered out of service, May 1983, semiannual rpt, 7552–15

Safety of domestic and foreign autos and light trucks, crash test results of selected new models for model year to date, press release series, 7766–7

Safety programs, and accidents, injuries, deaths, hazards, and property damage, by mode of transport, 1983, annual rpt, 7304–19

Sales of domestic and imported new autos and trucks, and US auto production and inventories, 1983-84, annual article, 2702–1.438

Sales, prices, and registrations of autos and auto products in US, and trade of 8 countries with US, by make and model, 1964-83, annual rpt, 9884–7

Scientists, engineers, and technicians employment in transportation, utilities, and retail and wholesale trade, by field of science and industry, 1982, 9628–72

Statistical Abstract of US, social, political, and economic data, 1950s-83 and trends, annual rpt, 2324–1.3

Tax (excise) collections of IRS, by source, quarterly press release, 8302–1

Tax provisions (State) for motor fuel, vehicle registration fees, and disposition of receipts, by State, as of Jan 1984, biennial rpt, 7554–37

Trailer shipments, exports, and firms, by trailer type, monthly Current Industrial Rpt, 2506–12.25

Washington State truck safety inspection program activities, and truck defects and accidents, various periods 1976-81, article, 7762–9.407

Water pollution fish kills, by State, location, and pollution source, monthly 1978-80, annual rpt, 9204–3

Wholesale trade census, 1982: employment, establishments, sales by commodity, and payroll, by SIC 4-digit kind of business and State, preliminary rpt, 2403–1.1

Index by Subjects and Names

see also Freight
see also Motor vehicle exhaust
see also Motor vehicle industry
see also under By Industry in the "Index by Categories"

Truman, Harry S., Scholarship Foundation

Budget of US Appendix, detailed budgets and personnel summaries, by agency, FY85, annual rpt, 104–3

Budget of US, appropriations, outlays, balances, and budget receipts, by govtl branch and agency, FY83, annual rpt, 8104–2

Scholarship awards by student characteristics, and program operation and financial status, 1983 with trends from 1977, annual rpt, 14314–1

Trust fund receipts by source, transfers, and investment holdings and transactions, monthly rpt, 14312–1

Truong, Tham V.

"Agricultural Subsidies in Portugal: Their Impact on Farm Income and Consumer Cost in the Context of Accession to the European Community", 1528–171

Trust funds

Assets of bank and trust company trust funds, by type of asset and fund and State, 1983, annual rpt, 13004–1

County Business Patterns: establishments, employees, and payrolls, by SIC 4-digit industry and county, 1981, annual State rpt series, 2326–8

County Business Patterns: establishments, employees, and payrolls, by SIC 4-digit industry and county, 1982, annual State rpt series, 2326–6

Credit union financial statements by region, State, and type of membership, for Federal and federally insured State unions, 1983, annual rpt, 9534–1

Flow-of-funds accounts, assets and liabilities by type and economic sector, year-end outstandings, 1960-83, annual rpt, 9364–3

Govt finances, by level of govt, State, and for large cities and counties, 1981-83, annual rpt series, 2466–2

Household income, home value and equity, and financial assets by type, by household characteristics, 1983 survey with trends from 1970, article, 9362–1.406

Income (legal) not reported on Federal income tax returns by source, and legal and illegal underground income, with bibl, 1974-81, article, 2702–1.419

Income tax returns of elderly, by income statement and tax item and income level, 1981 with trends from 1977, article, 8302–2.412

Income tax returns of individuals, detailed data, 1982, annual rpt, 8304–2

Japan-US Friendship Commission educational and cultural exchange activities, grants, and trust fund status, FY83, annual rpt, 14694–1

Mortgage loan activity, by type of lender, loan, and mortgaged property, monthly rpt, 5142–18

Mortgage loan originations, purchases, and acquisitions, for 11 lender types, selected years 1960-82, article, 9312–1.407

Mortgage loan transactions and holdings of State and local govt retirement funds and credit agencies, by type of property and loan, quarterly rpt, 5142–30

Pension fund assets, for public and private funds, 1971-82, annual rpt, 9364–5.12

State and local govt retirement systems, cash and security holdings and finances, quarterly rpt, 2462–2

Unemployment insurance system finances, claims, payments, and covered employment and wages, by State, 1938-82, 6408–5

see also Federal trust funds

Trust Territory of the Pacific Islands

Bank deposits in commercial and mutual savings banks and in US branches of foreign banks, by account type, instn, State, SMSA, and county, June 1983, annual rpt, 9295–3.18

Budget of US, funding under Compact of Free Association with Micronesia, FY85, annual rpt, 104–21

Environmental quality, pollutant discharge by type and source, and EPA protection activities and funding, 1970s-83, biennial regional rpt, 9184–15.9

Exports of US, detailed Schedule E commodities by mode of transport and world area and country of destination, 1983, annual rpts, 2424–5

Food distribution program participants on individual Indian reservations and in TTPI, irregular rpt, 1362–15

Govt financial data and audits by Interior Dept Inspector General, FY83, annual rpt, 5304–15

Imports of US, detailed Schedule A commodities by country and world area of origin, and mode of transport, 1983, annual rpts, 2424–2

Imports of US, detailed TSUSA commodities by country of origin, 1983, annual rpt, 2424–4

Loans and grants for economic and military assistance from US and intl agencies, by program and country, FY46-83, annual rpt, 9914–5

Medical referrals (off-island) of TTPI and American Samoa, costs, and potential savings, by govt, FY83 with comparisons from FY78, GAO rpt, 26123–72

Minerals Yearbook, 1982, Vol 2 preprints: State review of production and sales by commodity, and business activity, annual rpt, 5604–16.40

Minerals Yearbook, 1982, Vol 2: State reviews of production, sales, and firms, by commodity, and business activity, annual rpt, 5604–34

Population size and components of change, by outlying area, 1970-82, Current Population Rpt, 2546–3.127

Population size and components of change, by outlying area, 1980-83, Current Population Rpt, 2546–3.134

Population size and growth rates, and latest available benchmark demographic data, by country, 1950-83, biennial rpt, 2324–4

Population socioeconomic and political data, annual rpt, discontinued, 5304–3

Population socioeconomic, health, and govtl data, by TTPI govt, FY83 and selected trends, detailed annual rpt, 7004–6

Radiation from 1940s-70s nuclear weapons tests, levels in air and water, and personnel exposure by military unit and job category, series, 3906–1

Waterborne commerce of US with Pacific Island territories, 1982, annual rpt, 3754–3.4

see also Northern Mariana Islands
see also under By Outlying Area in the "Index by Categories"

Tryon, Ralph W.

"Current Account of the U.S., Japan, and Germany: A Cyclical Analysis", 9366–7.92

"Small Empirical Models of Exchange Market Intervention: A Review of the Literature", 9366–1.133

Tschetter, John

"Evaluation of BLS' Projections of 1980 Industry Employment", 6722–1.450

"1995 Labor Force: A Second Look", 6728–29

Tuberculosis

Cases and incidence of infectious notifiable diseases and other public health concerns, by census div and State, 1982, annual rpt, 4204–1

Cases of notifiable infectious diseases and current outbreaks, by region and State, weekly rpt, 4202–1

Cattle tuberculosis eradication and surveillance, cooperative Federal-State program activities, by State, FY83, annual rpt, 1394–13

Death rates from tuberculosis in NYC, UK, and Prussia, selected years 1865-1920, article, 4102–1.431

Deaths and death rates, by cause and age, provisional 1982-83, US Vital Statistics annual rpt, 4144–7

Deaths and death rates by detailed cause and demographic characteristics, 1979 and selected trends, US Vital Statistics annual rpt, 4144–2.1

Deaths and death rates, by detailed geographic area, cause, and demographic characteristics, 1979, US Vital Statistics annual rpt, 4144–3

Deaths and death rates, by selected cause and demographic characteristics, 1981, US Vital Statistics advance rpt, 4146–5.78

Deaths and death rates, by selected cause and demographic characteristics, 1982, US Vital Statistics advance rpt, 4146–5.81

Health condition and health care resources, use, and expenditures, 1970s-82 with trends and projections 1900-2000, annual compilation, 4144–11

Incidence, deaths, and treatment, by demographic characteristics, State, and city, 1982 and trends from 1953, annual rpt, 4204–2

Indian births, morbidity, and deaths and rates, and health services facilities and use, 1954-83, annual compilation, 4104–7

see also under By Disease in the "Index by Categories"

Tucker, John T.

"Publication of Employment Data for Additional Service-Producing Industries", 6742–2.410

Tucson, Ariz.

Census of Housing, 1980: occupancy and unit characteristics, by race, Hispanic origin, and city, SMSA rpt, 2473–1.355

Census of Population and Housing, 1980: detailed population and housing characteristics, by county, city, and census tract, SMSA rpt, 2551–2.355

Tucson, Ariz.

Homeless population and characteristics, and temporary shelter operations, use, and user characteristics, for selected cities, various periods 1979-84, hearing, 21248–85

Housing outlook and economic and demographic trends, FHLB 11th District, selected years 1969-82 and projected to 1992, urban area rpt, 9306–2.1

see also under By City and By SMSA or MSA in the "Index by Categories"

Tudor Engineering Co.

"Small-Scale Hydroelectric Power: A Brief Assessment", 3258–1

Tuition

Foreign military training of US, students, costs, and revenue losses from reduced tuition by country, by service branch, FY79-83, GAO rpt, 26123–56

Govt census, 1982: school districts revenues, expenditures, debt, and assets, by district and State, 2457–1

Health professionals supply and education, by occupation, demographic and professional characteristics, and location, 1950s-83 and projected to 2000, biennial rpt, 4114–8

Higher education enrollment of non-resident aliens, full- and part-time teaching staff, and average undergrad tuition, by instn type, selected years 1970/71-1992/93, annual rpt, 4824–1.2

Higher education instns, by type, location, and other characteristics, 1983/84 annual listing, 4844–3

Higher education instns, type, location, enrollment, and student charges, by State and congressional district, 1983/84, biennial listing, 4844–11

Higher education tuition and other student charges, for each public and private 2- and 4-year instn, by State, 1983/84, annual listing, 4844–10

Higher education tuition, fees, and other charges, 1974/75-1983/84, annual rpt, 4824–2.18

Personal consumption expenditures, natl income and product account, *Survey of Current Business,* monthly rpt, monthly and annual tables, 2702–1.23

Puerto Rico educational enrollment, finance, completions, curricula, and personnel by instn, and health and vital statistics, selected years 1970-83, hearings, 21348–93

see also Student aid

Tulare, Calif.

Census of Housing, 1980: occupancy and unit characteristics, by race, Hispanic origin, and city, SMSA rpt, 2473–1.363

Census of Population and Housing, 1980: detailed population and housing characteristics, by county, city, and census tract, SMSA rpt, 2551–2.363

Housing vacancy rates for single and multifamily units and mobile homes, by city and ZIP code, 1983, annual metro area rpt, 9304–20.10

Housing vacancy rates for single and multifamily units and mobile homes, by city and ZIP code, 1984, annual metro area rpt, 9304–20.18

see also under By SMSA or MSA in the "Index by Categories"

Tulsa, Okla.

Census of Housing, 1980: occupancy and unit characteristics, by race, Hispanic origin, and city, SMSA rpt, 2473–1.356

Census of Population and Housing, 1980: detailed population and housing characteristics, by county, city, and census tract, SMSA rpt, 2551–2.356

Homeless population and characteristics, and temporary shelter operations, use, and user characteristics, for selected cities, various periods 1979-84, hearing, 21248–85

Wages of office and plant workers, by occupation, 1984 labor market area survey rpt, 6785–3.6

see also under By City and By SMSA or MSA in the "Index by Categories"

Tung nuts and oil

see Oils, oilseeds, and fats

Tungsten

see Metals and metal industries

Tunisia

Agricultural and food production indexes, and production of selected commodities, by world region and country, 1974-83, annual rpt, 1524–5

Agricultural situation in Middle East and North Africa, by country and commodity, 1983 and outlook for 1984, annual rpt, 1524–4.3

Agricultural supply/demand, trade, and production, and socioeconomic data, by country, 1950s-77, 1528–179

AID activities and funding by project and function, FY85, and developing countries summary socioeconomic data, 1970s-83, by country, annual rpt, 9914–3

AID economic assistance to developing countries, obligations and disbursements by country, quarterly rpt, 9912–4

AID loan repayment status and terms by program and country, and status of predecessor agency loans, quarterly rpt, 9912–3

Background Notes, summary social, political, and economic data, 1984 rpt, 7006–2.54

Economic, social, and political summary data, by country, 1984, annual factbook, 244–11

Exports of US, detailed Schedule B commodities by country of destination, 1983, annual rpt, 2424–9

Exports of US, detailed Schedule E commodities by mode of transport and world area and country of destination, 1983, annual rpts, 2424–5

Imports of US, detailed Schedule A commodities by country and world area of origin, and mode of transport, 1983, annual rpts, 2424–2

Imports of US, detailed TSUSA commodities by country of origin, 1983, annual rpt, 2424–4

Loans and grants for economic and military assistance from US and intl agencies, by program and country, FY46-83, annual rpt, 9914–5

Military aid of US, arms sales, and training programs costs and budget requests by program, world region, and country, FY83-85, annual rpt, 7144–13

Military spending, arms trade, and armed forces size, with total govt spending and population, by country, 1972-82, annual rpt, 9824–1

Index by Subjects and Names

Minerals Yearbook, 1982, Vol 3: foreign country reviews of production, trade, and policies, by commodity, annual rpt, 5604–35

Minerals Yearbook, 1983, Vol 3 preprints: foreign country review of production, trade, and policies, by commodity, annual rpt, 5604–23.73

Oil and gas undiscovered recoverable resources, cumulative production, and identified reserves, as of 1982, preliminary oil basin rpt, 5666–17.13

Population size and growth rates, and latest available benchmark demographic data, by country, 1950-83, biennial rpt, 2324–4

see also under By Foreign Country in the "Index by Categories"

Turkey

Agricultural and food production indexes, and production of selected commodities, by world region and country, 1974-83, annual rpt, 1524–5

Agricultural situation in Middle East and North Africa, by country and commodity, 1983 and outlook for 1984, annual rpt, 1524–4.3

Agricultural supply/demand, trade, and production, and socioeconomic data, by country, 1950s-77, 1528–179

AID activities and funding by project and function, FY85, and developing countries summary socioeconomic data, 1970s-83, by country, annual rpt, 9914–3

AID economic assistance to developing countries, obligations and disbursements by country, quarterly rpt, 9912–4

AID loan repayment status and terms by program and country, and status of predecessor agency loans, quarterly rpt, 9912–3

Almond production and trade of US and selected countries, 1982/83-1983/84 and forecast 1985, article, 1925–34.425

Economic conditions, income, production, prices, employment, and trade, 1984 annual country rpt, 2046–4.120

Economic conditions, investment and export opportunities, and trade practices, 1983 country market research rpt, 2046–6.8

Economic, social, and political summary data, by country, 1984, annual factbook, 244–11

Exports and imports of NATO countries with Council for Mutual Economic Assistance Europe members, by country, 1980-83, annual rpt, 7144–5

Exports and imports of NATO countries with PRC, by country, 1980-83, annual rpt, 7144–14

Exports and imports of OECD countries, by country, 1983, annual rpt, 7144–10

Exports and imports of US with Western Europe, and US market share and export opportunities for selected commodities, by country, 1982-84, 2048–105

Exports of US, detailed Schedule B commodities by country of destination, 1983, annual rpt, 2424–9

Exports of US, detailed Schedule E commodities by mode of transport and world area and country of destination, 1983, annual rpts, 2424–5

Farm land improvement and farm machinery manufacturing in Turkey, impact of AID-Turkish govt joint assistance project, 1968-74, 9916–1.50

Index by Subjects and Names

Filbert production and trade of US and selected countries, 1981/82-1984/85, article, 1925–34.426

Imports of US, detailed Schedule A commodities by country and world area of origin, and mode of transport, 1983, annual rpts, 2424–2

Imports of US, detailed TSUSA commodities by country of origin, 1983, annual rpt, 2424–4

Loans and grants for economic and military assistance from US and intl agencies, by program and country, FY46-83, annual rpt, 9914–5

Military aid of US, arms sales, and training programs costs and budget requests by program, world region, and country, FY83-85, annual rpt, 7144–13

Military spending, arms trade, and armed forces size, with total govt spending and population, by country, 1972-82, annual rpt, 9824–1

Minerals Yearbook, 1982, Vol 3: foreign country reviews of production, trade, and policies, by commodity, annual rpt, 5604–35

Minerals Yearbook, 1982, Vol 3 preprints: foreign country review of production, trade, and policies, by commodity, annual rpt, 5604–17.73

Nuclear power plant construction and operation status, and capacity, by plant, region, State, and selected country, 1983 and projected to 2020, annual rpt, 3164–57

Population size and growth rates, and latest available benchmark demographic data, by country, 1950-83, biennial rpt, 2324–4

Raisin production, trade, consumption, and stocks of US and 3 countries, and US exports by country, various periods 1982/83-1984/85, article, 1925–34.434

Walnut production, stocks, use, and exports of US and 4 countries, and EC export subsidy, selected years 1977-1984/85, article, 1925–34.429

see also under By Foreign Country in the "Index by Categories"

Turkeys

see Poultry industry and products

Turnover of labor

see Labor turnover

Turpentine

see Gum and wood chemicals

Tuscaloosa, Ala.

Census of Housing, 1980: occupancy and unit characteristics, by race, Hispanic origin, and city, SMSA rpt, 2473–1.357

Census of Population and Housing, 1980: detailed population and housing characteristics, by county, city, and census tract, SMSA rpt, 2551–2.357

see also under By SMSA or MSA in the "Index by Categories"

Tuvalu

Economic, social, and political summary data, by country, 1984, annual factbook, 244–11

Population size and growth rates, and latest available benchmark demographic data, by country, 1950-83, biennial rpt, 2324–4

see also under By Foreign Country in the "Index by Categories"

TVA

see Tennessee Valley Authority

Twin Falls, Idaho

Traffic accidents alcohol-related in 3 Idaho counties, effect of reduction program, model results, 1970-80, article, 7762–9.404

Tyler, Tex.

Census of Housing, 1980: occupancy and unit characteristics, by race, Hispanic origin, and city, SMSA rpt, 2473–1.358

Census of Population and Housing, 1980: detailed population and housing characteristics, by county, city, and census tract, SMSA rpt, 2551–2.358

see also under By SMSA or MSA in the "Index by Categories"

Typewriters

see Office furniture and equipment

Uceda, Gustavo

"Louisiana: Hopes Ride on World Trade, Energy and World's Fair", 9371–1.407

Uganda

Agricultural and food production indexes, and production of selected commodities, by world region and country, 1974-83, annual rpt, 1524–5

Agricultural situation in sub-Saharan Africa, by country, 1982-83 and outlook for 1984, annual rpt, 1524–4.10

AID activities and funding by project and function, FY85, and developing countries summary socioeconomic data, 1970s-83, by country, annual rpt, 9914–3

AID economic assistance to developing countries, obligations and disbursements by country, quarterly rpt, 9912–4

AID loan repayment status and terms by program and country, and status of predecessor agency loans, quarterly rpt, 9912–3

Economic conditions and foreign marketing prospects in 46 Sub-Saharan countries, 1983 world region rpt, 2046–5.1

Economic, social, and political summary data, by country, 1984, annual factbook, 244–11

Exports of US, detailed Schedule B commodities by country of destination, 1983, annual rpt, 2424–9

Exports of US, detailed Schedule E commodities by mode of transport and world area and country of destination, 1983, annual rpts, 2424–5

Imports of US, detailed Schedule A commodities by country and world area of origin, and mode of transport, 1983, annual rpts, 2424–2

Imports of US, detailed TSUSA commodities by country of origin, 1983, annual rpt, 2424–4

Loans and grants for economic and military assistance from US and intl agencies, by program and country, FY46-83, annual rpt, 9914–5

Military aid of US, arms sales, and training programs costs and budget requests by program, world region, and country, FY83-85, annual rpt, 7144–13

Military spending, arms trade, and armed forces size, with total govt spending and population, by country, 1972-82, annual rpt, 9824–1

Unemployment insurance

Minerals Yearbook, 1982, Vol 3: foreign country reviews of production, trade, and policies, by commodity, annual rpt, 5604–35

Minerals Yearbook, 1982, Vol 3 preprints: foreign country review of production, trade, and policies, by commodity, annual rpt, 5604–17.83

Population size and growth rates, and latest available benchmark demographic data, by country, 1950-83, biennial rpt, 2324–4

see also under By Foreign Country in the "Index by Categories"

Uhrig, J. William

"Soybean Outlook Discussion", 1004–16.1

Ulcers

see Digestive diseases

Ulrich, Alice H.

"U.S. Timber Production, Trade, Consumption, and Price Statistics, 1950-83", 1204–29

Umm al-Qaiwain

see United Arab Emirates

Unconventional warfare

see Chemical and biological warfare agents

see Guerrilla warfare

see Underground movements

Underdeveloped countries

see Developing countries

Underground movements

Central America socioeconomic and political conditions in 6 countries, 1960s-83 with trends and projections 1930-2010, Commission rpt, 028–19.2

Terrorist (intl) incidents, casualties, and attacks on US targets, by attack type and world area, with chronology of events, 1983, annual rpt, 7004–13

Unemployment

see Employment and unemployment, general

see Employment and unemployment, local and regional

see Employment and unemployment, specific industries

see Public welfare programs

see Social security

see Unemployment insurance

see Unemployment insurance tax

see Work Incentive Program

Unemployment insurance

AFDC eligibility under Omnibus Budget Reconciliation Act, effect on caseloads and recipient benefits and living costs, 1981-83, GAO rpt, 26131–11

Beneficiaries of noncash public and employer-based transfer programs, by income source and socioeconomic characteristics, 1982, final Current Population Rpt, 2546–6.37

Beneficiaries, taxes collected, and State program operations by State, since 1940, monthly rpt, 4742–1.1, 4742–1.7

Benefit overpayment detection and recovery from random audit program in selected States, 1975-82 and projected to FY86, GAO rpt, 26121–77

Benefits and claims, by unemployment insurance program, Monthly Labor Review, 6722–1.4

Benefits, beneficiary characteristics, and trust funds of OASDHI, Medicaid, SSI, and other social insurance and public welfare programs, selected years 1950-82, annual rpt, 4744–3.9, 4744–3.10

Unemployment insurance

Benefits, claims, and exhaustions, 1946-83, annual rpt, 204–1.2

Budget of US Appendix, detailed budgets and personnel summaries, by agency, FY85, annual rpt, 104–3

Budget of US, CBO analysis and review of FY85 budget by function, annual rpt, 26304–2

Budget of US, compact budgets by function, agency, and account, FY85 with projections to FY89, annual rpt, 104–2

Budget of US, effects of Reagan Admin policy changes, by detailed program, FY85, annual rpt, 104–21

Budget of US, receipts by source and outlays by function, FY40-89 estimates revised for consistency with FY85 budget definitions, annual rpt, 104–12

Child support overdue payments deducted from income tax refunds and unemployment benefits, by State, FY83, annual rpt, 4004–16.3

Children and youth benefitting from Fed Govt public welfare programs and tax expenditures, participation and funding for 71 programs, FY81-83, 21968–30

Claims (weekly initial) under State programs, *Business Conditions Digest,* cyclical indicators, monthly rpt, 2702–3.3

Claims, insured unemployment, and exhaustions, by program, weekly rpt, 6402–14

Claims, weekly initial, under State programs, *Business Conditions Digest,* historical supplement and methodology, 1947-82, 2708–31

Economic indicators and components, current data and annual trends, monthly rpt, 23842–1.2

Employment and labor force statistics by major industry group and demographic characteristics, *Survey of Current Business,* monthly rpt, 2702–1.5

Employment and wages of workers covered by State unemployment insurance laws and Fed Govt unemployment compensation, by SIC 4-digit industry and State, 1982, annual rpt, 6744–16

Fed Govt aid to State and local govts, expenditures, and direct payments, by program, agency, and State, FY83, annual rpt, 2464–2

Fed Govt programs under Ways and Means Committee jurisdiction, program operations and financing data for assessing budgetary requirements, by State, FY70s-83, 21788–117

Fed Govt unemployment insurance trust fund, receipts, expenditures, assets, and liabilities, quarterly rpt, 8102–9.1

Finances, claims, benefits, and covered employment and wages, by State, including Federal-State extended benefits, 1938-82, 6408–5

Foreign social security programs coverage, funding, eligibility, and benefits, by country, 1983, biennial rpt, 4746–4.58

Fraud in Fed Govt benefit programs and other unreported taxable income from illegal activities, with methodology and bibl, 1970s-82, 8008–112

Govt expenditures for social welfare by program and level of govt, and private expenditures for health care, selected years FY50-82, annual article, 4742–1.425

Govt revenues by source, expenditures by function, debt, and assets, by level of govt, 1982-83, annual rpt, 2466–2.6

Income (household) and cash and noncash transfer program participation, by sociodemographic characteristics, quarterly rpt, 2542–2

Income (personal), and BEA and IRS calculations of adjusted gross income, by source, 1981-82, article, 2702–1.414

Income (personal) by source including transfer payments, and social insurance contributions by type, by region, 1982, 2708–40

Income from transfer payments, natl income and product account, *Survey of Current Business,* monthly rpt, monthly and annual tables, 2702–1.23

Income tax returns of individuals, by filing and deduction characteristics and income level, 1983, annual article, 8302–2.414

Income tax returns of individuals, detailed data, 1982, annual rpt, 8304–2

Income tax returns of individuals, selected income, deduction, and tax credit data by income, preliminary 1982, annual article, 8302–2.402

Labor Dept activities and staff, CETA participants characteristics, and employment service and unemployment insurance activities by State, FY83, annual rpt, 6304–1

Older persons income and income sources, by OASDI beneficiary and poverty status, labor force participation, and demographic characteristics, 1982, biennial rpt, 4744–26

Poverty-level persons and families, by income source, hours of work, earnings, taxes, and family characteristics, various periods 1959-84, 21788–131

Poverty rate by family composition, and effect of noncash transfers, taxes, unemployment benefits, and business cycles, selected years 1959-82, hearings, 21788–141

Railroad employee benefits and beneficiaries by type, and railroad employees and payrolls, FY82, annual rpt, 9704–2

Railroad employee benefits and beneficiaries by type, benefit program finances, and railroad employees and payroll, FY83, annual rpt, 9704–1

Railroad employee retirement, survivors, unemployment, and sickness insurance programs, monthly rpt, 9702–2

State and local govt productivity measurement, with background data and output indexes for 7 govt services, various periods 1955-82, 6728–27

State govt revenues by source, expenditures by function, debt, and holdings by type, FY83, annual rpt, 2466–2.5

State govt unemployment insurance program admin, quality appraisal results, FY84, annual rpt, 6404–16

State unemployment insurance benefits, coverage, and tax provisions, July 1984, semiannual listing, 6402–7

State unemployment insurance laws, changes in coverage, benefits, and tax rates, for 43 States and DC, 1983 annual article, 6722–1.414

State unemployment insurance laws, comparisons of provisions, as of Sept 1984, semiannual revision, 6402–2

Index by Subjects and Names

Texas border employment and economic impacts of Mexican peso devaluation, for 6 counties and 2 SMSAs, 1970s-May 1983, hearing, 21788–133

Veterans of Vietnam era, unemployment rates and compensation, compared with WW II and Korea veterans, FY83, annual rpt, 9924–8.2

Wages of workers covered by unemployment insurance, by industry div, State, and MSA, 1981-83, annual press releases, 6784–17

see also Unemployment insurance tax

Unemployment insurance tax

Budget of US, receipts by source and outlays by agency and program, monthly rpt, 8102–3

Employers by unemployment insurance tax rate category, with probability of changing categories, FY75-78, article, 6722–1.469

Fed Govt internal revenue, by type of tax, quarterly rpt, 8302–2.1

Fed Govt programs under Ways and Means Committee jurisdiction, program operations and financing data for assessing budgetary requirements, by State, FY70s-83, 21788–117

Fed Govt receipts by source and outlays by agency, *Treasury Bulletin,* quarterly rpt, 8002–4.1

Finances, claims, benefits, and covered employment and wages, by State, including Federal-State extended benefits, 1938-82, 6408–5

Foreign social security programs coverage, funding, eligibility, and benefits, by country, 1983, biennial rpt, 4746–4.58

Income (personal) by source including transfer payments, and social insurance contributions by type, by region, 1982, 2708–40

IRS collections, FY83, annual rpt, 8104–2.2

IRS tax collections by type of tax, procedures, and interest forgone through processing delay, for selected locations, FY81-82, GAO rpt, 26119–55

Natl income and product revised estimates, adjustment for misreporting of income tax returns info, 1977, article, 2702–1.422

Railroad employee retirement, survivors, unemployment, and sickness insurance programs, monthly rpt, 9702–2

State unemployment insurance benefits, coverage, and tax provisions, July 1984, semiannual listing, 6402–7

State unemployment insurance laws, changes in coverage, benefits, and tax rates, for 43 States and DC, 1983 annual article, 6722–1.414

State unemployment insurance laws, comparisons of provisions, as of Sept 1984, semiannual revision, 6402–2

Taxes collected and beneficiaries for social insurance programs, monthly rpt, 4742–1.1

see also Labor cost indexes

Unemployment Trust Fund

see Federal trust funds

Unions

see Labor unions

United Arab Emirates

Agricultural situation in Middle East and North Africa, by country and commodity, 1983 and outlook for 1984, annual rpt, 1524–4.3

Index by Subjects and Names

United Kingdom

AID economic assistance to developing countries, obligations and disbursements by country, quarterly rpt, 9912–4

AID loan repayment status and terms by program and country, and status of predecessor agency loans, quarterly rpt, 9912–3

Economic, social, and political summary data, by country, 1984, annual factbook, 244–11

Economic trends in income, production, prices, employment, finances, and trade, 1984 annual rpt, 2046–4.17

Exports and imports of US, by commodity and country, 1972-82, annual world region rpt, 244–13.1

Exports of US, detailed Schedule B commodities by country of destination, 1983, annual rpt, 2424–9

Exports of US, detailed Schedule E commodities by mode of transport and world area and country of destination, 1983, annual rpts, 2424–5

Imports of US, detailed Schedule A commodities by country and world area of origin, and mode of transport, 1983, annual rpts, 2424–2

Imports of US, detailed TSUSA commodities by country of origin, 1983, annual rpt, 2424–4

Military aid of US, arms sales, and training programs costs and budget requests by program, world region, and country, FY83-85, annual rpt, 7144–13

Military spending, arms trade, and armed forces size, with total govt spending and population, by country, 1972-82, annual rpt, 9824–1

Minerals Yearbook, 1982, Vol 3: foreign country reviews of production, trade, and policies, by commodity, annual rpt, 5604–35

Minerals Yearbook, 1983, Vol 3 preprints: foreign country review of production, trade, and policies, by commodity, annual rpt, 5604–23.75

Oil production and exports, by major exporting country, detailed data, monthly rpt, 3162–24

Population size and growth rates, and latest available benchmark demographic data, by country, 1950-83, biennial rpt, 2324–4

Telecommunication equipment market and trade, and user industry operations and demand, 1982 country market research rpt, 2045–12.32

see also under By Foreign Country in the "Index by Categories"

United Arab Republic

see Egypt

United Church of Christ

"Cable System Employment, 1980-81: A Report on the Status of Minorities and Women", 21368–45

United Kingdom

Agricultural and food production indexes, and production of selected commodities, by world region and country, 1974-83, annual rpt, 1524–5

Agricultural situation in Western Europe, by country and commodity, 1983 and outlook for 1984, annual rpt, 1524–4.6

Agricultural supply/demand, trade, and production, and socioeconomic data, by country, 1950s-77, 1528–179

AID loan repayment status and terms by program and country, and status of predecessor agency loans, quarterly rpt, 9912–3

Auto and auto products sales, prices, and registrations in US, and trade of 8 countries with US, by make and model, 1964-83, annual rpt, 9884–7

Auto safety and experimental vehicle designs, 1982, conf proceedings, annual rpt, 7764–3

Background Notes, summary social, political, and economic data, 1984 rpt, 7006–2.16

Biotechnology commercial uses, R&D funding and output, controls, and industry financial and operating data, for US and 5 countries, 1970s-83 and estimated 1984-85, 26358–98

Choline chloride from Canada and UK at less than fair value, imports injury to US industry, investigation with background financial and operating data, 1983 rpt, 9886–14.90

Computers and computer equipment market and trade, and user industry operations and demand, 1984 country market research rpt, 2045–1.50

Current account deficits, and financing by source, for US and 5 OECD countries, selected years 1973-1st qtr 1984, article, 9385–1.409

Dollar holdings rate of return related to domestic real money stock for 5 OECD countries, regression results, various periods 1966-84, article, 9391–1.418

Drug (animal) approval of govts, months to approval in US and 2 countries by drug brand and manufacturer, selected years 1965-83, hearing, 25528–98

Economic and monetary trends, compounded annual rates of change for US and 10 major trading partners, quarterly rpt, 9391–7

Economic conditions, consumer and stock prices and production indexes, 6 OECD countries and US, *Business Conditions Digest,* monthly rpt, 2702–3.10, 2708–31

Economic conditions in Communist, OECD, and selected other countries, 1960s-83, annual rpt, 244–5

Economic indicator performance in UK under Thatcher govt, with OECD comparisons, 1970-1983/84, article, 9391–1.414

Economic indicators and oil use and imports for US and 6 OECD countries, and oil production by country, biweekly rpt, 242–4

Economic indicators and trade balance of US and 4 countries, effect of US budget deficits, model results, various periods 1974-85, technical paper, 9366–7.102

Economic indicators for 7 OECD countries and US, quarterly rpt, 2042–10

Economic, social, and political summary data, by country, 1984, annual factbook, 244–11

Economic trends in income, production, prices, employment, finances, and trade, 1984 semiannual rpt, 2046–4.75

Employment, labor force, and participation and unemployment rates by sex, in US and 9 OECD countries, various periods 1970-3rd qtr 1983, annual article, 6722–1.404

Energy prices and taxes by energy source and end-use sector, for US and 9 OECD countries, quarterly 1979-83, annual rpt, 3164–71

Energy production by type, and oil prices, trade, and consumption, by country group and selected country, monthly rpt, 242–5

Export credit program activities of Eximbank and 6 OECD countries, 1982, annual rpt, 9254–3

Exports and imports, intl position of US and 4 OECD countries, and factors affecting US competition, quarterly pamphlet, 2042–25

Exports and imports of NATO countries with Council for Mutual Economic Assistance Europe members, by country, 1980-83, annual rpt, 7144–5

Exports and imports of NATO countries with PRC, by country, 1980-83, annual rpt, 7144–14

Exports and imports of OECD countries, by country, 1983, annual rpt, 7144–10

Exports and imports of OECD, total and for 4 major countries, and US trade by country, by commodity, 1972-82, annual world region rpt series, 244–13

Exports and imports of US, by commodity group, world area, selected country, US coastal area and port, and mode of transport, with seasonal adjustments, monthly rpt, 2422–9

Exports and imports of US, detailed SIC-based commodities by world area, 1983, annual rpts, 2424–6

Exports and imports of US with Western Europe, and US market share and export opportunities for selected commodities, by country, 1982-84, 2048–105

Exports of US, detailed Schedule B commodities by country of destination, 1983, annual rpt, 2424–9

Exports of US, detailed Schedule E commodities by mode of transport and world area and country of destination, 1983, annual rpts, 2424–5

Farmland (US) owned by foreigners, acreage, value, and use, by State and county, and for 5 leading investor countries, 1983, annual rpt, 1584–3

Finance (intl) and financial policy, external factors affecting US economy, econometric model methodology and results for US and 4 countries, various periods 1964-75, 9368–78

Fish and shellfish wholesale prices and market activity in 8 West Europe countries, weekly rpt, 2162–8

Food retail outlets in UK by type, 1970s-82, and US agricultural exports to UK by commodity, FY81-83, article, 1925–34.406

Food supply/demand and market and support prices, with exchange rates, fertilizer price index, GDP, and population, by EC country, 1960-83, 1528–173

Health care resources, use, and per capita public expenditures, and selected population characteristics, for US and 6 countries, selected years 1975-81, 21148–33

Imports of US, detailed Schedule A commodities by country and world area of origin, and mode of transport, 1983, annual rpts, 2424–2

ASI Annual Supplement 821

United Kingdom

Imports of US, detailed TSUSA commodities by country of origin, 1983, annual rpt, 2424–4

- Industrial production indexes of 7 OECD countries and US, biweekly rpt, periodic article, 2042–24
- Interest rates and budget balances of US and 6 OECD countries, 1973-83, annual rpt, 26304–3.1
- Investment (foreign direct) in US, major investors and investments by SIC 4-digit industry, transaction type and value, and location, 1983, annual rpt, 2044–20
- Loans and grants for economic and military assistance from US and intl agencies, by program and country, FY46-83, annual rpt, 9914–5
- Manufacturing labor productivity and cost indexes for US and 11 OECD countries, 1960-82, annual article, 6722–1.405
- Manufacturing productivity and unit labor cost indexes for US and 11 countries, 1950-82 and preliminary 1983, annual rpt, 6864–1
- Manufacturing wage growth in US and 2 countries, regression results, 1963-81, technical paper, 9381–10.34
- Manufacturing wage/price and wage/output adjustment in 6 OECD countries, 1960-81, technical paper, 9381–10.33
- Military aid of US, arms sales, and training programs costs and budget requests by program, world region, and country, FY83-85, annual rpt, 7144–13
- Military pension lifetime earnings in US and 7 countries, as of 1983, 26306–6.76
- Military spending, arms trade, and armed forces size, with total govt spending and population, by country, 1972-82, annual rpt, 9824–1
- Military weapons transfers to developing countries from US, USSR, and Europe, by weapon type and world region, 1974-82, 25948–3
- *Minerals Yearbook, 1982,* Vol 3: foreign country reviews of production, trade, and policies, by commodity, annual rpt, 5604–35
- *Minerals Yearbook, 1983,* Vol 3 preprints: foreign country review of production, trade, and policies, by commodity, annual rpt, 5604–23.76
- Monetary control policy of US and selected West European countries, and relation to credit, exchange rates, GNP, and other indicators, various periods 1960-82, conf papers, 9373–3.26
- Money supply growth and inflation rates related to public and private monetary control, 1694-1913, article, 9391–1.410
- Nuclear power generation in US and 18 non-Communist countries, monthly rpt, 3162–24.10
- Nuclear power plant construction and operation status, and capacity, by plant, region, State, and selected country, 1983 and projected to 2020, annual rpt, 3164–57
- Oil and gas undiscovered recoverable resources, cumulative production, and identified reserves, as of 1982, preliminary oil basin rpt, 5666–17.15
- Oil production, consumption, stocks, and exports and prices to US, by major exporting and consuming country, detailed data, monthly rpt, 3162–24

Population size and growth rates, and latest available benchmark demographic data, by country, 1950-83, biennial rpt, 2324–4

- Price indexes for consumer and producer goods, major commodities, exports, imports, nonfarm wages, and currency value, US and 4 countries, bimonthly rpt, 2042–11
- R&D expenditures and employment in science and technology, for US and 4 countries, selected years 1953-84, annual rpt, 9624–18.1
- Rail high-speed systems and railcar production of US and selected countries, with major cities population and land area, 1940s-82, 26358–97
- *Science Indicators,* R&D expenditures, innovations, research, and higher education, with foreign comparisons, 1960s- 83, annual rpt, 9624–10.1
- Ships in world merchant fleet, and tonnage, by country of registry, 1982, annual rpt, 7704–3.1
- Space launchings attaining Earth orbit or beyond, by country, 1957-83, annual rpt, 9504–9.1
- Space satellites and other objects launched since 1957, quarterly listing, 9502–2
- Sporting goods and recreational equipment and vehicles market and trade, 1984 country market research rpt, 2045–14.8
- Steel imports of US from EC and other countries, and US industry operating data, for 15 products limited under arrangement with EC, monthly rpt, 9882–10
- Telecommunication equipment market and trade, and user industry operations and demand, 1982 country market research rpt, 2045–12.37
- Titanium sponge from Japan and UK at less than fair value, imports injury to US industry, investigation with background financial and operating data, 1984 rpt, 9886–14.94, 9886–14.129
- Trade promotion policies and industry financing of EC, and effect on competing US industries, 1970s-82, 9886–4.73
- Travel to and from US, by world area and selected country, projected 1984-85, annual rpt, 2904–9
- Tuberculosis death rates in NYC, UK, and Prussia, selected years 1865-1920, article, 4102–1.431
- *see also* Gibraltar
- *see also* under By Foreign Country in the "Index by Categories"

United Mine Workers of America

"Employment Impacts of Acid Rain", 21368–52

United Nations

- AID activities and funding by project and function, FY85, and developing countries summary socioeconomic data, 1970s-83, by country, annual rpt, 9914–3
- *Background Notes,* UN history, structure, and programs, 1984 rpt, 7006–2.55
- Human rights conditions in 162 countries, economic and military aid of US, and economic aid of intl organizations, 1981-83, annual rpt, 21384–3
- Loans and grants for economic and military assistance from US and intl agencies, by program and country, FY46-83, annual rpt, 9914–5

Index by Subjects and Names

- PL 480 exports by commodity, and recipients, by program, sponsor, and country, FY82 and aggregate from FY55, annual rpt, 1924–7
- US participation in UN, and member and nonmember shares of UN budget by country, FY83-85, annual rpt, 7004–5
- *see also* International Atomic Energy Agency
- *see also* International Bank for Reconstruction and Development
- *see also* International Development Association
- *see also* International employees
- *see also* International Finance Corp.
- *see also* International Monetary Fund

Universities

see Higher education

University of Kentucky

Nursing continuing education in maternal and child health at University of Kentucky, course enrollment and student assessment of career value, 1983 article, 4102–1.405

University of Puerto Rico

Enrollment, tuition, construction costs, degrees granted, personnel by sex, and Fed Govt funding of medical research, 1970s-87, hearings, 21348–93

Unmanned space programs

- *see* Communications satellites
- *see* Meteorological satellites
- *see* Space programs

Upper Volta

- Agricultural and food production indexes, and production of selected commodities, by world region and country, 1974-83, annual rpt, 1524–5
- Agricultural situation in sub-Saharan Africa, by country, 1982-83 and outlook for 1984, annual rpt, 1524–4.10
- Agricultural supply/demand, trade, and production, and socioeconomic data, by country, 1950s-77, 1528–179
- AID activities and funding by project and function, FY85, and developing countries summary socioeconomic data, 1970s-83, by country, annual rpt, 9914–3
- AID economic assistance to developing countries, obligations and disbursements by country, quarterly rpt, 9912–4
- *Background Notes,* summary social, political, and economic data, 1984 rpt, 7006–2.30
- Economic conditions and foreign marketing prospects in 46 Sub-Saharan countries, 1983 world region rpt, 2046–5.1
- Economic, social, and political summary data, by country, 1984, annual factbook, 244–11
- Economic trends in income, production, prices, employment, finances, and trade, 1984 annual rpt, 2046–4.76
- Exports of US, detailed Schedule B commodities by country of destination, 1983, annual rpt, 2424–9
- Exports of US, detailed Schedule E commodities by mode of transport and world area and country of destination, 1983, annual rpts, 2424–5
- Imports of US, detailed Schedule A commodities by country and world area of origin, and mode of transport, 1983, annual rpts, 2424–2

Index by Subjects and Names

Urban areas

Imports of US, detailed TSUSA commodities by country of origin, 1983, annual rpt, 2424–4

Loans and grants for economic and military assistance from US and intl agencies, by program and country, FY46-83, annual rpt, 9914–5

Military aid of US, arms sales, and training programs costs and budget requests by program, world region, and country, FY83-85, annual rpt, 7144–13

Military spending, arms trade, and armed forces size, with total govt spending and population, by country, 1972-82, annual rpt, 9824–1

Minerals Yearbook, 1982, Vol 3: foreign country reviews of production, trade, and policies, by commodity, annual rpt, 5604–35

Minerals Yearbook, 1982, Vol 3 preprints: foreign country review of production, trade, and policies, by commodity, annual rpt, 5604–17.84

Population size and growth rates, and latest available benchmark demographic data, by country, 1950-83, biennial rpt, 2324–4

see also under By Foreign Country in the "Index by Categories"

Uranium

Alaska minerals resources, production, claims on wildlife refuges, oil and gas leases, and exploratory wells, with maps and bibl, 1983, annual rpt, 5664–11

Budget of US, effects of Reagan Admin policy changes, by detailed program, FY85, annual rpt, 104–21

County Business Patterns: establishments, employees, and payrolls, by SIC 4-digit industry and county, 1982, annual State rpt series, 2326–6

Electric power plant capital and operating detailed costs, capacity, and fuel use, by plant, plant type, utility, and State, 1982, annual rpt, 3164–9

Employment in nongovt nuclear industries by industry segment, occupation, and census div, with DOE and NRC nuclear employment, 1968-83, biennial rpt, 3004–11

Enrichment by DOE, prices under alternative TVA power rates and effects of TVA charges for power not taken, FY84-95, GAO rpt, 26113–114

Enrichment facilities operations, finances, uranium stocks, and energy use and capital investment by facility, FY83, annual rpt, 3354–7

Enrichment plants of DOE, production and other costs and selling prices, FY71-83 and projected to FY94, GAO rpt, 26113–137

Enrichment service and uranium fuel demand and spent fuel of nuclear power plants, for US and non-Communist country groups, 1983 and projected to 2020, annual rpt, 3164–72

Exploration, land acquisition expenditures, and employment, various periods 1966-83 and planned 1984-85, annual rpt, 3164–65

Exports and imports of US, detailed SIC-based commodities by world area, 1983, annual rpts, 2424–6

Exports and imports of US, totals and as percent of domestic production, by SIC 2- to 5-digit commodity, 1981, annual rpt, 2424–3

Exports, imports, tariffs, and industry operating data for uranium and uranium compounds, 1979-83, TSUSA commodity rpt supplement, 9885–4.47

Exports of US, detailed commodities by country of destination, monthly rpt, 2422–3

Exports of US, detailed Schedule E commodities by mode of transport and world area and country of destination, 1983, annual rpts, 2424–5

Fed Govt energy programs proposed budget appropriations, by office or dept and function, FY84-85, annual rpt, 3004–14

Foreign expenditures in US uranium exploration, 1975-82, annual rpt, 3024–2

Foreign minerals production, reserves, and industry role in domestic economy and world supply, country and world region rpt series, 5606–1

Great Lakes radioactivity discharges by source, and concentrations in environment, various periods 1963-82, annual rpt, 14644–1.2

Imports of US, detailed Schedule A commodities by country and world area of origin, and mode of transport, 1983, annual rpts, 2424–2

Imports of US, detailed Schedule A commodities by country, monthly rpt, 2422–2

Imports of US, detailed TSUSA commodities by country of origin, 1983, annual rpt, 2424–4

Inventory discrepancies for strategic nuclear materials at DOE facilities, 1st half FY83, semiannual rpt, 3002–4

Mineral industries census, 1982: financial and operating data, by SIC 2- to 4-digit industry, preliminary summary rpt, 2511–2.1

Mineral industries census, 1982: financial and operating data, including materials consumed, by SIC 4-digit industry and State, preliminary rpt, 2511–1.3

Minerals Yearbook, 1982, Vol 1: commodity reviews of production, reserves, supply, use, and trade, annual rpt, 5604–33

Minerals Yearbook, 1982, Vol 2 preprints: State reviews of production and sales by commodity, and business activity, annual rpt series, 5604–16

Minerals Yearbook, 1982, Vol 2: State reviews of production, sales, and firms, by commodity, and business activity, annual rpt, 5604–34

Minerals Yearbook, 1982, Vol 3: foreign country reviews of production, trade, and policies, by commodity, annual rpt, 5604–35

Minerals Yearbook, 1982, Vol 3 preprints: foreign country reviews of production, trade, and policies, by commodity, annual rpt series, 5604–17

Minerals Yearbook, 1983, Vol 3 preprints: foreign country reviews of production, trade, and policies, by commodity, annual rpt series, 5604–23

Mining and milling industries operations and finances, and reserves, with selected foreign comparisons, various periods 1964-83 and projected to 2000, 3008–95

Mining operations, finances, and costs of alternative methods to meet emissions

standards, for uranium industry and selected mines, selected years 1948-90, 9188–96

Nuclear fuel facilities inventory discrepancies, 2nd half 1983, semiannual rpt, 9632–3

Nuclear power and weapons policy, fuel supply/demand, waste disposal and siting, environmental effects of radiation, and public attitudes, 1970s-82 with projections to 2000, 3008–88

Nuclear power plant fuel assembly performance and failures, by fuel vendor for US and some foreign reactors, 1982, annual rpt, 9634–8

Nuclear reactor components and other atomic energy products and services, orders, total and Fed Govt shipments, and exports, 1983, annual Current Industrial Rpt, 2506–12.27

Prices, deliveries, trade, stocks, secondary marketing, investment, and employment, selected years 1967-83 and for commitments to 2001, annual rpt, 3164–66

Producers finances and operations, by energy type for US firms domestic and foreign operations, 1974-82, annual rpt, 3164–44.2

Production, reserves, and prices, by fuel type, and selected indicators of energy use, by State, 1982-83 with selected comparisons from 1971, annual rpt, 3164–60

Production, trade, and reserves of uranium, quarterly compilation, 3352–3

Production, trade, supply, use, conservation, and DOE activities, by energy type, FY83, annual rpt, 3024–2

Radioactive waste and spent fuel generation, inventory, disposal by site, reprocessing, and characteristics, by source, as of 1983 and projected to 2020, annual rpt, 3364–2

Research publications on uranium resources, 1976-83, listing, 3358–27

Reserves, exploration, production, and other industry data, annual rpt, discontinued, 3404–7

Supply/demand and prices, by fuel type and consuming sector with foreign comparisons, 1949-83, annual rpt, 3164–74

Supply/demand and prices, by fuel type, sector, and end use, with foreign comparisons, 1960-83 and projected to 1995, annual summary rpt, 3164–76

TVA expenditures for nuclear fuel, FY79-83, annual rpt, 9804–23.2

Western US Fed Govt lands by agency and mining restriction status, and energy resources on potential wilderness areas and other lands, 1970s-81 and projected to 1990, 3308–68

see also Radioactive waste

Urban areas

Air quality and transportation and related energy use, for urban areas and Chicago area, late 1970s-82 and projected under lower auto emission standards to 1995, 3408–31

Assaults, murders, and other deaths of law enforcement officers, by circumstances, level of govt, agency, victim and offender characteristics, and location, 1983, annual rpt, 6224–3

Urban areas

Census of Govts, 1982: properties, govt-assessed value, sales, and tax rates, by property type, State, SMSA, county, and city, 2453–1

Census of Housing, 1980: occupancy and unit characteristics of SMSAs and central cities, by race, Hispanic origin, and city, State and SMSA rpt series, 2473–1

Census of Population, 1980: detailed socioeconomic characteristics, by county, city, and inside-outside SMSAs and central cities, State rpt series, 2531–3

CPI by component for US city average, and by region, population size, and for 28 SMSAs, monthly press release, 6762–1

CPI by detailed component, for US city average, 28 SMSAs, and 4 regions by population size, monthly rpt, 6762–2

Crimes, arrests by offender characteristics, and rates, by offense, and law enforcement employees, by population size and jurisdiction, 1970s-83, annual rpt, 6224–2

Economic distress index and components, for 153 cities, 1975 and 1980, article, 9373–1.413

Economic, fiscal, and social trends and problems of urban areas, 1950-83 and Fed Govt funding estimates for FY84-87, biennial rpt, 5124–4

Environmental quality and protection programs, costs, and Fed Govt enforcement, 1983, detailed annual rpt, 484–1

Food consumption and nutrient intake by individuals, by food group, source, and socioeconomic characteristics, 1977-78 natl survey, final rpt series, 1356–4

Foreign and US population by age and percent urban, for 7 countries, selected years 1975-81, 21148–33

Foreign population size and growth rates, and latest available benchmark demographic data, by country, 1950-83, biennial rpt, 2324–4

Foreign women sociodemographic, economic, and fertility characteristics, with comparisons to men, by country, 1960s-85, world region rpt series, 2326–15

Housing and neighborhood quality indicators and attitudes, and occupant characteristics, by urban-rural location and region, 1981, annual survey, 2485–7

Housing completions, and new unit sales price, cost per square foot, and heating fuel use, by metro-nonmetro area, 1976-82, 1598–190

Hwy Statistics, detailed data on traffic, govt finances, fuel use, vehicles, driver licenses, and hwy characteristics, by State, 1983, annual rpt, 7554–1

Income of families and persons, by sociodemographic characteristics, 1983, advance annual Current Population Rpt, 2546–6.41

Older persons by demographic, socioeconomic, and health characteristics, selected years 1900-81 and projected to 2050, Current Population Rpt, 2546–2.125

Pest control firms in urban areas, pesticide use by type, employment, and sales, by type of service, 1981 survey, article, 1561–16.408

Population size and change for metro and nonmetro areas and central cities by census div, and growth of areas with large black and aged populations, 1970-82, 2328–47

Population size, Apr 1980 and July 1982, and per capita income, 1979 and 1981, by county and city, State Current Population Rpt series, 2546–11

Regional councils involved in service activities, by type of service and region population size, 1982 survey, hearing, 25408–88

Statistical Abstract of US, social, political, and economic data, 1950s-83 and trends, annual rpt, 2324–1.1

Teenage girls births and sexual experience by race, abortions, and birth control use, by age, 1970s-80 with birth trends from 1920, hearings, 21968–29

Water from urban runoff, quality, pollutant concentrations, and control cost-effectiveness, with monitoring sites rainfall and other characteristics, by city and region, 1978-83, 9208–122

Western States housing outlook and economic and demographic trends, FHLB 11th District, urban area rpt series, 9306–2

see also Central business districts
see also Central cities
see also City and town planning
see also Community development programs
see also Federal aid to local areas
see also Federal-local relations
see also Metropolitan Statistical Areas
see also Neighborhoods
see also New towns
see also Open space land programs
see also Relocation
see also State-local relations
see also Suburbs
see also Urban beautification
see also Urban renewal
see also Urban transportation
see also Zoning and zoning laws
see also under By City, By SMSA or MSA, and By Urban-Rural and Metro-Nonmetro in the "Index by Categories"

Urban beautification

HUD community dev programs funding and activities, for 5 programs, FY83, annual rpt, 5124–5

Urban, Francis

"Patterns and Trends in World Agricultural Land Use", 1528–180

"Trends in World Agricultural Land Use", 1522–3.401

Urban Mass Transportation Administration

Cost control proposals for Fed Govt programs and mgmt, 3-year savings by function and agency, and financial and operating data, 1960s-81, 16908–1.11

Employment at DOT, by subagency, State, and selected personnel characteristics, FY83, annual rpt, 7304–18

Fraud and abuse in DOT programs, audits and investigations, 1st half FY84, semiannual rpt, 7302–4

Grants of UMTA for equipment, construction, and operation, annual rpt, discontinued, 7884–3

Grants of UMTA to higher education instns for research and training, by project, FY84, annual rpt, 7884–7

Motor vehicle safety program funding of 4 DOT agencies, FY80, 7768–80

Railroad commuter systems financial and operating data for 7 systems, and public agency cost reimbursement, 1980, 7888–61

Research publications on public transit, 2nd half FY83, semiannual listing, 7882–1

Subway accidents, deaths, injuries, and property damage, by type of accident and victim and cause, for 11 systems, 1983, annual rpt, 7884–5

Transit system (automated guideway) characteristics and itemized costs, for 16 systems in operation or under construction, 1982, annual rpt, 7884–6

Transit system financial and operating data, by mode, function, fleet size, and individual system, FY82, annual rpt, 7884–4

Transit system mgmt training funded by Urban Mass Transportation Admin, participant characteristics and career impact, 1970-79, 7888–60

Transit system operations, tax burden related to ridership, fares, and govt funding, for selected States and cities, 1950s-82, reprint, 7888–59

Urban travel by purpose, effect of telecommunication advances, land use changes, and alternative work schedules, projected to 2000 with some trends 1950-80, 7888–63

Women's travel patterns, by employment and sociodemographic characteristics and type of child care used, 1980 survey, 7888–62

Urban planning

see City and town planning

Urban renewal

Budget of US, effects of Reagan Admin policy changes, by detailed program, FY85, annual rpt, 104–21

Enterprise zone and urban revitalization projects of State and local govts, effect on business and employment in selected areas, various dates 1972-83, hearing, 21788–140

Fed Govt aid to State and local govts, expenditures, and direct payments, by program, agency, and State, FY83, annual rpt, 2464–2

Fed Govt aid to State and local govts, selected years 1950-83 and estimated FY84-87, biennial rpt, 5124–4

Financing project notes sold by local authorities, monthly press release, suspended, 5142–36

Govt employment and payroll, by function, level of govt, and jurisdiction, 1983, annual rpt series, 2466–1

Govt finances, by level of govt, State, and for large cities and counties, 1981-83, annual rpt series, 2466–2

HUD community dev programs funding and activities, for 5 programs, FY83, annual rpt, 5124–5

Local govt finances and population characteristics for cities and suburbs, by region and selected SMSA, selected years 1957-FY83, 10048–61

Urban Dev Action Grant awards to local areas, preliminary approvals, with project descriptions, private investment, and jobs and taxes to be created, by city, quarterly press release series, 5002–7

Index by Subjects and Names

Urogenital diseases

Urban Dev Action Grant program effectiveness, and participation of small cities by State, 1978-82, GAO rpt, 26113–118

see also Community Development Block Grants

see also Open space land programs

see also Relocation

see also Urban beautification

Urban Systems Research & Engineering, Inc.

"State Community Development Block Grant Program: The First Year's Experience", 5188–106

Urban transportation

- Bond tax-exempt issues for private activity, by purpose, face value, major industry, and State, 1983, article, 8302–2.417
- Budget of US, effects of Reagan Admin policy changes, by detailed program, FY85, annual rpt, 104–21
- Business statistics, detailed data for major industries and economic indicators, *Survey of Current Business,* monthly rpt, 2702–1.8
- Capital needs and intergovtl financing for public works, by type of project and selected city, various periods 1950-83, 10048–60
- Census of Housing, 1980: structural, financial, and householder characteristics, by region and State, 2475–4
- Census of Population and Housing, 1980: data coverage, availability, and uses for urban and transportation planning, 1984 guide, 7558–101
- Census of Population and Housing, 1980: detailed population and housing characteristics, by county, city, and census tract, State and SMSA rpt series, 2551–2
- Census of Population, 1980: detailed socioeconomic and demographic characteristics, by age, sex, race, Hispanic origin, occupation, and industry, State rpt series, 2531–4
- Census of Population, 1980: detailed socioeconomic characteristics, by county, city, and inside-outside SMSAs and central cities, State rpt series, 2531–3
- City govt revenue sharing program allocations and use by function, and response to program cuts, by city size and region, 1982 survey, hearings, 25408–86.2
- Collective bargaining agreements expiring during year, covered workers by SIC 2-digit industry, firm, and union, with summary of key provisions, 1984, annual rpt, 6784–9
- Commuting to work, householder principal mode of transport, distance, and travel time, by race, Hispanic origin, tenure, urban-rural location, and region, 1981, annual survey, 2485–7
- Construction industries census, 1982: financial and operating data, by SIC 4-digit industry and State, preliminary rpt series, 2371–1
- County Business Patterns: establishments, employees, and payrolls, by SIC 4-digit industry and county, 1982, annual State rpt series, 2326–6
- CPI by detailed component, for US city average, 28 SMSAs, and 4 regions by population size, monthly rpt, 6762–2

DOT grant awards for transportation planning and safety programs, by region, State, and for 35 largest SMSAs, FY83, annual rpt, 7304–7

- Employment, earnings, and hours, by selected SIC 1- to 4-digit industry, State, and for 278 major labor areas, 1939-83, annual rpt, 6744–5
- Employment, earnings, and hours, by SIC 4-digit nonfarm industry, monthly 1974-Feb 1984, annual update, 6744–4
- Finances and operations of transit systems, by mode of transport, function, fleet size, and system, FY82, annual rpt, 7884–4
- Finances, operations, vehicles, equipment, accidents, and energy use, by mode of transport, 1955-84, annual rpt, 7304–2
- Financing methods of govts and private sector for hwy and urban transit systems, with case studies for selected metro areas, series, 7556–7
- Govt census, 1982: city govt revenues by source, expenditures by function, debt, and assets, by State and city, 2457–4
- Govt census, 1982: county govt revenues by source, expenditures by function, debt, and assets, by State and county, 2457–3
- Govt census, 1982: employment, payrolls, and average earnings, by function, level of govt, State, county, population size, and inside-outside SMSAs, 2455–2
- Govt census, 1982: local govt employment by function, payroll, and average earnings, for individual counties, cities, and school and special districts, 2455–1
- Govt census, 1982: State govt payments to local govts, by program, source of funds, level of govt, and State, with trends from 1902, 2460–3
- Govt employment and payroll, by function, level of govt, and jurisdiction, 1983, annual rpt series, 2466–1
- Govt transportation revenues by source and expenditures, by level of govt and mode of transport, and Fed Govt aid by type, FY77-82, 7308–185
- Income tax returns of corporations, detailed income and tax items by industry, 1981, annual rpt, 8304–4
- Income tax returns of sole proprietorships, detailed data by industry div and selected industry group, 1981, annual rpt, 8304–7
- Income tax returns of sole proprietorships, receipts, deductions by type, payroll, and net income, by major industry, 1982, annual article, 8302–2.413
- Input-output structure of US economy, detailed interindustry transactions for 537 industries, and components of final demand, 1977 benchmark data, 2708–17
- Minority group and women employment, by occupational group and SIC 2- to 3-digit industry, 1981, annual rpt, 9244–1.1
- Motor carriers (Class I interstate) finances, operations, equipment, employment, and payroll, by district, 1982, annual rpt, 9486–5.3
- Neighborhood and housing quality indicators and attitudes, by occupant and unit characteristics, region, and metro-nonmetro location, 1981, annual survey, 2485–2
- Neighborhood quality, indicators and attitudes by inside-outside central cities, 1979-82 surveys, SMSA rpt series, 2485–6

Occupational injury and illness rates, by SIC 2- to 4-digit industry, 1982, annual rpt, 6844–1

- Personal consumption expenditures, natl income and product account, *Survey of Current Business,* monthly rpt, monthly and annual tables, 2702–1.23
- Research publications on public transit, 2nd half FY83, semiannual listing, 7882–1
- Ridership for transit services, by service type, 1983 rpt, 7306–9.6
- Safety programs, and accidents, injuries, deaths, hazards, and property damage, by mode of transport, 1983, annual rpt, 7304–19
- State and local govt productivity measurement, with background data and output indexes for 7 govt services, various periods 1955-82, 6728–27
- Traffic volume on rural roads and city streets, by region, monthly rpt, 7552–8
- Transit system deficits, effect of cost and service increases and ridership and fare decreases, and govt aid and system operating ratios, 1970-80, 7308–184
- Transit system mgmt training funded by Urban Mass Transportation Admin, participant characteristics and career impact, 1970-79, 7888–60
- Transit system operations, tax burden related to ridership, fares, and govt funding, for selected States and cities, 1950s-82, reprint, 7888–59
- Transit systems, expenditures by level of govt, and revenues by source, with distribution of commuter trips by mode of transport, 1980-82, article, 10042–1.404
- Urban Mass Transportation Admin grants for equipment, construction, and operation, annual rpt, discontinued, 7884–3
- Urban Mass Transportation Admin grants to higher education instns for research and training, by project, FY84, annual rpt, 7884–7
- Women's travel patterns, by employment and sociodemographic characteristics and type of child care used, 1980 survey, 7888–62

see also Buses

see also Commuting

see also Subways

see also Taxicabs

see also Traffic engineering

Urbana, Ill.

- Census of Housing, 1980: occupancy and unit characteristics, by race, Hispanic origin, and city, SMSA rpt, 2473–1.113
- Census of Population and Housing, 1980: detailed population and housing characteristics, by county, city, and census tract, SMSA rpt, 2551–2.113
- Housing vacancy rates for single and multifamily units and mobile homes, by county, city, and ZIP code, 1983, annual metro area rpt, 9304–18.1
- Wages by occupation, and benefits for office and plant workers, 1984 labor market area survey rpt, 6785–3.7

see also under By SMSA or MSA in the "Index by Categories"

Urogenital diseases

Agent Orange exposed Air Force personnel diseases and disorders, by disease type, age, and officer status, 1984 rpt, 3604–3

Urogenital diseases

Deaths and death rates, by cause and age, provisional 1982-83, US Vital Statistics annual rpt, 4144–7

Deaths and death rates by detailed cause and demographic characteristics, 1979 and selected trends, US Vital Statistics annual rpt, 4144–2.1

Deaths and death rates, by detailed geographic area, cause, and demographic characteristics, 1979, US Vital Statistics annual rpt, 4144–3

Deaths and death rates, by selected cause and demographic characteristics, 1981, US Vital Statistics advance rpt, 4146–5.78

Deaths and death rates, by selected cause and demographic characteristics, 1982, US Vital Statistics advance rpt, 4146–5.81

Disability Insurance beneficiaries sociodemographic and medical characteristics, 1977-79, annual rpt, 4744–20

Economic indicators relation to measures of social pathology including crime and death rates, various periods 1950-80, 23848–76

Hospital discharges and length of stay, by patient characteristics, facility size, procedure performed, diagnosis, and region, 1982, annual rpt, 4147–13.78

Kidney end-stage disease Medicare and total patients, by treatment method, 1972-82, 26358–106

Kidney end-stage disease Medicare certified facilities, by facility type, service type, and region, 1980-83, article, 4652–1.434

Kidney end-stage disease, Medicare dialysis, transplants by facility, donor organ costs, deaths by age, and hospitalization, by region, 1981, annual rpt, 4654–5.2

Kidney end-stage disease Medicare enrollment, by age, sex, and region, 1973-82, annual rpt, 4744–3.7

Kidney end-stage disease Medicare enrollment, by beneficiary type and area of residence, 1980 with trends from 1966, 4656–1.18

Kidney end-stage disease Medicare program, new cases by State, total enrollment, and survival and death rates, by age, sex, and race, 1970s-81, article, 4652–1.408

Kidney end-stage disease Medicare reimbursement by treatment, diagnosis, outcome, and patient characteristics, with covered charges for transplants, 1974-79, article, 4652–1.421

Kidney end-stage disease patients and other Medicare enrollees covered services and use, and reimbursements, various periods 1966-82, annual rpt, 4654–1

Kidney end-stage disease patients by patient characteristics and country, and per capita spending for treatment, selected years 1973-81, article, 4102–1.450

Older persons by demographic, socioeconomic, and health characteristics, selected years 1900-81 and projected to 2050, Current Population Rpt, 2546–2.125

Uranium ore tailings at active mills, EPA radon and radionuclide emmission standards and US and foreign exposure and health effects, various periods 1957-83, hearings, 21208–17

see also Venereal diseases

Index by Subjects and Names

see also under By Disease in the "Index by Categories"

Urquhart, Michael

"Employment Shift to Services: Where Did It Come From?", 6722–1.425

Uruguay

- Agricultural and food production indexes, and production of selected commodities, by world region and country, 1974-83, annual rpt, 1524–5
- Agricultural situation in Latin America, by country, 1981-83 and outlook for 1984, annual rpt, 1524–4.9
- Agricultural supply/demand, trade, and production, and socioeconomic data, by country, 1950s-77, 1528–179
- AID economic assistance to developing countries, obligations and disbursements by country, quarterly rpt, 9912–4
- AID loan repayment status and terms by program and country, and status of predecessor agency loans, quarterly rpt, 9912–3
- Economic, social, and political summary data, by country, 1984, annual factbook, 244–11
- Economic trends in income, production, prices, employment, finances, and trade, 1984 annual rpt, 2046–4.97
- Exports and imports of US, by commodity and country, 1972-82, annual world region rpt, 244–13.2
- Exports of US, detailed Schedule B commodities by country of destination, 1983, annual rpt, 2424–9
- Exports of US, detailed Schedule E commodities by mode of transport and world area and country of destination, 1983, annual rpts, 2424–5
- Imports of US, detailed Schedule A commodities by country and world area of origin, and mode of transport, 1983, annual rpts, 2424–2
- Imports of US, detailed TSUSA commodities by country of origin, 1983, annual rpt, 2424–4
- Loans and grants for economic and military assistance from US and intl agencies, by program and country, FY46-83, annual rpt, 9914–5
- Military aid of US, arms sales, and training programs costs and budget requests by program, world region, and country, FY83-85, annual rpt, 7144–13
- Military spending, arms trade, and armed forces size, with total govt spending and population, by country, 1972-82, annual rpt, 9824–1
- *Minerals Yearbook, 1982,* Vol 3: foreign country reviews of production, trade, and policies, by commodity, annual rpt, 5604–35
- *Minerals Yearbook, 1983,* Vol 3 preprints: foreign country review of production, trade, and policies, by commodity, annual rpt, 5604–23.89
- Population size and growth rates, and latest available benchmark demographic data, by country, 1950-83, biennial rpt, 2324–4
- *see also* under By Foreign Country in the "Index by Categories"

U.S. Advisory Commission on Public Diplomacy

USIA activities, employment, and funding, FY83-84, annual rpt, 17594–1

U.S. Architectural and Transportation Barriers Compliance Board

- Budget of US Appendix, detailed budgets and personnel summaries, by agency, FY85, annual rpt, 104–3
- Budget of US, appropriations, outlays, balances, and budget receipts, by govtl branch and agency, FY83, annual rpt, 8104–2
- Building access for handicapped persons to Fed Govt or federally funded facilities, compliance activities and complaints by agency, FY83, annual rpt, 17614–1

U.S. Arms Control and Disarmament Agency

- Arms control treaties status, and Arms Control and Disarmament Agency activities, 1983, annual rpt, 9824–2
- Budget of US Appendix, detailed budgets and personnel summaries, by agency, FY85, annual rpt, 104–3
- Budget of US, appropriations, outlays, balances, and budget receipts, by govtl branch and agency, FY83, annual rpt, 8104–2
- DOD budget, FY85 weapons system requests consistency with US policy and specified treaties, with funding FY83-87, annual rpt, 21384–4
- Foreign military spending, arms trade, and armed forces size, with total govt spending and population, by country, 1972-82, annual rpt, 9824–1
- Foreign Service positions and union membership by agency, grievances, and pay rates, FY81-83 with ambassador appointments from 1961, GAO rpt, 26123–64
- R&D Fed Govt funding for all performers, by field and supporting agency, selected years FY60-84, annual rpt, 9627–20
- Soviet Union propaganda campaign against NATO nuclear missile deployment, and USSR and NATO nuclear arms and aircraft in place, 1977-83, narrative rpt, 9828–25
- Space and aeronautics programs and budgets of Fed Govt by agency, and foreign programs, 1957-FY85, annual rpt, 9504–9

U.S. Army Corps of Engineers *see* Army Corps of Engineers

U.S. Board of Parole *see* U.S. Parole Commission

U.S. Budget *see* Budget of the U.S.

U.S. Civil Service Commission *see* Office of Personnel Management

U.S. Coast Guard *see* Coast Guard

U.S. Commission on Civil Rights *see* Commission on Civil Rights

U.S. Customs Court *see* Court of International Trade

U.S. Customs Service

- Activities, operations, and staff of Customs Service, FY83, annual rpt, 8144–1
- Assaults, murders, and other deaths of law enforcement officers, by circumstances, level of govt, agency, victim and offender characteristics, and location, 1983, annual rpt, 6224–3
- Cost control proposals for Fed Govt programs and mgmt, 3-year savings by function and agency, and financial and operating data, 1960s-81, 16908–1.12, 16908–1.31

Index by Subjects and Names

Customs collections of 15 largest collection districts, by port, quarterly rpt, 8142-1

Import quotas and imports for selected commodities, by country of origin, monthly rpt, 8146-1

Law enforcement activities of Alcohol, Tobacco, and Firearms Bur in 20 cities and nationwide, funding, and jobs to be transferred to Customs and Secret Service, 1979-82, hearings, 21528-55

Virgin Islands import duty collections, and reimbursement of US Customs Service collections expenses, FY81-83, GAO rpt, 26119-54

U.S. Employment Service *see* Employment and Training Administration

U.S. Fire Administration *see* Federal Emergency Management Agency

U.S. Fish and Wildlife Service *see* Fish and Wildlife Service

U.S. Geological Survey *see* Geological Survey

U.S. Holocaust Memorial Council Budget of US Appendix, detailed budgets and personnel summaries, by agency, FY85, annual rpt, 104-3

Budget of US, appropriations, outlays, balances, and budget receipts, by govtl branch and agency, FY83, annual rpt, 8104-2

U.S. Information Agency Activities, employment, and funding of USIA, FY83-84, annual rpt, 17594-1

Budget of US Appendix, detailed budgets and personnel summaries, by agency, FY85, annual rpt, 104-3

Budget of US, appropriations, outlays, balances, and budget receipts, by govtl branch and agency, FY83, annual rpt, 8104-2

Cost control proposals for Fed Govt programs and mgmt, 3-year savings by function and agency, and financial and operating data, 1960s-81, 16908-1.10

Currency (foreign) holdings of US, detailed transactions and balances by program and country, 1st half FY84, semiannual rpt, 8102-7

English teaching programs and teacher seminars supported by USIA, by world region and country, FY83, annual rpt, 9854-2

Foreign Service positions and union membership by agency, grievances, and pay rates, FY81-83 with ambassador appointments from 1961, GAO rpt, 26123-64

Info centers and reading rooms of USIA, operations by world region, country, and city, FY83, annual rpt, 9854-4

Intl exchange and training programs of Fed Govt, participants by world region, and funding, by agency, FY83, annual rpt, 9854-8

Latin America students in US and Soviet bloc training programs, by program type and student country, and summary by world region, selected years 1972-82, GAO rpt, 26123-77

R&D Fed Govt funding for all performers, by field and supporting agency, selected years FY60-84, annual rpt, 9627-20

Space and aeronautics programs and budgets of Fed Govt by agency, and foreign programs, 1957-FY85, annual rpt, 9504-9

see also Voice of America

U.S. International Development Cooperation Agency

Developing countries economic aid of US, bilateral and through multilateral dev banks and intl agencies, by world area and country, 1970s-FY83, annual rpts, 9904-1

see also Agency for International Development

see also Overseas Private Investment Corp.

U.S. International Trade Commission

Agricultural products trade, tariffs, and industry operating data, 1979-83, TSUSA commodity rpt series, 9885-1

Analysts of USITC assigned to cover individual commodities, grouped by TSUSA schedule, 1983 listing, 9888-12

Auto and auto products sales, prices, and registrations in US, and trade of 8 countries with US, by make and model, 1964-83, annual rpt, 9884-7

Auto industry operations, and trade by country, monthly rpt, 9882-8

Brooms (broomcorn) shipments, trade, and apparent consumption data for USITC import quota determination, 1983, annual rpt, 9884-6

Budget of US Appendix, detailed budgets and personnel summaries, by agency, FY85, annual rpt, 104-3

Budget of US, appropriations, outlays, balances, and budget receipts, by govtl branch and agency, FY83, annual rpt, 8104-2

Chemicals (benzenoid), imports by country of origin and product, 1983, annual rpt, 9884-2

Chemicals (synthetic organic) production and sales by product, and listing of manufacturers, 1983, annual rpt, 9884-3

Chemicals (synthetic organic) production, by detailed product, monthly rpt, 9882-1

Chemicals and related products trade, tariffs, and industry operating data, TSUSA commodity rpt series, 9885-4

Communist country trade with US, by detailed commodity and country, quarterly rpt with articles, 9882-2

Exports and imports, agreement devs, US trade relations, and USITC investigations, 1983, annual rpt, 9884-5

Exports and imports of US by country, and trade shifts by commodity, USITC quarterly monitoring rpt, 9882-9

Footwear production, employment, consumption, prices, and US trade by country, quarterly rpt, 9882-6

Generalized System of Preferences status of 29 commodities, with US production, consumption, tariffs, and trade by country, selected years 1978-87, 9888-17

Import and tariff provisions effect on US industries and products, investigations with background financial and operating data, series, 9886-4

Imports from Communist countries, injury to US industries, investigations with background financial and operating data, selected industries and products, series, 9886-12

Imports injury to price-supported US agricultural industries, investigations with background financial and operating data for selected products, series, 9886-10

U.S. International Trade Commission

Imports injury to US industries from foreign subsidized products and sales in US at less than fair value, investigations with background financial and operating data, series, 9886-19

Imports injury to US industries from foreign subsidized products, investigations with background financial and operating data for selected industries and products, series, 9886-15

Imports injury to US industries from import sales at less than fair value, investigations with background financial and operating data, series, 9886-14

Imports injury to US industries from increased import sales, investigations with background financial and operating data, series, 9886-5

Imports injury to US industries from removal of duties on foreign subsidized products, investigations with background financial and operating data, series, 9886-18

Imports of US given duty-free treatment for value of US materials or parts sent abroad for processing or assembly, by country and commodity, 1979-82, biennial rpt, 9884-14

Investigations on trade and tariffs, publications issued, 1960-83, annual listing, 9884-12

Investigations, publications, and other USITC activities, FY83, annual rpt, 9884-1

Manufactured products (miscellaneous) trade, tariffs, and industry operating data, TSUSA commodity rpt series, 9885-7

Metals and metal products trade, tariffs, and industry operating data, TSUSA commodity rpt series, 9885-6

Minerals (nonmetallic) and mineral products trade, tariffs, and industry operating data, TSUSA commodity rpt series, 9885-5

Motorcycle imports, sales, and inventories of foreign make, and prices and employment for domestic makes, quarterly rpt, 9882-12

Mushroom imports injury to US industry, and stocks, production, sales, trade, and consumption, quarterly rpt, 9882-5

R&D Fed Govt funding for all performers, by field and supporting agency, selected years FY60-84, annual rpt, 9627-20

Rum production, trade by selected country, consumption, and shipments from Puerto Rico and Virgin Islands, Jan-June 1983-84, annual rpt, 9884-15

Steel (stainless and alloy tool) production, employment, prices, and US importer inventories and unfilled orders, quarterly rpt, 9882-3

Steel imports of US from EC and other countries, and US industry operating data, for 15 products limited under arrangement with EC, monthly rpt, 9882-10

Tariff Schedules of US, Annotated, classifications and rates of duty for detailed imported commodities, 1985 edition, 9886-13

Textile fiber and products trade, tariffs, and industry operating data, TSUSA commodity rpt series, 9885-3

Textile imports and import limits under Multifiber Arrangement by product and country, with US exports and use, 1970-83, semiannual rpt, 9882-11

U.S. International Trade Commission

Wood, paper, and printed matter trade, tariffs, and industry operating data, TSUSA commodity rpt series, 9885–2

U.S. Military Academy

see Service academies

U.S. Nuclear Regulatory Commission

see Nuclear Regulatory Commission

U.S. Parole Commission

Activities of Justice Dept, by subagency, FY82, annual rpt, 6004–1

Decisions for parole, guidelines validation and hearing examiner workloads, Parole Commission research rpt series, 6006–2

U.S. Postal Service

- Budget of US Appendix, detailed budgets and personnel summaries, by agency, FY85, annual rpt, 104–3
- Budget of US, appropriations, outlays, balances, and budget receipts, by govtl branch and agency, FY83, annual rpt, 8104–2
- Budget of US, CBO analysis of revenue and spending alternatives and projections of economic indicators, FY85-89, annual rpt, 26304–3.3
- Budget of US, object class analysis of obligations, by branch of Fed Govt and selected depts and agencies, FY85 estimates, annual rpt, 104–9
- Cost control proposals for Fed Govt programs and mgmt, 3-year savings by function and agency, and financial and operating data, 1960s-81, 16908–1.16
- Electronic mail system message volume and profitability under proposed rate and service increases, FY82 and projected to FY87, 21408–70
- Fed Govt off-budget outlays, by function FY62-89, and by entity FY73-89, annual rpt, 104–12
- Historical review of USPS organization, finances, and services since 1775, and current operations, FY81-82, annual rpt, 9864–6
- Input-output structure of US economy, detailed interindustry transactions for 537 industries, and components of final demand, 1977 benchmark data, 2708–17
- Mail operating costs itemized by class of mail, FY83, annual rpt, 9864–4
- Mail postage ratemaking and classification cases, processing, and participant costs and attitudes, 1970s-84, GAO rpt, 26119–63
- Mail revenue and volume by class of mail, and special service transactions, quarterly rpt, 9862–1
- Mail revenue, costs, and volume, by class of mail, FY83, annual rpt, 9864–2
- Operations, employment, productivity, and financial statements, FY79-83, annual rpt, 9864–1
- Operations, finances, and employee productivity, performance, and compensation, FY83 with projections to FY85, annual rpt, 9864–5
- Operations of USPS, revenues by source, and employee characteristics, 1970s-83, and electronic mail promotion costs, FY82-87, hearings, 21628–55
- Property (real) of Fed Govt, leased property inventory and rental costs, worldwide summary by location and agency, Sept 1983, annual rpt, 9454–10

Statistical Abstract of US, social, political, and economic data, 1950s-83 and trends, annual rpt, 2324–1.3

User fees to recover costs of 7 federally subsidized public service programs, by type of fee, user, and service, FY84-88, 26306–6.68

see also Postal employees

see also Postal service

U.S. Railway Association

- Budget of US Appendix, detailed budgets and personnel summaries, by agency, FY85, annual rpt, 104–3
- Budget of US, appropriations, outlays, balances, and budget receipts, by govtl branch and agency, FY83, annual rpt, 8104–2
- Finances of Federal off-budget entities, US Budget Appendix, FY85, detailed annual rpt, 104–3.3
- Operations of Conrail and finances and activities of US Railway Assn, FY81-83, annual rpt, 29604–1

U.S.-Saudi Arabian Joint Commission on Economic Cooperation

Project activities and costs of commission, and related contract awards by Fed Govt agency, as of 1983, GAO rpt, 26123–80

U.S. savings bonds

- Farm financial assets by type, 1940-84, annual rpt, 1544–16.2
- Fed Govt debt by holder, interest rates and costs, and financing mechanisms, projected FY84-89 with data for FY80-83, 26308–50
- Financial operations of Fed Govt, detailed data, *Treasury Bulletin,* quarterly rpt, 8002–4
- Issues, redemptions, and bonds outstanding, by series, monthly rpt, 8242–1
- Issues, redemptions, and bonds outstanding, monthly rpt, 8242–2
- Sales and redemptions, Treasury Bulletin quarterly rpt, 8002–4.6
- Sales, redemptions, exchanges, and bonds outstanding, for series EE and HH, monthly rpt, 8442–1

U.S. Savings Bonds Division

Savings bonds sold, redeemed, exchanged, and outstanding, for series EE and HH, monthly rpt, 8442–1

U.S. Secret Service

- Assaults, murders, and other deaths of law enforcement officers, by circumstances, level of govt, agency, victim and offender characteristics, and location, 1983, annual rpt, 6224–3
- Cost control proposals for Fed Govt programs and mgmt, 3-year savings by function and agency, and financial and operating data, 1960s-81, 16908–1.12
- Counterfeiting of currency and forgery of checks and bonds, Secret Service investigations and judicial disposition, FY74-84, annual rpt, 8464–1
- Law enforcement activities of Alcohol, Tobacco, and Firearms Bur in 20 cities and nationwide, funding, and jobs to be transferred to Customs and Secret Service, 1979-82, hearings, 21528–55

U.S. statutes

Court caseloads for Federal district, appeals, and bankruptcy courts, by type of suit and offense, circuit, and district, quarterly rpt, 18202–1

Index by Subjects and Names

Criminal offense citations manual of US criminal title and section codes, with corresponding detailed offenses and severity levels, 1984, annual rpt, 18204–14

U.S. Synthetic Fuels Corp.

- Budget of US, appropriations, outlays, balances, and budget receipts, by govtl branch and agency, FY83, annual rpt, 8104–2
- Budget of US, CBO analysis of revenue and spending alternatives and projections of economic indicators, FY85-89, annual rpt, 26304–3.3
- Cost control proposals for Fed Govt programs and mgmt, 3-year savings by function and agency, and financial and operating data, 1960s-81, 16908–1.14
- Finances of Federal off-budget entities, US Budget Appendix, FY85, detailed annual rpt, 104–3.3
- Financial statements, activities, and executive staff and salaries of Corp, FY83 annual rpt, 29654–1

U.S. Tariff Commission

see U.S. International Trade Commission

U.S. territories

see American Samoa

see Guam

see Puerto Rico

see Territories of the U.S.

see Trust Territory of the Pacific Islands

see Virgin Islands

see under By Outlying Area in the "Index by Categories"

U.S. Travel and Tourism Administration

- Budgets and permanent staff positions appropriated for Commerce Dept agencies, FY84-85, annual rpt, 2004–6
- Foreign travel to and from US and travel receipts and payments by world area, and travel to US by country, 1977-83, annual rpt, 2904–10
- Foreign travel to and from US, by world area and selected country, projected 1984-85, annual rpt, 2904–9
- Foreign travel to US and receipts by world area and selected country, 1960-83, and US Travel and Tourism Admin activities, 1983, annual rpt, 2904–6
- Foreign travel to US, by characteristics of visit and traveller, country, and State of destination, quarterly rpt, 2902–1
- Programs, funding, and employment of Commerce Dept agencies, FY83, annual rpt, 2004–1
- Publications of Commerce Dept, biweekly listing, 2002–1

U.S. Travel Service

see U.S. Travel and Tourism Administration

USDA

see Department of Agriculture

User fees

- Aircraft operating costs by component for privately owned small planes, and Fed Govt mileage reimbursement rates, 1983, annual rpt, 9454–13.2
- Airport financing by source, bond issues by region, and airport operations, by airport and operator type, FY75-83 and projected to FY93, 26306–6.75
- Budget of US, CBO analysis of revenue and spending alternatives and projections of economic indicators, FY85-89, annual rpt, 26304–3.3

Index by Subjects and Names

Utah

- Budget of US, receipts, outlays, and budget authority, by function and agency, FY84-89 revised estimates, midsession review of FY85 budget, annual rpt, 104–7
- Census of Govts, 1982: city govt revenues by source, expenditures by function, debt, and assets, by State and city, 2457–4
- Census of Govts, 1982: county govt revenues by source, expenditures by function, debt, and assets, by State and county, 2457–3
- Census of Govts, 1982: State govt payments to local govts, by program, source of funds, level of govt, and State, with trends from 1902, 2460–3
- City govt fiscal condition, revenue sharing program allocations, and responses to program cuts, FY81-83, surveys, hearings, 25408–86
- Fed Govt programs and mgmt cost control proposals, 3-year savings by function and agency, and financial and operating data, 1960s-81, 16908–1
- Fed Govt statistical agencies appropriations and missions, and effect of budget cuts on principal programs, FY80- 84, GAO rpt, 26125–28
- Fed Reserve payments services provided depository instns, financial statements, and costs and revenues by service and district bank, 1983, annual press release, 9364–9
- Forests (natl) receipts by type of use, *Agricultural Statistics, 1983,* annual rpt, 1004–1.2
- Freedom of Info Act, requests to HHS received and denied, costs, and fees collected, 1983, annual rpt, 4004–21
- Govt finances, by level of govt, State, and for large cities and counties, 1981-83, annual rpt series, 2466–2
- Hwy use taxes and Trust Fund revenues by tax type, and tax and truck size and weight limits effects on trucking industry, FY82-84 and projected to 1990, GAO rpt, 26117–31
- Hwy use taxes by tax type, and truck size and weight limits, economic effects on trucking industry, 1982-83 and projected 1984-87, hearings, 25328–24
- Hwy use taxes paid by trucking industry for Fed Govt and State hwys, 1972-82, annual rpt, 7304–2
- Land Mgmt Bur public lands admin and program activities in western States, FY82-84, annual rpt, 5724–13
- Local govt spending, reliance on State aid and local taxes by type, and excise tax growth by State, selected years FY57-83, article, 10042–1.403
- Nuclear power plant spent fuel permanent disposal site and transport costs, and Nuclear Waste Fund financing, alternative projections FY83-2037, 26308–49
- Nuclear Waste Fund obligations by function and receipts, and DOE Civilian Radioactive Mgmt Office activities and staff, quarterly GAO rpt, 26102–4
- Port dev costs and financing through user fees, and shipping industry impact on local economy, by State, other area, industry, commodity, and port, 1970s-2020, hearings, 21568–34
- Public opinion on taxes, tax policy, and intergovtl relations, 1972-84 surveys, annual rpt, 10044–2
- Public services subsidized by Fed Govt, user fees to recover costs of 7 programs, by type of fee, user, and service, FY84-88, 26306–6.68
- Radioactive waste mgmt activities and financing of DOE Office of Civilian Radioactive Waste Mgmt, FY83-85, annual rpt, 3364–1
- Recreation fees and collection costs, visitors, and capacity of outdoor Fed Govt, State, and private facilities, by managing agency and State, 1983, annual rpt, 5544–14
- Regulatory growth of Fed Govt effect on local compliance costs and funding, local officials assessment, and comparisons to State govt regulations, 1970s-82 with trends from 1900, 10048–58
- Transit system operations, tax burden related to ridership, fares, and govt funding, for selected States and cities, 1950s-82, reprint, 7888–59
- Transportation revenues by source and expenditures, by level of govt and mode of transport, and Fed Govt aid by type, FY77-82, 7308–185
- Washington State telephone rates including govt long-distance access charges, by company, 1983-89, hearing, 21148–32
- *see also* Tolls

USIA

see U.S. Information Agency

USMC

see Marine Corps

USSR

see Soviet Union

Utah

- Agriculture census, 1982: farms, farmland, production and costs, and operator characteristics, preliminary State summary and county rpts, 2330–1.49
- Agriculture census, 1982: farms, farmland, production, finances, and operator characteristics, by county, final State rpt, 2331–1.44
- Bank deposits in commercial and mutual savings banks and in US branches of foreign banks, by account type, instn, State, SMSA, and county, June 1983, annual rpt, 9295–3.17
- Cancer cases, incidence, deaths, and death rates, by body site, age, race, Hispanic origin, and sex, for 10 geographic areas, 1973-81, 4478–130
- Census of Housing, 1980: occupancy and unit characteristics of SMSAs and central cities, by race, Hispanic origin, and city, State rpt, 2473–1.46
- Census of Population, 1980: detailed socioeconomic and demographic characteristics, by age, sex, race, Hispanic origin, and industry, State rpt, 2531–4.46
- Coal dev plans on Fed Govt lease lands, environmental and socioeconomic impacts to 2000, final statement, 5726–4.6
- Coal Fed Govt leases, acreage, production, and prices, by State, and legal and mgmt issues, 1970s-83 with production projections to 2000, 11128–1
- County Business Patterns: establishments, employees, and payrolls, by SIC 4-digit industry and county, 1982, annual State rpt, 2326–6.46
- Employment, earnings, and hours, by selected SIC 1- to 4-digit industry, State, and for 278 major labor areas, 1939-83, annual rpt, 6744–5.2, 6744–5.3
- Environmental quality, pollutant discharge by type and source, and EPA protection activities and funding, 1970s-83, biennial regional rpt, 9184–15.8
- Exports of manufactured and agricultural commodities, manufacturing production, and export-related employment, 1960s-82, State rpt, 2046–3.44
- Forest biomass in Rocky Mountain States, conversion from volume to dry weight, for softwood and hardwood species, 1977, 1208–200
- Foster care children permanent placement, Fed Govt incentive program funding and operations in 7 States, FY80-82, GAO rpt, 26121–81
- Hay prices in 10 market areas, for baled alfalfa and prairie hay, weekly rpt, 1313–5
- HHS aid to each State and local govt or private instn, amount obligated, funding agency, and program, FY83, annual listing, 4004–3.8
- Income (personal) per capita and by source, and earnings by industry div, by State, MSA, and county, 1977-82, annual regional rpt, 2704–2.8
- Manufacturing census, 1982: financial and operating data, by SIC 2- to 4-digit industry, State, SMSA, and county, preliminary census div rpt, 2491–3.8
- Mineral Industry Surveys, State review of production, 1983, advance annual rpt, 5614–6.44
- *Minerals Yearbook, 1982,* Vol 2 preprints: State review of production and sales by commodity, and business activity, annual rpt, 5604–16.46
- *Minerals Yearbook, 1982,* Vol 2: State reviews of production, sales, and firms, by commodity, and business activity, annual rpt, 5604–34
- Oil shale dev projects in Green River area, production goals and cost estimates, as of 1983, article, 9381–1.409
- Phosphate rock reserves in southeastern and northwestern US, by location, 1984 rpt, 5668–74
- Population size and components of change, by MSA and county, 1980-82, annual State Current Population Rpt, 2546–4.44
- Population size, Apr 1980 and July 1982, and per capita income, 1979 and 1981, by county and city, State Current Population Rpt, 2546–11.44
- Retail trade census, 1982: employment, establishments, sales, and payroll, by SIC 2- to 4-digit kind of business, SMSA, and retail district, State rpt, 2401–1.45
- Salt Lake surface level, land coverage, water budget, salinity, and effects of human activity, various periods 1847-1983, 5668–70
- Savings and loan assns, FHLB 12th District members financial operations and housing industry indicators by State, monthly rpt, 9302–21
- Service industry census, 1982: employment, establishments, receipts, and payroll, by SIC 2- to 4-digit kind of business, SMSA, county, and city, State rpt, 2391–1.45

Utah

Small business mgmt counseling by university centers, costs, funding, and businesses served by industry, with detail for 2 States, 1980-83, hearing, 25728–36

Timber acreage and resources in Utah, by species, ownership class, and stand size, 1978, series, 1206–22

Timber resources and removals in 9 Rocky Mountain States, and forest and rangeland area, by ownership, forest and tree characteristics, and State, 1977, 1208–201

Water supply and quality in streams and lakes, and groundwater levels in wells, by drainage basin, 1983, annual State rpt, 5666–10.42

Water supply, and snow survey results, monthly State rpt, 1266–2.8

Water supply in Utah, streamflow, reservoir storage, and precipitation, 1984 water year, annual rpt, 1264–6

Wholesale trade census, 1982: employment, establishments, finances, and operations, by SIC 2- to 4-digit kind of business, SMSA, county, and city, State rpt, 2405–1.45

see also Ogden, Utah

see also Orem, Utah

see also Provo, Utah

see also Salt Lake City, Utah

see also under By State in the "Index by Categories"

Utica, N.Y.

Census of Housing, 1980: occupancy and unit characteristics, by race, Hispanic origin, and city, SMSA rpt, 2473–1.359

Census of Population and Housing, 1980: detailed population and housing characteristics, by county, city, and census tract, SMSA rpt, 2551–2.359

see also under By SMSA or MSA in the "Index by Categories"

Utilities

see Public utilities

Vacations and holidays

- Developing countries disaster preparedness and summary sociodemographic, political, and economic data, country rpt series, 9916–2
- Economic time series seasonal adjustment methodology, dev and design of Census Bur and other systems, with illustrative data, 1981 conf papers, 2626–7.5
- Employee benefits in private industry, coverage by benefit type and provisions and occupational group, 1983, annual rpt, 6784–19
- Employee benefits in private industry, percent of employers providing selected benefits, 1979-82, conf proceedings, 25408–89
- Fed Govt employee work-years by work schedule and for overtime and holidays, and compensation and leave used by category, various periods 1980-82, articles, 9842–1.401, 9842–1.402
- Fed Govt programs and mgmt cost control proposals, 3-year savings by function and agency, and financial and operating data, 1960s-81, 16908–1.16, 16908–1.27
- Foreign economic, social, and political summary data, by country, 1984, annual factbook, 244–11

Foreign holidays observed by businesses, by country, biweekly rpt, annual listing, 2042–24

- Labor force not at work on day of survey, employed part-time, or unemployed, by reason, sex, race, Hispanic origin, region, and State, 1983, annual rpt, 6744–7
- Railroad employee earnings, benefits, and hours, by occupation for Class I railroads, 1983, annual rpt, 9484–5
- Traffic fatal accidents detailed circumstances, and characteristics of persons and vehicles involved, 1982, annual rpt, 7764–10

see also Area wage surveys

see also Industry wage surveys

see also Labor cost indexes

Vaccination and vaccines

- Biotechnology commercial uses, R&D funding and output, controls, and industry financial and operating data, for US and 5 countries, 1970s-83 and estimated 1984-85, 26358–98
- Child immunization and preventive medicine programs in US and Mexico, disease cases, vaccine reactions, and deaths, 1984 conf papers, 4204–15
- Children and youth benefitting from Fed Govt public welfare programs and tax expenditures, participation and funding for 71 programs, FY81-83, 21968–30
- Exports and imports of US, detailed SIC-based commodities by world area, 1983, annual rpts, 2424–6
- Exports of US, detailed commodities by country of destination, monthly rpt, 2422–3
- Exports of US, detailed Schedule B commodities by country of destination, 1983, annual rpt, 2424–9
- Foreign travel vaccination requirements by country, and disease prevention recommendations, 1984 annual rpt, 4204–11
- Health condition and health care resources, use, and expenditures, 1970s-82 with trends and projections 1900-2000, annual compilation, 4144–11
- HHS aid to each State and local govt or private instn, amount obligated, funding agency, and program, FY83, annual listing, 4004–3
- Imports of US, detailed TSUSA commodities by country of origin, 1983, annual rpt, 2424–4
- Infectious notifiable diseases, cases and current outbreaks, by region and State, and recommended adult immunization supplement, weekly rpt, 4202–1
- Influenza deaths, viruses identified by State and country, epidemiology, and vaccine effects and recommended dosages by age, 1979/80-1980/81, annual rpt, 4205–3
- Measles immunization, natural immunity, and incidence rates in Israel, by age, 1965-83 and projected to 1990, article, 4102–1.429
- Producer prices and indexes, by stage of processing and detailed commodity, monthly rpt, 6762–6
- Producer prices and indexes, by stage of processing and detailed commodity, monthly 1983, annual supplement, 6764–2

Index by Subjects and Names

Public Health Service activities, and funding by function and subagency, FY83, annual rpt, 4044–2

Research publications on immunization, 1984 annual listing, 4204–16

TTPI vaccination program, and children aged 2 and 6 innoculated, FY82, annual rpt, 7004–6

Val Verde County, Tex.

Housing vacancy rates for single and multifamily units and mobile homes, by city and ZIP code, 1984, annual metro area rpt, 9304–19.16

Valente, Ralph J.

"Atmospheric Turbidity over the U.S. from 1967-76", 9198–106

Vallejo, Calif.

- Census of Population and Housing, 1980: detailed population and housing characteristics, by county, city, and census tract, SMSA rpt, 2551–2.360
- Housing vacancy rates for single and multifamily units and mobile homes, by city and ZIP code, 1983, annual metro area rpt, 9304–20.8
- Housing vacancy rates for single and multifamily units and mobile homes, by city and ZIP code, 1984, annual metro area rpt, 9304–20.20

see also under By SMSA or MSA in the "Index by Categories"

Van Arsdall, Roy N.

"U.S. Hog Industry", 1568–248

Van Den Avyle, Michael J.

- "Species Profiles: Life Histories and Environmental Requirements of Coastal Fishes and Invertebrates (South Atlantic), Atlantic Menhaden", 5506–8.15
- "Species Profiles: Life Histories and Environmental Requirements of Coastal Fishes and Invertebrates (South Atlantic), Blue Crab", 5506–8.24
- "Species Profiles: Life Histories and Environmental Requirements of Coastal Fishes and Invertebrates (South Atlantic), Summer Flounder", 5506–8.25

van Hees, Willem W.

- "Timber Resource Statistics for the Petersburg/Wrangell Inventory Unit, Alaska, 1972", 1206–9.11
- "Timber Resource Statistics for the Prince of Wales Inventory Unit, Alaska, 1973", 1206–9.12
- "Timber Resource Statistics for the Sitka Inventory Unit, Alaska, 1971", 1206–9.10
- "Timber Resource Statistics for the Tanana Inventory Unit, Alaska, 1971-75", 1206–9.13
- "Timber Resource Statistics for the Yakutat Inventory Unit, Alaska, 1975", 1206–9.15

Van Hooser, Dwane D.

"Forest Resources of the Rocky Mountain States", 1208–201

"Utah's Forest Resources, 1978", 1206–22.6

"Whole Tree Volume Estimates for the Rocky Mountain States", 1208–200

Van Meir, Lawrence W.

"Analyzing Feed and Residual Disappearance of Corn", 1561–4.402

"1984 Outlook for Feed Grains", 1004–16.1

Index by Subjects and Names

Vanadium
see Metals and metal industries

Vancouver, Canada
Fruit and vegetable shipments, and arrivals in 23 US and 5 Canada cities, by mode of transport and State or country of origin, 1983, annual rpt, 1311–4.2

Vancouver, Wash.
see also under By SMSA or MSA in the "Index by Categories"

Vandalism
Arrests and arrest rates, by offense, offender characteristics, population size, and State, 1970s-83, annual rpt, 6224–2.2
Arson investigation and prosecution, by incident characteristics and outcome, motive, and type of evidence, for 4 jurisdictions, 1981, 6068–184
Bombing (explosive and incendiary) and arson incidents by target, State, and circumstances, and explosives theft and recovery, 1982-83, annual rpt, 8484–4
Bombing (explosive and incendiary) incidents, damage, injuries, and deaths, by target, State, and circumstances, 1983, annual rpt, 6224–5
Pretrial citation release use, cost savings for law enforcement agencies, and failures to appear in court, by offense and selected jurisdiction, 1970s-82, 6068–187
Public housing under private mgmt, assessment by housing officials and managers, and tenants, with operating costs, crime, and rent delinquency by project type and location, 1982, 5188–103
School crime, assaults and robberies of secondary students and teachers, 1972-83, 4918–13
School crime, assaults and robberies of teachers and minority and all students, and vandalism incidents, 1976/77, 4808–12

Vandenbrink, Donna C.
"Did Usury Ceilings Hold Down Auto Sales?", 9375–1.409
"Effects of Usury Ceilings: The Economic Evidence", 9375–13.1
"High Speed Rail in the Midwest", 9375–1.406

Vanderlinden, Mark J.
"Deregulation: Is It the End of the 'Quiet Life'?", 9302–2.402
"Effects of New Competition in Local Markets: Fourth District Evidence", 9312–1.401

VanDeventer, Allan D.
"Three Studies of Biographical Factors Associated with Success in Air Traffic Control Specialist Screening/Training at the FAA Academy", 7506–10.24

Vankai, Thomas A.
"Eastern Europe: Agricultural Production and Trade Prospects Through 1990", 1528–178

Vanuatu
Economic, social, and political summary data, by country, 1984, annual factbook, 244–11
Minerals Yearbook, 1982, Vol 3 preprints: foreign country review of production, trade, and policies, by commodity, annual rpt, 5604–17.90
Minerals Yearbook, 1983, Vol 3 preprints: foreign country review of production, trade, and policies, by commodity, annual rpt, 5604–23.90

Population size and growth rates, and latest available benchmark demographic data, by country, 1950-83, biennial rpt, 2324–4
see also under By Foreign Country in the "Index by Categories"

Varnishes
see Paints and varnishes

Vasectomy
see Sexual sterilization

Vatican City
Economic, social, and political summary data, by country, 1984, annual factbook, 244–11

Vegetable oils
see Oils, oilseeds, and fats

Vegetable seeds
see Seeds

Vegetables and vegetable products
Acreage planted and harvested, by crop and State, 1982-83 and planned as of June 1984, annual rpt, 1621–23
Acreage planting intended for 19 crops, by State, as of Feb 1984, annual rpt, 1621–22
Acreage, yield, and production of field crops, by State, 1978-82 and preliminary 1983, 1641–7
Agricultural Statistics, 1983, annual rpt, 1004–1
Agriculture census, 1982: farms, farmland, production and costs, and operator characteristics, preliminary State and county rpt series, 2330–1
Agriculture census, 1982: farms, farmland, production, finances, and operator characteristics, by county, final State rpt series, 2331–1
Alcohol fuel (ethanol) production in Tennessee Valley, feedstocks, facilities, tax incentives, and related farming data, by State, 1970s-83 and projected to 1992, 9808–69
Bean (dried) prices by State, and foreign and US production, use, stocks, and trade, weekly rpt, 1311–17
California farm real estate market values, by use and crop, 1976-84, annual rpt, 1541–8.1
Canned and preserved vegetables industries, productivity, hours, and employment indexes, 1954-81, annual rpt, 6824–1.3
Celery acreage planted and growing, by major producing State and area, monthly rpt, 1621–14
Census of Population, 1980: detailed socioeconomic and demographic characteristics, by age, sex, race, Hispanic origin, occupation, and industry, State rpt series, 2531–4
China economic conditions, agricultural and industrial production, trade, and domestic and foreign investment, 1980-85, 2048–106
China exports and imports by SITC 1- to 5-digit commodity, 1970s-82, annual rpt, 244–12
Cold storage food stocks by commodity and census div, and warehouse cold storage space in use, by State, monthly rpt, 1631–5
Cold storage food stocks of 77 commodities, by region, 1983, annual rpt, 1631–11
Communist, OECD, and selected other countries agricultural production, by commodity, 1960s-83, annual rpt, 244–5.9

Vegetables and vegetable products

Consumer expenditures for fruit, vegetable, and potato products related to changes in income and other household characteristics, 1977-78, 1548–236
Consumption of food and nutrient intake by individuals, by food group, source, and socioeconomic characteristics, 1977-78 natl survey, final rpt series, 1356–4
Consumption, supply, trade, prices, expenditures, and indexes, by food commodity, 1963-83, annual rpt, 1544–4
Cooperatives finances and operations, aggregate for top 100 assns by principal product and revenue source, FY82, annual rpt, 1124–3
Cooperatives, membership, activities, and finances, by commodity and selected State, 1900-80 with trends from 1863, 1128–30
County Business Patterns: establishments, employees, and payrolls, by SIC 4-digit industry and county, 1981, annual State rpt series, 2326–8
County Business Patterns: establishments, employees, and payrolls, by SIC 4-digit industry and county, 1982, annual State rpt series, 2326–6
CPI by detailed component, for US city average, 28 SMSAs, and 4 regions by population size, monthly rpt, 6762–2
Cuba economic conditions, agricultural and industrial production and distribution, trade, and intl economic relations, 1970-82 and trends from 1957, 248–40
Eastern Europe agricultural production and trade by commodity, food consumption, and farm inputs, for 6 countries, 1960-80 with projections to 1991, 1528–178
EC fruit and vegetable product trade and tariffs, 1966-78, and effect of Greece, Spain, and Portugal entry into EC, projected to 1986, 1528–182
Employment, earnings, and hours, by selected SIC 1- to 4-digit industry, State, and for 278 major labor areas, 1939-83, annual rpt, 6744–5
Employment, earnings, and hours, by SIC 4-digit nonfarm industry, monthly 1974-Feb 1984, annual update, 6744–4
Exports and imports of US, by agricultural commodity and country, bimonthly rpt with articles, 1522–1
Exports and imports of US, by detailed agricultural commodity and country, FY83 and CY83, semiannual rpts, 1522–4
Exports and imports of US, by detailed agricultural commodity for 8 major commodity groups, monthly rpt, 1922–8
Exports and imports of US, detailed SIC-based commodities by world area, 1983, annual rpts, 2424–6
Exports and imports of US, totals and as percent of domestic production, by SIC 2- to 5-digit commodity, 1981, annual rpt, 2424–3
Exports, imports, tariffs, and industry operating data for fresh and frozen vegetables, 1979-83, TSUSA commodity rpt, 9885–1.69
Exports, imports, tariffs, and industry operating data for processed vegetables, foreign and US, 1978-82, TSUSA commodity rpt, 9885–1.61

Vegetables and vegetable products

Index by Subjects and Names

Exports of manufactured and agricultural commodities, manufacturing production, and export-related employment, 1960s-82, State rpt series, 2046–3

Exports of US, detailed commodities by country of destination, monthly rpt, 2422–3

Exports of US, detailed Schedule B commodities by country of destination, 1983, annual rpt, 2424–9

Exports of US, detailed Schedule E commodities by mode of transport and world area and country of destination, 1983, annual rpts, 2424–5

Exports under PL 480 concessional sales program, by commodity and country, 1978-83, semiannual rpt, 1922–10

Farm finances, assets, liabilities, income, receipts by commodity and State, and expenses, 1980-83 and trends from 1910, annual rpt, 1544–16

Farm production inputs, outputs, and productivity, by region, 1939-82, annual rpt, 1544–17

Foreign agricultural production, prices, and trade, by country, 1983 and outlook for 1984/85, annual world region rpt series, 1524–4

Foreign and US agricultural production, trade, and climatic devs, weekly press release, 1922–4

Foreign and US fresh and processed fruit, vegetable, and nut production and trade, FAS monthly rpt with articles, 1925–34

Futures trading by commodity and exchange, and Commodity Futures Trading Commission activities, funding, and employment, FY83, annual rpt, 11924–2

Gasohol production and costs by feedstock, prices, and market penetration rates and excise tax exemption by State, 1983, article, 1561–16.404

Genetic resource (plant and animal) conservation, commercial uses, causes of depletion, and geographic sources, 1984 rpt, 5548–13

Great Lakes trade, by SITC 3-digit commodity, port, vessel type, world area, and country, 1982, annual rpt, 7744–3

Imports of US, detailed Schedule A commodities by country and world area of origin, and mode of transport, 1983, annual rpts, 2424–2

Imports of US, detailed Schedule A commodities by country, monthly rpt, 2422–2

Imports of US, detailed TSUSA commodities by country of origin, 1983, annual rpt, 2424–4

Income tax returns of corporations, detailed income and tax items by industry, 1981, annual rpt, 8304–4

Income tax returns of partnerships, detailed data by industry, 1981 estimates, annual article, 8302–2.404

Income tax returns of partnerships, receipts by source, deductions by type, and establishments, by selected industry, 1982, annual article, 8302–2.416

Income tax returns of sole proprietorships, detailed data by industry div and selected industry group, 1981, annual rpt, 8304–7

Income tax returns of sole proprietorships, receipts, deductions by type, payroll, and net income, by major industry, 1982, annual article, 8302–2.413

Input-output structure of US economy, detailed interindustry transactions for 537 industries, and components of final demand, 1977 benchmark data, 2708–17

Manufacturing census, 1982: financial and operating data, by SIC 2- to 4-digit industry, State, SMSA, and county, preliminary census div rpt series, 2491–3

Manufacturing census, 1982: financial and operating data, for SIC 4-digit industries by product, preliminary rpt, 2491–1.10

Manufacturing census, 1982: financial and operating data, for SIC 4-digit industries by product, preliminary rpt series, 2491–1

Marketing cash receipts of farms, by detailed commodity and State, 1979-82, annual rpt, 1544–18

Minority group and women employment, by occupational group and SIC 2- to 3-digit industry, 1981, annual rpt, 9244–1.1

Mushroom imports injury to US industry, and stocks, production, sales, trade, and consumption, quarterly rpt, 9882–5

Mushroom production, sales, and prices, by State, 1981/82-1983/84 and planned 1984/85, annual rpt, 1631–9

Mushrooms (canned) trade by selected country, and US production, sales, and consumption, 1979/80-1982/83 and forecast 1984, article, 1925–34.423

Occupational injury and illness rates, by SIC 2- to 4-digit industry, 1982, annual rpt, 6844–1

OECD trade, total and for 4 major countries, and US trade by country, by commodity, 1972-82, annual world region rpt series, 244–13

Olives (bottled) from Spain, imports injury to US industry from removal of duties on foreign subsidized products, investigation with selected financial and operating data, 1984 rpt, 9886–18.15

Pesticide use and acreage treated, for 12 vegetable and melon crops, by type of pesticide, method of application, and region, 1979, 1588–82

Potato and sweet potato production, stocks, and prices, 1982-83, annual rpt, 1621–11

Potato and sweet potato production, stocks, prices, acreage, and yield, 1978-82 and preliminary 1983, 1641–14

Potato futures trading, NYC market activity, monthly rpt, 11922–2, 11922–5

Potato production, stocks, processing, yields, and harvest losses, by State, periodic rpt, 1621–10

Potatoes from Canada at less than fair value, imports injury to US industry, investigation with background financial and operating data, 1983 rpt, 9886–14.89

Prices (farm-retail) for foods, marketing cost components, and industry finances and productivity, selected years 1967-83, annual rpt, 1544–9

Prices (wholesale) for fresh fruit and vegetables in NYC, Chicago, and selected shipping points, by crop, 1983, annual rpt, 1311–8

Prices received by farmers and production value for detailed crops by State, 1981-83, annual rpt, 1621–2

Prices received by farmers for major products, and paid for farm inputs, by commodity and State, 1983, annual rpt, 1629–5

Producer prices and indexes, by stage of processing and detailed commodity, monthly rpt, 6762–6

Producer prices and indexes, by stage of processing and detailed commodity, monthly 1983, annual supplement, 6764–2

Production, acreage, and prices, for selected fresh and processing vegetables by State, 1981-84, annual rpts, 1621–25

Production, acreage, and yield, current and forecast for selected fresh and processing vegetables by State, periodic rpt, 1621–12

Production and farm finances, expenses by type, and domestic economic impact, selected years 1972-82 and preliminary 1983-84, annual rpt, 1544–19

Production, farms, acreage, and related data, by selected crop and State, monthly rpt, 1621–1

Production, prices, stocks, and consumption, for selected fresh and processed crops, periodic situation rpt with articles, 1561–11

Production, prices, trade, and marketing, by commodity, current situation and forecast, monthly rpt, 1502–4

Seed exports of US, by type of seed, world region, and country, FAS quarterly rpt, 1925–13

Shipments by mode of transport, arrivals, and imports, for fruit and vegetables by commodity and State and country of origin, weekly rpt, 1311–3

Shipments of fruits and vegetables, and arrivals in 23 US and 5 Canada cities, by mode of transport and State or country of origin, 1983, annual rpt series, 1311–4

Tomato (processing) acreage and production for 10 countries, and US imports of canned products by type and country, 1982-84, article, 1925–34.419

Tomato processor subsidies and minimum grower prices for Greece and total EC, 1981-83, article, 1925–34.404

Tomato products from Greece, imports injury to US industry from removal of duties on foreign subsidized products, investigation with financial and operating data, 1984 rpt, 9886–18.16

Truck transport of fruit and vegetables, costs per vehicle-mile by component for fleets and owner-operator trucks, monthly rpt, 1272–1

Truck transport of fruit and vegetables to 6 major markets, weekly rates by commodity and region, and monthly truck-mile costs, 1983 annual rpt, 1311–15

Underground economy, household expenditures and participation by type of goods or service and sociodemographic characteristics, with methodology and bibl, 1981 survey, 8308–27

USDA agricultural surplus direct purchase program finances, and purchases and food received by schools by commodity, various periods 1936-83, 1548–243

Virgin Islands economic censuses, 1982: employment, establishments, payroll, and receipts, by SIC 1- to 4-digit industry, island, and city, 2593–1

Index by Subjects and Names

Waterborne commerce of US (domestic and foreign), freight by commodity, traffic, and passengers, by port and waterway, 1982, annual rpt, 3754–3

Wholesale trade census, 1982: employment, establishments, sales by commodity, and payroll, by SIC 4-digit kind of business and State, preliminary rpt, 2403–1.32

see also under By Commodity in the "Index by Categories"

Vegetation

see Plants and vegetation

Vending machines and stands

- Blind-operated vending stand concessions on Federal and non-Federal property, and income, FY82-83, annual rpt, 4944–2
- Campground facilities privately owned, and financial and operating data, by region, 1982, annual rpt, 5544–14.5
- Census of Population, 1980: detailed socioeconomic and demographic characteristics, by age, sex, race, Hispanic origin, occupation, and industry, State rpt series, 2531–4
- Census of Retail Trade, 1982: employment, establishments, sales, and payroll, for automatic merchandising machine operators, by State, preliminary rpt, 2395–1.34
- County Business Patterns: establishments, employees, and payrolls, by SIC 4-digit industry and county, 1981, annual State rpt series, 2326–8
- Exports and imports of US, detailed SIC-based commodities by world area, 1983, annual rpts, 2424–6
- Exports and imports of US, totals and as percent of domestic production, by SIC 2- to 5-digit commodity, 1981, annual rpt, 2424–3
- Exports, imports, tariffs, and industry operating data for miscellaneous machines and equipment, 1979-83, TSUSA commodity rpt, 9885–6.84
- Exports of US, detailed commodities by country of destination, monthly rpt, 2422–3
- Exports of US, detailed Schedule B commodities by country of destination, 1983, annual rpt, 2424–9
- Food consumption and nutrient intake by individuals, by food group, source, and socioeconomic characteristics, 1977-78 natl survey, final rpt series, 1356–4
- Franchise business opportunities, by firm and kind of business, 1984 annual listing, 2044–27
- Imports of US, detailed Schedule A commodities by country, monthly rpt, 2422–2
- Imports of US, detailed TSUSA commodities by country of origin, 1983, annual rpt, 2424–4
- Income tax returns of sole proprietorships, detailed data by industry div and selected industry group, 1981, annual rpt, 8304–7
- Manufacturing census, 1982: financial and operating data, for SIC 4-digit industries by product, preliminary rpt, 2491–1.349
- Military post exchange operations, locations worldwide, sales by type of commodity or service and facility, and employment, FY83, annual rpt, 3504–10
- Occupational injury and illness rates, by SIC 2- to 4-digit industry, 1982, annual rpt, 6844–1

Occupational Outlook Handbook, 1984-85 biennial rpt, 6744–1

- Service industry census, 1982: employment, establishments, receipts, and payroll, by SIC 2- to 4-digit kind of business, SMSA, county, and city, State rpt series, 2391–1
- Shipments of coin-operated vending machines by product, and trade, 1982-83, annual Current Industrial Rpt, 2506–12.10
- Thefts, and total value of property stolen and recovered, by property type, 1983, annual rpt, 6224–2.1
- Video games and game software and components, effects of foreign imports on US industry, investigation with background financial and operating data, 1984 rpt, 9886–4.71

Venereal diseases

- Acquired immune deficiency syndrome (AIDS) cases, and research funding and activities, monthly rpt, 4042–2
- Acquired immune deficiency syndrome (AIDS) cases by patient sexual preference, 1979-83, article, 4102–1.431
- Acquired immune deficiency syndrome (AIDS) cases by sexual preference and intravenous drug use, and drug abusers characteristics, 1979-81, article, 4102–1.427
- Acquired immune deficiency syndrome (AIDS) inpatients at New York Hospital, by mental health and other characteristics, 1981-83, article, 4102–1.426
- Acquired immune deficiency syndrome (AIDS) research expenditures in 3 areas, by NIH inst, FY82, 4102–1.404
- Army active duty personnel health status and use of Army medical services in US and abroad, by treatment facility, monthly rpt, 3702–4.2
- Cases and control activities, annual rpt, suspended, 4204–5
- Cases and incidence of infectious notifiable diseases and other public health concerns, by census div and State, 1982, annual rpt, 4204–1
- Cases of notifiable infectious diseases and current outbreaks, by region and State, weekly rpt, 4202–1
- Cases reported and epidemiologic activities, by region, State, and large city, 1982, annual rpt, 4204–14
- Deaths and death rates by detailed cause and demographic characteristics, 1979 and selected trends, US Vital Statistics annual rpt, 4144–2.1
- Deaths and death rates, by detailed geographic area, cause, and demographic characteristics, 1979, US Vital Statistics annual rpt, 4144–3
- Deaths and death rates, by selected cause and demographic characteristics, 1981, US Vital Statistics advance rpt, 4146–5.78
- Deaths and death rates, by selected cause and demographic characteristics, 1982, US Vital Statistics advance rpt, 4146–5.81
- Health condition and health care resources, use, and expenditures, 1970s-82 with trends and projections 1900-2000, annual compilation, 4144–11
- Infant deaths by detailed cause, geographic location, age, race, and sex, 1979, US Vital Statistics annual rpt, 4144–2.2

Venezuela

- Pelvic inflammatory disease private physician diagnoses by age, race, and reason for visit, 1979-81, article, 4202–7.404
- *see also* under By Disease in the "Index by Categories"

Venezuela

- Agricultural and food production indexes, and production of selected commodities, by world region and country, 1974-83, annual rpt, 1524–5
- Agricultural exports of US to Latin America, by commodity, country group, and selected country, FY81-84 and forecast FY85, article, 1522–1.407
- Agricultural situation in Latin America, by country, 1981-83 and outlook for 1984, annual rpt, 1524–4.9
- Agricultural supply/demand and market for US exports, with socioeconomic indicators, selected years 1969-83 and projected to 1990, country rpt, 1526–6.5
- Agricultural supply/demand, trade, and production, and socioeconomic data, by country, 1950s-77, 1528–179
- AID economic assistance to developing countries, obligations and disbursements by country, quarterly rpt, 9912–4
- AID loan repayment status and terms by program and country, and status of predecessor agency loans, quarterly rpt, 9912–3
- *Background Notes,* summary social, political, and economic data, 1984 rpt, 7006–2.31
- Currency substitution and depreciation in Venezuela under free market conditions, Mar-Aug 1983, technical paper, 9366–7.98
- Economic conditions in Communist, OECD, and selected other countries, 1960s-83, annual rpt, 244–5
- Economic, social, and political summary data, by country, 1984, annual factbook, 244–11
- Economic trends in income, production, prices, employment, finances, and trade, 1984 semiannual rpt, 2046–4.40, 2046–4.99
- Exports and imports of US, by commodity and country, 1972-82, annual world region rpt, 244–13.2
- Exports of US, detailed Schedule B commodities by country of destination, 1983, annual rpt, 2424–9
- Exports of US, detailed Schedule E commodities by mode of transport and world area and country of destination, 1983, annual rpts, 2424–5
- Imports of US, detailed Schedule A commodities by country and world area of origin, and mode of transport, 1983, annual rpts, 2424–2
- Imports of US, detailed TSUSA commodities by country of origin, 1983, annual rpt, 2424–4
- Intl transactions of US with 10 countries, 1981-83, *Survey of Current Business,* monthly rpt, annual table, 2702–1.31
- Loans and grants for economic and military assistance from US and intl agencies, by program and country, FY46-83, annual rpt, 9914–5
- Military aid of US, arms sales, and training programs costs and budget requests by program, world region, and country, FY83-85, annual rpt, 7144–13

Venezuela

Military spending, arms trade, and armed forces size, with total govt spending and population, by country, 1972-82, annual rpt, 9824–1

Minerals Yearbook, 1982, Vol 3: foreign country reviews of production, trade, and policies, by commodity, annual rpt, 5604–35

Minerals Yearbook, 1983, Vol 3 preprints: foreign country review of production, trade, and policies, by commodity, annual rpt, 5604–23.77

Oil production, and exports and prices to US, by major exporting country, detailed data, monthly rpt, 3162–24

Population size and growth rates, and latest available benchmark demographic data, by country, 1950-83, biennial rpt, 2324–4

Sporting goods and recreational equipment and vehicles market and trade, 1982 country market research rpt, 2045–14.12

Travel to and from US, by world area and selected country, projected 1984-85, annual rpt, 2904–9

see also under By Foreign Country in the "Index by Categories"

Ventura, Calif.

- Census of Housing, 1980: occupancy and unit characteristics, by race, Hispanic origin, and city, SMSA rpt, 2473–1.275
- Census of Population and Housing, 1980: detailed population and housing characteristics, by county, city, and census tract, SMSA rpt, 2551–2.275
- Housing vacancy rates for single and multifamily units and mobile homes, by city and ZIP code, 1983, annual metro area rpt, 9304–20.12
- Wages of office and plant workers, by occupation, 1984 labor market area survey rpt, 6785–3.7

Ventura, Stephanie J.

- "Births of Hispanic Parentage, 1981", 4146–5.80
- "Infant Health Consequences of Childbearing by Teenagers and Older Mothers", 4102–1.420
- "Trends in Teenage Childbearing, U.S., 1970-81", 4147–21.41

Vermiculite

see Nonmetallic minerals and mines

Vermont

- Agriculture census, 1982: farms, farmland, production and costs, and operator characteristics, preliminary State summary and county rpts, 2330–1.50
- Agriculture census, 1982: farms, farmland, production, finances, and operator characteristics, by county, final State rpt, 2331–1.45
- Bank deposits in commercial and mutual savings banks and in US branches of foreign banks, by account type, instn, State, SMSA, and county, June 1983, annual rpt, 9295–3.1
- Census of Housing, 1980: occupancy and unit characteristics of SMSAs and central cities, by race, Hispanic origin, and city, State rpt, 2473–1.47
- Census of Population and Housing, 1980: detailed population and housing characteristics, by county, city, and census tract, State rpt, 2551–2.47
- County Business Patterns: establishments, employees, and payrolls, by SIC 4-digit industry and county, 1982, annual State rpt, 2326–6.47

Index by Subjects and Names

Economic indicators for New England States, Fed Reserve 1st District, monthly rpt with articles, 9373–2

Employment, earnings, and hours, by selected SIC 1- to 4-digit industry, State, and for 278 major labor areas, 1939-83, annual rpt, 6744–5.2, 6744–5.3

Environmental quality, pollutant discharge by type and source, and EPA protection activities and funding, 1970s-83, biennial regional rpt, 9184–15.1

Exports of manufactured and agricultural commodities, manufacturing production, and export-related employment, 1960s-82, State rpt, 2046–3.45

HHS aid to each State and local govt or private instn, amount obligated, funding agency, and program, FY83, annual listing, 4004–3.1

Income (personal) per capita and by source, and earnings by industry div, by State, MSA, and county, 1977-82, annual regional rpt, 2704–2.2

Mineral Industry Surveys, State review of production, 1983, advance annual rpt, 5614–6.45

Minerals Yearbook, 1982, Vol 2 preprints: State review of production and sales by commodity, and business activity, annual rpt, 5604–16.47

Minerals Yearbook, 1982, Vol 2: State reviews of production, sales, and firms, by commodity, and business activity, annual rpt, 5604–34

Population, births, deaths, and net migration, by MSA and county, 1980-82, annual State Current Population Rpt, 2546–4.45

Population size, Apr 1980 and July 1982, and per capita income, 1979 and 1981, by county and city, State Current Population Rpt, 2546–11.45

Retail trade census, 1982: employment, establishments, sales, and payroll, by SIC 2- to 4-digit kind of business, SMSA, county, and city, State rpt, 2397–1.46

Savings and loan assns, FHLB 1st District member instns financial operations and related economic and housing indicators, monthly rpt, 9302–4

Service industry census, 1982: employment, establishments, receipts, and payroll, by SIC 2- to 4-digit kind of business, SMSA, county, and city, State rpt, 2391–1.46

Wages by occupation, and benefits for office and plant workers, 1983 labor market area survey rpt, 6785–3.1

Wages for 3 occupational groups, relative average levels in 78 labor market areas, 1983, annual press release, 6785–13

Wages of office and plant workers, by occupation, 1984 labor market area survey rpt, 6785–3.10

Water supply and quality in streams and lakes, and groundwater levels in wells, by drainage basin, 1982, annual State rpt, 5666–20.28

Wholesale trade census, 1982: employment, establishments, finances, and operations, by SIC 2- to 4-digit kind of business, SMSA, county, and city, State rpt, 2405–1.46

see also Burlington, Vt.

see also under By State in the "Index by Categories"

Vernon, John M.

"Studies on Drug Substitution, Patent Policy and Innovation in the Pharmaceutical Industry", 25528–98

Vernon Parish, La.

- Housing vacancy rates for single and multifamily units and mobile homes, by city and ZIP code, 1984, annual metro area rpt, 9304–19.14

Vertrees, James G.

"Crop Price-Support Programs: Policy Options for Contemporary Agriculture", 26306–6.71

Vetch

see Seeds

Veterans

- Agent Orange exposed Air Force personnel diseases and disorders, by disease type, age, and officer status, 1984 rpt, 3604–3
- Census of Housing, 1980: structural, financial, and householder characteristics, by region and State, 2475–4
- Census of Population, 1980: detailed socioeconomic and demographic characteristics, by age, sex, race, Hispanic origin, occupation, and industry, State rpt series, 2531–4
- Census of Population, 1980: detailed socioeconomic characteristics, by county, city, and inside-outside SMSAs and central cities, State rpt series, 2531–3
- Health condition of veterans and nonveterans, and veteran use of VA and non-VA hospitals by disease, by age, race, income, and metro-nonmetro location, various periods 1971-81, 9926–1.18
- Homeless population and characteristics, and temporary shelter operations, use, and user characteristics, for selected cities, various periods 1979-84, hearing, 21248–85
- Income and educational attainment of veterans compared to nonveterans, by age, 1982-83, annual rpt, 9924–19
- Medicare population with supplemental private insurance coverage and mean annual premium, by selected characteristics of insured, 1977, 4186–3.18
- Older veterans aged 55 and over, socioeconomic characteristics, economic resources, health care and status, and actual and expected VA benefits use, 1983 survey, 9928–29
- Population and characteristics of veterans, and VA activities, FY83, annual rpt, 9924–1
- Population characteristics of veterans by period of service and age, and related issues, statistical rpt series, 9926–4
- Population of veterans, by period of service, age, and State, Sept 1984, semiannual rpt, 9922–3
- Red Cross program operations and financial statements, 1982/83, annual rpt, 29254–1
- *Statistical Abstract of US,* social, political, and economic data, 1950s-83 and trends, annual rpt, 2324–1.2
- Veteran population, by war or period of conflict, FY59-83, annual rpt, 9924–13.1
- Vietnam era veterans characteristics, and participation in VA programs, compared with WW II and Korea veterans, FY83, annual rpt, 9924–8

Index by Subjects and Names

Veterans benefits and pensions

Vietnam veterans health condition, methodology for 3 CDC studies on effects of military service and Agent Orange exposure, Nov 1983 rpt, 4208–22

Vietnam Veterans Memorial Fund receipts by source, and disbursements by item and payee, Apr 1979-Mar 1984, GAO rpt, 26111–21

War participants, deaths, veterans living, and compensation and pension recipients, for each US war, 1775-1983, semiannual rpt, 9922–8

Women veteran population, and use of benefits by type, by age, period of service, and State, with comparisons to men, FY83, annual rpt, 9924–24

Women veterans, by period of service, age, and State, Mar 1983 and projected to 2030, 9928–28

see also Retired military personnel

see also Servicemen's life insurance programs

see also Veterans benefits and pensions

see also Veterans employment

see also Veterans health facilities and services

see also Veterans housing

see also Veterans rehabilitation

Veterans Administration

Activities and programs, FY59-83, annual rpt, 9924–13

Activities and programs, monthly rpt, 9922–2

Activities and programs of VA, and veterans characteristics, FY83, annual rpt, 9924–1

Biostatistical data on VA patients and employees, special study series, 9926–1

Budget of US Appendix, detailed budgets and personnel summaries, by agency, FY85, annual rpt, 104–3

Budget of US, appropriations, outlays, balances, and budget receipts, by govtl branch and agency, FY83, annual rpt, 8104–2

Budget of US, compact budgets by function, agency, and account, FY85 with projections to FY89, annual rpt, 104–2

Budget of US, loans and loan guarantees, and Admin proposed limits on credit assistance, by program, FY83-89, annual rpt, 26306–3.65

Budget of US, object class analysis of obligations, by branch of Fed Govt and selected depts and agencies, FY85 estimates, annual rpt, 104–9

Compensation, pension, and retirement cases, by type of entitlement and period of service, monthly rpt, 9922–10

Cost control proposals for Fed Govt programs and mgmt, 3-year savings by function and agency, and financial and operating data, 1960s-81, 16908–1, 16908–1.10

Digestive Diseases Interagency Coordinating Committee activities, and related Federal research and funding, by agency, FY79-83, annual rpt, 4434–13

Disability and deaths not connected with service, pension cases for veterans, by sex, entitlement type, and period of service, as of Mar 1984, semiannual rpt, 9922–12

Disabled prisoners of war filing disability claims by period of service, and disability ratings by type and degree, various dates Oct 1981-May 1984, chartbook, 9928–30

Disabled veterans receiving VA compensation, by sex, type and degree of disability, and period of service, as of Mar 1984, semiannual rpt, 9922–9

Disabled veterans with VA vocational rehabilitation training, employment and other characteristics, and VA employment services, by regional office, as of 1983, GAO rpt, 26121–78

Educational assistance program participation and costs, under GI Bill and other veterans programs, WW II through Sept 1983, annual rpt, 9924–22

Employee workloads and productivity at Dept of Veterans Benefits field offices, quarterly rpt, 9922–7

Employment (civilian) of Fed Govt, by location, agency, and pay system, 1982, biennial rpt, 9844–8

Employment of disabled veterans in Fed Govt under noncompetitive temporary hiring authority, by pay system, grade, and agency, 2nd half FY82, semiannual rpt, 9842–4

Expenditures for VA programs, by county and congressional district, FY83, annual rpt, 9924–14

Fraud and abuse in VA programs, audits and investigations, 2nd half FY84, semiannual rpt, 9922–13

Health care for veterans, patients, visits, costs, and operating beds, by district and individual VA and contract facility, monthly rpt, 9922–5

Hearing aid performance evaluation, by model and manufacturer, 1984, annual rpt, 9924–5

Housing loan guarantee operations, monthly rpt, 9922–1

Income and employment status of veterans, by age and war or peacetime service, with comparisons to nonveterans, 1981, annual rpt, 9924–23

Land privately held, acreage and owners by owner characteristics, land use, and region, and purchase and improvement funding, 1978 survey, series, 1506–5

Life insurance for veterans and servicemen, actuarial analysis of 5 VA programs, 1982, annual rpt, 9924–16

Life insurance for veterans and servicemen, finances and coverage of 8 VA programs, 1983, annual rpt, 9924–2

Life insurance programs for servicemen's and veterans groups, income, expenses, and death rates, 1980-82, annual rpt, 9924–3

Medical care costs of VA, and amount recovered through billings, by facility, 1982, GAO rpt, 26121–66

Medical care costs, patients, and capacity of VA and non-Va facilties, by service type and patient age, 1970s-83 and projected to 2030, 26306–6.78

Medical facilities of Navy, use by active and retired military personnel, dependents, and others by facility and type, quarterly rpt, 3802–1

Medical facilities of VA, sharing agreement contracts, services, and costs by region and facility, FY83, annual rpt, 9924–18

Medicine and Surgery Dept of VA, trainees by detailed program and city, FY83, annual rpt, 9924–21

Mortgage holdings, transactions, and commitments, monthly rpt, 9312–1.1

Older veterans aged 55 and over, socioeconomic characteristics, economic resources, health care and status, and actual and expected VA benefits use, 1983 survey, 9928–29

Pay comparability of Fed Govt with private industry, and recommended pay rate adjustments, 1983, annual rpt, 104–16

Pay rates of Fed Govt civilian employees, by branch of govt, employee category, and pay level, as of 1984 with trends from 1789, 21628–54

Physicians, dentists, and nurses of VA, by age, selected employment characteristics, and VA district, quarterly rpt, 9922–11

Psychological services, staffing, research, and training programs in VA facilities, 1984 annual listing, 9924–10

R&D Fed Govt funding for all performers, by field and supporting agency, selected years FY60-84, annual rpt, 9627–20

Veteran population, by period of service, age, and State, Sept 1984, semiannual rpt, 9922–3

Veteran women, by period of service, age, and State, Mar 1983 and projected to 2030, 9928–28

Veterans characteristics by period of service and age, and related issues, statistical rpt series, 9926–4

Veterans income and educational attainment compared to nonveterans, by age, 1982-83, annual rpt, 9924–19

Vietnam era veterans characteristics, and participation in VA programs, compared with WW II and Korea veterans, FY83, annual rpt, 9924–8

War participants, deaths, veterans living, and compensation and pension recipients, for each US war, 1775-1983, semiannual rpt, 9922–8

Women veteran population, and use of benefits by type, by age, period of service, and State, with comparisons to men, FY83, annual rpt, 9924–24

Veterans benefits and pensions

Beneficiaries and taxes collected for social insurance programs since 1940, monthly rpt, 4742–1.1

Beneficiaries of noncash public and employer-based transfer programs, by income source and socioeconomic characteristics, 1982, final Current Population Rpt, 2546–6.37

Benefits, and beneficiaries with representative payees by age and relation to payee, by Fed Govt cash program, as of 1983, GAO rpt, 26121–85

Benefits, beneficiary characteristics, and trust funds of OASDHI, Medicaid, SSI, and other social insurance and public welfare programs, selected years 1950-82, annual rpt, 4744–3.9, 4744–3.10

Budget of US Appendix, detailed budgets and personnel summaries, by agency, FY85, annual rpt, 104–3

Budget of US, CBO analysis and review of FY85 budget by function, annual rpt, 26304–2

Budget of US, CBO analysis of revenue and spending alternatives and projections of economic indicators, FY85-89, annual rpt, 26304–3.3

Veterans benefits and pensions

Budget of US, compact budgets by function, agency, and account, FY85 with projections to FY89, annual rpt, 104–2

Budget of US, effects of Reagan Admin policy changes, by detailed program, FY85, annual rpt, 104–21

Budget of US, loans and loan guarantees, and Admin proposed limits on credit assistance, by program, FY83-89, annual rpt, 26306–3.65

Budget of US, receipts by source and outlays by agency and program, monthly rpt, 8102–3

Budget of US, receipts by source and outlays by function, FY40-89 estimates revised for consistency with FY85 budget definitions, annual rpt, 104–12

Budget of US, receipts, outlays, and budget authority, by function and agency, FY84-89 revised estimates, midsession review of FY85 budget, annual rpt, 104–7

Budget of US, receipts, outlays, and budget authority, by function and agency, 1st revision of FY85 budget, annual rpt, 104–17

Children and youth benefitting from Fed Govt public welfare programs and tax expenditures, participation and funding for 71 programs, FY81-83, 21968–30

Civil case processing of US Attorneys and amounts involved, by cause of action, FY83, annual rpt, 6004–2.5

Compensation, pension, and retirement cases, by type of entitlement and period of service, monthly rpt, 9922–10

Cost control proposals for Fed Govt programs and mgmt, CBO and GAO estimates of savings by function and agency, FY85-89, 26308–45

Cost control proposals for Fed Govt programs and mgmt, 3-year savings by function and agency, and financial and operating data, 1960s-81, 16908–1.10, 16908–1.23

Disability and deaths not connected with service, pension cases for veterans, by sex, entitlement type, and period of service, as of Mar 1984, semiannual rpt, 9922–12

Disabled prisoners of war filing disability claims by period of service, and disability ratings by type and degree, various dates Oct 1981-May 1984, chartbook, 9928–30

Disabled veterans, by age, race, employment status, period of service, and whether applied for VA benefits, 1979, 9926–4.6

Disabled veterans receiving VA compensation, by sex, type and degree of disability, and period of service, as of Mar 1984, semiannual rpt, 9922–9

Education Dept programs funding, operations, and effectiveness, FY83, annual rpt, 4804–5

Educational assistance, Pell grants and recipients, by educational costs, family income, instnl type and control, and State, 1981/82, annual rpt, 4804–1

Educational assistance program participation and costs, under GI Bill and other veterans programs, WW II through Sept 1983, annual rpt, 9924–22

Expenditures and beneficiaries of VA compensation, health, and rehabilitation programs, FY59-83, annual rpt, 9924–13

Fed Govt aid to State and local govts, expenditures, and direct payments, by program, agency, and State, FY83, annual rpt, 2464–2

Fed Govt consolidated financial statements based on business accounting methods, FY82-83, annual rpt, 8104–5

Fed Govt financial and nonfinancial domestic aid, 1984 annual comprehensive catalog, 104–5

Food stamp recipient households size and composition, income, and income deductions allowed, Aug 1981, annual rpt, 1364–8

Fraud and abuse in VA programs, audits and investigations, 2nd half FY84, semiannual rpt, 9922–13

Govt census, 1982: State govt payments to local govts, by program, source of funds, level of govt, and State, with trends from 1902, 2460–3

Govt expenditures for public welfare, by level of govt and type of program, selected years FY50-82, 4746–16.1

Govt expenditures for social welfare by program and level of govt, and private expenditures for health care, selected years FY50-82, annual article, 4742–1.425

Govt revenues by source and expenditures by function, natl income and product account, *Survey of Current Business,* monthly rpt, monthly and annual tables, 2702–1.24

Govt revenues by source, expenditures by function, debt, and assets, by level of govt, 1982-83, annual rpt, 2466–2.6

Income (household) and cash and noncash transfer program participation, by sociodemographic characteristics, quarterly rpt, 2542–2

Income (personal) by source including transfer payments, and social insurance contributions by type, by region, 1929 and 1982, 2708–40

Income from transfer payments, natl income and product account, *Survey of Current Business,* monthly rpt, monthly and annual tables, 2702–1.23

Life insurance for veterans and servicemen, actuarial analysis of 5 VA programs, 1982, annual rpt, 9924–16

Life insurance for veterans and servicemen, finances and coverage of 8 VA programs, 1983, annual rpt, 9924–2

Loan programs of Fed Govt, direct and guaranteed loans outstanding by agency and program, *Treasury Bulletin,* quarterly rpt, 8002–4.10

Older persons income and income sources, by OASDI beneficiary and poverty status, labor force participation, and demographic characteristics, 1982, biennial rpt, 4744–26

Older persons sociodemographic characteristics, and Fed Govt program participation and funding, 1983 with trends and projections 1900-2060, annual rpt, 25144–3.1

Older veterans aged 55 and over, socioeconomic characteristics, economic resources, health care and status, and actual and expected VA benefits use, 1983 survey, 9928–29

Index by Subjects and Names

Poverty-level persons and families, by income source, hours of work, earnings, taxes, and family characteristics, various periods 1959-84, 21788–131

Tax expenditures, Fed Govt revenues foregone through income tax deductions and exclusions by type, and effect of Deficit Reduction Act, FY84-89, annual rpt, 21784–10

VA program expenditures, by county and congressional district, FY83, annual rpt, 9924–14

VA programs and activities, and veterans characteristics, FY83, annual rpt, 9924–1

VA programs and activities, monthly rpt, 9922–2

VA workloads and productivity at each Dept of Veterans Benefits field office, with regional summaries, quarterly rpt, 9922–7

Veterans using VA services by number of programs used and program, 1979, 9926–4.10

Vietnam era veterans characteristics, and participation in VA programs, compared with WW II and Korea veterans, FY83, annual rpt, 9924–8

War participants, deaths, veterans living, and compensation and pension recipients, for each US war, 1775-1983, semiannual rpt, 9922–8

Women veteran population, and use of benefits by type, by age, period of service, and State, with comparisons to men, FY83, annual rpt, 9924–24

see also Military pensions

see also Servicemen's life insurance programs

see also Veterans health facilities and services

see also Veterans housing

Veterans employment

CETA participants by sociodemographic characteristics, and Labor Dept activities and staff, FY83, annual rpt, 6304–1

Disabled veterans, by age, race, employment status, period of service, and whether applied for VA benefits, 1979, 9926–4.6

Disabled veterans with VA vocational rehabilitation training, employment and other characteristics, and VA employment services, by regional office, as of 1983, GAO rpt, 26121–78

DOT employment by subagency, State, and selected personnel characteristics, FY83, annual rpt, 7304–18.2, 7304–18.3

Fed Govt appointments and separations of disabled and nondisabled veterans, by agency, 2nd half FY82, semiannual rpt, 9842–3

Fed Govt noncompetitive temporary hiring of disabled veterans, by pay system, grade, and agency, 2nd half FY82, semiannual rpt, 9842–4

Fed Govt personnel action appeals, decisions of Merit Systems Protection Board, by agency, veteran status, sex, and age, FY82, annual rpt, 9494–2.1

Health condition of veterans and nonveterans, and veteran use of VA and non-VA hospitals by disease, by age, race, income, and metro-nonmetro location, various periods 1971-81, 9926–1.18

Income and employment status of veterans, by age and war or peacetime service, with comparisons to nonveterans, 1981, annual rpt, 9924–23

Index by Subjects and Names

Veterans rehabilitation

Older veterans aged 55 and over, socioeconomic characteristics, economic resources, health care and status, and actual and expected VA benefits use, 1983 survey, 9928–29

Small Business Admin loan and contract activity by program, and balance sheets, FY83, annual rpt, 9764–1.1

Small business and all employees sociodemographic characteristics, by industry div and firm size, 1978-1979, annual rpt, 9764–6.3

Unemployment insurance benefits and claims, by program, Monthly Labor Review, 6722–1.4

Unemployment insurance claims, insured unemployment, and exhaustions, by program, weekly rpt, 6402–14

Unemployment rates and compensation, Vietnam era veterans compared with WW II and Korea veterans, FY83, annual rpt, 9924–8.2

VA employment characteristics and activities, FY83, annual rpt, 9924–1.8

Vietnam-era male veterans and nonveterans employment status, by age, monthly press release, 6742–5

Vietnam-era male veterans employment status, by age, race, and Hispanic origin, monthly rpt, 6742–2

Vietnam-era veterans and nonveterans employment status, by age, race, and Hispanic origin, annual averages, 1983, article, 6742–2.403

Vietnam era veterans and nonveterans employment status, 1980-82, annual rpt, 6724–1.1

Vietnam-era veterans employment status, BLS data, transcripts of BLS Commissioner's monthly testimony, periodic rpt, 23846–4

Veterans health facilities and services

Agent Orange exposure and Vietnam military service effects on veteran health condition, methodology for 3 CDC studies, Nov 1983 rpt, 4208–22

Budget of US, CBO analysis of revenue and spending alternatives and projections of economic indicators, FY85-89, annual rpt, 26304–3.3

Budget of US, effects of Reagan Admin policy changes, by detailed program, FY85, annual rpt, 104–21

Communicative disorders among VA patients, by age, disease and treatment characteristics, and facility type, 1981 survey, 9926–4.8, 9926–4.9

Cost control proposals for Fed Govt programs and mgmt, 3-year savings by function and agency, and financial and operating data, 1960s-81, 16908–1.10, 16908–1.24, 16908–1.28

Expenditures and beneficiaries of VA compensation, health, and rehabilitation programs, FY59-83, annual rpt, 9924–13

Expenditures by VA, by county and congressional district, FY83, annual rpt, 9924–14

Fraud and abuse in VA programs, audits and investigations, 2nd half FY84, semiannual rpt, 9922–13

Govt expenditures for social welfare by program and level of govt, and private expenditures for health care, selected years FY50-82, annual article, 4742–1.425

Health care expenditures, natl and personal total and per capita amounts, by type of service and source of funds, 1983 and trends from 1929, annual article, 4652–1.429

Health condition and health care resources, use, and expenditures, 1970s-82 with trends and projections 1900-2000, annual compilation, 4144–11

HHS aid to each State and local govt or private instn, amount obligated, funding agency, and program, FY83, annual listing, 4004–3

Medical care costs of VA, and amount recovered through billings, by facility, 1982, GAO rpt, 26121–66

Medical care costs, patients, and capacity of VA and non-Va facilties, by service type and patient age, 1970s-83 and projected to 2030, 26306–6.78

Medical facilities of VA, sharing agreement contracts, services, and costs by region and facility, FY83, annual rpt, 9924–18

Medicine and Surgery Dept of VA, trainees by detailed program and city, FY83, annual rpt, 9924–21

Mental health facilities, beds, and bed/population ratios, by facility type, region, and State, 1982 with trends from 1972, 4506–3.14

Mental health facilities of States and counties, inpatients, deaths, staff by occupation, and facilities, by State, 1970s-82, 4506–3.13

Mental health facilities, services, staff, and patient characteristics, 1970s-82 with trends from 1954, annual rpt, 4504–9

Nursing homes and hospitals of VA, discharges of aged veterans, 1982, article, 4652–1.420

Older veterans aged 55 and over, socioeconomic characteristics, economic resources, health care and status, and actual and expected VA benefits use, 1983 survey, 9928–29

Patients and employees, biostatistical data, special VA study series, 9926–1

Patients, visits, costs, and operating beds in VA and contract health facilities, by district and facility, monthly rpt, 9922–5

Psychological services, staffing, research, and training programs in VA facilities, 1984 annual listing, 9924–10

VA programs and activities, and veterans characteristics, FY83, annual rpt, 9924–1

VA programs and activities, monthly rpt, 9922–2

Veterans using VA services by number of programs used and program, 1979, 9926–4.10

Vietnam era veterans in VA medical centers, and outpatient medical and dental care, various periods FY68-83, annual rpt, 9924–8.4

Women veteran population, and use of benefits by type, by age, period of service, and State, with comparisons to men, FY83, annual rpt, 9924–24

see also Military hospitals

see also Veterans benefits and pensions

see also Veterans rehabilitation

Veterans hospitals

see Veterans health facilities and services

Veterans housing

Bond tax-exempt issues by purpose, and Fed Govt mortgage bond revenue losses and borrower characteristics, selected years 1971-85, hearings, 21788–135

Budget of US, effects of Reagan Admin policy changes, by detailed program, FY85, annual rpt, 104–21

Cost control proposals for Fed Govt programs and mgmt, 3-year savings by function and agency, and financial and operating data, 1960s-81, 16908–1.10

Home mortgages FHA-insured, financial, property, and mortgagor characteristics, 1983, annual rpt, 5144–17

Loan guarantee operations of VA, monthly rpt, 9922–1

Mortgage insurance of FHA and VA for new housing, bimonthly rpt, 2012–1.2

Mortgage loans guaranteed by VA, and other activities, FY83, annual rpt, 9924–1.7

Mortgage loans guaranteed by VA, loans defaulted, and property acquisition and mgmt, FY59-83, annual rpt, 9924–13.3

Mortgage transactions and holdings, by lender group and type of property and loan, quarterly rpt, 5142–30

New single and multifamily housing physical and financial characteristics, by region and metro-nonmetro location, 1979-83, annual rpt, 2384–1

New single-family housing units sold and sales price by type of financing, monthly rpt, quarterly tables, 2382–3.2

Older veterans aged 55 and over, socioeconomic characteristics, economic resources, health care and status, and actual and expected VA benefits use, 1983 survey, 9928–29

VA program expenditures, by county and congressional district, FY83, annual rpt, 9924–14

VA programs and activities, monthly rpt, 9922–2

Veterans using VA services by number of programs used and program, 1979, 9926–4.10

Vietnam era veterans participation in training, rehabilitation, and housing programs, compared with WW II and Korea veterans, FY83, annual rpt, 9924–8.6

Veterans loans

see Veterans benefits and pensions

Veterans pensions

see Veterans benefits and pensions

Veterans rehabilitation

Budget of US, effects of Reagan Admin policy changes, by detailed program, FY85, annual rpt, 104–21

Disabled American Veterans financial statements, 1982, GAO rpt, 26111–16

Employment and other characteristics of veterans with VA vocational rehabilitation training, and VA employment services, by regional office, as of 1983, GAO rpt, 26121–78

Expenditures and beneficiaries of VA compensation, health, and rehabilitation programs, FY59-83, annual rpt, 9924–13

Fed Govt appointments and separations of disabled and nondisabled veterans, by agency, 2nd half FY82, semiannual rpt, 9842–3

Veterans rehabilitation

Hearing aid performance evaluation, by model and manufacturer, 1984, annual rpt, 9924–5

Medicine and Surgery Dept of VA, trainees by detailed program and city, FY83, annual rpt, 9924–21

VA program expenditures, by county and congressional district, FY83, annual rpt, 9924–14

VA programs and activities, and veterans characteristics, FY83, annual rpt, 9924–1

VA programs and activities, monthly rpt, 9922–2

VA workloads and productivity at each Dept of Veterans Benefits field office, with regional summaries, quarterly rpt, 9922–7

Veterans using VA services by number of programs used and program, 1979, 9926–4.10

Vietnam era veterans participation in training, rehabilitation, and housing programs, compared with WW II and Korea veterans, FY83, annual rpt, 9924–8.6

Vocational rehabilitation program participation of disabled veterans, FY65-83, annual rpt, 9924–22

Vocationally rehabilitated persons under State agency programs, by sociodemographic characteristics and disabling condition, FY79-81, annual rpt, 4944–6

Veterinary medicine

Army morale, welfare, and recreation programs, revenue and expenses worldwide by activity and major command, FY82-83, annual rpt, 3704–12

Biotechnology commercial uses, R&D funding and output, controls, and industry financial and operating data, for US and 5 countries, 1970s-83 and estimated 1984-85, 26358–98

Census of Population, 1980: detailed socioeconomic and demographic characteristics, by age, sex, race, Hispanic origin, occupation, and industry, State rpt series, 2531–4

Census of Population, 1980: labor force, by sex, detailed occupation, and region, with comparison to 1970 census, supplementary rpt, 2535–1.12

County Business Patterns: establishments, employees, and payrolls, by SIC 4-digit industry and county, 1981, annual State rpt series, 2326–8

County Business Patterns: establishments, employees, and payrolls, by SIC 4-digit industry and county, 1982, annual State rpt series, 2326–6

Degrees conferred in higher education, by race, Hispanic origin, sex, level, and field, selected years 1949/50-1979/80, annual rpt, 4824–2.16

DOD medical personnel, trainees, and accessions by source, by occupation, specialty, and service branch, FY83, annual rpt, 3544–24

Drug (animal) approval of govts, months to approval in US and 2 countries by drug brand and manufacturer, selected years 1965-83, hearing, 25528–98

Drug shipments by region and selected census div and State, trade, and consumption, by product, 1983, annual Current Industrial Rpt, 2506–8.5

Farm production expenditures, detailed items by farm sales size and region, 1983, annual rpt, 1614–3

Farm production itemized costs, receipts, and net returns, for 13 crops, 4 livestock types, and milk, by region, 1981-83, annual rpt, 1544–20

Health condition and health care resources, use, and expenditures, 1970s-82 with trends and projections 1900-2000, annual compilation, 4144–11

Income tax returns of sole proprietorships, detailed data by industry div and selected industry group, 1981, annual rpt, 8304–7

Income tax returns of sole proprietorships, receipts, deductions by type, payroll, and net income, by major industry, 1982, annual article, 8302–2.413

Inspection of meat and poultry, Federal, State, and foreign govts activities and personnel, FY83, annual rpt, 1374–1

Manpower supply and education of health professionals, by occupation, demographic and professional characteristics, and location, 1950s-83 and projected to 2000, biennial rpt, 4114–8

Minority group and women employment and training in health professions, by field, selected years 1962/63-1983/84, 4118–18

Occupational Outlook Handbook, 1984-85 biennial rpt, 6744–1

R&D-employed scientists and engineers salaries by degree, type of establishment, age, experience, and field, 1984, annual rpt, 3004–1

Research grants awarded competitively by USDA for agricultural science, food and nutrition, and energy dev, FY83, annual listing, 1744–1

Science and engineering grad enrollment, fields of study, financial support, and other student and instn characteristics, 1975-82, annual survey, 9627–7

see also Animal diseases and zoonoses

Vicksburg, Miss.

Waterborne commerce of US (domestic and foreign), freight by commodity, traffic, and passengers, by port and waterway, 1982, annual rpt, 3754–3.2

Victoria, Tex.

Census of Housing, 1980: occupancy and unit characteristics, by race, Hispanic origin, and city, SMSA rpt, 2473–1.361

Census of Population and Housing, 1980: detailed population and housing characteristics, by county, city, and census tract, SMSA rpt, 2551–2.361

see also under By SMSA or MSA in the "Index by Categories"

Video cassette recorders

see Recording industry

see Television

Vietnam

Agricultural situation in Southeast Asia, by country and commodity, 1983 and outlook for 1984, annual rpt, 1524–4.5

AID economic assistance to developing countries, obligations and disbursements by country, quarterly rpt, 9912–4

AID loan repayment status and terms by program and country, and status of predecessor agency loans, quarterly rpt, 9912–3

Index by Subjects and Names

Background Notes, summary social, political, and economic data, 1984 rpt, 7006–2.35

Cuba economic conditions, agricultural and industrial production and distribution, trade, and intl economic relations, 1970-82 and trends from 1957, 248–40

Economic, social, and political summary data, by country, 1984, annual factbook, 244–11

Exports and imports of US with Communist countries, by detailed commodity and country, quarterly rpt with articles, 9882–2

Exports of US, detailed Schedule B commodities by country of destination, 1983, annual rpt, 2424–9

Exports of US, detailed Schedule E commodities by mode of transport and world area and country of destination, 1983, annual rpts, 2424–5

Imports of US, detailed Schedule A commodities by country and world area of origin, and mode of transport, 1983, annual rpts, 2424–2

Loans and grants for economic and military assistance from US and intl agencies, by program and country, FY46-83, annual rpt, 9914–5

Military spending, arms trade, and armed forces size, with total govt spending and population, by country, 1972-82, annual rpt, 9824–1

Minerals Yearbook, 1982, Vol 3: foreign country reviews of production, trade, and policies, by commodity, annual rpt, 5604–35

Minerals Yearbook, 1982, Vol 3 preprints: foreign country review of production, trade, and policies, by commodity, annual rpt, 5604–17.87

Population size and growth rates, and latest available benchmark demographic data, by country, 1950-83, biennial rpt, 2324–4

Refugee Indochinese population, arrivals, and departures, by country of origin and resettlement, camp, and ethnicity, monthly rpt, 7002–4

Refugee migration, settlement status, and assistance, by world area and country of origin and asylum, as of May 1984, annual rpt, 7004–15

Refugee resettlement program activities and funding, arrivals and population by country of origin and State, and employment and other characteristics, FY83, annual rpt, 4704–8

Science and technology dev and transfer between USSR and other members of Council for Mutual Economic Assistance, 1940s-81, 2326–9.7

see also under By Foreign Country in the "Index by Categories"

Vietnam conflict

see War

Vincennes, Ind.

Wages by occupation, and benefits for office and plant workers, 1983 labor market area survey rpt, 6785–3.2

Vineland, N.J.

Census of Housing, 1980: occupancy and unit characteristics, by race, Hispanic origin, and city, SMSA rpt, 2473–1.362

Census of Population and Housing, 1980: detailed population and housing characteristics, by county, city, and census tract, SMSA rpt, 2551–2.362

Index by Subjects and Names

see also under By SMSA or MSA in the "Index by Categories"

Vinyl chloride

see Chemicals and chemical industry

Vinyl materials

see Plastics and plastics industry

Virgin Islands

- Agriculture census, 1982: farms, farmland, production, finances, and operator characteristics, by island, final outlying area rpt, 2331–1.54
- Airlines (commuter and intrastate) operating in 1978 by region and State, and listing by city, by operation status in 1984, article, 9142–42.404
- Animal protection, licensing, and inspection activities of USDA, and animals used in research, by State, FY83, annual rpt, 1394–10
- Bank deposits in commercial and mutual savings banks and in US branches of foreign banks, by account type, instn, State, SMSA, and county, June 1983, annual rpt, 9295–3.2
- Births (live) by selected demographic characteristics, for 3 outlying areas, 1979, US Vital Statistics annual rpt, 4144–1.3
- Bombing (explosive and incendiary) incidents, damage, injuries, and deaths, by target, State, and circumstances, 1983, annual rpt, 6224–5
- Cattle brucellosis eradication, and testing of goats and swine, cooperative Federal-State program activities, by State, FY83, annual rpt, 1394–6
- Cattle tuberculosis eradication and surveillance, cooperative Federal-State program activities, by State, FY83, annual rpt, 1394–13
- Census of Population, 1980: detailed socioeconomic characteristics, by island, city, and urban-rural location, outlying area rpt, 2531–3.55
- Earthquake intensity, damage, and deaths, by location for major earthquakes since 1755, and hazard areas and natl reduction program activities, as of 1984, 5668–73
- Economic Censuses of Virgin Islands, 1982: employment, establishments, payroll, and receipts, by SIC 1- to 4-digit industry, island, and city, 2593–1
- Economic, social, and govtl data, FY81, annual rpt, 5304–4
- Employment and wages of workers covered by State unemployment insurance laws and Fed Govt unemployment compensation, by SIC 4-digit industry and State, 1982, annual rpt, 6744–16
- Employment by industry div, major manufacturing group, and State, Monthly Labor Review, 6722–1.2
- Employment, earnings, and hours, by selected SIC 1- to 4-digit industry, State, and for 278 major labor areas, 1939-83, annual rpt, 6744–5.2, 6744–5.3
- Environmental quality, pollutant discharge by type and source, and EPA protection activities and funding, 1970s-83, biennial regional rpt, 9184–15.2
- Exports and imports between US and outlying areas, by detailed commodity and mode of transport, monthly rpt, 2422–4
- Fishing (ocean sport) effort and catch, and Natl Marine Fisheries Service tagging and research activity, by species and location, 1983, annual rpt, 2164–7
- Govt census, 1982: properties, govt-assessed value, sales, and tax rates, by property type, State, SMSA, county, and city, 2453–1
- Govt financial data, audits of Interior Dept Inspector General, FY83, annual rpt, 5304–15.7
- Govt fiscal condition for Virgin Islands, FY81, annual rpt, 5304–10
- HHS aid to each State and local govt or private instn, amount obligated, funding agency, and program, FY83, annual listing, 4004–3.2
- Housing units authorized, by public and private ownership, State, and permit-issuing place, 1983, annual rpt, 2384–2
- HUD rental rehabilitation projects, local funding and Section 8 rent supplements for 22 States and 275 communities, 1984 press release, 5006–3.30
- Import duty collections of Virgin Islands, and reimbursement of US Customs Service collections expenses, FY81-83, GAO rpt, 26119–54
- Marriages, divorces, and rates, by detailed demographic characteristics, 1979 and trends, US Vital Statistics annual rpt, 4144–4.3
- Medicare program operations and admin efficiency, Blue Shield participants, and end-stage renal disease program activity, FY81, annual rpt, 4654–5
- *Minerals Yearbook,* 1982, Vol 2 preprints: State review of production and sales by commodity, and business activity, annual rpt, 5604–16.40
- *Minerals Yearbook,* 1982, Vol 2: State reviews of production, sales, and firms, by commodity, and business activity, annual rpt, 5604–34
- Mines, mills, and quarries occupational injuries, and employees and hours, by State, quarterly rpt, 6662–1
- Occupational injuries and illnesses, data available from NTIS, by State, 1981, annual rpt, 6704–2
- Oil and refined products imports into US and Virgin Islands, monthly rpt, 2422–6.2
- Oil exports to US by OPEC and non-OPEC countries, monthly rpt, 3162–24.3
- Population size and components of change, by outlying area, 1970-82, Current Population Rpt, 2546–3.127
- Population size and components of change, by outlying area, 1980-83, Current Population Rpt, 2546–3.134
- Population size and growth rates, and latest available benchmark demographic data, by country, 1950-83, biennial rpt, 2324–4
- Rum production, trade by selected country, consumption, and shipments from Puerto Rico and Virgin Islands, Jan-June 1983-84, annual rpt, 9884–15
- Rural Electrification Admin loans to power supply and distribution firms, and borrower operating and financial data, by firm and State, 1983, annual rpt, 1244–1
- Rural Electrification Program loan activities summary, by State, FY83 and cumulative from 1935, annual rpt, 1244–7
- Storms and unusual weather phenomena characteristics, casualties, and property damage, by State and outlying area, monthly listing, 2152–3

Virginia

- Unemployment insurance State govt program admin, quality appraisal results, FY84, annual rpt, 6404–16
- Unemployment insurance State govt program benefits, coverage, and tax provisions, July 1984, semiannual listing, 6402–7
- Unemployment insurance system finances, claims, payments, and covered employment and wages, by State, 1938-82, 6408–5
- US Attorneys civil and criminal case processing in district, appellate, and State courts, by district, FY83, annual rpt, 6004–2
- Wages for 3 occupational groups, relative average levels in 78 labor market areas, 1983, annual press release, 6785–13
- Wages of office and plant workers, by occupation, 1983 labor market area survey rpt, 6785–3.2
- Waterborne commerce of US (domestic and foreign), freight by commodity, traffic, and passengers, by port and waterway, 1982, annual rpt, 3754–3.2
- Wool textile product imports of US, transshipments through Virgin Islands, 1972-82, annual rpt, 2044–14
- Workers compensation law provisions of States and Fed Govt, by jurisdiction, as of July 1984, semiannual rpt, 6502–1
- Workers compensation laws, changes in coverage, benefits, and premium rates, for 49 States, DC, and Virgin Islands, 1983, annual article, 6722–1.415
- *see also* Charlotte Amalie, V.I.
- *see also* Christiansted, V.I.
- *see also* Frederiksted, V.I.
- *see also* under By Outlying Area in the "Index by Categories"

Virginia

- Agriculture census, 1982: farms, farmland, production and costs, and operator characteristics, preliminary State summary and county rpts, 2330–1.51
- Agriculture census, 1982: farms, farmland, production, finances, and operator characteristics, by county, final State rpt, 2331–1.46
- Apple production, marketing, and prices in 4 Appalachian States, 1983/84 crop year, annual rpt, 1311–13
- Bank deposits in commercial and mutual savings banks and in US branches of foreign banks, by account type, instn, State, SMSA, and county, June 1983, annual rpt, 9295–3.5
- Bank income and expenses, Fed Reserve 5th District member banks, by State, 1983, annual rpt, 9389–10
- Census of Housing, 1980: occupancy and unit characteristics of SMSAs and central cities, by race, Hispanic origin, and city, State rpt, 2473–1.48
- Census of Population and Housing, 1980: detailed population and housing characteristics, by county, city, and census tract, State rpt, 2551–2.48
- Census of Population, 1980: detailed socioeconomic and demographic characteristics, by age, sex, race, Hispanic origin, and industry, State rpt, 2531–4.48
- Coal (bituminous) mining production and related workers, wages by occupation, and benefits, by size of mine and union status,

Virginia

in 6 States and aggregate for Rocky Mountain States, July 1982 survey, 6787–6.198

- County Business Patterns: establishments, employees, and payrolls, by SIC 4-digit industry and county, 1982, annual State rpt, 2326–6.48
- Economic indicators by State, Fed Reserve 5th District, quarterly rpt, 9389–16
- Employment, earnings, and hours, by selected SIC 1- to 4-digit industry, State, and for 278 major labor areas, 1939-83, annual rpt, 6744–5.2, 6744–5.3
- Environmental quality, pollutant discharge by type and source, and EPA protection activities and funding, 1970s-83, biennial regional rpt, 9184–15.3
- Exports of manufactured and agricultural commodities, manufacturing production, and export-related employment, 1960s-82, State rpt, 2046–3.46
- Foster care children permanent placement, Fed Govt incentive program funding and operations in 7 States, FY80-82, GAO rpt, 26121–81
- HHS aid to each State and local govt or private instn, amount obligated, funding agency, and program, FY83, annual listing, 4004–3.3
- Higher education new enrollment in Virginia, and students needed to meet desegregation goals, by race and instn, selected years 1978-85, hearings, 21348–91
- Income (personal) per capita and by source, and earnings by industry div, by State, MSA, and county, 1977-82, annual regional rpt, 2704–2.6
- Manufacturing census, 1982: financial and operating data, by SIC 2- to 4-digit industry, State, SMSA, and county, preliminary census div rpt, 2491–3.5
- Mineral Industry Surveys, State review of production, 1983, advance annual rpt, 5614–6.46
- *Minerals Yearbook, 1982,* Vol 2 preprints: State review of production and sales by commodity, and business activity, annual rpt, 5604–16.48
- *Minerals Yearbook, 1982,* Vol 2: State reviews of production, sales, and firms, by commodity, and business activity, annual rpt, 5604–34
- Population, births, deaths, and net migration, by MSA and county, 1980-82, annual State Current Population Rpt, 2546–4.46
- Population size, Apr 1980 and July 1982, and per capita income, 1979 and 1981, by county and city, State Current Population Rpt, 2546–11.46
- Retail trade census, 1982: employment, establishments, sales, and payroll, by SIC 2- to 4-digit kind of business, SMSA, county, and city, State rpt, 2397–1.47
- Savings and loan assns, FHLB 4th District insured members financial condition and operations, by SMSA, monthly rpt, 9302–1
- Seat belt use by blue and white collar workers, results of Virginia projects to increase use, 1983, article, 7762–9.409
- Ships in Natl Defense Reserve Fleet at James River, Va, Jan 1984, semiannual inventory, 7702–2

Wages of office and plant workers in Lower Eastern Shore, Md-Va-Del, by occupation, 1984 labor market area survey rpt, 6785–3.9

- Wages of office and plant workers in Southwest Virginia, by occupation, 1983 labor market area survey rpt, 6785–3.2
- Water supply and quality, and effect of coal mining operations, for selected river basins in Eastern and Interior coal provinces, 1983 rpt, 5666–15.22, 5666–15.26
- Water supply and quality in streams and lakes, and groundwater levels in wells, by drainage basin, 1983, annual State rpt, 5666–10.43
- Wholesale trade census, 1982: employment, establishments, finances, and operations, by SIC 2- to 4-digit kind of business, SMSA, county, and city, State rpt, 2405–1.47
- *see also* Colonial Heights, Va.
- *see also* Danville, Va.
- *see also* Hampton, Va.
- *see also* Hopewell, Va.
- *see also* Lynchburg, Va.
- *see also* Newport News, Va.
- *see also* Norfolk, Va.
- *see also* Petersburg, Va.
- *see also* Portsmouth, Va.
- *see also* Richmond, Va.
- *see also* Roanoke, Va.
- *see also* Virginia Beach, Va.
- *see also* under By State in the "Index by Categories"

Virginia Beach, Va.

- Census of Housing, 1980: occupancy and unit characteristics, by race, Hispanic origin, and city, SMSA rpt, 2473–1.265
- Census of Population and Housing, 1980: detailed population and housing characteristics, by county, city, and census tract, SMSA rpt, 2551–2.265
- Home mortgage creative financing, effect on home sales price, model results for Virginia Beach, Va, July 1981-Mar 1982, article, 9412–2.408
- Wages of office and plant workers, by occupation, 1984 SMSA survey rpt, 6785–11.5
- *see also* under By City and By SMSA or MSA in the "Index by Categories"

Visalia, Calif.

- Census of Housing, 1980: occupancy and unit characteristics, by race, Hispanic origin, and city, SMSA rpt, 2473–1.363
- Census of Population and Housing, 1980: detailed population and housing characteristics, by county, city, and census tract, SMSA rpt, 2551–2.363
- Housing vacancy rates for single and multifamily units and mobile homes, by city and ZIP code, 1983, annual metro area rpt, 9304–20.10
- Housing vacancy rates for single and multifamily units and mobile homes, by city and ZIP code, 1984, annual metro area rpt, 9304–20.18
- *see also* under By SMSA or MSA in the "Index by Categories"

Viscount, Francis

- "City Fiscal Conditions in FY83: Dark Clouds on the Horizon", 25408–86.1
- "Importance of GRS Continues and the Need for Renewal Increases", 25408–86.2

Index by Subjects and Names

Vision

- Health care expenditures, natl and personal total and per capita amounts, by type of service and source of funds, 1983 and trends from 1929, annual article, 4652–1.429
- Older persons nutrition services program operations and assessment, and participant sociodemographic, health, and diet characteristics, 1976 and 1982, 4608–16
- Visual impairment survey methodology and results by age, in 3 SMSAs, Aug 1981-Dec 1982, 4478–147
- *see also* Blind
- *see also* Eye diseases and defects
- *see also* Optometry

VISTA

Activities, volunteer characteristics, and budget of ACTION, by program, FY82, annual rpt, 9024–2

Vital statistics

- Collection of vital and health statistics, and use in program and evaluation, Public Health Conf papers, 1983, biennial rpt, 4164–2
- *County and City Data Book,* detailed socioeconomic and demographic data for States, counties, and cities, selected years 1976-82, 2328–1
- Developing countries disaster preparedness and summary sociodemographic, political, and economic data, country rpt series, 9916–2
- Developing countries sociodemographic data, and AID dev assistance project activities, special study series, 9916–3
- Foreign aged population characteristics, with related health care data and vital statistics, by world area and selected country, 1950-80 and projected to 2020, 2546–10.12
- Foreign population size and growth rates, and latest available benchmark demographic data, by country, 1950-83, biennial rpt, 2324–4
- Foreign women sociodemographic, economic, and fertility characteristics, with comparisons to men, by country, 1960s-85, world region rpt series, 2326–15
- Health condition and health care resources, use, and expenditures, 1970s-82 with trends and projections 1900-2000, annual compilation, 4144–11
- Life tables, 1979 and trends from 1900, US Vital Statistics annual rpt, 4144–2.6
- Life tables, 1980 and trends from 1900, US Vital Statistics annual rpt, 4144–5
- Publications of NCHS, quarterly listing, 4122–2
- Publications of NCHS, 1979-83, annual listing, 4124–1
- *Statistical Abstract of US,* social, political, and economic data, 1950s-83 and trends, annual rpt, 2324–1.1
- TTPI socioeconomic, health, and govtl data, by TTPI govt, FY83 and selected trends, detailed annual rpt, 7004–6
- Vital and Health Statistics series: advance data rpts, 4146–8
- Vital and Health Statistics series: analytical studies, 4147–3
- Vital and Health Statistics series: foreign and US comparisons, analytical studies, 4147–5

Index by Subjects and Names

Vogt, Donna U.

Vital and Health Statistics series: natality, marriage, and divorce trends, 4147–21

Vital statistics, births, marriages, divorces, and deaths, provisional data, monthly rpt, 4142–1

Vital statistics, provisional 1982-83 with trends from 1950, annual rpt, 4144–7

Vital statistics records offices and availability of birth, death, marriage, and divorce certificates, by State, 1984 annual listing, 4124–7

Vital statistics, supplements to monthly rpts, series, 4146–5

Wisconsin public welfare programs caseloads, selected vital statistics, and households in poverty, 1970s-83, hearings, 21788–141

see also Births

see also Deaths

see also Life expectancy

see also Marriage and divorce

Vitamins

see Nutrition and malnutrition

Vocational Education Act

Bilingual vocational training projects, participants, characteristics, and costs, by program, FY82, annual rpt, 4804–26

Vocational education and training

Bilingual education programs, teachers, enrollment, and funding, selected years 1976-FY83, biennial rpt, 4804–14

Bilingual vocational training projects, participants, characteristics, and costs, by program, FY82, annual rpt, 4804–26

Census of Population, 1980: detailed socioeconomic and demographic characteristics, by age, sex, race, Hispanic origin, occupation, and industry, State rpt series, 2531–4

Census of Population, 1980: labor force, by sex, detailed occupation, and region, with comparison to 1970 census, supplementary rpt, 2535–1.12

Condition of Education, detailed data on enrollment, staff, achievement, finances, curricula, and education effects on employment, 1982-83, annual rpt, 4824–1.3

County Business Patterns: establishments, employees, and payrolls, by SIC 4-digit industry and county, 1981, annual State rpt series, 2326–8

County Business Patterns: establishments, employees, and payrolls, by SIC 4-digit industry and county, 1982, annual State rpt series, 2326–6

Degrees awarded in occupational programs, by sex and type of curriculum, 1973/74-1980/81, annual rpt, 4824–2.16

Education Dept programs funding, operations, and effectiveness, FY83, annual rpt, 4804–5

Employment, earnings, and hours, by SIC 4-digit nonfarm industry, monthly 1974-Feb 1984, annual update, 6744–4

Employment in vocational education programs, by State, program area, instn type, employment status, and type of position, annual rpt, suspended, 4864–5

Enrollment and other data for adult and vocational education programs, by student sociodemographic characteristics, selected years 1975-81, annual rpt, 4824–2.21

Enrollment and staff of vocational education programs, annual rpt, suspended, 4864–8

Enrollment in academic, vocational, and continuing education, by student characteristics, Oct 1982, 4848–16

Enrollment in vocational education programs, annual rpt, suspended, 4864–6

Fed Govt education block grants, State allocations by program and selected school district, FY82-84 and trends from FY60, hearing, 21408–75

Fed Govt funding for elementary and secondary education by agency, and Education Dept funding for special education by program, selected years FY60-84, 4808–9.3

Foreign and US educational enrollment and attainment, public expenditures, and vocational skills test scores, 1960s-76, 26358–105

Funding for vocational education by Federal, State, and local govts, annual rpt, discontinued, 4864–7

Funding of Natl Center for Research in Vocational Education, by purpose and source, selected years 1978-84, GAO rpt, 26121–79

Govt census, 1982: State govt payments to local govts, by program, source of funds, level of govt, and State, with trends from 1902, 2460–3

Handicapped children public education program enrollment, staff, and funding, by handicap, age, and State, 1981/82-1982/83, annual rpt, 4944–4

High school class of 1980: use of student aid and earnings to pay higher education costs, by instn type and family income, 1980-82, 4848–15

High school class of 1982: foreign language coursework, by language, course level, student and school characteristics, and location, 1984 rpt, 4828–17

High school classes of 1980 and 1982: educational and sociodemographic characteristics and expectations, natl longitudinal study, series, 4826–2

Jail capacities, conditions, expenditures, and services, and socioeconomic and other characteristics of inmates, various dates 1976-82, 10048–59

Kentucky Higher Education Student Loan Corp student loans, loan purchases and defaults by instn, and revenue bonds status, various dates 1979-84, hearing, 21348–92

Occupational manpower needs and supply by detailed occupation, and educational and training program enrollees and grads by detailed field, 1982 and 1995, biennial rpt, 6744–3

Occupational Outlook Handbook, 1984-85 biennial rpt, 6744–1

Prison Industries (Federal) operations and finances, FY83, annual rpt, 6244–3

Puerto Rico educational enrollment, finance, completions, curricula, and personnel by instn, and health and vital statistics, selected years 1970-83, hearings, 21348–93

Service industry census, 1982: employment, establishments, receipts, and payroll, by SIC 2- to 4-digit kind of business, SMSA, county, and city, State rpt series, 2391–1

Student aid Federal programs funding and participation, by instn type and control, State, and outlying area, with student loan defaults and collections, FY82, annual rpt, 4804–28

Teaching degrees conferred by specialty and State, required credit hours, and instn officials attitudes, by instn type, 1970s-83, hearings, 21348–89

Veterans education assistance program participation and costs under GI Bill and other programs, WW II through Sept 1983, annual rpt, 9924–22

Veterans education benefits and job training, and other VA activities, FY83, annual rpt, 9924–1.7

see also Apprenticeship

see also Employee development

see also Federal aid to vocational education

see also Industrial arts

see also Manpower training programs

see also Vocational guidance

see also Vocational rehabilitation

Vocational guidance

Occupational Outlook Handbook, 1984-85 biennial rpt, 6744–1

Occupational trends and outlook, quarterly rpt, 6742–1

Vocational rehabilitation State agency expenditures, caseloads, rehabilitations, and staff, under Section 110 of the Rehabilitation Act, by State, FY82, annual rpt, 4944–9

Vocational rehabilitation

Budget of US, effects of Reagan Admin policy changes, by detailed program, FY85, annual rpt, 104–21

Education Dept programs funding, operations, and effectiveness, FY83, annual rpt, 4804–5

HHS aid to each State and local govt or private instn, amount obligated, funding agency, and program, FY83, annual listing, 4004–3

Service industry census, 1982: employment, establishments, receipts, and payroll, by SIC 2- to 4-digit kind of business, SMSA, county, and city, State rpt series, 2391–1

State agency caseloads, by status and processing stage, region, and State, FY83 with trends from FY21, annual rpt, 4944–5

State agency clients following rehabilitation and employment, annual rpt, suspended, 4944–8

State agency expenditures, caseloads, rehabilitations, and staff, by State, FY82, annual rpt, 4944–9

State agency programs, vocationally rehabilitated persons by sociodemographic characteristics and disabling condition, FY79-81, annual rpt, 4944–6

Workshops for blind and handicapped, Fed Govt procurement of goods and services and participating workshops, FY78-82, annual rpt, 11714–1

see also Veterans rehabilitation

Voelker, A. H.

"Wilderness Designation of Bureau of Land Management Lands and Impacts on the Availability of Energy Resources", 3308–68

Vogel, Ronald J.

"Analysis of Structural Incentives in the Arizona Health Care Cost-Containment System", 4652–1.414

Vogt, Donna U.

"U.S. Government International Barter", 21208–20

Voice of America

Voice of America

Activities, employment, and funding of USIA, FY83-84, annual rpt, 17594–1

Broadcast data for Radio Free Europe, Radio Liberty, and other intl broadcasters, FY83, annual rpt, 10314–1

Volcanoes

Central America mineral, energy, and water resources, and natural hazards to resource dev, by country, 1981 with trends from 1977, 5668–71

Developing countries disaster preparedness and summary sociodemographic, political, and economic data, country rpt series, 9916–2

Foreign countries disasters, persons affected, deaths, damage, and aid by US and others, FY83 and trends from FY64, annual rpt, 9914–12

Mount St Helens, Wash, volcanic eruptions, effects on water quality and other environmental characteristics of Washington and Oregon watersheds, series, 5666–14

Volcanoes (worldwide) of climatological significance, 1956-82, and carbon dioxide hydrologic effects, projected for 26-35 years, 9188–95

Vollrath, Thomas

"Patterns and Trends in World Agricultural Land Use", 1528–180

"Selected Socioeconomic Development Indicators: Africa, Asia, Europe, Latin America, the Middle East, and North America/Oceania", 1528–179

"Trends in World Agricultural Land Use", 1522–3.401

Voluntary military service

Cost control proposals for Fed Govt programs and mgmt, 3-year savings by function and agency, and financial and operating data, 1960s-81, 16908–1.17

Enlistments and reenlistment rates, by service branch, monthly rpt, 3542–14.4

Enlistments and reenlistment rates, FY75-83, annual rpt, 3544–1.2

Health professionals supply and education, by occupation, demographic and professional characteristics, and location, 1950s-83 and projected to 2000, biennial rpt, 4114–8

High school classes of 1980 and 1982: educational and sociodemographic characteristics and expectations, natl longitudinal study, series, 4826–2

Manpower active duty strength, recruits, and reenlistment, by race, Hispanic origin, sex, and service branch, quarterly press release, 3542–7

Manpower of DOD, and organization, budget, weapons, and property, by service branch, State, and country, 1984 annual summary rpt, 3504–13

Navy budget and Navy and Marine Corps forces, equipment, and budget summary, planned FY84-85, semiannual pamphlet, 3802–3

Navy personnel by grade and length of service, reenlistment rate, and need for petty officers, FY72-83 and projected to FY88, GAO rpt, 26123–69

Reserve forces manpower strengths and characteristics, by component, quarterly rpt, 3542–4

Strategic military capability, force strengths, weapons, training, supplies, and requirements, by service branch, FY80-84 and projected to 1990, 3508–19

Women military personnel on active duty, by demographic and service characteristics and service branch, with comparisons to men, FY83, annual chartbook, 3544–26

Volunteers

Head Start Project enrollment, appropriations, and staff, FY65-84, annual rpt, 4604–8

Homeless population and characteristics, and temporary shelter operations, use, and user characteristics, by region and selected city, 1983, 5188–108

Homeless population and characteristics, and temporary shelter operations, use, and user characteristics, for selected cities, various periods 1979-84, hearing, 21248–85

Older persons nutrition services program operations and assessment, and participant sociodemographic, health, and diet characteristics, 1976 and 1982, 4608–16

Red Cross program operations and financial statements, 1982/83, annual rpt, 29254–1

see also ACTION

see also American National Red Cross

see also Retired Senior Volunteer Program

see also VISTA

see also Voluntary military service

Volunteers in Service to America

see VISTA

Voting

see Elections

Waco, Tex.

Census of Housing, 1980: occupancy and unit characteristics, by race, Hispanic origin, and city, SMSA rpt, 2473–1.364

Census of Population and Housing, 1980: detailed population and housing characteristics, by county, city, and census tract, SMSA rpt, 2551–2.364

Wages of office and plant workers, by occupation, 1984 labor market area survey rpt, 6785–3.7

see also under By City and By SMSA or MSA in the "Index by Categories"

Wade, Alice H.

"Life Tables for the U.S., 1900-2050", 4706–1.89

"Social Security Area Population Projections, 1984", 4706–1.92

Wage chronologies

see also Area wage surveys

see also Industry wage surveys

Wage controls

see also Minimum wage

Wage surveys

see also Area wage surveys

see also Industry wage surveys

see also National Survey of Professional, Administrative, Technical and Clerical Pay

Wages and salaries

see Agricultural wages

see Earnings, general

see Earnings, local and regional

see Earnings, specific industries

see Federal pay

Index by Subjects and Names

see Labor cost indexes

see Minimum wage

see Payroll

see State and local employees pay

Wainio, John T.

"Argentina: Farmers' Response to Grain Prices", 1528–170

Wakefield, Joseph C.

"Anatomy of a Federal Government Deficit, FY83", 2702–1.408

"Federal Budget Developments", 2702–1.411, 2702–1.429

"Federal Fiscal Programs", 2702–1.406

"National Defense Spending: A Review of Appropriations and Real Purchases", 2702–1.440

Waldman, Elizabeth

"Labor Force Statistics from a Family Perspective", 6746–1.253

"Most Women Who Maintain Families Receive Poor Labor Market Returns", 6746–1.253

Waldo, Daniel R.

"Demographic Characteristics and Health Care Use and Expenditures by the Aged in the U.S.: 1977-84", 4652–1.420

Wales

see United Kingdom

Walker, David B.

"Federalism in 1983: Mixed Results from Washington", 10042–1.402

Wall, Larry D.

"Commercial Bank Profitability in 1983", 9371–1.419

"Money Market Account Competition", 9371–1.431

"Risk Considerations in Deregulating Bank Activities", 9371–1.416

"Why Are Some Banks More Profitable than Others?", 9371–10.20

Walla Walla, Wash.

Housing vacancy rates for single and multifamily units and mobile homes, by city and ZIP code, 1983, annual metro area rpt, 9304–21.3

Housing vacancy rates for single and multifamily units and mobile homes, by city and ZIP code, 1984, annual metro area rpt, 9304–21.11

Waterborne commerce of US (domestic and foreign), freight by commodity, traffic, and passengers, by port and waterway, 1982, annual rpt, 3754–3.4

Wallich, Henry C.

"Capital Movements—The Tail That Wags the Dog", 9373–3.28

"International Monetary Policy", 1004–16.1

Walterboro, S.C.

Wages of office and plant workers, by occupation, 1984 labor market area survey rpt, 6785–3.7

War

Agent Orange exposure and Vietnam military service effects on veteran health condition, methodology for 3 CDC studies, Nov 1983 rpt, 4208–22

Census of Housing, 1980: structural, financial, and householder characteristics, by region and State, 2475–4

Claims against foreign govts by US natls, by country and type of claim, 1983, annual rpt, 6004–16

Foreign countries disasters, persons affected, deaths, damage, and aid by US and others, FY83 and trends from FY64, annual rpt, 9914–12

Index by Subjects and Names

Warehouses

Foreign debts to US for WWI assistance, by country and program, periodic rpt, 8002–6

Foreign military, social, and economic summary data by world area and country, 1960s-80s, hearing, 25388–47.1

Participants and casualties in principal US wars and conflicts, 1775-1973, annual rpt, 3544–1.2

Participants and casualties in principal US wars, 1775-1973, annual summary rpt, 3504–13

Participants, deaths, veterans living, and compensation and pension recipients, for each US war, 1775-1983, semiannual rpt, 9922–8

VA compensation, pension, and retirement cases, by type of entitlement and period of service, monthly rpt, 9922–10

Veteran population, by period of service, age, and State, Sept 1984, semiannual rpt, 9922–3

Veteran women, by period of service, age, and State, Mar 1983 and projected to 2030, 9928–28

Veteran women population, and use of benefits by type, by age, period of service, and State, with comparisons to men, FY83, annual rpt, 9924–24

Veterans aged 55 and over, socioeconomic characteristics, economic resources, health care and status, and actual and expected use of VA benefits, 1983 survey, 9928–29

Veterans characteristics and participation in VA programs, Vietnam era compared with WW II and Korea, FY83, annual rpt, 9924–8

Veterans characteristics by period of service and age, and related issues, statistical rpt series, 9926–4

Veterans disability and deaths not connected with service, pension cases by sex, entitlement type, and period of service, as of Mar 1984, semiannual rpt, 9922–12

Veterans disability by type, and deaths, by period of service, and VA activities, FY83, annual rpt, 9924–1.6

Veterans disability compensation from VA, cases by sex, type and degree of disability, and period of service, as of Mar 1984, semiannual rpt, 9922–9

Veterans education assistance program participation and costs under GI Bill and other programs, WW II through Sept 1983, annual rpt, 9924–22

Veterans income and educational attainment compared to nonveterans, by age and for Vietnam veterans, 1981-82, annual rpt, 9924–19

Veterans income and employment status, by age and war or peacetime service, with comparisons to nonveterans, 1981, annual rpt, 9924–23

Vietnam Agent Orange exposed Air Force personnel diseases and disorders, by disease type, age, and officer status, 1984 rpt, 3604–3

see also Arms control and disarmament

see also Civil defense

see also Guerrilla warfare

see also Military science

see also Military strategy

see also National defense

see also Prisoners of war

see also War casualties

see also War relief

War casualties

Casualties and participants in principal US wars, 1775-1973, annual rpt, 3544–1.2

Casualties and participants in principal US wars, 1775-1973, annual summary rpt, 3504–13

Deaths, participants, veterans living, and compensation and pension recipients, for each US war, 1775-1983, semiannual rpt, 9922–8

Foreign civilian and military war deaths by conflict, 1945-83, and summary military, social and economic data by world area and country, 1960s-80s, hearing, 25388–47.1

Foreign countries disasters, persons affected, deaths, damage, and aid by US and others, FY83 and trends from FY64, annual rpt, 9914–12

Vietnam conflict casualties of US military personnel, by service branch, 1961-80, annual rpt, 9924–8.1

War prisoners

see Prisoners of war

War relief

Foreign countries disasters, persons affected, deaths, damage, and aid by US and others, FY83 and trends from FY64, annual rpt, 9914–12

World War I debt to US of foreign govts, by country and program, periodic rpt, 8002–6

see also Refugees

Ward, Donn R.

"Processing Technologies and Their Effects on Microbiological Properties, Thermal Processing Efficiency, and Yield of Blue Crab", 2162–1.401

Warehouses

American Samoa minimum wage rates, employment, earnings, and benefits, by establishment and industry, Nov 1983, biennial rpt, 6504–6

Argentina grain production, exports by firm, storage by facility type and port, and shipments to ports by mode of transport, by grain type, selected years 1954-81, 1528–185

Arson incidents by occupancy of structure, average property value, and arrest rates, by type of property, 1983, annual rpt, 6224–2.1

Canada grain handling and rail transport system financial and operating data, and effects of limited capacity on grain and oilseed exports, selected years 1950-82, 1528–176

Census of Population, 1980: detailed socioeconomic and demographic characteristics, by age, sex, race, Hispanic origin, occupation, and industry, State rpt series, 2531–4

Census of Population, 1980: detailed socioeconomic characteristics, by county, city, and inside-outside SMSAs and central cities, State rpt series, 2531–3

Collective bargaining agreements expiring during year, covered workers by SIC 2-digit industry, firm, and union, with summary of key provisions, 1984, annual rpt, 6784–9

Construction industries census, 1982: financial and operating data, by SIC 4-digit industry and State, final rpt series, 2373–1

Construction industries census, 1982: financial and operating data, by SIC 4-digit industry and State, preliminary rpt series, 2371–1

Construction put in place, private and public nonresidential, by type, region, and census div, 1979-83, monthly rpt, annual tables, 2382–4.3

Cotton ginning charges and related data, by State, 1983/84, annual rpt, 1564–3

Cotton storage capacity, and total and chain operated warehouses, by region and State, selected years 1970-84, article, 1561–1.406

County Business Patterns: establishments, employees, and payrolls, by SIC 4-digit industry and county, 1981, annual State rpt series, 2326–8

County Business Patterns: establishments, employees, and payrolls, by SIC 4-digit industry and county, 1982, annual State rpt series, 2326–6

Earnings by major industry group, and personal income per capita and by source, by region and State, 1929-82, 2708–40

Employment, earnings, and hours, by selected SIC 1- to 4-digit industry, State, and for 278 major labor areas, 1939-83, annual rpt, 6744–5

Employment, earnings, and hours, by SIC 4-digit nonfarm industry, monthly 1974-Feb 1984, annual update, 6744–4

Energy use in nonresidential buildings, expenditures, and conservation, by building characteristics, EIA survey series, 3166–8

Farm production expenditures, detailed items by farm sales size and region, 1983, annual rpt, 1614–3

Fed Govt programs and mgmt cost control proposals, 3-year savings by function and agency, and financial and operating data, 1960s-81, 16908–1.23

Foreign trade zones, activities, and value of goods entering and leaving zones, 1973-82, GAO rpt, 26119–56

Grain cooperatives marketing, storage, and shipments by mode of transport, by grain type and region, FY80, 1128–28

Grain loan support programs of USDA, activity and status by type of grain and State, monthly rpt, 1802–3

Grain storage facilities off farms, capacity by State, 1978-83, 1641–17

Grain storage facility and equipment loans to farmers under CCC program, by State, FY68-84, annual table, 1804–14

Grain storage facility and equipment loans to farmers under CCC program, by State, monthly table, 1802–9

Income tax returns of sole proprietorships, detailed data by industry div and selected industry group, 1981, annual rpt, 8304–7

Income tax returns of sole proprietorships, receipts, deductions by type, payroll, and net income, by major industry, 1982, annual article, 8302–2.413

Input-output structure of US economy, detailed interindustry transactions for 85 industries, and components of final demand, 1977, article, 2702–1.421

Warehouses

Inventories of retail establishments, by SIC 2- to 4-digit kind of business, 1983, annual rpt, 2413–5

Korea (South) agricultural services projects of AID and Korea govt, economic impacts, 1950s-83, 9916–1.52

Minority group and women employment, by occupational group and SIC 2- to 3-digit industry, 1981, annual rpt, 9244–1.1

Occupational injury and illness rates, by SIC 2- to 4-digit industry, 1982, annual rpt, 6844–1

Oils and fats production, consumption by end use, and stocks, by type, monthly Current Industrial Rpt, 2506–4.4

Rice stocks on and off farms and total, periodic rpt, 1621–7

Scientists, engineers, and technicians employment in transportation, utilities, and retail and wholesale trade, by field of science and industry, 1982, 9628–72

Tobacco prices, marketing, grades, and types for 3 classes, 1983 crop and 1983/84 season, annual rpt series, 1319–5

see also Cold storage and refrigeration

Waring, George H.

"Survey of Federally-Funded Marine Mammal Research and Studies, FY70-82", 14734–2

Warner Robins, Ga.

see also under By SMSA or MSA in the "Index by Categories"

Warren, Marion K.

"AID and Education: A Sector Report on Lessons Learned", 9916–11.8

Warren, Mich.

see also under By City in the "Index by Categories"

Warren, Ohio

Census of Housing, 1980: occupancy and unit characteristics, by race, Hispanic origin, and city, SMSA rpt, 2473–1.379

Census of Population and Housing, 1980: detailed population and housing characteristics, by county, city, and census tract, SMSA rpt, 2551–2.379

see also under By SMSA or MSA in the "Index by Categories"

Warsaw Pact

Helsinki Final Act implementation by NATO, Warsaw Pact, and other signatory nations, Dec 1983-Mar 1984, semiannual rpt, 7002–1

Military, social, and economic summary data, by world area and country, 1960s-80s, hearing, 25388–47.1

Military spending, arms trade, and armed forces size, with total govt spending and population, by country, 1972-82, annual rpt, 9824–1

Military weapons and troop strength of US and NATO compared to USSR and Warsaw Pact, as of Jan 1984, annual rpt, 3564–1

Military weapons of USSR, Warsaw Pact, and NATO/Japan, selected years 1974-83, annual rpt, 3544–2

Military weapons systems of USSR and Warsaw Pact, assistance and presence worldwide, and force strengths, with selected US and NATO comparisons, as of 1984, 3508–14

Warships

see Naval vessels

Warwick, R.I.

Census of Housing, 1980: occupancy and unit characteristics, by race, Hispanic origin, and city, SMSA rpt, 2473–1.293

Census of Population and Housing, 1980: detailed population and housing characteristics, by county, city, and census tract, SMSA rpt, 2551–2.293

Housing and households detailed characteristics, and unit and neighborhood quality, by inside-outside central cities, 1980 survey, SMSA rpt, 2485–6.14

Wages of office and plant workers, by occupation, 1984 SMSA survey rpt, 6785–11.6

Washburn, D. K.

"Summary of Environmental Reports, Department of Energy Sites", 3004–23

Washington

see D.C.

see Washington State

Washington County, Miss.

Housing vacancy rates for single and multifamily units and mobile homes, by city and ZIP code, 1984, annual metro area rpt, 9304–19.28

Washington Metropolitan Area Transit Authority

Metrorail transit system effect on commuting patterns, population, business, land use, and environment, series, 7306–8

Washington National Airport

Cost control proposals for Fed Govt programs and mgmt, 3-year savings by function and agency, and financial and operating data, 1960s-81, 16908–1.11, 16908–1.28

Financial and operating data for DC metro airports, FY82-83, annual rpt, 7504–10

Washington Public Power Supply System

Nuclear power plants construction financing of Washington Public Power Supply System, with regional economic impacts and power supply/demand, 1980s-2035, hearing, 21448–29

Washington State

Agriculture census, 1982: farms, farmland, production and costs, and operator characteristics, preliminary State summary and county rpts, 2330–1.53

Agriculture census, 1982: farms, farmland, production, finances, and operator characteristics, by county, final State rpt, 2331–1.47

Bank deposits in commercial and mutual savings banks and in US branches of foreign banks, by account type, instn, State, SMSA, and county, June 1983, annual rpt, 9295–3.19

Census of Population and Housing, 1980: detailed population and housing characteristics, by county, city, and census tract, State rpt, 2551–2.49

Census of Population, 1980: detailed socioeconomic and demographic characteristics, by age, sex, race, Hispanic origin, and industry, State rpt, 2531–4.49

Coastal environmental and wildlife characteristics, use, and mgmt, for individual ecosystems, series, 5506–9

County Business Patterns: establishments, employees, and payrolls, by SIC 4-digit industry and county, 1982, annual State rpt, 2326–6.49

Index by Subjects and Names

Cranberry production, prices, area, and yield, for 5 States, 1982-83 and forecast 1984, annual rpt, 1621–18.4

Deaths, by sex, cause, and detailed occupation, summary data from occupational mortality study, 1950-79, 4248–47

Employment, earnings, and hours, by selected SIC 1- to 4-digit industry, State, and for 278 major labor areas, 1939-83, annual rpt, 6744–5.2, 6744–5.3

Environmental quality, pollutant discharge by type and source, and EPA protection activities and funding, 1970s-83, biennial regional rpt, 9184–15.10

Exports of manufactured and agricultural commodities, manufacturing production, and export-related employment, 1960s-82, State rpt, 2046–3.47

Fish and shellfish canned and frozen production, imports, landings, and prices, for Alaska and Northwest States, weekly rpt, 2162–6.5

Fishermen (ocean sport), fishing activities, and catch by species, by fisherman characteristics and State, for Pacific coast, 1979-80, 2166–17.1, 2166–17.3

Fishing for squid off Washington State with jig devices, catch and mean squid length, selected dates May-Sept 1981, article, 2162–1.401

Forests (natl) timber sales contract operations in Northwest US by forest and firm, and lumber supply/demand, FY76-1983 with trends from 1913, hearings, 25318–57

Hay prices in 10 market areas, for baled alfalfa and prairie hay, weekly rpt, 1313–5

HHS aid to each State and local govt or private instn, amount obligated, funding agency, and program, FY83, annual listing, 4004–3.10

Income (personal) per capita and by source, and earnings by industry div, by State, MSA, and county, 1977-82, annual regional rpt, 2704–2.9

Lumber production, prices, trade, and employment in Northwest US and British Columbia, quarterly rpt, 1202–3

Manufacturing census, 1982: financial and operating data, by SIC 2- to 4-digit industry, State, SMSA, and county, preliminary census div rpt, 2491–3.9

Mineral Industry Surveys, State review of production, 1983, advance annual rpt, 5614–6.47

Minerals Yearbook, 1982, Vol 2 preprints: State review of production and sales by commodity, and business activity, annual rpt, 5604–16.49

Minerals Yearbook, 1982, Vol 2: State reviews of production, sales, and firms, by commodity, and business activity, annual rpt, 5604–34

Mount St Helens, Wash, volcanic eruptions, effects on water quality and other environmental characteristics of Washington and Oregon watersheds, series, 5666–14

Nuclear power plants construction financing of Washington Public Power Supply System, with regional economic impacts and power supply/demand, 1980s-2035, hearing, 21448–29

Index by Subjects and Names

Population size and components of change, by MSA and county, 1980-82, annual State Current Population Rpt, 2546–4.47

Population size, Apr 1980 and July 1982, and per capita income, 1979 and 1981, by county and city, State Current Population Rpt, 2546–11.47

Retail trade census, 1982: employment, establishments, sales, and payroll, by SIC 2- to 4-digit kind of business, SMSA, county, and city, State rpt, 2397–1.48

Savings and loan assns, FHLB 12th District members financial operations and housing industry indicators by State, monthly rpt, 9302–21

Service industry census, 1982: employment, establishments, receipts, and payroll, by SIC 2- to 4-digit kind of business, SMSA, county, and city, State rpt, 2391–1.48

Shipping industry impact on local economy, and port dev financing through user fees, by State, other area, industry, and port, 1970s-2020, hearings, 21568–34

Telephone rates in Washington State, including govt long-distance access charges, by company, 1983-89, hearing, 21148–32

Timber acreage and resources, by species, ownership class, and county, 1980, and harvest, 1950-79, series, 1206–28

Truck safety inspection program activities in Washington State, and truck defects and accidents, various periods 1976-81, article, 7762–9.407

Water supply and quality in streams and lakes, and groundwater levels in wells, by drainage basin, 1981, annual State rpt, 5666–16.44

Water supply, and snow survey results, monthly State rpt, 1266–2.9

Wholesale trade census, 1982: employment, establishments, finances, and operations, by SIC 2- to 4-digit kind of business, SMSA, county, and city, State rpt, 2405–1.48

see also Bellingham, Wash.
see also Bremerton, Wash.
see also Everett, Wash.
see also Kennewick, Wash.
see also Olympia, Wash.
see also Pasco, Wash.
see also Richland, Wash.
see also Seattle, Wash.
see also Shelton, Wash.
see also Spokane, Wash.
see also Tacoma, Wash.
see also Walla Walla, Wash.
see also Wenatchee, Wash.
see also Yakima, Wash.
see also under By State in the "Index by Categories"

Waste management
see Radioactive waste
see Recycling of waste materials
see Refuse and refuse disposal
see Sewage and wastewater treatment systems

Wastewater treatment
see Sewage and wastewater treatment systems

Watches
see Instruments and measuring devices

Water and Power Resources Service
see Bureau of Reclamation

Water fluoridation

State govt preventive health services funding by program, Fed Govt block grants, and opinions on State program admin, for 13 States, FY81-84, GAO rpt, 26121–88

Water pollution

- Abatement capital and operating costs, by SIC 2- to 4-digit industry, State, and SMSA, 1982, annual Current Industrial Rpt, 2506–3.6
- Abatement capital and operating costs under Clean Air and Water Acts, for govts and selected industries, various periods 1970-2000, annual rpt, 9184–11
- Abatement capital expenditures, by pollution type and selected industry, 1973-84, annual article, 2702–1.423
- Abatement expenditures by govt, business, and consumers, 1972-82, annual article, 2702–1.407
- Abatement R&D industry funding, by pollution type and funding source, 1973-82, annual rpt, 9627–21
- Acid Precipitation Natl Assessment Program activities, and funding by Federal agency, 1983, annual rpt, 14354–1
- Acid rain and air pollution environmental effects, and methods for neutralizing acidified water bodies, summary research rpt series, 5506–5
- Acid rain causes and effects, air pollutant emissions by source, and control costs, by region and State, selected years 1977-83 and projected to 2000, 26358–104
- Acid rain causes and effects, air pollutant emissions by source in US and selected countries, and control costs, 1970s-83 and projected to 2000, 21368–52
- Acid rain causes and effects, air pollutant emissions by source in US and selected countries, control costs, and Fed Govt research funding, 1960s-82, 3408–27
- Central America mineral, energy, and water resources, and natural hazards to resource dev, by country, 1981 with trends from 1977, 5668–71
- Chemicals (volatile organic) in drinking water, monitoring results for each State and Puerto Rico, 1981, 9208–120
- Chesapeake Bay Program environmental research findings and water pollution control recommendations, as of 1983, narrative rpt, 9208–121
- Clinch River Breeder Reactor proposed site and nearby area, radiation levels in river water and sediment and ground water, 1983, annual rpt, 9804–24
- Coal dev plans on Fed Govt lease lands in 12 regions under Fed Coal Mgmt Program, environmental and socioeconomic impacts to 2000, final statement series, 5726–4
- Coal mining effect on water supply and quality in selected river basins of Eastern and Interior coal provinces, 1970s, series, 5666–15
- Coal mining effect on water supply and quality in selected river basins of Western coal provinces, series, 5666–19
- Coal transport environmental impacts by type and mode of transport, methodology for assessing alternative systems, 1983 rpt, 3408–28

Water pollution

- Coastal environmental and wildlife characteristics, use, and mgmt, for individual ecosystems, series, 5506–9
- Coastal environmental characteristics, fish, wildlife, and use, and population socioeconomic data, for individual areas, series, 5506–4
- Dissolved solids and water temperature in 6 rivers, by station, monthly rpt, 5662–3
- Environmental quality and protection programs, costs, and Fed Govt enforcement, 1983, detailed annual rpt, 484–1
- Environmental quality, pollutant discharge by type, and EPA protection activities, 1970s-83, biennial summary rpt, 9184–16
- Environmental quality, pollutant discharge by type and source, and EPA protection activities and funding, 1970s-83, biennial regional rpt series, 9184–15
- EPA budget and full-time staff positions by type of activity, and grants to States, by program, FY75-84 and proposed FY85, 26308–47
- EPA Office of R&D environmental research plans, and outlays by program, FY84-88, annual rpt, 9184–10
- EPA pollution control research and grant assistance program activities, monthly rpt, 9182–8
- EPA publications in NTIS collection, quarterly listing, 9182–5
- Estuary environmental characteristics, fish, wildlife, uses, and mgmt, for individual estuaries, series, 5506–7
- Farm production inputs, land mgmt, and environmental effects, for 4 crops, 1940s-80 and projected to 2010, 9188–94
- Fish kills from water pollution, by State, location, and pollution source, monthly 1978-80, annual rpt, 9204–3
- Great Lakes basin pollutant discharges by source, and control program activities, 1983 annual rpt, 14644–1
- Great Lakes fish concentrations of PCBs (polychlorinated biphenyls), for 29 species monitored at 24 sites, selected dates 1969-77, 9208–126
- Hudson River pollutant concentrations in sediments and fish and shellfish species, by pollutant type, late 1970s-82, hearings, 21568–36
- Idaho Natl Engineering Lab radiation monitoring results, for 4 onsite facilities and nearby areas, 1983, annual rpt, 3354–10
- Mount St Helens, Wash, volcanic eruptions, effects on water quality and other environmental characteristics of Washington and Oregon watersheds, series, 5666–14
- Nonpoint sources of water pollution, source land uses and acreage, and control program funding, by State or region, various periods 1974-FY84, 9208–123
- Oil enhanced recovery technologies use and environmental impacts, by oil field, county, and State, 1970s-80 and projected to 2000, 3408–29
- Phosphate rock industry environmental protection costs, by control type and selected State, with background operating data, 1977-81 with cost projections to 1990, 5608–143

Water pollution

Radiation and radionuclide concentrations in air, water, and milk, results of EPA and other monitoring programs, by State and site, quarterly rpt, 9232–2

Radiation exposure at DOE-contractor nuclear facilities and for surrounding population, and pollutant releases by type, by site, 1982, annual rpt, 3004–23

Radioactive strontium in NYC and San Francisco diet by food item, and in NYC tap water and milk, quarterly 1982 with trends from 1954, annual rpt, 3404–13

Radioactive waste from nuclear power plants, releases and waste composition by plant, 1981, annual rpt, 9634–1

Radionuclide concentrations in air, water, and biota near Nevada and other nuclear test sites, and in milk from western States, by location, 1983, annual rpt, 9234–4

Sedimentation control, surveillance, and research activity of Fed Govt, by project, agency, region, and State, 1982, annual rpt, 5664–9

Southeastern States soil conservation and water pollution reduction participants, costs, and acreage, by conservation method and State, selected years 1973-82, 1588–84

Southeastern US water supply and quality, with background socioeconomic data, for 8 States, 1960s-2020 with trends from 1930, 9208–119

TVA activities, financial and operating data by program and facility, and power sales by customer, FY83, annual rpt, 9804–1

Urban runoff water quality, pollutant concentrations, and control cost-effectiveness, with monitoring sites rainfall and other characteristics, by city and region, 1978-83, 9208–122

Utah Salt Lake surface level, land coverage, water budget, salinity, and effects of human activity, various periods 1847-1983, 5668–70

Wastewater discharge regulation system of EPA, operations and funding, various periods FY79-83, GAO rpt, 26113–113

Water quality, pollutant types and sources, and control program compliance, by State, 1982, biennial rpt, 9204–6

Water supply and quality, floods, drought, mudslides, and other hydrologic events, by State, 1983, annual rpt, 5664–12

Water supply and quality in streams and lakes, and groundwater levels in wells, by drainage basin, 1980, annual State rpt series, 5666–12

Water supply and quality in streams and lakes, and groundwater levels in wells, by drainage basin, 1981, annual State rpt series, 5666–16

Water supply and quality in streams and lakes, and groundwater levels in wells, by drainage basin, 1982, annual State rpt series, 5666–20

Water supply and quality in streams and lakes, and groundwater levels in wells, by drainage basin, 1983, annual State rpt series, 5666–10

see also Eutrophication

see also Food and waterborne diseases

see also Marine pollution

see also Oil spills

Water power

Natl Energy Policy Plan, energy supply, demand, and prices, by fuel and consuming sector, projected 1985-2010, biennial rpt, 3004–13

see also Dams

see also Hydroelectric power

Water Resources Council

Budget of US Appendix, detailed budgets and personnel summaries, by agency, FY85, annual rpt, 104–3

Budget of US, appropriations, outlays, balances, and budget receipts, by govtl branch and agency, FY83, annual rpt, 8104–2

Water resources development

Agricultural Conservation Program participation and payments, by State, FY83, annual rpt, 1804–7

Agricultural Stabilization and Conservation Service producer payments under 26 programs, monthly rpt, 1802–10

Army Corps of Engineers activities and projects, FY83 and trends from 1800s, annual rpt, 3754–1

Army Corps of Engineers water resources dev projects, recreation activities by district and project, 1982, annual rpt, 3754–5

Budget of US, effects of Reagan Admin policy changes, by detailed program, FY85, annual rpt, 104–21

Budget of US, receipts by source and outlays by function, FY40-89 estimates revised for consistency with FY85 budget definitions, annual rpt, 104–12

Colorado River Storage Project finances, water resource dev, power production, and other activities in western States, FY83, annual rpt, 5824–3

Construction industries census, 1982: financial and operating data, by SIC 4-digit industry and State, final rpt, 2373–1.7

Construction industries census, 1982: financial and operating data, by SIC 4-digit industry and State, preliminary rpt series, 2371–1

Developing countries economic dev projects funded by multilateral dev banks, environmental and cultural impacts, 1970s-83, hearings, 21248–80

Fed Govt aid to State and local govts, expenditures, and direct payments, by program, agency, and State, FY83, annual rpt, 2464–2

Fed Govt industrial dev funding by type, program, and agency, and State govt policies and support, selected years FY75-85, 26306–6.81

Fed Govt reclamation programs in western US, finances and operations by project and State, 1981-82, annual rpts, 5824–1

Forest, range, and associated waters use and mgmt assessment, and environmental impacts of Forest Service program options, 1977-2030 and trends from 1920, 1208–24

Geological Survey programs and funding, FY78-83, annual rpt, 5664–8

Govt census, 1982: State govt payments to local govts, by program, source of funds, level of govt, and State, with trends from 1902, 2460–3

Interior Dept programs, activities, and funding, various periods 1967-84, last issue of annual rpt, 5304–13

Land Mgmt Bur public lands admin and program activities in western States, FY82-84, annual rpt, 5724–13

Land Mgmt Bur public lands programs, FY83, annual rpt, 5724–1.2

Natl Forest System wildlife habitat and fishery improvements, use, and game population and harvest by species and forest, by region, FY83, annual rpt, 1204–31

Recreation construction for water resources dev projects of Army Corps of Engineers and Reclamation Bur, unfunded costs by project, FY82, GAO rpt, 26113–115

Satellite Landsat system proposed transfer to private sector, uses and product sales by user type, and university programs and personnel by instn, 1973-85, 26358–100

Soil and water conservation districts, farms, and area covered, by State, annual rpt, suspended, 1264–1

Soil Conservation Service activities, services, and acreage covered, by program, FY83, annual rpt, 1264–2

Water Bank Program agreements, acreage, and Fed Govt payments, by State, FY72-83, annual rpt, 1804–21

Water Bank Program agreements, acreage, and Fed Govt payments, by State, monthly rpt, 1802–5

Water supply and use in 3 areas with supply problems and total US, and methods to increase supply, selected years 1974-80 and projected to 2010, 9208–125

see also Aquaculture

see also Canals

see also Dredging

see also Flood control

see also Hydroelectric power

see also Inland water transportation

see also Irrigation

see also Marine resources

see also Saline water conversion

see also Water power

see also Water supply and use

see also Watershed projects

Water supply and use

Aerial survey R&D publications, and sources of natural resource and environmental data gathered by air- and spacecraft, quarterly listing, 9502–7

Agricultural research expenditures and scientist years, by topic, commodity, and performing organization, FY82, annual rpt, 1744–2

Agricultural Stabilization and Conservation Service producer payments under 26 programs, monthly rpt, 1802–10

Agriculture census, 1982: farms, farmland, production, finances, and operator characteristics, by county, final State rpt series, 2331–1

AID dev assistance activities, socioeconomic impacts, evaluation rpt series, 9916–1

Alaska Arctic Natl Wildlife Refuge resources, resident and visitor activities, and environmental impacts of energy exploration, 1983, annual update rpt, 5504–26

Army Corps of Engineers activities and projects, FY83 and trends from 1800s, annual rpt, 3754–1

Index by Subjects and Names

Water supply and use

Bond tax-exempt issues for private activity, by purpose, face value, major industry, and State, 1983, article, 8302–2.417

Capital (fixed), govt and private nonresidential structures and equipment, residential capital, and consumer-owned durable goods by item, 1980-83, annual article, 2702–1.433

Capital needs and financing for public works, by project type, level of govt, and selected jurisdiction, 1970s-83 and projected to 2000, hearing, 23848–181

Capital needs and intergovtl financing for public works, by type of project and selected city, various periods 1950-83, 10048–60

Carbon dioxide atmospheric concentration increase effects on hydrologic conditions, projected for 26-35 years, 9188–95

Census of Housing, 1980: inventory, occupancy, and unit characteristics, changes from 1973 by region and inside-outside SMSAs and central cities, series, 2473–3

Census of Housing, 1980: structural, financial, and householder characteristics, by region and State, 2475–4

Census of Population and Housing, 1980: detailed population and housing characteristics, by county, city, and census tract, State and SMSA rpt series, 2551–2

Census of Population, 1980: detailed socioeconomic and demographic characteristics, by age, sex, race, Hispanic origin, occupation, and industry, State rpt series, 2531–4

Central America mineral, energy, and water resources, and natural hazards to resource dev, by country, 1981 with trends from 1977, 5668–71

Coal dev plans on Fed Govt lease lands in 12 regions under Fed Coal Mgmt Program, environmental and socioeconomic impacts to 2000, final statement series, 5726–4

Coal mining effect on water supply and quality in selected river basins of Eastern and Interior coal provinces, 1970s, series, 5666–15

Coal mining effect on water supply and quality in selected river basins of Western coal provinces, series, 5666–19

Coastal environmental and wildlife characteristics, use, and mgmt, for individual ecosystems, series, 5506–9

Coastal environmental characteristics, fish, wildlife, and use, and population socioeconomic data, for individual areas, series, 5506–4

Colorado River Storage Project finances, water resource dev, power production, and other activities in western States, FY83, annual rpt, 5824–3

Construction industries census, 1982: financial and operating data, by SIC 4-digit industry and State, preliminary rpt series, 2371–1

Construction put in place, permits authorized by region, State, and MSA, and Federal contract awards, by construction type, bimonthly rpt with articles, 2012–1

Construction put in place, value of new public and private structures, by type, monthly rpt, 2382–4

County Business Patterns: establishments, employees, and payrolls, by SIC 4-digit industry and county, 1981, annual State rpt series, 2326–8

County Business Patterns: establishments, employees, and payrolls, by SIC 4-digit industry and county, 1982, annual State rpt series, 2326–6

Developing countries govt policy, and AID and other foreign assistance, effects on private sector dev and socioeconomic conditions, with case studies for 6 countries, 1960s-80, 9918–12

Developing countries PL 480 Title I funding and socioeconomic impacts, with case studies for 5 countries, 1950s- 81, 9918–13

Electric utility expenses for water, 1982, annual rpt, 3164–23

Environmental quality and protection programs, costs, and Fed Govt enforcement, 1983, detailed annual rpt, 484–1

Environmental quality, pollutant discharge by type, and EPA protection activities, 1970s-83, biennial summary rpt, 9184–16

Environmental quality, pollutant discharge by type and source, and EPA protection activities and funding, 1970s-83, biennial regional rpt series, 9184–15

EPA pollution control research and grant assistance program activities, monthly rpt, 9182–8

Farm production expenditures, detailed items by farm sales size and region, 1983, annual rpt, 1614–3

Fed Govt aid to State and local govts, expenditures, and direct payments, by program, agency, and State, FY83, annual rpt, 2464–2

Fed Govt reclamation programs in western US, finances and operations by project and State, 1981-82, annual rpts, 5824–1

FmHA loans and grants by program and State, and summary of services, FY83 with trends from FY63, annual rpt, 1184–17

FmHA soil and water loans, by race, Hispanic origin, and State, quarterly rpt, 1182–5

Foreign military, social, and economic summary data by world area and country, 1960s-80s, hearing, 25388–47.1

Franchise business opportunities, by firm and kind of business, 1984 annual listing, 2044–27

Geological Survey and other publications, 1983, annual listing, 5664–4

Geological Survey programs and funding, FY78-83, annual rpt, 5664–8

Govt census, 1982: city govt revenues by source, expenditures by function, debt, and assets, by State and city, 2457–4

Govt census, 1982: county govt revenues by source, expenditures by function, debt, and assets, by State and county, 2457–3

Govt census, 1982: employment, payrolls, and average earnings, by function, level of govt, State, county, population size, and inside-outside SMSAs, 2455–2

Govt census, 1982: local govt employment by function, payroll, and average earnings, for individual counties, cities, and school and special districts, 2455–1

Govt employment and payroll, by function, level of govt, and jurisdiction, 1983, annual rpt series, 2466–1

Govt finances, by level of govt, State, and for large cities and counties, 1981-83, annual rpt series, 2466–2

Great Lakes drinking water radionuclide concentrations, official standards, and human doses, 1981-82, annual rpt, 14644–1.2

Great Lakes water levels, daily and monthly averages by station, 1982 and summary 1900-82, annual rpt, 2174–3

Home mortgages (graduated payment) FHA-insured, financial, property, and mortgagor characteristics, for US and selected localities, quarterly rpt, 5142–42

Home mortgages (graduated payment) FHA-insured, financial, property, and mortgagor characteristics, for US and selected States, quarterly rpt, 5142–41

Home mortgages (graduated payment) FHA-insured, financial, property, and mortgagor characteristics, US summary, quarterly rpt, 5142–40

Home mortgages FHA-insured, financial, property, and mortgagor characteristics, for US and selected localities, quarterly rpt, 5142–2

Home mortgages FHA-insured, financial, property, and mortgagor characteristics, for US, selected States, and Puerto Rico, quarterly rpt, 5142–3

Home mortgages FHA-insured, financial, property, and mortgagor characteristics, quarterly rpt, 5142–1

Home mortgages FHA-insured, financial, property, and mortgagor characteristics, 1983, annual rpt, 5144–17

Home mortgages FHA-insured for low-cost homes, financial, construction, property, and mortgagor characteristics, quarterly rpt, 5142–4

Housing and financial characteristics, and unit and neighborhood quality, for 15 SMSAs, 1978, annual survey special supplement, 2485–8

Housing and households detailed characteristics, and unit and neighborhood quality, by inside-outside central cities, 1979-82 surveys, SMSA rpt series, 2485–6

Housing and neighborhood quality indicators and attitudes, and occupant characteristics, by urban-rural location and region, 1981, annual survey, 2485–7

Housing and neighborhood quality indicators and attitudes, by occupant and unit characteristics, region, and metro-nonmetro location, 1981, annual survey, 2485–2

Housing occupancy and unit and household characteristics, by region and metro-nonmetro residence, 1983, biennial survey, 2485–1

Housing water conservation programs and savings of water and energy, for selected cities and suburbs, 1980-83, 5188–109

Income tax returns of corporations, detailed income and tax items by industry, 1981, annual rpt, 8304–4

Income tax returns of sole proprietorships, detailed data by industry div and selected industry group, 1981, annual rpt, 8304–7

Water supply and use

Input-output structure of US economy, detailed interindustry transactions for 537 industries, and components of final demand, 1977 benchmark data, 2708–17

- Mexico and US range and wildlife characteristics, problems, and research strategies and needs, 1981 conf papers, 1208–197
- Montana water supply, snow water accumulations and reservoir storage, annual rpt, suspended, 1264–7
- Nevada water supply, streamflow, reservoir storage, and precipitation, 1984 water year, annual rpt, 1264–8
- New York State area snow depth and water equivalent, by site, winter 1982/83, annual rpt, 2184–2
- Northeastern US water supply, precipitation and stream runoff by station, monthly rpt, 2182–3
- Oil enhanced recovery technologies use and environmental impacts, by oil field, county, and State, 1970s-80 and projected to 2000, 3408–29
- Oregon water supply, streamflow by station and reservoir storage, 1984 water year, annual rpt, 1264–9
- Panama Canal water supply and use, by lake, FY81-82, annual rpt, 9664–3.3
- Quality and supply of water in streams and lakes, and groundwater levels in wells, by drainage basin, 1980, annual State rpt series, 5666–12
- Quality and supply of water in streams and lakes, and groundwater levels in wells, by drainage basin, 1981, annual State rpt series, 5666–16
- Quality and supply of water in streams and lakes, and groundwater levels in wells, by drainage basin, 1982, annual State rpt series, 5666–20
- Quality and supply of water in streams and lakes, and groundwater levels in wells, by drainage basin, 1983, annual State rpt series, 5666–10
- Reclamation Bur water storage and carriage facilities, by type, as of Sept 1983, annual listing, 5824–7
- Resources use and mgmt assessment and environmental impacts of Forest Service program options, 1977-2030 and trends from 1920, 1208–24
- Scientists, engineers, and technicians employment in transportation, utilities, and retail and wholesale trade, by field of science and industry, 1982, 9628–72
- Southeastern US water supply and quality, with background socioeconomic data, for 8 States, 1960s-2020 with trends from 1930, 9208–119
- State and local govt productivity measurement, with background data and output indexes for 7 govt services, various periods 1955-82, 6728–27
- *Statistical Abstract of US,* social, political, and economic data, 1950s-83 and trends, annual rpt, 2324–1.1
- TTPI budget, vital statistics, and health services data, often by TTPI govt, FY83 and selected trends, annual rpt, 7004–6.1
- Utah Salt Lake surface level, land coverage, water budget, salinity, and effects of human activity, various periods 1847-1983, 5668–70

Utah water supply, streamflow, reservoir storage, and precipitation, 1984 water year, annual rpt, 1264–6

- Water supply and quality, floods, drought, mudslides, and other hydrologic events, by State, 1983, annual rpt, 5664–12
- Water supply and use in 3 areas with supply problems and total US, and methods to increase supply, selected years 1974-80 and projected to 2010, 9208–125
- Water supply in US and Canada, streamflow, well and reservoir levels, and dissolved solids and temperature in 6 US rivers, by station, monthly rpt, 5662–3
- Waterborne commerce of US (domestic and foreign), freight by commodity, traffic, and passengers, by port and waterway, 1982, annual rpt, 3754–3
- Western US water supply, and snow survey results, monthly State rpt series, 1266–2
- Western US water supply, reservoir storage by large reservoir and State, and streamflow conditions, as of Oct 1984, annual rpt, 1264–4
- Western US water supply, snow depth measurements by station, State rpt series, 1266–3
- Western US water supply, streamflow and reservoir storage forecasts by stream and station, Jan-May monthly rpt, 1262–1

see also Dams

see also Food and waterborne diseases

see also Hydroelectric power

see also Irrigation

see also Reservoirs

see also Saline water conversion

see also Water fluoridation

see also Water pollution

see also Water power

see also Water resources development

see also Watershed projects

see also Weather

see also Wetlands

Waterbury, Conn.

- Census of Housing, 1980: occupancy and unit characteristics, by race, Hispanic origin, and city, SMSA rpt, 2473–1.366
- Census of Population and Housing, 1980: detailed population and housing characteristics, by county, city, and census tract, SMSA rpt, 2551–2.366

see also under By City and By SMSA or MSA in the "Index by Categories"

Waterloo, Iowa

- Census of Housing, 1980: occupancy and unit characteristics, by race, Hispanic origin, and city, SMSA rpt, 2473–1.367
- Census of Population and Housing, 1980: detailed population and housing characteristics, by county, city, and census tract, SMSA rpt, 2551–2.367

see also under By SMSA or MSA in the "Index by Categories"

Waters, Melvin E.

"Chemical Composition and Frozen Storage Stability of Weakfish", 2162–1.401

Watershed projects

- Agricultural Conservation Program participation and payments, by State, FY83, annual rpt, 1804–7
- Army Corps of Engineers activities and projects, FY83 and trends from 1800s, annual rpt, 3754–1
- Colorado River Storage Project finances, water resource dev, power production, and other activities in western States, FY83, annual rpt, 5824–3

Index by Subjects and Names

- Fed Govt aid to State and local govts, expenditures, and direct payments, by program, agency, and State, FY83, annual rpt, 2464–2
- Fed Govt reclamation programs in western US, finances and operations by project and State, 1981-82, annual rpts, 5824–1
- FmHA loans and grants by program and State, and summary of services, FY83 with trends from FY63, annual rpt, 1184–17
- Soil Conservation Service activities, services, and acreage covered, by program, FY83, annual rpt, 1264–2

Waterways

see Canals

see Harbors and ports

see Lakes and lakeshores

see Rivers and waterways

Watterson, Irene A.

"Residential Fuelwood Use in the U.S.: 1980-81", 1208–204

Wausau, Wis.

- Census of Housing, 1980: occupancy and unit characteristics, by race, Hispanic origin, and city, SMSA rpt, 2473–1.368
- Census of Population and Housing, 1980: detailed population and housing characteristics, by county, city, and census tract, SMSA rpt, 2551–2.368

see also under By SMSA or MSA in the "Index by Categories"

Wealth

- Financial and business statistics, historic trends, 1984 annual chartbook, 9364–2.11
- Financial and business statistics, quarterly chartbook, 9362–2.5
- Older persons by demographic, socioeconomic, and health characteristics, selected years 1900-81 and projected to 2050, Current Population Rpt, 2546–2.125
- Older persons long-term health care and financing alternatives, including nursing home insurance and use of home equity, 1984 conf papers, 4658–7
- Older persons sociodemographic characteristics, and Fed Govt program participation and funding, 1983 with trends and projections 1900-2060, annual rpt, 25144–3.1
- *Statistical Abstract of US,* social, political, and economic data, 1950s-83 and trends, annual rpt, 2324–1.3
- Women's employment and earnings, by labor force and socioeconomic characteristics, and compared to men, 1978-81 and trends from 1940s, 6568–29

see also Business assets and liabilities, general

see also Business assets and liabilities, specific industries

see also Gross National Product

see also Income taxes

see also Money supply

see also National income and product accounts

see also Personal and family income

see also Personal debt

see also Poverty

see also Property

see also Savings

see also Securities

Index by Subjects and Names

Weapons systems
see Arms sales
see Military assistance
see Military weapons
see Missiles and rockets

Weather

Air traffic control and airway facilities and equipment, FAA improvement activities and R&D under Natl Airspace System Plan, 1982-2000, annual rpt, 7504–12

Aircraft accident circumstances and severity, by type of flying and aircraft, 1981, annual rpt, 9614–3

Aircraft accidents of commuter carriers and air taxis by seating capacity and cause, and deaths, 1975-82, GAO rpt, 26113–116

Aircraft fatal accidents of commuter airlines, air taxis, and general aviation, alcohol involvement, circumstances, and pilot characteristics, 1975-81, 9618–11

Airline and general aviation accident circumstances, severity, and causes, for US operations of domestic and foreign aircraft, periodic rpt, 9612–1

Antarctic climatological data mgmt, 1983 workshop proceedings, 2156–18.15

Boat accidents, injuries, and fatalities, by age of operator and circumstances, 1983, annual rpt, 7404–1.2

Carbon dioxide atmospheric concentration increase effects on hydrologic conditions, projected for 26-35 years, 9188–95

Carbon dioxide atmospheric levels, climatic effects and impacts of fossil and synthetic fuels use, deforestation, and land use patterns, research rpt series, 3406–3

Carbon dioxide emissions, climatic effects, and control costs, projected under alternative emissions controls and energy use restrictions to 2100 with trends 1970s-80, reprint, 9188–88

Central cities and suburbs population and employment, effect of region, neighborhood, population, and labor characteristics, 1970-80, technical paper, 9387–8.89

Climatological data by census div and State, and departures from long-term mean, from 1895, series, 2156–17

Climatological data for surface and upper air, averages by foreign and US station, monthly rpt, 2152–4

Climatological data for 284 US and outlying stations, for period of record through 1982, annual rpt, 2154–8

Climatological data for 945 cities, *County and City Data Book,* 1980, 2328–1

Coastal environmental and socioeconomic conditions, and potential impacts of oil and gas OCS leases, final statement series, 5736–1

Coastal environmental characteristics, fish, wildlife, and use, and population socioeconomic data, for individual areas, series, 5506–4

Deaths due to cold weather and related causes, by age, race, State, and city, selected periods 1962-83, 21148–30

Developing countries disaster preparedness and summary sociodemographic, political, and economic data, country rpt series, 9916–2

Electric power demand of households in 136 SMSAs and other utility service areas,

with fuel prices, family income, and heating degree days, 1975 and projected to 1985, 1588–78

Energy production, reserves, and prices, by energy type, and selected indicators of energy use, by State, 1982-83 with selected comparisons from 1971, annual rpt, 3164–60

Estuary environmental characteristics, fish, wildlife, uses, and mgmt, for individual estuaries, series, 5506–7

Fed Govt services and research programs and funding, by agency, FY84-85, annual rpt, 2144–2

Forecast methodology, accuracy, and applications, technical rpt series, 2186–4

Foreign and US agricultural production, trade, and climatic devs, weekly press release, 1922–4

Foreign weather conditions and impact assessment, by world area and country, monthly rpt, 2152–9

Heating and cooling degree days, by census div, monthly and cumulative for season, monthly rpt, 3162–24.1

Heating and cooling degree days by State, and housing energy bills and departures from normal by fuel type, by census div, monthly rpt, 2152–11

Heating and cooling degree days, distribution for nonresidential buildings by building type, EIA survey series, 3166–8

Heating and cooling degree days, solar radiation, and residential electricity and gas costs, for 306 cities, fall 1982, 3308–67

Heating and cooling degree days weighted by population, by census div and State, with area-weighted temperature and precipitation, monthly rpt, 2152–13

Heating degree days, for 45 cities and total US, cumulative for season, weekly rpt, 3162–32.2

Hwy-railroad grade-crossing accidents, detailed data by State and railroad, 1982, annual rpt, 7604–2

Jamaica PL 480 Title I assistance effects on economic dev, with data on govt finance, economic indicators, demography, and dev programs, 1970s-81, 9916–1.51

Labor force not at work on day of survey, employed part-time, or unemployed, by reason, sex, race, Hispanic origin, region, and State, 1983, annual rpt, 6744–7

Lightning and other causes of fires on Forest Service land, by forest and State, 1983, annual rpt, 1204–6

Lightning and other causes of forest fires, and damage, by State and region, 1981, annual rpt, 1204–4

Marine weather and tropical cyclones, quarterly journal with articles, 2152–8

Marine weather broadcasts for US ships, by major ocean area, as of Jan 1984, biennial rpt, 2184–3

Natl Weather Service station locations and regular observations made, 1984 annual listing, 2184–5

Nevada water supply, streamflow, reservoir storage, and precipitation, 1984 water year, annual rpt, 1264–8

New York State area snow depth and water equivalent, by site, winter 1982/83, annual rpt, 2184–2

Weather control

NOAA scientific and technical publications, monthly listing, 2142–1

Northeastern US water supply, precipitation and stream runoff by station, monthly rpt, 2182–3

Precipitation and temperature outlook for US and Northern Hemisphere, and by US and selected foreign weather stations, semimonthly rpt, 2182–1

Precipitation forecast accuracy, by season, forecast period, and region, various periods 1966-82, technical memorandum, 2188–17

Railroad accidents, circumstances, severity, and railroad involved, quarterly rpt, 9612–3

Statistical Abstract of US, social, political, and economic data, 1950s-83 and trends, annual rpt, 2324–1.1

Temperature and precipitation, and effect on agriculture, by US region, State, and city, and world area, weekly rpt, 2152–2

Traffic fatal accidents detailed circumstances, and characteristics of persons and vehicles involved, 1982, annual rpt, 7764–10

Utah water supply, streamflow, reservoir storage, and precipitation, 1984 water year, annual rpt, 1264–6

Water supply and quality, and effect of coal mining operations, for selected river basins in Eastern and Interior coal provinces, series, 5666–15

Water supply and quality, and effect of coal mining operations, for selected river basins in Western coal provinces, series, 5666–19

Water supply and quality, floods, drought, mudslides, and other hydrologic events, by State, 1983, annual rpt, 5664–12

Weather events socioeconomic impacts and costs, heating and cooling degree days, and housing energy bills, by census div and State, monthly rpt, 2152–12

Weather phenomena and storm characteristics, casualties, and property damage, by State, monthly listing, 2152–3

Weather stations of Upper Air Observational Network, by US and foreign location, 1984 annual listing, 2184–6

Western US water supply, and snow survey results, monthly State rpt series, 1266–2

Western US water supply, snow depth measurements by station, State rpt series, 1266–3

Western US water supply, streamflow and reservoir storage forecasts by stream and station, Jan-May monthly rpt, 1262–1

see also Drought
see also Floods
see also Glaciers
see also Ice conditions
see also Meteorological satellites
see also Meteorology
see also Storms
see also Weather control

Weather Bureau
see National Environmental Satellite, Data, and Information Service
see National Weather Service

Weather control

Agricultural research expenditures and scientist years, by topic, commodity, and performing organization, FY82, annual rpt, 1744–2

Weather control

Modification activity rpts and summary, annual rpt, suspended, 2144–8

Weather satellites
see Meteorological satellites

Webb, Roy H.
"Forecasts 1984", 9389–1.404

Weber, Bruce R.
"U.S. Wheat Outlook", 1004–16.1

Webre, Philip
"Federal Support of U.S. Business", 26306–6.70

Weight
see Body measurements
see Obesity

Weights and measures
Natl Bur of Standards standard reference and research materials available, 1984-85, biennial catalog, 2214–2
Natl Standards Bur publications, 1983 annual listing, 2214–1
see also Industrial standards

Weinberg, Edgar
"BLS and the Economy: A Centennial Timetable", 6722–1.467

Weir, Paula
"Estimated Historic Time Series for the EIA-782", 3162–11.401

Weirton, W.Va.
Census of Housing, 1980: occupancy and unit characteristics, by race, Hispanic origin, and city, SMSA rpt, 2473–1.344
Census of Population and Housing, 1980: detailed population and housing characteristics, by county, city, and census tract, SMSA rpt, 2551–2.344
see also under By SMSA or MSA in the "Index by Categories"

Weisbrod, Glen
"Impacts of Downtown Revitalization Projects on Small Business", 21788–140.2

Weissert, William G.
"Care for the Chronically Ill: Nursing Home Incentive Payment Experiment", 4652–1.405
"Home Equity Financing of Long-Term Care for the Elderly", 4658–7

Weisskopf, Thomas E.
"Use of Hourly Earnings Proposed To Revive Spendable Earnings Series", 6722–1.468

Weitzman, Murray
"Trends in Employment and Earnings in the Philanthropic Sector", 6722–1.455

Welfare
see Aid to Families with Dependent Children
see Public welfare programs
see Social security

Welniak, Edward J.
"Money Income and Poverty Status of Families and Persons in the U.S.: 1983 (Advance Data from the Mar. 1984 Current Population Survey)", 2546–6.41
"Money Income of Households, Families, and Persons in the U.S.: 1982", 2546–6.39

Welsh, R. A.
"Analyses of Tipple and Delivered Samples of Coal Collected During FY82 and FY83", 3004–15

Wenatchee, Wash.
Housing vacancy rates for single and multifamily units and mobile homes, by city and ZIP code, 1983, annual metro area rpt, 9304–21.2

Housing vacancy rates for single and multifamily units and mobile homes, by city and ZIP code, 1984, annual metro area rpt, 9304–21.9

Wenninger, John
"M1-GNP Relationship: A Component Approach", 9385–1.413

Werneke, Diane
"Worker Participation and Productivity Change", 6722–1.457

Wesner, G. M.
"Assessment of Potential Environmental Problems Concerning Water Availability", 9208–125

West Haven, Conn.
Census of Housing, 1980: occupancy and unit characteristics, by race, Hispanic origin, and city, SMSA rpt, 2473–1.257
Census of Population and Housing, 1980: detailed population and housing characteristics, by county, city, and census tract, SMSA rpt, 2551–2.257

West Indies
see Caribbean area

West Lafayette, Ind.
Census of Housing, 1980: occupancy and unit characteristics, by race, Hispanic origin, and city, SMSA rpt, 2473–1.207
Census of Population and Housing, 1980: detailed population and housing characteristics, by county, city, and census tract, SMSA rpt, 2551–2.207

West, Margaret D.
"Projected Supply of Registered Nurses, 1990", 4102–1.439

West Palm Beach, Fla.
Census of Housing, 1980: occupancy and unit characteristics, by race, Hispanic origin, and city, SMSA rpt, 2473–1.369
Census of Population and Housing, 1980: detailed population and housing characteristics, by county, city, and census tract, SMSA rpt, 2551–2.369
Wages by occupation, and benefits for office and plant workers, 1984 labor market area survey rpt, 6785–3.3

West Point
see Service academies

West Virginia
Agriculture census, 1982: farms, farmland, production, finances, and operator characteristics, by county, final State rpt, 2331–1.48
Apple production, marketing, and prices in 4 Appalachian States, 1983/84 crop year, annual rpt, 1311–13
Bank deposits in commercial and mutual savings banks and in US branches of foreign banks, by account type, instn, State, SMSA, and county, June 1983, annual rpt, 9295–3.6
Bank income and expenses, Fed Reserve 5th District member banks, by State, 1983, annual rpt, 9389–10
Census of Housing, 1980: occupancy and unit characteristics of SMSAs and central cities, by race, Hispanic origin, and city, State rpt, 2473–1.50
Census of Population and Housing, 1980: detailed population and housing characteristics, by county, city, and census tract, State rpt, 2551–2.50
Census of Population, 1980: detailed socioeconomic and demographic characteristics, by age, sex, race, Hispanic origin, and industry, State rpt, 2531–4.50

Index by Subjects and Names

Coal (bituminous) mining production and related workers, wages by occupation, and benefits, by size of mine and union status, in 6 States and aggregate for Rocky Mountain States, July 1982 survey, 6787–6.198

Coal employment and economic losses from utility fuel switching to meet emissions standards, with detail for counties in 5 States, 1970s-83 and projected to 1990, 21368–52

County Business Patterns: establishments, employees, and payrolls, by SIC 4-digit industry and county, 1982, annual State rpt, 2326–6.50

Economic indicators by State, Fed Reserve 5th District, quarterly rpt, 9389–16

Employment, earnings, and hours, by selected SIC 1- to 4-digit industry, State, and for 278 major labor areas, 1939-83, annual rpt, 6744–5.2, 6744–5.3

Environmental quality, pollutant discharge by type and source, and EPA protection activities and funding, 1970s-83, biennial regional rpt, 9184–15.3

Exports of manufactured and agricultural commodities, manufacturing production, and export-related employment, 1960s-82, State rpt, 2046–3.48

HHS aid to each State and local govt or private instn, amount obligated, funding agency, and program, FY83, annual listing, 4004–3.3

HUD rental rehabilitation grants for low- and moderate-income housing, by community, 1984 press release, 5006–3.33

Income (personal) per capita and by source, and earnings by industry div, by State, MSA, and county, 1977-82, annual regional rpt, 2704–2.6

Manufacturing census, 1982: financial and operating data, by SIC 2- to 4-digit industry, State, SMSA, and county, preliminary census div rpt, 2491–3.5

Mineral Industry Surveys, State review of production, 1983, advance annual rpt, 5614–6.48

Minerals Yearbook, 1982, Vol 2 preprints: State review of production and sales by commodity, and business activity, annual rpt, 5604–16.50

Minerals Yearbook, 1982, Vol 2: State reviews of production, sales, and firms, by commodity, and business activity, annual rpt, 5604–34

Population, births, deaths, and net migration, by MSA and county, 1980-82, annual State Current Population Rpt, 2546–4.48

Population size, Apr 1980 and July 1982, and per capita income, 1979 and 1981, by county and city, State Current Population Rpt, 2546–11.48

Retail trade census, 1982: employment, establishments, sales, and payroll, by SIC 2- to 4-digit kind of business, SMSA, county, and city, State rpt, 2397–1.49

Transportation census, 1982: trucks, by detailed characteristics, miles traveled, and type of product carried, State rpt, 2573–1.49

Wages for 3 occupational groups, relative average levels in 78 labor market areas, 1983, annual press release, 6785–13

Index by Subjects and Names

Western States

Wages of office and plant workers, by occupation, 1984 labor market area survey rpt, 6785–3.9

Water supply and quality, and effect of coal mining operations, for selected river basins in Eastern and Interior coal provinces, 1983 rpt, 5666–15.22, 5666–15.26

Water supply and quality in streams and lakes, and groundwater levels in wells, by drainage basin, 1983, annual State rpt, 5666–10.45

Wholesale trade census, 1982: employment, establishments, finances, and operations, by SIC 2- to 4-digit kind of business, SMSA, county, and city, State rpt, 2405–1.49

see also Charleston, W.Va.
see also Huntington, W.Va.
see also Parkersburg, W.Va.
see also Weirton, W.Va.
see also Wheeling, W.Va.
see also under By State in the "Index by Categories"

Westcott, Paul C.

"Dynamic Corn Sector Adjustments to Changes in Selected Supply and Demand Variables", 1561–4.404

"Factors Affecting Quarterly Domestic Feed Demand for Corn", 1561–4.403

"Relationships Between Quarterly Wheat Prices and Stocks", 1561–12.401

Western Area Power Administration

Aircraft (jet) of WAPA, use, costs, and employee time savings, Oct 1981-May 1982 and Oct 1983-Feb 1984, 3006–5.8

Budget appropriations proposed for Fed Govt energy programs, by office or dept and function, FY84-85, annual rpt, 3004–14

Budget of US, effects of Reagan Admin policy changes, by detailed program, FY85, annual rpt, 104–21

Electric power sales, revenues, and prices of Bonneville Power Admin, by class of customer and individual purchaser, 1983, semiannual rpt, 3222–1

Electric power wholesale purchases and costs for individual REA borrowers, by supplier and State, 1940-83, annual rpt, 1244–5

Hydroelectric power small-scale potential generation, site inventory, and costs, by Western Area Power Admin State and county, 1984 rpt, 3258–1

Operations, financial statements, and sales by customer, FY83, annual rpt, 3254–1

Western Sahara

see Morocco

Western Samoa

Economic, social, and political summary data, by country, 1984, annual factbook, 244–11

Exports of US, detailed Schedule B commodities by country of destination, 1983, annual rpt, 2424–9

Exports of US, detailed Schedule E commodities by mode of transport and world area and country of destination, 1983, annual rpts, 2424–5

Imports of US, detailed Schedule A commodities by country and world area of origin, and mode of transport, 1983, annual rpts, 2424–2

Imports of US, detailed TSUSA commodities by country of origin, 1983, annual rpt, 2424–4

Loans and grants for economic and military assistance from US and intl agencies, by program and country, FY46-83, annual rpt, 9914–5

Population size and growth rates, and latest available benchmark demographic data, by country, 1950-83, biennial rpt, 2324–4

Western States

Army Corps of Engineers activities and projects, FY83 and trends from 1800s, annual rpt, 3754–1

Bank deposits, loans, investments, and borrowings, Fed Reserve 10th District depository instns, monthly rpt, 9381–2

Bank financial activity, Fed Reserve 10th District depository instns by State, and large commercial banks by city, monthly rpt, 9381–11

Bonneville Power Admin energy conservation program activities and funding data, FY82 and estimated FY83-87, 3228–2

Bonneville Power Admin operations, and Columbia River power system sales and financial statements, FY83, annual rpt, 3224–1

Bridges over navigable waters, with type of bridge and use, owner, dimensions, and location, 1984 regional listing, 7406–5.4

Census of Population, 1980: detailed socioeconomic and demographic characteristics, by age, sex, race, Hispanic origin, occupation, and industry, US summary rpt, 2531–4.1

Coal (bituminous) mining production and related workers, wages by occupation, and benefits, by size of mine and union status, in 6 States and aggregate for Rocky Mountain States, July 1982 survey, 6787–6.198

Coal dev on Fed Govt lease land in Western US, surface and mineral rights by State, and environmental protection adequacy, various periods 1978-85, 26358–103

Coal supply and Fed Govt coal leases, by owner, owner industry, and western State, various periods 1950-82 and projected to 2000, hearing, 25318–58

Coastal environmental and wildlife characteristics, use, and mgmt, for individual ecosystems, series, 5506–9

Colorado River Storage Project finances, water resource dev, power production, and other activities in western States, FY83, annual rpt, 5824–3

Commerce Dept regional center mgmt assistance operations, assessment, and procurement authority, by subagency, regional rpt series, 2006–4.1, 2006–4.2

Economic indicators, Fed Reserve 12th District, quarterly rpt, 9393–1

Electric and gas privately owned utilities, wages and employment by occupation, and benefits, by region, Oct 1982 survey, 6787–6.205

Electric power consumption and prices in Pacific Northwest by end-use sector, and economic and demographic data, 1960s-83 and projected to 2005, annual rpt, 3224–2

Electric power sales by customer, operations by plant, and financial statements of Western Area Power Admin, FY83, annual rpt, 3254–1

Electric power sales, revenues, and prices of Bonneville Power Admin, by class of customer and individual purchaser, 1983, semiannual rpt, 3222–1

Environmental quality, pollutant discharge by type and source, and EPA protection activities and funding, 1970s-83, biennial regional rpt, 9184–15.8, 9184–15.9, 9184–15.10

Farm production inputs, outputs, and productivity, by region, 1939-82, annual rpt, 1544–17

Farm real estate value per acre indexes, 15 western States, 1970s-84, annual rpt, 1541–8.1

Fed Govt lands in western US by agency and mining restriction status, and energy resources on potential wilderness areas and other lands, 1970s-81 and projected to 1990, 3308–68

Financial and economic devs, Fed Reserve Bank of San Francisco quarterly rpt articles, 9393–8

Financial and economic devs, Fed Reserve Bank of St Louis monthly rpt articles, 9391–1

Fish and shellfish landings, life cycles, and environmental needs, for selected species by region, with glossary and bibl, series, 5506–8

Fish landings, employment, gear used, and seafood production, for detailed species by State, 1977, annual rpt, 2164–2.7

Forest insect and disease incidence and damage, 1983, annual regional rpt, 1206–11.1, 1206–11.3

Forests (natl) below-cost timber sales and revenue by western forest, and volume, average price by species, and costs by western region, FY80-1982, GAO rpt, 26113–126

Fruit and vegetable shipments, and arrivals in 23 US and 5 Canada cities, by mode of transport and State or country of origin, 1983, annual rpt, 1311–4.2

Govt revenue and expenditures, surplus/deficit, and tax capacity and effort indexes, for US and 7 western States, selected years 1967-82, article, 9381–1.403

Grain mill production workers, wages, hours, and benefits, by occupation, mill product, and region, June 1982 survey, 6787–6.204

HHS aid to each State and local govt or private instn, amount obligated, funding agency, and program, FY83, annual listing, 4004–3

Horse and burro wild herd areas in western States, population, adoption, and protection and mgmt costs, as of 1984, biennial rpt, 5724–8

Housing and neighborhood quality indicators and attitudes, and occupant characteristics, by urban-rural location and region, 1981, annual survey, 2485–7.2

Housing and neighborhood quality indicators and attitudes, by occupant and unit characteristics, region, and metro-nonmetro location, 1981, annual survey, 2485–2

Housing census, 1980: inventory, occupancy, and unit characteristics, changes from 1973 by region and inside-outside SMSAs and central cities, series, 2473–3

Western States

Housing, employment, and economic indicators in FHLB 11th District, by SMSA, quarterly rpt, 9302–18

Housing finance studies, technical paper series, 9306–1

Housing occupancy and unit and household characteristics, by region and metro-nonmetro residence, 1983, biennial survey, 2485–1

Housing outlook and economic and demographic trends, FHLB 11th District, urban area rpt series, 9306–2

Housing vacancy rates for single and multifamily units and mobile homes in FHLB 10th District, by ZIP code, annual metro area rpt series, 9304–22

Housing vacancy rates for single and multifamily units and mobile homes in FHLB 11th District, by ZIP code, annual metro area rpt series, 9304–20

Housing vacancy rates for single and multifamily units and mobile homes in FHLB 12th District, by ZIP code, annual metro area rpt series, 9304–21

Hydroelectric power small-scale potential generation, site inventory, and costs, by Western Area Power Admin State and county, 1984 rpt, 3258–1

Income (personal) by industry group and region, percent change 1959-79 and 1979-83, article, 2702–1.443

Income (personal) per capita and by source, and earnings by industry div, by State, MSA, and county, 1977-82, annual regional rpt, 2704–2.8, 2704–2.9

Income (personal) per capita and by source, earnings by major industry group, and social insurance contributions, by region and State, 1929-82, 2708–40

Iron and steel production workers and wages by occupation, and benefits, by region, Aug 1983 survey, 6787–6.206

Land Mgmt Bur public lands admin and program activities in western States, FY82-84, annual rpt, 5724–13

Lumber and wood product production, consumption by end use, shipments, exports, and market channels, for Rocky Mountain States, 1974-76, 1208–208

Lumber production, prices, trade, and employment in Northwest US and British Columbia, quarterly rpt, 1202–3

Manufacturing census, 1982: financial and operating data, by SIC 2- to 4-digit industry, State, SMSA, and county, preliminary census div rpt, 2491–3.8, 2491–3.9

Mineral Industry Surveys, phosphate rock production, sales, exports, and use, 1984 crop year, annual rpt, 5614–20

Natl forest sales in Pacific Northwest by bidding method, harvest by company, and effects on local employment by community, 1974-77, 1208–194

Nuclear power plants construction financing of Washington Public Power Supply System, with regional economic impacts and power supply/demand, 1980s-2035, hearing, 21448–29

Oil and gas extraction production workers, wages, hours, and benefits, by occupation, region, and for 5 States, June 1982 survey, 6787–6.203

Oil and gas field itemized equipment and operating costs and cost indexes, for 10 producing areas, 1981-83, annual rpt, 3164–45

Index by Subjects and Names

Oil and gas potential reserves in Western States wilderness areas, for 11 States, 1982-83, compilation of papers, 5668–69

Phosphate rock reserves in southeastern and northwestern US, by location, 1984 rpt, 5668–74

Radionuclide concentrations in air, water, and biota near Nevada and other nuclear test sites, and in milk from western States, by location, 1983, annual rpt, 9234–4

Reclamation Bur water storage and carriage facilities, by type, as of Sept 1983, annual listing, 5824–7

Reclamation programs of Fed Govt in western US, finances and operations by project and State, 1981-82, annual rpts, 5824–1

Savings and loan assns, FHLB 10th District insured members finances and operations by SMSA, monthly rpt, 9302–22

Savings and loan assns, FHLB 10th District members, locations, assets, and savings, 1984, annual listing, 9304–17

Savings and loan assns, FHLB 11th District member offices, locations, savings balances, and accounts, quarterly listing, 9302–20

Savings and loan assns, FHLB 11th District members financial condition and operations by State, quarterly rpt, 9302–19

Savings and loan assns, FHLB 11th District members financial operations and housing industry indicators by State, monthly rpt, 9302–17

Savings and loan assns, FHLB 12th District members financial operations and housing industry indicators by State, monthly rpt, 9302–21

Shipbuilding costs and related employment, by coastal district, 1982, annual rpt, 7704–12

Shipping industry impact on local economy, and port dev financing through user fees, by State, other area, industry, and port, 1970s-2020, hearings, 21568–34

Tidal current tables, daily time and velocity by station for North America and Asia coasts, 1985, annual rpt, 2174–1.2

Tide height and time daily at worldwide coastal points, 1985 predictions, annual rpt, 2174–2.1

Timber resources and removals in 9 Rocky Mountain States, and forest and rangeland area, by ownership, forest and tree characteristics, and State, 1977, 1208–201

Uranium mining operations, finances, and costs of alternative methods to meet emissions standards, for industry and selected mines, selected years 1948-90, 9188–96

Uranium ore tailings at inactive mills and DOE remedial action program activities by site, and program funding, FY84, annual rpt, 3354–9

Water supply and quality, and effect of coal mining operations, for selected river basins in Western coal provinces, series, 5666–19

Water supply in Western US, and snow survey results, monthly State rpt series, 1266–2

Water supply in Western US, reservoir storage by large reservoir and State, and streamflow conditions, as of Oct 1984, annual rpt, 1264–4

Water supply in Western US, snow depth measurements by station, State rpt series, 1266–3

Water supply in Western US, streamflow and reservoir storage forecasts by stream and station, Jan-May monthly rpt, 1262–1

Waterborne commerce of US (domestic and foreign), freight by commodity, traffic, and passengers, by port and waterway, 1982, annual rpt, 3754–3.4

see also under names of individual States

Western Union International

Financial and operating data for 7 major telegraph carriers, quarterly rpt, 9282–1

Western Union Telegraph Co.

Financial and operating data for 7 major telegraph carriers, quarterly rpt, 9282–1

Financial, operating, and employment detailed data for telegraph carriers, domestic and overseas, 1982, annual rpt, 9284–6.5

Wages and employment in telephone and telegraph industry by occupation and sex, 1981, annual survey, 6787–6.199

Westrick, James J.

"Ground Water Supply Survey, Summary of Volatile Organic Contaminant Occurrence Data", 9208–120

Wetlands

Acreage and losses of wetlands, by wetland type and location, 1970s-83, 5508–89

Environmental characteristics, acreage, uses, and mgmt, by wetland type and region, 1950s-80, 26358–102

Environmental characteristics, fish, wildlife, and use, and population socioeconomic data, for individual coastal areas, series, 5506–4

Environmental characteristics, fish, wildlife, uses, and mgmt, for individual estuaries, series, 5506–7

Environmental characteristics, fish, wildlife, uses, and mgmt of individual coastal ecosystems, series, 5506–9

Environmental quality, pollutant discharge by type, and EPA protection activities, 1970s-83, biennial summary rpt, 9184–16

Environmental quality, pollutant discharge by type and source, and EPA protection activities and funding, 1970s-83, biennial regional rpt series, 9184–15

Fed Govt programs and mgmt cost control proposals, 3-year savings by function and agency, and financial and operating data, 1960s-81, 16908–1.22

Louisiana property tax on forest, agricultural, and marsh lands, impact of change from market to use valuation by parish, 1977-78, 1208–206

Natl Forest System wildlife habitat and fishery improvements, use, and game population and harvest by species and forest, by region, FY83, annual rpt, 1204–31

Oil spills in coastal and aquatic wildlife habitats, methodology for cleanup priority rating and listing of wildlife species of concern, 1984 rpt, 5508–87

Water Bank Program agreements, acreage, and Fed Govt payments, by State, FY72-83, annual rpt, 1804–21

Water Bank Program agreements, acreage, and Fed Govt payments, by State, monthly rpt, 1802–5

Index by Subjects and Names

Wheat

Whalen, Gary

"Nonbanking Operations of Bank Holding Companies", 9377–1.406

Whales

see Marine mammals

Whaley, Ross S.

"Longrun Timber Supply and Demand", 1004–16.1

Wharton, Charles H.

"Ecology of Bottomland Hardwood Swamps of the Southeast: A Community Profile", 5506–9.5

Wharton, Eric H.

"Biomass Statistics for the Northern U.S.", 1208–207

Wheat

- Acreage harvested and cropland area by crop and region, and potential for expansion, 1982-84 with trends from 1949, annual rpt, 1584–4
- Acreage planted and harvested, by crop and State, 1982-83 and planned as of June 1984, annual rpt, 1621–23
- Acreage planting intended for 19 crops, by State, as of Feb 1984, annual rpt, 1621–22
- Acreage reduction payment-in-kind program costs, requirements, producer and diversion payments, and loan interest forgiven, by crop, as of 1983, hearing, 21788–138
- Acreage, yield, and production of field crops, by State, 1978-82 and preliminary 1983, 1641–7
- Agricultural Stabilization and Conservation Service producer payments under 26 programs, monthly rpt, 1802–10
- Agricultural Stabilization and Conservation Service wheat program, 1960-84, annual fact sheet, 1806–4.9
- *Agricultural Statistics, 1983,* annual rpt, 1004–1
- Agriculture census, 1982: farms, farmland, production and costs, and operator characteristics, preliminary State and county rpt series, 2330–1
- Agriculture census, 1982: farms, farmland, production, finances, and operator characteristics, by county, final State rpt series, 2331–1
- *Agriculture Fact Book of US,* compilation of data for 1983 with trends from 1940, annual rpt, 1004–14
- Alcohol fuel (ethanol) production in Tennessee Valley, feedstocks, facilities, tax incentives, and related farming data, by State, 1970s-83 and projected to 1992, 9808–69
- Alcoholic beverage production, stocks, materials used, and taxable and tax-free removals, for beer and distilled spirits by State, monthly rpt, 8486–1.1, 8486–1.3
- Argentina grain and oilseed production, effect of agricultural price regulation, 1947-80, 1528–170
- Argentina grain production, exports by firm, storage by facility type and port, and shipments to ports by mode of transport, by grain type, selected years 1954-81, 1528–185
- China economic conditions, agricultural and industrial production, trade, and domestic and foreign investment, 1980-85, 2048–106

Communist, OECD, and selected other countries agricultural production, by commodity, 1960s-83, annual rpt, 244–5.9

- Consumption, supply, trade, prices, expenditures, and indexes, by food commodity, 1963-83, annual rpt, 1544–4
- Cooperatives grain marketing, storage, and shipments by mode of transport, by grain type and region, FY80, 1128–28
- Cuba economic conditions, agricultural and industrial production and distribution, trade, and intl economic relations, 1970-82 and trends from 1957, 248–40
- Developing countries food supply policies, with farm sector data, tariff income, and prices and imports of 5 grains, for 21 countries, 1960s-81, 1528–168
- Durum wheat acreage, production, prices, stocks, use, and US and Canada exports by country, quarterly rpt, 1313–6
- Eastern Europe agricultural production and trade by commodity, food consumption, and farm inputs, for 6 countries, 1960-80 with projections to 1991, 1528–178
- Eastern Europe grain production, consumption, and trade, and US farm cooperatives grain and oilseed export potential, for 4 countries, selected years 1960-90, 1128–27
- EC food supply/demand and market and support prices, with exchange rates, fertilizer price index, GDP, and population, by country, 1960-83, 1528–173
- Export licensing and monitoring activities under Export Admin Act, for selected commodities, and for Communist and other countries, FY83, annual rpt, 2044–22
- Export sales and shipments of US grains, oilseed products, hides, skins, and cotton, by country, weekly rpt, 1922–3
- Exports and imports of US, by agricultural commodity and country, bimonthly rpt with articles, 1522–1
- Exports and imports of US, by detailed agricultural commodity and country, FY83 and CY83, semiannual rpts, 1522–4
- Exports and imports of US, by detailed agricultural commodity for 8 major commodity groups, monthly rpt, 1922–8
- Exports and imports of US, detailed SIC-based commodities by world area, 1983, annual rpts, 2424–6
- Exports and imports of US, totals and as percent of domestic production, by SIC 2- to 5-digit commodity, 1981, annual rpt, 2424–3
- Exports of grain, prices and sales by type of grain, weekly rpt, 1272–2
- Exports of manufactured and agricultural commodities, manufacturing production, and export-related employment, 1960s-82, State rpt series, 2046–3
- Exports of US, detailed commodities by country of destination, monthly rpt, 2422–3
- Exports of US, detailed Schedule B commodities by country of destination, 1983, annual rpt, 2424–9
- Exports of US, detailed Schedule E commodities by mode of transport and world area and country of destination, 1983, annual rpts, 2424–5

Exports, stocks, and prices of wheat, corn, and soybeans, effects of appreciated dollar exchange rates, 1980-82 and for hypothetical 20-year period, 1528–174

- Exports under PL 480 concessional sales program, by commodity and country, 1955-83, semiannual rpt, 1922–6
- Exports under PL 480 concessional sales program, by commodity and country, 1978-83, semiannual rpt, 1922–10
- Farm finances, assets, liabilities, income, receipts by commodity and State, and expenses, 1980-83 and trends from 1910, annual rpt, 1544–16
- Flour mill production workers, wages, hours, and benefits, by occupation, mill product, and region, June 1982 survey, 6787–6.204
- Flour milling production by census div and State, daily capacity, and exports by country, monthly Current Industrial Rpt, 2506–4.1
- Foreign agricultural production, prices, and trade, by country, 1983 and outlook for 1984/85, annual world region rpt series, 1524–4
- Foreign and US agricultural production, prices, trade, and consumption, quarterly rpt with articles, 1522–3
- Foreign and US agricultural supply/demand and production data, for selected US and world crops, and for US livestock and dairy products, periodic rpt, 1522–5
- Foreign and US grain production, trade, stocks, consumption, and prices, FAS monthly and annual rpt series, 1925–2
- Foreign and US grain stocks, supply deviation, and effect on use, trade, and prices, by selected country, various periods 1960-83, 1528–184
- Foreign and US production, acreage, and yield for selected crops, forecasts by selected world region and country, FAS monthly rpt, 1925–28
- Foreign and US production, prices, trade, stocks, and use, periodic situation rpt with articles, 1561–12
- Foreign and US wheat and grain stocks, by world region, average 1979-83, 1528–183
- Futures contracts, stocks in deliverable position by type and grade, weekly tables, 11922–4
- Futures trading by commodity and exchange, and Commodity Futures Trading Commission activities, funding, and employment, FY83, annual rpt, 11924–2
- Futures trading in selected commodities, foreign currencies, and stock indexes, Chicago and other markets activity, monthly rpt, 11922–1
- Futures trading in selected commodities, foreign currencies, Treasury securities, and stock indexes, NYC, Chicago, and other markets activity, monthly rpt, 11922–5
- Great Lakes trade, by SITC 3-digit commodity, port, vessel type, world area, and country, 1982, annual rpt, 7744–3
- Imports of US, detailed Schedule A commodities by country and world area of origin, and mode of transport, 1983, annual rpts, 2424–2
- Imports of US, detailed Schedule A commodities by country, monthly rpt, 2422–2

January-December 1984

ASI Annual Supplement 853

Wheat

Imports of US, detailed TSUSA commodities by country of origin, 1983, annual rpt, 2424–4

Loan support programs of USDA for grains, activity and status by type of grain and State, monthly rpt, 1802–3

Marketing cash receipts of farms, by detailed commodity and State, 1979-82, annual rpt, 1544–18

OECD trade, total and for 4 major countries, and US trade by country, by commodity, 1972-82, annual world region rpt series, 244–13

Pesticide (ethylene dibromide) residue in grain and grain foods, and effect of processing and cooking, by selected product, 1984 hearing, 25168–62

PL 480 commodity allocations for long-term credit sales, by country, quarterly press release, 1922–7

Portugal agricultural subsidies, profits, marketing margins, and consumer prices, by commodity or product, and effects of prospective EC membership, 1981, 1528–171

Price levels of wheat, and 10-year moving averages, 1913-83, technical article, 1502–3.403

Prices on US farms and for imports at Rotterdam, and EC price supports, by type of grain, weekly press release, 1922–4

Prices received by farmers and production value for detailed crops by State, 1981-83, annual rpt, 1621–2

Prices received by farmers for major products, and paid for farm inputs and living items, by commodity and State, monthly rpt, 1629–1

Producer prices and indexes, by stage of processing and detailed commodity, monthly rpt, 6762–6

Producer prices and indexes, by stage of processing and detailed commodity, monthly 1983, annual supplement, 6764–2

Production, acreage, and yield, for selected grains by State, 1982-84 with wheat and rye seedings for 1985, annual rpt, 1621–24

Production and farm finances, expenses by type, and domestic economic impact, selected years 1972-82 and preliminary 1983-84, annual rpt, 1544–19

Production, farms, acreage, and related data, by selected crop and State, monthly rpt, 1621–1

Production inputs, land mgmt, and environmental effects, for 4 crops, 1940s-80 and projected to 2010, 9188–94

Production itemized costs, receipts, and net returns, for 13 crops, 4 livestock types, and milk, by region, 1981-83, annual rpt, 1544–20

Production, prices, trade, and export inspections by US port and country of destination, by grain type, weekly rpt, 1313–2

Production, prices, trade, and marketing, by commodity, current situation and forecast, monthly rpt, 1502–4

Soviet Union grain area, yield, production, trade, supply, and use forecasts, FAS monthly rpt, 1925–2.3

Stocks of grain by region and market city, and grain inspected for export, by type, weekly rpt, 1313–4

Stocks of grain on and off farms and total in all positions, by crop, periodic rpt, 1621–4

Stocks of grains, oilseeds, and hay on and off farms, by State, 1978-83, 1641–17

Supply/demand, prices, and commodity program operations, for selected crops and livestock, 1983 and outlook for 1984, annual article, 9381–1.402

Waterborne commerce of US (domestic and foreign), freight by commodity, traffic, and passengers, by port and waterway, 1982, annual rpt, 3754–3

see also under By Commodity in the "Index by Categories"

Wheelchairs

see Prosthetics and orthotics

Wheeling, W.Va.

Census of Housing, 1980: occupancy and unit characteristics, by race, Hispanic origin, and city, SMSA rpt, 2473–1.370

Census of Population and Housing, 1980: detailed population and housing characteristics, by county, city, and census tract, SMSA rpt, 2551–2.370

Housing vacancy rates for single and multifamily units and mobile homes, by city and ZIP code, 1984, annual metro area rpt, 9304–27.13

see also under By SMSA or MSA in the "Index by Categories"

Whichard, Obie G.

"U.S. International Trade and Investment in Services: Data Needs and Availability", 2706–5.30

Whigham, Pamela V.

"What Distinguishes Larger and More Efficient Credit Unions?", 9371–1.427

Whitcomb, Debra

"Citation Release", 6068–187

White collar crime

see Fraud

White collar workers

see Area wage surveys

see Clerical workers

see Executives

see Paraprofessionals

see Professional and technical workers

White House

Acreage of natl park system and other areas under Natl Park Service mgmt, by type of area, ownership, and site, as of Sept 1984, semiannual rpt, 5542–1

see also Executive Office of the President

White House Conference on Productivity

Productivity of labor and capital, costs, and prices, by selected industry, and compared to 6 OECD countries, selected years 1947-82, 17898–1

Whitehead, David D.

"Can Interstate Banking Increase Competitive Market Performance? An Empirical Test", 9371–1.401

"Firms Involved in ATM, POS, and Home Banking: A Survey", 9371–1.421

"Guide to Interstate Banking, 1983", 9371–13

Whitener, Leslie A.

"Statistical Portrait of Hired Farmworkers", 6722–1.440

Index by Subjects and Names

Whitlatch, Robert B.

"Ecology of New England Tidal Flats: A Community Profile", 5506–9.4

Whitton, Carolyn L.

"China's Cotton Prospects", 1561–1.405

Wholesale Price Index

see Producer Price Index

Wholesale trade

American Samoa minimum wage rates, employment, earnings, and benefits, by establishment and industry, Nov 1983, biennial rpt, 6504–6

Business Conditions Digest, current data on economic, business, and financial conditions and cyclical fluctuations, monthly rpt, 2702–3

Business Conditions Digest, historical supplement on economic, business, and financial conditions and cyclical fluctuations, with methodology, 1947-82, 2708–31

Business statistics, detailed data for major industries and economic indicators, *Survey of Current Business,* monthly rpt, 2702–1.4

Census of Population and Housing, 1980: detailed population and housing characteristics, by county, city, and census tract, State and SMSA rpt series, 2551–2

Census of Population, 1980: detailed socioeconomic and demographic characteristics, by age, sex, race, Hispanic origin, occupation, and industry, State rpt series, 2531–4

Census of Population, 1980: detailed socioeconomic characteristics, by county, city, and inside-outside SMSAs and central cities, State rpt series, 2531–3

Census of Population, 1980: labor force, by sex, detailed occupation, and region, with comparison to 1970 census, supplementary rpt, 2535–1.12

Coastal environmental characteristics, fish, wildlife, and use, and population socioeconomic data, for individual areas, series, 5506–4

Collective bargaining agreements expiring during year, covered workers by SIC 2-digit industry, firm, and union, with summary of key provisions, 1984, annual rpt, 6784–9

County and City Data Book, detailed socioeconomic and demographic data for States, counties, and cities, selected years 1976-82, 2328–1

County Business Patterns: establishments, employees, and payrolls, by SIC 4-digit industry and county, 1981, annual State rpt series, 2326–8

County Business Patterns: establishments, employees, and payrolls, by SIC 4-digit industry and county, 1982, annual State rpt series, 2326–6

Earnings by industry div, and personal income per capita and by source, by State, MSA, and county, 1977-82, annual regional rpts, 2704–2

Earnings by major industry group, and personal income per capita and by source, by region and State, 1929-82, 2708–40

Employment and earnings, detailed data, monthly rpt, 6742–2.5

Employment, earnings, and hours, by selected SIC 1- to 4-digit industry, State, and for 278 major labor areas, 1939-83, annual rpt, 6744–5

854 ASI Annual Supplement

January-December 1984

Index by Subjects and Names

Widows and widowers

Employment, earnings, and hours, by SIC 4-digit nonfarm industry, monthly 1974-Feb 1984, annual update, 6744–4

Employment, earnings, and hours, monthly press release, 6742–5

Employment situation, earnings, hours, and other BLS economic indicators, transcripts of BLS Commissioner's monthly testimony, periodic rpt, 23846–4

Employment, unemployment, and labor force, by demographic and employment characteristics, State, and for 30 metro areas and 11 large cities, 1983, annual rpt, 6744–7

Finances and operations, by SIC 2- to 4-digit industry, 1970s-83 and projected to 1988, annual rpt, 2014–4

Financial statements for manufacturing, mining, and trade corporations, by selected SIC 2- to 3-digit industry, quarterly rpt, 2502–1

Foreign direct investment in US, major investors and investments by SIC 4-digit industry, transaction type and value, and location, 1983, annual rpt, 2044–20

Franchisor sales of products and services to franchisees, by kind of business, 1982-84, annual rpt, 2014–5

Handbook of Labor Statistics, employment, earnings, hours, and labor force characteristics, 1982 and trends, detailed annual rpt, 6724–1

Income tax returns of corporations, detailed income and tax items by industry, 1981, annual rpt, 8304–4

Income tax returns of corporations, summary data by industry div, 1981 estimates, annual article, 8302–2.403

Income tax returns of corporations with foreign tax credit, income and deductions by type, asset size, and selected industry group, 1980, article, 8302–2.415

Income tax returns of foreign subsidiaries of US corporations, income and tax data, by industry and asset size, 1980, article, 8302–2.410

Income tax returns of partnerships, detailed data by industry, 1981 estimates, annual article, 8302–2.404

Income tax returns of partnerships, receipts by source, deductions by type, and establishments, by selected industry, 1982, annual article, 8302–2.416

Income tax returns of sole proprietorships, detailed data by industry div and selected industry group, 1981, annual rpt, 8304–7

Income tax returns of sole proprietorships, receipts, deductions by type, payroll, and net income, by major industry, 1982, annual article, 8302–2.413

Income tax returns with investment credits, for individuals by income, and for sole proprietorships by industry, 1981, article, 8302–2.409

Input-output structure of US economy, detailed interindustry transactions for 85 industries, and components of final demand, 1977, article, 2702–1.421

Input-output structure of US economy, detailed interindustry transactions for 537 industries, and components of final demand, 1977 benchmark data, 2708–17

Inventories, sales, and inventory/sales ratios for manufacturing and trade, quarterly article, 2702–1.34

Meat marketing and distribution establishments, sales, and per capita consumption, 1950s-82 with trends from 1929, 1548–232

Military post exchange operations, locations worldwide, sales by type of commodity or service and facility, and employment, FY83, annual rpt, 3504–10

Minority group and women's employment, by occupational group, SIC 2- to 3-digit industry, State, and SMSA, 1981, annual rpt, 9244–1

Natl income and product, comprehensive accounts and components, *Survey of Current Business,* monthly rpt, monthly and annual tables, 2702–1.27

Occupational injuries, illnesses, and workdays lost, by SIC 2-digit industry, 1982-83, annual press release, 6844–3

Occupational injury and illness rates, by SIC 2- to 4-digit industry, 1982, annual rpt, 6844–1

Occupational manpower needs and supply by detailed occupation, and educational and training program enrollees and grads by detailed field, 1982 and 1995, biennial rpt, 6744–3

Occupational Outlook Handbook, 1984-85 biennial rpt, 6744–1

Sales and inventories, by SIC 2- to 3-digit kind of business, monthly rpt, 2413–7

Sales and inventories, monthly rpt, 23842–1.3

Sales, inventories, purchases, and gross margins, by SIC 2- to 3-digit kind of business and type of ownership, 1983, annual rpt, 2413–13

Scientists, engineers, and technicians employment in transportation, utilities, and retail and wholesale trade, by field of science and industry, 1982, 9628–72

Seasonal adjustment methodology for economic time series, dev and design of Census Bur and other systems, with illustrative data, 1981 conf papers, 2626–7.5

Small and minority-owned businesses finances and operations, Federal contracts by agency, and worker characteristics, by industry, race, sex, and State, 1950s-83, annual rpt, 9764–6

Statistical Abstract of US, social, political, and economic data, 1950s-83 and trends, annual rpt, 2324–1.3

Transportation census, 1982: trucks, by detailed characteristics, miles traveled, and type of product carried, State rpt series, 2573–1

Virgin Islands economic censuses, 1982: employment, establishments, payroll, and receipts, by SIC 1- to 4-digit industry, island, and city, 2593–1

see also Agricultural marketing

see also Census of Wholesale Trade

see also Warehouses

see also under By Industry in the "Index by Categories"

see also under names of specific commodities or commodity groups

Wichita Falls, Tex.

Census of Housing, 1980: occupancy and unit characteristics, by race, Hispanic origin, and city, SMSA rpt, 2473–1.372

Census of Population and Housing, 1980: detailed population and housing characteristics, by county, city, and census tract, SMSA rpt, 2551–2.372

see also under By SMSA or MSA in the "Index by Categories"

Wichita, Kans.

Auto emissions control device tampering and fuel-switching incidence in 6 urban areas, 1983, annual rpt, 9194–15

Census of Housing, 1980: occupancy and unit characteristics, by race, Hispanic origin, and city, SMSA rpt, 2473–1.371

Census of Population and Housing, 1980: detailed population and housing characteristics, by county, city, and census tract, SMSA rpt, 2551–2.371

Housing and households detailed characteristics, and unit and neighborhood quality, by inside-outside central cities, 1981 survey, SMSA rpt, 2485–6.28

Housing vacancy rates for single and multifamily units and mobile homes, by county, city, and ZIP code, 1984, annual metro area rpt, 9304–22.11

Wages of office and plant workers, by occupation, 1984 SMSA survey rpt, 6785–11.4

see also under By City and By SMSA or MSA in the "Index by Categories"

Widmann, Richard H.

"Pulpwood Harvest Intensity in the Northeast, 1981", 9806–2.38

Widows and widowers

Census of Housing, 1980: structural, financial, and householder characteristics, by region and State, 2475–4

Census of Population and Housing, 1980: detailed population and housing characteristics, by county, city, and census tract, State and SMSA rpt series, 2551–2

Census of Population, 1980: detailed socioeconomic and demographic characteristics, by age, sex, race, Hispanic origin, occupation, and industry, State rpt series, 2531–4

Census of Population, 1980: detailed socioeconomic characteristics, by county, city, and inside-outside SMSAs and central cities, State rpt series, 2531–3

Fed Govt civil service retirees and survivors, and monthly benefit, for US territories and foreign countries, and by State, age, and sex, FY81-82, annual rpt, 9844–1.1

Foreign women sociodemographic, economic, and fertility characteristics, with comparisons to men, by country, 1960s-85, world region rpt series, 2326–15

OASDHI, Medicaid, SSI, and other social insurance and public welfare programs benefits, beneficiary characteristics, and trust funds, selected years 1937-83, annual rpt, 4744–3.4, 4744–3.6

Pension plan benefits for surviving spouses of workers in private industry, by benefit type and collective bargaining status, 1981, article, 6722–1.426

Remarriages, by detailed demographic and geographic characteristics, 1979 and trends, US Vital Statistics annual rpt, 4144–4

VA pensions for disability and death not connected with service, by entitlement type and veterans period of service, as of Mar 1984, semiannual rpt, 9922–12

War participants, deaths, veterans living, and compensation and pension recipients, for each US war, 1775-1983, semiannual rpt, 9922–8

ASI Annual Supplement 855

Widows and widowers

see also Old-Age, Survivors, Disability, and Health Insurance

see also under By Marital Status in the "Index by Categories"

Wiedemann, Alfred M.

"Ecology of Pacific Northwest Coastal Sand Dunes: A Community Profile", 5506–9.14

Wiener, James G.

"Comparative Analyses of Fish Populations in Naturally Acidic and Circumneutral Lakes in Northern Wisconsin", 5506–5.16

Wiggins, George R.

"Changes in Genetic Evaluation Procedures for Jan. 1984", 1702–2.403

"Counts of 305-Day Lactation Records Excluded from Genetic Evaluations for 1983", 1702–2.403

Wilder, Charles S.

"Health Characteristics by Geographic Region, Large Metropolitan Areas, and Other Places of Residence, U.S., 1980-81", 4147–10.146

Wilderness areas

- Acreage of natl park system and other areas under Natl Park System mgmt, by type of area, ownership, and site, as of Sept 1984, semiannual rpt, 5542–1
- Air quality protection classification of natl parks, acreage covered and recommended for redesignation by park, as of 1983, hearings, 25328–25
- Alaska Arctic Natl Wildlife Refuge resources, resident and visitor activities, and environmental impacts of energy exploration, 1983, annual update rpt, 5504–26
- Environmental quality and protection programs, costs, and Fed Govt enforcement, 1983, detailed annual rpt, 484–1
- Forest, range, and associated waters use and mgmt assessment, and environmental impacts of Forest Service program options, 1977-2030 and trends from 1920, 1208–24
- Interior Dept programs, activities, and funding, various periods 1967-84, last issue of annual rpt, 5304–13
- Land Mgmt Bur activities and finances, and public land acreage and use, annual State rpt series, 5724–11
- Land Mgmt Bur wilderness study areas and acreage, by State, as of Sept 1983, annual rpt, 5724–1.2
- Natl forests and other lands under Forest Service mgmt, by forest and location, Sept 1983, annual rpt, 1204–2
- Natl forests recreational use, visitor-days by type of activity, forest, and State, FY83 with trends from 1924, annual rpt series, 1204–17
- Natl Wilderness Preservation System acreage and additions, by State, FY83, annual rpt, 1204–1.1
- Natl Wilderness Preservation System acreage, by natl forest, wilderness and primitive area, and State, 1983, annual rpt, 5304–14
- Oil and gas potential reserves in Western States wilderness areas, for 11 States, 1982-83, compilation of papers, 5668–69
- State outdoor recreation units and acreage, by State, 1982/83, annual rpt, 5544–14.4

Wildlife and wildlife conservation

- Agricultural Conservation Program participation and payments, by State, FY83, annual rpt, 1804–7
- Air pollution and acid rain environmental effects, and methods of neutralizing acidified water bodies, summary research rpt series, 5506–5
- Alaska Arctic Natl Wildlife Refuge resources, resident and visitor activities, and environmental impacts of energy exploration, 1983, annual update rpt, 5504–26
- Coal dev plans on Fed Govt lease lands in 12 regions under Fed Coal Mgmt Program, environmental and socioeconomic impacts to 2000, final statement series, 5726–4
- Coastal environmental and socioeconomic conditions, and potential impacts of oil and gas OCS leases, final statement series, 5736–1
- Coastal environmental and wildlife characteristics, use, and mgmt, for individual ecosystems, series, 5506–9
- Coastal environmental characteristics, fish, wildlife, and use, and population socioeconomic data, for individual areas, series, 5506–4
- Colorado River Storage Project finances, water resource dev, power production, and other activities in western States, FY83, annual rpt, 5824–3
- Environmental quality and protection programs, costs, and Fed Govt enforcement, 1983, detailed annual rpt, 484–1
- Fed Govt aid to State and local govts, expenditures, and direct payments, by program, agency, and State, FY83, annual rpt, 2464–2
- Fed Govt fish and wildlife restoration program finances, funding by State, and hunting and fishing equipment excise tax revenue, FY84, annual rpt, 5504–13
- Fed Govt fish and wildlife restoration programs, including new sites, funding, and research, by State, FY81, annual rpt, 5504–1
- Fed Govt programs and mgmt cost control proposals, 3-year savings by function and agency, and financial and operating data, 1960s-81, 16908–1.22
- Fish and Wildlife Service conservation and research project descriptions and results, by program, FY83, annual rpt, 5504–20
- Forest, range, and associated waters use and mgmt assessment, and environmental impacts of Forest Service program options, 1977-2030 and trends from 1920, 1208–24
- Forest Service programs and activities, by State and region, FY83, annual rpt, 1204–1
- Genetic resource (plant and animal) conservation, commercial uses, causes of depletion, and geographic sources, 1984 rpt, 5548–13

Western US Fed Govt lands by agency and mining restriction status, and energy resources on potential wilderness areas and other lands, 1970s-81 and projected to 1990, 3308–68

Wisconsin forest fires damage to timber, crops, game, waterfowl, and recreation sites, economic effects by county, 1980-82, 1208–198

Index by Subjects and Names

- Grizzly bears in and around Yellowstone Natl Park, population, physical characteristics, diet, and movements, 1982, annual rpt, 5544–4
- Horse and burro wild herd areas in western States, population, adoption, and protection and mgmt costs, as of 1984, biennial rpt, 5724–8
- Land Mgmt Bur activities and finances, and public land acreage and use, annual State rpt series, 5724–11
- Land Mgmt Bur public lands admin and program activities in western States, FY82-84, annual rpt, 5724–13
- Livestock grazing on Natl Forest System lands, and losses from predators, poisonous plants, and other causes, by region and State, FY83, annual rpt, 1204–5
- Marine vertebrates off southeastern US coast, abundance and seasonal distribution, with oil and gas dev effects and lease status, early 1980s, 5508–85
- Mexico and US range and wildlife characteristics, problems, and research strategies and needs, 1981 conf papers, 1208–197
- Mount St Helens, Wash, volcanic eruptions, effects on water quality and other environmental characteristics of Washington and Oregon watersheds, series, 5666–14
- Natl Forest System wildlife habitat and fishery improvements, use, and game population and harvest by species and forest, by region, FY83, annual rpt, 1204–31
- Oil spills in coastal and aquatic wildlife habitats, methodology for cleanup priority rating and listing of wildlife species of concern, 1984 rpt, 5508–87
- Public lands game and waterfowl habitats, big game population, and wild horses and burros, FY83, annual rpt, 5724–1.2
- Rabies cases in animals and humans, for US and Mexico by State and for Canada by Province, 1980-82, annual rpt, 4205–28
- Radionuclide concentrations in cattle and wildlife near Nevada nuclear test site, 1957-81, last issue of annual rpt, 9234–5
- Research of State fish and wildlife agencies, federally funded wildlife and bird projects and costs, by species and State, 1984, annual rpt, 5504–24
- Satellite Landsat system proposed transfer to private sector, uses and product sales by user type, and university programs and personnel by instn, 1973-85, 26358–100
- TVA activities, financial and operating data by program and facility, and power sales by customer, FY83, annual rpt, 9804–1
- Utah timber acreage and resources, and forest recreational use and big game population by species, 1977-78, 1206–22.6
- Wetlands environmental characteristics, acreage, uses, and mgmt, by wetland type and region, 1950s-80, 26358–102
- Wisconsin forest fires damage to timber, crops, game, waterfowl, and recreation sites, economic effects by county, 1980-82, 1208–198

see also Birds and bird conservation

see also Endangered species

856 ASI Annual Supplement January-December 1984

Index by Subjects and Names

Wine and winemaking

see also Fish and fishing industry
see also Fishing, sport
see also Hunting and trapping
see also Marine mammals
see also Marine resources conservation
see also Wildlife refuges
see also Zoological parks

Wildlife refuges

Acreage of natl park system and other areas under Natl Park System mgmt, by type of area, ownership, and site, as of Sept 1984, semiannual rpt, 5542–1

Alaska Arctic Natl Wildlife Refuge resources, resident and visitor activities, and environmental impacts of energy exploration, 1983, annual update rpt, 5504–26

Alaska minerals resources, production, claims on wildlife refuges, oil and gas leases, and exploratory wells, with maps and bibl, 1983, annual rpt, 5664–11

Environmental quality and protection programs, costs, and Fed Govt enforcement, 1983, detailed annual rpt, 484–1

Fish and Wildlife Service restoration programs, including new sites, funding, and research, by State, FY81, annual rpt, 5504–1

Interior Dept programs, activities, and funding, various periods 1967-84, last issue of annual rpt, 5304–13

Natl forests and other lands under Forest Service mgmt, by forest and location, Sept 1983, annual rpt, 1204–2

Revenues from economic and recreational uses of wildlife refuges, and refuge managers attitudes toward expanded use, FY81-83, GAO rpt, 26113–128

Wilkes-Barre, Pa.

Dress industry production and related workers, wages, and benefits, by occupation, size of establishment, and union status, for 11 labor market areas, Aug 1982 survey, 6787–6.200

see also under By SMSA or MSA in the "Index by Categories"

Wilkin, John C.

"Economic Projections for OASDI Cost Estimates, 1983", 4706–1.90

Wilkins, Paul C.

"Marketing and Farm Supply Cooperatives: Commercial Farmer Membership and Use, 1980", 1128–32

"Marketing and Farm Supply Cooperatives: Livestock Producer Membership and Use, 1980", 1128–26

"Nation's Commercial Farmers Find Supply, Marketing Co-ops Useful", 1122–1.401

Wilkinson, Constance

"IPP Impacts on Small Business: Millard and Juab Counties", 25728–36

Wilkinson, Gary H.

"We, the Americans", 2326–1.1

Wilkinson, Robert

"Redesign of the Sample for the Current Population Survey", 6742–2.407

Willamette River

Bridges over navigable waters, with type of bridge and use, owner, dimensions, and location, 1984 regional listing, 7406–5.4

Freight (waterborne domestic and foreign) by commodity, traffic, and passengers, by port and waterway, 1982, annual rpt, 3754–3.4

Water supply and quality in streams and lakes, and groundwater levels in wells, by drainage basin, 1981, annual State rpt series, 5666–16

Water supply and quality in streams and lakes, and groundwater levels in wells, by drainage basin, 1982, annual State rpt series, 5666–20

Water supply and quality in streams and lakes, and groundwater levels in wells, by drainage basin, 1983, annual State rpt series, 5666–10

Water supply in US and Canada, streamflow, well and reservoir levels, and dissolved solids and temperature in 6 US rivers, by station, monthly rpt, 5662–3

Willer, W. D.

"Farm Finance: A Lenders Viewpoint", 1004–16.1

Williams, Austin B.

"Synopsis of Biological Data on the Blue Crab, Callinectes sapidus Rathbun", 2166–16.13

Williamson, John

"International Liquidity: Are the Supply and Composition Appropriate?", 9373–3.28

Williamsport, Pa.

Census of Housing, 1980: occupancy and unit characteristics, by race, Hispanic origin, and city, SMSA rpt, 2473–1.373

Census of Population and Housing, 1980: detailed population and housing characteristics, by county, city, and census tract, SMSA rpt, 2551–2.373

see also under By SMSA or MSA in the "Index by Categories"

Willms, Manfred

"Monetary Policy Decision Process in the Federal Republic of Germany", 9373–3.26

Wilmington, Del.

Census of Housing, 1980: occupancy and unit characteristics, by race, Hispanic origin, and city, SMSA rpt, 2473–1.374

Census of Population and Housing, 1980: detailed population and housing characteristics, by county, city, and census tract, SMSA rpt, 2551–2.374

Wages by occupation, and benefits for office and plant workers, 1984 labor market area survey rpt, 6785–3.5

see also under By SMSA or MSA in the "Index by Categories"

Wilmington, N.C.

Census of Housing, 1980: occupancy and unit characteristics, by race, Hispanic origin, and city, SMSA rpt, 2473–1.375

Census of Population and Housing, 1980: detailed population and housing characteristics, by county, city, and census tract, SMSA rpt, 2551–2.375

Waterborne commerce of US (domestic and foreign), freight by commodity, traffic, and passengers, by port and waterway, 1982, annual rpt, 3754–3.1

Wilson, David L.

"Economic Impacts of the Fort Union Coal Project on Farms and Ranches, Montana and North Dakota", 1588–79

Wilson, Elwyn E.

"Great Lakes Navigation Season, 1983", 2152–8.403

Wilson, John F.

"Foreign Sector in the U.S. Flow of Funds Accounts", 9366–7.95

Wilson, W. Gene

"Crucial Year for Southeastern Farmers", 9371–1.424

"Educational Inventory: Where Does the Southeast Stand?", 9371–1.428

"Mississippi: A State in Transition", 9371–1.409

Wind

see Meteorology
see Storms
see Weather
see Wind energy

Wind energy

Budget of US, effects of Reagan Admin policy changes, by detailed program, FY85, annual rpt, 104–21

Consumption by fuel type, and estimated supply from renewable resources, 1977 and projected 2000, hearing, 21448–30

Consumption, by fuel type, economic sector, and end use, 1983 and 2000, 2006–2.5

Electric power plants, by capacity, fuel used, unit type, region, State, and county, for plants added and retired, 1983 and planned through 1993, annual rpt, 3164–36

Natl Energy Policy Plan, energy supply, demand, and prices, by fuel and consuming sector, projected 1985-2010, biennial rpt, 3004–13

Production, trade, supply, use, conservation, and DOE activities, by energy type, FY83, annual rpt, 3024–2

Research publications on energy of DOE and other sources, monthly listing, 3002–2

Supply/demand and prices, by energy source and end-use sector and for 7 electric utilities, 1981-2000 with trends from 1960s, 3008–93

Supply/demand and prices, by fuel type and consuming sector with foreign comparisons, 1949-83, annual rpt, 3164–74

Wine and winemaking

Air pollutant emission factors, by detailed source, 3rd edition, 1983-84 supplements, 9198–13

Business statistics, detailed data for major industries and economic indicators, *Survey of Current Business,* monthly rpt, 2702–1.11

California farm real estate market values, by use and crop, 1976-84, annual rpt, 1541–8.1

Consumption of food and nutrient intake by individuals, by food group, source, and socioeconomic characteristics, 1977-78 natl survey, final rpt series, 1356–4

Consumption, supply, trade, prices, expenditures, and indexes, by food commodity, 1963-83, annual rpt, 1544–4

County Business Patterns: establishments, employees, and payrolls, by SIC 4-digit industry and county, 1981, annual State rpt series, 2326–8

County Business Patterns: establishments, employees, and payrolls, by SIC 4-digit industry and county, 1982, annual State rpt series, 2326–6

Employment, earnings, and hours, by SIC 4-digit nonfarm industry, monthly 1974-Feb 1984, annual update, 6744–4

Wine and winemaking

Exports and imports of US, by agricultural commodity and country, bimonthly rpt with articles, 1522–1

Exports and imports of US, by detailed agricultural commodity and country, FY83 and CY83, semiannual rpts, 1522–4

Exports and imports of US, detailed SIC-based commodities by world area, 1983, annual rpts, 2424–6

Exports and imports of US, totals and as percent of domestic production, by SIC 2- to 5-digit commodity, 1981, annual rpt, 2424–3

Exports, imports, tariffs, and industry operating data for selected alcoholic beverages, 1979-83, TSUSA commodity rpt, 9885–1.72

Exports of US, detailed commodities by country of destination, monthly rpt, 2422–3

Exports of US, detailed Schedule B commodities by country of destination, 1983, annual rpt, 2424–9

Exports of US, detailed Schedule E commodities by mode of transport and world area and country of destination, 1983, annual rpts, 2424–5

Foreign and US fresh and processed fruit, vegetable, and nut production and trade, FAS monthly rpt with articles, 1925–34

Imports of table wine from France and Italy, injury to US industry from sales covered by foreign govt grants, investigation with background financial and operating data, 1984 rpt, 9886–19.9

Imports of US, detailed Schedule A commodities by country and world area of origin, and mode of transport, 1983, annual rpts, 2424–2

Imports of US, detailed Schedule A commodities by country, monthly rpt, 2422–2

Imports of US, detailed TSUSA commodities by country of origin, 1983, annual rpt, 2424–4

Input-output structure of US economy, detailed interindustry transactions for 537 industries, and components of final demand, 1977 benchmark data, 2708–17

Inventory and supply of wine, by type of wine, source, and selected State, periodic situation rpt with articles, 1561–6

Israel and France urban youths use of selected drugs, alcohol, and cigarettes, by age and sex, 1977 and 1979, article, 4102–1.430

Manufacturing census, 1982: financial and operating data, by SIC 2- to 4-digit industry, State, SMSA, and county, preliminary census div rpt series, 2491–3

Manufacturing census, 1982: financial and operating data, for SIC 4-digit industries by product, preliminary rpt, 2491–1.34

Production, prices, and use of noncitrus fruit and nuts, by crop and State, 1981-83, annual rpt, 1621–18.1, 1621–18.3

Production, stocks, and taxable and tax-free removals, for wine by State, monthly rpt, 8486–1.2

Production, withdrawals, and stocks of wine, and materials used by type, by State, FY81-82, last issue of annual rpt, 8484–1.4

Retail trade census, 1982: employment, establishments, sales, and payroll, for liquor stores, by State, preliminary rpt, 2395–1.27

Tax (excise) collections of IRS, by source, quarterly press release, 8302–1

Taxation and revenue systems, by type of tax and system, level of govt, and State, selected years 1958-83, annual rpt, 10044–1.3

Winger, Alan R.

"Future Housing Demands and Sources of Mortgage Money", 9312–1.407

Wingo, William M.

"Species Profiles: Life Histories and Environmental Requirements of Coastal Fishes and Invertebrates (Gulf of Mexico), Sea Catfish and Gafftopsail Catfish", 5506–8.20

Winnipeg, Canada

Fruit and vegetable shipments, and arrivals in 23 US and 5 Canada cities, by mode of transport and State or country of origin, 1983, annual rpt, 1311–4.2

Winston-Salem, N.C.

Census of Housing, 1980: occupancy and unit characteristics, by race, Hispanic origin, and city, SMSA rpt, 2473–1.176

Census of Population and Housing, 1980: detailed population and housing characteristics, by county, city, and census tract, SMSA rpt, 2551–2.176

Wages of office and plant workers, by occupation, 1984 SMSA survey rpt, 6785–11.8

see also under By City and By SMSA or MSA in the "Index by Categories"

Winter Haven, Fla.

Census of Population and Housing, 1980: detailed population and housing characteristics, by county, city, and census tract, SMSA rpt, 2551–2.209

see also under By SMSA or MSA in the "Index by Categories"

Winter sports

Foreign market and trade for sporting goods and recreational equipment and vehicles, country market research rpts, 2045–14

Injuries and deaths from use of selected consumer products and related activity, by victim age and sex, 1982, annual rpt, 9164–7

Natl forests recreation sites, area, and capacity, by type of activity, as of Nov 1983, annual rpt, 1204–28

Natl forests recreational use, visitor-days by State and activity, FY79-83, annual rpt, 1204–1.1

Natl forests recreational use, visitor-days by type of activity, forest, and State, FY83 with trends from 1924, annual rpt series, 1204–17

Recreation (outdoor) participation, by type of activity, projected 1985-2030, 1208–195

Winterberger, Kenneth C.

"Timber Resource Statistics for the Wood-Salcha Block, Tanana Inventory Unit, Alaska, 1975", 1206–9.14

Wiretapping

see Electronic surveillance

Wiring (electrical)

see Electrical machinery and equipment *see* Electronics industry and products

Index by Subjects and Names

Wisconsin

Agricultural cooperatives, membership, activities, and finances, by commodity and selected State, 1900-80 with trends from 1863, 1128–30

Agriculture census, 1982: farms, farmland, production, finances, and operator characteristics, by county, final State rpt, 2331–1.49

Bank deposits in commercial and mutual savings banks and in US branches of foreign banks, by account type, instn, State, SMSA, and county, June 1983, annual rpt, 9295–3.12

Census of Housing, 1980: occupancy and unit characteristics of SMSAs and central cities, by race, Hispanic origin, and city, State rpt, 2473–1.51

Census of Population and Housing, 1980: detailed population and housing characteristics, by county, city, and census tract, State rpt, 2551–2.51

Census of Population, 1980: detailed socioeconomic and demographic characteristics, by age, sex, race, Hispanic origin, and industry, State rpt, 2531–4.51

Cheese wholesale prices in selected areas, 1983, annual rpt, 1317–1.3

County Business Patterns: establishments, employees, and payrolls, by SIC 4-digit industry and county, 1982, annual State rpt, 2326–6.51

Cranberry production, prices, area, and yield, for 5 States, 1982-83 and forecast 1984, annual rpt, 1621–18.4

Employment, earnings, and hours, by selected SIC 1- to 4-digit industry, State, and for 278 major labor areas, 1939-83, annual rpt, 6744–5.2, 6744–5.3

Environmental quality, pollutant discharge by type and source, and EPA protection activities and funding, 1970s-83, biennial regional rpt, 9184–15.5

Exports of manufactured and agricultural commodities, manufacturing production, and export-related employment, 1960s-82, State rpt, 2046–3.49

Farm investments, effective rates of Federal/State income and State/local property taxes, by category of structure and equipment, for 7 North Central States, 1981-82, 1548–237

Fish in northern Wisconsin acidic lakes, abundance and population characteristics, various dates 1979-83, 5506–5.16

Forest fires damage to timber, crops, game, waterfowl, and recreation sites in Wisconsin, economic effects by county, 1980-82, 1208–198

HHS aid to each State and local govt or private instn, amount obligated, funding agency, and program, FY83, annual listing, 4004–3.5

Home mortgages originated by S&Ls in Wisconsin and Illinois, effects of usury ceiling and market interest rates on supply and loan-to-price ratios, 1978-80, article, 9312–7.404

Housing vacancy rates for single and multifamily units and mobile homes in FHLB 7th District, by ZIP code, annual metro area rpt series, 9304–18

Hwy and bridge repair projects funded by Fed Govt, and costs, for 7 States, FY81-82, GAO rpt, 26113–121

Index by Subjects and Names

Women

Income (personal) per capita and by source, and earnings by industry div, by State, MSA, and county, 1977-82, annual regional rpt, 2704–2.4

Manufacturing census, 1982: financial and operating data, by SIC 2- to 4-digit industry, State, SMSA, and county, preliminary census div rpt, 2491–3.3

Mineral Industry Surveys, State review of production, 1983, advance annual rpt, 5614–6.49

Minerals Yearbook, 1982, Vol 2 preprints: State review of production and sales by commodity, and business activity, annual rpt, 5604–16.51

Minerals Yearbook, 1982, Vol 2: State reviews of production, sales, and firms, by commodity, and business activity, annual rpt, 5604–34

Mortgage interest fixed and adjustable rates and fees offered by Wisconsin S&Ls, monthly rpt, 9302–7

Population, births, deaths, and net migration, by MSA and county, 1980-82, annual State Current Population Rpt, 2546–4.49

Population size, Apr 1980 and July 1982, and per capita income, 1979 and 1981, by county and city, State Current Population Rpt, 2546–11.49

Public welfare programs caseloads, selected vital statistics, and households in poverty, for Wisconsin, 1970s-83, hearings, 21788–141

Pulpwood production by county, imports, and individual mill capacity, by species for 7 North Central States, 1982, annual rpt, 1204–19

Retail trade census, 1982: employment, establishments, sales, and payroll, by SIC 2- to 4-digit kind of business, SMSA, county, and city, State rpt, 2397–1.50

Savings and loan assns, FHLB 7th District insured members cost of funds, and savings flows and mortgage loans closed by SMSA, monthly rpt, 9302–5

Small business perceived burden of Fed Govt paperwork requirements, and burden for 4 Fed Govt agencies, FY83, 9768–14

Water supply and quality in streams and lakes, and groundwater levels in wells, by drainage basin, 1982, annual State rpt, 5666–20.46

see also Appleton, Wis.
see also Beloit, Wis.
see also Eau Claire, Wis.
see also Green Bay, Wis.
see also Janesville, Wis.
see also Kenosha, Wis.
see also La Crosse, Wis.
see also Madison, Wis.
see also Milwaukee, Wis.
see also Oshkosh, Wis.
see also Racine, Wis.
see also Sheboygan, Wis.
see also Superior, Wis.
see also Wausau, Wis.
see also under By State in the "Index by Categories"

Wisdom, Harold W.

"Wood Shipments to Puerto Rico", 1208–205

Wissman, Roger A.

"Co-op Share of Farm Marketings, Major Supply Purchases Climb", 1122–1.402

Withholding tax

see Income taxes
see Social security tax

Witkin, Michael J.

"State and County Mental Hospitals, U.S., 1980-81 and 1981-82", 4506–3.13

Witnesses

Crime and criminal justice statistics analysis, methodology, and use in courts, 1983 biennial conf proceedings, 6064–20

Criminal case processing from arrest to sentencing, cases and processing time by disposition, dismissal reason, and offense, for 14 cities, 1979, 6066–22.1

Justice Dept Witness Security Program operations, FY82, annual rpt, 6004–1

Protection under Witness Security Program, costs, participants by arrest record, and prosecutions by offense, offender type, and disposition, various periods FY70-83, GAO rpt, 26119–70

Wittwer, Sylvan H.

"New Agriculture", 1004–16.1

Wolfe, Harry B.

"Bedford-Stuyvesant/Crown Heights Demonstration Project", 4652–1.419

Wolfe, Raymond

"Sole Proprietorship Returns, 1982", 8302–2.413

Wolken, John D.

"Geographic Market Delineation: A Review of the Literature", 9366–1.138

Women

Body measurements of women, methodology and summary results, 1983 technical rpt, 7506–10.28

Census of Housing, 1980: inventory, occupancy, and unit characteristics, changes from 1973 by region and inside-outside SMSAs and central cities, series, 2473–3

Census of Housing, 1980: occupancy and unit characteristics of SMSAs and central cities, by race, Hispanic origin, and city, State and SMSA rpt series, 2473–1

Census of Population and Housing, 1980: detailed population and housing characteristics, by county, city, and census tract, State and SMSA rpt series, 2551–2

Census of Population, 1980: detailed socioeconomic and demographic characteristics, by age, sex, race, Hispanic origin, occupation, and industry, State rpt series, 2531–4

Census of Population, 1980: detailed socioeconomic characteristics, by county, city, and inside-outside SMSAs and central cities, State rpt series, 2531–3

Census of Population, 1980: women's socioeconomic characteristics, with trends and projections 1960-2050, young readers pamphlet, 2326–1.2

Contraceptives use by women, by method, marital status, age, and race, 1982, 4146–8.103

Criminal case disposition, effect of victim injury and other factors, and law enforcement official and victim attitudes, 1983 survey, 6068–185

Degrees (doctoral) of women and foreign students in science and engineering, and median years to degree attainment by sex, 1983 with trends from 1960, 9626–2.144

Disabled women, by socioeconomic and demographic characteristics, and compared to nondisabled women and disabled men, 1981, chartbook, 16598–4

Education Dept programs funding, operations, and effectiveness, FY83, annual rpt, 4804–5

Family planning and infertility services use by women, by source of service, marital status, age, race, and Hispanic origin, 1982, 4146–8.104

Food aid program of USDA for women, infants, and children, participants and costs by State and Indian agency, FY82 and trends from FY74, annual tables, 1364–12

Food aid programs of USDA, participants and costs by program and region, monthly rpt, 1362–14

Food aid programs of USDA, participants, monthly press release, 1362–13

Food aid special supplemental program for women, infants, and children, effectiveness and participant characteristics, 1973-82, GAO rpt, 26131–10

Foreign population size and growth rates, and latest available benchmark demographic data, by country, 1950-83, biennial rpt, 2324–4

Foreign women sociodemographic, economic, and fertility characteristics, with comparisons to men, by country, 1960s-85, world region rpt series, 2326–15

Health condition and health care resources, use, and expenditures, 1970s-82 with trends and projections 1900-2000, annual compilation, 4144–11

Married women in couples with wife as primary earner, socioeconomic and family characteristics, with comparative data for husbands, Mar 1982, 2326–11.9

Menopause symptoms treatment, estrogen prescribed by physicians by dosage and physician specialty, 1974 and 1981, article, 4102–1.444

Poverty population size, effect of counting public noncash transfers as income by recipient characteristics, 1979-83, 2626–2.52

Statistical Abstract of US, social, political, and economic data, 1950s-83 and trends, annual rpt, 2324–1.1

Travel patterns of women, by employment and sociodemographic characteristics and type of child care used, 1980 survey, 7888–62

Veteran women, by period of service, age, and State, Mar 1983 and projected to 2030, 9928–28

Veteran women population, and use of benefits by type, by age, period of service, and State, with comparisons to men, FY83, annual rpt, 9924–24

see also Families and households
see also Fertility
see also Maternity
see also Sex discrimination
see also Survey of Women-Owned Businesses
see also Women's employment
see also under By Sex in the "Index by Categories"

Women-Owned Business Enterprise Survey

Women-Owned Business Enterprise Survey *see* Survey of Women-Owned Businesses

Women's Bureau

- Employment and earnings of women, by labor force and socioeconomic characteristics, and compared to men, 1978-81 and trends from 1940s, 6568–29
- Labor force participation, earnings, and socioeconomic characteristics of women, 1983, annual fact sheet, 6564–1

Women's employment

- Agriculture census, 1982: farms, farmland, production and costs, and operator characteristics, preliminary State and county rpt series, 2330–1
- Agriculture census, 1982: farms, farmland, production, finances, and operator characteristics, by county, final State rpt series, 2331–1
- Apprenticeship of minorities and women in labor-mgmt, employer, and referral union programs, annual rpt, discontinued, 9244–7
- Births by outcome, and mother's sociodemographic, life style, and maternity characteristics, 1980, article, 4102–1.420, 4102–1.422
- Births, fertility rates, expected births, and childless women, by socioeconomic characteristics, June 1982, annual Current Population Rpt, 2546–1.386
- Births, fertility rates, expected births, and childless women, by socioeconomic characteristics, June 1983, advance annual Current Population Rpt, 2546–1.385
- Births, fertility rates, expected births, and childless women, by socioeconomic characteristics, June 1983, annual Current Population Rpt, 2546–1.393
- Breast-fed infants, by characteristics of mother and source of prenatal care, various periods 1970-75, article, 4102–1.442
- Breast-fed infants, by race and mother's sociodemographic characteristics, 1983 with trends from 1970, article, 4102–1.455
- Census of Population and Housing, 1980: detailed population and housing characteristics, by county, city, and census tract, State and SMSA rpt series, 2551–2
- Census of Population, 1980: detailed socioeconomic and demographic characteristics, by age, sex, race, Hispanic origin, occupation, and industry, State rpt series, 2531–4
- Census of Population, 1980: detailed socioeconomic characteristics, by county, city, and inside-outside SMSAs and central cities, State rpt series, 2531–3
- Census of Population, 1980: labor force, by sex, detailed occupation, and region, with comparison to 1970 census, supplementary rpt, 2535–1.12
- Census of Population, 1980: women's socioeconomic characteristics, with trends and projections 1960-2050, young readers pamphlet, 2326–1.2
- CETA participants by sociodemographic characteristics, and Labor Dept activities and staff, FY83, annual rpt, 6304–1
- Construction industry total and female workers, and construction worker earnings and hours, by selected SIC 2- to 3-digit industry, bimonthly rpt, 2012–1.7

Dallas-Fort Worth, Tex, SMSA employment, earnings, hours, and CPI changes, 1983 with trends from 1968, annual rpt, 6964–2

- Defense Fuel Supply Center procurement, prices, stocks, transport, and other activities and finances, FY83, annual rpt, 3904–8
- Disabled women, by socioeconomic and demographic characteristics, and compared to nondisabled women and disabled men, 1981, chartbook, 16598–4
- DOD engineering contract awards by function, contract type, and service branch, and oil and port dredging awards by company, 1970s-83, hearings, 21728–53
- DOD medical personnel and trainees, by occupation, sex, and service branch, FY83, annual rpt, 3544–24.1
- DOE procurement and assistance contracts, by State, contractor type, and top 100 instns, FY83, annual rpt, 3004–21
- DOT employment by subagency, State, and selected personnel characteristics, FY83, annual rpt, 7304–18.2, 7304–18.3
- DOT employment of minorities and women full-time, 1971-81, annual rpt, 7304–1
- Earnings of couples with both spouses working, by sociodemographic and employment characteristics and age of children, 1981, Current Population Rpt, 2546–2.120
- Earnings of families by number of earners, and earnings and employment status of individual family members, quarterly rpt, 6742–19
- Earnings of women and men, analysis of differential, selected years 1967-83, articles, 6722–1.436, 6722–1.437, 6722–1.438
- Educational attainment of labor force, by demographic and employment characteristics, 1982-83 with summary trends from 1940, 6746–1.251
- Educational attainment of labor force, by demographic and employment characteristics, 1983, article, 6722–1.423
- Educational attainment of labor force, by demographic and employment characteristics, 1984, press release, 6748–79
- Employment and earnings, detailed data, monthly rpt, 6742–2.5
- Employment and earnings of women, by labor force and socioeconomic characteristics, and compared to men, 1978-81 and trends from 1940s, 6568–29
- Employment change over business cycles, by worker characteristics and industry div, quarterly 1982-2nd qtr 1984 with trends from 1948, annual article, 6722–1.448
- Employment, earnings, and hours, by SIC 4-digit nonfarm industry, monthly 1974-Feb 1984, annual update, 6744–4
- Employment of minorities and and women, by occupational group, SIC 2- to 3-digit industry, State, and SMSA, 1981, annual rpt, 9244–1
- Employment situation, earnings, hours, and other BLS economic indicators, transcripts of BLS Commissioner's monthly testimony, periodic rpt, 23846–4
- Employment status of family members, by occupation, family composition, age of children, and other characteristics, 1983 and trends from 1940, 6746–1.253

Index by Subjects and Names

- Employment, unemployment, and labor force, by demographic and employment characteristics, State, and for 30 metro areas and 11 large cities, 1983, annual rpt, 6744–7
- Employment, unemployment, and labor force, detailed data by sociodemographic and employment characteristics, and industry, 1940s-83, 6748–72
- Employment, unemployment, hours, earnings, and productivity, selected years 1929-83, annual rpt, 204–1.2
- Families and households detailed socioeconomic characteristics, Mar 1982, annual Current Population Rpt, 2546–1.383
- Farm housesolds social security tax liability, alternative tax rates by type of legal organization, 1955-90, article, 1702–1.408
- Farm population employment by industry div, and unemployment, by region, 1983, annual rpt, 2544–1
- Fed Govt civilian employment of minority groups and women, by grade and agency, 1980 and 1983, 21348–41
- Fed Govt Equal Opportunity Recruitment Program implementation, and summary employment data, FY83, annual rpt, 9844–33
- Fed Govt minority group and handicapped employment, by race, Hispanic origin, disability, sex, and employment characteristics, as of Sept 1982, biennial rpt, 9844–27
- Fed Govt procurement contract awards to women-owned businesses, by agency, quarterly rpt, 102–6
- Foreign employment, labor force, and participation and unemployment rates by sex, in US and 9 OECD countries, various periods 1970-3rd qtr 1983, annual article, 6722–1.404
- Foreign women sociodemographic, economic, and fertility characteristics, with comparisons to men, by country, 1960s-85, world region rpt series, 2326–15
- *Handbook of Labor Statistics,* employment, earnings, hours, and labor force characteristics, 1982 and trends, detailed annual rpt, 6724–1
- Health professionals supply and education, by occupation, demographic and professional characteristics, and location, 1950s-83 and projected to 2000, biennial rpt, 4114–8
- Health professions employment and training of minorities and women, by field, selected years 1962/63-1983/84, 4118–18
- High school grads aged 17-21 percent distribution, by most recent occupation, sex, vocational education participation, May 1980, annual rpt, 4824–1.3
- Hispanic Americans socioeconomic and demographic characteristics, and compared to non-Hispanics, selected years 1970-83, chartbook, 2328–48
- Houston, Tex, SMSA employment, earnings, hours, and CPI changes, 1983 with trends from 1968, annual rpt, 6964–1
- Income (household) and cash and noncash transfer program participation, by sociodemographic characteristics, quarterly rpt, 2542–2

Index by Subjects and Names

Income of families and persons, by sociodemographic characteristics, 1983, advance annual Current Population Rpt, 2546–6.41

Income of households, families, and persons, by detailed socioeconomic characteristics and region, 1982, annual Current Population Rpt, 2546–6.39

Job Training Partnership Act participants, by program and socieconomic characteristics, Oct 1983-June 1984 with funding to 1985/86, 6408–63

Labor force and OASDHI participation of women by age, and pension coverage by sex, selected years 1939-82, hearing, 25368–131.1

Labor force characteristics and economic indicators, selected years 1880-1995, chartbook, 6728–30

Labor force experience of men and women by sociodemographic characteristics, and effect on earnings, 1979, Current Population Rpt, 2546–2.123

Labor force participation, by employment and demographic characteristics, 1982-83, annual article, 6722–1.472

Labor force participation, earnings, and socioeconomic characteristics of women, 1983, annual fact sheet, 6564–1

Labor force participation of women, by age, race, and family status, quarterly rpt, 6742–17

Labor force participation of women by marital status, and children by parent labor force status, by family composition, race, and Hispanic origin, Mar 1984 and trends from 1970, 6748–7&

Labor force status monthly changes, by selected worker characteristics, 1981-82, biennial rpt, 6744–17

Manufacturing employment, unemployment, hours, and women's employment, for all durables and for 5 metals industries, 1979-82, article, 6722–1.410

Married women in couples with wife as primary earner, socioeconomic and family characteristics, with comparative data for husbands, Mar 1982, 2326–11.9

Military active duty strength, recruits, and reenlistment, by race, Hispanic origin, sex, and service branch, quarterly press release, 3542–7

Military officers and enlisted personnel on active duty, May 1945-Sept 1983, annual rpt, 3544–1.2

Military women personnel on active duty, by demographic and service characteristics and service branch, with comparisons to men, FY83, annual chartbook, 3544–26

Military women personnel on active duty, by rank, grade, and service branch, monthly rpt, 3542–14.3

Minority business mgmt and financial assistance from federally funded organizations, by region, State, and business characteristics, FY83, annual rpt, 2104–6

Natl Guard (Army and Air) activities, manpower, and facilities, FY83, annual rpt, 3704–3

Navy personnel, detailed statistics, quarterly rpt, 3802–4

Navy procurement awards to disadvantaged and women-owned businesses, FY83, annual rpt, 3804–13.3

OASI beneficiaries by income level, and average income, by beneficiary characteristics and income source, before and after receipt of 1st benefit, 1969-77, article, 4742–1.418

Occupational employment and percent black, women, and part-time workers, by detailed occupation, 1982, biennial rpt, 6744–3

Older persons income and percent in poverty, by household composition and sex, with comparisons to nonaged, selected years 1950-82, article, 4742–1.413

Pilot and nonpilot certificates held and issued, by type of certificate, region, State, and for women, 1983, annual rpt, 7504–1.7

Pilots and nonpilots certified by FAA, by type of certificate, age, sex, region, and State, 1983, annual rpt, 7504–2

Poverty status of families and persons, by detailed socioeconomic characteristics, 1982, annual Current Population Rpt, 2546–6.40

Railroad employee benefits and beneficiaries by type, and railroad employees and payrolls, FY82, annual rpt, 9704–2

Science and engineering employment in higher education instns, by sex, field of science, and instn type, 1972-83, biennial rpt, 9627–24.2

Scientists and engineers employed at universities and colleges, by field, sex, State, and instn, Jan 1983 and selected trends from 1967, annual survey, 9627–11

Scientists and engineers employment by sector and activity, and share female, black, and Asian descent, by field, 1982, 9626–2.142

Scientists and engineers employment, salaries, and degrees, by field, type of employer, race, and sex, selected years 1960-81, annual rpt, 9624–18.5

Scientists and engineers supply, employment, and education, by sex, race, Hispanic origin, and field, selected years 1965-83, biennial rpt, 9624–20

Small Business Admin loan and contract activity by program, and balance sheets, FY83, annual rpt, 9764–1.1

Small business mgmt counseling by university centers, costs, funding, and businesses served by industry, with detail for 2 States, 1980-83, hearing, 25728–36

Small businesses owned by minorities and women, firms and receipts, owner characteristics, and Federal contracts by agency, by product or service, 1970s-82, annual rpt, 9764–6.4

State Dept and Foreign Service minority and women employment by pay level, and affirmative action plan, FY83, annual rpt, 7004–11

Statistical Abstract of US, social, political, and economic data, 1950s-83 and trends, annual rpt, 2324–1.3

Travel agency financial and operating data, and airline ticket sales by type of distributor, 1970s-82, hearing, 25268–81

Travel patterns of women, by employment and sociodemographic characteristics and type of child care used, 1980 survey, 7888–62

Wood fuel

TV and radio industry employment, total and for minorities, women, and youth, by job category and State, 1979-83, annual rpt, 9284–16

TV and radio industry minority and women employment by occupation, and business owners, by race and State, with revenues and stations, 1971-81, hearing, 21368–45

TV and radio station employment, total and for minorities and women, by full- and part-time status and individual station, 1983, annual rpt, 9284–7

TVA employment of minorities and women, by detailed occupation, pay level, and grade, FY83 and goals for FY84, annual rpt, 9804–17

Unemployment and part-time employment, by race, Hispanic origin, sex, family composition, income, and poverty status, 1980-82, annual report, 6744–15

Unemployment and part-time employment effects on family income, by socioeconomic and labor force characteristics, 1981-82, annual rpt, 6746–1.252

Unemployment, by duration, work experience during year, sex, race, and Hispanic origin, 1982-83, 6748–77

Unemployment duration and probability of employment or labor force withdrawal, by sex and race, 1982, article, 9373–1.410

Unemployment during business cycles, and by worker age, sex, occupation, industry div, reason, and duration, various periods 1969-82, article, 6722–1.444

Unemployment of men and women, by contributing factor, and change in industry share of labor force and unemployment, 1973-75 and 1981-82, article, 6722–1.432

Unemployment rates, current data and annual trends, monthly rpt, 23842–1.2

Unemployment rates for men and women under alternative assumptions, by industry div, 1964-82 with employment change projected to 1995, article, 6722–1.465

VA employment characteristics and activities, FY83, annual rpt, 9924–1.8

Wage growth and turnover rates related to marital status, sex, age, establishment type, and employer size, 1979/80, article, 9393–8.403

Women's employment share in selected occupations under 1970 and 1980 census classifications, 1970 and 1980, article, 6722–1.417

see also Survey of Women-Owned Businesses

see also under By Sex in the "Index by Categories"

Wood

see Lumber industry and products

see Wood fuel

Wood fuel

Agriculture census, 1982: farms, farmland, production, finances, and operator characteristics, by county, final State rpt series, 2331–1

Air pollutant emission factors, by detailed source, 3rd edition, 1983-84 supplements, 9198–13

Air pollution levels for 5 pollutants, by detailed source, State, and Air Quality Control Region, 1981, annual rpt, 9194–7

Wood fuel

Alaska electric power capacity and generation by fuel type, and marketing, by utility, type of ownership, and location, 1983, annual rpt, 3214–2

Consumption, by fuel type, economic sector, census div, and State, 1960-82, State Energy Data System annual rpt, 3164–39

Consumption of energy, by type of air pollutant source and fuel, and State, 1981, annual rpt, 9194–14

Consumption of wood fuel, by end-use sector, SIC 2-digit industry, region, State, and selected industrial and power plant, 1980-83, biennial rpt, 3164–78

Cuba economic conditions, agricultural and industrial production and distribution, trade, and intl economic relations, 1970-82 and trends from 1957, 248–40

DOD electric power plants and major fuel-burning facilities conversion from oil and gas, fuel use data, 1983, annual rpt, 3104–9

Electric power plants, by capacity, fuel used, unit type, region, State, and county, for plants added and retired, 1983 and planned through 1993, annual rpt, 3164–36

Exports, imports, tariffs, and industry operating data for fuelwood and other wood products, foreign and US, 1979-83, TSUSA commodity rpt, 9885–2.29

Exports of US, detailed commodities by country of destination, monthly rpt, 2422–3

Exports of US, detailed Schedule B commodities by country of destination, 1983, annual rpt, 2424–9

Fed Govt programs and mgmt cost control proposals, 3-year savings by function and agency, and financial and operating data, 1960s-81, 16908–1.31

Foreign and US tropical forests status by country and world region, conservation methods, and mgmt role of US, foreign, and intl groups, 1977-81 and projected to 2000, 26358–101.1

Forest Service itemized costs of wood fuel removal program in 3 central Appalachia natl forests, 1981, 1208–191

Home heating with wood, and wood acquired and used, by household characteristics and wood sources, 1980/81, 1208–204

Housing census, 1980: inventory, occupancy, and unit characteristics, changes from 1973 by region and inside-outside SMSAs and central cities, series, 2473–3

Housing energy use, costs, expenditures, and conservation, and household and housing characteristics, survey series, 3166–7

Housing occupancy and unit and household characteristics, by region and metro-nonmetro residence, 1983, biennial survey, 2485–1

Housing unit heating fuel, by type, occupant race, Hispanic origin, urban-rural location, and region, 1981, annual survey, 2485–7

Imports of US, detailed Schedule A commodities by country, monthly rpt, 2422–2

Mineral industries census, 1982: financial and operating data, including materials consumed, by SIC 4-digit industry and State, preliminary rpt series, 2511–1

Natl Energy Policy Plan, energy supply, demand, and prices, by fuel and consuming sector, projected 1985-2010, biennial rpt, 3004–13

North Central States natural gas residential use related to weather, fuels consumed by purpose, and energy share from wood, by State, various periods 1979-83, article, 3162–4.402

Prices and expenditures for fuels, by consuming sector, State, and fuel type, 1970-81, annual rpt, 3164–64

Production, prices by region and State, trade by country, and consumption, for timber by species and product, with industry earnings, 1950-83, annual rpt, 1204–29

Puerto Rico wood and wood product shipments from US by type, and from selected foreign sources, 1971-81, 1208–205

Supply/demand and prices, by fuel type and consuming sector with foreign comparisons, 1949-83, annual rpt, 3164–74

Supply/demand and prices, by fuel type, sector, and end use, with foreign comparisons, 1960-83 and projected to 1995, annual summary rpt, 3164–76

Underground economy, household expenditures and participation by type of goods or service and sociodemographic characteristics, with methodology and bibl, 1981 survey, 8308–27

Wood, Geoffrey E.

"Monetary Policy Decision Process in the UK", 9373–3.26

Wood, John H.

"Impact of Surveillance Fields on Crude Oil Production in the U.S.", 3164–58

Woodham, Douglas M.

"Potential Output Growth and the Long-Term Inflation Outlook", 9385–1.408

Wool and wool trade

Agricultural Stabilization and Conservation Service producer payments under 26 programs, monthly rpt, 1802–10

Agricultural Stabilization and Conservation Service wool and mohair programs, 1955-84, annual fact sheet, 1806–4.12, 1806–4.13

Agricultural Statistics, 1983, annual rpt, 1004–1

Agriculture census, 1982: farms, farmland, production and costs, and operator characteristics, preliminary State and county rpt series, 2330–1

Agriculture census, 1982: farms, farmland, production, finances, and operator characteristics, by county, final State rpt series, 2331–1

Business statistics, detailed data for major industries and economic indicators, *Survey of Current Business,* monthly rpt, 2702–1.19

China economic conditions, agricultural and industrial production, trade, and domestic and foreign investment, 1980-85, 2048–106

Communist, OECD, and selected other countries agricultural production, by commodity, 1960s-83, annual rpt, 244–5.9

Cooperatives, membership, activities, and finances, by commodity and selected State, 1900-80 with trends from 1863, 1128–30

Index by Subjects and Names

County Business Patterns: establishments, employees, and payrolls, by SIC 4-digit industry and county, 1981, annual State rpt series, 2326–8

County Business Patterns: establishments, employees, and payrolls, by SIC 4-digit industry and county, 1982, annual State rpt series, 2326–6

Employment, earnings, and hours, by SIC 4-digit nonfarm industry, monthly 1974-Feb 1984, annual update, 6744–4

Exports and imports of dairy, livestock, and poultry live animals, meat, and products, by commodity and country of destination, FAS quarterly rpt, 1925–32

Exports and imports of US, by agricultural commodity and country, bimonthly rpt with articles, 1522–1

Exports and imports of US, by detailed agricultural commodity and country, FY83 and CY83, semiannual rpts, 1522–4

Exports and imports of US, detailed SIC-based commodities by world area, 1983, annual rpts, 2424–6

Exports and imports of US, totals and as percent of domestic production, by SIC 2- to 5-digit commodity, 1981, annual rpt, 2424–3

Exports, imports, tariffs, and industry operating data for textile fiber and products, TSUSA commodity rpt series, 9885–3

Exports of textiles, by product and country of destination, monthly rpt, 2042–26

Exports of US, detailed commodities by country of destination, monthly rpt, 2422–3

Exports of US, detailed Schedule B commodities by country of destination, 1983, annual rpt, 2424–9

Exports of US, detailed Schedule E commodities by mode of transport and world area and country of destination, 1983, annual rpts, 2424–5

Farm finances, assets, liabilities, income, receipts by commodity and State, and expenses, 1980-83 and trends from 1910, annual rpt, 1544–16

Foreign agricultural production, prices, and trade, by country, 1983 and outlook for 1984/85, annual world region rpt series, 1524–4

Futures trading by commodity and exchange, and Commodity Futures Trading Commission activities, funding, and employment, FY83, annual rpt, 11924–2

Great Lakes trade, by SITC 3-digit commodity, port, vessel type, world area, and country, 1982, annual rpt, 7744–3

Imports and import limits for textiles under Multifiber Arrangement by product and country, with US exports and use, 1970-83, semiannual rpt, 9882–11

Imports of textiles, by country of origin, monthly rpt, 2042–27

Imports of textiles, by product and country of origin, monthly rpt, 2422–1

Imports of textiles, by product and country of origin, monthly rpt series, 2046–9

Imports of textiles, by product and country of origin, periodic rpt series, 2046–8

Imports of textiles, monthly rpt, 2042–18

Index by Subjects and Names

Imports of textiles, total and as percents of US production and use, by commodity, 1972-82, annual rpt, 2044–14

Imports of US, detailed Schedule A commodities by country and world area of origin, and mode of transport, 1983, annual rpts, 2424–2

Imports of US, detailed Schedule A commodities by country, monthly rpt, 2422–2

Imports of US, detailed TSUSA commodities by country of origin, 1983, annual rpt, 2424–4

Manufacturing census, 1982: financial and operating data, for SIC 4-digit industries by product, preliminary rpt series, 2491–1

Manufacturing census, 1982: textile mill machinery in place, by machine type and textile industry, special preliminary rpts, 2491–2

Market news summary statistics for livestock, meat, and wool, by animal type and market, weekly rpt, 1315–1

Marketing cash receipts of farms, by detailed commodity and State, 1979-82, annual rpt, 1544–18

Prices of foreign and domestic wool, and wool trade, weekly and biweekly rpt, 1315–2

Prices received by farmers for major products, and paid for farm inputs and living items, by commodity and State, monthly rpt, 1629–1

Prices received by farmers for major products, and paid for farm inputs, by commodity and State, 1983, annual rpt, 1629–5

Producer prices and indexes, by stage of processing and detailed commodity, monthly rpt, 6762–6

Producer prices and indexes, by stage of processing and detailed commodity, monthly 1983, annual supplement, 6764–2

Production and prices of wool and mohair, by State, 1982-83, annual release, 1623–6

Production, consumption, prices, and trade, periodic situation rpt with articles, 1561–1

Production, price, and value of wool and mohair, 1970-83, annual rpt, 1564–6.1, 1564–6.3

Production, prices, trade, and marketing, by commodity, current situation and forecast, monthly rpt, 1502–4

Production, stocks, materials used, and orders, by product and major State, and trade by country, periodic Current Industrial Rpt series, 2506–5

Sheep production receipts, itemized costs per ewe, and net returns, 1981-83, annual rpt, 1544–20

Wholesale trade census, 1982: employment, establishments, sales by commodity, and payroll, by SIC 4-digit kind of business and State, preliminary rpt, 2403–1.23

see also under By Commodity in the "Index by Categories"

Woolley, John T.

"Political Factors in Monetary Policy", 9373–3.26

Woonsocket, R.I.

see also under By SMSA or MSA in the "Index by Categories"

Worcester, Mass.

Census of Housing, 1980: occupancy and unit characteristics, by race, Hispanic origin, and city, SMSA rpt, 2473–1.376

Census of Population and Housing, 1980: detailed population and housing characteristics, by county, city, and census tract, SMSA rpt, 2551–2.376

Wages of office and plant workers, by occupation, 1984 SMSA survey rpt, 6785–11.3

see also under By City and By SMSA or MSA in the "Index by Categories"

Word processing

see Computer use

see Office furniture and equipment

Work Incentive Program

Budget of US, effects of Reagan Admin policy changes, by detailed program, FY85, annual rpt, 104–21

Fed Govt aid to State and local govts, expenditures, and direct payments, by program, agency, and State, FY83, annual rpt, 2464–2

Govt census, 1982: State govt payments to local govts, by program, source of funds, level of govt, and State, with trends from 1902, 2460–3

HHS aid to each State and local govt or private instn, amount obligated, funding agency, and program, FY83, annual listing, 4004–3

Income tax returns of corporations, detailed income and tax items by industry, 1981, annual rpt, 8304–4

Work stoppages

Employment and labor force statistics by major industry group and demographic characteristics, *Survey of Current Business,* monthly rpt, 2702–1.5

Foreign labor conditions in selected OECD countries, 1950-82, annual rpt, 6724–1.10

Monthly Labor Review, work stoppages involving 1,000 workers or more, workers involved, and days idle, 6722–1.8

Statistical Abstract of US, social, political, and economic data, 1950s-83 and trends, annual rpt, 2324–1.3

Wage and benefit changes from collective bargaining or employer decisions, by industry group, monthly rpt, 6782–1

Work stoppages involving 6 workers or more, workers and days idle by major issue, industry, and State, selected years 1930-82, annual rpt, 6724–1.8

Work-study programs

Education Dept programs funding, operations, and effectiveness, FY83, annual rpt, 4804–5

HHS aid to each State and local govt or private instn, amount obligated, funding agency, and program, FY83, annual listing, 4004–3

Student aid basic grant, loan, and work-study awards, Fed Govt share by instn and State, 1984/85, annual rpt, 4804–17

Student aid Federal programs funding and participation, by instn type and control, State, and outlying area, with student loan defaults and collections, FY82, annual rpt, 4804–28

Workers compensation

Work training

see Employee development

see Manpower training programs

see Vocational education and training

Worker adjustment assistance

see Trade adjustment assistance

Workers

see Agricultural labor

see Blue collar workers

see Clerical workers

see Employment and unemployment, general

see Employment and unemployment, specific industries

see Manpower

see Migrant workers

see Professional and technical workers

see Sales workers

Workers compensation

Asbestos-related occupational disease compensation paid and defendant and plaintiff litigation costs, with comparisons to other tort suits, selected years 1968-82, hearings, 21348–85

Beneficiaries and taxes collected for social insurance programs since 1940, monthly rpt, 4742–1.1

Benefits, beneficiary characteristics, and trust funds of OASDHI, Medicaid, SSI, and other social insurance and public welfare programs, selected years 1950-82, annual rpt, 4744–3.9, 4744–3.10

Benefits for workers compensation, degree of disability, coverage by State, employer costs, and insurance industry finances, selected years 1939-80, article, 4742–1.414

Benefits under each State and Federal workers compensation program by payment source, and State and black lung benefits by type, 1979-81, article, 4742–1.409

Benefits under State workers compensation programs, by benefit type, insurance source, and State, 1980-82, article, 4742–1.424

Budget of US, effects of Reagan Admin policy changes, by detailed program, FY85, annual rpt, 104–21

Children and youth benefitting from Fed Govt public welfare programs and tax expenditures, participation and funding for 71 programs, FY81-83, 21968–30

Fed Govt-administered compensation programs claims and dispositions by district, coverage, and expenditures, FY79-83, annual compilation, 6504–5

Fed Govt aid to State and local govts, expenditures, and direct payments, by program, agency, and State, FY83, annual rpt, 2464–2

Fed Govt cash benefits, and beneficiaries with representative payees by age and relation to payee, by program, as of 1983, GAO rpt, 26121–85

Fed Govt personnel action appeals, decisions of Merit Systems Protection Board, by region, agency, and employee characteristics, FY82, annual rpt, 9494–2

Fed Govt programs and mgmt cost control proposals, 3-year savings by function and agency, and financial and operating data, 1960s-81, 16908–1.3, 16908–1.34

Firefighters death benefits under workers compensation and local pension plans, by State and city, hearing, 21348–94

Workers compensation

Foreign social security programs coverage, funding, eligibility, and benefits, by country, 1983, biennial rpt, 4746–4.58

Govt census, 1982: State govt payments to local govts, by program, source of funds, level of govt, and State, with trends from 1902, 2460–3

Govt expenditures for social welfare by program and level of govt, and private expenditures for health care, selected years FY50-82, annual article, 4742–1.425

Health care expenditures, natl and personal total and per capita amounts, by type of service and source of funds, 1983 and trends from 1929, annual article, 4652–1.429

Income (personal) by source including transfer payments, and social insurance contributions by type, by region, 1982, 2708–40

Income of households, families, and persons, by detailed socioeconomic characteristics and region, 1982, annual Current Population Rpt, 2546–6.39

Occupational injuries and illnesses, data available from NTIS, by State, 1981, annual rpt, 6704–2

Older persons income and income sources, by OASDI beneficiary and poverty status, labor force participation, and demographic characteristics, 1982, biennial rpt, 4744–26

Postal workers compensation costs, and 3rd-party recovery program operations, FY83, annual rpt, 9864–5

Poverty-level persons and families, by income source, hours of work, earnings, taxes, and family characteristics, various periods 1959-84, 21788–131

State and Fed Govt workers compensation law provisions, by jurisdiction, as of July 1984, semiannual rpt, 6502–1

State govt revenues by source, expenditures by function, debt, and holdings by type, FY83, annual rpt, 2466–2.5

State workers compensation laws, changes in benefits, coverage, and premium rates, for 49 States, DC, and Virgin Islands, 1983, annual article, 6722–1.415

Traffic accidents and casualties detailed direct and indirect costs, by characteristics of persons and vehicles involved, 1979-80, 7768–80

see also Black lung

see also Disability insurance

see also Labor cost indexes

see also Unemployment insurance

Working mothers

see Women's employment

World Bank

see International Bank for Reconstruction and Development

see International Development Association

World Health Organization

Influenza deaths, viruses identified by State and country, epidemiology, and vaccine effects and recommended dosages by age, 1979/80-1980/81, annual rpt, 4205–3

World Meteorological Organization

Climatological data for surface and upper air, averages by foreign and US station, monthly rpt, 2152–4

World Wars

see War

Wrecking and demolition

Census of Housing, 1980: inventory, occupancy, and unit characteristics, changes from 1973 by region and inside-outside SMSAs and central cities, series, 2473–3

Construction industries census, 1982: financial and operating data, by SIC 4-digit industry and State, preliminary rpt series, 2371–1

County Business Patterns: establishments, employees, and payrolls, by SIC 4-digit industry and county, 1981, annual State rpt series, 2326–8

County Business Patterns: establishments, employees, and payrolls, by SIC 4-digit industry and county, 1982, annual State rpt series, 2326–6

Housing and householder selected characteristics, by urban-rural location, 1981, annual survey, 2485–7.1

HUD-acquired single family homes through mortgage default, and disposition, by city, monthly rpt, 5142–31

Ocean dumping of waste materials, EPA permit program and intl London Dumping Convention activities, 1981-83, annual rpt, 9204–8

Transportation census, 1982: trucks, by detailed characteristics, miles traveled, and type of product carried, State rpt series, 2573–1

Wright, Andrew

"Recent Developments in Papua New Guinea's Tuna Fishery", 2162–1.402

Wright, Douglas A.

"Instructional Use of Computers in Public Schools, Spring 1982", 4826–1.10

Writing

see Language and literature

WUI/Caribbean, Inc.

Financial and operating data for 7 major telegraph carriers, quarterly rpt, 9282–1

Wyckoff, Paul G.

"Economic Estimates of Urban Infrastructure Needs", 9377–9.9

"Estimating Infrastructure Needs: Methods and Controversies", 9377–1.405

Wynegar, Don

"International Travel to and from the U.S.: 1985 Outlook", 2904–9

Wynns, Peyton L.

"Changing Telephone Industry: Access Charges, Universal Service, and Local Rates", 26306–6.79

Wynveen, R. A.

"Post-Remedial-Action Radiological Survey of Kent Chemical Laboratory, the University of Chicago, Chicago, Ill.", 3406–1.40

"Radiological Survey of Chemicals Group, Olin Corporation (formerly Blockson Chemical Company), Joliet Ill., Mar. 27-Nov. 28, 1978", 3406–1.36

"Radiological Survey of the Albany Metallurgical Research Center, U.S. Bureau of Mines, Albany, Oreg.", 3406–1.39

"Radiological Survey of the Albany Metallurgical Research Center U.S. Bureau of Mines Biomass Facility and the 'Back Forty' Area, Albany, Oreg.", 3406–1.37

Index by Subjects and Names

"Radiological Survey of the National Guard Armory at Washington Park, 52nd Street and Cottage Grove Avenue, Chicago, Ill., Sept. 19, 1977-Oct. 11, 1978", 3406–1.35

Wyoming

Agriculture census, 1982: farms, farmland, production and costs, and operator characteristics, preliminary State summary and county rpts, 2330–1.56

Agriculture census, 1982: farms, farmland, production, finances, and operator characteristics, by county, final State rpt, 2331–1.50

Bank deposits in commercial and mutual savings banks and in US branches of foreign banks, by account type, instn, State, SMSA, and county, June 1983, annual rpt, 9295–3.15

Census of Housing, 1980: occupancy and unit characteristics of SMSAs and central cities, by race, Hispanic origin, and city, State rpt, 2473–1.52

Census of Population and Housing, 1980: detailed population and housing characteristics, by county, city, and census tract, State rpt, 2551–2.52

Coal Fed Govt leases, acreage, production, and prices, by State, and legal and mgmt issues, 1970s-83 with production projections to 2000, 11128–1

County Business Patterns: establishments, employees, and payrolls, by SIC 4-digit industry and county, 1982, annual State rpt, 2326–6.52

Employment, earnings, and hours, by selected SIC 1- to 4-digit industry, State, and for 278 major labor areas, 1939-83, annual rpt, 6744–5.2, 6744–5.3

Environmental quality, pollutant discharge by type and source, and EPA protection activities and funding, 1970s-83, biennial regional rpt, 9184–15.8

Exports of manufactured and agricultural commodities, manufacturing production, and export-related employment, 1960s-82, State rpt, 2046–3.50

Forest biomass in Rocky Mountain States, conversion from volume to dry weight, for softwood and hardwood species, 1977, 1208–200

Grizzly bears in and around Yellowstone Natl Park, population, physical characteristics, diet, and movements, 1982, annual rpt, 5544–4

HHS aid to each State and local govt or private instn, amount obligated, funding agency, and program, FY83, annual listing, 4004–3.8

Income (personal) per capita and by source, and earnings by industry div, by State, MSA, and county, 1977-82, annual regional rpt, 2704–2.8

Land Mgmt Bur activities and finances, and public land acreage and use, 1984 annual State rpt, 5724–11.1

Manufacturing census, 1982: financial and operating data, by SIC 2- to 4-digit industry, State, SMSA, and county, preliminary census div rpt, 2491–3.8

Mineral Industry Surveys, State review of production, 1983, advance annual rpt, 5614–6.50

Minerals Yearbook, 1982, Vol 2 preprints: State review of production and sales by commodity, and business activity, annual rpt, 5604–16.52

Minerals Yearbook, 1982, Vol 2: State reviews of production, sales, and firms, by commodity, and business activity, annual rpt, 5604–34

Oil and gas field itemized equipment and operating costs and cost indexes, for 10 producing areas, 1981-83, annual rpt, 3164–45

Oil shale dev projects in Green River area, production goals and cost estimates, as of 1983, article, 9381–1.409

Phosphate rock reserves in southeastern and northwestern US, by location, 1984 rpt, 5668–74

Population size and components of change, by MSA and county, 1980-82, annual State Current Population Rpt, 2546–4.50

Population size, Apr 1980 and July 1982, and per capita income, 1979 and 1981, by county and city, State Current Population Rpt, 2546–11.50

Retail trade census, 1982: employment, establishments, sales, and payroll, by SIC 2- to 4-digit kind of business, SMSA, and retail district, State rpt, 2401–1.51

Retail trade census, 1982: employment, establishments, sales, and payroll, by SIC 2- to 4-digit kind of business, SMSA, county, and city, State rpt, 2397–1.51

Savings and loan assns, FHLB 12th District members financial operations and housing industry indicators by State, monthly rpt, 9302–21

Service industry census, 1982: employment, establishments, receipts, and payroll, by SIC 2- to 4-digit kind of business, SMSA, county, and city, State rpt, 2391–1.51

Timber resources and removals in 9 Rocky Mountain States, and forest and rangeland area, by ownership, forest and tree characteristics, and State, 1977, 1208–201

Water supply and quality, and effect of coal mining operations, for selected river basins in Western coal provinces, 1983 rpt, 5666–19.4

Water supply and quality in streams and lakes, and groundwater levels in wells, by drainage basin, 1982, annual State rpt, 5666–20.47

Water supply and quality in streams and lakes, and groundwater levels in wells, by drainage basin, 1983, annual State rpt, 5666–10.47

Water supply, and snow survey results, monthly State rpt, 1266–2.10

Water supply, snow depth measurements by station, 1983-84, State rpt, 1266–3.10

Wholesale trade census, 1982: employment, establishments, finances, and operations, by SIC 2- to 4-digit kind of business, SMSA, county, and city, State rpt, 2405–1.51

see also Casper, Wyo.

see also Cheyenne, Wyo.

see also under By State in the "Index by Categories"

X-rays

Births by outcome, and mother's sociodemographic, life style, and maternity characteristics, 1980, article, 4102–1.421

Bone injury diagnoses from physical indicators and X-rays, by body site, 1977-79, 4186–2.6

CAT scan procedures on hospital inpatients, by body site and patient and hospital characteristics, 1979-82, 4146–8.102

China economic conditions, agricultural and industrial production, trade, and domestic and foreign investment, 1980-85, 2048–106

County Business Patterns: establishments, employees, and payrolls, by SIC 4-digit industry and county, 1981, annual State rpt series, 2326–8

County Business Patterns: establishments, employees, and payrolls, by SIC 4-digit industry and county, 1982, annual State rpt series, 2326–6

Exports and imports of US, detailed SIC-based commodities by world area, 1983, annual rpts, 2424–6

Exports of US, detailed commodities by country of destination, monthly rpt, 2422–3

Exports of US, detailed Schedule B commodities by country of destination, 1983, annual rpt, 2424–9

Imports of US, detailed Schedule A commodities by country, monthly rpt, 2422–2

Imports of US, detailed TSUSA commodities by country of origin, 1983, annual rpt, 2424–4

Input-output structure of US economy, detailed interindustry transactions for 537 industries, and components of final demand, 1977 benchmark data, 2708–17

Internist office visits and drugs provided, by characteristics of visit, patient, and physician, and location, 1980-81, 4147–13.80

Manufacturing census, 1982: financial and operating data, for SIC 4-digit industries by product, preliminary rpt, 2491–1.390

Medicare-participating facilities by control, beds, and terminated facilities, by facility type, region, and State, 1975-81, 4656–1.19

Medicare Supplementary Medical Insurance maximum charges reimbursable for specific services, by State and outlying area, 1983, annual rpt, 4654–4

Obstetrician-gynecologist office visits and drugs used, by visit reason, diagnosis, treatment, and patient and physician characteristics, 1980-81, 4147–13.76

Physicians (not office-based) visits by reason, diagnosis, treatment, patient and physician characteristics, and physician primary activity, 1980, 4147–13.77

Radiation control program activities, State and local expenditures, personnel, and NRC licenses, by State, FY80-82, annual rpt, 4064–3

Shipments, trade, and consumption of electronic equipment and associated products, by product, 1983, annual Current Industrial Rpt, 2506–12.21

Surgeon office visits and drugs provided, by characteristics of visit, patient, and physician, and location, 1980-81, 4147–13.79

Xylene

see Chemicals and chemical industry

Yager, Francis P.

"Marketing and Transportation of Grain by Local Cooperatives", 1128–28

Yakima, Wash.

Census of Housing, 1980: occupancy and unit characteristics, by race, Hispanic origin, and city, SMSA rpt, 2473–1.377

Census of Population and Housing, 1980: detailed population and housing characteristics, by county, city, and census tract, SMSA rpt, 2551–2.377

Wages of office and plant workers, by occupation, 1984 labor market area survey rpt, 6785–3.9

see also under By SMSA or MSA in the "Index by Categories"

Yaremchuk, Elizabeth H.

"Mergers in the Nonfuel Minerals Industry: Trends and Motives", 5608–145

Yarn

see Textile industry and fabrics

Yellowstone National Park

Acid rain effects on water quality, fish populations, and soils in Rocky Mountain and Yellowstone natl parks, as of 1983, summary research rpt, 5506–5.17

Grizzly bears in and around Yellowstone Natl Park, population, physical characteristics, diet, and movements, 1982, annual rpt, 5544–4

Yemen Arab Republic

see Yemen, North

Yemen, North

Agricultural situation in Middle East and North Africa, by country and commodity, 1983 and outlook for 1984, annual rpt, 1524–4.3

AID activities and funding by project and function, FY85, and developing countries summary socioeconomic data, 1970s-83, by country, annual rpt, 9914–3

AID economic assistance to developing countries, obligations and disbursements by country, quarterly rpt, 9912–4

AID loan repayment status and terms by program and country, and status of predecessor agency loans, quarterly rpt, 9912–3

Economic conditions, income, production, prices, employment, and trade, 1984 annual country rpt, 2046–4.121

Economic, social, and political summary data, by country, 1984, annual factbook, 244–11

Exports of US, detailed Schedule B commodities by country of destination, 1983, annual rpt, 2424–9

Exports of US, detailed Schedule E commodities by mode of transport and world area and country of destination, 1983, annual rpts, 2424–5

Imports of US, detailed Schedule A commodities by country and world area of origin, and mode of transport, 1983, annual rpts, 2424–2

Imports of US, detailed TSUSA commodities by country of origin, 1983, annual rpt, 2424–4

Loans and grants for economic and military assistance from US and intl agencies, by program and country, FY46-83, annual rpt, 9914–5

Yemen, North

Military aid of US, arms sales, and training programs costs and budget requests by program, world region, and country, FY83-85, annual rpt, 7144–13

Military spending, arms trade, and armed forces size, with total govt spending and population, by country, 1972-82, annual rpt, 9824–1

Minerals Yearbook, 1982, Vol 3: foreign country reviews of production, trade, and policies, by commodity, annual rpt, 5604–35

Minerals Yearbook, 1982, Vol 3 preprints: foreign country review of production, trade, and policies, by commodity, annual rpt, 5604–17.88

Population size and growth rates, and latest available benchmark demographic data, by country, 1950-83, biennial rpt, 2324–4

see also under By Foreign Country in the "Index by Categories"

Yemen, South

Agricultural situation in Middle East and North Africa, by country and commodity, 1983 and outlook for 1984, annual rpt, 1524–4.3

Economic, social, and political summary data, by country, 1984, annual factbook, 244–11

Exports of US, detailed Schedule B commodities by country of destination, 1983, annual rpt, 2424–9

Exports of US, detailed Schedule E commodities by mode of transport and world area and country of destination, 1983, annual rpts, 2424–5

Imports of US, detailed Schedule A commodities by country and world area of origin, and mode of transport, 1983, annual rpts, 2424–2

Imports of US, detailed TSUSA commodities by country of origin, 1983, annual rpt, 2424–4

Loans and grants for economic and military assistance from US and intl agencies, by program and country, FY46-83, annual rpt, 9914–5

Military spending, arms trade, and armed forces size, with total govt spending and population, by country, 1972-82, annual rpt, 9824–1

Minerals Yearbook, 1982, Vol 3: foreign country reviews of production, trade, and policies, by commodity, annual rpt, 5604–35

Minerals Yearbook, 1982, Vol 3 preprints: foreign country review of production, trade, and policies, by commodity, annual rpt, 5604–17.88

Population size and growth rates, and latest available benchmark demographic data, by country, 1950-83, biennial rpt, 2324–4

see also under By Foreign Country in the "Index by Categories"

Yinger, John

"Making Ends Meet: Boston's Budget in the 1980s", 9373–1.406

Yonkers, N.Y.

see also under By City in the "Index by Categories"

York, Pa.

Census of Housing, 1980: occupancy and unit characteristics, by race, Hispanic origin, and city, SMSA rpt, 2473–1.378

Census of Population and Housing, 1980: detailed population and housing characteristics, by county, city, and census tract, SMSA rpt, 2551–2.378

Wages by occupation, and benefits for office and plant workers, 1984 SMSA survey rpt, 6785–11.1

see also under By SMSA or MSA in the "Index by Categories"

Young, Anne M.

"Educational Attainment of Workers, Mar. 1982-83", 6746–1.251

"Fewer Students in Work Force as School Age Population Declines", 6722–1.446

"More U.S. Workers Are College Graduates", 6722–1.423

"Students, Graduates, and Dropouts, Oct. 1980-82", 6746–1.250

Young, Arthur F.

"Urban and Rural Housing Characteristics", 1004–16.1, 1702–1.407

Young, C. Edwin

"Investments in Soil Conservation Structures: The Role of Operator and Operation Characteristics", 1502–3.402

Young, Joseph W.

"Anthropometric and Mass Distribution Characteristics of the Adult Female", 7506–10.28

Young, Wanda W.

"Incorporating Severity of Illness and Comorbidity in Case-Mix Measurement", 4652–1.426

Youngstown, Ohio

Census of Housing, 1980: occupancy and unit characteristics, by race, Hispanic origin, and city, SMSA rpt, 2473–1.379

Census of Population and Housing, 1980: detailed population and housing characteristics, by county, city, and census tract, SMSA rpt, 2551–2.379

see also under By City and By SMSA or MSA in the "Index by Categories"

Youth

Abuse of adolescents, characteristics of victims and abuse, local agencies contacted, drug and alcohol involvement, and reciprocal violence, 1980-81 survey, 4608–18

Births and birth rates of teenage girls, and distribution of births with low birth weight and Apgar scores, by mother and infant characteristics, 1970-81, 4147–21.41

Births and sexual experience of teenage girls by race, abortions, and birth control use, by age, 1970s-80 with birth trends from 1920, hearings, 21968–29

Births by outcome, and mother's sociodemographic, life style, and maternity characteristics, 1980, article, 4102–1.420

Census of Housing, 1980: inventory, occupancy, and unit characteristics, changes from 1973 by region and inside-outside SMSAs and central cities, series, 2473–3

Census of Housing, 1980: occupancy and unit characteristics of SMSAs and central cities, by race, Hispanic origin, and city, State and SMSA rpt series, 2473–1

Census of Population and Housing, 1980: detailed population and housing characteristics, by county, city, and census tract, State and SMSA rpt series, 2551–2

Index by Subjects and Names

Crime and criminal justice data, including justice expenditures and employment by level of govt, 1970s-82 with some trends from 1875, 6068–174

Drug abuse and treatment research, highlights of studies by Natl Inst on Drug Abuse grant recipients, periodic rpt, 4492–4

Fed Govt public welfare programs and tax expenditures benefitting children and youth, participation and funding for 71 programs, FY81-83, 21968–30

FmHA loans, by type, race, Hispanic origin, and State, quarterly rpt, 1182–5

Health condition and health care resources, use, and expenditures, 1970s-82 with trends and projections 1900-2000, annual compilation, 4144–11

Homicide and suicide rates for youth, by sex, race, and circumstances, selected years 1970-79, and stress and violent behavior reduction goals for 1990, 4102–1.437

Housing and neighborhood quality indicators and attitudes, and occupant characteristics, by urban-rural location and region, 1981, annual survey, 2485–7

Income of families and persons, by sociodemographic characteristics, 1983, advance annual Current Population Rpt, 2546–6.41

Injuries, deaths, and medical costs from selected consumer products use, by victim age, 1981-83, annual rpt, 9164–2

Israel and France urban youths use of selected drugs, alcohol, and cigarettes, by age and sex, 1977 and 1979, article, 4102–1.430

Lead levels in blood by sociodemographic and behavioral characteristics, and potential workplace exposure, 1976-80, 4147–11.201

Married women in couples with wife as primary earner, socioeconomic and family characteristics, with comparative data for husbands, Mar 1982, 2326–11.9

Physician office visits of youths aged 11-20 by patient and visit characteristics and physician specialty, and drug mentions by brand, 1980-81, 4146–8.100

Poverty population size, effect of counting public noncash transfers as income by recipient characteristics, 1979-83, 2626–2.52

Poverty status of young adults related to motivation, psychological factors, and family characteristics, by race and sex, 1970s-82, longitudinal studies, 4008–65

Red Cross program operations and financial statements, 1982/83, annual rpt, 29254–1

Smoking and tobacco marketing legislation introduced and enacted in State legislatures, by State, 1982, annual rpt, 4204–13

Social services of State govts for youth, coordinating agencies activities, admin, membership, and funding sources, survey, 1984 rpt, 6068–182

see also Children

see also Elementary and secondary education

see also Foster home care

see also Higher education

Index by Subjects and Names

Yugoslavia

see also Juvenile delinquency
see also School dropouts
see also Seasonal and summer employment
see also Students
see also Youth employment
see also under By Age in the "Index by Categories"

Youth Conservation Corps

Activities, costs, and participant characteristics of Corps, by sponsoring agency, 1982, annual rpt, 5304–12

Forest Service programs and activities, by State and region, FY83, annual rpt, 1204–1

Youth Development and Delinquency Prevention Administration

see Office of Human Development Services

Youth employment

- Australia and US youth unemployment rates, by sex and age, Mar 1983 and trends from 1960s, article, 6722–1.462
- Business and financial statistics, historic trends, 1984 annual chartbook, 9364–2.4
- Census of Population and Housing, 1980: detailed population and housing characteristics, by county, city, and census tract, State and SMSA rpt series, 2551–2
- CETA participants by sociodemographic characteristics, and Labor Dept activities and staff, FY83, annual rpt, 6304–1
- Dallas-Fort Worth, Tex, SMSA employment, earnings, hours, and CPI changes, 1983 with trends from 1968, annual rpt, 6964–2
- Educational attainment of labor force, by demographic and employment characteristics, 1982-83 with summary trends from 1940, 6746–1.251
- Educational attainment of labor force, by demographic and employment characteristics, 1983, article, 6722–1.423
- Employment change over business cycles, by worker characteristics and industry div, quarterly 1982-2nd qtr 1984 with trends from 1948, annual article, 6722–1.448
- Employment of youth and hours worked, by high school and college enrollment status, sex, race, and Hispanic origin, 1982-83, annual article, 6722–1.446
- Employment of youth, by high school and college enrollment status, industry div, occupation, and selected demographic characteristics, 1980-82, 6746–1.250
- Employment situation, earnings, hours, and other BLS economic indicators, transcripts of BLS Commissioner's monthly testimony, periodic rpt, 23846–4
- Employment status of persons aged 16-19, annual averages, 1983, article, 6742–2.403
- Employment status of persons aged 16-21, monthly rpt, 6742–2.1
- Employment, unemployment, and labor force, by demographic and employment characteristics, State, and for 30 metro areas and 11 large cities, 1983, annual rpt, 6744–7
- Employment, unemployment, and labor force, detailed data by sociodemographic and employment characteristics, and industry, 1940s-83, 6748–72
- Employment, unemployment, hours, earnings, and productivity, selected years 1929-83, annual rpt, 204–1.2

Fed Govt employment and training program funding under Job Training Partnership Act, and required matching funds, for 3 programs by State, 1984/85, press release, 6408–58

Fed Govt public welfare programs and tax expenditures benefitting children and youth, participation and funding for 71 programs, FY81-83, 21968–30

Handbook of Labor Statistics, employment, earnings, hours, and labor force characteristics, 1982 and trends, detailed annual rpt, 6724–1

High school and college grads employment status, job opportunities, and income, selected years 1978-83, annual rpt, 4824–2.23

High school classes of 1980 and 1982: educational and sociodemographic characteristics and expectations, natl longitudinal study, series, 4826–2

High school grads aged 17-21 percent distribution, by most recent occupation, sex, vocational education participation, May 1980, annual rpt, 4824–1.3

Houston, Tex, SMSA employment, earnings, hours, and CPI changes, 1983 with trends from 1968, annual rpt, 6964–1

Income assistance, effects of experimental negative income tax program on employment, earnings, marital status, and other family characteristics in 2 cities, 1970-75, 4008–64

Income of families and persons, by sociodemographic characteristics, 1983, advance annual Current Population Rpt, 2546–6.41

Income of households, families, and persons, by detailed socioeconomic characteristics and region, 1982, annual Current Population Rpt, 2546–6.39

Job Training Partnership Act dislocated workers program performance standards guide for States, with data on previous programs, by State and client characteristics, FY81-82, 6408–59.2

Job Training Partnership Act participants, by program and socieconomic characteristics, Oct 1983-June 1984 with funding to 1985/86, 6408–63

Kentucky employment growth in 9-county rural area, labor force and establishment characteristics, 1979-80, 1598–194

Labor force characteristics and economic indicators, selected years 1880-1995, chartbook, 6728–30

Labor force participation of youth, by age group, Apr and July 1984 and change from 1983, annual press release, 6744–13

TV and radio industry employment, total and for minorities, women, and youth, by job category and State, 1979-83, annual rpt, 9284–16

Unemployment duration and probability of employment or labor force withdrawal, by sex and race, 1982, article, 9373–1.410

Unemployment during business cycles, and by worker age, sex, occupation, industry div, reason, and duration, various periods 1969-82, article, 6722–1.444

Wage growth and turnover rates related to marital status, sex, age, establishment type, and employer size, 1979/80, article, 9393–8.403

Youth Conservation Corps activities, costs, and participant characteristics, by sponsoring agency, 1982, annual rpt, 5304–12

see also Apprenticeship
see also Seasonal and summer employment

Yuba City, Calif.

Census of Housing, 1980: occupancy and unit characteristics, by race, Hispanic origin, and city, SMSA rpt, 2473–1.380

Census of Population and Housing, 1980: detailed population and housing characteristics, by county, city, and census tract, SMSA rpt, 2551–2.380

see also under By SMSA or MSA in the "Index by Categories"

Yugoslavia

- Agricultural and food production indexes, and production of selected commodities, by world region and country, 1974-83, annual rpt, 1524–5
- Agricultural situation in Eastern Europe, by country, 1983 and outlook for 1984, annual report, 1524–4.7
- Agricultural supply/demand, trade, and production, and socioeconomic data, by country, 1950s-77, 1528–179
- AID loan repayment status and terms by program and country, and status of predecessor agency loans, quarterly rpt, 9912–3
- Cuba economic conditions, agricultural and industrial production and distribution, trade, and intl economic relations, 1970-82 and trends from 1957, 248–40
- Economic conditions in Communist and OECD countries, 1982, annual rpt, 7144–11
- Economic conditions in Communist, OECD, and selected other countries, 1960s-83, annual rpt, 244–5
- Economic, social, and political summary data, by country, 1984, annual factbook, 244–11
- Electric power systems equipment market and trade, and user industry operations and demand, 1984 country market research rpt, 2045–15.5
- Exports and imports of US with Western Europe, and US market share and export opportunities for selected commodities, by country, 1982-84, 2048–105
- Exports of US, detailed Schedule B commodities by country of destination, 1983, annual rpt, 2424–9
- Exports of US, detailed Schedule E commodities by mode of transport and world area and country of destination, 1983, annual rpts, 2424–5
- Imports of US, detailed Schedule A commodities by country and world area of origin, and mode of transport, 1983, annual rpts, 2424–2
- Imports of US, detailed TSUSA commodities by country of origin, 1983, annual rpt, 2424–4
- Lab instruments market and trade, and user industry operations and demand, 1983 country market research rpt, 2045–10.17
- Loans and grants for economic and military assistance from US and intl agencies, by program and country, FY46-83, annual rpt, 9914–5
- Military aid of US, arms sales, and training programs costs and budget requests by program, world region, and country, FY83-85, annual rpt, 7144–13

Yugoslavia

Military spending, arms trade, and armed forces size, with total govt spending and population, by country, 1972-82, annual rpt, 9824–1

Minerals Yearbook, 1982, Vol 3: foreign country reviews of production, trade, and policies, by commodity, annual rpt, 5604–35

Minerals Yearbook, 1983, Vol 3 preprints: foreign country review of production, trade, and policies, by commodity, annual rpt, 5604–23.78

Mining industry equipment market and trade, and user industry operations and demand, 1983 country market research rpt, 2045–16.2

Nuclear power plant construction and operation status, and capacity, by plant, region, State, and selected country, 1983 and projected to 2020, annual rpt, 3164–57

Population size and growth rates, and latest available benchmark demographic data, by country, 1950-83, biennial rpt, 2324–4

Prune (dried) production, trade, consumption, and stocks of US and 2 countries, EC subsidies, and US exports by country, 1982/83-1984/85, article, 1925–34.435

see also under By Foreign Country in the "Index by Categories"

Zabrenski, Stephen T.

"Earnings of FSLIC-Insured Institutions: Second Half, 1983", 9312–6

Zaire

- Agricultural and food production indexes, and production of selected commodities, by world region and country, 1974-83, annual rpt, 1524–5
- Agricultural situation in sub-Saharan Africa, by country, 1982-83 and outlook for 1984, annual rpt, 1524–4.10
- AID activities and funding by project and function, FY85, and developing countries summary socioeconomic data, 1970s-83, by country, annual rpt, 9914–3
- AID economic assistance to developing countries, obligations and disbursements by country, quarterly rpt, 9912–4
- AID loan repayment status and terms by program and country, and status of predecessor agency loans, quarterly rpt, 9912–3
- *Background Notes,* summary social, political, and economic data, 1983 rpt, 7006–2.10
- Economic conditions and foreign marketing prospects in 46 Sub-Saharan countries, 1983 world region rpt, 2046–5.1
- Economic conditions, income, production, prices, employment, and trade, 1984 annual country rpt, 2046–4.122
- Economic conditions, investment and export opportunities, and trade practices, 1984 country market research rpt, 2046–6.2
- Economic, social, and political summary data, by country, 1984, annual factbook, 244–11
- Exports and imports of US, by commodity and country, 1972-82, annual world region rpt, 244–13.4
- Exports of US, detailed Schedule B commodities by country of destination, 1983, annual rpt, 2424–9

Exports of US, detailed Schedule E commodities by mode of transport and world area and country of destination, 1983, annual rpts, 2424–5

Imports of US, detailed Schedule A commodities by country and world area of origin, and mode of transport, 1983, annual rpts, 2424–2

Imports of US, detailed TSUSA commodities by country of origin, 1983, annual rpt, 2424–4

Loans and grants for economic and military assistance from US and intl agencies, by program and country, FY46-83, annual rpt, 9914–5

Military aid of US, arms sales, and training programs costs and budget requests by program, world region, and country, FY83-85, annual rpt, 7144–13

Military spending, arms trade, and armed forces size, with total govt spending and population, by country, 1972-82, annual rpt, 9824–1

Minerals Yearbook, 1982, Vol 3: foreign country reviews of production, trade, and policies, by commodity, annual rpt, 5604–35

Mining industry equipment market and trade, and user industry operations and demand, 1984 country market research rpt, 2045–16.4

Population size and growth rates, and latest available benchmark demographic data, by country, 1950-83, biennial rpt, 2324–4

see also under By Foreign Country in the "Index by Categories"

Zambia

- Agricultural and food production indexes, and production of selected commodities, by world region and country, 1974-83, annual rpt, 1524–5
- Agricultural situation in sub-Saharan Africa, by country, 1982-83 and outlook for 1984, annual rpt, 1524–4.10
- Agricultural supply/demand, trade, and production, and socioeconomic data, by country, 1950s-77, 1528–179
- AID activities and funding by project and function, FY85, and developing countries summary socioeconomic data, 1970s-83, by country, annual rpt, 9914–3
- AID economic assistance to developing countries, obligations and disbursements by country, quarterly rpt, 9912–4
- AID loan repayment status and terms by program and country, and status of predecessor agency loans, quarterly rpt, 9912–3
- *Background Notes,* summary social, political, and economic data, 1984 rpt, 7006–2.56
- Economic conditions and foreign marketing prospects in 46 Sub-Saharan countries, 1983 world region rpt, 2046–5.1
- Economic, social, and political summary data, by country, 1984, annual factbook, 244–11
- Economic trends in income, production, prices, employment, finances, and trade, 1984 semiannual rpt, 2046–4.41
- Exports of US, detailed Schedule B commodities by country of destination, 1983, annual rpt, 2424–9
- Exports of US, detailed Schedule E commodities by mode of transport and world area and country of destination, 1983, annual rpts, 2424–5

Index by Subjects and Names

Imports of US, detailed Schedule A commodities by country and world area of origin, and mode of transport, 1983, annual rpts, 2424–2

Imports of US, detailed TSUSA commodities by country of origin, 1983, annual rpt, 2424–4

Loans and grants for economic and military assistance from US and intl agencies, by program and country, FY46-83, annual rpt, 9914–5

Military aid of US, arms sales, and training programs costs and budget requests by program, world region, and country, FY83-85, annual rpt, 7144–13

Military spending, arms trade, and armed forces size, with total govt spending and population, by country, 1972-82, annual rpt, 9824–1

Minerals Yearbook, 1982, Vol 3: foreign country reviews of production, trade, and policies, by commodity, annual rpt, 5604–35

Minerals Yearbook, 1982, Vol 3 preprints: foreign country review of production, trade, and policies, by commodity, annual rpt, 5604–17.80

Population size and growth rates, and latest available benchmark demographic data, by country, 1950-83, biennial rpt, 2324–4

see also under By Foreign Country in the "Index by Categories"

Zanetos, M. A.

"Health Effects of Occupational Exposure to Hazardous Chemicals: A Comparative Assessment with Notes on Ionizing Radiation", 9638–50

Zarow, Linda

"1981 National Urban Pesticide Applicator Survey", 1561–16.408

Zieman, Joseph C.

"Ecology of the Seagrasses of South Florida: A Community Profile", 5506–9.8

Ziemer, Richard C.

"Federal Fiscal Programs", 2702–1.406

"Implicit Price Deflators for Military Construction", 2702–1.401

Zimbabwe

- Agricultural and food production indexes, and production of selected commodities, by world region and country, 1974-83, annual rpt, 1524–5
- Agricultural situation in sub-Saharan Africa, by country, 1982-83 and outlook for 1984, annual rpt, 1524–4.10
- AID activities and funding by project and function, FY85, and developing countries summary socioeconomic data, 1970s-83, by country, annual rpt, 9914–3
- AID economic assistance to developing countries, obligations and disbursements by country, quarterly rpt, 9912–4
- AID loan repayment status and terms by program and country, and status of predecessor agency loans, quarterly rpt, 9912–3
- Economic conditions and foreign marketing prospects in 46 Sub-Saharan countries, 1983 world region rpt, 2046–5.1
- Economic, social, and political summary data, by country, 1984, annual factbook, 244–11
- Employee stock ownership plans in developing countries, and firms finances and operations, with case studies of US and 3 countries, 1970s-82, 9916–3.19

Index by Subjects and Names

ZIP codes

Exports of US, detailed Schedule B commodities by country of destination, 1983, annual rpt, 2424–9

Exports of US, detailed Schedule E commodities by mode of transport and world area and country of destination, 1983, annual rpts, 2424–5

Imports of US, detailed Schedule A commodities by country and world area of origin, and mode of transport, 1983, annual rpts, 2424–2

Imports of US, detailed TSUSA commodities by country of origin, 1983, annual rpt, 2424–4

Loans and grants for economic and military assistance from US and intl agencies, by program and country, FY46-83, annual rpt, 9914–5

Medical and health care equipment market and trade, and user industry operations and demand, 1984 country market research rpt, 2045–2.52

Military aid of US, arms sales, and training programs costs and budget requests by program, world region, and country, FY83-85, annual rpt, 7144–13

Military spending, arms trade, and armed forces size, with total govt spending and population, by country, 1972-82, annual rpt, 9824–1

Minerals Yearbook, 1982, Vol 3: foreign country reviews of production, trade, and policies, by commodity, annual rpt, 5604–35

Minerals Yearbook, 1983, Vol 3 preprints: foreign country review of production, trade, and policies, by commodity, annual rpt, 5604–23.82

Population size and growth rates, and latest available benchmark demographic data, by country, 1950-83, biennial rpt, 2324–4

Telecommunication equipment market and trade, and user industry operations and demand, 1982 country market research rpt, 2045–12.38

see also under By Foreign Country in the "Index by Categories"

Zinc and zinc industry

Air pollutant emission factors, by detailed source, 3rd edition, 1983-84 supplements, 9198–13

Air pollutant metal levels, by monitoring site, State, and urban-rural location, 1977-79, last issue of annual rpt, 9194–10

Business statistics, detailed data for major industries and economic indicators, *Survey of Current Business,* monthly rpt, 2702–1.14

Castings (nonferrous) shipments and unfilled orders, by metal type, monthly Current Industrial Rpt, 2506–10.5

Communist, OECD, and selected other countries minerals and metals production, by commodity, 1960s-83, annual rpt, 244–5.6

County Business Patterns: establishments, employees, and payrolls, by SIC 4-digit industry and county, 1981, annual State rpt series, 2326–8

County Business Patterns: establishments, employees, and payrolls, by SIC 4-digit industry and county, 1982, annual State rpt series, 2326–6

Exports and imports of US, detailed SIC-based commodities by world area, 1983, annual rpts, 2424–6

Exports and imports of US, totals and as percent of domestic production, by SIC 2- to 5-digit commodity, 1981, annual rpt, 2424–3

Exports of US, detailed commodities by country of destination, monthly rpt, 2422–3

Exports of US, detailed Schedule B commodities by country of destination, 1983, annual rpt, 2424–9

Exports of US, detailed Schedule E commodities by mode of transport and world area and country of destination, 1983, annual rpts, 2424–5

Finances and operations, by SIC 2- to 4-digit industry, 1970s-83 and projected to 1988, annual rpt, 2014–4

Foreign and US supply under alternative market conditions, reserves, and background industry data, 1983 mineral rpt, 5606–4.10

Foreign minerals production, reserves, and industry role in domestic economy and world supply, country and world region rpt series, 5606–1

Futures trading by commodity and exchange, and Commodity Futures Trading Commission activities, funding, and employment, FY83, annual rpt, 11924–2

Great Lakes trade, by SITC 3-digit commodity, port, vessel type, world area, and country, 1982, annual rpt, 7744–3

Imports of US, detailed Schedule A commodities by country and world area of origin, and mode of transport, 1983, annual rpts, 2424–2

Imports of US, detailed Schedule A commodities by country, monthly rpt, 2422–2

Imports of US, detailed TSUSA commodities by country of origin, 1983, annual rpt, 2424–4

Input-output structure of US economy, detailed interindustry transactions for 537 industries, and components of final demand, 1977 benchmark data, 2708–17

Manufacturing census, 1982: financial and operating data, for SIC 4-digit industries by product, preliminary rpt, 2491–1.264

Mineral industries census, 1982: financial and operating data, by SIC 2- to 4-digit industry, preliminary summary rpt, 2511–2.1

Mineral industries census, 1982: financial and operating data, including materials consumed, by SIC 4-digit industry and State, preliminary rpt, 2511–1.2

Mineral Industry Surveys, commodity review of production, trade, stocks, and consumption, monthly rpt, 5612–1.27

Minerals Yearbook, 1982, Vol 1: commodity reviews of production, reserves, supply, use, and trade, annual rpt, 5604–33

Minerals Yearbook, 1982, Vol 2 preprints: State reviews of production and sales by commodity, and business activity, annual rpt series, 5604–16

Minerals Yearbook, 1982, Vol 2: State reviews of production, sales, and firms, by commodity, and business activity, annual rpt, 5604–34

Minerals Yearbook, 1982, Vol 3: foreign country reviews of production, trade, and policies, by commodity, annual rpt, 5604–35

Minerals Yearbook, 1982, Vol 3 preprints: foreign country reviews of production, trade, and policies, by commodity, annual rpt series, 5604–17

Minerals Yearbook, 1983, Vol 1 preprints: commodity review of production, reserves, supply, use, and trade, annual rpt, 5604–15.70

Minerals Yearbook, 1983, Vol 3 preprints: foreign country reviews of production, trade, and policies, by commodity, annual rpt series, 5604–23

Occupational injuries and incidence rates at metal mines and related operations, detailed analysis, 1982, annual rpt, 6664–3

Occupational injury and illness rates, by SIC 2- to 4-digit industry, 1982, annual rpt, 6844–1

Producer prices and indexes, by stage of processing and detailed commodity, monthly rpt, 6762–6

Producer prices and indexes, by stage of processing and detailed commodity, monthly 1983, annual supplement, 6764–2

Production, prices, trade, use, employment, tariffs, and stockpiling, by mineral commodity, with foreign comparisons, 1979-83, annual rpt, 5604–18

Productivity, hours, and employment indexes for selected SIC 3- and 4-digit industries, 1954-82, annual rpt, 6824–1.3

Stockpiling of strategic and critical materials, Fed Govt activities and inventories by commodity, Oct 1983-Mar 1984, semiannual rpt, 9432–1

Stockpiling of strategic materials, inventories, costs, and goals, by commodity, as of June 1984, semiannual rpt, 9452–7

Strategic minerals supply/demand, trade, and foreign and US industry devs by firm and country, by commodity, bimonthly rpt, 5602–4

Waterborne commerce of US (domestic and foreign), freight by commodity, traffic, and passengers, by port and waterway, 1982, annual rpt, 3754–3

see also under By Commodity in the "Index by Categories"

see also under By Industry in the "Index by Categories"

ZIP codes

Appalachian States, FHLB 5th District housing vacancy rates for single and multifamily units and mobile homes, by ZIP code, annual metro area rpt series, 9304–27

Cost control proposals for Fed Govt programs and mgmt, 3-year savings by function and agency, and financial and operating data, 1960s-81, 16908–1.16

Higher education instns, type, location, enrollment, and student charges, by State and congressional district, 1983/84, biennial listing, 4844–11

North Central States, FHLB 7th District housing vacancy rates for single and multifamily units and mobile homes, by ZIP code, annual metro area rpt series, 9304–18

ZIP codes

South Central States, FHLB 9th District housing vacancy rates for single and multifamily units and mobile homes by ZIP code, annual metro area rpt series, 9304–19

West Central States, FHLB 10th District housing vacancy rates for single and multifamily units and mobile homes, by ZIP code, annual metro area rpt series, 9304–22

Western States, FHLB 11th District housing vacancy rates for single and multifamily units and mobile homes, by ZIP code, annual metro area rpt series, 9304–20

Western States, FHLB 12th District housing vacancy rates for single and multifamily units and mobile homes, by ZIP code, annual metro area rpt series, 9304–21

Zipkin, A.

"Rural Primary Health Care Service in Israel: Some Measures of Utilization and Satisfaction", 4102–1.456

Zirconium

see Metals and metal industries

Zoning and zoning laws

California (southern) housing demand by county, prices and sales, and costs after homeowner tax deductions, 1970s-80, hearing, 21148–31

DC metro area Metrorail transit system, land use planning dev and impacts, 1984 narrative rpt, 7306–8.3

New Communities program of HUD, activities, costs, land sales, and community and population characteristics, for 13 communities, 1970s-83, 5188–107

see also Building permits

Zoological parks

Census of Population, 1980: detailed socioeconomic and demographic characteristics, by age, sex, race, Hispanic origin, occupation, and industry, State rpt series, 2531–4

Census of Service Industries, 1982: employment, establishments, receipts, and payroll, by SIC 2- to 4-digit kind of business, SMSA, county, and city, State rpt series, 2391–1

County Business Patterns: establishments, employees, and payrolls, by SIC 4-digit industry and county, 1982, annual State rpt series, 2326–6

Earnings by major industry group, and personal income per capita and by source, by region and State, 1929-82, 2708–40

Employment, earnings, and hours, by SIC 4-digit nonfarm industry, monthly 1974-Feb 1984, annual update, 6744–4

Endangered animals and plants foreign trade including reexports of live specimens and products, by purpose, country, and species, 1982, annual rpt, 5504–19

Minority group and women employment, by occupational group and SIC 2- to 3-digit industry, 1981, annual rpt, 9244–1.1

Natl Zoological Park in DC, species in collections and other activities, annual rpt, suspended, 9774–2

Zoology

High school class of 1982: science and math coursework and assessment, by sociodemographic and school characteristics and educational goal, 4826–2.14

Science and engineering doctoral degree recipients, by field, sex, race, age, citizenship, postgrad employment and study status, State, and instn, 1960-82, 9626–6.16

Science and engineering grad enrollment, fields of study, financial support, and other student and instn characteristics, 1975-82, annual survey, 9627–7

see also Animals

see also Birds and bird conservation

see also Wildlife and wildlife conservation

Index by Categories

Index by Categories

(This index contains references to publications, tables, and groups of tables that contain breakdowns of statistical data by State, by industry, by age, or by some other standard category.)

Geographic Breakdowns

By Census Division	871
By City	873
By County	877
By Foreign Country	880
By Outlying Area	887
By Region	890
By SMSA or MSA	898
By State	900
By Urban-Rural and Metro-Nonmetro	914

Economic Breakdowns

By Commodity	917
By Federal Agency	921
By Income	924
By Individual Company or Institution	926
By Industry	935
By Occupation	939

Demographic Breakdowns

By Age	942
By Disease	948
By Educational Attainment	949
By Marital Status	952
By Race	954
By Sex	959

Index by Categories

INTRODUCTION

The Index by Categories contains references to all publications, tables, and groups of tables that contain breakdowns of statistical data by any or several of the following 21 standard categories:

GEOGRAPHIC BREAKDOWNS

By Census Division	By Outlying Area
By City	By Region
By County	By SMSA or MSA
By Foreign Country	By State
	By Urban-Rural

ECONOMIC BREAKDOWNS

By Commodity	By Individual
By Federal Agency	Company
By Income	or Institution
By Industry	By Occupation

DEMOGRAPHIC BREAKDOWNS

By Age	By Marital Status
By Disease	By Race
By Educational	By Sex
Attainment	

SUBJECT SUBHEADINGS

Within each of the categories listed above, references have been grouped according to the subject matter of the publication or the statistical content being indexed. Nineteen subheadings have been used for this purpose; they are listed below. The kinds of material referenced under each subheading are noted, as well as cross-references to other, related subheadings.

Agriculture and Food — Covers all agricultural data, including commercial fishing and the fertilizer industry; agricultural credit of all kinds; agricultural land; farm population and labor; and all data on food except retail prices.

See also Natural Resources, Environment, and Pollution, for forestry data, additional conservation data Prices and Cost of Living, for retail food prices

Banking, Finance, and Insurance — Covers all data on financial institutions and their activities; all banking and insurance data; consumer credit; bankruptcy; securities markets; and money supply, interest rates, and other financial indicators.

See also Other specific subheadings, for Federal insurance programs Agriculture and Food, for agricultural credit Government and Defense, for Government debt and securities Health and Vital Statistics, for health insurance data Housing and Construction, for mortgage data Industry and Commerce, for general economic indicators

Communications and Transportation — Covers all data on industries in these sectors, including their finances, employment, occupational safety, and rates and regulation; highway data; Postal Service; all travel and tourism data, including accidents; advertising; and propaganda.

See also Energy Resources and Demand, for pipeline data Industry and Commerce, for equipment and parts manufacturing and trade

Education — Covers all data on education in general, including schools, faculty, students, graduates, and finances.

See also Government and Defense, for military academies Health and Vital Statistics, for medical and dental schools and all data on health manpower training Labor and Employment, for employment training programs, such as CETA and WIN, and for apprenticeships Science and Technology, for education exclusively in science and engineering Veterans Affairs, for GI Bill and other veterans' education

Energy Resources and Demand — Covers supply, consumption, and conservation of all types of energy. Includes exploration, extraction, R&D, transportation, distribution, and waste disposal of all energy forms; all data on energy industries; and energy use and costs.

See also Health and Vital Statistics, for accidents and occupational health in energy industries, including mines Natural Resources, Environment, and Pollution, for additional data exclusively on energy reserves, and for pollution and radioactivity from energy resources Prices and Cost of Living, for consumer utility bills

Geography and Climate — Covers all data on weather, climate, oceanography, and storms and other natural disasters.

See also Natural Resources, Environment, and Pollution, for data on water supply

Government and Defense — Covers all data on government in general, including activities, finances, programs, and personnel; all data on defense activities and foreign affairs; taxes; coinage; passports; and elections and voting.

See also Other specific subheadings for data on government aid, employment, or regulation in specific areas Health and Vital Statistics, for military medicine

Health and Vital Statistics — Covers all data on health condition, disease, and disability; occupational health and safety in general; medical care, costs, and insurance; medical facilities; health personnel and their education; and vital statistics.

See also Communications and Transportation, for all transportation accidents, including occupational accidents and health Public Welfare and Social Security, for data on Medicare, Medicaid, and social security disability recipients Veterans Affairs, for data on veterans' health and VA medical facilities

Housing and Construction — Covers all data on housing condition, finance, and occupancy; all data on the construction industry; all mortgages; urban renewal and community development; and government aid for housing or communities.

See also Communications and Transportation, for construction of highways and bridges Natural Resources, Environment, and Pollution, for construction of dams, sewer plants, etc.

Industry and Commerce — Covers all data on industry in general, including production, finances, payrolls, and profits; productivity; trade and marketing; foreign trade, tariffs, and balance of payments; and economic indicators in general.

See also Other more specific subheadings for data on specific industry sectors Government and Defense, for corporate income tax data

Labor and Employment — Covers all data on the labor force and employment in general, including characteristics, earnings, hours, working conditions, and employee benefits; unemployment; labor unions; and employment training programs, such as CETA and WIN.

See also Other more specific subheadings for employment and employees in specific disciplines, such as health or science, or in specific industry sectors, such as agriculture or transportation Industry and Commerce, for general industry data including employment and payrolls

Law Enforcement — Covers all data on crime and the characteristics of criminals; and all data on the criminal justice system, including police, lawyers, courts, prisons, and sentences.

See also Other specific subheadings for civil proceedings and government regulation in specific areas

Natural Resources, Environment, and Pollution — Covers all data on natural resource supply and conservation, including energy reserves, forests, public lands, and wildlife; land use; water supply, dams, and flood control; environmental quality; all types of pollutants; wastes in general, including sewage disposal; oil spills; and radioactivity in the environment.

See also Agriculture and Food, for conservation specifically related to agriculture Energy Resources and Demand, for additional data on energy reserves, disposal of wastes from energy production, and nuclear power Health and Vital Statistics, for occupational hazards and for the health effects of pollutants

Population—Covers all data on population size; characteristics of the population in general; demographic groups such as youth, women, or blacks; and migration.

See also Other specific subheadings for data on special population groups such as farmers, veterans, or mortgagors Health and Vital Statistics, for data on births and deaths

Prices and Cost of Living—Covers prices in general, both wholesale and retail; price indexes; consumer costs; and inflation.

See also Education, for tuition costs Health and Vital Statistics, for medical costs Industry and Commerce or other more specific subheadings, for data on production costs, farm value, etc.

Public Welfare and Social Security—Covers everything related to the social security program, including Medicare and disability insurance; everything related to welfare, public assistance, and medical assistance (Medicaid); food stamps and school lunch programs; and social services.

See also Health and Vital Statistics, for data on workers compensation and disabled persons in general Labor and Employment, for unemployment insurance

Recreation and Leisure—Covers all data on recreation activities and recreation industries. Includes sport fishing, hunting, parks, museums, and the arts; and tourist promotion.

See also Communications and Transportation, for data on travel Education, for libraries Energy Resources and Demand, for recreation areas at hydroelectric projects Natural Resources, Environment, and Pollution, for national forests, and for recreation areas at Corps of Engineers and similar projects

Science and Technology—Covers activities, private and government funding, employment, and education, exclusively in scientific fields; all data on space programs; and inventions and patents.

See also Agriculture and Food, for agricultural sciences Energy Resources and Demand, for R&D in energy fields Geography and Climate, for meteorology, oceanography, etc.

Veterans Affairs—Covers everything that relates exclusively to veterans, including education, health, VA hospitals, housing and VA home loans, employment and employment programs, pensions, and disability payments.

See also Government and Defense, for data on the armed services

USING THE INDEX

In using the Category Index, you must keep in mind that the amount of detail provided in the various tabular breakdowns may vary considerably.

Breakdowns "By sex" or "By urban-rural" are, by definition, complete. Breakdowns "By census division," "By region," or "By State" are generally complete unless specific limitations are noted.

Breakdowns "By race" generally show white and nonwhite or white, black, and other. When substantial data on race/ethnic breakdowns are included, they are indexed specifically in the Index of Subjects and Names (i.e. Black Americans, Indians, Hispanic Americans) as well as under the category "By race."

The greatest variation in the detail of category breakdowns occurs in such categories as "By city," "By country," "By foreign country," "By industry," "By commodity," and "By occupation." For these categories, we try, whenever possible, to indicate the degree of detail in the notations of content listed under the category terms and in the abstract of the publication.

For further information about using the Category Index, see the User Guide (Abstracts Volume, p. xxv; Index Volume, p. xv).

For use in conjunction with the Category Index, we have printed several standard classification systems that are frequently used in Federal statistical publications (see Index Volume, p. 1059). These classifications include regions of the U.S., SMSAs, Standard Industrial Classification, and Standard International Trade Classification.

Index by Categories

GEOGRAPHIC BREAKDOWNS

BY CENSUS DIVISION

Agriculture and Food

- Cold storage food stocks by commodity and census div, and warehouse cold storage space in use, by State, monthly rpt, 1631–5
- Fertilizer consumption, by fertilizer type and State, years ended June 1983-84, annual rpt, 1631–13
- Flour milling production by census div and State, daily capacity, and exports by country, monthly Current Industrial Rpt, 2506–4.1
- Meat marketing and distribution establishments, sales, and per capita consumption, 1950s-82 with trends from 1929, 1548–232

Education

- High school class of 1982: foreign language coursework, by language, course level, student and school characteristics, and location, 1984 rpt, 4828–17
- High school class of 1982: science and math coursework and assessment, by

sociodemographic and school characteristics and educational goal, 4826–2.14

Energy Resources and Demand

- Coal, coke, and breeze supply/demand, prices, trade, and stocks, by end-use sector and State, quarterly rpt with articles, 3162–37
- Coal production and stocks by district, and shipments by district of origin, State of destination, consuming sector, and mode of transport, quarterly rpt, 3162–8
- Coal stocks at electric utilities, by census div and State, weekly rpt, monthly data, 3162–1.2
- Electric power plant (coal-fired) capacity, coal demand, and coal supply by mode of transport and region of origin, by State, for units planned 1983-92, 3088–18
- Electric power plant (steam) fuel deliveries, costs, and quality, by fuel type, State, and utility, 1983, annual rpt, 3164–42
- Electric power plant capacity, production, retail sales, and fuel stocks, use, and costs, by State, 1979-83, annual rpt, 3164–11
- Electric power plants, by capacity, fuel used, unit type, region, State, and county, for plants added and retired, 1983 and planned through 1993, annual rpt, 3164–36

Electric utilities consumption of natural gas, by State, 1977 and 1983, annual rpt, 3104–8

- Electric utility fuel cost, quality, use, receipts, and stocks, and power plant production, by energy source, State and utility, quarterly rpt, 3162–39
- Electric utility production, fuel consumption, stocks, and costs by fuel type, and sales, by State, monthly rpt, 3162–35
- Energy use, by economic sector, State, census div, and detailed energy resource, 1960-82, State Energy Data System annual rpt, 3164–39
- Housing energy conservation programs of utilities, financing, costs, participation, and energy savings, various periods 1981-84, hearing, 21368–54
- Housing energy use, costs, expenditures, and conservation, and household and housing characteristics, survey series, 3166–7
- Nuclear industry nongovt employment by industry segment, occupation, and census div, and DOE and NRC nuclear employment, 1968-83, biennial rpt, 3004–11.1

BY CENSUS DIVISION

Geography and Climate

- Climatological data by census div and State, and departures from long-term mean, from 1895, series, 2156–17
- Heating and cooling degree days, by census div, monthly and cumulative for season, monthly rpt, 3162–24.1
- Heating and cooling degree days by State, and housing energy bills and departures from normal by fuel type, by census div, monthly rpt, 2152–11
- Heating and cooling degree days weighted by population, by census div and State, with area-weighted temperature and precipitation, monthly rpt, 2152–13
- Weather events socioeconomic impacts and costs, heating and cooling degree days, and housing energy bills, by census div and State, monthly rpt, 2152–12

Government and Defense

- DOD procurement, prime contract awards for 25 commodity categories and R&D, by State and census div, FY81-83, annual rpt, 3544–11
- Manufacturers under Fed Govt contract and owned by DOD, operating data by agency, selected SIC 2- to 4-digit industry, State, and SMSA, 1982, annual Current Industrial Rpt, 2506–3.4

Health and Vital Statistics

- Births and birth rates, by demographic and birth characteristics, 1981 with trends from 1940, US Vital Statistics advance rpt, 4146–5.73
- Births and birth rates, by parent and birth characteristics and infant condition at birth, 1982 and trends from 1940, US Vital Statistics annual advance rpt, 4146–5.79
- Births and birth rates, by selected demographic characteristics and geographic area, 1979 and trends, US Vital Statistics annual rpt, 4144–1.1
- Births, and birth rates for unmarried and all women, by race of child, age and Hispanic origin of mother, and State, 1980, 4147–21.42
- CAT scan procedures on hospital inpatients, by body site and patient and hospital characteristics, 1979-82, 4146–8.102
- *County and City Data Book,* detailed socioeconomic and demographic data for States, counties, and cities, selected years 1976-82, 2328–1
- Deaths and death rates by detailed cause and demographic characteristics, 1979 and selected trends, US Vital Statistics annual rpt, 4144–2.1
- Deaths and death rates, by selected cause and demographic characteristics, 1981, US Vital Statistics advance rpt, 4146–5.78
- Deaths and death rates, by selected cause and demographic characteristics, 1982, US Vital Statistics advance rpt, 4146–5.81
- Divorces, divorce rates, and characteristics, by region and State, 1981, US Vital Statistics advance rpt, 4146–5.74
- Health condition and health care resources, use, and expenditures, 1970s-82 with trends and projections 1900-2000, annual compilation, 4144–11
- Health professionals supply and education, by occupation, demographic and professional characteristics, and location, 1950s-83 and projected to 2000, biennial rpt, 4114–8

Hospital (community) occupancy rates by census div, and percent offering specialized facilities, by bed size, selected years 1978-81, article, 4652–1.418

- Hospital employment, vacancies, and vacancy rates, by occupation and by hospital specialty, region, census div, and State, 1980, annual rpt, 4114–12
- Hospitals and nursing homes, employees, and use, by ownership, bed size, region, and State, selected years 1969-80, 4147–14.30
- Infant deaths, 1979, US Vital Statistics annual rpt, 4144–2.2
- Infectious notifiable diseases, cases and incidence, by census div and State, 1982, annual rpt, 4204–1
- Marriages and marriage rates by State, and bride and groom characteristics, 1981, advance annual US Vital Statistics rpt, 4146–5.77
- Marriages, divorces, and rates, by detailed demographic and geographic characteristics, 1979 and trends, US Vital Statistics annual rpt, 4144–4
- Public health labs of States, personnel, finances, workloads, and other activities, by State, FY82, annual rpt, 4204–8

Housing and Construction

- Census of Housing, 1980: structural, financial, and householder characteristics, by region and State, 2475–4
- *County and City Data Book,* detailed socioeconomic and demographic data for States, counties, and cities, selected years 1976-82, 2328–1
- Mobile homes placed by structural characteristics, and sales price, by census div and State, monthly rpt, annual tables, 2382–1
- New construction (public and private) put in place, by type, region, and census div, monthly rpt, 2382–4.3
- New housing units authorized, by public and private ownership, by region, div, State, selected MSA, and 4,700 permit-issuing places, monthly rpt, 2382–5
- New housing units authorized, by public and private ownership, State, and permit-issuing place, 1983, annual rpt, 2384–2
- Window shipments and prices by market sector, and installation by unit type and State, for wood and aluminum frames, selected years 1967-82, article, 2012–1.403

Industry and Commerce

- Chemicals (inorganic) production by region, census div, and State, stocks, and trade, by product, monthly Current Industrial Rpt, 2506–8.1
- *County and City Data Book,* detailed socioeconomic and demographic data for States, counties, and cities, selected years 1976-82, 2328–1
- Drug shipments by region and selected census div and State, trade, and consumption, by product, 1983, annual Current Industrial Rpt, 2506–8.5
- Fabric (narrow) shipments, by census div and State, 1983, annual Current Industrial Rpt, 2506–5.6
- Iron and steel castings and scrap production, shipments, unfilled orders, stocks, receipts, and trade, by census div and State, monthly Current Industrial Rpt, 2506–10.1
- Lumber production and stocks of hardwood and softwood, by region, State, and species, 1982, annual Current Industrial Rpt, 2506–7.4

Index by Categories

- Manufacturing census, 1982: financial and operating data, by SIC 2- to 4-digit industry, State, SMSA, and county, preliminary census div rpt series, 2491–3
- Manufacturing employment and population, by region and census div, 1981, 26306–6.69
- Metalworking machinery industry computerized automation, by plant characteristics, for 6 industry groups and small plants, 1982 surveys, 23848–179
- Retail trade sales and inventories, by kind of business, region, census div, and selected State, SMSA, and city, and seasonal adjustments, monthly rpt, 2413–3
- Small and minority-owned businesses finances and operations, Federal contracts by agency, and worker characteristics, by industry, race, sex, and State, 1950s-83, annual rpt, 9764–6
- Small business loans and credit, operational expectations, and NYC metro area owners economic and professional attitudes, by industry div, 1980-83 surveys, hearings, 21728–52
- Sulfuric acid production, establishments, and shipments, by census div and State, and trade, 1983, annual Current Industrial Rpt, 2506–8.13

Labor and Employment

- *County and City Data Book,* detailed socioeconomic and demographic data for States, counties, and cities, selected years 1976-82, 2328–1
- Employment change by industry div, civilian labor force, and unemployment and rates, by region and State, 1983, article, 6722–1.454
- Employment, unemployment, and labor force, by demographic and employment characteristics, State, and for 30 metro areas and 11 large cities, 1983, annual rpt, 6744–7
- Small business and total employment, income, and number of firms, by State, industry, and size class, selected years 1967-83, annual rpt, 9764–6.1

Law Enforcement

- Assaults, murders, and other deaths of law enforcement officers, by circumstances, level of govt, agency, victim and offender characteristics, and location, 1983, annual rpt, 6224–3
- Bombing (explosive and incendiary) incidents, damage, injuries, and deaths, by target, State, and circumstances, 1983, annual rpt, 6224–5
- Crimes, arrests by offender characteristics, and rates, by offense, and law enforcement employees, by population size and jurisdiction, 1970s-83, annual rpt, 6224–2

Population

- Census of Population, 1980: Asian and Pacific Islander population, by detailed race and State, supplementary rpt, 2535–1.15
- Census of Population, 1980: detailed socioeconomic characteristics, by county, city, and inside-outside SMSAs and central cities, US summary rpt, 2531–3.1
- Census of Population, 1980: Indian and Alaska Native population and housing occupancy, by reservation, Alaska Native village, and other Indian area, supplementary rpt, 2535–1.16

Index by Categories

BY CITY

County and City Data Book, detailed socioeconomic and demographic data for States, counties, and cities, selected years 1976-82, 2328–1

Income (personal) totals, by region, census div, and State, quarterly article, 2702–1.32

Income of households, families, and persons, by detailed socioeconomic characteristics and region, 1982, annual Current Population Rpt, 2546–6.39

Metro and nonmetro areas and central cities population size and change by census div, and growth of areas with large black and aged populations, 1970-82, 2328–47

Older persons by demographic, socioeconomic, and health characteristics, selected years 1900-81 and projected to 2050, Current Population Rpt, 2546–2.125

Older persons sociodemographic characteristics, and Fed Govt program participation and funding, 1983 with trends and projections 1900-2060, annual rpt, 25144–3.1

Population estimates and projections, by region and State, Current Population Rpt series, 2546–3

Population size and components of change, by region, census div, and State, 1970s-83 with projections to 2050, annual Current Population Rpt, 2546–2.119

Voting age population for Nov 1984 election, by sex, age, race, Hispanic origin, region, and State, and percent voting during 1930-82, Current Population Rpt, 2546–3.129

Prices and Cost of Living

Electric power rate schedules, by user type, utility, and city, Jan 1984, annual rpt, 3164–40

Energy residential bills and departures from normal by fuel type, and heating and cooling degree days by State, by census div, monthly rpt, 2152–11, 2152–12

Natural gas average price, by end-use sector, census div, and State, 1982-83 with trends from 1978, annual article, 3162–4.413

Public Welfare and Social Security

Disability Insurance beneficiaries sociodemographic and medical characteristics, 1977-79, annual rpt, 4744–20

Medicare admissions to hospitals and other facilities, and enrollee reimbursement claims, by beneficiary type, 1966-83, annual rpt, 4744–3.7

Medicare and Medicaid eligibility, participation, covered services and use, and reimbursements and payments, various periods 1966-82, annual rpt, 4654–1

Medicare enrollment, reimbursement, and use and covered charges by type of service, by State and census div, 1978-82, 4658–8

Medicare facilities and services use, covered charges, and reimbursements, by beneficiary type and area of residence, series, 4656–1

Science and Technology

Computer specialists sociodemographic, educational, and employment characteristics, and Fed Govt support by agency, 1978, biennial Current Population Rpt, 2546–2.124

Employment of scientists and engineers at universities and colleges and federally funded R&D centers, by field, sex, State, and instn, Jan 1983 and selected trends from 1967, annual survey, 9627–11

Engineers sociodemographic, educational, and employment characteristics, and Federal support by agency, 1978, Current Population Rpt, 2546–2.121

Enrollment in grad science and engineering fields of study, financial support, and other student and instn characteristics, 1975-82, annual survey, 9627–7

R&D and science-related Fed Govt funding to higher education and nonprofit instns, by field, instn, agency, and State, FY82, annual rpt, 9627–17

R&D expenditures by higher education instns and federally funded centers, by field, source of funds, instn, and State, FY82, annual rpt, 9627–13

R&D expenditures of higher education instns, by source, field of science, census div, and State, 1972-83, biennial rpt, 9627–24.1

R&D Fed Govt funding for all performers, by field and supporting agency, selected years FY60-84, annual rpt, 9627–20

Veterans Affairs

Population of veterans and ratio to civilians, by census div and for 10 States with largest change, 1970 and 1980, 9926–4.7

BY CITY

Agriculture and Food

Argentina grain production, exports by firm, storage by facility type and port, and shipments to ports by mode of transport, by grain type, selected years 1954-81, 1528–185

Cotton prices at selected spot markets, futures prices at NYC exchange, and CCC loan rates, 1983/84 with some trends from 1920, annual rpt, 1309–2

Cotton prices in 8 spot markets, futures prices at NYC exchange, farm prices, and CCC loan stocks, monthly rpt, 1309–1

Dairy marketing and price data for selected cities, States, and regions, 1983, annual rpt, 1317–1

Fish landings by species and State, and value at leading ports and disposition, 1970s-83, annual rpt, 2164–1.1

Fruit and vegetable shipments, and arrivals in 23 US and 5 Canada cities, by mode of transport and State or country of origin, 1983, annual rpt series, 1311–4

Grain stocks by region and market city, and grain inspected for export, by type, weekly rpt, 1313–4

Molasses (feed) production, wholesale prices by market area, and US imports by customs district and country, weekly rpt, 1311–16

Banking, Finance, and Insurance

Banks requiring FDIC disbursement, depositors, deposits, and disbursements, by location and disbursement reason, 1983 with trends from 1934, annual rpt, 9294–1.2

Fed Financing Bank holdings and transactions, monthly press release, 9322–1

Fed Home Loan Bank System members, with assets of S&Ls, by instn, city, and State, 1983, annual listing, 9314–5

New England States, FHLB 1st District member savings instns, locations, and financial condition, 1984, annual listing, 9304–26

North Central States, FHLB 8th District member S&Ls, locations, assets, and savings, 1984, annual listing, 9304–9

North Central States tax exempt industrial revenue bonds issued by local govts, by Fed Reserve 7th District State, county, and city, with interest rate spread, 1975-80, 9375–13.2

Western States depository instns financial activity by State, and large commercial banks by city, Fed Reserve 10th District, monthly rpt, 9381–11

Western States, FHLB 11th District member S&L offices, locations, savings balances, and accounts, quarterly listing, 9302–20

Communications and Transportation

Air traffic levels at FAA-operated control facilities, by airport and State, FY83, annual rpt, 7504–27

Airline and general aviation accident circumstances, severity, and causes, for US operations of domestic and foreign aircraft, periodic rpt, 9612–1

Airline deregulation in 1978, effect on industry operations and finances, air traffic patterns, and CAB programs, various periods FY76-84, 9148–56

Airline deregulation in 1978, traffic and service changes by city, with market shares, fares, and load factors, quarterly rpt, 9142–42

Airline passenger and cargo traffic, and departures by aircraft type, by airline and US and foreign airport, 1982, annual rpt, 7504–35

Airport financing by source, bond issues by region, and airport operations, by airport and operator type, FY75-83 and projected to FY93, 26306–6.75

Airport planning and dev project grants of Fed Govt, by sponsor, airport, and location, periodic press release series, 7506–8

Airport size and safety, and accidents at or near airports by circumstance, for total and selected airports, various periods 1964-81, 9618–12

Aviation activity, detailed data on aircraft, air traffic, air carriers, personnel, airports, and FAA operations, 1974-83, annual rpt, 7504–1

Bridges and share structurally and functionally deficient, by bridge and city characteristics, region, and city, 1980, 10048–60

Bus industry collective ratemaking and regulatory reform impacts on operations, finances, and services to older persons and rural areas by State, 1970s-83, 14828–2

Coast Guard search and rescue activities, by district, station, and rescue vessel, FY83 and projected FY88, annual rpt, 7404–2

Eastern US local govt hwy expenditures, per capita aid, and bridges by condition, by selected county and city, various periods 1965-80, article, 9377–1.405

Railroad accidents, circumstances, severity, and railroad involved, quarterly rpt, 9612–3

Railroad accidents investigated by Fed Railroad Admin, casualties, damage, and circumstances, 1982, annual rpt, 7604–3

Ships and tonnage entering and clearing US Customs, by district and port of entry, 1983, annual rpt, 2424–7

BY CITY

Subway systems mileage by US city, electrified railroad mileage by country, and trolley and motor bus capital and operating costs, selected years 1960-80, 3006–7.7

Tanker offloading ports accessible to tankers of 200,000 deadweight tons and larger, by country, Jan 1984, annual rpt, 244–5.10

Taxicab licenses, density, fares, license prices, and deregulation effects, by selected city, various dates 1970-84, 9406–1.37

Telephone population, by type of use in large exchange areas, 1982, annual rpt, 9284–6.2

Transit system financial and operating data, by mode, function, fleet size, and individual system, FY82, annual rpt, 7884–4

Transit system mgmt training funded by Urban Mass Transportation Admin, participant characteristics and career impact, 1970-79, 7888–60

Transit system operations, tax burden related to ridership, fares, and govt funding, for selected States and cities, 1950s-82, reprint, 7888–59

Travel to and from US on US and foreign flag air carriers, by country, world area, and US port, monthly rpt, 7302–2

TV channels allocation and licensing status, for commercial and noncommercial UHF and VHF TV by market and community, as of Dec 1983, semiannual rpt, 9282–6

Education

- Fed Govt education block grants, State allocations by program and selected school district, FY82-84 and trends from FY60, hearing, 21408–75
- Higher education instns, type, location, enrollment, and student charges, by State and congressional district, 1983/84, biennial listing, 4844–11
- School employees health insurance plans in 7 cities, as of 1980, hearing, 21788–136

Energy Resources and Demand

- Alaska electric power capacity and generation by fuel type, and marketing, by utility, type of ownership, and location, 1983, annual rpt, 3214–2
- Bonneville Power Admin sales, revenues, and prices, by class of customer and individual purchaser, 1983, semiannual rpt, 3222–1
- Buildings (commercial) energy use under alternative heating, cooling, and air conditioning systems and control strategies, for 6 cities, 1983 rpt, 2218–68
- Bunker fuels, oil, and coal laden in US on vessels engaged in foreign trade, by port, monthly rpt, 2422–5
- Coal dev plans on Fed Govt lease lands in 12 regions under Fed Coal Mgmt Program, environmental and socioeconomic impacts to 2000, final statement series, 5726–4
- Coal purchases of Fed Govt, quality control analyses by mine and location, FY82-83, annual rpt, 3004–15
- Columbia River system electric power sales, by customer, FY83, annual rpt, 3224–1
- Electric power plant (nuclear and coal-fired) construction itemized cost estimates, and investment per kilowatt for 20 cities, 1980s-95, 9638–52
- Electric utility fuel cost, quality, use, receipts, and stocks, and power plant production, by energy source, State and utility, quarterly rpt, 3162–39

Foreign countries electric current characteristics, by country and selected city, 1984 rpt, 2018–8

- Housing (multifamily rental) energy use and costs, conservation effect on rental marketing, and effect of utility bill payment methods on conservation efforts, 1970s-80s, 3308–73
- Housing electricity and gas costs for 306 cities, by utility, with climatological data, fall 1982, 3308–67
- Nuclear reactors for domestic use and export by function, with owner, operating characteristics, and location, Apr 1984, semiannual listing, 3002–5
- Oil (Alaskan) potential exports to Japan, costs and benefits, with background data on oil prices, Pacific Basin supply/demand, and tankers, various periods 1918-99, hearings, 25388–45
- Oil refinery locations and capacities in US and territories, by company, Jan 1983, annual rpt, 3164–2
- OPEC oil refining capacity and production by city, and oil use and exports, by member, with comparisons to other countries, projected 1985-90, hearings, 25368–133.1
- Rural Electrification Admin financed electric power plants, with location, capacity, and owner, as of Jan 1984, annual listing, 1244–6
- Southeastern Power Admin sales by customer, plants, and capacity, and financial statements of Southeastern Fed Power Program, FY83, annual rpt, 3234–1
- Southwestern Fed Power System financial statements, electric power sales by customer, and project capacity, production, and costs, FY83, annual rpt, 3244–1
- TVA electric power purchases of municipal and cooperative distributors, and prices and consumption by distributor and consumer sector, monthly rpt, 9802–1
- TVA power distributors detailed operating and financial ratios, for individual municipal and cooperative distributors, FY79-83, annual rpt, 9804–19
- Western Area Power Admin operations by plant, financial statements, and electric power sales by customer, FY83, annual rpt, 3254–1

Geography and Climate

- Climatological data for surface and upper air, averages by foreign and US station, monthly rpt, 2152–4
- Climatological data for 284 US and outlying stations, for period of record through 1982, annual rpt, 2154–8
- Climatological data for 945 cities, *County and City Data Book,* 1980, 2328–1
- Earthquake and other ground motion intensity measured on USGS Natl Strong-Motion Network by station, and sources of foreign and US info, 1981, annual rpt, 5664–14
- Earthquake intensity, damage, and deaths, by location for major earthquakes since 1755, and hazard areas and natl reduction program activities, as of 1984, 5668–73
- Flood (flash) deaths, by flood circumstances, type of warning, cause of death, and location, Sept 1969-May 1981, article, 4102–1.406

Index by Categories

- Heating degree days, for 45 cities and total US, cumulative for season, weekly rpt, 3162–32.2
- Hurricanes and tropical storms in North Atlantic and Caribbean area, paths, surveillance, deaths, property damage, and landfall probabilities by city, 1983, annual rpt, 2184–7
- Precipitation and temperature outlook for US and Northern Hemisphere, and by US and selected foreign weather stations, semimonthly rpt, 2182–1
- Tidal current tables, daily time and velocity by station for North America and Asia coasts, 1985, annual rpt, 2174–1
- Tide height and time daily at worldwide coastal points, 1985 predictions, annual rpt series, 2174–2
- Weather conditions and effect on agriculture, by US region, State, and city, and world area, weekly rpt, 2152–2
- Weather stations of Natl Weather Service, locations and regular observations made, 1984 annual listing, 2184–5
- Weather stations of Upper Air Observational Network, by US and foreign location, 1984 annual listing, 2184–6

Government and Defense

- Census of Govts, 1982: city govt revenues by source, expenditures by function, debt, and assets, by State and city, 2457–4
- Census of Govts, 1982: local govt employment by function, payroll, and average earnings, for individual counties, cities, and school and special districts, 2455–1
- Census of Govts, 1982: properties, govt-assessed value, sales, and tax rates, by property type, State, SMSA, county, and city, 2453–1
- Commerce Dept regional center mgmt assistance operations, assessment, and procurement authority, by subagency, regional rpt series, 2006–4
- *County and City Data Book,* detailed socioeconomic and demographic data for States, counties, and cities, selected years 1976-82, 2328–1
- DOD base support costs by function, and personnel and acreage by installation, by service branch, FY85, annual rpt, 3504–11
- DOD contract and in-house commercial activities costs and work-years, by service branch, defense agency, State, and installation, FY83, annual rpt, 3544–25
- DOD prime contract awards, by individual contractor, service branch, State and city, and country, FY83, annual listing, 3544–22
- DOD prime contract awards for R&D to educational and nonprofit instns and Federal agencies, by instn and location, FY83, annual listing, 3544–17
- DOD prime contract awards in labor surplus areas, by service branch, State, and area, 1st half FY84, semiannual rpt, 3542–19
- Employment and payroll of city govts, by function and population size, for 447 largest cities, Oct 1983, annual rpt, 2466–1.1
- Fed Govt aid to State and local areas, by type of payment, State, county, and city, FY83, annual rpt, 2464–3.2
- Firefighters death benefits under workers compensation and local pension plans, by State and city, hearing, 21348–94

Index by Categories

BY CITY

Govt finances, by level of govt, State, and for large cities and counties, 1981-83, annual rpt series, 2466–2

Govt revenues by source, expenditures by function, debt, and cash and security holdings, for 447 cities, 1981-82, annual rpt, 2466–2.1

Immigration, and alien residents, workers, visitors, deportations, and naturalizations, by country of birth, FY81, annual rpt, 6264–2

Local govt spending, reliance on State aid and local taxes by type, and excise tax growth by State, selected years FY57-83, article, 10042–1.403

Navy procurement, by Navy field office, FY83, annual rpt, 3804–13.2

Property (real) of Fed Govt, leased property inventory and rental costs, worldwide summary by location and agency, Sept 1983, annual rpt, 9454–10

Public works capital needs and financing, by project type, level of govt, and selected jurisdiction, 1970s-83 and projected to 2000, hearing, 23848–181

Regulatory growth of Fed Govt effect on local compliance costs and funding, local officials assessment, and comparisons to State govt regulations, 1970s-82 with trends from 1900, 10048–58

Revenue sharing payments to States, local govts, Indian tribes, and Alaska Native villages, and entitlement computation data, FY84, series, 8066–1

Tax burden for average family by income level and selected city, and tax rates by selected jurisdiction, by type of tax, 1982, 10046–8.2

Tax collections of Fed Govt by type of tax, procedures, and interest forgone through processing delay, for selected locations, FY81-82, GAO rpt, 26119–55

Travel expenses of Fed Govt employees on official business, and reimbursement rates, for high rate cities, 1983, annual rpt, 9454–16

USIA info center and reading room operations, by world region, country, and city, FY83, annual rpt, 9854–4

Health and Vital Statistics

Alcohol, Drug Abuse, and Mental Health Admin research grants, awards, and fellowships by recipient, FY83, annual listing, 4044–13

Births and birth rates, by detailed demographic characteristics and geographic area, 1979 and trends, US Vital Statistics annual rpt, 4144–1

Cancer Natl Inst contracts and grants, by contractor, instn, State, and city, FY83, annual listing, 4474–28

County and City Data Book, detailed socioeconomic and demographic data for States, counties, and cities, selected years 1976-82, 2328–1

Deaths and death rates, by detailed geographic area, cause, and demographic characteristics, 1979, US Vital Statistics annual rpt, 4144–3

Deaths due to cold weather and related causes, by age, race, State, and city, selected periods 1962-83, 21148–30

Deaths recorded in 121 cities, weekly rpt, 4202–1

HHS aid to each State and local govt or private instn, amount obligated, funding agency, and program, FY83, annual listing, 4004–3

Indian and Alaska Native health program activities, and funding for scholarships, care services, and facilities construction, by city, FY82, annual rpt, 4104–11

Navy medical facility use by active and retired military personnel, dependents, and others, by facility and type, quarterly rpt, 3802–1

NIH grants and awards for R&D, training, construction, and medical libraries, by location and recipient, FY83, annual listings, 4434–7

Tuberculosis cases, deaths, and treatment, by demographic characteristics, State, and city, 1982 and trends from 1953, annual rpt, 4204–2

Venereal disease cases reported and epidemiologic activities, by region, State, and large city, 1982, annual rpt, 4204–14

Housing and Construction

Appalachian States, FHLB 5th District housing vacancy rates for single and multifamily units and mobile homes, by ZIP code, annual metro area rpt series, 9304–27

Bond tax-exempt issues by purpose, and Fed Govt mortgage bond revenue losses and borrower characteristics, selected years 1971-85, hearings, 21788–135

Bond tax-exempt issues for home mortgage subsidy, Fed Govt costs, and loans, mortgage value, and borrowers by jurisdiction, by borrower income, Dec 1981-July 1982, GAO rpt, 26113–127

Census of Housing, 1980: occupancy and unit characteristics of SMSAs and central cities, by race, Hispanic origin, and city, State and SMSA rpt series, 2473–1

Census of Population and Housing, 1980: detailed population and housing characteristics, by county, city, and census tract, State and SMSA rpt series, 2551–2

Community Dev Block Grants admin, allocation, and family social benefits, effect of policy changes to increase local admin responsibility, for 10 cities, as of 1982, 5188–105

County and City Data Book, detailed socioeconomic and demographic data for States, counties, and cities, selected years 1976-82, 2328–1

Discrimination in housing, complaints collected through HUD-sponsored fair housing study in 9 cities, with nationwide comparisons, 1978/79-1980/81, 5188–102

Home mortgage defaults, single family homes acquired by HUD and disposition by city, monthly rpt, 5142–31

Home mortgage terms on conventional loans by eligibility for Fed Govt secondary purchase, 1983, and alternative eligibility limits for 28 cities, 1984, GAO rpt, 26113–135

HUD programs for housing finance, construction, and improvement, periodic press releases, 5006–3

HUD rental rehabilitation grants for low- and moderate-income housing, by community, 1984 press release, 5006–3.33

HUD rental rehabilitation projects, local funding and Section 8 rent supplements for 22 States and 275 communities, 1984 press release, 5006–3.30

Low-rent housing project financing notes sold by local authorities, terms and individual issuers and purchasers, monthly listing, 5142–43

New Communities program of HUD, activities, costs, land sales, and community and population characteristics, for 13 communities, 1970s-83, 5188–107

New housing units authorized, by public and private ownership, by region, div, State, selected MSA, and 4,700 permit-issuing places, monthly rpt, 2382–5

New housing units authorized, by public and private ownership, State, and permit-issuing place, 1983, annual rpt, 2384–2

North Central States, FHLB 7th District housing vacancy rates for single and multifamily units and mobile homes, by ZIP code, annual metro area rpt series, 9304–18

Older and handicapped persons housing projects construction and rehabilitation loans of HUD, FY84, annual listing, 5004–6

Public building construction, acquisition, and alteration proposals, costs and tenure by city and project, as of 1983, hearings, 25328–23

Public building construction, alteration, and leasing projects, description and cost by location, Dec 1983, annual listing, 9454–12

Real estate broker industry structure and practices, sales commissions, and broker and consumer attitudes, selected years 1975-81, 9408–48

South Central States, FHLB 9th District housing vacancy rates for single and multifamily units and mobile homes by ZIP code, annual metro area rpt series, 9304–19

Urban Dev Action Grant awards, private and public investment, and jobs, housing units, and taxes generated, by city and project, FY83, annual rpt, 5124–5

Urban Dev Action Grant awards to local areas, preliminary approvals, with project descriptions, private investment, and jobs and taxes to be created, by city, quarterly press release series, 5002–7

Western States, FHLB 11th District housing vacancy rates for single and multifamily units and mobile homes, by ZIP code, annual metro area rpt series, 9304–20

Western States, FHLB 12th District housing vacancy rates for single and multifamily units and mobile homes, by ZIP code, annual metro area rpt series, 9304–21

Industry and Commerce

California business failures, plant closings, layoffs, and relocations, by plant, industry, county, and city, 1980-83, hearing, 21348–84.1

County and City Data Book, detailed socioeconomic and demographic data for States, counties, and cities, selected years 1976-82, 2328–1

Enterprise zone and urban revitalization projects of State and local govts, effect on business and employment in selected areas, various dates 1972-83, hearing, 21788–140

Exports and imports of US (airborne), by world area and US customs district and city, monthly rpt, 2422–8

BY CITY

Exports and imports of US, by commodity group, world area, selected country, US coastal area and port, and mode of transport, with seasonal adjustments, monthly rpt, 2422–9

Great Lakes trade, by SITC 3-digit commodity, port, vessel type, world area, and country, 1982, annual rpt, 7744–3

Retail trade census, 1982: employment, establishments, sales, and payroll, by SIC 2- to 4-digit kind of business, SMSA, and retail district, State rpt series, 2401–1

Retail trade census, 1982: employment, establishments, sales, and payroll, by SIC 2- to 4-digit kind of business, SMSA, county, and city, State rpt series, 2397–1

Retail trade sales and inventories, by kind of business, region, census div, and selected State, SMSA, and city, and seasonal adjustments, monthly rpt, 2413–3

Service industry census, 1982: employment, establishments, receipts, and payroll, by SIC 2- to 4-digit kind of business, SMSA, county, and city, State rpt series, 2391–1

Small Business Admin loans, contract awards, and surety bonds, by firm, State, and city, FY83, annual rpt, 9764–1.2

Tariff Schedules of US, Annotated, classifications and rates of duty for detailed imported commodities, and codes for ports and foreign countries, 1985 edition, 9886–13

Technology-intensive industry employment and establishments by industry and selected location, and venture capital investments by source, 1970s-82, 26358–107

Tennessee Valley industrial dev and effects on employment, investment, and TVA power demand, by location and company, 1983, annual rpt, 9804–3

Urban area economic distress index and components, for 153 cities, 1975 and 1980, article, 9373–1.413

Virgin Islands economic censuses, 1982: employment, establishments, payroll, and receipts, by SIC 1- to 4-digit industry, island, and city, 2593–1

Waterborne commerce of US (domestic and foreign), freight by commodity, traffic, and passengers, by port and waterway, 1982, annual rpt, 3754–3

Waterborne containerized cargo carried over principal trade routes, by flag of vessel, port, and US coastal district, 1982, annual rpt, 7704–8

Waterborne exports and imports of US, by type of service, customs district, port, and world area, monthly rpt, 2422–7

Waterborne trade of US, by type of service, commodity, country, route, and US port, 1982, annual rpt, 7704–2

Wholesale trade census, 1982: employment, establishments, finances, and operations, by SIC 2- to 4-digit kind of business, SMSA, county, and city, State rpt series, 2405–1

Labor and Employment

Building trades union wages, average hourly rates for 10 port cities, 1982, annual rpt, 7704–12.2

California business failures, plant closings, layoffs, and relocations, by plant, industry, county, and city, 1980-83, hearing, 21348–84.1

Collective bargaining calendar for Southeast US, 1984, annual rpt, 6946–1.68

County and City Data Book, detailed socioeconomic and demographic data for States, counties, and cities, selected years 1976-82, 2328–1

Employment and earnings, detailed data, monthly rpt, 6742–2.7

Employment, earnings, and hours, by selected SIC 1- to 4-digit industry, State, and for 278 major labor areas, 1939-83, annual rpt, 6744–5

Employment, unemployment, and labor force, by demographic and employment characteristics, State, and for 30 metro areas and 11 large cities, 1983, annual rpt, 6744–7

Job Training Partnership Act performance standards guide, and CETA job placements, unemployment rates, and average wages, by city or county, FY82, 6408–59.1

Labor unions reporting to Labor Dept, parent bodies and locals by State, city, and country, 1983 listing, 6468–17

Unemployment, labor surplus areas eligible for preferential Fed Govt contracts, and labor force data for 150 major labor markets, monthly listing, 6402–1

Law Enforcement

Aircraft hijackings, on-board explosions, other crimes against civil aviation, and circumstances, US and worldwide, 1931-83, annual rpt, 7504–31

Alcohol, Tobacco, and Firearms Bur activities nationwide and in 20 cities, funding, and jobs to be transferred to Customs and Secret Service, 1979-82, hearings, 21528–55

Assaults, murders, and other deaths of law enforcement officers, by circumstances, level of govt, agency, victim and offender characteristics, and location, 1983, annual rpt, 6224–3

Crime Index by population size and region, and offenses known to police by large city, Jan-June 1984, semiannual rpt, 6222–1

Crimes, arrests by offender characteristics, and rates, by offense, and law enforcement employees, by population size and jurisdiction, 1970s-83, annual rpt, 6224–2

Criminal case processing from arrest to sentencing, cases and processing time by disposition, dismissal reason, and offense, for 14 cities, 1979, 6066–22.1

Drug (illegal) treatment program and emergency room admissions in major cities, by drg type, 1982, annual rpt, 15894–1

Drug Enforcement Organized Crime Task Forces, funding and staff by agency, region, and city, as of FY83, GAO rpt, 26119–52

Federal Prison Industry locations, FY83, annual rpt, 6244–3

Pretrial citation release use, cost savings for law enforcement agencies, and failures to appear in court, by offense and selected jurisdiction, 1970s-82, 6068–187

Youth gang criminal activity control, police assessments, staff, and programs in 27 cities, with juvenile arrests nationwide for Crime Index offenses, 1980-81, 6068–175

Natural Resources, Environment, and Pollution

Air pollutant and radiation indoor levels by emissions source, and household exposure

Index by Categories

and health effects by pollutant type, various periods 1966-83, hearings, 21708–102

Air pollutant metal levels, by monitoring site, State, and urban-rural location, 1977-79, last issue of annual rpt, 9194–10

Air pollution levels for 6 pollutants, and measurements exceeding natl standards, by site, 1983, annual rpt, 9194–5

Air pollution levels for 132 hazardous organic chemicals, by urban-rural location, city, and for areas with many potential sources, 1970-80, 9198–109

Dams, reservoirs, and hydroelectric plants, listing of major foreign and US structures with location and characteristics, as of June 1983, 5828–13

Environmental quality, pollutant discharge by type and source, and EPA protection activities and funding, 1970s-83, biennial regional rpt series, 9184–15

Great Lakes basin pollutant discharges by source, and control program activities, 1983 annual rpt, 14644–1

Nevada and other nuclear test sites, radionuclide concentrations in nearby air, water, and biota and in milk from western States, by location, 1983, annual rpt, 9234–4

New York State area snow depth and water equivalent, by site, winter 1982/83, annual rpt, 2184–2

Northeastern US water supply, precipitation and stream runoff by station, monthly rpt, 2182–3

Nuclear power and weapons policy, fuel supply/demand, waste disposal and siting, environmental effects of radiation, and public attitudes, 1970s-82 with projections to 2000, 3008–88

Nuclear power plant siting population criteria and estimated compliance of selected regions and sites, 1983 rpt, 9638–54

Radiation and radionuclide concentrations in air, water, and milk, results of EPA and other monitoring programs, by State and site, quarterly rpt, 9232–2

Radioactive strontium fallout, monitoring results for 67 sites worldwide, quarterly 1976-82 with trends from 1958, annual rpt, 3404–12

Southwestern US atmospheric concentrations of sulfur dioxide by city or site, and copper smelter emissions by plant, selected years 1974-82, hearing, 21448–31

Uranium ore tailings at inactive mills and DOE remedial action program activities by site, and program funding, FY84, annual rpt, 3354–9

Water conservation, residential programs and savings of water and energy for selected cities and suburbs, 1980-83, 5188–109

Water from urban runoff, quality, pollutant concentrations, and control cost-effectiveness, with monitoring sites rainfall and other characteristics, by city and region, 1978-83, 9208–122

Water supply and quality in streams and lakes, and groundwater levels in wells, by drainage basin, 1980, annual State rpt series, 5666–12

Water supply and quality in streams and lakes, and groundwater levels in wells, by drainage basin, 1981, annual State rpt series, 5666–16

Index by Categories

BY COUNTY

Water supply and quality in streams and lakes, and groundwater levels in wells, by drainage basin, 1982, annual State rpt series, 5666–20

Water supply and quality in streams and lakes, and groundwater levels in wells, by drainage basin, 1983, annual State rpt series, 5666–10

Water supply in US and Canada, streamflow, well and reservoir levels, and dissolved solids and temperature in 6 US rivers, by station, monthly rpt, 5662–3

Western US water supply, snow depth measurements by station, State rpt series, 1266–3

Population

Census of Population and Housing, 1980: detailed population and housing characteristics, by county, city, and census tract, State and SMSA rpt series, 2551–2

Census of Population, 1980: detailed socioeconomic characteristics, by county, city, and inside-outside SMSAs and central cities, State rpt series, 2531–3

Census of Population, 1980: Indian and Alaska Native population and housing occupancy, by reservation, Alaska Native village, and other Indian area, supplementary rpt, 2535–1.16

County and City Data Book, detailed socioeconomic and demographic data for States, counties, and cities, selected years 1976-82, 2328–1

Developing countries disaster preparedness and summary sociodemographic, political, and economic data, country rpt series, 9916–2

Foreign and US population and land area of major cities and metro areas, for US, France, Japan, and UK, 1940s-82, 26358–97

Homeless population and characteristics, and temporary shelter operations, use, and user characteristics, by region and selected city, 1983, 5188–108

Homeless population and characteristics, and temporary shelter operations, use, and user characteristics, for selected cities, various periods 1979-84, hearing, 21248–85

Population size, Apr 1980 and July 1982, and per capita income, 1979 and 1981, by county and city, State Current Population Rpt series, 2546–11

Population size of top 25 cities, 1980 and 1982, press release, 2328–46

Prices and Cost of Living

CPI and PPI current statistics, Monthly Labor Review, 6722–1.5

CPI for selected areas, 1950-82, annual rpt, 6724–1.7

CPI planned 1987 revisions to urban areas sampled and index publication schedule, 1984 press release, 6888–29

Electric power average monthly residential bills, by city, *County and City Data Book,* 1982, 2328–1

Electric power rate schedules, by user type, utility, and city, Jan 1984, annual rpt, 3164–40

Electric power retail prices, by end-use sector in 40 large cities, monthly rpt, 3162–35

Electric power retail prices, by end-use sector in 40 large cities, 1979-83, annual rpt, 3164–11.3

Food price indexes (consumer and producer) and retail prices for selected items, and CPI for 25 cities, 1963-83, annual rpt, 1544–4.5

Foreign and US food prices for 15 items in DC and 15 foreign capital cities, weekly press release, periodic table, 1922–4

Foreign and US oil prices, tax, and customs duty, by refined product and major city, July 1983 and Jan 1984, annual rpt, 3164–50.4

Foreign living costs, State Dept indexes, housing allowances, and hardship differential rates by country and major city, quarterly rpt, 6862–1

Public Welfare and Social Security

AFDC eligibility under Omnibus Budget Reconciliation Act, effect on caseloads and recipient benefits and living costs, 1981-83, GAO rpt, 26131–11

Child Support Enforcement Program cost savings to AFDC, Federal and State govts, and public assistance programs, by State and selected city or county, FY76-85, 4748–37

Food aid programs of Fed Govt and others, funding, participant characteristics, and nutrition and poverty data, 1970s-83, 028–20

Food purchases for domestic aid programs, by commodity, firm, and shipping point or destination, weekly rpt, 1302–3

Recreation and Leisure

Fishing (ocean sport) effort and catch, and Natl Marine Fisheries Service tagging and research activity, by species and location, 1983, annual rpt, 2164–7

Museum grants of Natl Foundation on Arts and Humanities, by instn, State, and city, FY84, annual rpt series, 9564–6

Science and Technology

Computer systems and equipment of Fed Govt, inventory by manufacturer, type, agency, and location, FY83, last issue of annual rpt, 9454–4

Veterans Affairs

Health care for veterans, patients, visits, costs, and operating beds, by district and individual VA and contract facility, monthly rpt, 9922–5

Medical facilities of VA, sharing agreement contracts, services, and costs by region and facility, FY83, annual rpt, 9924–18

Medicine and Surgery Dept of VA, trainees by detailed program and city, FY83, annual rpt, 9924–21

Physicians, dentists, and nurses of VA, by age, selected employment characteristics, and VA district, quarterly rpt, 9922–11

BY COUNTY

Agriculture and Food

Agricultural Stabilization and Conservation Service payment-in-kind acreage reduction program, ineligible participants and acreage, and estimated incorrect payments, by State and selected county, 1983, 1008–46

Census of Agriculture, 1982: farms, farmland, production and costs, and operator characteristics, preliminary State and county rpt series, 2330–1

Census of Agriculture, 1982: farms, farmland, production, finances, and operator characteristics, by county, final State rpt series, 2331–1

Cotton acreage planted, by State and county, and fiber quality, by variety, 1980-84, annual rpt, 1309–6

Cotton ginnings and production for 18 States, by county, 1983 crop, annual rpt, 2344–1

Cotton ginnings, by State and county, seasonal monthly rpt, 2342–2

County and City Data Book, detailed socioeconomic and demographic data for States, counties, and cities, selected years 1976-82, 2328–1

Farmland (US) owned by foreigners, acreage, value, and use, by State and county, and for 5 leading investor countries, 1983, annual rpt, 1584–3

Farmland acquisitions of foreigners, by State and county, before 1980 and during 1980-82, 1588–77

Soil conservation program policies of Fed Govt, attitudes of farmers and ranchers in 6 central US counties, 1982/83 survey, hearing, 25168–61

Banking, Finance, and Insurance

Bank deposits in commercial and mutual savings banks and in US branches of foreign banks, by account type, instn, State, SMSA, and county, June 1983, annual rpt, 9295–3

County and City Data Book, detailed socioeconomic and demographic data for States, counties, and cities, selected years 1976-82, 2328–1

Michigan bankruptcy filings, by filer type, moving history, income, creditor action, debt and asset type, credit status, exemptions claimed, and county, 1979-81, hearings, 21528–57.3

North Central States, FHLB 7th District insured S&Ls cost of funds, and savings flows and mortgage loans closed by SMSA, monthly rpt, 9302–5

North Central States tax exempt industrial revenue bonds issued by local govts, by Fed Reserve 7th District State, county, and city, with interest rate spread, 1975-80, 9375–13.2

Savings instns FSLIC-insured, offices, and savings deposits, by State, SMSA, and county, 1983, annual rpt, 9314–4

Western States, FHLB 11th District member S&L offices, locations, savings balances, and accounts, quarterly listing, 9302–20

Communications and Transportation

Aircraft registered with FAA, by type and characteristics of aircraft, carrier, make, State, and county, 1983, annual rpt, 7504–3

DC metro area Metrorail transit system, effect on commuting patterns, population, business, land use, and environment, series, 7306–8

Eastern US local govt hwy expenditures, per capita aid, and bridges by condition, by selected county and city, various periods 1965-80, article, 9377–1.405

Hwy expenditures and aid per capita related to local area characteristics, for 10 eastern counties, annual averages 1965-76, technical paper, 9377–9.9

Education

Impacted area schools, Fed Govt funding by county and State, FY83, annual rpt, 4804–10

BY COUNTY

Energy Resources and Demand

- Coal dev plans on Fed Govt lease lands in 12 regions under Fed Coal Mgmt Program, environmental and socioeconomic impacts to 2000, final statement series, 5726–4
- Coal employment and economic losses from utility fuel switching to meet emissions standards, with detail for counties in 5 States, 1970s-83 and projected to 1990, 21368–52
- Coal production and mines by county, prices, productivity, miners, reserves, and stocks, by mining method and State, 1982-83, annual rpt, 3164–25
- Coal purchases of Fed Govt, quality control analyses by mine and location, FY82-83, annual rpt, 3004–15
- Columbia River system electric power sales, by customer, FY83, annual rpt, 3224–1
- Electric power plants, by capacity, fuel used, unit type, region, State, and county, for plants added and retired, 1983 and planned through 1993, annual rpt, 3164–36
- Oil enhanced recovery technologies use and environmental impacts, by oil field, county, and State, 1970s-80 and projected to 2000, 3408–29
- Western Area Power Admin small-scale potential hydroelectric generation, site inventory, characteristics, and costs, by State and county, 1984 rpt, 3258–1

Geography and Climate

Flood (flash) deaths, by flood circumstances, type of warning, cause of death, and location, Sept 1969-May 1981, article, 4102–1.406

Government and Defense

- Census of Govts, 1982: county govt revenues by source, expenditures by function, debt, and assets, by State and county, 2457–3
- Census of Govts, 1982: employment, payrolls, and average earnings, by function, level of govt, State, county, population size, and inside-outside SMSAs, 2455–2
- Census of Govts, 1982: local govt employment by function, payroll, and average earnings, for individual counties, cities, and school and special districts, 2455–1
- Census of Govts, 1982: properties, govt-assessed value, sales, and tax rates, by property type, State, SMSA, county, and city, 2453–1
- *County and City Data Book,* detailed socioeconomic and demographic data for States, counties, and cities, selected years 1976-82, 2328–1
- DOD prime contract awards in labor surplus areas, by service branch, State, and area, 1st half FY84, semiannual rpt, 3542–19
- Economic Dev Admin loans and grants, by program, State, county, and project or recipient, FY83 and cumulative FY66-83, annual rpt, 2064–2
- Employment and payrolls of county govts, by function and population size, for 375 largest counties, Oct 1983, annual rpt, 2466–1.2
- Fed Govt aid to State and local areas, by type of payment, State, county, and city, FY83, annual rpt, 2464–3
- Fed Govt civilian employment, by location, agency, and pay system, 1982, biennial rpt, 9844–8

Govt finances, by level of govt, State, and for large cities and counties, 1981-83, annual rpt series, 2466–2

- Govt revenues by source, expenditures by function, debt, and cash and security holdings, for individual large counties, 1981-82, annual rpt, 2466–2.2
- Local govt employment and payroll, by function and level of govt in 75 SMSAs and 69 large counties, Oct 1983, annual rpt, 2466–1.3
- Louisiana property tax on forest, agricultural, and marsh lands, impact of change from market to use valuation by parish, 1977-78, 1208–206
- Public works capital needs and financing, by project type, level of govt, and selected jurisdiction, 1970s-83 and projected to 2000, hearing, 23848–181
- Revenue sharing payments to States, local govts, Indian tribes, and Alaska Native villages, and entitlement computation data, FY84, series, 8066–1
- Tax revenues, by level of govt, type of tax, State, and selected large counties, quarterly rpt, 2462–3

Health and Vital Statistics

- Births, by State, county, and city, 1979, US Vital Statistics annual rpt, 4144–1.2
- Cancer deaths and death rates, by body site, race, sex, State, and county, 1950-79, 4478–146
- *County and City Data Book,* detailed socioeconomic and demographic data for States, counties, and cities, selected years 1976-82, 2328–1
- Deaths and death rates, by detailed geographic area, cause, and demographic characteristics, 1979, US Vital Statistics annual rpt, 4144–3
- Deaths in 50 largest SMSAs and their component counties, 1979 US Vital Statistics annual rpt, 4144–2.1
- Health manpower and facilities data, by county and SMSA, users guide to computerized area resource file, 1983, annual rpt, 4114–11
- HHS aid to each State and local govt or private instn, amount obligated, funding agency, and program, FY83, annual listing, 4004–3
- Infant deaths in 50 largest SMSAs and their component counties, 1979, US Vital Statistics annual rpt, 4144–2.2
- Marriages, divorces, and rates, by detailed demographic and geographic characteristics, 1979 and trends, US Vital Statistics annual rpt, 4144–4
- Plague (bubonic and pneumonia-inducing) deaths, and cases by onset date, patient characteristics, and source, 1983 and trends from 1950, article, 4202–7.408
- Tuberculosis cases, deaths, and treatment, by demographic characteristics, State, and city, 1982 and trends from 1953, annual rpt, 4204–2

Housing and Construction

- Appalachian States, FHLB 5th District housing vacancy rates for single and multifamily units and mobile homes, by ZIP code, annual metro area rpt series, 9304–27
- Bond tax-exempt issues by purpose, and Fed Govt mortgage bond revenue losses and borrower characteristics, selected years 1971-85, hearings, 21788–135

Bond tax-exempt issues for home mortgage subsidy, Fed Govt costs, and loans, mortgage value, and borrowers by jurisdiction, by borrower income, Dec 1981-July 1982, GAO rpt, 26113–127

- California (southern) housing demand by county, prices and sales, and costs after homeowner tax deductions, 1970s-80, hearing, 21148–31
- Census of Population and Housing, 1980: detailed population and housing characteristics, by county, city, and census tract, State and SMSA rpt series, 2551–2
- *County and City Data Book,* detailed socioeconomic and demographic data for States, counties, and cities, selected years 1976-82, 2328–1
- HUD programs for housing finance, construction, and improvement, periodic press releases, 5006–3
- HUD rental rehabilitation grants for low- and moderate-income housing, by community, 1984 press release, 5006–3.33
- HUD rental rehabilitation projects, local funding and Section 8 rent supplements for 22 States and 275 communities, 1984 press release, 5006–3.30
- Low-rent housing project financing notes sold by local authorities, terms and individual issuers and purchasers, monthly listing, 5142–43
- New housing units authorized, by public and private ownership, by region, div, State, selected MSA, and 4,700 permit-issuing places, monthly rpt, 2382–5
- New housing units authorized, by public and private ownership, State, and permit-issuing place, 1983, annual rpt, 2384–2
- North Central States, FHLB 7th District housing vacancy rates for single and multifamily units and mobile homes, by ZIP code, annual metro area rpt series, 9304–18
- Property improvement and mobile home loans FHA-insured, by State and county, 1983 and cumulative from 1934, annual rpt, 5144–16
- South Central States, FHLB 9th District housing vacancy rates for single and multifamily units and mobile homes by ZIP code, annual metro area rpt series, 9304–19
- West Central States, FHLB 10th District housing vacancy rates for single and multifamily units and mobile homes, by ZIP code, annual metro area rpt series, 9304–22
- Western States, FHLB 11th District housing vacancy rates for single and multifamily units and mobile homes, by ZIP code, annual metro area rpt series, 9304–20
- Western States, FHLB 12th District housing vacancy rates for single and multifamily units and mobile homes, by ZIP code, annual metro area rpt series, 9304–21

Industry and Commerce

- California business failures, plant closings, layoffs, and relocations, by plant, industry, county, and city, 1980-83, hearing, 21348–84.1
- *County and City Data Book,* detailed socioeconomic and demographic data for States, counties, and cities, selected years 1976-82, 2328–1

Index by Categories

BY COUNTY

County Business Patterns: establishments, employees, and payrolls, by SIC 4-digit industry and county, 1981, annual State rpt series, 2326–8

County Business Patterns: establishments, employees, and payrolls, by SIC 4-digit industry and county, 1982, annual State rpt series, 2326–6

Manufacturing census, 1982: financial and operating data, by SIC 2- to 4-digit industry, State, SMSA, and county, preliminary census div rpt series, 2491–3

Metals resource recovery through leaching technologies, characteristics of methods and operations, regulation, and research, series, 5606–6

Minerals Yearbook, 1982, Vol 2 preprints: State reviews of production and sales by commodity, and business activity, annual rpt series, 5604–16

Minerals Yearbook, 1982, Vol 2: State reviews of production, sales, and firms, by commodity, and business activity, annual rpt, 5604–34

North Central States pulpwood production by county, imports, and individual mill capacity, by species, 1982, annual rpt, 1204–19

North Central States timber removals, and mill receipts and production, by species, product, and county, series, 1206–10

NYC metro area small business owners and accountants, assessment of economy, professional activities, and community problems, by county and industry div, 1983 survey, hearings, 21728–52.3

Retail trade census, 1982: employment, establishments, sales, and payroll, by SIC 2- to 4-digit kind of business, SMSA, county, and city, State rpt series, 2397–1

Service industry census, 1982: employment, establishments, receipts, and payroll, by SIC 2- to 4-digit kind of business, SMSA, county, and city, State rpt series, 2391–1

Tennessee Valley industrial dev and effects on employment, investment, and TVA power demand, by location and company, 1983, annual rpt, 9804–3

Wholesale trade census, 1982: employment, establishments, finances, and operations, by SIC 2- to 4-digit kind of business, SMSA, county, and city, State rpt series, 2405–1

Labor and Employment

California business failures, plant closings, layoffs, and relocations, by plant, industry, county, and city, 1980-83, hearing, 21348–84.1

County and City Data Book, detailed socioeconomic and demographic data for States, counties, and cities, selected years 1976-82, 2328–1

Job Training Partnership Act performance standards guide, and CETA job placements, unemployment rates, and average wages, by city or county, FY82, 6408–59.1

Michigan health funding, Blue Cross-Blue Shield and welfare participation, and unemployment, poverty, and food assistance by county, 1979-83, hearing, 21348–86

Trade adjustment assistance eligibility, reemployment opportunities, and worker characteristics, investigations of industries injured by import competition, series, 6406–9

Law Enforcement

Crimes, arrests by offender characteristics, and rates, by offense, and law enforcement employees, by population size and jurisdiction, 1970s-83, annual rpt, 6224–2

Pretrial citation release use, cost savings for law enforcement agencies, and failures to appear in court, by offense and selected jurisdiction, 1970s-82, 6068–187

Wiretapping authorizations by offense, costs, persons involved, arrests, trials, and convictions, 1983, annual rpt, 18204–7

Natural Resources, Environment, and Pollution

Air pollutant metal levels, by monitoring site, State, and urban-rural location, 1977-79, last issue of annual rpt, 9194–10

Air pollution levels for 6 pollutants, and measurements exceeding natl standards, by site, 1983, annual rpt, 9194–5

Coastal environmental characteristics, fish, wildlife, and use, and population socioeconomic data, for individual areas, series, 5506–4

Estuary environmental characteristics, fish, wildlife, uses, and mgmt, for individual estuaries, series, 5506–7

Forests (natl) and other lands under Forest Service mgmt, by forest and location, Sept 1983, annual rpt, 1204–2

Northeast pulpwood production and yield per acre, for 14 States, by county, 1981, TVA technical paper, 9806–2.38

Oregon and California lands revested by Land Mgmt Bur, acreage and allocations by county, FY83, annual rpt, 5724–1.2

Phosphate rock reserves in southeastern and northwestern US, by location, 1984 rpt, 5668–74

Public land acreage and use, and Land Mgmt Bur activities and finances, annual State rpt series, 5724–11

Soil survey county descriptions and maps of USDA, 1899-1983, annual listing, 1264–11

Southeastern US water supply and quality, with background socioeconomic data, for 8 States, 1960s-2020 with trends from 1930, 9208–119

Timber (roundwood) production and residue volume in South Carolina, by species, product type, State region, and county, 1977-81, 1208–203

Timber acreage and resources in New Mexico, by species, ownership class, and county 1977-80, series, 1206–23

Timber acreage and resources in North Carolina, by species, ownership class, and county, 1982-83, series, 1206–4

Timber acreage and resources in Washington State, by species, ownership class, and county, 1980, and harvest, 1950-79, series, 1206–28

Timber acreage in Michigan, by ownership, county, and forest and tree characteristics, 1980, 1208–192

Timber acreage, resources, and removals in Minnesota, by species, county, and ownership class, series, 1206–24

Timber acreage, volume, growth, removals, and production in Michigan, by ownership, county, and forest and tree characteristics, 1980, series, 1206–31

Timber growth, removals, products output, and forest ownership and industries in Northeast States, State rpt series, 1206–16

Timber resources and removals in Georgia, by species, ownership class, and county, 1981-83, series, 1206–26

Timber resources and removals in Northeast States, by species, ownership class, and county, State rpt series, 1206–12

TVA region wood residue production and use, by tree species group and wood residue type, for 44 counties, 1979, technical paper, 9806–2.36

Waterfowl harvested during hunting season, by species, State, and county, annual average for 1971-80, decennial rpt, 5508–18

Wisconsin forest fires damage to timber, crops, game, waterfowl, and recreation sites, economic effects by county, 1980-82, 1208–198

Population

Alabama rural black population, education, employment, health services, and economic status, for 16 counties, selected years 1970-81, 11048–180

Appalachian States population, by county, 1980-81, annual rpt, 9084–1

Census of Population and Housing, 1980: detailed population and housing characteristics, by county, city, and census tract, State and SMSA rpt series, 2551–2

Census of Population, 1980: detailed socioeconomic characteristics, by county, city, and inside-outside SMSAs and central cities, State rpt series, 2531–3

Census of Population, 1980: Indian and Alaska Native population and housing occupancy, by reservation, Alaska Native village, and other Indian area, supplementary rpt, 2535–1.16

Census of Population, 1980: migration since 1975, by county and selected demographic characteristics, supplementary rpt, 2535–1.14

County and City Data Book, detailed socioeconomic and demographic data for States, counties, and cities, selected years 1976-82, 2328–1

Income (personal) per capita and by source, and earnings by industry div, by State, MSA, and county, 1977-82, annual regional rpts, 2704–2

Income (personal) per capita and total, by State, MSA, and county, with metro-nonmetro totals, 1980-82, annual article, 2702–1.413

Population size and components of change, by MSA and county, 1980-82, annual State Current Population Rpt series, 2546–4

Population size, Apr 1980 and July 1982, and per capita income, 1979 and 1981, by county and city, State Current Population Rpt series, 2546–11

Public Welfare and Social Security

Child Support Enforcement Program cost savings to AFDC, Federal and State govts, and public assistance programs, by State and selected city or county, FY76-85, 4748–37

Food stamp program participation and coupons distributed, by region, State, and project area, quarterly rpt, 1362–6

Michigan health funding, Blue Cross-Blue Shield and welfare participation, and unemployment, poverty, and food assistance by county, 1979-83, hearing, 21348–86

BY COUNTY

OASDI benefits and beneficiaries, by type of benefit, State, outlying area, and county, Dec 1982, 4748–38

Supplemental Security Income benefits and beneficiaries, by type of eligibility, State, and county, Dec 1983, annual rpt, 4744–27

Veterans Affairs

VA program expenditures, by county and congressional district, FY83, annual rpt, 9924–14

BY FOREIGN COUNTRY

Agriculture and Food

Agricultural research of US, scientist years by topic, performing organization, State, and for 12 countries, FY82, annual rpt, 1744–2.2

Agricultural Statistics, 1983, annual rpt, 1004–1

Bean (dried) prices by State, and foreign and US production, use, stocks, and trade, weekly rpt, 1311–17

Beef and veal consumption per capita, by selected country, 1977-83, annual rpt, 1544–4.2

Caribbean area fish landings and potential yield, consumption, and incidence of ciguatera, by island, 1984 article, 2162–1.403

Cheese and tobacco exports by country of origin, various periods 1974-82, strategic material stockpile mgmt hearings, 25208–27

Cocoa and cocoa products, foreign and US production, prices, and trade, FAS semiannual circular, 1925–9

Coffee production, trade and quotas, and consumption, by country, with US and intl prices, FAS periodic circular, 1925–5

Cotton production and trade, foreign and US, FAS monthly and annual rpt series, 1925–4

Cotton, wool, and synthetic fiber production, prices, consumption, and trade, periodic situation rpt with articles, 1561–1

Dairy imports subject to quota by commodity, and meat imports subject to Meat Import Law, by country of origin, FAS monthly circular, 1925–31

Dairy products foreign and US production, consumption, and trade, FAS annual circular series, 1925–10

Developing countries agricultural supply/demand and market for US exports, with socioeconomic indicators, country rpt series, 1526–6

Developing countries food production and needs, and related economic trends and outlook, for 67 countries, 1980-86, annual rpt, 1524–6

Developing countries food supply policies, with farm sector data, tariff income, and prices and imports of 5 grains, for 21 countries, 1960s-81, 1528–168

EC food supply/demand and market and support prices, with exchange rates, fertilizer price index, GDP, and population, by country, 1960-83, 1528–173

EC fruit and vegetable product trade and tariffs, 1966-78, and effect of Greece, Spain, and Portugal entry into EC, projected to 1986, 1528–182

Export sales and shipments of US grains, oilseed products, hides, skins, and cotton, by country, weekly rpt, 1922–3

Exports and imports of US, by agricultural commodity and country, bimonthly rpt with articles, 1522–1

Exports and imports of US, by detailed agricultural commodity and country, FY83 and CY83, semiannual rpts, 1522–4

Exports and personal expenditures of US and world for selected agricultural commodities, by country, and export share of US farm income, various periods 1926-82, 1528–172

Exports, imports, tariffs, and industry operating data for agricultural products, 1979-83, TSUSA commodity rpt series, 9885–1

Exports of selected agricultural products, for EC and selected other countries, 1960s-84, hearing, 25368–135

Exports of US agricultural products and dollar exchange rate, percent changes for 12 countries, 1981-83, article, 9391–1.421

Farm machinery and equipment foreign market and trade, and user industry operations and demand, country market research rpts, 2045–13

Farmland (US) owned by foreigners, acquisitions, dispositions, holdings, and use, by State and type and country of owner, 1983, annual rpt, 1584–2

Farmland (US) owned by foreigners, acreage, value, and use, by State and county, and for 5 leading investor countries, 1983, annual rpt, 1584–3

Farmland per capita, and total arable land area by use, by selected country and world region, selected years 1955-80, 1528–180

Farmland per capita by world region and selected country, and world arable land area by use, selected years 1955-80, article, 1522–3.401

Fats, oils, and related products foreign and US production and trade, FAS monthly and annual circular series, 1925–1

Feed and livestock trade by product and world region, and ocean freight rates between selected countries of origin and destination, selected years 1960-82, 1528–177

Fish and shellfish landings, prices, trade, consumption, and industry operating data, for US with foreign comparisons, 1982-83, annual rpt, 2164–1

Fish and shellfish of economic importance, biological, fishery, and mgmt data, literature review series, 2166–16

Fish catch quotas for US 200 mile zone, allocations by species and country, coastal area rpt series, 7006–5

Fish meal and oil, production and trade, monthly rpt, 2162–3

Fishing industry catch permits and quotas issued by US for incidental take of marine mammals, by applicant and species, 1984, annual rpt, 2164–11

Flour milling production by census div and State, daily capacity, and exports by country, monthly Current Industrial Rpt, 2506–4.1

Food aid contributions, by commodity group and country, 1975/76-83/84, 1528–181

Fruit and nut trade, by selected crop and country, periodic situation rpt with articles, 1561–6

Fruit and vegetable shipments, and arrivals in 23 US and 5 Canada cities, by mode of transport and State or country of origin, 1983, annual rpt series, 1311–4

Fruit and vegetable shipments by mode of transport, arrivals, and imports, by commodity and State and country of origin, weekly rpt, 1311–3

Fruits, vegetables, and nuts (fresh and processed) foreign and US production and trade, FAS monthly rpt with articles, 1925–34

Fruits, vegetables, and nuts (fresh and processed) foreign and US production and trade, FAS rpt supplement series, 1925–35

Grain production, prices, trade, and export inspections by US port and country of destination, by grain type, weekly rpt, 1313–2

Grain production, trade, stocks, and consumption, foreign and US, FAS monthly and annual rpt series, 1925–2

Grain shipment complaints investigated by country, and other activities of Federal Grain Inspection Service, FY83, annual rpt, 1294–1

Grain stocks, supply deviation, and effect on use, trade, and prices, for US and selected countries, various periods 1960-83, 1528–184

Honey and sugar production, prices, trade, stocks, and marketing, and honey loan activity and processing awards of CCC, weekly rpt, 1311–2

Hops production, stocks, use, and US trade by country, monthly rpt, 1313–7

Imports injury to price-supported US agricultural industries, investigations with background financial and operating data for selected products, series, 9886–10

Japan fish landings, prices, trade by country, cold storage, and market devs, periodic press release, 2162–7

Livestock and meat trade of US, by country, 1970-83, annual rpt, 1564–6.4

Livestock, poultry, and dairy live animals, meat, and products trade, by commodity and country of destination, FAS quarterly rpt, 1925–32

Livestock, poultry, and products foreign and US production, consumption, and trade, FAS semiannual circular, 1925–33

Meat and poultry inspection activities and personnel of Federal, State, and foreign govts, FY83, annual rpt, 1374–1

Meat imports subject to Meat Import Law, by country of origin, FAS monthly circular, 1925–31

Meat inspection for import or export, FY83, annual rpt, 1374–3

Meat plants inspected and certified for exporting products to US, by country, 1983, annual listing, 1374–2

Molasses (feed) production, wholesale prices by market area, and US imports by customs district and country, weekly rpt, 1311–16

Mushroom imports injury to US industry, and stocks, production, sales, trade, and consumption, quarterly rpt, 9882–5

Peanut and peanut oil exports of US, and foreign peanut production, by country, crop years 1979-83, annual rpt, 1311–5.2

Peanut production, prices, trade by country, and stocks, weekly rpt, 1311–1

Index by Categories

January-December 1984

Index by Categories

BY FOREIGN COUNTRY

Pests (plant) and pathogens found entering US, by country of origin, State, and method of interception, FY82, annual rpt, 1394–16

PL 480 and CCC export credit sales agreement terms, by commodity and country, FY83, annual rpt, 15344–1.11

PL 480 commodity allocations for long-term credit sales, by country, quarterly press release, 1922–7

PL 480 concessional sales agreements, market value and date signed, and shipping costs, by country, 1954-83, annual rpt, 1924–6

PL 480 concessional sales program, exports by commodity and country, 1955-83, semiannual rpt, 1922–6

PL 480 concessional sales program, exports by commodity and country, 1978-83, semiannual rpt, 1922–10

PL 480 exports by commodity, and recipients, by program, sponsor, and country, FY82 and aggregate from FY55, annual rpt, 1924–7

PL 480 Title I and III allocations, by commodity and country, FY85, semiannual rpt, 1542–6

Production, acreage, and yield for selected crops, forecasts by selected world region and country, FAS monthly rpt, 1925–28

Production and trade with US, by world region and selected country, 1960s-83, annual chartbook, 1504–3

Production, consumption, and policies for selected countries, and US export dev and promotion, monthly rpt, 1922–2

Production indexes and production of selected commodities, by world region and country, 1974-83, annual rpt, 1524–5

Production, prices, and trade of agricultural commodities, by country, 1983 and outlook for 1984/85, annual world region rpt series, 1524–4

Production, prices, trade, and consumption, foreign and US, quarterly rpt with articles, 1522–3

Production, trade, and supply/demand, with socioeconomic data, by country, 1950s-77, 1528–179

Rice market activities, prices, inspections, sales, trade, supply, and use, for US and selected foreign markets, weekly rpt, 1313–8

Rice production and trade, for selected countries and world regions, 1980/81-1983/84, semiannual rpt, 1561–8.4

Seed exports of US, by type of seed, world region, and country, FAS quarterly rpt, 1925–13

Spice, essential oil, and tea foreign and US production, prices, and trade, FAS annual rpt series, 1925–15

Statistical Abstract of US, selected social, political, and economic data, by country, 1945-83 and trends, annual rpt, 2324–1.4

Sugar and specialty sugar imports of US under quota, by country, weekly rpt, 1922–9

Sugar and sweeteners production, consumption, prices, supply, and trade, quarterly rpt with articles, 1561–14

Sugar, molasses, and honey foreign and US production, trade, and consumption, FAS annual rpt series, 1925–14

Sugar production, consumption, supply, and trade, quarterly rpt, 1621–28

Tobacco production and US trade, by country, quarterly situation rpt with articles, 1561–10

Tobacco production of selected countries, and US trade by country, 1978-83, annual rpt, 1319–1

Tobacco products foreign and US production, prices, trade, and acreage, FAS monthly rpt with articles, 1925–16

Tuna imports of US by country of origin, cannery receipts and production, and effect of reduced production on California economy, selected years 1977-82, article, 2162–1.403

Wheat (durum) acreage, production, prices, stocks, use, and US and Canada exports by country, quarterly rpt, 1313–6

Wheat and rye foreign and US production, prices, trade, stocks, and use, periodic situation rpt with articles, 1561–12

Wool market foreign and domestic prices and trade, weekly and biweekly rpt, 1315–2

Banking, Finance, and Insurance

Bank deposit concentration indicators, by State and for US and 7 OECD countries, various dates 1982-84, article, 9373–1.405

Banking and nonbanking firms liabilities to and claims on foreigners, by country, 1981-82, annual rpt, 9364–5.10

Banks (natl) foreign branches by world region and country, quarterly rpt, 8402–3.4

Banks (US) foreign branches assets and liabilities, by world region and country, quarterly rpt, 9365–3.7

Capital movements between US and foreign countries, *Treasury Bulletin,* quarterly rpt, 8002–4.12

Dollar exchange rate and US agricultural exports, percent change for 12 countries, 1981-83, article, 9391–1.421

Dollar exchange rates of 5 currencies, average current and 3-month forward rates, 1983, article, 9371–1.413

Dollar exchange rates of 35 countries, and interest rates and security yields for US and selected foreign countries, weekly chartbook, 9365–1.5

Eurocurrency syndicated loans, loan fees, and interest rate spread, by country group and selected country, 1981-83, technical paper, 9366–7.105

Exchange rates correlation with price and trade indicators, for 14 countries, 1977-83, article, 9373–1.418

Eximbank credits for energy-related products and services, by country and firm, 1982, annual rpt, 9254–3

Eximbank financial condition, and loan, credit, and insurance authorizations, by country, FY83, annual rpt, 9254–1

Fed Financing Bank holdings and transactions, monthly press release, 9322–1

Financial statistics, foreign and US, monthly rpt, 9362–1.3

Foreign exchange rates offered by US disbursing offices, by country, quarterly rpt, 8102–6

Intl financial instns funds by source and disbursements by purpose, by country, with US policy review, FY83, annual rpt, 15344–1

Loans and grants for economic and military assistance from US and intl agencies, by program and country, FY46-83, annual rpt, 9914–5

Loans of large US banks to foreigners at all US and foreign offices, by country group and country, quarterly rpt, 13002–1

Monetary control policy of US and selected West European countries, and relation to credit, exchange rates, GNP, and other indicators, various periods 1960-82, conf papers, 9373–3.26

OECD countries natl savings and current account balance ratios to GDP, by country, various periods 1963-81, technical paper, 9366–7.100

Overseas Private Investment Corp programs and finances, with list of insured projects and companies, FY83, annual rpt, 9904–2

Tax evasion through nonresidents bank claims and deposits, direct investments, income payments, and other transactions in 5 Caribbean countries, 1978-82, 8008–106

Communications and Transportation

Airline operations and passenger, cargo, and mail traffic, by type of service, air carrier, State, and country, 1974-83, annual rpt, 7504–1.4

Airline passenger and cargo traffic, and departures by aircraft type, by airline and US and foreign airport, 1982, annual rpt, 7504–35

Auto industry operations, and trade by country, monthly rpt, 9882–8

Communications satellite intl systems charges, operations, investment shares by country, and competition impacts, 1964-83 with projections to 2003, hearings, 25388–46

Developing countries disaster preparedness and summary sociodemographic, political, and economic data, country rpt series, 9916–2

Ocean freight rates for grain, by US loading port and country of destination, weekly rpt, 1272–2

Panama Canal commerce, by commodity, flag of vessel, and trade routes, FY82, annual rpt, 9664–3.2

Railroad electrified mileage by country, subway system mileage by US city, and trolley and motor bus capital and operating costs, selected years, 1960-80, 3006–7.7

Shipbuilding and deliveries, by type and by country of construction and registry, 1982, annual rpt, 7704–4

Shipping and shipbuilding subsidies and aid, and summary fleet, trade, and GNP data, for US and 47 countries, 1979-80, biennial rpt, 7704–18

Ships in US merchant fleet, shipping costs, construction, employment, military availability, and Fed Govt subsidies, 1970s-1984 and projected to 2000, 26306–6.83

Ships in world bulk carrier fleet, characteristics by country of registry, 1982, annual rpt, 7704–13

Ships in world merchant fleet, and tonnage, by country of registry, 1982, annual rpt, 7704–3

Ships in world merchant fleet, by selected characteristics and country of registry, as of Jan 1983, annual rpt, 7704–1

BY FOREIGN COUNTRY

Ships in world merchant fleet, US transfers to foreign firms, and deliveries, by vessel type and country, FY83, annual rpt, 7704–14.1, 7704–14.2

Ships in world tanker fleet, by selected characteristics and country of registry, 1982, annual rpt, 7704–17

St Lawrence Seaway ships, cargo and passenger volumes, and toll revenues, 1981-82 and trends from 1959, annual rpt, 7744–2

Statistical Abstract of US, selected social, political, and economic data, by country, 1945-83 and trends, annual rpt, 2324–1.4

Tanker fleet inventory, by country, selected years 1960-83, annual rpt, 244–5.10

Telecommunication equipment foreign market and trade, and user industry operations and demand, country market research rpts, 2045–12

Telegraph and telex messages, US and overseas, 1982, annual rpt, 9284–6.5

Telephone traffic and revenues, US and overseas, by world area and country, 1982, annual rpt, 9284–6.3

Traffic death rates for US and 8 OECD countries, 1980, annual rpt, 7764–1

Transportation finances, operations, vehicles, equipment, accidents, and energy use and transport, by mode of transport, 1955-84, annual rpt, 7304–2

Travel to and from US on US and foreign flag air carriers, by country, world area, and US port, monthly rpt, 7302–2

Travel to and from US, receipts and expenditures by world area and country, 1979-83, annual article, 2702–1.417

Travel to US and receipts, by selected country, 1983, annual rpt, 2904–10

Travel to US and receipts by world area and selected country, 1960-83, and US Travel and Tourism Admin activities, 1983, annual rpt, 2904–6

Travel to US, by characteristics of visit and traveler, country, and State of destination, quarterly rpt, 2902–1

Education

Education summary statistics by world area and country, and foreign students enrolled in US higher education instns, 1982 with trends, annual rpt, 4824–2.24

English teaching programs and teacher seminars supported by USIA, by world region and country, FY83, annual rpt, 9854–2

Latin America students in US and Soviet bloc training programs, by program type and student country, selected years 1972-82, GAO rpt, 26123–77

Microfiche from Educational Resources Info Center, holdings of US and foreign educational and other instns, as of 1983, listing, 4918–14

Statistical Abstract of US, selected social, political, and economic data, by country, 1945-83 and trends, annual rpt, 2324–1.4

Energy Resources and Demand

Coal exports and imports, and average price, by world area, country, and customs district, quarterly rpt, 3162–37

Coal exports, imports, and average price, by country of destination and origin and customs district, weekly rpt, monthly data, 3162–1.2

Coal import demand, by country, 1982 and projected to 2000, 3008–97

Coal imports from US, and price and demand elasticity, by country, 1981, 7308–182

Coal reserves, production, demand indicators, and trade, by country, selected years 1973-82 and alternative trade projections to 1995, annual rpt, 3164–77

Electric current characteristics, by country and selected city, 1984 rpt, 2018–8

Electric power systems equipment foreign market and trade, and user industry operations and demand, country market research rpts, 2045–15

Electric utility coal imports, by country of origin and utility, 1979-83, annual rpt, 3164–42

Energy production by type, and oil prices, trade, and consumption, by country group and selected country, monthly rpt, 242–5

Energy production, trade, and reserves, and oil and refined products supply and prices, by country, 1973-83, annual rpt, 3164–50

Energy supply/demand and prices, by energy resource and major producing and consuming country and sector, detailed data, monthly rpt, 3162–24

Energy supply/demand and prices, by fuel type and consuming sector with foreign comparisons, 1949-83, annual rpt, 3164–74

Energy supply/demand and prices, by fuel type, sector, and end use, with foreign comparisons, 1960-83 and projected to 1995, annual summary rpt, 3164–76

Energy use, oil supply and price, and nuclear generating capacity, for non-Communist markets, by country or country group, various periods 1960-95, annual rpt, 3164–75

Nuclear power generation in US and 18 non-Communist countries, monthly rpt, 3162–24.10

Nuclear power industry status and outlook, with reactor construction, utility financial and operating data, and foreign comparisons, 1970s-83 with projections to 2010, 26358–99

Nuclear power plant capacity, generation, shutdowns, operation status and costs, and fuel, quarterly rpt, 3352–3

Nuclear power plant construction and operation status, and capacity, by plant, region, State, and selected country, 1983 and projected to 2020, annual rpt, 3164–57

Nuclear reactors for domestic use and export by function, with owner, operating characteristics, and location, Apr 1984, semiannual listing, 3002–5

Oil (Alaskan) potential exports to Japan, costs and benefits, with background data on oil prices, Pacific Basin supply/demand, and tankers, various periods 1918-99, hearings, 25388–45

Oil (crude) prices, conservation, and real dollar exchange rates related to consumption, for 7 OECD countries, various periods 1975-83, article, 9379–1.405

Oil and gas OCS drilling rigs by country, rig losses, and worker injury and death rates, various periods 1966-83, hearing, 21568–35

Oil and gas undiscovered recoverable resources, cumulative production, and identified reserves, final oil basin rpt series, 5666–18

Index by Categories

Oil and gas undiscovered recoverable resources, cumulative production, and identified reserves, preliminary oil basin rpt series, 5666–17

Oil and refined products and natural gas liquids supply/demand, trade, stocks, and refining, by detailed product, State, and PAD district, monthly rpt with articles, 3162–6

Oil and refined products and natural gas liquids supply/demand, trade, stocks, and refining, by detailed product, State, and PAD district, 1983 annual rpt, 3164–2

Oil and refined products supply and prices, effects of 3 import disruptions, selected years 1972-82, 3108–28

Oil field equipment from 5 countries, injury to US industry from foreign subsidized imports and less than fair value sales, investigation with background financial and operating data, 1984 rpt, 9886–19.11

Oil identified and undiscovered reserves, by country and oil type, and cumulative production, as of 1981 and 1983, 5668–72

Oil prices impact on US oil trade and energy-intensive industries, with US and foreign reserves and industry operations, 1950-82 and projected to 2020, 9886–4.69

Oil prices of OPEC and non-OPEC countries, by crude type, weekly rpt, 3162–32

Oil production by country, consumption and imports for US and 6 OECD countries, and OPEC member prices, biweekly rpt, 242–4

Oil production, consumption, stocks, and exports and prices to US, by major exporting and consuming country, detailed data, monthly rpt, 3162–24

Oil refining capacity and production, and oil use and exports, by OPEC member, with comparisons to other countries, projected 1985-90, hearings, 25368–133.1

Oil reserves, production, and resource lifespan under alternative production rates, historic and projected, country rpt series, 3166–9

Strategic Petroleum Reserve, crude oil received, by source country, as of Dec 1983, annual rpt, 3004–20

Strategic Petroleum Reserve crude oil received, by source country, May 1983, 3008–91

Uranium from foreign sources delivered to DOE enrichment plants, by country of origin and US enrichment customer, 1983, annual rpt, 3164–66

Uranium reserves and mining and milling industries operations and finances, with selected foreign comparisons, various periods 1964-83 and projected to 2000, 3008–95

Geography and Climate

Classification codes for countries, dependencies, and areas of special sovereignty, 1983, 2216–2.120

Climatological data for surface and upper air, averages by foreign and US station, monthly rpt, 2152–4

Disasters, persons affected, deaths, damage, and aid by US and others, by country, FY83 and trends from FY64, annual rpt, 9914–12

Earthquake intensity, damage, time of origin, and seismic characteristics of all US and major foreign earthquakes, 1981, annual rpt, 5664–13

Index by Categories

BY FOREIGN COUNTRY

Oceanographic data, stations and cruises recording data for World Data Center A by country, ship, and type of data, 1983, annual rpt, 2144–15

Tide height and time daily at worldwide coastal points, 1985 predictions, annual rpt series, 2174–2

Weather conditions and impact assessment, by world area and country, monthly rpt, 2152–9

Government and Defense

- AID activities and funding by project and function, FY85, and developing countries summary socioeconomic data, 1970s-83, by country, annual rpt, 9914–3
- AID community dev assistance to local govts in developing countries, program activities and funding, 1960s-80s, 9918–11
- AID contracts and grants for technical and support services, by instn, country, and State, FY83, annual listing, 9914–7
- AID contracts and grants to universities for technical assistance to foreign countries and other services, FY83, annual listing, 9914–6
- AID dev assistance activities, socioeconomic impacts, evaluation rpt series, 9916–1
- AID dev assistance activities, special study series, 9916–3
- AID economic assistance to developing countries, obligations and disbursements by country, quarterly rpt, 9912–4
- AID Housing Guaranty Program financial statements, and projects by country, FY83, annual rpt, 9914–4
- AID loan repayment status and terms by program and country, and status of predecessor agency loans, quarterly rpt, 9912–3
- AID loans authorized, signed, and canceled, by country and world area, monthly rpt, 9912–2
- Arms control treaties status, and Arms Control and Disarmament Agency activities, 1983, annual rpt, 9824–2
- *Background Notes,* foreign countries summary social, political, and economic data, series, 7006–2
- Central America socioeconomic and political conditions in 6 countries, 1960s-83 with trends and projections 1930-2010, 028–19
- Chiefs of State and Cabinet members, by country, monthly listing, 242–7
- Claims against foreign govts by US natls, by country and type of claim, 1983, annual rpt, 6004–16
- Coin production of US Mint Bur, for US by denomination and mint, and for foreign countries, monthly table, 8202–1
- Copyright activities of Register of Copyrights, including intl relations, registrations, fees earned, and royalties collected, FY82, annual rpt, 26404–2
- Currency (foreign) accounts owned by US under AID admin and by foreign govts with joint AID control, status by program and country, quarterly rpt, 9912–1
- Currency (foreign) holdings of US, detailed transactions and balances by program and country, 1st half FY84, semiannual rpt, 8102–7
- Currency (foreign) purchases by US with dollars, by country, Oct 1983-Mar 1984, semiannual rpt, 8102–5

Current account balance related to budget balances, for US and 58 countries, various periods 1948-82, article, 9379–1.401

- Debt to US of foreign govts and private obligors, by country and program, periodic rpt, 8002–6
- Developing countries disaster preparedness and summary sociodemographic, political, and economic data, country rpt series, 9916–2
- Developing countries receiving US economic aid, total govt and defense expenditures, military imports, GNP, and intl reserves by country, 1976-81, annual rpt, 9914–1
- DOD base construction and renovation, budget authorization requests by DOD component, State, country, and project, FY85, annual rpt, 3544–15
- DOD base support costs by function, and personnel and acreage by installation, by service branch, FY85, annual rpt, 3504–11
- DOD budget, organization, personnel, weapons, and property, by service branch, State, and country, 1984 annual summary rpt, 3504–13
- DOD civilian indirect hires, by country, monthly rpt, 3542–16
- DOD military and civilian personnel and dependents, FY83, annual rpt, 3544–1
- DOD military personnel of US abroad, by service branch, world area, and country, quarterly news release, 3542–9
- DOD military personnel of US on active duty, by service branch, outlying area, and country, monthly rpt, 3542–14.5
- DOD prime contract awards, by individual contractor, service branch, State and city, and country, FY83, annual listing, 3544–22
- DOD prime contract awards for R&D to educational and nonprofit instns and Federal agencies, by instn and location, FY83, annual listing, 3544–17
- DOD supply inventory mgmt of for agencies, NATO, and foreign govts, 1970s-83, annual rpt, 21204–1
- Economic and military aid of US, by program and country, selected years 1940-82, annual rpt, 15344–1.1
- Economic and military aid of US, Reagan Admin budget requests by program and country, FY82-85, annual rpt, 7004–14
- Economic, social, and political summary data, by country, 1984, annual factbook, 244–11
- Helsinki Final Act implementation by NATO, Warsaw Pact, and other signatory nations, Dec 1983-Mar 1984, semiannual rpt, 7002–1
- Human rights conditions in 162 countries, economic and military aid of US, and economic aid of intl organizations, 1981-83, annual rpt, 21384–3
- Immigration, and alien residents, workers, visitors, deportations, and naturalizations, by country of birth, FY81, annual rpt, 6264–2
- Inter-American Foundation activities, grants, and fellowships, by country, FY83, annual rpt, 14424–1
- Latin America elections, votes and share of population voting by country and election type, selected years 1962-83, 7008–42
- Loans and grants for economic and military assistance from US and intl agencies, by program and country, FY46-83, annual rpt, 9914–5

Military aid of US, and sales of arms, equipment, and training, by item and country, FY50-83, annual rpt, 3904–3

- Military aid of US, arms sales, and training programs costs and budget requests by program, world region, and country, FY83-85, annual rpt, 7144–13
- Military aid of US by country and program, and developing countries with advanced weapons systems, FY85, annual rpt, 3544–2
- Military pension lifetime earnings in US and 7 countries, and comparisons to US civil and foreign service, as of 1983, hearings, 21208–19
- Military, social, and economic summary data, by world area and country, 1960s-80s, hearing, 25388–47.1
- Military spending, arms trade, and armed forces size, with total govt spending and population, by country, 1972-82, annual rpt, 9824–1
- Military training of US for foreign govts, students, costs, and revenue losses from reduced tuition by country, by service branch, FY79-83, GAO rpt, 26123–56
- Military units, by service branch, outlying area, and country, FY83-85, annual rpt, 3504–1.2
- Motor fuel taxes in US and selected countries, 1st qtr 1983, hearing, 21368–49
- Multinatl corporation income reallocation through regulation of intercorporate transactions, by tax item, treaty status, asset size, industry, and tax haven country, 1982, 8008–110
- NATO military expenditures, by country, selected years 1971-82, hearing, 21388–42
- Passports issued, by holder characteristics, travel purpose, and country of destination, quarterly rpt, 7182–1
- Sealift Military Command operations for naval fleet support, and transport of DOD and AID cargo by route, quarterly rpt, 3802–2
- Strategic materials stockpiles, and imports in exchange for CCC commodity exports by world region and country, various periods 1950-83, hearings, 21208–20
- Strategic materials stockpiling activities of Fed Govt, acquisitions by commodity and country of origin, as of Mar 1984, semiannual rpt, 9432–1.2
- Tax evasion through tax haven countries, with income, investments, and taxes withheld by country, various periods 1975-83, hearings, 21408–71
- Treaties and other bilateral and multilateral agreements of US in force, by country, Jan 1984, annual listing, 7004–1
- UN participation of US, and member and nonmember shares of UN budget by country, FY83-85, annual rpt, 7004–5
- US govt civilian employment abroad, by US citizenship, selected agency, and country, 1982, biennial rpt, 9844–8
- US govt contingent liabilities and claims paid on federally insured and guaranteed contracts with foreign obligors, by country and program, periodic rpt, 8002–12
- US govt-leased real property inventory and rental costs, worldwide summary by location and agency, 1983, annual rpt, 9454–10

BY FOREIGN COUNTRY

US govt-owned real property inventory and costs, worldwide summary by location, agency, and use, 1983, annual rpt, 9454–5

US Navy procurement, by contractor and location of work, FY83, annual rpt, 3804–13.1

USIA info center and reading room operations, by world region, country, and city, FY83, annual rpt, 9854–4

Visas of US issued and refused to immigrants and nonimmigrants, and status adjustments, by class and nationality, FY77, annual rpt, 7184–1

Warsaw Pact and USSR military weapons systems, assistance and presence worldwide, and force strengths, with selected US and NATO comparisons, as of 1984, 3508–14

Health and Vital Statistics

- Allergy and Infectious Diseases Natl Inst activities, grants by instn, State, and country, and disease incidence and costs, FY60s-84, annual rpt, 4474–30
- Cancer Natl Inst foreign research grants and contracts, FY83, annual fact book, 4474–13
- Caribbean area ciguatera incidence, by island, 1984 article, 2162–1.403
- Deaths in US by State and by outlying area or country of birth, 1979, US Vital Statistics annual rpt, 4144–2.1
- Health care natl expenditures in Israel, with comparisons to other budget sectors and expenditures of other countries, 1950s-83, article, 4102–1.446
- Health care resources, use, and per capita public expenditures, and selected population characteristics, for US and 6 countries, selected years 1975-81, 21148–33
- Heart, Lung, and Blood Natl Inst funds and recipients by instn, State, and foreign country, and heart disease death rates for US and 26 foreign countries by sex, 1960s-FY83, annual fact book, 4474–15
- Immunization and preventable disease elimination programs for children and pregnant women, 1983 conf papers, 4204–15
- Influenza deaths, viruses identified by State and country, epidemiology, and vaccine effects and recommended dosages by age, 1979/80-1980/81, annual rpt, 4205–3
- Kidney end-stage disease patients by patient characteristics and country, and per capita spending for treatment, selected years 1973-81, article, 4102–1.450
- Life expectancy and infant mortality rates, by selected country, 1975 and 1980, annual compilation, 4144–11.2
- Malaria cases in US, by country and world area of infection origin, 1982, annual rpt, 4205–4
- Medical and health care equipment foreign market and trade, and user industry operations and demand, country market research rpts, 2045–2
- Medical equipment and drugs trade, and US medical and dental equipment market shares of 5 countries, 1981-82, article, 4652–1.407
- NIH grants and awards for R&D, training, construction, and medical libraries, by location and recipient, FY83, annual listings, 4434–7

NIH intl program activities and funding, by inst and country, FY83, annual rpt, 4474–6

NIH intl research grants, by inst and recipient country and agency, historical data, 1984 annual rpt, 4434–1

Physicians practicing in US, by country of graduation, Dec 1980, biennial rpt, 4114–8

Statistical Abstract of US, selected social, political, and economic data, by country, 1945-83 and trends, annual rpt, 2324–1.4

Vaccination requirements for intl travel by country, and disease prevention recommendations, 1984 annual rpt, 4204–11

Industry and Commerce

- Aluminum primary production plant ownership, capacity, and type and source of raw material and energy used, by plant, State, and country, June 1984, semiannual listing, 5602–5
- Auto and auto products sales, prices, and registrations in US, and trade of 8 countries with US, by make and model, 1964-83, annual rpt, 9884–7
- Auto industry operations, trade, and registrations, foreign and US, selected years 1928-82, domestic content requirement hearings, 21788–134
- *Business America,* foreign and domestic commerce, and US investment and trade opportunities, biweekly rpt articles, 2042–24
- Chemicals (benzenoid), imports by country of origin and product, 1983, annual rpt, 9884–2
- Chemicals and related products trade, tariffs, and industry operating data, TSUSA commodity rpt series, 9885–4
- China economic conditions, agricultural and industrial production, trade, and domestic and foreign investment, 1980-85, 2048–106
- China exports and imports, by commodity, world area, and country, quarterly rpt, 242–6
- Communist, OECD, and selected other countries economic statistics, 1960s-83, annual rpt, 244–5
- Copper mine expansion in Cananea, Mexico, effects on US air pollution and copper industry, with US and foreign industry data, 1960s-95, hearing, 21448–31
- Cuba economic conditions, agricultural and industrial production and distribution, trade, and intl economic relations, 1970-82 and trends from 1957, 248–40
- Current account balance related to Fed Govt budget deficit, with balance for 14 OECD countries, various periods 1952-83, article, 9373–1.408
- Developing countries free zones, industry financial and operating data by country, with case studies for 5 countries, 1970s-82, 9918–10
- Developing countries govt policy, and AID and other foreign assistance, effects on private sector dev and socioeconomic conditions, with case studies for 6 countries, 1960s-80, 9918–12
- EC steel pipe and tube imports of US, by product type and country, various periods 1978-83 with US import duties to 1987, hearing, 25368–134

Index by Categories

- EC trade with US by country, and total agricultural and nonagricultural trade, selected years 1958-83, annual rpt, 7144–7
- Economic and monetary trends, compounded annual rates of change for US and 10 major trading partners, quarterly rpt, 9391–7
- Economic conditions, consumer and stock prices and production indexes, 6 OECD countries and US, *Business Conditions Digest,* historical supplement and methodology, 1947-82, 2708–31
- Economic conditions, consumer and stock prices and production indexes, 6 OECD countries and US, *Business Conditions Digest,* monthly rpt, 2702–3.10
- Economic conditions in Communist and OECD countries, 1982, annual rpt, 7144–11
- Economic indicators for 7 OECD countries and US, quarterly rpt, 2042–10
- Economic trends in foreign countries and implications for US, annual and semiannual country rpt series, 2046–4
- Economic trends of US with selected intl comparisons, selected years 1950-83, annual rpt, 204–1
- Electronic component equipment foreign market and trade, and user industry operations and demand, country market research rpts, 2045–4
- Electronic component manufacturing equipment foreign market and trade, and user industry operations and demand, country market research rpts, 2045–5
- Europe (Western) trade with US, and US market share and export opportunities for selected commodities, by country, 1982-84, 2048–105
- Export and import statistics country classifications, Census Bur codes and designations, revisions to 1981 base edition, 2428–3
- Export licensing and monitoring activities under Export Admin Act, for selected commodities, and for Communist and other countries, FY83, annual rpt, 2044–22
- Exports and imports, intl position of US and 4 OECD countries, and factors affecting US competition, quarterly pamphlet, 2042–25
- Exports and imports of US, and trade balance, by major commodity group, selected country, and world area, with seasonal adjustments, monthly rpt, 2422–6
- Exports and imports of US, by commodity group, world area, selected country, US coastal area and port, and mode of transport, with seasonal adjustments, monthly rpt, 2422–9
- Exports and imports of US by country, and trade shifts by commodity, USITC quarterly monitoring rpt, 9882–9
- Exports and imports of US, by world area, country, and commodity, *Survey of Current Business,* monthly rpt, 2702–1.7
- Exports and imports of US, detailed SIC-based commodities by world area, 1983, annual rpts, 2424–6
- Exports and imports of US with Communist countries, by detailed commodity and country, quarterly rpt with articles, 9882–2
- Exports, imports, and economic indicators by country and country group, and US trade policy actions, 1960s-83, annual rpt, 444–1

Index by Categories

BY FOREIGN COUNTRY

Exports, imports, and tariffs, USITC investigation publications issued, 1960-83, annual listing, 9884–12

Exports of US by selected commodity, and foreign and US economic and employment indicators and balance of payments, by world area and country, 1970s-83, annual rpt, 2044–26

Exports of US, detailed commodities by country of destination, monthly rpt, 2422–3

Exports of US, detailed Schedule B commodities by country of destination, 1983, annual rpt, 2424–9

Exports of US, detailed Schedule E commodities by mode of transport and world area and country of destination, 1983, annual rpts, 2424–5

Food processing and packaging equipment, foreign market and trade, and user industry operations and demand, country market research rpts, 2045–11

Footwear imports of US, by category, value class, and selected country, monthly rpt, 2042–29

Footwear production, employment, consumption, prices, and US trade by country, quarterly rpt, 9882–6

Foreign-owned US multiestablishment firms, employment, and payroll, by country, State, industry group, and foreign ownership share, 1981-82, annual rpt, 2324–6

Franchises of US firms engaged in distribution of goods and services, by country, 1982, annual rpt, 2014–5.1

Generalized System of Preferences status of 29 commodities, with US production, consumption, tariffs, and trade by country, selected years 1978-87, 9888–17

Graphic industries equipment foreign market and trade, and user industry operations and demand, country market research rpts, 2045–3

Great Lakes trade, by SITC 3-digit commodity, port, vessel type, world area, and country, 1982, annual rpt, 7744–3

Import and tariff provisions effect on US industries and products, investigations with background financial and operating data, series, 9886–4

Import quotas and imports for selected commodities, by country of origin, monthly rpt, 8146–1

Imports detained by FDA, by product, shipper or manufacturer, country, and detention reasons, monthly listing, 4062–2

Imports from Communist countries, injury to US industries, investigations with background financial and operating data, selected industries and products, series, 9886–12

Imports injury to US industries from foreign subsidized products and sales in US at less than fair value, investigations with background financial and operating data, series, 9886–19

Imports injury to US industries from foreign subsidized products, investigations with background financial and operating data for selected industries and products, series, 9886–15

Imports injury to US industries from import sales at less than fair value, investigations with background financial and operating data, series, 9886–14

Imports injury to US industries from increased import sales, investigations with background financial and operating data, series, 9886–5

Imports injury to US industries from removal of duties on foreign subsidized products, investigations with background financial and operating data, series, 9886–18

Imports of US, detailed Schedule A commodities by country and world area of origin, and mode of transport, 1983, annual rpts, 2424–2

Imports of US, detailed Schedule A commodities by country, monthly rpt, 2422–2

Imports of US, detailed TSUSA commodities by country of origin, 1983, annual rpt, 2424–4

Imports of US given duty-free treatment for value of US materials or parts sent abroad for processing or assembly, by country and commodity, 1979-82, biennial rpt, 9884–14

Industrial process control equipment foreign market and trade, and user industry operations and demand, country market research rpts, 2045–6

Industrial production indexes and CPI, for US and 6 OECD countries, current data and annual trends, monthly rpt, 23842–1.7

Investment (foreign direct) in and by US, by industry group and for selected countries and world regions, 1977 and 1980, article, 9373–1.411

Investment (foreign direct) in US by country, and finances, operations, and land owned, by industry group for businesses acquired and established, 1982-83, annual article, 2702–1.418

Investment (foreign direct) in US, by major industry group, world area, and selected country, 1980-83, annual article, 2702–1.439

Investment (foreign direct) in US, major investors and investments by SIC 4-digit industry, transaction type and value, and location, 1983, annual rpt, 2044–20

Investment (foreign direct) of US, by selected major industry group and world area, 1982-83, annual article, 2702–1.430

Investment (foreign direct) of US, by world area and country, 1977-83, article, 2702–1.442

Investment (intl direct) worldwide, and US investment flows by major industry, by world region and country, 1982 and trends from 1950, annual rpt, 2044–25

Japan specialty steel and ferroalloy raw material supply/demand, with industry market and manufacturing data, selected years 1970-81, 5608–144

Lumber and wood products exports of US, by commodity and country, FAS quarterly rpt, 1925–36

Lumber exports from Northwest US ports, by selected country, quarterly rpt, 1202–3

Machine tools and equipment foreign market and trade, and user industry operations and demand, country market research rpts, 2045–9

Manufactured products (miscellaneous) trade, tariffs, and industry operating data, TSUSA commodity rpt series, 9885–7

Metals and metal products trade, tariffs, and industry operating data, TSUSA commodity rpt series, 9885–6

Mineral Industry Surveys, commodity reviews of production, trade, and consumption, advance annual rpt series, 5614–5

Mineral Industry Surveys, commodity reviews of production, trade, stocks, and consumption, monthly rpt series, 5612–1

Mineral Industry Surveys, commodity reviews of production, trade, stocks, and consumption, quarterly rpt series, 5612–2

Minerals (nonfuel) foreign and US supply under alternative market conditions, reserves, and background industry data, series, 5606–4

Minerals (nonmetallic) and mineral products trade, tariffs, and industry operating data, TSUSA commodity rpt series, 9885–5

Minerals (strategic) supply/demand, trade, and foreign and US industry devs by firm and country, by commodity, bimonthly rpt, 5602–4

Minerals production and reserves, for 87 commodities by country, 1982-83, annual rpt, 5604–18

Minerals production, reserves, and industry role in domestic economy and world supply, country and world region rpt series, 5606–1

Minerals Yearbook, 1982, Vol 1: commodity reviews of production, reserves, supply, use, and trade, annual rpt, 5604–33

Minerals Yearbook, 1982, Vol 3: foreign country reviews of production, trade, and policies, by commodity, annual rpt, 5604–35

Minerals Yearbook, 1982, Vol 3 preprints: foreign country reviews of production, trade, and policies, by commodity, annual rpt series, 5604–17

Minerals Yearbook, 1983, Vol 1 preprints: commodity reviews of production, reserves, supply, use, and trade, annual rpt series, 5604–15

Minerals Yearbook, 1983, Vol 3 preprints: foreign country reviews of production, trade, and policies, by commodity, annual rpt series, 5604–23

Mining industry equipment foreign market and trade, and user industry operations and demand, country market research rpts, 2045–16

Money supply and velocity, prices, and real GNP, growth rates for 4 OECD countries and US, various periods 1954-81, article, 9391–1.401

Multinatl firms US affiliates, financial and operating data by country of parent and industry div, 1980-81, article, 2702–1.402

Multinatl US firms nonbank foreign affiliates, capital expenditures by major industry group and country, 1978-84, semiannual article, 2702–1.410

Multinatl US firms nonbank foreign affiliates, capital expenditures by major industry group and country, 1984-85, semiannual article, 2702–1.437

NATO countries trade with Council for Mutual Economic Assistance Europe members, by country, 1980-83, annual rpt, 7144–5

NATO countries trade with PRC, by country, 1983, annual rpt, 7144–14

OECD countries GNP and GNP growth, by country, 1973-83, annual rpt, 7144–8

BY FOREIGN COUNTRY

OECD economic indicators, for US and 6 countries, biweekly rpt, 242–4

OECD trade, by country, 1983, annual rpt, 7144–10

OECD trade, total and for 4 major countries, and US trade by country, by commodity, 1972-82, annual world region rpt series, 244–13

Overseas Business Reports: economic conditions, investment and export opportunities, and trade practices, annual country market research rpt series, 2046–6

Overseas Business Reports: economic conditions, investment and export opportunities, and trade practices, world region rpt series, 2046–5

Overseas Private Investment Corp activities, foreign and US project impacts, and list of insured projects and companies, FY83, annual rpt, 9904–3

Pacific Basin economic indicators, US and 12 countries, quarterly rpt, 9393–9

Productivity of labor and capital, costs, and prices, by selected industry, and compared to 6 OECD countries, selected years 1947-82, 17898–1

Rum production, trade by selected country, consumption, and shipments from Puerto Rico and Virgin Islands, Jan-June 1983-84, annual rpt, 9884–15

Services trade regulation proposals of US, with agreements, goods and services trade, intl investment, and GDP, by country, various periods 1970-82, 448–1

Statistical Abstract of US, selected social, political, and economic data, by country, 1945-83 and trends, annual rpt, 2324–1.4

Steel imports of US from EC and other countries, and US industry operating data, for 15 products limited under arrangement with EC, monthly rpt, 9882–10

Steel industry finances and operations under proposed import quota, projected 1985-89 with selected foreign comparisons and trends from 1950, 26306–6.80

Steel industry financial and operating data, steel imports by source, and employment situation at Fairless Hills, Pa, plant, 1970s-90, hearing, 25528–94

Tariff Schedules of US, Annotated, classifications and rates of duty for detailed imported commodities, and codes for ports and foreign countries, 1985 edition, 9886–13

Textile exports, by product and country of destination, monthly rpt, 2042–26

Textile fiber and products trade, tariffs, and industry operating data, TSUSA commodity rpt series, 9885–3

Textile imports and import limits under Multifiber Arrangement by product and country, with US exports and use, 1970-83, semiannual rpt, 9882–11

Textile imports, by country of origin, monthly rpt, 2042–27

Textile imports, by product and country of origin, monthly rpt, 2422–1

Textile imports, by product and country of origin, monthly rpt series, 2046–9

Textile imports, by product and country of origin, periodic rpt series, 2046–8

Textile mill production, stocks, materials used, orders, and trade by country, by product and major State, periodic Current Industrial Rpt series, 2506–5

Timber production, prices by region and State, trade by country, and consumption, by species and product, with industry earnings, 1950-83, annual rpt, 1204–29

Trade promotion costs and overseas staff of US and Foreign Commercial Service, by country, 1982-83, hearing, 21408–73

Waterborne containerized cargo carried over principal trade routes, by flag of vessel, port, and US coastal district, 1982, annual rpt, 7704–8

Waterborne trade of US, by type of service, commodity, country, route, and US port, 1982, annual rpt, 7704–2

Wood, paper, and printed matter trade, tariffs, and industry operating data, TSUSA commodity rpt series, 9885–2

Labor and Employment

Employment, labor force, and participation and unemployment rates by sex, in US and 9 OECD countries, various periods 1970-3rd qtr 1983, annual article, 6722–1.404

Labor force output and earnings, price indexes, and work stoppages, by selected country, 1950-82, annual rpt, 6724–1.10

Labor unions reporting to Labor Dept, parent bodies and locals by State, city, and country, 1983 listing, 6468–17

Manufacturing labor productivity and cost indexes for US and 11 OECD countries, 1960-82, annual article, 6722–1.405

Manufacturing productivity and unit labor cost indexes for US and 11 countries, 1950-82 and preliminary 1983, annual rpt, 6864–1

Statistical Abstract of US, selected social, political, and economic data, by country, 1945-83 and trends, annual rpt, 2324–1.4

Law Enforcement

Aircraft hijackings, on-board explosions, other crimes against civil aviation, and circumstances, US and worldwide, 1931-83, annual rpt, 7504–31

Drug (illegal) supply to US, by type of drug and world area and country of origin, 1982, annual rpt, 15894–1

Drug and narcotics foreign production, acreage, eradication, and seizures, by substance, with labs destroyed and US aid, by country, 1981-85, annual rpt, 7004–17

Kidnapping by parents over intl and interstate boundaries, characteristics of cases referred to State Dept and FBI by State and country, 1979-83, hearing, 25528–95

Terrorist (intl) incidents, casualties, and attacks on US targets, by attack type and world area, with chronology of events, 1983, annual rpt, 7004–13

Natural Resources, Environment, and Pollution

Acid rain and air pollution environmental effects, and methods for neutralizing acidified water bodies, summary research rpt series, 5506–5

Air pollutant and radiation indoor levels by emissions source, and household exposure and health effects by pollutant type, various periods 1966-83, hearings, 21708–102

Carbon dioxide emissions, climatic effects, and control costs, projected under alternative emissions controls and energy use restrictions to 2100 with trends 1970s-80, reprint, 9188–88

Index by Categories

Carbon dioxide emissions from fossil fuel combustion, and growth rates, by country and country group, 1950-80, 3006–7.6

Central America mineral, energy, and water resources, and natural hazards to resource dev, by country, 1981 with trends from 1977, 5668–71

Dams, reservoirs, and hydroelectric plants, listing of major foreign and US structures with location and characteristics, as of June 1983, 5828–13

Developing countries disaster preparedness and summary sociodemographic, political, and economic data, country rpt series, 9916–2

Developing countries economic dev projects funded by multilateral dev banks, environmental and cultural impacts, 1970s-83, hearings, 21248–80

Endangered animals and plants foreign trade including reexports of live specimens and products, by purpose, country, and species, 1982, annual rpt, 5504–19

Environmental quality and protection programs, costs, and Fed Govt enforcement, 1983, detailed annual rpt, 484–1

Forests (tropical) status by country and world region, conservation methods, and mgmt role of US, foreign, and intl groups, 1977-81 and projected to 2000, 26358–101

Genetic resource (plant and animal) conservation, commercial uses, causes of depletion, and geographic sources, 1984 rpt, 5548–13

Marine mammals taken incidentally with fish catch of foreign vessels, by species and country of vessel origin, 1978-81, article, 2162–1.401

Pollution control instruments and equipment foreign market and trade, and user industry operations and demand, country market research rpts, 2045–17

Uranium ore tailings at active mills, EPA radon and radionuclide ermission standards and US and foreign exposure and health effects, various periods 1957-83, hearings, 21208–17

Population

Central America socioeconomic and political conditions in 6 countries, 1960s-83 with trends and projections 1930-2010, Commission rpt, 028–19.2

Developing countries disaster preparedness and summary sociodemographic, political, and economic data, country rpt series, 9916–2

Developing countries summary socioeconomic data, 1970s-83, and AID activities and funding by project and function, FY82-85, by country, annual rpt, 9914–3

Economic, social, and political summary data, by country, 1984, annual factbook, 244–11

Older persons characteristics, with related health care data and vital statistics, by world area and selected country, 1950-80 and projected to 2020, 2546–10.12

Older population death rates by age and sex, life expectancy, and birthplace of US aged, by selected country, 1976-78 and projected to 2050, Current Population Rpt, 2546–2.125

January-December 1984

Index by Categories

Population, and agricultural and food production indexes, by country and world region, 1974-83, annual rpt, 1524–5

Population by age and percent urban, for 7 countries, selected years 1975-81, 21148–33

Population size and growth rates, and latest available benchmark demographic data, by country, 1950-83, biennial rpt, 2324–4

Population socioeconomic data, and agricultural production, supply/demand, and trade, by country, 1950-77, 1528–179

Refugee and alien arrivals and resettlements in US, by State, outlying area, country of birth and citizenship, age, sex, and sponsoring agency, monthly rpt, 4702–3

Refugee arrivals in US, and worldwide Indochinese refugee population and resettlement, by country of origin, monthly rpt, 7002–4

Refugee arrivals in US, by world area of origin and processing and nationality, monthly rpt, 7002–5

Refugee migration, settlement status, and assistance, by world area and country of origin and asylum, as of May 1984, annual rpt, 7004–15

Refugee resettlement program activities and funding, arrivals and population by country of origin and State, and employment and other characteristics, FY83, annual rpt, 4704–8

Refugees from Central America by country of origin and asylum, and aid from US and Mexico, FY82-1984, GAO rpt, 26123–70

Refugees from Indochina, arrivals in US by country of origin and State of destination, tuberculosis cases, and unexplained sudden deaths, 1982, annual rpt, 4204–1.3

Statistical Abstract of US, selected social, political, and economic data, by country, 1945-83 and trends, annual rpt, 2324–1.4

US citizens birthplace inside-outside State of residence, by region and for Puerto Rico, other outlying areas, and abroad, 1980 Census of Population, State rpt series, 2531–4

US population and housing detailed characteristics, including ancestral origin, by census tract, 1980 Census of Population and Housing, State and SMSA rpt series, 2551–2

US population detailed socioeconomic characteristics, by county, city, and inside-outside SMSAs and central cities, 1980 Census of Population, State rpt series, 2531–3

Women sociodemographic, economic, and fertility characteristics, with comparisons to men, by country, 1960s-85, world region rpt series, 2326–15

Prices and Cost of Living

Living costs abroad, State Dept indexes, housing allowances, and hardship differential rates by country and major city, quarterly rpt, 6862–1

OECD energy prices and taxes by energy source and end-use sector, for US and 9 countries, quarterly 1979-83, annual rpt, 3164–71

Postal rates for domestic letters in US and 14 countries, 1983, annual rpt, 9864–1, 9864–5.3

Price indexes for consumer and producer goods, major commodities, exports,

imports, nonfarm wages, and currency value, US and 4 countries, bimonthly rpt, 2042–11

Telecommunications service rates for messages sent within US and to selected countries, by type and country, as of May 1982-Oct 1983, annual rpt, 9284–6.6

Public Welfare and Social Security

OASDHI, Medicaid, SSI, and other social insurance and public welfare programs benefits, beneficiary characteristics, and trust funds, selected years 1937-82, annual rpt, 4744–3.6

Social security programs benefits and expenditures, unemployment rate, and economic indicators growth, for 9 EC countries, 1960-82, article, 4742–1.405

Social security programs coverage, funding, eligibility, and benefits, by country, 1983, biennial rpt, 4746–4.58

Recreation and Leisure

Sporting goods and recreational equipment and vehicles foreign market and trade, country market research rpts, 2045–14

Science and Technology

Astronautic and aeronautic events, foreign and US, comprehensive chronology, 1976, annual rpt, 9504–2

Biotechnology commercial uses, R&D funding and output, controls, and industry financial and operating data, for US and 5 countries, 1970s-83 and estimated 1984-85, 26358–98

Biotechnology firms, patents, and trade by country, and effect of industry growth on US drug and chemical trade, selected years 1979-2000, 9886–4.78

Computers and computer equipment foreign market and trade, and user industry operations and demand, country market research rpts, 2045–1

Computers and other equipment with nuclear weapons applications, approvals for export to PRC by item and to other foreign markets, July 1981-June 1982, GAO rpt, 26123–76

Degree (doctoral) recipients in science and engineering, by field, sex, race, age, citizenship, postgrad employment and study status, State, and instn, 1960-82, 9626–6.16

Lab instruments foreign market and trade, and user industry operations and demand, country market research rpts, 2045–10

NASA procurement contract awards, by type, contractor, State, and country, FY84, semiannual rpt, 9502–6

NASA R&D funding to colleges and universities, by State, field of science, and instn, FY83, annual listing, 9504–7

Patents (US) granted to US and foreign applicants, by applicant type, firm, State, and country, subject rpt series, 2246–2

Patents (US) granted to US and foreign applicants, by patent type, State, and country, 1983, annual press release, 2244–2

Patents (US) granted to US and foreign applicants, by year of grant and application, country, and type of applicant, 1960s-83, annual rpt, 2244–3

Patents and trademarks (US), foreign resident applications and issuances by country, FY76-83, annual rpt, 2244–1.2, 2244–1.3

BY OUTLYING AREA

R&D expenditures and employment in science and technology, for US and 4 countries, selected years 1953-84, annual rpt, 9624–18.1

R&D Fed Govt funding for foreign performers, by world region and country, FY82-84, annual rpt, 9627–20.2

Robots for industrial use, R&D, training, and employment impacts, US with comparisons to foreign countries, 1980s with projections to 1992, 26358–105

Satellite systems (foreign and US) for civil observation, data product revenue, and proposed transfer of Fed Govt system to private sector, selected years 1978-FY84, 2148–47

Science Indicators, R&D expenditures, innovations, research, and higher education, with foreign comparisons, 1960s- 83, annual rpt, 9624–10.1

Space launchings attaining Earth orbit or beyond, by country, 1957-83, annual rpt, 9504–9.1

BY OUTLYING AREA

Agriculture and Food

Agricultural research expenditures and scientist years, by topic, commodity, and performing organization, FY82, annual rpt, 1744–2

Census of Agriculture, 1982: farms, farmland, production and costs, and operator characteristics, preliminary State and county rpt series, 2330–1

Census of Agriculture, 1982: farms, farmland, production, finances, and operator characteristics, by county, final State rpt series, 2331–1

Conservation practices in rural areas, Agricultural Conservation Program participation and payments, by State, FY83, annual rpt, 1804–7

Fish and fish products production by region and State, and trade, by species and product, 1982-83, annual rpt series, 2166–6

Fishery resources mgmt and R&D, Fed Govt grants by project and resulting publications, 1983, annual listing, 2164–3

FmHA loans and borrower supervision activities in farm and housing programs, by type and State, monthly rpt, 1182–1

FmHA loans, by type, race, Hispanic origin, and State, quarterly rpt, 1182–5

Research funding for agriculture from Fed Govt and States, by region, State, and outlying area, FY78-82, GAO rpt, 26113–111

Tobacco production, prices, stocks, taxes by State, and trade and foreign production by country, 1983, annual rpt, 1319–1

Banking, Finance, and Insurance

Credit union membership, shares and loans, and asset size, for Federal and federally insured State unions by State, 1984 annual listing, 9534–6

Savings and loan assn balance sheet items by State and SMSA, and finances of FHLBs, 1983, annual rpt, 9314–3

Savings instns FSLIC-insured, offices, and savings deposits, by State, SMSA, and county, 1983, annual rpt, 9314–4

BY OUTLYING AREA

Communications and Transportation

- Air passenger traffic, and aircraft operations by type, by airport, region, and State, projected FY82-95 and trends from FY76, annual rpt, 7504–7
- Aircraft registered with FAA, by type and characteristics of aircraft, carrier, make, State, and county, 1983, annual rpt, 7504–3
- Airline passenger and cargo traffic, and departures by aircraft type, by airline and US and foreign airport, 1982, annual rpt, 7504–35
- Airport improvement program grants and activities, by State and airport, FY83, annual rpt, 7504–38
- Airport planning and dev project grants of Fed Govt, by sponsor, airport, and location, periodic press release series, 7506–8
- DOT employment by subagency, State, and selected personnel characteristics, FY83, annual rpt, 7304–18.1
- DOT grant awards for transportation planning and safety programs, by region, State, and for 35 largest SMSAs, FY83, annual rpt, 7304–7
- Drivers license requirements and admin, by State and Canada Province, 1984, biennial rpt, 7554–18
- Hwy safety program Fed Govt appropriations, by State and program, quarterly rpt, 7552–9
- *Hwy Statistics,* detailed data on traffic, govt finances, fuel use, vehicles, driver licenses, and hwy characteristics, by State, 1983, annual rpt, 7554–1
- Hwy Trust Fund status and net revenues, FY57-83, annual summary rpt, 7554–24
- Port dev costs and financing through user fees, and shipping industry impact on local economy, by State, other area, industry, commodity, and port, 1970s-82, hearings, 21568–34.1
- Rural Telephone Program loan activities summary, by State, FY83, annual rpt, 1244–8
- Telephone facilities and use, by State and outlying area, 1982, annual rpt, 9284–6.2
- Telephone operating data, costs, and billings for American Telephone and Telegraph Co local and long distance lines, by State, 1980-82 with trends from 1970, 23848–176
- TV and radio industry minority and women employment by occupation, and business owners, by race and State, with revenues and stations, 1971-81, hearing, 21368–45

Education

- Bilingual education funding of States, FY83, and Spanish and other minority language population and children with limited English proficiency, 1980, by State, biennial rpt, 4804–14
- *Digest of Education Statistics,* detailed data on students, staff, finances, and facilities, 1982 and selected trends, annual rpt, 4824–2
- Handicapped children public education program enrollment, staff, and funding, by handicap, age, and State, 1981/82-1982/83, annual rpt, 4944–4
- Head Start Project enrollment of handicapped children, by handicap, State, and for Indian and migrant programs, 1982, annual rpt, 4604–1
- Higher education enrollment, by student characteristics, instn type, State, and for 150 instns, fall 1982, annual rpt, 4844–2
- Higher education instns, by type, location, and other characteristics, 1983/84 annual listing, 4844–3
- Higher education instns, type, location, enrollment, and student charges, by State and congressional district, 1983/84, biennial listing, 4844–11
- Higher education student aid sources, by selected school and student characteristics, 1967-83, annual rpt, 4804–5
- Impacted area schools, Fed Govt funding by county and State, FY83, annual rpt, 4804–10
- Microfiche from Educational Resources Info Center, holdings of US and foreign educational and other instns, as of 1983, listing, 4918–14
- Student aid basic grant, loan, and work-study awards, Fed Govt share by instn and State, 1984/85, annual rpt, 4804–17
- Student aid Federal programs funding and participation, by instn type and control, State, and outlying area, with student loan defaults and collections, FY82, annual rpt, 4804–28

Energy Resources and Demand

- Conservation aid of DOE, activities, funding, and grants by State, by program, FY84, annual rpt, 3304–21
- Conservation grants of Fed Govt to public and nonprofit private instns, by building type and State, 1983, annual rpt, 3304–15
- Conservation programs of State govts, Fed Govt financial and technical aid, and reported energy savings, by State, 1983, annual rpt, 3304–1
- Electric power wholesale purchases and costs for individual REA borrowers, by supplier and State, 1940-83, annual rpt, 1244–5
- Energy use, by type of air pollutant source and fuel, and State, 1981, annual rpt, 9194–14
- Oil and refined products and natural gas liquids supply/demand, trade, stocks, and refining, by detailed product, State, and PAD district, 1983 annual rpt, 3164–2

Geography and Climate

- Climatological data for 284 US and outlying stations, for period of record through 1982, annual rpt, 2154–8

Government and Defense

- Census of Govts, 1982: properties, govt-assessed value, sales, and tax rates, by property type, State, SMSA, county, and city, 2453–1
- DOD base construction and renovation, budget authorization requests by DOD component, State, country, and project, FY85, annual rpt, 3544–15
- DOD base support costs by function, and personnel and acreage by installation, by service branch, FY85, annual rpt, 3504–11
- DOD contract and in-house commercial activities costs and work-years, by service branch, defense agency, State, and installation, FY83, annual rpt, 3544–25
- DOD military and civilian personnel and dependents, FY83, annual rpt, 3544–1
- DOD military personnel of US abroad, by service branch, world area, and country, quarterly news release, 3542–9

Index by Categories

- DOD military personnel of US on active duty, by service branch, outlying area, and country, monthly rpt, 3542–14.5
- DOD prime contract awards, by individual contractor, service branch, State and city, and country, FY83, annual listing, 3544–22
- Economic Dev Admin loans and grants, by program, State, county, and project or recipient, FY83 and cumulative FY66-83, annual rpt, 2064–2
- Election campaign presidential candidate expenditure limits and voting age population, by State, 1984 Federal elections, press release, 9276–1.19
- Fed Govt aid to State and local areas, by type of payment, State, county, and city, FY83, annual rpt, 2464–3
- Fed Govt aid to State and local govts, expenditures, and direct payments, by program, agency, and State, FY83, annual rpt, 2464–2
- Fed Govt civilian employment, by US citizenship, selected agency, and outlying area, 1982, biennial rpt, 9844–8
- Immigration, and alien residents, workers, visitors, deportations, and naturalizations, by country of birth, FY81, annual rpt, 6264–2
- Income tax receipts of IRS, by State and district, FY83, annual rpt, 8104–2.2
- IRS collections by type of tax, refunds, and taxes due, by region and State, FY83, annual rpt, 8304–3.3
- Local govt receipts from Fed Govt in lieu of property taxes on public lands, by State, FY84, annual press release, 5724–9
- Military draft registrants, by State, 2nd half FY84, semiannual rpt, 9742–1
- Military reserve forces manpower strengths and characteristics, by component, quarterly rpt, 3542–4
- Military units, by service branch, outlying area, and country, FY83-85, annual rpt, 3504–1.2
- Navy procurement, by contractor and location of work, FY83, annual rpt, 3804–13
- Outlying areas govt financial data and audits by Interior Dept Inspector General, by area, FY83, annual rpt, 5304–15
- Property (real) of Fed Govt, inventory and costs, worldwide summary by location, agency, and use, 1983, annual rpt, 9454–5
- Property (real) of Fed Govt, leased property inventory and rental costs, worldwide summary by location and agency, Sept 1983, annual rpt, 9454–10

Health and Vital Statistics

- Abortions performed in 12 States and NYC, by State of residence and for non-US residents by selected area, 1980, US Vital Statistics final rpt, 4146–5.72
- Births (live) by selected demographic characteristics, for 3 outlying areas, 1979, US Vital Statistics annual rpt, 4144–1.3
- Deaths by cause and demographic characteristics 1979, and number and rates 1940-79, US Vital Statistics annual rpt, 4144–3.2
- Deaths in US by State and by outlying area or country of birth, 1979, US Vital Statistics annual rpt, 4144–2.1
- HHS aid to each State and local govt or private instn, amount obligated, funding agency, and program, FY83, annual listing, 4004–3

Index by Categories

BY OUTLYING AREA

Infectious notifiable diseases, cases and current outbreaks, by region and State, weekly rpt, 4202–1

Infectious notifiable diseases, cases and incidence, by census div and State, 1982, annual rpt, 4204–1

Influenza deaths, viruses identified by State and country, epidemiology, and vaccine effects and recommended dosages by age, 1979/80-1980/81, annual rpt, 4205–3

Mines (sand and gravel) and related operations, occupational injuries and incidence rates, detailed analysis, 1982, annual rpt, 6664–2

Mines (stone) and related operations, occupational injuries and incidence rates, detailed analysis, 1982, annual rpt, 6664–5

NIH grants and awards for R&D, training, construction, and medical libraries, by location and recipient, FY83, annual listings, 4434–7

Occupational Safety and Health Admin enforcement activities and funding, and State programs and staff, 1982, annual rpt, 6604–2.1

Public health labs of States, pay scales and job requirements by occupation and State, FY81-83, annual rpt, 4204–7

Public health labs of States, personnel, finances, workloads, and other activities, by State, FY82, annual rpt, 4204–8

Tuberculosis cases, deaths, and treatment, by demographic characteristics, State, and city, 1982 and trends from 1953, annual rpt, 4204–2

Venereal disease cases reported and epidemiologic activities, by region, State, and large city, 1982, annual rpt, 4204–14

Vital statistics records offices and availability of birth, death, marriage, and divorce certificates, by State, 1984 annual listing, 4124–7

Housing and Construction

Home mortgage loans, and other balance sheet items of S&Ls, by FHLB district, State, and SMSA, 1983, annual rpt, 9314–3

Housing solar energy and energy conservation projects, HUD grants by State and outlying area, 1984 press release, 5006–3.36

Industry and Commerce

Exports and imports between US and outlying areas, by detailed commodity and mode of transport, monthly rpt, 2422–4

Foreign-owned US multiestablishment firms, employment, and payroll, by country, State, industry group, and foreign ownership share, 1981-82, annual rpt, 2324–6

Mineral Industry Surveys, commodity reviews of production, trade, stocks, and consumption, monthly rpt series, 5612–1

Mineral Industry Surveys, commodity reviews of production, trade, stocks, and consumption, quarterly rpt series, 5612–2

Minerals Yearbook, 1982, Vol 1: commodity reviews of production and trade, by State, annual rpt, 5604–33.2

Minerals Yearbook, 1982, Vol 2 preprints: State reviews of production and sales by commodity, and business activity, annual rpt series, 5604–16

Minerals Yearbook, 1982, Vol 2: State reviews of production, sales, and firms, by commodity, and business activity, annual rpt, 5604–34

Small Business Admin loans, contract awards, and surety bonds, by firm, State, and city, FY83, annual rpt, 9764–1.2

Waterborne commerce of US (domestic and foreign), freight by commodity, traffic, and passengers, by port and waterway, 1982, annual rpt, 3754–3

Waterborne trade of US, by type of service, commodity, country, route, and US port, 1982, annual rpt, 7704–2

Labor and Employment

Employment and training program funding under Job Training Partnership Act, and required matching funds, for 3 programs by State, 1984/85, press release, 6408–58

Older persons community service part-time employment and program funding, by State and outlying area, FY84, press release, 6408–60

Unemployment insurance laws, comparisons of State provisions, as of Sept 1984, semiannual revision, 6402–2

Vocational rehabilitation, State agency caseloads by status and processing stage, region, and State, FY83 with trends from FY21, annual rpt, 4944–5

Vocational rehabilitation State agency expenditures, caseloads, rehabilitations, and staff, under Section 110 of the Rehabilitation Act, by State, FY82, annual rpt, 4944–9

Wages by occupation, for office and plant workers in selected labor market areas, 1983 surveys, annual summary rpt, 6785–6

Wages for 3 occupational groups, relative average levels in 78 labor market areas, 1983, annual press release, 6785–13

Youth summer job program of Fed Govt, funding and jobs by State and for Indians, summer 1984, press release, 6408–62

Law Enforcement

Assaults, murders, and other deaths of law enforcement officers, by circumstances, level of govt, agency, victim and offender characteristics, and location, 1983, annual rpt, 6224–3

Bombing (explosive and incendiary) incidents, damage, injuries, and deaths, by target, State, and circumstances, 1983, annual rpt, 6224–5

Court caseloads, actions, procedure duration, judges, and jurors, by Federal district and appeals court, 1979-84, annual rpt, 18204–3

Court caseloads for Federal district, appeals, and bankruptcy courts, by type of suit and offense, circuit, and district, quarterly rpt, 18202–1

Crimes against financial instns, by State, semiannual article, 9312–1

Juror (grand and petit) usage and costs, trials, and trial days, by Federal district court, years ended June 1980-84, annual rpt, 18204–4

Natural Resources, Environment, and Pollution

Air pollution levels for 5 pollutants, by detailed source, State, and Air Quality Control Region, 1981, annual rpt, 9194–7

Air pollution levels for 6 pollutants, and measurements exceeding natl standards, by site, 1983, annual rpt, 9194–5

Environmental quality, pollutant discharge by type and source, and EPA protection activities and funding, 1970s-83, biennial regional rpt series, 9184–15

EPA pollution control research and grant assistance program activities, monthly rpt, 9182–8

Fish and wildlife restoration program of Fed Govt, finances, funding by State, and hunting and fishing equipment excise tax revenue, FY84, annual rpt, 5504–13

Fish and Wildlife Service restoration programs, including new sites, funding, and research, by State, FY81, annual rpt, 5504–1

Forest and windbarrier planting and seeding, by State, FY83, annual rpt, 1204–7

Forests (natl) and other lands under Forest Service mgmt, by forest and location, Sept 1983, annual rpt, 1204–2

Forests (tropical) status by country and world region, conservation methods, and mgmt role of US, foreign, and intl groups, 1977-80s and projected to 2000, 26358–101.1

Water quality, pollutant types and sources, and control program compliance, by State, 1982, biennial rpt, 9204–6

Water supply and quality in streams and lakes, and groundwater levels in wells, by drainage basin, 1980, annual State rpt series, 5666–12

Water supply and quality in streams and lakes, and groundwater levels in wells, by drainage basin, 1981, annual State rpt series, 5666–6

Water supply and quality in streams and lakes, and groundwater levels in wells, by drainage basin, 1982, annual State rpt series, 5666–20

Water supply and quality in streams and lakes, and groundwater levels in wells, by drainage basin, 1983, annual State rpt series, 5666–10

Population

Census of Population, 1980: detailed socioeconomic and demographic characteristics, by age, sex, race, Hispanic origin, occupation, and industry, State rpt series, 2531–4

Census of Population, 1980: detailed socioeconomic characteristics, by county, city, and inside-outside SMSAs and central cities, State rpt series, 2531–3

Population size and components of change, by outlying area, 1970-82, Current Population Rpt, 2546–3.127

Population size and components of change, by outlying area, 1980-83, Current Population Rpt, 2546–3.134

Refugee and alien arrivals and resettlements in US, by State, outlying area, country of birth and citizenship, age, sex, and sponsoring agency, monthly rpt, 4702–3

Refugee arrivals in US by world area of origin and State of settlement, and Fed Govt intl and domestic assistance costs, FY85, annual rpt, 7004–16

Refugee resettlement program activities and funding, arrivals and population by country of origin and State, and employment and other characteristics, FY83, annual rpt, 4704–8

Statistical Abstract of US, selected social, political, and economic data, by country, 1945-83 and trends, annual rpt, 2324–1.4

BY OUTLYING AREA

Public Welfare and Social Security

Abortions funded by Medicaid by justification, and expenditures, by State, FY78-83, annual rpt, 4654–9

AFDC and aid to aged, blind, and disabled, programs in outlying areas under Social Security Act, FY82, annual rpt, 4704–9

AFDC recipients and payments, applications by disposition, payment discontinuances by reason, and hearings by outcome, by State, quarterly rpt, 4742–6

Child Support Enforcement Program costs, cases, and collections, by State, FY82, semiannual rpt, 4002–5

Child Support Enforcement Program costs, cases, and collections, by State, FY83, annual rpt, 4004–29

Child Support Enforcement Program financial and operating data, FY79-83, annual rpt, 4004–16

Fed Govt aid to State and local govts, expenditures, and direct payments, by program, agency, and State, FY83, annual rpt, 2464–2

Food aid program of USDA for women, infants, and children, participants, clinics, and costs, by State and Indian agency, FY82, annual table, 1364–12.1

Food stamp program participation and coupons distributed, by region, State, and project area, quarterly rpt, 1362–6

Medicare and Medicaid eligibility, participation, covered services and use, and reimbursements and payments, various periods 1966-82, annual rpt, 4654–1

Medicare facilities and services use, covered charges, and reimbursements, by beneficiary type and area of residence, series, 4656–1

OASDHI, Medicaid, SSI, and other social insurance and public welfare programs benefits, beneficiary characteristics, and trust funds, selected years 1937-83, annual rpt, 4744–3

OASDI benefits and beneficiaries, by type of benefit, State, outlying area, and county, Dec 1982, 4748–38

School breakfast and other USDA child nutrition programs, participation and finances, by region and State, annual rpt series, 1364–13

Social Security Bulletin, OASDHI and other program operations and beneficiary characteristics, from 1940, monthly rpt with articles, 4742–1

Recreation and Leisure

Arts and humanities funding, by source and State, FY82-83 with trends from FY66, 21408–69

Boat registrations, use, and accident deaths, injuries, and property damage, by detailed cause and State, 1983, annual rpt, 7404–1

Historic Preservation Fund grants, by State, FY85, annual press release, 5544–9

Natl park area visits and overnight stays, visitors, and vehicles, by State and park, 1983, annual rpt, 5544–12

Outdoor recreation area dev, Interior Dept Land and Water Conservation Fund grants by State, FY85, annual press release, 5544–15

Science and Technology

Patents (US) granted to US and foreign applicants, by patent type, State, and country, 1983, annual press release, 2244–2

Patents issued to US residents, by State, FY76-83, annual rpt, 2244–1.2

R&D and science-related Fed Govt funding to higher education and nonprofit instns, by field, instn, agency, and State, FY82, annual rpt, 9627–17

BY REGION

Agriculture and Food

Acreage harvested and cropland area by crop and region, and potential for expansion, 1982-84 with trends from 1949, annual rpt, 1584–4

Agricultural cooperatives commercial farmer membership and use, by type and sales size of farm and region, 1980, 1128–32

Agricultural cooperatives, membership, and activities, by type of service, commodity, and State, FY51-1982, annual survey rpt, 1124–1

Agricultural cooperatives membership, by farm sales size and type, by region, 1980, article, 1122–1.401

Agricultural research expenditures and scientist years, by topic, commodity, and performing organization, FY82, annual rpt, 1744–2

Cold storage food stocks of 77 commodities, by region, 1983, annual rpt, 1631–11

Corn and soybean yields, itemized production costs, and input use, effects of alternative tillage systems, by region and for 10 States, 1980, 1588–80

Cotton fiber and processing test results, by staple, region, State, and production area, seasonal biweekly rpt, 1309–3

Cotton fiber and processing test results, by State, 1983, annual rpt, 1309–4

Cotton, wool, and synthetic fiber production, prices, consumption, and trade, periodic situation rpt with articles, 1561–1

Dairy cooperatives and percent share of producers and deliveries, by region, 1982 with trends from 1965, article, 1317–4.403

Dairy cooperatives sales volume and market shares by commodity, and finances, by region, 1980 with trends from 1957, 1128–29

Dairy marketing and price data for selected cities, States, and regions, 1983, annual rpt, 1317–1

Dairy products household expenditures, effects of income and other sociodemographic characteristics, modeling results, 1977/78, 1561–2.404

Egg production by type of product, and shell eggs broken under Fed Govt inspection by region, monthly rpt, 1625–2

Exports of agricultural products, for 17 commodity groups, by region and State, 1978/79-1983/84, article, 1522–1.403

Farm Credit System mortgage and other loans, and financial statements, 1982 and selected trends from 1961, annual rpt, 9264–2

Farm finances, assets, expenses, cash flow, receipts, and loans, selected years 1971-85, annual rpt, 1544–13

Farm finances, expenses by type, loans by purpose and source, and credit detail by Fed Reserve District, quarterly rpt, 9365–3.10

Farm labor, wages, hours, and perquisites, by State, quarterly rpt, 1631–1

Index by Categories

Farm mortgage debt outstanding, by type of lender and district, as of Jan 1983, annual rpt, 9264–3

Farm non-real estate debt outstanding, by type of lender and district, as of Jan 1983, annual rpt, 9264–4

Farm population, by employment and socioeconomic characteristics, 1983, annual rpt, 2544–1

Farm population, by farm type and sales size and selected other characteristics, 1975-80, 1598–144

Farm production expenditures, detailed items by farm sales size and region, 1983, annual rpt, 1614–3

Farm production inputs, land mgmt, and environmental effects, for 4 crops, 1940s-80 and projected to 2010, 9188–94

Farm production inputs, outputs, and productivity, by region, 1939-82, annual rpt, 1544–17

Farm production itemized costs, receipts, and net returns, for 13 crops, 4 livestock types, and milk, by region, 1981-83, annual rpt, 1544–20

Farm real estate value, sales, financing, taxes, and proposed use after purchase, by State, 1970s-84, annual rpt, 1541–8

Farms with sales under $2,500, acreage, finances, operations, and operator characteristics, by region and for 6 States, 1978, 1548–241

Fertilizer production and trade, and consumption by region and State, 1983, annual rpt, 1804–6

Fish and eggs for stocking distributed from natl hatcheries, by species, hatchery, and jurisdiction, FY83, annual rpt, 5504–10

Fish and fish products production by region and State, and trade, by species and product, 1982-83, annual rpt series, 2166–6

Fish hatchery production, deliveries, and operating costs, and fishery assistance, by region, hatchery, and Fed Govt assistance station, FY82, annual rpt, 5504–9

Fish landings by species and State, and value at leading ports and disposition, 1970s-83, annual rpt, 2164–1.1

Fish landings by species, State, and at leading ports, and industry operating data, by region, 1970s-83, annual rpt, 2164–1.10

Fish landings, employment, gear used, and seafood production, for detailed species by State, 1977, annual rpt, 2164–2

FmHA loans for rural home mortgages, eligibility of current recipients under revised income limit, by State, 1983, GAO rpt, 26113–134

Food expenditures for fruit, vegetable, and potato products related to changes in income and other household characteristics, 1977-78, 1548–236

Fruit and vegetable shipments, and arrivals in 23 US and 5 Canada cities, by mode of transport and State or country of origin, 1983, annual rpt series, 1311–4

Grain cooperatives marketing, storage, and shipments by mode of transport, by grain type and region, FY80, 1128–28

Grain cooperatives storage and handling facilities, sales, exports, and financial condition, selected years 1974-82, 1128–31

Index by Categories

BY REGION

Grain mill production workers, wages, hours, and benefits, by occupation, mill product, and region, June 1982 survey, 6787–6.204

Grain production, prices, trade, and export inspections by US port and country of destination, by grain type, weekly rpt, 1313–2

Grain stocks by region and market city, and grain inspected for export, by type, weekly rpt, 1313–4

Health insurance coverage of farmers, farm population, and managers, by insurance type and selected sociodemographic characteristics, 1976, 1598–191

Hog production, producer characteristics, facilities, and marketing, by type and size of enterprise and region, 1975 and 1980, 1568–248

Honey and sugar production, prices, trade, stocks, and marketing, and honey loan activity and processing awards of CCC, weekly rpt, 1311–2

Livestock grazing on Natl Forest System lands, and losses from predators, poisonous plants, and other causes, by region and State, FY83, annual rpt, 1204–5

Livestock packers purchases and feeding, and livestock markets, dealers, and sales, by region and State, 1981-82, annual rpt, 1384–1

Livestock producers membership in agricultural cooperatives, and patronage for marketing and supplies purchase, by region and farm sales size, 1980, 1128–26

Livestock slaughter by species, meat production, and number of slaughtering plants, by State, 1983, annual rpt, 1623–10

Livestock slaughter under Fed Govt inspection, by livestock type and region, monthly rpt, 1623–9

Livestock slaughter under Federal inspection, by type, monthly 1983, annual rpt, 1564–6.2

Milk order market major provisions, summary by Federal marketing area, as of July 1984, annual rpt, 1317–11

Milk order market prices and detailed operations, by State and market area, monthly 1982-83, annual rpt, 1317–3

Milk order market prices and detailed operations, monthly rpt with articles, 1317–4

Milk pasteurized by ultra-high temperature, sales, production, stocks, costs, market shares, and prices, 1980, 1568–247

Milk price supports effect on production, use, prices, and farm receipts, by region and State, 1940s-83 and alternative projections to 1988/89, 1568–245

Molasses (feed) production, wholesale prices by market area, and US imports by customs district and country, weekly rpt, 1311–16

Mushroom production, sales, and prices, by State, 1981/82-1983/84 and planned 1984/85, annual rpt, 1631–9

Peanut production, prices, stocks, exports, use, inspection, and quality, by region and State, selected crop years 1974-83, annual rpt, 1311–5

Peanut production, prices, trade by country, and stocks, weekly rpt, 1311–1

Pesticide use and acreage treated, for 12 vegetable and melon crops, by type of pesticide, method of application, and region, 1979, 1588–82

Pesticide use for selected crops, periodic situation rpt with articles, 1561–16

Poultry (egg, chicken, and turkey) production and inventories, monthly rpt, 1625–1

Poultry and egg marketing and price data for selected regions, States, and SMSAs, monthly 1983, annual rpt, 1317–2

Poultry layer inventory, by region, 1982-83, annual rpt, 1625–7

Poultry Natl Improvement Plan, hatchery participation and flocks included, by disease program, region, and State, 1981-83, annual rpt, 1394–15

Prices received by farmers for major products, and paid for farm inputs and living items, by commodity and State, monthly rpt, 1629–1

Prices received by farmers for major products, and paid for farm inputs, by commodity and State, 1983, annual rpt, 1629–5

Research funding for agriculture from Fed Govt and States, by region, State, and outlying area, FY78-82, GAO rpt, 26113–111

Sugar and sweeteners production, consumption, prices, supply, and trade, quarterly rpt with articles, 1561–14

Turkey hatcheries incubator egg inventory and poult placements, by region, monthly rpt, 1625–10

Turkey hatchery production, by region, monthly 1982-83, annual rpt, 1625–8.2

Vegetable production, prices, stocks, and consumption, for selected fresh and processed crops, periodic situation rpt with articles, 1561–11

Banking, Finance, and Insurance

Bank deposits in commercial and mutual savings banks and in US branches of foreign banks, by account type, instn, State, SMSA, and county, June 1983, annual rpt, 9295–3

Bankruptcy caseloads in Federal district courts and new judges needed, by circuit and district, and characteristics of bankruptcy filers, 1978-83, hearing, 25528–97

Credit union financial statements by region, State, and type of membership, for Federal and federally insured State unions, 1983, annual rpt, 9534–1

Fed Home Loan Mortgage Corp activities and financial statements, 1983, annual rpt, 9414–1

Fed Reserve payments services provided depository instns, financial statements, and costs and revenues by service and district bank, 1983, annual press release, 9364–9

Interest and dividend rates paid and return on mortgages at FSLIC-insured S&Ls, by FHLB district, monthly rpt, 9312–1

Investment companies classification, assets, and location, Sept 1982, annual directory, 9734–1

Savings and loan assn auditing firms concentration ratios, by FHLB district, 1976-80, article, 9312–1.403

Savings and loan assn balance sheet items by State and SMSA, and finances of FHLBs, 1983, annual rpt, 9314–3

Savings and loan assns assets and liabilities, by FHLB district and State, selected years 1955-82, annual rpt, 9314–1

Savings instns FSLIC-insured, offices, and savings deposits, by State, SMSA, and county, 1983, annual rpt, 9314–4

Small Business Investment Companies finances, funding, licensing, and loan activity, 2nd half FY84, semiannual rpt, 9762–3

Treasury bill offerings and auction results, by Fed Reserve district and term to maturity, periodic releases, 8002–7

Communications and Transportation

Air passenger traffic, and aircraft operations by type, by airport, region, and State, projected FY82-95 and trends from FY76, annual rpt, 7504–7

Air traffic levels at FAA-operated control facilities, by airport and State, FY83, annual rpt, 7504–27

Aircraft (general aviation), hours flown, and equipment, by type, use, and model of aircraft, region, and State, 1982, annual rpt, 7504–29

Aircraft active in general aviation, by region, as of Jan 1979-83 and forecast FY84-95, annual rpt, 7504–6

Aircraft handled by instrument flight rule, by user type, FAA traffic control center, and region, FY69-83 and forecast to FY95, annual rpt, 7504–15

Aircraft pilots and nonpilots certified by FAA, by type of certificate, age, sex, region, and State, 1983, annual rpt, 7504–2

Aircraft registered with FAA, by type and characteristics of aircraft, carrier, make, State, and county, 1983, annual rpt, 7504–3

Airlines (commuter and intrastate) operating in 1978 by region and State, and listing by city, by operation status in 1984, article, 9142–42.404

Airport financing by source, bond issues by region, and airport operations, by airport and operator type, FY75-83 and projected to FY93, 26306–6.75

Auto registrations for domestic and imported new cars, by region and State, 1964-83, annual rpt, 9884–7.4

Aviation activity, detailed data on aircraft, air carriers, personnel, airports, and FAA operations, 1974-83, annual rpt, 7504–1

Bridges and share structurally and functionally deficient, by bridge and city characteristics, region, and city, 1980, 10048–60

Bridges over navigable waters, with type of bridge and use, owner, dimensions, and location, 1984 regional listing series, 7406–5

Coast Guard search and rescue activities, by district, station, and rescue vessel, FY83 and projected FY88, annual rpt, 7404–2

DOT grant awards for transportation planning and safety programs, by region, State, and for 35 largest SMSAs, FY83, annual rpt, 7304–7

FAA activities and finances, and employees by region, FY82-83, annual rpt, 7504–10

Grain ocean freight rates by route, and waterborne trade of grain and selected other commodities worldwide, 1966-82, 1548–235

Hwy construction material prices and indexes for Federal-aid system, by type of material and urban-rural location, quarterly rpt, 7552–7

BY REGION

Hwy safety program Fed Govt appropriations, by State and program, quarterly rpt, 7552–9

Hwy traffic volume on rural roads and city streets, by region, monthly rpt, 7552–8

ICC enforcement of motor carrier regulations, staff by position, and caseload by violation type, by ICC region, selected years FY80-85, GAO rpt, 26113–133

Motor carriers (Class I) of property financial and operating data, by region and firm, quarterly rpt, 9482–5

Motor carriers (Class I interstate) finances, operations, equipment, employment, and payroll, by district, 1982, annual rpt, 9486–5.3

Motor carriers (Class II) of property financial and operating data, by region, 1982, annual rpt, 9484–10

Ocean freight rates for grain, by US loading port and country of destination, weekly rpt, 1272–2

Pipeline safety regulations enforcement of DOT and States by pipeline type and State, and accidents and commodity losses, selected years 1973-FY84, GAO rpt, 26113–130

Port dev costs and financing through user fees, and shipping industry impact on local economy, by State, other area, industry, commodity, and port, 1970s-2020, hearings, 21568–34

Port dredging contract awards of Army Corps of Engineers, by region and company, FY82-83, hearings, 21728–53

Ports, port facilities by type, and inland waterways by size, by location, 1982-83, annual rpt, 7704–16

Railroad finances and operations, detailed data by firm, class of service, and district, 1983, annual rpt, 9486–6.1

Railroad freight volume and revenues, by commodity and region of origin and destination, 1982, annual rpt, 7604–6

Railroad revenue, income, freight, and rate of return, by Class I freight railroad and district, quarterly rpt, 9482–2

Shipbuilding costs and related employment, by coastal district, 1982, annual rpt, 7704–12

Ships and tonnage entering and clearing US Customs, by district and port of entry, 1983, annual rpt, 2424–7

Ships in US merchant fleet, shipping costs, construction, employment, military availability, and Fed Govt subsidies, 1970s-1984 and projected to 2000, 26306–6.83

Traffic deaths by region, and death rates for miles traveled, monthly rpt, 7762–7

Travel patterns, personal and household characteristics, auto use, and public transport availability, 1977 survey, series, 7556–6

Truck transport of fruit and vegetables to 6 major markets, weekly rates by commodity and region, and monthly truck-mile costs, 1983 annual rpt, 1311–15

Education

Computer access and use in elementary and secondary schools, by region, urban-rural location, and Title I status, spring 1982, 4826–1.10

Condition of Education, detailed data on enrollment, staff, achievement, finances, curricula, and education effects on employment, 1982-83, annual rpt, 4824–1

Educational progress, natl assessment summary data for 7 learning areas, by characteristics of participants, selected years 1971-82, annual rpt, 4824–2.6

Elementary and secondary enrollment, households with children enrolled by school control, householder characteristics, and region, Oct 1982, 4838–13

Fed Govt education block grants, State allocations by program and selected school district, FY82-84 and trends from FY60, hearing, 21408–75

High school class of 1982: coursework compared to graduation criteria of natl commission, by student and school characteristics, 4828–16

High school class of 1982: foreign language course enrollment, by language, student and school characteristics, and location, 1984 rpt, 4838–11

High school classes of 1980 and 1982: educational and sociodemographic characteristics and expectations, natl longitudinal study, series, 4826–2

Indian Education Act grants to local agencies, Education Dept audit results by region, FY82, annual rpt, 4804–29

Postsecondary enrollment in academic, vocational, and continuing education, by student characteristics, Oct 1982, 4848–16

Energy Resources and Demand

Agricultural cooperatives oil and gas production, supply, and reserves, 1979 and 1982, article, 1561–16.403

Buildings heating and air conditioning fuel by type, for new private nonresidential and public buildings, by region, 1979-83, monthly rpt, annual tables, 2382–4.4

Coal exports and imports, and average price, by world area, country, and customs district, quarterly rpt, 3162–37

Coal Fed Govt leases, acreage, production, and prices, by State, and legal and mgmt issues, 1970s-83 with production projections to 2000, 11128–1

Coal production and mines by county, prices, productivity, miners, reserves, and stocks, by mining method and State, 1982-83, annual rpt, 3164–25

Coal production and stocks by district, and shipments by district of origin, State of destination, consuming sector, and mode of transport, quarterly rpt, 3162–8

Coal production by State and region, trade, consumption, and stocks, weekly rpt, 3162–1

Coal supply/demand, projected 1983-95 with summary trends from 1865, annual rpt, 3164–68

Coal surface mining reclamation costs and Interior Dept regulatory enforcement activities, impacts on industry in 5 States and 3 regions, various periods 1978-82, 6068–177

Electric and gas privately owned utilities, wages and employment by occupation, and benefits, by region, Oct 1982 survey, 6787–6.205

Electric power peak demand, generating and interregional transfer capability, and reserve margins, detailed data by region, 1984-93, annual rpt, 3404–6

Electric power plant (coal-fired) capacity, coal demand, and coal supply by mode of transport and region of origin, by State, for units planned 1983-92, 3088–18

Index by Categories

Electric power plant capacity, by plant type, age, and DOE region, 1982, and new and replacement capacity trends and projections, 1900-2020, 3008–98

Electric power plant capacity, production, retail sales, and fuel stocks, use, and costs, by State, 1979-83, annual rpt, 3164–11

Electric power plants, by capacity, fuel used, unit type, region, State, and county, for plants added and retired, 1983 and planned through 1993, annual rpt, 3164–36

Electric power transactions of US with Canada and Mexico, by utility and US region, 1983, annual rpt, 3104–10

Electric utility production, by North American Electric Reliability Council region, monthly rpt, 3162–35

Energy use in nonresidential buildings, expenditures, and conservation, by building characteristics, EIA survey series, 3166–8

Energy use, prices, and conservation and efficiency measures, by fuel type, end-use sector, selected industry, and region, 1960-83, annual rpt, 3164–73

Household energy use, appliances, motor vehicles, and vehicle fuel economy, by census region and urban-rural location, various periods Oct 1980-Mar 1983, annual rpt, 3164–74

Household energy use by socioeconomic characteristics, impact of energy price increases, selected years 1978-95, 3004–13.3

Housing (multifamily rental) energy use and costs, conservation effect on rental marketing, and effect of utility bill payment methods on conservation efforts, 1970s-80s, 3308–73

Housing electricity and gas costs for 306 cities, by utility, with climatological data, fall 1982, 3308–67

Housing energy conservation programs of utilities, financing, costs, participation, and energy savings, various periods 1981-84, hearing, 21368–54

Housing energy use, and savings under alternative conservation strategies, by State, with model methodology and energy prices, selected years 1970-81, 21368–48

Housing energy use, costs, expenditures, and conservation, and household and housing characteristics, survey series, 3166–7

Industrial electric power cogeneration in 5 industries, and fuel use and utility supply/demand effects, by region, 1983-93, 3008–92

Irrigation system energy use and costs, and irrigated farm acreage by fuel and region, selected years 1974-84 and trends from 1900, article, 1561–16.406

Natural gas interstate pipeline sales, total and under minimum fee contract provision, by service type, contract date, and region, 1981, 3168–91

Natural gas interstate pipeline sales, total and under minimum fee contract provision by service type, contract date, and region, 1981, summary article, 3162–4.408

Natural gas pipeline and compressor station construction costs, 1979-82, annual rpt, 3084–3

Natural gas production, wells drilled, and contract prices, by Natural Gas Policy Act section, producer and well characteristics, State, and field, selected years 1968-83, 3168–90

Index by Categories

Nuclear engineering student enrollments and degrees granted, by State, instn, and subfield, and placements by sector, 1983, annual rpt, 3004–5

Nuclear power plant capacity, generation, shutdowns, operation status and costs, and fuel, quarterly rpt, 3352–3

Nuclear power plant construction and operation status, and capacity, by plant, region, State, and selected country, 1983 and projected to 2020, annual rpt, 3164–57

Nuclear reactors at central station power plants, operating status and other characteristics by plant, utility, and State, as of Jan 1984, annual rpt, 3354–11

Oil and gas drilling costs and cost indexes for onshore wells and dry holes, by depth and region, 1983-84, annual rpt, 3164–67

Oil and gas extraction production workers, wages, hours, and benefits, by occupation, region, and for 5 States, June 1982 survey, 6787–6.203

Oil and refined products and natural gas liquids supply/demand, trade, stocks, and refining, by detailed product, State, and PAD district, monthly rpt with articles, 3162–6

Oil and refined products and natural gas liquids supply/demand, trade, stocks, and refining, by detailed product, State, and PAD district, 1983 annual rpt, 3164–2

Oil enhanced recovery technologies use and environmental impacts, by oil field, county, and State, 1970s-80 and projected to 2000, 3408–29

Oil pipeline industry competition, market shares and throughput capacity by firm and market area, as of 1983, 6008–18

Oil product surveys, lab analyses of aviation, heating, diesel, and gasoline fuel properties, last issues of annual and semiannual rpt series, 3006–2

Oil refined products sales of gas plant operators, refiners, and resellers, price and volume for 13 products, by end-use sector, PAD district, and State, monthly rpt, 3162–11

Oil refineries financial and operating impacts from auto use of alcohol fuels, projected to 2000 with trends 1964-80, 3308–75

Rural Electrification Admin loans to power supply and distribution firms, and borrower operating and financial data, by firm and State, 1983, annual rpt, 1244–1

Uranium reserves and mining and milling industries operations and finances, with selected foreign comparisons, various periods 1964-83 and projected to 2000, 3008–95

Wood acquired and used for home heating, by household characteristics and wood sources, 1980/81, 1208–204

Wood fuel consumption, by end-use sector, SIC 2-digit industry, region, State, and selected industrial and power plant, 1980-83, biennial rpt, 3164–78

Geography and Climate

Meteorological forecast methodology, accuracy, and applications, technical rpt series, 2186–4

Precipitation forecast accuracy, by season, forecast period, and region, various periods 1966-82, technical memorandum, 2188–17

BY REGION

Government and Defense

Budget of US, special analysis of grants-in-aid outlays, by agency, function, and region, FY83-87, annual rpt, 104–1.8

Collective bargaining agreements of Federal employees, unions involved, and employees covered, by agency for agreements expiring July 1984-June 1985, annual listing, 9847–1

Customs collections, by district, FY79-83, annual rpt, 8144–1

Customs collections of 15 largest collection districts, by port, quarterly rpt, 8142–1

Defense Fuel Supply Center procurement, prices, stocks, transport, and other activities and finances, FY83, annual rpt, 3904–8

DOD military post exchange operations, locations worldwide, sales by type of commodity or service and facility, and employment, FY83, annual rpt, 3504–10

Election campaign Fed Govt funding, reform and tax deduction proposals, and TV and political action committee influence, opinion surveys, various dates 1977-83, hearings, 21428–7.1

Fed Govt personnel action appeals, decisions of Merit Systems Protection Board, by region, agency, and employee characteristics, FY82, annual rpt, 9494–2

Govt finances, by level of govt and State, selected years 1929-83, annual rpt, 10044–1

Immigration, and alien residents, workers, visitors, deportations, and naturalizations, by country of birth, FY81, annual rpt, 6264–2

Income tax returns and collections, for IRS regions, districts, and service centers, 1972-82 and projections to 1990, annual rpt, 8304–8

Income tax returns filed by type, for US, IRS regions, and service center cities, 1972-82 and projected 1983-90, annual rpt, 8304–9.1

Income tax returns filed by type of filer, selected income items, summary data, quarterly rpt, 8302–2.1

Income tax returns of individuals by tax return item, State, and occupation, and income by source and tax owed, by income level, selected years 1916-80, conf papers, 8308–28.1

IRS collections by type of tax, refunds, and taxes due, by region and State, FY83, annual rpt, 8304–3.3

Local govt finances and population characteristics for cities and suburbs, by region and selected SMSA, selected years 1957-FY83, 10048–61

Passports issued, by holder characteristics, travel purpose, and country of destination, quarterly rpt, 7182–1

Property (surplus personal) of Fed Govt donated to State and local agencies and nonprofit instns, by region and State, FY83, annual rpt, 9454–22

Revenue sharing and other Fed Govt grant program alternative allocations, with city govt finances and responses to program cuts, FY79-83, hearings, 25408–86

Sealift Military Command operations for naval fleet support, and transport of DOD and AID cargo by route, quarterly rpt, 3802–2

Taxes, tax policy, and intergovtl relations, public opinion survey results, 1972-84, annual rpt, 10044–2

Voting age population selected characteristics and participation in presidential elections, 1964-80 with projections to 2000, Current Population Rpt, 2546–2.117

Health and Vital Statistics

Alcohol, Drug Abuse and Mental Health Admin staff, contract awards, and grants, by Inst, program, and State, FY83, annual factbook, 4044–1

Asian and Pacific Islands Americans births by ethnic origin and sociodemographic and birth characteristics, with comparisons to blacks and whites, 1978-80, 4146–5.75

Births (cesarean and total) in hospitals affiliated and not affiliated with medical schools, by characteristics of mother, birth, and hospital, 1977, 4186–6.4

Births and birth rates, by selected demographic characteristics and geographic area, 1979 and trends, US Vital Statistics annual rpt, 4144–1.1

Births attended by midwives and in nonhospital settings, by mother's sociodemographic and prenatal care characteristics and infant race and birthweight, 1978-79 with trends from 1935, 4147–21.40

Births, fertility rates, expected births, and childless women, by socioeconomic characteristics, June 1982, annual Current Population Rpt, 2546–1.386

Births, fertility rates, expected births, and childless women, by socioeconomic characteristics, June 1983, advance annual Current Population Rpt, 2546–1.385

Births, fertility rates, expected births, and childless women, by socioeconomic characteristics, June 1983, annual Current Population Rpt, 2546–1.393

Blood program collection, production, and distribution activities, technical services, and research, 1982/83, Red Cross annual rpt, 29254–3

Breast-fed infants, by race and mother's sociodemographic characteristics, 1983 with trends from 1970, article, 4102–1.455

Children's hospital use by Canada Province and US region, and death rates, by diagnosis and sex, selected years 1977-79, 4147–5.1

Correctional instns (Federal) health services employment, by occupation, instn, and region, monthly rpt, 6242–2

County and City Data Book, detailed socioeconomic and demographic data for States, counties, and cities, selected years 1976-82, 2328–1

Deaths and death rates by detailed cause and demographic characteristics, 1979 and selected trends, US Vital Statistics annual rpt, 4144–2.1

Deaths and death rates, by region and State, provisional 1982-83 with trends from 1950, US Vital Statistics annual rpt, 4144–7

Deaths and death rates, by selected cause and demographic characteristics, 1981, US Vital Statistics advance rpt, 4146–5.78

Deaths and death rates, by selected cause and demographic characteristics, 1982, US Vital Statistics advance rpt, 4146–5.81

Deaths due to cold weather and related causes, by age, race, State, and city, selected periods 1962-83, 21148–30

BY REGION

Dental malpractice claims, by amount, procedure type, region, State, and provider and patient characteristics, 1970, article, 4102–1.416

Disabled women, by socioeconomic and demographic characteristics, and compared to nondisabled women and disabled men, 1981, chartbook, 16598–4

Divorces, divorce rates, and characteristics, by region and State, 1981, US Vital Statistics advance rpt, 4146–5.74

Drugs, alcohol, and cigarettes, high school seniors use and assessment by drug type, sex, and region, 1975-83 surveys, annual rpt, 4494–4

Fetal deaths and rates, by gestation period, birth weight and order, race, age of mother, and geographic area, 1979, US Vital Statistics annual rpt, 4144–2.3

Health care expenditures, natl survey on services use, costs, and sources of payment, by patient and physician characteristics, 1977-78, series, 4186–3

Health care services of selected medical practitioners, use by patient characteristics, 1980 survey with trends from 1963, 4146–12.4

Health condition and health care resources, use, and expenditures, 1970s-82 with trends and projections 1900-2000, annual compilation, 4144–11

Health condition, hospitalization, disability, and medical costs, by demographic characteristics, Vital and Health Statistics series, 4147–10

Health maintenance organizations for employee health insurance, enrollment, premiums, coverage, and employer attitudes, by region and industry div, 1982, 4108–32

Health professionals supply and education, by occupation, demographic and professional characteristics, and location, 1950s-83 and projected to 2000, biennial rpt, 4114–8

HHS aid to each State and local govt or private instn, amount obligated, funding agency, and program, FY83, annual listing, 4004–3

Hospital discharges and length of stay, by patient age and sex, facility size and ownership, procedure performed, and region, 1982, 4146–8.96

Hospital discharges and length of stay, by patient age and sex, facility size and ownership, procedure performed, and region, 1983, 4146–8.101

Hospital discharges and length of stay, by patient characteristics, facility size, procedure performed, diagnosis, and region, 1982, annual rpt, 4147–13.78

Hospital discharges and length of stay of aged and nonaged persons, by region, facility size, and diagnosis, 1981, 4146–8.98

Hospital employment, vacancies, and vacancy rates, by occupation and by hospital specialty, region, census div, and State, 1980, annual rpt, 4114–12

Hospitals and nursing homes, employees, and use, by ownership, bed size, region, and State, selected years 1969-80, 4147–14.30

Infant deaths, 1979, US Vital Statistics annual rpt, 4144–2.2

Infectious notifiable diseases, cases and current outbreaks, by region and State, weekly rpt, 4202–1

Infectious notifiable diseases, cases and incidence, by census div and State, 1982, annual rpt, 4204–1

Internist office visits and drugs provided, by characteristics of visit, patient, and physician, and location, 1980-81, 4147–13.80

Marriages and marriage rates by State, and bride and groom characteristics, 1981, advance annual US Vital Statistics rpt, 4146–5.77

Marriages, divorces, and rates, by detailed demographic and geographic characteristics, 1979 and trends, US Vital Statistics annual rpt, 4144–4

Mental health office and clinic visits, average charges, and total expenditures for services, by type of provider and patient characteristics, 1980, 4146–11.5

NIH extramural grant and contract awards for research, R&D, and construction, FY72-83, annual rpt, 4434–9

NIH grants and awards for R&D, training, construction, and medical libraries, by location and recipient, FY83, annual listings, 4434–7

Nursing home facilities use and characteristics, and nurses employed, by region and State, 1980, 4147–14.29

Obstetrician-gynecologist office visits and drugs used, by visit reason, diagnosis, treatment, and patient and physician characteristics, 1980-81, 4147–13.76

Occupational Safety and Health Admin enforcement activities and funding, and State programs and staff, 1982, annual rpt, 6604–2.1

Older persons health care total and out-of-pocket expenditures, by sociodemographic characteristics, poverty and health status, and degree of functional limitation, 1980, 4146–11.4

Pharmacists employment and sociodemographic characteristics, and reasons for not working in field, by State and overseas, as of 1979, 4147–14.28

Radiation protection and health physics enrollments and degrees granted by State and instn, and grads employment, 1983, annual rpt, 3004–7

Surgeon office visits and drugs provided, by characteristics of visit, patient, and physician, and location, 1980-81, 4147–13.79

Tuberculosis cases, deaths, and treatment, by demographic characteristics, State, and city, 1982 and trends from 1953, annual rpt, 4204–2

Venereal disease cases reported and epidemiologic activities, by region, State, and large city, 1982, annual rpt, 4204–14

Vital statistics, births, marriages, divorces, and deaths, provisional data, monthly rpt, 4142–1

Workers compensation under Fed Govt-administered programs, coverage, expenditures, and claims and dispositions by district, FY83, annual compilation, 6504–5

Housing and Construction

Apartment market absorption rates and characteristics for nonsubsidized privately financed furnished and unfurnished units completed in 1982, annual Current Housing Rpt, 2484–2

Index by Categories

Apartment market absorption rates and characteristics for nonsubsidized privately financed units completed in 1983, preliminary annual Current Housing Rpt, 2484–3

Census of Housing, 1980: inventory, occupancy, and unit characteristics, changes from 1973 by region and inside-outside SMSAs and central cities, series, 2473–3

Census of Housing, 1980: structural, financial, and householder characteristics, by region and State, 2475–4

Community dev programs funding and activities, for 5 HUD programs, FY83, annual rpt, 5124–5

Construction put in place, permits authorized by region, State, and MSA, and Federal contract awards, by construction type, bimonthly rpt with articles, 2012–1

County and City Data Book, detailed socioeconomic and demographic data for States, counties, and cities, selected years 1976-82, 2328–1

Home mortgage default prospects by mortgage type and borrower characteristics, various periods 1967-82, technical paper, 9381–10.39

Home mortgage defaults, single family homes acquired by HUD and disposition by city, monthly rpt, 5142–31

Home mortgage loans, and other balance sheet items of S&Ls, by FHLB district, State, and SMSA, 1983, annual rpt, 9314–3

Home mortgages FHA-insured, secondary market prices and interest rates on conventional loans, by region, monthly press release, 5142–20

Home ownership rates and unit age, by region and urban-rural location, 1980, article, 1702–1.407

Homeless population and characteristics, and temporary shelter operations, use, and user characteristics, by region and selected city, 1983, 5188–108

Housing alteration and repair expenditures by characteristics of property and region, 1983, annual rpt, 2384–4

Housing and financial characteristics, and unit and neighborhood quality, by inside-outside central cities and SMSAs, and for 4 regions and 15 SMSAs, 1978, annual survey special supplement, 2485–8

Housing occupancy and unit and household characteristics, by region and metro-nonmetro residence, 1983, biennial survey, 2485–1

Housing units, by region and metro-nonmetro location, 1973 and 1981, biennial rpt, 5124–4

Indian and Alaska Native housing and community dev program operations, FY82 with Community Dev Block Grant funding by tribe and State for FY81, annual rpt, 5004–5

New construction (public and private) put in place, by type, region, and census div, monthly rpt, 2382–4.3

New housing unit starts, by units per structure and metro-nonmetro location, and mobile home placements and sales price, by region, monthly rpt, 2382–1

New housing units authorized, by public and private ownership, by region, div, State, selected MSA, and 4,700 permit-issuing places, monthly rpt, 2382–5

Index by Categories

BY REGION

New housing units authorized, by public and private ownership, State, and permit-issuing place, 1983, annual rpt, 2384–2

New housing units completed and under construction, by units per structure, region, and inside-outside SMSAs, monthly rpt, 2382–2

New single and multifamily housing physical and financial characteristics, by region and metro-nonmetro location, 1979-83, annual rpt, 2384–1

New single-family homes sold and for sale, by price, stage of construction, months on market, and region, and seasonal adjustments, monthly rpt, 2382–3

Older and handicapped persons housing projects construction and rehabilitation loans of HUD, FY84, annual listing, 5004–6

Older persons rural housing condition, selected householder and housing characteristics with comparisons to urban and nonaged population, 1979, 1598–193

Quality of housing and neighborhoods, indicators and attitudes, and occupant characteristics, by urban-rural location and region, 1981, annual survey, 2485–7.2

Quality of housing and neighborhoods, indicators and attitudes, by occupant and unit characteristics, region, and metro-nonmetro location, 1981, annual survey, 2485–2

Vacancy and occupancy rates, and vacant unit characteristics, by metro-nonmetro location and region, selected years 1960-83, annual rpt, 2484–1.1

Vacant housing characteristics and costs, and occupancy and vacancy rates, by region and metro-nonmetro location, quarterly rpt, 2482–1

Industry and Commerce

Asphalt and tar roofing and siding shipments, by product and region, 1983, annual Current Industrial Rpt, 2506–8.6

Chemical, oil, rubber, and plastic production, shipments, stocks, and materials used, by detailed product, periodic Current Industrial Rpt series, 2506–8

Clay construction products production and shipments by region, trade, and consumption, by product, monthly Current Industrial Rpt, 2506–9.2

County and City Data Book, detailed socioeconomic and demographic data for States, counties, and cities, selected years 1976-82, 2328–1

Drug shipments by region and selected census div and State, trade, and consumption, by product, 1983, annual Current Industrial Rpt, 2506–8.5

Exports and imports of US (airborne), by world area and US customs district and city, monthly rpt, 2422–8

Exports and imports of US, by commodity group, world area, selected country, US coastal area and port, and mode of transport, with seasonal adjustments, monthly rpt, 2422–9

Foreign corporation US affiliates, assets and employment by region and State, 1977 and 1981, annual rpt, 2044–25

Foreign firms US affiliates, land and mineral rights, plant and equipment, and employment, by region and State, 1980-81, article, 2702–1.402

Foreign-owned US multiestablishment firms, employment, and payroll, by country, State, industry group, and foreign ownership share, 1981-82, annual rpt, 2324–6

Imports detained by FDA, by product, shipper or manufacturer, country, and detention reasons, monthly listing, 4062–2

Lumber, furniture, and paper products production and shipments by region and State, inventories, trade, and consumption, periodic Current Industrial Rpt series, 2506–7

Lumber production and stocks of hardwood and softwood, by region, State, and species, 1982, annual Current Industrial Rpt, 2506–7.4

Lumber production, prices, trade, and employment in Northwest US and British Columbia, quarterly rpt, 1202–3

Manufacturing employment and population, by region and census div, 1981, 26306–6.69

Metalworking machinery industry computerized automation, by plant characteristics, for 6 industry groups and small plants, 1982 surveys, 23848–179

Minority business mgmt and financial assistance from federally funded organizations, by region, State, and business characteristics, FY83, annual rpt, 2104–6

Payroll (nonfarm) effect of economic recovery, by industry div and region, 4th qtr 1982-4th qtr 1983, article, 2702–1.412

Plywood (hardwood) production and shipments by region, trade, and consumption, by product, 1983, annual Current Industrial Rpt, 2506–7.1

Plywood (softwood) production, shipments by region and State, trade, and consumption, by product, 1983, annual Current Industrial Rpt, 2506–7.2

Retail trade sales and inventories, by kind of business, region, census div, and selected State, SMSA, and city, and seasonal adjustments, monthly rpt, 2413–3

Steel import trigger prices to prevent Japan dumping, and domestic steel prices, employment, and imports, by product and region, various dates 1977-1983, hearings, 21368–51

Steel mill shipments, by product class, 1981-82, annual Current Industrial Rpt, 2506–10.2

Tariff Schedules of US, Annotated, classifications and rates of duty for detailed imported commodities, and codes for ports and foreign countries, 1985 edition, 9886–13

Technology-intensive industry employment and establishments by industry and selected location, and venture capital investments by source, 1970s-82, 26358–107

Textile mill production, stocks, materials used, orders, and trade by country, by product and major State, periodic Current Industrial Rpt series, 2506–5

Timber production, prices by region and State, trade by country, and consumption, by species and product, with industry earnings, 1950-83, annual rpt, 1204–29

Waterborne commerce of US (domestic and foreign), freight by commodity, traffic, and passengers, by port and waterway, 1982, annual rpt, 3754–3

Waterborne containerized cargo carried over principal trade routes, by flag of vessel, port, and US coastal district, 1982, annual rpt, 7704–8

Waterborne exports and imports of US, by type of service, customs district, port, and world area, monthly rpt, 2422–7

Waterborne trade of US, by type of service, commodity, country, route, and US port, 1982, annual rpt, 7704–2

Labor and Employment

Census of Population, 1980: labor force, by sex, detailed occupation, and region, with comparison to 1970 census, supplementary rpt, 2535–1.12

County and City Data Book, detailed socioeconomic and demographic data for States, counties, and cities, selected years 1976-82, 2328–1

Discrimination against Hispanics and other minorities in employment, Equal Employment Opportunity Commission enforcement activities, personnel, and litigation, 1970s-FY83, 9248–18

Earnings by major industry group, and personal income per capita and by source, by region and State, 1929-82, 2708–40

Earnings by sex and region related to wages in South, with adjustments for job comparability and union membership status, 1978, 1981, and 1983, article, 9389–1.406

Employment change by industry div, civilian labor force, and unemployment and rates, by region and State, 1983, article, 6722–1.454

Employment Cost Index and percent change by occupational group, industry div, region, and metro-nonmetro area, quarterly press release, 6782–5

Employment Cost Index changes for nonfarm workers, by occupation, industry div, region, and bargaining status, monthly rpt, 6782–1

Employment, total and manufacturing, change in metro-nonmetro counties by region and county size, various periods 1951-79, technical paper, 9387–8.90

Employment, unemployment, and labor force, by demographic and employment characteristics, State, and for 30 metro areas and 11 large cities, 1983, annual rpt, 6744–7

Handbook of Labor Statistics, employment, earnings, hours, and labor force characteristics, 1982 and trends, detailed annual rpt, 6724–1

Labor Dept activities and staff, CETA participants characteristics, and employment service and unemployment insurance activities by State, FY83, annual rpt, 6304–1

Longshoremen available in 4 coastal regions, monthly rpt, 7702–1

Small business and total employment, income, and number of firms, by State, industry, and size class, selected years 1967-83, annual rpt, 9764–6.1

Vocational rehabilitation, State agency caseloads by status and processing stage, region, and State, FY83 with trends from FY21, annual rpt, 4944–5

Vocational rehabilitation State agency expenditures, caseloads, rehabilitations, and staff, under Section 110 of the Rehabilitation Act, by State, FY82, annual rpt, 4944–9

BY REGION

Wages by occupation, and benefits for office and plant workers in 70 SMSAs, 1983, annual rpt, 6785–1

Wages by occupation, for office and plant workers in metro areas, by sex and region, July 1983, annual summary rpt, 6785–9

Wages by occupation, for office and plant workers in selected SMSAs, 1983 and 1984 surveys, annual rpt, 6785–5

Wages, hours, benefits, and employment, by occupation and selected geographic areas, industry surveys series, 6787–6

Law Enforcement

Assaults, murders, and other deaths of law enforcement officers, by circumstances, level of govt, agency, victim and offender characteristics, and location, 1983, annual rpt, 6224–3

Bankruptcy court cases and admin in districts with and without case trustees, and staff and potential costs of nationwide trustee program, various periods 1979-83, annual rpt, 6004–15

Bombing (explosive and incendiary) incidents, damage, injuries, and deaths, by target, State, and circumstances, 1983, annual rpt, 6224–5

Corrupt govt officials prosecutions and convictions, by judicial district and level of govt, 1976-83, annual rpt, 6004–13

Court caseloads, actions, procedure duration, judges, and jurors, by Federal district and appeals court, 1979-84, annual rpt, 18204–3

Court caseloads for Federal district, appeals, and bankruptcy courts, by type of suit and offense, circuit, and district, quarterly rpt, 18202–1

Crime Index by population size and region, and offenses known to police by large city, Jan-June 1984, semiannual rpt, 6222–1

Crimes, arrests by offender characteristics, and rates, by offense, and law enforcement employees, by population size and jurisdiction, 1970s-83, annual rpt, 6224–2

Drug Enforcement Organized Crime Task Forces, funding and staff by agency, region, and city, as of FY83, GAO rpt, 26119–52

Drug enforcement regional task force program investigation activities, funding, and personnel, with nationwide drug abuse data, 1983 annual rpt, 6004–17

Habeas corpus writs filed by State prisoners in Federal district and appeals courts by circuit, and petition disposition, selected years 1961-82, 6066–19.4

Homicides and homicide rates, by victim characteristics, location, and circumstances, and years of life lost from homicide and other leading causes of death, 1970-78, 4205–38

Jail capacities, conditions, expenditures, and services, and socioeconomic and other characteristics of inmates, various dates 1976-82, 10048–59

Juror (grand and petit) usage and costs, trials, and trial days, by Federal district court, years ended June 1980-84, annual rpt, 18204–4

Parole and probation population, and entries and exits by reason, by State, 1983, periodic rpt, 6062–2.408

Parole examiner workloads and decisions, and hearings with legal representation for inmate, FY80-82, 6006–2.32

Prison expansion plans of States, beds and construction costs by region, 1984 survey, 6066–20.6

Prison population, capacity, and construction and operating costs, for individual Federal instns by region, 1983 and projected 1984-90, GAO rpt, 26119–59

Prisoners in Federal and State correctional instns, by sex, region, and State, quarterly release, 6062–3

Prisoners in Federal correctional instns, by prison, security level, contract facility type, sex, and region, monthly and weekly rpts, 6242–1

Prisoners under death sentence, and executions since 1930, by prisoner characteristics, region, and State, 1982, annual rpt, 6065–1

Prisoners under death sentence, by prison control, sex, and region, 1972-83 with executions from 1930, by State, periodic rpt, 6062–2.406

Public defender systems, costs, cases, and expenditures by level of govt and State, with system characteristics and lawyer fee ranges, 1981, 6066–19.8

Natural Resources, Environment, and Pollution

Acid rain causes and effects, air pollutant emissions by source, and control costs, by region and State, selected years 1977-83 and projected to 2000, 26358–104

Acid rain causes and effects, air pollutant emissions by source in US and selected countries, control costs, and Fed Govt research funding, 1960s-82, 3408–27

Air pollutant emission effects of solar and biomass energy use, by region, and projected to 2000, 3408–30

Air pollutant sulfur dioxide emissions of coal-fired power plants in eastern US, effect of alternative geographic area limits on power and coal industries, 1983 rpt, 3408–32

Air pollutant sulfur dioxide emissions reduction proposal, effects on polluting industries and coal production by region and State, projected to 2010, 9188–97

Air pollution levels for 5 pollutants, by detailed source, State, and Air Quality Control Region, 1981, annual rpt, 9194–7

Air pollution levels for 6 pollutants, by source, region, and for large SMSAs, 1975-82, annual rpt, 9194–1

Army Corps of Engineers activities and projects, FY83 and trends from 1800s, annual rpt, 3754–1

Carbon dioxide atmospheric concentration increase effects on hydrologic conditions, projected for 26-35 years, 9188–95

Coal dev plans on Fed Govt lease lands in 12 regions under Fed Coal Mgmt Program, environmental and socioeconomic impacts to 2000, final statement series, 5726–4

Coastal environmental and wildlife characteristics, use, and mgmt, for individual ecosystems, series, 5506–9

Coastal environmental characteristics, fish, wildlife, and use, and population socioeconomic data, for individual areas, series, 5506–4

Dams, reservoirs, and hydroelectric plants, listing of major foreign and US structures with location and characteristics, as of June 1983, 5828–13

Index by Categories

Environmental quality and protection programs, costs, and Fed Govt enforcement, 1983, detailed annual rpt, 484–1

Environmental quality, pollutant discharge by type and source, and EPA protection activities and funding, 1970s-83, biennial regional rpt series, 9184–15

EPA pollution control research and grant assistance program activities, monthly rpt, 9182–8

Fish and wildlife restoration program of Fed Govt, finances, funding by State, and hunting and fishing equipment excise tax revenue, FY84, annual rpt, 5504–13

Forest fire damage and causes, by State and region, 1981, annual rpt, 1204–4

Forest fires on Forest Service land and acres burned, by cause, forest, and State, 1983, annual rpt, 1204–6

Forest insect and disease incidence, by region or State, 1983, annual rpt, 1204–8

Forest Natl System wildlife habitat and fishery improvements, use, and game population and harvest by species and forest, by region, FY83, annual rpt, 1204–31

Forest, range, and associated waters use and mgmt assessment, and environmental impacts of Forest Service program options, 1977-2030 and trends from 1920, 1208–24

Forest Service programs and activities, by State and region, FY83, annual rpt, 1204–1

Forestry activities on State and private lands, Fed Govt and State funding by project and State, FY83, annual tables, 1204–32

Forestry Incentives Program, Fed Govt cost-sharing funds for private timberland improvement, by region and State, monthly rpt, 1802–11

Forests (natl) and other lands under Forest Service mgmt, by forest and location, Sept 1983, annual rpt, 1204–2

Forests (natl) below-cost timber sales and revenue by western forest, and volume, average price by species, and costs by western region, FY80-1982, GAO rpt, 26113–126

Forests (natl) recreational use, visitor-days by type of activity, forest, and State, FY83 with trends from 1924, annual rpt series, 1204–17

Forests (natl) sawtimber stumpage prices, by species and region, quarterly rpt, 1202–1

Hazardous waste sites and activities of Fed Govt civil agencies, and EPA data mgmt, by waste location, 1984, GAO rpt, 26113–139

Land privately held, acreage and owners by owner characteristics, land use, and region, and purchase and improvement funding, 1978 survey, series, 1506–5

Mourning dove population, by region and hunting and nonhunting State, 1984, annual rpt, 5504–15

Nuclear power plant siting population criteria and estimated compliance of selected regions and sites, 1983 rpt, 9638–54

Ocean dumping of waste materials, EPA permit program and intl London Dumping Convention activities, 1981-83, annual rpt, 9204–8

Phosphate rock industry environmental protection costs, by control type and

Index by Categories

BY REGION

selected State, with background operating data, 1977-81 with cost projections to 1990, 5608–143

- Radiation exposure at DOE and DOE-contractor sites, by facility type and contractor, 1982, annual rpt, 3404–1
- Sedimentation control, surveillance, and research activity of Fed Govt, by project, agency, region, and State, 1982, annual rpt, 5664–9
- Water from urban runoff, quality, pollutant concentrations, and control cost-effectiveness, with monitoring sites rainfall and other characteristics, by city and region, 1978-83, 9208–122
- Water pollution from nonpoint sources, source land uses and acreage, and control program funding, by State or region, various periods 1974-FY84, 9208–123
- Water supply and quality, floods, drought, mudslides, and other hydrologic events, by State, 1983, annual rpt, 5664–12
- Water supply and use in 3 areas with supply problems and total US, and methods to increase supply, selected years 1974-80 and projected to 2010, 9208–125
- Wetlands environmental characteristics, acreage, uses, and mgmt, by wetland type and region, 1950s-80, 26358–102
- Woodcock population and hunter harvest, by region and State, 1984 and trends from 1966, annual rpt, 5504–11
- Youth Conservation Corps activities, costs, and participant characteristics, by sponsoring agency, 1982, annual rpt, 5304–12

Population

- Census of Population and Housing, 1980: detailed population and housing characteristics, by county, city, and census tract, State and SMSA rpt series, 2551–2
- Census of Population, 1980: Asian and Pacific Islander population, by detailed race and State, supplementary rpt, 2535–1.15
- Census of Population, 1980: detailed socioeconomic and demographic characteristics, by age, sex, race, Hispanic origin, occupation, and industry, US summary rpt, 2531–4.1
- Census of Population, 1980: detailed socioeconomic characteristics, by county, city, and inside-outside SMSAs and central cities, US summary rpt, 2531–3.1
- Census of Population, 1980: Indian and Alaska Native population and housing occupancy, by reservation, Alaska Native village, and other Indian area, supplementary rpt, 2535–1.16
- Census of Population, 1980: migration since 1975, by State and selected demographic characteristics, supplementary rpt, 2535–1.13
- City and suburb population characteristics and local govt finances, by region and selected SMSA, 1950s-FY83, 10048–61
- *County and City Data Book,* detailed socioeconomic and demographic data for States, counties, and cities, selected years 1976-82, 2328–1
- Economic and demographic trends for IRS regions, districts, and service centers, 1972-82 and projected to 1990, annual rpt, 8304–8
- Educational attainment of population, by sociodemographic characteristics and for

large States and SMSAs, 1981 and trends from 1940, biennial Current Population Rpt, 2546–1.390

- Household living arrangements, family relationships, and marital status, by demographic characteristics, Mar 1983, annual Current Population Rpt, 2546–1.388
- Income (household) and cash and noncash transfer program participation, by sociodemographic characteristics, quarterly rpt, 2542–2
- Income (household) before and after taxes, by socioeconomic characteristics, type of tax paid, and region, 1981, Current Population Rpt, 2546–2.118
- Income (household) before and after taxes, by socioeconomic characteristics, type of tax paid, and region, 1982, annual Current Population Rpt, 2546–2.122
- Income (personal) by industry group and region, percent change 1959-79 and 1979-83, article, 2702–1.443
- Income (personal) per capita and by source, and earnings by industry div, by State, MSA, and county, 1977-82, annual regional rpts, 2704–2
- Income (personal) per capita and by source, earnings by major industry group, and social insurance contributions, by region and State, 1929-82, 2708–40
- Income (personal) per capita and total, and earnings by major industry group, by region and State, 1981-83, annual article, 2702–1.432
- Income (personal) totals, by region, census div, and State, quarterly article, 2702–1.32
- Income and socioeconomic characteristics of persons, families, and households, detailed cross-tabulations, Current Population Rpt series, 2546–6
- Metro and nonmetro areas and central cities population size and change by census div, and growth of areas with large black and aged populations, 1970-82, 2328–47
- Mobility of population, detailed data by demographic and socioeconomic characteristics of movers and nonmovers, Mar 1981-82, annual Current Population Rpt, 2546–1.384
- Older persons by demographic, socioeconomic, and health characteristics, selected years 1900-81 and projected to 2050, Current Population Rpt, 2546–2.125
- Older persons population characteristics, and needs and costs of social services by type, by metro-nonmetro status, 1970s-82 with trends from 1900, 21148–28
- Older persons sociodemographic characteristics, and Fed Govt program participation and funding, 1983 with trends and projections 1900-2060, annual rpt, 25144–3.1
- Population estimates and projections, by region and State, Current Population Rpt series, 2546–3
- Population size and components of change, by region, census div, and State, 1970s-83 with projections to 2050, annual Current Population Rpt, 2546–2.119
- Refugee resettlement program activities and funding, arrivals and population by country of origin and State, and employment and other characteristics, FY83, annual rpt, 4704–8

Voting age population for Nov 1984 election, by sex, age, race, Hispanic origin, region, and State, and percent voting during 1930-82, Current Population Rpt, 2546–3.129

Prices and Cost of Living

- Child raising itemized costs in urban and rural nonfarm areas, by age and region, quarterly rpt, 1702–1
- CPI by component for US city average, and by region, population size, and for 28 SMSAs, monthly press release, 6762–1
- CPI by detailed component, for US city average, 28 SMSAs, and 4 regions by population size, monthly rpt, 6762–2.2
- CPI components relative importance, for selected SMSAs, and US city average by region and population size, 1983, annual rpt, 6884–1
- CPI current statistics, Monthly Labor Review, 6722–1.5
- Housing prices and price index for new single-family units sold, by region, quarterly rpt, 2382–8
- Oil refined products sales of gas plant operators, refiners, and resellers, price and volume for 13 products, by end-use sector, PAD district, and State, monthly rpt, 3162–11
- Prices received by farmers for major products, and paid for farm inputs, by commodity and State, 1983, annual rpt, 1629–5
- Producer prices and indexes, by stage of processing and detailed commodity, monthly rpt, 6762–6
- Producer prices and indexes, by stage of processing and detailed commodity, monthly 1983, annual supplement, 6764–2
- Retail prices for energy and food, and housing fuel consumption, by region, and for 28 SMSAs and US city average, monthly press release, 6762–8
- Vegetable and potato per capita weekly expenditures, by commodity, season, race, age, and region, 1977-78, article, 1561–11.401

Public Welfare and Social Security

- Disability Insurance beneficiaries sociodemographic and medical characteristics, 1977-79, annual rpt, 4744–20
- Farm households receiving social security income, farms and amount by characteristics of farm and operator, 1978-82, article, 1702–1.410
- Food aid program of USDA for women, infants, and children, participants, clinics, and costs, by State and Indian agency, FY82, annual table, 1364–12.1
- Food aid programs of Fed Govt and others, funding, participant characteristics, and nutrition and poverty data, 1970s-83, 028–20
- Food aid programs of USDA, participants and costs by program and region, monthly rpt, 1362–14
- Food stamp program participation and coupons distributed, by region, State, and project area, quarterly rpt, 1362–6
- Kidney end-stage disease Medicare certified facilities, by facility type, service type, and region, 1980-83, article, 4652–1.434
- Medicare admissions to hospitals and other facilities, and enrollee reimbursement claims, by beneficiary type, 1966-83, annual rpt, 4744–3.7

BY REGION

Medicare aged beneficiaries activity restriction, untreated health conditions, and perceived health status, by sociodemographic characteristics, 1980, 4146–12.2

Medicare aged beneficiaries medical care by usual source, and untreated health conditions, by sociodemographic characteristics, 1980, 4146–12.3

Medicare end-stage renal disease dialysis, transplants by facility, donor organ costs, deaths by age, and hospitalization, by region, 1981, annual rpt, 4654–5.2

Medicare facilities and services use, covered charges, and reimbursements, by beneficiary type and area of residence, series, 4656–1

Medicare physician charges and reimbursement by enrollee characteristics and carrier, payment limits effects on charges in California, and physician earnings, by specialty, 1950s-84, 25368–127

Noncash public and employer-based transfer program recipients, by income source and socioeconomic characteristics, 1982, advance Current Population Rpt, 2546–6.38

Noncash public and employer-based transfer program recipients, by income source and socioeconomic characteristics, 1982, final Current Population Rpt, 2546–6.37

Poverty population size, effect of counting public noncash transfers as income by recipient characteristics, 1979-83, 2626–2.52

Poverty population size, effects of counting public noncash transfers as income by recipient characteristics, 1979-82, 2626–2.50

Runaway and other homeless youth programs, funding by source, activities, and participant characteristics, FY82, annual rpt, 4604–3

School breakfast and other USDA child nutrition programs, participation and finances, by region and State, annual rpt series, 1364–13

Supplementary Security Income beneficiary socioeconomic characteristics and health service use, 1970s-83 and SSI program projections to 1995, 25148–29

Recreation and Leisure

Army Corps of Engineers water resources dev projects, recreation activities by district and project, 1982, annual rpt, 3754–5

Campground facilities privately owned, and financial and operating data, by region, 1982, annual rpt, 5544–14.5

Fishermen (ocean sport), fishing activities, and catch by species, by fisherman characteristics, State, and coastal region, series, 2166–17

Natl park area visits and overnight stays, visitors, and vehicles, by State and park, 1983, annual rpt, 5544–12

Natl park system visitor deaths, by park and type of accident, 1973-83, annual rpt, 5544–6

Science and Technology

Computer specialists sociodemographic, educational, and employment characteristics, and Fed Govt support by agency, 1978, biennial Current Population Rpt, 2546–2.124

Engineers sociodemographic, educational, and employment characteristics, and Federal support by agency, 1978, Current Population Rpt, 2546–2.121

GSA computers and automatic data processing systems costs, cost savings, and employment, by activity, subagency, and regional office, FY83-88, 9458–17

Veterans Affairs

Medical facilities of VA, sharing agreement contracts, services, and costs by region and facility, FY83, annual rpt, 9924–18

Physicians, dentists, and nurses of VA, by age, selected employment characteristics, and VA district, quarterly rpt, 9922–11

Population of veterans and ratio to civilians, by census div and for 10 States with largest change, 1970 and 1980, 9926–4.7

Unemployment rates and compensation, Vietnam era veterans compared with WW II and Korea veterans, FY83, annual rpt, 9924–8.2

VA employment services for disabled veterans with VA vocational rehabilitation training, and veteran characteristics and employment, by regional office, as of 1983, GAO rpt, 26121–78

VA workloads and productivity at each Dept of Veterans Benefits field office, with regional summaries, quarterly rpt, 9922–7

Women veteran population, and use of benefits by type, by age, period of service, and State, with comparisons to men, FY83, annual rpt, 9924–24

BY SMSA OR MSA

Agriculture and Food

Poultry and egg marketing and price data for selected regions, States, and SMSAs, monthly 1983, annual rpt, 1317–2

Banking, Finance, and Insurance

Appalachian States, FHLB 5th District member S&Ls financial condition and operations by SMSA, monthly rpt, 9302–8

Bank deposits in commercial and mutual savings banks and in US branches of foreign banks, by account type, instn, State, SMSA, and county, June 1983, annual rpt, 9295–3

New England States economic indicators, Fed Reserve 1st District, monthly rpt with articles, 9373–2

New England States, FHLB 1st District member instns financial operations and housing industry indicators, monthly rpt, 9302–4

North Central States, FHLB 7th District insured S&Ls cost of funds, and savings flows and mortgage loans closed by SMSA, monthly rpt, 9302–5

North Central States, FHLB 8th District member S&Ls financial operations by State and SMSA, monthly rpt, 9302–9

Savings and loan assn balance sheet items by State and SMSA, and finances of FHLBs, 1983, annual rpt, 9314–3

Savings instns FSLIC-insured, offices, and savings deposits, by State, SMSA, and county, 1983, annual rpt, 9314–4

South Central States, FHLB 9th District insured S&Ls financial condition and operations by SMSA, monthly rpt, 9302–13

Index by Categories

Southeastern States, FHLB 4th District insured S&Ls financial condition and operations, by SMSA, monthly rpt, 9302–1

West Central States, FHLB 10th District insured S&Ls finances and operations by SMSA, monthly rpt, 9302–22

Western States, FHLB 11th District member S&L offices, locations, savings balances, and accounts, quarterly listing, 9302–20

Communications and Transportation

DOT grant awards for transportation planning and safety programs, by region, State, and for 35 largest SMSAs, FY83, annual rpt, 7304–7

Hwy and urban transit systems financing methods of govts and private sector, with case studies for selected metro areas, series, 7556–7

Energy Resources and Demand

Electric power demand of households in 136 SMSAs and other utility service areas, with fuel prices, family income, and heating degree days, 1975 and projected to 1985, 1588–78

Gasoline average prices in selected SMSAs, Dec 1981, annual rpt, 3304–5.1

Housing energy consumption and retail prices, by energy type, region, and for 28 SMSAs and US city average, monthly press release, 6762–8

Geography and Climate

Heating degree days and household electric power demand, by SMSA, 1975 and projected to 1985, 1588–78

Government and Defense

Census of Govts, 1982: properties, govt-assessed value, sales, and tax rates, by property type, State, SMSA, county, and city, 2453–1

Fed Govt civilian employment, by location, agency, and pay system, 1982, biennial rpt, 9844–8

Local govt employment and payroll, by function and level of govt in 75 SMSAs and 69 large counties, Oct 1983, annual rpt, 2466–1.3

Local govt finances and population characteristics for cities and suburbs, by region and selected SMSA, selected years 1957-FY83, 10048–61

Manufacturers under Fed Govt contract and owned by DOD, operating data by agency, selected SIC 2- to 4-digit industry, State, and SMSA, 1982, annual Current Industrial Rpt, 2506–3.4

Passports issued, by holder characteristics, travel purpose, and country of destination, quarterly rpt., 7182–1

Property (real) of Fed Govt, own-to-lease ratios by State and for 25 SMSAs, as of 1983, hearings, 25328–23

Health and Vital Statistics

Births and birth rates, by selected demographic characteristics and geographic area, 1979 and trends, US Vital Statistics annual rpt, 4144–1.1

Deaths and death rates, by detailed geographic area, cause, and demographic characteristics, 1979, US Vital Statistics annual rpt, 4144–3

Deaths in 50 largest SMSAs and their component counties, 1979 US Vital Statistics annual rpt, 4144–2.1

Index by Categories

BY SMSA OR MSA

Disability days, injury and illness rates by type, and use of health services and Medicaid, by age, region, metro-nonmetro location, and selected SMSA, 1980-81, 4147–10.146

Health manpower and facilities data, by county and SMSA, users guide to computerized area resource file, 1983, annual rpt, 4114–11

Hospital worker wages by sex and occupation, and benefits, for 22 MSAs, Oct 1981 survey, 6787–6.201

Infant deaths in 50 largest SMSAs and their component counties, 1979, US Vital Statistics annual rpt, 4144–2.2

Nurses in hospitals and nursing homes, earnings by position and selected metro area, 1978 and 1981, biennial rpt, 4114–8

Southeastern States health care resource availability, and employment by occupation, by facility type, by State and SMSA in Fed Reserve 6th District, 1970s-81, article, 9371–1.425

Housing and Construction

Appalachian States, FHLB 5th District housing vacancy rates for single and multifamily units and mobile homes, by ZIP code, annual metro area rpt series, 9304–27

Bonds for home mortgage subsidy, purchase price limit for tax-exempt status, by State and MSA, 1984 annual press release, 8304–16.2

Census of Housing, 1980: occupancy and unit characteristics of SMSAs and central cities, by race, Hispanic origin, and city, State and SMSA rpt series, 2473–1

Census of Population and Housing, 1980: detailed population and housing characteristics, by county, city, and census tract, State and SMSA rpt series, 2551–2

Construction put in place, permits authorized by region, State, and MSA, and Federal contract awards, by construction type, bimonthly rpt with articles, 2012–1

Earth-sheltered housing design, energy efficiency, natural and nuclear hazard reduction, and costs, by selected SMSA, 1983 rpt, 3308–71

Florida economic indicators, and residential and nonresidential construction by SMSA, various periods 1970-84, article, 9371–1.404

Home mortgage (conventional) terms on loans closed, and commitment rates, by type of loan and lender and for 32 SMSAs, monthly rpt, 9312–2

Home mortgage loan-to-price ratios and interest rates, by type of lender and MSA, various dates 1982-83, hearing, 21968–28

Home mortgages (graduated payment) FHA-insured, financial, property, and mortgagor characteristics, for US and selected localities, quarterly rpt, 5142–42

Home mortgages FHA-insured, financial, property, and mortgagor characteristics, for US and selected localities, quarterly rpt, 5142–2

Housing and financial characteristics, and unit and neighborhood quality, for 15 SMSAs, 1978, annual survey special supplement, 2485–8

Housing and households detailed characteristics, and unit and neighborhood quality, by inside-outside central cities, 1979-82 surveys, SMSA rpt series, 2485–6

Housing financing of S&Ls and others, mortgage terms and debt outstanding, and balance sheets of S&Ls and FHLBs, 1983, annual rpt, 9314–3

New housing unit starts and completions authorized by building permits in 20 MSAs, quarterly rpt, 2382–9

New housing units authorized, by public and private ownership, by region, div, State, selected MSA, and 4,700 permit-issuing places, monthly rpt, 2382–5

New housing units authorized, by public and private ownership, State, and permit-issuing place, 1983, annual rpt, 2384–2

North Central States, FHLB 7th District housing vacancy rates for single and multifamily units and mobile homes, by ZIP code, annual metro area rpt series, 9304–18

South Central States, FHLB 9th District housing vacancy rates for single and multifamily units and mobile homes by ZIP code, annual metro area rpt series, 9304–19

West Central States, FHLB 10th District housing vacancy rates for single and multifamily units and mobile homes, by ZIP code, annual metro area rpt series, 9304–22

Western States, FHLB 11th District housing, employment, and economic indicators, by SMSA, quarterly rpt, 9302–18

Western States, FHLB 11th District housing vacancy rates for single and multifamily units and mobile homes, by ZIP code, annual metro area rpt series, 9304–20

Western States, FHLB 12th District housing vacancy rates for single and multifamily units and mobile homes, by ZIP code, annual metro area rpt series, 9304–21

Industry and Commerce

Cold storage capacity of warehouses, by State and SMSA, Oct 1983, biennial rpt, 1614–2

Manufacturing capacity utilization, by SIC 2- to 4-digit industry, State, and SMSA, 1982, annual Current Industrial Rpt, 2506–3.7

Manufacturing census, 1982: financial and operating data, by SIC 2- to 4-digit industry, State, SMSA, and county, preliminary census div rpt series, 2491–3

New England States economic indicators, Fed Reserve 1st District, monthly rpt with articles, 9373–2

Retail trade census, 1982: employment, establishments, sales, and payroll, by SIC 2- to 4-digit kind of business, SMSA, and retail district, State rpt series, 2401–1

Retail trade census, 1982: employment, establishments, sales, and payroll, by SIC 2- to 4-digit kind of business, SMSA, county, and city, State rpt series, 2397–1

Retail trade sales and inventories, by kind of business, region, census div, and selected State, SMSA, and city, and seasonal adjustments, monthly rpt, 2413–3

Service industry census, 1982: employment, establishments, receipts, and payroll, by SIC 2- to 4-digit kind of business, SMSA, county, and city, State rpt series, 2391–1

Technology-intensive industry employment and establishments by industry and selected location, and venture capital investments by source, 1970s-82, 26358–107

Wholesale trade census, 1982: employment, establishments, finances, and operations, by SIC 2- to 4-digit kind of business, SMSA, county, and city, State rpt series, 2405–1

Labor and Employment

Alabama employment and unemployment by SMSA and industry div, and planned capital investment and new jobs by selected firm, 1982-83, article, 9371–1.408

Earnings, annual average percent changes for selected occupational groups, selected SMSAs, monthly rpt, 6782–1

Earnings for selected industries and interarea pay comparisons, 1945-82, annual rpt, 6724–1.6

Earnings of factory production workers in 12 port SMSAs, 1982, annual rpt, 7704–12.2

Employment (nonagricultural) by industry div, manufacturing hours and earnings, labor force, and unemployment, by selected labor market area, 1981-83, article, 6742–2.408

Employment and earnings, detailed data, monthly rpt, 6742–2.5, 6742–2.6

Employment, earnings, and hours, by selected SIC 1- to 4-digit industry, State, and for 278 major labor areas, 1939-83, annual rpt, 6744–5

Employment, unemployment, and labor force, by demographic and employment characteristics, State, and for 30 metro areas and 11 large cities, 1983, annual rpt, 6744–7

Louisiana employment and unemployment, by SMSA and major manufacturing industry group, 1970s-83, article, 9371–1.407

Minority group and women employment, by occupational group, SIC 2-digit industry group, and SMSA, 1981, annual rpt, 9244–1.2

New England States employment, wages, and price conditions by State and selected SMSA, 1983, annual rpt, 6916–7.1

North Carolina employment and unemployment by SMSA, and export-related employment share, by major industry group, various periods 1967-83, article, 9371–1.410

Southeastern States nonagricultural employment by industry div and SMSA, earnings, and hours, for 8 States, monthly press release, 6942–7

Trade adjustment assistance eligibility, reemployment opportunities, and worker characteristics, investigations of industries injured by import competition, series, 6406–9

Unemployment levels and rates, by State and for 240 large SMSAs, monthly press release with Current Population Survey annual benchmark averages, 6742–12

Wages by occupation, and benefits for office and plant workers, annual labor market survey rpt series, 6785–3

Wages by occupation, and benefits for office and plant workers in 70 SMSAs, 1983, annual rpt, 6785–1

Wages by occupation, and benefits for office and plant workers, 1983, annual SMSA survey rpt series, 6785–12

Wages by occupation, and benefits for office and plant workers, 1984, annual SMSA survey rpt series, 6785–11

BY SMSA OR MSA

Wages by occupation, for office and plant workers in selected labor market areas, 1983 surveys, annual summary rpt, 6785–6

- Wages by occupation, for office and plant workers in selected SMSAs, 1983 and 1984 surveys, annual rpt, 6785–5
- Wages for 3 occupational groups, relative average levels in 78 labor market areas, 1983, annual press release, 6785–13
- Wages for 4 occupational groups, relative average levels in 70 SMSAs, 1983, annual press release, 6785–8
- Wages, hours, benefits, and employment, by occupation and selected geographic areas, industry surveys series, 6787–6
- Wages of workers covered by unemployment insurance, by MSA, 1981-82, annual press release, 6784–17.1
- Wages of workers covered by unemployment insurance, by MSA, 1982-83, annual press release, 6784–17.3
- Western States, FHLB 11th District housing, employment, and economic indicators, by SMSA, quarterly rpt, 9302–18

Law Enforcement

- Crime and crime rates, by offense, MSA, and central city, 1983, annual rpt, 6224–2.5
- Homicides and homicide rates, by victim characteristics, location, and circumstances, and years of life lost from homicide and other leading causes of death, 1970-78, 4205–38

Natural Resources, Environment, and Pollution

- Air pollution levels for 5 pollutants, by detailed source, State, and Air Quality Control Region, 1981, annual rpt, 9194–7
- Air pollution levels for 6 pollutants, by source, region, and for large SMSAs, 1975-82, annual rpt, 9194–1
- Pollution abatement capital and operating costs, by SIC 2- to 4-digit industry, State, and SMSA, 1982, annual Current Industrial Rpt, 2506–3.6

Population

- Census of Population and Housing, 1980: detailed population and housing characteristics, by county, city, and census tract, State and SMSA rpt series, 2551–2
- Census of Population, 1980: detailed socioeconomic and demographic characteristics, by age, sex, race, Hispanic origin, occupation, and industry, State rpt series, 2531–4
- Census of Population, 1980: detailed socioeconomic characteristics, by county, city, and inside-outside SMSAs and central cities, State rpt series, 2531–3
- City and suburb population characteristics and local govt finances, by region and selected SMSA, 1950s-FY83, 10048–61
- Educational attainment of population, by sociodemographic characteristics and for large States and SMSAs, 1981 and trends from 1940, biennial Current Population Rpt, 2546–1.390
- Income (personal) per capita and by source, and earnings by industry div, by State, MSA, and county, 1977-82, annual regional rpts, 2704–2
- Income (personal) per capita and total, by State, MSA, and county, with metro-nonmetro totals, 1980-82, annual article, 2702–1.413

Population size and components of change, by MSA and county, 1980-82, annual State Current Population Rpt series, 2546–4

- Poverty status of families and persons, by detailed socioeconomic characteristics, 1982, annual Current Population Rpt, 2546–6.40
- **Prices and Cost of Living**
- CPI by component for US city average, and by region, population size, and for 28 SMSAs, monthly press release, 6762–1
- CPI by detailed component, for US city average, 28 SMSAs, and 4 regions by population size, monthly rpt, 6762–2
- CPI components relative importance, for selected SMSAs, and US city average by region and population size, 1983, annual rpt, 6884–1
- CPI for selected areas, 1950-82, annual rpt, 6724–1.7
- Energy retail prices, by energy type, region, and for 28 SMSAs and US city average, monthly press release, 6762–8
- Natural gas average residential prices, by metro area, monthly rpt, 3162–4.2

BY STATE

Agriculture and Food

- Acreage planted and harvested, by crop and State, 1982-83 and planned as of June 1984, annual rpt, 1621–23
- Acreage planting intended for 19 crops, by State, as of Feb 1984, annual rpt, 1621–22
- Acreage, yield, and production of field crops, by State, 1978-82 and preliminary 1983, 1641–7
- Agricultural cooperatives, membership, activities, and finances, by commodity and selected State, 1900-80 with trends from 1863, 1128–30
- Agricultural cooperatives, membership, and activities, by type of service, commodity, and State, FY51-1982, annual survey rpt, 1124–1
- Agricultural cooperatives, membership, and sales, by State, 1983, article, 1122–1.409
- Agricultural research expenditures and scientist years, by topic, commodity, and performing organization, FY82, annual rpt, 1744–2
- Agricultural Stabilization and Conservation Service payment-in-kind acreage reduction program, ineligible participants and acreage, and estimated incorrect payments, by State and selected county, 1983, 1008–46
- *Agricultural Statistics, 1983,* annual rpt, 1004–1
- *Agriculture Fact Book of US,* compilation of data for 1983 with trends from 1940, annual rpt, 1004–14
- Agriculture-related employment by State, 1979, article, 1541–7.403
- Alcohol and tobacco production, removals, stocks, and materials used, by State, monthly rpts, 8486–1
- Alcoholic beverages and tobacco production, stocks, and Fed Govt tax and enforcement activities, by State, FY81-82, last issue of annual rpt, 8484–1
- Animal protection, licensing, and inspection activities of USDA, and animals used in research, by State, FY83, annual rpt, 1394–10

Index by Categories

- Bean (dried) prices by State, and foreign and US production, use, stocks, and trade, weekly rpt, 1311–17
- Cattle and calves for beef and milk, inventory and value by State, 1982-84, semiannual press release, 1623–1
- Cattle and calves on feed, inventory and marketings by State, monthly release, 1623–2
- Cattle brucellosis eradication, and testing of goats and swine, cooperative Federal-State program activities, by State, FY83, annual rpt, 1394–6
- Cattle tuberculosis eradication and surveillance, cooperative Federal-State program activities, by State, FY83, annual rpt, 1394–13
- Census of Agriculture, 1982: farms, farmland, production and costs, and operator characteristics, preliminary State and county rpt series, 2330–1
- Census of Agriculture, 1982: farms, farmland, production, finances, and operator characteristics, by county, final State rpt series, 2331–1
- Cherry production, prices, and use, by producer State, 1981-83, annual rpt, 1621–18.6
- Cherry production, prices, and use, by producer State, 1982-84, annual rpt, 1621–18.2
- Chicken and turkey hatchery production, by State, 1983, annual rpt, 1625–8
- Cold storage food stocks by commodity and census div, and warehouse cold storage space in use, by State, monthly rpt, 1631–5
- Conservation practices in rural areas, Agricultural Conservation Program participation and payments, by State, FY83, annual rpt, 1804–7
- Corn and soybean yields, itemized production costs, and input use, effects of alternative tillage systems, by region and for 10 States, 1980, 1588–80
- Cotton acreage planted, by State and county, and fiber quality, by variety, 1980-84, annual rpt, 1309–6
- Cotton fiber and processing test results, by staple, region, State, and production area, seasonal biweekly rpt, 1309–3
- Cotton fiber and processing test results, by State, 1983, annual rpt, 1309–4
- Cotton fiber grade, staple, and mike, for upland and American Pima cotton by State, monthly rpt, 1309–11
- Cotton ginning charges and related data, by State, 1983/84, annual rpt, 1564–3
- Cotton ginnings and production for 18 States, by county, 1983 crop, annual rpt, 2344–1
- Cotton ginnings, by State and county, seasonal monthly rpt, 2342–2
- Cotton ginnings, by State, seasonal semimonthly rpt, 2342–1
- Cotton quality specifications, by State, 1983/84, annual rpt, 1309–7
- Cotton storage capacity, and total and chain operated warehouses, by region and State, selected years 1970-84, article, 1561–1.406
- Cottonseed quality factors, by State, 1983 crop, annual rpt, 1309–5
- *County and City Data Book,* detailed socioeconomic and demographic data for States, counties, and cities, selected years 1976-82, 2328–1

January-December 1984

Index by Categories

BY STATE

Dairy Herd Improvement Program activities and research, periodic rpt, 1702–2

Dairy marketing and price data for selected cities, States, and regions, 1983, annual rpt, 1317–1

Dairy production by State, stocks, prices, and CCC price support activities, by product type, monthly rpt, 1627–3

Dairy products production by type, and plants, by State, 1983, annual rpt, 1627–5

Egg production and layer inventory, by State, 1982-83, annual rpt, 1625–7

Exports of agricultural products, for 17 commodity groups, by region and State, 1978/79-1983/84, article, 1522–1.403

Exports of manufactured and agricultural commodities, manufacturing production, and export-related employment, 1960s-82, State rpt series, 2046–3

Farm business legal organization, finances, operations, tax rates, and State laws restricting farm corporations, 1960s-82, 1548–233

Farm Credit System mortgage and other loans, and financial statements, 1982 and selected trends from 1961, annual rpt, 9264–2

Farm debt, loans outstanding, and interest rates, by type of lender and State, 1960-83 with trends from 1940, biennial rpt, 1544–2

Farm finances, assets, liabilities, income, receipts by commodity and State, and expenses, 1980-83 and trends from 1910, annual rpt, 1544–16

Farm labor, farms, and labor costs, by labor and farm type and State, with immigrant labor law effect on farm work force, 1978, 1598–192

Farm labor, wages, hours, and perquisites, by State, quarterly rpt, 1631–1

Farm real estate value, sales, financing, taxes, and proposed use after purchase, by State, 1970s-84, annual rpt, 1541–8

Farmland (US) owned by foreigners, acquisitions, dispositions, holdings, and use, by State and type and country of owner, 1983, annual rpt, 1584–2

Farmland (US) owned by foreigners, acreage, value, and use, by State and county, and for 5 leading investor countries, 1983, annual rpt, 1584–3

Farmland acquisitions of foreigners, by State and county, before 1980 and during 1980-82, 1588–77

Farmland restoration from natural disaster, Emergency Conservation Program participation and payments, by practice and State, FY83, annual rpt, 1804–22

Farms, production, acreage, and related data, by selected crop and State, monthly rpt, 1621–1

Fats, oils, and oilseed production, prices, trade, and consumption, periodic situation rpt with articles, 1561–3

Fertilizer consumption, by fertilizer type and State, years ended June 1983-84, annual rpt, 1631–13

Fertilizer production and trade, and consumption by region and State, 1983, annual rpt, 1804–6

Fertilizer use for selected crops, and pesticide expenditures, by State, periodic situation rpt with articles, 1561–16

Fish and eggs for stocking distributed from natl hatcheries, by species, hatchery, and jurisdiction, FY83, annual rpt, 5504–10

Fish and fish products production by region and State, and trade, by species and product, 1982-83, annual rpt series, 2166–6

Fish landings by species and State, and value at leading ports and disposition, 1970s-83, annual rpt, 2164–1.1

Fish landings by species, State, and at leading ports, and industry operating data, by region, 1970s-83, annual rpt, 2164–1.10

Fish landings, employment, gear used, and seafood production, for detailed species by State, 1977, annual rpt, 2164–2

Fishery resources mgmt and R&D, Fed Govt grants by project and resulting publications, 1983, annual listing, 2164–3

FmHA loans and borrower supervision activities in farm and housing programs, by type and State, monthly rpt, 1182–1

FmHA loans, by type, race, Hispanic origin, and State, quarterly rpt, 1182–5

FmHA loans for rural home mortgages, eligibility of current recipients under revised income limit, by State, 1983, GAO rpt, 26113–134

Food products (processed) production and stocks by State, shipments, exports, materials used, and consumption, periodic Current Industrial Rpt series, 2506–4

Fruit (citrus) production and use, by crop and State, 1977/78-1981/82, 1641–4

Fruit (citrus) production, prices, and use, by producer State, 1981/82-1983/84, annual rpt, 1621–18.5

Fruit (noncitrus) and nut production, prices, and use, by crop and State, 1981-83, annual rpt, 1621–18.1, 1621–18.3

Fruit and nut production, prices, trade, stocks, and use, by selected crop, periodic situation rpt with articles, 1561–6

Fruit and vegetable shipments, and arrivals in 23 US and 5 Canada cities, by mode of transport and State or country of origin, 1983, annual rpt series, 1311–4

Fruit and vegetable shipments by mode of transport, arrivals, and imports, by commodity and State and country of origin, weekly rpt, 1311–3

Grain loan support programs of USDA, activity and status by type of grain and State, monthly rpt, 1802–3

Grain, oilseed, and hay stocks on and off farms, and capacity of off-farm grain storage facilities, by State, 1978-83, 1641–17

Grain production, acreage, and yield, by selected crop and State, 1982-84 with wheat and rye seedings for 1985, annual rpt, 1621–24

Grain stocks on and off farms and total in all positions, by crop, periodic rpt, 1621–4

Hog and pig inventory, value, farrowings, and farms, by State, quarterly release, 1623–3

Hog and pig production and farm sales, by type and size of enterprise and State, selected years 1950-80, 1568–248

Hog and pig production, inventory, and farms, by State, 1979-82, 1641–10

Honey and sugar production, prices, trade, stocks, and marketing, and honey loan activity and processing awards of CCC, weekly rpt, 1311–2

Income (gross and net) and cash marketing receipts for farms, by detailed commodity, and production expenses, by State, 1979-82, annual rpt, 1544–18

Livestock and livestock production, 1983, annual rpt, 1564–6

Livestock grazing on Natl Forest System lands, and losses from predators, poisonous plants, and other causes, by region and State, FY83, annual rpt, 1204–5

Livestock inspected by Fed Govt, by type, weekly rpt, 1315–1

Livestock packers purchases and feeding, and livestock markets, dealers, and sales, by region and State, 1981-82, annual rpt, 1384–1

Livestock slaughter and meat production, by livestock type and State, monthly rpt, 1623–9

Livestock slaughter by species, meat production, and number of slaughtering plants, by State, 1983, annual rpt, 1623–10

Meat and poultry inspection activities and personnel of Federal, State, and foreign govts, FY83, annual rpt, 1374–1

Meat and poultry inspection by Food Safety and Inspection Service, FY83, annual rpt, 1374–3

Meat animal production, marketing, slaughter, prices, and producers gross income, by animal type and State, 1982-83, annual rpt, 1623–8

Milk and dairy production, prices, consumption, and trade, quarterly situation rpt with articles, 1561–2

Milk cows, and milk and cream production and marketings, by State, 1981-83, annual rpt, 1627–4

Milk cows and milk production, and grain and other concentrates fed, by State, monthly rpt, 1627–1

Milk deliveries to Fed Govt order plants, by State and marketing area of origin and destination, 1982-83, article, 1317–4.405

Milk order market major provisions, summary by Federal marketing area, as of July 1984, annual rpt, 1317–11

Milk order market prices and detailed operations, by State and market area, monthly 1982-83, annual rpt, 1317–3

Milk price supports effect on production, use, prices, and farm receipts, by region and State, 1940s-83 and alternative projections to 1988/89, 1568–245

Mink and mink pelt production, by State, 1983-84 with trends from 1969, annual rpt, 1631–7

Mushroom production, sales, and prices, by State, 1981/82-1983/84 and planned 1984/85, annual rpt, 1631–9

North Central States farm investments, effective rates of Federal/State income and State/local property taxes, by category of structure and equipment and State, 1981-82, 1548–237

Peach production, marketing, and prices in 4 Southeastern States and Appalachia, 1983, annual rpt, 1311–12

Peanut production, prices, stocks, exports, use, inspection, and quality, by region and State, selected crop years 1974-83, annual rpt, 1311–5

Peanut production, prices, trade by country, and stocks, weekly rpt, 1311–1

BY STATE

Peppermint and spearmint oil area, production, yield, farm value, and grower prices, by State, 1982-83, FAS annual rpt, 1925–15.2

Pests (plant) and pathogens found entering US, by country of origin, State, and method of interception, FY82, annual rpt, 1394–16

Potato and sweet potato production, stocks, and prices, 1982-83, annual rpt, 1621–11

Potato and sweet potato production, stocks, prices, acreage, and yield, 1978-82 and preliminary 1983, 1641–14

Potato production, stocks, processing, yields, and harvest losses, by State, periodic rpt, 1621–10

Poultry (egg, chicken, and turkey) production and inventories, monthly rpt, 1625–1

Poultry and egg marketing and price data for selected regions, States, and SMSAs, monthly 1983, annual rpt, 1317–2

Poultry Natl Improvement Plan, hatchery participation and flocks included, by disease program, region, and State, 1981-83, annual rpt, 1394–15

Poultry prices received by farmers, for chickens, turkeys, and eggs, by State, monthly and annual average, 1959-78, 1651–3

Poultry production, prices, and producers gross income, by State, 1982-83, annual rpt, 1625–5

Poultry slaughtered under Fed Govt inspection, pounds certified, and condemnations by cause, by State, monthly rpt, 1625–3

Prices received by farmers and production value for detailed crops by State, 1981-83, annual rpt, 1621–2

Prices received by farmers for major products, and paid for farm inputs and living items, by commodity and State, monthly rpt, 1629–1

Prices received by farmers for major products, and paid for farm inputs, by commodity and State, 1983, annual rpt, 1629–5

Research funding for agriculture from Fed Govt and States, by region, State, and outlying area, FY78-82, GAO rpt, 26113–111

Rice market activities, prices, inspections, sales, trade, supply, and use, for US and selected foreign markets, weekly rpt, 1313–8

Rice production, prices, trade, stocks, and use, 1978-July 1984 and 1984/85 outlook, semiannual situation rpt, 1561–8

Sheep and lambs by State, and goats in Texas, inventories and operations, 1981-84, annual press release, 1623–4

Southeastern States soil conservation and water pollution reduction participants, costs, and acreage, by conservation method and State, selected years 1973-82, 1588–84

Soybean stocks on and off farms, by State, various dates 1983-84, annual rpt, 1621–5

Storage facility and equipment loans to farmers under CCC grain program, by State, FY68-84, annual table, 1804–14

Storage facility and equipment loans to farmers under CCC grain program, by State, monthly table, 1802–9

Sugar and sweeteners production, consumption, prices, supply, and trade, quarterly rpt with articles, 1561–14

Sugar production, consumption, supply, and trade, quarterly rpt, 1621–28

Tobacco prices, marketing, grades, and types for 3 classes, 1983 crop and 1983/84 season, annual rpt series, 1319–5

Tobacco production, prices, stocks, taxes by State, and trade and foreign production by country, 1983, annual rpt, 1319–1

Tobacco sales cash receipts, quarterly situation rpt with articles, 1561–10

Turkey inventories and production, by State, 1981-83 with 1984 breeding intentions, annual release, 1625–6

TVA fertilizer distribution in farmer education programs by State, dev costs, and shipments by type and purpose, FY83, annual rpt, 9804–1.2

Vegetable and fruit production, acreage, and prices, for selected fresh and processing crops by State, 1981-84, annual rpts, 1621–25

Vegetable and fruit production, acreage, and yield, current and forecast for selected fresh and processing crops by State, periodic rpt, 1621–12

Vegetable production, prices, stocks, and consumption, for selected fresh and processed crops, periodic situation rpt with articles, 1561–11

Water Bank Program agreements, acreage, and Fed Govt payments, by State, monthly rpt, 1802–5

Wool and mohair production and prices, by State, 1982-83, annual release, 1623–6

Banking, Finance, and Insurance

Appalachian States, FHLB 5th District member S&Ls financial condition and operations by SMSA, monthly rpt, 9302–8

Automated teller machines and point of sale debit card systems offered by retailers, by firm, firm type, and State, 1984 survey, article, 9371–1.421

Automated teller machines shared networks by State, and membership and characteristics of top 16 regional and natl networks, Nov 1983, article, 9373–1.403

Bank deposits in commercial and mutual savings banks and in US branches of foreign banks, by account type, instn, State, SMSA, and county, June 1983, annual rpt, 9295–3

Bank interstate offices by type, and electronic funds transfer networks, for Fed Reserve 7th District by State of origin and coverage, 1981-83, article, 9375–1.403

Bank interstate service offices, including S&Ls, bank branches, and nonbank subsidiaries offering financial services, by instn and State, 1981-83, 9371–13

Bank investment returns on capital assets for leasing, and municipal bond holdings, for 16 States, 1982, article, 9385–1.402

Bank offices, branches, earnings, assets, and deposits, 1982, annual rpt, 9364–5.11

Banking intl facilities by State and ownership, and aggregate assets and liabilities, various dates 1981-83, article, 9391–1.409

Bankruptcy caseloads in Federal district courts and new judges needed, by circuit and district, and characteristics of bankruptcy filers, 1978-83, hearing, 25528–97

Index by Categories

Banks (natl) domestic and intl operations, charters, mergers, and liquidations, by State and instn, and Comptroller of Currency activities, quarterly rpt, 8402–3

Banks requiring FDIC disbursement, depositors, deposits, and disbursements, by location and disbursement reason, 1983 with trends from 1934, annual rpt, 9294–1.2

Bond tax-exempt issues for private activity, by purpose, face value, major industry, and State, 1983, article, 8302–2.417

County and City Data Book, detailed socioeconomic and demographic data for States, counties, and cities, selected years 1976-82, 2328–1

Credit union financial statements by region, State, and type of membership, for Federal and federally insured State unions, 1983, annual rpt, 9534–1

Credit union membership, shares and loans, and asset size, for Federal and federally insured State unions by State, 1984 annual listing, 9534–6

Fed Home Loan Bank System members, with assets of S&Ls, by instn, city, and State, 1983, annual listing, 9314–5

Middle Atlantic States, FHLB 2nd District member savings instns financial operations, by State, monthly rpt, 9302–14

Midwest States, FHLB of Des Moines members by type and State, 1982-83, annual rpt, 9304–7

Negotiable orders of withdrawal accounts authorized and offered at industrial banks, S&Ls, and savings banks, and instns and deposits, by State, as of Dec 1983, press release, 9368–75

New England States economic indicators, Fed Reserve 1st District, monthly rpt with articles, 9373–2

New England States, FHLB 1st District member instns financial operations and housing industry indicators, monthly rpt, 9302–4

New England States, FHLB 1st District member savings instns, locations, and financial condition, 1984, annual listing, 9304–26

New England States thrift and commercial banking instns financial statements, by type of instn and State, 1972 and 1982, annual rpt, 9304–3

North Central States, Fed Reserve 7th District, economic issues, working paper series, 9375–13

North Central States, FHLB 6th District insured S&Ls financial condition and operations by State, monthly rpt, 9302–11

North Central States, FHLB 8th District member S&Ls financial operations by State and SMSA, monthly rpt, 9302–9

North Central States, FHLB 8th District member S&Ls, locations, assets, and savings, 1984, annual listing, 9304–9

Northeast States savings bank deposits by type, and commercial banks share of savings in depository instns, by State, various dates 1970-83, hearing, 21248–83

Savings and loan assn balance sheet items by State and SMSA, and finances of FHLBs, 1983, annual rpt, 9314–3

Savings and loan assns assets and liabilities, by FHLB district and State, selected years 1955-82, annual rpt, 9314–1

Index by Categories

BY STATE

Savings instns FSLIC-insured, offices, and savings deposits, by State, SMSA, and county, 1983, annual rpt, 9314–4

Small Business Investment Companies finances, funding, licensing, and loan activity, 2nd half FY84, semiannual rpt, 9762–3

South Central States, FHLB 9th District insured S&Ls financial condition and operations by SMSA, monthly rpt, 9302–13

Southeastern States, FHLB 4th District insured S&Ls financial condition and operations, by SMSA, monthly rpt, 9302–1

Southeastern States, FHLB 4th District member S&Ls financial ratios and mortgage portfolios by State, 2nd half 1983, semiannual rpt, 9302–3

Southeastern States financial and economic devs, Fed Reserve 6th District, monthly rpt with articles, 9371–1

Stockbroker firms by type of organization and State, finances, and SEC applications and registrations, 1978-FY83, annual rpt, 9734–2.1

Trust assets of banks and trust companies, by type of asset and fund and State, 1983, annual rpt, 13004–1

West Central States, FHLB 10th District insured S&Ls finances and operations by SMSA, monthly rpt, 9302–22

Western States depository instns financial activity by State, and large commercial banks by city, Fed Reserve 10th District, monthly rpt, 9381–11

Western States, FHLB 11th District member S&L offices, locations, savings balances, and accounts, quarterly listing, 9302–20

Western States, FHLB 11th District member S&Ls financial condition and operations by State, quarterly rpt, 9302–19

Western States, FHLB 11th District member S&Ls financial operations and housing industry indicators, by State monthly rpt, 9302–17

Western States, FHLB 12th District member S&Ls financial operations and housing industry indicators by State, monthly rpt, 9302–21

Communications and Transportation

Air passenger traffic, and aircraft operations by type, by airport, region, and State, projected FY82-95 and trends from FY76, annual rpt, 7504–7

Air traffic levels at FAA-operated control facilities, by airport and State, FY83, annual rpt, 7504–27

Aircraft (general aviation), hours flown, and equipment, by type, use, and model of aircraft, region, and State, 1982, annual rpt, 7504–29

Aircraft accidents in general aviation by State, circumstances, and pilots involved by age and blood alcohol level, 1981, annual rpt, 9614–3.1

Aircraft collisions, and near collisions by circumstances and State, by type of aircraft, various periods 1980-84, 7508–61

Aircraft pilots and nonpilots certified by FAA, by type of certificate, age, sex, region, and State, 1983, annual rpt, 7504–2

Aircraft registered with FAA, by type and characteristics of aircraft, carrier, make, State, and county, 1983, annual rpt, 7504–3

Airline and general aviation accident circumstances, severity, and causes, for US operations of domestic and foreign aircraft, periodic rpt, 9612–1

Airline deregulation in 1978, effect on industry operations and finances, air traffic patterns, and CAB programs, various periods FY76-84, 9148–56

Airline passenger and cargo traffic, and departures by aircraft type, by airline and US and foreign airport, 1982, annual rpt, 7504–35

Airlines (commuter and intrastate) operating in 1978 by region and State, and listing by city, by operation status in 1984, article, 9142–42.404

Airport improvement program grants and activities, by State and airport, FY83, annual rpt, 7504–38

Airport planning and dev project grants of Fed Govt, by sponsor, airport, and location, periodic press release series, 7506–8

Appalachia hwy system and access roads funding and completion status, by State, quarterly tables, 9082–1

Auto registrations for domestic and imported new cars, by region and State, 1964-83, annual rpt, 9884–7.4

Aviation activity, detailed data on aircraft, air traffic, air carriers, personnel, airports, and FAA operations, 1974-83, annual rpt, 7504–1

Bridge replacement and rehabilitation program of Fed Govt, funding by bridge and bridge status by State, 1983, annual rpt, 7554–27

Bus industry collective ratemaking and regulatory reform impacts on operations, finances, and services to older persons and rural areas by State, 1970s-83, 14828–2

DOT employment by subagency, State, and selected personnel characteristics, FY83, annual rpt, 7304–18.1

DOT grant awards for transportation planning and safety programs, by region, State, and for 35 largest SMSAs, FY83, annual rpt, 7304–7

Drivers license requirements and admin, by State and Canada Province, 1984, biennial rpt, 7554–18

Drivers licensed by age and sex, and licensing policies, by State, 1982, annual rpt, 7554–16

Hwy and urban transit systems financing methods of govts and private sector, with case studies for selected metro areas, series, 7556–7

Hwy construction bids and contracts for Federal-aid interstate and secondary hwys, by State, 1st half 1984, semiannual rpt, 7552–12

Hwy construction expenditures and contracts awarded for Federal-aid system, by type of material used and State, various periods 1944-83, annual rpts, 7554–29

Hwy construction material prices and indexes for Federal-aid system, by type of material and urban-rural location, quarterly rpt, 7552–7

Hwy interstate system mileage, costs, and Fed Govt funding, by hwy completion status and State, as of June 1984, 7556–3.4

Hwy-railroad grade-crossing accidents, detailed data by State and railroad, 1982, annual rpt, 7604–2

Hwy safety improvement, federally funded programs implementation by State, FY83, annual rpt, 7554–26

Hwy safety program Fed Govt appropriations, by State and program, quarterly rpt, 7552–9

Hwy speed averages and vehicles exceeding 55 mph, by State, quarterly rpt, 7552–14

Hwy Statistics, detailed data on traffic, govt finances, fuel use, vehicles, driver licenses, and hwy characteristics, by State, 1983, annual rpt, 7554–1

Hwy Statistics, summary data on traffic, govt finances, fuel use, vehicles, and driver licenses, by State, 1982, annual rpt, 7554–24

Hwy traffic volume on rural roads and city streets, by region, monthly rpt, 7552–8

Hwys designated for use by large trucks, mileage by State, as of June 1984, press release, 7556–3.1

Pipeline safety regulations enforcement of DOT and States by pipeline type and State, and accidents and commodity losses, selected years 1973-FY84, GAO rpt, 26113–130

Ports, port facilities by type, and inland waterways by size, by location, 1982-83, annual rpt, 7704–16

Railroad accidents, casualties, and property damage, Fed Railroad Admin activities, and safety inspectors by State, 1982, annual rpt, 7604–12

Railroad accidents investigated by Fed Railroad Admin, casualties, damage, and circumstances, 1982, annual rpt, 7604–3

Railroad employee benefits and beneficiaries by type, and railroad employees and payrolls, FY82, annual rpt, 9704–2

Railroad employee benefits and beneficiaries by type, benefit program finances, and railroad employees and payroll, FY83, annual rpt, 9704–1

Rural Telephone Program loan activities summary, by State, FY83, annual rpt, 1244–8

Telephone companies borrowing under rural telephone loan program, and financial and operating data, 1983, annual rpt, 1244–2.3

Telephone facilities and use, by State and outlying area, 1982, annual rpt, 9284–6.2

Telephone operating and financial data by company type, with fixed cost recovery from interstate revenue by Bell company and State, 1981-82 with trends from 1945, 26306–6.79

Telephone operating data, costs, and billings for American Telephone and Telegraph Co local and long distance lines, by State, 1980-82 with trends from 1970, 23848–176

Traffic accidents and deaths by characteristics of persons and vehicles involved and State, and Natl Hwy Traffic Safety Admin activities, 1961-81, annual rpt, 7764–1

Traffic accidents, deaths, injuries, and rates, by hwy type and State, 1982, annual rpt, 7554–2

Traffic deaths, total and alcohol-related, and drunk driver license revocations and other deterrence measures in selected States, 1980-82, 9618–10

BY STATE

Traffic fatal accidents, circumstances, and characteristics of persons and vehicles involved, 1983, annual rpt, 7764–14

Traffic fatal accidents detailed circumstances, and characteristics of persons and vehicles involved, 1982, annual rpt, 7764–10

Traffic fatal accidents total and alcohol-related, model results by State, 1976-81, article, 7762–9.405

Traffic safety projects research and evaluation, quarterly rpt articles, 7762–9

Transit system operations, tax burden related to ridership, fares, and govt funding, for selected States and cities, 1950s-82, reprint, 7888–59

Transportation census, 1982: trucks, by detailed characteristics, miles traveled, and type of product carried, State rpt series, 2573–1

Travel to US, by characteristics of visit and traveler, country, and State of destination, quarterly rpt, 2902–1

Truck accidents, injuries, deaths, and property damage, by circumstances, carrier type, and driver age and condition, 1983, annual rpt, 7554–9

TV and radio industry employment, total and for minorities, women, and youth, by job category and State, 1979-83, annual rpt, 9284–16

TV and radio industry minority and women employment by occupation, and business owners, by race and State, with revenues and stations, 1971-81, hearing, 21368–45

Education

Bilingual education funding of States, FY83, and Spanish and other minority language population and children with limited English proficiency, 1980, by State, biennial rpt, 4804–14

Census of Govts, 1982: school districts revenues, expenditures, debt, and assets, by district and State, 2457–1

Condition of Education, detailed data on enrollment, staff, achievement, finances, curricula, and education effects on employment, 1982-83, annual rpt, 4824–1

Digest of Education Statistics, detailed data on students, staff, finances, and facilities, 1982 and selected trends, annual rpt, 4824–2

Education of teachers, teaching degrees and salaries, high school seniors achievement test scores, and school enrollment and finances, 1970s-83, hearings, 21348–89

Elementary and secondary public school districts, schools, enrollment, staff, and finances, by State, 1981/82, annual rpt, 4834–13

Elementary and secondary public school enrollment, by grade level and State, fall 1982, annual rpt, 4834–10

Fed Govt education block grants, State allocations by program and selected school district, FY82-84 and trends from FY60, hearing, 21408–75

Fed Govt educational grants, State allocations by program, type of recipient agency, and State, FY83, annual rpt, 4804–8

Handicapped children early education research and service project activities and characteristics, and grants to States for program dev, 1983-84, annual listing, 4804–30

Handicapped children public education program enrollment, staff, and funding, by handicap, age, and State, 1981/82-1982/83, annual rpt, 4944–4

Head Start Project enrollment of handicapped children, by handicap, State, and for Indian and migrant programs, 1982, annual rpt, 4604–1

High school grads and 12th grade enrollment, by State, 1981/82, annual rpt, 4834–12

Higher education enrollment, by student characteristics, instn type, State, and for 150 instns, fall 1982, annual rpt, 4844–2

Higher education instns, by type, location, and other characteristics, 1983/84 annual listing, 4844–3

Higher education instns, type, location, enrollment, and student charges, by State and congressional district, 1983/84, biennial listing, 4844–11

Impacted area schools, Fed Govt funding by county and school and congressional district, and eligible pupils, by State, FY83, annual rpt, 4804–10

Indian Education Act, Fed Govt grants and fellowships awarded by State, FY83, and natl advisory council funding, FY73-84, annual rpt, 14874–1

Library (research) funding of Education Dept, by project, program area, instn, and State, FY84, annual listing, 4804–22

Mentally retarded and developmentally disabled treatment and services, university-affiliated facility funding, activities, and clients, 1980-FY83, 4608–19

Microfiche from Educational Resources Info Center, holdings of US and foreign educational and other instns, as of 1983, listing, 4918–14

Student aid basic grant, loan, and work-study awards, Fed Govt share by instn and State, 1984/85, annual rpt, 4804–17

Student aid Federal programs funding and participation, by instn type and control, State, and outlying area, with student loan defaults and collections, FY82, annual rpt, 4804–28

Student aid need-based program funding, and State Student Incentive Grant funding, recipients, and average income and award, by State, FY67-82, GAO rpt, 26121–69

Student aid Pell grants and recipients, by educational costs, family income, instnl type and control, and State, 1981/82, annual rpt, 4804–1

Teachers salaries in schools and colleges by State, 1982/83, and school employees health insurance plans in 7 cities, as of 1980, hearing, 21788–136

Truman, Harry S, Scholarship Foundation, program operation, financial status, and awards by student characteristics, 1983 with trends from 1977, annual rpt, 14314–1

Tuition and other student charges at each public and private 2- and 4-year higher education instn, by State, 1983/84, annual listing, 4844–10

Vocational training bilingual projects, participants, characteristics, and costs, by program, FY82, annual rpt, 4804–26

Index by Categories

Energy Resources and Demand

Coal, coke, and breeze supply/demand, prices, trade, and stocks, by end-use sector and State, quarterly rpt with articles, 3162–37

Coal Fed Govt leases, acreage, production, and prices, by State, and legal and mgmt issues, 1970s-83 with production projections to 2000, 11128–1

Coal lands of Fed Govt leasing activity, acreage, and reserves, by State, coal region, and tract, FY83, annual rpt, 5724–10

Coal production and mines by county, prices, productivity, miners, reserves, and stocks, by mining method and State, 1982-83, annual rpt, 3164–25

Coal production and stocks, and electric utility generation, capacity, and coal use, alternative estimates 1977-82, annual rpt, 3164–63

Coal production and stocks by district, and shipments by district of origin, State of destination, consuming sector, and mode of transport, quarterly rpt, 3162–8

Coal production by State and region, trade, consumption, and stocks, weekly rpt, 3162–1

Coal purchases of Fed Govt, quality control analyses by mine and location, FY82-83, annual rpt, 3004–15

Coal supply and Fed Govt coal leases, by owner, owner industry, and western State, various periods 1950-82 and projected to 2000, hearing, 25318–58

Coal supply/demand, projected 1983-95 with summary trends from 1865, annual rpt, 3164–68

Coal surface mining reclamation costs and Interior Dept regulatory enforcement activities, impacts on industry in 5 States and 3 regions, various periods 1978-82, 6068–177

Conservation aid of DOE, activities, funding, and grants by State, by program, FY84, annual rpt, 3304–21

Conservation grants of Fed Govt to public and nonprofit private instns, by building type and State, 1983, annual rpt, 3304–15

Conservation programs of State govts, Fed Govt financial and technical aid, and reported energy savings, by State, 1983, annual rpt, 3304–1

DOE procurement and assistance contracts, by State, contractor type, and top 100 instns, FY83, annual rpt, 3004–21

Electric power plant (coal-fired) capacity, coal demand, and coal supply by mode of transport and region of origin, by State, for units planned 1983-92, 3088–18

Electric power plant (steam) fuel deliveries, costs, and quality, by fuel type, State, and utility, 1983, annual rpt, 3164–42

Electric power plant capacity, production, retail sales, and fuel stocks, use, and costs, by State, 1979-83, annual rpt, 3164–11

Electric power plant capital and operating detailed costs, capacity, and fuel use, by plant, plant type, utility, and State, 1982, annual rpt, 3164–9

Electric power plants, by capacity, fuel used, unit type, region, State, and county, for plants added and retired, 1983 and planned through 1993, annual rpt, 3164–36

Electric power sold by privately owned utilities to other utilities, municipals, and

Index by Categories

BY STATE

cooperatives for resale to consumers, by State and company, 1982, annual rpt, 3164–23.2

Electric power wholesale purchases and costs for individual REA borrowers, by supplier and State, 1940-83, annual rpt, 1244–5

Electric utilities consumption of natural gas, by State, 1977 and 1983, annual rpt, 3104–8

Electric utility fuel cost, quality, use, receipts, and stocks, and power plant production, by energy source, State and utility, quarterly rpt, 3162–39

Electric utility production, fuel consumption, stocks, and costs by fuel type, and sales, by State, monthly rpt, 3162–35

Energy production, reserves, and prices, by energy type, and selected indicators of energy use, by State, 1982-83 with selected comparisons from 1971, annual rpt, 3164–60

Energy use, by economic sector, State, census div, and detailed energy resource, 1960-82, State Energy Data System annual rpt, 3164–39

Energy use, by type of air pollutant source and fuel, and State, 1981, annual rpt, 9194–14

Energy use, per capita and by economic sector, State, and major energy resource, 1960-82, State Energy Data System annual supplement, 3164–55

Fed Govt and Indian lands oil, gas, coal, and other mineral production and revenues, by State, 1983 with trends from 1920, annual rpt, 5734–2

Fed Govt OCS oil, gas, and mineral production, revenues, and reserves, by State and ocean region, 1950s-82, annual rpt, 5734–3

Gasohol and ethanol plant capacity and production, tax exemptions and sales by State, and prices, 1983, annual rpt, 3304–9

Gasohol production and costs by feedstock, prices, and market penetration rates and excise tax exemption by State, 1983, article, 1561–16.404

Gasoline and gasohol consumption, and motor fuel tax rates by fuel type, by State, monthly rpt, 7552–1

Home heating costs of low-income households, natural gas price decontrol effects, aid programs, and gas supply/demand data, by income level and State, 1970s-95, hearing, 25148–26

Housing (low-income) energy aid of Fed Govt, allocations and average benefits in 13 States, and public interest group assessment, FY81-83, GAO rpt, 26121–75

Housing (low-income) energy aid of Fed Govt, by income, aid type, and State, FY83, annual rpt, 4744–3.13

Housing electricity and gas costs for 306 cities, by utility, with climatological data, fall 1982, 3308–67

Housing energy conservation programs of utilities, financing, costs, participation, and energy savings, various periods 1981-84, hearing, 21368–54

Housing energy use, and savings under alternative conservation strategies, by State, with model methodology and energy prices, selected years 1970-81, 21368–48

Natural and supplemental gas production, prices, trade, use, reserves, and pipeline company finances, by firm and State, monthly rpt with articles, 3162–4

Natural gas composition and occurrence of helium, analyses of samples from individual wells and pipelines in 26 States and 2 countries, 1983, annual survey, 5604–2

Natural gas consumer prices, by consumer sector, census div, and State, 1983, preliminary annual rpt, 3164–4

Natural gas interstate pipeline company supplies, reserves, production, purchases, and contracts, by firm, 1983 with projected deliverability to 2003, annual rpt, 3164–33

Natural gas pipeline safety, Fed Govt expenditures, FY81, and State inspection personnel, enforcement actions, and accidents investigated, by State, 1982, annual rpt, 7304–5

Natural gas production and trade by State, and underground storage changes, EIA estimates based on alternative data sources, 1980-81, 3008–90

Natural gas production, wells drilled, and contract prices, by Natural Gas Policy Act section, producer and well characteristics, State, and field, selected years 1968-83, 3168–90

Nuclear engineering student enrollments and degrees granted, by State, instn, and subfield, and placements by sector, 1983, annual rpt, 3004–5

Nuclear power industry status and outlook, with reactor construction, utility financial and operating data, and foreign comparisons, 1970s-83 with projections to 2010, 26358–99

Nuclear power plant construction and operation status, and capacity, by plant, region, State, and selected country, 1983 and projected to 2020, annual rpt, 3164–57

Nuclear power plant construction costs and status, and capacity, by plant and State, as of Mar 1984, annual rpt, 3164–69

Nuclear reactors at central station power plants, operating status and other characteristics by plant, utility, and State, as of Jan 1984, annual rpt, 3354–11

Nuclear reactors for domestic use and export by function, with owner, operating characteristics, and location, Apr 1984, semiannual listing, 3002–5

Nuclear Regulatory Commission activities, employment, and finances, and operations of individual power plants by State, FY83, annual rpt, 9634–2

Oil (Alaskan) potential exports to Japan, costs and benefits, with background data on oil prices, Pacific Basin supply/demand, and tankers, various periods 1918-99, hearings, 25388–45

Oil and gas extraction production workers, wages, hours, and benefits, by occupation, region, and for 5 States, June 1982 survey, 6787–6.203

Oil and gas fields by State and EIA field code, 1983, annual listing, 3164–70

Oil and refined products and natural gas liquids supply/demand, trade, stocks, and refining, by detailed product, State, and PAD district, monthly rpt with articles, 3162–6

Oil and refined products and natural gas liquids supply/demand, trade, stocks, and refining, by detailed product, State, and PAD district, 1983 annual rpt, 3164–2

Oil and refined products supply and prices, effects of 3 import disruptions, selected years 1972-82, 3108–28

Oil enhanced recovery technologies use and environmental impacts, by oil field, county, and State, 1970s-80 and projected to 2000, 3408–29

Oil, gas, and gas liquids reserves and production, by State and selected substate area, 1983, annual rpt, 3164–46

Oil price and allocation regulations enforcement by DOE, and overcharge allegations, settlements, and refunds to States, by company, as of June 1983, hearing, 21368–50

Oil production, total and for surveillance fields, by State and inland and Federal offshore area, 1980-82, biennial rpt, 3164–58

Oil refined products sales of gas plant operators, refiners, and resellers, price and volume for 13 products, by end-use sector, PAD district, and State, monthly rpt, 3162–11

Pacific Northwest electricity consumption and prices by end-use sector, and economic and demographic data, 1960s-83 and projected to 2005, annual rpt, 3224–2

Rural Electrification Admin financed electric power plants, with location, capacity, and owner, as of Jan 1984, annual listing, 1244–6

Rural Electrification Admin loans to power supply and distribution firms, and borrower operating and financial data, by firm and State, 1983, annual rpt, 1244–1

Rural Electrification Program loan activities summary, by State, FY83 and cumulative from 1935, annual rpt, 1244–7

Solar collector and photovoltaic module production, sales, and use, with listing of manufacturers, 1983, annual rpt, 3164–62

Southeastern Power Admin sales by customer, plants, and capacity, and financial statements of Southeastern Fed Power Program, FY83, annual rpt, 3234–1

Tennessee Valley ethanol production, feedstocks, facilities, tax incentives, and related farming data, by State, 1970s-83 and projected to 1992, 9808–69

TVA Biomass Fuels Program, technologies and processes dev, costs, and resource requirements, 1970s-90s, series, 9806–9

TVA procurement contract awards, by State, FY83 and cumulative from FY34, annual rpt, 9804–1.2

Uranium mining and milling employment, by State and type of activity, 1983, annual rpt, 3164–66

Uranium mining operations, finances, and costs of alternative methods to meet emissions standards, for industry and selected mines, selected years 1948-90, 9188–96

Uranium reserves and mining and milling industries operations and finances, with selected foreign comparisons, various periods 1964-83 and projected to 2000, 3008–95

Western Area Power Admin operations by plant, financial statements, and electric power sales by customer, FY83, annual rpt, 3254–1

Western Area Power Admin small-scale potential hydroelectric generation, site inventory, characteristics, and costs, by State and county, 1984 rpt, 3258–1

ASI Annual Supplement 905

BY STATE

Wood acquired and used for home heating, by household characteristics and wood sources, 1980/81, 1208–204

Wood fuel consumption, by end-use sector, SIC 2-digit industry, region, State, and selected industrial and power plant, 1980-83, biennial rpt, 3164–78

Geography and Climate

Climatological data by census div and State, and departures from long-term mean, from 1895, series, 2156–17

Earthquake and other ground motion intensity measured on USGS Natl Strong-Motion Network by station, and sources of foreign and US info, 1981, annual rpt, 5664–14

Earthquake intensity, damage, and deaths, by location for major earthquakes since 1755, and hazard areas and natl reduction program activities, as of 1984, 5668–73

Earthquake intensity, damage, time of origin, and seismic characteristics of all US and major foreign earthquakes, 1981, annual rpt, 5664–13

Earthquake intensity, time of origin, seismic characteristics, and location, by State, quarterly rpt, 5662–4

Heating and cooling degree days by State, and housing energy bills and departures from normal by fuel type, by census div, monthly rpt, 2152–11

Heating and cooling degree days weighted by population, by census div and State, with area-weighted temperature and precipitation, monthly rpt, 2152–13

Storms and unusual weather phenomena characteristics, casualties, and property damage, by State and outlying area, monthly listing, 2152–3

Weather conditions and effect on agriculture, by US region, State, and city, and world area, weekly rpt, 2152–2

Weather events socioeconomic impacts and costs, heating and cooling degree days, and housing energy bills, by census div and State, monthly rpt, 2152–12

Weather stations of Natl Weather Service, locations and regular observations made, 1984 annual listing, 2184–5

Government and Defense

AID contracts and grants for technical and support services, by instn, country, and State, FY83, annual listing, 9914–7

Appalachia regional dev spending, by program area and source of funds, FY82, annual rpt, 9084–1

Census of Govts, 1982: city govt revenues by source, expenditures by function, debt, and assets, by State and city, 2457–4

Census of Govts, 1982: county govt revenues by source, expenditures by function, debt, and assets, by State and county, 2457–3

Census of Govts, 1982: employment, payrolls, and average earnings, by function, level of govt, State, county, population size, and inside-outside SMSAs, 2455–2

Census of Govts, 1982: properties, govt-assessed value, sales, and tax rates, by property type, State, SMSA, county, and city, 2453–1

Census of Govts, 1982: State govt payments to local govts, by program, source of funds, level of govt, and State, with trends from 1902, 2460–3

Collective bargaining agreements of Federal employees, unions involved, and employees covered, by agency for agreements expiring July 1984-June 1985, annual listing, 9847–1

County and City Data Book, detailed socioeconomic and demographic data for States, counties, and cities, selected years 1976-82, 2328–1

DOD base construction and renovation, budget authorization requests by DOD component, State, country, and project, FY85, annual rpt, 3544–15

DOD base support costs by function, and personnel and acreage by installation, by service branch, FY85, annual rpt, 3504–11

DOD budget, expenditures for each service branch and total defense agencies, by function and State, FY85, annual rpt, 3544–23

DOD budget, organization, personnel, weapons, and property, by service branch, State, and country, 1984 annual summary rpt, 3504–13

DOD civilian and military employment, by State, service branch, and major installation, as of Sept 1983, annual rpt, 3544–7

DOD contract and in-house commercial activities costs and work-years, by service branch, defense agency, State, and installation, FY83, annual rpt, 3544–25

DOD military and civilian employment, by State, FY83, annual rpt, 3544–1.1

DOD prime contract awards, by individual contractor, service branch, State and city, and country, FY83, annual listing, 3544–22

DOD prime contract awards for military and civil functions, by service branch and State, 1st half FY84, semiannual rpt, 3542–5

DOD prime contract awards in labor surplus areas, by service branch, State, and area, 1st half FY84, semiannual rpt, 3542–19

DOD procurement, prime contract awards for 25 commodity categories and R&D, by State and census div, FY81-83, annual rpt, 3544–11

Economic Dev Admin loans and grants, by program, State, county, and project or recipient, FY83 and cumulative FY66-83, annual rpt, 2064–2

Election campaign finances and Fed Election Commission monitoring activities, 1984 Federal elections, biennial rpt series, 9276–2

Election campaign funding by political action committee and candidate, proposed candidate spending limits, voting rates by party, and political opinions, by State, 1960-82, hearings, 25688–6

Election campaign political action committee funding, by House and Senate candidate, 1978-82 Federal elections, biennial rpt, 9274–4

Election campaign presidential candidate expenditure limits and voting age population, by State, 1984 Federal elections, press release, 9276–1.19

Fed Govt aid to State and local areas, by type of payment, State, county, and city, FY83, annual rpt, 2464–3

Fed Govt aid to State and local govts, expenditures, and direct payments, by program, agency, and State, FY83, annual rpt, 2464–2

Index by Categories

Fed Govt civil service retirees and survivors, and monthly benefit, for US territories and foreign countries, and by State, age, and sex, FY81-82, annual rpt, 9844–1.1

Fed Govt civilian employment and aggregate and average pay, by pay system and State, Mar 1983, annual article, 9842–1.404

Fed Govt civilian employment, by location, agency, and pay system, 1982, biennial rpt, 9844–8

Fed Govt programs under Ways and Means Committee jurisdiction, program operations and financing data for assessing budgetary requirements, by State, FY70s-83, 21788–117

Firefighters death benefits under workers compensation and local pension plans, by State and city, hearing, 21348–94

Govt finances, by level of govt and State, selected years 1929-83, annual rpt, 10044–1

Govt finances, by level of govt, State, and for large cities and counties, 1981-83, annual rpt series, 2466–2

Immigration, and alien residents, workers, visitors, deportations, and naturalizations, by country of birth, FY81, annual rpt, 6264–2

Income tax receipts of IRS, by State and district, FY83, annual rpt, 8104–2.2

Income tax returns and collections, for IRS regions, districts, and service centers, 1972-82 and projections to 1990, annual rpt, 8304–8

Income tax returns filed by type of filer, selected income items, summary data, quarterly rpt, 8302–2.1

Income tax returns of individuals by tax return item, State, and occupation, and income by source and tax owed, by income level, selected years 1916-80, conf papers, 8308–28.1

Income tax returns of individuals, selected income, deduction, and tax credit data by income, preliminary 1982, annual article, 8302–2.402

Income tax returns of sole proprietorships, detailed data by industry div and selected industry group, 1981, annual rpt, 8304–7

Intergovernmental Perspective, quarterly rpt, 10042–1

IRS collections by type of tax, refunds, and taxes due, by region and State, FY83, annual rpt, 8304–3.3

Local govt receipts from Fed Govt in lieu of property taxes on public lands, by State, FY84, annual press release, 5724–9

Manufacturers under Fed Govt contract and owned by DOD, operating data by agency, selected SIC 2- to 4-digit industry, State, and SMSA, 1982, annual Current Industrial Rpt, 2506–3.4

Military draft registrants, by State, 2nd half FY84, semiannual rpt, 9742–1

Military reserve forces manpower strengths and characteristics, by component, quarterly rpt, 3542–4

Motor fuel State tax provisions, motor vehicle registration fees, and disposition of receipts, by State, as of Jan 1984, biennial rpt, 7554–37

Motor fuel tax rates, by State, 1975-83, annual table, 7554–32

Natl Guard (Army and Air) activities, manpower, and facilities, FY83, annual rpt, 3704–3

Index by Categories

BY STATE

Navy procurement, by contractor and location of work, FY83, annual rpt, 3804–13

New England State govts revenues, expenditures, and year-end closing balances, for 6 States, FY83 and projected FY84, article, 9373–2.401

Passports issued, by holder characteristics, travel purpose, and country of destination, quarterly rpt, 7182–1

Procurement contract awards of Fed Govt, by State, agency, procurement and contractor type, and for top 100 contractors, quarterly rpt, 102–6

Property (real) of Fed Govt, inventory and costs, worldwide summary by location, agency, and use, 1983, annual rpt, 9454–5

Property (real) of Fed Govt, leased property inventory and rental costs, worldwide summary by location and agency, Sept 1983, annual rpt, 9454–10

Property (real) of Fed Govt, own-to-lease ratios by State and for 25 SMSAs, as of 1983, hearings, 25328–23

Property (surplus personal) of Fed Govt donated to State and local agencies and nonprofit instns, by region and State, FY83, annual rpt, 9454–22

Revenue sharing and other Fed Govt grant program alternative allocations, with city govt finances and responses to program cuts, FY79-83, hearings, 25408–86

Revenue sharing entitlements by State, and noncompliance audit cases by type, FY83 and cumulative through FY82, annual rpt, 8064–1.1

Revenue sharing payments to States, local govts, Indian tribes, and Alaska Native villages, and entitlement computation data, FY84, series, 8066–1

Statistical Abstract of US, social, political, and economic data, 1950s-83 and trends, annual rpt, 2324–1.2

Tax (excise) revenue of local govts, by excise type and State, average annual growth FY72-82, article, 10042–1.403

Tax burden for average family by income level and selected city, and tax rates by selected jurisdiction, by type of tax, 1982, 10046–8.2

Tax revenues, by level of govt, type of tax, State, and selected large counties, quarterly rpt, 2462–3

Taxes on mineral production, State severance tax and royalty revenue by selected State, selected years FY73-83, article, 9375–1.407

Western States govt revenues and expenditures, surplus/deficit, and tax capacity and effort indexes, for 7 States, selected years 1967-82, article, 9381–1.403

Health and Vital Statistics

Abortions performed in 12 States and NYC, by State of residence and for non-US residents by selected area, 1980, US Vital Statistics final rpt, 4146–5.72

Alcohol, Drug Abuse, and Mental Health Admin research grants, awards, and fellowships by recipient, FY83, annual listing, 4044–13

Alcohol, Drug Abuse and Mental Health Admin staff, contract awards, and grants, by Inst, program, and State, FY83, annual factbook, 4044–1

Allergy and Infectious Diseases Natl Inst activities, grants by instn, State, and country, and disease incidence and costs, FY60s-84, annual rpt, 4474–30

Asian and Pacific Islands Americans births by ethnic origin and sociodemographic and birth characteristics, with comparisons to blacks and whites, 1978-80, 4146–5.75

Births and birth rates, by demographic and birth characteristics, 1981 with trends from 1940, US Vital Statistics advance rpt, 4146–5.73

Births and birth rates, by detailed demographic characteristics and geographic area, 1979 and trends, US Vital Statistics annual rpt, 4144–1

Births and birth rates, by parent and birth characteristics and infant condition at birth, 1982 and trends from 1940, US Vital Statistics annual advance rpt, 4146–5.79

Births, and birth rates for unmarried and all women, by race of child, age and Hispanic origin of mother, and State, 1980, 4147–21.42

Births attended by midwives and in nonhospital settings, by mother's sociodemographic and prenatal care characteristics and infant race and birthweight, 1978-79 with trends from 1935, 4147–21.40

Cancer deaths and death rates, by body site, race, sex, State, and county, 1950-79, 4478–146

Cancer Natl Inst contracts and grants, by contractor, instn, State, and city, FY83, annual listing, 4474–28

Coal mines and related operations, occupational injuries and incidence rates, detailed analysis, 1982, annual rpt, 6664–4

County and City Data Book, detailed socioeconomic and demographic data for States, counties, and cities, selected years 1976-82, 2328–1

Deaths and death rates by detailed cause and demographic characteristics, 1979 and selected trends, US Vital Statistics annual rpt, 4144–2.1, 4144–2.5

Deaths and death rates, by detailed geographic area, cause, and demographic characteristics, 1979, US Vital Statistics annual rpt, 4144–3

Deaths and death rates, by selected cause and demographic characteristics, 1981, US Vital Statistics advance rpt, 4146–5.78

Deaths and death rates, by selected cause and demographic characteristics, 1982, US Vital Statistics advance rpt, 4146–5.81

Deaths due to cold weather and related causes, by age, race, State, and city, selected periods 1962-83, 21148–30

Dengue and dengue-like illness cases reported and confirmed in Puerto Rico by month or week of onset, and cases•by State, 1982, article, 4202–7.407

Dental malpractice claims, by amount, procedure type, region, State, and provider and patient characteristics, 1970, article, 4102–1.416

Dental Research Natl Inst research and training funds awarded, by recipient instn, FY83, annual listing, 4474–19

Divorces, divorce rates, and characteristics, by region and State, 1981, US Vital Statistics advance rpt, 4146–5.74

Fed Govt civilian health benefit plans enrollment and premiums, for individual private and employee organization plans, FY81-82, annual rpt, 9844–1.2

Fetal deaths and rates, by gestation period, birth weight and order, race, age of mother, and geographic area, 1979, US Vital Statistics annual rpt, 4144–2.3

Health condition and health care resources, use, and expenditures, 1970s-82 with trends and projections 1900-2000, annual compilation, 4144–11

Health habits associated with 10 major death causes, prevalence of 8 risk factors in selected States, 1981-83 surveys, article, 4202–7.405

Health maintenance organizations and prepaid health plans enrollment, use, and Fed Govt aid, FY83, annual rpt, 4104–8

Health manpower and facilities data, by county and SMSA, users guide to computerized area resource file, 1983, annual rpt, 4114–11

Health professionals supply and education, by occupation, demographic and professional characteristics, and location, 1950s-83 and projected to 2000, biennial rpt, 4114–8

Heart, Lung, and Blood Natl Inst organization, disease and mortality data, and funds and recipients, FY83 with trends from 1900, annual fact book, 4474–15

HHS aid to each State and local govt or private instn, amount obligated, funding agency, and program, FY83, annual listing, 4004–3

Hispanic Americans births and birth and fertility rates, by detailed Hispanic origin, characteristics of mother, birth, and prenatal care, and for 22 States, 1981, 4146–5.80

Hispanic Americans with disabilities, by disability type and severity and for 5 States, selected years 1970-78, conf proceedings, 16598–5

Hospital employment, vacancies, and vacancy rates, by occupation and by hospital specialty, region, census div, and State, 1980, annual rpt, 4114–12

Hospitals and nursing homes, employees, and use, by ownership, bed size, region, and State, selected years 1969-80, 4147–14.30

Infant deaths by detailed cause, geographic location, age, race, and sex, 1979, US Vital Statistics annual rpt, 4144–2.2

Infectious notifiable diseases, cases and current outbreaks, by region and State, weekly rpt, 4202–1

Infectious notifiable diseases, cases and incidence, by census div and State, 1982, annual rpt, 4204–1

Influenza deaths, viruses identified by State and country, epidemiology, and vaccine effects and recommended dosages by age, 1979/80-1980/81, annual rpt, 4205–3

Marriages and marriage rates by State, and bride and groom characteristics, 1981, advance annual US Vital Statistics rpt, 4146–5.77

Marriages, divorces, and rates, by detailed demographic and geographic characteristics, 1979 and trends, US Vital Statistics annual rpt, 4144–4

Maternal and child health, State govt spending and admin of Fed Govt block grants, by program for 13 States, 1981-83, GAO rpt, 26121–70

BY STATE

Mental health and drug and alcohol abuse treatment funding of State govts, and admin of Fed Govt block grants, for 13 States, FY80-84, GAO rpt, 26121–87

Mental health facilities, services, staff, and patient characteristics, *Statistical Notes* series, 4506–3

Mental health facilities, services, staff, and patient characteristics, 1970s-82 with trends from 1954, annual rpt, 4504–9

Mental hospitals of States and counties, patients and admissions by diagnosis, age, and State, FY81, annual rpt, 4504–2

Metal mines and related operations, occupational injuries and incidence rates, detailed analysis, 1982, annual rpt, 6664–3

Minerals (nonmetallic) mining and related operations injury, employment, and worktime data, 1982, annual rpt, 6664–1

Mines (sand and gravel) and related operations, occupational injuries and incidence rates, detailed analysis, 1982, annual rpt, 6664–2

Mines (stone) and related operations, occupational injuries and incidence rates, detailed analysis, 1982, annual rpt, 6664–5

Mines, mills, and quarries occupational injuries, and employees and hours, by State, quarterly rpt, 6662–1

NIH grants and awards for R&D, training, construction, and medical libraries, by location and recipient, FY83, annual listings, 4434–7

NIH grants, awards, and obligations by State and type of recipient, and full-time personnel, by inst, FY83, annual rpt, 4434–3

Nursing home facilities use and characteristics, and nurses employed, by region and State, 1980, 4147–14.29

Occupational health and safety State govt program staffing requirements, and occupational injury data, for selected States, selected years 1973-81, hearings, 21348–88

Occupational injuries and illnesses, data available from NTIS, by State, 1981, annual rpt, 6704–2

Occupational Safety and Health Admin enforcement activities and funding, and State programs and staff, 1982, annual rpt, 6604–2.1

Perinatal deaths and death rates, by State, urban-rural location, sex, and race, 1979, US Vital Statistics annual rpt, 4144–2.4

Pharmacists employment and sociodemographic characteristics, and reasons for not working in field, by State and overseas, as of 1979, 4147–14.28

Physician supply and ratio to population by State and county population size, and counties with shortages and needs, 1960-79 and projected 1982-94, 4118–52

Plague (bubonic and pneumonia-inducing) deaths, and cases by onset date, patient characteristics, and source, 1983 and trends from 1950, article, 4202–7.408

Preventive health services block grants of Fed Govt, State funding by program, and opinions on State program admin, for 13 States, FY81-84, GAO rpt, 26121–88

Public health labs of States, pay scales and job requirements by occupation and State, FY81-83, annual rpt, 4204–7

Index by Categories

Public health labs of States, personnel, finances, workloads, and other activities, by State, FY82, annual rpt, 4204–8

Rabies cases in animals and humans, for US and Mexico by State and for Canada by Province, 1980-82, annual rpt, 4205–28

Radiation protection and health physics enrollments and degrees granted by State and instn, and grads employment, 1983, annual rpt, 3004–7

Reye syndrome cases by State, and mortality rate by influenza strain, with patient characteristics, various years 1974-82, article, 4202–7.402

Smoking and tobacco marketing legislation introduced and enacted in State legislatures, by State, 1982, annual rpt, 4204–13

Southeastern States health care resource availability, and employment by occupation, by facility type, by State and SMSA in Fed Reserve 6th District, 1970s-81, article, 9371–1.425

Tuberculosis cases, deaths, and treatment, by demographic characteristics, State, and city, 1982 and trends from 1953, annual rpt, 4204–2

Venereal disease cases reported and epidemiologic activities, by region, State, and large city, 1982, annual rpt, 4204–14

Vital statistics, births, marriages, divorces, and deaths, provisional data, monthly rpt, 4142–1

Vital statistics, provisional 1982-83 with trends from 1950, annual rpt, 4144–7

Vital statistics records offices and availability of birth, death, marriage, and divorce certificates, by State, 1984 annual listing, 4124–7

Waterborne disease outbreaks and cases, by type, source, and location, 1983, annual rpt, 4205–35

Workers compensation benefits under each State and Federal program by payment source, and State and black lung benefits by type, 1979-81, article, 4742–1.409

Workers compensation benefits under State programs, by benefit type, insurance source, and State, and Fed Govt black lung program payments, 1980-82, article, 4742–1.424

Workers compensation coverage by State, benefits, degree of disability, employer costs, and insurance industry finances, 1939-80, article, 4742–1.414

Workers compensation law provisions of States and Fed Govt, by jurisdiction, as of July 1984, semiannual rpt, 6502–1

Workers compensation laws, changes in coverage, benefits, and premium rates, for 49 States, DC, and Virgin Islands, 1983, annual article, 6722–1.415

Housing and Construction

Bond tax-exempt issues by purpose, and Fed Govt mortgage bond revenue losses and borrower characteristics, selected years 1971-85, hearings, 21788–135

Bond tax-exempt issues for home mortgage subsidy, Fed Govt costs, and loans, mortgage value, and borrowers by jurisdiction, by borrower income, Dec 1981-July 1982, GAO rpt, 26113–127

Bond tax-exempt issues for home mortgage subsidy, issuance and purchase price limits for tax-exempt status, by State and MSA, 1984 annual press releases, 8304–16

Census of Construction Industries, 1982: financial and operating data, by SIC 4-digit industry and State, final rpt series, 2373–1

Census of Construction Industries, 1982: financial and operating data, by SIC 4-digit industry and State, preliminary rpt series, 2371–1

Census of Housing, 1980: occupancy and unit characteristics of SMSAs and central cities, by race, Hispanic origin, and city, State and SMSA rpt series, 2473–1

Census of Housing, 1980: structural, financial, and householder characteristics, by region and State, 2475–4

Census of Population and Housing, 1980: detailed population and housing characteristics, by county, city, and census tract, State and SMSA rpt series, 2551–2

Community Dev Block Grants to small cities, State admin, project characteristics, and assessments of local officials, 1982, 5188–106

Community dev programs funding and activities, for 5 HUD programs, FY83, annual rpt, 5124–5

Construction put in place, permits authorized by region, State, and MSA, and Federal contract awards, by construction type, bimonthly rpt with articles, 2012–1

County and City Data Book, detailed socioeconomic and demographic data for States, counties, and cities, selected years 1976-82, 2328–1

Home mortgage loan originations, by State and for Puerto Rico, 1978-83, press release, 5148–6

Home mortgage loans, and other balance sheet items of S&Ls, by FHLB district, State, and SMSA, 1983, annual rpt, 9314–3

Home mortgages (graduated payment) FHA-insured, financial, property, and mortgagor characteristics, for US and selected States, quarterly rpt, 5142–41

Home mortgages FHA-insured, financial, property, and mortgagor characteristics, for US, selected States, and Puerto Rico, quarterly rpt, 5142–3

Housing solar energy and energy conservation projects, HUD grants by State and outlying area, 1984 press release, 5006–3.36

HUD rental rehabilitation program allocations, by State, county, and city, FY85, press release, 5006–3.39

HUD rental rehabilitation projects, local funding and Section 8 rent supplements for 22 States and 275 communities, 1984 press release, 5006–3.30

Indian and Alaska Native housing and community dev program operations, FY82 with Community Dev Block Grant funding by tribe and State for FY81, annual rpt, 5004–5

Mobile and manufactured home safety standards, program inspections, enforcement actions, and accidents and casualties by victim characteristics, 1982-83, biennial rpt, 5004–4

Mobile home shipments from manufacturers, by State, monthly rpt, periodic table, 2382–5

Mobile homes placed by structural characteristics, and sales price, by census div and State, monthly rpt, annual tables, 2382–1

Index by Categories

BY STATE

New housing units authorized, by public and private ownership, by region, div, State, selected MSA, and 4,700 permit-issuing places, monthly rpt, 2382–5

New housing units authorized, by public and private ownership, State, and permit-issuing place, 1983, annual rpt, 2384–2

Older and handicapped persons housing projects construction and rehabilitation loans of HUD, FY84, annual listing, 5004–6

Property improvement and mobile home loans FHA-insured, by State and county, 1983 and cumulative from 1934, annual rpt, 5144–16

Public building construction, alteration, and leasing projects, description and cost by location, Dec 1983, annual listing, 9454–12

Real estate broker govt certification requirements, licenses, and exam results, by State and Canada Province, 1977-78, 9408–48

Southeastern States S&Ls adjustable- and fixed-rate, and other home mortgages issued, by State and asset size, 4th qtr 1983, survey results, article, 9302–2.401

Urban Dev Action Grant program effectiveness, and participation of small cities by State, 1978-82, GAO rpt, 26113–118

Window shipments and prices by market sector, and installation by unit type and State, for wood and aluminum frames, selected years 1967-82, article, 2012–1.403

Industry and Commerce

Aluminum primary production plant ownership, capacity, and type and source of raw material and energy used, by plant, State, and country, June 1984, semiannual listing, 5602–5

Chemical, oil, rubber, and plastic production, shipments, stocks, and materials used, by detailed product, periodic Current Industrial Rpt series, 2506–8

Clay construction products production and shipments by region, trade, and consumption, by product, monthly Current Industrial Rpt, 2506–9.2

Cold storage capacity of warehouses, by State and SMSA, Oct 1983, biennial rpt, 1614–2

County and City Data Book, detailed socioeconomic and demographic data for States, counties, and cities, selected years 1976-82, 2328–1

County Business Patterns: establishments, employees, and payrolls, by SIC 4-digit industry and county, 1981, annual State rpt series, 2326–8

County Business Patterns: establishments, employees, and payrolls, by SIC 4-digit industry and county, 1982, annual State rpt series, 2326–6

Drug shipments by region and selected census div and State, trade, and consumption, by product, 1983, annual Current Industrial Rpt, 2506–8.5

Enterprise zone and urban revitalization projects of State and local govts, effect on business and employment in selected areas, various dates 1972-83, hearing, 21788–140

Exports of manufactured and agricultural commodities, manufacturing production, and export-related employment, 1960s-82, State rpt series, 2046–3

Foreign corporation US affiliates, assets and employment by region and State, 1977 and 1981, annual rpt, 2044–25

Foreign direct investment in US, major investors and investments by SIC 4-digit industry, transaction type and value, and location, 1983, annual rpt, 2044–20

Foreign firms US affiliates, land and mineral rights, plant and equipment, and employment, by region and State, 1980-81, article, 2702–1.402

Foreign-owned US multiestablishment firms, employment, and payroll, by country, State, industry group, and foreign ownership share, 1981-82, annual rpt, 2324–6

Franchises of firms engaged in distribution of goods and services, by State, 1982, annual rpt, 2014–5

Industrial dev Fed Govt funding by type, program, and agency, and State govt policies and support, selected years FY75-85, 26306–6.81

Iron and steel castings and scrap production, shipments, unfilled orders, stocks, receipts, and trade, by census div and State, monthly Current Industrial Rpt, 2506–10.1

Lumber, furniture, and paper products production and shipments by region and State, inventories, trade, and consumption, periodic Current Industrial Rpt series, 2506–7

Lumber production and stocks of hardwood and softwood, by region, State, and species, 1982, annual Current Industrial Rpt, 2506–7.4

Manufacturing capacity utilization, by SIC 2- to 4-digit industry, State, and SMSA, 1982, annual Current Industrial Rpt, 2506–3.7

Manufacturing census, 1982: financial and operating data, by SIC 2- to 4-digit industry, State, SMSA, and county, preliminary census div rpt series, 2491–3

Manufacturing census, 1982: financial and operating data, for SIC 4-digit industries by product, preliminary rpt series, 2491–1

Manufacturing operating and financial data, 1980-81 Annual Survey of Manufactures rpt reprints, hardbound vol, 2504–1

Metals resource recovery through leaching technologies, characteristics of methods and operations, regulation, and research, series, 5606–6

Mineral industries census, 1982: financial and operating data, by State and for 4 offshore regions, preliminary summary rpt, 2511–2.2

Mineral industries census, 1982: financial and operating data, including materials consumed, by SIC 4-digit industry and State, preliminary rpt series, 2511–1

Mineral Industry Surveys, commodity reviews of production, trade, and consumption, advance annual rpt series, 5614–5

Mineral Industry Surveys, commodity reviews of production, trade, stocks, and consumption, monthly rpt series, 5612–1

Mineral Industry Surveys, commodity reviews of production, trade, stocks, and consumption, quarterly rpt series, 5612–2

Mineral Industry Surveys, explosives and blasting agents consumption by type, industry, and State, 1983, annual rpt, 5614–22

Mineral Industry Surveys, State reviews of production, 1983, advance annual rpt series, 5614–6

Minerals Yearbook, 1982, Vol 1: commodity reviews of production, reserves, supply, use, and trade, annual rpt, 5604–33

Minerals Yearbook, 1982, Vol 2 preprints: State reviews of production and sales by commodity, and business activity, annual rpt series, 5604–16

Minerals Yearbook, 1982, Vol 2: State reviews of production, sales, and firms, by commodity, and business activity, annual rpt, 5604–34

Minerals Yearbook, 1983, Vol 1 preprints: commodity reviews of production, reserves, supply, use, and trade, annual rpt series, 5604–15

Minority business mgmt and financial assistance from federally funded organizations, by region, State, and business characteristics, FY83, annual rpt, 2104–6

New England States economic indicators, Fed Reserve 1st District, monthly rpt with articles, 9373–2

New England States gross product by industry sector and State, and compared to GNP, 1981-82, annual article, 9373–2.403

North Central States pulpwood production by county, imports, and individual mill capacity, by species, 1982, annual rpt, 1204–19

North Central States timber removals, and mill receipts and production, by species, product, and county, series, 1206–10

Northwest US and British Columbia forest industry production, prices, trade, and employment, quarterly rpt, 1202–3

Plywood (softwood) production, shipments by region and State, trade, and consumption, by product, 1983, annual Current Industrial Rpt, 2506–7.2

Retail trade census, 1982: employment, establishments, sales, and payroll, by SIC 2- to 4-digit kind of business, SMSA, and retail district, State rpt series, 2401–1

Retail trade census, 1982: employment, establishments, sales, and payroll, by SIC 2- to 4-digit kind of business, SMSA, county, and city, State rpt series, 2397–1

Retail trade census, 1982: employment, establishments, sales, and payroll, by SIC 4-digit kind of business and State, preliminary rpt series, 2395–1

Retail trade sales and inventories, by kind of business, region, census div, and selected State, SMSA, and city, and seasonal adjustments, monthly rpt, 2413–3

Service industry census, 1982: employment, establishments, receipts, and payroll, by SIC 2- to 4-digit kind of business, SMSA, county, and city, State rpt series, 2391–1

Service industry census, 1982: employment, establishments, receipts, and payroll, by SIC 4-digit kind of business and State, preliminary rpt series, 2390–2

Small and minority-owned businesses finances and operations, Federal contracts by agency, and worker characteristics, by industry, race, sex, and State, 1950s-83, annual rpt, 9764–6

Small Business Admin loans, contract awards, and surety bonds, by firm, State, and city, FY83, annual rpt, 9764–1.2

BY STATE

Southeastern States and 5 SMSAs economic indicators, Fed Reserve 8th District, quarterly rpt, 9391–15

Southeastern States economic indicators, by State, Fed Reserve 5th District, quarterly rpt, 9389–16

Southeastern States industrial robots by major industry, and State share of manufacturing employment, by State, 1984 survey, article, 9371–1.423

Steel mill shipments, by product class, 1981-82, annual Current Industrial Rpt, 2506–10.2

Sulfuric acid production, establishments, and shipments, by census div and State, and trade, 1983, annual Current Industrial Rpt, 2506–8.13

Technology-intensive industry employment and establishments by industry and selected location, and venture capital investments by source, 1970s-82, 26358–107

Textile mill production, stocks, materials used, orders, and trade by country, by product and major State, periodic Current Industrial Rpt series, 2506–5

Timber production, prices by region and State, trade by country, and consumption, by species and product, with industry earnings, 1950-83, annual rpt, 1204–29

Trade-related employment and production by industry, occupation, and State, and US trade policy actions, 1960s-83, annual rpt, 444–1

TVA region wood residue production and use, by tree species group and wood residue type, for 44 counties, 1979, technical paper, 9806–2.36

Western States economic indicators, Fed Reserve 12th District, quarterly rpt, 9393–1

Wholesale trade census, 1982: employment, establishments, finances, and operations, by SIC 2- to 4-digit kind of business, SMSA, county, and city, State rpt series, 2405–1

Wholesale trade census, 1982: employment, establishments, sales by commodity, and payroll, by SIC 4-digit kind of business and State, preliminary rpt series, 2403–1

Labor and Employment

Collective bargaining agreements expiring during year, covered workers by SIC 2-digit industry, firm, and union, with summary of key provisions, 1984, annual rpt, 6784–9

Collective bargaining calendar for Southeast US, 1984, annual rpt, 6946–1.68

County and City Data Book, detailed socioeconomic and demographic data for States, counties, and cities, selected years 1976-82, 2328–1

Earnings by major industry group, and personal income per capita and by source, by region and State, 1929-82, 2708–40

Earnings of manufacturing production workers, by State, with adjustments for industrial mix variations, selected years 1973-82, article, 9373–1.407

Employment (nonagricultural) by industry div, manufacturing hours and earnings, labor force, and unemployment, by selected labor market area, 1981-83, article, 6742–2.408

Employment and earnings, detailed data, monthly rpt, 6742–2.5, 6742–2.6, 6742–2.7

Employment and training program funding under Job Training Partnership Act, and required matching funds, for 3 programs by State, 1984/85, press release, 6408–58

Employment and unemployment, 10 largest States, monthly press release, 6742–5

Employment and wages of workers covered by State unemployment insurance laws and Fed Govt unemployment compensation, by SIC 4-digit industry and State, 1982, annual rpt, 6744–16

Employment by industry div, major manufacturing group, and State, Monthly Labor Review, 6722–1.2

Employment change by industry div, civilian labor force, and unemployment and rates, by region and State, 1983, article, 6722–1.454

Employment, earnings, and hours, by selected SIC 1- to 4-digit industry, State, and for 278 major labor areas, 1939-83, annual rpt, 6744–5

Employment in regionally concentrated and all industries, and population size, by State, 1970-82, article, 6722–1.413

Employment, unemployment, and labor force, by demographic and employment characteristics, State, and for 30 metro areas and 11 large cities, 1983, annual rpt, 6744–7

Handbook of Labor Statistics, employment, earnings, hours, and labor force characteristics, 1982 and trends, detailed annual rpt, 6724–1

Job Training Partnership Act allotments for migrant and seasonal farm workers retraining assistance, by State and administering organization, as of July 1984, press release, 6408–64

Job Training Partnership Act dislocated workers program performance standards guide for States, with data on previous programs, by State and client characteristics, FY81-82, 6408–59.2

Labor Dept activities and staff, CETA participants characteristics, and employment service and unemployment insurance activities by State, FY83, annual rpt, 6304–1

Labor legislation enacted by 48 States, DC, and Guam, 1983, annual summary article, 6722–1.406

Labor unions reporting to Labor Dept, parent bodies and locals by State, city, and country, 1983 listing, 6468–17

Minority group and women employment, by occupational group, SIC 2-digit industry, and State, 1981, annual rpt, 9244–1.1

New England States employment, wages, and price conditions by State and selected SMSA, 1983, annual rpt, 6916–7.1

North Central States employment in durable goods manufacturing by industry group and State, and Fed Govt outlays, for Fed Reserve 7th District, 1978-FY82, article, 9375–1.402

North Central States manufacturing and total employment, percent change for Fed Reserve 7th District States, various periods 1969-84, article, 9375–1.408

Older persons community service part-time employment and program funding, by State and outlying area, FY84, press release, 6408–60

Index by Categories

Small business and total employment, income, and number of firms, by State, industry, and size class, selected years 1967-83, annual rpt, 9764–6.1

Southeastern States high technology employment and share of total employment, by State, 1982 and percent change 1975-82, press release, 6948–6

Southeastern States nonagricultural employment by industry div and SMSA, earnings, and hours, for 8 States, monthly press release, 6942–7

Southeastern States textile mill employment and average hours and earnings, for 8 States, monthly press release, 6942–1

Southwestern States employment by major nonagricultural industry, and average hours and earnings of manufacturing production workers, monthly rpt, 6962–2

Trade adjustment assistance eligibility, reemployment opportunities, and worker characteristics, investigations of industries injured by import competition, series, 6406–9

Trade adjustment assistance for workers, petitions, investigations, and determinations, by major industry group, union, and State, monthly rpt, 6402–13

Unemployed displaced workers training and placement program of Fed Govt, funding and enrollment for 13 States and Guam, June 1984, press release, 6408–61

Unemployment insurance laws, changes in coverage, benefits, and tax rates, for 43 States and DC, 1983, annual article, 6722–1.414

Unemployment insurance laws, comparisons of State provisions, as of Sept 1984, semiannual revision, 6402–2

Unemployment insurance overpayments detection and recovery from random audit program in selected States, 1975-82 and projected to FY86, GAO rpt, 26121–77

Unemployment insurance State govt program admin, quality appraisal results, FY84, annual rpt, 6404–16

Unemployment insurance State govt program benefits, coverage, and tax provisions, July 1984, semiannual listing, 6402–7

Unemployment insurance system finances, claims, payments, and covered employment and wages, by State, 1938-82, 6408–5

Unemployment, labor surplus areas eligible for preferential Fed Govt contracts, and labor force data for 150 major labor markets, monthly listing, 6402–1

Unemployment levels and rates, by State and for 240 large SMSAs, monthly press release with Current Population Survey annual benchmark averages, 6742–12

Vocational rehabilitation, State agency caseloads by status and processing stage, region, and State, FY83 with trends from FY21, annual rpt, 4944–5

Vocational rehabilitation State agency expenditures, caseloads, rehabilitations, and staff, under Section 110 of the Rehabilitation Act, by State, FY82, annual rpt, 4944–9

Wages for 3 occupational groups, relative average levels in 78 labor market areas, 1983, annual press release, 6785–13

Wages, hours, benefits, and employment, by occupation and selected geographic areas, industry surveys series, 6787–6

Index by Categories

BY STATE

Wages of workers covered by unemployment insurance, by State and industry div, 1982-83, annual press release, 6784–17.2
Work stoppages involving 6 workers or more, workers and days idle by major issue, industry, and State, selected years 1930-82, annual rpt, 6724–1.8
Youth summer job program of Fed Govt, funding and jobs by State and for Indians, summer 1984, press release, 6408–62

Law Enforcement

Alcohol, tobacco, firearms, and explosives arrests and seizures, by State, FY82, last issue of annual rpt, 8484–1.6
Arrests for serious crimes, disposition in 5 States, and criminal justice employment nationwide by job category and level of govt, Dec 1983 rpt, 6062–2.401
Assaults, murders, and other deaths of law enforcement officers, by circumstances, level of govt, agency, victim and offender characteristics, and location, 1983, annual rpt, 6224–3
Bankruptcy court cases and admin in districts with and without case trustees, and staff and potential costs of nationwide trustee program, various periods 1979-83, annual rpt, 6004–15
Bombing (explosive and incendiary) and arson incidents by target, State, and circumstances, and explosives theft and recovery, 1982-83, annual rpt, 8484–4
Bombing (explosive and incendiary) incidents, damage, injuries, and deaths, by target, State, and circumstances, 1983, annual rpt, 6224–5
Convictions, prison sentences, and average sentence lengths, by offense, offender class, and selected State, various periods 1971-84, 6066–19.10
Corrupt govt officials prosecutions and convictions, by judicial district and level of govt, 1976-83, annual rpt, 6004–13
Court case filings in State trial courts by case type, and appellate court filings and dispositions by court type, by State, 1978-83, periodic rpt, 6062–2.409
Court caseloads, actions, procedure duration, judges, and jurors, by Federal district and appeals court, 1979-84, annual rpt, 18204–3
Court caseloads for Federal district, appeals, and bankruptcy courts, by type of suit and offense, circuit, and district, quarterly rpt, 18202–1
Court cases disposition and convictions in Federal district courts, as of June 1983, annual rpt, 18204–1
Crime and criminal justice data, including justice expenditures and employment by level of govt, 1970s-82 with some trends from 1875, 6068–174
Crime victim compensation costs, by State, 1979-81, GAO rpt, 26119–70
Crimes against financial instns, by State, semiannual article, 9312–1
Crimes, arrests by offender characteristics, and rates, by offense, and law enforcement employees, by population size and jurisdiction, 1970s-83, annual rpt, 6224–2
Drug enforcement regional task force program investigation activities, funding, and personnel, with nationwide drug abuse data, 1983 annual rpt, 6004–17

Executions since 1930, and prisoners under death sentence by prison control, sex, and region, by State, 1972-82, periodic rpt, 6062–2.406
Executions since 1930, and prisoners under death sentence, by prisoner characteristics, region, and State, 1982, annual rpt, 6065–1
Federal district court staff by position, and visiting judges, visits, and visit days, by large district, various dates 1982-84, 18408–25
Homicides and homicide rates, by victim characteristics, location, and circumstances, and years of life lost from homicide and other leading causes of death, 1970-78, 4205–38
Jail capacities, conditions, expenditures, and services, and socioeconomic and other characteristics of inmates, various dates 1976-82, 10048–59
Juror (grand and petit) usage and costs, trials, and trial days, by Federal district court, years ended June 1980-84, annual rpt, 18204–4
Kidnapping by parents over intl and interstate boundaries, characteristics of cases referred to State Dept and FBI by State and country, 1979-83, hearing, 25528–95
Magistrate case processing duties assigned in Fed Govt district courts, by type of case, duty, and district, 1983 rpt, 18408–24
Marijuana cultivation control, DEA funding by State, 1983, GAO rpt, 26119–64
Parole and probation population, and entries and exits by reason, by State, 1983, periodic rpt, 6062–2.408
Prison population and capacity by State and individual DC and Federal instn, construction costs, and Fed Govt operating costs, 1983 and projected to 1990, GAO rpt, 26119–59
Prison terms actually served by selected State, and Illinois pretrial detention time credited to sentence, by offense, various periods 1977-83, 6066–19.7
Prisoners in Federal and State correctional instns, by sex, region, and State, quarterly release, 6062–3
Prisoners in State prisons median sentence, and admissions and releases by prisoner and sentencing characteristics, by offense and State, 1981 and trends from 1926, 6066–19.9
Public defender systems, costs, cases, and expenditures by level of govt and State, with system characteristics and lawyer fee ranges, 1981, 6066–19.8
US Attorneys civil and criminal case processing in district, appellate, and State courts, by district, FY83, annual rpt, 6004–2
Wiretapping authorizations by offense, costs, persons involved, arrests, trials, and convictions, 1983, annual rpt, 18204–7

Natural Resources, Environment, and Pollution

Acid rain causes and effects, air pollutant emissions by source, and control costs, by region and State, selected years 1977-83 and projected to 2000, 26358–104
Acid rain causes and effects, air pollutant emissions by source in US and selected countries, and control costs, 1970s-83 and projected to 2000, 21368–52

Acid rain causes and effects, air pollutant emissions by source in US and selected countries, control costs, and Fed Govt research funding, 1960s-82, 3408–27
Air pollutant metal levels, by monitoring site, State, and urban-rural location, 1977-79, last issue of annual rpt, 9194–10
Air pollutant sulfur dioxide emissions of coal-fired power plants in eastern US, effect of alternative geographic area limits on power and coal industries, 1983 rpt, 3408–32
Air pollutant sulfur dioxide emissions reduction proposal, effects on polluting industries and coal production by region and State, projected to 2010, 9188–97
Air pollution levels for 5 pollutants, by detailed source, State, and Air Quality Control Region, 1981, annual rpt, 9194–7
Army Corps of Engineers activities and projects, FY83 and trends from 1800s, annual rpt, 3754–1
Birds (marine) on southeastern US coast, distribution, abundance, and oil spill effects, by species and State, 1820s-1982, 5508–72
Coastal environmental and wildlife characteristics, use, and mgmt, for individual ecosystems, series, 5506–9
Coastal environmental characteristics, fish, wildlife, and use, and population socioeconomic data, for individual areas, series, 5506–4
Colorado River Storage Project finances, water resource dev, power production, and other activities in western States, FY83, annual rpt, 5824–3
Dams, reservoirs, and hydroelectric plants, listing of major foreign and US structures with location and characteristics, as of June 1983, 5828–13
Environmental quality and protection programs, costs, and Fed Govt enforcement, 1983, detailed annual rpt, 484–1
Environmental quality, pollutant discharge by type and source, and EPA protection activities and funding, 1970s-83, biennial regional rpt series, 9184–15
EPA pollution control research and grant assistance program activities, monthly rpt, 9182–8
Fish and wildlife restoration program of Fed Govt, finances, funding by State, and hunting and fishing equipment excise tax revenue, FY84, annual rpt, 5504–13
Fish and Wildlife Service restoration programs, including new sites, funding, and research, by State, FY81, annual rpt, 5504–1
Fishery research of State fish and wildlife agencies, federally funded projects and costs by species and State, 1984, annual rpt, 5504–23
Forest and windbarrier planting and seeding, by State, FY83, annual rpt, 1204–7
Forest fire damage and causes, by State and region, 1981, annual rpt, 1204–4
Forest fires on Forest Service land and acres burned, by cause, forest, and State, 1983, annual rpt, 1204–6
Forest insect and disease incidence, by region or State, 1983, annual rpt, 1204–8
Forest Natl System wildlife habitat and fishery improvements, use, and game

BY STATE

population and harvest by species and forest, by region, FY83, annual rpt, 1204–31

Forest, range, and associated waters use and mgmt assessment, and environmental impacts of Forest Service program options, 1977-2030 and trends from 1920, 1208–24

Forest Service programs and activities, by State and region, FY83, annual rpt, 1204–1

Forestry activities on State and private lands, Fed Govt and State funding by project and State, FY83, annual tables, 1204–32

Forestry Incentives Program, Fed Govt cost-sharing funds for private timberland improvement, by region and State, monthly rpt, 1802–11

Forests (natl) and other lands under Forest Service mgmt, by forest and location, Sept 1983, annual rpt, 1204–2

Forests (natl) recreational use, visitor-days by type of activity, forest, and State, FY83 with trends from 1924, annual rpt series, 1204–17

Great Lakes basin pollutant discharges by source, and control program activities, 1983 annual rpt, 14644–1

Horse and burro wild herd areas in western States, population, adoption, and protection and mgmt costs, as of 1984, biennial rpt, 5724–8

Land Mgmt Bur activities, and grants, sales, and use of public lands, by State, FY83 and historical, annual rpt, 5724–1

Land privately held, acreage and owners by owner characteristics, land use, and region, and purchase and improvement funding, 1978 survey, series, 1506–5

Mineral leases on Fed Govt and Indian lands, by State, as of Dec 1983, annual rpt, 5734–2

Mourning dove population, by region and hunting and nonhunting State, 1984, annual rpt, 5504–15

Northeast and North Central regions biomass timber, green weight by biomass component and State, 1981, 1208–207

Nuclear power and weapons policy, fuel supply/demand, waste disposal and siting, environmental effects of radiation, and public attitudes, 1970s-82 with projections to 2000, 3008–88

Nuclear power plant siting population criteria and estimated compliance of selected regions and sites, 1983 rpt, 9638–54

Phosphate rock industry environmental protection costs, by control type and selected State, with background operating data, 1977-81 with cost projections to 1990, 5608–143

Phosphate rock reserves in southeastern and northwestern US, by location, 1984 rpt, 5668–74

Pollution abatement capital and operating costs, by SIC 2- to 4-digit industry, State, and SMSA, 1982, annual Current Industrial Rpt, 2506–3.6

Public land acreage and use, and Land Mgmt Bur activities and finances, annual State rpt series, 5724–11

Radiation and radionuclide concentrations in air, water, and milk, results of EPA and other monitoring programs, by State and site, quarterly rpt, 9232–2

Radiation control program activities, State and local expenditures, personnel, and NRC licenses, by State, FY80-82, annual rpt, 4064–3

Radioactive materials transport surveillance program activities and results, State survey rpt series, 9636–1

Radioactive waste and spent fuel generation, inventory, disposal by site, reprocessing, and characteristics, by source, as of 1983 and projected to 2020, annual rpt, 3364–2

Radioactive waste generation, by northeast State and reactor and nonreactor source, 1979-81 and projected to 2000, hearing, 25528–93

Reclamation programs of Fed Govt in western US, finances and operations by project and State, 1981-82, annual rpts, 5824–1

Rocky Mountain forest and rangeland area, and timber resources and removals, by ownership, forest and tree characteristics, and State, 1977, 1208–201

Sedimentation control, surveillance, and research activity of Fed Govt, by project, agency, region, and State, 1982, annual rpt, 5664–9

Soil survey county descriptions and maps of USDA, 1899-1983, annual listing, 1264–11

Southeastern US water supply and quality, with background socioeconomic data, for 8 States, 1960s-2020 with trends from 1930, 9208–119

Timber growth, removals, products output, and forest ownership and industries in Northeast States, State rpt series, 1206–16

Timber resources and removals in Northeast States, by species, ownership class, and county, State rpt series, 1206–12

Water Bank Program agreements, acreage, and Fed Govt payments, by State, FY72-83, annual rpt, 1804–21

Water pollution fish kills, by State, location, and pollution source, monthly 1978-80, annual rpt, 9204–3

Water pollution from nonpoint sources, source land uses and acreage, and control program funding, by State or region, various periods 1974-FY84, 9208–123

Water pollution regulation under EPA wastewater discharge system, operations and funding, various periods FY79-83, GAO rpt, 26113–113

Water quality, pollutant types and sources, and control program compliance, by State, 1982, biennial rpt, 9204–6

Water supply and quality, floods, drought, mudslides, and other hydrologic events, by State, 1983, annual rpt, 5664–12

Water supply and quality in streams and lakes, and groundwater levels in wells, by drainage basin, 1980, annual State rpt series, 5666–12

Water supply and quality in streams and lakes, and groundwater levels in wells, by drainage basin, 1981, annual State rpt series, 5666–16

Water supply and quality in streams and lakes, and groundwater levels in wells, by drainage basin, 1982, annual State rpt series, 5666–20

Water supply and quality in streams and lakes, and groundwater levels in wells, by drainage basin, 1983, annual State rpt series, 5666–10

Index by Categories

Water supply contamination by volatile organic chemicals, monitoring results for each State and Puerto Rico, 1981, 9208–120

Waterfowl harvested during hunting season, by species, State, and county, annual average for 1971-80, decennial rpt, 5508–18

Western States wilderness areas potential oil and natural gas reserves, for 11 States, 1982-83, compilation of papers, 5668–69

Western US water supply, and snow survey results, monthly State rpt series, 1266–2

Western US water supply, reservoir storage by large reservoir and State, and streamflow conditions, as of Oct 1984, annual rpt, 1264–4

Western US water supply, snow depth measurements by station, State rpt series, 1266–3

Wetlands acreage and losses, by wetland type and location, 1970s-83, 5508–89

Wilderness Preservation Natl System acreage, by natl forest, wilderness and primitive area, and State, 1983, annual rpt, 5304–14

Wildlife and bird research of State fish and wildlife agencies, federally funded projects and costs, by species and State, 1984, annual rpt, 5504–24

Woodcock population and hunter harvest, by region and State, 1984 and trends from 1966, annual rpt, 5504–11

Youth Conservation Corps activities, costs, and participant characteristics, by sponsoring agency, 1982, annual rpt, 5304–12

Population

Census of Population and Housing, 1980: detailed population and housing characteristics, by county, city, and census tract, State and SMSA rpt series, 2551–2

Census of Population, 1980: Asian and Pacific Islander population, by detailed race and State, supplementary rpt, 2535–1.15

Census of Population, 1980: detailed socioeconomic and demographic characteristics, by age, sex, race, Hispanic origin, occupation, and industry, State rpt series, 2531–4

Census of Population, 1980: detailed socioeconomic characteristics, by county, city, and inside-outside SMSAs and central cities, State rpt series, 2531–3

Census of Population, 1980: Indian and Alaska Native population and housing occupancy, by reservation, Alaska Native village, and other Indian area, supplementary rpt, 2535–1.16

Census of Population, 1980: migration since 1975, by county and selected demographic characteristics, supplementary rpt, 2535–1.14

Census of Population, 1980: migration since 1975, by State and selected demographic characteristics, supplementary rpt, 2535–1.13

County and City Data Book, detailed socioeconomic and demographic data for States, counties, and cities, selected years 1976-82, 2328–1

Economic and demographic trends for IRS regions, districts, and service centers, 1972-82 and projected to 1990, annual rpt, 8304–8

Index by Categories

BY STATE

Educational attainment of population, by sociodemographic characteristics and for large States and SMSAs, 1981 and trends from 1940, biennial Current Population Rpt, 2546–1.390

Florida and California elderly migration by selected State of origin or destination, and Florida elderly, by sociodemographic and housing characteristics, 1970 and 1980, 4478–150

Hispanic Americans socioeconomic and demographic characteristics, and compared to non-Hispanics, selected years 1970-83, chartbook, 2328–48

Income (personal) per capita and by source, and earnings by industry div, by State, MSA, and county, 1977-82, annual regional rpts, 2704–2

Income (personal) per capita and by source, earnings by major industry group, and social insurance contributions, by region and State, 1929-82, 2708–40

Income (personal) per capita and total, and earnings by major industry group, by region and State, 1981-83, annual article, 2702–1.432

Income (personal) per capita and total, by State, MSA, and county, with metro-nonmetro totals, 1980-82, annual article, 2702–1.413

Income (personal) totals, by region, census div, and State, quarterly article, 2702–1.32

Older persons by demographic, socioeconomic, and health characteristics, selected years 1900-81 and projected to 2050, Current Population Rpt, 2546–2.125

Older persons population characteristics, and needs and costs of social services by type, by metro-nonmetro status, 1970s-82 with trends from 1900, 21148–28

Older persons sociodemographic characteristics, and Fed Govt program participation and funding by agency, 1983 with trends and projections 1900-2080, annual rpt, 25144–3

Older persons sociodemographic characteristics and transportation needs, selected years 1900-2040, 7308–183

Population estimates and projections, by region and State, Current Population Rpt series, 2546–3

Population size and components of change, by MSA and county, 1980-82, annual State Current Population Rpt series, 2546–4

Population size and components of change, by region, census div, and State, 1970s-83 with projections to 2050, annual Current Population Rpt, 2546–2.119

Refugee and alien arrivals and resettlements in US, by State, outlying area, country of birth and citizenship, age, sex, and sponsoring agency, monthly rpt, 4702–3

Refugee arrivals in US by world area of origin and State of settlement, and Fed Govt intl and domestic assistance costs, FY85, annual rpt, 7004–16

Refugee resettlement program activities and funding, arrivals and population by country of origin and State, and employment and other characteristics, FY83, annual rpt, 4704–8

Refugees from Indochina, arrivals in US by country of origin and State of destination, tuberculosis cases, and unexplained sudden deaths, 1982, annual rpt, 4204–1.3

Statistical Abstract of US, social, political, and economic data, 1950s-83 and trends, annual rpt, 2324–1.1

Voting age population for Nov 1984 election, by sex, age, race, Hispanic origin, region, and State, and percent voting during 1930-82, Current Population Rpt, 2546–3.129

Prices and Cost of Living

Electric power average residential bills, State rankings, as of Jan 1983, annual rpt, 1244–1.6

Electric power rate schedules, by user type, utility, and city, Jan 1984, annual rpt, 3164–40

Energy prices and expenditures for fuels and electricity, by consuming sector, State, and fuel type, 1970-81, annual rpt, 3164–64

Energy use, prices, and conservation and efficiency measures, by fuel type, end-use sector, selected industry, and region, 1960-83, annual rpt, 3164–73

Fruit and vegetable wholesale prices in NYC, Chicago, and selected shipping points, by crop, 1983, annual rpt, 1311–8

Heating oil retail prices, by State, and wholesale prices and dealer margins, monthly rpt, 3162–24.9

Natural gas average price, by end-use sector, census div, and State, 1982-83 with trends from 1978, annual article, 3162–4.413

Oil refined products sales of gas plant operators, refiners, and resellers, price and volume for 13 products, by end-use sector, PAD district, and State, monthly rpt, 3162–11

Prices received by farmers for major products, and paid for farm inputs, by commodity and State, 1983, annual rpt, 1629–5

Public Welfare and Social Security

Abortions funded by Medicaid by justification, and expenditures, by State, FY78-83, annual rpt, 4654–9

AFDC and food stamp program costs and productivity in 8 States, 1973-82, GAO rpt, 26111–18

AFDC and foster home care benefits per child, for selected States, 1974 and 1982, hearing, 21968–28

AFDC, food stamp, and SSI overpayments, payment error rates, and sanctions imposed, by State, various dates 1980-82, GAO rpt, 26113–136

AFDC programs and provisions of States under Social Security Act, FY82, annual rpt, 4704–9

AFDC recipients and payments, applications by disposition, payment discontinuances by reason, and hearings by outcome, by State, quarterly rpt, 4742–6

AFDC State admin agencies performance measures, caseloads, payments, and costs, by State, FY81, annual rpt, 4704–10

AFDC workfare program participation and requirements in 16 States, Feb 1983, GAO rpt, 26131–9

Black lung benefit claims and benefits by State, and trust fund receipts by source and disbursements, 1982, annual rpt, 6504–3

Child Support Enforcement Program cost savings to AFDC, Federal and State govts, and public assistance programs, by State and selected city or county, FY76-85, 4748–37

Child Support Enforcement Program costs, cases, and collections, by State, FY82, semiannual rpt, 4002–5

Child Support Enforcement Program costs, cases, and collections, by State, FY83, annual rpt, 4004–29

Child Support Enforcement Program financial and operating data, FY79-83, annual rpt, 4004–16

Community services block grants by type of service provider, State mgmt, and opinions of officials and groups involved, for 13 States, FY81-83, GAO rpt, 26121–84

Disability Insurance beneficiaries sociodemographic and medical characteristics, 1977-79, annual rpt, 4744–20

Fed Govt aid to State and local govts, expenditures, and direct payments, by program, agency, and State, FY83, annual rpt, 2464–2

Food aid program of USDA for women, infants, and children, participants, clinics, and costs, by State and Indian agency, FY82, annual table, 1364–12.1

Food aid programs of Fed Govt and others, funding, participant characteristics, and nutrition and poverty data, 1970s-83, 028–20

Food aid programs of USDA, participants and costs by program, region, and State, monthly rpt, 1362–14

Food distribution program participants on individual Indian reservations and in TTPI, irregular rpt, 1362–15

Food stamp program participation and coupons distributed, by region, State, and project area, quarterly rpt, 1362–6

Foster care children permanent placement, Fed Govt incentive program funding and operations in 7 States, FY80-82, GAO rpt, 26121–81

Medicaid physician reimbursement schedules for general practitioners and specialists, and estimated change in total reimbursement, by State, as of 1979, article, 4652–1.410

Medicare and Medicaid costs and market value, by type of beneficiary and State, 1979-82, 2626–2.50

Medicare and Medicaid eligibility, participation, covered services and use, and reimbursements and payments, various periods 1966-82, annual rpt, 4654–1

Medicare end-stage renal disease program enrollment, new cases by State, and survival and death rates, by age, sex, and race, 1970s-81, article, 4652–1.408

Medicare enrollment, reimbursement, and use and covered charges by type of service, by State and census div, 1978-82, 4658–8

Medicare facilities and services use, covered charges, and reimbursements, by beneficiary type and area of residence, series, 4656–1

Medicare Hospital Insurance and Supplementary Medical Insurance benefits and beneficiaries, by State, FY81, annual rpt, 4654–5.1

Medicare physician charges and reimbursement by enrollee characteristics and carrier, payment limits effects on charges in California, and physician earnings, by specialty, 1950s-84, 25368–127

BY STATE

Medicare Supplementary Medical Insurance maximum charges reimbursable for specific services, by State and outlying area, 1983, annual rpt, 4654–4

OASDHI beneficiaries with direct deposit of benefit checks, by age, sex, race, benefit amount, and State, as of Dec 1983, article, 4742–1.412

OASDHI, Medicaid, SSI, and other social insurance and public welfare programs benefits, beneficiary characteristics, and trust funds, selected years 1937-83, annual rpt, 4744–3

OASDI benefits and beneficiaries, by type of benefit, State, outlying area, and county, Dec 1982, 4748–38

School breakfast and other USDA child nutrition programs, participation and finances, by region and State, annual rpt series, 1364–13

Social Security Bulletin, OASDHI and other program operations and beneficiary characteristics, from 1940, monthly rpt with articles, 4742–1

Social service spending of State govts by service type and funding source, and admin of Fed Govt block grants, for 13 States, selected years FY80-84, GAO rpt, 26121–76

Supplemental Security Income and other income maintenance program benefits and beneficiaries, by State, monthly rpt, 4742–2

Supplemental Security Income and 3 earlier programs benefits, beneficiaries below poverty level, and State program expenditures, various periods 1972-83, article, 4742–1.402

Supplemental Security Income benefits and beneficiaries, by type of eligibility, State, and county, Dec 1983, annual rpt, 4744–27

Supplemental Security Income payments, and recipients by other income source, eligibility type, and other characteristics, by State, 1982, annual rpt, 4744–16

Supplementary Security Income beneficiary socioeconomic characteristics and health service use, 1970s-83 and SSI program projections to 1995, 25148–29

Recreation and Leisure

Arts and humanities funding, by source and State, FY82-83 with trends from FY66, 21408–69

Boat registrations, use, and accident deaths, injuries, and property damage, by detailed cause and State, 1983, annual rpt, 7404–1

Fishermen (ocean sport), fishing activities, and catch by species, by fisherman characteristics, State, and coastal region, series, 2166–17

Fishing (ocean sport) effort and catch, and Natl Marine Fisheries Service tagging and research activity, by species and location, 1983, annual rpt, 2164–7

Historic Preservation Fund grants, by State, FY85, annual press release, 5544–9

Licenses for fishing and hunting issued and gross cost to sportsmen, by State, FY83, annual rpt, 5504–16

Museum grants of Natl Foundation on Arts and Humanities, by instn, State, and city, FY84, annual rpt series, 9564–6

Natl park area visits and overnight stays, visitors, and vehicles, by State and park, 1983, annual rpt, 5544–12

Outdoor recreation area dev, Interior Dept Land and Water Conservation Fund grants by State, FY85, annual press release, 5544–15

Recreation fees and collection costs, visitors, and capacity of outdoor Fed Govt, State, and private facilities, by managing agency and State, 1983, annual rpt, 5544–14

Science and Technology

Computer systems and equipment of Fed Govt, inventory by manufacturer, type, agency, and location, FY83, last issue of annual rpt, 9454–4

Degree (doctoral) recipients in science and engineering, by field, sex, race, age, citizenship, postgrad employment and study status, State, and instn, 1960-82, 9626–6.16

Employment of scientists and engineers at universities and colleges and federally funded R&D centers, by field, sex, State, and instn, Jan 1983 and selected trends from 1967, annual survey, 9627–11

Enrollment in grad science and engineering, fields of study, financial support, and other student and instn characteristics, 1975-82, annual survey, 9627–7

NASA contract awards, by State, FY83, annual rpt, 9504–6.2

NASA procurement contract awards, by type, contractor, State, and country, FY84, semiannual rpt, 9502–6

NASA R&D funding to colleges and universities, by State, field of science, and instn, FY83, annual listing, 9504–7

NSF grant and award recipients, by State, FY83, annual listing, 9624–11

Patents (US) granted to US and foreign applicants, by applicant type, firm, State, and country, subject rpt series, 2246–2

Patents (US) granted to US and foreign applicants, by patent type, State, and country, 1983, annual press release, 2244–2

Patents issued to US residents, by State, FY76-83, annual rpt, 2244–1.2

R&D and science-related Fed Govt funding to higher education and nonprofit instns, by field, instn, agency, and State, FY82, annual rpt, 9627–17

R&D expenditures by higher education instns and federally funded centers, by field, source of funds, instn, and State, FY82, annual rpt, 9627–13

R&D expenditures of higher education instns, by source, field of science, census div, and State, 1972-83, biennial rpt, 9627–24.1

R&D Fed Govt facilities and services available for private sector use, by field of science, 1984 biennial listing, 2224–4

R&D Fed Govt funding by agency and State, and expenditures by subject, for Federal research centers, 1972-81, annual rpt, 9624–10.5

R&D Fed Govt funding for all performers, by field and supporting agency, selected years FY60-84, annual rpt, 9627–20

Robotics degrees and courses offered, by State and school level, 1982, 26358–105

Veterans Affairs

Educational assistance program participation and costs under GI Bill and other veterans programs, WW II through Sept 1983, annual rpt, 9924–22

Index by Categories

Life insurance of VA for veterans and servicemen, programs combined coverage and payments by State, 1983, annual rpt, 9924–2

Medical facilities of VA, sharing agreement contracts, services, and costs by region and facility, FY83, annual rpt, 9924–18

Population and characteristics of veterans, and VA hospital and other activities, by State, FY83, annual rpt, 9924–1

Population of veterans and ratio to civilians, by census div and for 10 States with largest change, 1970 and 1980, 9926–4.7

Population of veterans, by period of service, age, and State, Sept 1984, semiannual rpt, 9922–3

Psychological services, staffing, research, and training programs in VA facilities, 1984 annual listing, 9924–10

VA program expenditures, by county and congressional district, FY83, annual rpt, 9924–14

Vietnam era veterans, demographic and service characteristics, compared with WW II and Korea veterans, FY83, annual rpt, 9924–8.1

Women veteran population, and use of benefits by type, by age, period of service, and State, with comparisons to men, FY83, annual rpt, 9924–24

Women veterans, by period of service, age, and State, Mar 1983 and projected to 2030, 9928–28

BY URBAN-RURAL AND METRO-NONMETRO

Agriculture and Food

Farm population, by employment and socioeconomic characteristics, 1983, annual rpt, 2544–1

Food consumption and nutrient intake by individuals, by food group, source, and socioeconomic characteristics, 1977-78 natl survey, final rpt series, 1356–4

Food expenditures for fruit, vegetable, and potato products related to changes in income and other household characteristics, 1977-78, 1548–236

Grain mill production workers, wages, hours, and benefits, by occupation, mill product, and region, June 1982 survey, 6787–6.204

Rural area situation and dev, periodic rpt articles, 1502–7

Communications and Transportation

Hwy construction expenditures and contracts awarded for Federal-aid system, by type of material used and State, various periods 1944-83, annual rpts, 7554–29

Hwy construction material prices and indexes for Federal-aid system, by type of material and urban-rural location, quarterly rpt, 7552–7

Hwy-railroad grade-crossing accidents, detailed data by State and railroad, 1982, annual rpt, 7604–2

Hwy safety, accident, and traffic data from Natl Statistics and Analysis Center, series, 7766–10

Hwy Statistics, summary data on traffic, govt finances, fuel use, vehicles, and driver licenses, by State, 1982, annual rpt, 7554–24

Traffic accidents and casualties detailed direct and indirect costs, by characteristics of persons and vehicles involved, 1979-80, 7768–80

Index by Categories

BY URBAN-RURAL AND METRO-NONMETRO

Traffic accidents, circumstances, injuries, deaths, and characteristics of persons and vehicles involved, 1982, annual rpt, 7764–13

Traffic accidents, deaths, injuries, and rates, by hwy type and State, 1982, annual rpt, 7554–2

Traffic deaths and rates, by urban-rural location, 1975-84, 7766–13.9

Traffic fatal accidents, circumstances, and characteristics of persons and vehicles involved, 1983, annual rpt, 7764–14

Traffic fatal accidents detailed circumstances, and characteristics of persons and vehicles involved, 1982, annual rpt, 7764–10

Travel patterns, personal and household characteristics, auto use, and public transport availability, 1977 survey, series, 7556–6

Women's travel patterns, by employment and sociodemographic characteristics and type of child care used, 1980 survey, 7888–62

Education

Computer access and use in elementary and secondary schools, by region, urban-rural location, and Title I status, spring 1982, 4826–1.10

Condition of Education, detailed data on enrollment, staff, achievement, finances, curricula, and education effects on employment, 1982-83, annual rpt, 4824–1

Educational progress, natl assessment summary data for 7 learning areas, by characteristics of participants, selected years 1971-82, annual rpt, 4824–2.6

Head Start Project enrollment, appropriations, and staff, FY65-84, annual rpt, 4604–8

Head Start Project programs effect on child dev, by characteristics of program, child, and family, literature review, selected years 1965-81, 4608–20

High school class of 1982: foreign language course enrollment, by language, student and school characteristics, and location, 1984 rpt, 4838–11

High school class of 1982: foreign language coursework, by language, course level, student and school characteristics, and location, 1984 rpt, 4828–17

High school classes of 1980 and 1982: educational and sociodemographic characteristics and expectations, natl longitudinal study, series, 4826–2

Indian education program operations, funding, student progress measures, and opinions of school staff, parents, and students, selected years 1973-83, 4808–13

Energy Resources and Demand

Household energy use, appliances, motor vehicles, and vehicle fuel economy, by census region and urban-rural location, various periods Oct 1980-Mar 1983, annual rpt, 3164–74

Household energy use by socioeconomic characteristics, impact of energy price increases, selected years 1978-95, 3004–13.3

Housing energy use, costs, expenditures, and conservation, and household and housing characteristics, survey series, 3166–7

Wood acquired and used for home heating, by household characteristics and wood sources, 1980/81, 1208–204

Government and Defense

Census of Govts, 1982: employment, payrolls, and average earnings, by function, level of govt, State, county, population size, and inside-outside SMSAs, 2455–2

Census of Govts, 1982: properties, govt-assessed value, sales, and tax rates, by property type, State, SMSA, county, and city, 2453–1

Election campaign Fed Govt funding, reform and tax deduction proposals, and TV and political action committee influence, opinion surveys, various dates 1977-83, hearings, 21428–7.1

Immigration, and alien residents, workers, visitors, deportations, and naturalizations, by country of birth, FY81, annual rpt, 6264–2

Property (real) of Fed Govt, inventory and costs, worldwide summary by location, agency, and use, 1983, annual rpt, 9454–5

Property (real) of Fed Govt, leased property inventory and rental costs, worldwide summary by location and agency, Sept 1983, annual rpt, 9454–10

Taxes, tax policy, and intergovtl relations, public opinion survey results, 1972-84, annual rpt, 10044–2

Health and Vital Statistics

Abortions, by patient sociodemographic characteristics, pregnancy history, and procedure, 1980, US Vital Statistics final rpt, 4146–5.72

Arizona nursing home patients aged 55 and older in urban and rural areas, impairment levels for specified functions, 1980, article, 4102–1.413

Births and birth rates, by detailed demographic characteristics and geographic area, 1979 and trends, US Vital Statistics annual rpt, 4144–1

Births attended by midwives and in nonhospital settings, by mother's sociodemographic and prenatal care characteristics and infant race and birthweight, 1978-79 with trends from 1935, 4147–21.40

Births, fertility rates, expected births, and childless women, by socioeconomic characteristics, June 1982, annual Current Population Rpt, 2546–1.386

Births, fertility rates, expected births, and childless women, by socioeconomic characteristics, June 1983, advance annual Current Population Rpt, 2546–1.385

Births, fertility rates, expected births, and childless women, by socioeconomic characteristics, June 1983, annual Current Population Rpt, 2546–1.393

Blood lead levels by sociodemographic and behavioral characteristics, and potential workplace exposure, 1976-80, 4147–11.201

Deaths and death rates, by detailed geographic area, cause, and demographic characteristics, 1979, US Vital Statistics annual rpt, 4144–3

Disabled women, by socioeconomic and demographic characteristics, and compared to nondisabled women and disabled men, 1981, chartbook, 16598–4

Drugs, alcohol, and cigarettes, high school seniors use and assessment by drug type, sex, and region, 1975-83 surveys, annual rpt, 4494–4

Fetal deaths and rates, by gestation period, birth weight and order, race, age of mother, and geographic area, 1979, US Vital Statistics annual rpt, 4144–2.3

Health care services of selected medical practitioners, use by patient characteristics, 1980 survey with trends from 1963, 4146–12.4

Health condition and health care resources, use, and expenditures, 1970s-82 with trends and projections 1900-2000, annual compilation, 4144–11

Health condition, hospitalization, disability, and medical costs, by demographic characteristics, Vital and Health Statistics series, 4147–10

Infant deaths by detailed cause, geographic location, age, race, and sex, 1979, US Vital Statistics annual rpt, 4144–2.2

Internist office visits and drugs provided, by characteristics of visit, patient, and physician, and location, 1980-81, 4147–13.80

Massachusetts parents awareness and use of safety measures to protect their children from accidents, for 9 communities by urban-rural location, Sept 1980-June 1982 survey, article, 4102–1.402

Mental health office and clinic visits, average charges, and total expenditures for services, by type of provider and patient characteristics, 1980, 4146–11.5

Nigeria native and Western health care use, by sociodemographic characteristics, 1984 article, 4102–1.417

Obstetrician-gynecologist office visits and drugs used, by visit reason, diagnosis, treatment, and patient and physician characteristics, 1980-81, 4147–13.76

Older persons health care total and out-of-pocket expenditures, by sociodemographic characteristics, poverty and health status, and degree of functional limitation, 1980, 4146–11.4

Perinatal deaths and death rates, by State, urban-rural location, sex, and race, 1979, US Vital Statistics annual rpt, 4144–2.4

Physician supply and ratio to population by State and county population size, and counties with shortages and needs, 1960-79 and projected 1982-94, 4118–52

Physicians (not office-based) visits by reason, diagnosis, treatment, patient and physician characteristics, and physician primary activity, 1980, 4147–13.77

Surgeon office visits and drugs provided, by characteristics of visit, patient, and physician, and location, 1980-81, 4147–13.79

Housing and Construction

Apartment market absorption rates and characteristics for nonsubsidized privately financed furnished and unfurnished units completed in 1982, annual Current Housing Rpt, 2484–2

Apartment market absorption rates and characteristics for nonsubsidized privately financed units completed in 1983, preliminary annual Current Housing Rpt, 2484–3

Census of Housing, 1980: inventory, occupancy, and unit characteristics, changes from 1973 by region and inside-outside SMSAs and central cities, series, 2473–3

BY URBAN-RURAL AND METRO-NONMETRO

Census of Housing, 1980: occupancy and unit characteristics of SMSAs and central cities, by race, Hispanic origin, and city, State and SMSA rpt series, 2473–1

Census of Population and Housing, 1980: detailed population and housing characteristics, by county, city, and census tract, State and SMSA rpt series, 2551–2

Community Dev Block Grants to small cities, State admin, project characteristics, and assessments of local officials, 1982, 5188–106

Home mortgages (graduated payment) FHA-insured, financial, property, and mortgagor characteristics, for US and selected localities, quarterly rpt, 5142–42

Home mortgages (graduated payment) FHA-insured, financial, property, and mortgagor characteristics, for US and selected States, quarterly rpt, 5142–41

Home mortgages (graduated payment) FHA-insured, financial, property, and mortgagor characteristics, US summary, quarterly rpt, 5142–40

Home mortgages FHA-insured, financial, property, and mortgagor characteristics, for US and selected localities, quarterly rpt, 5142–2

Home mortgages FHA-insured, financial, property, and mortgagor characteristics, for US, selected States, and Puerto Rico, quarterly rpt, 5142–3

Home mortgages FHA-insured, financial, property, and mortgagor characteristics, quarterly rpt, 5142–1

Home mortgages FHA-insured, financial, property, and mortgagor characteristics, 1983, annual rpt, 5144–17

Home mortgages FHA-insured for low-cost homes, financial, construction, property, and mortgagor characteristics, quarterly rpt, 5142–4

Home ownership rates and unit age, by region and urban-rural location, 1980, article, 1702–1.407

Housing adequacy, quality, and affordability by condition and age of unit, rent paid or owner expense and share of income, and metro-nonmetro location, 1980, article, 1702–1.406

Housing and financial characteristics, and unit and neighborhood quality, by inside-outside central cities and SMSAs, and for 4 regions and 15 SMSAs, 1978, annual survey special supplement, 2485–8

Housing and households characteristics, and low-income housing construction and availability, 1970s-83, hearing, 21968–28.1

Housing occupancy and unit and household characteristics, by region and metro-nonmetro residence, 1983, biennial survey, 2485–1

Housing units, by region and metro-nonmetro location, 1973 and 1981, biennial rpt, 5124–4

New housing completions, sales price, cost per square foot, and heating fuel use, by metro-nonmetro area, 1976-82, 1598–190

New housing starts and completions by number of units and inside-outside MSA, new and existing home sales, and new home prices, by region, bimonthly rpt, 2012–1.2

New housing unit starts, by units per structure and metro-nonmetro location, and mobile home placements and sales price, by region, monthly rpt, 2382–1

New housing units authorized, by public and private ownership, by region, div, State, selected MSA, and 4,700 permit-issuing places, monthly rpt, 2382–5

New housing units completed and under construction, by units per structure, region, and inside-outside SMSAs, monthly rpt, 2382–2

New single and multifamily housing physical and financial characteristics, by region and metro-nonmetro location, 1979-83, annual rpt, 2384–1

Older persons rural housing condition, selected householder and housing characteristics with comparisons to urban and nonaged population, 1979, 1598–193

Public housing under private mgmt, assessment by housing officials and managers, and tenants, with operating costs, crime, and rent delinquency by project type and location, 1982, 5188–103

Quality of housing and neighborhoods, indicators and attitudes, and occupant characteristics, by urban-rural location and region, 1981, annual survey, 2485–7

Quality of housing and neighborhoods, indicators and attitudes, by occupant and unit characteristics, region, and metro-nonmetro location, 1981, annual survey, 2485–2

Vacancy and occupancy rates, and vacant unit characteristics, by metro-nonmetro location and region, selected years 1960-83, annual rpt, 2484–1

Vacant housing characteristics and costs, and occupancy and vacancy rates, by region and metro-nonmetro location, quarterly rpt, 2482–1

Industry and Commerce

Metalworking machinery industry computerized automation, by plant characteristics, for 6 industry groups and small plants, 1982 surveys, 23848–179

Retail trade census, 1982: employment, establishments, sales, and payroll, by SIC 2- to 4-digit kind of business, SMSA, county, and city, State rpt series, 2397–1

Service industry census, 1982: employment, establishments, receipts, and payroll, by SIC 2- to 4-digit kind of business, SMSA, county, and city, State rpt series, 2391–1

Small business loan and credit activities and assessment, effect of bank deregulation by business characteristics, 1980 and 1982 surveys, hearings, 21728–52.1

Wholesale trade census, 1982: employment, establishments, finances, and operations, by SIC 2- to 4-digit kind of business, SMSA, county, and city, State rpt series, 2405–1

Labor and Employment

Employment and unemployment in metro and nonmetro areas, monthly rpt, quarterly data, 6742–2.8

Employment and unemployment in metro and nonmetro poverty and nonpoverty areas, annual averages, 1983, article, 6742–2.403

Employment Cost Index and percent change by occupational group, industry div, region, and metro-nonmetro area, quarterly press release, 6782–5

Employment Cost Index, quarterly article, 6782–1

Employment, total and manufacturing, change in metro-nonmetro counties by region and county size, various periods 1951-79, technical paper, 9387–8.90

Index by Categories

Metal (nonferrous) manufacturing wages and benefits, by occupation, size of establishment, and for metro-nonmetro areas, 1981 survey, 6787–6.196

Unemployment of men and women, by contributing factor, and change in industry share of labor force and unemployment, 1973-75 and 1981-82, article, 6722–1.432

Law Enforcement

Assaults, murders, and other deaths of law enforcement officers, by circumstances, level of govt, agency, victim and offender characteristics, and location, 1983, annual rpt, 6224–3

Bombing (explosive and incendiary) incidents, damage, injuries, and deaths, by target, State, and circumstances, 1983, annual rpt, 6224–5

Crime Index by population size and region, and offenses known to police by large city, Jan-June 1984, semiannual rpt, 6222–1

Crime victimization of households, by offense type, race of household head, and family income and urban-rural residence, 1975-83, periodic rpt, 6062–2.404

Crime victimization rates by type of offense, and victim and offense characteristics, Natl Crime Survey series, 6066–3

Crimes, arrests by offender characteristics, and rates, by offense, and law enforcement employees, by population size and jurisdiction, 1970s-83, annual rpt, 6224–2

Peru cocaine addicts and arrested traffickers and users socioeconomic characteristics, and cocaine confiscated, 1974-78, intl conf papers, 7008–40

Robbery rates and circumstances, medical costs and property losses of victims, and offender and victim characteristics, 1960s-81, 6068–180

Natural Resources, Environment, and Pollution

Air pollutant metal levels, by monitoring site, State, and urban-rural location, 1977-79, last issue of annual rpt, 9194–10

Air pollutant nitrate and sulfate emissions, monitoring results by surveillance station, 1979 with trends by urban-rural area from 1971, 9198–107

Air pollution levels for 132 hazardous organic chemicals, by urban-rural location, city, and for areas with many potential sources, 1970-80, 9198–109

Chicago area air pollution levels by location, late 1970s-82 and projected under lower auto emission standards to 1995, 3408–31

Environmental quality, pollutant discharge by type and source, and EPA protection activities and funding, 1970s-83, biennial regional rpt series, 9184–15

New Jersey and NYC atmospheric levels of 28 volatile organic compounds, by site and urban-rural location, 1979-June 1981, 9198–108

Population

Appalachia population by age and urban-rural location, and employment and net employment change by industry, selected years 1960-90, article, 9088–33

Census of Population and Housing, 1980: detailed population and housing characteristics, by county, city, and census tract, State and SMSA rpt series, 2551–2

Census of Population, 1980: detailed socioeconomic characteristics, by county, city, and inside-outside SMSAs and central cities, State rpt series, 2531–3

Index by Categories

Educational attainment of population, by sociodemographic characteristics and for large States and SMSAs, 1981 and trends from 1940, biennial Current Population Rpt, 2546–1.390

Families and households detailed socioeconomic characteristics, Mar 1982, annual Current Population Rpt, 2546–1.383

Foreign aged population characteristics, with related health care data and vital statistics, by world area and selected country, 1950-80 and projected to 2020, 2546–10.12

Foreign population size and growth rates, and latest available benchmark demographic data, by country, 1950-83, biennial rpt, 2324–4

Foreign women sociodemographic, economic, and fertility characteristics, with comparisons to men, by country, 1960s-85, world region rpt series, 2326–15

Hispanic Americans socioeconomic and demographic characteristics, and compared to non-Hispanics, selected years 1970-83, chartbook, 2328–48

Homeless population and characteristics, and temporary shelter operations, use, and user characteristics, by region and selected city, 1983, 5188–108

Household living arrangements, family relationships, and marital status, by demographic characteristics, Mar 1983, annual Current Population Rpt, 2546–1.388

Income (household) and cash and noncash transfer program participation, by sociodemographic characteristics, quarterly rpt, 2542–2

Income (personal) per capita and by source, and earnings by industry div, by State, MSA, and county, 1977-82, annual regional rpts, 2704–2

Income (personal) per capita and total, by State, MSA, and county, with metro-nonmetro totals, 1980-82, annual article, 2702–1.413

Income and socioeconomic characteristics of persons, families, and households, detailed cross-tabulations, Current Population Rpt series, 2546–6

Migration, population, employment, income, housing, health, and education, rural and urban comparisons, 1960s-83, annual chartbook, 1504–3

Mobility of population, detailed data by demographic and socioeconomic characteristics of movers and nonmovers, Mar 1981-82, annual Current Population Rpt, 2546–1.384

Older persons by demographic, socioeconomic, and health characteristics, selected years 1900-81 and projected to 2050, Current Population Rpt, 2546–2.125

Older persons population characteristics, and needs and costs of social services by type, by metro-nonmetro status, 1970s-82 with trends from 1900, 21148–28

Population demographic and economic characteristics, 1982 with projections of population size to 2050, annual Current Population Rpt, 2546–2.119

Population size and change for metro and nonmetro areas and central cities by census div, and growth of areas with large black and aged populations, 1970-82, 2328–47

Poverty status of families and persons, by detailed socioeconomic characteristics, 1982, annual Current Population Rpt, 2546–6.40

Poverty status of families and persons by selected characteristics, public welfare funding, and effect of counting transfer payments as income, selected years 1950-83, 25928–4

Prices and Cost of Living

Child raising itemized costs in urban and rural nonfarm areas, by age and region, quarterly rpt, 1702–1

Public Welfare and Social Security

Colorado Medicare beneficiaries with partial coverage, 1978, article, 4652–1.404

Food aid programs of Fed Govt and others, funding, participant characteristics, and nutrition and poverty data, 1970s-83, 028–20

Medicare aged beneficiaries activity restriction, untreated health conditions, and perceived health status, by sociodemographic characteristics, 1980, 4146–12.2

Medicare aged beneficiaries medical care by usual source, and untreated health conditions, by sociodemographic characteristics, 1980, 4146–12.3

Medicare and Medicaid nursing home patient cost-allocation based on case-mix and other facility characteristics, 1980, article, 4652–1.432

Noncash public and employer-based transfer program recipients, by income source and socioeconomic characteristics, 1982, advance Current Population Rpt, 2546–6.38

Noncash public and employer-based transfer program recipients, by income source and socioeconomic characteristics, 1982, final Current Population Rpt, 2546–6.37

Poverty population size, effect of counting public noncash transfers as income by recipient characteristics, 1979-83, 2626–2.52

Poverty population size, effects of counting public noncash transfers as income by recipient characteristics, 1979-82, 2626–2.50

Supplemental Security Income payments, and recipients by other income source, eligibility type, and other characteristics, by State, 1982, annual rpt, 4744–16

Supplementary Security Income beneficiary socioeconomic characteristics and health service use, 1970s-83 and SSI program projections to 1995, 25148–29

Science and Technology

Engineers sociodemographic, educational, and employment characteristics, and Federal support by agency, 1978, Current Population Rpt, 2546–2.121

Veterans Affairs

Health condition of veterans and nonveterans, and veteran use of VA and non-VA hospitals by disease, by age, race, income, and metro-nonmetro location, various periods 1971-81, 9926–1.18

BY COMMODITY

ECONOMIC BREAKDOWNS

BY COMMODITY

Agriculture and Food

Acreage harvested and cropland area by crop and region, and potential for expansion, 1982-84 with trends from 1949, annual rpt, 1584–4

Acreage planted and harvested, by crop and State, 1982-83 and planned as of June 1984, annual rpt, 1621–23

Acreage planting intended for 19 crops, by State, as of Feb 1984, annual rpt, 1621–22

Acreage reduction payment-in-kind program costs, requirements, producer and diversion payments, and loan interest forgiven, by crop, as of 1983, hearing, 21788–138

Advertising (generic) for agricultural commodities, activities and funding by source, selected years 1972-83, 1548–242

Agricultural cooperative finances and operations, aggregate for top 100 assns by principal product and revenue source, FY82, annual rpt, 1124–3

Agricultural cooperatives activities, operations, finances, and current issues, monthly rpt articles, 1122–1

Agricultural cooperatives, membership, activities, and finances, by commodity and selected State, 1900-80 with trends from 1863, 1128–30

Agricultural cooperatives, membership, and activities, by type of service, commodity, and State, FY51-1982, annual survey rpt, 1124–1

Agricultural policies of US effect on trade, with US and foreign trade by commodity and grain stocks by world area, various periods 1979-83, 1528–183

Agricultural production, marketing, trade, supply, food consumption, and food and nutrition programs, 1960s-83, annual chartbook, 1504–3

Agricultural research expenditures and scientist years, by topic, commodity, and performing organization, FY82, annual rpt, 1744–2

Agricultural Stabilization and Conservation Service programs, annual commodity fact sheet series, 1806–4

Agricultural Statistics, 1983, annual rpt, 1004–1

Agriculture Fact Book of US, compilation of data for 1983 with trends from 1940, annual rpt, 1004–14

Business statistics, detailed data for major industries and economic indicators, *Survey of Current Business,* monthly rpt, 2702–1.11

Canada agricultural trade with US, effects of nontariff trade barriers, selected years 1955-81, 1528–175

CCC commodities for sale, and prices, monthly press release, 1802–4

CCC finances and program operations, FY83, annual rpt, 1824–1

CCC inventories by commodity, 1979-83, and borrowing authority appropriations, FY72-83, strategic material stockpile mgmt hearings, 25208–27

CCC loan activities by commodity, and agency operating results, monthly press release, 1802–7

BY COMMODITY

Index by Categories

Census of Agriculture, 1982: farms, farmland, production and costs, and operator characteristics, preliminary State and county rpt series, 2330–1

Census of Agriculture, 1982: farms, farmland, production, finances, and operator characteristics, by county, final State rpt series, 2331–1

China economic conditions, agricultural and industrial production, trade, and domestic and foreign investment, 1980-85, 2048–106

Coastal environmental characteristics, fish, wildlife, and use, and population socioeconomic data, for individual areas, series, 5506–4

Cold storage food stocks by commodity and census div, and warehouse cold storage space in use, by State, monthly rpt, 1631–5

Cold storage food stocks of 77 commodities, by region, 1983, annual rpt, 1631–11

Communist, OECD, and selected other countries agricultural production, by commodity, 1960s-83, annual rpt, 244–5.9

Crop insurance participation and operations in 2 States by crop, and Fed Crop Insurance Corp finances, 1980-84, GAO rpt, 26113–132

Crop Reporting Board commodity publications, 1984 releases, annual listing, 1614–1

Crop support levels by program, and Fed Govt policy issues effect on agricultural and food prices, income, and trade, Nov 1984, semiannual rpt, 1542–6

Developing countries agricultural supply/demand and market for US exports, with socioeconomic indicators, country rpt series, 1526–6

Developing countries food production and needs, and related economic trends and outlook, for 67 countries, 1980-86, annual rpt, 1524–6

Developing countries food supply policies, with farm sector data, tariff income, and prices and imports of 5 grains, for 21 countries, 1960s-81, 1528–168

Eastern Europe agricultural production and trade by commodity, food consumption, and farm inputs, for 6 countries, 1960-80 with projections to 1991, 1528–178

EC agricultural self-sufficiency and trade by selected product, with comparisons to other countries, selected years 1959/60-1983/84, hearing, 25368–135

EC food supply/demand and market and support prices, with exchange rates, fertilizer price index, GDP, and population, by country, 1960-83, 1528–173

Economic Research Service activities, funding, and staff in DC and other locations, by detailed branch and section, FY83, annual rpt, 1504–7

Economic Research Service activities, funding, and staff in DC and other locations, by detailed branch and section, FY84, annual rpt, 1504–6

Export sales and shipments of US grains, oilseed products, hides, skins, and cotton, by country, weekly rpt, 1922–3

Exports and imports of agricultural commodities, outlook and current situation, quarterly rpt, 1542–4

Exports and imports of US, by agricultural commodity and country, bimonthly rpt with articles, 1522–1

Exports and imports of US, by detailed agricultural commodity and country, FY83 and CY83, semiannual rpts, 1522–4

Exports and imports of US, by detailed agricultural commodity for 8 major commodity groups, monthly rpt, 1922–8

Exports and personal expenditures of US and world for selected agricultural commodities, by country, and export share of US farm income, various periods 1926-82, 1528–172

Exports, imports, tariffs, and industry operating data for agricultural products, 1979-83, TSUSA commodity rpt series, 9885–1

Exports of manufactured and agricultural commodities, manufacturing production, and export-related employment, 1960s-82, State rpt series, 2046–3

Farm business legal organization, finances, operations, tax rates, and State laws restricting farm corporations, 1960s-82, 1548–233

Farm finance and credit conditions, forecast 1984, conf papers, annual rpt, 1004–16

Farm finance and credit conditions, forecast 1984, conf summary, annual rpt, 9264–9

Farm finances, assets, expenses, cash flow, receipts, and loans, selected years 1971-85, annual rpt, 1544–13

Farm finances, assets, liabilities, income, receipts by commodity and State, and expenses, 1980-83 and trends from 1910, annual rpt, 1544–16

Farm finances, production, expenses by type, and domestic economic impact, selected years 1972-82 and preliminary 1983-84, annual rpt, 1544–19

Farm labor, farms, and labor costs, by labor and farm type and State, with immigrant labor law effect on farm work force, 1978, 1598–192

Farm population, by farm type and sales size and selected other characteristics, 1975-80, 1598–144

Farm production inputs, outputs, and productivity, by region, 1939-82, annual rpt, 1544–17

Farm production itemized costs, receipts, and net returns, for 13 crops, 4 livestock types, and milk, by region, 1981-83, annual rpt, 1544–20

Farm production, prices, marketing, and trade, by commodity, forecast and current situation, monthly rpt, 1502–4

Farmland eroded by rainfall, acreage by crop, and farm operators by selected characteristics, by soil erosion class, 1977-78, 1588–83

Farms, production, acreage, and related data, by selected crop and State, monthly rpt, 1621–1

Fertilizer and pesticide use for selected crops, periodic situation rpt with articles, 1561–16

Food consumption, supply, trade, prices, expenditures, and indexes, by commodity, 1963-83, annual rpt, 1544–4

Food expenditures for fruit, vegetable, and potato products related to changes in income and other household characteristics, 1977-78, 1548–236

Food industry advertising expenditures by media type, and advertising to sales ratio by selected food item, 1970-79 with some trends from 1955, 1548–234

Food products (processed) production and stocks by State, shipments, exports, materials used, and consumption, periodic Current Industrial Rpt series, 2506–4

Food weekly allowances for households under USDA thrifty food plan, by age and sex, 1983 with comparisons to 1975, article, 1702–1.402

Foreign agricultural and food production indexes, and production of selected commodities, by world region and country, 1974-83, annual rpt, 1524–5

Foreign agricultural production, prices, and trade, by country, 1983 and outlook for 1984/85, annual world region rpt series, 1524–4

Foreign Agriculture, production, consumption, and policies, and US export dev and promotion, monthly rpt, 1922–2

Foreign and US agricultural production, prices, trade, and consumption, quarterly rpt with articles, 1522–3

Foreign and US agricultural supply/demand and production data, for selected US and world crops, and for US livestock and dairy products, periodic rpt, 1522–5

Foreign and US agricultural supply/demand indicators by commodity and world area, and related research and extension program needs, 1950s-2020, 1008–47

Foreign and US feed and livestock trade by product and world region, and ocean freight rates between selected countries of origin and destination, selected years 1960-82, 1528–177

Foreign and US fresh and processed fruit, vegetable, and nut production and trade, FAS monthly rpt with articles, 1925–34

Foreign and US livestock, poultry, and trade, FAS semiannual circular, 1925–33

Fruit (noncitrus) and nut production, prices, and use, by crop and State, 1981-83, annual rpt, 1621–18.1, 1621–18.3

Fruit and nut production, prices, trade, stocks, and use, by selected crop, periodic situation rpt with articles, 1561–6

Fruit and vegetable shipments, and arrivals in 23 US and 5 Canada cities, by mode of transport and State or country of origin, 1983, annual rpt series, 1311–4

Fruit and vegetable shipments by mode of transport, arrivals, and imports, by commodity and State and country of origin, weekly rpt, 1311–3

Imports injury to price-supported US agricultural industries, investigations with background financial and operating data for selected products, series, 9886–10

Income (gross and net) and cash marketing receipts for farms, by detailed commodity, and production expenses, by State, 1979-82, annual rpt, 1544–18

Livestock, poultry, and dairy live animals, meat, and products trade, by commodity and country of destination, FAS quarterly rpt, 1925–32

Natural gas price decontrol alternatives effect on farm production by crop, prices, and fertilizer use and costs, 1982-90, model results, 1548–239

Index by Categories

BY COMMODITY

Pesticide use and acreage treated, for 12 vegetable and melon crops, by type of pesticide, method of application, and region, 1979, 1588–82

Pesticide use for crops and livestock, acreage treated, application methods, and use of safety equipment and professional services, 1982 survey, 1588–76

PL 480 and CCC export credit sales agreement terms, by commodity and country, FY83, annual rpt, 15344–1.11

PL 480 commodity allocations for long-term credit sales, by country, quarterly press release, 1922–7

PL 480 concessional sales program, exports by commodity and country, 1955-83, semiannual rpt, 1922–6

PL 480 concessional sales program, exports by commodity and country, 1978-83, semiannual rpt, 1922–10

PL 480 exports by commodity, and recipients, by program, sponsor, and country, FY82 and aggregate from FY55, annual rpt, 1924–7

Portugal agricultural subsidies, profits, marketing margins, and consumer prices, by commodity or product, and effects of prospective EC membership, 1981, 1528–171

Prices received by farmers and production value for detailed crops by State, 1981-83, annual rpt, 1621–2

Prices received by farmers for major products, and paid for farm inputs and living items, by commodity and State, monthly rpt, 1629–1

Prices received by farmers for major products, and paid for farm inputs, by commodity and State, 1983, annual rpt, 1629–5

Southeastern States agricultural conditions, Fed Reserve 8th District, quarterly rpt, 9391–13

Stocks of grains, oilseeds, and hay on and off farms, and capacity of off-farm grain storage facilities, by State, 1978-83, 1641–17

Tennessee Valley ethanol production, feedstocks, facilities, tax incentives, and related farming data, by State, 1970s-83 and projected to 1992, 9808–69

TTPI socioeconomic, health, and govtl data, by TTPI govt, FY83 and selected trends, detailed annual rpt, 7004–6

Underground economy, household expenditures and participation by type of goods or service and sociodemographic characteristics, with methodology and bibl, 1981 survey, 8308–27

USDA agricultural surplus direct purchase program finances, and purchases and food received by schools by commodity, various periods 1936-83, 1548–243

Vegetable and fruit production, acreage, and prices, for selected fresh and processing crops by State, 1981-84, annual rpts, 1621–25

Vegetable and fruit production, acreage, and yield, current and forecast for selected fresh and processing crops by State, periodic rpt, 1621–12

Vegetable production, prices, stocks, and consumption, for selected fresh and processed crops, periodic situation rpt with articles, 1561–11

Banking, Finance, and Insurance

Futures trading by commodity and exchange, and Commodity Futures Trading Commission activities, funding, and employment, FY83, annual rpt, 11924–2

Futures trading in selected commodities, foreign currencies, and stock indexes, Chicago and other markets activity, monthly rpt, 11922–1

Futures trading in selected commodities, foreign currencies, Treasury securities, and stock indexes, NYC, Chicago, and other markets activity, monthly rpt, 11922–5

Futures trading in selected commodities, Treasury securities, and stock indexes, NYC market activity, monthly rpt, 11922–2

Communications and Transportation

Advertising in periodicals, costs by type of product, *Survey of Current Business,* monthly rpt, 2702–1.4

Freight and distance hauled, by commodity and mode of transport, selected years 1970-82, annual rpt, 3304–5.3

Panama Canal commerce, by commodity, flag of vessel, and trade routes, FY82, annual rpt, 9664–3.2

Pipeline safety regulations enforcement of DOT and States by pipeline type and State, and accidents and commodity losses, selected years 1973-FY84, GAO rpt, 26113–130

Port dev costs and financing through user fees, and shipping industry impact on local economy, by State, other area, industry, commodity, and port, 1970s-82, hearings, 21568–34.1

Port impact on local employment through transport of 5 commodities, by industry for 3 eastern ports, and demand for US coal by country, 1981, 7308–182

Railroad finances, operations, and freight rates and shares, by commodity and railroad, 1970s-82, hearings, 25268–80

Railroad freight volume and revenues, by commodity and region of origin and destination, 1982, annual rpt, 7604–6

St Lawrence Seaway Dev Corp finances and activities, and seaway toll charges and cargo tonnage by type of cargo, 1983, annual rpt, 7744–1

St Lawrence Seaway ships, cargo and passenger volumes, and toll revenues, 1981-82 and trends from 1959, annual rpt, 7744–2

Transportation census, 1982: trucks, by detailed characteristics, miles traveled, and type of product carried, State rpt series, 2573–1

Truck transport of fruit and vegetables to 6 major markets, weekly rates by commodity and region, and monthly truck-mile costs, 1983 annual rpt, 1311–15

Energy Resources and Demand

Gasohol production and costs by feedstock, prices, and market penetration rates and excise tax exemption by State, 1983, article, 1561–16.404

Government and Defense

DOD military post exchange operations, locations worldwide, sales by type of commodity or service and facility, and employment, FY83, annual rpt, 3504–10

DOD procurement, prime contract awards by detailed procurement category, FY80-83, annual rpt, 3544–18

DOD procurement, prime contract awards for 25 commodity categories and R&D, by State and census div, FY81-83, annual rpt, 3544–11

DOD shipments of military and personal property, loss claims, passenger traffic, and costs, by mode of transport, quarterly rpt, 3702–1

Foreign military aid of US and sales of arms, equipment, and training, by item and country, FY50-83, annual rpt, 3904–3

Navy procurement, by contractor and location of work, FY83, annual rpt, 3804–13

Strategic and critical materials stockpiling activities and inventories of Fed Govt, by commodity, as of Mar 1984, semiannual rpt, 9432–1

Strategic materials stockpile inventories, costs, and goals, by commodity, as of June 1984, semiannual rpt, 9452–7

Strategic materials stockpiles, and imports in exchange for CCC commodity exports by world region and country, various periods 1950-83, hearings, 21208–20

Tax (excise) collections of IRS, by source, quarterly press release, 8302–1

Health and Vital Statistics

Injuries and deaths from use of selected consumer products and related activity, by victim age and sex, 1982, annual rpt, 9164–7

Injuries and deaths from use of selected consumer products, by victim age and medical treatment status, 1982, annual rpt, 9164–6

Injuries, deaths, and medical costs from consumer products use, and Consumer Product Safety Commission activities and recalls, by product type and brand, FY83, annual rpt, 9164–2

Minerals (nonmetallic) mining and related operations injury, employment, and worktime data, 1982, annual rpt, 6664–1

Industry and Commerce

Alaska minerals resources, production, claims on wildlife refuges, oil and gas leases, and exploratory wells, with maps and bibl, 1983, annual rpt, 5664–11

Business statistics, detailed data for major industries and economic indicators, *Survey of Current Business,* monthly rpt, 2702–1

Capital investment net costs for 35 types of structures and equipment, under 1980-82 tax laws, article, 9387–1.405

Chemicals and related products trade, tariffs, and industry operating data, TSUSA commodity rpt series, 9885–4

China economic and business investment conditions, trade practices, and trade with US by detailed commodity, 1978-82, 2048–72

China economic conditions, agricultural and industrial production, trade, and domestic and foreign investment, 1980-85, 2048–106

China exports and imports, by commodity, world area, and country, quarterly rpt, 242–6

China exports and imports by SITC 1- to 5-digit commodity, 1970s-82, annual rpt, 244–12

Communist, OECD, and selected other countries industrial production and trade, by commodity, 1960s-83, annual rpt, 244–5

BY COMMODITY

Index by Categories

Cuba economic conditions, agricultural and industrial production and distribution, trade, and intl economic relations, 1970-82 and trends from 1957, 248–40

Europe (Western) trade with US, and US market share and export opportunities for selected commodities, by country, 1982-84, 2048–105

Export licensing and monitoring activities under Export Admin Act, for selected commodities, and for Communist and other countries, FY83, annual rpt, 2044–22

Exports and imports, agreement devs, US trade relations, and USITC investigations, 1983, annual rpt, 9884–5

Exports and imports between US and outlying areas, by detailed commodity and mode of transport, monthly rpt, 2422–4

Exports and imports of US, and trade balance, by major commodity group, selected country, and world area, with seasonal adjustments, monthly rpt, 2422–6

Exports and imports of US, by commodity group, world area, selected country, US coastal area and port, and mode of transport, with seasonal adjustments, monthly rpt, 2422–9

Exports and imports of US by country, and trade shifts by commodity, USITC quarterly monitoring rpt, 9882–9

Exports and imports of US, detailed SIC-based commodities by world area, 1983, annual rpts, 2424–6

Exports and imports of US, totals and as percent of domestic production, by SIC 2- to 5-digit commodity, 1981, annual rpt, 2424–3

Exports and imports of US with Communist countries, by detailed commodity and country, quarterly rpt with articles, 9882–2

Exports, imports, and economic indicators by country and country group, and US trade policy actions, 1960s-83, annual rpt, 444–1

Exports, imports, and tariffs, USITC investigation publications issued, 1960-83, annual listing, 9884–12

Exports of manufactured and agricultural commodities, manufacturing production, and export-related employment, 1960s-82, State rpt series, 2046–3

Exports of US by selected commodity, and foreign and US economic and employment indicators and balance of payments, by world area and country, 1970s-83, annual rpt, 2044–26

Exports of US, detailed commodities by country of destination, monthly rpt, 2422–3

Exports of US, detailed Schedule B commodities by country of destination, 1983, annual rpt, 2424–9

Exports of US, detailed Schedule E commodities by mode of transport and world area and country of destination, 1983, annual rpts, 2424–5

Foreign economic trends and implications for US, annual and semiannual country rpt series, 2046–4

Foreign trade balance of US, by commodity group, FY80-83, annual rpt, 26304–3.1

Generalized System of Preferences status of 29 commodities, with US production, consumption, tariffs, and trade by country, selected years 1978-87, 9888–17

Great Lakes trade, by SITC 3-digit commodity, port, vessel type, world area, and country, 1982, annual rpt, 7744–3

Import and tariff provisions effect on US industries and products, investigations with background financial and operating data, series, 9886–4

Import quotas and imports for selected commodities, by country of origin, monthly rpt, 8146–1

Imports detained by FDA, by product, shipper or manufacturer, country, and detention reasons, monthly listing, 4062–2

Imports from Communist countries, injury to US industries, investigations with background financial and operating data, selected industries and products, series, 9886–12

Imports injury to US industries from foreign subsidized products, investigations with background financial and operating data for selected industries and products, series, 9886–15

Imports injury to US industries from import sales at less than fair value, investigations with background financial and operating data, series, 9886–14

Imports injury to US industries from increased import sales, investigations with background financial and operating data, series, 9886–5

Imports injury to US industries from removal of duties on foreign subsidized products, investigations with background financial and operating data, series, 9886–18

Imports of US, detailed Schedule A commodities by country and world area of origin, and mode of transport, 1983, annual rpts, 2424–2

Imports of US, detailed Schedule A commodities by country, monthly rpt, 2422–2

Imports of US, detailed TSUSA commodities by country of origin, 1983, annual rpt, 2424–4

Imports of US given duty-free treatment for value of US materials or parts sent abroad for processing or assembly, by country and commodity, 1979-82, biennial rpt, 9884–14

Input-output structure of US economy, detailed interindustry transactions for 537 industries, and components of final demand, 1977 benchmark data, 2708–17

Jamaica PL 480 Title I assistance effects on economic dev, with data on govt finance, economic indicators, demography, and dev programs, 1970s-81, 9916–1.51

Manufactured products (miscellaneous) trade, tariffs, and industry operating data, TSUSA commodity rpt series, 9885–7

Manufacturing census, 1982: financial and operating data, for SIC 4-digit industries by product, preliminary rpt series, 2491–1

Manufacturing operating and financial data, 1980-81 Annual Survey of Manufactures rpt reprints, hardbound vol, 2504–1

Metals and metal products trade, tariffs, and industry operating data, TSUSA commodity rpt series, 9885–6

Mineral industries census, 1982: financial and operating data, including materials consumed, by SIC 4-digit industry and State, preliminary rpt series, 2511–1

Mineral Industry Surveys, commodity reviews of production, trade, and consumption, advance annual rpt series, 5614–5

Mineral Industry Surveys, commodity reviews of production, trade, stocks, and consumption, monthly rpt series, 5612–1

Mineral Industry Surveys, commodity reviews of production, trade, stocks, and consumption, quarterly rpt series, 5612–2

Mineral Industry Surveys, State reviews of production, 1983, advance annual rpt series, 5614–6

Minerals (nonfuel) foreign and US supply under alternative market conditions, reserves, and background industry data, series, 5606–4

Minerals (nonfuel) from marine sources, demand by mineral type, selected years 1978-83 with projections to 2000, 15048–4

Minerals (nonmetallic) and mineral products trade, tariffs, and industry operating data, TSUSA commodity rpt series, 9885–5

Minerals production, prices, trade, use, employment, tariffs, and stockpiling, by commodity, with foreign comparisons, 1979-83, annual rpt, 5604–18

Minerals production, reserves, and industry role in domestic economy and world supply, country and world region rpt series, 5606–1

Minerals Yearbook, 1982, Vol 1: commodity reviews of production, reserves, supply, use, and trade, annual rpt, 5604–33

Minerals Yearbook, 1982, Vol 2 preprints: State reviews of production and sales by commodity, and business activity, annual rpt series, 5604–16

Minerals Yearbook, 1982, Vol 3: foreign country reviews of production, trade, and policies, by commodity, annual rpt, 5604–35

Minerals Yearbook, 1982, Vol 3 preprints: foreign country reviews of production, trade, and policies, by commodity, annual rpt series, 5604–17

Minerals Yearbook, 1983, Vol 1 preprints: commodity reviews of production, reserves, supply, use, and trade, annual rpt series, 5604–15

Minerals Yearbook, 1983, Vol 3 preprints: foreign country reviews of production, trade, and policies, by commodity, annual rpt series, 5604–23

OECD trade, total and for 4 major countries, and US trade by country, by commodity, 1972-82, annual world region rpt series, 244–13

Overseas Business Reports: economic conditions, investment and export opportunities, and trade practices, annual country market research rpt series, 2046–6

Overseas Business Reports: economic conditions, investment and export opportunities, and trade practices, world region rpt series, 2046–5

Personal stocks of durable goods, by type, in current and constant dollars, 1980-83, annual article, 2702–1.433

Retail trade census, 1982: employment, establishments, sales, and payroll, by SIC 4-digit kind of business and State, preliminary rpt series, 2395–1

Service industry census, 1982: employment, establishments, receipts, and payroll, by SIC 4-digit kind of business and State, preliminary rpt series, 2390–2

Index by Categories

Soviet Union industrial and agricultural production by selected commodity, and demographic trends and projections by Republic, 1950s-2000, hearings, 23848–180

Statistical Abstract of US, social, political, and economic data, 1950s-83 and trends, annual rpt, 2324–1.3

Tariff Schedules of US, Annotated, classifications and rates of duty for detailed imported commodities, 1985 edition, 9886–13

Tariff Schedules of US, Annotated, commodity classification revisions under proposed internatl system, 1984 rpt, 9886–4.66

Textile exports, by product and country of destination, monthly rpt, 2042–26

Textile fiber and products trade, tariffs, and industry operating data, TSUSA commodity rpt series, 9885–3

Textile imports and import limits under Multifiber Arrangement by product and country, with US exports and use, 1970-83, semiannual rpt, 9882–11

Textile imports, by product and country of origin, monthly rpt, 2422–1

Textile imports, by product and country of origin, monthly rpt series, 2046–9

Textile imports, by product and country of origin, periodic rpt series, 2046–8

USITC analysts assigned to cover individual commodities, grouped by TSUSA schedule, 1983 listing, 9888–12

Waterborne commerce of US (domestic and foreign), freight by commodity, traffic, and passengers, by port and waterway, 1982, annual rpt, 3754–3

Waterborne trade of grain and selected other commodities worldwide, and grain shipping rates by route, 1966-82, 1548–235

Waterborne trade of US, by type of service, commodity, country, route, and US port, 1982, annual rpt, 7704–2

Wholesale trade census, 1982: employment, establishments, sales by commodity, and payroll, by SIC 4-digit kind of business and State, preliminary rpt series, 2403–1

Wholesale trade sales and inventories, by SIC 2- to 3-digit kind of business, monthly rpt, 2413–7

Wood, paper, and printed matter trade, tariffs, and industry operating data, TSUSA commodity rpt series, 9885–2

Natural Resources, Environment, and Pollution

Endangered animals and plants foreign trade including reexports of live specimens and products, by purpose, country, and species, 1982, annual rpt, 5504–19

Mineral leases on Fed Govt and Indian lands, by State, as of Dec 1983, annual rpt, 5734–2

Radioactive strontium in NYC and San Francisco diet by food item, and in NYC tap water and milk, quarterly 1982 with trends from 1954, annual rpt, 3404–13

Prices and Cost of Living

CPI and PPI current statistics, detailed data, Monthly Labor Review, 6722–1.5

CPI by component for US city average, and by region, population size, and for 28 SMSAs, monthly press release, 6762–1

CPI by detailed component, for US city average, 28 SMSAs, and 4 regions by population size, monthly rpt, 6762–2

BY FEDERAL AGENCY

CPI components relative importance, for selected SMSAs, and US city average by region and population size, 1983, annual rpt, 6884–1

CPI, 1935-82, annual rpt, 6724–1.7

Department store inventory price indexes, July 1984, semiannual rpt, 6762–7

Export and import price indexes for food and manufactured products, quarterly press release, 6762–13

Export and import price indexes for selected commodities, 1st half 1984, semiannual article, 6722–1.459

Export and import price indexes for selected commodities, 1983, semiannual article, 6722–1.424

Food price indexes (consumer and producer) and retail prices for selected items, and CPI for 25 cities, 1963-83, annual rpt, 1544–4.5

Food prices (farm-retail), marketing cost components, and industry finances and productivity, selected years 1967-83, annual rpt, 1544–9

Food prices and consumption trends, quarterly rpt with articles, 1541–7

Foreign and US food prices for 15 items in DC and 15 foreign capital cities, weekly press release, periodic table, 1922–4

Fruit and vegetable wholesale prices in NYC, Chicago, and selected shipping points, by crop, 1983, annual rpt, 1311–8

North Central States farm credit conditions and economic devs, Fed Reserve 7th District, biweekly rpt, 9375–10

OECD economic indicators, for US and 6 countries, biweekly rpt, 242–4

Price indexes (consumer and producer) by commodity and service group, and expenditure class, selected years 1929-83, annual rpt, 204–1.4

Prices received by farmers for major products, and paid for farm inputs, by commodity and State, 1983, annual rpt, 1629–5

Producer Price Index, by major commodity group and subgroup, and processing stage, monthly press release, 6762–5

Producer prices and indexes, by stage of processing and detailed commodity, monthly rpt, 6762–6

Producer prices and indexes, by stage of processing and detailed commodity, monthly 1983, annual supplement, 6764–2

Retail prices for energy and food, and housing fuel consumption, by region, and for 28 SMSAs and US city average, monthly press release, 6762–8

Retail prices set by manufacturers under fair-trade law by brand and product, with manufacturers, market concentration, and sales, by industry, selected years 1952-82, 9406–1.38

Vegetable and potato per capita weekly expenditures, by commodity, season, race, age, and region, 1977-78, article, 1561–11.401

Public Welfare and Social Security

Food purchases for domestic aid programs, by commodity, firm, and shipping point or destination, weekly rpt, 1302–3

Recreation and Leisure

Foreign market and trade for sporting goods and recreational equipment and vehicles, country market research rpts, 2045–14

Science and Technology

China export licenses from US for computers and other equipment with nuclear weapons applications, July 1981-June 1982, GAO rpt, 26123–76

Lab instruments foreign market and trade, and user industry operations and demand, country market research rpts, 2045–10

BY FEDERAL AGENCY

Banking, Finance, and Insurance

Fed Financing Bank holdings and transactions, monthly press release, 9322–1

Communications and Transportation

Chauffeur services of Fed Govt used by officials for commuting, driver overtime hours and pay by agency, 4th qtr 1982, GAO rpt, 26123–63

Hwy funding provisions of Fed Govt by agency and program, and State motor fuel tax provisions and vehicle registration fees, as of Jan 1984, biennial rpt, 7554–37

Motor vehicle fleet of Fed Govt, costs and operating data by agency, FY83, annual rpt, 9454–9

Radio frequency assignments for Federal agency use, 2nd half 1983, semiannual rpt, 2802–1

Shipping costs and foreign cargo shipments of Fed Govt by agency or program and route, and employment and economic impacts of US vessel preference, 1980, GAO rpt, 26117–30

Waterborne cargo sponsored by Fed Govt, total and US-flag share by agency and program, 1982, annual rpt, 7704–14.3

Education

Fed Govt funding for education, by agency, program, and State, selected years FY79-85, annual rpt, 4824–2.22

Vocational Education Research Natl Center funding, by purpose and source, selected years 1978-84, GAO rpt, 26121–79

Energy Resources and Demand

Energy use and efficiency of Fed Govt, by agency and fuel type, FY83, annual rpt, 3304–22

Energy use by Fed Govt, by agency and fuel type, FY75-83, annual rpt, 3164–74.1

Motor vehicle fleet of Fed Govt, auto and light truck fuel use by agency, FY77-83, hearing, 21368–49

Geography and Climate

Meteorological services and research of Fed Govt, programs and funding by agency, FY84-85, annual rpt, 2144–2

Weather-related disaster programs of Fed Govt, costs by agency, monthly rpt, annual data, 2152–12

Government and Defense

Advisory committees of Fed Govt, and members, staff, meetings, and costs, by agency, FY83, annual rpt, 9454–18

Audit activities, funding, and staff of Fed Govt agencies without inspectors general, by agency, FY83, GAO rpt, 26111–23

Audits of Fed Govt agencies and resolution of questioned costs, by selected agency, FY81-83, GAO rpt, 26111–24

Budget authority rescissions and deferrals, monthly rpt, 102–2

Budget of US Appendix, detailed budgets and personnel summaries, by agency, FY85, annual rpt, 104–3

BY FEDERAL AGENCY

Index by Categories

Budget of US, appropriations, outlays, balances, and budget receipts, by govtl branch and agency, FY83, annual rpt, 8104–2

Budget of US, authority balances in FY85 budget, by agency, FY83-85, annual rpt, 104–8

Budget of US, brief overview, FY85, annual rpt, 104–6

Budget of US, CBO analysis of revenue and spending alternatives and projections of economic indicators, FY85-89, annual rpt, 26304–3

Budget of US, compact budgets by function, agency, and account, FY85 with projections to FY89, annual rpt, 104–2

Budget of US, effects of Reagan Admin policy changes, by detailed program, FY85, annual rpt, 104–21

Budget of US, object class analysis of obligations, by branch of Fed Govt and selected depts and agencies, FY85 estimates, annual rpt, 104–9

Budget of US, receipts by source and outlays by agency and program, monthly rpt, 8102–3

Budget of US, receipts by source and outlays by function, FY40-89 estimates revised for consistency with FY85 budget definitions, annual rpt, 104–12

Budget of US, receipts, outlays, and budget authority, by function and agency, FY84-89 revised estimates, midsession review of FY85 budget, annual rpt, 104–7

Budget of US, receipts, outlays, and budget authority, by function and agency, 1st revision of FY85 budget, annual rpt, 104–17

Budget of US, special analyses of economic and social impact, FY85, annual rpt, 104–1

Civil rights enforcement offices funding and staff, for 6 Federal agencies, FY80-84, 11048–179

Collective bargaining agreements of Federal employees, unions involved, and employees covered, by agency for agreements expiring July 1984-June 1985, annual listing, 9847–1

Collective bargaining multi-unit agreements of Federal employees, by labor union and agency, as of July 1983, annual listing, 9847–4

Cost control proposals for Fed Govt programs and mgmt, CBO and GAO estimates of savings by function and agency, FY85-89, 26308–45

Cost control proposals for Fed Govt programs and mgmt, 3-year savings by function and agency, and financial and operating data, 1960s-81, 16908–1

Currency (foreign) holdings of US, detailed transactions and balances by program and country, 1st half FY84, semiannual rpt, 8102–7

DOD supply inventory mgmt of for agencies, NATO, and foreign govts, 1970s-83, annual rpt, 21204–1

Employee appeals of personnel actions, decisions of Merit Systems Protection Board, by region, agency, and employee characteristics, FY82, annual rpt, 9494–2

Employment (civilian) of Fed Govt, by location, agency, and pay system, 1982, biennial rpt, 9844–8

Employment and payroll (civilian) of Fed Govt, by agency in DC metro area, total US, and abroad, monthly rpt, 9842–1

Executive employee dev programs of Fed Govt, employee and candidate attitudes in 5 agencies, 1983 survey, GAO rpt, 26119–69

Expenditures of Fed Govt in States and local areas, Census Bur data collection, limitation, contributing agency costs, and opinions of congressional users, 1984 GAO rpt, 26111–20

Fed Govt aid to State and local govts, expenditures, and direct payments, by program, agency, and State, FY83, annual rpt, 2464–2

Financial consolidated statements of Fed Govt based on business accounting methods, FY82-83, annual rpt, 8104–5

Financial operations of Fed Govt, detailed data, *Treasury Bulletin,* quarterly rpt, 8002–4

GAO activities and operations, and resulting Fed Govt cost savings, FY83, annual rpt, 26104–1

GAO evaluations of Federal programs, 1984 listing, 26106–5.1

GAO publications issued, 2nd half 1983, semiannual listing, 26102–1

Info security clearances of Fed Govt and contractor employees, polygraph use, and prepublication reviews, by agency, 1979-83, GAO rpt, 26123–66

Info Security Oversight Office monitoring of Fed Govt classified info security measures and classification actions, FY83, annual rpt, 9454–21

Inspectors General investigations and audits of Fed Govt agencies fraud and abuse, by agency, 1st half FY84, semiannual rpt, 102–5

Intl exchange and training programs of Fed Govt, participants by world region, and funding, by agency, FY83, annual rpt, 9854–8

Investigations of Fed Govt civil agencies operations, summaries of GAO rpts published 1975-83, annual rpt, 26104–5

Labor unions recognized in Fed Govt, agreements and membership by agency and office or installation, Jan 1983, annual listing, 9844–14

Labor unions recognized in Fed Govt, membership by agency and union, as of Jan 1983, annual rpt, 9844–17

Liabilities and other financial commitments, by Federal agency, as of Sept 1983, annual rpt, 8104–3

Loans and loan guarantees of Fed Govt issued and outstanding, by agency, off-budget entity, or program, FY82, article, 9391–1.403

Minority group and handicapped employment of Fed Govt, by race, Hispanic origin, disability, sex, and employment characteristics, as of Sept 1982, biennial rpt, 9844–27

Minority group and women civilian employment of Fed Govt, by grade and agency, 1980 and 1983, 21348–41

Paperwork Reduction Act effects on Fed Govt info collection requirements and respondent burden, by agency, FY80-84, annual rpt, 104–19

Paperwork requirements of Fed Govt, small business perceived burden, and burden for 4 Fed Govt agencies, FY83, 9768–14

Polygraph lie detection test accuracy, and Fed Govt use by agency, selected years 1947-83, 26358–96

Procurement contract awards of Fed Govt, by State, agency, procurement and contractor type, and for top 100 contractors, quarterly rpt, 102–6

Property (real) of Fed Govt, inventory and costs, worldwide summary by location, agency, and use, 1983, annual rpt, 9454–5

Property (real) of Fed Govt, leased property inventory and rental costs, worldwide summary by location and agency, Sept 1983, annual rpt, 9454–10

Saudi Arabia-US Joint Commission on Economic Cooperation project activities and costs, and related contract awards by Fed Govt agency, as of 1983, GAO rpt, 26123–80

Senior Executive Service of Fed Govt, employee admin, and program status and effectiveness, by agency and by executive and job characteristics, July 1979-Sept 1983, GAO rpt, 26119–51

Small business and minority- and women-owned businesses Federal contracts, by agency, FY81-82, annual rpt, 9764–6.4, 9764–6.5

Health and Vital Statistics

Diabetes programs and expenditures of Fed Govt, by agency and NIH inst, FY84, annual rpt, 4434–8

Digestive Diseases Interagency Coordinating Committee activities, and related Federal research and funding, by agency, FY79-83, annual rpt, 4434–13

Drug abuse and trafficking reduction plan of Fed Govt, funding by agency and background data on drug use by substance, selected years FY81-85, biennial rpt, 024–1

Health care expenditures by type and source, and govt aid to health R&D by level of govt and Federal agency, 1970s-83, annual compilation, 4144–11.5

Occupational injuries, deaths, and illnesses, by agency, 1982, annual rpt, 6604–1

Housing and Construction

Building access for handicapped persons to Fed Govt or federally funded facilities, compliance activities and complaints by agency, FY83, annual rpt, 17614–1

Construction mgmt of Fed Govt, cost control proposals 3-year savings by project and agency, and financial and operating data, 1960s-81, 16908–1.22

Public building construction, acquisition, and alteration proposals, costs and tenure by city and project, as of 1983, hearings, 25328–23

Industry and Commerce

Industrial dev Fed Govt funding by type, program, and agency, and State govt policies and support, selected years FY75-85, 26306–6.81

Manufacturers under Fed Govt contract and owned by DOD, operating data by agency, selected SIC 2- to 4-digit industry, State, and SMSA, 1982, annual Current Industrial Rpt, 2506–3.4

Minority business Fed Govt funding, procurement, and subsidies, and deposits in minority-owned banks, by agency, FY69-83, annual rpt, 2104–5

Index by Categories

BY FEDERAL AGENCY

Labor and Employment

Employment and wages of workers covered by State unemployment insurance laws and Fed Govt unemployment compensation, by industry div and State, 1981, annual rpt, 6744–16

Fed Labor Relations Authority and Fed Service Impasses Panel activities, and cases by region, union, and agency, FY79-82, annual rpt, 13364–1

Public service job creation program of Fed Govt for unemployed, funding by agency, as of June 1983, GAO rpt, 26115–51

Law Enforcement

Assaults, murders, and other deaths of law enforcement officers, by circumstances, level of govt, agency, victim and offender characteristics, and location, 1983, annual rpt, 6224–3

Civil case processing of US Attorneys and amounts involved, by agency, FY83, annual rpt, 6004–2.5

Drug abuse and trafficking reduction plan of Fed Govt, funding by agency and background data on drug use by substance, selected years FY81-85, biennial rpt, 024–1

Drug enforcement regional task force program investigation activities, funding, and personnel, with nationwide drug abuse data, 1983 annual rpt, 6004–17

Juvenile delinquency prevention, Fed Govt programs funding by Federal agency and block grant, FY82, annual rpt, 6064–11

Natural Resources, Environment, and Pollution

Acid Precipitation Natl Assessment Program activities, and funding by Federal agency, 1983, annual rpt, 14354–1

Environmental quality and protection programs, costs, and Fed Govt enforcement, 1983, detailed annual rpt, 484–1

Fish and eggs for stocking distributed from natl hatcheries, by species, hatchery, and jurisdiction, FY83, annual rpt, 5504–10

Forests (tropical) conservation, mgmt role of public and private US, foreign, and intl groups, 1983 rpt, 26358–101.3

Geological Survey reimbursable program funds from other Federal agencies, by program and agency, FY78-83, annual rpt, 5664–8

Hazardous waste sites and activities of Fed Govt civil agencies, and EPA data mgmt, by waste location, 1984, GAO rpt, 26113–139

Land federally owned, by agency and State, FY83, annual rpt, 5724–1.1

Sedimentation control, surveillance, and research activity of Fed Govt, by project, agency, region, and State, 1982, annual rpt, 5664–9

Western US Fed Govt lands by agency and mining restriction status, and energy resources on potential wilderness areas and other lands, 1970s-81 and projected to 1990, 3308–68

Public Welfare and Social Security

Benefits and beneficiaries with representative payees by Fed Govt cash benefit program, and OASDI and SSI fraud and misuse, various periods FY74-81, GAO rpt, 26121–85

Budget of US, loans and loan guarantees, and Admin proposed limits on credit assistance, by program, FY83-89, annual rpt, 26306–3.65

Cost control proposals for Fed Govt programs and mgmt, 3-year savings by function and agency, and financial and operating data, 1960s-81, 16908–1.23

Fed Govt aid to State and local govts, expenditures, and direct payments, by program, agency, and State, FY83, annual rpt, 2464–2

Fed Govt financial and nonfinancial domestic aid, 1984 annual comprehensive catalog, 104–5

Older persons discrimination in Fed Govt aid programs, Age Discrimination Act enforcement by 28 agencies, FY83, annual rpt, 4004–27

Older persons programs, funding and participation by agency, FY83 with trends from FY79, annual rpt, 25144–3.2

Recreation and Leisure

Recreation fees and collection costs, visitors, and capacity of outdoor Fed Govt, State, and private facilities, by managing agency and State, 1983, annual rpt, 5544–14

Science and Technology

Acid rain causes and effects, air pollutant emissions by source in US and selected countries, control costs, and Fed Govt research funding, 1960s-82, 3408–27

Biotechnology commercial uses, R&D funding and output, controls, and industry financial and operating data, for US and 5 countries, 1970s-83 and estimated 1984-85, 26358–98

Computer data files available from NTIS, by subject, 1984 annual listing, 2224–3

Computer data files of NTIS, by agency, periodic listing, 2222–1

Computer software and documentation available from NTIS, by agency and program characteristics, 1984 annual listing, 2224–2

Computer specialists sociodemographic, educational, and employment characteristics, and Fed Govt support by agency, 1978, biennial Current Population Rpt, 2546–2.124

Computer systems and equipment of Fed Govt, inventory by manufacturer, type, agency, and location, FY83, last issue of annual rpt, 9454–4

Computer systems, equipment, and use of Fed Govt, 3-year cost control proposal savings by agency, and financial and operating data, 1960s-81, 16908–1.21

Computers and telecommunications systems major acquisition plans and obligations of Fed Govt, by agency, FY84-89, annual listing, 104–20

DOD prime contract awards for R&D to educational and nonprofit instns and Federal agencies, by instn and location, FY83, annual listing, 3544–17

DOD procurement, prime contractors for R&D, top 500 and value of contracts, FY83, annual listing, 3544–4

Engineers sociodemographic, educational, and employment characteristics, and Federal support by agency, 1978, Current Population Rpt, 2546–2.121

Marine mammals research, Fed Govt funding by agency, topic, and performing instn, FY82, annual rpt, 14734–2

NASA-launched communications and other satellites, and USSR launches by type, 1957-83, annual rpt, 9504–6.1

NASA procurement contract awards to or through Fed Govt agencies, FY84, semiannual rpt, 9502–6

Oceanographic research cruise schedules and ship characteristics, by academic instn or Federal agency, 1984, annual rpt, 3804–6

Patents issued to Federal agencies, FY73-83, annual rpt, 2244–1.2

R&D and science-related Fed Govt funding to higher education and nonprofit instns, by field, instn, agency, and State, FY82, annual rpt, 9627–17

R&D expenditures of higher education instns, and science and engineering employment and grad students, by field, 1972-83, biennial rpt, 9627–24

R&D Fed Govt expenditures, by agency, performer, and field of science, FY75-84, annual rpt, 9624–18.2

R&D Fed Govt funding, by agency and performer, FY83-84, 9626–2.132

R&D Fed Govt funding, by function, agency, and program, selected years FY80-84 and proposed FY85, 26308–46

R&D Fed Govt funding for all performers, by field and supporting agency, selected years FY60-84, annual rpt, 9627–20

R&D Fed Govt labs required technology transfer to public and private sector, labs complying, funding, and requests, by agency, FY82, GAO rpt, 26113–141

R&D funding by industry, program, and Federal agency, and high-technology trade performance, selected years 1960-FY84, 26306–6.77

Robots for industrial use, R&D, training, and employment impacts, US with comparisons to foreign countries, 1980s with projections to 1992, 26358–105

Satellite Landsat system proposed transfer to private sector, uses and product sales by user type, and university programs and personnel by instn, 1973-85, 26358–100

Satellite systems (foreign and US) for civil observation, data product revenue, and proposed transfer of Fed Govt system to private sector, selected years 1978-FY84, 2148–47

Science Indicators, R&D expenditures, innovations, research, and higher education, with foreign comparisons, 1960s- 83, annual rpt, 9624–10

Space and aeronautics programs and budgets of Fed Govt by agency, and foreign programs, 1957-FY85, annual rpt, 9504–9

Space shuttle launch guests by type, and itemized Fed Govt costs by agency, Apr 1981-Nov 1983, GAO rpt, 26123–78

Statistical agencies of Fed Govt missions and appropriations, and effect of budget cuts on principal programs, FY80-84, GAO rpt, 26125–28

Statistical programs of Fed Govt, funding by subject and agency, FY74-85, annual rpt, 104–10

Veterans Affairs

Employment appointments and separations of disabled and nondisabled veterans, by agency, 2nd half FY82, semiannual rpt, 9842–3

Employment of disabled veterans in Fed Govt under noncompetitive temporary

BY FEDERAL AGENCY

hiring authority, by pay system, grade, and agency, 2nd half FY82, semiannual rpt, 9842–4

BY INCOME

Agriculture and Food

Census of Agriculture, 1982: farms, farmland, production and costs, and operator characteristics, preliminary State and county rpt series, 2330–1

Dairy products household expenditures, effects of income and other sociodemographic characteristics, modeling results, 1977/78, 1561–2.404

Farm finances, assets, liabilities, income, receipts by commodity and State, and expenses, 1980-83 and trends from 1910, annual rpt, 1544–16

Farm finances, production, expenses by type, and domestic economic impact, selected years 1972-82 and preliminary 1983-84, annual rpt, 1544–19

Farm operators by selected characteristics, cropland eroded by rainfall, and acreage by crop, by soil erosion class, 1977-78, 1588–83

Farm population, by employment and socioeconomic characteristics, 1983, annual rpt, 2544–1

Farm production expenditures, detailed items by farm sales size and region, 1983, annual rpt, 1614–3

Food consumption and nutrient intake by individuals, by food group, source, and socioeconomic characteristics, 1977-78 natl survey, final rpt series, 1356–4

Food expenditures for fruit, vegetable, and potato products related to changes in income and other household characteristics, 1977-78, 1548–236

Health insurance coverage of farmers, farm population, and managers, by insurance type and selected sociodemographic characteristics, 1976, 1598–191

Banking, Finance, and Insurance

Banking in-home services, consumer expected use and acceptable costs, 1983 survey, article, 9371–1.422

Debt (mortgage and consumer) and net worth, by householder characteristics and family income, 1983 survey, article, 9362–1.411

Financial services household use and preferred provider, by respondent age and income, 1982-84 surveys, article, 9371–1.417

Michigan bankruptcy filings, by filer type, moving history, income, creditor action, debt and asset type, credit status, exemptions claimed, and county, 1979-81, hearings, 21528–57.3

Communications and Transportation

Bus riders by age, income, and trip purpose, and impacts of regulatory reform on bus industry operations, finances, and services, 1970s-83, 14828–2.2

Transit system operations, tax burden related to ridership, fares, and govt funding, for selected States and cities, 1950s-82, reprint, 7888–59

Travel patterns, personal and household characteristics, auto use, and public transport availability, 1977 survey, series, 7556–6

Women's travel patterns, by employment and sociodemographic characteristics and type of child care used, 1980 survey, 7888–62

Education

Elementary and secondary enrollment, households with children enrolled by school control, householder characteristics, and region, Oct 1982, 4838–13

High school class of 1980: use of student aid and earnings to pay higher education costs, by instn type and family income, 1980-82, 4848–15

High school class of 1982: foreign language coursework, by language, course level, student and school characteristics, and location, 1984 rpt, 4828–17

High school classes of 1980 and 1982: educational and sociodemographic characteristics and expectations, natl longitudinal study, series, 4826–2

Higher education student aid sources, by selected school and student characteristics, 1967-83, annual rpt, 4804–5

Student aid Pell grants and recipients, by educational costs, family income, instnl type and control, and State, 1981/82, annual rpt, 4804–1

Energy Resources and Demand

Home heating costs of low-income households, natural gas price decontrol effects, aid programs, and gas supply/demand data, by income level and State, 1970s-95, hearing, 25148–26

Household energy use by socioeconomic characteristics, impact of energy price increases, selected years 1978-95, 3004–13.3

Household, housing, and fuel use characteristics, EIA survey series, 3166–7

Housing (low-income) energy aid of Fed Govt, by income, aid type, and State, FY83, annual rpt, 4744–3.13

TVA employment of minorities and women, by detailed occupation, pay level, and grade, FY83 and goals for FY84, annual rpt, 9804–17

Wood acquired and used for home heating, by household characteristics and wood sources, 1980/81, 1208–204

Government and Defense

Election campaign Fed Govt funding, reform and tax deduction proposals, and TV and political action committee influence, opinion surveys, various dates 1977-83, hearings, 21428–7.1

Fed Govt minority group and handicapped employment, by race, Hispanic origin, disability, sex, and employment characteristics, as of Sept 1982, biennial rpt, 9844–27

Income tax and social security tax burden of households and effect of indexing by income level, 1982, and Fed Govt revenues by source, FY60-89, press release, 8008–109

Income tax returns and filers, by income level, filing and tax payment status, and amount of tax owed or refund, selected years 1978-82, article, 8302–2.408

Income tax returns filed by type, for US, IRS regions, and service center cities, 1972-82 and projected 1983-90, annual rpt, 8304–9.1

Income tax returns filed by type of filer, selected income items, summary data, quarterly rpt, 8302–2.1

Index by Categories

Income tax returns of elderly, by income statement and tax item and income level, 1981 with trends from 1977, article, 8302–2.412

Income tax returns of individuals, by filing and deduction characteristics and income level, 1983, annual article, 8302–2.414

Income tax returns of individuals by tax return item, State, and occupation, and income by source and tax owed, by income level, selected years 1916-80, conf papers, 8308–28.1

Income tax returns of individuals, detailed data, 1982, annual rpt, 8304–2

Income tax returns of individuals, selected income, deduction, and tax credit data by income, preliminary 1982, annual article, 8302–2.402

Income tax returns with investment credits, for individuals by income, and for sole proprietorships by industry, 1981, article, 8302–2.409

Income tax returns with oil depletion allowances and royalty income, and aged exemption, 1980, hearing, 21788–132

Income taxes and rates, by type of filer, income, level of govt, and State, 1976-83, annual rpt, 10044–1.3

Tax burden for average family by income level and selected city, and tax rates by selected jurisdiction, by type of tax, 1982, 10046–8.2

Tax expenditures from employee benefit plans, for income and payroll tax by benefit type and income, with benefits by industry, 1950-83 and projected to 1988, article, 9373–1.404

Taxes, tax policy, and intergovtl relations, public opinion survey results, 1972-84, annual rpt, 10044–2

Health and Vital Statistics

Births by outcome, and mother's sociodemographic, life style, and maternity characteristics, 1980, article, 4102–1.422, 4102–1.424

Births, fertility rates, expected births, and childless women, by socioeconomic characteristics, June 1982, annual Current Population Rpt, 2546–1.386

Births, fertility rates, expected births, and childless women, by socioeconomic characteristics, June 1983, advance annual Current Population Rpt, 2546–1.385

Births, fertility rates, expected births, and childless women, by socioeconomic characteristics, June 1983, annual Current Population Rpt, 2546–1.393

Blood lead levels by sociodemographic and behavioral characteristics, and potential workplace exposure, 1976-80, 4147–11.201

Breast-fed infants, by race and mother's sociodemographic characteristics, 1983 with trends from 1970, article, 4102–1.455

Disability (work-related), incidence among men aged 22-64 related to sociodemographic and employment characteristics and to self-evaluated mental stress, 1972-74, 4746–5.43

Disabled women, by socioeconomic and demographic characteristics, and compared to nondisabled women and disabled men, 1981, chartbook, 16598–4

Health care expenditures, natl survey on services use, costs, and sources of payment, by patient and physician characteristics, 1977-78, series, 4186–3

Index by Categories

BY INCOME

Health care services of selected medical practitioners, use by patient characteristics, 1980 survey with trends from 1963, 4146–12.4

Health condition and health care resources, use, and expenditures, 1970s-82 with trends and projections 1900-2000, annual compilation, 4144–11

Health condition, hospitalization, disability, and medical costs, by demographic characteristics, Vital and Health Statistics series, 4147–10

Life expectancy increase impacts on OASDI and pension policy, with alternative sociodemographic projections to 2100, hearing, 25368–130

Mental health office and clinic visits, average charges, and total expenditures for services, by type of provider and patient characteristics, 1980, 4146–11.5

Nigeria native and Western health care use, by sociodemographic characteristics, 1984 article, 4102–1.417

Older persons health care total and out-of-pocket expenditures, by sociodemographic characteristics, poverty and health status, and degree of functional limitation, 1980, 4146–11.4

Pregnancy health counseling effect on smoking, diet, delivery costs, and birth weight, by sociodemographic characteristics and pregnancy history, 1983 article, 4102–1.401

Housing and Construction

Bond tax-exempt issues by purpose, and Fed Govt mortgage bond revenue losses and borrower characteristics, selected years 1971-85, hearings, 21788–135

Bond tax-exempt issues for home mortgage subsidy, Fed Govt costs, and loans, mortgage value, and borrowers by jurisdiction, by borrower income, Dec 1981-July 1982, GAO rpt, 26113–127

Census of Housing, 1980: inventory, occupancy, and unit characteristics, changes from 1973 by region and inside-outside SMSAs and central cities, series, 2473–3

Census of Housing, 1980: structural, financial, and householder characteristics, by region and State, 2475–4

Census of Population and Housing, 1980: detailed population and housing characteristics, by county, city, and census tract, State and SMSA rpt series, 2551–2

Home mortgages (graduated payment) FHA-insured, financial, property, and mortgagor characteristics, for US and selected States, quarterly rpt, 5142–41

Home mortgages (graduated payment) FHA-insured, financial, property, and mortgagor characteristics, US summary, quarterly rpt, 5142–40

Home mortgages FHA-insured, financial, property, and mortgagor characteristics, for US and selected localities, quarterly rpt, 5142–2

Home mortgages FHA-insured, financial, property, and mortgagor characteristics, quarterly rpt, 5142–1

Home mortgages FHA-insured, financial, property, and mortgagor characteristics, 1983, annual rpt, 5144–17

Home mortgages FHA-insured for low-cost homes, financial, construction, property, and mortgagor characteristics, quarterly rpt, 5142–4

Housing and financial characteristics, and unit and neighborhood quality, for 15 SMSAs, 1978, annual survey special supplement, 2485–8

Housing and households characteristics, and low-income housing construction and availability, 1970s-83, hearing, 21968–28.1

Housing and households detailed characteristics, and unit and neighborhood quality, by inside-outside central cities, 1979-82 surveys, SMSA rpt series, 2485–6

Housing occupancy and unit and household characteristics, by region and metro-nonmetro residence, 1983, biennial survey, 2485–1

Older persons rural housing condition, selected householder and housing characteristics with comparisons to urban and nonaged population, 1979, 1598–193

Quality of housing and neighborhoods, indicators and attitudes, and occupant characteristics, by urban-rural location and region, 1981, annual survey, 2485–7

Quality of housing and neighborhoods, indicators and attitudes, by occupant and unit characteristics, region, and metro-nonmetro location, 1981, annual survey, 2485–2.2

Rental housing, effects of Fed Govt tax policies on real estate investment, 1969-81, 5188–104

Industry and Commerce

Underground economy, household expenditures and participation by type of goods or service and sociodemographic characteristics, with methodology and bibl, 1981 survey, 8308–27

Labor and Employment

Employment and earnings, detailed data, monthly rpt, 6742–2.8

Employment, earnings, and hours, by SIC 4-digit nonfarm industry, monthly 1974-Feb 1984, annual update, 6744–4

Employment status of family members, by occupation, family composition, age of children, and other characteristics, 1983 and trends from 1940, 6746–1.253

Labor force characteristics and economic indicators, selected years 1880-1995, chartbook, 6728–30

NYC wages by occupation, for office and plant workers, 1983, annual rpt, 6926–1.75

Unemployment and part-time employment, by race, Hispanic origin, sex, family composition, income, and poverty status, 1980-82, annual report, 6744–15

Unemployment insurance system finances, claims, payments, and covered employment and wages, by State, 1938-82, 6408–5

Vocationally rehabilitated persons under State agency programs, by sociodemographic characteristics and disabling condition, FY79-81, annual rpt, 4944–6

Wages by occupation, and benefits for office and plant workers, annual labor market survey rpt series, 6785–3

Wages by occupation, and benefits for office and plant workers in 70 SMSAs, 1983, annual rpt, 6785–1

Wages by occupation, and benefits for office and plant workers, 1983, annual SMSA survey rpt series, 6785–12

Wages by occupation, and benefits for office and plant workers, 1984, annual SMSA survey rpt series, 6785–11

Wages by occupation, for office and plant workers in selected labor market areas, 1983 surveys, annual summary rpt, 6785–6

Wages, hours, benefits, and employment, by occupation and selected geographic areas, industry surveys series, 6787–6

Wages of white-collar workers, by occupation, work level, and industry div, Mar 1984, annual rpt, 6784–2

Women's employment and earnings, by labor force and socioeconomic characteristics, and compared to men, 1978-81 and trends from 1940s, 6568–29

Law Enforcement

Bank robbery court cases by case processing, sentencing, and offender characteristics, and compared to other Fed Govt felony cases, 1979-80, periodic rpt, 6062–2.407

Crime and criminal justice data, including justice expenditures and employment by level of govt, 1970s-82 with some trends from 1875, 6068–174

Crime victim medical expenses and property loss, and median loss by victim characteristics, by offense type, 1975-81, 6066–19.6

Crime victimization of households, by offense type, race of household head, and family income and urban-rural residence, 1975-83, periodic rpt, 6062–2.404

Crime victimization rates by type of offense, and victim and offense characteristics, Natl Crime Survey series, 6066–3

Crimes of violence involving relatives, by victim-offender relationship, circumstances, and victim characteristics, aggregate 1973-81, 6066–19.5

Drug defendants, by sociodemographic and case processing characteristics, with comparisons to Federal fraud and bank robbery defendants, 1979, 6062–2.403

Jail capacities, conditions, expenditures, and services, and socioeconomic and other characteristics of inmates, various dates 1976-82, 10048–59

Natural Resources, Environment, and Pollution

Forest land owner characteristics in Northeast States, owners and acreage, series, 1206–7

Youth Conservation Corps activities, costs, and participant characteristics, by sponsoring agency, 1982, annual rpt, 5304–12

Population

Census of Population and Housing, 1980: detailed population and housing characteristics, by county, city, and census tract, State and SMSA rpt series, 2551–2

Census of Population, 1980: detailed socioeconomic and demographic characteristics, by age, sex, race, Hispanic origin, occupation, and industry, State rpt series, 2531–4

Census of Population, 1980: detailed socioeconomic characteristics, by county, city, and inside-outside SMSAs and central cities, State rpt series, 2531–3

Coastal environmental characteristics, fish, wildlife, and use, and population socioeconomic data, for individual areas, series, 5506–4

Consumer Income, socioeconomic characteristics of persons, families, and households, detailed cross-tabulations, Current Population Rpt series, 2546–6

BY INCOME

County and City Data Book, detailed socioeconomic and demographic data for States, counties, and cities, selected years 1976-82, 2328–1

Homeless population and characteristics, and temporary shelter operations, use, and user characteristics, for selected cities, various periods 1979-84, hearing, 21248–85

Income (household) and cash and noncash transfer program participation, by sociodemographic characteristics, quarterly rpt, 2542–2

Income (household) before and after taxes, by socioeconomic characteristics, type of tax paid, and region, 1981, Current Population Rpt, 2546–2.118

Income (household) before and after taxes, by socioeconomic characteristics, type of tax paid, and region, 1982, annual Current Population Rpt, 2546–2.122

Income (household), home value and equity, and financial assets by type, by household characteristics, 1983 survey with trends from 1970, article, 9362–1.406

Mobility of population, detailed data by demographic and socioeconomic characteristics of movers and nonmovers, Mar 1981-82, annual Current Population Rpt, 2546–1.384

Older persons by demographic, socioeconomic, and health characteristics, selected years 1900-81 and projected to 2050, Current Population Rpt, 2546–2.125

Older persons income and income sources, by OASDI beneficiary and poverty status, labor force participation, and demographic characteristics, 1982, biennial rpt, 4744–26

Older persons income and income sources, including retirement benefits by plan type, by age and marital status, 1950s-82, conf proceedings, 25408–87

Older persons sociodemographic characteristics, and Fed Govt program participation and funding, 1983 with trends and projections 1900-2060, annual rpt, 25144–3.1

Poverty status of families and persons, by detailed socioeconomic characteristics, 1982, annual Current Population Rpt, 2546–6.40

Women in couples with wife as primary earner, socioeconomic and family characteristics, with comparative data for husbands, Mar 1982, 2326–11.9

Prices and Cost of Living

Foreign living costs, State Dept indexes, housing allowances, and hardship differential rates by country and major city, quarterly rpt, 6862–1

Public Welfare and Social Security

Farm households receiving social security income, farms and amount by characteristics of farm and operator, 1978-82, article, 1702–1.410

Food stamp recipient households size and composition, income, and income deductions allowed, Aug 1981, annual rpt, 1364–8

Income assistance, effects of experimental negative income tax program on employment, earnings, marital status, and other family characteristics in 2 cities, 1970-75, 4008–64

Medicare aged beneficiaries activity restriction, untreated health conditions, and

perceived health status, by sociodemographic characteristics, 1980, 4146–12.2

Medicare aged beneficiaries medical care by usual source, and untreated health conditions, by sociodemographic characteristics, 1980, 4146–12.3

Noncash public and employer-based transfer program recipients, by income source and socioeconomic characteristics, 1982, advance Current Population Rpt, 2546–6.38

Noncash public and employer-based transfer program recipients, by income source and socioeconomic characteristics, 1982, final Current Population Rpt, 2546–6.37

Nutrition services for elderly, program operations and assessment, and participant sociodemographic, health, and diet characteristics, 1976 and 1982, 4608–16

OASDHI, Medicaid, SSI, and other social insurance and public welfare programs benefits, beneficiary characteristics, and trust funds, selected years 1937-83, annual rpt, 4744–3

OASI beneficiaries by income level, and average income, by beneficiary characteristics and income source, before and after receipt of 1st benefit, 1969-77, article, 4742–1.418

OASI benefits, survivor family knowledge of provisions by educational attainment and income, with responses to each survey question, 1978, article, 4742–1.401

Older persons entitled to both Medicare and Medicaid, demographic characteristics, and health condition and services use, 1980, article, 4652–1.433

Poverty population size, effects of counting public noncash transfers as income by recipient characteristics, 1979-82, 2626–2.50

Rhode Island State health insurance claims and benefit-cost ratio by income and Medicare eligibility status, various periods 1975-79, article, 4652–1.423

Supplementary Security Income beneficiary socioeconomic characteristics and health service use, 1970s-83 and SSI program projections to 1995, 25148–29

Widows with minor children receiving OASI survivor benefits, health insurance coverage and health care services and expenses, 1976-78, article, 4742–1.404

Science and Technology

Computer specialists sociodemographic, educational, and employment characteristics, and Fed Govt support by agency, 1978, biennial Current Population Rpt, 2546–2.124

Engineers sociodemographic, educational, and employment characteristics, and Federal support by agency, 1978, Current Population Rpt, 2546–2.121

R&D-employed scientists and engineers salaries by degree, type of establishment, age, experience, and field, 1984, annual rpt, 3004–1

Salaries of scientists and engineers in R&D at DOE labs and non-DOE facilities, Aug 1982-Feb 1984, annual rpt, 3004–9

Veterans Affairs

Fed Govt appointments and separations of disabled and nondisabled veterans, by agency, 2nd half FY82, semiannual rpt, 9842–3

Index by Categories

Fed Govt noncompetitive temporary hiring of disabled veterans, by pay system, grade, and agency, 2nd half FY82, semiannual rpt, 9842–4

Health condition of veterans and nonveterans, and veteran use of VA and non-VA hospitals by disease, by age, race, income, and metro-nonmetro location, various periods 1971-81, 9926–1.18

Income and educational attainment of veterans compared to nonveterans, by age, 1982-83, annual rpt, 9924–19

Income and employment status of veterans, by age and war or peacetime service, with comparisons to nonveterans, 1981, annual rpt, 9924–23

Older veterans aged 55 and over, socioeconomic characteristics, economic resources, health care and status, and actual and expected VA benefits use, 1983 survey, 9928–29

Vietnam era veterans, educational attainment and personal and family income, 1975-81, annual rpt, 9924–8.3

BY INDIVIDUAL COMPANY OR INSTITUTION

Agriculture and Food

Agricultural research expenditures and scientist years, by topic, commodity, and performing organization, FY82, annual rpt, 1744–2

Animal drug approval of govts, months to approval in US and 2 countries by drug brand and manufacturer, selected years 1965-83, hearing, 25528–98

Argentina grain production, exports by firm, storage by facility type and port, and shipments to ports by mode of transport, by grain type, selected years 1954-81, 1528–185

Cooperative sales volume and ranking, for 9 cooperatives on *Fortune* Service 100 list, 1983-84, article, 1122–1.406

Cooperative sales volume and ranking, for 10 cooperatives on *Fortune* 500 list, 1981-83, article, 1122–1.405

Fish and eggs for stocking distributed from natl hatcheries, by species, hatchery, and jurisdiction, FY83, annual rpt, 5504–10

Fish hatchery production, deliveries, and operating costs, and fishery assistance, by region, hatchery, and Fed Govt assistance station, FY82, annual rpt, 5504–9

Fishery resources mgmt and R&D, Fed Govt grants by project and resulting publications, 1983, annual listing, 2164–3

Food retailers after-tax profits, aggregate and for 13 supermarket chains, 1983, annual rpt, 1544–9.2

Grain handling facility explosions, injuries, deaths, and cause, by company, FY83, annual rpt, 1294–1

Honey processing contracts of CCC, by contractor, weekly rpt, monthly tables, 1311–2

Livestock, meat, and wool, market news summary statistics by animal type and market, weekly rpt, 1315–1

Meat plants inspected and certified for exporting products to US, by country, 1983, annual listing, 1374–2

Pesticide manufacturers listing, 1982, annual rpt, 1804–5

Index by Categories

BY INDIVIDUAL COMPANY OR INSTITUTION

PL 480 exports by commodity, and recipients, by program, sponsor, and country, FY82 and aggregate from FY55, annual rpt, 1924–7

Banking, Finance, and Insurance

Automated teller machines and point of sale debit card systems offered by retailers, by firm, firm type, and State, 1984 survey, article, 9371–1.421

Automated teller machines shared networks by State, and membership and characteristics of top 16 regional and natl networks, Nov 1983, article, 9373–1.403

Bank deposits in commercial and mutual savings banks and in US branches of foreign banks, by account type, instn, State, SMSA, and county, June 1983, annual rpt, 9295–3

Bank holding company income, actual and in event of Argentina nonpayment of debt interest, for 7 US multinatls, 1st qtr 1984, 9368–77

Bank holding company interstate service applications, and New England acquisitions and mergers effect on assets, by firm, Dec 1974-Sept 1983, article, 9373–1.409

Bank interstate offices by type, and electronic funds transfer networks, for Fed Reserve 7th District by State of origin and coverage, 1981-83, article, 9375–1.403

Bank interstate service offices, including S&Ls, bank branches, and nonbank subsidiaries offering financial services, by instn and State, 1981-83, 9371–13

Bank merger proposals receiving adverse Justice Dept appraisals, bank deposits, market shares and ratios, and merger disposition, June 1982-Dec 1983, article, 9375–1.404

Bank mergers and consolidations approved by Fed Reserve Board of Governors during 1983, annual rpt, 9364–1.2

Bank mergers approved and denied by FDIC, and resources, deposits, and offices of merged banks, 1982, annual rpt, 9294–1.1

Bankruptcy filings with SEC participation, by firm, FY83, annual rpt, 9734–2.7

Banks (natl) domestic and intl operations, charters, mergers, and liquidations, by State and instn, and Comptroller of Currency activities, quarterly rpt, 8402–3

Banks requiring FDIC disbursement, depositors, deposits, and disbursements, by location and disbursement reason, 1983 with trends from 1934, annual rpt, 9294–1.2

Brokered certificates of deposit in acquired and closed individual banks and S&Ls, and disposition of instns, 1982-Oct 1983, hearing, 21248–83

Corporate Eurobonds issued by US firms and their finance subsidiaries, value and average yields and rates by firm, various periods 1975-82, hearings, 21408–71

Credit union membership, shares and loans, and asset size, for Federal and federally insured State unions by State, 1984 annual listing, 9534–6

Credit Union Natl Admin insurance fund financial activity, and insured instns financial and operating data, FY83, annual rpt with semiannual update for 1st qtr FY84, 9534–7

Eurodollar bond market issues of US corporations, and amount raised and savings relative to domestic market, by company, 1975-82, hearing, 25368–132

Eximbank credits for energy-related products and services, by country and firm, 1982, annual rpt, 9254–3

Eximbank financial condition, and loan, credit, and insurance authorizations, by country, FY83, annual rpt, 9254–1

Fed Financing Bank holdings and transactions, monthly press release, 9322–1

Fed Home Loan Bank System members, with assets of S&Ls, by instn, city, and State, 1983, annual listing, 9314–5

Financial instns income taxes, effective rates, and selected financial data, by instn type and firm, with comparisons to other industries, selected years 1960-82, hearing, 25368–129

Financial services of nonbank firms and bank holding companies, with financial and operating data by firm, 1981-82 with trends from 1962, technical paper, 9375–11.3

Futures trading by commodity and exchange, and Commodity Futures Trading Commission activities, funding, and employment, FY83, annual rpt, 11924–2

Intl financial instns funds by source and disbursements by purpose, by country, with US policy review, FY83, annual rpt, 15344–1

Investment companies classification, assets, and location, Sept 1982, annual directory, 9734–1

New England States, FHLB 1st District member savings instns, locations, and financial condition, 1984, annual listing, 9304–26

North Central States, FHLB 8th District member S&Ls, locations, assets, and savings, 1984, annual listing, 9304–9

Overseas Private Investment Corp programs and finances, with list of insured projects and companies, FY83, annual rpt, 9904–2

Securities brokerage services and finances of brokerage firms and New England banks and thrifts, and brokerage acquisitions by firm, selected years 1977-84, article, 9373–1.417

Securities purchases, sales, and holdings, by issuer and type and ownership of security, monthly listing, 9732–2

Small Business Investment Companies finances, funding, licensing, and loan activity, 2nd half FY84, semiannual rpt, 9762–3

Stock exchange trading volume, securities listed by type, and exchange finances, by exchange, selected years 1935-82, annual rpt, 9734–2.1, 9734–2.2

Stock market transactions volume and proceeds and new issue registrations, for US registered exchanges, SEC monthly rpt, 9732–1

Surety companies authorized to post bonds with Fed Govt, location and bonding limits, as of July 1984, annual listing, 8104–4

Trust assets by type of asset and fund, for 500 largest banks, 1983, annual rpt, 13004–1

Western States, FHLB 10th District member S&Ls, locations, assets, and savings, 1984, annual listing, 9304–17

Western States, FHLB 11th District member S&L offices, locations, savings balances, and accounts, quarterly listing, 9302–20

Communications and Transportation

Air passenger and shipper complaints to CAB, by US and foreign air carrier and type of complaint, monthly rpt, 9142–20

Air passenger traffic, and aircraft operations by type, by airport, region, and State, projected FY82-95 and trends from FY76, annual rpt, 7504–7

Air passengers denied confirmed space on commercial flights, by carrier, monthly rpt, 9142–23

Air traffic control facilities of FAA, operations and services by service type, aviation category, and facility, 1974-83, annual rpt, 7504–1.2

Air traffic levels at FAA-operated control facilities, by airport and State, FY83, annual rpt, 7504–27

Aircraft (general aviation), hours flown, and equipment, by type, use, and model of aircraft, region, and State, 1982, annual rpt, 7504–29

Aircraft accidents and deaths for airlines and general aviation, 1983, preliminary annual rpt, 9614–9

Aircraft handled by instrument flight rule, by user type, FAA traffic control center, and region, FY69-83 and forecast to FY95, annual rpt, 7504–15

Aircraft in civil air carrier fleet, by carrier, make, and model, 1983, annual rpt, 7504–1.5

Aircraft registered with FAA, by type and characteristics of aircraft, carrier, make, State, and county, 1983, annual rpt, 7504–3

Airline and general aviation accident circumstances, severity, and causes, for US operations of domestic and foreign aircraft, periodic rpt, 9612–1

Airline deregulation in 1978, effect on industry operations and finances, air traffic patterns, and CAB programs, various periods FY76-84, 9148–56

Airline deregulation in 1978, traffic and service changes by city, with market shares, fares, and load factors, quarterly rpt, 9142–42

Airline financial and operating data for certificated, charter, and cargo carriers, quarterly rpt, 9142–30

Airline financial data, by carrier, carrier group, and for total certificated system, quarterly rpt, 9142–12

Airline flight and engine hours, and shutdown rates, by aircraft and engine model for each air carrier, monthly rpt, 7502–13

Airline income and profitability, by major carrier, 1972-83, annual rpt, 9144–37

Airline income taxes paid, net income, and effective tax rates, by major carrier, 1968-83, annual rpt, 9144–34

Airline indebtedness by type of holder, and debt shares of major holders, by carrier, as of Dec 1982, annual rpt, 9144–1.4

Airline intl operations, traffic and financial data for US combination carriers in Atlantic, Pacific, and Latin America regions, quarterly rpt, 9142–41

Airline operating unit costs for each system major and short-haul natl carrier, quarterly rpt, 9142–37

Airline operations and passenger, cargo, and mail traffic, by type of service, air carrier, State, and country, 1974-83, annual rpt, 7504–1.4, 7504–1.6

BY INDIVIDUAL COMPANY OR INSTITUTION

Index by Categories

Airline passenger and cargo traffic, and departures by aircraft type, by airline and US and foreign airport, 1982, annual rpt, 7504–35

Airline passenger traffic, capacity, yields, and load factors, changes for each system major and short-haul natl carrier, periodic rpt, 9142–45

Airline passenger traffic since 1978 deregulation, by major carrier, quarterly rpt, 9142–49

Airline pilots medically disqualified for service, by airline, disease, affected body site, and age, 1978-80, 7506–10.23

Airline pilots terminated for medical reasons and reinstated by carrier, and aircraft accidents by age of flight crew, selected years 1960-81, hearing, 21148–34

Airline profit margins, for major operators of large aircraft by carrier group and carrier, quarterly rpt, 9142–43

Airline subsidies of Fed Govt paid since 1979 to air carriers serving small communities, by carrier, monthly rpt, 9142–48

Airline traffic and financial data, by carrier, FY83 with trends from FY73, annual rpt, 9144–1

Airline traffic, capacity, and performance, by carrier and type of operation, monthly rpt, 9142–13

Airline traffic, capacity, and performance for medium regionals, by carrier and certification status, quarterly rpt, 9142–44

Airport improvement program grants and activities, by State and airport, FY83, annual rpt, 7504–38

Airport planning and dev project grants of Fed Govt, by sponsor, airport, and location, periodic press release series, 7506–8

Airport size and safety, and accidents at or near airports by circumstance, for total and selected airports, various periods 1964-81, 9618–12

Auto and light truck safety, crash test results of selected new domestic and foreign models for model year to date, press release series, 7766–7

Bridges over navigable waters, with type of bridge and use, owner, dimensions, and location, 1984 regional listing series, 7406–5

Bus industry collective ratemaking and regulatory reform impacts on operations, finances, and services to older persons and rural areas by State, 1970s-83, 14828–2

Coast Guard search and rescue activities, by district, station, and rescue vessel, FY83 and projected FY88, annual rpt, 7404–2

Communications satellite intl systems charges, operations, investment shares by country, and competition impacts, 1964-83 with projections to 2003, hearings, 25388–46

Hwy toll facilities of State and local govts, receipts and disbursements by facility, 1983, annual rpt, 7554–1.4

Intermodal containers and equipment owned by US shipping and leasing companies, inventory by type and size, 1983, annual rpt, 7704–10

Maritime Commission mgmt and enforcement activities, filings by type and disposition, and civil penalties by shipper, FY83, annual rpt, 9334–1

Motor carrier passengers and selected revenue data, for individual large Class I motor carriers, quarterly rpt, 9482–13

Motor carriers (Class I) of household goods operating revenues, net income, and revenue tons, by firm, quarterly rpt, 9482–14

Motor carriers (Class I) of property financial and operating data, by region and firm, quarterly rpt, 9482–5

Motor vehicle safety research and funding of Natl Hwy Traffic Safety Admin and Federal Hwy Admin, 1981, annual rpt, 7764–1

Motorcycle operating costs by component, for 5 makes, and Fed Govt mileage reimbursement rates, 1983, annual rpt, 9454–13.3

Port dev costs and financing through user fees, and shipping industry impact on local economy, by State, other area, industry, commodity, and port, 1970s-2020, hearings, 21568–34

Radio broadcasts of marine weather for US ships, by radio station and major ocean area, as of Jan 1984, biennial rpt, 2184–3

Rail line storage capacity of grain cooperatives, by rail line abandonment status, railroad, and region, FY80, 1128–28

Railroad accidents, circumstances, severity, and railroad involved, quarterly rpt, 9612–3

Railroad accidents investigated by Fed Railroad Admin, casualties, damage, and circumstances, 1982, annual rpt, 7604–3

Railroad commuter systems financial and operating data for 7 systems, and public agency cost reimbursement, 1980, 7888–61

Railroad finances and operations, detailed data by firm, class of service, and district, 1983, annual rpt, 9486–6.1

Railroad finances, operations, and freight rates and shares, by commodity and railroad, 1970s-82, hearings, 25268–80

Railroad-hwy grade crossing accidents, detailed data by State and railroad, 1982, annual rpt, 7604–2

Railroad retiree annuities in current-payment status and awarded, by last railroad employer, 1982, annual rpt, 9704–2.2

Railroad revenue, income, freight, and rate of return, by Class I freight railroad and district, quarterly rpt, 9482–2

Ship weather reports, and gale and wave observations of US and foreign ships, quarterly journal, 2152–8

Shipbuilding and operating subsidies of MarAd, by vessel type and firm, FY83, annual rpt, 7704–14.1, 7704–14.2

Shipbuilding and repair facilities, construction capability, number and value of ships under construction, and employment, by shipyard, 1983, annual rpt, 7704–9

Shipbuilding deliveries, contracts, and Merchant Marine Act awards, and wage rates at Navy shipyards, 1971-81, annual rpt, 7704–12

Ships in active US merchant fleet and Natl Defense Reserve Fleet, number and tonnage by name and owner/operator, Jan 1984, semiannual inventory, 7702–2

Ships in US merchant fleet, shipping costs, construction, employment, military

availability, and Fed Govt subsidies, 1970s-1984 and projected to 2000, 26306–6.83

Ships in world bulk carrier fleet, characteristics by country of registry, 1982, annual rpt, 7704–13

Ships in world merchant fleet, by selected characteristics and country of registry, as of Jan 1983, annual rpt, 7704–1

Ships in world tanker fleet, by selected characteristics and country of registry, 1982, annual rpt, 7704–17

Subway accidents, deaths, injuries, and property damage, by type of accident and victim and cause, for 11 systems, 1983, annual rpt, 7884–5

Telegraph carriers financial and operating data, for 7 firms, quarterly rpt, 9282–1

Telephone and telegraph firms detailed financial, operating, and employment statistics, 1982, annual rpt, 9284–6

Telephone companies borrowing under rural telephone loan program, and financial and operating data, 1983, annual rpt, 1244–2

Telephone operating and financial data by company type, with fixed cost recovery from interstate revenue by Bell company and State, 1981-82 with trends from 1945, 26306–6.79

Transit services for commuting and other purposes, dev and effects, series, 7306–9

Transit system (automated guideway) characteristics and itemized costs, for 16 systems in operation or under construction, 1982, annual rpt, 7884–6

Transit system financial and operating data, by mode, function, fleet size, and individual system, FY82, annual rpt, 7884–4

Transit system mgmt training funded by Urban Mass Transportation Admin, participant characteristics and career impact, 1970-79, 7888–60

TV and radio station employment, total and for minorities and women, by full- and part-time status and individual station, 1983, annual rpt, 9284–7

TV channels allocation and licensing status, for commercial and noncommercial UHF and VHF TV by market and community, as of Dec 1983, semiannual rpt, 9282–6

Urban Mass Transportation Admin grants to higher education instns for research and training, by project, FY84, annual rpt, 7884–7

Washington State telephone rates including govt long-distance access charges, by company, 1983-89, hearing, 21148–32

Waterborne commerce of US (domestic and foreign), freight by commodity, traffic, and passengers, by port and waterway, 1982, annual rpt, 3754–3

Education

Census of Govts, 1982: school districts revenues, expenditures, debt, and assets, by district and State, 2457–1

Digest of Education Statistics, detailed data on students, staff, finances, and facilities, 1982 and selected trends, annual rpt, 4824–2

Education Dept financial aid programs for educational instns and individuals, 1984 annual listing, 4804–3

Education Natl Inst activities and education research grants awarded by recipient, and Education Dept expenditures by function, FY81-82, annual rpt, 4914–4

Index by Categories

BY INDIVIDUAL COMPANY OR INSTITUTION

Endowment funds of 100 higher education instns with largest amounts, FY81, annual rpt, 4824–2.20

Handicapped children early education research and service project activities and characteristics, and grants to States for program dev, 1983-84, annual listing, 4804–30

Higher education desegregation, Louisiana black instn funding, and Virginia students needed to meet desegregation goals, by instn, late 1970s-85, hearings, 21348–91

Higher education enrollment, by student characteristics, instn type, State, and for 150 instns, fall 1982, annual rpt, 4844–2

Higher education instns, by type, location, and other characteristics, 1983/84 annual listing, 4844–3

Higher education instns, type, location, enrollment, and student charges, by State and congressional district, 1983/84, biennial listing, 4844–11

Impacted area schools, Fed Govt funding by school and congressional district and State, FY83, annual rpt, 4804–10

Japan-US Friendship Commission educational and cultural exchange activities, grants, and trust fund status, FY83, annual rpt, 14694–1

Kentucky Higher Education Student Loan Corp student loans, loan purchases and defaults by instn, and revenue bonds status, various dates 1979-84, hearing, 21348–92

Libraries, depository for Fed Govt publications, 1983 annual listing, 2214–1

Libraries selected characteristics, for largest public, 1974 and 1978, and for 50 largest higher education, 1981/82, annual rpt, 4824–2.25

Library (research) funding of Education Dept, by project, program area, instn, and State, FY84, annual listing, 4804–22

Mentally retarded and developmentally disabled treatment and services, university-affiliated facility funding, activities, and clients, 1980-FY83, 4608–19

Microfiche from Educational Resources Info Center, holdings of US and foreign educational and other instns, as of 1983, listing, 4918–14

Natl Endowment for Arts activities and grants, FY83, annual rpt, 9564–3

Natl Endowment for Humanities activities and grants, FY83, annual rpt, 9564–2

Puerto Rico educational enrollment, finance, completions, curricula, and personnel by instn, and health and vital statistics, selected years 1970-83, hearings, 21348–93

Student aid basic grant, loan, and work-study awards, Fed Govt share by instn and State, 1984/85, annual rpt, 4804–17

Truman, Harry S, Scholarship Foundation, program operation, financial status, and awards by student characteristics, 1983 with trends from 1977, annual rpt, 14314–1

Tuition and other student charges at each public and private 2- and 4-year higher education instn, by State, 1983/84, annual listing, 4844–10

Vocational Education Research Natl Center funding, by purpose and source, selected years 1978-84, GAO rpt, 26121–79

Vocational training bilingual projects, participants, characteristics, and costs, by program, FY82, annual rpt, 4804–26

Energy Resources and Demand

Alaska electric power capacity and generation by fuel type, and marketing, by utility, type of ownership, and location, 1983, annual rpt, 3214–2

Alaska minerals resources, production, claims on wildlife refuges, oil and gas leases, and exploratory wells, with maps and bibl, 1983, annual rpt, 5664–11

Alcohol fuel (ethanol) production in Tennessee Valley, feedstocks, facilities, tax incentives, and related farming data, by State, 1970s-83 and projected to 1992, 9808–69

Army Corps of Engineers activities and projects, FY83 and trends from 1800s, annual rpt, 3754–1

Auto and light truck fuel economy performance by make, and standards, 1978-85 model years, annual rpt, 7764–9

Auto and light truck fuel use, economy standards and manufacturer compliance, and gas prices and taxes, with selected foreign comparisons, FY80-83 and projected to 2000, hearing, 21368–49

Auto engine and power train R&D projects, DOE contracts and funding by recipient, FY83, annual rpt, 3304–17

Auto fuel economy test results for models complying with California emission standards, 1984 model year, annual rpt, 3304–13

Auto fuel economy test results, 1985 model year, annual rpt, 3304–11

Bonneville Power Admin sales, revenues, and prices, by class of customer and individual purchaser, 1983, semiannual rpt, 3222–1

Bunker fuels, oil, and coal laden in US on vessels engaged in foreign trade, by port, monthly rpt, 2422–5

Coal distribution firms and producing districts served, quarterly rpt, annual listing, 3162–8

Coal lands of Fed Govt leasing activity, acreage, and reserves, by State, coal region, and tract, FY83, annual rpt, 5724–10

Coal purchases of Fed Govt, quality control analyses by mine and location, FY82-83, annual rpt, 3004–15

Coal supply and Fed Govt coal leases, by owner, owner industry, and western State, various periods 1950-82 and projected to 2000, hearing, 25318–58

Columbia River system electric power sales, by customer, FY83, annual rpt, 3224–1

Conservation grants of Fed Govt to public and nonprofit private instns, by building type and State, 1983, annual rpt, 3304–15

DOD electric power plants and major fuel-burning facilities conversion from oil and gas, fuel use data, 1983, annual rpt, 3104–9

DOE in-house energy use, conservation investments, and savings, by type of use and fuel and field office, FY83, annual rpt, 3024–3

DOE procurement and assistance contracts, by State, contractor type, and top 100 instns, FY83, annual rpt, 3004–21

Electric and gas utility diversification activity by type, and finances and bond ratings by selected firm, various periods 1970-83, hearing, 21368–53

Electric power demand of households in 136 SMSAs and other utility service areas, with fuel prices, family income, and heating degree days, 1975 and projected to 1985, 1588–78

Electric power generating capacity, demand, and cost, by energy source and end-use sector and for 7 electric utilities, 1981-2000 with trends from 1960s, 3008–93

Electric power plant (coal-fired) capacity, coal demand, and coal supply by mode of transport and region of origin, by State, for units planned 1983-92, 3088–18

Electric power plant (steam) fuel deliveries, costs, and quality, by fuel type, State, and utility, 1983, annual rpt, 3164–42

Electric power plant capital and operating detailed costs, capacity, and fuel use, by plant, plant type, utility, and State, 1982, annual rpt, 3164–9

Electric power plants (nuclear and fossil steam), new units and capacity, projected 1984-93, 3404–6

Electric power plants and industrial facilities prohibited from oil and gas primary use, and exemption petitions, by facility, with summary fuel use, 1983, annual rpt, 3104–8

Electric power plants, by capacity, fuel used, unit type, region, State, and county, for plants added and retired, 1983 and planned through 1993, annual rpt, 3164–36

Electric power transactions of US with Canada and Mexico, by utility and US region, 1983, annual rpt, 3104–10

Electric power wholesale purchases and costs for individual REA borrowers, by supplier and State, 1940-83, annual rpt, 1244–5

Electric utilities privately owned, common stock performance measures for companies with and without nuclear facilities, 1963-82, 3168–88

Electric utilities privately owned, detailed financial and operating data, by company, 1982, annual rpt, 3164–23.2

Electric utility fuel cost, quality, use, receipts, and stocks, and power plant production, by energy source, State and utility, quarterly rpt, 3162–39

Electric utility rate minimization from improved efficiency, proposed FERC incentive program operations and costs, with comparisons to 3 State programs, 1950s-82, 3088–17

Energy production, trade, supply, use, conservation, and DOE activities, by energy type, FY83, annual rpt, 3024–2

Energy-related inventions recommended for possible DOE support by Natl Bur of Standards, with DOE evaluation status, 1984, annual listing, 2214–5

Fed Govt reclamation projects in western US, electric power capacities and transmission miles, and water storage and carriage facilities, by State, FY81, annual rpt, 5824–1.1

Housing electricity and gas costs for 306 cities, by utility, with climatological data, fall 1982, 3308–67

Housing energy conservation programs of utilities, financing, costs, participation, and energy savings, various periods 1981-84, hearing, 21368–54

Hydroelectric power projects with licenses expiring Jan 1984-Dec 1989 annual rpt, 3084–9

BY INDIVIDUAL COMPANY OR INSTITUTION

Index by Categories

Hydrogen energy R&D activities of DOE, and description and funding of 24 projects, FY83, annual rpt, 3304–18

Montana and North Dakota coal production, impact of mining on agricultural land availability and on farm income and production costs, by mining tract, 1982 rpt, 1588–79

Natural and supplemental gas production, prices, trade, use, reserves, and pipeline company finances, by firm and State, monthly rpt with articles, 3162–4

Natural gas composition and occurrence of helium, analyses of samples from individual wells and pipelines in 26 States and 2 countries, 1983, annual survey, 5604–2

Natural gas interstate pipeline company detailed financial and operating data, by firm, 1983, annual rpt, 3164–38

Natural gas interstate pipeline company supplies, reserves, production, purchases, and contracts, by firm, 1983 with projected deliverability to 2003, annual rpt, 3164–33

Natural gas pipeline and compressor station construction costs, 1979-82, annual rpt, 3084–3

Natural gas price decontrol effect on prices, Iowa supply/demand, and economic indicators, with US imports from Canada, various periods 1969-95, hearings, 23848–177

Natural gas supply, contract prices, pipeline operations and finances, and residential use, various periods 1966-1983/84, 3168–89

Natural gas volume and prices for interstate pipeline market activities, and price decontrol effects, 1978-80s, 3168–50

Nuclear engineering student enrollments and degrees granted, by State, instn, and subfield, and placements by sector, 1983, annual rpt, 3004–5

Nuclear fuel facilities inventory discrepancies, 2nd half 1983, semiannual rpt, 9632–3

Nuclear power accident liability insurance under Price-Anderson Act, effects on industry finances and operations, with insurance coverage, claims, and costs, various periods 1957-82, 9638–49

Nuclear power industry status and outlook, with reactor construction, utility financial and operating data, and foreign comparisons, 1970s-83 with projections to 2010, 26358–99

Nuclear power plant and reactor construction costs, by plant and reactor, for start-up dates 1960-82 and projected to 1995, 3006–7.5

Nuclear power plant capacity, generation, shutdowns, operation status and costs, and fuel, quarterly rpt, 3352–3

Nuclear power plant construction and operation status, and capacity, by plant, region, State, and selected country, 1983 and projected to 2020, annual rpt, 3164–57

Nuclear power plant construction costs and status, and capacity, by plant and State, as of Mar 1984, annual rpt, 3164–69

Nuclear power plant construction costs and status, capacity, and revenue requirements, by plant and utility, various dates Dec 1983-Mar 1984, article, 9385–1.412

Nuclear power plant electrical systems, errors in operation and maintenance by circumstance, plant type, and system, 1977-81, 9638–51

Nuclear power plant fuel assembly performance and failures, by fuel vendor for US and some foreign reactors, 1982, annual rpt, 9634–8

Nuclear power plant licensing actions and status, by action type and plant, monthly rpt, 9632–5

Nuclear power plant operating and safety data, by plant, 1981, annual rpt, 9634–6

Nuclear power plant safety standards and research, design, licensing, construction, operation, and finances, with data by reactor, bimonthly rpt, 3352–4

Nuclear power plant spent fuel discharges and additional storage capacity required, by reactor, projected 1984-93, annual rpt, 3354–2

Nuclear reactor operating and inspection data for individual commercial facilities, monthly rpt, 9632–1

Nuclear reactors at central station power plants, operating status and other characteristics by plant, utility, and State, as of Jan 1984, annual rpt, 3354–11

Nuclear reactors for domestic use and export by function, with owner, operating characteristics, and location, Apr 1984, semiannual listing, 3002–5

Nuclear Regulatory Commission activities, employment, and finances, and operations of individual power plants by State, FY83, annual rpt, 9634–2

Nuclear strategic materials, inventory discrepancies at DOE facilities, 1st half FY83, semiannual rpt, 3002–4

Oil and gas fields by State and EIA field code, 1983, annual listing, 3164–70

Oil and gas finances by firm, and effect of income and excise tax provisions on firms, Fed Govt revenues, and investor tax returns, 1980 and projected to 1992, hearing, 21788–132

Oil and gas OCS reserves of Fed Govt, leasing and exploration activities, production, revenues, and costs, by ocean region, FY83, annual rpt, 5734–4

Oil enhanced recovery technologies use and environmental impacts, by oil field, county, and State, 1970s-80 and projected to 2000, 3408–29

Oil, gas, and liquefied petroleum gas sales from Naval Petroleum Reserves fields, by purchaser, FY83, annual rpt, 3004–22

Oil pipeline industry competition, market shares and throughput capacity by firm and market area, as of 1983, 6008–18

Oil price and allocation regulations enforcement by DOE, and overcharge allegations, settlements, and refunds to States, by company, as of June 1983, hearing, 21368–50

Oil production, historic data by field, country rpt series, 3166–9

Oil refineries in operation, and refineries bought and sold by company, by capacity, various dates 1980-85, article, 3162–6.401

Oil refinery locations and capacities in US and territories, by company, Jan 1983, annual rpt, 3164–2

Public utility holding company finances, securities issued, and subsidiaries by type, by firm, FY83, annual rpt, 9734–2.6

R&D and science and engineering education related to energy, DOE and DOE natl labs aid to selected higher education instns, 1960s-84, 3008–89.2

R&D projects and funding of DOE at natl labs, universities, and other instns, annual summary rpts, 3004–18

Radioactive wastes from DOE defense facilities, interim storage inventories by site and permanent disposal plan costs, 1982 with projections to 2015, 3358–32

Rural Electrification Admin financed electric power plants, with location, capacity, and owner, as of Jan 1984, annual listing, 1244–6

Rural Electrification Admin loans to power supply and distribution firms, and borrower operating and financial data, by firm and State, 1983, annual rpt, 1244–1

Solar collector and photovoltaic module manufacturers, 1983, annual listing, 3164–62

Solar photovoltaic system R&D sponsored by DOE, project descriptions and publications, FY83, annual listing, 3304–20

Southeastern Power Admin sales by customer, plants, and capacity, and financial statements of Southeastern Fed Power Program, FY83, annual rpt, 3234–1

Southwestern Fed Power System financial statements, electric power sales by customer, and project capacity, production, and costs, FY83, annual rpt, 3244–1

Strategic Petroleum Reserve activities and funding, by supplier and site, quarterly GAO rpt, 26102–3

Tennessee Valley river control and reservoir elevations, storage, flows, and hydroelectric generating capacity use, 1981, annual rpt, 9804–7

Trans-Alaska Pipeline System owner companies financial data, and retail gasoline competitive position in 2 States, by company, 1980-83, hearing, 21728–51

TVA construction projects employment, and impacts on nearby areas, survey rpt series, 9806–7

TVA electric power purchases of municipal and cooperative distributors, and prices and consumption by distributor and consumer sector, monthly rpt, 9802–1

TVA electric power sales to distributor systems, industrial users, and Fed Govt, and revenues and rates, FY83, annual rpt, 9804–1.2

TVA power distributors detailed operating and financial ratios, for individual municipal and cooperative distributors, FY79-83, annual rpt, 9804–19

TVA power distributors purchases and resales of TVA power, and rates charged, by consumer class, 1983, annual rpt, 9804–14

TVA power program finances and operations, by plant and distributor, FY83, annual rpt, 9804–23

Uranium from foreign sources delivered to DOE enrichment plants, by country of origin and US enrichment customer, 1983, annual rpt, 3164–66

Uranium mining operations, finances, and costs of alternative methods to meet emissions standards, for industry and selected mines, selected years 1948-90, 9188–96

Uranium reserves and mining and milling industries operations and finances, with selected foreign comparisons, various periods 1964-83 and projected to 2000, 3008–95

Index by Categories

BY INDIVIDUAL COMPANY OR INSTITUTION

Washington Public Power Supply System nuclear reactors construction financing, with regional economic impacts and power supply/demand, 1980s-2035, hearing, 21448–29

Western Area Power Admin operations by plant, financial statements, and electric power sales by customer, FY83, annual rpt, 3254–1

Wood fuel consumption, by end-use sector, SIC 2-digit industry, region, State, and selected industrial and power plant, 1980-83, biennial rpt, 3164–78

Geography and Climate

Climatological data for surface and upper air, averages by foreign and US station, monthly rpt, 2152–4

Climatological data for 284 US and outlying stations, for period of record through 1982, annual rpt, 2154–8

Disasters, persons affected, deaths, damage, and aid by US and others, by country, FY83 and trends from FY64, annual rpt, 9914–12

Earthquake and other ground motion intensity measured on USGS Natl Strong-Motion Network by station, and sources of foreign and US info, 1981, annual rpt, 5664–14

Weather stations of Natl Weather Service, locations and regular observations made, 1984 annual listing, 2184–5

Weather stations of Upper Air Observational Network, by US and foreign location, 1984 annual listing, 2184–6

Government and Defense

AID activities and funding by project and function, FY85, and developing countries summary socioeconomic data, 1970s-83, by country, annual rpt, 9914–3

AID contracts and grants for technical and support services, by instn, country, and State, FY83, annual listing, 9914–7

AID contracts and grants to universities for technical assistance to foreign countries and other services, FY83, annual listing, 9914–6

AID loan repayment status and terms by program and country, and status of predecessor agency loans, quarterly rpt, 9912–3

Army morale, welfare, and recreation programs, revenue and expenses worldwide by activity and major command, FY82-83, annual rpt, 3704–12

Capitol Architect detailed expenditures for buildings and grounds, salaries, supplies, and services, 1st half FY84, semiannual rpt, 25922–2

Coin production of US Mint Bur, for US by denomination and mint, and for foreign countries, monthly table, 8202–1

Collective bargaining agreements of Federal employees, unions involved, and employees covered, by agency for agreements expiring July 1984-June 1985, annual listing, 9847–1

Collective bargaining multi-unit agreements of Federal employees, by labor union and agency, as of July 1983, annual listing, 9847–4

DOD base construction and renovation, budget authorization requests by DOD component, State, country, and project, FY85, annual rpt, 3544–15

DOD civilian and military employment, by State, service branch, and major installation, as of Sept 1983, annual rpt, 3544–7

DOD contractor subcontract awards to small and disadvantaged business, by firm and service branch, quarterly listing, 3542–17

DOD engineering contract awards by function, contract type, and service branch, and oil and port dredging awards by company, 1970s-83, hearings, 21728–53

DOD military post exchange operations, locations worldwide, sales by type of commodity or service and facility, and employment, FY83, annual rpt, 3504–10

DOD prime contract awards, by individual contractor, service branch, State and city, and country, FY83, annual listing, 3544–22

DOD prime contract awards, dollar volume for 100 leading contractors and subsidiaries, FY83, annual rpt, 3544–5

DOD prime contract awards for R&D to educational and nonprofit instns and Federal agencies, by instn and location, FY83, annual listing, 3544–17

DOD prime contract awards, for 100 leading contractors, FY83, annual summary rpt, 3504–13

DOD training and education programs funding, staff, students, and facilities, by service branch and reserve component, FY85, annual rpt, 3504–5

DOD weapons budget, description, prime contractor, and costs of individual weapons or systems, FY83-85, annual rpt, 3504–2

Economic Dev Admin loans and grants, by program, State, county, and project or recipient, FY83 and cumulative FY66-83, annual rpt, 2064–2

Election campaign Fed Govt funding, reform and tax deduction proposals, and TV and political action committee influence, opinion surveys, various dates 1977-83, hearings, 21428–7.1

Election campaign finances, election procedures, and Fed Election Commission monitoring activities, press release series, 9276–1

Election campaign financial activities of individual party committees and political action committees for 1984 elections, 1983-84, 9276–2.7

Election campaign funding and activities of Fed Election Commission, and political action committees funding, 1983, annual rpt, 9274–1

Election campaign funding by political action committee and candidate, proposed candidate spending limits, voting rates by party, and political opinions, by State, 1960-82, hearings, 25688–6

Election campaign funding of maritime and other labor unions for congressional campaigns, by party, 1981-82, hearings, 25388–45

FTC budget authority and expenditures for regulatory analysis, by prospective regulation and contractor, 1983, hearings, 21528–56

GPO document sales program mgmt and finances, and bookstore operations by location, FY78-82, GAO rpt, 26111–17

House of Representatives salaries, expenses, and contingent fund disbursement, detailed listings, quarterly rpt, 21942–1

Human rights conditions in 162 countries, economic and military aid of US, and economic aid of intl organizations, 1981-83, annual rpt, 21384–3

Labor unions recognized in Fed Govt, agreements and membership by agency and office or installation, Jan 1983, annual listing, 9844–14

Labor unions recognized in Fed Govt, membership by agency and union, as of Jan 1983, annual rpt, 9844–17

Missile experimental (MX) procurement funding, and contract awards by company, FY84 with procurement projections to FY89, GAO rpt, 26123–75

Navy procurement, by contractor and location of work, FY83, annual rpt, 3804–13

Procurement contract awards of Fed Govt, by State, agency, procurement and contractor type, and for top 100 contractors, quarterly rpt, 102–6

Revenue sharing payments to States, local govts, Indian tribes, and Alaska Native villages, and entitlement computation data, FY84, series, 8066–1

Senate salaries, expenses, and contingent fund disbursements, by payee, detailed listings, 1st half FY84, semiannual rpt, 25922–1

Health and Vital Statistics

Alcohol, Drug Abuse, and Mental Health Admin research grants, awards, and fellowships by recipient, FY83, annual listing, 4044–13

Allergy and Infectious Diseases Natl Inst activities, grants by instn, State, and country, and disease incidence and costs, FY60s-84, annual rpt, 4474–30

Arizona hospitals and nursing homes, finances and operations for specified facilities, and itemized expenses for selected cases, 1978-83, hearing, 21148–29

Cancer Natl Inst contracts and grants, by contractor, instn, State, and city, FY83, annual listing, 4474–28

Cancer Natl Inst epidemiology and biometry activities, staff, budget, and contract awards by project and recipient instn, FY83, annual rpt, 4474–29

Cancer research and treatment, instns receiving Natl Cancer Inst support, FY83, annual fact book, 4474–13

Cigarette tar, nicotine, and carbon monoxide content in 207 varieties, 1982, periodic rpt, 9402–2

Consumer Product Safety Commission activities, recalls, and product-related injuries, deaths, and medical costs, by product type and brand, FY83, annual rpt, 9164–2

Correctional instns (Federal) health services employment, by occupation, instn, and region, monthly rpt, 6242–2

Dental Research Natl Inst research and training funds awarded, by recipient instn, FY83, annual listing, 4474–19

DOE and contractor facility accidents, deaths, illnesses, radiation exposure, and property damage, by facility, 1982, annual rpt, 3004–24

Drug (prescription) use by outpatient characteristics and generic or brand name, and hospital and drugstore costs by drug class, 1982, annual rpt, 4064–12

BY INDIVIDUAL COMPANY OR INSTITUTION

Drugs (prescription) invoice costs to pharmacists, and Medicare maximum allowable costs, by drug class and manufacturer, July/Aug 1983, 4658–6

Drugs prescribed or provided by office-based physicians most often, by brand or generic name and therapeutic category, 1981, 4146–8.99, 4146–8.100

Fed Employees Health Benefits Program finances, benefit reductions, and rate increases, by plan, 1981-82, GAO rpt, 26121–67

Fed Govt civilian health benefit plans enrollment and premiums, for individual private and employee organization plans, FY81-82, annual rpt, 9844–1.2

Health and population research funded by 4 private organizations, project listing by topic, with funding data, 1981, annual rpt, 4474–16

Health Care Financing Admin research activities and grants by research area, as of June 1984, semiannual listing, 4652–8

Health maintenance organizations and prepaid health plans enrollment, use, and Fed Govt aid, FY83, annual rpt, 4104–8

Health maintenance organizations enrollment (total, Medicare, and Medicaid), finances, Fed Govt qualification status, and PHS loan activity, by HMO, FY83, annual rpt, 4044–2

Health professions schools minority group and women enrollment and grads, by field and instn, selected years 1962/63-1983/84, 4118–18

Health Services Research Natl Center grants and contracts, by program area, FY83, annual listing, 4184–2

Hearing aid performance evaluation, by model and manufacturer, 1984, annual rpt, 9924–5

Heart, Lung, and Blood Natl Inst organization, disease and mortality data, and funds and recipients, FY83 with trends from 1900, annual fact book, 4474–15

HHS aid to each State and local govt or private instn, amount obligated, funding agency, and program, FY83, annual listing, 4004–3

HHS program evaluations and funding, 1970-83, listing, 4008–60

Indian Health Service hospital admissions, discharges, births, total and occupied beds, length of stay, and outpatient visits, by area and facility, quarterly rpt, 4102–3

Mental health facilities, services, and costs in DC, and effect of St Elizabeths Hospital operations and finances transfer to DC govt, FY83, GAO rpt, 26121–72

Navy and Marine Corps disease incidence, medical care, and deaths, by detailed diagnosis, and medical personnel and workloads, 1978-79, annual rpt, 3804–1

Navy medical facility use by active and retired military personnel, dependents, and others, by facility and type, quarterly rpt, 3802–1

NIH extramural grant and contract awards to top instns and top 20 medical schools, FY82, annual rpt, 4434–9

NIH grants and awards for R&D, training, construction, and medical libraries, by location and recipient, FY83, annual listings, 4434–7

NIH newly announced grants and awards, quarterly listing, 4432–1

Nursing home cost insurance premiums by age, and benefit provisions, for policies of 16 companies, 1984 conf paper, 4658–7

NYC health care demonstration project for reorganization of 6 facilities in Brooklyn, Federal and State govt funding by facility, 1979-82, article, 4652–1.419

Physician visits for new pain symptoms, by diagnosis, physician specialty, and patient characteristics, and drugs prescribed or used, 1980-81, 4146–8.97

Radiation occupational exposure at individual commercial nuclear power plants, 1969-82, annual rpt, 9634–3

Radiation protection and health physics enrollments and degrees granted by State and instn, and grads employment, 1983, annual rpt, 3004–7

Smoke alarm sound levels by brand, and response time by circumstances and for older and mentally retarded persons, 1983 rpt, 2218–70

Housing and Construction

Broward County, Fla, property ownership by individual Netherlands Antilles firms, various periods 1978-83, hearings, 21408–71

Construction and building materials industries trade assns, professional societies, and labor unions, 1984 listing, article, 2012–1.405

Homeless population and characteristics, and temporary shelter operations, use, and user characteristics, for selected cities, various periods 1979-84, hearing, 21248–85

HUD rental rehabilitation projects, owner minority status, funding, assisted units, and location for 141 projects, 1984 press release, 5006–3.38

Indian and Alaska Native housing and community dev program operations, FY82 with Community Dev Block Grant funding by tribe and State for FY81, annual rpt, 5004–5

Low-rent housing project financing notes sold by local authorities, terms and individual issuers and purchasers, monthly listing, 5142–43

Low-rent housing project financing notes sold by local authorities, terms and individual purchasers, monthly press release, 5142–37

NYC South Bronx housing and economic dev, HUD grants to 4 neighborhood organizations, 1984 press release, 5006–3.31

Older and handicapped persons housing projects construction and rehabilitation loans of HUD, FY84, annual listing, 5004–6

Public building construction, acquisition, and alteration proposals, costs and tenure by city and project, as of 1983, hearings, 25328–23

Public building construction, alteration, and leasing projects, description and cost by location, Dec 1983, annual listing, 9454–12

Industry and Commerce

Alabama employment and unemployment by SMSA and industry div, and planned capital investment and new jobs by selected firm, 1982-83, article, 9371–1.408

Index by Categories

Aluminum industry electricity use, operations, and energy and labor efficiency by plant, for Pacific Northwest, projected 1984-2003, annual rpt, 3224–2.4

Aluminum primary production plant ownership, capacity, and type and source of raw material and energy used, by plant, State, and country, June 1984, semiannual listing, 5602–5

Auto and auto equipment recalls for safety-related defects, by make, quarterly listing, 7762–2

Auto and auto products sales, prices, and registrations in US, and trade of 8 countries with US, by make and model, 1964-83, annual rpt, 9884–7

Auto industry finances and operations by manufacturer, foreign competition, and consumer auto expenditures and attitudes toward car buying, selected years 1968-85, annual rpt, 2004–8

Auto industry operations, trade, and registrations, foreign and US, selected years 1928-82, domestic content requirement hearings, 21788–134

Auto safety and experimental vehicle designs, 1982, conf proceedings, annual rpt, 7764–3

California business failures, plant closings, layoffs, and relocations, by plant, industry, county, and city, 1980-83, hearing, 21348–84.1

Chemicals (synthetic organic) production and sales by product, and listing of manufacturers, 1983, annual rpt, 9884–3

Coastal environmental characteristics, fish, wildlife, and use, and population socioeconomic data, for individual areas, series, 5506–4

Copper mine expansion in Cananea, Mexico, effects on US air pollution and copper industry, with US and foreign industry data, 1960s-95, hearing, 21448–31

Export Admin Act antiboycott provisions, violations and fines by company, and boycotts by firm type and country, FY83, annual rpt, 2044–22

Forecasts for selected business activities and natl economic indicators, compilation of representative opinions, 1984, annual rpt, 9389–3

Foreign direct investment in US, major investors and investments by SIC 4-digit industry, transaction type and value, and location, 1983, annual rpt, 2044–20

Foreign minerals production, reserves, and industry role in domestic economy and world supply, country and world region rpt series, 5606–1

Foreign trade zones operations and economic effects, with data on merchandise shipments, value added, employment, hours, and customs revenue, 1978-83, 9886–4.70

Franchise business opportunities by firm and kind of business, and sources of aid and info, 1984 annual listing, 2044–27

Imports detained by FDA, by product, shipper or manufacturer, country, and detention reasons, monthly listing, 4062–2

Japan semiconductor industry govt subsidies by program, with financial and operating data by firm, R&D, and comparisons to US industry, 1970s-83, hearings, 21368–46.1

Index by Categories

BY INDIVIDUAL COMPANY OR INSTITUTION

Japan specialty steel and ferroalloy raw material supply/demand, with industry market and manufacturing data, selected years 1970-81, 5608–144

Manufactured goods relative market shares of largest US and foreign firms by selected industry and firm, 1960, 1970, and 1981, hearing, 21248–79

Metals resource recovery through leaching technologies, characteristics of methods and operations, regulation, and research, series, 5606–6

Minerals (nonfuel) foreign and US supply under alternative market conditions, reserves, and background industry data, series, 5606–4

Minerals (strategic) supply/demand, trade, and foreign and US industry devs by firm and country, by commodity, bimonthly rpt, 5602–4

Minerals Yearbook, 1982, Vol 2: State reviews of production, sales, and firms, by commodity, and business activity, annual rpt, 5604–34

Minerals Yearbook, 1982, Vol 3 preprints: foreign country reviews of production, trade, and policies, by commodity, annual rpt series, 5604–17

Minerals Yearbook, 1983, Vol 1 preprints: commodity reviews of production, reserves, supply, use, and trade, annual rpt series, 5604–15

Minerals Yearbook, 1983, Vol 3 preprints: foreign country reviews of production, trade, and policies, by commodity, annual rpt series, 5604–23

North Central States pulpwood production by county, imports, and individual mill capacity, by species, 1982, annual rpt, 1204–19

Overseas Private Investment Corp activities, foreign and US project impacts, and list of insured projects and companies, FY83, annual rpt, 9904–3

Pacific Northwest natl forest sales by bidding method, harvest by company, and effects on local employment by community, 1974-77, 1208–194

Pension fund terminations and value of reversion to sponsor, for 12 largest private terminations, 1980-83, article, 9385–1.406

Robots for industrial use and computer aided design, sales by vendor, 1980-83, 26358–105

Ship construction and conversion costs by owner and builder, fleet size, and employment, monthly rpt, 7702–1

Small Business Admin loans, contract awards, and surety bonds, by firm, State, and city, FY83, annual rpt, 9764–1.2

Small business mgmt counseling by university centers, costs, funding, and businesses served by industry, with detail for 2 States, 1980-83, hearing, 25728–36

Southeastern States, financial and operating characteristics of 22 high performance firms and 10 largest banks, 1982-83, article, 9371–1.414

Steel industry market shares and return on sales, by major manufacturer, selected years 1950-83, 26306–6.80

Steel plant modernization capital investment under Clean Air Act compliance extension program, by firm, 1981-83, GAO rpt, 26113–138

Steel plant modernization projects, Urban Dev Action Grant and private funding and jobs created, by plant and city, 1984 press release, 5006–3.37

Tennessee Valley industrial dev and effects on employment, investment, and TVA power demand, by location and company, 1983, annual rpt, 9804–3

Waterborne exports and imports of US, by type of service, customs district, port, and world area, monthly rpt, 2422–7

Labor and Employment

American Samoa minimum wage rates, employment, earnings, and benefits, by establishment and industry, Nov 1983, biennial rpt, 6504–6

California business failures, plant closings, layoffs, and relocations, by plant, industry, county, and city, 1980-83, hearing, 21348–84.1

Collective bargaining agreements expiring during year, covered workers by SIC 2-digit industry, firm, and union, with summary of key provisions, 1984, annual rpt, 6784–9

Collective bargaining calendar for Southeast US, 1984, annual rpt, 6946–1.68

Collective bargaining contract expirations and wage increases, scheduled and under cost-of-living escalator provisions, by SIC 2-digit industry and selected firm and union, 1984, annual article, 6722–1.402

Fed Labor Relations Authority and Fed Service Impasses Panel activities, and cases by region, union, and agency, FY79-82, annual rpt, 13364–1

Indian and Alaska Native employment and training program funding allocation under Job Training Partnership Act, by individual tribe and group, FY84, press release, 6408–57

Intl Labor Affairs Bur research contracts, by project and contractor, FY73-84, annual listing, 6364–1

Job Training Partnership Act allotments for migrant and seasonal farm workers retraining assistance, by State and administering organization, as of July 1984, press release, 6408–64

Labor union mergers, and affiliation and membership at time of merger, Jan 1979-Apr 1984, article, 6722–1.456

Labor union representation elections conducted by NLRB, results, monthly rpt, 9582–2

Labor unions reporting to Labor Dept, parent bodies and locals by State, city, and country, 1983 listing, 6468–17

New England States collective bargaining contract terminations and workers covered, by industry and firm, 1984, annual rpt, 6916–7.2

Trade adjustment assistance for workers, petitions, investigations, and determinations, by major industry group, union, and State, monthly rpt, 6402–13

Law Enforcement

Aircraft hijackings, on-board explosions, other crimes against civil aviation, and circumstances, US and worldwide, 1931-83, annual rpt, 7504–31

Higher education instns crime and crime rates by offense, and law enforcement employees, by instn, 1983, annual rpt, 6224–2

Jail inmates in 100 largest jails, as of June 1982, and characteristics of 10 regional jails, 1979, 10048–59

Juvenile Justice and Delinquency Prevention Natl Inst programs and research project funding, FY81-82, annual rpt, 6064–19

New Jersey and Maryland prison capacity and population, and New Jersey construction costs by type and funding source, by facility, 1977-82 and projected to 1988, 25528–99

Prison population and capacity by State and individual DC and Federal instn, construction costs, and Fed Govt operating costs, 1983 and projected to 1990, GAO rpt, 26119–59

Prisoners in Federal correctional instns, by prison, security level, contract facility type, sex, and region, monthly and weekly rpts, 6242–1

Natural Resources, Environment, and Pollution

Air pollutant nitrate and sulfate emissions, monitoring results by surveillance station, 1979 with trends by urban-rural area from 1971, 9198–107

Air pollution abatement under Clean Air Act, air quality protection classification of natl parks, emissions of copper smelters in 2 States, and diesel car sales, 1970s-83, hearings, 25328–25

Air pollution monitoring results for atmospheric turbidity by station and season, with description of model predicting urbanization effects, 1960s-76, 9198–106

Coal dev plans on Fed Govt lease lands in 12 regions under Fed Coal Mgmt Program, environmental and socioeconomic impacts to 2000, final statement series, 5726–4

Colorado River Storage Project finances, water resource dev, power production, and other activities in western States, FY83, annual rpt, 5824–3

Dams, reservoirs, and hydroelectric plants, listing of major foreign and US structures with location and characteristics, as of June 1983, 5828–13

Environmental quality, pollutant discharge by type and source, and EPA protection activities and funding, 1970s-83, biennial regional rpt series, 9184–15

Fish and Wildlife Service restoration programs, including new sites, funding, and research, by State, FY81, annual rpt, 5504–1

Forest fires on Forest Service land and acres burned, by cause, forest, and State, 1983, annual rpt, 1204–6

Forests (natl) and other lands under Forest Service mgmt, by forest and location, Sept 1983, annual rpt, 1204–2

Forests (natl) timber sales contract operations in Northwest US by forest and firm, and lumber supply/demand, FY76-1983 with trends from 1913, hearings, 25318–57

Forests (tropical) conservation, mgmt role of public and private US, foreign, and intl groups, 1983 rpt, 26358–101.3

Great Lakes basin pollutant discharges by source, and control program activities, 1983 annual rpt, 14644–1

Hazardous waste sites and activities of Fed Govt civil agencies, and EPA data mgmt, by waste location, 1984, GAO rpt, 26113–139

BY INDIVIDUAL COMPANY OR INSTITUTION

Nevada water supply, streamflow, reservoir storage, and precipitation, 1984 water year, annual rpt, 1264–8

New York Bight pollutant loadings from ocean dumping of municipal wastes by type and source, and concentrations in fish and sediments, 1970s-82, hearings, 21568–36

Northeastern US water supply, precipitation and stream runoff by station, monthly rpt, 2182–3

Nuclear power plant siting population criteria and estimated compliance of selected regions and sites, 1983 rpt, 9638–54

Ocean dumping of waste materials, EPA permit program and intl London Dumping Convention activities, 1981-83, annual rpt, 9204–8

Oregon water supply, streamflow by station and reservoir storage, 1984 water year, annual rpt, 1264–9

Radiation and radionuclide concentrations in air, water, and milk, results of EPA and other monitoring programs, by State and site, quarterly rpt, 9232–2

Radiation exposure at DOE and DOE-contractor sites, by facility type and contractor, 1982, annual rpt, 3404–1

Radiation exposure at DOE-contractor nuclear facilities and for surrounding population, and pollutant releases by type, by site, 1982, annual rpt, 3004–23

Radiation from 1940s-70s nuclear weapons tests, levels in air and water, and personnel exposure by military unit and job category, series, 3906–1

Radioactive contamination of former AEC and Manhattan Project research and storage sites, test results series, 3406–1

Radioactive materials transport surveillance program activities and results, State survey rpt series, 9636–1

Radioactive waste and spent fuel generation, inventory, disposal by site, reprocessing, and characteristics, by source, as of 1983 and projected to 2020, annual rpt, 3364–2

Radioactive waste from nuclear power plants, releases and waste composition by plant, 1981, annual rpt, 9634–1

Radionuclide concentrations in air, water, and biota near Nevada and other nuclear test sites, and in milk from western States, by location, 1983, annual rpt, 9234–4

Reclamation Bur water storage and carriage facilities, by type, as of Sept 1983, annual listing, 5824–7

Reclamation programs of Fed Govt in western US, finances and operations by project and State, 1981-82, annual rpts, 5824–1

Recreation construction for water resources dev projects of Army Corps of Engineers and Reclamation Bur, unfunded costs by project, FY82, GAO rpt, 26113–115

Sedimentation control, surveillance, and research activity of Fed Govt, by project, agency, region, and State, 1982, annual rpt, 5664–9

Tennessee Valley river control and reservoir elevations, storage, flows, and hydroelectric generating capacity use, 1981, annual rpt, 9804–7

Utah water supply, streamflow, reservoir storage, and precipitation, 1984 water year, annual rpt, 1264–6

Western US water supply, reservoir storage by large reservoir and State, and streamflow conditions, as of Oct 1984, annual rpt, 1264–4

Western US water supply, snow depth measurements by station, State rpt series, 1266–3

Western US water supply, streamflow and reservoir storage forecasts by stream and station, Jan-May monthly rpt, 1262–1

Youth Conservation Corps activities, costs, and participant characteristics, by sponsoring agency, 1982, annual rpt, 5304–12

Population

Census of Population, 1980: Indian and Alaska Native population and housing occupancy, by reservation, Alaska Native village, and other Indian area, supplementary rpt, 2535–1.16

Population and health research funded by 4 private organizations, project listing by topic, with funding data, 1981, annual rpt, 4474–16

Prices and Cost of Living

Auto manufacturers suggested retail prices of selected US and Japan models by firm, and US auto industry operating and trade data, monthly rpt, 9882–8

Drug prices by brand and generic category, patent life, FDA approval time, and industry R&D costs and finances, selected years 1962-83, hearing, 25528–98

Electric power rate schedules, by user type, utility, and city, Jan 1984, annual rpt, 3164–40

Retail prices set by manufacturers under fair-trade law by brand and product, with manufacturers, market concentration, and sales, by industry, selected years 1952-82, 9406–1.38

Public Welfare and Social Security

Food distribution program participants on individual Indian reservations and in TTPI, irregular rpt, 1362–15

Food purchases for domestic aid programs, by commodity, firm, and shipping point or destination, weekly rpt, 1302–3

Medicare end-stage renal disease dialysis, transplants by facility, donor organ costs, deaths by age, and hospitalization, by region, 1981, annual rpt, 4654–5.2

Medicare physician charges and reimbursement by enrollee characteristics and carrier, payment limits effects on charges in California, and physician earnings, by specialty, 1950s-84, 25368–127

Medicare reimbursement rates in Massachusetts, and rates used and physicians not certified in designated specialty by selected carrier, various periods 1981-82, GAO rpt, 26121–82

Philanthropic foundations assets and grants for 50 largest foundations, and for selected foundations by recipient, selected years 1975-82, hearings, 21788–137

Philanthropic foundations detailed financial and operating data, and stock holdings by instn, 1979 with selected trends from 1920, GAO rpt, 26119–53

Refugee and alien arrivals and resettlements in US, by State, outlying area, country of birth and citizenship, age, sex, and sponsoring agency, monthly rpt, 4702–3

Index by Categories

Refugee assistance, Fed Govt contributions to intl agencies, FY84-85, annual rpt, 7004–16

Refugee Indochinese population, arrivals, and departures, by country of origin and resettlement, camp, and ethnicity, monthly rpt, 7002–4

Refugee resettlement program activities and funding, arrivals and population by country of origin and State, and employment and other characteristics, FY83, annual rpt, 4704–8

Runaway and other homeless youth programs, funding by source, activities, and participant characteristics, FY82, annual rpt, 4604–3

Voluntary agencies overseas foreign aid programs funding and expenditures, by agency, 1982/83, annual rpt, 9914–9

Recreation and Leisure

Army Corps of Engineers water resources dev projects, recreation activities by district and project, 1982, annual rpt, 3754–5

Fishing (ocean sport) effort and catch, and Natl Marine Fisheries Service tagging and research activity, by species and location, 1983, annual rpt, 2164–7

Museum grants of Natl Foundation on Arts and Humanities, by instn, State, and city, FY84, annual rpt series, 9564–6

Natl park system visitor deaths, by park and type of accident, 1973-83, annual rpt, 5544–6

Park natl system and other areas under Natl Park Service mgmt, acreage by type of area, ownership, and site, as of Sept 1984, semiannual rpt, 5542–1

Smithsonian Instn finances, activities, and visitors, FY83, annual rpt, 9774–3

Science and Technology

Astronautic and aeronautic events, foreign and US, comprehensive chronology, 1976, annual rpt, 9504–2

Biotechnology commercial uses, R&D funding and output, controls, and industry financial and operating data, for US and 5 countries, 1970s-83 and estimated 1984-85, 26358–98

Computer systems and equipment of Fed Govt, inventory by manufacturer, type, agency, and location, FY83, last issue of annual rpt, 9454–4

Degree (doctoral) recipients in science and engineering, by field, sex, race, age, citizenship, postgrad employment and study status, State, and instn, 1960-82, 9626–6.16

DOD procurement, prime contractors for R&D, top 500 and value of contracts, FY83, annual listing, 3544–4

Employment of scientists and engineers at universities and colleges and federally funded R&D centers, by field, sex, State, and instn, Jan 1983 and selected trends from 1967, annual survey, 9627–11

Employment of scientists and engineers at universities and colleges, by field, sex, and instn, 1973-82, 9626–2.140

Enrollment in grad science and engineering, fields of study, financial support, and other student and instn characteristics, 1975-82, annual survey, 9627–7

Marine mammals research, Fed Govt funding by agency, topic, and performing instn, FY82, annual rpt, 14734–2

Index by Categories

NASA procurement contract awards, by type, contractor, State, and country, FY84, semiannual rpt, 9502–6

NASA R&D funding to colleges and universities, by State, field of science, and instn, FY83, annual listing, 9504–7

NSF grant and award recipients, by State, FY83, annual listing, 9624–11

NSF research programs, activities, and funding, FY82-83, annual rpt, 9624–6

Oceanographic research cruise schedules and ship characteristics, by academic instn or Federal agency, 1984, annual rpt, 3804–6

Patents (US) granted to US and foreign applicants, by applicant type, firm, State, and country, subject rpt series, 2246–2

Patents (US) granted to US and foreign applicants, by year of grant and application, country, and type of applicant, 1960s-83, annual rpt, 2244–3

R&D and science-related Fed Govt funding and total and federally funded expenditures of universities and colleges, by instn and field of science, FY82, 9626–2.135, 9626–2.136

R&D and science-related Fed Govt funding to higher education and nonprofit instns, by field, instn, agency, and State, FY82, annual rpt, 9627–17

R&D expenditures by higher education instns and federally funded centers, by field, source of funds, instn, and State, FY82, annual rpt, 9627–13

R&D Fed Govt facilities and services available for private sector use, by field of science, 1984 biennial listing, 2224–4

Satellite Landsat system proposed transfer to private sector, uses and product sales by user type, and university programs and personnel by instn, 1973-85, 26358–100

Satellite systems (foreign and US) for civil observation, data product revenue, and proposed transfer of Fed Govt system to private sector, selected years 1978-FY84, 2148–47

Veterans Affairs

Health care for veterans, patients, visits, costs, and operating beds, by district and individual VA and contract facility, monthly rpt, 9922–5

Hospital and nursing home use, beds, daily census, and construction projects, by VA facility, FY83, annual rpt, 9924–1

Medical care costs of VA, and amount recovered through billings, by facility, 1982, GAO rpt, 26121–66

Medical facilities of VA, sharing agreement contracts, services, and costs by region and facility, FY83, annual rpt, 9924–18

Medicine and Surgery Dept of VA, trainees by detailed program and city, FY83, annual rpt, 9924–21

Psychological services, staffing, research, and training programs in VA facilities, 1984 annual listing, 9924–10

Speech disorders among patients in VA facilities, by severity, patient characteristics, diagnostician occupation, and facility type, FY81, 9926–1.17

Vietnam Veterans Memorial Fund receipts by source, and disbursements by item and payee, Apr 1979-Mar 1984, GAO rpt, 26111–21

BY INDUSTRY

Banking, Finance, and Insurance

Bond tax-exempt issues for private activity, by purpose, face value, major industry, and State, 1983, article, 8302–2.417

Credit union financial statements by region, State, and type of membership, for Federal and federally insured State unions, 1983, annual rpt, 9534–1

Small Business Investment Companies finances, funding, licensing, and loan activity, 2nd half FY84, semiannual rpt, 9762–3

Stock (common) performance measures, for privately owned electric utilities and selected industry groups, selected years 1970-82, GAO rpt, 26113–129

Stock market transactions volume and proceeds and new issue registrations, for US registered exchanges, SEC monthly rpt, 9732–1

Communications and Transportation

Port dev costs and financing through user fees, and shipping industry impact on local economy, by State, other area, industry, commodity, and port, 1970s-2020, hearings, 21568–34

Port impact on local employment through transport of 5 commodities, by industry for 3 eastern ports, and demand for US coal by country, 1981, 7308–182

Transportation census, 1982: trucks, by detailed characteristics, miles traveled, and type of product carried, State rpt series, 2573–1

Energy Resources and Demand

Coal consumption, average prices, and stocks at manufacturing plants, by SIC 2-digit industry, quarterly rpt, 3162–37.2

Coal export-related employment, by industry, 1981-82, 3008–97

Electric power use indexes, by SIC 2- and 3-digit industry, monthly rpt, 9365–2.10

Energy demand in industry, forecasting model description, detailed technology specifications, and energy use, for 27 SIC 2- to 4-digit industries, 1970s-80 and projected to 2000, 3308–66

Energy use, prices, and conservation and efficiency measures, by fuel type, end-use sector, selected industry, and region, 1960-83, annual rpt, 3164–73

Manufacturing energy efficiency progress, and energy use by type, by SIC 2-digit industry, 1982, annual rpt, 3304–8

Manufacturing fuel and electricity demand growth and price elasticities, input data and model estimates by SIC 2-digit industry, 1958-78, 3006–7.4

Natural gas interstate pipeline company sales and prices, by individual industrial customer, SIC 2-digit industry group, and State, monthly rpt, annual tables, 3162–4.6

Oil prices impact on US oil trade and energy-intensive industries, with US and foreign reserves and industry operations, 1950-82 and projected to 2020, 9886–4.69

Pacific Northwest electricity consumption and prices by end-use sector, and economic and demographic data, 1960s-83 and projected to 2005, annual rpt, 3224–2

Wood fuel consumption, by end-use sector, SIC 2-digit industry, region, State, and selected industrial and power plant, 1980-83, biennial rpt, 3164–78

BY INDUSTRY

Government and Defense

DOD contract and in-house commercial activities costs and work-years, by service branch, defense agency, State, and installation, FY83, annual rpt, 3544–25

Income tax credit for corporate investments, with data on returns, income, taxes, and investment value, by industry div and selected major group, 1974-80, article, 8302–2.405

Income tax returns filed by type of filer, selected income items, summary data, quarterly rpt, 8302–2.1

Income tax returns of corporations, detailed income and tax items by industry, 1981, annual rpt, 8304–4

Income tax returns of corporations, summary data by industry div, 1981 estimates, annual article, 8302–2.403

Income tax returns of corporations with foreign tax credit, income and deductions by type, asset size, and selected industry group, 1980, article, 8302–2.415

Income tax returns of foreign subsidiaries of US corporations, income and tax data, by industry and asset size, 1980, article, 8302–2.410

Income tax returns of partnerships, detailed data by industry, 1981 estimates, annual article, 8302–2.404

Income tax returns of partnerships, receipts by source, deductions by type, and establishments, by selected industry, 1982, annual article, 8302–2.416

Income tax returns of sole proprietorships, detailed data by industry div and selected industry group, 1981, annual rpt, 8304–7

Income tax returns of sole proprietorships, receipts, deductions by type, payroll, and net income, by major industry, 1982, annual article, 8302–2.413

Income tax returns with investment credits, for individuals by income, and for sole proprietorships by industry, 1981, article, 8302–2.409

Income taxes and effective rates on corporate US, foreign, and worldwide income, by major industry group, and share of Fed Govt receipts, 1980-82, 23868–14

Income taxes, effective rates, and selected financial data, for financial instns by type and individual firm, with comparisons to other industries, selected years 1960-82, hearing, 25368–129

Loans, grants, and tax benefits of Fed Govt to business, by program and economic sector, projected FY84-88 with effective tax rates for FY80-82, 26306–6.70

Manufacturers under Fed Govt contract and owned by DOD, operating data by agency, selected SIC 2- to 4-digit industry, State, and SMSA, 1982, annual Current Industrial Rpt, 2506–3.4

Multinatl corporation income reallocation through regulation of intercorporate transactions, by tax item, treaty status, asset size, industry, and tax haven country, 1982, 8008–110

Retail store sales tax as percent of sales, by SIC 2- to 4-digit kind of business, 1983, annual rpt, 2413–5

Small business employment and receipts size standards for Fed Govt contract awards by industry, and DOD contract awards data, 1970s-83, hearings, 21728–53

BY INDUSTRY

Wholesale trade sales tax as a percent of sales, by SIC 2- to 3-digit kind of business, 1983, annual rpt, 2413–13

Health and Vital Statistics

Asbestos workers, exposure levels, cancer incidence, and deaths, by industry and occupation, and asbestos regulation enforcement and costs/benefits, various periods 1940-2027, hearing, 21408–72

Births by outcome, and mother's sociodemographic, life style, and maternity characteristics, 1980, article, 4102–1.422

Health maintenance organizations for employee health insurance, enrollment, premiums, coverage, and employer attitudes, by region and industry div, 1982, 4108–32

Injuries, detailed accident circumstances and safety data, by body part injured, type of equipment used, or industry, series, 6846–1

Occupational deaths, by industry div and cause, 1981-82, article, 6722–1.422

Occupational health and safety State govt program staffing requirements, and occupational injury data, for selected States, selected years 1973-81, hearings, 21348–88

Occupational health risks from hazardous substances and radiation, by industry, occupation, age, and sex, with bibl and glossary, 1920s-82, 9638–50

Occupational injuries and illnesses, incidence rates by employment size and industry, workdays lost, and deaths, 1980-81, annual rpt, 6604–2.2

Occupational injuries, illnesses, and workdays lost, by SIC 2-digit industry, 1982-83, annual press release, 6844–3

Occupational injury and illness rates, by industry, 1972-81, annual rpt, 6724–1.9

Occupational injury and illness rates, by SIC 2- to 4-digit industry, 1982, annual rpt, 6844–1

South Carolina manufacturing plants with selected employee health care services, by SIC 2-digit industry, 1982, article, 4102–1.408

Industry and Commerce

Business activity indicators (nonfinancial), 1982, annual rpt, 9364–5.9

Business Conditions Digest, current data on economic, business, and financial conditions and cyclical fluctuations, monthly rpt, 2702–3

Business failures by industry div, 1978 and 1983, article, 9381–1.414

Business statistics, detailed data for major industries and economic indicators, *Survey of Current Business,* monthly rpt, 2702–1

California business failures, plant closings, layoffs, and relocations, by plant, industry, county, and city, 1980-83, hearing, 21348–84.1

Capacity utilization in 15 manufacturing industries, mining, electric and all utilities, and industrial materials including energy, monthly rpt, 9365–2.19

Capital expenditures and prices for plant and equipment, actual and expected, by major industry group, 1981-84, annual article, 2702–1.404

Capital expenditures for plant and equipment, actual and expected, by major industry group, quarterly article, 2702–1.33

Capital expenditures for plant and equipment, by major industry group, 1982, annual rpt, 9364–5.6

Corporations financial statements for manufacturing, mining, and trade, by selected SIC 2- to 3-digit industry, quarterly rpt, 2502–1

Corporations profits, by industry, 1929-83, annual rpt, 204–1.7

County and City Data Book, detailed socioeconomic and demographic data for States, counties, and cities, selected years 1976-82, 2328–1

County Business Patterns: establishments, employees, and payrolls, by SIC 4-digit industry and county, 1981, annual State rpt series, 2326–8

County Business Patterns: establishments, employees, and payrolls, by SIC 4-digit industry and county, 1982, annual State rpt series, 2326–6

Economic conditions and employment, alternative BLS projections to 1995 with selected trends for 1959-82, 6728–29

Economic conditions of US, with some foreign comparisons, 1960s-82 and alternative projections to 1992, hearing, 21248–79

Enterprise zone and urban revitalization projects of State and local govts, effect on business and employment in selected areas, various dates 1972-83, hearing, 21788–140

Exports and imports of US, detailed SIC-based commodities by world area, 1983, annual rpts, 2424–6

Exports of manufactured and agricultural commodities, manufacturing production, and export-related employment, 1960s-82, State rpt series, 2046–3

Foreign direct investment in and by US, by industry group and for selected countries and world regions, 1977 and 1980, article, 9373–1.411

Foreign direct investment in US by country, and finances, operations, and land ownership, by industry group for businesses acquired and established, 1982-83, annual article, 2702–1.418

Foreign direct investment in US, by major industry group, world area, and selected country, 1980-83, annual article, 2702–1.439

Foreign direct investment in US, major investors and investments by SIC 4-digit industry, transaction type and value, and location, 1983, annual rpt, 2044–20

Foreign direct investment of US, by selected major industry group and world area, 1980-82, annual article, 2702–1.430

Foreign direct investment worldwide, and US investment flows by major industry, by world region and selected country, 1982 and trends from 1950, annual rpt, 2044–25

Foreign firms US affiliates financial and operating data, by country of parent firm and industry div, 1980-81, article, 2702–1.402

Foreign minerals production, reserves, and industry role in domestic economy and world supply, country and world region rpt series, 5606–1

Foreign-owned US multiestablishment firms, employment, and payroll, by country, State, industry group, and foreign ownership share, 1981-82, annual rpt, 2324–6

Index by Categories

Franchise business opportunities by firm and kind of business, and sources of aid and info, 1984 annual listing, 2044–27

Franchises of firms engaged in distribution of goods and services by kind of business, establishments by State, and sales, 1982-84, annual rpt, 2014–5

GNP by industry div, in current and 1972 dollars, 1947-82, annual rpt, 204–1.1

GNP in current and constant dollars, and implicit price deflators, by industry div, 1981-83, article, 2702–1.416

Import and tariff provisions effect on US industries and products, investigations with background financial and operating data, series, 9886–4

Import quotas and tariffs, jobs protected and cost per job for selected products, and foreign trade balance by industry div, various periods 1958-81, article, 9381–1.412

Imports injury to US industries from foreign subsidized products, investigations with background financial and operating data for selected industries and products, series, 9886–15

Imports injury to US industries from import sales at less than fair value, investigations with background financial and operating data, series, 9886–14

Imports injury to US industries from increased import sales, investigations with background financial and operating data, series, 9886–5

Imports injury to US industries from removal of duties on foreign subsidized products, investigations with background financial and operating data, series, 9886–18

Industry finances and operations, by SIC 2- to 4-digit industry, 1970s-83 and projected to 1988, annual rpt, 2014–4

Input-output structure of US economy, detailed interindustry transactions for 537 industries, and components of final demand, 1977 benchmark data, 2708–17

Jamaica PL 480 Title I assistance effects on economic dev, with data on govt finance, economic indicators, demography, and dev programs, 1970s-81, 9916–1.51

Manufacturing census, 1982: financial and operating data, by SIC 2- to 4-digit industry, State, SMSA, and county, preliminary census div rpt series, 2491–3

Manufacturing census, 1982: financial and operating data, for SIC 4-digit industries by product, preliminary rpt series, 2491–1

Manufacturing operating and financial data, 1980-81 Annual Survey of Manufactures rpt reprints, hardbound vol, 2504–1

Manufacturing production and selected measures of capacity utilization, for 16 industry groups, monthly rpt, 23842–1.3

Manufacturing production, shipments, inventories, orders, and pollution control expenses, periodic Current Industrial Rpt series, 2506–3

Mineral Industry Surveys, explosives and blasting agents consumption by type, industry, and State, 1983, annual rpt, 5614–22

Minerals (nonfuel) company mergers by SIC 1- to 4-digit industry of acquired and acquiring firm, assets, and earnings measures, various periods 1960-79, 5608–145

Index by Categories

BY INDUSTRY

Minority business mgmt and financial assistance from federally funded organizations, by region, State, and business characteristics, FY83, annual rpt, 2104–6

Multinatl and multistate corporations income under alternative State income tax treatment methods, by major industry, 1977, article, 9373–1.412

Multinatl US firms nonbank foreign affiliates, capital expenditures by major industry group and country, 1978-84, semiannual article, 2702–1.410

Multinatl US firms nonbank foreign affiliates, capital expenditures by major industry group and country, 1984-85, semiannual article, 2702–1.437

Natl income and product, comprehensive accounts and components, *Survey of Current Business,* monthly rpt, monthly and annual tables, 2702–1.27

New England States gross product by industry sector and State, and compared to GNP, 1981-82, annual article, 9373–2.403

Overseas Business Reports: economic conditions, investment and export opportunities, and trade practices, annual country market research rpt series, 2046–6

Overseas Business Reports: economic conditions, investment and export opportunities, and trade practices, world region rpt series, 2046–5

Partnership finances, tax deductions, and employment, by industry div and size, 1979, article, 8302–2.411

Payroll (nonfarm) effect of economic recovery, by industry div and region, 4th qtr 1982-4th qtr 1983, article, 2702–1.412

Production and electric power use indexes, by SIC 2- to 4-digit industry, monthly rpt, 9365–2.10

Production trends from 1919, financial and business statistics, 1984 annual chartbook, 9364–2.5

Productivity, hours, and employment indexes for selected SIC 3- and 4-digit industries, 1954-82, annual rpt, 6824–1

Productivity of labor and capital, costs, and prices, by selected industry, and compared to 6 OECD countries, selected years 1947-82, 17898–1

Productivity of labor and capital, growth by SIC 1- to 2-digit industry, and measurement methods and bibl, various periods 1948-78 with trends from 1800, 2218–69

Productivity of labor, economic growth, and industrial policy dev, selected years 1947-82 with some projections to 1986, 26306–6.69

Retail trade census, 1982: employment, establishments, sales, and payroll, by SIC 2- to 4-digit kind of business, SMSA, and retail district, State rpt series, 2401–1

Retail trade census, 1982: employment, establishments, sales, and payroll, by SIC 2- to 4-digit kind of business, SMSA, county, and city, State rpt series, 2397–1

Retail trade sales and inventories, by kind of business, region, census div, and selected State, SMSA, and city, and seasonal adjustments, monthly rpt, 2413–3

Retail trade sales, by kind of business, advance monthly rpt, 2413–2

Retail trade sales, inventories, purchases, gross margin, and accounts receivable, by SIC 2- to 4-digit kind of business and type of ownership, 1983, annual rpt, 2413–5

Service industry census, 1982: employment, establishments, receipts, and payroll, by SIC 2- to 4-digit kind of business, SMSA, county, and city, State rpt series, 2391–1

Service industry receipts, by SIC 2- to 4-digit kind of business, 1983, annual rpt, 2413–8

Services intl transactions, and operations of US multinatl service firms and foreign affiliates, by industry and world region, 1977-82, 2706–5.30

Small and minority-owned businesses finances and operations, Federal contracts by agency, and worker characteristics, by industry, race, sex, and State, 1950s-83, annual rpt, 9764–6

Small business capital formation under securities law exemptions, effects on stocks offered, issuers, and purchasers, series, 9736–2

Small business economic conditions, with comparisons to larger businesses, selected years 1979-83, annual rpt, 9764–1.1

Small business loans and credit, operational expectations, and NYC metro area owners economic and professional attitudes, by industry div, 1980-83 surveys, hearings, 21728–52

Small business mgmt counseling by university centers, costs, funding, and businesses served by industry, with detail for 2 States, 1980-83, hearing, 25728–36

Southeastern States and 5 SMSAs economic indicators, Fed Reserve 8th District, quarterly rpt, 9391–15

Soviet Union industrial production annual growth rate, by major industry, 1960s-83, annual rpt, 244–5.3

Statistical Abstract of US, social, political, and economic data, 1950s-83 and trends, annual rpt, 2324–1.3

Technology-intensive industry employment and establishments by industry and selected location, and venture capital investments by source, 1970s-82, 26358–107

Tennessee Valley industrial dev and effects on employment, investment, and TVA power demand, by location and company, 1983, annual rpt, 9804–3

Trade policy of Fed Govt, with data on US industry foreign trade and revenues, and Japan semiconductor industry subsidies, 1970s-83, hearings, 21368–46

Trade-related employment and production by industry, occupation, and State, and US trade policy actions, 1960s-83, annual rpt, 444–1

Virgin Islands economic censuses, 1982: employment, establishments, payroll, and receipts, by SIC 1- to 4-digit industry, island, and city, 2593–1

Wholesale trade census, 1982: employment, establishments, finances, and operations, by SIC 2- to 4-digit kind of business, SMSA, county, and city, State rpt series, 2405–1

Wholesale trade census, 1982: employment, establishments, sales by commodity, and payroll, by SIC 4-digit kind of business and State, preliminary rpt series, 2403–1

Wholesale trade sales, inventories, purchases, and gross margins, by SIC 2- to 3-digit kind of business and type of ownership, 1983, annual rpt, 2413–13

Wood used in manufacturing, by type of wood, end use, and SIC 4-digit industry, 1977 with summary trends from 1928, 1208–3

Labor and Employment

American Samoa minimum wage rates, employment, earnings, and benefits, by establishment and industry, Nov 1983, biennial rpt, 6504–6

Appalachia population by age and urban-rural location, and employment and net employment change by industry, selected years 1960-90, article, 9088–33

BLS projections of employment by industry and GNP by component, analysis of projections to 1980 made selected years 1970-76, article, 6722–1.450

California business failures, plant closings, layoffs, and relocations, by plant, industry, county, and city, 1980-83, hearing, 21348–84.1

Census of Population and Housing, 1980: detailed population and housing characteristics, by county, city, and census tract, State and SMSA rpt series, 2551–2

Census of Population, 1980: detailed socioeconomic and demographic characteristics, by age, sex, race, Hispanic origin, occupation, and industry, State rpt series, 2531–4

Census of Population, 1980: detailed socioeconomic characteristics, by county, city, and inside-outside SMSAs and central cities, State rpt series, 2531–3

Coastal environmental characteristics, fish, wildlife, and use, and population socioeconomic data, for individual areas, series, 5506–4

Collective bargaining agreements expiring during year, covered workers by SIC 2-digit industry, firm, and union, with summary of key provisions, 1984, annual rpt, 6784–9

Collective bargaining calendar for Southeast US, 1984, annual rpt, 6946–1.68

Collective bargaining contract expirations and wage increases, scheduled and under cost-of-living escalator provisions, by SIC 2-digit industry and selected firm and union, 1984, annual article, 6722–1.402

Cuba economic conditions, agricultural and industrial production and distribution, trade, and intl economic relations, 1970-82 and trends from 1957, 248–40

Dallas-Fort Worth, Tex, SMSA employment, earnings, hours, and CPI changes, 1983 with trends from 1968, annual rpt, 6964–2

Denver-Boulder, Colo, SMSA employment, earnings, and CPI changes, 1983, annual rpt, 6974–2

Earnings and hours, by industry div and major manufacturing group, Monthly Labor Review, 6722–1.3

Earnings by industry div, and personal income per capita and by source, by State, MSA, and county, 1977-82, annual regional rpts, 2704–2

Earnings by major industry group, and personal income per capita and by source, by region and State, 1929-82, 2708–40

Earnings, hourly and weekly averages and Hourly Earnings Index, by industry div, monthly press release, 6742–3

Economic dev assistance of Fed Govt, generation of jobs by industry div, model methodology and outputs, various periods FY69-78, GAO rpt, 26117–32

BY INDUSTRY

Index by Categories

Employee benefit plans effects on income and payroll tax revenue by benefit type and income, with benefits by industry, 1950-83 and projected to 1988, article, 9373–1.404

Employment and earnings, detailed data, monthly rpt, 6742–2

Employment and economic conditions, alternative BLS projections to 1995 with selected trends for 1959-82, 6728–29

Employment and labor force statistics by major industry group and demographic characteristics, *Survey of Current Business,* monthly rpt, 2702–1.5

Employment and unemployment current statistics, Monthly Labor Review, 6722–1.1

Employment and wages of workers covered by State unemployment insurance laws and Fed Govt unemployment compensation, by SIC 4-digit industry and State, 1982, annual rpt, 6744–16

Employment by detailed occupation, for 29 SIC 2-digit nonmanufacturing industries, 1981 BLS survey, 6748–60

Employment by industry div, major manufacturing group, and State, Monthly Labor Review, 6722–1.2

Employment, by sector, major industry group, and sex, selected years 1850-1982, article, 6722–1.425

Employment change by industry div, civilian labor force, and unemployment and rates, by region and State, 1983, article, 6722–1.454

Employment change over business cycles, by worker characteristics and industry div, quarterly 1982-2nd qtr 1984 with trends from 1948, annual article, 6722–1.448

Employment Cost Index and percent change by occupational group, industry div, region, and metro-nonmetro area, quarterly press release, 6782–5

Employment Cost Index changes for nonfarm workers, by occupation, industry div, region, and bargaining status, monthly rpt, 6782–1

Employment Cost Index wage and salary component changes by occupational group, industry div, and collective bargaining status, and CPI changes, selected periods Sept 1975-Dec 1983, article, 6722–1.430

Employment, earnings, and hours, by selected SIC 1- to 4-digit industry, State, and for 278 major labor areas, 1939-83, annual rpt, 6744–5

Employment, earnings, and hours, by SIC 4-digit nonfarm industry, monthly 1974-Feb 1984, annual update, 6744–4

Employment, earnings, and hours, monthly press release, 6742–5

Employment situation, earnings, hours, and other BLS economic indicators, transcripts of BLS Commissioner's monthly testimony, periodic rpt, 23846–4

Employment, unemployment, and labor force, by demographic and employment characteristics, State, and for 30 metro areas and 11 large cities, 1983, annual rpt, 6744–7

Employment, unemployment, and labor force, detailed data by sociodemographic and employment characteristics, and industry, 1940s-83, 6748–72

Employment, unemployment, labor force participation, and discouraged workers, by

demographic and employment characteristics, quarterly 1981-83, annual article, 6722–1.409

Farm population employment by industry div, and unemployment, by region, 1983, annual rpt, 2544–1

Georgia job expansion in southern rural 10-county area, employment and establishments by worker and industry characteristics, 1976-81, article, 1502–7.401

Handbook of Labor Statistics, employment, earnings, hours, and labor force characteristics, 1982 and trends, detailed annual rpt, 6724–1

Hispanic Americans socioeconomic and demographic characteristics, and compared to non-Hispanics, selected years 1970-83, chartbook, 2328–48

Hours at work and hours paid ratios and impacts on productivity measures, by firm size and major industry group, with survey methodology, 1981-82, article, 6722–1.434

Houston, Tex, SMSA employment, earnings, hours, and CPI changes, 1983 with trends from 1968, annual rpt, 6964–1

Import-sensitive industries employment and wage adjustments, for 25 SIC 3-digit industries, selected years 1960-82, article, 6722–1.439

Japan worker earnings, by years of service and other characteristics, selected years 1955-80, article, 6722–1.427

Japan workers wages in smaller firms relative to wages in larger firms, by worker characteristics, firm size, and industry div, 1950s-81, article, 6722–1.461

Job tenure and occupational mobility of workers, by sociodemographic characteristics and industry div, as of Jan 1983, press release, 6748–76

Kansas City, Mo-Kans, SMSA employment, earnings, and CPI changes, with comparisons to total US, 1983, annual rpt, 6974–1

Kentucky employment growth in 9-county rural area, labor force and establishment characteristics, 1979-80, 1598–194

Labor force participation, by employment and demographic characteristics, 1982-83, annual article, 6722–1.472

Labor force status monthly changes, by selected worker characteristics, 1981-82, biennial rpt, 6744–17

Manufacturing computerized automation dev, R&D, training, and employment impacts, with comparisons to foreign countries, selected years 1960-83, 26358–105

Massachusetts employment in traditional and high technology industry by occupation, and wages by industry, and compared to US and 3 SMSAs, various periods 1976-82, article, 9373–1.416

Minority group and women's employment, by occupational group, SIC 2- to 3-digit industry, State, and SMSA, 1981, annual rpt, 9244–1

New England States collective bargaining contract terminations and workers covered, by industry and firm, 1984, annual rpt, 6916–7.2

New England States college grads employment prospects in 1984, annual narrative rpt, 6916–7.3

NYC metro area employment and prices, 1983, annual rpt, 6924–2

Occupational Outlook Handbook, 1984-85 biennial rpt, 6744–1

Older persons sociodemographic characteristics, and Fed Govt program participation and funding, 1983 with trends and projections 1900-2060, annual rpt, 25144–3.1

Oregon and Montana earnings by SIC 1- to 3-digit industry and payments to retirees by type, for 4 timber dependent communities, 1970, 1208–196

Population demographic and economic characteristics, 1982 with projections of population size to 2050, annual Current Population Rpt, 2546–2.119

Pregnant women's employment, by occupation, major industry, and sociodemographic characteristics, 1980, article, 4144–11.1

Productivity indexes for 128 SIC 2- to 4-digit industries, 1977-82, article, 6722–1.408

Self-employed, wage and salary, and unpaid family workers, employment, earnings, and hours, by industry div and occupation, 1970-83, article, 6722–1.443

Small and minority-owned businesses finances and operations, Federal contracts by agency, and worker characteristics, by industry, race, sex, and State, 1950s-83, annual rpt, 9764–6

Southeastern States employment, prices, earnings, and union membership in 8 States, Oct 1982-83, annual rpt, 6944–2

Southeastern States financial and economic devs, Fed Reserve 6th District, monthly rpt with articles, 9371–1

Southwestern States employment by major nonagricultural industry, and average hours and earnings of manufacturing production workers, monthly rpt, 6962–2

St Louis, Mo, SMSA employment, earnings, and CPI changes, 1983, annual rpt, 6974–3

Technology-intensive manufacturing employment by selected industry group, 1982, article, 9373–2.402

Trade adjustment assistance eligibility, reemployment opportunities, and worker characteristics, investigations of industries injured by import competition, series, 6406–9

Trade adjustment assistance for workers, petitions, investigations, and determinations, by major industry group, union, and State, monthly rpt, 6402–13

Unemployment and part-time employment effects on family income, by socioeconomic and labor force characteristics, 1981-82, annual rpt, 6746–1.252

Unemployment, by duration, selected demographic characteristics, industry div, and reason for job loss, various periods 1979-June 1983, article, 6722–1.411

Unemployment during business cycles, and by worker age, sex, occupation, industry div, reason, and duration, various periods 1969-82, article, 6722–1.444

Unemployment effect on family income and poverty status, by demographic, employment, and unemployment characteristics, 1981-82, annual article, 6722–1.412

Index by Categories

BY OCCUPATION

Unemployment of men and women, by contributing factor, and change in industry share of labor force and unemployment, 1973-75 and 1981-82, article, 6722–1.432

Wage and benefit changes from collective bargaining or employer decisions, by industry group, monthly rpt, 6782–1

Wage differential due to unionization, effect on production and prices by industry div, 1971, technical paper, 9387–8.81

Wages by occupation, and benefits for office and plant workers in 70 SMSAs, 1983, annual rpt, 6785–1

Wages by occupation, for office and plant workers in selected labor market areas, 1983 surveys, annual summary rpt, 6785–6

Wages, hours, benefits, and employment, by occupation and selected geographic areas, industry surveys series, 6787–6

Wages of white-collar workers, by occupation, work level, and industry div, Mar 1984, annual rpt, 6784–2

Wages of workers covered by unemployment insurance, by State and industry div, 1982-83, annual press release, 6784–17.2

Western States, FHLB 11th District housing, employment, and economic indicators, by SMSA, quarterly rpt, 9302–18

Western States housing outlook and economic and demographic trends, FHLB 11th District, urban area rpt series, 9306–2

Women's employment and earnings, by labor force and socioeconomic characteristics, and compared to men, 1978-81 and trends from 1940s, 6568–29

Work stoppages involving 6 workers or more, workers and days idle by major issue, industry, and State, selected years 1930-82, annual rpt, 6724–1.8

Youth employment, by high school and college enrollment status, industry div, occupation, and selected demographic characteristics, 1980-82, 6746–1.250

Law Enforcement

Security services expenditures, by level of govt and for private business by major industry, 1981, 6066–20.8

Natural Resources, Environment, and Pollution

Acid rain causes and effects, air pollutant emissions by source, and control costs, by region and State, selected years 1977-83 and projected to 2000, 26358–104

Air pollutant emission factors, by detailed source, 3rd edition, 1983-84 supplements, 9198–13

Air pollution abatement equipment shipments by industry, exports, and new and backlog orders, by product, 1983, annual Current Industrial Rpt, 2506–12.5

Air pollution levels for 5 pollutants, by detailed source, State, and Air Quality Control Region, 1981, annual rpt, 9194–7

Air pollution levels for 5 pollutants, by source, 1970- 82 with trends from 1940, annual rpt, 9194–13

Environmental quality and protection programs, costs, and Fed Govt enforcement, 1983, detailed annual rpt, 484–1

Foreign market and trade for pollution control instruments and equipment, and user industry operations and demand, country market research rpts, 2045–17

Hazardous waste generated in 8 southeastern States, by SIC 2-digit industry, 1960s-2020 with some trends from 1930, 9208–119

Pollution abatement capital and operating costs, by SIC 2- to 4-digit industry, State, and SMSA, 1982, annual Current Industrial Rpt, 2506–3.6

Pollution abatement capital and operating costs under Clean Air and Water Acts, for govts and selected industries, various periods 1970-2000, annual rpt, 9184–11

Pollution abatement capital expenditures, by pollution type and selected industry, 1973-84, annual article, 2702–1.423

Pollution abatement expenditures, and effect on economic indicators and industry operations, by major industry, projected under 3 pollution regulation alternatives 1983-95, 9188–84

Water pollution fish kills, by State, location, and pollution source, monthly 1978-80, annual rpt, 9204–3

Population

Income (personal) by industry group and region, percent change 1959-79 and 1979-83, article, 2702–1.443

Income (personal) per capita and by source, and earnings by industry div, by State, MSA, and county, 1977-82, annual regional rpts, 2704–2

Income (personal) per capita and total, and earnings by major industry group, by region and State, 1981-83, annual article, 2702–1.432

Income of households, families, and persons, by detailed socioeconomic characteristics and region, 1982, annual Current Population Rpt, 2546–6.39

Prices and Cost of Living

Producer Price Index current statistics, Monthly Labor Review, 6722–1.5

Producer prices and indexes, by stage of processing and detailed commodity, monthly rpt, 6762–6

Producer prices and indexes, by stage of processing and detailed commodity, monthly 1983, annual supplement, 6764–2

Retail prices set by manufacturers under fair-trade law by brand and product, with manufacturers, market concentration, and sales, by industry, selected years 1952-82, 9406–1.38

Public Welfare and Social Security

Noncash public and employer-based transfer program recipients, by income source and socioeconomic characteristics, 1982, final Current Population Rpt, 2546–6.37

OASDHI, Medicaid, SSI, and other social insurance and public welfare programs benefits, beneficiary characteristics, and trust funds, selected years 1937-83, annual rpt, 4744–3.4

OASI beneficiaries by income level, and average income, by beneficiary characteristics and income source, before and after receipt of 1st benefit, 1969-77, article, 4742–1.418

Science and Technology

Computer specialists sociodemographic, educational, and employment characteristics, and Fed Govt support by agency, 1978, biennial Current Population Rpt, 2546–2.124

Computers and computer equipment foreign market and trade, and user industry operations and demand, country market research rpts, 2045–1

Employment of scientists, engineers, and technicians in private industry, by occupation and industry group, 1980-81, biennial rpt, 9627–23

Employment of scientists, engineers, and technicians in transportation, utilities, and retail and wholesale trade, by field of science and industry, 1982, 9628–72

Engineers sociodemographic, educational, and employment characteristics, and Federal support by agency, 1978, Current Population Rpt, 2546–2.121

R&D expenditures of industry by funding source, and projected impact on output, employment, and hours of labor, by selected industry, various periods 1953-90, hearings, 25368–133

R&D funding by industry, program, and Federal agency, and high-technology trade performance, selected years 1960-FY84, 26306–6.77

R&D industry expenditures by funding source, and scientists and engineers employed, by SIC 2- and 3-digit industry, 1982 with trends from 1962, annual rpt, 9626–2.139

R&D industry expenditures, funding sources, and employment of scientists, by field and selected SIC 2- to 4-digit industry, 1971-83, annual rpt, 9624–18.3

R&D industry expenditures, total and for 6 leading industries, projected 1984-85 with trends from 1975, 9626–2.145

R&D industry funding and employment of scientists and engineers, by industry group, firm size, and funding source, 1956-82, annual rpt, 9627–21

Science Indicators, R&D expenditures, innovations, research, and higher education, with foreign comparisons, 1960s- 83, annual rpt, 9624–10

Scientist, engineer, and technician shortages by field and selected industry, 1981-83, 9626–2.133

BY OCCUPATION

Agriculture and Food

Farmland eroded by rainfall, acreage by crop, and farm operators by selected characteristics, by soil erosion class, 1977-78, 1588–83

Grain mill production workers, wages, hours, and benefits, by occupation, mill product, and region, June 1982 survey, 6787–6.204

Communications and Transportation

Railroad employee benefits and beneficiaries by type, and railroad employees and payrolls, FY82, annual rpt, 9704–2

Travel patterns, personal and household characteristics, auto use, and public transport availability, 1977 survey, series, 7556–6

TV and radio industry minority and women employment by occupation, and business owners, by race and State, with revenues and stations, 1971-81, hearing, 21368–45

Education

Elementary and secondary enrollment, households with children enrolled by school control, householder characteristics, and region, Oct 1982, 4838–13

High school classes of 1980 and 1982: educational and sociodemographic characteristics and expectations, natl longitudinal study, series, 4826–2

BY OCCUPATION

High school grads aged 17-21 percent distribution, by most recent occupation, sex, vocational education participation, May 1980, annual rpt, 4824–1.3

Special education programs for handicapped children, enrollment, staff, and funding, by handicap and State, 1981/82 and 1982/83, annual rpt, 4944–4

Vocational training bilingual projects, participants, characteristics, and costs, by program, FY82, annual rpt, 4804–26

Energy Resources and Demand

Electric and gas privately owned utilities, wages and employment by occupation, and benefits, by region, Oct 1982 survey, 6787–6.205

Nuclear industry nongovt employment by industry segment, occupation, and census div, and DOE and NRC nuclear employment, 1968-83, biennial rpt, 3004–11

Oil and gas extraction production workers, wages, hours, and benefits, by occupation, region, and for 5 States, June 1982 survey, 6787–6.203

TVA employment of minorities and women, by detailed occupation, pay level, and grade, FY83 and goals for FY84, annual rpt, 9804–17

Government and Defense

Advisory committees of Fed Govt, and members, staff, meetings, and costs, by agency, FY83, annual rpt, 9454–18

Army personnel assigned to critical occupation specialties by skill type, and working outside specialty at 5 installations, as of Mar 1982, GAO rpt, 26123–59

DOD medical personnel, trainees, and accessions by source, by occupation, specialty, and service branch, FY83, annual rpt, 3544–24

Election campaign Fed Govt funding, reform and tax deduction proposals, and TV and political action committee influence, opinion surveys, various dates 1977-83, hearings, 21428–7.1

Fed Govt civilian employment by occupation, total and for 25 agencies, as of Oct 1983, annual article, 9842–1.405

Fed Govt Equal Opportunity Recruitment Program implementation, and summary employment data, FY83, annual rpt, 9844–33

Fed Govt minority group and handicapped employment, by race, Hispanic origin, disability, sex, and employment characteristics, as of Sept 1982, biennial rpt, 9844–27

Fed Govt pay comparability with private industry, and recommended pay rate adjustments, 1983, annual rpt, 104–16

Income tax returns of individuals by tax return item, State, and occupation, and income by source and tax owed, by income level, selected years 1916-80, conf papers, 8308–28.1

Military personnel in US, and civilian employment, by age, sex, occupation, and educational attainment, 1982 and summary trends from 1950, article, 6722–1.441

Military reserve forces manpower strengths and characteristics, by component, quarterly rpt, 3542–4

Military women personnel on active duty, by demographic and service characteristics and service branch, with comparisons to men, FY83, annual chartbook, 3544–26

Navy personnel, detailed statistics, quarterly rpt, 3802–4

Passports issued, by holder characteristics, travel purpose, and country of destination, quarterly rpt, 7182–1

Taxes, tax policy, and intergovtl relations, public opinion survey results, 1972-84, annual rpt, 10044–2

Health and Vital Statistics

Air pollutant and radiation indoor levels by emissions source, and household exposure and health effects by pollutant type, various periods 1966-83, hearings, 21708–102

Asbestos workers, exposure levels, cancer incidence, and deaths, by industry and occupation, and asbestos regulation enforcement and costs/benefits, various periods 1940-2027, hearing, 21408–72

Births by outcome, and mother's sociodemographic, life style, and maternity characteristics, 1980, article, 4102–1.420, 4102–1.422

Births, fertility rates, expected births, and childless women, by socioeconomic characteristics, June 1982, annual Current Population Rpt, 2546–1.386

Births, fertility rates, expected births, and childless women, by socioeconomic characteristics, June 1983, advance annual Current Population Rpt, 2546–1.385

Births, fertility rates, expected births, and childless women, by socioeconomic characteristics, June 1983, annual Current Population Rpt, 2546–1.393

Correctional instns (Federal) health services employment, by occupation, instn, and region, monthly rpt, 6242–2

Disabled women, by socioeconomic and demographic characteristics, and compared to nondisabled women and disabled men, 1981, chartbook, 16598–4

Hazardous substances and radiation effects on workers health, by industry, occupation, age, and sex, with bibl and glossary, 1920s-82, 9638–50

Health professionals supply and education, by occupation, demographic and professional characteristics, and location, 1950s-83 and projected to 2000, biennial rpt, 4114–8

Hospital worker wages by sex and occupation, and benefits, for 22 MSAs, Oct 1981 survey, 6787–6.201

Injuries, detailed accident circumstances and safety data, by body part injured, type of equipment used, or industry, series, 6846–1

Malaria cases reported in US, including military personnel and foreign civilians, 1966-82, annual rpt, 4205–4

Peru cocaine addicts and arrested traffickers and users socioeconomic characteristics, and cocaine confiscated, 1974-78, intl conf papers, 7008–40

Puerto Rico health professionals, by occupation, 1980 and 1982, hearings, 21348–93

Washington State deaths by sex, cause, and detailed occupation, summary data from occupational mortality study, 1950-79, 4248–47

Housing and Construction

Census of Housing, 1980: structural, financial, and householder characteristics, by region and State, 2475–4

Index by Categories

Home mortgage default prospects by mortgage type and borrower characteristics, various periods 1967-82, technical paper, 9381–10.39

Industry and Commerce

Machine tool orders by selected industry, trade, and shipments and Japan share of US market by type of tool, various dates 1972-84, hearing, 25388–48

Underground economy, household expenditures and participation by type of goods or service and sociodemographic characteristics, with methodology and bibl, 1981 survey, 8308–27

Labor and Employment

Census of Population and Housing, 1980: detailed population and housing characteristics, by county, city, and census tract, State and SMSA rpt series, 2551–2

Census of Population, 1980: detailed socioeconomic and demographic characteristics, by age, sex, race, Hispanic origin, occupation, and industry, State rpt series, 2531–4

Census of Population, 1980: detailed socioeconomic characteristics, by county, city, and inside-outside SMSAs and central cities, State rpt series, 2531–3

Census of Population, 1980: labor force, by sex, detailed occupation, and region, with comparison to 1970 census, supplementary rpt, 2535–1.12

Coastal environmental characteristics, fish, wildlife, and use, and population socioeconomic data, for individual areas, series, 5506–4

Denver-Boulder, Colo, SMSA employment, earnings, and CPI changes, 1983, annual rpt, 6974–2

Earnings, annual average percent changes for selected occupational groups, selected SMSAs, monthly rpt, 6782–1

Earnings for selected industries and occupations, and interarea pay comparisons, 1945-82, annual rpt, 6724–1.6

Earnings of couples with both spouses working, by sociodemographic and employment characteristics and age of children, 1981, Current Population Rpt, 2546–2.120

Earnings of wage and salary workers, quarterly rpt, 6742–19

Earnings of women and men, analysis of differential, selected years 1967-83, articles, 6722–1.437, 6722–1.438

Educational attainment of labor force, by demographic and employment characteristics, 1982-83 with summary trends from 1940, 6746–1.251

Educational attainment of labor force, by demographic and employment characteristics, 1983, article, 6722–1.423

Educational attainment of labor force, by demographic and employment characteristics, 1984, press release, 6748–79

Employee benefits in private industry, coverage by benefit type and provisions and occupational group, 1983, annual rpt, 6784–19

Employment and earnings, detailed data, monthly rpt, 6742–2

Employment and economic conditions, alternative BLS projections to 1995 with selected trends for 1959-82, 6728–29

Index by Categories

BY OCCUPATION

Employment and labor force statistics by major industry group and demographic characteristics, *Survey of Current Business,* monthly rpt, 2702–1.5

Employment by detailed occupation, for 29 SIC 2-digit nonmanufacturing industries, 1981 BLS survey, 6748–60

Employment Cost Index and percent change by occupational group, industry div, region, and metro-nonmetro area, quarterly press release, 6782–5

Employment Cost Index changes for nonfarm workers, by occupation, industry div, region, and bargaining status, monthly rpt, 6782–1

Employment Cost Index wage and salary component changes by occupational group, industry div, and collective bargaining status, and CPI changes, selected periods Sept 1975-Dec 1983, article, 6722–1.430

Employment, revisions based on 1983 classification system, by sex and major occupational group, 1972-82, article, 6742–2.402

Employment status of family members, by occupation, family composition, age of children, and other characteristics, 1983 and trends from 1940, 6746–1.253

Employment, unemployment, and labor force, by demographic and employment characteristics, State, and for 30 metro areas and 11 large cities, 1983, annual rpt, 6744–7

Employment, unemployment, labor force participation, and discouraged workers, by demographic and employment characteristics, quarterly 1981-83, annual article, 6722–1.409

Foreign women sociodemographic, economic, and fertility characteristics, with comparisons to men, by country, 1960s-85, world region rpt series, 2326–15

Fresno, Calif, economic, population, labor, and housing indicators, various periods 1974-85, hearing, 21248–84

Handbook of Labor Statistics, employment, earnings, hours, and labor force characteristics, 1982 and trends, detailed annual rpt, 6724–1

High school and college grads employment status, job opportunities, and income, selected years 1978-83, annual rpt, 4824–2.23

Hispanic Americans socioeconomic and demographic characteristics, and compared to non-Hispanics, selected years 1970-83, chartbook, 2328–48

Japan workers wages in smaller firms relative to wages in larger firms, by worker characteristics, firm size, and industry div, 1950s-81, article, 6722–1.461

Job tenure and occupational mobility of workers, by sociodemographic characteristics and occupation, as of Jan 1983, article, 6722–1.460

Kansas City, Mo-Kans, SMSA employment, earnings, and CPI changes, with comparisons to total US, 1983, annual rpt, 6974–1

Kentucky employment growth in 9-county rural area, labor force and establishment characteristics, 1979-80, 1598–194

Labor force characteristics and economic indicators, selected years 1880-1995, chartbook, 6728–30

Labor force experience of men and women by sociodemographic characteristics, and effect on earnings, 1979, Current Population Rpt, 2546–2.123

Manufacturing computerized automation dev, R&D, training, and employment impacts, with comparisons to foreign countries, selected years 1960-83, 26358–105

Massachusetts employment in traditional and high technology industry by occupation, and wages by industry, and compared to US and 3 SMSAs, various periods 1976-82, article, 9373–1.416

Minority group and women's employment, by occupational group, SIC 2- to 3-digit industry, State, and SMSA, 1981, annual rpt, 9244–1

New England States college grads employment prospects in 1984, annual narrative rpt, 6916–7.3

NYC wages by occupation, for office and plant workers, 1983, annual rpt, 6926–1.75

Occupational manpower needs and supply by detailed occupation, and educational and training program enrollees and grads by detailed field, 1982 and 1995, biennial rpt, 6744–3

Occupational Outlook Handbook, 1984-85 biennial rpt, 6744–1

Occupational separation rates by worker characteristics, and replacement rates, 1980-81 with projections to 1990, article, 6722–1.416

Older persons sociodemographic characteristics, and Fed Govt program participation and funding, 1983 with trends and projections 1900-2060, annual rpt, 25144–3.1

Population demographic and economic characteristics, 1982 with projections of population size to 2050, annual Current Population Rpt, 2546–2.119

Pregnant women's employment, by occupation, major industry, and sociodemographic characteristics, 1980, article, 4144–11.1

Self-employed, wage and salary, and unpaid family workers, employment, earnings, and hours, by industry div and occupation, 1970-83, article, 6722–1.443

Southeastern States employment measures by occupation, for Fed Reserve 6th District States, 1982 and projected to 1995, article, 9371–1.430

St Louis, Mo, SMSA employment, earnings, and CPI changes, 1983, annual rpt, 6974–3

Statistical Abstract of US, social, political, and economic data, 1950s-83 and trends, annual rpt, 2324–1.3

Trade adjustment assistance eligibility, reemployment opportunities, and worker characteristics, investigations of industries injured by import competition, series, 6406–9

Trade-related employment and production by industry, occupation, and State, and US trade policy actions, 1960s-83, annual rpt, 444–1

Unemployment and part-time employment effects on family income, by socioeconomic and labor force characteristics, 1981-82, annual rpt, 6746–1.252

Unemployment during business cycles, and by worker age, sex, occupation, industry div, reason, and duration, various periods 1969-82, article, 6722–1.444

Unemployment effect on family income and poverty status, by demographic, employment, and unemployment characteristics, 1981-82, annual article, 6722–1.412

Unemployment major indicators by BLS, transcripts of BLS Commissioner's monthly testimony, periodic rpt, 23846–4

Unemployment major indicators, by occupational group, monthly press release, 6742–5

Vocationally rehabilitated persons under State agency programs, by sociodemographic characteristics and disabling condition, FY79-81, annual rpt, 4944–6

Wages by occupation, and benefits for office and plant workers, annual labor market survey rpt series, 6785–3

Wages by occupation, and benefits for office and plant workers in 70 SMSAs, 1983, annual rpt, 6785–1

Wages by occupation, and benefits for office and plant workers, 1983, annual SMSA survey rpt series, 6785–12

Wages by occupation, and benefits for office and plant workers, 1984, annual SMSA survey rpt series, 6785–11

Wages by occupation, for office and plant workers in metro areas, by sex and region, July 1983, annual summary rpt, 6785–9

Wages by occupation, for office and plant workers in selected labor market areas, 1983 surveys, annual summary rpt, 6785–6

Wages by occupation, for office and plant workers in selected SMSAs, 1983 and 1984 surveys, annual rpt, 6785–5

Wages, hours, benefits, and employment, by occupation and selected geographic areas, industry surveys series, 6787–6

Wages of white-collar workers, by occupation, work level, and industry div, Mar 1984, annual rpt, 6784–2

Women in couples with wife as primary earner, socioeconomic and family characteristics, with comparative data for husbands, Mar 1982, 2326–11.9

Women's employment and earnings, by labor force and socioeconomic characteristics, and compared to men, 1978-81 and trends from 1940s, 6568–29

Women's employment share in selected occupations under 1970 and 1980 census classifications, 1970 and 1980, article, 6722–1.417

Youth employment, by high school and college enrollment status, industry div, occupation, and selected demographic characteristics, 1980-82, 6746–1.250

Youth summer employment, by sex, race, and class of worker, 1979-84, annual press release, 6744–14

Law Enforcement

Crime victimization rates by type of offense, and victim and offense characteristics, Natl Crime Survey series, 6066–3

Peru cocaine addicts and arrested traffickers and users socioeconomic characteristics, and cocaine confiscated, 1974-78, intl conf papers, 7008–40

Natural Resources, Environment, and Pollution

Forest land owner characteristics in Northeast States, owners and acreage, series, 1206–7

BY OCCUPATION

Land privately held, acreage and owners by owner characteristics, land use, and region, and purchase and improvement funding, 1978 survey, series, 1506–5

Radiation from 1940s-70s nuclear weapons tests, levels in air and water, and personnel exposure by military unit and job category, series, 3906–1

Population

Educational attainment of population, by sociodemographic characteristics and for large States and SMSAs, 1981 and trends from 1940, biennial Current Population Rpt, 2546–1.390

Families and households detailed socioeconomic characteristics, Mar 1982, annual Current Population Rpt, 2546–1.383

Income (household) and cash and noncash transfer program participation, by sociodemographic characteristics, quarterly rpt, 2542–2

Income (household), home value and equity, and financial assets by type, by household characteristics, 1983 survey with trends from 1970, article, 9362–1.406

Income and socioeconomic characteristics of persons, families, and households, detailed cross-tabulations, Current Population Rpt series, 2546–6

Mobility of population, detailed data by demographic and socioeconomic characteristics of movers and nonmovers, Mar 1981-82, annual Current Population Rpt, 2546–1.384

Poverty status of families and persons, by detailed socioeconomic characteristics, 1982, annual Current Population Rpt, 2546–6.40

Public Welfare and Social Security

Disability Insurance beneficiaries sociodemographic and medical characteristics, 1977-79, annual rpt, 4744–20

Noncash public and employer-based transfer program recipients, by income source and socioeconomic characteristics, 1982, final Current Population Rpt, 2546–6.37

OASI beneficiaries by income level, and average income, by beneficiary characteristics and income source, before and after receipt of 1st benefit, 1969-77, article, 4742–1.418

Science and Technology

Computer specialists sociodemographic, educational, and employment characteristics, and Fed Govt support by agency, 1978, biennial Current Population Rpt, 2546–2.124

Employment of scientists, engineers, and technicians in defense and nondefense industries, and supply/demand, by field, 1981-87, 9628–71

Employment of scientists, engineers, and technicians in private industry, by occupation and industry group, 1980-81, biennial rpt, 9627–23

Employment of scientists, engineers, and technicians in transportation, utilities, and retail and wholesale trade, by field of science and industry, 1982, 9628–72

Engineers sociodemographic, educational, and employment characteristics, and Federal support by agency, 1978, Current Population Rpt, 2546–2.121

Robots installed for manufacturing, and jobs displaced and created by occupation, by type of robot use, 1980s-2000, hearings, 21728–54

Veterans Affairs

Medicine and Surgery Dept of VA, trainees by detailed program and city, FY83, annual rpt, 9924–21

Older veterans aged 55 and over, socioeconomic characteristics, economic resources, health care and status, and actual and expected VA benefits use, 1983 survey, 9928–29

DEMOGRAPHIC BREAKDOWNS

BY AGE

Agriculture and Food

Census of Agriculture, 1982: farms, farmland, production and costs, and operator characteristics, preliminary State and county rpt series, 2330–1

Census of Agriculture, 1982: farms, farmland, production, finances, and operator characteristics, by county, final State rpt series, 2331–1

Dairy products household expenditures, effects of income and other sociodemographic characteristics, modeling results, 1977/78, 1561–2.404

Farm hired workers, sociodemographic characteristics, and farm/nonfarm income and workdays, by whether worked in Mar 1981, article, 6722–1.440

Farm population, by employment and socioeconomic characteristics, 1983, annual rpt, 2544–1

Farmland eroded by rainfall, acreage by crop, and farm operators by selected characteristics, by soil erosion class, 1977-78, 1588–83

Food consumption and nutrient intake by individuals, by food group, source, and socioeconomic characteristics, 1977-78 natl survey, final rpt series, 1356–4

Food expenditures for fruit, vegetable, and potato products related to changes in income and other household characteristics, 1977-78, 1548–236

Health insurance coverage of farmers, farm population, and managers, by insurance type and selected sociodemographic characteristics, 1976, 1598–191

Banking, Finance, and Insurance

Banking in-home services, consumer expected use and acceptable costs, 1983 survey, article, 9371–1.422

Debt (mortgage and consumer) and net worth, by householder characteristics and family income, 1983 survey, article, 9362–1.411

Financial services household use and preferred provider, by respondent age and income, 1982-84 surveys, article, 9371–1.417

Communications and Transportation

Aircraft accidents in general aviation by State, circumstances, and pilots involved by age and blood alcohol level, 1981, annual rpt, 9614–3.1

Index by Categories

Aircraft fatal accidents of commuter airlines, air taxis, and general aviation, alcohol involvement, circumstances, and pilot characteristics, 1975-81, 9618–11

Airline and general aviation accident circumstances, severity, and causes, for US operations of domestic and foreign aircraft, periodic rpt, 9612–1

Airline pilots medically disqualified for service, by airline, disease, affected body site, and age, 1978-80, 7506–10.23

Airline pilots terminated for medical reasons and reinstated by carrier, and aircraft accidents by age of flight crew, selected years 1960-81, hearing, 21148–34

Bus riders by age, income, and trip purpose, and impacts of regulatory reform on bus industry operations, finances, and services, 1970s-83, 14828–2.2

DOT employment by subagency, State, and selected personnel characteristics, FY83, annual rpt, 7304–18.1

Drivers licensed by age and sex, and licensing policies, by State, 1982, annual rpt, 7554–16

Drivers licenses in force, by age, sex, and State, 1982-83, annual summary rpt, 7554–24

Drivers licenses in force by license type, sex, and age, and revenues, by State, 1983, annual rpt, 7554–1.2

Drivers licenses renewed by mail and in person at California Motor Vehicles Dept, by driver age and accident and conviction rates, 1980-83, article, 7762–9.401

Pilots and nonpilots certified by FAA, by type of certificate, age, sex, region, and State, 1983, annual rpt, 7504–2.2

Railroad employee benefits and beneficiaries by type, and railroad employees and payrolls, FY82, annual rpt, 9704–2

Railroad employee benefits and beneficiaries by type, benefit program finances, and railroad employees and payroll, FY83, annual rpt, 9704–1

Seat belt use, effects of driving circumstances and driver characteristics and attitudes, 1981 survey, 7768–82

Traffic accidents and casualties detailed direct and indirect costs, by characteristics of persons and vehicles involved, 1979-80, 7768–80

Traffic accidents and deaths by characteristics of persons and vehicles involved and State, and Natl Hwy Traffic Safety Admin activities, 1961-81, annual rpt, 7764–1

Traffic accidents, circumstances, injuries, deaths, and characteristics of persons and vehicles involved, 1982, annual rpt, 7764–13

Traffic deaths, by victim occupancy, age, and sex, 1975-83, 7766–13.7

Traffic fatal accidents, circumstances, and characteristics of persons and vehicles involved, 1983, annual rpt, 7764–14

Traffic fatal accidents detailed circumstances, and characteristics of persons and vehicles involved, 1982, annual rpt, 7764–10

Travel patterns, personal and household characteristics, auto use, and public transport availability, 1977 survey, series, 7556–6

Travel to US, by characteristics of visit and traveler, country, and State of destination, quarterly rpt, 2902–1

Index by Categories

BY AGE

Truck accidents, injuries, deaths, and property damage, by circumstances, carrier type, and driver age and condition, 1983, annual rpt, 7554–9

Education

Condition of Education, detailed data on enrollment, staff, achievement, finances, curricula, and education effects on employment, 1982-83, annual rpt, 4824–1

Digest of Education Statistics, detailed data on students, staff, finances, and facilities, 1982 and selected trends, annual rpt, 4824–2

Enrollment of persons aged 3-34, by grade level and student characteristics, Oct 1982, advance annual Current Population Rpt, 2546–1.391

Enrollment of persons aged 3-34, by grade level, instn control, and student characteristics, Oct 1983, advance annual Current Population Rpt, 2546–1.392

Handicapped children public education program enrollment, staff, and funding, by handicap, age, and State, 1981/82-1982/83, annual rpt, 4944–4

Head Start Project enrollment, appropriations, and staff, FY65-84, annual rpt, 4604–8

High school classes of 1980 and 1982: educational and sociodemographic characteristics and expectations, natl longitudinal study, series, 4826–2

Postsecondary enrollment in academic, vocational, and continuing education, by student characteristics, Oct 1982, 4848–16

Energy Resources and Demand

Employment of scientists and engineers in energy-related fields, supply/demand and effects of R&D funding, by sector, energy type, and age, 1962-91, annual rpt, 3004–19

Household energy use by socioeconomic characteristics, impact of energy price increases, selected years 1978-95, 3004–13.3

Household, housing, and fuel use characteristics, EIA survey series, 3166–7

Government and Defense

Election campaign Fed Govt funding, reform and tax deduction proposals, and TV and political action committee influence, opinion surveys, various dates 1977-83, hearings, 21428–7.1

Fed Govt civil service retirees and survivors, and monthly benefit, for US territories and foreign countries, and by State, age, and sex, FY81-82, annual rpt, 9844–1.1

Fed Govt personnel action appeals, decisions of Merit Systems Protection Board, by agency, veteran status, sex, and age, FY82, annual rpt, 9494–2.1

Immigration, and alien residents, workers, visitors, deportations, and naturalizations, by country of birth, FY81, annual rpt, 6264–2

Military personnel, by selected sociodemographic characteristics, 1984 annual summary rpt, 3504–13

Military personnel in US, and civilian employment, by age, sex, occupation, and educational attainment, 1982 and summary trends from 1950, article, 6722–1.441

Military personnel on active duty, by age and education, 1960-83, annual rpt, 3544–1.2

Military reserve forces manpower strengths and characteristics, by component, quarterly rpt, 3542–4

Navy personnel, detailed statistics, quarterly rpt, 3802–4

Passports issued, by holder characteristics, travel purpose, and country of destination, quarterly rpt, 7182–1

Servicemen's life insurance program participants, death rates by age and service branch, 1980-82, annual rpt, 9924–3

Taxes, tax policy, and intergovtl relations, public opinion survey results, 1972-84, annual rpt, 10044–2

Voting age population selected characteristics and participation in presidential elections, 1964-80 with projections to 2000, Current Population Rpt, 2546–2.117

Health and Vital Statistics

Abortions (legal), and deaths from abortion and childbirth, by medical and sociodemographic characteristics, 1972-83, hearings, 21368–47

Abortions, by patient sociodemographic characteristics, pregnancy history, and procedure, 1980, US Vital Statistics final rpt, 4146–5.72

Air pollutant and radiation indoor levels by emissions source, and household exposure and health effects by pollutant type, various periods 1966-83, hearings, 21708–102

Alaska Native Medical Center visits and ambulatory high use patients by age and sex, and patient deaths, 1972-78, article, 4102–1.440

Asian and Pacific Islands Americans births by ethnic origin and sociodemographic and birth characteristics, with comparisons to blacks and whites, 1978-80, 4146–5.75

Births (cesarean and total) in hospitals affiliated and not affiliated with medical schools, by characteristics of mother, birth, and hospital, 1977, 4186–6.4

Births and birth rates, by demographic and birth characteristics, 1981 with trends from 1940, US Vital Statistics advance rpt, 4146–5.73

Births and birth rates, by parent and birth characteristics and infant condition at birth, 1982 and trends from 1940, US Vital Statistics annual advance rpt, 4146–5.79

Births, and birth rates for unmarried and all women, by race of child, age and Hispanic origin of mother, and State, 1980, 4147–21.42

Births and birth rates of teenage girls, and distribution of births with low birth weight and Apgar scores, by mother and infant characteristics, 1970-81, 4147–21.41

Births attended by midwives and in nonhospital settings, by mother's sociodemographic and prenatal care characteristics and infant race and birthweight, 1978-79 with trends from 1935, 4147–21.40

Births, birth rates, and birth characteristics, by age of parents, 1979 and trends, US Vital Statistics annual rpt, 4144–1

Births, by outcome, and mother's sociodemographic, life style, and maternity characteristics, 1980, article, 4102–1

Births, fertility rates, expected births, and childless women, by socioeconomic characteristics, June 1982, annual Current Population Rpt, 2546–1.386

Births, fertility rates, expected births, and childless women, by socioeconomic characteristics, June 1983, advance annual Current Population Rpt, 2546–1.385

Births, fertility rates, expected births, and childless women, by socioeconomic characteristics, June 1983, annual Current Population Rpt, 2546–1.393

Birthspacing by period of woman's birth and marriage, period of child's birth, and sociodemographic characteristics, June 1980, Current Population Rpt, 2546–1.387

Cancer cases, incidence, deaths, and death rates, by body site, age, race, Hispanic origin, and sex, for 10 geographic areas, 1973-81, 4478–130

Cancer deaths by age, 1980, and deaths and new cases, 1983, by sex and body site, annual fact book, 4474–13

CAT scan procedures on hospital inpatients, by body site and patient and hospital characteristics, 1979-82, 4146–8.102

Child obesity and low height-for-age, for public food program participants aged 1-4, by race and Hispanic origin, 1982, article, 4202–7.403

Contraceptives use by women, by method, marital status, age, and race, 1982, 4146–8.103

Coxsackie B virus cases, by isolate, associated clinical syndrome and patient age and sex, US and Nassau County, NY, 1970-79, article, 4102–1.452

Death rates by age and sex, and persons aged 65 and 80 and older share of population and deaths, selected years 1900-80, article, 4102–1.447

Death rates by sex, race, and age for 40 causes, projected for 10-year period, 1982 rpt, 4208–21

Death rates for persons 65 and over, by major cause, sex, and age, selected years 1940-80, 4147–3.25

Deaths and death rates, by cause, age, sex, and race, provisional 1982-83 with trends from 1950, US Vital Statistics annual rpt, 4144–7

Deaths and death rates by detailed cause and demographic characteristics, 1979 and selected trends, US Vital Statistics annual rpt, 4144–2.1, 4144–2.5

Deaths and death rates, by detailed geographic area, cause, and demographic characteristics, 1979, US Vital Statistics annual rpt, 4144–3

Deaths and death rates, by selected cause and demographic characteristics, 1981, US Vital Statistics advance rpt, 4146–5.78

Deaths and death rates, by selected cause and demographic characteristics, 1982, US Vital Statistics advance rpt, 4146–5.81

Deaths and death rates, provisional data, monthly rpt, 4142–1

Deaths by principal or contributing cause, with type of injury reported in accidental, poisoning, and violent deaths, by age, sex, and race, 1978, 4146–5.76

Deaths due to cold weather and related causes, by age, race, State, and city, selected periods 1962-83, 21148–30

Deaths recorded in 121 cities, by age group and for infants, weekly rpt, 4202–1

Dental malpractice claims, by amount, procedure type, region, State, and provider and patient characteristics, 1970, article, 4102–1.416

BY AGE

Index by Categories

Disability (work-related), incidence among men aged 22-64 related to sociodemographic and employment characteristics and to self-evaluated mental stress, 1972-74, 4746–5.43

Disabled women, by socioeconomic and demographic characteristics, and compared to nondisabled women and disabled men, 1981, chartbook, 16598–4

Divorces, divorce rates, and characteristics, by region and State, 1981, US Vital Statistics advance rpt, 4146–5.74

Drug (prescription) use by outpatient characteristics and generic or brand name, and hospital and drugstore costs by drug class, 1982, annual rpt, 4064–12

Drug abuse treatment programs, methods, and policy issues, series, 4496–5

Drug abusers characteristics, and acquired immune deficiency syndrome (AIDS) cases by sexual preference and intravenous drug use, 1979-81, article, 4102–1.427

Drugs (analgesic) provided during visits to office-based physicians, by patient characteristics, drug brand and type, and physician specialty, 1980-81, 4146–8.99

Family planning and infertility services use by women, by source of service, marital status, age, race, and Hispanic origin, 1982, 4146–8.104

Fetal deaths and rates, by gestation period, birth weight and order, race, age of mother, and geographic area, 1979, US Vital Statistics annual rpt, 4144–2.3

Health and Nutrition Examination Natl Survey, health and dental condition and body measurements by age, sex, and race, Vital and Health Statistics series, 4147–11

Health care expenditures, natl survey on services use, costs, and sources of payment, by patient and physician characteristics, 1977-78, series, 4186–3

Health care services of selected medical practitioners, use by patient characteristics, 1980 survey with trends from 1963, 4146–12.4

Health condition and health care resources, use, and expenditures, 1970s-82 with trends and projections 1900-2000, annual compilation, 4144–11

Health condition, hospitalization, disability, and medical costs, by demographic characteristics, Vital and Health Statistics series, 4147–10

Health habits associated with 10 major death causes, prevalence of 8 risk factors in selected States, 1981-83 surveys, article, 4202–7.405

Hispanic Americans births and birth and fertility rates, by detailed Hispanic origin, characteristics of mother, birth, and prenatal care, and for 22 States, 1981, 4146–5.80

Hospital and nursing home discharges, by age, sex, marital status, and selected diagnosis, 1976 and 1979, article, 4102–1.443

Hospital discharges and length of stay, by patient age and sex, facility size and ownership, procedure performed, and region, 1982, 4146–8.96

Hospital discharges and length of stay, by patient age and sex, facility size and ownership, procedure performed, and region, 1983, 4146–8.101

Hospital discharges and length of stay, by patient characteristics, facility size, procedure performed, diagnosis, and region, 1982, annual rpt, 4147–13.78

Infant deaths by detailed cause, geographic location, age, race, and sex, 1979, US Vital Statistics annual rpt, 4144–2.2

Infectious notifiable diseases, cases and incidence, by census div and State, 1982, annual rpt, 4204–1

Influenza deaths, viruses identified by State and country, epidemiology, and vaccine effects and recommended dosages by age, 1979/80-1980/81, annual rpt, 4205–3

Injuries and deaths from use of selected consumer products and related activity, by victim age and sex, 1982, annual rpt, 9164–7

Injuries and deaths from use of selected consumer products, by victim age and medical treatment status, 1982, annual rpt, 9164–6

Injuries, deaths, and medical costs from selected consumer products use, by victim age, 1981-83, annual rpt, 9164–2

Internist office visits and drugs provided, by characteristics of visit, patient, and physician, and location, 1980-81, 4147–13.80

Israel and France urban youths use of selected drugs, alcohol, and cigarettes, by age and sex, 1977 and 1979, article, 4102–1.430

Israel, Tel Aviv Medical Center services and use, by patient age and condition, selected years 1976-83, article, 4102–1.445

Kidney end-stage disease patients by patient characteristics and country, and per capita spending for treatment, selected years 1973-81, article, 4102–1.450

Life expectancy, and deaths by cause, by sex and age, 1900-2050, SSA actuarial rpt, 4706–1.89

Life expectancy increase impacts on OASDI and pension policy, with alternative sociodemographic projections to 2100, hearing, 25368–130

Life tables, 1979 and trends from 1900, US Vital Statistics annual rpt, 4144–2.6

Life tables, 1980 and trends from 1900, US Vital Statistics annual rpt, 4144–5

Marriages and marriage rates by State, and bride and groom characteristics, 1981, advance annual US Vital Statistics rpt, 4146–5.77

Marriages, divorces, and rates, by detailed demographic and geographic characteristics, 1979 and trends, US Vital Statistics annual rpt, 4144–4

Measles immunization, natural immunity, and incidence rates in Israel, by age, 1965-83 and projected to 1990, article, 4102–1.429

Medicare coverage of new medical technologies and reimbursements, and health services use and costs, selected years 1966-82, 26358–106

Mental health facilities, services, staff, and patient characteristics, 1970s-82 with trends from 1954, annual rpt, 4504–9

Mental health office and clinic visits, average charges, and total expenditures for services, by type of provider and patient characteristics, 1980, 4146–11.5

Mental hospitals of States and counties, patients and admissions by diagnosis, age, and State, FY81, annual rpt, 4504–2

Mentally retarded and developmentally disabled treatment and services, university-affiliated facility funding, activities, and clients, 1980-FY83, 4608–19

Navy and Marine Corps disease incidence, medical care, and deaths, by detailed diagnosis, and medical personnel and workloads, 1978-79, annual rpt, 3804–1

New York State spontaneous fetal death rates, by period of gestation, 1968-78, article, 4102–1.428

Nigeria native and Western health care use, by sociodemographic characteristics, 1984 article, 4102–1.417

Nurses (registered) population and employment by age and education, and nursing program admissions and grads, projected 1981-90, article, 4102–1.439

Nursing home cost insurance premiums by age, and benefit provisions, for policies of 16 companies, 1984 conf paper, 4658–7

Nutrient intake, by age and sex, various periods 1971-80, 028–20

Nutrition status of infants and children, blood and height-weight indicators, and low birth weight risk factors, by age, race, and Hispanic origin, 1981, annual rpt, 4205–24

Nutrition surveillance, blood values and other nutrition indicators by age, race, and Hispanic origin, 1982, annual rpt, 4204–1.3

Obstetrician-gynecologist office visits and drugs used, by visit reason, diagnosis, treatment, and patient and physician characteristics, 1980-81, 4147–13.76

Occupational health risks from hazardous substances and radiation, by industry, occupation, age, and sex, with bibl and glossary, 1920s-82, 9638–50

Occupational injuries, detailed accident circumstances and safety data, by body part injured, type of equipment used, or industry, series, 6846–1

Older persons health care total and out-of-pocket expenditures, by sociodemographic characteristics, poverty and health status, and degree of functional limitation, 1980, 4146–11.4

Older persons health status, health services use and expenditures by type, Medicare enrollment and reimbursement, and private insurance coverage, 1977-84, article, 4652–1.420

Pelvic inflammatory disease private physician diagnoses by age, race, and reason for visit, 1979-81, article, 4202–7.404

Peru cocaine addicts and arrested traffickers and users socioeconomic characteristics, and cocaine confiscated, 1974-78, intl conf papers, 7008–40

Pharmacists employment and sociodemographic characteristics, and reasons for not working in field, by State and overseas, as of 1979, 4147–14.28

Physician visits for new pain symptoms, by diagnosis, physician specialty, and patient characteristics, and drugs prescribed or used, 1980-81, 4146–8.97

Physicians (not office-based) visits by reason, diagnosis, treatment, patient and physician characteristics, and physician primary activity, 1980, 4147–13.77

Pregnancy health counseling effect on smoking, diet, delivery costs, and birth

Index by Categories

BY AGE

weight, by sociodemographic characteristics and pregnancy history, 1983 article, 4102–1.401

Pregnancy-related deaths and death rates, by age and race, 1974-78, article, 4202–7.406

Smoking related to chronic obstructive lung disease and deaths, by sociodemographic and smoking characteristics, literature review, 1984 annual Surgeon General rpt, 4044–6

Soviet Union industrial and agricultural production by selected commodity, and demographic trends and projections by Republic, 1950s-2000, hearings, 23848–180

Statistical Abstract of US, social, political, and economic data, 1950s-83 and trends, annual rpt, 2324–1.1

Sterilization of women following hospital delivery of live or stillborn infants, by sociodemographic and maternity characteristics, 1972 and 1980, article, 4102–1.419

Surgeon office visits and drugs provided, by characteristics of visit, patient, and physician, and location, 1980-81, 4147–13.79

Teenage girls births and sexual experience by race, abortions, and birth control use, by age, 1970s-80 with birth trends from 1920, hearings, 21968–29

TTPI births by age of mother and deaths by age and sex, selected years 1965-82, annual rpt, 7004–6.1

Tuberculosis cases, deaths, and treatment, by demographic characteristics, State, and city, 1982 and trends from 1953, annual rpt, 4204–2

Visual impairment survey methodology and results by age, in 3 SMSAs, Aug 1981-Dec 1982, 4478–147

Youth office visits to physicians by patient and visit characteristics and physician specialty, and drug mentions by brand, 1980-81, 4146–8.100

Housing and Construction

Census of Housing, 1980: inventory, occupancy, and unit characteristics, changes from 1973 by region and inside-outside SMSAs and central cities, series, 2473–3

Census of Housing, 1980: occupancy and unit characteristics of SMSAs and central cities, by race, Hispanic origin, and city, State and SMSA rpt series, 2473–1

Census of Housing, 1980: structural, financial, and householder characteristics, by region and State, 2475–4

Home mortgages (graduated payment) FHA-insured, financial, property, and mortgagor characteristics, for US and selected States, quarterly rpt, 5142–41

Home mortgages (graduated payment) FHA-insured, financial, property, and mortgagor characteristics, US summary, quarterly rpt, 5142–40

Home mortgages FHA-insured, financial, property, and mortgagor characteristics, quarterly rpt, 5142–1

Home mortgages FHA-insured, financial, property, and mortgagor characteristics, 1983, annual rpt, 5144–17

Housing characteristics of recent movers for new and previous unit, and household characteristics, by inside-outside central cities, 1979-82 surveys, SMSA rpt series, 2485–6

Housing occupancy and unit and household characteristics, by region and metro-nonmetro residence, 1983, biennial survey, 2485–1

Mobile and manufactured home safety standards, program inspections, enforcement actions, and accidents and casualties by victim characteristics, 1982-83, biennial rpt, 5004–4

Quality of housing and neighborhoods, indicators and attitudes, and occupant characteristics, by urban-rural location and region, 1981, annual survey, 2485–7

Industry and Commerce

Underground economy, household expenditures and participation by type of goods or service and sociodemographic characteristics, with methodology and bibl, 1981 survey, 8308–27

Labor and Employment

Australia and US youth unemployment rates, by sex and age, Mar 1983 and trends from 1960s, article, 6722–1.462

CETA participants by sociodemographic characteristics, and Labor Dept activities and staff, FY83, annual rpt, 6304–1

Earnings of couples with both spouses working, by sociodemographic and employment characteristics and age of children, 1981, Current Population Rpt, 2546–2.120

Earnings of full- and part-time workers, quarterly rpt, 6742–19

Earnings of women and men, analysis of differential, by sociodemographic characteristics, hours worked, and occupation, selected years 1967-83, article, 6722–1.437

Employment and earnings, detailed data, monthly rpt, 6742–2

Employment and economic conditions, alternative BLS projections to 1995 with selected trends for 1959-82, 6728–29

Employment and unemployment current statistics, Monthly Labor Review, 6722–1.1

Employment change over business cycles, by worker characteristics and industry div, quarterly 1982-2nd qtr 1984 with trends from 1948, annual article, 6722–1.448

Employment, earnings, and hours, monthly press release, 6742–5

Employment-population ratios and unemployment rates, for total and civilian male labor force, by age and race, 1963-82, article, 6722–1.442

Employment situation, earnings, hours, and other BLS economic indicators, transcripts of BLS Commissioner's monthly testimony, periodic rpt, 23846–4

Employment status of family members, by family composition, age of children, and other characteristics, 1983 and trends from 1940, 6746–1.253

Employment, unemployment, and labor force, by demographic and employment characteristics, State, and for 30 metro areas and 11 large cities, 1983, annual rpt, 6744–7

Employment, unemployment, and labor force, detailed data by sociodemographic and employment characteristics, and industry, 1940s-83, 6748–72

Employment, unemployment, hours, earnings, and productivity, selected years 1929-83, annual rpt, 204–1.2

Employment, unemployment, labor force participation, and discouraged workers, by demographic and employment characteristics, quarterly 1981-83, annual article, 6722–1.409

Handbook of Labor Statistics, employment, earnings, hours, and labor force characteristics, 1982 and trends, detailed annual rpt, 6724–1

Japan worker earnings, by years of service and other characteristics, selected years 1955-80, article, 6722–1.427

Japan workers wages in smaller firms relative to wages in larger firms, by worker characteristics, firm size, and industry div, 1950s-81, article, 6722–1.461

Job tenure and occupational mobility of workers, by sociodemographic characteristics and industry div, as of Jan 1983, press release, 6748–76

Job tenure and occupational mobility of workers, by sociodemographic characteristics and occupation, as of Jan 1983, article, 6722–1.460

Job Training Partnership Act dislocated workers program performance standards guide for States, with data on previous programs, by State and client characteristics, FY81-82, 6408–59.2

Kentucky employment growth in 9-county rural area, labor force and establishment characteristics, 1979-80, 1598–194

Labor force and participation rates, and unemployed persons, by age and sex, *Business Conditions Digest,* historical supplement and methodology, 1947-82, 2708–31

Labor force and participation rates, and unemployed persons, by age and sex, *Business Conditions Digest,* monthly rpt, 2702–3.7

Labor force characteristics and economic indicators, selected years 1880-1995, chartbook, 6728–30

Labor force experience of men and women by sociodemographic characteristics, and effect on earnings, 1979, Current Population Rpt, 2546–2.123

Labor force participation, by employment and demographic characteristics, 1982-83, annual article, 6722–1.472

Labor force status monthly changes, by selected worker characteristics, 1981-82, biennial rpt, 6744–17

Occupational separation rates by worker characteristics, and replacement rates, 1980-81 with projections to 1990, article, 6722–1.416

Pension benefits and after-tax salary replacement rates by plan type, and older persons income and income sources, by age and marital status, 1950s-82, conf proceedings, 25408–87

Retirement status of older white men, and 2-year transition and continuation rates, by age, selected years 1969-75, article, 6722–1.445

Small business and all employees sociodemographic characteristics, by industry div and firm size, 1978-1979, annual rpt, 9764–6.3

Trade adjustment assistance eligibility, reemployment opportunities, and worker characteristics, investigations of industries injured by import competition, series, 6406–9

BY AGE

Unemployment and part-time employment, by race, Hispanic origin, sex, family composition, income, and poverty status, 1980-82, annual report, 6744–15

Unemployment and part-time employment effects on family income, by socioeconomic and labor force characteristics, 1981-82, annual rpt, 6746–1.252

Unemployment, by duration, selected demographic characteristics, industry div, and reason for job loss, various periods 1979-June 1983, article, 6722–1.411

Unemployment duration questions of Current Population Survey, response consistency, and results, 1984 article, 6722–1.421

Unemployment during business cycles, and by worker age, sex, occupation, industry div, reason, and duration, various periods 1969-82, article, 6722–1.444

Unemployment rates, current data and annual trends, monthly rpt, 23842–1.2

Vocationally rehabilitated persons under State agency programs, by sociodemographic characteristics and disabling condition, FY79-81, annual rpt, 4944–6

Women's employment and earnings, by labor force and socioeconomic characteristics, and compared to men, 1978-81 and trends from 1940s, 6568–29

Women's labor force and OASDHI participation by age, and pension coverage by sex, selected years 1939-82, hearing, 25368–131.1

Women's labor force participation, by age, race, and family status, quarterly rpt, 6742–17

Youth employment and hours worked, by high school and college enrollment status, sex, race, and Hispanic origin, 1982-83, annual article, 6722–1.446

Youth employment, by high school and college enrollment status, industry div, occupation, and selected demographic characteristics, 1980-82, 6746–1.250

Youth labor force participation, by age group, Apr and July 1984 and change from 1983, annual press release, 6744–13

Law Enforcement

Aircraft hijackers, and date and place of birth and race or ethnic group, 1961-83, annual rpt, 7504–31.3

Arrests and arrest rates, by offense, offender characteristics, population size, and State, 1970s-83, annual rpt, 6224–2.2

Assaults, murders, and other deaths of law enforcement officers, by circumstances, level of govt, agency, victim and offender characteristics, and location, 1983, annual rpt, 6224–3

Bank robbery court cases by case processing, sentencing, and offender characteristics, and compared to other Fed Govt felony cases, 1979-80, periodic rpt, 6062–2.407

Convicted Federal offenders, by offense and district, as of June 1983, annual rpt, 18204–1

Crime and criminal justice data, including justice expenditures and employment by level of govt, 1970s-82 with some trends from 1875, 6068–174

Crime victim medical expenses and property loss, and median loss by victim characteristics, by offense type, 1975-81, 6066–19.6

Crime victimization rates by type of offense, and victim and offense characteristics, Natl Crime Survey series, 6066–3

Crimes of violence involving relatives, by victim-offender relationship, circumstances, and victim characteristics, aggregate 1973-81, 6066–19.5

Drug defendants, by sociodemographic and case processing characteristics, with comparisons to Federal fraud and bank robbery defendants, 1979, 6062–2.403

Homicides and homicide rates, by victim characteristics, location, and circumstances, and years of life lost from homicide and other leading causes of death, 1970-78, 4205–38

Jail capacities, conditions, expenditures, and services, and socioeconomic and other characteristics of inmates, various dates 1976-82, 10048–59

Kidnapping by parents over intl and interstate boundaries, characteristics of cases referred to State Dept and FBI by State and country, 1979-83, hearing, 25528–95

Parolees from Federal instns, favorable release outcomes after 2 years by age and recidivism risk category, 1970/72 and 1978, 6006–2.31

Peru cocaine addicts and arrested traffickers and users socioeconomic characteristics, and cocaine confiscated, 1974-78, intl conf papers, 7008–40

Physicians employed in prisons by sociodemographic, employment, and professional characteristics, and compared to all physicians, 1979, article, 4102–1.407

Prisoners in State prisons median sentence, and admissions and releases by prisoner and sentencing characteristics, by offense and State, 1981 and trends from 1926, 6066–19.9

Prisoners under death sentence, and executions since 1930, by prisoner characteristics, region, and State, 1982, annual rpt, 6065–1

Robbery rates and circumstances, medical costs and property losses of victims, and offender and victim characteristics, 1960s-81, 6068–180

Statistical Abstract of US, social, political, and economic data, 1950s-83 and trends, annual rpt, 2324–1.1

Natural Resources, Environment, and Pollution

Forest land owner characteristics in Northeast States, owners and acreage, series, 1206–7

Land privately held, acreage and owners by owner characteristics, land use, and region, and purchase and improvement funding, 1978 survey, series, 1506–5

Uranium ore tailings at active mills, EPA radon and radionuclide emmission standards and US and foreign exposure and health effects, various periods 1957-83, hearings, 21208–17

Population

Appalachia population by age and urban-rural location, and employment and net employment change by industry, selected years 1960-90, article, 9088–33

Census of Population and Housing, 1980: detailed population and housing characteristics, by county, city, and census tract, State and SMSA rpt series, 2551–2

Index by Categories

Census of Population, 1980: detailed socioeconomic and demographic characteristics, by age, sex, race, Hispanic origin, occupation, and industry, State rpt series, 2531–4

Census of Population, 1980: detailed socioeconomic characteristics, by county, city, and inside-outside SMSAs and central cities, State rpt series, 2531–3

Census of Population, 1980: migration since 1975, by county and selected demographic characteristics, supplementary rpt, 2535–1.14

Census of Population, 1980: migration since 1975, by State and selected demographic characteristics, supplementary rpt, 2535–1.13

City and suburb population characteristics and local govt finances, by region and selected SMSA, 1950s-FY83, 10048–61

Coastal environmental characteristics, fish, wildlife, and use, and population socioeconomic data, for individual areas, series, 5506–4

County and City Data Book, detailed socioeconomic and demographic data for States, counties, and cities, selected years 1976-82, 2328–1

Economic and demographic factors used in OASDI program cost estimates, selected years 1913-82 with alternative projections to 2060, 4706–1.90

Educational attainment of population, by sociodemographic characteristics and for large States and SMSAs, 1981 and trends from 1940, biennial Current Population Rpt, 2546–1.390

Educational trends, 1972/73-1992/93, biennial pocket-size card, 4824–3

Florida and California elderly migration by selected State of origin or destination, and Florida elderly, by sociodemographic and housing characteristics, 1970 and 1980, 4478–150

Foreign and US population by age and percent urban, for 7 countries, selected years 1975-81, 21148–33

Foreign women sociodemographic, economic, and fertility characteristics, with comparisons to men, by country, 1960s-85, world region rpt series, 2326–15

Hispanic Americans socioeconomic and demographic characteristics, and compared to non-Hispanics, selected years 1970-83, chartbook, 2328–48

Homeless population and characteristics, and temporary shelter operations, use, and user characteristics, for selected cities, various periods 1979-84, hearing, 21248–85

Household living arrangements, family relationships, and marital status, by age and sex, Mar 1984, advance annual Current Population Rpt, 2546–1.389

Household living arrangements, family relationships, and marital status, by demographic characteristics, Mar 1983, annual Current Population Rpt, 2546–1.388

Income (household) and cash and noncash transfer program participation, by sociodemographic characteristics, quarterly rpt, 2542–2

Income (household) before and after taxes, by socioeconomic characteristics, type of tax paid, and region, 1981, Current Population Rpt, 2546–2.118

Index by Categories

BY AGE

Income (household) before and after taxes, by socioeconomic characteristics, type of tax paid, and region, 1982, annual Current Population Rpt, 2546–2.122

Income (household), home value and equity, and financial assets by type, by household characteristics, 1983 survey with trends from 1970, article, 9362–1.406

Income and socioeconomic characteristics of persons, families, and households, detailed cross-tabulations, Current Population Rpt series, 2546–6

Mobility of population, detailed data by demographic and socioeconomic characteristics of movers and nonmovers, Mar 1981-82, annual Current Population Rpt, 2546–1.384

Older persons by demographic, socioeconomic, and health characteristics, selected years 1900-81 and projected to 2050, Current Population Rpt, 2546–2.125

Older persons income and income sources, by OASDI beneficiary and poverty status, labor force participation, and demographic characteristics, 1982, biennial rpt, 4744–26

Older persons income and percent in poverty, by household composition and sex, with comparisons to nonaged, selected years 1950-82, article, 4742–1.413

Older persons population characteristics, and needs and costs of social services by type, by metro-nonmetro status, 1970s-82 with trends from 1900, 21148–28

Older persons sociodemographic characteristics, and Fed Govt program participation and funding by agency, 1983 with trends and projections 1900-2080, annual rpt, 25144–3

Older persons sociodemographic characteristics and transportation needs, selected years 1900-2040, 7308–183

Population demographic and economic characteristics, 1982 with projections of population size to 2050, annual Current Population Rpt, 2546–2.119

Population demographic, social, and economic characteristics, Current Population Rpt series, 2546–1

Population estimates for States, by age group, July 1981-83, Current Population Rpt, 2546–3.131

Population size and components of change, projected under 3 fertility assumptions, 1982-2080 with trends from 1900, SSA actuarial rpt, 4706–1.92

Population size by single years of age, and components of change, by sex and race, projected 1983-2080, final Current Population Rpt, 2546–3.132

Population size, by single years of age, sex, and race, 1980-83, annual Current Population Rpt, 2546–3.130

Poverty status of families and persons, by detailed socioeconomic characteristics, 1982, annual Current Population Rpt, 2546–6.40

Refugee and alien arrivals and resettlements in US, by State, outlying area, country of birth and citizenship, age, sex, and sponsoring agency, monthly rpt, 4702–3

Refugee resettlement program activities and funding, arrivals and population by country of origin and State, and employment and other characteristics, FY83, annual rpt, 4704–8

Southeastern States public pension payments and disposable income, and family income by age of household head, by State, selected years 1959-80, article, 9371–1.420

Statistical Abstract of US, social, political, and economic data, 1950s-83 and trends, annual rpt, 2324–1.1, 2324–1.3

Voting age population for Nov 1984 election, by sex, age, race, Hispanic origin, region, and State, and percent voting during 1930-82, Current Population Rpt, 2546–3.129

Western States housing outlook and economic and demographic trends, FHLB 11th District, urban area rpt series, 9306–2

Prices and Cost of Living

Child raising itemized costs in urban and rural nonfarm areas, by age and region, quarterly rpt, 1702–1

Vegetable and potato per capita weekly expenditures, by commodity, season, race, age, and region, 1977-78, article, 1561–11.401

Public Welfare and Social Security

ACTION activities, volunteer characteristics, and budget, by program, FY82, annual rpt, 9024–2

Colorado Medicare beneficiaries with partial coverage, 1978, article, 4652–1.404

Disability Insurance awards, death and recovery termination rates, and life expectancy of disabled, by age and sex, 1965-83 and projected to 2000, 4706–1.93

Disability Insurance beneficiaries sociodemographic and medical characteristics, 1977-79, annual rpt, 4744–20

Farm households receiving social security income, farms and amount by characteristics of farm and operator, 1978-82, article, 1702–1.410

Fed Govt cash benefit program beneficiaries with representative payees, by age, relation to payee, and program, as of 1983, GAO rpt, 26121–85

Food aid special supplemental program for women, infants, and children, effectiveness and participant characteristics, 1973-82, GAO rpt, 26131–10

Food stamp recipient households size and composition, income, and income deductions allowed, Aug 1981, annual rpt, 1364–8

Hospital and physician reimbursement by patient disease type and severity category, and patients in 2 or more categories by coverage type, FY80-83, article, 4652–1.426

Income assistance, effects of experimental negative income tax program on employment, earnings, marital status, and other family characteristics in 2 cities, 1970-75, 4008–64

Medicare aged beneficiaries activity restriction, untreated health conditions, and perceived health status, by sociodemographic characteristics, 1980, 4146–12.2

Medicare aged beneficiaries medical care by usual source, and untreated health conditions, by sociodemographic characteristics, 1980, 4146–12.3

Medicare aged enrollees in last year of life, reimbursement by type of service, hospital use, and discharges by diagnosis, 1977-78, article, 4652–1.412

Medicare and Medicaid eligibility, participation, covered services and use, and reimbursements and payments, various periods 1966-82, annual rpt, 4654–1

Medicare end-stage renal disease dialysis, transplants by facility, donor organ costs, deaths by age, and hospitalization, by region, 1981, annual rpt, 4654–5.2

Medicare end-stage renal disease program enrollment, new cases by State, and survival and death rates, by age, sex, and race, 1970s-81, article, 4652–1.408

Medicare hospital reimbursement based on disease severity and patient age, 1979-81, article, 4652–1.425

Medicare kidney end-stage program, reimbursement by treatment, diagnosis, outcome, and patient characteristics, with covered charges for transplants, 1974-79, article, 4652–1.421

Medicare physician charges and reimbursement by enrollee characteristics and carrier, payment limits effects on charges in California, and physician earnings, by specialty, 1950s-84, 25368–127

Noncash public and employer-based transfer program recipients, by income source and socioeconomic characteristics, 1982, advance Current Population Rpt, 2546–6.38

Noncash public and employer-based transfer program recipients, by income source and socioeconomic characteristics, 1982, final Current Population Rpt, 2546–6.37

Nutrition services for elderly, program operations and assessment, and participant sociodemographic, health, and diet characteristics, 1976 and 1982, 4608–16

OASDHI beneficiaries with direct deposit of benefit checks, by age, sex, race, benefit amount, and State, as of Dec 1983, article, 4742–1.412

OASDHI benefits wage replacement rate and delayed retirement credits, by retirement age, selected years 1986-2050, article, 4742–1.420

OASDHI, Medicaid, SSI, and other social insurance and public welfare programs benefits, beneficiary characteristics, and trust funds, selected years 1937-83, annual rpt, 4744–3

OASDHI, SSI, and other social security programs and recipient characteristics, *Research and Statistics Notes,* series, 4746–16

OASDI beneficiaries by age and sex, and program operations and costs, projected 1983-2060 with trends from 1940, SSA actuarial rpt, 4706–1.91

OASDI benefit eligibility, hypothetical impact of 1978 law change on 1977 workers quarters of coverage, by age and sex, 1977, article, 4742–1.408

Older persons entitled to both Medicare and Medicaid, demographic characteristics, and health condition and services use, 1980, article, 4652–1.433

Poverty population size, effect of counting public noncash transfers as income by recipient characteristics, 1979-83, 2626–2.52

Poverty population size, effects of counting public noncash transfers as income by recipient characteristics, 1979-82, 2626–2.50

BY AGE

Runaway and other homeless youth programs, funding by source, activities, and participant characteristics, FY82, annual rpt, 4604–3

Supplemental Security Income payments, and recipients by other income source, eligibility type, and other characteristics, by State, 1982, annual rpt, 4744–16

Supplementary Security Income beneficiary socioeconomic characteristics and health service use, 1970s-83 and SSI program projections to 1995, 25148–29

Recreation and Leisure

- Boat accidents, injuries, and fatalities, by age of operator and circumstances, 1983, annual rpt, 7404–1.2
- Fishermen (ocean sport), fishing activities, and catch by species, by fisherman characteristics, State, and coastal region, series, 2166–17
- Natl park system visitor deaths, by park and type of accident, 1973-83, annual rpt, 5544–6

Science and Technology

- Computer specialists sociodemographic, educational, and employment characteristics, and Fed Govt support by agency, 1978, biennial Current Population Rpt, 2546–2.124
- Degree (doctoral) recipients in science and engineering, by field, sex, race, age, citizenship, postgrad employment and study status, State, and instn, 1960-82, 9626–6.16
- Employment, salaries, and degrees of scientists and engineers, by field, type of employer, race, and sex, selected years 1960-81, annual rpt, 9624–18.5
- Employment, supply, and education of scientists and engineers, by sex, race, Hispanic origin, and field, selected years 1965-83, biennial rpt, 9624–20
- Engineers sociodemographic, educational, and employment characteristics, and Federal support by agency, 1978, Current Population Rpt, 2546–2.121
- Salaries of scientists and engineers in R&D at DOE labs and non-DOE facilities, Aug 1982-Feb 1984, annual rpt, 3004–9
- Salaries of scientists and engineers in R&D, by degree, type of establishment, age, experience, and field, 1984, annual rpt, 3004–1

Veterans Affairs

- Agent Orange exposed Air Force personnel diseases and disorders, by disease type, age, and officer status, 1984 rpt, 3604–3
- Disabled veterans with VA vocational rehabilitation training, employment and other characteristics, and VA employment services, by regional office, as of 1983, GAO rpt, 26121–78
- Health condition of veterans and nonveterans, and veteran use of VA and non-VA hospitals by disease, by age, race, income, and metro-nonmetro location, various periods 1971-81, 9926–1.18
- Income and educational attainment of veterans compared to nonveterans, by age, 1982-83, annual rpt, 9924–19
- Income and employment status of veterans, by age and war or peacetime service, with comparisons to nonveterans, 1981, annual rpt, 9924–23

Life insurance for veterans and servicemen, actuarial analysis of 5 VA programs, 1982, annual rpt, 9924–16

- Life insurance programs for veterans groups, participant death rates by age and service branch, 1980-82, annual rpt, 9924–3
- Medical care costs, patients, and capacity of VA and non-Va facilties, by service type and patient age, 1970s-83 and projected to 2030, 26306–6.78
- Older veterans aged 55 and over, socioeconomic characteristics, economic resources, health care and status, and actual and expected VA benefits use, 1983 survey, 9928–29
- Physicians, dentists, and nurses of VA, by age, selected employment characteristics, and VA district, quarterly rpt, 9922–11
- Population and characteristics of veterans, and VA hospital and other activities, by State, FY83, annual rpt, 9924–1
- Population characteristics of veterans by period of service and age, and related issues, statistical rpt series, 9926–4
- Population of veterans, by period of service, age, and State, Sept 1984, semiannual rpt, 9922–3
- Speech disorders among patients in VA facilties, by severity, patient characteristics, diagnostician occupation, and facility type, FY81, 9926–1.17
- Vietnam era veterans characteristics, and participation in VA programs, compared with WW II and Korea veterans, FY83, annual rpt, 9924–8
- Women veteran population, and use of benefits by type, by age, period of service, and State, with comparisons to men, FY83, annual rpt, 9924–24
- Women veterans, by period of service, age, and State, Mar 1983 and projected to 2030, 9928–28

BY DISEASE

Communications and Transportation

- Airline pilots medically disqualified for service, by airline, disease, affected body site, and age, 1978-80, 7506–10.23
- Railroad employees sickness benefits and beneficiaries, by age, occupation, and sickness type, 1981/82, annual rpt, 9704–2.3

Education

- Handicapped children early education research and service project activities and characteristics, and grants to States for program dev, 1983-84, annual listing, 4804–30
- Handicapped children public education program enrollment, staff, and funding, by handicap, age, and State, 1981/82-1982/83, annual rpt, 4944–4
- Head Start Project enrollment of handicapped children, by handicap, State, and for Indian and migrant programs, 1982, annual rpt, 4604–1

Government and Defense

- Army active duty personnel health status and use of Army medical services in US and abroad, by treatment facility, monthly rpt, 3702–4.2
- DOD Civilian Health and Medical Program of the Uniformed Services costs for care for top 10 inpatient diagnoses, FY83, semiannual rpt, 3502–2.4

Navy and Marine Corps disease incidence, medical care, and deaths, by detailed diagnosis, and medical personnel and workloads, 1978-79, annual rpt, 3804–1

Health and Vital Statistics

- Abortions (legal), and deaths from abortion and childbirth, by medical and sociodemographic characteristics, 1972-83, hearings, 21368–47
- Allergy and Infectious Diseases Natl Inst activities, grants by instn, State, and country, and disease incidence and costs, FY60s-84, annual rpt, 4474–30
- Canada and US hospital use by children by Canada Province and US region, and death rates, by diagnosis and sex, selected years 1977-79, 4147–5.1
- CAT scan procedures on hospital inpatients, by body site and patient and hospital characteristics, 1979-82, 4146–8.102
- Costs of disease, direct and indirect, by diagnosis, 1981, annual fact book, 4474–15
- Death rates by cause, age, and sex, average 1968-80, SSA actuarial rpt, 4706–1.92
- Death rates by sex, race, and age for 40 causes, projected for 10-year period, 1982 rpt, 4208–21
- Deaths and death rates, by cause and age, provisional 1982-83, US Vital Statistics annual rpt, 4144–7
- Deaths and death rates, by detailed cause and demographic characteristics, 1979 and summary trends from 1900, US Vital Statistics annual rpt, 4144–2
- Deaths and death rates, by detailed geographic area, cause, and demographic characteristics, 1979, US Vital Statistics annual rpt, 4144–3
- Deaths and death rates, by selected cause and demographic characteristics, 1981, US Vital Statistics advance rpt, 4146–5.78
- Deaths and death rates, by selected cause and demographic characteristics, 1982, US Vital Statistics advance rpt, 4146–5.81
- Deaths and death rates from homicide, by location, circumstances, and victim characteristics, and years of life lost from homicide and other leading causes of death, 1970-78, 4205–38
- Deaths and death rates, provisional data, monthly rpt, 4142–1
- Deaths and death rates, years of potential life lost, and physician contacts, for 9 diagnoses, weekly rpt, monthly data, 4202–1
- Deaths by principal or contributing cause, with type of injury reported in accidental, poisoning, and violent deaths, by age, sex, and race, 1978, 4146–5.76
- Deaths from 10 leading causes, selected years 1900-82, annual fact book, 4474–15
- DOE and contractor facility accidents, deaths, illnesses, radiation exposure, and property damage, by facility, 1982, annual rpt, 3004–24
- Drug (prescription) use by outpatient characteristics and generic or brand name, and hospital and drugstore costs by drug class, 1982, annual rpt, 4064–12
- Drugs (analgesic) provided during visits to office-based physicians, by patient characteristics, drug brand and type, and physician specialty, 1980-81, 4146–8.99
- Health care expenditures per capita, by type of service and patient age and sex, for 10-15 medical conditions, 1980, article, 4652–1.413

Index by Categories

Health condition and health care resources, use, and expenditures, 1970s-82 with trends and projections 1900-2000, annual compilation, 4144–11

Heart, Lung, and Blood Natl Inst activities and funding, with morbidity and mortality data, various periods 1940-88, annual rpt, 4474–22

Hispanic Americans with disabilities, by disability type and severity and for 5 States, selected years 1970-78, conf proceedings, 16598–5

Hospital and nursing home discharges, by age, sex, marital status, and selected diagnosis, 1976 and 1979, article, 4102–1.443

Hospital discharges and length of stay, by patient age and sex, facility size and ownership, procedure performed, and region, 1982, 4146–8.96

Hospital discharges and length of stay, by patient age and sex, facility size and ownership, procedure performed, and region, 1983, 4146–8.101

Hospital discharges and length of stay, by patient characteristics, facility size, procedure performed, diagnosis, and region, 1982, annual rpt, 4147–13.78

Hospital discharges and length of stay of aged and nonaged persons, by region, facility size, and diagnosis, 1981, 4146–8.98

Indian births, morbidity, and deaths and rates, and health services facilities and use, 1954-83, annual compilation, 4104–7

Infant deaths by detailed cause, geographic location, age, race, and sex, 1979, US Vital Statistics annual rpt, 4144–2.2

Infectious diseases reported to public health depts, physician reasons for underreporting, 1982 survey, article, 4102–1.411

Infectious notifiable diseases and other public health concerns, cases and mortality trends, quarterly rpt articles, 4202–7

Infectious notifiable diseases, cases and current outbreaks, by region and State, weekly rpt, 4202–1

Infectious notifiable diseases, cases and incidence, by census div and State, and deaths by cause, 1982, annual rpt, 4204–1

Israel, Tel Aviv Medical Center services and use, by patient age and condition, selected years 1976-83, article, 4102–1.445

Life expectancy, and deaths by cause, by sex and age, 1900-2050, SSA actuarial rpt, 4706–1.89

Life expectancy increase impacts on OASDI and pension policy, with alternative sociodemographic projections to 2100, hearing, 25368–130

Mental health facilities, services, staff, and patient characteristics, 1970s-82 with trends from 1954, annual rpt, 4504–9

Mental hospitals of States and counties, patients and admissions by diagnosis, age, and State, FY81, annual rpt, 4504–2

New Jersey nursing care by nursing unit type, level of care related to length of stay, and costs by diagnosis under 2 allocation methods, as of 1981, article, 4652–1.424

Occupational health risks from hazardous substances and radiation, by industry, occupation, age, and sex, with bibl and glossary, 1920s-82, 9638–50

Older persons by demographic, socioeconomic, and health characteristics, selected years 1900-81 and projected to 2050, Current Population Rpt, 2546–2.125

Older persons health status, health services use and expenditures by type, Medicare enrollment and reimbursement, and private insurance coverage, 1977-84, article, 4652–1.420

Physician visits for new pain symptoms, by diagnosis, physician specialty, and patient characteristics, and drugs prescribed or used, 1980-81, 4146–8.97

Physicians (not office-based) visits by reason, diagnosis, treatment, patient and physician characteristics, and physician primary activity, 1980, 4147–13.77

Surgeon office visits and drugs provided, by characteristics of visit, patient, and physician, and location, 1980-81, 4147–13.79

TTPI socioeconomic, health, and govtl data, by TTPI govt, FY83 and selected trends, detailed annual rpt, 7004–6

Washington State deaths by sex, cause, and detailed occupation, summary data from occupational mortality study, 1950-79, 4248–47

Waterborne disease outbreaks and cases, by type, source, and location, 1983, annual rpt, 4205–35

Waterborne diseases from drinking water, cases and outbreaks, by type and cause, aggregate 1971-80, 9208–124

Youth office visits to physicians by patient and visit characteristics and physician specialty, and drug mentions by brand, 1980-81, 4146–8.100

Labor and Employment

Vocationally rehabilitated persons under State agency programs, by sociodemographic characteristics and disabling condition, FY79-81, annual rpt, 4944–6

Natural Resources, Environment, and Pollution

Uranium ore tailings at active mills, EPA radon and radionuclide emmission standards and US and foreign exposure and health effects, various periods 1957-83, hearings, 21208–17

Public Welfare and Social Security

Disability Insurance beneficiaries sociodemographic and medical characteristics, 1977-79, annual rpt, 4744–20

Medicare aged enrollees in last year of life, reimbursement by type of service, hospital use, and discharges by diagnosis, 1977-78, article, 4652–1.412

Medicare hospital reimbursement based on disease severity and patient age, 1979-81, article, 4652–1.425

Medicare kidney end-stage program, reimbursement by treatment, diagnosis, outcome, and patient characteristics, with covered charges for transplants, 1974-79, article, 4652–1.421

OASDHI, Medicaid, SSI, and other social insurance and public welfare programs benefits, beneficiary characteristics, and trust funds, selected years 1937-83, annual rpt, 4744–3.4

Supplementary Security Income beneficiary socioeconomic characteristics and health service use, 1970s-83 and SSI program projections to 1995, 25148–29

BY EDUCATIONAL ATTAINMENT

Veterans Affairs

Agent Orange exposed Air Force personnel diseases and disorders, by disease type, age, and officer status, 1984 rpt, 3604–3

Communicative disorders among VA patients, by age, disease and treatment characteristics, and facility type, 1981 survey, 9926–4.8

Disabled prisoners of war filing disability claims by period of service, and disability ratings by type and degree, various dates Oct 1981-May 1984, chartbook, 9928–30

Health condition of veterans and nonveterans, and veteran use of VA and non-VA hospitals by disease, by age, race, income, and metro-nonmetro location, various periods 1971-81, 9926–1.18

Hospital patients of VA discharged, by compensation and pension status, patient type and sex, and VA activities, FY83, annual rpt, 9924–1.3

Older veterans aged 55 and over, socioeconomic characteristics, economic resources, health care and status, and actual and expected VA benefits use, 1983 survey, 9928–29

Vietnam era veterans in VA medical centers, and outpatient medical and dental care, various periods FY68-83, annual rpt, 9924–8.4

Women veteran population, and use of benefits by type, by age, period of service, and State, with comparisons to men, FY83, annual rpt, 9924–24

BY EDUCATIONAL ATTAINMENT

Agriculture and Food

Farmland eroded by rainfall, acreage by crop, and farm operators by selected characteristics, by soil erosion class, 1977-78, 1588–83

Communications and Transportation

Seat belt use, effects of driving circumstances and driver characteristics and attitudes, 1981 survey, 7768–82

Traffic fatal accidents, alcohol levels of drivers and pedestrians by driver age and sex and time of accident, 1980, 7768–81

Education

Condition of Education, detailed data on enrollment, staff, achievement, finances, curricula, and education effects on employment, 1982-83, annual rpt, 4824–1

Digest of Education Statistics, detailed data on students, staff, finances, and facilities, 1982 and selected trends, annual rpt, 4824–2

Elementary and secondary enrollment, households with children enrolled by school control, householder characteristics, and region, Oct 1982, 4838–13

Enrollment of persons aged 3-34, by grade level and student characteristics, Oct 1982, advance annual Current Population Rpt, 2546–1.391

Enrollment of persons aged 3-34, by grade level, instn control, and student characteristics, Oct 1983, advance annual Current Population Rpt, 2546–1.392

Head Start Project programs effect on child dev, by characteristics of program, child, and family, literature review, selected years 1965-81, 4608–20

BY EDUCATIONAL ATTAINMENT

High school classes of 1980 and 1982: educational and sociodemographic characteristics and expectations, natl longitudinal study, series, 4826–2

Energy Resources and Demand

Employment of scientists and engineers in energy-related fields, supply/demand and effects of R&D funding, by sector, energy type, and age, 1962-91, annual rpt, 3004–19

Household, housing, and fuel use characteristics, EIA survey series, 3166–7

Government and Defense

Election campaign Fed Govt funding, reform and tax deduction proposals, and TV and political action committee influence, opinion surveys, various dates 1977-83, hearings, 21428–7.1

Military personnel, by selected sociodemographic characteristics, 1984 annual summary rpt, 3504–13

Military personnel in US, and civilian employment, by age, sex, occupation, and educational attainment, 1982 and summary trends from 1950, article, 6722–1.441

Military personnel on active duty, by age and education, 1960-83, annual rpt, 3544–1.2

Military reserve forces manpower strengths and characteristics, by component, quarterly rpt, 3542–4

Military women personnel on active duty, by demographic and service characteristics and service branch, with comparisons to men, FY83, annual chartbook, 3544–26

Navy personnel, detailed statistics, quarterly rpt, 3802–4

Taxes, tax policy, and intergovtl relations, public opinion survey results, 1972-84, annual rpt, 10044–2

Voting age population selected characteristics and participation in presidential elections, 1964-80 with projections to 2000, Current Population Rpt, 2546–2.117

Health and Vital Statistics

Abortions, by patient sociodemographic characteristics, pregnancy history, and procedure, 1980, US Vital Statistics final rpt, 4146–5.72

Asian and Pacific Islands Americans births by ethnic origin and sociodemographic and birth characteristics, with comparisons to blacks and whites, 1978-80, 4146–5.75

Births and birth rates, by demographic and birth characteristics, 1981 with trends from 1940, US Vital Statistics advance rpt, 4146–5.73

Births and birth rates, by detailed demographic characteristics and geographic area, 1979 and trends, US Vital Statistics annual rpt, 4144–1

Births and birth rates, by parent and birth characteristics and infant condition at birth, 1982 and trends from 1940, US Vital Statistics annual advance rpt, 4146–5.79

Births and birth rates of teenage girls, and distribution of births with low birth weight and Apgar scores, by mother and infant characteristics, 1970-81, 4147–21.41

Births attended by midwives and in nonhospital settings, by mother's sociodemographic and prenatal care characteristics and infant race and birthweight, 1978-79 with trends from 1935, 4147–21.40

Births, by birth weight, Apgar score, infant and mother characteristics, birthplace, and attendant, 1978, article, 4102–1.414

Births, by outcome, and mother's sociodemographic, life style, and maternity characteristics, 1980, article, 4102–1

Births, fertility rates, expected births, and childless women, by socioeconomic characteristics, June 1982, annual Current Population Rpt, 2546–1.386

Births, fertility rates, expected births, and childless women, by socioeconomic characteristics, June 1983, advance annual Current Population Rpt, 2546–1.385

Births, fertility rates, expected births, and childless women, by socioeconomic characteristics, June 1983, annual Current Population Rpt, 2546–1.393

Birthspacing by period of woman's birth and marriage, period of child's birth, and sociodemographic characteristics, June 1980, Current Population Rpt, 2546–1.387

Blood lead levels by sociodemographic and behavioral characteristics, and potential workplace exposure, 1976-80, 4147–11.201

Breast-fed infants, by characteristics of mother and source of prenatal care, various periods 1970-75, article, 4102–1.442

Breast-fed infants, by race and mother's sociodemographic characteristics, 1983 with trends from 1970, article, 4102–1.455

Disability (work-related), incidence among men aged 22-64 related to sociodemographic and employment characteristics and to self-evaluated mental stress, 1972-74, 4746–5.43

Disabled women, by socioeconomic and demographic characteristics, and compared to nondisabled women and disabled men, 1981, chartbook, 16598–4

Health care expenditures, natl survey on services use, costs, and sources of payment, by patient and physician characteristics, 1977-78, series, 4186–3

Health care services of selected medical practitioners, use by patient characteristics, 1980 survey with trends from 1963, 4146–12.4

Health condition and health care resources, use, and expenditures, 1970s-82 with trends and projections 1900-2000, annual compilation, 4144–11

Health condition, hospitalization, disability, and medical costs, by demographic characteristics, Vital and Health Statistics series, 4147–10

Health professionals supply and education, by occupation, demographic and professional characteristics, and location, 1950s-83 and projected to 2000, biennial rpt, 4114–8

Hispanic Americans births and birth and fertility rates, by detailed Hispanic origin, characteristics of mother, birth, and prenatal care, and for 22 States, 1981, 4146–5.80

Kidney end-stage disease patients by patient characteristics and country, and per capita spending for treatment, selected years 1973-81, article, 4102–1.450

Marriages, divorces, and rates, by detailed demographic and geographic characteristics, 1979 and trends, US Vital Statistics annual rpt, 4144–4

Mental health office and clinic visits, average charges, and total expenditures for services, by type of provider and patient characteristics, 1980, 4146–11.5

Index by Categories

Mental health workers, nursing and social work degrees, psychologists by degree level, and psychiatry residencies, 1950s-81, annual rpt, 4504–9.4

Nigeria native and Western health care use, by sociodemographic characteristics, 1984 article, 4102–1.417

Nurses (registered) population and employment by age and education, and nursing program admissions and grads, projected 1981-90, article, 4102–1.439

Peru cocaine addicts and arrested traffickers and users socioeconomic characteristics, and cocaine confiscated, 1974-78, intl conf papers, 7008–40

Pregnancy health counseling effect on smoking, diet, delivery costs, and birth weight, by sociodemographic characteristics and pregnancy history, 1983 article, 4102–1.401

Sterilization of women following hospital delivery of live or stillborn infants, by sociodemographic and maternity characteristics, 1972 and 1980, article, 4102–1.419

Housing and Construction

Census of Housing, 1980: inventory, occupancy, and unit characteristics, changes from 1973 by region and inside-outside SMSAs and central cities, series, 2473–3

Home mortgage default prospects by mortgage type and borrower characteristics, various periods 1967-82, technical paper, 9381–10.39

Housing occupancy and unit and household characteristics, by region and metro-nonmetro residence, 1983, biennial survey, 2485–1

Older persons rural housing condition, selected householder and housing characteristics with comparisons to urban and nonaged population, 1979, 1598–193

Quality of housing and neighborhoods, indicators and attitudes, and occupant characteristics, by urban-rural location and region, 1981, annual survey, 2485–7

Industry and Commerce

Underground economy, household expenditures and participation by type of goods or service and sociodemographic characteristics, with methodology and bibl, 1981 survey, 8308–27

Labor and Employment

CETA participants by sociodemographic characteristics, and Labor Dept activities and staff, FY83, annual rpt, 6304–1

Earnings of couples with both spouses working, by sociodemographic and employment characteristics and age of children, 1981, Current Population Rpt, 2546–2.120

Earnings of women and men, analysis of differential, by sociodemographic characteristics, hours worked, and occupation, selected years 1967-83, article, 6722–1.437

Educational attainment of labor force, by demographic and employment characteristics, 1984, press release, 6748–79

Japan workers wages in smaller firms relative to wages in larger firms, by worker characteristics, firm size, and industry div, 1950s-81, article, 6722–1.461

950 ASI Annual Supplement

January-December 1984

Index by Categories

Job Training Partnership Act dislocated workers program performance standards guide for States, with data on previous programs, by State and client characteristics, FY81-82, 6408–59.2

Kentucky employment growth in 9-county rural area, labor force and establishment characteristics, 1979-80, 1598–194

Labor force characteristics and economic indicators, selected years 1880-1995, chartbook, 6728–30

Labor force educational attainment, by demographic and employment characteristics, 1982-83 with summary trends from 1940, 6746–1.251

Labor force educational attainment, by demographic and employment characteristics, 1983, article, 6722–1.423

Labor force experience of men and women by sociodemographic characteristics, and effect on earnings, 1979, Current Population Rpt, 2546–2.123

Labor force, special characteristics, Labor Statistics Handbook, 1947-82, annual rpt, 6724–1.2

Occupational manpower needs and supply by detailed occupation, and educational and training program enrollees and grads by detailed field, 1982 and 1995, biennial rpt, 6744–3

Occupational separation rates by worker characteristics, and replacement rates, 1980-81 with projections to 1990, article, 6722–1.416

Small business and all employees sociodemographic characteristics, by industry div and firm size, 1978-1979, annual rpt, 9764–6.3

Trade adjustment assistance eligibility, reemployment opportunities, and worker characteristics, investigations of industries injured by import competition, series, 6406–9

Vocationally rehabilitated persons under State agency programs, by sociodemographic characteristics and disabling condition, FY79-81, annual rpt, 4944–6

Women maintaining families, by labor force status, occupation, marital status, education, presence and age of children, race, and Hispanic origin, 1983, article, 6746–1.253

Women's employment and earnings, by labor force and socioeconomic characteristics, and compared to men, 1978-81 and trends from 1940s, 6568–29

Youth employment and hours worked, by high school and college enrollment status, sex, race, and Hispanic origin, 1982-83, annual article, 6722–1.446

Youth employment, by high school and college enrollment status, industry div, occupation, and selected demographic characteristics, 1980-82, 6746–1.250

Law Enforcement

Bank robbery court cases by case processing, sentencing, and offender characteristics, and compared to other Fed Govt felony cases, 1979-80, periodic rpt, 6062–2.407

Crime victimization rates by type of offense, and victim and offense characteristics, Natl Crime Survey series, 6066–3

Drug defendants, by sociodemographic and case processing characteristics, with comparisons to Federal fraud and bank robbery defendants, 1979, 6062–2.403

Jail capacities, conditions, expenditures, and services, and socioeconomic and other characteristics of inmates, various dates 1976-82, 10048–59

Peru cocaine addicts and arrested traffickers and users socioeconomic characteristics, and cocaine confiscated, 1974-78, intl conf papers, 7008–40

Prisoners under death sentence, and executions since 1930, by prisoner characteristics, region, and State, 1982, annual rpt, 6065–1

Natural Resources, Environment, and Pollution

Forest land owner characteristics in Northeast States, owners and acreage, series, 1206–7

Land privately held, acreage and owners by owner characteristics, land use, and region, and purchase and improvement funding, 1978 survey, series, 1506–5

Youth Conservation Corps activities, costs, and participant characteristics, by sponsoring agency, 1982, annual rpt, 5304–12

Population

Census of Population and Housing, 1980: detailed population and housing characteristics, by county, city, and census tract, State and SMSA rpt series, 2551–2

Census of Population, 1980: detailed socioeconomic and demographic characteristics, by age, sex, race, Hispanic origin, occupation, and industry, State rpt series, 2531–4

Census of Population, 1980: detailed socioeconomic characteristics, by county, city, and inside-outside SMSAs and central cities, State rpt series, 2531–3

Coastal environmental characteristics, fish, wildlife, and use, and population socioeconomic data, for individual areas, series, 5506–4

County and City Data Book, detailed socioeconomic and demographic data for States, counties, and cities, selected years 1976-82, 2328–1

Hispanic Americans socioeconomic and demographic characteristics, and compared to non-Hispanics, selected years 1970-83, chartbook, 2328–48

Homeless population and characteristics, and temporary shelter operations, use, and user characteristics, for selected cities, various periods 1979-84, hearing, 21248–85

Income (household), home value and equity, and financial assets by type, by household characteristics, 1983 survey with trends from 1970, article, 9362–1.406

Income and socioeconomic characteristics of persons, families, and households, detailed cross-tabulations, Current Population Rpt series, 2546–6

Mobility of population, detailed data by demographic and socioeconomic characteristics of movers and nonmovers, Mar 1981-82, annual Current Population Rpt, 2546–1.384

Older persons by demographic, socioeconomic, and health characteristics, selected years 1900-81 and projected to 2050, Current Population Rpt, 2546–2.125

Older persons population characteristics, and needs and costs of social services by type, by metro-nonmetro status, 1970s-82 with trends from 1900, 21148–28

BY EDUCATIONAL ATTAINMENT

Older persons sociodemographic characteristics and transportation needs, selected years 1900-2040, 7308–183

Population demographic, social, and economic characteristics, Current Population Rpt series, 2546–1

Poverty status of families and persons, by detailed socioeconomic characteristics, 1982, annual Current Population Rpt, 2546–6.40

Southeastern States economic dev effect on education, for Fed Reserve 6th District States, selected years 1900-82, article, 9371–1.428

Statistical Abstract of US, social, political, and economic data, 1950s-83 and trends, annual rpt, 2324–1.1, 2324–1.3

TTPI socioeconomic, health, and govtl data, by TTPI govt, FY83 and selected trends, detailed annual rpt, 7004–6

Women in couples with wife as primary earner, socioeconomic and family characteristics, with comparative data for husbands, Mar 1982, 2326–11.9

Public Welfare and Social Security

AFDC eligibility under Omnibus Budget Reconciliation Act, effect on caseloads and recipient benefits and living costs, 1981-83, GAO rpt, 26131–11

Disability Insurance beneficiaries sociodemographic and medical characteristics, 1977-79, annual rpt, 4744–20

Food aid special supplemental program for women, infants, and children, effectiveness and participant characteristics, 1973-82, GAO rpt, 26131–10

Income assistance, effects of experimental negative income tax program on employment, earnings, marital status, and other family characteristics in 2 cities, 1970-75, 4008–64

Medicare aged beneficiaries activity restriction, untreated health conditions, and perceived health status, by sociodemographic characteristics, 1980, 4146–12.2

Medicare aged beneficiaries medical care by usual source, and untreated health conditions, by sociodemographic characteristics, 1980, 4146–12.3

OASI benefits, survivor family knowledge of provisions by educational attainment and income, with responses to each survey question, 1978, article, 4742–1.401

Older persons entitled to both Medicare and Medicaid, demographic characteristics, and health condition and services use, 1980, article, 4652–1.433

Science and Technology

Computer specialists sociodemographic, educational, and employment characteristics, and Fed Govt support by agency, 1978, biennial Current Population Rpt, 2546–2.124

Employment, salaries, and degrees of scientists and engineers, by field, type of employer, race, and sex, selected years 1960-81, annual rpt, 9624–18.5

Employment, supply, and education of scientists and engineers, by sex, race, Hispanic origin, and field, selected years 1965-83, biennial rpt, 9624–20

Engineers sociodemographic, educational, and employment characteristics, and Federal support by agency, 1978, Current Population Rpt, 2546–2.121

BY EDUCATIONAL ATTAINMENT

Salaries of scientists and engineers in R&D at DOE labs and non-DOE facilities, Aug 1982-Feb 1984, annual rpt, 3004–9

Salaries of scientists and engineers in R&D, by degree, type of establishment, age, experience, and field, 1984, annual rpt, 3004–1

Scientists and engineers employment, unemployment, and earnings, by field, sex, race, and Hispanic origin, 1970s-82, annual rpt, 9624–10.3

Veterans Affairs

Educational attainment and income of veterans compared to nonveterans, by age, 1982-83, annual rpt, 9924–19

Older veterans aged 55 and over, socioeconomic characteristics, economic resources, health care and status, and actual and expected VA benefits use, 1983 survey, 9928–29

Vietnam era veterans educational attainment at separation from armed forces compared with WW II and Korea veterans, and at present, FY83, annual rpt, 9924–8.1, 9924–8.3

BY MARITAL STATUS

Agriculture and Food

Farm population, by employment and socioeconomic characteristics, 1983, annual rpt, 2544–1

Banking, Finance, and Insurance

Debt (mortgage and consumer) and net worth, by householder characteristics and family income, 1983 survey, article, 9362–1.411

Communications and Transportation

Women's travel patterns, by employment and sociodemographic characteristics and type of child care used, 1980 survey, 7888–62

Education

Elementary and secondary enrollment, households with children enrolled by school control, householder characteristics, and region, Oct 1982, 4838–13

High school classes of 1980 and 1982: educational and sociodemographic characteristics and expectations, natl longitudinal study, series, 4826–2

Postsecondary enrollment in academic, vocational, and continuing education, by student characteristics, Oct 1982, 4848–16

Teachers in public elementary and secondary schools, demographic and employment characteristics, 1961-81, annual rpt, 4824–2.8

Energy Resources and Demand

Household, housing, and fuel use characteristics, EIA survey series, 3166–7

Government and Defense

Immigration, and alien residents, workers, visitors, deportations, and naturalizations, by country of birth, FY81, annual rpt, 6264–2

Income tax returns of individuals, detailed data, 1982, annual rpt, 8304–2

Taxes, tax policy, and intergovtl relations, public opinion survey results, 1972-84, annual rpt, 10044–2

Health and Vital Statistics

Abortions (legal), and deaths from abortion and childbirth, by medical and sociodemographic characteristics, 1972-83, hearings, 21368–47

Abortions, by patient sociodemographic characteristics, pregnancy history, and procedure, 1980, US Vital Statistics final rpt, 4146–5.72

Births and birth rates, by detailed demographic characteristics and geographic area, 1979 and trends, US Vital Statistics annual rpt, 4144–1

Births and birth rates of teenage girls, and distribution of births with low birth weight and Apgar scores, by mother and infant characteristics, 1970-81, 4147–21.41

Births attended by midwives and in nonhospital settings, by mother's sociodemographic and prenatal care characteristics and infant race and birthweight, 1978-79 with trends from 1935, 4147–21.40

Births by outcome, and mother's sociodemographic, life style, and maternity characteristics, 1980, article, 4102–1.421, 4102–1.424

Births, fertility rates, expected births, and childless women, by socioeconomic characteristics, June 1982, annual Current Population Rpt, 2546–1.386

Births, fertility rates, expected births, and childless women, by socioeconomic characteristics, June 1983, advance annual Current Population Rpt, 2546–1.385

Births, fertility rates, expected births, and childless women, by socioeconomic characteristics, June 1983, annual Current Population Rpt, 2546–1.393

Birthspacing by period of woman's birth and marriage, period of child's birth, and sociodemographic characteristics, June 1980, Current Population Rpt, 2546–1.387

Contraceptives use by women, by method, marital status, age, and race, 1982, 4146–8.103

Disability (work-related), incidence among men aged 22-64 related to sociodemographic and employment characteristics and to self-evaluated mental stress, 1972-74, 4746–5.43

Disabled women, by socioeconomic and demographic characteristics, and compared to nondisabled women and disabled men, 1981, chartbook, 16598–4

Family planning and infertility services use by women, by source of service, marital status, age, race, and Hispanic origin, 1982, 4146–8.104

Health care services of selected medical practitioners, use by patient characteristics, 1980 survey with trends from 1963, 4146–12.4

Health condition and health care resources, use, and expenditures, 1970s-82 with trends and projections 1900-2000, annual compilation, 4144–11

Hispanic Americans births and birth and fertility rates, by detailed Hispanic origin, characteristics of mother, birth, and prenatal care, and for 22 States, 1981, 4146–5.80

Hospital and nursing home discharges, by age, sex, marital status, and selected diagnosis, 1976 and 1979, article, 4102–1.443

Marriages, divorces, and rates, by detailed demographic and geographic characteristics, 1979 and trends, US Vital Statistics annual rpt, 4144–4

Index by Categories

Peru cocaine addicts and arrested traffickers and users socioeconomic characteristics, and cocaine confiscated, 1974-78, intl conf papers, 7008–40

Pregnancy health counseling effect on smoking, diet, delivery costs, and birth weight, by sociodemographic characteristics and pregnancy history, 1983 article, 4102–1.401

Housing and Construction

Census of Housing, 1980: structural, financial, and householder characteristics, by region and State, 2475–4

Home mortgages (graduated payment) FHA-insured, financial, property, and mortgagor characteristics, for US and selected localities, quarterly rpt, 5142–42

Home mortgages (graduated payment) FHA-insured, financial, property, and mortgagor characteristics, for US and selected States, quarterly rpt, 5142–41

Home mortgages (graduated payment) FHA-insured, financial, property, and mortgagor characteristics, US summary, quarterly rpt, 5142–40

Home mortgages FHA-insured, financial, property, and mortgagor characteristics, for US and selected localities, quarterly rpt, 5142–2

Home mortgages FHA-insured, financial, property, and mortgagor characteristics, for US, selected States, and Puerto Rico, quarterly rpt, 5142–3

Home mortgages FHA-insured, financial, property, and mortgagor characteristics, quarterly rpt, 5142–1

Home mortgages FHA-insured, financial, property, and mortgagor characteristics, 1983, annual rpt, 5144–17

Home mortgages FHA-insured for low-cost homes, financial, construction, property, and mortgagor characteristics, quarterly rpt, 5142–4

Housing and households characteristics, and low-income housing construction and availability, 1970s-83, hearing, 21968–28.1

Older persons rural housing condition, selected householder and housing characteristics with comparisons to urban and nonaged population, 1979, 1598–193

Industry and Commerce

Underground economy, household expenditures and participation by type of goods or service and sociodemographic characteristics, with methodology and bibl, 1981 survey, 8308–27

Labor and Employment

Earnings of families by number of earners, and earnings and employment status of individual family members, quarterly rpt, 6742–19

Educational attainment of labor force, by demographic and employment characteristics, 1982-83 with summary trends from 1940, 6746–1.251

Employment and earnings, detailed data, monthly rpt, 6742–2.2, 6742–2.3

Employment and economic conditions, alternative BLS projections to 1995 with selected trends for 1959-82, 6728–29

Employment and labor force statistics by major industry group and demographic characteristics, *Survey of Current Business*, monthly rpt, 2702–1.5

Index by Categories

BY MARITAL STATUS

Employment and price changes during recession and recovery, by selected employee characteristics, 1979-Jan 1984, 6728–28

Employment and unemployment by selected worker characteristics, annual averages, 1983, article, 6742–2.403

Employment and unemployment current statistics, Monthly Labor Review, 6722–1.1

Employment status of family members, by occupation, family composition, age of children, and other characteristics, 1983 and trends from 1940, 6746–1.253

Employment, unemployment, and labor force, by demographic and employment characteristics, State, and for 30 metro areas and 11 large cities, 1983, annual rpt, 6744–7

Employment, unemployment, and labor force, detailed data by sociodemographic and employment characteristics, and industry, 1940s-83, 6748–72

Employment, unemployment, labor force participation, and discouraged workers, by demographic and employment characteristics, quarterly 1981-83, annual article, 6722–1.409

Handbook of Labor Statistics, employment, earnings, hours, and labor force characteristics, 1982 and trends, detailed annual rpt, 6724–1

Labor force experience of men and women by sociodemographic characteristics, and effect on earnings, 1979, Current Population Rpt, 2546–2.123

Pension benefits and after-tax salary replacement rates by plan type, and older persons income and income sources, by age and marital status, 1950s-82, conf proceedings, 25408–87

Unemployment and part-time employment, by race, Hispanic origin, sex, family composition, income, and poverty status, 1980-82, annual report, 6744–15

Unemployment and part-time employment effects on family income, by socioeconomic and labor force characteristics, 1981-82, annual rpt, 6746–1.252

Vocationally rehabilitated persons under State agency programs, by sociodemographic characteristics and disabling condition, FY79-81, annual rpt, 4944–6

Women's employment and earnings, by labor force and socioeconomic characteristics, and compared to men, 1978-81 and trends from 1940s, 6568–29

Women's labor force participation, by age, race, and family status, quarterly rpt, 6742–17

Women's labor force participation by marital status, and children by parent labor force status, by family composition, race, and Hispanic origin, Mar 1984 and trends from 1970, 6748–78

Law Enforcement

Bank robbery court cases by case processing, sentencing, and offender characteristics, and compared to other Fed Govt felony cases, 1979-80, periodic rpt, 6062–2.407

Crime and criminal justice data, including justice expenditures and employment by level of govt, 1970s-82 with some trends from 1875, 6068–174

Crime victim medical expenses and property loss, and median loss by victim characteristics, by offense type, 1975-81, 6066–19.6

Crime victimization rates by type of offense, and victim and offense characteristics, Natl Crime Survey series, 6066–3

Crimes of violence involving relatives, by victim-offender relationship, circumstances, and victim characteristics, aggregate 1973-81, 6066–19.5

Drug defendants, by sociodemographic and case processing characteristics, with comparisons to Federal fraud and bank robbery defendants, 1979, 6062–2.403

Jail capacities, conditions, expenditures, and services, and socioeconomic and other characteristics of inmates, various dates 1976-82, 10048–59

Peru cocaine addicts and arrested traffickers and users socioeconomic characteristics, and cocaine confiscated, 1974-78, intl conf papers, 7008–40

Prisoners under death sentence, and executions since 1930, by prisoner characteristics, region, and State, 1982, annual rpt, 6065–1

Population

Census of Population and Housing, 1980: detailed population and housing characteristics, by county, city, and census tract, State and SMSA rpt series, 2551–2

Census of Population, 1980: detailed socioeconomic and demographic characteristics, by age, sex, race, Hispanic origin, occupation, and industry, State rpt series, 2531–4

Census of Population, 1980: detailed socioeconomic characteristics, by county, city, and inside-outside SMSAs and central cities, State rpt series, 2531–3

Educational attainment of population, by sociodemographic characteristics and for large States and SMSAs, 1981 and trends from 1940, biennial Current Population Rpt, 2546–1.390

Florida and California elderly migration by selected State of origin or destination, and Florida elderly, by sociodemographic and housing characteristics, 1970 and 1980, 4478–150

Foreign women sociodemographic, economic, and fertility characteristics, with comparisons to men, by country, 1960s-85, world region rpt series, 2326–15

Homeless population and characteristics, and temporary shelter operations, use, and user characteristics, for selected cities, various periods 1979-84, hearing, 21248–85

Household living arrangements, family relationships, and marital status, by age and sex, Mar 1984, advance annual Current Population Rpt, 2546–1.389

Household living arrangements, family relationships, and marital status, by demographic characteristics, Mar 1983, annual Current Population Rpt, 2546–1.388

Income (household), home value and equity, and financial assets by type, by household characteristics, 1983 survey with trends from 1970, article, 9362–1.406

Income and socioeconomic characteristics of persons, families, and households, detailed cross-tabulations, Current Population Rpt series, 2546–6

Mobility of population, detailed data by demographic and socioeconomic characteristics of movers and nonmovers, Mar 1981-82, annual Current Population Rpt, 2546–1.384

Older persons by demographic, socioeconomic, and health characteristics, selected years 1900-81 and projected to 2050, Current Population Rpt, 2546–2.125

Older persons income and income sources, by OASDI beneficiary and poverty status, labor force participation, and demographic characteristics, 1982, biennial rpt, 4744–26

Older persons population characteristics, and needs and costs of social services by type, by metro-nonmetro status, 1970s-82 with trends from 1900, 21148–28

Population demographic and economic characteristics, 1982 with projections of population size to 2050, annual Current Population Rpt, 2546–2.119

Population demographic, social, and economic characteristics, Current Population Rpt series, 2546–1

Population size and components of change, projected under 3 fertility assumptions, 1982-2080 with trends from 1900, SSA actuarial rpt, 4706–1.92

Poverty status of families and persons, by detailed socioeconomic characteristics, 1982, annual Current Population Rpt, 2546–6.40

Statistical Abstract of US, social, political, and economic data, 1950s-83 and trends, annual rpt, 2324–1.1

Public Welfare and Social Security

Food aid special supplemental program for women, infants, and children, effectiveness and participant characteristics, 1973-82, GAO rpt, 26131–10

Income assistance, effects of experimental negative income tax program on employment, earnings, marital status, and other family characteristics in 2 cities, 1970-75, 4008–64

Medicare aged beneficiaries activity restriction, untreated health conditions, and perceived health status, by sociodemographic characteristics, 1980, 4146–12.2

Medicare aged beneficiaries medical care by usual source, and untreated health conditions, by sociodemographic characteristics, 1980, 4146–12.3

Noncash public and employer-based transfer program recipients, by income source and socioeconomic characteristics, 1982, advance Current Population Rpt, 2546–6.38

Noncash public and employer-based transfer program recipients, by income source and socioeconomic characteristics, 1982, final Current Population Rpt, 2546–6.37

Nutrition services for elderly, program operations and assessment, and participant sociodemographic, health, and diet characteristics, 1976 and 1982, 4608–16

OASI beneficiaries by income level, and average income, by beneficiary characteristics and income source, before and after receipt of 1st benefit, 1969-77, article, 4742–1.418

Supplemental Security Income payments, and recipients by other income source, eligibility type, and other characteristics, by State, 1982, annual rpt, 4744–16

BY MARITAL STATUS

Supplementary Security Income beneficiary socioeconomic characteristics and health service use, 1970s-83 and SSI program projections to 1995, 25148–29

Veterans Affairs

Hospital patients of VA discharged, by compensation and pension status, patient type and sex, and VA activities, FY83, annual rpt, 9924–1.3

Older veterans aged 55 and over, socioeconomic characteristics, economic resources, health care and status, and actual and expected VA benefits use, 1983 survey, 9928–29

BY RACE

Agriculture and Food

- Census of Agriculture, 1982: farms, farmland, production and costs, and operator characteristics, preliminary State and county rpt series, 2330–1
- Census of Agriculture, 1982: farms, farmland, production, finances, and operator characteristics, by county, final State rpt series, 2331–1
- Dairy products household expenditures, effects of income and other sociodemographic characteristics, modeling results, 1977/78, 1561–2.404
- Farm hired workers, sociodemographic characteristics, and farm/nonfarm income and workdays, by whether worked in Mar 1981, article, 6722–1.440
- Farm population, by employment and socioeconomic characteristics, 1983, annual rpt, 2544–1
- Farm population, by farm type and sales size and selected other characteristics, 1975-80, 1598–144
- FmHA loans, by type, race, Hispanic origin, and State, quarterly rpt, 1182–5
- Food consumption and nutrient intake by individuals, by food group, source, and socioeconomic characteristics, 1977-78 natl survey, final rpt series, 1356–4
- Food consumption expenditures and nutrient intake of low-income households, by food stamp program participation and race, 1979-80, article, 1541–7.402
- Food expenditures for fruit, vegetable, and potato products related to changes in income and other household characteristics, 1977-78, 1548–236

Banking, Finance, and Insurance

Debt (mortgage and consumer) and net worth, by householder characteristics and family income, 1983 survey, article, 9362–1.411

Communications and Transportation

- DOT employment by subagency, State, and selected personnel characteristics, FY83, annual rpt, 7304–18.2
- Postal Service operations, revenues by source, and employee characteristics, 1970s-83, and electronic mail promotion costs, FY82-87, hearings, 21628–55
- Seat belt use, effects of driving circumstances and driver characteristics and attitudes, 1981 survey, 7768–82
- TV and radio industry employment, total and for minorities, women, and youth, by job category and State, 1979-83, annual rpt, 9284–16

TV and radio industry minority and women employment by occupation, and business owners, by race and State, with revenues and stations, 1971-81, hearing, 21368–45

TV and radio station employment, total and for minorities and women, by full- and part-time status and individual station, 1983, annual rpt, 9284–7

Education

- *Condition of Education,* detailed data on enrollment, staff, achievement, finances, curricula, and education effects on employment, 1982-83, annual rpt, 4824–1
- *Digest of Education Statistics,* detailed data on students, staff, finances, and facilities, 1982 and selected trends, annual rpt, 4824–2
- Education Dept programs funding, operations, and effectiveness, FY83, annual rpt, 4804–5
- Elementary and secondary enrollment, households with children enrolled by school control, householder characteristics, and region, Oct 1982, 4838–13
- Enrollment of persons aged 3-34, by grade level and student characteristics, Oct 1982, advance annual Current Population Rpt, 2546–1.391
- Enrollment of persons aged 3-34, by grade level, instn control, and student characteristics, Oct 1983, advance annual Current Population Rpt, 2546–1.392
- Handicapped children early education research and service project activities and characteristics, and grants to States for program dev, 1983-84, annual listing, 4804–30
- Head Start Project enrollment, appropriations, and staff, FY65-84, annual rpt, 4604–8
- High school class of 1982: coursework compared to graduation criteria of natl commission, by student and school characteristics, 4828–16
- High school class of 1982: foreign language course enrollment, by language, student and school characteristics, and location, 1984 rpt, 4838–11
- High school class of 1982: foreign language coursework, by language, course level, student and school characteristics, and location, 1984 rpt, 4828–17
- High school classes of 1980 and 1982: educational and sociodemographic characteristics and expectations, natl longitudinal study, series, 4826–2
- Higher education enrollment, by student characteristics, instn type, State, and for 150 instns, fall 1982, annual rpt, 4844–2
- Postsecondary enrollment in academic, vocational, and continuing education, by student characteristics, Oct 1982, 4848–16
- Truman, Harry S, Scholarship Foundation, program operation, financial status, and awards by student characteristics, 1983 with trends from 1977, annual rpt, 14314–1
- Virginia higher education new enrollment, and students needed to meet desegregation goals, by race and instn, selected years 1978-85, hearings, 21348–91
- Vocational training bilingual projects, participants, characteristics, and costs, by program, FY82, annual rpt, 4804–26

Energy Resources and Demand

- Household energy use by socioeconomic characteristics, impact of energy price increases, selected years 1978-95, 3004–13.3
- Household, housing, and fuel use characteristics, EIA survey series, 3166–7
- Nuclear engineering student enrollments and degrees granted, by State, instn, and subfield, and placements by sector, 1983, annual rpt, 3004–5
- TVA employment of minorities and women, by detailed occupation, pay level, and grade, FY83 and goals for FY84, annual rpt, 9804–17

Government and Defense

- Customs Service activities, operations, and staff, FY79-83, annual rpt, 8144–1
- Election campaign Fed Govt funding, reform and tax deduction proposals, and TV and political action committee influence, opinion surveys, various dates 1977-83, hearings, 21428–7.1
- Fed Govt civilian employment in selected agencies by handicap status, and worldwide by pay plan and grade, by race, Hispanic origin, and sex, as of Sept 1982, article, 9842–1.403
- Fed Govt Equal Opportunity Recruitment Program implementation, and summary employment data, FY83, annual rpt, 9844–33
- Fed Govt minority group and handicapped employment, by race, Hispanic origin, disability, sex, and employment characteristics, as of Sept 1982, biennial rpt, 9844–27
- Fed Govt Senior Executive Service employee admin, and program status and effectiveness, by agency and by executive and job characteristics, July 1979-Sept 1983, GAO rpt, 26119–51
- Military active duty strength, recruits, and reenlistment, by race, Hispanic origin, sex, and service branch, quarterly press release, 3542–7
- Military officers aides, enlisted personnel authorized and assigned to perform personal services by race and sex, and program costs, by service branch, 1982-83, GAO rpt, 26123–53
- Military personnel, by selected sociodemographic characteristics, 1984 annual summary rpt, 3504–13
- Military reserve forces manpower strengths and characteristics, by component, quarterly rpt, 3542–4
- Minority group and women civilian employment of Fed Govt, by grade and agency, 1980 and 1983, 21348–41
- Natl Guard (Army and Air) activities, manpower, and facilities, FY83, annual rpt, 3704–3
- State Dept and Foreign Service minority and women employment by pay level, and affirmative action plan, FY83, annual rpt, 7004–11
- Taxes, tax policy, and intergovtl relations, public opinion survey results, 1972-84, annual rpt, 10044–2
- Voting age population selected characteristics and participation in presidential elections, 1964-80 with projections to 2000, Current Population Rpt, 2546–2.117

Index by Categories

Health and Vital Statistics

BY RACE

Abortions (legal), and deaths from abortion and childbirth, by medical and sociodemographic characteristics, 1972-83, hearings, 21368–47

Abortions, by patient sociodemographic characteristics, pregnancy history, and procedure, 1980, US Vital Statistics final rpt, 4146–5.72

Births (cesarean and total) in hospitals affiliated and not affiliated with medical schools, by characteristics of mother, birth, and hospital, 1977, 4186–6.4

Births among Asian and Pacific Islands Americans by ethnic origin and sociodemographic and birth characteristics, with comparisons to blacks and whites, 1978-80, 4146–5.75

Births and birth rates, by demographic and birth characteristics, 1981 with trends from 1940, US Vital Statistics advance rpt, 4146–5.73

Births and birth rates, by detailed demographic characteristics and geographic area, 1979 and trends, US Vital Statistics annual rpt, 4144–1

Births and birth rates, by parent and birth characteristics and infant condition at birth, 1982 and trends from 1940, US Vital Statistics annual advance rpt, 4146–5.79

Births, and birth rates for unmarried and all women, by race of child, age and Hispanic origin of mother, and State, 1980, 4147–21.42

Births and birth rates of teenage girls, and distribution of births with low birth weight and Apgar scores, by mother and infant characteristics, 1970-81, 4147–21.41

Births attended by midwives and in nonhospital settings, by mother's sociodemographic and prenatal care characteristics and infant race and birthweight, 1978-79 with trends from 1935, 4147–21.40

Births, by birth weight, Apgar score, infant and mother characteristics, birthplace, and attendant, 1978, article, 4102–1.414

Births, by outcome, and mother's sociodemographic, life style, and maternity characteristics, 1980, article, 4102–1

Births, fertility rates, expected births, and childless women, by socioeconomic characteristics, June 1982, annual Current Population Rpt, 2546–1.386

Births, fertility rates, expected births, and childless women, by socioeconomic characteristics, June 1983, advance annual Current Population Rpt, 2546–1.385

Births, fertility rates, expected births, and childless women, by socioeconomic characteristics, June 1983, annual Current Population Rpt, 2546–1.393

Birthspacing by period of woman's birth and marriage, period of child's birth, and sociodemographic characteristics, June 1980, Current Population Rpt, 2546–1.387

Breast-fed infants, by characteristics of mother and source of prenatal care, various periods 1970-75, article, 4102–1.442

Breast-fed infants, by race and mother's sociodemographic characteristics, 1983 with trends from 1970, article, 4102–1.455

Cancer cases, incidence, deaths, and death rates, by body site, age, race, Hispanic origin, and sex, for 10 geographic areas, 1973-81, 4478–130

Cancer deaths and death rates, by body site, race, sex, State, and county, 1950-79, 4478–146

Child obesity and low height-for-age, for public food program participants aged 1-4, by race and Hispanic origin, 1982, article, 4202–7.403

Contraceptives use by women, by method, marital status, age, and race, 1982, 4146–8.103

Death rates by sex, race, and age for 40 causes, projected for 10-year period, 1982 rpt, 4208–21

Deaths and death rates by age, and life expectancy, by sex and race, provisional 1982-83 with trends from 1950, US Vital Statistics annual rpt, 4144–7

Deaths and death rates by detailed cause and demographic characteristics, 1979 and selected trends, US Vital Statistics annual rpt, 4144–2.1, 4144–2.5

Deaths and death rates, by detailed geographic area, cause, and demographic characteristics, 1979, US Vital Statistics annual rpt, 4144–3

Deaths and death rates, by selected cause and demographic characteristics, 1981, US Vital Statistics advance rpt, 4146–5.78

Deaths and death rates, by selected cause and demographic characteristics, 1982, US Vital Statistics advance rpt, 4146–5.81

Deaths and death rates, provisional data, monthly rpt, 4142–1

Deaths by principal or contributing cause, with type of injury reported in accidental, poisoning, and violent deaths, by age, sex, and race, 1978, 4146–5.76

Deaths due to cold weather and related causes, by age, race, State, and city, selected periods 1962-83, 21148–30

Drug abuse treatment programs, methods, and policy issues, series, 4496–5

Drug abusers characteristics, and acquired immune deficiency syndrome (AIDS) cases by sexual preference and intravenous drug use, 1979-81, article, 4102–1.427

Drugs (analgesic) provided during visits to office-based physicians, by patient characteristics, drug brand and type, and physician specialty, 1980-81, 4146–8.99

Family planning and infertility services use by women, by source of service, marital status, age, race, and Hispanic origin, 1982, 4146–8.104

Fetal deaths and rates, by gestation period, birth weight and order, race, age of mother, and geographic area, 1979, US Vital Statistics annual rpt, 4144–2.3

Health and Nutrition Examination Natl Survey, health and dental condition and body measurements by age, sex, and race, Vital and Health Statistics series, 4147–11

Health care expenditures, natl survey on services use, costs, and sources of payment, by patient and physician characteristics, 1977-78, series, 4186–3

Health care services for elderly, knowledge, use, and factors affecting service quality, by race and Hispanic origin, 1984 article, 4652–1.406

Health care services of selected medical practitioners, use by patient characteristics, 1980 survey with trends from 1963, 4146–12.4

Health condition and health care resources, use, and expenditures, 1970s-82 with trends and projections 1900-2000, annual compilation, 4144–11

Health condition, hospitalization, disability, and medical costs, by demographic characteristics, Vital and Health Statistics series, 4147–10

Health professionals supply and education, by occupation, demographic and professional characteristics, and location, 1950s-83 and projected to 2000, biennial rpt, 4114–8

Health professions employment and training of minorities and women, by field, selected years 1962/63-1983/84, 4118–18

Hispanic Americans births and birth and fertility rates, by detailed Hispanic origin, characteristics of mother, birth, and prenatal care, and for 22 States, 1981, 4146–5.80

Hospital discharges and length of stay, by patient characteristics, facility size, procedure performed, diagnosis, and region, 1982, annual rpt, 4147–13.78

Infant and fetal deaths, and women with no prenatal care during 1st trimester, by race and Hispanic origin, 1960-80 and reduction goals for 1990, article, 4102–1.425

Infant deaths by detailed cause, geographic location, age, race, and sex, 1979, US Vital Statistics annual rpt, 4144–2.2

Kidney end-stage disease patients by patient characteristics and country, and per capita spending for treatment, selected years 1973-81, article, 4102–1.450

Life expectancy increase impacts on OASDI and pension policy, with alternative sociodemographic projections to 2100, hearing, 25368–130

Life tables, 1979 and trends from 1900, US Vital Statistics annual rpt, 4144–2.6

Life tables, 1980 and trends from 1900, US Vital Statistics annual rpt, 4144–5

Marriages, divorces, and rates, by detailed demographic and geographic characteristics, 1979 and trends, US Vital Statistics annual rpt, 4144–4

Mental health facilities, services, staff, and patient characteristics, 1970s-82 with trends from 1954, annual rpt, 4504–9

Mental health office and clinic visits, average charges, and total expenditures for services, by type of provider and patient characteristics, 1980, 4146–11.5

Mentally retarded and developmentally disabled treatment and services, university-affiliated facility funding, activities, and clients, 1980-FY83, 4608–19

Nutrition status of infants and children, blood and height-weight indicators, and low birth weight risk factors, by age, race, and Hispanic origin, 1981, annual rpt, 4205–24

Nutrition surveillance, blood values and other nutrition indicators by age, race, and Hispanic origin, 1982, annual rpt, 4204–1.3

Obstetrician-gynecologist office visits and drugs used, by visit reason, diagnosis, treatment, and patient and physician characteristics, 1980-81, 4147–13.76

Older persons health care total and out-of-pocket expenditures, by sociodemographic characteristics, poverty and health status, and degree of functional limitation, 1980, 4146–11.4

BY RACE

Pelvic inflammatory disease private physician diagnoses by age, race, and reason for visit, 1979-81, article, 4202–7.404

Perinatal deaths and death rates, by State, urban-rural location, sex, and race, 1979, US Vital Statistics annual rpt, 4144–2.4

Pharmacists employment and sociodemographic characteristics, and reasons for not working in field, by State and overseas, as of 1979, 4147–14.28

Physician visits for new pain symptoms, by diagnosis, physician specialty, and patient characteristics, and drugs prescribed or used, 1980-81, 4146–8.97

Physicians (not office-based) visits by reason, diagnosis, treatment, patient and physician characteristics, and physician primary activity, 1980, 4147–13.77

Pregnancy health counseling effect on smoking, diet, delivery costs, and birth weight, by sociodemographic characteristics and pregnancy history, 1983 article, 4102–1.401

Pregnancy-related deaths and death rates, by age and race, 1974-78, article, 4202–7.406

Radiation protection and health physics enrollments and degrees granted by State and instn, and grads employment, 1983, annual rpt, 3004–7

Reye syndrome cases by State, and mortality rate by influenza strain, with patient characteristics, various years 1974-82, article, 4202–7.402

Sterilization of women following hospital delivery of live or stillborn infants, by sociodemographic and maternity characteristics, 1972 and 1980, article, 4102–1.419

Surgeon office visits and drugs provided, by characteristics of visit, patient, and physician, and location, 1980-81, 4147–13.79

Teenage girls births and sexual experience by race, abortions, and birth control use, by age, 1970s-80 with birth trends from 1920, hearings, 21968–29

Tuberculosis cases, deaths, and treatment, by demographic characteristics, State, and city, 1982 and trends from 1953, annual rpt, 4204–2

Youth office visits to physicians by patient and visit characteristics and physician specialty, and drug mentions by brand, 1980-81, 4146–8.100

Housing and Construction

Census of Housing, 1980: inventory, occupancy, and unit characteristics, changes from 1973 by region and inside-outside SMSAs and central cities, series, 2473–3

Census of Housing, 1980: occupancy and unit characteristics of SMSAs and central cities, by race, Hispanic origin, and city, State and SMSA rpt series, 2473–1

Census of Housing, 1980: structural, financial, and householder characteristics, by region and State, 2475–4

Census of Population and Housing, 1980: detailed population and housing characteristics, by county, city, and census tract, State and SMSA rpt series, 2551–2

Fresno, Calif, economic, population, labor, and housing indicators, various periods 1974-85, hearing, 21248–84

Home mortgage default prospects by mortgage type and borrower characteristics, various periods 1967-82, technical paper, 9381–10.39

Home mortgages (graduated payment) FHA-insured, financial, property, and mortgagor characteristics, for US and selected localities, quarterly rpt, 5142–42

Home mortgages (graduated payment) FHA-insured, financial, property, and mortgagor characteristics, for US and selected States, quarterly rpt, 5142–41

Home mortgages (graduated payment) FHA-insured, financial, property, and mortgagor characteristics, US summary, quarterly rpt, 5142–40

Home mortgages FHA-insured, financial, property, and mortgagor characteristics, for US and selected localities, quarterly rpt, 5142–2

Home mortgages FHA-insured, financial, property, and mortgagor characteristics, for US, selected States, and Puerto Rico, quarterly rpt, 5142–3

Home mortgages FHA-insured, financial, property, and mortgagor characteristics, quarterly rpt, 5142–1

Home mortgages FHA-insured, financial, property, and mortgagor characteristics, 1983, annual rpt, 5144–17

Home mortgages FHA-insured for low-cost homes, financial, construction, property, and mortgagor characteristics, quarterly rpt, 5142–4

Housing (rental) unit choice of Pittsburgh, Pa, recent movers related to unit, neighborhood, and town characteristics, 1967 survey, 9306–1.7

Housing and financial characteristics, and unit and neighborhood quality, for 15 SMSAs, 1978, annual survey special supplement, 2485–8

Housing and households characteristics, and low-income housing construction and availability, 1970s-83, hearing, 21968–28.1

Housing and households detailed characteristics, and unit and neighborhood quality, by inside-outside central cities, 1979-82 surveys, SMSA rpt series, 2485–6

Housing occupancy and unit and household characteristics, by region and metro-nonmetro residence, 1983, biennial survey, 2485–1

Mobile and manufactured home safety standards, program inspections, enforcement actions, and accidents and casualties by victim characteristics, 1982-83, biennial rpt, 5004–4

Older persons rural housing condition, selected householder and housing characteristics with comparisons to urban and nonaged population, 1979, 1598–193

Quality of housing and neighborhoods, indicators and attitudes, and occupant characteristics, by urban-rural location and region, 1981, annual survey, 2485–7

Quality of housing and neighborhoods, indicators and attitudes, by occupant and unit characteristics, region, and metro-nonmetro location, 1981, annual survey, 2485–2

Industry and Commerce

Franchise businesses minority-owned, by kind of business, 1982, annual rpt, 2014–5.1

Index by Categories

Minority business mgmt and financial assistance from federally funded organizations, by region, State, and business characteristics, FY83, annual rpt, 2104–6

Small businesses owned by minorities and women, firms and receipts, owner characteristics, and Federal contracts by agency, by product or service, 1970s-82, annual rpt, 9764–6.4

Underground economy, household expenditures and participation by type of goods or service and sociodemographic characteristics, with methodology and bibl, 1981 survey, 8308–27

Labor and Employment

CETA participants by sociodemographic characteristics, and Labor Dept activities and staff, FY83, annual rpt, 6304–1

Dallas-Fort Worth, Tex, SMSA employment, earnings, hours, and CPI changes, 1983 with trends from 1968, annual rpt, 6964–2

Discrimination against Hispanics and other minorities in employment, Equal Employment Opportunity Commission enforcement activities, personnel, and litigation, 1970s-FY83, 9248–18

Earnings of full- and part-time workers, and of families by number of earners, quarterly rpt, 6742–19

Earnings of women and men, analysis of differential, by sociodemographic characteristics, hours worked, and occupation, selected years 1967-83, article, 6722–1.437

Educational attainment of labor force, by demographic and employment characteristics, 1982-83 with summary trends from 1940, 6746–1.251

Educational attainment of labor force, by demographic and employment characteristics, 1983, article, 6722–1.423

Educational attainment of labor force, by demographic and employment characteristics, 1984, press release, 6748–79

Employment and earnings, detailed data, monthly rpt, 6742–2

Employment and economic conditions, alternative BLS projections to 1995 with selected trends for 1959-82, 6728–29

Employment and labor force statistics by major industry group and demographic characteristics, *Survey of Current Business,* monthly rpt, 2702–1.5

Employment and price changes during recession and recovery, by selected employee characteristics, 1979-Jan 1984, 6728–28

Employment and unemployment current statistics, Monthly Labor Review, 6722–1.1

Employment change over business cycles, by worker characteristics and industry div, quarterly 1982-2nd qtr 1984 with trends from 1948, annual article, 6722–1.448

Employment, earnings, and hours, monthly press release, 6742–5

Employment-population ratios and unemployment rates, for total and civilian male labor force, by age and race, 1963-82, article, 6722–1.442

Employment situation, earnings, hours, and other BLS economic indicators, transcripts of BLS Commissioner's monthly testimony, periodic rpt, 23846–4

Index by Categories

BY RACE

Employment status of family members, by occupation, family composition, age of children, and other characteristics, 1983 and trends from 1940, 6746–1.253

Employment, unemployment, and labor force, by demographic and employment characteristics, State, and for 30 metro areas and 11 large cities, 1983, annual rpt, 6744–7

Employment, unemployment, and labor force, detailed data by sociodemographic and employment characteristics, and industry, 1940s-83, 6748–72

Employment, unemployment, and labor force participation, by detailed Hispanic origin, race, and sex, quarterly rpt, 6742–18

Employment, unemployment, labor force participation, and discouraged workers, by demographic and employment characteristics, quarterly 1981-83, annual article, 6722–1.409

Fresno, Calif, economic, population, labor, and housing indicators, various periods 1974-85, hearing, 21248–84

Handbook of Labor Statistics, employment, earnings, hours, and labor force characteristics, 1982 and trends, detailed annual rpt, 6724–1

Houston, Tex, SMSA employment, earnings, hours, and CPI changes, 1983 with trends from 1968, annual rpt, 6964–1

Income of families, by household type, race and Hispanic origin, farm-nonfarm residence, region, and number of earners, and change in real income, 1981-82, article, 1702–1.404

Job tenure and occupational mobility of workers, by sociodemographic characteristics and industry div, as of Jan 1983, press release, 6748–76

Job tenure and occupational mobility of workers, by sociodemographic characteristics and occupation, as of Jan 1983, article, 6722–1.460

Job Training Partnership Act dislocated workers program performance standards guide for States, with data on previous programs, by State and client characteristics, FY81-82, 6408–59.2

Labor force characteristics and economic indicators, selected years 1880-1995, chartbook, 6728–30

Labor force experience of men and women by sociodemographic characteristics, and effect on earnings, 1979, Current Population Rpt, 2546–2.123

Labor force participation, by employment and demographic characteristics, 1982-83, annual article, 6722–1.472

Minority group and women's employment, by occupational group, SIC 2- to 3-digit industry, State, and SMSA, 1981, annual rpt, 9244–1

Occupational separation rates by worker characteristics, and replacement rates, 1980-81 with projections to 1990, article, 6722–1.416

Small business and all employees sociodemographic characteristics, by industry div and firm size, 1978-1979, annual rpt, 9764–6.3

Unemployment and part-time employment, by race, Hispanic origin, sex, family composition, income, and poverty status, 1980-82, annual report, 6744–15

Unemployment and part-time employment effects on family income, by socioeconomic and labor force characteristics, 1981-82, annual rpt, 6746–1.252

Unemployment, by duration, selected demographic characteristics, industry div, and reason for job loss, various periods 1979-June 1983, article, 6722–1.411

Unemployment, by duration, work experience during year, sex, race, and Hispanic origin, 1982-83, 6748–77

Unemployment duration and probability of employment or labor force withdrawal, by sex and race, 1982, article, 9373–1.410

Unemployment duration questions of Current Population Survey, response consistency, and results, 1984 article, 6722–1.421

Unemployment effect on family income and poverty status, by demographic, employment, and unemployment characteristics, 1981-82, annual article, 6722–1.412

Unemployment rates, current data and annual trends, monthly rpt, 23842–1.2

Unemployment rates, 1948-83, annual rpt, 204–1.2

Vocationally rehabilitated persons under State agency programs, by sociodemographic characteristics and disabling condition, FY79-81, annual rpt, 4944–6

Women's employment and earnings, by labor force and socioeconomic characteristics, and compared to men, 1978-81 and trends from 1940s, 6568–29

Women's labor force participation, by age, race, and family status, quarterly rpt, 6742–17

Women's labor force participation by marital status, and children by parent labor force status, by family composition, race, and Hispanic origin, Mar 1984 and trends from 1970, 6748–78

Women's labor force participation, earnings, and socioeconomic characteristics, 1983, annual fact sheet, 6564–1

Youth employment and hours worked, by high school and college enrollment status, sex, race, and Hispanic origin, 1982-83, annual article, 6722–1.446

Youth employment, by high school and college enrollment status, industry div, occupation, and selected demographic characteristics, 1980-82, 6746–1.250

Youth summer employment, by sex, race, and class of worker, 1979-84, annual press release, 6744–14

Law Enforcement

Aircraft hijackers, and date and place of birth and race or ethnic group, 1961-83, annual rpt, 7504–31.3

Arrests and arrest rates, by offense, offender characteristics, population size, and State, 1970s-83, annual rpt, 6224–2.2

Assaults, murders, and other deaths of law enforcement officers, by circumstances, level of govt, agency, victim and offender characteristics, and location, 1983, annual rpt, 6224–3

Crime and criminal justice data, including justice expenditures and employment by level of govt, 1970s-82 with some trends from 1875, 6068–174

Crime victim medical expenses and property loss, and median loss by victim characteristics, by offense type, 1975-81, 6066–19.6

Crime victimization of households, by offense type, race of household head, and family income and urban-rural residence, 1975-83, periodic rpt, 6062–2.404

Crime victimization rates by type of offense, and victim and offense characteristics, Natl Crime Survey series, 6066–3

Crimes of violence involving relatives, by victim-offender relationship, circumstances, and victim characteristics, aggregate 1973-81, 6066–19.5

Homicide and suicide rates for youth, by sex, race, and circumstances, selected years 1970-79, and stress and violent behavior reduction goals for 1990, 4102–1.437

Homicides and homicide rates, by victim characteristics, location, and circumstances, and years of life lost from homicide and other leading causes of death, 1970-78, 4205–38

Jail capacities, conditions, expenditures, and services, and socioeconomic and other characteristics of inmates, various dates 1976-82, 10048–59

Kidnapping by parents over intl and interstate boundaries, characteristics of cases referred to State Dept and FBI by State and country, 1979-83, hearing, 25528–95

Prisoners in State prisons median sentence, and admissions and releases by prisoner and sentencing characteristics, by offense and State, 1981 and trends from 1926, 6066–19.9

Prisoners under death sentence, and executions since 1930, by prisoner characteristics, region, and State, 1982, annual rpt, 6065–1

Robbery rates and circumstances, medical costs and property losses of victims, and offender and victim characteristics, 1960s-81, 6068–180

School crime against students, teachers, and others, by offense, circumstances, and offender sex and race, 1974-76, 6066–20.2

Statistical Abstract of US, social, political, and economic data, 1950s-83 and trends, annual rpt, 2324–1.1

Natural Resources, Environment, and Pollution

Land privately held, acreage and owners by owner characteristics, land use, and region, and purchase and improvement funding, 1978 survey, series, 1506–5

Youth Conservation Corps activities, costs, and participant characteristics, by sponsoring agency, 1982, annual rpt, 5304–12

Population

Alabama rural black population, education, employment, health services, and economic status, for 16 counties, selected years 1970-81, 11048–180

Census of Population and Housing, 1980: detailed population and housing characteristics, by county, city, and census tract, State and SMSA rpt series, 2551–2

Census of Population, 1980: Asian and Pacific Islander population, by detailed race and State, supplementary rpt, 2535–1.15

Census of Population, 1980: detailed socioeconomic and demographic characteristics, by age, sex, race, Hispanic origin, occupation, and industry, State rpt series, 2531–4

BY RACE

Census of Population, 1980: detailed socioeconomic characteristics, by county, city, and inside-outside SMSAs and central cities, State rpt series, 2531–3

Census of Population, 1980: migration since 1975, by county and selected demographic characteristics, supplementary rpt, 2535–1.14

Census of Population, 1980: migration since 1975, by State and selected demographic characteristics, supplementary rpt, 2535–1.13

City and suburb population characteristics and local govt finances, by region and selected SMSA, 1950s-FY83, 10048–61

Coastal environmental characteristics, fish, wildlife, and use, and population socioeconomic data, for individual areas, series, 5506–4

County and City Data Book, detailed socioeconomic and demographic data for States, counties, and cities, selected years 1976-82, 2328–1

Educational attainment of population, by sociodemographic characteristics and for large States and SMSAs, 1981 and trends from 1940, biennial Current Population Rpt, 2546–1.390

Florida and California elderly migration by selected State of origin or destination, and Florida elderly, by sociodemographic and housing characteristics, 1970 and 1980, 4478–150

Fresno, Calif, economic, population, labor, and housing indicators, various periods 1974-85, hearing, 21248–84

Homeless population and characteristics, and temporary shelter operations, use, and user characteristics, for selected cities, various periods 1979-84, hearing, 21248–85

Household living arrangements, family relationships, and marital status, by demographic characteristics, Mar 1983, annual Current Population Rpt, 2546–1.388

Income (household) and cash and noncash transfer program participation, by sociodemographic characteristics, quarterly rpt, 2542–2

Income (household) before and after taxes, by socioeconomic characteristics, type of tax paid, and region, 1981, Current Population Rpt, 2546–2.118

Income (household) before and after taxes, by socioeconomic characteristics, type of tax paid, and region, 1982, annual Current Population Rpt, 2546–2.122

Income (household), home value and equity, and financial assets by type, by household characteristics, 1983 survey with trends from 1970, article, 9362–1.406

Income and socioeconomic characteristics of persons, families, and households, detailed cross-tabulations, Current Population Rpt series, 2546–6

Income of families and persons in 1982 dollars, and poverty status, by race, 1947-82, annual rpt, 204–1.1

Mobility of population, detailed data by demographic and socioeconomic characteristics of movers and nonmovers, Mar 1981-82, annual Current Population Rpt, 2546–1.384

Older persons by demographic, socioeconomic, and health characteristics, selected years 1900-81 and projected to 2050, Current Population Rpt, 2546–2.125

Older persons income and income sources, by OASDI beneficiary and poverty status, labor force participation, and demographic characteristics, 1982, biennial rpt, 4744–26

Older persons population characteristics, and needs and costs of social services by type, by metro-nonmetro status, 1970s-82 with trends from 1900, 21148–28

Older persons sociodemographic characteristics, and Fed Govt program participation and funding, 1983 with trends and projections 1900-2060, annual rpt, 25144–3.1

Older persons sociodemographic characteristics and transportation needs, selected years 1900-2040, 7308–183

Population demographic and economic characteristics, 1982 with projections of population size to 2050, annual Current Population Rpt, 2546–2.119

Population demographic, social, and economic characteristics, Current Population Rpt series, 2546–1

Population size by single years of age, and components of change, by sex and race, projected 1983-2080, final Current Population Rpt, 2546–3.132

Population size, by single years of age, sex, and race, 1980-83, annual Current Population Rpt, 2546–3.130

Poverty-level persons and families, by income source, hours of work, earnings, taxes, and family characteristics, various periods 1959-84, 21788–131

Poverty status of families and persons, by detailed socioeconomic characteristics, 1982, annual Current Population Rpt, 2546–6.40

Poverty status of families and persons by selected characteristics, public welfare funding, and effect of counting transfer payments as income, selected years 1950-83, 25928–4

Poverty status of young adults related to motivation, psychological factors, and family characteristics, by race and sex, 1970s-82, longitudinal study, 4008–65.1

Statistical Abstract of US, social, political, and economic data, 1950s-83 and trends, annual rpt, 2324–1.1, 2324–1.3

Voting age population for Nov 1984 election, by sex, age, race, Hispanic origin, region, and State, and percent voting during 1930-82, Current Population Rpt, 2546–3.129

Women in couples with wife as primary earner, socioeconomic and family characteristics, with comparative data for husbands, Mar 1982, 2326–11.9

Prices and Cost of Living

Vegetable and potato per capita weekly expenditures, by commodity, season, race, age, and region, 1977-78, article, 1561–11.401

Public Welfare and Social Security

ACTION activities, volunteer characteristics, and budget, by program, FY82, annual rpt, 9024–2

Colorado Medicare beneficiaries with partial coverage, 1978, article, 4652–1.404

Farm households receiving social security income, farms and amount by characteristics of farm and operator, 1978-82, article, 1702–1.410

Index by Categories

Food aid programs of Fed Govt and others, funding, participant characteristics, and nutrition and poverty data, 1970s-83, 028–20

Food aid special supplemental program for women, infants, and children, effectiveness and participant characteristics, 1973-82, GAO rpt, 26131–10

Income assistance, effects of experimental negative income tax program on employment, earnings, marital status, and other family characteristics in 2 cities, 1970-75, 4008–64

Medicare aged beneficiaries activity restriction, untreated health conditions, and perceived health status, by sociodemographic characteristics, 1980, 4146–12.2

Medicare aged beneficiaries medical care by usual source, and untreated health conditions, by sociodemographic characteristics, 1980, 4146–12.3

Medicare and Medicaid eligibility, participation, covered services and use, and reimbursements and payments, various periods 1966-82, annual rpt, 4654–1

Medicare end-stage renal disease program enrollment, new cases by State, and survival and death rates, by age, sex, and race, 1970s-81, article, 4652–1.408

Medicare kidney end-stage program, reimbursement by treatment, diagnosis, outcome, and patient characteristics, with covered charges for transplants, 1974-79, article, 4652–1.421

Medicare physician charges and reimbursement by enrollee characteristics and carrier, payment limits effects on charges in California, and physician earnings, by specialty, 1950s-84, 25368–127

Noncash public and employer-based transfer program recipients, by income source and socioeconomic characteristics, 1982, advance Current Population Rpt, 2546–6.38

Noncash public and employer-based transfer program recipients, by income source and socioeconomic characteristics, 1982, final Current Population Rpt, 2546–6.37

Nutrition services for elderly, program operations and assessment, and participant sociodemographic, health, and diet characteristics, 1976 and 1982, 4608–16

OASDHI beneficiaries with direct deposit of benefit checks, by age, sex, race, benefit amount, and State, as of Dec 1983, article, 4742–1.412

OASDHI, Medicaid, SSI, and other social insurance and public welfare programs benefits, beneficiary characteristics, and trust funds, selected years 1937-83, annual rpt, 4744–3

OASDHI, SSI, and other social security programs and recipient characteristics, *Research and Statistics Notes,* series, 4746–16

Older persons entitled to both Medicare and Medicaid, demographic characteristics, and health condition and services use, 1980, article, 4652–1.433

Poverty population size, effect of counting public noncash transfers as income by recipient characteristics, 1979-83, 2626–2.52

Index by Categories

BY SEX

Poverty population size, effects of counting public noncash transfers as income by recipient characteristics, 1979-82, 2626–2.50

Runaway and other homeless youth programs, funding by source, activities, and participant characteristics, FY82, annual rpt, 4604–3

Supplemental Security Income and 3 earlier programs benefits, beneficiaries below poverty level, and State program expenditures, various periods 1972-83, article, 4742–1.402

Supplemental Security Income payments, and recipients by other income source, eligibility type, and other characteristics, by State, 1982, annual rpt, 4744–16

Supplementary Security Income beneficiary socioeconomic characteristics and health service use, 1970s-83 and SSI program projections to 1995, 25148–29

Science and Technology

Computer specialists sociodemographic, educational, and employment characteristics, and Fed Govt support by agency, 1978, biennial Current Population Rpt, 2546–2.124

Degree (doctoral) recipients in science and engineering, by field, sex, race, age, citizenship, postgrad employment and study status, State, and instn, 1960-82, 9626–6.16

Employment characteristics or grad enrollment of science and engineering grads of 1980-81, by degree level, field, sex, and race, 1982, 9627–25

Employment, salaries, and degrees of scientists and engineers, by field, type of employer, race, and sex, selected years 1960-81, annual rpt, 9624–18.5

Employment, supply, and education of scientists and engineers, by sex, race, Hispanic origin, and field, selected years 1965-83, biennial rpt, 9624–20

Engineers sociodemographic, educational, and employment characteristics, and Federal support by agency, 1978, Current Population Rpt, 2546–2.121

Enrollment in grad science and engineering, fields of study, financial support, and other student and instn characteristics, 1975-82, annual survey, 9627–7

Enrollment in science and engineering grad programs, by field, degree level, source of financial support, race, and Hispanic origin, 1975-81, 9626–2.134

Higher education instns science and engineering grad students, by field, type of financial aid, sex, race, Hispanic origin, and citizenship, 1972-83, biennial rpt, 9627–24.3

Scientists and engineers employment, unemployment, and earnings, by field, sex, race, and Hispanic origin, 1970s-82, annual rpt, 9624–10.3

Veterans Affairs

Disabled veterans, by age, race, employment status, period of service, and whether applied for VA benefits, 1979, 9926–4.6

Health condition of veterans and nonveterans, and veteran use of VA and non-VA hospitals by disease, by age, race, income, and metro-nonmetro location, various periods 1971-81, 9926–1.18

Older veterans aged 55 and over, socioeconomic characteristics, economic resources, health care and status, and actual and expected VA benefits use, 1983 survey, 9928–29

Speech disorders among patients in VA facilties, by severity, patient characteristics, diagnostician occupation, and facility type, FY81, 9926–1.17

Unemployment rates and compensation, Vietnam era veterans compared with WW II and Korea veterans, FY83, annual rpt, 9924–8.2

VA employment characteristics and activities, FY83, annual rpt, 9924–1.8

BY SEX

Agriculture and Food

Census of Agriculture, 1982: farms, farmland, production and costs, and operator characteristics, preliminary State and county rpt series, 2330–1

Census of Agriculture, 1982: farms, farmland, production, finances, and operator characteristics, by county, final State rpt series, 2331–1

Farm hired workers, sociodemographic characteristics, and farm/nonfarm income and workdays, by whether worked in Mar 1981, article, 6722–1.440

Farm population, by employment and socioeconomic characteristics, 1983, annual rpt, 2544–1

Food consumption and nutrient intake by individuals, by food group, source, and socioeconomic characteristics, 1977-78 natl survey, final rpt series, 1356–4

Banking, Finance, and Insurance

Bankruptcy (personal), filers by debt type and other characteristics, and impacts in Connecticut and Michigan, various dates 1946-82, hearings, 21528–57

Bankruptcy (personal), filers by debt type and other characteristics, selected years 1978-81, hearing, 25528–97.1

Communications and Transportation

Aircraft pilots and nonpilots certified by FAA, by type of certificate, age, sex, region, and State, 1983, annual rpt, 7504–2

DOT employment by subagency, State, and selected personnel characteristics, FY83, annual rpt, 7304–18

Drivers licensed by age and sex, and licensing policies, by State, 1982, annual rpt, 7554–16

Drivers licenses in force, by age, sex, and State, 1982-83, annual summary rpt, 7554–24

Drivers licenses in force by license type, sex, and age, and revenues, by State, 1983, annual rpt, 7554–1.2

Postal Service operations, revenues by source, and employee characteristics, 1970s-83, and electronic mail promotion costs, FY82-87, hearings, 21628–55

Railroad employee benefits and beneficiaries by type, and railroad employees and payrolls, FY82, annual rpt, 9704–2

Telephone and telegraph industry employment and wages, by occupation and sex, 1981, annual survey, 6787–6.199

Telephone company employees, by sex and individual company, Dec 1982, annual rpt, 9284–6.4

Traffic accidents and casualties detailed direct and indirect costs, by characteristics of persons and vehicles involved, 1979-80, 7768–80

Traffic accidents and deaths by characteristics of persons and vehicles involved and State, and Natl Hwy Traffic Safety Admin activities, 1961-81, annual rpt, 7764–1

Traffic accidents, circumstances, injuries, deaths, and characteristics of persons and vehicles involved, 1982, annual rpt, 7764–13

Traffic deaths, by victim occupancy, age, and sex, 1975-83, 7766–13.7

Traffic fatal accidents, alcohol levels of drivers and pedestrians by driver age and sex and time of accident, 1980, 7768–81

Traffic fatal accidents, circumstances, and characteristics of persons and vehicles involved, 1983, annual rpt, 7764–14

Traffic fatal accidents detailed circumstances, and characteristics of persons and vehicles involved, 1982, annual rpt, 7764–10

Travel patterns, personal and household characteristics, auto use, and public transport availability, 1977 survey, series, 7556–6

TV and radio industry employment, total and for minorities, women, and youth, by job category and State, 1979-83, annual rpt, 9284–16

TV and radio industry minority and women employment by occupation, and business owners, by race and State, with revenues and stations, 1971-81, hearing, 21368–45

TV and radio station employment, total and for minorities and women, by full- and part-time status and individual station, 1983, annual rpt, 9284–7

Education

Condition of Education, detailed data on enrollment, staff, achievement, finances, curricula, and education effects on employment, 1982-83, annual rpt, 4824–1

Digest of Education Statistics, detailed data on students, staff, finances, and facilities, 1982 and selected trends, annual rpt, 4824–2

DOD Dependents Schools students higher education admissions tests scores by sex and subject, and educational goals and attitudes, 1983, annual rpt, 3504–17

Education Dept programs funding, operations, and effectiveness, FY83, annual rpt, 4804–5

Enrollment of persons aged 3-34, by grade level and student characteristics, Oct 1982, advance annual Current Population Rpt, 2546–1.391

Enrollment of persons aged 3-34, by grade level, instn control, and student characteristics, Oct 1983, advance annual Current Population Rpt, 2546–1.392

Grads and degrees, secondary and higher education, 1972/73-1992/93, biennial pocket-size card, 4824–3

High school class of 1982: foreign language course enrollment, by language, student and school characteristics, and location, 1984 rpt, 4838–11

High school class of 1982: foreign language coursework, by language, course level, student and school characteristics, and location, 1984 rpt, 4828–17

BY SEX

High school classes of 1972 and 1980: achievement test scores by sex and whether planning education major, hearings, 21348–89

High school classes of 1980 and 1982: educational and sociodemographic characteristics and expectations, natl longitudinal study, series, 4826–2

Higher education enrollment, by student characteristics, instn type, State, and for 150 instns, fall 1982, annual rpt, 4844–2

Indian education program operations, funding, student progress measures, and opinions of school staff, parents, and students, selected years 1973-83, 4808–13

Libraries of colleges and universities, expenditures, holdings by type, use, staff by sex, and Federal grants received, 1979-82, biennial rpt, 4854–1

Postsecondary enrollment in academic, vocational, and continuing education, by student characteristics, Oct 1982, 4848–16

Puerto Rico University personnel, and degrees earned by Hispanics, by sex, selected years 1970-83, hearings, 21348–93

Truman, Harry S, Scholarship Foundation, program operation, financial status, and awards by student characteristics, 1983 with trends from 1977, annual rpt, 14314–1

Energy Resources and Demand

Household, housing, and fuel use characteristics, EIA survey series, 3166–7

Nuclear engineering student enrollments and degrees granted, by State, instn, and subfield, and placements by sector, 1983, annual rpt, 3004–5

TVA employment of minorities and women, by detailed occupation, pay level, and grade, FY83 and goals for FY84, annual rpt, 9804–17

Government and Defense

Army active duty personnel health status and use of Army medical services in US and abroad, by treatment facility, monthly rpt, 3702–4.2

Customs Service activities, operations, and staff, FY79-83, annual rpt, 8144–1

DOD medical personnel and trainees, by occupation, sex, and service branch, FY83, annual rpt, 3544–24.1

Election campaign Fed Govt funding, reform and tax deduction proposals, and TV and political action committee influence, opinion surveys, various dates 1977-83, hearings, 21428–7.1

Fed Govt civil service retirees and survivors, and monthly benefit, for US territories and foreign countries, and by State, age, and sex, FY81-82, annual rpt, 9844–1.1

Fed Govt civilian employment in selected agencies by handicap status, and worldwide by pay plan and grade, by race, Hispanic origin, and sex, as of Sept 1982, article, 9842–1.403

Fed Govt Equal Opportunity Recruitment Program implementation, and summary employment data, FY83, annual rpt, 9844–33

Fed Govt minority group and handicapped employment, by race, Hispanic origin, disability, sex, and employment characteristics, as of Sept 1982, biennial rpt, 9844–27

Fed Govt personnel action appeals, decisions of Merit Systems Protection Board, by agency, veteran status, sex, and age, FY82, annual rpt, 9494–2.1

Fed Govt Senior Executive Service employee admin, and program status and effectiveness, by agency and by executive and job characteristics, July 1979-Sept 1983, GAO rpt, 26119–51

Immigration, and alien residents, workers, visitors, deportations, and naturalizations, by country of birth, FY81, annual rpt, 6264–2

Military active duty strength, recruits, and reenlistment, by race, Hispanic origin, sex, and service branch, quarterly press release, 3542–7

Military manpower levels, by grade, sex, and service branch, FY80-84 and projected to 1990, 3508–19

Military officers aides, enlisted personnel authorized and assigned to perform personal services by race and sex, and program costs, by service branch, 1982-83, GAO rpt, 26123–53

Military personnel, by selected sociodemographic characteristics, 1984 annual summary rpt, 3504–13

Military personnel in US, and civilian employment, by age, sex, occupation, and educational attainment, 1982 and summary trends from 1950, article, 6722–1.441

Military reserve forces manpower strengths and characteristics, by component, quarterly rpt, 3542–4

Military women personnel on active duty, by demographic and service characteristics and service branch, with comparisons to men, FY83, annual chartbook, 3544–26

Minority group and women civilian employment of Fed Govt, by grade and agency, 1980 and 1983, 21348–41

Navy personnel, detailed statistics, quarterly rpt, 3802–4

Passports issued, by holder characteristics, travel purpose, and country of destination, quarterly rpt, 7182–1

State Dept and Foreign Service minority and women employment by pay level, and affirmative action plan, FY83, annual rpt, 7004–11

Taxes, tax policy, and intergovtl relations, public opinion survey results, 1972-84, annual rpt, 10044–2

Voting age population selected characteristics and participation in presidential elections, 1964-80 with projections to 2000, Current Population Rpt, 2546–2.117

Health and Vital Statistics

Alaska Native Medical Center visits and ambulatory high use patients by age and sex, and patient deaths, 1972-78, article, 4102–1.440

Births and birth rates, by demographic and birth characteristics, 1981 with trends from 1940, US Vital Statistics advance rpt, 4146–5.73

Births and birth rates, by parent and birth characteristics and infant condition at birth, 1982 and trends from 1940, US Vital Statistics annual advance rpt, 4146–5.79

Births, by sex and sex ratio, 1940-79, US Vital Statistics annual rpt, 4144–1

Canada and US hospital use by children by Canada Province and US region, and death rates, by diagnosis and sex, selected years 1977-79, 4147–5.1

Index by Categories

Cancer cases, incidence, deaths, and death rates, by body site, age, race, Hispanic origin, and sex, for 10 geographic areas, 1973-81, 4478–130

Cancer deaths and death rates, by body site, race, sex, State, and county, 1950-79, 4478–146

Cancer deaths by age, 1980, and deaths and new cases, 1983, by sex and body site, annual fact book, 4474–13

CAT scan procedures on hospital inpatients, by body site and patient and hospital characteristics, 1979-82, 4146–8.102

Coxsackie B virus cases, by isolate, associated clinical syndrome and patient age and sex, US and Nassau County, NY, 1970-79, article, 4102–1.452

Death rates by age and sex, and persons aged 65 and 80 and older share of population and deaths, selected years 1900-80, article, 4102–1.447

Death rates by sex, race, and age for 40 causes, projected for 10-year period, 1982 rpt, 4208–21

Death rates for persons 65 and over, by major cause, sex, and age, selected years 1940-80, 4147–3.25

Deaths and death rates by age, and life expectancy, by sex and race, provisional 1982-83 with trends from 1950, US Vital Statistics annual rpt, 4144–7

Deaths and death rates by detailed cause and demographic characteristics, 1979 and selected trends, US Vital Statistics annual rpt, 4144–2.1, 4144–2.5

Deaths and death rates, by detailed geographic area, cause, and demographic characteristics, 1979, US Vital Statistics annual rpt, 4144–3

Deaths and death rates, by selected cause and demographic characteristics, 1981, US Vital Statistics advance rpt, 4146–5.78

Deaths and death rates, by selected cause and demographic characteristics, 1982, US Vital Statistics advance rpt, 4146–5.81

Deaths and death rates, provisional data, monthly rpt, 4142–1

Deaths by principal or contributing cause, with type of injury reported in accidental, poisoning, and violent deaths, by age, sex, and race, 1978, 4146–5.76

Dental malpractice claims, by amount, procedure type, region, State, and provider and patient characteristics, 1970, article, 4102–1.416

Disabled women, by socioeconomic and demographic characteristics, and compared to nondisabled women and disabled men, 1981, chartbook, 16598–4

Drug (prescription) use by outpatient characteristics and generic or brand name, and hospital and drugstore costs by drug class, 1982, annual rpt, 4064–12

Drug abuse treatment programs, methods, and policy issues, series, 4496–5

Drug abusers characteristics, and acquired immune deficiency syndrome (AIDS) cases by sexual preference and intravenous drug use, 1979-81, article, 4102–1.427

Drugs (analgesic) provided during visits to office-based physicians, by patient characteristics, drug brand and type, and physician specialty, 1980-81, 4146–8.99

Drugs, alcohol, and cigarettes, high school seniors use and assessment by drug type, sex, and region, 1975-83 surveys, annual rpt, 4494–4

Index by Categories

BY SEX

Foreign and US life expectancy by sex, for 7 countries, selected years 1975-81, 21148–33

Health and Nutrition Examination Natl Survey, health and dental condition and body measurements by age, sex, and race, Vital and Health Statistics series, 4147–11

Health care expenditures, natl survey on services use, costs, and sources of payment, by patient and physician characteristics, 1977-78, series, 4186–3

Health care expenditures per capita, by type of service and patient age and sex, for 10-15 medical conditions, 1980, article, 4652–1.413

Health care services of selected medical practitioners, use by patient characteristics, 1980 survey with trends from 1963, 4146–12.4

Health condition and health care resources, use, and expenditures, 1970s-82 with trends and projections 1900-2000, annual compilation, 4144–11

Health condition, hospitalization, disability, and medical costs, by demographic characteristics, Vital and Health Statistics series, 4147–10

Health habits associated with 10 major death causes, prevalence of 8 risk factors in selected States, 1981-83 surveys, article, 4202–7.405

Health habits of adults, including physical activity, smoking, alcohol use, hypertension, and seat belt use, by age and sex, 1982, annual rpt, 4204–1.3

Health professionals supply and education, by occupation, demographic and professional characteristics, and location, 1950s-83 and projected to 2000, biennial rpt, 4114–8

Health professions employment and training of minorities and women, by field, selected years 1962/63-1983/84, 4118–18

Heart, Lung, and Blood Natl Inst funds and recipients by instn, State, and foreign country, and heart disease death rates for US and 26 foreign countries by sex, 1960s-FY83, annual fact book, 4474–15

Hospital and nursing home discharges, by age, sex, marital status, and selected diagnosis, 1976 and 1979, article, 4102–1.443

Hospital discharges and length of stay, by patient age and sex, facility size and ownership, procedure performed, and region, 1982, 4146–8.96

Hospital discharges and length of stay, by patient age and sex, facility size and ownership, procedure performed, and region, 1983, 4146–8.101

Hospital discharges and length of stay, by patient characteristics, facility size, procedure performed, diagnosis, and region, 1982, annual rpt, 4147–13.78

Hospital worker wages by sex and occupation, and benefits, for 22 MSAs, Oct 1981 survey, 6787–6.201

Infant deaths by detailed cause, geographic location, age, race, and sex, 1979, US Vital Statistics annual rpt, 4144–2.2

Injuries and deaths from use of selected consumer products and related activity, by victim age and sex, 1982, annual rpt, 9164–7

Internist office visits and drugs provided, by characteristics of visit, patient, and physician, and location, 1980-81, 4147–13.80

Israel and France urban youths use of selected drugs, alcohol, and cigarettes, by age and sex, 1977 and 1979, article, 4102–1.430

Kidney end-stage disease patients by patient characteristics and country, and per capita spending for treatment, selected years 1973-81, article, 4102–1.450

Life expectancy, and deaths by cause, by sex and age, 1900-2050, SSA actuarial rpt, 4706–1.89

Life expectancy increase impacts on OASDI and pension policy, with alternative sociodemographic projections to 2100, hearing, 25368–130

Life tables, 1979 and trends from 1900, US Vital Statistics annual rpt, 4144–2.6

Life tables, 1980 and trends from 1900, US Vital Statistics annual rpt, 4144–5

Mental health office and clinic visits, average charges, and total expenditures for services, by type of provider and patient characteristics, 1980, 4146–11.5

Mental health short-stay hospitals discharges by diagnosis, and physician office visits, by sex, selected years 1975-80, annual rpt, 4504–9.2

Mentally retarded and developmentally disabled treatment and services, university-affiliated facility funding, activities, and clients, 1980-FY83, 4608–19

Navy and Marine Corps disease incidence, medical care, and deaths, by detailed diagnosis, and medical personnel and workloads, 1978-79, annual rpt, 3804–1

Nigeria native and Western health care use, by sociodemographic characteristics, 1984 article, 4102–1.417

Obstetrician-gynecologist office visits and drugs used, by visit reason, diagnosis, treatment, and patient and physician characteristics, 1980-81, 4147–13.76

Occupational health risks from hazardous substances and radiation, by industry, occupation, age, and sex, with bibl and glossary, 1920s-82, 9638–50

Occupational injuries, detailed accident circumstances and safety data, by body part injured, type of equipment used, or industry, series, 6846–1

Older persons health care total and out-of-pocket expenditures, by sociodemographic characteristics, poverty and health status, and degree of functional limitation, 1980, 4146–11.4

Perinatal deaths and death rates, by State, urban-rural location, sex, and race, 1979, US Vital Statistics annual rpt, 4144–2.4

Peru cocaine addicts and arrested traffickers and users socioeconomic characteristics, and cocaine confiscated, 1974-78, intl conf papers, 7008–40

Pharmacists employment and sociodemographic characteristics, and reasons for not working in field, by State and overseas, as of 1979, 4147–14.28

Physician visits for new pain symptoms, by diagnosis, physician specialty, and patient characteristics, and drugs prescribed or used, 1980-81, 4146–8.97

Physicians (not office-based) visits by reason, diagnosis, treatment, patient and physician characteristics, and physician primary activity, 1980, 4147–13.77

Radiation protection and health physics enrollments and degrees granted by State and instn, and grads employment, 1983, annual rpt, 3004–7

Reye syndrome cases by State, and mortality rate by influenza strain, with patient characteristics, various years 1974-82, article, 4202–7.402

Smoke alarm sound levels by brand, and response time by circumstances and for older and mentally retarded persons, 1983 rpt, 2218–70

Smoking related to chronic obstructive lung disease and deaths, by sociodemographic and smoking characteristics, literature review, 1984 annual Surgeon General rpt, 4044–6

Surgeon office visits and drugs provided, by characteristics of visit, patient, and physician, and location, 1980-81, 4147–13.79

TTPI deaths by age and sex, and health service training participants by sex, selected years 1965-82, annual rpt, 7004–6.1

Tuberculosis cases, deaths, and treatment, by demographic characteristics, State, and city, 1982 and trends from 1953, annual rpt, 4204–2

Venereal disease cases and incidence, 1982, annual rpt, 4204–1

Venereal disease cases reported and epidemiologic activities, by region, State, and large city, 1982, annual rpt, 4204–14

Washington State deaths by sex, cause, and detailed occupation, summary data from occupational mortality study, 1950-79, 4248–47

Youth office visits to physicians by patient and visit characteristics and physician specialty, and drug mentions by brand, 1980-81, 4146–8.100

Housing and Construction

Census of Housing, 1980: inventory, occupancy, and unit characteristics, changes from 1973 by region and inside-outside SMSAs and central cities, series, 2473–3

Census of Housing, 1980: occupancy and unit characteristics of SMSAs and central cities, by race, Hispanic origin, and city, State and SMSA rpt series, 2473–1

Home mortgages (graduated payment) FHA-insured, financial, property, and mortgagor characteristics, for US and selected localities, quarterly rpt, 5142–42

Home mortgages (graduated payment) FHA-insured, financial, property, and mortgagor characteristics, for US and selected States, quarterly rpt, 5142–41

Home mortgages (graduated payment) FHA-insured, financial, property, and mortgagor characteristics, US summary, quarterly rpt, 5142–40

Home mortgages FHA-insured, financial, property, and mortgagor characteristics, for US and selected localities, quarterly rpt, 5142–2

Home mortgages FHA-insured, financial, property, and mortgagor characteristics, for US, selected States, and Puerto Rico, quarterly rpt, 5142–3

Home mortgages FHA-insured, financial, property, and mortgagor characteristics, quarterly rpt, 5142–1

BY SEX

Index by Categories

Home mortgages FHA-insured, financial, property, and mortgagor characteristics, 1983, annual rpt, 5144–17

Home mortgages FHA-insured for low-cost homes, financial, construction, property, and mortgagor characteristics, quarterly rpt, 5142–4

Homeless population and characteristics, and temporary shelter operations, use, and user characteristics, by region and selected city, 1983, 5188–108

Housing occupancy and unit and household characteristics, by region and metro-nonmetro residence, 1983, biennial survey, 2485–1

Mobile and manufactured home safety standards, program inspections, enforcement actions, and accidents and casualties by victim characteristics, 1982-83, biennial rpt, 5004–4

Older persons rural housing condition, selected householder and housing characteristics with comparisons to urban and nonaged population, 1979, 1598–193

Quality of housing and neighborhoods, indicators and attitudes, and occupant characteristics, by urban-rural location and region, 1981, annual survey, 2485–7

Industry and Commerce

Small businesses owned by minorities and women, firms and receipts, owner characteristics, and Federal contracts by agency, by product or service, 1970s-82, annual rpt, 9764–6.4

Labor and Employment

- Australia and US youth unemployment rates, by sex and age, Mar 1983 and trends from 1960s, article, 6722–1.462
- Census of Population, 1980: labor force, by sex, detailed occupation, and region, with comparison to 1970 census, supplementary rpt, 2535–1.12
- CETA participants by sociodemographic characteristics, and Labor Dept activities and staff, FY83, annual rpt, 6304–1
- Dallas-Fort Worth, Tex, SMSA employment, earnings, hours, and CPI changes, 1983 with trends from 1968, annual rpt, 6964–2
- Disability (short-term) earnings lost, insurance benefits, sick leave, and work days lost by sex, by type of worker, 1948-81, article, 4742–1.417
- Discrimination against Hispanics and other minorities in employment, Equal Employment Opportunity Commission enforcement activities, personnel, and litigation, 1970s-FY83, 9248–18
- Earnings by sex and region related to wages in South, with adjustments for job comparability and union membership status, 1978, 1981, and 1983, article, 9389–1.406
- Earnings of full- and part-time workers, quarterly rpt, 6742–19
- Earnings of women and men, analysis of differential, by sociodemographic characteristics, hours worked, and occupation, selected years 1967-83, article, 6722–1.437
- Educational attainment of labor force, by demographic and employment characteristics, 1982-83 with summary trends from 1940, 6746–1.251
- Educational attainment of labor force, by demographic and employment characteristics, 1983, article, 6722–1.423

Educational attainment of labor force, by demographic and employment characteristics, 1984, press release, 6748–79

Employment and earnings, detailed data, monthly rpt, 6742–2

Employment and earnings of women, by labor force and socioeconomic characteristics, and compared to men, 1978-81 and trends from 1940s, 6568–29

Employment and economic conditions, alternative BLS projections to 1995 with selected trends for 1959-82, 6728–29

Employment and labor force statistics by major industry group and demographic characteristics, *Survey of Current Business,* monthly rpt, 2702–1.5

Employment and price changes during recession and recovery, by selected employee characteristics, 1979-Jan 1984, 6728–28

Employment and unemployment current statistics, Monthly Labor Review, 6722–1.1

Employment, by sector, major industry group, and sex, selected years 1850-1982, article, 6722–1.425

Employment change over business cycles, by worker characteristics and industry div, quarterly 1982-2nd qtr 1984 with trends from 1948, annual article, 6722–1.448

Employment, earnings, and hours, monthly press release, 6742–5

Employment share of women in selected occupations under 1970 and 1980 census classifications, 1970 and 1980, article, 6722–1.417

Employment situation, earnings, hours, and other BLS economic indicators, transcripts of BLS Commissioner's monthly testimony, periodic rpt, 23846–4

Employment status of family members, by occupation, family composition, age of children, and other characteristics, 1983 and trends from 1940, 6746–1.253

Employment, unemployment, and labor force, by demographic and employment characteristics, State, and for 30 metro areas and 11 large cities, 1983, annual rpt, 6744–7

Employment, unemployment, and labor force, detailed data by sociodemographic and employment characteristics, and industry, 1940s-83, 6748–72

Employment, unemployment, hours, earnings, and productivity, selected years 1929-83, annual rpt, 204–1.2

Employment, unemployment, labor force participation, and discouraged workers, by demographic and employment characteristics, quarterly 1981-83, annual article, 6722–1.409

Foreign employment, labor force, and participation and unemployment rates by sex, in US and 9 OECD countries, various periods 1970-3rd qtr 1983, annual article, 6722–1.404

Fresno, Calif, economic, population, labor, and housing indicators, various periods 1974-85, hearing, 21248–84

Handbook of Labor Statistics, employment, earnings, hours, and labor force characteristics, 1982 and trends, detailed annual rpt, 6724–1

Houston, Tex, SMSA employment, earnings, hours, and CPI changes, 1983 with trends from 1968, annual rpt, 6964–1

Japan worker earnings, by years of service and other characteristics, selected years 1955-80, article, 6722–1.427

Job tenure and occupational mobility of workers, by sociodemographic characteristics and industry div, as of Jan 1983, press release, 6748–76

Job tenure and occupational mobility of workers, by sociodemographic characteristics and occupation, as of Jan 1983, article, 6722–1.460

Job Training Partnership Act dislocated workers program performance standards guide for States, with data on previous programs, by State and client characteristics, FY81-82, 6408–59.2

Job Training Partnership Act participants, by program and socieeconomic characteristics, Oct 1983-June 1984 with funding to 1985/86, 6408–63

Kentucky employment growth in 9-county rural area, labor force and establishment characteristics, 1979-80, 1598–194

Labor force and participation rates, and unemployed persons, by age and sex, *Business Conditions Digest,* historical supplement and methodology, 1947-82, 2708–31

Labor force and participation rates, and unemployed persons, by age and sex, *Business Conditions Digest,* monthly rpt, 2702–3.7

Labor force characteristics and economic indicators, selected years 1880-1995, chartbook, 6728–30

Labor force experience of men and women by sociodemographic characteristics, and effect on earnings, 1979, Current Population Rpt, 2546–2.123

Labor force participation, by employment and demographic characteristics, 1982-83, annual article, 6722–1.472

Labor force status monthly changes, by selected worker characteristics, 1981-82, biennial rpt, 6744–17

Minority group and women's employment, by occupational group, SIC 2- to 3-digit industry, State, and SMSA, 1981, annual rpt, 9244–1

Minority group labor force participation, employment, and unemployment, by race, detailed Hispanic origin, and sex, quarterly rpt, 6742–18

NYC wages by occupation, for office and plant workers, 1983, annual rpt, 6926–1.75

Occupational separation rates by worker characteristics, and replacement rates, 1980-81 with projections to 1990, article, 6722–1.416

Pension coverage by sex, and women's labor force and OASDHI participation by age, selected years 1939-82, hearing, 25368–131.1

Small business and all employees sociodemographic characteristics, by industry div and firm size, 1978-1979, annual rpt, 9764–6.3

Unemployed discouraged workers, by sex, employment history, and job search effort, 1979-83, article, 6722–1.449

Unemployment and part-time employment, by race, Hispanic origin, sex, family composition, income, and poverty status, 1980-82, annual report, 6744–15

Index by Categories

BY SEX

Unemployment and part-time employment effects on family income, by socioeconomic and labor force characteristics, 1981-82, annual rpt, 6746–1.252

Unemployment, by duration, selected demographic characteristics, industry div, and reason for job loss, various periods 1979-June 1983, article, 6722–1.411

Unemployment, by duration, work experience during year, sex, race, and Hispanic origin, 1982-83, 6748–77

Unemployment duration and probability of employment or labor force withdrawal, by sex and race, 1982, article, 9373–1.410

Unemployment duration questions of Current Population Survey, response consistency, and results, 1984 article, 6722–1.421

Unemployment during business cycles, and by worker age, sex, occupation, industry div, reason, and duration, various periods 1969-82, article, 6722–1.444

Unemployment effect on family income and poverty status, by demographic, employment, and unemployment characteristics, 1981-82, annual article, 6722–1.412

Unemployment of men and women, by contributing factor, and change in industry share of labor force and unemployment, 1973-75 and 1981-82, article, 6722–1.432

Unemployment rates, current data and annual trends, monthly rpt, 23842–1.2

Vocationally rehabilitated persons under State agency programs, by sociodemographic characteristics and disabling condition, FY79-81, annual rpt, 4944–6

Wages by occupation, and benefits for office and plant workers, 1983, annual SMSA survey rpt series, 6785–12

Wages by occupation, and benefits for office and plant workers, 1984, annual SMSA survey rpt series, 6785–11

Wages by occupation, for office and plant workers in metro areas, by sex and region, July 1983, annual summary rpt, 6785–9

Wages, hours, benefits, and employment, by occupation and selected geographic areas, industry surveys series, 6787–6

Youth employment and hours worked, by high school and college enrollment status, sex, race, and Hispanic origin, 1982-83, annual article, 6722–1.446

Youth employment, by high school and college enrollment status, industry div, occupation, and selected demographic characteristics, 1980-82, 6746–1.250

Youth summer employment, by sex, race, and class of worker, 1979-84, annual press release, 6744–14

Law Enforcement

Assaults, murders, and other deaths of law enforcement officers, by circumstances, level of govt, agency, victim and offender characteristics, and location, 1983, annual rpt, 6224–3

Convicted Federal offenders, by offense and district, as of June 1983, annual rpt, 18204–1

Crime and criminal justice data, including justice expenditures and employment by level of govt, 1970s-82 with some trends from 1875, 6068–174

Crime victim medical expenses and property loss, and median loss by victim characteristics, by offense type, 1975-81, 6066–19.6

Crime victimization rates by type of offense, and victim and offense characteristics, Natl Crime Survey series, 6066–3

Crimes, arrests by offender characteristics, and rates, by offense, and law enforcement employees, by population size and jurisdiction, 1970s-83, annual rpt, 6224–2

Crimes of violence involving relatives, by victim-offender relationship, circumstances, and victim characteristics, aggregate 1973-81, 6066–19.5

Employment of State and local law enforcement personnel and officers, by sex, population size, census div, and jurisdiction, 1983, annual rpt, 6224–2.3

Homicide and suicide rates for youth, by sex, race, and circumstances, selected years 1970-79, and stress and violent behavior reduction goals for 1990, 4102–1.437

Homicides and homicide rates, by victim characteristics, location, and circumstances, and years of life lost from homicide and other leading causes of death, 1970-78, 4205–38

Jail capacities, conditions, expenditures, and services, and socioeconomic and other characteristics of inmates, various dates 1976-82, 10048–59

Kidnapping by parents over intl and interstate boundaries, characteristics of cases referred to State Dept and FBI by State and country, 1979-83, hearing, 25528–95

Peru cocaine addicts and arrested traffickers and users socioeconomic characteristics, and cocaine confiscated, 1974-78, intl conf papers, 7008–40

Physicians employed in prisons by sociodemographic, employment, and professional characteristics, and compared to all physicians, 1979, article, 4102–1.407

Prisoners in Federal and State correctional instns, by sex, region, and State, quarterly release, 6062–3

Prisoners in Federal correctional instns, by prison, security level, contract facility type, sex, and region, monthly and weekly rpts, 6242–1

Prisoners in State prisons median sentence, and admissions and releases by prisoner and sentencing characteristics, by offense and State, 1981 and trends from 1926, 6066–19.9

Prisoners under death sentence, and executions since 1930, by prisoner characteristics, region, and State, 1982, annual rpt, 6065–1

Prisoners under death sentence, by prison control, sex, and region, 1972-83 with executions from 1930, by State, periodic rpt, 6062–2.406

Robbery rates and circumstances, medical costs and property losses of victims, and offender and victim characteristics, 1960s-81, 6068–180

School crime against students, teachers, and others, by offense, circumstances, and offender sex and race, 1974-76, 6066–20.2

Statistical Abstract of US, social, political, and economic data, 1950s-83 and trends, annual rpt, 2324–1.1

Natural Resources, Environment, and Pollution

Land privately held, acreage and owners by owner characteristics, land use, and region, and purchase and improvement funding, 1978 survey, series, 1506–5

Youth Conservation Corps activities, costs, and participant characteristics, by sponsoring agency, 1982, annual rpt, 5304–12

Population

Census of Population and Housing, 1980: detailed population and housing characteristics, by county, city, and census tract, State and SMSA rpt series, 2551–2

Census of Population, 1980: detailed socioeconomic and demographic characteristics, by age, sex, race, Hispanic origin, occupation, and industry, State rpt series, 2531–4

Census of Population, 1980: detailed socioeconomic characteristics, by county, city, and inside-outside SMSAs and central cities, State rpt series, 2531–3

Census of Population, 1980: migration since 1975, by county and selected demographic characteristics, supplementary rpt, 2535–1.14

Census of Population, 1980: migration since 1975, by State and selected demographic characteristics, supplementary rpt, 2535–1.13

Coastal environmental characteristics, fish, wildlife, and use, and population socioeconomic data, for individual areas, series, 5506–4

County and City Data Book, detailed socioeconomic and demographic data for States, counties, and cities, selected years 1976-82, 2328–1

Economic and demographic factors used in OASDI program cost estimates, selected years 1913-82 with alternative projections to 2060, 4706–1.90

Educational attainment of population, by sociodemographic characteristics and for large States and SMSAs, 1981 and trends from 1940, biennial Current Population Rpt, 2546–1.390

Florida and California elderly migration by selected State of origin or destination, and Florida elderly, by sociodemographic and housing characteristics, 1970 and 1980, 4478–150

Foreign aged population characteristics, with related health care data and vital statistics, by world area and selected country, 1950-80 and projected to 2020, 2546–10.12

Foreign population size and growth rates, and latest available benchmark demographic data, by country, 1950-83, biennial rpt, 2324–4

Foreign women sociodemographic, economic, and fertility characteristics, with comparisons to men, by country, 1960s-85, world region rpt series, 2326–15

Homeless population and characteristics, and temporary shelter operations, use, and user characteristics, for selected cities, various periods 1979-84, hearing, 21248–85

Household living arrangements, family relationships, and marital status, by age and sex, Mar 1984, advance annual Current Population Rpt, 2546–1.389

Household living arrangements, family relationships, and marital status, by demographic characteristics, Mar 1983, annual Current Population Rpt, 2546–1.388

BY SEX

Income (household) and cash and noncash transfer program participation, by sociodemographic characteristics, quarterly rpt, 2542–2

Income and socioeconomic characteristics of persons, families, and households, detailed cross-tabulations, Current Population Rpt series, 2546–6

Married women in couples with wife as primary earner, socioeconomic and family characteristics, with comparative data for husbands, Mar 1982, 2326–11.9

Mobility of population, detailed data by demographic and socioeconomic characteristics of movers and nonmovers, Mar 1981-82, annual Current Population Rpt, 2546–1.384

Older persons by demographic, socioeconomic, and health characteristics, selected years 1900-81 and projected to 2050, Current Population Rpt, 2546–2.125

Older persons income and income sources, by OASDI beneficiary and poverty status, labor force participation, and demographic characteristics, 1982, biennial rpt, 4744–26

Older persons income and percent in poverty, by household composition and sex, with comparisons to nonaged, selected years 1950-82, article, 4742–1.413

Older persons population characteristics, and needs and costs of social services by type, by metro-nonmetro status, 1970s-82 with trends from 1900, 21148–28

Older persons sociodemographic characteristics, and Fed Govt program participation and funding, 1983 with trends and projections 1900-2060, annual rpt, 25144–3.1

Older persons sociodemographic characteristics and transportation needs, selected years 1900-2040, 7308–183

Population demographic and economic characteristics, 1982 with projections of population size to 2050, annual Current Population Rpt, 2546–2.119

Population demographic, social, and economic characteristics, Current Population Rpt series, 2546–1

Population size and components of change, projected under 3 fertility assumptions, 1982-2080 with trends from 1900, SSA actuarial rpt, 4706–1.92

Population size by single years of age, and components of change, by sex and race, projected 1983-2080, final Current Population Rpt, 2546–3.132

Population size, by single years of age, sex, and race, 1980-83, annual Current Population Rpt, 2546–3.130

Poverty status of families and persons, by detailed socioeconomic characteristics, 1982, annual Current Population Rpt, 2546–6.40

Poverty status of families and persons by selected characteristics, public welfare funding, and effect of counting transfer payments as income, selected years 1950-83, 25928–4

Poverty status of young adults related to motivation, psychological factors, and family characteristics, by race and sex, 1970s-82, longitudinal study, 4008–65.1

Refugee and alien arrivals and resettlements in US, by State, outlying area, country of birth and citizenship, age, sex, and sponsoring agency, monthly rpt, 4702–3

Voting age population for Nov 1984 election, by sex, age, race, Hispanic origin, region, and State, and percent voting during 1930-82, Current Population Rpt, 2546–3.129

Public Welfare and Social Security

ACTION activities, volunteer characteristics and budget, by program, FY82, annual rpt, 9024–2

Colorado Medicare beneficiaries with partial coverage, 1978, article, 4652–1.404

Disability Insurance awards, death and recovery termination rates, and life expectancy of disabled, by age and sex, 1965-83 and projected to 2000, 4706–1.93

Disability Insurance beneficiaries sociodemographic and medical characteristics, 1977-79, annual rpt, 4744–20

Farm households receiving social security income, farms and amount by characteristics of farm and operator, 1978-82, article, 1702–1.410

Food aid programs of Fed Govt and others, funding, participant characteristics, and nutrition and poverty data, 1970s-83, 028–20

Food stamp recipient households size and composition, income, and income deductions allowed, Aug 1981, annual rpt, 1364–8

Medicare aged beneficiaries activity restriction, untreated health conditions, and perceived health status, by sociodemographic characteristics, 1980, 4146–12.2

Medicare aged beneficiaries medical care by usual source, and untreated health conditions, by sociodemographic characteristics, 1980, 4146–12.3

Medicare and Medicaid eligibility, participation, covered services and use, and reimbursements and payments, various periods 1966-82, annual rpt, 4654–1

Medicare end-stage renal disease program enrollment, new cases by State, and survival and death rates, by age, sex, and race, 1970s-81, article, 4652–1.408

Medicare kidney end-stage program, reimbursement by treatment, diagnosis, outcome, and patient characteristics, with covered charges for transplants, 1974-79, article, 4652–1.421

Medicare physician charges and reimbursement by enrollee characteristics and carrier, payment limits effects on charges in California, and physician earnings, by specialty, 1950s-84, 25368–127

Noncash public and employer-based transfer program recipients, by income source and socioeconomic characteristics, 1982, advance Current Population Rpt, 2546–6.38

Noncash public and employer-based transfer program recipients, by income source and socioeconomic characteristics, 1982, final Current Population Rpt, 2546–6.37

Nutrition services for elderly, program operations and assessment, and participant sociodemographic, health, and diet characteristics, 1976 and 1982, 4608–16

OASDHI beneficiaries with direct deposit of benefit checks, by age, sex, race, benefit amount, and State, as of Dec 1983, article, 4742–1.412

Index by Categories

OASDHI, Medicaid, SSI, and other social insurance and public welfare programs benefits, beneficiary characteristics, and trust funds, selected years 1937-83, annual rpt, 4744–3

OASDHI, SSI, and other social security programs and recipient characteristics, *Research and Statistics Notes,* series, 4746–16

OASDI beneficiaries by age and sex, and program operations and costs, projected 1983-2060 with trends from 1940, SSA actuarial rpt, 4706–1.91

OASDI benefit eligibility, hypothetical impact of 1978 law change on 1977 workers quarters of coverage, by age and sex, 1977, article, 4742–1.408

OASDI retirement age proposed revisions based on increased life expectancy, by sex under 4 measurement methods, selected years 1940-2050, article, 4742–1.406

OASI beneficiaries by income level, and average income, by beneficiary characteristics and income source, before and after receipt of 1st benefit, 1969-77, article, 4742–1.418

Older persons entitled to both Medicare and Medicaid, demographic characteristics, and health condition and services use, 1980, article, 4652–1.433

Poverty population size, effects of counting public noncash transfers as income by recipient characteristics, 1979-82, 2626–2.50

Runaway and other homeless youth programs, funding by source, activities, and participant characteristics, FY82, annual rpt, 4604–3

Supplemental Security Income and 3 earlier programs benefits, beneficiaries below poverty level, and State program expenditures, various periods 1972-83, article, 4742–1.402

Supplemental Security Income payments, and recipients by other income source, eligibility type, and other characteristics, by State, 1982, annual rpt, 4744–16

Supplementary Security Income beneficiary socioeconomic characteristics and health service use, 1970s-83 and SSI program projections to 1995, 25148–29

Recreation and Leisure

Fishermen (ocean sport), fishing activities, and catch by species, by fisherman characteristics, State, and coastal region, series, 2166–17

Science and Technology

Computer specialists sociodemographic, educational, and employment characteristics, and Fed Govt support by agency, 1978, biennial Current Population Rpt, 2546–2.124

Degree (doctoral) recipients in science and engineering, by field, sex, race, age, citizenship, postgrad employment and study status, State, and instn, 1960-82, 9626–6.16

Degrees (doctoral) of women and foreign students in science and engineering, and median years to degree attainment by sex, 1983 with trends from 1960, 9626–2.144

Employment characteristics or grad enrollment of science and engineering grads of 1980-81, by degree level, field, sex, and race, 1982, 9627–25

Index by Categories

BY SEX

Employment of scientists and engineers at universities and colleges and federally funded R&D centers, by field, sex, State, and instn, Jan 1983 and selected trends from 1967, annual survey, 9627–11

Employment of scientists and engineers at universities and colleges, by field, sex, and instn, 1973-82, 9626–2.140

Employment, salaries, and degrees of scientists and engineers, by field, type of employer, race, and sex, selected years 1960-81, annual rpt, 9624–18.5

Employment, supply, and education of scientists and engineers, by sex, race, Hispanic origin, and field, selected years 1965-83, biennial rpt, 9624–20

Engineers sociodemographic, educational, and employment characteristics, and Federal support by agency, 1978, Current Population Rpt, 2546–2.121

Enrollment in grad science and engineering, fields of study, financial support, and other student and instn characteristics, 1975-82, annual survey, 9627–7

R&D expenditures of higher education instns, and science and engineering employment and grad students, by field, 1972-83, biennial rpt, 9627–24

Salaries of scientists and engineers in R&D, by degree, type of establishment, age, experience, and field, 1984, annual rpt, 3004–1

Scientists and engineers employment, unemployment, and earnings, by field, sex, race, and Hispanic origin, 1970s-82, annual rpt, 9624–10.3

Veterans Affairs

Disability and deaths not connected with service, pension cases for veterans, by sex, entitlement type, and period of service, as of Mar 1984, semiannual rpt, 9922–12

Disabled veterans receiving VA compensation, by sex, type and degree of disability, and period of service, as of Mar 1984, semiannual rpt, 9922–9

Hospital patients of VA discharged, by compensation and pension status, patient type and sex, and VA activities, FY83, annual rpt, 9924–1.3

Older veterans aged 55 and over, socioeconomic characteristics, economic resources, health care and status, and actual and expected VA benefits use, 1983 survey, 9928–29

Population of women veterans, and use of benefits by type, by age, period of service, and State, with comparisons to men, FY83, annual rpt, 9924–24

Speech disorders among patients in VA facilties, by severity, patient characteristics, diagnostician occupation, and facility type, FY81, 9926–1.17

VA employment characteristics and activities, FY83, annual rpt, 9924–1.8

Index by Titles

Index by Titles

Titles are listed alphabetically in natural word order, as they appear in the Abstracts Volume, Titles beginning with numbers (e.g., "1980 Census...") appear at the end of the Index. Where appropriate, alternate word-orders of titles have also been provided.

In addition to publication titles, titles of individual monographs within a publication series are indexed, as are the titles of all periodical articles receiving individual abstracts.

AAFES Facts for Vendors, FY83, 3504–10
Abrasive Materials: Minerals Yearbook Preprint, Vol. 1, 1983, 5604–15.3
Abrasive Products (Industry 3291): 1982 Census of Manufactures. Preliminary Report. Industry Series, 2491–1.243
Academic Science/Engineering: Graduate Enrollment and Support, Fall 1982, Detailed Statistical Tables, 9627–7
Academic Science/Engineering: R&D Funds, FY82, 9627–13
Academic Science/Engineering: Scientists and Engineers, Jan. 1983, 9627–11
Academic Science/Engineering: 1972-83. R&D Funds, Federal Support, Scientists and Engineers, Graduate Enrollment and Support, 9627–24
Access to Health Care Among Aged Medicare Beneficiaries, 4146–12.3
Accidents Involving Injuries, 6846–1
Accidents of Motor Carriers of Property, 1983, 7554–9
Accomplishments of FBI Undercover Operations, 26119–67
Accounting and Budgeting Systems for Mental Health Organizations, 4506–2.6
Accounting, Auditing, and Bookkeeping Services (Industry 893): 1982 Census of Service Industries. Preliminary Report. Industry Series, 2390–2.19
Accuracy, Cost, and Users of the Consolidated Federal Funds Report, 26111–20
Acid Rain: A Survey of Data and Current Analyses, 21368–52
Acid Rain and Transported Air Pollutants, Implications for Public Policy, 26358–104
Acid Rain Information Book, Second Edition, 3408–27
Acidification Impact on Fisheries: Substitution and the Valuation of Recreation Resources, 21368–52
ACIR: The Year in Review, 25th Annual Report, 10044–3
Acreage, 1621–23
Acreage Reduction Programs Report, 1802–12
Acrylic Sheet from Taiwan: Determination of the Commission in Investigation No. 731-TA-139 (Final) Under the Tariff Act of 1930, Together with the Information Obtained in the Investigation, 9886–14.105
Action Plan for Debt Collection, 5004–7
ACTION, 1982 Annual Report, 9024–2
Active Compensation, Pension and Retirement Cases by Period of Service, 9922–10
Active Duty Military Personnel Strengths By Regional Area and by Country as of (Date), 3542–9
Activities of EPA Assistance Programs And Interagency-Intergovernmental Agreements, 9182–8

Activities of the Grants Assistance Programs, 9182–8
Actual and Forecasted Conservation in the Residential Gas Space Heating Market Through 1990, 21368–54
Actuarial Analysis of 1982 Operations Department of Veterans Benefits, 9924–16
Actuarial Notes, 4706–2
Actuarial Status of the HI and SMI Trust Funds, 4742–1.411
Actuarial Status of the OASI and DI Trust Funds, 4742–1.410
Actuarial Studies, 4706–1
ADAMHA Data Book, FY82, 4044–1
ADAMHA Data Book, FY83, 4044–1
Adana Area of Turkey Benefits from Rising Demand for Foodstuffs from Nearby Middle East Markets, 1925–34.430
Additions and Resident Patients at End of Year, State and County Mental Hospitals: By Age and Diagnosis, by State, U.S., 1981, 4504–2
Adhesives and Sealants (Industry 2891): 1982 Census of Manufactures. Preliminary Report. Industry Series, 2491–1.197
Adjusting In-Area Fluid Milk Sales for Calendar Composition, 1317–4.401
Adjustments in World Payments: An Evaluation, 9373–3.28
Administration and Service Delivery in the SSI Program: The First 10 Years, 4742–1.416
Administration of Public Laws 81-874 and 81-815: Thirty-third Annual Report, FY83, 4804–10
Administration of the Marine Mammal Protection Act of 1972, Annual Report, Jan. 1-Dec. 31, 1983, 5504–12
Administration of the Marine Protection, Research, and Sanctuaries Act of 1972, as Amended (P.L. 92-532) and Implementing the International London Dumping Convention: Report to Congress, Jan.1981-Dec. 1983, 9204–8
Administration of the Public Health Service Report to Congress, FY82, 4044–2
Administration of the Public Health Service Report to Congress, FY83, 4044–2
Administration of the Wild Free-Roaming Horse and Burro Act, 5th Report to Congress, 5724–8
Administration's Proposal To Extend Mandatory Retirement to Flight Engineers, 21148–34
Administrative Law Judge Corps Act, 25528–96
Administrator of Veterans Affairs, Annual Report, 1983, 9924–1
Adolescent Maltreatment: Issues and Program Models, 4608–18
ADP, IRM & Telecommunications, 26104–11.1

Adult Basic and Secondary Education Programs, 4864–4
Advance Data from Vital and Health Statistics Of the National Center for Health Statistics, 4146–8
Advance Monthly Retail Sales, Current Business Reports, 2413–2
Advance Report of Final Divorce Statistics, 1981, 4146–5.74
Advance Report of Final Marriage Statistics, 1981, 4146–5.77
Advance Report of Final Mortality Statistics, 1981, 4146–5.78
Advance Report of Final Mortality Statistics, 1982, 4146–5.81
Advance Report of Final Natality Statistics, 1981, 4146–5.73
Advance Report of Final Natality Statistics, 1982, 4146–5.79
Advanced Energy Projects, FY84 Research Summaries, 3004–18.7
Advertising Agencies (Industry 7311): 1982 Census of Service Industries. Preliminary Report. Industry Series, 2390–2.5
Advertising and Promotion in Food Marketing, 1548–234
Advisory Commission on Intergovernmental Relations Staff Working Papers, 10046–8
Aeronautics and Space Report of the President, 1983 Activities, 9504–9
Affirmative Action (Equal Employment Opportunity) Program Plan for Minorities and Women, 9804–17
Affirmative Action FY83 Accomplishment Report And FY84 Update for Minorities and Women, 9804–17
Affirmative Employment Statistics: Federal Civilian Workforce Statistics, 9844–27
Affirmative Employment Statistics for Executive Branch Agencies, Sept. 30, 1982, 9842–1.403
Affordability of Alternative Mortgage Instruments: A Household Analysis, 9312–7.401
After-Tax Money Income Estimates of Households: 1981, 2546–2.118
After-Tax Money Income Estimates of Households: 1982, 2546–2.122
Ag Decline Prompts Top 100 To Cut Debt, Prune Assets, 1122–1.410
Age, Altitude, and Workload Effects on Complex Performance, 7506–10.27
Age and Capacity Profile of Electric Generation Plants in the U.S., 3008–98
Age Discrimination in Employment Act of 1967, As Amended: A Report Covering Activities Under the Act, 9244–8
Agency Supported English Teaching Programs, 9854–2
Aggregate Energy Demand Patterns in the Manufacturing Sector, 3006–7.4

Aggregate Reserves of

Aggregate Reserves of Depository Institutions and Monetary Base, 9365–1

Aggregate Statistics: Accurate or Misleading?, 3162–24.401

Aging of the Population of a City and Its Implications for Hospital-Based services: The Example of Tel Aviv-Yaffo, 4102–1.445

Agricultural and Credit Outlook '84, 9264–9

Agricultural and Horticultural Machinery, Lawnmowers, and Tractors, TSUS Items 666(pt.) and 692(pt.): Summary of Trade and Tariff Information, 9885–6.68

Agricultural Chemicals, N.E.C. (Industry 2879): 1982 Census of Manufactures. Preliminary Report. Industry Series, 2491–1.196

Agricultural Conservation Program, FY83 Statistical Summary, 1804–7

Agricultural Credit Conditions Survey: Federal Reserve Bank of Minneapolis, 9383–11

Agricultural Economics Research, 1502–3

Agricultural Finance Databook, Quarterly Series, 9365–3.10

Agricultural Finance Outlook and Situation Report, 1544–13

Agricultural Finance Situation and Outlook, 1004–16.1

Agricultural Finance Statistics, 1960-83, 1544–2

Agricultural Fuel Crops, 201-County Tennessee Valley Region, 9808–69

Agricultural Implications of Natural Gas Deregulation, 1548–239

Agricultural Letter, Federal Reserve Bank of Chicago, 9375–10

Agricultural Machinery and Equipment: Country Market Survey, 2045–13

Agricultural Outlook, 1004–16.1

Agricultural Outlook, 1502–4

Agricultural Outlook Conference Proceedings, 1984, 1004–16

Agricultural Policy: Objectives for a New Environment, 9381–1.411

Agricultural Prices, Monthly Report, 1629–1

Agricultural Prices, 1983 Summary, 1629–5

Agricultural Stabilization and Conservation Service: Commodity Fact Sheets, 1806–4

Agricultural Stabilization and Conservation Service Payment-In-Kind (PIK) Program: A Review of PIK Program Compliance and Effectiveness, 1008–46

Agricultural Statistics, 1983, 1004–1

Agricultural Subsidies in Portugal: Their Impact on Farm Income and Consumer Cost in the Context of Accession to the European Community, 1528–171

Agricultural Tillage Tools from Brazil: Determination of the Commission in Investigation No. 701-TA-223 (Preliminary) Under Section 703(a) Together with the Information Obtained in the Investigation, 9886–15.55

Agricultural Trade: 1984 and Beyond, 1004–16.1

Agriculture: An Eighth District Perspective, 9391–13

AID and Education: A Sector Report on Lessons Learned, 9916–11.8

AID Assistance to Local Government: Experience and Issues, 9918–11

AID Congressional Presentation, FY85, 9914–3

AID Evaluation Special Studies, 9916–3

Titles

AID-Financed University Contracts and Grants Active During the Period Oct. 1, 1982 Through Sept. 30, 1983, 9914–6

AID Program Evaluation Reports, 9916–11

AID Project Impact Evaluation Reports, 9916–1

AIDS Information Bulletin, 4042–2

Air and Gas Compressors (Industry 3563): 1982 Census of Manufactures. Preliminary Report. Industry Series, 2491–1.338

Air Carrier Financial Statistics, 9142–12

Air Carrier Industry Scheduled Service Traffic Statistics: Medium Regional Air Carrier Details, 9142–44

Air Carrier Traffic Statistics, 9142–13

Air-Conditioning and Refrigeration Equipment Including Warm Air Furnaces, 1983, Current Industrial Report, 2506–12.7

Air Conditioning, Commercial and Industrial Refrigeration Equipment Trade Data, 2014–2

Air Force Comptroller, 3602–1

Air Pollution and Acid Rain Reports, 5506–5

Air Quality Data for Metals, 1977 Through 1979, from the National Air Surveillance Networks, 9194–10

Air Quality Data for Nonmetallic Inorganic Ions: Nitrate and Sulfate for 1979 from the National Air Surveillance Networks, 9198–107

Air Quality Data: 1983 Annual Statistics, Including Summaries with Reference to Standards, 9194–5

Air Route Traffic Control Center Forecasts, FY84-95, 7504–15

Air Service in Alaska: An Update, 9142–42.405

Air Service in Hawaii, 9142–42.406

Air Travelers Security Act of 1983, 25268–81

Aircraft (Industry 3721): 1982 Census of Manufactures. Preliminary Report. Industry Series, 2491–1.398

Aircraft Accident Reports: Brief Format, U.S. Civil and Foreign Aviation, 9612–1

·Aircraft Engines and Engine Parts (Industry 3724): 1982 Census of Manufactures. Preliminary Report. Industry Series, 2491–1.399

Aircraft Equipment, N.E.C. (Industry 3728): 1982 Census of Manufactures. Preliminary Report. Industry Series, 2491–1.400

Aircraft Hijackings and Other Criminal Acts Against Civil Aviation, Statistical and Narrative Reports, Updated to Jan. 1, 1984, 7504–31

Aircraft Propellers, 1983, Current Industrial Report, 2506–12.23

Aircraft Utilization and Propulsion Reliability Report, 7502–13

Airport Activity Statistics of Certificated Route Air Carriers, 12 Months Ending Dec. 31, 1982, 7504–35

Airport Improvement Program, Second Annual Report of Accomplishments, FY83, 7504–38

Airport Improvement Program, Third Quarter FY84, 7506–8.31

Airport Improvement Program, Fourth Quarter FY84, 7506–8.33

Alabama: Prospects Brighten for 1984, 9371–1.408

Alaska Electric Power Statistics, 1960-83, 3214–2

Alaska Land Conveyance Program, A Slow, Complex, and Costly Process, 26113–125

Alaska Power Administration, Annual Report, 3214–1

Alcohol and Health: Fifth Special Report to the U.S. Congress from the Secretary of Health and Human Services, 4488–4

Alcohol, Drug Abuse, Mental Health, Research Grant Awards, FY83, 4044–13

Alcohol Fuels in the U.S.: Status and Prospects, 1561–16.404

Alcohol Health and Research World, 4482–1

Alcohol in Fatal Accidents, National Estimates, U.S.A., 7768–81

Alcohol in Fatal Accidents, National Estimates, U.S.A.: Executive Summary, 7768–81

Alcohol, Tobacco and Firearms Summary Statistics, FY81-82 Distilled Spirits, Wine, Beer, Tobacco, Firearms, Enforcement, Taxes, 8484–1

Alcoholic Beverages, TSUS Items 167.10-169.59: Summary of Trade and Tariff Information, 9885–1.72

Alkalies and Chlorine (Industry 2812): 1982 Census of Manufactures. Preliminary Report. Industry Series, 2491–1.174

Alternative Energy Futures: A Review of Low-Energy-Growth Forecasts and Least-Cost Planning Studies, 3008–93

Alternative Estimates of Capital Consumption and Domestic Profits of Nonfinancial Corporations, 1980-83, 2702–1.434

Alternative Financial Strategies: The Results of Some Policy Simulations with the Multi-Country Model, 9366–7.90

Alternative Reverse Mortgages: A Simulation Analysis of Initial Benefits in Baltimore, 9312–7.402

Alternatives to Intervention: Domestic Instruments and External Objectives, 9373–3.26

Alternatives to the Current Individual Income Tax, 9381–1.415

Aluminum Extruded Products (Industry 3354): 1982 Census of Manufactures. Preliminary Report. Industry Series, 2491–1.270

Aluminum Foundries (Industry 3361): 1982 Census of Manufactures. Preliminary Report. Industry Series, 2491–1.259

Aluminum Industry: Mineral Industry Surveys, 5612–1.1

Aluminum Ingot and Mill Products, Current Industrial Report, 2506–10.9

Aluminum: Minerals Yearbook Preprint, Vol. 1, 1983, 5604–15.4

Aluminum Rolling and Drawing, N.E.C. (Industry 3355): 1982 Census of Manufactures. Preliminary Report. Industry Series, 2491–1.271

Aluminum Sheet, Plate, and Foil (Industry 3353): 1982 Census of Manufactures. Preliminary Report. Industry Series, 2491–1.269

Amending the Mineral Leasing Act of 1920, 25318–58

American Centers and Reading Rooms Abroad Annual Statistics: FY83 Summary, 9854–4

American Indian Areas and Alaska Native Villages: 1980. 1980 Census of Population. Supplementary Report, 2535–1.16

American Red Cross, 1983 Annual Report, 29254–1

American Samoa Government Annual Report, FY83, 5304–15.4

American Woodcock, 1984 Status, 5504–11

Titles

America's Renewable Resources: A Supplement to the 1979 Assessment of the Forest and Range Land Situation in the U.S., 1208–24.4

America's Wars, 9922–8

AMS Food Purchases: Weekly Summary, 1302–3

An Overview of the Criminal Justice System: The American Response to Crime, 6062–2.401

Anaerobic Fermentation of Beef Cattle Manure and Crop Residues, 3304–14

Analyses of Natural Gases, 1983, 5604–2

Analyses of Tipple and Delivered Samples of Coal Collected During FY82 and FY83, 3004–15

Analysis of a Senate Emission Reduction Bill (S-3041), 9188–97

Analysis of Administration Strategic Arms Reduction and Modernization Proposals, 26306–6.73

Analysis of Chapter Seven and Eleven Bankruptcies Filed in the Northern Division of Eastern District of Michigan, from Oct. 1979-Feb. 1981, 21528–57.3

Analysis of Commuter Rail Costs and Cost Allocation Methods, 7888–61

Analysis of Congressional Budget Estimates for FY80-82, Special Study, 26308–48

Analysis of Data and Report on Union Recognition in the Federal Service, 9844–17

Analysis of DOD's FY85 Multiyear Procurement Candidates, 26123–83

Analysis of Electrical Fire Investigations in Ten Cities, 2218–71

Analysis of HUD-Acquired Home Mortgage Properties, 5142–31

Analysis of IHS and U.S. Hospital Discharge Rates: By Age and Primary Diagnosis, 4104–9

Analysis of New York's Timber Resources, 1206–16.7

Analysis of Regulation D, 9736–2.5

Analysis of Special Tax Provisions Affecting Independent Oil and Gas Producers, Special Study, 21788–132

Analysis of Structural Incentives in the Arizona Health Care Cost-Containment System, 4652–1.414

Analysis of Tax-Exempt Pollution Control Financing, 21788–135

Analysis of the Financial Health of the Electric Utility Industry, 26113–129

Analysis of the Grace Commission's Major Proposals for Cost Control, 26308–45

Analysis of the Natural Gas Policy Act and Several Alternatives, 3168–50

Analysis of the President's Budgetary Proposals for FY85, 26304–2

Analysis of the President's Credit Budget for FY85, 26306–3.65

Analysis of the Reversal in Breast Feeding Trends in the Early 1970s, 4102–1.442

Analytical and Epidemiological Studies. Vital and Health Statistics Series 3, 4147–3

Analyzing Feed and Residual Disappearance of Corn, 1561–4.402

Analyzing Machinery Purchases and Sales by Producers According to Acreage Operated, 1544–19.403

Anatomy of a Federal Government Deficit, FY83, 2702–1.408

Animal and Marine Fats and Oils (Industry 2077): 1982 Census of Manufactures. Preliminary Report. Industry Series, 2491–1.30

Animal Drug Lag, 25528–98

Animal Fats, Hardened or Hydrogenated Oils, and Greases, TSUS Items 177(pt.) and 178(pt.): Summary of Trade and Tariff Information, 9885–1.62

Animal Feeds and Animal Feed Ingredients, TSUS Items 184(pt.): Summary of Trade and Tariff Information, 9885–1.64

Animal Investigation Program for the Nevada Test Site: 1957-81, 9234–5

Animal Welfare Enforcement, FY83, Report of the Secretary of Agriculture to the President of the Senate and the Speaker of the House of Representatives, 1394–10

Annual Accomplishment Report and Update of the Affirmative Action (Equal Employment Opportunity) Programs for Minorities and Women for FY83, 7004–11

Annual Data and Verification Tabulation, Atlantic Tropical Cyclones, 1983, 2184–7

Annual Data and Verification Tabulation, Eastern North Pacific Tropical Storms and Hurricanes, 1983, 2184–8

Annual Energy Outlook, 1983, With Projections to 1995, 3164–75

Annual Energy Review, 1983, 3164–74

Annual Evaluation Report, FY83, 4804–5

Annual Financial Report, FY83, 7504–10

Annual Financial Report of the National Credit Union Share Insurance Fund, FY83, 9534–7

Annual Grazing Statistical Use Summary, 1204–5

Annual Housing Survey:

Annual Housing Survey: Housing Characteristics for Selected Metropolitan Areas, 2485–6

Annual Housing Survey: 1978, Supplementary Report No. 1. Summary of Housing Characteristics for Selected Metropolitan Areas, 2485–8

Annual Housing Survey: 1979, Housing Characteristics for Selected Metropolitan Areas, Honolulu, Hawaii SMSA, 2485–6.1

Annual Housing Survey: 1980, Housing Characteristics for Selected Metropolitan Areas, Albany-Schenectady-Troy, N.Y. SMSA, 2485–6.2

Annual Housing Survey: 1980, Housing Characteristics for Selected Metropolitan Areas, Allentown-Bethlehem-Easton, Pa. SMSA, 2485–6.7

Annual Housing Survey: 1980, Housing Characteristics for Selected Metropolitan Areas, Birmingham, Ala. SMSA, 2485–6.8

Annual Housing Survey: 1980, Housing Characteristics for Selected Metropolitan Areas, Grand Rapids, Mich. SMSA, 2485–6.9

Annual Housing Survey: 1980, Housing Characteristics for Selected Metropolitan Areas, Indianapolis, Ind. SMSA, 2485–6.10

Annual Housing Survey: 1980, Housing Characteristics for Selected Metropolitan Areas, Los Angeles-Long Beach, Calif. SMSA, 2485–6.3

Annual Housing Survey: 1980, Housing Characteristics for Selected Metropolitan Areas, Louisville, Ky.-Ind. SMSA, 2485–6.11

Annual Housing Survey: 1980, Housing Characteristics for Selected Metropolitan Areas, Memphis, Tenn.-Ark. SMSA, 2485–6.4

Annual Housing Survey: 1980, Housing Characteristics for Selected Metropolitan Areas, New York, N.Y. SMSA, 2485–6.12

Annual Housing Survey: 1980, Housing Characteristics for Selected Metropolitan Areas, Oklahoma City, Okla. SMSA, 2485–6.13

Annual Housing Survey: 1980, Housing Characteristics for Selected Metropolitan Areas, Providence-Pawtucket-Warwick, R.I.-Mass. SMSA, 2485–6.14

Annual Housing Survey: 1980, Housing Characteristics for Selected Metropolitan Areas, Sacramento, Calif. SMSA, 2485–6.15

Annual Housing Survey: 1980, Housing Characteristics for Selected Metropolitan Areas, Saginaw, Mich. SMSA, 2485–6.5

Annual Housing Survey: 1980, Housing Characteristics for Selected Metropolitan Areas, Salt Lake City, Utah SMSA, 2485–6.6

Annual Housing Survey: 1980, Housing Characteristics for Selected Metropolitan Areas, St. Louis, Mo.-Ill. SMSA, 2485–6.16

Annual Housing Survey: 1981, Housing Characteristics for Selected Metropolitan Areas, Anaheim-Santa Ana-Garden Grove, Calif. SMSA, 2485–6.19

Annual Housing Survey: 1981, Housing Characteristics for Selected Metropolitan Areas, Boston, Mass. SMSA, 2485–6.30

Annual Housing Survey: 1981, Housing Characteristics for Selected Metropolitan Areas, Dallas, Tex. SMSA, 2485–6.21

Annual Housing Survey: 1981, Housing Characteristics for Selected Metropolitan Areas, Detroit, Mich. SMSA, 2485–6.17

Annual Housing Survey: 1981, Housing Characteristics for Selected Metropolitan Areas, Fort Worth, Tex. SMSA, 2485–6.22

Annual Housing Survey: 1981, Housing Characteristics for Selected Metropolitan Areas, Madison, Wis. SMSA, 2485–6.20

Annual Housing Survey: 1981, Housing Characteristics for Selected Metropolitan Areas, Minneapolis-St. Paul, Minn. SMSA, 2485–6.29

Annual Housing Survey: 1981, Housing Characteristics for Selected Metropolitan Areas, Newark, N.J. SMSA, 2485–6.31

Annual Housing Survey: 1981, Housing Characteristics for Selected Metropolitan Areas, Orlando, Fla. SMSA, 2485–6.23

Annual Housing Survey: 1981, Housing Characteristics for Selected Metropolitan Areas, Phoenix, Ariz. SMSA, 2485–6.24

Annual Housing Survey: 1981, Housing Characteristics for Selected Metropolitan Areas, Pittsburgh, Pa. SMSA, 2485–6.25

Annual Housing Survey: 1981, Housing Characteristics for Selected Metropolitan Areas, Spokane, Wash. SMSA, 2485–6.26

Annual Housing Survey: 1981, Housing Characteristics for Selected Metropolitan Areas, Tacoma, Wash. SMSA, 2485–6.27

Annual Housing Survey: 1981, Housing Characteristics for Selected Metropolitan Areas, Washington, D.C.-Md.-Va. SMSA, 2485–6.18

Annual Housing Survey: 1981, Housing Characteristics for Selected Metropolitan Areas, Wichita, Kans. SMSA, 2485–6.28

Annual Housing Survey: 1981, Part B, Indicators of Housing and Neighborhood Quality by Financial Characteristics, 2485–2

Annual Housing Survey: Titles

Annual Housing Survey: 1981, Part E, Urban and Rural Housing Characteristics, U.S. and Regions, 2485–7

Annual Housing Survey: 1982, Housing Characteristics for Selected Metropolitan Areas, Atlanta, Ga. SMSA, 2485–6.32

Annual Housing Survey: 1982, Housing Characteristics for Selected Metropolitan Areas, Cincinnati, OH-KY-IN SMSA, 2485–6.35

Annual Housing Survey: 1982, Housing Characteristics for Selected Metropolitan Areas, Columbus, OH SMSA, 2485–6.36

Annual Housing Survey: 1982, Housing Characteristics for Selected Metropolitan Areas, Kansas City, MO-KS SMSA, 2485–6.37

Annual Housing Survey: 1982, Housing Characteristics for Selected Metropolitan Areas, New Orleans, LA SMSA, 2485–6.43

Annual Housing Survey: 1982, Housing Characteristics for Selected Metropolitan Areas, Paterson-Clifton-Passaic, NJ SMSA, 2485–6.38

Annual Housing Survey: 1982, Housing Characteristics for Selected Metropolitan Areas, Philadelphia, Pa.-N.J. SMSA, 2485–6.33

Annual Housing Survey: 1982, Housing Characteristics for Selected Metropolitan Areas, Rochester, NY SMSA, 2485–6.39

Annual Housing Survey: 1982, Housing Characteristics for Selected Metropolitan Areas, San Antonio, TX SMSA, 2485–6.40

Annual Housing Survey: 1982, Housing Characteristics for Selected Metropolitan Areas, San Bernardino-Riverside-Ontario, CA SMSA, 2485–6.41

Annual Housing Survey: 1982, Housing Characteristics for Selected Metropolitan Areas, San Diego, CA SMSA, 2485–6.42

Annual Housing Survey: 1982, Housing Characteristics for Selected Metropolitan Areas, San Francisco-Oakland, Calif. SMSA, 2485–6.34

Annual Housing Survey: 1983, Part A. General Housing Characteristics, 2485–1

Annual Line of Business Report: Statistical Report of the Bureau of Economics to the Federal Trade Commission, 9404–5

Annual of the Federal Trade Commission, FY82, 9404–1

Annual Outlook for U.S. Coal, 1984 With Projections to 1995, 3164–68

Annual Pay Levels for Metropolitan Areas, 1982, 6784–17.1

Annual Pay Levels in Metropolitan Areas, 1983, 6784–17.3

Annual Prospects for World Coal Trade, 1984, With Projections to 1995, 3164–77

Annual Report and Summaries of FY84 Activities Supported by the Division of Biological Energy Research, 3004–18.2

Annual Report, Bureau of Reclamation, 5824–1

Annual Report, Bureau of Reclamation, 1981: Appendix II, Finance and Physical Features, 5824–1.1

Annual Report by the Administrator of Veterans Affairs on Sharing Medical Resources, FY83, 9924–18

Annual Report for the U.S. Small Business Administration, FY82, 9764–1

Annual Report from the Secretary of Health and Human Services to the President and Congress On Drug Abuse Prevention, Treatment, and Rehabilitation, FY82, 4004–26

Annual Report, FY83, Outer Continental Shelf Oil and Gas Leasing and Production Program, 5734–4

Annual Report FY83 of the Chief of Engineers on Civil Works Activities, 3754–1

Annual Report: Minerals Accountability in the Department of the Interior, 5734–1

Annual Report of Characteristics of Initial Farm Ownership Loan Applicants, 1184–7

Annual Report of Characteristics of Initial Operating Loan Applicants, 1184–9

Annual Report of Characteristics of Initial Soil and Water Loan Applicants, 1184–8

Annual Report of Energy Conservation Indicators for 1982, 3164–73

Annual Report of Energy Conservation Indicators for 1982, Supplement, 3164–73.2

Annual Report of Energy Purchased by REA Borrowers, 1983, 1244–5

Annual Report of International Activities, FY83, National Institutes of Health, 4474–6

Annual Report of the Attorney General of the U.S., 1982, 6004–1

Annual Report of the Board of the National Credit Union Administration, 9534–3

Annual Report of the Board of Trustees of the Federal Hospital Insurance Trust Fund, 1984, 4704–5

Annual Report of the Board of Trustees of the Federal Old-Age and Survivors Insurance and Disability Insurance Trust Funds, 1984, 4704–4

Annual Report of the Board of Trustees of the Federal Supplementary Medical Insurance Trust Fund, 1984, 4704–3

Annual Report of the Chairman of the Development Coordination Committee, 1983 Statistical Annex 1, 9914–5

Annual Report of the Community Relations Service, 1983, 6004–9

Annual Report of the Director of the Administrative Office of the U.S. Courts, 1983, 18204–8

Annual Report of the Director of the Mint, Fiscal Year Ended Sept. 30, 1982, 8204–1

Annual Report of the Director of the Mint, Fiscal Year Ended Sept. 30, 1983, 8204–1

Annual Report of the Governor of the Virgin Islands, 1981, 5304–4

Annual Report of the Immigration and Naturalization Service, 6264–2

Annual Report of the Marine Mammal Commission, 1983, 14734–1

Annual Report of the Office of Inspector General, Trust Territories of the Pacific Islands, 5304–15

Annual Report of the Office of Revenue Sharing, FY83, 8064–1

Annual Report of the Organized Crime Drug Enforcement Task Force Program, 6004–17

Annual Report of the Postmaster General, 1983, 9864–1

Annual Report of the Register of Copyrights, 1982, 26404–2

Annual Report of the Secretary of Commerce, FY83, 2004–1

Annual Report of the U.S. Court of Military Appeals and the Judge Advocates General of the Armed Forces and the General Counsel of the Department of Transportation, Oct. 1, 1982-Sept. 30, 1983, 3504–3

Annual Report of the U.S. Government Printing Office, FY83, 26204–1

Annual Report on Federal Government Energy Management, FY82, 3304–22

Annual Report on Federal Government Energy Management, FY83, 3304–22

Annual Report on Hazardous Materials Transportation, 1983, 7304–4

Annual Report on In-House Energy Management, FY83, 3024–3

Annual Report on Michigan-Ontario Air Pollution, 14644–5

Annual Report on Pipeline Safety, 1982, 7304–5

Annual Report on the Administration of the Radiation Control for Health and Safety Act of 1968, Public Law 90-602, 1983, 4064–13

Annual Report on the Implementation of Section 403 of the Powerplant and Industrial Fuel Use Act of 1978, 3104–9

Annual Report on the Use of Alcohol in Fuels, 3304–9

Annual Report on Tobacco Statistics, 1983, 1319–1

Annual Report Submitted to the Committees on Armed Services of the Senate and of the House of Representatives and to the Secretary of Defense and Secretary of Transportation and the Secretaries of the Departments of the Army, Navy, and Air Force, Oct. 1, 1982-Sept. 30, 1983, 3504–3

Annual Report, Title IV, Part B of the Elementary and Secondary Education Act (Public Law 93-380), 4804–12

Annual Report to Congress: Office of Civilian Radioactive Waste Management, 3364–1

Annual Report to Congress, 1983, 1294–1

Annual Report to the Congress, Jan. 1 to Sept. 30, 1983, 26354–3

Annual Report to the Congress and the President On 1981 Industrial Energy Efficiency Improvement, 3304–8

Annual Report to the Congress and the President On 1982 Industrial Energy Efficiency Improvement Program, 3304–8

Annual Report to the President and the Congress On the State Energy Conservation Program, 1983, 3304–1

Annual Report to the President, FY83, Information Security Oversight Office, 9454–21

Annual Report, U.S. Department of Education, FY83, 4804–6

Annual Report 1982 to the President and Congress: National Acid Precipitation Assessment Program, 14354–1

Annual Report 1983 to the President and Congress: National Acid Precipitation Assessment Program, 14354–1

Annual Review of Aircraft Accident Data, U.S. General Aviation, 1980, 9614–3

Annual Review of Aircraft Accident Data, U.S. General Aviation, 1981, 9614–3

Annual Revisions to the Money Stock, 9362–1.404

Annual Sales and Year-End Inventories, Purchases, and Gross Margin Estimates of Merchant Wholesalers, 1983 Wholesale Trade, Current Business Reports, 2413–13

Annual Sales, Year-End Inventories, Purchases, Gross Margin, and Accounts

Titles

Receivable, by Kind of Retail Store, 1983 Retail Trade, Current Business Reports, 2413–5

Annual Southwestern Region Pest Conditions Report, 1983, 1206–11.2

Annual Statistical Digest, 1982, 9364–5

Annual Statistical Summary, FY74-84 U.S. Secret Service, 8464–1

Annual Status Report On the Uranium Mill Tailings Remedial Action Program, 3354–9

Annual Survey of Manufactures, 1980-81, 2504–1

Annual Survey of Oil and Gas, 1982, Current Industrial Report, 2506–8.11

Annual Tropical Cyclone Report, 1983, 3804–8

Annual U.S. Economic Data, 1964-83, 9391–9

Anthropometric and Mass Distribution Characteristics of the Adult Female, 7506–10.28

Anticipated Economic Effects of the Surface Transportation Assistance Act of 1982, 25328–24

Antifriction Bearings, 1983, Current Industrial Report, 2506–12.28

Antimony: Mineral Industry Surveys, 5612–2.1

Antimony: Minerals Yearbook Preprint, Vol. 1, 1983, 5604–15.5

Antitrust Implications of Thrifts' Expanded Commercial Loan Powers, 9387–1.404

Antitrust Laws, Justice Department Guidelines, and the Limits of Concentration in Local Banking Markets, 9366–1.136

Appalachia: Journal of the Appalachian Regional Commission, Vol. 17, No. 2, 9088–33

Appalachia: The Economic Outlook Through the Eighties, 9088–33

Appalachian Access Roads Mileage Summary by States, 9082–1.4

Appalachian Development Highway System, 9082–1

Appalachian Development Highway System Mileage Summary by Corridor, 9082–1.3

Appalachian Development Highway System Mileage Summary by States, 9082–1.2

Appalachian Highway Program Funding Requirements, 9082–1.1

Appalachian Land Stabilization and Conservation Program: Status Report, 1804–3

Appalachian Regional Commission Annual Report, 1982, 9084–1

Apparel and Accessories, N.E.C. (Industry 2389): 1982 Census of Manufactures. Preliminary Report. Industry Series, 2491–1.102

Apparel Belts (Industry 2387): 1982 Census of Manufactures. Preliminary Reports. Industry Series, 2491–1.101

Apparel Stores Display Above-Average Productivity, 6722–1.463

Apparent Consumption of Industrial Explosives and Blasting Agents in the U.S., 1983: Mineral Industry Survey, 5614–22

Appearances of Soviet Leaders, Jan.-Dec. 1983, 244–8

Appendix to the Report of the National Bipartisan Commission on Central America, 028–19.2

Appliance Repair, Nov. 1981. Industry Wage Survey, 6787–6.197

Applications for Initial Insured and Guaranteed Loans Received from Individuals, By Type of Loan and Race or Ethnic Group, 1184–1

Applied Time Series Analysis of Economic Data, 2626–7.5

Approaches to Developing Questionnaires, 106–4.4

Approval of Awards to Institutions Participating In the College Work-Study, the Supplemental Educational Opportunity Grants, and the National Direct Student Loan Programs: Notification to Members of Congress, 4804–17

Architect of the Capitol, Semiannual Report for the Period Oct. 1, 1983-Mar. 31, 1984, 25922–2

Architectural Metal Work (Industry 3446): 1982 Census of Manufactures. Preliminary Report. Industry Series, 2491–1.289

Arctic National Wildlife Refuge Coastal Plain Resource Assessment: 1983 Update Report, Baseline Study of the Fish, Wildlife, and Their Habitats, 5504–26

Are Options on Treasury Bond Futures Priced Efficiently?, 9391–1.404

Are Unions Facing a Crisis? Labor Officials Are Divided, 6722–1.451

Area Development in Liberia: Toward Integration and Participation, 9916–1.53

Area Resource File: A Health Professions Planning and Research Tool, 4114–11

Area Resource File System, 4114–11

Area Trends, A Supplement to FHA Trends, Section 203 Home Mortgages Insured by FHA, 5142–2

Area Trends, A Supplement to FHA Trends, Section 245 Home Mortgages Insured by FHA, 5142–42

Area Trends in Employment and Unemployment, 6402–1

Area Wage Surveys, 6785–3

Area Wage Surveys: Bull. 3020 Series, 6785–12

Area Wage Surveys: Bull. 3025 Series, 6785–11

Area Wage Surveys, Selected Metropolitan Areas, 1983, 6785–1

Argentina: Farmers' Response to Grain Prices, 1528–170

Argentina's Grain Marketing System, 1528–185

Arms Control Impact Statements, FY84, 21384–4

Army Can Better Use Its Soldiers Trained in Critical Shortage Occupations, 26123–59

Army Can Do More To Assure War Reserve Funds Are Spent Effectively, 26123–58

Army Morale, Welfare and Recreation, Annual Report, FY83, 3704–12

Army Needs To Better Plan To Meet Its Civilian Personnel Needs in Wartime, 26123–82

Arson Investigation and Prosecution: A Study of Four Major American Cities, 6068–184

Articles Containing Sugar: Report to the President on Investigation No. 22-46 Under Section 22 of the Agricultural Adjustment Act, 9886–10.7

Artificial Flowers (Industry 3962): 1982 Census of Manufactures. Preliminary Report. Industry Series, 2491–1.436

Artists' Colors, Inks and Ink Powders, and Paints, Coating, and Related Items, TSUS Items 408(pt.), 413(pt.), and 474(pt.): Summary of Trade and Tariff Information, 9885–4.46

Asset and Liability Trends,

Asbestos and Asbestos Products, TSUS Items 518(pt.): Summary of Trade and Tariff Information, 9885–5.16

Asbestos: Minerals Yearbook Preprint, Vol. 1, 1983, 5604–15.6

Asbestos Products (Industry 3292): 1982 Census of Manufactures. Preliminary Report. Industry Series, 2491–1.244

ASCS Needs Better Information To Adequately Assess Proposed County and State Office Automation, 26125–27

Asian and Pacific Islander Population by State, 1980: 1980 Census of Population. Supplementary Report, 2535–1.15

Asian Rice Situation and Outlook, 1925–2.6

Asphalt and Tar Roofing and Siding Products, 1983, Current Industrial Report, 2506–8.6

Asphalt Felts and Coatings (Industry 2952): 1982 Census of Manufactures. Preliminary Report. Industry Series, 2491–1.204

Assessing Criminal Justice Needs, 6066–20.4

Assessing Erosion on U.S. Cropland, Land Management and Physical Features, 1588–83

Assessing the Social Costs of Oil Spills: The AMOCO CADIZ Case Study, 2178–13

Assessment of Environmental Problems Associated with Increased Enhanced Oil Recovery in the U.S.: 1980-2000, 3408–29

Assessment of Factors Affecting Industrial Electricity Demand, Final Report, 3008–87

Assessment of Level of Care: Implications of Interrater Reliability on Health Policy, 4652–1.431

Assessment of Potential Environmental Problems Concerning Water Availability, 9208–125

Assessment of Random Audit, A New Department of Labor Program To Improve the Accuracy of Unemployment Insurance Benefit Payments, 26121–77

Assessment of SES Performance Appraisal Systems, 26119–61

Assessment of Special Rules Exempting Employers Withdrawing from Multiemployer Pension Plans from Withdrawal Liability, 26121–73

Assessment of the Quality of Selected EIA Data Series, Coal and Electric Power from 1977-82, 3164–63

Assessment of the Relationships Between the Department of Energy and Universities and Colleges, 3008–89

Assessment of Undiscovered Conventionally Recoverable Petroleum Resources, 5666–17

Assessment of Undiscovered Conventionally Recoverable Petroleum Resources, 5666–18

Assessment of Undiscovered Conventionally Recoverable Petroleum Resources of Northwestern, Central, and Northeastern Africa (Including Morocco, Northern and Western Algeria, Northeastern Tunisia, Mauritania, Mali, Niger, Eastern Nigeria, Chad, Central African Republic, Sudan, Ethiopia, Somalia, and Southeastern Egypt), 5666–17.13

Assessment of Undiscovered Conventionally Recoverable Petroleum Resources of Onshore China, 5666–17.14

Assessment of Undiscovered Conventionally Recoverable Petroleum Resources of the Northwest European Assessment Region, 5666–17.15

Asset and Liability Trends, 1982: All Operating Savings and Loan Associations by Type of Association and Area, 9314–1

Asset/Liability Management:

Asset/Liability Management: An Overview, 9306–1.4

Assets and Liabilities of Domestically Chartered and Foreign Related Banking Institutions, 9365–1

Assumable Loan Value in Creative Financing, 9412–2.404

Astronautics and Aeronautics, 1976, 9504–2

Atlantic Tropical Cyclones, 1983, Annual Data and Verification Tabulation, 2184–7

Atlas of Mean Winter Temperature Departures from the Long-Term Mean over the Contiguous U.S., 1895-1983, 2156–17.12

Atlas of Monthly and Seasonal Temperature Departures from the Long-Term Mean (1895-1983) for the Contiguous U.S., Fall, 2156–17.16

Atlas of Monthly and Seasonal Temperature Departures from the Long-Term Mean (1895-1983) for the Contiguous U.S., Spring, 2156–17.14

Atlas of Monthly and Seasonal Temperature Departures from the Long-Term Mean (1895-1983) for the Contiguous U.S., Summer, 2156–17.15

Atlas of Monthly and Seasonal Temperature Departures from the Long-Term Mean (1895-1983) for the Contiguous U.S., Winter, 2156–17.13

Atmospheric Turbidity over the U.S. from 1967-76, 9198–106

Attitudes Toward Campaign Financing: A CSI Survey Report, 25688–6

Attorney General of the U.S., Annual Report, 1981, 6004–1

Audit, Inspection and Investigative Operations, Department of Defense, Office of Inspector General, Report to the Congress for the Six-Month Period Oct. 1, 1983-Mar. 31, 1984, 3542–18

Audits of Federal Programs: Reasons for the Disparity Between Costs Questioned by Auditors and Amounts Agencies Disallow, 26111–24

Auto Dealer Repair Shops, Nov. 1982: Industry Wage Survey, 6787–6.202

Auto Fuel Efficiency Standards, 21368–49

Automatic Data Processing Activities Summary in the U.S. Government, 9454–7

Automatic Data Processing Equipment Inventory in the U.S. Government As of the End of FY83, 9454–4

Automatic Merchandising Machine Operators (Industry 5962): 1982 Census of Retail Trade. Preliminary Report. Industry Series, 2395–1.34

Automatic Merchandising Machines (Industry 3581): 1982 Census of Manufactures. Preliminary Report. Industry Series, 2491–1.349

Automobiles and Other Motor Vehicles (Industry 5012): 1982 Census of Wholesale Trade. Preliminary Report. Industry Series, 2403–1.1

Automobiles, Trucks, Buses, and Bodies and Chassis of the Foregoing Motor Vehicles, TSUS Items 692(pt.): Summary of Trade and Tariff Information, 9885–6.63

Automotive and Apparel Trimmings (Industry 2396): 1982 Census of Manufactures. Preliminary Report. Industry Series, 2491–1.108

Automotive Fuel Economy Program, Eighth Annual Report to the Congress, 7764–9

Automotive Repair Shops (Industry 753): 1982 Census of Service Industries. Preliminary Report. Industry Series, 2390–2.9

Automotive Stampings (Industry 3465): 1982 Census of Manufactures. Preliminary Report. Industry Series, 2491–1.296

Average Annual Pay, 6784–17

Average Annual Pay by State and Industry, 1983, 6784–17.2

Average Area Purchase Price Safe Harbor Limitations for Single-Family Residences, 8304–16.2

Average Bankrupt: A Description and Analysis of 753 Personal Bankruptcy Filings in Nine States, 25528–97.1

Average Price of Natural Gas Delivered to Consumers, 1983 (Preliminary Data Report), 3164–4

Average Price of Natural Gas Delivered to Consumers, 1983 (Preliminary), 3162–4.413

Average Wages for 1982 for Indexing Under the Social Security Act and the Automatic Determinations for 1984, 4706–2.119

Aviation Fuels, 1983: Petroleum Products Survey, 3006–2.2

Back to School Forecast: Fall 1984, 4804–19

Background Data on Physician Reimbursement Under Medicare, 25368–127

Background Material and Data on Programs Within the Jurisdiction of the Committee on Ways and Means, 21788–117

Background Material on Poverty, 21788–131

Background Notes on the Countries of the World, 7006–2

Background on the Tax Treatment of Property and Casualty Insurance Companies, 25368–128

Backlog of Orders for Aerospace Companies, Current Industrial Report, 2506–12.22

Bags, Except Textile Bags (Industry 2643): 1982 Census of Manufactures. Preliminary Report. Industry Series, 2491–1.147

Balances of Budget Authority: Budget for FY85, 104–8

Ball and Roller Bearings (Industry 3562): 1982 Census of Manufactures. Preliminary Report. Industry Series, 2491–1.337

Bank Entry into Securities Brokerage: Competitive and Legal Aspects, 9373–1.417

Bank Lending to Developing Countries: Recent Developments and Some Considerations for the Future, 9362–1.407

Bank Mergers Today: New Guidelines, Changing Markets, 9375–1.404

Bank Regulation and Deposit Insurance: Controlling the FDIC's Losses, 9393–8.407

Bank Robbery, 6062–2.407

Bankers' Banks: An Institution Whose Time Has Come?, 9371–1.415

Banking and Finance: An Eighth District Perspective, 9391–14

Bankruptcy Improvements Act, 25528–97

Banks and Branches Data Book: Summary of Deposits in All Commercial and Mutual Savings Banks and Domestic Branches of Foreign Banks, Operating Banks and Branches, 9295–3

Bargaining Calendar, 1984, 6784–9

Bargaining Co-ops Remain Stable, Strongest in West Coast States, 1122–1.403

Titles

Barite: Minerals Yearbook Preprint, Vol. 1, 1983, 5604–15.7

Barium Chloride from the People's Republic of China: Determination of the Commission in Investigation No. 731-TA-149 (Final) Under the Tariff Act of 1930, Together with the Information Obtained in the Investigation, 9886–14.122

Barriers to Trade in Agricultural Products Between Canada and the U.S., 1528–175

Base Structure Annex to Manpower Requirements Report for FY85, 3504–11

Baseline Budget Projections for FY85-89. A Report to the Senate and House Committees on the Budget, Part II, 26304–3.2

Basic Data Relating to NIH, 4434–3

Basic Iron and Steel, Aug. 1983, Industry Wage Survey, 6787–6.206

Bauxite and Alumina: Mineral Industry Surveys, 5612–2.2

Bauxite and Alumina: Minerals Yearbook Preprint, Vol. 1, 1983, 5604–15.8

Bauxite, Ferroalloy Ores, Metal Mining Services, and Miscellaneous Metal Ores (Industry 1051, 1061, 1081, 1092, 1094, and 1099): 1982 Census of Mineral Industries. Preliminary Report. Industry Series, 2511–1.3

Bean Market News, 1311–17

Bedford-Stuyvesant/Crown Heights Demonstration Project, 4652–1.419

Beef and Pork: Capacity of Marketing Services, 1561–7.401

Beer and Ale (Industry 5181): 1982 Census of Wholesale Trade. Preliminary Report. Industry Series, 2403–1.37

Beer: Statistical Release, 8486–1.1

Beet Sugar (Industry 2063): 1982 Census of Manufactures. Preliminary Report. Industry Series, 2491–1.24

Behavior of the Spread Between Treasury Bill Rates and Private Money Market Rates Since 1978, 9389–1.401

Behavioral, Health, and Cost Outcomes of an HMO-Based Prenatal Health Education Program, 4102–1.401

Behavioral Risk Factor Surveillance, 1981-83, 4202–7.405

Benefits and Beneficiaries Under Public Employee Retirement Programs, 1980, 4742–1.403

Benefits and Costs of the Federal Asbestos Standard, 21408–72

Benefits to Federal Law Enforcement Officers and Firefighters, 21348–94

Benzenoid Cyclic Intermediates-Commodity Chemicals, TSUS Items 401(pt.), 402(pt.), 404(pt.), and 406(pt.): Summary of Trade and Tariff Information, 9885–4.42

Benzenoid Cyclic Intermediates, Specialty Chemicals: TSUS Items 401(pt.), 402(pt.), 407(pt.), 408(pt.), 408(pt.), and 409(pt.): Summary of Trade and Tariff Information, 9885–4.45

Beryllium: Minerals Yearbook Preprint, Vol. 1, 1983, 5604–15.9

Better Federal Program Administration Can Contribute To Improving State Foster Care Programs, 26121–81

Better Times Ahead for Agriculture, 9381–1.402

Beyond Crime: Law Enforcement Operational and Cost Data, 6066–21.1

BHPr Support, Directory of Awards, 4114–1

Titles — Budget of the U.S.

Bibliography of Documents Issued by the GAO on Matters Related to ADP, IRM & Telecommunications, 26104–11.1

Bibliography on Shift Work Research: 1950-82, 7506–10.29

Bibliography on Smoking and Health, 1983, 4044–8

Bicycle Tires and Tubes from Taiwan: Determinations of the Commission in Investigation No. 731-TA-166 (Final) Under the Tariff Act of 1930, Together with the Information Obtained in the Investigation, 9886–14.106

Bid Opening Report: Federal-Aid Highway Construction Contracts, 1983, 7552–12

Bid Opening Report: Federal-Aid Highway Construction Contracts, First Six Months 1984, 7552–12

Biennial Report of Employment by Geographic Area: Federal Civilian Workforce Statistics, Dec. 31, 1982, 9844–8

Biological Products (Industry 2831): 1982 Census of Manufactures. Preliminary Report. Industry Series, 2491–1.182

Biomass Statistics for the Northern U.S., 1208–207

Biometric Monographs, 9926–1

Birth and Fertility Rates for States: U.S., 1980, 4147–21.42

Births of Hispanic Parentage, 1981, 4146–5.80

Bismuth: Mineral Industry Surveys, 5612–2.3

Bismuth: Minerals Yearbook Preprint, Vol. 1, 1983, 5604–15.10

Bituminous Coal, July 1982. Industry Wage Survey, 6787–6.198

BJS/NACJP Statistical Series Project Reports, 6066–21

Black Lung Benefits Act: Annual Report on Administration of the Act During 1982, 6504–3

Blankbooks and Looseleaf Binders (Industry 2782): 1982 Census of Manufactures. Preliminary Report. Industry Series, 2491–1.169

Blast Furnaces and Steel Mills (Industry 3312): 1982 Census of Manufactures. Preliminary Report. Industry Series, 2491–1.250

BLM in Wyoming: A Report to the Public, 1984, 5724–11.1

Blood Lead Levels for Persons Ages 6 Months-74 Years, U.S., 1976-80, 4147–11.201

Blood Pressure and Heart Rate Changes in Children when They Read Aloud, 4102–1.415

Blood Services Operations Report, 1982-83, 29254–3

Blowers and Fans (Industry 3564): 1982 Census of Manufactures. Preliminary Report. Industry Series, 2491–1.339

BLS and the Economy: A Centennial Timetable, 6722–1.467

BLS Establishment Estimates Revised to March 1983 Benchmarks, 6742–2.409

BLS Handbook of Methods, 6888–1

BLS Handbook of Methods: Vol. II, The Consumer Price Index, 6888–1.2

BLS Regional Reports, Middle Atlantic Region, 6926–1

BLS Regional Reports, New England Region, 6916–7

BLS Regional Reports, Southeast Region, 6946–1

BLS Sets Plans for Improving CPI in 1987, 6888–29

BLS Working Papers, 6886–6

BLS' 1982 Survey of Work-Related Deaths, 6722–1.422

BMCS National Roadside Inspection, 7554–35

BMCS National Roadside Inspection, May 2-5, 1983, 7552–15

Board for International Broadcasting, 1984 Annual Report, 10314–1

Board of Governors of the Federal Reserve System, 70th Annual Report, 1983, 9364–1

Boat Building and Repairing (Industry 3732): 1982 Census of Manufactures. Preliminary Report. Industry Series, 2491–1.405

Boat Dealers (Industry 5551): 1982 Census of Retail Trade. Preliminary Report. Industry Series, 2395–1.13

Boating Statistics, 1983, 7404–1

Body Supporting Garments, TSUS Items 376(pt.): Summary of Trade and Tariff Information, 9885–3.48

Bolts, Nuts, Rivets, and Washers (Industry 3452): 1982 Census of Manufactures. Preliminary Report. Industry Series, 2491–1.293

Bomb Summary, 1983, 6224–5

Bonneville Power Administration, 1983 Annual Report, 3224–1

Bonneville Power Administration Forecasts of Electricity Consumption in the Pacific Northwest: Technical Documentation, 3224–2

Book Printing (Industry 2732): 1982 Census of Manufactures. Preliminary Report. Industry Series, 2491–1.161

Book Publishing (Industry 2731): 1982 Census of Manufactures. Preliminary Report. Industry Series, 2491–1.160

Bookbinding and Related Work (Industry 2789): 1982 Census of Manufactures. Preliminary Report. Industry Series, 2491–1.170

Books, Magazines, Newspapers, and Other Cultural Printed Matter, TSUS Items 270(pt.) and 273(pt.): Summary of Trade and Tariff Information, 9885–2.28

Boot and Shoe Cut Stock and Findings (Industry 3131): 1982 Census of Manufactures. Preliminary Report. Industry Series, 2491–1.213

Boron: Minerals Yearbook Preprint, Vol. 1, 1983, 5604–15.11

Borrowers Pay Lower Effective Interest Rates for Large Conventional Mortgage Loans, 26113–135

Bottled and Canned Soft Drinks (Industry 2086): 1982 Census of Manufactures. Preliminary Report. Industry Series, 2491–1.36

Bottled Green Olives from Spain: Determination of the Commission in Investigation No. 104-TAA-122 Under Section 104(b) of the Trade Agreements Act of 1979, Together with the Information Obtained in the Investigation, 9886–18.15

Bowling Alleys (Industry 7933): 1982 Census of Service Industries. Preliminary Report. Industry Series, 2390–2.13

Brass, Bronze, and Copper Foundries (Industry 3362): 1982 Census of Manufactures. Preliminary Report. Industry Series, 2491–1.260

Brassieres and Allied Garments (Industry 2342): 1982 Census of Manufactures. Preliminary Report. Industry Series, 2491–1.90

Brassieres, Girdles, and Allied Garments, Current Industrial Report, 2506–6.5

Brazil: An Export Market Profile, 1526–6.4

Bread, Cake, and Related Products (Industry 2051): 1982 Census of Manufactures. Preliminary Report. Industry Series, 2491–1.20

Breast Feeding—the Community Norm. Report of a Workshop, 4102–1.455

Brick and Structural Clay Tile (Industry 3251): 1982 Census of Manufactures. Preliminary Report. Industry Series, 2491–1.228

Bridge, Tunnel, and Elevated Highway Construction Contractors (Industry 1622): 1982 Census of Construction Industries. Preliminary Report. Industry Series, 2371–1.7

Bridge, Tunnel, and Elevated Highway Construction Contractors, Industry 1622. 1982 Census of Construction Industries. Industry Series, 2373–1.7

Bridges over the Navigable Waters of the U.S., 7406–5

Bridges over the Navigable Waters of the U.S., Atlantic Coast, 7406–5.1

Bridges over the Navigable Waters of the U.S., Great Lakes, 7406–5.3

Bridges over the Navigable Waters of the U.S., Gulf Coast and Mississippi River System, 7406–5.2

Bridges over Navigable Waters of the U.S., Pacific Coast, 7406–5.4

Brief History of Farmers Home Administration, 1184–17

Broadcast Station Totals, 9282–4

Broadwoven Fabrics (Gray), Current Industrial Report, 2506–5.11

Broadwoven Fabrics of Manmade Fibers, TSUS Items 338(pt.): Summary of Trade and Tariff Information, 9885–3.42

Brokered Deposits: Issues and Alternatives, 9371–1.412

Bromine: Minerals Yearbook Preprint, Vol. 1, 1983, 5604–15.12

Bromine, 1983: Mineral Industry Surveys Annual Advance Summary, 5614–5.3

Broom Corn Brooms: U.S. Producer's Shipments, Imports for Consumption, Exports, and Apparent Consumption, 1983, 9884–6

Brooms and Brushes (Industry 3991): 1982 Census of Manufactures. Preliminary Report. Industry Series, 2491–1.439

Budget and Forces Summary, 3802–3

Budget Deficit: Are the International Consequences Unfavorable?, 9373–1.408

Budget Deficit Mythology, 9383–6.401

Budget Estimates, FY85, Appropriation: Salaries and Expenses, 9634–9

Budget in Brief, FY85, Department of Transportation, 7304–10

Budget of the Environmental Protection Agency: An Overview of Selected Proposals for 1985, 26308–47

Budget of the U.S. Government, FY85, 104–2

Budget of the U.S. Government, FY85 Appendix, 104–3

Budget of the U.S. Government, FY85. Special Analysis, 104–1

Building and Sustaining the Titles

Building and Sustaining the Economic Recovery: Credit Conditions, Employment, and Economic Prospects. Part 2: Fresno, Calif., 21248–84

Building Paper and Board Mills (Industry 2661): 1982 Census of Manufactures. Preliminary Report. Industry Series, 2491–1.144

Bulk Carriers in the World Fleet Oceangoing Merchant Type Ships of 1,000 Gross Tons and Over (Excludes Vessels on the Great Lakes), as of Jan. 1, 1983, 7704–13

Bumper World Cocoa Bean Crop Forecast for 1984/85, 1925–9.2

Bunker Fuels: Oil and Coal Laden in the U.S. on Vessels Engaged in Foreign Trade, 2422–5

Bureau of Economic Analysis Staff Papers, 2706–5

Bureau of Engraving and Printing, Annual Statistical Report, 8164–1

Bureau of Justice Statistics Bulletin, 6062–2

Bureau of Justice Statistics Special Reports, 6066–19

Bureau of Land Management Should Follow Fair Market Value Requirements in Selling Land in Las Vegas, Nevada, 26113–122

Bureau of Land Management State Offices, Facts and Statistics, 5724–11

Bureau of Prisons Reports, 6242–1

Bureau of Reclamation, Annual Report, 5824–1

Bureau of the Census Catalog, 1984, 2304–2

Burial Caskets (Industry 3995): 1982 Census of Manufactures. Preliminary Report. Industry Series, 2491–1.441

Burley Tobacco: ASCS Commodity Fact Sheet, 1984, 1806–4.14

Burnout: Age at Release from Prison and Recidivism, 6006–2.31

Business America, 2042–24

Business: An Eighth District Perspective, 9391–15

Business Conditions Digest, 2702–3

Business Cycles and the Eighth District, 9391–1.402

Business Forecasts, 1984, 9389–3

Business Forms, Binders, Carbon Paper, and Inked Ribbons, 1983, Current Industrial Report, 2506–7.11

Business Plan for Home Banking, 9371–1.422

Business Review, Federal Reserve Bank of Philadelphia, 9387–1

Buttons (Industry 3963): 1982 Census of Manufactures. Preliminary Report. Industry Series, 2491–1.437

Cable System Employment, 1980-81: A Report on the Status of Minorities and Women, 21368–45

Cable Television Industry Annual Data, 9284–15

Cadmium: Mineral Industry Surveys, 5612–2.5

Cadmium: Minerals Yearbook Preprint, Vol. 1, 1983, 5604–15.13

Calcium and Calcium Compounds: Minerals Yearbook Preprint, Vol. 1, 1983, 5604–15.14

Calcium Hypochlorite from Japan: Determination of the Commission in Investigation No. 731-TA-189 (Preliminary) Under the Tariff Act of 1930, Together with the Information Obtained in the Investigation, 9886–14.107

Calculating and Accounting Machines (Industry 3574): 1982 Census of Manufactures. Preliminary Report. Industry Series, 2491–1.346

Calculating the Adjusted Monetary Base Under Contemporaneous Reserve Requirements, 9391–1.407

Calculations of Profitability for U.S. Dollar-Deutsche Mark Intervention, 9366–1.130

California and National Economic Conditions, 21248–84

California Gas Mileage Guide, 1984, 3304–13

Californians, Japanese Lead List of '83 Patentees, 2244–2

California's Prospects for the Rest of the 1980's: Economic Growth and Housing Production, 9306–1.1

Camera and Photographic Supply Stores (Industry 5946): 1982 Census of Retail Trade. Preliminary Report. Industry Series, 2395–1.32

Cameroon: An Export Market Profile, 1526–6.6

Campaign Finance Reform, 21428–7

Campaign Finance Reform Proposals of 1983, 25688–6

Can Exchange Rate Predictability Be Achieved Without Monetary Convergence? Evidence from the EMS, 9366–7.101

Can Interstate Banking Increase Competitive Market Performance? An Empirical Test, 9371–1.401

Can We Delay a Greenhouse Warming? The Effectiveness and Feasibility of Options To Slow a Build-Up of Carbon Dioxide in the Atmosphere, 9188–88

Canada's Fruit and Vegetable Imports Continue To Grow, 1925–34.418

Canada's Grain Handling and Transportation System, 1528–176

Cancer Prevention Awareness Survey, Summary Report, 4478–149

Cane Sugar Refining (Industry 2062): 1982 Census of Manufactures. Preliminary Report. Industry Series, 2491–1.23

Canned and Cured Seafoods (Industry 2091): 1982 Census of Manufactures. Preliminary Report. Industry Series, 2491–1.38

Canned Fishery Products, Annual Summary 1982, 2166–6.1

Canned Fruits and Vegetables (Industry 2033): 1982 Census of Manufactures. Preliminary Report. Industry Series, 2491–1.9

Canned Specialties (Industry 2032): 1982 Census of Manufactures. Preliminary Report. Industry Series, 2491–1.8

Canned Tuna Fish: Public Version of Report to the President, Investigation No. TA-224-53 Under Section 224 of the Trade Act of 1974, 6406–9.6

Canned Tuna Fish: Report to the President on Investigation No. TA-201-53 Under Section 201 of the Trade Act of 1974, 9886–5.52

Canvas and Related Products (Industry 2394): 1982 Census of Manufactures. Preliminary Report. Industry Series, 2491–1.106

Capacity of Refrigerated Warehouses in the U.S., Oct. 1, 1983, 1614–2

Capacity Shares at the Medium Hubs, 1978-84, 9142–42.408

Capacity Utilization: Manufacturing, Mining, Utilities, and Industrial Materials, 9365 2.19

Capital Expenditures by Majority-Owned Foreign Affiliates of U.S. Companies, 1984, 2702–1.410

Capital Expenditures by Majority-Owned Foreign Affiliates of U.S. Companies, 1984 and 1985, 2702–1.437

Capital Movements—The Tail That Wags the Dog, 9373–3.28

Capital Punishment, 1982. National Prisoner Statistics, 6065–1

Capital Punishment 1983, 6062–2.406

Capitalizing Workers: The Impact of Employee Stock Ownership Plans in Selected Developing Countries, 9916–3.19

Capsule Review of the DOE Research and Development Field Facilities, 3004–4

Car Washes (Industry 7542): 1982 Census of Service Industries. Preliminary Report. Industry Series, 2390–2.10

Carbon and Certain Alloy Steel Products: Public Version of Report to the President, Investigation No. TA-224-51 Under Section 224 of the Trade Act of 1974, 6406–9.5

Carbon and Certain Alloy Steel Products: Report to the President on Investigation No. TA-201-51 Under Section 201 of the Trade Act of 1930, 9886–5.51

Carbon and Graphite Products (Industry 3624): 1982 Census of Manufactures. Preliminary Report. Industry Series, 2491–1.361

Carbon Dioxide and Climate: Summaries of Research in FY83 and FY84, 3004–18.1

Carbon Dioxide Effects Research and Assessment Program, 3406–3

Carbon Dioxide Emissions from Fossil Fuels: A Procedure for Estimation and Results for 1950-81, 3008–94

Carbon Monoxide Concentrations in Four U.S. Cities During the Winter of 1981, 9198–110

Carbon Paper and Inked Ribbons (Industry 3955): 1982 Census of Manufactures. Preliminary Report. Industry Series, 2491–1.434

Carbon Steel Products from Argentina, Australia, Finland, South Africa, and Spain: Determination of the Commission in Investigations Nos. 701-TA-212 (Preliminary) and 731-TA-169 through 182 (Preliminary) Under the Tariff Act of 1930, Together with the Information Obtained in the Investigations, 9886–19.8

Carbon Steel Products from Brazil: Determinations of the Commission in Investigations Nos. 701-TA-205-207 (Final) Under the Tariff Act of 1930, Together with the Information Obtained in the Investigations, 9886–15.49

Carbon Steel Products from Brazil: Determinations of the Commission in Investigations Nos. 701-TA-205-207 (Preliminary) and 731-TA-153 and 154 (Preliminary) Under the Tariff Act of 1930, Together with the Information Obtained in the Investigations, 9886–19.7

Carbon Steel Wire Rod from Argentina and Spain: Determinations of the Commission in Investigations No. 731-TA-157 and 160 (Final) Under the Tariff Act of 1930, Together with the Information Obtained in the Investigations, 9886–14.126

Carbon Steel Wire Rod from Argentina, Mexico, Poland, and Spain: Determination of the Commission in Investigations Nos.

Titles

701-TA-209 and 731-TA-157-160 (Preliminary) Under the Tariff Act of 1930, Together with the Information Obtained in the Investigations, 9886–15.47

- Carbon Steel Wire Rod from Poland: Determination of the Commission in Investigation No. 731-TA-159 (Final) Under the Tariff Act of 1930, Together with the Information Obtained in the Investigation, 9886–14.116
- Carbon Steel Wire Rod from Spain: Determination of the Commission in Investigation No. 701-TA-209 (Final) Under the Tariff Act of 1930, Together with the Information Obtained in the Investigation, 9886–15.50
- Carbon Steel Wire Rod from the German Democratic Republic: Determination of the Commission in Investigation No. 731-TA-205 (Preliminary) Under the Tariff Act of 1930, Together with the Information Obtained in the Investigation, 9886–14.127
- Carburetors, Pistons, Rings, and Valves (Industry 3592): 1982 Census of Manufactures. Preliminary Report. Industry Series, 2491–1.354
- Care for the Chronically Ill: Nursing Home Incentive Payment Experiment, 4652–1.405
- Carload Waybill Statistics, 1982, 7604–6
- Carpentering Special Trade Contractors (Industry 1751): 1982 Census of Construction Industries. Preliminary Report. Industry Series, 2371–1.16
- Carpet and Rugs, Current Industrial Report, 2506–5.9
- Carpets and Rugs, N.E.C. (Industry 2279): 1982 Census of Manufactures. Preliminary Report. Industry Series, 2491–1.64
- Carrying Costs and Treasury Bill Futures, 9387–8.88
- Case Filings in State Courts, 1983, 6062–2.409
- Case Mix, Quality, and Cost Relationships in Colorado Nursing Homes, 4652–1.432
- Caseload Statistics, State Vocational Rehabilitation Agencies, FY83, 4944–5
- Cash and Non-Cash Benefits for Persons with Limited Income, 25928–4
- Cash Benefits for Short-Term Sickness, 1948-81, 4742–1.417
- Cast-Iron Pipe Fittings from Brazil: Determinations of the Commission in Investigation No. 701-TA-221 (Preliminary) Under the Tariff Act of 1930, Together with the Information Obtained in the Investigation, 9886–15.53
- Castor Oil Products from Brazil: Determination of the Commission in Investigation No. 104-TAA-20 Under Section 104(b) of the Trade Agreements Act of 1979, Together with the Information Obtained in the Investigation, 9886–18.13
- CAT Scan Use in Short-Stay Non-Federal Hospitals: U.S., 1979-82, 4146–8.102
- Catalog of Cell Lines, 1984: NIGMS Human Genetic Mutant Cell Repository, NIA Aging Cell Repository, 4474–23
- Catalog of DIOR Reports, 3544–16
- Catalog of Federal Domestic Assistance, Update to the 1983 Report, 104–5
- Catalog of Federal Domestic Assistance, 1984, 104–5
- Catalog of Publications of the National Center for Health Statistics, 1979-83, 4124–1

Catfish, 1631–14
Cattle, 1623–1
Cattle on Feed, 1623–2
Cattle Outlook Discussion, 1004–16.1
Causes of Rising Transit Operating Deficits, 7308–184
CBO Studies, 26306–6
CCC Milk Support Program Activities, 1802–2
Celery, 1621–14
Cell-Site Radio Apparatus and Subassemblies Thereof from Japan: Determination of the Commission in Investigation No. 731-TA-163 (Preliminary) Under the Tariff Act of 1930, Together with the Information Obtained in the Investigation, 9886–14.95
Cell-Site Transceivers and Subassemblies Thereof from Japan: Determination of the Commission in Investigation No. 731-TA-163 (Final) Under the Tariff Act of 1930, Together with the Information Obtained in the Investigation, 9886–14.130
Cellulosic Manmade Fibers (Industry 2823): 1982 Census of Manufactures. Preliminary Report. Industry Series, 2491–1.180
Cement, Hydraulic (Industry 3241): 1982 Census of Manufactures. Preliminary Report. Industry Series, 2491–1.227
Cement: Mineral Industry Surveys, 5612–1.2
Cement: Minerals Yearbook Preprint, Vol. 1, 1983, 5604–15.15
Cement, 1983: Mineral Industry Surveys Annual Advance Summary, 5614–5.5
Census of Agriculture, 1982. Preliminary Reports, 2330–1
Census of Agriculture, 1982. Vol. 1. Geographic Area Series, 2331–1
Census of Construction Industries, 1982. Industry Series, 2373–1
Census of Construction Industries, 1982. Preliminary Reports. Industry Series, 2371–1
Census of Governments, 1982. Vol. 2. Taxable Property Values and Assessment-Sales Price Ratios, 2453–1
Census of Governments, 1982. Vol. 3. Government Employment. No. 1: Employment of Major Local Governments, 2455–1
Census of Governments, 1982. Vol. 3. Public Employment. No. 2: Compendium of Public Employment, 2455–2
Census of Governments, 1982. Vol. 4. Governmental Finances. No. 1: Finances of Public School Systems, 2457–1
Census of Governments, 1982. Vol. 4. Governmental Finances. No. 3: Finances of County Governments, 2457–3
Census of Governments, 1982. Vol. 4. Governmental Finances. No. 4: Finances of Municipal and Township Governments, 2457–4
Census of Governments, 1982. Vol. 6. Topical Studies. No. 3: State Payments to Local Governments, 2460–3
Census of Housing, 1980. Vol. 2. Metropolitan Housing Characteristics, 2473–1
Census of Housing, 1980. Vol. 4. Characteristics of Housing Units. Components of Inventory Change, 2473–3
Census of Housing, 1980. Vol. 4. Characteristics of Housing Units. Components of Inventory Change. Part I: U.S. and Regions, 2473–3.1

Ceramic Wall and Floor Tile

Census of Housing, 1980. Vol. 4. Characteristics of Housing Units. Components of Inventory Change. Part II: SMSA Groupings with Populations of Less than One Million in 1970, 2473–3.2
Census of Manufactures, 1982. Preliminary Reports. Geographic Area Series, 2491–3
Census of Manufactures, 1982. Preliminary Reports. Industry Series, 2491–1
Census of Manufactures, 1982. Preliminary Reports. Subject Series, 2491–2
Census of Mineral Industries, 1982. Preliminary Reports. Industry Series, 2511–1
Census of Mineral Industries, 1982. Preliminary Reports. Summary Series, 2511–2
Census of Population and Housing, 1980. Census Tracts, 2551–2
Census of Population, 1980. Supplementary Reports, 2535–1
Census of Population, 1980. Vol. 1. Characteristics of the Population. Chapter C: General Social and Economic Characteristics, 2531–3
Census of Population, 1980. Vol. 1. Characteristics of the Population. Chapter D: Detailed Population Characteristics, 2531–4
Census of Retail Trade, 1982. Geographic Area Series, 2397–1
Census of Retail Trade, 1982. Major Retail Centers in Standard Metropolitan Statistical Areas, 2401–1
Census of Retail Trade, 1982. Preliminary Reports. Industry Series, 2395–1
Census of Service Industries, 1982. Geographic Area Series, 2391–1
Census of Service Industries, 1982. Preliminary Reports. Industry Series, 2390–2
Census of State Government Initiatives for High-Technology Industrial Development, Background Paper, 26358–107.2
Census of Transportation, 1982. Truck Inventory and Use Survey, 2573–1
Census of U.S. Civil Aircraft, 1983, 7504–3
Census of Wholesale Trade, 1982. Geographic Area Series, 2405–1
Census of Wholesale Trade, 1982. Preliminary Reports. Industry Series, 2403–1
Census Tracts. 1980 Census of Population and Housing, 2551–2
Center for Research for Mothers and Children, 1983 Progress Report, 4474–31
Central America: The Effects of Population on Economic and Social Development, 028–19.2
Central American Refugees: Regional Conditions and Prospects and Potential Impact on the U.S., 26123–70
Central North Pacific Tropical Cyclones, 1983, 2152–8.402
Centrifuges and Filtering and Purifying Equipment, TSUS Items 661(pt.): Summary of Trade and Tariff Information, 9885–6.60
Century of Wage Statistics: The BLS Contribution, 6722–1.466
Ceramic Table and Kitchen Articles, TSUS Items 533(pt.): Summary of Trade and Tariff Information, 9885–5.13
Ceramic Wall and Floor Tile (Industry 3253): 1982 Census of Manufactures. Preliminary Report. Industry Series, 2491–1.229

Cereal Breakfast Foods

Cereal Breakfast Foods (Industry 2043): 1982 Census of Manufactures. Preliminary Report. Industry Series, 2491–1.15

Certain Textile and Leather Products: Imports from China and the U.S. Market, 9882–2.401

CFTC Databook, 11924–3

Challenger's Sixth Flight Highlights Earth Science, 9506–2.120

CHAMPUS Chartbook of Statistics, 3502–2

Changes in Air Traffic Hub Classifications, 1978-1982, 9142–42.401

Changes in Genetic Evaluation Procedures for Jan. 1984, 1702–2.403

Changes in Heart Disease Risk Factors, 4144–11.1

Changes in Mortality Among the Elderly: U.S., 1940-78. Supplement to 1980, 4147–3.25

Changes in Rates of Spontaneous Fetal Deaths Reported in Upstate New York Vital Records by Gestational Age, 1968-78, 4102–1.428

Changes in Scheduled Airline Flights by Number of Intermediate Stops, Dec. 1978 to Dec. 1983, 9142–42.403

Changes in the AIPL Genetic Evaluation Procedures, 1702–2.401

Changes in the Factor Requirements of U.S. Foreign Trade, 9381–10.30

Changes in the Number of Carriers Serving Domestic Points, Dec. 1983 vs. Dec. 1978, 9142–42.402

Changes in the U.S. Telecommunications Industry and the Impact on U.S. Telecommunications Trade: Report to the Committee on Finance, U.S. Senate, on Investigation No. 332-172 Under Section 332 of the Tariff Act of 1930, 9886–4.75

Changes in the Use of Adjustable-Rate Mortgages in the Fourth FHLB District, 9302–2.403

Changes in Unemployment Insurance Legislation During 1983, 6722–1.414

Changing Asset/Liability Structure of Savings Institutions in a Deregulated Environment, 9306–1.3

Changing Composition of the Military and the Effect on Labor Force Data, 6722–1.442

Changing Pattern of CO_2 Emissions, 3006–7.6

Changing Public Attitudes on Governments and Taxes, 1984, 10044–2

Changing Role of Real and Nominal Interest Rates, 9381–1.405

Changing Technology in Cotton Classing, 1004–16.1

Changing Telephone Industry: Access Charges, Universal Service, and Local Rates, 26306–6.79

Changing the Method for Calculating Quarters of Coverage: The Impact on Workers' Insured Status, 4742–1.408

Changing Trends in the Red Meat Distribution System, 1548–232

Characteristics of Apartments Completed, 1983, Current Housing Report, 2484–3

Characteristics of Asian Births: U.S., 1980, 4146–5.75

Characteristics of Federal Land Bank Loans, 9264–8

Characteristics of FHA Single-Family Mortgages: Selected Sections of National Housing Act, 5144–17

Characteristics of Food Stamp Households, Aug. 1981, 1364–8

Characteristics of Households and Persons Receiving Selected Noncash Benefits: 1982, 2546–6.37

Characteristics of Households Receiving Selected Noncash Benefits: 1982 (Advance Data from the Mar. 1983 Current Population Survey), 2546–6.38

Characteristics of Households with Children Enrolled in Elementary and Secondary Schools, 4838–13

Characteristics of Housing Units. Components of Inventory Change. Part I: U.S. and Regions. 1980 Census of Housing, Vol. 4, 2473–3.1

Characteristics of Housing Units. Components of Inventory Change. Part II: SMSA Groupings with Populations of Less than One Million in 1970. 1980 Census of Housing, Vol. 4, 2473–3.2

Characteristics of Housing Units. Components of Inventory Change. 1980 Census of Housing, Vol. 4, 2473–3

Characteristics of Medically Disqualified Airline Pilots, 7506–10.23

Characteristics of New Housing, 1982, Construction Reports, 2384–1

Characteristics of Persons Rehabilitated in FY81, State-Federal Program of Vocational Rehabilitation, 4944–6

Characteristics of Pharmacists, U.S., 4147–14.28

Characteristics of Recent Science/Engineering Graduates: 1982, Detailed Statistical Tables, 9627–25

Characteristics of Social Security Disability Insurance Beneficiaries, 4744–20

Characteristics of State Plans for Aid to Families with Dependent Children 1983 Edition, 4704–9

Characteristics of the Population Below the Poverty Level: 1982, 2546–6.40

Characteristics of the Population. Chapter C: General Social and Economic Characteristics. 1980 Census of Population, Vol. 1, 2531–3

Characteristics of the Population. Chapter D: Detailed Population Characteristics. 1980 Census of Population, Vol. 1, 2531–4

Characterizations of Coastal Ecosystems, 5506–4

Charging for Federal Services, 26306–6.68

Cheese, Natural and Processed (Industry 2022): 1982 Census of Manufactures. Preliminary Report. Industry Series, 2491–1.4

Chemical and Fertilizer Mineral Mining (Industries 1472-1477 and 1479): 1982 Census of Mineral Industries. Preliminary Report. Industry Series, 2511–1.11

Chemical Composition and Frozen Storage Stability of Weakfish, 2162–1.401

Chemical Preparations, N.E.C. (Industry 2899): 1982 Census of Manufactures. Preliminary Report. Industry Series, 2491–1.201

Chemicals and Allied Products (Industry 5161): 1982 Census of Wholesale Trade. Preliminary Report. Industry Series, 2403–1.35

Cherokee Indian Agency: Annual Council Report, 1981, 5704–4

Cherokee Indian Agency: Annual Council Report, 1982, 5704–4

Cherokee Indian Agency: Annual Council Report, 1983, 5704–4

Cherry Production: Tart Cherry Production Up Substantially, 1621–18.2

Chesapeake Bay Program: Findings and Recommendations, 9208–121

Chewing and Smoking Tobacco (Industry 2131): 1982 Census of Manufactures. Preliminary Report. Industry Series, 2491–1.46

Chewing Gum (Industry 2067): 1982 Census of Manufactures. Preliminary Report. Industry Series, 2491–1.26

Chiefs of State and Cabinet Members of Foreign Governments, 242–7

Child-Care Services: A National Picture, 6746–1.253

Child Nutrition Programs, 1364–13

Child Support Enforcement, 8th Annual Report to Congress for the Period Ending Sept. 30, 1983, 4004–16

Child Support Enforcement Statistics, FY82, 4002–5

Child Support Enforcement Statistics, FY83, 4004–29

Children's Coats and Suits (Industry 2363): 1982 Census of Manufactures. Preliminary Report. Industry Series, 2491–1.94

Children's Dresses and Blouses (Industry 2361): 1982 Census of Manufactures. Preliminary Report. Industry Series, 2491–1.93

Children's Outerwear, N.E.C. (Industry 2369): 1982 Census of Manufactures. Preliminary Report. Industry Series, 2491–1.95

Childspacing Among Birth Cohorts of American Women: 1905-59, 2546–1.387

China: International Trade Annual Statistical Supplement, 244–12

China: International Trade Quarterly Review, 242–6

China: Outlook and Situation Report, 1524–4.8

China's Cotton Prospects, 1561–1.405

China's Economy and Foreign Trade, 2044–13

China's Economy and Foreign Trade, 1981-85, 2048–106

Chloropicrin from People's Republic of China: Determination of the Commission in Investigation No. 731-TA-130 (Final) Under the Tariff Act of 1930, Together with the Information Obtained in the Investigation, 9886–14.98

Choline Chloride from Canada and the United Kingdom: Determinations of the Commission in Investigations Nos. 731-TA-155 and 731-TA-156 (Preliminary) Under the Tariff Act of 1930, Together with the Information Obtained in the Investigations, 9886–14.90

Choline Chloride from Canada: Determination of the Commission in Investigation No. 731-TA-155 (Final) Under the Tariff Act of 1930, Together with the Information Obtained in the lvestigation, 9886–14.123

Chromium Availability, Market Economy Countries. A Minerals Availability Program Appraisal, 5606–4.12

Chromium: Mineral Industry Surveys, 5612–1.3

Chromium: Minerals Yearbook Preprint, Vol. 1, 1983, 5604–15.16

Chronology of Hijackings of U.S. Registered Aircraft and Legal Status of Hijackers, 7504–31.3

Titles

Chrysler Corporation Loan Guarantee Board, Report to Congress, Oct. 1, 1982-Sept. 30, 1983, 8004–14

Cigarettes and Cigars: Statistical Release, 8486–1.4

Cigars (Industry 2121): 1982 Census of Manufactures. Preliminary Report. Industry Series, 2491–1.45

Ciguatera in the Eastern Caribbean, 2162–1.403

Circular Knit Fabric Mills (Industry 2257): 1982 Census of Manufactures. Preliminary Report. Industry Series, 2491–1.56

Citation Release, 6068–187

Citrus Fruits: Revised Estimates by States, 1977-78 Through 1981-82, 1641–4

Citrus Fruits: 1984 Summary, 1621–18.5

Citrus Situation, 1925–34.401

City Employment in 1983, 2466–1.1

City Fiscal Conditions in FY83: Dark Clouds on the Horizon, 25408–86.1

City Government Finances in 1981-82, 2466–2.1

City Government Finances in 1982-83, 2466–2.7

Civil Aeronautics Board: Consumer Complaint Report, 9142–20

Civil Aeronautics Board Reports to Congress, FY83, 9144–1

Civil Pilot Taxonomy: Implications for Flight Safety, 21148–34

Civilian Manpower Statistics, 3542–16

Class I Freight Railroads Selected Earnings Data, 9482–2

Class I Line-Haul Railroads Selected Earnings Data, 9482–2

Classification and Estimation of Alcohol Involvement in Fatalities, 7762–9.405

Classification, Assets and Location of Registered Investment Companies Under the Investment Company Act of 1940, As of Sept. 30, 1982, 9734–1

Classification, Assets and Location of Registered Investment Companies Under the Investment Company Act of 1940, As of Sept. 30, 1983, 9734–1

Classification Criteria for Size and Type of Farm, 1544–19.402

Classification of Reasons Why Persons Seek Primary Care: Pilot Study of a New System, 4102–1.460

Clay, Ceramic, and Refractory Minerals (Industries 1452, 1453, 1454, 1455, and 1459): 1982 Census of Mineral Industries. Preliminary Report. Industry Series, 2511–1.10

Clay Construction Products, Current Industrial Report, 2506–9.2

Clay Refractories (Industry 3255): 1982 Census of Manufactures. Preliminary Report. Industry Series, 2491–1.230

Clays: Minerals Yearbook Preprint, Vol. 1, 1983, 5604–15.17

Clays, 1983: Mineral Industry Surveys Annual Advance Summary, 5614–5.11

Clean Air Amendments of 1983, 25328–25

Clearinghouse on Health Indexes, 4122–1

Climate Impact Assessment, Foreign Countries, 2152–9

Climate Impact Assessment, U.S., 2152–12

Climate Impact Assessment, U.S.: Energy Section, 2152–11

Clinical Research Notes, NIDA, 4492–4

Clinical Research Notes, NIDA, 4494–9

Closures for Containers, Current Industrial Report, 2506–11.4

Co-op Share of Farm Marketings, Major Supply Purchases Climb, 1122–1.402

Co-ops' Production of Crude Oil Down, but Reserve Protection Increased, 1122–1.407

Co-ops Un"Fortune"ately Lose Ground on '500' List, 1122–1.405

Coal and Other Carbonaceous Materials, TSUS Item 521.31: Summary of Trade and Tariff Information, 9885–5.15

Coal and Other Minerals and Ores (Industry 5052): 1982 Census of Wholesale Trade. Preliminary Report. Industry Series, 2403–1.7

Coal Distribution, 3162–8

Coal-Fired Capacity Additions System, 3166–11

Coal-Fired Capacity Additions System: Evaluation and Testing, 3166–11.1

Coal from the Nation: Household Demand for Electricity, 1588–78

Coal Mining (Industry 1111, 1112, 1211, and 1213): 1982 Census of Mineral Industries. Preliminary Report. Industry Series, 2511–1.4

Coal Production, 1983, 3164–25

Coal Quarterly Report, 3162–37

Coast Guard SAR Statistics, 1983, 7404–2

Coated Fabrics, Not Rubberized (Industry 2295): 1982 Census of Manufactures. Preliminary Report. Industry Series, 2491–1.73

Cobalt: Mineral Industry Surveys, 5612–1.4

Cobalt: Minerals Yearbook Preprint, Vol. 1, 1983, 5604–15.18

Coca Production in Peru, 7008–40

Cocaine 1980, 7008–40

Cocoa, Chocolate, and Confectionery, TSUS Items 156(pt.) and 157(pt.): Summary of Trade and Tariff Information, 9885–1.67

Cocoa: Foreign Agriculture Circular, 1925–9

Codes for the Identification of Hydrologic Units in the U.S. and the Caribbean Outlying Areas: Data Standards and Guidelines, 2216–2.126

Coffee: Foreign Agriculture Circular, 1925–5

Coinage Executed During (Month), 8202–1

Cold Finishing of Steel Shapes (Industry 3316): 1982 Census of Manufactures. Preliminary Report. Industry Series, 2491–1.253

Cold-Rolled Carbon Steel Sheet and Carbon Steel Structural Shapes from the Republic of Korea: Determinations of the Commission in Investigations Nos. 701-TA-218 and 219 (Preliminary) Under the Tariff Act of 1930, Together with the Information Obtained in the Investigation, 9886–15.51

Cold-Rolled Carbon Steel Sheet from Brazil: Determination of the Commission in Investigation No. 731-TA-154 (Final) Under the Tariff Act of 1930, Together with the Information Obtained in the Investigation, 9886–14.120

Cold Storage, 1631–5

Cold Storage, 1983 Summary, 1631–11

Collective Bargaining Calendar Crowded Again in 1984, 6722–1.402

Collective Bargaining Calendar for the Southeast, 1984, 6946–1.68

College Admissions Testing Programs, Summary Report for Students in the Department of Defense Dependents Schools (DoDDS), 1983, 3504–17

Committee for Purchase from

College Costs: Basic Student Charges, 2-Year and 4-Year Institutions, 1983-84, 4844–10

Color Perception and ATC Job Performance, 7506–10.26

Color Television Receivers from the Republic of Korea and Taiwan: Determinations of the Commission in Investigations Nos. 731-TA-134 and 135 (Final) Under the Tariff Act of 1930, Together with the Information Obtained in the Investigations, 9886–14.101

Colorado River Storage Project and Participating Projects in FY83, 27th Annual Report, 5824–3

Columbium and Tantalum: Minerals Yearbook Preprint, Vol. 1, 1983, 5604–15.19

Combined Effective Income and Property Tax Rates for Farm Capital, 1548–237

Coming Soon: Taxpayer Data Classified by Occupation, 8308–28.1

Commentary, Federal Home Loan Bank of San Francisco, 9302–17

Commerce Budget in Brief, FY85, 2004–6

Commerce Publications Update, 2002–1

Commercial Activities Inventory Report and Five Year Review Schedule, FY83, 3544–25

Commercial and Industrial Loan Commitments at Selected Large Commercial Banks, 9365–2.18

Commercial Bank Investment in Municipal Securities, 9385–1.402

Commercial Bank Profitability in 1983, 9371–1.419

Commercial Biotechnology, An International Analysis, 26358–98

Commercial Fertilizers, Total Fertilizer Consumption Up 20 Percent, 1631–13

Commercial Lighting Fixtures (Industry 3646): 1982 Census of Manufactures. Preliminary Report. Industry Series, 2491–1.374

Commercial Machines and Equipment (Industry 5081): 1982 Census of Wholesale Trade. Preliminary Report. Industry Series, 2403–1.12

Commercial Nuclear Power, 1984: Prospects for the U.S. and the World, 3164–57

Commercial Printing, Gravure (Industry 2754): 1982 Census of Manufactures. Preliminary Report. Industry Series, 2491–1.166

Commercial Printing, Letterpress (Industry 2751): 1982 Census of Manufactures. Preliminary Report. Industry Series, 2491–1.163

Commercial Printing, Lithographic (Offset) (Industry 2752): 1982 Census of Manufactures. Preliminary Report. Industry Series, 2491–1.164

Commissioner and Chief Counsel, Internal Revenue Service: 1983 Annual Report, 8304–3

Commissioner of Patents and Trademarks, Annual Report, FY83, 2244–1

Commitments and Discharges for the Fiscal Year: Bureau of Prisons, 6242–1.3

Commitments and Discharges for the Month: Bureau of Prisons, 6242–1.2

Commitments of Traders in Commodity Futures, Chicago, 11922–1

Commitments of Traders in Commodity Futures, Chicago and New York, 11922–5

Commitments of Traders in Commodity Futures, New York, 11922–2

Committee for Purchase from the Blind and Other Severely Handicapped, Annual Report, 1983, 11714–1

Commodity Credit Corp. Titles

Commodity Credit Corp. Monthly Sales List, 1802–4

Commodity Credit Corporation, Report of the President, Sept. 30, 1983, 1824–1

Commodity Futures Trading Commission, Annual Report, 1983, 11924–2

Commodity Only Program, FY77-80, 1364–13.4

Commodity Only Program, FY81, 1364–13.4

Commodity Price Relationships in the Southern Plains, 1561–4.401

Commodity/Country Allocations Under Title I, P.L. 480, 1922–7

Commonwealth of the Northern Mariana Islands Annual Report, FY83, 5304–15.1

Communications, Oct.-Dec. 1981. Industry Wage Survey, 6787–6.199

Communicative Disorders Among Patients in VA Medical Facilities, 9926–1.17

Community Services Block Grant: New State Role Brings Program and Administrative Changes, 26121–84

Commuter Airline Industry Since Deregulation, 9142–42.404

Companies Participating in the DOD Subcontracting Program, 3542–17

Companies Receiving the Largest Dollar Volume of Prime Contract Awards, FY83, 3544–5

Comparability of the Federal Statutory Pay Systems with Private Enterprise Pay Rates: Annual Report of the President's Pay Agent, 1983, 104–16

Comparative Analyses of Fish Populations in Naturally Acidic and Circumneutral Lakes in Northern Wisconsin, 5506–5.16

Comparative Analysis of Cosmetic Contact Lens Fitting by Ophthalmologists, Optometrists, and Opticians: Report of the Staff to the Federal Trade Commission, 9408–49

Comparative Analysis of Five PL 480 Title I Impact Evaluation Studies, 9918–13

Comparative Analysis of Policies and Other Factors Which Affect the Role of the Private Sector in Economic Development, 9918–12

Comparative Climatic Data for the U.S. Through 1982, 2154–8

Comparative International Vital and Health Statistics Reports. Vital and Health Statistics Series 5, 4147–5

Comparative Performance of Multiple Reaction Function Equations Estimated by Canonical Methods, 9373–3.26

Comparative Trend Analysis, Federal Home Loan Bank of Topeka, 9302–22

Comparing Distributions of Foreign Investment in U.S. Agricultural Land, 1588–77

Comparison of Actual and Predicted Energy Savings In Minnesota Gas-Heated Single-Family Homes, 3308–74

Comparison of Compensation Paid Scientists and Engineers in Research and Development, DOE Laboratories Compared to National Survey of Compensation, Aug. 1982-Feb. 1984 Data, 3004–9

Comparison of Direct Deposit and Check Payment Costs, 9366–1.139

Comparison of Nurses' Smoking Habits: The 1975 DHEW Survey and Connecticut Nurses, 1981, 4102–1.403

Comparison of State Unemployment Insurance Laws, 6402–2

Comparison of Youth Unemployment in Australia and the U.S., 6722–1.462

Comparisons Between Ship and Buoy Climatologies, 2152–8.403

Compendium of HHS Evaluation Studies, 4008–60

Compendium of Public Employment. 1982 Census of Governments, Vol. 3. Public Employment, No. 2, 2455–2

Compensation Report, FY81-82, 9844–1

Competition and Other Current Issues in the Natural Gas Market, 3168–89

Competition for National Forest Timber: Effects on Timber-Dependent Communities, 1208–194

Competition in the Coal Industry: Report of the U.S. Department of Justice Pursuant to Section 8 of the Federal Coal Leasing Amendments Act of 1976, 6004–12

Competition in the Oil Pipeline Industry: A Preliminary Report, 6008–18

Competitive Assessment of the U.S. Foundry Industry: Report to the President on Investigation No. 332-176 Under Section 332 of the Tariff Act of 1930, 9886–4.77

Competitive Assessment of the U.S. Video Game Industry: Report on Investigation No. 332-160 Under Section 332(b) of the Tariff Act of 1930, 9886–4.71

Competitive Assessment of the U.S. Wood and Upholstered Household Furniture Industry: Report to Subcommittee on Trade, Committee on Ways and Means, U.S. House of Representatives Investigation No. 332-170, Under Section 332(b) of the Tariff Act of 1930, as Amended, 9886–4.74

Competitive Conditions Relating to the Importation of Industrial Molds into the U.S. from Canada: Report to the Subcommittee on Trade of the House Ways and Means Committee on Investigation No. 332-169 Under Section 332 of the Tariff Act of 1930, 9886–4.72

Competitive Position of U.S. Producers of Robotics in Domestic and World Markets: Report on Investigation No. 332-155, Under Section 332(b) of the Tariff Act of 1930, 9886–4.65

Compilation of Air Pollutant Emission Factors, Third Edition, 9198–13

Compliance, Enforcement and Reporting Under the Labor-Management Reporting and Disclosure Act, 6464–2

Components of Inventory Change. Part I: U.S. and Regions. 1980 Census of Housing, Vol. 4. Characteristics of Housing Units, 2473–3.1

Components of Inventory Change. Part II: SMSA Groupings with Populations of Less than One Million in 1970. 1980 Census of Housing, Vol. 4. Characteristics of Housing Units, 2473–3.2

Components of Inventory Change. 1980 Census of Housing, Vol. 4. Characteristics of Housing Units, 2473–3

Composition, Nutritive Value, and Sensory Attributes of Fish Sticks Prepared from Minced Fish Flesh Fortified with Textured Soy Proteins, 2162–1.401

Comprehensive Federal Crop Insurance: Issues After Two Years of Experience, 21168–28

Comprehensive Statement on Postal Operations, 1983, 9864–5

Computer and Data Processing Services (Industry 737): 1982 Census of Service Industries. Preliminary Report. Industry Series, 2390–2.7

Computerization of Market News Reports, 1004–16.1

Computerized Manufacturing Automation: Employment, Education, and the Workplace, 26358–105

Computers and Office and Accounting Machines, 1983, Current Industrial Report, 2506–12.2

Computers and Peripheral Equipment: Country Market Survey, 2045–1

Concentrated Apple Juice, 1925–34.411

Concordance of Statistics, Available in Selected Federal Reserve Publications, 9364–8

Concrete Block and Brick (Industry 3271): 1982 Census of Manufactures. Preliminary Report. Industry Series, 2491–1.237

Concrete Products, N.E.C. (Industry 3272): 1982 Census of Manufactures. Preliminary Report. Industry Series, 2491–1.238

Concrete Work Special Trade Contractors (Industry 1771): 1982 Census of Construction Industries. Preliminary Report. Industry Series, 2371–1.19

Concrete Work Special Trade Contractors, Industry 1771. 1982 Census of Construction Industries. Industry Series, 2373–1.19

Condensed and Evaporated Milk (Industry 2023): 1982 Census of Manufactures. Preliminary Report. Industry Series, 2491–1.5

Condition of Bilingual Education in the Nation, 1984: A Report from the Secretary of Education to the President and the Congress, 4804–14

Condition of Education: Statistical Report, 1984 Edition, 4824–1

Condition of Hispanics in America Today, 2328–48

Conditional Variance and the Risk Premium in the Foreign Exchange Market, 9381–10.32

Conditions Attached to Adjustment Financing: Evolution of the IMF Practice, 9373–3.28

Conditions of Competition Between Certain Domestic and Imported Fabricated Structural Steel Products: Report to the Subcommittee on Trade, Committee on Ways and Means, U.S. House of Representatives on Investigation No. 332-181 Under Section 332(b) of the Tariff Act of 1930, 9886–4.79

Conditions of Competition Between the U.S. and Canadian Live Swine and Pork Industries: Report to the U.S. Senate Committee on Finance on Investigation No. 332-186 Under Section 332 of the Tariff Act of 1930, 9886–4.80

Confectionery Products; Chocolate and Cocoa Products (Industry 2065 and 2066): 1982 Census of Manufactures. Preliminary Report. Industry Series, 2491–1.25

Confectionery, 1983, Current Industrial Report, 2506–4.5

Conference Series, Federal Reserve Bank of Boston, 9373–3

Conflicting Measures of Private Saving, 2702–1.441

Confusion over Validity and Effects of Purported Petty Officer Shortage, 26123–69

Congress Needs Better Information on Forest Service's Below-Cost Timber Sales, 26113–126

Congressional Presentation, FY85, Agency for International Development. Annex 1: Africa, 9914–3.2

Titles

Congressional Presentation, FY85, Agency for International Development. Annex 2: Asia, 9914–3.3

Congressional Presentation, FY85, Agency for International Development. Annex 3: Latin America and the Caribbean, Vol. 1, South America and the Caribbean, 9914–3.4

Congressional Presentation, FY85, Agency for International Development. Annex 3: Latin America and the Caribbean, Vol. 2, Central America, 9914–3.5

Congressional Presentation, FY85, Agency for International Development. Annex 4: Near East, 9914–3.6

Congressional Presentation, FY85, Agency for International Development. Annex 5: Centrally Funded Programs, 9914–3.7

Congressional Presentation, FY85, Agency for International Development. International Organizations and Programs, 9914–3.8

Congressional Presentation, FY85, Agency for International Development. Main Volume, 9914–3.1

Congressional Presentation, FY85, Agency for International Development. U.S. Trade and Development Program, 9914–3.9

Congressional Sourcebook Series, 26106–5

Congressionally Mandated Study of School Finance, A Final Report to Congress from the Secretary of Education, 4808–9

Consequences of Imposing the U.S. 30 Percent Withholding Tax on Interest Paid to or by Netherlands Antilles Finance Subsidiaries of U.S. Corporations, 21408–71

Conservation Highlights, 1983, 1264–2

Conservation Sourcebook, 3228–2

Conservation Sourcebook, Appendix, 3228–2.2

Considering Departures from Current Timber Harvesting Policies: Case Studies of Four Communities in the Pacific Northwest, 1208–196

Consolidated Annual Report on State and Territorial Public Health Laboratories, FY82, 4204–8

Consolidated Annual Report to Congress on Community Development Programs, 1984, 5124–5

Consolidated Federal Funds Report, FY83, 2464–3

Consolidated Federal Funds Report, FY83. Vol. I: County Areas, 2464–3.1

Consolidated Federal Funds Report, FY83. Vol. II: Subcounty Areas, 2464–3.2

Consolidated Financial Statements of the U.S. Government: FY83 Prototype, 8104–5

Constant Market Share Analysis of Latin America's Agricultural Export Growth, 1528–169

Construction and Mining Machinery and Equipment (Industry 5082): 1982 Census of Wholesale Trade. Preliminary Report. Industry Series, 2403–1.13

Construction Machinery (Industry 3531): 1982 Census of Manufactures. Preliminary Report. Industry Series, 2491–1.316

Construction Machinery, Current Industrial Report, 2506–12.3

Construction Outlook for 1984, 2012–1.402

Construction Reports: Characteristics of New Housing, 1983, 2384–1

Construction Reports: Housing Completions, 2382–2

Construction Reports: Housing Starts, 2382–1

Corporation Income Tax

Construction Reports: Housing Units Authorized by Building Permits and Public Contracts, 2382–5

Construction Reports: Housing Units Authorized by Building Permits and Public Contracts, Annual 1983, 2384–2

Construction Reports: New One-Family Houses Sold and for Sale, 2382–3

Construction Reports: New Residential Construction in Selected SMSAs, 2382–9

Construction Reports: Price Index of New One-Family Houses Sold, 2382–8

Construction Reports: Residential Alterations and Repairs, 2382–7

Construction Reports: Residential Alterations and Repairs, Annual 1983, 2384–4

Construction Reports: Value of New Construction Put in Place, 2382–4

Construction Review, 2012–1

Consumer and Industrial Electrical Products, TSUS Items 678(pt.), 683(pt.), 685(pt.), and 688(pt.): Summary of Trade and Tariff Information, 9885–6.65

Consumer Choice of Dwelling, Neighborhood, and Public Services, 9306–1.7

Consumer Demand for Product Deregulation, 9371–1.417

Consumer Income, Current Population Reports, 2546–6

Consumer Installment Credit, 9365–2.6

Consumer Price Index, 6762–1

Consumer Price Trends in Dallas/Fort Worth and Houston, 1978-82, 6966–1.12

Consumer Prices: Energy and Food, 6762–8

Consumer Product Safety Commission, 1983 Annual Report, 9164–2

Consumer, Scientific, Technical, and Industrial Glassware, 1983, Current Industrial Report, 2506–9.3

Consumer Spending: Recovery and Beyond, 1004–16.1

Consumer Spending: Recovery and Beyond, 1702–1.405

Consumers' Experience with Real Estate Brokers: A Report on the Consumer Survey of the FTC's Residential Real Estate Brokerage Investigation, 9408–48

Consumers' Right to Bankruptcy: Origins and Effects, 21528–57.2

Consumption on the Cotton System and Stocks, Current Industrial Report, 2506–5.8

Consumption on the Woolen System and Worsted Combing, Current Industrial Report, 2506–5.2

Containerized Cargo Statistics, 1982, 7704–8

Contingent Foreign Liabilities of the U.S. Government, 8002–12

Continuing Education and the American Workforce, 15214–1

Continuing Education for Maternal Child Health Nurses: A Means To Improve the Health Care of Mothers and Children, 4102–1.405

Contracted Research Listing: U.S. Department of Labor/Bureau of International Labor Affairs, FY73-84, 6364–1

Contracting for Surveys, 106–4.3

Contracts Between Interstate Pipelines and Their Customers, 3162–4.408

Contracts for the Sale of Federal Timber, 25318–57

Contribution of the Family to the Economic Support of the Elderly, 1702–1.409

Controlled Foreign Corporations, 1980, 8302–2.410

Convention on International Trade in Endangered Species of Wild Fauna and Flora: Annual Report for 1982, 5504–19

Conventional Home Mortgage Rates, 9312–2

Conversion of the Tariff Schedules of the U.S. Annotated into the Nomenclature Structure of the Harmonized System: Report on Investigation No. 332-131 Under Section 332 of the Tariff Act of 1930, 9886–4.66

Converted Flexible Materials for Packaging and Other Uses, 1983, Current Industrial Report, 2506–7.7

Converted Paper Products, N.E.C. (Industry 2649): 1982 Census of Manufactures. Preliminary Report. Industry Series, 2491–1.152

Conveyors and Conveying Equipment (Industry 3535): 1982 Census of Manufactures. Preliminary Report. Industry Series, 2491–1.320

Cookies and Crackers (Industry 2052): 1982 Census of Manufactures. Preliminary Report. Industry Series, 2491–1.21

Cooperative Grain Trade Opportunities in Eastern Europe, 1128–27

Cooperative Historical Statistics, 1128–30

Cooperative Involvement in Grain Marketing, 1128–31

Cooperative State-Federal Bovine Tuberculosis Eradication Program Statistical Tables of FY83, 1394–13

Cooperative State-Federal Brucellosis Eradication Program, Statistical Tables of FY83, 1394–6

Cooperative Vessel Still Afloat; Losses Slashed, Net Margins Tripled, 1122–1.412

Cooperatives in Federal Milk Order Markets, 1317–4.403

Copper Availability, Market Economy Countries. A Minerals Availability Program Appraisal, 5606–4.11

Copper Controlled Materials, Current Industrial Report, 2506–10.10

Copper in the U.S. and Copper Sulfate: Mineral Industry Surveys, 5612–1.6

Copper: Minerals Yearbook Preprint, Vol. 1, 1983, 5604–15.20

Copper Ores, Lead and Zinc Ores, Gold Ores, and Silver Ores (Industry 1021, 1031, 1041, and 1044): 1982 Census of Mineral Industries. Preliminary Report. Industry Series, 2511–1.2

Copper Rolling and Drawing (Industry 3351): 1982 Census of Manufactures. Preliminary Report. Industry Series, 2491–1.268

Cordage and Twine (Industry 2298): 1982 Census of Manufactures. Preliminary Report. Industry Series, 2491–1.76

Corn and Soybean Fertilizer Use for Alternative Tillage Practices, 1561–16.401

Corn and Soybean Production Losses from Potential Pesticide Regulatory Actions, 1561–16.407

Corporate and Personal Taxation of Capital Income in an Open Economy, 8006–3.51

Corporate Farming: Importance, Incentives, and State Restrictions, 1548–233

Corporate Foreign Tax Credit, 1980: An Industry Focus, 8302–2.415

Corporate Use of Pension Overfunding, 9385–1.406

Corporation Income Tax Returns: Statistics of Income, 1981, 8304–4

Corporation Income Tax Returns, 1981, 8302–2.403

Corporation Source Book of

Corporation Source Book of Statistics of Income, 1981, 8304–4
Corps of Engineers' and Bureau of Reclamation's Recreation Construction Backlogs, 26113–115
Correctional Crisis: Prison Populations and Public Policy, 6068–176
Corrections and the Private Sector, 6066–20.6
Correlates and Consequences of Marijuana Use, 4496–1.31
Corrugated and Solid Fiber Boxes (Industry 2653): 1982 Census of Manufactures. Preliminary Report. Industry Series, 2491–1.155
Cost and Quality of Fuels for Electric Utility Plants, 1983, 3164–42
Cost-Effectiveness Considerations in Corridor Planning and Project Programming, Report 1. Financing Urban Transportation Improvements, 7556–7.1
Cost Effectiveness of Dual Sourcing for Production Price Competition Is Uncertain, 26123–67
Cost Experience of Automated Guideway Transit Systems, Supplement V Costs and Trends for the Period 1976-82, 7884–6
Cost Information on USDA's Tobacco Program, 26113–117
Cost of Clean Air and Water, Report to Congress, 1984, 9184–11
Cost of Owning and Operating Automobiles and Vans, 1984, 7554–21
Cost of Pipeline and Compressor Station Construction Under Non-Budget Pipeline Certificate Authorization For the Years 1979-82, 3084–3
Cost Study of the Small Business Development Center Delivery System and the Small Business Administration's (SBA's) Management Assistance Delivery System, 25728–36
Costs and Benefits of Single-Family Mortgage Revenue Bonds: Preliminary Report, 26113–127
Costs and Effects of Environmental Protection Controls Regulating U.S. Phosphate Rock Mining, 5608–143
Costs and Indexes For Domestic Oil and Gas Field Equipment and Production Operations, 1983, 3164–45
Costs for Developed Recreation Sites In the Northern Region, USDA Forest Service, 1208–202
Costs of Asbestos Litigation, 21348–85
Costs of Government Funded Trips for Invitees To Attend Space Shuttle Launches at Kennedy Space Center, Florida, 26123–78
Costs of Producing and Selling Flue-Cured Tobacco: 1982, Preliminary 1983, and Projected 1984, 1561–10.402
Costs of Producing Burley Tobacco: 1982 and 1983 and Projected 1984, 1561–10.401
Costs of Watermelon Handling from Grower to Retailer, 1308–18
Costume Jewelry (Industry 3961): 1982 Census of Manufactures. Preliminary Report. Industry Series, 2491–1.435
Cotton and Cotton Waste: Quota Information, 8146–1.2
Cotton and Wool Outlook and Situation Report, 1561–1
Cotton Fiber and Processing Test Results, 1309–3

Cotton: Foreign Agriculture Circular, 1925–4
Cotton Ginning Charges, Harvesting Practices, and Selected Marketing Costs, 1983/84 Season, 1564–3
Cotton Ginnings, by Counties, 2342–2
Cotton Ginnings, by States, 2342–1
Cotton Ginnings in the U.S., Crop of 1983, 2344–1
Cotton Manufactures. Agreement Category by Country of Origin and TSUSA Number by Country of Origin: U.S. General Imports, 2046–9.4
Cotton Manufactures. Agreement Category: U.S. General Imports, 2046–9.6
Cotton Manufactures. Agreement Category: U.S. General Imports, 2046–9.5
Cotton Manufactures. Country of Origin by Agreement Category: U.S. General Imports, 2046–9.7
Cotton Price Statistics, 1309–1
Cotton Price Statistics, 1983-84, Vol. 65, No. 13, 1309–2
Cotton Quality: Supply, Disappearance, Carryover, 1983-84, 1309–8
Cotton Quality: Crop of 1983, 1309–7
Cotton Shop Towels from Pakistan: Determination of the Commission in Investigation No. 701-TA-202 (Final) Under the Tariff Act of 1930, Together with the Information Obtained in the Investigation, 9886–15.48
Cotton Varieties Planted, 1984 Crop, 1309–6
Cotton, Wool and Manmade Fiber Textile Products: Quota Information, 8146–1.4
Cotton Yarn from Brazil: Determinations of the Commission in Investigation No. 104-TA-21 Under Section 104(b) of the Trade Agreements Act of 1979, Together with the Information Obtained in the Investigation, 9886–18.14
Cottonseed Oil Mills (Industry 2074): 1982 Census of Manufactures. Preliminary Report. Industry Series, 2491–1.27
Cottonseed Quality, Crop of 1983, 1309–5
Council of State Housing Agencies Response to the General Accounting Office Study "The Costs and Benefits of Mortgage Revenue Bonds: Preliminary Report", 21788–135
Counting Community Capital: The Status of Rural Infrastructure, 1004–16.1
Country Exposure Lending Survey, 13002–1
Country Financial Report: Economic Assistance, 9912–4
Country Market Survey: Agricultural Machinery and Equipment, 2045–13
Country Market Survey: Computers and Peripheral Equipment, 2045–1
Country Market Survey: Electric Power Systems, 2045–15
Country Market Survey: Electronic Components, 2045–4
Country Market Survey: Equipment and Materials for Electronic Components Production, 2045–5
Country Market Survey: Food Processing and Packaging Equipment, 2045–11
Country Market Survey: Graphic Industries Equipment, 2045–3
Country Market Survey: Industrial Process Controls, 2045–6
Country Market Survey: Laboratory Instruments, 2045–10
Country Market Survey: Machine Tools, 2045–9

Titles

Country Market Survey: Medical Equipment, 2045–2
Country Market Survey: Mining Industry Equipment, 2045–16
Country Market Survey: Pollution Control Instrumentation and Equipment, 2045–17
Country Market Survey: Sporting Goods and Recreational Equipment, 2045–14
Country Market Survey: Telecommunications Equipment, 2045–12
Country Reports on Human Rights Practices for 1983, 21384–3
Country Reports on the World Refugee Situation: Report to the Congress for FY85, 7004–15
Country/Regional Profiles, Office of U.S. Foreign Disaster Assistance, 9916–2
Counts of 305-Day Lactation Records Excluded from Genetic Evaluations for 1983, 1702–2.403
County and City Data Book, 1983: A Statistical Abstract Supplement, 2328–1
County and Metropolitan Area Personal Income, 1980-82, 2702–1.413
County Business Patterns, 1981, 2326–8
County Business Patterns, 1982, 2326–6
County Government Employment in 1983, 2466–1.2
County Government Finances in 1981-82, 2466–2.2
County Government Finances in 1982-83, 2466–2.8
CPI Detailed Report, 6762–2
Cranberries: 1984 Production Forecast Up 4 Percent, 1621–18.4
Creamery Butter (Industry 2021): 1982 Census of Manufactures. Preliminary Report. Industry Series, 2491–1.3
Creative Finance: Measures, Sources, and Tests, 9412–2.401
Creative Financing and House Prices: A Study of Capitalization Effects, 9412–2.402
Creative Financing "Concessions" in Residential Sales: Effects and Implications, 9412–2.405
Credit, Banks and Small Business, 21728–52.1
Credit Union Directory, 1984, 9534–6
Crime and Mental Disorder, 6066–20.5
Crime in the U.S., 1983: Uniform Crime Reports, 6224–2
Criminal Defense Systems, 6066–19.8
Criminal Justice Response to Victim Harm, 6068–185
Criminal Victimization in the U.S., 1981, 6066–3.32
Criminal Victimization 1983, 6062–2.405
Crisis in Central America: Economic Problems, Prospects and Proposals, 028–19.2
Crop Price-Support Programs: Policy Options for Contemporary Agriculture, 26306–6.71
Crop Production, 1621–1
Crop Quality Differences and Estimates of Corn for Feed Use, 1561–4.405
Crop Reporting Board Catalog, 1984 Releases, 1614–1
Crop Values, 1981-83, Season Average Prices Received by Farmers and Value of Production, 1621–2
Cropland Use and Supply Outlook and Situation Report, 1584–4
Cross-Hedging Rice Bran and Millfeed, 1561–8.401

Titles

Cross Sections: A Review of Business and Economic Developments Published Quarterly by the Federal Reserve Bank of Richmond, 9389–16

Crowns and Closures (Industry 3466): 1982 Census of Manufactures. Preliminary Report. Industry Series, 2491–1.297

CRR and Excess Reserves: An Early Appraisal, 9385–1.414

Crucial Year for Southeastern Farmers, 9371–1.424

Crude Petroleum and Natural Gas (Industry 1311): 1982 Census of Mineral Industries. Preliminary Report. Industry Series, 2511–1.5

Crushed Stone: Minerals Yearbook Preprint, Vol. 1, 1983, 5604–15.61

Cuban Economy: A Statistical Review, 248–40

Cumulative Report on Rescissions and Deferrals, 102–2

Currency Misalignments: The Case of the Dollar and the Yen, 9385–1.404

Currency Substitution: A Test of Its Importance, 9391–1.418

Currency Substitution, Duality, and Exchange Rate Indeterminancy: An Empirical Analysis of the Venezuelan Experience, 9366–7.98

Current Account of the U.S., Japan, and Germany: A Cyclical Analysis, 9366–7.92

Current Budget Estimates, 104–17

Current Business Reports: Advance Monthly Retail Sales, 2413–2

Current Business Reports: Monthly Retail Trade Sales and Inventories, 2413–3

Current Business Reports: Monthly Wholesale Trade, Sales and Inventories, 2413–7

Current Business Reports: Retail Trade, Annual Sales, Year-End Inventories, and Accounts Receivable, by Kind of Retail Store, 2413–5

Current Business Reports: Wholesale Trade, Annual Sales and Year-End Inventories of Merchant Wholesalers, 2413–13

Current Business Reports: 1983 Retail Trade. Annual Sales, Year-End Inventories, Purchases, Gross Margin, and Accounts Receivable, by Kind of Retail Store, 2413–5

Current Business Reports: 1983 Service Annual Survey, 2413–8

Current Business Reports: 1983 Wholesale Trade. Annual Sales and Year-End Inventories, Purchases, and Gross Margin Estimates of Merchant Wholesalers, 2413–13

Current Federal Aid Research Report: Fish, Spring 1984, 5504–23

Current Federal Aid Research Report: Wildlife, Spring 1984, 5504–24

Current Federal Retirement System, 25408–87

Current Housing Reports. Characteristics of Apartments Completed: 1983, 2484–3

Current Housing Reports. Housing Vacancies: Vacant Housing Units in the U.S., 2482–1

Current Housing Reports. Market Absorption of Apartments, 2482–2

Current Housing Reports. Series H-111: Housing Vacancies: Vacancy Rates and Characteristics of Housing in the U.S., Annual Statistics 1983, 2484–1

Current Housing Reports. Series H-121: Housing Characteristics, 2486–1

Dairy Product Manufacturing

Current Housing Reports. Series H-130: Market Absorption of Apartments, Annual, 1983 Absorptions (Completions in 1982), 2484–2

Current Housing Reports. Annual Housing Survey: 1981. Part B, Indicators of Housing and Neighborhood Quality by Financial Characteristics, 2485–2

Current Housing Reports. Annual Housing Survey: 1981. Part E, Urban and Rural Housing Characteristics, U.S. and Regions, 2485–7

Current Housing Reports. Annual Housing Survey: 1983. Part A: General Housing Characteristics, 2485–1

Current Industrial Reports: All Manufacturing Industries, 2506–3

Current Industrial Reports: Apparel and Leather, 2506–6

Current Industrial Reports: Intermediate Metal Products, 2506–11

Current Industrial Reports: Lumber, Furniture, and Paper Products, 2506–7

Current Industrial Reports: Machinery and Equipment, 2506–12

Current Industrial Reports: Oil, Chemicals, Rubber, and Plastics, 2506–8

Current Industrial Reports: Primary Metals, 2506–10

Current Industrial Reports: Processed Food, 2506–4

Current Industrial Reports: Stone, Clay, and Glass Products, 2506–9

Current Industrial Reports: Textile Mill Products, 2506–5

Current International Trade Position of the U.S., 2042–25

Current Population Reports. Series P-20: Population Characteristics, 2546–1

Current Population Reports. Series P-23: Special Studies, 2546–2

Current Population Reports. Series P-25: Population Estimates and Projections, 2546–3

Current Population Reports. Series P-25: Population Estimates and Projections. Estimates of the Population of Puerto Rico and the Outlying Areas: 1980-83, 2546–3.134

Current Population Reports. Series P-25: Population Estimates and Projections; Estimates of the Population of the U.S. to (Date), 2542–1

Current Population Reports. Series P-26: Local Population Estimates. Estimates of the Population of Counties and Metropolitan Areas: July 1, 1981 and 1982 (Provisional), 2546–4

Current Population Reports. Series P-26: Local Population Estimates. 1982 Population Estimates and 1981 Per Capita Income Estimates for Counties, Incorporated Places, and Selected Minor Civil Divisions, 2546–11

Current Population Reports. Series P-27: Farm Population. Farm Population of the U.S.: 1982, 2544–1

Current Population Reports. Series P-27: Farm Population. Farm Population of the U.S.: 1983, 2544–1

Current Population Reports. Series P-60: Consumer Income, 2546–6

Current Population Reports. Series P-70: Household Economic Studies. Economic Characteristics of Households in the U.S., 2542–2

Current Population Survey: A Historical Perspective and BLS' Role, 6722–1.435

Current Price Developments In the U.S. and Major Foreign Countries, 2042–11

Current Salary Schedules of Federal Officers and Employees Together with a History of Salary and Retirement Annuity Adjustments, 21628–54

Current Status of the Mule Deer on Tiburon Island, Sonora, 1208–197

Current Status of the Natural Resources in the Northwest of Mexico, 1208–197

Current Technical Service Contracts and Grants Active During the Period Oct. 1, 1982 Through Sept. 30, 1983, 9914–7

Current Wage Developments, 6782–1

Current World Fertilizer Situation and Outlook, 1982/83-1992/93, 1004–16.1

Curtailing Indirect Federal Subsidies to the U.S. Postal Service, 26306–6.82

Curtains and Draperies (Industry 2391): 1982 Census of Manufactures. Preliminary Report. Industry Series, 2491–1.103

Customs Collections Quarterly, 8142–1

Customs U.S.A.: A Report on the Activities of the U.S. Customs Service During FY83, 8144–1

Cut Stone and Stone Products (Industry 3281): 1982 Census of Manufactures. Preliminary Report. Industry Series, 2491–1.242

Cut-to-Length Carbon Steel Plate from the Federal Republic of Germany: Determination of the Commission in Investigation No. 731-TA-147 (Preliminary-Remand) Under the Tariff Act of 1930, 9886–14.108

Cutlery (Industry 3421): 1982 Census of Manufactures. Preliminary Report. Industry Series, 2491–1.278

CWEP's Implementation Results to Date Raise Questions About the Administration's Proposed Mandatory Workfare Program, 26131–9

Cyanuric Acid and Its Chlorinated Derivatives from Japan: Determination of the Commission in Investigation No. 731-TA-136 (Final) Under the Tariff Act of 1930, Together with the Information Obtained in the Investigation, 9886–14.102

Cyclical Adjustment of the Federal Budget and Federal Debt, 2702–1.403

Cyclical Adjustment of the Federal Budget and Federal Debt: Detailed Methodology and Estimates, 2706–5.31

Cyclical Productivity and the Returns to Labor: A Vector Autoregressive Analysis, 9381–10.35

Daily Treasury Statement, 8102–4

Dairy and Livestock: Foreign Agriculture Circular. Meat and Dairy Imports, 1925–31

Dairy: ASCS Commodity Fact Sheet, 1806–4.1

Dairy: Foreign Agriculture Circular, 1925–10

Dairy Herd Improvement Letter, 1702–2

Dairy, Livestock and Poultry: Foreign Agriculture Circular, 1925–32

Dairy Market Statistics, 1983 Annual Summary, 1317–1

Dairy Outlook, 1004–16.1

Dairy Outlook and Situation, 1561–2

Dairy Product Manufacturing Costs at Cooperative Plants, 1128–25

Dairy Products

Titles

Dairy Products, 1627–3
Dairy Products (Industry 5143): 1982 Census of Wholesale Trade. Preliminary Report. Industry Series, 2403–1.29
Dairy Products: Quota Information, 8146–1.3
Dairy Products, 1983 Summary, 1627–5
Dairy Program Alternatives for the 1980's, 1568–246
Data Book, Operating Banks and Branches June 30, 1983: Summary of Deposits in All Commercial and Mutual Savings Banks and Domestic Branches of Foreign Banks, 9295–3
Data File User's Manual, High School and Beyond Course Offerings and Course Enrollments Survey (1982), 4826–2.17
Data File User's Manual, High School and Beyond Transcripts Survey (1982), 4826–2.16
Data from the National Health Examination Survey and the National Health and Nutrition Examination Survey. Vital and Health Statistics Series 11, 4147–11
Data from the National Health Interview Survey. Vital and Health Statistics Series 10, 4147–10
Data on Female Veterans, FY83, 9924–24
Data on Health Resources: Manpower and Facilities. Vital and Health Statistics Series 14, 4147–14
Data on Health Resources Utilization. Vital and Health Statistics Series 13, 4147–13
Data on Natality, Marriage, and Divorce. Vital and Health Statistics Series 21, 4147–21
Data on Vietnam Era Veterans, 9924–8
Data User News, 2302–3
Deadly Cold: Health Hazards Due to Cold Weather, 21148–30
Dealing with Deficits—Striking a New Fiscal Balance?, 10042–1.401
Debits and Deposit Turnover at Commercial Banks, 9365–2.5
Debt Collection Action Plans Update, 5004–7
Decline in Competitiveness of the U.S. Copper Industry, 21368–55
Declining City Productivity and the Growth of Rural Regions: A Test of Alternative Explanations, 9387–8.90
Defense Base Act, Annual Statistical Report by District Office, FY83, 6504–5.3
Defense Cataloging and Standardization Act of 1952, Fifty-third Report to Congress, Jan. 1-Sept. 30, 1983, 21204–1
Defense Fuel Supply Center, Annual Historical Summary, FY83, 3904–6
Defense Plans/Reality Mismatch Study: An Update, 21268–36
Defense Research and Development Emphasized in 1985 Budget, 9626–2.146
Defense Waste Management Plan, 3358–32
Defense '84: Almanac, 3504–13
Deficit and the Fiscal and Monetary Policy Mix, 9373–3.27
Deficit Reduction Act of 1984: Provisions Related to the AFDC Program, 4742–1.423
Deficit Reduction Act of 1984: Provisions Related to the Medicare and Medicaid Programs, 4742–1.422
Deficit Reduction Act of 1984: Provisions Related to the OASDI and SSI Programs, 4742–1.421
Deficit-Savings Ratios as Indicators of Interest-Rate Pressure: A Collection of Notes, 9366–7.89

Deficits and Monetary Growth, 9371–1.402
Defined Benefit Plans, 25408–87
Definition and Measurement of Exchange Market Intervention, 9366–1.126
Degree Awards to Women, 4844–9
Dehydrated Fruits, Vegetables, and Soups (Industry 2034): 1982 Census of Manufactures. Preliminary Report. Industry Series, 2491–1.10
Demand Deposit Equity Act of 1983, 21248–83
Democracy in Latin America and the Caribbean, 7008–42
Demographic and Socioeconomic Aspects of Aging in the U.S., 2546–2.125
Demographic Characteristics and Health Care Use and Expenditures by the Aged in the U.S.: 1977-84, 4652–1.420
Demographic Estimates for Countries with a Population of 10 Million or More, 2324–4
Dengue in the U.S., 1982, 4202–7.407
Dental Equipment and Supplies (Industry 3843): 1982 Census of Manufactures. Preliminary Report. Industry Series, 2491–1.420
Dental Malpractice: Baseline Data from Insurance Claims Closed in 1970, with Analysis, 4102–1.416
Dental Record Documentation in Selected Ambulatory Care Facilities, 4102–1.458
Denver Economic Report, 1983, 6974–2
Department of Commerce Office of Inspector General, Semiannual Report to the Congress, Oct. 1, 1983-Mar. 31, 1984, 2002–5
Department of Defense Annual Report to Congress, 3544–2
Department of Defense Budget, FY85: Procurement Programs (P-1), 3504–14
Department of Defense Budget, FY85: R, D, T & E Programs (R-1), 3504–15
Department of Defense Congressional Action on FY84 Appropriation Request, 3504–7
Department of Defense Military Functions, Status of Funds, 3542–3
Department of Defense, Office of Inspector General, Report to the Congress: Audit, Inspection and Investigative Operations for the Six Month Period Oct. 1, 1983-Mar. 31, 1984, 3542–18
Department of Defense Prime Contract Awards By Region and State, FY81-83, 3544–11
Department of Defense Prime Contract Awards, First Half, FY84, 3542–1
Department of Defense Prime Contract Awards in Labor Surplus Areas, FY83, 3542–19
Department of Defense Prime Contract Awards in Labor Surplus Areas, First Half FY84, 3542–19
Department of Defense Program for Research, Development and Acquisition, FY85, 3504–6
Department of Defense Real and Personal Property, Sept. 30, 1983, 3544–6
Department of Defense Selected Medical Care Statistics, 3542–15
Department of Defense Space Programs, 3504–9
Department of Energy Annual Procurement and Federal Assistance Report, FY83, 3004–21
Department of the Treasury News, 8002–7

Department Store Inventory Price Indexes: Jan. 1984, 6762–7
Department Store Inventory Price Indexes: July 1984, 6762–7
Department Stores (Industry 5311): 1982 Census of Retail Trade. Preliminary Report. Industry Series, 2395–1.5
Deposit Insurance, Moral Hazard, and Credit Unions, 9379–1.404
Depository Librarians' Views on GPO's Administration of the Depository Library Program, 26111–19
Deregulated Deposit Rates and Monetary Policy, 9393–8.402
Deregulating Community Development, 5188–105
Deregulation: Is It the End of the "Quiet Life"?, 9302–2.402
Deregulation of Financial Institutions and Its Impact on Small Business Financing, 21728–52
Despite Recession, Companies' Own R&D Funding Rose 13% During 1982, 9626–2.139
Detailed Input-Output Structure of the U.S. Economy, Vol. I: Use and Make of Commodities by Industries, 2708–17.1
Detailed Input-Output Structure of the U.S. Economy, Vol. II: Total Requirements for Commodities and Industries, 2708–17.2
Detailed Input-Output Structure of the U.S. Economy, 1977, 2708–17
Detailed Occupation of the Experienced Civilian Labor Force by Sex for the U.S. and Regions; 1980 and 1970. 1980 Census of Population. Supplementary Report, 2535–1.12
Detailed Population Characteristics. 1980 Census of Population, Vol. 1. Characteristics of the Population, Chapter D, 2531–4
Determinants of Monetary Policy in France, The Federal Republic of Germany, Italy and the UK: A Comparative Analysis, 9373–3.26
Determinants of Physician Assignment Rates by Type of Service, 4652–1.416
Determinants of Stock Savings and Loan Value, 9316–2.46
Determination of Front-End Fees on Syndicated Eurocurrency Credits, 9366–7.105
Developing a Regulatory Bureaucracy: The Office of Surface Mining Reclamation and Enforcement, 6068–177
Development and Design of Private Employer Pensions, 25408–89
Development and Evaluation of a Community Cancer Resource Directory, 4102–1.459
Development Coordination Committee, 1983 Annual Report of the Chairman, 9904–1
Development Issues: U.S. Actions Affecting Developing Countries, 9904–1.1
Development of Alternative Technologies for Quarantine Treatment of Fruits and Vegetables, 21168–29
Development of Corporate Incentive Programs for Motivating Safety Belt Use: A Review, 7762–9.409
Development of Terminal-Based EFT Delivery Systems in the Eighties, 9312–1.409
Development Report, FY83: Overseas Private Investment Corporation, 9904–3
Developments in Aging: 1983, 25144–3
Developments in Europe, September 1983, 21388–42

Titles

Developments in Farm to Retail Price Spreads for Food Products, 1544–9

Diabetes Mellitus Interagency Coordinating Committee, 10th Annual Report, FY83, 4434–8

Diabetes Mellitus Interagency Coordinating Committee, 11th Annual Report, FY84, 4434–8

Diagnosis-Related Groups Using Data from the National Hospital Discharge Survey: U.S., 1981, 4146–8.98

Diatomite: Minerals Yearbook Preprint, Vol. 1, 1983, 5604–15.21

Did Financial Markets in 1983 Point to Recession?, 9385–1.410

Did Usury Ceilings Hold Down Auto Sales?, 9375–1.409

Die-Cut Paper and Board (Industry 2645): 1982 Census of Manufactures. Preliminary Report. Industry Series, 2491–1.148

Differences Among Black, Hispanic, and White People in Knowledge About Long-Term Care Services, 4652–1.406

Differences Between Operating and Net Financial Results With Emphasis on the Relationship Between Operating Profit Margin and Corporate Rate of Return, System Majors, 1972-83, 9144–37

Differences Between the 9-City and 12-City Broiler Price Reports, 1561–7.404

Diffusion and the Changing Geographic Distribution of Primary Care Physicians, 4118–52

Digest of Education Statistics, 1983-84, 4824–2

Digestive Diseases Coordinating Committee, Fourth Annual Report, FY81, 4434–13

Digestive Diseases Coordinating Committee, Fifth Annual Report, FY82, 4434–13

Digestive Diseases Interagency Coordinating Committee, Sixth Annual Report, FY83, 4434–13

Dimension Stone: Minerals Yearbook Preprint, Vol. 1, 1983, 5604–15.61

Dimension Stone, 1983: Mineral Industry Surveys Annual Advance Summary, 5614–5.6

Direct Selling Establishments (Industry 5963): 1982 Census of Retail Trade. Preliminary Report. Industry Series, 2395–1.35

Directory of Commodity Assignments, 9888–12

Directory of Computer Software, 1984, 2224–2

Directory of Computerized Data Files, 1982, 2224–3

Directory of Computerized Data Files, 1984, 2224–3

Directory of Data Files, 2302–5

Directory of ERIC Microfiche Collection, 4914–3

Directory of ERIC Microfiche Collections, 4918–14

Directory of Federal Technology Resources, 1984, 2224–4

Directory of National Trade Associations, Professional Societies, and Labor Unions of the Construction and Building Materials Industries, 2012–1.405

Directory of Psychology Staffing and Services, 1984, 9924–10

Disability and Death Pension Data, 9922–12

Disability Compensation Data, 9922–9

Disabled Veterans and Their Usage of VA Programs, 9926–4.6

Disabled Women in America, 16598–4

Disabled-Worker Projections for OASDI Cost Estimates, 1984, 4706–1.93

Discouraged Workers: How Strong Are Their Links to the Job Market?, 6722–1.449

Discovery To Make Maiden Flight on Mission 41-D, 9506–2.119

Discovery To Make Maiden Flight on STS 41-D, 9506–2.118

Discovery's Second Mission Scheduled, 9506–2.121

Discriminant Analysis of S&L Accounting Profits: 1976-81, 9316–2.47

Disease Staging: Implications for Hospital Reimbursement and Management, 4652–1.425

Dismantling of the Bureau of Alcohol, Tobacco and Firearms, 21528–55

Disorder in Our Public Schools, 4808–12

Distilled Spirits: Statistical Release, 8486–1.3

Distributing Acid Rain Mitigation Costs: Analysis of a Three-Mill User Fee on Fossil Fuel Electricity Generation, 21368–52

Distribution and Quantitative Assessment of World Crude-Oil Reserves and Resources, 5668–72

Distribution of Employment Growth in Nine Kentucky Counties: A Case Study, 1598–194

Distribution of Loans by Six Specified Types, By Race or Ethnic Group, 1182–5

Distribution of Personnel by State and by Selected Locations, Sept. 30, 1983, 3544–7

Distribution of Psychiatric Beds, U.S. and Each State, 1982, 4506–3.14

Distribution of Waterfowl Species Harvested in States and Counties During 1971-80 Hunting Seasons, 5508–18

Distributional Assessment of Rhode Island's Catastrophic Health Insurance Plan (CHIP), 4652–1.423

Distributors of TVA Power: Statistics, FY79-83, 9804–19

District Court Executive Pilot Program: A Report on the Preliminary Experience in Five Federal Courts, 18408–25

District Data Highlights, Federal Home Loan Bank of Dallas, 9302–13

District of Columbia Workmen's Compensation Act, Annual Statistical Report, FY83, 6504–5.6

Division of Hatcheries and Fishery Resources Management, Annual Report, FY82 Statistical Appendix, 5504–9

Division of Research Resources, Annual Report, FY83, 4434–12

Divorce Process: Developing Educational Programs for Individuals and Families, 1004–16.1

Do Macroeconomic Policy Decisions Affect the Private Sector Ex Ante?—The EEC Experience with Crowding Out, 9373–3.26

Do We Want Large Social Security Surpluses?, 9373–1.414

Doctoral Scientists and Engineers Working in Energy-Related Activities, 3004–2

DOD Justification of Aircraft for Noncombat Missions, 21408–76

DOD Needs To Provide More Credible Weapon Systems Cost Estimates to the Congress, 26123–62

DoDDS First Grade School Readiness Testing Program: Summary of Results, School Year 1983/84, 3504–18

Drug Abuse Prevention,

Does Higher Inflation Lead to More Uncertain Inflation?, 9391–1.406

Dog, Cat, and Other Pet Food (Industry 2047): 1982 Census of Manufactures. Preliminary Report. Industry Series, 2491–1.18

Doing Business with China, 2048–72

Doing Business with Panama, 2046–6.6

Dollar Intervention and the Deutschemark-Dollar Exchange Rate: A Daily Time-Series Model, 9377–9.12

Dollar Value of U.S. R&D Expenditures Overseas Declined in 1982, 9626–2.131

Dolls (Industry 3942): 1982 Census of Manufactures. Preliminary Report. Industry Series, 2491–1.428

Domestic Cotton Outlook, 1004–16.1

Domestic Freight Yields and Traffic, Major and All-Cargo Groups, 9142–35

Domestic Natural Gas Reserves and Production Dedicated to Interstate Pipeline Companies, 1983, 3162–4.405

Domestic Natural Gas Reserves and Production Dedicated to Interstate Pipeline Companies, 1983 (Preliminary Data Report), 3164–33

Domestic Saving, Current Accounts, and International Capital Mobility, 9366–7.100

Domestic Soybean Outlook, 1004–16.1

Domestic Steel Industry and the Antitrust Laws, 25528–94

Donation of Federal Surplus Personal Property, 9454–22

Donovan Allocates $47 Million for Indian, Native American Training Programs, 6408–57

Donovan Allocates $58 Million for Migrant/Seasonal Farmworker Programs, 6408–64

Donovan Allots $3 Billion To Train 1 Million Jobless for Work, 6408–58

Donovan Announces Allocation of $317 Million for 62,000 Older Worker Jobs, 6408–60

Donovan Grants $6.8 Million To Aid 4,300 Jobless Dislocated Workers, 6408–61

Donovan Salutes Progress of Job Training Act: 500,000 Trainees in First 6 Months of Operations, 6408–63

DOT Employment Facts, FY83, 7304–18

Drapery Hardware and Blinds and Shades (Industry 2591): 1982 Census of Manufactures. Preliminary Report. Industry Series, 2491–1.139

Dried Prune Situation, 1925–34.435

Dried Salted Codfish from Canada: Determination of the Commission in Investigation No. 731-TA-199 (Preliminary) Under the Tariff Act of 1930, Together with the Information Obtained in the Investigation, 9886–14.115

Drilling and Production Under Title I of the Natural Gas Policy Act, 3168–90

Drinking Places (Alcoholic Beverages) (Industry 5813): 1982 Census of Retail Trade. Preliminary Report. Industry Series, 2395–1.25

Driver License Administration Requirements and Fees: Status as of Jan. 1, 1984, 7554–18

Drivers Licenses, 1982, 7554–16

Drug Abuse Prevention, Treatment, and Rehabilitation, FY82: Annual Report from the Secretary of Health and Human Services to the President and Congress, 4004–26

Drug and Proprietary Stores

Drug and Proprietary Stores (Industry 5912): 1982 Census of Retail Trade. Preliminary Report. Industry Series, 2395–1.26

Drug Use and Pretrial Crime in the District of Columbia, 6066–20.7

Drug Utilization in the U.S., 1982, 4064–12

Drugs, Drug Proprietaries, and Druggists' Sundries (Industry 5122): 1982 Census of Wholesale Trade. Preliminary Report. Industry Series, 2403–1.22

Dually Entitled Elderly Medicare and Medicaid Population Living in the Community, 4652–1.433

Duck Stamp Data, 5504–25

Dungeness Crab Leg Loss in the Columbia River Estuary, 2162–1.403

Dutch Disease or Monetarist Medicine?: The British Economy Under Mrs. Thatcher, 9391–1.414

Dynamic Adjustment in Money Demand, 9393–8.404

Dynamic Corn Sector Adjustments to Changes in Selected Supply and Demand Variables, 1561–4.404

Dynamics of Growth and Change in the Health-Care Industry, 9371–1.425

Early Look at the Volatility of Money and Interest Rates under CRR, 9391–1.422

Earned Degrees Conferred, 4844–5

Earnings Differences Between Men and Women: An Introductory Note, 6722–1.436

Earnings in 1981 of Married-Couple Families, by Selected Characteristics of Husbands and Wives, 2546–2.120

Earnings of FSLIC-Insured Institutions: Second Half, 1983, 9312–6

Earnings of Workers and Their Families, 6742–19

Earth and Water Resources and Hazards in Central America, 5668–71

Earth Resources: A Continuing Bibliography with Indexes, 9502–7

Earthquakes in the U.S., 5662–4

East Asia Markets Promising, 1522–1.406

East Asia: Outlook and Situation Report, 1524–4.2

East-West Trade Statistics Monitoring System: Third Annual Analysis of Manufactured Imports from the NME's and the World, 9882–2.403

Eastern Europe: Agricultural Production and Trade Prospects Through 1990, 1528–178

Eastern Europe: Outlook and Situation Report, 1524–4.7

Eastern North Pacific Tropical Cyclones, 1983, 2152–8.402

Eastern North Pacific Tropical Storms and Hurricanes, 1983, Annual Data and Verification Tabulation, 2184–8

EC Grains, Oilseeds, and Livestock: Selected Statistics, 1960-80, 1528–173

Ecological Characterization of the Mississippi Deltaic Plain Region: A Narrative with Management Recommendations, 5506–4.2

Ecological Profiles of Selected Estuaries, 5506–7

Ecology: Coastal Community Profiles, 5506–9

Ecology of Albemarle Sound, North Carolina: An Estuarine Profile, 5506–7.1

Ecology of Bottomland Hardwood Swamps of the Southeast: A Community Profile, 5506–9.5

Ecology of Estuarine Channels of the Pacific Northwest Coast: A Community Profile, 5506–9.12

Ecology of Intertidal Flats of North Carolina: A Community Profile, 5506–9.1

Ecology of Intertidal Oyster Reefs of the South Atlantic Coast: A Community Profile, 5506–9.2

Ecology of New England High Salt Marshes: A Community Profile, 5506–9.6

Ecology of New England Tidal Flats: A Community Profile, 5506–9.4

Ecology of Pacific Northwest Coastal Sand Dunes: A Community Profile, 5506–9.14

Ecology of Petroleum Platforms in the Northwestern Gulf of Mexico: A Community Profile, 5506–9.7

Ecology of San Francisco Bay Tidal Marshes: A Community Profile, 5506–9.10

Ecology of Southeastern Shrub Bogs (Pocosins) and Carolina Bays: A Community Profile, 5506–9.9

Ecology of the Mangroves of South Florida: A Community Profile, 5506–9.3

Ecology of the Seagrasses of South Florida: A Community Profile, 5506–9.8

Ecology of Tidal Freshwater Marshes of the U.S. East Coast: A Community Profile, 5506–9.13

Ecology of Tidal Marshes of the Pacific Northwest Coast: A Community Profile, 5506–9.11

Econometric Models and the Study of the Economic Effects of Social Security, 4742–1.419

Economic Analysis of Taxicab Regulation, 9406–1.37

Economic and Budget Outlook: An Update, 26304–3.4

Economic and Energy Indicators, 242–4

Economic and Housing Indicators, Eleventh District, Federal Home Loan Bank of San Francisco, 9302–18

Economic Appraisal of Sail-Assisted Commercial Fishing Vessels in Hawaiian Waters, 2162–1.401

Economic Censuses of Outlying Areas, 1982. Virgin Islands of the U.S., 2593–1

Economic Characteristics of Households in the U.S. Current Population Reports. Series P-70. Household Economic Studies, 2542–2

Economic Cost of Crime to Victims, 6066–19.6

Economic Cost to Society of Motor Vehicle Accidents, 7768–80

Economic Crisis in Mexico, 21248–82

Economic, Demographic and Related Tax Statistics: Districts, Regions, and Service Centers, 1983 Update, 8304–8

Economic Development Administration, 1983 Annual Report, 2064–2

Economic Effects of Cargo Preference Laws, 26117–30

Economic Effects of Levying a User Charge on Foreign and Domestic Commerce To Finance Harbor Maintenance, 21568–34

Economic Estimates of Urban Infrastructure Needs, 9377–9.9

Economic Growth: How Much Is Too Much?, 9373–1.402

Economic Growth of OECD Countries, 1973-83, 7144–8

Economic Impacts of Increased Price Variability: A Case Study with Rice, 1502–3.404

Titles

Economic Impacts of the Avian Influenza Outbreak, 1561–7.402

Economic Impacts of the Fort Union Coal Project on Farms and Ranches, Montana and North Dakota, 1588–79

Economic Implications of Alternative Home Financing, 9412–2.406

Economic Indicators, 23842–1

Economic Indicators of the Farm Sector: Costs of Production, 1983, 1544–20

Economic Indicators of the Farm Sector: Farm Sector Review, 1983, 1544–19

Economic Indicators of the Farm Sector: Income and Balance Sheet Statistics, 1983, 1544–16

Economic Indicators of the Farm Sector: Production and Efficiency Statistics, 1982, 1544–17

Economic Indicators of the Farm Sector: State Income and Balance Sheet Statistics, 1982, 1544–18

Economic Influence of Retirees on Selected Southeastern Communities, 9371–1.420

Economic Issues of a Changing Telecommunications Industry, 23848–176

Economic Outlook. A Report to the Senate and House Committees on the Budget, Part I, 26304–3.1

Economic Outlook for Families, 1984, 1004–16.1

Economic Outlook for Families, 1984, 1702–1.404

Economic Outlook for Fifth District States in 1984: Forecasts from Vector Autoregression Models, 9389–1.403

Economic Outlook for the 1990's: Three Scenarios for Economic Growth, 6728–29

Economic Perspectives: Federal Reserve Bank of Chicago, 9375–1

Economic Potential for Utilizing Minced Fish in Cooked Sausage Products, 2162–1.401

Economic Profile of the Dallas/Fort Worth Metropolitan Area, 1983, 6964–2

Economic Profile of the Houston Metropolitan Area, 1983, 6964–1

Economic Projections for OASDI Cost Estimates, 1983, 4706–1.90

Economic Prosperity: An Eclectic View, 9383–2

Economic Recovery and Jobs in the Seventh District, 9375–1.408

Economic Report of the President, Transmitted to the Congress Feb. 1984, 204–1

Economic Report of the President, 1984, 23844–4

Economic Reports of the Federal Trade Commission, 9406–1

Economic Research Reports, 2626–7

Economic Research Service Accomplishments in 1983, 1504–7

Economic Research Service in 1984, 1504–6

Economic Review, Federal Reserve Bank of Atlanta, 9371–1

Economic Review, Federal Reserve Bank of Cleveland, 9377–1

Economic Review, Federal Reserve Bank of Dallas, 9379–1

Economic Review, Federal Reserve Bank of Kansas City, 9381–1

Economic Review, Federal Reserve Bank of Richmond, 9389–1

Economic Review, Federal Reserve Bank of San Francisco, 9393–8

Titles

Economic Support Fund Assistance to the Philippines, 26123–54

Economic Trends, Federal Reserve Bank of Cleveland, 9377–10

Economic Upheaval in the Midwest, 9375–1.402

Economic Uses of the National Wildlife Refuge System Unlikely To Increase Significantly, 26113–128

Economic Well-Being of Farms: Annual Report to Congress on the Status of Family Farms, 1504–4

Economics of Firm Size: Implications from Labor-Market Studies, 9393–8.403

Economics of Large Government Deficits, 9373–3.27

Economics of Natural Gas Deregulation, 23848–177

Economics of Nuclear Power: Past Record, Present Trends, and Future Prospects, 3006–7.5

Economy, 1004–16.1

Economy and the Federal Budget: Guides to the Automatic Effects, 2702–1.427

Economy Improves; Bargaining Problems Persist in 1983, 6722–1.403

Education and Income Characteristics of Male War Veterans and Nonveterans, Mar. 1982, 9924–19

Education Directory, Colleges and Universities, 1983-84, 4844–3

Education for All Handicapped Children Act: Sixth Annual Report to Congress on the Implementation of Public Law 94-142, 4944–4

Educational and Nonprofit Institutions Receiving Prime Contract Awards for Research, Development, Test, and Evaluation, FY83, 3544–17

Educational Attainment in the U.S.: Mar. 1981 and 1980, 2546–1.390

Educational Attainment of Workers, Mar. 1982-83, 6746–1.251

Educational Inventory: Where Does the Southeast Stand?, 9371–1.428

Educational Programs for Other Cultured Families, 1004–16.1

Effect of Changes in the Cap on U.S. Agricultural Trade, 1004–16.1

Effect of Government Targeting on World Semiconductor Competition: A Case History of Japanese Industrial Strategy and Its Costs for America, 21368–46.1

Effect of Illinois and Wisconsin Usuary Laws on the Supply and Quality of Mortgage Credit Offered, 9312–7.404

Effect of Interest Rates on Mortgage Prepayments, 9306–1.6

Effect of the AML Index on the Borrower, 9312–7.403

Effect of the Head Start Program on Children's Cognitive Development, Preliminary Report, 4608–20

Effect of U.S. Coal Exports on Domestic Economic Growth and on U.S. National Security, 3008–97

Effect of Water Meters on Water Use, 5188–109.2

Effect of Water Pressure on Water Use, 5188–109.3

Effective Income Tax Rates for Farm Capital, 1950-84, 1548–231

Effectiveness of Mental Health Clinical Training Programs Cannot Be Evaluated, 26121–86

Electronic Connectors

Effects of Deficits on Prices of Financial Assets: Theory and Evidence, 8008–111

Effects of Delaying the Operation of a Nuclear Power Plant, 9638–53

Effects of Exchange Rate Uncertainty on German and U.S. Trade, 9385–1.405

Effects of Exchange Rate Variability on International Trade and Other Economic Variables: A Review of the Literature, 9366–1.129

Effects of Exchange Rate Variability on Output and Employment, 9366–7.97

Effects of Fiscal Policy on the U.S. Economy, 9366–1.134

Effects of Foreign Product Counterfeiting on U.S. Industry: Final Report on Investigation No. 332-158 Under Section 332(b) of the Tariff Act of 1930, 9886–4.67

Effects of Import Quotas on the Steel Industry, 26306–6.80

Effects of Natural Gas Decontrol on Farming Costs and Income, 1548–240

Effects of New Competition in Local Markets: Fourth District Evidence, 9312–1.401

Effects of OASDI Benefit Increase, Dec. 1983, 4742–1.407

Effects of Oil Prices and Exchange Rates on World Oil Consumption, 9379–1.405

Effects of Relaxing Automobile Emission Standards: A Generic Analysis and an Urban Case Study, 3408–31

Effects of Simulated Changes in Consumer Preference on the Meat and Poultry Industries, 1502–3.402

Effects of Strong Dollar, Economic Recovery Apparent in First-Half Import and Export Prices, 6722–1.459

Effects of the Omnibus Budget Reconciliation Act of 1981 (OBRA) Welfare Changes and the Recession on Poverty, 21788–139

Effects of Usury Ceilings: The Economic Evidence, 9375–13.1

Efficacy of the Federal Drug Abuse Control Strategy: State and Local Perspectives, 21968–27

Efficiency of the Treasury Bill Futures Market: Some Alternative Test Results, 9316–1.105

Efforts To Prevent Fraud, Waste and Mismanagement, a Progress Report to the President, First Six Months FY84, 102–5

Egg Filler Flats from Canada: Determination of the Commission in Investigation No. 731-TA-201 (Preliminary) Under the Tariff Act of 1930, Together with the Information Obtained in the Investigation, 9886–14.119

Egg Products, 1625–2

Eggs, Chickens, and Turkeys, 1625–1

Eighth Annual FAA Forecast Conference Proceedings, 7504–28

El Nino-Southern Oscillation Episode of 1982-83, 2152–8.402

El Salvador: Revolution or Reform?, 7008–39

Elasticity of Substitution and Land Use in Agricultural Production: A Cause for Optimism?, 1502–3.403

Electric and Gas Utilities, Oct. 1982, Industry Wage Survey, 6787–6.205

Electric and Hybrid Vehicles Program, Seventh Annual Report to Congress for FY83, 3304–2

Electric Current Abroad 1984 Edition, 2018–8

Electric Housewares and Fans (Industry 3634): 1982 Census of Manufactures. Preliminary Report. Industry Series, 2491–1.366

Electric Housewares and Fans, 1983, Current Industrial Report, 2506–12.15

Electric Lamps (Industry 3641): 1982 Census of Manufactures. Preliminary Report. Industry Series, 2491–1.370

Electric Lamps, Current Industrial Report, 2506–12.13

Electric Lighting Fixtures, 1983, Current Industrial Report, 2506–12.19

Electric Power Annual, 1983, 3164–11

Electric Power Machinery and Equipment, TSUS Items 682(pt.), 686(pt.), and 688(pt.): Summary of Trade and Tariff Information, 9885–6.62

Electric Power Monthly, 3162–35

Electric Power Quarterly, 3162–39

Electric Power Supply and Demand for the Contiguous U.S., 1984-93: Staff Report, 3404–6

Electric Power Systems: Country Market Survey, 2045–15

Electric Railroads and Trolley Systems: Past, Present, and Future, 3006–7.7

Electrical Apparatus and Equipment (Industry 5063): 1982 Census of Wholesale Trade. Preliminary Report. Industry Series, 2403–1.8

Electrical Appliances, Television and Radio Sets (Industry 5064): 1982 Census of Wholesale Trade. Preliminary Report. Industry Series, 2403–1.9

Electrical Industrial Apparatus, N.E.C. (Industry 3629): 1982 Census of Manufactures. Preliminary Report. Industry Series, 2491–1.362

Electrical Work Special Trade Contractors (Industry 1731): 1982 Census of Construction Industries. Preliminary Report. Industry Series, 2371–1.12

Electrical Work Special Trade Contractors, Industry 1731. 1982 Census of Construction Industries. Industry Series, 2373–1.12

Electricity Exchanges Across International Borders, 1983, 3104–10

Electricity, Gas, and Liquid Supply and Production Meters, TSUS Items 713(pt.): Summary of Trade and Tariff Information, 9885–7.63

Electricity Sales Statistics, 9802–1

Electricity Sales Statistics, 1983, 9804–14

Electrometallurgical Products (Industry 3313): 1982 Census of Manufactures. Preliminary Report. Industry Series, 2491–1.251

Electron Tubes, All Types (Industry 3671): 1982 Census of Manufactures. Preliminary Report. Industry Series, 2491–1.381

Electronic Capacitors (Industry 3675): 1982 Census of Manufactures. Preliminary Report. Industry Series, 2491–1.383

Electronic Coils and Transformers (Industry 3677): 1982 Census of Manufactures. Preliminary Report. Industry Series, 2491–1.385

Electronic Components: Country Market Survey, 2045–4

Electronic Components, N.E.C. (Industry 3679): 1982 Census of Manufactures. Preliminary Report. Industry Series, 2491–1.387

Electronic Computing Equipment (Industry 3573): 1982 Census of Manufactures. Preliminary Report. Industry Series, 2491–1.345

Electronic Connectors (Industry 3678): 1982 Census of Manufactures. Preliminary Report. Industry Series, 2491–1.386

Electronic Fetal Monitoring

Electronic Fetal Monitoring in Relation to Cesarean Section Delivery, for Live Births and Stillbirths in the U.S., 1980, 4102–1.424

Electronic Fund Transfer and Crime, 6066–19.3

Electronic Marketing Developments, 1004–16.1

Elevators and Moving Stairways (Industry 3534): 1982 Census of Manufactures. Preliminary Report. Industry Series, 2491–1.319

Eleventh Annual Report of the Diabetes Mellitus Interagency Coordinating Committee, FY84, 4434–8

Eleventh Report of the National Heart, Lung, and Blood Advisory Council, 4474–11

Eliminating Fraud, Waste and Abuse in the Federal Government, A Progress Report to the President, FY83, Second Six Months, 102–5

Emergency Conservation Program, FY83 Summary, 1804–22

Empirical Comparisons of Credit and Monetary Aggregates Using Vector Autoregressive Methods, 9389–1.402

Empirical Estimates of Investment in Employment, Inventories of Finished Goods and Unfilled Orders, 9387–8.80

Empirical Yields of Timber and Forest Biomass in the Southeast, 1208–199

Employee Benefits and the Tax Base, 9373–1.404

Employee Benefits in Medium and Large Firms, 1983, 6784–19

Employee Retirement Income Security Act, 1982 Report to Congress, 6464–4

Employer Attitudes Toward Health Maintenance Organizations, 4108–32

Employment and Earnings, 6742–2

Employment and Training Report of the President, 6404–2

Employment and Unemployment: Area Trends, 6402–1

Employment and Unemployment Improvements Widespread in 1983, 6722–1.409

Employment and Wages, Annual Average 1981, 6744–16

Employment and Wages, Annual Averages 1982, 6744–16

Employment Characteristics of Mothers During Pregnancy, 4144–11.1

Employment Cost Index, 6782–5

Employment Data on Title 38 Physicians, Dentists and Nurses, 9922–11

Employment, Hours, and Earnings, States and Areas, 1939-82, 6744–5

Employment, Hours, and Earnings, States and Areas, Data for 1980-83, Supplement, 6744–5.3

Employment, Hours, and Earnings, States and Areas, 1939-82. Vol. I: Alabama-Nevada, 6744–5.1

Employment, Hours, and Earnings, States and Areas, 1939-82. Vol. II: New Hampshire-Wyoming, 6744–5.2

Employment Impacts of Acid Rain, 21368–52

Employment in Durable Goods Anything but Durable in 1979-82, 6722–1.410

Employment in Perspective: Minority Workers, 6742–18

Employment in Perspective: Working Women, 6742–17

Employment in the First Half: Robust Recovery Continues, 6722–1.448

Employment of Major Local Governments, 1982 Census of Governments, 2455–1

Employment Outlook for 1984 New England College Graduates, 6916–7.3

Employment Projections for 1995, 6728–29

Employment Security Administration Account, Statement of Receipts and Expenditures, 8102–9.1

Employment Shift to Services: Where Did It Come From?, 6722–1.425

Employment Situation, 6742–5

Employment Situation for New York-Northeastern New Jersey, 6922–4

Employment Trends in St. Louis: 1954-82, 9391–1.405

Employment-Unemployment, Monthly Hearings, 23846–4

Encouraging High-Technology Development, Background Paper No. 2., 26358 107.3

End-Stage Renal Disease Annual Report to Congress, 4654–7

End-Stage Renal Disease: A Profile of Facilities Furnishing Treatment, 4652–1.434

End Uses of Sulfur and Sulfuric Acid, 1983: Mineral Industry Surveys Annual Advance Summary, 5614–5.7

Energy: A Continuing Bibliography with Indexes, 9502–4

Energy Abstracts for Policy Analysis, 3002–2

Energy Activity and Its Impact Upon the Economy: A Technical Report in Support of the National Energy Policy Plan, 3004–13.3

Energy and Irrigation, 1561–16.406

Energy and the Aged: The Impact of Natural Gas Deregulation, 25148–26

Energy Conservation Indicators, Annual Report, 3304–19

Energy Conservation Indicators Annual Report, 3164–73

Energy Conservation Indicators, 1983 Annual Report, 3164–73.3

Energy Information Administration Annual Report to Congress, 1983, 3164–29

Energy-Related Manpower, 1983, 3004–19

Energy Use and Conservation in the Construction Materials Industries, 2012–1.401

Enforcement Activity: General Aviation, 7504–25

Engine Electrical Equipment (Industry 3694): 1982 Census of Manufactures. Preliminary Report. Industry Series, 2491–1.391

Engineering and Scientific Instruments (Industry 3811): 1982 Census of Manufactures. Preliminary Report. Industry Series, 2491–1.411

Engineering, Architectural, and Surveying Services (Industry 891): 1982 Census of Service Industries. Preliminary Report. Industry Series, 2390–2.18

Engraving and Plate Printing (Industry 2753): 1982 Census of Manufactures. Preliminary Report. Industry Series, 2491–1.165

Enhancing Governmental Productivity Through Competition: Targeting for Annual Savings of One Billion Dollars by 1988, 108–39

Enterprise Zone Activity in the States: Summary of Survey Findings, 21788–140.1

Envelopes (Industry 2642): 1982 Census of Manufactures. Preliminary Report. Industry Series, 2491–1.146

Environment, Safety, Health at DOE Facilities, 3404–4

Environment, Safety, Health at DOE Facilities, 1982, 3004–24

Environmental Cancer and Heart and Lung Disease, Sixth Annual Report to Congress, 9184–9

Environmental Controls (Industry 3822): 1982 Census of Manufactures. Preliminary Report. Industry Series, 2491–1.412

Environmental Impact of Multilateral Development Bank-Funded Projects, 21248–80

Environmental Implications of Solar and Biomass Energy Growth, 3408–30

Environmental Levels of PCB in Great Lakes Fish, 9208–126

Environmental Management Reports, 9184–15

Environmental Progress and Challenges: An EPA Perspective, 9184–16

Environmental Protection in the Federal Coal Leasing Program, 26358–103

Environmental Quality Profile: Region 7, 9184–13

Environmental Quality 1983: 14th Annual Report of the Council on Environmental Quality, 484–1

Environmental Radiation Data, 9232–2

Environmental Surveillance for the INEL Radioactive Waste Management Complex and Other Areas, Annual Report, 1983, 3354–10

EPA Economic Dislocation Early Warning System, Quarterly Summary Report, 9182–6

EPA Publications Bibliography, Quarterly Abstract Bulletin, 9182–5

EPA Radon and Radionuclide Emission Standards, 21208–17

Ephemeris of the Sun, Polaris and Other Selected Stars, With Companion Data and Tables, 1984, 5724–7

Epidemic of Gynecomastia Among Illegal Haitian Entrants, 4102–1.451

Epidemiologic, Clinical, and Laboratory Features of Coxsackie B1-B5 Infections in the U.S., 1970-79, 4102–1.452

Epidemiologic Investigation of Health Effects in Air Force Personnel Following Exposure to Herbicides, Baseline Morbidity Study Results, 3604–3

Epidemiology and Health Service Resource Allocation Policy for Alcohol, Drug Abuse, and Mental Disorders, 4102–1.449

Epidemiology, Health Policy, and Resource Allocation: The Israeli Perspective, 4102–1.446

Epidemiology of Cancer and the Delivery of Medical Care Services, 4102–1.448

Epidemiology of End Stage Renal Disease and Implications for Public Policy, 4102–1.450

Epidemiology of Haemophilus Influenzae Type B Disease Among Navajo Indians, 4102–1.441

Equal Employment Opportunity Commission and Hispanics: An Analysis of the Equal Employment Opportunity Commission's Services to Hispanics in the U.S., 9248–18

Equal Employment Opportunity Program Affirmative Action Plan for Minorities and Women, FY83 Annual Update, 9804–17

Equal Employment Opportunity Statistics, 9844–27

Titles

FAA Approves $247 Million

Equal Employment Opportunity Trend Report, Prepared by State, Station Class, Job Category, and Year, 9284–16

Equalizing Regional Differences in Wages: A Study of Wages and Migration in the South and Other Regions, 9389–1.406

Equipment and Materials for Electronic Components Production: Country Market Survey, 2045–5

Equipment Rental and Leasing Services (Industry 7394): 1982 Census of Service Industries. Preliminary Report. Industry Series, 2390–2.8

ERISA—The First Decade: Was the Legislation Consistent with Other National Goals?, 9373–1.419

Errata: National Income and Product Accounts, 2702–1.426

Estimated Effect of Eliminating TVA Electricity Demand Charges On the Price of Enriched Uranium, 26113–114

Estimated Expenditures for States and Selected Areas, FY85, 3544–23

Estimated Historic Time Series for the EIA-782, 3162–11.401

Estimated Potato Stocks, 1621–10

Estimates of Federal Tax Expenditures for FY84-89, 21784–10

Estimates of Losses from Short Puts, 9316–1.102

Estimates of Poverty Including the Value of Noncash Benefits: 1979 to 1982, 2626–2.50

Estimates of Poverty Including the Value of Noncash Benefits: 1983, 2626–2.52

Estimates of the Population of Counties and Metropolitan Areas: July 1, 1981, and 1982 (Provisional). Current Population Reports. Series P-26. Local Population Estimates, 2546–4

Estimates of the Population of Puerto Rico and the Outlying Areas: 1970-82, 2546–3.127

Estimates of the Population of Puerto Rico and the Outlying Areas: 1980-83. Current Population Reports. Series P-25. Population Estimates and Projections, 2546–3.134

Estimates of the Population of States, by Age: July 1, 1981, to 1983, 2546–3.131

Estimates of the Population of States: July 1, 1981 to 1983 (Advance Report), 2546–3.128

Estimates of the Population of States: 1970-83. Current Population Reports. Series P-25. Population Estimates and Projections, 2546–3.133

Estimates of the Population of the U.S., by Age, Sex, and Race: 1980-83, 2546–3.130

Estimates of the Total Population and the Population of Voting Age for States and Congressional Districts, 2544–2

Estimates of Tip Income in Eating Places, 1982, 8302–2.406

Estimates of U.S. Wood Energy Consumption, 1980-83, 3164–78

Estimating Distributed Lag Relationships Using Near-Minimax Procedures, 9366–6.79

Estimating Infrastructure Needs: Methods and Controversies, 9377–1.405

Estimating Retail and Farm Marketing Relationships for U.S. Processed and Fresh Apples, 1561–6.401

Estimating the Effects of Economic Change on National Health and Social Well-Being, 23848–76

Estimating the Input-Output Tables from Scarce Data: Experiences of the U.S. Census Bureau's Center for International Research, 2546–10.13

Estimation and Sampling Procedures in the NMCES Insurance Surveys, 4186–4.3

Estimation of Mortgage Prepayment Rates, 9316–1.103

European Communities' Proposals To Reform Common Agricultural Policy, 25368–135

European Monetary System: Tombstone or Cornerstone?, 9373–3.28

European Weekly Frozen Fish Report, 2162–8

Evaluation of BLS' Projections of 1980 Industry Employment, 6722–1.450

Evaluation of Boise Selective Traffic Enforcement Project, 7762–9.406

Evaluation of Logging Systems Designed To Recover Harvesting Residues for Energy, 9806–2.37

Evaluation of Selected Provisions of the Federal Coal Leasing Amendments Act of 1976, 25318–58.1

Evaluation of the Bonneville County DUI Accident Prevention Program (Project Safety), 7762–9.404

Evaluation of the Child Support Enforcement Program, Final Report, 4748–37

Evaluation of the Department of Commerce Administrative Support Centers, 2006–4

Evaluation of the Department of Commerce Mountain Administrative Support Center, Boulder, Colo., July 1, 1983-Feb. 29, 1984, 2006–4.2

Evaluation of the Department of Commerce Western Administrative Support Center, Seattle, Wash., Oct. 1-Dec. 31, 1983, 2006–4.1

Evaluation of the Federal New Communities Program, 5188–107

Evaluation of the Impact of the Part A Entitlement Program Funded Under Title IV of the Indian Education Act, Final Report, 4808–13

Evaluation of the Nutrition Services for the Elderly, 4608–16

Evaluation of the Operation of the Trade Adjustment Assistance Center Program, 2044–24

Evaluation of the 1981 AFDC Changes: Initial Analyses, 26131–11

Evaluation of Utility Home Energy Audit (RCS) Programs, 3308–69

Evidence on Possible Default and the Tilt Problem Under Three Mortgage Contracts, 9381–10.39

Evolution of the Bank Regulatory Structure: A Reappraisal, 9389–2

Examination of Auditor Concentration in the Savings and Loan Industry, 9312–1.403

Examination of Distributed Lag Model Coefficients Estimated with Smoothness Priors, 9366–6.77

Examining the Recent Behavior of Inflation, 9391–1.420

Excavating and Foundation Work Special Trade Contractors (Industry 1794): 1982 Census of Construction Industries. Preliminary Report. Industry Series, 2371–1.23

Excess Navy Ships Sold to Foreign Countries at Understated Prices, 26123–60

Exchange Market Intervention in Four European Countries, 9373–3.26

Exchange Rate Arrangements in the Eighties, 9373–3.28

Exchange Rate Determination and Real Interest Rate Differentials Under Uncertainty, 9366–7.91

Exchange Rate Volatility and Federal Reserve Policy, 9381–1.413

Exclusive Dealing and Vertical Integration: The Efficiency of Contracts in the Tuna Industry, 9406–1.39

Executive Summary: 5-Year (1984-88) General Services Strategic Plan for ADP, 9458–17

Executive Summary for the Affirmative Action Multi-Year Plan (MYP), 7004–11

Expanded Federal Authority Needed To Protect Medicare and Medicaid Patients from Health Practitioners Who Lose Their Licenses, 26121–80

Expediting Tax Deposits Can Increase the Government's Interest Earnings, 26119–55

Expenditures for Public Assistance Programs, 4744–22

Expenditures for the Medical Care of Elderly People Living in the Community Throughout 1980, 4146–11.4

Expenditures for Vocational Education, 4864–7

Experience with the Shift Technical Advisor Position: Interviews with Personnel from Nine Plants, 9638–55

Experimental Squid Jigging Off the Washington Coast, 2162–1.401

Explosions Aboard Aircraft, 7504–31.6

Explosives (Industry 2892): 1982 Census of Manufactures. Preliminary Report. Industry Series, 2491–1.198

Explosives Incidents, 1983, 8484–4

Export Administration Annual Report, FY83, 2044–22

Export-Import Bank of the U.S., 1983 Annual Report, 9254–1

Export-Import Bank Proposal of Credit to Brazil and Mexico, 25248–97

Export Market Profiles, 1526–6

Export Markets for U.S. Grain and Feed Commodities, 1925–2.4

Export of Alaskan Crude Oil, 25388–45

Export Outlook for Horticultural Products, 1925–34.433

Export Promotion Programs of the Foreign Commercial Service and the Export-Import Bank, 21408–73

Export Trade and Prospects: Dairy, Livestock, and Poultry, 1925–32.1

Exports of Dual-Use, Nuclear-Related Equipment to the People's Republic of China, 26123–76

Exports Under the Concessional Sales Program: Title I (III), Public Law 480, 1922–6

Extending Driver Licenses by Mail: A 36-Month Follow-Up, 7762–9.401

Extra Long Staple Cotton: ASCS Commodity Fact Sheet, 1984, 1806–4.11

Extramural Trends, FY72-83, 4434–9

Eye Glasses or Contact Lenses: U.S., 1979 and 1980, 4147–10.145

FAA Air Traffic Activity, FY83, 7504–27

FAA Apportions $531 Million in Airport Funds in FY85, 7506–8.32

FAA Approves $247 Million in Allocations for Second Quarter of FY84, 7506–8.30

FAA Approves $58 Million

FAA Approves $58 Million for First Quarter in FY84, 7506–8.29

FAA Aviation Forecasts, FY84-95, 7504–6

FAA News, 7506–8

FAA Statistical Handbook of Aviation, 1983, 7504–1

Fabric and Expanded Neoprene Laminate from Japan: Determination of the Commission in Investigation No. 731-TA-206 (Preliminary) Under the Tariff Act of 1930, Together with the Information Obtained in the Investigation, 9886–14.128

Fabric Dress and Work Gloves (Industry 2381): 1982 Census of Manufactures. Preliminary Report. Industry Series, 2491–1.97

Fabricated Plate Work (Boiler Shops) (Industry 3443): 1982 Census of Manufactures. Preliminary Report. Industry Series, 2491–1.287

Fabricated Rubber Products, N.E.C. (Industry 3069): 1982 Census of Manufactures. Preliminary Report. Industry Series, 2491–1.210

Fabricated Structural Metal (Industry 3441): 1982 Census of Manufactures. Preliminary Report. Industry Series, 2491–1.285

Fabricated Textile Products, N.E.C. (Industry 2399): 1982 Census of Manufactures. Preliminary Report. Industry Series, 2491–1.110

Fact Book, FY83: Defense Fuel Supply Center, 3904–8

Fact Book of U.S. Agriculture, 1004–14

Fact Book, 1982, New England Thrift Industry, 9304–3

Fact Sheet on Child Feeding Programs, 1362–12

Fact Sheet on Child Feeding Programs, 1364–14

Fact Sheet: U.S. Military Strengths Worldwide, 3542–9

Factfinder for the Nation, 2326–7

Factors Affecting Domestic Soybean Meal Use, 1561–3.401

Factors Affecting Laboratory Test Use and Prices, 4652–1.415

Factors Affecting Quarterly Domestic Feed Demand for Corn, 1561–4.403

Factors Affecting Reserves of Depository Institutions and Condition Statement of Federal Reserve Banks, 9365–1

Facts for Vendors, FY83, AAFES, 3504–10

Facts, Projections, and Gaps Concerning Data on Aging, 4102–1.447

Failure To Regulate, Asbestos: A Lethal Legacy, 21408–72

Fair Housing Enforcement Demonstration, 5188–102

Fair Market Value Policy for Federal Coal Leasing, Report of the Commission, 11128–1

Fair Practices in Automotive Products Act of 1983, 21788–134

Fall Enrollment in Colleges and Universities, Preliminary Estimates, 4844–1

Fall Enrollment in Colleges and Universities, 1982, 4844–2

Fall-Harvested Round White Potatoes from Canada: Determination of the Commission in Investigation No. 731-TA-124 (Final) Under the Tariff Act of 1930, Together with the Information Obtained in the Investigation, 9886–14.89

Fall Water Supply Summary, 1984, 1264–4

Families at Work: The Jobs and the Pay, 6746–1.253

Family Caregiving for the Elderly, 1004–16.1

Family Clothing Stores (Industry 5651): 1982 Census of Retail Trade. Preliminary Report. Industry Series, 2395–1.17

Family Economics Review, 1702–1

Family Farm: Government and Private Responsibilities, 1004–16.1

Family Physicians' Beliefs About Screening for Colorectal Cancer Using the Stool Guaiac Slide Test, 4102–1.433

Family Violence, 6066–19.5

Fans, Blowers, Compressors, Air Pumps and Vacuum Pumps, and Air-Conditioning and Refrigeration Machines, TSUS Items 661(pt.): Summary of Trade and Tariff Information, 9885–6.83

Farm and Garden Machinery and Equipment (Industry 5083): 1982 Census of Wholesale Trade. Preliminary Report. Industry Series, 2403–1.14

Farm and Housing Activity Report, 1182–1

Farm Credit Administration and Cooperative Farm Credit System, 49th Annual Report, 1982, 9264–2

Farm Credit Banks Report to Investors, 1983, 9264–5

Farm Credit Conditions in the Fifth District, 9389–17

Farm Finance: A Lender's Viewpoint, 1004–16.1

Farm Income Situation and Outlook, 1004–16.1

Farm Labor, 1631–1

Farm Machinery and Lawn and Garden Equipment, 1983, Current Industrial Report, 2506–12.1

Farm Nonreal Estate Debt, Jan. 1, 1983, 9264–4

Farm Operator Households Receiving Social Security Income, 1979, 1702–1.410

Farm People's Health Insurance Coverage, 1598–191

Farm Population of the U.S.: 1982. Current Population Reports. Series P-27. Farm Population, 2544–1

Farm Population of the U.S.: 1983. Current Population Reports. Series P-27. Farm Population, 2544–1

Farm Population Trends by Farm Characteristics, 1975-80, 1598–144

Farm Production Expenditures 1983 Summary, 1614–3

Farm Programs and the Congressional Subcommittees, 1004–16.1

Farm Real Estate Debt, Jan. 1, 1983, 9264–3

Farm Real Estate Market Developments Outlook and Situation Report, 1541–8

Farm Storage, Drying Equipment, Wet Storage, Forage and Silage, Hay Storage, and Solar Equipment Loans, 1802–9

Farm Storage Facility and Equipment, FY68-84, New Loan Data, 1804–14

Farm Supplies (Industry 5191): 1982 Census of Wholesale Trade. Preliminary Report. Industry Series, 2403–1.38

Farmer Cooperative Statistics, 1982, 1124–1

Farmer Cooperatives, 1122–1

Farmer Owned Share of Market Up Despite Fewer Dairy Co-ops, 1122–1.404

Farmers and Economic Shocks: Ranking Texas Agricultural Production Regions, 9379–1.406

Titles

Farmers' Perceptions and Information Sources: A Quantitative Analysis, 1502–3.401

Farmline, 1502–6

Fast Response Survey System, 4826–1

Fasteners and Hardware, TSUS Items 646.02-647.10: Summary of Trade and Tariff Information, 9885–6.82

Fatal Accident Reporting System, 1982, 7764–10

Fatal and Injury Accident Rates on Federal-Aid and Other Highway Systems, 7554–2

Fatality Trends, 7766–13

Fatality Trends: Car Size, 7766–13.8

Fatality Trends: Totals and Rates, 7766–13.9

Fatality Trends: Victim Age, 7766–13.7

Fats and Oils: Oilseed Crushings, Current Industrial Report, 2506–4.3

Fats and Oils Outlook and Situation, 1561–3

Fats and Oils Production, Consumption, and Factory and Warehouse Stocks, Current Industrial Report, 2506–4.4

Fats and Oils Production, Consumption, and Stocks, Current Industrial Report, 2506–4.4

Fatty Substances; Certain Natural Chemicals and Chemical Products; and Radioactive Elements, Compounds, and Isotopes, and Nonradioactive Isotopes and Their Compounds, TSUS Items 490(pt.), 491(pt.), 493(pt.), and 494(pt.): Summary of Trade and Tariff Information, 9885–4.38

FDA Compliance Program Report of Findings: Pesticides and Metals in Fish Program, 4064–8

FDA Quarterly Activities Report, 4062–3

FDIC Annual Report, 9294–1

FEC Announces Spending Limits for 1984 Primary Season, 9276–1.19

FEC Approves Matching Funds for 1984 Presidential Candidates, 9276–1.20

FEC Issues 1984 Mid-Year PAC Growth Figures, 9276–1.22

FEC Releases New PAC Figures, 9276–1.18

FEC Reports on Financial Activity, 9276–2

FEC Reports on Financial Activity, 1983-84: Interim Report No. 1, Presidential Pre-Nomination Campaigns, 9276–2.1

FEC Reports on Financial Activity, 1983-84: Interim Report No. 2, Presidential Pre-Nomination Campaigns, 9276–2.2

FEC Reports on Financial Activity, 1983-84: Interim Report No. 3, Presidential Pre-Nomination Campaigns, 9276–2.3

FEC Reports on Financial Activity, 1983-84: Interim Report No. 4, Presidential Pre-Nomination Campaigns, 9276–2.4

FEC Reports on Financial Activity, 1983-84: Interim Report No. 5, Presidential Pre-Nomination Campaigns, 9276–2.5

FEC Reports on Financial Activity, 1983-84: Interim Report No. 7, U.S. Senate and House Campaigns, 9276–2.6

FEC Reports on Financial Activity, 1983-84: Interim Report No. 8, Party and Non-Party Political Committees, 9276–2.7

Federal Academic Obligations Increased by 13% in 1982, 5% in Real Dollars, 9626–2.135

Federal Advisory Committees, Twelfth Annual Report of the President, FY83, 9454–18

Federal Agencies' Actions To Implement Section 11 of the Stevenson-Wydler Technology Innovation Act of 1980, 26113–141

Titles

Federal Reserve Bank of

Federal Agencies' Implementation of the 1983 Emergency Jobs Appropriations Act, 26115–51

Federal Agency Performance for Minority Business Development, FY83, 2104–5

Federal Agricultural Research Funding: Issues and Concerns, 26113–111

Federal Aid in Fish and Wildlife Restoration, 1981, 5504–1

Federal Aid to States, 8104–1

Federal and State Initiatives Needed To Improve Productivity and Reduce Administrative Costs of the Aid to Families with Dependent Children and Food Stamp Programs, 26111–18

Federal and State Liability for Inaccurate Payments of Food Stamp, AFDC, and SSI Program Benefits, 26113–136

Federal Budget Developments, 2702–1.411

Federal Budget Developments, 2702–1.429

Federal Civil Rights Commitments: An Assessment of Enforcement Resources and Performance, 11048–179

Federal Civilian Leave Data for the Executive Branch, Leave Year 1981, 9842–1.402

Federal Civilian Work Force Statistics, Monthly Release, Employment and Trends, 9842–1

Federal Civilian Work Years and Personnel Costs in the Executive Branch for FY82, 9842–1.401

Federal Civilian Workforce Statistics: Affirmative Employment Statistics, 9844–27

Federal Civilian Workforce Statistics: Biennial Report of Employment by Geographic Area, Dec. 31, 1982, 9844–8

Federal Coal Management Program: Final Environmental Impact Statements, 5726–4

Federal Coal Management Program Final Environmental Impact Statement: San Juan River Region, 5726–4.7

Federal Coal Management Program Final Environmental Impact Statement: Southern Appalachian Coal Region, 5726–4.8

Federal Coal Management Program Final Environmental Impact Statement: Uinta-Southwestern Utah Coal Region, 5726–4.6

Federal Coal Management Report, FY83, 5724–10

Federal Construction-Related Expenditures, 1980-85, 2012–1.404

Federal Court Management Statistics, 1984, 18204–3

Federal Debt and Interest Costs, Special Study, 26308–50

Federal Deposit Insurance as a Call Option: Implications for Depository Institution and Insurer Behavior, 9316–1.107

Federal, District of Columbia, and States Future Prison and Correctional Institution Populations and Capacities, 26119–59

Federal Drug Law Violators, 6062–2.403

Federal Economic Development Assistance Programs: An Econometric Analysis of Their Employment Effects, 1974-78, 26117–32

Federal Education Assistance: Are Block Grants Meeting the Need?, 21408–75

Federal Education Policies and Programs: Intergovernmental Issues in Their Design, Operation, and Effects, 4808–9.3

Federal Election Commission, Annual Report, 1983, 9274–1

Federal Emergency Management Agency Publications Catalog, 9434–5

Federal Emergency Management Agency's Plan for Revitalizing U.S. Civil Defense: A Review of Three Major Plan Components, 26123–61

Federal Employees' Compensation Act and the Longshoremen's and Harbor Workers' Compensation Act and Extensions, Annual Statistical Report for All Districts Combined, FY83, 6504–5.1

Federal Employees' Compensation Act and the Longshoremen's and Harbor Workers' Compensation Act and Extensions, Annual Statistical Reports, FY83, 6504–5

Federal Energy Regulatory Commission: 1982 Annual Report, 3084–9

Federal Energy Regulatory Commission: 1983 Annual Report, 3084–9

Federal Evaluations 1983: A Directory Issued by the Comptroller General, 26106–5.1

Federal Expenditures by State for FY83, 2464–2

Federal Financial Institutions Examination Council, Annual Report 1983, 13004–2

Federal Financing Bank Activity: Federal Financing Bank News, 9322–1

Federal Financing Bank News: Federal Financing Bank Activity, 9322–1

Federal Fiscal Programs, 2702–1.406

Federal Flood Insurance, 1983, 21248–81

Federal Fringe Benefit Facts, 9844–1

Federal Funds for Research and Development, 9627–20

Federal Government Energy Management, Annual Report, 3024–1

Federal Government Energy Management, Annual Report, 3304–22

Federal Government Finances, 1985 Budget Data, 104–12

Federal Highway Administration News, 7556–3

Federal Home Loan Bank Board, Invited Research Working Papers, 9316–2

Federal Home Loan Bank Board, Research Working Papers, 9316–1

Federal Home Loan Bank Board Journal, 9312–1

Federal Home Loan Bank, Ninth District, Annual Report, 9304–11

Federal Home Loan Bank of Atlanta, Annual Report, 1983, 9304–1

Federal Home Loan Bank of Boston, Annual Report, 1983, 9304–2

Federal Home Loan Bank of Boston, Membership Directory 1984, 9304–26

Federal Home Loan Bank of Chicago, 1983 Annual Report, 9304–4

Federal Home Loan Bank of Cincinnati, 1983 Annual Report, 9304–6

Federal Home Loan Bank of Dallas, 1983 Annual Report, 9304–11

Federal Home Loan Bank of Des Moines, 1983 Annual Report, 9304–7

Federal Home Loan Bank of Des Moines, 1984 Membership Directory, 9304–9

Federal Home Loan Bank of Indianapolis, Annual Report, 1983, 9304–10

Federal Home Loan Bank of New York, 51st Annual Report, 1983, 9304–12

Federal Home Loan Bank of Pittsburgh, 1983 Annual Report, 9304–13

Federal Home Loan Bank of San Francisco, 1983 Annual Report, 9304–14

Federal Home Loan Bank of Seattle, Annual Report, 1983, 9304–15

Federal Home Loan Bank of Topeka, Annual Report, 1983, 9304–16

Federal Home Loan Bank of Topeka, Membership Directory, 1984, 9304–17

Federal Home Loan Mortgage Corporation, Annual Report 1983, 9414–1

Federal Hospital Insurance Trust Fund, 1984 Annual Report of the Board of Trustees, 4704–5

Federal Information Processing Standards Publications, 2216–2

Federal Judicial Workload Statistics, 18202–1

Federal Juvenile Delinquency Programs, Sixth Analysis and Evaluation, 6064–11

Federal Labor Relations Authority, Fifth Annual Report, 13364–1

Federal Maritime Commission, 22nd Annual Report, FY83, 9334–1

Federal Meat and Poultry Inspection, FY83, Statistical Summary, 1374–3

Federal Milk Order Market Statistics, 1317–4

Federal Milk Order Market Statistics, 1983 Annual Summary, 1317–3

Federal Mine Health Program, 4244–1

Federal Motor Vehicle Fleet Report, FY83, 9454–9

Federal Offenders in U.S. District Courts, 1983, 18204–1

Federal Offshore Statistics: Leasing, Exploration, Production, Revenue, 5734–3

Federal Old-Age and Survivors Insurance and Disability Insurance Trust Funds, 1984 Annual Report of the Board of Trustees, 4704–4

Federal Personal Income Taxes: Liabilities and Payments, 1980-82, 2702–1.415

Federal Personnel Should Be Better Informed of How Undesignated Contributions to the Combined Federal Campaign Will Be Distributed, 26119–66

Federal Plan for Meteorological Services and Supporting Research, FY85, 2144–2

Federal Prisoners Confined on (date): Bureau of Prisons, 6242–1.1

Federal Procurement Data System Standard Report, 102–6

Federal Programs Affecting Children, 21968–30

Federal Recreation Fee Report, 1983 Including Federal and State and Private Sector Recreation Visitation and Fee Data, a Report to Congress, 5544–14

Federal Reserve Bank of Atlanta, 1983 Annual Report, 9371–4

Federal Reserve Bank of Atlanta Economic Review, 9371–1

Federal Reserve Bank of Boston, New England Economic Review, 9373–1

Federal Reserve Bank of Chicago, 1983 Annual Report, 9375–5

Federal Reserve Bank of Chicago, Economic Perspectives, 9375–1

Federal Reserve Bank of Cleveland, Annual Report 1983, 9377–5

Federal Reserve Bank of Cleveland, Economic Review, 9377–1

Federal Reserve Bank of Dallas, 1983 Annual Report, 9379–2

Federal Reserve Bank of Dallas Economic Review, 9379–1

Federal Reserve Bank of Kansas City, Annual Report, 1983, 9381–3

Federal Reserve Bank of

Federal Reserve Bank of Kansas City Economic Review, 9381–1

Federal Reserve Bank of Minneapolis, Annual Report, 1983, 9383–2

Federal Reserve Bank of Minneapolis Quarterly Review, 9383–6

Federal Reserve Bank of New York, Sixty-Ninth Annual Report for the Year Ended Dec. 31, 1983, 9385–2

Federal Reserve Bank of New York Quarterly Review, 9385–1

Federal Reserve Bank of Philadelphia, Annual Report 1983, 9387–3

Federal Reserve Bank of Philadelphia Business Review, 9387–1

Federal Reserve Bank of Richmond, 1983 Annual Report, 9389–2

Federal Reserve Bank of Richmond Economic Review, 9389–1

Federal Reserve Bank of San Francisco, Annual Report, 1983, 9393–2

Federal Reserve Bank of San Francisco Economic Review, 9393–8

Federal Reserve Bank of San Francisco, Western Economic Indicators, 9393–1

Federal Reserve Bank of St. Louis Review, 9391–1

Federal Reserve Bulletin, 9362–1

Federal Reserve Chart Book, 9362–2

Federal Reserve Monthly Statistical Releases, 9365–2

Federal Reserve Quarterly Statistical Releases, 9365–3

Federal Reserve Weekly Statistical Releases, 9365–1

Federal Reserve's New Operating Procedures: A Post Mortem, 9366–6.78

Federal Role in State Industrial Development Programs, 26306–6.81

Federal State and Local Transportation Financial Statistics, FY77-82, 7308–185

Federal Statistics: A Special Report on the Statistical Programs and Activities of the U.S. Government, FY85, 104–10

Federal Strategy for Prevention of Drug Abuse and Drug Trafficking, 024–1

Federal Supplementary Medical Insurance Trust Fund, 1984 Annual Report, 4704–3

Federal Support for R&D and Innovation, 26306–6.77

Federal Support of U.S. Business, 26306–6.70

Federal Support to Universities, Colleges, and Selected Nonprofit Institutions, FY82, Final Report, 9627–17

Federal Tax Incentives and Rental Housing, 5188–104

Federal Taxation and the Domestic-Foreign Asset Choice of a U.S. Bank, 9366–7.99

Federal Trade Commission, FY82 Annual Report, 9404–1

Federal Trust Fund Reports, 8102–9

Federalism in 1983: Mixed Results from Washington, 10042–1.402

Federated States of Micronesia Annual Report, FY83, 5304–15.5

Feed Grains: ASCS Commodity Fact Sheet, 1984, 1806–4.10

Feed Outlook and Situation Report, 1561–4

Feldspar, Nepheline Syenite, and Aplite: Minerals Yearbook Preprint, Vol. 1, 1983, 5604–15.22

Felt Goods, Except Woven Felts and Hats (Industry 2291): 1982 Census of Manufactures. Preliminary Report. Industry Series, 2491–1.69

Titles

Female-Male Unemployment Differential: Effects of Changes in Industry Employment, 6722–1.465

Female Veteran Population, 9928–28

Ferroalloys: Minerals Yearbook Preprint, Vol. 1, 1983, 5604–15.23

Ferrosilicon from the Union of Soviet Socialist Republics: Report to the President on Investigation No. TA-406-10 Under Section 406 of the Trade Act of 1974, 9886–12.8

Fertility of American Women. Current Population Reports. Series P-20. Population Characteristics, 2546–1.393

Fertility of American Women: June 1982, 2546–1.386

Fertility of American Women: June 1983 (Advance Report), 2546–1.385

Fertilizer Outlook and Situation, 1561–5

Fertilizer Supply, 1983-84 Nitrogen, Phosphate, Potash for USDA State and County Emergency Records, 1804–6

Fertilizers, Mixing Only (Industry 2875): 1982 Census of Manufactures. Preliminary Report. Industry Series, 2491–1.195

Fertilizers, Other than Nitrogenous, TSUS Items 480(pt.): Summary of Trade and Tariff Information, 9885–4.44

Fewer Students in Work Force as School Age Population Declines, 6722–1.446

FHA Home Mortgage Claims Rates, Cumulative Total Foreclosures, 5142–27

FHA Interest Rate Changes, 5002–6

FHA Low Cost Housing Trends of 1-Family Homes, 5142–4

FHA Mobile Home and Property Improvement Loans Insured, Title I, Section 2, 5142–10

FHA Property Improvement and Mobile Home Activity Report, By State and by County for 1983 and Cumulative Through Dec. 31, 1983, 5144–16

FHA Report of Operations, 5142–5

FHA Trends of Home Mortgage Characteristics, Mortgages Insured, Section 203b, 5142–1

FHA Trends of Home Mortgage Characteristics: Mortgages Insured—Section 245 GPM, 5142–40

FHWA Allocates More than $1 Billion in Special Highway and Bridge Funds for FY85, 7556–3.2

FHWA Designates Final Highway Network for Commercial Motor Vehicle Use, 7556–3.1

FHWA Reports Increase in Road Construction Costs for Third Quarter of 1984, 7556–3.3

FHWA Reports Over 96 Percent of the Interstate Highway System Is Now in Service, 7556–3.4

Fiber Cans, Drums, and Similar Products (Industry 2655): 1982 Census of Manufactures. Preliminary Report. Industry Series, 2491–1.157

Fibrous Glass, 1983, Current Industrial Report, 2506–9.5

Field Crops: Final Estimates by States, 1978-82, Preliminary 1983, 1641–7

Field Studies and Statistics Program, FY83, 4474–29

Fifteen Years Ago, Rural Alabama Revisited, 11048–180

Fifteenth Annual Report on Medicare Covering FY81 Including Reports on the Medigap Program and the End Stage Renal Disease Program, 4654–5

Fifteenth Period Entitlements, Revenue Sharing: Oct. 1, 1983-Sept. 30, 1984, 8066–1.94

Fifteenth Semiannual Report by the President To the Commission on Security and Cooperation in Europe on the Implementation of the Helsinki Final Act, June 1-Nov. 30, 1983, 7002–1

Fifth Annual Report of the Federal Labor Relations Authority, 13364–1

Fifth Annual Report on the Implementation of the Federal Equal Opportunity Recruitment Program, Report to Congress, 9844–33

Fifth Annual Report on the Use of Alcohol in Fuels, 3304–9

Fifth Annual Report to Congress on the Automotive Technology Development Program, 3304–17

Fifth Special Report to the U.S. Congress on Alcohol and Health From the Secretary of Health and Human Services, 4488–4

Fifty-fourth Report to Congress (Jan. 1 Through Sept 30, 1983) of the Department of Defense In Accordance with Section 2455, Title 10, U.S.C. of the Defense Cataloging and Standardization Act of 1952, 21204–1

Final Environmental Impact Statement, Proposed Diapir Field Lease Offering (June 1984), 5736–1.10

Final Marriage Statistics, 1981, Advance Report, 4146–5.77

Final Mortality Statistics, 1981, Advance Report, 4146–5.78

Final Mortality Statistics, 1982, Advance Report, 4146–5.81

Final Natality Statistics, 1981, Advance Report, 4146–5.73

Final Natality Statistics, 1982, Advance Report, 4146–5.79

Final Report for Inflation and Pension Benefits, 6468–18

Final Report of the Nationwide Urban Runoff Program, 9208–122

Final Report of the Project: Motivation and Economic Mobility of the Poor, 4008–65

Final Report of the Seattle-Denver Income Maintenance Experiment, 4008–64

Final Report of the Seattle-Denver Income Maintenance Experiment. Vol. 1: Design and Results, 4008–64.2

Final Report of the Seattle-Denver Income Maintenance Experiment. Vol. 2: Administration, 4008–64.3

Final Report of the SEC Government-Business Forum on Small Business Capital Formation, 1983, 9734–4

Finance Companies, 9365–2.7

Finances of County Governments. 1982 Census of Governments, Vol. 4. Governmental Finances, No. 3, 2457–3

Finances of Employee-Retirement Systems of State and Local Governments in 1982-83, 2466–2.4

Finances of Municipal and Township Governments. 1982 Census of Governments, Vol. 4. Governmental Finances, No. 4, 2457–4

Finances of Public School Systems. 1982 Census of Governments, Vol. 4. Governmental Finances, No. 1, 2457–1

Finances of Selected Public Employee Retirement Systems, 2462–2

Financial and Other Problems Facing the Federal Employees Health Insurance Program, 26121–67

Titles

Financial and Traffic Results: U.S. Combination Carriers, 9142–41

Financial and Traffic Results: U.S. Combination Carriers, Atlantic Operations, 9142–41.1

Financial and Traffic Results: U.S. Combination Carriers, Latin American Operations, 9142–41.2

Financial and Traffic Results: U.S. Combination Carriers, Pacific Operations, 9142–41.3

Financial Assistance by Geographic Area, FY83, 4004–3

Financial Characteristics of Member Savings Institutions, 2nd Half 1982-2nd Half 1983, 9302–3

Financial Condition of the Government of the Virgin Islands, As of Sept. 30, 1981, 5304–10

Financial Highlights by Insurance Funds, 5002–9

Financial Information Report, Federal Home Loan Bank of Indianapolis, 9302–11

Financial Information Report, Quarterly Report Aggregates: Federal Home Loan Bank of Indianapolis, 9302–23

Financial Letter, Federal Reserve Bank of Kansas City, 9381–2

Financial Perspective on Agriculture, 9362–1.401

Financial Problems of the John F. Kennedy Center for the Performing Arts Need To Be Addressed, 26119–60

Financial Services in Transition: The Effects of Nonbank Competitors, 9375–11.3

Financial Statistics of Institutions of Higher Education: State Data, 4844–6

Financial Statistics of Selected Electric Utilities, 1982, 3164–23

Financing Education in the Southeast, 9371–1.429

Financing Public Physical Infrastructure, 10048–60

Financing the U.S. Current Account Deficit, 9385–1.409

Financing Urban Transportation Improvements, 7556–7

Financing U.S. Airports in the 1980s, 26306–6.75

Finished Broadwoven Fabric Production, 1983, Current Industrial Report, 2506–5.10

Finished Fabrics: Production, Inventories, and Unfilled Orders, Current Industrial Report, 2506–5.1

Finishing Mills, Cotton (Industry 2261): 1982 Census of Manufactures. Preliminary Report. Industry Series, 2491–1.59

Finishing Mills, Manmade (Industry 2262): 1982 Census of Manufactures. Preliminary Report. Industry Series, 2491–1.60

Finishing Mills, N.E.C. (Industry 2269): 1982 Census of Manufactures. Preliminary Report. Industry Series, 2491–1.61

FIPS Pubs Index, 2216–2.121

Fire Effects Appraisal System for Wisconsin, 1208–198

Firms Involved in ATM, POS, and Home Banking: A Survey, 9371–1.421

First District Facts, Federal Home Loan Bank of Boston, 9302–4

First Rental Rehabilitation Grants Awarded to 76 Areas, One State, 5006–3.33

First Report Required by Section 123 of the Natural Gas Policy Act of 1978, 3008–96

Forces Shaping the Future of

Fiscal Condition of Tenth District States, 9381–1.403

Fiscal Disparities: Central Cities and Suburbs, 1981. An Information Report, 10048–61

Fish Kill Statistics Summary, 1978-80, 9204–3

Fish Kills Caused by Pollution, 9204–3

Fish Meal and Oil, 2162–3

Fish Netting and Fishing Nets of Textile Materials, TSUS Items 355(pt.): Summary of Trade and Tariff Information, 9885–3.44

Fish Sticks, Fish Portions, and Breaded Shrimp, 2162–4

Fish Sticks, Fish Portions, and Breaded Shrimp, Annual Summary 1983, 2166–6.5

Fisheries and Wildlife Research and Development, 1983, 5504–20

Fisheries of the U.S., 1983, 2164–1

Fisheries Synopses, 2166–16

Fishery Market News Reports, 2162–6

Fishery Statistics of the U.S., 1977, 2164–2

Five-Year Plan for Meeting the Automatic Data Processing and Telecommunications Needs of the Federal Government, 104–20

Five-Year Plan for Meeting the Automatic Data Processing and Telecommunications Needs of the Federal Government. Vol. 1: Planning Strategies, 104–20.1

Five-Year Plan for Meeting the Automatic Data Processing and Telecommunications Needs of the Federal Government. Vol. 2: Major Information Technology Systems Acquisition Plans of Federal Executive Agencies, 1984-1989, 104–20.2

Fixed Reproducible Tangible Wealth in the U.S., 1980-83, 2702–1.433

Flat Glass (Industry 3211): 1982 Census of Manufactures. Preliminary Report. Industry Series, 2491–1.223

Flat Glass, Current Industrial Report, 2506–9.6

Flat-Rolled Carbon Steel Products from Brazil: Determination of the Commission in Investigation No. 731-TA-123 (Final) Under the Tariff Act of 1930, Together with the Information Obtained in the Investigation, 9886–14.99

Flavoring Extracts and Syrups, N.E.C. (Industry 2087): 1982 Census of Manufactures. Preliminary Report. Industry Series, 2491–1.37

Flavors, Odoriferous Compounds, Perfumery, Cosmetics, and Toilet Preparations, TSUS Items 412(pt.), 413(pt.), 425(pt.), 437(pt.), 450(pt.)-452(pt.), 460(pt.), 461(pt.), and 493(pt.): Summary of Trade and Tariff Information, 9885–4.40

Floor Covering Stores (Industry 5713): 1982 Census of Retail Trade. Preliminary Report. Industry Series, 2395–1.20

Floor Laying and Other Floorwork Special Trade Contractors, N.E.C. (Industry 1752): 1982 Census of Construction Industries. Preliminary Report. Industry Series, 2371–1.17

Florida Coastal Ecological Characterization: A Socioeconomic Study of the Northwestern Region, 5506–4.9

Florida Coastal Ecological Characterization: A Socioeconomic Study of the Southwestern Region, 5506–4.8

Florida: Expecting a Boom, 9371–1.404

Florists (Industry 5992): 1982 Census of Retail Trade. Preliminary Report. Industry Series, 2395–1.38

Flour and Other Grain Mill Products; Blended and Prepared Flour (Industries 2041 and 2045): 1982 Census of Manufactures. Preliminary Report. Industry Series, 2491–1.14

Flour Milling Products, Current Industrial Report, 2506–4.1

Flow of Funds Accounts, Assets and Liabilities Outstanding, 1960-83, 9364–3

Flow of Funds Accounts, Seasonally Adjusted and Unadjusted, 9365–3.3

Flue-Cured Tobacco: ASCS Commodity Fact Sheet, 1984, 1806–4.15

Fluid Meters and Counting Devices (Industry 3824): 1982 Census of Manufactures. Preliminary Report. Industry Series, 2491–1.414

Fluid Milk (Industry 2026): 1982 Census of Manufactures. Preliminary Report. Industry Series, 2491–1.7

Fluid Power Products, Including Aerospace, 1983, Current Industrial Report, 2506–12.31

Fluorescent Lamp Ballasts, Current Industrial Report, 2506–12.14

Fluorspar: Mineral Industry Surveys, 5612–2.10

Fluorspar: Minerals Yearbook Preprint, Vol. 1, 1983, 5604–15.24

Food and Agriculture Competitively Awarded Research Grants, FY83, 1744–1

Food and Drug Administration, Annual Report, 4064–2

Food Bibliography, 26104–11.2

Food Consumption, Prices, and Expenditures, 1963-83, 1544–4

Food Cost Review, 1983, 1544–9

Food for Peace: 1982 Annual Report on Public Law 480, 1924–7

Food Habits and Trophic Relationships of a Community of Fishes on the Outer Continental Shelf, 2168–78

Food Intakes: Individuals in 48 States, 1977-78, 1356–4.1

Food Policies in Developing Countries, 1528–168

Food Preparations, N.E.C. (Industry 2099): 1982 Census of Manufactures. Preliminary Report. Industry Series, 2491–1.43

Food Prices and Marketing, 1004–16.1

Food Processing and Packaging Equipment: Country Market Survey, 2045–11

Food Products Machinery (Industry 3551): 1982 Census of Manufactures. Preliminary Report. Industry Series, 2491–1.330

Food Program Update, 1362–14

Food Retail Trends in the United Kingdom, 1925–34.406

Food Stamp Program: Statistical Summary of Operations, 1362–6

Foods for Health: Report of the Pilot Program, 4478–144

Footwear (Industry 5139): 1982 Census of Wholesale Trade. Preliminary Report. Industry Series, 2403–1.26

Footwear, Current Industrial Report, 2506–6.7

Footwear, Except Rubber, N.E.C. (Industry 3149): 1982 Census of Manufactures. Preliminary Report. Industry Series, 2491–1.217

Footwear, 1983, Current Industrial Report, 2506–6.8

Forces Shaping the Future of U.S. Agriculture, 1004–16.1

Forecast of Citizen

Titles

Forecast of Citizen Departures to Europe for (Date), 7182–2

Forecast of Likely U.S. Energy Supply/Demand Balances for 1985 and 2000, 2006–2

Forecasting the Money Supply in Time Series Models, 9377–9.8

Forecasting Using Contemporaneous Correlations, 9377–9.11

Forecasts 1984, 9389–1.404

Foreign Agricultural Service: Special Reports, 1924–1

Foreign Agricultural Trade of the U.S., 1522–1

Foreign Agriculture, 1922–2

Foreign Agriculture Circular: Wood Products. International Trade and Foreign Markets, 1925–36

Foreign Agriculture Circular: Cocoa, 1925–9

Foreign Agriculture Circular: Coffee, 1925–5

Foreign Agriculture Circular: Cotton, 1925–4

Foreign Agriculture Circular: Dairy, 1925–10

Foreign Agriculture Circular: Dairy and Livestock. Meat and Dairy Imports, 1925–31

Foreign Agriculture Circular: Dairy, Livestock and Poultry, 1925–32

Foreign Agriculture Circular: Grains, 1925–2

Foreign Agriculture Circular: Horticultural Products, 1925–34

Foreign Agriculture Circular: Horticultural Products, Supplements, 1925–35

Foreign Agriculture Circular: Livestock and Poultry Situation. World Meat and Egg Situation and Outlook, 1925–33

Foreign Agriculture Circular: Oilseeds and Products, 1925–1

Foreign Agriculture Circular: Seeds, Field and Vegetable, 1925–13

Foreign Agriculture Circular: Sugar, Molasses and Honey, 1925–14

Foreign Agriculture Circular: Tea, Spices, and Essential Oils, 1925–15

Foreign Agriculture Circular: Tobacco. World Tobacco Situation, 1925–16

Foreign Agriculture Circular: World Crop Production, 1925–28

Foreign Aid and U.S. Policy Objectives, 7008–38

Foreign Animal Disease Report, 1392–3

Foreign Claims Settlement Commission of the U.S., 1983 Annual Report, 6004–16

Foreign Currency Futures: Some Further Aspects, 9375–1.401

Foreign Direct Investment in the U.S.: 1982 Transactions, 2044–20

Foreign Direct Investment in the U.S.: 1983 Transactions, 2044–20

Foreign Direct Investment in the U.S. in 1983, 2702–1.439

Foreign Economic Reports, 2326–9

Foreign Economic Trends And Their Implications for the U.S., 2046–4

Foreign Energy Supply Assessment Series, 3166–9

Foreign Exchange Constraints and Growth Possibilities in LDCs, 9366–7.106

Foreign Fishery Information Releases: Supplements to Market News Report, 2162–7

Foreign Industrial Targeting and Its Effects on U.S. Industries Phase II: The European Community and Member States: Report to the Subcommittee on Trade, Committee on Ways and Means, U.S. House of

Representatives on Investigation No. 332-162 Under Section 332(b) of the Tariff Act of 1930, 9886–4.73

Foreign Language Education in American High Schools, 4838–11

Foreign Military Sales, Foreign Military Construction Sales and Military Assistance Facts, As of Sept. 30, 1983, 3904–3

Foreign Ownership of U.S. Agricultural Land Through Dec. 31, 1983, 1584–2

Foreign Ownership of U.S. Agricultural Land Through Dec. 31, 1982: County Level Data, 1584–3

Foreign Ownership of U.S. Agricultural Land Through Dec. 31, 1983: County Level Data, 1584–3

Foreign Plants Certified To Export Meat to the U.S., Report of the Secretary of Agriculture to the U.S. Congress, 1374–2

Foreign Sector in the U.S. Flow of Funds Accounts, 9366–7.95

Foreign Service Act of 1980: Implementation, Status, Progress, and Problems, 26123–64

Foreign Trade Zone Growth Primarily Benefits Users Who Import for Domestic Commerce, 26119–56

Forest Area and Timber Resource Statistics for State and Private Lands in Montana, 1206–25

Forest Area and Timber Resource Statistics for State and Private Lands in New Mexico, 1206–23

Forest Area and Timber Resource Statistics for State and Private Lands in New Mexico, 1980, 1206–23.7

Forest Area and Timber Resource Statistics for State and Private Lands in Southwestern Montana, 1978, 1206–25.6

Forest Area and Timber Resource Statistics for Utah, 1975-78, 1206–22

Forest Insect and Disease Conditions in the U.S., 1983, 1204–8

Forest Insect and Disease Conditions, Intermountain Region, 1983, 1206–11.3

Forest Insect and Disease Conditions: USDA Forest Service Regions, 1206–11

Forest-Land Owners in the Northeast Region, 1206–7

Forest-Land Owners of New York, 1206–7.10

Forest Pest Conditions in the Rocky Mountain Region for 1983, 1206–11.1

Forest Resources: Northeastern Region, 1206–16

Forest Resources of the Rocky Mountain States, 1208–201

Forest Service 1982 Research Accomplishments, 1204–14

Forest Statistics for Georgia, 1206–26

Forest Statistics for Maine, 1971 and 1982, 1206–12.7

Forest Statistics for the Northern Coastal Plain of North Carolina, 1984, 1206–4.6

Forest Statistics for the Southern Coastal Plain of North Carolina, 1983, 1206–4.5

Forest Statistics of North Carolina, 1206–4

Forest Statistics of the Northeastern Region, 1206–12

Forestry Incentives Program (FIP), Monthly Progress Report Summary, 1802–11

Forged Undercarriage Components from Italy: Determination of the Commission in Investigation No. 701-TA-201 (Final) Under the Tariff Act of 1930, Together with the Information Obtained in the Investigation, 9886–15.46

Formerly Utilized MED/AEC Sites Remedial Action Program, 3406–1

Forums on Federal Pensions. Part 1: Economic Security Programs, 25408–87

Forums on Federal Pensions. Part 2. The Retirement Income System: Design Issues, 25408–89

Foundation Garments, 1983, Current Industrial Report, 2506–6.5

Foundations of Econometrics, Are There Any?, 9366–6.76

Foundry Machinery and Metal Rolling Mills, TSUS Items 674(pt.): Summary of Trade and Tariff Information, 9885–6.71

Four Bronx Groups Selected To Share $1.3 Million for South Bronx Development, 5006–3.31

Four Discussions, 9366–6.75

Franchise Opportunities Handbook, 2014–6

Franchise Opportunities Handbook, 2044–27

Franchising in the Economy, 1982-84, 2014–5

Free Zones in Developing Countries: Expanding Opportunities for the Private Sector, 9918–10

Freedom of Information Activities, Annual Report of the Department of Health and Human Services, 1983, 4004–21

Fresh Cut Roses from Colombia: Determination of the Commission in Investigation No. 731-TA-148 (Final) Under the Tariff Act of 1930, Together with the Information Obtained in the Investigation, 9886–14.118

Fresh Fruit and Vegetable Arrival Totals, for 23 Cities, 1311–4.3

Fresh Fruit and Vegetable Arrivals and Shipments, 1983, 1311–4

Fresh Fruit and Vegetable Arrivals in Eastern Cities, by Commodities, States, and Months, 1311–4.1

Fresh Fruit and Vegetable Arrivals in Western Cities, by Commodities, States, and Months, 1311–4.2

Fresh Fruit and Vegetable Prices, 1983: Wholesale Chicago and New York City, F.o.b. Leading Shipping Points, 1311–8

Fresh Fruit and Vegetable Shipments, by Commodities, States, and Months, 1311–4.4

Fresh Fruit and Vegetables, Ornamental Crops. Weekly Summary: Shipments and Arrivals, 1311–3

Fresh Fruits and Vegetables (Industry 5148): 1982 Census of Wholesale Trade. Preliminary Report. Industry Series, 2403–1.32

Fresh or Frozen Packaged Fish (Industry 2092): 1982 Census of Manufactures. Preliminary Report. Industry Series, 2491–1.39

Frozen Fishery Products, Preliminary, 2162–2

Frozen Foods (Industry 5142): 1982 Census of Wholesale Trade. Preliminary Report. Industry Series, 2403–1.28

Frozen Fruits and Vegetables (Industry 2037): 1982 Census of Manufactures. Preliminary Report. Industry Series, 2491–1.12

Frozen Specialties (Industry 2038): 1982 Census of Manufactures. Preliminary Report. Industry Series, 2491–1.13

Fruit and Vegetable Truck Cost Report, 1272–1

Fruit and Vegetable Truck Rate and Cost Summary, 1983, 1311–15

Titles

Fruit Juices, TSUS Items 165(pt.): Summary of Trade and Tariff Information, 9885–1.70
Fruit Outlook and Situation, 1561–6
Fruits: Production, Use and Value, 1621–18
FSLIC-Insured Institutions Net Income, 9312–6
FTC Report to Congress Pursuant to the Federal Cigarette Labeling and Advertising Act, for the Year 1981, 9404–4
Fuel Cost and Consumption: Certificated Carriers, Domestic and International Operations, 9142–21
Fuel Oil Dealers (Industry 5983): 1982 Census of Retail Trade. Preliminary Report. Industry Series, 2395–1.36
Fuel Performance Annual Report for 1982, 9634–8
Fuelwood, Wood Waste, Wood Excelsior, Wood Flour, and Wood Charcoal, TSUS Items 200(pt.): Summary of Trade and Tariff Information, 9885–2.29
Full-Time Civilian Employment and Salary Statistics, Mar. 31, 1984, 9842–1.404
Full-Time Federal Civilian Employment in White- and Blue-Collar Occupations as of Oct. 31, 1983, 9842–1.405
Functional Cost Analysis, 9364–6
Functional Cost Analysis, 1982 Average Banks, 9364–6.1
Fund Flows, Historic Trends: Total Certificated Industry, 9142–34
Funding Information on the State Student Incentive Grant Program And Other Need-Based Student Aid Programs of Selected States, 26121–69
Funeral Service and Crematories (Industry 7261): 1982 Census of Service Industries. Preliminary Report. Industry Series, 2390–2.4
Fur Goods (Industry 2371): 1982 Census of Manufactures. Preliminary Report. Industry Series, 2491–1.96
Furniture (Industry 5021): 1982 Census of Wholesale Trade. Preliminary Report. Industry Series, 2403–1.3
Furniture and Fixtures, N.E.C. (Industry 2599): 1982 Census of Manufactures. Preliminary Report. Industry Series, 2491–1.140
Furniture Stores (Industry 5712): 1982 Census of Retail Trade. Preliminary Report. Industry Series, 2395–1.19
Furniture, TSUS Items 727(pt.): Summary of Trade and Tariff Information, 9885–7.62
Further Experience with the Syndromes Produced by Coca Paste Smoking, 7008–40
Future Consumption of Timber Growth in Northern Minnesota: 1980-2030, 1206–24.9
Future Family Farm Needs, 1004–16.1
Future Farm Program Needs, 1004–16.1
Future Food Imports of the Soviet Union and Other Centrally Planned Economies, 1004–16.1
Future Housing Demands and Sources of Mortgage Money, 9312–1.407
Future of University Affiliated Facilities for the Developmentally Disabled, 4608–19
Future of U.S. Basic Industries, 25368–133
FY82 Annual Report to the Congress on the Status and Accomplishments of the Centers Funded Under the Runaway and Homeless Youth Act, 4604–3
FY83 Annual Report of the Chief of Engineers on Civil Works Activities, 3754–1

Global Dynamics of Biospheric

FY83 Annual Report on In-House Energy Management, 3024–3
FY83 Federal Agency Performance for Minority Business Development, 2104–5
FY85 Arms Control Impact Statements, 21384–4
FY85 Budget in Brief, Department of Transportation, 7304–10
FY85 Department of Defense Program for Research, Development and Acquisition, 3504–6
FY85 Military Construction Report, 3544–15
FY85 Rental Rehabilitation Amounts, Application Dates Announced, 5006–3.39

Gains Reported for Minorities, Women in the Federal Workforce, 9844–29
Gallium: Minerals Yearbook Preprint, Vol. 1, 1983, 5604–15.25
Games, Toys, and Children's Vehicles (Industry 3944): 1982 Census of Manufactures. Preliminary Report. Industry Series, 2491–1.429
GAO Annual Report, 1983, 26104–1
GAO Bibliographies, 26104–11
GAO Views on the Methodology Used in an SSA Title II Study of Representative Payment, 26121–85
Gas Mileage Guide, 1985, 3304–11
Gas Supplies of Interstate Natural Gas Pipeline Companies, 1983, 3164–33
Gaskets, Packing and Sealing Devices (Industry 3293): 1982 Census of Manufactures. Preliminary Report. Industry Series, 2491–1.245
Gasoline Service Stations (Industry 5541): 1982 Census of Retail Trade. Preliminary Report. Industry Series, 2395–1.12
Gem Stones: Minerals Yearbook Preprint, Vol. 1, 1983, 5604–15.26
General Accounting Office Publications List, July-Dec. 1983, 26102–1
General Aviation Activity and Avionics Survey, 7504–29
General Contractors, Industrial Buildings and Warehouses (Industry 1541): 1982 Census of Construction Industries. Preliminary Report. Industry Series, 2371–1.4
General Contractors: Industrial Buildings and Warehouses, Industry 1541. 1982 Census of Construction Industries. Industry Series, 2373–1.4
General Contractors—Nonresidential Buildings, Other than Industrial Buildings and Warehouses, Industry 1542. 1982 Census of Construction Industries. Industry Series, 2373–1.5
General Contractors, Residential Buildings, Other than Single-Family Houses (Industry 1522): 1982 Census of Construction Industries. Preliminary Report. Industry Series, 2371–1.2
General Contractors: Residential Buildings, Other than Single-Family Houses, Industry 1522. 1982 Census of Construction Industries. Industry Series, 2373–1.2
General Contractors, Single-Family Houses (Industry 1521): 1982 Census of Construction Industries. Preliminary Report. Industry Series, 2371–1.1
General Contractors: Single-Family Houses, Industry 1521. 1982 Census of Construction Industries. Industry Series, 2373–1.1

General Description of the Corporation Source Book, Statistics of Income Division, 8304–4
General Equilibrium Properties of the Term Structure of Interest Rates, 9387–8.91
General Housing Characteristics, Annual Housing Survey, 1983, 2485–1
General Imports of Cotton, Wool, and Manmade Fiber Manufactures, 2422–1
General Industrial Machinery, N.E.C. (Industry 3569): 1982 Census of Manufactures. Preliminary Report. Industry Series, 2491–1.344
General-Line Groceries (Industry 5141): 1982 Census of Wholesale Trade. Preliminary Report. Industry Series, 2403–1.27
General Revenue Sharing. Payments Reports, 8066–1
General Services Administration Annual Report, 9454–1
General Services Administration Operating Summary: 1983, 9454–23
General Social and Economic Characteristics. 1980 Census of Population, Vol. 1. Characteristics of the Population, Chapter C, 2531–3
General Trade Policy, 21368–46
Generating Nutrient Data, 1004–16.1
Generation and Sales Statistics, 1983, 3222–1
Generation of Behavioral Lags for ISTUM2, 3308–66.8
Generic Advertising of Farm Products, 1548–242
Geographic Area Series. 1982 Census of Agriculture, Vol. 1, 2331–1
Geographic Distribution of VA Expenditures, FY82: County and Congressional District, 9924–14
Geographic Distribution of VA Expenditures, FY83: County and Congressional District, 9924–14
Geographic Market Delineation: A Review of the Literature, 9366–1.138
Geographic Profile of Employment and Unemployment, 1983, 6744–7
Geographic Shifts in the Veteran Population During the 1970's, 9926–4.7
Geographical Distribution of Assets and Liabilities of Major Foreign Branches of U.S. Banks, 9365–3.7
Geographical Mobility: Mar. 1981 to Mar. 1982, 2546–1.384
Georgia: A Healthy Economy Looks for Solid Growth, 9371–1.405
Georgia's Forests, 1206–26.7
Glaciological Data, 2156–18
Glass and Glazing Work Special Trade Contractors (Industry 1793): 1982 Census of Construction Industries. Preliminary Report. Industry Series, 2371–1.22
Glass and Glazing Work Special Trade Contractors, Industry 1793. 1982 Census of Construction Industries. Industry Series, 2373–1.22
Glass Containers (Industry 3221): 1982 Census of Manufactures. Preliminary Report. Industry Series, 2491–1.224
Glass Containers, Current Industrial Report, 2506–9.4
Glass Containers, TSUS Items 545(pt.): Summary of Trade and Tariff Information, 9885–5.14
Global Dynamics of Biospheric Carbon, 3406–3.36

Global Perspective for Crop Titles

Global Perspective for Crop Insurance in 1984, 1004–16.1

Global Stocks of Grain: Implications for U.S. Policy, 1528–184

Gloves and Mittens, 1983, Current Industrial Report, 2506–6.4

Glue, Gelatin, and Related Products, TSUS Items 455(pt.): Summary of Trade and Tariff Information, 9885–4.48

GNMA Annual Report, 1983, 5144–6

Gold and Silver Leaching Practices in the U.S., 5606–6.1

Gold and Silver: Mineral Industry Surveys, 5612–1.10

Gold: Minerals Yearbook Preprint, Vol. 1, 1983, 5604–15.27

Government Employment, 2466–1

Government Finances Series, 2466–2

Government Life Insurance Programs for Veterans and Members of the Services, Annual Report, 1983, 9924–2

Government Loan and Guarantee Programs, 9391–1.403

Government National Mortgage Association (GNMA) Annual Report, 1983, 5144–6

Government of Guam Annual Report, FY83, 5304–15.6

Government of the Virgin Islands Annual Report, FY83, 5304–15.7

Government-Owned Surplus Dairy Products Held in Inventory, 26113–120

Government Printing Office Can More Effectively Manage Its General Sales Program, 26111–17

Governmental Actors and Factors in Mass Transit, 10042–1.404

Governmental Finances in 1982-83, 2466–2.6

Governmental Finances. No. 1: Finances of Public School Systems. 1982 Census of Governments, Vol. 4, 2457–1

Governmental Finances. No. 3: Finances of County Governments. 1982 Census of Governments, Vol. 4, 2457–3

Governmental Finances. No. 4: Finances of Municipal and Township Governments. 1982 Census of Governments, Vol. 4, 2457–4

Graduate Science/Engineering Enrollment Grew by 2% Between Fall 1981 and 1982, with Computer Sciences, Up 20%, Leading Growth, 9626–2.141

Graduate Science/Engineering Enrollment Rose 2% in 1981, Mostly in "High-Tech" Fields, 9626–2.134

Grain (Industry 5153): 1982 Census of Wholesale Trade. Preliminary Report. Industry Series, 2403–1.33

Grain and Feed Market News, Weekly Summary and Statistics, 1313–2

Grain Loan Activity Through (Month), 1802–3

Grain Market News: Quarterly Durum Report, 1313–6

Grain Mill Products, June 1982: Industry Wage Survey, 6787–6.204

Grain Stocks, 1621–4

Grain Transportation Situation, 1272–2

Grains: Foreign Agriculture Circular, 1925–2

Grand and Petit Juror Service in U.S. District Courts, 1983, 18204–4

Grand and Petit Juror Service in U.S. District Courts, 1984, 18204–4

Grand and Upright Pianos from the Republic of Korea: Determination of the Commission in Investigation No. 731-TA-204

(Preliminary) Under the Tariff Act of 1930, Together with the Information Obtained in the Investigation, 9886–14.124

Grant Awards, FY83, 7304–7

Grant-In-Aid for Fisheries: Program Activities, 1983, 2164–3

Graphic Industries Equipment: Country Market Survey, 2045–3

Graphite: Minerals Yearbook Preprint, Vol. 1, 1983, 5604–15.28

Graphite, 1983: Mineral Industry Surveys Annual Advance Summary, 5614–5.8

Grassroots Development: Journal of the Inter-American Foundation, Vol. 8:1, 14422–2

Gray Iron Foundries (Industry 3321): 1982 Census of Manufactures. Preliminary Report. Industry Series, 2491–1.255

Grazing Statistical Summary, FY83, 1204–5

Great Lakes and Connecting Channels: Water Levels and Depths, 3752–2

Great Lakes Navigation Season, 1983, 2152–8.403

Great Lakes Water Level Facts, 3758–6

Great Lakes Water Levels, 1982, 2174–3

Great Lakes Water Quality, 1983 Report, 14644–1

"Great Velocity Decline" of 1982-83: A Comparative Analysis of M1 and M2, 9393–8.410

Greeting Card Publishing (Industry 2771): 1982 Census of Manufactures. Preliminary Report. Industry Series, 2491–1.168

Grocery Stores (Industry 5411): 1982 Census of Retail Trade. Preliminary Report. Industry Series, 2395–1.8

Gross Flow Data from the Current Population Survey, 1970-80, 6744–17

Gross Flows in the Labor Force, 1980-82, 6744–17

Gross Migration for Counties: 1975 to 1980. 1980 Census of Population. Supplementary Report, 2535–1.14

Gross Mortgage Originations for Owner-Occupied Homes, 8304–16.1

Gross Product by Industry, 1983, 2702–1.416

Gross State Product in New England, 9373–2.403

Ground Water Management in the Southeastern U.S., Final Report, 9208–119

Ground Water Supply Survey, Summary of Volatile Organic Contaminant Occurrence Data, 9208–120

Groundwater Contamination from Underground Fuel Tanks, 1561–16.405

Growing Role of Private Security, 6066–20.8

Growth in Nonmetropolitan Areas Slows, 2328–47

Growth Markets of the 1980's: Western Europe, 2048–105

Growth of the Underground Economy, 1950-81: Some Evidence from the Current Population Survey, 23848–178

Guide for Setting Title II-A Performance Standards, 6408–59.1

Guide to Alternative Financing Mechanisms for Urban Highways, Report 3. Financing Urban Transportation Improvements, 7556–7.3

Guide to Department of Education Programs, 1984, 4804–3

Guide to Interstate Banking, 1983, 9371–13

Guide to the 1982 Census of Agriculture And Related Statistics, 2308–55

Guide to the 1982 Economic Censuses And Related Statistics, 2308–5

Guided Missiles and Space Vehicles (Industry 3761): 1982 Census of Manufactures. Preliminary Report. Industry Series, 2491–1.401

Guideline, a Framework for the Evaluation and Comparison of Software Development Tools: Software, 2216–2.115

Guideline, American National Dictionary for Information Processing Systems: Software, 2216–2.125

Guideline, Codes for Named Populated Places, Primary County Divisions, and Other Locational Entities of the U.S.: Data Standards and Guidelines, 2216–2.122

Guideline for Computer Security Certification and Accreditation: Computer Security, 2216–2.124

Guideline for Implementation of ANSI Codes for the Representation of Names of Countries, Dependencies, and Areas of Special Sovereignty: Data Standards and Guidelines, 2216–2.120

Guideline for Lifecycle Validation, Verification, and Testing of Computer Software, 2216–2.123

Guideline for Optical Character Recognition (OCR) Print Quality: Hardware Standard, 2216–2.114

Guideline on Electrical Power for ADP Installations: Hardware, 2216–2.117

Guideline on Software Maintenance: Software, 2216–2.127

Gum and Wood Chemicals (Industry 2861): 1982 Census of Manufactures. Preliminary Report. Industry Series, 2491–1.190

Gypsum: Mineral Industry Surveys, 5612–1.31

Gypsum: Minerals Yearbook Preprint, Vol. 1, 1983, 5604–15.29

Gypsum Products (Industry 3275): 1982 Census of Manufactures. Preliminary Report. Industry Series, 2491–1.241

Habeas Corpus, 6066–19.4

Hand-Directed or -Controlled Power Tools, TSUS Items 674(pt.) and 683(pt.): Summary of Trade and Tariff Information, 9885–6.79

Hand Saws and Saw Blades (Industry 3425): 1982 Census of Manufactures. Preliminary Report. Industry Series, 2491–1.280

Handbags, TSUS Items 706(pt.): Summary of Trade and Tariff Information, 9885–7.60

Handbook of Agricultural Charts, 1983, 1504–3

Handbook of Cyclical Indicators: A Supplement to the Business Conditions Digest, 2708–31

Handbook of Economic Statistics, 1984, 244–5

Handbook of Hearing Aid Measurement, 1984, 9924–5

Handbook of Labor Statistics, 6724–1

Handbook on Women Workers, 1983, Time of Change, 6568–29

Handicapped Children's Early Education Program, 1982-83 Overview and Directory, 4804–30

Handicapped Children's Early Education Program, Directory, 1983-84 Edition, 4804–30

Handkerchiefs, Neckwear, Hosiery and Underwear, TSUS Items 370(pt.), 374(pt.), 378(pt.), and 379(pt.): Summary of Trade and Tariff Information, 9885–3.46

Titles — Hispanic Charge Study

Hardware (Industry 5072): 1982 Census of Wholesale Trade. Preliminary Report. Industry Series, 2403–1.10

Hardware, N.E.C. (Industry 3429): 1982 Census of Manufactures. Preliminary Report. Industry Series, 2491–1.281

Hardware Stores (Industry 5251): 1982 Census of Retail Trade. Preliminary Report. Industry Series, 2395–1.3

Hardwood Dimension and Flooring (Industry 2426): 1982 Census of Manufactures. Preliminary Report. Industry Series, 2491–1.113

Hardwood Plywood, 1983, Current Industrial Report, 2506–7.1

Hardwood Veneer and Plywood (Industry 2435): 1982 Census of Manufactures. Preliminary Report. Industry Series, 2491–1.117

Harry S. Truman Memorial Scholarship Fund: Status of Account, 14312–1

Harry S. Truman Scholarship Foundation, Annual Report, 1983, 14314–1

Has the Deregulation of Deposit Interest Rates Raised Mortgage Rates?, 9391–1.412

Hatchery Production, 1983 Summary, 1625–8

Hats and Caps, Except Millinery (Industry 2352): 1982 Census of Manufactures. Preliminary Report. Industry Series, 2491–1.92

Hay Market News, 1313–5

Hazard Mitigation Potential of Earth-Sheltered Residences, 3308–71

Hazardous Materials Transportation, Annual Report, 1983, 7304–4

Health and Prevention Profile: U.S., 1983, 4144–11

Health and the Environment Miscellaneous, Part 1, 21368–47

Health Care Cost Control Act of 1983, 21788–136

Health Care Coverage of Survivor Families with Children: Determinants and Consequences, 4742–1.404

Health Care Expenditures for Major Diseases, 4144–11.1

Health Care Expenditures for Major Diseases in 1980, 4652–1.413

Health Care Financing Notes, 4656–1

Health Care Financing Program Statistics: The Medicare and Medicaid Data Book, 1983, 4654–1

Health Care Financing Review, 4652–1

Health Care Financing Status Report, Research and Demonstrations in Health Care Financing, 4652–8

Health Care of Adolescents by Office-Based Physicians: National Ambulatory Medical Care Survey, 1980-81, 4146–8.100

Health Characteristics by Geographic Region, Large Metropolitan Areas, and Other Places of Residence, U.S., 1980-81, 4147–10.146

Health Characteristics of Male Veterans and Nonveterans, Health Interview Surveys, 1971-81, 9926–1.18

Health Consequences of Smoking: Chronic Obstructive Lung Disease. A Report of the Surgeon General, 4044–6

Health Data Inventory, FY83-84, 4044–3

Health Demographic Profile System's Inventory of Small Area Social Indicators, 4506–8.4

Health Effects of Occupational Exposure to Hazardous Chemicals: A Comparative Assessment with Notes on Ionizing Radiation, 9638–50

Health Effects of Occupational Exposure to Hazardous Chemicals: A Comparative Assessment with Notes on Ionizing Radiation. Abstracts of NIOSH Criteria Documents, 9638–50.3

Health Effects of Occupational Exposure to Hazardous Chemicals: A Comparative Assessment with Notes on Ionizing Radiation. Executive Summary, 9638–50.1

Health Effects of Occupational Exposure to Hazardous Chemicals: A Comparative Assessment with Notes on Ionizing Radiation. Supporting Documentation and Review of Epidemiologic Studies of Specific Chemicals, 9638–50.2

Health Indicators for Hispanic, Black, and White Americans, 4147–10.147

Health Information for International Travel, 1984: Supplement to the Morbidity and Mortality Weekly Report, 4204–11

Health Information Resources In the Department of Health and Human Services, 4044–11

Health Information Resources in the Federal Government, 1984, 4048–18

Health Insurance Coverage and Physician Visits Among Hispanic and Non-Hispanic People, 4144–11.1

Health Manpower Statistics, FY83, 3544–24

Health of the Army, 3702–4

Health Physics/Radiation Protection Enrollments and Degrees, 1983, 3004–7

Health Services Personnel: Bureau of Prisons, 6242–2

Health Spending in the 1980s: Integration of Clinical Practice Patterns with Management, 4652–1.407

Health Status of Aged Medicare Beneficiaries, 4146–12.2

Health Survey Research Methods, 4184–1

Hearing on Follow Through Amendments of 1983, 21348–87

Hearing on H.R. 3073, People Protection Act, 21208–18

Hearing on Loan Consolidation Legislation, 21348–92

Hearings on Higher Education Civil Rights Enforcement, 21348–91

Hearings on H.R. 3980, H.R. 3544, H.R. 626, 21208–20

Hearings on the Occupational Disease Compensation Act of 1983, 21348–85

Heating Equipment, Except Electric (Industry 3433): 1982 Census of Manufactures. Preliminary Report. Industry Series, 2491–1.284

Heating Oils, 1984: Petroleum Products Survey, 3006–2.4

Heavy Construction Contractors, N.E.C. (Industry 1629): 1982 Census of Construction Industries. Preliminary Report. Industry Series, 2371–1.9

Heavy Rail Transit Safety, 1983 Annual Report, 7884–5

Heavyweight Motorcycles: Quarterly Report on Selected Indicators, 9882–12

Helium: Minerals Yearbook Preprint, Vol. 1, 1983, 5604–15.30

Helmand Valley Project in Afghanistan, 9916–3.18

Helping Labor and Management Set Up a Quality-of-Worklife Program, 6722–1.419

Herbs and Spices, TSUS Items 161(pt.) and 162(pt.): Summary of Trade and Tariff Information, 9885–1.66

HFCS Competition: A Year of Transition, 1004–16.1

High-Performance Companies in the Southeast: What Can They Teach Us?, 9371–1.414

High School and Beyond: A National Longitudinal Study for the 1980's, 4826–2

High School and Beyond Course Offerings and Course Enrollments Survey (1982), Data File User's Manual, 4826–2.17

High School and Beyond Tabulation: Foreign Language Course Taking by 1980 High School Sophomores Who Graduated in 1982, 4828–17

High School and Beyond Transcripts Survey (1982), Data File User's Manual, 4826–2.16

High School Course Grade Standards, 4826–2.21

High School Seniors: A Comparative Study of the Classes of 1972 and 1980, 4826–2.15

High Speed Rail in the Midwest, 9375–1.406

High Technology and Regional Economic Development, 9373–2.402

High Technology in the Southeast, 6948–6

High Technology Industries: Economic Indicators, 2042–28

High Utilizers of Ambulatory Care Services: 6-Year Followup at Alaska Native Medical Center, 4102–1.440

Higher Education Act, Title II-C, FY84 Abstracts: Strengthening Research Library Resources Program, 4804–22

Highlights, Federal Home Loan Bank of Cincinnati, 9302–8

Highlights from Drugs and American High-School Students, 1975-83, 4494–4

Highlights of U.S. Export and Import Trade, 2422–9

Highway and Street Construction Contractors (Industry 1611): 1982 Census of Construction Industries. Preliminary Report. Industry Series, 2371–1.6

Highway and Street Construction Contractors, Industry 1611. 1982 Census of Construction Industries. Industry Series, 2373–1.6

Highway Bridge Replacement and Rehabilitation Program, Fifth Annual Report to Congress, 7554–27

Highway Construction Usage Factors for Construction Materials, 7554–29

Highway Safety Facts, 7766–10

Highway Safety Improvement Programs, 1984 Annual Report of the Secretary of Transportation to the U.S. Congress, Pursuant to Section 203, P.L. 93-87 and 23 U.S.C. 151 and 152, 7554–26

Highway Safety Performance, 1982: Fatal and Injury Accident Rates on Public Roads in the U.S., 7554–2

Highway Safety, 1981, 7764–1

Highway Safety 1981: A Report on Activities Under the Highway Safety Act of 1966, 7764–1.1

Highway Statistics, 1983, 7554–1

Highway Taxes and Fees: How They Are Collected and Distributed, 7554–37

Highway, Transport Fatalities Down for Fourth Year, But Declines Are Far Below 1982, 9614–6

Hispanic Access to Higher Education, 21348–93

Hispanic Charge Study Executive Summary, 9248–18

Hispanic Population: An

Hispanic Population: An Overview, 16598–5
Historic Preservation Fund, FY84 Apportionment to the States, Territories, and the National Trust Under P.L. 98-146, 5544–9
Historic Preservation Fund, FY85 Apportionment to the States, Territories, and the National Trust Under P.L. 98-473, 5544–9
Historical Chart Book, 1984, Board of Governors of the Federal Reserve System, 9364–2
Historical Climatology Series, 2156–17
Historical Financial Analysis of the Investor-Owned Electric Utility Industry, 3168–87
Historical Perspective, 1004–16.1
Historical Plant Cost and Annual Production Expenses for Selected Electric Plants, 1982, 3164–9
Historically Black Colleges and Universities Fact Book, 4004–28
History of the U.S. National Reporting Program for Mental Health Statistics, 1840-1983. Mental Health Service System Reports, Series HN, 4508–5
History of the U.S. Postal Service, 1775-1982, 9864–6
Hog Operations Becoming Fewer, Larger, and More Efficient, 1561–7.405
Hogs and Pigs, 1623–3
Hogs and Pigs, Final Estimates for 1979-82, 1641–10
Hoists, Cranes, and Monorails (Industry 3536): 1982 Census of Manufactures. Preliminary Report. Industry Series, 2491–1.321
Home Equity Financing of Long-Term Care for the Elderly, 4658–7
Home Health Care Cost-Function Analysis, 4652–1.411
Home Mortgage Commitment Rates in Illinois, Federal Home Loan Bank of Chicago, 9302–6
Home Mortgage Commitment Rates in Wisconsin, Federal Home Loan Bank of Chicago, 9302–7
Home Taping in America: 1983, Extent and Impact, 25528–100.1
Homelessness in America: II, Appendixes, 21248–85
Homeownership Trends: 1983, 2486–1.6
Homicide Surveillance: Summary, 1970-78, 4205–38
Honduras: An Export Market Profile, 1526–6.3
Honey: ASCS Commodity Fact Sheet, 1984, 1806–4.7
Hong Kong Market, 1925–34.408
Hop Stocks, 1621–8
Hops Market News, 1313–7
Horticultural Exports Down 3 Percent in FY84, 1925–34.428
Horticultural Markets: Finland, Norway, and Sweden, 1925-34.431
Horticultural Markets: New Zealand, 1925–34.402
Horticultural Markets: U.S. Exports to the Caribbean Islands, 1925–34.413
Horticultural Products: Foreign Agriculture Circular, 1925–34
Hosiery, N.E.C. (Industry 2252): 1982 Census of Manufactures. Preliminary Report. Industry Series, 2491–1.53

Hospital Cost and Utilization Project Research Notes, 4186–6
Hospital Merger Increased Medicare and Medicaid Payments for Capital Costs, 26121–65
Hospital Use by Children in the U.S. and Canada, 4147–5.1
Hospitals: Industry Wage Survey, 6787–6.201
Hot-Rolled Carbon Steel Plate from the Republic of Korea: Determination of the Commission in Investigation No. 731-TA-151 (Final) Under the Tariff Act of 1930, Together with the Information Obtained in the Investigation, 9886–14.111
Hot-Rolled Carbon Steel Plate from the Republic of Korea: Determination of the Commission in Investigation No. 731-TA-151 (Preliminary) Under the Tariff Act of 1930, Together with the Information Obtained in the Investigation, 9886–14.91
Hot-Rolled Carbon Steel Sheet from Brazil: Determination of the Commission in Investigation No. 731-TA-153 (Final) Under the Tariff Act of 1930, Together with the Information Obtained in the Investigation, 9886–14.113
Hotels, Motor Hotels, and Motels (Industry 7011): 1982 Census of Service Industries. Preliminary Report. Industry Series, 2390–2.1
Hourly Flight Operations at 32 Selected Airports, Sept. 1984, 9142–42.411
House Furnishings, N.E.C. (Industry 2392): 1982 Census of Manufactures. Preliminary Report. Industry Series, 2491–1.104
House Slippers (Industry 3142): 1982 Census of Manufactures. Preliminary Report. Industry Series, 2491–1.214
Household and Family Characteristics: Mar. 1982, 2546–1.383
Household Appliance Stores (Industry 5722): 1982 Census of Retail Trade. Preliminary Report. Industry Series, 2395–1.21
Household Appliances, N.E.C. (Industry 3639): 1982 Census of Manufactures. Preliminary Report. Industry Series, 2491–1.369
Household Characteristics and the Demand for Vegetables and Potatoes, 1561–11.401
Household Characteristics, Frequency of Use, and the Demand for Dairy Products, 1561–2.404
Household Economic Studies. Economic Characteristics of Households in the U.S. Current Population Reports. Series P-70, 2542–2
Household Expenditures for Fruits, Vegetables, and Potatoes, 1548–236
Household Furniture, N.E.C. (Industry 2519): 1982 Census of Manufactures. Preliminary Report. Industry Series, 2491–1.133
Household Glassware, TSUS Items 546(pt.): Summary of Trade and Tariff Information, 9885–5.18
Household Refrigerators and Freezers (Industry 3632): 1982 Census of Manufactures. Preliminary Report. Industry Series, 2491–1.364
Household Vacuum Cleaners (Industry 3635): 1982 Census of Manufactures. Preliminary Report. Industry Series, 2491–1.367
Households, Families, Marital Status, and Living Arrangements: Mar. 1984 (Advance Report), 2546–1.389

Households Touched by Crime, 1983, 6062–2.404
Housing: An Overview, 21968–28
Housing and Housing Finance in the Republic of Korea: Part 1, 9312–1.404
Housing and Housing Finance in the Republic of Korea: Part 2, 9312–1.406
Housing Assistance Plan, 1982-85, 21248–84
Housing Authorized by Building Permits and Public Contracts, Construction Reports, 2382–5
Housing Characteristics for Selected Metropolitan Areas, Annual Housing Survey, 1979, 2485–6
Housing Characteristics for Selected Metropolitan Areas, Annual Housing Survey, 1980, 2485–6
Housing Characteristics for Selected Metropolitan Areas, Annual Housing Survey, 1981, 2485–6
Housing Characteristics for Selected Metropolitan Areas, Annual Housing Survey, 1982, 2485–6
Housing Completions, Construction Reports, 2382–2
Housing Finance Review, 9312–7
Housing Finance Review, 9412–2
Housing Guaranty Program, Annual Report, FY83, 9914–4
Housing of the Rural Elderly, 1598–193
Housing Quality and Affordability, 1702–1.406
Housing Quality and Affordability, 1980, 1004–16.1
Housing Starts, Construction Reports, 2382–1
Housing Tenure, Uncertainty, and Taxation, 8006–3.50
Housing Units Authorized by Building Permits and Public Contracts, Annual 1983, Construction Report, 2384–2
Housing Vacancies: Vacancy Rates and Characteristics of Housing in the U.S., Annual Statistics 1983, 2484–1
Housing Vacancies: Vacant Housing Units in the U.S., Current Housing Reports, 2482–1
Housing Vacancy Survey, Federal Home Loan Bank Board of Cincinnati, 9304–27
Housing Vacancy Survey, Federal Home Loan Bank of Chicago, 9304–18
Housing Vacancy Survey, Federal Home Loan Bank of Dallas, 9304–19
Housing Vacancy Survey, Federal Home Loan Bank of San Francisco, 9304–20
Housing Vacancy Survey, Federal Home Loan Bank of Seattle, 9304–21
Housing Vacancy Survey, Federal Home Loan Bank of Topeka, 9304–22
How Can the Federal Government Best Decrease Poverty in the U.S.? National Debate Topic for High Schools, 1984-85, 25928–4
How Different Are Regional Wages? A Second Look, 9373–1.407
How Do Families Fare when the Breadwinner Retires?, 6746–1.253
How Federal Milk Order Market Statistics Are Developed and What They Mean, 1317–4.402
How Robust Are the Policy Conclusions of the St. Louis Equation?: Some Further Evidence, 9391–1.417
How Social Security Payments Affect Private Pensions, 6722–1.431
How Soon Will the U.S. Reach Full Employment? An Assessment Based on Okun's Law, 9393–8.408

Titles

How the Content of the Agricultural and Economic Censuses Is Determined and Used, 26125–26

HUD Awards $1.7 Million To Promote Equal Housing Opportunity, 5006–3.34

HUD News: Miscellaneous Press Releases, 5006–3

HUD News Release: HUD Secretary Announces Financing for Elderly and Handicapped Housing, 5004–6

HUD Pension Fund Survey, Mortgage Related Investments of Private Pension Funds, 5002–10

HUD Secretary Announces Financing for Elderly and Handicapped Housing News Release, 5004–6

HUD Secretary Announces Housing Development Grants, 5006–3.38

HUD Solar Bank Announces Awards of $18 Million, 5006–3.36

HUD Under Secretary Outlines Assistance to Steel Industry, 5006–3.37

Human Resources, 21968–28

Hydraulic Cement, TSUS Items 511(pt.): Summary of Trade and Tariff Information, 9885–5.17

Hydrocarbon Processing in OPEC Countries: Excess Capacities and Readjustment Pains in the World Refining Industry, 25368–133.1

Hydroelectic Plant Construction Cost and Annual Production Expenses, 3164–37

Hydroelectric Power: 1983 Was a Record Year, 3162–39.401

Hydrogen Energy Coordinating Committee Annual Report: Summary of DOE Hydrogen Programs for FY83, 3304–18

Hydrologic Assessment, Selected Basins in the Eastern and Interior Coal Provinces, 5666–15

Hydrologic Assessment, Selected Basins in the Western, Interior, Northern Great Plains, and Rocky Mountain Coal Provinces, 5666–19

Hydrologic Effects of the Eruptions of Mount St. Helens, Wash., 1980, 5666–14

Hydrology of Area 1, Eastern Coal Province, Pennsylvania, 5666–15.24

Hydrology of Area 2, Eastern Coal Province, Pennsylvania and New York, 5666–15.25

Hydrology of Area 10, Eastern Coal Province, West Virginia and Virginia, 5666–15.26

Hydrology of Area 13, Eastern Coal Province, Kentucky, Virginia, and West Virginia, 5666–15.22

Hydrology of Area 21, Eastern Coal Province, Tennessee, Alabama and Georgia, 5666–15.23

Hydrology of Area 54, Northern Great Plains, and Rocky Mountain Coal Provinces, Colorado, and Wyoming, 5666–19.4

Hydrology of Area 61, Northern Great Plains and Rocky Mountain Coal Provinces, Colorado and New Mexico, 5666–19.5

Hypertension Control: Meeting the 1990 Objectives for the Nation, 4102–1.432

I/O Channel Interface: Hardware Standard, 2216–2.119

Ice Cream and Frozen Desserts (Industry 2024): 1982 Census of Manufactures. Preliminary Report. Industry Series, 2491–1.6

Income Changes at and After

Ichthyoplankton and Fish Recruitment Studies in Large Marine Ecosystems, 2162–1.402

Identical Bidding in Public Procurement: Report of the Attorney General Under Executive Order 10936, 6004–8

Identification and Analysis of Human Errors Underlying Electrical/Electronic Component Related Events Reported by Nuclear Power Plant Licensees, 9638–51

Illicit Traffic and Undue Use of Coca and Cocaine in Peru in 1978, 7008–40

Immigrants Admitted as Professional, Technical, and Kindred Workers, 6264–1

Immigration and Naturalization Service Annual Report, 6264–2

Immigration Reform and Agricultural Labor, 1598–192

Immunization Conference Proceedings, Atlanta, Ga., May 16-19, 1983, 4204–15

Immunization Conference Proceedings, Boston, Mass., May 21-24, 1984, 4204–15

Immunization: Survey of Recent Research, No. 2, 4204–16

Impact of Changing Women's Roles on Transportation Needs and Usage, Final Report, 7888–62

Impact of Discount Rate Changes on Market Interest Rates, 9381–1.404

Impact of Federally Sponsored Credit Agencies' Policy Instruments on Housing and Credit Markets, 9316–2.45

Impact of Robots and Computers on the Work Force of the 1980's, 21728–54

Impact of Surveillance Fields on Crude Oil Production in the U.S., 3164–58

Impact of Tariff and Nontariff Barriers on the U.S. Sheet Vinyl Flooring Industry: Report to the Subcommittee on Trade, Committee on Ways and Means, U.S. House of Representatives, Investigation No. 332-179, Under Section 332(b) of the Tariff Act of 1930, as Amended, 9886–4.76

Impact of Ultra-High Temperature Milk on the U.S. Dairy Industry, 1568–247

Impact of Unemployment on Children and Families, 21348–86

Impact on Low Income and Elderly Consumers of Take-or-Pay and Indefinite Price Escalator Clauses in Gas Contracts, 25148–26

Impacts of Alcohol Fuels on the U.S. Refining Industry, 3308–75

Impacts of Automation on Employment, 1963-2000, 21728–54

Impacts of Coal Surface Mining on 25 Migratory Bird Species of High Federal Interest, 5508–88

Impacts of Downtown Revitalization Projects on Small Business, 21788–140.2

Impacts of Nationwide Adoption of the California Solids Standards for Fluid Milk Product, 1561–2.405

Impacts of Oil Disturbances: Lessons from Experience, 3108–28

Implementation of Helsinki Accord, June 1-Nov. 30, 1983. Fifteenth Semiannual Report, 7002–1

Implementation of Helsinki Accord, Dec. 1, 1983-Mar. 31, 1984. Sixteenth Semiannual Report, 7002–1

Implementation of Section 620(s) of the Foreign Assistance Act of 1961, As Amended: A Report to Congress, 1983, 9914–1

Implementation of the Provisions of the Airline Deregulation Act of 1978, 9148–56

Implications for Bank Merger Policy of Financial Deregulation, Interstate Banking, and Financial Supermarkets, 9366–1.135

Implications of Foreign-Trade Zones for U.S. Industries and for Competitive Conditions Between U.S. and Foreign Firms: Report to the Committee on Ways and Means, U.S. House of Representatives, on Investigation No. 332-165 Under Section 332(g) of the Tariff Act of 1930, 9886–4.70

Implications of Land Contracts for Property Tax Assessment Practices, 9412–2.407

Implications of the Government Deficit for U.S. Capital Formation, 9373–3.27

Implications of the Motor Carrier Act of 1980, 1548–238

Implicit Price Deflators for Military Construction, 2702–1.401

Importance and Impact of Federal Alcohol Fuel Tax Incentives, 26113–140

Importance of GRS Continues and the Need for Renewal Increases, 25408–86.2

Importance of Nutrient Data, 1004–16.1

Imports and Exports of Fishery Products, Annual Summary 1983, 2166–6.6

Imports of Benzenoid Chemicals and Products, 1983, 9884–2

Imports Under Items 806.30 and 807.00 of the Tariff Schedules of the U.S., 1979-82, 9884–14

Impossibility of Causality Testing, 1502–3.403

Improper Use of Industrial Funds by Defense Extended the Life of Appropriations Which Otherwise Would Have Expired, 26111–22

Improved Adjustments for Misreporting of Tax Return Information Used To Estimate the National Income and Product Accounts, 1977, 2702–1.422

Improved Forest and Range Land Productivity Through Research, 1982 Research Accomplishments, 1204–14

Improvements in U.S. Warfighting Capability, FY80-84, 3508–19

Improving U.S. Farmland, 1506–5.20

IMS Awards $2,890,534 for Conservation Project Support, 9564–6.3

IMS Awards $305,245 for Educational and Management Improvement Projects in Museums, 9564–6.2

In-Store ATMs: Steppingstone to POS, 9371–1.403

In the National Interest: Continuing Education, 15214–1

Incapacitating Criminals: Recent Research Findings, 6066–20.3

Incentive Regulation in the Electric Utility Industry, Final Report, 3088–17

Incentives in Manufacturing: The Carrot and the Stick, 6722–1.447

Incidental Catch of Marine Mammals by Foreign Fishing Vessels, 1978-81, 2162–1.401

Income Analysis of Farmers Home Administration Subsidized Rural Homebuyers, 1983, 26113–134

Income and Expenses, 1983: Member Banks and Foreign and Domestic Subsidiaries in the Fifth Federal Reserve District, 9389–10

Income Changes at and After Social Security Benefit Receipt: Evidence from the Retirement History Study, 4742–1.418

Income of the Population 55

Income of the Population 55 and Over, 1982, 4744–26

Income Tax Compliance Research, Estimates for 1973-81, 8308–26

Income Taxes and Income Tax Rates for Financial Reporting Purposes: 1968-83 System Majors, 9144–34

Incomes of the Aged and Nonaged, 1950-82, 4742–1.413

Incomplete Experience Rating in State Unemployment Insurance, 6722–1.469

Incomplete Participant Data Affect Reliability of Values Placed by Actuaries on Multiemployer Pension Plans, 26121–83

Incorporating Severity of Illness and Comorbidity in Case-Mix Measurement, 4652–1.426

Indexes and Estimates of Domestic Well Drilling Costs, 1983 and 1984, 3164–67

Indian and Alaska Native Housing and Community Development Programs: Annual Report to Congress, FY80, 5004–5

Indian and Alaska Native Housing and Community Development Programs: Annual Report to Congress, FY81, 5004–5

Indian and Alaska Native Housing and Community Development Programs: Annual Report to Congress (As of Dec. 1, 1982), 5004–5

Indian Education Act: Indian Students Have the Right to Excellence in Education, 14874–1

Indian Education Act, Part A: Report to the Congress on the Annual Program Audit for FY82, 4804–29

Indian Health Care Improvement Act, P.L. 94-437, Annual Report, FY82, 4104–11

Indian Health Service, FY85 Budget Appropriation: "Chart Series" Tables, 4104–7

Indicators of Comparative East-West Economic Strength, 1982, 7144–11

Indicators of Housing and Neighborhood Quality by Financial Characteristics. Annual Housing Survey: 1981. Part B, 2485–2

Indicators of Long-Term Real Interest Rates, 9393–8.406

Individual Income Tax Returns: Selected Characteristics from the 1983 Taxpayer Usage Study, 8302–2.414

Individual Income Tax Returns, 1982, Statistics of Income, 8304–2

Indochinese Refugee Program, 7002–4

Indoor Air Quality Research, 21708–102

Induced Terminations of Pregnancy: Reporting States, 1980, 4146–5.72

Industrial and Personal Service Paper (Industry 5113): 1982 Census of Wholesale Trade. Preliminary Report. Industry Series, 2403–1.21

Industrial Composition of Foreign Direct Investment in the U.S. and Abroad: A Preliminary Look, 9373–1.411

Industrial Consequences of Alternative Pollution Regulation Scenarios, 9188–84

Industrial Controls (Industry 3622): 1982 Census of Manufactures. Preliminary Report. Industry Series, 2491–1.359

Industrial Democracy: Made in the U.S.A., 6722–1.433

Industrial Development: Tennessee Valley Region, 1983, 9804–3

Industrial Diversification, Exchange Rate Shocks, and the Texas-Mexico Border, 9379–1.402

Industrial Energy Productivity Project, Final Report, 3308–66

Industrial Energy Productivity Project, Final Report: Computer Code Documentation for the Industrial Sector Technology Use Model (ISTUM-2), 3308–66.9

Industrial Energy Productivity Project, Final Report: Generic Energy Services, 3308–66.7

Industrial Energy Productivity Project, Final Report: Introduction, 3308–66.1

Industrial Energy Productivity Project, Final Report: Other Industries, 3308–66.6

Industrial Energy Productivity Project, Final Report: Overall Study Methodology, 3308–66.8

Industrial Energy Productivity Project, Final Report: The Chemicals Industry, 3308–66.5

Industrial Energy Productivity Project, Final Report: The Iron and Steel Industry, 3308–66.4

Industrial Energy Productivity Project, Final Report: The Petroleum Refining Industry, 3308–66.3

Industrial Energy Productivity Project, Final Report: The Pulp and Paper Industry, 3308–66.2

Industrial Fishery Products, Annual Summary 1982, 2166–6.2

Industrial Gases (Industry 2813): 1982 Census of Manufactures. Preliminary Report. Industry Series, 2491–1.175

Industrial Gases, Current Industrial Report, 2506–8.3

Industrial Heat Treatment Equipment, TSUS Items 661(pt.): Summary of Trade and Tariff Information, 9885–6.72

Industrial Inorganic Chemicals, N.E.C. (Industry 2819): 1982 Census of Manufactures. Preliminary Report. Industry Series, 2491–1.177

Industrial Machinery and Equipment (Industry 5084): 1982 Census of Wholesale Trade. Preliminary Report. Industry Series, 2403–1.15

Industrial Organic Chemicals, N.E.C. (Industry 2869): 1982 Census of Manufactures. Preliminary Report. Industry Series, 2491–1.192

Industrial Patent Activity in the U.S., 2244–3

Industrial Patent Activity in the U.S., Part 1: Time Series Profile by Company and Country of Origin, 1969-82, 2244–3.1

Industrial Patent Activity in the U.S., Part 1: Time Series Profile by Company and Country of Origin, 1969-83, 2244–3.3

Industrial Patent Activity in the U.S., Part 2: Alphabetical Listing by Company, 1970-82, 2244–3.2

Industrial Patent Activity in the U.S., Part 2: Alphabetical Listing by Company, 1969-83, 2244–3.4

Industrial Policy Debate, 26306–6.69

Industrial Process Controls: Country Market Survey, 2045–6

Industrial Production, 9365–2.10

Industrial Supplies (Industry 5085): 1982 Census of Wholesale Trade. Preliminary Report. Industry Series, 2403–1.16

Industrial Trucks and Tractors (Industry 3537): 1982 Census of Manufactures. Preliminary Report. Industry Series, 2491–1.322

Industries Series. 1982 Census of Construction Industries, 2373–1

Titles

Industry Reports Shortages of Scientists and Engineers Down Substantially from 1982 to 1983, 9626–2.133

Industry Summary: Quarterly Financial Review, 9142–30.5

Industry Wage Survey: Appliance Repair, Nov. 1981, 6787–6.197

Industry Wage Survey: Auto Dealer Repair Shops, Nov. 1982, 6787–6.202

Industry Wage Survey: Basic Iron and Steel, Aug. 1983, 6787–6.206

Industry Wage Survey: Bituminous Coal, July 1982, 6787–6.198

Industry Wage Survey: Communications, Oct.-Dec. 1981, 6787–6.199

Industry Wage Survey: Electric and Gas Utilities, Oct. 1982, 6787–6.205

Industry Wage Survey: Grain Mill Products, June 1982, 6787–6.204

Industry Wage Survey: Hospitals, 6787–6.201

Industry Wage Survey: Nonferrous Metal Manufacturing Industries, Feb. 1981, 6787–6.196

Industry Wage Survey: Oil and Gas Extraction, June 1982, 6787–6.203

Industry Wage Survey: Women's and Misses' Dresses, Aug. 1982, 6787–6.200

Industry Wage Surveys, 6787–6

Infant Health Consequences of Childbearing by Teenagers and Older Mothers, 4102–1.420

Inflation and the Business Cycle During the Postwar Period, 6722–1.464

Inflation and the Choice of "Monetary" Guidelines, 9373–1.401

Inflation Remained Low in 1983 in Face of Strong Recovery, 6722–1.429

Inflationary Expectations and the Consumer, 9387–8.92

Influences on U.S. Direct Food Purchase Program, 1548–243

Influenza Surveillance, Report No. 94, 4205–3

Information Collection Budget of the U.S. Government, FY84, 104–19

Information Contained in Local Assessment Records, 1972 to 1982, 1588–81

Information Explosion, 1004–16.1

Information on DOE's Costing and Pricing of Uranium Enrichment Services, 26113–137

Information on Forest Service Below-Cost Timber Sales for National Forests in Colorado, 26113–131

Information on the Federal Crop Insurance Program in North Carolina and Iowa, 26113–132

Information on the Military Services' Enlisted Aide Program, 26123–53

Information Security Oversight Office, Annual Report to the President, FY83, 9454–21

Information Systems Reports. Mental Health Service System Reports, Series FN, 4506–2

Initial State & Local Data Elements, Revenue Sharing Entitlement Period 15: Oct. 1, 1983-Sept. 30,1984, 8066–1.95

Injuries in the Logging Industry, 6846–1.14

Injuries Resulting from Falls from Elevations, 6846–1.13

Injuries Resulting from Falls on Stairs, 6846–1.15

Injury and Illness Data Available from 1981 Workers' Compensation Records, 6704–2

Injury Experience in Coal Mining, 1982, 6664–4

Titles

Injury Experience in Metallic Mineral Mining, 1982, 6664–3

Injury Experience in Nonmetallic Mineral Mining (Except Stone and Coal), 1982, 6664–1

Injury Experience in Sand and Gravel Mining, 1982, 6664–2

Injury Experience in Stone Mining, 1982, 6664–5

Inland Transport Modes for Coal and Coal-Derived Energy: An Evaluation Method for Comparing Environmental Impacts, 3408–28

Inorganic Chemicals, Current Industrial Report, 2506–8.1

Inorganic Chemicals, 1982, Current Industrial Report, 2506–8.14

Inorganic Fertilizer Materials and Related Products, Current Industrial Report, 2506–8.2

Inorganic Pigments (Industry 2816): 1982 Census of Manufactures. Preliminary Report. Industry Series, 2491–1.176

Inpatient and Outpatient Summary Data For Indian Health Service Hospitals, 4102–3

Input-Output Structure of the U.S. Economy, 1977, 2702–1.421

Inputs Outlook and Situation Report, 1561–16

Insights into Major Urban Development Action Grant Issues, 26113–118

Inspector General Semiannual Report to the Congress, Oct. 1, 1983-Mar. 31, 1984, 7302–4

Installation or Erection of Building Equipment Special Trade Contractors, N.E.C. (Industry 1796): 1982 Census of Construction Industries. Preliminary Report. Industry Series, 2371–1.25

Institute for Energy Analysis, Research Memoranda, 3006–7

Institute of Museum Services Grant Awards, FY84, 9564–6

Institutions of Higher Education: Index by State and Congressional District, 1983-84, 4844–11

Instructional Use of Computers in Public Schools, Spring 1982, 4826–1.10

Instruments of Monetary Policy, 9381–1.408

Instruments To Measure Electricity (Industry 3825): 1982 Census of Manufactures. Preliminary Report. Industry Series, 2491–1.415

Insulated Wire and Cable, 1982, Current Industrial Report, 2506–10.8

Integration of Science and Technology in CEMA, 2326–9.7

Inter-American Foundation, Annual Report, 1983, 14424–1

Interagency Task Force on Acid Precipitation: First Annual Report to the President and the Congress of the U.S., 14354–1

Interest Rate Risk and the Stock Prices of Financial Institutions, 9391–1.419

Interest Rate Uncertainty and Corporate Debt Maturity, 9381–10.29

Interface Between Data Terminal Equipment (DTE) and Data Circuit-Terminating Equipment (DCE) for Operation with Packet-Switched Data Communication Networks: Hardware Standard, 2216–2.116

Intergovernmental Perspective, 10042–1

Intergovernmental Responsibilities for Financing Public Transit Services, 7888–59

Interim Investigation of Average Daily Subsistence Costs For Selected Localities Within the Conterminous U.S., Part 1, 9454–16

Interim Surveys of Forest Resources in the Southeast, 1206–32

Internal Combustion Engines, N.E.C. (Industry 3519): 1982 Census of Manufactures. Preliminary Report. Industry Series, 2491–1.313

Internal Combustion Engines, 1983, Current Industrial Report, 2506–12.6

Internal Revenue Collections of Excise Taxes, 8302–1

Internal Revenue Report of Excise Taxes, 8302–1

Internal Revenue Service Study of International Cases Involving Section 482 of the Internal Revenue Code, 8008–110

International Aspects of U.S. Monetary and Fiscal Policy, 9373–3.27

International Banking Facilities, 9391–1.409

International Capital Mobility and the Coordination of Monetary Rules, 9387–8.85

International Communication and Information Policy, 25388–46

International Comparisons of Manufacturing Productivity and Labor Cost Trends, Preliminary Measures for 1983, 6864–1

International Developments in Biotechnology and Their Possible Impact on Certain Sectors of the U.S. Chemical Industry: Report on Investigation No. 332-174 Under Section 332(b) of the Tariff Act of 1930, 9886–4.78

International Differences in Wage Behavior: Real, Nominal, or Exaggerated?, 9381–10.34

International Direct Investment, Global Trends and the U.S. Role, 2044–25

International Economic Conditions, 9391–7

International Economic Indicators, 2042–10

International Emergency Lending Facilities—Are They Adequate?, 9373–3.28

International Energy Annual, 1983, 3164–50

International Energy Prices, 1978-82, 3164–71

International Energy Prices, 1979-83, 3164–71

International Energy Statistical Review, 242–5

International Exchange and Training Programs of the U.S. Government, Annual Report, FY82, 9854–8

International Exchange and Training Programs of the U.S. Government, Annual Report, FY83, 9854–8

International Finance: The National Advisory Council on International Monetary and Financial Policies, Annual Report to the President and to the Congress for FY83, 15344–1

International Finance Discussion Papers, 9366–7

International Investment Position of the U.S. in 1983, 2702–1.424

International Investment Position of the U.S., 1970-83, 2702–1.431

International Liquidity: Are the Supply and Composition Appropriate?, 9373–3.28

International Market for Ornamental Plants, 1925–34.417

International Monetary Policy, 1004–16.1

Investment Banking:

International Monetary System: Forty Years After Bretton Woods, 9373–3.28

International Narcotics Control Strategy Report to Committee on Foreign Relations, Committee on Foreign Affairs, 7004–17

International Narcotics Control Strategy Report Mid Year Update, 7004–17

International Network of Food Data Systems (INFOODS), 1004–16.1

International Pesticide Outlook, 1004–16.1

International Repercussions of the U.S. Budget Deficit, 9366–7.102

International Research Documents, 2546–10

International Security and Development Cooperation Program, 7004–14

International Technical Conference on Experimental Safety Vehicles, 7764–3

International Trade and Foreign Markets: Foreign Agriculture Circular, Wood Products, 1925–36

International Travel and Passenger Fares, 1983, 2702–1.417

International Travel to and from the U.S.: 1985 Outlook, 2904–9

International Trends and Perspectives: Aging, 2546–10.12

Interrelationship of Funding for the Arts At the Federal, State, and Local Levels, 21408–69

Interstate Banking: The Drive To Consolidate, 9373–1.409

Interstate Commerce Commission, 1983 Annual Report, 9484–1

Interstate Commerce Commission Can Better Manage Its Enforcement Program, 26113–133

Interstate Movements of Natural Gas, 1982, 3162–4.409

Intertemporal Asset Pricing and the Term Structure of Exchange and Interest Rates: The Eurocurrency Market, 9381–10.40

Intervention, Deficit Finance and Real Exchange Rates: The Case of Japan, 9393–8.405

Intravenous Drug Users and the Acquired Immune Deficiency Syndrome, 4102–1.427

Introduction to the Guide to ED Programs, 4804–3

Inventories of Steel Mill Shapes, Current Industrial Report, 2506–10.3

Inventory of Agricultural Research, FY82, 1744–2

Inventory of American Intermodal Equipment, 1984, 7704–10

Inventory of Power Plants in the U.S., 1983 Annual, 3164–36

Inventory of Private Agency Population Research, 1981, 4474–16

Investigating the Differences in Weekly Earnings of Women and Men, 6722–1.437

Investigation of Average Daily Subsistence Costs Incurred During Travel Within the Conterminous U.S., 9454–16

Investigation of Average Daily Subsistence Costs Incurred During Travel Within the Conterminous U.S., Part 2, 9454–16

Investigation of Cash Management Practices and Their Effects on the Demand for Money, 9389–1.409

Investigation of Operating Costs for Privately Owned Vehicles, 9454–13

Investigations of Major Drug Trafficking Organizations, 26119–57

Investment Banking: Commercial Banks' Inroads, 9371–1.418

Investment Tax Credit for

Investment Tax Credit for Individual Taxpayers, 1981, 8302–2.409
Investment Tax Credit on Corporation Returns, 1980, 8302–2.405
Investments in Soil Conservation Structures: The Role of Operator and Operation Characteristics, 1502–3.402
Investor Perceptions of Nuclear Power, 3168–88
Iodine: Minerals Yearbook Preprint, Vol. 1, 1983, 5604–15.74
Iodine, 1983: Mineral Industry Surveys Annual Advance Summary, 5614–5.9
IPP Impacts on Small Businesses: Millard and Juab Counties, 25728–36
Iron and Steel Castings, Current Industrial Reports, 2506–10.1
Iron and Steel Forgings (Industry 3462): 1982 Census of Manufactures. Preliminary Report. Industry Series, 2491–1.294
Iron and Steel Foundries and Steel Ingot Producers, Current Industrial Reports, 2506–10.1
Iron and Steel: Minerals Yearbook Preprint, Vol. 1, 1983, 5604–15.33
Iron and Steel Scrap: Mineral Industry Surveys, 5612–1.11
Iron and Steel Scrap: Minerals Yearbook Preprint, Vol. 1, 1983, 5604–15.34
Iron Bars from Brazil: Determination of the Commission in Investigation No. 701-TA-208 (Preliminary) Under the Tariff Act of 1930, Together with the Information Obtained in the Investigation, 9886–15.45
Iron Ore: Mineral Industry Surveys, 5612–1.12
Iron Ore: Minerals Yearbook Preprint, Vol. 1, 1983, 5604–15.31
Iron Oxide Pigments: Minerals Yearbook Preprint, Vol. 1, 1983, 5604–15.32
IRS' Administration of the Crude Oil Windfall Profit Tax Act of 1980, 26119–65
IRS Generally Does a Good Job when Abating Civil Penalties, and Has Made Recent Improvements, 26119–68
Is the Dollar Overvalued in Foreign Exchange Markets?, 9371–1.413
Is There a Need for Reform?, 9373–3.28
Issues Facing Cotton Producers, 1004–16.1
Issues in World Agricultural Trade, 1004–16.1

Jails: Intergovernmental Dimensions of a Local Problem, A Commission Report, 10048–59
Jamaica: The Impact and Effectiveness of the PL 480 Title I Program, 9916–1.51
Japan-U.S. Friendship Commission Annual Report, 1983, 14694–1
Japan's Low Unemployment: An In-Depth Analysis, 6722–1.418
Jet and Non-Jet Service in the 48 States, June 1978-June 1984, 9142–42.409
Jewelers' Materials and Lapidary Work (Industry 3915): 1982 Census of Manufactures. Preliminary Report. Industry Series, 2491–1.426
Jewelry, Precious Metal (Industry 3911): 1982 Census of Manufactures. Preliminary Report. Industry Series, 2491–1.424
Jewelry Stores (Industry 5944): 1982 Census of Retail Trade. Preliminary Report. Industry Series, 2395–1.30
Jewelry, Watches, Diamonds and Other Precious Stones (Industry 5094): 1982 Census of Wholesale Trade. Preliminary Report. Industry Series, 2403–1.19

Job Attitudes Toward the New Maintenance Concept of the Airway Facilities Service, 7506–10.25
Job Cuts Are Only One Means Firms Use To Counter Imports, 6722–1.439
Job Outlook Through 1995: Industry Output and Employment Projections, 6728–29
Job Patterns for Minorities and Women In Apprenticeship Programs and Referral Unions, 9244–7
Job Patterns for Minorities and Women In Private Industry, 1981, 9244–1
Job Training Partnership Act, CETA, and Rural Communities, 1502–7.403
Jobs and Prices in a Recovering Economy, 6728–28
Joint Economic Report, 1984, 23844–2
Joint Hearing on Plant Closing, 21348–84
Joint Production, Quasi-Fixed Factors of Production and Investment in Finished Goods Inventories, 9387–8.79
Journal of the Inter-American Foundation: Grassroots Development, 14422–2

Kalecki-Keynes Model of World Trade, Finance, and Economic Growth, 9366–7.94
Kansas City Economic Report, 1983, 6974–1
Kinds and Abundances of Fish Larvae in the Caribbean Sea and Adjacent Areas, 2168–80
Kiwifruit Trade Is Set for Dramatic Growth, 1925–34.410
Knit Fabric Production, 1983, Current Industrial Report, 2506–5.7
Knit Outerwear Mills (Industry 2253): 1982 Census of Manufactures. Preliminary Report. Industry Series, 2491–1.54
Knit Underwear Mills (Industry 2254): 1982 Census of Manufactures. Preliminary Report. Industry Series, 2491–1.55
Knitting Mills, N.E.C. (Industry 2259): 1982 Census of Manufactures. Preliminary Report. Industry Series, 2491–1.58
Knowledge of Accident Prevention Among Parents of Young Children in Nine Massachusetts Towns, 4102–1.402
Knowledge of Social Security: Survivor Families with Young Children, 4742–1.401
Koch's Postulates and the Search for the AIDS Agent, 4102–1.431
Korean Agricultural Services: The Invisible Hand in the Iron Glove. Market and Nonmarket Forces in Korean Rural Development, 9916–1.52
Kyanite and Related Materials: Minerals Yearbook Preprint, Vol. 1, 1983, 5604–15.36

Labor Agreement Expirations in the Federal Service, July 1, 1984-June 30, 1985, 9847–1
Labor Contract Negotiations Under the Civil Service Reform Act of 1978, 26119–62
Labor Force Participation of Older Workers, 6886–6.8
Labor Force Statistics Derived from the Current Population Survey: A Databook, 6748–72
Labor Force Statistics from a Family Perspective, 6746–1.253
Labor Market Advantages Continue for College Graduates, 6748–79

Titles

Labor Organization Mergers 1979-84: Adapting to Change, 6722–1.456
Laboratory Instruments: Country Market Survey, 2045–10
Lamb Meat from New Zealand: Determination of the Commission in Investigations Nos. 701-TA-214 and 731-TA-188 (Preliminary) Under the Tariff Act of 1930, Together with the Information Obtained in the Investigations, 9886–19.10
Land and Water Conservation Fund Distributed to States for FY85, 5544–15
Land Areas of the National Forest System, As of Sept. 30, 1983, 1204–2
Land Use Bibliography, 26104–11.3
Large Class I Household Goods Carriers Selected Earnings Data, 9482–14
Large Class I Motor Carriers of Passengers Selected Earnings Data, 9482–13
Large Class I Motor Carriers of Property Selected Earnings Data, 9482–5
Large Diameter Carbon Steel Welded Pipes from Brazil: Determination of the Commission in Investigation No. 731-TA-183 (Preliminary) Under the Tariff Act of 1930, Together with the Information Obtained in the Investigation, 9886–14.103
Large Trucks in Fatal Accidents, 7766–10.10
Latin America: Outlook and Situation Report, 1524–4.9
Laundry, Cleaning, and Garment Services (Industry 721): 1982 Census of Service Industries. Preliminary Report. Industry Series, 2390–2.2
Law Enforcement Efforts To Control Domestically Grown Marijuana, 26119–64
Law Enforcement Officers Killed and Assaulted, 1983, 6224–3
Lawn and Garden Equipment (Industry 3524): 1982 Census of Manufactures. Preliminary Report. Industry Series, 2491–1.315
Layers and Egg Production, Annual Revisions 1982-83, by Months, 1625–7
Lead and Zinc Availability, Domestic: A Minerals Availability Program Appraisal, 5606–4.10
Lead Industry: Mineral Industry Surveys, 5612–1.13
Lead: Minerals Yearbook Preprint, Vol. 1, 1983, 5604–15.37
Lead Pencils and Art Goods (Industry 3952): 1982 Census of Manufactures. Preliminary Report. Industry Series, 2491–1.432
Leasing of Agricultural Inputs, 1544–19.406
Leather and Sheep Lined Clothing (Industry 2386): 1982 Census of Manufactures. Preliminary Report. Industry Series, 2491–1.100
Leather Gloves and Mittens (Industry 3151): 1982 Census of Manufactures. Preliminary Report. Industry Series, 2491–1.218
Leather Goods, N.E.C. (Industry 3199): 1982 Census of Manufactures. Preliminary Report. Industry Series, 2491–1.222
Leather Tanning and Finishing (Industry 3111): 1982 Census of Manufactures. Preliminary Report. Industry Series, 2491–1.212
Legal Services (Industry 81): 1982 Census of Service Industries. Preliminary Report. Industry Series, 2390–2.17
Legal Status of Hijackers, Summarization, 7504–31.5
Legislative Proposals Linking Commodity and Conservation Programs, 25168–61

Titles

Library Statistics of Colleges and Universities, Institutional Data, 4854–1

Licensed Fuel Facility Status Report, Vol. 4, No. 1, 9632–3

Licensed Fuel Facility Status Report, Vol. 4, No. 2, 9632–3

Licensed Operating Reactors, Status Summary Report, 9632–1

Licensed Physicians Who Work in Prisons: A Profile, 4102–1.407

Life Cycle of Individual Income Tax Returns, 8302–2.408

Life Tables for the U.S., 1900-2050, 4706–1.89

"Lifetime Earnings" in Japan for the Class of 1955, 6722–1.427

Lifetime Work Experience and Its Effect on Earnings: Retrospective Data from the 1979 Income Survey Development Program, 2546–2.123

Lime (Industry 3274): 1982 Census of Manufactures. Preliminary Report. Industry Series, 2491–1.240

Lime: Mineral Industry Surveys, 5612–1.15

Lime: Minerals Yearbook Preprint, Vol. 1, 1983, 5604–15.38

Liming of Acidified Waters: A Review of Methods and Effects on Aquatic Ecosystems, 5506–5.13

Liming of Acidified Waters: Issues and Research. A Report of the International Liming Workshop, 5506–5.14

Linking Employment Problems to Economic Status, 6744–15

Lipid Research Clinics Coronary Primary Prevention Trial, 4478–145

Liquefied Petroleum Gas (Bottled Gas) Dealers (Industry 5984): 1982 Census of Retail Trade. Preliminary Report. Industry Series, 2395–1.37

Liquor Stores (Industry 5921): 1982 Census of Retail Trade. Preliminary Report. Industry Series, 2395–1.27

List of Available Publications of USDA, 1004–13

List of Bureau of Mines Publications and Articles, Jan. 1-Dec. 31, 1982, with Subject and Author Index, 5604–40

List of Intercepted Plant Pests, FY82, 1394–16

List of Published Soil Surveys: Jan. 1984, 1264–11

Lithium: Minerals Yearbook Preprint, Vol. 1, 1983, 5604–15.39

Lithographic Platemaking Services (Industry 2795): 1982 Census of Manufactures. Preliminary Report. Industry Series, 2491–1.173

Livestock (Industry 5154): 1982 Census of Wholesale Trade. Preliminary Report. Industry Series, 2403–1.34

Livestock and Meat Statistics, 1983, 1564–6

Livestock and Poultry Outlook and Situation Report, 1561–7

Livestock and Poultry Situation: Foreign Agriculture Circular, 1925–33

Livestock, Meat, and Wool Market News, Weekly Summary and Statistics, 1315–1

Livestock Slaughter, 1623–9

Livestock Slaughter, 1983 Summary, 1623–10

Loan Activity Report, 9912–2

Loan Commitments at Selected Large Commercial Banks, 9365–2.18

Loan Impacts in Home Energy Audit Programs: A Minnesota Example, 3308–72

Main Line Natural Gas Sales

Local Area Personal Income, 1977-82, 2704–2

Local Area Personal Income, 1977-82. Vol. 1: Summary, 2704–2.1

Local Area Personal Income, 1977-82. Vol. 2: New England Region, 2704–2.2

Local Area Personal Income, 1977-82. Vol. 3: Mideast Region, 2704–2.3

Local Area Personal Income, 1977-82. Vol. 4: Great Lakes Region, 2704–2.4

Local Area Personal Income, 1977-82. Vol. 5: Plains Region, 2704–2.5

Local Area Personal Income, 1977-82. Vol. 6: Southeast Region, 2704–2.6

Local Area Personal Income, 1977-82. Vol. 7: Southwest Region, 2704–2.7

Local Area Personal Income, 1977-82. Vol. 8: Rocky Mountain Region, 2704–2.8

Local Area Personal Income, 1977-82. Vol. 9: Far West Region, Including Alaska and Hawaii, 2704–2.9

Local Finance: A Bootstraps Operation, 10042–1.403

Local Government Employment in Selected Metropolitan Areas and Large Counties: 1983, 2466–1.3

Local Governments To Receive Record Payments for Tax-Exempt Federal Lands, 5724–9

Local Population Estimates. Estimates of the Population of Counties and Metropolitan Areas: July 1, 1981, and 1982 (Provisional). Current Population Reports. Series P-26, 2546–4

Local Population Estimates. 1982 Population Estimates and 1981 Per Capita Income Estimates for Counties, Incorporated Places, and Selected Minor Civil Divisions. Current Population Reports. Series P-26., 2546–11

Logging Camps and Logging Contractors (Industry 2411): 1982 Census of Manufactures. Preliminary Report. Industry Series, 2491–1.111

Logistics Support Costs for the B-1B Aircraft Can Be Reduced, 26123–79

Long-Range Estimates of the Financial Status of the Old-Age, Survivors, and Disability Insurance Program, 1983, 4706–1.91

Long-Range Projections of Social Security Trust Fund Operations in Dollars, 4706–2.120

Long Staple Cotton Review, 1309–12

Long-Term Care Financing and Delivery Systems: Exploring Some Alternatives, 4658–7

Long-Term Developments in Trade in Feeds and Livestock Products, 1528–177

Longitudinal Study of Black Youth: Issues, Scope and Findings. Part II, Final Report of the Project: Motivation and Economic Mobility of the Poor, 4008–65.2

Longrun Changes in World Food Supply and Demand: Implications for Development Assistance Policy, 1528–181

Longrun Timber Supply and Demand, 1004–16.1

Longshoremen's and Harbor Workers' Compensation Act and Extensions and the Federal Employees' Compensation Act, Annual Statistical Report for All Districts Combined, FY83, 6504–5.1

Longshoremen's and Harbor Workers' Compensation Act and Extensions, Injuries Reported by District Office, Month, and Act, FY83, 6504–5.7

Longshoremen's and Harbor Workers' Compensation Act, Annual Statistical Report by District Office, FY83, 6504–5.2

Los Angeles Tops Chicago as Second Largest City; Houston Surpasses Philadelphia as Fourth Largest, Census Bureau Estimates, 2328–46

Louisiana: Hopes Ride on World Trade, Energy and World's Fair, 9371–1.407

Low-Income Housing Project Note Sale, 5142–37

Low-Level Radioactive Waste in the Northeast: Disposal Volume Projections, 25528–93

Lowell: A High Technology Success Story, 9373–1.416

Luggage (Industry 3161): 1982 Census of Manufactures. Preliminary Report. Industry Series, 2491–1.219

Lumber, Plywood and Millwork (Industry 5031): 1982 Census of Wholesale Trade. Preliminary Report. Industry Series, 2403–1.4

Lumber Production and Mill Stocks, 1982, Current Industrial Report, 2506–7.4

Lumber Yards (Industry 5211): 1982 Census of Retail Trade. Preliminary Report. Industry Series, 2395–1.1

Macaroni and Spaghetti (Industry 2098): 1982 Census of Manufactures. Preliminary Report. Industry Series, 2491–1.42

Machine Tool Accessories (Industry 3545): 1982 Census of Manufactures. Preliminary Report. Industry Series, 2491–1.326

Machine Tools: Country Market Survey, 2045–9

Machine Tools, Metal Cutting Types (Industry 3541): 1982 Census of Manufactures. Preliminary Report. Industry Series, 2491–1.323

Machine Tools, Metal Forming Types (Industry 3542): 1982 Census of Manufactures. Preliminary Report. Industry Series, 2491–1.324

Machinery, Except Electrical, N.E.C. (Industry 3599): 1982 Census of Manufactures. Preliminary Report. Industry Series, 2491–1.355

Machines Used for Molding and Forming Rubber or Plastics, TSUS Item 678.35: Summary of Trade and Tariff Information, 9885–6.61

Macroeconomic and Energy Supply Integration, 3308–66.8

Macroeconomic Implications of Labor Contracting with Asymmetric Information, 9366–7.104

Magnesium Compounds: Minerals Yearbook Preprint, Vol. 1, 1983, 5604–15.41

Magnesium Mill Products, 1983, Current Industrial Report, 2506–10.6

Magnesium: Mineral Industry Surveys, 5612–2.12

Magnesium: Minerals Yearbook Preprint, Vol. 1, 1983, 5604–15.40

Mail Order Houses (Industry 5961): 1982 Census of Retail Trade. Preliminary Report. Industry Series, 2395–1.33

Main Line Natural Gas Sales to Industrial Users, 1982, 3162–4.401

Main Line Natural Gas Sales to Industrial Users, 1983, 3162–4.412

Major Collective Bargaining

Major Collective Bargaining Settlements in Private Industry, 6782–2

Major Dams, Reservoirs, and Hydroelectric Plants: Worldwide and Bureau of Reclamation, 5824–11

Major Dams, Reservoirs, and Hydroelectric Plants: Worldwide and Bureau of Reclamation, 5828–13

Major Household Appliances, 1983, Current Industrial Report, 2506–12.16

Major Information Technology Systems Acquisition Plans of Federal Executive Agencies, 104–20

Major International Markets for Agricultural Products, 1522–1.402

Major Programs, Bureau of Labor Statistics, 6704–1

Major Themes and Additional Budget Details, FY85, 104–21

Majors: Quarterly Financial Review, 9142–30.1

Making Ends Meet: Boston's Budget in the 1980s, 9373–1.406

Malaria Surveillance, Annual Summary, 1982, 4205–4

Malleable Iron Foundries (Industry 3322): 1982 Census of Manufactures. Preliminary Report. Industry Series, 2491–1.256

Malt (Industry 2083): 1982 Census of Manufactures. Preliminary Report. Industry Series, 2491–1.33

Malt Beverages (Industry 2082): 1982 Census of Manufactures. Preliminary Report. Industry Series, 2491–1.32

Management Information Report: Worker Adjustment Assistance Under the Trade Act of 1974, 6402–13

Management of New Pain in Office-Based Ambulatory Care: National Ambulatory Medical Care Survey, 1980 and 1981, 4146–8.97

Management of Northern Fur Seals on the Pribilof Islands, Alaska, 1786-1981, 2168–79

Managing Federal Information Resources, Annual Report Under the Paperwork Reduction Act of 1980, 104–19

Managing Programs for the Elderly: Design of a Social Information System, 4652–1.402

Managing the Nation's Public Lands: A Program Report Pursuant to Requirements of the Federal Land Policy and Management Act of 1976, 5724–13

Manganese: Mineral Industry Surveys, 5612–1.16

Manganese: Minerals Yearbook Preprint, Vol. 1, 1983, 5604–15.42

Manifold Business Forms (Industry 2761): 1982 Census of Manufactures. Preliminary Report. Industry Series, 2491–1.167

Manpower Assessment Briefs, 3006–8

Manpower Requirements Report for FY85, 3504–1

Manufactured Ice (Industry 2097): 1982 Census of Manufactures. Preliminary Report. Industry Series, 2491–1.41

Manufacturers' Shipments, Inventories, and Orders, Current Industrial Report, 2506–3.1

Manufacturing Industries, N.E.C. (Industry 3999): 1982 Census of Manufactures. Preliminary Report. Industry Series, 2491–1.443

MARAD '82: Annual Report of the Maritime Administration, FY82, 7704–14

MARAD '83: Annual Report of the Maritime Administration, FY83, 7704–14

Marijuana and Health Report to the U.S. Congress from the Secretary of Health and Human Services, 4494–1

Marine Birds of the Southeastern U.S. and Gulf of Mexico, 5508–72

Marine Birds of the Southeastern U.S. and Gulf of Mexico. Part III: Charadriiformes, 5508–72.3

Marine Fisheries Review, 2162–1

Marine Mammal Commission Annual Report, 1983, 14734–1

Marine Mammal Protection Act of 1972 Annual Report, Apr. 1, 1983-Mar. 31, 1984, 2164–11

Marine Minerals: An Alternative Mineral Supply, National Ocean Goals and Objectives for the 1980's, 15048–4

Marine Recreational Fishery Statistics Survey, 2164–13

Marine Recreational Fishery Statistics Survey, 2166–17

Marine Recreational Fishery Statistics Survey, Atlantic and Gulf Coasts, 1979(Revised)-1980, 2166–17.2

Marine Recreational Fishery Statistics Survey, Pacific Coast, 1979-80, 2166–17.1

Marine Recreational Fishery Statistics Survey, Pacific Coast, 1981-82, 2166–17.3

Mariners Weather Log, 2152–8

Marital Status and Its Relation to the Use of Short-Stay Hospitals and Nursing Homes, 4102–1.443

Marital Status and Living Arrangements: Mar. 1983, 2546–1.388

Maritime Policy and Regional Economic Development: Port Development, 21568–34

Maritime Subsidies, 7704–18

Market Absorption of Apartments, Annual, 1983 Absorptions (Completions in 1982), Current Housing Reports, Series H-130, 2484–2

Market Absorption of Apartments, Current Housing Reports, 2482–2

Market Evidence on the Effective Maturity of Bank Assets and Liabilities, 9387–8.82

Market Perceptions of Monetary Policy and the Weekly M1 Announcements, 9387–8.93

Market Profiles for Africa, 2046–5.1

Market Trends in the U.S. Window Industry, 2012–1.403

Marketable Phosphate Rock: Mineral Industry Surveys, 5612–1.30

Marketing and Farm Supply Cooperatives: Commercial Farmer Membership and Use, 1980, 1128–32

Marketing and Farm Supply Cooperatives: Livestock Producer Membership and Use, 1980, 1128–26

Marketing and Transportation of Grain by Local Cooperatives, 1128–28

Marketing Appalachian District Apples, 1983 Crop, 1311–13

Marketing Florida, Georgia, South Carolina, North Carolina, and Appalachian District Peaches, 1983 Crop, 1311–12

Marketing in Bangladesh, 2046–6.9

Marketing in Cameroon, 2046–6.4

Marketing in Canada, 2046–6.1

Marketing in France, 2046–6.5

Marketing in Peru, 2046–6.7

Marketing in South Africa, 2046–6.10

Marketing in Thailand, 2046–6.3

Marketing in Turkey, 2046–6.8

Marketing Methods, Pricing Arrangements, and Marketing Channels Used by Southern Soybean Producers in 1982/83, 1561–3.402

Marketing Operations of Dairy Cooperatives, 1128–29

Married Couples: Work and Income Patterns, 6746–1.253

Masonry, Stone Setting, and Other Stonework Special Trade Contractors (Industry 1741): 1982 Census of Construction Industries. Preliminary Report. Industry Series, 2371–1.13

Materials Sciences Programs, FY84, 3004–18.3

Maternal and Child Health Block Grant: Program Changes Emerging Under State Administration, 26121–70

Maternal and Infant Characteristics Associated with Cesarean Section Delivery, 4144–11.1

Maternal Mortality Surveillance, 1974-78, 4202–7.406

Maternal Occupation and Industry and the Pregnancy Outcome of U.S. Married Women, 1980, 4102–1.422

Maternal Smoking and Drinking Behavior Before and During Pregnancy, 4144–11.1

Mattresses and Bedsprings (Industry 2515): 1982 Census of Manufactures. Preliminary Report. Industry Series, 2491–1.131

Maturity Distribution of Outstanding Negotiable Time Certificates of Deposit at Large Commercial Banks, 9365–2.13

Measurement and Analysis of Productivity Growth: A Synthesis of Thought, 2218–69

Measurement of Nursing Intensity, 4652–1.427

Measurement of Selected Income Flows in Informal Markets, 8308–27

Measuring and Analyzing the Cyclically Adjusted Budget, 9373–3.27

Measuring and Controlling Devices (Industry 3829): 1982 Census of Manufactures. Preliminary Report. Industry Series, 2491–1.416

Measuring and Dispensing Pumps (Industry 3586): 1982 Census of Manufactures. Preliminary Report. Industry Series, 2491–1.352

Measuring Productivity in State and Local Government, 6728–27

Measuring State OSHA Effectiveness Using Occupational Injury Rates: Problems and Prospects, 21348–88

Meat and Dairy Imports, 1925–31

Meat and Meat Products (Industry 5147): 1982 Census of Wholesale Trade. Preliminary Report. Industry Series, 2403–1.31

Meat and Poultry Inspection, 1983, Report of the Secretary of Agriculture to the U.S. Congress, 1374–1

Meat Animals Production, Disposition, and Income, 1983 Summary, 1623–8

Meat Packing Plants; Sausages and Other Prepared Meats (Industry 2011 and 2013): 1982 Census of Manufactures. Preliminary Report. Industry Series, 2491–1.1

Meatpacking and Prepared Meats Industry: Above-Average Productivity Gains, 6722–1.428

Mechanical Power Transmission Equipment, TSUS Items 680(pt.) and 681(pt.): Summary of Trade and Tariff Information, 9885–6.64

Titles

Military Women in the

Medicaid Financed Abortions, Quarterly Report, 4652–6

Medicaid Nursing Home Reimbursement Policies, Rates, and Expenditures, 4652–1.422

Medical Care Advisory Committee for State Medicaid Programs: Current Status and Trends, 4652–1.409

Medical Equipment: Country Market Survey, 2045–2

Medical Statistics, U.S. Navy, 1978 and 1979: 109th Annual Summary, 3804–1

Medical Technology and Costs of the Medicare Program, 26358–106

Medicare: Use of Hospital Outpatient Services by the Disabled, 4657–7

Medicare and Medicaid Data Book, 1983. Health Care Financing Program Statistics, 4654–1

Medicare and the Health Costs of Older Americans: The Extent and Effects of Cost Sharing, 25148–27

Medicare Benefits and Financing: Report of the 1982 Advisory Council on Social Security, 10178–1

Medicare Directory of Prevailing Charges, 1983, 4654–4

Medicare Experience with End-Stage Renal Disease: Trends in Incidence, Prevalence, and Survival, 4652–1.408

Medicare Fifteenth Annual Report Covering FY81, Including Reports on the Medigap Program and the End Stage Renal Disease Program, 4654–5

Medicare: Participating Providers and Suppliers of Health Services, 1981, 4656–1.19

Medicare: Persons Enrolled, 1980, 4656–1.18

Medicare Program Statistics Annual, Selected State Data, 1978-82, 4658–8

Medicare: Use and Reimbursement for Aged Persons by Survival Status, 1979, 4656–1.17

Medicare: Use of Short-Stay Hospitals By Aged and Disabled Inpatients, 4657–9

Medicare: Use of Skilled Nursing Facilities, 1980, 4656–1.20

Medicinals and Botanicals (Industry 2833): 1982 Census of Manufactures. Preliminary Report. Industry Series, 2491–1.183

Mediterranean Citrus Outlook, 1925–34.432

Meeting Future Needs for U.S. Food, Fiber, and Forest Products, 1008–47.2

Member Activity Report, Second District, Federal Home Loan Bank of New York, 9302–14

Members of the Federal Home Loan Bank System, 1983, 9314–5

Men's and Boys' Clothing and Furnishings (Industry 5136): 1982 Census of Wholesale Trade. Preliminary Report. Industry Series, 2403–1.24

Men's and Boys' Clothing, N.E.C. (Industry 2329): 1982 Census of Manufactures. Preliminary Report. Industry Series, 2491–1.84

Men's and Boys' Neckwear (Industry 2323): 1982 Census of Manufactures. Preliminary Report. Industry Series, 2491–1.81

Men's and Boys' Outerwear, 1983, Current Industrial Report, 2506–6.10

Men's and Boys' Separate Trousers (Industry 2327): 1982 Census of Manufactures. Preliminary Report. Industry Series, 2491–1.82

Men's and Boys' Shirts and Nightwear (Industry 2321): 1982 Census of Manufactures. Preliminary Report. Industry Series, 2491–1.79

Men's and Boys' Suits and Coats (Industry 2311): 1982 Census of Manufactures. Preliminary Report. Industry Series, 2491–1.78

Men's and Boys' Underwear (Industry 2322): 1982 Census of Manufactures. Preliminary Report. Industry Series, 2491–1.80

Men's and Boys' Work Clothing (Industry 2328): 1982 Census of Manufactures. Preliminary Report. Industry Series, 2491–1.83

Men's, Women's, Misses', and Juniors' Selected Apparel, Current Industrial Report, 2506–6.2

Mental Health Service System, Series FN. Information Systems Reports, 4506–2

Mental Health, U.S., 1983, 4504–9

Merchant Fleets of the World: Oceangoing Steam and Motor Ships of 1,000 Gross Tons and Over, as of Jan. 1, 1983, 7704–3

Mercury: Mineral Industry Surveys, 5612–2.13

Mercury: Minerals Yearbook Preprint, Vol. 1, 1983, 5604–15.43

Merger Decisions: FDIC Annual Report, 1982, 9294–1.1

Mergers in the Nonfuel Minerals Industry: Trends and Motives, 5608–145

Merging of the Savings and Loan Industry, 9312–1.402

Message Format for Computer-Based Message Systems: Software Standard, 2216–2.118

Metal and Nonmetal Mining Fatalities, 6664–7

Metal Barrels, Drums, and Pails (Industry 3412): 1982 Census of Manufactures. Preliminary Report. Industry Series, 2491–1.277

Metal Cans (Industry 3411): 1982 Census of Manufactures. Preliminary Report. Industry Series, 2491–1.276

Metal Coating and Allied Services (Industry 3479): 1982 Census of Manufactures. Preliminary Report. Industry Series, 2491–1.300

Metal Doors, Sash, and Trim (Industry 3442): 1982 Census of Manufactures. Preliminary Report. Industry Series, 2491–1.286

Metal Foil and Leaf (Industry 3497): 1982 Census of Manufactures. Preliminary Report. Industry Series, 2491–1.309

Metal Heat Treating (Industry 3398): 1982 Census of Manufactures. Preliminary Report. Industry Series, 2491–1.274

Metal Household Furniture (Industry 2514): 1982 Census of Manufactures. Preliminary Report. Industry Series, 2491–1.130

Metal Office Furniture (Industry 2522): 1982 Census of Manufactures. Preliminary Report. Industry Series, 2491–1.135

Metal Partitions and Fixtures (Industry 2542): 1982 Census of Manufactures. Preliminary Report. Industry Series, 2491–1.138

Metal Sanitary Ware (Industry 3431): 1982 Census of Manufactures. Preliminary Report. Industry Series, 2491–1.282

Metal Stampings, N.E.C. (Industry 3469): 1982 Census of Manufactures. Preliminary Report. Industry Series, 2491–1.298

Metalworking Machinery, Current Industrial Report, 2506–12.12

Metalworking Machinery, N.E.C. (Industry 3549): 1982 Census of Manufactures. Preliminary Report. Industry Series, 2491–1.329

Method for Ranking Biological Habitats in Oil Spill Response Planning and Impact Assessment, 5508–87

Methods of Monetary Control in Italy, 1974-83, 9373–3.26

Metropolitan Central City Population and Employment Growth During the 1970's, 9387–8.89

Metropolitan Housing Characteristics. 1980 Census of Housing, Vol. 1, 2473–1

Metropolitan Regional Governance, 25408–88

Metrorail Before-and-After Study Reports, 7306–8

Metrorail Station Area Planning, 7306–8.3

Mexican Citrus Update, 1925–34.405

Mexican Economic Crisis: Policy Implications for the U.S., 21248–82

Mica: Minerals Yearbook Preprint, Vol. 1, 1983, 5604–15.44

Michigan Forest Statistics, 1980, 1206–31.5

Michigan's Fourth Forest Inventory: Area, 1208–192

Michigan's Fourth Forest Inventory: Timber Volumes and Projections of Timber Supply, 1206–31.6

Michigan's Predicted Timber Yields, 1981-2010, 1208–193

Microcomputer as Home Equipment: A Role for Home Economists, 1004–16.1

Microcomputer Program for the Calculation of a Trawlnet Section Taper, 2162–1.402

Microphones, Loudspeakers, and Electric Sound and Visual Signaling Apparatus, TSUS Items 684(pt.) and 685(pt.): Summary of Trade and Tariff Information, 9885–6.81

Mid-Session Review of the 1985 Budget, 104–7

Middle Atlantic Regional Reports, 6926–1

Middle East and North Africa: Outlook and Situation Report, 1524–4.3

Midwest Prepares for Interstate Banking, 9375–1.403

Midwest Update, 9375–9

Midwife and Out-of-Hospital Deliveries: U.S., 4147–21.40

Military and Federal Civilian Disposable Income Comparisons and Extra Pays Received by Military Personnel, 26123–65

Military Construction Program, FY85, 3544–15

Military Manpower Statistics, 3542–14

Military Manpower Strength Assessment and Active Force Recruiting Results, 3542–7

Military Manpower Strength Assessment, Recruiting and Reenlistment Results, Active Force, 3542–7

Military Manpower Training Report for FY85. Vol. IV: Force Readiness Report, 3504–5

Military Sealift Command, Parts 1 and 2, 3802–2

Military Strength Figures Summarized by DOD, 3542–2

Military Traffic Management Command: Worldwide Traffic Management Summary, 3702–1

Military Traffic Management Report, 3702–1

Military Women in the Department of Defense, Manpower Installations and Logistics, 3544–26

Milk Processor-Distributors' Titles

Milk Processor-Distributors' Sales, Costs, and Margins, 1544–15

Milk Production, 1627–1

Milk Production, Disposition, and Income, 1983 Summary, Milk Production Series, 1627–4

Millinery (Industry 2351): 1982 Census of Manufactures. Preliminary Report. Industry Series, 2491–1.91

Millwork (Industry 2431): 1982 Census of Manufactures. Preliminary Report. Industry Series, 2491–1.115

Millwork, TSUS Items 200(pt.), 202(pt.), 206(pt.), and 207(pt.): Summary of Trade and Tariff Information, 9885–2.35

Mine Injuries and Worktime, Quarterly, 6662–1

Mineral Commodity Summaries, 1984, 5604–18

Mineral Industries of Africa, 5606–1.11

Mineral Industry Surveys: Annual Advance Summaries by Commodity, 5614–5

Mineral Industry Surveys: Apparent Consumption of Industrial Explosives and Blasting Agents in the U.S., 1983, 5614–22

Mineral Industry Surveys: Monthly Mineral Surveys, 5612–1

Mineral Industry Surveys: Phosphate Rock, 1984 Crop Year, 5614–20

Mineral Industry Surveys: Quarterly Mineral Surveys, 5612–2

Mineral Industry Surveys: 1983 Annual Preliminary Summaries by State, 5614–6

Mineral Leaching Practices in the U.S., 5606–6

Mineral Perspectives, 5606–1

Mineral Revenues: The 1983 Report on Receipts from Federal and Indian Leases, with Summary Data from 1920 to 1983, 5734–2

Mineral Wool (Industry 3296): 1982 Census of Manufactures. Preliminary Report. Industry Series, 2491–1.247

Minerals Accountability in the Department of the Interior, Annual Report, 5734–1

Minerals and Materials: A Bimonthly Survey, 5602–4

Minerals Availability Program Appraisals, 5606–4

Minerals in the World Economy, 5604–35.1

Minerals in the World Economy, 1982, 5604–17.1

Minerals Yearbook, 1982. Vol. 1. Metals and Minerals, 5604–33

Minerals Yearbook, 1982. Vol. 2. Annual Preprints by State, 5604–16

Minerals Yearbook, 1982. Vol. 2. Area Reports: Domestic, 5604–34

Minerals Yearbook, 1982. Vol. 3. Annual Preprints by Country, 5604–17

Minerals Yearbook, 1982. Vol. 3. Area Reports: International, 5604–35

Minerals Yearbook, 1983. Vol. 1. Annual Preprints by Commodity, 5604–15

Minerals Yearbook, 1983. Vol. 3. Annual Preprints by Country, 5604–23

Minifarms: Farm Business or Rural Residence?, 1548–241

Mining and Quarrying Trends in the Metal and Nonmetal Industries: Minerals Yearbook Preprint, Vol. 1, 1983, 5604–15.1

Mining Industry Equipment: Country Market Survey, 2045–16

Mining Machinery (Industry 3532): 1982 Census of Manufactures. Preliminary Report. Industry Series, 2491–1.317

Mining Machinery and Mineral Processing Equipment, 1983, Current Industrial Report, 2506–12.4

Mink, 1631–7

Minnesota—Wisconsin Manufacturing Grade Milk Price, 1629–6

Minnesota-Wisconsin Manufacturing Grade Milk Price Series, 1317–4.404

Minnesota-Wisconsin Milk Prices, 1629–2

Minorities and Women in Apprenticeship Programs and Referral Unions, 9244–7

Minorities and Women in Federal Employment, 9844–13

Minorities and Women in the Health Fields, 1984 Edition, 4118–18

Minority Business Development Agency, Annual Performance Report, FY83, 2104–6

Minority Employment Report By States, Number of Employees, 9284–7

Miscellaneous Articles of Wood, TSUS Items 200(pt.), 203(pt.), 206(pt.), and 207(pt.): Summary of Trade and Tariff Information, 9885–2.30

Miscellaneous Chemicals and Chemical Products, TSUS Items 409(pt.), 410(pt.), 432(pt.), 470(pt.), 493(pt.), 494(pt.), and 495(pt.): Summary of Trade and Tariff Information, 9885–4.43

Miscellaneous Fabricated Wire Products (Industry 3496): 1982 Census of Manufactures. Preliminary Report. Industry Series, 2491–1.308

Miscellaneous General Merchandise Stores (Industry 5399): 1982 Census of Retail Trade. Preliminary Report. Industry Series, 2395–1.7

Miscellaneous Legislation Concerning Various Foreign Policy Issues, 21388–43

Miscellaneous Machines and Equipment, TSUS Items 660(pt.), 661(pt.), 662(pt.), 674(pt.), and 678(pt.): Summary of Trade and Tariff Information, 9885–6.84

Miscellaneous Metal Work (Industry 3449): 1982 Census of Manufactures. Preliminary Report. Industry Series, 2491–1.291

Miscellaneous Non-Metalworking and Non-Metal Processing Machines, TSUS Items 674(pt.) and 678(pt.): Summary of Trade and Tariff Information, 9885–6.80

Miscellaneous Nonmetallic Minerals (Except Fuels) and Services (Industry 1481, 1492, 1496, and 1499): 1982 Census of Mineral Industries. Preliminary Report. Industry Series, 2511–1.12

Miscellaneous Parts of Machines, N.S.P.F., TSUS Items 680(pt.) and 681(pt.): Summary of Trade and Tariff Information, 9885–6.70

Miscellaneous Plastics Products (Industry 3079): 1982 Census of Manufactures. Preliminary Report. Industry Series, 2491–1.211

Miscellaneous Printed Matter, TSUS Items 270(pt.), 273(pt.), and 274(pt.): Summary of Trade and Tariff Information, 9885–2.33

Miscellaneous Publishing (Industry 2741): 1982 Census of Manufactures. Preliminary Report. Industry Series, 2491–1.162

Miscellaneous Vehicles and Transportation Related Equipment, TSUS Items 678(pt.), 692(pt.), and 694(pt.): Summary of Trade and Tariff Information, 9885–6.78

Miscellanous Grains and Grain Products, TSUS Items 130(pt.) and 131(pt.): Summary of Trade and Tariff Information, 9885–1.68

Mississippi: A State in Transition, 9371–1.409

Mitigating Acid Rain: Implications for High-Sulfur Coal Regions, 21368–52

Mobile Home Dealers (Industry 5271): 1982 Census of Retail Trade. Preliminary Report. Industry Series, 2395–1.4

Mobile Homes (Industry 2451): 1982 Census of Manufactures. Preliminary Report. Industry Series, 2491–1.126

Modeling the Retirement Process for Policy Evaluation and Research, 6722–1.445

Modifying Military Retirement: Alternative Approaches, 26306–6.76

Mohair: ASCS Commodity Fact Sheet, 1984, 1806–4.12

Molasses Market News, 1311–16

Molasses, TSUS Items 155(pt.): Summary of Trade and Tariff Information, 9885–1.60

Molybdenum: Mineral Industry Surveys, 5612–1.17

Molybdenum: Minerals Yearbook Preprint, Vol. 1, 1983, 5604–15.45

Monetary and Credit Targets in an Open Economy, 9373–3.26

Monetary Authorities' Reaction Functions and the European Monetary System, 9373–3.26

Monetary Control: A Comparison of the U.S. and Canadian Experiences, 1975-79, 9381–10.38

Monetary Perspective on Underground Economic Activity in the U.S., 9362–1.402

Monetary Policy and Open Market Operations in 1983, 9385–1.407

Monetary Policy Decision Process in the Federal Republic of Germany, 9373–3.26

Monetary Policy Decision Process in the UK, 9373–3.26

Monetary Policy Games and the Role of Private Information, 9366–7.103

Monetary Policy Objectives for 1984, 9362–4

Monetary Policy Regimes and International Term Structures of Interest Rates, 9393–8.401

Monetary Policy Report to Congress Pursuant to the Full Employment and Balanced Growth Act of 1978, 9362–4

Monetary Trends, 9391–2

Money and Inflation in Colonial Massachusetts, 9383–6.402

Money, Debt and Economic Activity, 9391–1.416

Money-GNP Link: Assessing Alternative Transaction Measures, 9391–1.408

Money Growth Variability and GNP, 9391–1.411

Money Income and Poverty Status of Families and Persons in the U.S.: 1983 (Advance Data from the Mar. 1984 Current Population Survey), 2546–6.41

Money Income of Households, Families, and Persons in the U.S.: 1982, 2546–6.39

Money Market Account Competition, 9371–1.431

Money Market Mutual Funds Are Hardly Money, 9383–6.403

Money Stock, Liquid Assets, and Debit Measures, 9365–1

Monohydric Alcohols, TSUS Items 427(pt.), 428(pt.), and 430(pt.): Summary of Trade and Tariff Information, 9885–4.37

Monthly and Seasonal Weather Outlook, 2182–1

Monthly Benefit Statistics, 9702–2

Titles

Monthly Benefit Statistics: Summary Program Data. Old-Age Survivors, Disability, and Health Insurance; Supplemental Security Income; Aid to Families with Dependent Children, 4742–2

Monthly Benefit Statistics, Railroad Retirement and Unemployment Insurance Programs, 9702–2

Monthly Bulletin of Lake Levels for the Great Lakes, 3752–1

Monthly Climatic Data for the World, 2152–4

Monthly Comparative Statistical Analysis of Member Institutions, Federal Home Loan Bank of Seattle, 9302–21

Monthly Cotton Linters Review, 1309–10

Monthly Energy Review, 3162–24

Monthly Fatality Report, 7762–7

Monthly Gasoline Reported by States, 7552–1

Monthly Import Detention List, 4062–2

Monthly Labor Review, 6722–1

Monthly Product Announcement, 2302–6

Monthly Report of Assets and Liabilities of International Banking Facilities, 9365–2.22

Monthly Report on Selected Steel Industry Data, 9882–10

Monthly Report on Selected Steel Industry Data: Report to the Subcommittee on Trade, Committee on Ways and Means, on Investigation No. 332-153 Under Section 332 of the Tariff Act of 1930, 9882–10

Monthly Retail Trade Sales and Inventories, Current Business Reports, 2413–3

Monthly State, Regional and National Heating/Cooling Degree Days Weighted by Population, 2152–13

Monthly Statement of the Public Debt of the U.S., 8242–2

Monthly Statistical Report, Federal Home Loan Bank of Pittsburgh, 9302–16

Monthly Treasury Statement of Receipts and Outlays of the U.S. Government, 8102–3

Monthly Vital Statistics Report, Annual Summary of Births, Deaths, Marriages, and Divorces: U.S., 1983, 4144–7

Monthly Vital Statistics Report. Provisional Data, 4142–1

Monthly Vital Statistics Report Supplements, 4146–5

Monthly Wholesale Trade: Sales and Inventories, Current Business Reports, 2413–7

Morbidity and Mortality, Weekly Report, 4202–1

Morbidity and Mortality Weekly Report: CDC Surveillance Summaries, 4202–7

More Attention Needed in Key Areas of the Expanded Crop Insurance Program, 26113–119

More Coursework in the New Basics Is Needed To Meet Standards of National Commission on Excellence in Education, 4828–16

More U.S. Workers Are College Graduates, 6722–1.423

Mortality from Flash Floods: A Review of National Weather Service Reports, 1969-81, 4102–1.406

Mortgage Industry in the Federal Republic of Germany, 9312–1.405

Mortgage Loan Commitment Rates in Illinois, 9302–6

Mortgage Loan Commitment Rates in Wisconsin, 9302–7

National Credit Union

Mortgage Rate Buydowns: Further Evidence, 9412–2.408

Mortgage-Related Investments of Selected Financial Institutions, 5008–33

Most Women Who Maintain Families Receive Poor Labor Market Returns, 6746–1.253

Motion Picture Theatres (Industry 783): 1982 Census of Service Industries. Preliminary Report. Industry Series, 2390–2.12

Motivation and Economic Mobility of the Poor, Final Report of the Project, 4008–65

Motor Gasolines, Summer 1983: Petroleum Products Survey, 3006–2.1

Motor Gasolines, Winter 1983-84: Petroleum Products Survey, 3006–2.3

Motor Homes Produced on Purchased Chassis (Industry 3716): 1982 Census of Manufactures. Preliminary Report. Industry Series, 2491–1.397

Motor Vehicle Parts and Accessories (Industry 3714): 1982 Census of Manufactures. Preliminary Report. Industry Series, 2491–1.395

Motor Vehicle Safety 1981: A Report on Activities Under the National Traffic and Motor Vehicle Safety Act of 1966 as Amended and the Motor Vehicle Information and Cost Savings Act of 1972 as Amended and the Energy Policy and Conservation Act of 1975, 7764–1.2

Motor Vehicle Tampering Survey, 1983, 9194–15

Motor Vehicles and Car Bodies (Industry 3711): 1982 Census of Manufactures. Preliminary Report. Industry Series, 2491–1.393

Motor Vehicles, Model Year 1984, 2702–1.438

Motorcycles, Bicycles, and Parts (Industry 3751): 1982 Census of Manufactures. Preliminary Report. Industry Series, 2491–1.407

Motorcycles, TSUS Items 692(pt.): Summary of Trade and Tariff Information, 9885–6.76

Motors and Generators (Industry 3621): 1982 Census of Manufactures. Preliminary Report. Industry Series, 2491–1.358

Motors and Generators, 1983, Current Industrial Report, 2506–12.17

Mourning Dove Breeding Population Status, 1984, 5504–15

Multi-Unit Agreements in the Federal Service, 9847–4

Multifactor Productivity Measures: Private Business, Private Nonfarm Business, and Manufacturing Sectors, Annual Measures for 1983, 6824–2

Multiple Causes of Death in the U.S., 4146–5.76

Museum General Operating Support Grants Announced, 9564–6.1

Mushrooms, 1631–9

Musical Instruments (Industry 3931): 1982 Census of Manufactures. Preliminary Report. Industry Series, 2491–1.427

M1-GNP Relationship: A Component Approach, 9385–1.413

NAEP Newsletter, 4892–1

Nailed Wood Boxes and Shook (Industry 2441): 1982 Census of Manufactures. Preliminary Report. Industry Series, 2491–1.120

Narcotics Intelligence Estimate: The Supply of Drugs to the U.S. Illicit Market from Foreign and Domestic Sources in 1982 (with Projections Through 1983), 15894–1

Narrow Fabric Mills (Industry 2241): 1982 Census of Manufactures. Preliminary Report. Industry Series, 2491–1.51

Narrow Fabrics, 1983, Current Industrial Report, 2506–5.6

NASA News Press Kits, 9506–2

NASA Pocket Statistics, 9504–6

NASA Semiannual Procurement Report, FY84, 9502–6

NASA Semiannual Procurement Report, Oct. 1, 1983-Mar. 31, 1984, 9502–6

NASA To Launch New Earth Resources Satellite for NOAA, 9506–2.116

NASA University Program Management Information System, FY83, 9504–7

NASA's University Program: Active Projects, FY83, 9504–7

National Accident Sampling Systems, 1982: A Report on Traffic Accidents and Injuries in the U.S. Collected in NASS in the Year 1982, 7764–13

National Acid Precipitation Assessment Program: 1982 Annual Report to the President and Congress, 14354–1

National Acid Precipitation Assessment Program: 1983 Annual Report to the President and Congress, 14354–1

National Air Pollutant Emission Estimates, 1940-82, 9194–13

National Air Quality and Emissions Trends Report, 1982, 9194–1

National Airspace System Plan: Facilities, Equipment and Associated Development, 7504–12

National Airway System, Annual Report, FY83. The FAA at 25: People, Performance, Progress, 7504–37

National Ambulatory Medical Care Complement Survey: U.S., 1980, 4147–13.77

National and Regional Costs and Returns of Producing Milk, 1561–2.401

National Annual Medicaid Statistics, 4657–10

National Assessment of Educational Progress Reconsidered: A New Design for a New Era, 4898–15

National Bipartisan Commission on Central America, Report, 028–19

National Bureau of Standards Publications, 1983 Catalog, 2214–1

National Cancer Institute Extramural Grant and Contract Awards, FY83, 4474–28

National Cancer Institute Fact Book, 4474–13

National Commission on Libraries and Information Science: Annual Report, 1982-83, 15634–1

National Cooperative Dairy Herd Improvement Program Participation Report, State Activities as of Jan. 1, 1984, 1702–2.402

National Council on Educational Research, Seventh Annual Report, FY81 and FY82, 4914–4

National Credit Union Administration, 1983 Annual Report, 9534–1

National Credit Union Administration, 1983 Mid-Year Statistics, 9534–1

National Credit Union Administration, 1983 Year End Statistics, 9534–1

National Credit Union

National Credit Union Administration Central Liquidity Facility Report for the Quarter, 9532–4

National Credit Union Administration Credit Union Directory, 1984, 9534–6

National Credit Union Share Insurance Fund Semiannual Report, 9534–7

National Crime Survey, 6066–3

National Defense Executive Reserve: Annual Report to the President, 9434–1

National Defense Spending: A Review of Appropriations and Real Purchases, 2702–1.440

National Defense Stockpile, 25208–27

National Earthquake Hazards Reduction Program: Report to the U.S. Congress, Overview, 5668–73

National Economic Trends, 9391–3

National Endowment for the Arts: Annual Report 1983, 9564–3

National Endowment for the Humanities: Eighteenth Annual Report, 1983, 9564–2

National Energy Policy Plan: A Report to the Congress Required by Title VIII of the Department of Energy Organization Act (Public Law 95-91), 3004–13

National Food Review, 1541–7

National Forest Fire Report, 1983, 1204–6

National Forest Recreation Use Reports, 1204–17

National Guard Bureau, 1983 Annual Review of the Chief, 3704–3

National Health Care Expenditures Study: Instruments and Procedures, 4186–4

National Health Expenditures, 1983, 4652–1.429

National Heart, Lung, and Blood Advisory Council, Eleventh Report, 4474–11

National Heart, Lung, and Blood Institute Demonstration Projects in Workplace High Blood Pressure Control, Summary Report, 4478–148

National Heart, Lung, and Blood Institute FY83 Fact Book, 4474–15

National Heart, Lung, and Blood Institute, Ninth Report of the Director: Research Pathways to Modern Medicine, 4474–22.1

National Heart, Lung, and Blood Institute, Tenth Report of the Director: Ten-Year Review and Five-Year Plan. Vol. 1: Progress and Promise, 4474–22.2

National Heart, Lung, and Blood Institute, Tenth Report of the Director: Ten-Year Review and Five-Year Plan. Vol. 2: Heart and Vascular Diseases, 4474–22.3

National Heart, Lung, and Blood Institute, Tenth Report of the Director: Ten-Year Review and Five-Year Plan. Vol. 3: Lung Diseases, 4474–22.4

National Heart, Lung, and Blood Institute, Tenth Report of the Director: Ten-Year Review and Five-Year Plan. Vol. 4: Blood Diseases and Resources, 4474–22.5

National Heart, Lung, and Blood Institute, Tenth Report of the Director: Ten-Year Review and Five-Year Plan. Vol. 5: Companion Issues, 4474–22.6

National Highway Traffic Safety Administration News, 7766–7

National Honey Report, 1311–2

National Hospital Discharge Survey: 1982 Summary, 4146–8.96

National Hospital Discharge Survey: 1983 Summary, 4146–8.101

Titles

National Income and Product Accounts: Preliminary Revised Estimates, 1977, 2702–1.420

National Institute of Allergy and Infectious Diseases Profile, FY84, 4474–30

National Institute of Dental Research Programs, FY82 Funds, 4474–19

National Institute of Dental Research Programs, FY83 Funds, 4474–19

National Institute of General Medical Sciences, Annual Report, FY83, 4474–12

National Institute of Mental Health Survey and Reports Branch, Statistical Notes, 4506–3

National Institutes of Health Grants for Training, Construction, Medical Libraries, FY83 Funds, 4434–7.2

National Institutes of Health New Grants and Awards: Arranged by State, City and Institution, 4432–1

National Institutes of Health Research and Development Contracts, FY83 Funds, 4434–7.1

National Institutes of Health Research Grants, FY83 Funds, 4434–7.3

National Library of Medicine Programs and Services, FY83, 4464–1

National Medical Care Utilization and Expenditure Survey: Data Reports, 4146–11

National Medical Care Utilization and Expenditure Survey, Series A-C, 4146–12

National Oceanographic Fleet Operating Schedules for 1984, 3804–6

National Park Service: Summary of Acreages, 5542–1

National Park Service Scientific Activities in the Southwestern U.S., 1208–197

National Park Statistical Abstract, 1983, 5544–12

National Patterns of Science and Technology Resources, 1984, 9624–18

National Poultry Improvement Plan: Tables on Hatchery and Flock Participation, 1981-82 and 1982-83, 1394–15

National Science Foundation, Thirty-third Annual Report for FY83, 9624–6

National Science Foundation Grants and Awards for FY83, 9624–11

National 'Self-Sufficiency' Project Awards Announced, 5006–3.35

National Status on Control of Garbage-Feeding, 1392–5

National Survey of Compensation Paid Scientists and Engineers Engaged in Research and Development Activities, 3004–1

National Survey of Professional, Administrative, Technical, and Clerical Pay, Mar. 1984, 6784–2

National Transportation Safety Board, Annual Report to Congress, 1983, 9614–1

National Transportation Statistics, 7304–2

National Urban Mass Transportation Statistics: 1982, Section 15 Annual Report, 7884–4

National Water Conditions, 5662–3

National Water Quality Inventory: 1982 Report to Congress, 9204–6

National Water Summary 1983, Hydrologic Events and Issues, 5664–12

National Weather Service: A Strategy and Organization Concept for the Future, Results of a Study for the National Oceanic and Atmospheric Administration, 2188–16

National Weather Service and Cooperative Upper Air Stations, 2184–6

National Weather Service Offices and Stations, 2184–5

National Wool Market Review, Livestock Division, 1315–2

National Zoological Park Annual Report, 9774–2

Nationals: Quarterly Financial Review, 9142–30.2

Nation's Commercial Farmers Find Supply, Marketing Co-ops Useful, 1122–1.401

Nation's Farm Co-op Margins Climb, but Sales Decline Continues in 1983, 1122–1.409

Nationwide Food Consumption Survey, Food Intakes: Individuals in 48 States, 1977-78, 1356–4.1

Nationwide Food Consumption Survey, 1977-78: Final Reports, 1356–4

Natural Gas Annual, 3164–4

Natural Gas Liquids, (Industry 1321): 1982 Census of Mineral Industries. Preliminary Report. Industry Series, 2511–1.6

Natural Gas Monthly, 3162–4

Natural Gas Overview: Winter 1984-85, 3162–4.411

Natural Gas Policy and the Midwest Region, 9375–13.3

Natural Gas Production and Wellhead Price, 1983 (Preliminary), 3162–4.410

Natural Gas Production and Wellhead Price, 1983 (Preliminary Data Report), 3164–4

Natural Gas Wellhead Markets: Structures and Trends, 3162–4.403

Nature and Impact of TVA's Agricultural Resource Development Program, 9808–68

Naval Petroleum and Oil Shale Reserves, Annual Report of Operations, 3404–10

Naval Petroleum and Oil Shale Reserves, Annual Report of Operations, FY83, 3004–22

Naval Stores (Turpentine, Rosin, and Pine Gum), TSUS Item 188.50: Summary of Trade and Tariff Information, 9885–1.59

Navy Alcohol and Drug Program Highlights, FY83, 3804–12

Navy Can Reduce Its Stated Requirements for F/A-18 Weapons Tactics Trainers, 26123–73

Navy Military Personnel Statistics, 3802–4

NBS Standard Reference Materials Catalog, 1984-85, 2214–2

NCHS Publication Note: Publications Issued, 4122–2

NCHSR National Health Care Expenditures Study: Data Preview Series, 4186–3

NCHSR Research Proceedings Series: Health Survey Research Methods, 4184–1

NCHSR Research Reports, 4186–2

NCI Fact Book: National Cancer Program, 1983, 4474–13

NCI Grants Financial Data, 4474–28

NECIP Annual Report, 1983, 7604–9

Need for Care Among the Noninstitutionalized Elderly, 4144–11.1

Need To Assess Federal Role in Regulating and Enforcing Pipeline Safety, 26113–130

Need To Better Assess Consequences Before Reducing Taxpayer Assistance, 26119–58

Needs Assessment and Evaluation: Mental Health Service System Series BN, 4506–8

Needs Assessment for the Food and Agricultural Sciences: A Report to the Congress from the Secretary of Agriculture, 1008–47

Titles

Number of Returns To Be

Needy Family Program Participation: Indian Reservations and Territories, 1362–15

Neighborhood Changes in New York City During the 1970s: Are the 'Gentry' Returning?, 9385–1.403

NEISS Data Highlights, 9162–1

NEISS Data Highlights, 9164–7

Net Payments Made to Producers, 1802–10

New Agriculture, 1004–16.1

New and Expanding Firms Provide New Jobs in Rural Georgia, 1502–7.401

New Approaches to the Budgetary Treatment of Federal Credit Assistance, 26306–6.72

New BLS Survey Measures the Ratio of Hours Worked to Hours Paid, 6722–1.434

New Complete Aircraft and Aircraft Engines (Except Military), Current Industrial Report, 2506–12.24

New Directions in Youth Services: Experiences with State-Level Coordination, 6068–182

New England Economic Indicators, 9373–2

New England Economic Review, 9373–1

New England Economy and the Development of High Technology Industries, 9373–2.404

"New England Experiment" in Interstate Banking, 9373–1.405

New England Labor and the Economy at the Year-End 1983, 6916–7.1

New England Regional Reports, 6916–7

New England State Governments—Looking Ahead to a Better Fiscal Year, 9373–2.401

New England Thrift Industry, Fact Book 1982, 9304–3

New Evidence on the Diversity of Agricultural Income and Expense Accounts, 1544–19.401

New Loan Data: Farm Storage Facility and Equipment, FY68-84, 1804–14

New Occupational Separation Data Improve Estimates of Job Replacement Needs, 6722–1.416

New One-Family Houses Sold and for Sale, Construction Reports, 2382–3

New Publications, Bureau of Mines, 5602–2

New Publications of the Geological Survey, 5662–1

New Residential Construction in Selected SMSAs, Construction Reports, 2382–9

New Savings and Transaction Instruments, 1702–1.401

New Seasonal Adjustment Factors for Household Data Series, 6742–2.411

New Ship Construction, 1982, 7704–4

New Technology in the American Machinery Industry: Trends and Implications, 23848–179

New York-Northeastern New Jersey Area Economy, 1983 Year-End Review, 6924–2

New York State Police Controlled Access Highway Task Force, 7762–9.403

News from the Federal Election Commission, 9276–1

Newspapers (Industry 2711): 1982 Census of Manufactures. Preliminary Report. Industry Series, 2491–1.158

NFIB Quarterly Economic Report for Small Business, July 1983, 21728–52.2

NHTSA Releases Crash Test Results of 1984 Model Vehicles, 7766–7.9

NHTSA Releases Five More Crash Test Results of 1984 Model Vehicles, 7766–7.8

NHTSA Releases Five More Crash Test Results of 1984 Model Vehicles, 7766–7.10

NHTSA Releases Five More Crash Test Results of 1984 Model Vehicles, 7766–7.11

Nickel: Mineral Industry Surveys, 5612–1.20

Nickel: Minerals Yearbook Preprint, Vol. 1, 1983, 5604–15.46

Nigerians' Use of Native and Western Medicine for the Same Illness, 4102–1.417

NIH Almanac, 1984, 4434–1

NIH Annual Report of International Activities, FY83, 4474–6

NIH Data Book, 1984 Basic Data Relating to the National Institutes of Health, 4434–3

NIH Grants and Awards, 4434–7

NIH Publications List, 4434–2

Nine Co-ops Make Fortune 'Service 100', 1122–1.406

Nineteenth Annual Report on the Status of the National Wilderness Preservation System, 5304–14

Ninth International Technical Conference on Experimental Safety Vehicles, 7764–3

Ninth Report of the Director, National Heart, Lung, and Blood Institute: Research Pathways to Modern Medicine, 4474–22.1

NIOSH Research and Demonstration Grants Awarded, 4244–2

Nitrogen: Minerals Yearbook Preprint, Vol. 1, 1983, 5604–15.47

Nitrogenous Fertilizers (Industry 2873): 1982 Census of Manufactures. Preliminary Report. Industry Series, 2491–1.193

N.L.R.B. Election Report, 9582–2

NOAA Scientific and Technical Publications Announcement, 2142–1

NOAA Technical Memoranda, National Weather Service, Weather Analysis and Prediction Division Series, 2186–4

Nominal and Real Wage Stickiness in Six Large OECD Countries, 9381–10.33

Non-Federal Funding for Academic R&D Activities Increased at Faster Pace than Federal Funding in FY82, 9626–2.136

Non-Real Estate and Real Estate Farm Debt Held by Individuals and Others: 1980 Benchmark and Revisions, 1972-82, 1548–230

Nonagricultural Employment in the Southeast, 6942–7

Nonappropriated Fund Instrumentalities Act, Annual Statistical Report by District Office, FY83, 6504–5.5

Nonbanking Operations of Bank Holding Companies, 9377–1.406

Noncitrus Fruits and Nuts: 1983 Annual Summary, Production, Use, Value, 1621–18.1

Noncitrus Fruits and Nuts: 1983 Midyear Supplement. Fruit Production and Value Down, 1621–18.3

Nonclay Refractories (Industry 3297): 1982 Census of Manufactures. Preliminary Report. Industry Series, 2491–1.248

Noncurrent-Carrying Wiring Devices (Industry 3644): 1982 Census of Manufactures. Preliminary Report. Industry Series, 2491–1.372

Nonferrous Castings, Current Industrial Report, 2506–10.5

Nonferrous Forgings (Industry 3463): 1982 Census of Manufactures. Preliminary Report. Industry Series, 2491–1.295

Nonferrous Foundries, N.E.C. (Industry 3369): 1982 Census of Manufactures. Preliminary Report. Industry Series, 2491–1.261

Nonferrous Metal Manufacturing Industries, Feb. 1981. Industry Wage Survey, 6787–6.196

Nonferrous Rolling and Drawing, N.E.C. (Industry 3356): 1982 Census of Manufactures. Preliminary Report. Industry Series, 2491–1.272

Nonferrous Wire Drawing and Insulating (Industry 3357): 1982 Census of Manufactures. Preliminary Report. Industry Series, 2491–1.273

Nonmetallic Mineral Products, N.E.C. (Industry 3299): 1982 Census of Manufactures. Preliminary Report. Industry Series, 2491–1.249

Nonmetro Areas Gain in New Housing Market, 1598–190

Nonreal Estate Farm Debt, 9264–4

Nonresidential Buildings Energy Consumption Survey, 3166–8

Nonresidential Buildings Energy Consumption Survey: 1979 Consumption and Expenditures. Part 2: Steam, Fuel Oil, LPG, and All Fuels, 3166–8.4

Nonrubber Footwear Quarterly Statistical Report: Report to the Senate Committee on Finance on Investigation No. 332-191, Under Section 332 of the Tariff Act of 1930, 9882–6

Nonrubber Footwear: Report to the President on Investigation No. TA-201-50 Under Section 201 of the Trade Act of 1974, 9886–5.49

Nonwoven Fabrics (Industry 2297): 1982 Census of Manufactures. Preliminary Report. Industry Series, 2491–1.75

North America and Oceania: Outlook and Situation Report, 1524–4.1

North Atlantic Tropical Cyclones, 1983, 2152–8.401

North Carolina: Impressive Growth, Long-Term Questions, 9371–1.410

Northeast Corridor Improvement Project, Annual Report, 1983, 7604–9

Nosocomial Infection Surveillance, 1980-82, 4202–7.401

Notes on Sedimentation Activities, 1982, 5664–9

NSF Special Reports, 9626–6

NTIS Data Files Listing, 2222–1

Nuclear Engineering Enrollments and Degrees, 1983, 3004–5

Nuclear Fact Book, 3008–88

Nuclear Power in an Age of Uncertainty, 26358–99

Nuclear Power Plant Construction: Paying the Bill, 9385–1.412

Nuclear Power Plant Operating Experience, 1981, 9634–6

Nuclear Power Program Information and Data, Update, 3352–3

Nuclear Reactors Built, Being Built, or Planned in the U.S., 3002–5

Nuclear-Related Engineering and Technician Employment Increased Substantially Between 1981 and 1983, Although Total Employment Slowed, 3006–8.2

Nuclear Safety Technical Progress Review, 3352–4

Nuclear Test Personnel Review Series, 3906–1

Nuclear Waste Disposal: Achieving Adequate Financing, Special Study, 26308–49

Number of Returns To Be Filed: Calendar Year Projections, 1983-90, 8304–9

Number of Working Mothers Now

Number of Working Mothers Now at Record Levels, 6748–78

Nursing and Related Care Homes as Reported from the 1980 NMFI Survey, 4147–14.29

Nutrition Monitoring and Research in the Department of Health and Human Services, 4102–1.454

Nutrition Surveillance, Annual Summary 1981, 4205–24

Object Class Analysis: Budget for FY85, 104–9

Observations on the Distribution, Abundance, and Productivity of the Osprey in the Ojo de Liebre-Guerrero Negro Lagoon, B.C.S., Mexico, 1208–197

Occupational Earnings and Wage Trends in Metropolitan Areas, 6785–5

Occupational Earnings in All Metropolitan Areas, July 1983, 6785–9

Occupational Earnings in Selected Areas, 6785–6

Occupational Employment in Mining, Construction, Finance, and Services, 6748–60

Occupational Employment in Nuclear-Related Activities, 1983, 3004–11

Occupational Employment Projections Through 1995, 6728–29

Occupational Employment Statistics for 1972-82, 6742–2.402

Occupational Exposure to Asbestos: Population at Risk and Projected Mortality, 1980-2030, 21408–72

Occupational Fatalities As Found in Reports of OSHA Fatality/Catastrophe Investigations, 6606–2

Occupational Health Services in South Carolina Manufacturing Plants: Results of a Survey, 4102–1.408

Occupational Injuries and Illnesses in the U.S., By Industry, 1982, 6844–1

Occupational Injuries and Illnesses in 1983, 6844–3

Occupational Mobility and Job Tenure in 1983, 6722–1.460

Occupational Mortality in Washington State, 1950-79, 4248–47

Occupational Outlook Handbook, 1984-85 Edition, 6744–1

Occupational Outlook Quarterly, 6742–1

Occupational Projections and Training Data, 1984 Edition, 6744–3

Occupational Radiation Exposure at Commercial Nuclear Power Reactors, 1982, 9634–3

Occupational Reclassification and Changes in Distribution by Gender, 6722–1.417

Occupational Safety and Health Statistics of the Federal Government, 1982, 6604–1

Ocean Fleet Shipping Rates, Capacity, and Utilization for Grains, 1548–235

Ocean Pollution, 21568–36

Oceanic Gamefish Investigations: Statistical Results of Billfish Data Collected, 2164–7

Oceanic Pelagics Program Summary, 1983, 2164–7

Oceanographic Data Exchange, 1983, 2144–15

Oceanographic Monthly Summary, 2182–5

Oceanographic Observations Off the Pacific Northwest Following the 1982 El Nino Event, 2162–1.403

OECD Trade with Asia, 244–13.5

OECD Trade with Mexico and Central America, 244–13.3

OECD Trade with Persian Gulf Oil Producers, 244–13.1

OECD Trade with Regions of the World, 244–13

OECD Trade with South America, 244–13.2

OECD Trade with Sub-Saharan Africa, 244–13.4

Office Machines, N.E.C., and Typewriters (Industry 3579): 1982 Census of Manufactures. Preliminary Report. Industry Series, 2491–1.348

Office of Aviation Medicine Reports, 7506–10

Office of Energy Research Program Summaries, 3004–18

Office of Health Maintenance Organizations, 9th Annual Report to the Congress, FY83, 4104–8

Office of Inspector General, Annual Reports for the U.S. Territories, 5304–15

Office of Inspector General, Semiannual Report to the Congress, Apr. 1-Sept. 30, 1984, 2002–5

Office of Inspector General, FY84-I Semiannual Report, 3002–12

Office of Inspector General, FY84-II Semiannual Report, 3002–12

Office of Inspector General Report to the Congress, For the Six Month Period Oct. 1, 1983-Mar. 31, 1984, Pursuant to Section 5(b) of Public Law 95-452, 5002–8

Office of Inspector General Report to the Congress, For the Six Month Period Apr. 1-Sept. 30, 1984, Pursuant to Section 5(b) of Public Law 95-452, 5002–8

Office of Inspector General Semi-Annual Report to Congress: U.S. Department of Education, Oct. 1, 1983-Mar. 31, 1984, 4802–1

Office of Inspector General Semi-Annual Report to Congress: U.S. Department of Education, Apr. 1-Sept. 30, 1984, 4802–1

Office of Inspector General, Semiannual Report to Congress, April 1-Sept. 30, 1983, 9452–8

Office of Inspector General, Semiannual Report to Congress, Oct. 1, 1983-Mar. 31, 1984, 9452–8

Office of Inspector General, Semiannual Report to Congress, Apr. 1-Sept. 30, 1984, 9452–8

Office of Inspector General Semiannual Report, Oct. 1983-Mar. 1984, 4002–6

Office of Inspector General Semiannual Report: Oct. 1, 1983-Mar. 31, 1984, 5302–2

Office of Inspector General Semiannual Report, Apr.-Sept. 1984, 4002–6

Office of Inspector General U.S. Department of Interior. Annual Report: American Samoa Government, FY83, 5304–15.4

Office of Inspector General U.S. Department of Interior. Annual Report: Commonwealth of the Northern Mariana Islands, FY83, 5304–15.1

Office of Inspector General U.S. Department of Interior. Annual Report: Federated States of Micronesia, FY83, 5304–15.5

Office of Inspector General U.S. Department of Interior. Annual Report: Government of Guam, FY83, 5304–15.6

Titles

Office of Inspector General U.S. Department of Interior. Annual Report: Government of the Virgin Islands, FY83, 5304–15.7

Office of Inspector General U.S. Department of Interior. Annual Report: Republic of the Marshall Islands, FY83, 5304–15.3

Office of Inspector General U.S. Department of the Interior. Annual Report: Republic of Palau, FY83, 5304–15.2

Office of Inspector General Semiannual Report, Apr. 1-Sept. 30, 1983, 9182–10

Office of Inspector General Report to the Congress, for the Six Month Period Oct. 1, 1983-Mar. 31, 1984, Pursuant to Section 5(b) of Public Law 95-452, 9182–10

Office of Refugee Resettlement Monthly Data Report, 4702–3

Office of Revenue Sharing, Annual Report, FY83, 8064–1

Office of Tax Analysis Papers, 8006–3

Office of the Inspector General Semiannual Report, Apr. 1-Sept. 30, 1984, 9182–10

Office of the Inspector General, Semiannual Report, Apr. 1-Sept. 30, 1984, 9502–9

Office of U.S. Foreign Disaster Assistance, Annual Report, FY83, 9914–12

Offices of Dentists (Industry 8021): 1982 Census of Service Industries. Preliminary Report. Industry Series, 2390–2.15

Offices of Optometrists (Industry 8042): 1982 Census of Service Industries. Preliminary Report. Industry Series, 2390–2.16

Offices of Physicians (Industry 801): 1982 Census of Service Industries. Preliminary Report. Industry Series, 2390–2.14

Official Guard and Reserve Manpower: Strengths and Statistics, 3542–4

Official Summary of Security Transactions and Holdings, 9732–2

Offshore Petroleum Exploration: Capabilities and Constraints, 21448–30

Offshore Safety, 21568–35

Offsite Environmental Monitoring Report, Radiation Monitoring Around U.S. Nuclear Test Areas, 1983, 9234–4

Oil and Gas Extraction: Industry Wage Survey, June 1982, 6787–6.203

Oil and Gas Field Code Master List, 1983, 3164–70

Oil and Gas Field Services (Industry 1381, 1382, and 1389): 1982 Census of Mineral Industries. Preliminary Report. Industry Series, 2511–1.7

Oil and Gas, plus Mining Statistics, 5664–3

Oil Country Tubular Goods from Argentina, Brazil, Korea, Mexico, and Spain: Determinations of the Commission in Investigations Nos. 701-TA-215 Through 217 (Preliminary) and 731-TA-191 Through 195 (Preliminary) Under the Tariff Act of 1930, Together with the Information Obtained in the Investigations, 9886–19.11

Oil Crops Outlook and Situation Report, 1561–3

Oil Drilling Prohibitions at the Channel Islands and Pt. Reyes-Farallon Islands National Marine Sanctuaries: Some Costs and Benefits, 21448–30.1

Oil Field Machinery (Industry 3533): 1982 Census of Manufactures. Preliminary Report. Industry Series, 2491–1.318

Oil Overcharges, 21368–50

Oil Price Effects in Theory and Practice, 9366–7.93

Titles

Oil Prices, Welfare Tradeoffs, and International Policy Coordination in a Three Region World Model: An Optimizing Approach, 9366–7.96

Oil Shale in the U.S.: Prospects for Development, 9381–1.409

Oilseeds and Products: Foreign Agriculture Circular, 1925–1

Oilspill Risk Analyses, 5736–2

Oilspill Risk Analysis for the Gulf of Alaska/Cook Inlet Lease Offering (Oct. 1984), 5736–2.7

Oilspill Risk Analysis for the St. George Basin (Dec. 1984) and North Aleutian Basin (Apr. 1985) Outer Continental Shelf Lease Offerings, 5736–2.8

Older Americans and the Federal Budget: Past, Present, and Future, 25148–28

"On Call" Positions in Spot Cotton Based on New York Cotton Futures Reported by Merchants in Special Account Status, 11922–3

On-Farm Water Management in Aegean Turkey, 1968-74, 9916–1.50

One American Worker in Ten Has Been with the Same Employer More than 20 Years, 6748–76

One-fourth of Academic Research Equipment Classified Obsolete, 9626–2.138

OPEC Direct Investment in the U.S., 2044–23

Operating Reactors Licensing Actions Summary, 9632–5

Operation and Status of the State and Local Fiscal Assistance Trust Fund and the Antirecession Fiscal Assistance Trust Fund, FY83, 8064–1.2

Operation CROSSROADS, 1946, 3906–1.42

Operation of the Trade Agreements Program, 35th Report, 1983, 9884–5

Operation of TVA Reservoirs: Annual 1981, 9804–7

Operation SANDSTONE, 1948, 3906–1.41

Operations of the the National Weather Service, 2184–1

Operative Builders (Industry 1531): 1982 Census of Construction Industries. Preliminary Report. Industry Series, 2371–1.3

Operative Builders, Industry 1531. 1982 Census of Construction Industries. Industry Series, 2373–1.3

Ophthalmic Goods (Industry 3851): 1982 Census of Manufactures. Preliminary Report. Industry Series, 2491–1.421

Opportunities To Improve the Postal Ratemaking Process, 26119–63

Opportunities To Increase VA's Medical Care Cost Recoveries, 26121–66

Optical Goods Stores (Industry 5999 pt.): 1982 Census of Retail Trade. Preliminary Report. Industry Series, 2395–1.39

Optical Instruments and Lenses (Industry 3832): 1982 Census of Manufactures. Preliminary Report. Industry Series, 2491–1.417

Options for Change in Military Medical Care, 26306–6.74

Ordnance and Accessories, N.E.C. (Industry 3489): 1982 Census of Manufactures. Preliminary Report. Industry Series, 2491–1.304

Organic Chemical Crudes, TSUS Items 401(pt.): Summary of Trade and Tariff Information, 9885–4.39

Organic Fibers, Noncellulosic (Industry 2824): 1982 Census of Manufactures. Preliminary Report. Industry Series, 2491–1.181

Organized Crime Drug Enforcement Task Forces: Status and Observations, 26119–52

OSFA Program Book, FY82, 4804–28

OSHA Oversight: Staffing Levels for OSHA Approved State Plans, 21348–88

Other Metals: Minerals Yearbook Preprint, Vol. 1, 1983, 5604–15.72

Other Nonmetals: Minerals Yearbook Preprint, Vol. 1, 1983, 5604–15.73

Other Tobaccos: ASCS Commodity Fact Sheet, 1984, 1806–4.16

Our Changing Economy: A BLS Centennial Chartbook, 6728–30

Our Nation's Infrastructure, 23848–181

Out in the Cold: The Expected Impact of Rising Natural Gas Prices on the Poor, the Elderly, and the Unemployed, 25148–26.401

Out-of-Hospital Births, U.S., 1978: Birth Weight and Apgar Score as Measures of Outcome, 4102–1.414

Outcomes of a Diabetes Education Program, 4102–1.457

Outer Continental Shelf Lands Act, Annual Statistical Report by District Office, FY83, 6504–5.4

Outer Continental Shelf Lease Sales and the Department of the Interior's 5-Year Leasing Plan, Part 1, 21448–30

Outer Continental Shelf, O.C.S. Oil and Gas Leasing, and Marine Sanctuaries: A Comparison of Areas, 21448–30

Outlook for Canned Tomato Products, 1925–34.419

Outlook for Collective Bargaining in New England in 1984, 6916–7.2

Outlook for Feed Grains, 1004–16.1

Outlook for Fruit and Tree Nuts, 1004–16.1

Outlook for Inflation, 9377–1.404

Outlook for Participation in the 1985 Upland Cotton Program, 1561–1.404

Outlook for Timber Products, 1004–16.1

Outlook for U.S. Agricultural Exports, 1542–4

Outlook for U.S. Agricultural Trade, 1004–16.1

Outlook '84, Proceedings, 1004–16

Output and Employment Trends in Basic Manufacturing Industries: The Role of R&D, 25368–133

Over-the-Counter Drugs: Factors in Adult Use of Sedatives, Tranquilizers, and Stimulants, 4102–1.435

Overseas Business Reports: Marketing in Individual Countries, 2046–6

Overseas Business Reports: Trade and Marketing in World Regions, 2046–5

Overseas Private Investment Corporation 1983 Annual Report, 9904–2

Overseas Private Investment Corporation, Development Report, FY83, 9904–3

Oversight Hearing on Full Employment and Balanced Growth Act, 21348–90

Oversight of General Revenue Sharing, 25408–86

Oversight on Operation of Postal Service, 21628–55

Oversight on Teacher Preparation, 21348–89

Overview of the Intramural Projects, FY84-86, Of the Office of Research, Statistics, and International Policy, 4744–11

Passengers Denied Boarding:

Overview of the Military Retirement System, 21208–19

Overview of the Natural Gas Reserves and Resources of North America, 3162–4.404

PAC Money Contributed to U.S. Senate and House Candidates, 1977-82, 9274–4

Pacific Basin Economic Indicators, 9393–9

Packaging of Grants, Loans, and Earnings for Financing Postsecondary Education, 4848–15

Packers and Stockyards' Statistical Resume, Reporting Years 1981-82, 1384–1

Paddings and Upholstery Filling (Industry 2293): 1982 Census of Manufactures. Preliminary Report. Industry Series, 2491–1.71

Pads for Woodwind Instrument Keys from Italy: Determination of the Commission in Investigation No. 731-TA-152 (Final) Under the Tariff Act of 1930, Together with the Information Obtained in the Investigation, 9886–14.114

Pads for Woodwind Instrument Keys from Italy: Determination of the Commission in Investigations Nos. 701-TA-203 and 731-TA-152 (Preliminary) Under the Tariff Act of 1930, Together with the Information Obtained in the Investigations, 9886–19.6

Paint and Allied Products, 1983, Current Industrial Report, 2506–8.16

Paint, Varnish, and Lacquer, Current Industrial Report, 2506–8.4

Painting, Paper Hanging, and Decorating Special Trade Contractors (Industry 1721): 1982 Census of Construction Industries. Preliminary Report. Industry Series, 2371–1.11

Paints and Allied Products (Industry 2851): 1982 Census of Manufactures. Preliminary Report. Industry Series, 2491–1.189

Panama Canal Commission, Annual Report, Fiscal Year Ended Sept. 30, 1982, 9664–3

Paper Coating and Glazing (Industry 2641): 1982 Census of Manufactures. Preliminary Report. Industry Series, 2491–1.145

Paper Industries Machinery (Industry 3554): 1982 Census of Manufactures. Preliminary Report. Industry Series, 2491–1.333

Paperboard Mills (Industry 2631): 1982 Census of Manufactures. Preliminary Report. Industry Series, 2491–1.143

Paratransit: Options for the Future, 7306–9

Paratransit: Options for the Future. The Overview Report, 7306–9.6

Parental Kidnapping, 25528–95

Parity for Minorities in the Media, 21368–45

Parole in the U.S., 6064–14

Participants in Postsecondary Education: Oct. 1982, 4848–16

Participation in the Milk Diversion Program, 1561–2.402

Participation in the National School Lunch Program, 26113–123

Particleboard (Industry 2492): 1982 Census of Manufactures. Preliminary Report. Industry Series, 2491–1.124

Partnership Employment and Payroll, 1979, 8302–2.411

Partnership Returns for 1981 Reflect Tax Shelter Activity, 8302–2.404

Partnership Returns, 1982, 8302–2.416

Passengers Denied Boarding: CAB Bumping Report, 9142–23

Patent Profiles

Patent Profiles, 2246–2
Patent Profiles: Telecommunications, 2246–2.7
Patent Term Restoration Act of 1983, 25528–98
Patents Issued by the Patent and Trademark Office, 2244–2
Patients in Public General Hospitals, 4144–11.1
Patterns and Trends in World Agricultural Land Use, 1528–180
Patterns of Ambulatory Care in Internal Medicine: The National Ambulatory Medical Care Survey, U.S., Jan. 1980-Dec. 1981, 4147–13.80
Patterns of Ambulatory Care in Obstetrics and Gynecology: The National Ambulatory Medical Care Survey, U.S., Jan. 1980-Dec. 1981, 4147–13.76
Patterns of Ambulatory Care in Office Visits to General Surgeons: The National Ambulatory Medical Care Survey, U.S., Jan. 1980-Dec. 1981, 4147–13.79
Patterns of Global Terrorism: 1983, 7004–13
Patterns of International Terrorism, 7004–13
Patterns of Participation in Secondary Vocational Education, 1978-82, 4826–2.18
Paving Mixtures and Blocks (Industry 2951): 1982 Census of Manufactures. Preliminary Report. Industry Series, 2491–1.203
Pay Differentials: The Case of Japan, 6722–1.461
Paying for Physician Services in State Medicaid Programs, 4652–1.410
Payment-in-Kind Program, 21788–138
Payments to Air Carriers 419 Subsidy, Summary of Obligations and Disbursements Covering Operations, 9142–48
Peanut Marketing Summary, 1982 Crop, 1311–5
Peanut Marketing Summary, 1983 Crop, 1311–5
Peanut Report, 1311–1
Peanut Stocks and Processing, Aug. 1983-Jan. 1984, 1621–6
Peanut Stocks and Processing, Feb.-July 1984., 1621–6
Peanuts: ASCS Commodity Fact Sheet, 1984, 1806–4.2
Peat: Minerals Yearbook Preprint, Vol. 1, 1983, 5604–15.48
Pell Grants, End of Year Report, 1981-82, 4804–1
Pelvic Inflammatory Disease: Incidence and Trends in Private Practice, 4202–7.404
Pending Public Buildings Proposals, 25328–23
Pens and Mechanical Pencils (Industry 3951): 1982 Census of Manufactures. Preliminary Report. Industry Series, 2491–1.431
Pens, Pencils, and Marking Devices, 1983, Current Industrial Report, 2506–7.12
Pensions and Mortgages: Housing Investment Opportunities for the 80's, 5008–32
Performance Capabilities of the C-5 and C-17 Cargo Aircraft, 26123–81
Performance Evaluation of the Energy Information Administration, Department of Energy, Professional Audit Review Team's Report to the President and the Congress, 26104–14
Performance Measures for Dislocated Worker Programs, 6408–59.2
Performance of Thin Futures Markets: Rice and Sunflower Seed Futures, 1502–3.404

Titles

Performance Profiles of Major Energy Producers, 1982, 3164–44
Periodicals (Industry 2721): 1982 Census of Manufactures. Preliminary Report. Industry Series, 2491–1.159
Perlite: Minerals Yearbook Preprint, Vol. 1, 1983, 5604–15.49
Person Trip Characteristics, 7556–6.11
Personal Bankruptcy, 21528–57
Personal Bankruptcy Data for Opt-Out Hearings and Other Purposes, 21528–57.1
Personal Income and Adjusted Gross Income, 1980-82, 2702–1.414
Personal Income and Educational Attainment of Male War Veterans and Nonveterans, Mar. 1983, 9924–19
Personal Leather Goods, N.E.C. (Industry 3172): 1982 Census of Manufactures. Preliminary Report. Industry Series, 2491–1.221
Personal-Use Firewood Program on Three National Forests: A Cost Analysis, 1208–191
Persons Receiving Care from Selected Health Care Practitioners: U.S., 1980, 4146–12.4
Persons with Limitations of Activity: Health Insurance, Expenditures and Use of Services, 4186–3.19
Perspective on the Federal Deficit Problem, 9391–1.415
Pest Conditions Annual Report, 1983: Southwestern Region, 1206–11.2
Pesticide Review, 1982 For USDA State and County Emergency Records, 1804–5
Pesticide Use and Practices, 1982, 1588–76
Petroleum and Coal Products, N.E.C. (Industry 2999): 1982 Census of Manufactures. Preliminary Report. Industry Series, 2491–1.205
Petroleum Bulk Stations and Terminals (Industry 5171): 1982 Census of Wholesale Trade. Preliminary Report. Industry Series, 2403–1.36
Petroleum Consumption by Electric Utilities: 10 Years After the Arab Oil Embargo, 3162–39.402
Petroleum Geology and Resources of Southeastern Mexico, Northern Guatemala, and Belize, 5666–18.4
Petroleum Marketing Monthly, 3162–11
Petroleum Potential of Wilderness Lands In the Western U.S., 5668–69
Petroleum Products Survey, 3006–2
Petroleum Refining; Lubricating Oils and Greases (Industries 2911 and 2992): 1982 Census of Manufactures. Preliminary Report. Industry Series, 2491–1.202
Petroleum Resources of Indonesia, Malaysia, Brunei, and Thailand, 3166–9.9
Petroleum Resources of Libya, Algeria, and Egypt, 3166–9.8
Petroleum Supply Annual, 1983, 3164–2
Petroleum Supply Monthly, 3162–6
Pharmaceutical Preparations (Industry 2834): 1982 Census of Manufactures. Preliminary Report. Industry Series, 2491–1.184
Pharmaceutical Preparations, Except Biologicals, 1983, Current Industrial Report, 2506–8.5
Philadelphia Research Working Papers, 9387–8
Phipps Bend Nuclear Plant, Socioeconomic Monitoring and Mitigation Report, Sept. 30, 1982, 9806–7.2

Phipps Bend Nuclear Plant, Socioeconomic Monitoring Report, Dec. 31, 1981, 9806–7.1
Phonograph Records and Prerecorded Tape (Industry 3652): 1982 Census of Manufactures. Preliminary Report. Industry Series, 2491–1.378
Phosphate Rock, Crop Year Annual, Mineral Industry Survey, 5614–20
Phosphate Rock: Minerals Yearbook Preprint, Vol. 1, 1983, 5604–15.50
Phosphate-Rock Resources of the U.S., 5668–74
Phosphate Rock, 1983: Mineral Industry Surveys Annual Advance Summary, 5614–5.1
Phosphatic Fertilizers (Industry 2874): 1982 Census of Manufactures. Preliminary Report. Industry Series, 2491–1.194
Photoengraving (Industry 2793) and Electrotyping and Stereotyping (Industry 2794): 1982 Census of Manufactures. Preliminary Report. Industry Series, 2491–1.172
Photographic Equipment and Supplies (Industry 3861): 1982 Census of Manufactures. Preliminary Report. Industry Series, 2491–1.422
Photovoltaic Energy Systems: Program Summary, FY83, 3304–20
Pianos and Other Keyboard Stringed Instruments, TSUS Items 725(pt.) and 726(pt.): Summary of Trade and Tariff Information, 9885–7.55
Pickles, Sauces, and Salad Dressings (Industry 2035): 1982 Census of Manufactures. Preliminary Report. Industry Series, 2491–1.11
Piece Goods (Industry 5133): 1982 Census of Wholesale Trade. Preliminary Report. Industry Series, 2403–1.23
Pile Fabrics and Tufted Fabrics, TSUS Items 346(pt.): Summary of Trade and Tariff Information, 9885–3.43
Pillows, Cushions, Mattresses, and Bedsprings; and Nontextile Floor Coverings, TSUS Items 727(pt.) and 728(pt.): Summary of Trade and Tariff Information, 9885–7.61
Pine Resource in South Carolina: An Interim Assessment, 1983, 1206–32.1
Pistachios: A New Addition to U.S. Exports, 1925–34.424
Pitfalls in Analyzing Deficits and Inflation, 9387–8.86
Plague in the U.S., 1983, 4202–7.408
Plans for Company-Funded Research and Development Show 12% Annual Increases Through 1985, 9626–2.145
Plant and Equipment Expenditures by Business for Pollution Abatement, 1983 and Planned 1984, 2702–1.423
Plant and Equipment Expenditures, 1984, 2702–1.404
Plant Biology Research Expenditures Totaled $200 Million and Were Concentrated in Land-Grant Institutions, 1983, 9626–2.143
Plant Closings and Worker Dislocation, 9377–1.401
Plastering, Drywall, Acoustical and Insulation Work Special Trade Contractors (Industry 1742): 1982 Census of Construction Industries. Preliminary Report. Industry Series, 2371–1.14
Plastics Bottles, 1983, Current Industrial Report, 2506–8.10

Titles

Prescribing Estrogen During

Plastics Materials and Resins (Industry 2821): 1982 Census of Manufactures. Preliminary Report. Industry Series, 2491–1.178

Plating and Polishing (Industry 3471): 1982 Census of Manufactures. Preliminary Report. Industry Series, 2491–1.299

Platinum-Group Metals: Mineral Industry Surveys, 5612–2.14

Platinum-Group Metals: Minerals Yearbook Preprint, Vol. 1, 1983, 5604–15.51

Pleating and Stitching (Industry 2395): 1982 Census of Manufactures. Preliminary Report. Industry Series, 2491–1.107

Plumbing and Heating Equipment and Supplies (Hydronics) (Industry 5074): 1982 Census of Wholesale Trade. Preliminary Report. Industry Series, 2403–1.11

Plumbing Fittings and Brass Goods (Industry 3432): 1982 Census of Manufactures. Preliminary Report. Industry Series, 2491–1.283

Plumbing Fixtures, Current Industrial Report, 2506–11.2

Plumbing, Heating (Except Electric), and Air Conditioning Special Trade Contractors (Industry 1711): 1982 Census of Construction Industries. Preliminary Report. Industry Series, 2371–1.10

Pocket Data Book: USA, 2324–2

Police Handling of Youth Gangs, 6068–175

Policy Research Notes, 1542–6

Polishes and Sanitation Goods (Industry 2842): 1982 Census of Manufactures. Preliminary Report. Industry Series, 2491–1.186

Political Economy of Central Banking in the U.S. or Quis Custodiet Ipsos Custodes, 9373–3.26

Political Economy of French Monetary Policy, 9373–3.26

Political Economy of Monetary Policy: National and International Aspects, 9373–3.26

Political Economy of the Soviet Union, 23848–180

Political Factors in Monetary Policy, 9373–3.26

Pollution Abatement and Control Expenditures, 1972-82, 2702–1.407

Pollution Abatement Costs and Expenditures, 1982, Current Industrial Report, 2506–3.6

Pollution Control Instrumentation and Equipment: Country Market Survey, 2045–17

Polygraph and Prepublication Review Policies of Federal Agencies, 26123–66

Population Attributable Risk of Hypertension from Heavy Alcohol Consumption, 4102–1.434

Population Characteristics. Current Population Reports. Series P-20, 2546–1

Population Characteristics. Fertility of American Women. Current Population Reports. Series P-20, 2546–1.393

Population Distribution Analyses for Nuclear Power Plant Siting, 9638–54

Population Estimates and Projections. Estimates of the Population of Puerto Rico and the Outlying Areas: 1980-83. Current Population Reports. Series P-25, 2546–3.134

Population Profile of the U.S.: 1982, 2546–2.119

Porcelain Electrical Supplies (Industry 3264): 1982 Census of Manufactures. Preliminary Report. Industry Series, 2491–1.235

Port Requirements for the San Francisco Bay Area, 21568–34

Portrait Photography Studios (Industry 722): 1982 Census of Service Industries. Preliminary Report. Industry Series, 2390–2.3

Position Classification and Pay In State and Territorial Public Health Laboratories, 4204–7

Possible Effects of Changing World Crude Oil Prices: Final Report on Investigation No. 332-161 Under Section 332(b) of the Tariff Act of 1930, 9886–4.69

Post-Remedial-Action Radiological Survey of Kent Chemical Laboratory, the University of Chicago, Chicago, Ill., 3406–1.40

Post-Remedial-Action Radiological Survey of the Westinghouse Advanced Reactors Division, Plutonium Fuel Laboratories, Cheswick, Pa., Oct. 1-8, 1981, 3406–1.38

Postal Service Electronic Mail: The Price Still Isn't Right, 21408–70

Postmaster General, FY83 Annual Report, 9864–1

Postretirement Increases Under Private Pension Plans, 6722–1.453

Potash: Minerals Yearbook Preprint, Vol. 1, 1983, 5604–15.52

Potassium Chloride from East Germany, Israel, Spain, and the USSR: Determinations of the Commission in Investigations Nos. 303-TA-15 and 701-TA-213 (Preliminary), and 731-TA-184 through 187 (Preliminary) Under the Tariff Act of 1930, Together with the Information Obtained in the Investigations, 9886–15.52

Potassium Chloride from Israel and Spain: Determinations of the Commission in Investigations Nos. 303-TA-15 and 701-TA-213 (Final) Under the Tariff Act of 1930, Together with the Information Obtained in the Investigations, 9886–15.54

Potassium Permanganate from Spain: Determination of the Commission in Investigation No. 731-TA-126 (Final) Under the Tariff Act of 1930, Together with the Information Obtained in the Investigation, 9886–14.92

Potassium Permanganate from the People's Republic of China: Determination of the Commission in Investigation No. 731-TA-125 (Final) Under the Tariff Act of 1930, Together with the Information Obtained in the Investigation, 9886–14.93

Potatoes and Sweetpotatoes, Final Estimates 1978-82, Preliminary 1983, 1641–14

Potatoes and Sweetpotatoes, 1982-83, 1621–11

Potential Climatic Impacts of Increasing Atmospheric Carbon Dioxide With Emphasis on Water Availability and Hydrology in the U.S., 9188–95

Potential for Industrial Cogeneration Development To Defer New-Utility Electric-Power Capacity over the Next Decade, 3008–92

Potential Health Effects in Human Populations from Exposure to Ethylene Dibromide, 25168–62

Potential Impact of Fiber Optics on Copper Consumption, 2048–104

Potential Inequities Affecting Women, Part 1 of 3, 25368–131

Potential Output Growth and the Long-Term Inflation Outlook, 9385–1.408

Pottery Products, N.E.C. (Industry 3269): 1982 Census of Manufactures. Preliminary Report. Industry Series, 2491–1.236

Poultry and Egg Outlook, 1004–16.1

Poultry and Poultry Products (Industry 5144): 1982 Census of Wholesale Trade. Preliminary Report. Industry Series, 2403–1.30

Poultry Dressing Plants; Poultry and Egg Processing (Industries 2016 and 2017): 1982 Census of Manufactures. Preliminary Report. Industry Series, 2491–1.2

Poultry Market Statistics: 1983 Annual Summary, Federal-State Market News in Cooperation with State Departments of Agriculture, 1317–2

Poultry Production, Disposition, and Income, 1983 Summary, 1625–5

Poultry Slaughter, 1625–3

Poverty in the U.S.: Where Do We Stand Now?, 25928–4

Poverty Rate Increase, 21788–141

Power Driven Hand Tools (Industry 3546): 1982 Census of Manufactures. Preliminary Report. Industry Series, 2491–1.327

Power Program Summary, 1982, Tennessee Valley Authority, 9804–23

Power Program Summary, 1983, Tennessee Valley Authority, 9804–23

Power Transmission Equipment, N.E.C. (Industry 3568): 1982 Census of Manufactures. Preliminary Report. Industry Series, 2491–1.343

Powerplant and Industrial Fuel Use Act, Annual Report, 3104–8

Preconstruction Radioactivity Levels In the Vicinity of the Proposed Clinch River Breeder Reactor Project, 1983, 9804–24

Prefabricated Metal Buildings (Industry 3448): 1982 Census of Manufactures. Preliminary Report. Industry Series, 2491–1.290

Prefabricated Wood Buildings (Industry 2452): 1982 Census of Manufactures. Preliminary Report. Industry Series, 2491–1.127

Preferences of Temporary Workers: Time, Variety, and Flexibility, 6722–1.452

Pregnancy and Infant Health: Progress Toward the 1990 Objectives, 4102–1.425

Preliminary Income and Tax Statistics for 1982 Individual Income Tax Returns, 8302–2.402

Preliminary Report on U.S. Production of Selected Synthetic Organic Chemicals, 9882–1

Preliminary Statistics on Aircraft Accident Data, 9614–9

Preliminary Statistics on Compensation Claims from Former Prisoners of War, Oct. 1, 1981-May 1, 1984, 9928–30

Preliminary Summary of Food Assistance Program Results, 1362–13

Premature Institutionalization Among the Rural Elderly in Arizona, 4102–1.413

Prepared Feeds, N.E.C. (Industry 2048): 1982 Census of Manufactures. Preliminary Report. Industry Series, 2491–1.19

Prepayment Implications of Mortgage-Backed Security Prices, 9316–1.106

Prepayment of Section 202 Loan: Concord-Pasadena Elderly Housing Project Part 1, 21148–31

Preprimary Enrollment, 4834–7

Prescribing Estrogen During Menopause: Physician Survey of Practices in 1974 and 1981, 4102–1.444

Present Policies and Methods

Titles

Present Policies and Methods Regarding the Long-Term Adjustment of Benefits, 4742–1.420

Presidential Report to the Congress on the Implementation of Section 403 of the Powerplant and Industrial Fuel Use Act of 1978, 3104–9

President's Annual Report To the Congress on the Administration of the Federal Railroad Safety Act of 1970, 7304–15

President's List of Articles Which May Be Designated or Modified as Eligible Articles for Purposes of the U.S. Generalized System of Preferences: Report to the President on Investigation Nos. TA-503(a)-11 and 332-166, 9888–17

President's National Urban Policy Report, 1984, 5124–4

President's Private Sector Survey on Cost Control, 16908–1

President's Private Sector Survey on Cost Control: Management Office Selected Issues. Vol. I: Publishing, Printing, Reproduction, and Audiovisual Activities, 16908–1.32

President's Private Sector Survey on Cost Control: Management Office Selected Issues. Vol. II: Travel and Traffic Management, 16908–1.32

President's Private Sector Survey on Cost Control: Management Office Selected Issues. Vol. III: Financial Management in the Federal Government, 16908–1.33

President's Private Sector Survey on Cost Control: Management Office Selected Issues. Vol. IV: Wage Setting Laws, Impact on the Federal Government, 16908–1.33

President's Private Sector Survey on Cost Control: Management Office Selected Issues. Vol. V: Anomalies in the Federal Work Environment, 16908–1.34

President's Private Sector Survey on Cost Control: Management Office Selected Issues. Vol. VI: Federal Retirement Systems, 16908–1.34

President's Private Sector Survey on Cost Control: Management Office Selected Issues. Vol. VII: Information Gap in the Federal Government, 16908–1.35

President's Private Sector Survey on Cost Control: Management Office Selected Issues. Vol. VIII: Cost of Congressional Encroachment, 16908–1.36

President's Private Sector Survey on Cost Control: Management Office Selected Issues. Vol. IX: Federal Health Care Costs, 16908–1.36

President's Private Sector Survey on Cost Control: Management Office Selected Issues. Vol. X: Opportunities Beyond PPSSCC, 16908–1.37

President's Private Sector Survey on Cost Control: Management Office Selected Issues. Vol. X: Federally Subsidized Programs, 16908–1.37

President's Private Sector Survey on Cost Control: Report on Automatic Data Processing and Office Automation, 16908–1.21

President's Private Sector Survey on Cost Control: Report on Boards and Commissions. Banking and Investment, 16908–1.14

President's Private Sector Survey on Cost Control: Report on Boards and Commissions. Business Related, Vol. I, 16908–1.15

President's Private Sector Survey on Cost Control: Report on Boards and Commissions. Business Related, Vol. II, 16908–1.16

President's Private Sector Survey on Cost Control: Report on Federal Construction Management, 16908–1.22

President's Private Sector Survey on Cost Control: Report on Federal Feeding, 16908 1.23

President's Private Sector Survey on Cost Control: Report on Federal Hospital Management, 16908–1.24

President's Private Sector Survey on Cost Control: Report on Federal Management Systems, 16908–1.25

President's Private Sector Survey on Cost Control: Report on Financial Asset Management, 16908–1.26

President's Private Sector Survey on Cost Control: Report on Land, Facilities, Personal Property, 16908–1.29

President's Private Sector Survey on Cost Control: Report on Low Income Standards and Benefits, 16908–1.23

President's Private Sector Survey on Cost Control: Report on Personnel Management, 16908–1.27

President's Private Sector Survey on Cost Control: Report on Privatization, 16908–1.28

President's Private Sector Survey on Cost Control: Report on Procurement, Contracts, Inventory Management, 16908–1.29

President's Private Sector Survey on Cost Control: Report on Real Property Management, 16908–1.29

President's Private Sector Survey on Cost Control: Report on Research and Development, 16908–1.30

President's Private Sector Survey on Cost Control: Report on the Department of Agriculture, 16908–1.2

President's Private Sector Survey on Cost Control: Report on the Department of Commerce, 16908–1.3

President's Private Sector Survey on Cost Control: Report on the Department of Education, 16908–1.5

President's Private Sector Survey on Cost Control: Report on the Department of Energy, the Federal Energy Regulatory Commission and the Nuclear Regulatory Commission, 16908–1.4

President's Private Sector Survey on Cost Control: Report on the Department of Health and Human Services. Department Management, Office of Development Services, ACTION, 16908–1.5

President's Private Sector Survey on Cost Control: Report on the Department of Health and Human Services. Public Health Service, Health Care Financing Administration, 16908–1.7

President's Private Sector Survey on Cost Control: Report on the Department of Health and Human Services. Social Security Administration, 16908–1.6

President's Private Sector Survey on Cost Control: Report on the Department of Housing and Urban Development, 16908–1.8

President's Private Sector Survey on Cost Control: Report on the Department of Justice, 16908–1.9

President's Private Sector Survey on Cost Control: Report on the Department of Labor, 16908–1.3

President's Private Sector Survey on Cost Control: Report on the Department of State, AID, USIA, 16908–1.10

President's Private Sector Survey on Cost Control: Report on the Department of the Air Force, 16908–1.20

President's Private Sector Survey on Cost Control: Report on the Department of the Army, 16908–1.18

President's Private Sector Survey on Cost Control: Report on the Department of the Interior, 16908–1.9

President's Private Sector Survey on Cost Control: Report on the Department of the Navy, 16908–1.19

President's Private Sector Survey on Cost Control: Report on the Department of the Treasury, 16908–1.12

President's Private Sector Survey on Cost Control: Report on the Department of Transportation, 16908–1.11

President's Private Sector Survey on Cost Control: Report on the Environmental Protection Agency, the Small Business Administration and the Federal Emergency Management Agency, 16908–1.13

President's Private Sector Survey on Cost Control: Report on the Office of the Secretary of Defense, 16908–1.17

President's Private Sector Survey on Cost Control: Report on the Veterans Administration, 16908–1.10

President's Private Sector Survey on Cost Control: Report on User Charges, 16908–1.31

President's Private Sector Survey on Cost Control: Report to the President, 16908–1.1

President's Report on Occupational Safety and Health, 1982, 6604–2

President's 1981 Annual Report to the Congress On the Administration of the Federal Railroad Safety Act of 1970, 7604–12

President's 1982 Annual Report to the Congress On the Administration of the Federal Railroad Safety Act of 1970, 7604–12

Pressed and Blown Glass, N.E.C. (Industry 3229): 1982 Census of Manufactures. Preliminary Report. Industry Series, 2491–1.225

Pressed and Molded Pulp Goods (Industry 2646): 1982 Census of Manufactures. Preliminary Report. Industry Series, 2491–1.149

Prevailing Wage Laws, the Federal Reserve, and the Service Contract Act, 9377–1.402

Prevalence of Growth Stunting and Obesity: Pediatric Nutrition Surveillance System, 1982, 4202–7.403

Preventing Substance Abuse: The State of the Art, 4102–1.410

Prevention of Measles in Israel: Implications of a Long-Term Partial Immunization Program, 4102–1.429

Price-Anderson Act, the Third Decade: Report to Congress, 9638–49

Price Behavior During Balance of Payments Adjustment, 9373–1.418

Price Index of New One-Family Houses Sold, Construction Reports, 2382–8

Titles

Price Information for Drug Products, Invoice Level Prices, 4652–7

Price Information for Drug Products, Invoice Level Prices, Aug. 1983, 4658–6

Price Trends for Federal-Aid Highway Construction, 7552–7

Prices Received by Farmers: Eggs, Chickens, and Turkeys, by State and U.S., 1959-78, 1651–3

Prices Received by Farmers: Minnesota-Wisconsin Manufacturing Grade Milk Price Series and Final Two-State Estimates, 1629–2

Primary Aluminum (Industry 3334): 1982 Census of Manufactures. Preliminary Report. Industry Series, 2491–1.265

Primary Aluminum Plants, Worldwide Dec. 31, 1981, 5602–5

Primary Aluminum Plants, Worldwide June 30, 1982, 5602–5

Primary Aluminum Plants, Worldwide Dec. 31, 1982, 5602–5

Primary Aluminum Plants, Worldwide June 30, 1983, 5602–5

Primary Aluminum Plants, Worldwide Dec. 31, 1983, 5602–5

Primary Aluminum Plants, Worldwide June 30, 1984, 5602–5

Primary Batteries, Dry and Wet (Industry 3692): 1982 Census of Manufactures. Preliminary Report. Industry Series, 2491–1.389

Primary Copper (Industry 3331): 1982 Census of Manufactures. Preliminary Report. Industry Series, 2491–1.262

Primary Forest Products Industry and Timber Use, Missouri, 1980, 1206–10.6

Primary Forest Products Industry and Timber Use: North Central Region, 1206–10

Primary Lead (Industry 3332): 1982 Census of Manufactures. Preliminary Report. Industry Series, 2491–1.263

Primary Metal Products, N.E.C. (Industry 3399): 1982 Census of Manufactures. Preliminary Report. Industry Series, 2491–1.275

Primary Nonferrous Metals, N.E.C. (Industry 3339): 1982 Census of Manufactures. Preliminary Report. Industry Series, 2491–1.266

Primary Zinc (Industry 3333): 1982 Census of Manufactures. Preliminary Report. Industry Series, 2491–1.264

Prime Contract Awards by Service Category and Federal Supply Classification, FY80-83, 3544–18

Prime Contract Awards by State, First Half, FY84, 3542–5

Prime Contract Awards by State, FY83, 3542–5

Prime Contract Awards Over $10,000 by State, Place, and Contractor, 3544–22

Prime Contract Awards, Size Distribution, FY83, 3544–19

Prime Contracts by State, City, Contractor, FY83, 3544–22

Principal Federal Statistical Programs: Special Report on Statistics Related to the Budget of the U.S. Government, 104–10

Printing and Typesetting Machinery and Printing Plates, TSUS Items 668(pt.): Summary of Trade and Tariff Information, 9885–6.74

Printing and Writing Papers, TSUS Items 252(pt.), 254(pt.), and 256(pt.): Summary of Trade and Tariff Information, 9885–2.34

Printing Ink (Industry 2893): 1982 Census of Manufactures. Preliminary Report. Industry Series, 2491–1.199

Printing Trades Machinery (Industry 3555): 1982 Census of Manufactures. Preliminary Report. Industry Series, 2491–1.334

Priorities in Health Statistics: Proceedings of the 19th National Meeting of the Public Health Conference on Records and Statistics, Aug. 1983, 4164–2

Prison Admissions and Releases, 1981, 6066–19.9

Prison Overcrowding, 25528–99

Prisoners Under Jurisdiction of State and Federal Correctional Authorities, 6062–3

Private Activity Tax-Exempt Bonds, 1983, 8302–2.417

Private Central Bank: Some Olde English Lessons, 9391–1.410

Private Health Insurance Coverage of the Medicare Population, 4186–3.18

Private Health Insurance: New Measures of a Complex and Changing Industry, 4652–1.430

Private Mortgage Insurance Activity, 5142–38

Private Sector Financing of Family Farms, 1004–16.1

Probability of Dying Within the Next 10 Years At Selected Ages for 40 Major Causes, 4208–21

Probation and Parole 1983, 6062–2.408

Problems and Potentials of Genetic Engineering, 1004–16.1

Problems and Prospects of the Mexican Economy in 1983-88, 21248–82

Problems in Alerting and Preparing Army Reservists for Mobilization, 26123–57

Proceedings, National Workshop on Welfare Research and Statistics, 4744–21

Proceedings of a Conference on Bank Structure and Competition Federal Reserve Bank of Chicago, May 2-4, 1983, 9375–7

Proceedings of a Conference on Bank Structure and Competition Federal Reserve Bank of Chicago, Apr. 23-25, 1984, 9375–7

Proceedings of the Conference on Applied Time Series Analysis of Economic Data, 2626–7.5

Proceedings of the First General Conference on Social Graphics, 2626–2.51

Proceedings of the Second Workshop on Law and Justice Statistics, 1983, 6064–20

Proceedings of the 19th National Meeting of the Public Health Conference on Records and Statistics Priorities in Health Statistics, 4164–2

Proceedings, 23rd National Workshop on Welfare Research and Statistics. Theme: Growing To Meet the Needs, 4704–11

Proceedings: 3rd Asian Conference on Low-Income Shelter and Housing Finance, Oct. 11-14, 1982, 9914–11

Process Control Instruments (Industry 3823): 1982 Census of Manufactures. Preliminary Report. Industry Series, 2491–1.413

Processed Fishery Products, Current Fishery Statistics, 2166–6

Processed Fishery Products, Annual Summary 1982, 2166–6.4

Processed Mushrooms: U.S. Producers' Production, Sales, Inventories, and U.S. Imports, Exports, and Apparent Consumption; Report to the President on Investigation No. 332-84 Under Section 332 of the Tariff Act of 1930, 9882–5

Program Acquisition Costs by

Processed Textile Waste (Industry 2294): 1982 Census of Manufactures. Preliminary Report. Industry Series, 2491–1.72

Processed Vegetables, N.E.C., TSUS Items 140(pt). and 141(pt.): Summary of Trade and Tariff Information, 9885–1.61

Processing and Refining Capacity of the Domestic Sugar Industry, 1561–14.401

Processing Technologies and Their Effects on Microbiological Properties, Thermal Processing Efficiency, and Yield of Blue Crab, 2162–1.401

Procurement from Small and Other Business Firms, 3542–10

Procurement Program (P-1), Department of Defense Budget for FY85, 3504–14

Producer Milk Marketed Under Federal Milk Orders by State of Origin, 1317–4.405

Producer Price Indexes, 6762–5

Producer Price Trends Continue Moderate in the Third Quarter, 6722–1.407

Producer Prices and Price Indexes, 6762–6

Producer Prices and Price Indexes, Supplement to Data, 6764–2

Product Summary Report and NEISS Estimates of National Injury Incidents, 9164–6

Production and Use of Industrial Wood and Bark Residues for 44 Counties in Alabama, Georgia, Kentucky, and Mississippi, 9806–2.36

Production Decline of U.S. Surveillance Oil Fields, 3164–58

Production of Housing Services and the Derived Demand for Residential Energy, 9306–1.2

Production, Prices, Employment, and Trade in Northwest Forest Industries, 1202–3

Productivity and Costs Nonfinancial Corporate Sector, 6822–1

Productivity and Costs, Private Business, Nonfarm Business, and Manufacturing Sectors, 6822–2

Productivity Declined in 1982 in a Majority of Industries Measured, 6722–1.408

Productivity Growth: A Better Life for America, Report to the President of the U.S., 17898–1

Productivity Growth in the Switchgear Industry Slows After 1973, 6722–1.420

Productivity in Making Air Conditioners, Refrigeration Equipment, and Furnaces, 6722–1.471

Productivity Measures for Selected Industries, 1954-82, 6824–1

Productivity 'Slowdown': A Sectoral Analysis, 9381–1.407

Productivity Trends in Manufacturing in the U.S. and 11 Other Countries, 6722–1.405

Products of Purchased Glass (Industry 3231): 1982 Census of Manufactures. Preliminary Report. Industry Series, 2491–1.226

Profile, FY84, National Institute of Allergy and Infectious Diseases, 4474–30

Profile of State Performance in the Aid to Families with Dependent Children Program, 1981, 4704–10

Profiles of the Problems of Coca in Bolivia, 7008–40

Profitability of Insured Commercial Banks in 1983, 9362–1.409

Profitability of Milk Production in Selected States, 1561–2.403

Program Acquisition Costs by Weapon System: Department of Defense Budget for FY85, 3504–2

Program Activities: DOE State

Program Activities: DOE State and Local Assistance Programs, 1983 Report, 3304–21

Program Activities: DOE State and Local Assistance Programs, 1984 Report, 3304–21

Program and Demographic Characteristics of Supplemental Security Income Beneficiaries, Dec. 1982, 4744–16

Program Outlook for Crop Insurance in 1984, 1004–16.1

Program Tables, 6004–16.1

Programs of the Office of Energy Research, 3004–18.6

Programs of the Office of Energy Research, 3004–18.8

Progress in Energy, 1983-84, 3024–4

Progress in the Prevention and Control of Air Pollution in 1982, 9194–4

Progress of Education in the U.S., 1980-81 Through 1982-83, 4804–27

Progress Report on Federal Executive Development Programs, 26119–69

Progress Report to the President, Efforts To Prevent Fraud, Waste and Mismanagement, First Six Months FY84, 102–5

Project Head Start Statistical Fact Sheet, 4604–8

Project Ranch Hand II: An Epidemiologic Investigation of Health Effects in Air Force Personnel Following Exposure to Herbicides, Baseline Morbidity Study Results, 3604–3

Project Summaries: FY83, 9624–21

Projected Response of the Science, Engineering, and Technical Labor Market to Defense and Nondefense Needs: 1982-87, 9628–71

Projected Supply of Registered Nurses, 1990, 4102–1.439

Projections of Future Forest Recreation Use, 1208–195

Projections of the Population of the U.S., by Age, Sex, and Race: 1983-2080, 2546–3.132

Projections of the Population of Voting Age for States: Nov. 1984, 2546–3.129

Promising Outlook for Soil and Water Conservation, 1004–16.1

Propagation and Distribution of Fishes from National Fish Hatcheries, FY82, 5504–10

Propagation and Distribution of Fishes from National Fish Hatcheries, FY83, 5504–10

Property Improvement and Mobile Home Loans Insured and Claims Paid, Title I, Section 2, Classes 1 and 2 Combined, 5142–9

Proposal for Transferring St. Elizabeths Hospital to the District of Columbia, 26121–72

Proposed Outer Continental Shelf Oil and Gas Lease Sales: Final Environmental Impact Statements, 5736–1

Proposed Refugee Admissions and Allocations for FY85, Report to the Congress, 7004–16

Pros and Cons of Worldwide Unitary Taxation, 9373–1.412

Prosecution of Felony Arrests, 1979, 6066–22.1

Prospective Plantings, 1621–22

Prospects for Primary Health Care in Africa: Another Look at the Sine Saloum Rural Health Project in Senegal, 9916–3.20

Protecting American Agriculture: APHIS, 1004–16.1

Protecting American Agriculture: The PPQ Role, 1004–16.1

Protecting American Agriculture: The VS Role, 1004–16.1

Protocol for Epidemiologic Studies of the Health of Vietnam Veterans, 4208–22

Provision of Post-Employment Services (PES), 4944–8

Provisional Data on Federally Funded Community Mental Centers, 4504–5

Proximate Chemical Composition and Fatty Acids of Three Small Coastal Pelagic Species, 2162–1.403

Psychiatric Problems of AIDS Inpatients at the New York Hospital: Preliminary Report, 4102–1.426

Public Building and Related Furniture (Industry 2531): 1982 Census of Manufactures. Preliminary Report. Industry Series, 2491–1.136

Public Buildings Projects Authorized by the Public Buildings Act of 1959, Status Report as of Dec. 31, 1983, 9454–12

Public Elementary and Secondary Education in the U.S., 1981-82: A Statistical Compendium, 4834–13

Public Employee Pension Benefit Plans, 21788–142

Public Health Personnel in the U.S., 4114–10

Public Health Reports, 4102–1

Public High School Graduates, 1981-82, 4834–12

Public Housing Authority Experience with Private Management, 5188–103

Public Land Statistics, 1983, 5724–1

Public Law 480, Concessional Sales Agreements Signed Through Dec. 31, 1983, 1924–6

Public Law 480, Title I and III, Exports by Commodity and Country, FY78-83, 1922–10

Public Law 480, Title I and III, Exports by Commodity and Country, 1978-83, 1922–10

Public Response to Hurricane Probability Forecasts, 2186–4.11

Public Roads, A Journal of Highway Research and Development, 7552–3

Public School Enrollment, U.S., Fall 1982, 4834–10

Public Social Welfare Expenditures, FY81-82, 4746–16.1

Public Utility Holding Company Act Amendments, 21368–53

Public Utility Regulatory Policies Act of 1978 Annual Report to Congress, 3104–7

Public/Private Cooperation in Rural Roadway Improvements, 1004–16.1

Publication of Employment Data for Additional Service-Producing Industries, 6742–2.410

Publications Abstracts, FY83, 2804–3

Publications Catalog of the U.S. Department of Commerce, 2004–4

Publications of the Geological Survey, 1983, 5664–4

Publications of the National Bureau of Standards, 1983 Catalog, 2214–1

Publications of the National Institute of Justice: A Comprehensive Bibliography, 6064–8

Pulp and Paper Machinery and Bookbinding Machinery, TSUS Items 668(pt.): Summary of Trade and Tariff Information, 9885–6.77

Pulp Mills (Industry 2611): 1982 Census of Manufactures. Preliminary Report. Industry Series, 2491–1.141

Pulpwood Harvest Intensity in the Northeast, 1981, 9806–2.38

Pulpwood Prices in the Southeast, 1982, 1204–22

Pulpwood Production in the North-Central Region, By County, 1982, 1204–19

Pumice and Pumicite: Minerals Yearbook Preprint, Vol. 1, 1983, 5604–15.53

Pumps and Compressors, 1983, Current Industrial Report, 2506–12.8

Pumps and Pumping Equipment (Industry 3561): 1982 Census of Manufactures. Preliminary Report. Industry Series, 2491–1.336

Pumps for Liquids and Parts, TSUS Items 660(pt.): Summary of Trade and Tariff Information, 9885–6.75

Quality Assessment of National Defense Stockpile Cobalt Inventory, 25208–27

Quality of Responses of High School Students to Questionniare Items, 4826–2.22

Quarterly Coal Report, 3162–37

Quarterly Financial Report for Manufacturing, Mining, and Trade Corporations, 2502–1

Quarterly Financial Review, 9142–30

Quarterly Journal Comptroller of the Currency, Administrator of National Banks, 8402–3

Quarterly Operating Data of Telegraph Carriers, 9282–1

Quarterly Operating Data of Telephone Carriers, 9282–2

Quarterly Public Assistance Statistics, 4742–6

Quarterly Review, Federal Reserve Bank of Minneapolis, 9383–6

Quarterly Review, Federal Reserve Bank of New York, 9385–1

Quarterly Speed Summary, 7552–14

Quarterly Status Report of Federal Funds Used for Highway Safety Improvements, 7552–9

Quarterly Summary of Federal, State, and Local Tax Revenue, 2462–3

Quarterly Survey of Agricultural Credit Conditions In Eleventh Federal Reserve District, 9379–11

Quarterly Survey on Certain Stainless Steel and Alloy Tool Steel, Report to the President on Investigation No. 332-162 Under Section 332 of the Tariff Act of 1930, 9882–3

Quota Information, 8146–1

Quota Information: Cotton and Cotton Waste, 8146–1.2

Quota Information: Cotton, Wool and Manmade Fiber Textile Products, 8146–1.4

Quota Information: Dairy Products, 8146–1.3

Quota Information: Sugars, Sirups, and Molasses, 8146–1.9

Quota Information: Various Commodities, 8146–1.1

R, D, T & E Programs (R-1), Department of Defense Budget for FY85, 3504–15

Rabies Surveillance, Annual Summary, 1980-82, 4205–28

Racial, Ethnic and Sex Enrollment Data from Institutions of Higher Education, 4804–23

Titles

Regulatory Reform Act:

Radial Ply Tires for Passenger Cars from the Republic of Korea: Determination of the Commission in Investigation No. 731-TA-200 (Preliminary) Under the Tariff Act of 1930, Together with the Information Obtained in the Investigation, 9886–14.117

Radiation Exposures for DOE and DOE Contractor Employees, 1982: Fifteenth Annual Report, 3404–1

Radiation Procedures Performed on U.S. Women During Pregnancy: Findings from Two 1980 Surveys, 4102–1.421

Radio and Television Receivers, Phonographs, and Related Equipment, 1983, Current Industrial Report, 2506–12.20

Radio and TV Communication Equipment (Industry 3662): 1982 Census of Manufactures. Preliminary Report. Industry Series, 2491–1.380

Radio and TV Receiving Sets (Industry 3651): 1982 Census of Manufactures. Preliminary Report. Industry Series, 2491–1.377

Radio and TV Repair Shops (Industry 7622): 1982 Census of Service Industries. Preliminary Report. Industry Series, 2390–2.11

Radioactive Materials Released from Nuclear Power Plants, Annual Report, 1981, 9634–1

Radiological Survey of Chemicals Group, Olin Corporation (formerly Blockson Chemical Company) Joliet, Ill., Mar. 27-Nov. 28, 1978, 3406–1.36

Radiological Survey of the Albany Metallurgical Research Center, U.S. Bureau of Mines, Albany, Oreg., 3406–1.39

Radiological Survey of the Albany Metallurgical Research Center U.S. Bureau of Mines Biomass Facility and the "Back Forty" Area, Albany, Oreg., 3406–1.37

Radiological Survey of the National Guard Armory at Washington Park, 52nd Street and Cottage Grove Avenue, Chicago, Ill., Sept. 19, 1977-Oct. 11, 1978, 3406–1.35

Rail-Highway Crossing Accident/Incident and Inventory Bulletin, No. 5, 1982, 7604–2

Rail Transit Safety, Annual Report, 7884–5

Railroad Accident Reports, Brief Format, 9612–3

Railroad Equipment (Industry 3743): 1982 Census of Manufactures. Preliminary Report. Industry Series, 2491–1.406

Railroad Retirement Board, Annual Report FY83, 9704–1

Railroad Retirement Board 1982 Annual Report, Statistical Supplement, 9704–2

Randolph-Sheppard Vending Facility Program: Summary, FY83, 4944–2

Rankings of Air Carriers by Number of Stations Served, New Stations Added and Stations Closed in the Past Year, 9142–42.410

Rare-Earth Minerals and Metals: Minerals Yearbook Preprint, Vol. 1, 1983, 5604–15.54

REA Financed Generating Plants, As of Jan. 1, 1984, 1244–6

Readiness Assessment of the Reserve Components, FY83, 3544–27

Ready-Mixed Concrete (Industry 3273): 1982 Census of Manufactures. Preliminary Report. Industry Series, 2491–1.239

Real Earnings, 6742–3

Real Growth in Federal R&D Funds Estimated at 12% in 1984, Largest Increase Since Midsixties, 9626–2.132

Recap of International Travel to and from the U.S. in 1983, 2904–10

Receipts and Expenditures of State Governments and of Local Governments, 1980-83, 2702–1.436

Recent CAP Changes: Will They Reduce Subsidized Exports?, 1522–3.402

Recent Decline in Agricultural Exports: Is the Exchange Rate the Culprit?, 9391–1.421

Recent Developments in Papua New Guinea's Tuna Fishery, 2162–1.402

Recent Developments in the Credit Union Industry, 9381–1.410

Recent Developments in the State and Local Government Sector, 9362–1.408

Recent Experience with M1 as a Policy Guide, 9381–1.406

Recent Financing Activity of Nonfinancial Corporations, 9362–1.405

Recent Labor Market Developments in the U.S. and Nine Other Countries, 6722–1.404

Recent Market Activities of Major Interstate Pipeline Companies, 3168–50.5

Recent Recessions Swell Ranks of the Long-Term Unemployed, 6722–1.411

Recent Residential Sales of Natural Gas in the North Central U.S., 3162–4.402

Recent Shifts in the Location of U.S. Egg Production, 1561–7.403

Recent Trends in Adjustable and Other Mortgage Lending: A Survey of the Eleventh District, 9306–1.5

Recent Trends in Airline Cost Elements, U.S. Certificated Route Carriers by Group, 9142–47

Recent Trends in Clothing and Textiles, 1702–1.403

Recent Trends in Operating Profit Margins: Major Large Aircraft Operators, 9142–43

Recent Trends in the U.S. Foreign Exchange Market, 9385–1.411

Recessionary Impacts on the Unemployment of Men and Women, 6722–1.432

Reclaimed Rubber (Industry 3031): 1982 Census of Manufactures. Preliminary Report. Industry Series, 2491–1.208

Reconciling Two Measures of Consumer Price Change: Second Quarter 1984, 6762–2.401

Recreation Sites, Areas, Improvements, and Services in the National Forest System, As of Nov. 1, 1983, 1204–28

Recreation Statistics, 1982, 3754–5

Recreational and Utility Trailer Dealers (Industry 5561): 1982 Census of Retail Trade. Preliminary Report. Industry Series, 2395–1.14

Recreational Billfish Survey Newsletter: Oceanic Gamefish Investigations, 1982, 2164–7

Red Meats Outlook, 1004–16.1

Red Raspberries from Canada: Determination of the Commission in Investigation No. 731-TA-196 (Preliminary) Under the Tariff Act of 1930, Together with the Information Obtained in the Investigation, 9886–14.112

Redesign of the Sample for the Current Population Survey, 6742–2.407

Reducing Grades of the General Schedule Work Force, 26306–6.84

Reducing the Deficit: Spending and Revenue Options. A Report to the Senate and House Committees on the Budget, Part III, 26304–3.3

Reductions in U.S. Costs to Station Forces in the Federal Republic of Germany and the United Kingdom Are Unlikely, 26123–71

Reexamination of Occurrence Rates for Accidental Oil Spills On the U.S. Outer Continental Shelf, 5738–1

Reexamination of Purchasing Power Parity: A Multi-Country and Multi-Period Study, 9381–10.36

Reference Sources, Census Bureau, 2326–7.62

Reference Tables and Graphs for World Wheat Trade, 1925–2.7

Reference Tables on Sugar Supply/Distribution for Individual Countries, 1974/75-1983/84, 1925–14.4

Reference Tables on the Major Producing, Consuming, and Trading Countries of Cottonseed, Cottonseed Meal and Oil, 1925–1.2

Reference Tables on U.S. Grain Exports by Destination, 1925–2.5

Refinery Capacity Trends and Outlook, 3162–6.401

Reflections on Bretton Woods, 9373–3.28

Reflections on Money and Inflation, 9377–1.403

Refractories, Current Industrial Report, 2506–9.1

Refreshment Places (Industry 5812 Pt. B): 1982 Census of Retail Trade. Preliminary Report. Industry Series, 2395–1.24

Refrigeration and Heating Equipment (Industry 3585): 1982 Census of Manufactures. Preliminary Report. Industry Series, 2491–1.351

Refugee Arrivals in the U.S., 7002–5

Refugee Resettlement Program, Report to the Congress, 4704–8

Regional Administrator's Annual Report: Environmental Quality in New England, 9184–6

Regional Economic Forecasting Procedure Applied to Texas, 9377–9.10

Regional, New-Source Bubble Policy for Sulfur Dioxide Emissions in the Eastern U.S., 3408–32

Regional Nonfarm Wages and Salaries Thus Far in the Recovery, 2702–1.412

Regional Report, Special Publication Series, Federal Home Loan Bank of San Francisco, 9306–2

Regional Shifts in Personal Income by Industrial Component, 1959-83, 2702–1.443

Regional Survey of the Chemistry of Headwater Lakes and Streams in New England: Vulnerability to Acidification, 5506–5.15

Regional Variations in Employment and Uemployment During 1970-82, 6722–1.413

Regionals, All Cargo and Charter: Quarterly Financial Review, 9142–30.4

Regionals, Scheduled Combination Carriers: Quarterly Financial Review, 9142–30.3

Register of Reporting Labor Organizations, 1983, 6468–17

Regulation of Safety on Panamanian Flag Vessels: The Panama Offshore Industry Advisory Committee as a Model for Successful Government Industry Interface, 21568–35

Regulatory Federalism: Policy, Process, Impact, and Reform, 10048–58

Regulatory Reform Act: Supplement, Part 3, 21528–56

Reimbursing Physicians Under Titles

Reimbursing Physicians Under Medicare on the Basis of Their Specialty, 26121–82

Relationships Among Exchange Rates, Intervention, and Interest Rates: An Empirical Investigation, 9366–1.132

Relationships Between Quarterly Wheat Prices and Stocks, 1561–12.401

Relative Cost of Shipbuilding: A Report to the Congress on the Relative Cost of Shipbuilding in the Various Coastal Districts of the U.S., 7704–12

Relative Importance of Components in the Consumer Price Indexes, 1983, 6884–1

Relative Intensity Measures: Pricing of Inpatient Nursing Services Under Diagnosis-Related Group Prospective Hospital Payment, 4652–1.424

Reliability in Guideline Application: Initial Hearings, 1982, 6006–2.33

Remote Sensing and the Private Sector, Issues for Discussion, 26358–100

Removing Barriers to the Market Penetration of Methanol Fuels, 26113–112

Rental Housing for the Large Family, 21968–28

Rental Rehabilitation Amounts, FY85, Application Dates Announced, 5006–3.39

Rental Rehabilitation Demonstration Selects 275 Communities, 22 States in 3rd Round, 5006–3.30

Report of Mandays for the Month: Bureau of Prisons, 6242–1.4

Report of NIJJDP, FY81-82, 6064–19

Report of Railroad Employment, Class I Line-Haul Railroads, 9482–3

Report of State and Local Radiological Health Programs, FY82, 4064–3

Report of "Tar," Nicotine and Carbon Monoxide of the Smoke of 207 Varieties of Domestic Cigarettes, 9402–2

Report of the Attorney General on the U.S. Trustee System Established in the Bankruptcy Reform Act of 1978, for the Period Oct. 1, 1979-Dec. 31, 1983, 6004–15

Report of the Clerk of the House, 21942–1

Report of the Director, National Heart, Lung, and Blood Institute, 4474–22

Report of the Field Studies and Statistics Program, FY83, 4474–29

Report of the Forest Service, FY83, 1204–1

Report of the Interdepartment Radio Advisory Committee, July 1-Dec. 31, 1983, 2802–1

Report of the National Bipartisan Commission on Central America, 028–19

Report of the President of the Commodity Credit Corporation, Sept. 30, 1983, 1824–1

Report of the President's Commission on Strategic Forces, 3508–17

Report of the President's Task Force on Food Assistance, 028–20

Report of the Proceedings of the Judicial Conference of the U.S., 18204–5

Report of the Secretary of Agriculture, 1983, 1004–3

Report of the Secretary of Defense Caspar W. Weinberger to the Congress On the FY85 Budget, FY86 Authorization Request and FY85-89 Defense Programs, 3544–2

Report of the Secretary of the Senate, From Oct. 1, 1983 to Mar. 31, 1984, 25922–1

Report of the U.S. Advisory Commission on Public Diplomacy, 1983, 17594–1

Report of the U.S. Architectural and Transportation Barriers Compliance Board To the President and the Congress for 1982, 17614–1

Report of the U.S. Architectural and Transportation Barriers Compliance Board To the President and the Congress for 1983, 17614–1

Report of the U.S. Claims Court For the Court Year Ending Sept. 30, 1983, 18224–1

Report of the U.S. Department of Justice Pursuant to Section 8 of the Federal Coal Leasing Amendments Act of 1976, 6004–12

Report of the 1982 Advisory Council on Social Security: Medicare Benefits and Financing, 10178–1

Report on Airline Service, Fares, Traffic, Load Factors and Market Shares, A Staff Study, 9142–42

Report on Applications for Orders Authorizing or Approving the Interception of Wire or Oral Communications (Wiretap Report) Jan. 1-Dec. 31, 1983, 18204–7

Report on Foreign Currencies Held by the U.S. Government, Oct. 1, 1983-Mar. 31, 1984, 8102–7

Report on Great Lakes Water Quality, 1983. Appendix: Great Lakes Surveillance, 14644–1.1

Report on Great Lakes Water Quality, 1983. Appendix on Radioactivity, 14644–1.2

Report on Medicaid Financed Abortions, Oct. 1, 1982-Sept. 30, 1983, 4654–9

Report on Population and Family Planning Activities: A Report to the House Committee on Appropriations, 4044–4

Report on Priced Services Activities for 1983, 9364–9

Report on Survey of U.S. Shipbuilding and Repair Facilities, 1983, 7704–9

Report on the FY85 Pay Increase Under the Federal Statutory Pay Systems, Annual Report of the Advisory Committee on Federal Pay, 10104–1

Report on the Implementation of the Magnuson Fishery Conservation and Management Act of 1976, 2164–12

Report on the National Eye Institute's Visual Acuity Impairment Survey Pilot Study, 4478–147

Report on the Noncompetitive Employment of 30 Percent or More Disabled Veterans in the Federal Government Apr.-Sept. 1982, 9842–4

Report on the Significant Actions of the Office of Personnel Management During 1982, 9494–1

Report on U.S. Government International Exchange and Training Programs, FY82, 9854–8

Report on U.S. Government International Exchange and Training Programs, FY83, 9854–8

Report on 1984 National Survey of Compensation Paid Scientists and Engineers Engaged in Research and Development Activities, 3004–1

Report to Congress, Annual Report on the Implementation of the Federal Equal Opportunity Recruitment Program, 9844–33

Report to Congress, Jan. 1981-Dec. 1983: On Administration of the Marine Protection, Research, and Sanctuaries Act of 1972, as Amended (P.L. 92-532) and Implementing the International London Dumping Convention, 9204–8

Report to Congress: Nonpoint Source Pollution in the U.S., 9208–123

Report to Congress on the Activities and Operations of the Public Integrity Section for 1983, 6004–13

Report to Congress on the Manufactured Housing Program: Title VI of the Housing and Community Development Act of 1974, 5004–4

Report to Congress on the National Manufactured Housing Construction and Safety Standards Program, 5004–4

Report to Congress on the Nation's Renewable Resources, 1980, 1208–24

Report to Congress, Scientific Exchange Activities with the Soviet Union, FY81 and FY82, Department of State Authorization Act, Sec. 126.(a) and (b), 7008–41

Report to the Congress and the Trade Policy Committee On Trade Between the U.S. and the Nonmarket Economy Countries, 9882–2

Report to the Congress on Matters Contained in the Helium Act (Public Law 86-777), FY83, 5604–32

Report to the Congress on Ocean Pollution, Monitoring and Research, Oct. 1982 Through Sept. 1983, 2144–9

Report to the Congress on the Implementation of the Age Discrimination Act of 1975 During FY83, As Required by Section 308(b) of the Age Discrimination Act of 1975, as Amended, 4004–27

Report to the Congress on the Status of the Public Ports of the U.S., 7704–16

Report to the Congress, Refugee Resettlement Program, 4704–8

Report to the Nation on Crime and Justice, The Data, 6068–174

Report to the President and Congress On the Status of Health Personnel in the U.S., 4114–8

Report to the President and the Congress of the U.S., Part One: Collective Ratemaking in the Bus Industry, the Need for Antitrust Immunity; Part Two: Implementation of the Bus Regulatory Reform Act of 1982, the Impact on Older Americans and the Effect on Intrastate Bus Services, 14828–2

Report to the President on Emergency Management in the U.S. Annual Report, 1983, 9434–2

Report to the President on Investigations Under Section 22 of the Agricultural Adjustment Act, As Amended, 9886–10

Report to the Secretary on the Homeless and Emergency Shelters, 5188–108

Report to the Senate and House Committees on the Budget, 26304–3

Report to the U.S. Congress on Export Credit Competition and the Export-Import Bank of the U.S., For the Period Jan. 1-Dec. 31, 1982, 9254–3

Reported Morbidity and Mortality in the U.S., Annual Summary, 1982, 4204–1

Reports of the Office of the Inspector General, 3006–5

Reports of the Proceedings of the Judicial Conference of the U.S., 1983, and Annual Report of the Director of the Administrative Office of the U.S. Courts, 1983, 18204–8

Reports to the President on Investigations Under Section 201 of the Trade Act of 1974, 9886–5

Titles

Reports to the President on Investigations Under Section 406 of the Trade Act of 1974, 9886–12

Republic of Palau Annual Report, FY83, 5304–15.2

Republic of the Marshall Islands Annual Report, FY83, 5304–15.3

Resale Price Maintenance: Economic Theories and Empirical Evidence, 9406–1.38

Research and Development Funding in the Proposed FY85 Budget, Special Study, 26308–46

Research and Development in Industry: Funds, Scientists and Engineers, 9627–21

Research and Development in Industry, 1981: Funds, 1981; Scientists and Engineers, Jan. 1982, 9627–21.1

Research and Development in Industry, 1982: Funds, 1982; Scientists and Engineers, Jan. 1983, 9627–21.1

Research and Statistics Notes, 4746–16

Research in Brief, 6066–20

Research Issues, National Institute on Drug Abuse, 4496–1

Research Outlook, 1984, 9184–10

Research Reports, Special Publication Series, Federal Home Loan Bank of San Francisco, 9306–1

Research Reports, SSA, 4746–4

Research Tables Based on Characteristics of State Plans for Aid to Families with Dependent Children: Eligibility, Assistance, Administration in Effect Oct. 1, 1982, 1983 Edition, 4704–9.2

Research Working Papers, Federal Reserve Bank of Kansas City, 9381–10

Residence in 1975 for States by Age, Sex, Race, and Spanish Origin. 1980 Census of Population. Supplementary Report, 2535–1.13

Residential Alterations and Repairs, 2012–1.406

Residential Alterations and Repairs, Construction Reports, 2382–7

Residential Alterations and Repairs, 1983 Annual Report, Construction Reports, 2384–4

Residential Conservation Service, 21368–54

Residential Conservation Service in Connecticut: Evaluation of the CONN SAVE Program, 3308–77

Residential Energy Conservation: How Far Have We Progressed and How Much Farther Can We Go?, 21368–48

Residential Energy Consumption Survey, 3166–7

Residential Energy Consumption Survey. Consumption and Expenditures, Apr. 1982-Mar. 1983, Part 1: National Data, 3166–7.20

Residential Energy Consumption Survey. Consumption and Expenditures, Apr. 1982-Mar. 1983. Part 2: Regional Data, 3166–7.22

Residential Energy Consumption Survey. Housing Characteristics, 1982, 3166–7.19

Residential Energy Costs for SOLCOST Data Bank Cities, Winter 1982-83, 3308–67

Residential Fuelwood Use in the U.S.: 1980-81, 1208–204

Residential Lighting Fixtures (Industry 3645): 1982 Census of Manufactures. Preliminary Report. Industry Series, 2491–1.373

Residential Real Estate Brokerage Industry, Vols. I and II And the Butters Report, 9408–48

Rolling Mill Machinery

Residential Water Conservation Projects, 5188–109

Residential Water Conservation Projects, Summary Report, 5188–109.1

Resource and Environmental Impacts of Trends in U.S. Agriculture, 9188–94

Response Variation in the CPS: Caveats for the Unemployment Analyst, 6722–1.421

Restaurants and Lunchrooms (Industry 5812 Pt. A): 1982 Census of Retail Trade. Preliminary Report. Industry Series, 2395–1.23

Results of Coverage and Processing Changes to the 1980 Individual Statistics of Income Program, 8308–28.1

Results of Note and Bond Auctions, 8002–7.3

Results of the Nationwide Urban Runoff Program, Vol. 1: Final Report, 9208–122

Results of Treasury's [ ]-Day Bill Auction, 8002–7.4

Results of Treasury's Weekly Bill Auctions, 8002–7.1

Results of Treasury's 52-Week Bill Auction, 8002–7.2

Retail Trade: Annual Sales, Year-End Inventories, Purchases, Gross Margin, and Accounts Receivable, by Kind of Retail Store, 1983, Current Business Reports, 2413–5

Retailing in Tennessee: A Report on Number of Firms and Sales in the Retail Sector for the Calendar Year, 9804–15

Return Banks Have Paid on NOW Accounts, 9387–1.403

Return to Nursing Home Investment: Issues for Public Policy, 4652–1.417

Returns to Corn and Soybean Tillage Practices, 1588–80

Revenue, Pieces and Weight By Classes of Mail and Special Services, 9862–1

Revenue Sharing. Quarterly Payment, Quarter 1, Entitlement Period 15, 8066–1.96

Revenue Sharing. Quarterly Payment, Quarter 2, Entitlement Period 15, 8066–1.97

Revenue Sharing. Quarterly Payment, Quarter 3, Entitlement Period 15, 8066–1.98

Revenues Rise but Participation Drops Slightly in Latest Hunting and Fishing Figures, 5504–16

Review, Federal Reserve Bank of St. Louis, 9391–1

Review, Fourth District, Federal Home Loan Bank of Atlanta, 9302–2

Review of Bank Performance in the Fifth District, 1983, 9389–1.408

Review of Existing and Alternative Federal Dairy Programs, 1568–245

Review of Federal Crop Insurance Program, 21168–28

Review of Head Start Research Since 1970, 4608–17

Review of Industry Coding Systems, 106–4.5

Review of the Audit of the Disabled American Veterans National Headquarters' Financial Statements For the Year Ended Dec. 31, 1982, 26111–16

Review of the Department of Defense Dec. 31, 1983, Selected Acquisition Reports (SARs), 26304–5

Review of the Federal Home Loan Bank Board's Adjustable-Rate Mortgage Regulations and the Current ARM Proposal, 9316–1.104

Review of the National Center for Research in Vocational Education, 26121–79

Review of the Procurement Actions of the Department of Defense During the One-Week Period Ending Sept. 30, 1983, 108–38

Review of the Upland Cotton Acreage Base, 1561–1.403

Revised Manufacturing and Trade Inventories and Sales, 2702–1.34

Revised Monthly Retail Sales and Inventories: Jan. 1974-Dec. 1983, 2413–3

Revised Monthly Wholesale Trade: Sales and Inventories, Jan. 1974-Dec. 1983, Current Business Reports, 2413–7

Revised Seasonally Adjusted Labor Force Series, 6742–2.404

Revision of IRS Tax Deductions for the Arts, 21408–74

Revision of Seasonally Adjusted Labor Force Series, 6742–2.401

Revolutionary Terrorism in El Salvador over 20,000 Victims, 21388–41

Reye Syndrome Surveillance, 1981-82, 4202–7.402

Rice and Milled Rice Products, TSUS Items 130(pt.) and 131(pt.): Summary of Trade and Tariff Information, 9885–1.63

Rice: ASCS Commodity Fact Sheet, 1984, 1806–4.6

Rice Market News, 1313–8

Rice Milling (Industry 2044): 1982 Census of Manufactures. Preliminary Report. Industry Series, 2491–1.16

Rice Outlook and Situation Report, 1561–8

Rice Stocks, 1621–7

Right Rabbit: Which Intermediate Target Should the Fed Pursue?, 9375–1.405

Rising Protectionism and U.S. International Trade Policy, 9381–1.412

Risk Considerations in Deregulating Bank Activities, 9371–1.416

Roadside Vehicle Inspection Report, 1982, 7554–35

Roasted Coffee (Industry 2095): 1982 Census of Manufactures. Preliminary Report. Industry Series, 2491–1.40

Robbery in the U.S.: An Analysis of Recent Trends and Patterns, 6068–180

Robes and Dressing Gowns (Industry 2384): 1982 Census of Manufactures. Preliminary Report. Industry Series, 2491–1.98

Robot Corps in Southeastern Industry, 9371–1.423

Robust Growth and the Strong Dollar Set Pattern for 1983 Import and Export Prices, 6722–1.424

Rocky Mountain Acidification Study, 5506–5.17

Role of Epidemiology in the Regulation of Oral Contraceptives, 4102–1.436

Role of Securities Act Exemptions in Business Financing, 9736–2

Role of the Discount Window in Monetary Policy Under Alternative Operating Procedures and Reserve Requirement Systems, 9387–8.87

Role of the Fund, 9373–3.28

Role of Traditional Mortgage Lenders in Future Mortgage Lending: Problems and Prospects, 9375–11.4

Roles of Magistrates in Federal District Courts, 18408–24

Rolling Mill Machinery (Industry 3547): 1982 Census of Manufactures. Preliminary Report. Industry Series, 2491–1.328

Route Strategies at the Large Titles

Route Strategies at the Large Hubs, 1978-84, 9142-42.407

Rubber and Plastics Footwear (Industry 3021): 1982 Census of Manufactures. Preliminary Report. Industry Series, 2491-1.207

Rubber and Plastics Hose and Belting, 1983, Current Industrial Report, 2506-8.12

Rubber Footwear, TSUS Items 700(pt.): Summary of Trade and Tariff Information, 9885-7.59

Rubber: Production, Shipments, and Stocks, 1983, Current Industrial Report, 2506-8.7

Rum: Initial Report (Covering Jan.-June of 1983 and 1984) on Selected Economic Indicators, 9884-15

Rural Development Perspectives, 1502-7

Rural Electric Borrowers, 1983 Statistical Report, 1244-1

Rural Electrification Program: Fiscal Year Statistical Summary, 1244-7

Rural Fire Prevention and Control Program Financing: Federal, State, and Private Lands, 1204-10

Rural Primary Health Care Service in Israel: Some Measures of Utilization and Satisfaction, 4102-1.456

Rural Telephone Borrowers, 1983 Statistical Report, 1244-2

Rural Telephone Program: Fiscal Year Statistical Summary, 1244-8

Rye: ASCS Commodity Fact Sheet, 1984, 1806-4.5

S&L Use of New Powers: A Comparative Study of State- and Federal-Chartered Associations, 9371-1.426

S&L Use of New Powers: Consumer and Commercial Loan Expansion, 9371-1.432

Safety Related Recall Campaigns for Motor Vehicles And Motor Vehicle Equipment, Including Tires, 7762-2

Safety Standards for Mobile Homes Make a Difference, 1502-7.402

Safety Standards on Small Passenger Aircraft, with Nine or Fewer Seats, Are Significantly Less Stringent than on Larger Aircraft, 26113-116

Safety Study: Airport Certification and Operations, 9618-12

Safety Study. Deterrence of Drunk Driving: The Role of Sobriety Checkpoints and Administrative License Revocations, 9618-10

Safety Study: Statistical Review of Alcohol-Involved Aviation Accidents, 9618-11

Saint Lawrence Seaway Development Corporation, 1983 Annual Report, 7744-1

Sales Programs of Nine Regional Supply Cooperatives, 1128-24

Salt: Minerals Yearbook Preprint, Vol. 1, 1983, 5604-15.56

Salt, 1983: Mineral Industry Surveys Annual Advance Summary, 5614-5.10

San Juan River Regional Coal Environmental Impact Statement, Final, 5726-4.7

Sand and Gravel (Industry 1442 and 1446): 1982 Census of Mineral Industries. Preliminary Report. Industry Series, 2511-1.9

Sand and Gravel: Minerals Yearbook Preprint, Vol. 1, 1983, 5604-15.57

Sanitary Paper Products (Industry 2647): 1982 Census of Manufactures. Preliminary Report. Industry Series, 2491-1.150

SAR Statistics, 1983, U.S. Coast Guard, 7404-2

Satellite Indicators of Rapid Cyclogenesis, 2152-8.401

Satellite Situation Report, 9502-2

Savings and Home Financing Source Book, 1983, 9314-3

Savings and Loan Association Activity, 9312-4

Savings and Loan Summary Statistics, Federal Home Loan Bank of San Francisco, 9302-19

Savings Balances and Accounts, Federal Home Loan Bank of San Francisco, 9302-20

Sawmills and Planing Mills, General (Industry 2421): 1982 Census of Manufactures. Preliminary Report. Industry Series, 2491-1.112

SBIC Digest: The Equity Financing Arm of the U.S. Small Business Administration, 9762-3

Scales and Balances, Except Laboratory (Industry 3576): 1982 Census of Manufactures. Preliminary Report. Industry Series, 2491-1.347

Scaling Household Nutrient Data, 1502-3.401

Scheduled Passenger Traffic (RPM'S) Among the Majors (System Operations) Since Deregulation, 9142-49

Schiffli Machine Embroideries (Industry 2397): 1982 Census of Manufactures. Preliminary Report. Industry Series, 2491-1.109

School Breakfast Program, FY77-80, 1364-13.1

School Breakfast Program, FY81, 1364-13.1

School Enrollment—Social and Economic Characteristics of Students: Oct. 1982 (Advance Report). Current Population Reports. Series P-20. Population Characteristics, 2546-1.391

School Enrollment—Social and Economic Characteristics of Students: Oct. 1983 (Advance Report). Current Population Reports. Series P-20. Population Characteristics, 2546-1.392

Schools and Hospitals Grant Awards Listing (Cycle 5), Data Compiled Through Dec. 1983, 3304-15

Science and Engineering Doctorates: 1960-82, 9626-6.16

Science and Engineering Employment in Academia Grew 3% in 1983, 9626-2.140

Science and Engineering Jobs Grew Twice as Fast as Overall U.S. Employment with Industry Taking the Lead, 9626-2.142

Science and Mathematics Education in American High Schools: Results from the High School and Beyond Study, 4826-2.14

Science Base Underlying Research on Acquired Immune Deficiency Syndrome, 4102-1.404

Science Indicators, 1982, 9624-10

Science Resources Studies Highlights, 9626-2

Scientific Exchange Activities with the Soviet Union, FY81 and FY82, Department of State Authorization Act, Sec. 126.(a) and (b), Report to Congress, 7008-41

Scientific Validity of Polygraph Testing, A Research Review and Evaluation, 26358-96

Scientists' Acid Deposition Survey, 25328-25

Scientists, Engineers, and Technicians in Manufacturing and Nonmanufacturing Industries: 1980-81, Detailed Statistical Tables, 9627-23

Scientists, Engineers and Technicians in Private Industry: Detailed Statistical Tables, 9627-23

Scientists, Engineers, and Technicians in Trade and Regulated Industries: 1982, 9628-72

Scissors and Shears from Brazil: Determination of the Commission in Investigation No. 104-TAA-19 Under Section 104(b) of the Trade Agreements Act of 1979, Together with the Information Obtained in the Investigation, 9886-18.12

Scrap and Waste Materials (Industry 5093): 1982 Census of Wholesale Trade. Preliminary Report. Industry Series, 2403-1.18

Screw Machine Products (Industry 3451): 1982 Census of Manufactures. Preliminary Report. Industry Series, 2491-1.292

Seasonal Abundance and Habitat-Use Patterns of Coastal Bird Populations On Padre and Mustang Island Barrier Beaches, 5508-86

Seasonally Adjusted Traffic and Capacity: Majors, Scheduled Service; System, Domestic and International Operations, 9142-19

Seattle-Denver Income Maintenance Experiment, Final Report, 4008-64

SEC Government-Business Forum on Small Business Capital Formation, 1983, Final Report, 9734-4

SEC Monthly Statistical Review, 9732-1

Second Annual Report of Accomplishments Under the Airport Improvement Program, FY83, 7504-38

Secondary Market Activities of the Student Loan Marketing Association, 26121-71

Secondary Market Prices and Yields, 5142-20

Secondary Mortgage Markets: Recent Trends and Research Results, 9312-1.408

Secondary Nonferrous Metals (Industry 3341): 1982 Census of Manufactures. Preliminary Report. Industry Series, 2491-1.267

Secretary of Energy Annual Report to Congress, 3024-2

Securities and Exchange Commission 48th Annual Report For the Fiscal Year Ended Sept. 30, 1982, 9734-2

Securities and Exchange Commission 49th Annual Report For the Fiscal Year Ended Sept. 30, 1983, 9734-2

Security Assistance Programs, FY85, 7144-13

Seeds, Field and Vegetable: Foreign Agriculture Circular, 1925-13

SEER Program: Cancer Incidence and Mortality in the U.S., 1973-81, 4478-130

Seismic Engineering Program Report, 5662-2

Seismic Engineering Program Report, 5664-14

Selected Acquisition Reports, 3502-1

Selected Aspects of Construction Cost Management, 3006-5.7

Selected Aspects of Howard University's Operations And Use of Federally Appropriated Funds, 26121-74

Selected Atomic Energy Products, 1983, Current Industrial Report, 2506-12.27

Selected Balance Sheet Data, Fourth Federal Home Loan Bank District, Federal Home Loan Bank of Atlanta, 9302-1

Selected Borrowings in Immediately Available Funds of Large Member Banks, 9365-1

Selected Characteristics of Foreign-Owned U.S. Firms: 1982, 2324-6

Titles

Selected Characteristics of Persons in Computer Specialties: 1978, 2546–2.124

Selected Characteristics of Persons in Engineering: 1978, 2546–2.121

Selected Electronic and Associated Products, Including Telephone and Telegraph Apparatus, 1983, Current Industrial Report, 2506–12.21

Selected Heating Equipment, 1982, Current Industrial Report, 2506–11.6

Selected Heating Equipment, 1983, Current Industrial Report, 2506–11.6

Selected Highway Statistics and Charts, 1982, 7554–24

Selected Industrial Air Pollution Control Equipment, 1983, Current Industrial Report, 2506–12.5

Selected Instruments and Related Products, 1982, Current Industrial Report, 2506–12.26

Selected Interest and Exchange Rates: Weekly Series of Charts; and Foreign Exchange Rates, 9365–1.5

Selected Interest Rates, 9365–2.14

Selected Manpower Statistics, FY83, 3544–1

Selected Occupational Fatalities Related to Oil/Gas Well Drilling and Servicing as Found in Report of OSHA Fatality/Catastrophe Investigations, 6606–2.11

Selected Office Supplies and Accessories, 1983, Current Industrial Report, 2506–7.13

Selected Publications of the U.S. International Trade Commission, Through Dec. 1983, 9884–12

Selected Raw Material Requirements for Japan's Specialty Steel Industry, 5608–144

Selected Socioeconomic Development Indicators: Africa, Asia, Europe, Latin America, the Middle East, and North America/Oceania, 1528–179

Selected Statistics Concerning Near Midair and Midair Collisions, 7508–61

Selected Statistics of Class II Motor Carriers of Property, Year Ended Dec. 31, 1981, 9484–10

Selected Statistics of Class II Motor Carriers of Property, Year Ended Dec. 31, 1982, 9484–10

Selected Worldwide Marine Weather Broadcasts, 2184–3

Selective Service, Semiannual Report of the Director, Oct. 1, 1983-Mar. 31, 1984, 9742–1

Selective Service, Semiannual Report of the Director to the Congress, Apr. 1-Sept. 30, 1984, 9742–1

Selenium: Mineral Industry Surveys, 5612–2.15

Self-Employed Workers: An Update to 1983, 6722–1.443

Semi-Annual Report of the Inspector General, U.S. Small Business Administration, 9762–5

Semi-Annual Report on Strategic Special Nuclear Material Inventory Differences, 3002–4

Semiannual Report of the Architect of the Capitol, For the Period Oct. 1, 1983-Mar. 31, 1984, 25922–2

Semiannual Report of the Director of Selective Service, Oct. 1, 1983-Mar. 31, 1984., 9742–1

Semiannual Report of the Director of Selective Service to the Congress, Apr. 1-Sept. 30, 1984, 9742–1

Sixth Report to Congress on

Semiannual Report of the Inspector General, 6302–2

Semiannual Report of the Inspector General, Oct. 1, 1983-Mar. 31, 1984, 9922–13

Semiannual Report of the Inspector General, Apr. 1- Sept. 30, 1984, 9922–13

Semiannual Report, Office of Inspector General, Oct. 1, 1983-Mar. 31, 1984, 1002–4

Semiannual Report, Office of Inspector General, Apr. 1- Sept. 30, 1984, 1002–4

Semiannual Report on Operations of the Office of Inspector General, Oct. 1, 1983-Mar. 31, 1984, 5302–2

Semiannual Report to Congress on the Effectiveness of the Civil Aviation Security Program, July 1-Dec. 31, 1983, 7502–5

Semiannual Report to Congress on the Effectiveness of the Civil Aviation Security Program, Jan. 1-June 30, 1984, 7502–5

Semiannual Report, 1st Half FY84, Office of Inspector General, 3002–12

Semiannual Report, 2nd Half FY84, Office of Inspector General, 3002–12

Semiconductors and Related Devices (Industry 3674): 1982 Census of Manufactures. Preliminary Report. Industry Series, 2491–1.382

Semiconductors, TSUS Items 687(pt.): Summary of Trade and Tariff Information, 9885–6.67

Sentencing Practices in 13 States, 6066–19.10

Series EE and HH Savings Bonds, Statistical Summary, 8442–1

Serious Juvenile Crime: A Redirected Federal Effort, 6068–179

Service Annual Survey, Current Business Reports, 2413–8

Service Establishment Equipment and Supplies (Industry 5087): 1982 Census of Wholesale Trade. Preliminary Report. Industry Series, 2403–1.17

Service Industry Machinery, N.E.C. (Industry 3589): 1982 Census of Manufactures. Preliminary Report. Industry Series, 2491–1.353

Servicemen's and Veterans Group Life Insurance Programs, Eighteenth Annual Report, Year Ending June 30, 1983, 9924–3

Services to Dwellings and Other Buildings (Industry 734): 1982 Census of Service Industries. Preliminary Report. Industry Series, 2390–2.6

Set-Up Paperboard Boxes (Industry 2652): 1982 Census of Manufactures. Preliminary Report. Industry Series, 2491–1.154

Seventh Annual Report of the National Council on Educational Research, FY81 and FY82, 4914–4

Seventh District Letter, Federal Home Loan Bank of Chicago, 9302–5

Severe Need Breakfast Program, FY77-80, 1364–13.2

Severe Need Breakfast Program, FY81, 1364–13.2

Severity of Crime, 6062–2.402

Sewing for Profit Utilizes Home Economics Skills, 1004–16.1

Sewing Machines (Industry 3636): 1982 Census of Manufactures. Preliminary Report. Industry Series, 2491–1.368

Sewing Machines, TSUS Items 672(pt.): Summary of Trade and Tariff Information, 9885–6.66

Sex-Specific Equivalent Retirement Ages: 1940-2050, 4742–1.406

Sexually Transmitted Disease Fact Sheet, 4204–5

Sexually Transmitted Disease (STD) Statistical Letter, 1982, No. 132, 4204–14

Shaping and Assembling Webbing, 2162–1.402

Shared ATM Networks: Market Structure and Public Policy, 9373–1.403

Sharing Medical Resources, FY83, Annual Report by the Administrator of Veterans Affairs, 9924–18

Sheep and Goats, 1623–4

Sheet Metal Work (Industry 3444): 1982 Census of Manufactures. Preliminary Report. Industry Series, 2491–1.288

Sheets, Pillowcases, and Towels, Current Industrial Report, 2506–6.6

Ship Building and Repairing (Industry 3731): 1982 Census of Manufactures. Preliminary Report. Industry Series, 2491–1.404

Shipments of Selected Plastics Products, 1982, Current Industrial Report, 2506–8.9

Shipments of Selected Plastics Products, 1983, Current Industrial Report, 2506–8.9

Shipments to Federal Government Agencies, 1982, Current Industrial Report, 2506–3.4

Shoe Stores (Industry 5661): 1982 Census of Retail Trade. Preliminary Report. Industry Series, 2395–1.18

Short-Term Energy Outlook, 3162–34

Shortening and Cooking Oils (Industry 2079): 1982 Census of Manufactures. Preliminary Report. Industry Series, 2491–1.31

Shutdowns and Job Loss in California: The Need for New National Priorities, 21348–84.1

Significant Features of Fiscal Federalism, 1982-83 Edition, 10044–1

Significant Provisions of State Unemployment Insurance Laws, Jan. 1, 1984, 6402–7

Significant Provisions of State Unemployment Insurance Laws, July 1, 1984, 6402–7

Signs and Advertising Displays (Industry 3993): 1982 Census of Manufactures. Preliminary Report. Industry Series, 2491–1.440

Silicon: Mineral Industry Surveys, 5612–1.34

Silicon: Minerals Yearbook Preprint, Vol. 1, 1983, 5604–15.58

Silver and Gold: Mineral Industry Surveys, 5612–1.10

Silver: Minerals Yearbook Preprint, Vol. 1, 1983, 5604–15.59

Silverware and Plated Ware (Industry 3914): 1982 Census of Manufactures. Preliminary Report. Industry Series, 2491–1.425

Singapore's Fresh Vegetable Market, 1925–34.422

Single Family Insurance Activities, 5142–6

Sixteenth Semiannual Report by the President To the Commission on Security and Cooperation in Europe on the Implementation of the Helsinki Final Act, Dec. 1, 1983-Mar. 31, 1984, 7002–1

Sixth Analysis and Evaluation of Federal Juvenile Delinquency Programs, 6064–11

Sixth Annual Report to Congress on the Implementation of Public Law 94-142: The Education for All Handicapped Children Act, 4944–4

Sixth Report to Congress on the National Manufactured Housing Construction and Safety Standards Program, 5004–4

Size Characteristics and Titles

Size Characteristics and Spending Patterns for Corn Belt Grain Farms in 1982, from the Farm Production Expenditure Survey, 1544–19.404

Size Standards, 21728–53

Sizing Up the Deficit: An Efficient Tax Perspective, 9387–1.402

Skyrocketing Health Care Costs, Causes and Solutions: Phoenix, Ariz., 21148–29

Slag-Iron and Steel: Minerals Yearbook Preprint, Vol. 1, 1983, 5604–15.35

Small Arms (Industry 3484): 1982 Census of Manufactures. Preliminary Report. Industry Series, 2491–1.303

Small Arms Ammunition (Industry 3482): 1982 Census of Manufactures. Preliminary Report. Industry Series, 2491–1.301

Small Arms and Parts, TSUS Items 730(pt.): Summary of Trade and Tariff Information, 9885–7.53

Small Business Administration's Small Business Development Center Program, 25728–36

Small Business Paperwork: Problems and Progress, 9768–14

Small Business Speaks: The Chemical Bank Report, 21728–52.3

Small Empirical Models of Exchange Market Intervention: A Review of the Literature, 9366–1.133

Small Grains, 1984 Annual Summary and 1985 Crop Winter Wheat and Rye Seedings, 1621–24

Small Issue Industrial Revenue Bond Financing in the Seventh Federal Reserve District, 9375–13.2

Small-Scale Hydroelectric Power: A Brief Assessment, 3258–1

Smithsonian Year, 1983, Annual Report of the Smithsonian Institution for the Year Ended Sept. 30, 1983, 9774–3

Smoking and Drinking Behavior Before and During Pregnancy of Married Mothers of Live-Born Infants and Stillborn Infants, 4102–1.418

Smoking and Health Bulletin, 4042–1

SMSA Groupings with Populations of Less than One Million in 1970. 1980 Census of Housing, Vol. 4. Characteristics of Housing Units. Components of Inventory Change, Part II, 2473–3.2

Snow Cover Surveys, 1982-83 Eastern Snow Conference, 2184–2

Snow Surveys and Water Supply Outlook for Alaska, 1266–2.1

Soap and Other Detergents (Industry 2841): 1982 Census of Manufactures. Preliminary Report. Industry Series, 2491–1.185

Social and Clinical Correlates of Postpartum Sterilization in the U.S., 1972 and 1980, 4102–1.419

Social and Economic Incentives for Family Caregivers, 4652–1.403

Social Desirability of Preventive Health Behavior, 4102–1.438

Social Dimensions of Rangeland Management, 1208–197

Social Security Administration, 1984 Annual Report to the Congress, 4704–6

Social Security Area Population Projections, 1984, 4706–1.92

Social Security Beneficiaries by State and County, Dec. 1982, 4748–38

Social Security Beneficiaries Enrolled in the Direct Deposit Program, Dec. 1983, 4742–1.412

Social Security Beneficiaries in Metropolitan Areas, 4744–10

Social Security Bulletin, 4742–1

Social Security Bulletin, Annual Statistical Supplement, 1983, 4744–3

Social Security Could Improve Its Management and Detection of Postentitlement Changes by Using Postadjudicative Appraisal Data, 26121–68

Social Security Problems in Western European Countries, 4742–1.405

Social Security Program of Self-Employed Farm Operator Families, 1702–1.408

Social Security Programs Throughout the World, 1983, 4746–4.58

Social Welfare Expenditures, 1981 and 1982, 4742–1.425

Society's Coming New Age, 1004–16.1

Soda Ash and Natural Sodium Sulfate: Mineral Industry Surveys, 5612–1.33

Sodium Compounds: Minerals Yearbook Preprint, Vol. 1, 1983, 5604–15.60

Sodium Compounds, 1983: Mineral Industry Surveys Annual Advance Summary, 5614–5.4

Softwood Plywood, 1983, Current Industrial Report, 2506–7.2

Softwood Veneer and Plywood (Industry 2436): 1982 Census of Manufactures. Preliminary Report. Industry Series, 2491–1.118

Solar Collector Manufacturing Activity, 1983, 3164–62

Sole Proprietorship Returns, 1981: Statistics of Income, 8304–7.1

Sole Proprietorship Returns, 1982, 8302–2.413

Some Aspects of the Work Environment and Subsequent Disability Among Working-Age Men, 4746–5.43

Some Chemical Effects of the Mount St. Helens Eruption on Selected Streams in the State of Washington, 5666–14.9

Some Implications of Financial Innovations in the U.S., 9366–1.137

Sources of Economic Security, 25408–87

Sources of Revenue for Public School Support, 4838–12

Sources of Secular Increases in the Unemployment Rate, 1969-82, 6722–1.444

South Asia: Outlook and Situation Report, 1524–4.11

South Carolina: A Strong Recovery, but Problems Remain, 9371–1.411

South Carolina's Industrial Timber Products Output, 1977-81, 1208–203

Southeast Asia: Outlook and Situation Report, 1524–4.5

Southeast Regional Reports, 6946–1

Southeastern Economy in 1983, 6944–2

Southeastern Power Administration, Annual Report, 1983, 3234–1

Southeast's Occupational Employment Outlook, 9371–1.430

Southern Appalachian Coal Region, Draft Environmental Impact Statement II, 5726–4.8

Southern Appalachian Coal Region, Final Environmental Impact Statement II, 5726–4.8

Southern Hemisphere Citrus Situation, 1925–34.420

Southern Hemisphere Raisin and Dried Prune Situation, 1925–34.416

Southwest Employment and Earnings, 6962–2

Southwest Regional Reports, 6966–1

Southwestern Power Administration, 1983 Annual Report, 3244–1

Soviet Military Power, 1984, 3508–14

Soviet Propaganda Campaign Against NATO, 9828–25

Soybean Oil Mills (Industry 2075): 1982 Census of Manufactures. Preliminary Report. Industry Series, 2491–1.28

Soybean Outlook Discussion, 1004–16.1

Soybean Stocks, 1621–5

Soybeans: ASCS Commodity Fact Sheet, 1984, 1806–4.4

Space Propulsion Units and Parts (Industry 3764): 1982 Census of Manufactures. Preliminary Report. Industry Series, 2491–1.402

Space Shuttle Mission 41-C, 9506–2.117

Space Shuttle Mission 41-D, 9506–2.118

Space Shuttle Mission 41-D, 9506–2.119

Space Shuttle Mission 41-G, 9506–2.120

Space Shuttle Mission 51-A, 9506–2.121

Space Vehicle Equipment, N.E.C. (Industry 3769): 1982 Census of Manufactures. Preliminary Report. Industry Series, 2491–1.403

Special Analyses, Budget of the U.S. Government, FY85, 104–1

Special Demographic Analyses, 2326–11

Special Dies, Tools, Jigs, and Fixtures (Industry 3544): 1982 Census of Manufactures. Preliminary Report. Industry Series, 2491–1.325

Special Industry Machinery, N.E.C. (Industry 3559): 1982 Census of Manufactures. Preliminary Report. Industry Series, 2491–1.335

Special Labor Force Reports, 6746–1

Special Milk Program, FY76-80, 1364–13.3

Special Milk Program, FY81, 1364–13.3

Special Product Sawmills, N.E.C. (Industry 2429): 1982 Census of Manufactures. Preliminary Report. Industry Series, 2491–1.114

Special Rehabilitation and Research Needs of Disabled Hispanic Persons, 16598–5

Special Report on the Statistical Programs and Activities of the U.S. Government, FY85. Federal Statistics, 104–10

Special Studies, Current Population Reports. Series P-23, 2546–2

Special Studies Papers, 9366–6

Special Supplemental Food Program for Women, Infants and Children (WIC), 1364–12

Special Trade Contractors, N.E.C. (Industry 1799): 1982 Census of Construction Industries. Preliminary Report. Industry Series, 2371–1.26

Species Profiles: Life Histories and Environmental Requirements of Coastal Fishes and Invertebrates, 5506–8

Species Profiles: Life Histories and Environmental Requirements of Coastal Fishes and Invertebrates (Gulf of Mexico), Atlantic Croaker, 5506–8.16

Species Profiles: Life Histories and Environmental Requirements of Coastal Fishes and Invertebrates (Gulf of Mexico), Bay Anchovy and Striped Anchovy, 5506–8.17

Species Profiles: Life Histories and Environmental Requirements of Coastal Fishes and Invertebrates (Gulf of Mexico), Brown Shrimp, 5506–8.18

Titles

Species Profiles: Life Histories and Environmental Requirements of Coastal Fishes and Invertebrates (Gulf of Mexico), Gulf Menhaden, 5506–8.19

Species Profiles: Life Histories and Environmental Requirements of Coastal Fishes and Invertebrates (Gulf of Mexico), Sea Catfish and Gafftopsail Catfish, 5506–8.20

Species Profiles: Life Histories and Environmental Requirements of Coastal Fishes and Invertebrates (Gulf of Mexico), Spotted Seatrout, 5506–8.21

Species Profiles: Life Histories and Environmental Requirements of Coastal Fishes and Invertebrates (Mid-Atlantic), Alewife/Blueback Herring, 5506–8.10

Species Profiles: Life Histories and Environmental Requirements of Coastal Fishes and Invertebrates (Mid-Atlantic), Atlantic Silverside, 5506–8.11

Species Profiles: Life Histories and Environmental Requirements of Coastal Fishes and Invertebrates (Mid-Atlantic), Bay Scallop, 5506–8.12

Species Profiles: Life Histories and Environmental Requirements of Coastal Fishes and Invertebrates (Mid-Atlantic), Striped Bass, 5506–8.13

Species Profiles: Life Histories and Environmental Requirements of Coastal Fishes and Invertebrates (Mid-Atlantic), Surf Clam, 5506–8.14

Species Profiles: Life Histories and Environmental Requirements of Coastal Fishes and Invertebrates (North Atlantic), Hard Clam, 5506–8.23

Species Profiles: Life Histories and Environmental Requirements of Coastal Fishes and Invertebrates (North Atlantic), White Perch, 5506–8.9

Species Profiles: Life Histories and Environmental Requirements of Coastal Fishes and Invertebrates (Pacific Northwest), Chinook Salmon, 5506–8.22

Species Profiles: Life Histories and Environmental Requirements of Coastal Fishes and Invertebrates (South Atlantic), Atlantic Menhaden, 5506–8.15

Species Profiles: Life Histories and Environmental Requirements of Coastal Fishes and Invertebrates (South Atlantic), Blue Crab, 5506–8.24

Species Profiles: Life Histories and Environmental Requirements of Coastal Fishes and Invertebrates (South Atlantic), Summer Flounder, 5506–8.25

Species Profiles: Life Histories and Environmental Requirements of Coastal Fishes and Invertebrates (South Florida), Pink Shrimp, 5506–8.26

Species Profiles: Life Histories and Environmental Requirements of Coastal Fishes and Invertebrates (South Florida), Snook, 5506–8.27

Species Profiles: Life Histories and Environmental Requirements of Coastal Fishes and Invertebrates (South Florida), Stone Crab, 5506–8.28

Speech Pathology: Communicative Disorders Among Patients in VA Hospitals. Part 1: The Prevalence of Communicative Disorders, 9926–4.8

Speech Pathology: Communicative Disorders Among Patients in VA Medical Facilities. Part 2: Treatment, Type, and Severity of Communicative Disorders, 9926–4.9

Spent Fuel and Radioactive Waste Inventories, Projections, and Characteristics, 3354–5

Spent Fuel and Radioactive Waste Inventories, Projections, and Characteristics, 3364–2

Spent Fuel Storage Requirements, 3354–2

Sporting Goods and Recreational Equipment: Country Market Survey, 2045–14

Sporting Goods Stores and Bicycle Shops (Industry 5941): 1982 Census of Retail Trade. Preliminary Report. Industry Series, 2395–1.28

Sporting Goods, TSUS Items 731(pt.), 734(pt.), and 735(pt.): Summary of Trade and Tariff Information, 9885–7.56

Spun Yarn Production, 1983, Current Industrial Report, 2506–5.5

St. Lawrence Seaway: Traffic Report for the 1982 Navigation Season, 7744–2

St. Louis Economic Report, 1983, 6974–3

Staff Economic Studies, Board of Governors of the Federal Reserve System, 9366–1

Staff Memoranda, Federal Reserve Bank of Chicago, 9375–11

Staff Papers, SSA, 4746–5

Staff Report on the Securities Industry, 9734–3

Staff Studies, Board of Governors of the Federal Reserve System, 9366–1

Staff Working Papers, 26306–3

Staffing Patterns Prominent in Female-Male Earnings Gap, 6722–1.438

Staggers Rail Act of 1980, 25268–80

Stainless Steel Sheet and Strip from Spain: Determination of the Commission in Investigation No. 731-TA-164 (Final) Under the Tariff Act of 1930, Together with the Information Obtained in the Investigation, 9886–14.125

Stainless Steel Sheet and Strip from Spain: Determination of the Commission in Investigation No. 731-TA-164 (Preliminary) Under the Tariff Act of 1930, Together with the Information Obtained in the Investigation, 9886–14.97

Stainless Steel Table Flatware: Report to the President on Investigation No. TA-201-49 Under Section 201 of the Trade Act of 1974, 9886–5.48

Stainless Steel Wire Cloth from Japan: Determination of the Commission in Investigation No. 731-TA-190 (Preliminary) Under the Tariff Act of 1930, Together with the Information Obtained in the Investigation, 9886–14.109

State and County Mental Hospitals, U.S., 1980-81 and 1981-82, 4506–3.13

State and Federal Motor-Fuel Tax Rates By Years, 1975-83, 7554–32

State and Local Government Collective Bargaining Settlements, 1983, 6782–6

State and Local Government Collective Bargaining Settlements, First 6 Months 1984, 6782–6

State and Local Government Employment and Payrolls, 6742–4

State and Local Government Fiscal Position: An Alternative Measure, 2702–1.409

State and Local Government Fiscal Position in 1983, 2702–1.405

State and Local Governments: An Assessment of Their Financial Position and Fiscal Policies, 9385–1.401

State and Metropolitan Area Employment and Unemployment, 6742–12

State Workers' Compensation

State and National Standardized Lactation Averages by Breed for Cows on Official Test, Calving in 1982, 1702–2.403

State and Private Forestry Funding Trends, FY83, 1204–32

State and Regional Employment and Unemployment in 1983, 6722–1.454

State Ceiling Safe Harbor Limitations, 1984, 8304–16

State-Chartered Credit Unions, Annual Report, 9534–2

State Community Development Block Grant Program: The First Year's Experience, 5188–106

State Energy Conservation Program, 1983, Annual Report to the President and the Congress, 3304–1

State Energy Data Report, Consumption Estimates, 1960-82, 3164–39

State Energy Data Report Supplement, Consumption Estimates, 1960-82, 3164–55

State Energy Overview 1982, 3164–60

State Energy Price and Expenditure Report, 1970-81, 3164–64

State Experiences with Taxes on Generators or Disposers of Hazardous Waste, 26113–124

State Export Series, 2046–3

State Government Finances in 1983, 2466–2.5

State Government Tax Collections in 1983, 2466–2.3

State Labor Legislation Enacted in 1983, 6722–1.406

State Legislation on Smoking and Health, 1982, 4204–13

State of Affirmative Action in the Federal Government: Staff Report Analyzing 1980 and 1983 Employment Profiles, 21348–41

State of Civil Rights, 1957-83: The Final Report of the U.S. Commission on Civil Rights, 11044–3

State of Small Business: A Report of the President, Transmitted to the Congress Together with the Annual Report on Small Business and Competition of the U.S. Small Business Administration, 9764–6

State of the Art in Long-Term Care Insurance, 4658–7

State Payments to Local Governments. 1982 Census of Governments, Vol. 6. Topical Studies, No. 3, 2460–3

State Personal Income: Estimates for 1929-82 and a Statement of Sources and Methods, 2708–40

State Personal Income, 1977-83: Revised Estimates, 2702–1.432

State Programs and Services in Food and Drug Control, 4064–11

State Surveillance of Radioactive Material Transportation, Final Report, 9636–1.23

State Taxation of Energy Production: Regional and National Issues, 9375–1.407

State Trends, A Supplement to FHA Trends, Section 203 Home Mortgages Insured by FHA, 5142–3

State Trends, A Supplement to FHA Trends, Section 245 Home Mortgages Insured by FHA, 5142–41

State Vocational Rehabilitation Agency, Program Data, FY82, 4944–9

State Workers' Compensation Laws, 6502–1

Statement by Anthony M. Solomon, President, Federal Reserve Bank of New York, Before the Subcommittee on International Trade,

Statement by Anthony M.

Investment and Monetary Policy, Committee on Banking, Finance and Urban Affairs, U.S. House of Representatives, 9368–77

Statement by Beryl W. Sprinkel, Under Secretary of the Treasury for Monetary Affairs, Before the Senate Committee on Banking, Housing, and Urban Affairs, Washington, D.C., 8008–108

Statement by Paul A. Volcker, Chairman, Board of Governors of the Federal Reserve System, Before the Committee on Banking, Housing and Urban Affairs, U.S. Senate, 9368–75

Statement by Preston Martin, Vice Chairman, Board of Governors of the Federal Reserve System, Before the Subcommittee on Financial Institutions Supervision, Regulation and Insurance of the Committee on Banking, Finance and Urban Affairs, U.S. House of Representatives, 9368–76

Statement of Carol E. Dinkins, Deputy Attorney General, Before the Subcommittee on the Constitution, Committee on the Judiciary, U.S. Senate, Concerning S. 2802, the Legal Fees Equity Act, 6008–19

Statement of Charles E. McLure, Jr., Deputy Assistant Secretary for Tax Analysis, Before the Subcommittee on Oversight, Committee on Ways and Means, U.S. House of Representatives, 8008–109

Statement of Foreign Currencies Purchased with Dollars, FY83, 8102–5

Statement of Foreign Currencies Purchased with Dollars, Oct. 1, 1983-Mar. 31, 1984, 8102–5

Statement of Liabilities and Other Financial Commitments of the U.S. Government, As of Sept. 30, 1983, 8104–3

Statement of Receipts and Expenditures, Federal Old Age and Survivors, Disability Insurance and Hospital Insurance Trust Funds, 8102–9.2

Statement of Receipts and Expenditures, Federal Supplementary Medical Insurance Trust Fund, 8102–9.3

States Fund an Expanded Range of Activities Under Low-Income Home Energy Assistance Block Grant, 26121–75

States Have Made Few Changes in Implementing the Alcohol, Drug Abuse, and Mental Health Service Block Grant, 26121–87

States Use Added Flexibility Offered by the Preventive Health and Health Services Block Grant, 26121–88

States Use Several Strategies To Cope with Funding Reductions Under Social Services Block Grant, 26121–76

Stationery Products (Industry 2648): 1982 Census of Manufactures. Preliminary Report. Industry Series, 2491–1.151

Stationery Supplies (Industry 5112): 1982 Census of Wholesale Trade. Preliminary Report. Industry Series, 2403–1.20

Statistical Abstract of the U.S.: 1984, 2324–1

Statistical Analysis of the Operations and Activities of Private Foundations, 26119–53

Statistical Analysis of the World's Merchant Fleets: Showing Age, Size, Speed, and Draft by Frequency Grouping as of Jan. 1, 1983, 7704–1

Statistical Briefs, 9926–4

Titles

Statistical Compilation of Engineering Features on Bureau of Reclamation Projects Sept. 30, 1983, 5824–7

Statistical Data of the Uranium Industry, 3404–7

Statistical Highlight, 4822–1

Statistical Notes, NIMH Survey and Reports Branch, 4506–3

Statistical Policy Working Papers, 106–4

Statistical Portrait of Hired Farmworkers, 6722–1.440

Statistical Profile of Handicapped Federal Civilian Employees, 9844–23

Statistical Profile of Older Floridians, For State and Area Agency Planners, 4478–150

Statistical Release: Beer, 8486–1.1

Statistical Release: Cigarettes and Cigars, 8486–1.4

Statistical Release: Distilled Spirits, 8486–1.3

Statistical Release: Wines, 8486–1.2

Statistical Releases: Bureau of Alcohol, Tobacco and Firearms, 8486–1

Statistical Review of Alcohol-Involved Aviation Accidents, Safety Study, 9618–11

Statistical Summary: Federal Meat and Poultry Inspection for FY83, 1374–3

Statistical Summary for Fish and Wildlife Restoration, FY84, 5504–13

Statistical Summary: Minerals Yearbook Preprint, Vol. 1, 1983, 5604–15.2

Statistical Summary of VA Activities, 9922–2

Statistical Supplement, 1982 Annual Report, U.S. Railroad Retirement Board, 9704–2

Statistical Uses of Administrative Records: Recent Research and Present Prospects, 8308–28

Statistical Yearbook of the Immigration and Naturalization Service, 1981, 6264–2.1

Statistics: Distributors of TVA Power, FY79-83, 9804–19

Statistics for U.S. Exports and Imports: Dairy, Livestock, and Poultry, 1925–32.2

Statistics of Communications Common Carriers, 1982, 9284–6

Statistics of Income, Corporation Income Tax Returns, 1981, 8304–4

Statistics of Income, Individual Income Tax Returns, 1982, 8304–2

Statistics of Income, Sole Proprietorship and Partnership Returns, 8304–7

Statistics of Income and Related Administrative Record Research: 1984, 8304–17

Statistics of Income Bulletin, 8302–2

Statistics of Income for Individuals: A Historical Perspective, 8308–28.1

Statistics of Interstate Natural Gas Pipeline Companies, 1982, 3164–38

Statistics of Interstate Natural Gas Pipeline Companies, 1983, 3164–38

Statistics of Navy Medicine, 3802–1

Statistics of Privately Owned Electric Utilities, Annual (Classes A and B Companies), 3164–23

Statistics of Public School Systems in the Twenty Largest U.S. Cities, 4834–11

Statistics of Publicly Owned Electric Utilities, Annual, 3164–24

Statistics on Hospital Personnel, From the American Hospital Association's 1980 Annual Survey of Hospitals, 4114–12

Statistics on Immigrant and Nonimmigrant Visa Issuances, 7184–1

Statistics on Oilseeds and Related Data, 1564–12

Status of Account: Harry S. Truman Memorial Scholarship Fund, 14312–1

Status of Active Foreign Credits of the U.S. Government: Foreign Credits by U.S. Government Agencies, 8002–6

Status of Airport and Airway Trust Fund, 8102–9.5

Status of American Woodcock, 1984, 5504–11

Status of Bilingual Vocational Training, FY82: A Joint Report from the Secretary of Labor and the Secretary of Education to the President and to the Congress, 4804–26

Status of Black Lung Disability Trust Fund, 8102–9.10

Status of Civilian Federal Agencies' Efforts To Address Hazardous Waste Problems on Their Lands, 26113–139

Status of Coal Supply Contracts for New Electric Generating Units, 3084–4

Status of Coal Supply Contracts for New Electric Generating Units, 1983-92, 3088–18

Status of Conservation Districts, 1264–1

Status of Defense Materials Inventories As of Dec. 31, 1983, 9452–7

Status of Defense Materials Inventories, As of June 30, 1984, 9452–7

Status of Foreign Currency Funds Administered by the Agency for International Development, 9912–1

Status of Handicapped Children in Head Start Programs, 4604–1

Status of Hazardous Substance Response Trust Fund, 8102–9.6

Status of Highway Trust Fund, 8102–9.7

Status of Inland Waterways Trust Fund, 8102–9.8

Status of Internal Audit Capabilities of Federal Agencies Without Statutory Inspectors General, 26111–23

Status of Interstate Compacts for the Disposal of Low-Level Radioactive Waste, 25528–93

Status of Loan Agreements, 9912–3

Status of Peacekeeper (MX) FY84 Procurement Funding, 26123–75

Status of Reforestation Trust Fund, 8102–9.9

Status of Strategic Petroleum Reserve Activities, 26102–3

Status of the Department of Energy's Implementation of the Nuclear Waste Policy Act of 1982, 26102–4

Status of the Economy, 21248–79

Status of the Fishery Resources Off the Northeastern U.S. for 1983, 2164–14

Status of the National Wilderness Preservation System, Annual Report, 5304–14

Status of the Peacekeeper (MX) Weapon System, 26123–74

Status of the Rural Elderly, 21148–28

Status of the Statistical Community After Sustaining Budget Reductions, 26125–28

Status of U.S. Sugar Import Quotas, 1922–9

Status Report as of Dec. 31, 1983, Of Public Buildings Projects Authorized by the Public Buildings Act of 1959, 9454–12

Status Report of the Energy-Related Inventions Program, As of Mar. 1, 1984, 2214–5

Status Report, Research and Demonstrations in Health Care Financing, 4652–8

Steel Foundries, N.E.C. (Industry 3325): 1982 Census of Manufactures. Preliminary Report. Industry Series, 2491–1.258

Titles

Steel Industry Compliance Extension Act Brought About Some Modernization and Unexpected Benefits, 26113–138

Steel Mill Products, 1982, Current Industrial Report, 2506–10.2

Steel Pipes and Tubes (Industry 3317): 1982 Census of Manufactures. Preliminary Report. Industry Series, 2491–1.254

Steel Shipping Drums and Pails, Current Industrial Report, 2506–11.5

Steel Springs, Except Wire (Industry 3493): 1982 Census of Manufactures. Preliminary Report. Industry Series, 2491–1.305

Steel Valves and Certain Parts Thereof from Japan: Determination of the Commission in Investigation No. 731-TA-145 (Final) Under the Tariff Act of 1930, Together with the Information Obtained in the Investigation, 9886–14.110

Steel Wire and Related Products (Industry 3315): 1982 Census of Manufactures. Preliminary Report. Industry Series, 2491–1.252

Stock Market Performance, Majors, 9142–36

Stock Prices and Economic News, 9381–10.37

Stockpile Report to the Congress, 9432–1

Stockpile Report to the Congress, Apr.-Sept. 1983, 9432–1.1

Stockpile Report to the Congress, Oct.1983-Mar. 1984, 9432–1.1

Stockpile Report to the Congress. Statistical Supplement, Mar. 31, 1984, 9432–1.2

Stockpiling U.S. Agricultural Commodities with Volatile World Markets: The Case of Soybeans, 1502–3.402

Stocks of Grain, 11922–4

Stocks of Grain At Selected Terminal and Elevator Sites, 1313–4

Stocks of Grains, Oilseeds, and Hay: Final Estimates by States, 1978-83, 1641–17

Stone (Industry 1411, 1422, 1423, and 1429): 1982 Census of Mineral Industries. Preliminary Report. Industry Series, 2511–1.8

Storage Batteries (Industry 3691): 1982 Census of Manufactures. Preliminary Report. Industry Series, 2491–1.388

Storm Data, 2152–3

Strategic Petroleum Reserve, Annual Report, 3004–20

Strategic Petroleum Reserve, Annual Report, 3404–9

Strategic Petroleum Reserve, Quarterly Report, 3002–13

Strategic Petroleum Reserve, Quarterly Report, 3402–4

Strategic Planning and Management System, 9182–11

Strategic Special Nuclear Material Inventory Differences, Semi-Annual Report, 3002–4

Strategies for Energy Conservation for a Large Office Building, 2218–68

Strengthening Research Library Resources Program, Higher Education Act, Title II-C, FY84 Abstracts, 4804–22

Strong Dollar Dampens Demand for U.S. Farm Exports, 1528–174

Strong Dollar, the Current Account, and Federal Deficits: Cause and Effect, 9379–1.401

Strong-Motion Program Report, Jan.-Dec. 1981, 5664–14

Strong Post-Recession Gain in Productivity Contributes to Slow Growth in Labor Costs, 6722–1.470

Strontium-90 in the U.S. Diet, 1982, 3404–13

Structural Characteristics of the Housing Inventory. 1980 Census of Housing. Vol. 3. Subject Reports. Chapter 4, 2475–4

Structural Steel Erection Special Trade Contractors (Industry 1791): 1982 Census of Construction Industries. Preliminary Report. Industry Series, 2371–1.21

Structural Wood Members, N.E.C. (Industry 2439): 1982 Census of Manufactures. Preliminary Report. Industry Series, 2491–1.119

Structure, Parameterization and Solution of a Multicountry Simulation Model, 9387–8.84

Student Drug Use, Attitudes and Beliefs, National Trends, 4494–4

Students, Graduates, and Dropouts, Oct. 1980-82, 6746–1.250

Studies in Port Facilities and Urban Economic Development, 7308–182

Studies of Felony Case Processing in Prosecutors' Offices, 6066–22

Studies on Drug Substitution, Patent Policy and Innovation in the Pharmaceutical Industry, 25528–98

Study of Contracts Between Interstate Pipelines and Their Customers, 3168–91

Study of Demographic, Situational, and Motivational Factors Affecting Restraint Usage in Automobiles, 7768–82

Study of MSPB Appeals Decisions for FY82, 9494–2

Study of the Careers of Participants in UMTA's Transit Management Programs (Section 10), 7888–60

Study of 1982 Effective Tax Rates of Selected Large U.S. Corporations, 23868–14

Sub-Saharan Africa: Outlook and Situation Report, 1524–4.10

Substance Abuse by Adolescents in Israel and France: A Cross-Cultural Perspective, 4102–1.430

Sugar and Other Sweeteners, TSUS Items 155(pt.): Summary of Trade and Tariff Information, 9885–1.71

Sugar and Sweetener Outlook and Situation Report, 1561–14

Sugar: ASCS Commodity Fact Sheet, 1983, 1806–4.3

Sugar Market Statistics, 1621–28

Sugar, Molasses and Honey: Foreign Agriculture Circular, 1925–14

Sugarbeet and Sugarcane Grower Receipts, Production Costs, and Net Returns, 1981-83 Crops, 1561–14.403

Sugarbeet and Sugarcane Production and Processing Costs: 1982 Crop, 1561–14.402

Sugars, Sirups, and Molasses: Quota Information, 8146–1.9

Sulfur: Mineral Industry Surveys, 5612–1.23

Sulfur: Minerals Yearbook Preprint, Vol. 1, 1983, 5604–15.62

Sulfur Oxides and Public Health: Evidence of Greater Risks, 25328–25

Sulfur, 1983: Mineral Industry Surveys Annual Advance Summary, 5614–5.2

Sulfuric Acid, 1983, Current Industrial Report, 2506–8.13

Summaries of Conclusions and Recommendations On Department of Defense Operations, 26104–6

Summaries of Conclusions and Recommendations On the Operations of Civil Departments and Agencies, 26104–5

Summary of Trade and Tariff

Summaries of FY84 Research in the Chemical Sciences, 3004–18.5

Summaries of Physical Research in the Geosciences, 3004–18.4

Summary and Analysis of International Travel to the U.S., 2902–1

Summary National Income and Product Series, Annually and Quarterly, 1952-83, 2702–1.435

Summary of Accidents Investigated by the Federal Railroad Administration, 1982, 7604–3

Summary of Acid Rain Analyses Undertaken by ICF for the Edison Electric Institute, National Wildlife Federation and Environmental Protection Agency, 21368–52

Summary of Annual Environmental Reports: Department of Energy Nuclear Sites, 3404–11

Summary of Annual Environmental Reports: Department of Energy Nuclear Sites, 3004–23

Summary of Claims Based on Alleged Violations of Federal Railroad Safety Statutes and Regulations Settled During the Period Oct. 1982 Through Sept. 30, 1983, 7604–10

Summary of Cotton Fiber and Processing Test Results, Crop of 1983, 1309–4

Summary of DM&S Trainees By Major Programs, FY83, 9924–21

Summary of Environmental Reports, Department of Energy Sites, 3004–23

Summary of Equity Security Transactions, 9365–2.15

Summary of Grants and Contracts Active On Sept. 30, 1983, 4184–2

Summary of Housing Characteristics for Selected Metropolitan Areas. Supplementary Report No. 1. Annual Housing Survey: 1978, 2485–8

Summary of Loan Activity and Operating Results Through (Month), Issued by CCC, 1802–7

Summary of Major Provisions in Federal Milk Marketing Orders, July 1, 1984, 1317–11

Summary of Mortgage Insurance Operations, 5002–3

Summary of Passport Statistics, 7182–1

Summary of Returns, Survey of 4th District Manufacturing, 9377–4

Summary of Safety Management Audits, 1982, 7554–38

Summary of Savings Accounts by Geographic Area: FSLIC-Insured Institutions, Sept. 1983, 9314–4

Summary of Snow Survey Measurements: Federal-State-Private Cooperative Snow Surveys, 1266–3

Summary of Snow Survey Measurements: Wyoming, 1983-84, 1266–3.10

Summary of the 1983 Annual Reports of the Medicare Board of Trustees, 4652–1.401

Summary of the 1984 Annual Reports of the Medicare Board of Trustees, 4654–8

Summary of Trade and Tariff Information: Schedule 1, Animal and Vegetable Products, 9885–1

Summary of Trade and Tariff Information: Schedule 2, Wood and Paper; Printed Matter, 9885–2

Summary of Trade and Tariff Information: Schedule 3, Textile Fibers and Textile Products, 9885–3

Summary of Trade and Tariff

Summary of Trade and Tariff Information: Schedule 4, Chemicals and Related Materials, 9885–4

Summary of Trade and Tariff Information: Schedule 5, Nonmetallic Minerals and Products, 9885–5

Summary of Trade and Tariff Information: Schedule 6, Metals and Metal Products, 9885–6

Summary of Trade and Tariff Information: Schedule 7, Specified Products; Miscellaneous and Nonenumerated Products, 9885–7

Summary of U.S. Export and Import Merchandise Trade: Seasonally Adjusted and Unadjusted Data, 2422–6

Summary of Weather Modification Activities Reported, 2144–8

Summary Report of Real Property Leased to the U.S. Throughout the World, As of Sept. 30, 1983, 9454–10

Summary Report of Real Property Owned by the U.S. Throughout the World, As of Sept. 30, 1983, 9454–5

Summer Youth Employment Situation, 6744–14

Supplement to Employment and Earnings, Revised Establishment Data, 6744–4

Supplement to Employment and Earnings, States and Areas, Data, 6744–5.3

Supplement to Employment, Hours, and Earnings, States and Areas, Data for 1980-83, 6744–5.3

Supplement to Producer Prices and Price Indexes, Data for 1983, 6764–2

Supplement to Statistics on Cotton and Related Data, 1564–10

Supplement to the 1979 Assessment of the Forest and Range Land Situation in the U.S.: America's Renewable Resources, 1208–24.4

Supplement V: Cost Experience of Automated Guideway Transit Systems, Costs and Trends for the Period 1976-82, 7884–6

Supplemental Analysis of Natural Gas Consumer Regulatory Reform Legislation, 25148–26

Supplemental Security Income: State and County Data, Dec. 1983., 4744–27

Supplemental Security Income Program: A 10-Year Overview, 25148–29

Supplemental Security Income Program 10-Year Review, 4742–1.402

Supply of Drugs to the U.S. Illicit Market from Foreign and Domestic Sources in 1982 (with Projections Through 1983), Narcotics Intelligence Estimate, 15894–1

Supporting a Family: Providing the Basics, 21968–28

Surety Companies Acceptable on Federal Bonds, 1984 Revision, 8104–4

Surface Transportation Assistance Act of 1982: Comparative Economic Effects on the Trucking Industry, 26117–31

Surge in Bankruptcies: Is the New Law Responsible?, 21528–57

Surgical and Medical Instruments (Industry 3841): 1982 Census of Manufactures. Preliminary Report. Industry Series, 2491–1.418

Surgical Appliances and Supplies (Industry 3842): 1982 Census of Manufactures. Preliminary Report. Industry Series, 2491–1.419

Survey of Aging Veterans: A Study of the Means, Resources, and Future Expectations of Veterans Aged 55 and Over, 9928–29

Survey of Community Water Systems, 23848–181

Survey of Consumer Finances, 1983, 9362–1.406

Survey of Consumer Finances, 1983: A Second Report, 9362–1.411

Survey of Contracting Statistics, 3802–5

Survey of Contracting Statistics, 3804–13

Survey of Current Business, 2702–1

Survey of Federally-Funded Marine Mammal Research and Studies, FY70-82, 14734–2

Survey of Mortgage Lending Activity, State Estimates 1978-83, 5148–6

Survey of Mortgage Lending Activity, 5142–18

Survey of Mortgage Lending Activity, Gross Flow, 5142–30

Survey of Nuclear Power Plant Construction Costs, 1983, 3164–69

Survey of Nuclear Power Plant Construction Costs, 1984, 3164–69

Survey of Plant Capacity, 1982, Current Industrial Report, 2506–3.7

Survey of Plant Capacity, 1983, Current Industrial Report, 2506–3.7

Survey of U.S. Uranium Exploration Activity, 1983, 3164–65

Survey of U.S. Uranium Marketing Activity, 1983, 3164–66

Survey of Water Fixture Use, 5188–109.4

Survey Results: Profile of 1983 Regional Council Activities, 25408–88.1

Surviving Spouse's Benefits in Private Pension Plans, 6722–1.426

Sustaining Tropical Forest Resources: Reforestation of Degraded Lands, 26358–101.2

Sustaining Tropical Forest Resources: U.S. and International Institutions, 26358–101.3

Swimwear, Nightwear, Robes, Playsuits, and Disposable Wearing Apparel, TSUS Items 379(pt.)-383(pt.), 700(pt.), and 703(pt.): Summary of Trade and Tariff Information, 9885–3.47

Switchgear and Switchboard Apparatus (Industry 3613): 1982 Census of Manufactures. Preliminary Report. Industry Series, 2491–1.357

Switchgear, Switchboard Apparatus, Relays, and Industrial Controls, 1983, Current Industrial Report, 2506–12.11

Synopsis of Biological Data on Shortnose Sturgeon, Acipenser brevirostrum LeSueur 1818, 2166–16.14

Synopsis of Biological Data on Skipjack Tuna, 2166–16.12

Synopsis of Biological Data on the Blue Crab, Callinectes sapidus Rathbun, 2166–16.13

Synopsis of the Annual Energy Review and Outlook, 1983, 3164–76

Synthetic Organic Chemicals: U.S. Production and Sales, 1983, 9884–3

Synthetic Organic Pigments, TSUS Items 410(pt.): Summary of Trade and Tariff Information, 9885–4.41

Synthetic Rubber (Industry 2822): 1982 Census of Manufactures. Preliminary Report. Industry Series, 2491–1.179

Table Wine from France and Italy: Determinations of the Commission in

Titles

Investigations Nos. 701-TA-210 and 211 (Preliminary) and 731-TA-167 and 168 (Preliminary) Under the Tariff Act of 1930, Together with the Information Obtained in the Investigations, 9886–19.9

Tabulation of Project Note Sales for Low-Income Housing, 5142–43

"Taking a Bite Out of Crime": The Impact of a Mass Media Crime Prevention Campaign, 6068–183

Talc and Pyrophyllite: Minerals Yearbook Preprint, Vol. 1, 1983, 5604–15.63

Tankers in the World Fleet, As of Jan. 1, 1983, 7704–17

Tanks and Tank Components (Industry 3795): 1982 Census of Manufactures. Preliminary Report. Industry Series, 2491–1.409

Tapered Roller Bearings and Parts Thereof from Japan and Italy: Determinations of the Commission in Investigations Nos. 731-TA-120 and 122 (Final) Under Section 735 of the Tariff Act of 1930, Together with the Information Obtained in the Investigations, 9886–14.96

Taps, Cocks, Valves, and Similar Devices and Parts, TSUS Items 680(pt.): Summary of Trade and Tariff Information, 9885–6.73

Targeting High Tech in the Delaware Valley, 9387–1.401

Tariff Schedules of the U.S. Annotated, 1984 Supplements, 9886–13

Tariff Schedules of the U.S. Annotated, 1985, 9886–13

Task Force on Environmental Cancer and Heart and Lung Disease, Sixth Annual Report to Congress, 9184–9

Tax Burdens for Families Residing in the Largest City in Each State, 1982, 10046–8.2

Tax Effect, and the Recent Behaviour of the After-Tax Real Rate: Is It Too High?, 9389–1.407

Tax Evasion Through the Netherlands Antilles And Other Tax Haven Countries, 21408–71

Tax Havens in the Caribbean Basin, 8008–106

Tax Incentives for Saving, 8302–2.407

Tax Incentives Targeted to Distressed Areas, 21788–140

Tax Policy Effects on Investment: The 1981 and 1982 Tax Acts, 9387–1.405

Tax Rules Governing Private Foundations, Part 2, 21788–137

Tax Treatment of Producers of Oil and Gas, 21788–132

Taxable Property Values and Assessment-Sales Price Ratios. 1982 Census of Governments. Vol. 2, 2453–1

Taxation of Financial Services Industry, 25368–129

Taxation of Income Flowing Through Life Insurance Companies, 8006–3.49

Taxation of Property and Casualty Insurance Companies, 25368–128

Taxpayers Age 65 or Over, 1977-81, 8302–2.412

Tea, Spices, and Essential Oils: Foreign Agriculture Circular, 1925–15

Technical Assistance Guide For Setting Job Training Partnership Act Performance Standards, 6408–59

Technical Papers: Census Bureau, 2626–2

Technological Change and Its Labor Impact in Four Industries, 6828–23

Titles

Technologies To Sustain Tropical Forest Resources, 26358–101

Technology and Household Production, 1004–16.1

Technology, Innovation, and Regional Economic Development, 26358–107

Technology, Innovation, and Regional Economic Development. Background Paper: Census of State Government Initiatives for High-Technology Industrial Development, 26358–107.2

Technology, Innovation, and Regional Economic Development. Background Paper No. 2: Encouraging High-Technology Development, 26358–107.3

Teen Parents and Their Children: Issues and Programs, 21968–29

Telecommunications Equipment: Country Market Survey, 2045–12

Telephone and Telegraph Apparatus (Industry 3661): 1982 Census of Manufactures. Preliminary Report. Industry Series, 2491–1.379

Telephone Conferencing in Civil and Criminal Court Cases, 6068–186

Telephone Rate Increases and the Elderly, 21148–32

Television Apparatus, Except Cameras, TSUS Items 685(pt.): Summary of Trade and Tariff Information, 9885–6.69

Television Channel Utilization, 9282–6

Tenant-Paid Energy Costs in Multifamily Rental Housing: Effects on Energy Use, Owner Investment, and the Market Value of Energy, 3308–73

Tennessee: Continuing the Momentum of Recovery, 9371–1.406

Tennessee Valley Authority 1983 Annual Report, 9804–1

Tenth Annual Report of the Diabetes Mellitus Interagency Coordinating Committee, FY83, 4434–8

Tenth District Depository Institution and Large Commercial Bank Statistics, 9381–11

Tenth Report of the Director, National Heart, Lung, and Blood Institute: Ten-Year Review and Five-Year Plan. Vol. 1: Progress and Promise, 4474–22.2

Tenth Report of the Director, National Heart, Lung, and Blood Institute: Ten-Year Review and Five-Year Plan. Vol. 2: Heart and Vascular Diseases, 4474–22.3

Tenth Report of the Director, National Heart, Lung, and Blood Institute: Ten-Year Review and Five-Year Plan. Vol. 3: Lung Diseases, 4474–22.4

Tenth Report of the Director, National Heart, Lung, and Blood Institute: Ten-Year Review and Five-Year Plan. Vol. 4: Blood Diseases and Resources, 4474–22.5

Tenth Report of the Director, National Heart, Lung, and Blood Institute: Ten-Year Review and Five-Year Plan. Vol. 5: Companion Issues, 4474–22.6

Terminal Area Forecasts, FY84-95, 7504–7

Testimony of the Comptroller General On the Impact of the Senior Executive Service, 26119–51

Testimony of the Hon. Donald T. Regan, Secretary of the Treasury, Before the Joint Economic Committee, 8008–107

Testing for Serial Correlation in the Presence of Heteroscedasticity with Applications to Exchange Rate Models, 9381–10.31

Titanium: Minerals Yearbook

Testing in Our Schools, 4918–15

Tests of Consistency Among Five EIA Natural Gas Data Collections, 3008–90

Textile Bags (Industry 2393): 1982 Census of Manufactures. Preliminary Report. Industry Series, 2491–1.105

Textile Goods, N.E.C. (Industry 2299): 1982 Census of Manufactures. Preliminary Report. Industry Series, 2491–1.77

Textile Machinery (Industry 3552): 1982 Census of Manufactures. Preliminary Report. Industry Series, 2491–1.331

Textile Machinery in Place (Major Group 22). 1982 Census of Manufactures. Preliminary Report. Subject Series, 2491–2.1

Textile Manufactures, Except Cotton. Agreement Categories by Commodity: U.S. General Imports, 2046–9.3

Textile Manufactures, Except Cotton. Agreement Category by Country of Origin and TSUSA Number by Country of Origin: U.S. General Imports, 2046–9.1

Textile Manufactures, Except Cotton. Country of Origin by Agreement Category and Country of Origin Totals: U.S. General Imports, 2046–9.2

Textile Plant Employment in the Southeast, 6942–1

Textile Plant Employment in the Southeast, 1983, 6944–1

Textured Yarn Production, 1983, Current Industrial Report, 2506–5.4

Thailand's Rice Export Potential, 1561–8.402

The "Underground Economy" and BLS Statistical Data, 6722–1.401

Theft by Employees in Work Organizations, Executive Summary, 6068–178

Theory of Optimum Deficits and Debt, 9373–3.27

Therapeutic Community; Study of Effectiveness, 4496–5.18

Thermal-Electric Plant Construction Cost and Annual Production Expenses, 1981, 3164–9

Third Asian Conference on Low-Income Shelter and Housing Finance, Oct. 11-14, 1982: Proceedings, 9914–11

Third Party Candidate To Receive Federal Funds, 9276–1.21

Thorium: Minerals Yearbook Preprint, Vol. 1, 1983, 5604–15.64

Thread Mills (Industry 2284): 1982 Census of Manufactures. Preliminary Report. Industry Series, 2491–1.68

Three Studies Evaluating the Effectiveness of Incentives for Increasing Safety Belt Use, 7762–9.408

Three Studies of Biographical Factors Associated with Success in Air Traffic Control Specialist Screening/Training at the FAA Academy, 7506–10.24

Three Years of Change in College and University Libraries, 1978-79 to 1981-82, 4854–1

Thrift Institution Activity, 9312–4

Throwing and Winding Mills (Industry 2282): 1982 Census of Manufactures. Preliminary Report. Industry Series, 2491–1.66

Tidal Current Tables, 2174–1

Tidal Current Tables, 1985: Atlantic Coast of North America, 2174–1.1

Tidal Current Tables, 1985: Pacific Coast of North America and Asia, 2174–1.2

Tide Tables 1985, High and Low Water Predictions, 2174–2

Tide Tables 1985, High and Low Water Predictions: Central and Western Pacific Ocean and Indian Ocean, 2174–2.4

Tide Tables 1985, High and Low Water Predictions: East Coast of North and South America, Including Greenland, 2174–2.2

Tide Tables 1985, High and Low Water Predictions: Europe and West Coast of Africa, Including the Mediterranean Sea, 2174–2.3

Tide Tables 1985, High and Low Water Predictions: West Coast of North and South America Including the Hawaiian Islands, 2174–2.1

Timber Resource Statistics for Alaska, 1206–9

Timber Resource Statistics for Eastern Washington, 1206–28.3

Timber Resource Statistics for the Petersburg/Wrangell Inventory Unit, Alaska, 1972, 1206–9.11

Timber Resource Statistics for the Prince of Wales Inventory Unit, Alaska, 1973, 1206–9.12

Timber Resource Statistics for the Sitka Inventory Unit, Alaska, 1971, 1206–9.10

Timber Resource Statistics for the Tanana Inventory Unit, Alaska, 1971-75, 1206–9.13

Timber Resource Statistics for the Upper Tanana Block, Tanana Inventory Unit, Alaska, 1974, 1206–9.9

Timber Resource Statistics for the Wood-Salcha Block, Tanana Inventory Unit, Alaska, 1975, 1206–9.14

Timber Resource Statistics for the Yakutat Inventory Unit, Alaska, 1975", 1206–9.15

Timber Resource Statistics for Washington, 1206–28

Timber Resources of Michigan, 1206–31

Timber Resources of Minnesota, 1206–24

Time of Change: 1983 Handbook on Women Workers, 6568–29

Time Series Forecasting Models of the Texas Economy: A Comparison, 9379–1.403

Time-Series of the Relationship Between Exchange Rates and Intervention: A Review of the Techniques and Literature, 9366–1.131

Time Served in Prison, 6066–19.7

Tin: Mineral Industry Surveys, 5612–1.24

Tin: Minerals Yearbook Preprint, Vol. 1, 1983, 5604–15.65

Tire, Battery, and Accessory Dealers (Industry 5531 pt.): 1982 Census of Retail Trade. Preliminary Report. Industry Series, 2395–1.11

Tire Cord and Fabric (Industry 2296): 1982 Census of Manufactures. Preliminary Report. Industry Series, 2491–1.74

Tires and Inner Tubes (Industry 3011): 1982 Census of Manufactures. Preliminary Report. Industry Series, 2491–1.206

Titanium Ingot, Mill Products, and Castings, Current Industrial Report, 2506–10.11

Titanium Mill Products, Ingot, and Castings, Current Industrial Report, 2506–10.11

Titanium: Mineral Industry Surveys, 5612–2.16

Titanium: Minerals Yearbook Preprint, Vol. 1, 1983, 5604–15.66

Titanium Sponge from Japan and the United Kingdom: Determinations of the Commission in Investigations Nos. 731-TA-161 and 162 (Final) Under the

Titanium Sponge from Japan — Titles

Tariff Act of 1930, Together with the Information Obtained in the Investigations, 9886–14.129

Titanium Sponge from Japan and the United Kingdom: Determinations of the Commission in Investigations Nos. 731-TA-161 and 162 (Preliminary) Under the Tariff Act of 1930, Together with the Information Obtained in the Investigations, 9886–14.94

Tobacco and Tobacco Products, TSUS Items 170(pt.): Summary of Trade and Tariff Information, 9885–1.65

Tobacco: Foreign Agriculture Circular, 1925–16

Tobacco Market Review, 1319–5

Tobacco Market Review, Burley, 1983 Crop, 1319–5.2

Tobacco Market Review, Fire-Cured and Dark Air-Cured, 1983 Crop, 1319–5.3

Tobacco Market Review: Flue-Cured, 1983 Crop, 1319–5.1

Tobacco Outlook and Situation Report, 1561–10

Tobacco Stemming and Redrying (Industry 2141): 1982 Census of Manufactures. Preliminary Report. Industry Series, 2491–1.47

Tobacco Stocks, 1319–3

Toilet Preparations (Industry 2844): 1982 Census of Manufactures. Preliminary Report. Industry Series, 2491–1.188

Tomato Products from Greece: Determination of the Commission in Investigation No. 104-TAA-23 Under Section 104(b) of the Trade Agreements Act of 1979, Together with the Information Obtained in the Investigation, 9886–18.16

Top 100 Boost Margins Despite Lower Volume, 1122–1.408

Top 100 Cooperatives, 1982 Financial Profile, 1124–3

Top 100 Raise Cash Refunds, Retains; Reduce Borrowings from Co-op Banks, 1122–1.411

Total Active Individual Borrowers by Race or Ethnic Group, 1184–11

Total Enrollment in Institutions of Higher Education, 4844–4

Toward a Better Understanding of Hospital Occupancy Rates, 4652–1.418

Toward an Improved Seafood Nomenclature System, 2162–1.401

Toys and Hobby Goods and Supplies (Industry 5042): 1982 Census of Wholesale Trade. Preliminary Report. Industry Series, 2403–1.6

Tractors (Except Garden Tractors), Current Industrial Report, 2506–12.9

Trade Adjustment Assistance Industry Reports Under Section 224 of the Trade Act of 1974, 6406–9

Trade in 1983 Between the U.S. and the Nonmarket Economy Countries, 9882–2.402

Trade of European Non-NATO Countries and Japan with China, 7144–15

Trade of European Non-NATO Countries and Japan with European CEMA Countries, 7144–6

Trade of NATO Countries with China, 1980-83, 7144–14

Trade of NATO Countries with European CEMA Countries, 1980-83, 7144–5

Trade Patterns of the West, 1983, 7144–10

Traffic Safety Evaluation Research Review: A Quarterly Supplement to the Traffic Safety Newsletter, 7762–9

Traffic Safety Impact of Two Experimental Motorcycle Licensing Programs, 7762–9.402

Traffic Volume Trends, 7552–8

Transfer of the Civil Operational Earth Observation Satellites to the Private Sector, 2148–47

Transformers (Industry 3612): 1982 Census of Manufactures. Preliminary Report. Industry Series, 2491–1.356

Transformers, 1983, Current Industrial Report, 2506–12.29

Transmission of Data Noise into Policy Noise in Monetary Control, 9366–6.74

Transport Statistics in the U.S.: Railroad Companies and Motor Carriers Subject to the Interstate Commerce Act, for the Year Ended Dec. 31, 1982, 9486–5

Transport Statistics in the U.S.: Railroad Companies and Motor Carriers Subject to the Interstate Commerce Act, for the Year Ended Dec. 31, 1983, 9486–6

Transport Statistics in the U.S. for the Year Ended Dec. 31, 1983. Part 1: Railroads, 9486–6.1

Transport Statistics in the U.S., Year Ended Dec. 31, 1982. Part 2: Motor Carriers, Release 2, 9486–5.3

Transportation Accident Fatalities, Preliminary Statistics, 9614–6

Transportation and Agricultural Export Expansion, 1004–16.1

Transportation Energy Data Book: Edition 6, 3304–5

Transportation Energy Data Book: Edition 7, 3304–5

Transportation Equipment, N.E.C. (Industry 3799): 1982 Census of Manufactures. Preliminary Report. Industry Series, 2491–1.410

Transportation for Older Americans: Issues and Options for the Decade of the 1980's, 7308–183

Transportation of Radioactive Materials in (State), 9636–1

Transportation Planners' Guide to Using the 1980 Census, 7558–101

Transportation Safety Information Report, 1983 Annual Summary, 7304–19

Transportation Statistics, 2326–7.61

Travel Trailers and Campers (Industry 3792): 1982 Census of Manufactures. Preliminary Report. Industry Series, 2491–1.408

Treasury Bulletin, 8002–4

Treasury Combined Statement Of Receipts, Expenditures and Balances of the U.S. Government, FY83, 8104–2

Treasury Reporting Rates of Exchange, 8102–6

Treaties in Force: A List of Treaties and Other International Agreements of the U.S. in Force on Jan. 1, 1984, 7004–1

Treatment Research Monograph Series, 4496–5

Trend Data, 1959-83, 9924–13

Trends, Federal Home Loan Bank of Des Moines, 9302–9

Trends in Education, 1972-73 to 1992-93, 4824–3

Trends in Employment and Earnings in the Philanthropic Sector, 6722–1.455

Trends in Employment and Unemployment in Families, 6746–1.253

Trends in Health Personnel, 4144–11.1

Trends in Heavy Truck Energy Use and Efficiency, 3308–70

Trends in International Trade in Nonpowered Handtools: Report to the Committee on Ways and Means, U.S. House of Representatives on Investigation No. 332-163 Under Section 332 of the Tariff Act of 1930, 9886–4.68

Trends in Interpersonal Crimes in Schools, 4918–13

Trends in Maternal and Infant Health Factors Associated with Low Infant Birth Weight, U.S., 1972 and 1980, 4102–1.423

Trends in Medicare Reimbursement for End-Stage Renal Disease: 1974-79, 4652–1.421

Trends in Multifactor Productivity, 6824–2

Trends in Municipal Financing and the Use of Tax-Exempt Bonds To Finance Private Activities, 21788–135

Trends in Nuclear Power Plant Capital Investment Cost Estimates, 1976-82, 9638–52

Trends in Nursing and Related Care Homes and Hospitals: U.S., Selected Years, 1969-80, 4147–14.30

Trends in Skill and Accuracy of National Weather Service POP Forecasts, 2188–17

Trends in Teenage Childbearing, U.S., 1970-81, 4147–21.41

Trends in the Real After-Tax Cost of Farm Machinery, 1960-83, 1561–16.402

Trends in Traffic, Capacity, Load Factor and Yields, Scheduled Passenger Service, 9142–45

Trends in Traffic, Capacity, Load Factor, and Yields, Scheduled Passenger Service: Short-Haul Nationals (System), 9142–45.2

Trends in Traffic, Capacity, Load Factor, and Yields, Scheduled Passenger Service: System Majors, 9142–45.1

Trends in U.S. Life Expectancy, 25368–130

Trends in World Agricultural Land Use, 1522–3.401

Tropical Fruit and Products Trade Statistics in Selected Countries, 1925–35.1

Truck Inventory and Use Survey. 1982 Census of Transportation, 2573–1

Truck Trailers (Industry 3715): 1982 Census of Manufactures. Preliminary Report. Industry Series, 2491–1.396

Truck Trailers, Current Industrial Report, 2506–12.25

Trust Assets of Banks and Trust Companies, 1983, 13004–1

Trust Territory of the Pacific Islands: Annual Report to the Secretary of the Interior, 5304–3

Trust Territory of the Pacific Islands, 1983, 7004–6

Tuberculosis Statistics: States and Cities, 1982, 4204–2

Tubular Metal Framed Stacking Chairs from Italy and Taiwan: Determinations of the Commission in Investigations Nos. 731-TA-202 and 203 (Preliminary) Under the Tariff Act of 1930, Together with the Information Obtained in the Investigation, 9886–14.121

Tucson Area Economy and Housing Market: Outlook to 1992, 9306–2.1

Titles

Tufted Carpets and Rugs (Industry 2272): 1982 Census of Manufactures. Preliminary Report. Industry Series, 2491–1.63

Tuition Rates Charged Foreign Governments for Military Training Should Be Revised, 26123–56

Tungsten: Mineral Industry Surveys, 5612–1.25

Tungsten: Minerals Yearbook Preprint, Vol. 1, 1983, 5604–15.67

Turbines and Turbine Generator Sets (Industry 3511): 1982 Census of Manufactures. Preliminary Report. Industry Series, 2491–1.312

Turkey Hatchery, 1625–10

Turkeys, 1625–6

Turtles, Birds, and Mammals in the Northern Gulf of Mexico and Nearby Atlantic Waters: An Overview Based on Aerial Surveys of OCS Areas, with Emphasis on Oil and Gas Effects, 5508–85

TVA Biomass Fuels Update II, 9806–9.8

TVA Socioeconomic Monitoring and Mitigation Reports, 9806–7

TVA Technical Notes, 9806–2

TVA's Biomass Fuels Program, 9806–9

Twentieth Annual Report on the Status of the National Wilderness Preservation System, 5304–14

Twenty-second Annual Report of the Federal Maritime Commission to the Congress of the U.S. for FY83, 9334–1

Twenty-seventh Annual Report of the President of the U.S. on the Trade Agreements Program, 1983, 444–1

Two Years After High School: A Capsule Description of 1980 Seniors, 4826–2.19

Two Years in High School: The Status of 1980 Sophomores in 1982, 4826–2.20

Types of Work Performed Using Resurfacing, Restoration, Rehabilitation, and Reconstruction Federal Highway Funds, 26113–121

Typesetting (Industry 2791): 1982 Census of Manufactures. Preliminary Report. Industry Series, 2491–1.171

Typical Electric Bills, Jan. 1, 1984, 3164–40

Uinta-Southwestern Utah Coal Region: Round 2, Final Environmental Impact Statement, 5726–4.6

Umbrellas, Whips, Riding Crops, and Canes: Matches, Pyrotechnics, and Candles: and Smokers' Articles: TSUS Items 751(pt.), 755(pt.), and 756(pt.): Summary of Trade and Tariff Information, 9885–7.54

UMTA Transit Assistance Grants, 7884–3

UMTA University Research and Training Program, FY84 Grant Awards, 7884–7

Unconventional Arms Policy: Selling Ourselves Short. Promotion of Foreign Military Sales to the Developing World Under the Reagan Administration, 25948–3

Underestimation of Funding Requirements in Five Year Procurement Plans Briefing Paper, 26123–68

Underground Economy: An Introduction, 2702–1.419

Underground Economy: An Introduction, 2702–1.428

Underground Natural Gas Storage in the U.S., 1983-84 Heating Year (Apr. 1983-Mar. 1984), 3162–4.407

Underground Storage of Large Volumes of Crude Oil: The U.S. Strategic Petroleum Reserve Program, 3008–91

Underreporting of Disease and Physicians' Knowledge of Reporting Requirements, 4102–1.411

Underrepresented in Graduate Medical Education and Medical Research, 4102–1.412

Understanding Police Agency Performance, 6068–181

Underwear and Nightwear, 1983, Current Industrial Report, 2506–6.9

Unemployment in 1982: Beyond the Official Labor Force Statistics, 9373–1.410

Unemployment in 1982: The Cost to Workers and Their Families, 6722–1.412

Unemployment Insurance Financial Data, 6408–5

Unemployment Insurance Quality Appraisal Results, FY83, 6404–16

Unemployment Insurance Quality Appraisal Results, FY84, 6404–16

Unemployment Insurance Weekly Claims Report, 6402–14

Unfair Foreign Trade Practices (Part 2), 21368–51

UNICOR Federal Prisons Industries, Inc. Annual Report, 1983, 6244–3

Uniform Crime Report, 1983 Preliminary Annual Release, 6222–1

Uniform Crime Report, 1984 Preliminary Annual Release, 6222–1

Uniform Crime Reports: Bomb Summary, 1983, 6224–5

Uniform Crime Reports: Crime in the U.S., 1983, 6224–2

Union-Nonunion Wage Differentials and the Functional Distribution of Income: Some Simulation Results from a General Equilibrium Model, 9387–8.83

Union Recognition in the Federal Government, Statistical Summary, Summary Reports Within Agencies and Listings Within Agencies of Exclusive Recognitions and Agreements, As of Jan. 1983, 9844–14

Union Settlements and Aggregate Wage Behavior in the 1980s, 9362–1.410

Unions, Relative Wages, and Economic Efficiency, 9387–8.81

Unit Costs and Unit Cost Changes, 9142–37

Unit Costs and Unit Cost Changes: Short-Haul Nationals, 9142–37.2

Unit Costs and Unit Cost Changes: System Majors, 9142–37.1

United States (Geographic Area Statistics): 1982 Census of Mineral Industries. Preliminary Report. Summary Series, 2511–2.2

United States (Industry Statistics): 1982 Census of Mineral Industries. Preliminary Report. Summary Series, 2511–2.1

Universe of Operating and Nonoperating Local Public School Systems, 4834–1

Unmounted Ophthalmic Lenses, TSUS Item 708.01: Summary of Trade and Tariff Information, 9885–7.57

Unrecognized Redistributions of Revenue in Diagnosis-Related Group-Based Prospective Payment Systems, 4652–1.428

Unreported Taxable Income from Selected Illegal Activities, 8008–112

Unwrought Copper: Public Version of Report to the President, Investigation No. TA-224-52 Under Section 224 of the Trade Act of 1974, 6406–9.4

U.S. and Soviet Bloc Training

Unwrought Copper: Report to the President on Investigation No. TA-201-52 Under Section 201 of the Trade Act of 1974, 9886–5.50

Update, Nuclear Power Program Information and Data, 3352–3

Update of the Affirmative Action Plan and Annual Accomplishment Report of Equal Employment Activities, FY83, 7004–11

Upholstered Household Furniture (Industry 2512): 1982 Census of Manufactures. Preliminary Report. Industry Series, 2491–1.129

Upland Cotton: ASCS Commodity Fact Sheet, 1984, 1806–4.8

Uranium and Uranium Compounds, TSUS Items 421(pt.), 422(pt.), 601(pt.), 629(pt.), and 660(pt.): Summary of Trade and Tariff Information, 9885–4.47

Uranium Enrichment, 1983 Annual Report, 3354–7

Uranium Marketing Survey, 3164–66

Urban and Rural Housing Characteristics, 1004–16.1

Urban and Rural Housing Characteristics, 1702–1.407

Urban and Rural Housing Characteristics, U.S. and Regions. Annual Housing Survey: 1981. Part E, 2485–7

Urban Decline and Distress: An Update, 9373–1.413

Urban Development Action Grants, Quarterly Awards, 5002–7

Urban Renewal Project Note Sale, 5142–36

Urban Transportation Abstracts, Winter 1983, Vol. 2, No. 2, 7882–1

Urban Travel Trends: Historical Observations and Future Forecasts, Final Report, May 1984, 7888–63

U.S. (Industry Statistics), Firms Subject to Federal Income Tax: 1982 Census of Service Industries. Preliminary Report. Industry Series, 2390–2.20

U.S. (Industry Statistics): 1982 Census of Manufactures. Preliminary Report. Industry Series, 2491–1.444

U.S. (Industry Statistics): 1982 Census of Retail Trade. Preliminary Report. Industry Series, 2395–1.40

U.S. (Industry Statistics): 1982 Census of Wholesale Trade. Preliminary Report. Industry Series, 2403–1.40

U.S. Affiliates of Foreign Companies: Operations in 1981, 2702–1.402

U.S. Agricultural Export Contributions by State, FY83, 1522–1.403

U.S. Agricultural Exports to Latin America Up in 1984, May Drop in 1985, 1522–1.407

U.S. Agricultural Exports to Sub-Saharan Africa To Increase in FY84, 1522–1.401

U.S. Agricultural Imports To Help Developing Countries' Earnings, 1522–1.405

U.S. Airborne Exports and General Imports: Shipping Weight and Value; Customs District and Continent, 2422–8

U.S. and Foreign Registered Aircraft Hijackings, 7504–31.2

U.S. and Foreign Registered Aircraft Hijackings, Summarization, 7504–31.1

U.S. and Regions. 1980 Census of Housing, Vol. 4. Characteristics of Housing Units. Components of Inventory Change, Part I, 2473–3.1

U.S. and Soviet Bloc Training of Latin American and Caribbean Students: Considerations in Developing Future U.S. Programs, 26123–77

U.S. Arms Control and Titles

- U.S. Arms Control and Disarmament Agency 1983 Annual Report, Message from the President of the U.S., 9824–2
- U.S. Assistance to Foreign Copper Producers and the Effects on Domestic Industries and Environmental Standards, 21448–31
- U.S. Attorney's Office Statistical Report, FY83, 6004–2
- U.S. Auto Industry: U.S. Factory Sales, Retail Sales, Imports, Exports, Apparent Consumption, Suggested Retail Prices, and Trade Balances with Selected Countries for Motor Vehicles, 1964-83, 9884–7
- U.S. Automobile Industry: Monthly Report on Selected Economic Indicators, 9882–8
- U.S. Automobile Industry: Monthly Report on Selected Economic Indicators. Report to the Subcommittee on Trade, Committee on Ways and Means, on Investigation No. 332-177 Under Section 332 of the Tariff Act of 1930, 9882–8
- U.S. Automobile Industry: Report to the Congress from the Secretary of Transportation, 7304–17
- U.S. Automobile Industry, 1982: Report to the Congress from the Secretary of Commerce, 2004–8
- U.S. Budget in Brief, FY85, 104–6
- U.S. Business Enterprises Acquired or Established by Foreign Direct Investors in 1983, 2702–1.418
- U.S. Cancer Mortality Rates and Trends, 1950-79, 4478–146
- U.S. Central Station Nuclear Electric Generating Units: Significant Milestones, 3352–1
- U.S. Central Station Nuclear Electric Generating Units: Significant Milestones, 3354–11
- U.S. Civil Airmen Statistics, 1983, 7504–2
- U.S. Civil Service Retirement System, Annual Report, Sept. 30, 1983, 9844–34
- U.S. Commodity Exports and Imports as Related to Output 1981 and 1980, 2424–3
- U.S. Consumer Product Safety Commission, 1983 Annual Report, 9164–2
- U.S. Cooperative Involvement in the Petroleum Industry, 1982, 1561–16.403
- U.S. Cotton Quality Report for Ginnings Prior to (Date), 1309–11
- U.S. Court of International Trade Report for the Fiscal Year Ending Sept. 1984, 18224–2
- U.S. Court of Military Appeals and the Judge Advocates General of the Armed Forces and the General Counsel of the Department of Transportation, Annual Report, Oct. 1, 1982-Sept. 30, 1983, 3504–3
- U.S. Courts: A Pictorial Summary for the Twelve Month Period Ended June 30, 1984, 18204–9
- U.S. Crude Oil, Natural Gas, and Natural Gas Liquids Reserves, 1983 Annual Report, 3164–46
- U.S. Customs Service's Collection of Duties on Imports to the Virgin Islands, 26119–54
- U.S. Department of Commerce: Annual Report of the Secretary, FY83, 2004–1
- U.S. Department of Education, Annual Report, FY83, 4804–6
- U.S. Department of Energy, FY85 Budget Highlights, 3004–14
- U.S. Department of Energy, Grand Junction Area Office Reports, 3358–27
- U.S. Department of Labor, Seventy-First Annual Report, FY83, 6304–1
- U.S. Department of State Indexes of Living Costs Abroad, Quarters Allowances, and Hardship Differentials, 6862–1
- U.S. Department of Transportation, 15th Annual Report, FY81, 7304–1
- U.S. Department of Transportation: Grant Awards, 7304–7
- U.S. Direct Investment Abroad: Country Detail for Selected Items, 1977-83, 2702–1.442
- U.S. Direct Investment Abroad in 1983, 2702–1.430
- U.S. Earthquakes, 2154–1
- U.S. Earthquakes, 1981, 5664–13
- U.S. Economic Assistance to Central America, 26123–55
- U.S. Economy and Monetary Policy in 1983, 9381–1.401
- U.S. Economy in an Interdependent World: A Multicountry Model, 9368–78
- U.S. Energy for the Rest of the Century, 1984 Edition, 2006–2.5
- U.S. Energy Industry Financial Developments, 3162–38
- U.S. Essential Oil Trade Increases in 1983, 1925–15.2
- U.S.-European Communities Steel Pipe and Tube Imports Agreement, 25368–134
- U.S. Experience with Exchange Market Intervention: Jan.-Mar. 1975, 9366–1.127
- U.S. Experience with Exchange Market Intervention: Sept. 1977-Dec. 1979, 9366–1.140
- U.S. Experience with Exchange Market Intervention: Oct. 1980-Sept. 1981, 9366–1.128
- U.S. Export Sales, 1922–3
- U.S. Exports and Imports, SIC-Based Products: Annual, 1983, 2424–6
- U.S. Exports: Domestic Merchandise, SIC-Based Products by World Areas, 2424–6.1
- U.S. Exports of Cotton, Wool and Man-Made Fiber Manufactures: Subgroup by Country of Destination, 2042–26
- U.S. Exports, Schedule B Commodity by Country, 2424–9
- U.S. Exports: Schedule E, Commodity by Country, 2422–3
- U.S. Exports: Schedule E Commodity Groupings by World Area and Country, 2424–5.1
- U.S. Exports to Japan Continue To Grow, 1925–34.421
- U.S. Exports: World Area and Country by Schedule E Commodity Groupings, 2424–5.2
- U.S. Exports, 1983, 2424–5
- U.S. Farm Exports to Eastern Europe Rose Slightly in 1983, 1522–1.404
- U.S. Farmer and World Market Development, 1528–172
- U.S. Fertilizer and Pesticide Outlook and Situation, 1982/83-1983/84, 1004–16.1
- U.S. Financial Data, 9391–4
- U.S. Footwear Imports, Summary Tables, 2042–29
- U.S. Foreign Agricultural Trade Statistical Report, 1522–4
- U.S. Foreign Agricultural Trade Statistical Report, CY83, 1522–4.2
- U.S. Foreign Agricultural Trade Statistical Report, FY83, 1522–4.1
- U.S. Foreign Fishery Allocations, 7006–5
- U.S. Foreign Trade: Airborne Exports and General Imports. Shipping Weight and Value; Customs District and Continent, 2422–8
- U.S. Foreign Trade, Changes in Schedule C: Classification of Country and Territory Designations for U.S. Import/Export Statistics, 2428–3
- U.S. Foreign Trade: Export and Import Merchandise, Seasonally Adjusted and Unadjusted Data, 2422–6
- U.S. Foreign Trade: General Imports of Cotton, Wool, and Manmade Fiber Manufactures, 2422–1
- U.S. Foreign Trade: Summary Charts, 2044–17
- U.S. Foreign Trade: Waterborne Exports and General Imports. Trade Area, District, Port, Type Service, and U.S. Flag, 2422–7
- U.S. Forest Planting Report, 1983, 1204–7
- U.S. Foundations Responsiveness to Puerto Rican Needs and Concerns: Foundation Giving to Puerto Rican Organizations 1979-81, 21788–137.1
- U.S. General Accounting Office, 1983, Annual Report, 26104–1
- U.S. General Imports and Imports for Consumption: Schedule A, Commodity by Country, 2422–2
- U.S. General Imports: Cotton Manufactures, 2046–8.1
- U.S. General Imports: Cotton, Wool, and Man-Made Fiber Textile Manufactures. Country of Origin by Textile Category, by Date of Exportation, 2046–8.4
- U.S. General Imports: Customs Import Value, 2046–9
- U.S. General Imports: Man-Made Fibers and Manufactures, 2046–8.3
- U.S. General Imports of Cotton Manufactures. Agreement Category, 2046–9.6
- U.S. General Imports of Cotton Manufactures. Agreement Category by Country of Origin and TSUSA Number by Country of Origin, 2046–9.4
- U.S. General Imports of Cotton Manufactures. Country of Origin, 2046–9.7
- U.S. General Imports of Cotton Manufactures. Country of Origin by Agreement Category, 2046–9.5
- U.S. General Imports of Cotton, Wool and Man-Made Fiber Manufactures: Subgroup by Country of Origin, 2042–27
- U.S. General Imports of Cotton, Wool and Man-Made Fiber Textiles (Major Subgroups in Equivalent Square Yards), 2042–18
- U.S. General Imports of Textile Manufactures, Except Cotton. Agreement Categories by Commodity, 2046–9.3
- U.S. General Imports of Textile Manufactures, Except Cotton. Agreement Category by Country of Origin and TSUSA Number by Country of Origin, 2046–9.1
- U.S. General Imports of Textile Manufactures, Except Cotton. Country of Origin by Agreement Category and Country of Origin Totals, 2046–9.2
- U.S. General Imports: Quantity Totals, 2046–8
- U.S. General Imports: Schedule A, Commodity by Country, 2422–2
- U.S. General Imports: Schedule A Commodity Groupings by World Area and Country, 2424–2.3

Titles

U.S. General Imports: Textile Manufactures Other than Cotton, Wool or Man-Made Fibers, 2046–8.5

U.S. General Imports: Textile Manufactures Other than Cotton, Wool or Man-Made Fibers, Dec. 1983, 2046–8.5

U.S. General Imports: Wool Manufactures, 2046–8.2

U.S. General Imports: World Area and Country of Origin by Schedule A Commodity Groupings, Vol. 1, 2424–2.1

U.S. General Imports: World Area and Country of Origin by Schedule A Commodity Groupings, Vol. 2, 2424–2.2

U.S. General Imports, 1983, 2424–2

U.S. Geological Survey Yearbook, FY83, 5664–8

U.S. Government International Barter, 21208–20

U.S. Government Printing Office, Annual Report FY83, 26204–1

U.S. Great Lakes Ports Statistics For Overseas and Canadian Waterborne Commerce for 1982, 7744–3

U.S. Hog Industry, 1568–248

U.S. Import and Export Price Indexes, 6762–13

U.S. Imports and Exports of Natural Gas: 1983, 3162–4.406

U.S. Imports: Consumption and General SIC-Based Products by World Areas, 2424–6.2

U.S. Imports for Consumption and General Imports: TSUSA Commodity by Country of Origin, 1983, 2424–4

U.S. Imports of Fresh Cut Flowers Continue To Grow, 1925–34.412

U.S. Imports of Textile and Apparel Products Under the Multifiber Arrangement, 1976-82 and Jan.-June 1983, 9882–11

U.S. Imports of Textile and Apparel Products Under the Multifiber Arrangement, 1976-83, 9882–11

U.S. Industrial Outlook 1984, Prospects for over 300 Industries, 2014–4

U.S. International Air Travel Statistics, 7302–2

U.S. International Trade and Investment in Services: Data Needs and Availability, 2706–5.30

U.S. International Trade Commission, 1983 Annual Report, 9884–1

U.S. International Transactions in 1983, 9362–1.403

U.S.-Japan Agricultural Relations, 1004–16.1

U.S. Landownership Survey, 1506–5

U.S. Machine Tool Industry: Its Relation to National Security, 25388–48

U.S. Merchant Marine Data Sheet, 7702–1

U.S.-Mexico Border Issues and the Peso Devaluation, 21788–133

U.S. Military Posture for FY85, 3564–1

U.S. Military Strengths Worldwide: Fact Sheet, 3542–9

U.S. National Income and Product Accounts: Revised Estimates, 1981-83, First and Second Quarter 1984, 2702–1.425

U.S. National Study on Trade in Services, 448–1

U.S. Nuclear Regulatory Commission, 1983 Annual Report, 9634–2

U.S. Oceanborne Foreign Trade Routes, 1982, 7704–2

U.S. Outlook for Sweeteners and Tropical Products, 1004–16.1

U.S. Overseas Loans and Grants And Assistance from International Organizations, 9914–5

U.S. Parole Commission Research Unit, Research Reports, 6006–2

U.S. Participation in the UN: Report by the President to the Congress for the Year 1982, 7004–5

U.S. Participation in the UN: Report by the President to the Congress for the Year 1983, 7004–5

U.S. Passenger Rail Technologies, 26358–97

U.S. Policy in Central America, 21388–41

U.S. Postal Service Cost Segments and Components, FY83, 9864–4

U.S. Postal Service Revenue and Cost Analysis, FY83, 9864–2

U.S. Production, Imports & Import/Production Ratios For Cotton, Wool & Man-Made Fiber Textiles & Apparel, 2044–14

U.S. Production of Fish Fillets and Steaks, Annual Summary 1982, 2166–6.3

U.S. Production of Soda Ash and Natural Sodium Sulfate: Mineral Industry Surveys, 5612–1.33

U.S. Public Health Service Annual Report to the Congress, 4044–2

U.S. Railway Association, Annual Report, 1981-83, 29604–1

U.S. Raw Cotton Content of Textile Imports by Country of Origin, 1983, 1561–1.401

U.S. Registered Aircraft Hijacking Statistics, 1961 to Present: Summarization by Year, 7504–31.4

U.S. Role as Contracting Agent for the U.S.-Saudi Arabian Joint Commission on Economic Cooperation, 26123–80

U.S. Savings Bonds Issued and Redeemed Through (Month), 8242–1

U.S. Secret Service Annual Statistical Summary, FY83, 8464–1

U.S. Shipping and Shipbuilding: Trends and Policy Choices, 26306–6.83

U.S. Small Business Administration, Annual Report FY82, 9764–1

U.S. Small Business Administration, Annual Report FY83, 9764–1

U.S.-Soviet Relations, Part 3, 25388–47

U.S. Spice Trade at Record Levels in 1983, 1925–15.1

U.S. Synthetic Fuels Corporation, Annual Report, 1983, 29654–1

U.S. Timber Production, Trade, Consumption, and Price Statistics, 1950-83, 1204–29

U.S. Title and Code Criminal Offense Citations, 18204–14

U.S. Tobacco Prices, 1983, 1925–16.406

U.S. Tobacco Trade: 1983, 1925–16.401

U.S. Trade in Dairy, Livestock, and Poultry Commodities, 1925–32.2

U.S. Trade Performance in 1983 and Outlook, 2044–26

U.S. Trade: Record of the 1970s—Challenge of the 1980s, 21368–46

U.S. Trade Shifts in Selected Commodity Areas, 9882–9

U.S. Trade with Puerto Rico and U.S. Possessions, 2422–4

U.S. Trade with the European Community, 1958-83, 7144–7

U.S. Travel and Tourism Administration, 2nd Program Report, 1983, 2904–6

U.S. Tuna Trade Summary, 1982, 2162–1.403

U.S. Uranium Mining and Milling Industry, A Comprehensive Review, 3008–95

USITC Investigations Under

U.S. Uranium Mining Industry: Background Information on Economics and Emissions, 9188–96

U.S. Waterborne Exports and General Imports: Trade Area, District, Port, Type Service, and U.S. Flag, 2422–7

U.S. Wheat Outlook, 1004–16.1

U.S. Wine Trade, 1925–34.409

USA Statistics in Brief, 1984, 2324–1

Usage of Multiple VA Programs, 9926–4.10

USDA Summary of 1982 U.S. Cow Herd Averages, 1702–2.401

USDA Summary of 1982 U.S. Goat Herd Averages, 1702–2.401

USDA 1983 Thrifty Food Plan, 1702–1.402

USDA's Nutrient Data Bases, 1004–16.1

USDA's Revised Truck Fleet Cost, 1311–15

Use and Cost of Soil Conservation and Water Quality Practices in the Southeast, 1588–84

Use and Costs of Medicare Services in the Last Years of Life, 4144–11.1

Use and Costs of Medicare Services in the Last 2 Years of Life, 4652–1.412

Use of Contraception in the U.S., 1982, 4146–8.103

Use of Electricity Billing Data To Determine Household Energy Use "Fingerprints", 3308–76

Use of Employment Data To Estimate Office Space Demand, 6722–1.474

Use of Government Vehicles for Home-to-Work Transportation, 26123–63

Use of Hourly Earnings Proposed To Revive Spendable Earnings Series, 6722–1.468

Use of Operating Loans and Other Credit Funds, FmHA Operating Loans, 1184–4

Use of Private Funds for Highway Improvements, Report 2. Financing Urban Transportation Improvements, 7556–7.2

Use of Services for Family Planning and Infertility: U.S., 1982, 4146–8.104

Use Valuation of Louisiana's Rural Lands: Short-Run Fiscal Impacts, 1208–206

Uses and Impacts of Hospital Tax-Exempt Financing, 21788–135

Uses of Adjustable-Rate and Other Mortgages in the Fourth FHLB District, 9302–2.401

Uses of Livestock Futures Markets by Large Hedgers, 11924–2.401

Uses of State-Administered Federal Education Funds, FY83 Grants (A Report Required by Section 406(a), General Education Provisions Act, as Amended): Eighth Annual Report of the U.S. Secretary of Education to the Senate Committee on Labor and Human Resources, House Committee on Education and Labor, 4804–8

USITC Investigations of Steel Imports, 9886–19

USITC Investigations Under Section 104(b) of the Trade Agreements Act of 1979, 9886–18

USITC Investigations Under Section 332 of the Tariff Act of 1930, 9886–4

USITC Investigations Under Sections 703(a) and 705(b) of the Tariff Act of 1930, As Amended, 9886–15

USITC Investigations Under Sections 703(a), 733(a), 705(b), and 735(b) of the Tariff Act of 1930, As Amended, 9886–19

USITC Investigations Under Sections 733(a) and 735(b) of the Tariff Act of 1930, As Amended, 9886–14

USSR Grain Situation and

USSR Grain Situation and Outlook, 1925–2.3
USSR Outlook and Situation Report, 1524–4.4
Utah's Forest Resources, 1978, 1206–22.6
Utilization and Expenditures for Ambulatory Mental Health Care During 1980, 4146–11.5
Utilization and Ownership of U.S. Cotton Storage Capacity, 1561–1.406
Utilization of Analgesic Drugs in Office-Based Ambulatory Care: National Ambulatory Medical Care Survey, 1980-81, 4146–8.99
Utilization of Medicare Services by Beneficiaries Having Partial Medicare Coverage, 4652–1.404
Utilization of Short-Stay Hospitals, U.S., 1982 Annual Summary, 4147–13.78

VA Can Provide More Employment Assistance to Veterans Who Complete Its Vocational Rehabilitation Program, 26121–78
VA Field Station Summary, Department of Veterans Benefits, 9922–7
VA Loan Guaranty Highlights, 9922–1
Vacancy Rates and Characteristics of Housing in the U.S.: Annual Statistics 1983, Current Housing Reports, Series H-111, 2484–1
Vacant Housing Units in the U.S., Current Housing Reports, 2482–1
Valuation of Creative Financing in Housing, 9412–2.403
Value of Conserving Genetic Resources, 5548–13
Value of Net Change in Farm Inventories, 1974-83, 1544–19.405
Value of New Construction Put in Place, Construction Reports, 2382–4
Value to Visitors of Improving Visibility at Mesa Verde and Great Smoky National Parks, 21368–52
Valves and Pipe Fittings (Industry 3494): 1982 Census of Manufactures. Preliminary Report. Industry Series, 2491–1.306
Valves, Nozzles, and Connectors of Brass from Italy for Use in Fire Protection Systems: Determination of the Commission in Investigation No. 731-TA-165 (Preliminary) Under the Tariff Act of 1930, Together with the Information Obtained in the Investigation, 9886–14.100
Vanadium: Mineral Industry Surveys, 5612–1.26
Vanadium: Minerals Yearbook Preprint, Vol. 1, 1983, 5604–15.68
Variation in Use of Obstetric Technology, 4144–11.1
Variety Stores (Industry 5331): 1982 Census of Retail Trade. Preliminary Report. Industry Series, 2395–1.6
Various Commodities: Quota Information, 8146–1.1
Various Industries in American Samoa, An Economic Report, 6504–6
Vector Autoregressions: A User's Guide, 9381–10.41
VEDS Update: Preliminary Data, 4864–8
Vegetable Oil Mills, N.E.C. (Industry 2076): 1982 Census of Manufactures. Preliminary Report. Industry Series, 2491–1.29
Vegetable Outlook and Situation, 1561–11
Vegetables, 1621–12
Vegetables, Annual Summary, 1621–25

Vegetables, Fresh, Chilled, or Frozen, TSUS Items 135(pt.), 137(pt.), and 138(pt.): Summary of Trade and Tariff Information, 9885–1.69
Vegetables: 1983 Summary, 1621–25.1
Vegetables: 1984 Preliminary Acreage, Yield, Production and Value, 1621–25.2
Vehicular Lighting Equipment (Industry 3647): 1982 Census of Manufactures. Preliminary Report. Industry Series, 2491–1.375
Velocity: A Multivariate Time-Series Approach, 9377–9.13
Velocity and Inflation Expectations: 1922-1983, 9393–8.409
Vending Machines (Coin-Operated), 1983, Current Industrial Report, 2506–12.10
Veneer Log Production and Receipts, North Central Region, 1204–24
Venezuela: An Export Market Profile, 1526–6.5
Vermiculite: Minerals Yearbook Preprint, Vol. 1, 1983, 5604–15.69
Vessel Entrances and Clearances, 1983 Annual Report: Type of Vessel and Tonnage, 2424–7
Vessel Inventory Report, As of January 1, 1984, 7702–2
Veteran Population, Sept. 30, 1983, 9922–3
Veteran Population, Mar. 31, 1984, 9922–3
Veteran Population, Sept. 30, 1984, 9922–3
Veterans Administration Health Care: Planning for Future Years, 26306–6.78
Veterans Administration Summary of Medical Programs, 9922–5
Veterans Benefits Under Current Educational Programs, FY83, 9924–22
Veterans Readjustment Appointments in the Federal Government, Apr.-Sept. 1982, 9842–3
Video and Audio Home Taping, 25528–100
Vietnam Veterans Memorial Fund's Financial Operations Were Properly Accounted for and Reported, 26111–21
View from Congress, 1004–16.1
Violence in School, 6066–20.2
Virgin Islands of the U.S. 1982 Economic Censuses of Outlying Areas, 2593–1
Visitor Fatalities, 1973-83 Inclusive, 5544–6
Visits to Physicians and Other Health Care Practitioners, 4144–11.1
Visual Acuity Impairment Survey Pilot Study, 4478–147
Vital and Health Statistics Series 3: Analytical and Epidemiological Studies, 4147–3
Vital and Health Statistics Series 10: Data from the Health Interview Survey, 4147–10
Vital and Health Statistics Series 11: Data from the Health Examination Survey and the Health and Nutrition Examination Survey, 4147–11
Vital and Health Statistics Series 13: Data on Health Resources Utilization, 4147–13
Vital and Health Statistics Series 14: Data on Health Resources: Manpower and Facilities, 4147–14
Vital and Health Statistics Series 21: Data on Natality, Marriage, and Divorce, 4147–21
Vital Statistics of the U.S., 1979. Vol. I, Natality, 4144–1
Vital Statistics of the U.S., 1979. Vol. II, Mortality, Part A, 4144–2
Vital Statistics of the U.S., 1979. Vol. II, Mortality, Part B, 4144–3
Vital Statistics of the U.S., 1979. Vol. III, Marriage and Divorce, 4144–4

Titles

Vital Statistics of the U.S., 1980. Life Tables: Vol. II, Section 6, 4144–5
Vitreous China Food Utensils (Industry 3262): 1982 Census of Manufactures. Preliminary Report. Industry Series, 2491–1.233
Vitreous Plumbing Fixtures (Industry 3261): 1982 Census of Manufactures. Preliminary Report. Industry Series, 2491–1.232
Vocational Education Program Enrollment, 4864–6
Vocational Education Staff, 4864–5
Volatile Organic Chemicals in the Atmosphere: An Assessment of Available Data, 9198–109
Volatile Organic Compounds in the Ambient Atmosphere of the New Jersey, New York Area, 9198–108
Volume and Value of Sawtimber Stumpage Sold from National Forests: By Selected Species and Region, 1202–1
Voluntary Export Restraints: The Cost of Building Walls, 9377–1.407
Voluntary Foreign Aid Programs, Reports of American Voluntary Agencies Engaged in Overseas Relief and Development Registered with the Agency for International Development, 9914–9
Voting and Registration Highlights from the Current Population Survey: 1964-80, 2546–2.117

Wage Differences Among Metropolitan Areas, 1983, 6785–8
Wage Differences Among Selected Areas, 1983, 6785–13
Wage Statistics of Class I Railroads in the U.S., 1983, 9484–5
Wages in New York City, May 1983, 6926–1.75
Waking Effectiveness of Household Smoke and Fire Detection Devices, 2218–70
Warm Core Cyclones in the Mediterranean, 2152–8.401
Warp Knit Fabric Mills (Industry 2258): 1982 Census of Manufactures. Preliminary Report. Industry Series, 2491–1.57
Washington Public Power Supply System: Financial Meltdown, 21448–29
Washington State Patrol Heavy Truck Inspection Program, 7762–9.407
Wastewater Discharges Are Not Complying with EPA Pollution Control Permits, 26113–113
Watches and Watch Movements from Insular Possessions, 9884–6
Watches, Clocks, and Watchcases (Industry 3873): 1982 Census of Manufactures. Preliminary Report. Industry Series, 2491–1.423
Water Bank Program: Compilation of Status of Agreements, 1802–5
Water Bank Program 1972 Through Sept. 30, 1983, 1804–21
Water Conservation Retrofit Effectiveness, 5188–109.5
Water in America 1983, 5664–12
Water-Level and Water-Quality Changes in Great Salt Lake, Utah, 1847-1983, 5668–70
Water-Related Disease Outbreaks Surveillance: Annual Summary 1983, 4205–35
Water Resources Data for (State), Water Year 1980, 5666–12
Water Resources Data for (State), Water Year 1981, 5666–16

Titles

Water Resources Data for (State), Water Year 1982, 5666–20
Water Resources Data for (State), Water Year 1983, 5666–10
Water Saved by Low-Flush Toilets and Low-Flow Shower Heads, 5188–109.6
Water, Sewer, Pipe Line, Communication and Power Line Construction Contractors (Industry 1623): 1982 Census of Construction Industries. Preliminary Report. Industry Series, 2371–1.8
Water, Sewer, Pipe Line, Communication and Power Line Construction Contractors, Industry 1623. 1982 Census of Construction Industries. Industry Series, 2373–1.8
Water Supply Outlook, And Federal-State-Private Cooperative Snow Surveys, 1266–2
Water Supply Outlook For the Northeastern U.S., 2182–3
Water Supply Outlook for Arizona, 1266–2.2
Water Supply Outlook for Colorado and New Mexico, 1266–2.3
Water Supply Outlook for Idaho, 1266–2.4
Water Supply Outlook for Montana, 1264–7
Water Supply Outlook for Montana, 1266–2.5
Water Supply Outlook for Nevada, 1266–2.6
Water Supply Outlook for Nevada, As of Oct. 1, 1984, 1264–8
Water Supply Outlook for Oregon, 1266–2.7
Water Supply Outlook for Oregon, As of Oct. 1, 1984, 1264–9
Water Supply Outlook for the Western U.S., 1262–1
Water Supply Outlook for Utah, 1266–2.8
Water Supply Outlook for Utah, As of Oct. 1, 1984, 1264–6
Water Supply Outlook for Washington, 1266–2.9
Water Supply Outlook for Wyoming, 1266–2.10
Water Supply Summary, Fall 1984, 1264–4
Water Well Drilling Special Trade Contractors (Industry 1781): 1982 Census of Construction Industries. Preliminary Report. Industry Series, 2371–1.20
Waterborne Commerce of the U.S., 1982, 3754–3
Waterborne Outbreaks in the U.S., 1971-81, 9208–124
Waterproof Outergarments (Industry 2385): 1982 Census of Manufactures. Preliminary Report. Industry Series, 2491–1.99
Ways To Reduce the Cost of Medical Referral Programs in Micronesia and American Samoa, 26123–72
We, the American Women, 2326–1.2
We, the Americans, 2326–1
Weather and Crop Prospects, 1984, 1004–16.1
Weaving and Finishing Mills, Wool (Industry 2231): 1982 Census of Manufactures. Preliminary Report. Industry Series, 2491–1.50
Weaving Mills, Cotton (Industry 2211): 1982 Census of Manufactures. Preliminary Report. Industry Series, 2491–1.48
Weaving Mills, Manmade Fiber and Silk (Industry 2221): 1982 Census of Manufactures. Preliminary Report. Industry Series, 2491–1.49
Weekly Coal Production, 3162–1
Weekly Consolidated Condition Report of Large Commercial Banks and Domestic Subsidiaries, 9365–1.3

Women's, Children's and

Weekly Petroleum Status Report, 3162–32
Weekly Roundup of World Production and Trade, 1922–4
Weekly Roundup of World Production and Trade, Supplement, 1922–8
Weekly Summary of Reserves and Interest Rates, 9365–1.6
Weekly Weather and Crop Bulletin, 2152–2
Weight Frequencies for Striped Marlin Caught Off Southern California, 2162–1.401
Welded Carbon Steel Pipes and Tubes from Brazil and Spain: Determinations of the Commission in Investigations No. 701-TA-120 (Preliminary) and Nos. 731-TA-197 and 198 (Preliminary) Under the Tariff Act of 1930, Together with the Information Obtained in the Investigations, 9886–19.12
Welded Carbon Steel Pipes and Tubes from the Republic of Korea and Taiwan: Determinations of the Commission in Investigations Nos. 731-TA-131, 132, and 138 (Final) Under the Tariff Act of 1930, Together with the Information Obtained in the Investigations, 9886–14.104
Welding Apparatus, Electric (Industry 3623): 1982 Census of Manufactures. Preliminary Report. Industry Series, 2491–1.360
Western Area Power Administration, 1983 Annual Report, 3254–1
Western Area Power Administration's Purchase of a Jet Fixed-Winged Aircraft, 3006–5.8
Western Economic Indicators, Federal Reserve Bank of San Francisco, 9393–1
Western Europe: Outlook and Situation Report, 1524–4.6
Wet Corn Milling (Industry 2046): 1982 Census of Manufactures. Preliminary Report. Industry Series, 2491–1.17
Wetlands of the U.S.: Current Status and Recent Trends, 5508–89
Wetlands: Their Use and Regulation, 26358–102
What Can Central Banks Do About the Value of the Dollar?, 9391–1.413
What Distinguishes Larger and More Efficient Credit Unions?, 9371–1.427
What Is the Rule for Financing Public Debt?, 9379–1.407
Wheat: ASCS Commodity Fact Sheet, 1984, 1806–4.9
Wheat Outlook and Situation, 1561–12
Wheat Price: Past and Future Levels and Volatility, 1502–3.403
When Are Export Subsidies Rational?, 1502–3.401
Where To Write for Vital Records: Births, Deaths, Marriages, and Divorces, 4124–7
White-Collar Pay Determination Under Range-of-Rate Systems, 6722–1.473
Who Gets Rural Jobs?, 1004–16.1
Who Receives Cesareans: Patient and Hospital Characteristics, 4186–6.4
Whole Tree Volume Estimates for the Rocky Mountain States, 1208–200
Wholesale Trade: Annual Sales and Year-End Inventories, Purchases, and Gross Margin Estimates of Merchant Wholesalers, 1983, Current Business Reports, 2413–13
Why Are Some Banks More Profitable than Others?, 9371–10.20
Why Does Velocity Matter?, 9391–1.401
Why Has the Unemployment Rate Declined So Rapidly?, 9373–1.415

WIC Evaluations Provide Some Favorable but No Conclusive Evidence on the Effects Expected for the Special Supplemental Program for Women, Infants, and Children, 26131–10
Wilderness Designation of Bureau of Land Management Lands And Impacts on the Availability of Energy Resources, 3308–68
Wildfire Statistics, 1981, 1204–4
Wildlife and Fish Habitat Management in the Forest Service, FY82, 1204–31
Wildlife and Fish Habitat Management in the Forest Service, FY83, 1204–31
Wildlife and Fisheries Report, 1982, 1204–31
Wildlife and Fisheries Report, 1983, 1204–31
Wildlife and Range Research Needs in Northern Mexico and Southwestern U.S.: Workshop Proceedings, 1208–197
Will Big Deficits Spoil the Recovery?, 9373–3.27
Will Big Deficits Spoil the Recovery?, 21248–79
Windfall Profits Tax Collections and Independent Gasoline Marketers, 21728–51
Wines, Brandy, and Brandy Spirits (Industry 2084): 1982 Census of Manufactures. Preliminary Report. Industry Series, 2491–1.34
Wines: Statistical Release, 8486–1.2
Wire Springs (Industry 3495): 1982 Census of Manufactures. Preliminary Report. Industry Series, 2491–1.307
Wiring Devices and Supplies, 1983, Current Industrial Report, 2506–12.18
Witness Security Program: Prospective Results and Participant Arrest Data, 26119–70
Wives Who Earn More than Their Husbands, 2326–11.9
Women and Minorities in Science and Engineering, 9624–20
Women and Non-U.S. Citizens Responsible for Increase in Production of Science and Engineering Doctorates in 1983, 9626–2.144
Women of the World, 2326–15
Women of the World: Latin America and the Caribbean, 2326–15.1
Women of the World: Sub-Saharan Africa, 2326–15.2
Women Workers: 20 Facts, 6564–1
Women's and Children's Outerwear, 1983, Current Industrial Report, 2506–6.11
Women's and Children's Underwear (Industry 2341): 1982 Census of Manufactures. Preliminary Report. Industry Series, 2491–1.89
Women's and Misses' Blouses (Industry 2331): 1982 Census of Manufactures. Preliminary Report. Industry Series, 2491–1.85
Women's and Misses' Dresses (Industry 2335): 1982 Census of Manufactures. Preliminary Report. Industry Series, 2491–1.86
Women's and Misses' Dresses, Aug. 1982. Industry Wage Survey, 6787–6.200
Women's and Misses' Outerwear, N.E.C. (Industry 2339): 1982 Census of Manufactures. Preliminary Report. Industry Series, 2491–1.88
Women's and Misses' Suits and Coats (Industry 2337): 1982 Census of Manufactures. Preliminary Report. Industry Series, 2491–1.87
Women's, Children's and Infants' Clothing and Accessories (Industry 5137): 1982 Census of Wholesale Trade. Preliminary Report. Industry Series, 2403–1.25

Women's Footwear, Except

Women's Footwear, Except Athletic (Industry 3144): 1982 Census of Manufactures. Preliminary Report. Industry Series, 2491–1.216

Women's, Girls', and Infants' Dresses, Suits, and Skirts, TSUS Items 383(pt.): Summary of Trade and Tariff Information, 9885–3.41

Women's Handbags and Purses (Industry 3171): 1982 Census of Manufactures. Preliminary Report. Industry Series, 2491–1.220

Women's Hosiery, Except Socks (Industry 2251): 1982 Census of Manufactures. Preliminary Report. Industry Series, 2491–1.52

Women's Ready-to-Wear Stores (Industry 5621): 1982 Census of Retail Trade. Preliminary Report. Industry Series, 2395–1.16

Wood Containers, N.E.C. (Industry 2449): 1982 Census of Manufactures. Preliminary Report. Industry Series, 2491–1.122

Wood Household Furniture (Industry 2511): 1982 Census of Manufactures. Preliminary Report. Industry Series, 2491–1.128

Wood Kitchen Cabinets (Industry 2434): 1982 Census of Manufactures. Preliminary Report. Industry Series, 2491–1.116

Wood Office Furniture (Industry 2521): 1982 Census of Manufactures. Preliminary Report. Industry Series, 2491–1.134

Wood Pallets and Skids (Industry 2448): 1982 Census of Manufactures. Preliminary Report. Industry Series, 2491–1.121

Wood Partitions and Fixtures (Industry 2541): 1982 Census of Manufactures. Preliminary Report. Industry Series, 2491–1.137

Wood Poles, Wood Fencing, Wood Railroad Ties, and Similar Articles, TSUS Items 200(pt.): Summary of Trade and Tariff Information, 9885–2.31

Wood Preserving (Industry 2491): 1982 Census of Manufactures. Preliminary Report. Industry Series, 2491–1.123

Wood Product Flows and Market Structure in the Rocky Mountain States, 1208–208

Wood Products: Foreign Agriculture Circular, 1925–36

Wood Products, N.E.C. (Industry 2499): 1982 Census of Manufactures. Preliminary Report. Industry Series, 2491–1.125

Wood Pulp and Other Paper-Making Materials, TSUS Items 250(pt.): Summary of Trade and Tariff Information, 9885–2.32

Wood Shipments to Puerto Rico, 1208–205

Wood Used in U.S. Manufacturing Industries, 1977, 1208–3

Woodworking Machinery (Industry 3553): 1982 Census of Manufactures. Preliminary Report. Industry Series, 2491–1.332

Wool and Mohair, 1623–6

Wool and Related Animal Hair and Waste, and Processed Fibers and Yarns of Wool and Related Animal Hair, TSUS Items 306(pt.) and 307(pt.): Summary of Trade and Tariff Information, 9885–3.45

Wool: ASCS Commodity Fact Sheet, 1984, 1806–4.13

Wool Yarn Mills (Industry 2283): 1982 Census of Manufactures. Preliminary Report. Industry Series, 2491–1.67

Work Experience and Income of Male Veterans and Nonveterans in 1981, 9924–23

Titles

Work Experience in 1983 Reflects the Effects of the Recovery, 6722–1.472

Work Experience of the Population in 1981-82, 6746–1.252

Work Injury Reports, 6846–1

Work Plan, 4744–11

Work-Sharing Approaches: Past and Present, 6722–1.458

Worker Participation and Productivity Change, 6722–1.457

Workers' Compensation: Coverage, Benefits, and Costs, 1982, 4742–1.424

Workers' Compensation Program Experience, 1981, 4742–1.409

Workers' Compensation: Significant Enactments in 1983, 6722–1.415

Workers' Compensation: 1976-80 Benchmark Revisions, 4742–1.414

Workers' Purchasing Power Rises Despite Slowdown in Wage and Salary Gains, 6722–1.430

Working Data for Demand Analysis, 1544–21

Working for Uncle Sam: A Look at Members of the Armed Forces, 6722–1.441

Working Paper Series, Federal Reserve Bank of Atlanta, 9371–10

Working Paper Series on Regional Economic Issues, Federal Reserve Bank of Chicago, 9375–13

Working Papers, Federal Reserve Bank of Cleveland, 9377–9

Workload and Decision Trends: Statistical Highlights, FY80-82, 6006–2.32

Works of Art and Antiques; Articles of Carving or Molding Material; and Waste and Scrap and Nonenumerated Products, TSUS Items 765(pt.), 766(pt.), 792(pt.), 793(pt.), 798(pt.), and 799(pt.): Summary of Trade and Tariff Information, 9885–7.58

Workshop on Antarctic Climate Data, 2156–18.15

Worksite Health Promotion in Colorado, 4102–1.453

World Agricultural Supply and Demand Estimates, 1522–5

World Agriculture Outlook and Situation Report, 1522–3

World Agriculture Regional Outlook and Situation Reports, 1524–4

World Agriculture Regional Supplements: Review and Outlook, 1524–4

World Almond Situation, 1925–34.425

World Canned Deciduous Fruit Situation, 1925–34.414

World Canned Mushroom Situation, 1925–34.423

World Centrifugal Sugar Situation and Outlook, 1925–14.1

World Centrifugal Sugar Situation and Outlook, 1925-14.3

World Cigarette Production and Trade, 1925–16.403

World Cocoa Bean Production Below Consumption Needs, 1925–9.1

World Cotton Outlook, 1004–16.1

World Cotton Situation, 1925–4.2

World Cotton Trade Declines, 1925–4.3

World Cotton Trends and Competition, 1561–1.402

World Crop Production: Foreign Agriculture Circular, 1925–28

World Dairy Situation and Outlook, 1925–10.1

World Dairy Situation and Outlook, 1925–10.2

World Deciduous Fruit and Table Grape Situation, 1925–34.407

World Factbook, 1984, 244–11

World Filbert Situation, 1925–34.426

World Food Aid Needs and Availabilities, 1984, 1524–6

World Food Grain Outlook, 1004–16.1

World Fresh Citrus Fruit Production and Trade Statistics, 1925–35.2

World Grain Situation/Outlook, 1925–2.1

World Health Systems, Lessons for the U.S., 21148–33

World Honey Situation, 1925–14.2

World Indices of Agricultural and Food Production, 1974-83, 1524–5

World Leaf Tobacco Trade in 1983, 1925–16.405

World Meat and Egg Situation and Outlook: Foreign Agriculture Circular, 1925–33

World Military and Social Expenditures, 1983: An Annual Report on World Priorities, 25388–47.1

World Military Expenditures and Arms Transfers, 1972-82, 9824–1

World Nuclear Fuel Cycle Requirements, 1983, 3164–72

World Nuclear Fuel Cycle Requirements, 1984, 3164–72

World Oilseed Situation and U.S. Export Opportunities, 1925–1.1

World Oilseeds Outlook, 1004–16.1

World Outlook for Livestock and Poultry, 1004–16.1

World Outlook for Sugar and Tropical Products, 1004–16.1

World Pineapple Situation, 1925–34.415

World Population: 1983 Recent Demographic Estimates for the Countries and Regions of the World, 2324–4

World Population: 1984 Recent Demographic Estimates for Countries and Regions of the World, 2324–4

World Raisin Situation, 1925–34.434

World Raisin Trade, 1925–34.427

World Tea Supplies Tighten, Prices Rise Sharply, 1925–15.3

World Tobacco Outlook, 1004–16.1

World Tobacco Production, 1925–16.402

World Tobacco Production, 1925–16.407

World Tobacco Situation, 1925–16

World Tobacco Supply and Distribution, 1925–16.404

World Tomato Products Situation, 1925–34.404

World Trade and U.S. Farm Policy, 1528–183

World Trade in Fruits and Vegetables: Projections for an Enlarged European Community, 1528–182

World Tree Nut Update, 1925–34.403

World Walnut Situation, 1925–34.429

Worldwide Deposition of Strontium-90 Through 1982, 3404–12

Worldwide Significant Criminal Acts Involving Civil Aviation, 1983, 7504–31.7

Woven Carpets and Rugs (Industry 2271): 1982 Census of Manufactures. Preliminary Report. Industry Series, 2491–1.62

Wrecking and Demolition Work Special Trade Contractors (Industry 1795): 1982 Census of Construction Industries. Preliminary Report. Industry Series, 2371–1.24

Titles

X-Ray, Electromedical, and Electrotherapeutic Apparatus (Industry 3693): 1982 Census of Manufactures. Preliminary Report. Industry Series, 2491–1.390

X-Ray Screening Protocol for Extremity Injuries, 4186–2.6

Yarn Mills, Except Wool (Industry 2281): 1982 Census of Manufactures. Preliminary Report. Industry Series, 2491–1.65

YCC Program Report, 1982, 5304–12

Year of Enrichment, 1983: Improving the Quality of Life for All Americans, 5304–13

Year of Progress: Preparing for the 21st Century, 5304–13

Yellowstone Grizzly Bear Investigations, Report of the Interagency Study Team, 1982, 5544–4

Your Money Saving Guide, Generic Prescription Drugs You Can Trust, 25528–98

Youth Labor Force Expected To Be Smaller This Summer than Last, 6744–13

Zinc Industry and Smelter Production: Mineral Industry Surveys, 5612–1.27

Zinc: Minerals Yearbook Preprint, Vol. 1, 1983, 5604–15.70

Zirconium and Hafnium: Minerals Yearbook Preprint, Vol. 1, 1983, 5604–15.71

2nd Program Report of the U.S. Travel and Tourism Administration, 1983, 2904–6

2.7 Million Fewer Persons Experienced Unemployment in 1983 than in 1982, 6748–77

10-Year Review of the Supplemental Security Income Program, 4742–1.402

15 Groups Share $825,000 for New Horizons Housing Opportunity Program, 5006–3.32

18th Immunization Conference Proceedings, Atlanta, Ga., May 16-19, 1983, 4204–15

19th Immunization Conference Proceedings, Boston, Mass., May 21-24, 1984, 4204–15

20 Facts on Women Workers, 6564–1

$25.5 Million in Historic Preservation Grant Funds Apportioned, 5544–9

45th Annual Report of Energy Purchased by REA Borrowers, 1244–5

48th Annual Report of the Securities and Exchange Commission for the Fiscal Year Ended Sept. 30, 1982, 9734–2

49th Annual Report, Farm Credit Administration and the Cooperative Farm Credit System, 1982, 9264–2

49th Annual Report of the Securities and Exchange Commission for the Fiscal Year Ended Sept. 30, 1983, 9734–2

70th Annual Report, 1983, Board of Governors of the Federal Reserve System, 9364–1

70th Year of Individual Income and Tax Statistics, 1913-82, 8302–2.401

100 Companies Receiving the Largest Dollar Volume of Prime Contract Awards, FY83, 3544–5

$100 Million Added to Summer Youth Jobs Program; 875,000 Federally Supported Summer Youth Jobs Now Available, 6408–62

500 Contractors Receiving the Largest Dollar Volume of Prime Contract Awards For Research, Development, Test, and Evaluation, FY83, 3544–4

1977 Nationwide Personal Transportation Study, 7556–6

1977 Report of the Visa Office, 7184–1

1978 Annual Housing Survey. Supplementary Report No. 1. Summary of Housing Characteristics for Selected Metropolitan Areas, 2485–8

1978 Survey of A.G.A. Gas Utility Merchandising Companies, 21368–54

1978-83 Increase in U.S. Business Failures, 9381–1.414

1979 Annual Housing Survey. Housing Characteristics for Selected Metropolitan Areas, 2485–6

1979 Pesticide Use on Vegetables in Five Regions, 1588–82

1980 and 1981 Accident Experience of Civil Airmen with Selected Visual Pathology, 7506–10.30

1980 Annual Housing Survey. Housing Characteristics for Selected Metropolitan Areas, 2485–6

1980 Census of Housing. Vol. 2. Metropolitan Housing Characteristics, 2473–1

1980 Census of Housing. Vol. 3. Subject Reports. Chapter 4: Structural Characteristics of the Housing Inventory, 2475–4

1980 Census of Housing. Vol. 4. Characteristics of Housing Units. Components of Inventory Change, 2473–3

1980 Census of Housing. Vol. 4. Characteristics of Housing Units. Components of Inventory Change. Part I: U.S. and Regions, 2473–3.1

1980 Census of Housing. Vol. 4. Characteristics of Housing Units. Components of Inventory Change. Part II: SMSA Groupings with Populations of Less than One Million in 1970, 2473–3.2

1980 Census of Population. Supplementary Reports, 2535–1

1980 Census of Population and Housing. Census Tracts, 2551–2

1980 Census of Population. Vol. 1. Characteristics of the Population. Chapter C: General Social and Economic Characteristics, 2531–3

1980 Census of Population. Vol. 1. Characteristics of the Population. Chapter D: Detailed Population Characteristics, 2531–4

1980 Report to Congress on the Nation's Renewable Resources, 1208–24

1980-81 Annual Survey of Manufactures, 2504–1

1981 Annual Housing Survey. Housing Characteristics for Selected Metropolitan Areas, 2485–6

1981 Annual Housing Survey. Part B, Indicators of Housing and Neighborhood Quality by Financial Characteristics, 2485–2

1981 Annual Housing Survey. Part E, Urban and Rural Housing Characteristics, U.S. and Regions, 2485–7

1981 Annual Report of the Governor of the Virgin Islands To the Secretary of the Interior for the Fiscal Year Ended Sept. 30, 5304–4

1982 Census of Service

1981 National Emissions Data System (NEDS) Fuel Use Report, 9194–14

1981 National Emissions Report: National Emissions Data System of the Aerometric and Emissions Reporting System, 9194–7

1981 National Urban Pesticide Applicator Survey, 1561–16.408

1981 Statistical Yearbook of the Immigration and Naturalization Service, 6264–2.1

1981 Wildfire Statistics, 1204–4

1982 Annual Housing Survey. Housing Characteristics for Selected Metropolitan Areas, 2485–6

1982 Annual Report, Appalachian Regional Commission, 9084–1

1982 Annual Wildlife and Fisheries Report, 1204–31

1982 Carload Waybill Statistics, 7604–6

1982 Census of Agriculture. Preliminary Reports, 2330–1

1982 Census of Agriculture. Vol. 1. Geographic Area Series, State and County Data, 2331–1

1982 Census of Construction Industries. Industry Series, 2373–1

1982 Census of Construction Industries. Preliminary Reports. Industry Series, 2371–1

1982 Census of Governments. Vol. 2. Taxable Property Values and Assessment-Sales Price Ratios, 2453–1

1982 Census of Governments. Vol. 3. Government Employment. No. 1: Employment of Major Local Governments, 2455–1

1982 Census of Governments. Vol. 3. Government Employment. No. 2: Compendium of Public Employment, 2455–2

1982 Census of Governments. Vol. 4. Governmental Finances. No. 1: Finances of Public School Systems, 2457–1

1982 Census of Governments. Vol. 4. Governmental Finances. No. 3: Finances of County Governments, 2457–3

1982 Census of Governments. Vol. 4. Governmental Finances. No. 4: Finances of Municipal and Township Governments, 2457–4

1982 Census of Governments. Vol. 6. Topical Studies. No. 3: State Payments to Local Governments, 2460–3

1982 Census of Manufactures. Preliminary Report. Geographic Area Series, 2491–3

1982 Census of Manufactures. Preliminary Reports. Industry Series, 2491–1

1982 Census of Manufactures. Preliminary Reports. Subject Series, 2491–2

1982 Census of Mineral Industries. Preliminary Reports. Industry Series, 2511–1

1982 Census of Mineral Industries: Preliminary Reports. Summary Series, 2511–2

1982 Census of Retail Trade. Geographic Area Series, 2397–1

1982 Census of Retail Trade. Major Retail Centers in Standard Metropolitan Statistical Areas, 2401–1

1982 Census of Retail Trade. Preliminary Reports. Industry Series, 2395–1

1982 Census of Service Industries. Geographic Area Series, 2391–1

1982 Census of Service Industries. Preliminary Reports. Industry Series, 2390–2

1982 Census of

Titles

1982 Census of Transportation: Truck Inventory and Use Survey, 2573–1

1982 Census of Wholesale Trade. Geographic Area Series, 2405–1

1982 Census of Wholesale Trade. Preliminary Reports. Industry Series, 2403–1

1982 Economic Censuses of Outlying Areas, Virgin Islands of the U.S., 2593–1

1982 Job Market for New Science and Engineering Graduates About the Same as That of Previous Years, 9626–2.137

1982 Population Estimates and 1981 Per Capita Income Estimates for Counties, Incorporated Places, and Selected Minor Civil Divisions. Current Population Reports. Series P-26. Local Population Estimates, 2546–11

1982 Power Program Summary, Tennessee Valley Authority, 9804–23

1982 Roadside Vehicle Inspection Report, 7554–35

1982 Summary: National Hospital Discharge Survey, 4146–8.96

1982 Tuberculosis Statistics: States and Cities, 4204–2

1983, a Year of Enrichment: Improving the Quality of Life for All Americans, 5304–13

1983 Annual Housing Survey. Part A: General Housing Characteristics. Current Housing Reports, 2485–1

1983 Annual Report, Economic Development Administration, 2064–2

1983 Annual Report, Federal Deposit Insurance Corporation, 9294–1

1983 Annual Report of the Chairman of the Development Coordination Committee; Statistical Annex 1, 9914–5

1983 Annual Report on the Administration of the Radiation Control for Health and Safety Act of 1968, Public Law 90-602., 4064–13

1983 Annual Review of the Chief, National Guard Bureau, 3704–3

1983 Annual Tropical Cyclone Report, 3804–8

1983 Annual Wildlife and Fisheries Report, 1204–31

1983 Columbus Physical Improvements Needs Survey, 23848–181

1983 Denver Economic Report, 6974–2

1983 Federally Coordinated Program of Highway Research, Development, and Technology, 7554–14

1983 Grand and Petit Juror Service In U.S. District Courts, 18204–4

1983 Handbook of Agricultural Charts, 1504–3

1983 Handbook on Women Workers, Time of Change, 6568–29

1983 Income and Expenses: Member Banks and Foreign and Domestic Subsidiaries in the Fifth Federal Reserve District, 9389–10

1983 International Energy Annual, 3164–50

1983 Kansas City Economic Report, 6974–1

1983 M1 Seasonal Factor Revisions: An Illustration of Problems That May Arise in Using Seasonally Adjusted Data for Policy Purposes, 9389–1.405

1983 Plant Biology Research Expenditures Totaled $200 Million and Were Concentrated in Land-Grant Institutions, 9626–2.143

1983 Power Program Summary, Tennessee Valley Authority, 9804 23

1983 Promotional Activities Under Federal Milk Orders, 1317–4.406

1983 RCS Evaluation Highlights: Cost-Benefit Evaluation of the Residential Conservation Service Program, 21368–54

1983 Report of the U.S. Advisory Commission on Public Diplomacy, 17594–1

1983 Report on Great Lakes Water Quality, 14644–1

1983 Report on Great Lakes Water Quality, Appendix: Great Lakes Surveillance, 14644–1.1

1983 Report on Great Lakes Water Quality: Appendix on Radioactivity, 14644–1.2

1983 SAR Statistics, U.S. Coast Guard, 7404–2

1983 Service Annual Survey, Current Business Reports, 2413–8

1983 St. Louis Economic Report, 6974–3

1983 Statistical Report, Rural Electric Borrowers, 1244–1

1983 Statistical Report, Rural Telephone Borrowers, 1244–2

1983 Summary: National Hospital Discharge Survey, 4146–8.101

1983 Survey of Nuclear Power Plant Construction Costs, 3164–69

1983 Traffic Fatalities Early Assessment, 7764–14

1983 Trust Territory of the Pacific Islands, 7004–6

1983 Update Report, Baseline Study of the Fish, Wildlife, and Their Habitats: Arctic National Wildlife Refuge Coastal Plain Resource Assessment, 5504–26

1983 U.S. Forest Planting Report, 1204–7

1983 Year-End Review of the New York-Northeastern New Jersey Area Economy, 6924–2

1983-84 Education Directory, Colleges and Universities, 4844–3

1983-84 Miscellaneous Tax Bills, VI: S. 1066, S. 1550, S. 1557, and S. 1666, 25368–132

1984 Annual Report Of the Board of Trustees of the Federal Hospital Insurance Trust Fund, 4704–5

1984 Annual Report Of the Board of Trustees of the Federal Old-Age and Survivors Insurance and Disability Insurance Trust Funds, 4704–4

1984 Annual Report of the Board of Trustees of the Federal Supplementary Medical Insurance Trust Fund, 4704–3

1984 Annual Report of the Chairman of the Development Coordination Committee, 9904–1

1984 Annual Report on Alaska's Mineral Resources, 5664–11

1984 Annual Report on Highway Safety Improvement Programs, Report of the Secretary of Transportation to the U.S. Congress, Pursuant to Section 203, P.L. 93-87 and 23 U.S.C. 151 and 152, 7554–26

1984 Catalog of Cell Lines: NIGMS Human Genetic Mutant Cell Repository, NIA Aging Cell Repository, 4474–23

1984 Catalog of Federal Domestic Assistance, 104–5

1984 Economic Report of the President, 23844–4

1984 Fact Book of U.S. Agriculture, 1004–14

1984 Fall Water Supply Summary, 1264–4

1984 Federal Poverty and Income Guidelines, 4742–1.415

1984 Gas Mileage Guide: California EPA Fuel Economy Estimates, 3304–13

1984 Grand and Petit Juror Service In U.S. District Courts, 18204–4

1984 Guide to Department of Education Programs, 4804–3

1984 Historical Chart Book, Board of Governors of the Federal Reserve System, 9364–2

1984 Joint Economic Report, 23844–2

1984 Mourning Dove Breeding Population Status, 5504–15

1984 National Strategy for Prevention of Drug Abuse and Drug Trafficking, 024–1

1984 National Survey of Compensation Paid Scientists and Engineers Engaged in Research and Development Activities, 3004–1

1984 NIH Almanac, 4434–1

1984 Outlook for Feed Grains, 1004–16.1

1984 Outlook for Food Prices and Consumption, 1004–16.1

1984 Outlook for Tobacco, 1004–16.1

1984 Outlook for Vegetables, 1004–16.1

1984 Status of American Woodcock, 5504–11

1984 Summer Youth Employment Situation Improves, 6744–14

1984 U.S. Industrial Outlook, Prospects for over 300 Industries, 2014–4

1985 Gas Mileage Guide: EPA Fuel Economy Estimates, 3304–11

1990 Objectives for the Nation for Control of Stress and Violent Behavior: Progress Report, 4102–1.437

1990 Objectives for the Nation for Injury Prevention: A Progress Review, 4102–1.409

1995 Labor Force: A Second Look, 6728–29

Index by Agency Report Numbers

Index by Agency Report Numbers

Agency report number practices vary from agency to agency, and even from publication to publication within an agency. Sometimes they are noted on the publication, sometimes they are not. We have attempted to list every agency report number available to us in the form that appears on the publications.

A number of publications abstracted did not have identifiable assigned numbers and are not included in this list.

EXECUTIVE OFFICE OF THE PRESIDENT Office of Management and Budget

Stat. Policy Working Paper No. 9	106–4.3
Stat. Policy Working Paper No. 10	106–4.4

Central Intelligence Agency

CR WF 84-001	244–11
DI 84-10033	244–13.5
DI EEI (yr.-nos.)	242–4
DI IESR (yr.-nos.)	242–5
GI 84-10162	244–13.5
Ref. Aid ALA 84-10052	248–40
Ref. Aid CPAS 84-10002	244–5
Ref. Aid CR 84-10820	244–8
Ref. Aid CR CS (yr.-nos.)	242–7
Ref. Aid DI 84-10022	244–13.1
Ref. Aid DI 84-10024	244–13.2
Ref. Aid DI 84-10025	244–13.3
Ref. Aid DI 84-10127	244–13.4
Ref. Aid EA 84-10070	244–12
Ref. Aid EA CIT (yr.-nos.)	242–6
Ref. Aid GI 84-10111	244–13.1
Ref. Aid GI 84-10130	244–13.2
Ref. Aid GI 84-10131	244–13.3
Ref. Aid GI 84-10136	244–13.4

DEPARTMENT OF AGRICULTURE

ACS Res. Rpt. 21	1128–27
ACS Res. Rpt. 32	1128–24
ACS Res. Rpt. 33	1128–26
ACS Res. Rpt. 34	1128–25
ACS Res. Rpt. 35	1128–28
ACS Res. Rpt. 38	1128–31
ACS Res. Rpt. 40	1128–29
ACS Res. Rpt. 42	1128–32
AER 506	1548–233
AER 508	1588–80
AER 509	1548–232
AER 510	1598–192
AER 511	1568–248
AER 512	1548–239
AER 513	1588–83
AER 514	1544–9
AER 516	1568–247
AFO-25	1544–13
Agric. Hndbk. 619	1504–3
Agric. Info. Bull. 462	1588–76
Agric. Info. Bull. 480	1548–241
Agric. Info. Bull. 481	1548–242
Agric. Info. Bull. 482	1506–5.20
AO-(nos.)	1502–4
APHIS 82-9	1394–16
APHIS 91-43	1394–15
Audit Rpt. No. 3621-4-KC	1008–46
CD-89	1541–8
CO-1-(yr.)	1364–13.4

CO-1-81	1364–13.4
Cooperative Info. Rpt. 1, Section 26	1128–30
Cooperative Info. Rpt. 1, Section 27	1124–1
CoSt 1(date)	1631–5
CoSt 2(4-84)	1614–2
CoSt 3(84)	1631–11
CrPr 2-1(date)	1621–1
CrPr 2-1(84)	1621–2
CrPr 2-2(date)	1621–1
CrPr 2-2(6-84)	1621–23
CrPr 2-2(84)	1621–24
CrPr 2-4(2-84)	1621–22
CUS-1	1584–4
CWS-(nos.)	1561–1
Da 1-1(date)	1627–1
Da 1-2(84)	1627–4
Da 2-1(84)	1627–5
Da 2-6(date)	1627–3
DS-(nos.)	1561–2
ECIFS 2-4	1544–18
ECIFS 2-5	1544–17
ECIFS 3-1	1544–20
ECIFS 3-2	1544–19
ECIFS 3-3	1544–16
ERS Staff Rpt. AGES820421	1588–79
ERS Staff Rpt. AGES820517	1588–78
ERS Staff Rpt. AGES830414	1528–175
ERS Staff Rpt. AGES830502	1528–169
ERS Staff Rpt. AGES830519	1548–230
ERS Staff Rpt. AGES830621	1548–231
ERS Staff Rpt. AGES830701	1584–3
ERS Staff Rpt. AGES830720	1528–171
ERS Staff Rpt. AGES830726	1528–170
ERS Staff Rpt. AGES830810	1528–172
ERS Staff Rpt. AGES830824	1588–77
ERS Staff Rpt. AGES830909	1548–238
ERS Staff Rpt. AGES830912	1548–235
ERS Staff Rpt. AGES830916	1528–185
ERS Staff Rpt. AGES830920	1588–82
ERS Staff Rpt. AGES831007	1548–234
ERS Staff Rpt. AGES831028	1588–84
ERS Staff Rpt. AGES831202	1548–237

ERS Staff Rpt. AGES831207	1548–240
ERS Staff Rpt. AGES831216	1588–81
ERS Staff Rpt. AGES840110	1568–246
ERS Staff Rpt. AGES840111	1528–181
ERS Staff Rpt. AGES840112	1548–243
ERS Staff Rpt. AGES840121	1568–245
ERS Staff Rpt. AGES840217	1544–21
ERS Staff Rpt. AGES840319	1528–184
ERS Staff Rpt. AGES840328	1584–2
ERS Staff Rpt. AGES840502	1584–3
ERS Staff Rpt. AGES840521	1528–183
ERS Tech. Bull. 1690	1548–236
FAER 192	1528–176
FAER 193	1528–174
FAER 194	1528–168
FAER 195	1528–178
FAER 196	1526–6.3
FAER 197	1526–6.4
FAER 198	1528–180
FAER 199	1528–177
FAER 201	1526–6.5
FAER 202	1528–182
FAER 205	1526–6.6
FC (nos.)	1925–4.2
FC 1-84	1925–4.3
FCB 1-84	1925–9.1
FCB 2-84	1925–9.2
FCOF (nos.)	1925–5
FD 1-84	1925–10.1
FD 2-84	1925–10.2
FDL-MT (nos.)	1925–31
FDLP (nos.)	1925–32
FdS-(nos.)	1561–4
FFVS (nos.)	1925–13
FG (nos.)	1925–2
FG 2-84	1925–2.5
FG 4-84	1925–2.6
FG 16-84	1925–2.7
FHORT (nos.)	1925–34
FL&P 1-84	1925–33
FL&P 2-84	1925–33
FMOS (nos.)	1317–4
FOP (nos.)	1925–1
FOP Supp. 6-84	1925–1.2
FrNt 1-3(7-84)	1621–18.3
FrNt 1-3(84)	1621–18.1
FrNt 2-4(6-84)	1621–18.2
FrNt 2-4(10-84)	1621–18.6
FrNt 3-1(84)	1621–18.5
FS 1-84	1925–14.1
FS 2-84	1925–14.2

Report Numbers

FS 3-84	1925-14.3
FS 4-84 Supp	1925-14.4
FS-383	1204-2
FS-386	1208-24.4
FSIS-14	1374-3
FT (nos.)	1925-16
FTEA 1-84	1925-15.1
FTEA 2-84	1925-15.2
FTEA 3-84	1925-15.3
FVAS-1(1983)	1311-4.1
FVAS-2(1983)	1311-4.2
FVAS-3(1983)	1311-4.3
FVAS-4(1983)	1311-4.4
Gen. Tech. Rpt. NC-90	1208-198
Gen. Tech. Rpt. PNW-148	1208-194
Gen. Tech. Rpt. WO-35	1204-14
Gen. Tech. Rpt. WO-36	1208-197
GrLg 11-1(date)	1621-4
GrLg 11-1(9-84)	1621-5
GrLg 11-2-1(3-84)	1621-6
GrLg 11-2-1(9-84)	1621-6
GrLg 11-3(date)	1621-7
IOS-(nos.)	1561-16
La 1(8-84)	1631-1
LPS-(nos.)	1561-7
LvGn 1(1-84)	1623-4
LvGn 1(1-84)	1623-1.1
LvGn 1(7-84)	1623-1.2
Misc. Pub. 1063	1004-14
Misc. Pub. 1442	1204-29
Mktg. Res. Rpt. 1141	1308-18
MtAn 1-1(84)	1623-8
MtAn 1-2(date)	1623-9
MtAn 1-2(84)	1623-10
MtAn 2-1(date)	1623-2
MtAn 4(date)	1623-3
MtAn 5-3(3-84)	1623-6
MtAn 6(7-84)	1631-7
NFCS 1977-78, Rpt. No.	
I-1	1356-4.1
NFCS 1977-78, Rpt. No.	
I-2	1356-4.2
NFR-(nos.)	1541-7
OCS-(nos.)	1561-3
P&SA 84-1	1384-1
Policy Res. Note 17	1542-6
Policy Res. Note 18	1542-6
Pot 1-2(date)	1621-10
Pot 6(9-84)	1621-11
Pou 1-1(date)	1625-1
Pou 2-1(date)	1625-3
Pou 2-3(84)	1625-5
Pou 2-4(84)	1625-7
Pou 2-5(date)	1625-2
Pou 2-7(84)	1625-8
Pou 3(date)	1625-10
Pou 3(1-84)	1625-6
PR (nos.)	1922-7
Pr 1(date)	1629-1
Pr 1-3(84)	1629-5
R-3 84-13	1206-11.2
REA Bull. 1-1	1244-1
REA Bull. 300-4	1244-2
REA Elec. Prog. Stat.	
Bull. 330	1244-7
REA Tel. Prog. Stat. Bull.	
T-212	1244-8
Res. Note NE-318	1208-207
Res. Note SE-322	1204-22
Res. Paper INT-317	1208-202
Res. Paper NC-243	1208-193
Res. Paper NC-244	1206-24.9
Res. Paper NE-527	1208-191
Res. Paper PNW-306	1208-196
Res. Paper SE-244	1206-32.1
Res. Paper SE-245	1208-199
Res. Paper SO-197	1208-206
Res. Paper SO-201	1208-205
Resource Bull. FPL-12	1208-3
Resource Bull. INT-28	1206-25.6
Resource Bull. INT-29	1208-200
Resource Bull. INT-30	1206-22.6
Resource Bull. INT-32	1206-23.7
Resource Bull. INT-33	1208-201
Resource Bull. NC-67	1206-31.5
Resource Bull. NC-68	1208-192
Resource Bull. NC-71	1206-10.6
Resource Bull. NC-72	1206-31.6
Resource Bull. NC-79	1204-19
Resource Bull. NE-78	1206-7.10
Resource Bull. NE-80	1206-16.7
Resource Bull. NE-81	1206-12.7
Resource Bull. PNW-100	1206-9.9
Resource Bull. PNW-101	1206-9.10
Resource Bull. PNW-102	1206-9.11
Resource Bull. PNW-103	1206-9.12
Resource Bull. PNW-104	1206-28.3
Resource Bull. PNW-105	1206-9.15
Resource Bull. PNW-107	1206-9.14
Resource Bull. PNW-109	1206-9.13
Resource Bull. RM-6	1208-208
Resource Bull. SE-71	1208-203
Resource Bull. SE-72	1206-4.5
Resource Bull. SE-73	1206-26.7
Resource Bull. SE-74	1206-4.6
Resource Bull. WO-2	1208-195
RS-43	1561-8
RS-44	1561-8
RS-84-1	1524-4.1
RS-84-2	1524-4.2
RS-84-3	1524-4.3
RS-84-4	1524-4.4
RS-84-5	1524-4.5
RS-84-6	1524-4.6
RS-84-7	1524-4.7
RS-84-8	1524-4.8
RS-84-9	1524-4.9
RS-84-10	1524-4.10
RS-84-11	1524-4.11
Rural Dev. Res. Rpt. 38	1598-190
Rural Dev. Res. Rpt. 39	1598-191
Rural Dev. Res. Rpt. 40	1598-144
Rural Dev. Res. Rpt. 41	1598-194
Rural Dev. Res. Rpt. 42	1598-193
SB-2(yr.)	1364-13.1
SB-2-81	1364-13.1
SBSN-2(yr.)	1364-13.2
SBSN-2-81	1364-13.2
SDS 1-84	1922-6
SDS 2-83	1924-6
SM-2(yr.)	1364-13.3
SM-2-81	1364-13.3
SpCr 1(8-84)	1621-18.4
SpCr 2(3-84)	1621-8
SpCr 2(9-84)	1621-8
SpCr 4(date)	1621-28
SpCr 7(11-84)	1631-13
SpCr 8(date)	1631-14
Specialty Sugar Import	
Notice (nos.-yr.)	1922-9
SpSy (date)	1631-1
SpSy 5(7-84)	1614-3
SSR-(v.nos. & nos.)	1561-14
Stat. Bull. 703	1528-173
Stat. Bull. 704	1651-3
Stat. Bull. 705	1528-179
Stat. Bull. 706	1544-2
Stat. Bull. 707	1641-17
Stat. Bull. 708	1641-7
Stat. Bull. 709	1641-14
Stat. Bull. 710	1524-5
Stat. Bull. 711	1317-3
Stat. Bull. 712	1641-4
Stat. Bull. 713	1544-4
Stat. Bull. 715	1564-6
Stat. Bull. 716	1641-10
Sugar Import Notice	
(nos.-yr.)	1922-9
TFS-(nos.)	1561-6
TOB-(nos.)	1319-3
TOB-FDA-27	1319-5.3
TOB-FL-27	1319-5.1
TOB-LA-28	1319-5.2
TS-(nos.)	1561-10
TVS-(nos.)	1561-11
Vg 1-1(12-84)	1621-25.2
Vg 1-2(6-84)	1621-25.1
Vg 2-1(date)	1621-12
Vg 2-1-1(date)	1621-14
Vg 2-1-2(8-84)	1631-9
Vg 3-1(date)	1621-12
WAS-(nos.)	1522-3
WASDE-(nos.)	1522-5
WCP (nos.)	1925-28
WIC-1-82	1364-12.1
WIC-2-82	1364-12.2
WP(nos.)	1925-36
WR-(nos.)	1922-4
WR Supp. (nos.-yr.)	1922-8
WS-(nos.)	1561-12
WS-(nos.-yr.)	1311-3

DEPARTMENT OF COMMERCE

BEA-SP84-040	2706-5.31
BEA-SP84-041	2706-5.30
Census A30-83	2344-1
Census A10-(nos.)	2342-1
Census A20-(nos.)	2342-2
Census AC82-A-00-000(P)	2330-1.57
Census AC82-A-1	2331-1.1
Census AC82-A-1(P)	2330-1.1
Census AC82-A-2	2331-1.2
Census AC82-A-2(P)	2330-1.2
Census AC82-A-3	2331-1.3
Census AC82-A-4	2331-1.4
Census AC82-A-04(P)	2330-1.4
Census AC82-A-5	2331-1.5
Census AC82-A-5(P)	2330-1.5
Census AC82-A-6	2331-1.6
Census AC82-A-06(P)	2330-1.6
Census AC82-A-7	2331-1.7
Census AC82-A-8	2331-1.8
Census AC82-A-08(P)	2330-1.8
Census AC82-A-9	2331-1.9
Census AC82-A-09(P)	2330-1.9
Census AC82-A-10	2331-1.10
Census AC82-A-11	2331-1.11
Census AC82-A-12	2331-1.12
Census AC82-A-12(P)	2330-1.12
Census AC82-A-13	2331-1.13
Census AC82-A-13(P)	2330-1.13
Census AC82-A-14	2331-1.14
Census AC82-A-15	2331-1.15
Census AC82-A-15(P)	2330-1.15
Census AC82-A-16	2331-1.16
Census AC82-A-16(P)	2330-1.16
Census AC82-A-17	2331-1.17
Census AC82-A-18	2331-1.18
Census AC82-A-19	2331-1.19
Census AC82-A-19(P)	2330-1.19
Census AC82-A-20	2331-1.20
Census AC82-A-20(P)	2330-1.20
Census AC82-A-21	2331-1.21
Census AC82-A-21(P)	2330-1.21
Census AC82-A-22	2331-1.22
Census AC82-A-22(P)	2330-1.22
Census AC82-A-23(P)	2330-1.23

Report Numbers

Entry	Number
Census AC82-A-24	2331-1.24
Census AC82-A-25	2331-1.25
Census AC82-A-26	2331-1.26
Census AC82-A-26(P)	2330-1.26
Census AC82-A-27	2331-1.27
Census AC82-A-27(P)	2330-1.27
Census AC82-A-28	2331-1.28
Census AC82-A-29	2331-1.29
Census AC82-A-29(P)	2330-1.29
Census AC82-A-30	2331-1.30
Census AC82-A-30(P)	2330-1.30
Census AC82-A-31	2331-1.31
Census AC82-A-31(P)	2330-1.31
Census AC82-A-32	2331-1.32
Census AC82-A-32(P)	2330-1.32
Census AC82-A-33	2331-1.33
Census AC82-A-33(P)	2330-1.33
Census AC82-A-34	2331-1.34
Census AC82-A-35(P)	2330-1.35
Census AC82-A-36	2331-1.36
Census AC82-A-36(P)	2330-1.36
Census AC82-A-37	2331-1.37
Census AC82-A-37(P)	2330-1.37
Census AC82-A-38	2331-1.38
Census AC82-A-38(P)	2330-1.38
Census AC82-A-39(P)	2330-1.39
Census AC82-A-40	2331-1.40
Census AC82-A-40(P)	2330-1.40
Census AC82-A-41	2331-1.41
Census AC82-A-41(P)	2330-1.41
Census AC82-A-42	2331-1.42
Census AC82-A-43	2331-1.43
Census AC82-A-44	2331-1.44
Census AC82-A-45	2331-1.45
Census AC82-A-45(P)	2330-1.45
Census AC82-A-46	2331-1.46
Census AC82-A-46(P)	2330-1.46
Census AC82-A-47	2331-1.47
Census AC82-A-47(P)	2330-1.47
Census AC82-A-48	2331-1.48
Census AC82-A-49	2331-1.49
Census AC82-A-49(P)	2330-1.49
Census AC82-A-50	2331-1.50
Census AC82-A-50(P)	2330-1.50
Census AC82-A-51	2331-1.51
Census AC82-A-51(P)	2330-1.51
Census AC82-A-52	2331-1.52
Census AC82-A-53	2331-1.53
Census AC82-A-53(P)	2330-1.53
Census AC82-A-54	2331-1.54
Census AC82-A-56(P)	2330-1.56
Census BR-(yr.-nos.)	2413-3
Census BR-13-82S	2413-3
Census BR-83-13	2413-5
Census BS-83-01	2413-8
Census BW-(yr.-nos.)	2413-7
Census BW-13-82S	2413-7
Census BW-83-13	2413-13
Census C20-(yr.-nos.)	2382-1
Census C21-(yr.-nos.)	2382-9
Census C22-(yr.-nos.)	2382-2
Census C25-(yr.-nos.)	2382-3
Census C25-83-13	2384-1
Census C27-(yr.-nos.)	2382-8
Census C30-(yr.-nos.)	2382-4
Census C40-(yr.-nos.)	2382-5
Census C40-83-13	2384-2
Census C50-(yr.-Q nos.)	2382-7
Census C50-83-A	2384-4
Census CB84-72	2328-46
Census CBP-81-53	2326-8.53
Census CBP-82-1	2326-6.1
Census CBP-82-2	2326-6.2
Census CBP-82-3	2326-6.3
Census CBP-82-4	2326-6.4
Census CBP-82-6	2326-6.6
Census CBP-82-7	2326-6.7
Census CBP-82-8	2326-6.8
Census CBP-82-9	2326-6.9
Census CBP-82-10	2326-6.10
Census CBP-82-11	2326-6.11
Census CBP-82-12	2326-6.12
Census CBP-82-13	2326-6.13
Census CBP-82-14	2326-6.14
Census CBP-82-15	2326-6.15
Census CBP-82-16	2326-6.16
Census CBP-82-17	2326-6.17
Census CBP-82-18	2326-6.18
Census CBP-82-19	2326-6.19
Census CBP-82-20	2326-6.20
Census CBP-82-21	2326-6.21
Census CBP-82-22	2326-6.22
Census CBP-82-23	2326-6.23
Census CBP-82-24	2326-6.24
Census CBP-82-25	2326-6.25
Census CBP-82-26	2326-6.26
Census CBP-82-27	2326-6.27
Census CBP-82-28	2326-6.28
Census CBP-82-29	2326-6.29
Census CBP-82-30	2326-6.30
Census CBP-82-31	2326-6.31
Census CBP-82-32	2326-6.32
Census CBP-82-33	2326-6.33
Census CBP-82-34	2326-6.34
Census CBP-82-35	2326-6.35
Census CBP-82-36	2326-6.36
Census CBP-82-37	2326-6.37
Census CBP-82-38	2326-6.38
Census CBP-82-39	2326-6.39
Census CBP-82-40	2326-6.40
Census CBP-82-41	2326-6.41
Census CBP-82-42	2326-6.42
Census CBP-82-43	2326-6.43
Census CBP-82-44	2326-6.44
Census CBP-82-45	2326-6.45
Census CBP-82-46	2326-6.46
Census CBP-82-47	2326-6.47
Census CBP-82-48	2326-6.48
Census CBP-82-49	2326-6.49
Census CBP-82-50	2326-6.50
Census CBP-82-51	2326-6.51
Census CBP-82-52	2326-6.52
Census CBP-82-53	2326-6.53
Census CC82-I-1	2373-1.1
Census CC82-I-1(P)	2371-1.1
Census CC82-I-2	2373-1.2
Census CC82-I-2(P)	2371-1.2
Census CC82-I-3	2373-1.3
Census CC82-I-3(P)	2371-1.3
Census CC82-I-4	2373-1.4
Census CC82-I-4(P)	2371-1.4
Census CC82-I-5	2373-1.5
Census CC82-I-6	2373-1.6
Census CC82-I-6(P)	2371-1.6
Census CC82-I-7	2373-1.7
Census CC82-I-7(P)	2371-1.7
Census CC82-I-8	2373-1.8
Census CC82-I-8(P)	2371-1.8
Census CC82-I-9(P)	2371-1.9
Census CC82-I-10(P)	2371-1.10
Census CC82-I-11(P)	2371-1.11
Census CC82-I-12	2373-1.12
Census CC82-I-12(P)	2371-1.12
Census CC82-I-13(P)	2371-1.13
Census CC82-I-14(P)	2371-1.14
Census CC82-I-16(P)	2371-1.16
Census CC82-I-17(P)	2371-1.17
Census CC82-I-19	2373-1.19
Census CC82-I-19(P)	2371-1.19
Census CC82-I-20(P)	2371-1.20
Census CC82-I-21(P)	2371-1.21
Census CC82-I-22	2373-1.22
Census CC82-I-22(P)	2371-1.22
Census CC82-I-23(P)	2371-1.23
Census CC82-I-24(P)	2371-1.24
Census CC82-I-25(P)	2371-1.25
Census CC82-I-26(P)	2371-1.26
Census CDS-80-9	2326-11.9
Census CFF No. 5(Rev)	2326-7.62
Census CFF No. 13(Rev.)	2326-7.61
Census Economic Res.	
Rpt. ER-5	2626-7.5
Census ES2-18	2424-3
Census FER 21	2326-9.7
Census FOF No. 6	2324-6
Census FT130-(yr.-nos.)	2422-1
Census FT135-(date)	2422-2
Census FT150/1983	2424-2.3
Census FT155/1983, Vol.	
1	2424-2.1
Census FT155/1983, Vol.	
2	2424-2.2
Census FT210/1983	2424-6.2
Census FT246/1983	2424-4
Census FT410-(date)	2422-3
Census FT446/1983	2424-9
Census FT450/1983	2424-5.1
Census FT455/1983, Vol.	
1	2424-5.2
Census FT455/1983, Vol.	
2	2424-5.2
Census FT610/1983	2424-6.1
Census FT800-(date)	2422-4
Census FT810-(yr.-nos.)	2422-5
Census FT900-(yr.-nos.)	2422-6
Census FT975-83	2424-7
Census FT985-(yr.-nos.)	2422-7
Census FT986-(yr.-nos.)	2422-8
Census FT990-(date)	2422-9
Census GC82(2)	2453-1
Census GC82(3)-2	2455-2
Census GC82(4)-1	2457-1
Census GC82(4)-3	2457-3
Census GC82(4)-4	2457-4
Census GC82(6)-3	2460-3
Census GE83, No. 2	2466-1.1
Census GE83, No. 3	2466-1.3
Census GE83, No. 4	2466-1.2
Census GF82, No. 4	2466-2.1
Census GF82, No. 8	2466-2.2
Census GF83, No. 1	2466-2.3
Census GF83, No. 2	2466-2.4
Census GF83, No. 3	2466-2.5
Census GF83, No. 4	2466-2.7
Census GF83, No. 5	2466-2.6
Census GF83, No. 8	2466-2.8
Census GR (yr.-nos.)	2462-2
Census GT (yr.-nos.)	2462-3
Census H-111-(yr.-nos.)	2482-1
Census H-111-83-5	2484-1
Census H-121, No. 18	2486-1.6
Census H-130-(yr.-nos.)	2482-2
Census H-130-83-5	2484-2
Census H-131-83-A	2484-3
Census H-150-81, pt.B	2485-2
Census H-150-81, pt.E	2485-7
Census H-150-83, pt.A	2485-1
Census H-170-79-48	2485-6.1
Census H-170-80-1	2485-6.2
Census H-170-80-7	2485-6.3
Census H-170-80-8	2485-6.4
Census H-170-80-14	2485-6.5
Census H-170-80-15	2485-6.6
Census H-170-80-41	2485-6.7
Census H-170-80-43	2485-6.8
Census H-170-80-47	2485-6.9
Census H-170-80-50	2485-6.10
Census H-170-80-52	2485-6.11
Census H-170-80-53	2485-6.12
Census H-170-80-54	2485-6.13
Census H-170-80-56	2485-6.14

Report Numbers

Census H-170-80-58	2485-6.15	Census HC80-2-61	2473-1.61	Census HC80-2-141	2473-1.141
Census H-170-80-59	2485-6.16	Census HC80-2-62	2473-1.62	Census HC80-2-142	2473-1.142
Census H-170-81-2	2485-6.19	Census HC80-2-63	2473-1.63	Census HC80-2-143	2473-1.143
Census H-170-81-3	2485-6.30	Census HC80-2-64	2473-1.64	Census HC80-2-144	2473-1.144
Census H-170-81-4	2485-6.21	Census HC80-2-65	2473-1.65	Census HC80-2-145	2473-1.145
Census H-170-81-5	2485-6.17	Census HC80-2-66	2473-1.66	Census HC80-2-146	2473-1.146
Census H-170-81-6	2485-6.22	Census HC80-2-67	2473-1.67	Census HC80-2-147	2473-1.147
Census H-170-81-9	2485-6.29	Census HC80-2-68	2473-1.68	Census HC80-2-148	2473-1.148
Census H-170-81-10	2485-6.31	Census HC80-2-69	2473-1.69	Census HC80-2-149	2473-1.149
Census H-170-81-11	2485-6.23	Census HC80-2-70	2473-1.70	Census HC80-2-150	2473-1.150
Census H-170-81-12	2485-6.24	Census HC80-2-71	2473-1.71	Census HC80-2-151	2473-1.151
Census H-170-81-13	2485-6.25	Census HC80-2-72	2473-1.72	Census HC80-2-152	2473-1.152
Census H-170-81-16	2485-6.26	Census HC80-2-73	2473-1.73	Census HC80-2-153	2473-1.153
Census H-170-81-17	2485-6.27	Census HC80-2-75	2473-1.75	Census HC80-2-154	2473-1.154
Census H-170-81-18	2485-6.18	Census HC80-2-76	2473-1.76	Census HC80-2-155	2473-1.155
Census H-170-81-19	2485-6.28	Census HC80-2-77	2473-1.77	Census HC80-2-156	2473-1.156
Census H-170-81-20	2485-6.20	Census HC80-2-78	2473-1.78	Census HC80-2-157	2473-1.157
Census H-170-82-21	2485-6.32	Census HC80-2-79	2473-1.79	Census HC80-2-158	2473-1.158
Census H-170-82-23	2485-6.35	Census HC80-2-80	2473-1.80	Census HC80-2-159	2473-1.159
Census H-170-82-25	2485-6.36	Census HC80-2-81	2473-1.81	Census HC80-2-160	2473-1.160
Census H-170-82-27	2485-6.37	Census HC80-2-82	2473-1.82	Census HC80-2-161	2473-1.161
Census H-170-82-30	2485-6.43	Census HC80-2-83	2473-1.83	Census HC80-2-162	2473-1.162
Census H-170-82-32	2485-6.38	Census HC80-2-84	2473-1.84	Census HC80-2-163	2473-1.163
Census H-170-82-33	2485-6.33	Census HC80-2-85	2473-1.85	Census HC80-2-164	2473-1.164
Census H-170-82-35	2485-6.39	Census HC80-2-86	2473-1.86	Census HC80-2-165	2473-1.165
Census H-170-82-36	2485-6.40	Census HC80-2-87	2473-1.87	Census HC80-2-166	2473-1.166
Census H-170-82-37	2485-6.41	Census HC80-2-88	2473-1.88	Census HC80-2-167	2473-1.167
Census H-170-82-38	2485-6.42	Census HC80-2-89	2473-1.89	Census HC80-2-168	2473-1.168
Census H-170-82-39	2485-6.34	Census HC80-2-90	2473-1.90	Census HC80-2-169	2473-1.169
Census H-171-78, No. 1	2485-8	Census HC80-2-91	2473-1.91	Census HC80-2-170	2473-1.170
Census HC80-2-2	2473-1.2	Census HC80-2-92	2473-1.92	Census HC80-2-171	2473-1.171
Census HC80-2-3	2473-1.3	Census HC80-2-93	2473-1.93	Census HC80-2-172	2473-1.172
Census HC80-2-5	2473-1.5	Census HC80-2-94	2473-1.94	Census HC80-2-173	2473-1.173
Census HC80-2-7	2473-1.7	Census HC80-2-95	2473-1.95	Census HC80-2-174	2473-1.174
Census HC80-2-8	2473-1.8	Census HC80-2-96	2473-1.96	Census HC80-2-175	2473-1.175
Census HC80-2-9	2473-1.9	Census HC80-2-97	2473-1.97	Census HC80-2-176	2473-1.176
Census HC80-2-11	2473-1.11	Census HC80-2-98	2473-1.98	Census HC80-2-177	2473-1.177
Census HC80-2-12	2473-1.12	Census HC80-2-99	2473-1.99	Census HC80-2-178	2473-1.178
Census HC80-2-13	2473-1.13	Census HC80-2-100	2473-1.100	Census HC80-2-179	2473-1.179
Census HC80-2-14	2473-1.14	Census HC80-2-101	2473-1.101	Census HC80-2-180	2473-1.180
Census HC80-2-15	2473-1.15	Census HC80-2-102	2473-1.102	Census HC80-2-181	2473-1.181
Census HC80-2-16	2473-1.16	Census HC80-2-103	2473-1.103	Census HC80-2-183	2473-1.183
Census HC80-2-17	2473-1.17	Census HC80-2-104	2473-1.104	Census HC80-2-184	2473-1.184
Census HC80-2-18	2473-1.18	Census HC80-2-105	2473-1.105	Census HC80-2-185	2473-1.185
Census HC80-2-19	2473-1.19	Census HC80-2-106	2473-1.106	Census HC80-2-186	2473-1.186
Census HC80-2-20	2473-1.20	Census HC80-2-107	2473-1.107	Census HC80-2-187	2473-1.187
Census HC80-2-21	2473-1.21	Census HC80-2-108	2473-1.108	Census HC80-2-188	2473-1.188
Census HC80-2-22	2473-1.22	Census HC80-2-110	2473-1.110	Census HC80-2-189	2473-1.189
Census HC80-2-23	2473-1.23	Census HC80-2-111	2473-1.111	Census HC80-2-190	2473-1.190
Census HC80-2-25	2473-1.25	Census HC80-2-112	2473-1.112	Census HC80-2-191	2473-1.191
Census HC80-2-26	2473-1.26	Census HC80-2-113	2473-1.113	Census HC80-2-192	2473-1.192
Census HC80-2-27	2473-1.27	Census HC80-2-114	2473-1.114	Census HC80-2-193	2473-1.193
Census HC80-2-28	2473-1.28	Census HC80-2-115	2473-1.115	Census HC80-2-194	2473-1.194
Census HC80-2-29	2473-1.29	Census HC80-2-116	2473-1.116	Census HC80-2-195	2473-1.195
Census HC80-2-30	2473-1.30	Census HC80-2-117	2473-1.117	Census HC80-2-196	2473-1.196
Census HC80-2-31	2473-1.31	Census HC80-2-118	2473-1.118	Census HC80-2-197	2473-1.197
Census HC80-2-32	2473-1.32	Census HC80-2-120	2473-1.120	Census HC80-2-198	2473-1.198
Census HC80-2-33	2473-1.33	Census HC80-2-121	2473-1.121	Census HC80-2-199	2473-1.199
Census HC80-2-34	2473-1.34	Census HC80-2-122	2473-1.122	Census HC80-2-200	2473-1.200
Census HC80-2-35	2473-1.35	Census HC80-2-123	2473-1.123	Census HC80-2-201	2473-1.201
Census HC80-2-36	2473-1.36	Census HC80-2-124	2473-1.124	Census HC80-2-202	2473-1.202
Census HC80-2-38	2473-1.38	Census HC80-2-125	2473-1.125	Census HC80-2-203	2473-1.203
Census HC80-2-39	2473-1.39	Census HC80-2-126	2473-1.126	Census HC80-2-204	2473-1.204
Census HC80-2-40	2473-1.40	Census HC80-2-127	2473-1.127	Census HC80-2-205	2473-1.205
Census HC80-2-41	2473-1.41	Census HC80-2-128	2473-1.128	Census HC80-2-206	2473-1.206
Census HC80-2-42	2473-1.42	Census HC80-2-129	2473-1.129	Census HC80-2-207	2473-1.207
Census HC80-2-44	2473-1.44	Census HC80-2-130	2473-1.130	Census HC80-2-208	2473-1.208
Census HC80-2-45	2473-1.45	Census HC80-2-131	2473-1.131	Census HC80-2-210	2473-1.210
Census HC80-2-46	2473-1.46	Census HC80-2-132	2473-1.132	Census HC80-2-211	2473-1.211
Census HC80-2-47	2473-1.47	Census HC80-2-133	2473-1.133	Census HC80-2-212	2473-1.212
Census HC80-2-48	2473-1.48	Census HC80-2-134	2473-1.134	Census HC80-2-213	2473-1.213
Census HC80-2-50	2473-1.50	Census HC80-2-135	2473-1.135	Census HC80-2-214	2473-1.214
Census HC80-2-51	2473-1.51	Census HC80-2-136	2473-1.136	Census HC80-2-215	2473-1.215
Census HC80-2-52	2473-1.52	Census HC80-2-137	2473-1.137	Census HC80-2-216	2473-1.216
Census HC80-2-58	2473-1.58	Census HC80-2-138	2473-1.138	Census HC80-2-217	2473-1.217
Census HC80-2-59	2473-1.59	Census HC80-2-139	2473-1.139	Census HC80-2-218	2473-1.218
Census HC80-2-60	2473-1.60	Census HC80-2-140	2473-1.140	Census HC80-2-219	2473-1.219

Report Numbers

Census HC80-2-220	2473-1.220	Census HC80-2-301	2473-1.301	Census HC80-4-I	2473-3.1
Census HC80-2-221	2473-1.221	Census HC80-2-302	2473-1.302	Census HC80-4-IIB	2473-3.2
Census HC80-2-222	2473-1.222	Census HC80-2-303	2473-1.303	Census Intl. Res. Doc. 12	2546-10.12
Census HC80-2-223	2473-1.223	Census HC80-2-304	2473-1.304	Census Intl. Res. Doc. 13	2546-10.13
Census HC80-2-224	2473-1.224	Census HC80-2-305	2473-1.305	Census ISP-RD-12	2546-10.12
Census HC80-2-225	2473-1.225	Census HC80-2-306	2473-1.306	Census ISP-RD-13	2546-10.13
Census HC80-2-226	2473-1.226	Census HC80-2-307	2473-1.307	Census ISP-WP-83	2324-4
Census HC80-2-227	2473-1.227	Census HC80-2-308	2473-1.308	Census ISP-WP-84	2324-4
Census HC80-2-228	2473-1.228	Census HC80-2-309	2473-1.309	Census M3-1(yr.-nos.)	2506-3.1
Census HC80-2-230	2473-1.230	Census HC80-2-310	2473-1.310	Census M20A(yr.-nos.)	2506-4.1
Census HC80-2-231	2473-1.231	Census HC80-2-311	2473-1.311	Census M20J(yr.-nos.)	2506-4.3
Census HC80-2-232	2473-1.232	Census HC80-2-312	2473-1.312	Census M20K(yr.-nos.)	2506-4.4
Census HC80-2-233	2473-1.233	Census HC80-2-313	2473-1.313	Census M22A(yr.-nos.)	2506-5.1
Census HC80-2-234	2473-1.234	Census HC80-2-315	2473-1.315	Census M22D(yr.-nos.)	2506-5.2
Census HC80-2-236	2473-1.236	Census HC80-2-316	2473-1.316	Census M22P(yr.-nos.)	2506-5.8
Census HC80-2-237	2473-1.237	Census HC80-2-317	2473-1.317	Census M23I(yr.-nos.)	2506-6.2
Census HC80-2-238	2473-1.238	Census HC80-2-318	2473-1.318	Census M28A(yr.-nos.)	2506-8.1
Census HC80-2-239	2473-1.239	Census HC80-2-319	2473-1.319	Census M28B(yr.-nos.)	2506-8.2
Census HC80-2-240	2473-1.240	Census HC80-2-320	2473-1.320	Census M28C(yr.-nos.)	2506-8.3
Census HC80-2-241	2473-1.241	Census HC80-2-321	2473-1.321	Census M28F(yr.-nos.)	2506-8.4
Census HC80-2-242	2473-1.242	Census HC80-2-322	2473-1.322	Census M30E(83)-13	2506-8.10
Census HC80-2-243	2473-1.243	Census HC80-2-324	2473-1.324	Census M31A(yr.-nos.)	2506-6.7
Census HC80-2-244	2473-1.244	Census HC80-2-325	2473-1.325	Census M32D(yr.-nos.)	2506-9.2
Census HC80-2-245	2473-1.245	Census HC80-2-326	2473-1.326	Census M32G(yr.-nos.)	2506-9.4
Census HC80-2-246	2473-1.246	Census HC80-2-327	2473-1.327	Census M33-2(yr.-nos.)	2506-10.9
Census HC80-2-247	2473-1.247	Census HC80-2-328	2473-1.328	Census M33-3(yr.-nos.)	2506-10.3
Census HC80-2-248	2473-1.248	Census HC80-2-329	2473-1.329	Census M33A(yr.-nos.)	2506-10.1
Census HC80-2-249	2473-1.249	Census HC80-2-330	2473-1.330	Census M33E(yr.-nos.)	2506-10.5
Census HC80-2-250	2473-1.250	Census HC80-2-331	2473-1.331	Census M34H(yr.-nos.)	2506-11.4
Census HC80-2-251	2473-1.251	Census HC80-2-332	2473-1.332	Census M35S(yr.-nos.)	2506-12.9
Census HC80-2-252	2473-1.252	Census HC80-2-333	2473-1.333	Census M36D(yr.-nos.)	2506-12.13
Census HC80-2-253	2473-1.253	Census HC80-2-334	2473-1.334	Census M37G(yr.-nos.)	2506-12.24
Census HC80-2-254	2473-1.254	Census HC80-2-336	2473-1.336	Census M37L(yr.-nos.)	2506-12.25
Census HC80-2-255	2473-1.255	Census HC80-2-337	2473-1.337	Census MA13K(82)-1	2506-8.11
Census HC80-2-256	2473-1.256	Census HC80-2-338	2473-1.338	Census MA20D(83)-1	2506-4.5
Census HC80-2-257	2473-1.257	Census HC80-2-339	2473-1.339	Census MA22F.1(83)-1	2506-5.4
Census HC80-2-258	2473-1.258	Census HC80-2-340	2473-1.340	Census MA22F.2(83)-1	2506-5.5
Census HC80-2-259	2473-1.259	Census HC80-2-341	2473-1.341	Census MA22G(83)-1	2506-5.6
Census HC80-2-260	2473-1.260	Census HC80-2-342	2473-1.342	Census MA22K(83)-1	2506-5.7
Census HC80-2-261	2473-1.261	Census HC80-2-343	2473-1.343	Census MA22S(83)-1	2506-5.10
Census HC80-2-262	2473-1.262	Census HC80-2-344	2473-1.344	Census MA23D(83)-1	2506-6.4
Census HC80-2-263	2473-1.263	Census HC80-2-345	2473-1.345	Census MA23E(83)-1	2506-6.10
Census HC80-2-264	2473-1.264	Census HC80-2-346	2473-1.346	Census MA23F(83)-1	2506-6.11
Census HC80-2-265	2473-1.265	Census HC80-2-347	2473-1.347	Census MA23G(83)-1	2506-6.9
Census HC80-2-266	2473-1.266	Census HC80-2-348	2473-1.348	Census MA23J(83)-1	2506-6.5
Census HC80-2-267	2473-1.267	Census HC80-2-349	2473-1.349	Census MA24F(83)-1	2506-7.1
Census HC80-2-268	2473-1.268	Census HC80-2-350	2473-1.350	Census MA24H(83)-1	2506-7.2
Census HC80-2-269	2473-1.269	Census HC80-2-351	2473-1.351	Census MA24T(82)-1	2506-7.4
Census HC80-2-270	2473-1.270	Census HC80-2-352	2473-1.352	Census MA26B(83)-1	2506-7.13
Census HC80-2-271	2473-1.271	Census HC80-2-353	2473-1.353	Census MA26F(83)-1	2506-7.7
Census HC80-2-272	2473-1.272	Census HC80-2-354	2473-1.354	Census MA27A(83)-1	2506-7.11
Census HC80-2-273	2473-1.273	Census HC80-2-355	2473-1.355	Census MA28A(82)-1	2506-8.14
Census HC80-2-274	2473-1.274	Census HC80-2-356	2473-1.356	Census MA28B(83)-1	2506-8.13
Census HC80-2-275	2473-1.275	Census HC80-2-357	2473-1.357	Census MA28F(83)-1	2506-8.16
Census HC80-2-276	2473-1.276	Census HC80-2-358	2473-1.358	Census MA28G(83)-1	2506-8.5
Census HC80-2-277	2473-1.277	Census HC80-2-359	2473-1.359	Census MA29A(83)-1	2506-8.6
Census HC80-2-278	2473-1.278	Census HC80-2-361	2473-1.361	Census MA30A(83)-1	2506-8.7
Census HC80-2-279	2473-1.279	Census HC80-2-362	2473-1.362	Census MA30B(83)-1	2506-8.12
Census HC80-2-280	2473-1.280	Census HC80-2-363	2473-1.363	Census MA30D(82)-1	2506-8.9
Census HC80-2-281	2473-1.281	Census HC80-2-364	2473-1.364	Census MA30D(83)-1	2506-8.9
Census HC80-2-282	2473-1.282	Census HC80-2-365	2473-1.365	Census MA31A(83)-1	2506-6.8
Census HC80-2-283	2473-1.283	Census HC80-2-366	2473-1.366	Census MA32E(83)-1	2506-9.3
Census HC80-2-284	2473-1.284	Census HC80-2-367	2473-1.367	Census MA32J(83)-1	2506-9.5
Census HC80-2-285	2473-1.285	Census HC80-2-368	2473-1.368	Census MA33B(82)-1	2506-10.2
Census HC80-2-286	2473-1.286	Census HC80-2-369	2473-1.369	Census MA33G(83)-1	2506-10.6
Census HC80-2-287	2473-1.287	Census HC80-2-370	2473-1.370	Census MA33L(82)-1	2506-10.8
Census HC80-2-289	2473-1.289	Census HC80-2-371	2473-1.371	Census MA34N(82)-1	2506-11.6
Census HC80-2-291	2473-1.291	Census HC80-2-372	2473-1.372	Census MA34N(83)-1	2506-11.6
Census HC80-2-292	2473-1.292	Census HC80-2-373	2473-1.373	Census MA35A(83)-1	2506-12.1
Census HC80-2-293	2473-1.293	Census HC80-2-374	2473-1.374	Census MA35D(82)-1	2506-12.3
Census HC80-2-294	2473-1.294	Census HC80-2-375	2473-1.375	Census MA35F(83)-1	2506-12.4
Census HC80-2-295	2473-1.295	Census HC80-2-376	2473-1.376	Census MA35J(83)-1	2506-12.5
Census HC80-2-296	2473-1.296	Census HC80-2-377	2473-1.377	Census MA35L(83)-1	2506-12.6
Census HC80-2-297	2473-1.297	Census HC80-2-378	2473-1.378	Census MA35M(83)-1	2506-12.7
Census HC80-2-298	2473-1.298	Census HC80-2-379	2473-1.379	Census MA35N(83)-1	2506-12.31
Census HC80-2-299	2473-1.299	Census HC80-2-380	2473-1.380	Census MA35P(83)-1	2506-12.8
Census HC80-2-300	2473-1.300	Census HC80-3-4	2475-4	Census MA35Q(83)-1	2506-12.28

January-December 1984

ASI Annual Supplement 1039

Report Numbers

Census MA35R(83)-1 .... 2506-12.2
Census MA35U(83)-1 .... 2506-12.10
Census MA36A(83)-1 .... 2506-12.11
Census MA36E(83)-1 .... 2506-12.15
Census MA36F(83)-1 .... 2506-12.16
Census MA36G(83)-1 .... 2506-12.29
Census MA36H(83)-1 .... 2506-12.17
Census MA36K(83)-1 .... 2506-12.18
Census MA36L(83)-1 .... 2506-12.19
Census MA36M(83)-1 .... 2506-12.20
Census MA36N(83)-1 .... 2506-12.21
Census MA37E(83)-1 .... 2506-12.23
Census MA38B(82)-1 .... 2506-12.26
Census MA38Q(83)-1 .... 2506-12.27
Census MA39A(83)-1 .... 2506-7.12
Census MA175(82)-1 .... 2506-3.4
Census MA200(82)-1 .... 2506-3.6
Census MC82-A-2(P) 2491-3.2
Census MC82-A-3(P) 2491-3.3
Census MC82-A-4(P) 2491-3.4
Census MC82-A-5(P) 2491-3.5
Census MC82-A-6(P) 2491-3.6
Census MC82-A-7(P) 2491-3.7
Census MC82-A-8(P) 2491-3.8
Census MC82-A-9(P) 2491-3.9
Census
MC82-1-20A-1(P)(Rev.) 2491-1.1
Census MC82-1-20A-2(P) 2491-1.2
Census MC82-1-20B-1(P) 2491-1.3
Census MC82-1-20B-2(P) 2491-1.4
Census MC82-1-20B-3(P) 2491-1.5
Census MC82-1-20B-4(P) 2491-1.6
Census MC82-1-20B-5(P) 2491-1.7
Census MC82-1-20C-1(P) 2491-1.8
Census MC82-1-20C-2(P) 2491-1.9
Census MC82-1-20C-3(P) 2491-1.10
Census MC82-1-20C-4(P) 2491-1.11
Census MC82-1-20C-5(P) 2491-1.12
Census MC82-1-20C-6(P) 2491-1.13
Census MC82-1-20D-1(P) 2491-1.14
Census MC82-1-20D-2(P) 2491-1.15
Census MC82-1-20D-3(P) 2491-1.16
Census MC82-1-20D-4(P) 2491-1.17
Census MC82-1-20D-5(P) 2491-1.18
Census MC82-1-20D-6(P) 2491-1.19
Census MC82-1-20E-1(P) 2491-1.20
Census MC82-1-20E-2(P) 2491-1.21
Census MC82-1-20F-2(P) 2491-1.23
Census MC82-1-20F-3(P) 2491-1.24
Census MC82-1-20F-4(P) 2491-1.25
Census MC82-1-20F-5(P) 2491-1.26
Census MC82-1-20G-1(P) 2491-1.27
Census MC82-1-20G-2(P) 2491-1.28
Census MC82-1-20G-3(P) 2491-1.29
Census MC82-1-20G-4(P) 2491-1.30
Census MC82-1-20G-5(P) 2491-1.31
Census MC82-1-20H-1(P) 2491-1.32
Census MC82-1-20H-2(P) 2491-1.33
Census MC82-1-20H-3(P) 2491-1.34
Census MC82-1-20H-5(P) 2491-1.36
Census MC82-1-20H-6(P) 2491-1.37
Census MC82-1-20I-1(P) 2491-1.38
Census MC82-1-20I-2(P) 2491-1.39
Census MC82-1-20I-3(P) 2491-1.40
Census MC82-1-20I-4(P) 2491-1.41
Census MC82-1-20I-5(P) 2491-1.42
Census MC82-1-20I-6(P) 2491-1.43
Census MC82-1-21A-2(P) 2491-1.45
Census MC82-1-21A-3(P) 2491-1.46
Census MC82-1-21A-4(P) 2491-1.47
Census MC82-1-22A-1(P) 2491-1.48
Census MC82-1-22A-2(P) 2491-1.49
Census MC82-1-22A-3(P) 2491-1.50
Census MC82-1-22A-4(P) 2491-1.51
Census MC82-1-22B-1(P) 2491-1.52
Census MC82-1-22B-2(P) 2491-1.53
Census MC82-1-22B-3(P) 2491-1.54
Census MC82-1-22B-4(P) 2491-1.55
Census MC82-1-22B-5(P) 2491-1.56
Census MC82-1-22B-6(P) 2491-1.57
Census MC82-1-22B-7(P) 2491-1.58
Census MC82-1-22C-1(P) 2491-1.59
Census MC82-1-22C-2(P) 2491-1.60
Census MC82-1-22C-3(P) 2491-1.61
Census MC82-1-22D-1(P) 2491-1.62
Census MC82-1-22D-2(P) 2491-1.63
Census MC82-1-22D-3(P) 2491-1.64
Census MC82-1-22E-1(P) 2491-1.65
Census MC82-1-22E-2(P) 2491-1.66
Census MC82-1-22E-3(P) 2491-1.67
Census MC82-1-22E-4(P) 2491-1.68
Census MC82-1-22F-1(P) 2491-1.69
Census MC82-1-22F-3(P) 2491-1.71
Census MC82-1-22F-4(P) 2491-1.72
Census MC82-1-22F-5(P) 2491-1.73
Census MC82-1-22F-6(P) 2491-1.74
Census MC82-1-22F-7(P) 2491-1.75
Census MC82-1-22F-8(P) 2491-1.76
Census MC82-1-22F-9(P) 2491-1.77
Census MC82-1-23A-1(P) 2491-1.78
Census MC82-1-23A-2(P) 2491-1.79
Census MC82-1-23A-3(P) 2491-1.80
Census MC82-1-23A-4(P) 2491-1.81
Census MC82-1-23A-5(P) 2491-1.82
Census MC82-1-23A-6(P) 2491-1.83
Census MC82-1-23A-7(P) 2491-1.84
Census MC82-1-23B-1(P) 2491-1.85
Census MC82-1-23B-2(P) 2491-1.86
Census MC82-1-23B-3(P) 2491-1.87
Census MC82-1-23B-4(P) 2491-1.88
Census MC82-1-23C-1(P) 2491-1.89
Census MC82-1-23C-2(P) 2491-1.90
Census MC82-1-23C-3(P) 2491-1.91
Census MC82-1-23C-4(P) 2491-1.92
Census MC82-1-23C-5(P) 2491-1.93
Census MC82-1-23C-6(P) 2491-1.94
Census MC82-1-23C-7(P) 2491-1.95
Census MC82-1-23D-1(P) 2491-1.96
Census MC82-1-23D-2(P) 2491-1.97
Census MC82-1-23D-3(P) 2491-1.98
Census MC82-1-23D-4(P) 2491-1.99
Census MC82-1-23D-5(P) 2491-1.100
Census MC82-1-23D-6(P) 2491-1.101
Census MC82-1-23D-7(P) 2491-1.102
Census MC82-1-23E-1(P) 2491-1.103
Census MC82-1-23E-2(P) 2491-1.104
Census MC82-1-23E-3(P) 2491-1.105
Census MC82-1-23E-4(P) 2491-1.106
Census MC82-1-23E-5(P) 2491-1.107
Census MC82-1-23E-6(P) 2491-1.108
Census MC82-1-23E-7(P) 2491-1.109
Census MC82-1-23E-8(P) 2491-1.110
Census MC82-1-24A-1(P) 2491-1.111
Census MC82-1-24A-2(P) 2491-1.112
Census MC82-1-24A-3(P) 2491-1.113
Census MC82-1-24A-4(P) 2491-1.114
Census MC82-1-24B-1(P) 2491-1.115
Census MC82-1-24B-2(P) 2491-1.116
Census MC82-1-24B-3(P) 2491-1.117
Census MC82-1-24B-4(P) 2491-1.118
Census MC82-1-24B-5(P) 2491-1.119
Census MC82-1-24C-1(P) 2491-1.120
Census MC82-1-24C-2(P) 2491-1.121
Census MC82-1-24C-3(P) 2491-1.122
Census MC82-1-24C-4(P) 2491-1.123
Census MC82-1-24C-5(P) 2491-1.124
Census MC82-1-24C-6(P) 2491-1.125
Census MC82-1-24D-1(P) 2491-1.126
Census MC82-1-24D-2(P) 2491-1.127
Census MC82-1-25A-1(P) 2491-1.128
Census MC82-1-25A-2(P) 2491-1.129
Census MC82-1-25A-3(P) 2491-1.130
Census MC82-1-25A-4(P) 2491-1.131
Census MC82-1-25A-6(P) 2491-1.133
Census MC82-1-25B-1(P) 2491-1.134
Census MC82-1-25B-2(P) 2491-1.135
Census MC82-1-25B-3(P) 2491-1.136
Census MC82-1-25A-4(P) 2491-1.137
Census MC82-1-25B-5(P) 2491-1.138
Census MC82-1-25B-6(P) 2491-1.139
Census MC82-1-25B-7(P) 2491-1.140
Census MC82-1-26A-1(P) 2491-1.141
Census MC82-1-26A-3(P) 2491-1.143
Census MC82-1-26A-4(P) 2491-1.144
Census MC82-1-26B-1(P) 2491-1.145
Census MC82-1-26B-2(P) 2491-1.146
Census MC82-1-26B-3(P) 2491-1.147
Census MC82-1-26B-4(P) 2491-1.148
Census
MC82-1-26B-5(P)(Rev.) 2491-1.149
Census MC82-1-26B-6(P) 2491-1.150
Census MC82-1-26B-7(P) 2491-1.151
Census MC82-1-26B-8(P) 2491-1.152
Census MC82-1-26C-2(P) 2491-1.154
Census MC82-1-26C-3(P) 2491-1.155
Census MC82-1-26C-5(P) 2491-1.157
Census MC82-1-27A-1(P) 2491-1.158
Census MC82-1-27A-2(P) 2491-1.159
Census MC82-1-27A-3(P) 2491-1.160
Census MC82-1-27A-4(P) 2491-1.161
Census MC82-1-27A-5(P) 2491-1.162
Census MC82-1-27B-1(P) 2491-1.163
Census MC82-1-27B-2(P) 2491-1.164
Census MC82-1-27B-3(P) 2491-1.165
Census MC82-1-27B-4(P) 2491-1.166
Census MC82-1-27B-5(P) 2491-1.167
Census MC82-1-27C-1(P) 2491-1.168
Census MC82-1-27C-2(P) 2491-1.169
Census MC82-1-27C-3(P) 2491-1.170
Census MC82-1-27C-4(P) 2491-1.171
Census MC82-1-27C-5(P) 2491-1.172
Census MC82-1-27C-6(P) 2491-1.173
Census MC82-1-28A-1(P) 2491-1.174
Census MC82-1-28A-2(P) 2491-1.175
Census MC82-1-28A-3(P) 2491-1.176
Census MC82-1-28A-4(P) 2491-1.177
Census MC82-1-28B-1(P) 2491-1.178
Census MC82-1-28B-2(P) 2491-1.179
Census MC82-1-28B-3(P) 2491-1.180
Census MC82-1-28B-4(P) 2491-1.181
Census MC82-1-28C-1(P) 2491-1.182
Census MC82-1-28C-2(P) 2491-1.183
Census MC82-1-28C-3(P) 2491-1.184
Census MC82-1-28D-1(P) 2491-1.185
Census MC82-1-28D-2(P) 2491-1.186
Census MC82-1-28D-4(P) 2491-1.188
Census MC82-1-28E(P) 2491-1.189
Census MC82-1-28F-1(P) 2491-1.190
Census MC82-1-28F-3(P) 2491-1.192
Census MC82-1-28G-1(P) 2491-1.193
Census MC82-1-28G-2(P) 2491-1.194
Census MC82-1-28G-3(P) 2491-1.195
Census MC82-1-28G-4(P) 2491-1.196
Census MC82-1-28H-1(P) 2491-1.197
Census MC82-1-28H-2(P) 2491-1.198
Census MC82-1-28H-3(P) 2491-1.199
Census MC82-1-28H-5(P) 2491-1.201
Census
MC82-1-29A-1(P)(Rev.) 2491-1.202
Census
MC82-1-29A-2(P)(Rev.) 2491-1.203
Census MC82-1-29A-3(P) 2491-1.204
Census MC82-1-29A-4(P) 2491-1.205
Census MC82-1-30A-1(P) 2491-1.206
Census MC82-1-30A-2(P) 2491-1.207
Census MC82-1-30A-3(P) 2491-1.208
Census MC82-1-30A-5(P) 2491-1.210
Census MC82-1-30A-6(P) 2491-1.211
Census MC82-1-31A-1(P) 2491-1.212
Census MC82-1-31A-2(P) 2491-1.213
Census MC82-1-31A-3(P) 2491-1.214

Report Numbers

Entry	Number
Census MC82-I-31A-5(P)	2491-1.216
Census MC82-I-31A-6(P)	2491-1.217
Census MC82-I-31B-1(P)	2491-1.218
Census MC82-I-31B-2(P)	2491-1.219
Census MC82-I-31B-3(P)	2491-1.220
Census MC82-I-31B-4(P)	2491-1.221
Census MC82-I-31B-5(P)	2491-1.222
Census MC82-I-32A-1(P)	2491-1.223
Census MC82-I-32A-2(P)	2491-1.224
Census MC82-I-32A-3(P)	2491-1.225
Census MC82-I-32A-4(P)	2491-1.226
Census MC82-I-32B-1(P)	2491-1.227
Census MC82-I-32B-2(P)	2491-1.228
Census MC82-I-32B-3(P)	2491-1.229
Census MC82-I-32B-4(P)	2491-1.230
Census MC82-I-32C-1(P)	2491-1.232
Census MC82-I-32C-2(P)	2491-1.233
Census MC82-I-32C-4(P)	2491-1.235
Census MC82-I-32C-5(P)	2491-1.236
Census MC82-I-32D-1(P)	2491-1.237
Census MC82-I-32D-2(P)	2491-1.238
Census MC82-I-32D-3(P)	2491-1.239
Census MC82-I-32D-4(P)	2491-1.240
Census MC82-I-32D-5(P)	2491-1.241
Census MC82-I-32D-6(P)	2491-1.242
Census MC82-I-32E-1(P)	2491-1.243
Census MC82-I-32E-2(P)	2491-1.244
Census MC82-I-32E-3(P)	2491-1.245
Census MC82-I-32E-5(P)	2491-1.247
Census MC82-I-32E-6(P)	2491-1.248
Census MC82-I-32E-7(P)	2491-1.249
Census MC82-I-33A-1(P)	2491-1.250
Census MC82-I-33A-2(P)	2491-1.251
Census MC82-I-33A-3(P)	2491-1.252
Census MC82-I-33A-4(P)	2491-1.253
Census MC82-I-33A-5(P)	2491-1.254
Census MC82-I-33B-1(P)	2491-1.255
Census MC82-I-33B-2(P)	2491-1.256
Census MC82-I-33B-4(P)	2491-1.258
Census MC82-I-33B-5(P)	2491-1.259
Census MC82-I-33B-6(P)	2491-1.260
Census MC82-I-33B-7(P)	2491-1.261
Census MC82-I-33C-1(P)	2491-1.262
Census MC82-I-33C-2(P)	2491-1.263
Census MC82-I-33C-3(P)	2491-1.264
Census MC82-I-33C-4(P)	2491-1.265
Census MC82-I-33C-5(P)	2491-1.266
Census MC82-I-33C-6(P)	2491-1.267
Census MC82-I-33D-1(P)	2491-1.268
Census MC82-I-33D-2(P)	2491-1.269
Census MC82-I-33D-3(P)	2491-1.270
Census MC82-I-33D-4(P)	2491-1.271
Census MC82-I-33D-5(P)	2491-1.272
Census MC82-I-33D-6(P)	2491-1.273
Census MC82-I-33D-7(P)	2491-1.274
Census MC82-I-33D-8(P)	2491-1.275
Census MC82-I-34A-1(P)	2491-1.276
Census MC82-I-34A-2(P)	2491-1.277
Census MC82-I-34A-3(P)	2491-1.278
Census MC82-I-34A-5(P)	2491-1.280
Census MC82-I-34A-6(P)	2491-1.281
Census MC82-I-34B-1(P)	2491-1.282
Census MC82-I-34B-2(P)	2491-1.283
Census MC82-I-34B-3(P)	2491-1.284
Census MC82-I-34C-1(P)	2491-1.285
Census MC82-I-34C-2(P)	2491-1.286
Census MC82-I-34C-3(P)	2491-1.287
Census MC82-I-34C-4(P)	2491-1.288
Census MC82-I-34C-5(P)	2491-1.289
Census MC82-I-34C-6(P)	2491-1.290
Census MC82-I-34C-7(P)	2491-1.291
Census MC82-I-34D-1(P)	2491-1.292
Census MC82-I-34D-2(P)	2491-1.293
Census MC82-I-34D-3(P)	2491-1.294
Census MC82-I-34D-4(P)	2491-1.295
Census MC82-I-34D-5(P)	2491-1.296
Census MC82-I-34D-6(P)	2491-1.297
Census MC82-I-34D-7(P)	2491-1.298
Census MC82-I-34D-8(P)	2491-1.299
Census MC82-I-34D-9(P)	2491-1.300
Census MC82-I-34E-1(P)	2491-1.301
Census MC82-I-34E-3(P)	2491-1.303
Census MC82-I-34E-4(P)	2491-1.304
Census MC82-I-34F-1(P)	2491-1.305
Census MC82-I-34F-2(P)	2491-1.306
Census MC82-I-34F-3(P)	2491-1.307
Census MC82-I-34F-4(P)	2491-1.308
Census MC82-I-34F-5(P)	2491-1.309
Census MC82-I-35A-1(P)	2491-1.312
Census MC82-I-35A-1(P)	2491-1.313
Census MC82-I-35A-4(P)	2491-1.315
Census MC82-I-35B-1(P)	2491-1.316
Census MC82-I-35B-2(P)	2491-1.317
Census MC82-I-35B-3(P)	2491-1.318
Census MC82-I-35B-4(P)	2491-1.319
Census MC82-I-35B-5(P)	2491-1.320
Census MC82-I-35B-6(P)	2491-1.321
Census MC82-I-35B-7(P)	2491-1.322
Census MC82-I-35C-1(P)	2491-1.323
Census MC82-I-35C-2(P)	2491-1.324
Census MC82-I-35C-3(P)	2491-1.325
Census MC82-I-35C-4(P)	2491-1.326
Census MC82-I-35C-5(P)	2491-1.327
Census MC82-I-35C-6(P)	2491-1.328
Census MC82-I-35C-7(P)	2491-1.329
Census MC82-I-35D-1(P)	2491-1.330
Census MC82-I-35D-2(P)	2491-1.331
Census MC82-I-35D-3(P)	2491-1.332
Census MC82-I-35D-4(P)	2491-1.333
Census MC82-I-35D-5(P)	2491-1.334
Census MC82-I-35D-6(P)	2491-1.335
Census MC82-I-35E-1(P)	2491-1.336
Census MC82-I-35E-2(P)	2491-1.337
Census MC82-I-35E-3(P)	2491-1.338
Census MC82-I-35E-4(P)	2491-1.339
Census MC82-I-35E-8(P)	2491-1.343
Census MC82-I-35E-9(P)	2491-1.344
Census MC82-I-35F-1(P)	2491-1.345
Census MC82-I-35F-2(P)	2491-1.346
Census MC82-I-35F-3(P)	2491-1.347
Census MC82-I-35F-4(P)	2491-1.348
Census MC82-I-35G-1(P)	2491-1.349
Census MC82-I-35G-3(P)	2491-1.351
Census MC82-I-35G-4(P)	2491-1.352
Census MC82-I-35G-5(P)	2491-1.353
Census MC82-I-35G-6(P)	2491-1.354
Census MC82-I-35G-7(P)	2491-1.355
Census MC82-I-36A-1(P)	2491-1.356
Census MC82-I-36A-2(P)	2491-1.357
Census MC82-I-36A-3(P)	2491-1.358
Census MC82-I-36A-4(P)	2491-1.359
Census MC82-I-36A-5(P)	2491-1.360
Census MC82-I-36A-6(P)	2491-1.361
Census MC82-I-36A-7(P)	2491-1.362
Census MC82-I-36B-2(P)	2491-1.364
Census MC82-I-36B-4(P)	2491-1.366
Census MC82-I-36B-5(P)	2491-1.367
Census MC82-I-36B-6(P)	2491-1.368
Census MC82-I-36B-7(P)	2491-1.369
Census MC82-I-36C-1(P)	2491-1.370
Census MC82-I-36C-3(P)	2491-1.372
Census MC82-I-36C-4(P)	2491-1.373
Census MC82-I-36C-5(P)	2491-1.374
Census MC82-I-36C-6(P)	2491-1.375
Census MC82-I-36D-1(P)	2491-1.377
Census MC82-I-36D-2(P)	2491-1.378
Census MC82-I-36D-3(P)	2491-1.379
Census MC82-I-36D-4(P)	2491-1.380
Census MC82-I-36E-1(P)	2491-1.381
Census MC82-I-36E-2(P)	2491-1.382
Census MC82-I-36E-3(P)	2491-1.383
Census MC82-I-36E-5(P)	2491-1.385
Census MC82-I-36E-6(P)	2491-1.386
Census MC82-I-36E-7(P)	2491-1.387
Census MC82-I-36F-1(P)	2491-1.388
Census MC82-I-36F-2(P)	2491-1.389
Census MC82-I-36F-3(P)	2491-1.390
Census MC82-I-36F-4(P)	2491-1.391
Census MC82-I-37A-1(P)	2491-1.393
Census MC82-I-37A-3(P)	2491-1.395
Census MC82-I-37A-4(P)	2491-1.396
Census MC82-I-37A-5(P)	2491-1.397
Census MC82-I-37B-1(P)	2491-1.398
Census MC82-I-37B-2(P)	2491-1.399
Census MC82-I-37B-3(P)	2491-1.400
Census MC82-I-37B-4(P)	2491-1.401
Census MC82-I-37B-5(P)	2491-1.402
Census MC82-I-37B-6(P)	2491-1.403
Census MC82-I-37C-1(P)	2491-1.404
Census MC82-I-37C-2(P)	2491-1.405
Census MC82-I-37C-3(P)	2491-1.406
Census MC82-I-37C-4(P)	2491-1.407
Census MC82-I-37C-5(P)	2491-1.408
Census MC82-I-37C-6(P)	2491-1.409
Census MC82-I-37C-7(P)	2491-1.410
Census MC82-I-38A-1(P)	2491-1.411
Census MC82-I-38A-2(P)	2491-1.412
Census MC82-I-38A-3(P)	2491-1.413
Census MC82-I-38A-4(P)	2491-1.414
Census MC82-I-38A-5(P)	2491-1.415
Census MC82-I-38A-6(P)	2491-1.416
Census MC82-I-38A-7(P)	2491-1.417
Census MC82-I-38B-1(P)	2491-1.418
Census MC82-I-38B-2(P)	2491-1.419
Census MC82-I-38B-3(P)	2491-1.420
Census MC82-I-38B-4(P)	2491-1.421
Census MC82-I-38B-5(P)	2491-1.422
Census MC82-I-38B-6(P)	2491-1.423
Census MC82-I-39A-1(P)	2491-1.424
Census MC82-I-39A-2(P)	2491-1.425
Census MC82-I-39A-3(P)	2491-1.426
Census MC82-I-39B-1(P)	2491-1.427
Census MC82-I-39B-2(P)	2491-1.428
Census MC82-I-39B-3(P)	2491-1.429
Census MC82-I-39C-1(P)	2491-1.431
Census MC82-I-39C-2(P)	2491-1.432
Census MC82-I-39C-4(P)	2491-1.434
Census MC82-I-39C-5(P)	2491-1.435
Census MC82-I-39C-6(P)	2491-1.436
Census MC82-I-39C-7(P)	2491-1.437
Census MC82-I-39D-1(P)	2491-1.439
Census MC82-I-39D-2(P)	2491-1.440
Census MC82-I-39D-3(P)	2491-1.441
Census MC82-I-39D-5(P)	2491-1.443
Census MC82-SUM-1(P)	2491-1.444
Census MC82-S-3(P)	2491-2.1
Census MIC82-SUM-1(P)	2511-2.1
Census MIC82-SUM-2(P)	2511-2.2
Census MIC82-I-10B(P)	2511-1.2
Census MIC82-I-10C(P)	2511-1.3
Census MIC82-I-12A(P)	2511-1.4
Census MIC82-I-13A(P)	2511-1.5
Census MIC82-I-13B(P)	2511-1.6
Census MIC82-I-13C(P)	2511-1.7
Census MIC82-I-14A(P)	2511-1.8
Census MIC82-I-14B(P)	2511-1.9
Census MIC82-I-14C(P)	2511-1.10
Census MIC82-I-14D(P)	2511-1.11
Census MIC82-I-14E(P)	2511-1.12
Census MQ-22Q(yr.-nos.)	2506-5.9
Census MQ-22T(yr.-nos.)	2506-5.11
Census MQ-23X(yr.-nos.)	2506-6.6
Census MQ-32A(yr.-nos.)	2506-9.6
Census MQ-32C(yr.-nos.)	2506-9.1
Census MQ-34E(yr.-nos.)	2506-11.2
Census MQ-34K(yr.-nos.)	2506-11.5
Census MQ-35D(yr.-nos.)	2506-12.3
Census MQ-35W(yr.-nos.)	2506-12.12
Census MQ-36B(yr.-nos.)	2506-12.13
Census MQ-36C(yr.-nos.)	2506-12.14
Census MQ-37D(yr.-nos.)	2506-12.22

January-December 1984

ASI Annual Supplement 1041

Report Numbers

Census MQ-C1(82)-1 .... 2506-3.7
Census MQ-C1(83)-1 .... 2506-3.7
Census OAC82-5 2593-1
Census P-20, No. 381 .... 2546-1.383
Census P-20, No. 384 .... 2546-1.384
Census P-20, No. 385 .... 2546-1.387
Census P-20, No. 386 .... 2546-1.385
Census P-20, No. 387 .... 2546-1.386
Census P-20, No. 389 .... 2546-1.388
Census P-20, No. 390 .... 2546-1.390
Census P-20, No. 391 .... 2546-1.389
Census P-20, No. 392 .... 2546-1.391
Census P-20, No. 394 .... 2546-1.392
Census P-20, No. 395 .... 2546-1.393
Census P-23, No. 130 .... 2546-2.119
Census P-23, No. 131 .... 2546-2.117
Census P-23, No. 132 .... 2546-2.118
Census P-23, No. 133 .... 2546-2.120
Census P-23, No. 134 .... 2546-2.124
Census P-23, No. 135 .... 2546-2.121
Census P-23, No. 136 .... 2546-2.123
Census P-23, No. 137 .... 2546-2.122
Census P-23, No. 138 .... 2546-2.125
Census P-25, No. 942 2542-1
Census P-25, No. 943 .... 2546-3.127
Census P-25, No. 944 .... 2546-3.128
Census P-25, No. 945 2542-1
Census P-25, No. 946 2542-1
Census P-25, No. 947 2542-1
Census P-25, No. 948 .... 2546-3.129
Census P-25, No. 949 .... 2546-3.130
Census P-25, No. 950 2542-1
Census P-25, No. 951 .... 2546-3.131
Census P-25, No. 952 .... 2546-3.132
Census P-25, No. 953 2542-1
Census P-25, No. 954 2542-1
Census P-25, No. 955 2542-1
Census P-25, No. 956 2542-1
Census P-25, No. 957 .... 2546-3.133
Census P-25, No. 958 2542-1
Census P-25, No. 959 2542-1
Census P-25, No. 960 .... 2546-3.134
Census P-26, No. 82-1-SC 2546-11.1
Census P-26, No. 82-2-SC 2546-11.2
Census P-26, No. 82-2-C 2546-4.2
Census P-26, No. 82-3-SC 2546-11.3
Census P-26, No. 82-4-SC 2546-11.4
Census P-26, No. 82-4-C 2546-4.4
Census P-26, No. 82-5-SC 2546-11.5
Census P-26, No. 82-5-C 2546-4.5
Census P-26, No. 82-6-SC 2546-11.6
Census P-26, No. 82-6-C 2546-4.6
Census P-26, No. 82-7-C 2546-4.7
Census P-26, No. 82-8-SC 2546-11.8
Census P-26, No. 82-8-C 2546-4.8
Census P-26, No. 82-9-SC 2546-11.9
Census P-26, No. 82-9-C 2546-4.9
Census P-26, No.
82-10-SC 2546-11.10
Census P-26, No.
82-11-SC 2546-11.11
Census P-26, No.
82-12-SC 2546-11.12
Census P-26, No. 82-12-C 2546-4.12
Census P-26, No. 82-13-C 2546-4.13
Census P-26, No.
82-14-SC 2546-11.14
Census P-26, No. 82-14-C 2546-4.14
Census P-26, No.
82-15-SC 2546-11.15
Census P-26, No. 82-15-C 2546-4.15
Census P-26, No.
82-16-SC 2546-11.16
Census P-26, No. 82-16-C 2546-4.16
Census P-26, No.
82-17-SC 2546-11.17
Census P-26, No. 82-17-C 2546-4.17

Census P-26, No.
82-18-SC 2546-11.18
Census P-26, No. 82-18-C 2546-4.18
Census P-26, No.
82-19-SC 2546-11.19
Census P-26, No. 82-19-C 2546-4.19
Census P-26, No.
82-20-SC 2546-11.20
Census P-26, No. 82-20-C 2546-4.20
Census P-26, No.
82-21-SC 2546-11.21
Census P-26, No. 82-21-C 2546-4.21
Census P-26, No.
82-22-SC 2546-11.22
Census P-26, No.
82-23-SC 2546-11.23
Census P-26, No. 82-23-C 2546-4.23
Census P-26, No.
82-24-SC 2546-11.24
Census P-26, No. 82-24-C 2546-4.24
Census P-26, No.
82-25-SC 2546-11.25
Census P-26, No. 82-25-C 2546-4.25
Census P-26, No.
82-26-SC 2546-11.26
Census P-26, No. 82-26-C 2546-4.26
Census P-26, No.
82-27-SC 2546-11.27
Census P-26, No. 82-27-C 2546-4.27
Census P-26, No.
82-28-SC 2546-11.28
Census P-26, No. 82-28-C 2546-4.28
Census P-26, No.
82-29-SC 2546-11.29
Census P-26, No. 82-29-C 2546-4.29
Census P-26, No.
82-30-SC 2546-11.30
Census P-26, No. 82-30-C 2546-4.30
Census P-26, No.
82-31-SC 2546-11.31
Census P-26, No. 82-31-C 2546-4.31
Census P-26, No.
82-32-SC 2546-11.32
Census P-26, No. 82-32-C 2546-4.32
Census P-26, No.
82-33-SC 2546-11.33
Census P-26, No. 82-33-C 2546-4.33
Census P-26, No.
82-34-SC 2546-11.34
Census P-26, No. 82-34-C 2546-4.34
Census P-26, No.
82-35-SC 2546-11.35
Census P-26, No. 82-35-C 2546-4.35
Census P-26, No.
82-36-SC 2546-11.36
Census P-26, No. 82-36-C 2546-4.36
Census P-26, No.
82-37-SC 2546-11.37
Census P-26, No. 82-37-C 2546-4.37
Census P-26, No.
82-38-SC 2546-11.38
Census P-26, No. 82-38-C 2546-4.38
Census P-26, No.
82-39-SC 2546-11.39
Census P-26, No. 82-39-C 2546-4.39
Census P-26, No.
82-40-SC 2546-11.40
Census P-26, No. 82-40-C 2546-4.40
Census P-26, No.
82-41-SC 2546-11.41
Census P-26, No. 82-41-C 2546-4.41
Census P-26, No.
82-42-SC 2546-11.42
Census P-26, No. 82-42-C 2546-4.42
Census P-26, No.
82-43-SC 2546-11.43
Census P-26, No. 82-43-C 2546-4.43

Census P-26, No.
82-44-SC 2546-11.44
Census P-26, No. 82-44-C 2546-4.44
Census P-26, No.
82-45-SC 2546-11.45
Census P-26, No. 82-45-C 2546-4.45
Census P-26, No.
82-46-SC 2546-11.46
Census P-26, No. 82-46-C 2546-4.46
Census P-26, No.
82-47-SC 2546-11.47
Census P-26, No. 82-47-C 2546-4.47
Census P-26, No.
82-48-SC 2546-11.48
Census P-26, No. 82-48-C 2546-4.48
Census P-26, No.
82-49-SC 2546-11.49
Census P-26, No. 82-49-C 2546-4.49
Census P-26, No.
82-50-SC 2546-11.50
Census P-26, No. 82-50-C 2546-4.50
Census P-27, No. 56 2544-1
Census P-27, No. 57 2544-1
Census P-60, No. 141 .... 2546-6.38
Census P-60, No. 142 .... 2546-6.39
Census P-60, No. 143 .... 2546-6.37
Census P-60, No. 144 .... 2546-6.40
Census P-60, No. 145 .... 2546-6.41
Census P-70, (nos.) 2542-2
Census PC80-S1-12 .... 2535-1.15
Census PC80-S1-13 .... 2535-1.16
Census PC80-S1-15 .... 2535-1.12
Census PC80-S1-16 .... 2535-1.13
Census PC80-S1-17 .... 2535-1.14
Census PC80-1-C1 .... 2531-3.1
Census PC80-1-C53A 2531-3.53
Census PC80-1-C55 .... 2531-3.55
Census PC80-1-D1-A 2531-4.1
Census PC80-1-D1-B 2531-4.1
Census PC80-1-D1-C 2531-4.1
Census PC80-1-D2 .... 2531-4.2
Census PC80-1-D4 .... 2531-4.4
Census PC80-1-D5 .... 2531-4.5
Census PC80-1-D6 .... 2531-4.6
Census PC80-1-D7 .... 2531-4.7
Census PC80-1-D8 .... 2531-4.8
Census PC80-1-D9 .... 2531-4.9
Census PC80-1-D10 .... 2531-4.10
Census PC80-1-D11 .... 2531-4.11
Census PC80-1-D12 .... 2531-4.12
Census PC80-1-D13 .... 2531-4.13
Census PC80-1-D14 .... 2531-4.14
Census PC80-1-D15 .... 2531-4.15
Census PC80-1-D16 .... 2531-4.16
Census PC80-1-D17 .... 2531-4.17
Census PC80-1-D18 .... 2531-4.18
Census PC80-1-D19 .... 2531-4.19
Census PC80-1-D20 .... 2531-4.20
Census PC80-1-D22 .... 2531-4.22
Census PC80-1-D23 .... 2531-4.23
Census PC80-1-D24 .... 2531-4.24
Census PC80-1-D25 .... 2531-4.25
Census PC80-1-D26 .... 2531-4.26
Census PC80-1-D27 .... 2531-4.27
Census PC80-1-D29 .... 2531-4.29
Census PC80-1-D30 .... 2531-4.30
Census PC80-1-D31 .... 2531-4.31
Census PC80-1-D32 .... 2531-4.32
Census PC80-1-D33 .... 2531-4.33
Census PC80-1-D34 .... 2531-4.34
Census PC80-1-D35 .... 2531-4.35
Census PC80-1-D36 .... 2531-4.36
Census PC80-1-D37 .... 2531-4.37
Census PC80-1-D38 .... 2531-4.38
Census PC80-1-D39 .... 2531-4.39
Census PC80-1-D40 .... 2531-4.40
Census PC80-1-D42 .... 2531-4.42

Report Numbers

Census PC80-1-D43	2531-4.43	Census PHC80-2-79	2551-2.79	Census PHC80-2-157	2551-2.157
Census PC80-1-D44	2531-4.44	Census PHC80-2-80	2551-2.80	Census PHC80-2-158	2551-2.158
Census PC80-1-D45	2531-4.45	Census PHC80-2-81	2551-2.81	Census PHC80-2-159	2551-2.159
Census PC80-1-D46	2531-4.46	Census PHC80-2-82	2551-2.82	Census PHC80-2-160	2551-2.160
Census PC80-1-D48	2531-4.48	Census PHC80-2-83	2551-2.83	Census PHC80-2-161	2551-2.161
Census PC80-1-D49	2531-4.49	Census PHC80-2-84	2551-2.84	Census PHC80-2-162	2551-2.162
Census PC80-1-D50	2531-4.50	Census PHC80-2-85	2551-2.85	Census PHC80-2-163	2551-2.163
Census PC80-1-D51	2531-4.51	Census PHC80-2-86	2551-2.86	Census PHC80-2-164	2551-2.164
Census PC80-1-D53	2531-4.53	Census PHC80-2-87	2551-2.87	Census PHC80-2-165	2551-2.165
Census PHC80-2-2	2551-2.2	Census PHC80-2-88	2551-2.88	Census PHC80-2-166	2551-2.166
Census PHC80-2-3	2551-2.3	Census PHC80-2-89	2551-2.89	Census PHC80-2-167	2551-2.167
Census PHC80-2-4	2551-2.4	Census PHC80-2-90	2551-2.90	Census PHC80-2-168	2551-2.168
Census PHC80-2-5	2551-2.5	Census PHC80-2-91	2551-2.91	Census PHC80-2-169	2551-2.169
Census PHC80-2-6	2551-2.6	Census PHC80-2-92	2551-2.92	Census PHC80-2-170	2551-2.170
Census PHC80-2-7	2551-2.7	Census PHC80-2-93	2551-2.93	Census PHC80-2-171	2551-2.171
Census PHC80-2-8	2551-2.8	Census PHC80-2-94	2551-2.94	Census PHC80-2-172	2551-2.172
Census PHC80-2-9	2551-2.9	Census PHC80-2-95	2551-2.95	Census PHC80-2-173	2551-2.173
Census PHC80-2-11	2551-2.11	Census PHC80-2-96	2551-2.96	Census PHC80-2-174	2551-2.174
Census PHC80-2-12	2551-2.12	Census PHC80-2-97	2551-2.97	Census PHC80-2-175	2551-2.175
Census PHC80-2-13	2551-2.13	Census PHC80-2-98	2551-2.98	Census PHC80-2-176	2551-2.176
Census PHC80-2-14	2551-2.14	Census PHC80-2-99	2551-2.99	Census PHC80-2-177	2551-2.177
Census PHC80-2-15	2551-2.15	Census PHC80-2-100	2551-2.100	Census PHC80-2-178	2551-2.178
Census PHC80-2-16	2551-2.16	Census PHC80-2-101	2551-2.101	Census PHC80-2-179	2551-2.179
Census PHC80-2-17	2551-2.17	Census PHC80-2-102	2551-2.102	Census PHC80-2-180	2551-2.180
Census PHC80-2-18	2551-2.18	Census PHC80-2-103	2551-2.103	Census PHC80-2-181	2551-2.181
Census PHC80-2-19	2551-2.19	Census PHC80-2-104	2551-2.104	Census PHC80-2-182	2551-2.182
Census PHC80-2-20	2551-2.20	Census PHC80-2-105	2551-2.105	Census PHC80-2-183	2551-2.183
Census PHC80-2-21	2551-2.21	Census PHC80-2-106	2551-2.106	Census PHC80-2-184	2551-2.184
Census PHC80-2-22	2551-2.22	Census PHC80-2-107	2551-2.107	Census PHC80-2-185	2551-2.185
Census PHC80-2-23	2551-2.23	Census PHC80-2-108	2551-2.108	Census PHC80-2-186	2551-2.186
Census PHC80-2-24	2551-2.24	Census PHC80-2-110	2551-2.110	Census PHC80-2-187	2551-2.187
Census PHC80-2-25	2551-2.25	Census PHC80-2-111	2551-2.111	Census PHC80-2-188	2551-2.188
Census PHC80-2-26	2551-2.26	Census PHC80-2-112	2551-2.112	Census PHC80-2-189	2551-2.189
Census PHC80-2-27	2551-2.27	Census PHC80-2-113	2551-2.113	Census PHC80-2-190	2551-2.190
Census PHC80-2-28	2551-2.28	Census PHC80-2-114	2551-2.114	Census PHC80-2-191	2551-2.191
Census PHC80-2-29	2551-2.29	Census PHC80-2-115	2551-2.115	Census PHC80-2-192	2551-2.192
Census PHC80-2-30	2551-2.30	Census PHC80-2-116	2551-2.116	Census PHC80-2-193	2551-2.193
Census PHC80-2-31	2551-2.31	Census PHC80-2-117	2551-2.117	Census PHC80-2-194	2551-2.194
Census PHC80-2-32	2551-2.32	Census PHC80-2-118	2551-2.118	Census PHC80-2-195	2551-2.195
Census PHC80-2-33	2551-2.33	Census PHC80-2-119	2551-2.119	Census PHC80-2-196	2551-2.196
Census PHC80-2-34	2551-2.34	Census PHC80-2-120	2551-2.120	Census PHC80-2-197	2551-2.197
Census PHC80-2-35	2551-2.35	Census PHC80-2-121	2551-2.121	Census PHC80-2-198	2551-2.198
Census PHC80-2-37	2551-2.37	Census PHC80-2-122	2551-2.122	Census PHC80-2-199	2551-2.199
Census PHC80-2-38	2551-2.38	Census PHC80-2-123	2551-2.123	Census PHC80-2-200	2551-2.200
Census PHC80-2-39	2551-2.39	Census PHC80-2-124	2551-2.124	Census PHC80-2-201	2551-2.201
Census PHC80-2-40	2551-2.40	Census PHC80-2-125	2551-2.125	Census PHC80-2-202	2551-2.202
Census PHC80-2-41	2551-2.41	Census PHC80-2-126	2551-2.126	Census PHC80-2-203	2551-2.203
Census PHC80-2-42	2551-2.42	Census PHC80-2-127	2551-2.127	Census PHC80-2-204	2551-2.204
Census PHC80-2-43	2551-2.43	Census PHC80-2-128	2551-2.128	Census PHC80-2-205	2551-2.205
Census PHC80-2-44	2551-2.44	Census PHC80-2-129	2551-2.129	Census PHC80-2-206	2551-2.206
Census PHC80-2-45	2551-2.45	Census PHC80-2-130	2551-2.130	Census PHC80-2-207	2551-2.207
Census PHC80-2-47	2551-2.47	Census PHC80-2-131	2551-2.131	Census PHC80-2-208	2551-2.208
Census PHC80-2-48	2551-2.48	Census PHC80-2-132	2551-2.132	Census PHC80-2-209	2551-2.209
Census PHC80-2-49	2551-2.49	Census PHC80-2-133	2551-2.133	Census PHC80-2-210	2551-2.210
Census PHC80-2-50	2551-2.50	Census PHC80-2-134	2551-2.134	Census PHC80-2-211	2551-2.211
Census PHC80-2-51	2551-2.51	Census PHC80-2-135	2551-2.135	Census PHC80-2-212	2551-2.212
Census PHC80-2-52	2551-2.52	Census PHC80-2-136	2551-2.136	Census PHC80-2-213	2551-2.213
Census PHC80-2-58	2551-2.58	Census PHC80-2-137	2551-2.137	Census PHC80-2-214	2551-2.214
Census PHC80-2-59	2551-2.59	Census PHC80-2-138	2551-2.138	Census PHC80-2-215	2551-2.215
Census PHC80-2-60	2551-2.60	Census PHC80-2-139	2551-2.139	Census PHC80-2-216	2551-2.216
Census PHC80-2-61	2551-2.61	Census PHC80-2-140	2551-2.140	Census PHC80-2-217	2551-2.217
Census PHC80-2-62	2551-2.62	Census PHC80-2-141	2551-2.141	Census PHC80-2-218	2551-2.218
Census PHC80-2-63	2551-2.63	Census PHC80-2-142	2551-2.142	Census PHC80-2-219	2551-2.219
Census PHC80-2-64	2551-2.64	Census PHC80-2-143	2551-2.143	Census PHC80-2-220	2551-2.220
Census PHC80-2-65	2551-2.65	Census PHC80-2-144	2551-2.144	Census PHC80-2-221	2551-2.221
Census PHC80-2-66	2551-2.66	Census PHC80-2-145	2551-2.145	Census PHC80-2-222	2551-2.222
Census PHC80-2-67	2551-2.67	Census PHC80-2-146	2551-2.146	Census PHC80-2-223	2551-2.223
Census PHC80-2-68	2551-2.68	Census PHC80-2-147	2551-2.147	Census PHC80-2-224	2551-2.224
Census PHC80-2-69	2551-2.69	Census PHC80-2-148	2551-2.148	Census PHC80-2-225	2551-2.225
Census PHC80-2-70	2551-2.70	Census PHC80-2-149	2551-2.149	Census PHC80-2-226	2551-2.226
Census PHC80-2-71	2551-2.71	Census PHC80-2-150	2551-2.150	Census PHC80-2-227	2551-2.227
Census PHC80-2-72	2551-2.72	Census PHC80-2-151	2551-2.151	Census PHC80-2-228	2551-2.228
Census PHC80-2-73	2551-2.73	Census PHC80-2-152	2551-2.152	Census PHC80-2-229	2551-2.229
Census PHC80-2-75	2551-2.75	Census PHC80-2-153	2551-2.153	Census PHC80-2-230	2551-2.230
Census PHC80-2-76	2551-2.76	Census PHC80-2-154	2551-2.154	Census PHC80-2-231	2551-2.231
Census PHC80-2-77	2551-2.77	Census PHC80-2-155	2551-2.155	Census PHC80-2-232	2551-2.232
Census PHC80-2-78	2551-2.78	Census PHC80-2-156	2551-2.156	Census PHC80-2-233	2551-2.233

Report Numbers

Census PHC80-2-234 .... 2551–2.234
Census PHC80-2-236 .... 2551–2.236
Census PHC80-2-237 .... 2551–2.237
Census PHC80-2-238 .... 2551–2.238
Census PHC80-2-239 .... 2551–2.239
Census PHC80-2-240 .... 2551–2.240
Census PHC80-2-241 .... 2551–2.241
Census PHC80-2-242 .... 2551–2.242
Census PHC80-2-243 .... 2551–2.243
Census PHC80-2-244 .... 2551–2.244
Census PHC80-2-245 .... 2551–2.245
Census PHC80-2-246 .... 2551–2.246
Census PHC80-2-247 .... 2551–2.247
Census PHC80-2-248 .... 2551–2.248
Census PHC80-2-249 .... 2551–2.249
Census PHC80-2-250 .... 2551–2.250
Census PHC80-2-251 .... 2551–2.251
Census PHC80-2-252 .... 2551–2.252
Census PHC80-2-253 .... 2551–2.253
Census PHC80-2-254 .... 2551–2.254
Census PHC80-2-255 .... 2551–2.255
Census PHC80-2-256 .... 2551–2.256
Census PHC80-2-257 .... 2551–2.257
Census PHC80-2-258 .... 2551–2.258
Census PHC80-2-259 .... 2551–2.259
Census PHC80-2-260 .... 2551–2.260
Census PHC80-2-261 .... 2551–2.261
Census PHC80-2-262 .... 2551–2.262
Census PHC80-2-263 .... 2551–2.263
Census PHC80-2-264 .... 2551–2.264
Census PHC80-2-265 .... 2551–2.265
Census PHC80-2-266 .... 2551–2.266
Census PHC80-2-267 .... 2551–2.267
Census PHC80-2-268 .... 2551–2.268
Census PHC80-2-269 .... 2551–2.269
Census PHC80-2-270 .... 2551–2.270
Census PHC80-2-271 .... 2551–2.271
Census PHC80-2-272 .... 2551–2.272
Census PHC80-2-273 .... 2551–2.273
Census PHC80-2-274 .... 2551–2.274
Census PHC80-2-275 .... 2551–2.275
Census PHC80-2-276 .... 2551–2.276
Census PHC80-2-277 .... 2551–2.277
Census PHC80-2-278 .... 2551–2.278
Census PHC80-2-279 .... 2551–2.279
Census PHC80-2-280 .... 2551–2.280
Census PHC80-2-281 .... 2551–2.281
Census PHC80-2-282 .... 2551–2.282
Census PHC80-2-283 .... 2551–2.283
Census PHC80-2-284 .... 2551–2.284
Census PHC80-2-285 .... 2551–2.285
Census PHC80-2-286 .... 2551–2.286
Census PHC80-2-287 .... 2551–2.287
Census PHC80-2-289 .... 2551–2.289
Census PHC80-2-290 .... 2551–2.290
Census PHC80-2-291 .... 2551–2.291
Census PHC80-2-292 .... 2551–2.292
Census PHC80-2-293 .... 2551–2.293
Census PHC80-2-294 .... 2551–2.294
Census PHC80-2-295 .... 2551–2.295
Census PHC80-2-296 .... 2551–2.296
Census PHC80-2-297 .... 2551–2.297
Census PHC80-2-298 .... 2551–2.298
Census PHC80-2-299 .... 2551–2.299
Census PHC80-2-300 .... 2551–2.300
Census PHC80-2-301 .... 2551–2.301
Census PHC80-2-302 .... 2551–2.302
Census PHC80-2-303 .... 2551–2.303
Census PHC80-2-304 .... 2551–2.304
Census PHC80-2-305 .... 2551–2.305
Census PHC80-2-306 .... 2551–2.306
Census PHC80-2-307 .... 2551–2.307
Census PHC80-2-308 .... 2551–2.308
Census PHC80-2-309 .... 2551–2.309
Census PHC80-2-310 .... 2551–2.310
Census PHC80-2-311 .... 2551–2.311
Census PHC80-2-312 .... 2551–2.312
Census PHC80-2-313 .... 2551–2.313
Census PHC80-2-314 .... 2551–2.314
Census PHC80-2-315 .... 2551–2.315
Census PHC80-2-316 .... 2551–2.316
Census PHC80-2-317 .... 2551–2.317
Census PHC80-2-318 .... 2551–2.318
Census PHC80-2-319 .... 2551–2.319
Census PHC80-2-320 .... 2551–2.320
Census PHC80-2-321 .... 2551–2.321
Census PHC80-2-322 .... 2551–2.322
Census PHC80-2-324 .... 2551–2.324
Census PHC80-2-325 .... 2551–2.325
Census PHC80-2-326 .... 2551–2.326
Census PHC80-2-327 .... 2551–2.327
Census PHC80-2-328 .... 2551–2.328
Census PHC80-2-329 .... 2551–2.329
Census PHC80-2-330 .... 2551–2.330
Census PHC80-2-331 .... 2551–2.331
Census PHC80-2-332 .... 2551–2.332
Census PHC80-2-333 .... 2551–2.333
Census PHC80-2-334 .... 2551–2.334
Census PHC80-2-335 .... 2551–2.335
Census PHC80-2-336 .... 2551–2.336
Census PHC80-2-337 .... 2551–2.337
Census PHC80-2-338 .... 2551–2.338
Census PHC80-2-339 .... 2551–2.339
Census PHC80-2-340 .... 2551–2.340
Census PHC80-2-341 .... 2551–2.341
Census PHC80-2-342 .... 2551–2.342
Census PHC80-2-343 .... 2551–2.343
Census PHC80-2-344 .... 2551–2.344
Census PHC80-2-345 .... 2551–2.345
Census PHC80-2-346 .... 2551–2.346
Census PHC80-2-347 .... 2551–2.347
Census PHC80-2-348 .... 2551–2.348
Census PHC80-2-349 .... 2551–2.349
Census PHC80-2-350 .... 2551–2.350
Census PHC80-2-351 .... 2551–2.351
Census PHC80-2-352 .... 2551–2.352
Census PHC80-2-353 .... 2551–2.353
Census PHC80-2-354 .... 2551–2.354
Census PHC80-2-355 .... 2551–2.355
Census PHC80-2-356 .... 2551–2.356
Census PHC80-2-357 .... 2551–2.357
Census PHC80-2-358 .... 2551–2.358
Census PHC80-2-359 .... 2551–2.359
Census PHC80-2-360 .... 2551–2.360
Census PHC80-2-361 .... 2551–2.361
Census PHC80-2-362 .... 2551–2.362
Census PHC80-2-363 .... 2551–2.363
Census PHC80-2-364 .... 2551–2.364
Census PHC80-2-365 .... 2551–2.365
Census PHC80-2-366 .... 2551–2.366
Census PHC80-2-367 .... 2551–2.367
Census PHC80-2-368 .... 2551–2.368
Census PHC80-2-369 .... 2551–2.369
Census PHC80-2-370 .... 2551–2.370
Census PHC80-2-371 .... 2551–2.371
Census PHC80-2-372 .... 2551–2.372
Census PHC80-2-373 .... 2551–2.373
Census PHC80-2-374 .... 2551–2.374
Census PHC80-2-375 .... 2551–2.375
Census PHC80-2-376 .... 2551–2.376
Census PHC80-2-377 .... 2551–2.377
Census PHC80-2-378 .... 2551–2.378
Census PHC80-2-379 .... 2551–2.379
Census PHC80-2-380 .... 2551–2.380
Census Pub. Bull. C-E-1 .... 2428–3.1
Census Pub. Bull. C-E-2 .... 2428–3.3
Census Pub. Bull. C-I-1 .... 2428–3.2
Census Pub. Bull. C-I-2 .... 2428–3.4
Census QFR-(yr.-nos.) 2502–1
Census RC82-A-1 .... 2397–1.1
Census RC82-A-2 .... 2397–1.2
Census RC82-A-4 .... 2397–1.4
Census RC82-A-6 .... 2397–1.6
Census RC82-A-7 .... 2397–1.7
Census RC82-A-8 .... 2397–1.8
Census RC82-A-9 .... 2397–1.9
Census RC82-A-10 .... 2397–1.10
Census RC82-A-11 .... 2397–1.11
Census RC82-A-12 .... 2397–1.12
Census RC82-A-14 .... 2397–1.14
Census RC82-A-15 .... 2397–1.15
Census RC82-A-16 .... 2397–1.16
Census RC82-A-17 .... 2397–1.17
Census RC82-A-18 .... 2397–1.18
Census RC82-A-19 .... 2397–1.19
Census RC82-A-20 .... 2397–1.20
Census RC82-A-21 .... 2397–1.21
Census RC82-A-22 .... 2397–1.22
Census RC82-A-23 .... 2397–1.23
Census RC82-A-24 .... 2397–1.24
Census RC82-A-25 .... 2397–1.25
Census RC82-A-26 .... 2397–1.26
Census RC82-A-27 .... 2397–1.27
Census RC82-A-28 .... 2397–1.28
Census RC82-A-29 .... 2397–1.29
Census RC82-A-30 .... 2397–1.30
Census RC82-A-31 .... 2397–1.31
Census RC82-A-32 .... 2397–1.32
Census RC82-A-33 .... 2397–1.33
Census RC82-A-34 .... 2397–1.34
Census RC82-A-35 .... 2397–1.35
Census RC82-A-36 .... 2397–1.36
Census RC82-A-37 .... 2397–1.37
Census RC82-A-38 .... 2397–1.38
Census RC82-A-39 .... 2397–1.39
Census RC82-A-40 .... 2397–1.40
Census RC82-A-41 .... 2397–1.41
Census RC82-A-42 .... 2397–1.42
Census RC82-A-43 .... 2397–1.43
Census RC82-A-44 .... 2397–1.44
Census RC82-A-46 .... 2397–1.46
Census RC82-A-47 .... 2397–1.47
Census RC82-A-48 .... 2397–1.48
Census RC82-A-49 .... 2397–1.49
Census RC82-A-50 .... 2397–1.50
Census RC82-A-51 .... 2397–1.51
Census RC82-C-2 .... 2401–1.2
Census RC82-C-3 .... 2401–1.3
Census RC82-C-12 .... 2401–1.12
Census RC82-C-13 .... 2401–1.13
Census RC82-C-27 .... 2401–1.27
Census RC82-C-29 .... 2401–1.29
Census RC82-C-45 .... 2401–1.45
Census RC82-C-51 .... 2401–1.51
Census RC82-I-1(P) 2395–1.1
Census RC82-I-3(P) 2395–1.3
Census RC82-I-4(P) 2395–1.4
Census RC82-I-5(P) 2395–1.5
Census RC82-I-6(P) 2395–1.6
Census RC82-I-7(P) 2395–1.7
Census RC82-I-8(P) 2395–1.8
Census RC82-I-11(P) 2395–1.11
Census RC82-I-12(P) 2395–1.12
Census RC82-I-13(P) 2395–1.13
Census RC82-I-14(P) 2395–1.14
Census RC82-I-16(P) 2395–1.16
Census RC82-I-17(P) 2395–1.17
Census RC82-I-18(P) 2395–1.18
Census RC82-I-19(P) 2395–1.19
Census RC82-I-20(P) 2395–1.20
Census RC82-I-21(P) 2395–1.21
Census RC82-I-23(P) 2395–1.23
Census RC82-I-24(P) 2395–1.24
Census RC82-I-25(P) 2395–1.25
Census RC82-I-26(P) 2395–1.26
Census RC82-I-27(P) 2395–1.27
Census RC82-I-28(P) 2395–1.28
Census RC82-I-30(P) 2395–1.30
Census RC82-I-32(P) 2395–1.32
Census RC82-I-33(P) 2395–1.33
Census RC82-I-34(P) 2395–1.34

Report Numbers

Census RC82-I-35(P) 2395–1.35
Census RC82-I-36(P) 2395–1.36
Census RC82-I-37(P) 2395–1.37
Census RC82-I-38(P) 2395–1.38
Census RC82-I-39(P) 2395–1.39
Census WC82-SUM-1(P) 2403–1.40
Census SC82-A-2 .... 2391–1.2
Census SC82-A-3 .... 2391–1.3
Census SC82-A-4 .... 2391–1.4
Census SC82-A-6 .... 2391–1.6
Census SC82-A-10 .... 2391–1.10
Census SC82-A-12 .... 2391–1.12
Census SC82-A-13 .... 2391–1.13
Census SC82-A-19 .... 2391–1.19
Census SC82-A-20 .... 2391–1.20
Census SC82-A-22 .... 2391–1.22
Census SC82-A-25 .... 2391–1.25
Census SC82-A-27 .... 2391–1.27
Census SC82-A-28 .... 2391–1.28
Census SC82-A-29 .... 2391–1.29
Census SC82-A-30 .... 2391–1.30
Census SC82-A-32 .... 2391–1.32
Census SC82-A-35 .... 2391–1.35
Census SC82-A-37 .... 2391–1.37
Census SC82-A-38 .... 2391–1.38
Census SC82-A-40 .... 2391–1.40
Census SC82-A-42 .... 2391–1.42
Census SC82-A-44 .... 2391–1.44
Census SC82-A-45 .... 2391–1.45
Census SC82-A-46 .... 2391–1.46
Census SC82-A-48 .... 2391–1.48
Census SC82-A-51 .... 2391–1.51
Census SC82-I-1(P) 2390–2.1
Census SC82-I-2(P) 2390–2.2
Census SC82-I-3(P) 2390–2.3
Census SC82-I-4(P) 2390–2.4
Census SC82-I-5(P) 2390–2.5
Census SC82-I-6(P) 2390–2.6
Census SC82-I-7(P) 2390–2.7
Census SC82-I-8(P) 2390–2.8
Census SC82-I-9(P) 2390–2.9
Census SC82-I-10(P) 2390–2.10
Census SC82-I-11(P) 2390–2.11
Census SC82-I-12(P) 2390–2.12
Census SC82-I-13(P) 2390–2.13
Census SC82-I-14(P) 2390–2.14
Census SC82-I-15(P) 2390–2.15
Census SC82-I-16(P) 2390–2.16
Census SC82-I-17(P) 2390–2.17
Census SC82-I-18(P) 2390–2.18
Census SC82-I-19(P) 2390–2.19
Census SC82-SUM-1(P) 2390–2.20
Census TC82-T-3 .... 2573–1.3
Census TC82-T-4 .... 2573–1.4
Census TC82-T-9 .... 2573–1.9
Census TC82-T-14 .... 2573–1.14
Census TC82-T-18 .... 2573–1.18
Census TC82-T-20 .... 2573–1.20
Census TC82-T-21 .... 2573–1.21
Census TC82-T-24 .... 2573–1.24
Census TC82-T-28 .... 2573–1.28
Census TC82-T-33 .... 2573–1.33
Census TC82-T-40 .... 2573–1.40
Census TC82-T-42 .... 2573–1.42
Census TC82-T-49 .... 2573–1.49
Census Tech. Paper 49 .... 2626–2.51
Census Tech. Paper 51 .... 2626–2.50
Census Tech. Paper 52 .... 2626–2.52
Census WC82-A-2 .... 2405–1.2
Census WC82-A-3 .... 2405–1.3
Census WC82-A-4 .... 2405–1.4
Census WC82-A-5 .... 2405–1.5
Census WC82-A-6 .... 2405–1.6
Census WC82-A-7 .... 2405–1.7
Census WC82-A-8 .... 2405–1.8
Census WC82-A-9 .... 2405–1.9
Census WC82-A-12 .... 2405–1.12
Census WC82-A-13 .... 2405–1.13
Census WC82-A-19 .... 2405–1.19
Census WC82-A-20 .... 2405–1.20
Census WC82-A-21 .... 2405–1.21
Census WC82-A-22 .... 2405–1.22
Census WC82-A-27 .... 2405–1.27
Census WC82-A-28 .... 2405–1.28
Census WC82-A-29 .... 2405–1.29
Census WC82-A-30 .... 2405–1.30
Census WC82-A-31 .... 2405–1.31
Census WC82-A-32 .... 2405–1.32
Census WC82-A-33 .... 2405–1.33
Census WC82-A-34 .... 2405–1.34
Census WC82-A-35 .... 2405–1.35
Census WC82-A-37 .... 2405–1.37
Census WC82-A-38 .... 2405–1.38
Census WC82-A-39 .... 2405–1.39
Census WC82-A-40 .... 2405–1.40
Census WC82-A-41 .... 2405–1.41
Census WC82-A-42 .... 2405–1.42
Census WC82-A-45 .... 2405–1.45
Census WC82-A-46 .... 2405–1.46
Census WC82-A-47 .... 2405–1.47
Census WC82-A-48 .... 2405–1.48
Census WC82-A-49 .... 2405–1.49
Census WC82-A-51 .... 2405–1.51
Census WC82-I-1(P) 2403–1.1
Census WC82-I-3(P) 2403–1.3
Census WC82-I-4(P) 2403–1.4
Census WC82-I-6(P) 2403–1.6
Census WC82-I-7(P) 2403–1.7
Census WC82-I-8(P) 2403–1.8
Census WC82-I-9(P) 2403–1.9
Census WC82-I-10(P) 2403–1.10
Census WC82-I-11(P) 2403–1.11
Census WC82-I-12(P) 2403–1.12
Census WC82-I-13(P) 2403–1.13
Census WC82-I-14(P) 2403–1.14
Census WC82-I-15(P) 2403–1.15
Census WC82-I-16(P) 2403–1.16
Census WC82-I-17(P) 2403–1.17
Census
WC82-I-18(P)(Revised) 2403–1.18
Census WC82-I-19(P) 2403–1.19
Census WC82-I-20(P) 2403–1.20
Census WC82-I-21(P) 2403–1.21
Census WC82-I-22(P) 2403–1.22
Census WC82-I-23(P) 2403–1.23
Census WC82-I-24(P) 2403–1.24
Census WC82-I-25(P) 2403–1.25
Census WC82-I-26(P) 2403–1.26
Census WC82-I-27(P) 2403–1.27
Census WC82-I-28(P) 2403–1.28
Census WC82-I-29(P) 2403–1.29
Census WC82-I-30(P) 2403–1.30
Census WC82-I-31(P) 2403–1.31
Census WC82-I-32(P) 2403–1.32
Census WC82-I-33(P) 2403–1.33
Census WC82-I-34(P) 2403–1.34
Census WC82-I-35(P) 2403–1.35
Census WC82-I-36(P) 2403–1.36
Census WC82-I-37(P) 2403–1.37
Census WC82-I-38(P) 2403–1.38
Census RC82-SUM-1(P) 2395–1.40
Census WID-1 .... 2326–15.1
Census WID-2 .... 2326–15.2
CMS/AGM/602/83 .... 2045–13.3
CMS/CPE/122/84 .... 2045–1.51
CMS/CPE/401/84 .... 2045–1.49
CMS/CPE/409/83 .... 2045–1.42
CMS/CPE/412/84 .... 2045–1.50
CMS/CPE/513/84 .... 2045–1.48
CMS/CPE/517/84 .... 2045–1.45
CMS/CPE/525/84 .... 2045–1.47
CMS/CPE/582/83 .... 2045–1.44
CMS/CPE/602/83 .... 2045–1.46
CMS/CPE/729/83 .... 2045–1.43
CMS/ECP/582/79 .... 2045–5.16
CMS/ELC/421/83 .... 2045–4.24
CMS/ELC/588/83 .... 2045–4.23
CMS/EPS/469/84 .... 2045–15.8
CMS/EPS/479/84 .... 2045–15.5
CMS/EPS/549/84 .... 2045–15.4
CMS/EPS/560/83 .... 2045–15.3
CMS/EPS/565/84 .... 2045–15.7
CMS/EPS/753/84 .... 2045–15.6
CMS/FPP/351/84 .... 2045–11.20
CMS/FPP/423/82 .... 2045–11.24
CMS/FPP/427/81 .... 2045–11.25
CMS/FPP/517/83 .... 2045–11.19
CMS/FPP/549/84 .... 2045–11.23
CMS/FPP/565/84 .... 2045–11.22
CMS/FPP/580/84 .... 2045–11.21
CMS/GIE/201/84 .... 2045–3.28
CMS/GIE/421/84 .... 2045–3.30
CMS/GIE/428/82 .... 2045–3.31
CMS/GIE/588/84 .... 2045–3.29
CMS/GIE/791/84 .... 2045–3.32
CMS/IPC/351/84 .... 2045–6.34
CMS/IPC/427/84 .... 2045–6.40
CMS/IPC/428/82 .... 2045–6.39
CMS/IPC/469/84 .... 2045–6.36
CMS/IPC/559/84 .... 2045–6.41
CMS/IPC/580/84 .... 2045–6.35
CMS/IPC/583/84 .... 2045–6.38
CMS/IPC/602/84 .... 2045–6.37
CMS/LAB/403/83 .... 2045–10.16
CMS/LAB/423/83 .... 2045–10.15
CMS/LAB/479/83 .... 2045–10.17
CMS/LAB/588/84 .... 2045–10.19
CMS/LAB/602/83 .... 2045–10.18
CMS/MED/351/84 .... 2045–2.53
CMS/MED/357/84 .... 2045–2.47
CMS/MED/560/77 .... 2045–2.50
CMS/MED/580/83 .... 2045–2.51
CMS/MED/582/83 .... 2045–2.48
CMS/MED/588/84 .... 2045–2.49
CMS/MED/796/83 .... 2045–2.52
CMS/MIE/479/83 .... 2045–16.2
CMS/MIE/533/83 .... 2045–16.3
CMS/MIE/535/84 .... 2045–16.5
CMS/MIE/766/84 .... 2045–16.4
CMS/MTL/471/84 .... 2045–9.3
CMS/PCE/565/84 .... 2045–17.1
CMS/SGR/201/83 .... 2045–14.11
CMS/SGR/307/82 .... 2045–14.12
CMS/SGR/401/84 .... 2045–14.6
CMS/SGR/412/84 .... 2045–14.8
CMS/SGR/441/84 .... 2045–14.7
CMS/SGR/517/84 .... 2045–14.5
CMS/SGR/588/82 .... 2045–14.10
CMS/SGR/602/83 .... 2045–14.9
CMS/TCE/351/82 .... 2045–12.34
CMS/TCE/357/84 .... 2045–12.31
CMS/TCE/401/82 .... 2045–12.36
CMS/TCE/409/83 .... 2045–12.30
CMS/TCE/412/82 .... 2045–12.37
CMS/TCE/51X/82 .... 2045–12.32
CMS/TCE/602/83 .... 2045–12.33
CMS/TCE/753/82 .... 2045–12.35
CMS/TCE/796/82 .... 2045–12.38
E84-(nos.) 2162–8
FAO Fisheries Synopsis
No. 136 .... 2166–16.12
FAO Fisheries Synopsis
No. 138 .... 2166–16.13
FAO Fisheries Synopsis
No. 140 .... 2166–16.14
FCM P1-1984 2144–2
FET 83-102 .... 2046–4.8
FET 83-108 .... 2046–4.3
FET 83-109 .... 2046–4.2
FET 83-110 .... 2046–4.1
FET 83-111 .... 2046–4.7

Report Numbers

FET 83-112	2046-4.12
FET 83-113	2046-4.6
FET 83-114	2046-4.5
FET 84-01	2046-4.4
FET 84-02	2046-4.14
FET 84-03	2046-4.15
FET 84-04	2046-4.11
FET 84-05	2046-4.9
FET 84-06	2046-4.16
FET 84-07	2046-4.13
FET 84-08	2046-4.17
FET 84-09	2046-4.10
FET 84-10	2046-4.23
FET 84-11	2046-4.26
FET 84-12	2046-4.18
FET 84-13	2046-4.30
FET 84-14	2046-4.21
FET 84-15	2046-4.27
FET 84-16	2046-4.25
FET 84-17	2046-4.29
FET 84-18	2046-4.20
FET 84-19	2046-4.22
FET 84-20	2046-4.37
FET 84-21	2046-4.31
FET 84-22	2046-4.33
FET 84-23	2046-4.36
FET 84-24	2046-4.39
FET 84-25	2046-4.19
FET 84-26	2046-4.32
FET 84-27	2046-4.28
FET 84-28	2046-4.43
FET 84-29	2046-4.24
FET 84-30	2046-4.40
FET 84-32	2046-4.38
FET 84-33	2046-4.35
FET 84-34	2046-4.41
FET 84-35	2046-4.34
FET 84-36	2046-4.45
FET 84-37	2046-4.44
FET 84-38	2046-4.42
FET 84-39	2046-4.48
FET 84-40	2046-4.46
FET 84-41	2046-4.47
FET 84-42	2046-4.54
FET 84-43	2046-4.52
FET 84-44	2046-4.53
FET 84-45	2046-4.50
FET 84-46	2046-4.49
FET 84-47	2046-4.51
FET 84-48	2046-4.62
FET 84-49	2046-4.63
FET 84-50	2046-4.60
FET 84-51	2046-4.55
FET 84-52	2046-4.56
FET 84-53	2046-4.64
FET 84-54	2046-4.57
FET 84-55	2046-4.58
FET 84-56	2046-4.59
FET 84-57	2046-4.61
FET 84-58	2046-4.74
FET 84-59	2046-4.72
FET 84-60	2046-4.75
FET 84-61	2046-4.67
FET 84-62	2046-4.71
FET 84-63	2046-4.73
FET 84-64	2046-4.68
FET 84-65	2046-4.69
FET 84-66	2046-4.70
FET 84-67	2046-4.76
FET 84-68	2046-4.65
FET 84-69	2046-4.66
FET 84-70	2046-4.95
FET 84-71	2046-4.88
FET 84-72	2046-4.77
FET 84-73	2046-4.84
FET 84-74	2046-4.87
FET 84-75	2046-4.79
FET 84-76	2046-4.89
FET 84-77	2046-4.92
FET 84-78	2046-4.86
FET 84-79	2046-4.81
FET 84-80	2046-4.94
FET 84-81	2046-4.90
FET 84-82	2046-4.93
FET 84-83	2046-4.83
FET 84-84	2046-4.80
FET 84-85	2046-4.82
FET 84-86	2046-4.91
FET 84-87	2046-4.85
FET 84-88	2046-4.78
FET 84-89	2046-4.99
FET 84-90	2046-4.96
FET 84-91	2046-4.98
FET 84-92	2046-4.106
FET 84-93	2046-4.97
FET 84-94	2046-4.102
FET 84-95	2046-4.107
FET 84-96	2046-4.103
FET 84-97	2046-4.110
FET 84-98	2046-4.104
FET 84-99	2046-4.100
FET 84-100	2046-4.105
FET 84-101	2046-4.101
FET 84-103	2046-4.109
FET 84-104	2046-4.111
FET 84-105	2046-4.112
FET 84-106	2046-4.119
FET 84-107	2046-4.116
FET 84-108	2046-4.122
FET 84-109	2046-4.120
FET 84-110	2046-4.118
FET 84-111	2046-4.115
FET 84-112	2046-4.108
FET 84-113	2046-4.121
FET 84-114	2046-4.114
FET 84-116	2046-4.113
FET 84-117	2046-4.124
FET 84-118	2046-4.125
FET 84-119	2046-4.123
FET 84-120	2046-4.126
FIPS Pub. 11-2	2216-2.125
FIPS Pub. 55-1	2216-2.122
FIPS Pub. 58(Rev.)	2216-2.121
FIPS Pub. 60-2	2216-2.119
FIPS Pub. 90	2216-2.114
FIPS Pub. 94	2216-2.117
FIPS Pub. 98	2216-2.118
FIPS Pub. 99	2216-2.115
FIPS Pub. 100	2216-2.116
FIPS Pub. 101	2216-2.123
FIPS Pub. 102	2216-2.124
FIPS Pub. 103	2216-2.126
FIPS Pub. 104	2216-2.120
FIPS Pub. 106	2216-2.127
Fishery Market News Rpt.	
B-(nos.)	2162-6.2
Fishery Market News Rpt.	
N-(nos.)	2162-6.1
Fishery Market News Rpt.	
O-(nos.)	2162-6.3
Fishery Market News Rpt.	
P-(nos.)	2162-6.4
Fishery Market News Rpt.	
SW-(nos.)	2162-6.5
GD-15	2156-18.15
Historical Climatology	
Series 3-1	2156-17.12
Historical Climatology	
Series 3-2	2156-17.13
Historical Climatology	
Series 3-3	2156-17.14
Historical Climatology	
Series 3-4	2156-17.15
Historical Climatology	
Series 3-5	2156-17.16
ITA-991(yr.-nos.)	2506-10.11
ITA-9008(yr.-nos.)	2506-10.10
NBS-GCR-83-439	2218-70
NBS Planning Rpt. 17	2218-69
NBS Spec. Pub. 260	2214-2
NBS Spec. Pub. 305,	
Supp. 15	2214-1
NBS Spec. Pub. 660	2218-69
NBSIR 83-2746	2218-68
NBSIR 83-2803	2218-71
NOAA CFS (nos.) FF	2162-2
NOAA CFS (nos.) FM	2162-3
NOAA CFS 8301. MF-1	2166-6.1
NOAA CFS 8302. MF-2	2166-6.2
NOAA CFS 8303. MF-4	2166-6.4
NOAA CFS 8308. MF-3	2166-6.3
NOAA CFS 8315. MF-6	2166-6.6
NOAA CFS 8316. MF-5	2166-6.5
NOAA CFS 8320	2164-1
NOAA CFS 8321	2166-17.1
NOAA CFS 8322	2166-17.2
NOAA CFS 8323	2166-17.3
NOAA TM NMFS	
F/NEC-29	2164-14
NOAA TM NWS FCST	
29	2186-4.11
NOAA TM NWS	
NHC-21	2184-7
NOAA TM NWS TDL	
73	2188-17
NOAA TM NWS	
WR-186	2184-8
NOAA TR NMFS 1	2166-16.13
NOAA TR NMFS 4	2168-79
NOAA TR NMFS 14	2166-16.14
NOAA TR NMFS Circ.	
451	2166-16.12
NOAA TR NMFS	
SSRF-773	2168-78
NOAA TR NMFS	
SSRF-776	2168-80
OBR 83-09	2046-6.1
OBR 83-10	2046-5.1
OBR 83-14	2046-6.8
OBR 84-01	2046-6.2
OBR 84-02	2046-6.3
OBR 84-03	2046-6.5
OBR 84-04	2046-6.6
OBR 84-05	2046-6.7
OBR 84-06	2046-6.4
OBR 84-07	2046-6.9
OBR 84-08	2046-6.10
PAT 84-6	2244-2
Stat. Digest 71	2164-2
TQ 2010	2046-8.1
TQ 2196	2042-26
TQ 2210	2046-8.2
TQ 2310	2046-8.3
TQ 2493	2046-8.4
TQ 2496	2042-27
TQ 2510	2046-8.5
TQ 2709	2046-9.4
TQ 2710	2046-9.5
TQ 2711	2046-9.6
TQ 2712	2046-9.7
TQ 2750	2046-9.1
TQ 2751	2046-9.2
TQ 2752	2046-9.3
WDCA-OC-84-1	2144-15

DEPARTMENT OF ENERGY

ANL-OHS/HP-83-100	3406-1.35
ANL-OHS/HP-83-101	3406-1.37
ANL-OHS/HP-83-102	3406-1.39

Report Numbers

ANL-OHS/HP-83-103 .... 3406–1.36
ANL-OHS/HP-83-107 .... 3406–1.40
ANL-OHS/HP-84-100 .... 3406–1.38
ANL/EES-TM-232 3408–28
ANL/EES-TM-239 3408–32
ANL/ES-133 3408–31
BNL-51528 3408–29
Carbon Dioxide Effects
Res. and Assessment
Program No. 019 .... 3406–3.36
CONF-830583-3 3408–30
CONF-8108131 .... 3406–3.36
DOE/AD-11151-T1 3008–97
DOE/BP-205 3224–1
DOE/BP-307 3224–2
DOE/CE-0015/2 3304–8
DOE/CE-0015/3 3304–8
DOE/CE-0016/3 3304–1
DOE/CE-0019/4 3304–11
DOE/CE-0020/3 3304–13
DOE/CE-0027/2 3304–17
DOE/CE-0033/2 3304–20
DOE/CE-0034/2 3304–18
DOE/CE-0043/1 3304–22
DOE/CE-0043/2 3304–22
DOE/CE-0050 3304–21
DOE/CE-0118 3304–21
DOE/CS-20050/1 3308–73
DOE/CS-30013-T9 3308–67
DOE/CS-40151/1, Vol.1 .... 3308–66.1
DOE/CS-40151/1, Vol.2 .... 3308–66.2
DOE/CS-40151/1, Vol.3 .... 3308–66.3
DOE/CS-40151/1, Vol.4 .... 3308–66.4
DOE/CS-40151/1, Vol.5 .... 3308–66.5
DOE/CS-40151/1, Vol.6 .... 3308–66.6
DOE/CS-40151/1, Vol.7 .... 3308–66.7
DOE/CS-40151/1, Vol.8 .... 3308–66.8
DOE/CS-40151/1, Vol.9 .... 3308–66.9
DOE/CS-50007-T2 3308–75
DOE/DP-0001/13 3002–4
DOE/DP-0015 3358–32
DOE/DP-0539/050 9234–5
DOE/DP-0539/051 9234–4
DOE/EGG-2312 3354–10
DOE/EIA-0035(yr./nos.) 3162–24
DOE/EIA-0040(84) 3164–40
DOE/EIA-0095(83) 3164–36
DOE/EIA-0109(yr./nos.) 3162–6
DOE/EIA-0118(83) 3164–25
DOE/EIA-0121(yr./nos.) 3162–37
DOE/EIA-0125(yr./nos.) 3162–8
DOE/EIA-0130(yr./nos.) 3162–4
DOE/EIA-0131(83)P 3164–4
DOE/EIA-0131(83)P/2 3164–4
DOE/EIA-0145(82) 3164–38
DOE/EIA-0145(83) 3164–38
DOE/EIA-0167(83) 3164–33
DOE/EIA-0167(83)P 3164–33
DOE/EIA-0173(83) 3164–29
DOE/EIA-0174(83) 3164–62
DOE/EIA-0185(83) 3164–45
DOE/EIA-0191(83) 3164–42
DOE/EIA-0202/(nos.) 3162–34
DOE/EIA-0206(82) 3164–44
DOE/EIA-0208(yr./nos.) 3162–32
DOE/EIA-0214(82) 3164–39
DOE/EIA-0214(82)S 3164–55
DOE/EIA-0216(83) 3164–46
DOE/EIA-0218(nos.) 3162–1
DOE/EIA-0219(83) 3164–50
DOE/EIA-0226(yr./nos.) 3162–35
DOE/EIA-0292(83) 3164–63
DOE/EIA-0314(82) 3166–7.19
DOE/EIA-0318(79)/2 .... 3166–8.4
DOE/EIA-0321/1(82) 3166–7.20
DOE/EIA-0321/2(82) 3166–7.22
DOE/EIA-0323(81) 3164–9
DOE/EIA-0333(84) 3164–68
DOE/EIA-0340(83)/1 .... 3164–2.1
DOE/EIA-0340(83)/2 .... 3164–2.2
DOE/EIA-0341(83) 3164–78
DOE/EIA-0347(83-84) 3164–67
DOE/EIA-0348(83) 3164–11
DOE/EIA-0354(82/2) 3164–60
DOE/EIA-0363(84) 3164–77
DOE/EIA-0370(83) 3164–70
DOE/EIA-0376(81) 3164–64
DOE/EIA-0380(yr./nos.) 3162–11
DOE/EIA-0383(83) 3164–75
DOE/EIA-0384(83) 3164–74
DOE/EIA-0385(83) 3164–76
DOE/EIA-0397(yr./nos.) 3162–39
DOE/EIA-0402(83) 3164–65
DOE/EIA-0403(83) 3164–66
DOE/EIA-0424(82) 3164–71
DOE/EIA-0424(83) 3164–71
DOE/EIA-0435 .... 3166–9.8
DOE/EIA-0436(83) 3164–72
DOE/EIA-0436(84) 3164–72
DOE/EIA-0437(82) 3164–23
DOE/EIA-0438(84) 3164–57
DOE/EIA-0439(83) 3164–69
DOE/EIA-0439(84) 3164–69
DOE/EIA-0440 .... 3168–50.5
DOE/EIA-0441(82) 3164–73.1
DOE/EIA-0441(83) 3164–73.3
DOE/EIA-0443 3168–87
DOE/EIA-0446 3168–88
DOE/EIA-0447 .... 3166–9.9
DOE/EIA-0448 3168–90
DOE/EIA-0449 3168–91
DOE/EIA-0451 .... 3166–11.1
DOE/EIA-0455(82) 3164–9
DOE/EIA-0458 .... 3166–7.21
DOE/EIA-0459 3164–58
DOE/EIA-0489 3168–89
DOE/EML-429 3404–13
DOE/EML-430 3404–12
DOE/EP-0018/1 3408–27
DOE/EP-0040/2 3404–1
DOE/ER-0134/1 3004–19
DOE/ER-0143/2 .... 3004–18.3
DOE/ER-0144/2 .... 3004–18.5
DOE/ER-0145/2 .... 3004–18.4
DOE/ER-0147/2 .... 3004–18.2
DOE/ER-0150/2 .... 3004–18.7
DOE/ER-0165/1 3004–5
DOE/ER-0175/2 .... 3006–8.2
DOE/ER-0191 .... 3004–18.6
DOE/ER-0191/1 .... 3004–18.8
DOE/ER-0193 3004–7
DOE/ER-0202 .... 3004–18.1
DOE/EV-0005/22 .... 3406–1.35
DOE/EV-0005/35 .... 3406–1.36
DOE/EV-0005/36 .... 3406–1.38
DOE/EV-0005/39 .... 3406–1.37
DOE/EV-0005/40 .... 3406–1.39
DOE/EV-0005/43 .... 3406–1.40
DOE/FE-(nos.) 3002–13
DOE/FE-0036 3004–20
DOE/FE-0039 3004–22
DOE/IE-0003 3404–6
DOE/IG-0008/6 3002–12
DOE/IG-0208 .... 3006–5.7
DOE/IG-0214 .... 3006–5.8
DOE/MA-0004/3 3024–3
DOE/MA-0062/2 3004–14
DOE/MA-0142 3004–21
DOE/NBB-0024/1 3004–1
DOE/NBB-0036 3008–94
DOE/NBM-3014042 3008–91
DOE/NBM-3015045 3008–93
DOE/NE-0025/2 3354–9
DOE/NE-0025/3 3354–9
DOE/NE-0030/11 3354–11
DOE/OR-00033-T26 3008–90
DOE/PE-0030/1 .... 3004–13.3
DOE/PE-0049 3004–23
DOE/PE-0054 3008–96
DOE/PE-0055 3004–24
DOE/PE-70039/1 3008–87
DOE/PE-70042/1 3008–92
DOE/PETC/TR-84/7 3004–15
DOE/RG-0062 3104–10
DOE/RL-84-1 3354–2
DOE/RW-0004 3364–1
DOE/RW-0006 3364–2
DOE/S-0010(84) 3024–2
DOE/S-0025, Vol. I 3008–89.1
DOE/S-0025, Vol. II 3008–89.2
DOE/S-0028 3008–95
DOE/S-0030/1 3024–4
DOE/SWP-0001/2 3244–1
DOE/TIC-8200-R48 3002–5
FERC-0105 3084–9
FERC-0107 3084–9
Manpower Assessment
Brief 2 .... 3006–8.2
NIPER-133-PPS 84/1 .... 3006–2.1
NIPER-134 PPS 84/2 .... 3006–2.2
NIPER-135 PPS 84/3 .... 3006–2.3
NIPER-136 PPS 84/4 .... 3006–2.4
ORAU-227 3004–11
ORAU/IEA-83-8(M) 3006–7.4
ORAU/IEA-83-12(M) 3006–7.7
ORAU/IEA-83-13(M) 3006–7.5
ORAU/IEA-84-1(M) 3006–7.6
ORNL-5957 3308–71
ORNL-6050 3304–5
ORNL/CON-132 3308–77
ORNL/CON-145 3308–72
ORNL/CON-147 3308–74
ORNL/CON-164 3308–76
ORNL/TM-8310 3308–68
ORNL/TM-8492 3108–28
ORNL/TM-8510 3008–98
ORNL/TM-8843 3308–70
ORO-842 3354–7
PNL-4239-Ed.2 3008–88
SR/EAFD/84-01 .... 3164–73.2

DEPARTMENT OF DEFENSE

CHAMPUS 5400.2-CB 3502–2
DNA 6032F 3906–1.42
DNA 6033F 3906–1.41
DOD 4100.33-INV 3544–25
DoDDS Pamphlet
83-P-0017 3504–17
DoDDS Pamphlet
84-C-0001 3504–18
F01 3544–6
F02 3544–23
FAD 728/84 3504–7
FAD 748/(yr.) 3542–3
L02 3542–15
M01 3544–1
M02 3544–7
M03 3542–14
M04 3542–16
M06 3544–24
MSC Rpt. 7700-2 3802–2
NAVMAT P-4200 3804–13
NAVMED P-5027 3804–1
NAVMED P-5028 3802–1
NAVPERS 15658 3802–4
NAVSO P-3523 3802–3
P-1 3504–14
P01 3544–5
P02 3544–4
P03 3542–1

January-December 1984
ASI Annual Supplement 1047

Report Numbers

P04	3544–17
P05	3542–19
P06	3544–11
P07	3544–18
P08	3544–19
P09	3542–5
P14	3542–17
P16	3542–10
R-1	3504–15
Release No. 27-84	3544–15
RP-34(84)	3804–6
ST24	3544–22
WRSC-WCUS-82-(nos.)	3754–3

DEPARTMENT OF HEALTH AND HUMAN SERVICES

Actuarial Note No. 120	4706–2.120
Actuarial Study No. 89	4706–1.89
Actuarial Study No. 90	4706–1.90
Actuarial Study No. 91	4706–1.91
Actuarial Study No. 92	4706–1.92
Actuarial Study No. 93	4706–1.93
ADM (yr.)-151	4482–1
ADM (yr.)-158	4506–3
ADM 83-662	4044–1
ADM 83-1046	4506–2.6
ADM 83-1275	4504–9
ADM 83-1296	4508–5
ADM 84-319	4044–13
ADM 84-662	4044–1
ADM 84-1276	4496–1.31
ADM 84-1286	4496–5.18
ADM 84-1291	4488–4
ADM 84-1317	4494–4
AoA 83-20915	4608–16.1
AoA 83-20916	4608–16.2
AoA 83-20917	4608–16.3
CDC (yr.)-8017	4202–1
CDC 84-8017	4202–7
CDC 84-8111	4204–8
CDC 84-8241	4204–1
CDC 84-8249	4204–2
CDC 84-8255	4205–28
CDC 84-8280	4204–11
CDC 84-8295	4205–3
CDC 84-8295	4205–24
CDC 84-8385	4205–35
CDC 84-8391	4204–16
DHHS 82-20202	4146–12.2
DHHS 84-20203	4146–12.3
DHHS 84-20206	4146–12.4
HCFA 02156	4654–5
HCFA 03156	4654–1
HCFA 03160	4656–1.18
HCFA 03161	4656–1.19
HCFA 03162	4656–1.20
HCFA 03165	4652–8
HCFA 03166	4656–1.17
HCFA 03171	4652–8
HCFA 03172	4658–8
HCFA 03174	4658–7
HCFA 03185	4652–8
HCFA 10015	4654–4
HRS-DV-84-5	4118–18
HRS-M-HM-83-2	4108–32
HRS-M-HM-84-1	4104–8
HRS-P-OD-84-1	4118–52
HRS-P-OD-84-4	4114–8.1
HRS-P-OD-84-4	4114–8.2
Influenza Rpt. No. 94	4205–3
Mental Health Stat. Note	
166	4506–3.13
Mental Health Stat. Note	
167	4506–3.14
National Medical Care	
Utilization and	

Expenditure Survey,	
Data Rpt. No. 4	4146–11.4
National Medical Care	
Utilization and	
Expenditure Survey,	
Data Rpt. No. 5	4146–11.5
NCHSR 84-74	4186–4.3
NCHSR Data Preview	
No. 18	4186–3.18
NCHSR Instruments and	
Procedures 3	4186–4.3
NIDA Res. Issues 34	4496–1.31
NIH 83-1967	4474–11
NIH 83-2036	4478–144
NIH 84-5	4434–1
NIH 84-7	4434–2
NIH 84-694a	4474–16
NIH 84-1042	4434–7.3
NIH 84-1043	4434–7.2
NIH 84-1044	4434–7.1
NIH 84-1261	4434–3
NIH 84-2011	4474–23
NIH 84-2335	4474–22.1
NIH 84-2356	4474–22.2
NIH 84-2357	4474–22.3
NIH 84-2358	4474–22.4
NIH 84-2359	4474–22.5
NIH 84-2360	4474–22.6
NIH 84-2676	4478–149
NIH 85-1837	4478–130
NIMH Series BN, No. 4	4506–8.4
NIMH Series FN, No. 6	4506–2.6
NIMH Series HN, No. 3	4508–5
NIOSH 83-116	4248–47
OCSE Pub. 0005	4002–5
OCSE Pub. 0005	4004–29
ODAM 5-83	4114–12
ODAM 18-84	4114–11
OHDS 83-31184	4608–17
OHDS 83-31186	4608–20
OHDS 84-29002	4608–19
OHDS 84-30339	4608–18
OS 83-12	4004–3
PHS (yr.)-1120	4142–1
PHS (yr.)-1309-(nos.)	4122–2
PHS (yr.)-50193	4102–1
PHS 81-1214	4164–2
PHS 84-1100	4144–1
PHS 84-1101	4144–2
PHS 84-1102	4144–3
PHS 84-1103	4144–4
PHS 84-1104	4144–5
PHS 84-1120, Vol. 32,	
No. 8, Supp	4146–5.72
PHS 84-1120, Vol. 32,	
No. 9, Supp	4146–5.73
PHS 84-1120, Vol. 32,	
No. 9, Supp.(2)	4146–5.74
PHS 84-1120, Vol. 32,	
No. 10, Supp	4146–5.75
PHS 84-1120, Vol. 32,	
No. 10, Supp	4146–5.76
PHS 84-1120, Vol. 32,	
No. 11, Supp	4146–5.77
PHS 84-1120, Vol. 32,	
No. 13	4144–7
PHS 84-1120, Vol. 33,	
No. 3, Supp	4146–5.78
PHS 84-1120, Vol. 33,	
No. 6, Supp	4146–5.79
PHS 84-1142	4124–7
PHS 84-1232	4144–11
PHS 84-1250, No. 95	4146–8.96
PHS 84-1250, No. 96	4146–8.99
PHS 84-1250, No. 97	4146–8.97
PHS 84-1250, No. 98	4146–8.98
PHS 84-1250, No. 99	4146–8.100

PHS 84-1250, No. 100	4146–8.102
PHS 84-1250, No. 101	4146–8.101
PHS 84-1301	4124–1
PHS 84-1406a	4147–3.25
PHS 84-1477	4147–5.1
PHS 84-1573	4147–10.145
PHS 84-1574	4147–10.146
PHS 84-1576	4147–10.147
PHS 84-1683	4147–11.201
PHS 84-1737	4147–13.76
PHS 84-1738	4147–13.77
PHS 84-1739	4147–13.78
PHS 84-1740	4147–13.79
PHS 84-1741	4147–13.80
PHS 84-1823	4147–14.28
PHS 84-1824	4147–14.29
PHS 84-1825	4147–14.30
PHS 84-1918	4147–21.40
PHS 84-1919	4147–21.41
PHS 84-1920	4147–21.42
PHS 84-3345	4186–6.4
PHS 84-3346	4184–1
PHS 84-3347	4186–2.6
PHS 84-3362	4186–3.18
PHS 84-3363	4186–3.19
PHS 84-3368	4184–2
PHS 84-3369	4186–4.3
PHS 84-5024	4044–6
PHS 84-20000	4146–11
PHS 84-50146	4048–18
PHS 84-50196	4044–8
PHS 84-50205	4044–6
PHS 85-1120, Vol. 33,	
No. 8, Supp	4146–5.80
PHS 85-1120, Vol. 33,	
No. 9, Supp	4146–5.81
PHS 85-1250, No. 102	4146–8.103
PHS 85-1250, No. 103	4146–8.104
PHS Bibliography Series	
No. 45	4044–8
Res. Rpt. (SSA) 59	4746–4.58
Rpt. 19M	4432–1
Series B, Descriptive Rpt.	
2	4146–12.2
Series B, Descriptive Rpt.	
3	4146–12.3
Series B, Descriptive Rpt.	
6	4146–12.4
SSA 11-11500, No. 119	4706–2.119
SSA 11-11536	4706–1.89
SSA 11-11537	4706–1.90
SSA 11-11538	4706–1.91
SSA 11-11539	4706–1.92
SSA 11-11540	4706–1.93
SSA 13-11700	4742–1
SSA 13-11700	4744–3
SSA 13-11701, No. 1	4746–16.1
SSA 13-11703	4742–2
SSA 13-11705	4742–6
SSA 13-11805	4746–4.58
SSA 13-11871	4744–26
SSA 13-11873	4746–5.43
SSA 13-11947	4744–20
SSA 13-11954	4748–38
SSA 13-11976	4744–27
SSA 13-11977	4744–16
SSA 80-08005	4704–9.2
SSA 80-08011	4704–11
SSA 80-08032	4704–10
SSA 80-21235	4704–9.1
SSA Staff Paper 43	4746–5.43
Vital and Health Statistics	
Series 3, No. 22a	4147–3.25
Vital and Health Statistics	
Series 5, No. 1	4147–5.1
Vital and Health Statistics	
Series 10, No. 145	4147–10.145

Report Numbers

Vital and Health Statistics Series 10, No. 146 .... 4147-10.146 Vital and Health Statistics Series 10, No. 148 .... 4147-10.147 Vital and Health Statistics Series 11, No. 233 .... 4147-11.201 Vital and Health Statistics Series 13, No. 76 .... 4147-13.76 Vital and Health Statistics Series 13, No. 77 .... 4147-13.77 Vital and Health Statistics Series 13, No. 78 .... 4147-13.78 Vital and Health Statistics Series 13, No. 79 .... 4147-13.79 Vital and Health Statistics Series 13, No. 80 .... 4147-13.80 Vital and Health Statistics Series 14, No. 28 .... 4147-14.28 Vital and Health Statistics Series 14, No. 29 .... 4147-14.29 Vital and Health Statistics Series 14, No. 30 .... 4147-14.30 Vital and Health Statistics Series 21, No. 40 .... 4147-21.40 Vital and Health Statistics Series 21, No. 41 .... 4147-21.41 Vital and Health Statistics Series 21, No. 42 .... 4147-21.42

DEPARTMENT OF EDUCATION

ED 240 747 .... 4804-5 FRSS Rpt. 14 .... 4826-1.10 LSB 84-4-16 .... 4828-17 NAEP Rpt. 83-1 .... 4898-15 NCES 83-220b .... 4848-15 NCES 83-407 .... 4824-2 NCES 84-101b .... 4834-10 NCES 84-102 .... 4834-12 NCES 84-104 .... 4834-13 NCES 84-105b .... 4838-13 NCES 84-106b .... 4838-12 NCES 84-201 .... 4826-1.10 NCES 84-202 .... 4826-2.15 NCES 84-204b .... 4828-16 NCES 84-205 .... 4826-2.16 NCES 84-206 .... 4826-2.17 NCES 84-207 .... 4826-2.20 NCES 84-208b .... 4854-1 NCES 84-209 .... 4826-2.19 NCES 84-211b .... 4826-2.14 NCES 84-212b .... 4838-11 NCES 84-213b .... 4826-2.18 NCES 84-216 .... 4826-2.22 NCES 84-221b .... 4826-2.21 NCES 84-300 .... 4844-3 NCES 84-304 .... 4844-11 NCES 84-305 .... 4844-2 NCES 84-307 .... 4844-10 NCES 84-309 .... 4848-16 NCES 84-401 .... 4824-1 NCES 84-406 .... 4824-3 Rpt. No. 85-1 .... 4804-17 RSA-IM-83-43 .... 4944-9 RSA-IM-84-08 .... 4944-6 RSA-IM-84-17 .... 4944-5 RSA-IM-84-22 4944-2

DEPARTMENT OF HOUSING AND URBAN DEVELOPMENT

HUD 84-120 .... 5006-3.30 HUD 84-129 .... 5006-3.31 HUD 84-162 .... 5006-3.32 HUD 84-199 .... 5006-3.33 HUD 84-216 .... 5006-3.34 HUD 84-223 .... 5006-3.35

HUD 84-237 .... 5006-3.36 HUD 84-238 .... 5004-6 HUD 84-252 .... 5148-6 HUD 84-258 .... 5006-3.37 HUD 84-259 .... 5006-3.38 HUD 84-271 .... 5006-3.39 HUD 927-16 .... 5002-8 HUD-85-12-N .... 5144-6 HUD-758-PDR .... 5188-103.2 HUD-759-PDR .... 5188-103.1 HUD-CPD-697-2 .... 5124-5 HUD-IG-428-11 .... 5002-8 HUD-PDR-636 .... 5188-106 HUD-PDR-647 .... 5188-105 HUD-PDR-731 .... 5188-104 HUD-PDR-750 .... 5188-102 HUD-PDR-903 .... 5188-109.1 HUD-UI-767 .... 5008-32 R33MJCA .... 5142-6 RR: S0102 .... 5144-17 RR: S0403 .... 5142-1 RR: S0404 .... 5142-2 RR: S0405 .... 5142-3 RR: S0406 .... 5142-4 RR: S0433 .... 5142-40 RR: S0434 .... 5142-42 RR: S0435 .... 5142-41 RR: S0535 .... 5142-41 RR: S1210 .... 5142-5 RR: S1216 .... 5142-31 RRT: 1215 .... 5142-9 Sale 84-(nos.) 5142-43

DEPARTMENT OF INTERIOR

Air Pollution and Acid Rain Rpt. 13 .... 5506-5.13 Air Pollution and Acid Rain Rpt. 14 .... 5506-5.14 Air Pollution and Acid Rain Rpt. 15 .... 5506-5.15 Air Pollution and Acid Rain Rpt. 16 .... 5506-5.16 Air Pollution and Acid Rain Rpt. 17 .... 5506-5.17 Bur. Mines IC 8930 .... 5606-4.11 Bur. Mines IC 8932 .... 5608-143 Bur. Mines IC 8946 .... 5608-144 Bur. Mines IC 8962 .... 5606-4.10 Bur. Mines IC 8969 .... 5606-6.1 Bur. Mines IC 8977 .... 5606-4.12 Bur. Mines IC 8979 .... 5608-145 Bur. Mines IC 8993 .... 5604-2 Fish Distribution Rpt. 17 .... 5504-10 Fish Distribution Rpt. 18 .... 5504-10 FWS/OBS-79/39 .... 5506-9.1 FWS/OBS-80/40.13 .... 5506-5.13 FWS/OBS-80/40.14 .... 5506-5.14 FWS/OBS-80/40.15 .... 5506-5.15 FWS/OBS-80/40.16 .... 5506-5.16 FWS/OBS-80/40.17 .... 5506-5.17 FWS/OBS-81/01 .... 5506-9.4 FWS/OBS-81/15 .... 5506-9.2 FWS/OBS-81/24 .... 5506-9.3 FWS/OBS-81/37 .... 5506-9.5 FWS/OBS-81/55 .... 5506-9.6 FWS/OBS-82/04 .... 5506-9.9 FWS/OBS-82/11.(nos.) .... 5506-8 FWS/OBS-82/11.1 .... 5506-8.18 FWS/OBS-82/11.2 .... 5506-8.19 FWS/OBS-82/11.3 .... 5506-8.16 FWS/OBS-82/11.4 .... 5506-8.21 FWS/OBS-82/11.5 .... 5506-8.20 FWS/OBS-82/11.6 .... 5506-8.22 FWS/OBS-82/11.7 .... 5506-8.9 FWS/OBS-82/11.8 .... 5506-8.13 FWS/OBS-82/11.9 .... 5506-8.10

FWS/OBS-82/11.10 .... 5506-8.11 FWS/OBS-82/11.11 .... 5506-8.15 FWS/OBS-82/11.12 .... 5506-8.12 FWS/OBS-82/11.13 .... 5506-8.14 FWS/OBS-82/11.14 .... 5506-8.17 FWS/OBS-82/11.15 .... 5506-8.25 FWS/OBS-82/11.16 .... 5506-8.27 FWS/OBS-82/11.17 .... 5506-8.26 FWS/OBS-82/11.18 .... 5506-8.23 FWS/OBS-82/11.19 .... 5506-8.24 FWS/OBS-82/11.21 .... 5506-8.28 FWS/OBS-82/25 .... 5506-9.8 FWS/OBS-82/27 .... 5506-9.7 FWS/OBS-82/32 .... 5506-9.11 FWS/OBS-82/61 .... 5508-87 FWS/OBS-82/65 .... 5508-85 FWS/OBS-82/69 .... 5506-4.2 FWS/OBS-83/01 .... 5506-7.1 FWS/OBS-83/05 .... 5506-9.12 FWS/OBS-83/14 .... 5506-4.8 FWS/OBS-83/14 .... 5506-4.8 FWS/OBS-83/14 .... 5506-4.8 FWS/OBS-83/14 .... 5506-4.8 FWS/OBS-83/15 .... 5506-4.9 FWS/OBS-83/15 .... 5506-4.9 FWS/OBS-83/15 .... 5506-4.9 FWS/OBS-83/17 .... 5506-9.13 FWS/OBS-83/23 .... 5506-9.10 FWS/OBS-83/30 .... 5508-72.3 FWS/OBS-83/31 .... 5508-86 FWS/OBS-83/35 .... 5508-88 FWS/OBS-84/04 .... 5506-9.14 GS Circ. 760 .... 5666-18.4 GS Circ. 850-E .... 5666-14.9 GS Circ. 888 .... 5668-74 GS Circ. 896-(ltrs.) .... 5662-4 GS Circ. 902-A-P .... 5668-69 GS Circ. 913 .... 5668-70 GS Circ. 914 .... 5664-14 GS Circ. 918 .... 5668-73 GS Circ. 925 .... 5668-71 GS Circ. 940 .... 5664-11 GS List (nos.) .... 5662-1 GS Open-File Rpt. 82-223 .... 5666-15.24 GS Open-File Rpt. 82-505 .... 5666-15.22 GS Open-File Rpt. 82-647 .... 5666-15.25 GS Open-File Rpt. 82-679 .... 5666-15.23 GS Open-File Rpt. 82-864 .... 5666-15.26 GS Open File Rpt. 83-132 .... 5666-19.5 GS Open-File Rpt. 83-146 .... 5666-19.4 GS Water-Data Rpt. AL-82-1 .... 5666-20.1 GS Water-Data Rpt. AL-83-1 .... 5666-10.1 GS Water-Data Rpt. AR-82-1 .... 5666-20.4 GS Water-Data Rpt. AZ-82-1 .... 5666-20.3 GS Water-Data Rpt. CA-82-1 .... 5666-20.5 GS Water-Data Rpt. CA-82-2 .... 5666-20.5 GS Water-Data Rpt. CA-82-3 .... 5666-20.5 GS Water-Data Rpt. CA-82-4 .... 5666-20.5 GS Water-Data Rpt. CO-83-1 .... 5666-10.6 GS Water-Data Rpt. CO-83-2 .... 5666-10.6 GS Water-Data Rpt. FL-82-3A .... 5666-20.8 GS Water-Data Rpt. FL-82-3B .... 5666-20.8 GS Water-Data Rpt. FL-82-4 .... 5666-20.8

Report Numbers

GS Water-Data Rpt.	
HI-83-1	5666-10.10
GS Water-Data Rpt.	
HI-83-2	5666-10.10
GS Water-Data Rpt.	
IA-83-1	5666-10.14
GS Water-Data Rpt.	
IL-82-1	5666-20.12
GS Water-Data Rpt.	
IL-83-1	5666-10.12
GS Water-Data Rpt.	
IL-83-2	5666-10.12
GS Water-Data Rpt.	
IN-83-1	5666-10.13
GS Water-Data Rpt.	
KY-82-1	5666-20.16
GS Water-Data Rpt.	
KY-83-1	5666-10.16
GS Water-Data Rpt.	
LA-82-1	5666-20.17
GS Water-Data Rpt.	
LA-83-1	5666-10.17
GS Water-Data Rpt.	
MA-RI-82-1	5666-20.20
GS Water-Data Rpt.	
MD-DE-83-1	5666-10.19
GS Water-Data Rpt.	
ME-83-1	5666-10.18
GS Water-Data Rpt.	
MI-83-1	5666-10.21
GS Water-Data Rpt.	
MN-82-1	5666-20.22
GS Water-Data Rpt.	
MN-82-2	5666-20.22
GS Water-Data Rpt.	
MO-80-1	5666-12.24
GS Water-Data Rpt.	
MS-82-1	5666-20.23
GS Water-Data Rpt.	
MT-83-2	5666-10.25
GS Water-Data Rpt.	
NC-83-1	5666-10.32
GS Water-Data Rpt.	
NE-82-1	5666-20.26
GS Water-Data Rpt.	
NH-VT-82-1	5666-20.28
GS Water-Data Rpt.	
NJ-80-2	5666-12.29
GS Water-Data Rpt.	
NJ-81-2	5666-16.29
GS Water-Data Rpt.	
NJ-83-1	5666-10.29
GS Water-Data Rpt.	
NJ-83-2	5666-10.29
GS Water-Data Rpt.	
NY-83-1	5666-10.31
GS Water-Data Rpt.	
NY-83-2	5666-10.31
GS Water-Data Rpt.	
NY-83-3	5666-10.31
GS Water-Data Rpt.	
OH-80-1	5666-12.34
GS Water-Data Rpt.	
OH-83-1	5666-10.34
GS Water-Data Rpt.	
OH-83-2	5666-10.34
GS Water-Data Rpt.	
OR-81-2	5666-16.36
GS Water-Data Rpt.	
OR-82-1	5666-20.36
GS Water-Data Rpt.	
OR-82-2	5666-20.36
GS Water-Data Rpt.	
PA-82-1	5666-20.37
GS Water-Data Rpt.	
PA-82-2	5666-20.37

GS Water-Data Rpt.	
PA-83-2	5666-10.37
GS Water-Data Rpt.	
PA-83-3	5666-10.37
GS Water-Data Rpt.	
PR-81-82-1	5666-20.48
GS Water-Data Rpt.	
SC-82-1	5666-20.38
GS Water-Data Rpt.	
SD-83-1	5666-10.39
GS Water-Data Rpt.	
TN-83-1	5666-10.40
GS Water-Data Rpt.	
UT-83-1	5666-10.42
GS Water-Data Rpt.	
VA-83-1	5666-10.43
GS Water-Data Rpt.	
WA-81-2	5666-16.44
GS Water-Data Rpt.	
WI-82-1	5666-20.46
GS Water-Data Rpt.	
WV-83-1	5666-10.45
GS Water-Data Rpt.	
WY-82-1	5666-20.47
GS Water-Data Rpt.	
WY-83-1	5666-10.47
N-MO-MOI-12-84-B	5304-15.5
N-MO-MOI-12-84-C	5304-15.6
N-MO-MOI-12-84-D	5304-15.1
N-MO-MOI-12-84-E	5304-15.2
N-MO-MOI-12-84-F	5304-15.3
NPS 2200	5544-12
OCS EIS MMS 84-0009	5736-1.10
OCS EIS MMS 84-0009	5736-1.10
OCS Rpt. MMS 84-0004	5736-2.8
OCS Rpt. MMS 84-0010	5734-4
Open-File Rpt. 83-598	5666-17.13
Open-File Rpt. 83-728	5668-72
Open-File Rpt. 83-801	5666-17.14
Open-File Rpt. 83-882	5736-2.7
Open-File Rpt. 84-94	5666-17.15
S-MO-MOI-12-84	5304-15.4
Spec. Scientific Rpt.,	
Wildlife 254	5508-18
TR EL-82-4	5506-8
USGS Water-Supply Paper	
2250	5664-12
USGS/WRD/HD-81/001	5666-12.24
USGS/WRD/HD-81/051	5666-12.34
USGS/WRD/HD-81/058	5666-12.29
USGS/WRD/HD-82/021	5666-20.5
USGS/WRD/HD-82/026	5666-16.36
USGS/WRD/HD-82/027	5666-20.48
USGS/WRD/HD-82/034	5666-16.44
USGS/WRD/HD-82/039	5666-16.29
USGS/WRD/HD-82/042	5666-20.16
USGS/WRD/HD-82/044	5666-20.46
USGS/WRD/HD-82/047	5666-20.37
USGS/WRD/HD-82/066	5666-20.17
USGS/WRD/HD-82/071	5666-20.12
USGS/WRD/HD-82/078	5666-20.38
USGS/WRD/HD-83/068	5666-20.47
USGS/WRD/HD-84/003	5666-20.22
USGS/WRD/HD-84/004	5666-20.22
USGS/WRD/HD-84/005	5666-20.36
USGS/WRD/HD-84/006	5666-20.36
USGS/WRD/HD-84/007	5666-20.37
USGS/WRD/HD-84/008	5666-20.1
USGS/WRD/HD-84/009	5666-20.28
USGS/WRD/HD-84/010	5666-20.4
USGS/WRD/HD-84/011	5666-20.8
USGS/WRD/HD-84/012	5666-20.8
USGS/WRD/HD-84/013	5666-20.20
USGS/WRD/HD-84/014	5666-20.26
USGS/WRD/HD-84/015	5666-20.8
USGS/WRD/HD-84/016	5666-10.21

USGS/WRD/HD-84/017	5666-20.5
USGS/WRD/HD-84/018	5666-20.5
USGS/WRD/HD-84/019	5666-20.23
USGS/WRD/HD-84/020	5666-20.5
USGS/WRD/HD-84/022	5666-10.19
USGS/WRD/HD-84/023	5666-10.18
USGS/WRD/HD-84/024	5666-10.34
USGS/WRD/HD-84/025	5666-10.34
USGS/WRD/HD-84/026	5666-10.16
USGS/WRD/HD-84/029	5666-10.17
USGS/WRD/HD-84/030	5666-10.43
USGS/WRD/HD-84/031	5666-20.3
USGS/WRD/HD-84/032	5666-10.25
USGS/WRD/HD-84/033	5666-10.10
USGS/WRD/HD-84/034	5666-10.31
USGS/WRD/HD-84/035	5666-10.6
USGS/WRD/HD-84/036	5666-10.6
USGS/WRD/HD-84/038	5666-10.42
USGS/WRD/HD-84/042	5666-10.31
USGS/WRD/HD-84/044	5666-10.13
USGS/WRD/HD-84/048	5666-10.47
USGS/WRD/HD-84/049	5666-10.37
USGS/WRD/HD-84/051	5666-10.31
USGS/WRD/HD-84/052	5666-10.14
USGS/WRD/HD-84/053	5666-10.29
USGS/WRD/HD-84/054	5666-10.29
USGS/WRD/HD-84/055	5666-10.32
USGS/WRD/HD-84/056	5666-10.40
USGS/WRD/HD-84/057	5666-10.12
USGS/WRD/HD-84/058	5666-10.12
USGS/WRD/HD-84/059	5666-10.1
USGS/WRD/HD-84/060	5666-10.37
USGS/WRD/HD-84/062	5666-10.10
USGS/WRD/HD-84/063	5666-10.39
USGS/WRD/HD-84/064	5666-10.45
V-MO-MOI-12-84	5304-15.7
V-TG-VIS-08-83	5304-10

DEPARTMENT OF JUSTICE

Rpt. 1-21	6004-2
U.S. Parole Commission	
Res. Rpt. 33	6006-2.31
U.S. Parole Commission	
Res. Rpt. 34	6006-2.32
U.S. Parole Commission	
Res. Rpt. 35	6006-2.33

DEPARTMENT OF LABOR

BLS Announcement 83-2	6704-2
BLS Bull. 1370-17/Vol. 1	6744-5.1
BLS Bull. 1370-17/Vol. 2	6744-5.2
BLS Bull. 1370-18	6744-5.3
BLS Bull. 2096-1	6748-72
BLS Bull. 2134-2	6888-1.2
BLS Bull. 2166	6728-27
BLS Bull. 2167	6787-6.196
BLS Bull. 2175	6724-1
BLS Bull. 2177	6787-6.197
BLS Bull. 2182	6828-23
BLS Bull. 2185	6787-6.198
BLS Bull. 2186	6748-60
BLS Bull. 2187	6787-6.200
BLS Bull. 2188	6787-6.199
BLS Bull. 2189	6824-1
BLS Bull. 2191	6746-1.251
BLS Bull. 2192	6746-1.250
BLS Bull. 2193	6787-6.203
BLS Bull. 2194	6784-9
BLS Bull. 2195	6846-1.13
BLS Bull. 2196	6844-1
BLS Bull. 2197	6728-29
BLS Bull. 2198	6787-6.202
BLS Bull. 2199	6746-1.252
BLS Bull. 2201	6744-15
BLS Bull. 2203	6846-1.14

Report Numbers

BLS Bull. 2204 ... 6787–6.201
BLS Bull. 2205 ... 6744–1
BLS Bull. 2206 ... 6744–3
BLS Bull. 2207 ... 6787–6.204
BLS Bull. 2208 ... 6784–2
BLS Bull. 2209 ... 6746–1.253
BLS Bull. 2210 ... 6884–1
BLS Bull. 2211 ... 6728–30
BLS Bull. 2213 ... 6784–19
BLS Bull. 2214 ... 6846–1.15
BLS Bull. 2215 ... 6744–16
BLS Bull. 2216 ... 6744–7
BLS Bull. 2218 ... 6787–6.205
BLS Bull. 2221 ... 6787–6.206
BLS Bull. 3020-51 ... 6785–12.1
BLS Bull. 3020-52 ... 6785–12.1
BLS Bull. 3020-53 ... 6785–12.2
BLS Bull. 3020-54 ... 6785–12.1
BLS Bull. 3020-55 ... 6785–12.1
BLS Bull. 3020-56 ... 6785–12.1
BLS Bull. 3020-57 ... 6785–12.2
BLS Bull. 3020-58 ... 6785–12.1
BLS Bull. 3020-59 ... 6785–12.2
BLS Bull. 3020-60 ... 6785–12.2
BLS Bull. 3020-61 ... 6785–12.2
BLS Bull. 3020-62 ... 6785–12.2
BLS Bull. 3020-63 ... 6785–12.2
BLS Bull. 3020-64 ... 6785–12.2
BLS Bull. 3020-65 ... 6785–12.3
BLS Bull. 3020-66 ... 6785–12.3
BLS Bull. 3020-67 ... 6785–12.3
BLS Bull. 3020-68 ... 6785–12.3
BLS Bull. 3020-69 ... 6785–12.4
BLS Bull. 3020-70 ... 6785–12.3
BLS Bull. 3020-71 ... 6785–12.4
BLS Bull. 3020-72 ... 6785–12.5
BLS Bull. 3020-73 ... 6785–1
BLS Bull. 3025-1 ... 6785–11.1
BLS Bull. 3025-2 ... 6785–11.1
BLS Bull. 3025-3 ... 6785–11.1
BLS Bull. 3025-4 ... 6785–11.1
BLS Bull. 3025-5 ... 6785–11.2
BLS Bull. 3025-6 ... 6785–11.3
BLS Bull. 3025-7 ... 6785–11.4
BLS Bull. 3025-8 ... 6785–11.3
BLS Bull. 3025-9 ... 6785–11.3
BLS Bull. 3025-10 ... 6785–11.4
BLS Bull. 3025-11 ... 6785–11.4
BLS Bull. 3025-12 ... 6785–11.4
BLS Bull. 3025-13 ... 6785–11.4
BLS Bull. 3025-14 ... 6785–11.5
BLS Bull. 3025-15 ... 6785–11.5
BLS Bull. 3025-16 ... 6785–11.5
BLS Bull. 3025-17 ... 6785–11.5
BLS Bull. 3025-18 ... 6785–11.5
BLS Bull. 3025-19 ... 6785–11.6
BLS Bull. 3025-20 ... 6785–11.5
BLS Bull. 3025-21 ... 6785–11.6
BLS Bull. 3025-22 ... 6785–11.6
BLS Bull. 3025-23 ... 6785–11.6
BLS Bull. 3025-24 ... 6785–11.6
BLS Bull. 3025-25 ... 6785–11.6
BLS Bull. 3025-26 ... 6785–11.6
BLS Bull. 3025-27 ... 6785–11.6
BLS Bull. 3025-28 ... 6785–11.8
BLS Bull. 3025-29 ... 6785–11.8
BLS Bull. 3025-30 ... 6785–11.7
BLS Bull. 3025-31 ... 6785–11.7
BLS Bull. 3025-32 ... 6785–11.8
BLS Bull. 3025-33 ... 6785–11.8
BLS Bull. 3025-34 ... 6785–11.8
BLS Bull. 3025-35 ... 6785–11.8
BLS Bull. 3025-36 ... 6785–11.8
BLS Bull. 3025-37 ... 6785–11.8
BLS Bull. 3025-38 ... 6785–11.8
BLS Bull. 3025-39 ... 6785–11.8
BLS Bull. 3025-40 ... 6785–11.9
BLS Bull. 3025-41 ... 6785–11.9
BLS Bull. 3025-42 ... 6785–11.9
BLS Bull. 3025-43 ... 6785–11.9
BLS Bull. 3025-44 ... 6785–11.10
BLS Bull. 3025-45 ... 6785–11.10
BLS Bull. 3025-46 ... 6785–11.10
BLS Bull. 3025-47 ... 6785–11.10
BLS Bull. 3025-48 ... 6785–11.10
BLS Bull. 3025-49 ... 6785–11.10
BLS Bull. 3025-50 ... 6785–11.10
BLS Bull. 3025-51 ... 6785–11.10
BLS Bull. 3025-52 ... 6785–11.10
BLS Bull. 3025-53 ... 6785–11.10
BLS Middle Atlantic Region Rpt. No. 75 ... 6926–1.75
BLS New England Region Rpt. No. 84-1 ... 6916–7.1
BLS New England Region Rpt. No. 84-2 ... 6916–7.2
BLS New England Region Rpt. No. 84-3 ... 6916–7.3
BLS Rpt. 704 ... 6728–28
BLS Southeast Region Rpt. No. 65 ... 6946–1.68
BLS Southwest Region Rpt. No. 22 ... 6966–1.12
BLS Summary 83-8 ... 6785–6.1
BLS Summary 83-9 ... 6785–5.1
BLS Summary 84-1 ... 6785–6.2
BLS Summary 84-2 ... 6785–5.2
BLS Summary 84-3 ... 6785–9
BLS Summary 84-4 ... 6785–13
BLS Summary 84-5 ... 6785–8
BLS Summary 84-7 ... 6785–5.3
BLS Summary 84-8 ... 6785–6.3
BLS Summary 84-9 ... 6785–6.4
BLS Working Paper 139 ... 6886–6.8
Comparison Revision 4 ... 6402–2
Comparison Revision 5 ... 6402–2
ET Hndbk 394 ... 6408–5
GR FLOW-80 ... 6744–17
GR FLOW-82 ... 6744–17
IR 1143 ... 6664–4
IR 1144 ... 6664–3
IR 1145 ... 6664–1
IR 1146 ... 6664–5
IR 1147 ... 6664–2
OSHA 2066 ... 6604–1
OSHA 3082 ... 6604–2
OSHA 3087 ... 6606–2.11
USDL 83-525 ... 6408–57
USDL 84-1 ... 6408–58
USDL 84-42 ... 6784–17.3
USDL 84-71 ... 6784–17.1
USDL 84-75 ... 6782–6
USDL 84-86 ... 6748–76
USDL 84-89 ... 6888–29
USDL 84-238 ... 6744–13
USDL 84-245 ... 6864–1
USDL 84-262 ... 6408–60
USDL 84-284 ... 6408–61
USDL 84-290 ... 6748–77
USDL 84-302 ... 6408–62
USDL 84-313 ... 6408–64
USDL 84-321 ... 6748–78
USDL 84-329 ... 6408–63
USDL 84-352 ... 6782–6
USDL 84-371 ... 6744–14
USDL 84-378 ... 6784–17.2
USDL 84-388 ... 6748–79
USDL 84-431 ... 6824–2
USDL 84-472 ... 6844–3
Women's Bur. Bull. 298 ... 6568–29

DEPARTMENT OF STATE

Current Policy 546 ... 7008–39
Current Policy 548 ... 7008–38
Current Policy 605 ... 7008–42
Intl. Organization and Conf. Series 162 ... 7004–6
Intl. Organization and Conf. Series 163 ... 7004–5
Intl. Organization and Conf. Series 165 ... 7004–5
Pub. 7748 ... 7006–2.26
Pub. 7749 ... 7006–2.31
Pub. 7751 ... 7006–2.11
Pub. 7753 ... 7006–2.8
Pub. 7758 ... 7006–2.4
Pub. 7761 ... 7006–2.15
Pub. 7782 ... 7006–2.6
Pub. 7793 ... 7006–2.10
Pub. 7820 ... 7006–2.51
Pub. 7836 ... 7006–2.32
Pub. 7841 ... 7006–2.56
Pub. 7856 ... 7006–2.58
Pub. 7857 ... 7006–2.30
Pub. 7881 ... 7006–2.27
Pub. 7904 ... 7006–2.59
Pub. 7931 ... 7006–2.44
Pub. 7953 ... 7006–2.60
Pub. 7970 ... 7006–2.2
Pub. 7974 ... 7006–2.29
Pub. 7991 ... 7006–2.39
Pub. 7998 ... 7006–2.3
Pub. 8025 ... 7006–2.37
Pub. 8026 ... 7006–2.34
Pub. 8032 ... 7006–2.1
Pub. 8056 ... 7006–2.19
Pub. 8069 ... 7006–2.20
Pub. 8070 ... 7006–2.14
Pub. 8091 ... 7006–2.48
Pub. 8097 ... 7006–2.21
Pub. 8099 ... 7006–2.16
Pub. 8126 ... 7006–2.5
Pub. 8142 ... 7006–2.54
Pub. 8149 ... 7006–2.36
Pub. 8184 ... 7006–2.57
Pub. 8209 ... 7006–2.17
Pub. 8217 ... 7006–2.40
Pub. 8223 ... 7006–2.7
Pub. 8227 ... 7006–2.46
Pub. 8228 ... 7006–2.25
Pub. 8240 ... 7006–2.52
Pub. 8242 ... 7006–2.43
Pub. 8251 ... 7006–2.49
Pub. 8287 ... 7006–2.38
Pub. 8298 ... 7006–2.28
Pub. 8301 ... 7006–2.24
Pub. 8306 ... 7006–2.62
Pub. 8318 ... 7006–2.13
Pub. 8325 ... 7006–2.61
Pub. 8396 ... 7006–2.23
Pub. 8698 ... 7006–2.42
Pub. 8822 ... 7006–2.18
Pub. 8824 ... 7006–2.50
Pub. 8856 ... 7006–2.12
Pub. 8874 ... 7006–2.45
Pub. 8874 ... 7006–2.47
Pub. 8933 ... 7006–2.55
Pub. 8955 ... 7006–2.35
Pub. 8992 ... 7006–2.41
Pub. 9234 ... 7006–2.53
Pub. 9351 ... 7004–1
Pub. 9375 ... 7006–2.9
Pub. 9379 ... 7004–6
Pub. 9382 ... 7004–5
Pub. 9406 ... 7004–5
Rpt. 770-AR ... 7144–11
Rpt. 809-AR ... 7144–8
Rpt. 835-AR ... 7144–7
Rpt. 928-AR ... 7144–10
Rpt. 944-AR ... 7144–5
Rpt. 945-AR ... 7144–14

January-December 1984
ASI Annual Supplement 1051

Report Numbers

Spec. Rpt. 113	7002–1
Spec. Rpt. 116	7004–14
Spec. Rpt. 117	7002–1

DEPARTMENT OF TRANSPORTATION

AMS-420	7504–3
APO-110	7504–15
COMDTINST	
M16107.2C	7404–2
COMDTINST	
M16754.1E	7404–1
COMDTPUB P16590.1	7406–5.1
COMDTPUB P16590.2	7406–5.2
COMDTPUB P16590.3	7406–5.3
COMDTPUB P16590.4	7406–5.4
DOT-FAA-APO-84-2	7504–37
DOT HS (nos.)	7762–2
DOT HS 806 342	7768–80
DOT HS 806 370	7768–81
DOT HS 806 371	7768–81
DOT HS 806 402	7768–82
DOT HS 806 530	7764–13
DOT HS 806 541	7764–14
DOT HS 806 566	7764–10
DOT HS 806 570	7764–1.2
DOT HS 806 571	7764–1.1
DOT-I-83-8	7306–9.6
DOT-I-83-30	7888–59
DOT-I-83-42	7308–183
DOT-I-83-47	7308–184
DOT-I-83-50	7306–8.3
DOT-RSPA-DMA-50-84-	
12	7308–182
DOT-TSC-FAA-83-3	7504–29
DOT-TSC-RSPA-83-9	7304–2
DOT-TSC-RSPA-84-2	7304–19
DOT-TSC-RSPA-84-3	7304–2
DOT-TSC-UMTA-83-28	7888–61
DOT-TSC-UMTA-83-40	7888–60
DOT-TSC-UMTA-84-8	7884–6
DOT-TSC-UMTA-84-23	7884–5
FAA 04-84	7506–8.29
FAA 19-84	7506–8.30
FAA 33-84	7506–8.31
FAA 42-84	7506–8.32
FAA 44-84	7506–8.33
FAA-AM-83-5	7506–10.23
FAA-AM-83-6	7506–10.24
FAA-AM-83-7	7506–10.25
FAA-AM-83-11	7506–10.26
FAA-AM-83-15	7506–10.27
FAA-AM-83-16	7506–10.28
FAA-AM-83-17	7506–10.29
FAA-AM-83-18	7506–10.30
FAA-APO-83-7	7504–28
FAA-APO-84-1	7504–6
FAA APO-84-2	7504–15
FAA-MS-83-5	7504–29
FHWA 10-84	7556–3.1
FHWA 22-84	7556–3.2
FHWA 23-84	7556–3.3
FHWA 24-84	7556–3.4
FHWA/PL/83/001	7556–7.1
FHWA/PL/83/017	7556–7.2
FHWA/PL/84/001	7556–7.3
HHP-41	7554–16
MF-205	7554–32
Nationwide Personal	
Transportation Study,	
1977, Rpt. 11	7556–6.11
NHTSA 03-84	7766–7.9
NHTSA 07-84	7766–7.8
NHTSA 15-84	7766–7.10

NHTSA 17-84	7766–7.11
Rpt. DC-06-0439-84-1	7888–63
Statement TD-1, 1982	7604–6
UMTA-CA-11-0024-1	7888–62
UMTA-DC-06-0258-84-1	7882–1
UMTA-MA-06-0049-83-3	7888–61
UMTA-MA-06-0107-84-1	7884–4
UMTA-MA-06-0126-83-3	7888–60
UMTA-MA-06-0126-84-5	7884–6
UMTA-MA-06-0152-84-1	7884–5

DEPARTMENT OF TREASURY

ATF P 1323.1(6/84)	8484–1
ATF P 5400.10(6/84)	8484–4
Dept of Treasury Doc.	
3285	8104–2
IR-84-78	8304–16.1
IR-84-86	8304–16.2
IRS Doc. 6011(Rev.12-83)	8304–8
IRS Doc.	
6186-A(Rev.11-83)	8304–9.1
IRS Pub. 16(Rev.7-84)	8304–4
IRS Pub. 55	8304–3
IRS Pub. 79(10-84)	8304–2
IRS Pub. 647(Rev.6-84)	8304–4
IRS Pub. 1131(11-83)	8304–7.1
IRS Pub. 1136(date)	8302–2
IRS Pub. 1243(4-84)	8008–110
OTA Paper 53	8006–3.49
OTA Paper 54	8006–3.50
R-2504	8008–107
R-2633	8008–109
Rpt. Symbol 76	8486–1.3

INDEPENDENT AGENCIES Environmental Protection Agency

AP-42, Supp. 14	9198–13.8
AP-42, Supp. 15	9198–13.9
EPA-230/05-84-008	9184–11
EPA-450/4-83-022	9194–7
EPA-450/4-83-023	9194–14
EPA-450/4-83-024	9194–13
EPA-450/4-84-002	9194–1
EPA-450/4-84-018	9194–5
EPA-520/1-(yr.-nos.)	9232–2
EPA-520/5-(yr.-nos.)	9232–2
EPA-600/D-83-111	9208–124
EPA-600/1-83-015a	4478–146.1
EPA-600/1-83-015b	4478–146.2
EPA-600/1-83-015c	4478–146.3
EPA-600/3-83-027a	9198–109
EPA-600/2-83-090	9208–119
EPA-600/3-82-031	9188–94
EPA-600/3-82-076	9198–106
EPA-600/3-83-022	9198–108
EPA-600/3-83-094	9208–126
EPA-600/4-83-005	9198–107
EPA-600/4-83-025	9198–110
EPA-600/4-83-053	9194–10
EPA-600/4-84-040	9234–4
EPA-600/6-83-002	9208–125
EPA-600/6-84-020	9234–5
EPA-600/9-84-004	9184–10
EPA-904/9-83-112a	9184–15.4
EPA-904/9-83-112b	9184–15.4
EPA-908/9-83-001	9184–15.8
EPA-910/9-83-102c.5	9184–15.10
PNL-5035	9188–96

Federal Deposit Insurance Corp.

P-7700-01-83	9295–3.1
P-7700-02-83	9295–3.2

P-7700-03-83	9295–3.3
P-7700-04-83	9295–3.4
P-7700-05-83	9295–3.5
P-7700-06-83	9295–3.6
P-7700-07-83	9295–3.7
P-7700-08-83	9295–3.8
P-7700-09-83	9295–3.9
P-7700-10-83	9295–3.10
P-7700-11-83	9295–3.11
P-7700-12-83	9295–3.12
P-7700-13-83	9295–3.13
P-7700-14-83	9295–3.14
P-7700-15-83	9295–3.15
P-7700-16-83	9295–3.16
P-7700-17-83	9295–3.17
P-7700-18-83	9295–3.18
P-7700-19-83	9295–3.19

Federal Home Loan Bank Board

Invited Res. Working	
Paper 44	9316–2.46
Invited Res. Working	
Paper 45	9316–2.45
Invited Res. Working	
Paper 50	9316–2.47
Res. Working Paper 111	9316–1.102
Res. Working Paper 112	9316–1.103
Res. Working Paper 113	9316–1.104
Res. Working Paper 114	9316–1.105
Res. Working Paper 115	9316–1.106
Res. Working Paper 116	9316–1.107

Federal Reserve Board of Governors

E.11	9365–3.7
E.15	9365–3.10
G.3	9365–2.19
G.5	9365–2.5
G.6	9365–2.13
G.9	9365–2.14
G.12.3	9365–2.14
G.13	9365–2.22
G.16	9365–2.15
G.19	9365–2.6
G.20	9365–2.7
G.21	9365–2.18
H.3	9365–1
H.4.1	9365–1
H.4.2	9365–1.3
H.5	9365–1
H.6	9365–1
H.8	9365–1
H.10	9365–1.5
Intl. Finance Discussion	
Paper 232	9366–7.91
Intl. Finance Discussion	
Paper 234	9366–7.89
Intl. Finance Discussion	
Paper 235	9366–7.90
Intl. Finance Discussion	
Paper 236	9366–7.92
Intl. Finance Discussion	
Paper 237	9366–7.93
Intl. Finance Discussion	
Paper 238	9366–7.94
Intl. Finance Discussion	
Paper 239	9366–7.95
Intl. Finance Discussion	
Paper 240	9366–7.97
Intl. Finance Discussion	
Paper 241	9366–7.96
Intl. Finance Discussion	
Paper 242	9366–7.98

Report Numbers

Intl. Finance Discussion Paper 243 .... 9366–7.99
Intl. Finance Discussion Paper 244 .... 9366–7.100
Intl. Finance Discussion Paper 245 .... 9366–7.101
Intl. Finance Discussion Paper 246 .... 9366–7.102
Intl. Finance Discussion Paper 248 .... 9366–7.104
Intl. Finance Discussion Paper 249 .... 9366–7.103
Intl. Finance Discussion Paper 250 .... 9366–7.105
Intl. Finance Discussion Paper 251 .... 9366–7.106
K.7 9366–7
Spec. Studies Paper 182 .... 9366–6.76
Spec. Studies Paper 183 .... 9366–6.75
Spec. Studies Paper 184 .... 9366–6.74
Spec. Studies Paper 185 .... 9366–6.77
Spec. Studies Paper 186 .... 9366–6.78
Spec. Studies Paper 187 .... 9366–6.79
Staff Study 126 .... 9366–1.126
Staff Study 127 .... 9366–1.127
Staff Study 128 .... 9366–1.140
Staff Study 129 .... 9366–1.128
Staff Study 130 .... 9366–1.129
Staff Study 131 .... 9366–1.130
Staff Study 132 .... 9366–1.131
Staff Study 133 .... 9366–1.132
Staff Study 134 .... 9366–1.133
Staff Study 136 .... 9366–1.134
Staff Study 137 .... 9366–1.135
Staff Study 138 .... 9366–1.136
Staff Study 139 .... 9366–1.137
Staff Study 140 .... 9366–1.138
Staff Study 141 .... 9366–1.139
Z.1 9364–3
Z.1 .... 9365–3.3
Z.11 9366–6

Federal Reserve Bank of Boston

Conf. Series 26 .... 9373–3.26
Conf. Series 27 .... 9373–3.27
Conf. Series 28 .... 9373–3.28

Federal Reserve Bank of Chicago

SM-84-1 .... 9375–11.3
SM-84-4 .... 9375–11.4

Federal Reserve Bank of Cleveland

Working Paper 8304 .... 9377–9.8
Working Paper 8401 .... 9377–9.9
Working Paper 8402 .... 9377–9.10
Working Paper 8403 .... 9377–9.11
Working Paper 8404 .... 9377–9.12
Working Paper 8405 .... 9377–9.13

Federal Reserve Bank of Kansas City

RWP 83-11 .... 9381–10.31
RWP 83-12 .... 9381–10.32
RWP 83-13 .... 9381–10.33
RWP 84-01 .... 9381–10.34
RWP 84-02 .... 9381–10.29
RWP 84-03 .... 9381–10.30
RWP 84-04 .... 9381–10.35
RWP 84-05 .... 9381–10.36

RWP 84-06 .... 9381–10.37
RWP 84-07 .... 9381–10.38
RWP 84-08 .... 9381–10.39
RWP 84-09 .... 9381–10.40
RWP 84-10 .... 9381–10.41

Federal Reserve Bank of Philadelphia

Working Paper No. 82-9 .... 9387–8.79
Working Paper No. 82-10 .... 9387–8.80
Working Paper No. 82-11 .... 9387–8.81
Working Paper No. 82-12 .... 9387–8.82
Working Paper No. 83-1 .... 9387–8.83
Working Paper No. 83-2 .... 9387–8.84
Working Paper No. 83-3 .... 9387–8.85
Working Paper No. 83-4 .... 9387–8.86
Working Paper No. 83-5 .... 9387–8.87
Working Paper No. 83-6 .... 9387–8.88
Working Paper No. 83-7 .... 9387–8.89
Working Paper No. 83-8 .... 9387–8.90
Working Paper No. 83-9 .... 9387–8.91
Working Paper No. 84-1 .... 9387–8.92
Working Paper No. 84-2 .... 9387–8.93

Federal Home Loan Mortgage Corp.

Pub. 16 9414–1

Federal Emergency Management Agency

FEMA-36 .... 9432–1.1
LAW-26-AP 9432–1.2

General Services Administration

AP-3 9452–7

Interstate Commerce Commission

Statement A-300 9484–5
Statement M-350 9482–3

National Aeronautics and Space Administration

NASA SP-4021 9504–2
NASA SP-7041(nos.) 9502–7
NASA SP-7043(nos.) 9502–4
NASA TM-86245 9504–7
Release 84-22 .... 9506–2.116
Release 84-38 .... 9506–2.117
Release 84-69 .... 9506–2.118
Release 84-117 .... 9506–2.119
Release 84-133 .... 9506–2.120
Release 84-149 .... 9506–2.121

National Credit Union Administration

NCUA 8060 9534–1
NCUA 8602 9534–6

National Transportation Safety Board

NTSB/AAB-(yr./nos.) 9612–1
NTSB/ARG-84/01 9614–3
NTSB/ARG-84/02 9614–3
NTSB/RAB-(yr./nos.) 9612–3
NTSB/SS-84/01 9618–10
NTSB/SS-84/02 9618–12
NTSB/SS-84/03 9618–11

SB 84-3 9614–9
SB 84-18 9614–6

National Science Foundation

NSB 83-1 9624–10
NSF 83-310 .... 9626–2.134
NSF 83-319 .... 9627–20.2
NSF 83-320 .... 9627–20.1
NSF 83-324 9627–23
NSF 83-325 .... 9627–21.1
NSF 83-326 9624–21
NSF 83-328 .... 9626–6.16
NSF 83-329 .... 9626–2.131
NSF 84-1 9624–6
NSF 84-2 9624–11
NSF 84-300 9624–20
NSF 84-302 .... 9626–2.132
NSF 84-303 .... 9626–2.133
NSF 84-304 9628–71
NSF 84-305 .... 9626–2.135
NSF 84-306 9627–7
NSF 84-307 .... 9626–2.136
NSF 84-308 9627–13
NSF 84-309 9627–11
NSF 84-310 .... 9626–2.137
NSF 84-311 9624–18
NSF 84-312 .... 9626–2.138
NSF 84-313 .... 9626–2.141
NSF 84-314 .... 9626–2.139
NSF 84-315 9627–17
NSF 84-317 .... 9626–2.140
NSF 84-318 9627–25
NSF 84-319 .... 9626–2.142
NSF 84-320 9628–72
NSF 84-322 9627–24
NSF 84-325 .... 9627–21.1
NSF 84-327 .... 9626–2.143
NSF 84-328 .... 9626–2.144
NSF 84-329 .... 9626–2.145
NSF 84-333 .... 9626–2.146

Nuclear Regulatory Commission

BNL-NUREG-51592 9638–51
NUREG-0020-(nos.) 9632–1
NUREG-0430, Vol. 4,
No. 1 9632–3
NUREG-0430, Vol. 4,
No. 2 9632–3
NUREG-0713, Vol. 4 9634–3
NUREG-0748 9632–5
NUREG-0957 9638–49
NUREG-1015 .... 9636–1.23
NUREG-1040 9634–9
NUREG-1090 9634–2
NUREG/CR-2907, Vol. 2 9634–1
NUREG/CR-2987 9638–51
NUREG/CR-3056 9638–54
NUREG/CR-3118, Vol. 1 .... 9638–50.1
NUREG/CR-3118, Vol. 2 .... 9638–50.2
NUREG/CR-3118, Vol. 3 .... 9638–50.3
NUREG/CR-3396 9638–55
NUREG/CR-3430 9634–6
NUREG/CR-3500 9638–52
NUREG/CR-3501 9638–53
NUREG/CR-3602 9634–8
ORNL/CSD/TM-197 9638–54
ORNL/NSIC-215, Vol. 1 9634–6
ORNL/TM-8684 9638–53
ORNL/TM-8898 9638–52
PNL-4783 9638–55

Tennessee Valley Authority

Bull. Y-184 .... 9806–9.8

Report Numbers

Circ. Z-158	9808–69
Circ. Z-159	9808–68
Monthly Rpt. (nos.)	9802–1
PBNP-SMR-9	9806–7.1
PBNP-SMR-10	9806–7.2
Tech. Rpt. No. 29-1-45	9804–7
TVA Tech. Note B49	9806–2.36
TVA Tech. Note B50	9806–2.37
TVA Tech. Note B51	9806–2.38
TVA/OACD-84/2	9808–68
TVA/OACD-84/3	9806–9.8
TVA/OGM/IO-84/2	9804–1.1
TVA/ONR/LFR-83/18	9806–2.36
TVA/ONR/LFR-83/33	9806–2.37
TVA/ONRED/AWR-84/	
30	9804–7
TVA/ONRED/ID-84/3	9804–3
TVA/ONRED/LFR-84/1	9806–2.38
TVA/OP/EUDR-81/2	9804–14
TVA/OP/EUDR-81/4	9804–19
TVA/OP/PINF-83/5	9804–23.2
TVA/OP/PINFO-84/7	9804–23."

U.S. Arms Control and Disarmament Agency

ACDA Pub. 117	9824–1

Office of Personnel Management

AR (nos.)-13	9842–1
BRI 40-93	9844–1
FPM Bull. 711-89	9844–17
MW 68-16	9844–8
OALMR 83-1	9844–14
OPM/ALMR 83-03	9847–4
OPM/ELAR 84-02	9847–1
OPM/OLMR 81-14	9847–4
OPM/OLMR 82-06	9847–4
OPM/WEV-DV-82-2	9842–4
OPM/WEV-VRA-82-2	9842–3
Pamphlet CIG-82-71	9844–27

U.S. Postal Service

Pub. 100	9864–6

U.S. International Trade Commission

SOC Series C/P (yr.-nos.)	9882–1
USITC Pub. (nos.)	9882–3
USITC Pub. (nos.)	9882–5
USITC Pub. (nos.)	9882–6
USITC Pub. 841, Control No. 1-7-44	9885–1.63
USITC Pub. 841, Control No. 1-7-49	9885–1.68
USITC Pub. 841, Control No. 1-8-43	9885–1.61
USITC Pub. 841, Control No. 1-8-51	9885–1.69
USITC Pub. 841, Control No. 1-10-12(Supp.)	9885–1.60
USITC Pub. 841, Control No. 1-10-48	9885–1.67
USITC Pub. 841, Control No. 1-10-52	9885–1.71
USITC Pub. 841, Control No. 1-11-47	9885–1.66
USITC Pub. 841, Control No. 1-12-50	9885–1.70
USITC Pub. 841, Control No. 1-12-53	9885–1.72
USITC Pub. 841, Control No. 1-13-46	9885–1.65
USITC Pub. 841, Control No. 1-14-42	9885–1.62
USITC Pub. 841, Control No. 1-15-6(Supp.)	9885–1.59
USITC Pub. 841, Control No. 1-15-45	9885–1.64
USITC Pub. 841, Control No. 2-1-11(Supp.)	9885–2.35
USITC Pub. 841, Control No. 2-1-20	9885–2.29
USITC Pub. 841, Control No. 2-1-21	9885–2.30
USITC Pub. 841, Control No. 2-1-23	9885–2.31
USITC Pub. 841, Control No. 2-4-22	9885–2.32
USITC Pub. 841, Control No. 2-4-25	9885–2.34
USITC Pub. 841, Control No. 2-5-19	9885–2.28
USITC Pub. 841, Control No. 2-5-24	9885–2.33
USITC Pub. 841, Control No. 3-1-19(Supp.)	9885–3.45
USITC Pub. 841, Control No. 3-3-4(Supp. 2)	9885–3.42
USITC Pub. 841, Control No. 3-4-1(Supp.)	9885–3.44
USITC Pub. 841, Control No. 3-4-30	9885–3.43
USITC Pub. 841, Control No. 3-6-3(Second Supp.)	9885–3.48
USITC Pub. 841, Control No. 3-6-29	9885–3.41
USITC Pub. 841, Control No. 3-6-31	9885–3.47
USITC Pub. 841, Control No. 3-6-32	9885–3.46
USITC Pub. 841, Control No. 4-X-29	9885–4.40
USITC Pub. 841, Control No. 4-1,9-15(Supp.)	9885–4.46
USITC Pub. 841, Control No. 4-1-12(Supp.)	9885–4.42
USITC Pub. 841, Control No. 4-1-16(Supp.)	9885–4.45
USITC Pub. 841, Control No. 4-1-17(Supp.)	9885–4.41
USITC Pub. 841, Control No. 4-1-28	9885–4.39
USITC Pub. 841, Control No. 4-2-3(Second Supp.)	9885–4.47
USITC Pub. 841, Control No. 4-2-8(Supp.)	9885–4.37
USITC Pub. 841, Control No. 4-6-13(Supp.)	9885–4.48
USITC Pub. 841, Control No. 4-11-31	9885–4.44
USITC Pub. 841, Control No. 4-13-27	9885–4.38
USITC Pub. 841, Control No. 4-13-30	9885–4.43
USITC Pub. 841, Control No. 5-1-4(Supp.)	9885–5.16
USITC Pub. 841, Control No. 5-1-5(Supp.)	9885–5.17
USITC Pub. 841, Control No. 5-1-12	9885–5.15
USITC Pub. 841, Control No. 5-2-6(Supp.)	9885–5.13
USITC Pub. 841, Control No. 5-3-1(Supp.)	9885–5.14
USITC Pub. 841, Control No. 5-3-10(Supp.)	9885–5.18
USITC Pub. 841, Control No. 6-3-29(Supp.)	9885–6.82
USITC Pub. 841, Control No. 6-4, 5-20(Supp.)	9885–6.65
USITC Pub. 841, Control No. 6-4-7(Supp.)	9885–6.74
USITC Pub. 841, Control No. 6-4-14(Supp.)	9885–6.66
USITC Pub. 841, Control No. 6-4-20(Supp.)	9885–6.71
USITC Pub. 841, Control No. 6-4-27(Supp.)	9885–6.77
USITC Pub. 841, Control No. 6-4-48	9885–6.60
USITC Pub. 841, Control No. 6-4-50	9885–6.61
USITC Pub. 841, Control No. 6-4-51	9885–6.64
USITC Pub. 841, Control No. 6-4-52	9885–6.68
USITC Pub. 841, Control No. 6-4-53	9885–6.70
USITC Pub. 841, Control No. 6-4-54	9885–6.72
USITC Pub. 841, Control No. 6-4-55	9885–6.75
USITC Pub. 841, Control No. 6-4-56	9885–6.73
USITC Pub. 841, Control No. 6-4-58	9885–6.83
USITC Pub. 841, Control No. 6-4-59	9885–6.79
USITC Pub. 841, Control No. 6-4-60	9885–6.84
USITC Pub. 841, Control No. 6-4-61	9885–6.80
USITC Pub. 841, Control No. 6-5-22(Supp.)	9885–6.67
USITC Pub. 841, Control No. 6-5-23(Supp.)	9885–6.81
USITC Pub. 841, Control No. 6-5-32(Supp.)	9885–6.62
USITC Pub. 841, Control No. 6-5-33(Supp.)	9885–6.69
USITC Pub. 841, Control No. 6-6-6(Supp.)	9885–6.76
USITC Pub. 841, Control No. 6-6-49	9885–6.63
USITC Pub. 841, Control No. 6-6-57	9885–6.78
USITC Pub. 841, Control No. 7-X-34	9885–7.54
USITC Pub. 841, Control No. 7-X-35	9885–7.58
USITC Pub. 841, Control No. 7-1-8(Second Supp.)	9885–7.60
USITC Pub. 841, Control No. 7-1-11(Second Supp.)	9885–7.59
USITC Pub. 841, Control No. 7-2-6(Second Supp.)	9885–7.57
USITC Pub. 841, Control No. 7-2-8(Second Supp.)	9885–7.63
USITC Pub. 841, Control No. 7-3-5(Second supp.)	9885–7.55
USITC Pub. 841, Control No. 7-4-9(Second Supp.)	9885–7.62
USITC Pub. 841, Control No. 7-4-19(Supp.)	9885–7.61

Report Numbers

USITC Pub. 841, Control No. 7-5-15(Supp.) 9885-7.53
USITC Pub. 841, Control No. 7-5-16(Supp.) 9885-7.56
USITC Pub. 1400 .... 9886-4.66
USITC Pub. 1400 .... 9886-4.66
USITC Pub. 1400 .... 9886-4.66
USITC Pub. 1400 .... 9886-4.66
USITC Pub. 1448 .... 9886-13.3
USITC Pub. 1448 .... 9886-13.1
USITC Pub. 1448 .... 9886-13.2
USITC Pub. 1456 .... 9886-18.12
USITC Pub. 1459 .... 9886-14.91
USITC Pub. 1462 .... 9886-10.7
USITC Pub. 1463 .... 9886-14.89
USITC Pub. 1465 .... 9886-15.46
USITC Pub. 1466 .... 9886-19.6
USITC Pub. 1467 9884-14
USITC Pub. 1470 .... 9886-19.7
USITC Pub. 1471 9882-11
USITC Pub. 1472 .... 9886-15.45
USITC Pub. 1473 .... 9886-14.90
USITC Pub. 1474 .... 9886-14.92
USITC Pub. 1475 .... 9886-4.65
USITC Pub. 1476 .... 9886-15.47
USITC Pub. 1477 .... 9886-14.94
USITC Pub. 1479 .... 9886-4.67
USITC Pub. 1480 .... 9886-14.93
USITC Pub. 1483 .... 9886-18.13
USITC Pub. 1484 .... 9886-12.8
USITC Pub. 1485 .... 9886-4.68
USITC Pub. 1488 .... 9886-14.95
USITC Pub. 1490 .... 9886-15.48
USITC Pub. 1494 .... 9886-4.69
USITC Pub. 1495 .... 9886-14.97
USITC Pub. 1496 .... 9886-4.70
USITC Pub. 1497 .... 9886-14.96
USITC Pub. 1499 .... 9886-14.99
USITC Pub. 1500 .... 9886-14.100
USITC Pub. 1501 .... 9886-4.71
USITC Pub. 1502 .... 9886-19.9
USITC Pub. 1505 .... 9886-14.98
USITC Pub. 1510 .... 9886-19.8
USITC Pub. 1511 .... 9882-2.402
USITC Pub. 1513 .... 9886-14.102
USITC Pub. 1514 .... 9886-14.101
USITC Pub. 1517 .... 9886-4.73
USITC Pub. 1518 9884-6
USITC Pub. 1519 .... 9886-14.104
USITC Pub. 1520 9884-12
USITC Pub. 1522 .... 9886-4.72
USITC Pub. 1524 .... 9886-14.103
USITC Pub. 1525 .... 9886-14.105
USITC Pub. 1526 9888-17
USITC Pub. 1529 .... 9886-15.52
USITC Pub. 1530 .... 9886-18.14
USITC Pub. 1531 .... 9886-18.15
USITC Pub. 1532 .... 9886-14.106
USITC Pub. 1535 9884-5
USITC Pub. 1538 .... 9886-15.49
USITC Pub. 1539 9882-11
USITC Pub. 1540 .... 9886-14.107
USITC Pub. 1542 .... 9886-4.75
USITC Pub. 1543 .... 9886-4.74
USITC Pub. 1544 .... 9886-15.50
USITC Pub. 1545 .... 9886-5.49
USITC Pub. 1548 9884-2
USITC Pub. 1549 .... 9886-5.50
USITC Pub. 1550 .... 9886-14.108
USITC Pub. 1552 .... 9886-14.109
USITC Pub. 1553 .... 9886-5.51
USITC Pub. 1555 .... 9886-19.11
USITC Pub. 1556 .... 9886-14.110
USITC Pub. 1558 .... 9886-5.52
USITC Pub. 1559 .... 9886-15.51
USITC Pub. 1561 .... 9886-14.111

USITC Pub. 1562 .... 9886-4.76
USITC Pub. 1565 .... 9886-14.112
USITC Pub. 1566 .... 9886-14.114
USITC Pub. 1568 .... 9886-14.113
USITC Pub. 1569 .... 9886-19.12
USITC Pub. 1571 .... 9886-14.115
USITC Pub. 1572 .... 9886-14.117
USITC Pub. 1574 .... 9886-14.116
USITC Pub. 1575 .... 9886-14.118
USITC Pub. 1577 .... 9886-14.119
USITC Pub. 1579 .... 9886-14.120
USITC Pub. 1580 9884-1
USITC Pub. 1581 .... 9886-14.121
USITC Pub. 1582 .... 9886-4.77
USITC Pub. 1583 .... 9882-2.403
USITC Pub. 1584 .... 9886-14.122
USITC Pub. 1585 9884-7
USITC Pub. 1588 9884-3
USITC Pub. 1589 .... 9886-4.78
USITC Pub. 1593 .... 9886-14.125
USITC Pub. 1594 .... 9886-18.16
USITC Pub. 1595 .... 9886-14.123
USITC Pub. 1596 .... 9886-15.54
USITC Pub. 1597 .... 9886-15.53
USITC Pub. 1598 .... 9886-14.126
USITC Pub. 1599 .... 9886-14.124
USITC Pub. 1600 .... 9886-14.129
USITC Pub. 1601 .... 9886-4.79
USITC Pub. 1607 .... 9886-14.127
USITC Pub. 1608 .... 9886-14.128
USITC Pub. 1609 .... 9886-15.55
USITC Pub. 1610 .... 9886-13.4
USITC Pub. 1613 9884-15
USITC Pub. 1615 .... 9886-4.80
USITC Pub. 1618 .... 9886-14.130
USITC Pub. 1534 .... 9886-19.10
USITC Pub. 1536 .... 9886-5.48

U.S. International Development Cooperation Agency

AID Evaluation Special Study No. 18 .... 9916-3.18
AID Evaluation Special Study No. 19 .... 9916-3.19
AID Evaluation Special Study No. 20 .... 9916-3.20
AID Program Evaluation Discussion Paper 17 9918-11
AID Program Evaluation Discussion Paper 18 9918-10
AID Program Evaluation Discussion Paper 19 9918-13
AID Program Evaluation Discussion Paper 20 9918-12
AID Program Evaluation Rpt. No. 12 .... 9916-11.8
AID Project Impact Evaluation Rpt. No. 50 .... 9916-1.50
AID Project Impact Evaluation Rpt. No. 51 .... 9916-1.51
AID Project Impact Evaluation Rpt. No. 52 .... 9916-1.52
AID Project Impact Evaluation Rpt. No. 53 .... 9916-1.53
CONG-R-0105 9914-5
PN-AAL-024 9918-10
PN-AAL-026 9918-11
PN-AAL-028 .... 9916-3.18
PN-AAL-029 .... 9916-1.50
PN-AAL-030 9918-13
PN-AAL-031 9918-12
PN-AAL-033 .... 9916-3.19
PN-AAL-034 .... 9916-11.8
PN-AAL-035 .... 9916-1.51

PN-AAL-036 .... 9916-1.52
PN-AAL-037 .... 9916-3.20
PN-AAL-038 .... 9916-1.53
W-209 9912-4
W-213 9912-1
W-224 9912-3
W-244 9912-2
W-442 9914-6
W-443 9914-7

Veterans Administration

Biometrics Mono. 17 .... 9926-1.17
Biometrics Mono. 18 .... 9926-1.18
IB 11-76 9924-5
IB 70-83-4 9922-9
IB 70-83-5 9922-12
IB 70-84-3 9922-9
IB 70-84-4 9922-12
IM&S M 70-84-6 9924-22
IM&S M 70-84-7 9924-19
RCS 15-10 9924-21
RCS 70-0561 9922-3
RSM 70-84-1 9928-28
RSM 70-84-2 9924-23
RSM 70-84-3 9928-29
RSM 70-84-4 9924-19
SB 70-83-1 .... 9926-4.6
SB 70-83-2 .... 9926-4.7
SB 70-83-3 .... 9926-4.8
SB 70-83-4 .... 9926-4.9
SB 70-83-5 .... 9926-4.10

SPECIAL BOARDS, COMMITTEES, AND COMMISSIONS

Advisory Commission on Intergovernmental Relations

A-94 10048-59
A-95 10048-58
A-96 10048-60
ACIR Rpt. S-13 10044-2
B7 10048-58
B8 10048-59
M-137 10044-1
Staff Working Paper 3R 10046-8.2

Commission on Civil Rights

Clearinghouse Pub. 82 11048-179
Clearinghouse Pub. 82 11048-180

Federal Financial Institutions Examination Council

Rpt. E.16 13002-1

Marine Mammal Commission

MMC-82/02 14734-2

UNITED STATES COURTS Federal Judicial Center

FJC-R-83-1 18408-24
FJC-SP-84-6 18408-25

CONGRESS House

H. Doc. 98-138 104-2
H. Doc. 98-139 104-3

Report Numbers

H. Doc. 98-140	204-1
H. Doc. 98-198	4704-3
H. Doc. 98-199	4704-5
H. Doc. 98-200	4704-4
H. Rpt. 98-547	21408-69
H. Rpt. 98-552	21408-70

Senate

S. Doc. 98-25	25928-4
S. Doc. 98-28, Pt. 1	25922-1.1
S. Doc. 98-28, Pt. 2	25922-1.2
S. Doc. 98-30	25922-2
S. Hrg. 98-174, Pt. 3	25388-47
S. Hrg. 98-180	23848-177
S. Hrg. 98-214	25318-57
S. Hrg. 98-223	25328-23
S. Hrg. 98-271, Pt. 24	23846-4.18
S. Hrg. 98-278	25368-129
S. Hrg. 98-313	25368-131
S. Hrg. 98-322	25408-86
S. Hrg. 98-331	25528-93
S. Hrg. 98-339	25368-128
S. Hrg. 98-340	25148-26
S. Hrg. 98-359	25368-130
S. Hrg. 98-363	25388-45
S. Hrg. 98-379	25268-80
S. Hrg. 98-418	25728-36
S. Hrg. 98-435	25528-94
S. Hrg. 98-442	25248-97
S. Hrg. 98-447	25328-24
S. Hrg. 98-450	25268-81
S. Hrg. 98-472	25528-95
S. Hrg. 98-483	25388-46
S. Hrg. 98-496	25168-61
S. Hrg. 98-537	25368-132
S. Hrg. 98-543	25328-25
S. Hrg. 98-555	25528-96
S. Hrg. 98-574	25528-97
S. Hrg. 98-578	25528-98
S. Hrg. 98-588	25688-6
S. Hrg. 98-591	25368-133
S. Hrg. 98-597	25528-100
S. Hrg. 98-605	25368-134
S. Hrg. 98-621	25528-99
S. Hrg. 98-622	25208-27
S. Hrg. 98-643	25388-48
S. Hrg. 98-647	23848-181
S. Hrg. 98-651	25408-88
S. Hrg. 98-659	25318-58
S. Hrg. 98-660	25168-62
S. Hrg. 98-661	25368-135
S. Hrg. 98-691	23848-180
S. Hrg. 98-873, Pt. 1	23844-4.1
S. Hrg. 98-873, Pt. 2	23844-4.2
S. Prt. 98-68	25948-3
S. Prt. 98-98	23848-176
S. Prt. 98-106	25368-127
S. Prt. 98-122	23848-178
S. Prt. 98-148	23848-179
S. Prt. 98-149	21384-4
S. Prt. 98-159, Pt. 1	25408-87
S. Prt. 98-159, Pt. 2	25408-89
S. Prt. 98-166	25148-27
S. Prt. 98-168	25148-28
S. Prt. 98-194	25148-29
S. Prt. 98-198	23848-76
S. Rpt. 98-360, Vol. 1	25144-3.1
S. Rpt. 98-360, Vol. 2	25144-3.2
S. Rpt. 98-362	23844-2

General Accounting Office

GAO/AFMD-83-103	26111-16
GAO/AFMD-84-18	26111-18
GAO/AFMD-84-20	26111-17
GAO/AFMD-84-34	26111-22
GAO/AFMD-84-45	26111-23
GAO/AFMD 84-50	26111-19
GAO/AFMD-84-57	26111-24
GAO/AFMD-84-59	26111-21
GAO/AFMD-85-1	26111-20
GAO/GGD-84-10	26119-63
GAO/GGD-84-13	26119-58
GAO/GGD-84-14	26119-55
GAO/GGD-84-15	26119-65
GAO/GGD-84-16	26119-61
GAO/GGD-84-21	26119-68
GAO/GGD-84-26	26119-54
GAO/GGD-84-32	26119-51
GAO/GGD-84-35	26119-52
GAO/GGD-84-36	26119-57
GAO/GGD-84-38	26119-53
GAO/GGD-84-50	26119-60
GAO/GGD-84-52	26119-56
GAO/GGD-84-56	26119-59
GAO/GGD-84-68	26119-62
GAO/GGD-84-77	26119-64
GAO/GGD-84-79	26119-67
GAO/GGD-84-84	26119-66
GAO/GGD-84-87	26119-70
GAO/GGD-84-92	26119-69
GAO/HRD-83-21	26121-67
GAO/HRD-84-1	26121-73
GAO/HRD-84-2	26121-81
GAO/HRD-84-10	26121-65
GAO/HRD-84-19	26121-69
GAO/HRD-84-26	26121-77
GAO/HRD-84-27	26121-68
GAO/HRD-84-31	26121-66
GAO/HRD-84-34	26121-85
GAO/HRD-84-35	26121-70
GAO/HRD-84-37	26121-86
GAO/HRD-84-38	26121-83
GAO/HRD-84-39	26121-78
GAO/HRD-84-41	26121-88
GAO/HRD-84-43	26121-74
GAO/HRD-84-48	26121-72
GAO/HRD-84-51	26121-71
GAO/HRD-84-52	26121-87
GAO/HRD-84-53	26121-80
GAO/HRD-84-64	26121-75
GAO/HRD-84-68	26121-76
GAO/HRD-84-76	26121-84
GAO/HRD-84-78	26121-79
GAO/HRD-84-94	26121-82
GAO/IMTEC-83-4	26125-26
GAO/IMTEC-84-9	26104-11.1
GAO/IMTEC-84-11	26125-27
GAO/IMTEC-84-17	26125-28
GAO/NSIAD-84-7	26123-60
GAO/NSIAD-84-11	26123-61
GAO/NSIAD-84-12	26123-53
GAO/NSIAD-84-17	26123-59
GAO/NSIAD-84-27	26123-63
GAO/NSIAD-84-30	26123-69
GAO/NSIAD-84-36	26123-79
GAO/NSIAD-84-41	26123-65
GAO/NSIAD-84-44	26123-54
GAO/NSIAD-84-48	26123-80
GAO/NSIAD-84-50	26123-58
GAO/NSIAD-84-52	26123-57
GAO/NSIAD-84-61	26123-56
GAO/NSIAD-84-65	26123-64
GAO/NSIAD-84-70	26123-62
GAO/NSIAD-84-71	26123-55
GAO/NSIAD-84-77	26123-78
GAO/NSIAD-84-84	26123-73
GAO/NSIAD-84-88	26123-68
GAO/NSIAD-84-106	26123-70
GAO/NSIAD-84-107	26123-82
GAO/NSIAD-84-109	26123-77
GAO/NSIAD-84-111	26123-67
GAO/NSIAD 84-112	26123-74
GAO/NSIAD-84-113	26123-75
GAO/NSIAD-84-115	26123-76
GAO/NSIAD-84-119	26123-81
GAO/NSIAD-84-130	26123-71
GAO/NSIAD-84-135	26123-66
GAO/NSIAD-84-139	26123-72
GAO/NSIAD-85-9	26123-83
GAO/OACG-84-1	26115-51
GAO/OACG-84-3	26106-5.1
GAO/OADPS-84-1	26104-5
GAO/OADPS-84-2	26104-6
GAO/OCE-84-2	26117-31
GAO/OCE-84-3	26117-30
GAO/OCE-84-5	26117-32
GAO/PART-84-1	26104-14
GAO/PEMD-84-2	26131-9
GAO/PEMD-84-4	26131-10
GAO/PEMD-84-6	26131-11
GAO/RCED-(yr.-nos.)	26102-3
GAO/RCED-83-145	26113-127
GAO/RCED-84-1	26113-140
GAO/RCED-84-2	26113-116
GAO/RCED-84-14	26113-125
GAO/RCED-84-18	26113-114
GAO/RCED-84-20	26113-111
GAO/RCED-84-22	26113-129
GAO/RCED-84-33	26113-117
GAO/RCED-84-36	26113-112
GAO/RCED-84-53	26113-113
GAO/RCED-84-54	26113-115
GAO/RCED-84-55	26113-118
GAO/RCED-84-60	26113-141
GAO/RCED-84-65	26113-119
GAO/RCED-84-72	26113-120
GAO/RCED-84-83	26113-121
GAO/RCED-84-96	26113-126
GAO/RCED-84-102	26113-130
GAO/RCED-84-103	26113-138
GAO/RCED-84-108	26113-128
GAO/RCED-84-120	26113-132
GAO/RCED-84-127	26113-122
GAO/RCED-84-130	26104-11.2
GAO/RCED-84-131	26113-133
GAO/RCED-84-132	26113-123
GAO/RCED-84-145	26113-134
GAO/RCED-84-146	26113-124
GAO/RCED-84-151	26113-135
GAO/RCED-84-153	26104-11.3
GAO/RCED-84-155	26113-136
GAO/RCED-84-156	26113-137
GAO/RCED-84-184	26113-131
GAO/RCED-84-188	26113-139
GAO/RCED-(yr.-nos.)	26102-4

Office of Technology Assessment

OTA-A-226	26354-3
OTA-BA-218	26358-98
OTA-BA-219	26358-98
OTA-BP-F-18	26358-101.2
OTA-BP-F-19	26358-101.3
OTA-BP-STI-21	26358-107.2
OTA-BP-STI-25	26358-107.3
OTA-CIT-235	26358-105
OTA-CIT-236	26358-105
OTA-E-216	26358-99
OTA-E-217	26358-99
OTA-E-237	26358-103
OTA-F-214	26358-101.1
OTA-F-215	26358-101.1
OTA-H-227	26358-106

	Report Numbers
OTA-H-228	26358–106
OTA-O-204	26358–104
OTA-O-205	26358–104
OTA-O-206	26358–102
OTA-O-207	26358–102
OTA-STI-222	26358–97
OTA-STI-223	26358–97
OTA-STI-238	26358–107.1
OTA-TM-H-15	26358–96
OTA-TM-ISC-20	26358–100

QUASI OFFICIAL AGENCIES American National Red Cross

ARC 501	29254–1
ARC 591	29254–3

Guide to Selected Standard Classifications

Guide to Selected Standard Classifications
(This guide outlines the major standard classification systems used by various Federal agencies to arrange and present social and economic statistical data.)

Census Regions and Divisions	1059
Outlying Areas of the U.S.	1059
Standard Federal Administrative Regions	1059
Farm Production Regions	1059
Federal Reserve Districts	1060
Federal Home Loan Bank Districts	1060
Bureau of Labor Statistics Regions (and Regional Offices)	1060
Metropolitan Statistical Areas	1061
Consolidated Metropolitan Statistical Areas	1062
Cities with Population over 100,000	1063
Consumer Price Index Cities	1063
Standard Industrial Classification	1064
Standard Occupational Classification	1075
Standard International Trade Classification, Revision 2	1078

Census Regions and Divisions

CENSUS REGIONS SHOWING DIVISIONS INCLUDED IN EACH:

Northeast
New England, Middle Atlantic

North Central
East North Central, West North Central

South
South Atlantic, East South Central, West South Central

West
Mountain, Pacific

CENSUS DIVISIONS SHOWING STATES INCLUDED IN EACH:

New England
Maine, New Hampshire, Vermont, Massachusetts, Rhode Island, Connecticut

Middle Atlantic
New York, New Jersey, Pennsylvania

East North Central
Ohio, Indiana, Illinois, Michigan, Wisconsin

West North Central
Minnesota, Iowa, Missouri, North Dakota, South Dakota, Nebraska, Kansas

South Atlantic
Delaware, Maryland, District of Columbia, Virginia, West Virginia, North Carolina, South Carolina, Georgia, Florida

East South Central
Kentucky, Tennessee, Alabama, Mississippi

West South Central
Arkansas, Louisiana, Oklahoma, Texas

Mountain
Montana, Idaho, Wyoming, Colorado, New Mexico, Arizona, Utah, Nevada

Pacific
Washington, Oregon, California, Alaska, Hawaii

Outlying Areas of the United States

American Samoa
Guam

Northern Mariana Islands
Puerto Rico

Trust Territory of the Pacific Islands
Virgin Islands

Standard Federal Administrative Regions

Region I
Connecticut, Maine, Massachusetts, New Hampshire, Rhode Island, and Vermont

Region II
New Jersey, New York, Puerto Rico, and the Virgin Islands

Region III
Delaware, District of Columbia, Maryland, Pennsylvania, Virginia, and West Virginia

Region IV
Alabama, Florida, Georgia, Kentucky, Mississippi, North Carolina, South Carolina, and Tennessee

Region V
Illinois, Indiana, Michigan, Minnesota, Ohio, and Wisconsin

Region VI
Arkansas, Louisiana, New Mexico, Oklahoma, and Texas

Region VII
Iowa, Kansas, Missouri, and Nebraska

Region VIII
Colorado, Montana, North Dakota, South Dakota, Utah, and Wyoming

Region IX
American Samoa, Arizona, California, Guam, Hawaii, and Nevada

Region X
Alaska, Idaho, Oregon, and Washington

Farm Production Regions

National agricultural data are frequently grouped into 10 farm production regions, covering the 48 contiguous States. Alaska, Hawaii, and Puerto Rico are each shown separately, if included.

Appalachian
Kentucky, North Carolina, Tennessee, Virginia, West Virginia

Corn Belt
Illinois, Indiana, Iowa, Missouri, Ohio

Delta States
Arkansas, Louisiana, Mississippi

Lake States
Michigan, Minnesota, Wisconsin

Mountain
Arizona, Colorado, Idaho, Montana, Nevada, New Mexico, Utah, Wyoming

Northeast
Connecticut, Delaware, Maine, Maryland, Massachusetts, New Hampshire, New Jersey, New York, Pennsylvania, Rhode Island, Vermont

Northern Plains
Kansas, Nebraska, North Dakota, South Dakota

Pacific
California, Oregon, Washington

Southeast
Alabama, Florida, Georgia, South Carolina

Southern Plains
Oklahoma, Texas

Federal Reserve Districts

District 1 (Boston)
Maine, Massachusetts, New Hampshire, Rhode Island, Vermont; most of Connecticut

District 2 (New York)
New York, Puerto Rico, Virgin Islands; portions of New Jersey; Fairfield Co., Connecticut

District 3 (Philadelphia)
Delaware; portions of New Jersey and Pennsylvania

District 4 (Cleveland)
Ohio; portions of Kentucky, Pennsylvania, West Virginia

District 5 (Richmond)
District of Columbia, Maryland, North & South Carolina, Virginia; portions of West Virginia

District 6 (Atlanta)
Alabama, Florida, Georgia; portions of Louisiana, Mississippi, Tennessee

District 7 (Chicago)
Iowa; portions of Michigan, Illinois, Indiana, Wisconsin

District 8 (St. Louis)
Arkansas; portions of Kentucky, Illinois, Indiana, Mississippi, Missouri, Tennessee

District 9 (Minneapolis)
Minnesota, Montana, North & South Dakota; portions of Michigan and Wisconsin

District 10 (Kansas City)
Colorado, Kansas, Nebraska, Oklahoma, Wyoming; portions of Missouri, New Mexico

District 11 (Dallas)
Texas; portions of Louisiana, New Mexico

District 12 (San Francisco)
Alaska, Arizona, California, Guam, Hawaii, Idaho, Nevada, Oregon, Utah, Washington

Federal Home Loan Bank Districts

District 1 (Boston)
Connecticut, Maine, Massachusetts, New Hampshire, Rhode Island, and Vermont

District 2 (New York)
New Jersey, New York, Puerto Rico, and Virgin Islands

District 3 (Pittsburgh)
Delaware, Pennsylvania, and West Virginia

District 4 (Atlanta)
Alabama, District of Columbia, Florida, Georgia, Maryland, North Carolina, South Carolina, and Virginia

District 5 (Cincinnati)
Kentucky, Ohio, and Tennessee

District 6 (Indianapolis)
Indiana and Michigan

District 7 (Chicago)
Illinois and Wisconsin

District 8 (Des Moines)
Iowa, Minnesota, Missouri, North Dakota, and South Dakota

District 9 (Dallas)
Arkansas, Louisiana, Mississippi, New Mexico, and Texas

District 10 (Topeka)
Colorado, Kansas, Nebraska, and Oklahoma

District 11 (San Francisco)
Arizona, Nevada, and California

District 12 (Seattle)
Alaska, Hawaii, Guam, Idaho, Montana, Oregon, Utah, Washington, and Wyoming

Bureau of Labor Statistics Regions (And Regional Offices)

Region 1: New England (Boston)
Connecticut, Maine, Massachusetts, New Hampshire, Rhode Island, Vermont

Region 2: Middle Atlantic Region (New York)
New Jersey, New York, Puerto Rico, Virgin Islands

Region 3: Mideast Region (Philadelphia)
Delaware, District of Columbia, Maryland, Pennsylvania, Virginia, West Virginia

Region 4: Southeast Region (Atlanta)
Alabama, Florida, Georgia, Kentucky, Mississippi, North Carolina, South Carolina, Tennessee

Region 5: North Central Region (Chicago)
Illinois, Indiana, Michigan, Minnesota, Ohio, Wisconsin

Region 6: Southwest Region (Dallas)
Arkansas, Louisiana, New Mexico, Oklahoma, Texas

Region 7 and 8: Mountain-Plains Region (Kansas City)
Colorado, Iowa, Kansas, Missouri, Montana, Nebraska, North Dakota, South Dakota, Utah, Wyoming

Region 9 and 10: Pacific Region (San Francisco)
Alaska, American Samoa, Arizona, California, Guam, Hawaii, Idaho, Nevada, Oregon, Trust Territory of the Pacific Islands, Washington

Metropolitan Statistical Areas

Metropolitan Statistical Areas (MSAs) were developed to enable all Federal statistical agencies to use the same boundaries in publishing urban data.

As part of the Federal Government's July 1983 revision of its metropolitan area classification, Standard Metropolitan Statistical Areas (SMSAs) were replaced by MSAs and Primary Metropolitan Statistical Areas (PSMAs). In addition, some new areas were designated, and the titles or definitions of several areas were changed.

MSAs and PSMAs are listed below. SMSA titles in use through June 1983 are listed in ASI 1982 Annual.

Area Code	Area Title	Area Code	Area Title	Area Code	Area Title
0040	Abilene, Tex.	1140	Bradenton, Fla.	2180	Dothan, Ala.
0060	Aguadilla, P.R.	1145	Brazoria, Tex.	2200	Dubuque, Iowa
0080	Akron, Ohio	1150	Bremerton, Wash.	2240	Duluth, Minn.-Wis.
0120	Albany, Ga.	1160	Bridgeport-Milford, Conn.		
0160	Albany-Schenectady-Troy, N.Y.	1170	Bristol, Conn.	2285	East St. Louis-Belleville, Ill.
		1200	Brockton, Mass.	2290	Eau Claire, Wis.
0200	Albuquerque, N. Mex.	1240	Brownsville-Harlingen, Tex.	2320	El Paso, Tex.
0220	Alexandria, La.	1260	Bryan-College Station, Tex.	2330	Elkhart-Goshen, Ind.
0240	Allentown-Bethlehem, Pa.-N.J.			2335	Elmira, N.Y.
		1280	Buffalo, N.Y.	2340	Enid, Okla.
0275	Alton-Granite City, Ill.	1300	Burlington, N.C.	2360	Erie, Pa.
0280	Altoona, Pa.	1305	Burlington, Vt.	2400	Eugene-Springfield, Oreg.
0320	Amarillo, Tex.			2440	Evansville, Ind.-Ky.
0360	Anaheim-Santa Ana, Calif.	1310	Caguas, P.R.		
0380	Anchorage, Alaska	1320	Canton, Ohio	2480	Fall River, Mass.-R.I.
0400	Anderson, Ind.	1350	Casper, Wyo.	2520	Fargo-Moorhead, N. Dak.-Minn.
0405	Anderson, S.C.	1360	Cedar Rapids, Iowa		
0440	Ann Arbor, Mich.	1400	Champaign-Urbana-Rantoul, Ill.	2560	Fayetteville, N.C.
0450	Anniston, Ala.			2580	Fayetteville-Springdale, Ark.
0460	Appleton-Oshkosh-Neenah, Wis.	1440	Charleston, S.C.	2600	Fitchburg-Leominster, Mass.
		1480	Charleston, W.Va.	2640	Flint, Mich.
0470	Arecibo, P.R.	1520	Charlotte-Gastonia-Rock Hill, N.C.-S.C.	2650	Florence, Ala.
0480	Asheville, N.C.			2655	Florence, S.C.
0500	Athens, Ga.	1540	Charlottesville, Va.	2670	Fort Collins-Loveland, Colo.
0520	Atlanta, Ga.	1560	Chattanooga, Tenn.-Ga.		
0560	Atlantic City, N.J.	1600	Chicago, Ill.	2680	Fort Lauderdale-Hollywood-Pompano Beach, Fla.
0600	Augusta, Ga.-S.C.	1620	Chico, Calif.		
0620	Aurora-Elgin, Ill.	1640	Cincinnati, Ohio-Ky.-Ind.	2700	Fort Myers, Fla.
0640	Austin, Tex.	1660	Clarksville-Hopkinsville, Tenn.-Ky.	2710	Fort Pierce, Fla.
				2720	Fort Smith, Ark.-Okla.
0680	Bakersfield, Calif.	1680	Cleveland, Ohio	2750	Fort Walton Beach, Fla.
0720	Baltimore, Md.	1720	Colorado Springs, Colo.	2760	Fort Wayne, Ind.
0730	Bangor, Maine	1740	Columbia, Mo.	2800	Fort Worth-Arlington, Tex.
0760	Baton Rouge, La.	1760	Columbia, S.C.	2840	Fresno, Calif.
0780	Battle Creek, Mich.	1800	Columbus, Ga.-Ala.		
0840	Beaumont-Port Arthur, Tex.	1840	Columbus, Ohio	2880	Gadsden, Ala.
		1880	Corpus Christi, Tex.	2900	Gainesville, Fla.
0845	Beaver County, Pa.	1900	Cumberland, Md.-W.Va.	2920	Galveston-Texas City, Tex.
0860	Bellingham, Wash.			2960	Gary-Hammond, Ind.
0870	Benton Harbor, Mich.	1920	Dallas, Tex.	2975	Glens Falls, N.Y.
0875	Bergen-Passaic, N.J.	1930	Danbury, Conn.	2985	Grand Forks, N.Dak.
0880	Billings, Mont.	1950	Danville, Va.	3000	Grand Rapids, Mich.
0920	Biloxi-Gulfport, Miss.	1960	Davenport-Rock Island-Moline, Iowa-Ill.	3040	Great Falls, Mont.
0960	Binghamton, N.Y.			3060	Greeley, Colo.
1000	Birmingham, Ala.	2000	Dayton-Springfield, Ohio	3080	Green Bay, Wis.
1010	Bismarck, N.Dak.	2020	Daytona Beach, Fla.	3120	Greensboro-Winston-Salem-High Point, N.C.
1020	Bloomington, Ind.	2040	Decatur, Ill.		
1040	Bloomington-Normal, Ill.	2080	Denver, Colo.	3160	Greenville-Spartanburg, S.C.
1080	Boise City, Idaho	2120	Des Moines, Iowa		
1120	Boston, Mass.	2160	Detroit, Mich.	3180	Hagerstown, Md.
1125	Boulder-Longmont, Colo.			3200	Hamilton-Middletown, Ohio
				3240	Harrisburg-Lebanon-Carlisle, Pa.
				3280	Hartford, Conn.
				3290	Hickory, N.C.
				3320	Honolulu, Hawaii
				3350	Houma-Thibodaux, La.
				3360	Houston, Tex.

Area Code	Area Title
3400	Huntington-Ashland, W.Va.-Ky.-Ohio
3440	Huntsville, Ala.
3480	Indianapolis, Ind.
3500	Iowa City, Iowa
3520	Jackson, Mich.
3560	Jackson, Miss.
3600	Jacksonville, Fla.
3605	Jacksonville, N.C.
3620	Janesville-Beloit, Wis.
3640	Jersey City, N.J.
3660	Johnson City-Kingsport-Bristol, Tenn.-Va.
3680	Johnstown, Pa.
3690	Joliet, Ill.
3710	Joplin, Mo.
3720	Kalamazoo, Mich.
3740	Kankakee, Ill.
3755	Kansas City, Kans.
3760	Kansas City, Mo.
3800	Kenosha, Wis.
3810	Killeen-Temple, Tex.
3840	Knoxville, Tenn.
3850	Kokomo, Ind.
3870	LaCrosse, Wis.
3880	Lafayette, La.
3920	Lafayette, Ind.
3960	Lake Charles, La.
3965	Lake County, Ill.
3980	Lakeland-Winter Haven, Fla.
4000	Lancaster, Pa.
4040	Lansing-East Lansing, Mich.
4080	Laredo, Tex.
4100	Las Cruces, N. Mex.
4120	Las Vegas, Nev.
4150	Lawrence, Kans.
4160	Lawrence-Haverhill, Mass.-N.H.
4200	Lawton, Okla.
4240	Lewiston-Auburn, Maine
4280	Lexington-Fayette, Ky.
4320	Lima, Ohio
4360	Lincoln, Nebr.
4400	Little Rock-North Little Rock, Ark.
4420	Longview-Marshall, Tex.
4440	Lorain-Elyria, Ohio
4480	Los Angeles-Long Beach, Calif.
4520	Louisville, Ky.-Ind.
4560	Lowell, Mass.-N.H.
4600	Lubbock, Tex.
4640	Lynchburg, Va.
4680	Macon-Warner Robins, Ga.
4720	Madison, Wis.

January-December 1984

ASI Annual Supplement 1061

Metropolitan Statistical Areas

Guide to Selected Standard Classifications

Code	Area	Code	Area	Code	Area	Code	Area
4760	Manchester, N.H.	5880	Oklahoma City, Okla.	6920	Sacramento, Calif.	8280	Tampa-St. Petersburg-
4800	Mansfield, Ohio	5910	Olympia, Wash.	6960	Saginaw-Bay City-Midland,		Clearwater, Fla.
4840	Mayaguez, P.R.	5920	Omaha, Nebr.-Iowa		Mich.	8320	Terre Haute, Ind.
4880	McAllen-Edinburg-Mission,	5950	Orange County, N.Y.	6980	St. Cloud, Minn.	8360	Texarkana, Tex.-Ark.
	Tex.	5960	Orlando, Fla.	7000	St. Joseph, Mo.	8400	Toledo, Ohio
4890	Medford, Oreg.	5990	Owensboro, Ky.	7040	St. Louis, Mo.-Ill.	8440	Topeka, Kans.
4900	Melbourne-Titusville-Palm	6000	Oxnard-Ventura, Calif.	7080	Salem, Oreg.	8480	Trenton, N.J.
	Bay, Fla.			7090	Salem-Gloucester, Mass.	8520	Tucson, Ariz.
4920	Memphis, Tenn.-Ark.-Miss.			7120	Salinas-Seaside-	8560	Tulsa, Okla.
5000	Miami-Hialeah, Fla.	6015	Panama City, Fla.		Monterey, Calif.	8600	Tuscaloosa, Ala.
5015	Middlesex-Somerset-	6020	Parkersburg-Marietta,	7160	Salt Lake City-Ogden,	8640	Tyler, Tex.
	Hunterdon, N.J.		W.Va.-Ohio		Utah		
5020	Middletown, Conn.	6025	Pascagoula, Miss.	7200	San Angelo, Tex.	8680	Utica-Rome, N.Y.
5040	Midland, Tex.	6060	Pawtucket-Woonsocket-	7240	San Antonio, Tex.		
5080	Milwaukee, Wis.		Attleboro, R.I.-Mass.	7320	San Diego, Calif.	8720	Vallejo-Fairfield-
5120	Minneapolis-St. Paul,	6080	Pensacola, Fla.	7360	San Francisco, Calif.		Napa, Calif.
	Minn.-Wis.	6120	Peoria, Ill.	7400	San Jose, Calif.	8725	Vancouver, Wash.
5160	Mobile, Ala.	6160	Philadelphia, Pa.-N.J.	7440	San Juan, P.R.	8750	Victoria, Tex.
5170	Modesto, Calif.	6200	Phoenix, Ariz.	7480	Santa Barbara-Santa Maria-	8760	Vineland-Millville-
5190	Monmouth-Ocean, N.J.	6240	Pine Bluff, Ark.		Lompoc, Calif.		Bridgeton, N.J.
5200	Monroe, La.	6280	Pittsburgh, Pa.	7485	Santa Cruz, Calif.	8780	Visalia-Tulare-Porterville,
5240	Montgomery, Ala.	6320	Pittsfield, Mass.	7500	Santa Rosa-Petaluma,		Calif.
5280	Muncie, Ind.	6360	Ponce, P.R.		Calif.		
5320	Muskegon, Mich.	6400	Portland, Maine	7510	Sarasota, Fla.	8800	Waco, Tex.
		6440	Portland, Oreg.	7520	Savannah, Ga.	8840	Washington, D.C.-Md.-Va.
5350	Nashua, N.H.	6450	Portsmouth-Dover-	7560	Scranton-Wilkes-Barre, Pa.	8880	Waterbury, Conn.
5360	Nashville, Tenn.		Rochester, N.H.-Maine	7600	Seattle, Wash.	8920	Waterloo-Cedar Falls,
5380	Nassau-Suffolk, N.Y.	6460	Poughkeepsie, N.Y.	7610	Sharon, Pa.		Iowa
5400	New Bedford, Mass.	6480	Providence, R.I.	7620	Sheboygan, Wis.	8940	Wausau, Wis.
5440	New Britain, Conn.	6520	Provo-Orem, Utah	7640	Sherman-Denison, Tex.	8960	West Palm Beach-Boca
5480	New Haven-Meriden,	6560	Pueblo, Colo.	7680	Shreveport, La.		Raton-Delray Beach, Fla.
	Conn.			7720	Sioux City, Iowa-Nebr.	9000	Wheeling, W.Va.-Ohio
5520	New London-Norwich,	6600	Racine, Wis.	7760	Sioux Falls, S.Dak.	9040	Wichita, Kans.
	Conn.-R.I.	6640	Raleigh-Durham, N.C.	7800	South Bend-Mishawaka,	9080	Wichita Falls, Tex.
5560	New Orleans, La.	6680	Reading, Pa.		Ind.	9140	Williamsport, Pa.
5600	New York, N.Y.	6690	Redding, Calif.	7840	Spokane, Wash.	9160	Wilmington, Del.-N.J.-Md.
5640	Newark, N.J.	6720	Reno, Nev.	7880	Springfield, Ill.	9200	Wilmington, N.C.
5700	Niagara Falls, N.Y.	6740	Richland-Kennewick-	7920	Springfield, Mo.	9240	Worcester, Mass.
5720	Norfolk-Virginia Beach-		Pasco, Wash.	8000	Springfield, Mass.		
	Newport News, Va.	6760	Richmond-Petersburg, Va.	8040	Stamford, Conn.	9260	Yakima, Wash.
5760	Norwalk, Conn.	6780	Riverside-San Bernardino,	8050	State College, Pa.	9280	York, Pa.
			Calif.	8080	Steubenville-Weirton,	9320	Youngstown-Warren,
5775	Oakland, Calif.	6800	Roanoke, Va.		Ohio-W. Va.		Ohio
5790	Ocala, Fla.	6820	Rochester, Minn.	8120	Stockton, Calif.	9340	Yuba City, Calif.
5800	Odessa, Tex.	6840	Rochester, N.Y.	8160	Syracuse, N.Y.		
		6880	Rockford, Ill.	8200	Tacoma, Wash.		
				8240	Tallahassee, Fla.		

Consolidated Metropolitan Statistical Areas

Consolidated Metropolitan Statistical Areas (CSMAs) consist of component Primary Metropolitan Statistical Areas.

As part of the Federal Government's July 1983 revision of its metropolitan area classification, the term CSMA replaced "Standard Consolidated Statistical Areas." In addition, some new areas were designated, and the titles or definitions of several areas were changed. CSMAs are listed below. Standard Consolidated Statistical Area titles in use through June 1983 are listed in ASI 1982 Annual.

Area Code	Area Title	Area Code	Area Title	Area Code	Area Title
07	Boston-Lawrence-Salem, Mass.-N.H.	34	Denver-Boulder, Colo.	77	Philadelphia-Wilmington-Trenton, Pa.-Del.-N.J.-Md.
10	Buffalo-Niagara Falls, N.Y.	35	Detroit-Ann Arbor, Mich.	78	Pittsburgh-Beaver Valley, Pa.
14	Chicago-Gary-Lake County, Ill.-Ind.-Wis.	41	Hartford-New Britain-Middletown, Conn.	79	Portland-Vancouver, Oreg.-Wash.
21	Cincinnati-Hamilton, Ohio-Ky.-Ind.	42	Houston-Galveston-Brazoria, Tex.	80	Providence-Fall River, R.I.-Mass.
28	Cleveland-Akron-Lorain, Ohio	47	Kansas City, Mo.-Kans.	82	St. Louis-East St. Louis-Alton, Mo.-Ill.
31	Dallas-Fort Worth, Tex.	49	Los Angeles-Anaheim-Riverside, Calif.	84	San Francisco-Oakland-San Jose, Calif.
		56	Miami-Fort Lauderdale, Fla.	87	San Juan-Caguas, P.R.
		63	Milwaukee-Racine, Wis.	91	Seattle-Tacoma, Wash.
		70	New York-Northern New Jersey-Long Island, N.Y.-N.J.-Conn.		

1062 **ASI Annual Supplement** **January-December 1984**

Cities With Population Over 100,000

1982 Rank and Population

Rank	City	Population
1	New York, NY	7,086,096
2	Los Angeles, CA	3,022,247
3	Chicago, IL	2,997,155
4	Houston, TX	1,725,617
5	Philadelphia, PA	1,665,382
6	Detroit, MI	1,138,717
7	Dallas, TX	943,848
8	San Diego, CA	915,956
9	Phoenix, AZ	824,230
10	San Antonio, TX	819,021
11	Honolulu, HI	781,899
12	Baltimore, MD	774,113
13	Indianapolis, IN	707,655
14	San Francisco, CA	691,637
15	San Jose, CA...........	659,181
16	Memphis, TN	645,760
17	Washington, DC.......	633,425
18	Milwaukee, WI	631,509
19	Columbus, OH	570,588
20	New Orleans, LA	564,561
21	Boston, MA	560,847
22	Cleveland, OH	558,869
23	Jacksonville, FL	556,370
24	Denver, CO	505,563
25	Seattle, WA	490,077
26	Nashville-Davidson, TN	455,252
27	Kansas City, MO	445,222
28	El Paso, TX............	445,071
29	St. Louis, MO	437,354
30	Atlanta, GA	428,153
31	Oklahoma City, OK....	427,714
32	Pittsburgh, PA	414,936
33	Fort Worth, TX	401,402
34	Miami, FL	382,726
35	Cincinnati, OH	380,118
36	Tulsa, OK	375,300
37	Long Beach, CA.......	371,426
38	Minneapolis, MN	369,161
39	Austin, TX	368,135
40	Portland, OR	367,530
41	Baton Rouge, LA......	361,572
42	Tucson, AZ	352,455
43	Toledo, OH............	350,565
44	Buffalo, NY	348,035
45	Oakland, CA...........	344,652
46	Albuquerque, NM	341,978
47	Omaha, NE	328,557
48	Charlotte, NC	323,972
49	Newark, NJ............	320,512
50	Louisville, KY	293,531
51	Wichita, KS	288,723
52	Sacramento, CA	288,597
53	Birmingham, AL	283,239
54	Virginia Beach, VA	282,588
55	Tampa, FL	276,413
56	St. Paul, MN..........	270,443
57	Norfolk, VA	266,874
58	Corpus Christi, TX	246,081
59	Fresno, CA	244,623
60	Rochester, NY	244,094
61	St. Petersburg, FL	241,214
62	Colorado Springs, CO ..	231,699
63	Akron, OH	231,659
64	Anaheim, CA	226,467
65	Jersey City, NJ	222,881
66	Richmond, VA	218,237
67	Santa Ana, CA	217,219
68	Shreveport, LA........	210,881
69	Lexington-Fayette, KY .	207,668
70	Mobile, AL	204,586
71	Jackson, MS	204,195
72	Anchorage, AK	194,675
73	Yonkers, NY..........	192,342
74	Des Moines, IA........	191,506
75	Dayton, OH	188,499
76	Aurora, CO............	184,372
77	Arlington, TX.........	182,975
78	Grand Rapids, MI	182,774
79	Montgomery, AL......	182,406
80	Las Vegas, NV.........	179,587
81	Lincoln, NE	177,340
82	Lubbock, TX	176,588
83	Huntington Beach, CA	176,314
84	Knoxville, TN	175,298
85	Columbus, GA	174,348
86	Riverside, CA	174,023
87	Madison, WI	172,640
88	Spokane, WA	171,903
89	Mesa, AZ..............	171,695
90	Chattanooga, TN	168,016
91	Little Rock, AR	167,974
92	Fort Wayne, IN	167,633
93	Syracuse, NY	166,187
94	Salt Lake City, UT	163,859
95	Kansas City, KS	162,211
96	Stockton, CA	161,815
97	Tacoma, WA	161,351
98	Worcester, MA	161,049
99	Greensboro, NC	157,337
100	Warren, MI	156,131
101	Providence, RI	155,717
102	Amarillo, TX	155,356
103	Hialeah, FL............	154,713
104	Raleigh, NC	154,211
105	Flint, MI	154,019
106	Fort Lauderdale, FL ...	153,755
107	Springfield, MA	151,586
108	Newport News, VA	151,240
109	Garland, TX	148,975
110	Gary, IN	147,537
111	Savannah, GA	145,699
112	Huntsville, AL	145,421
113	Bridgeport, CT	143,745
114	Glendale, CA	142,148
115	Winston-Salem, NC....	140,846
116	Paterson, NJ	138,986
117	Rockford, IL..........	138,334
118	Fremont, CA	137,925
119	Hartford, CT	136,334
120	Springfield, MO	134,453
121	Orlando, FL	134,255
122	Evansville, IN	130,275
123	Torrance, CA	130,213
124	Lansing, MI...........	128,338
125	Garden Grove, CA.....	126,340
126	New Haven, CT	125,348
127	Hampton, VA..........	124,966
128	San Bernardino, CA ...	124,319
129	Beaumont, TX	123,477
130	Peoria, IL	122,261
131	Hollywood, FL.........	122,051
132	Brownsville, TX	122,010
133	Pasadena, CA	120,954
134	Topeka, KS	120,269
135	Chesapeake, VA	119,749
136	Macon, GA	118,730
137	Lakewood, CO	118,498
138	Erie, PA	118,493
139	Oxnard, CA	115,657
140	Bakersfield, CA	115,528
141	Irving, TX	114,305
142	Modesto, CA	114,076
143	Tempe, AZ	112,514
144	Independence, MO	111,617
145	Youngstown, OH	111,391
146	Cedar Rapids, IA	109,086
147	Sterling Heights, MI...	108,482
148	South Bend, IN	107,690
149	Sunnyvale, CA	107,110
150	Elizabeth, NJ	106,803
151	Reno, NV	106,748
152	Glendale, AZ	106,420
153	Portsmouth, VA.......	105,807
154	Ann Arbor, MI........	104,880
155	Boise City, ID	104,586
156	Fullerton, CA	104,532
157	Allentown, PA	104,324
158	Abilene, TX	104,302
159	Alexandria, VA........	104,276
160	Concord, CA	104,061
161	Davenport, IA	103,799
162	Eugene, OR............	103,709
163	Stamford, CT	103,614
164	Berkeley, CA...........	103,479
165	Waterbury, CT	102,940
166	Tallahassee, FL	102,579
167	Odessa, TX	102,465
168	Waco, TX	102,200
169	Columbia, SC	101,457
170	Livonia, MI...........	101,366
171	Durham, NC	101,242
172	Pueblo, CO	100,934
173	Pomona, CA...........	100,465
174	Houma, LA	100,346
175	Roanoke, VA	100,187
176	Albany, NY	100,048

Consumer Price Index Cities

Since January 1978, Consumer Price Index data have been collected, and shown separately in CPI reports, for the following 28 Standard Metropolitan Statistical Areas:

Anchorage, Alaska
Atlanta, Ga.
Baltimore, Md.
Boston, Mass.
Buffalo, N.Y.
Chicago, Ill.-Northwestern Ind.
Cincinnati, Ohio-Ky.-Ind.
Cleveland, Ohio
Dallas-Ft. Worth, Tex.
Denver-Boulder, Colo.
Detroit, Mich.
Honolulu, Hawaii
Houston, Tex.
Kansas City, Mo.-Kans.
Los Angeles-Long Beach, Anaheim, Calif.
Miami, Fla.
Milwaukee, Wis.
Minneapolis-St. Paul, Minn.-Wis.
New York, N.Y.-Northeastern N.J.
Northeast Pa. (Scranton)
Philadelphia, Pa.-N.J.
Pittsburgh, Pa.
Portland, Oreg.-Wash.
St. Louis, Mo.-Ill.
San Diego, Calif.
Seattle-Everett, Wash.
San Francisco-Oakland, Calif.
Washington, D.C.-Md.-Va.

January-December 1984

Standard Industrial Classification

The Standard Industrial Classification (SIC) was developed to classify industrial establishments by the type of activity in which they are engaged, for the purpose of promoting uniformity and comparability of statistical data collected by Federal and State agencies, trade associations, and others. The classification system is at 4 levels: industry division, major groups, groups, and individual industries—represented by 1- to 4-digit codes. The following list is taken from the 1972 *Standard Industrial Classification Manual* and its 1977 supplement, which revise 1967 and 1957 editions. For description of the *Manual* see ASI Retrospective Edition, 108-4; for description of the 1977 supplement to the *Manual*, see ASI 1978 Annual, 2088-5.

Group and Industry Code

AGRICULTURE, FORESTRY, AND FISHING

- **01 AGRICULTURAL PRODUCTION— CROPS**
- **011 Cash Grains**
  - 0111 Wheat
  - 0112 Rice
  - 0115 Corn
  - 0116 Soybeans
  - 0119 Cash grains, not elsewhere classified
- **013 Field Crops, Except Cash Grains**
  - 0131 Cotton
  - 0132 Tobacco
  - 0133 Sugar crops
  - 0134 Irish potatoes
  - 0139 Field crops, except cash grains, not elsewhere classified
- **016 Vegetables and Melons**
  - 0161 Vegetables and melons
- **017 Fruits and Tree Nuts**
  - 0171 Berry crops
  - 0172 Grapes
  - 0173 Tree nuts
  - 0174 Citrus fruits
  - 0175 Deciduous tree fruits
  - 0179 Fruits and tree nuts, not elsewhere classified
- **018 Horticultural Specialties**
  - 0181 Ornamental floriculture and nursery products
  - 0182 Food crops grown under cover
  - 0189 Horticultural specialties, not elsewhere classified
- **019 General Farms, Primarily Crop**
  - 0191 General farms, primarily crop
- **02 AGRICULTURAL PRODUCTION— LIVESTOCK**
- **021 Livestock, Except Dairy, Poultry, and Animal Specialties**
  - 0211 Beef cattle feedlots
  - 0212 Beef cattle, except feedlots
  - 0213 Hogs
  - 0214 Sheep and goats
  - 0219 General livestock, except dairy, poultry, and animal specialties
- **024 Dairy Farms**
  - 0241 Dairy farms
- **025 Poultry and Eggs**
  - 0251 Broiler, fryer, and roaster chickens
  - 0252 Chicken eggs
  - 0253 Turkeys and turkey eggs
  - 0254 Poultry hatcheries
  - 0259 Poultry and eggs, not elsewhere classified
- **027 Animal Specialties**
  - 0271 Fur-bearing animals and rabbits
  - 0272 Horses and other equines
  - 0279 Animal specialties, not elsewhere classified
- **029 General Farms, Primarily Livestock**
  - 0291 General farms, primarily livestock
- **07 AGRICULTURAL SERVICES**
- **071 Soil Preparation Services**
  - 0711 Soil preparation services
- **072 Crop Services**
  - 0721 Crop planting, cultivating, and protection
  - 0722 Crop harvesting, primarily by machine
  - 0723 Crop preparation services for market, except cotton ginning
  - 0724 Cotton ginning
  - 0729 General crop services
- **074 Veterinary Services**
  - 0741 Veterinary services for livestock, except animal specialties
  - 0742 Veterinary services for animal specialties
- **075 Animal Services, Except Veterinary**
  - 0751 Livestock services, except services for animal specialties
  - 0752 Animal specialty services
- **076 Farm Labor and Management Services**
  - 0761 Farm labor contractors and crew leaders
  - 0762 Farm management services
- **078 Landscape and Horticultural Services**
  - 0781 Landscape counseling and planning
  - 0782 Lawn and garden services
  - 0783 Ornamental shrub and tree services
- **08 FORESTRY**
- **081 Timber tracts**
  - 0811 Timber tracts
- **082 Forest Nurseries and Tree Seed Gathering and Extracting**
  - 0821 Forest nurseries and tree seed gathering and extracting
- **084 Gathering of Miscellaneous Forest Products, Except Tree Seeds**
  - 0843 Extraction of pine gum
  - 0849 Gathering of forest products, not elsewhere classified
- **085 Forestry Services**
  - 0851 Forestry services
- **09 FISHING, HUNTING, AND TRAPPING**
- **091 Commercial Fishing**
  - 0912 Finfish
  - 0913 Shellfish
  - 0919 Miscellaneous marine products
- **092 Fish Hatcheries and Preserves**
  - 0921 Fish hatcheries and preserves
- **097 Hunting and Trapping, and Game Propagation**
  - 0971 Hunting and trapping, and game propagation

MINING

- **10 METAL MINING**
- **101 Iron Ores**
  - 1011 Iron ores
- **102 Copper Ores**
  - 1021 Copper ores
- **103 Lead and Zinc Ores**
  - 1031 Lead and zinc ores
- **104 Gold and Silver Ores**
  - 1041 Gold ores
  - 1044 Silver ores
- **105 Bauxite and Other Aluminum Ores**
  - 1051 Bauxite and other aluminum ores
- **106 Ferroalloy Ores, Except Vanadium**
  - 1061 Ferroalloy ores, except vanadium
- **108 Metal Mining Services**
  - 1081 Metal mining services
- **109 Miscellaneous Metal Ores**
  - 1092 Mercury ores
  - 1094 Uranium-radium-vanadium ores
  - 1099 Metal ores, not elsewhere classified
- **11 ANTHRACITE MINING**
- **111 Anthracite Mining**
  - 1111 Anthracite
  - 1112 Anthracite mining services
- **12 BITUMINOUS COAL AND LIGNITE MINING**
- **121 Bituminous Coal and Lignite Mining**
  - 1211 Bituminous coal and lignite
  - 1213 Bituminous coal and lignite mining services
- **13 OIL AND GAS EXTRACTION**
- **131 Crude Petroleum and Natural Gas**
  - 1311 Crude petroleum and natural gas
- **132 Natural Gas Liquids**
  - 1321 Natural gas liquids
- **138 Oil and Gas Field Services**
  - 1381 Drilling oil and gas wells
  - 1382 Oil and gas field exploration services
  - 1389 Oil and gas field services, not elsewhere classified
- **14 MINING AND QUARRYING OF NON-METALLIC MINERALS, EXCEPT FUELS**
- **141 Dimension Stone**
  - 1411 Dimension stone
- **142 Crushed and Broken Stone, Including Riprap**
  - 1422 Crushed and broken limestone
  - 1423 Crushed and broken granite
  - 1429 Crushed and broken stone, not elsewhere classified

Guide to Selected Standard Classifications — Standard Industrial Classification

- **144 Sand and Gravel**
  - 1442 Construction sand and gravel
  - 1446 Industrial sand

- **145 Clay, Ceramic, and Refractory Minerals**
  - 1452 Bentonite
  - 1453 Fire clay
  - 1454 Fuller's earth
  - 1455 Kaolin and ball clay
  - 1459 Clay, ceramic, and refractory minerals, not elsewhere classified

- **147 Chemical and Fertilizer Mineral Mining**
  - 1472 Barite
  - 1473 Fluorspar
  - 1474 Potash, soda, and borate minerals
  - 1475 Phosphate rock
  - 1476 Rock salt
  - 1477 Sulfur
  - 1479 Chemical and fertilizer mineral mining, not elsewhere classified

- **148 Nonmetallic Minerals (Except Fuels) Services**
  - 1481 Nonmetallic minerals (except fuels) services

- **149 Miscellaneous Nonmetallic Minerals, Except Fuels**
  - 1492 Gypsum
  - 1496 Talc, soapstone, and pyrophyllite
  - 1499 Miscellaneous nonmetallic minerals, not elsewhere classified

---

CONSTRUCTION

- **15 BUILDING CONSTRUCTION—GENERAL CONTRACTORS AND OPERATIVE BUILDERS**

- **152 General Building Contractors—Residential Buildings**
  - 1521 General contractors—single-family houses
  - 1522 General contractors—residential buildings, other than single-family

- **153 Operative Builders**
  - 1531 Operative builders

- **154 General Building Contractors—Nonresidential Buildings**
  - 1541 General contractors—industrial buildings and warehouses
  - 1542 General contractors—nonresidential buildings, other than industrial buildings and warehouses

- **16 CONSTRUCTION OTHER THAN BUILDING CONSTRUCTION—GENERAL CONTRACTORS**

- **161 Highway and Street Construction, Except Elevated Highways**
  - 1611 Highway and street construction, except elevated highways

- **162 Heavy Construction, Except Highway and Street Construction**
  - 1622 Bridge, tunnel, and elevated highway construction
  - 1623 Water, sewer, pipe line, communication and power line construction
  - 1629 Heavy construction, not elsewhere classified

- **17 CONSTRUCTION—SPECIAL TRADE CONTRACTORS**

- **171 Plumbing, Heating (Except Electric), and Air Conditioning**
  - 1711 Plumbing, heating (except electric), and air conditioning

- **172 Painting, Paper Hanging, and Decorating**
  - 1721 Painting, paper hanging, and decorating

- **173 Electrical Work**
  - 1731 Electrical work

- **174 Masonry, Stonework, Tile Setting, and Plastering**
  - 1741 Masonry, stone setting, and other stonework
  - 1742 Plastering, drywall, acoustical and insulation work
  - 1743 Terrazzo, tile, marble, and mosaic work

- **175 Carpentering and Flooring**
  - 1751 Carpentering
  - 1752 Floor laying and other floorwork, not elsewhere classified

- **176 Roofing and Sheet Metal Work**
  - 1761 Roofing and sheet metal work

- **177 Concrete Work**
  - 1771 Concrete work

- **178 Water Well Drilling**
  - 1781 Water well drilling

- **179 Miscellaneous Special Trade Contractors**
  - 1791 Structural steel erection
  - 1793 Glass and glazing work
  - 1794 Excavating and foundation work
  - 1795 Wrecking and demolition work
  - 1796 Installation or erection of building equipment, not elsewhere classified
  - 1799 Special trade contractors, not elsewhere classified

MANUFACTURING

- **20 FOOD AND KINDRED PRODUCTS**

- **201 Meat Products**
  - 2011 Meat packing plants
  - 2013 Sausages and other prepared meat products
  - 2016 Poultry dressing plants
  - 2017 Poultry and egg processing

- **202 Dairy Products**
  - 2021 Creamery butter
  - 2022 Cheese, natural and processed
  - 2023 Condensed and evaporated milk
  - 2024 Ice cream and frozen desserts
  - 2026 Fluid milk

- **203 Canned and Preserved Fruits and Vegetables**
  - 2032 Canned specialties
  - 2033 Canned fruits, vegetables, preserves, jams, and jellies
  - 2034 Dried and dehydrated fruits, vegetables and soup mixes
  - 2035 Pickled fruits and vegetables, vegetable sauces and seasonings, and salad dressings
  - 2037 Frozen fruits, fruit juices and vegetables
  - 2038 Frozen specialties

- **204 Grain Mill Products**
  - 2041 Flour and other grain mill products
  - 2043 Cereal breakfast foods
  - 2044 Rice milling
  - 2045 Blended and prepared flour
  - 2046 Wet corn milling
  - 2047 Dog, cat and other pet food
  - 2048 Prepared feeds and feed ingredients for animals and fowls, not elsewhere classified

- **205 Bakery Products**
  - 2051 Bread and other bakery products, except cookies and crackers
  - 2052 Cookies and crackers

- **206 Sugar and Confectionery Products**
  - 2061 Cane sugar, except refining only
  - 2062 Cane sugar refining
  - 2063 Beet sugar
  - 2065 Candy and other confectionery products
  - 2066 Chocolate and cocoa products
  - 2067 Chewing gum

- **207 Fats and Oils**
  - 2074 Cottonseed oil mills
  - 2075 Soybean oil mills
  - 2076 Vegetable oil mills, except corn, cottonseed, and soybean
  - 2077 Animal and marine fats and oils
  - 2079 Shortening, table oils, margarine and other edible fats and oils, not elsewhere classified

- **208 Beverages**
  - 2082 Malt beverages
  - 2083 Malt
  - 2084 Wines, brandy, and brandy spirits
  - 2085 Distilled, rectified, and blended liquors
  - 2086 Bottled and canned soft drinks and carbonated waters
  - 2087 Flavoring extracts and flavoring sirups, not elsewhere classified

- **209 Miscellaneous Food Preparations and Kindred Products**
  - 2091 Canned and cured fish and seafoods
  - 2092 Fresh or frozen packaged fish and seafoods
  - 2095 Roasted coffee
  - 2097 Manufactured ice
  - 2098 Macaroni, spaghetti, vermicelli, and noodles
  - 2099 Food preparations, not elsewhere classified

- **21 TOBACCO MANUFACTURES**

- **211 Cigarettes**
  - 2111 Cigarettes

- **212 Cigars**
  - 2121 Cigars

- **213 Tobacco (Chewing and Smoking) and Snuff**
  - 2131 Tobacco (chewing and smoking) and snuff

- **214 Tobacco Stemming and Redrying**
  - 2141 Tobacco stemming and redrying

- **22 TEXTILE MILL PRODUCTS**

- **221 Broad Woven Fabric Mills, Cotton**
  - 2211 Broad woven fabric mills, cotton

- **222 Broad Woven Fabric Mills, Man-made Fiber and Silk**
  - 2221 Broad woven fabric mills, man-made fiber and silk

- **223 Broad Woven Fabric Mills, Wool (Including Dyeing and Finishing)**
  - 2231 Broad woven fabric mills, wool (including dyeing and finishing)

- **224 Narrow Fabrics and Other Smallwares Mills: Cotton, Wool, Silk, and Man-made Fiber**
  - 2241 Narrow fabrics and other smallwares mills: cotton, wool, silk, and man-made fiber

- **225 Knitting Mills**
  - 2251 Women's full length and knee length hosiery
  - 2252 Hosiery, except women's full length and knee length hosiery

Standard Industrial Classification

Guide to Selected Standard Classifications

- 2253 Knit outerwear mills
- 2254 Knit underwear mills
- 2257 Circular knit fabric mills
- 2258 Warp knit fabric mills
- 2259 Knitting mills, not elsewhere classified

226 Dyeing and Finishing Textiles, Except Wool Fabrics and Knit Goods

- 2261 Finishers of broad woven fabrics of cotton
- 2262 Finishers of broad woven fabrics of man-made fiber and silk
- 2269 Finishers of textiles, not elsewhere classified

227 Floor Covering Mills

- 2271 Woven carpets and rugs
- 2272 Tufted carpets and rugs
- 2279 Carpets and rugs, not elsewhere classified

228 Yarn and Thread Mills

- 2281 Yarn spinning mills: cotton, man-made fibers and silk
- 2282 Yarn texturizing, throwing, twisting, and winding mills: cotton, man-made fibers, and silk
- 2283 Yarn mills, wool, including carpet and rug yarn
- 2284 Thread mills

229 Miscellaneous Textile Goods

- 2291 Felt goods, except woven felts and hats
- 2292 Lace goods
- 2293 Paddings and upholstery filling
- 2294 Processed waste and recovered fibers and flock
- 2295 Coated fabrics, not rubberized
- 2296 Tire cord and fabric
- 2297 Nonwoven fabrics
- 2298 Cordage and twine
- 2299 Textile goods, not elsewhere classified

23 APPAREL AND OTHER FINISHED PRODUCTS MADE FROM FABRICS AND SIMILAR MATERIALS

231 Men's, Youths', and Boys' Suits, Coats, and Overcoats

- 2311 Men's, youths', and boys' suits, coats, and overcoats

232 Men's, Youths', and Boys' Furnishings, Work Clothing, and Allied Garments

- 2321 Men's, youths', and boys' shirts (except work shirts) and nightwear
- 2322 Men's, youths', and boys' underwear
- 2323 Men's, youths', and boys' neckwear
- 2327 Men's, youths', and boys' separate trousers
- 2328 Men's, youths', and boys' work clothing
- 2329 Men's, youths', and boys' clothing, not elsewhere classified

233 Women's, Misses', and Juniors' Outerwear

- 2331 Women's, misses', and juniors' blouses, waists, and shirts
- 2335 Women's, misses', and juniors' dresses
- 2337 Women's, misses', and juniors' suits, skirts, and coats
- 2339 Women's, misses', and juniors' outerwear, not elsewhere classified

234 Women's, Misses', Children's, and Infants' Undergarments

- 2341 Women's, misses', children's, and infants' underwear and nightwear
- 2342 Brassieres, girdles, and allied garments

235 Hats, Caps, and Millinery

- 2351 Millinery
- 2352 Hats and caps, except millinery

236 Girls', Children's, and Infants' Outerwear

- 2361 Girls', children's, and infants' dresses, blouses, waists, and shirts
- 2363 Girls', children's, and infants' coats and suits
- 2369 Girls', children's, and infants' outerwear, not elsewhere classified

237 Fur Goods

- 2371 Fur goods

238 Miscellaneous Apparel and Accessories

- 2381 Dress and work gloves, except knit and all-leather
- 2384 Robes and dressing gowns
- 2385 Raincoats and other waterproof outer garments
- 2386 Leather and sheep lined clothing
- 2387 Apparel belts
- 2389 Apparel and accessories, not elsewhere classified

239 Miscellaneous Fabricated Textile Products

- 2391 Curtains and draperies
- 2392 Housefurnishings, except curtains and draperies
- 2393 Textile bags
- 2394 Canvas and related products
- 2395 Pleating, decorative and novelty stitching, and tucking for the trade
- 2396 Automotive trimmings, apparel findings, and related products
- 2397 Schiffli machine embroideries
- 2399 Fabricated textile products, not elsewhere classified

24 LUMBER AND WOOD PRODUCTS, EXCEPT FURNITURE

241 Logging Camps and Logging Contractors

- 2411 Logging camps and logging contractors

242 Sawmills and Planing Mills

- 2421 Sawmills and planing mills, general
- 2426 Hardwood dimension and flooring mills
- 2429 Special product sawmills, not elsewhere classified

243 Millwork, Veneer, Plywood, and Structural Wood Members

- 2431 Millwork
- 2434 Wood kitchen cabinets
- 2435 Hardwood veneer and plywood
- 2436 Softwood veneer and plywood
- 2439 Structural wood members, not elsewhere classified

244 Wood Containers

- 2441 Nailed and lock corner wood boxes and shook
- 2448 Wood pallets and skids
- 2449 Wood containers, not elsewhere classified

245 Wood Buildings and Mobile Homes

- 2451 Mobile homes
- 2452 Prefabricated wood buildings and components

249 Miscellaneous Wood Products

- 2491 Wood preserving
- 2492 Particleboard
- 2499 Wood products, not elsewhere classified

25 FURNITURE AND FIXTURES

251 Household Furniture

- 2511 Wood household furniture, except upholstered
- 2512 Wood household furniture, upholstered
- 2514 Metal household furniture
- 2515 Mattresses and bedsprings
- 2517 Wood television, radio, phonograph, and sewing machine cabinets
- 2519 Household furniture, not elsewhere classified

252 Office Furniture

- 2521 Wood office furniture
- 2522 Metal office furniture

253 Public Building and Related Furniture

- 2531 Public building and related furniture

254 Partitions, Shelving, Lockers, and Office and Store Fixtures

- 2541 Wood partitions, shelving, lockers, and office and store fixtures
- 2542 Metal partitions, shelving, lockers, and office and store fixtures

259 Miscellaneous Furniture and Fixtures

- 2591 Drapery hardware and window blinds and shades
- 2599 Furniture and fixtures, not elsewhere classified

26 PAPER AND ALLIED PRODUCTS

261 Pulp Mills

- 2611 Pulp mills

262 Paper Mills, Except Building Paper Mills

- 2621 Paper mills, except building paper mills

263 Paperboard Mills

- 2631 Paperboard mills

264 Converted Paper and Paperboard Products, Except Containers and Boxes

- 2641 Paper coating and glazing
- 2642 Envelopes
- 2643 Bags, except textile bags
- 2645 Die-cut paper and paperboard and cardboard
- 2646 Pressed and molded pulp goods
- 2647 Sanitary paper products
- 2648 Stationery, tablets and related products
- 2649 Converted paper and paperboard products, not elsewhere classified

265 Paperboard Containers and Boxes

- 2651 Folding paperboard boxes
- 2652 Set-up paperboard boxes
- 2653 Corrugated and solid fiber boxes
- 2654 Sanitary food containers
- 2655 Fiber cans, tubes, drums, and similar products

266 Building Paper and Building Board Mills

- 2661 Building paper and building board mills

27 PRINTING, PUBLISHING, AND ALLIED INDUSTRIES

271 Newspapers: Publishing, Publishing and Printing

- 2711 Newspapers: publishing, publishing and printing

Guide to Selected Standard Classifications

Standard Industrial Classification

272 Periodicals: Publishing, Publishing and Printing
2721 Periodicals: publishing, publishing and printing

273 Books
2731 Books: publishing, publishing and printing
2732 Book printing

274 Miscellaneous Publishing
2741 Miscellaneous publishing

275 Commercial Printing
2751 Commercial printing, letterpress and screen
2752 Commercial printing, lithographic
2753 Engraving and plate printing
2754 Commercial printing, gravure

276 Manifold Business Forms
2761 Manifold business forms

277 Greeting Card Publishing
2771 Greeting card publishing

278 Blankbooks, Looseleaf Binders, and Bookbinding and Related Work
2782 Blankbooks, looseleaf binders and devices
2789 Bookbinding and related work

279 Service Industries for the Printing Trade
2791 Typesetting
2793 Photoengraving
2794 Electrotyping and stereotyping
2795 Lithographic platemaking and related services

28 CHEMICALS AND ALLIED PRODUCTS

281 Industrial Inorganic Chemicals
2812 Alkalies and chlorine
2813 Industrial gases
2816 Inorganic pigments
2819 Industrial inorganic chemicals, not elsewhere classified

282 Plastics Materials and Synthetic Resins, Synthetic Rubber, Synthetic and Other Man-Made Fibers, Except Glass
2821 Plastics materials, synthetic resins, and nonvulcanizable elastomers
2822 Synthetic rubber (vulcanizable elastomers)
2823 Cellulosic man-made fibers
2824 Synthetic organic fibers, except cellulosic

283 Drugs
2831 Biological products
2833 Medicinal chemicals and botanical products
2834 Pharmaceutical preparations

284 Soap, Detergents, and Cleaning Preparations, Perfumes, Cosmetics, and Other Toilet Preparations
2841 Soap and other detergents, except specialty cleaners
2842 Specialty cleaning, polishing, and sanitation preparations
2843 Surface active agents, finishing agents, sulfonated oils and assistants
2844 Perfumes, cosmetics, and other toilet preparations

285 Paints, Varnishes, Lacquers, Enamels, and Allied Products
2851 Paints, varnishes, lacquers, enamels, and allied products

286 Industrial Organic Chemicals
2861 Gum and wood chemicals

2865 Cyclic (coal tar) crudes, and cyclic intermediates, dyes, and organic pigments (lakes and toners)
2869 Industrial organic chemicals, not elsewhere classified

287 Agricultural Chemicals
2873 Nitrogenous fertilizers
2874 Phosphatic fertilizers
2875 Fertilizers, mixing only
2879 Pesticides and agricultural chemicals, not elsewhere classified

289 Miscellaneous Chemical Products
2891 Adhesives and sealants
2892 Explosives
2893 Printing ink
2895 Carbon black
2899 Chemicals and chemical preparations, not elsewhere classified

29 PETROLEUM REFINING AND RELATED INDUSTRIES

291 Petroleum Refining
2911 Petroleum refining

295 Paving and Roofing Materials
2951 Paving mixtures and blocks
2952 Asphalt felts and coatings

299 Miscellaneous Products of Petroleum and Coal
2992 Lubricating oils and greases
2999 Products of petroleum and coal, not elsewhere classified

30 RUBBER AND MISCELLANEOUS PLASTICS PRODUCTS

301 Tires and Inner Tubes
3011 Tires and inner tubes

302 Rubber and Plastics Footwear
3021 Rubber and plastics footwear

303 Reclaimed Rubber
3031 Reclaimed rubber

304 Rubber and Plastics Hose and Belting
3041 Rubber and plastics hose and belting

306 Fabricated Rubber Products, Not Elsewhere Classified
3069 Fabricated rubber products, not elsewhere classified

307 Miscellaneous Plastics Products
3079 Miscellaneous plastics products

31 LEATHER AND LEATHER PRODUCTS

311 Leather Tanning and Finishing
3111 Leather tanning and finishing

313 Boot and Shoe Cut Stock and Findings
3131 Boot and shoe cut stock and findings

314 Footwear, Except Rubber
3142 House slippers
3143 Men's footwear, except athletic
3144 Women's footwear, except athletic
3149 Footwear, except rubber, not elsewhere classified

315 Leather Gloves and Mittens
3151 Leather gloves and mittens

316 Luggage
3161 Luggage

317 Handbags and Other Personal Leather Goods
3171 Women's handbags and purses

3172 Personal leather goods, except women's handbags and purses

319 Leather Goods, Not Elsewhere Classified
3199 Leather goods, not elsewhere classified

32 STONE, CLAY, GLASS AND CONCRETE PRODUCTS

321 Flat Glass
3211 Flat glass

322 Glass and Glassware, Pressed or Blown
3221 Glass containers
3229 Pressed and blown glass and glassware, not elsewhere classified

323 Glass Products, Made of Purchased Glass
3231 Glass products, made of purchased glass

324 Cement, Hydraulic
3241 Cement, hydraulic

325 Structural Clay Products
3251 Brick and structural clay tile
3253 Ceramic wall and floor tile
3255 Clay refractories
3259 Structural clay products, not elsewhere classified

326 Pottery and Related Products
3261 Vitreous china plumbing fixtures and china and earthenware fittings and bathroom accessories
3262 Vitreous china table and kitchen articles
3263 Fine earthenware (whiteware) table and kitchen articles
3264 Porcelain electrical supplies
3269 Pottery products, not elsewhere classified

327 Concrete, Gypsum, and Plaster Products
3271 Concrete block and brick
3272 Concrete products, except block and brick
3273 Ready-mixed concrete
3274 Lime
3275 Gypsum products

328 Cut Stone and Stone Products
3281 Cut stone and stone products

329 Abrasive, Asbestos, and Miscellaneous Nonmetallic Mineral Products
3291 Abrasive products
3292 Asbestos products
3293 Gaskets, packing, and sealing devices
3295 Minerals and earths, ground or otherwise treated
3296 Mineral wool
3297 Nonclay refractories
3299 Nonmetallic mineral products, not elsewhere classified

33 PRIMARY METAL INDUSTRIES

331 Blast Furnaces, Steel Works, and Rolling and Finishing Mills
3312 Blast furnaces (including coke ovens), steel works, and rolling mills
3313 Electrometallurgical products
3315 Steel wire drawing and steel nails and spikes
3316 Cold rolled steel sheet, strip, and bars
3317 Steel pipe and tubes

332 Iron and Steel Foundries
3321 Gray iron foundries
3322 Malleable iron foundries

Standard Industrial Classification

Guide to Selected Standard Classifications

- 3324 Steel inventment foundries
- 3325 Steel foundries, not elsewhere classified

333 Primary Smelting and Refining of Nonferrous Metals

- 3331 Primary smelting and refining of copper
- 3332 Primary smelting and refining of lead
- 3333 Primary smelting and refining of zinc
- 3334 Primary production of aluminum
- 3339 Primary smelting and refining of nonferrous metals, not elsewhere classified

334 Secondary Smelting and Refining of Nonferrous Metals

- 3341 Secondary smelting and refining of nonferrous metals

335 Rolling, Drawing, and Extruding of Nonferrous Metals

- 3351 Rolling, drawing, and extruding of copper
- 3353 Aluminum sheet, plate, and foil
- 3354 Aluminum extruded products
- 3355 Aluminum rolling and drawing, not elsewhere classified
- 3356 Rolling, drawing, and extruding of nonferrous metals, except copper and aluminum
- 3357 Drawing and insulating of nonferrous wire

336 Nonferrous Foundries (Castings)

- 3361 Aluminum foundries (castings)
- 3362 Brass, bronze, copper, copper base alloy foundries (castings)
- 3369 Nonferrous foundries (castings), not elsewhere classified

339 Miscellaneous Primary Metal Products

- 3398 Metal heat treating
- 3399 Primary metal products, not elsewhere classified

34 FABRICATED METAL PRODUCTS, EXCEPT MACHINERY AND TRANSPORTATION EQUIPMENT

341 Metal Cans and Shipping Containers

- 3411 Metal cans
- 3412 Metal shipping barrels, drums, kegs, and pails

342 Cutlery, Hand Tools, and General Hardware

- 3421 Cutlery
- 3423 Hand and edge tools, except machine tools and hand saws
- 3425 Hand saws and saw blades
- 3429 Hardware, not elsewhere classified

343 Heating Equipment, Except Electric and Warm Air; and Plumbing Fixtures

- 3431 Enameled iron and metal sanitary ware
- 3432 Plumbing fixture fittings and trim (brass goods)
- 3433 Heating equipment, except electric and warm air furnaces

344 Fabricated Structural Metal Products

- 3441 Fabricated structural metal
- 3442 Metal doors, sash, frames, molding, and trim
- 3443 Fabricated plate work (boiler shops)
- 3444 Sheet metal work
- 3446 Architectural and ornamental metal work
- 3448 Prefabricated metal buildings and components
- 3449 Miscellaneous metal work

345 Screw Machine Products, and Bolts, Nuts, Screws, Rivets, and Washers

- 3451 Screw machine products
- 3452 Bolts, nuts, screws, rivets, and washers

346 Metal Forgings and Stampings

- 3462 Iron and steel forgings
- 3463 Nonferrous forgings
- 3465 Automotive stampings
- 3466 Crowns and closures
- 3469 Metal stampings, not elsewhere classified

347 Coating, Engraving, and Allied Services

- 3471 Electroplating, plating, polishing, anodizing and coloring
- 3479 Coating, engraving, and allied services, not elsewhere classified

348 Ordnance and Accessories, Except Vehicles and Guided Missiles

- 3482 Small arms ammunition
- 3483 Ammunition, except for small arms, not elsewhere classified
- 3484 Small arms
- 3489 Ordnance and accessories, not elsewhere classified

349 Miscellaneous Fabricated Metal Products

- 3493 Steel springs, except wire
- 3494 Valves and pipe fittings, except plumbers' brass goods
- 3495 Wire springs
- 3496 Miscellaneous fabricated wire products
- 3497 Metal foil and leaf
- 3498 Fabricated pipe and fabricated pipe fittings
- 3499 Fabricated metal products, not elsewhere classified

35 MACHINERY, EXCEPT ELECTRICAL

351 Engines and Turbines

- 3511 Steam, gas, and hydraulic turbines, and turbine generator set units
- 3519 Internal combustion engines, not elsewhere classified

352 Farm and Garden Machinery and Equipment

- 3523 Farm machinery and equipment
- 3524 Garden tractors and lawn and garden equipment

353 Construction, Mining, and Materials Handling Machinery and Equipment

- 3531 Construction machinery and equipment
- 3532 Mining machinery and equipment, except oil field machinery and equipment
- 3533 Oil field machinery and equipment
- 3534 Elevators and moving stairways
- 3535 Conveyors and conveying equipment
- 3536 Hoists, industrial cranes, and monorail systems
- 3537 Industrial trucks, tractors, trailers, and stackers

354 Metalworking Machinery and Equipment

- 3541 Machine tools, metal cutting types
- 3542 Machine tools, metal forming types
- 3544 Special dies and tools, die sets, jigs and fixtures, and industrial molds
- 3545 Machine tool accessories and measuring devices
- 3546 Power driven hand tools
- 3547 Rolling mill machinery and equipment
- 3549 Metalworking machinery, not elsewhere classified

355 Special Industry Machinery, Except Metalworking Machinery

- 3551 Food products machinery
- 3552 Textile machinery
- 3553 Woodworking machinery
- 3554 Paper industries machinery
- 3555 Printing trades machinery and equipment
- 3559 Special industry machinery, not elsewhere classified

356 General Industrial Machinery and Equipment

- 3561 Pumps and pumping equipment
- 3562 Ball and roller bearings
- 3563 Air and gas compressors
- 3564 Blowers and exhaust and ventilation fans
- 3565 Industrial patterns
- 3566 Speed changers, industrial high speed drives, and gears
- 3567 Industrial process furnaces and ovens
- 3568 Mechanical power transmission equipment, not elsewhere classified
- 3569 General industrial machinery and equipment, not elsewhere classified

357 Office, Computing, and Accounting Machines

- 3572 Typewriters
- 3573 Electronic computing equipment
- 3574 Calculating and accounting machines, except electronic computing equipment
- 3576 Scales and balances, except laboratory
- 3579 Office machines, not elsewhere classified

358 Refrigeration and Service Industry Machinery

- 3581 Automatic merchandising machines
- 3582 Commercial laundry, dry cleaning, and pressing machines
- 3585 Air conditioning and warm air heating equipment and commercial and industrial refrigeration equipment
- 3586 Measuring and dispensing pumps
- 3589 Service industry machines, not elsewhere classified

359 Miscellaneous Machinery, Except Electrical

- 3592 Carburetors, pistons, piston rings and valves
- 3599 Machinery, except electrical, not elsewhere classified

36 ELECTRICAL AND ELECTRONIC MACHINERY, EQUIPMENT, AND SUPPLIES

361 Electric Transmission and Distribution Equipment

- 3612 Power, distribution, and specialty transformers

Guide to Selected Standard Classifications — Standard Industrial Classification

3613 Switchgear and switchboard apparatus

362 Electrical Industrial Apparatus
3621 Motors and generators
3622 Industrial controls
3623 Welding apparatus, electric
3624 Carbon and graphite products
3629 Electrical industrial apparatus, not elsewhere classified

363 Household Appliances
3631 Household cooking equipment
3632 Household refrigerators and home and farm freezers
3633 Household laundry equipment
3634 Electric housewares and fans
3635 Household vacuum cleaners
3636 Sewing machines
3639 Household appliances, not elsewhere classified

364 Electric Lighting and Wiring Equipment
3641 Electric lamps
3643 Current-carrying wiring devices
3644 Noncurrent-carrying wiring devices
3645 Residential electric lighting fixtures
3646 Commercial, industrial, and institutional electric lighting fixtures
3647 Vehicular lighting equipment
3648 Lighting equipment, not elsewhere classified

365 Radio and Television Receiving Equipment, Except Communication Types
3651 Radio and television receiving sets, except communication types
3652 Phonograph records and prerecorded magnetic tape

366 Communication Equipment
3661 Telephone and telegraph apparatus
3662 Radio and television transmitting, signaling, and detection equipment and apparatus

367 Electronic Components and Accessories
3671 Radio and television receiving type electron tubes, except cathode ray
3672 Cathode ray television picture tubes
3673 Transmitting, industrial, and special purpose electron tubes
3674 Semiconductors and related devices
3675 Electronic capacitors
3676 Resistors, for electronic applications
3677 Electronic coils, transformers and other inductors
3678 Connectors, for electronic applications
3679 Electronic components, not elsewhere classified

369 Miscellaneous Electrical Machinery, Equipment, and Supplies
3691 Storage batteries
3692 Primary batteries, dry and wet
3693 Radiographic X-ray, fluoroscopic X-ray, therapeutic X-ray, and other X-ray apparatus and tubes; electromedical and electrotherapeutic apparatus
3694 Electric equipment for internal combustion engines

3699 Electrical machinery, equipment and supplies, not elsewhere classified

37 TRANSPORTATION EQUIPMENT

371 Motor Vehicles and Motor Vehicle Equipment
3711 Motor vehicles and passenger car bodies
3713 Truck and bus bodies
3714 Motor vehicle parts and accessories
3715 Truck trailers
3716 Motor homes

372 Aircraft and Parts
3721 Aircraft
3724 Aircraft engines and engine parts
3728 Aircraft parts and auxiliary equipment, not elsewhere classified

373 Ship and Boat Building and Repairing
3731 Ship building and repairing
3732 Boat building and repairing

374 Railroad Equipment
3743 Railroad equipment

375 Motorcycles, Bicycles, and Parts
3751 Motorcycles, bicycles, and parts

376 Guided Missiles and Space Vehicles and Parts
3761 Guided missiles and space vehicles
3764 Guided missile and space vehicle propulsion units and propulsion unit parts
3769 Guided missile and space vehicle parts and auxiliary equipment, not elsewhere classified

379 Miscellaneous Transportation Equipment
3792 Travel trailers and campers
3795 Tanks and tank components
3799 Transportation equipment, not elsewhere classified

38 MEASURING, ANALYZING, AND CONTROLLING INSTRUMENTS; PHOTOGRAPHIC, MEDICAL, AND OPTICAL GOODS; WATCHES AND CLOCKS

381 Engineering, Laboratory, Scientific, and Research Instruments, and Associated Equipment
3811 Engineering, laboratory, scientific, and research instruments, and associated equipment

382 Measuring and Controlling Instruments
3822 Automatic controls for regulating residential and commercial environments and appliances
3823 Industrial instruments for measurement, display, and control of process variables; and related products
3824 Totalizing fluid meters and counting devices
3825 Instruments for measuring and testing of electricity and electrical signals
3829 Measuring and controlling devices, not elsewhere classified

383 Optical Instruments and Lenses
3832 Optical instruments and lenses

384 Surgical, Medical, and Dental Instruments and Supplies
3841 Surgical and medical instruments and apparatus
3842 Orthopedic, prosthetic, and surgical appliances and supplies
3843 Dental equipment and supplies

385 Ophthalmic Goods
3851 Ophthalmic goods

386 Photographic Equipment and Supplies
3861 Photographic equipment and supplies

387 Watches, Clocks, Clockwork Operated Devices, and Parts
3873 Watches, clocks, clockwork operated devices, and parts

39 MISCELLANEOUS MANUFACTURING INDUSTRIES

391 Jewelry, Silverware, and Plated Ware
3911 Jewelry, precious metal
3914 Silverware, plated ware, and stainless steel ware
3915 Jewelers' findings and materials, and lapidary work

393 Musical Instruments
3931 Musical instruments

394 Toys and Amusement, Sporting, and Athletic Goods
3942 Dolls
3944 Games, toys, and children's vehicles; except dools and bicycles
3949 Sporting and athletic goods, not elsewhere classified

395 Pens, Pencils, and Other Office and Artists' Materials
3951 Pens, mechanical pencils, and parts
3952 Lead pencils, crayons, and artists' materials
3953 Marking devices
3955 Carbon paper and inked ribbons

396 Costume Jewelry, Costume Novelties, Buttons, and Miscellaneous Notions, Except Precious Metal
3961 Costume jewelry and costume novelties, except precious metal
3962 Feathers, plumes, and artificial trees and flowers
3963 Buttons
3964 Needles, pins, hooks and eyes, and similar notions

399 Miscellaneous Manufacturing Industries
3991 Brooms and brushes
3993 Signs and advertising displays
3995 Burial caskets
3996 Linoleum, asphalted-felt-base, and other hard surface floor coverings, not elsewhere classified
3999 Manufacturing industries, not elsewhere classified

TRANSPORTATION AND PUBLIC UTILITIES

40 RAILROAD TRANSPORTATION

401 Railroads
4011 Railroads, line-haul operating
4013 Switching and terminal establishments

41 LOCAL AND SUBURBAN TRANSIT AND INTERURBAN HIGHWAY PASSENGER TRANSPORTATION

411 Local and Suburban Passenger Transportation
4111 Local and suburban transit
4119 Local passenger transportation, not elsewhere classified

January-December 1984 — ASI Annual Supplement 1069

Standard Industrial Classification

Guide to Selected Standard Classifications

- **412 Taxicabs**
  - 4121 Taxicabs
- **413 Intercity and Rural Highway Passenger Transportation**
  - 4131 Intercity and rural highway passenger transportation
- **414 Passenger Transportation Charter Service**
  - 4141 Local passenger transportation charter service
  - 4142 Passenger transportation charter service, except local
- **415 School Buses**
  - 4151 School buses
- **417 Terminal and Service Facilities for Motor Vehicle Passenger Transportation**
  - 4171 Terminal and joint terminal maintenance facilities for motor vehicle passenger transportation
  - 4172 Maintenance and service facilities for motor vehicle passenger transportation
- **42 MOTOR FREIGHT TRANSPORTA-TION AND WAREHOUSING**
- **421 Trucking, Local and Long Distance**
  - 4212 Local trucking without storage
  - 4213 Trucking, except local
  - 4214 Local trucking with storage
- **422 Public Warehousing**
  - 4221 Farm product warehousing and storage
  - 4222 Refrigerated warehousing
  - 4224 Household goods warehousing and storage
  - 4225 General warehousing and storage
  - 4226 Special warehousing and storage, not elsewhere classified
- **423 Terminal and Joint Terminal Maintenance Facilities for Motor Freight Transportation**
  - 4231 Terminal and joint terminal maintenance facilities for motor freight transportation
- **43 U.S. POSTAL SERVICE**
- **431 U.S. Postal Service**
  - 4311 U.S. Postal Service
- **44 WATER TRANSPORTATION**
- **441 Deep Sea Foreign Transportation**
  - 4411 Deep sea foreign transportation
- **442 Deep Sea Domestic Transportation**
  - 4421 Transportation to and between noncontiguous territories
  - 4422 Coastwise transportation
  - 4423 Intercoastal transportation
- **443 Great Lakes-St. Lawrence Seaway Transportation**
  - 4431 Great Lakes-St. Lawrence Seaway Transportation
- **444 Transportation on Rivers and Canals**
  - 4441 Transportation on rivers and canals
- **445 Local Water Transportation**
  - 4452 Ferries
  - 4453 Lighterage
  - 4454 Towing and tugboat service
  - 4459 Local water transportation, not elsewhere classified
- **446 Services Incidental to Water Transportation**
  - 4463 Marine cargo handling
  - 4464 Canal operation

- 4469 Water transportation services, not elsewhere classified

- **45 TRANSPORTATION BY AIR**
- **451 Air Transportation, Certificated Carriers**
  - 4511 Air transportation, certificated carriers
- **452 Air Transportation, Noncertificated Carriers**
  - 4521 Air transportation, noncertificated carriers
- **458 Fixed Facilities and Services Related to Air Transportation**
  - 4582 Airports and flying fields
  - 4583 Airport terminal services
- **46 PIPE LINES, EXCEPT NATURAL GAS**
- **461 Pipe Lines, Except Natural Gas**
  - 4612 Crude petroleum pipe lines
  - 4613 Refined petroleum pipe lines
  - 4619 Pile lines, not elsewhere classified
- **47 TRANSPORTATION SERVICES**
- **471 Freight Forwarding**
  - 4712 Freight forwarding
- **472 Arrangement of Transportation**
  - 4722 Arrangement of passenger transportation
  - 4723 Arrangement of transportation of freight and cargo
- **474 Rental of Railroad Cars**
  - 4742 Rental of railroad cars with care of lading
  - 4743 Rental of railroad cars without care of lading
- **478 Miscellaneous Services Incidental to Transportation**
  - 4782 Inspection and weighing services connected with transportation
  - 4783 Packing and crating
  - 4784 Fixed facilities for handling motor vehicle transportation, not elsewhere classified
  - 4789 Services incidental to transportation, not elsewhere classified
- **48 COMMUNICATION**
- **481 Telephone Communication (Wire or Radio)**
  - 4811 Telephone communication (wire or radio)
- **482 Telegraph Communication (Wire or Radio)**
  - 4821 Telegraph communication (wire or radio)
- **483 Radio and Television Broadcasting**
  - 4832 Radio broadcasting
  - 4833 Television broadcasting
- **489 Communication Services, Not Elsewhere Classified**
  - 4899 Communications services, not elsewhere classified
- **49 ELECTRIC, GAS, AND SANITARY SERVICES**
- **491 Electric Services**
  - 4911 Electric services
- **492 Gas Production and Distribution**
  - 4922 Natural gas transmission
  - 4923 Natural gas transmission and distribution
  - 4924 Natural gas distribution
  - 4925 Mixed, manufactured or liquified petroleum gas production and/or distribution

- **493 Combination Electric and Gas, and Other Utility Services**
  - 4931 Electric and other services combined
  - 4932 Gas and other services combined
  - 4939 Combination utilities, not elsewhere classified
- **494 Water Supply**
  - 4941 Water supply
- **495 Sanitary Services**
  - 4952 Sewerage systems
  - 4953 Refuse systems
  - 4959 Sanitary services, not elsewhere classified
- **496 Steam Supply**
  - 4961 Steam supply
- **497 Irrigation Systems**
  - 4971 Irrigation systems

WHOLESALE TRADE

- **50 WHOLESALE TRADE–DURABLE GOODS**
- **501 Motor Vehicles and Automotive Parts and Supplies**
  - 5012 Automobiles and other motor vehicles
  - 5013 Automotive parts and supplies
  - 5014 Tires and tubes
- **502 Furniture and Home Furnishings**
  - 5021 Furniture
  - 5023 Home furnishings
- **503 Lumber and Other Construction Materials**
  - 5031 Lumber, plywood and millwork
  - 5039 Construction materials, not elsewhere classified
- **504 Sporting, Recreational, Photographic, and Hobby Goods, Toys and Supplies**
  - 5041 Sporting and recreational goods and supplies
  - 5042 Toys and hobby goods and supplies
  - 5043 Photographic equipment and supplies
- **505 Metals and Minerals, Except Petroleum**
  - 5051 Metals service centers and offices
  - 5052 Coal and other minerals and ores
- **506 Electrical Goods**
  - 5063 Electrical apparatus and equipment, wiring supplies and construction materials
  - 5064 Electrical appliances, television and radio sets
  - 5065 Electronic parts and equipment
- **507 Hardware, and Plumbing and Heating Equipment and Supplies**
  - 5072 Hardware
  - 5074 Plumbing and heating equipment and supplies (hydronics)
  - 5075 Warm air heating and air conditioning equipment and supplies
  - 5078 Refrigeration equipment and supplies
- **508 Machinery, Equipment, and Supplies**
  - 5081 Commercial machines and equipment
  - 5082 Construction and mining machinery and equipment

Guide to Selected Standard Classifications

Standard Industrial Classification

5083 Farm and garden machinery and equipment
5084 Industrial machinery and equipment
5085 Industrial supplies
5086 Professional equipment and supplies
5087 Service establishment equipment and supplies
5088 Transportation equipment and supplies, except motor vehicles

509 Miscellaneous Durable Goods
5093 Scrap and waste materials
5094 Jewelry, watches, diamonds and other precious stones
5099 Durable goods, not elsewhere classified

51 WHOLESALE TRADE–NONDURABLE GOODS

511 Paper and Paper Products
5111 Printing and writing paper
5112 Stationery supplies
5113 Industrial and personal service paper

512 Drugs, Drug Proprietaries and Druggists' Sundries
5122 Drugs, drug proprietaries, and druggists' sundries

513 Apparel, Piece Goods, and Notions
5133 Piece goods (woven fabrics)
5134 Notions and other dry goods
5136 Men's and boys' clothing and furnishings
5137 Women's, children's and infants' clothing and accessories
5139 Footwear

514 Groceries and Related Products
5141 Groceries, general line
5142 Frozen foods
5143 Dairy products
5144 Poultry and poultry products
5145 Confectionery
5146 Fish and seafoods
5147 Meats and meat products
5148 Fresh fruits and vegetables
5149 Groceries and related products, not elsewhere classified

515 Farm-Product Raw Materials
5152 Cotton
5153 Grain
5154 Livestock
5159 Farm-product raw materials, not elsewhere classified

516 Chemicals and Allied Products
5161 Chemicals and allied products

517 Petroleum and Petroleum Products
5171 Petroleum bulk stations and terminals
5172 Petroleum and petroleum products wholesalers, except bulk stations and terminals

518 Beer, Wine and Distilled Alcoholic Beverages
5181 Beer and ale
5182 Wines and distilled alcoholic beverages

519 Miscellaneous Nondurable Goods
5191 Farm supplies
5194 Tobacco and tobacco products
5198 Paints, varnishes, and supplies
5199 Nondurable goods, not elsewhere classified

RETAIL TRADE

52 BUILDING MATERIALS, HARDWARE, GARDEN SUPPLY, AND MOBILE HOME DEALERS

521 Lumber and Other Building Materials Dealers
5211 Lumber and other building materials dealers

523 Paint, Glass, and Wallpaper Stores
5231 Paint, glass, and wallpaper stores

525 Hardware Stores
5251 Hardware stores

526 Retail Nurseries, Lawn and Garden Supply Stores
5261 Retail nurseries, lawn and garden supply stores

527 Mobile Home Dealers
5271 Mobile home dealers

53 GENERAL MERCHANDISE STORES

531 Department Stores
5311 Department stores

533 Variety Stores
5331 Variety stores

539 Miscellaneous General Merchandise Stores
5399 Miscellaneous general merchandise stores

54 FOOD STORES

541 Grocery Stores
5411 Grocery stores

542 Meat and Fish (Seafood) Markets, Including Freezer Provisioners
5422 Freezer and locker meat provisioners
5423 Meat and fish (seafood) markets

543 Fruit Stores and Vegetable Markets
5431 Fruit stores and vegetable markets

544 Candy, Nut, and Confectionery Stores
5441 Candy, nut, and confectionery stores

545 Dairy Products Stores
5451 Dairy products stores

546 Retail Bakeries
5462 Retail bakeries–baking and selling
5463 Retail bakeries–selling only

549 Miscellaneous Food Stores
5499 Miscellaneous food stores

55 AUTOMOTIVE DEALERS AND GASOLINE SERVICE STATIONS

551 Motor Vehicle Dealers (New and Used)
5511 Motor vehicle dealers (new and used)

552 Motor Vehicle Dealers (Used Only)
5521 Motor vehicle dealers (used only)

553 Auto and Home Supply Stores
5531 Auto and home supply stores

554 Gasoline Service Stations
5541 Gasoline service stations

555 Boat Dealers
5551 Boat dealers

556 Recreational and Utility Trailer Dealers
5561 Recreational and utility trailer dealers

557 Motorcycle Dealers
5571 Motorcycle dealers

559 Automotive Dealers, Not Elsewhere Classified
5599 Automotive dealers, not elsewhere classified

56 APPAREL AND ACCESSORY STORES

561 Men's and Boys' Clothing and Furnishings Stores
5611 Men's and boys' clothing and furnishings stores

562 Women's Ready-to-Wear Stores
5621 Women's ready-to-wear stores

563 Women's Accessory and Specialty Stores
5631 Women's accessory and specialty stores

564 Children's and Infants' Wear Stores
5641 Children's and infants' wear stores

565 Family Clothing Stores
5651 Family clothing stores

566 Shoe Stores
5661 Shoe stores

568 Furriers and Fur Shops
5681 Furriers and fur shops

569 Miscellaneous Apparel and Accessory Stores
5699 Miscellaneous apparel and accessory stores

57 FURNITURE, HOME FURNISHINGS AND EQUIPMENT STORES

571 Furniture, Home Furnishings, and Equipment Stores, Except Appliances
5712 Furniture stores
5713 Floor covering stores
5714 Drapery, curtain, and upholstery stores
5719 Miscellaneous home furnishing stores

572 Household Appliance Stores
5722 Household appliance stores

573 Radio, Television, and Music Stores
5732 Radio and television stores
5733 Music stores

58 EATING AND DRINKING PLACES

581 Eating and Drinking Places
5812 Eating places
5813 Drinking places (alcoholic beverages)

59 MISCELLANEOUS RETAIL

591 Drug Stores and Proprietary Stores
5912 Drug stores and proprietary stores

592 Liquor Stores
5921 Liquor stores

593 Used Merchandise Stores
5931 Used merchandise stores

594 Miscellaneous Shopping Goods Stores
5941 Sporting goods stores and bicycle shops
5942 Book stores
5943 Stationery stores
5944 Jewelry stores
5945 Hobby, toy, and game shops
5946 Camera and photographic supply stores
5947 Gift, novelty, and souvenir shops
5948 Luggage and leather goods stores
5949 Sewing, needlework, and piece goods stores

Standard Industrial Classification

Guide to Selected Standard Classifications

596 Nonstore Retailers
- 5961 Mail order houses
- 5962 Automatic merchandising machine operators
- 5963 Direct selling establishments

598 Fuel and Ice Dealers
- 5982 Fuel and ice dealers, except fuel oil dealers and bottled gas dealers
- 5983 Fuel oil dealers
- 5984 Liquified petroleum gas (bottled gas) dealers

599 Retail Stores, Not Elsewhere Classified
- 5992 Florist
- 5993 Cigar stores and stands
- 5994 News dealers and newsstands
- 5999 Miscellaneous retail stores, not elsewhere classified

FINANCE, INSURANCE, AND REAL ESTATE

60 BANKING

601 Federal Reserve Banks
- 6011 Federal Reserve banks

602 Commercial and Stock Savings Banks
- 6022 State banks, members of the Federal Reserve System
- 6023 State banks, not members of the Federal Reserve System, insured by the Federal Deposit Insurance Corporation
- 6024 State banks, not members of the Federal Reserve System, not insured by the Federal Deposit Insurance Corporation
- 6025 National banks, members of the Federal Reserve System
- 6026 National banks, not members of the Federal Reserve System, insured by the Federal Deposit Insurance Corporation
- 6027 National banks, not insured by the Federal Deposit Insurance Corporation
- 6028 Unincorporated private banks, not insured by the Federal Deposit Insurance Corporation

603 Mutual Savings Banks
- 6032 Mutual savings banks, members of the Federal Reserve System
- 6033 Mutual savings banks, not members of the Federal Reserve System, insured by the Federal Deposit Insurance Corporation
- 6034 Mutual savings banks, not insured by the Federal Deposit Insurance Corporation

604 Trust Companies Not Engaged in Deposit Banking
- 6042 State nondeposit trust companies, members of the Federal Reserve System, insured and not insured
- 6044 State nondeposit trust companies, not insured by the Federal Deposit Insurance Corporation

605 Establishments Performing Functions Closely Related to Banking
- 6052 Foreign exchange establishments
- 6054 Safe deposit companies
- 6055 Clearinghouse associations
- 6056 Corporations for banking abroad
- 6059 Establishments performing functions closely related to deposit banking, not elsewhere classified

61 CREDIT AGENCIES OTHER THAN BANKS

611 Rediscount and Financing Institutions for Credit Agencies Other Than Banks
- 6112 Rediscount and financing institutions for credit agencies (other than banks) not primarily associated with agricultural credit
- 6113 Rediscount and financing institutions for credit agencies (other than banks) primarily associated with agricultural credit

612 Savings and Loan Associations
- 6122 Federal savings and loan associations
- 6123 State savings and loan associations, insured by the Federal Savings and Loan Insurance Corporation
- 6124 State savings and loan associations, not insured, members of the Federal Home Loan Bank System
- 6125 State savings and loan associations, not insured, not members of the Federal Home Loan Bank System

613 Agricultural Credit Institutions
- 6131 Agricultural credit institutions

614 Personal Credit Institutions
- 6142 Federal credit unions
- 6143 State credit unions
- 6144 Industrial loan companies not engaged in deposit banking
- 6145 Licensed small loan lenders
- 6146 Installment sales finance companies
- 6149 Miscellaneous personal credit institutions

615 Business Credit Institutions
- 6153 Short-term business credit institutions
- 6159 Miscellaneous business credit institutions

616 Mortgage Bankers and Brokers
- 6162 Mortgage bankers and loan correspondents
- 6163 Loan brokers

62 SECURITY AND COMMODITY BROKERS, DEALERS, EXCHANGES, AND SERVICES

621 Security Brokers, Dealers, and Flotation Companies
- 6211 Security brokers, dealers, and flotation companies

622 Commodity Contracts Brokers and Dealers
- 6221 Commodity contracts brokers and dealers

623 Security and Commodity Exchanges
- 6231 Security and commodity exchanges

628 Services Allied With the Exchange of Securities or Commodities
- 6281 Services allied with the exchange of securities or commodities

63 INSURANCE

631 Life Insurance
- 6311 Life insurance

632 Accident and Health Insurance and Medical Service Plans
- 6321 Accident and health insurance
- 6324 Hospital and medical service plans

633 Fire, Marine, and Casualty Insurance
- 6331 Fire, marine, and casualty insurance

635 Surety Insurance
- 6351 Surety insurance

636 Title Insurance
- 6361 Title insurance

637 Pension, Health, and Welfare Funds
- 6371 Pension, health, and welfare funds

639 Insurance Carriers, Not Elsewhere Classified
- 6399 Insurance carriers, not elsewhere classified

64 INSURANCE AGENTS, BROKERS, AND SERVICE

641 Insurance Agents, Brokers, and Service
- 6411 Insurance agents, brokers, and service

65 REAL ESTATE

651 Real Estate Operators (Except Developers) and Lessors
- 6512 Operators of nonresidential buildings
- 6513 Operators of apartment buildings
- 6514 Operators of dwellings other than apartment buildings
- 6515 Operators of residential mobile home sites
- 6517 Lessors of railroad property
- 6519 Lessors of real property, not elsewhere classified

653 Real Estate Agents and Managers
- 6531 Real estate agents and managers

654 Title Abstract Offices
- 6541 Title abstract offices

655 Subdividers and Developers
- 6552 Subdividers and developers, except cemeteries
- 6553 Cemetery subdividers and developers

66 COMBINATIONS OF REAL ESTATE, INSURANCE, LOANS, LAW OFFICES

661 Combinations of Real Estate, Insurance, Loans, Law Offices
- 6611 Combinations of real estate, insurance, loans, law offices

67 HOLDING AND OTHER INVESTMENT OFFICES

671 Holding Offices
- 6711 Holding offices

672 Investment Offices
- 6722 Management investment offices, open-end
- 6723 Management investment offices, closed-end
- 6724 Unit investment trusts
- 6725 Face-amount certificate offices

673 Trusts
- 6732 Educational, religious, and charitable trusts
- 6733 Trusts, except educational, religious, and charitable

679 Miscellaneous Investing
- 6792 Oil royalty traders
- 6793 Commodity traders
- 6794 Patent owners and lessors
- 6798 Real Estate Investment Trusts
- 6799 Investors, not elsewhere classified

SERVICES

70 HOTELS, ROOMING HOUSES, CAMPS, AND OTHER LODGING PLACES

701 Hotels, Motels, and Tourist Courts
- 7011 Hotels, motels, and tourist courts

Guide to Selected Standard Classifications

Standard Industrial Classification

702 Rooming and Boarding Houses
7021 Rooming and boarding houses

703 Camps and Trailering Parks
7032 Sporting and recreational camps
7033 Trailering parks and camp sites for transients

704 Organization Hotels and Lodging Houses, on Membership Basis
7041 Organization hotels and lodging houses, on membership basis

72 PERSONAL SERVICES

721 Laundry, Cleaning, and Garment Services
7211 Power laundries, family and commercial
7212 Garment pressing, and agents for laundries and dry cleaners
7213 Linen supply
7214 Diaper service
7215 Coin-operated laundries and dry cleaning
7216 Dry cleaning plants, except rug cleaning
7217 Carpet and upholstery cleaning
7218 Industrial launderers
7219 Laundry and garment services, not elsewhere classified

722 Photographic Studios, Portrait
7221 Photographic studios, portrait

723 Beauty Shops
7231 Beauty shops

724 Barber Shops
7241 Barber shops

725 Shoe Repair Shops, Shoe Shine Parlors, and Hat Cleaning Shops
7251 Shoe repair shops, shoe shine parlors, and hat cleaning shops

726 Funeral Service and Crematories
7261 Funeral service and crematories

729 Miscellaneous Personal Services
7299 Miscellaneous personal services

73 BUSINESS SERVICES

731 Advertising
7311 Advertising agencies
7312 Outdoor advertising services
7313 Radio, television, and publishers' advertising representatives
7319 Advertising, not elsewhere classified

732 Consumer Credit Reporting Agencies, Mercantile Reporting Agencies, and Adjustment and Collection Agencies
7321 Consumer credit reporting agencies, mercantile reporting agencies, and adjustment and collection agencies

733 Mailing, Reproduction, Commercial Art and Photography, and Stenographic Services
7331 Direct mail advertising services
7332 Blueprinting and photocopying services
7333 Commercial photography, art, and graphics
7339 Stenographic services; and reproduction services, not elsewhere classified

734 Services to Dwellings and Other Buildings
7341 Window cleaning
7342 Disinfecting and exterminating services
7349 Cleaning and maintenance services to dwellings and other buildings, not elsewhere classified

735 News Syndicates
7351 News syndicates

736 Personnel Supply Services
7361 Employment agencies
7362 Temporary help supply services
7369 Personnel supply services, not elsewhere classified

737 Computer and Data Processing Services
7372 Computer programming and other software services
7374 Data processing services
7379 Computer related services, not elsewhere classified

739 Miscellaneous Business Services
7391 Research and development laboratories
7392 Management, consulting, and public relations services
7393 Detective agencies and protective services
7394 Equipment rental and leasing services
7395 Photofinishing laboratories
7396 Trading stamp services
7397 Commercial testing laboratories
7399 Business services, not elsewhere classified

75 AUTOMOTIVE REPAIR, SERVICES, AND GARAGES

751 Automotive Rental and Leasing, Without Drivers
7512 Passenger car rental and leasing, without drivers
7513 Truck rental and leasing, without drivers
7519 Utility trailer and recreational vehicle rental

752 Automobile Parking
7523 Parking lots
7525 Parking structures

753 Automotive Repair Shops
7531 Top and body repair shops
7534 Tire retreading and repair shops
7535 Paint shops
7538 General automotive repair shops
7539 Automotive repair shops, not elsewhere classified

754 Automotive Services, Except Repair
7542 Car washes
7549 Automotive services, except repair and car washes

76 MISCELLANEOUS REPAIR SERVICES

762 Electrical Repair Shops
7622 Radio and television repair shops
7623 Refrigeration and air conditioning service and repair shops
7629 Electrical and electronic repair shops, not elsewhere classified

763 Watch, Clock, and Jewelry Repair
7631 Watch, clock, and jewelry repair

764 Reupholstery and Furniture Repair
7641 Reupholstery and furniture repair

769 Miscellaneous Repair Shops and Related Services
7692 Welding repair shops
7694 Armature rewinding shops
7699 Repair shops and related services, not elsewhere classified

78 MOTION PICTURES

781 Motion Picture Production and Allied Services
7813 Motion picture production, except for television

7814 Motion picture and tape production for television
7819 Services allied to motion picture production

782 Motion Picture Distribution and Allied Services
7823 Motion picture film exchanges
7824 Film or tape distribution for television
7829 Services allied to motion picture distribution

783 Motion Picture Theaters
7832 Motion picture theaters, except drive-in
7833 Drive-in motion picture theaters

79 AMUSEMENT AND RECREATION SERVICES, EXCEPT MOTION PICTURES

791 Dance Halls, Studios, and Schools
7911 Dance halls, studios, and schools

792 Theatrical Producers (Except Motion Pictures), Bands, Orchestras, and Entertainers
7922 Theatrical producers (except motion picture) and miscellaneous theatrical services
7929 Bands, orchestras, actors, and other entertainers and entertainment groups

793 Bowling Alleys and Billiard and Pool Establishments
7932 Billiard and pool establishments
7933 Bowling alleys

794 Commercial Sports
7941 Professional sports clubs and promoters
7948 Racing, including track operation

799 Miscellaneous Amusement and Recreation Services
7992 Public golf courses
7993 Coin-operated amusement devices
7996 Amusement parks
7997 Membership sports and recreation clubs
7999 Amusement and recreation services, not elsewhere classified

80 HEALTH SERVICES

801 Offices of Physicians
8011 Offices of physicians

802 Offices of Dentists
8021 Offices of dentists

803 Offices of Osteopathic Physicians
8031 Offices of osteopathic physicians

804 Offices of Other Health Practitioners
8041 Offices of chiropractors
8042 Offices of optometrists
8049 Offices of health practitioners, not elsewhere classified

805 Nursing and Personal Care Facilities
8051 Skilled nursing care facilities
8059 Nursing and personal care facilities, not elsewhere classified

806 Hospitals
8062 General medical and surgical hospitals
8063 Psychiatric hospitals
8069 Specialty hospitals, except psychiatric

807 Medical and Dental Laboratories
8071 Medical laboratories
8072 Dental laboratories

Standard Industrial Classification

Guide to Selected Standard Classifications

- **808 Outpatient Care Facilities**
  - 8081 Outpatient care facilities
- **809 Health and Allied Services, Not Elsewhere Classified**
  - 8091 Health and allied services, not elsewhere classified
- **81 LEGAL SERVICES**
- **811 Legal Services**
  - 8111 Legal services
- **82 EDUCATIONAL SERVICES**
- **821 Elementary and Secondary Schools**
  - 8211 Elementary and secondary schools
- **822 Colleges, Universities, Professional Schools, and Junior Colleges**
  - 8221 Colleges, universities, and professional schools
  - 8222 Junior colleges and technical institutes
- **823 Libraries and Information Centers**
  - 8231 Libraries and information centers
- **824 Correspondence Schools and Vocational Schools**
  - 8241 Correspondence schools
  - 8243 Data processing schools
  - 8244 Business and secretarial schools
  - 8249 Vocational schools, except vocational high schools, not elsewhere classified
- **829 Schools and Educational Services, Not Elsewhere Classified**
  - 8299 Schools and educational services, not elsewhere classified
- **83 SOCIAL SERVICES**
- **832 Individual and Family Social Services**
  - 8321 Individual and family social services
- **833 Job Training and Vocational Rehabilitation Services**
  - 8331 Job training and vocational rehabilitation services
- **835 Child Day Care Services**
  - 8351 Child day care services
- **836 Residential Care**
  - 8361 Residential care
- **839 Social Services, Not Elsewhere Classified**
  - 8399 Social services, not elsewhere classified
- **84 MUSEUMS, ART GALLERIES, BOTANICAL AND ZOOLOGICAL GARDENS**
- **841 Museums and Art Galleries**
  - 8411 Museums and art galleries
- **842 Arboreta, Botanical and Zoological Gardens**
  - 8421 Arboreta, botanical and zoological gardens
- **86 MEMBERSHIP ORGANIZATIONS**
- **861 Business Associations**
  - 8611 Business associations
- **862 Professional Membership Organizations**
  - 8621 Professional membership organizations
- **863 Labor Unions and Similar Labor Organizations**
  - 8631 Labor unions and similar labor organizations
- **864 Civic, Social, and Fraternal Associations**
  - 8641 Civic, social, and fraternal associations
- **865 Political Organizations**
  - 8651 Political organizations
- **866 Religious Organizations**
  - 8661 Religious organizations
- **869 Membership Organizations, Not Elsewhere Classified**
  - 8699 Membership organizations, not elsewhere classified
- **88 PRIVATE HOUSEHOLDS**
- **881 Private Households**
  - 8811 Private households
- **89 MISCELLANEOUS SERVICES**
- **891 Engineering, Architectural, and Surveying Services**
  - 8911 Engineering, architectural, and surveying services
- **892 Noncommercial Educational, Scientific, and Research Organizations**
  - 8922 Noncommercial educational, scientific, and research organizations
- **893 Accounting, Auditing, and Bookkeeping Services**
  - 8931 Accounting, auditing, and bookkeeping services
- **899 Services, Not Elsewhere Classified**
  - 8999 Services, not elsewhere classified

PUBLIC ADMINISTRATION

- **91 EXECUTIVE, LEGISLATIVE, AND GENERAL GOVERNMENT, EXCEPT FINANCE**
- **911 Executive Offices**
  - 9111 Executive offices
- **912 Legislative Bodies**
  - 9121 Legislative bodies
- **913 Executive and Legislative Offices Combined**
  - 9131 Executive and legislative offices combined
- **919 General Government, Not Elsewhere Classified**
  - 9199 General government, not elsewhere classified
- **92 JUSTICE, PUBLIC ORDER, AND SAFETY**
- **921 Courts**
  - 9211 Courts
- **922 Public Order and Safety**
  - 9221 Police protection
  - 9222 Legal counsel and prosecution
  - 9223 Correctional institutions
  - 9224 Fire protection
  - 9229 Public order and safety, not elsewhere classified
- **93 PUBLIC FINANCE, TAXATION, AND MONETARY POLICY**
- **931 Public Finance, Taxation, and Monetary Policy**
  - 9311 Public finance, taxation, and monetary policy
- **94 ADMINISTRATION OF HUMAN RESOURCES PROGRAMS**
- **941 Administration of Educational Programs**
  - 9411 Administration of educational programs
- **943 Administration of Public Health Programs**
  - 9431 Administration of public health programs
- **944 Administration of Social, Manpower, and Income Maintenance Programs**
  - 9441 Administration of social, manpower, and income maintenance programs
- **945 Administration of Veterans' Affairs, Except Health and Insurance**
  - 9451 Administration of veterans' affairs, except health and insurance
- **95 ADMINISTRATION OF ENVIRONMENTAL QUALITY AND HOUSING PROGRAMS**
- **951 Administration of Environmental Quality Programs**
  - 9511 Air and water resource and solid waste management
  - 9512 Land, mineral, wildlife, and forest conservation
- **953 Administration of Housing and Urban Development Programs**
  - 9531 Administration of housing programs
  - 9532 Administration of urban planning and community and rural development
- **96 ADMINISTRATION OF ECONOMIC PROGRAMS**
- **961 Administration of General Economic Programs**
  - 9611 Administration of general economic programs
- **962 Regulation and Administration of Transportation Programs**
  - 9621 Regulation and administration of transportation programs
- **963 Regulation and Administration of Communication, Electric, Gas, and Other Utilities**
  - 9631 Regulation and administration of communication, electric, gas, and other utilities
- **964 Regulation of Agricultural Marketing and Commodities**
  - 9641 Regulation of agricultural marketing and commodities
- **965 Regulation, Licensing, and Inspection of Miscellaneous Commercial Sectors**
  - 9651 Regulation, licensing, and inspection of miscellaneous commercial sectors
- **966 Space Research and Technology**
  - 9661 Space research and technology
- **97 NATIONAL SECURITY AND INTERNATIONAL AFFAIRS**
- **971 National Security**
  - 9711 National security
- **972 International Affairs**
  - 9721 International affairs
- **99 NONCLASSIFIABLE ESTABLISHMENTS**
- **999 Nonclassifiable Establishments**
  - 9999 Nonclassifiable establishments

Standard Occupational Classification

The Standard Occupational Classification was developed to provide a standardized system of job descriptions and classification codes for all occupations performed for pay or profit, for use in the presentation and analysis of statistical data about occupations. The classification system is at 4 levels, with division titles, 2- and 3-digit occupation group codes, and 4-digit unit group codes. The classification was used in the 1980 Census of Population and in Labor Department programs.

The classification is presented in the revised 1980 *Standard Occupational Classification Manual,* from which the following list is taken (for description, see ASI 1981 Annual, 2088-2).

Occupation Group Code

EXECUTIVE, ADMINISTRATIVE AND MANAGERIAL OCCUPATIONS

- **11 Officials and Administrators, Public Administration**
  - 111 Legislators
  - 112 Chief Executives and General Administrators
  - 113 Officials and Administrators, Government Agencies

- **12-13 Officials and Administrators, Other**
  - 121 General Managers and Other Top Executives
  - 122 Financial Managers
  - 123 Personnel and Labor Relations Managers
  - 124 Purchasing Managers
  - 125 Managers; Marketing, Advertising, and Public Relations
  - 126 Managers; Engineering, Mathematics, and Natural Sciences
  - 127 Managers; Social Sciences and Related Fields
  - 128 Administrators; Education and Related Fields
  - 131 Managers; Medicine and Health
  - 132 Production Managers, Industrial
  - 133 Construction Managers
  - 134 Public Utilities Managers
  - 135 Managers; Service Organizations
  - 136 Managers; Mining, Quarrying, Well Drilling, and Similar Operations
  - 137 Managers; Administrative Services
  - 139 Officials and Administrators; Other, Not Elsewhere Classified

- **14 Management Related Occupations**
  - 141 Accountants, Auditors, and Other Financial Specialists
  - 142 Management Analysts
  - 143 Personnel, Training, and Labor Relations Specialists
  - 144 Purchasing Agents and Buyers
  - 145 Business and Promotion Agents
  - 147 Inspectors and Compliance Officers
  - 149 Management Related Occupations, Not Elsewhere Classified

ENGINEERS, SURVEYORS AND ARCHITECTS

- **16 Engineers, Surveyors and Architects**
  - 161 Architects
  - 162-3 Engineers
  - 164 Surveyors and Mapping Scientists

NATURAL SCIENTISTS AND MATHEMATICIANS

- **17 Computer, Mathematical, and Operations Research Occupations**
  - 171 Computer Scientists
  - 172 Operations and Systems Researchers and Analysts
  - 173 Mathematical Scientists

- **18 Natural Scientists**
  - 184 Physical Scientists
  - 185 Life Scientists

SOCIAL SCIENTISTS, SOCIAL WORKERS, RELIGIOUS WORKERS, AND LAWYERS

- **19 Social Scientists and Urban Planners**
  - 191 Social Scientists
  - 192 Urban and Regional Planners

- **20 Social, Recreation, and Religious Workers**
  - 203 Social and Recreation Workers
  - 204 Religious Workers

- **21 Lawyers and Judges**
  - 211 Lawyers
  - 212 Judges

TEACHERS, LIBRARIANS, AND COUNSELORS

- **22 Teachers; College, University and Other Postsecondary Institution**

- **23 Teachers, Except Postsecondary Institution**
  - 231 Prekindergarten and Kindergarten Teachers
  - 232 Elementary School Teachers
  - 233 Secondary School Teachers
  - 235 Teachers; Special Education
  - 236 Instructional Coordinators
  - 239 Adult Education and Other Teachers, Not Elsewhere Classified

- **24 Vocational and Educational Counselors**

- **25 Librarians, Archivists, and Curators**
  - 251 Librarians
  - 252 Archivists and Curators

HEALTH DIAGNOSING AND TREATING PRACTITIONERS

- **26 Physicians and Dentists**
  - 261 Physicians
  - 262 Dentists

- **27 Veterinarians**

- **28 Other Health Diagnosing and Treating Practitioners**
  - 281 Optometrists
  - 283 Podiatrists
  - 289 Health Diagnosing and Treating Practitioners, Not Elsewhere Classified

REGISTERED NURSES, PHARMACISTS, DIETITIANS, THERAPISTS, AND PHYSICIAN'S ASSISTANTS

- **29 Registered Nurses**

- **30 Pharmacists, Dietitians, Therapists, and Physician's Assistants**
  - 301 Pharmacists
  - 302 Dietitians
  - 303 Therapists
  - 304 Physician's Assistants

WRITERS, ARTISTS, ENTERTAINERS, AND ATHLETES

- **32 Writers, Artists, Performers, and Related Workers**
  - 321 Authors
  - 322 Designers
  - 323 Musicians and Composers
  - 324 Actors and Directors
  - 325 Painters, Sculptors, Craft-Artists and Artist-Printmakers
  - 326 Photographers
  - 327 Dancers
  - 328 Performers, Not Elsewhere Classified
  - 329 Writers, Artists, and Related Workers; Not Elsewhere Classified

- **33 Editors, Reporters, Public Relations Specialists, and Announcers**
  - 331 Editors and Reporters
  - 332 Public Relations Specialists and Publicity Writers
  - 333 Radio, Television and Other Announcers

- **34 Athletes and Related Workers**

Standard Occupational Classification

Guide to Selected Standard Classifications

HEALTH TECHNOLOGISTS AND TECHNICIANS

36 Health Technologists and Technicians
- 362 Clinical Laboratory Technologists and Technicians
- 363 Dental Hygienists
- 364 Health Record Technologists and Technicians
- 365 Radiologic Technologists and Technicians
- 366 Licensed Practical Nurses
- 369 Health Technologists and Technicians, Not Elsewhere Classified

TECHNOLOGISTS AND TECHNICIANS, EXCEPT HEALTH

37 Engineering and Related Technologists and Technicians
- 371 Engineering Technologists and Technicians
- 372 Drafting Occupations
- 373 Surveying and Mapping Technicians

38 Science Technologists and Technicians
- 382 Biological Technologists and Technicians, Except Health
- 383 Chemical and Nuclear Technologists and Technicians
- 384 Mathematical Technicians
- 389 Science Technologists and Technicians, Not Elsewhere Classified

39 Technicians; Except Health, Engineering, and Science
- 392 Air Traffic Controllers
- 393 Radio and Related Operators
- 396 Legal Technicians
- 397 Programmers
- 398 Technical Writers
- 399 Technicians, Not Elsewhere Classified

MARKETING AND SALES OCCUPATIONS

40 Supervisors; Marketing and Sales Occupations
- 401 Supervisors; Sales Occupations, Insurance, Real Estate, and Business Services
- 402 Supervisors; Sales Occupations, Commodities Except Retail
- 403 Supervisors; Sales Occupations, Retail

41 Insurance, Securities, Real Estate, and Business Service Sales Occupations
- 412 Insurance, Real Estate, and Securities Sales Occupations
- 415 Business Service Sales Occupations

42 Sales Occupations, Commodities Except Retail
- 421 Sales Engineers
- 423 Technical Sales Workers and Service Advisors
- 424 Sales Representatives

43 Sales Occupations, Retail
- 434-5 Salespersons, Commodities
- 436 Sales Occupations; Other

44 Sales Related Occupations
- 444 Appraisers and Related Occupations
- 445 Demonstrators, Promoters, and Models
- 446 Shoppers
- 447 Auctioneers
- 449 Sales Occupations; Other, Not Elsewhere Classified

ADMINISTRATIVE SUPPORT OCCUPATIONS, INCLUDING CLERICAL

45 Supervisors; Administrative Support Occupations, Including Clerical

46-47 Administrative Support Occupations, Including Clerical
- 461 Computer and Peripheral Equipment Operators
- 462 Secretaries, Stenographers and Typists
- 463 General Office Occupations
- 464 Information Clerks
- 466 Correspondence Clerks and Order Clerks
- 469 Record Clerks
- 471 Financial Record Processing Occupations
- 472 Duplicating, Mail and Other Office Machine Operators
- 473 Communications Equipment Operators
- 474 Mail and Message Distributing Occupations
- 475 Material Recording, Scheduling, and Distributing Clerks
- 478 Adjusters, Investigators, and Collectors
- 479 Miscellaneous Administrative Support Occupations, Including Clerical

SERVICE OCCUPATIONS

50 Private Household Occupations
- 502 Day Workers
- 503 Launderers and Ironers
- 504 Cooks, Private Household
- 505 Housekeepers and Butlers
- 506 Child Care Workers, Private Household
- 507 Private Household Cleaners and Servants
- 509 Private Household Occupations, Not Elsewhere Classified

51 Protective Service Occupations
- 511 Supervisors; Service Occupations, Protective
- 512 Firefighting and Fire Prevention Occupations
- 513 Police and Detectives
- 514 Guards

52 Service Occupations, Except Private Household and Protective
- 521 Food and Beverage Preparation and Service Occupations
- 523 Health Service Occupations
- 524 Cleaning and Building Service Occupations, Except Private Household
- 525-6 Personal Service Occupations

AGRICULTURAL, FORESTRY AND FISHING OCCUPATIONS

55 Farm Operators and Managers
- 551 Farmers (Working Proprietors)
- 552 Farm Managers

56 Other Agricultural and Related Occupations
- 561 Farm Occupations, Except Managerial
- 562 Related Agricultural Occupations

57 Forestry and Logging Occupations
- 571 Supervisors; Forestry and Logging Workers
- 572 Forestry Workers, Except Logging
- 573 Timber Cutting and Related Occupations
- 579 Logging Occupations, Not Elsewhere Classified

58 Fishers, Hunters, and Trappers
- 583 Fishers
- 584 Hunters and Trappers

MECHANICS AND REPAIRERS

60 Supervisors; Mechanics and Repairers

61 Mechanics and Repairers
- 611 Vehicle and Mobile Equipment Mechanics and Repairers
- 613 Industrial Machinery Repairers
- 614 Machinery Maintenance Occupations
- 615 Electrical and Electronic Equipment Repairers
- 616 Heating, Air-Conditioning, and Refrigeration Mechanics
- 617 Miscellaneous Mechanics and Repairers

CONSTRUCTION AND EXTRACTIVE OCCUPATIONS

63 Supervisors; Construction and Extractive Occupations
- 631 Supervisors; Construction
- 632 Supervisors; Extractive Occupations

64 Construction Trades
- 641 Brickmasons, Stonemasons, and Hard Tile Setters
- 642 Carpenters and Related Workers
- 643 Electricians and Power Transmission Installers
- 644 Painters, Paperhangers, and Plasterers
- 645 Plumbers, Pipefitters and Steamfitters
- 646-7 Other Construction Trades

65 Extractive Occupations
- 652 Drillers, Oil Well
- 653 Explosive Workers
- 654 Mining Machine Operators
- 656 Extractive Occupations, Not Elsewhere Classified

PRECISION PRODUCTION OCCUPATIONS

67 Supervisors; Precision Production Occupations

68 Precision Production Occupations
- 681-2 Precision Metal Workers
- 683 Precision Woodworkers
- 684 Precision Printing Occupations
- 685 Precision Textile, Apparel and Furnishings Workers
- 686 Precision Workers; Assorted Materials
- 687 Precision Food Production Occupations
- 688 Precision Inspectors, Testers, and Related Workers

69 Plant and System Operators
- 691 Water and Sewage Treatment Plant Operators
- 692 Gas Plant Operators
- 693 Power Plant Operators
- 694 Chemical Plant Operators
- 695 Petroleum Plant Operators
- 696 Miscellaneous Plant or System Operators

PRODUCTION WORKING OCCUPATIONS

71 Supervisors; Production Occupations

73-74 Machine Setup Operators
- 731-2 Metalworking and Plastic Working Machine Setup Operators
- 733 Metal Fabricating Machine Setup Operators
- 734 Metal and Plastic Processing Machine Setup Operators
- 743 Woodworking Machine Setup Operators
- 744 Printing Machine Setup Operators
- 745 Textile Machine Setup Operators
- 746-7 Assorted Materials: Machine Setup Operators

75-76 Machine Operators and Tenders
- 751-2 Metalworking and Plastic Working Machine Operators and Tenders
- 753 Metal Fabricating Machine Operators and Tenders
- 754 Metal and Plastic Processing Machine Operators and Tenders
- 763 Woodworking Machine Operators and Tenders
- 764 Printing Machine Operators and Tenders
- 765 Textile, Apparel and Furnishings Machine Operators and Tenders
- 766-7 Machine Operators and Tenders; Assorted Materials

77 Fabricators, Assemblers, and Hand Working Occupations
- 771 Welders and Solderers
- 772 Assemblers
- 774 Fabricators, Not Elsewhere Classified
- 775 Hand Working Occupations

78 Production Inspectors, Testers, Samplers, and Weighers
- 782 Production Inspectors, Checkers and Examiners
- 783 Production Testers
- 784 Production Samplers and Weighers
- 785 Graders and Sorters, Except Agricultural
- 787 Production Expediters

TRANSPORTATION AND MATERIAL MOVING OCCUPATIONS

81 Supervisors; Transportation and Material Moving Occupations
- 811 Supervisors; Motorized Equipment Operators
- 812 Supervisors; Material Moving Equipment Operators

82 Transportation Occupations
- 821 Motor Vehicle Operators
- 823 Rail Transportation Occupations
- 824 Water Transportation Occupations
- 825 Airplane Pilots and Navigators
- 828 Transportation Inspectors

83 Material Moving Occupations, Except Transportation
- 831 Material Moving Equipment Operators

HANDLERS, EQUIPMENT CLEANERS, HELPERS AND LABORERS

85 Supervisors; Handlers, Equipment Cleaners, Helpers, and Laborers

86 Helpers
- 861 Helpers; Machine Operators and Tenders
- 862 Helpers; Fabricators and Inspectors
- 863 Helpers; Mechanics and Repairers
- 864 Helpers; Construction Trades
- 865 Helpers; Extractive Occupations

87 Handlers, Equipment Cleaners and Laborers
- 871 Construction Laborers
- 872 Freight, Stock, and Material Movers; Hand
- 873 Garage and Service Station Related Occupations
- 874 Parking Lot Attendants
- 875 Vehicle Washers and Equipment Cleaners
- 876 Miscellaneous Manual Occupations

MILITARY OCCUPATIONS

91 Military Occupations

MISCELLANEOUS OCCUPATIONS

99 Miscellaneous Occupations

Standard International Trade Classification, Revision 2

The Standard International Trade Classification (SITC) is a statistical classification of commodities in world trade, developed by the United Nations to facilitate international comparison of commodity trade data. Revision 2 was published in 1975.

In U.S. foreign trade statistics, commodities are primarily classified according to two systems developed and maintained by the Census Bureau: *Schedule A, Statistical Classification of Commodities Imported into the U.S.*, and *Schedule E, SITC Based Classification of Domestic and Foreign Commodities Exported from the U.S.*

Import data are initially collected in terms of the 10,000 codes of the *Tariff Schedules of the U.S., Annotated* (TSUSA). These data are then rearranged and reported in terms of 1978 Schedule A, which is based on SITC Revision 2.

Export data are initially collected in terms of 1978 Schedule B, which is consistent with the TSUSA classification used for imports. These data are then rearranged and reported in terms of 1978 Schedule E, which is also based on SITC Revision 2.

Both Schedules A and E, which provide commodity codes to the detailed 7-digit level, are essentially identical at the 1-, 2-, and 3-digit level to the SITC, Revision 2, whose 3-digit commodity codes are listed below. Schedule A was revised and Schedule E was introduced in January 1978 to make U.S. data comparable to foreign country trade data.

Section, Division, and Group Codes

0 FOOD AND LIVE ANIMALS CHIEFLY FOR FOOD

- **00 Live Animals Chiefly for Food**
  - 001 Live animals chiefly for food
- **01 Meat and Meat Preparations**
  - 011 Meat and edible meat offals, fresh, chilled or frozen
  - 012 Meat and edible meat offals (except poultry liver), salted, in brine, dried or smoked
  - 014 Meat and edible meat offals, prepared or preserved, n.e.s.; fish extracts
- **02 Dairy Products and Birds' Eggs**
  - 022 Milk and cream
  - 023 Butter
  - 024 Cheese and curd
  - 025 Eggs, birds', and egg yolks, fresh, dried, or otherwise preserved, sweetened or not
- **03 Fish, Crustaceans and Molluscs, and Preparations Thereof**
  - 034 Fish, fresh (live or dead), chilled or frozen
  - 035 Fish, dried, salted or in brine; smoked fish
  - 036 Crustaceans and molluscs, whether in shell or not, fresh (live or dead), chilled, frozen, salted, in brine or dried; crustaceans, in shell, simply boiled in water
  - 037 Fish, crustaceans and molluscs, prepared or preserved, n.e.s.
- **04 Cereals and Cereal Preparations**
  - 041 Wheat (including spelt) and meslin, unmilled
  - 042 Rice
  - 043 Barley, unmilled
  - 044 Maize (corn), unmilled
  - 045 Cereals, unmilled (other than wheat, rice, barley and maize)
  - 046 Meal and flour of wheat and flour of meslin
  - 047 Other cereal meals and flours
  - 048 Cereal preparations and preparations of flour or starch of fruits or vegetables
- **05 Vegetables and Fruit**
  - 054 Vegetables, fresh, chilled, frozen or simply preserved
  - 056 Vegetables, roots and tubers, prepared or preserved, n.e.s.
  - 057 Fruit and nuts (not including oil nuts), fresh or dried
  - 058 Fruit, preserved, and fruit preparations
- **06 Sugar, Sugar Preparations and Honey**
  - 061 Sugar and honey
  - 062 Sugar confectionery (except chocolate confectionery) and other sugar preparations
- **07 Coffee, Tea, Cocoa, Spices, and Manufacturers Thereof**
  - 071 Coffee and coffee substitutes
  - 072 Cocoa
  - 073 Chocolate and other food preparations containing cocoa, n.e.s.
  - 074 Tea and mate
  - 075 Spices
- **08 Feeding Stuff for Animals (Not Including Unmilled Cereals)**
  - 081 Feeding stuff for animals (not including unmilled cereals)
- **09 Miscellaneous Edible Products and Preparations**
  - 091 Margarine and shortening
  - 098 Edible products and preparations, n.e.s.

1 BEVERAGES AND TOBACCO

- **11 Beverages**
  - 111 Non-alcoholic beverages, n.e.s.
  - 112 Alcoholic beverages
- **12 Tobacco and Tobacco Manufactures**
  - 121 Tobacco, unmanufactured; tobacco refuse
  - 122 Tobacco, manufactured

2 CRUDE MATERIALS, INEDIBLE, EXCEPT FUELS

- **21 Hides, Skins and Furskins, Raw**
  - 211 Hides and skins (except furskins), raw
  - 212 Furskins, raw (including astrakhan, caracul, Persian lamb, broadtail and similar skins)
- **22 Oil Seeds and Oleaginous Fruit**
  - 222 Oil seeds and oleaginous fruit, whole or broken, of a kind used for the extraction of 'soft' fixed vegetable oils (excluding flours and meals)
  - 223 Oilseeds and oleaginous fruit, whole or broken, of a kind used for the extraction of other fixed vegetable oils
- **23 Crude Rubber (Including Synthetic and Reclaimed)**
  - 232 Natural rubber latex; natural rubber and similar natural gums
  - 233 Synthetic rubber latex; synthetic rubber and reclaimed rubber; waste and scrap of unhardened rubber
- **24 Cork and Wood**
  - 244 Cork, natural, raw and waste (including natural cork in blocks or sheets)
  - 245 Fuel wood (excluding wood waste) and wood charcoal
  - 246 Pulpwood (including chips and wood waste)
  - 247 Other wood in the rough or roughly squared
  - 248 Wood, simply worked, and railway sleepers of wood
- **25 Pulp and Waste Paper**
  - 251 Pulp and waste paper
- **26 Textile Fibres (Other Than Wool Tops) and Their Wastes (Not Manufactured Into Yarn or Fabric)**
  - 261 Silk
  - 263 Cotton
  - 264 Jute and other textile bast fibres, n.e.s., raw or processed but not spun; tow and waste thereof
  - 265 Vegetable textile fibres (other)
  - 266 Synthetic fibres suitable for spinning
  - 267 Other man-made fibres suitable for spinning and waste of man-made fibres
  - 268 Wool and other animal hair (excluding wool tops)
  - 269 Old clothing and other old textile articles; rags
- **27 Crude Fertilizers and Crude Minerals (excluding Coal, and Precious Stones)**
  - 271 Fertilizers, crude
  - 273 Stone, sand and gravel
  - 274 Sulphur and unroasted iron pyrites

Guide to Selected Standard Classifications

SITC, Revision 2

- 277 Natural abrasives, n.e.s. (including industrial diamonds)
- 278 Other crude minerals

28 Metalliferous Ores and Metal Scrap

- 281 Iron ore and concentrates
- 282 Waste and scrap metal of iron or steel
- 286 Ores and concentrates of uranium and thorium
- 287 Ores and concentrates of base metals, n.e.s.
- 288 Non-ferrous base metal waste and scrap, n.e.s.
- 289 Ores and concentrates of precious metals; waste, scrap and sweepings of precious metals (other than of gold)

29 Crude Animal and Vegetable Materials, n.e.s.

- 291 Crude animal materials, n.e.s.
- 292 Crude vegetable materials, n.e.s.

3 MINERAL FUELS, LUBRICANTS AND RELATED MATERIALS

32 Coal, Coke and Briquettes

- 322 Coal, lignite and peat
- 323 Briquettes; coke and semi-coke of coal, lignite or peat; retort carbon

33 Petroleum, Petroleum Products and Related Materials

- 333 Petroleum oils, crude, and crude oils obtained from bituminous minerals
- 334 Petroleum products, refined
- 335 Residual petroleum products, n.e.s. and related materials

34 Gas, Natural and Manufactured

- 341 Gas, natural and manufactured

35 Electric Current

- 351 Electric current

4 ANIMAL AND VEGETABLE OILS, FATS AND WAXES

41 Animal Oils and Fats

- 411 Animal oils and fats

42 Fixed Vegetable Oils and Fats

- 423 Fixed vegetable oils, 'soft', crude, refined or purified
- 424 Other fixed vegetable oils, fluid or solid, crude, refined or purified

43 Animal and Vegetable Oils and Fats, Processed, and Waxes of Animal or Vegetable Origin

- 431 Animal and vegetable oils and fats, processed, and waxes of animal or vegetable origin

5 CHEMICALS AND RELATED PRODUCTS, N.E.S.

51 Organic Chemicals

- 511 Hydrocarbons, n.e.s., and their halogenated, sulphonated, nitrated or nitrosated derivatives

- 512 Alcohols, phenols, phenol-alcohols, and their halogenated, sulphonated, nitrated or nitrosated derivatives
- 513 Carboxylic acids, and their anhydrides, halides, peroxides and peracids, and their halogenated, sulphonated, nitrated or nitrosated derivatives
- 514 Nitrogen-function compounds
- 515 Organo-inorganic and heterocyclic compounds
- 516 Other organic chemicals

52 Inorganic Chemicals

- 522 Inorganic chemical elements, oxides, and halogen salts
- 523 Other inorganic chemicals; organic and inorganic compounds of precious metals
- 524 Radio-active and associated materials

53 Dyeing, Tanning and Colouring Materials

- 531 Synthetic organic dyestuffs, etc., natural indigo and colour lakes
- 532 Dyeing and tanning extracts, and synthetic tanning materials
- 533 Pigments, paints, varnishes and related materials

54 Medicinal and Pharmaceutical Products

- 541 Medicinal and pharmaceutical products

55 Essential Oils and Perfume Materials; Toilet, Polishing and Cleansing Preparations

- 551 Essential oils, perfume and flavour materials
- 553 Perfumery, cosmetics and toilet preparations (excluding soaps)
- 554 Soap, cleansing and polishing preparations

56 Fertilizers, Manufactured

- 562 Fertilizers, manufactured

57 Explosives and Pyrotechnic Products

- 572 Explosives and pyrotechnic products

58 Artificial Resins and Plastic Materials, and Cellulose Esters and Ethers

- 582 Condensation, polycondensation and polyaddition products
- 583 Polymerization and copolymerization products
- 584 Regenerated cellulose; cellulose nitrate, cellulose acetate and other cellulose esters, cellulose ethers and other chemical derivatives of cellulose, plasticized or not (e.g., collodions, celluloid); vulcanized fibre
- 585 Other artificial resins and plastic materials

59 Chemical Materials and Products, n.e.s.

- 591 Disinfectants, insecticides, fungicides, weed killers, anti-sprouting products, rat poisons and similar products, put up in forms or packings for sale by retail
- 592 Starches, inulin and wheat gluten; albuminoidal substances; glues
- 598 Miscellaneous chemical products, n.e.s.

6 MANUFACTURED GOODS CLASSIFIED CHIEFLY BY MATERIAL

61 Leather, Leather Manufactures, n.e.s., and Dressed Furskins

- 611 Leather
- 612 Manufactures of leather or of composition leather, n.e.s; saddlery and harness; parts of footwear, n.e.s.
- 613 Furskins, tanned or dressed

62 Rubber Manufactures, n.e.s.

- 621 Materials of rubber (e.g., pastes, plates, sheets, rods, thread, tubes, of rubber)
- 625 Rubber tyres, tyre cases, interchangeable tyre treads, inner tubes and tyre flaps, for wheels of all kinds
- 628 Articles of rubber, n.e.s.

63 Cork and Wood Manufactures (Excluding Furniture)

- 633 Cork manufactures
- 634 Veneers, plywood, "improved" or reconstituted wood, and other wood, worked, n.e.s.
- 635 Wood manufactures, n.e.s.

64 Paper, Paperboard, and Articles of Paper Pulp, of Paper or of Paperboard

- 641 Paper and paperboard
- 642 Paper and paperboard, cut to size or shape, and articles of paper or paperboard

65 Textile Yarn, Fabrics, Made-Up Articles, n.e.s., and Related Products

- 651 Textile yarn
- 652 Cotton fabrics, woven (not including narrow or special fabrics)
- 653 Fabrics, woven, of man-made fibres (not including narrow or special fabrics)
- 654 Textile fabrics, woven, other than of cotton or man-made fibres
- 655 Knitted or crocheted fabrics (including tubular knit fabrics, pile fabrics and open-work fabrics)
- 656 Tulle, lace, embroidery, ribbons, trimmings and other small wares
- 657 Special textile fabrics and related products
- 658 Made-up articles, wholly or chiefly of textile materials, n.e.s.
- 659 Floor coverings, etc.

66 Non-Metallic Mineral Manufactures, n.e.s.

- 661 Lime, cement, and fabricated construction materials (except glass and clay materials)
- 662 Clay construction materials and refractory construction materials
- 663 Mineral manufactures, n.e.s.
- 664 Glass
- 665 Glassware
- 666 Pottery
- 667 Pearls, precious and semi-precious stones, unworked or worked

67 Iron and Steel

- 671 Pig iron, spiegeleisen, sponge iron, iron or steel powders and shot, and ferro-alloys

SITC, Revision 2

Guide to Selected Standard Classifications

- 672 Ingots and other primary forms, of iron or steel
- 673 Iron and steel bars, rods, angles, shapes and sections (including sheet piling)
- 674 Universals, plates and sheets, of iron or steel
- 675 Hoop and strip, of iron or steel, hot-rolled or cold-rolled
- 676 Rails and railway track construction material, of iron or steel
- 677 Iron or steel wire (excluding wire rod), whether or not coated, but not insulated
- 678 Tubes, pipes and fittings, of iron or steel
- 679 Iron and steel castings, forgings and stampings, in the rough state, n.e.s.

68 **Non-Ferrous Metals**

- 681 Silver, platinum and other metals of the platinum group
- 682 Copper
- 683 Nickel
- 684 Aluminum
- 685 Lead
- 686 Zinc
- 687 Tin
- 688 Uranium depleted in U235 and thorium, and their alloys, unwrought or wrought, and articles thereof, n.e.s.
- 689 Miscellaneous non-ferrous base metals employed in metallurgy, and cermets

69 **Manufactures of Metal, n.e.s.**

- 691 Structures and parts of structures, n.e.s., of iron, steel or aluminum
- 692 Metal containers for storage and transport
- 693 Wire products (excluding insulated electrical wiring) and fencing grills
- 694 Nails, screws, nuts, bolts, rivets and the like, of iron, steel or copper
- 695 Tools for use in the hand or in machines
- 696 Cutlery
- 697 Household equipment of base metal, n.e.s.
- 699 Manufactures of base metal, n.e.s.

7 MACHINERY AND TRANSPORT EQUIPMENT

71 **Power Generating Machinery and Equipment**

- 711 Steam and other vapour generating boilers, superheated water boilers, and auxiliary plant for use therewith; and parts thereof, n.e.s.
- 712 Steam and other vapour power units, not incorporating boilers; steam engines (including mobile engines) with self-contained boilers; and parts thereof, n.e.s.
- 713 Internal combustion piston engines, and parts thereof, n.e.s.
- 714 Engines and motors, non-electric (other); parts, n.e.s.
- 716 Rotating electric plant and parts thereof, n.e.s.

- 718 Other power generating machinery and parts thereof, n.e.s.

72 **Machinery Specialized For Particular Industries**

- 721 Agricultural machinery (excluding tractors) and parts thereof, n.e.s.
- 722 Tractors (other), whether or not fitted with power take-offs, winches or pulleys
- 723 Civil engineering and contractors' plant and equipment and parts thereof, n.e.s.
- 724 Textile and leather machinery, and parts thereof, n.e.s.
- 725 Paper mill and pulp mill machinery, paper cutting machines and other machinery for the manufacture of paper articles; and parts thereof, n.e.s.
- 726 Printing and bookbinding machinery, and parts thereof, n.e.s.
- 727 Food-processing machines (excluding domestic) and parts thereof, n.e.s.
- 728 Other machinery and equipment specialized for particular industries, and parts thereof, n.e.s.

73 **Metalworking Machinery**

- 736 Machine-tools for working metal or metal carbides, and parts and accessories thereof, n.e.s.
- 737 Metalworking machinery (other than machine-tools), and parts thereof, n.e.s.

74 **General Industrial Machinery and Equipment, n.e.s., and Machine Parts, n.e.s.**

- 741 Heating and cooling equipment and parts thereof, n.e.s.
- 742 Pumps (including motor and turbo pumps) for liquids, whether or not fitted with measuring devices; liquid elevators of bucket, chain, screw, band and similar kinds; parts, n.e.s.
- 743 Pumps (other than pumps for liquids) and compressors; fans and blowers; centrifuges; filtering and purifying apparatus; and parts thereof, n.e.s.
- 744 Mechanical handling equipment, and parts thereof, n.e.s.
- 745 Other non-electrical machinery, tools and mechanical apparatus, and parts thereof, n.e.s.
- 749 Non-electric parts and accessories of machinery, n.e.s.

75 **Office Machines and Automatic Data Processing Equipment**

- 751 Office machines
- 752 Automatic data processing machines and units thereof; magnetic or optical readers, machines for transcribing data onto data media in coded form and machines for processing such data, n.e.s.
- 759 Parts, n.e.s. of and accessories (other than covers, carrying cases and the like) suitable for use with machines of a kind falling within heading 751 or 752

76 **Telecommunications and Sound Recording and Reproducing Apparatus and Equipment**

- 761 Television receivers (including receivers incorporating radio-broadcast receivers or sound recorders or reproducers)
- 762 Radio-broadcast receivers (including receivers incorporating sound recorders or reproducers)
- 763 Gramophones (phonographs), dictating machines and other sound recorders and reproducers (including record players and tape decks, with or without sound-heads); television image and sound recorders and reproducers, magnetic
- 764 Telecommunications equipment, n.e.s.; and parts, n.e.s. of and accessories for the apparatus and equipment falling within division 76

77 **Electrical Machinery, Apparatus and Appliances, n.e.s., and Electrical Parts Thereof (Including Non-Electrical Counterparts, n.e.s. of Electrical Household Type Equipment)**

- 771 Electric power machinery (other), and parts thereof, n.e.s.
- 772 Electrical apparatus for making and breaking electrical circuits
- 773 Equipment for distributing electricity
- 774 Electric apparatus for medical purposes and radiological apparatus
- 775 Household type, electrical and non-electrical equipment, n.e.s.
- 776 Thermionic, cold cathode and photo-cathode valves and tubes; photocells; mounted piezoelectric crystals; diodes, transistors and similar semi-conductor devices; electronic microcircuits; and parts thereof, n.e.s.
- 778 Electrical machinery and apparatus, n.e.s.

78 **Road Vehicles (Including Air-Cushion Vehicles)**

- 781 Passenger motor cars (other than public-service type vehicles), including vehicles designed for the transport of both passengers and goods
- 782 Motor vehicles for the transport of goods or materials and special purpose motor vehicles
- 783 Road motor vehicles, n.e.s.
- 784 Parts and accessories, n.e.s.
- 785 Motorcycles, motor scooters and other cycles, motorized and non-motorized; invalid carriages
- 786 Trailers and other vehicles, not motorized, n.e.s. and specially designed and equipped transport containers

79 **Other Transport Equipment**

- 791 Railway vehicles (including hovertrains) and associated equipment

Guide to Selected Standard Classifications SITC, Revision 2

- 792 Aircraft and associated equipment, and parts thereof, n.e.s.
- 793 Ships, boats (including hovercraft) and floating structures

---

8 MISCELLANEOUS MANUFACTURED ARTICLES

- **81 Sanitary, Plumbing, Heating and Lighting Fixtures and Fittings, n.e.s.**
  - 812 Sanitary, plumbing, heating and lighting fixtures and fittings, n.e.s.
- **82 Furniture and Parts Thereof**
  - 821 Furniture and parts thereof
- **83 Travel Goods, Handbags and Similar Containers**
  - 831 Travel goods, shopping bags, handbags, satchels, brief-cases, wallets, purses, etc.
- **84 Articles of Apparel and Clothing Accessories**
  - 842 Outer garments, men's and boys', of textile fabrics (other than knitted or crocheted goods)
  - 843 Outer garments, women's, girls' and infants', of textile fabrics (other than knitted or crocheted)
  - 844 Under garments of textile fabrics (other than knitted or crocheted goods)
  - 845 Outer garments and other articles, knitted or crocheted, not elastic nor rubberized
  - 846 Under garments, knitted or crocheted
  - 847 Clothing accessories, of textile fabrics, n.e.s.
  - 848 Articles of apparel and clothing accessories of other than textile fabrics; headgear of all materials
- **85 Footwear**
  - 851 Footwear
- **87 Professional, scientific and Controlling Instruments and Apparatus, n.e.s.**
  - 871 Optical instruments and apparatus
  - 872 Medical instruments and appliances, n.e.s.
  - 873 Meters and counters, n.e.s.
  - 874 Measuring, checking, analysing and controlling instruments and apparatus, n.e.s.; parts and accessories, n.e.s.
- **88 Photographic Apparatus, Equipment and Supplies and Optical Goods, n.e.s.; Watches and Clocks**
  - 881 Photographic apparatus and equipment, n.e.s.
  - 882 Photographic and cinematographic supplies
  - 883 Cinematograph film, exposed and developed, whether or not incorporating sound track or consisting only of sound track, negative or positive
  - 884 Optical goods, n.e.s.
  - 885 Watches and clocks
- **89 Miscellaneous Manufactured Articles, n.e.s.**
  - 892 Printed matter
  - 893 Articles, n.e.s. of materials of the kinds described in division 58
  - 894 Baby carriages, toys, games and sporting goods
  - 895 Office and stationery supplies, n.e.s.
  - 896 Works of art, collectors' pieces and antiques
  - 897 Jewellery, goldsmiths' and silversmiths' wares, and other articles of precious or semi-precious materials, n.e.s.
  - 898 Musical instruments and parts and accessories thereof (including phonograph records and the like)
  - 899 Other miscellaneous manufactured articles, n.e.s.

---

9 COMMODITIES AND TRANSACTIONS NOT CLASSIFIED ELSEWHERE IN THE SITC

- 911.0 Postal packages not classified according to kind
- 931.0 Special transactions and commodities not classified according to kind
- 941.0 Animals, live, n.e.s. (including zoo animals, dogs, cats, insects, etc.)
- 951.0 Armoured fighting vehicles, arms of war and ammunition therefor, and parts of arms, n.e.s.
- 961.0 Coin (other than gold coin), not being legal tender
- 971.0 Gold, non-monetary (excluding gold ores and concentrates)